תורה · נביאים · כתובים

THE KOREN TANAKH

HEBREW-ENGLISH

קוֹרֵן ירושלים

THE MAGERMAN EDITION

תורה · נביאים · כתובים
THE KOREN TANAKH
HEBREW-ENGLISH

כי מציון תצא תורה ודבר ה׳ מירושלים

KOREN PUBLISHERS JERUSALEM

The Koren Tanakh
The Magerman Edition
First Hebrew–English Edition

Koren Publishers Jerusalem Ltd.
POB 4044, Jerusalem 91040, ISRAEL
POB 8531, New Milford, CT 06776-8531, USA

www.korenpub.com

Compact size, Paperback, ISBN 978-965-7766-39-2
Ma'alot with thumb index, Compact size, Flex Binding, ISBN 978-965-7766-49-1
Ma'alot with thumb index, Standard size, Hardcover, ISBN 978-965-7766-40-8
Ma'alot with thumb index, Standard size, Leather, ISBN 978-965-7766-50-7
Ma'alot with thumb index, Large size, Hardcover, ISBN 978-965-7766-46-0
Ma'alot with thumb index, Large size, Leather, ISBN 978-965-7766-51-4

Printed in PRC

The Torah is eternal.

Humanity is ephemeral and dynamic.

The Torah is the cornerstone of the world, of our People, and it forms the baseline of the Tanakh, the holy writings of God and His prophets. The changing nature of human society demands a fresh Tanakh translation which speaks to each and every one of us while remaining rooted in the eternal essence of the Torah. The Tanakh is a living script, the screenplay of the history of humanity from Creation to the present.

Rabbi Lord Jonathan Sacks זצ״ל was the authentic Torah voice for our generation, simultaneously steeped in Torah tradition and deeply engaged with people of all faiths. He succinctly understood and eloquently conveyed both the particular Jewish identity of our sacred writings as well as their universal relevance.

We pray that this unique, traditional, and painstakingly researched and annotated translation of Tanakh animates and enlivens Torah for *Klal Yisrael*, uniting us in our traditions, exposing us to new ways of thinking, and ultimately bringing us closer to the Redemption.

אֲנִי מַאֲמִין בֶּאֱמוּנָה שְׁלֵמָה
בְּבִיאַת הַמָּשִׁיחַ
וְאַף עַל פִּי שֶׁיִּתְמַהְמֵהַּ עִם כָּל זֶה אֲחַכֶּה לּוֹ
בְּכָל יוֹם שֶׁיָּבוֹא.

I believe with perfect faith
in the coming of the Messiah,
and though he may delay,
I wait daily for his coming.

We are pleased that we were able to contribute to this critically important edition of the Tanakh which will reach so, so many Jews and non-Jews alike.

Debra and David Magerman
Philadelphia, Pennsylvania

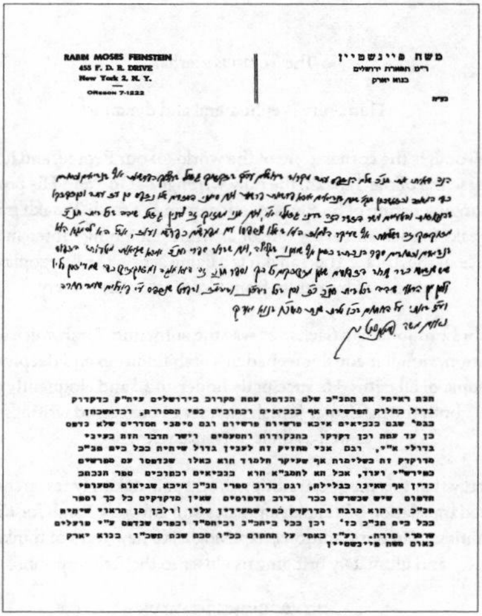

RABBI MOSES FEINSTEIN
455 F. D. R. DRIVE
New York 2, N. Y.
ORegon 7-1222

משה פיינשטיין
ר"מ תפארת ירושלים
בנוא יארק

בע"ה

הנה ראיתי את התנ"ך שלם הנדפס עתה מקורן בירושלים עיה"ק בדקדוק
גדול בחלוק הפרשיות אף בנביאים וכתובים כפי המסורה, וכדאשכחן
בגמ' שגם בנביאים איכא פרשיות וגם סימני הסדרים שלא נדפס
כן עד עתה וכן דקדקו בהנקודות והטעמים וישר הדבר הזה בעיני
גדולי א"י, וגם אני מחזיק זה לענין גדול שיהיה בכל בית תנ"ך
מדוקדק זה בשלימות אף שעיקר הלמוד הוא באלו שנדפסו עם מפרשים
כפירש"י ועוד, אבל הא לתנ"ך הוא בנביאים וכתובים ספר הנכתב
כדין אף שאינו בגלילה, וגם ברוב ספרי תנ"ך איכא שגיאות מטעותי
הדפוס שיש שנשרשו כבר מרוב הדפוסים שאין מדקדקים כל כך וספר
תנ"ך זה הוא מוגה ומדוקדק כפי שמעידין עליו ולכן מן הראוי שיהיה
בכל בית תנ"ך כזה וכן בכל ביהכ"נ וביהמ"ד ובפרט שנדפס ע"י פועלים
שומרי תורה. ועל זה באתי על החתום בכ"ו טבת שנת תשכ"ו בנוא יארק
נאום משה פיינשטיין

I have just viewed the full Koren Tanakh printed in Jerusalem. I was impressed by the great meticulousness with which the passages are laid out, even in the Prophets and Writings, according to the Masora. As we know from the Talmud, the books of the Prophets, too, are divided into *parashot* as well as *sedarim,* divisions which have not been conveyed in previous printed editions. In addition, Koren's editors were very scrupulous regarding the placement of vocalization and cantillation marks, and their work in this respect has met with the approval of the greatest rabbis of Israel. I too consider it of great importance that every Jewish home own such a comprehensive Tanakh … Most Tanakhs include mistakes and typographic errors which have become entrenched over time and printing in many successive editions. Yet the Koren Tanakh is accurate and reliable, as testified by its users. Therefore it is advisable that such a Tanakh be found in every household, synagogue, and *beit midrash,* all the more since it was published by a Torah-observant firm.

26th of Tevet, 5726 (1966), New York
Moses Feinstein

This haskama refers to the first Hebrew edition of this work.

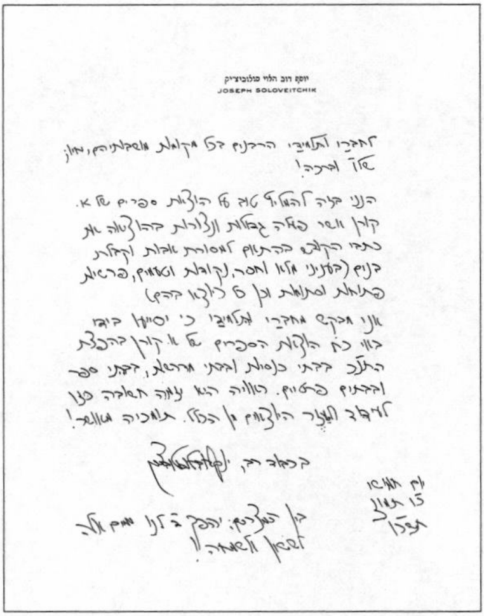

יוסף דוב הלוי סולובייצ׳יק
JOSEPH SOLOVEITCHIK

To my rabbinical colleagues and students throughout the world,

I hereby recommend the publications of Eliyahu Koren, who has performed a great service in publishing the Holy Scriptures according to Jewish tradition, with careful regard for accuracy in spelling, vowels and accentuation, paragraph divisions, and the like.

I call upon my friends and students to assist the representatives of Koren Publishers Jerusalem by distributing the Tanakh in synagogues and *batei midrash*, in schools and in private homes. Such an important initiative is worthy of outstanding encouragement and assistance.

"... and joyous are those who hold her fast!"

Respectfully,
Joseph B. Soloveitchik
Thursday, 26 Tammuz, 5726 (1966)
Between the straits:
May God transform these days into ones of joy and happiness!

This haskama refers to the first Hebrew edition of this work.

CONTENTS

WEEKLY TORAH PORTIONS

NUMBERS

DEUTERONOMY

FOREWORD
RABBI LORD JONATHAN SACKS

"When God began creating heaven and earth, the earth was void and desolate, there was darkness on the face of the deep, and the spirit of God moved over the waters...." Thus unfolds the most revolutionary as well as the most influential account of creation in the history of the human spirit.

Yet what I find so profound and counterintuitive is how the Torah frames creation. It does so not from a vantage point of physics or cosmology, but rather through a phrase we hear repeatedly in the opening verses: "And God said, Let there be... And there was...." What is truly creative, we learn, is not science or technology per se, but rather the word. That is what forms all being.

Judaism treats mere words with a great degree of seriousness: "Life and death are in the power of the tongue," says the book of Proverbs (18:21). Likewise the verses in Psalms (34:13–14), "Whoever of you loves life and desires to see many good days, keep your tongue from evil and your lips from telling lies."

There are ancient cultures who worshipped the gods because they saw them as powers: lightning, thunder, the rain and sun, the sea and ocean that epitomized the forces of chaos, and sometimes wild animals that represented danger and fear. Judaism was not a religion that worshipped power, despite the fact that God is more powerful than any pagan deity. Judaism, like other religions, has holy places, holy people, sacred times, and consecrated rituals. What made Judaism different, however, is that it is supremely *a religion of holy words*.

Creation, revelation, and the moral life begin with the creative word, the idea, the vision, the dream. Language – and with it the ability to remember a distant past and conceptualize a distant future – lies at the heart of our uniqueness as the image of God. Just as God makes the natural world by words, so we make the human world by words. Already at the opening of the Torah, at the very beginning of creation, the Jewish doctrine of revelation is foretold: that God reveals Himself to humanity not in the sun, the stars, the wind or the storm but in and through words – sacred words that establish eternal covenant between heaven and earth, and thus become co-partners with God in the work of redemption.

This new translation of our foundational texts, this collection of words, has been a true partnership. First, with the outstanding team at Koren Publishers inspirationally led by Matthew Miller, its tireless and visionary driving force. What Koren have achieved in reviving Jewish publishing is remarkable, and particular thanks must be paid to Rabbi Tzvi Hersh Weinreb, Jessica Sacks, Sara Daniel, Rabbi Reuven Ziegler, and Ashirah Yosefah Firszt, together with the other Koren professionals and translators who have contributed so much to this particular project.

Second, with Debra and David Magerman, whose friendship I cherish, and whose support for this project and the Koren Ḥumash is so deeply appreciated. Their generosity will benefit generations of Jews around the world who will make use of these publications for decades to come.

My deepest thanks, as always, are to Elaine and my family, who remain my inspiration and strength, and who have taught me to be open to the Divine Other.

Ultimately, though, all thanks belong to God, whose timeless words continue to provide endless guidance for us today.

Rabbi Lord Jonathan Sacks
London, 5781 (2020)

PUBLISHER'S PREFACE

"One generation will praise Your works to the next…" (Ps. 145:4)

To undertake a new English translation of the Tanakh – the Jewish scriptures comprising the Torah, Nevi'im (Prophets), and Ketuvim (Writings) – requires chutzpah and humility in equal measure, but neither more than *yirat Shamayim* – fear and trembling before God. In translating God's words and those of His prophets, one assumes the precarious position of mediator between Him and the reader, searching for the formulation that will do His work the greatest measure of justice, while simultaneously bringing the reader closer to the text. While there are already numerous English translations of the Bible in the Jewish world, ours aims to stand out through its emphasis on authentically conveying the *hadrat kodesh*, the sacred majesty, of the original Hebrew. More specifically, we have created a translation which

- is readable and stylistically sound to the modern eye and ear, without compromising accuracy or scholarly integrity,
- whispers the tonality of the Hebrew original,
- maintains the beauty and the majestic quality of the poetry and prose of Tanakh,
- is faithful to the classical Jewish interpretive tradition, while cognizant of contemporary scholarship,
- invites the contemporary reader to experience afresh the timeless stories and wisdom contained in the Hebrew scriptures.

This work has been the fruit of a happy collaboration between many people. While this preface cannot list everyone involved, we must acknowledge the contributions of those few without whom the new *Koren Tanakh* simply would not have been produced.

Rabbi Lord Jonathan Sacks, זצ״ל, translated the Torah and much of Psalms. His profound learning, moral depth, and sheer eloquence, expressed in his many published works, made him a leading religious figure not only within contemporary Judaism, but throughout the greater religious world. His untimely passing as the first edition went to press was an irreparable loss to the Jewish people, but we take a measure of consolation in the knowledge that this brilliant translation, to which he devoted his final years, will help carry on his legacy for generations to come. We are honored to have been Rabbi Sacks's publishers, students, and friends.

Rabbi Dr. Tzvi Hersh Weinreb, *שליט״א*, translated the books of Jeremiah and Proverbs and reviewed many of the other translations. A leading American rabbi and former Chief Executive of the Orthodox Union, Rabbi Weinreb spans the divide between the publishing world in Israel and the needs of American Jewry. We have benefitted greatly from both his scholarship and his sage advice.

Debra and David Magerman, whose unfailing support for this edition as well as the accompanying new *Koren Ḥumash* has demonstrated their faith and friendship – and no small amount of patience – for the invaluable work contained therein. We thank you both, on behalf not only of the many dozens of professionals involved, but of the generations of Jews who will use and cherish this groundbreaking publication.

Translation Team Manager and Senior Translator Jessica Sacks, Sara Daniel, and the other translators, who have invested inestimable time, scholarship, and their prodigious literary talents in this Tanakh.

Rabbi Reuven Ziegler, Ashirah Yosefah Firszt, Rabbi Avishai Magence, and Rabbi Yedidya Naveh, whose management and guidance of scores of translators, scholars, editors, proofreaders, and designers have been superb. Without their skills, no fruit of the above literary talents would have seen the light of publication, and without their expertise, the final product would not have attained the same exacting standards of quality.

Typographer Esther Be'er – who studied under Eliyahu Koren himself – and her colleagues **Rina Ben Gal** and **Tomi Mager** designed the clear, elegant, and functional layout of this Tanakh, which is worthy of our founder's name and of the superb typographical quality of past Koren titles.

In addition to the above, the new *Koren Tanakh* is a testament to the many gifted professionals who had a role in its creation: consulting experts, reviewing scholars, editors, and proofreaders. Their names and contributions are in the Acknowledgments pages which follow.

We are presently developing an extensive range of publications built around this new translation as a core text: the forthcoming **Magerman Edition of the Koren Ḥumash** with extensive commentaries by Rabbi Sacks, the **Rohr Edition of the Koren Mikraot HaDorot**, the **Hertog Edition of the Koren Tanakh of the Land of Israel**, the **Nagel Edition of the Koren Ḥumash Lev Ladaat for Young Adults**, and more. Each of these will fulfill different needs and address specific purposes. What they will share is this intelligent, eloquent translation. It is our hope that the new *Koren Tanakh* will provide its readers with insights beyond and behind the text, and perhaps even a glimpse into their own story.

Matthew Miller, Publisher
Jerusalem, 5781 (2020)

ABOUT THIS EDITION

THE KOREN TANAKH IN HISTORY

Early Printed Hebrew Bibles

Hebrew biblical texts were first printed in Italy in Bologna (1477), with other publications soon following in Soncino, Casale, and Naples. The first complete Hebrew Bible, in folio, was printed in 1488 at Soncino, without any commentary, and was riddled with errors. Further Jewish editions were soon published – one in 1490 in Isola del Liri, with Rashi's commentaries; a very accurate edition of the Ḥumash in Lisbon in 1491; and a second complete edition of the Tanakh in 1494 at Brescia.

But soon thereafter – from 1514 onwards – biblical books in Hebrew began to be printed by Christians, the most notable among them being the Catholic Venetian printer Daniel Bomberg. Bomberg's second edition (1524–25), known as the *Mikraot Gedolot*, was printed in a large format with commentaries and philological notes, and in a smaller format without commentaries. This edition formed the basis of almost every subsequent edition of the Hebrew Bible to this day, including many of those printed by Jews.

Since then, many Hebrew editions of the Tanakh have been brought out by Christian publishers, who dominated the editorial and textual scholarship of Hebrew printing for almost 450 years. Most Jews in the nineteenth century used Bibles published by Christian missionaries (or reprinted from such editions). While this may be difficult to imagine today, for much of modern history the only books available to the Jewish student of Torah were those printed by gentiles intent on converting them.

The Hebrew Koren Tanakh

Along with the establishment of the State of Israel, the spiritual reconstitution of the Jewish people in their ancient homeland was expressed in no way more than by the preparation and printing of the famous *Koren Tanakh*. Mr. Eliyahu Koren understood that the miracle of the nation's return to the land of Israel demanded a clear spiritual response, one which struck to the heart of the question – still debated to this day – of what drives the spirit of the Jewish people. This response would take the shape of a new Tanakh – with text meticulously researched by Torah scholars and free of errors, and with a new typeface that combined classical aesthetic sensibilities with a meticulously modern insistence on clarity and legibility – printed by a Jewish publishing house in Jerusalem, in the modern State of Israel.

Over the course of the 1950s, Eliyahu Koren, along with scholar Meir Medan and a team that included Dr. Daniel Goldschmidt and Avraham Meir Haberman, worked to create an unprecedentedly accurate edition of the Hebrew scriptures. The *Koren Tanakh*, first published in Jerusalem in 1962, was the first fully Jewish bible to be published since the end of the fifteenth century, with Jewish scholars and editors, type designers, printers and binders. It was remarkable also for being the first publication ever set in the famous Koren Tanakh typeface, which was painstakingly designed especially for it. Since that first printing, the publication of Jewish texts worldwide has made great strides. Koren Publishers too has continually updated and improved its editions, of which this new volume joins a long and worthy tradition.

◂ *Notable*

Notable Features of the Hebrew Koren Text

The Hebrew text of the original *Koren Tanakh* was meticulously researched and reviewed by some of the foremost Masoretic scholars of the generation. The text itself was based for the most part on the earlier work of Rabbi Wolf Heidenheim and *Minḥat Shai,* as well as the Leningrad Codex, the oldest complete surviving manuscript of the Tanakh in Hebrew. The text was met with critical acclaim on its publication and received the approbation of rabbinic luminaries such as Rabbi Joseph B. Soloveitchik and Rabbi Moshe Feinstein.

The *Koren Tanakh* also stands out in its presentation and organization of the text. In early modern bibles printed by gentiles and used by Jews, the chapter divisions were not based on any Jewish tradition, but on a Christian one. Because this system has by now become an accepted standard of reference even for Jews, it is retained on the inside margin of the page. However, the *Koren Tanakh* is the first to also mark and number the division of the biblical text into the traditional Jewish system of *sedarim*. These appear on the outer margin of the page, as do the divisions for *aliyot* and weekly *parashot*. These distinctions are more than mere intellectual curiosity: they have significant theological import. Many of the disputes between Judaism and Christianity are reflected in the different designation of chapters and sections. The page itself is printed in the style of a *sefer Torah,* including proper graphical representation of the *petuḥa* and *setuma* line breaks according to the Masora, as opposed to the placeholder letters *peh* and *samekh* typically used by older editions to save paper.

In other editions of the Tanakh, the *keri* and *ketiv* – words that are not pronounced as written – are presented in a confusing manner, with the letters of the word printed as written but attended by the vocalization marks of the word pronounced. This can often lead to mispronunciation when the discrepancy between the two is purely consonantal; for example, in Esther 3:4, there might be no indication that the word is pronounced *ke'omram* rather than *be'omram,* as it is written. In the *Koren Tanakh,* the *ketiv* will always appear in the body of the text with no vowels at all, immediately sending the reader to the margin, where the word as it is pronounced is written in full, guaranteeing correct recitation. The tetragrammaton (spelled *yod-heh-vav-heh*) is also rendered without the vowel marks of *Adonai* so often applied in other editions, both highlighting the sanctity of the name and helping to dispel the common but erroneous notion that the name itself might properly be pronounced "Jehovah."

The award-winning Koren Tanakh typeface, designed by Eliyahu Koren especially for the *Koren Tanakh,* instantly became a classic of Hebrew typography. Designed for crystal clarity and classical elegance, it draws on the balance and dignity of the Sephardic calligraphic tradition, and subtly and uncompromisingly accommodates the forms of all the Hebrew letters and vocalization and cantillation marks without crowding or confusion. For example, the marks distinguishing between the letters *shin* and *sin* are notoriously confused in other typefaces with the vocalization mark *ḥolam* (before or after the letter, respectively), which makes an "o" sound; the Koren typeface clearly differentiates between the two. Furthermore, the proportions of the letterforms allow for a *lamed* that never needs to "bow" its head (or to be decapitated entirely), as was so often the case in older typefaces. In addition, the vowel mark for a *pataḥ genuva* (which is uncharacteristically pronounced *before* the consonant to which it is appended –

◂ always a

always a guttural letter at the end of a word, as in *siaḥ* or *Yehoshua*) is positioned slightly to the right as a reminder of its correct pronunciation. Finally, subtle distinctions are made between distinct but orthographically similar cantillation marks such as *mahpakh* and *yetiv*, or *pashta* and *kadma*. The most recent editions of the Hebrew *Koren Tanakh* also include typographical distinctions between *sheva na* and *sheva naḥ*, and between *kamatz gadol* and *kamatz katan*, to further aid correct pronunciation.

The First Koren English Edition

The translation used for the first English *Koren Tanakh* of 1967 was not entirely new. It was, rather, a thoroughly corrected, modernized, and revised version of the Anglo-Jewish bibles that had long been accepted for home and synagogue use throughout the English-speaking world. The Koren translation was based upon *The Jewish Family Bible*, edited by M. Friedlander and published in 1881 with the sanction of the Chief Rabbi of the British Empire, Dr. N. M. Adler. The translation had two important merits: it was faithful to the Masora, while retaining as much of the excellent language and rhythm of the King James "Authorized Version" of 1611 as Jewish sentiment permitted.

That translation was revised for Koren by Professor Harold Fisch, a renowned scholar of English literature and Rector of Bar Ilan University. The language of the older versions was modernized to some extent, and fresh translations and interpretations were included based on comparisons with other Jewish bible translations, *targumim*, and classical and contemporary scholarship. Names of biblical characters, until then invariably rendered in their Hellenized/anglicized versions such as "Eve" and "Jeconiah," were newly presented as they are pronounced in Hebrew, using a transliteration scheme approved by the Academy of the Hebrew Language. Still, more than fifty years later, the language of that translation – especially the retention of the pronouns "thee," "thou," "thy," and "thine" – can feel archaic to the contemporary reader, and the academic, technical style of transliterating names dry and detached.

Now, Koren Publishers has had the great privilege of partnering with Rabbi Lord Jonathan Sacks, who was perhaps the most eloquent spokesman for Judaism in our times, in publishing a completely new and fully Jewish translation of the Tanakh – one which aims to wed the Masoretic authenticity and attention to detail that are the hallmarks of Koren with the literary majesty and elegance that characterize all of Rabbi Sacks's English works. It is the fruit of this great undertaking which you hold in your hands.

NAMES IN THE NEW KOREN TANAKH

The system used by the 1967 Fisch translation for transliterating names possessed the advantage of authenticity and a more Hebrew feel. However, the style was technical and academic, and it sometimes had the opposite of its desired effect by making the characters appear foreign. In this edition, we have opted for a middle path. We transliterate personal names – as well as those of places and tribes – using a simpler, more popular style, eschewing doubled letters and apostrophes except where needed to ensure correct pronunciation. The result is that personal names are spelled much as contemporary Israelis might spell their names in English – e.g., Yaakov (not Ya'aqov) or Rivka (not Rivqa). Whether with respect to august figures such as Moshe – "drawn from the water" – or minor ones such as Ikhavod – "without honor" (contrast to the comic Ichabod of Washington Irving) – we see the rendering of names in contemporary transliteration as imparting a new dimension of the Tanakh that weds cultural authenticity with intimacy.

In certain rare cases where anything but the common anglicized version of a name would feel jarring – e.g., "Israel" or "Pharaoh" – the anglicizations have been preserved, as well as with demonyms (such as "Moabites") whose suffixes indelibly mark them as English words. In addition, the names of many places and geographical features with straightforward meanings that describe them have been translated outright – for example, the Mount of Olives.

As regards names of God, we have followed Rabbi Sacks's direction in maintaining the elegant and accurate distinction between "God," used for *Elohim*, and "Lord" for the tetragrammaton (the ineffable name of God spelled *yod-heh-vav-heh*). This reflects the Almighty's twin roles as Creator of the universe and God of Israel. The appellation "Lord" is set in block capitals to symbolize how the name in Hebrew, while pronounced *Adonai* (which literally means "my Lord"), is in fact written as God's personal name, which may not be uttered. Thus, in those cases where the tetragrammaton is traditionally pronounced *Elohim* rather than *Adonai*, the name is rendered in English as "God," in block capitals.

THE PROCESS OF TRANSLATION

The translators who took part in this project, all of whom have deep understanding of the Hebrew texts, were chosen primarily for their uniformly superb literary abilities. After translation, each text was edited and reviewed several times by leading scholars of biblical history, language, and literature to ensure the high level of accuracy and integrity readers should expect from a flagship Koren publication. This process provided our translators with clear parameters in which to creatively render into contemporary English the beauty, drama, and nuances of the original Hebrew texts. With consummate skill and close attention to style, our literary editors helped craft the translations in dialogue with the translators, followed by the attentions of copy editors and consistency editors, as well as multiple rounds of proofreading. Throughout, we have prioritized the experience of the English, with the aim that those holding this volume will forget that they are reading a translation and lose themselves in the drama of the narrative, the elegance of the poetry, the holiness of the law, and the relevance of the wisdom.

Our translation adheres to the Masoretic text of Tanakh. In cases where the Masoretic text distinguishes between the way the word is written (*ketiv*) and the way it is pronounced (*keri*), the translation follows the latter.

Hebrew is a grammatically gendered language, and masculine words and forms are often used to refer to both sexes. In such cases, we have favored the use of gender-neutral forms in English – for example, "people" and "children" rather than "men" and "sons."

To fit the requirements of English style, we occasionally replaced names with pronouns and vice versa, and changed the position of speech markers ("she said") in the sentence, thereby ensuring the clarity and fluidity of the dialogue.

◂ In the case

In the case of prophecy, introducing modern punctuation to the ancient text is especially difficult. The prophets often shift between the first and third person when conveying God's word, identifying so closely with their message that it is difficult at times to distinguish between God's voice and the prophet's own. The approach we found most organic to the text was to use quotation marks when God appears in direct "dialogue" with the prophet. When, however, the prophet conveys or is asked to convey a message to others, that message is introduced merely by the use of a colon: "The Lord said to Moshe, 'This is what you shall tell the Israelites: You yourselves have seen ....'"

Every translation is an interpretation. While we have made use of contemporary approaches to understanding Tanakh, we are also committed to the way the Tanakh, and in particular the Torah, has been received and understood in the Jewish tradition. The acute discernments of Rashi and other commentators, especially those of the school of the *pashtanim*, will be felt in many parts of the translation. In the instances where a rabbinic reading was chosen against the apparent grain of the literal one, we have marked this with a footnote.

This edition of the new *Koren Tanakh* is intentionally sparing in its use of footnotes and explanatory texts. Rather than producing a comprehensive commentary (which would be a titanic undertaking in its own right), we have largely restricted ourselves to pointing out elements of the Hebrew – such as wordplay – that cannot come across in translation, or crucial background information without which the reader might find him- or herself simply unable to understand the text at hand.

To aid the reader further, we have appended to this volume a selection of maps, charts, timelines, genealogies, and illustrations. Drawing upon the extensive collection of high-quality supplementary material developed over the past six decades by Koren Publishers Jerusalem, we have thoroughly updated the material to reflect contemporary graphic sensibilities and to facilitate comprehension.

We sincerely pray that our efforts will "find favor and approval in the eyes of God" (Prov. 3:4) and in the eyes of all to whom the word of God is dear.

THE NEW **KOREN TANAKH** TRANSLATORS

The responsibility of a translator cannot be overstated: for normal books, the best translators are those who transmit words and concepts fluidly from one language to another, from one culture to another, seamlessly, quietly, innocuously. Indeed, it is those translations which jar the reader, which call attention to the text being a translation, that may be considered failures. The success of a translator is his or her very anonymity.

To translate the words of God and His prophets only heightens the responsibilities. Beyond the standard requirements, Bible translators must rephrase these ancient words for the eye and the ear of the contemporary English-speaking reader, conveying the true sense of each word with respect, reverence, love, belief, erudition, elegance, and fluency. Such challenges require translators gifted with extraordinary abilities and sensitivities.

We are truly blessed to have worked with a team of brilliantly literate and highly educated professionals, and are proud to acknowledge their contribution – together with that of our consulting scholars, editors, managers, and staff – to the Jews of the English-speaking world and their *avodat Hashem.*

Rabbi Lord Jonathan Sacks: Genesis, Exodus, Leviticus, Numbers, Deuteronomy, Psalms 1–4, 6, 9, 15, 16, 19, 20, 23, 24, 27, 29, 30, 33, 34, 47, 48, 49, 67, 81, 82, 90–100, 103, 104, 113–118, 120–137, 139, 144–150

Rabbi Dr. Tzvi Hirsch Weinreb: Jeremiah, Proverbs

Jessica Sacks: Isaiah, Jonah, Song of Songs, Ruth, Lamentations, Ecclesiastes, Esther

Sara Daniel: Joshua, Judges, I and II Samuel, I and II Kings, I and II Chronicles, Psalms 5, 7, 8, 10–14, 17, 18, 21, 22, 25, 26, 28, 31, 32, 35–46, 50–66, 68–80, 83–89, 101, 102, 105, 106–112, 119, 138, 140–143

Rachel Ebner: Ezekiel 40–48, Daniel

Lauren Gordon: Ezekiel 1–39

Serylle Horwitz: Ezra 2, Nehemiah

Annie Kantar: Job 3–31, 38–42:6

Tichye Krakowski: Joel, Amos, Obadiah, Haggai, Zechariah, Malachi, Job 1–2, 32–37, 42:7–17

Adina Luber: Ezra 1, 3–10

Dafna Renbaum: Nahum, Habakkuk, Micah, Hosea, Zephaniah

THE NEW **KOREN TANAKH** TRANSLATION SCHOLARS

We extend heartfelt appreciation to the esteemed scholars of Tanakh who invested many hours reviewing draft translations and providing our translators with valuable corrections, translation guidance, and textual and historical insights. The scholars are listed in alphabetical order, followed by the translations they reviewed.

Rabbi Dr. Tzvi Hersh Weinreb: Consultancy scholar for translation queries and final decisions

Dr. Baruch Alster: Haggai

Prof. Joseph L. Angel: I and II Kings, Ezekiel 1–39, Psalms, Daniel

Rabbi Prof. Elie Assis: Joel

Prof. Michael Avioz: Bibliography and resources scholar

Prof. Shawn Zelig Aster: Isaiah, Hosea, Amos, Micah, Haggai

Rabbi Prof. Yitzhak Berger: Genesis, Exodus, Leviticus, Numbers, Deuteronomy, Jeremiah 1–26, Jonah, Malachi

Prof. Emerita Adele Berlin: Jeremiah 27–52, Proverbs, Lamentations

Rabbi Dr. Ezra Frazer: Zechariah, Ezra, Nehemiah

Dr. Tova Ganzel: Ezekiel

Dr. Binyamin Goldstein: I and II Samuel, I and II Chronicles

Rabbi Prof. Isaac B. Gottlieb: I Kings 1–21, Ecclesiastes

Prof. Emeritus Edward Greenstein: Job

Rabbi Michael Hattin: Joshua, Song of Songs

Prof. Aaron Koller: Judges, Esther

Dr. Yael Landman: Nahum

Dr. Bryna Jocheved Levy: Obadiah, Habakkuk, Zephaniah

Dr. Yael Ziegler: Ruth

THE NEW **KOREN TANAKH** FOOTNOTE SCHOLARS

As noted above, the footnote style chosen for our initial editions of the new *Koren Tanakh* is one of brief clarification. The Tanakh scholars listed below, in alphabetical order, spent many hours researching and composing richly informative footnotes from which we have drawn and adapted the short footnotes appearing in this Tanakh edition.

Prof. Joseph L. Angel: I and II Kings, Ezekiel, Psalms, Daniel

Prof. Shawn Zelig Aster: Joshua, Judges, Isaiah, Jeremiah, Ezekiel, Hosea, Joel, Amos, Obadiah, Micah, Nahum, Habakkuk, Zephaniah Haggai, Zechariah, Malachi

Rabbi Prof. Yitzhak Berger: Genesis, Exodus, Leviticus, Numbers, Deuteronomy

Prof. Emerita Adele Berlin: Jonah, Proverbs, Job, Song of Songs, Ruth, Lamentations, Ecclesiastes, Esther

Rabbi Dr. Ezra Frazer: Ezra, Nehemiah

Dr. Binyamin Goldstein: I and II Samuel, I and II Chronicles

Rabbi Yedidya Naveh: Selection and editing of footnotes

THE NEW **KOREN TANAKH**
EDITORS, TYPESETTERS, AND GRAPHIC DESIGNERS

EDITOR IN CHIEF
Rabbi Reuven Ziegler

MANAGING EDITORS
Ashirah Yosefah Firszt (Project)
Rabbi Avishai Magence (Production)

LITERARY EDITORS
Prof. Emeritus William L. Lee: Joshua, Judges, I and II Samuel, I and II Kings, Isaiah, Jeremiah, Ezekiel, Hosea, Joel, Amos, Obadiah, Jonah, Micah, Nahum, Habakkuk, Zephaniah, Haggai, Zechariah, Malachi, Psalms, Proverbs, Job, Song of Songs, Ruth, Lamentations, Ecclesiastes, Esther, Daniel, Ezra, Nehemiah, I and II Chronicles
Jessica Sacks: Genesis, Exodus, Leviticus, Numbers, Deuteronomy

COPY EDITORS
Shira Finson
Debbie Ismailoff
Rachel Meghnagi
Ita Olesker

CONSISTENCY EDITORS
Caryn Meltz
Rabbi Yedidya Naveh

PROOFREADERS
English:
Sara Daniel
Debbie Ismailoff
Caryn Meltz
Ita Olesker
Dvora Rhein

Hebrew:
Avichai Gamdani
Efrat Gross

REFERENCE MATERIAL
Editors:
David Arnovitz
Rabbi Alan Haber (translator)
Caryn Meltz

Content:
Rabbi Dan Beeri
Rabbi Yinon Chen
Efrat Gross
Tamar Hayardeni
Dr. Neriah Klein
Rabbi Menachem Makover
Hanan Moses
Rabbi David Nativ
Eliav Stollman

Graphic Designers:
Tani Bayer
Eliyahu Misgav

Map Designers:
A. D. Riddle
Jay Rosenberg

TYPESETTERS
Esther Be'er
Rina Ben Gal
Estie Dishon
Tomi Mager
Sara Bluma Weinstock

TORAH READINGS FOR SPECIAL DAYS

Rosh Ḥodesh	Numbers 28:1–15, p. 389
Fast Days	Exodus 32:11–14, p. 205 Continues with Exodus 34:1–10, p. 209
Ninth of Av	Shaḥarit: Deuteronomy 4:25–40, p. 427 Minḥa: See Fast Days, above.
Ḥanukka – Day 1	Ashkenazim: Numbers 7:1–17, p. 329 Sepharadim: Numbers 6:22–7:17, p. 329
Ḥanukka – Days 2–7	Read the offering for the respective day, Numbers 7:18–53, p. 331 On Rosh Ḥodesh, read the Rosh Ḥodesh reading from the first Torah scroll, and the Ḥanukka reading from the second Torah scroll.
Ḥanukka – Day 8	Numbers 7:54–8:4, p. 333
Purim	Exodus 17:8–16, p. 169

TORAH READINGS FOR SPECIAL SHABBATOT
(READ FROM THE SECOND TORAH SCROLL)

Shabbat Rosh Ḥodesh	Numbers 28:9–15, p. 389
Shabbat Ḥanukka	Read the the passage for Shabbat Rosh Ḥodesh from the second Torah scroll and for Ḥanukka from the third Torah scroll.
Parashat Shekalim	Exodus 30:11–16, p. 201 If Rosh Ḥodesh falls on Parashat Shekalim, the passage for Rosh Ḥodesh is read from the second Torah scroll and Parashat Shekalim from the third Torah scroll.
Parashat Zakhor	Deuteronomy 25:17–19, p. 475
Parashat Para	Numbers 19:1–22, p. 365
Parashat HaḤodesh	Exodus 12:1–20, p. 153 If Parashat HaḤodesh falls on Rosh Ḥodesh, the passage for Rosh Ḥodesh is read from the second Torah scroll and Parashat HaḤodesh from the third Torah scroll.
Purim on Shabbat (in Walled Cities)	Exodus 17:8–16, p. 169 *Haftara*: Same as Shabbat Zakhor.

TORAH READINGS FOR FESTIVALS

Pesaḥ – Day 1	Exodus 12:21–51, p. 155 On Shabbat, Sepharadim read Exodus 12:14–51, p. 153 *Maftir*: Numbers 28:16–25, p. 389
Day 2	Leviticus 22:26–23:44, p. 289 In Israel: *Revi'i* (second Torah scroll): Numbers 28:19–25, p. 389 In the Diaspora: *Maftir*: Same as Day 1.
Day 3	Exodus 13:1–16, p. 157 *Revi'i* (second Torah scroll): Numbers 28:19–25, p. 389
Day 4	Exodus 22:24–23:19, p. 181 (If it falls on a Sunday, Sepharadim read the passage for Day 3.) *Revi'i* (second Torah scroll): Numbers 28:19–25, p. 389
Day 5	Exodus 34:1–26, p. 209 (If it falls on a Monday, Sepharadim read the passage for Day 4.) *Revi'i* (second Torah scroll): Numbers 28:19–25, p. 389
Day 6	Numbers 9:1–14, p. 339 *Revi'i* (second Torah scroll): Numbers 28:19–25, p. 389
Shabbat Ḥol HaMoed Pesaḥ	Exodus 33:12–34:26, p. 209 *Maftir*: Numbers 28:19–25, p. 389
Day 7	Exodus 13:17–15:26, p. 159 *Maftir*: Numbers 28:19–25, p. 389
Day 8 (Diaspora)	Deuteronomy 15:19–16:17, p. 455 On Shabbat: Deuteronomy 14:22–16:17, p. 453 *Maftir*: Numbers 28:19–25, p. 389
Shavuot – Day 1	Exodus 19:1–20:23, p. 173 *Maftir*: Numbers 28:26–31, p. 391
Day 2 (Diaspora)	Deuteronomy 15:19–16:17, p. 455 On Shabbat: Deuteronomy 14:22–16:17, p. 453 *Maftir*: Same as Day 1.
Rosh HaShana – Day 1	Genesis 21:1–34, p. 43 *Maftir*: Numbers 29:1–6, p. 391
Day 2	Genesis 22:1–24, p. 47 *Maftir*: Same as Day 1.
Yom Kippur – Shaḥarit	Leviticus 16:1–34, p. 273 *Maftir*: Numbers 29:7–11, p. 391

Minḥa	Leviticus 18:1–30, p. 279
Sukkot – Day 1	Leviticus 22:26–23:44, p. 289 *Maftir*: Numbers 29:12–16, p. 391
Day 2	Israel: Numbers 29:17–19, p. 391 Diaspora: Same as day 1.
Day 3	Israel: Numbers 29:20–22, p. 391 Diaspora: Numbers 29:17–25, p. 391
Day 4	Israel: Numbers 29:23–25, p. 393 Diaspora: Numbers 29:20–28, p. 391
Day 5	Israel: Numbers 29:26–28, p. 393 Diaspora: Numbers 29:23–31, p. 393
Day 6	Israel: Numbers 29:29–31, p. 393 Diaspora: Numbers 29:26–34, p. 393
Hoshana Rabba	Israel: Numbers 29:32–34, p. 393 Diaspora: Numbers 29:26–34, p. 393
Shabbat Ḥol HaMoed Sukkot	Exodus 33:12–34:26, p. 209 *Maftir*: Read the offering for the respective day (in the Diaspora adding the offering for the previous day).
Shemini Atzeret (Diaspora)	Deuteronomy 15:19–16:17, p. 455 On Shabbat: Deuteronomy 14:22–16:17, p. 453 *Maftir*: Numbers 29:35–30:1, p. 393
Simḥat Torah (Israel and Diaspora)	First Torah scroll: Deuteronomy 33:1–34:12, p. 499 Second Torah scroll: Genesis 1:1–2:3, p. 5 Third Torah scroll (*Maftir*): Numbers 29:35–30:1, p. 393

HAFTAROT (WITH VARIATIONS FOR ASHKENAZIM, SEPHARADIM, YEMENITES, AND MINHAG ANGLIA)

Bereshit	Ashkenazim:	Isaiah 42:5–43:10, p. 1009
	Sephardim:	Isaiah 32:5–21, p. 991
	Yemenites:	Isaiah 32:5–16, p. 991
Noaḥ	Ashkenazim:	Isaiah 54:1–55:5, p. 1031
	Sephardim:	Isaiah 54:1–54:10, p. 1031
	Yemenites:	Isaiah 54:1–55:3, p. 1031
Lekh Lekha	Ashkenazim & Sephardim:	Isaiah 40:27–41:16, p. 1007
	Yemenites:	Isaiah 40:25–41:16, p. 1005
Vayera	Ashkenazim & Yemenites:	II Kings 4:1–37, p. 871
	Sephardim:	II Kings 4:1–23, p. 871
Ḥayei Sara		I Kings 1:1–31, p. 787
Toledot	Ashkenazim & Sephardim:	Malachi 1:1–2:7, p. 1407
	Yemenites:	Malachi 1:1–3:4, p. 1047
Vayetze	Ashkenazim:	Hosea 12:13–14:10, p. 1329 (some add Joel 2:26–27, p. 1335)
	Sephardim:	Hosea 11:7–12:12 / –13:5, p. 1327
	Yemenites:	Hosea 11:7–12:14, p. 1327
Vayishlaḥ		Obadiah 1:1–21, p. 1351 (Minhag Anglia: Hosea 11:7–12:12, p. 1327)
Vayeshev		Amos 2:6–3:8, p. 1341
Miketz		I Kings 3:15–4:1, p. 797
Vayigash		Ezekiel 37:15–28, p. 1277
Vayeḥi		I Kings 2:1–12, p. 791
Shemot	Ashkenazim:	Isaiah 27:6–28:13, p. 981, and 29:22–23, p. 987
	Sephardim:	Jeremiah 1:1–2:3, p. 1055
	Yemenites:	Ezekiel 16:1–14, p. 1219
Vaera	Ashkenazim & Sephardim:	Ezekiel 28:25–29:21, p. 1255
	Yemenites:	Ezekiel 28:24–29:21, p. 1255
Bo	Ashkenazim & Sephardim:	Jeremiah 46:13–28, p. 1167
	Yemenites:	Isaiah 19:1–25, p. 969
Beshalaḥ	Ashkenazim:	Judges 4:4–5:31, p. 583
	Sephardim:	Judges 5:1–31, p. 585
	Yemenites:	Judges 4:23–5:31, p. 585

Yitro	Ashkenazim:	Isaiah 6:1–7:6, p. 949, and 9:5–6, p. 955
	Sephardim:	Isaiah 6:1–13, p. 949
	Yemenites:	Isaiah 6:1–13, p. 949, and 9:5–6, p. 955
Mishpatim	Ashkenazim & Sephardim:	Jeremiah 34:8–22, p. 1139, and 33:25–26, p. 1137
	Yemenites:	Jeremiah 34:8–35:19, p. 1139
Teruma		I Kings 5:26–6:13, p. 803
Tetzaveh		Ezekiel 43:10–27, p. 1293
Ki Tisa	Ashkenazim:	I Kings 18:1–39, p. 845
	Sephardim:	I Kings 18:20–39, p. 847
	Yemenites:	I Kings 18:1–45, p. 845
Vayak'hel	Ashkenazim:	I Kings 7:40–50, p. 809
	Sephardim:	I Kings 7:13–26, p. 807
	Yemenites:	I Kings 7:13–22, p. 807
Pekudei	Ashkenazim:	I Kings 7:51–8:21, p. 811
	Sephardim & Yemenites:	I Kings 7:40–50, p. 809
Vayikra	Ashkenazim & Sephardim:	Isaiah 43:21–44:23, p. 1013
	Yemenites:	Isaiah 43:21–44:6, p. 1013
Tzav	Ashkenazim & Sephardim:	Jeremiah 7:21–8:3, p. 1071, and 9:22–23, p. 1077
	Yemenites:	Jeremiah 7:21–28, p. 1071, and 9:22–23, p. 1077
Shemini	Ashkenazim:	II Samuel 6:1–7:17, p. 729
	Sephardim:	II Samuel 6:1–19, p. 729
	Yemenites:	II Samuel 6:1–7:3, p. 729
Tazria		II Kings 4:42–5:19, p. 875
Metzora	Ashkenazim & Sephardim:	II Kings 7:3–20, p. 881
	Yemenites:	II Kings 7:1–20, p. 881, and 13:23, p. 903
Aḥarei Mot		Ezekiel 22:1–16, p. 1239 (Minhag Anglia ends at 22:19)
Kedoshim	Ashkenazim:	Amos 9:7–9:15, p. 1351
	Sephardim:	Ezekiel 20:2–20, p. 1231
	Yemenites:	Ezekiel 20:1–15, p. 1231
Emor		Ezekiel 44:15–31, p. 1297
Behar	Ashkenazim & Sephardim:	Jeremiah 32:6–27, p. 1131
	Yemenites:	Jeremiah 16:19-17:14, p. 1093

Beḥukotai	Ashkenazim & Sephardim:	Jeremiah 16:19–17:14, p. 1093
	Yemenites:	Ezekiel 34:1–27, p. 1269
Bemidbar		Hosea 2:1–22, p. 1315
Naso	Ashkenazim & Sephardim:	Judges 13:2–25, p. 611
	Yemenites:	Judges 13:2–24, p. 611
Behaalotekha	Ashkenazim & Sephardim:	Zechariah 2:14–4:7, p. 1393
	Yemenites:	Zechariah 2:14–4:9, p. 1393
Shelaḥ		Joshua 2:1–24, p. 509
Koraḥ		1 Samuel 11:14–12:22, p. 661
Ḥukat	Ashkenazim & Sephardim:	Judges 11:1–33, p. 605
	Yemenites:	Judges 11:1–40, p. 605
Balak		Micah 5:6–6:8, p. 1365
Pinḥas (before 17 Tamuz)		1 Kings 18:46–19:21, p. 851
Shabbat following 17 Tamuz (Pinḥas or Mattot)		Jeremiah 1:1–2:3, p. 1055
Masei	Ashkenazim & Sephardim:	Jeremiah 2:4–28, p. 1055, and (for Ashkenazim) 3:4, p. 1059, or (for Sephardim) 4:1–2, p. 1061 (Minhag Anglia includes both additions.)
	Yemenites:	Isaiah 1:1–20, p. 941
Devarim	Ashkenazim & Sephardim:	Isaiah 1:1–27, p. 941
	Yemenites:	Isaiah 1:21–31, p. 941
Vaetḥanan	Ashkenazim & Sephardim:	Isaiah 40:1–26, p. 1005
	Yemenites:	Isaiah 40:1–27, p. 1005, and 41:17, p. 1007
Ekev		Isaiah 49:14–51:3, p. 1023
Re'eh		Isaiah 54:11–55:5, p. 1031
Shofetim		Isaiah 51:12–52:12, p. 1027
Ki Tetzeh		Isaiah 54:1–10, p. 1031
Ki Tavo		Isaiah 60:1–22, p. 1039
Nitzavim (or Nitzavim-Vayelekh)	Ashkenazim & Sephardim:	Isaiah 61:10–63:9, p. 1043
	Yemenites:	Isaiah 61:9–63:9, p. 1043

Shabbat Shuva (Vayelekh or Haazinu)	Ashkenazim:	Hosea 14:2–10, p. 1331, and Joel 2:15–27 p. (some begin at 2:11). Some also read Micah 7:18–20, p. 1367 (Minhag Anglia reads in the order: Hosea, Micah, Joel.)
	Sepharadim:	Hosea 14:2–10, p. 1331, and Micah 7:18–20, p. 1367
	Yemenites:	Hosea 14:2–10, p. 1331
Haazinu (after Yom Kippur)	Ashkenazim & Sepharadim:	II Samuel 22:1–51, p. 773
	Yemenites:	Ezekiel 17:22–18:32, p. 1227
Special Shabbatot and Holidays		
Shabbat Rosh Ḥodesh		Isaiah 66:1–24, p. 1049
Shabbat Erev Rosh Ḥodesh		I Samuel 20:18–42, p. 689
Shabbat Ḥanukka	(1)	Zechariah 2:14–4:7, p. 1389 (Yemenites read until 4:9)
	(2)	I Kings 7:40–50, p. 809
Fast Day Minḥa		Isaiah 55:6–56:8, p. 1033
Ninth of Av – Shaḥarit	Ashkenazim & Sepharadim:	Jeremiah 8:13–9:23, p. 1075
	Yemenites:	Jeremiah 6:16–17, p. 1069, and 8:13–9:23, p. 1075
Ninth of Av – Minḥa	Ashkenazim:	Isaiah 55:6–56:8, p. 1033
	Sepharadim:	Hosea 14:2–10, p. 1331
	Yemenites:	Hosea 14:2–10, p. 1331, and Micah 7:18–20, p. 1367
Parashat Shekalim	Ashkenazim & Yemenites:	II Kings 12:1–17, p. 897 (Minhag Anglia begins at 11:17, p. 895)
	Sepharadim:	II Kings 11:17–12:17, p. 895
Parashat Zakhor	Ashkenazim:	I Samuel 15:2–34, p. 671
	Sepharadim and Minhag Anglia:	I Samuel 15:1–34, p. 671
	Yemenites:	I Samuel 14:52–15:33, p. 671
Parashat Para	Ashkenazim:	Ezekiel 36:16–38, p. 1275
	Sepharadim & Yemenites:	Ezekiel 36:16–36, p. 1275
Parashat HaḤodesh	Ashkenazim:	Ezekiel 45:16–46:18, p. 1301
	Sepharadim:	Ezekiel 45:18–46:15, p. 1301
	Yemenites:	Ezekiel 45:9–46:11, p. 1299
Shabbat HaGadol		Malachi 3:4–24, p. 1049

Pesaḥ Day 1		(Some begin with Joshua 3:5–7, p. 513) Joshua 5:2–6:1, p. 517, and 6:27, p. 521
Pesaḥ Day 2 (Diaspora)	Ashkenazim & Sepharadim:	II Kings 23:1–9, p. 927 and 21–25, p. 931
	Yemenites:	II Kings 22:1–7, p. 925 and 23:21–25, p. 931
Shabbat Ḥol HaMoed Pesaḥ	Ashkenazim & Sepharadim:	Ezekiel 37:1–14, p. 1275
	Yemenites:	Ezekiel 36:37–37:14, p. 1275
Pesaḥ Day 7		II Samuel 22:1–51, p. 773
Pesaḥ Day 8 (Diaspora)		Isaiah 10:32–12:6, p. 959
Shavuot Day 1	Ashkenazim & Sepharadim:	Ezekiel 1:1–28, p. 1193 and 3:12, p. 1197
	Yemenites:	Ezekiel 1:1–2:2, p. 1193 and 3:12, p. 1197
Shavuot Day 2 (Diaspora)		Habakkuk 2:20–3:19, p. 1375
Rosh HaShana Day 1		I Samuel 1:1–2:10, p. 639
Rosh HaShana Day 2		Jeremiah 31:1–19, p. 1155
Yom Kippur – Shaḥarit		Isaiah 57:14–58:14, p. 1035 (Yemenites add 59:20–21, p. 1039)
Yom Kippur – Minḥa		The Book of Jonah, p. 1353 and Micah 7:18–20, p. 1367
Sukkot Day 1	Ashkenazim & Sepharadim:	Zechariah 14:1–21, p. 1405
	Yemenites:	Zechariah 13:9–14:21, p. 1403
Sukkot Day 2 (Diaspora)	Ashkenazim & Sepharadim:	I Kings 8:2–21, p. 811
	Yemenites:	I Kings 7:51–8:21, p. 811
Shabbat Ḥol HaMoed Sukkot	Ashkenazim & Sepharadim:	Ezekiel 38:18–39:16, p. 1279
	Yemenites:	Ezekiel 38:1–23, p. 1279
Shemini Atzeret (Diaspora)	Ashkenazim:	I Kings 8:54–9:1, p. 817
	Sepharadim, Yemenites, & Minhag Anglia:	I Kings 8:54–66, p. 817
Simḥat Torah	Ashkenazim:	Joshua 1:1–18, p. 509
	Sepharadim & Yemenites:	Joshua 1:1–9, p. 509 (Yemenites add 6:27, p. 521)

BLESSINGS BEFORE AND AFTER READING THE TORAH

Before the Torah is read, the Oleh says:

בָּרְכוּ Bless the LORD, the blessed One.

Cong: Bless the LORD, the blessed One, for ever and all time.

Bless the LORD, the blessed One, for ever and all time.

Blessed are You, LORD our God, King of the Universe,
who has chosen us from all peoples
and has given us His Torah.
Blessed are You, LORD, Giver of the Torah.

After the reading, the Oleh says:

Blessed are You, LORD our God, King of the Universe,
who has given us (His Torah ,) the Torah of truth,
planting everlasting life in our midst.
Blessed are You, LORD, Giver of the Torah.

BLESSINGS BEFORE AND AFTER READING THE HAFTARA

Before reading the Haftara, the person called up for Maftir says:

בָּרוּךְ Blessed are You, LORD our God, King of the Universe,
who chose good prophets
and was pleased with their words, spoken in truth.
Blessed are You, LORD, who chose the Torah, His servant Moshe,
His people Israel, and the prophets of truth and righteousness.

After the Haftara, the person called up for Maftir says the following blessings:

(גֹּאֲלֵנוּ As for our redeemer, the LORD of hosts is His name,
the Holy One of Israel.)

בָּרוּךְ Blessed are You, LORD our God, King of the Universe,
Rock of all worlds, righteous for all generations,
the faithful God who says and does, speaks and fulfills,
all of whose words are truth and righteousness.
You are faithful, LORD our God,
and faithful are Your words,
not one of which returns unfulfilled,
for You, God, are a faithful (and compassionate) King.
Blessed are You, LORD, faithful in all His words.

ברכות התורה

Before קריאת התורה*, the* עולה *says:*

בָּרְכוּ אֶת יהוה הַמְבֹרָךְ.

קהל: בָּרוּךְ יהוה הַמְבֹרָךְ לְעוֹלָם וָעֶד.

בָּרוּךְ יהוה הַמְבֹרָךְ לְעוֹלָם וָעֶד.
בָּרוּךְ אַתָּה יהוה, אֱלֹהֵינוּ מֶלֶךְ הָעוֹלָם
אֲשֶׁר בָּחַר בָּנוּ מִכָּל הָעַמִּים וְנָתַן לָנוּ אֶת תּוֹרָתוֹ.
בָּרוּךְ אַתָּה יהוה, נוֹתֵן הַתּוֹרָה.

After קריאת התורה*, the* עולה *says:*

בָּרוּךְ אַתָּה יהוה אֱלֹהֵינוּ מֶלֶךְ הָעוֹלָם
אֲשֶׁר נָתַן לָנוּ (אֶת תּוֹרָתוֹ) תּוֹרַת אֱמֶת וְחַיֵּי עוֹלָם נָטַע בְּתוֹכֵנוּ.
בָּרוּךְ אַתָּה יהוה, נוֹתֵן הַתּוֹרָה.

ברכות ההפטרה

Before reading the הפטרה*, the person called up for* מפטיר *says:*

בָּרוּךְ אַתָּה יהוה אֱלֹהֵינוּ מֶלֶךְ הָעוֹלָם
אֲשֶׁר בָּחַר בִּנְבִיאִים טוֹבִים
וְרָצָה בְדִבְרֵיהֶם הַנֶּאֱמָרִים בֶּאֱמֶת.
בָּרוּךְ אַתָּה יהוה, הַבּוֹחֵר בַּתּוֹרָה וּבְמֹשֶׁה עַבְדּוֹ
וּבְיִשְׂרָאֵל עַמּוֹ וּבִנְבִיאֵי הָאֱמֶת וָצֶדֶק (וְהַצֶּדֶק).

After the הפטרה*, the person called up for* מפטיר *says the following blessings:*

(גֹּאֲלֵנוּ יהוה צְבָאוֹת שְׁמוֹ, קְדוֹשׁ יִשְׂרָאֵל:) ישעיה מז

בָּרוּךְ אַתָּה יהוה אֱלֹהֵינוּ מֶלֶךְ הָעוֹלָם
צוּר כָּל הָעוֹלָמִים, צַדִּיק בְּכָל הַדּוֹרוֹת
הָאֵל הַנֶּאֱמָן, הָאוֹמֵר וְעוֹשֶׂה, הַמְדַבֵּר וּמְקַיֵּם
שֶׁכָּל דְּבָרָיו אֱמֶת וָצֶדֶק.
נֶאֱמָן אַתָּה הוּא יהוה אֱלֹהֵינוּ וְנֶאֱמָנִים דְּבָרֶיךָ
וְדָבָר אֶחָד מִדְּבָרֶיךָ אָחוֹר לֹא יָשׁוּב רֵיקָם,
כִּי אֵל מֶלֶךְ נֶאֱמָן (וְרַחֲמָן) אָתָּה.
בָּרוּךְ אַתָּה יהוה, הָאֵל הַנֶּאֱמָן בְּכָל דְּבָרָיו.

רַחֵם Have compassion on Zion for it is the source of our life,
and save the one grieved in spirit swiftly in our days.
Blessed are You, Lord, who makes Zion rejoice in her children.

שַׂמְּחֵנוּ Grant us joy, Lord our God,
through Eliyahu the prophet Your servant,
and through the kingdom of the house of David Your anointed –
may he soon come and make our hearts glad.
May no stranger sit on his throne,
and may others not continue to inherit his glory,
for You promised him by Your holy name
that his light would never be extinguished.
Blessed are You, Lord, Shield of David.

On Shabbat, including Shabbat Ḥol HaMo'ed Pesaḥ, say:

עַל הַתּוֹרָה For the Torah, for Divine worship,
for the prophets, and for this Sabbath day
which You, Lord our God, have given us for holiness and rest,
honor and glory –
for all these we thank and bless You, Lord our God,
and may Your name be blessed by the mouth of all that lives,
continually, for ever and all time.
Blessed are You, Lord, who sanctifies the Sabbath. (Amen.)

On Yom Tov and on Shabbat Ḥol HaMo'ed Sukkot, say (adding on Shabbat the words in parentheses):

עַל הַתּוֹרָה For the Torah, for Divine worship, for the prophets,
(for this Sabbath day) and for this day of
On Pesaḥ: the Festival of Matzot
On Shavuot: the Festival of Shavuot
On Sukkot: the Festival of Sukkot
On Shemini Atzeret and Simḥat Torah: the Festival of Shemini Atzeret

which You, Lord our God, have given us (for holiness and rest), for joy and gladness,
honor and glory – for all these we thank and bless You, Lord our God,
and may Your name be blessed by the mouth of all that lives,
continually, for ever and all time.
Blessed are You, Lord, who sanctifies (the Sabbath), Israel and the festivals. (Amen.)

רַחֵם עַל צִיּוֹן כִּי הִיא בֵּית חַיֵּינוּ
וְלַעֲלוּבַת נֶפֶשׁ תּוֹשִׁיעַ בִּמְהֵרָה בְיָמֵינוּ.
בָּרוּךְ אַתָּה יהוה, מְשַׂמֵּחַ צִיּוֹן בְּבָנֶיהָ.
שַׂמְּחֵנוּ יהוה אֱלֹהֵינוּ בְּאֵלִיָּהוּ הַנָּבִיא עַבְדֶּךָ
וּבְמַלְכוּת בֵּית דָּוִד מְשִׁיחֶךָ
בִּמְהֵרָה יָבוֹא וְיָגֵל לִבֵּנוּ.
עַל כִּסְאוֹ לֹא יֵשֶׁב זָר, וְלֹא יִנְחֲלוּ עוֹד אֲחֵרִים אֶת כְּבוֹדוֹ
כִּי בְשֵׁם קָדְשְׁךָ נִשְׁבַּעְתָּ לּוֹ שֶׁלֹּא יִכְבֶּה נֵרוֹ לְעוֹלָם וָעֶד.
בָּרוּךְ אַתָּה יהוה, מָגֵן דָּוִד.

On שבת*, including* שבת חול המועד פסח*, say:*

עַל הַתּוֹרָה וְעַל הָעֲבוֹדָה וְעַל הַנְּבִיאִים וְעַל יוֹם הַשַּׁבָּת הַזֶּה
שֶׁנָּתַתָּ לָּנוּ יהוה אֱלֹהֵינוּ לִקְדֻשָּׁה וְלִמְנוּחָה, לְכָבוֹד וּלְתִפְאָרֶת.
עַל הַכֹּל יהוה אֱלֹהֵינוּ אֲנַחְנוּ מוֹדִים לָךְ וּמְבָרְכִים אוֹתָךְ.
יִתְבָּרַךְ שִׁמְךָ בְּפִי כָּל חַי תָּמִיד לְעוֹלָם וָעֶד.
בָּרוּךְ אַתָּה יהוה, מְקַדֵּשׁ הַשַּׁבָּת. (אָמֵן.)

On יום טוב *and on* שבת חול המועד סוכות*, say (adding on* שבת *the words in parentheses):*

עַל הַתּוֹרָה וְעַל הָעֲבוֹדָה וְעַל הַנְּבִיאִים (בשבת: וְעַל יוֹם הַשַּׁבָּת הַזֶּה), וְעַל יוֹם

בפסח: חַג הַמַּצּוֹת הַזֶּה
בשבועות: חַג הַשָּׁבוּעוֹת הַזֶּה
בסוכות: חַג הַסֻּכּוֹת הַזֶּה
בשמיני עצרת ובש״ת: (הַ)שְּׁמִינִי חַג (הָ)עֲצֶרֶת הַזֶּה

שֶׁנָּתַתָּ לָּנוּ, יהוה אֱלֹהֵינוּ (בשבת: לִקְדֻשָּׁה וְלִמְנוּחָה) לְשָׂשׂוֹן וּלְשִׂמְחָה
לְכָבוֹד וּלְתִפְאָרֶת. עַל הַכֹּל יהוה אֱלֹהֵינוּ אֲנַחְנוּ מוֹדִים לָךְ וּמְבָרְכִים אוֹתָךְ.
יִתְבָּרַךְ שִׁמְךָ בְּפִי כָּל חַי תָּמִיד לְעוֹלָם וָעֶד.
בָּרוּךְ אַתָּה יהוה, מְקַדֵּשׁ (בשבת: הַשַּׁבָּת וְ)יִשְׂרָאֵל וְהַזְּמַנִּים. (אָמֵן.)

CANTILLATION NAMES AND MARKS FOR TORAH READING (*TE'AMIM*)

In addition to determining the melody for reading the verses, the *te'amim* serve to break them into their constituent clauses to aid understanding, much like punctuation. As with syntax and punctuation in any language, the *te'amim* follow a strict and complex set of rules governing their order and usage. The *te'amim* presented below roughly follow the order in which they might appear in a hypothetical verse (although no sound verse could contain every *taam* exactly once). The *te'amim* are presented three times to convey the names given them by Ashkenazim, Sepharadim, and Yemenites.

Ashkenazim

זַרְקָא֮ סֶגּוֹל֒ רְבִ֗יעַ מַהְפַּ֤ךְ פַּשְׁטָא֙ יְ֚תִיב זָקֵף־קָטֹ֔ן זָקֵף־
גָּד֕וֹל מֵרְכָ֥א טִפְּחָ֖א מֻנַּ֣ח אֶתְנַחְתָּ֑א פָּזֵ֡ר תְּ֠לִישָא־גְדוֹלָה
תְּלִישָא־קְטַנָּה֩ קַדְמָ֨א וְאַזְלָ֜א גֵּרְשַׁ֞יִם דַּרְגָּ֧א תְּבִ֛יר סוֹף־פָּסוּק׃

Sepharadim

זַרְקָא֮ שׁוֹפָר־הוֹלֵךְ סְגוֹלְתָּא֒ פָּזֵר־גָּדוֹל תְּ֠לִשָׁא
תִּילְשָׁא֩ אַזְלָא גֵּרִ֜ישׁ רָבִ֗יעַ שְׁנֵי־גֵרְשִׁין֞ דַּרְגָּ֧א תְּבִ֛יר
מַאֲרִ֥יךְ טַרְחָ֖א אַתְנָ֑ח שׁוֹפָר־מְהֻפָּ֤ךְ קַדְמָא֙ יְ֚תִיב
זָקֵף־קָטֹ֔ן זָקֵף־גָּד֕וֹל סוֹף־פָּסוּק׃

Yemenites

זַרְקָא֮ שׁוֹפָר־הוֹלֵךְ סְגֻלְתָּא֒ פָּזֵ֡ר תְּ֠לִשָׁא־יָמִין
תִּלְשָׁא־שְׂמֹאל֩ אַזֵּ֨ל וְאָ֜תֵי רְבִ֗יעַ תְּרֵין־טַרְסִין֞ דַּרְגָּ֧א תְּבִ֛יר
מַאֲרְכָ֥ה טִפְּחָ֖א אַתְנָחָ֑א שׁוֹפָר־הָפוּ֤ךְ פַּשְׁטָא֙ יְ֚תִיב
זָקֵף־קָטֹ֔ן זָקֵף־גָּד֕וֹל סוֹף־פָּסוּק׃

The following *te'amim* appear only rarely:

שַׁלְשֶׁ֓לֶת ׀ גַּלְגַּ֪ל קַרְנֵי־פָרָ֟ה מֵרְכָא־כְפוּלָ֦ה

The following signs are not *te'amim*, but aid in proper reading:

מֶֽתֶג מַקַּף־ פְּסִיק ׀

Te'amim for the books of Psalms, Proverbs, and Job – טעמי אמ״ת

גַּלְגַּל פָּזֵר מַהְפַּךְ־לְגַרְמֵהּ ׀ צִנּוֹר רְבִיעַ־קָטֹן
אֶתְנַח־הָפוּךְ עוֹלֶה וְיוֹרֵד שַׁלְשֶׁלֶת־קְטַנָּה צִנּוֹרִית מַהְפַּךְ אַזְלָא־לְגַרְמֵהּ ׀
עִלּוּי רְבִיעַ־גָּדוֹל דְּחִי אֶתְנַחְתָּא שַׁלְשֶׁלֶת־גְּדוֹלָה ׀
מֵרְכָא רְבִיעַ־מֻגְרָשׁ קַדְמָא טַרְחָא מֻנַּח סִלּוּק׃

תורה
TORAH

בראשית BERESHIT / GENESIS

שמות SHEMOT / EXODUS

ויקרא VAYIKRA / LEVITICUS

במדבר BEMIDBAR / NUMBERS

דברים DEVARIM / DEUTERONOMY

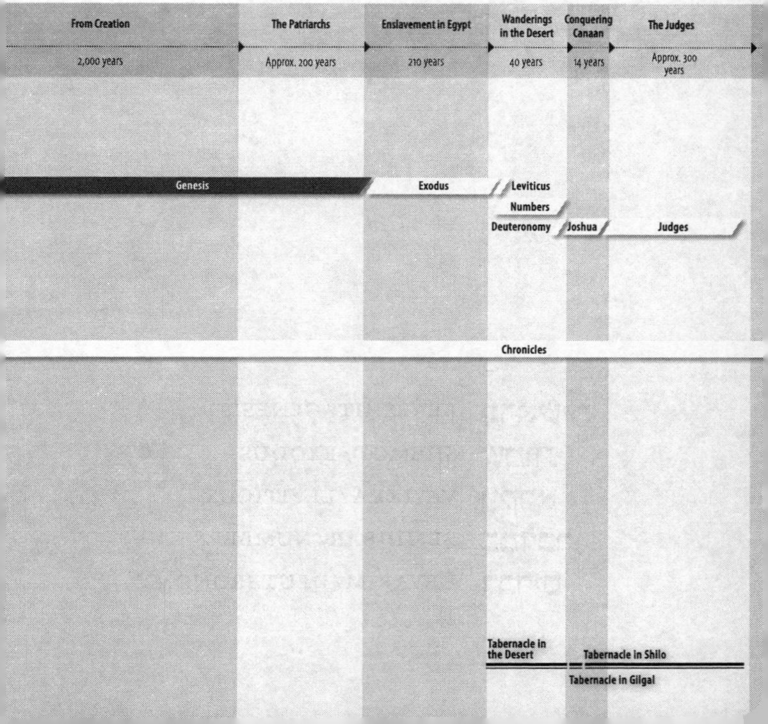
From Creation
2,000 years
The Patriarchs
Approx. 200 years
Enslavement in Egypt
210 years
Wanderings in the Desert
40 years
Conquering Canaan
14 years
The Judges
Approx. 300 years
Genesis
Exodus
Leviticus
Numbers
Deuteronomy
Joshua
Judges
Chronicles
Tabernacle in the Desert
Tabernacle in Shilo
Tabernacle in Gilgal

בראשית

BERESHIT / GENESIS

GENESIS	Beginning of humanity – from Adam to Avraham	Avraham	Yitzḥak	Yaakov	Yosef and his brothers – the descent to Egypt
	Chs. 1–11	12:1–25:18	25:19–26:34	27–36	37–50
	2,309 years				

BERESHIT

1 1 2 When God began creating heaven and earth, the earth was void and desolate,
there was darkness on the face of the deep, and the spirit of God moved over
3 4 the waters. God said, "Let there be light." And there was light. God saw the
5 light: it was good; and God separated the light from the darkness. And God
called the light "day," and the darkness He called "night." There was evening,
and there was morning – one day.
6 Then God said, "Let an expanse stretch through the water; let it separate water
7 from water." So God made the expanse, and it separated the water beneath
8 the expanse from the water above. And so it was. God called the expanse
"heavens." There was evening, and there was morning – a second day.
9 Then God said, "Let the water beneath the heavens be gathered to one place,
10 and let dry ground appear." And so it was. God called the dry ground "earth,"
11 and the gathered waters He called "seas." And God saw: it was good. Then
God said, "Let the earth produce vegetation: seed-bearing plants and trees of
12 all the kinds on earth that grow seed-bearing fruit." And so it was. The earth
produced vegetation: plants bearing seeds, each of its kind, and trees bearing
13 fruit containing seeds, each of its kind. And God saw: it was good. There was
evening, and there was morning – a third day.
14 Then God said, "Let there be lights in the heavens' expanse to separate day
15 from night and to serve for signs and seasons, days and years. They shall be
16 lights in the heavens' expanse, shining upon the earth." And so it was. God
made the two great lights – the greater light to rule by day and the lesser light
17 to rule by night – and the stars. God set them in the heavens' expanse to
18 shine upon the earth, to rule by day and by night and to separate light from
19 darkness. And God saw that it was good. There was evening, and there was
morning – a fourth day.
20 Then God said, "Let the water teem with swarms of living creatures, and let
21 birds fly over the earth across the heavens' expanse." So God created the great
sea creatures, and all the kinds of crawling, living things that swarm in the
water, and all the kinds of winged, flying creatures. And God saw that it was
22 good. God blessed them, saying: "Be fertile and multiply and fill the waters
23 of the seas, and let flying creatures multiply on earth." There was evening, and
there was morning – a fifth day.
24 Then God said, "Let the land produce every kind of living thing: all the
different species of cattle, crawling things and wild animals of the earth."
25 And so it was. God made the different kinds of wild animals of the earth,

א

א ב בְּרֵאשִׁית בָּרָא אֱלֹהִים אֵת הַשָּׁמַיִם וְאֵת הָאָרֶץ׃ וְהָאָרֶץ הָיְתָה תֹהוּ
וָבֹהוּ וְחֹשֶׁךְ עַל־פְּנֵי תְהוֹם וְרוּחַ אֱלֹהִים מְרַחֶפֶת עַל־פְּנֵי הַמָּיִם׃
ג ד וַיֹּאמֶר אֱלֹהִים יְהִי־אוֹר וַיְהִי־אוֹר׃ וַיַּרְא אֱלֹהִים אֶת־הָאוֹר כִּי־טוֹב
ה וַיַּבְדֵּל אֱלֹהִים בֵּין הָאוֹר וּבֵין הַחֹשֶׁךְ׃ וַיִּקְרָא אֱלֹהִים ׀ לָאוֹר יוֹם
וְלַחֹשֶׁךְ קָרָא לָיְלָה וַיְהִי־עֶרֶב וַיְהִי־בֹקֶר יוֹם אֶחָד׃

ו וַיֹּאמֶר אֱלֹהִים יְהִי רָקִיעַ בְּתוֹךְ הַמָּיִם וִיהִי מַבְדִּיל בֵּין מַיִם לָמָיִם׃
ז וַיַּעַשׂ אֱלֹהִים אֶת־הָרָקִיעַ וַיַּבְדֵּל בֵּין הַמַּיִם אֲשֶׁר מִתַּחַת לָרָקִיעַ
ח וּבֵין הַמַּיִם אֲשֶׁר מֵעַל לָרָקִיעַ וַיְהִי־כֵן׃ וַיִּקְרָא אֱלֹהִים לָרָקִיעַ שָׁמָיִם
וַיְהִי־עֶרֶב וַיְהִי־בֹקֶר יוֹם שֵׁנִי׃

ט וַיֹּאמֶר אֱלֹהִים יִקָּווּ הַמַּיִם מִתַּחַת הַשָּׁמַיִם אֶל־מָקוֹם אֶחָד וְתֵרָאֶה
י הַיַּבָּשָׁה וַיְהִי־כֵן׃ וַיִּקְרָא אֱלֹהִים ׀ לַיַּבָּשָׁה אֶרֶץ וּלְמִקְוֵה הַמַּיִם קָרָא
יא יַמִּים וַיַּרְא אֱלֹהִים כִּי־טוֹב׃ וַיֹּאמֶר אֱלֹהִים תַּדְשֵׁא הָאָרֶץ דֶּשֶׁא עֵשֶׂב
מַזְרִיעַ זֶרַע עֵץ פְּרִי עֹשֶׂה פְּרִי לְמִינוֹ אֲשֶׁר זַרְעוֹ־בוֹ עַל־הָאָרֶץ וַיְהִי־
יב כֵן׃ וַתּוֹצֵא הָאָרֶץ דֶּשֶׁא עֵשֶׂב מַזְרִיעַ זֶרַע לְמִינֵהוּ וְעֵץ עֹשֶׂה־פְּרִי
יג אֲשֶׁר זַרְעוֹ־בוֹ לְמִינֵהוּ וַיַּרְא אֱלֹהִים כִּי־טוֹב׃ וַיְהִי־עֶרֶב וַיְהִי־בֹקֶר
יוֹם שְׁלִישִׁי׃

יד וַיֹּאמֶר אֱלֹהִים יְהִי מְאֹרֹת בִּרְקִיעַ הַשָּׁמַיִם לְהַבְדִּיל בֵּין הַיּוֹם וּבֵין
טו הַלָּיְלָה וְהָיוּ לְאֹתֹת וּלְמוֹעֲדִים וּלְיָמִים וְשָׁנִים׃ וְהָיוּ לִמְאוֹרֹת בִּרְקִיעַ
טז הַשָּׁמַיִם לְהָאִיר עַל־הָאָרֶץ וַיְהִי־כֵן׃ וַיַּעַשׂ אֱלֹהִים אֶת־שְׁנֵי הַמְּאֹרֹת
הַגְּדֹלִים אֶת־הַמָּאוֹר הַגָּדֹל לְמֶמְשֶׁלֶת הַיּוֹם וְאֶת־הַמָּאוֹר הַקָּטֹן
יז לְמֶמְשֶׁלֶת הַלַּיְלָה וְאֵת הַכּוֹכָבִים׃ וַיִּתֵּן אֹתָם אֱלֹהִים בִּרְקִיעַ
יח הַשָּׁמָיִם לְהָאִיר עַל־הָאָרֶץ׃ וְלִמְשֹׁל בַּיּוֹם וּבַלַּיְלָה וּלְהַבְדִּיל בֵּין
יט הָאוֹר וּבֵין הַחֹשֶׁךְ וַיַּרְא אֱלֹהִים כִּי־טוֹב׃ וַיְהִי־עֶרֶב וַיְהִי־בֹקֶר יוֹם
רְבִיעִי׃

כ וַיֹּאמֶר אֱלֹהִים יִשְׁרְצוּ הַמַּיִם שֶׁרֶץ נֶפֶשׁ חַיָּה וְעוֹף יְעוֹפֵף עַל־הָאָרֶץ
כא עַל־פְּנֵי רְקִיעַ הַשָּׁמָיִם׃ וַיִּבְרָא אֱלֹהִים אֶת־הַתַּנִּינִם הַגְּדֹלִים וְאֵת
כָּל־נֶפֶשׁ הַחַיָּה ׀ הָרֹמֶשֶׂת אֲשֶׁר שָׁרְצוּ הַמַּיִם לְמִינֵהֶם וְאֵת כָּל־עוֹף
כב כָּנָף לְמִינֵהוּ וַיַּרְא אֱלֹהִים כִּי־טוֹב׃ וַיְבָרֶךְ אֹתָם אֱלֹהִים לֵאמֹר פְּרוּ
כג וּרְבוּ וּמִלְאוּ אֶת־הַמַּיִם בַּיַּמִּים וְהָעוֹף יִרֶב בָּאָרֶץ׃ וַיְהִי־עֶרֶב וַיְהִי־
בֹקֶר יוֹם חֲמִישִׁי׃

כד וַיֹּאמֶר אֱלֹהִים תּוֹצֵא הָאָרֶץ נֶפֶשׁ חַיָּה לְמִינָהּ בְּהֵמָה וָרֶמֶשׂ וְחַיְתוֹ־
כה אֶרֶץ לְמִינָהּ וַיְהִי־כֵן׃ וַיַּעַשׂ אֱלֹהִים אֶת־חַיַּת הָאָרֶץ לְמִינָהּ וְאֶת־

and cattle, and all the species of creature that creep upon land. And God saw
26 that it was good. Then God said, "Let us make humankind in our image, our
likeness, that they may rule over the fish of the sea and the flying creatures of
the heavens, the cattle and all the earth, and every living creature that moves
27 upon the earth." So God created humankind in His image: in the image of
28 God He created him; male and female He created them. God blessed them,
saying, "Be fertile and multiply. Fill the earth and subdue it. Rule over the
fish of the sea, and the flying creatures of the heavens, and every living thing
29 that moves upon the earth." Then God said, "I give you all these seed-bearing
plants on the face of the earth and every tree with seed-bearing fruit. They
30 shall be yours to eat. And to all the beasts of the earth and birds of the heavens
and everything that crawls over the earth and has within it living spirit – I
31 give every green plant for food." And so it was. Then God saw all that He had
made: and it was very good. There was evening, and there was morning – the
sixth day.

2 1 So the heavens and the earth were finished, and all their vast array. On the
2 seventh day God finished the work that He had done, and on the seventh
3 day He rested from all the work that He had done. God blessed the seventh
day and sanctified it, because on it He rested from all His work, from all that
God had created and done.

4 This is the story of the heavens and the earth when they were created, on the
5 day the Lord God made earth and heaven. No shrub of the field yet grew on
earth, and no plant had yet sprouted, for the Lord God had not yet brought
6 rain upon the earth, and there was no one to work the land. A mist would
7 rise up from the earth and water all the face of the land. Then the Lord God
formed man from the dust of the land[1] and breathed the breath of life into
8 his nostrils, and the man became a living being. The Lord God planted a
9 garden in Eden, in the east, and there he put the man He had formed. And
from the land, the Lord God caused all kinds of trees to grow, pleasant to
look at and good to eat from, and the Tree of Life stood in the middle of
10 the garden, and the Tree of Knowledge of good and evil. A river flows from
11 Eden to water this garden, and from there divides into four headwaters. The
name of the first is Pishon. It surrounds the land of Ḥavila, where there is
12 gold. And the gold of that land is good; bdellium and rock crystal are there
13 also. The name of the second river is Giḥon; it is the one that surrounds the
14 land of Kush. The name of the third river is the Tigris, and it flows to the east
15 of Assyria. The fourth river is the Euphrates. The Lord God took the man
16 and placed him in the Garden of Eden to work it and safeguard it. And the
Lord God commanded the man: "You are free to eat from any tree in the
17 garden. But the Tree of Knowledge of good and evil – you may not eat from

1 | The Hebrew *adam* (man) resonates with *adama* (land).

הַבְּהֵמָה לְמִינָהּ וְאֵת כָּל־רֶמֶשׂ הָאֲדָמָה לְמִינֵהוּ וַיַּרְא אֱלֹהִים כִּי־טוֹב:
כו וַיֹּאמֶר אֱלֹהִים נַעֲשֶׂה אָדָם בְּצַלְמֵנוּ כִּדְמוּתֵנוּ וְיִרְדּוּ בִדְגַת הַיָּם וּבְעוֹף
הַשָּׁמַיִם וּבַבְּהֵמָה וּבְכָל־הָאָרֶץ וּבְכָל־הָרֶמֶשׂ הָרֹמֵשׂ עַל־הָאָרֶץ:
כז וַיִּבְרָא אֱלֹהִים ׀ אֶת־הָאָדָם בְּצַלְמוֹ בְּצֶלֶם אֱלֹהִים בָּרָא אֹתוֹ זָכָר
כח וּנְקֵבָה בָּרָא אֹתָם: וַיְבָרֶךְ אֹתָם אֱלֹהִים וַיֹּאמֶר לָהֶם אֱלֹהִים פְּרוּ וּרְבוּ
וּמִלְאוּ אֶת־הָאָרֶץ וְכִבְשֻׁהָ וּרְדוּ בִּדְגַת הַיָּם וּבְעוֹף הַשָּׁמַיִם וּבְכָל־חַיָּה
כט הָרֹמֶשֶׂת עַל־הָאָרֶץ: וַיֹּאמֶר אֱלֹהִים הִנֵּה נָתַתִּי לָכֶם אֶת־כָּל־עֵשֶׂב ׀
זֹרֵעַ זֶרַע אֲשֶׁר עַל־פְּנֵי כָל־הָאָרֶץ וְאֶת־כָּל־הָעֵץ אֲשֶׁר־בּוֹ פְרִי־עֵץ
ל זֹרֵעַ זָרַע לָכֶם יִהְיֶה לְאָכְלָה: וּלְכָל־חַיַּת הָאָרֶץ וּלְכָל־עוֹף הַשָּׁמַיִם
וּלְכֹל ׀ רוֹמֵשׂ עַל־הָאָרֶץ אֲשֶׁר־בּוֹ נֶפֶשׁ חַיָּה אֶת־כָּל־יֶרֶק עֵשֶׂב לְאָכְלָה
לא וַיְהִי־כֵן: וַיַּרְא אֱלֹהִים אֶת־כָּל־אֲשֶׁר עָשָׂה וְהִנֵּה־טוֹב מְאֹד וַיְהִי־עֶרֶב
וַיְהִי־בֹקֶר יוֹם הַשִּׁשִּׁי:
ב א ב וַיְכֻלּוּ הַשָּׁמַיִם וְהָאָרֶץ וְכָל־צְבָאָם: וַיְכַל אֱלֹהִים בַּיּוֹם הַשְּׁבִיעִי
מְלַאכְתּוֹ אֲשֶׁר עָשָׂה וַיִּשְׁבֹּת בַּיּוֹם הַשְּׁבִיעִי מִכָּל־מְלַאכְתּוֹ אֲשֶׁר
ג עָשָׂה: וַיְבָרֶךְ אֱלֹהִים אֶת־יוֹם הַשְּׁבִיעִי וַיְקַדֵּשׁ אֹתוֹ כִּי בוֹ שָׁבַת מִכָּל־
מְלַאכְתּוֹ אֲשֶׁר־בָּרָא אֱלֹהִים לַעֲשׂוֹת:
ד אֵלֶּה תוֹלְדוֹת הַשָּׁמַיִם וְהָאָרֶץ בְּהִבָּרְאָם בְּיוֹם עֲשׂוֹת יְהוָה אֱלֹהִים ב שני
ה אֶרֶץ וְשָׁמָיִם: וְכֹל ׀ שִׂיחַ הַשָּׂדֶה טֶרֶם יִהְיֶה בָאָרֶץ וְכָל־עֵשֶׂב הַשָּׂדֶה
טֶרֶם יִצְמָח כִּי לֹא הִמְטִיר יְהוָה אֱלֹהִים עַל־הָאָרֶץ וְאָדָם אַיִן לַעֲבֹד
ו אֶת־הָאֲדָמָה: וְאֵד יַעֲלֶה מִן־הָאָרֶץ וְהִשְׁקָה אֶת־כָּל־פְּנֵי־הָאֲדָמָה:
ז וַיִּיצֶר יְהוָה אֱלֹהִים אֶת־הָאָדָם עָפָר מִן־הָאֲדָמָה וַיִּפַּח בְּאַפָּיו נִשְׁמַת
ח חַיִּים וַיְהִי הָאָדָם לְנֶפֶשׁ חַיָּה: וַיִּטַּע יְהוָה אֱלֹהִים גַּן בְּעֵדֶן מִקֶּדֶם וַיָּשֶׂם
ט שָׁם אֶת־הָאָדָם אֲשֶׁר יָצָר: וַיַּצְמַח יְהוָה אֱלֹהִים מִן־הָאֲדָמָה כָּל־
עֵץ נֶחְמָד לְמַרְאֶה וְטוֹב לְמַאֲכָל וְעֵץ הַחַיִּים בְּתוֹךְ הַגָּן וְעֵץ הַדַּעַת
י טוֹב וָרָע: וְנָהָר יֹצֵא מֵעֵדֶן לְהַשְׁקוֹת אֶת־הַגָּן וּמִשָּׁם יִפָּרֵד וְהָיָה
יא לְאַרְבָּעָה רָאשִׁים: שֵׁם הָאֶחָד פִּישׁוֹן הוּא הַסֹּבֵב אֵת כָּל־אֶרֶץ הַחֲוִילָה
יב אֲשֶׁר־שָׁם הַזָּהָב: וּזֲהַב הָאָרֶץ הַהִוא טוֹב שָׁם הַבְּדֹלַח וְאֶבֶן הַשֹּׁהַם:
יג יד וְשֵׁם־הַנָּהָר הַשֵּׁנִי גִּיחוֹן הוּא הַסּוֹבֵב אֵת כָּל־אֶרֶץ כּוּשׁ: וְשֵׁם הַנָּהָר
הַשְּׁלִישִׁי חִדֶּקֶל הוּא הַהֹלֵךְ קִדְמַת אַשּׁוּר וְהַנָּהָר הָרְבִיעִי הוּא פְרָת:
טו וַיִּקַּח יְהוָה אֱלֹהִים אֶת־הָאָדָם וַיַּנִּחֵהוּ בְגַן־עֵדֶן לְעָבְדָהּ וּלְשָׁמְרָהּ:
טז יז וַיְצַו יְהוָה אֱלֹהִים עַל־הָאָדָם לֵאמֹר מִכֹּל עֵץ־הַגָּן אָכֹל תֹּאכֵל: וּמֵעֵץ
הַדַּעַת טוֹב וָרָע לֹא תֹאכַל מִמֶּנּוּ כִּי בְּיוֹם אֲכָלְךָ מִמֶּנּוּ מוֹת תָּמוּת:

18 that, for on the day you eat of it, you shall die." Then the LORD God said, "It
19 is not good for man to be alone. I will make a fitting partner for him." The
LORD God formed all the wild animals, and all the birds of the heavens, out
of the land. He brought them to the man to see what he would call them, and
20 whatever he called each living thing, that became its name. So the man gave
names to all the animals, the birds of the heavens, and all the wild creatures.
21 But he found no fitting partner for himself. Then the LORD God made the
man fall into a deep sleep, and while he was sleeping He took one of his ribs
22 and closed the flesh in its place. And the LORD God built the rib He had
23 taken from the man into a woman. He brought her to the man. And the
man said: "This, at last is bone of my bones and flesh of my flesh. This shall
24 be called Woman, for from Man was this one taken."[2] That is why a man
leaves his father and mother and cleaves to his wife and they become one
25 flesh. The man and his wife were both naked, but they were not ashamed.
3 1 The serpent was the slyest of all the wild animals the LORD God had made.
"Did God say," it asked the woman, "that you must not eat from any tree in
2 the garden?" The woman told the serpent, "We may eat the fruit of the trees
3 in the garden, but God did say, 'You must not eat fruit from the tree in the
4 middle of the garden, and you must not touch it, or you will die." But the
5 serpent told the woman, "You will not die; God knows that on the day you
eat from it your eyes will be opened, and you will be like God, knowing good
6 and evil." The woman saw that the tree was ripe for eating, enticing to the
eyes, and desirable too for granting insight. She took some of its fruit and
7 ate, and she gave some to her husband and he too ate. The eyes of both of
them were opened, and they realized that they were naked. So they sewed
8 fig leaves together and made coverings for themselves. They heard the sound
of the LORD God walking in the garden in the cool of the day, and the man
9 and his wife hid from the LORD God among the trees of the garden. The
10 LORD God called to the man: "Where are you?" He answered, "I heard
Your voice in the garden, and I was afraid, because I was naked. So I hid."
11 "Who told you," God asked, "that you were naked? Have you eaten from the
12 tree from which I commanded you not to eat?" The man said, "The woman
13 You put here with me – she gave me fruit from the tree and I ate." Then the
LORD God said to the woman, "What is this you have done?" The woman
14 said, "The serpent beguiled me and I ate." And the LORD God said to the
serpent, "Because you have done this, you are accursed more than all the
animals and all wild beasts. You will creep on your belly and dust will you
15 eat all the days of your life. I will plant hostility between you and the woman,
between your children and hers. And man will strike your head, and you will
16 strike his heel." To the woman He said, "I will make your pain in
pregnancy searingly great; in sorrow will you bear children. You will long for

2 | *Isha* (woman) resonates with *ish* (man).

יח וַיֹּאמֶר יְהוָה אֱלֹהִים לֹא־טוֹב הֱיוֹת הָאָדָם לְבַדּוֹ אֶעֱשֶׂה־לּוֹ עֵזֶר
יט כְּנֶגְדּוֹ: וַיִּצֶר יְהוָה אֱלֹהִים מִן־הָאֲדָמָה כָּל־חַיַּת הַשָּׂדֶה וְאֵת כָּל־עוֹף
הַשָּׁמַיִם וַיָּבֵא אֶל־הָאָדָם לִרְאוֹת מַה־יִּקְרָא־לוֹ וְכֹל אֲשֶׁר יִקְרָא־לוֹ
כ הָאָדָם נֶפֶשׁ חַיָּה הוּא שְׁמוֹ: וַיִּקְרָא הָאָדָם שֵׁמוֹת לְכָל־הַבְּהֵמָה שלישי
כא וּלְעוֹף הַשָּׁמַיִם וּלְכֹל חַיַּת הַשָּׂדֶה וּלְאָדָם לֹא־מָצָא עֵזֶר כְּנֶגְדּוֹ: וַיַּפֵּל
יְהוָה אֱלֹהִים ׀ תַּרְדֵּמָה עַל־הָאָדָם וַיִּישָׁן וַיִּקַּח אַחַת מִצַּלְעֹתָיו וַיִּסְגֹּר
כב בָּשָׂר תַּחְתֶּנָּה: וַיִּבֶן יְהוָה אֱלֹהִים ׀ אֶת־הַצֵּלָע אֲשֶׁר־לָקַח מִן־הָאָדָם
כג לְאִשָּׁה וַיְבִאֶהָ אֶל־הָאָדָם: וַיֹּאמֶר הָאָדָם זֹאת הַפַּעַם עֶצֶם מֵעֲצָמַי
כד וּבָשָׂר מִבְּשָׂרִי לְזֹאת יִקָּרֵא אִשָּׁה כִּי מֵאִישׁ לֻקְחָה־זֹּאת: עַל־כֵּן
יַעֲזָב־אִישׁ אֶת־אָבִיו וְאֶת־אִמּוֹ וְדָבַק בְּאִשְׁתּוֹ וְהָיוּ לְבָשָׂר אֶחָד:
כה ג א וַיִּהְיוּ שְׁנֵיהֶם עֲרוּמִּים הָאָדָם וְאִשְׁתּוֹ וְלֹא יִתְבֹּשָׁשׁוּ: וְהַנָּחָשׁ הָיָה
עָרוּם מִכֹּל חַיַּת הַשָּׂדֶה אֲשֶׁר עָשָׂה יְהוָה אֱלֹהִים וַיֹּאמֶר אֶל־הָאִשָּׁה
ב אַף כִּי־אָמַר אֱלֹהִים לֹא תֹאכְלוּ מִכֹּל עֵץ הַגָּן: וַתֹּאמֶר הָאִשָּׁה אֶל־
ג הַנָּחָשׁ מִפְּרִי עֵץ־הַגָּן נֹאכֵל: וּמִפְּרִי הָעֵץ אֲשֶׁר בְּתוֹךְ־הַגָּן אָמַר
ד אֱלֹהִים לֹא תֹאכְלוּ מִמֶּנּוּ וְלֹא תִגְּעוּ בּוֹ פֶּן תְּמֻתוּן: וַיֹּאמֶר הַנָּחָשׁ
ה אֶל־הָאִשָּׁה לֹא־מוֹת תְּמֻתוּן: כִּי יֹדֵעַ אֱלֹהִים כִּי בְּיוֹם אֲכָלְכֶם מִמֶּנּוּ
ו וְנִפְקְחוּ עֵינֵיכֶם וִהְיִיתֶם כֵּאלֹהִים יֹדְעֵי טוֹב וָרָע: וַתֵּרֶא הָאִשָּׁה כִּי
טוֹב הָעֵץ לְמַאֲכָל וְכִי תַאֲוָה־הוּא לָעֵינַיִם וְנֶחְמָד הָעֵץ לְהַשְׂכִּיל
ז וַתִּקַּח מִפִּרְיוֹ וַתֹּאכַל וַתִּתֵּן גַּם־לְאִישָׁהּ עִמָּהּ וַיֹּאכַל: וַתִּפָּקַחְנָה
עֵינֵי שְׁנֵיהֶם וַיֵּדְעוּ כִּי עֵירֻמִּם הֵם וַיִּתְפְּרוּ עֲלֵה תְאֵנָה וַיַּעֲשׂוּ לָהֶם
ח חֲגֹרֹת: וַיִּשְׁמְעוּ אֶת־קוֹל יְהוָה אֱלֹהִים מִתְהַלֵּךְ בַּגָּן לְרוּחַ הַיּוֹם
ט וַיִּתְחַבֵּא הָאָדָם וְאִשְׁתּוֹ מִפְּנֵי יְהוָה אֱלֹהִים בְּתוֹךְ עֵץ הַגָּן: וַיִּקְרָא
י יְהוָה אֱלֹהִים אֶל־הָאָדָם וַיֹּאמֶר לוֹ אַיֶּכָּה: וַיֹּאמֶר אֶת־קֹלְךָ שָׁמַעְתִּי
יא בַּגָּן וָאִירָא כִּי־עֵירֹם אָנֹכִי וָאֵחָבֵא: וַיֹּאמֶר מִי הִגִּיד לְךָ כִּי עֵירֹם אָתָּה
יב הֲמִן־הָעֵץ אֲשֶׁר צִוִּיתִיךָ לְבִלְתִּי אֲכָל־מִמֶּנּוּ אָכָלְתָּ: וַיֹּאמֶר הָאָדָם
יג הָאִשָּׁה אֲשֶׁר נָתַתָּה עִמָּדִי הִוא נָתְנָה־לִּי מִן־הָעֵץ וָאֹכֵל: וַיֹּאמֶר
יְהוָה אֱלֹהִים לָאִשָּׁה מַה־זֹּאת עָשִׂית וַתֹּאמֶר הָאִשָּׁה הַנָּחָשׁ הִשִּׁיאַנִי
יד וָאֹכֵל: וַיֹּאמֶר יְהוָה אֱלֹהִים ׀ אֶל־הַנָּחָשׁ כִּי עָשִׂיתָ זֹּאת אָרוּר אַתָּה
מִכָּל־הַבְּהֵמָה וּמִכֹּל חַיַּת הַשָּׂדֶה עַל־גְּחֹנְךָ תֵלֵךְ וְעָפָר תֹּאכַל כָּל־
טו יְמֵי חַיֶּיךָ: וְאֵיבָה ׀ אָשִׁית בֵּינְךָ וּבֵין הָאִשָּׁה וּבֵין זַרְעֲךָ וּבֵין זַרְעָהּ
טז הוּא יְשׁוּפְךָ רֹאשׁ וְאַתָּה תְּשׁוּפֶנּוּ עָקֵב: אֶל־הָאִשָּׁה
אָמַר הַרְבָּה אַרְבֶּה עִצְּבוֹנֵךְ וְהֵרֹנֵךְ בְּעֶצֶב תֵּלְדִי בָנִים וְאֶל־אִישֵׁךְ

17 your husband, but he will rule over you." To Adam[3] He said, "Because
you listened to your wife and ate of the tree from which I commanded you not
to eat – cursed will be the land on your account. By painful toil you will eat
18 from it all the days of your life. It will sprout thorns and thistles for you, and
19 you shall eat plants of the field. By the sweat of your brow will you eat bread
until you return to the land, for from there you were taken. You are dust, and
20 you will return to dust." Then the man named his wife Ḥava, for she would
21 become the mother of all life.[4] Then the LORD God made garments of skins
for Adam and his wife and clothed them.
22 The LORD God then said, "Now that man has become like one of us, knowing
good and evil, he must not be allowed to reach out his hand and take also
23 from the Tree of Life, eat, and live forever." So the LORD God sent him
away from the Garden of Eden to work the land from which he had been
24 taken. He drove out the man, and east of the Garden of Eden He placed the
cherubim and the flaming, whirling sword to guard the way to the Tree of
4 1 Life. The man knew[5] his wife Ḥava, and she conceived and gave
2 birth to Kayin. She said, "With the LORD's help I have made a man."[6] Later,
she gave birth to his brother Hevel.[7] Hevel became a shepherd, while Kayin
3 was a worker of the land. Time passed, and Kayin brought fruit of the land as
4 an offering to the LORD. Hevel too brought an offering: fat portions from the
firstborn of his flock. The LORD looked favorably on Hevel and his offering,
5 but upon Kayin and his offering He did not look with favor. Kayin became
6 very angry, and his face downcast. The LORD said to Kayin: "Why are you
7 angry; why is your face downcast? If you act well, will you not be uplifted? If
you fail to act well, sin is crouching at the door; it longs to have you, but you
8 must rule over it." Then Kayin said to his brother Hevel[8] – and when they
9 were in the field, Kayin rose up against his brother Hevel and killed him. The
LORD asked Kayin, "Where is your brother, Hevel?" "I do not know," he said.
10 "Am I my brother's keeper?" He said, "What is it you have done? The voice
11 of your brother's blood cries out to Me from the land! Now you are cursed,
more so than the land[9] that has opened its mouth to receive your brother's
12 blood from your hand. When you work the land, it will no longer grant you
13 its powers. You will be a fugitive wanderer over the land." Kayin said to the
14 LORD, "My sin is more than I can bear. You have banished me today from the
face of the land, and from Your face too I will be hidden. I will be a fugitive
15 wanderer over the land, and whoever finds me will kill me." The LORD said
to him, "Whoever then kills Kayin will suffer vengeance seven times over."
Then the LORD put a mark on Kayin so that none who found him would kill
16 him. So Kayin departed from the LORD's presence and lived in the land of

---

3 | The Hebrew *adam* can be read, depending on usage, as a common noun (man; cf. 2:7) or as a proper name.
4 | The name Ḥava resonates with *ḥai* (life).
5 | A euphemism for sexual relations.
6 | The name Kayin resonates with *kaniti* (I have made).
7 | *Hevel* means "breath" and carries connotations of transience.
8 | It is not specified what Kayin told Hevel.
9 | Cf. 3:17.

יז תְּשׁוּקָתֵךְ וְהוּא יִמְשָׁל־בָּךְ׃ וּלְאָדָם אָמַר כִּי שָׁמַעְתָּ לְקוֹל
אִשְׁתֶּךָ וַתֹּאכַל מִן־הָעֵץ אֲשֶׁר צִוִּיתִיךָ לֵאמֹר לֹא תֹאכַל מִמֶּנּוּ אֲרוּרָה
יח הָאֲדָמָה בַּעֲבוּרֶךָ בְּעִצָּבוֹן תֹּאכֲלֶנָּה כֹּל יְמֵי חַיֶּיךָ׃ וְקוֹץ וְדַרְדַּר תַּצְמִיחַ
יט לָךְ וְאָכַלְתָּ אֶת־עֵשֶׂב הַשָּׂדֶה׃ בְּזֵעַת אַפֶּיךָ תֹּאכַל לֶחֶם עַד שׁוּבְךָ
כ אֶל־הָאֲדָמָה כִּי מִמֶּנָּה לֻקָּחְתָּ כִּי־עָפָר אַתָּה וְאֶל־עָפָר תָּשׁוּב׃ וַיִּקְרָא
כא הָאָדָם שֵׁם אִשְׁתּוֹ חַוָּה כִּי הִוא הָיְתָה אֵם כָּל־חָי׃ וַיַּעַשׂ יְהוָה אֱלֹהִים
לְאָדָם וּלְאִשְׁתּוֹ כָּתְנוֹת עוֹר וַיַּלְבִּשֵׁם׃
כב וַיֹּאמֶר ׀ יְהוָה אֱלֹהִים הֵן הָאָדָם הָיָה כְּאַחַד מִמֶּנּוּ לָדַעַת טוֹב ג רביעי
וָרָע וְעַתָּה ׀ פֶּן־יִשְׁלַח יָדוֹ וְלָקַח גַּם מֵעֵץ הַחַיִּים וְאָכַל וָחַי לְעֹלָם׃
כג וַיְשַׁלְּחֵהוּ יְהוָה אֱלֹהִים מִגַּן־עֵדֶן לַעֲבֹד אֶת־הָאֲדָמָה אֲשֶׁר לֻקַּח מִשָּׁם׃
כד וַיְגָרֶשׁ אֶת־הָאָדָם וַיַּשְׁכֵּן מִקֶּדֶם לְגַן־עֵדֶן אֶת־הַכְּרֻבִים וְאֵת לַהַט
ד א הַחֶרֶב הַמִּתְהַפֶּכֶת לִשְׁמֹר אֶת־דֶּרֶךְ עֵץ הַחַיִּים׃ וְהָאָדָם
יָדַע אֶת־חַוָּה אִשְׁתּוֹ וַתַּהַר וַתֵּלֶד אֶת־קַיִן וַתֹּאמֶר קָנִיתִי אִישׁ אֶת־
ב יְהוָה׃ וַתֹּסֶף לָלֶדֶת אֶת־אָחִיו אֶת־הָבֶל וַיְהִי־הֶבֶל רֹעֵה צֹאן וְקַיִן
ג הָיָה עֹבֵד אֲדָמָה׃ וַיְהִי מִקֵּץ יָמִים וַיָּבֵא קַיִן מִפְּרִי הָאֲדָמָה מִנְחָה
ד לַיהוָה׃ וְהֶבֶל הֵבִיא גַם־הוּא מִבְּכֹרוֹת צֹאנוֹ וּמֵחֶלְבֵהֶן וַיִּשַׁע יְהוָה
ה אֶל־הֶבֶל וְאֶל־מִנְחָתוֹ׃ וְאֶל־קַיִן וְאֶל־מִנְחָתוֹ לֹא שָׁעָה וַיִּחַר לְקַיִן
ו מְאֹד וַיִּפְּלוּ פָּנָיו׃ וַיֹּאמֶר יְהוָה אֶל־קָיִן לָמָּה חָרָה לָךְ וְלָמָּה נָפְלוּ
ז פָנֶיךָ׃ הֲלוֹא אִם־תֵּיטִיב שְׂאֵת וְאִם לֹא תֵיטִיב לַפֶּתַח חַטָּאת רֹבֵץ
ח וְאֵלֶיךָ תְּשׁוּקָתוֹ וְאַתָּה תִּמְשָׁל־בּוֹ׃ וַיֹּאמֶר קַיִן אֶל־הֶבֶל אָחִיו וַיְהִי
ט בִּהְיוֹתָם בַּשָּׂדֶה וַיָּקָם קַיִן אֶל־הֶבֶל אָחִיו וַיַּהַרְגֵהוּ׃ וַיֹּאמֶר יְהוָה אֶל־
י קַיִן אֵי הֶבֶל אָחִיךָ וַיֹּאמֶר לֹא יָדַעְתִּי הֲשֹׁמֵר אָחִי אָנֹכִי׃ וַיֹּאמֶר מֶה
יא עָשִׂיתָ קוֹל דְּמֵי אָחִיךָ צֹעֲקִים אֵלַי מִן־הָאֲדָמָה׃ וְעַתָּה אָרוּר אָתָּה
יב מִן־הָאֲדָמָה אֲשֶׁר פָּצְתָה אֶת־פִּיהָ לָקַחַת אֶת־דְּמֵי אָחִיךָ מִיָּדֶךָ׃ כִּי
תַעֲבֹד אֶת־הָאֲדָמָה לֹא־תֹסֵף תֵּת־כֹּחָהּ לָךְ נָע וָנָד תִּהְיֶה בָאָרֶץ׃
יג יד וַיֹּאמֶר קַיִן אֶל־יְהוָה גָּדוֹל עֲוֺנִי מִנְּשֹׂא׃ הֵן גֵּרַשְׁתָּ אֹתִי הַיּוֹם מֵעַל
פְּנֵי הָאֲדָמָה וּמִפָּנֶיךָ אֶסָּתֵר וְהָיִיתִי נָע וָנָד בָּאָרֶץ וְהָיָה כָל־מֹצְאִי
טו יַהַרְגֵנִי׃ וַיֹּאמֶר לוֹ יְהוָה לָכֵן כָּל־הֹרֵג קַיִן שִׁבְעָתַיִם יֻקָּם וַיָּשֶׂם יְהוָה
טז לְקַיִן אוֹת לְבִלְתִּי הַכּוֹת־אֹתוֹ כָּל־מֹצְאוֹ׃ וַיֵּצֵא קַיִן מִלִּפְנֵי יְהוָה וַיֵּשֶׁב

17 Nod,[10] east of Eden. Kayin knew his wife, and she conceived and gave birth
18 to Ḥanokh. He built a city, naming it Ḥanokh after his son. Ḥanokh had a
son Irad, and Irad had a son Meḥuyael. Meḥiyael had a son Metushael, and
19 Metushael had a son Lemekh. Lemekh married two women, one named Ada
20 and the other Tzila. Ada gave birth to Yaval. He was the ancestor of those
21 who live in tents and raise livestock. His brother's name was Yuval. He was
22 the ancestor of all those who play the lyre and the pipe. Tzila, too, had a son,
Tuval-Kayin, who forged all kinds of bronze and iron tools. Tuval-Kayin's
23 sister was Naama. Lemekh said to his wives: "Ada and Tzila, listen to my voice;
wives of Lemekh, heed my words. I killed a man for wounding me, killed a boy
24 for bruising me. If Kayin will be avenged seven times, then Lemekh, seventy-
25 seven." Adam knew his wife again, and she gave birth to a son and named
him Shet, "because God has granted[11] me another child in place of Hevel,"
26 for Kayin had killed him. And Shet too had a son, and named him Enosh.
5 1 That was when people began to pray in the name of the LORD. This
is the book of Adam's descendants: On the day God created humankind, He
2 made them in the likeness of God. Male and female He created them, and
on the day they were created, He blessed them and called them Humankind.[12]
3 Adam lived one hundred and thirty years and then had a son in his own
4 likeness and image, and named him Shet. After Shet was born, Adam lived
5 eight hundred years and had other sons and daughters. Altogether Adam
6 lived nine hundred and thirty years, and then he died. Shet lived
7 one hundred and five years and then had a son, Enosh. After Enosh was
born, Shet lived eight hundred and seven years and had other sons and
8 daughters. Altogether, Shet lived nine hundred and twelve years, and then
9 10 he died. Enosh lived ninety years and then had a son, Keinan. After
Keinan was born, Enosh lived eight hundred and fifteen years and had other
11 sons and daughters. Altogether, Enosh lived nine hundred and five years, and
12 then he died. Keinan lived seventy years and had a son, Mahalalel.
13 After Mahalalel was born, Keinan lived eight hundred and forty years and
14 had other sons and daughters. Altogether, Keinan lived nine hundred and
15 ten years, and then he died. Mahalalel lived sixty-five years and had a
16 son, Yered. After Yered was born, Mahalalel lived eight hundred and thirty
17 years and had other sons and daughters. Altogether, Mahalalel lived eight
18 hundred and ninety-five years, and then he died. Yered lived
19 one hundred and sixty-two years and had a son, Ḥanokh. After Ḥanokh was
born, Yered lived eight hundred years and had other sons and daughters.

---

10 | "Land of Nod" bears the simultaneous meaning "land of wandering."

11 | The name Shet resonates with *shat* (granted).

12 | Hebrew *adam*.

יז בְּאֶרֶץ־נוֹד קִדְמַת־עֵדֶן: וַיֵּדַע קַיִן אֶת־אִשְׁתּוֹ וַתַּהַר וַתֵּלֶד אֶת־חֲנוֹךְ
יח וַיְהִי בֹּנֶה עִיר וַיִּקְרָא שֵׁם הָעִיר כְּשֵׁם בְּנוֹ חֲנוֹךְ: וַיִּוָּלֵד לַחֲנוֹךְ אֶת־
עִירָד וְעִירָד יָלַד אֶת־מְחוּיָאֵל וּמְחִיָּיאֵל יָלַד אֶת־מְתוּשָׁאֵל וּמְתוּשָׁאֵל
יט יָלַד אֶת־לָמֶךְ: וַיִּקַּח־לוֹ לֶמֶךְ שְׁתֵּי נָשִׁים שֵׁם הָאַחַת עָדָה וְשֵׁם חמישי
כ הַשֵּׁנִית צִלָּה: וַתֵּלֶד עָדָה אֶת־יָבָל הוּא הָיָה אֲבִי יֹשֵׁב אֹהֶל וּמִקְנֶה:
כא כב וְשֵׁם אָחִיו יוּבָל הוּא הָיָה אֲבִי כָּל־תֹּפֵשׂ כִּנּוֹר וְעוּגָב: וְצִלָּה גַם־הִוא
יָלְדָה אֶת־תּוּבַל קַיִן לֹטֵשׁ כָּל־חֹרֵשׁ נְחֹשֶׁת וּבַרְזֶל וַאֲחוֹת תּוּבַל־קַיִן
כג נַעֲמָה: וַיֹּאמֶר לֶמֶךְ לְנָשָׁיו עָדָה וְצִלָּה שְׁמַעַן קוֹלִי נְשֵׁי לֶמֶךְ הַאְזֵנָּה
כד אִמְרָתִי כִּי אִישׁ הָרַגְתִּי לְפִצְעִי וְיֶלֶד לְחַבֻּרָתִי: כִּי שִׁבְעָתַיִם יֻקַּם־קָיִן
כה וְלֶמֶךְ שִׁבְעִים וְשִׁבְעָה: וַיֵּדַע אָדָם עוֹד אֶת־אִשְׁתּוֹ וַתֵּלֶד בֵּן וַתִּקְרָא
אֶת־שְׁמוֹ שֵׁת כִּי שָׁת־לִי אֱלֹהִים זֶרַע אַחֵר תַּחַת הֶבֶל כִּי הֲרָגוֹ קָיִן:
כו וּלְשֵׁת גַּם־הוּא יֻלַּד־בֵּן וַיִּקְרָא אֶת־שְׁמוֹ אֱנוֹשׁ אָז הוּחַל לִקְרֹא בְּשֵׁם
ה א יְהוָה: זֶה סֵפֶר תּוֹלְדֹת אָדָם בְּיוֹם בְּרֹא אֱלֹהִים אָדָם ד ששי
ב בִּדְמוּת אֱלֹהִים עָשָׂה אֹתוֹ: זָכָר וּנְקֵבָה בְּרָאָם וַיְבָרֶךְ אֹתָם וַיִּקְרָא
ג אֶת־שְׁמָם אָדָם בְּיוֹם הִבָּרְאָם: וַיְחִי אָדָם שְׁלֹשִׁים וּמְאַת שָׁנָה וַיּוֹלֶד
ד בִּדְמוּתוֹ כְּצַלְמוֹ וַיִּקְרָא אֶת־שְׁמוֹ שֵׁת: וַיִּהְיוּ יְמֵי־אָדָם אַחֲרֵי הוֹלִידוֹ
ה אֶת־שֵׁת שְׁמֹנֶה מֵאֹת שָׁנָה וַיּוֹלֶד בָּנִים וּבָנוֹת: וַיִּהְיוּ כָּל־יְמֵי אָדָם
ו אֲשֶׁר־חַי תְּשַׁע מֵאוֹת שָׁנָה וּשְׁלֹשִׁים שָׁנָה וַיָּמֹת: וַיְחִי־
ז שֵׁת חָמֵשׁ שָׁנִים וּמְאַת שָׁנָה וַיּוֹלֶד אֶת־אֱנוֹשׁ: וַיְחִי־שֵׁת אַחֲרֵי
הוֹלִידוֹ אֶת־אֱנוֹשׁ שֶׁבַע שָׁנִים וּשְׁמֹנֶה מֵאוֹת שָׁנָה וַיּוֹלֶד בָּנִים
ח וּבָנוֹת: וַיִּהְיוּ כָּל־יְמֵי־שֵׁת שְׁתֵּים עֶשְׂרֵה שָׁנָה וּתְשַׁע מֵאוֹת שָׁנָה
ט וַיָּמֹת: וַיְחִי אֱנוֹשׁ תִּשְׁעִים שָׁנָה וַיּוֹלֶד אֶת־קֵינָן: וַיְחִי
י אֱנוֹשׁ אַחֲרֵי הוֹלִידוֹ אֶת־קֵינָן חֲמֵשׁ עֶשְׂרֵה שָׁנָה וּשְׁמֹנֶה מֵאוֹת שָׁנָה
יא וַיּוֹלֶד בָּנִים וּבָנוֹת: וַיִּהְיוּ כָּל־יְמֵי אֱנוֹשׁ חָמֵשׁ שָׁנִים וּתְשַׁע מֵאוֹת
יב שָׁנָה וַיָּמֹת: וַיְחִי קֵינָן שִׁבְעִים שָׁנָה וַיּוֹלֶד אֶת־מַהֲלַלְאֵל:
יג וַיְחִי קֵינָן אַחֲרֵי הוֹלִידוֹ אֶת־מַהֲלַלְאֵל אַרְבָּעִים שָׁנָה וּשְׁמֹנֶה מֵאוֹת
יד שָׁנָה וַיּוֹלֶד בָּנִים וּבָנוֹת: וַיִּהְיוּ כָּל־יְמֵי קֵינָן עֶשֶׂר שָׁנִים וּתְשַׁע מֵאוֹת
טו שָׁנָה וַיָּמֹת: וַיְחִי מַהֲלַלְאֵל חָמֵשׁ שָׁנִים וְשִׁשִּׁים שָׁנָה
טז וַיּוֹלֶד אֶת־יָרֶד: וַיְחִי מַהֲלַלְאֵל אַחֲרֵי הוֹלִידוֹ אֶת־יֶרֶד שְׁלֹשִׁים שָׁנָה
יז וּשְׁמֹנֶה מֵאוֹת שָׁנָה וַיּוֹלֶד בָּנִים וּבָנוֹת: וַיִּהְיוּ כָּל־יְמֵי מַהֲלַלְאֵל חָמֵשׁ
יח וְתִשְׁעִים שָׁנָה וּשְׁמֹנֶה מֵאוֹת שָׁנָה וַיָּמֹת: וַיְחִי־יֶרֶד שְׁתַּיִם
יט וְשִׁשִּׁים שָׁנָה וּמְאַת שָׁנָה וַיּוֹלֶד אֶת־חֲנוֹךְ: וַיְחִי־יֶרֶד אַחֲרֵי הוֹלִידוֹ

20 Altogether, Yered lived nine hundred and sixty-two years, and then he
21 died. Ḥanokh lived sixty-five years and had a son, Metushelaḥ.
22 Ḥanokh walked faithfully with God for three hundred years after Metushelaḥ
23 was born, and had other sons and daughters. Altogether, Ḥanokh lived for
24 three hundred and sixty-five years. Ḥanokh walked faithfully with God and
25 then he was no more, for God took him. Metushelaḥ lived one
26 hundred and eighty-seven years and had a son, Lemekh. After Lemekh was
born, Metushelaḥ lived seven hundred and eighty-two years and had other
27 sons and daughters. Altogether, Metushelaḥ lived nine hundred and sixty-
28 nine years, and then he died. Lemekh lived one hundred and eighty-
29 two years and had a son. He named him Noaḥ, saying, "This one will bring us
comfort[13] after all our labor and the sorrow of our hands on the land the LORD
30 has cursed." After Noaḥ was born, Lemekh lived five hundred and ninety-five
31 years and had other sons and daughters. Altogether, Lemekh lived seven
32 hundred and seventy-seven years, and then he died. After Noaḥ was
6 1 five hundred years old, Noaḥ had three sons: Shem, Ḥam, and Yefet. Humans
2 began to multiply on earth, and daughters were born to them. When the
sons of God[14] saw that the daughters of man were lovely, they began to take
3 whomever they chose to be wives to them. Then the LORD said, "My spirit
will not forever judge man; he is of flesh. His life shall be but one hundred
4 and twenty years." In those days the Nefilim[15] were on earth, and later also,
for the sons of God had gone to the daughters of man and had children with
them. These were the heroes of old, men of legends.
5 The LORD saw how great man's wickedness was upon the earth, and that his
6 thoughts constantly inclined toward evil. Then the LORD regretted that He
7 had made man on earth, and His heart was touched with sorrow. The LORD
said, "I will erase My creation, humankind, from the face of the land – man,
even animals and creeping things, even birds of the heavens – for I regret
8 having made them." But Noaḥ found favor in the LORD's sight.

NOAḤ

9 This is the story of Noaḥ. Noaḥ was a righteous man, a person of integrity in
10 his generation; Noaḥ walked with God. And Noaḥ had three sons: Shem,
11 Ḥam, and Yefet. The earth had become corrupt in God's sight, full of violence.
12 And when God saw how corrupt the earth had become, all flesh corrupting
13 its ways upon the earth, God said to Noaḥ, "The end of all flesh has
come before Me, for the earth is full of violence because of them. I am about
14 to destroy them, along with all the earth. So make yourself an ark of cypress

13 | *Noaḥ* resonates with *yenaḥamenu* (will bring us comfort).
14 | Opinions vary regarding the meaning and proper translation of this phrase.
15 | Apparently giants (see Num. 13:33).

כ אֶת־חֲנוֹךְ שְׁמֹנֶה מֵאוֹת שָׁנָה וַיּוֹלֶד בָּנִים וּבָנוֹת: וַיִּהְיוּ כָּל־יְמֵי־יֶרֶד
כא שְׁתַּיִם וְשִׁשִּׁים שָׁנָה וּתְשַׁע מֵאוֹת שָׁנָה וַיָּמֹת: וַיְחִי חֲנוֹךְ
כב חָמֵשׁ וְשִׁשִּׁים שָׁנָה וַיּוֹלֶד אֶת־מְתוּשָׁלַח: וַיִּתְהַלֵּךְ חֲנוֹךְ אֶת־הָאֱלֹהִים
אַחֲרֵי הוֹלִידוֹ אֶת־מְתוּשֶׁלַח שְׁלֹשׁ מֵאוֹת שָׁנָה וַיּוֹלֶד בָּנִים וּבָנוֹת:
כג כד וַיְהִי כָּל־יְמֵי חֲנוֹךְ חָמֵשׁ וְשִׁשִּׁים שָׁנָה וּשְׁלֹשׁ מֵאוֹת שָׁנָה: וַיִּתְהַלֵּךְ
כה חֲנוֹךְ אֶת־הָאֱלֹהִים וְאֵינֶנּוּ כִּי־לָקַח אֹתוֹ אֱלֹהִים: וַיְחִי שביעי
כו מְתוּשֶׁלַח שֶׁבַע וּשְׁמֹנִים שָׁנָה וּמְאַת שָׁנָה וַיּוֹלֶד אֶת־לָמֶךְ: וַיְחִי
מְתוּשֶׁלַח אַחֲרֵי הוֹלִידוֹ אֶת־לֶמֶךְ שְׁתַּיִם וּשְׁמוֹנִים שָׁנָה וּשְׁבַע מֵאוֹת
כז שָׁנָה וַיּוֹלֶד בָּנִים וּבָנוֹת: וַיִּהְיוּ כָּל־יְמֵי מְתוּשֶׁלַח תֵּשַׁע וְשִׁשִּׁים שָׁנָה
כח וּתְשַׁע מֵאוֹת שָׁנָה וַיָּמֹת: וַיְחִי־לֶמֶךְ שְׁתַּיִם וּשְׁמֹנִים
כט שָׁנָה וּמְאַת שָׁנָה וַיּוֹלֶד בֵּן: וַיִּקְרָא אֶת־שְׁמוֹ נֹחַ לֵאמֹר זֶה יְנַחֲמֵנוּ
ל מִמַּעֲשֵׂנוּ וּמֵעִצְּבוֹן יָדֵינוּ מִן־הָאֲדָמָה אֲשֶׁר אֵרְרָהּ יְהוָה: וַיְחִי־לֶמֶךְ
אַחֲרֵי הוֹלִידוֹ אֶת־נֹחַ חָמֵשׁ וְתִשְׁעִים שָׁנָה וַחֲמֵשׁ מֵאֹת שָׁנָה וַיּוֹלֶד
לא בָּנִים וּבָנוֹת: וַיְהִי כָּל־יְמֵי־לֶמֶךְ שֶׁבַע וְשִׁבְעִים שָׁנָה וּשְׁבַע מֵאוֹת שָׁנָה
לב וַיָּמֹת: וַיְהִי־נֹחַ בֶּן־חֲמֵשׁ מֵאוֹת שָׁנָה וַיּוֹלֶד נֹחַ אֶת־שֵׁם
ו א אֶת־חָם וְאֶת־יָפֶת: וַיְהִי כִּי־הֵחֵל הָאָדָם לָרֹב עַל־פְּנֵי הָאֲדָמָה וּבָנוֹת
ב יֻלְּדוּ לָהֶם: וַיִּרְאוּ בְנֵי־הָאֱלֹהִים אֶת־בְּנוֹת הָאָדָם כִּי טֹבֹת הֵנָּה וַיִּקְחוּ
ג לָהֶם נָשִׁים מִכֹּל אֲשֶׁר בָּחָרוּ: וַיֹּאמֶר יְהוָה לֹא־יָדוֹן רוּחִי בָאָדָם לְעֹלָם
ד בְּשַׁגַּם הוּא בָשָׂר וְהָיוּ יָמָיו מֵאָה וְעֶשְׂרִים שָׁנָה: הַנְּפִלִים הָיוּ בָאָרֶץ
בַּיָּמִים הָהֵם וְגַם אַחֲרֵי־כֵן אֲשֶׁר יָבֹאוּ בְּנֵי הָאֱלֹהִים אֶל־בְּנוֹת הָאָדָם
וְיָלְדוּ לָהֶם הֵמָּה הַגִּבֹּרִים אֲשֶׁר מֵעוֹלָם אַנְשֵׁי הַשֵּׁם:
ה וַיַּרְא יְהוָה כִּי רַבָּה רָעַת הָאָדָם בָּאָרֶץ וְכָל־יֵצֶר מַחְשְׁבֹת לִבּוֹ רַק מפטיר
ו רַע כָּל־הַיּוֹם: וַיִּנָּחֶם יְהוָה כִּי־עָשָׂה אֶת־הָאָדָם בָּאָרֶץ וַיִּתְעַצֵּב
ז אֶל־לִבּוֹ: וַיֹּאמֶר יְהוָה אֶמְחֶה אֶת־הָאָדָם אֲשֶׁר־בָּרָאתִי מֵעַל פְּנֵי
הָאֲדָמָה מֵאָדָם עַד־בְּהֵמָה עַד־רֶמֶשׂ וְעַד־עוֹף הַשָּׁמָיִם כִּי נִחַמְתִּי
ח כִּי עֲשִׂיתִם: וְנֹחַ מָצָא חֵן בְּעֵינֵי יְהוָה:

ט אֵלֶּה תּוֹלְדֹת נֹחַ נֹחַ אִישׁ צַדִּיק תָּמִים הָיָה בְּדֹרֹתָיו אֶת־הָאֱלֹהִים ה נח
י הִתְהַלֶּךְ־נֹחַ: וַיּוֹלֶד נֹחַ שְׁלֹשָׁה בָנִים אֶת־שֵׁם אֶת־חָם וְאֶת־יָפֶת:
יא יב וַתִּשָּׁחֵת הָאָרֶץ לִפְנֵי הָאֱלֹהִים וַתִּמָּלֵא הָאָרֶץ חָמָס: וַיַּרְא אֱלֹהִים
אֶת־הָאָרֶץ וְהִנֵּה נִשְׁחָתָה כִּי־הִשְׁחִית כָּל־בָּשָׂר אֶת־דַּרְכּוֹ עַל־
יג הָאָרֶץ: וַיֹּאמֶר אֱלֹהִים לְנֹחַ קֵץ כָּל־בָּשָׂר בָּא לְפָנַי
יד כִּי־מָלְאָה הָאָרֶץ חָמָס מִפְּנֵיהֶם וְהִנְנִי מַשְׁחִיתָם אֶת־הָאָרֶץ: עֲשֵׂה

15 wood. Make it with compartments and coat it in pitch inside and out. This is
how you shall make it: the ark shall be three hundred cubits long, fifty cubits
16 wide, and thirty cubits high. Make a window for the ark, and taper the latter
to within a cubit of the top.[16] Put a door in the side of the ark and make lower,
17 middle, and upper decks. And I – I am about to bring floodwaters over the
earth to destroy all flesh that has within it the breath of life under the heavens.
18 Everything on earth will die. But I will establish My covenant with you, and
you will enter the ark – you, your sons, your wife, and your sons' wives with
19 you. And you shall take two of each living creature, male and female, into the
20 ark to keep alive with you. Of every kind of bird, animal, and wild beast, bring
21 two to keep alive. As for you, take all the food to be eaten and store it: it will
22 be for food for you and for them." Noaḥ did so: all that God commanded
7 1 him, he fulfilled. Then the LORD said to Noaḥ, "Enter the ark, you and all
your household, for I have seen you alone to be righteous before Me in this
2 generation. Take seven and seven of every pure animal, seven pairs, and two
3 of every animal that is not pure, of each kind a pair. Also take seven pairs of
each kind of bird, male and female, to keep their kind alive across the earth.
4 For in seven days' time I will send rain on the earth for forty days and forty
nights, and I will wipe from the face of the earth every living creature I have
5 6 made." Noaḥ did all that the LORD commanded him. Noaḥ was six hundred
7 years old when the floodwaters came upon the earth. Noaḥ, with his sons, his
wife, and his sons' wives, came into the ark to escape the waters of the flood.
8 The pure animals, the animals that were not pure, the birds, and all that
9 walked the earth came two by two to Noaḥ into the ark, male and female, as
10 God had commanded Noaḥ. Thus, after seven days the floodwaters came
11 upon the earth. In the six hundredth year of Noaḥ's life, in the second month,
on the seventeenth of the month – on that day, all the wellsprings of the great
12 deep burst, and heavens' floodgates opened. The rain fell on the earth for
13 forty days and forty nights. On that very day, Noaḥ, his sons, Shem, Ḥam,
14 and Yefet, Noaḥ's wife, and his sons' three wives entered the ark. With them
came every kind of wild beast, every kind of animal, every creeping, crawling
creature of the land, every kind of flying creature, every bird, and each winged
15 thing. They came to Noaḥ, to the ark, two by two, of all flesh that had within
16 it the breath of life. They came, male and female of all flesh, as God had

16 | That is, the ark should slant upward, becoming narrower as it approaches the top.

לְךָ֙ תֵּבַ֣ת עֲצֵי־גֹ֔פֶר קִנִּ֖ים תַּעֲשֶׂ֣ה אֶת־הַתֵּבָ֑ה וְכָֽפַרְתָּ֥ אֹתָ֛הּ מִבַּ֥יִת
טו וּמִח֖וּץ בַּכֹּֽפֶר׃ וְזֶ֕ה אֲשֶׁ֥ר תַּעֲשֶׂ֖ה אֹתָ֑הּ שְׁלֹ֨שׁ מֵא֤וֹת אַמָּה֙ אֹ֣רֶךְ הַתֵּבָ֔ה
טז חֲמִשִּׁ֤ים אַמָּה֙ רָחְבָּ֔הּ וּשְׁלֹשִׁ֥ים אַמָּ֖ה קוֹמָתָֽהּ׃ צֹ֣הַר ׀ תַּעֲשֶׂ֣ה לַתֵּבָ֗ה
וְאֶל־אַמָּה֙ תְּכַלֶּ֣נָּה מלמעלה ופתח התבה בְּצִדָּ֣הּ תָּשִׂ֑ים תַּחְתִּיִּ֛ם
יז שְׁנִיִּ֥ם וּשְׁלִשִׁ֖ים תַּעֲשֶֽׂהָ׃ וַאֲנִ֗י הִנְנִי֩ מֵבִ֨יא אֶת־הַמַּבּ֥וּל מַ֙יִם֙ עַל־הָאָ֔רֶץ
לְשַׁחֵ֣ת כָּל־בָּשָׂ֗ר אֲשֶׁר־בּוֹ֙ ר֣וּחַ חַיִּ֔ים מִתַּ֖חַת הַשָּׁמָ֑יִם כֹּ֥ל אֲשֶׁר־בָּאָ֖רֶץ
יח יִגְוָֽע׃ וַהֲקִמֹתִ֥י אֶת־בְּרִיתִ֖י אִתָּ֑ךְ וּבָאתָ֙ אֶל־הַתֵּבָ֔ה אַתָּ֕ה וּבָנֶ֛יךָ וְאִשְׁתְּךָ֥
יט וּנְשֵֽׁי־בָנֶ֖יךָ אִתָּֽךְ׃ וּמִכָּל־הָ֠חַי מִֽכָּל־בָּשָׂ֞ר שְׁנַ֧יִם מִכֹּ֛ל תָּבִ֥יא אֶל־הַתֵּבָ֖ה
כ לְהַחֲיֹ֣ת אִתָּ֑ךְ זָכָ֥ר וּנְקֵבָ֖ה יִהְיֽוּ׃ מֵהָע֣וֹף לְמִינֵ֗הוּ וּמִן־הַבְּהֵמָה֙ לְמִינָ֔הּ
כא מִכֹּ֛ל רֶ֥מֶשׂ הָאֲדָמָ֖ה לְמִינֵ֑הוּ שְׁנַ֧יִם מִכֹּ֛ל יָבֹ֥אוּ אֵלֶ֖יךָ לְהַחֲיֽוֹת׃ וְאַתָּ֣ה
קַח־לְךָ֗ מִכָּל־מַאֲכָל֙ אֲשֶׁ֣ר יֵֽאָכֵ֔ל וְאָסַפְתָּ֖ אֵלֶ֑יךָ וְהָיָ֥ה לְךָ֛ וְלָהֶ֖ם
כב ז א לְאָכְלָֽה׃ וַיַּ֖עַשׂ נֹ֑חַ כְּ֠כֹל אֲשֶׁ֨ר צִוָּ֥ה אֹת֛וֹ אֱלֹהִ֖ים כֵּ֥ן עָשָֽׂה׃ וַיֹּ֤אמֶר יהוה֙ שני
לְנֹ֔חַ בֹּֽא־אַתָּ֥ה וְכָל־בֵּיתְךָ֖ אֶל־הַתֵּבָ֑ה כִּֽי־אֹתְךָ֥ רָאִ֛יתִי צַדִּ֥יק לְפָנַ֖י
ב בַּדּ֥וֹר הַזֶּֽה׃ מִכֹּ֣ל ׀ הַבְּהֵמָ֣ה הַטְּהוֹרָ֗ה תִּֽקַּח־לְךָ֛ שִׁבְעָ֥ה שִׁבְעָ֖ה אִ֣ישׁ
ג וְאִשְׁתּ֑וֹ וּמִן־הַבְּהֵמָ֡ה אֲ֠שֶׁר לֹ֣א טְהֹרָ֥ה הִ֛וא שְׁנַ֖יִם אִ֥ישׁ וְאִשְׁתּֽוֹ׃ גַּ֣ם
מֵע֧וֹף הַשָּׁמַ֛יִם שִׁבְעָ֥ה שִׁבְעָ֖ה זָכָ֣ר וּנְקֵבָ֑ה לְחַיּ֥וֹת זֶ֖רַע עַל־פְּנֵ֥י כָל־
ד הָאָֽרֶץ׃ כִּי֩ לְיָמִ֨ים ע֜וֹד שִׁבְעָ֗ה אָנֹכִי֙ מַמְטִ֣יר עַל־הָאָ֔רֶץ אַרְבָּעִ֣ים
י֔וֹם וְאַרְבָּעִ֖ים לָ֑יְלָה וּמָחִ֗יתִי אֶת־כָּל־הַיְקוּם֙ אֲשֶׁ֣ר עָשִׂ֔יתִי מֵעַ֖ל פְּנֵ֥י
ה ו הָֽאֲדָמָֽה׃ וַיַּ֖עַשׂ נֹ֑חַ כְּכֹ֥ל אֲשֶׁר־צִוָּ֖הוּ יהוה׃ וְנֹ֕חַ בֶּן־שֵׁ֥שׁ מֵא֖וֹת שָׁנָ֑ה
ז וְהַמַּבּ֣וּל הָיָ֔ה מַ֖יִם עַל־הָאָֽרֶץ׃ וַיָּ֣בֹא נֹ֗חַ וּ֠בָנָיו וְאִשְׁתּ֧וֹ וּנְשֵֽׁי־בָנָ֛יו אִתּ֖וֹ
ח אֶל־הַתֵּבָ֑ה מִפְּנֵ֖י מֵ֥י הַמַּבּֽוּל׃ מִן־הַבְּהֵמָה֙ הַטְּהוֹרָ֔ה וּמִן־הַ֨בְּהֵמָ֔ה
ט אֲשֶׁ֥ר אֵינֶ֖נָּה טְהֹרָ֑ה וּמִ֨ן־הָע֔וֹף וְכֹ֥ל אֲשֶׁר־רֹמֵ֖שׂ עַל־הָאֲדָמָֽה׃ שְׁנַ֨יִם
שְׁנַ֜יִם בָּ֧אוּ אֶל־נֹ֛חַ אֶל־הַתֵּבָ֖ה זָכָ֣ר וּנְקֵבָ֑ה כַּאֲשֶׁ֛ר צִוָּ֥ה אֱלֹהִ֖ים אֶת־
י יא נֹֽחַ׃ וַיְהִ֖י לְשִׁבְעַ֣ת הַיָּמִ֑ים וּמֵ֣י הַמַּבּ֔וּל הָי֖וּ עַל־הָאָֽרֶץ׃ בִּשְׁנַ֨ת שֵׁשׁ־
מֵא֤וֹת שָׁנָה֙ לְחַיֵּי־נֹ֔חַ בַּחֹ֙דֶשׁ֙ הַשֵּׁנִ֔י בְּשִׁבְעָֽה־עָשָׂ֥ר י֖וֹם לַחֹ֑דֶשׁ בַּיּ֣וֹם
יב הַזֶּ֗ה נִבְקְעוּ֙ כָּֽל־מַעְיְנֹת֙ תְּה֣וֹם רַבָּ֔ה וַאֲרֻבֹּ֥ת הַשָּׁמַ֖יִם נִפְתָּֽחוּ׃ וַיְהִ֥י
יג הַגֶּ֖שֶׁם עַל־הָאָ֑רֶץ אַרְבָּעִ֣ים י֔וֹם וְאַרְבָּעִ֖ים לָֽיְלָה׃ בְּעֶ֨צֶם הַיּ֤וֹם הַזֶּה֙ בָּ֣א
נֹ֔חַ וְשֵׁם־וְחָ֥ם וָיֶ֖פֶת בְּנֵי־נֹ֑חַ וְאֵ֣שֶׁת נֹ֗חַ וּשְׁלֹ֧שֶׁת נְשֵֽׁי־בָנָ֛יו אִתָּ֖ם אֶל־
יד הַתֵּבָֽה׃ הֵ֜מָּה וְכָל־הַחַיָּ֣ה לְמִינָ֗הּ וְכָל־הַבְּהֵמָה֙ לְמִינָ֔הּ וְכָל־הָרֶ֛מֶשׂ
הָֽרֹמֵ֥שׂ עַל־הָאָ֖רֶץ לְמִינֵ֑הוּ וְכָל־הָע֣וֹף לְמִינֵ֔הוּ כֹּ֖ל צִפּ֥וֹר כָּל־כָּנָֽף׃
טו וַיָּבֹ֥אוּ אֶל־נֹ֖חַ אֶל־הַתֵּבָ֑ה שְׁנַ֤יִם שְׁנַ֙יִם֙ מִכָּל־הַבָּשָׂ֔ר אֲשֶׁר־בּ֖וֹ ר֥וּחַ
טז חַיִּֽים׃ וְהַבָּאִ֗ים זָכָ֨ר וּנְקֵבָ֤ה מִכָּל־בָּשָׂר֙ בָּ֔אוּ כַּאֲשֶׁ֛ר צִוָּ֥ה אֹת֖וֹ אֱלֹהִ֑ים

17 commanded him. Then the LORD shut him in. For forty days the flood came
upon the earth. The waters swelled, lifting the ark so that it rose above the
18 land. The waters surged, swelling enormously on the earth, and the ark
19 began to drift on the surface of the water. The waters surged ever more, until
20 all the high mountains beneath all the heavens were covered. Fifteen cubits
21 above them the waters surged as the mountains were covered. All flesh that
moved upon the earth perished – birds, animals, wild beasts, and all the
22 creatures that swarm on the earth, and all humankind. Everything on dry land
23 that had breath of life in its nostrils died. Every living thing on the face of the
earth was wiped out: from humans to animals, from creeping creatures to
winged birds of the heavens, all were wiped from the earth. Only Noaḥ and
24 those with him in the ark survived. For one hundred fifty days, the waters
8 1 surged over the earth. Then God remembered Noaḥ and all the wild beasts
and animals with him in the ark. God sent a wind over the earth, and the
2 waters began to subside. The wellsprings of the deep and heavens' floodgates
3 closed, and the heavens' rains were reined in. The water steadily receded from
4 the earth, and by the end of one hundred fifty days, the water had abated. In
the seventh month, on the seventeenth day of the month, the ark came to
5 rest on the mountains of Ararat. The water continued to abate until the
tenth month, and on the first day of the tenth month, the mountaintops
6 became visible. After forty days Noaḥ opened the window he had made
7 in the ark and sent a raven forth. It flew to and fro until the water on the
8 earth had dried. After that he sent forth a dove to see whether the water had
9 subsided from the face of the land. But the dove found no resting place to
plant its foot, and so it returned to him, to the ark, for water still covered the
face of the earth completely. He reached out his hand and brought the dove
10 back to him, into the ark. Then he waited another seven days, and again he
11 sent the dove forth from the ark. The dove came back to him in the evening
– and in its beak was a freshly picked olive leaf. Noaḥ knew then that the
12 water had subsided from the earth. He waited another seven days and again
13 sent forth the dove – and it returned to him no more. So it was that, by the
first day of the first month of Noaḥ's six hundred and first year, the water on
the earth dried up. Noaḥ removed the covering of the ark and saw that the
14 face of the land was dry. By the twenty-seventh day of the second month,
15 16 the earth had dried completely. Then God said to Noaḥ, "Leave
17 the ark – you, and your wife, your sons, and your sons' wives with you. And
every living thing with you – birds, animals, and all wild beasts that walk
the earth – bring them out with you. Let them swarm again on the earth
18 and be fertile and multiply upon it." So Noaḥ came out with his sons, his
19 wife, and his sons' wives. Every beast, creeping thing, winged creature,

יז וַיִּסְגֹּר יְהוָה בַּעֲדוֹ: וַיְהִי הַמַּבּוּל אַרְבָּעִים יוֹם עַל־הָאָרֶץ וַיִּרְבּוּ הַמַּיִם שלישי
יח וַיִּשְׂאוּ אֶת־הַתֵּבָה וַתָּרָם מֵעַל הָאָרֶץ: וַיִּגְבְּרוּ הַמַּיִם וַיִּרְבּוּ מְאֹד עַל־
יט הָאָרֶץ וַתֵּלֶךְ הַתֵּבָה עַל־פְּנֵי הַמָּיִם: וְהַמַּיִם גָּבְרוּ מְאֹד מְאֹד עַל־
כ הָאָרֶץ וַיְכֻסּוּ כָּל־הֶהָרִים הַגְּבֹהִים אֲשֶׁר־תַּחַת כָּל־הַשָּׁמָיִם: חֲמֵשׁ
כא עֶשְׂרֵה אַמָּה מִלְמַעְלָה גָּבְרוּ הַמָּיִם וַיְכֻסּוּ הֶהָרִים: וַיִּגְוַע כָּל־בָּשָׂר ׀
הָרֹמֵשׂ עַל־הָאָרֶץ בָּעוֹף וּבַבְּהֵמָה וּבַחַיָּה וּבְכָל־הַשֶּׁרֶץ הַשֹּׁרֵץ עַל־
כב הָאָרֶץ וְכֹל הָאָדָם: כֹּל אֲשֶׁר נִשְׁמַת־רוּחַ חַיִּים בְּאַפָּיו מִכֹּל אֲשֶׁר
כג בֶּחָרָבָה מֵתוּ: וַיִּמַח אֶת־כָּל־הַיְקוּם ׀ אֲשֶׁר ׀ עַל־פְּנֵי הָאֲדָמָה מֵאָדָם
עַד־בְּהֵמָה עַד־רֶמֶשׂ וְעַד־עוֹף הַשָּׁמַיִם וַיִּמָּחוּ מִן־הָאָרֶץ וַיִּשָּׁאֶר אַךְ־
כד נֹחַ וַאֲשֶׁר אִתּוֹ בַּתֵּבָה: וַיִּגְבְּרוּ הַמַּיִם עַל־הָאָרֶץ חֲמִשִּׁים וּמְאַת יוֹם:
ח א וַיִּזְכֹּר אֱלֹהִים אֶת־נֹחַ וְאֵת כָּל־הַחַיָּה וְאֶת־כָּל־הַבְּהֵמָה אֲשֶׁר אִתּוֹ ו
ב בַּתֵּבָה וַיַּעֲבֵר אֱלֹהִים רוּחַ עַל־הָאָרֶץ וַיָּשֹׁכּוּ הַמָּיִם: וַיִּסָּכְרוּ מַעְיְנֹת
ג תְּהוֹם וַאֲרֻבֹּת הַשָּׁמָיִם וַיִּכָּלֵא הַגֶּשֶׁם מִן־הַשָּׁמָיִם: וַיָּשֻׁבוּ הַמַּיִם מֵעַל
ד הָאָרֶץ הָלוֹךְ וָשׁוֹב וַיַּחְסְרוּ הַמַּיִם מִקְצֵה חֲמִשִּׁים וּמְאַת יוֹם: וַתָּנַח
הַתֵּבָה בַּחֹדֶשׁ הַשְּׁבִיעִי בְּשִׁבְעָה־עָשָׂר יוֹם לַחֹדֶשׁ עַל הָרֵי אֲרָרָט:
ה וְהַמַּיִם הָיוּ הָלוֹךְ וְחָסוֹר עַד הַחֹדֶשׁ הָעֲשִׂירִי בָּעֲשִׂירִי בְּאֶחָד לַחֹדֶשׁ
ו נִרְאוּ רָאשֵׁי הֶהָרִים: וַיְהִי מִקֵּץ אַרְבָּעִים יוֹם וַיִּפְתַּח נֹחַ אֶת־חַלּוֹן
ז הַתֵּבָה אֲשֶׁר עָשָׂה: וַיְשַׁלַּח אֶת־הָעֹרֵב וַיֵּצֵא יָצוֹא וָשׁוֹב עַד־יְבֹשֶׁת
ח הַמַּיִם מֵעַל הָאָרֶץ: וַיְשַׁלַּח אֶת־הַיּוֹנָה מֵאִתּוֹ לִרְאוֹת הֲקַלּוּ הַמַּיִם
ט מֵעַל פְּנֵי הָאֲדָמָה: וְלֹא־מָצְאָה הַיּוֹנָה מָנוֹחַ לְכַף־רַגְלָהּ וַתָּשָׁב אֵלָיו
אֶל־הַתֵּבָה כִּי־מַיִם עַל־פְּנֵי כָל־הָאָרֶץ וַיִּשְׁלַח יָדוֹ וַיִּקָּחֶהָ וַיָּבֵא אֹתָהּ
י אֵלָיו אֶל־הַתֵּבָה: וַיָּחֶל עוֹד שִׁבְעַת יָמִים אֲחֵרִים וַיֹּסֶף שַׁלַּח אֶת־
יא הַיּוֹנָה מִן־הַתֵּבָה: וַתָּבֹא אֵלָיו הַיּוֹנָה לְעֵת עֶרֶב וְהִנֵּה עֲלֵה־זַיִת טָרָף
יב בְּפִיהָ וַיֵּדַע נֹחַ כִּי־קַלּוּ הַמַּיִם מֵעַל הָאָרֶץ: וַיִּיָּחֶל עוֹד שִׁבְעַת יָמִים
יג אֲחֵרִים וַיְשַׁלַּח אֶת־הַיּוֹנָה וְלֹא־יָסְפָה שׁוּב־אֵלָיו עוֹד: וַיְהִי בְּאַחַת
וְשֵׁשׁ־מֵאוֹת שָׁנָה בָּרִאשׁוֹן בְּאֶחָד לַחֹדֶשׁ חָרְבוּ הַמַּיִם מֵעַל הָאָרֶץ
יד וַיָּסַר נֹחַ אֶת־מִכְסֵה הַתֵּבָה וַיַּרְא וְהִנֵּה חָרְבוּ פְּנֵי הָאֲדָמָה: וּבַחֹדֶשׁ
טו הַשֵּׁנִי בְּשִׁבְעָה וְעֶשְׂרִים יוֹם לַחֹדֶשׁ יָבְשָׁה הָאָרֶץ: וַיְדַבֵּר ז רביעי
טז אֱלֹהִים אֶל־נֹחַ לֵאמֹר: צֵא מִן־הַתֵּבָה אַתָּה וְאִשְׁתְּךָ וּבָנֶיךָ וּנְשֵׁי־בָנֶיךָ
יז אִתָּךְ: כָּל־הַחַיָּה אֲשֶׁר־אִתְּךָ מִכָּל־בָּשָׂר בָּעוֹף וּבַבְּהֵמָה וּבְכָל־הָרֶמֶשׂ
הָרֹמֵשׂ עַל־הָאָרֶץ הוצא אִתָּךְ וְשָׁרְצוּ בָאָרֶץ וּפָרוּ וְרָבוּ עַל־הָאָרֶץ: הַיְצֵא
יח יט וַיֵּצֵא־נֹחַ וּבָנָיו וְאִשְׁתּוֹ וּנְשֵׁי־בָנָיו אִתּוֹ: כָּל־הַחַיָּה כָּל־הָרֶמֶשׂ וְכָל־

everything that creeps across the earth, emerged from the ark by families.
20 Then Noaḥ built an altar to the Lord and, taking of each of the kinds of pure
21 animals and pure birds, sacrificed burnt offerings on the altar. The Lord
smelled the fragrant aroma and said in His heart, "Never again will I curse the
land because of man;[17] the devisings of the human heart are evil from its
22 youth. And never again will I destroy all life as I have done. As long as earth
and time endure – sowing time and harvest, cold and heat, summer, winter,
9 1 day, and night will not cease." Then God blessed Noaḥ and his sons, saying
2 to them, "Be fertile, multiply, fill the earth. Fear and dread of you shall fall
upon all beasts of the earth, upon all winged creatures of the heavens, upon
all that creeps upon the land and all fish of the sea. Into your hand they are
3 given. Every moving thing that lives shall be food for you; I allow them all to
4 you, like green plants. But flesh with its lifeblood still in it you may not eat.
5 And for your own lifeblood I will demand account; I will demand it from
every wild beast. For human life I will demand account, of every man toward
6 his fellow man: One who sheds the blood of man – by man shall his blood
7 be shed, for in God's image man was made. As for you, be fertile and multiply,
8 abound on earth and become many on it." Then God said to Noaḥ
9 and to his sons with him: "I – I am about to establish My covenant with you
10 and your descendants after you, and with every living creature that is with
you – the birds, the animals, and all the wild beasts of earth that are with you,
11 everything that left the ark, every living creature on earth. I will establish My
covenant with you, that never again may all life be destroyed by the waters of
12 a flood; never again will there be a flood to destroy the earth." God said, "This
is the sign of the covenant I am making between Me and you – and every
13 living creature with you – for all generations to come. I have laid down My
bow in the clouds to be the sign of the covenant between Me and the earth.
14 Whenever I bring clouds over the earth and the rainbow appears in the
15 clouds, I will remember My covenant that binds Me and you and every living
creature of all flesh so that never again will the waters become a flood to
16 destroy all life. The rainbow will be there in the cloud, and I will see it,
remembering the eternal covenant between God and every living creature,
17 all flesh upon the earth." So said God to Noaḥ: "This is the sign of the covenant
that I have established between Me and all flesh that is on earth."
18 Noaḥ's sons who came out from the ark were Shem, Ḥam, and Yefet. Ḥam
19 was the father of Kenaan.[18] These three were Noaḥ's sons; and from them all
20 the world branched out. Noaḥ began to be a man of the land, and he planted
21 a vineyard. He drank some of the wine, became drunk, and lay uncovered
22 in his tent. Ḥam, father of Kenaan, saw his father's nakedness and told his
23 two brothers who were outside. Shem and Yefet then took a cloak and put it
over both their shoulders. They walked backward and covered their father's

17 | Cf. 3:17, 5:29.

18 | The ancestor of the Canaanites, whose land would ultimately be given to Israel, descendants of Shem.

כ הָעוֹף כֹּל רוֹמֵשׂ עַל־הָאָרֶץ לְמִשְׁפְּחֹתֵיהֶם יָצְאוּ מִן־הַתֵּבָה: וַיִּבֶן נֹחַ
מִזְבֵּחַ לַיהוָה וַיִּקַּח מִכֹּל ׀ הַבְּהֵמָה הַטְּהֹרָה וּמִכֹּל הָעוֹף הַטָּהֹר וַיַּעַל
כא עֹלֹת בַּמִּזְבֵּחַ: וַיָּרַח יהוה אֶת־רֵיחַ הַנִּיחֹחַ וַיֹּאמֶר יהוה אֶל־לִבּוֹ לֹא
אֹסִף לְקַלֵּל עוֹד אֶת־הָאֲדָמָה בַּעֲבוּר הָאָדָם כִּי יֵצֶר לֵב הָאָדָם רַע
כב מִנְּעֻרָיו וְלֹא־אֹסִף עוֹד לְהַכּוֹת אֶת־כָּל־חַי כַּאֲשֶׁר עָשִׂיתִי: עֹד כָּל־יְמֵי
ט א הָאָרֶץ זֶרַע וְקָצִיר וְקֹר וָחֹם וְקַיִץ וָחֹרֶף וְיוֹם וָלַיְלָה לֹא יִשְׁבֹּתוּ: וַיְבָרֶךְ
אֱלֹהִים אֶת־נֹחַ וְאֶת־בָּנָיו וַיֹּאמֶר לָהֶם פְּרוּ וּרְבוּ וּמִלְאוּ אֶת־הָאָרֶץ:
ב וּמוֹרַאֲכֶם וְחִתְּכֶם יִהְיֶה עַל כָּל־חַיַּת הָאָרֶץ וְעַל כָּל־עוֹף הַשָּׁמָיִם בְּכֹל
ג אֲשֶׁר תִּרְמֹשׂ הָאֲדָמָה וּבְכָל־דְּגֵי הַיָּם בְּיֶדְכֶם נִתָּנוּ: כָּל־רֶמֶשׂ אֲשֶׁר
ד הוּא־חַי לָכֶם יִהְיֶה לְאָכְלָה כְּיֶרֶק עֵשֶׂב נָתַתִּי לָכֶם אֶת־כֹּל: אַךְ־בָּשָׂר
ה בְּנַפְשׁוֹ דָמוֹ לֹא תֹאכֵלוּ: וְאַךְ אֶת־דִּמְכֶם לְנַפְשֹׁתֵיכֶם אֶדְרֹשׁ מִיַּד
כָּל־חַיָּה אֶדְרְשֶׁנּוּ וּמִיַּד הָאָדָם מִיַּד אִישׁ אָחִיו אֶדְרֹשׁ אֶת־נֶפֶשׁ
ו הָאָדָם: שֹׁפֵךְ דַּם הָאָדָם בָּאָדָם דָּמוֹ יִשָּׁפֵךְ כִּי בְּצֶלֶם אֱלֹהִים עָשָׂה
ז ח אֶת־הָאָדָם: וְאַתֶּם פְּרוּ וּרְבוּ שִׁרְצוּ בָאָרֶץ וּרְבוּ־בָהּ: וַיֹּאמֶר חמישי
ט אֱלֹהִים אֶל־נֹחַ וְאֶל־בָּנָיו אִתּוֹ לֵאמֹר: וַאֲנִי הִנְנִי מֵקִים אֶת־בְּרִיתִי
י אִתְּכֶם וְאֶת־זַרְעֲכֶם אַחֲרֵיכֶם: וְאֵת כָּל־נֶפֶשׁ הַחַיָּה אֲשֶׁר אִתְּכֶם בָּעוֹף
בַּבְּהֵמָה וּבְכָל־חַיַּת הָאָרֶץ אִתְּכֶם מִכֹּל יֹצְאֵי הַתֵּבָה לְכֹל חַיַּת הָאָרֶץ:
יא וַהֲקִמֹתִי אֶת־בְּרִיתִי אִתְּכֶם וְלֹא־יִכָּרֵת כָּל־בָּשָׂר עוֹד מִמֵּי הַמַּבּוּל
יב וְלֹא־יִהְיֶה עוֹד מַבּוּל לְשַׁחֵת הָאָרֶץ: וַיֹּאמֶר אֱלֹהִים זֹאת אוֹת־הַבְּרִית
אֲשֶׁר־אֲנִי נֹתֵן בֵּינִי וּבֵינֵיכֶם וּבֵין כָּל־נֶפֶשׁ חַיָּה אֲשֶׁר אִתְּכֶם לְדֹרֹת
יג עוֹלָם: אֶת־קַשְׁתִּי נָתַתִּי בֶּעָנָן וְהָיְתָה לְאוֹת בְּרִית בֵּינִי וּבֵין הָאָרֶץ:
יד טו וְהָיָה בְּעַנְנִי עָנָן עַל־הָאָרֶץ וְנִרְאֲתָה הַקֶּשֶׁת בֶּעָנָן: וְזָכַרְתִּי אֶת־בְּרִיתִי
אֲשֶׁר בֵּינִי וּבֵינֵיכֶם וּבֵין כָּל־נֶפֶשׁ חַיָּה בְּכָל־בָּשָׂר וְלֹא־יִהְיֶה עוֹד הַמַּיִם
טז לְמַבּוּל לְשַׁחֵת כָּל־בָּשָׂר: וְהָיְתָה הַקֶּשֶׁת בֶּעָנָן וּרְאִיתִיהָ לִזְכֹּר בְּרִית
עוֹלָם בֵּין אֱלֹהִים וּבֵין כָּל־נֶפֶשׁ חַיָּה בְּכָל־בָּשָׂר אֲשֶׁר עַל־הָאָרֶץ:
יז וַיֹּאמֶר אֱלֹהִים אֶל־נֹחַ זֹאת אוֹת־הַבְּרִית אֲשֶׁר הֲקִמֹתִי בֵּינִי וּבֵין
כָּל־בָּשָׂר אֲשֶׁר עַל־הָאָרֶץ:

יח וַיִּהְיוּ בְנֵי־נֹחַ הַיֹּצְאִים מִן־הַתֵּבָה שֵׁם וְחָם וָיָפֶת וְחָם הוּא אֲבִי כְנָעַן: ח ששי
יט כ שְׁלֹשָׁה אֵלֶּה בְּנֵי־נֹחַ וּמֵאֵלֶּה נָפְצָה כָל־הָאָרֶץ: וַיָּחֶל נֹחַ אִישׁ הָאֲדָמָה
כא כב וַיִּטַּע כָּרֶם: וַיֵּשְׁתְּ מִן־הַיַּיִן וַיִּשְׁכָּר וַיִּתְגַּל בְּתוֹךְ אָהֳלֹה: וַיַּרְא חָם אֲבִי
כג כְנַעַן אֵת עֶרְוַת אָבִיו וַיַּגֵּד לִשְׁנֵי־אֶחָיו בַּחוּץ: וַיִּקַּח שֵׁם וָיֶפֶת אֶת־
הַשִּׂמְלָה וַיָּשִׂימוּ עַל־שְׁכֶם שְׁנֵיהֶם וַיֵּלְכוּ אֲחֹרַנִּית וַיְכַסּוּ אֵת עֶרְוַת

nakedness, averting their faces so as not to see the nakedness of their father.
24 Noaḥ woke from his wine and realized what his youngest son had done to
25 him. He said, "Cursed be Kenaan! The lowest of slaves shall he be to his
26 brothers." Then he said, "Blessed be the LORD, God of Shem; Kenaan shall
27 be his slave. May God enlarge Yefet, and let him dwell in the tents of Shem;
28 Kenaan shall be his slave." After the flood Noaḥ lived three hundred and fifty
29 years. Noaḥ lived a total of nine hundred and fifty years, and he died.
10 1 These are the descendants of Noaḥ's sons, Shem, Ḥam, and Yefet; after
2 the flood, children were born to them.[19] Yefet's sons were Gomer, Magog,
3 Madai, Yavan, Tuval, Meshekh, and Tiras. Gomer's sons were Ashkenaz,
4 Rifat, and Togarma. Yavan's sons were Elisha, Tarshish, Kitim, and Dodanim.
5 From these the seagoing nations spread out to their territories, each with
6 its own language, by their clans and their nations. Ḥam's sons were Kush,
7 Mitzrayim,[20] Put, and Kenaan. Kush's sons were Seva, Ḥavila, Savta, Raama,
8 and Savtekha. Raama's sons were Sheva and Dedan. Kush was the father of
9 Nimrod, the first mighty warrior on earth. He was a mighty hunter before the
LORD, which is why people still say, "Like Nimrod, a mighty hunter before
10 the LORD." His kingdom began with Babylon, Erekh, Akad, and Kalneh
11 in the land of Shinar. From that land, Ashur went out and built Nineveh,
12 Reḥovot Ir, Kalaḥ, and Resen between Nineveh and Kalaḥ; that is the great
13 city. Mitzrayim fathered the Ludim, Anamim, Lehavim and Naftuḥim,
14 Patrusim, Kasluḥim – from whom the Philistines descended – and the
15, 16 Kaftorim. Kenaan fathered Tzidon, his firstborn, and Ḥet, and the
17, 18 Jebusites, Amorites, and Girgashites, the Hivites, Arkites, and Sinites, the
Arvadites, Zemarites, and Hamatites. Later, the Canaanite families were
19 dispersed. The Canaanite borders were from Sidon toward Gerar near Aza,
20 and toward Sedom, Amora, Adma, and Tzevoyim, near Lasha. These were
the descendants of Ḥam, by their clans and their languages, with their lands
21 and their nations. Sons were also born to Shem. The older brother
22 of Yefet, he was the ancestor of all the sons of Ever. Shem's sons were Elam,
23 Ashur, Arpakhshad, Lud, and Aram. Aram's sons were Utz, Ḥul, Geter, and
24 Mash. Arpakhshad was the father of Shelaḥ, and Shelaḥ was the father of
25 Ever. To Ever, two sons were born. One was named Peleg, for in his time the
26 earth was divided.[21] His brother was named Yoktan. Yoktan was the father of
27, 28 Almodad, Shelef, Ḥatzarmavet, Yeraḥ, Hadoram, Uzal, Dikla, Oval, Avimael,
29, 30 Sheva, Ofir, Ḥavila, and Yovav; all these were Yoktan's sons. Their settlements
31 extended from Mesha toward Sefar, in the eastern hill country. These were the
descendants of Shem, by their clans and their languages, with their lands and

19 | The following are the eponymous ancestors of various nations.

20 | In this translation, Ḥam's son is rendered "Mitzrayim," while the nation is called "Egypt"; see introduction.

21 | Peleg evokes the Hebrew *niflega* (divided). This is often understood to refer to the dispersion recounted in 11:1–9.

כד אֲבִיהֶם וּפְנֵיהֶם אֲחֹרַנִּית וְעֶרְוַת אֲבִיהֶם לֹא רָאוּ: וַיִּיקֶץ נֹחַ מִיֵּינוֹ
כה וַיֵּדַע אֵת אֲשֶׁר־עָשָׂה לוֹ בְּנוֹ הַקָּטָן: וַיֹּאמֶר אָרוּר כְּנָעַן עֶבֶד עֲבָדִים
כו יִהְיֶה לְאֶחָיו: וַיֹּאמֶר בָּרוּךְ יְהוָה אֱלֹהֵי שֵׁם וִיהִי כְנַעַן עֶבֶד לָמוֹ:
כז כח יַפְתְּ אֱלֹהִים לְיֶפֶת וְיִשְׁכֹּן בְּאָהֳלֵי־שֵׁם וִיהִי כְנַעַן עֶבֶד לָמוֹ: וַיְחִי־נֹחַ
כט אַחַר הַמַּבּוּל שְׁלֹשׁ מֵאוֹת שָׁנָה וַחֲמִשִּׁים שָׁנָה: וַיְהִי כָּל־יְמֵי־נֹחַ תְּשַׁע
מֵאוֹת שָׁנָה וַחֲמִשִּׁים שָׁנָה וַיָּמֹת:

י א וְאֵלֶּה תּוֹלְדֹת בְּנֵי־נֹחַ שֵׁם חָם וָיָפֶת וַיִּוָּלְדוּ לָהֶם בָּנִים אַחַר הַמַּבּוּל:
ב ג בְּנֵי יֶפֶת גֹּמֶר וּמָגוֹג וּמָדַי וְיָוָן וְתֻבָל וּמֶשֶׁךְ וְתִירָס: וּבְנֵי גֹּמֶר אַשְׁכְּנַז
ד ה וְרִיפַת וְתֹגַרְמָה: וּבְנֵי יָוָן אֱלִישָׁה וְתַרְשִׁישׁ כִּתִּים וְדֹדָנִים: מֵאֵלֶּה
ו נִפְרְדוּ אִיֵּי הַגּוֹיִם בְּאַרְצֹתָם אִישׁ לִלְשֹׁנוֹ לְמִשְׁפְּחֹתָם בְּגוֹיֵהֶם: וּבְנֵי
ז חָם כּוּשׁ וּמִצְרַיִם וּפוּט וּכְנָעַן: וּבְנֵי כוּשׁ סְבָא וַחֲוִילָה וְסַבְתָּה וְרַעְמָה
ח וְסַבְתְּכָא וּבְנֵי רַעְמָה שְׁבָא וּדְדָן: וְכוּשׁ יָלַד אֶת־נִמְרֹד הוּא הֵחֵל
ט לִהְיוֹת גִּבֹּר בָּאָרֶץ: הוּא־הָיָה גִבֹּר־צַיִד לִפְנֵי יְהוָה עַל־כֵּן יֵאָמַר
י כְּנִמְרֹד גִּבּוֹר צַיִד לִפְנֵי יְהוָה: וַתְּהִי רֵאשִׁית מַמְלַכְתּוֹ בָּבֶל וְאֶרֶךְ
יא וְאַכַּד וְכַלְנֵה בְּאֶרֶץ שִׁנְעָר: מִן־הָאָרֶץ הַהִוא יָצָא אַשּׁוּר וַיִּבֶן אֶת־
יב נִינְוֵה וְאֶת־רְחֹבֹת עִיר וְאֶת־כָּלַח: וְאֶת־רֶסֶן בֵּין נִינְוֵה וּבֵין כָּלַח
יג הִוא הָעִיר הַגְּדֹלָה: וּמִצְרַיִם יָלַד אֶת־לוּדִים וְאֶת־עֲנָמִים וְאֶת־
יד לְהָבִים וְאֶת־נַפְתֻּחִים: וְאֶת־פַּתְרֻסִים וְאֶת־כַּסְלֻחִים אֲשֶׁר יָצְאוּ
טו מִשָּׁם פְּלִשְׁתִּים וְאֶת־כַּפְתֹּרִים: וּכְנַעַן יָלַד אֶת־צִידֹן
טז יז בְּכֹרוֹ וְאֶת־חֵת: וְאֶת־הַיְבוּסִי וְאֶת־הָאֱמֹרִי וְאֵת הַגִּרְגָּשִׁי: וְאֶת־הַחִוִּי
יח וְאֶת־הַעַרְקִי וְאֶת־הַסִּינִי: וְאֶת־הָאַרְוָדִי וְאֶת־הַצְּמָרִי וְאֶת־הַחֲמָתִי
יט וְאַחַר נָפֹצוּ מִשְׁפְּחוֹת הַכְּנַעֲנִי: וַיְהִי גְּבוּל הַכְּנַעֲנִי מִצִּידֹן בֹּאֲכָה גְרָרָה
כ עַד־עַזָּה בֹּאֲכָה סְדֹמָה וַעֲמֹרָה וְאַדְמָה וּצְבֹיִם עַד־לָשַׁע: אֵלֶּה בְנֵי־
כא חָם לְמִשְׁפְּחֹתָם לִלְשֹׁנֹתָם בְּאַרְצֹתָם בְּגוֹיֵהֶם: וּלְשֵׁם יֻלַּד
כב גַּם־הוּא אֲבִי כָּל־בְּנֵי־עֵבֶר אֲחִי יֶפֶת הַגָּדוֹל: בְּנֵי שֵׁם עֵילָם וְאַשּׁוּר
כג כד וְאַרְפַּכְשַׁד וְלוּד וַאֲרָם: וּבְנֵי אֲרָם עוּץ וְחוּל וְגֶתֶר וָמַשׁ: וְאַרְפַּכְשַׁד
כה יָלַד אֶת־שָׁלַח וְשֶׁלַח יָלַד אֶת־עֵבֶר: וּלְעֵבֶר יֻלַּד שְׁנֵי בָנִים שֵׁם הָאֶחָד
כו פֶּלֶג כִּי בְיָמָיו נִפְלְגָה הָאָרֶץ וְשֵׁם אָחִיו יָקְטָן: וְיָקְטָן יָלַד אֶת־אַלְמוֹדָד
כז וְאֶת־שָׁלֶף וְאֶת־חֲצַרְמָוֶת וְאֶת־יָרַח: וְאֶת־הֲדוֹרָם וְאֶת־אוּזָל וְאֶת־
כח כט דִּקְלָה: וְאֶת־עוֹבָל וְאֶת־אֲבִימָאֵל וְאֶת־שְׁבָא: וְאֶת־אוֹפִר וְאֶת־חֲוִילָה
ל וְאֶת־יוֹבָב כָּל־אֵלֶּה בְּנֵי יָקְטָן: וַיְהִי מוֹשָׁבָם מִמֵּשָׁא בֹּאֲכָה סְפָרָה
לא הַר הַקֶּדֶם: אֵלֶּה בְנֵי־שֵׁם לְמִשְׁפְּחֹתָם לִלְשֹׁנֹתָם בְּאַרְצֹתָם לְגוֹיֵהֶם:

32 their nations. These, then, are the clans of the sons of Noaḥ, by their lines, in
their nations. And from these, the nations spread out across the earth after
the flood.
11 1 2 The whole world spoke the same language, the same words. And as the people
migrated from the east they found a valley in the land of Shinar and settled
3 there. They said to each other, "Come, let us make bricks, let us bake them
4 thoroughly." They used bricks for stone and tar for mortar. And they said,
"Come, let us build ourselves a city and a tower that reaches the heavens,
and make a name for ourselves. Otherwise we will be scattered across the
5 face of the earth." But the LORD came down to see the city and the tower
6 being built by the children of men. The LORD said, "If, as one people with
one language, they have begun to do this, nothing they plan to do will be
7 impossible for them. Let us go down and confuse their language so that one
8 will not understand the speech of another." From there the LORD scattered
9 them all over the earth, and they abandoned the building of the city. That is
why it was called Bavel, because it was there that the LORD confused[22] the
language of all the earth; and from there the LORD scattered them all across
the face of the earth.
10 These are the descendants of Shem. When Shem was one hundred years
11 old, he had a son, Arpakhshad, two years after the flood. After Arpakhshad
was born, Shem lived five hundred years and had other sons and
12 daughters. When Arpakhshad was thirty-five years old, he had a son,
13 Shelaḥ. After Shelaḥ was born, Arpakhshad lived four hundred and three years
14 and had other sons and daughters. When Shelaḥ was thirty years
15 old, he had a son, Ever. After Ever was born, Shelaḥ lived four hundred and
16 three years and had other sons and daughters. Ever lived thirty-four
17 years and then had a son, Peleg. After Peleg was born, Ever lived four hundred
18 and thirty years and had other sons and daughters. Peleg lived thirty
19 years and then had a son, Reu. After Reu was born, Peleg lived two hundred
20 and nine years and had other sons and daughters. Reu lived thirty-
21 two years and then had a son, Serug. After Serug was born, Reu lived two
22 hundred and seven years and had other sons and daughters. Serug
23 lived thirty years and then had a son, Naḥor. After Naḥor was born, Serug
24 lived two hundred years and had other sons and daughters. Naḥor
25 lived twenty-nine years and then had a son, Teraḥ. After Teraḥ was born,
Naḥor lived one hundred and nineteen years and had other sons and
26 daughters. Teraḥ lived seventy years and fathered Avram, Naḥor,
27 and Haran. These are the descendants of Teraḥ. Teraḥ was the father of Avram,

22 | The name Bavel (Babylon) resonates with *balal* (confused).

לב אֵ֣לֶּה מִשְׁפְּחֹ֧ת בְּנֵי־נֹ֛חַ לְתוֹלְדֹתָ֖ם בְּגוֹיֵהֶ֑ם וּמֵאֵ֜לֶּה נִפְרְד֧וּ הַגּוֹיִ֛ם
בָּאָ֖רֶץ אַחַ֥ר הַמַּבּֽוּל׃
יא א ב וַֽיְהִ֥י כָל־הָאָ֖רֶץ שָׂפָ֣ה אֶחָ֑ת וּדְבָרִ֖ים אֲחָדִֽים׃ וַֽיְהִ֖י בְּנָסְעָ֣ם מִקֶּ֑דֶם ט שביעי
ג וַֽיִּמְצְא֥וּ בִקְעָ֛ה בְּאֶ֥רֶץ שִׁנְעָ֖ר וַיֵּ֥שְׁבוּ שָֽׁם׃ וַיֹּאמְר֞וּ אִ֣ישׁ אֶל־רֵעֵ֗הוּ הָ֚בָה
נִלְבְּנָ֣ה לְבֵנִ֔ים וְנִשְׂרְפָ֖ה לִשְׂרֵפָ֑ה וַתְּהִ֨י לָהֶ֤ם הַלְּבֵנָה֙ לְאָ֔בֶן וְהַ֣חֵמָ֔ר הָיָ֥ה
ד לָהֶ֖ם לַחֹֽמֶר׃ וַיֹּאמְר֞וּ הָ֣בָה ׀ נִבְנֶה־לָּ֣נוּ עִ֗יר וּמִגְדָּל֙ וְרֹאשׁ֣וֹ בַשָּׁמַ֔יִם
ה וְנַֽעֲשֶׂה־לָּ֖נוּ שֵׁ֑ם פֶּן־נָפ֖וּץ עַל־פְּנֵ֥י כָל־הָאָֽרֶץ׃ וַיֵּ֣רֶד יְהוָ֔ה לִרְאֹ֥ת אֶת־
ו הָעִ֖יר וְאֶת־הַמִּגְדָּ֑ל אֲשֶׁ֥ר בָּנ֖וּ בְּנֵ֥י הָאָדָֽם׃ וַיֹּ֣אמֶר יְהוָ֗ה הֵ֣ן עַ֤ם אֶחָד֙
וְשָׂפָ֤ה אַחַת֙ לְכֻלָּ֔ם וְזֶ֖ה הַחִלָּ֣ם לַעֲשׂ֑וֹת וְעַתָּה֙ לֹֽא־יִבָּצֵ֣ר מֵהֶ֔ם כֹּ֛ל אֲשֶׁ֥ר
ז יָזְמ֖וּ לַעֲשֽׂוֹת׃ הָ֚בָה נֵֽרְדָ֔ה וְנָבְלָ֥ה שָׁ֖ם שְׂפָתָ֑ם אֲשֶׁר֙ לֹ֣א יִשְׁמְע֔וּ אִ֖ישׁ
ח שְׂפַ֥ת רֵעֵֽהוּ׃ וַיָּ֨פֶץ יְהוָ֥ה אֹתָ֛ם מִשָּׁ֖ם עַל־פְּנֵ֣י כָל־הָאָ֑רֶץ וַֽיַּחְדְּל֖וּ לִבְנֹ֥ת
ט הָעִֽיר׃ עַל־כֵּ֞ן קָרָ֤א שְׁמָהּ֙ בָּבֶ֔ל כִּי־שָׁ֛ם בָּלַ֥ל יְהוָ֖ה שְׂפַ֣ת כָּל־הָאָ֑רֶץ
וּמִשָּׁם֙ הֱפִיצָ֣ם יְהוָ֔ה עַל־פְּנֵ֖י כָּל־הָאָֽרֶץ׃
י אֵ֚לֶּה תּוֹלְדֹ֣ת שֵׁ֔ם שֵׁ֚ם בֶּן־מְאַ֣ת שָׁנָ֔ה וַיּ֖וֹלֶד אֶת־אַרְפַּכְשָׁ֑ד שְׁנָתַ֖יִם
יא אַחַ֥ר הַמַּבּֽוּל׃ וַֽיְחִי־שֵׁ֗ם אַֽחֲרֵי֙ הוֹלִיד֣וֹ אֶת־אַרְפַּכְשָׁ֔ד חֲמֵ֥שׁ מֵא֖וֹת
יב שָׁנָ֑ה וַיּ֥וֹלֶד בָּנִ֖ים וּבָנֽוֹת׃ וְאַרְפַּכְשַׁ֣ד חַ֔י חָמֵ֥שׁ וּשְׁלֹשִׁ֖ים שָׁנָ֑ה
יג וַיּ֖וֹלֶד אֶת־שָֽׁלַח׃ וַיְחִ֣י אַרְפַּכְשַׁ֗ד אַֽחֲרֵי֙ הוֹלִיד֣וֹ אֶת־שֶׁ֔לַח שָׁלֹ֣שׁ שָׁנִ֔ים
יד וְאַרְבַּ֥ע מֵא֖וֹת שָׁנָ֑ה וַיּ֥וֹלֶד בָּנִ֖ים וּבָנֽוֹת׃ וְשֶׁ֥לַח חַ֖י שְׁלֹשִׁ֣ים
טו שָׁנָ֑ה וַיּ֖וֹלֶד אֶת־עֵֽבֶר׃ וַֽיְחִי־שֶׁ֗לַח אַֽחֲרֵי֙ הוֹלִיד֣וֹ אֶת־עֵ֔בֶר שָׁלֹ֣שׁ שָׁנִ֔ים
טז וְאַרְבַּ֥ע מֵא֖וֹת שָׁנָ֑ה וַיּ֥וֹלֶד בָּנִ֖ים וּבָנֽוֹת׃ וַֽיְחִי־עֵ֕בֶר אַרְבַּ֥ע
יז וּשְׁלֹשִׁ֖ים שָׁנָ֑ה וַיּ֖וֹלֶד אֶת־פָּֽלֶג׃ וַֽיְחִי־עֵ֗בֶר אַֽחֲרֵי֙ הוֹלִיד֣וֹ אֶת־פֶּ֔לֶג
יח שְׁלֹשִׁ֣ים שָׁנָ֔ה וְאַרְבַּ֥ע מֵא֖וֹת שָׁנָ֑ה וַיּ֥וֹלֶד בָּנִ֖ים וּבָנֽוֹת׃ וַֽיְחִי־
יט פֶ֖לֶג שְׁלֹשִׁ֣ים שָׁנָ֑ה וַיּ֖וֹלֶד אֶת־רְעֽוּ׃ וַֽיְחִי־פֶ֗לֶג אַֽחֲרֵי֙ הוֹלִיד֣וֹ אֶת־רְע֔וּ
כ תֵּ֥שַׁע שָׁנִ֖ים וּמָאתַ֣יִם שָׁנָ֑ה וַיּ֥וֹלֶד בָּנִ֖ים וּבָנֽוֹת׃ וַיְחִ֣י רְע֔וּ
כא שְׁתַּ֥יִם וּשְׁלֹשִׁ֖ים שָׁנָ֑ה וַיּ֖וֹלֶד אֶת־שְׂרֽוּג׃ וַיְחִ֣י רְע֗וּ אַֽחֲרֵי֙ הוֹלִיד֣וֹ אֶת־
כב שְׂר֔וּג שֶׁ֥בַע שָׁנִ֖ים וּמָאתַ֣יִם שָׁנָ֑ה וַיּ֥וֹלֶד בָּנִ֖ים וּבָנֽוֹת׃ וַיְחִ֥י
כג שְׂר֖וּג שְׁלֹשִׁ֣ים שָׁנָ֑ה וַיּ֖וֹלֶד אֶת־נָחֽוֹר׃ וַיְחִ֣י שְׂר֗וּג אַחֲרֵ֛י הוֹלִיד֥וֹ אֶת־
כד נָח֖וֹר מָאתַ֣יִם שָׁנָ֑ה וַיּ֥וֹלֶד בָּנִ֖ים וּבָנֽוֹת׃ וַיְחִ֣י נָח֔וֹר תֵּ֥שַׁע
כה וְעֶשְׂרִ֖ים שָׁנָ֑ה וַיּ֖וֹלֶד אֶת־תָּֽרַח׃ וַיְחִ֣י נָח֗וֹר אַֽחֲרֵי֙ הוֹלִיד֣וֹ אֶת־תֶּ֔רַח
כו תְּשַֽׁע־עֶשְׂרֵ֥ה שָׁנָ֖ה וּמְאַ֣ת שָׁנָ֑ה וַיּ֥וֹלֶד בָּנִ֖ים וּבָנֽוֹת׃ וַֽיְחִי־
כז תֶ֖רַח שִׁבְעִ֣ים שָׁנָ֑ה וַיּוֹלֶד֙ אֶת־אַבְרָ֔ם אֶת־נָח֖וֹר וְאֶת־הָרָֽן׃ וְאֵ֙לֶּה֙
תּוֹלְדֹ֣ת תֶּ֔רַח תֶּ֚רַח הוֹלִ֣יד אֶת־אַבְרָ֔ם אֶת־נָח֖וֹר וְאֶת־הָרָ֑ן וְהָרָ֖ן

28 Naḥor, and Haran, and Haran had a son, Lot. While his father Teraḥ was
29 still alive, Haran died in the land of his birth, Ur Kasdim. Avram and Naḥor
married; the name of Avram's wife was Sarai, and the name of Naḥor's wife
30 was Milka. She was the daughter of Haran, father of Milka and Yiska. And
31 Sarai was barren – she had no child. Teraḥ took his son Avram, and his
grandson Lot, son of Haran, and his daughter-in-law Sarai, his son Avram's
wife, and together they set out from Ur Kasdim to go to the land of Canaan.
32 But when they arrived at Ḥaran, they settled there. Teraḥ lived two hundred
and five years, and he died in Ḥaran.

LEKH LEKHA

12 1 The LORD said to Avram, "Go – from your land, your birthplace, and your
2 father's house – to the land that I will show you. I will make you a great
nation, and I will bless you and make your name great. You will become a
3 blessing. And I will bless those who bless you, and those who curse you I
4 will curse. And through you, all the families of the earth will be blessed." So
Avram went, as the LORD had told him, and with him went Lot. Avram was
5 seventy-five years old when he left Ḥaran. Avram took Sarai his wife, and
Lot his nephew, and all the wealth they had acquired and the people they
had gathered in Ḥaran. They set out to go to the land of Canaan, and they
6 entered the land of Canaan.Avram traveled through the land to the region of
7 Shekhem, to the Oak of Moreh. The Canaanites were then in the land. Then
the LORD appeared to Avram and said, "To your descendants I will give this
8 land." There he built an altar to the LORD, who had appeared to him. And from
there he moved on to the hills east of Beit El, and pitched his tent with Beit El
to the west and Ai to the east. There he built an altar to the LORD and called
9 on the name of the LORD. Then Avram journeyed on, traveling toward the
Negev.
10 There was a famine in the land. Avram went down to Egypt to stay there for
11 a while because the famine in the land was severe. And as his arrival in Egypt
drew close, he said to Sarai his wife, "I know what a beautiful woman you are.
12 When the Egyptians see you, they will say, 'She is his wife'; they will kill me
13 and keep you alive. Please, say you are my sister. Then I will be treated well for
14 your sake, and because of you my life will be spared." When Avram came to
Egypt, the Egyptians saw the woman, saw that she was very beautiful indeed.
15 And when Pharaoh's officials saw her, they praised her to Pharaoh, and the
16 woman was taken into Pharaoh's palace. He treated Avram well for her sake:
he acquired flocks, herds, donkeys, male and female servants, she-donkeys,
17 and camels. But the LORD struck Pharaoh and his household with terrible
18 afflictions because of Avram's wife Sarai. Pharaoh summoned Avram and said,
"What have you done to me? Why did you not tell me she was your wife?
19 Why did you say 'She is my sister,' so that I took her as a wife? Now – here is
20 your wife. Take her. Go." Pharaoh gave orders to his men about him, and they
13 1 sent him on his way, together with his wife and all that he had. Then Avram

כח הוֹלִיד אֶת־לוֹט׃ וַיָּמָת הָרָן עַל־פְּנֵי תֶּרַח אָבִיו בְּאֶרֶץ מוֹלַדְתּוֹ בְּאוּר
כט כַּשְׂדִּים׃ וַיִּקַּח אַבְרָם וְנָחוֹר לָהֶם נָשִׁים שֵׁם אֵשֶׁת־אַבְרָם שָׂרָי וְשֵׁם מפטיר
ל אֵשֶׁת־נָחוֹר מִלְכָּה בַּת־הָרָן אֲבִי־מִלְכָּה וַאֲבִי יִסְכָּה׃ וַתְּהִי שָׂרַי
לא עֲקָרָה אֵין לָהּ וָלָד׃ וַיִּקַּח תֶּרַח אֶת־אַבְרָם בְּנוֹ וְאֶת־לוֹט בֶּן־הָרָן
בֶּן־בְּנוֹ וְאֵת שָׂרַי כַּלָּתוֹ אֵשֶׁת אַבְרָם בְּנוֹ וַיֵּצְאוּ אִתָּם מֵאוּר כַּשְׂדִּים
לב לָלֶכֶת אַרְצָה כְּנַעַן וַיָּבֹאוּ עַד־חָרָן וַיֵּשְׁבוּ שָׁם׃ וַיִּהְיוּ יְמֵי־תֶרַח חָמֵשׁ
שָׁנִים וּמָאתַיִם שָׁנָה וַיָּמָת תֶּרַח בְּחָרָן׃

יב א וַיֹּאמֶר יהוה אֶל־אַבְרָם לֶךְ־לְךָ מֵאַרְצְךָ וּמִמּוֹלַדְתְּךָ וּמִבֵּית אָבִיךָ י לך לך
ב אֶל־הָאָרֶץ אֲשֶׁר אַרְאֶךָּ׃ וְאֶעֶשְׂךָ לְגוֹי גָּדוֹל וַאֲבָרֶכְךָ וַאֲגַדְּלָה שְׁמֶךָ
ג וֶהְיֵה בְּרָכָה׃ וַאֲבָרְכָה מְבָרְכֶיךָ וּמְקַלֶּלְךָ אָאֹר וְנִבְרְכוּ בְךָ כֹּל מִשְׁפְּחֹת
ד הָאֲדָמָה׃ וַיֵּלֶךְ אַבְרָם כַּאֲשֶׁר דִּבֶּר אֵלָיו יהוה וַיֵּלֶךְ אִתּוֹ לוֹט וְאַבְרָם
ה בֶּן־חָמֵשׁ שָׁנִים וְשִׁבְעִים שָׁנָה בְּצֵאתוֹ מֵחָרָן׃ וַיִּקַּח אַבְרָם אֶת־שָׂרַי
אִשְׁתּוֹ וְאֶת־לוֹט בֶּן־אָחִיו וְאֶת־כָּל־רְכוּשָׁם אֲשֶׁר רָכָשׁוּ וְאֶת־הַנֶּפֶשׁ
ו אֲשֶׁר־עָשׂוּ בְחָרָן וַיֵּצְאוּ לָלֶכֶת אַרְצָה כְּנַעַן וַיָּבֹאוּ אַרְצָה כְּנָעַן׃ וַיַּעֲבֹר
אַבְרָם בָּאָרֶץ עַד מְקוֹם שְׁכֶם עַד אֵלוֹן מוֹרֶה וְהַכְּנַעֲנִי אָז בָּאָרֶץ׃
ז וַיֵּרָא יהוה אֶל־אַבְרָם וַיֹּאמֶר לְזַרְעֲךָ אֶתֵּן אֶת־הָאָרֶץ הַזֹּאת וַיִּבֶן שָׁם
ח מִזְבֵּחַ לַיהוה הַנִּרְאֶה אֵלָיו׃ וַיַּעְתֵּק מִשָּׁם הָהָרָה מִקֶּדֶם לְבֵית־אֵל
וַיֵּט אָהֳלֹה בֵּית־אֵל מִיָּם וְהָעַי מִקֶּדֶם וַיִּבֶן־שָׁם מִזְבֵּחַ לַיהוה וַיִּקְרָא
ט בְּשֵׁם יהוה׃ וַיִּסַּע אַבְרָם הָלוֹךְ וְנָסוֹעַ הַנֶּגְבָּה׃
י וַיְהִי רָעָב בָּאָרֶץ וַיֵּרֶד אַבְרָם מִצְרַיְמָה לָגוּר שָׁם כִּי־כָבֵד הָרָעָב
יא בָּאָרֶץ׃ וַיְהִי כַּאֲשֶׁר הִקְרִיב לָבוֹא מִצְרָיְמָה וַיֹּאמֶר אֶל־שָׂרַי אִשְׁתּוֹ
יב הִנֵּה־נָא יָדַעְתִּי כִּי אִשָּׁה יְפַת־מַרְאֶה אָתְּ׃ וְהָיָה כִּי־יִרְאוּ אֹתָךְ
יג הַמִּצְרִים וְאָמְרוּ אִשְׁתּוֹ זֹאת וְהָרְגוּ אֹתִי וְאֹתָךְ יְחַיּוּ׃ אִמְרִי־נָא אֲחֹתִי
יד אָתְּ לְמַעַן יִיטַב־לִי בַעֲבוּרֵךְ וְחָיְתָה נַפְשִׁי בִּגְלָלֵךְ׃ וַיְהִי כְּבוֹא אַבְרָם שני
טו מִצְרָיְמָה וַיִּרְאוּ הַמִּצְרִים אֶת־הָאִשָּׁה כִּי־יָפָה הִוא מְאֹד׃ וַיִּרְאוּ אֹתָהּ
שָׂרֵי פַרְעֹה וַיְהַלְלוּ אֹתָהּ אֶל־פַּרְעֹה וַתֻּקַּח הָאִשָּׁה בֵּית פַּרְעֹה׃
טז וּלְאַבְרָם הֵיטִיב בַּעֲבוּרָהּ וַיְהִי־לוֹ צֹאן־וּבָקָר וַחֲמֹרִים וַעֲבָדִים וּשְׁפָחֹת
יז וַאֲתֹנֹת וּגְמַלִּים׃ וַיְנַגַּע יהוה ׀ אֶת־פַּרְעֹה נְגָעִים גְּדֹלִים וְאֶת־בֵּיתוֹ
יח עַל־דְּבַר שָׂרַי אֵשֶׁת אַבְרָם׃ וַיִּקְרָא פַרְעֹה לְאַבְרָם וַיֹּאמֶר מַה־זֹּאת
יט עָשִׂיתָ לִּי לָמָּה לֹא־הִגַּדְתָּ לִּי כִּי אִשְׁתְּךָ הִוא׃ לָמָה אָמַרְתָּ אֲחֹתִי
כ הִוא וָאֶקַּח אֹתָהּ לִי לְאִשָּׁה וְעַתָּה הִנֵּה אִשְׁתְּךָ קַח וָלֵךְ׃ וַיְצַו עָלָיו
יג א פַּרְעֹה אֲנָשִׁים וַיְשַׁלְּחוּ אֹתוֹ וְאֶת־אִשְׁתּוֹ וְאֶת־כָּל־אֲשֶׁר־לוֹ׃ וַיַּעַל

went up from Egypt to the Negev with his wife and all he had, and with him
2 went Lot. And Avram had become very wealthy in cattle, silver, and gold.
3 From the Negev he continued on his journey to Beit El, to the site between
4 Beit El and Ai where his tent had previously been, and where he had first made
5 an altar. There Avram called on the name of the LORD. Lot, who went with
6 Avram, had flocks, herds, and tents as well, and the land could not support
them living together; so many were their possessions that they were unable
7 to live side by side. A dispute broke out between Avram's herdsmen and those
of Lot; and the Canaanites and the Perizzites were then too living in the land.
8 Avram said to Lot, "Please, let there be no friction between me and you, and
9 between my herdsmen and yours, for we are brothers. The whole land lies
before you; please separate yourself from me. If you go to the left, I will go to
10 the right; if you go to the right, I will go to the left." Lot raised his eyes and
saw that the whole plain of the Jordan up to Tzoar was well watered. It was
like the garden of the LORD, like the land of Egypt; this was before the LORD
11 destroyed Sedom and Amora.[23] So Lot chose for himself the entire plain of
12 the Jordan. He traveled eastward, and the two men separated. Avram settled
in the land of Canaan while Lot settled in the cities of the plain, pitching his
13 tent near Sedom. But the people of Sedom were evil, great sinners against
14 the LORD. After Lot had separated from him, the LORD said to Avram, "Raise
your eyes and look around from where you are to the north, south, east, and
15 16 west. All the land you see I will give to you and your descendants forever. I
will make your descendants like the dust of the earth: if anyone could count
17 the dust of the earth, then could your descendants be counted. Get up and
18 walk through the length and breadth of the land, for to you shall I give it." So
Avram took his tent and came to settle by the Oaks of Mamre, in Ḥevron.
There he built an altar to the LORD.
14 1 In the days of Amrafel, king of Shinar, Aryokh, king of Elasar, Kedorlaomer,
2 king of Eilam, and Tidal, king of Goyim, they all waged war against Bera,
king of Sedom, Birsha, king of Amora, Shinav, king of Adma, and Shemever,
3 king of Tzevoyim, and the king of Bela – that is, Tzoar. These had all come
4 together in Siddim Valley – now the Dead Sea; for twelve years they had
5 served Kedorlaomer, but in the thirteenth year they had rebelled. In the
fourteenth year Kedorlaomer and his allied kings came and defeated the
Refaim in Ashterot Karnayim, the Zuzim in Ham, the Eimim in Shaveh
6 Kiryatayim,[24] and the Horites in the hill country of Se'ir as far as Eil Paran
7 by the wilderness. Then they swung back and came to Ein Mishpat – that
is, Kadesh – conquering the whole territory of the Amalekites, as well as
8 the Amorites living in Ḥatzetzon Tamar. Then the kings of Sedom, Amora,

---

23 | See chapter 19.

24 | Concerning these peoples, see Deuteronomy 2:10–11, 20.

ב אַבְרָם מִמִּצְרַיִם הוּא וְאִשְׁתּוֹ וְכָל־אֲשֶׁר־לוֹ וְלוֹט עִמּוֹ הַנֶּגְבָּה׃ וְאַבְרָם
ג כָּבֵד מְאֹד בַּמִּקְנֶה בַּכֶּסֶף וּבַזָּהָב׃ וַיֵּלֶךְ לְמַסָּעָיו מִנֶּגֶב וְעַד־בֵּית־אֵל
עַד־הַמָּקוֹם אֲשֶׁר־הָיָה שָׁם אָהֳלֹה בַּתְּחִלָּה בֵּין בֵּית־אֵל וּבֵין הָעָי׃
ד אֶל־מְקוֹם הַמִּזְבֵּחַ אֲשֶׁר־עָשָׂה שָׁם בָּרִאשֹׁנָה וַיִּקְרָא שָׁם אַבְרָם
ה בְּשֵׁם יְהוָה׃ וְגַם־לְלוֹט הַהֹלֵךְ אֶת־אַבְרָם הָיָה צֹאן־וּבָקָר וְאֹהָלִים׃ שלישי
ו וְלֹא־נָשָׂא אֹתָם הָאָרֶץ לָשֶׁבֶת יַחְדָּו כִּי־הָיָה רְכוּשָׁם רָב וְלֹא יָכְלוּ
ז לָשֶׁבֶת יַחְדָּו׃ וַיְהִי־רִיב בֵּין רֹעֵי מִקְנֵה־אַבְרָם וּבֵין רֹעֵי מִקְנֵה־לוֹט
ח וְהַכְּנַעֲנִי וְהַפְּרִזִּי אָז יֹשֵׁב בָּאָרֶץ׃ וַיֹּאמֶר אַבְרָם אֶל־לוֹט אַל־נָא תְהִי
ט מְרִיבָה בֵּינִי וּבֵינֶךָ וּבֵין רֹעַי וּבֵין רֹעֶיךָ כִּי־אֲנָשִׁים אַחִים אֲנָחְנוּ׃ הֲלֹא
כָל־הָאָרֶץ לְפָנֶיךָ הִפָּרֶד נָא מֵעָלָי אִם־הַשְּׂמֹאל וְאֵימִנָה וְאִם־הַיָּמִין
י וְאַשְׂמְאִילָה׃ וַיִּשָּׂא־לוֹט אֶת־עֵינָיו וַיַּרְא אֶת־כָּל־כִּכַּר הַיַּרְדֵּן כִּי כֻלָּהּ
מַשְׁקֶה לִפְנֵי ׀ שַׁחֵת יְהוָה אֶת־סְדֹם וְאֶת־עֲמֹרָה כְּגַן־יְהוָה כְּאֶרֶץ
יא מִצְרַיִם בֹּאֲכָה צֹעַר׃ וַיִּבְחַר־לוֹ לוֹט אֵת כָּל־כִּכַּר הַיַּרְדֵּן וַיִּסַּע לוֹט
יב מִקֶּדֶם וַיִּפָּרְדוּ אִישׁ מֵעַל אָחִיו׃ אַבְרָם יָשַׁב בְּאֶרֶץ־כְּנָעַן וְלוֹט יָשַׁב
יג בְּעָרֵי הַכִּכָּר וַיֶּאֱהַל עַד־סְדֹם׃ וְאַנְשֵׁי סְדֹם רָעִים וְחַטָּאִים לַיהוָה
יד מְאֹד׃ וַיהוָה אָמַר אֶל־אַבְרָם אַחֲרֵי הִפָּרֶד־לוֹט מֵעִמּוֹ שָׂא־נָא עֵינֶיךָ
טו וּרְאֵה מִן־הַמָּקוֹם אֲשֶׁר־אַתָּה שָׁם צָפֹנָה וָנֶגְבָּה וָקֵדְמָה וָיָמָּה׃ כִּי
אֶת־כָּל־הָאָרֶץ אֲשֶׁר־אַתָּה רֹאֶה לְךָ אֶתְּנֶנָּה וּלְזַרְעֲךָ עַד־עוֹלָם׃
טז וְשַׂמְתִּי אֶת־זַרְעֲךָ כַּעֲפַר הָאָרֶץ אֲשֶׁר ׀ אִם־יוּכַל אִישׁ לִמְנוֹת אֶת־
יז עֲפַר הָאָרֶץ גַּם־זַרְעֲךָ יִמָּנֶה׃ קוּם הִתְהַלֵּךְ בָּאָרֶץ לְאָרְכָּהּ וּלְרָחְבָּהּ
יח כִּי לְךָ אֶתְּנֶנָּה׃ וַיֶּאֱהַל אַבְרָם וַיָּבֹא וַיֵּשֶׁב בְּאֵלֹנֵי מַמְרֵא אֲשֶׁר בְּחֶבְרוֹן
וַיִּבֶן־שָׁם מִזְבֵּחַ לַיהוָה׃

יד א וַיְהִי בִּימֵי אַמְרָפֶל מֶלֶךְ־שִׁנְעָר אַרְיוֹךְ מֶלֶךְ אֶלָּסָר כְּדָרְלָעֹמֶר מֶלֶךְ יא רביעי
ב עֵילָם וְתִדְעָל מֶלֶךְ גּוֹיִם׃ עָשׂוּ מִלְחָמָה אֶת־בֶּרַע מֶלֶךְ סְדֹם וְאֶת־
בִּרְשַׁע מֶלֶךְ עֲמֹרָה שִׁנְאָב ׀ מֶלֶךְ אַדְמָה וְשֶׁמְאֵבֶר מֶלֶךְ צביים וּמֶלֶךְ צְבוֹיִם
ג בֶּלַע הִיא־צֹעַר׃ כָּל־אֵלֶּה חָבְרוּ אֶל־עֵמֶק הַשִּׂדִּים הוּא יָם הַמֶּלַח׃
ד שְׁתֵּים עֶשְׂרֵה שָׁנָה עָבְדוּ אֶת־כְּדָרְלָעֹמֶר וּשְׁלֹשׁ־עֶשְׂרֵה שָׁנָה מָרָדוּ׃
ה וּבְאַרְבַּע עֶשְׂרֵה שָׁנָה בָּא כְדָרְלָעֹמֶר וְהַמְּלָכִים אֲשֶׁר אִתּוֹ וַיַּכּוּ אֶת־
רְפָאִים בְּעַשְׁתְּרֹת קַרְנַיִם וְאֶת־הַזּוּזִים בְּהָם וְאֵת הָאֵימִים בְּשָׁוֵה
ו קִרְיָתָיִם׃ וְאֶת־הַחֹרִי בְּהַרְרָם שֵׂעִיר עַד אֵיל פָּארָן אֲשֶׁר עַל־הַמִּדְבָּר׃
ז וַיָּשֻׁבוּ וַיָּבֹאוּ אֶל־עֵין מִשְׁפָּט הִוא קָדֵשׁ וַיַּכּוּ אֶת־כָּל־שְׂדֵה הָעֲמָלֵקִי
ח וְגַם אֶת־הָאֱמֹרִי הַיֹּשֵׁב בְּחַצְצֹן תָּמָר׃ וַיֵּצֵא מֶלֶךְ־סְדֹם וּמֶלֶךְ עֲמֹרָה

Adma, Tzevoyim, and Bela – that is, Tzoar – marched out and drew up their
9 battle lines in Siddim Valley against Kedorlaomer, king of Eilam, Tidal, king
of Goyim, Amrafel, king of Shinar, and Aryokh, king of Elasar: four kings
10 battling five. The Siddim Valley was riddled with tar pits, and when the kings
of Sedom and Amora tried to flee, they fell into them. The others fled to the
11 mountains. The victors seized all the possessions of Sedom and Amora and
12 all the food, and they left, taking with them – since he had been living in
13 Sedom – Avram's nephew, Lot, and his possessions. A fugitive came and
reported this to Avram the Hebrew, who was then living near the Oaks of
14 Mamre the Amorite, a kinsman of Avram's allies, Eshkol and Aner. When
Avram heard that his own kinsman had been taken captive, he marshaled the
three hundred eighteen trained men born in his household, and went in
15 pursuit as far as Dan. He divided his forces against the captors at night and
16 defeated them, pursuing them to Ḥova, north of Damascus. He recovered all
the plunder, as well as his kinsman Lot and his possessions, the women, and
17 the other survivors as well. When he returned from defeating Kedorlaomer
and the kings with him, the king of Sedom came out to greet him at Shaveh
18 Valley – that is, the Valley of the King. And Malki Tzedek, king of Shalem,
19 offered bread and wine. He was a priest of God Most High, and he blessed
Avram, saying: "Blessed be Avram by God Most High, Maker of heaven and
20 earth, and blessed be God Most High who delivered your foes into your
21 hand." Then Avram gave him a tenth of everything. And the king of Sedom
said to Avram, "Give me the people, and keep the possessions for yourself."
22 But Avram said to the king of Sedom, "I raise my hand in oath to the LORD,
23 God Most High, Maker of heaven and earth, that I will not accept anything
of yours, not even a thread or a shoe strap, so that you never shall say, 'I made
24 Avram rich.' I will accept nothing but what my young men have eaten and the
share that belongs to the men who went with me – Aner, Eshkol, and Mamre;
15 1 let them have their share." After these events the word of the LORD
came to Avram in a vision, saying: "Do not be afraid, Avram. I am your
2 shield. Your reward shall be very great." But Avram said, "My Lord GOD, what
will You have given me if I remain childless, and the one who will take charge
3 of my household is Eliezer of Damascus?"[25] Avram said, "You have given me
4 no children. A man of my household will be my heir." Then the word of the
LORD came to him: "That man will not be your heir; one who comes forth
5 from your own loins will be your heir." He took him outside and said, "Look
at the heavens and count the stars – if indeed you can count them." He said
6 to him, "That is how your descendants will be." And because Avram put his
7 trust in the LORD, He reckoned it to him as righteousness.[26] And He told him,
"I am the LORD who brought you out from Ur Kasdim to give you this land
8 to possess it." And he said, "My Lord GOD, how shall I know that I will
9 possess it?" And he said to him, "Take for me a three-year-old heifer, and a

---

25 | Eliezer is understood to have been a prominent servant of Avram.

26 | Alternatively, Avram recognized the righteousness of God.

וּמֶלֶךְ אַדְמָה וּמֶלֶךְ צְבֹיִים וּמֶלֶךְ בֶּלַע הִוא־צֹעַר וַיַּעַרְכוּ אִתָּם מִלְחָמָה צְבוֹיִם
ט בְּעֵמֶק הַשִּׂדִּים׃ אֵת כְּדָרְלָעֹמֶר מֶלֶךְ עֵילָם וְתִדְעָל מֶלֶךְ גּוֹיִם וְאַמְרָפֶל
י מֶלֶךְ שִׁנְעָר וְאַרְיוֹךְ מֶלֶךְ אֶלָּסָר אַרְבָּעָה מְלָכִים אֶת־הַחֲמִשָּׁה׃ וְעֵמֶק
הַשִּׂדִּים בֶּאֱרֹת בֶּאֱרֹת חֵמָר וַיָּנֻסוּ מֶלֶךְ־סְדֹם וַעֲמֹרָה וַיִּפְּלוּ־שָׁמָּה
יא וְהַנִּשְׁאָרִים הֶרָה נָּסוּ׃ וַיִּקְחוּ אֶת־כָּל־רְכֻשׁ סְדֹם וַעֲמֹרָה וְאֶת־כָּל־
יב אָכְלָם וַיֵּלֵכוּ׃ וַיִּקְחוּ אֶת־לוֹט וְאֶת־רְכֻשׁוֹ בֶּן־אֲחִי אַבְרָם וַיֵּלֵכוּ וְהוּא
יג יֹשֵׁב בִּסְדֹם׃ וַיָּבֹא הַפָּלִיט וַיַּגֵּד לְאַבְרָם הָעִבְרִי וְהוּא שֹׁכֵן בְּאֵלֹנֵי
יד מַמְרֵא הָאֱמֹרִי אֲחִי אֶשְׁכֹּל וַאֲחִי עָנֵר וְהֵם בַּעֲלֵי בְרִית־אַבְרָם׃ וַיִּשְׁמַע
אַבְרָם כִּי נִשְׁבָּה אָחִיו וַיָּרֶק אֶת־חֲנִיכָיו יְלִידֵי בֵיתוֹ שְׁמֹנָה עָשָׂר וּשְׁלֹשׁ
טו מֵאוֹת וַיִּרְדֹּף עַד־דָּן׃ וַיֵּחָלֵק עֲלֵיהֶם ׀ לַיְלָה הוּא וַעֲבָדָיו וַיַּכֵּם וַיִּרְדְּפֵם
טז עַד־חוֹבָה אֲשֶׁר מִשְּׂמֹאל לְדַמָּשֶׂק׃ וַיָּשֶׁב אֵת כָּל־הָרְכֻשׁ וְגַם אֶת־
יז לוֹט אָחִיו וּרְכֻשׁוֹ הֵשִׁיב וְגַם אֶת־הַנָּשִׁים וְאֶת־הָעָם׃ וַיֵּצֵא מֶלֶךְ־סְדֹם
לִקְרָאתוֹ אַחֲרֵי שׁוּבוֹ מֵהַכּוֹת אֶת־כְּדָרְלָעֹמֶר וְאֶת־הַמְּלָכִים אֲשֶׁר
יח אִתּוֹ אֶל־עֵמֶק שָׁוֵה הוּא עֵמֶק הַמֶּלֶךְ׃ וּמַלְכִּי־צֶדֶק מֶלֶךְ שָׁלֵם הוֹצִיא
יט לֶחֶם וָיָיִן וְהוּא כֹהֵן לְאֵל עֶלְיוֹן׃ וַיְבָרְכֵהוּ וַיֹּאמַר בָּרוּךְ אַבְרָם לְאֵל
כ עֶלְיוֹן קֹנֵה שָׁמַיִם וָאָרֶץ׃ וּבָרוּךְ אֵל עֶלְיוֹן אֲשֶׁר־מִגֵּן צָרֶיךָ בְּיָדֶךָ
כא וַיִּתֶּן־לוֹ מַעֲשֵׂר מִכֹּל׃ וַיֹּאמֶר מֶלֶךְ־סְדֹם אֶל־אַבְרָם תֶּן־לִי הַנֶּפֶשׁ חמישי
כב וְהָרְכֻשׁ קַח־לָךְ׃ וַיֹּאמֶר אַבְרָם אֶל־מֶלֶךְ סְדֹם הֲרִמֹתִי יָדִי אֶל־יְהוָה
כג אֵל עֶלְיוֹן קֹנֵה שָׁמַיִם וָאָרֶץ׃ אִם־מִחוּט וְעַד שְׂרוֹךְ־נַעַל וְאִם־אֶקַּח
כד מִכָּל־אֲשֶׁר־לָךְ וְלֹא תֹאמַר אֲנִי הֶעֱשַׁרְתִּי אֶת־אַבְרָם׃ בִּלְעָדַי רַק
אֲשֶׁר אָכְלוּ הַנְּעָרִים וְחֵלֶק הָאֲנָשִׁים אֲשֶׁר הָלְכוּ אִתִּי עָנֵר אֶשְׁכֹּל
טו א וּמַמְרֵא הֵם יִקְחוּ חֶלְקָם׃ אַחַר ׀ הַדְּבָרִים הָאֵלֶּה הָיָה יב
דְבַר־יְהוָה אֶל־אַבְרָם בַּמַּחֲזֶה לֵאמֹר אַל־תִּירָא אַבְרָם אָנֹכִי מָגֵן לָךְ
ב שְׂכָרְךָ הַרְבֵּה מְאֹד׃ וַיֹּאמֶר אַבְרָם אֲדֹנָי יֱהוִה מַה־תִּתֶּן־לִי וְאָנֹכִי
ג הוֹלֵךְ עֲרִירִי וּבֶן־מֶשֶׁק בֵּיתִי הוּא דַּמֶּשֶׂק אֱלִיעֶזֶר׃ וַיֹּאמֶר אַבְרָם הֵן
ד לִי לֹא נָתַתָּה זָרַע וְהִנֵּה בֶן־בֵּיתִי יוֹרֵשׁ אֹתִי׃ וְהִנֵּה דְבַר־יְהוָה אֵלָיו
ה לֵאמֹר לֹא יִירָשְׁךָ זֶה כִּי־אִם אֲשֶׁר יֵצֵא מִמֵּעֶיךָ הוּא יִירָשֶׁךָ׃ וַיּוֹצֵא
אֹתוֹ הַחוּצָה וַיֹּאמֶר הַבֶּט־נָא הַשָּׁמַיְמָה וּסְפֹר הַכּוֹכָבִים אִם־תּוּכַל
ו לִסְפֹּר אֹתָם וַיֹּאמֶר לוֹ כֹּה יִהְיֶה זַרְעֶךָ׃ וְהֶאֱמִן בַּיהוָה וַיַּחְשְׁבֶהָ לּוֹ
ז צְדָקָה׃ וַיֹּאמֶר אֵלָיו אֲנִי יְהוָה אֲשֶׁר הוֹצֵאתִיךָ מֵאוּר כַּשְׂדִּים לָתֶת ששי
ח לְךָ אֶת־הָאָרֶץ הַזֹּאת לְרִשְׁתָּהּ׃ וַיֹּאמַר אֲדֹנָי יֱהוִה בַּמָּה אֵדַע כִּי
ט אִירָשֶׁנָּה׃ וַיֹּאמֶר אֵלָיו קְחָה לִי עֶגְלָה מְשֻׁלֶּשֶׁת וְעֵז מְשֻׁלֶּשֶׁת וְאַיִל

three-year-old goat, and a three-year-old ram, and a turtledove, and a young
10 pigeon." And he took all these and cut them in two and put each half opposite
11 its other half, but the birds he did not cut.[27] Birds of prey descended on the
12 carcasses, but Avram drove them away. And so it was that, as the sun went
down, a deep sleep fell upon Avram and a deep, dark dread came upon him.
13 And God said to Avram, "Know with certainty that your descendants will
be migrants in a land not their own, and there they will be enslaved and
14 oppressed for four hundred years. But I will bring judgment on the nation
15 they will serve, and afterward they will go free with great wealth. As for you,
16 you will join your ancestors in peace; you will be buried in ripe old age. And
the fourth generation will return here, for the guilt of the Amorites is not yet
17 resolved."[28] And when the sun set and it was very dark, a smoking furnace
18 appeared and a blazing torch passed between these pieces. On that day the
LORD made a covenant with Avram: "To your descendants I will give this land,
19 from the River of Egypt to the great river Euphrates, the land of the Kenites,
20 21 the Kenizzites, the Kadmonites, the Hittites, the Perizzites, the Refaim, the
16 1 Amorites, the Canaanites, the Girgashites, and the Jebusites." Sarai,
Avraham's wife, had borne him no children; but she had an Egyptian
2 maidservant named Hagar. Sarai said to Avram, "The LORD has kept me from
having children. Come now to my maid. Perhaps through her I might build
3 a family." And Avram listened to Sarai. So it was that, after living in Canaan
for ten years, Avram's wife Sarai took Hagar, her Egyptian maidservant, and
4 gave her to her husband Avram to be his wife. He came to Hagar and she
conceived. And when she realized that she was pregnant, she began to look
5 upon her mistress with contempt. Sarai said to Avram, "The abuse I suffer is
your fault. I laid my servant in your arms and now that she knows she is
pregnant, she looks upon me with contempt. Let the LORD judge between
6 me and you!" Avram said to Sarai, "Your maid is in your own hands. Do with
her whatever you think best." Sarai treated her harshly – and Hagar ran away
7 from her. An angel of the LORD found her near a spring of water in the desert,
8 the spring by the road to Shur. He said, "Hagar, maidservant of Sarai, where
have you come from and where are you going?" She said, "I am running away
9 from my mistress Sarai." The angel of the LORD said to her, "Go back to your
10 mistress; submit yourself under her hand." And the angel of the LORD added:
"I will greatly multiply your descendants; they will be too many to count."
11 Said the angel of the LORD: "You are pregnant and will give birth to a son.
12 You shall name him Yishmael, for the LORD has heard your affliction.[29] He
will become a wild donkey of a man; his hand will be against everyone, and
13 everyone's hand against him. He will live up against all his brothers." She gave
a name to the LORD who had spoken to her: "You are the God who sees me,"
14 for she said: "Have I not here seen Him who sees me?" That is why the well

---

27 | This was a covenant ceremony (cf., e.g., Jer. 34:18).
28 | The accumulated guilt of the inhabitants of Canaan does not yet warrant their displacement.
29 | The name Yishmael means "God hears."

י מְשֻׁלֶּשׁ וְתֹר וְגוֹזָל: וַיִּקַּח־לוֹ אֶת־כׇּל־אֵלֶּה וַיְבַתֵּר אֹתָם בַּתָּוֶךְ וַיִּתֵּן
יא אִישׁ־בִּתְרוֹ לִקְרַאת רֵעֵהוּ וְאֶת־הַצִּפֹּר לֹא בָתָר: וַיֵּרֶד הָעַיִט עַל־
יב הַפְּגָרִים וַיַּשֵּׁב אֹתָם אַבְרָם: וַיְהִי הַשֶּׁמֶשׁ לָבוֹא וְתַרְדֵּמָה נָפְלָה
יג עַל־אַבְרָם וְהִנֵּה אֵימָה חֲשֵׁכָה גְדֹלָה נֹפֶלֶת עָלָיו: וַיֹּאמֶר לְאַבְרָם
יָדֹעַ תֵּדַע כִּי־גֵר ׀ יִהְיֶה זַרְעֲךָ בְּאֶרֶץ לֹא לָהֶם וַעֲבָדוּם וְעִנּוּ אֹתָם
יד אַרְבַּע מֵאוֹת שָׁנָה: וְגַם אֶת־הַגּוֹי אֲשֶׁר יַעֲבֹדוּ דָּן אָנֹכִי וְאַחֲרֵי־כֵן
טו יֵצְאוּ בִּרְכֻשׁ גָּדוֹל: וְאַתָּה תָּבוֹא אֶל־אֲבֹתֶיךָ בְּשָׁלוֹם תִּקָּבֵר בְּשֵׂיבָה
טז טוֹבָה: וְדוֹר רְבִיעִי יָשׁוּבוּ הֵנָּה כִּי לֹא־שָׁלֵם עֲוֺן הָאֱמֹרִי עַד־הֵנָּה:
יז וַיְהִי הַשֶּׁמֶשׁ בָּאָה וַעֲלָטָה הָיָה וְהִנֵּה תַנּוּר עָשָׁן וְלַפִּיד אֵשׁ אֲשֶׁר
יח עָבַר בֵּין הַגְּזָרִים הָאֵלֶּה: בַּיּוֹם הַהוּא כָּרַת יהוה אֶת־אַבְרָם בְּרִית
לֵאמֹר לְזַרְעֲךָ נָתַתִּי אֶת־הָאָרֶץ הַזֹּאת מִנְּהַר מִצְרַיִם עַד־הַנָּהָר הַגָּדֹל
יט כ נְהַר־פְּרָת: אֶת־הַקֵּינִי וְאֶת־הַקְּנִזִּי וְאֵת הַקַּדְמֹנִי: וְאֶת־הַחִתִּי וְאֶת־
כא הַפְּרִזִּי וְאֶת־הָרְפָאִים: וְאֶת־הָאֱמֹרִי וְאֶת־הַכְּנַעֲנִי וְאֶת־הַגִּרְגָּשִׁי
טז א וְאֶת־הַיְבוּסִי: וְשָׂרַי אֵשֶׁת אַבְרָם לֹא יָלְדָה לוֹ וְלָהּ יג
ב שִׁפְחָה מִצְרִית וּשְׁמָהּ הָגָר: וַתֹּאמֶר שָׂרַי אֶל־אַבְרָם הִנֵּה־נָא עֲצָרַנִי
יהוה מִלֶּדֶת בֹּא־נָא אֶל־שִׁפְחָתִי אוּלַי אִבָּנֶה מִמֶּנָּה וַיִּשְׁמַע אַבְרָם
ג לְקוֹל שָׂרָי: וַתִּקַּח שָׂרַי ׀ אֵשֶׁת אַבְרָם אֶת־הָגָר הַמִּצְרִית שִׁפְחָתָהּ
מִקֵּץ עֶשֶׂר שָׁנִים לְשֶׁבֶת אַבְרָם בְּאֶרֶץ כְּנָעַן וַתִּתֵּן אֹתָהּ לְאַבְרָם
ד אִישָׁהּ לוֹ לְאִשָּׁה: וַיָּבֹא אֶל־הָגָר וַתַּהַר וַתֵּרֶא כִּי הָרָתָה וַתֵּקַל גְּבִרְתָּהּ
ה בְּעֵינֶיהָ: וַתֹּאמֶר שָׂרַי אֶל־אַבְרָם חֲמָסִי עָלֶיךָ אָנֹכִי נָתַתִּי שִׁפְחָתִי
ו בְּחֵיקֶךָ וַתֵּרֶא כִּי הָרָתָה וָאֵקַל בְּעֵינֶיהָ יִשְׁפֹּט יהוה בֵּינִי וּבֵינֶיךָ: וַיֹּאמֶר
אַבְרָם אֶל־שָׂרַי הִנֵּה שִׁפְחָתֵךְ בְּיָדֵךְ עֲשִׂי־לָהּ הַטּוֹב בְּעֵינָיִךְ וַתְּעַנֶּהָ
ז שָׂרַי וַתִּבְרַח מִפָּנֶיהָ: וַיִּמְצָאָהּ מַלְאַךְ יהוה עַל־עֵין הַמַּיִם בַּמִּדְבָּר
ח עַל־הָעַיִן בְּדֶרֶךְ שׁוּר: וַיֹּאמַר הָגָר שִׁפְחַת שָׂרַי אֵי־מִזֶּה בָאת וְאָנָה
ט תֵלֵכִי וַתֹּאמֶר מִפְּנֵי שָׂרַי גְּבִרְתִּי אָנֹכִי בֹּרַחַת: וַיֹּאמֶר לָהּ מַלְאַךְ יהוה
י שׁוּבִי אֶל־גְּבִרְתֵּךְ וְהִתְעַנִּי תַּחַת יָדֶיהָ: וַיֹּאמֶר לָהּ מַלְאַךְ יהוה הַרְבָּה
יא אַרְבֶּה אֶת־זַרְעֵךְ וְלֹא יִסָּפֵר מֵרֹב: וַיֹּאמֶר לָהּ מַלְאַךְ יהוה הִנָּךְ הָרָה
יב וְיֹלַדְתְּ בֵּן וְקָרָאת שְׁמוֹ יִשְׁמָעֵאל כִּי־שָׁמַע יהוה אֶל־עׇנְיֵךְ: וְהוּא
יג יִהְיֶה פֶּרֶא אָדָם יָדוֹ בַכֹּל וְיַד כֹּל בּוֹ וְעַל־פְּנֵי כׇל־אֶחָיו יִשְׁכֹּן: וַתִּקְרָא
שֵׁם־יהוה הַדֹּבֵר אֵלֶיהָ אַתָּה אֵל רֳאִי כִּי אָמְרָה הֲגַם הֲלֹם רָאִיתִי
יד אַחֲרֵי רֹאִי: עַל־כֵּן קָרָא לַבְּאֵר בְּאֵר לַחַי רֹאִי הִנֵּה בֵין־קָדֵשׁ וּבֵין

15 is called Be'er Laḥai Ro'i.[30] It is still there between Kadesh and Bered. So
Hagar bore Avram a son, and Avram gave the name Yishmael to the son
16 that she had borne. Avram was eighty-six years old when Hagar bore him
17 1 Yishmael. When Avram was ninety-nine years old, the LORD
2 appeared to him and said, "I am El Shaddai. Walk before Me in integrity, and
I will establish My covenant between Me and you, and make you exceedingly
3 4 numerous." Avram fell facedown. And God said to him, "As for Me – this is
5 My covenant with you: you shall be father to a multitude of nations. No longer
shall you be called Avram. Your name will be Avraham, for I have made you
6 father to a multitude of nations.[31] I will make you exceptionally fertile, I will
7 turn you into nations; kings will come from you. I will establish My covenant
between Me and you and your descendants after you throughout the
generations: an eternal covenant. I will be God to you and your descendants
8 after you, and I will give you and your descendants after you the land where
you now live as strangers, the whole land of Canaan, an everlasting possession,
9 and I will be their God." Then God said to Avraham, "As for you, you shall
keep My covenant, you and your descendants after you throughout their
10 generations. This is My covenant, kept between Me and you and your
11 descendants after you: every male among you shall be circumcised. You must
circumcise the flesh of your foreskin – this shall be the sign of the covenant
12 between Me and you. Throughout the generations, every male among you
shall be circumcised at the age of eight days, including the slave born in your
household, including one acquired from a stranger not descended from you.
13 All must be circumcised – those born in your household, those acquired with
your money – and My covenant in your flesh will be a covenant everlasting.
14 Any uncircumcised male, whose foreskin has not been circumcised, shall be
15 severed from his people; he has broken My covenant." God
then said to Avraham, "As for Sarai your wife, you shall no longer call her Sarai.
16 Her name will be Sara.[32] I will bless her and give you a son by her. I will
bless her so that she shall birth nations; kings of peoples shall descend from
17 her." Avraham fell on his face and laughed. "Can a hundred-year-old man
18 become a father?" he said to himself. "Can Sara, at ninety, bear a child?" To
19 God Avraham said, "If only Yishmael might live before you!" God said,
"Nonetheless, Sara your wife will bear you a son, and you shall name him
Yitzḥak.[33] I will establish My covenant with him as an everlasting covenant
20 for his descendants after him. As for Yishmael – I have heard you.[34] I will bless
him and make him fertile and multiply him exceedingly. He will become
21 father of twelve princes, and I will make of him a great nation. But I will
establish My covenant[35] with Yitzḥak, whom Sara will bear to you this time

30 | Meaning "Well of the Living One Who Sees Me."

31 | The name Avraham resonates with *av hamon* (father of a multitude).

32 | Meaning "noblewoman."

33 | The name Yitzḥak derives from the verb *vayitzḥak* (to laugh), referring to Avraham's mirth in verse 17.

34 | The name Yishmael means "God hears" (cf. 16:10).

35 | The covenant affirming that Avraham's progeny will take possession of the land of Canaan.

טו בָּרֶד: וַתֵּלֶד הָגָר לְאַבְרָם בֵּן וַיִּקְרָא אַבְרָם שֶׁם־בְּנוֹ אֲשֶׁר־יָלְדָה הָגָר
טז יִשְׁמָעֵאל: וְאַבְרָם בֶּן־שְׁמֹנִים שָׁנָה וְשֵׁשׁ שָׁנִים בְּלֶדֶת־הָגָר אֶת־
יז א יִשְׁמָעֵאל לְאַבְרָם: וַיְהִי אַבְרָם בֶּן־תִּשְׁעִים שָׁנָה וְתֵשַׁע יד
שָׁנִים וַיֵּרָא יְהוָה אֶל־אַבְרָם וַיֹּאמֶר אֵלָיו אֲנִי־אֵל שַׁדַּי הִתְהַלֵּךְ לְפָנַי
ב וֶהְיֵה תָמִים: וְאֶתְּנָה בְרִיתִי בֵּינִי וּבֵינֶךָ וְאַרְבֶּה אוֹתְךָ בִּמְאֹד מְאֹד:
ג ד וַיִּפֹּל אַבְרָם עַל־פָּנָיו וַיְדַבֵּר אִתּוֹ אֱלֹהִים לֵאמֹר: אֲנִי הִנֵּה בְרִיתִי
ה אִתָּךְ וְהָיִיתָ לְאַב הֲמוֹן גּוֹיִם: וְלֹא־יִקָּרֵא עוֹד אֶת־שִׁמְךָ אַבְרָם וְהָיָה
ו שִׁמְךָ אַבְרָהָם כִּי אַב־הֲמוֹן גּוֹיִם נְתַתִּיךָ: וְהִפְרֵתִי אֹתְךָ בִּמְאֹד מְאֹד
ז וּנְתַתִּיךָ לְגוֹיִם וּמְלָכִים מִמְּךָ יֵצֵאוּ: וַהֲקִמֹתִי אֶת־בְּרִיתִי בֵּינִי וּבֵינֶךָ שביעי
וּבֵין זַרְעֲךָ אַחֲרֶיךָ לְדֹרֹתָם לִבְרִית עוֹלָם לִהְיוֹת לְךָ לֵאלֹהִים וּלְזַרְעֲךָ
ח אַחֲרֶיךָ: וְנָתַתִּי לְךָ וּלְזַרְעֲךָ אַחֲרֶיךָ אֵת ׀ אֶרֶץ מְגֻרֶיךָ אֵת כָּל־אֶרֶץ
ט כְּנַעַן לַאֲחֻזַּת עוֹלָם וְהָיִיתִי לָהֶם לֵאלֹהִים: וַיֹּאמֶר אֱלֹהִים אֶל־אַבְרָהָם
י וְאַתָּה אֶת־בְּרִיתִי תִשְׁמֹר אַתָּה וְזַרְעֲךָ אַחֲרֶיךָ לְדֹרֹתָם: זֹאת בְּרִיתִי
אֲשֶׁר תִּשְׁמְרוּ בֵּינִי וּבֵינֵיכֶם וּבֵין זַרְעֲךָ אַחֲרֶיךָ הִמּוֹל לָכֶם כָּל־זָכָר:
יא יב וּנְמַלְתֶּם אֵת בְּשַׂר עָרְלַתְכֶם וְהָיָה לְאוֹת בְּרִית בֵּינִי וּבֵינֵיכֶם: וּבֶן־
שְׁמֹנַת יָמִים יִמּוֹל לָכֶם כָּל־זָכָר לְדֹרֹתֵיכֶם יְלִיד בָּיִת וּמִקְנַת־כֶּסֶף
יג מִכֹּל בֶּן־נֵכָר אֲשֶׁר לֹא מִזַּרְעֲךָ הוּא: הִמּוֹל ׀ יִמּוֹל יְלִיד בֵּיתְךָ וּמִקְנַת
יד כַּסְפֶּךָ וְהָיְתָה בְרִיתִי בִּבְשַׂרְכֶם לִבְרִית עוֹלָם: וְעָרֵל ׀ זָכָר אֲשֶׁר לֹא־
יִמּוֹל אֶת־בְּשַׂר עָרְלָתוֹ וְנִכְרְתָה הַנֶּפֶשׁ הַהִוא מֵעַמֶּיהָ אֶת־בְּרִיתִי
טו הֵפַר: וַיֹּאמֶר אֱלֹהִים אֶל־אַבְרָהָם שָׂרַי אִשְׁתְּךָ לֹא־תִקְרָא
טז אֶת־שְׁמָהּ שָׂרָי כִּי שָׂרָה שְׁמָהּ: וּבֵרַכְתִּי אֹתָהּ וְגַם נָתַתִּי מִמֶּנָּה לְךָ בֵּן
יז וּבֵרַכְתִּיהָ וְהָיְתָה לְגוֹיִם מַלְכֵי עַמִּים מִמֶּנָּה יִהְיוּ: וַיִּפֹּל אַבְרָהָם עַל־
פָּנָיו וַיִּצְחָק וַיֹּאמֶר בְּלִבּוֹ הַלְּבֶן מֵאָה־שָׁנָה יִוָּלֵד וְאִם־שָׂרָה הֲבַת־
יח תִּשְׁעִים שָׁנָה תֵּלֵד: וַיֹּאמֶר אַבְרָהָם אֶל־הָאֱלֹהִים לוּ יִשְׁמָעֵאל יִחְיֶה
יט לְפָנֶיךָ: וַיֹּאמֶר אֱלֹהִים אֲבָל שָׂרָה אִשְׁתְּךָ יֹלֶדֶת לְךָ בֵּן וְקָרָאתָ אֶת־
שְׁמוֹ יִצְחָק וַהֲקִמֹתִי אֶת־בְּרִיתִי אִתּוֹ לִבְרִית עוֹלָם לְזַרְעוֹ אַחֲרָיו:
כ וּלְיִשְׁמָעֵאל שְׁמַעְתִּיךָ הִנֵּה ׀ בֵּרַכְתִּי אֹתוֹ וְהִפְרֵיתִי אֹתוֹ וְהִרְבֵּיתִי
כא אֹתוֹ בִּמְאֹד מְאֹד שְׁנֵים־עָשָׂר נְשִׂיאִם יוֹלִיד וּנְתַתִּיו לְגוֹי גָּדוֹל: וְאֶת־
בְּרִיתִי אָקִים אֶת־יִצְחָק אֲשֶׁר תֵּלֵד לְךָ שָׂרָה לַמּוֹעֵד הַזֶּה בַּשָּׁנָה

22 next year." When He finished speaking with him, God went up from Avraham.
23 On that very day, Avraham took his son Yishmael, along with all those born
in his house or acquired with money, every male in Avraham's household, and
24 circumcised the flesh of their foreskins as God had instructed him. Avraham
25 was ninety-nine years old when he was circumcised, and his son Yishmael
26 was thirteen. That very day, Avraham and his son Yishmael were circumcised;
27 and all the men of his household, whether home-born or acquired from
strangers, were circumcised together with him.
18 1 The LORD appeared to him by the Oaks of Mamre as he was sitting at the VAYERA
2 entrance to his tent in the heat of the day. Avraham looked up and saw three
men standing nearby. The moment he saw them, he ran from the opening of
3 his tent to greet them, and bowed down low to the ground. He said, "My lords,
4 if I have found favor in your sight, please do not pass your servant by. Let a
little water be brought so that you can wash your feet and rest under the tree.
5 Since you are passing by your servant, let me bring a morsel of bread so that
you can be refreshed before you go on your way." They replied. "Do just as
6 you say." Avraham rushed to Sara in the tent and said, "Hurry – three *se'a*[36] of
7 fine flour; knead it and bake bread." Avraham himself ran to the herd and took
a tender choice calf and gave it to the young man, who hurried to prepare it.
8 He brought curds and milk and the calf that had been prepared, and set them
9 before them, standing by them as they ate, under the tree. They asked him,
10 "Where is your wife Sara?" "There, in the tent," he replied. Then one of them
said, "I will return to you this time next year, and your wife Sara will have a
11 son." Sara was listening at the opening of the tent behind him. Avraham and
Sara were already old, advanced in years; the way of women no longer visited
12 Sara. So Sara laughed to herself, saying, "Now that I am worn out, can I have
13 this pleasure? With my lord an old man?" Then the LORD said to Avraham,
14 "Why did Sara laugh and say, 'Can I really have a child, now that I am old?' Is
anything beyond the LORD's powers? At the due time next year I will return
15 to you, and Sara will have a son." Sara, because she was afraid, denied it: "I
16 did not laugh," she said. But He said, "Not so. You laughed." The men got up
to leave and looked down toward Sedom. Avraham accompanied them to see
17 them on their way. The LORD said, "Shall I hide from Avraham what I am
18 about to do? Avraham is about to become a great and mighty nation, and
19 through him all the nations on earth will be blessed. For I have chosen him
so that he may direct his children and his household after him to keep the way
of the LORD by doing what is right and just, that the LORD may bring about
20 for Avraham what He spoke of for him." Then the LORD said, "The outcry
21 against Sedom and Amora is great, and their sin is very grave. I shall go down
now and see if they have really done as much as the outcry that has reached
22 Me. If not, I will know." The men turned from there and went toward Sedom,

36 | See note on I Kings 18:32.

כב כג הָאַחֶרֶת׃ וַיְכַל לְדַבֵּר אִתּוֹ וַיַּעַל אֱלֹהִים מֵעַל אַבְרָהָם׃ וַיִּקַּח אַבְרָהָם
אֶת־יִשְׁמָעֵאל בְּנוֹ וְאֵת כָּל־יְלִידֵי בֵיתוֹ וְאֵת כָּל־מִקְנַת כַּסְפּוֹ כָּל־
זָכָר בְּאַנְשֵׁי בֵּית אַבְרָהָם וַיָּמָל אֶת־בְּשַׂר עָרְלָתָם בְּעֶצֶם הַיּוֹם הַזֶּה
כד כַּאֲשֶׁר דִּבֶּר אִתּוֹ אֱלֹהִים׃ וְאַבְרָהָם בֶּן־תִּשְׁעִים וָתֵשַׁע שָׁנָה בְּהִמֹּלוֹ מפטיר
כה בְּשַׂר עָרְלָתוֹ׃ וְיִשְׁמָעֵאל בְּנוֹ בֶּן־שְׁלֹשׁ עֶשְׂרֵה שָׁנָה בְּהִמֹּלוֹ אֵת בְּשַׂר
כו כז עָרְלָתוֹ׃ בְּעֶצֶם הַיּוֹם הַזֶּה נִמּוֹל אַבְרָהָם וְיִשְׁמָעֵאל בְּנוֹ׃ וְכָל־אַנְשֵׁי
בֵיתוֹ יְלִיד בָּיִת וּמִקְנַת־כֶּסֶף מֵאֵת בֶּן־נֵכָר נִמֹּלוּ אִתּוֹ׃

יח א וַיֵּרָא אֵלָיו יהוה בְּאֵלֹנֵי מַמְרֵא וְהוּא יֹשֵׁב פֶּתַח־הָאֹהֶל כְּחֹם הַיּוֹם׃ טו וירא
ב וַיִּשָּׂא עֵינָיו וַיַּרְא וְהִנֵּה שְׁלֹשָׁה אֲנָשִׁים נִצָּבִים עָלָיו וַיַּרְא וַיָּרָץ לִקְרָאתָם
ג מִפֶּתַח הָאֹהֶל וַיִּשְׁתַּחוּ אָרְצָה׃ וַיֹּאמַר אֲדֹנָי אִם־נָא מָצָאתִי חֵן בְּעֵינֶיךָ
ד אַל־נָא תַעֲבֹר מֵעַל עַבְדֶּךָ׃ יֻקַּח־נָא מְעַט־מַיִם וְרַחֲצוּ רַגְלֵיכֶם וְהִשָּׁעֲנוּ
ה תַּחַת הָעֵץ׃ וְאֶקְחָה פַת־לֶחֶם וְסַעֲדוּ לִבְּכֶם אַחַר תַּעֲבֹרוּ כִּי־עַל־כֵּן
ו עֲבַרְתֶּם עַל־עַבְדְּכֶם וַיֹּאמְרוּ כֵּן תַּעֲשֶׂה כַּאֲשֶׁר דִּבַּרְתָּ׃ וַיְמַהֵר אַבְרָהָם
הָאֹהֱלָה אֶל־שָׂרָה וַיֹּאמֶר מַהֲרִי שְׁלֹשׁ סְאִים קֶמַח סֹלֶת לוּשִׁי וַעֲשִׂי
ז עֻגוֹת׃ וְאֶל־הַבָּקָר רָץ אַבְרָהָם וַיִּקַּח בֶּן־בָּקָר רַךְ וָטוֹב וַיִּתֵּן אֶל־הַנַּעַר
ח וַיְמַהֵר לַעֲשׂוֹת אֹתוֹ׃ וַיִּקַּח חֶמְאָה וְחָלָב וּבֶן־הַבָּקָר אֲשֶׁר עָשָׂה וַיִּתֵּן
ט לִפְנֵיהֶם וְהוּא עֹמֵד עֲלֵיהֶם תַּחַת הָעֵץ וַיֹּאכֵלוּ׃ וַיֹּאמְרוּ אֵלָיו אַיֵּה
י שָׂרָה אִשְׁתֶּךָ וַיֹּאמֶר הִנֵּה בָאֹהֶל׃ וַיֹּאמֶר שׁוֹב אָשׁוּב אֵלֶיךָ כָּעֵת חַיָּה
וְהִנֵּה־בֵן לְשָׂרָה אִשְׁתֶּךָ וְשָׂרָה שֹׁמַעַת פֶּתַח הָאֹהֶל וְהוּא אַחֲרָיו׃
יא וְאַבְרָהָם וְשָׂרָה זְקֵנִים בָּאִים בַּיָּמִים חָדַל לִהְיוֹת לְשָׂרָה אֹרַח כַּנָּשִׁים׃
יב וַתִּצְחַק שָׂרָה בְּקִרְבָּהּ לֵאמֹר אַחֲרֵי בְלֹתִי הָיְתָה־לִּי עֶדְנָה וַאדֹנִי זָקֵן׃
יג וַיֹּאמֶר יהוה אֶל־אַבְרָהָם לָמָּה זֶּה צָחֲקָה שָׂרָה לֵאמֹר הַאַף אֻמְנָם
יד אֵלֵד וַאֲנִי זָקַנְתִּי׃ הֲיִפָּלֵא מֵיהוה דָּבָר לַמּוֹעֵד אָשׁוּב אֵלֶיךָ כָּעֵת חַיָּה
טו וּלְשָׂרָה בֵן׃ וַתְּכַחֵשׁ שָׂרָה ׀ לֵאמֹר לֹא צָחַקְתִּי כִּי ׀ יָרֵאָה וַיֹּאמֶר ׀ לֹא שני
טז כִּי צָחָקְתְּ׃ וַיָּקֻמוּ מִשָּׁם הָאֲנָשִׁים וַיַּשְׁקִפוּ עַל־פְּנֵי סְדֹם וְאַבְרָהָם הֹלֵךְ
יז עִמָּם לְשַׁלְּחָם׃ וַיהוה אָמָר הַמְכַסֶּה אֲנִי מֵאַבְרָהָם אֲשֶׁר אֲנִי עֹשֶׂה׃
יח יט וְאַבְרָהָם הָיוֹ יִהְיֶה לְגוֹי גָּדוֹל וְעָצוּם וְנִבְרְכוּ־בוֹ כֹּל גּוֹיֵי הָאָרֶץ׃ כִּי
יְדַעְתִּיו לְמַעַן אֲשֶׁר יְצַוֶּה אֶת־בָּנָיו וְאֶת־בֵּיתוֹ אַחֲרָיו וְשָׁמְרוּ דֶּרֶךְ
יהוה לַעֲשׂוֹת צְדָקָה וּמִשְׁפָּט לְמַעַן הָבִיא יהוה עַל־אַבְרָהָם אֵת
כ אֲשֶׁר־דִּבֶּר עָלָיו׃ וַיֹּאמֶר יהוה זַעֲקַת סְדֹם וַעֲמֹרָה כִּי־רָבָּה וְחַטָּאתָם
כא כִּי כָבְדָה מְאֹד׃ אֵרֲדָה־נָּא וְאֶרְאֶה הַכְּצַעֲקָתָהּ הַבָּאָה אֵלַי עָשׂוּ ׀
כב כָּלָה וְאִם־לֹא אֵדָעָה׃ וַיִּפְנוּ מִשָּׁם הָאֲנָשִׁים וַיֵּלְכוּ סְדֹמָה וְאַבְרָהָם

23 while Avraham still stood before the LORD. Then Avraham stepped forward
24 and said: "Would You really sweep away the righteous with the wicked? What
if there are fifty righteous people in the city? Would You really sweep it away
25 and not spare the place for the sake of the fifty righteous people in it? Far be
it from You to do such a thing – to kill the righteous with the wicked, treating
the righteous like the wicked. Far be it from You! Shall the judge of all the
26 earth not do justice?" The LORD said, "If I find fifty righteous people in the
27 city of Sedom, I will spare the whole place for their sake." Then Avraham
spoke up again and said, "Now that I have dared to speak to the Lord, though
28 I am mere dust and ashes, what if the righteous are five less than fifty? Will
You destroy the whole city for the lack of five people?" He said, "If I find
29 forty-five there, I will not destroy it." He spoke to Him yet again, saying,
"What if only forty are found there?" He said, "I will refrain for the sake of
30 the forty." Then he said, "Please, may the Lord not be angry, but let me speak.
What if only thirty are found there?" He answered, "I will refrain if I find thirty
31 there." "Now that I have dared to speak to the Lord," he said, "what if only
twenty are found there?" He said, "I will not destroy, for the sake of the
32 twenty." Then he said, "Please, may the Lord not be angry, but let me speak
just once more. What if only ten are found there?" He said, "I will not destroy,
33 for the sake of the ten." When the LORD had finished speaking with Avraham,
19 1 He left. And Avraham went back to his place. The two angels arrived at Sedom
in the evening, while Lot was sitting in the city gate. Lot saw them, and rose
2 to greet them, bowing with his face to the ground. He said, "Please, my lords,
turn aside to your servant's house, stay the night, wash your feet, and then go
on your way early in the morning." "No," they said, "we will spend the night
3 in the square." But he was so insistent that they followed him to his house and
came in. He made a feast for them and baked unleavened bread, and they ate.
4 They had not yet gone to bed when all the townsmen, the men of Sedom –
young and old, all the people from every quarter – surrounded the house.
5 They called to Lot, "Where are the men who came to you tonight? Bring them
6 out to us so that we may know them."[37] Lot went out to speak to them,
7 shutting the door behind him,and said, "My brothers, please do not do this
8 evil. I have two daughters who have never known a man. Let me bring them
out to you; you may do what you like with them. But do not do anything to
9 these men, for they have come under the protection of my roof." "Get
out of our way," they replied. "This fellow came here as a migrant and now he
is setting himself up as a judge! We will treat you worse than them." They
10 pressed hard against Lot and moved forward to break down the door. But the
men inside reached out and pulled Lot back into the house and shut the door
11 behind him. Then they struck the men at the door, young and old, with
blindness so that they wore themselves out trying in vain to find the door.
12 The visitors said to Lot, "Who else do you have here – children-in-law, sons,

---

37 | That is, violate them.

כג עוֹדֶנּוּ עֹמֵד לִפְנֵי יהוה: וַיִּגַּשׁ אַבְרָהָם וַיֹּאמַר הַאַף תִּסְפֶּה צַדִּיק עִם־
כד רָשָׁע: אוּלַי יֵשׁ חֲמִשִּׁים צַדִּיקִם בְּתוֹךְ הָעִיר הַאַף תִּסְפֶּה וְלֹא־תִשָּׂא
כה לַמָּקוֹם לְמַעַן חֲמִשִּׁים הַצַּדִּיקִם אֲשֶׁר בְּקִרְבָּהּ: חָלִלָה לְּךָ מֵעֲשֹׂת ׀
כַּדָּבָר הַזֶּה לְהָמִית צַדִּיק עִם־רָשָׁע וְהָיָה כַצַּדִּיק כָּרָשָׁע חָלִלָה לָּךְ
כו הֲשֹׁפֵט כָּל־הָאָרֶץ לֹא יַעֲשֶׂה מִשְׁפָּט: וַיֹּאמֶר יהוה אִם־אֶמְצָא בִסְדֹם
כז חֲמִשִּׁים צַדִּיקִם בְּתוֹךְ הָעִיר וְנָשָׂאתִי לְכָל־הַמָּקוֹם בַּעֲבוּרָם: וַיַּעַן
אַבְרָהָם וַיֹּאמַר הִנֵּה־נָא הוֹאַלְתִּי לְדַבֵּר אֶל־אֲדֹנָי וְאָנֹכִי עָפָר וָאֵפֶר:
כח אוּלַי יַחְסְרוּן חֲמִשִּׁים הַצַּדִּיקִם חֲמִשָּׁה הֲתַשְׁחִית בַּחֲמִשָּׁה אֶת־כָּל־
כט הָעִיר וַיֹּאמֶר לֹא אַשְׁחִית אִם־אֶמְצָא שָׁם אַרְבָּעִים וַחֲמִשָּׁה: וַיֹּסֶף
עוֹד לְדַבֵּר אֵלָיו וַיֹּאמַר אוּלַי יִמָּצְאוּן שָׁם אַרְבָּעִים וַיֹּאמֶר לֹא אֶעֱשֶׂה
ל בַּעֲבוּר הָאַרְבָּעִים: וַיֹּאמֶר אַל־נָא יִחַר לַאדֹנָי וַאֲדַבֵּרָה אוּלַי יִמָּצְאוּן
לא שָׁם שְׁלֹשִׁים וַיֹּאמֶר לֹא אֶעֱשֶׂה אִם־אֶמְצָא שָׁם שְׁלֹשִׁים: וַיֹּאמֶר
הִנֵּה־נָא הוֹאַלְתִּי לְדַבֵּר אֶל־אֲדֹנָי אוּלַי יִמָּצְאוּן שָׁם עֶשְׂרִים וַיֹּאמֶר
לב לֹא אַשְׁחִית בַּעֲבוּר הָעֶשְׂרִים: וַיֹּאמֶר אַל־נָא יִחַר לַאדֹנָי וַאֲדַבְּרָה
אַךְ־הַפַּעַם אוּלַי יִמָּצְאוּן שָׁם עֲשָׂרָה וַיֹּאמֶר לֹא אַשְׁחִית בַּעֲבוּר
לג הָעֲשָׂרָה: וַיֵּלֶךְ יהוה כַּאֲשֶׁר כִּלָּה לְדַבֵּר אֶל־אַבְרָהָם וְאַבְרָהָם שָׁב
יט א לִמְקֹמוֹ: וַיָּבֹאוּ שְׁנֵי הַמַּלְאָכִים סְדֹמָה בָּעֶרֶב וְלוֹט יֹשֵׁב בְּשַׁעַר־סְדֹם טז שלישי
ב וַיַּרְא־לוֹט וַיָּקָם לִקְרָאתָם וַיִּשְׁתַּחוּ אַפַּיִם אָרְצָה: וַיֹּאמֶר הִנֶּה נָּא־
אֲדֹנַי סוּרוּ נָא אֶל־בֵּית עַבְדְּכֶם וְלִינוּ וְרַחֲצוּ רַגְלֵיכֶם וְהִשְׁכַּמְתֶּם
ג וַהֲלַכְתֶּם לְדַרְכְּכֶם וַיֹּאמְרוּ לֹּא כִּי בָרְחוֹב נָלִין: וַיִּפְצַר־בָּם מְאֹד וַיָּסֻרוּ
ד אֵלָיו וַיָּבֹאוּ אֶל־בֵּיתוֹ וַיַּעַשׂ לָהֶם מִשְׁתֶּה וּמַצּוֹת אָפָה וַיֹּאכֵלוּ: טֶרֶם
יִשְׁכָּבוּ וְאַנְשֵׁי הָעִיר אַנְשֵׁי סְדֹם נָסַבּוּ עַל־הַבַּיִת מִנַּעַר וְעַד־זָקֵן כָּל־
ה הָעָם מִקָּצֶה: וַיִּקְרְאוּ אֶל־לוֹט וַיֹּאמְרוּ לוֹ אַיֵּה הָאֲנָשִׁים אֲשֶׁר־בָּאוּ
ו אֵלֶיךָ הַלָּיְלָה הוֹצִיאֵם אֵלֵינוּ וְנֵדְעָה אֹתָם: וַיֵּצֵא אֲלֵהֶם לוֹט הַפֶּתְחָה
ז ח וְהַדֶּלֶת סָגַר אַחֲרָיו: וַיֹּאמַר אַל־נָא אַחַי תָּרֵעוּ: הִנֵּה־נָא לִי שְׁתֵּי
בָנוֹת אֲשֶׁר לֹא־יָדְעוּ אִישׁ אוֹצִיאָה־נָּא אֶתְהֶן אֲלֵיכֶם וַעֲשׂוּ לָהֶן
כַּטּוֹב בְּעֵינֵיכֶם רַק לָאֲנָשִׁים הָאֵל אַל־תַּעֲשׂוּ דָבָר כִּי־עַל־כֵּן בָּאוּ
ט בְּצֵל קֹרָתִי: וַיֹּאמְרוּ ׀ גֶּשׁ־הָלְאָה וַיֹּאמְרוּ הָאֶחָד בָּא־לָגוּר וַיִּשְׁפֹּט
שָׁפוֹט עַתָּה נָרַע לְךָ מֵהֶם וַיִּפְצְרוּ בָאִישׁ בְּלוֹט מְאֹד וַיִּגְּשׁוּ לִשְׁבֹּר
י הַדָּלֶת: וַיִּשְׁלְחוּ הָאֲנָשִׁים אֶת־יָדָם וַיָּבִיאוּ אֶת־לוֹט אֲלֵיהֶם הַבָּיְתָה
יא וְאֶת־הַדֶּלֶת סָגָרוּ: וְאֶת־הָאֲנָשִׁים אֲשֶׁר־פֶּתַח הַבַּיִת הִכּוּ בַּסַּנְוֵרִים
יב מִקָּטֹן וְעַד־גָּדוֹל וַיִּלְאוּ לִמְצֹא הַפָּתַח: וַיֹּאמְרוּ הָאֲנָשִׁים אֶל־לוֹט עֹד

13 daughters, or anyone else in the city? Bring them out of here, because we
are about to destroy this place. So great is the outcry against them before
14 the Lord that He has sent us to destroy it." Lot went out and spoke to his
sons-in-law, the men who were betrothed to his daughters, and told them,
"Get up and leave this place: the Lord is about to destroy the city!" But his
15 sons-in-law thought him laughable. As dawn was breaking, the angels hurried
Lot. "Get up," they said. "Take your wife and your two daughters here, or
16 you will be swept away amid the city's sin." Still he hesitated. So the men
seized him, his wife, and his two daughters by the hand and led them safely
17 outside the city, for the Lord had mercy upon him. As soon as they had
brought them out, one said, "Run for your life. Do not look back. Do not stop
18 anywhere in the plain. Flee to the mountains or you will be swept away." But
19 Lot said to them, "No, my lords, please. Your servant has found favor in your
eyes, and you have done me great kindness in saving my life. But I cannot flee
20 to the mountains; the disaster would overtake me, and I would die.[38] There
is a town here close enough for refuge. It is small. Let me flee there – is it not
21 small? – so that I might survive." "Very well," he said, "I will grant this request
22 also; I will not overthrow the town of which you speak. But hurry. Flee there,
because I cannot do anything until you reach it." That is why the town is called
23 24 Tzoar.[39] By the time Lot reached Tzoar, the sun had risen over the land. Then
the Lord rained down sulfur and fire on Sedom and Amora. Out of the
25 heavens it came from the Lord. He overthrew those cities, and the whole
26 plain, and all the cities' inhabitants, and the vegetation on the land. But Lot's
27 wife looked back – and she was turned into a pillar of salt. Avraham rose early
the next morning and returned to the place where he had stood before the
28 Lord. He looked down toward Sedom and Amora and all the land of the
29 plain, and he saw thick smoke rising from the land like smoke from a kiln. So
it was, that when God destroyed the cities of the plain, He remembered
Avraham and brought Lot out of the overthrow that overturned the cities
30 where Lot had lived. Lot went up from Tzoar and settled in the hills together
with his two daughters because he was afraid to stay in Tzoar. He and his two
31 daughters settled in a cave. The elder said to the younger, "Our father is old,
and there is no man left on earth to come to us in the normal way of the world.
32 Let us get our father drunk with wine and then sleep with him, so that we
33 may raise a new generation through our father." That night they gave their
father wine to drink. Then the elder daughter went in and slept with him. He
34 was unaware when she lay down and when she arose. The next day, the elder
said to the younger, "Last night I slept with my father. Let us get him to drink
wine again tonight, then you go in and sleep with him. So may we preserve
35 our family line through our father." So that night they got their father to drink

---

38 | Lot does not regard the mountains as a safe haven from the impending source of destruction.

39 | Tzoar resonates with *mitzar* (small) in verse 20.

מִי־לְךָ פֹה חָתָן וּבָנֶיךָ וּבְנֹתֶיךָ וְכֹל אֲשֶׁר־לְךָ בָּעִיר הוֹצֵא מִן־הַמָּקוֹם׃
יג כִּי־מַשְׁחִתִים אֲנַחְנוּ אֶת־הַמָּקוֹם הַזֶּה כִּי־גָדְלָה צַעֲקָתָם אֶת־פְּנֵי
יד יהוה וַיְשַׁלְּחֵנוּ יהוה לְשַׁחֲתָהּ׃ וַיֵּצֵא לוֹט וַיְדַבֵּר ׀ אֶל־חֲתָנָיו ׀ לֹקְחֵי
בְנֹתָיו וַיֹּאמֶר קוּמוּ צְּאוּ מִן־הַמָּקוֹם הַזֶּה כִּי־מַשְׁחִית יהוה אֶת־הָעִיר
טו וַיְהִי כִמְצַחֵק בְּעֵינֵי חֲתָנָיו׃ וּכְמוֹ הַשַּׁחַר עָלָה וַיָּאִיצוּ הַמַּלְאָכִים בְּלוֹט
לֵאמֹר קוּם קַח אֶת־אִשְׁתְּךָ וְאֶת־שְׁתֵּי בְנֹתֶיךָ הַנִּמְצָאֹת פֶּן־תִּסָּפֶה
טז בַּעֲוֺן הָעִיר׃ וַיִּתְמַהְמָהּ ׀ וַיַּחֲזִיקוּ הָאֲנָשִׁים בְּיָדוֹ וּבְיַד־אִשְׁתּוֹ וּבְיַד
יז שְׁתֵּי בְנֹתָיו בְּחֶמְלַת יהוה עָלָיו וַיֹּצִאֻהוּ וַיַּנִּחֻהוּ מִחוּץ לָעִיר׃ וַיְהִי
כְהוֹצִיאָם אֹתָם הַחוּצָה וַיֹּאמֶר הִמָּלֵט עַל־נַפְשֶׁךָ אַל־תַּבִּיט אַחֲרֶיךָ
יח וְאַל־תַּעֲמֹד בְּכָל־הַכִּכָּר הָהָרָה הִמָּלֵט פֶּן־תִּסָּפֶה׃ וַיֹּאמֶר לוֹט אֲלֵהֶם
יט אַל־נָא אֲדֹנָי׃ הִנֵּה־נָא מָצָא עַבְדְּךָ חֵן בְּעֵינֶיךָ וַתַּגְדֵּל חַסְדְּךָ אֲשֶׁר
עָשִׂיתָ עִמָּדִי לְהַחֲיוֹת אֶת־נַפְשִׁי וְאָנֹכִי לֹא אוּכַל לְהִמָּלֵט הָהָרָה
כ פֶּן־תִּדְבָּקַנִי הָרָעָה וָמַתִּי׃ הִנֵּה־נָא הָעִיר הַזֹּאת קְרֹבָה לָנוּס שָׁמָּה
כא וְהִוא מִצְעָר אִמָּלְטָה נָּא שָׁמָּה הֲלֹא מִצְעָר הִוא וּתְחִי נַפְשִׁי׃ וַיֹּאמֶר רביעי
אֵלָיו הִנֵּה נָשָׂאתִי פָנֶיךָ גַּם לַדָּבָר הַזֶּה לְבִלְתִּי הָפְכִּי אֶת־הָעִיר אֲשֶׁר
כב דִּבַּרְתָּ׃ מַהֵר הִמָּלֵט שָׁמָּה כִּי לֹא אוּכַל לַעֲשׂוֹת דָּבָר עַד־בֹּאֲךָ שָׁמָּה
כג עַל־כֵּן קָרָא שֵׁם־הָעִיר צוֹעַר׃ הַשֶּׁמֶשׁ יָצָא עַל־הָאָרֶץ וְלוֹט בָּא
כד צֹעֲרָה׃ וַיהוה הִמְטִיר עַל־סְדֹם וְעַל־עֲמֹרָה גָּפְרִית וָאֵשׁ מֵאֵת יהוה
כה מִן־הַשָּׁמָיִם׃ וַיַּהֲפֹךְ אֶת־הֶעָרִים הָאֵל וְאֵת כָּל־הַכִּכָּר וְאֵת כָּל־יֹשְׁבֵי
כו הֶעָרִים וְצֶמַח הָאֲדָמָה׃ וַתַּבֵּט אִשְׁתּוֹ מֵאַחֲרָיו וַתְּהִי נְצִיב מֶלַח׃
כז וַיַּשְׁכֵּם אַבְרָהָם בַּבֹּקֶר אֶל־הַמָּקוֹם אֲשֶׁר־עָמַד שָׁם אֶת־פְּנֵי יהוה׃
כח וַיַּשְׁקֵף עַל־פְּנֵי סְדֹם וַעֲמֹרָה וְעַל כָּל־פְּנֵי אֶרֶץ הַכִּכָּר וַיַּרְא וְהִנֵּה עָלָה
כט קִיטֹר הָאָרֶץ כְּקִיטֹר הַכִּבְשָׁן׃ וַיְהִי בְּשַׁחֵת אֱלֹהִים אֶת־עָרֵי הַכִּכָּר
וַיִּזְכֹּר אֱלֹהִים אֶת־אַבְרָהָם וַיְשַׁלַּח אֶת־לוֹט מִתּוֹךְ הַהֲפֵכָה בַּהֲפֹךְ
ל אֶת־הֶעָרִים אֲשֶׁר־יָשַׁב בָּהֵן לוֹט׃ וַיַּעַל לוֹט מִצּוֹעַר וַיֵּשֶׁב בָּהָר וּשְׁתֵּי
בְנֹתָיו עִמּוֹ כִּי יָרֵא לָשֶׁבֶת בְּצוֹעַר וַיֵּשֶׁב בַּמְּעָרָה הוּא וּשְׁתֵּי בְנֹתָיו׃
לא וַתֹּאמֶר הַבְּכִירָה אֶל־הַצְּעִירָה אָבִינוּ זָקֵן וְאִישׁ אֵין בָּאָרֶץ לָבוֹא
לב עָלֵינוּ כְּדֶרֶךְ כָּל־הָאָרֶץ׃ לְכָה נַשְׁקֶה אֶת־אָבִינוּ יַיִן וְנִשְׁכְּבָה עִמּוֹ
לג וּנְחַיֶּה מֵאָבִינוּ זָרַע׃ וַתַּשְׁקֶיןָ אֶת־אֲבִיהֶן יַיִן בַּלַּיְלָה הוּא וַתָּבֹא
לד הַבְּכִירָה וַתִּשְׁכַּב אֶת־אָבִיהָ וְלֹא־יָדַע בְּשִׁכְבָהּ וּבְקוּמָהּ׃ וַיְהִי מִמָּחֳרָת
וַתֹּאמֶר הַבְּכִירָה אֶל־הַצְּעִירָה הֵן־שָׁכַבְתִּי אֶמֶשׁ אֶת־אָבִי נַשְׁקֶנּוּ יַיִן
לה גַּם־הַלַּיְלָה וּבֹאִי שִׁכְבִי עִמּוֹ וּנְחַיֶּה מֵאָבִינוּ זָרַע׃ וַתַּשְׁקֶיןָ גַּם בַּלַּיְלָה

wine again, and the younger went and slept with him. And he was unaware
36 when she lay down and when she arose. And so both of Lot's daughters
37 became pregnant by their father. The elder had a son, whom she named
38 Moav.[40] He is the ancestor of the Moabites of today. The younger also had a
son, whom she named Ben Ami.[41] And he is the ancestor of the Amonites of
20 1 today. Avraham then journeyed on to the Negev region, settling
2 between Kadesh and Shur. For a while he lived as a stranger in Gerar. There
Avraham said of his wife Sara, "She is my sister." Avimelekh, king of Gerar,
3 sent for Sara and took her as his own. But God came to Avimelekh in a dream
one night and told him, "You will die because of the woman you have taken.
4 She is already married." Avimelekh had not gone near her, so he said, "Lord,
5 would You destroy an innocent nation? Did he not tell me, 'She is my sister'?
Did she not say, 'He is my brother'? I have acted from an innocent heart, with
6 clean hands." Then, in the dream, God said to him, "I too knew that you acted
from an innocent heart, and so I kept you from sinning against Me. That is
7 why I did not let you touch her. But now, give back the man's wife. He is a
prophet. He will pray for you and you will live. But if you do not give her
8 back, know that you and all your people are to die." Early the next morning,
Avimelekh summoned all his servants and told them all this – they were very
9 afraid. Then Avimelekh summoned Avraham and said, "What have you
done to us? What wrong have I done you? Why have you brought such
onerous guilt upon me and my kingdom? You have done to me that which
10 should never be done. What were you thinking of," asked Avimelekh, "that
11 you did such a thing?" Avraham replied, "I thought, 'There is no fear of God
12 in this place. They will kill me because of my wife.' Besides, she really is my
sister. She is the daughter of my father though not of my mother, and she
13 became my wife. When God made me wander from my father's house, I
said to her, 'Do me this kindness: wherever we go, say of me, "He is my
14 brother."'" Avimelekh gave Avraham sheep, cattle, and male and female slaves,
15 and returned his wife Sara to him. Avimelekh said, "Here is my land. Live
16 wherever you wish." To Sara he said, "I am giving your brother a thousand
pieces of silver. This will allay the suspicions of everyone who is with you.
17 You are fully vindicated." Then Avraham prayed to God, and God healed
Avimelekh, his wife, and his female slaves so they could again have children,
18 for the Lord had prevented all the women in Avimelekh's household from
21 1 bearing children, because of Sara, Avraham's wife. The Lord
remembered Sara as He had said He would, and acted for Sara as He had
2 promised. Sara became pregnant and bore a son to Avraham in his old age
3 at the very time God had promised. Avraham named his newborn son, whom

40 | The name Moav resonates with *me'av* (from father).

41 | Literally "son of my kin."

הַהוּא אֶת־אֲבִיהֶן יָיִן וַתָּקָם הַצְּעִירָה וַתִּשְׁכַּב עִמּוֹ וְלֹא־יָדַע בְּשִׁכְבָהּ
לו לז וּבְקֻמָהּ: וַתַּהֲרֶיןָ שְׁתֵּי בְנוֹת־לוֹט מֵאֲבִיהֶן: וַתֵּלֶד הַבְּכִירָה בֵּן וַתִּקְרָא
לח שְׁמוֹ מוֹאָב הוּא אֲבִי־מוֹאָב עַד־הַיּוֹם: וְהַצְּעִירָה גַם־הִוא יָלְדָה בֵּן
כ א וַתִּקְרָא שְׁמוֹ בֶּן־עַמִּי הוּא אֲבִי בְנֵי־עַמּוֹן עַד־הַיּוֹם: וַיִּסַּע יז
מִשָּׁם אַבְרָהָם אַרְצָה הַנֶּגֶב וַיֵּשֶׁב בֵּין־קָדֵשׁ וּבֵין שׁוּר וַיָּגָר בִּגְרָר:
ב וַיֹּאמֶר אַבְרָהָם אֶל־שָׂרָה אִשְׁתּוֹ אֲחֹתִי הִוא וַיִּשְׁלַח אֲבִימֶלֶךְ מֶלֶךְ
ג גְּרָר וַיִּקַּח אֶת־שָׂרָה: וַיָּבֹא אֱלֹהִים אֶל־אֲבִימֶלֶךְ בַּחֲלוֹם הַלָּיְלָה
וַיֹּאמֶר לוֹ הִנְּךָ מֵת עַל־הָאִשָּׁה אֲשֶׁר־לָקַחְתָּ וְהִוא בְּעֻלַת בָּעַל:
ד ה וַאֲבִימֶלֶךְ לֹא קָרַב אֵלֶיהָ וַיֹּאמַר אֲדֹנָי הֲגוֹי גַּם־צַדִּיק תַּהֲרֹג: הֲלֹא
הוּא אָמַר־לִי אֲחֹתִי הִוא וְהִיא־גַם־הִוא אָמְרָה אָחִי הוּא בְּתָם־לְבָבִי
ו וּבְנִקְיֹן כַּפַּי עָשִׂיתִי זֹאת: וַיֹּאמֶר אֵלָיו הָאֱלֹהִים בַּחֲלֹם גַּם אָנֹכִי יָדַעְתִּי
כִּי בְתָם־לְבָבְךָ עָשִׂיתָ זֹּאת וָאֶחְשֹׂךְ גַּם־אָנֹכִי אוֹתְךָ מֵחֲטוֹ־לִי עַל־
ז כֵּן לֹא־נְתַתִּיךָ לִנְגֹּעַ אֵלֶיהָ: וְעַתָּה הָשֵׁב אֵשֶׁת־הָאִישׁ כִּי־נָבִיא הוּא
וְיִתְפַּלֵּל בַּעַדְךָ וֶחְיֵה וְאִם־אֵינְךָ מֵשִׁיב דַּע כִּי־מוֹת תָּמוּת אַתָּה וְכָל־
ח אֲשֶׁר־לָךְ: וַיַּשְׁכֵּם אֲבִימֶלֶךְ בַּבֹּקֶר וַיִּקְרָא לְכָל־עֲבָדָיו וַיְדַבֵּר אֶת־
ט כָּל־הַדְּבָרִים הָאֵלֶּה בְּאָזְנֵיהֶם וַיִּירְאוּ הָאֲנָשִׁים מְאֹד: וַיִּקְרָא אֲבִימֶלֶךְ
לְאַבְרָהָם וַיֹּאמֶר לוֹ מֶה־עָשִׂיתָ לָּנוּ וּמֶה־חָטָאתִי לָךְ כִּי־הֵבֵאתָ עָלַי
וְעַל־מַמְלַכְתִּי חֲטָאָה גְדֹלָה מַעֲשִׂים אֲשֶׁר לֹא־יֵעָשׂוּ עָשִׂיתָ עִמָּדִי:
י וַיֹּאמֶר אֲבִימֶלֶךְ אֶל־אַבְרָהָם מָה רָאִיתָ כִּי עָשִׂיתָ אֶת־הַדָּבָר הַזֶּה:
יא וַיֹּאמֶר אַבְרָהָם כִּי אָמַרְתִּי רַק אֵין־יִרְאַת אֱלֹהִים בַּמָּקוֹם הַזֶּה וַהֲרָגוּנִי
יב עַל־דְּבַר אִשְׁתִּי: וְגַם־אָמְנָה אֲחֹתִי בַת־אָבִי הִוא אַךְ לֹא בַת־אִמִּי
יג וַתְּהִי־לִי לְאִשָּׁה: וַיְהִי כַּאֲשֶׁר הִתְעוּ אֹתִי אֱלֹהִים מִבֵּית אָבִי וָאֹמַר
לָהּ זֶה חַסְדֵּךְ אֲשֶׁר תַּעֲשִׂי עִמָּדִי אֶל כָּל־הַמָּקוֹם אֲשֶׁר נָבוֹא שָׁמָּה
יד אִמְרִי־לִי אָחִי הוּא: וַיִּקַּח אֲבִימֶלֶךְ צֹאן וּבָקָר וַעֲבָדִים וּשְׁפָחֹת וַיִּתֵּן
טו לְאַבְרָהָם וַיָּשֶׁב לוֹ אֵת שָׂרָה אִשְׁתּוֹ: וַיֹּאמֶר אֲבִימֶלֶךְ הִנֵּה אַרְצִי
טז לְפָנֶיךָ בַּטּוֹב בְּעֵינֶיךָ שֵׁב: וּלְשָׂרָה אָמַר הִנֵּה נָתַתִּי אֶלֶף כֶּסֶף לְאָחִיךְ
יז הִנֵּה הוּא־לָךְ כְּסוּת עֵינַיִם לְכֹל אֲשֶׁר אִתָּךְ וְאֵת כֹּל וְנֹכָחַת: וַיִּתְפַּלֵּל
אַבְרָהָם אֶל־הָאֱלֹהִים וַיִּרְפָּא אֱלֹהִים אֶת־אֲבִימֶלֶךְ וְאֶת־אִשְׁתּוֹ
יח וְאַמְהֹתָיו וַיֵּלֵדוּ: כִּי־עָצֹר עָצַר יהוה בְּעַד כָּל־רֶחֶם לְבֵית אֲבִימֶלֶךְ
כא א עַל־דְּבַר שָׂרָה אֵשֶׁת אַבְרָהָם: וַיהוה פָּקַד אֶת־ יח
ב שָׂרָה כַּאֲשֶׁר אָמָר וַיַּעַשׂ יהוה לְשָׂרָה כַּאֲשֶׁר דִּבֵּר: וַתַּהַר וַתֵּלֶד שָׂרָה
ג לְאַבְרָהָם בֵּן לִזְקֻנָיו לַמּוֹעֵד אֲשֶׁר־דִּבֶּר אֹתוֹ אֱלֹהִים: וַיִּקְרָא אַבְרָהָם

4 Sara had borne him, Yitzḥak. And when Yitzḥak his son was eight days old,
5 Avraham circumcised him as God had commanded. Avraham was one
6 hundred years old when his son Yitzḥak was born to him. Sara said, "God has
7 brought me laughter; all those who hear will laugh with me."[42] Then she said,
"Who would have told Avraham, 'Sara will nurse children'? Yet I have borne
8 a son in his old age." The child grew and was weaned; on the day Yitzḥak was
9 weaned, Avraham held a great feast. But Sara saw the son whom Hagar the
10 Egyptian had borne Avraham mocking.[43] She said to Avraham, "Drive out
that slave woman and her son, for the son of that slave woman must not share
11 the inheritance with my son, with Yitzḥak." This distressed Avraham greatly
12 because of his son. But God told Avraham, "Do not be distressed about the
boy or about your slave. Listen to whatever Sara tells you, because it is through
13 Yitzḥak that your descendants will be reckoned. But I will make the slave's
14 son too into a nation, because he is your child." Early the next morning
Avraham took bread and a skin of water and gave them to Hagar. He placed
them on her shoulder, and together with the child, he sent her away. She went
15 wandering in the Be'er Sheva desert. When the water in the skin was all gone,
16 she cast the child away under one of the bushes and went and sat down at a
distance, about a bowshot away, saying, "I cannot watch the child die." Sitting
17 there, at a distance, she raised her voice and wept. God heard the boy crying,
and an angel of God called to Hagar from the heavens and said to her, "Hagar,
18 what is wrong? Fear not. God has heard the boy's cry there, where he is. Go,
raise up the boy and take him by the hand, for I will make of him a great
19 nation." Then God opened her eyes and she saw a well of water. She went and
20 filled the skin with water and gave the boy to drink. God was with the boy as
21 he grew. He lived in the desert and became an expert with the bow. In the
Paran desert he lived, and his mother took him a wife from Egypt.
22 At that time, Avimelekh and Pikhol, commander of his troops, said to
23 Avraham, "God is with you in all you do. Now swear to me here before God
that you will not deal falsely with me or with my children or grandchildren.
Show me and the land where you have lived as a stranger the same kindness
24 25 I have shown to you."[44] Avraham said, "I swear." Then Avraham rebuked
26 Avimelekh for the well of water that Avimelekh's servants had seized. But
Avimelekh said, "I do not know who has done this. You did not tell me; I had
27 not heard about it until today." Avraham then brought sheep and cattle and
28 gave them to Avimelekh, and the two of them forged a covenant. Avraham
29 set apart seven ewe lambs from the flock. Avimelekh asked him, "What is the

42 | The name Yitzḥak derives from the verb denoting laughter (cf. 17:17–19, 18:12–14).

43 | Hebrew *metzaḥek* – again bearing a connection to the name Yitzḥak.

44 | See 20:14–16.

ד אֶת־שֶׁם־בְּנוֹ הַנּוֹלַד־לוֹ אֲשֶׁר־יָלְדָה־לּוֹ שָׂרָה יִצְחָק: וַיָּמָל אַבְרָהָם
ה אֶת־יִצְחָק בְּנוֹ בֶּן־שְׁמֹנַת יָמִים כַּאֲשֶׁר צִוָּה אֹתוֹ אֱלֹהִים: וְאַבְרָהָם חמישי
ו בֶּן־מְאַת שָׁנָה בְּהִוָּלֶד לוֹ אֵת יִצְחָק בְּנוֹ: וַתֹּאמֶר שָׂרָה צְחֹק עָשָׂה
ז לִי אֱלֹהִים כָּל־הַשֹּׁמֵעַ יִצְחַק־לִי: וַתֹּאמֶר מִי מִלֵּל לְאַבְרָהָם הֵינִיקָה
ח בָנִים שָׂרָה כִּי־יָלַדְתִּי בֵן לִזְקֻנָיו: וַיִּגְדַּל הַיֶּלֶד וַיִּגָּמַל וַיַּעַשׂ אַבְרָהָם
ט מִשְׁתֶּה גָדוֹל בְּיוֹם הִגָּמֵל אֶת־יִצְחָק: וַתֵּרֶא שָׂרָה אֶת־בֶּן־הָגָר
י הַמִּצְרִית אֲשֶׁר־יָלְדָה לְאַבְרָהָם מְצַחֵק: וַתֹּאמֶר לְאַבְרָהָם גָּרֵשׁ
הָאָמָה הַזֹּאת וְאֶת־בְּנָהּ כִּי לֹא יִירַשׁ בֶּן־הָאָמָה הַזֹּאת עִם־בְּנִי עִם־
יא יב יִצְחָק: וַיֵּרַע הַדָּבָר מְאֹד בְּעֵינֵי אַבְרָהָם עַל אוֹדֹת בְּנוֹ: וַיֹּאמֶר אֱלֹהִים
אֶל־אַבְרָהָם אַל־יֵרַע בְּעֵינֶיךָ עַל־הַנַּעַר וְעַל־אֲמָתֶךָ כֹּל אֲשֶׁר תֹּאמַר
יג אֵלֶיךָ שָׂרָה שְׁמַע בְּקֹלָהּ כִּי בְיִצְחָק יִקָּרֵא לְךָ זָרַע: וְגַם אֶת־בֶּן־הָאָמָה
יד לְגוֹי אֲשִׂימֶנּוּ כִּי זַרְעֲךָ הוּא: וַיַּשְׁכֵּם אַבְרָהָם ׀ בַּבֹּקֶר וַיִּקַּח־לֶחֶם וְחֵמַת
מַיִם וַיִּתֵּן אֶל־הָגָר שָׂם עַל־שִׁכְמָהּ וְאֶת־הַיֶּלֶד וַיְשַׁלְּחֶהָ וַתֵּלֶךְ וַתֵּתַע
טו בְּמִדְבַּר בְּאֵר שָׁבַע: וַיִּכְלוּ הַמַּיִם מִן־הַחֵמֶת וַתַּשְׁלֵךְ אֶת־הַיֶּלֶד תַּחַת
טז אַחַד הַשִּׂיחִם: וַתֵּלֶךְ וַתֵּשֶׁב לָהּ מִנֶּגֶד הַרְחֵק כִּמְטַחֲוֵי קֶשֶׁת כִּי אָמְרָה
יז אַל־אֶרְאֶה בְּמוֹת הַיָּלֶד וַתֵּשֶׁב מִנֶּגֶד וַתִּשָּׂא אֶת־קֹלָהּ וַתֵּבְךְּ: וַיִּשְׁמַע
אֱלֹהִים אֶת־קוֹל הַנַּעַר וַיִּקְרָא מַלְאַךְ אֱלֹהִים ׀ אֶל־הָגָר מִן־הַשָּׁמַיִם
וַיֹּאמֶר לָהּ מַה־לָּךְ הָגָר אַל־תִּירְאִי כִּי־שָׁמַע אֱלֹהִים אֶל־קוֹל הַנַּעַר
יח בַּאֲשֶׁר הוּא־שָׁם: קוּמִי שְׂאִי אֶת־הַנַּעַר וְהַחֲזִיקִי אֶת־יָדֵךְ בּוֹ כִּי־לְגוֹי
יט גָּדוֹל אֲשִׂימֶנּוּ: וַיִּפְקַח אֱלֹהִים אֶת־עֵינֶיהָ וַתֵּרֶא בְּאֵר מָיִם וַתֵּלֶךְ
כ וַתְּמַלֵּא אֶת־הַחֵמֶת מַיִם וַתַּשְׁקְ אֶת־הַנָּעַר: וַיְהִי אֱלֹהִים אֶת־הַנַּעַר
כא וַיִּגְדָּל וַיֵּשֶׁב בַּמִּדְבָּר וַיְהִי רֹבֶה קַשָּׁת: וַיֵּשֶׁב בְּמִדְבַּר פָּארָן וַתִּקַּח־לוֹ
אִמּוֹ אִשָּׁה מֵאֶרֶץ מִצְרָיִם:
כב וַיְהִי בָּעֵת הַהִוא וַיֹּאמֶר אֲבִימֶלֶךְ וּפִיכֹל שַׂר־צְבָאוֹ אֶל־אַבְרָהָם ששי
כג לֵאמֹר אֱלֹהִים עִמְּךָ בְּכֹל אֲשֶׁר־אַתָּה עֹשֶׂה: וְעַתָּה הִשָּׁבְעָה לִּי
בֵאלֹהִים הֵנָּה אִם־תִּשְׁקֹר לִי וּלְנִינִי וּלְנֶכְדִּי כַּחֶסֶד אֲשֶׁר־עָשִׂיתִי
כד עִמְּךָ תַּעֲשֶׂה עִמָּדִי וְעִם־הָאָרֶץ אֲשֶׁר־גַּרְתָּה בָּהּ: וַיֹּאמֶר אַבְרָהָם
כה אָנֹכִי אִשָּׁבֵעַ: וְהוֹכִחַ אַבְרָהָם אֶת־אֲבִימֶלֶךְ עַל־אֹדוֹת בְּאֵר הַמַּיִם
כו אֲשֶׁר גָּזְלוּ עַבְדֵי אֲבִימֶלֶךְ: וַיֹּאמֶר אֲבִימֶלֶךְ לֹא יָדַעְתִּי מִי עָשָׂה אֶת־
הַדָּבָר הַזֶּה וְגַם־אַתָּה לֹא־הִגַּדְתָּ לִּי וְגַם אָנֹכִי לֹא שָׁמַעְתִּי בִּלְתִּי
כז הַיּוֹם: וַיִּקַּח אַבְרָהָם צֹאן וּבָקָר וַיִּתֵּן לַאֲבִימֶלֶךְ וַיִּכְרְתוּ שְׁנֵיהֶם בְּרִית:
כח כט וַיַּצֵּב אַבְרָהָם אֶת־שֶׁבַע כִּבְשֹׂת הַצֹּאן לְבַדְּהֶן: וַיֹּאמֶר אֲבִימֶלֶךְ אֶל־

30 meaning of these seven ewe lambs you have set apart?" He replied, "Accept
31 these seven lambs from me as testimony that I dug this well." That is why
that place is called Be'er Sheva, because there the two men swore an oath.[45]
32 Thus they made a pact at Be'er Sheva. And then Avimelekh and Pikhol,
33 commander of his troops, returned to the land of the Philistines. Avraham
planted a tamarisk tree in Be'er Sheva, and there he called on the name of the
34 LORD, the Everlasting God. Avraham stayed on in the land of the Philistines
for many days.
22 1 After these things, God tested Avraham. "Avraham!" He said. And Avraham
2 replied, "Here I am." Then God said, "Take your son, your only one, the one
whom you love – Yitzḥak – and go to the land of Moria. There, offer him up
as a burnt offering on one of the mountains, the one that I will show you."
3 Early the next morning Avraham rose and saddled his donkey. With him he
took two of his young men and Yitzḥak his son. He cut wood for the offering
4 and set out toward the place of which God had told him. On the third day
5 Avraham looked up and, in the distance, he saw the place. He told his young
men, "Stay here with the donkey. I and the boy will go there and worship.
6 Then we will come back to you." Avraham took the wood for the offering and
placed it on Yitzḥak his son. He himself took the fire and the knife. The two
7 of them walked together. Then Yitzḥak said to his father, Avraham, "Father?"
Avraham said, "Here I am, my son." Yitzḥak said, "Here is the fire and the
8 wood, but where is the lamb for the burnt offering?" And Avraham replied,
"God will see to a lamb for an offering, my son." The two of them walked on
9 together. They came to the place of which God had spoken. There Avraham
built an altar and arranged the wood. Then he bound Yitzḥak his son and
10 laid him on the altar on top of the wood. Avraham reached out his hand
11 and took hold of the knife to slay his son. But an angel of the LORD called out
12 to him from the heavens, "Avraham! Avraham!" He said, "Here I am." "Do
not lift your hand against the boy; do nothing to him, for now I know that
you fear God: for you have not withheld from Me your son, your only one."
13 Avraham looked up and saw a ram caught in a thicket by its horns. Avraham
went, took hold of the ram, and offered it up as a burnt offering in place of his
14 son. And Avraham named the place The LORD Will See.[46] To this day it is said,
15 "On the mountain of the LORD, He will be seen." Then the angel of the LORD
16 called to Avraham from the heavens a second time and said, "By My own Self
I swear, says the LORD, that because you have done this and have not withheld
17 your son, your only one, I will bless you greatly and make your descendants
as many as the stars of the heavens, as the sand on the seashore. Your

---

45 | The name Be'er Sheva resonates with both *sheva* (seven) and *nishbe'u* (swore).
46 | Cf. verse 8: "God will see to a lamb for an offering."

ל אַבְרָהָם מָה הֵנָּה שֶׁבַע כְּבָשֹׂת הָאֵלֶּה אֲשֶׁר הִצַּבְתָּ לְבַדָּנָה: וַיֹּאמֶר
כִּי אֶת־שֶׁבַע כְּבָשֹׂת תִּקַּח מִיָּדִי בַּעֲבוּר תִּהְיֶה־לִּי לְעֵדָה כִּי חָפַרְתִּי
לא אֶת־הַבְּאֵר הַזֹּאת: עַל־כֵּן קָרָא לַמָּקוֹם הַהוּא בְּאֵר שָׁבַע כִּי שָׁם
לב נִשְׁבְּעוּ שְׁנֵיהֶם: וַיִּכְרְתוּ בְרִית בִּבְאֵר שָׁבַע וַיָּקָם אֲבִימֶלֶךְ וּפִיכֹל
לג שַׂר־צְבָאוֹ וַיָּשֻׁבוּ אֶל־אֶרֶץ פְּלִשְׁתִּים: וַיִּטַּע אֶשֶׁל בִּבְאֵר שָׁבַע
לד וַיִּקְרָא־שָׁם בְּשֵׁם יהוה אֵל עוֹלָם: וַיָּגָר אַבְרָהָם בְּאֶרֶץ פְּלִשְׁתִּים
יָמִים רַבִּים:
כב א וַיְהִי אַחַר הַדְּבָרִים הָאֵלֶּה וְהָאֱלֹהִים נִסָּה אֶת־אַבְרָהָם וַיֹּאמֶר אֵלָיו יט שביעי
ב אַבְרָהָם וַיֹּאמֶר הִנֵּנִי: וַיֹּאמֶר קַח־נָא אֶת־בִּנְךָ אֶת־יְחִידְךָ אֲשֶׁר־
אָהַבְתָּ אֶת־יִצְחָק וְלֶךְ־לְךָ אֶל־אֶרֶץ הַמֹּרִיָּה וְהַעֲלֵהוּ שָׁם לְעֹלָה
ג עַל אַחַד הֶהָרִים אֲשֶׁר אֹמַר אֵלֶיךָ: וַיַּשְׁכֵּם אַבְרָהָם בַּבֹּקֶר וַיַּחֲבֹשׁ
אֶת־חֲמֹרוֹ וַיִּקַּח אֶת־שְׁנֵי נְעָרָיו אִתּוֹ וְאֵת יִצְחָק בְּנוֹ וַיְבַקַּע עֲצֵי עֹלָה
ד וַיָּקָם וַיֵּלֶךְ אֶל־הַמָּקוֹם אֲשֶׁר־אָמַר־לוֹ הָאֱלֹהִים: בַּיּוֹם הַשְּׁלִישִׁי וַיִּשָּׂא
ה אַבְרָהָם אֶת־עֵינָיו וַיַּרְא אֶת־הַמָּקוֹם מֵרָחֹק: וַיֹּאמֶר אַבְרָהָם אֶל־
נְעָרָיו שְׁבוּ־לָכֶם פֹּה עִם־הַחֲמוֹר וַאֲנִי וְהַנַּעַר נֵלְכָה עַד־כֹּה וְנִשְׁתַּחֲוֶה
ו וְנָשׁוּבָה אֲלֵיכֶם: וַיִּקַּח אַבְרָהָם אֶת־עֲצֵי הָעֹלָה וַיָּשֶׂם עַל־יִצְחָק בְּנוֹ
ז וַיִּקַּח בְּיָדוֹ אֶת־הָאֵשׁ וְאֶת־הַמַּאֲכֶלֶת וַיֵּלְכוּ שְׁנֵיהֶם יַחְדָּו: וַיֹּאמֶר
יִצְחָק אֶל־אַבְרָהָם אָבִיו וַיֹּאמֶר אָבִי וַיֹּאמֶר הִנֶּנִּי בְנִי וַיֹּאמֶר הִנֵּה
ח הָאֵשׁ וְהָעֵצִים וְאַיֵּה הַשֶּׂה לְעֹלָה: וַיֹּאמֶר אַבְרָהָם אֱלֹהִים יִרְאֶה־לּוֹ
ט הַשֶּׂה לְעֹלָה בְּנִי וַיֵּלְכוּ שְׁנֵיהֶם יַחְדָּו: וַיָּבֹאוּ אֶל־הַמָּקוֹם אֲשֶׁר אָמַר־
לוֹ הָאֱלֹהִים וַיִּבֶן שָׁם אַבְרָהָם אֶת־הַמִּזְבֵּחַ וַיַּעֲרֹךְ אֶת־הָעֵצִים וַיַּעֲקֹד
י אֶת־יִצְחָק בְּנוֹ וַיָּשֶׂם אֹתוֹ עַל־הַמִּזְבֵּחַ מִמַּעַל לָעֵצִים: וַיִּשְׁלַח אַבְרָהָם
יא אֶת־יָדוֹ וַיִּקַּח אֶת־הַמַּאֲכֶלֶת לִשְׁחֹט אֶת־בְּנוֹ: וַיִּקְרָא אֵלָיו מַלְאַךְ
יב יהוה מִן־הַשָּׁמַיִם וַיֹּאמֶר אַבְרָהָם ׀ אַבְרָהָם וַיֹּאמֶר הִנֵּנִי: וַיֹּאמֶר אַל־
תִּשְׁלַח יָדְךָ אֶל־הַנַּעַר וְאַל־תַּעַשׂ לוֹ מְאוּמָה כִּי ׀ עַתָּה יָדַעְתִּי כִּי־יְרֵא
יג אֱלֹהִים אַתָּה וְלֹא חָשַׂכְתָּ אֶת־בִּנְךָ אֶת־יְחִידְךָ מִמֶּנִּי: וַיִּשָּׂא אַבְרָהָם
אֶת־עֵינָיו וַיַּרְא וְהִנֵּה־אַיִל אַחַר נֶאֱחַז בַּסְּבַךְ בְּקַרְנָיו וַיֵּלֶךְ אַבְרָהָם
יד וַיִּקַּח אֶת־הָאַיִל וַיַּעֲלֵהוּ לְעֹלָה תַּחַת בְּנוֹ: וַיִּקְרָא אַבְרָהָם שֵׁם־
טו הַמָּקוֹם הַהוּא יהוה ׀ יִרְאֶה אֲשֶׁר יֵאָמֵר הַיּוֹם בְּהַר יהוה יֵרָאֶה: וַיִּקְרָא
טז מַלְאַךְ יהוה אֶל־אַבְרָהָם שֵׁנִית מִן־הַשָּׁמָיִם: וַיֹּאמֶר בִּי נִשְׁבַּעְתִּי
נְאֻם־יהוה כִּי יַעַן אֲשֶׁר עָשִׂיתָ אֶת־הַדָּבָר הַזֶּה וְלֹא חָשַׂכְתָּ אֶת־
יז בִּנְךָ אֶת־יְחִידֶךָ: כִּי־בָרֵךְ אֲבָרֶכְךָ וְהַרְבָּה אַרְבֶּה אֶת־זַרְעֲךָ כְּכוֹכְבֵי

18 descendants will possess their enemies' gate,[47] and through your descendants
will all nations of the earth be blessed, because you have listened to My voice."
19 Avraham returned to his young men, and together they set out and went to
Be'er Sheva, and Avraham stayed on in Be'er Sheva.
20 Some time later, Avraham was told, "Milka too has had children with your
21 brother Naḥor: Utz, his firstborn, his brother Buz, Kemuel, father of Aram,
22 23 Kesed, Ḥazo, Pildash, Yidlaf, and Betuel." Betuel had a daughter Rivka. Milka
24 bore these eight sons to Avraham's brother Naḥor. His concubine, named
Reuma, also had children: Tevaḥ, Gaḥam, Taḥash, and Maakha.

23 1 Sara's lifetime – the years of Sara's life – were one hundred and twenty-seven. ḤAYEI SARA
2 Sara died in Kiryat Arba – that is, Ḥevron – in the land of Canaan. And
3 Avraham came to mourn for Sara and to weep for her. Then Avraham rose
4 from beside his dead and spoke to the Hittites. He said, "I am a migrant and
a visitor among you. Sell me a burial site here so that I can bury my dead."
5 6 The Hittites answered Avraham, "Hear us, my lord. You are a prince of God
in our midst. Bury your dead in the choicest of our tombs. None of us will
7 refuse you his tomb to bury your dead." Avraham rose and bowed down to
8 the Hittites, the people of the land, and said to them, "If you are willing to
allow me to bury the dead that lies before me, then hear me and intercede on
9 my behalf with Efron son of Tzoḥar. Let him sell me the cave of Makhpela
that he owns, at the edge of his field. Ask him to sell it to me at the full price
10 as a burial site in your midst." Efron was sitting among the Hittites. Efron the
Hittite answered Avraham in the hearing of all the Hittites who had come to
11 the city gate. He said, "No, my lord, hear me. I give you the field and I give
you the cave that is in it. In the presence of my people, I give it to you. Bury
12 13 your dead." Avraham bowed down again before the people of the land and
said to Efron in their hearing, "Please, would that you would hear me. I give
you the money for the field. Take it from me so that I can bury my dead there."
14 15 Efron answered Avraham and said to him, "My lord, hear me. A piece of land
worth four hundred silver shekel – what is that between you and me? Bury
16 your dead." Avraham heard Efron.[48] He weighed out for him the price he
had mentioned in the Hittites' hearing: four hundred silver shekel at the
17 merchants' standard rate. So Efron's field in Makhpela near Mamre – the field,
18 its cave, and all the trees within the field's borders – passed to Avraham as his
possession, in the presence of all the Hittites who had come to the city gate.

47 | That is, their cities.

48 | Avraham discerned Efron's real intention: that he be paid the specified amount.

הַשָּׁמַיִם וְכַחוֹל אֲשֶׁר עַל־שְׂפַת הַיָּם וְיִרַשׁ זַרְעֲךָ אֵת שַׁעַר אֹיְבָיו׃
יח יט וְהִתְבָּרְכוּ בְזַרְעֲךָ כֹּל גּוֹיֵי הָאָרֶץ עֵקֶב אֲשֶׁר שָׁמַעְתָּ בְּקֹלִי׃ וַיָּשָׁב
אַבְרָהָם אֶל־נְעָרָיו וַיָּקֻמוּ וַיֵּלְכוּ יַחְדָּו אֶל־בְּאֵר שָׁבַע וַיֵּשֶׁב אַבְרָהָם
בִּבְאֵר שָׁבַע׃
כ וַיְהִי אַחֲרֵי הַדְּבָרִים הָאֵלֶּה וַיֻּגַּד לְאַבְרָהָם לֵאמֹר הִנֵּה יָלְדָה מִלְכָּה מפטיר
כא גַם־הִוא בָּנִים לְנָחוֹר אָחִיךָ׃ אֶת־עוּץ בְּכֹרוֹ וְאֶת־בּוּז אָחִיו וְאֶת־
כב קְמוּאֵל אֲבִי אֲרָם׃ וְאֶת־כֶּשֶׂד וְאֶת־חֲזוֹ וְאֶת־פִּלְדָּשׁ וְאֶת־יִדְלָף וְאֵת
כג בְּתוּאֵל׃ וּבְתוּאֵל יָלַד אֶת־רִבְקָה שְׁמֹנָה אֵלֶּה יָלְדָה מִלְכָּה לְנָחוֹר
כד אֲחִי אַבְרָהָם׃ וּפִילַגְשׁוֹ וּשְׁמָהּ רְאוּמָה וַתֵּלֶד גַּם־הִוא אֶת־טֶבַח
וְאֶת־גַּחַם וְאֶת־תַּחַשׁ וְאֶת־מַעֲכָה׃
כג א וַיִּהְיוּ חַיֵּי שָׂרָה מֵאָה שָׁנָה וְעֶשְׂרִים שָׁנָה וְשֶׁבַע שָׁנִים שְׁנֵי חַיֵּי חיי שרה
ב שָׂרָה׃ וַתָּמָת שָׂרָה בְּקִרְיַת אַרְבַּע הִוא חֶבְרוֹן בְּאֶרֶץ כְּנָעַן וַיָּבֹא
ג אַבְרָהָם לִסְפֹּד לְשָׂרָה וְלִבְכֹּתָהּ׃ וַיָּקָם אַבְרָהָם מֵעַל פְּנֵי מֵתוֹ וַיְדַבֵּר
ד אֶל־בְּנֵי־חֵת לֵאמֹר׃ גֵּר־וְתוֹשָׁב אָנֹכִי עִמָּכֶם תְּנוּ לִי אֲחֻזַּת־קֶבֶר
ה עִמָּכֶם וְאֶקְבְּרָה מֵתִי מִלְּפָנָי׃ וַיַּעֲנוּ בְנֵי־חֵת אֶת־אַבְרָהָם לֵאמֹר לוֹ׃
ו שְׁמָעֵנוּ ׀ אֲדֹנִי נְשִׂיא אֱלֹהִים אַתָּה בְּתוֹכֵנוּ בְּמִבְחַר קְבָרֵינוּ קְבֹר
ז אֶת־מֵתֶךָ אִישׁ מִמֶּנּוּ אֶת־קִבְרוֹ לֹא־יִכְלֶה מִמְּךָ מִקְּבֹר מֵתֶךָ׃ וַיָּקָם
ח אַבְרָהָם וַיִּשְׁתַּחוּ לְעַם־הָאָרֶץ לִבְנֵי־חֵת׃ וַיְדַבֵּר אִתָּם לֵאמֹר אִם־יֵשׁ
אֶת־נַפְשְׁכֶם לִקְבֹּר אֶת־מֵתִי מִלְּפָנַי שְׁמָעוּנִי וּפִגְעוּ־לִי בְּעֶפְרוֹן בֶּן־
ט צֹחַר׃ וְיִתֶּן־לִי אֶת־מְעָרַת הַמַּכְפֵּלָה אֲשֶׁר־לוֹ אֲשֶׁר בִּקְצֵה שָׂדֵהוּ
י בְּכֶסֶף מָלֵא יִתְּנֶנָּה לִּי בְּתוֹכְכֶם לַאֲחֻזַּת־קָבֶר׃ וְעֶפְרוֹן יֹשֵׁב בְּתוֹךְ
בְּנֵי־חֵת וַיַּעַן עֶפְרוֹן הַחִתִּי אֶת־אַבְרָהָם בְּאָזְנֵי בְנֵי־חֵת לְכֹל בָּאֵי
יא שַׁעַר־עִירוֹ לֵאמֹר׃ לֹא־אֲדֹנִי שְׁמָעֵנִי הַשָּׂדֶה נָתַתִּי לָךְ וְהַמְּעָרָה
יב אֲשֶׁר־בּוֹ לְךָ נְתַתִּיהָ לְעֵינֵי בְנֵי־עַמִּי נְתַתִּיהָ לָּךְ קְבֹר מֵתֶךָ׃ וַיִּשְׁתַּחוּ
יג אַבְרָהָם לִפְנֵי עַם־הָאָרֶץ׃ וַיְדַבֵּר אֶל־עֶפְרוֹן בְּאָזְנֵי עַם־הָאָרֶץ לֵאמֹר
אַךְ אִם־אַתָּה לוּ שְׁמָעֵנִי נָתַתִּי כֶּסֶף הַשָּׂדֶה קַח מִמֶּנִּי וְאֶקְבְּרָה אֶת־
יד טו מֵתִי שָׁמָּה׃ וַיַּעַן עֶפְרוֹן אֶת־אַבְרָהָם לֵאמֹר לוֹ׃ אֲדֹנִי שְׁמָעֵנִי אֶרֶץ
טז אַרְבַּע מֵאֹת שֶׁקֶל־כֶּסֶף בֵּינִי וּבֵינְךָ מַה־הִוא וְאֶת־מֵתְךָ קְבֹר׃ וַיִּשְׁמַע
אַבְרָהָם אֶל־עֶפְרוֹן וַיִּשְׁקֹל אַבְרָהָם לְעֶפְרֹן אֶת־הַכֶּסֶף אֲשֶׁר דִּבֶּר
יז בְּאָזְנֵי בְנֵי־חֵת אַרְבַּע מֵאוֹת שֶׁקֶל כֶּסֶף עֹבֵר לַסֹּחֵר׃ וַיָּקָם ׀ שְׂדֵה שני
עֶפְרוֹן אֲשֶׁר בַּמַּכְפֵּלָה אֲשֶׁר לִפְנֵי מַמְרֵא הַשָּׂדֶה וְהַמְּעָרָה אֲשֶׁר־בּוֹ
יח וְכָל־הָעֵץ אֲשֶׁר בַּשָּׂדֶה אֲשֶׁר בְּכָל־גְּבֻלוֹ סָבִיב׃ לְאַבְרָהָם לְמִקְנָה

19 Avraham then buried Sara his wife in the cave in the field of Makhpela near
20 Mamre – that is, Ḥevron – in the land of Canaan. Thus the field and its cave
24 1 passed from the Hittites to Avraham as a burial site. Avraham was
2 old, advanced in years, and the LORD had blessed him in all things. And
Avraham said to the senior servant of his household, who was in charge of all
3 he had, "Place your hand under my thigh.[49] I want you to swear by the LORD,
God of heaven and earth, that you will not take a wife for my son from among
4 the daughters of the Canaanites among whom I live. Instead, go to my land
5 and birthplace, and there find a wife for Yitzḥak my son." The servant asked,
"What if the woman does not want to come back with me to this land? Shall
6 I bring your son back to the land from which you came?" Avraham said to
7 him, "Be sure not to take my son back there. The LORD, God of the heavens,
took me from my father's house and from the land of my birth. He spoke to
me and swore to me, 'To your descendants I will give this land.' He will send
8 His angel before you, and there you will find a wife for my son. But if the
woman does not want to come back with you, then you will be released from
9 this oath to me. Just do not take my son back there." So the servant placed his
10 hand under his master Avraham's thigh and swore this by an oath to him. The
servant then took ten of his master's camels, laden with all his master's bounty,
11 and set out to Aram Naharayim, to the city of Naḥor. By the well outside the
city, he had the camels kneel. It was evening, the time when the women came
12 out to draw water. "LORD, God of my master Avraham," he said, "please, grant
13 me success today and show kindness to my master Avraham. I am standing
here by the spring and the daughters of the townspeople are coming out to
14 draw water. If I say to a young woman, 'Please lower your jar so that I can
drink,' and she replies, 'Drink, and I will water your camels also,' let her be the
one You have chosen for Your servant Yitzḥak. By this I will know that You
15 have shown kindness to my master." Before he had even finished speaking,
Rivka, daughter of Betuel son of Milka, the wife of Avraham's brother Naḥor,
16 came out with her jar on her shoulder. The young woman was very beautiful,
a virgin whom no man had known. She went down to the spring, filled her
17 jar, and came up. The servant ran to meet her and said, "Please let me sip a
18 little water from your jar." She said, "Drink, my lord," and quickly lowered her
19 jar to her hand and let him drink. When she had let him drink his fill, she said,
"I will draw water for your camels, too, until they have had enough to drink."
20 Quickly she emptied her jar into the trough and ran back to the well to draw
21 more water; she drew for all his camels. The man stood gazing at her, silently
22 wondering whether the LORD had made his journey successful. When the

---

49 | An act sometimes performed in conjunction with an oath.

יט לְעֵינֵי בְנֵי־חֵת בְּכֹל בָּאֵי שַׁעַר־עִירוֹ: וְאַחֲרֵי־כֵן קָבַר אַבְרָהָם אֶת־
שָׂרָה אִשְׁתּוֹ אֶל־מְעָרַת שְׂדֵה הַמַּכְפֵּלָה עַל־פְּנֵי מַמְרֵא הִוא חֶבְרוֹן
כ בְּאֶרֶץ כְּנָעַן: וַיָּקָם הַשָּׂדֶה וְהַמְּעָרָה אֲשֶׁר־בּוֹ לְאַבְרָהָם לַאֲחֻזַּת־קָבֶר
כד א מֵאֵת בְּנֵי־חֵת: וְאַבְרָהָם זָקֵן בָּא בַּיָּמִים וַיהוָה בֵּרַךְ כ
ב אֶת־אַבְרָהָם בַּכֹּל: וַיֹּאמֶר אַבְרָהָם אֶל־עַבְדּוֹ זְקַן בֵּיתוֹ הַמֹּשֵׁל בְּכָל־
ג אֲשֶׁר־לוֹ שִׂים־נָא יָדְךָ תַּחַת יְרֵכִי: וְאַשְׁבִּיעֲךָ בַּיהוָה אֱלֹהֵי הַשָּׁמַיִם
וֵאלֹהֵי הָאָרֶץ אֲשֶׁר לֹא־תִקַּח אִשָּׁה לִבְנִי מִבְּנוֹת הַכְּנַעֲנִי אֲשֶׁר אָנֹכִי
ד יוֹשֵׁב בְּקִרְבּוֹ: כִּי אֶל־אַרְצִי וְאֶל־מוֹלַדְתִּי תֵּלֵךְ וְלָקַחְתָּ אִשָּׁה לִבְנִי
ה לְיִצְחָק: וַיֹּאמֶר אֵלָיו הָעֶבֶד אוּלַי לֹא־תֹאבֶה הָאִשָּׁה לָלֶכֶת אַחֲרַי
אֶל־הָאָרֶץ הַזֹּאת הֶהָשֵׁב אָשִׁיב אֶת־בִּנְךָ אֶל־הָאָרֶץ אֲשֶׁר־יָצָאתָ
ו מִשָּׁם: וַיֹּאמֶר אֵלָיו אַבְרָהָם הִשָּׁמֶר לְךָ פֶּן־תָּשִׁיב אֶת־בְּנִי שָׁמָּה:
ז יְהוָה ׀ אֱלֹהֵי הַשָּׁמַיִם אֲשֶׁר לְקָחַנִי מִבֵּית אָבִי וּמֵאֶרֶץ מוֹלַדְתִּי וַאֲשֶׁר
דִּבֶּר־לִי וַאֲשֶׁר נִשְׁבַּע־לִי לֵאמֹר לְזַרְעֲךָ אֶתֵּן אֶת־הָאָרֶץ הַזֹּאת הוּא
ח יִשְׁלַח מַלְאָכוֹ לְפָנֶיךָ וְלָקַחְתָּ אִשָּׁה לִבְנִי מִשָּׁם: וְאִם־לֹא תֹאבֶה
הָאִשָּׁה לָלֶכֶת אַחֲרֶיךָ וְנִקִּיתָ מִשְּׁבֻעָתִי זֹאת רַק אֶת־בְּנִי לֹא תָשֵׁב
ט שָׁמָּה: וַיָּשֶׂם הָעֶבֶד אֶת־יָדוֹ תַּחַת יֶרֶךְ אַבְרָהָם אֲדֹנָיו וַיִּשָּׁבַע לוֹ עַל־
י הַדָּבָר הַזֶּה: וַיִּקַּח הָעֶבֶד עֲשָׂרָה גְמַלִּים מִגְּמַלֵּי אֲדֹנָיו וַיֵּלֶךְ וְכָל־טוּב שלישי
יא אֲדֹנָיו בְּיָדוֹ וַיָּקָם וַיֵּלֶךְ אֶל־אֲרַם נַהֲרַיִם אֶל־עִיר נָחוֹר: וַיַּבְרֵךְ הַגְּמַלִּים
יב מִחוּץ לָעִיר אֶל־בְּאֵר הַמָּיִם לְעֵת עֶרֶב לְעֵת צֵאת הַשֹּׁאֲבֹת: וַיֹּאמַר ׀
יְהוָה אֱלֹהֵי אֲדֹנִי אַבְרָהָם הַקְרֵה־נָא לְפָנַי הַיּוֹם וַעֲשֵׂה־חֶסֶד עִם
יג אֲדֹנִי אַבְרָהָם: הִנֵּה אָנֹכִי נִצָּב עַל־עֵין הַמָּיִם וּבְנוֹת אַנְשֵׁי הָעִיר יֹצְאֹת
יד לִשְׁאֹב מָיִם: וְהָיָה הַנַּעֲרָ אֲשֶׁר אֹמַר אֵלֶיהָ הַטִּי־נָא כַדֵּךְ וְאֶשְׁתֶּה
וְאָמְרָה שְׁתֵה וְגַם־גְּמַלֶּיךָ אַשְׁקֶה אֹתָהּ הֹכַחְתָּ לְעַבְדְּךָ לְיִצְחָק וּבָהּ
טו אֵדַע כִּי־עָשִׂיתָ חֶסֶד עִם־אֲדֹנִי: וַיְהִי־הוּא טֶרֶם כִּלָּה לְדַבֵּר וְהִנֵּה
רִבְקָה יֹצֵאת אֲשֶׁר יֻלְּדָה לִבְתוּאֵל בֶּן־מִלְכָּה אֵשֶׁת נָחוֹר אֲחִי אַבְרָהָם
טז וְכַדָּהּ עַל־שִׁכְמָהּ: וְהַנַּעֲרָ טֹבַת מַרְאֶה מְאֹד בְּתוּלָה וְאִישׁ לֹא יְדָעָהּ
יז וַתֵּרֶד הָעַיְנָה וַתְּמַלֵּא כַדָּהּ וַתָּעַל: וַיָּרָץ הָעֶבֶד לִקְרָאתָהּ וַיֹּאמֶר
יח הַגְמִיאִינִי נָא מְעַט־מַיִם מִכַּדֵּךְ: וַתֹּאמֶר שְׁתֵה אֲדֹנִי וַתְּמַהֵר וַתֹּרֶד
יט כַּדָּהּ עַל־יָדָהּ וַתַּשְׁקֵהוּ: וַתְּכַל לְהַשְׁקֹתוֹ וַתֹּאמֶר גַּם לִגְמַלֶּיךָ אֶשְׁאָב
כ עַד אִם־כִּלּוּ לִשְׁתֹּת: וַתְּמַהֵר וַתְּעַר כַּדָּהּ אֶל־הַשֹּׁקֶת וַתָּרָץ עוֹד
כא אֶל־הַבְּאֵר לִשְׁאֹב וַתִּשְׁאַב לְכָל־גְּמַלָּיו: וְהָאִישׁ מִשְׁתָּאֵה לָהּ מַחֲרִישׁ
כב לָדַעַת הַהִצְלִיחַ יְהוָה דַּרְכּוֹ אִם־לֹא: וַיְהִי כַּאֲשֶׁר כִּלּוּ הַגְּמַלִּים

camels had finished drinking, the man took a gold ring weighing a half shekel
23 and two gold bracelets for her arms weighing ten shekel, and he asked,
"Whose daughter are you? Please tell me, is there room in your father's house
24 for us to spend the night?" She answered him, "I am the daughter of Betuel,
25 the son Milka bore to Naḥor." She added, "We have plenty of straw and
26 fodder, as well as room for you to spend the night." The man bowed low,
27 prostrating himself to the LORD. He said, "Blessed be the LORD, God of my
master Avraham, who has not withheld His kindness and faithfulness from
my master. As for me – the LORD has guided me on the way to the house of
28 my master's close family." The young woman ran and told all this to her
29 mother's household. Rivka had a brother named Lavan; he ran outside to the
30 man at the spring. He had seen the ring, and the bracelets on his sister's arms,
and had heard his sister Rivka tell what the man had said to her. He came up
31 to the man who was still standing by the camels at the spring, and said,
"Come. The LORD bless you! Why are you standing outside? I have made
32 room in the house and prepared a place for the camels." So the man entered
the house, the camels were unloaded, straw and fodder were brought for the
33 camels, and water was brought for him and his men to wash their feet. Food
was set before him to eat, but he said, "I will not eat until I have said what I
34 35 have to say." "Speak, then," said Lavan. "I am Avraham's servant," he said. "The
LORD has blessed my master greatly, and he has prospered. He has given
him sheep and cattle, silver and gold, male and female servants, camels and
36 donkeys. My master's wife Sara bore my master a son in her old age, and he
37 committed to his son all that is his. My master made me swear, saying, 'You
must not take a wife for my son from among the daughters of the Canaanites
38 in whose land I live. Instead you must go to my father's house and family and
39 there find a wife for my son.' I asked my master, 'What if the woman does not
40 want to come back with me?' He answered, 'The LORD before whom I have
walked will send His angel with you to make your journey a success, so that
41 you may find a wife for my son from my family and father's house. You are
released from this vow only if you come to my family and they refuse to give
42 her to you. Then you are released from my vow.' Today, when I came to the
spring, I said, 'LORD, God of my master Avraham, if You will, please grant
43 success to this journey on which I have come. I am standing here by a spring
of water. The woman who comes out to draw water, to whom I say, "Please
44 let me sip a little water from your jar," and who says to me, "Drink, and I will
also draw for your camels" – let her be the one the LORD has chosen for my
45 master's son.' Before I had even finished speaking to myself, Rivka came out
with her jar on her shoulder. She went down to the spring and drew water,
46 and I asked her, 'Please, let me drink.' She immediately lowered her jar and
said, 'Drink, and I will also water your camels.' So I drank, and she gave the
47 camels water too. I asked her, 'Whose daughter are you?' She said, 'The
daughter of Betuel son of Naḥor, whom Milka bore to him.' So I placed a ring

לִשְׁתּוֹת וַיִּקַּח הָאִישׁ נֶזֶם זָהָב בֶּקַע מִשְׁקָלוֹ וּשְׁנֵי צְמִידִים עַל־יָדֶיהָ
כג עֲשָׂרָה זָהָב מִשְׁקָלָם׃ וַיֹּאמֶר בַּת־מִי אַתְּ הַגִּידִי נָא לִי הֲיֵשׁ בֵּית־אָבִיךְ
כד מָקוֹם לָנוּ לָלִין׃ וַתֹּאמֶר אֵלָיו בַּת־בְּתוּאֵל אָנֹכִי בֶּן־מִלְכָּה אֲשֶׁר יָלְדָה
כה לְנָחוֹר׃ וַתֹּאמֶר אֵלָיו גַּם־תֶּבֶן גַּם־מִסְפּוֹא רַב עִמָּנוּ גַּם־מָקוֹם לָלוּן׃
כו כז וַיִּקֹּד הָאִישׁ וַיִּשְׁתַּחוּ לַיהוה׃ וַיֹּאמֶר בָּרוּךְ יהוה אֱלֹהֵי אֲדֹנִי אַבְרָהָם רביעי
אֲשֶׁר לֹא־עָזַב חַסְדּוֹ וַאֲמִתּוֹ מֵעִם אֲדֹנִי אָנֹכִי בַּדֶּרֶךְ נָחַנִי יהוה בֵּית
כח כט אֲחֵי אֲדֹנִי׃ וַתָּרָץ הַנַּעֲרָ וַתַּגֵּד לְבֵית אִמָּהּ כַּדְּבָרִים הָאֵלֶּה׃ וּלְרִבְקָה
ל אָח וּשְׁמוֹ לָבָן וַיָּרָץ לָבָן אֶל־הָאִישׁ הַחוּצָה אֶל־הָעָיִן׃ וַיְהִי ׀ כִּרְאֹת
אֶת־הַנֶּזֶם וְאֶת־הַצְּמִדִים עַל־יְדֵי אֲחֹתוֹ וּכְשָׁמְעוֹ אֶת־דִּבְרֵי רִבְקָה
אֲחֹתוֹ לֵאמֹר כֹּה־דִבֶּר אֵלַי הָאִישׁ וַיָּבֹא אֶל־הָאִישׁ וְהִנֵּה עֹמֵד עַל־
לא הַגְּמַלִּים עַל־הָעָיִן׃ וַיֹּאמֶר בּוֹא בְּרוּךְ יהוה לָמָּה תַעֲמֹד בַּחוּץ וְאָנֹכִי
לב פִּנִּיתִי הַבַּיִת וּמָקוֹם לַגְּמַלִּים׃ וַיָּבֹא הָאִישׁ הַבַּיְתָה וַיְפַתַּח הַגְּמַלִּים
וַיִּתֵּן תֶּבֶן וּמִסְפּוֹא לַגְּמַלִּים וּמַיִם לִרְחֹץ רַגְלָיו וְרַגְלֵי הָאֲנָשִׁים אֲשֶׁר
לג אִתּוֹ׃ ויישם לְפָנָיו לֶאֱכֹל וַיֹּאמֶר לֹא אֹכַל עַד אִם־דִּבַּרְתִּי דְּבָרָי וַיֹּאמֶר וַיּוּשַׂם
לד לה דַּבֵּר׃ וַיֹּאמַר עֶבֶד אַבְרָהָם אָנֹכִי׃ וַיהוה בֵּרַךְ אֶת־אֲדֹנִי מְאֹד וַיִּגְדָּל
לו וַיִּתֶּן־לוֹ צֹאן וּבָקָר וְכֶסֶף וְזָהָב וַעֲבָדִם וּשְׁפָחֹת וּגְמַלִּים וַחֲמֹרִים׃ וַתֵּלֶד
שָׂרָה אֵשֶׁת אֲדֹנִי בֵן לַאדֹנִי אַחֲרֵי זִקְנָתָהּ וַיִּתֶּן־לוֹ אֶת־כָּל־אֲשֶׁר־לוֹ׃
לז וַיַּשְׁבִּעֵנִי אֲדֹנִי לֵאמֹר לֹא־תִקַּח אִשָּׁה לִבְנִי מִבְּנוֹת הַכְּנַעֲנִי אֲשֶׁר
לח אָנֹכִי יֹשֵׁב בְּאַרְצוֹ׃ אִם־לֹא אֶל־בֵּית־אָבִי תֵּלֵךְ וְאֶל־מִשְׁפַּחְתִּי וְלָקַחְתָּ
לט מ אִשָּׁה לִבְנִי׃ וָאֹמַר אֶל־אֲדֹנִי אֻלַי לֹא־תֵלֵךְ הָאִשָּׁה אַחֲרָי׃ וַיֹּאמֶר אֵלָי
יהוה אֲשֶׁר־הִתְהַלַּכְתִּי לְפָנָיו יִשְׁלַח מַלְאָכוֹ אִתָּךְ וְהִצְלִיחַ דַּרְכֶּךָ
מא וְלָקַחְתָּ אִשָּׁה לִבְנִי מִמִּשְׁפַּחְתִּי וּמִבֵּית אָבִי׃ אָז תִּנָּקֶה מֵאָלָתִי כִּי
מב תָבוֹא אֶל־מִשְׁפַּחְתִּי וְאִם־לֹא יִתְּנוּ לָךְ וְהָיִיתָ נָקִי מֵאָלָתִי׃ וָאָבֹא כא
הַיּוֹם אֶל־הָעָיִן וָאֹמַר יהוה אֱלֹהֵי אֲדֹנִי אַבְרָהָם אִם־יֶשְׁךָ־נָּא מַצְלִיחַ
מג דַּרְכִּי אֲשֶׁר אָנֹכִי הֹלֵךְ עָלֶיהָ׃ הִנֵּה אָנֹכִי נִצָּב עַל־עֵין הַמָּיִם וְהָיָה
הָעַלְמָה הַיֹּצֵאת לִשְׁאֹב וְאָמַרְתִּי אֵלֶיהָ הַשְׁקִינִי־נָא מְעַט־מַיִם
מד מִכַּדֵּךְ׃ וְאָמְרָה אֵלַי גַּם־אַתָּה שְׁתֵה וְגַם לִגְמַלֶּיךָ אֶשְׁאָב הִוא הָאִשָּׁה
מה אֲשֶׁר־הֹכִיחַ יהוה לְבֶן־אֲדֹנִי׃ אֲנִי טֶרֶם אֲכַלֶּה לְדַבֵּר אֶל־לִבִּי וְהִנֵּה
רִבְקָה יֹצֵאת וְכַדָּהּ עַל־שִׁכְמָהּ וַתֵּרֶד הָעַיְנָה וַתִּשְׁאָב וָאֹמַר אֵלֶיהָ
מו הַשְׁקִינִי נָא׃ וַתְּמַהֵר וַתּוֹרֶד כַּדָּהּ מֵעָלֶיהָ וַתֹּאמֶר שְׁתֵה וְגַם־גְּמַלֶּיךָ
מז אַשְׁקֶה וָאֵשְׁתְּ וְגַם הַגְּמַלִּים הִשְׁקָתָה׃ וָאֶשְׁאַל אֹתָהּ וָאֹמַר בַּת־מִי
אַתְּ וַתֹּאמֶר בַּת־בְּתוּאֵל בֶּן־נָחוֹר אֲשֶׁר יָלְדָה־לּוֹ מִלְכָּה וָאָשִׂם הַנֶּזֶם

48 on her nose and bracelets on her arms. I bowed low and prostrated myself to
the Lord, and blessed the Lord, God of my master Avraham, who led me
49 on the right way to take the daughter of my master's brother for his son. Now,
if you are willing to show kindness and faithfulness to my master, tell me; and
50 if not, tell me that, so that I may move on, right or left." Lavan and Betuel
answered, "This is surely from the Lord: there is nothing for us to say to you,
51 bad or good. Here is Rivka in front of you. Take her; go. Let her be the wife
52 of your master's son, as the Lord has spoken." When Avraham's servant heard
53 these words, he bowed down to the ground before the Lord. The servant
brought out gold and silver jewelry and clothes and gave them to Rivka. He
54 also gave costly gifts to her brother and her mother. Then he and his men ate
and drank and spent the night there. When they got up the next morning he
55 said, "Send me on my way to my master." But her brother and her mother
replied, "Let the young woman stay with us a year or ten months. Then she
56 may go." "Do not delay me," he said, "now that the Lord has made my journey
57 a success. Let me leave so that I may go back to my master." They replied, "Let
58 us call the young woman and ask her." So they called Rivka and asked her,
59 "Will you go with this man?" She replied, "I will." So they sent their sister
Rivka on her way, together with her nurse and Avraham's servant and his men.
60 They blessed Rivka and said to her, "Our sister, may you grow into thousands
61 of myriads, and may your descendants possess their enemies' gates." Then
Rivka set off with her maids, riding on camels and following the man. The
62 servant took Rivka and went. Yitzḥak was just coming back from the direction
63 of Be'er Laḥai Ro'i, for he was then living in the Negev. He had gone out in
the field toward evening to meditate. Looking up, he saw – there were camels
64 approaching. Rivka too looked up – and saw Yitzḥak. She jumped down from
65 the camel and asked the servant, "Who is that man walking in the field toward
us?" The servant replied, "That is my master." And she took her veil and
66 67 covered herself. The servant told Yitzḥak all he had done. And Yitzḥak
brought her into the tent of his mother Sara. He took Rivka as his wife, and
he loved her. And Yitzḥak was comforted after his mother's death.
25 1 2 Avraham took another wife, whose name was Ketura. She bore him Zimran,
3 Yokshan, Medan, Midyan, Yishbak, and Shuaḥ; Yokshan was the father of
Sheva and Dedan. The sons of Dedan were Ashurim, Letushim, and Leumim.
4 The sons of Midyan were Eifa, Efer, Ḥanokh, Avida, and Eldaa; all these
5 6 were descendants of Ketura. Avraham left all that was his to Yitzḥak – while
he was still living he gave gifts to the sons of his concubines and sent them
7 eastward, away from his son Yitzḥak, to the land of the East. These are the
days, the years of Avraham's life: he lived one hundred and seventy-five years.

מח עַל־אַפָּהּ וְהַצְּמִידִים עַל־יָדֶיהָ: וָאֶקֹּד וָאֶשְׁתַּחֲוֶה לַיהוָה וָאֲבָרֵךְ
אֶת־יהוָה אֱלֹהֵי אֲדֹנִי אַבְרָהָם אֲשֶׁר הִנְחַנִי בְּדֶרֶךְ אֱמֶת לָקַחַת אֶת־
מט בַּת־אֲחִי אֲדֹנִי לִבְנוֹ: וְעַתָּה אִם־יֶשְׁכֶם עֹשִׂים חֶסֶד וֶאֱמֶת אֶת־אֲדֹנִי
נ הַגִּידוּ לִי וְאִם־לֹא הַגִּידוּ לִי וְאֶפְנֶה עַל־יָמִין אוֹ עַל־שְׂמֹאל: וַיַּעַן לָבָן
וּבְתוּאֵל וַיֹּאמְרוּ מֵיהוָה יָצָא הַדָּבָר לֹא נוּכַל דַּבֵּר אֵלֶיךָ רַע אוֹ־טוֹב:
נא הִנֵּה־רִבְקָה לְפָנֶיךָ קַח וָלֵךְ וּתְהִי אִשָּׁה לְבֶן־אֲדֹנֶיךָ כַּאֲשֶׁר דִּבֶּר יהוָה:
נב וַיְהִי כַּאֲשֶׁר שָׁמַע עֶבֶד אַבְרָהָם אֶת־דִּבְרֵיהֶם וַיִּשְׁתַּחוּ אַרְצָה לַיהוָה:
נג וַיּוֹצֵא הָעֶבֶד כְּלֵי־כֶסֶף וּכְלֵי זָהָב וּבְגָדִים וַיִּתֵּן לְרִבְקָה וּמִגְדָּנֹת נָתַן חמישי
נד לְאָחִיהָ וּלְאִמָּהּ: וַיֹּאכְלוּ וַיִּשְׁתּוּ הוּא וְהָאֲנָשִׁים אֲשֶׁר־עִמּוֹ וַיָּלִינוּ
נה וַיָּקוּמוּ בַבֹּקֶר וַיֹּאמֶר שַׁלְּחֻנִי לַאדֹנִי: וַיֹּאמֶר אָחִיהָ וְאִמָּהּ תֵּשֵׁב הַנַּעֲרָ
נו אִתָּנוּ יָמִים אוֹ עָשׂוֹר אַחַר תֵּלֵךְ: וַיֹּאמֶר אֲלֵהֶם אַל־תְּאַחֲרוּ אֹתִי
נז וַיהוָה הִצְלִיחַ דַּרְכִּי שַׁלְּחוּנִי וְאֵלְכָה לַאדֹנִי: וַיֹּאמְרוּ נִקְרָא לַנַּעֲרָ
נח וְנִשְׁאֲלָה אֶת־פִּיהָ: וַיִּקְרְאוּ לְרִבְקָה וַיֹּאמְרוּ אֵלֶיהָ הֲתֵלְכִי עִם־הָאִישׁ
נט הַזֶּה וַתֹּאמֶר אֵלֵךְ: וַיְשַׁלְּחוּ אֶת־רִבְקָה אֲחֹתָם וְאֶת־מֵנִקְתָּהּ וְאֶת־
ס עֶבֶד אַבְרָהָם וְאֶת־אֲנָשָׁיו: וַיְבָרְכוּ אֶת־רִבְקָה וַיֹּאמְרוּ לָהּ אֲחֹתֵנוּ
סא אַתְּ הֲיִי לְאַלְפֵי רְבָבָה וְיִירַשׁ זַרְעֵךְ אֵת שַׁעַר שֹׂנְאָיו: וַתָּקָם רִבְקָה
וְנַעֲרֹתֶיהָ וַתִּרְכַּבְנָה עַל־הַגְּמַלִּים וַתֵּלַכְנָה אַחֲרֵי הָאִישׁ וַיִּקַּח הָעֶבֶד
סב אֶת־רִבְקָה וַיֵּלַךְ: וְיִצְחָק בָּא מִבּוֹא בְּאֵר לַחַי רֹאִי וְהוּא יוֹשֵׁב בְּאֶרֶץ
סג הַנֶּגֶב: וַיֵּצֵא יִצְחָק לָשׂוּחַ בַּשָּׂדֶה לִפְנוֹת עָרֶב וַיִּשָּׂא עֵינָיו וַיַּרְא וְהִנֵּה
סד גְמַלִּים בָּאִים: וַתִּשָּׂא רִבְקָה אֶת־עֵינֶיהָ וַתֵּרֶא אֶת־יִצְחָק וַתִּפֹּל
סה מֵעַל הַגָּמָל: וַתֹּאמֶר אֶל־הָעֶבֶד מִי־הָאִישׁ הַלָּזֶה הַהֹלֵךְ בַּשָּׂדֶה
סו לִקְרָאתֵנוּ וַיֹּאמֶר הָעֶבֶד הוּא אֲדֹנִי וַתִּקַּח הַצָּעִיף וַתִּתְכָּס: וַיְסַפֵּר
סז הָעֶבֶד לְיִצְחָק אֵת כָּל־הַדְּבָרִים אֲשֶׁר עָשָׂה: וַיְבִאֶהָ יִצְחָק הָאֹהֱלָה
שָׂרָה אִמּוֹ וַיִּקַּח אֶת־רִבְקָה וַתְּהִי־לוֹ לְאִשָּׁה וַיֶּאֱהָבֶהָ וַיִּנָּחֵם יִצְחָק
אַחֲרֵי אִמּוֹ:
כה א ב וַיֹּסֶף אַבְרָהָם וַיִּקַּח אִשָּׁה וּשְׁמָהּ קְטוּרָה: וַתֵּלֶד לוֹ אֶת־זִמְרָן וְאֶת־ כב ששי
ג יָקְשָׁן וְאֶת־מְדָן וְאֶת־מִדְיָן וְאֶת־יִשְׁבָּק וְאֶת־שׁוּחַ: וְיָקְשָׁן יָלַד אֶת־
ד שְׁבָא וְאֶת־דְּדָן וּבְנֵי דְדָן הָיוּ אַשּׁוּרִם וּלְטוּשִׁם וּלְאֻמִּים: וּבְנֵי מִדְיָן
ה עֵיפָה וָעֵפֶר וַחֲנֹךְ וַאֲבִידָע וְאֶלְדָּעָה כָּל־אֵלֶּה בְּנֵי קְטוּרָה: וַיִּתֵּן
ו אַבְרָהָם אֶת־כָּל־אֲשֶׁר־לוֹ לְיִצְחָק: וְלִבְנֵי הַפִּילַגְשִׁים אֲשֶׁר לְאַבְרָהָם
נָתַן אַבְרָהָם מַתָּנֹת וַיְשַׁלְּחֵם מֵעַל יִצְחָק בְּנוֹ בְּעוֹדֶנּוּ חַי קֵדְמָה אֶל־
ז אֶרֶץ קֶדֶם: וְאֵלֶּה יְמֵי שְׁנֵי־חַיֵּי אַבְרָהָם אֲשֶׁר־חָי מְאַת שָׁנָה וְשִׁבְעִים

8 Avraham breathed his last and died in his ripe old age, aged and satisfied, and
9 was gathered to his people. His sons, Yitzḥak and Yishmael, buried him in
the cave of Makhpela, near Mamre, in the field of Efron son of Tzoḥar the
10 Hittite – the field Avraham had bought from the Hittites. There Avraham was
11 buried with Sara his wife. After Avraham's death, God blessed Yitzḥak his son,
who was then living near Be'er Laḥai Ro'i.
12 These are the descendants of Avraham's son Yishmael, whom Sara's maid-
13 servant, Hagar the Egyptian, bore to Avraham. The the names of Yishmael's
sons, in the order of their birth, are: Nevayot – Yishmael's firstborn, Kedar,
14 15 Adbe'el, Mivsam, Mishma, Duma, Massa, Ḥadad, Teima, Yetur, Nafish,
16 and Kedma. These were Yishmael's sons, and these are their names by their
17 villages and encampments: twelve princes and their tribes. These were the
years of Yishmael's life: he lived one hundred and thirty-seven years. He
18 breathed his last and died, and was gathered to his people. The Ishmaelites
dwelt from Ḥavila to Shur, up against Egypt, all the way to Assyria, settling
up against all their brothers.

TOLEDOT

19 This is the story of Yitzḥak, son of Avraham: Avraham was Yitzḥak's father.
20 When Yitzḥak was forty he married Rivka, daughter of Betuel the Aramean
21 of Padan Aram, sister of Lavan the Aramean. And Yitzḥak pleaded with the
Lord on behalf of his wife, for she was childless. The Lord granted his plea
22 and Rivka became pregnant. But the children clashed within her. She said,
23 "If this is so, why am I living?" So she went to inquire of the Lord. The Lord
said to her, "Two nations are inside your womb; two peoples are to part from
you. People will overpower people, and the greater shall the younger serve."[50]
24 When the time came for her to give birth, there were twins in her womb.
25 The first came out red. His whole body was like a hairy cloak, so they named
26 him Esav.[51] Then his brother emerged, his hand grasping Esav's heel, so he
27 named him Yaakov.[52] Yitzḥak was sixty years old when they were born. The
boys grew up. Esav became a skilled hunter, a man of the field, while Yaakov
28 was an innocent man who stayed among the tents. Yitzḥak loved Esav because
29 he ate of his game, but Rivka loved Yaakov. Once when Yaakov was cooking
30 a stew, Esav came in exhausted from the field. He said to Yaakov, "Let me
gulp down some of that red stuff. I am starved!" – that is how he came to be
31 32 named Edom.[53] Yaakov said, "First sell me your birthright." And Esav said,
33 "Look, I am about to die. What use to me is a birthright?" But Yaakov said,
34 "Swear to me first." So he swore, and sold Yaakov his birthright. Yaakov then
gave Esav bread and lentil stew. He ate, drank, got up, and left. Thus – Esav
disdained his birthright.

50 | The ambiguity as to who will serve whom reflects the Hebrew.

51 | The name Esav may bear the sense of "covered" or "concealed" (cf. Ob. 1:6). The word *se'ar* (hair) resonates with Se'ir, the land inhabited by Esav's descendants.

52 | The name Yaakov resonates with *akev* (heel).

53 | The name Edom resonates with *adom* (red) here, as well as with *admoni* (red) in verse 25.

ח שָׁנָה וְחָמֵשׁ שָׁנִים: וַיִּגְוַע וַיָּמָת אַבְרָהָם בְּשֵׂיבָה טוֹבָה זָקֵן וְשָׂבֵעַ
ט וַיֵּאָסֶף אֶל־עַמָּיו: וַיִּקְבְּרוּ אֹתוֹ יִצְחָק וְיִשְׁמָעֵאל בָּנָיו אֶל־מְעָרַת
הַמַּכְפֵּלָה אֶל־שְׂדֵה עֶפְרֹן בֶּן־צֹחַר הַחִתִּי אֲשֶׁר עַל־פְּנֵי מַמְרֵא:
י הַשָּׂדֶה אֲשֶׁר־קָנָה אַבְרָהָם מֵאֵת בְּנֵי־חֵת שָׁמָּה קֻבַּר אַבְרָהָם וְשָׂרָה
יא אִשְׁתּוֹ: וַיְהִי אַחֲרֵי מוֹת אַבְרָהָם וַיְבָרֶךְ אֱלֹהִים אֶת־יִצְחָק בְּנוֹ וַיֵּשֶׁב
יִצְחָק עִם־בְּאֵר לַחַי רֹאִי:
יב וְאֵלֶּה תֹּלְדֹת יִשְׁמָעֵאל בֶּן־אַבְרָהָם אֲשֶׁר יָלְדָה הָגָר הַמִּצְרִית שִׁפְחַת שביעי
יג שָׂרָה לְאַבְרָהָם: וְאֵלֶּה שְׁמוֹת בְּנֵי יִשְׁמָעֵאל בִּשְׁמֹתָם לְתוֹלְדֹתָם בְּכֹר
יד טו יִשְׁמָעֵאל נְבָיֹת וְקֵדָר וְאַדְבְּאֵל וּמִבְשָׂם: וּמִשְׁמָע וְדוּמָה וּמַשָּׂא: חֲדַד
טז וְתֵימָא יְטוּר נָפִישׁ וָקֵדְמָה: אֵלֶּה הֵם בְּנֵי יִשְׁמָעֵאל וְאֵלֶּה שְׁמֹתָם מפטיר
יז בְּחַצְרֵיהֶם וּבְטִירֹתָם שְׁנֵים־עָשָׂר נְשִׂיאִם לְאֻמֹּתָם: וְאֵלֶּה שְׁנֵי חַיֵּי
יִשְׁמָעֵאל מְאַת שָׁנָה וּשְׁלֹשִׁים שָׁנָה וְשֶׁבַע שָׁנִים וַיִּגְוַע וַיָּמָת וַיֵּאָסֶף
יח אֶל־עַמָּיו: וַיִּשְׁכְּנוּ מֵחֲוִילָה עַד־שׁוּר אֲשֶׁר עַל־פְּנֵי מִצְרַיִם בֹּאֲכָה
אַשּׁוּרָה עַל־פְּנֵי כָל־אֶחָיו נָפָל:
יט כ וְאֵלֶּה תּוֹלְדֹת יִצְחָק בֶּן־אַבְרָהָם אַבְרָהָם הוֹלִיד אֶת־יִצְחָק: וַיְהִי כג תולדת
יִצְחָק בֶּן־אַרְבָּעִים שָׁנָה בְּקַחְתּוֹ אֶת־רִבְקָה בַּת־בְּתוּאֵל הָאֲרַמִּי מִפַּדַּן
כא אֲרָם אֲחוֹת לָבָן הָאֲרַמִּי לוֹ לְאִשָּׁה: וַיֶּעְתַּר יִצְחָק לַיהוה לְנֹכַח אִשְׁתּוֹ
כב כִּי עֲקָרָה הִוא וַיֵּעָתֶר לוֹ יהוה וַתַּהַר רִבְקָה אִשְׁתּוֹ: וַיִּתְרֹצְצוּ הַבָּנִים
כג בְּקִרְבָּהּ וַתֹּאמֶר אִם־כֵּן לָמָּה זֶּה אָנֹכִי וַתֵּלֶךְ לִדְרֹשׁ אֶת־יהוה: וַיֹּאמֶר
יהוה לָהּ שְׁנֵי גיים בְּבִטְנֵךְ וּשְׁנֵי לְאֻמִּים מִמֵּעַיִךְ יִפָּרֵדוּ וּלְאֹם מִלְאֹם גוֹיִם
כד יֶאֱמָץ וְרַב יַעֲבֹד צָעִיר: וַיִּמְלְאוּ יָמֶיהָ לָלֶדֶת וְהִנֵּה תוֹמִם בְּבִטְנָהּ:
כה כו וַיֵּצֵא הָרִאשׁוֹן אַדְמוֹנִי כֻּלּוֹ כְּאַדֶּרֶת שֵׂעָר וַיִּקְרְאוּ שְׁמוֹ עֵשָׂו: וְאַחֲרֵי־כֵן
יָצָא אָחִיו וְיָדוֹ אֹחֶזֶת בַּעֲקֵב עֵשָׂו וַיִּקְרָא שְׁמוֹ יַעֲקֹב וְיִצְחָק בֶּן־שִׁשִּׁים
כז שָׁנָה בְּלֶדֶת אֹתָם: וַיִּגְדְּלוּ הַנְּעָרִים וַיְהִי עֵשָׂו אִישׁ יֹדֵעַ צַיִד אִישׁ שָׂדֶה
כח וְיַעֲקֹב אִישׁ תָּם יֹשֵׁב אֹהָלִים: וַיֶּאֱהַב יִצְחָק אֶת־עֵשָׂו כִּי־צַיִד בְּפִיו
כט וְרִבְקָה אֹהֶבֶת אֶת־יַעֲקֹב: וַיָּזֶד יַעֲקֹב נָזִיד וַיָּבֹא עֵשָׂו מִן־הַשָּׂדֶה וְהוּא
ל עָיֵף: וַיֹּאמֶר עֵשָׂו אֶל־יַעֲקֹב הַלְעִיטֵנִי נָא מִן־הָאָדֹם הָאָדֹם הַזֶּה כִּי
לא עָיֵף אָנֹכִי עַל־כֵּן קָרָא־שְׁמוֹ אֱדוֹם: וַיֹּאמֶר יַעֲקֹב מִכְרָה כַיּוֹם אֶת־
לב בְּכֹרָתְךָ לִי: וַיֹּאמֶר עֵשָׂו הִנֵּה אָנֹכִי הוֹלֵךְ לָמוּת וְלָמָּה־זֶּה לִי בְּכֹרָה:
לג וַיֹּאמֶר יַעֲקֹב הִשָּׁבְעָה לִּי כַּיּוֹם וַיִּשָּׁבַע לוֹ וַיִּמְכֹּר אֶת־בְּכֹרָתוֹ לְיַעֲקֹב:
לד וְיַעֲקֹב נָתַן לְעֵשָׂו לֶחֶם וּנְזִיד עֲדָשִׁים וַיֹּאכַל וַיֵּשְׁתְּ וַיָּקָם וַיֵּלַךְ וַיִּבֶז
עֵשָׂו אֶת־הַבְּכֹרָה:

26 1 Another famine afflicted the land, apart from the earlier famine in Avraham's
2 days, and Yitzḥak went to Avimelekh, king of the Philistines, in Gerar. The
Lord had appeared to him: "Do not go down to Egypt," He had said. "Stay
3 in the land I tell you of. Bide in this land and I will be with you and bless you,
for I am going to give all these lands to you and your descendants, fulfilling
4 the oath I swore to Avraham your father. I will make your descendants as
many as the stars of the heavens, and I will give them all these lands. All the
5 nations of the earth will bless themselves by your descendants, because
Avraham listened to My voice and kept My charge: My commandments, My
6 7 statutes, and My laws." So Yitzḥak now settled in Gerar. The men of the place
inquired after his wife; "She is my sister," he said. He was terrified to say "She
is my wife." "The men of the place might kill me for Rivka," he thought, "she
8 is so beautiful." When he had already been there for some time, Avimelekh,
king of the Philistines, looked down from a window and saw Yitzḥak enjoying
9 himself with his wife Rivka. Avimelekh summoned Yitzḥak. "She is your
wife," he said. "Why did you say, 'She is my sister'?" Yitzḥak replied, "I thought
10 I might die because of her." "What is this you have done to us?" said
Avimelekh. "One of the people might have slept with your wife, and you
11 would have brought guilt upon us." Avimelekh then issued an order to all the
12 people: "Whoever touches this man or his wife shall be put to death." Yitzḥak
planted crops in that land, and that year he reaped a hundredfold because the
13 Lord had blessed him. The man became rich; he prospered more and more
14 until he became very wealthy. He had flocks and herds and a large retinue of
15 servants, and the Philistines envied him. So the Philistines stopped up all the
wells that his father's servants had dug in the time of his father Avraham, filling
16 them with earth. Avimelekh said to Yitzḥak, "Move away from us. You have
17 become much too powerful for us." So Yitzḥak left and camped in the valley
18 of Gerar and settled there. And he reopened the wells that had been dug in
the time of his father Avraham, which the Philistines had stopped up after
Avraham died, and gave them the same names his father had given them.
19 20 Yitzḥak's servants dug in the valley and discovered a well of fresh water, but
the shepherds of Gerar quarreled with Yitzḥak's shepherds, claiming that the
water was theirs. So he called the well Esek,[54] because they contended with
21 him there. They dug another well, and there was a quarrel about that too; so
22 he called it Sitna.[55] He moved on from there and dug another well, and this
time they did not quarrel over it; so he named this one Reḥovot.[56] "Now the
23 Lord has given us space," he said, "and we will flourish in the land." From
24 there he went up to Be'er Sheva. That night the Lord appeared to him and
said, "I am the God of your father Avraham. Do not be afraid, for I am with
you. I will bless you and multiply your descendants for the sake of Avraham
25 My servant." Yitzḥak built an altar there and called on the name of the Lord.

54 | Meaning "contention."
55 | Meaning "hostility."
56 | Meaning "wide spaces."

כו א ויהי רעב בארץ מלבד הרעב הראשון אשר היה בימי אברהם וילך
ב יצחק אל־אבימלך מלך־פלשתים גררה: וירא אליו יהוה ויאמר
ג אל־תרד מצרימה שכן בארץ אשר אמר אליך: גור בארץ הזאת
ואהיה עמך ואברכך כי־לך ולזרעך אתן את־כל־הארצת האל
ד והקמתי את־השבעה אשר נשבעתי לאברהם אביך: והרביתי
את־זרעך ככוכבי השמים ונתתי לזרעך את כל־הארצת האל
ה והתברכו בזרעך כל גויי הארץ: עקב אשר־שמע אברהם בקלי
ו ז וישמר משמרתי מצותי חקותי ותורתי: וישב יצחק בגרר: וישאלו שני
אנשי המקום לאשתו ויאמר אחתי הוא כי ירא לאמר אשתי פן־
ח יהרגני אנשי המקום על־רבקה כי־טובת מראה הוא: ויהי כי־ארכו־
לו שם הימים וישקף אבימלך מלך פלשתים בעד החלון וירא והנה
ט יצחק מצחק את רבקה אשתו: ויקרא אבימלך ליצחק ויאמר אך
הנה אשתך הוא ואיך אמרת אחתי הוא ויאמר אליו יצחק כי
י אמרתי פן־אמות עליה: ויאמר אבימלך מה־זאת עשית לנו כמעט
יא שכב אחד העם את־אשתך והבאת עלינו אשם: ויצו אבימלך
יב את־כל־העם לאמר הנגע באיש הזה ובאשתו מות יומת: ויזרע
יצחק בארץ ההוא וימצא בשנה ההוא מאה שערים ויברכהו יהוה:
יג יד ויגדל האיש וילך הלוך וגדל עד כי־גדל מאד: ויהי־לו מקנה־צאן שלישי
טו ומקנה בקר ועבדה רבה ויקנאו אתו פלשתים: וכל־הבארת אשר
חפרו עבדי אביו בימי אברהם אביו סתמום פלשתים וימלאום
טז עפר: ויאמר אבימלך אל־יצחק לך מעמנו כי־עצמת ממנו מאד:
יז יח וילך משם יצחק ויחן בנחל־גרר וישב שם: וישב יצחק ויחפר ׀
את־בארת המים אשר חפרו בימי אברהם אביו ויסתמום פלשתים
אחרי מות אברהם ויקרא להן שמות כשמת אשר־קרא להן אביו:
יט כ ויחפרו עבדי־יצחק בנחל וימצאו־שם באר מים חיים: ויריבו רעי
גרר עם־רעי יצחק לאמר לנו המים ויקרא שם־הבאר עשק כי
כא התעשקו עמו: ויחפרו באר אחרת ויריבו גם־עליה ויקרא שמה
כב שטנה: ויעתק משם ויחפר באר אחרת ולא רבו עליה ויקרא שמה
כג רחבות ויאמר כי־עתה הרחיב יהוה לנו ופרינו בארץ: ויעל רביעי
כד משם באר שבע: וירא אליו יהוה בלילה ההוא ויאמר אנכי אלהי
אברהם אביך אל־תירא כי־אתך אנכי וברכתיך והרביתי את־זרעך
כה בעבור אברהם עבדי: ויבן שם מזבח ויקרא בשם יהוה ויט־שם

26 There he pitched his tent, and there his servants dug a well. Avimelekh came
to him from Gerar, with Aḥuzat his advisor and Pikhol the commander of his
27 troops. Yitzḥak said to them, "Why have you come to me? You hate me; you
28 sent me away from you." They said, "We have seen clearly that the Lord is
with you, so we say: Let there be a pact between you and us. Let us make a
29 covenant with you that you will do us no harm, just as we did not touch you,
just as we have done you nothing but good and we sent you on your way in
30 peace. And now – the Lord bless you." Yitzḥak made them a feast, and they
31 ate and drank. Early in the morning they rose and exchanged oaths, and
32 Yitzḥak sent them on their way. They parted from him in peace. That day,
Yitzḥak's servants came and told him about the well that they had dug; they
33 said, "We have found water." He named it Shiva,[57] which is why the town is
34 called Be'er Sheva to this day.[58] When Esav was forty years old,
he married Yehudit daughter of Be'eri the Hittite, and Basmat daughter
35 of Eilon the Hittite. These were a source of bitter sorrow to Yitzḥak and
27 1 Rivka. When Yitzḥak had grown old, when his eyes had grown so
dim that he could not see, he summoned his elder son Esav. "My son," he said.
2 Esav replied, "Here I am." He said, "I am old, and I do not know when I will
3 die. So now, take your weapons, your quiver and bow, and go out into the
4 field and hunt me some game. Then make me delicious food, prepared in the
way that I love, and bring it to me to eat so that my soul may bless you before
5 I die." When Yitzḥak was speaking to Esav his son, Rivka was listening. Esav
6 went out into the field to hunt game to bring back. And Rivka said to her son
7 Yaakov, "I overheard your father say to your brother Esav, 'Fetch me some
game and make me delicious food so that I may eat and give you my blessing
8 before the Lord before I die.' Now, my son, listen carefully to my instructions.
9 Go to the flock and bring me two choice young goats. I will make them into
10 delicious food, in the way he loves. Then take it to your father to eat so that
11 he may give you his blessing before he dies." Yaakov said to Rivka his mother,
12 "My brother Esav is hairy, but I have smooth skin. What if my father touches
me? I will look to him like a fraud and bring upon myself not a blessing but a
13 curse." But his mother replied, "Your curse will be on me, my son. Do as I say.
14 Go; fetch them for me." So he went, took the goats, and brought them to his
mother, and his mother prepared delicious food in the way his father loved.
15 Then Rivka took her elder son Esav's best clothes, which were with her in the
16 house, and put them on Yaakov, her younger son. She put the goatskins on
17 his hands and the smooth part of his neck. She then handed her son Yaakov
18 the delicious food and bread that she had prepared. He went in to his father;
"My father," he said. His father replied, "Here I am. Who are you, my son?"
19 Yaakov said to his father, "I am Esav your firstborn. I have done as you asked.

57 | The name Shiva resonates with *vayishave'u* (exchanged oaths) in verse 31.

58 | Be'er denotes a well, and Sheva resonates with Shiva and *vayishave'u*.

כו אֹהָלוֹ וַיִּכְרוּ־שָׁם עַבְדֵי־יִצְחָק בְּאֵר׃ וַאֲבִימֶלֶךְ הָלַךְ אֵלָיו מִגְּרָר
כז וַאֲחֻזַּת מֵרֵעֵהוּ וּפִיכֹל שַׂר־צְבָאוֹ׃ וַיֹּאמֶר אֲלֵהֶם יִצְחָק מַדּוּעַ בָּאתֶם
כח אֵלָי וְאַתֶּם שְׂנֵאתֶם אֹתִי וַתְּשַׁלְּחוּנִי מֵאִתְּכֶם׃ וַיֹּאמְרוּ רָאוֹ רָאִינוּ
כִּי־הָיָה יְהוָה ׀ עִמָּךְ וַנֹּאמֶר תְּהִי נָא אָלָה בֵּינוֹתֵינוּ בֵּינֵינוּ וּבֵינֶךָ
כט וְנִכְרְתָה בְרִית עִמָּךְ׃ אִם־תַּעֲשֵׂה עִמָּנוּ רָעָה כַּאֲשֶׁר לֹא נְגַעֲנוּךָ
וְכַאֲשֶׁר עָשִׂינוּ עִמְּךָ רַק־טוֹב וַנְּשַׁלֵּחֲךָ בְּשָׁלוֹם אַתָּה עַתָּה בְּרוּךְ
ל לא יְהוָה׃ וַיַּעַשׂ לָהֶם מִשְׁתֶּה וַיֹּאכְלוּ וַיִּשְׁתּוּ׃ וַיַּשְׁכִּימוּ בַבֹּקֶר וַיִּשָּׁבְעוּ חמישי
לב אִישׁ לְאָחִיו וַיְשַׁלְּחֵם יִצְחָק וַיֵּלְכוּ מֵאִתּוֹ בְּשָׁלוֹם׃ וַיְהִי ׀ בַּיּוֹם הַהוּא
וַיָּבֹאוּ עַבְדֵי יִצְחָק וַיַּגִּדוּ לוֹ עַל־אֹדוֹת הַבְּאֵר אֲשֶׁר חָפָרוּ וַיֹּאמְרוּ לוֹ
לג מָצָאנוּ מָיִם׃ וַיִּקְרָא אֹתָהּ שִׁבְעָה עַל־כֵּן שֵׁם־הָעִיר בְּאֵר שֶׁבַע עַד
לד הַיּוֹם הַזֶּה׃ וַיְהִי עֵשָׂו בֶּן־אַרְבָּעִים שָׁנָה וַיִּקַּח אִשָּׁה אֶת־
לה יְהוּדִית בַּת־בְּאֵרִי הַחִתִּי וְאֶת־בָּשְׂמַת בַּת־אֵילֹן הַחִתִּי׃ וַתִּהְיֶיןָ מֹרַת
כז א רוּחַ לְיִצְחָק וּלְרִבְקָה׃ וַיְהִי כִּי־זָקֵן יִצְחָק וַתִּכְהֶיןָ עֵינָיו כד
מֵרְאֹת וַיִּקְרָא אֶת־עֵשָׂו ׀ בְּנוֹ הַגָּדֹל וַיֹּאמֶר אֵלָיו בְּנִי וַיֹּאמֶר אֵלָיו
ב ג הִנֵּנִי׃ וַיֹּאמֶר הִנֵּה־נָא זָקַנְתִּי לֹא יָדַעְתִּי יוֹם מוֹתִי׃ וְעַתָּה שָׂא־נָא
ד כֵלֶיךָ תֶּלְיְךָ וְקַשְׁתֶּךָ וְצֵא הַשָּׂדֶה וְצוּדָה לִּי צידה׃ וַעֲשֵׂה־לִי מַטְעַמִּים צָיִד
כַּאֲשֶׁר אָהַבְתִּי וְהָבִיאָה לִּי וְאֹכֵלָה בַּעֲבוּר תְּבָרֶכְךָ נַפְשִׁי בְּטֶרֶם
ה אָמוּת׃ וְרִבְקָה שֹׁמַעַת בְּדַבֵּר יִצְחָק אֶל־עֵשָׂו בְּנוֹ וַיֵּלֶךְ עֵשָׂו הַשָּׂדֶה
ו לָצוּד צַיִד לְהָבִיא׃ וְרִבְקָה אָמְרָה אֶל־יַעֲקֹב בְּנָהּ לֵאמֹר הִנֵּה שָׁמַעְתִּי
ז אֶת־אָבִיךָ מְדַבֵּר אֶל־עֵשָׂו אָחִיךָ לֵאמֹר׃ הָבִיאָה לִּי צַיִד וַעֲשֵׂה־לִי
ח מַטְעַמִּים וְאֹכֵלָה וַאֲבָרֶכְכָה לִפְנֵי יְהוָה לִפְנֵי מוֹתִי׃ וְעַתָּה בְנִי שְׁמַע
ט בְּקֹלִי לַאֲשֶׁר אֲנִי מְצַוָּה אֹתָךְ׃ לֶךְ־נָא אֶל־הַצֹּאן וְקַח־לִי מִשָּׁם שְׁנֵי
י גְּדָיֵי עִזִּים טֹבִים וְאֶעֱשֶׂה אֹתָם מַטְעַמִּים לְאָבִיךָ כַּאֲשֶׁר אָהֵב׃ וְהֵבֵאתָ
יא לְאָבִיךָ וְאָכָל בַּעֲבֻר אֲשֶׁר יְבָרֶכְךָ לִפְנֵי מוֹתוֹ׃ וַיֹּאמֶר יַעֲקֹב אֶל־רִבְקָה
יב אִמּוֹ הֵן עֵשָׂו אָחִי אִישׁ שָׂעִר וְאָנֹכִי אִישׁ חָלָק׃ אוּלַי יְמֻשֵּׁנִי אָבִי
יג וְהָיִיתִי בְעֵינָיו כִּמְתַעְתֵּעַ וְהֵבֵאתִי עָלַי קְלָלָה וְלֹא בְרָכָה׃ וַתֹּאמֶר לוֹ
יד אִמּוֹ עָלַי קִלְלָתְךָ בְּנִי אַךְ שְׁמַע בְּקֹלִי וְלֵךְ קַח־לִי׃ וַיֵּלֶךְ וַיִּקַּח וַיָּבֵא
טו לְאִמּוֹ וַתַּעַשׂ אִמּוֹ מַטְעַמִּים כַּאֲשֶׁר אָהֵב אָבִיו׃ וַתִּקַּח רִבְקָה אֶת־
בִּגְדֵי עֵשָׂו בְּנָהּ הַגָּדֹל הַחֲמֻדֹת אֲשֶׁר אִתָּהּ בַּבָּיִת וַתַּלְבֵּשׁ אֶת־יַעֲקֹב
טז בְּנָהּ הַקָּטָן׃ וְאֵת עֹרֹת גְּדָיֵי הָעִזִּים הִלְבִּישָׁה עַל־יָדָיו וְעַל חֶלְקַת
יז צַוָּארָיו׃ וַתִּתֵּן אֶת־הַמַּטְעַמִּים וְאֶת־הַלֶּחֶם אֲשֶׁר עָשָׂתָה בְּיַד יַעֲקֹב
יח יט בְּנָהּ׃ וַיָּבֹא אֶל־אָבִיו וַיֹּאמֶר אָבִי וַיֹּאמֶר הִנֶּנִּי מִי אַתָּה בְּנִי׃ וַיֹּאמֶר

20 Please sit up and eat some of my game so that your soul may bless me." Yitzḥak
asked his son, "How did you find it so quickly, my son?" He replied, "The
21 Lord your God brought it about for me." Then Yitzḥak said to Yaakov, "Come
close and let me feel you, my son, to know – are you really my son Esav?"
22 Yaakov came close to Yitzḥak his father, who felt him and said, "The voice is
23 the voice of Yaakov, but the hands are the hands of Esav." He did not recognize
him, because his hands were hairy like those of his brother Esav. And he
24 25 blessed him. "Are you really my son Esav?" he asked. He replied, "I am." "Then
serve me and let me eat some of my son's game so that my soul may bless you."
26 He served him food and he ate, he brought him wine and he drank. Then
27 Yaakov's father Yitzḥak said to him, "Come close and kiss me, my son." So he
came close and kissed him, and Yitzḥak smelled the smell of his clothes and
blessed him, saying: "The smell of my son is the smell of a field the Lord has
28 blessed. God endow you with dew of heaven, the cream of the land, much
29 grain and wine. May peoples serve you; may nations bow down to you. Be
lord over your brothers, and may your mother's sons bow down to you. A
30 curse on those who curse you; on those who bless you, blessing." Yitzḥak had
finished blessing Yaakov, and Yaakov had just left his father Yitzḥak, when his
31 brother Esav came back from the hunt. He too had prepared delicious food
and brought it to his father. And he said to his father, "Let my father sit up
32 and eat some of his son's game so that your soul may bless me." "Who are
you?" asked his father Yitzḥak. "I am your son, your firstborn, Esav," he
33 replied. Yitzḥak was seized with a violent fit of trembling. "Who then was it
that hunted game and brought it to me? I ate it all before you came, and I
34 blessed him – and he will be blessed." When Esav heard his father's words,
he burst into a loud and bitter cry. He said to his father, "Bless me, me too, my
35 36 father!" "Your brother came in deceit and took your blessing," he replied. Esav
said, "Is he not rightly named Yaakov? Twice he has supplanted me.[59] He took
my birthright and now he has taken my blessing." And then, "Do you not have
37 any blessing left for me?" Yitzḥak answered Esav, "I have made him lord over
you and given him all his brothers as servants. I have endowed him with
38 grain and wine. What then can I do for you, my son?" Esav said to his father,
"Have you only one blessing, father? Bless me, me too, my father!" And Esav
39 wept aloud. His father Yitzḥak answered him and said: "Of the cream of the
40 land your home shall be, of the dew of heaven above. By your sword you will
live, and your brother you will serve; but when you break loose, you will
41 throw off his yoke from your neck." Esav resented Yaakov because of the
blessing his father had given him. "The days of mourning for my father are
approaching," he said to himself, "and then I will kill my brother Yaakov."
42 When Rivka was told what her elder son Esav had said, she summoned her
younger son Yaakov and said, "Your brother Esav is consoling himself with
43 the thought of killing you. Now, my son, listen to me. Flee at once to my

59 | Hebrew *vayakeveni*, resonating with the name Yaakov.

יַעֲקֹב אֶל־אָבִיו אָנֹכִי עֵשָׂו בְּכֹרֶךָ עָשִׂיתִי כַּאֲשֶׁר דִּבַּרְתָּ אֵלָי קוּם־נָא
כ שְׁבָה וְאָכְלָה מִצֵּידִי בַּעֲבוּר תְּבָרְכַנִּי נַפְשֶׁךָ: וַיֹּאמֶר יִצְחָק אֶל־בְּנוֹ
כא מַה־זֶּה מִהַרְתָּ לִמְצֹא בְּנִי וַיֹּאמֶר כִּי הִקְרָה יהוה אֱלֹהֶיךָ לְפָנָי: וַיֹּאמֶר
יִצְחָק אֶל־יַעֲקֹב גְּשָׁה־נָּא וַאֲמֻשְׁךָ בְּנִי הַאַתָּה זֶה בְּנִי עֵשָׂו אִם־לֹא:
כב וַיִּגַּשׁ יַעֲקֹב אֶל־יִצְחָק אָבִיו וַיְמֻשֵּׁהוּ וַיֹּאמֶר הַקֹּל קוֹל יַעֲקֹב וְהַיָּדַיִם
כג יְדֵי עֵשָׂו: וְלֹא הִכִּירוֹ כִּי־הָיוּ יָדָיו כִּידֵי עֵשָׂו אָחִיו שְׂעִרֹת וַיְבָרְכֵהוּ:
כד כה וַיֹּאמֶר אַתָּה זֶה בְּנִי עֵשָׂו וַיֹּאמֶר אָנִי: וַיֹּאמֶר הַגִּשָׁה לִּי וְאֹכְלָה מִצֵּיד
כו בְּנִי לְמַעַן תְּבָרֶכְךָ נַפְשִׁי וַיַּגֶּשׁ־לוֹ וַיֹּאכַל וַיָּבֵא לוֹ יַיִן וַיֵּשְׁתְּ: וַיֹּאמֶר
כז אֵלָיו יִצְחָק אָבִיו גְּשָׁה־נָּא וּשְׁקָה־לִּי בְּנִי: וַיִּגַּשׁ וַיִּשַּׁק־לוֹ וַיָּרַח אֶת־
רֵיחַ בְּגָדָיו וַיְבָרְכֵהוּ וַיֹּאמֶר רְאֵה רֵיחַ בְּנִי כְּרֵיחַ שָׂדֶה אֲשֶׁר בֵּרְכוֹ
כח יהוה: וְיִתֶּן־לְךָ הָאֱלֹהִים מִטַּל הַשָּׁמַיִם וּמִשְׁמַנֵּי הָאָרֶץ וְרֹב דָּגָן כה ששי
כט וְתִירֹשׁ: יַעַבְדוּךָ עַמִּים וְיִשְׁתַּחֲוֻ לְךָ לְאֻמִּים הֱוֵה גְבִיר לְאַחֶיךָ וְיִשְׁתַּחֲווּ
ל לְךָ בְּנֵי אִמֶּךָ אֹרְרֶיךָ אָרוּר וּמְבָרֲכֶיךָ בָּרוּךְ: וַיְהִי כַּאֲשֶׁר כִּלָּה יִצְחָק
לְבָרֵךְ אֶת־יַעֲקֹב וַיְהִי אַךְ יָצֹא יָצָא יַעֲקֹב מֵאֵת פְּנֵי יִצְחָק אָבִיו וְעֵשָׂו
לא אָחִיו בָּא מִצֵּידוֹ: וַיַּעַשׂ גַּם־הוּא מַטְעַמִּים וַיָּבֵא לְאָבִיו וַיֹּאמֶר לְאָבִיו
לב יָקֻם אָבִי וְיֹאכַל מִצֵּיד בְּנוֹ בַּעֲבֻר תְּבָרְכַנִּי נַפְשֶׁךָ: וַיֹּאמֶר לוֹ יִצְחָק
לג אָבִיו מִי־אָתָּה וַיֹּאמֶר אֲנִי בִּנְךָ בְכֹרְךָ עֵשָׂו: וַיֶּחֱרַד יִצְחָק חֲרָדָה גְּדֹלָה
עַד־מְאֹד וַיֹּאמֶר מִי־אֵפוֹא הוּא הַצָּד־צַיִד וַיָּבֵא לִי וָאֹכַל מִכֹּל בְּטֶרֶם
לד תָּבוֹא וָאֲבָרְכֵהוּ גַּם־בָּרוּךְ יִהְיֶה: כִּשְׁמֹעַ עֵשָׂו אֶת־דִּבְרֵי אָבִיו וַיִּצְעַק
צְעָקָה גְּדֹלָה וּמָרָה עַד־מְאֹד וַיֹּאמֶר לְאָבִיו בָּרְכֵנִי גַם־אָנִי אָבִי:
לה לו וַיֹּאמֶר בָּא אָחִיךָ בְּמִרְמָה וַיִּקַּח בִּרְכָתֶךָ: וַיֹּאמֶר הֲכִי קָרָא שְׁמוֹ יַעֲקֹב
וַיַּעְקְבֵנִי זֶה פַעֲמַיִם אֶת־בְּכֹרָתִי לָקָח וְהִנֵּה עַתָּה לָקַח בִּרְכָתִי וַיֹּאמַר
לז הֲלֹא־אָצַלְתָּ לִּי בְּרָכָה: וַיַּעַן יִצְחָק וַיֹּאמֶר לְעֵשָׂו הֵן גְּבִיר שַׂמְתִּיו לָךְ
וְאֶת־כָּל־אֶחָיו נָתַתִּי לוֹ לַעֲבָדִים וְדָגָן וְתִירֹשׁ סְמַכְתִּיו וּלְכָה אֵפוֹא
לח מָה אֶעֱשֶׂה בְּנִי: וַיֹּאמֶר עֵשָׂו אֶל־אָבִיו הַבְרָכָה אַחַת הִוא־לְךָ אָבִי
לט בָּרְכֵנִי גַם־אָנִי אָבִי וַיִּשָּׂא עֵשָׂו קֹלוֹ וַיֵּבְךְּ: וַיַּעַן יִצְחָק אָבִיו וַיֹּאמֶר
מ אֵלָיו הִנֵּה מִשְׁמַנֵּי הָאָרֶץ יִהְיֶה מוֹשָׁבֶךָ וּמִטַּל הַשָּׁמַיִם מֵעָל: וְעַל־
חַרְבְּךָ תִחְיֶה וְאֶת־אָחִיךָ תַּעֲבֹד וְהָיָה כַּאֲשֶׁר תָּרִיד וּפָרַקְתָּ עֻלּוֹ מֵעַל
מא צַוָּארֶךָ: וַיִּשְׂטֹם עֵשָׂו אֶת־יַעֲקֹב עַל־הַבְּרָכָה אֲשֶׁר בֵּרְכוֹ אָבִיו וַיֹּאמֶר
מב עֵשָׂו בְּלִבּוֹ יִקְרְבוּ יְמֵי אֵבֶל אָבִי וְאַהַרְגָה אֶת־יַעֲקֹב אָחִי: וַיֻּגַּד לְרִבְקָה
אֶת־דִּבְרֵי עֵשָׂו בְּנָהּ הַגָּדֹל וַתִּשְׁלַח וַתִּקְרָא לְיַעֲקֹב בְּנָהּ הַקָּטָן וַתֹּאמֶר
מג אֵלָיו הִנֵּה עֵשָׂו אָחִיךָ מִתְנַחֵם לְךָ לְהָרְגֶךָ: וְעַתָּה בְנִי שְׁמַע בְּקֹלִי

44 brother Lavan in Ḥaran. Stay with him a while, until your brother's rage
45 subsides. When your brother is no longer angry with you and has forgotten
what you did to him, I will send word to you to come back. Why should I lose
46 you both in one day?" Rivka then said to Yitzḥak, "I loathe my life because
of these Hittite women. If Yaakov marries a Hittite woman like them, one
28 1 of the women of the land, why should I go on living?" So Yitzḥak called
Yaakov to him. He blessed him and charged him: "You are not to marry a
2 Canaanite woman. Go at once to Padan Aram, to the house of your mother's
father Betuel, and there marry a daughter of your mother's brother Lavan.
3 May El Shaddai bless you, make you fertile, and multiply you so that you
4 become a community of peoples. May He grant Avraham's blessing to you
and your descendants, that you may possess the land where of your wayfaring
5 you live as a stranger, which God gave to Avraham." Then Yitzḥak sent Yaakov
on his way. He went toward Padan Aram, to Lavan son of Betuel the Aramean,
6 brother of Rivka, Yaakov and Esav's mother. Esav learned that Yitzḥak had
blessed Yaakov and sent him to Padan Aram to find a wife, and that when he
7 blessed him, he commanded him not to marry a Canaanite woman, and that
8 Yaakov had obeyed his father and mother and had gone to Padan Aram. Esav
9 realized then that the Canaanite women displeased his father Yitzḥak. So Esav
went to Yishmael and took Maḥalat, daughter of Avraham's son Yishmael, a
10 sister of Nevayot, to be his wife, with his other wives. Yaakov left VAYETZE
11 Be'er Sheva and journeyed toward Ḥaran. In time he chanced upon a certain
place and decided to spend the night there, because the sun had set. He took
some stones of the place and put them under his head, and in that place lay
12 down to sleep. And he dreamed: He saw a ladder set upon the ground, whose
13 top reached the heavens. On it, angels of God went up and came down. The
Lord stood over him there and said, "I am the Lord, the God of Avraham
your father, and the God of Yitzḥak. The land on which you lie I will give
14 to you and your descendants. Your descendants shall be like the dust of
the earth, and you will spread out to the west, the east, the north, and the
south. Through you and your descendants, all the families of the earth will
15 be blessed. I am with you. I will protect you wherever you go and I will bring
you back to this land, for I will not leave you until I have done what I have
16 spoken of to you." Then Yaakov awoke from his sleep and said, "Truly, the
17 Lord is in this place – and I did not know it!" He was afraid and said, "How
full of awe is this place! This is none other than the House of God, and this
18 the gate of the heavens!" Yaakov rose early the next morning, took the stone
he had placed under his head, set it up as a pillar, and poured oil on top of it.
19 He named the place Beit El;[60] the town was originally called Luz. Yaakov then
20 made a vow. "If God will be with me," he said, "protecting me on this journey

60 | Meaning "House of God."

מד וְקוּם בְּרַח־לְךָ אֶל־לָבָן אָחִי חָרָנָה׃ וְיָשַׁבְתָּ עִמּוֹ יָמִים אֲחָדִים עַד
מה אֲשֶׁר־תָּשׁוּב חֲמַת אָחִיךָ׃ עַד־שׁוּב אַף־אָחִיךָ מִמְּךָ וְשָׁכַח אֵת אֲשֶׁר־
עָשִׂיתָ לּוֹ וְשָׁלַחְתִּי וּלְקַחְתִּיךָ מִשָּׁם לָמָה אֶשְׁכַּל גַּם־שְׁנֵיכֶם יוֹם אֶחָד׃
מו וַתֹּאמֶר רִבְקָה אֶל־יִצְחָק קַצְתִּי בְחַיַּי מִפְּנֵי בְּנוֹת חֵת אִם־לֹקֵחַ יַעֲקֹב
כח א אִשָּׁה מִבְּנוֹת־חֵת כָּאֵלֶּה מִבְּנוֹת הָאָרֶץ לָמָּה לִּי חַיִּים׃ וַיִּקְרָא יִצְחָק
אֶל־יַעֲקֹב וַיְבָרֶךְ אֹתוֹ וַיְצַוֵּהוּ וַיֹּאמֶר לוֹ לֹא־תִקַּח אִשָּׁה מִבְּנוֹת כְּנָעַן׃
ב קוּם לֵךְ פַּדֶּנָה אֲרָם בֵּיתָה בְתוּאֵל אֲבִי אִמֶּךָ וְקַח־לְךָ מִשָּׁם
ג אִשָּׁה מִבְּנוֹת לָבָן אֲחִי אִמֶּךָ׃ וְאֵל שַׁדַּי יְבָרֵךְ אֹתְךָ וְיַפְרְךָ וְיַרְבֶּךָ וְהָיִיתָ
ד לִקְהַל עַמִּים׃ וְיִתֶּן־לְךָ אֶת־בִּרְכַּת אַבְרָהָם לְךָ וּלְזַרְעֲךָ אִתָּךְ לְרִשְׁתְּךָ
ה אֶת־אֶרֶץ מְגֻרֶיךָ אֲשֶׁר־נָתַן אֱלֹהִים לְאַבְרָהָם׃ וַיִּשְׁלַח יִצְחָק אֶת־ שביעי
יַעֲקֹב וַיֵּלֶךְ פַּדֶּנָה אֲרָם אֶל־לָבָן בֶּן־בְּתוּאֵל הָאֲרַמִּי אֲחִי רִבְקָה אֵם
ו יַעֲקֹב וְעֵשָׂו׃ וַיַּרְא עֵשָׂו כִּי־בֵרַךְ יִצְחָק אֶת־יַעֲקֹב וְשִׁלַּח אֹתוֹ פַּדֶּנָה
אֲרָם לָקַחַת־לוֹ מִשָּׁם אִשָּׁה בְּבָרְכוֹ אֹתוֹ וַיְצַו עָלָיו לֵאמֹר לֹא־תִקַּח
ז אִשָּׁה מִבְּנוֹת כְּנָעַן׃ וַיִּשְׁמַע יַעֲקֹב אֶל־אָבִיו וְאֶל־אִמּוֹ וַיֵּלֶךְ פַּדֶּנָה מפטיר
ח ט אֲרָם׃ וַיַּרְא עֵשָׂו כִּי רָעוֹת בְּנוֹת כְּנָעַן בְּעֵינֵי יִצְחָק אָבִיו׃ וַיֵּלֶךְ עֵשָׂו
אֶל־יִשְׁמָעֵאל וַיִּקַּח אֶת־מָחֲלַת ׀ בַּת־יִשְׁמָעֵאל בֶּן־אַבְרָהָם אֲחוֹת
י נְבָיוֹת עַל־נָשָׁיו לוֹ לְאִשָּׁה׃ וַיֵּצֵא יַעֲקֹב מִבְּאֵר כו ויצא
יא שָׁבַע וַיֵּלֶךְ חָרָנָה׃ וַיִּפְגַּע בַּמָּקוֹם וַיָּלֶן שָׁם כִּי־בָא הַשֶּׁמֶשׁ וַיִּקַּח מֵאַבְנֵי
יב הַמָּקוֹם וַיָּשֶׂם מְרַאֲשֹׁתָיו וַיִּשְׁכַּב בַּמָּקוֹם הַהוּא׃ וַיַּחֲלֹם וְהִנֵּה סֻלָּם
מֻצָּב אַרְצָה וְרֹאשׁוֹ מַגִּיעַ הַשָּׁמָיְמָה וְהִנֵּה מַלְאֲכֵי אֱלֹהִים עֹלִים וְיֹרְדִים
יג בּוֹ׃ וְהִנֵּה יהוה נִצָּב עָלָיו וַיֹּאמַר אֲנִי יהוה אֱלֹהֵי אַבְרָהָם אָבִיךָ וֵאלֹהֵי
יד יִצְחָק הָאָרֶץ אֲשֶׁר אַתָּה שֹׁכֵב עָלֶיהָ לְךָ אֶתְּנֶנָּה וּלְזַרְעֶךָ׃ וְהָיָה זַרְעֲךָ
כַּעֲפַר הָאָרֶץ וּפָרַצְתָּ יָמָּה וָקֵדְמָה וְצָפֹנָה וָנֶגְבָּה וְנִבְרְכוּ בְךָ כָּל־
טו מִשְׁפְּחֹת הָאֲדָמָה וּבְזַרְעֶךָ׃ וְהִנֵּה אָנֹכִי עִמָּךְ וּשְׁמַרְתִּיךָ בְּכֹל אֲשֶׁר־
תֵּלֵךְ וַהֲשִׁבֹתִיךָ אֶל־הָאֲדָמָה הַזֹּאת כִּי לֹא אֶעֱזָבְךָ עַד אֲשֶׁר אִם־
טז עָשִׂיתִי אֵת אֲשֶׁר־דִּבַּרְתִּי לָךְ׃ וַיִּיקַץ יַעֲקֹב מִשְּׁנָתוֹ וַיֹּאמֶר אָכֵן יֵשׁ
יז יהוה בַּמָּקוֹם הַזֶּה וְאָנֹכִי לֹא יָדָעְתִּי׃ וַיִּירָא וַיֹּאמַר מַה־נּוֹרָא הַמָּקוֹם
יח הַזֶּה אֵין זֶה כִּי אִם־בֵּית אֱלֹהִים וְזֶה שַׁעַר הַשָּׁמָיִם׃ וַיַּשְׁכֵּם יַעֲקֹב
בַּבֹּקֶר וַיִּקַּח אֶת־הָאֶבֶן אֲשֶׁר־שָׂם מְרַאֲשֹׁתָיו וַיָּשֶׂם אֹתָהּ מַצֵּבָה וַיִּצֹק
יט שֶׁמֶן עַל־רֹאשָׁהּ׃ וַיִּקְרָא אֶת־שֵׁם־הַמָּקוֹם הַהוּא בֵּית־אֵל וְאוּלָם לוּז
כ שֵׁם־הָעִיר לָרִאשֹׁנָה׃ וַיִּדַּר יַעֲקֹב נֶדֶר לֵאמֹר אִם־יִהְיֶה אֱלֹהִים עִמָּדִי
וּשְׁמָרַנִי בַּדֶּרֶךְ הַזֶּה אֲשֶׁר אָנֹכִי הוֹלֵךְ וְנָתַן־לִי לֶחֶם לֶאֱכֹל וּבֶגֶד

21 I am taking, giving me bread to eat and clothes to wear, and if I return in peace
22 to my father's house, then the Lord will be my God. This stone I set up as a
pillar will become a house of God, and of all that You give me I will dedicate
29 1 a tenth to You." Yaakov began traveling again and came to the land of the
2 people of the East. There he saw a well in a field. Three flocks of sheep were
lying beside it because this was the well from which the flocks were watered.
3 The top of it was covered with a large stone. When all the flocks were gathered
there, the stone would be rolled from the mouth of the well and the sheep
4 watered. The stone would then be put back in place on top of the well. Yaakov
asked the shepherds, "Brothers, where are you from?" "We are from Ḥaran,"
5 they replied. He asked, "Do you know Lavan son of Naḥor?" "We know him,"
6 they said. He asked, "Is he well?" "He is well," they said, "and look, here is his
7 daughter Raḥel coming with the sheep." "Look," he said, "it is still broad
daylight. It is not yet time to gather in the animals. Water the flocks and take
8 them back to pasture." But they said, "We cannot do that until all the flocks
are gathered and the stone is rolled from the top of the well. Only then can
9 we water the flocks." While he was still talking with them, Raḥel came with
10 her father's sheep; she was a shepherdess. When Yaakov saw Raḥel, daughter
of his mother's brother Lavan, with Lavan's sheep, he stepped forward, rolled
11 the stone from the top of the well, and watered his uncle's sheep. And Yaakov
12 kissed Raḥel – and wept aloud. And Yaakov told Raḥel that he was related to
13 her father: he was Rivka's son. She ran to tell her father. When Lavan heard
the news about Yaakov, his sister's son, he ran to meet him. He embraced and
kissed him and brought him to his house. Yaakov told Lavan all that had
14 happened. Lavan said to him, "You are truly of my own bones, my own flesh."
15 And Yaakov stayed with him for a month. Then Lavan said to him, "If you are
my brother, does that mean you should work for me for nothing? Tell me
16 what your hire should be." Lavan had two daughters. The elder was called
17 Leah and the younger Raḥel. Leah had sensitive eyes; Raḥel was beautiful
18 and lovely. And Yaakov was in love with Raḥel, so he said, "I will work for you
19 seven years for your younger daughter Raḥel." Lavan replied, "Better that I
20 give her to you than to some other man. Stay on with me." So Yaakov worked
for Raḥel seven years. But so great was his love for her that they seemed to
21 him but a few days. Then Yaakov said to Lavan, "Give me my wife – my time
22 is done, let me come to her." So Lavan brought together all the local people
23 and made a feast. In the evening he took his daughter Leah and brought her
24 in to him, and he came to her. Lavan also gave his servant Zilpa to his daughter
25 Leah as her maid. Then came morning – and it was Leah. Yaakov said to
Lavan, "What is this you have done to me? I served you for Raḥel, did I not?
26 Why did you deceive me?" Lavan said, "This is not done in our country – to
27 marry off the younger before the firstborn. Wait until the bridal week of this
one is over and then we will give you the other one also, in return for your

כא כב לִלְבֹּשׁ׃ וְשַׁבְתִּי בְשָׁלוֹם אֶל־בֵּית אָבִי וְהָיָה יְהוָה לִי לֵאלֹהִים׃ וְהָאֶבֶן
הַזֹּאת אֲשֶׁר־שַׂמְתִּי מַצֵּבָה יִהְיֶה בֵּית אֱלֹהִים וְכֹל אֲשֶׁר תִּתֶּן־לִי עַשֵּׂר
כט א ב אֲעַשְּׂרֶנּוּ לָךְ׃ וַיִּשָּׂא יַעֲקֹב רַגְלָיו וַיֵּלֶךְ אַרְצָה בְנֵי־קֶדֶם׃ וַיַּרְא וְהִנֵּה שני
בְאֵר בַּשָּׂדֶה וְהִנֵּה־שָׁם שְׁלֹשָׁה עֶדְרֵי־צֹאן רֹבְצִים עָלֶיהָ כִּי מִן־הַבְּאֵר
ג הַהִוא יַשְׁקוּ הָעֲדָרִים וְהָאֶבֶן גְּדֹלָה עַל־פִּי הַבְּאֵר׃ וְנֶאֶסְפוּ־שָׁמָּה
כָל־הָעֲדָרִים וְגָלְלוּ אֶת־הָאֶבֶן מֵעַל פִּי הַבְּאֵר וְהִשְׁקוּ אֶת־הַצֹּאן
ד וְהֵשִׁיבוּ אֶת־הָאֶבֶן עַל־פִּי הַבְּאֵר לִמְקֹמָהּ׃ וַיֹּאמֶר לָהֶם יַעֲקֹב אַחַי
ה מֵאַיִן אַתֶּם וַיֹּאמְרוּ מֵחָרָן אֲנָחְנוּ׃ וַיֹּאמֶר לָהֶם הַיְדַעְתֶּם אֶת־לָבָן
ו בֶּן־נָחוֹר וַיֹּאמְרוּ יָדָעְנוּ׃ וַיֹּאמֶר לָהֶם הֲשָׁלוֹם לוֹ וַיֹּאמְרוּ שָׁלוֹם וְהִנֵּה
ז רָחֵל בִּתּוֹ בָּאָה עִם־הַצֹּאן׃ וַיֹּאמֶר הֵן עוֹד הַיּוֹם גָּדוֹל לֹא־עֵת הֵאָסֵף
ח הַמִּקְנֶה הַשְׁקוּ הַצֹּאן וּלְכוּ רְעוּ׃ וַיֹּאמְרוּ לֹא נוּכַל עַד אֲשֶׁר יֵאָסְפוּ
ט כָּל־הָעֲדָרִים וְגָלְלוּ אֶת־הָאֶבֶן מֵעַל פִּי הַבְּאֵר וְהִשְׁקִינוּ הַצֹּאן׃ עוֹדֶנּוּ
י מְדַבֵּר עִמָּם וְרָחֵל ׀ בָּאָה עִם־הַצֹּאן אֲשֶׁר לְאָבִיהָ כִּי רֹעָה הִוא׃ וַיְהִי
כַּאֲשֶׁר רָאָה יַעֲקֹב אֶת־רָחֵל בַּת־לָבָן אֲחִי אִמּוֹ וְאֶת־צֹאן לָבָן אֲחִי
אִמּוֹ וַיִּגַּשׁ יַעֲקֹב וַיָּגֶל אֶת־הָאֶבֶן מֵעַל פִּי הַבְּאֵר וַיַּשְׁקְ אֶת־צֹאן לָבָן
יא יב אֲחִי אִמּוֹ׃ וַיִּשַּׁק יַעֲקֹב לְרָחֵל וַיִּשָּׂא אֶת־קֹלוֹ וַיֵּבְךְּ׃ וַיַּגֵּד יַעֲקֹב לְרָחֵל
יג כִּי אֲחִי אָבִיהָ הוּא וְכִי בֶן־רִבְקָה הוּא וַתָּרָץ וַתַּגֵּד לְאָבִיהָ׃ וַיְהִי כִשְׁמֹעַ
לָבָן אֶת־שֵׁמַע ׀ יַעֲקֹב בֶּן־אֲחֹתוֹ וַיָּרָץ לִקְרָאתוֹ וַיְחַבֶּק־לוֹ וַיְנַשֶּׁק־לוֹ
יד וַיְבִיאֵהוּ אֶל־בֵּיתוֹ וַיְסַפֵּר לְלָבָן אֵת כָּל־הַדְּבָרִים הָאֵלֶּה׃ וַיֹּאמֶר לוֹ
טו לָבָן אַךְ עַצְמִי וּבְשָׂרִי אָתָּה וַיֵּשֶׁב עִמּוֹ חֹדֶשׁ יָמִים׃ וַיֹּאמֶר לָבָן לְיַעֲקֹב
טז הֲכִי־אָחִי אַתָּה וַעֲבַדְתַּנִי חִנָּם הַגִּידָה לִּי מַה־מַּשְׂכֻּרְתֶּךָ׃ וּלְלָבָן שְׁתֵּי
יז בָנוֹת שֵׁם הַגְּדֹלָה לֵאָה וְשֵׁם הַקְּטַנָּה רָחֵל׃ וְעֵינֵי לֵאָה רַכּוֹת וְרָחֵל
יח הָיְתָה יְפַת־תֹּאַר וִיפַת מַרְאֶה׃ וַיֶּאֱהַב יַעֲקֹב אֶת־רָחֵל וַיֹּאמֶר אֶעֱבָדְךָ שלישי
יט שֶׁבַע שָׁנִים בְּרָחֵל בִּתְּךָ הַקְּטַנָּה׃ וַיֹּאמֶר לָבָן טוֹב תִּתִּי אֹתָהּ לָךְ
כ מִתִּתִּי אֹתָהּ לְאִישׁ אַחֵר שְׁבָה עִמָּדִי׃ וַיַּעֲבֹד יַעֲקֹב בְּרָחֵל שֶׁבַע שָׁנִים
כא וַיִּהְיוּ בְעֵינָיו כְּיָמִים אֲחָדִים בְּאַהֲבָתוֹ אֹתָהּ׃ וַיֹּאמֶר יַעֲקֹב אֶל־לָבָן
כב הָבָה אֶת־אִשְׁתִּי כִּי מָלְאוּ יָמָי וְאָבוֹאָה אֵלֶיהָ׃ וַיֶּאֱסֹף לָבָן אֶת־כָּל־
כג אַנְשֵׁי הַמָּקוֹם וַיַּעַשׂ מִשְׁתֶּה׃ וַיְהִי בָעֶרֶב וַיִּקַּח אֶת־לֵאָה בִתּוֹ וַיָּבֵא
כד אֹתָהּ אֵלָיו וַיָּבֹא אֵלֶיהָ׃ וַיִּתֵּן לָבָן לָהּ אֶת־זִלְפָּה שִׁפְחָתוֹ לְלֵאָה בִתּוֹ
כה שִׁפְחָה׃ וַיְהִי בַבֹּקֶר וְהִנֵּה־הִוא לֵאָה וַיֹּאמֶר אֶל־לָבָן מַה־זֹּאת עָשִׂיתָ
כו לִּי הֲלֹא בְרָחֵל עָבַדְתִּי עִמָּךְ וְלָמָּה רִמִּיתָנִי׃ וַיֹּאמֶר לָבָן לֹא־יֵעָשֶׂה
כז כֵן בִּמְקוֹמֵנוּ לָתֵת הַצְּעִירָה לִפְנֵי הַבְּכִירָה׃ מַלֵּא שְׁבֻעַ זֹאת וְנִתְּנָה

28 serving me another seven years." Yaakov did so. He completed Leah's bridal
29 week; then Lavan gave him his daughter Raḥel as a wife. Lavan gave his
30 servant Bilha to his daughter Raḥel as her maid. And Yaakov came also to
Raḥel; and he loved Raḥel more than Leah. And he served him for another
31 seven years. When the Lord saw that Leah was unloved, He opened her
32 womb, but Raḥel was barren. Leah became pregnant and had a son. She
named him Reuven, saying, "The Lord has seen my affliction. Now my
33 husband will love me."[61] She became pregnant again and had a son. She said,
"The Lord has heard that I am unloved, so He has given me this son also,"
34 and she named him Shimon.[62] She became pregnant again and had a son and
said, "Now that I have borne him three sons, my husband will walk with me."
35 That is why he was named Levi.[63] She became pregnant again and had a son.
She said, "This time I will praise the Lord," so she named him Yehuda.[64] Then
30 1 she ceased having children. Aware that she had borne Yaakov no children,
Raḥel became envious of her sister. To Yaakov she said, "Give me children!
2 If not, let me die!" Yaakov grew angry with Raḥel, and said, "Am I in place of
3 God, who has kept you from having children?" "Here is Bilha my slave," she
said. "Come to her. Let her give birth on my knees[65] so that I too can build a
4 family through her." So she gave him her maid Bilha as a wife. Yaakov came
5 6 to her, and she became pregnant and bore Yaakov a son. Then Raḥel said,
"God has vindicated me. He has listened to my voice and given me a son." So
7 she named him Dan.[66] Bilha, Raḥel's maid, became pregnant again and bore
8 Yaakov a second son. And Raḥel said, "I have struggled hard with my sister
9 and I have won." So she named him Naftali.[67] Leah realized that she was no
longer having children, so she took her maid Zilpa and gave her to Yaakov as
10 11 a wife. And Leah's maid Zilpa bore Yaakov a son. Leah said, "Good fortune
12 has come!" So she named him Gad.[68] Then Zilpa, Leah's maid, bore Yaakov
13 a second son. Leah said, "How blessed I am; young girls will call me blessed."
14 So she named him Asher.[69] During the wheat harvest, Reuven went for a walk
and found mandrakes in the field. He brought them to his mother Leah. Raḥel
15 said to Leah, "Please give me some of your son's mandrakes." She replied, "Is
it not enough that you have taken away my husband? Now you want to take
my son's mandrakes too!" "Very well," said Raḥel. "Let him sleep with you
16 tonight in exchange for your son's mandrakes." When Yaakov came back from
the field that evening, Leah went out to meet him and said, "You are to come
to me, for I have hired you with my son's mandrakes." So that night he slept

---

61 | The name Reuven resonates with *raa* (has seen) and *ben* (son).

62 | The name Shimon resonates with *shama* (has heard).

63 | The name Levi resonates with *yillaveh* (will walk with).

64 | The name Yehuda resonates with *odeh* (I will praise).

65 | Meaning "I will raise the child as my own."

66 | The name Dan resonates with *dananni* (has vindicated me).

67 | The name Naftali resonates with *niftalti* (I have struggled hard).

68 | *Gad* is the word used to denote "good fortune."

69 | The name Asher resonates with *be'oshri* (how blessed I am).

לָךְ גַּם־אֶת־זֹאת בַּעֲבֹדָה אֲשֶׁר תַּעֲבֹד עִמָּדִי עוֹד שֶׁבַע־שָׁנִים אֲחֵרוֹת:
כח וַיַּעַשׂ יַעֲקֹב כֵּן וַיְמַלֵּא שְׁבֻעַ זֹאת וַיִּתֶּן־לוֹ אֶת־רָחֵל בִּתּוֹ לוֹ לְאִשָּׁה:
כט ל וַיִּתֵּן לָבָן לְרָחֵל בִּתּוֹ אֶת־בִּלְהָה שִׁפְחָתוֹ לָהּ לְשִׁפְחָה: וַיָּבֹא גַּם
אֶל־רָחֵל וַיֶּאֱהַב גַּם־אֶת־רָחֵל מִלֵּאָה וַיַּעֲבֹד עִמּוֹ עוֹד שֶׁבַע־שָׁנִים
לא אֲחֵרוֹת: וַיַּרְא יהוה כִּי־שְׂנוּאָה לֵאָה וַיִּפְתַּח אֶת־רַחְמָהּ וְרָחֵל עֲקָרָה: כז
לב וַתַּהַר לֵאָה וַתֵּלֶד בֵּן וַתִּקְרָא שְׁמוֹ רְאוּבֵן כִּי אָמְרָה כִּי־רָאָה יהוה
לג בְּעָנְיִי כִּי עַתָּה יֶאֱהָבַנִי אִישִׁי: וַתַּהַר עוֹד וַתֵּלֶד בֵּן וַתֹּאמֶר כִּי־שָׁמַע
יהוה כִּי־שְׂנוּאָה אָנֹכִי וַיִּתֶּן־לִי גַּם־אֶת־זֶה וַתִּקְרָא שְׁמוֹ שִׁמְעוֹן:
לד וַתַּהַר עוֹד וַתֵּלֶד בֵּן וַתֹּאמֶר עַתָּה הַפַּעַם יִלָּוֶה אִישִׁי אֵלַי כִּי־יָלַדְתִּי
לה לוֹ שְׁלֹשָׁה בָנִים עַל־כֵּן קָרָא־שְׁמוֹ לֵוִי: וַתַּהַר עוֹד וַתֵּלֶד בֵּן וַתֹּאמֶר
הַפַּעַם אוֹדֶה אֶת־יהוה עַל־כֵּן קָרְאָה שְׁמוֹ יְהוּדָה וַתַּעֲמֹד מִלֶּדֶת:
ל א וַתֵּרֶא רָחֵל כִּי לֹא יָלְדָה לְיַעֲקֹב וַתְּקַנֵּא רָחֵל בַּאֲחֹתָהּ וַתֹּאמֶר אֶל־
ב יַעֲקֹב הָבָה־לִּי בָנִים וְאִם־אַיִן מֵתָה אָנֹכִי: וַיִּחַר־אַף יַעֲקֹב בְּרָחֵל
ג וַיֹּאמֶר הֲתַחַת אֱלֹהִים אָנֹכִי אֲשֶׁר־מָנַע מִמֵּךְ פְּרִי־בָטֶן: וַתֹּאמֶר הִנֵּה
אֲמָתִי בִלְהָה בֹּא אֵלֶיהָ וְתֵלֵד עַל־בִּרְכַּי וְאִבָּנֶה גַם־אָנֹכִי מִמֶּנָּה:
ד ה וַתִּתֶּן־לוֹ אֶת־בִּלְהָה שִׁפְחָתָהּ לְאִשָּׁה וַיָּבֹא אֵלֶיהָ יַעֲקֹב: וַתַּהַר בִּלְהָה
ו וַתֵּלֶד לְיַעֲקֹב בֵּן: וַתֹּאמֶר רָחֵל דָּנַנִּי אֱלֹהִים וְגַם שָׁמַע בְּקֹלִי וַיִּתֶּן־לִי
ז בֵּן עַל־כֵּן קָרְאָה שְׁמוֹ דָּן: וַתַּהַר עוֹד וַתֵּלֶד בִּלְהָה שִׁפְחַת רָחֵל בֵּן
ח שֵׁנִי לְיַעֲקֹב: וַתֹּאמֶר רָחֵל נַפְתּוּלֵי אֱלֹהִים ׀ נִפְתַּלְתִּי עִם־אֲחֹתִי גַּם־
ט יָכֹלְתִּי וַתִּקְרָא שְׁמוֹ נַפְתָּלִי: וַתֵּרֶא לֵאָה כִּי עָמְדָה מִלֶּדֶת וַתִּקַּח
י אֶת־זִלְפָּה שִׁפְחָתָהּ וַתִּתֵּן אֹתָהּ לְיַעֲקֹב לְאִשָּׁה: וַתֵּלֶד זִלְפָּה שִׁפְחַת
יא יב לֵאָה לְיַעֲקֹב בֵּן: וַתֹּאמֶר לֵאָה בגד וַתִּקְרָא אֶת־שְׁמוֹ גָּד: וַתֵּלֶד זִלְפָּה בָּא גָד
יג שִׁפְחַת לֵאָה בֵּן שֵׁנִי לְיַעֲקֹב: וַתֹּאמֶר לֵאָה בְּאָשְׁרִי כִּי אִשְּׁרוּנִי בָּנוֹת
יד וַתִּקְרָא אֶת־שְׁמוֹ אָשֵׁר: וַיֵּלֶךְ רְאוּבֵן בִּימֵי קְצִיר־חִטִּים וַיִּמְצָא רביעי
דוּדָאִים בַּשָּׂדֶה וַיָּבֵא אֹתָם אֶל־לֵאָה אִמּוֹ וַתֹּאמֶר רָחֵל אֶל־לֵאָה
טו תְּנִי־נָא לִי מִדּוּדָאֵי בְּנֵךְ: וַתֹּאמֶר לָהּ הַמְעַט קַחְתֵּךְ אֶת־אִישִׁי וְלָקַחַת
גַּם אֶת־דּוּדָאֵי בְּנִי וַתֹּאמֶר רָחֵל לָכֵן יִשְׁכַּב עִמָּךְ הַלַּיְלָה תַּחַת דּוּדָאֵי
טז בְנֵךְ: וַיָּבֹא יַעֲקֹב מִן־הַשָּׂדֶה בָּעֶרֶב וַתֵּצֵא לֵאָה לִקְרָאתוֹ וַתֹּאמֶר
אֵלַי תָּבוֹא כִּי שָׂכֹר שְׂכַרְתִּיךָ בְּדוּדָאֵי בְּנִי וַיִּשְׁכַּב עִמָּהּ בַּלַּיְלָה הוּא:

17 with her. God listened to Leah, and she became pregnant and bore Yaakov
18 a fifth son. Leah said, "God has rewarded me for giving my maid to my
19 husband," so she named him Yissakhar.[70] Leah became pregnant again and
20 bore Yaakov a sixth son. "God has given me a precious gift," said Leah. "This
time my husband will honor me, for I have borne him six sons," so she named
21 22 him Zevulun.[71] Later she gave birth to a daughter and named her Dina. Then
23 God remembered Raḥel and listened to her and enabled her to conceive. She
became pregnant and gave birth to a son. She said, "God has taken away my
24 shame," and she named him Yosef, saying, "May the Lord grant me another
25 son also."[72] After Raḥel had given birth to Yosef, Yaakov said to Lavan, "Release
26 me to go home to my own land. Give me my wives and my children for whom
I have worked for you, and let me go. You know very well how much work I
27 have done for you." But Lavan said to him, "If you will allow me to say so, I
have learned by divination that it is because of you that the Lord has blessed
28 29 me." He added, "Name your hire and I will pay it." Yaakov said, "You know
well how I have worked for you and how your livestock have fared under my
30 care. You had little before I came, but it has swelled into much. The Lord has
blessed you wherever I have been. Now, when can I do likewise for my own
31 household?" Lavan asked, "What shall I give you?" Yaakov replied, "Do not
give me anything. If you do this one thing for me, I will continue to shepherd
32 and guard your flocks. Let me go through all your flocks today and remove
every speckled or spotted sheep, every dark-colored lamb, and every spotted
33 or speckled goat. They shall be my hire. Let my honesty testify for me in the
future, whenever you come to check the wages you have paid me. Any goat
not speckled or spotted or any lamb not dark colored in my possession
34 shall be considered stolen." Lavan said, "Agreed. Let it be as you have said."
35 That day Lavan removed the streaked or spotted goats, all the speckled or
spotted female goats – every one that had a trace of white – and every dark-
36 colored lamb. These he placed in the care of his sons. Then he put a three-
day-journey's distance between him and Yaakov. Yaakov tended the rest of
37 Lavan's flock. Yaakov took fresh shoots of poplar, almond, and plane trees and
38 peeled white strips in them, exposing the white of the shoots. Then he set the
peeled shoots in all the water troughs so that they would be in front of the
flocks when they came to drink. They would mate when they came to drink,
39 and since they mated by the shoots, they bore streaked, speckled, and spotted
40 young.[73] Yaakov set apart the young of the flock, and he made the others
belonging to Lavan face the streaked and dark-colored animals. Thus he bred
separate flocks for himself, and he did not let them breed with Lavan's flocks.
41 Whenever the stronger animals were mating, Yaakov would place the shoots
42 in the troughs facing them so that they mated facing the shoots. But the

70 | The name Yissakhar resonates with *natan sekhari* (has rewarded me).

71 | The name Zevulun resonates with *zeved* (gift) and *yizbeleni* (will honor me).

72 | *Yosef* is the word used by Raḥel to denote "grant." The name also resonates with *asaf* (has taken away, v. 23).

73 | The animals produced offspring that exhibited the designs seen during the mating process.

יז יח וַיִּשְׁמַע אֱלֹהִים אֶל־לֵאָה וַתַּהַר וַתֵּלֶד לְיַעֲקֹב בֵּן חֲמִישִׁי: וַתֹּאמֶר
לֵאָה נָתַן אֱלֹהִים שְׂכָרִי אֲשֶׁר־נָתַתִּי שִׁפְחָתִי לְאִישִׁי וַתִּקְרָא שְׁמוֹ
יט כ יִשָּׂשכָר: וַתַּהַר עוֹד לֵאָה וַתֵּלֶד בֵּן־שִׁשִּׁי לְיַעֲקֹב: וַתֹּאמֶר לֵאָה זְבָדַנִי
אֱלֹהִים ׀ אֹתִי זֵבֶד טוֹב הַפַּעַם יִזְבְּלֵנִי אִישִׁי כִּי־יָלַדְתִּי לוֹ שִׁשָּׁה בָנִים
כא וַתִּקְרָא אֶת־שְׁמוֹ זְבֻלוּן: וְאַחַר יָלְדָה בַּת וַתִּקְרָא אֶת־שְׁמָהּ דִּינָה:
כב וַיִּזְכֹּר אֱלֹהִים אֶת־רָחֵל וַיִּשְׁמַע אֵלֶיהָ אֱלֹהִים וַיִּפְתַּח אֶת־רַחְמָהּ: כח
כג כד וַתַּהַר וַתֵּלֶד בֵּן וַתֹּאמֶר אָסַף אֱלֹהִים אֶת־חֶרְפָּתִי: וַתִּקְרָא אֶת־שְׁמוֹ
כה יוֹסֵף לֵאמֹר יֹסֵף יְהוָה לִי בֵּן אַחֵר: וַיְהִי כַּאֲשֶׁר יָלְדָה רָחֵל אֶת־יוֹסֵף
כו וַיֹּאמֶר יַעֲקֹב אֶל־לָבָן שַׁלְּחֵנִי וְאֵלְכָה אֶל־מְקוֹמִי וּלְאַרְצִי: תְּנָה אֶת־
נָשַׁי וְאֶת־יְלָדַי אֲשֶׁר עָבַדְתִּי אֹתְךָ בָּהֵן וְאֵלֵכָה כִּי אַתָּה יָדַעְתָּ אֶת־
כז עֲבֹדָתִי אֲשֶׁר עֲבַדְתִּיךָ: וַיֹּאמֶר אֵלָיו לָבָן אִם־נָא מָצָאתִי חֵן בְּעֵינֶיךָ
כח נִחַשְׁתִּי וַיְבָרְכֵנִי יְהוָה בִּגְלָלֶךָ: וַיֹּאמַר נָקְבָה שְׂכָרְךָ עָלַי וְאֶתֵּנָה: חמישי
כט וַיֹּאמֶר אֵלָיו אַתָּה יָדַעְתָּ אֵת אֲשֶׁר עֲבַדְתִּיךָ וְאֵת אֲשֶׁר־הָיָה מִקְנְךָ
ל אִתִּי: כִּי מְעַט אֲשֶׁר־הָיָה לְךָ לְפָנַי וַיִּפְרֹץ לָרֹב וַיְבָרֶךְ יְהוָה אֹתְךָ לְרַגְלִי
לא וְעַתָּה מָתַי אֶעֱשֶׂה גַם־אָנֹכִי לְבֵיתִי: וַיֹּאמֶר מָה אֶתֶּן־לָךְ וַיֹּאמֶר יַעֲקֹב
לֹא־תִתֶּן־לִי מְאוּמָה אִם־תַּעֲשֶׂה־לִּי הַדָּבָר הַזֶּה אָשׁוּבָה אֶרְעֶה צֹאנְךָ
לב אֶשְׁמֹר: אֶעֱבֹר בְּכָל־צֹאנְךָ הַיּוֹם הָסֵר מִשָּׁם כָּל־שֶׂה ׀ נָקֹד וְטָלוּא
לג וְכָל־שֶׂה־חוּם בַּכְּשָׂבִים וְטָלוּא וְנָקֹד בָּעִזִּים וְהָיָה שְׂכָרִי: וְעָנְתָה־בִּי
צִדְקָתִי בְּיוֹם מָחָר כִּי־תָבוֹא עַל־שְׂכָרִי לְפָנֶיךָ כֹּל אֲשֶׁר־אֵינֶנּוּ נָקֹד
לד וְטָלוּא בָּעִזִּים וְחוּם בַּכְּשָׂבִים גָּנוּב הוּא אִתִּי: וַיֹּאמֶר לָבָן הֵן לוּ יְהִי
לה כִדְבָרֶךָ: וַיָּסַר בַּיּוֹם הַהוּא אֶת־הַתְּיָשִׁים הָעֲקֻדִּים וְהַטְּלֻאִים וְאֵת
כָּל־הָעִזִּים הַנְּקֻדּוֹת וְהַטְּלֻאֹת כֹּל אֲשֶׁר־לָבָן בּוֹ וְכָל־חוּם בַּכְּשָׂבִים
לו וַיִּתֵּן בְּיַד־בָּנָיו: וַיָּשֶׂם דֶּרֶךְ שְׁלֹשֶׁת יָמִים בֵּינוֹ וּבֵין יַעֲקֹב וְיַעֲקֹב רֹעֶה
לז אֶת־צֹאן לָבָן הַנּוֹתָרֹת: וַיִּקַּח־לוֹ יַעֲקֹב מַקַּל לִבְנֶה לַח וְלוּז וְעַרְמוֹן
לח וַיְפַצֵּל בָּהֵן פְּצָלוֹת לְבָנוֹת מַחְשֹׂף הַלָּבָן אֲשֶׁר עַל־הַמַּקְלוֹת: וַיַּצֵּג
אֶת־הַמַּקְלוֹת אֲשֶׁר פִּצֵּל בָּרֳהָטִים בְּשִׁקְתוֹת הַמָּיִם אֲשֶׁר תָּבֹאןָ הַצֹּאן
לט לִשְׁתּוֹת לְנֹכַח הַצֹּאן וַיֵּחַמְנָה בְּבֹאָן לִשְׁתּוֹת: וַיֶּחֱמוּ הַצֹּאן אֶל־
מ הַמַּקְלוֹת וַתֵּלַדְןָ הַצֹּאן עֲקֻדִּים נְקֻדִּים וּטְלֻאִים: וְהַכְּשָׂבִים הִפְרִיד
יַעֲקֹב וַיִּתֵּן פְּנֵי הַצֹּאן אֶל־עָקֹד וְכָל־חוּם בְּצֹאן לָבָן וַיָּשֶׁת לוֹ עֲדָרִים
מא לְבַדּוֹ וְלֹא שָׁתָם עַל־צֹאן לָבָן: וְהָיָה בְּכָל־יַחֵם הַצֹּאן הַמְקֻשָּׁרוֹת
וְשָׂם יַעֲקֹב אֶת־הַמַּקְלוֹת לְעֵינֵי הַצֹּאן בָּרְהָטִים לְיַחְמֵנָּה בַּמַּקְלוֹת:
מב וּבְהַעֲטִיף הַצֹּאן לֹא יָשִׂים וְהָיָה הָעֲטֻפִים לְלָבָן וְהַקְּשֻׁרִים לְיַעֲקֹב:

weaker animals he did not put there, so the weaker went to Lavan and the
43 stronger to Yaakov. Thus the man's wealth swelled into a fortune. He had large
31 1 flocks, female and male servants, camels and donkeys. Yaakov heard that
Lavan's sons were saying, "Yaakov has taken everything our father owned; of
2 what belonged to our father, he has made all these riches." And Yaakov saw
3 that Lavan's manner toward him was not what it had been. The LORD said to
Yaakov, "Go back to the land of your fathers where you were born; I will be
4 with you." So Yaakov sent word to Raḥel and Leah to come out to the field
5 where his flock was. He said to them, "I see that your father's manner toward
6 me is not what it used to be. But the God of my father has been with me. You
7 well know how I have worked for your father with all my strength. Your father
cheated me, changing my wages ten times, but God has not let him harm me.
8 If he said, 'The speckled animals shall be your hire,' then all the flock would
give birth to speckled young. If he said, 'The streaked animals shall be your
9 hire,' then all the flock would give birth to streaked young. God has taken
10 your father's livestock and given it to me. Once, during the breeding season,
I had a dream: I saw that the rams mounting the flock were streaked, speckled,
11 or spotted. And in the dream an angel of God said to me, 'Yaakov.' I replied,
12 'Here I am.' He said, 'Look up and see that all the rams mounting the flock
are streaked, speckled, or spotted, for I have seen all that Lavan is doing to
13 you. I am the God of Beit El, where you anointed a pillar and made a vow to
Me. Now – leave this land at once and return to the land where you were
14 born.'" Raḥel and Leah answered him, "Do we still have a share in the
15 inheritance of our father's estate? He treats us like strangers. He has sold us
16 and spent the money. All the wealth that God has taken from our father
17 belongs to us and our children. So do whatever God has told you." So Yaakov
18 put his children and wives on camels and drove all the livestock and wealth
he had accumulated – the livestock he had acquired in Padan Aram – heading
19 for his father Yitzḥak in the land of Canaan. Meanwhile, when Lavan had gone
20 to shear his sheep, Raḥel had stolen her father's household gods. Yaakov
21 deceived Lavan the Aramean by not telling him that he was running away. He
fled with all he had, crossed the Euphrates, and headed for the hill country of
22 23 Gilad. On the third day, Lavan was told that Yaakov had fled. Taking his
kinsmen with him, he pursued him for seven days, catching up with him in
24 the hill country of Gilad. That night God came to Lavan the Aramean in a
dream and said to him, "Take care not to say anything to Yaakov for good or
25 for bad." When Lavan overtook him, Yaakov had pitched his tent in the hill
country, and Lavan and his kinsmen too encamped in the hill country of
26 Gilad. Lavan said to Yaakov, "What have you done? You have deceived me,

מג וַיִּפְרֹץ הָאִישׁ מְאֹד מְאֹד וַיְהִי־לוֹ צֹאן רַבּוֹת וּשְׁפָחוֹת וַעֲבָדִים וּגְמַלִּים
לא א וַחֲמֹרִים: וַיִּשְׁמַע אֶת־דִּבְרֵי בְנֵי־לָבָן לֵאמֹר לָקַח יַעֲקֹב אֵת כָּל־אֲשֶׁר
ב לְאָבִינוּ וּמֵאֲשֶׁר לְאָבִינוּ עָשָׂה אֵת כָּל־הַכָּבֹד הַזֶּה: וַיַּרְא יַעֲקֹב אֶת־
ג פְּנֵי לָבָן וְהִנֵּה אֵינֶנּוּ עִמּוֹ כִּתְמוֹל שִׁלְשׁוֹם: וַיֹּאמֶר יהוה אֶל־יַעֲקֹב כט
ד שׁוּב אֶל־אֶרֶץ אֲבוֹתֶיךָ וּלְמוֹלַדְתֶּךָ וְאֶהְיֶה עִמָּךְ: וַיִּשְׁלַח יַעֲקֹב וַיִּקְרָא
ה לְרָחֵל וּלְלֵאָה הַשָּׂדֶה אֶל־צֹאנוֹ: וַיֹּאמֶר לָהֶן רֹאֶה אָנֹכִי אֶת־פְּנֵי
ו אֲבִיכֶן כִּי־אֵינֶנּוּ אֵלַי כִּתְמֹל שִׁלְשֹׁם וֵאלֹהֵי אָבִי הָיָה עִמָּדִי: וְאַתֵּנָה
ז יְדַעְתֶּן כִּי בְּכָל־כֹּחִי עָבַדְתִּי אֶת־אֲבִיכֶן: וַאֲבִיכֶן הֵתֶל בִּי וְהֶחֱלִף
ח אֶת־מַשְׂכֻּרְתִּי עֲשֶׂרֶת מֹנִים וְלֹא־נְתָנוֹ אֱלֹהִים לְהָרַע עִמָּדִי: אִם־כֹּה
יֹאמַר נְקֻדִּים יִהְיֶה שְׂכָרֶךָ וְיָלְדוּ כָל־הַצֹּאן נְקֻדִּים וְאִם־כֹּה יֹאמַר
ט עֲקֻדִּים יִהְיֶה שְׂכָרֶךָ וְיָלְדוּ כָל־הַצֹּאן עֲקֻדִּים: וַיַּצֵּל אֱלֹהִים אֶת־מִקְנֵה
י אֲבִיכֶם וַיִּתֶּן־לִי: וַיְהִי בְּעֵת יַחֵם הַצֹּאן וָאֶשָּׂא עֵינַי וָאֵרֶא בַּחֲלוֹם וְהִנֵּה
יא הָעַתֻּדִים הָעֹלִים עַל־הַצֹּאן עֲקֻדִּים נְקֻדִּים וּבְרֻדִּים: וַיֹּאמֶר אֵלַי
יב מַלְאַךְ הָאֱלֹהִים בַּחֲלוֹם יַעֲקֹב וָאֹמַר הִנֵּנִי: וַיֹּאמֶר שָׂא־נָא עֵינֶיךָ
וּרְאֵה כָּל־הָעַתֻּדִים הָעֹלִים עַל־הַצֹּאן עֲקֻדִּים נְקֻדִּים וּבְרֻדִּים כִּי
יג רָאִיתִי אֵת כָּל־אֲשֶׁר לָבָן עֹשֶׂה לָּךְ: אָנֹכִי הָאֵל בֵּית־אֵל אֲשֶׁר מָשַׁחְתָּ
שָּׁם מַצֵּבָה אֲשֶׁר נָדַרְתָּ לִּי שָׁם נֶדֶר עַתָּה קוּם צֵא מִן־הָאָרֶץ הַזֹּאת
יד וְשׁוּב אֶל־אֶרֶץ מוֹלַדְתֶּךָ: וַתַּעַן רָחֵל וְלֵאָה וַתֹּאמַרְנָה לוֹ הַעוֹד לָנוּ
טו חֵלֶק וְנַחֲלָה בְּבֵית אָבִינוּ: הֲלוֹא נָכְרִיּוֹת נֶחְשַׁבְנוּ לוֹ כִּי מְכָרָנוּ וַיֹּאכַל
טז גַּם־אָכוֹל אֶת־כַּסְפֵּנוּ: כִּי כָל־הָעֹשֶׁר אֲשֶׁר הִצִּיל אֱלֹהִים מֵאָבִינוּ לָנוּ
יז הוּא וּלְבָנֵינוּ וְעַתָּה כֹּל אֲשֶׁר אָמַר אֱלֹהִים אֵלֶיךָ עֲשֵׂה: וַיָּקָם יַעֲקֹב ששי
יח וַיִּשָּׂא אֶת־בָּנָיו וְאֶת־נָשָׁיו עַל־הַגְּמַלִּים: וַיִּנְהַג אֶת־כָּל־מִקְנֵהוּ וְאֶת־
כָּל־רְכֻשׁוֹ אֲשֶׁר רָכָשׁ מִקְנֵה קִנְיָנוֹ אֲשֶׁר רָכַשׁ בְּפַדַּן אֲרָם לָבוֹא אֶל־
יט יִצְחָק אָבִיו אַרְצָה כְּנָעַן: וְלָבָן הָלַךְ לִגְזֹז אֶת־צֹאנוֹ וַתִּגְנֹב רָחֵל
כ אֶת־הַתְּרָפִים אֲשֶׁר לְאָבִיהָ: וַיִּגְנֹב יַעֲקֹב אֶת־לֵב לָבָן הָאֲרַמִּי עַל־בְּלִי
כא הִגִּיד לוֹ כִּי בֹרֵחַ הוּא: וַיִּבְרַח הוּא וְכָל־אֲשֶׁר־לוֹ וַיָּקָם וַיַּעֲבֹר אֶת־
כב הַנָּהָר וַיָּשֶׂם אֶת־פָּנָיו הַר הַגִּלְעָד: וַיֻּגַּד לְלָבָן בַּיּוֹם הַשְּׁלִישִׁי כִּי בָרַח
כג יַעֲקֹב: וַיִּקַּח אֶת־אֶחָיו עִמּוֹ וַיִּרְדֹּף אַחֲרָיו דֶּרֶךְ שִׁבְעַת יָמִים וַיַּדְבֵּק
כד אֹתוֹ בְּהַר הַגִּלְעָד: וַיָּבֹא אֱלֹהִים אֶל־לָבָן הָאֲרַמִּי בַּחֲלֹם הַלָּיְלָה
כה וַיֹּאמֶר לוֹ הִשָּׁמֶר לְךָ פֶּן־תְּדַבֵּר עִם־יַעֲקֹב מִטּוֹב עַד־רָע: וַיַּשֵּׂג לָבָן
אֶת־יַעֲקֹב וְיַעֲקֹב תָּקַע אֶת־אָהֳלוֹ בָּהָר וְלָבָן תָּקַע אֶת־אֶחָיו בְּהַר
כו הַגִּלְעָד: וַיֹּאמֶר לָבָן לְיַעֲקֹב מֶה עָשִׂיתָ וַתִּגְנֹב אֶת־לְבָבִי וַתְּנַהֵג אֶת־

27 and carried off my daughters like captives of the sword. Why did you leave
secretly? Why did you deceive me by not telling me? I would have sent you
28 off with celebration and song, with tambourines and harps. You did not even
let me kiss my grandchildren and daughters goodbye. You have behaved
29 foolishly. I have the power to harm you, but last night your father's God spoke
to me and said, 'Take care not to say anything to Yaakov for good or for bad.'
30 I realize you left because you longed so much for your father's house. But why
31 did you steal my gods?" Yaakov answered Lavan, saying, "I was afraid; I
32 thought you would take your daughters away from me by force. But if you
find your gods with anyone here, they shall not live. In the presence of our
kinsmen, see if there is anything of yours here, and take it." Yaakov did not
33 know that Raḥel was the one who had stolen them. So Lavan went into
Yaakov's tent, Leah's tent, and the tents of the two female slaves, but found
34 nothing. Leaving Leah's tent, he entered Raḥel's. But Raḥel had taken the
household gods and put them inside a camel cushion, and was sitting on
35 them; and Lavan rummaged through the tent but found nothing. She said to
her father, "Do not be angry, my lord, but I cannot get up for you, for the way
of women is with me now." So he searched but did not find his household
36 gods. Yaakov became indignant and confronted Lavan. "What is my crime?"
37 he asked Lavan. "What wrong did I do that you come chasing after me? You
have rummaged through all my possessions. What have you found that
belongs to your house? Put it here in front of my kinsmen and yours and let
38 them decide between the two of us! For the twenty years I was with you, your
sheep and goats did not miscarry. Not once did I take a ram from your flock
39 as food. I never brought you an animal torn by wild beasts. I bore the loss
myself. Whether it was stolen by day or by night you demanded payment
40 from me. By day I was ravaged by the heat; at night by the freezing cold. Sleep
41 fled from my eyes. Twenty years I spent working in your household – fourteen
for your two daughters and six for your flock – and ten times you changed my
42 wages. Had the God of my father – the God of Avraham, the Fear of Yitzḥak
– not been with me, you would have sent me away empty-handed. But God
43 saw my plight and the toil of my hands, and He rebuked you last night." Then
Lavan spoke up and said to Yaakov, "The daughters are my daughters. The
children are my children. The flocks are my flocks. All that you see is mine.
But what can I do now about my daughters or the children they have borne?
44 Come now, let us make a covenant, you and I, and let it be a witness between
45 46 us." So Yaakov took a stone and set it up as a pillar. Yaakov said to his kinsmen,
"Gather stones." They took stones and made a mound, and there by the
47 mound they ate. Lavan called it Yegar Sahaduta, while Yaakov called it Galed.[74]
48 Lavan said, "This mound is a witness between me and you this day." That is
49 why it is called Galed. It is also called Mitzpa because he said, "May the Lord
50 keep watch between me and you when we are out of each other's sight.[75] If

---

74 | Both names mean "mound of testimony," the former in Aramaic, the latter in Hebrew (cf. also the name Gilad in v. 25).

75 | The name Mitzpa derives from the same root as *yitzef* (keep watch).

כז בְּנֹתַי כִּשְׁבֻיוֹת חָרֶב: לָמָּה נַחְבֵּאתָ לִבְרֹחַ וַתִּגְנֹב אֹתִי וְלֹא־הִגַּדְתָּ לִּי
כח וָאֲשַׁלֵּחֲךָ בְּשִׂמְחָה וּבְשִׁרִים בְּתֹף וּבְכִנּוֹר: וְלֹא נְטַשְׁתַּנִי לְנַשֵּׁק לְבָנַי
כט וְלִבְנֹתָי עַתָּה הִסְכַּלְתָּ עֲשׂוֹ: יֶשׁ־לְאֵל יָדִי לַעֲשׂוֹת עִמָּכֶם רָע וֵאלֹהֵי
אֲבִיכֶם אֶמֶשׁ | אָמַר אֵלַי לֵאמֹר הִשָּׁמֶר לְךָ מִדַּבֵּר עִם־יַעֲקֹב מִטּוֹב
ל עַד־רָע: וְעַתָּה הָלֹךְ הָלַכְתָּ כִּי־נִכְסֹף נִכְסַפְתָּה לְבֵית אָבִיךָ לָמָּה
לא גָנַבְתָּ אֶת־אֱלֹהָי: וַיַּעַן יַעֲקֹב וַיֹּאמֶר לְלָבָן כִּי יָרֵאתִי כִּי אָמַרְתִּי פֶּן־
לב תִּגְזֹל אֶת־בְּנוֹתֶיךָ מֵעִמִּי: עִם אֲשֶׁר תִּמְצָא אֶת־אֱלֹהֶיךָ לֹא יִחְיֶה נֶגֶד
אַחֵינוּ הַכֶּר־לְךָ מָה עִמָּדִי וְקַח־לָךְ וְלֹא־יָדַע יַעֲקֹב כִּי רָחֵל גְּנָבָתַם:
לג וַיָּבֹא לָבָן בְּאֹהֶל־יַעֲקֹב | וּבְאֹהֶל לֵאָה וּבְאֹהֶל שְׁתֵּי הָאֲמָהֹת וְלֹא
לד מָצָא וַיֵּצֵא מֵאֹהֶל לֵאָה וַיָּבֹא בְּאֹהֶל רָחֵל: וְרָחֵל לָקְחָה אֶת־הַתְּרָפִים
וַתְּשִׂמֵם בְּכַר הַגָּמָל וַתֵּשֶׁב עֲלֵיהֶם וַיְמַשֵּׁשׁ לָבָן אֶת־כָּל־הָאֹהֶל וְלֹא
לה מָצָא: וַתֹּאמֶר אֶל־אָבִיהָ אַל־יִחַר בְּעֵינֵי אֲדֹנִי כִּי לוֹא אוּכַל לָקוּם
לו מִפָּנֶיךָ כִּי־דֶרֶךְ נָשִׁים לִי וַיְחַפֵּשׂ וְלֹא מָצָא אֶת־הַתְּרָפִים: וַיִּחַר לְיַעֲקֹב
וַיָּרֶב בְּלָבָן וַיַּעַן יַעֲקֹב וַיֹּאמֶר לְלָבָן מַה־פִּשְׁעִי מַה חַטָּאתִי כִּי דָלַקְתָּ
לז אַחֲרָי: כִּי־מִשַּׁשְׁתָּ אֶת־כָּל־כֵּלַי מַה־מָּצָאתָ מִכֹּל כְּלֵי־בֵיתֶךָ שִׂים כֹּה
לח נֶגֶד אַחַי וְאַחֶיךָ וְיוֹכִיחוּ בֵּין שְׁנֵינוּ: זֶה עֶשְׂרִים שָׁנָה אָנֹכִי עִמָּךְ רְחֵלֶיךָ
לט וְעִזֶּיךָ לֹא שִׁכֵּלוּ וְאֵילֵי צֹאנְךָ לֹא אָכָלְתִּי: טְרֵפָה לֹא־הֵבֵאתִי אֵלֶיךָ
מ אָנֹכִי אֲחַטֶּנָּה מִיָּדִי תְּבַקְשֶׁנָּה גְּנֻבְתִי יוֹם וּגְנֻבְתִי לָיְלָה: הָיִיתִי בַיּוֹם
מא אֲכָלַנִי חֹרֶב וְקֶרַח בַּלָּיְלָה וַתִּדַּד שְׁנָתִי מֵעֵינָי: זֶה־לִּי עֶשְׂרִים שָׁנָה
בְּבֵיתֶךָ עֲבַדְתִּיךָ אַרְבַּע־עֶשְׂרֵה שָׁנָה בִּשְׁתֵּי בְנֹתֶיךָ וְשֵׁשׁ שָׁנִים בְּצֹאנֶךָ
מב וַתַּחֲלֵף אֶת־מַשְׂכֻּרְתִּי עֲשֶׂרֶת מֹנִים: לוּלֵי אֱלֹהֵי אָבִי אֱלֹהֵי אַבְרָהָם
וּפַחַד יִצְחָק הָיָה לִי כִּי עַתָּה רֵיקָם שִׁלַּחְתָּנִי אֶת־עָנְיִי וְאֶת־יְגִיעַ כַּפַּי
מג רָאָה אֱלֹהִים וַיּוֹכַח אָמֶשׁ: וַיַּעַן לָבָן וַיֹּאמֶר אֶל־יַעֲקֹב הַבָּנוֹת בְּנֹתַי שביעי
וְהַבָּנִים בָּנַי וְהַצֹּאן צֹאנִי וְכֹל אֲשֶׁר־אַתָּה רֹאֶה לִי־הוּא וְלִבְנֹתַי מָה־
מד אֶעֱשֶׂה לָאֵלֶּה הַיּוֹם אוֹ לִבְנֵיהֶן אֲשֶׁר יָלָדוּ: וְעַתָּה לְכָה נִכְרְתָה בְרִית
מה אֲנִי וָאָתָּה וְהָיָה לְעֵד בֵּינִי וּבֵינֶךָ: וַיִּקַּח יַעֲקֹב אָבֶן וַיְרִימֶהָ מַצֵּבָה:
מו וַיֹּאמֶר יַעֲקֹב לְאֶחָיו לִקְטוּ אֲבָנִים וַיִּקְחוּ אֲבָנִים וַיַּעֲשׂוּ־גָל וַיֹּאכְלוּ
מז שָׁם עַל־הַגָּל: וַיִּקְרָא־לוֹ לָבָן יְגַר שָׂהֲדוּתָא וְיַעֲקֹב קָרָא לוֹ גַּלְעֵד:
מח וַיֹּאמֶר לָבָן הַגַּל הַזֶּה עֵד בֵּינִי וּבֵינְךָ הַיּוֹם עַל־כֵּן קָרָא־שְׁמוֹ גַּלְעֵד:
מט וְהַמִּצְפָּה אֲשֶׁר אָמַר יִצֶף יְהוָה בֵּינִי וּבֵינֶךָ כִּי נִסָּתֵר אִישׁ מֵרֵעֵהוּ:
נ אִם־תְּעַנֶּה אֶת־בְּנֹתַי וְאִם־תִּקַּח נָשִׁים עַל־בְּנֹתַי אֵין אִישׁ עִמָּנוּ רְאֵה

you mistreat my daughters or take other wives besides my daughters, even
though no one else is present, remember that God is the witness between me
51 and you." Lavan said to Yaakov, "Here is the mound and here is the pillar I
52 have set up between us. This mound is a witness, and the pillar is a witness,
that I will not go past this mound on your side and that you will not go past
53 this mound and pillar on my side with intent to do harm. May the God of
Avraham, the god of Naḥor, and the god of their father be our judge." Yaakov
54 swore by the Fear of his father Yitzḥak. He offered a sacrifice on the hill and
invited his kinsmen to break bread. And they ate and spent the night upon
55 that hill. Lavan rose early the next morning. He kissed his grandchildren and
daughters goodbye and blessed them. Lavan then left to return home.
32 1 Yaakov continued on his way – and angels of God encountered him. When
2 he saw them, Yaakov said, "This is God's own camp," and he named the place
Maḥanayim.[76]
3 Yaakov sent messengers ahead of him to his brother Esav in the land of VAYISHLAḤ
4 Se'ir, the country of Edom. He instructed them, "Say the following to my lord
Esav: 'Your servant Yaakov says, "I have been staying with Lavan; until now
5 I have remained there. And I have acquired cattle, donkeys, sheep, and male
and female servants. I am sending this message to my lord to find favor in
6 your eyes."'" And when the messengers returned to Yaakov, they said, "We
came to your brother Esav. He is on his way to meet you, and with him, four
7 hundred men." Yaakov was acutely afraid and distressed. He divided the
people with him into two camps,[77] along with the flocks, the cattle, and the
8 camels. "If Esav comes and attacks one camp," he thought, "the other camp
9 may still survive." Then Yaakov prayed, "God of my father Avraham and
God of my father Yitzḥak, LORD, You who said to me, 'Go back to the land
10 where you were born and I will deal well with you,' I am unworthy of all the
kindnesses and the faithfulness that You have bestowed upon Your servant.
When I crossed the Jordan I had only my staff, and now I have become two
11 camps. Rescue me, I pray, from my brother's hand, from the hand of Esav. I
12 am afraid he will come and kill us all, mothers and children alike. Yet You said,
'I will deal well with you and make your descendants countless, like the sand
13 of the sea.'" He spent the night there. Then, from what he had at hand, he
14 selected a gift for his brother Esav: two hundred female goats, twenty male
15 goats, two hundred ewes, twenty rams, thirty milk camels and their young,
16 forty cows, ten bulls, twenty female donkeys, and ten male donkeys. He put
them in the care of his servants, each herd by itself, and he told the servants,
17 "Go on ahead of me. Keep a space between the herds." He instructed the first,
"When my brother Esav meets you and asks, 'To whom do you belong?
18 Where are you going? Who owns all these animals ahead of you?' you must
say, 'They belong to your servant Yaakov; they are a gift sent to my lord
19 Esav – and he is coming behind us.'" He likewise instructed the second and

76 | Literally "two camps."
77 | Cf. previous note.

נא אֱלֹהִים עֵד בֵּינִי וּבֵינֶךָ׃ וַיֹּאמֶר לָבָן לְיַעֲקֹב הִנֵּה ׀ הַגַּל הַזֶּה וְהִנֵּה
נב הַמַּצֵּבָה אֲשֶׁר יָרִיתִי בֵּינִי וּבֵינֶךָ׃ עֵד הַגַּל הַזֶּה וְעֵדָה הַמַּצֵּבָה אִם־אָנִי
לֹא־אֶעֱבֹר אֵלֶיךָ אֶת־הַגַּל הַזֶּה וְאִם־אַתָּה לֹא־תַעֲבֹר אֵלַי אֶת־
נג הַגַּל הַזֶּה וְאֶת־הַמַּצֵּבָה הַזֹּאת לְרָעָה׃ אֱלֹהֵי אַבְרָהָם וֵאלֹהֵי נָחוֹר
נד יִשְׁפְּטוּ בֵינֵינוּ אֱלֹהֵי אֲבִיהֶם וַיִּשָּׁבַע יַעֲקֹב בְּפַחַד אָבִיו יִצְחָק׃ וַיִּזְבַּח
יַעֲקֹב זֶבַח בָּהָר וַיִּקְרָא לְאֶחָיו לֶאֱכָל־לָחֶם וַיֹּאכְלוּ לֶחֶם וַיָּלִינוּ בָּהָר׃
נה וַיַּשְׁכֵּם לָבָן בַּבֹּקֶר וַיְנַשֵּׁק לְבָנָיו וְלִבְנוֹתָיו וַיְבָרֶךְ אֶתְהֶם וַיֵּלֶךְ וַיָּשָׁב מפטיר
לב א ב לָבָן לִמְקֹמוֹ׃ וְיַעֲקֹב הָלַךְ לְדַרְכּוֹ וַיִּפְגְּעוּ־בוֹ מַלְאֲכֵי אֱלֹהִים׃ וַיֹּאמֶר
יַעֲקֹב כַּאֲשֶׁר רָאָם מַחֲנֵה אֱלֹהִים זֶה וַיִּקְרָא שֵׁם־הַמָּקוֹם הַהוּא
מַחֲנָיִם׃

ג וַיִּשְׁלַח יַעֲקֹב מַלְאָכִים לְפָנָיו אֶל־עֵשָׂו אָחִיו אַרְצָה שֵׂעִיר שְׂדֵה אֱדוֹם׃ ל וישלח
ד וַיְצַו אֹתָם לֵאמֹר כֹּה תֹאמְרוּן לַאדֹנִי לְעֵשָׂו כֹּה אָמַר עַבְדְּךָ יַעֲקֹב
ה עִם־לָבָן גַּרְתִּי וָאֵחַר עַד־עָתָּה׃ וַיְהִי־לִי שׁוֹר וַחֲמוֹר צֹאן וְעֶבֶד וְשִׁפְחָה
ו וָאֶשְׁלְחָה לְהַגִּיד לַאדֹנִי לִמְצֹא־חֵן בְּעֵינֶיךָ׃ וַיָּשֻׁבוּ הַמַּלְאָכִים אֶל־
יַעֲקֹב לֵאמֹר בָּאנוּ אֶל־אָחִיךָ אֶל־עֵשָׂו וְגַם הֹלֵךְ לִקְרָאתְךָ וְאַרְבַּע־
ז מֵאוֹת אִישׁ עִמּוֹ׃ וַיִּירָא יַעֲקֹב מְאֹד וַיֵּצֶר לוֹ וַיַּחַץ אֶת־הָעָם אֲשֶׁר־אִתּוֹ
ח וְאֶת־הַצֹּאן וְאֶת־הַבָּקָר וְהַגְּמַלִּים לִשְׁנֵי מַחֲנוֹת׃ וַיֹּאמֶר אִם־יָבוֹא
עֵשָׂו אֶל־הַמַּחֲנֶה הָאַחַת וְהִכָּהוּ וְהָיָה הַמַּחֲנֶה הַנִּשְׁאָר לִפְלֵיטָה׃
ט וַיֹּאמֶר יַעֲקֹב אֱלֹהֵי אָבִי אַבְרָהָם וֵאלֹהֵי אָבִי יִצְחָק יְהוָה הָאֹמֵר
י אֵלַי שׁוּב לְאַרְצְךָ וּלְמוֹלַדְתְּךָ וְאֵיטִיבָה עִמָּךְ׃ קָטֹנְתִּי מִכֹּל הַחֲסָדִים
וּמִכָּל־הָאֱמֶת אֲשֶׁר עָשִׂיתָ אֶת־עַבְדֶּךָ כִּי בְמַקְלִי עָבַרְתִּי אֶת־הַיַּרְדֵּן
יא הַזֶּה וְעַתָּה הָיִיתִי לִשְׁנֵי מַחֲנוֹת׃ הַצִּילֵנִי נָא מִיַּד אָחִי מִיַּד עֵשָׂו כִּי־
יב יָרֵא אָנֹכִי אֹתוֹ פֶּן־יָבוֹא וְהִכַּנִי אֵם עַל־בָּנִים׃ וְאַתָּה אָמַרְתָּ הֵיטֵב
יג אֵיטִיב עִמָּךְ וְשַׂמְתִּי אֶת־זַרְעֲךָ כְּחוֹל הַיָּם אֲשֶׁר לֹא־יִסָּפֵר מֵרֹב׃ וַיָּלֶן שני
יד שָׁם בַּלַּיְלָה הַהוּא וַיִּקַּח מִן־הַבָּא בְיָדוֹ מִנְחָה לְעֵשָׂו אָחִיו׃ עִזִּים
טו מָאתַיִם וּתְיָשִׁים עֶשְׂרִים רְחֵלִים מָאתַיִם וְאֵילִים עֶשְׂרִים׃ גְּמַלִּים
מֵינִיקוֹת וּבְנֵיהֶם שְׁלֹשִׁים פָּרוֹת אַרְבָּעִים וּפָרִים עֲשָׂרָה אֲתֹנֹת עֶשְׂרִים
טז וַעְיָרִם עֲשָׂרָה׃ וַיִּתֵּן בְּיַד־עֲבָדָיו עֵדֶר עֵדֶר לְבַדּוֹ וַיֹּאמֶר אֶל־עֲבָדָיו
יז עִבְרוּ לְפָנַי וְרֶוַח תָּשִׂימוּ בֵּין עֵדֶר וּבֵין עֵדֶר׃ וַיְצַו אֶת־הָרִאשׁוֹן לֵאמֹר
כִּי יִפְגָּשְׁךָ עֵשָׂו אָחִי וּשְׁאֵלְךָ לֵאמֹר לְמִי־אַתָּה וְאָנָה תֵלֵךְ וּלְמִי אֵלֶּה
יח לְפָנֶיךָ׃ וְאָמַרְתָּ לְעַבְדְּךָ לְיַעֲקֹב מִנְחָה הִוא שְׁלוּחָה לַאדֹנִי לְעֵשָׂו
יט וְהִנֵּה גַם־הוּא אַחֲרֵינוּ׃ וַיְצַו גַּם אֶת־הַשֵּׁנִי גַּם אֶת־הַשְּׁלִישִׁי גַּם אֶת־

third and all the others who followed the herds, "You shall say the same thing
20 to Esav when you meet him. Also say, 'Your servant Yaakov is coming behind
us.'" He thought, "I will pacify him with these gifts I am sending on ahead.
21 Then I will face him. Perhaps he will accept me." So the gifts went on ahead
22 of him, while he remained in the camp that night. That night Yaakov got up
and took his two wives, two maidservants, and eleven sons and crossed the
23 ford of the Yabok. He took them and crossed the stream with them and then
24 brought across all that he had. And Yaakov was left alone. And a man wrestled
25 with him until dawn. When he saw that he could not overpower him, the man
wrenched Yaakov's hip in its socket so that the socket of Yaakov's hip was
26 strained as he wrestled with the man. "Let me go," said the man, "for dawn is
27 breaking." But he replied, "I will not let you go unless you bless me." "What
28 is your name?" asked the man. "Yaakov," he replied. "No longer will your
name be Yaakov, but Yisrael," said the man, "for you have struggled with God
29 and with men and have prevailed."[78] Yaakov asked, "Please tell me your name."
30 But he said, "Why do you ask my name?" and he blessed him there.[79] Yaakov
named the place Peniel, "for I have seen God face-to-face and yet my life has
31 been spared."[80] The sun was rising on him as he moved on from Penuel,
32 limping on his thigh. That is why, to this day, the Israelites do not eat the
sciatic nerve by the hip socket: because he wrenched Yaakov's hip socket at
33 1 the sciatic nerve. Yaakov looked up – and saw Esav coming with his four
hundred men. So he divided the children among Leah, Raḥel, and the two
2 maidservants. He put the maidservants and their children first, Leah and her
3 children behind, and Raḥel and Yosef at the rear. And he went ahead of them,
bowing down to the ground seven times until he came close to his brother.
4 Esav ran to meet him and embraced him. He threw his arms around his neck
5 and kissed him, and they wept. Esav looked up and saw the women and
children. He asked, "Who are these with you?" Yaakov answered, "They are
6 the children God has graciously given your servant." Then the maidservants
7 and their children came forward and bowed down. Leah and her children
came forward and bowed down. And last, Yosef and Raḥel approached and
8 bowed down. Esav asked, "What did you mean by all the procession that I
9 met before?" He said, "To find favor in your eyes, my lord." But Esav said, "I
10 have plenty, my brother. Let what is yours remain yours." "No, please," said
Yaakov. "If I have found favor in your eyes, accept this gift from me, for seeing
11 your face is like seeing the face of God, and you have shown me favor. Please
accept my blessing that was brought to you, for God has been gracious to me,
12 and I have everything." Yaakov pressed him, and he accepted. Then Esav said,
13 "Let us be on our way. I will go beside you." But Yaakov said, "My lord knows
that the children are fragile, and I must care for the nursing sheep and cattle.
14 If they are driven hard even for one day, all the flocks will die. Let my lord go

---

78 | The first part of the name Yisrael resonates with *sarita* (you have struggled). The ending "el" is a divine name.

79 | This response implies that the "man" is an angel; cf. Judges 13:18.

80 | The first part of the name Peniel resonates with *panim* (face). The ending "el" is a reference to God.

כָּל־הַהֹלְכִים אַחֲרֵי הָעֲדָרִים לֵאמֹר כַּדָּבָר הַזֶּה תְּדַבְּרוּן אֶל־עֵשָׂו
כ בְּמֹצַאֲכֶם אֹתוֹ: וַאֲמַרְתֶּם גַּם הִנֵּה עַבְדְּךָ יַעֲקֹב אַחֲרֵינוּ כִּי־אָמַר
אֲכַפְּרָה פָנָיו בַּמִּנְחָה הַהֹלֶכֶת לְפָנָי וְאַחֲרֵי־כֵן אֶרְאֶה פָנָיו אוּלַי יִשָּׂא
כא כב פָנָי: וַתַּעֲבֹר הַמִּנְחָה עַל־פָּנָיו וְהוּא לָן בַּלַּיְלָה־הַהוּא בַּמַּחֲנֶה: וַיָּקָם ׀
בַּלַּיְלָה הוּא וַיִּקַּח אֶת־שְׁתֵּי נָשָׁיו וְאֶת־שְׁתֵּי שִׁפְחֹתָיו וְאֶת־אַחַד עָשָׂר
כג יְלָדָיו וַיַּעֲבֹר אֵת מַעֲבַר יַבֹּק: וַיִּקָּחֵם וַיַּעֲבִרֵם אֶת־הַנָּחַל וַיַּעֲבֵר אֶת־
כד כה אֲשֶׁר־לוֹ: וַיִּוָּתֵר יַעֲקֹב לְבַדּוֹ וַיֵּאָבֵק אִישׁ עִמּוֹ עַד עֲלוֹת הַשָּׁחַר: וַיַּרְא
כִּי לֹא יָכֹל לוֹ וַיִּגַּע בְּכַף־יְרֵכוֹ וַתֵּקַע כַּף־יֶרֶךְ יַעֲקֹב בְּהֵאָבְקוֹ עִמּוֹ:
כו וַיֹּאמֶר שַׁלְּחֵנִי כִּי עָלָה הַשָּׁחַר וַיֹּאמֶר לֹא אֲשַׁלֵּחֲךָ כִּי אִם־בֵּרַכְתָּנִי:
כז כח וַיֹּאמֶר אֵלָיו מַה־שְּׁמֶךָ וַיֹּאמֶר יַעֲקֹב: וַיֹּאמֶר לֹא יַעֲקֹב יֵאָמֵר עוֹד
שִׁמְךָ כִּי אִם־יִשְׂרָאֵל כִּי־שָׂרִיתָ עִם־אֱלֹהִים וְעִם־אֲנָשִׁים וַתּוּכָל:
כט וַיִּשְׁאַל יַעֲקֹב וַיֹּאמֶר הַגִּידָה־נָּא שְׁמֶךָ וַיֹּאמֶר לָמָּה זֶּה תִּשְׁאַל לִשְׁמִי
ל וַיְבָרֶךְ אֹתוֹ שָׁם: וַיִּקְרָא יַעֲקֹב שֵׁם הַמָּקוֹם פְּנִיאֵל כִּי־רָאִיתִי אֱלֹהִים שלישי
לא פָּנִים אֶל־פָּנִים וַתִּנָּצֵל נַפְשִׁי: וַיִּזְרַח־לוֹ הַשֶּׁמֶשׁ כַּאֲשֶׁר עָבַר אֶת־פְּנוּאֵל
לב וְהוּא צֹלֵעַ עַל־יְרֵכוֹ: עַל־כֵּן לֹא־יֹאכְלוּ בְנֵי־יִשְׂרָאֵל אֶת־גִּיד הַנָּשֶׁה
אֲשֶׁר עַל־כַּף הַיָּרֵךְ עַד הַיּוֹם הַזֶּה כִּי נָגַע בְּכַף־יֶרֶךְ יַעֲקֹב בְּגִיד הַנָּשֶׁה:

לג א וַיִּשָּׂא יַעֲקֹב עֵינָיו וַיַּרְא וְהִנֵּה עֵשָׂו בָּא וְעִמּוֹ אַרְבַּע מֵאוֹת אִישׁ וַיַּחַץ
ב אֶת־הַיְלָדִים עַל־לֵאָה וְעַל־רָחֵל וְעַל שְׁתֵּי הַשְּׁפָחוֹת: וַיָּשֶׂם אֶת־
הַשְּׁפָחוֹת וְאֶת־יַלְדֵיהֶן רִאשֹׁנָה וְאֶת־לֵאָה וִילָדֶיהָ אַחֲרֹנִים וְאֶת־
ג רָחֵל וְאֶת־יוֹסֵף אַחֲרֹנִים: וְהוּא עָבַר לִפְנֵיהֶם וַיִּשְׁתַּחוּ אַרְצָה שֶׁבַע
ד פְּעָמִים עַד־גִּשְׁתּוֹ עַד־אָחִיו: וַיָּרָץ עֵשָׂו לִקְרָאתוֹ וַיְחַבְּקֵהוּ וַיִּפֹּל עַל־
ה צַוָּארָו וַיִּשָּׁקֵהוּ וַיִּבְכּוּ: וַיִּשָּׂא אֶת־עֵינָיו וַיַּרְא אֶת־הַנָּשִׁים וְאֶת־הַיְלָדִים
וַיֹּאמֶר מִי־אֵלֶּה לָּךְ וַיֹּאמַר הַיְלָדִים אֲשֶׁר־חָנַן אֱלֹהִים אֶת־עַבְדֶּךָ:
ו ז וַתִּגַּשְׁןָ הַשְּׁפָחוֹת הֵנָּה וְיַלְדֵיהֶן וַתִּשְׁתַּחֲוֶיןָ: וַתִּגַּשׁ גַּם־לֵאָה וִילָדֶיהָ רביעי
ח וַיִּשְׁתַּחֲווּ וְאַחַר נִגַּשׁ יוֹסֵף וְרָחֵל וַיִּשְׁתַּחֲווּ: וַיֹּאמֶר מִי לְךָ כָּל־הַמַּחֲנֶה
ט הַזֶּה אֲשֶׁר פָּגָשְׁתִּי וַיֹּאמֶר לִמְצֹא־חֵן בְּעֵינֵי אֲדֹנִי: וַיֹּאמֶר עֵשָׂו יֶשׁ־לִי
י רָב אָחִי יְהִי לְךָ אֲשֶׁר־לָךְ: וַיֹּאמֶר יַעֲקֹב אַל־נָא אִם־נָא מָצָאתִי חֵן
בְּעֵינֶיךָ וְלָקַחְתָּ מִנְחָתִי מִיָּדִי כִּי עַל־כֵּן רָאִיתִי פָנֶיךָ כִּרְאֹת פְּנֵי אֱלֹהִים
יא וַתִּרְצֵנִי: קַח־נָא אֶת־בִּרְכָתִי אֲשֶׁר הֻבָאת לָךְ כִּי־חַנַּנִי אֱלֹהִים וְכִי
יב יג יֶשׁ־לִי־כֹל וַיִּפְצַר־בּוֹ וַיִּקָּח: וַיֹּאמֶר נִסְעָה וְנֵלֵכָה וְאֵלְכָה לְנֶגְדֶּךָ: וַיֹּאמֶר
אֵלָיו אֲדֹנִי יֹדֵעַ כִּי־הַיְלָדִים רַכִּים וְהַצֹּאן וְהַבָּקָר עָלוֹת עָלָי וּדְפָקוּם
יד יוֹם אֶחָד וָמֵתוּ כָּל־הַצֹּאן: יַעֲבָר־נָא אֲדֹנִי לִפְנֵי עַבְדּוֹ וַאֲנִי אֶתְנַהֲלָה

on ahead of his servant, and I will go slowly at the pace of the livestock before
15 me and the pace of the children until I come to my lord in Se'ir." Esav said,
"Let me leave some of my people with you." "Why do that?" he said. "Just let
16 me find favor in the eyes of my lord." So that day Esav started back on his
17 way to Se'ir, and Yaakov journeyed on to Sukkot. There he built himself
a house and made huts for his livestock; that is why he named the place
18 Sukkot.[81] Thus Yaakov, having come from Padan Aram, arrived safely
at the town of Shekhem in Canaan, and he set up camp within sight of the
19 town. He bought the plot of ground where he pitched his tent from the sons
20 of Ḥamor, father of Shekhem, for one hundred *kesita*[82] of silver. There he
34 1 erected an altar and named it El Elohei Yisrael.[83] Dina, the daughter
whom Leah had borne to Yaakov, went out to see the daughters of the land.
2 When Shekhem son of Ḥamor the Hivite, prince of the land, saw her, he took
3 hold of her, lay with her, and violated her. He became deeply drawn to Dina,
Yaakov's daughter, and, in love with the young woman, he spoke to her heart.
4 5 Shekhem said to his father Ḥamor, "Take this girl as a wife for me." When
Yaakov heard that he had defiled his daughter Dina, his sons were in the field
6 with his livestock, and so he stayed silent until they came home. Shekhem's
7 father Ḥamor came to Yaakov to speak with him. Meanwhile, Yaakov's sons,
having heard what had happened, came back from the field. They were
shocked and furious, for Shekhem had committed an outrage in Israel by
8 sleeping with Yaakov's daughter. Such a thing cannot be done! But Ḥamor
spoke with them and said, "My son Shekhem has his heart set upon your
9 daughter. Please give her to him as his wife. Intermarry with us. Give us your
10 daughters and take our daughters for yourselves. Settle with us. The land is
11 open to you. Live here, trade here, acquire property here." Then Shekhem
said to Dina's father and brothers, "Let me but find favor in your eyes and I
12 will give whatever you ask. Set the bridal price and gifts as high as you like. I
will give whatever you ask of me; only give me the young woman as my
13 wife." Yaakov's sons responded to Shekhem and his father Ḥamor, and they
14 spoke deceptively: he had, after all, defiled their sister Dina. They told them,
"We cannot do this. To give our sister to an uncircumcised man would be a
15 disgrace to us. Only on one condition will we agree with you: If you become
16 like us, circumcising all your males, then we will give you our daughters and
take your daughters for ourselves. We will live with you and become one
17 people. If you do not agree to be circumcised, we will take our daughter and
18 19 go." Their words gratified Ḥamor and his son Shekhem. The young man, the
most honored of his father's family, lost no time in doing it, because he longed
20 for Yaakov's daughter. Ḥamor and his son Shekhem came to the town gate
21 and spoke to their fellow townsmen. "These people are friendly toward us,"

---

81 | Meaning "huts."

82 | Apparently a unit of silver.

83 | Meaning "God, the God of Yisrael."

לְאִטִּי לְרֶגֶל הַמְּלָאכָה אֲשֶׁר־לְפָנַי וּלְרֶגֶל הַיְלָדִים עַד אֲשֶׁר־אָבֹא
טו אֶל־אֲדֹנִי שֵׂעִירָה׃ וַיֹּאמֶר עֵשָׂו אַצִּיגָה־נָּא עִמְּךָ מִן־הָעָם אֲשֶׁר אִתִּי
טז וַיֹּאמֶר לָמָּה זֶּה אֶמְצָא־חֵן בְּעֵינֵי אֲדֹנִי׃ וַיָּשָׁב בַּיּוֹם הַהוּא עֵשָׂו לְדַרְכּוֹ
יז שֵׂעִירָה׃ וְיַעֲקֹב נָסַע סֻכֹּתָה וַיִּבֶן לוֹ בָּיִת וּלְמִקְנֵהוּ עָשָׂה סֻכֹּת עַל־כֵּן
יח קָרָא שֵׁם־הַמָּקוֹם סֻכּוֹת׃ וַיָּבֹא יַעֲקֹב שָׁלֵם עִיר לא
שְׁכֶם אֲשֶׁר בְּאֶרֶץ כְּנַעַן בְּבֹאוֹ מִפַּדַּן אֲרָם וַיִּחַן אֶת־פְּנֵי הָעִיר׃
יט וַיִּקֶן אֶת־חֶלְקַת הַשָּׂדֶה אֲשֶׁר נָטָה־שָׁם אָהֳלוֹ מִיַּד בְּנֵי־חֲמוֹר
כ אֲבִי שְׁכֶם בְּמֵאָה קְשִׂיטָה׃ וַיַּצֶּב־שָׁם מִזְבֵּחַ וַיִּקְרָא־לוֹ אֵל אֱלֹהֵי
לד א יִשְׂרָאֵל׃ וַתֵּצֵא דִינָה בַּת־לֵאָה אֲשֶׁר יָלְדָה לְיַעֲקֹב לִרְאוֹת חמישי
ב בִּבְנוֹת הָאָרֶץ׃ וַיַּרְא אֹתָהּ שְׁכֶם בֶּן־חֲמוֹר הַחִוִּי נְשִׂיא הָאָרֶץ וַיִּקַּח
ג אֹתָהּ וַיִּשְׁכַּב אֹתָהּ וַיְעַנֶּהָ׃ וַתִּדְבַּק נַפְשׁוֹ בְּדִינָה בַּת־יַעֲקֹב וַיֶּאֱהַב
ד אֶת־הַנַּעֲרָ וַיְדַבֵּר עַל־לֵב הַנַּעֲרָ׃ וַיֹּאמֶר שְׁכֶם אֶל־חֲמוֹר אָבִיו לֵאמֹר
ה קַח־לִי אֶת־הַיַּלְדָּה הַזֹּאת לְאִשָּׁה׃ וְיַעֲקֹב שָׁמַע כִּי טִמֵּא אֶת־דִּינָה
ו בִתּוֹ וּבָנָיו הָיוּ אֶת־מִקְנֵהוּ בַּשָּׂדֶה וְהֶחֱרִשׁ יַעֲקֹב עַד־בֹּאָם׃ וַיֵּצֵא
ז חֲמוֹר אֲבִי־שְׁכֶם אֶל־יַעֲקֹב לְדַבֵּר אִתּוֹ׃ וּבְנֵי יַעֲקֹב בָּאוּ מִן־הַשָּׂדֶה
כְּשָׁמְעָם וַיִּתְעַצְּבוּ הָאֲנָשִׁים וַיִּחַר לָהֶם מְאֹד כִּי נְבָלָה עָשָׂה בְיִשְׂרָאֵל
ח לִשְׁכַּב אֶת־בַּת־יַעֲקֹב וְכֵן לֹא יֵעָשֶׂה׃ וַיְדַבֵּר חֲמוֹר אִתָּם לֵאמֹר שְׁכֶם
ט בְּנִי חָשְׁקָה נַפְשׁוֹ בְּבִתְּכֶם תְּנוּ נָא אֹתָהּ לוֹ לְאִשָּׁה׃ וְהִתְחַתְּנוּ אֹתָנוּ
י בְּנֹתֵיכֶם תִּתְּנוּ־לָנוּ וְאֶת־בְּנֹתֵינוּ תִּקְחוּ לָכֶם׃ וְאִתָּנוּ תֵּשֵׁבוּ וְהָאָרֶץ
יא תִּהְיֶה לִפְנֵיכֶם שְׁבוּ וּסְחָרוּהָ וְהֵאָחֲזוּ בָּהּ׃ וַיֹּאמֶר שְׁכֶם אֶל־אָבִיהָ
יב וְאֶל־אַחֶיהָ אֶמְצָא־חֵן בְּעֵינֵיכֶם וַאֲשֶׁר תֹּאמְרוּ אֵלַי אֶתֵּן׃ הַרְבּוּ עָלַי
מְאֹד מֹהַר וּמַתָּן וְאֶתְּנָה כַּאֲשֶׁר תֹּאמְרוּ אֵלָי וּתְנוּ־לִי אֶת־הַנַּעֲרָ
יג לְאִשָּׁה׃ וַיַּעֲנוּ בְנֵי־יַעֲקֹב אֶת־שְׁכֶם וְאֶת־חֲמוֹר אָבִיו בְּמִרְמָה וַיְדַבֵּרוּ
יד אֲשֶׁר טִמֵּא אֵת דִּינָה אֲחֹתָם׃ וַיֹּאמְרוּ אֲלֵיהֶם לֹא נוּכַל לַעֲשׂוֹת הַדָּבָר
הַזֶּה לָתֵת אֶת־אֲחֹתֵנוּ לְאִישׁ אֲשֶׁר־לוֹ עָרְלָה כִּי־חֶרְפָּה הִוא לָנוּ׃
טו טז אַךְ־בְּזֹאת נֵאוֹת לָכֶם אִם תִּהְיוּ כָמֹנוּ לְהִמֹּל לָכֶם כָּל־זָכָר׃ וְנָתַנּוּ
אֶת־בְּנֹתֵינוּ לָכֶם וְאֶת־בְּנֹתֵיכֶם נִקַּח־לָנוּ וְיָשַׁבְנוּ אִתְּכֶם וְהָיִינוּ לְעַם
יז אֶחָד׃ וְאִם־לֹא תִשְׁמְעוּ אֵלֵינוּ לְהִמּוֹל וְלָקַחְנוּ אֶת־בִּתֵּנוּ וְהָלָכְנוּ׃
יח יט וַיִּיטְבוּ דִבְרֵיהֶם בְּעֵינֵי חֲמוֹר וּבְעֵינֵי שְׁכֶם בֶּן־חֲמוֹר׃ וְלֹא־אֵחַר הַנַּעַר
כ לַעֲשׂוֹת הַדָּבָר כִּי חָפֵץ בְּבַת־יַעֲקֹב וְהוּא נִכְבָּד מִכֹּל בֵּית אָבִיו׃ וַיָּבֹא
חֲמוֹר וּשְׁכֶם בְּנוֹ אֶל־שַׁעַר עִירָם וַיְדַבְּרוּ אֶל־אַנְשֵׁי עִירָם לֵאמֹר׃
כא הָאֲנָשִׁים הָאֵלֶּה שְׁלֵמִים הֵם אִתָּנוּ וְיֵשְׁבוּ בָאָרֶץ וְיִסְחֲרוּ אֹתָהּ וְהָאָרֶץ

they said. "Let them live in the land and trade in it. We have space enough for
22 them. We can marry their daughters and they can marry ours. But only on
one condition will they agree to dwell with us as one people. Every male
23 among us must be circumcised as they are. Will not their livestock, property,
and all their animals be ours? Let us, then, agree to their terms and let them
24 settle among us." All the people who went out by the town gate listened to
Ḥamor and his son Shekhem, and all the males who went out by the town
25 gate were circumcised. On the third day, when the people were weak from
pain, two of Yaakov's sons, Shimon and Levi, Dina's brothers, took their
26 swords, entered the unsuspecting town, and killed every single male. They
killed Ḥamor and his son Shekhem by the sword, took Dina from Shekhem's
27 house and left. Yaakov's sons came upon the dead and plundered the town
28 that had defiled their sister. They took their flocks, their cattle, their donkeys,
29 and everything else of theirs in the town and out in the field. Their wealth,
their children, and their women they took captive and looted, and all that was
30 in the houses. Yaakov said to Shimon and Levi, "You have brought trouble
upon me – you have made me odious to the inhabitants of the land, the
Canaanites and Perizzites. I am few in number, and if they join forces and
31 attack me, I and my household will be destroyed." But they said, "Should our
sister be treated like a whore?"
35 1 God said to Yaakov, "Arise, go up to Beit El. Stay there, and there build an altar
2 to God, who appeared to you as you fled your brother Esav." Yaakov told his
household and everyone with him, "Be rid of the alien gods you have with
3 you. Purify yourselves and change your clothes. Then come, let us go up to
Beit El, and there I will make an altar to God, who answered me in my time of
4 trouble and who has been with me wherever I have gone." They gave Yaakov
all the alien gods they had, and even the rings in their ears,[84] and Yaakov
5 buried them under a terebinth near Shekhem. As they set out, the terror of
God fell on the surrounding towns so that no one pursued Yaakov's sons.
6 Yaakov and all the people with him came to Luz – that is, Beit El – in the land
7 of Canaan. There he built an altar and called the place El Beit El,[85] because it
8 was there that God had revealed Himself to him as he fled his brother. Devora,
Rivka's nurse, died and was buried under the oak outside Beit El. And so it
was named Oak of Weeping.
9 After Yaakov had returned from Padan Aram God appeared to him again and
10 blessed him. God said to him, "Your name is Yaakov; no longer shall you be
11 called Yaakov; Yisrael shall be your name." Thus He named him Yisrael. God
said to him: "I am El Shaddai. Be fertile and multiply. A nation, a community
12 of nations will come to be from you. Of your loins, kings shall come forth. The
land I gave to Avraham and Yitzḥak I surely give to you; to your descendants

84 | Earrings may have been associated with idol worship (cf. Ex. 32:2–4).
85 | Literally "God, the House of God."

הִנֵּה רַחֲבַת־יָדַיִם לִפְנֵיהֶם אֶת־בְּנֹתָם נִקַּח־לָנוּ לְנָשִׁים וְאֶת־בְּנֹתֵינוּ
כב נִתֵּן לָהֶם׃ אַךְ־בְּזֹאת יֵאֹתוּ לָנוּ הָאֲנָשִׁים לָשֶׁבֶת אִתָּנוּ לִהְיוֹת לְעַם
כג אֶחָד בְּהִמּוֹל לָנוּ כָּל־זָכָר כַּאֲשֶׁר הֵם נִמֹּלִים׃ מִקְנֵהֶם וְקִנְיָנָם וְכָל־
כד בְּהֶמְתָּם הֲלוֹא לָנוּ הֵם אַךְ נֵאוֹתָה לָהֶם וְיֵשְׁבוּ אִתָּנוּ׃ וַיִּשְׁמְעוּ אֶל־
חֲמוֹר וְאֶל־שְׁכֶם בְּנוֹ כָּל־יֹצְאֵי שַׁעַר עִירוֹ וַיִּמֹּלוּ כָּל־זָכָר כָּל־יֹצְאֵי
כה שַׁעַר עִירוֹ׃ וַיְהִי בַיּוֹם הַשְּׁלִישִׁי בִּהְיוֹתָם כֹּאֲבִים וַיִּקְחוּ שְׁנֵי־בְנֵי־יַעֲקֹב
שִׁמְעוֹן וְלֵוִי אֲחֵי דִינָה אִישׁ חַרְבּוֹ וַיָּבֹאוּ עַל־הָעִיר בֶּטַח וַיַּהַרְגוּ כָּל־
כו זָכָר׃ וְאֶת־חֲמוֹר וְאֶת־שְׁכֶם בְּנוֹ הָרְגוּ לְפִי־חָרֶב וַיִּקְחוּ אֶת־דִּינָה
כז מִבֵּית שְׁכֶם וַיֵּצֵאוּ׃ בְּנֵי יַעֲקֹב בָּאוּ עַל־הַחֲלָלִים וַיָּבֹזּוּ הָעִיר אֲשֶׁר
כח טִמְּאוּ אֲחוֹתָם׃ אֶת־צֹאנָם וְאֶת־בְּקָרָם וְאֶת־חֲמֹרֵיהֶם וְאֵת אֲשֶׁר־
כט בָּעִיר וְאֶת־אֲשֶׁר בַּשָּׂדֶה לָקָחוּ׃ וְאֶת־כָּל־חֵילָם וְאֶת־כָּל־טַפָּם וְאֶת־
ל נְשֵׁיהֶם שָׁבוּ וַיָּבֹזּוּ וְאֵת כָּל־אֲשֶׁר בַּבָּיִת׃ וַיֹּאמֶר יַעֲקֹב אֶל־שִׁמְעוֹן
וְאֶל־לֵוִי עֲכַרְתֶּם אֹתִי לְהַבְאִישֵׁנִי בְּיֹשֵׁב הָאָרֶץ בַּכְּנַעֲנִי וּבַפְּרִזִּי וַאֲנִי
לא מְתֵי מִסְפָּר וְנֶאֶסְפוּ עָלַי וְהִכּוּנִי וְנִשְׁמַדְתִּי אֲנִי וּבֵיתִי׃ וַיֹּאמְרוּ הַכְזוֹנָה
יַעֲשֶׂה אֶת־אֲחוֹתֵנוּ׃

לה א וַיֹּאמֶר אֱלֹהִים אֶל־יַעֲקֹב קוּם עֲלֵה בֵית־אֵל וְשֶׁב־שָׁם וַעֲשֵׂה־שָׁם
ב מִזְבֵּחַ לָאֵל הַנִּרְאֶה אֵלֶיךָ בְּבָרְחֲךָ מִפְּנֵי עֵשָׂו אָחִיךָ׃ וַיֹּאמֶר יַעֲקֹב
אֶל־בֵּיתוֹ וְאֶל כָּל־אֲשֶׁר עִמּוֹ הָסִרוּ אֶת־אֱלֹהֵי הַנֵּכָר אֲשֶׁר בְּתֹכְכֶם
ג וְהִטַּהֲרוּ וְהַחֲלִיפוּ שִׂמְלֹתֵיכֶם׃ וְנָקוּמָה וְנַעֲלֶה בֵּית־אֵל וְאֶעֱשֶׂה־שָּׁם
מִזְבֵּחַ לָאֵל הָעֹנֶה אֹתִי בְּיוֹם צָרָתִי וַיְהִי עִמָּדִי בַּדֶּרֶךְ אֲשֶׁר הָלָכְתִּי׃
ד וַיִּתְּנוּ אֶל־יַעֲקֹב אֵת כָּל־אֱלֹהֵי הַנֵּכָר אֲשֶׁר בְּיָדָם וְאֶת־הַנְּזָמִים אֲשֶׁר
ה בְּאָזְנֵיהֶם וַיִּטְמֹן אֹתָם יַעֲקֹב תַּחַת הָאֵלָה אֲשֶׁר עִם־שְׁכֶם׃ וַיִּסָּעוּ וַיְהִי ׀
חִתַּת אֱלֹהִים עַל־הֶעָרִים אֲשֶׁר סְבִיבוֹתֵיהֶם וְלֹא רָדְפוּ אַחֲרֵי בְּנֵי
ו יַעֲקֹב׃ וַיָּבֹא יַעֲקֹב לוּזָה אֲשֶׁר בְּאֶרֶץ כְּנַעַן הִוא בֵּית־אֵל הוּא וְכָל־הָעָם
ז אֲשֶׁר־עִמּוֹ׃ וַיִּבֶן שָׁם מִזְבֵּחַ וַיִּקְרָא לַמָּקוֹם אֵל בֵּית־אֵל כִּי שָׁם נִגְלוּ
ח אֵלָיו הָאֱלֹהִים בְּבָרְחוֹ מִפְּנֵי אָחִיו׃ וַתָּמָת דְּבֹרָה מֵינֶקֶת רִבְקָה וַתִּקָּבֵר
מִתַּחַת לְבֵית־אֵל תַּחַת הָאַלּוֹן וַיִּקְרָא שְׁמוֹ אַלּוֹן בָּכוּת׃
ט י וַיֵּרָא אֱלֹהִים אֶל־יַעֲקֹב עוֹד בְּבֹאוֹ מִפַּדַּן אֲרָם וַיְבָרֶךְ אֹתוֹ׃ וַיֹּאמֶר־לוֹ לב
אֱלֹהִים שִׁמְךָ יַעֲקֹב לֹא־יִקָּרֵא שִׁמְךָ עוֹד יַעֲקֹב כִּי אִם־יִשְׂרָאֵל יִהְיֶה
יא שְׁמֶךָ וַיִּקְרָא אֶת־שְׁמוֹ יִשְׂרָאֵל׃ וַיֹּאמֶר לוֹ אֱלֹהִים אֲנִי אֵל שַׁדַּי פְּרֵה
יב וּרְבֵה גּוֹי וּקְהַל גּוֹיִם יִהְיֶה מִמֶּךָּ וּמְלָכִים מֵחֲלָצֶיךָ יֵצֵאוּ׃ וְאֶת־הָאָרֶץ ששי
אֲשֶׁר נָתַתִּי לְאַבְרָהָם וּלְיִצְחָק לְךָ אֶתְּנֶנָּה וּלְזַרְעֲךָ אַחֲרֶיךָ אֶתֵּן אֶת־

13 after you I will give the land." God went up from him at the place where He
14 had spoken with him. Yaakov set up a stone pillar at the place where God had
15 talked with him, and on it he offered a libation and poured oil. And Yaakov
16 named the place where God had spoken to him Beit El.[86] From Beit El they
moved on. While they were still some distance from Efrat, Raḥel began to
17 give birth; her labor pains were intense. When her labor was at its worst, the
18 midwife said to her, "Don't be afraid. You have another son." But she was
dying. With her last breath, she named him Ben Oni;[87] but his father called
19 him Binyamin.[88] So Raḥel died and was buried on the road to Efrat – that is,
20 Beit Leḥem. Yaakov erected a pillar at her grave. To this day, that pillar marks
21 of Raḥel's grave. Yisrael traveled on, pitching his tent beyond Migdal Eder.
22 While Yisrael was staying in that region, Reuven went and lay with his father's
concubine Bilha. And Yisrael heard –[89]
23 Yaakov had twelve sons. The sons of Leah were Reuven, Yaakov's firstborn,
24 Shimon, Levi, Yehuda, Yissakhar, and Zevulun. The sons of Raḥel were Yosef
25 26 and Binyamin. The sons of Raḥel's maid Bilha were Dan and Naftali. The sons
of Leah's maid Zilpa were Gad and Asher. These were the sons of Yaakov, born
27 to him in Padan Aram. Yaakov came home to his father Yitzḥak at Mamre,
near Kiryat Arba – that is, Ḥevron – where Avraham and Yitzḥak had lived as
28 29 strangers. Yitzḥak lived one hundred and eighty years. Then he breathed his
last, and died, and was gathered to his people, aged, satisfied with his years.
His sons Esav and Yaakov buried him.
36 1 2 These are the descendants of Esav – that is, Edom. Esav took wives from
among the daughters of Canaan: Ada daughter of Eilon the Hittite, and
3 Oholivama daughter of Ana, granddaughter of Tzivon the Hivite – and
4 also Basmat, daughter of Yishmael and sister of Nevayot. Ada bore Elifaz
5 to Esav, and Basmat bore Reuel. Oholivama bore Yeush, Yalam, and Koraḥ.
6 These were the sons of Esav, born in the land of Canaan. Esav took his wives,
sons and daughters, and all the members of his household, together with
his livestock, his other animals, and all the possessions he had acquired in
7 Canaan, and he moved to another region, away from his brother Yaakov, for
their possessions were too great for them to remain together; because of all
their livestock, the land where they were living could not support them both.
8 9 So Esav settled in the hill country of Se'ir. Esav is Edom. These, then, are the
descendants of Esav, ancestor of the Edomites, in the hill country of Se'ir.
10 These are the names of Esav's sons: Elifaz, son of Esav's wife Ada, and Reuel,
11 son of Esav's wife Basmat. The sons of Elifaz were Teiman, Omar, Tzefo,
12 Gatam, and Kenaz. Timna, a concubine of Esav's son Elifaz, bore him Amalek.
13 These are the descendants of Esav's wife Ada. The sons of Reuel were Naḥat,

---

86 | Meaning "House of God."

87 | Meaning "son of my sorrow," but it may also denote "son of my strength."

88 | Meaning "son of the right side." The right side signifies strength.

89 | A break appears here in the middle of the verse, implying that the ensuing passage bears a connection to the present one.

יג יד הָאָרֶץ׃ וַיַּעַל מֵעָלָיו אֱלֹהִים בַּמָּקוֹם אֲשֶׁר־דִּבֶּר אִתּוֹ׃ וַיַּצֵּב יַעֲקֹב
מַצֵּבָה בַּמָּקוֹם אֲשֶׁר־דִּבֶּר אִתּוֹ מַצֶּבֶת אָבֶן וַיַּסֵּךְ עָלֶיהָ נֶסֶךְ וַיִּצֹק
טו עָלֶיהָ שָׁמֶן׃ וַיִּקְרָא יַעֲקֹב אֶת־שֵׁם הַמָּקוֹם אֲשֶׁר דִּבֶּר אִתּוֹ שָׁם אֱלֹהִים
טז בֵּית־אֵל׃ וַיִּסְעוּ מִבֵּית אֵל וַיְהִי־עוֹד כִּבְרַת־הָאָרֶץ לָבוֹא אֶפְרָתָה
יז וַתֵּלֶד רָחֵל וַתְּקַשׁ בְּלִדְתָּהּ׃ וַיְהִי בְהַקְשֹׁתָהּ בְּלִדְתָּהּ וַתֹּאמֶר לָהּ
יח הַמְיַלֶּדֶת אַל־תִּירְאִי כִּי־גַם־זֶה לָךְ בֵּן׃ וַיְהִי בְּצֵאת נַפְשָׁהּ כִּי מֵתָה
יט וַתִּקְרָא שְׁמוֹ בֶּן־אוֹנִי וְאָבִיו קָרָא־לוֹ בִנְיָמִין׃ וַתָּמָת רָחֵל וַתִּקָּבֵר
כ בְּדֶרֶךְ אֶפְרָתָה הִוא בֵּית לָחֶם׃ וַיַּצֵּב יַעֲקֹב מַצֵּבָה עַל־קְבֻרָתָהּ הִוא
כא מַצֶּבֶת קְבֻרַת־רָחֵל עַד־הַיּוֹם׃ וַיִּסַּע יִשְׂרָאֵל וַיֵּט אָהֳלֹה מֵהָלְאָה
כב לְמִגְדַּל־עֵדֶר׃ וַיְהִי בִּשְׁכֹּן יִשְׂרָאֵל בָּאָרֶץ הַהִוא וַיֵּלֶךְ רְאוּבֵן וַיִּשְׁכַּב
אֶת־בִּלְהָה פִּילֶגֶשׁ אָבִיו וַיִּשְׁמַע יִשְׂרָאֵל
כג וַיִּהְיוּ בְנֵי־יַעֲקֹב שְׁנֵים עָשָׂר׃ בְּנֵי לֵאָה בְּכוֹר יַעֲקֹב רְאוּבֵן וְשִׁמְעוֹן וְלֵוִי
כד כה וִיהוּדָה וְיִשָּׂשכָר וּזְבוּלֻן׃ בְּנֵי רָחֵל יוֹסֵף וּבִנְיָמִן׃ וּבְנֵי בִלְהָה שִׁפְחַת
כו רָחֵל דָּן וְנַפְתָּלִי׃ וּבְנֵי זִלְפָּה שִׁפְחַת לֵאָה גָּד וְאָשֵׁר אֵלֶּה בְּנֵי יַעֲקֹב
כז אֲשֶׁר יֻלַּד־לוֹ בְּפַדַּן אֲרָם׃ וַיָּבֹא יַעֲקֹב אֶל־יִצְחָק אָבִיו מַמְרֵא קִרְיַת
כח הָאַרְבַּע הִוא חֶבְרוֹן אֲשֶׁר־גָּר־שָׁם אַבְרָהָם וְיִצְחָק׃ וַיִּהְיוּ יְמֵי יִצְחָק
כט מְאַת שָׁנָה וּשְׁמֹנִים שָׁנָה׃ וַיִּגְוַע יִצְחָק וַיָּמָת וַיֵּאָסֶף אֶל־עַמָּיו זָקֵן
וּשְׂבַע יָמִים וַיִּקְבְּרוּ אֹתוֹ עֵשָׂו וְיַעֲקֹב בָּנָיו׃
לו א ב וְאֵלֶּה תֹּלְדוֹת עֵשָׂו הוּא אֱדוֹם׃ עֵשָׂו לָקַח אֶת־נָשָׁיו מִבְּנוֹת כְּנָעַן
אֶת־עָדָה בַּת־אֵילוֹן הַחִתִּי וְאֶת־אָהֳלִיבָמָה בַּת־עֲנָה בַּת־צִבְעוֹן
ג ד הַחִוִּי׃ וְאֶת־בָּשְׂמַת בַּת־יִשְׁמָעֵאל אֲחוֹת נְבָיוֹת׃ וַתֵּלֶד עָדָה לְעֵשָׂו
ה אֶת־אֱלִיפָז וּבָשְׂמַת יָלְדָה אֶת־רְעוּאֵל׃ וְאָהֳלִיבָמָה יָלְדָה אֶת־יעיש יְעוּשׁ
וְאֶת־יַעְלָם וְאֶת־קֹרַח אֵלֶּה בְּנֵי עֵשָׂו אֲשֶׁר יֻלְּדוּ־לוֹ בְּאֶרֶץ כְּנָעַן׃
ו וַיִּקַּח עֵשָׂו אֶת־נָשָׁיו וְאֶת־בָּנָיו וְאֶת־בְּנֹתָיו וְאֶת־כָּל־נַפְשׁוֹת בֵּיתוֹ
וְאֶת־מִקְנֵהוּ וְאֶת־כָּל־בְּהֶמְתּוֹ וְאֵת כָּל־קִנְיָנוֹ אֲשֶׁר רָכַשׁ בְּאֶרֶץ כְּנָעַן
ז וַיֵּלֶךְ אֶל־אֶרֶץ מִפְּנֵי יַעֲקֹב אָחִיו׃ כִּי־הָיָה רְכוּשָׁם רָב מִשֶּׁבֶת יַחְדָּו וְלֹא
ח יָכְלָה אֶרֶץ מְגוּרֵיהֶם לָשֵׂאת אֹתָם מִפְּנֵי מִקְנֵיהֶם׃ וַיֵּשֶׁב עֵשָׂו בְּהַר
ט שֵׂעִיר עֵשָׂו הוּא אֱדוֹם׃ וְאֵלֶּה תֹּלְדוֹת עֵשָׂו אֲבִי אֱדוֹם בְּהַר שֵׂעִיר׃
י אֵלֶּה שְׁמוֹת בְּנֵי־עֵשָׂו אֱלִיפַז בֶּן־עָדָה אֵשֶׁת עֵשָׂו רְעוּאֵל בֶּן־בָּשְׂמַת
יא יב אֵשֶׁת עֵשָׂו׃ וַיִּהְיוּ בְּנֵי אֱלִיפָז תֵּימָן אוֹמָר צְפוֹ וְגַעְתָּם וּקְנַז׃ וְתִמְנַע
הָיְתָה פִילֶגֶשׁ לֶאֱלִיפַז בֶּן־עֵשָׂו וַתֵּלֶד לֶאֱלִיפַז אֶת־עֲמָלֵק אֵלֶּה בְּנֵי
יג עָדָה אֵשֶׁת עֵשָׂו׃ וְאֵלֶּה בְּנֵי רְעוּאֵל נַחַת וָזֶרַח שַׁמָּה וּמִזָּה אֵלֶּה הָיוּ

Zeraḥ, Shama, and Miza. These were the descendants of Esav's wife Basmat.
14 The sons of Oholivama, daughter of Ana and granddaughter of Esav's wife
15 Tzivon, whom she bore to Esav, were Yeush, Yalam, and Koraḥ. These were
the tribal chiefs among Esav's descendants. The sons of Elifaz, Esav's firstborn,
16 were the chiefs Teiman, Omar, Tzefo, Kenaz, Koraḥ, Gatam, and Amalek.
These were the chiefs descended from Elifaz in Edom; they were grandsons
17 of Ada. The sons of Esav's son Reuel were the chiefs Naḥat, Zeraḥ, Shama,
and Miza. These were the chiefs descended from Reuel in Edom; they were
18 grandsons of Esav's wife Basmat. The sons of Esav's wife Oholivama were
the chiefs Yeush, Yalam, and Koraḥ. These were the chiefs descended from
19 Esav's wife Oholivama daughter of Ana. These were the sons of Esav – that
20 is, Edom – and these were their chiefs. These are the sons of Se'ir
21 the Horite who were settled in the land: Lotan, Shoval, Tzivon, Ana, Dishon,
Etzer, and Dishan. These were the chiefs of the Horites, descendants of Se'ir
22 in the land of Edom. Lotan's sons were Ḥori and Heimam. Timna was Lotan's
23 24 sister. Shoval's sons were Alvan, Manaḥat, Eival, Shefo, and Onam. Tzivon's
sons were Aya and Ana. This is the Ana who discovered hot springs in the
25 desert while pasturing the donkeys of his father Tzivon. Ana's children were
26 Dishon and Oholivama daughter of Ana. Dishon's sons were Ḥemdan,
27 Eshban, Yitran, and Keran. Etzer's sons were Bilhan, Zaavan, and Akan.
28 29 Dishan's sons were Utz and Aran. These were the tribal chiefs of the Horites:
30 chiefs Lotan, Shoval, Tzivon, Ana, Dishon, Etzer, and Dishan. These were the
Horite chiefs by their divisions in the land of Se'ir.
31 These were the kings who reigned in Edom before any king reigned over
32 the Israelites. Bela son of Beor became king in Edom. His city was named
33 Dinhava. When Bela died, Yovav son of Zeraḥ from Botzra succeeded him as
34 king. When Yovav died, Ḥusham from the land of the Temanites succeeded
35 him as king. When Ḥusham died, Hadad son of Bedad, who defeated Midyan
in the country of Moav, succeeded him as king. His city was named Avit.
36 37 When Hadad died, Samla from Masreka succeeded him as king. When Samla
38 died, Sha'ul from Reḥovot HaNahar succeeded him as king. When Sha'ul
39 died, Baal Ḥanan son of Akhbor succeeded him as king. When Baal Ḥanan
son of Akhbor died, Hadar succeeded him as king. His city was named Pa'u,
and his wife's name was Meheitavel, daughter of Matred, daughter of Mei
40 Zahav. These were the chiefs descended from Esav, by their clans, localities,
41 42 and names: the chiefs Timna, Alva, Yetet, Oholivama, Ela, Pinon, Kenaz,
43 Teiman, Mivtzar, Magdiel, and Iram. These were the chiefs of Edom – of
Esav, ancestor of the Edomites – each with their own settlements in the land
that they held.

יד בְּנֵי בָשְׂמַת אֵשֶׁת עֵשָׂו: וְאֵלֶּה הָיוּ בְּנֵי אָהֳלִיבָמָה בַת־עֲנָה בַּת־צִבְעוֹן
טו אֵשֶׁת עֵשָׂו וַתֵּלֶד לְעֵשָׂו את־יעיש וְאֶת־יַעְלָם וְאֶת־קֹרַח: אֵלֶּה אַלּוּפֵי יְעוּשׁ
בְנֵי־עֵשָׂו בְּנֵי אֱלִיפַז בְּכוֹר עֵשָׂו אַלּוּף תֵּימָן אַלּוּף אוֹמָר אַלּוּף צְפוֹ
טז אַלּוּף קְנַז: אַלּוּף־קֹרַח אַלּוּף גַּעְתָּם אַלּוּף עֲמָלֵק אֵלֶּה אַלּוּפֵי אֱלִיפַז
יז בְּאֶרֶץ אֱדוֹם אֵלֶּה בְּנֵי עָדָה: וְאֵלֶּה בְּנֵי רְעוּאֵל בֶּן־עֵשָׂו אַלּוּף נַחַת
אַלּוּף זֶרַח אַלּוּף שַׁמָּה אַלּוּף מִזָּה אֵלֶּה אַלּוּפֵי רְעוּאֵל בְּאֶרֶץ אֱדוֹם
יח אֵלֶּה בְּנֵי בָשְׂמַת אֵשֶׁת עֵשָׂו: וְאֵלֶּה בְּנֵי אָהֳלִיבָמָה אֵשֶׁת עֵשָׂו אַלּוּף
יְעוּשׁ אַלּוּף יַעְלָם אַלּוּף קֹרַח אֵלֶּה אַלּוּפֵי אָהֳלִיבָמָה בַּת־עֲנָה אֵשֶׁת
יט כ עֵשָׂו: אֵלֶּה בְנֵי־עֵשָׂו וְאֵלֶּה אַלּוּפֵיהֶם הוּא אֱדוֹם: אֵלֶּה שביעי
כא בְנֵי־שֵׂעִיר הַחֹרִי יֹשְׁבֵי הָאָרֶץ לוֹטָן וְשׁוֹבָל וְצִבְעוֹן וַעֲנָה: וְדִשׁוֹן וְאֵצֶר
כב וְדִישָׁן אֵלֶּה אַלּוּפֵי הַחֹרִי בְּנֵי שֵׂעִיר בְּאֶרֶץ אֱדוֹם: וַיִּהְיוּ בְנֵי־לוֹטָן חֹרִי
כג וְהֵימָם וַאֲחוֹת לוֹטָן תִּמְנָע: וְאֵלֶּה בְּנֵי שׁוֹבָל עַלְוָן וּמָנַחַת וְעֵיבָל שְׁפוֹ
כד וְאוֹנָם: וְאֵלֶּה בְנֵי־צִבְעוֹן וְאַיָּה וַעֲנָה הוּא עֲנָה אֲשֶׁר מָצָא אֶת־הַיֵּמִם
כה בַּמִּדְבָּר בִּרְעֹתוֹ אֶת־הַחֲמֹרִים לְצִבְעוֹן אָבִיו: וְאֵלֶּה בְנֵי־עֲנָה דִּשֹׁן
כו וְאָהֳלִיבָמָה בַּת־עֲנָה: וְאֵלֶּה בְּנֵי דִישָׁן חֶמְדָּן וְאֶשְׁבָּן וְיִתְרָן וּכְרָן:
כז כח כט אֵלֶּה בְּנֵי־אֵצֶר בִּלְהָן וְזַעֲוָן וַעֲקָן: אֵלֶּה בְנֵי־דִישָׁן עוּץ וַאֲרָן: אֵלֶּה
ל אַלּוּפֵי הַחֹרִי אַלּוּף לוֹטָן אַלּוּף שׁוֹבָל אַלּוּף צִבְעוֹן אַלּוּף עֲנָה: אַלּוּף
דִּשֹׁן אַלּוּף אֵצֶר אַלּוּף דִּישָׁן אֵלֶּה אַלּוּפֵי הַחֹרִי לְאַלֻּפֵיהֶם בְּאֶרֶץ
שֵׂעִיר:
לא וְאֵלֶּה הַמְּלָכִים אֲשֶׁר מָלְכוּ בְּאֶרֶץ אֱדוֹם לִפְנֵי מְלָךְ־מֶלֶךְ לִבְנֵי
לב לג יִשְׂרָאֵל: וַיִּמְלֹךְ בֶּאֱדוֹם בֶּלַע בֶּן־בְּעוֹר וְשֵׁם עִירוֹ דִּנְהָבָה: וַיָּמָת בָּלַע
לד וַיִּמְלֹךְ תַּחְתָּיו יוֹבָב בֶּן־זֶרַח מִבָּצְרָה: וַיָּמָת יוֹבָב וַיִּמְלֹךְ תַּחְתָּיו חֻשָׁם
לה מֵאֶרֶץ הַתֵּימָנִי: וַיָּמָת חֻשָׁם וַיִּמְלֹךְ תַּחְתָּיו הֲדַד בֶּן־בְּדַד הַמַּכֶּה אֶת־
לו מִדְיָן בִּשְׂדֵה מוֹאָב וְשֵׁם עִירוֹ עֲוִית: וַיָּמָת הֲדָד וַיִּמְלֹךְ תַּחְתָּיו שַׂמְלָה
לז לח מִמַּשְׂרֵקָה: וַיָּמָת שַׂמְלָה וַיִּמְלֹךְ תַּחְתָּיו שָׁאוּל מֵרְחֹבוֹת הַנָּהָר: וַיָּמָת
לט שָׁאוּל וַיִּמְלֹךְ תַּחְתָּיו בַּעַל חָנָן בֶּן־עַכְבּוֹר: וַיָּמָת בַּעַל חָנָן בֶּן־עַכְבּוֹר
וַיִּמְלֹךְ תַּחְתָּיו הֲדַר וְשֵׁם עִירוֹ פָּעוּ וְשֵׁם אִשְׁתּוֹ מְהֵיטַבְאֵל בַּת־מַטְרֵד
מ בַּת מֵי זָהָב: וְאֵלֶּה שְׁמוֹת אַלּוּפֵי עֵשָׂו לְמִשְׁפְּחֹתָם לִמְקֹמֹתָם בִּשְׁמֹתָם מפטיר
מא אַלּוּף תִּמְנָע אַלּוּף עַלְוָה אַלּוּף יְתֵת: אַלּוּף אָהֳלִיבָמָה אַלּוּף אֵלָה
מב מג אַלּוּף פִּינֹן: אַלּוּף קְנַז אַלּוּף תֵּימָן אַלּוּף מִבְצָר: אַלּוּף מַגְדִּיאֵל אַלּוּף
עִירָם אֵלֶּה ׀ אַלּוּפֵי אֱדוֹם לְמֹשְׁבֹתָם בְּאֶרֶץ אֲחֻזָּתָם הוּא עֵשָׂו אֲבִי
אֱדוֹם:

37 1 Yaakov settled where his father had lived as a stranger, in the land of Canaan. VAYESHEV
2 This is the story of Yaakov. Yosef, seventeen years old, was shepherding the
flock with his brothers, an assistant to the sons of his father's wives Bilha
3 and Zilpa. And Yosef brought his father bad reports of them. Now, Yisrael
loved Yosef more than all his other sons, for he was a child of his old age;
4 he made him an ornately colored robe. But when his brothers saw that their
father loved him more than any of them, they hated him and could not say
5 a peaceful word to him. Then Yosef had a dream, and when he told it to his
6 brothers, they hated him still more. "Listen to this dream I had," he said.
7 "We were binding sheaves in the field when my sheaf rose and stood upright
8 and your sheaves gathered around mine and bowed down to it." His brothers
said to him, "Do you mean to be king over us? Do you mean to rule over us?"
9 Then they hated him even more for his dreams and for what he said. Then
he had another dream and told it to his brothers. "I had another dream," he
said. "This time, the sun, moon, and eleven stars were bowing down to me."
10 When he told his father as well as his brothers, his father rebuked him and
said, "What kind of dream is this that you have had? Shall we really come, I
11 and your mother and your brothers, to bow to the ground before you?" His
12 brothers were jealous of him; but his father kept the matter in mind. When
13 his brothers had gone to pasture their father's flock near Shekhem, Yisrael
said to Yosef, "Come, your brothers are pasturing the flocks near Shekhem; I
14 will send you to them." Yosef said, "Here I am." He said to him, "Go and see
how your brothers and the flocks are doing, and bring me back word," and
15 he sent him from the Ḥevron Valley, from where he walked to Shekhem. A
man found him wandering lost among the fields and asked him, "What are
16 you looking for?" He replied, "I'm looking for my brothers. Can you tell
17 me where they are pasturing the sheep?" "They have moved on from here,"
said the man. "I heard them say, 'Let us go to Dotan.'" So Yosef went after
18 his brothers and found them at Dotan. They saw him in the distance, and
19 by the time he reached them, they had plotted to kill him. "Here comes the
20 dreamer!" they said to one another. "Now let us kill him and throw him into
one of the pits – we can say that a wild animal ate him – then we shall see
21 what will come of his dreams!" When Reuven heard this, he tried to save him
22 from them. "Let us not kill him," he said. "Do not shed blood," said Reuven.
"Throw him into this pit in the desert, but do not lay hands on him." His plan
23 was to rescue him and bring him back to his father. So when Yosef came to
his brothers, they stripped him of his robe, the ornately colored robe he was
24 wearing, and they took him and threw him into the pit. The pit was empty;
25 there was no water in it. And they sat down and ate their meal. Looking up,
they saw a caravan of Ishmaelites coming from Gilad, their camels laden with

לז א וַיֵּשֶׁב יַעֲקֹב בְּאֶרֶץ מְגוּרֵי אָבִיו בְּאֶרֶץ כְּנָעַן: ב אֵלֶּה ׀ תֹּלְדוֹת יַעֲקֹב יוֹסֵף לג וישב
בֶּן־שְׁבַע־עֶשְׂרֵה שָׁנָה הָיָה רֹעֶה אֶת־אֶחָיו בַּצֹּאן וְהוּא נַעַר אֶת־בְּנֵי
בִלְהָה וְאֶת־בְּנֵי זִלְפָּה נְשֵׁי אָבִיו וַיָּבֵא יוֹסֵף אֶת־דִּבָּתָם רָעָה אֶל־
ג אֲבִיהֶם: וְיִשְׂרָאֵל אָהַב אֶת־יוֹסֵף מִכָּל־בָּנָיו כִּי־בֶן־זְקֻנִים הוּא לוֹ וְעָשָׂה
ד לוֹ כְּתֹנֶת פַּסִּים: וַיִּרְאוּ אֶחָיו כִּי־אֹתוֹ אָהַב אֲבִיהֶם מִכָּל־אֶחָיו וַיִּשְׂנְאוּ
ה אֹתוֹ וְלֹא יָכְלוּ דַּבְּרוֹ לְשָׁלֹם: וַיַּחֲלֹם יוֹסֵף חֲלוֹם וַיַּגֵּד לְאֶחָיו וַיּוֹסִפוּ
ו עוֹד שְׂנֹא אֹתוֹ: וַיֹּאמֶר אֲלֵיהֶם שִׁמְעוּ־נָא הַחֲלוֹם הַזֶּה אֲשֶׁר חָלָמְתִּי:
ז וְהִנֵּה אֲנַחְנוּ מְאַלְּמִים אֲלֻמִּים בְּתוֹךְ הַשָּׂדֶה וְהִנֵּה קָמָה אֲלֻמָּתִי
ח וְגַם־נִצָּבָה וְהִנֵּה תְסֻבֶּינָה אֲלֻמֹּתֵיכֶם וַתִּשְׁתַּחֲוֶיןָ לַאֲלֻמָּתִי: וַיֹּאמְרוּ
לוֹ אֶחָיו הֲמָלֹךְ תִּמְלֹךְ עָלֵינוּ אִם־מָשׁוֹל תִּמְשֹׁל בָּנוּ וַיּוֹסִפוּ עוֹד שְׂנֹא
ט אֹתוֹ עַל־חֲלֹמֹתָיו וְעַל־דְּבָרָיו: וַיַּחֲלֹם עוֹד חֲלוֹם אַחֵר וַיְסַפֵּר אֹתוֹ
לְאֶחָיו וַיֹּאמֶר הִנֵּה חָלַמְתִּי חֲלוֹם עוֹד וְהִנֵּה הַשֶּׁמֶשׁ וְהַיָּרֵחַ וְאַחַד
י עָשָׂר כּוֹכָבִים מִשְׁתַּחֲוִים לִי: וַיְסַפֵּר אֶל־אָבִיו וְאֶל־אֶחָיו וַיִּגְעַר־בּוֹ
אָבִיו וַיֹּאמֶר לוֹ מָה הַחֲלוֹם הַזֶּה אֲשֶׁר חָלָמְתָּ הֲבוֹא נָבוֹא אֲנִי וְאִמְּךָ
יא וְאַחֶיךָ לְהִשְׁתַּחֲוֹת לְךָ אָרְצָה: וַיְקַנְאוּ־בוֹ אֶחָיו וְאָבִיו שָׁמַר אֶת־
יב יג הַדָּבָר: וַיֵּלְכוּ אֶחָיו לִרְעוֹת אֶת־צֹאן אֲבִיהֶם בִּשְׁכֶם: וַיֹּאמֶר יִשְׂרָאֵל שני
אֶל־יוֹסֵף הֲלוֹא אַחֶיךָ רֹעִים בִּשְׁכֶם לְכָה וְאֶשְׁלָחֲךָ אֲלֵיהֶם וַיֹּאמֶר
יד לוֹ הִנֵּנִי: וַיֹּאמֶר לוֹ לֶךְ־נָא רְאֵה אֶת־שְׁלוֹם אַחֶיךָ וְאֶת־שְׁלוֹם הַצֹּאן
טו וַהֲשִׁבֵנִי דָּבָר וַיִּשְׁלָחֵהוּ מֵעֵמֶק חֶבְרוֹן וַיָּבֹא שְׁכֶמָה: וַיִּמְצָאֵהוּ אִישׁ
טז וְהִנֵּה תֹעֶה בַּשָּׂדֶה וַיִּשְׁאָלֵהוּ הָאִישׁ לֵאמֹר מַה־תְּבַקֵּשׁ: וַיֹּאמֶר אֶת־
יז אַחַי אָנֹכִי מְבַקֵּשׁ הַגִּידָה־נָּא לִי אֵיפֹה הֵם רֹעִים: וַיֹּאמֶר הָאִישׁ נָסְעוּ
מִזֶּה כִּי שָׁמַעְתִּי אֹמְרִים נֵלְכָה דֹּתָיְנָה וַיֵּלֶךְ יוֹסֵף אַחַר אֶחָיו וַיִּמְצָאֵם
יח בְּדֹתָן: וַיִּרְאוּ אֹתוֹ מֵרָחֹק וּבְטֶרֶם יִקְרַב אֲלֵיהֶם וַיִּתְנַכְּלוּ אֹתוֹ לַהֲמִיתוֹ:
יט כ וַיֹּאמְרוּ אִישׁ אֶל־אָחִיו הִנֵּה בַּעַל הַחֲלֹמוֹת הַלָּזֶה בָּא: וְעַתָּה ׀ לְכוּ
וְנַהַרְגֵהוּ וְנַשְׁלִכֵהוּ בְּאַחַד הַבֹּרוֹת וְאָמַרְנוּ חַיָּה רָעָה אֲכָלָתְהוּ וְנִרְאֶה
כא מַה־יִּהְיוּ חֲלֹמֹתָיו: וַיִּשְׁמַע רְאוּבֵן וַיַּצִּלֵהוּ מִיָּדָם וַיֹּאמֶר לֹא נַכֶּנּוּ נָפֶשׁ:
כב וַיֹּאמֶר אֲלֵהֶם ׀ רְאוּבֵן אַל־תִּשְׁפְּכוּ־דָם הַשְׁלִיכוּ אֹתוֹ אֶל־הַבּוֹר הַזֶּה
אֲשֶׁר בַּמִּדְבָּר וְיָד אַל־תִּשְׁלְחוּ־בוֹ לְמַעַן הַצִּיל אֹתוֹ מִיָּדָם לַהֲשִׁיבוֹ
כג אֶל־אָבִיו: וַיְהִי כַּאֲשֶׁר־בָּא יוֹסֵף אֶל־אֶחָיו וַיַּפְשִׁיטוּ אֶת־יוֹסֵף אֶת־ שלישי
כד כֻּתָּנְתּוֹ אֶת־כְּתֹנֶת הַפַּסִּים אֲשֶׁר עָלָיו: וַיִּקָּחֻהוּ וַיַּשְׁלִכוּ אֹתוֹ הַבֹּרָה
כה וְהַבּוֹר רֵק אֵין בּוֹ מָיִם: וַיֵּשְׁבוּ לֶאֱכָל־לֶחֶם וַיִּשְׂאוּ עֵינֵיהֶם וַיִּרְאוּ וְהִנֵּה
אֹרְחַת יִשְׁמְעֵאלִים בָּאָה מִגִּלְעָד וּגְמַלֵּיהֶם נֹשְׂאִים נְכֹאת וּצְרִי וָלֹט

26 spices, balm, and myrrh, to be taken to Egypt. Yehuda said to his brothers,
27 "What do we gain by killing our brother and covering his blood? Let's sell
him to the Ishmaelites and not harm him with our own hands. After all, he is
28 our brother, our own flesh and blood." His brothers agreed. Some Midianite
traders passed by and they pulled Yosef up out of the pit, and they sold him
to the Ishmaelites for twenty pieces of silver. They then brought Yosef to
29 Egypt. Reuven returned to the pit – and Yosef was not there. He tore his
30 clothes, went back to his brothers, and said, "The boy is gone, and I – where
31 can I turn?" They took Yosef's robe, slaughtered a goat, and dipped the robe
32 in the blood. They had the ornately colored robe brought to their father,
and they said, "We found this. Try to identify it. Is it your son's robe or not?"
33 He recognized it and said, "It is my son's robe! A wild animal must have
34 eaten him! Yosef has been torn limb from limb!" Yaakov tore his clothes, put
35 sackcloth on his loins, and mourned for his son for many days. All his sons
and daughters tried to comfort him, but he refused to be comforted and said,
"I will go down to Sheol[90] mourning for my son." His father wept for him.
36 Meanwhile, the Medanites had sold him in Egypt to Potifar, one of Pharaoh's
officials, captain of the guard.

38 1 Around that time, Yehuda left his brothers and camped near an Adulamite
2 named Ḥira. There, Yehuda met the daughter of Shua, a Canaanite, and he
3 married her and came to her. She became pregnant and had a son, whom he
4 named Er. She became pregnant again and had another son, and she named
5 him Onan. She had yet another son and named him Shela; Yehuda was in
6 Keziv when she gave birth to him. Yehuda took a wife for his firstborn, Er;
7 her name was Tamar. But Er, Yehuda's firstborn, was wicked in the Lord's
8 sight, and the Lord took his life. Yehuda then said to Onan, "Go in to your
brother's wife and fulfill your duty as her brother-in-law.[91] Provide children
9 for your brother." But Onan knew that the children would not be considered
his. Whenever he came to his brother's wife, he let his seed go to waste on
10 the ground so as not to have children in his brother's name. What he did was
11 wicked in the Lord's sight, and so He took his life also. Then Yehuda said to
his daughter-in-law Tamar, "Live as a widow in your father's house until my
son Shela grows up" – for he thought he too might die like his brothers. So
12 Tamar went to live in her father's house. A long time passed, and Yehuda's
wife, Shua's daughter, died. When he had completed his time of mourning,
he and his neighbor Ḥira the Adulamite went to join his sheepshearers in
13 Timna. Tamar was told, "Your father-in-law is going to Timna to shear his
14 sheep." And she took off her widow's clothes and covered herself with a veil.
Disguised, she sat at the entrance to Einayim on the road to Timna, for she
had seen that Shela was now grown up and yet she had not been given to him
15 as a wife. Yehuda saw her and thought she was a prostitute, because she had
16 covered her face. Not realizing that she was his daughter-in-law, he turned
aside to her on the road and said, "Come, let me sleep with you." She said,

90 | The netherworld.

91 | On levirate marriage, see Deuteronomy 25:5–10.

כו הֹלְכִים לְהוֹרִיד מִצְרָיְמָה׃ וַיֹּאמֶר יְהוּדָה אֶל־אֶחָיו מַה־בֶּצַע כִּי
כז נַהֲרֹג אֶת־אָחִינוּ וְכִסִּינוּ אֶת־דָּמוֹ׃ לְכוּ וְנִמְכְּרֶנּוּ לַיִּשְׁמְעֵאלִים וְיָדֵנוּ
כח אַל־תְּהִי־בוֹ כִּי־אָחִינוּ בְשָׂרֵנוּ הוּא וַיִּשְׁמְעוּ אֶחָיו׃ וַיַּעַבְרוּ אֲנָשִׁים
מִדְיָנִים סֹחֲרִים וַיִּמְשְׁכוּ וַיַּעֲלוּ אֶת־יוֹסֵף מִן־הַבּוֹר וַיִּמְכְּרוּ אֶת־יוֹסֵף
כט לַיִּשְׁמְעֵאלִים בְּעֶשְׂרִים כָּסֶף וַיָּבִיאוּ אֶת־יוֹסֵף מִצְרָיְמָה׃ וַיָּשָׁב רְאוּבֵן
ל אֶל־הַבּוֹר וְהִנֵּה אֵין־יוֹסֵף בַּבּוֹר וַיִּקְרַע אֶת־בְּגָדָיו׃ וַיָּשָׁב אֶל־אֶחָיו
לא וַיֹּאמַר הַיֶּלֶד אֵינֶנּוּ וַאֲנִי אָנָה אֲנִי־בָא׃ וַיִּקְחוּ אֶת־כְּתֹנֶת יוֹסֵף וַיִּשְׁחֲטוּ
לב שְׂעִיר עִזִּים וַיִּטְבְּלוּ אֶת־הַכֻּתֹּנֶת בַּדָּם׃ וַיְשַׁלְּחוּ אֶת־כְּתֹנֶת הַפַּסִּים
וַיָּבִיאוּ אֶל־אֲבִיהֶם וַיֹּאמְרוּ זֹאת מָצָאנוּ הַכֶּר־נָא הַכְּתֹנֶת בִּנְךָ הִוא
לג אִם־לֹא׃ וַיַּכִּירָהּ וַיֹּאמֶר כְּתֹנֶת בְּנִי חַיָּה רָעָה אֲכָלָתְהוּ טָרֹף טֹרַף
לד יוֹסֵף׃ וַיִּקְרַע יַעֲקֹב שִׂמְלֹתָיו וַיָּשֶׂם שַׂק בְּמָתְנָיו וַיִּתְאַבֵּל עַל־בְּנוֹ
לה יָמִים רַבִּים׃ וַיָּקֻמוּ כָל־בָּנָיו וְכָל־בְּנֹתָיו לְנַחֲמוֹ וַיְמָאֵן לְהִתְנַחֵם וַיֹּאמֶר
לו כִּי־אֵרֵד אֶל־בְּנִי אָבֵל שְׁאֹלָה וַיֵּבְךְּ אֹתוֹ אָבִיו׃ וְהַמְּדָנִים מָכְרוּ אֹתוֹ
אֶל־מִצְרָיִם לְפוֹטִיפַר סְרִיס פַּרְעֹה שַׂר הַטַּבָּחִים׃

לח א וַיְהִי בָּעֵת הַהִוא וַיֵּרֶד יְהוּדָה מֵאֵת אֶחָיו וַיֵּט עַד־אִישׁ עֲדֻלָּמִי וּשְׁמוֹ לד רביעי
ב חִירָה׃ וַיַּרְא־שָׁם יְהוּדָה בַּת־אִישׁ כְּנַעֲנִי וּשְׁמוֹ שׁוּעַ וַיִּקָּחֶהָ וַיָּבֹא
ג ד אֵלֶיהָ׃ וַתַּהַר וַתֵּלֶד בֵּן וַיִּקְרָא אֶת־שְׁמוֹ עֵר׃ וַתַּהַר עוֹד וַתֵּלֶד בֵּן
ה וַתִּקְרָא אֶת־שְׁמוֹ אוֹנָן׃ וַתֹּסֶף עוֹד וַתֵּלֶד בֵּן וַתִּקְרָא אֶת־שְׁמוֹ שֵׁלָה
ו וְהָיָה בִכְזִיב בְּלִדְתָּהּ אֹתוֹ׃ וַיִּקַּח יְהוּדָה אִשָּׁה לְעֵר בְּכוֹרוֹ וּשְׁמָהּ
ז ח תָּמָר׃ וַיְהִי עֵר בְּכוֹר יְהוּדָה רַע בְּעֵינֵי יהוה וַיְמִתֵהוּ יהוה׃ וַיֹּאמֶר
יְהוּדָה לְאוֹנָן בֹּא אֶל־אֵשֶׁת אָחִיךָ וְיַבֵּם אֹתָהּ וְהָקֵם זֶרַע לְאָחִיךָ׃
ט וַיֵּדַע אוֹנָן כִּי לֹּא לוֹ יִהְיֶה הַזָּרַע וְהָיָה אִם־בָּא אֶל־אֵשֶׁת אָחִיו וְשִׁחֵת
י אַרְצָה לְבִלְתִּי נְתָן־זֶרַע לְאָחִיו׃ וַיֵּרַע בְּעֵינֵי יהוה אֲשֶׁר עָשָׂה וַיָּמֶת
יא גַּם־אֹתוֹ׃ וַיֹּאמֶר יְהוּדָה לְתָמָר כַּלָּתוֹ שְׁבִי אַלְמָנָה בֵית־אָבִיךְ עַד־
יִגְדַּל שֵׁלָה בְנִי כִּי אָמַר פֶּן־יָמוּת גַּם־הוּא כְּאֶחָיו וַתֵּלֶךְ תָּמָר וַתֵּשֶׁב
יב בֵּית אָבִיהָ׃ וַיִּרְבּוּ הַיָּמִים וַתָּמָת בַּת־שׁוּעַ אֵשֶׁת־יְהוּדָה וַיִּנָּחֶם יְהוּדָה
יג וַיַּעַל עַל־גֹּזְזֵי צֹאנוֹ הוּא וְחִירָה רֵעֵהוּ הָעֲדֻלָּמִי תִּמְנָתָה׃ וַיֻּגַּד לְתָמָר
יד לֵאמֹר הִנֵּה חָמִיךְ עֹלֶה תִמְנָתָה לָגֹז צֹאנוֹ׃ וַתָּסַר בִּגְדֵי אַלְמְנוּתָהּ
מֵעָלֶיהָ וַתְּכַס בַּצָּעִיף וַתִּתְעַלָּף וַתֵּשֶׁב בְּפֶתַח עֵינַיִם אֲשֶׁר עַל־דֶּרֶךְ
טו תִּמְנָתָה כִּי רָאֲתָה כִּי־גָדַל שֵׁלָה וְהִוא לֹא־נִתְּנָה לוֹ לְאִשָּׁה׃ וַיִּרְאֶהָ
טז יְהוּדָה וַיַּחְשְׁבֶהָ לְזוֹנָה כִּי כִסְּתָה פָּנֶיהָ׃ וַיֵּט אֵלֶיהָ אֶל־הַדֶּרֶךְ וַיֹּאמֶר

17 "What will you give me to sleep with you?" He said, "I will send you a young
goat from my flock." "Only if you give me something as a pledge until you
18 send it," she said. "What pledge should I give you?" he asked. She answered,
"Your seal and cord, and the staff in your hand." He gave them to her and went
19 in to her – and she became pregnant by him. She got up and left, removed her
20 veil, and put on her widow's clothes again. And Yehuda sent the young goat
by his neighbor the Adulamite, to recover the pledge from the woman, but
21 he could not find her. He asked the local men, "Where is the cult prostitute,[92]
the one by the roadside at Einayim?" They said, "No cult prostitute has been
22 here." So he went back to Yehuda and said, "I could not find her. Besides, the
23 local men said that there was no cult prostitute there." Yehuda said, "Let her
keep what she has or we will become a laughingstock. I tried to send her this
24 young goat, but you could not find her." About three months later, Yehuda
was told, "Your daughter-in-law Tamar has behaved as a loose woman; in
fact she has become pregnant by her harlotry." "Take her out and let her be
25 burned," Yehuda said. As she was being brought out, she sent her father-
in-law a message: "I am pregnant by the man to whom these belong." She
26 added, "Please identify to whom this seal and cord and staff belong." Yehuda
recognized them and said, "She is more righteous than I. It was because I did
27 not give her to Shela my son." He did not know her intimately again. When
28 the time came for her to give birth, there were twins in her womb. As she was
in labor one child put out a hand, so the midwife took a crimson thread and
29 tied it to his wrist, saying, "This one came out first." But he pulled his hand
back and then his brother came out. She said, "How you have burst through!"
30 So he was named Peretz.[93] Then his brother came out with the crimson thread
39 1 on his wrist. He was named Zeraḥ.[94] Meanwhile, Yosef had been
brought down to Egypt. Potifar, an Egyptian, one of Pharaoh's officials and
captain of the guard, had bought him from the Ishmaelites who had brought
2 him there. The Lord was with Yosef, and he became a successful man. He
3 lived in the house of his Egyptian master. And his master saw that the Lord
4 was with him and that the Lord granted him success in all he did; Yosef
found favor in his eyes and became his personal attendant. Potifar put him
5 in charge of his household, giving him responsibility for all he owned. From
the moment he put him in charge of his household and all he owned, the
Lord blessed the Egyptian because of Yosef. The Lord's blessing was in all
6 he owned, in house and field. And so he left all he had in Yosef's hands and,
with him there, he had no concern for anything but the food he ate.[95] Now,
7 Yosef was well built and handsome, and after a while, his master's wife cast
8 her eyes on Yosef. "Lie with me," she said. But he refused. "With me here," he
told her, "my master does not concern himself with the running of the house;
9 he has entrusted me with all that he owns. No one in this house has greater

92 | A type of prostitute associated with religious worship.

93 | Meaning "bursting through."

94 | The term *zeraḥ* means "shining," an apparent reference to the color of the thread.

95 | Possibly a euphemism for his wife (cf. v. 9).

הָבָה נָּא אָבוֹא אֵלַיִךְ כִּי לֹא יָדַע כִּי כַלָּתוֹ הִוא וַתֹּאמֶר מַה־תִּתֶּן־לִּי
יז כִּי תָבוֹא אֵלָי: וַיֹּאמֶר אָנֹכִי אֲשַׁלַּח גְּדִי־עִזִּים מִן־הַצֹּאן וַתֹּאמֶר אִם־
יח תִּתֵּן עֵרָבוֹן עַד שָׁלְחֶךָ: וַיֹּאמֶר מָה הָעֵרָבוֹן אֲשֶׁר אֶתֶּן־לָּךְ וַתֹּאמֶר
חֹתָמְךָ וּפְתִילֶךָ וּמַטְּךָ אֲשֶׁר בְּיָדֶךָ וַיִּתֶּן־לָהּ וַיָּבֹא אֵלֶיהָ וַתַּהַר לוֹ:
יט כ וַתָּקָם וַתֵּלֶךְ וַתָּסַר צְעִיפָהּ מֵעָלֶיהָ וַתִּלְבַּשׁ בִּגְדֵי אַלְמְנוּתָהּ: וַיִּשְׁלַח
יְהוּדָה אֶת־גְּדִי הָעִזִּים בְּיַד רֵעֵהוּ הָעֲדֻלָּמִי לָקַחַת הָעֵרָבוֹן מִיַּד
כא הָאִשָּׁה וְלֹא מְצָאָהּ: וַיִּשְׁאַל אֶת־אַנְשֵׁי מְקֹמָהּ לֵאמֹר אַיֵּה הַקְּדֵשָׁה
כב הִוא בָעֵינַיִם עַל־הַדָּרֶךְ וַיֹּאמְרוּ לֹא־הָיְתָה בָזֶה קְדֵשָׁה: וַיָּשָׁב אֶל־
יְהוּדָה וַיֹּאמֶר לֹא מְצָאתִיהָ וְגַם אַנְשֵׁי הַמָּקוֹם אָמְרוּ לֹא־הָיְתָה בָזֶה
כג קְדֵשָׁה: וַיֹּאמֶר יְהוּדָה תִּקַּח־לָהּ פֶּן נִהְיֶה לָבוּז הִנֵּה שָׁלַחְתִּי הַגְּדִי הַזֶּה
כד וְאַתָּה לֹא מְצָאתָהּ: וַיְהִי ׀ כְּמִשְׁלֹשׁ חֳדָשִׁים וַיֻּגַּד לִיהוּדָה לֵאמֹר זָנְתָה
תָּמָר כַּלָּתֶךָ וְגַם הִנֵּה הָרָה לִזְנוּנִים וַיֹּאמֶר יְהוּדָה הוֹצִיאוּהָ וְתִשָּׂרֵף:
כה הִוא מוּצֵאת וְהִיא שָׁלְחָה אֶל־חָמִיהָ לֵאמֹר לְאִישׁ אֲשֶׁר־אֵלֶּה לּוֹ
אָנֹכִי הָרָה וַתֹּאמֶר הַכֶּר־נָא לְמִי הַחֹתֶמֶת וְהַפְּתִילִים וְהַמַּטֶּה הָאֵלֶּה:
כו וַיַּכֵּר יְהוּדָה וַיֹּאמֶר צָדְקָה מִמֶּנִּי כִּי־עַל־כֵּן לֹא־נְתַתִּיהָ לְשֵׁלָה בְנִי
כז כח וְלֹא־יָסַף עוֹד לְדַעְתָּהּ: וַיְהִי בְּעֵת לִדְתָּהּ וְהִנֵּה תְאוֹמִים בְּבִטְנָהּ: וַיְהִי
בְלִדְתָּהּ וַיִּתֶּן־יָד וַתִּקַּח הַמְיַלֶּדֶת וַתִּקְשֹׁר עַל־יָדוֹ שָׁנִי לֵאמֹר זֶה יָצָא
כט רִאשֹׁנָה: וַיְהִי ׀ כְּמֵשִׁיב יָדוֹ וְהִנֵּה יָצָא אָחִיו וַתֹּאמֶר מַה־פָּרַצְתָּ עָלֶיךָ
ל פָּרֶץ וַיִּקְרָא שְׁמוֹ פָּרֶץ: וְאַחַר יָצָא אָחִיו אֲשֶׁר עַל־יָדוֹ הַשָּׁנִי וַיִּקְרָא
לט א שְׁמוֹ זָרַח: וְיוֹסֵף הוּרַד מִצְרָיְמָה וַיִּקְנֵהוּ פּוֹטִיפַר סְרִיס לה חמישי
פַּרְעֹה שַׂר הַטַּבָּחִים אִישׁ מִצְרִי מִיַּד הַיִּשְׁמְעֵאלִים אֲשֶׁר הוֹרִדֻהוּ
ב שָׁמָּה: וַיְהִי יְהוָה אֶת־יוֹסֵף וַיְהִי אִישׁ מַצְלִיחַ וַיְהִי בְּבֵית אֲדֹנָיו הַמִּצְרִי:
ג וַיַּרְא אֲדֹנָיו כִּי יְהוָה אִתּוֹ וְכֹל אֲשֶׁר־הוּא עֹשֶׂה יְהוָה מַצְלִיחַ בְּיָדוֹ:
ד וַיִּמְצָא יוֹסֵף חֵן בְּעֵינָיו וַיְשָׁרֶת אֹתוֹ וַיַּפְקִדֵהוּ עַל־בֵּיתוֹ וְכָל־יֶשׁ־לוֹ
ה נָתַן בְּיָדוֹ: וַיְהִי מֵאָז הִפְקִיד אֹתוֹ בְּבֵיתוֹ וְעַל כָּל־אֲשֶׁר יֶשׁ־לוֹ וַיְבָרֶךְ
יְהוָה אֶת־בֵּית הַמִּצְרִי בִּגְלַל יוֹסֵף וַיְהִי בִּרְכַּת יְהוָה בְּכָל־אֲשֶׁר יֶשׁ־לוֹ
ו בַּבַּיִת וּבַשָּׂדֶה: וַיַּעֲזֹב כָּל־אֲשֶׁר־לוֹ בְּיַד־יוֹסֵף וְלֹא־יָדַע אִתּוֹ מְאוּמָה
כִּי אִם־הַלֶּחֶם אֲשֶׁר־הוּא אוֹכֵל וַיְהִי יוֹסֵף יְפֵה־תֹאַר וִיפֵה מַרְאֶה:
ז וַיְהִי אַחַר הַדְּבָרִים הָאֵלֶּה וַתִּשָּׂא אֵשֶׁת־אֲדֹנָיו אֶת־עֵינֶיהָ אֶל־יוֹסֵף ששי
ח וַתֹּאמֶר שִׁכְבָה עִמִּי: וַיְמָאֵן ׀ וַיֹּאמֶר אֶל־אֵשֶׁת אֲדֹנָיו הֵן אֲדֹנִי לֹא־
ט יָדַע אִתִּי מַה־בַּבָּיִת וְכֹל אֲשֶׁר־יֶשׁ־לוֹ נָתַן בְּיָדִי: אֵינֶנּוּ גָדוֹל בַּבַּיִת

authority than I. He has withheld nothing from me except you, because you
are his wife. How could I do so great a wrong? It would be a sin against God!"
10 And though she spoke to Yosef day after day, he would not consent to lie
11 with her or be with her. One day he came into the house to do his work and
12 none of the other servants were there. She caught him by his cloak and said,
13 "Lie with me!" He ran away from her and fled outside. When she saw that
14 he had left his cloak in her hand and had run out of the house, she called out
to her servants and said to them, "Look! He brought us a Hebrew to mock[96]
15 us! He came to me to lie with me, but I screamed. And when he heard me
16 scream and cry for help, he left his cloak with me and ran outside." She kept
17 his cloak beside her until his master came home. Then she told him the same
18 story: "The Hebrew slave you brought us came to me to mock me. I screamed
19 and called for help, and he left his cloak with me and ran outside." When his
master heard the story his wife told him – "This is what your servant did to
20 me!" – he was incensed. Yosef's master had him put in prison, where the
21 king's prisoners were confined. He remained there in prison. But the LORD
was with Yosef and showed him kindness, granting him favor in the eyes of
22 the prison warden. The warden put Yosef in charge of all the prisoners in the
23 jail. Everything done there was under his direction. The warden did not need
to pay attention to anything he had entrusted to him, because the LORD was
with him, giving him success in all he did.
40 1 Some time later, the Egyptian kings' cupbearer and baker gave offense to
2 their master, the king of Egypt. Pharaoh was angry with the two officials,
3 his chief cupbearer, and his chief baker, and he placed them in custody in
the house of the captain of the guard, in the very place where Yosef was
4 confined. The captain of the guard assigned them to Yosef and it was he who
5 attended them. When they had been in custody for some time, the two of
them – the imprisoned cupbearer and baker of the king of Egypt – each had
6 a dream on the same night, each dream seeming to carry its own meaning.
When Yosef came to them the next morning, he saw that they were both
7 distressed. He asked Pharaoh's officials who were in custody with him in his
8 master's house, "Why are you looking so troubled today?" "We both had
dreams," they told him, "but there is no one to interpret them." Yosef replied,
9 "Interpretation belongs to God. Tell me your dreams." So the chief cupbearer
told his dream to Yosef and said to him, "In my dream I saw a vine in front
10 of me. The vine had three branches. As soon as it budded, it blossomed, and
11 its clusters ripened into grapes. Pharaoh's cup was in my hand; I took the

96 | This verb (*letzaḥek*) can have sexual connotations (cf., e.g., v. 17, 21:9, 26:8; Ex. 32:6).

הַזֶּה מִמֶּנִּי וְלֹא־חָשַׂךְ מִמֶּנִּי מְאוּמָה כִּי אִם־אוֹתָךְ בַּאֲשֶׁר אַתְּ־אִשְׁתּוֹ
י וְאֵיךְ אֶעֱשֶׂה הָרָעָה הַגְּדֹלָה הַזֹּאת וְחָטָאתִי לֵאלֹהִים: וַיְהִי כְּדַבְּרָהּ
יא אֶל־יוֹסֵף יוֹם ׀ יוֹם וְלֹא־שָׁמַע אֵלֶיהָ לִשְׁכַּב אֶצְלָהּ לִהְיוֹת עִמָּהּ: וַיְהִי
כְּהַיּוֹם הַזֶּה וַיָּבֹא הַבַּיְתָה לַעֲשׂוֹת מְלַאכְתּוֹ וְאֵין אִישׁ מֵאַנְשֵׁי הַבַּיִת
יב שָׁם בַּבָּיִת: וַתִּתְפְּשֵׂהוּ בְּבִגְדוֹ לֵאמֹר שִׁכְבָה עִמִּי וַיַּעֲזֹב בִּגְדוֹ בְּיָדָהּ
יג וַיָּנָס וַיֵּצֵא הַחוּצָה: וַיְהִי כִּרְאוֹתָהּ כִּי־עָזַב בִּגְדוֹ בְּיָדָהּ וַיָּנָס הַחוּצָה:
יד וַתִּקְרָא לְאַנְשֵׁי בֵיתָהּ וַתֹּאמֶר לָהֶם לֵאמֹר רְאוּ הֵבִיא לָנוּ אִישׁ עִבְרִי
טו לְצַחֶק בָּנוּ בָּא אֵלַי לִשְׁכַּב עִמִּי וָאֶקְרָא בְּקוֹל גָּדוֹל: וַיְהִי כְשָׁמְעוֹ כִּי־
טז הֲרִימֹתִי קוֹלִי וָאֶקְרָא וַיַּעֲזֹב בִּגְדוֹ אֶצְלִי וַיָּנָס וַיֵּצֵא הַחוּצָה: וַתַּנַּח בִּגְדוֹ
יז אֶצְלָהּ עַד־בּוֹא אֲדֹנָיו אֶל־בֵּיתוֹ: וַתְּדַבֵּר אֵלָיו כַּדְּבָרִים הָאֵלֶּה לֵאמֹר
יח בָּא אֵלַי הָעֶבֶד הָעִבְרִי אֲשֶׁר־הֵבֵאתָ לָּנוּ לְצַחֶק בִּי: וַיְהִי כַּהֲרִימִי קוֹלִי
יט וָאֶקְרָא וַיַּעֲזֹב בִּגְדוֹ אֶצְלִי וַיָּנָס הַחוּצָה: וַיְהִי כִשְׁמֹעַ אֲדֹנָיו אֶת־דִּבְרֵי
אִשְׁתּוֹ אֲשֶׁר דִּבְּרָה אֵלָיו לֵאמֹר כַּדְּבָרִים הָאֵלֶּה עָשָׂה לִי עַבְדֶּךָ וַיִּחַר
כ אַפּוֹ: וַיִּקַּח אֲדֹנֵי יוֹסֵף אֹתוֹ וַיִּתְּנֵהוּ אֶל־בֵּית הַסֹּהַר מְקוֹם אֲשֶׁר־אסורי אֲסִירֵי
כא הַמֶּלֶךְ אֲסוּרִים וַיְהִי־שָׁם בְּבֵית הַסֹּהַר: וַיְהִי יהוה אֶת־יוֹסֵף וַיֵּט אֵלָיו
כב חָסֶד וַיִּתֵּן חִנּוֹ בְּעֵינֵי שַׂר בֵּית־הַסֹּהַר: וַיִּתֵּן שַׂר בֵּית־הַסֹּהַר בְּיַד־יוֹסֵף
אֵת כָּל־הָאֲסִירִם אֲשֶׁר בְּבֵית הַסֹּהַר וְאֵת כָּל־אֲשֶׁר עֹשִׂים שָׁם הוּא
כג הָיָה עֹשֶׂה: אֵין ׀ שַׂר בֵּית־הַסֹּהַר רֹאֶה אֶת־כָּל־מְאוּמָה בְּיָדוֹ בַּאֲשֶׁר
יהוה אִתּוֹ וַאֲשֶׁר־הוּא עֹשֶׂה יהוה מַצְלִיחַ:

מ א וַיְהִי אַחַר הַדְּבָרִים הָאֵלֶּה חָטְאוּ מַשְׁקֵה מֶלֶךְ־מִצְרַיִם וְהָאֹפֶה שביעי
ב לַאֲדֹנֵיהֶם לְמֶלֶךְ מִצְרָיִם: וַיִּקְצֹף פַּרְעֹה עַל שְׁנֵי סָרִיסָיו עַל שַׂר
ג הַמַּשְׁקִים וְעַל שַׂר הָאוֹפִים: וַיִּתֵּן אֹתָם בְּמִשְׁמַר בֵּית שַׂר הַטַּבָּחִים
ד אֶל־בֵּית הַסֹּהַר מְקוֹם אֲשֶׁר יוֹסֵף אָסוּר שָׁם: וַיִּפְקֹד שַׂר הַטַּבָּחִים אֶת־
ה יוֹסֵף אִתָּם וַיְשָׁרֶת אֹתָם וַיִּהְיוּ יָמִים בְּמִשְׁמָר: וַיַּחַלְמוּ חֲלוֹם שְׁנֵיהֶם
אִישׁ חֲלֹמוֹ בְּלַיְלָה אֶחָד אִישׁ כְּפִתְרוֹן חֲלֹמוֹ הַמַּשְׁקֶה וְהָאֹפֶה אֲשֶׁר
ו לְמֶלֶךְ מִצְרַיִם אֲשֶׁר אֲסוּרִים בְּבֵית הַסֹּהַר: וַיָּבֹא אֲלֵיהֶם יוֹסֵף בַּבֹּקֶר
ז וַיַּרְא אֹתָם וְהִנָּם זֹעֲפִים: וַיִּשְׁאַל אֶת־סְרִיסֵי פַרְעֹה אֲשֶׁר אִתּוֹ בְמִשְׁמַר
ח בֵּית אֲדֹנָיו לֵאמֹר מַדּוּעַ פְּנֵיכֶם רָעִים הַיּוֹם: וַיֹּאמְרוּ אֵלָיו חֲלוֹם חָלַמְנוּ
וּפֹתֵר אֵין אֹתוֹ וַיֹּאמֶר אֲלֵהֶם יוֹסֵף הֲלוֹא לֵאלֹהִים פִּתְרֹנִים סַפְּרוּ־נָא
ט לִי: וַיְסַפֵּר שַׂר־הַמַּשְׁקִים אֶת־חֲלֹמוֹ לְיוֹסֵף וַיֹּאמֶר לוֹ בַּחֲלוֹמִי וְהִנֵּה־
י גֶפֶן לְפָנָי: וּבַגֶּפֶן שְׁלֹשָׁה שָׂרִיגִם וְהִוא כְפֹרַחַת עָלְתָה נִצָּהּ הִבְשִׁילוּ
יא אַשְׁכְּלֹתֶיהָ עֲנָבִים: וְכוֹס פַּרְעֹה בְּיָדִי וָאֶקַּח אֶת־הָעֲנָבִים וָאֶשְׂחַט

grapes and squeezed them into Pharaoh's cup, and I placed the cup in his
12 hand." "This is what it means," Yosef said. "The three branches are three days.
13 In three days Pharaoh will lift your head and restore you to your position.
You will place Pharaoh's cup in his hand again, as you did when you were
14 his cupbearer. When it goes well with you, remember me and do me this
15 kindness: mention me to Pharaoh so as to free me from this place. The truth
is that I was kidnapped from the land of the Hebrews. Here too, I have done
16 nothing to deserve being placed in this pit." The chief baker saw that he had
given a favorable interpretation, so he said to Yosef, "I too had a dream. There
17 were three baskets of white bread on my head. In the top basket were all
sorts of baked food that Pharaoh eats, but birds were eating them out of the
18 basket above my head." "This is what it means," Yosef said. "The three baskets
19 are three days. In three days Pharaoh will lift your head from your body; he
20 will hang you from a stake, and birds will eat your flesh." The third day was
Pharaoh's birthday. He made a feast for all his servants, and from among
21 them he singled out his chief cupbearer and chief baker. He restored the chief
cupbearer to his position so that, as before, he placed the cup in Pharaoh's
22 23 hand. But he hung up the chief baker, as Yosef had predicted. Still, the chief
cupbearer did not remember Yosef; he forgot him.

41 1 Two years passed. Then Pharaoh had a dream: he was standing by the Nile MIKETZ
2 when seven handsome, healthy cows came up out of the river and grazed
3 among the reeds. Then seven other cows came up from the river after them,
4 ugly and gaunt, and stood beside them by the riverbank. The ugly, gaunt cows
5 ate up the seven handsome, healthy cows. Pharaoh awoke. Falling back to
sleep, he had a second dream: he saw seven ears of grain, ripe and robust,
6 growing on a single stalk. Suddenly, seven other ears sprouted after them, thin
7 and scorched by the east wind. The thin ears swallowed up the seven ripe,
8 full ears. Pharaoh awoke – and realized it had been a dream. In the morning
his mind was troubled, so he sent for all the magicians and sages of Egypt.
Pharaoh told them his dream, but no one could offer an interpretation that
9 satisfied him. Then the chief cupbearer said to Pharaoh, "I must recall my sins
10 today. Once, Pharaoh was angry with his servants and placed me and the chief
11 baker in custody in the house of the captain of the guard. One night he and
12 I each had a dream, and each dream seemed to have its own meaning. With
us was a young Hebrew, a slave of the captain of the guard. We told him

יב אֹתָם אֶל־כּוֹס פַּרְעֹה וָאֶתֵּן אֶת־הַכּוֹס עַל־כַּף פַּרְעֹה: וַיֹּאמֶר לוֹ יוֹסֵף
יג זֶה פִּתְרֹנוֹ שְׁלֹשֶׁת הַשָּׂרִגִים שְׁלֹשֶׁת יָמִים הֵם: בְּעוֹד | שְׁלֹשֶׁת יָמִים
יִשָּׂא פַרְעֹה אֶת־רֹאשֶׁךָ וַהֲשִׁיבְךָ עַל־כַּנֶּךָ וְנָתַתָּ כוֹס־פַּרְעֹה בְּיָדוֹ
יד כַּמִּשְׁפָּט הָרִאשׁוֹן אֲשֶׁר הָיִיתָ מַשְׁקֵהוּ: כִּי אִם־זְכַרְתַּנִי אִתְּךָ כַּאֲשֶׁר
יִיטַב לָךְ וְעָשִׂיתָ־נָּא עִמָּדִי חָסֶד וְהִזְכַּרְתַּנִי אֶל־פַּרְעֹה וְהוֹצֵאתַנִי
טו מִן־הַבַּיִת הַזֶּה: כִּי־גֻנֹּב גֻּנַּבְתִּי מֵאֶרֶץ הָעִבְרִים וְגַם־פֹּה לֹא־עָשִׂיתִי
טז מְאוּמָה כִּי־שָׂמוּ אֹתִי בַּבּוֹר: וַיַּרְא שַׂר־הָאֹפִים כִּי טוֹב פָּתָר וַיֹּאמֶר
יז אֶל־יוֹסֵף אַף־אֲנִי בַּחֲלוֹמִי וְהִנֵּה שְׁלֹשָׁה סַלֵּי חֹרִי עַל־רֹאשִׁי: וּבַסַּל
הָעֶלְיוֹן מִכֹּל מַאֲכַל פַּרְעֹה מַעֲשֵׂה אֹפֶה וְהָעוֹף אֹכֵל אֹתָם מִן־הַסַּל
יח מֵעַל רֹאשִׁי: וַיַּעַן יוֹסֵף וַיֹּאמֶר זֶה פִּתְרֹנוֹ שְׁלֹשֶׁת הַסַּלִּים שְׁלֹשֶׁת
יט יָמִים הֵם: בְּעוֹד | שְׁלֹשֶׁת יָמִים יִשָּׂא פַרְעֹה אֶת־רֹאשְׁךָ מֵעָלֶיךָ וְתָלָה
כ אוֹתְךָ עַל־עֵץ וְאָכַל הָעוֹף אֶת־בְּשָׂרְךָ מֵעָלֶיךָ: וַיְהִי | בַּיּוֹם הַשְּׁלִישִׁי מפטיר
יוֹם הֻלֶּדֶת אֶת־פַּרְעֹה וַיַּעַשׂ מִשְׁתֶּה לְכָל־עֲבָדָיו וַיִּשָּׂא אֶת־רֹאשׁ |
כא שַׂר הַמַּשְׁקִים וְאֶת־רֹאשׁ שַׂר הָאֹפִים בְּתוֹךְ עֲבָדָיו: וַיָּשֶׁב אֶת־שַׂר
כב הַמַּשְׁקִים עַל־מַשְׁקֵהוּ וַיִּתֵּן הַכּוֹס עַל־כַּף פַּרְעֹה: וְאֵת שַׂר הָאֹפִים
כג תָּלָה כַּאֲשֶׁר פָּתַר לָהֶם יוֹסֵף: וְלֹא־זָכַר שַׂר־הַמַּשְׁקִים אֶת־יוֹסֵף
וַיִּשְׁכָּחֵהוּ:

מא א ב וַיְהִי מִקֵּץ שְׁנָתַיִם יָמִים וּפַרְעֹה חֹלֵם וְהִנֵּה עֹמֵד עַל־הַיְאֹר: וְהִנֵּה לו מקץ
מִן־הַיְאֹר עֹלֹת שֶׁבַע פָּרוֹת יְפוֹת מַרְאֶה וּבְרִיאֹת בָּשָׂר וַתִּרְעֶינָה
ג בָּאָחוּ: וְהִנֵּה שֶׁבַע פָּרוֹת אֲחֵרוֹת עֹלוֹת אַחֲרֵיהֶן מִן־הַיְאֹר רָעוֹת
מַרְאֶה וְדַקּוֹת בָּשָׂר וַתַּעֲמֹדְנָה אֵצֶל הַפָּרוֹת עַל־שְׂפַת הַיְאֹר:
ד וַתֹּאכַלְנָה הַפָּרוֹת רָעוֹת הַמַּרְאֶה וְדַקֹּת הַבָּשָׂר אֵת שֶׁבַע הַפָּרוֹת
ה יְפֹת הַמַּרְאֶה וְהַבְּרִיאֹת וַיִּיקַץ פַּרְעֹה: וַיִּישָׁן וַיַּחֲלֹם שֵׁנִית וְהִנֵּה | שֶׁבַע
ו שִׁבֳּלִים עֹלוֹת בְּקָנֶה אֶחָד בְּרִיאוֹת וְטֹבוֹת: וְהִנֵּה שֶׁבַע שִׁבֳּלִים דַּקּוֹת
ז וּשְׁדוּפֹת קָדִים צֹמְחוֹת אַחֲרֵיהֶן: וַתִּבְלַעְנָה הַשִּׁבֳּלִים הַדַּקּוֹת אֵת
ח שֶׁבַע הַשִּׁבֳּלִים הַבְּרִיאוֹת וְהַמְּלֵאוֹת וַיִּיקַץ פַּרְעֹה וְהִנֵּה חֲלוֹם: וַיְהִי
בַבֹּקֶר וַתִּפָּעֶם רוּחוֹ וַיִּשְׁלַח וַיִּקְרָא אֶת־כָּל־חַרְטֻמֵּי מִצְרַיִם וְאֶת־
כָּל־חֲכָמֶיהָ וַיְסַפֵּר פַּרְעֹה לָהֶם אֶת־חֲלֹמוֹ וְאֵין־פּוֹתֵר אוֹתָם לְפַרְעֹה:
ט וַיְדַבֵּר שַׂר הַמַּשְׁקִים אֶת־פַּרְעֹה לֵאמֹר אֶת־חֲטָאַי אֲנִי מַזְכִּיר הַיּוֹם:
י פַּרְעֹה קָצַף עַל־עֲבָדָיו וַיִּתֵּן אֹתִי בְּמִשְׁמַר בֵּית שַׂר הַטַּבָּחִים אֹתִי
יא וְאֵת שַׂר הָאֹפִים: וַנַּחַלְמָה חֲלוֹם בְּלַיְלָה אֶחָד אֲנִי וָהוּא אִישׁ כְּפִתְרוֹן
יב חֲלֹמוֹ חָלָמְנוּ: וְשָׁם אִתָּנוּ נַעַר עִבְרִי עֶבֶד לְשַׂר הַטַּבָּחִים וַנְּסַפֶּר־לוֹ

our dreams and he interpreted them for us, telling each of us the meaning of
13 his dream. Things turned out exactly as he interpreted them to us. I was
14 restored to my position, and the baker was hung up." So Pharaoh sent for
Yosef. He was rushed from the dungeon, had his hair cut, changed his clothes,
15 and came before Pharaoh. Pharaoh said to Yosef, "I had a dream and no one
can interpret it; I have heard that when you hear a dream you can interpret
16 it." "Not I," replied Yosef to Pharaoh. "God will give Pharaoh the answer that
17 he needs." Pharaoh told Yosef: "In my dream, I was standing by the bank of
18 the Nile when seven handsome, healthy cows came up out of the river and
19 grazed among the reeds. Then after them came seven other cows, scrawny,
20 very sickly, and thin – I never saw such sickly cows in all Egypt. Then the thin,
21 sickly cows ate up the first seven healthy cows. But when they had eaten them
you could not tell that they had eaten them, for they still looked as bad as
22 before. Then I awoke. In my dream I then saw seven ears of grain, ripe and
23 full, growing on a single stalk. Suddenly, seven other ears sprouted after them,
24 shriveled, thin, and scorched by the east wind, and the thin ears swallowed
the seven good ears. I told this to the magicians, but none could explain it to
25 me." Yosef said to Pharaoh, "The two dreams of Pharaoh are one and the same.
26 God has told Pharaoh what He is about to do. The seven good cows are seven
years, and so too the seven good ears are seven years. It is one and the same
27 dream. The seven thin, sickly cows that came up after them are seven years,
as are the seven empty ears scorched by the east wind. They are seven years
28 of famine. It is as I have told Pharaoh: God has shown Pharaoh what He is
29 about to do. Seven years are coming when there will be great abundance
30 throughout the land of Egypt. But after them will come seven years of famine,
when all the abundance in Egypt will be forgotten. Famine will ravage the
31 land. So devastating will the famine be that no one in the land will know
32 anything of abundance anymore. As for Pharaoh having the same dream
twice, this means that the matter has already been decided by God, and He
33 is soon to bring it about. So now let Pharaoh seek out an astute, wise man and
34 set him over the land of Egypt. Let Pharaoh appoint overseers across the land
35 and take a fifth of Egypt's harvest during the seven years of abundance. Let
them gather all that food in these coming good years, storing the grain under
36 Pharaoh's aegis so that there is food under guard in all the cities. The food
should be held in reserve for the land when the seven years of famine come
37 to Egypt, so that the country is not ruined by the famine." The plan seemed
38 good to Pharaoh and all his officials. Pharaoh said to them, "Could we find

יג וַיִּפְתָּר־לָנוּ אֶת־חֲלֹמֹתֵינוּ אִישׁ כַּחֲלֹמוֹ פָּתָר: וַיְהִי כַּאֲשֶׁר פָּתַר־לָנוּ
יד כֵּן הָיָה אֹתִי הֵשִׁיב עַל־כַּנִּי וְאֹתוֹ תָלָה: וַיִּשְׁלַח פַּרְעֹה וַיִּקְרָא אֶת־
טו יוֹסֵף וַיְרִיצֻהוּ מִן־הַבּוֹר וַיְגַלַּח וַיְחַלֵּף שִׂמְלֹתָיו וַיָּבֹא אֶל־פַּרְעֹה: וַיֹּאמֶר שני
פַּרְעֹה אֶל־יוֹסֵף חֲלוֹם חָלַמְתִּי וּפֹתֵר אֵין אֹתוֹ וַאֲנִי שָׁמַעְתִּי עָלֶיךָ
טז לֵאמֹר תִּשְׁמַע חֲלוֹם לִפְתֹּר אֹתוֹ: וַיַּעַן יוֹסֵף אֶת־פַּרְעֹה לֵאמֹר בִּלְעָדָי
יז אֱלֹהִים יַעֲנֶה אֶת־שְׁלוֹם פַּרְעֹה: וַיְדַבֵּר פַּרְעֹה אֶל־יוֹסֵף בַּחֲלֹמִי הִנְנִי
יח עֹמֵד עַל־שְׂפַת הַיְאֹר: וְהִנֵּה מִן־הַיְאֹר עֹלֹת שֶׁבַע פָּרוֹת בְּרִיאוֹת
יט בָּשָׂר וִיפֹת תֹּאַר וַתִּרְעֶינָה בָּאָחוּ: וְהִנֵּה שֶׁבַע־פָּרוֹת אֲחֵרוֹת עֹלוֹת
אַחֲרֵיהֶן דַּלּוֹת וְרָעוֹת תֹּאַר מְאֹד וְרַקּוֹת בָּשָׂר לֹא־רָאִיתִי כָהֵנָּה
כ בְּכָל־אֶרֶץ מִצְרַיִם לָרֹעַ: וַתֹּאכַלְנָה הַפָּרוֹת הָרַקּוֹת וְהָרָעוֹת אֵת שֶׁבַע
כא הַפָּרוֹת הָרִאשֹׁנוֹת הַבְּרִיאֹת: וַתָּבֹאנָה אֶל־קִרְבֶּנָה וְלֹא נוֹדַע כִּי־בָאוּ
כב אֶל־קִרְבֶּנָה וּמַרְאֵיהֶן רַע כַּאֲשֶׁר בַּתְּחִלָּה וָאִיקָץ: וָאֵרֶא בַּחֲלֹמִי
כג וְהִנֵּה ׀ שֶׁבַע שִׁבֳּלִים עֹלֹת בְּקָנֶה אֶחָד מְלֵאֹת וְטֹבוֹת: וְהִנֵּה שֶׁבַע
כד שִׁבֳּלִים צְנֻמוֹת דַּקּוֹת שְׁדֻפוֹת קָדִים צֹמְחוֹת אַחֲרֵיהֶם: וַתִּבְלַעְןָ
הַשִּׁבֳּלִים הַדַּקֹּת אֵת שֶׁבַע הַשִּׁבֳּלִים הַטֹּבוֹת וָאֹמַר אֶל־הַחַרְטֻמִּים
כה וְאֵין מַגִּיד לִי: וַיֹּאמֶר יוֹסֵף אֶל־פַּרְעֹה חֲלוֹם פַּרְעֹה אֶחָד הוּא אֵת
כו אֲשֶׁר הָאֱלֹהִים עֹשֶׂה הִגִּיד לְפַרְעֹה: שֶׁבַע פָּרֹת הַטֹּבֹת שֶׁבַע שָׁנִים
כז הֵנָּה וְשֶׁבַע הַשִּׁבֳּלִים הַטֹּבֹת שֶׁבַע שָׁנִים הֵנָּה חֲלוֹם אֶחָד הוּא: וְשֶׁבַע
הַפָּרוֹת הָרַקּוֹת וְהָרָעֹת הָעֹלֹת אַחֲרֵיהֶן שֶׁבַע שָׁנִים הֵנָּה וְשֶׁבַע
כח הַשִּׁבֳּלִים הָרֵקוֹת שְׁדֻפוֹת הַקָּדִים יִהְיוּ שֶׁבַע שְׁנֵי רָעָב: הוּא הַדָּבָר
אֲשֶׁר דִּבַּרְתִּי אֶל־פַּרְעֹה אֲשֶׁר הָאֱלֹהִים עֹשֶׂה הֶרְאָה אֶת־פַּרְעֹה:
כט ל הִנֵּה שֶׁבַע שָׁנִים בָּאוֹת שָׂבָע גָּדוֹל בְּכָל־אֶרֶץ מִצְרָיִם: וְקָמוּ שֶׁבַע
שְׁנֵי רָעָב אַחֲרֵיהֶן וְנִשְׁכַּח כָּל־הַשָּׂבָע בְּאֶרֶץ מִצְרָיִם וְכִלָּה הָרָעָב
לא אֶת־הָאָרֶץ: וְלֹא־יִוָּדַע הַשָּׂבָע בָּאָרֶץ מִפְּנֵי הָרָעָב הַהוּא אַחֲרֵי־כֵן
לב כִּי־כָבֵד הוּא מְאֹד: וְעַל הִשָּׁנוֹת הַחֲלוֹם אֶל־פַּרְעֹה פַּעֲמָיִם כִּי־נָכוֹן
לג הַדָּבָר מֵעִם הָאֱלֹהִים וּמְמַהֵר הָאֱלֹהִים לַעֲשֹׂתוֹ: וְעַתָּה יֵרֶא פַרְעֹה
לד אִישׁ נָבוֹן וְחָכָם וִישִׁיתֵהוּ עַל־אֶרֶץ מִצְרָיִם: יַעֲשֶׂה פַרְעֹה וְיַפְקֵד
פְּקִדִים עַל־הָאָרֶץ וְחִמֵּשׁ אֶת־אֶרֶץ מִצְרַיִם בְּשֶׁבַע שְׁנֵי הַשָּׂבָע:
לה וְיִקְבְּצוּ אֶת־כָּל־אֹכֶל הַשָּׁנִים הַטֹּבֹת הַבָּאֹת הָאֵלֶּה וְיִצְבְּרוּ־בָר תַּחַת
לו יַד־פַּרְעֹה אֹכֶל בֶּעָרִים וְשָׁמָרוּ: וְהָיָה הָאֹכֶל לְפִקָּדוֹן לָאָרֶץ לְשֶׁבַע
שְׁנֵי הָרָעָב אֲשֶׁר תִּהְיֶיןָ בְּאֶרֶץ מִצְרָיִם וְלֹא־תִכָּרֵת הָאָרֶץ בָּרָעָב:
לז לח וַיִּיטַב הַדָּבָר בְּעֵינֵי פַרְעֹה וּבְעֵינֵי כָּל־עֲבָדָיו: וַיֹּאמֶר פַּרְעֹה אֶל־עֲבָדָיו לז

39 another like him, a man who has within him the spirit of God?" So Pharaoh
said to Yosef, "Since God has made all this known to you, there can be no one
40 else as astute or as wise as you. You shall be in charge of my court, and by your
command shall all my people be directed. Only the throne itself will make
41 me greater than you." Then Pharaoh said to Yosef, "I hereby place you in
42 charge of all the land of Egypt." Pharaoh removed his signet ring from his
hand and placed it on Yosef's. He had him robed in garments of the finest
43 linen, and placed a gold chain around his neck. He had him ride in the chariot
of his second-in-command, and ahead of him people proclaimed, "*Avrekh*."[97]
44 Thus was he given authority over all Egypt. Pharaoh told Yosef, "I am
Pharaoh, but without your consent no one will lift hand or foot in all Egypt."
45 And Pharaoh gave Yosef the name Tzafenat Pane'ah[98] and gave him Asnat,
daughter of Potifera, priest of On, as his wife. Thus Yosef went out to oversee
46 Egypt. When he entered the service of Pharaoh, king of Egypt, Yosef was
thirty years old. Leaving Pharaoh's presence, Yosef traveled throughout
47 the land of Egypt. During the seven years of plenty the land produced in
48 profusion. He gathered all the grain produced during the seven years of plenty
in Egypt and stored it in the cities. In each city he stored the grain grown in
49 the surrounding fields. Yosef stored so much grain that it was like the sand of
the sea. They had to stop keeping records because it was beyond measure.
50 Before the years of famine came, two sons were born to Yosef by Asnat
51 daughter of Potifera, priest of On. Yosef named his firstborn Menashe, saying,
52 "God has made me forget all my troubles and all my father's family."[99] The
second son he named Efrayim, saying, "God has made me fruitful in the land
53 of my affliction."[100] The seven years of abundance in Egypt came to an end,
54 and the seven years of famine began, just as Yosef had said they would. There
55 was famine in all the other lands, but throughout Egypt there was food. When
all Egypt began to feel the famine, the people cried to Pharaoh for food.
56 Pharaoh told all the Egyptians, "Go to Yosef. Whatever he tells you – do." The
famine spread over the entire country. Yosef then opened all the storehouses
and sold grain to the Egyptians, for the famine was worsening throughout
57 Egypt. People from all over the region came to Egypt to buy grain from Yosef,
42 1 because all across the land the famine was devastating. Knowing that there
was grain in Egypt, Yaakov said to his sons, "Why do you keep looking at one
2 another?" He said, "I have heard that there is grain in Egypt. Go down there
3 and buy some for us so that we may live and not die." So ten of Yosef's brothers
4 went down to buy grain in Egypt. But Yaakov did not send Yosef's brother
5 Binyamin with them, for he was afraid that harm might come to him. So
Yisrael's sons were among those who came to buy grain, the famine having
6 reached as far as the land of Canaan. Yosef was the governor of the land; it

---

97 | Possibly meaning "bow" or "kneel," or in Egyptian "make way."

98 | Possibly "interpreter of secrets," or in Egyptian related to a word meaning "life."

99 | The name Menashe resonates with *nashani* (made me forget).

100 | The name Efrayim resonates with *hifrani* (made me fruitful).

לט הֲנִמְצָא כָזֶה אִישׁ אֲשֶׁר רוּחַ אֱלֹהִים בּוֹ: וַיֹּאמֶר פַּרְעֹה אֶל־יוֹסֵף אַחֲרֵי שלישי
מ הוֹדִיעַ אֱלֹהִים אוֹתְךָ אֶת־כָּל־זֹאת אֵין־נָבוֹן וְחָכָם כָּמוֹךָ: אַתָּה
מא תִּהְיֶה עַל־בֵּיתִי וְעַל־פִּיךָ יִשַּׁק כָּל־עַמִּי רַק הַכִּסֵּא אֶגְדַּל מִמֶּךָּ: וַיֹּאמֶר
מב פַּרְעֹה אֶל־יוֹסֵף רְאֵה נָתַתִּי אֹתְךָ עַל כָּל־אֶרֶץ מִצְרָיִם: וַיָּסַר פַּרְעֹה
אֶת־טַבַּעְתּוֹ מֵעַל יָדוֹ וַיִּתֵּן אֹתָהּ עַל־יַד יוֹסֵף וַיַּלְבֵּשׁ אֹתוֹ בִּגְדֵי־שֵׁשׁ
מג וַיָּשֶׂם רְבִד הַזָּהָב עַל־צַוָּארוֹ: וַיַּרְכֵּב אֹתוֹ בְּמִרְכֶּבֶת הַמִּשְׁנֶה אֲשֶׁר־לוֹ
מד וַיִּקְרְאוּ לְפָנָיו אַבְרֵךְ וְנָתוֹן אֹתוֹ עַל כָּל־אֶרֶץ מִצְרָיִם: וַיֹּאמֶר פַּרְעֹה
אֶל־יוֹסֵף אֲנִי פַרְעֹה וּבִלְעָדֶיךָ לֹא־יָרִים אִישׁ אֶת־יָדוֹ וְאֶת־רַגְלוֹ בְּכָל־
מה אֶרֶץ מִצְרָיִם: וַיִּקְרָא פַרְעֹה שֵׁם־יוֹסֵף צָפְנַת פַּעְנֵחַ וַיִּתֶּן־לוֹ אֶת־אָסְנַת
מו בַּת־פּוֹטִי פֶרַע כֹּהֵן אֹן לְאִשָּׁה וַיֵּצֵא יוֹסֵף עַל־אֶרֶץ מִצְרָיִם: וְיוֹסֵף
בֶּן־שְׁלֹשִׁים שָׁנָה בְּעָמְדוֹ לִפְנֵי פַּרְעֹה מֶלֶךְ־מִצְרָיִם וַיֵּצֵא יוֹסֵף מִלִּפְנֵי
מז פַרְעֹה וַיַּעֲבֹר בְּכָל־אֶרֶץ מִצְרָיִם: וַתַּעַשׂ הָאָרֶץ בְּשֶׁבַע שְׁנֵי הַשָּׂבָע
מח לִקְמָצִים: וַיִּקְבֹּץ אֶת־כָּל־אֹכֶל ׀ שֶׁבַע שָׁנִים אֲשֶׁר הָיוּ בְּאֶרֶץ מִצְרַיִם
וַיִּתֶּן־אֹכֶל בֶּעָרִים אֹכֶל שְׂדֵה־הָעִיר אֲשֶׁר סְבִיבֹתֶיהָ נָתַן בְּתוֹכָהּ:
מט וַיִּצְבֹּר יוֹסֵף בָּר כְּחוֹל הַיָּם הַרְבֵּה מְאֹד עַד כִּי־חָדַל לִסְפֹּר כִּי־אֵין
נ מִסְפָּר: וּלְיוֹסֵף יֻלַּד שְׁנֵי בָנִים בְּטֶרֶם תָּבוֹא שְׁנַת הָרָעָב אֲשֶׁר יָלְדָה־
נא לּוֹ אָסְנַת בַּת־פּוֹטִי פֶרַע כֹּהֵן אוֹן: וַיִּקְרָא יוֹסֵף אֶת־שֵׁם הַבְּכוֹר מְנַשֶּׁה
נב כִּי־נַשַּׁנִי אֱלֹהִים אֶת־כָּל־עֲמָלִי וְאֵת כָּל־בֵּית אָבִי: וְאֵת שֵׁם הַשֵּׁנִי
נג קָרָא אֶפְרָיִם כִּי־הִפְרַנִי אֱלֹהִים בְּאֶרֶץ עָנְיִי: וַתִּכְלֶינָה שֶׁבַע שְׁנֵי רביעי
נד הַשָּׂבָע אֲשֶׁר הָיָה בְּאֶרֶץ מִצְרָיִם: וַתְּחִלֶּינָה שֶׁבַע שְׁנֵי הָרָעָב לָבוֹא
כַּאֲשֶׁר אָמַר יוֹסֵף וַיְהִי רָעָב בְּכָל־הָאֲרָצוֹת וּבְכָל־אֶרֶץ מִצְרַיִם הָיָה
נה לָחֶם: וַתִּרְעַב כָּל־אֶרֶץ מִצְרַיִם וַיִּצְעַק הָעָם אֶל־פַּרְעֹה לַלָּחֶם וַיֹּאמֶר
נו פַּרְעֹה לְכָל־מִצְרַיִם לְכוּ אֶל־יוֹסֵף אֲשֶׁר־יֹאמַר לָכֶם תַּעֲשׂוּ: וְהָרָעָב
הָיָה עַל כָּל־פְּנֵי הָאָרֶץ וַיִּפְתַּח יוֹסֵף אֶת־כָּל־אֲשֶׁר בָּהֶם וַיִּשְׁבֹּר
נז לְמִצְרַיִם וַיֶּחֱזַק הָרָעָב בְּאֶרֶץ מִצְרָיִם: וְכָל־הָאָרֶץ בָּאוּ מִצְרַיְמָה
מב א לִשְׁבֹּר אֶל־יוֹסֵף כִּי־חָזַק הָרָעָב בְּכָל־הָאָרֶץ: וַיַּרְא יַעֲקֹב כִּי יֶשׁ־שֶׁבֶר
ב בְּמִצְרָיִם וַיֹּאמֶר יַעֲקֹב לְבָנָיו לָמָּה תִּתְרָאוּ: וַיֹּאמֶר הִנֵּה שָׁמַעְתִּי
כִּי יֶשׁ־שֶׁבֶר בְּמִצְרָיִם רְדוּ־שָׁמָּה וְשִׁבְרוּ־לָנוּ מִשָּׁם וְנִחְיֶה וְלֹא נָמוּת:
ג ד וַיֵּרְדוּ אֲחֵי־יוֹסֵף עֲשָׂרָה לִשְׁבֹּר בָּר מִמִּצְרָיִם: וְאֶת־בִּנְיָמִין אֲחִי יוֹסֵף
ה לֹא־שָׁלַח יַעֲקֹב אֶת־אֶחָיו כִּי אָמַר פֶּן־יִקְרָאֶנּוּ אָסוֹן: וַיָּבֹאוּ בְּנֵי
ו יִשְׂרָאֵל לִשְׁבֹּר בְּתוֹךְ הַבָּאִים כִּי־הָיָה הָרָעָב בְּאֶרֶץ כְּנָעַן: וְיוֹסֵף הוּא
הַשַּׁלִּיט עַל־הָאָרֶץ הוּא הַמַּשְׁבִּיר לְכָל־עַם הָאָרֶץ וַיָּבֹאוּ אֲחֵי יוֹסֵף

was he who dispensed food to all its people. When Yosef's brothers arrived,
7 they bowed down to him, their faces to the ground. Yosef recognized his
brothers as soon as he saw them, but he acted like a stranger and spoke harshly
to them. "Where have you come from?" he asked. They replied, "From the
8 land of Canaan – to buy food." Yosef recognized his brothers, but they did
9 not recognize him. Then Yosef remembered the dreams he had dreamed
about them. "You are spies!" he said. "You have come to see where our land
10 is exposed." "No, my lord," they said. "Your servants have come to buy food.
11 We all are sons of the same man. We are honest men. Your servants are not
12 13 spies." "Lies," he said. "You have come to see where our land is exposed." "We
were once twelve brothers," they replied, "sons of one man in Canaan. The
14 youngest is now with our father, and one is gone." But Yosef said, "It is as I
15 said to you – you are spies. This is how you will be tested. By Pharaoh's life,
16 you will not leave this place unless your youngest brother comes here. Let
one of you go and fetch your brother. The rest of you will remain confined
here. This will test whether or not you are telling the truth. If not, by Pharaoh's
17 18 life, you are spies." He had them placed in custody for three days. On the third
day, Yosef said to them, "If you do this you will live, for I am a God-fearing
19 man. If you are honest, let one of your brothers stay here in prison while the
20 rest of you go and take back grain for your starving households. Then bring
your youngest brother to me so that your words can be verified and you will
21 not die." They agreed. And they said to one another, "We are guilty, guilty
because of what we did to our brother. We saw his suffering when he pleaded
with us but we did not listen. That is why this trouble has come upon us."
22 Then Reuven spoke up: "Did I not tell you not to sin against the boy? But
23 you would not listen. Now comes the reckoning for his blood." They did not
realize that Yosef could understand them, for a translator stood between them.
24 And Yosef turned away from them and wept. Then he turned back to them
and spoke again. He had Shimon taken from them and placed in chains before
25 their eyes. Yosef gave orders to fill their bags with grain and put each man's
money back in his sack. They were to be given provisions for the journey.
26 After this was done for them, they loaded their grain on their donkeys and
27 left. As one of them was opening his sack to feed his donkey at the place where
they stopped for the night, he saw his money right there at the top of his pack.
28 "My money has been returned!" he told his brothers. "There it is in my pack!"
Their hearts sank. Trembling, they turned to one another, saying, "What is
29 this that God has done to us?" When they came to their father Yaakov in the
30 land of Canaan, they told him all that had happened to them. They said, "The
man who is the lord of the land spoke to us harshly. He accused us of spying
31 32 on the land. We said to him, 'We are honest men; we are not spies. We were
twelve brothers, sons of the same father. One is gone, and the youngest is now
33 with our father in Canaan.' Then the man who is lord of the land said to us,

ז וַיִּשְׁתַּחֲווּ־לוֹ אַפַּיִם אָרְצָה׃ וַיַּרְא יוֹסֵף אֶת־אֶחָיו וַיַּכִּרֵם וַיִּתְנַכֵּר אֲלֵיהֶם
וַיְדַבֵּר אִתָּם קָשׁוֹת וַיֹּאמֶר אֲלֵהֶם מֵאַיִן בָּאתֶם וַיֹּאמְרוּ מֵאֶרֶץ כְּנַעַן
ח ט לִשְׁבָּר־אֹכֶל׃ וַיַּכֵּר יוֹסֵף אֶת־אֶחָיו וְהֵם לֹא הִכִּרֻהוּ׃ וַיִּזְכֹּר יוֹסֵף אֵת
הַחֲלֹמוֹת אֲשֶׁר חָלַם לָהֶם וַיֹּאמֶר אֲלֵהֶם מְרַגְּלִים אַתֶּם לִרְאוֹת אֶת־
י עֶרְוַת הָאָרֶץ בָּאתֶם׃ וַיֹּאמְרוּ אֵלָיו לֹא אֲדֹנִי וַעֲבָדֶיךָ בָּאוּ לִשְׁבָּר־
יא אֹכֶל׃ כֻּלָּנוּ בְּנֵי אִישׁ־אֶחָד נָחְנוּ כֵּנִים אֲנַחְנוּ לֹא־הָיוּ עֲבָדֶיךָ מְרַגְּלִים׃
יב יג וַיֹּאמֶר אֲלֵהֶם לֹא כִּי־עֶרְוַת הָאָרֶץ בָּאתֶם לִרְאוֹת׃ וַיֹּאמְרוּ שְׁנֵים
עָשָׂר עֲבָדֶיךָ אַחִים ׀ אֲנַחְנוּ בְּנֵי אִישׁ־אֶחָד בְּאֶרֶץ כְּנָעַן וְהִנֵּה הַקָּטֹן
יד אֶת־אָבִינוּ הַיּוֹם וְהָאֶחָד אֵינֶנּוּ׃ וַיֹּאמֶר אֲלֵהֶם יוֹסֵף הוּא אֲשֶׁר דִּבַּרְתִּי
טו אֲלֵכֶם לֵאמֹר מְרַגְּלִים אַתֶּם׃ בְּזֹאת תִּבָּחֵנוּ חֵי פַרְעֹה אִם־תֵּצְאוּ מִזֶּה
טז כִּי אִם־בְּבוֹא אֲחִיכֶם הַקָּטֹן הֵנָּה׃ שִׁלְחוּ מִכֶּם אֶחָד וְיִקַּח אֶת־אֲחִיכֶם
וְאַתֶּם הֵאָסְרוּ וְיִבָּחֲנוּ דִּבְרֵיכֶם הַאֱמֶת אִתְּכֶם וְאִם־לֹא חֵי פַרְעֹה כִּי
יז יח מְרַגְּלִים אַתֶּם׃ וַיֶּאֱסֹף אֹתָם אֶל־מִשְׁמָר שְׁלֹשֶׁת יָמִים׃ וַיֹּאמֶר אֲלֵהֶם לח
יט יוֹסֵף בַּיּוֹם הַשְּׁלִישִׁי זֹאת עֲשׂוּ וִחְיוּ אֶת־הָאֱלֹהִים אֲנִי יָרֵא׃ אִם־כֵּנִים חמישי
אַתֶּם אֲחִיכֶם אֶחָד יֵאָסֵר בְּבֵית מִשְׁמַרְכֶם וְאַתֶּם לְכוּ הָבִיאוּ שֶׁבֶר
כ רַעֲבוֹן בָּתֵּיכֶם׃ וְאֶת־אֲחִיכֶם הַקָּטֹן תָּבִיאוּ אֵלַי וְיֵאָמְנוּ דִבְרֵיכֶם וְלֹא
כא תָמוּתוּ וַיַּעֲשׂוּ־כֵן׃ וַיֹּאמְרוּ אִישׁ אֶל־אָחִיו אֲבָל אֲשֵׁמִים ׀ אֲנַחְנוּ
עַל־אָחִינוּ אֲשֶׁר רָאִינוּ צָרַת נַפְשׁוֹ בְּהִתְחַנְנוֹ אֵלֵינוּ וְלֹא שָׁמָעְנוּ עַל־
כב כֵּן בָּאָה אֵלֵינוּ הַצָּרָה הַזֹּאת׃ וַיַּעַן רְאוּבֵן אֹתָם לֵאמֹר הֲלוֹא אָמַרְתִּי
אֲלֵיכֶם ׀ לֵאמֹר אַל־תֶּחֶטְאוּ בַיֶּלֶד וְלֹא שְׁמַעְתֶּם וְגַם־דָּמוֹ הִנֵּה נִדְרָשׁ׃
כג כד וְהֵם לֹא יָדְעוּ כִּי שֹׁמֵעַ יוֹסֵף כִּי הַמֵּלִיץ בֵּינֹתָם׃ וַיִּסֹּב מֵעֲלֵיהֶם וַיֵּבְךְּ
וַיָּשָׁב אֲלֵהֶם וַיְדַבֵּר אֲלֵהֶם וַיִּקַּח מֵאִתָּם אֶת־שִׁמְעוֹן וַיֶּאֱסֹר אֹתוֹ
כה לְעֵינֵיהֶם׃ וַיְצַו יוֹסֵף וַיְמַלְאוּ אֶת־כְּלֵיהֶם בָּר וּלְהָשִׁיב כַּסְפֵּיהֶם אִישׁ
כו אֶל־שַׂקּוֹ וְלָתֵת לָהֶם צֵדָה לַדָּרֶךְ וַיַּעַשׂ לָהֶם כֵּן׃ וַיִּשְׂאוּ אֶת־שִׁבְרָם
כז עַל־חֲמֹרֵיהֶם וַיֵּלְכוּ מִשָּׁם׃ וַיִּפְתַּח הָאֶחָד אֶת־שַׂקּוֹ לָתֵת מִסְפּוֹא
כח לַחֲמֹרוֹ בַּמָּלוֹן וַיַּרְא אֶת־כַּסְפּוֹ וְהִנֵּה־הוּא בְּפִי אַמְתַּחְתּוֹ׃ וַיֹּאמֶר
אֶל־אֶחָיו הוּשַׁב כַּסְפִּי וְגַם הִנֵּה בְאַמְתַּחְתִּי וַיֵּצֵא לִבָּם וַיֶּחֶרְדוּ אִישׁ
כט אֶל־אָחִיו לֵאמֹר מַה־זֹּאת עָשָׂה אֱלֹהִים לָנוּ׃ וַיָּבֹאוּ אֶל־יַעֲקֹב אֲבִיהֶם
ל אַרְצָה כְּנָעַן וַיַּגִּידוּ לוֹ אֵת כָּל־הַקֹּרֹת אֹתָם לֵאמֹר׃ דִּבֶּר הָאִישׁ אֲדֹנֵי
לא הָאָרֶץ אִתָּנוּ קָשׁוֹת וַיִּתֵּן אֹתָנוּ כִּמְרַגְּלִים אֶת־הָאָרֶץ׃ וַנֹּאמֶר אֵלָיו
לב כֵּנִים אֲנָחְנוּ לֹא הָיִינוּ מְרַגְּלִים׃ שְׁנֵים־עָשָׂר אֲנַחְנוּ אַחִים בְּנֵי אָבִינוּ
לג הָאֶחָד אֵינֶנּוּ וְהַקָּטֹן הַיּוֹם אֶת־אָבִינוּ בְּאֶרֶץ כְּנָעַן׃ וַיֹּאמֶר אֵלֵינוּ

'This is how I will know that you are honest men. Leave one of your brothers
34 with me, take something for your starving households, and go. Then bring
your youngest brother to me. Then I will know that you are not spies but
honest men. And then I will give you back your brother, and you can trade in
35 the land.'" They began emptying their sacks, and there in each one's sack was
his money bag. When they and their father saw the money bags, they were
36 afraid. Their father Yaakov said to them, "You have taken my children away
from me. Yosef is gone. Shimon is gone. Now you want to take Binyamin? All
37 this I must suffer!" Reuven said to his father, "You may kill my two sons if I
do not bring him back to you; entrust him to my care and I will bring him
38 back to you." "My son will not go down with you," said Yaakov. "His brother
is dead, and he is all I have left. If any harm comes to him on the way, you will
43 1 bring down my gray head in grief to Sheol." The famine in the land continued
2 to be severe. When they had eaten all the grain they had brought from Egypt,
3 their father said to them, "Go back and buy us some more food." But Yehuda
said to him, "The man warned us, 'Do not appear before me unless your
4 brother is with you.' If you agree to send our brother with us, we will go and
5 buy you food. But if you will not send him, we cannot go. The man told us,
6 'Do not appear before me unless your brother is with you.'" Yisrael said, "Why
did you bring this trouble on me by telling the man you had another brother?"
7 They replied, "The man kept asking about us and our family: 'Is your father
still alive?' he asked. 'Do you have a brother?' We simply answered his
questions. How could we know that he would say, 'Bring your brother here'?"
8 And Yehuda said to his father Yisrael, "Send the boy with me. Let us be on
9 our way so that we, you, and our children may live and not die. I myself am
the guarantee for his safety: you may hold me personally responsible. If I do
not bring him back and set him before you, I will have sinned against you for
10 all time. We could have been there and back twice if we had not hesitated so
11 long." And then their father Yisrael said to them, "If that is how it must be,
then do this. Take some of the best produce of the land in your bags, and bring
them to the man as a gift – a little balm and a little honey, some spices and
12 myrrh, pistachio nuts and almonds. Take with you double the money. Return
13 the money that was put back into your sacks. Perhaps it was a mistake. And
14 take your brother. Go back to the man at once. May El Shaddai grant you
mercy before the man, that he may send your other brother forth to you, and
15 Binyamin. And as for me, if I am to be bereaved, I will be bereaved." So the
men took the gift and double the money and set out with Binyamin. They
16 went to Egypt and presented themselves to Yosef. When Yosef saw Binyamin

הָאִישׁ אֲדֹנֵי הָאָרֶץ בְּזֹאת אֵדַע כִּי כֵנִים אַתֶּם אֲחִיכֶם הָאֶחָד הַנִּיחוּ
לד אִתִּי וְאֶת־רַעֲבוֹן בָּתֵּיכֶם קְחוּ וָלֵכוּ׃ וְהָבִיאוּ אֶת־אֲחִיכֶם הַקָּטֹן אֵלַי
וְאֵדְעָה כִּי לֹא מְרַגְּלִים אַתֶּם כִּי כֵנִים אַתֶּם אֶת־אֲחִיכֶם אֶתֵּן לָכֶם
לה וְאֶת־הָאָרֶץ תִּסְחָרוּ׃ וַיְהִי הֵם מְרִיקִים שַׂקֵּיהֶם וְהִנֵּה־אִישׁ צְרוֹר־כַּסְפּוֹ
לו בְּשַׂקּוֹ וַיִּרְאוּ אֶת־צְרֹרוֹת כַּסְפֵּיהֶם הֵמָּה וַאֲבִיהֶם וַיִּירָאוּ׃ וַיֹּאמֶר
אֲלֵהֶם יַעֲקֹב אֲבִיהֶם אֹתִי שִׁכַּלְתֶּם יוֹסֵף אֵינֶנּוּ וְשִׁמְעוֹן אֵינֶנּוּ וְאֶת־
לז בִּנְיָמִן תִּקָּחוּ עָלַי הָיוּ כֻלָּנָה׃ וַיֹּאמֶר רְאוּבֵן אֶל־אָבִיו לֵאמֹר אֶת־שְׁנֵי
בָנַי תָּמִית אִם־לֹא אֲבִיאֶנּוּ אֵלֶיךָ תְּנָה אֹתוֹ עַל־יָדִי וַאֲנִי אֲשִׁיבֶנּוּ
לח אֵלֶיךָ׃ וַיֹּאמֶר לֹא־יֵרֵד בְּנִי עִמָּכֶם כִּי־אָחִיו מֵת וְהוּא לְבַדּוֹ נִשְׁאָר
וּקְרָאָהוּ אָסוֹן בַּדֶּרֶךְ אֲשֶׁר תֵּלְכוּ־בָהּ וְהוֹרַדְתֶּם אֶת־שֵׂיבָתִי בְּיָגוֹן
מג א ב שְׁאוֹלָה׃ וְהָרָעָב כָּבֵד בָּאָרֶץ׃ וַיְהִי כַּאֲשֶׁר כִּלּוּ לֶאֱכֹל אֶת־הַשֶּׁבֶר
אֲשֶׁר הֵבִיאוּ מִמִּצְרָיִם וַיֹּאמֶר אֲלֵיהֶם אֲבִיהֶם שֻׁבוּ שִׁבְרוּ־לָנוּ מְעַט־
ג אֹכֶל׃ וַיֹּאמֶר אֵלָיו יְהוּדָה לֵאמֹר הָעֵד הֵעִד בָּנוּ הָאִישׁ לֵאמֹר לֹא־
ד תִרְאוּ פָנַי בִּלְתִּי אֲחִיכֶם אִתְּכֶם׃ אִם־יֶשְׁךָ מְשַׁלֵּחַ אֶת־אָחִינוּ אִתָּנוּ
ה נֵרְדָה וְנִשְׁבְּרָה לְךָ אֹכֶל׃ וְאִם־אֵינְךָ מְשַׁלֵּחַ לֹא נֵרֵד כִּי־הָאִישׁ אָמַר
ו אֵלֵינוּ לֹא־תִרְאוּ פָנַי בִּלְתִּי אֲחִיכֶם אִתְּכֶם׃ וַיֹּאמֶר יִשְׂרָאֵל לָמָה
ז הֲרֵעֹתֶם לִי לְהַגִּיד לָאִישׁ הַעוֹד לָכֶם אָח׃ וַיֹּאמְרוּ שָׁאוֹל שָׁאַל־הָאִישׁ
לָנוּ וּלְמוֹלַדְתֵּנוּ לֵאמֹר הַעוֹד אֲבִיכֶם חַי הֲיֵשׁ לָכֶם אָח וַנַּגֶּד־לוֹ עַל־
ח פִּי הַדְּבָרִים הָאֵלֶּה הֲיָדוֹעַ נֵדַע כִּי יֹאמַר הוֹרִידוּ אֶת־אֲחִיכֶם׃ וַיֹּאמֶר
יְהוּדָה אֶל־יִשְׂרָאֵל אָבִיו שִׁלְחָה הַנַּעַר אִתִּי וְנָקוּמָה וְנֵלֵכָה וְנִחְיֶה
ט וְלֹא נָמוּת גַּם־אֲנַחְנוּ גַם־אַתָּה גַּם־טַפֵּנוּ׃ אָנֹכִי אֶעֶרְבֶנּוּ מִיָּדִי
תְּבַקְשֶׁנּוּ אִם־לֹא הֲבִיאֹתִיו אֵלֶיךָ וְהִצַּגְתִּיו לְפָנֶיךָ וְחָטָאתִי לְךָ כָּל־
י יא הַיָּמִים׃ כִּי לוּלֵא הִתְמַהְמָהְנוּ כִּי־עַתָּה שַׁבְנוּ זֶה פַעֲמָיִם׃ וַיֹּאמֶר
אֲלֵהֶם יִשְׂרָאֵל אֲבִיהֶם אִם־כֵּן ׀ אֵפוֹא זֹאת עֲשׂוּ קְחוּ מִזִּמְרַת הָאָרֶץ
בִּכְלֵיכֶם וְהוֹרִידוּ לָאִישׁ מִנְחָה מְעַט צֳרִי וּמְעַט דְּבַשׁ נְכֹאת וָלֹט
יב בָּטְנִים וּשְׁקֵדִים׃ וְכֶסֶף מִשְׁנֶה קְחוּ בְיֶדְכֶם וְאֶת־הַכֶּסֶף הַמּוּשָׁב בְּפִי
יג אַמְתְּחֹתֵיכֶם תָּשִׁיבוּ בְיֶדְכֶם אוּלַי מִשְׁגֶּה הוּא׃ וְאֶת־אֲחִיכֶם קָחוּ
יד וְקוּמוּ שׁוּבוּ אֶל־הָאִישׁ׃ וְאֵל שַׁדַּי יִתֵּן לָכֶם רַחֲמִים לִפְנֵי הָאִישׁ וְשִׁלַּח לט
לָכֶם אֶת־אֲחִיכֶם אַחֵר וְאֶת־בִּנְיָמִין וַאֲנִי כַּאֲשֶׁר שָׁכֹלְתִּי שָׁכָלְתִּי׃
טו וַיִּקְחוּ הָאֲנָשִׁים אֶת־הַמִּנְחָה הַזֹּאת וּמִשְׁנֶה־כֶּסֶף לָקְחוּ בְיָדָם וְאֶת־
טז בִּנְיָמִן וַיָּקֻמוּ וַיֵּרְדוּ מִצְרַיִם וַיַּעַמְדוּ לִפְנֵי יוֹסֵף׃ וַיַּרְא יוֹסֵף אִתָּם אֶת־ ששי
בִּנְיָמִין וַיֹּאמֶר לַאֲשֶׁר עַל־בֵּיתוֹ הָבֵא אֶת־הָאֲנָשִׁים הַבָּיְתָה וּטְבֹחַ

with them, he said to his house steward, "Take these men to my house.
Slaughter an animal and prepare a meal, for they will dine with me at noon."
17 18 The man did as Yosef said and brought them to Yosef's house. The men were
frightened that they were being brought to Yosef's house. They said, "We have
been brought here because of the money that was put back in our sacks the
19 first time. He wants to attack us, seize us as slaves, and take our donkeys." So
they went up to Yosef's steward and spoke to him at the entrance to the house.
20 "If you please, my lord," they said, "we came here once before to buy food.
21 But at the place where we stopped for the night, we opened our bags and each
of us found his money, in its exact weight, in the mouth of his bag. So we have
22 brought it back with us. We have also brought additional money to buy food.
23 We do not know who put our money in our bags." He replied, "All is well. Do
not be afraid. Your God, the God of your father, must have placed a hidden
gift in your bags. I received the money you paid." Then he brought Shimon
24 out to them. He brought the brothers into Yosef's house, gave them water to
25 bathe their feet, and had fodder brought for their donkeys. They set out their
gifts in preparation for Yosef's arrival at noon, because they had heard that
26 they were going to eat there. When Yosef entered the house, they presented
him with the gifts they had brought and bowed low to the ground before him.
27 He asked them how they were. Then he asked, "How is the elderly father
28 about whom you spoke? Is he still alive?" They said, "Your servant our father
29 is alive and well." They bowed down and prostrated themselves. Then he
looked up and saw his brother Binyamin, his mother's son, and asked, "Is this
your youngest brother, the one you mentioned to me?" And he said, "God be
30 gracious to you, my son." At that, he hurried out, for he was overcome with
feeling toward his brother and was on the verge of tears. He went into a private
31 room and there he wept. He washed his face and came out, controlling
32 himself. "Serve the food," he said. They served him apart, them apart, and the
Egyptians who ate with him apart, for the Egyptians could not eat with
33 Hebrews, since to Egyptians that was considered abhorrent. Seated by his
direction in order of age, oldest to youngest, they looked at one another in
34 amazement. He sent them portions from his table, giving Binyamin five times
44 1 as much as anyone else. And they drank and grew merry with him. Then Yosef
instructed his steward, "Fill the men's bags with as much food as they can
2 carry, and put each one's money in the mouth of his bag. Then put my
chalice – the silver chalice – in the mouth of the youngest one's bag, along
3 with the money for his grain." He did as Yosef told him. As morning showed
4 its first light, the men were sent on their way with their donkeys. They had
not gone far from the city when Yosef said to his steward, "Go after the men
at once. When you catch up with them, say to them, 'Why have you repaid
5 good with evil? Is it not from this that my master drinks and that he uses for

יז טֶבַח וְהָכֵן כִּי אִתִּי יֹאכְלוּ הָאֲנָשִׁים בַּצׇּהֳרָיִם: וַיַּעַשׂ הָאִישׁ כַּאֲשֶׁר
יח אָמַר יוֹסֵף וַיָּבֵא הָאִישׁ אֶת־הָאֲנָשִׁים בֵּיתָה יוֹסֵף: וַיִּירְאוּ הָאֲנָשִׁים
כִּי הוּבְאוּ בֵּית יוֹסֵף וַיֹּאמְרוּ עַל־דְּבַר הַכֶּסֶף הַשָּׁב בְּאַמְתְּחֹתֵינוּ
בַּתְּחִלָּה אֲנַחְנוּ מוּבָאִים לְהִתְגֹּלֵל עָלֵינוּ וּלְהִתְנַפֵּל עָלֵינוּ וְלָקַחַת
יט אֹתָנוּ לַעֲבָדִים וְאֶת־חֲמֹרֵינוּ: וַיִּגְּשׁוּ אֶל־הָאִישׁ אֲשֶׁר עַל־בֵּית יוֹסֵף
כ וַיְדַבְּרוּ אֵלָיו פֶּתַח הַבָּיִת: וַיֹּאמְרוּ בִּי אֲדֹנִי יָרֹד יָרַדְנוּ בַּתְּחִלָּה לִשְׁבׇּר־
כא אֹכֶל: וַיְהִי כִּי־בָאנוּ אֶל־הַמָּלוֹן וַנִּפְתְּחָה אֶת־אַמְתְּחֹתֵינוּ וְהִנֵּה כֶסֶף־
כב אִישׁ בְּפִי אַמְתַּחְתּוֹ כַּסְפֵּנוּ בְּמִשְׁקָלוֹ וַנָּשֶׁב אֹתוֹ בְּיָדֵנוּ: וְכֶסֶף אַחֵר
הוֹרַדְנוּ בְיָדֵנוּ לִשְׁבׇּר־אֹכֶל לֹא יָדַעְנוּ מִי־שָׂם כַּסְפֵּנוּ בְּאַמְתְּחֹתֵינוּ:
כג וַיֹּאמֶר שָׁלוֹם לָכֶם אַל־תִּירָאוּ אֱלֹהֵיכֶם וֵאלֹהֵי אֲבִיכֶם נָתַן לָכֶם
מַטְמוֹן בְּאַמְתְּחֹתֵיכֶם כַּסְפְּכֶם בָּא אֵלָי וַיּוֹצֵא אֲלֵהֶם אֶת־שִׁמְעוֹן:
כד וַיָּבֵא הָאִישׁ אֶת־הָאֲנָשִׁים בֵּיתָה יוֹסֵף וַיִּתֶּן־מַיִם וַיִּרְחֲצוּ רַגְלֵיהֶם וַיִּתֵּן
כה מִסְפּוֹא לַחֲמֹרֵיהֶם: וַיָּכִינוּ אֶת־הַמִּנְחָה עַד־בּוֹא יוֹסֵף בַּצׇּהֳרָיִם כִּי
כו שָׁמְעוּ כִּי־שָׁם יֹאכְלוּ לָחֶם: וַיָּבֹא יוֹסֵף הַבַּיְתָה וַיָּבִיאוּ לוֹ אֶת־הַמִּנְחָה
כז אֲשֶׁר־בְּיָדָם הַבָּיְתָה וַיִּשְׁתַּחֲווּ־לוֹ אָרְצָה: וַיִּשְׁאַל לָהֶם לְשָׁלוֹם וַיֹּאמֶר
כח הֲשָׁלוֹם אֲבִיכֶם הַזָּקֵן אֲשֶׁר אֲמַרְתֶּם הַעוֹדֶנּוּ חָי: וַיֹּאמְרוּ שָׁלוֹם
כט לְעַבְדְּךָ לְאָבִינוּ עוֹדֶנּוּ חָי וַיִּקְּדוּ וַיִּשְׁתַּחֲוֻּ: וַיִּשָּׂא עֵינָיו וַיַּרְא אֶת־בִּנְיָמִין
אָחִיו בֶּן־אִמּוֹ וַיֹּאמֶר הֲזֶה אֲחִיכֶם הַקָּטֹן אֲשֶׁר אֲמַרְתֶּם אֵלָי וַיֹּאמַר
ל אֱלֹהִים יׇחְנְךָ בְּנִי: וַיְמַהֵר יוֹסֵף כִּי־נִכְמְרוּ רַחֲמָיו אֶל־אָחִיו וַיְבַקֵּשׁ שביעי
לא לִבְכּוֹת וַיָּבֹא הַחַדְרָה וַיֵּבְךְּ שָׁמָּה: וַיִּרְחַץ פָּנָיו וַיֵּצֵא וַיִּתְאַפַּק וַיֹּאמֶר
לב שִׂימוּ לָחֶם: וַיָּשִׂימוּ לוֹ לְבַדּוֹ וְלָהֶם לְבַדָּם וְלַמִּצְרִים הָאֹכְלִים אִתּוֹ
לְבַדָּם כִּי לֹא יוּכְלוּן הַמִּצְרִים לֶאֱכֹל אֶת־הָעִבְרִים לֶחֶם כִּי־תוֹעֵבָה
לג הִוא לְמִצְרָיִם: וַיֵּשְׁבוּ לְפָנָיו הַבְּכֹר כִּבְכֹרָתוֹ וְהַצָּעִיר כִּצְעִרָתוֹ וַיִּתְמְהוּ
לד הָאֲנָשִׁים אִישׁ אֶל־רֵעֵהוּ: וַיִּשָּׂא מַשְׂאֹת מֵאֵת פָּנָיו אֲלֵהֶם וַתֵּרֶב
מד א מַשְׂאַת בִּנְיָמִן מִמַּשְׂאֹת כֻּלָּם חָמֵשׁ יָדוֹת וַיִּשְׁתּוּ וַיִּשְׁכְּרוּ עִמּוֹ: וַיְצַו
אֶת־אֲשֶׁר עַל־בֵּיתוֹ לֵאמֹר מַלֵּא אֶת־אַמְתְּחֹת הָאֲנָשִׁים אֹכֶל כַּאֲשֶׁר
ב יוּכְלוּן שְׂאֵת וְשִׂים כֶּסֶף־אִישׁ בְּפִי אַמְתַּחְתּוֹ: וְאֶת־גְּבִיעִי גְּבִיעַ הַכֶּסֶף
תָּשִׂים בְּפִי אַמְתַּחַת הַקָּטֹן וְאֵת כֶּסֶף שִׁבְרוֹ וַיַּעַשׂ כִּדְבַר יוֹסֵף אֲשֶׁר
ג ד דִּבֵּר: הַבֹּקֶר אוֹר וְהָאֲנָשִׁים שֻׁלְּחוּ הֵמָּה וַחֲמֹרֵיהֶם: הֵם יָצְאוּ אֶת־
הָעִיר לֹא הִרְחִיקוּ וְיוֹסֵף אָמַר לַאֲשֶׁר עַל־בֵּיתוֹ קוּם רְדֹף אַחֲרֵי
הָאֲנָשִׁים וְהִשַּׂגְתָּם וְאָמַרְתָּ אֲלֵהֶם לָמָּה שִׁלַּמְתֶּם רָעָה תַּחַת טוֹבָה:
ה הֲלוֹא זֶה אֲשֶׁר יִשְׁתֶּה אֲדֹנִי בּוֹ וְהוּא נַחֵשׁ יְנַחֵשׁ בּוֹ הֲרֵעֹתֶם אֲשֶׁר

6 divination? It is a wicked thing you have done.'" He caught up with them and
7 repeated those words to them. But they said to him, "How can my lord say
8 such things? Heaven forbid that we should do such a thing! Look, we brought
back to you from Canaan the money we found in the mouths of our bags.
9 Why would we steal silver or gold from your master's house? If any of your
servants is found with it, he shall die, and the rest of us will become my lord's
10 slaves." "Let it be as you say," he replied, "but only the one with whom it is
11 found shall be my slave. The rest of you can go free." Each of them quickly
12 lowered his bag to the ground, and each opened his bag. He searched,
beginning with the oldest and ending with the youngest. The chalice was found
13 in Binyamin's bag. The brothers tore their clothes. Each loaded his donkey
14 again, and they returned to the city. Yehuda and his brothers came to Yosef's
house – he was still there – and they threw themselves on the ground before
15 him. Yosef said to them, "What is this thing you have done? Do you not know
16 that a man like me can find out the truth by divination?" Yehuda replied,
"What can we say to my lord? What can we speak? How can we prove our
innocence? God has uncovered your servants' guilt! We are now my lord's
17 slaves – we and the one in whose possession the chalice was found." "Heaven
forbid that I should do such a thing," he said. "The man in whose possession
the chalice was found will become my slave. As for the rest of you, go back to
18 your father in peace." But Yehuda stepped forward to him. "If you VAYIGASH
please, my lord," he said, "let your servant speak a word in my lord's hearing.
19 Do not be angry with me, you who are the equal of Pharaoh. My lord asked
20 his servants, 'Do you have a father or a brother?' And we told my lord, 'We
have an elderly father and there is a young son, a child of his old age. When
his brother died, he was the only one of his mother's sons left, and his father
21 loves him.' Then you said to your servants, 'Bring him to me that I may set
22 eyes on him.' But we said to my lord, 'The boy cannot leave his father. If he
23 left him, his father would die.' Then you told your servants, 'Unless your
24 youngest brother comes with you, you shall not see my face again.' When we
25 went back to your servant my father, we told him what my lord had said. Then
26 our father said, 'Go back and buy a little more food.' We said, 'We cannot go.
We can go only if our youngest brother is with us. If he is not with us, we
27 cannot see the man's face.' Then your servant, my father, said to us, 'You know
28 that my wife bore me two sons. One is gone from me, and I said, "He must
29 have been torn to pieces." I have not seen him since. If you take this one from
me and harm befalls him, you will bring down my gray head in grief to Sheol.'
30 So now, if the boy is not with us when I go back to your servant my father, so
31 bound together are their lives that when he sees that the boy is not with us,
he will die. Your servants will have brought down the gray head of your
32 servant, our father, in grief to Sheol. Your servant offered himself to my father
as a guarantee for the boy. I said, 'If I do not bring him back to you, I will have

ו ז עֲשִׂיתֶם: וַיַּשִּׂגֵם וַיְדַבֵּר אֲלֵהֶם אֶת־הַדְּבָרִים הָאֵלֶּה: וַיֹּאמְרוּ אֵלָיו
לָמָּה יְדַבֵּר אֲדֹנִי כַּדְּבָרִים הָאֵלֶּה חָלִילָה לַעֲבָדֶיךָ מֵעֲשׂוֹת כַּדָּבָר
ח הַזֶּה: הֵן כֶּסֶף אֲשֶׁר מָצָאנוּ בְּפִי אַמְתְּחֹתֵינוּ הֱשִׁיבֹנוּ אֵלֶיךָ מֵאֶרֶץ
ט כְּנָעַן וְאֵיךְ נִגְנֹב מִבֵּית אֲדֹנֶיךָ כֶּסֶף אוֹ זָהָב: אֲשֶׁר יִמָּצֵא אִתּוֹ מֵעֲבָדֶיךָ
י וָמֵת וְגַם־אֲנַחְנוּ נִהְיֶה לַאדֹנִי לַעֲבָדִים: וַיֹּאמֶר גַּם־עַתָּה כְדִבְרֵיכֶם
יא כֶּן־הוּא אֲשֶׁר יִמָּצֵא אִתּוֹ יִהְיֶה־לִּי עָבֶד וְאַתֶּם תִּהְיוּ נְקִיִּם: וַיְמַהֲרוּ
יב וַיּוֹרִדוּ אִישׁ אֶת־אַמְתַּחְתּוֹ אָרְצָה וַיִּפְתְּחוּ אִישׁ אַמְתַּחְתּוֹ: וַיְחַפֵּשׂ
יג בַּגָּדוֹל הֵחֵל וּבַקָּטֹן כִּלָּה וַיִּמָּצֵא הַגָּבִיעַ בְּאַמְתַּחַת בִּנְיָמִן: וַיִּקְרְעוּ
יד שִׂמְלֹתָם וַיַּעֲמֹס אִישׁ עַל־חֲמֹרוֹ וַיָּשֻׁבוּ הָעִירָה: וַיָּבֹא יְהוּדָה וְאֶחָיו מפטיר
טו בֵּיתָה יוֹסֵף וְהוּא עוֹדֶנּוּ שָׁם וַיִּפְּלוּ לְפָנָיו אָרְצָה: וַיֹּאמֶר לָהֶם יוֹסֵף
מָה־הַמַּעֲשֶׂה הַזֶּה אֲשֶׁר עֲשִׂיתֶם הֲלוֹא יְדַעְתֶּם כִּי־נַחֵשׁ יְנַחֵשׁ אִישׁ
טז אֲשֶׁר כָּמֹנִי: וַיֹּאמֶר יְהוּדָה מַה־נֹּאמַר לַאדֹנִי מַה־נְּדַבֵּר וּמַה־נִּצְטַדָּק
הָאֱלֹהִים מָצָא אֶת־עֲוֹן עֲבָדֶיךָ הִנֶּנּוּ עֲבָדִים לַאדֹנִי גַּם־אֲנַחְנוּ גַּם
יז אֲשֶׁר־נִמְצָא הַגָּבִיעַ בְּיָדוֹ: וַיֹּאמֶר חָלִילָה לִּי מֵעֲשׂוֹת זֹאת הָאִישׁ
אֲשֶׁר נִמְצָא הַגָּבִיעַ בְּיָדוֹ הוּא יִהְיֶה־לִּי עָבֶד וְאַתֶּם עֲלוּ לְשָׁלוֹם אֶל־
יח אֲבִיכֶם: וַיִּגַּשׁ אֵלָיו יְהוּדָה וַיֹּאמֶר בִּי אֲדֹנִי יְדַבֶּר־נָא מ ויגש
עַבְדְּךָ דָבָר בְּאָזְנֵי אֲדֹנִי וְאַל־יִחַר אַפְּךָ בְּעַבְדֶּךָ כִּי כָמוֹךָ כְּפַרְעֹה:
יט כ אֲדֹנִי שָׁאַל אֶת־עֲבָדָיו לֵאמֹר הֲיֵשׁ־לָכֶם אָב אוֹ־אָח: וַנֹּאמֶר אֶל־
אֲדֹנִי יֶשׁ־לָנוּ אָב זָקֵן וְיֶלֶד זְקֻנִים קָטָן וְאָחִיו מֵת וַיִּוָּתֵר הוּא לְבַדּוֹ
כא לְאִמּוֹ וְאָבִיו אֲהֵבוֹ: וַתֹּאמֶר אֶל־עֲבָדֶיךָ הוֹרִדֻהוּ אֵלָי וְאָשִׂימָה עֵינִי
כב עָלָיו: וַנֹּאמֶר אֶל־אֲדֹנִי לֹא־יוּכַל הַנַּעַר לַעֲזֹב אֶת־אָבִיו וְעָזַב אֶת־אָבִיו
כג וָמֵת: וַתֹּאמֶר אֶל־עֲבָדֶיךָ אִם־לֹא יֵרֵד אֲחִיכֶם הַקָּטֹן אִתְּכֶם לֹא
כד תֹסִפוּן לִרְאוֹת פָּנָי: וַיְהִי כִּי עָלִינוּ אֶל־עַבְדְּךָ אָבִי וַנַּגֶּד־לוֹ אֵת דִּבְרֵי
כה כו אֲדֹנִי: וַיֹּאמֶר אָבִינוּ שֻׁבוּ שִׁבְרוּ־לָנוּ מְעַט־אֹכֶל: וַנֹּאמֶר לֹא נוּכַל
לָרֶדֶת אִם־יֵשׁ אָחִינוּ הַקָּטֹן אִתָּנוּ וְיָרַדְנוּ כִּי־לֹא נוּכַל לִרְאוֹת פְּנֵי
כז הָאִישׁ וְאָחִינוּ הַקָּטֹן אֵינֶנּוּ אִתָּנוּ: וַיֹּאמֶר עַבְדְּךָ אָבִי אֵלֵינוּ אַתֶּם
כח יְדַעְתֶּם כִּי שְׁנַיִם יָלְדָה־לִּי אִשְׁתִּי: וַיֵּצֵא הָאֶחָד מֵאִתִּי וָאֹמַר אַךְ טָרֹף
כט טֹרָף וְלֹא רְאִיתִיו עַד־הֵנָּה: וּלְקַחְתֶּם גַּם־אֶת־זֶה מֵעִם פָּנַי וְקָרָהוּ
ל אָסוֹן וְהוֹרַדְתֶּם אֶת־שֵׂיבָתִי בְּרָעָה שְׁאֹלָה: וְעַתָּה כְּבֹאִי אֶל־עַבְדְּךָ
לא אָבִי וְהַנַּעַר אֵינֶנּוּ אִתָּנוּ וְנַפְשׁוֹ קְשׁוּרָה בְנַפְשׁוֹ: וְהָיָה כִּרְאוֹתוֹ כִּי־אֵין שני
הַנַּעַר וָמֵת וְהוֹרִידוּ עֲבָדֶיךָ אֶת־שֵׂיבַת עַבְדְּךָ אָבִינוּ בְּיָגוֹן שְׁאֹלָה:
לב כִּי עַבְדְּךָ עָרַב אֶת־הַנַּעַר מֵעִם אָבִי לֵאמֹר אִם־לֹא אֲבִיאֶנּוּ אֵלֶיךָ

33 sinned against my father for all time.' So, please, let your servant stay as my
34 lord's slave in place of the boy, and let the boy go back with his brothers. For
how can I go back to my father if the boy is not with me? I could not bear to
45 1 see the misery that would overwhelm my father!" Yosef could no longer
control himself in the company of all his attendants. He cried out, "Have
everyone leave my presence!" So no one else was with Yosef when he revealed
2 himself to his brothers. He wept so loudly that the Egyptians could hear him,
3 and the news reached Pharaoh's palace. Yosef said to his brothers, "I am Yosef.
Is my father really still alive?" His brothers were so bewildered at his presence
4 that they could not answer him. "Come close to me, please," said Yosef to his
brothers. They came close, and he said, "I am your brother Yosef, whom you
5 sold into Egypt. And now, do not be distressed or angry with yourselves that
6 you sold me here, for God sent me ahead of you to save lives. For two years
now there has been famine in the land, and for another five years there will
7 be no plowing or reaping. So God sent me ahead of you to ensure your
8 survival in the land, and to save your lives by a great deliverance. So then, it
was not you who sent me here, but God. He has made me a father to Pharaoh,
9 lord of his whole household and ruler of all Egypt. Hurry back to my father
and tell him, 'This is what your son Yosef says: God has made me lord of all
10 Egypt. Come down to me without delay. You may live in the region of Goshen
where you will be close to me, you, your children, and your grandchildren,
11 your flocks and herds and all that is yours. I will provide for you there, for
there are still five years of famine to come. Otherwise you, your household,
12 and all who belong to you will be destitute.' You and my brother Binyamin
13 can see with your own eyes that it is I who am speaking to you. Tell my father
about all the honor accorded to me in Egypt and about everything you have
14 seen. Hurry now – bring my father here." Then he threw his arms around his
15 brother Binyamin's neck and wept, and Binyamin wept on his neck; he kissed
all his brothers and wept over them. Only after that could his brothers speak
16 to him. When the news reached Pharaoh's palace that Yosef's brothers had
17 come, Pharaoh and his officials were gratified. Pharaoh said to Yosef, "Tell
18 your brothers, 'Do this: Load your animals and go back to Canaan. Bring your
father and your families and come to me. I will give you the best of the land
19 of Egypt; you shall live off the cream of the land. You are also instructed to
do this: Take wagons from Egypt for your children and wives. Bring your
20 father and come. Do not trouble yourselves about your belongings, for the
21 best of all Egypt will be yours.'" Yisrael's sons did so. Yosef gave them wagons
22 as Pharaoh had ordered, and gave them provisions for the journey. To each
he gave new clothes, but to Binyamin he gave three hundred pieces of silver
23 and five sets of clothes. To his father he sent the following: ten donkeys

לג וְחָטָאתִי לְאָבִי כָּל־הַיָּמִים: וְעַתָּה יֵשֶׁב־נָא עַבְדְּךָ תַּחַת הַנַּעַר עֶבֶד
לד לַאדֹנִי וְהַנַּעַר יַעַל עִם־אֶחָיו: כִּי־אֵיךְ אֶעֱלֶה אֶל־אָבִי וְהַנַּעַר אֵינֶנּוּ
מה א אִתִּי פֶּן אֶרְאֶה בָרָע אֲשֶׁר יִמְצָא אֶת־אָבִי: וְלֹא־יָכֹל יוֹסֵף לְהִתְאַפֵּק
לְכֹל הַנִּצָּבִים עָלָיו וַיִּקְרָא הוֹצִיאוּ כָל־אִישׁ מֵעָלָי וְלֹא־עָמַד אִישׁ
ב אִתּוֹ בְּהִתְוַדַּע יוֹסֵף אֶל־אֶחָיו: וַיִּתֵּן אֶת־קֹלוֹ בִּבְכִי וַיִּשְׁמְעוּ מִצְרַיִם
ג וַיִּשְׁמַע בֵּית פַּרְעֹה: וַיֹּאמֶר יוֹסֵף אֶל־אֶחָיו אֲנִי יוֹסֵף הַעוֹד אָבִי חָי
ד וְלֹא־יָכְלוּ אֶחָיו לַעֲנוֹת אֹתוֹ כִּי נִבְהֲלוּ מִפָּנָיו: וַיֹּאמֶר יוֹסֵף אֶל־אֶחָיו
גְּשׁוּ־נָא אֵלַי וַיִּגָּשׁוּ וַיֹּאמֶר אֲנִי יוֹסֵף אֲחִיכֶם אֲשֶׁר־מְכַרְתֶּם אֹתִי
ה מִצְרָיְמָה: וְעַתָּה | אַל־תֵּעָצְבוּ וְאַל־יִחַר בְּעֵינֵיכֶם כִּי־מְכַרְתֶּם אֹתִי
ו הֵנָּה כִּי לְמִחְיָה שְׁלָחַנִי אֱלֹהִים לִפְנֵיכֶם: כִּי־זֶה שְׁנָתַיִם הָרָעָב בְּקֶרֶב
ז הָאָרֶץ וְעוֹד חָמֵשׁ שָׁנִים אֲשֶׁר אֵין־חָרִישׁ וְקָצִיר: וַיִּשְׁלָחֵנִי אֱלֹהִים
לִפְנֵיכֶם לָשׂוּם לָכֶם שְׁאֵרִית בָּאָרֶץ וּלְהַחֲיוֹת לָכֶם לִפְלֵיטָה גְּדֹלָה:
ח וְעַתָּה לֹא־אַתֶּם שְׁלַחְתֶּם אֹתִי הֵנָּה כִּי הָאֱלֹהִים וַיְשִׂימֵנִי לְאָב לְפַרְעֹה שלישי
ט וּלְאָדוֹן לְכָל־בֵּיתוֹ וּמֹשֵׁל בְּכָל־אֶרֶץ מִצְרָיִם: מַהֲרוּ וַעֲלוּ אֶל־אָבִי
וַאֲמַרְתֶּם אֵלָיו כֹּה אָמַר בִּנְךָ יוֹסֵף שָׂמַנִי אֱלֹהִים לְאָדוֹן לְכָל־מִצְרָיִם
י רְדָה אֵלַי אַל־תַּעֲמֹד: וְיָשַׁבְתָּ בְאֶרֶץ־גֹּשֶׁן וְהָיִיתָ קָרוֹב אֵלַי אַתָּה
יא וּבָנֶיךָ וּבְנֵי בָנֶיךָ וְצֹאנְךָ וּבְקָרְךָ וְכָל־אֲשֶׁר־לָךְ: וְכִלְכַּלְתִּי אֹתְךָ שָׁם
יב כִּי־עוֹד חָמֵשׁ שָׁנִים רָעָב פֶּן־תִּוָּרֵשׁ אַתָּה וּבֵיתְךָ וְכָל־אֲשֶׁר־לָךְ: וְהִנֵּה
יג עֵינֵיכֶם רֹאוֹת וְעֵינֵי אָחִי בִנְיָמִין כִּי־פִי הַמְדַבֵּר אֲלֵיכֶם: וְהִגַּדְתֶּם לְאָבִי
אֶת־כָּל־כְּבוֹדִי בְּמִצְרַיִם וְאֵת כָּל־אֲשֶׁר רְאִיתֶם וּמִהַרְתֶּם וְהוֹרַדְתֶּם
יד אֶת־אָבִי הֵנָּה: וַיִּפֹּל עַל־צַוְּארֵי בִנְיָמִן־אָחִיו וַיֵּבְךְּ וּבִנְיָמִן בָּכָה עַל־
טו צַוָּארָיו: וַיְנַשֵּׁק לְכָל־אֶחָיו וַיֵּבְךְּ עֲלֵהֶם וְאַחֲרֵי כֵן דִּבְּרוּ אֶחָיו אִתּוֹ:
טז וְהַקֹּל נִשְׁמַע בֵּית פַּרְעֹה לֵאמֹר בָּאוּ אֲחֵי יוֹסֵף וַיִּיטַב בְּעֵינֵי פַרְעֹה
יז וּבְעֵינֵי עֲבָדָיו: וַיֹּאמֶר פַּרְעֹה אֶל־יוֹסֵף אֱמֹר אֶל־אַחֶיךָ זֹאת עֲשׂוּ
יח טַעֲנוּ אֶת־בְּעִירְכֶם וּלְכוּ־בֹאוּ אַרְצָה כְּנָעַן: וּקְחוּ אֶת־אֲבִיכֶם וְאֶת־
בָּתֵּיכֶם וּבֹאוּ אֵלָי וְאֶתְּנָה לָכֶם אֶת־טוּב אֶרֶץ מִצְרַיִם וְאִכְלוּ אֶת־חֵלֶב
יט הָאָרֶץ: וְאַתָּה צֻוֵּיתָה זֹאת עֲשׂוּ קְחוּ־לָכֶם מֵאֶרֶץ מִצְרַיִם עֲגָלוֹת רביעי
כ לְטַפְּכֶם וְלִנְשֵׁיכֶם וּנְשָׂאתֶם אֶת־אֲבִיכֶם וּבָאתֶם: וְעֵינְכֶם אַל־תָּחֹס
כא עַל־כְּלֵיכֶם כִּי־טוּב כָּל־אֶרֶץ מִצְרַיִם לָכֶם הוּא: וַיַּעֲשׂוּ־כֵן בְּנֵי יִשְׂרָאֵל
כב וַיִּתֵּן לָהֶם יוֹסֵף עֲגָלוֹת עַל־פִּי פַרְעֹה וַיִּתֵּן לָהֶם צֵדָה לַדָּרֶךְ: לְכֻלָּם
נָתַן לָאִישׁ חֲלִפוֹת שְׂמָלֹת וּלְבִנְיָמִן נָתַן שְׁלֹשׁ מֵאוֹת כֶּסֶף וְחָמֵשׁ
כג חֲלִפֹת שְׂמָלֹת: וּלְאָבִיו שָׁלַח כְּזֹאת עֲשָׂרָה חֲמֹרִים נֹשְׂאִים מִטּוּב

loaded with the best things of Egypt and ten female donkeys loaded with
24 grain, bread, and food for his father's journey. He sent his brothers on their
way; and as they were leaving, he said to them, "Do not quarrel on the way."
25 So they went up out of Egypt and came to their father Yaakov in Canaan.
26 They told him, "Yosef is still alive; in fact, he is ruler over all Egypt." His heart
27 stood still; he did not believe them. But when they told him everything
Yosef had said to them, and when he saw the wagons that Yosef had sent to
28 carry him back, Yaakov's spirit was filled with new life. Yisrael said, "It is
46 1 enough: Yosef my son is still alive. I must go and see him before I die." So
Yisrael set out with all he had. When he reached Be'er Sheva, he offered up
2 sacrifices to the God of his father Yitzḥak. And God spoke to Yisrael in a
3 night vision: "Yaakov, Yaakov." He replied, "Here I am." "I am God, the God
of your father," He said. "Do not be afraid to go down to Egypt, for there I
4 will make of you a great nation. I Myself will go down to Egypt with you, and
5 I Myself will also bring you back; and Yosef's hand will close your eyes." Then
Yaakov left Be'er Sheva. Yisrael's sons took their father Yaakov and their
6 children and wives in the wagons that Pharaoh had sent to carry him. They
took their livestock and all the possessions they had acquired in Canaan.
7 So Yaakov and all his descendants came to Egypt. He brought with him to
Egypt his sons and grandsons, daughters and granddaughters, and all his
8 descendants. These are the names of the children of Israel – Yaakov
9 and his descendants – who came to Egypt: Reuven, Yaakov's firstborn, and
10 Reuven's sons, Ḥanokh, Palu, Ḥetzron, and Karmi. Shimon's sons were
Yemuel, Yamin, Ohad, Yakhin, Tzoḥar, and Sha'ul, son of the Canaanite
11 12 woman. Levi's sons were Gershon, Kehat, and Merari. Yehuda's sons were Er,
Onan, Shela, Peretz, and Zeraḥ – but Er and Onan had died in Canaan.[101]
13 Peretz's sons were Ḥetzron and Ḥamul. Yissakhar's sons were Tola, Puva, Yov,
14 15 and Shimron. Zevulun's sons were Sered, Elon, and Yaḥliel. These were the
sons whom Leah bore to Yaakov in Padan Aram, besides his daughter Dina.
16 In all, male and female, they numbered thirty-three. Gad's sons were Tzifyon,
17 Ḥagi, Shuni, Etzbon, Eri, Arodi, and Areli. Asher's sons were Yimna, Yishva,
Yishvi, and Beria. Their sister was Seraḥ. Beria's sons were Ḥever and Malkiel.
18 These were the children of Zilpa, whom Lavan had given to his daughter
19 Leah; these she bore to Yaakov – sixteen in all. The sons of Yaakov's wife Raḥel
20 were Yosef and Binyamin. In Egypt Menashe and Efrayim were born to Yosef;
21 Asnat, daughter of Potifera priest of On, bore them to him. Binyamin's sons
were Bela, Bekher, Ashbel, Gera, Naaman, Eḥi, Rosh, Mupim, Ḥupim, and
22 23 Ard. These are the children Raḥel bore to Yaakov – fourteen in all. Dan's son
24 25 was Ḥushim. Naftali's sons were Yaḥtze'el, Guni, Yetzer, and Shilem. These

101 | See 38:7–10.

כד מִצְרָיִם וְעֶשֶׂר אֲתֹנֹת נֹשְׂאֹת בָּר וָלֶחֶם וּמָזוֹן לְאָבִיו לַדָּרֶךְ: וַיְשַׁלַּח
כה אֶת־אֶחָיו וַיֵּלֵכוּ וַיֹּאמֶר אֲלֵהֶם אַל־תִּרְגְּזוּ בַּדָּרֶךְ: וַיַּעֲלוּ מִמִּצְרָיִם
כו וַיָּבֹאוּ אֶרֶץ כְּנַעַן אֶל־יַעֲקֹב אֲבִיהֶם: וַיַּגִּדוּ לוֹ לֵאמֹר עוֹד יוֹסֵף חַי
וְכִי־הוּא מֹשֵׁל בְּכָל־אֶרֶץ מִצְרָיִם וַיָּפָג לִבּוֹ כִּי לֹא־הֶאֱמִין לָהֶם:
כז וַיְדַבְּרוּ אֵלָיו אֵת כָּל־דִּבְרֵי יוֹסֵף אֲשֶׁר דִּבֶּר אֲלֵהֶם וַיַּרְא אֶת־הָעֲגָלוֹת
כח אֲשֶׁר־שָׁלַח יוֹסֵף לָשֵׂאת אֹתוֹ וַתְּחִי רוּחַ יַעֲקֹב אֲבִיהֶם: וַיֹּאמֶר חמישי
מו א יִשְׂרָאֵל רַב עוֹד־יוֹסֵף בְּנִי חָי אֵלְכָה וְאֶרְאֶנּוּ בְּטֶרֶם אָמוּת: וַיִּסַּע
יִשְׂרָאֵל וְכָל־אֲשֶׁר־לוֹ וַיָּבֹא בְּאֵרָה שָּׁבַע וַיִּזְבַּח זְבָחִים לֵאלֹהֵי אָבִיו
ב יִצְחָק: וַיֹּאמֶר אֱלֹהִים ׀ לְיִשְׂרָאֵל בְּמַרְאֹת הַלַּיְלָה וַיֹּאמֶר יַעֲקֹב ׀
ג יַעֲקֹב וַיֹּאמֶר הִנֵּנִי: וַיֹּאמֶר אָנֹכִי הָאֵל אֱלֹהֵי אָבִיךָ אַל־תִּירָא מֵרְדָה
ד מִצְרַיְמָה כִּי־לְגוֹי גָּדוֹל אֲשִׂימְךָ שָׁם: אָנֹכִי אֵרֵד עִמְּךָ מִצְרַיְמָה וְאָנֹכִי
ה אַעַלְךָ גַם־עָלֹה וְיוֹסֵף יָשִׁית יָדוֹ עַל־עֵינֶיךָ: וַיָּקָם יַעֲקֹב מִבְּאֵר
שָׁבַע וַיִּשְׂאוּ בְנֵי־יִשְׂרָאֵל אֶת־יַעֲקֹב אֲבִיהֶם וְאֶת־טַפָּם וְאֶת־נְשֵׁיהֶם
ו בָּעֲגָלוֹת אֲשֶׁר־שָׁלַח פַּרְעֹה לָשֵׂאת אֹתוֹ: וַיִּקְחוּ אֶת־מִקְנֵיהֶם וְאֶת־
רְכוּשָׁם אֲשֶׁר רָכְשׁוּ בְּאֶרֶץ כְּנַעַן וַיָּבֹאוּ מִצְרָיְמָה יַעֲקֹב וְכָל־זַרְעוֹ
ז אִתּוֹ: בָּנָיו וּבְנֵי בָנָיו אִתּוֹ בְּנֹתָיו וּבְנוֹת בָּנָיו וְכָל־זַרְעוֹ הֵבִיא אִתּוֹ
ח מִצְרָיְמָה: וְאֵלֶּה שְׁמוֹת בְּנֵי־יִשְׂרָאֵל הַבָּאִים מִצְרַיְמָה
ט יַעֲקֹב וּבָנָיו בְּכֹר יַעֲקֹב רְאוּבֵן: וּבְנֵי רְאוּבֵן חֲנוֹךְ וּפַלּוּא וְחֶצְרֹן וְכַרְמִי:
י יא וּבְנֵי שִׁמְעוֹן יְמוּאֵל וְיָמִין וְאֹהַד וְיָכִין וְצֹחַר וְשָׁאוּל בֶּן־הַכְּנַעֲנִית: וּבְנֵי
יב לֵוִי גֵּרְשׁוֹן קְהָת וּמְרָרִי: וּבְנֵי יְהוּדָה עֵר וְאוֹנָן וְשֵׁלָה וָפֶרֶץ וָזָרַח וַיָּמָת
יג עֵר וְאוֹנָן בְּאֶרֶץ כְּנַעַן וַיִּהְיוּ בְנֵי־פֶרֶץ חֶצְרֹן וְחָמוּל: וּבְנֵי יִשָּׂשכָר תּוֹלָע
יד טו וּפֻוָּה וְיוֹב וְשִׁמְרֹן: וּבְנֵי זְבֻלוּן סֶרֶד וְאֵלוֹן וְיַחְלְאֵל: אֵלֶּה ׀ בְּנֵי לֵאָה
אֲשֶׁר יָלְדָה לְיַעֲקֹב בְּפַדַּן אֲרָם וְאֵת דִּינָה בִתּוֹ כָּל־נֶפֶשׁ בָּנָיו וּבְנוֹתָיו
טז שְׁלֹשִׁים וְשָׁלֹשׁ: וּבְנֵי גָד צִפְיוֹן וְחַגִּי שׁוּנִי וְאֶצְבֹּן עֵרִי וַאֲרוֹדִי וְאַרְאֵלִי:
יז וּבְנֵי אָשֵׁר יִמְנָה וְיִשְׁוָה וְיִשְׁוִי וּבְרִיעָה וְשֶׂרַח אֲחֹתָם וּבְנֵי בְרִיעָה חֶבֶר
יח וּמַלְכִּיאֵל: אֵלֶּה בְּנֵי זִלְפָּה אֲשֶׁר־נָתַן לָבָן לְלֵאָה בִתּוֹ וַתֵּלֶד אֶת־אֵלֶּה
יט כ לְיַעֲקֹב שֵׁשׁ עֶשְׂרֵה נָפֶשׁ: בְּנֵי רָחֵל אֵשֶׁת יַעֲקֹב יוֹסֵף וּבִנְיָמִן: וַיִּוָּלֵד
לְיוֹסֵף בְּאֶרֶץ מִצְרַיִם אֲשֶׁר יָלְדָה־לּוֹ אָסְנַת בַּת־פּוֹטִי פֶרַע כֹּהֵן אֹן
כא אֶת־מְנַשֶּׁה וְאֶת־אֶפְרָיִם: וּבְנֵי בִנְיָמִן בֶּלַע וָבֶכֶר וְאַשְׁבֵּל גֵּרָא וְנַעֲמָן
כב אֵחִי וָרֹאשׁ מֻפִּים וְחֻפִּים וָאָרְדְּ: אֵלֶּה בְּנֵי רָחֵל אֲשֶׁר יֻלַּד לְיַעֲקֹב כָּל־
כג כד נֶפֶשׁ אַרְבָּעָה עָשָׂר: וּבְנֵי־דָן חֻשִׁים: וּבְנֵי נַפְתָּלִי יַחְצְאֵל וְגוּנִי וְיֵצֶר
כה וְשִׁלֵּם: אֵלֶּה בְּנֵי בִלְהָה אֲשֶׁר־נָתַן לָבָן לְרָחֵל בִּתּוֹ וַתֵּלֶד אֶת־אֵלֶּה

were the sons born to Yaakov by Bilha, whom Lavan had given to his daughter
26 Raḥel – seven in all. So the number of people who came to Egypt with
Yaakov – his direct descendants, not including his sons' wives – were sixty-six
27 in all. Yosef's sons, born to him in Egypt, were two in number. Thus the total
28 number of Yaakov's family who came to Egypt was seventy. He
sent Yehuda ahead of him to Yosef to show him the way to Goshen. When
29 they came to the region of Goshen, Yosef harnessed his chariot and rode to
Goshen to greet his father Yisrael. He presented himself to him, threw his
30 arms around his neck, and wept on his shoulder for a long time. "Now I can
31 die," said Yisrael to Yosef. "I have seen your face! You are still alive!" Yosef said
to his brothers and his father's household, "I will go and speak to Pharaoh. I
will tell him, 'My brothers and my father's household have come to me from
32 Canaan. The men are shepherds. They tend livestock. They have brought their
33 sheep and cattle and all they have.' When Pharaoh summons you and asks,
34 'What is your occupation?' you should say, 'We and our fathers have tended
livestock all our lives.' Then you will be allowed to settle in the region of
47 1 Goshen, because the Egyptians abominate all who keep sheep."[102] So Yosef
went and told Pharaoh. He said, "My father and brothers, together with their
flocks, herds, and all they have, have come from Canaan and are now in the
2 region of Goshen." He chose five of his brothers and presented them to
3 Pharaoh. Pharaoh asked the brothers, "What is your occupation?" They
4 replied, "Your servants are shepherds, as our fathers were before." And they
said to Pharaoh, "We have come to stay for a while in your land because the
famine is severe in Canaan and there is no pasture for your servants' flocks.
5 Please, then, let your servants settle in the region of Goshen." Pharaoh said
6 to Yosef, "Your father and brothers have come to you. The land of Egypt is
open before you. Settle your father and brothers in the best part of the land.
Let them live in the region of Goshen, and if there are able men among them,
7 you may give them charge of my own livestock." Then Yosef brought his father
8 Yaakov and presented him before Pharaoh. Yaakov blessed Pharaoh, and
9 Pharaoh asked Yaakov, "How old are you?" Yaakov said to Pharaoh, "The years
of my wandering are one hundred and thirty. Few and hard have been the
years of my life, and I have not reached the age my fathers reached in their
10 11 own wanderings." Yaakov blessed Pharaoh and left his presence. Yosef settled
his father and brothers, giving them holdings in the best part of Egypt, in the
12 region of Ramesses,[103] as Pharaoh had instructed. And Yosef provided his
father, his brothers, and all his father's household with food, befitting the
13 numbers of their dependents. And there was no food across the land, because
the famine was so severe. Egypt and Canaan languished because of the
14 famine. Yosef collected all the money that was to be found in Egypt and
Canaan in payment for the grain the people were buying, and he brought it

---

102 | In other words, because of this consideration, Pharaoh will agree to have you live in a peripheral location such as Goshen.

103 | Ramesses evidently comprised all or part of Goshen.

כו לְיַעֲקֹב כָּל־נֶפֶשׁ שִׁבְעָה׃ כָּל־הַנֶּפֶשׁ הַבָּאָה לְיַעֲקֹב מִצְרַיְמָה יֹצְאֵי
כז יְרֵכוֹ מִלְּבַד נְשֵׁי בְנֵי־יַעֲקֹב כָּל־נֶפֶשׁ שִׁשִּׁים וָשֵׁשׁ׃ וּבְנֵי יוֹסֵף אֲשֶׁר־
יֻלַּד־לוֹ בְמִצְרַיִם נֶפֶשׁ שְׁנָיִם כָּל־הַנֶּפֶשׁ לְבֵית־יַעֲקֹב הַבָּאָה מִצְרַיְמָה
כח שִׁבְעִים׃ וְאֶת־יְהוּדָה שָׁלַח לְפָנָיו אֶל־יוֹסֵף לְהוֹרֹת לְפָנָיו מא ששי
כט גֹּשְׁנָה וַיָּבֹאוּ אַרְצָה גֹּשֶׁן׃ וַיֶּאְסֹר יוֹסֵף מֶרְכַּבְתּוֹ וַיַּעַל לִקְרַאת־יִשְׂרָאֵל
ל אָבִיו גֹּשְׁנָה וַיֵּרָא אֵלָיו וַיִּפֹּל עַל־צַוָּארָיו וַיֵּבְךְּ עַל־צַוָּארָיו עוֹד׃ וַיֹּאמֶר
יִשְׂרָאֵל אֶל־יוֹסֵף אָמוּתָה הַפָּעַם אַחֲרֵי רְאוֹתִי אֶת־פָּנֶיךָ כִּי עוֹדְךָ חָי׃
לא וַיֹּאמֶר יוֹסֵף אֶל־אֶחָיו וְאֶל־בֵּית אָבִיו אֶעֱלֶה וְאַגִּידָה לְפַרְעֹה וְאֹמְרָה
לב אֵלָיו אַחַי וּבֵית־אָבִי אֲשֶׁר בְּאֶרֶץ־כְּנַעַן בָּאוּ אֵלָי׃ וְהָאֲנָשִׁים רֹעֵי צֹאן
לג כִּי־אַנְשֵׁי מִקְנֶה הָיוּ וְצֹאנָם וּבְקָרָם וְכָל־אֲשֶׁר לָהֶם הֵבִיאוּ׃ וְהָיָה כִּי־
לד יִקְרָא לָכֶם פַּרְעֹה וְאָמַר מַה־מַּעֲשֵׂיכֶם׃ וַאֲמַרְתֶּם אַנְשֵׁי מִקְנֶה הָיוּ
עֲבָדֶיךָ מִנְּעוּרֵינוּ וְעַד־עַתָּה גַּם־אֲנַחְנוּ גַּם־אֲבֹתֵינוּ בַּעֲבוּר תֵּשְׁבוּ
מז א בְּאֶרֶץ גֹּשֶׁן כִּי־תוֹעֲבַת מִצְרַיִם כָּל־רֹעֵה צֹאן׃ וַיָּבֹא יוֹסֵף וַיַּגֵּד לְפַרְעֹה
וַיֹּאמֶר אָבִי וְאַחַי וְצֹאנָם וּבְקָרָם וְכָל־אֲשֶׁר לָהֶם בָּאוּ מֵאֶרֶץ כְּנָעַן
ב וְהִנָּם בְּאֶרֶץ גֹּשֶׁן׃ וּמִקְצֵה אֶחָיו לָקַח חֲמִשָּׁה אֲנָשִׁים וַיַּצִּגֵם לִפְנֵי
ג פַרְעֹה׃ וַיֹּאמֶר פַּרְעֹה אֶל־אֶחָיו מַה־מַּעֲשֵׂיכֶם וַיֹּאמְרוּ אֶל־פַּרְעֹה
ד רֹעֵה צֹאן עֲבָדֶיךָ גַּם־אֲנַחְנוּ גַּם־אֲבוֹתֵינוּ׃ וַיֹּאמְרוּ אֶל־פַּרְעֹה לָגוּר
בָּאָרֶץ בָּאנוּ כִּי־אֵין מִרְעֶה לַצֹּאן אֲשֶׁר לַעֲבָדֶיךָ כִּי־כָבֵד הָרָעָב
ה בְּאֶרֶץ כְּנָעַן וְעַתָּה יֵשְׁבוּ־נָא עֲבָדֶיךָ בְּאֶרֶץ גֹּשֶׁן׃ וַיֹּאמֶר פַּרְעֹה אֶל־
ו יוֹסֵף לֵאמֹר אָבִיךָ וְאַחֶיךָ בָּאוּ אֵלֶיךָ׃ אֶרֶץ מִצְרַיִם לְפָנֶיךָ הִוא בְּמֵיטַב
הָאָרֶץ הוֹשֵׁב אֶת־אָבִיךָ וְאֶת־אַחֶיךָ יֵשְׁבוּ בְּאֶרֶץ גֹּשֶׁן וְאִם־יָדַעְתָּ
ז וְיֶשׁ־בָּם אַנְשֵׁי־חַיִל וְשַׂמְתָּם שָׂרֵי מִקְנֶה עַל־אֲשֶׁר־לִי׃ וַיָּבֵא יוֹסֵף
ח אֶת־יַעֲקֹב אָבִיו וַיַּעֲמִדֵהוּ לִפְנֵי פַרְעֹה וַיְבָרֶךְ יַעֲקֹב אֶת־פַּרְעֹה׃ וַיֹּאמֶר
ט פַּרְעֹה אֶל־יַעֲקֹב כַּמָּה יְמֵי שְׁנֵי חַיֶּיךָ׃ וַיֹּאמֶר יַעֲקֹב אֶל־פַּרְעֹה יְמֵי
שְׁנֵי מְגוּרַי שְׁלֹשִׁים וּמְאַת שָׁנָה מְעַט וְרָעִים הָיוּ יְמֵי שְׁנֵי חַיַּי וְלֹא
י הִשִּׂיגוּ אֶת־יְמֵי שְׁנֵי חַיֵּי אֲבֹתַי בִּימֵי מְגוּרֵיהֶם׃ וַיְבָרֶךְ יַעֲקֹב אֶת־פַּרְעֹה
יא וַיֵּצֵא מִלִּפְנֵי פַרְעֹה׃ וַיּוֹשֵׁב יוֹסֵף אֶת־אָבִיו וְאֶת־אֶחָיו וַיִּתֵּן לָהֶם אֲחֻזָּה שביעי
בְּאֶרֶץ מִצְרַיִם בְּמֵיטַב הָאָרֶץ בְּאֶרֶץ רַעְמְסֵס כַּאֲשֶׁר צִוָּה פַרְעֹה׃
יב וַיְכַלְכֵּל יוֹסֵף אֶת־אָבִיו וְאֶת־אֶחָיו וְאֵת כָּל־בֵּית אָבִיו לֶחֶם לְפִי הַטָּף׃
יג וְלֶחֶם אֵין בְּכָל־הָאָרֶץ כִּי־כָבֵד הָרָעָב מְאֹד וַתֵּלַהּ אֶרֶץ מִצְרַיִם וְאֶרֶץ
יד כְּנַעַן מִפְּנֵי הָרָעָב׃ וַיְלַקֵּט יוֹסֵף אֶת־כָּל־הַכֶּסֶף הַנִּמְצָא בְאֶרֶץ־מִצְרַיִם
וּבְאֶרֶץ כְּנַעַן בַּשֶּׁבֶר אֲשֶׁר־הֵם שֹׁבְרִים וַיָּבֵא יוֹסֵף אֶת־הַכֶּסֶף בֵּיתָה

15 into Pharaoh's palace. When the money in Egypt and Canaan was gone, all
the Egyptians came to Yosef, saying, "Give us food. Why should we die before
16 your eyes just because there is no more money left?" "Bring your livestock,"
said Yosef, "and I will sell you food in exchange for your livestock since there
17 is no more money left." So they brought their livestock to Yosef, and he gave
them food in exchange for horses, sheep, cattle, and donkeys. He supplied
18 them with food that year in exchange for all their livestock. That year passed,
and they came to him the following year and said, "We cannot hide from my
lord that the money is gone and the livestock belongs to you. There is nothing
19 left for my lord except our bodies and our land. Why should we and our land
die before your eyes? Acquire us and our land in exchange for food, and we
with our land will be slaves to Pharaoh. Give us seed so that we can live and
20 not die and so that the land does not become desolate." Thus Yosef acquired
all the land of Egypt for Pharaoh. Each Egyptian sold his field, because the
21 famine had become too much for them. So the land became Pharaoh's. As
for the people, he transferred them town by town from one end of Egypt to
22 the other.[104] The only land he did not acquire was that of the priests, because
they received an allotment of food from Pharaoh; they were able to live on
the allotment that Pharaoh gave them, and so they did not sell their land.
23 Yosef said to the people, "Today I have acquired you and your land for Pharaoh.
24 Here is seed for you to sow the land. When the harvest comes, give one-fifth
to Pharaoh. Four-fifths shall be yours as seed for your fields and as food for
25 you, your households, and your children." "You have saved our lives," they said.
26 "May we find favor in the eyes of my lord – we shall be slaves to Pharaoh." So
Yosef made it a law, as it is to this day, governing land in Egypt, that one-fifth
of all produce belongs to Pharaoh. Only the land of the priests did not become
27 Pharaoh's. Thus Yisrael settled in the land of Egypt, in the region of Goshen.
They acquired holdings in it and were fertile and greatly increased in number.
28 Yaakov lived in Egypt for seventeen years; the years of his life were one VAYEḤI
29 hundred and forty-seven. As the time of his death drew near, he summoned
his son Yosef and said to him, "If I have found favor in your eyes, place your
hand under my thigh[105] and promise to deal kindly and truly with me: do not
30 bury me in Egypt. Let me lie with my fathers. Carry me from Egypt and bury
31 me where they are buried." "I will do as you say," he replied. Yaakov said, "Swear
to me," and Yosef swore. Then, at the head of the bed, Yisrael bowed.
48 1 Some time later, Yosef was told, "Your father is ill." He brought with him
2 his two sons, Menashe and Efrayim. And when Yaakov was told, "Your son
Yosef has come to see you," Yisrael summoned his strength and sat up in the
3 bed. Yaakov said to Yosef, "El Shaddai appeared to me in Luz in the land of

---

104 | To help ensure that the people would not try to reclaim their land.
105 | Sometimes performed in conjunction with an oath (cf. 24:2).

טו פַּרְעֹה: וַיִּתֹּם הַכֶּסֶף מֵאֶרֶץ מִצְרַיִם וּמֵאֶרֶץ כְּנַעַן וַיָּבֹאוּ כָל־מִצְרַיִם
אֶל־יוֹסֵף לֵאמֹר הָבָה־לָּנוּ לֶחֶם וְלָמָּה נָמוּת נֶגְדֶּךָ כִּי אָפֵס כָּסֶף:
טז וַיֹּאמֶר יוֹסֵף הָבוּ מִקְנֵיכֶם וְאֶתְּנָה לָכֶם בְּמִקְנֵיכֶם אִם־אָפֵס כָּסֶף:
יז וַיָּבִיאוּ אֶת־מִקְנֵיהֶם אֶל־יוֹסֵף וַיִּתֵּן לָהֶם יוֹסֵף לֶחֶם בַּסּוּסִים וּבְמִקְנֵה
הַצֹּאן וּבְמִקְנֵה הַבָּקָר וּבַחֲמֹרִים וַיְנַהֲלֵם בַּלֶּחֶם בְּכָל־מִקְנֵהֶם בַּשָּׁנָה
יח הַהִוא: וַתִּתֹּם הַשָּׁנָה הַהִוא וַיָּבֹאוּ אֵלָיו בַּשָּׁנָה הַשֵּׁנִית וַיֹּאמְרוּ לוֹ
לֹא־נְכַחֵד מֵאֲדֹנִי כִּי אִם־תַּם הַכֶּסֶף וּמִקְנֵה הַבְּהֵמָה אֶל־אֲדֹנִי לֹא
יט נִשְׁאַר לִפְנֵי אֲדֹנִי בִּלְתִּי אִם־גְּוִיָּתֵנוּ וְאַדְמָתֵנוּ: לָמָּה נָמוּת לְעֵינֶיךָ
גַּם־אֲנַחְנוּ גַּם־אַדְמָתֵנוּ קְנֵה־אֹתָנוּ וְאֶת־אַדְמָתֵנוּ בַּלָּחֶם וְנִהְיֶה
אֲנַחְנוּ וְאַדְמָתֵנוּ עֲבָדִים לְפַרְעֹה וְתֶן־זֶרַע וְנִחְיֶה וְלֹא נָמוּת וְהָאֲדָמָה
כ לֹא תֵשָׁם: וַיִּקֶן יוֹסֵף אֶת־כָּל־אַדְמַת מִצְרַיִם לְפַרְעֹה כִּי־מָכְרוּ מִצְרַיִם
כא אִישׁ שָׂדֵהוּ כִּי־חָזַק עֲלֵהֶם הָרָעָב וַתְּהִי הָאָרֶץ לְפַרְעֹה: וְאֶת־הָעָם
כב הֶעֱבִיר אֹתוֹ לֶעָרִים מִקְצֵה גְבוּל־מִצְרַיִם וְעַד־קָצֵהוּ: רַק אַדְמַת
הַכֹּהֲנִים לֹא קָנָה כִּי חֹק לַכֹּהֲנִים מֵאֵת פַּרְעֹה וְאָכְלוּ אֶת־חֻקָּם
כג אֲשֶׁר נָתַן לָהֶם פַּרְעֹה עַל־כֵּן לֹא מָכְרוּ אֶת־אַדְמָתָם: וַיֹּאמֶר יוֹסֵף
אֶל־הָעָם הֵן קָנִיתִי אֶתְכֶם הַיּוֹם וְאֶת־אַדְמַתְכֶם לְפַרְעֹה הֵא־לָכֶם
כד זֶרַע וּזְרַעְתֶּם אֶת־הָאֲדָמָה: וְהָיָה בַּתְּבוּאֹת וּנְתַתֶּם חֲמִישִׁית לְפַרְעֹה
וְאַרְבַּע הַיָּדֹת יִהְיֶה לָכֶם לְזֶרַע הַשָּׂדֶה וּלְאָכְלְכֶם וְלַאֲשֶׁר בְּבָתֵּיכֶם
כה וְלֶאֱכֹל לְטַפְּכֶם: וַיֹּאמְרוּ הֶחֱיִתָנוּ נִמְצָא־חֵן בְּעֵינֵי אֲדֹנִי וְהָיִינוּ עֲבָדִים מפטיר
כו לְפַרְעֹה: וַיָּשֶׂם אֹתָהּ יוֹסֵף לְחֹק עַד־הַיּוֹם הַזֶּה עַל־אַדְמַת מִצְרַיִם
כז לְפַרְעֹה לַחֹמֶשׁ רַק אַדְמַת הַכֹּהֲנִים לְבַדָּם לֹא הָיְתָה לְפַרְעֹה: וַיֵּשֶׁב
כח יִשְׂרָאֵל בְּאֶרֶץ מִצְרַיִם בְּאֶרֶץ גֹּשֶׁן וַיֵּאָחֲזוּ בָהּ וַיִּפְרוּ וַיִּרְבּוּ מְאֹד: וַיְחִי ויחי
יַעֲקֹב בְּאֶרֶץ מִצְרַיִם שְׁבַע עֶשְׂרֵה שָׁנָה וַיְהִי יְמֵי־יַעֲקֹב שְׁנֵי חַיָּיו שֶׁבַע
כט שָׁנִים וְאַרְבָּעִים וּמְאַת שָׁנָה: וַיִּקְרְבוּ יְמֵי־יִשְׂרָאֵל לָמוּת וַיִּקְרָא ׀ לִבְנוֹ
לְיוֹסֵף וַיֹּאמֶר לוֹ אִם־נָא מָצָאתִי חֵן בְּעֵינֶיךָ שִׂים־נָא יָדְךָ תַּחַת יְרֵכִי
ל וְעָשִׂיתָ עִמָּדִי חֶסֶד וֶאֱמֶת אַל־נָא תִקְבְּרֵנִי בְּמִצְרָיִם: וְשָׁכַבְתִּי עִם־
אֲבֹתַי וּנְשָׂאתַנִי מִמִּצְרַיִם וּקְבַרְתַּנִי בִּקְבֻרָתָם וַיֹּאמַר אָנֹכִי אֶעֱשֶׂה
לא כִדְבָרֶךָ: וַיֹּאמֶר הִשָּׁבְעָה לִי וַיִּשָּׁבַע לוֹ וַיִּשְׁתַּחוּ יִשְׂרָאֵל עַל־רֹאשׁ
הַמִּטָּה:

מח א וַיְהִי אַחֲרֵי הַדְּבָרִים הָאֵלֶּה וַיֹּאמֶר לְיוֹסֵף הִנֵּה אָבִיךָ חֹלֶה וַיִּקַּח מב
ב אֶת־שְׁנֵי בָנָיו עִמּוֹ אֶת־מְנַשֶּׁה וְאֶת־אֶפְרָיִם: וַיַּגֵּד לְיַעֲקֹב וַיֹּאמֶר הִנֵּה
ג בִּנְךָ יוֹסֵף בָּא אֵלֶיךָ וַיִּתְחַזֵּק יִשְׂרָאֵל וַיֵּשֶׁב עַל־הַמִּטָּה: וַיֹּאמֶר יַעֲקֹב

4 Canaan. He blessed me and said to me, 'I will make you fruitful and increase
your numbers. I will make you a community of peoples, and I will give this
5 land to your descendants as an everlasting possession.' Now, the two sons
who were born to you in Egypt before I came here shall be considered mine:
6 Efrayim and Menashe will be like Reuven and Shimon to me. Any child born
to you after shall be yours; in any inheritance they will be reckoned under the
7 names of their brothers.[106] For I – as I was returning from Padan, Raḥel died
beside me in Canaan while we were still on the way, a short distance from
Efrat. And I buried her there beside the road to Efrat – that is, Beit Leḥem."
8 9 Then Yisrael looked at Yosef's sons and said, "Who are these?" Yosef told
his father, "They are my sons God has given me here." "Please bring them to
10 me," Yaakov said, "so that I can bless them." Yisrael's eyes were heavy with age
and he could not see. So Yosef brought them close to him, and he kissed and
11 embraced them. Yisrael said to Yosef, "I never expected to see you again, and
12 now God has shown me your children as well." Yosef then took them from
13 between his knees and bowed low, his face to the ground. Yosef took both of
them, Efrayim on his right to Yisrael's left, and Menashe on his left to Yisrael's
14 right, and brought them close. Yisrael reached out his right hand and put it
on Efrayim's head, even though he was the younger. And, crossing his hands,
15 he put his left hand on Menashe's head even though he was the firstborn. He
blessed Yosef and said, "God before whom my fathers walked – Avraham and
16 Yitzḥak – God who has been my shepherd all my life to now, the angel who
has delivered me from all harm, may He bless the boys. Through them may
my name be recalled, and the names of my fathers, Avraham and Yitzḥak.
17 May they grow to a multitude upon the land." When Yosef saw that his father
had placed his right hand on Efrayim's head, he was displeased. He took hold
18 of his father's hand to move it from Efrayim's head to Menashe's head. Yosef
said to his father, "Not so, father. This is the firstborn. Put your right hand on
19 his head." But his father refused: "I know, my son, I know. He too will be a
people, and he too will become great, but his younger brother will become
20 even greater, and his descendants will become an abundance of nations." On
that day, he blessed them: "By you shall Israel bless,[107] saying: May God make
21 you like Efrayim and Menashe." He put Efrayim before Menashe. Then Yisrael
said to Yosef, "I am about to die, but God will be with you and will bring you
22 back to the land of your fathers. And to you I give one portion more than your
brothers, which I took from the Amorites by my sword and my bow."
49 1 Then Yaakov called for his sons and said, "Gather together so that I can
2 tell you what will happen to you in the days to come. Assemble and listen,

106 | Descendants of Yosef through any other sons would thus be incorporated into the tribes of Efrayim and Menashe.

107 | When the Israelites offer blessings, they will invoke Efrayim and Menashe.

ד אֶל־יוֹסֵף אֵל שַׁדַּי נִרְאָה־אֵלַי בְּלוּז בְּאֶרֶץ כְּנָעַן וַיְבָרֶךְ אֹתִי׃ וַיֹּאמֶר
אֵלַי הִנְנִי מַפְרְךָ וְהִרְבִּיתִךָ וּנְתַתִּיךָ לִקְהַל עַמִּים וְנָתַתִּי אֶת־הָאָרֶץ
ה הַזֹּאת לְזַרְעֲךָ אַחֲרֶיךָ אֲחֻזַּת עוֹלָם׃ וְעַתָּה שְׁנֵי־בָנֶיךָ הַנּוֹלָדִים לְךָ
בְּאֶרֶץ מִצְרַיִם עַד־בֹּאִי אֵלֶיךָ מִצְרַיְמָה לִי־הֵם אֶפְרַיִם וּמְנַשֶּׁה כִּרְאוּבֵן
ו וְשִׁמְעוֹן יִהְיוּ־לִי׃ וּמוֹלַדְתְּךָ אֲשֶׁר־הוֹלַדְתָּ אַחֲרֵיהֶם לְךָ יִהְיוּ עַל שֵׁם
ז אֲחֵיהֶם יִקָּרְאוּ בְּנַחֲלָתָם׃ וַאֲנִי ׀ בְּבֹאִי מִפַּדָּן מֵתָה עָלַי רָחֵל בְּאֶרֶץ
כְּנַעַן בַּדֶּרֶךְ בְּעוֹד כִּבְרַת־אֶרֶץ לָבֹא אֶפְרָתָה וָאֶקְבְּרֶהָ שָּׁם בְּדֶרֶךְ
ח אֶפְרָת הִוא בֵּית לָחֶם׃ וַיַּרְא יִשְׂרָאֵל אֶת־בְּנֵי יוֹסֵף וַיֹּאמֶר מִי־אֵלֶּה׃
ט וַיֹּאמֶר יוֹסֵף אֶל־אָבִיו בָּנַי הֵם אֲשֶׁר־נָתַן־לִי אֱלֹהִים בָּזֶה וַיֹּאמַר
י קָחֶם־נָא אֵלַי וַאֲבָרְכֵם׃ וְעֵינֵי יִשְׂרָאֵל כָּבְדוּ מִזֹּקֶן לֹא יוּכַל לִרְאוֹת שני
יא וַיַּגֵּשׁ אֹתָם אֵלָיו וַיִּשַּׁק לָהֶם וַיְחַבֵּק לָהֶם׃ וַיֹּאמֶר יִשְׂרָאֵל אֶל־יוֹסֵף
יב רְאֹה פָנֶיךָ לֹא פִלָּלְתִּי וְהִנֵּה הֶרְאָה אֹתִי אֱלֹהִים גַּם אֶת־זַרְעֶךָ׃ וַיּוֹצֵא
יג יוֹסֵף אֹתָם מֵעִם בִּרְכָּיו וַיִּשְׁתַּחוּ לְאַפָּיו אָרְצָה׃ וַיִּקַּח יוֹסֵף אֶת־שְׁנֵיהֶם
אֶת־אֶפְרַיִם בִּימִינוֹ מִשְּׂמֹאל יִשְׂרָאֵל וְאֶת־מְנַשֶּׁה בִשְׂמֹאלוֹ מִימִין
יד יִשְׂרָאֵל וַיַּגֵּשׁ אֵלָיו׃ וַיִּשְׁלַח יִשְׂרָאֵל אֶת־יְמִינוֹ וַיָּשֶׁת עַל־רֹאשׁ אֶפְרַיִם
וְהוּא הַצָּעִיר וְאֶת־שְׂמֹאלוֹ עַל־רֹאשׁ מְנַשֶּׁה שִׂכֵּל אֶת־יָדָיו כִּי מְנַשֶּׁה
טו הַבְּכוֹר׃ וַיְבָרֶךְ אֶת־יוֹסֵף וַיֹּאמַר הָאֱלֹהִים אֲשֶׁר הִתְהַלְּכוּ אֲבֹתַי לְפָנָיו
טז אַבְרָהָם וְיִצְחָק הָאֱלֹהִים הָרֹעֶה אֹתִי מֵעוֹדִי עַד־הַיּוֹם הַזֶּה׃ הַמַּלְאָךְ
הַגֹּאֵל אֹתִי מִכָּל־רָע יְבָרֵךְ אֶת־הַנְּעָרִים וְיִקָּרֵא בָהֶם שְׁמִי וְשֵׁם אֲבֹתַי
יז אַבְרָהָם וְיִצְחָק וְיִדְגּוּ לָרֹב בְּקֶרֶב הָאָרֶץ׃ וַיַּרְא יוֹסֵף כִּי־יָשִׁית אָבִיו שלישי
יַד־יְמִינוֹ עַל־רֹאשׁ אֶפְרַיִם וַיֵּרַע בְּעֵינָיו וַיִּתְמֹךְ יַד־אָבִיו לְהָסִיר אֹתָהּ
יח מֵעַל רֹאשׁ־אֶפְרַיִם עַל־רֹאשׁ מְנַשֶּׁה׃ וַיֹּאמֶר יוֹסֵף אֶל־אָבִיו לֹא־כֵן
יט אָבִי כִּי־זֶה הַבְּכֹר שִׂים יְמִינְךָ עַל־רֹאשׁוֹ׃ וַיְמָאֵן אָבִיו וַיֹּאמֶר יָדַעְתִּי
בְנִי יָדַעְתִּי גַּם־הוּא יִהְיֶה־לְּעָם וְגַם־הוּא יִגְדָּל וְאוּלָם אָחִיו הַקָּטֹן יִגְדַּל
כ מִמֶּנּוּ וְזַרְעוֹ יִהְיֶה מְלֹא־הַגּוֹיִם׃ וַיְבָרְכֵם בַּיּוֹם הַהוּא לֵאמוֹר בְּךָ יְבָרֵךְ
יִשְׂרָאֵל לֵאמֹר יְשִׂמְךָ אֱלֹהִים כְּאֶפְרַיִם וְכִמְנַשֶּׁה וַיָּשֶׂם אֶת־אֶפְרַיִם
כא לִפְנֵי מְנַשֶּׁה׃ וַיֹּאמֶר יִשְׂרָאֵל אֶל־יוֹסֵף הִנֵּה אָנֹכִי מֵת וְהָיָה אֱלֹהִים
כב עִמָּכֶם וְהֵשִׁיב אֶתְכֶם אֶל־אֶרֶץ אֲבֹתֵיכֶם׃ וַאֲנִי נָתַתִּי לְךָ שְׁכֶם אַחַד
עַל־אַחֶיךָ אֲשֶׁר לָקַחְתִּי מִיַּד הָאֱמֹרִי בְּחַרְבִּי וּבְקַשְׁתִּי׃

מט א וַיִּקְרָא יַעֲקֹב אֶל־בָּנָיו וַיֹּאמֶר הֵאָסְפוּ וְאַגִּידָה לָכֶם אֵת אֲשֶׁר־יִקְרָא מג רביעי
ב אֶתְכֶם בְּאַחֲרִית הַיָּמִים׃ הִקָּבְצוּ וְשִׁמְעוּ בְּנֵי יַעֲקֹב וְשִׁמְעוּ אֶל־יִשְׂרָאֵל

3 Yaakov's sons. Listen to your father Yisrael. Reuven, you are my firstborn,
my strength, first fruit of my manhood, excelling in rank, excelling in power.
4 Unstable as water, you shall not excel, for you went up onto your father's bed
and defiled it – went up onto my couch.[108]
5 6 Shimon and Levi are brothers; weapons of violence their wares.[109] Let me
never join their council, nor my honor be of their assembly. For in their anger
7 they killed men; at their whim they hamstrung oxen. Cursed be their anger,
for it is most fierce, and their fury, for it is most cruel. I will divide them up
in Yaakov, and scatter them in Israel.[110]
8 Yehuda, your brothers shall praise you. Your hand will be on the neck of your
9 foes. To you will your father's sons bow.[111] Yehuda is a lion's cub. From the prey,
my son, you have risen. Like a lion he crouches, lies down, like a lioness; who
10 dares to rouse him? The scepter shall not pass from Yehuda, nor the staff from
between his feet, so that tribute will come to him and the homage of nations
11 be his. He tethers his donkey to vines, to the vine bough his donkey's colt;
12 he washes his clothes in wine, his robe in the blood of grapes.[112] His eyes are
darker than wine, and his teeth whiter than milk.[113]
13 Zevulun will live by the seashore; he will be a haven for ships. To Sidon his
border will reach.
14 15 Yissakhar is a strong-boned donkey, lying down among the sheep pens. Seeing
how good is his resting place, and how pleasant is the land, he will bend his
16 shoulder to the load, and work like a slave in harness. Dan will seek
17 justice[114] for his people as one of Israel's tribes. Dan: a snake by the roadside, a
viper upon the path that bites the horse's heel, so that its rider falls backward.[115]
18 19 I wait for Your salvation, LORD. Gad will be raided by raiders, but
20 he then will raid at their heels.[116] From Asher will come rich food,
21 he will proffer the king's delights. Naftali is a deer set free, bearing
22 loveliest fawns. Yosef is a fruitful vine, a fruitful vine by a spring,
23 whose branches spread over a wall. Archers attacked him with bitterness,
24 shot at him, harassed him. But his bow stopped steady, and his arms held firm
because of the hand of the Mighty One of Yaakov, the Shepherd, Yisrael's Rock,
25 because of the God of your father who will help you, because of Shaddai who
will bless you with blessings of heaven above, blessings of the deep that lies
26 under, blessings of breast and of womb. May your father's blessing surpass even
the blessings of my forebears – to the bounds of the everlasting hills. May they
rest on the head of Yosef, on the brow of the elect of his brothers.

---

108 | See 35:22.

109 | See 34:25–26.

110 | Neither tribe would receive a contiguous portion of territory in the land of Israel.

111 | The tribe of Yehuda would later give rise to King David and his dynasty.

112 | These images suggest luxuriant wealth.

113 | From the abundance of wine and milk.

114 | The word *yadin* (seek justice) plays on the name Dan.

115 | This image suggests a type of military prowess.

116 | The phrase *gedud yegudenu* (will be raided by raiders) and the word *yagud* (will raid) play on the name Gad.

ג אֲבִיכֶם: רְאוּבֵן בְּכֹרִי אַתָּה כֹּחִי וְרֵאשִׁית אוֹנִי יֶתֶר שְׂאֵת וְיֶתֶר עָז:
ד פַּחַז כַּמַּיִם אַל־תּוֹתַר כִּי עָלִיתָ מִשְׁכְּבֵי אָבִיךָ אָז חִלַּלְתָּ יְצוּעִי
עָלָה:
ה ו שִׁמְעוֹן וְלֵוִי אַחִים כְּלֵי חָמָס מְכֵרֹתֵיהֶם: בְּסֹדָם אַל־תָּבֹא נַפְשִׁי
בִּקְהָלָם אַל־תֵּחַד כְּבֹדִי כִּי בְאַפָּם הָרְגוּ אִישׁ וּבִרְצֹנָם עִקְּרוּ־שׁוֹר:
ז אָרוּר אַפָּם כִּי עָז וְעֶבְרָתָם כִּי קָשָׁתָה אֲחַלְּקֵם בְּיַעֲקֹב וַאֲפִיצֵם
בְּיִשְׂרָאֵל:
ח יְהוּדָה אַתָּה יוֹדוּךָ אַחֶיךָ יָדְךָ בְּעֹרֶף אֹיְבֶיךָ יִשְׁתַּחֲווּ לְךָ בְּנֵי אָבִיךָ:
ט גּוּר אַרְיֵה יְהוּדָה מִטֶּרֶף בְּנִי עָלִיתָ כָּרַע רָבַץ כְּאַרְיֵה וּכְלָבִיא מִי
י יְקִימֶנּוּ: לֹא־יָסוּר שֵׁבֶט מִיהוּדָה וּמְחֹקֵק מִבֵּין רַגְלָיו עַד כִּי־יָבֹא
יא שִׁילֹה וְלוֹ יִקְּהַת עַמִּים: אֹסְרִי לַגֶּפֶן עִירֹה וְלַשֹּׂרֵקָה בְּנִי אֲתֹנוֹ כִּבֵּס
יב בַּיַּיִן לְבֻשׁוֹ וּבְדַם־עֲנָבִים סוּתֹה: חַכְלִילִי עֵינַיִם מִיָּיִן וּלְבֶן־שִׁנַּיִם
מֵחָלָב:
יג זְבוּלֻן לְחוֹף יַמִּים יִשְׁכֹּן וְהוּא לְחוֹף אֳנִיֹּת וְיַרְכָתוֹ עַל־צִידֹן:
יד טו יִשָּׂשכָר חֲמֹר גָּרֶם רֹבֵץ בֵּין הַמִּשְׁפְּתָיִם: וַיַּרְא מְנֻחָה כִּי טוֹב וְאֶת־
טז הָאָרֶץ כִּי נָעֵמָה וַיֵּט שִׁכְמוֹ לִסְבֹּל וַיְהִי לְמַס־עֹבֵד: דָּן
יז יָדִין עַמּוֹ כְּאַחַד שִׁבְטֵי יִשְׂרָאֵל: יְהִי־דָן נָחָשׁ עֲלֵי־דֶרֶךְ שְׁפִיפֹן
יח עֲלֵי־אֹרַח הַנֹּשֵׁךְ עִקְּבֵי־סוּס וַיִּפֹּל רֹכְבוֹ אָחוֹר: לִישׁוּעָתְךָ קִוִּיתִי
יט כ יְהוָה: גָּד גְּדוּד יְגוּדֶנּוּ וְהוּא יָגֻד עָקֵב: מֵאָשֵׁר חמישי
כא שְׁמֵנָה לַחְמוֹ וְהוּא יִתֵּן מַעֲדַנֵּי־מֶלֶךְ: נַפְתָּלִי אַיָּלָה
כב שְׁלֻחָה הַנֹּתֵן אִמְרֵי־שָׁפֶר: בֵּן פֹּרָת יוֹסֵף בֵּן פֹּרָת
כג עֲלֵי־עָיִן בָּנוֹת צָעֲדָה עֲלֵי־שׁוּר: וַיְמָרֲרֻהוּ וָרֹבּוּ וַיִּשְׂטְמֻהוּ בַּעֲלֵי
כד חִצִּים: וַתֵּשֶׁב בְּאֵיתָן קַשְׁתּוֹ וַיָּפֹזּוּ זְרֹעֵי יָדָיו מִידֵי אֲבִיר יַעֲקֹב מִשָּׁם
כה רֹעֶה אֶבֶן יִשְׂרָאֵל: מֵאֵל אָבִיךָ וְיַעְזְרֶךָּ וְאֵת שַׁדַּי וִיבָרְכֶךָּ בִּרְכֹת
כו שָׁמַיִם מֵעָל בִּרְכֹת תְּהוֹם רֹבֶצֶת תָּחַת בִּרְכֹת שָׁדַיִם וָרָחַם: בִּרְכֹת
אָבִיךָ גָּבְרוּ עַל־בִּרְכֹת הוֹרַי עַד־תַּאֲוַת גִּבְעֹת עוֹלָם תִּהְיֶיןָ לְרֹאשׁ
יוֹסֵף וּלְקָדְקֹד נְזִיר אֶחָיו:

27 Binyamin is a ravening wolf, devouring prey in the morning, and by evening
28 dividing the plunder." All these are the twelve tribes of Israel, and this is what
their father said to them when he blessed them, giving each his particular
29 blessing. Then he gave them instruction, saying, "I am about to be gathered
to my people. Bury me with my fathers in the cave in the field of Efron the
30 Hittite, the cave in the field of Makhpela near Mamre in Canaan, which
Avraham bought, together with the field, from Efron the Hittite as a burial
31 place.[117] There Avraham and his wife Sara are buried, there Yitzḥak and his
32 wife Rivka are buried, and there I buried Leah. The field and the cave in it
33 were bought from the Hittites." There Yaakov finished instructing his sons.
And he drew his feet back onto the bed, breathed his last, and was gathered
50 1 to his people. Yosef fell on his father's face and wept over him and kissed
2 him. Then Yosef instructed his servants the physicians to embalm his father.
3 So the physicians embalmed Yisrael. It took them forty days; that was the
time required for embalming. The Egyptians mourned him for seventy days.
4 When the period of mourning was over, Yosef spoke to Pharaoh's court: "If
I have found favor in your eyes, please speak to Pharaoh on my behalf. Tell
5 him, 'My father made me swear an oath, saying, "I am about to die. Bury me in
the grave I prepared for myself in the land of Canaan." Now let me go up and
6 bury my father; then I will return.'" Pharaoh said, "Go and bury your father
7 as he had you swear." So Yosef went up to bury his father. With him went all
Pharaoh's officials, the elders of his palace, and all the other elders of Egypt,
8 together with all Yosef's household, his brothers, and his father's household.
9 They left only their children and flocks and herds in Goshen. With them too
10 went a chariot brigade and horsemen; it was a very large retinue. When they
reached the threshing floor of Atad, beyond the Jordan, they held a great and
solemn lamentation, and Yosef observed a seven-day period of mourning
11 for his father. When the Canaanites who lived there saw the mourning at the
threshing floor of Atad they said, "Egypt is in deep mourning here"; that is
12 why the place beyond the Jordan was called Avel Mitzrayim.[118] So his sons
13 did as he had instructed them. They carried him to Canaan and buried him
in the cave of the field of Makhpela, near Mamre, which Avraham had bought
14 as a burial site from Efron the Hittite. After burying his father, Yosef returned
to Egypt together with his brothers and all those who had accompanied him
15 to his father's burial. When Yosef's brothers knew that their father was dead,
they said, "What if Yosef really hates us and decides to pay us back for all the
16 wrong we did to him?" So they sent word to Yosef saying, "Your father gave
17 these instructions before his death: 'This is what you are to say to Yosef:
"Please forgive the crime and sin of your brothers who inflicted such harm
upon you."' That being so, please forgive the crime of these servants of your

117 | See 23:16–18.

118 | Meaning "mourning of Egypt."

כז כח בִּנְיָמִין זְאֵב יִטְרָף בַּבֹּקֶר יֹאכַל עַד וְלָעֶרֶב יְחַלֵּק שָׁלָל׃ כָּל־אֵלֶּה שִׁבְטֵי ששי
יִשְׂרָאֵל שְׁנֵים עָשָׂר וְזֹאת אֲשֶׁר־דִּבֶּר לָהֶם אֲבִיהֶם וַיְבָרֶךְ אוֹתָם אִישׁ
כט אֲשֶׁר כְּבִרְכָתוֹ בֵּרַךְ אֹתָם׃ וַיְצַו אוֹתָם וַיֹּאמֶר אֲלֵהֶם אֲנִי נֶאֱסָף אֶל־
עַמִּי קִבְרוּ אֹתִי אֶל־אֲבֹתָי אֶל־הַמְּעָרָה אֲשֶׁר בִּשְׂדֵה עֶפְרוֹן הַחִתִּי׃
ל בַּמְּעָרָה אֲשֶׁר בִּשְׂדֵה הַמַּכְפֵּלָה אֲשֶׁר־עַל־פְּנֵי מַמְרֵא בְּאֶרֶץ כְּנָעַן
אֲשֶׁר קָנָה אַבְרָהָם אֶת־הַשָּׂדֶה מֵאֵת עֶפְרֹן הַחִתִּי לַאֲחֻזַּת־קָבֶר׃
לא שָׁמָּה קָבְרוּ אֶת־אַבְרָהָם וְאֵת שָׂרָה אִשְׁתּוֹ שָׁמָּה קָבְרוּ אֶת־יִצְחָק
לב וְאֵת רִבְקָה אִשְׁתּוֹ וְשָׁמָּה קָבַרְתִּי אֶת־לֵאָה׃ מִקְנֵה הַשָּׂדֶה וְהַמְּעָרָה
לג אֲשֶׁר־בּוֹ מֵאֵת בְּנֵי־חֵת׃ וַיְכַל יַעֲקֹב לְצַוֺּת אֶת־בָּנָיו וַיֶּאֱסֹף רַגְלָיו
נ א אֶל־הַמִּטָּה וַיִּגְוַע וַיֵּאָסֶף אֶל־עַמָּיו׃ וַיִּפֹּל יוֹסֵף עַל־פְּנֵי אָבִיו וַיֵּבְךְּ
ב עָלָיו וַיִּשַּׁק־לוֹ׃ וַיְצַו יוֹסֵף אֶת־עֲבָדָיו אֶת־הָרֹפְאִים לַחֲנֹט אֶת־אָבִיו
ג וַיַּחַנְטוּ הָרֹפְאִים אֶת־יִשְׂרָאֵל׃ וַיִּמְלְאוּ־לוֹ אַרְבָּעִים יוֹם כִּי כֵּן יִמְלְאוּ
ד יְמֵי הַחֲנֻטִים וַיִּבְכּוּ אֹתוֹ מִצְרַיִם שִׁבְעִים יוֹם׃ וַיַּעַבְרוּ יְמֵי בְכִיתוֹ
וַיְדַבֵּר יוֹסֵף אֶל־בֵּית פַּרְעֹה לֵאמֹר אִם־נָא מָצָאתִי חֵן בְּעֵינֵיכֶם
ה דַּבְּרוּ־נָא בְּאָזְנֵי פַרְעֹה לֵאמֹר׃ אָבִי הִשְׁבִּיעַנִי לֵאמֹר הִנֵּה אָנֹכִי מֵת
בְּקִבְרִי אֲשֶׁר כָּרִיתִי לִי בְּאֶרֶץ כְּנַעַן שָׁמָּה תִּקְבְּרֵנִי וְעַתָּה אֶעֱלֶה־נָּא
ו וְאֶקְבְּרָה אֶת־אָבִי וְאָשׁוּבָה׃ וַיֹּאמֶר פַּרְעֹה עֲלֵה וּקְבֹר אֶת־אָבִיךָ
ז כַּאֲשֶׁר הִשְׁבִּיעֶךָ׃ וַיַּעַל יוֹסֵף לִקְבֹּר אֶת־אָבִיו וַיַּעֲלוּ אִתּוֹ כָּל־עַבְדֵי
ח פַרְעֹה זִקְנֵי בֵיתוֹ וְכֹל זִקְנֵי אֶרֶץ־מִצְרָיִם׃ וְכֹל בֵּית יוֹסֵף וְאֶחָיו וּבֵית
ט אָבִיו רַק טַפָּם וְצֹאנָם וּבְקָרָם עָזְבוּ בְּאֶרֶץ גֹּשֶׁן׃ וַיַּעַל עִמּוֹ גַּם־רֶכֶב
י גַּם־פָּרָשִׁים וַיְהִי הַמַּחֲנֶה כָּבֵד מְאֹד׃ וַיָּבֹאוּ עַד־גֹּרֶן הָאָטָד אֲשֶׁר בְּעֵבֶר
הַיַּרְדֵּן וַיִּסְפְּדוּ־שָׁם מִסְפֵּד גָּדוֹל וְכָבֵד מְאֹד וַיַּעַשׂ לְאָבִיו אֵבֶל שִׁבְעַת
יא יָמִים׃ וַיַּרְא יוֹשֵׁב הָאָרֶץ הַכְּנַעֲנִי אֶת־הָאֵבֶל בְּגֹרֶן הָאָטָד וַיֹּאמְרוּ
אֵבֶל־כָּבֵד זֶה לְמִצְרָיִם עַל־כֵּן קָרָא שְׁמָהּ אָבֵל מִצְרַיִם אֲשֶׁר בְּעֵבֶר
יב יג הַיַּרְדֵּן׃ וַיַּעֲשׂוּ בָנָיו לוֹ כֵּן כַּאֲשֶׁר צִוָּם׃ וַיִּשְׂאוּ אֹתוֹ בָנָיו אַרְצָה כְּנַעַן
וַיִּקְבְּרוּ אֹתוֹ בִּמְעָרַת שְׂדֵה הַמַּכְפֵּלָה אֲשֶׁר קָנָה אַבְרָהָם אֶת־הַשָּׂדֶה
יד לַאֲחֻזַּת־קֶבֶר מֵאֵת עֶפְרֹן הַחִתִּי עַל־פְּנֵי מַמְרֵא׃ וַיָּשָׁב יוֹסֵף מִצְרַיְמָה
הוּא וְאֶחָיו וְכָל־הָעֹלִים אִתּוֹ לִקְבֹּר אֶת־אָבִיו אַחֲרֵי קָבְרוֹ אֶת־אָבִיו׃
טו וַיִּרְאוּ אֲחֵי־יוֹסֵף כִּי־מֵת אֲבִיהֶם וַיֹּאמְרוּ לוּ יִשְׂטְמֵנוּ יוֹסֵף וְהָשֵׁב יָשִׁיב
טז לָנוּ אֵת כָּל־הָרָעָה אֲשֶׁר גָּמַלְנוּ אֹתוֹ׃ וַיְצַוּוּ אֶל־יוֹסֵף לֵאמֹר אָבִיךָ
יז צִוָּה לִפְנֵי מוֹתוֹ לֵאמֹר׃ כֹּה־תֹאמְרוּ לְיוֹסֵף אָנָּא שָׂא נָא פֶּשַׁע אַחֶיךָ
וְחַטָּאתָם כִּי־רָעָה גְמָלוּךָ וְעַתָּה שָׂא נָא לְפֶשַׁע עַבְדֵי אֱלֹהֵי אָבִיךָ

18 father's God." Yosef wept as they spoke to him. Then his brothers came and
19 threw themselves down before him and said, "We are your slaves." But Yosef
20 said to them, "Do not be afraid. Am I in place of God? You intended to harm
me, but God intended it for good, to bring about what is now being done:
21 the saving of many lives. So, do not be afraid. I myself will provide for you
22 and your children." And he comforted them and spoke to their hearts. Yosef
remained in Egypt together with his father's family, and he lived one hundred
23 and ten years. Yosef saw the third generation of Efrayim's children, and the
24 children of Menashe's son Makir were also born on Yosef's knees.[119] Yosef
said to his brothers, "I am about to die. But God will surely take note of you
and bring you out of this land to the land He promised to Avraham, Yitzḥak,
25 and Yaakov." Then Yosef bound the children of Israel by an oath: "When God
26 takes note of you, carry my bones up from this place." Yosef died at the age of
one hundred and ten. He was embalmed and placed in a coffin there, in Egypt.

119 | That is, they were born during Yosef's lifetime.

יח וַיֵּ֥בְךְּ יוֹסֵ֖ף בְּדַבְּרָ֥ם אֵלָֽיו׃ וַיֵּלְכוּ֙ גַּם־אֶחָ֔יו וַיִּפְּל֖וּ לְפָנָ֑יו וַיֹּ֣אמְר֔וּ הִנֶּ֥נּוּ
יט לְךָ֖ לַעֲבָדִֽים׃ וַיֹּ֧אמֶר אֲלֵהֶ֛ם יוֹסֵ֖ף אַל־תִּירָ֑אוּ כִּ֛י הֲתַ֥חַת אֱלֹהִ֖ים אָֽנִי׃
כ וְאַתֶּ֕ם חֲשַׁבְתֶּ֥ם עָלַ֖י רָעָ֑ה אֱלֹהִים֙ חֲשָׁבָ֣הּ לְטֹבָ֔ה לְמַ֗עַן עֲשֹׂ֛ה כַּיּ֥וֹם הַזֶּ֖ה
כא לְהַחֲיֹ֥ת עַם־רָֽב׃ וְעַתָּה֙ אַל־תִּירָ֔אוּ אָנֹכִ֛י אֲכַלְכֵּ֥ל אֶתְכֶ֖ם וְאֶֽת־טַפְּכֶ֑ם שביעי
כב וַיְנַחֵ֣ם אוֹתָ֔ם וַיְדַבֵּ֖ר עַל־לִבָּֽם׃ וַיֵּ֤שֶׁב יוֹסֵף֙ בְּמִצְרַ֔יִם ה֖וּא וּבֵ֣ית אָבִ֑יו
כג וַיְחִ֣י יוֹסֵ֔ף מֵאָ֥ה וָעֶ֖שֶׂר שָׁנִֽים׃ וַיַּ֤רְא יוֹסֵף֙ לְאֶפְרַ֔יִם בְּנֵ֖י שִׁלֵּשִׁ֑ים גַּ֗ם בְּנֵ֤י מפטיר
כד מָכִיר֙ בֶּן־מְנַשֶּׁ֔ה יֻלְּד֖וּ עַל־בִּרְכֵּ֥י יוֹסֵֽף׃ וַיֹּ֤אמֶר יוֹסֵף֙ אֶל־אֶחָ֔יו אָנֹכִ֖י
מֵ֑ת וֵֽאלֹהִ֞ים פָּקֹ֧ד יִפְקֹ֣ד אֶתְכֶ֗ם וְהֶעֱלָ֤ה אֶתְכֶם֙ מִן־הָאָ֣רֶץ הַזֹּ֔את אֶל־
כה הָאָ֕רֶץ אֲשֶׁ֥ר נִשְׁבַּ֛ע לְאַבְרָהָ֥ם לְיִצְחָ֖ק וּֽלְיַעֲקֹֽב׃ וַיַּשְׁבַּ֣ע יוֹסֵ֔ף אֶת־בְּנֵ֥י
יִשְׂרָאֵ֖ל לֵאמֹ֑ר פָּקֹ֨ד יִפְקֹ֤ד אֱלֹהִים֙ אֶתְכֶ֔ם וְהַעֲלִתֶ֥ם אֶת־עַצְמֹתַ֖י מִזֶּֽה׃
כו וַיָּ֣מָת יוֹסֵ֔ף בֶּן־מֵאָ֥ה וָעֶ֖שֶׂר שָׁנִ֑ים וַיַּחַנְט֣וּ אֹת֔וֹ וַיִּ֥ישֶׂם בָּאָר֖וֹן בְּמִצְרָֽיִם׃

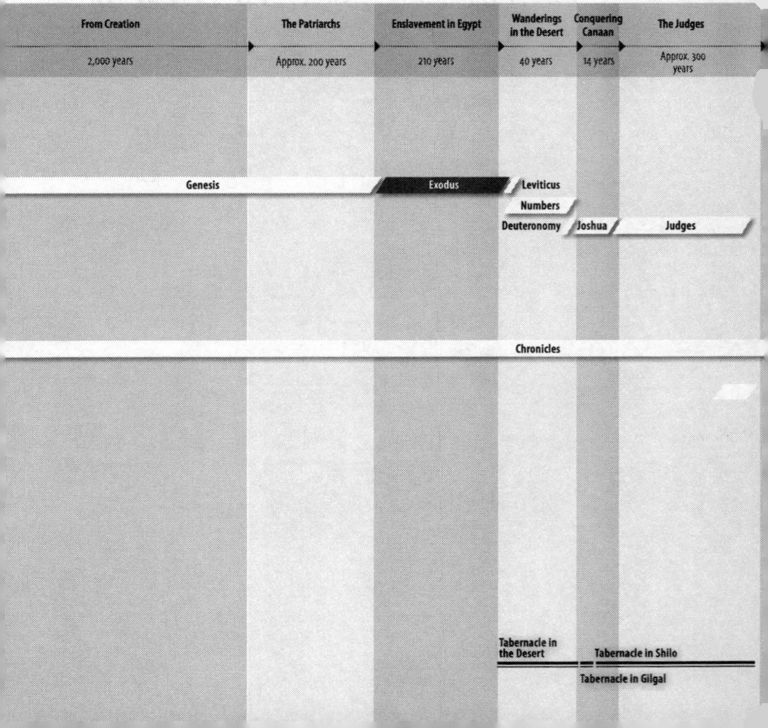

From Creation
2,000 years
The Patriarchs
Approx. 200 years
Enslavement in Egypt
210 years
Wanderings in the Desert
40 years
Conquering Canaan
14 years
The Judges
Approx. 300 years
Genesis
Exodus
Leviticus
Numbers
Deuteronomy
Joshua
Judges
Chronicles
Tabernacle in the Desert
Tabernacle in Shilo
Tabernacle in Gilgal

שמות
SHEMOT / EXODUS

EXODUS	Suffering in Egypt and the arrival of Moshe	The exodus from Egypt	The assembly at Mount Sinai	The Tabernacle
	Chs. 1–2	3–17	18–24	25–40

1 1 And these are the names of the sons of Yisrael who came to Egypt with Yaakov, SHEMOT
2 each with his household: Reuven, Shimon, Levi and Yehuda; Yissakhar,
3 4 5 Zevulun and Binyamin; Dan and Naftali; Gad and Asher. The descendants of
6 Yaakov were seventy in all, and Yosef was already in Egypt. Then Yosef died,
7 and all his brothers, and all that generation. But the Israelites were fruitful
and burgeoned; they multiplied and became exceptionally strong, until the
land was filled with them.

8 9 Then a new king arose over Egypt, who had not known Yosef. And he said
to his people, "You see that the Israelite people are many and more powerful
10 than we. Come, let us deal wisely with them in case they increase, and if war
breaks out they may join our enemies and fight against us and escape from
11 the land." So they placed slave masters over the Israelites to oppress them
with forced labor; they built supply cities for Pharaoh: Pitom and Ramesses.
12 But the more they were oppressed, the more they increased and spread; and
13 the Egyptians came to dread the Israelites. The Egyptians imposed back-
14 breaking labor on the Israelites, embittering their lives with harsh work in
mortar and brick and all field labors; all the work they forced upon them
15 was intended to break them. Then the king of Egypt said to the midwives
16 of the Hebrews – one named Shifra, the other Puah – "When you help a
Hebrew woman give birth, look on the birth stool. If it is a boy, kill him, and
17 if it is a girl, let her live." But the midwives feared God, and did not do as the
18 king of Egypt ordered them. They let the babies live. Then the king of Egypt
summoned the midwives and demanded, "Why have you done this; why
19 have you let the children live?" But "Hebrew women," the midwives replied,
"are not like Egyptians. They are full of vigor, and have already given birth by
20 the time the midwife arrives." God was good to the midwives; and the people
21 multiplied and grew very strong. And because the midwives feared God, He
22 granted them households.[1] Then Pharaoh commanded his entire people,
saying, "Throw every boy that is born into the Nile, and let all the girls live."
2 1 2 A man of the house of Levi went and married a daughter of Levi. And she
became pregnant and gave birth to a son. She saw what a fine child he was, and
3 for three months she kept him hidden. And when she could no longer hide
him, she took a papyrus basket and coated it with tar and pitch. She laid the
4 child in it and placed it among the reeds by the bank of the Nile, and his sister
5 stood by at a distance to see what would happen to him. Pharaoh's daughter
came down to bathe in the Nile, while her attendants walked by the riverbank.
6 She saw the basket among the reeds and sent her maid to fetch it. When she
opened it she saw him there, the child; the boy was crying, and she was moved
7 to pity for him: "This must be one of the Hebrew boys." Then his sister asked
Pharaoh's daughter, "Shall I go and fetch one of the Hebrew women to nurse
8 the child for you?" "Go," said Pharaoh's daughter. So the girl went away and

---

1 | As generally understood, this means that they were blessed with progeny.

א א ב וְאֵלֶּה שְׁמוֹת בְּנֵי יִשְׂרָאֵל הַבָּאִים מִצְרָיְמָה אֵת יַעֲקֹב אִישׁ וּבֵיתוֹ בָּאוּ׃ א
ג ד רְאוּבֵן שִׁמְעוֹן לֵוִי וִיהוּדָה׃ יִשָּׂשכָר זְבוּלֻן וּבִנְיָמִן׃ דָּן וְנַפְתָּלִי גָּד וְאָשֵׁר׃
ה וַיְהִי כָּל־נֶפֶשׁ יֹצְאֵי יֶרֶךְ־יַעֲקֹב שִׁבְעִים נָפֶשׁ וְיוֹסֵף הָיָה בְמִצְרָיִם׃
ו ז וַיָּמָת יוֹסֵף וְכָל־אֶחָיו וְכֹל הַדּוֹר הַהוּא׃ וּבְנֵי יִשְׂרָאֵל פָּרוּ וַיִּשְׁרְצוּ
וַיִּרְבּוּ וַיַּעַצְמוּ בִּמְאֹד מְאֹד וַתִּמָּלֵא הָאָרֶץ אֹתָם׃
ח ט וַיָּקָם מֶלֶךְ־חָדָשׁ עַל־מִצְרָיִם אֲשֶׁר לֹא־יָדַע אֶת־יוֹסֵף׃ וַיֹּאמֶר אֶל־עַמּוֹ
י הִנֵּה עַם בְּנֵי יִשְׂרָאֵל רַב וְעָצוּם מִמֶּנּוּ׃ הָבָה נִתְחַכְּמָה לוֹ פֶּן־יִרְבֶּה
וְהָיָה כִּי־תִקְרֶאנָה מִלְחָמָה וְנוֹסַף גַּם־הוּא עַל־שֹׂנְאֵינוּ וְנִלְחַם־בָּנוּ
יא וְעָלָה מִן־הָאָרֶץ׃ וַיָּשִׂימוּ עָלָיו שָׂרֵי מִסִּים לְמַעַן עַנֹּתוֹ בְּסִבְלֹתָם
יב וַיִּבֶן עָרֵי מִסְכְּנוֹת לְפַרְעֹה אֶת־פִּתֹם וְאֶת־רַעַמְסֵס׃ וְכַאֲשֶׁר יְעַנּוּ אֹתוֹ
יג כֵּן יִרְבֶּה וְכֵן יִפְרֹץ וַיָּקֻצוּ מִפְּנֵי בְּנֵי יִשְׂרָאֵל׃ וַיַּעֲבִדוּ מִצְרַיִם אֶת־בְּנֵי
יד יִשְׂרָאֵל בְּפָרֶךְ׃ וַיְמָרְרוּ אֶת־חַיֵּיהֶם בַּעֲבֹדָה קָשָׁה בְּחֹמֶר וּבִלְבֵנִים
טו וּבְכָל־עֲבֹדָה בַּשָּׂדֶה אֵת כָּל־עֲבֹדָתָם אֲשֶׁר־עָבְדוּ בָהֶם בְּפָרֶךְ׃ וַיֹּאמֶר
מֶלֶךְ מִצְרַיִם לַמְיַלְּדֹת הָעִבְרִיֹּת אֲשֶׁר שֵׁם הָאַחַת שִׁפְרָה וְשֵׁם הַשֵּׁנִית
טז פּוּעָה׃ וַיֹּאמֶר בְּיַלֶּדְכֶן אֶת־הָעִבְרִיּוֹת וּרְאִיתֶן עַל־הָאָבְנָיִם אִם־בֵּן הוּא
יז וַהֲמִתֶּן אֹתוֹ וְאִם־בַּת הִוא וָחָיָה׃ וַתִּירֶאןָ הַמְיַלְּדֹת אֶת־הָאֱלֹהִים וְלֹא
יח עָשׂוּ כַּאֲשֶׁר דִּבֶּר אֲלֵיהֶן מֶלֶךְ מִצְרָיִם וַתְּחַיֶּיןָ אֶת־הַיְלָדִים׃ וַיִּקְרָא שני
מֶלֶךְ־מִצְרַיִם לַמְיַלְּדֹת וַיֹּאמֶר לָהֶן מַדּוּעַ עֲשִׂיתֶן הַדָּבָר הַזֶּה וַתְּחַיֶּיןָ
יט אֶת־הַיְלָדִים׃ וַתֹּאמַרְןָ הַמְיַלְּדֹת אֶל־פַּרְעֹה כִּי לֹא כַנָּשִׁים הַמִּצְרִיֹּת
כ הָעִבְרִיֹּת כִּי־חָיוֹת הֵנָּה בְּטֶרֶם תָּבוֹא אֲלֵהֶן הַמְיַלֶּדֶת וְיָלָדוּ׃ וַיֵּיטֶב
כא אֱלֹהִים לַמְיַלְּדֹת וַיִּרֶב הָעָם וַיַּעַצְמוּ מְאֹד׃ וַיְהִי כִּי־יָרְאוּ הַמְיַלְּדֹת
כב אֶת־הָאֱלֹהִים וַיַּעַשׂ לָהֶם בָּתִּים׃ וַיְצַו פַּרְעֹה לְכָל־עַמּוֹ לֵאמֹר כָּל־הַבֵּן
הַיִּלּוֹד הַיְאֹרָה תַּשְׁלִיכֻהוּ וְכָל־הַבַּת תְּחַיּוּן׃

ב א ב וַיֵּלֶךְ אִישׁ מִבֵּית לֵוִי וַיִּקַּח אֶת־בַּת־לֵוִי׃ וַתַּהַר הָאִשָּׁה וַתֵּלֶד בֵּן וַתֵּרֶא
ג אֹתוֹ כִּי־טוֹב הוּא וַתִּצְפְּנֵהוּ שְׁלֹשָׁה יְרָחִים׃ וְלֹא־יָכְלָה עוֹד הַצְּפִינוֹ
וַתִּקַּח־לוֹ תֵּבַת גֹּמֶא וַתַּחְמְרָה בַחֵמָר וּבַזָּפֶת וַתָּשֶׂם בָּהּ אֶת־הַיֶּלֶד
ד וַתָּשֶׂם בַּסּוּף עַל־שְׂפַת הַיְאֹר׃ וַתֵּתַצַּב אֲחֹתוֹ מֵרָחֹק לְדֵעָה מַה־יֵּעָשֶׂה
ה לוֹ׃ וַתֵּרֶד בַּת־פַּרְעֹה לִרְחֹץ עַל־הַיְאֹר וְנַעֲרֹתֶיהָ הֹלְכֹת עַל־יַד הַיְאֹר
ו וַתֵּרֶא אֶת־הַתֵּבָה בְּתוֹךְ הַסּוּף וַתִּשְׁלַח אֶת־אֲמָתָהּ וַתִּקָּחֶהָ׃ וַתִּפְתַּח
וַתִּרְאֵהוּ אֶת־הַיֶּלֶד וְהִנֵּה־נַעַר בֹּכֶה וַתַּחְמֹל עָלָיו וַתֹּאמֶר מִיַּלְדֵי
ז הָעִבְרִים זֶה׃ וַתֹּאמֶר אֲחֹתוֹ אֶל־בַּת־פַּרְעֹה הַאֵלֵךְ וְקָרָאתִי לָךְ אִשָּׁה
ח מֵינֶקֶת מִן הָעִבְרִיֹּת וְתֵינִק לָךְ אֶת־הַיָּלֶד׃ וַתֹּאמֶר־לָהּ בַּת־פַּרְעֹה לֵכִי

9 called the child's mother. "Take this child," Pharaoh's daughter told her. "Nurse
him for me, and I will pay you your wage." So the woman took the child and
10 nursed him. The child grew, and she brought him to Pharaoh's daughter and he
became her son. She named him Moshe, "because," she said, "I drew him out of
11 the water."[2] One day, when Moshe had grown up, he went out to his people and
saw their forced labor. And he noticed an Egyptian striking a Hebrew: one of
12 his brothers. Looking this way and that and seeing no one, he struck down the
13 Egyptian and hid his body in the sand. The next day he went out and saw two
Hebrews fighting. He asked the guilty one, "Why are you striking your own
14 neighbor?" The man said, "Who made you a ruler and judge over us? Do you
intend to kill me as you killed the Egyptian?" Then Moshe was afraid. "Surely,"
15 he thought, "the thing has become known." Word reached Pharaoh and he
sought to kill Moshe. But Moshe fled his presence and went to live in the land
16 of Midyan. There he sat down beside a well. The priest of Midyan had seven
daughters; they came to draw water and filled the troughs to water their father's
17 flock. Then the shepherds arrived and started to drive the young women away.
18 But Moshe stood up to defend them, and then watered their flock. When the
sisters returned to Reuel their father, he asked them, "How is it that you have
19 come back so quickly today?" They said, "An Egyptian rescued us from the
20 shepherds. He even drew water for us and watered the flock." "Where is he?"
he asked his daughters. "Why did you leave him there? Invite him in to have
21 something to eat." Moshe accepted an invitation to stay with the man, and
22 he gave Moshe his daughter Tzipora in marriage. She gave birth to a son, and
Moshe named him Gershom, saying, "I have been a stranger in an alien land."[3]
23 Years passed, and the king of Egypt died. The Israelites sighed in their
enslavement and cried out, and from their servitude their plea for help rose up
24 to God. And God heard their groaning, and remembered His covenant with
25 Avraham, with Yitzḥak, and with Yaakov. God saw the Israelites, and God
3 1 knew.[4] One day Moshe was tending the flock of his father-in-law
Yitro, priest of Midyan. He led the flock to the far side of the wilderness and
2 came to Ḥorev, the mountain of God. Then an angel of the LORD appeared
to him in flames of fire from the midst of a bush – and he saw – the bush
3 was ablaze with fire but was not consumed. Moshe said, "I must turn aside
4 to see this wonder. Why does the bush not burn up?" The LORD saw that
he had turned aside to look, and God called to him from within the bush:[5]
5 "Moshe, Moshe." He answered, "Here I am." Then God said, "Do not come
close. Remove the shoes from your feet, for the place where you stand is holy
6 ground. I," He said, "am the God of your father, the God of Avraham, the God
of Yitzḥak, and the God of Yaakov." Then Moshe hid his face, for he was afraid

2 | The name Moshe resonates with *meshitihu* (I drew him out).
3 | The name Gershom resonates with *ger sham* (a stranger there).
4 | God noted their suffering and took it to heart.
5 | When describing divine interaction with a human being, the text may variously refer to an "angel," as in verse 2, or to "God," as in the present verse.

ט וַתֵּלֶךְ הָעַלְמָה וַתִּקְרָא אֶת־אֵם הַיָּלֶד: וַתֹּאמֶר לָהּ בַּת־פַּרְעֹה הֵילִיכִי
אֶת־הַיֶּלֶד הַזֶּה וְהֵינִקִהוּ לִי וַאֲנִי אֶתֵּן אֶת־שְׂכָרֵךְ וַתִּקַּח הָאִשָּׁה הַיֶּלֶד
י וַתְּנִיקֵהוּ: וַיִּגְדַּל הַיֶּלֶד וַתְּבִאֵהוּ לְבַת־פַּרְעֹה וַיְהִי־לָהּ לְבֵן וַתִּקְרָא
יא שְׁמוֹ מֹשֶׁה וַתֹּאמֶר כִּי מִן־הַמַּיִם מְשִׁיתִהוּ: וַיְהִי | בַּיָּמִים הָהֵם וַיִּגְדַּל שלישי
מֹשֶׁה וַיֵּצֵא אֶל־אֶחָיו וַיַּרְא בְּסִבְלֹתָם וַיַּרְא אִישׁ מִצְרִי מַכֶּה אִישׁ־
יב עִבְרִי מֵאֶחָיו: וַיִּפֶן כֹּה וָכֹה וַיַּרְא כִּי אֵין אִישׁ וַיַּךְ אֶת־הַמִּצְרִי וַיִּטְמְנֵהוּ
יג בַּחוֹל: וַיֵּצֵא בַּיּוֹם הַשֵּׁנִי וְהִנֵּה שְׁנֵי־אֲנָשִׁים עִבְרִים נִצִּים וַיֹּאמֶר
יד לָרָשָׁע לָמָּה תַכֶּה רֵעֶךָ: וַיֹּאמֶר מִי שָׂמְךָ לְאִישׁ שַׂר וְשֹׁפֵט עָלֵינוּ
הַלְהָרְגֵנִי אַתָּה אֹמֵר כַּאֲשֶׁר הָרַגְתָּ אֶת־הַמִּצְרִי וַיִּירָא מֹשֶׁה וַיֹּאמַר
טו אָכֵן נוֹדַע הַדָּבָר: וַיִּשְׁמַע פַּרְעֹה אֶת־הַדָּבָר הַזֶּה וַיְבַקֵּשׁ לַהֲרֹג אֶת־
מֹשֶׁה וַיִּבְרַח מֹשֶׁה מִפְּנֵי פַרְעֹה וַיֵּשֶׁב בְּאֶרֶץ־מִדְיָן וַיֵּשֶׁב עַל־הַבְּאֵר:
טז וּלְכֹהֵן מִדְיָן שֶׁבַע בָּנוֹת וַתָּבֹאנָה וַתִּדְלֶנָה וַתְּמַלֶּאנָה אֶת־הָרְהָטִים
יז לְהַשְׁקוֹת צֹאן אֲבִיהֶן: וַיָּבֹאוּ הָרֹעִים וַיְגָרְשׁוּם וַיָּקָם מֹשֶׁה וַיּוֹשִׁעָן
יח וַיַּשְׁקְ אֶת־צֹאנָם: וַתָּבֹאנָה אֶל־רְעוּאֵל אֲבִיהֶן וַיֹּאמֶר מַדּוּעַ מִהַרְתֶּן
יט בֹּא הַיּוֹם: וַתֹּאמַרְןָ אִישׁ מִצְרִי הִצִּילָנוּ מִיַּד הָרֹעִים וְגַם־דָּלֹה דָלָה
כ לָנוּ וַיַּשְׁקְ אֶת־הַצֹּאן: וַיֹּאמֶר אֶל־בְּנֹתָיו וְאַיּוֹ לָמָּה זֶּה עֲזַבְתֶּן אֶת־
כא הָאִישׁ קִרְאֶן לוֹ וְיֹאכַל לָחֶם: וַיּוֹאֶל מֹשֶׁה לָשֶׁבֶת אֶת־הָאִישׁ וַיִּתֵּן
כב אֶת־צִפֹּרָה בִתּוֹ לְמֹשֶׁה: וַתֵּלֶד בֵּן וַיִּקְרָא אֶת־שְׁמוֹ גֵּרְשֹׁם כִּי אָמַר
גֵּר הָיִיתִי בְּאֶרֶץ נָכְרִיָּה:
כג וַיְהִי בַיָּמִים הָרַבִּים הָהֵם וַיָּמָת מֶלֶךְ מִצְרַיִם וַיֵּאָנְחוּ בְנֵי־יִשְׂרָאֵל
מִן־הָעֲבֹדָה וַיִּזְעָקוּ וַתַּעַל שַׁוְעָתָם אֶל־הָאֱלֹהִים מִן־הָעֲבֹדָה:
כד וַיִּשְׁמַע אֱלֹהִים אֶת־נַאֲקָתָם וַיִּזְכֹּר אֱלֹהִים אֶת־בְּרִיתוֹ אֶת־אַבְרָהָם
כה אֶת־יִצְחָק וְאֶת־יַעֲקֹב: וַיַּרְא אֱלֹהִים אֶת־בְּנֵי יִשְׂרָאֵל וַיֵּדַע
ג א אֱלֹהִים: וּמֹשֶׁה הָיָה רֹעֶה אֶת־צֹאן יִתְרוֹ חֹתְנוֹ כֹּהֵן ב רביעי
מִדְיָן וַיִּנְהַג אֶת־הַצֹּאן אַחַר הַמִּדְבָּר וַיָּבֹא אֶל־הַר הָאֱלֹהִים חֹרֵבָה:
ב וַיֵּרָא מַלְאַךְ יְהוָה אֵלָיו בְּלַבַּת־אֵשׁ מִתּוֹךְ הַסְּנֶה וַיַּרְא וְהִנֵּה הַסְּנֶה
ג בֹּעֵר בָּאֵשׁ וְהַסְּנֶה אֵינֶנּוּ אֻכָּל: וַיֹּאמֶר מֹשֶׁה אָסֻרָה־נָּא וְאֶרְאֶה
ד אֶת־הַמַּרְאֶה הַגָּדֹל הַזֶּה מַדּוּעַ לֹא־יִבְעַר הַסְּנֶה: וַיַּרְא יְהוָה כִּי סָר
לִרְאוֹת וַיִּקְרָא אֵלָיו אֱלֹהִים מִתּוֹךְ הַסְּנֶה וַיֹּאמֶר מֹשֶׁה מֹשֶׁה וַיֹּאמֶר
ה הִנֵּנִי: וַיֹּאמֶר אַל־תִּקְרַב הֲלֹם שַׁל־נְעָלֶיךָ מֵעַל רַגְלֶיךָ כִּי הַמָּקוֹם
ו אֲשֶׁר אַתָּה עוֹמֵד עָלָיו אַדְמַת־קֹדֶשׁ הוּא: וַיֹּאמֶר אָנֹכִי אֱלֹהֵי אָבִיךָ
אֱלֹהֵי אַבְרָהָם אֱלֹהֵי יִצְחָק וֵאלֹהֵי יַעֲקֹב וַיַּסְתֵּר מֹשֶׁה פָּנָיו כִּי יָרֵא

7 to look at God. The LORD continued, "I have seen My people's suffering in
Egypt; I have heard them cry out amid their oppressors; I know their anguish.
8 So I have come to rescue them from the hand of the Egyptians and bring them
up from that land to one that is good, spacious, a land flowing with milk and
honey, the place of the Canaanites, Hittites, Amorites, Perizzites, Hivites,
9 and Jebusites. Now the cry of the Israelites has reached Me; I have seen the
10 oppression the Egyptians subject them to. So go: I am sending you to Pharaoh
11 to bring My people, the Israelites, out of Egypt." But "who am I," said Moshe
12 to God, "to go to Pharaoh, to bring the Israelites out of Egypt?" God replied,
"I will be with you. Proof that I have sent you will come when, having brought
13 the people out of Egypt, you come to serve God upon this mountain." Moshe
said to God, "When I go to the Israelites and tell them, 'Your fathers' God
has sent me to you,' they will ask me, 'What is His name?' What shall I say?"
14 God replied to Moshe, "I will be what I will be."[6] He said, "This is what you
15 shall tell the Israelites: I will be sent me to you." Then God said to Moshe,
"You shall say this to the Israelites: The LORD[7] God of your fathers, the God
of Avraham, the God of Yitzḥak, and the God of Yaakov, has sent me to you.
This is My name forever, and this is how I will be remembered through the
16 ages. Go, gather the elders of Israel and tell them: The LORD God of your
fathers appeared to me – the God of Avraham, Yitzḥak, and Yaakov – saying:
I have taken note of you and I have seen what is being inflicted upon you in
17 Egypt. And I promise to bring you out of the misery of Egypt to the land
of the Canaanites and Hittites, the Amorites and Perizzites, the Hivites and
18 Jebusites, to a land flowing with milk and honey. They will listen to you. Then
you and the elders of Israel shall go to the king of Egypt and tell him, 'The
LORD God of the Hebrews has revealed Himself to us. Send us forth now for
a three-day journey into the wilderness to sacrifice to the LORD our God.'
19 But I know that even by a mighty hand the king of Egypt would not send you
20 forth. So I will stretch out My hand and strike Egypt with all the wonders I
21 will do there. After that, he will send you forth. And I will grant this people
favor in the eyes of the Egyptians, so that when you leave, you will not leave
22 empty-handed. Every woman shall ask her neighbor, ask any woman lodging
with her, for objects of silver and gold, and clothing, and you shall put these
4 1 on your sons and daughters, and despoil the Egyptians." But Moshe replied,
"They will not believe me. They will not listen to me. They will say, 'The LORD
2 has not appeared to you.'" "What is that in your hand?" asked the LORD. "A
3 staff," he replied. "Throw it to the ground." He threw it, and it turned into a
4 snake; and Moshe fled back from it. The LORD told Moshe, "Reach out your
hand and take hold of its tail." He reached out his hand and grasped it, and

6 | Several other translations are possible, for example, "I am who I am." The name seems to relate to being or eternity.

7 | This is the four-letter name of God (the tetragrammaton), which essentially means "He will be." This name is commonly represented in English by the phrase "the LORD."

ז מֵהַבִּיט אֶל־הָאֱלֹהִים: וַיֹּאמֶר יְהוָה רָאֹה רָאִיתִי אֶת־עֳנִי עַמִּי אֲשֶׁר
בְּמִצְרָיִם וְאֶת־צַעֲקָתָם שָׁמַעְתִּי מִפְּנֵי נֹגְשָׂיו כִּי יָדַעְתִּי אֶת־מַכְאֹבָיו:
ח וָאֵרֵד לְהַצִּילוֹ ׀ מִיַּד מִצְרַיִם וּלְהַעֲלֹתוֹ מִן־הָאָרֶץ הַהִוא אֶל־אֶרֶץ
טוֹבָה וּרְחָבָה אֶל־אֶרֶץ זָבַת חָלָב וּדְבָשׁ אֶל־מְקוֹם הַכְּנַעֲנִי וְהַחִתִּי
ט וְהָאֱמֹרִי וְהַפְּרִזִּי וְהַחִוִּי וְהַיְבוּסִי: וְעַתָּה הִנֵּה צַעֲקַת בְּנֵי־יִשְׂרָאֵל בָּאָה
י אֵלָי וְגַם־רָאִיתִי אֶת־הַלַּחַץ אֲשֶׁר מִצְרַיִם לֹחֲצִים אֹתָם: וְעַתָּה לְכָה
יא וְאֶשְׁלָחֲךָ אֶל־פַּרְעֹה וְהוֹצֵא אֶת־עַמִּי בְנֵי־יִשְׂרָאֵל מִמִּצְרָיִם: וַיֹּאמֶר
מֹשֶׁה אֶל־הָאֱלֹהִים מִי אָנֹכִי כִּי אֵלֵךְ אֶל־פַּרְעֹה וְכִי אוֹצִיא אֶת־בְּנֵי
יב יִשְׂרָאֵל מִמִּצְרָיִם: וַיֹּאמֶר כִּי־אֶהְיֶה עִמָּךְ וְזֶה־לְּךָ הָאוֹת כִּי אָנֹכִי
שְׁלַחְתִּיךָ בְּהוֹצִיאֲךָ אֶת־הָעָם מִמִּצְרַיִם תַּעַבְדוּן אֶת־הָאֱלֹהִים עַל
יג הָהָר הַזֶּה: וַיֹּאמֶר מֹשֶׁה אֶל־הָאֱלֹהִים הִנֵּה אָנֹכִי בָא אֶל־בְּנֵי יִשְׂרָאֵל
וְאָמַרְתִּי לָהֶם אֱלֹהֵי אֲבוֹתֵיכֶם שְׁלָחַנִי אֲלֵיכֶם וְאָמְרוּ־לִי מַה־שְּׁמוֹ
יד מָה אֹמַר אֲלֵהֶם: וַיֹּאמֶר אֱלֹהִים אֶל־מֹשֶׁה אֶהְיֶה אֲשֶׁר אֶהְיֶה וַיֹּאמֶר
טו כֹּה תֹאמַר לִבְנֵי יִשְׂרָאֵל אֶהְיֶה שְׁלָחַנִי אֲלֵיכֶם: וַיֹּאמֶר עוֹד אֱלֹהִים
אֶל־מֹשֶׁה כֹּה תֹאמַר אֶל־בְּנֵי יִשְׂרָאֵל יְהוָה אֱלֹהֵי אֲבֹתֵיכֶם אֱלֹהֵי
אַבְרָהָם אֱלֹהֵי יִצְחָק וֵאלֹהֵי יַעֲקֹב שְׁלָחַנִי אֲלֵיכֶם זֶה־שְּׁמִי לְעֹלָם
טז וְזֶה זִכְרִי לְדֹר דֹּר: לֵךְ וְאָסַפְתָּ אֶת־זִקְנֵי יִשְׂרָאֵל וְאָמַרְתָּ אֲלֵהֶם יְהוָה חמישי
אֱלֹהֵי אֲבֹתֵיכֶם נִרְאָה אֵלַי אֱלֹהֵי אַבְרָהָם יִצְחָק וְיַעֲקֹב לֵאמֹר פָּקֹד
יז פָּקַדְתִּי אֶתְכֶם וְאֶת־הֶעָשׂוּי לָכֶם בְּמִצְרָיִם: וָאֹמַר אַעֲלֶה אֶתְכֶם מֵעֳנִי
מִצְרַיִם אֶל־אֶרֶץ הַכְּנַעֲנִי וְהַחִתִּי וְהָאֱמֹרִי וְהַפְּרִזִּי וְהַחִוִּי וְהַיְבוּסִי
יח אֶל־אֶרֶץ זָבַת חָלָב וּדְבָשׁ: וְשָׁמְעוּ לְקֹלֶךָ וּבָאתָ אַתָּה וְזִקְנֵי יִשְׂרָאֵל
אֶל־מֶלֶךְ מִצְרַיִם וַאֲמַרְתֶּם אֵלָיו יְהוָה אֱלֹהֵי הָעִבְרִיִּים נִקְרָה עָלֵינוּ
וְעַתָּה נֵלְכָה־נָּא דֶּרֶךְ שְׁלֹשֶׁת יָמִים בַּמִּדְבָּר וְנִזְבְּחָה לַיהוָה אֱלֹהֵינוּ:
יט וַאֲנִי יָדַעְתִּי כִּי לֹא־יִתֵּן אֶתְכֶם מֶלֶךְ מִצְרַיִם לַהֲלֹךְ וְלֹא בְּיָד חֲזָקָה:
כ וְשָׁלַחְתִּי אֶת־יָדִי וְהִכֵּיתִי אֶת־מִצְרַיִם בְּכֹל נִפְלְאֹתַי אֲשֶׁר אֶעֱשֶׂה
כא בְּקִרְבּוֹ וְאַחֲרֵי־כֵן יְשַׁלַּח אֶתְכֶם: וְנָתַתִּי אֶת־חֵן הָעָם־הַזֶּה בְּעֵינֵי
כב מִצְרָיִם וְהָיָה כִּי תֵלֵכוּן לֹא תֵלְכוּ רֵיקָם: וְשָׁאֲלָה אִשָּׁה מִשְּׁכֶנְתָּהּ
וּמִגָּרַת בֵּיתָהּ כְּלֵי־כֶסֶף וּכְלֵי זָהָב וּשְׂמָלֹת וְשַׂמְתֶּם עַל־בְּנֵיכֶם וְעַל־
ד א בְּנֹתֵיכֶם וְנִצַּלְתֶּם אֶת־מִצְרָיִם: וַיַּעַן מֹשֶׁה וַיֹּאמֶר וְהֵן לֹא־יַאֲמִינוּ לִי
ב וְלֹא יִשְׁמְעוּ בְּקֹלִי כִּי יֹאמְרוּ לֹא־נִרְאָה אֵלֶיךָ יְהוָה: וַיֹּאמֶר אֵלָיו יְהוָה
ג מַזֶּה בְיָדֶךָ וַיֹּאמֶר מַטֶּה: וַיֹּאמֶר הַשְׁלִיכֵהוּ אַרְצָה וַיַּשְׁלִיכֵהוּ אַרְצָה מַה־זֶּה
ד וַיְהִי לְנָחָשׁ וַיָּנָס מֹשֶׁה מִפָּנָיו: וַיֹּאמֶר יְהוָה אֶל־מֹשֶׁה שְׁלַח יָדְךָ וֶאֱחֹז

5 in his hand it turned back into a staff. "This is so that they will believe that
the LORD God of their fathers, the God of Avraham, Yitzḥak, and Yaakov,
6 appeared to you." The LORD spoke to him again: "Put your hand inside your
cloak." He put his hand inside his cloak; when he took it out it was as white
7 as snow.[8] "Put it back inside your cloak," He said. Moshe put his hand back
8 inside his cloak, and when he took it out the skin color had returned. "If they
do not believe you and are not persuaded by the first sign, they will believe
9 the evidence of the second sign. And if they do not believe either of these
signs, and will not listen to you, then take some water from the Nile and spill
it on the ground. The water you take from the Nile will become blood on the
10 ground." Then Moshe said to the LORD, "Please, my LORD, I am not a man
of words; I was not yesterday, nor the day before, and still I am not since You
11 spoke to Your servant. I am slow of speech and tongue." "Who gives man
speech?" said the LORD to him. "Who makes people dumb or deaf? Who
12 gives them sight or blindness? Is it not I, the LORD? Now go. I will help you
13 speak and I will teach you what to say." But "Please, my LORD," he said, "send
14 someone else." Then the LORD's anger blazed against Moshe. "Have you not
a brother, Aharon the Levite? He, I know, is able to speak. Even now he is
15 setting out to meet you, and when he sees you his heart will rejoice. You shall
speak to him and place words in his mouth. I will help you both to speak, and
16 I will teach you what to do. He will speak on your behalf to the people – he
17 will be your voice; and you will be his access to God.[9] Take this staff in your
hand. With it, you shall perform the signs."
18 Moshe left and returned to Yeter his father-in-law. He said to him, "Let me
go back to my brothers in Egypt, to see if they are still alive." Yitro said to
19 him, "Go in peace." While Moshe was still in Midyan, the LORD said to him,
20 "Go, return to Egypt. All those who sought your life have died." So Moshe
took his wife and sons and put them on a donkey, and he set out to return to
21 Egypt, taking in his hand the staff of God. The LORD said to Moshe, "When
you return to Egypt, see that you perform for Pharaoh all the wonders I have
placed in your power. But still I will strengthen his heart and he will not send
22 the people forth. Tell Pharaoh: This is what the LORD says, 'Israel is My son,
23 My firstborn. I have told you: Send forth My son, so that he may serve Me.
24 If you refuse to let him go, I will kill your son, your firstborn.'" At a lodging
25 place on the way, the LORD confronted Moshe and was about to kill him. But
Tzipora took a flint knife and cut off her son's foreskin, throwing it down at
26 his feet, and said, "You are a bridegroom of blood to me." So He let him go.
Then "A bridegroom of blood," she said, "because of circumcision."[10]

---

8 | The Hebrew denotes a scale disease associated with a white discoloration of the skin.

9 | Literally "you will be to him as God," i.e., you will instruct him what to convey. Cf. 7:1.

10 | Tzipora's statements here, as well as their intended addressee, are cryptic in the Hebrew; interpretations vary.

ה בִּזְנָבוֹ וַיִּשְׁלַח יָדוֹ וַיַּחֲזֶק־בּוֹ וַיְהִי לְמַטֶּה בְּכַפּוֹ: לְמַעַן יַאֲמִינוּ כִּי־נִרְאָה
אֵלֶיךָ יהוה אֱלֹהֵי אֲבֹתָם אֱלֹהֵי אַבְרָהָם אֱלֹהֵי יִצְחָק וֵאלֹהֵי יַעֲקֹב:
ו וַיֹּאמֶר יהוה לוֹ עוֹד הָבֵא־נָא יָדְךָ בְּחֵיקֶךָ וַיָּבֵא יָדוֹ בְּחֵיקוֹ וַיּוֹצִאָהּ
ז וְהִנֵּה יָדוֹ מְצֹרַעַת כַּשָּׁלֶג: וַיֹּאמֶר הָשֵׁב יָדְךָ אֶל־חֵיקֶךָ וַיָּשֶׁב יָדוֹ אֶל־
ח חֵיקוֹ וַיּוֹצִאָהּ מֵחֵיקוֹ וְהִנֵּה־שָׁבָה כִּבְשָׂרוֹ: וְהָיָה אִם־לֹא יַאֲמִינוּ לָךְ
ט וְלֹא יִשְׁמְעוּ לְקֹל הָאֹת הָרִאשׁוֹן וְהֶאֱמִינוּ לְקֹל הָאֹת הָאַחֲרוֹן: וְהָיָה
אִם־לֹא יַאֲמִינוּ גַּם לִשְׁנֵי הָאֹתוֹת הָאֵלֶּה וְלֹא יִשְׁמְעוּן לְקֹלֶךָ וְלָקַחְתָּ
מִמֵּימֵי הַיְאֹר וְשָׁפַכְתָּ הַיַּבָּשָׁה וְהָיוּ הַמַּיִם אֲשֶׁר תִּקַּח מִן־הַיְאֹר וְהָיוּ
י לְדָם בַּיַּבָּשֶׁת: וַיֹּאמֶר מֹשֶׁה אֶל־יהוה בִּי אֲדֹנָי לֹא אִישׁ דְּבָרִים אָנֹכִי
גַּם מִתְּמוֹל גַּם מִשִּׁלְשֹׁם גַּם מֵאָז דַּבֶּרְךָ אֶל־עַבְדֶּךָ כִּי כְבַד־פֶּה וּכְבַד
יא לָשׁוֹן אָנֹכִי: וַיֹּאמֶר יהוה אֵלָיו מִי שָׂם פֶּה לָאָדָם אוֹ מִי־יָשׂוּם אִלֵּם אוֹ
יב חֵרֵשׁ אוֹ פִקֵּחַ אוֹ עִוֵּר הֲלֹא אָנֹכִי יהוה: וְעַתָּה לֵךְ וְאָנֹכִי אֶהְיֶה עִם־פִּיךָ
יג יד וְהוֹרֵיתִיךָ אֲשֶׁר תְּדַבֵּר: וַיֹּאמֶר בִּי אֲדֹנָי שְׁלַח־נָא בְּיַד־תִּשְׁלָח: וַיִּחַר־
אַף יהוה בְּמֹשֶׁה וַיֹּאמֶר הֲלֹא אַהֲרֹן אָחִיךָ הַלֵּוִי יָדַעְתִּי כִּי־דַבֵּר יְדַבֵּר
טו הוּא וְגַם הִנֵּה־הוּא יֹצֵא לִקְרָאתֶךָ וְרָאֲךָ וְשָׂמַח בְּלִבּוֹ: וְדִבַּרְתָּ אֵלָיו
וְשַׂמְתָּ אֶת־הַדְּבָרִים בְּפִיו וְאָנֹכִי אֶהְיֶה עִם־פִּיךָ וְעִם־פִּיהוּ וְהוֹרֵיתִי
טז אֶתְכֶם אֵת אֲשֶׁר תַּעֲשׂוּן: וְדִבֶּר־הוּא לְךָ אֶל־הָעָם וְהָיָה הוּא יִהְיֶה־לְּךָ
יז לְפֶה וְאַתָּה תִּהְיֶה־לּוֹ לֵאלֹהִים: וְאֶת־הַמַּטֶּה הַזֶּה תִּקַּח בְּיָדֶךָ אֲשֶׁר
תַּעֲשֶׂה־בּוֹ אֶת־הָאֹתֹת:
יח וַיֵּלֶךְ מֹשֶׁה וַיָּשָׁב ׀ אֶל־יֶתֶר חֹתְנוֹ וַיֹּאמֶר לוֹ אֵלְכָה־נָּא וְאָשׁוּבָה ג ששי
אֶל־אַחַי אֲשֶׁר־בְּמִצְרַיִם וְאֶרְאֶה הַעוֹדָם חַיִּים וַיֹּאמֶר יִתְרוֹ לְמֹשֶׁה
יט לֵךְ לְשָׁלוֹם: וַיֹּאמֶר יהוה אֶל־מֹשֶׁה בְּמִדְיָן לֵךְ שֻׁב מִצְרָיִם כִּי־מֵתוּ
כ כָּל־הָאֲנָשִׁים הַמְבַקְשִׁים אֶת־נַפְשֶׁךָ: וַיִּקַּח מֹשֶׁה אֶת־אִשְׁתּוֹ וְאֶת־
בָּנָיו וַיַּרְכִּבֵם עַל־הַחֲמֹר וַיָּשָׁב אַרְצָה מִצְרָיִם וַיִּקַּח מֹשֶׁה אֶת־מַטֵּה
כא הָאֱלֹהִים בְּיָדוֹ: וַיֹּאמֶר יהוה אֶל־מֹשֶׁה בְּלֶכְתְּךָ לָשׁוּב מִצְרַיְמָה
רְאֵה כָּל־הַמֹּפְתִים אֲשֶׁר־שַׂמְתִּי בְיָדֶךָ וַעֲשִׂיתָם לִפְנֵי פַרְעֹה וַאֲנִי
כב אֲחַזֵּק אֶת־לִבּוֹ וְלֹא יְשַׁלַּח אֶת־הָעָם: וְאָמַרְתָּ אֶל־פַּרְעֹה כֹּה אָמַר
כג יהוה בְּנִי בְכֹרִי יִשְׂרָאֵל: וָאֹמַר אֵלֶיךָ שַׁלַּח אֶת־בְּנִי וְיַעַבְדֵנִי וַתְּמָאֵן
כד לְשַׁלְּחוֹ הִנֵּה אָנֹכִי הֹרֵג אֶת־בִּנְךָ בְּכֹרֶךָ: וַיְהִי בַדֶּרֶךְ בַּמָּלוֹן וַיִּפְגְּשֵׁהוּ
כה יהוה וַיְבַקֵּשׁ הֲמִיתוֹ: וַתִּקַּח צִפֹּרָה צֹר וַתִּכְרֹת אֶת־עָרְלַת בְּנָהּ וַתַּגַּע
כו לְרַגְלָיו וַתֹּאמֶר כִּי חֲתַן־דָּמִים אַתָּה לִי: וַיִּרֶף מִמֶּנּוּ אָז אָמְרָה חֲתַן
דָּמִים לַמּוּלֹת:

27 The LORD said to Aharon, "Go and meet Moshe in the wilderness." And
28 he went and met him at God's mountain, and kissed him. And Moshe told
Aharon all that the LORD had said about his mission, and all the miraculous
29 signs He had commanded him to perform. So Moshe and Aharon went and
30 gathered all the elders of Israel. Aharon told them everything the LORD had
31 said to Moshe, and he performed the signs before the people. And the people
believed. When they heard that the LORD was watching over the Israelites,
and that He had seen their misery, they bowed their heads and prostrated
5 1 themselves. After this, Moshe and Aharon came to Pharaoh; they said, "Thus
says the LORD, God of Israel: Send My people forth so that they may hold
2 a festival for Me in the wilderness." But Pharaoh said, "Who is this LORD
that I should obey Him and send Israel forth? I do not know the LORD, and
3 I will not send Israel forth." "The God of the Hebrews has revealed Himself
to us," they said. "Let us take a three-day journey into the wilderness and
sacrifice to the LORD our God, or He may strike us with the plague or with
4 the sword." The king of Egypt said to them, "Why, Moshe and Aharon,
5 would you take the people from their work? Get back to your labor! Look,"
said Pharaoh, "how numerous the people of the land have become; and yet
6 you would have them rest from their labors." That day, Pharaoh gave orders
7 to the people's taskmasters and foremen: "Do not give the people straw for
8 bricks as before. Let them go and gather their own straw. But require them
to make the same quota of bricks as before. Do not reduce it. They are lazy.
9 That is why they are crying out, 'Send us forth to sacrifice to our God.' Make
the work harder for the people; and make sure they do it instead of listening
10 to lies." So the taskmasters and foremen went out and told the people, "This
11 is what Pharaoh says: I will no longer give you straw. You must go and get
your own straw wherever you can find it. Your production must not fall short
12 of what it was." So the people spread out all over Egypt to collect stubble for
13 straw. The taskmasters kept pressuring them, saying, "Complete your daily
14 work quota just as when there was straw." And the Israelite foremen whom
Pharaoh's slave drivers had appointed were flogged. "Why have you not
fulfilled your quota of bricks," they were asked, "either yesterday or today
15 as you did before?" The Israelite foremen came and protested to Pharaoh,
16 "Why are you treating your servants like this? Your servants are given no
straw, yet they tell us, 'Make bricks!' We are being flogged for your people's
17 failing." But he said, "Lazy, that is what you are – lazy! That is why you keep
18 saying, 'Send us forth to sacrifice to the LORD.' Now go. Get to work. Straw
19 will not be given you, and you must complete your count of bricks." When
the Israelite foremen saw that they were not to reduce each day's quota, they
20 knew that harm was coming to them. Leaving Pharaoh, they met Moshe and
21 Aharon, who stood awaiting them. They said to them, "May the LORD look

כז וַיֹּאמֶר יהוה אֶל־אַהֲרֹן לֵךְ לִקְרַאת מֹשֶׁה הַמִּדְבָּרָה וַיֵּלֶךְ וַיִּפְגְּשֵׁהוּ
כח בְּהַר הָאֱלֹהִים וַיִּשַּׁק־לוֹ: וַיַּגֵּד מֹשֶׁה לְאַהֲרֹן אֵת כָּל־דִּבְרֵי יהוה אֲשֶׁר
כט שְׁלָחוֹ וְאֵת כָּל־הָאֹתֹת אֲשֶׁר צִוָּהוּ: וַיֵּלֶךְ מֹשֶׁה וְאַהֲרֹן וַיַּאַסְפוּ אֶת־
ל כָּל־זִקְנֵי בְּנֵי יִשְׂרָאֵל: וַיְדַבֵּר אַהֲרֹן אֵת כָּל־הַדְּבָרִים אֲשֶׁר־דִּבֶּר יהוה
לא אֶל־מֹשֶׁה וַיַּעַשׂ הָאֹתֹת לְעֵינֵי הָעָם: וַיַּאֲמֵן הָעָם וַיִּשְׁמְעוּ כִּי־פָקַד
ה א יהוה אֶת־בְּנֵי יִשְׂרָאֵל וְכִי רָאָה אֶת־עָנְיָם וַיִּקְּדוּ וַיִּשְׁתַּחֲווּ: וְאַחַר שביעי
בָּאוּ מֹשֶׁה וְאַהֲרֹן וַיֹּאמְרוּ אֶל־פַּרְעֹה כֹּה־אָמַר יהוה אֱלֹהֵי יִשְׂרָאֵל
ב שַׁלַּח אֶת־עַמִּי וְיָחֹגּוּ לִי בַּמִּדְבָּר: וַיֹּאמֶר פַּרְעֹה מִי יהוה אֲשֶׁר אֶשְׁמַע
בְּקֹלוֹ לְשַׁלַּח אֶת־יִשְׂרָאֵל לֹא יָדַעְתִּי אֶת־יהוה וְגַם אֶת־יִשְׂרָאֵל לֹא
ג אֲשַׁלֵּחַ: וַיֹּאמְרוּ אֱלֹהֵי הָעִבְרִים נִקְרָא עָלֵינוּ נֵלְכָה־נָּא דֶּרֶךְ שְׁלֹשֶׁת
יָמִים בַּמִּדְבָּר וְנִזְבְּחָה לַיהוה אֱלֹהֵינוּ פֶּן־יִפְגָּעֵנוּ בַּדֶּבֶר אוֹ בֶחָרֶב:
ד וַיֹּאמֶר אֲלֵהֶם מֶלֶךְ מִצְרַיִם לָמָּה מֹשֶׁה וְאַהֲרֹן תַּפְרִיעוּ אֶת־הָעָם
ה מִמַּעֲשָׂיו לְכוּ לְסִבְלֹתֵיכֶם: וַיֹּאמֶר פַּרְעֹה הֵן־רַבִּים עַתָּה עַם הָאָרֶץ
ו וְהִשְׁבַּתֶּם אֹתָם מִסִּבְלֹתָם: וַיְצַו פַּרְעֹה בַּיּוֹם הַהוּא אֶת־הַנֹּגְשִׂים בָּעָם
ז וְאֶת־שֹׁטְרָיו לֵאמֹר: לֹא תֹאסִפוּן לָתֵת תֶּבֶן לָעָם לִלְבֹּן הַלְּבֵנִים
ח כִּתְמוֹל שִׁלְשֹׁם הֵם יֵלְכוּ וְקֹשְׁשׁוּ לָהֶם תֶּבֶן: וְאֶת־מַתְכֹּנֶת הַלְּבֵנִים
אֲשֶׁר הֵם עֹשִׂים תְּמוֹל שִׁלְשֹׁם תָּשִׂימוּ עֲלֵיהֶם לֹא תִגְרְעוּ מִמֶּנּוּ כִּי־
ט נִרְפִּים הֵם עַל־כֵּן הֵם צֹעֲקִים לֵאמֹר נֵלְכָה נִזְבְּחָה לֵאלֹהֵינוּ: תִּכְבַּד
י הָעֲבֹדָה עַל־הָאֲנָשִׁים וְיַעֲשׂוּ־בָהּ וְאַל־יִשְׁעוּ בְּדִבְרֵי־שָׁקֶר: וַיֵּצְאוּ
נֹגְשֵׂי הָעָם וְשֹׁטְרָיו וַיֹּאמְרוּ אֶל־הָעָם לֵאמֹר כֹּה אָמַר פַּרְעֹה אֵינֶנִּי
יא נֹתֵן לָכֶם תֶּבֶן: אַתֶּם לְכוּ קְחוּ לָכֶם תֶּבֶן מֵאֲשֶׁר תִּמְצָאוּ כִּי אֵין נִגְרָע
יב מֵעֲבֹדַתְכֶם דָּבָר: וַיָּפֶץ הָעָם בְּכָל־אֶרֶץ מִצְרָיִם לְקֹשֵׁשׁ קַשׁ לַתֶּבֶן:
יג וְהַנֹּגְשִׂים אָצִים לֵאמֹר כַּלּוּ מַעֲשֵׂיכֶם דְּבַר־יוֹם בְּיוֹמוֹ כַּאֲשֶׁר בִּהְיוֹת
יד הַתֶּבֶן: וַיֻּכּוּ שֹׁטְרֵי בְּנֵי יִשְׂרָאֵל אֲשֶׁר־שָׂמוּ עֲלֵהֶם נֹגְשֵׂי פַרְעֹה לֵאמֹר
מַדּוּעַ לֹא כִלִּיתֶם חָקְכֶם לִלְבֹּן כִּתְמוֹל שִׁלְשֹׁם גַּם־תְּמוֹל גַּם־הַיּוֹם:
טו וַיָּבֹאוּ שֹׁטְרֵי בְּנֵי יִשְׂרָאֵל וַיִּצְעֲקוּ אֶל־פַּרְעֹה לֵאמֹר לָמָּה תַעֲשֶׂה
טז כֹה לַעֲבָדֶיךָ: תֶּבֶן אֵין נִתָּן לַעֲבָדֶיךָ וּלְבֵנִים אֹמְרִים לָנוּ עֲשׂוּ וְהִנֵּה
יז עֲבָדֶיךָ מֻכִּים וְחָטָאת עַמֶּךָ: וַיֹּאמֶר נִרְפִּים אַתֶּם נִרְפִּים עַל־כֵּן אַתֶּם
יח אֹמְרִים נֵלְכָה נִזְבְּחָה לַיהוה: וְעַתָּה לְכוּ עִבְדוּ וְתֶבֶן לֹא־יִנָּתֵן לָכֶם
יט וְתֹכֶן לְבֵנִים תִּתֵּנוּ: וַיִּרְאוּ שֹׁטְרֵי בְנֵי־יִשְׂרָאֵל אֹתָם בְּרָע לֵאמֹר לֹא־
כ תִגְרְעוּ מִלִּבְנֵיכֶם דְּבַר־יוֹם בְּיוֹמוֹ: וַיִּפְגְּעוּ אֶת־מֹשֶׁה וְאֶת־אַהֲרֹן נִצָּבִים
כא לִקְרָאתָם בְּצֵאתָם מֵאֵת פַּרְעֹה: וַיֹּאמְרוּ אֲלֵהֶם יֵרֶא יהוה עֲלֵיכֶם

on you and judge, because you have made us repellent in the eyes of Pharaoh
22 and his officials; you have put a sword in their hands to kill us." Then Moshe
returned to the LORD and said, "Why, LORD, have You brought harm to this
23 people? Is this why You sent me? Ever since I came to Pharaoh to speak in
Your name, he has dealt worse with this people; and You have done nothing
6 1 to deliver Your people." But the LORD said to Moshe, "Now you are about
to see what I will do to Pharaoh. By a mighty hand he will send them forth,
2 and by a mighty hand he will drive them from his land." Then God VAERA
3 spoke to Moshe. "I am the LORD," He said to him. "As El Shaddai I appeared to
Avraham, Yitzḥak, and Yaakov – but by My name the LORD[11] I did not make
4 Myself known to them. And I made a covenant with them to give them the
5 land of Canaan, the land where they lived as strangers. And now, I have heard
the groaning of the Israelites whom the Egyptians are holding as slaves, and I
6 remember My covenant. Therefore, say to the Israelites: I am the LORD, and
I will free you from the forced labor of the Egyptians, I will rescue you from
slavery. I will liberate you with an arm stretched forth and with great acts of
7 judgment. I will take you as My people and I will be your God. Then you will
know that I am the LORD your God, freeing you from Egyptian forced labor.
8 And I will bring you to the land that I promised to give to Avraham, Yitzḥak,
9 and Yaakov; to you I will give it as a possession. I am the LORD." Moshe told
this to the Israelites, but in the brokenness of their spirit and the brutal labor
they did not listen to him.
10 11 Then the LORD said to Moshe, "Go, tell Pharaoh, king of Egypt, to send the
12 Israelites forth from his land." But Moshe said to the LORD, "The Israelites,
You see, have not listened to me. How then will Pharaoh listen? And I am a
man of uncircumcised lips."[12]
13 The LORD spoke to Moshe and Aharon; and He charged them with regard to
the Israelites and to Pharaoh, king of Egypt, to bring the Israelites out of the
14 land of Egypt. These were the heads of their ancestral houses. The
sons of Reuven, Yisrael's firstborn, were Ḥanokh, Palu, Ḥetzron, and Karmi;
15 these were the families of Reuven. Shimon's sons were Yemuel, Yamin, Ohad,
Yakhin, Tzoḥar, and Sha'ul, son of a Canaanite woman; these are the families
16 of Shimon. These are the names of Levi's sons by their lineage: Gershon,
17 Kehat, and Merari. Levi lived one hundred thirty-seven years. The sons of
18 Gershon were Livni and Shimi, by their families. The sons of Kehat were
Amram, Yitzhar, Ḥevron, and Uziel. Kehat lived one hundred thirty-three
19 years. The sons of Merari were Maḥli and Mushi. These are the families of
20 the Levites by their lineage. Amram married Yokheved, his father's sister,
who bore him Aharon and Moshe. Amram lived one hundred thirty-seven
21 22 years. The sons of Yitzhar were Koraḥ, Nefeg, and Zikhri. The sons of Uziel

11 | See note on 3:15.
12 | This seems to denote some difficulty in speaking; cf. 4:10.

וְיִשְׁפֹּט אֲשֶׁר הִבְאַשְׁתֶּם אֶת־רֵיחֵנוּ בְּעֵינֵי פַרְעֹה וּבְעֵינֵי עֲבָדָיו לָתֶת־
כב חֶרֶב בְּיָדָם לְהָרְגֵנוּ: וַיָּשָׁב מֹשֶׁה אֶל־יְהוָה וַיֹּאמַר אֲדֹנָי לָמָה הֲרֵעֹתָה מפטיר
כג לָעָם הַזֶּה לָמָּה זֶּה שְׁלַחְתָּנִי: וּמֵאָז בָּאתִי אֶל־פַּרְעֹה לְדַבֵּר בִּשְׁמֶךָ
ו א הֵרַע לָעָם הַזֶּה וְהַצֵּל לֹא־הִצַּלְתָּ אֶת־עַמֶּךָ: וַיֹּאמֶר יְהוָה אֶל־מֹשֶׁה
עַתָּה תִרְאֶה אֲשֶׁר אֶעֱשֶׂה לְפַרְעֹה כִּי בְיָד חֲזָקָה יְשַׁלְּחֵם וּבְיָד חֲזָקָה
ב יְגָרְשֵׁם מֵאַרְצוֹ: וַיְדַבֵּר אֱלֹהִים אֶל־מֹשֶׁה וַיֹּאמֶר אֵלָיו אֲנִי ד וארא
ג יְהוָה: וָאֵרָא אֶל־אַבְרָהָם אֶל־יִצְחָק וְאֶל־יַעֲקֹב בְּאֵל שַׁדָּי וּשְׁמִי יְהוָה
ד לֹא נוֹדַעְתִּי לָהֶם: וְגַם הֲקִמֹתִי אֶת־בְּרִיתִי אִתָּם לָתֵת לָהֶם אֶת־אֶרֶץ
ה כְּנָעַן אֵת אֶרֶץ מְגֻרֵיהֶם אֲשֶׁר־גָּרוּ בָהּ: וְגַם ׀ אֲנִי שָׁמַעְתִּי אֶת־נַאֲקַת
ו בְּנֵי יִשְׂרָאֵל אֲשֶׁר מִצְרַיִם מַעֲבִדִים אֹתָם וָאֶזְכֹּר אֶת־בְּרִיתִי: לָכֵן
אֱמֹר לִבְנֵי־יִשְׂרָאֵל אֲנִי יְהוָה וְהוֹצֵאתִי אֶתְכֶם מִתַּחַת סִבְלֹת מִצְרַיִם
וְהִצַּלְתִּי אֶתְכֶם מֵעֲבֹדָתָם וְגָאַלְתִּי אֶתְכֶם בִּזְרוֹעַ נְטוּיָה וּבִשְׁפָטִים
ז גְּדֹלִים: וְלָקַחְתִּי אֶתְכֶם לִי לְעָם וְהָיִיתִי לָכֶם לֵאלֹהִים וִידַעְתֶּם כִּי אֲנִי
ח יְהוָה אֱלֹהֵיכֶם הַמּוֹצִיא אֶתְכֶם מִתַּחַת סִבְלוֹת מִצְרָיִם: וְהֵבֵאתִי אֶתְכֶם
אֶל־הָאָרֶץ אֲשֶׁר נָשָׂאתִי אֶת־יָדִי לָתֵת אֹתָהּ לְאַבְרָהָם לְיִצְחָק וּלְיַעֲקֹב
ט וְנָתַתִּי אֹתָהּ לָכֶם מוֹרָשָׁה אֲנִי יְהוָה: וַיְדַבֵּר מֹשֶׁה כֵּן אֶל־בְּנֵי יִשְׂרָאֵל
וְלֹא שָׁמְעוּ אֶל־מֹשֶׁה מִקֹּצֶר רוּחַ וּמֵעֲבֹדָה קָשָׁה:
י יא וַיְדַבֵּר יְהוָה אֶל־מֹשֶׁה לֵּאמֹר: בֹּא דַבֵּר אֶל־פַּרְעֹה מֶלֶךְ מִצְרָיִם
יב וִישַׁלַּח אֶת־בְּנֵי־יִשְׂרָאֵל מֵאַרְצוֹ: וַיְדַבֵּר מֹשֶׁה לִפְנֵי יְהוָה לֵאמֹר
הֵן בְּנֵי־יִשְׂרָאֵל לֹא־שָׁמְעוּ אֵלַי וְאֵיךְ יִשְׁמָעֵנִי פַרְעֹה וַאֲנִי עֲרַל
שְׂפָתָיִם:
יג וַיְדַבֵּר יְהוָה אֶל־מֹשֶׁה וְאֶל־אַהֲרֹן וַיְצַוֵּם אֶל־בְּנֵי יִשְׂרָאֵל וְאֶל־פַּרְעֹה
יד מֶלֶךְ מִצְרָיִם לְהוֹצִיא אֶת־בְּנֵי־יִשְׂרָאֵל מֵאֶרֶץ מִצְרָיִם: אֵלֶּה שני
רָאשֵׁי בֵית־אֲבֹתָם בְּנֵי רְאוּבֵן בְּכֹר יִשְׂרָאֵל חֲנוֹךְ וּפַלּוּא חֶצְרֹן וְכַרְמִי
טו אֵלֶּה מִשְׁפְּחֹת רְאוּבֵן: וּבְנֵי שִׁמְעוֹן יְמוּאֵל וְיָמִין וְאֹהַד וְיָכִין וְצֹחַר
טז וְשָׁאוּל בֶּן־הַכְּנַעֲנִית אֵלֶּה מִשְׁפְּחֹת שִׁמְעוֹן: וְאֵלֶּה שְׁמוֹת בְּנֵי־לֵוִי
לְתֹלְדֹתָם גֵּרְשׁוֹן וּקְהָת וּמְרָרִי וּשְׁנֵי חַיֵּי לֵוִי שֶׁבַע וּשְׁלֹשִׁים וּמְאַת
יז יח שָׁנָה: בְּנֵי גֵרְשׁוֹן לִבְנִי וְשִׁמְעִי לְמִשְׁפְּחֹתָם: וּבְנֵי קְהָת עַמְרָם וְיִצְהָר
יט וְחֶבְרוֹן וְעֻזִּיאֵל וּשְׁנֵי חַיֵּי קְהָת שָׁלֹשׁ וּשְׁלֹשִׁים וּמְאַת שָׁנָה: וּבְנֵי מְרָרִי
כ מַחְלִי וּמוּשִׁי אֵלֶּה מִשְׁפְּחֹת הַלֵּוִי לְתֹלְדֹתָם: וַיִּקַּח עַמְרָם אֶת־יוֹכֶבֶד
דֹּדָתוֹ לוֹ לְאִשָּׁה וַתֵּלֶד לוֹ אֶת־אַהֲרֹן וְאֶת־מֹשֶׁה וּשְׁנֵי חַיֵּי עַמְרָם שֶׁבַע
כא כב וּשְׁלֹשִׁים וּמְאַת שָׁנָה: וּבְנֵי יִצְהָר קֹרַח וָנֶפֶג וְזִכְרִי: וּבְנֵי עֻזִּיאֵל מִישָׁאֵל

23 were Mishael, Eltzafan, and Sitri. Aharon married Elisheva, daughter of
Aminadav and sister of Naḥshon, and she bore him Nadav and Avihu, Elazar
24 and Itamar. The sons of Koraḥ were Asir, Elkana, and Aviasaf; these are the
25 families of the Korahites. Elazar, Aharon's son, married one of the daughters
of Putiel, and she bore him Pinḥas. These were the heads of the Levite clans
26 by their families. These were the Aharon and Moshe to whom the LORD said,
27 "Bring the Israelites out of Egypt, by their battalions." It was they who spoke
up to Pharaoh, king of Egypt, to bring the Israelites out of Egypt – this same
28 Moshe and Aharon. So it came to pass on the day the LORD spoke to Moshe
29 in Egypt. The LORD said to Moshe, "I am the LORD. Tell Pharaoh,
30 king of Egypt, all that I am telling you." But Moshe replied to the LORD, "You
know that I have uncircumcised lips.[13] How then will Pharaoh listen to me?"
7 1 Then the LORD said to Moshe, "I am making you now like a god to Pharaoh,
2 and your brother Aharon will be your prophet.[14] All that I command you, you
are to speak, and your brother Aharon to convey to Pharaoh, that he send the
3 Israelites forth from his land. But I will harden Pharaoh's heart and multiply
4 My signs and wonders in the land of Egypt. Still Pharaoh will not listen to you.
Then I will set My hand against Egypt and, with great acts of judgment, bring
5 My battalions, My people the Israelites, forth out of the land of Egypt. When
I stretch out My hand against Egypt and bring the Israelites out from among
6 them, the Egyptians will know that I am the LORD." Moshe and Aharon did
7 so; they did exactly as the LORD commanded them. Moshe was eighty years
old, and Aharon eighty-three, when they spoke to Pharaoh.
8 9 Then the LORD said to Moshe, and to Aharon, "When Pharaoh says to you,
'Perform a miracle,' tell Aharon: Take your staff and throw it down before
10 Pharaoh and it will become a crocodile." So Moshe and Aharon went to
Pharaoh and did just as the LORD had commanded. Aharon threw down his
11 staff before Pharaoh and his officials, and it became a snake. Pharaoh then
summoned his sages and sorcerers, and the Egyptian magicians did the same
12 thing by their sorcery. Each threw down his staff, and they became snakes – but
13 Aharon's staff swallowed up theirs. Pharaoh, nonetheless, was obstinate, and
14 he would not listen to them, just as the LORD had predicted. Then
the LORD said to Moshe, "Pharaoh's heart is unyielding. He refuses to send
15 the people forth. So go to Pharaoh in the morning as he goes out to the water.
Place yourself by the bank of the Nile where you will encounter him, taking
16 in your hand the staff that turned into a snake. Say to him: The LORD, God
of the Hebrews, has sent me to tell you: Send My people forth, so that they
17 may serve Me in the wilderness. So far, you have not listened. This is what the

13 | See note on verse 22.
14 | See note on 4:16.

כג וְאֶלְצָפָן וְסִתְרִי׃ וַיִּקַּח אַהֲרֹן אֶת־אֱלִישֶׁבַע בַּת־עַמִּינָדָב אֲחוֹת נַחְשׁוֹן
לוֹ לְאִשָּׁה וַתֵּלֶד לוֹ אֶת־נָדָב וְאֶת־אֲבִיהוּא אֶת־אֶלְעָזָר וְאֶת־אִיתָמָר׃
כד כה וּבְנֵי קֹרַח אַסִּיר וְאֶלְקָנָה וַאֲבִיאָסָף אֵלֶּה מִשְׁפְּחֹת הַקָּרְחִי׃ וְאֶלְעָזָר
בֶּן־אַהֲרֹן לָקַח־לוֹ מִבְּנוֹת פּוּטִיאֵל לוֹ לְאִשָּׁה וַתֵּלֶד לוֹ אֶת־פִּינְחָס
כו אֵלֶּה רָאשֵׁי אֲבוֹת הַלְוִיִּם לְמִשְׁפְּחֹתָם׃ הוּא אַהֲרֹן וּמֹשֶׁה אֲשֶׁר אָמַר
יהוה לָהֶם הוֹצִיאוּ אֶת־בְּנֵי יִשְׂרָאֵל מֵאֶרֶץ מִצְרַיִם עַל־צִבְאֹתָם׃
כז הֵם הַמְדַבְּרִים אֶל־פַּרְעֹה מֶלֶךְ־מִצְרַיִם לְהוֹצִיא אֶת־בְּנֵי־יִשְׂרָאֵל
כח מִמִּצְרָיִם הוּא מֹשֶׁה וְאַהֲרֹן׃ וַיְהִי בְּיוֹם דִּבֶּר יהוה אֶל־מֹשֶׁה בְּאֶרֶץ
כט מִצְרָיִם׃ וַיְדַבֵּר יהוה אֶל־מֹשֶׁה לֵּאמֹר אֲנִי יהוה דַּבֵּר אֶל־ שלישי
ל פַּרְעֹה מֶלֶךְ מִצְרַיִם אֵת כָּל־אֲשֶׁר אֲנִי דֹּבֵר אֵלֶיךָ׃ וַיֹּאמֶר מֹשֶׁה לִפְנֵי
יהוה הֵן אֲנִי עֲרַל שְׂפָתַיִם וְאֵיךְ יִשְׁמַע אֵלַי פַּרְעֹה׃
ז א וַיֹּאמֶר יהוה אֶל־מֹשֶׁה רְאֵה נְתַתִּיךָ אֱלֹהִים לְפַרְעֹה וְאַהֲרֹן אָחִיךָ
ב יִהְיֶה נְבִיאֶךָ׃ אַתָּה תְדַבֵּר אֵת כָּל־אֲשֶׁר אֲצַוֶּךָּ וְאַהֲרֹן אָחִיךָ יְדַבֵּר
ג אֶל־פַּרְעֹה וְשִׁלַּח אֶת־בְּנֵי־יִשְׂרָאֵל מֵאַרְצוֹ׃ וַאֲנִי אַקְשֶׁה אֶת־לֵב
ד פַּרְעֹה וְהִרְבֵּיתִי אֶת־אֹתֹתַי וְאֶת־מוֹפְתַי בְּאֶרֶץ מִצְרָיִם׃ וְלֹא־יִשְׁמַע
אֲלֵכֶם פַּרְעֹה וְנָתַתִּי אֶת־יָדִי בְּמִצְרָיִם וְהוֹצֵאתִי אֶת־צִבְאֹתַי אֶת־עַמִּי
ה בְנֵי־יִשְׂרָאֵל מֵאֶרֶץ מִצְרַיִם בִּשְׁפָטִים גְּדֹלִים׃ וְיָדְעוּ מִצְרַיִם כִּי־אֲנִי
יהוה בִּנְטֹתִי אֶת־יָדִי עַל־מִצְרָיִם וְהוֹצֵאתִי אֶת־בְּנֵי־יִשְׂרָאֵל מִתּוֹכָם׃
ו ז וַיַּעַשׂ מֹשֶׁה וְאַהֲרֹן כַּאֲשֶׁר צִוָּה יהוה אֹתָם כֵּן עָשׂוּ׃ וּמֹשֶׁה בֶּן־שְׁמֹנִים
שָׁנָה וְאַהֲרֹן בֶּן־שָׁלֹשׁ וּשְׁמֹנִים שָׁנָה בְּדַבְּרָם אֶל־פַּרְעֹה׃
ח ט וַיֹּאמֶר יהוה אֶל־מֹשֶׁה וְאֶל־אַהֲרֹן לֵאמֹר׃ כִּי יְדַבֵּר אֲלֵכֶם פַּרְעֹה ה רביעי
לֵאמֹר תְּנוּ לָכֶם מוֹפֵת וְאָמַרְתָּ אֶל־אַהֲרֹן קַח אֶת־מַטְּךָ וְהַשְׁלֵךְ
י לִפְנֵי־פַרְעֹה יְהִי לְתַנִּין׃ וַיָּבֹא מֹשֶׁה וְאַהֲרֹן אֶל־פַּרְעֹה וַיַּעֲשׂוּ־כֵן
כַּאֲשֶׁר צִוָּה יהוה וַיַּשְׁלֵךְ אַהֲרֹן אֶת־מַטֵּהוּ לִפְנֵי פַרְעֹה וְלִפְנֵי עֲבָדָיו
יא וַיְהִי לְתַנִּין׃ וַיִּקְרָא גַּם־פַּרְעֹה לַחֲכָמִים וְלַמְכַשְּׁפִים וַיַּעֲשׂוּ גַם־הֵם
יב חַרְטֻמֵּי מִצְרַיִם בְּלַהֲטֵיהֶם כֵּן׃ וַיַּשְׁלִיכוּ אִישׁ מַטֵּהוּ וַיִּהְיוּ לְתַנִּינִם
יג וַיִּבְלַע מַטֵּה־אַהֲרֹן אֶת־מַטֹּתָם׃ וַיֶּחֱזַק לֵב פַּרְעֹה וְלֹא שָׁמַע אֲלֵהֶם
יד כַּאֲשֶׁר דִּבֶּר יהוה׃ וַיֹּאמֶר יהוה אֶל־מֹשֶׁה כָּבֵד לֵב פַּרְעֹה
טו מֵאֵן לְשַׁלַּח הָעָם׃ לֵךְ אֶל־פַּרְעֹה בַּבֹּקֶר הִנֵּה יֹצֵא הַמַּיְמָה וְנִצַּבְתָּ
לִקְרָאתוֹ עַל־שְׂפַת הַיְאֹר וְהַמַּטֶּה אֲשֶׁר־נֶהְפַּךְ לְנָחָשׁ תִּקַּח בְּיָדֶךָ׃
טז וְאָמַרְתָּ אֵלָיו יהוה אֱלֹהֵי הָעִבְרִים שְׁלָחַנִי אֵלֶיךָ לֵאמֹר שַׁלַּח אֶת־
יז עַמִּי וְיַעַבְדֻנִי בַּמִּדְבָּר וְהִנֵּה לֹא־שָׁמַעְתָּ עַד־כֹּה׃ כֹּה אָמַר יהוה בְּזֹאת

Lord says: This will make it known to you that I am the Lord. With the staff
18 in my hand I will strike the water in the Nile and it will become blood. The
fish in the Nile will die; the Nile will stink and the Egyptians will be unable to
19 drink its water." Then the Lord said to Moshe, "Tell Aharon: Take
your staff and stretch out your hand over the waters of Egypt, their rivers,
canals, ponds, and reservoirs, and they will turn into blood. There will be
20 blood throughout Egypt, even inside vessels of wood and of stone." Moshe
and Aharon did just as the Lord commanded. Aharon raised his staff, in full
view of Pharaoh and his officials, and struck the water of the Nile, and all the
21 Nile's water turned into blood. The Nile fish died, and the river stank so that
the Egyptians could not drink its water. Throughout the land of Egypt, blood
22 appeared. But the Egyptian magicians did the same thing by their sorcery.
So Pharaoh's heart remained adamant, and he would not listen to them, just
23 as the Lord had predicted. Pharaoh turned and went back into his palace
24 and did not take even this to heart. The Egyptians all dug along the Nile to
25 get drinking water, unable to drink of the waters of the Nile. And seven days
went by after the Lord's striking of the Nile.
26 Then the Lord said to Moshe, "Go to Pharaoh and say to him: This is what
27 the Lord says: Send My people forth, so that they may serve Me. And if you
should refuse to send them forth – I will scourge your land with frogs from
28 end to end. The Nile will teem with frogs. They will come up into your palace,
into your bedroom and up onto your bed, into the houses of your officials and
29 of all your people, into your ovens and your kneading pans. The frogs shall
8 1 climb up onto you and your people and all your officials." The Lord said to
Moshe, "Speak to Aharon: Stretch out your hand that holds your staff over the
rivers, the canals, and the pools, and cause frogs to climb up and out onto the
2 land of Egypt." So Aharon stretched out his hand over the waters of Egypt,
3 and frogs climbed up and covered the Egyptian land. But the magicians used
their sorcery and did the same, making frogs climb up over the land of Egypt.
4 Then Pharaoh called for Moshe and Aharon and said, "Pray to the Lord to
take the frogs away from me and from my people, and I will send your people
5 forth to sacrifice to the Lord." Moshe said to Pharaoh, "Gloat over me:[15] you
name the time when I should pray that the frogs be removed, for you and your
officials, and your people, from you and your homes, remaining only in the
6 Nile." "Tomorrow," he replied. Moshe said, "It will be as you say. Then you
7 will know that there is none like the Lord our God. The frogs will depart
from you and from your homes, your officials, all your people. They will only
8 remain in the Nile." Moshe and Aharon departed Pharaoh's presence, and
Moshe cried out to the Lord about the frogs He had brought upon Pharaoh.
9 The Lord did as Moshe said, and the frogs in the houses, courtyards, and
10 fields died; they gathered them up into heaping piles, and the stench filled

---

15 | Interpretations of the phrase vary. According to this rendering, Moshe challenges Pharaoh to set a time when God would be unable to stop the plague. Should the plague persist then, Pharaoh would be able to "gloat."

תֵּדַע כִּי אֲנִי יהוה הִנֵּה אָנֹכִי מַכֶּה ׀ בַּמַּטֶּה אֲשֶׁר־בְּיָדִי עַל־הַמַּיִם אֲשֶׁר
יח בַּיְאֹר וְנֶהֶפְכוּ לְדָם׃ וְהַדָּגָה אֲשֶׁר־בַּיְאֹר תָּמוּת וּבָאַשׁ הַיְאֹר וְנִלְאוּ
יט מִצְרַיִם לִשְׁתּוֹת מַיִם מִן־הַיְאֹר׃ וַיֹּאמֶר יהוה אֶל־מֹשֶׁה
אֱמֹר אֶל־אַהֲרֹן קַח מַטְּךָ וּנְטֵה־יָדְךָ עַל־מֵימֵי מִצְרַיִם עַל־נַהֲרֹתָם ׀
עַל־יְאֹרֵיהֶם וְעַל־אַגְמֵיהֶם וְעַל כָּל־מִקְוֵה מֵימֵיהֶם וְיִהְיוּ־דָם וְהָיָה
כ דָם בְּכָל־אֶרֶץ מִצְרַיִם וּבָעֵצִים וּבָאֲבָנִים׃ וַיַּעֲשׂוּ־כֵן מֹשֶׁה וְאַהֲרֹן
כַּאֲשֶׁר ׀ צִוָּה יהוה וַיָּרֶם בַּמַּטֶּה וַיַּךְ אֶת־הַמַּיִם אֲשֶׁר בַּיְאֹר לְעֵינֵי פַרְעֹה
כא וּלְעֵינֵי עֲבָדָיו וַיֵּהָפְכוּ כָּל־הַמַּיִם אֲשֶׁר־בַּיְאֹר לְדָם׃ וְהַדָּגָה אֲשֶׁר־בַּיְאֹר
מֵתָה וַיִּבְאַשׁ הַיְאֹר וְלֹא־יָכְלוּ מִצְרַיִם לִשְׁתּוֹת מַיִם מִן־הַיְאֹר וַיְהִי
כב הַדָּם בְּכָל־אֶרֶץ מִצְרָיִם׃ וַיַּעֲשׂוּ־כֵן חַרְטֻמֵּי מִצְרַיִם בְּלָטֵיהֶם וַיֶּחֱזַק
כג לֵב־פַּרְעֹה וְלֹא־שָׁמַע אֲלֵהֶם כַּאֲשֶׁר דִּבֶּר יהוה׃ וַיִּפֶן פַּרְעֹה וַיָּבֹא
כד אֶל־בֵּיתוֹ וְלֹא־שָׁת לִבּוֹ גַּם־לָזֹאת׃ וַיַּחְפְּרוּ כָל־מִצְרַיִם סְבִיבֹת הַיְאֹר
כה מַיִם לִשְׁתּוֹת כִּי לֹא יָכְלוּ לִשְׁתֹּת מִמֵּימֵי הַיְאֹר׃ וַיִּמָּלֵא שִׁבְעַת יָמִים
אַחֲרֵי הַכּוֹת־יהוה אֶת־הַיְאֹר׃
כו וַיֹּאמֶר יהוה אֶל־מֹשֶׁה בֹּא אֶל־פַּרְעֹה וְאָמַרְתָּ אֵלָיו כֹּה אָמַר יהוה
כז שַׁלַּח אֶת־עַמִּי וְיַעַבְדֻנִי׃ וְאִם־מָאֵן אַתָּה לְשַׁלֵּחַ הִנֵּה אָנֹכִי נֹגֵף אֶת־
כח כָּל־גְּבוּלְךָ בַּצְפַרְדְּעִים׃ וְשָׁרַץ הַיְאֹר צְפַרְדְּעִים וְעָלוּ וּבָאוּ בְּבֵיתֶךָ
וּבַחֲדַר מִשְׁכָּבְךָ וְעַל־מִטָּתֶךָ וּבְבֵית עֲבָדֶיךָ וּבְעַמֶּךָ וּבְתַנּוּרֶיךָ
ח כט א וּבְמִשְׁאֲרוֹתֶיךָ׃ וּבְכָה וּבְעַמְּךָ וּבְכָל־עֲבָדֶיךָ יַעֲלוּ הַצְפַרְדְּעִים׃ וַיֹּאמֶר
יהוה אֶל־מֹשֶׁה אֱמֹר אֶל־אַהֲרֹן נְטֵה אֶת־יָדְךָ בְּמַטֶּךָ עַל־הַנְּהָרֹת
עַל־הַיְאֹרִים וְעַל־הָאֲגַמִּים וְהַעַל אֶת־הַצְפַרְדְּעִים עַל־אֶרֶץ מִצְרָיִם׃
ב וַיֵּט אַהֲרֹן אֶת־יָדוֹ עַל מֵימֵי מִצְרָיִם וַתַּעַל הַצְּפַרְדֵּעַ וַתְּכַס אֶת־אֶרֶץ
ג מִצְרָיִם׃ וַיַּעֲשׂוּ־כֵן הַחַרְטֻמִּים בְּלָטֵיהֶם וַיַּעֲלוּ אֶת־הַצְפַרְדְּעִים עַל־
ד אֶרֶץ מִצְרָיִם׃ וַיִּקְרָא פַרְעֹה לְמֹשֶׁה וּלְאַהֲרֹן וַיֹּאמֶר הַעְתִּירוּ אֶל־יהוה
וְיָסֵר הַצְפַרְדְּעִים מִמֶּנִּי וּמֵעַמִּי וַאֲשַׁלְּחָה אֶת־הָעָם וְיִזְבְּחוּ לַיהוה׃
ה וַיֹּאמֶר מֹשֶׁה לְפַרְעֹה הִתְפָּאֵר עָלַי לְמָתַי ׀ אַעְתִּיר לְךָ וְלַעֲבָדֶיךָ
וּלְעַמְּךָ לְהַכְרִית הַצְפַרְדְּעִים מִמְּךָ וּמִבָּתֶּיךָ רַק בַּיְאֹר תִּשָּׁאַרְנָה׃
ו וַיֹּאמֶר לְמָחָר וַיֹּאמֶר כִּדְבָרְךָ לְמַעַן תֵּדַע כִּי־אֵין כַּיהוה אֱלֹהֵינוּ׃
ז וְסָרוּ הַצְפַרְדְּעִים מִמְּךָ וּמִבָּתֶּיךָ וּמֵעֲבָדֶיךָ וּמֵעַמֶּךָ רַק בַּיְאֹר תִּשָּׁאַרְנָה׃ חמישי
ח וַיֵּצֵא מֹשֶׁה וְאַהֲרֹן מֵעִם פַּרְעֹה וַיִּצְעַק מֹשֶׁה אֶל־יהוה עַל־דְּבַר
ט הַצְפַרְדְּעִים אֲשֶׁר־שָׂם לְפַרְעֹה׃ וַיַּעַשׂ יהוה כִּדְבַר מֹשֶׁה וַיָּמֻתוּ
י הַצְפַרְדְּעִים מִן־הַבָּתִּים מִן־הַחֲצֵרֹת וּמִן־הַשָּׂדֹת׃ וַיִּצְבְּרוּ אֹתָם חֳמָרִם

11 the whole land. But when Pharaoh saw that respite had come, he hardened
12 his heart and would not listen, just as the Lord had predicted. Then
the Lord said to Moshe, "Tell Aharon: Extend your staff and strike the dust of
13 the earth; all over Egypt it will be transformed into lice." They did so. Aharon
extended the hand that held his staff and struck the dust of the earth, and
suddenly there were lice on the people, on the animals. The dust of the earth
14 was turned to lice all across Egypt. The magicians tried to produce lice with
their sorcery, but they could not. Meanwhile the lice still infested people and
15 animals alike. "This," the magicians told Pharaoh, "is the finger of God." But
Pharaoh's heart was toughened, and – as the Lord had predicted – he would
16 not listen to them. Then the Lord said to Moshe, "Rise up early in
the morning and confront Pharaoh as he goes out to the water; tell him: This
17 is what the Lord says: Send My people forth, so that they may serve Me. If
you refuse to send them forth, I will send swarms of insects[16] onto you, your
officials, your people, and your houses. The Egyptians' houses will be filled
with swarms of insects; the ground they stand upon will be covered by them.
18 On that day, I will set the land of Goshen, where My people live, apart – there,
there will be no swarms – and then you will know that I am the Lord, here on
19 earth. Between My people and yours I will mark out a separation; tomorrow,
20 this sign will come to be." The Lord did so. Great swarms of insects infested
Pharaoh's palace and the houses of his officials. All across Egypt, swarms of
21 insects devastated the land. Pharaoh called for Moshe and Aharon. "Go,"
22 he said, "and sacrifice to your God here in the land." But Moshe replied,
"That would not be right for us to do; our sacrifice to the Lord our God
is an abomination to the Egyptians. If, before the Egyptians' eyes, we offer
the sacrifice they consider an abomination, will they not stone us to death?[17]
23 Send us forth, three days' journey into the wilderness, to sacrifice there to the
24 Lord our God, as He will instruct us." Pharaoh said, "I will send you forth;
you shall sacrifice to the Lord your God in the wilderness. Just do not go far
25 away. Pray for me." Moshe said, "I am going to leave you and pray to the Lord.
Tomorrow, the swarms of insects will move on from Pharaoh, his officials, and
his people. But let Pharaoh no more deceive us, refusing to send the people
26 forth to make their sacrifice to the Lord." Moshe left Pharaoh and prayed to
27 the Lord. And the Lord did what Moshe asked. He diverted the swarms of
28 insects from Pharaoh, his officials, his people – not one was left behind. But
this time too, Pharaoh hardened his heart and did not send the people forth.
9 1 Then the Lord said to Moshe, "Go to Pharaoh. Tell him: This is what the
2 Lord, God of the Hebrews, says: Send My people forth to serve Me. If you
3 refuse to send them forth, if you continue to hold them back, the Lord's
hand will turn against your livestock in the field. A deadly epidemic will strike
4 horses, donkeys, and camels, cattle and flocks. But the Lord will set Israel's

16 | Alternatively "wild animals."

17 | The sense seems to be that sheep, goats, and cattle were sacred to the Egyptians, and it would have offended them to witness the Israelites slaughtering them for their own rites.

יא חֳמָרִם וַתִּבְאַשׁ הָאָרֶץ: וַיַּרְא פַּרְעֹה כִּי הָיְתָה הָרְוָחָה וְהַכְבֵּד אֶת־
יב לִבּוֹ וְלֹא שָׁמַע אֲלֵהֶם כַּאֲשֶׁר דִּבֶּר יהוה: וַיֹּאמֶר יהוה
אֶל־מֹשֶׁה אֱמֹר אֶל־אַהֲרֹן נְטֵה אֶת־מַטְּךָ וְהַךְ אֶת־עֲפַר הָאָרֶץ וְהָיָה
יג לְכִנִּם בְּכָל־אֶרֶץ מִצְרָיִם: וַיַּעֲשׂוּ־כֵן וַיֵּט אַהֲרֹן אֶת־יָדוֹ בְמַטֵּהוּ וַיַּךְ
אֶת־עֲפַר הָאָרֶץ וַתְּהִי הַכִּנָּם בָּאָדָם וּבַבְּהֵמָה כָּל־עֲפַר הָאָרֶץ הָיָה
יד כִנִּים בְּכָל־אֶרֶץ מִצְרָיִם: וַיַּעֲשׂוּ־כֵן הַחַרְטֻמִּים בְּלָטֵיהֶם לְהוֹצִיא
טו אֶת־הַכִּנִּים וְלֹא יָכֹלוּ וַתְּהִי הַכִּנָּם בָּאָדָם וּבַבְּהֵמָה: וַיֹּאמְרוּ הַחַרְטֻמִּם
אֶל־פַּרְעֹה אֶצְבַּע אֱלֹהִים הִוא וַיֶּחֱזַק לֵב־פַּרְעֹה וְלֹא־שָׁמַע אֲלֵהֶם
טז כַּאֲשֶׁר דִּבֶּר יהוה: וַיֹּאמֶר יהוה אֶל־מֹשֶׁה הַשְׁכֵּם בַּבֹּקֶר ו
וְהִתְיַצֵּב לִפְנֵי פַרְעֹה הִנֵּה יוֹצֵא הַמָּיְמָה וְאָמַרְתָּ אֵלָיו כֹּה אָמַר יהוה
יז שַׁלַּח עַמִּי וְיַעַבְדֻנִי: כִּי אִם־אֵינְךָ מְשַׁלֵּחַ אֶת־עַמִּי הִנְנִי מַשְׁלִיחַ בְּךָ
וּבַעֲבָדֶיךָ וּבְעַמְּךָ וּבְבָתֶּיךָ אֶת־הֶעָרֹב וּמָלְאוּ בָּתֵּי מִצְרַיִם אֶת־הֶעָרֹב
יח וְגַם הָאֲדָמָה אֲשֶׁר־הֵם עָלֶיהָ: וְהִפְלֵיתִי בַיּוֹם הַהוּא אֶת־אֶרֶץ גֹּשֶׁן
אֲשֶׁר עַמִּי עֹמֵד עָלֶיהָ לְבִלְתִּי הֱיוֹת־שָׁם עָרֹב לְמַעַן תֵּדַע כִּי אֲנִי
יט יהוה בְּקֶרֶב הָאָרֶץ: וְשַׂמְתִּי פְדֻת בֵּין עַמִּי וּבֵין עַמֶּךָ לְמָחָר יִהְיֶה ששי
כ הָאֹת הַזֶּה: וַיַּעַשׂ יהוה כֵּן וַיָּבֹא עָרֹב כָּבֵד בֵּיתָה פַרְעֹה וּבֵית עֲבָדָיו
כא וּבְכָל־אֶרֶץ מִצְרַיִם תִּשָּׁחֵת הָאָרֶץ מִפְּנֵי הֶעָרֹב: וַיִּקְרָא פַרְעֹה אֶל־
כב מֹשֶׁה וּלְאַהֲרֹן וַיֹּאמֶר לְכוּ זִבְחוּ לֵאלֹהֵיכֶם בָּאָרֶץ: וַיֹּאמֶר מֹשֶׁה לֹא
נָכוֹן לַעֲשׂוֹת כֵּן כִּי תּוֹעֲבַת מִצְרַיִם נִזְבַּח לַיהוה אֱלֹהֵינוּ הֵן נִזְבַּח
כג אֶת־תּוֹעֲבַת מִצְרַיִם לְעֵינֵיהֶם וְלֹא יִסְקְלֻנוּ: דֶּרֶךְ שְׁלֹשֶׁת יָמִים נֵלֵךְ
כד בַּמִּדְבָּר וְזָבַחְנוּ לַיהוה אֱלֹהֵינוּ כַּאֲשֶׁר יֹאמַר אֵלֵינוּ: וַיֹּאמֶר פַּרְעֹה
אָנֹכִי אֲשַׁלַּח אֶתְכֶם וּזְבַחְתֶּם לַיהוה אֱלֹהֵיכֶם בַּמִּדְבָּר רַק הַרְחֵק
כה לֹא־תַרְחִיקוּ לָלֶכֶת הַעְתִּירוּ בַּעֲדִי: וַיֹּאמֶר מֹשֶׁה הִנֵּה אָנֹכִי יוֹצֵא
מֵעִמָּךְ וְהַעְתַּרְתִּי אֶל־יהוה וְסָר הֶעָרֹב מִפַּרְעֹה מֵעֲבָדָיו וּמֵעַמּוֹ מָחָר
כו רַק אַל־יֹסֵף פַּרְעֹה הָתֵל לְבִלְתִּי שַׁלַּח אֶת־הָעָם לִזְבֹּחַ לַיהוה: וַיֵּצֵא
כז מֹשֶׁה מֵעִם פַּרְעֹה וַיֶּעְתַּר אֶל־יהוה: וַיַּעַשׂ יהוה כִּדְבַר מֹשֶׁה וַיָּסַר
כח הֶעָרֹב מִפַּרְעֹה מֵעֲבָדָיו וּמֵעַמּוֹ לֹא נִשְׁאַר אֶחָד: וַיַּכְבֵּד פַּרְעֹה אֶת־
לִבּוֹ גַּם בַּפַּעַם הַזֹּאת וְלֹא שִׁלַּח אֶת־הָעָם:
ט א וַיֹּאמֶר יהוה אֶל־מֹשֶׁה בֹּא אֶל־פַּרְעֹה וְדִבַּרְתָּ אֵלָיו כֹּה־אָמַר יהוה
ב אֱלֹהֵי הָעִבְרִים שַׁלַּח אֶת־עַמִּי וְיַעַבְדֻנִי: כִּי אִם־מָאֵן אַתָּה לְשַׁלֵּחַ
ג וְעוֹדְךָ מַחֲזִיק בָּם: הִנֵּה יַד־יהוה הוֹיָה בְּמִקְנְךָ אֲשֶׁר בַּשָּׂדֶה בַּסּוּסִים
ד בַּחֲמֹרִים בַּגְּמַלִּים בַּבָּקָר וּבַצֹּאן דֶּבֶר כָּבֵד מְאֹד: וְהִפְלָה יהוה בֵּין

5 livestock apart from Egypt's; none belonging to the Israelites will die. The
Lord has set His appointed time; tomorrow the Lord will bring this about
6 in the land." And the next day, the Lord brought it to be. All the livestock of
the Egyptians perished, but of the Israelites' livestock, not one creature died.
7 Pharaoh investigated the matter and discovered that not one among Israel's
livestock had died. But still Pharaoh's heart remained hard, and he would not
send the people forth.
8 Then the Lord said to Moshe and Aharon, "Take a handful of soot from a
9 furnace and throw it up in the air before Pharaoh's eyes. It will become a cloud
of dust over all the land of Egypt, and on people and animals it will become
a rash, breaking out into boils on people and animals throughout the land of
10 Egypt." So they took soot from the furnace and stood before Pharaoh. Moshe
threw it up in the air, and it became a rash that broke into boils on people and
11 animals. The magicians could not stand before Moshe because of their boils;
12 for the boils had affected them as they had the rest of the Egyptians. But the
Lord strengthened Pharaoh's heart, and he would not listen to them, just as
13 the Lord had told Moshe. Then the Lord said to Moshe, "Rise up
early in the morning and confront Pharaoh. Tell him: This is what the Lord,
14 God of the Hebrews, says: Send My people forth to serve Me, or this time I
will set the full force of My plagues upon you, your officials, and your people
15 so that you will know that there is none like Me in all the world. By now I
could have stretched out My hand and struck you and your people with an
16 epidemic that would have wiped you off the face of the earth. But I have let
you survive for this purpose – to show you My power, and to have My name
17 known throughout the land. You are still abusing your power over My people,
18 refusing to let them go. And so this time tomorrow I will bring a hailstorm
on Egypt heavier than any it has suffered, from the day Egypt was established
19 until now. Give an order now to bring in your livestock and all else you have
in the field. Anyone or any animal in the open, any not brought under shelter,
20 will die when the hail beats down." Those of Pharaoh's officials who feared
21 the Lord's word hurried to bring in their slaves and livestock. And those
who set no stock in the Lord's word kept their slaves and livestock where
they were in the fields.
22 The Lord said to Moshe, "Reach your hand out to the sky, that hail may
fall on all the land of Egypt, on the people and the animals and everything
23 growing in Egypt's fields." Moshe raised his staff toward the sky; the Lord
sent thunderclaps and hail. Fire struck the ground, and the Lord rained
24 down hail on the land of Egypt. The hail, with fire blazing inside it, battered
so hard that there had been nothing like it anywhere in Egypt since it first
25 became a nation. The hail struck everything in the open field throughout all
Egypt: people, animals, and everything growing in the fields, and it smashed

מקנה ישראל ובין מקנה מצרים ולא ימות מכל־לבני ישראל דבר:
ה ו וישם יהוה מועד לאמר מחר יעשה יהוה הדבר הזה בארץ: ויעש
יהוה את־הדבר הזה ממחרת וימת כל מקנה מצרים וממקנה בני־
ז ישראל לא־מת אחד: וישלח פרעה והנה לא־מת ממקנה ישראל
עד־אחד ויכבד לב פרעה ולא שלח את־העם:
ח ויאמר יהוה אל־משה ואל־אהרן קחו לכם מלא חפניכם פיח כבשן
ט וזרקו משה השמימה לעיני פרעה: והיה לאבק על כל־ארץ מצרים
והיה על־האדם ועל־הבהמה לשחין פרח אבעבעת בכל־ארץ
י מצרים: ויקחו את־פיח הכבשן ויעמדו לפני פרעה ויזרק אתו משה
יא השמימה ויהי שחין אבעבעת פרח באדם ובבהמה: ולא־יכלו
החרטמים לעמד לפני משה מפני השחין כי־היה השחין בחרטמם
יב ובכל־מצרים: ויחזק יהוה את־לב פרעה ולא שמע אלהם כאשר
יג דבר יהוה אל־משה: ויאמר יהוה אל־משה השכם בבקר
והתיצב לפני פרעה ואמרת אליו כה־אמר יהוה אלהי העברים
יד שלח את־עמי ויעבדני: כי ׀ בפעם הזאת אני שלח את־כל־מגפתי
טו אל־לבך ובעבדיך ובעמך בעבור תדע כי אין כמני בכל־הארץ: כי
עתה שלחתי את־ידי ואך אותך ואת־עמך בדבר ותכחד מן־הארץ:
טז ואולם בעבור זאת העמדתיך בעבור הראתך את־כחי ולמען ספר
יז יח שמי בכל־הארץ: עודך מסתולל בעמי לבלתי שלחם: הנני ממטיר שביעי
כעת מחר ברד כבד מאד אשר לא־היה כמהו במצרים למן־היום
יט הוסדה ועד־עתה: ועתה שלח העז את־מקנך ואת כל־אשר לך
בשדה כל־האדם והבהמה אשר־ימצא בשדה ולא יאסף הביתה
כ וירד עלהם הברד ומתו: הירא את־דבר יהוה מעבדי פרעה הניס
כא את־עבדיו ואת־מקנהו אל־הבתים: ואשר לא־שם לבו אל־דבר
יהוה ויעזב את־עבדיו ואת־מקנהו בשדה:
כב ויאמר יהוה אל־משה נטה את־ידך על־השמים ויהי ברד בכל־ארץ
מצרים על־האדם ועל־הבהמה ועל כל־עשב השדה בארץ מצרים:
כג ויט משה את־מטהו על־השמים ויהוה נתן קלת וברד ותהלך־אש
כד ארצה וימטר יהוה ברד על־ארץ מצרים: ויהי ברד ואש מתלקחת
בתוך הברד כבד מאד אשר לא־היה כמהו בכל־ארץ מצרים מאז
כה היתה לגוי: ויך הברד בכל־ארץ מצרים את כל־אשר בשדה מאדם
ועד־בהמה ואת כל־עשב השדה הכה הברד ואת־כל־עץ השדה

26 asunder every tree. Only in Goshen, where the Israelites lived, no hail fell.
27 Then Pharaoh sent for Moshe and Aharon and said to them, "This time I
28 have sinned. The LORD is in the right, and I and my people are guilty. Pray
to the LORD. Enough of God's thunder and hail – I will send you forth. You
29 need not wait any longer." Moshe said to him, "As I leave the city, I will spread
out my hands to the LORD. The thunder will stop and there will be no more
30 hail. You will then know that the world belongs to the LORD. But I know that
31 you and your officials still do not hold the LORD God in awe." By then the
flax and barley had been destroyed, because the barley was ripe and the flax
32 in bud. But the wheat and spelt had not been destroyed, because they ripen
33 later. Moshe left Pharaoh and the city and spread out his hands to the LORD.
34 The thunder and hail stopped; the rain did not pound the earth anymore. But
when Pharaoh saw that the rain, hail, and thunder had stopped, he once more
35 turned to sinfulness. He hardened his heart; his officials likewise. Pharaoh's
heart was strengthened and he refused to send the Israelites forth, just as the
LORD had predicted at Moshe's hand.
10 1 Then the LORD said to Moshe, "Go to Pharaoh. I have hardened his heart BO
2 and his officials', that I may display these My signs before him, and so that
you may tell your children and grandchildren how I made the Egyptians a
laughingstock by the signs I revealed among them; and know that I am the
3 LORD." Moshe and Aharon came to Pharaoh and said to him, "Thus says the
LORD, God of the Hebrews: How much longer will you refuse to submit to
4 Me? Send My people forth to serve Me. For if you refuse to send My people
5 forth, tomorrow I bring locusts to your land. They will cover the landscape so
that you will not be able to see the ground. They will eat what little remains
6 after the hail, including all the trees that grow up from your soil. They will fill
your palaces, your officials' houses, and all the houses of Egypt. Your parents
and grandparents never saw anything like this, from the day they arrived
7 upon this earth until today." Then Moshe turned and left Pharaoh. Pharaoh's
officials then said to him, "How long must we leave this man to ensnare us?
Send the people forth to serve the LORD their God. Do you not yet know
8 that Egypt is being destroyed?" Moshe and Aharon were summoned back
to Pharaoh, and he said to them, "Go and serve the LORD your God. Who
9 exactly will be going?" "With our youths and our elderly folk we will go," said
Moshe, "with our sons and our daughters, our sheep and our cattle, we all
10 must go, for it will be our festival of the LORD." He replied, "The LORD be with
you if I let you and your children go! Look – evil is staring you in the face.[18]
11 No! Let the men go and serve the LORD. That is what you are asking for." Then
12 Pharaoh had Moshe and Aharon expelled from his presence. The
LORD said to Moshe, "Reach out your hand over Egypt so that locusts swarm

---

18 | Explanations of this verse vary widely. According to this rendering, which is close to the original Hebrew, Pharaoh's words are defiant and threatening.

כו כז שָׁבֵר: רַק בְּאֶרֶץ גֹּשֶׁן אֲשֶׁר־שָׁם בְּנֵי יִשְׂרָאֵל לֹא הָיָה בָּרָד: וַיִּשְׁלַח
פַּרְעֹה וַיִּקְרָא לְמֹשֶׁה וּלְאַהֲרֹן וַיֹּאמֶר אֲלֵהֶם חָטָאתִי הַפָּעַם יהוה
כח הַצַּדִּיק וַאֲנִי וְעַמִּי הָרְשָׁעִים: הַעְתִּירוּ אֶל־יהוה וְרַב מִהְיֹת קֹלֹת
כט אֱלֹהִים וּבָרָד וַאֲשַׁלְּחָה אֶתְכֶם וְלֹא תֹסִפוּן לַעֲמֹד: וַיֹּאמֶר אֵלָיו מֹשֶׁה
כְּצֵאתִי אֶת־הָעִיר אֶפְרֹשׂ אֶת־כַּפַּי אֶל־יהוה הַקֹּלוֹת יֶחְדָּלוּן וְהַבָּרָד
ל לֹא יִהְיֶה־עוֹד לְמַעַן תֵּדַע כִּי לַיהוה הָאָרֶץ: וְאַתָּה וַעֲבָדֶיךָ יָדַעְתִּי
לא כִּי טֶרֶם תִּירְאוּן מִפְּנֵי יהוה אֱלֹהִים: וְהַפִּשְׁתָּה וְהַשְּׂעֹרָה נֻכָּתָה כִּי
לב הַשְּׂעֹרָה אָבִיב וְהַפִּשְׁתָּה גִּבְעֹל: וְהַחִטָּה וְהַכֻּסֶּמֶת לֹא נֻכּוּ כִּי אֲפִילֹת
לג הֵנָּה: וַיֵּצֵא מֹשֶׁה מֵעִם פַּרְעֹה אֶת־הָעִיר וַיִּפְרֹשׂ כַּפָּיו אֶל־יהוה וַיַּחְדְּלוּ מפטיר
לד הַקֹּלוֹת וְהַבָּרָד וּמָטָר לֹא־נִתַּךְ אָרְצָה: וַיַּרְא פַּרְעֹה כִּי־חָדַל הַמָּטָר
לה וְהַבָּרָד וְהַקֹּלֹת וַיֹּסֶף לַחֲטֹא וַיַּכְבֵּד לִבּוֹ הוּא וַעֲבָדָיו: וַיֶּחֱזַק לֵב פַּרְעֹה
וְלֹא שִׁלַּח אֶת־בְּנֵי יִשְׂרָאֵל כַּאֲשֶׁר דִּבֶּר יהוה בְּיַד־מֹשֶׁה:
י א וַיֹּאמֶר יהוה אֶל־מֹשֶׁה בֹּא אֶל־פַּרְעֹה כִּי־אֲנִי הִכְבַּדְתִּי אֶת־לִבּוֹ וְאֶת־ ז בא
ב לֵב עֲבָדָיו לְמַעַן שִׁתִי אֹתֹתַי אֵלֶּה בְּקִרְבּוֹ: וּלְמַעַן תְּסַפֵּר בְּאָזְנֵי בִנְךָ
וּבֶן־בִּנְךָ אֵת אֲשֶׁר הִתְעַלַּלְתִּי בְּמִצְרַיִם וְאֶת־אֹתֹתַי אֲשֶׁר־שַׂמְתִּי בָם
ג וִידַעְתֶּם כִּי־אֲנִי יהוה: וַיָּבֹא מֹשֶׁה וְאַהֲרֹן אֶל־פַּרְעֹה וַיֹּאמְרוּ אֵלָיו
כֹּה־אָמַר יהוה אֱלֹהֵי הָעִבְרִים עַד־מָתַי מֵאַנְתָּ לֵעָנֹת מִפָּנָי שַׁלַּח
ד עַמִּי וְיַעַבְדֻנִי: כִּי אִם־מָאֵן אַתָּה לְשַׁלֵּחַ אֶת־עַמִּי הִנְנִי מֵבִיא מָחָר
ה אַרְבֶּה בִּגְבֻלֶךָ: וְכִסָּה אֶת־עֵין הָאָרֶץ וְלֹא יוּכַל לִרְאֹת אֶת־הָאָרֶץ
וְאָכַל ׀ אֶת־יֶתֶר הַפְּלֵטָה הַנִּשְׁאֶרֶת לָכֶם מִן־הַבָּרָד וְאָכַל אֶת־כָּל־
ו הָעֵץ הַצֹּמֵחַ לָכֶם מִן־הַשָּׂדֶה: וּמָלְאוּ בָתֶּיךָ וּבָתֵּי כָל־עֲבָדֶיךָ וּבָתֵּי
כָל־מִצְרַיִם אֲשֶׁר לֹא־רָאוּ אֲבֹתֶיךָ וַאֲבוֹת אֲבֹתֶיךָ מִיּוֹם הֱיוֹתָם עַל־
ז הָאֲדָמָה עַד הַיּוֹם הַזֶּה וַיִּפֶן וַיֵּצֵא מֵעִם פַּרְעֹה: וַיֹּאמְרוּ עַבְדֵי פַרְעֹה
אֵלָיו עַד־מָתַי יִהְיֶה זֶה לָנוּ לְמוֹקֵשׁ שַׁלַּח אֶת־הָאֲנָשִׁים וְיַעַבְדוּ
ח אֶת־יהוה אֱלֹהֵיהֶם הֲטֶרֶם תֵּדַע כִּי אָבְדָה מִצְרָיִם: וַיּוּשַׁב אֶת־מֹשֶׁה
וְאֶת־אַהֲרֹן אֶל־פַּרְעֹה וַיֹּאמֶר אֲלֵהֶם לְכוּ עִבְדוּ אֶת־יהוה אֱלֹהֵיכֶם מִי
ט וָמִי הַהֹלְכִים: וַיֹּאמֶר מֹשֶׁה בִּנְעָרֵינוּ וּבִזְקֵנֵינוּ נֵלֵךְ בְּבָנֵינוּ וּבִבְנוֹתֵנוּ
י בְּצֹאנֵנוּ וּבִבְקָרֵנוּ נֵלֵךְ כִּי חַג־יהוה לָנוּ: וַיֹּאמֶר אֲלֵהֶם יְהִי כֵן יהוה
יא עִמָּכֶם כַּאֲשֶׁר אֲשַׁלַּח אֶתְכֶם וְאֶת־טַפְּכֶם רְאוּ כִּי רָעָה נֶגֶד פְּנֵיכֶם: לֹא
כֵן לְכוּ־נָא הַגְּבָרִים וְעִבְדוּ אֶת־יהוה כִּי אֹתָהּ אַתֶּם מְבַקְשִׁים וַיְגָרֶשׁ
יב אֹתָם מֵאֵת פְּנֵי פַרְעֹה: וַיֹּאמֶר יהוה אֶל־מֹשֶׁה נְטֵה יָדְךָ שני
עַל־אֶרֶץ מִצְרַיִם בָּאַרְבֶּה וְיַעַל עַל־אֶרֶץ מִצְרָיִם וְיֹאכַל אֶת־כָּל־עֵשֶׂב

13 over the land and eat everything growing there, all that is left after the hail." So
Moshe stretched out his staff over Egypt, and the LORD caused an east wind
to blow across the land all that day and night. By morning, the east wind had
14 brought the locusts. They invaded all of Egypt and settled throughout its land
in a dense swarm. Never before had there been such a plague of locusts, nor
15 will there ever be again. They covered all the landscape until the ground was
black. They ate all that was left after the hail: all the plants and all the fruit.
16 Nothing green remained on trees or plants throughout all Egypt. In haste,
Pharaoh summoned Moshe and Aharon and said, "I have sinned against
17 the LORD your God and you. Forgive my sin now, one more time. Pray to
18 the LORD your God to take this death away from me." Moshe left Pharaoh's
19 presence and prayed to the LORD. And the LORD turned the wind, westerly
and very strong, and lifted the locusts and swept them into the Sea of Reeds.[19]
20 Not one locust remained anywhere in Egypt. But the LORD strengthened
Pharaoh's heart and he would not send the Israelites forth.
21 Then the LORD said to Moshe, "Reach out your hand toward the sky to bring
22 darkness down over Egypt – darkness so deep it can be felt." Moshe reached
out his hand toward the sky, and all across Egypt it was pitch dark for three
23 days. For three days, no one could see anyone else or even move. But in the
24 Israelites' homes, they had light. Then Pharaoh summoned Moshe and said,
"Go, serve the LORD. Just leave your flocks and herds. Your children may
25 go with you." "Then give us sacrifices and burnt offerings to present to the
26 LORD our God," said Moshe. "Our livestock must go with us. Not a hoof can
be left behind. We must take them to serve the LORD our God, for until we
27 arrive, we will not know what we must use to serve the LORD." But the LORD
strengthened Pharaoh's heart, and he would not agree to send the people
28 forth. "Leave my presence," said Pharaoh. "Take care never to see my face
29 again, because on the day you do, that day you will die!" Moshe replied, "As
you say: I will not see your face again."
11 1 Then the LORD said to Moshe, "One last plague will I send against Pharaoh,
against Egypt. After that, he will send you forth from here, and when he does,
2 he will drive you out completely. Now tell the people, men and women, to
3 ask of their neighbors articles of silver and of gold." The LORD granted the
people favor in the eyes of the Egyptians. And the man Moshe, too, was held
in high regard in the land of Egypt, among both Pharaoh's officials and the
4 people. Moshe said, "This is what the LORD says: Around midnight
5 I will move throughout Egypt, and every firstborn son in Egypt will die, from
Pharaoh's firstborn presiding on his throne to the firstborn of the slave girl

19 | The popular translation "Red Sea" is now regarded as incorrect.

יג הָאָרֶץ אֵת כָּל־אֲשֶׁר הִשְׁאִיר הַבָּרָד: וַיֵּט מֹשֶׁה אֶת־מַטֵּהוּ עַל־אֶרֶץ
מִצְרַיִם וַיהוָה נִהַג רוּחַ־קָדִים בָּאָרֶץ כָּל־הַיּוֹם הַהוּא וְכָל־הַלָּיְלָה
יד הַבֹּקֶר הָיָה וְרוּחַ הַקָּדִים נָשָׂא אֶת־הָאַרְבֶּה: וַיַּעַל הָאַרְבֶּה עַל כָּל־
אֶרֶץ מִצְרַיִם וַיָּנַח בְּכֹל גְּבוּל מִצְרָיִם כָּבֵד מְאֹד לְפָנָיו לֹא־הָיָה כֵן
טו אַרְבֶּה כָּמֹהוּ וְאַחֲרָיו לֹא יִהְיֶה־כֵּן: וַיְכַס אֶת־עֵין כָּל־הָאָרֶץ וַתֶּחְשַׁךְ
הָאָרֶץ וַיֹּאכַל אֶת־כָּל־עֵשֶׂב הָאָרֶץ וְאֵת כָּל־פְּרִי הָעֵץ אֲשֶׁר הוֹתִיר
הַבָּרָד וְלֹא־נוֹתַר כָּל־יֶרֶק בָּעֵץ וּבְעֵשֶׂב הַשָּׂדֶה בְּכָל־אֶרֶץ מִצְרָיִם:
טז וַיְמַהֵר פַּרְעֹה לִקְרֹא לְמֹשֶׁה וּלְאַהֲרֹן וַיֹּאמֶר חָטָאתִי לַיהוָה אֱלֹהֵיכֶם
יז וְלָכֶם: וְעַתָּה שָׂא נָא חַטָּאתִי אַךְ הַפַּעַם וְהַעְתִּירוּ לַיהוָה אֱלֹהֵיכֶם
יח וְיָסֵר מֵעָלַי רַק אֶת־הַמָּוֶת הַזֶּה: וַיֵּצֵא מֵעִם פַּרְעֹה וַיֶּעְתַּר אֶל־יְהוָה:
יט וַיַּהֲפֹךְ יְהוָה רוּחַ־יָם חָזָק מְאֹד וַיִּשָּׂא אֶת־הָאַרְבֶּה וַיִּתְקָעֵהוּ יָמָּה סּוּף
כ לֹא נִשְׁאַר אַרְבֶּה אֶחָד בְּכֹל גְּבוּל מִצְרָיִם: וַיְחַזֵּק יְהוָה אֶת־לֵב פַּרְעֹה
וְלֹא שִׁלַּח אֶת־בְּנֵי יִשְׂרָאֵל:
כא וַיֹּאמֶר יְהוָה אֶל־מֹשֶׁה נְטֵה יָדְךָ עַל־הַשָּׁמַיִם וִיהִי חֹשֶׁךְ עַל־אֶרֶץ
כב מִצְרָיִם וְיָמֵשׁ חֹשֶׁךְ: וַיֵּט מֹשֶׁה אֶת־יָדוֹ עַל־הַשָּׁמָיִם וַיְהִי חֹשֶׁךְ־אֲפֵלָה
כג בְּכָל־אֶרֶץ מִצְרַיִם שְׁלֹשֶׁת יָמִים: לֹא־רָאוּ אִישׁ אֶת־אָחִיו וְלֹא־קָמוּ
אִישׁ מִתַּחְתָּיו שְׁלֹשֶׁת יָמִים וּלְכָל־בְּנֵי יִשְׂרָאֵל הָיָה אוֹר בְּמוֹשְׁבֹתָם:
כד וַיִּקְרָא פַרְעֹה אֶל־מֹשֶׁה וַיֹּאמֶר לְכוּ עִבְדוּ אֶת־יְהוָה רַק צֹאנְכֶם שלישי
כה וּבְקַרְכֶם יֻצָּג גַּם־טַפְּכֶם יֵלֵךְ עִמָּכֶם: וַיֹּאמֶר מֹשֶׁה גַּם־אַתָּה תִּתֵּן
כו בְּיָדֵנוּ זְבָחִים וְעֹלֹת וְעָשִׂינוּ לַיהוָה אֱלֹהֵינוּ: וְגַם־מִקְנֵנוּ יֵלֵךְ עִמָּנוּ
לֹא תִשָּׁאֵר פַּרְסָה כִּי מִמֶּנּוּ נִקַּח לַעֲבֹד אֶת־יְהוָה אֱלֹהֵינוּ וַאֲנַחְנוּ
כז לֹא־נֵדַע מַה־נַּעֲבֹד אֶת־יְהוָה עַד־בֹּאֵנוּ שָׁמָּה: וַיְחַזֵּק יְהוָה אֶת־לֵב
כח פַּרְעֹה וְלֹא אָבָה לְשַׁלְּחָם: וַיֹּאמֶר־לוֹ פַרְעֹה לֵךְ מֵעָלָי הִשָּׁמֶר לְךָ
כט אַל־תֹּסֶף רְאוֹת פָּנַי כִּי בְּיוֹם רְאֹתְךָ פָנַי תָּמוּת: וַיֹּאמֶר מֹשֶׁה כֵּן דִּבַּרְתָּ
לֹא־אֹסִף עוֹד רְאוֹת פָּנֶיךָ:
ח יא א וַיֹּאמֶר יְהוָה אֶל־מֹשֶׁה עוֹד נֶגַע אֶחָד אָבִיא עַל־פַּרְעֹה וְעַל־מִצְרַיִם
אַחֲרֵי־כֵן יְשַׁלַּח אֶתְכֶם מִזֶּה כְּשַׁלְּחוֹ כָּלָה גָּרֵשׁ יְגָרֵשׁ אֶתְכֶם מִזֶּה:
ב דַּבֶּר־נָא בְּאָזְנֵי הָעָם וְיִשְׁאֲלוּ אִישׁ ׀ מֵאֵת רֵעֵהוּ וְאִשָּׁה מֵאֵת רְעוּתָהּ
ג כְּלֵי־כֶסֶף וּכְלֵי זָהָב: וַיִּתֵּן יְהוָה אֶת־חֵן הָעָם בְּעֵינֵי מִצְרָיִם גַּם ׀
הָאִישׁ מֹשֶׁה גָּדוֹל מְאֹד בְּאֶרֶץ מִצְרַיִם בְּעֵינֵי עַבְדֵי־פַרְעֹה וּבְעֵינֵי
ד הָעָם: וַיֹּאמֶר מֹשֶׁה כֹּה אָמַר יְהוָה כַּחֲצֹת הַלַּיְלָה אֲנִי רביעי
ה יוֹצֵא בְּתוֹךְ מִצְרָיִם: וּמֵת כָּל־בְּכוֹר בְּאֶרֶץ מִצְרַיִם מִבְּכוֹר פַּרְעֹה

6 at her hand mill; the firstborn of the cattle as well. A scream will ring out
7 across Egypt, unlike any that has been before, or any that will be again. But
among the Israelites not a dog will bare its tongue at man or beast.[20] Then
8 you will know that the LORD is setting Israel apart from Egypt. And all these
officials of yours will come and bow down to me, saying, 'Leave, you and all
the people behind you.' After that, I will leave." He turned and left Pharaoh,
9 blazing with anger. The LORD said to Moshe, "Pharaoh will not listen
10 to you, that My wonders may be multiplied in Egypt." Moshe and Aharon
had produced all these wonders before Pharaoh, but the LORD strengthened
12 1 Pharaoh's heart, and he did not let the Israelites leave his land. Then
2 the LORD spoke to Moshe and Aharon in the land of Egypt. He said, "This
month shall be to you the beginning of months; the opening of the year, this
3 month will be for you.[21] Speak to the entire community of Israel and say: On
the tenth of this month each man must take a lamb for his family; one for
4 every household. If the household is too small for a lamb, let him and a close
neighbor take a lamb together, to suit the number of people involved; they
5 shall be counted for the lamb in proportion to their eating. A one-year-old
6 male shall you take, flawless, from among the sheep or goats. You shall guard
it until the fourteenth day of this month. And then, in the afternoon, all the
7 community of Israel shall slaughter it. They shall then take some of the blood
and put it on the two sides and top of the doorframes of the houses where
8 they are to eat the lamb. They shall eat the meat that night, roasted over a
9 fire; with unleavened bread and bitter herbs they shall eat it. Do not eat it raw
or boiled in water; it must be roasted over fire with its head, its legs, and its
10 inner parts. Do not leave any of it until morning; any left over until morning
11 you shall burn with fire. This is how you shall eat it: your belt secured, the
sandals on your feet, your staff in your hand. Eat it in haste. It is the LORD's
12 Passover.[22] I will pass through the land of Egypt that night, and will kill every
firstborn in Egypt, man and beast. Against all the gods of Egypt I will execute
13 judgments. I am the LORD. The blood will be your sign on the houses where
you are. I will see the blood and I will pass over you.[23] No deadly plague will
14 touch you when I strike the land of Egypt. This day will become a memorial
for you; you will celebrate it as a festival to the LORD for all generations,
15 a celebration that will be an everlasting law. For seven days you shall eat
unleavened bread. By the first day you shall have removed leaven from your
houses, for the soul of anyone who eats leavened bread from the first day to the
16 seventh will be severed from Israel.[24] The first day shall be a sacred assembly
and the seventh day shall be a sacred assembly. On them no work may be

---

20 | The Israelites will not face any threat of harm.

21 | The month in question – Nisan on the later Jewish calendar – coincides with the early part of spring. See note on 13:4.

22 | Cf. verse 13: "I will pass over you."

23 | Others translate "I will protect you." Cf. Isaiah 31:5.

24 | This punishment appears frequently in the Torah and is interpreted in various ways. According to this rendering, God warns of a spiritual dissolution.

הַיֹּשֵׁב עַל־כִּסְאוֹ עַד בְּכוֹר הַשִּׁפְחָה אֲשֶׁר אַחַר הָרֵחָיִם וְכֹל בְּכוֹר
ו בְּהֵמָה: וְהָיְתָה צְעָקָה גְדֹלָה בְּכָל־אֶרֶץ מִצְרָיִם אֲשֶׁר כָּמֹהוּ לֹא
ז נִהְיָתָה וְכָמֹהוּ לֹא תֹסִף: וּלְכֹל ׀ בְּנֵי יִשְׂרָאֵל לֹא יֶחֱרַץ־כֶּלֶב לְשֹׁנוֹ
לְמֵאִישׁ וְעַד־בְּהֵמָה לְמַעַן תֵּדְעוּן אֲשֶׁר יַפְלֶה יהוה בֵּין מִצְרַיִם וּבֵין
ח יִשְׂרָאֵל: וְיָרְדוּ כָל־עֲבָדֶיךָ אֵלֶּה אֵלַי וְהִשְׁתַּחֲווּ־לִי לֵאמֹר צֵא אַתָּה
וְכָל־הָעָם אֲשֶׁר־בְּרַגְלֶיךָ וְאַחֲרֵי־כֵן אֵצֵא וַיֵּצֵא מֵעִם־פַּרְעֹה בָּחֳרִי־
ט אָף: וַיֹּאמֶר יהוה אֶל־מֹשֶׁה לֹא־יִשְׁמַע אֲלֵיכֶם פַּרְעֹה לְמַעַן
י רְבוֹת מוֹפְתַי בְּאֶרֶץ מִצְרָיִם: וּמֹשֶׁה וְאַהֲרֹן עָשׂוּ אֶת־כָּל־הַמֹּפְתִים
הָאֵלֶּה לִפְנֵי פַרְעֹה וַיְחַזֵּק יהוה אֶת־לֵב פַּרְעֹה וְלֹא־שִׁלַּח אֶת־בְּנֵי־
יב א יִשְׂרָאֵל מֵאַרְצוֹ: וַיֹּאמֶר יהוה אֶל־מֹשֶׁה וְאֶל־אַהֲרֹן בְּאֶרֶץ
ב מִצְרַיִם לֵאמֹר: הַחֹדֶשׁ הַזֶּה לָכֶם רֹאשׁ חֳדָשִׁים רִאשׁוֹן הוּא לָכֶם
ג לְחָדְשֵׁי הַשָּׁנָה: דַּבְּרוּ אֶל־כָּל־עֲדַת יִשְׂרָאֵל לֵאמֹר בֶּעָשֹׂר לַחֹדֶשׁ
ד הַזֶּה וְיִקְחוּ לָהֶם אִישׁ שֶׂה לְבֵית־אָבֹת שֶׂה לַבָּיִת: וְאִם־יִמְעַט הַבַּיִת
מִהְיוֹת מִשֶּׂה וְלָקַח הוּא וּשְׁכֵנוֹ הַקָּרֹב אֶל־בֵּיתוֹ בְּמִכְסַת נְפָשֹׁת
ה אִישׁ לְפִי אָכְלוֹ תָּכֹסּוּ עַל־הַשֶּׂה: שֶׂה תָמִים זָכָר בֶּן־שָׁנָה יִהְיֶה לָכֶם
ו מִן־הַכְּבָשִׂים וּמִן־הָעִזִּים תִּקָּחוּ: וְהָיָה לָכֶם לְמִשְׁמֶרֶת עַד אַרְבָּעָה
עָשָׂר יוֹם לַחֹדֶשׁ הַזֶּה וְשָׁחֲטוּ אֹתוֹ כֹּל קְהַל עֲדַת־יִשְׂרָאֵל בֵּין
ז הָעַרְבָּיִם: וְלָקְחוּ מִן־הַדָּם וְנָתְנוּ עַל־שְׁתֵּי הַמְּזוּזֹת וְעַל־הַמַּשְׁקוֹף עַל
ח הַבָּתִּים אֲשֶׁר־יֹאכְלוּ אֹתוֹ בָּהֶם: וְאָכְלוּ אֶת־הַבָּשָׂר בַּלַּיְלָה הַזֶּה צְלִי־
ט אֵשׁ וּמַצּוֹת עַל־מְרֹרִים יֹאכְלֻהוּ: אַל־תֹּאכְלוּ מִמֶּנּוּ נָא וּבָשֵׁל מְבֻשָּׁל
י בַּמָּיִם כִּי אִם־צְלִי־אֵשׁ רֹאשׁוֹ עַל־כְּרָעָיו וְעַל־קִרְבּוֹ: וְלֹא־תוֹתִירוּ
יא מִמֶּנּוּ עַד־בֹּקֶר וְהַנֹּתָר מִמֶּנּוּ עַד־בֹּקֶר בָּאֵשׁ תִּשְׂרֹפוּ: וְכָכָה תֹּאכְלוּ
אֹתוֹ מָתְנֵיכֶם חֲגֻרִים נַעֲלֵיכֶם בְּרַגְלֵיכֶם וּמַקֶּלְכֶם בְּיֶדְכֶם וַאֲכַלְתֶּם
יב אֹתוֹ בְּחִפָּזוֹן פֶּסַח הוּא לַיהוה: וְעָבַרְתִּי בְאֶרֶץ־מִצְרַיִם בַּלַּיְלָה הַזֶּה
וְהִכֵּיתִי כָל־בְּכוֹר בְּאֶרֶץ מִצְרַיִם מֵאָדָם וְעַד־בְּהֵמָה וּבְכָל־אֱלֹהֵי
יג מִצְרַיִם אֶעֱשֶׂה שְׁפָטִים אֲנִי יהוה: וְהָיָה הַדָּם לָכֶם לְאֹת עַל הַבָּתִּים
אֲשֶׁר אַתֶּם שָׁם וְרָאִיתִי אֶת־הַדָּם וּפָסַחְתִּי עֲלֵכֶם וְלֹא־יִהְיֶה בָכֶם
יד נֶגֶף לְמַשְׁחִית בְּהַכֹּתִי בְּאֶרֶץ מִצְרָיִם: וְהָיָה הַיּוֹם הַזֶּה לָכֶם לְזִכָּרוֹן
טו וְחַגֹּתֶם אֹתוֹ חַג לַיהוה לְדֹרֹתֵיכֶם חֻקַּת עוֹלָם תְּחָגֻּהוּ: שִׁבְעַת יָמִים
מַצּוֹת תֹּאכֵלוּ אַךְ בַּיּוֹם הָרִאשׁוֹן תַּשְׁבִּיתוּ שְּׂאֹר מִבָּתֵּיכֶם כִּי ׀ כָּל־
אֹכֵל חָמֵץ וְנִכְרְתָה הַנֶּפֶשׁ הַהִוא מִיִּשְׂרָאֵל מִיּוֹם הָרִאשֹׁן עַד־יוֹם
טז הַשְּׁבִעִי: וּבַיּוֹם הָרִאשׁוֹן מִקְרָא־קֹדֶשׁ וּבַיּוֹם הַשְּׁבִיעִי מִקְרָא־קֹדֶשׁ

done but preparing the food for everyone to eat. That alone may you do.
17 Safeguard the unleavened bread,[25] because on this very day I will have brought
your battalions out of Egypt. You shall observe this day for all generations;
18 it is an everlasting law. From the fourteenth day of the first month in the
evening until the twenty-first day of the month in the evening, you may eat
19 only unleavened bread. During these seven days, leaven must not be found in
your houses. Anyone, whether newcomer or native born, who eats leavened
20 food will have his soul severed from the community of Israel. Eat nothing
leavened. Wherever you may live, you shall eat unleavened bread."
21 Then Moshe called together all the elders of Israel and instructed them, "Each
select or acquire one of the flock for yourselves, for your families and slaughter
22 the Passover sacrifice. Take a bunch of hyssop, dip it in the blood in the bowl,
and put some of the blood on the top and two sides of the doorframe. None
23 of you shall leave by the doors of your houses until morning. When the Lord
passes through to strike Egypt and sees the blood on the top and sides of a
doorframe, He will pass over that doorway and will not let the destroyer
24 enter your houses to strike you down. Keep this as a law for you and for your
25 children forever. When you enter the land the Lord will give you as He has
26 promised, you shall keep this ceremony. And when your children say to you,
27 'What does this ceremony mean to you?' you shall say, 'It is the Passover
sacrifice to the Lord who passed over the houses of the Israelites in Egypt, for
He struck the Egyptians; but our homes, He spared.'" Then the people bowed
28 down and prostrated themselves. The Israelites proceeded to do exactly as
29 the Lord had commanded Moshe and Aharon. It happened at
midnight: the Lord struck down all the firstborn in Egypt, from the firstborn
of Pharaoh, presiding on his throne, to the firstborn of the prison captives,
30 and all the firstborn cattle. Pharaoh arose that night, he and all his officials
and all Egypt – for a great scream rang out across Egypt, for there was no
31 house without its dead. That night, Pharaoh summoned Moshe and Aharon
and said, "Get up, get out from among my people, you and the Israelites. Go.
32 Serve the Lord exactly as you requested; take your sheep and cattle also, just
33 as you said. Just go. But bless me too." The Egyptians too urged the people to
34 make haste and leave the land. "All of us will die," they said. The people took
their dough before it could rise, carrying it on their shoulders in kneading
35 pans wrapped in their clothing. As Moshe had told them, the Israelites had
36 requested items of silver and gold, and clothing, of the Egyptians, and the
Lord had given the people favor in the eyes of the Egyptians and they had
granted their request. Thus they despoiled Egypt.

25 | That is, ensure that it does not become leavened, or more generally, scrupulously observe the commandment.

יִהְיֶה לָכֶם כָּל־מְלָאכָה לֹא־יֵעָשֶׂה בָהֶם אַךְ אֲשֶׁר יֵאָכֵל לְכָל־נֶפֶשׁ
יז הוּא לְבַדּוֹ יֵעָשֶׂה לָכֶם: וּשְׁמַרְתֶּם אֶת־הַמַּצּוֹת כִּי בְּעֶצֶם הַיּוֹם הַזֶּה
הוֹצֵאתִי אֶת־צִבְאוֹתֵיכֶם מֵאֶרֶץ מִצְרָיִם וּשְׁמַרְתֶּם אֶת־הַיּוֹם הַזֶּה
יח לְדֹרֹתֵיכֶם חֻקַּת עוֹלָם: בָּרִאשֹׁן בְּאַרְבָּעָה עָשָׂר יוֹם לַחֹדֶשׁ בָּעֶרֶב
יט תֹּאכְלוּ מַצֹּת עַד יוֹם הָאֶחָד וְעֶשְׂרִים לַחֹדֶשׁ בָּעָרֶב: שִׁבְעַת יָמִים
שְׂאֹר לֹא יִמָּצֵא בְּבָתֵּיכֶם כִּי ׀ כָּל־אֹכֵל מַחְמֶצֶת וְנִכְרְתָה הַנֶּפֶשׁ הַהִוא
כ מֵעֲדַת יִשְׂרָאֵל בַּגֵּר וּבְאֶזְרַח הָאָרֶץ: כָּל־מַחְמֶצֶת לֹא תֹאכֵלוּ בְּכֹל
מוֹשְׁבֹתֵיכֶם תֹּאכְלוּ מַצּוֹת:
כא וַיִּקְרָא מֹשֶׁה לְכָל־זִקְנֵי יִשְׂרָאֵל וַיֹּאמֶר אֲלֵהֶם מִשְׁכוּ וּקְחוּ לָכֶם חמישי
כב צֹאן לְמִשְׁפְּחֹתֵיכֶם וְשַׁחֲטוּ הַפָּסַח: וּלְקַחְתֶּם אֲגֻדַּת אֵזוֹב וּטְבַלְתֶּם
בַּדָּם אֲשֶׁר־בַּסַּף וְהִגַּעְתֶּם אֶל־הַמַּשְׁקוֹף וְאֶל־שְׁתֵּי הַמְּזוּזֹת מִן־הַדָּם
כג אֲשֶׁר בַּסָּף וְאַתֶּם לֹא תֵצְאוּ אִישׁ מִפֶּתַח־בֵּיתוֹ עַד־בֹּקֶר: וְעָבַר יהוה
לִנְגֹּף אֶת־מִצְרַיִם וְרָאָה אֶת־הַדָּם עַל־הַמַּשְׁקוֹף וְעַל שְׁתֵּי הַמְּזוּזֹת
וּפָסַח יהוה עַל־הַפֶּתַח וְלֹא יִתֵּן הַמַּשְׁחִית לָבֹא אֶל־בָּתֵּיכֶם לִנְגֹּף:
כד כה וּשְׁמַרְתֶּם אֶת־הַדָּבָר הַזֶּה לְחָק־לְךָ וּלְבָנֶיךָ עַד־עוֹלָם: וְהָיָה כִּי־תָבֹאוּ
אֶל־הָאָרֶץ אֲשֶׁר יִתֵּן יהוה לָכֶם כַּאֲשֶׁר דִּבֵּר וּשְׁמַרְתֶּם אֶת־הָעֲבֹדָה
כו הַזֹּאת: וְהָיָה כִּי־יֹאמְרוּ אֲלֵיכֶם בְּנֵיכֶם מָה הָעֲבֹדָה הַזֹּאת לָכֶם:
כז וַאֲמַרְתֶּם זֶבַח־פֶּסַח הוּא לַיהוה אֲשֶׁר פָּסַח עַל־בָּתֵּי בְנֵי־יִשְׂרָאֵל
בְּמִצְרַיִם בְּנָגְפּוֹ אֶת־מִצְרַיִם וְאֶת־בָּתֵּינוּ הִצִּיל וַיִּקֹּד הָעָם וַיִּשְׁתַּחֲווּ:
כח וַיֵּלְכוּ וַיַּעֲשׂוּ בְּנֵי יִשְׂרָאֵל כַּאֲשֶׁר צִוָּה יהוה אֶת־מֹשֶׁה וְאַהֲרֹן כֵּן
כט עָשׂוּ: וַיְהִי ׀ בַּחֲצִי הַלַּיְלָה וַיהוה הִכָּה כָל־בְּכוֹר בְּאֶרֶץ ט ששי
מִצְרַיִם מִבְּכֹר פַּרְעֹה הַיֹּשֵׁב עַל־כִּסְאוֹ עַד בְּכוֹר הַשְּׁבִי אֲשֶׁר בְּבֵית
ל הַבּוֹר וְכֹל בְּכוֹר בְּהֵמָה: וַיָּקָם פַּרְעֹה לַיְלָה הוּא וְכָל־עֲבָדָיו וְכָל־
מִצְרַיִם וַתְּהִי צְעָקָה גְדֹלָה בְּמִצְרָיִם כִּי־אֵין בַּיִת אֲשֶׁר אֵין־שָׁם מֵת:
לא וַיִּקְרָא לְמֹשֶׁה וּלְאַהֲרֹן לַיְלָה וַיֹּאמֶר קוּמוּ צְּאוּ מִתּוֹךְ עַמִּי גַּם־אַתֶּם
לב גַּם־בְּנֵי יִשְׂרָאֵל וּלְכוּ עִבְדוּ אֶת־יהוה כְּדַבֶּרְכֶם: גַּם־צֹאנְכֶם גַּם־
לג בְּקַרְכֶם קְחוּ כַּאֲשֶׁר דִּבַּרְתֶּם וָלֵכוּ וּבֵרַכְתֶּם גַּם־אֹתִי: וַתֶּחֱזַק מִצְרַיִם
לד עַל־הָעָם לְמַהֵר לְשַׁלְּחָם מִן־הָאָרֶץ כִּי אָמְרוּ כֻּלָּנוּ מֵתִים: וַיִּשָּׂא
הָעָם אֶת־בְּצֵקוֹ טֶרֶם יֶחְמָץ מִשְׁאֲרֹתָם צְרֻרֹת בְּשִׂמְלֹתָם עַל־שִׁכְמָם:
לה וּבְנֵי־יִשְׂרָאֵל עָשׂוּ כִּדְבַר מֹשֶׁה וַיִּשְׁאֲלוּ מִמִּצְרַיִם כְּלֵי־כֶסֶף וּכְלֵי זָהָב
לו וּשְׂמָלֹת: וַיהוה נָתַן אֶת־חֵן הָעָם בְּעֵינֵי מִצְרַיִם וַיַּשְׁאִלוּם וַיְנַצְּלוּ
אֶת־מִצְרָיִם:

37 The Israelites traveled from Ramesses to Sukkot. There were about six
38 hundred thousand men on foot, quite apart from the children. And a great
variety of other people went up with them, as well as large droves of livestock,
39 flocks and cattle. With the dough they had brought from Egypt, they baked
cakes of unleavened bread, not risen. They had been driven out of Egypt and
40 could not delay, and had prepared no other provisions. The Israelites had
41 lived in Egypt for four hundred thirty years. At the end of four hundred thirty
42 years, to the very day, all the LORD's battalions left Egypt. All that night, the
LORD watched over them to bring them out of Egypt; and still this night
is kept as one of watchfulness for the LORD[26] throughout the generations
of Israel.
43 The LORD said to Moshe and Aharon, "This is the law of the Passover sacrifice.
44 No foreigner may eat of it. But any slave who has been acquired for money
45 and circumcised may eat it. No gentile resident or hired laborer may eat of it.
46 It should be eaten in a single house; bring none of the meat outside the house.
47 Do not break any of its bones. All the community of Israel shall observe this.
48 If a stranger lives among you and wishes to offer a Passover sacrifice to the
LORD, every male in his household must be circumcised. Then he may join in
49 observing it and be like a native born. But no uncircumcised man may eat of it.
There shall be one and the same law for the native born and the stranger who
50 lives among you." All the Israelites did exactly as the LORD had commanded
51 Moshe and Aharon. And on that very day the LORD brought the
Israelites out of Egypt in their battalions.
13 1 2 The LORD said to Moshe, "Consecrate every firstborn to Me. Man and beast,
3 the first to emerge from every womb among the Israelites is Mine." Moshe
said to the people, "Remember this day, the day you left Egypt, the house of
slaves, when with a mighty hand the LORD rescued you from here. No leaven
4 5 may be eaten. Today, in the month of Aviv,[27] you are leaving. And when the
LORD brings you into the land of the Canaanites, Hittites, Amorites, Hivites,
and Jebusites, the land that He promised your ancestors He would give
you – one flowing with milk and with honey – you shall keep this ceremony
6 in this month. For seven days you shall eat unleavened bread; the seventh
7 day shall be a festival to the LORD. Unleavened bread shall be eaten for those
8 seven days; no bread or leavening shall be seen in all your land. On that
day you must tell your child, 'This is because of what the LORD did for me
9 when I left Egypt.' It shall be a sign on your arm, a reminder between your
eyes,[28] so that the LORD's teaching be on your tongue, for with a mighty
10 hand the LORD brought you out of Egypt. Celebrate this law each year at its
set time.

---

26 | Meaning watchful observance of the prescribed ritual. Alternatively, "watchfulness *by* the LORD," i.e., a night of special divine protection.

27 | In early spring, when certain crops begin to form – equivalent to Nisan on the later Jewish calendar. *Aviv* literally means kernels of ripening grain.

28 | An idiom meaning something constantly remembered. Traditionally it is understood as a reference to tefillin, which are worn on the arm and just above the forehead.

לז וַיִּסְעוּ בְנֵי־יִשְׂרָאֵל מֵרַעְמְסֵס סֻכֹּתָה כְּשֵׁשׁ־מֵאוֹת אֶלֶף רַגְלִי הַגְּבָרִים
לח לְבַד מִטָּף: וְגַם־עֵרֶב רַב עָלָה אִתָּם וְצֹאן וּבָקָר מִקְנֶה כָּבֵד מְאֹד:
לט וַיֹּאפוּ אֶת־הַבָּצֵק אֲשֶׁר הוֹצִיאוּ מִמִּצְרַיִם עֻגֹת מַצּוֹת כִּי לֹא חָמֵץ
כִּי־גֹרְשׁוּ מִמִּצְרַיִם וְלֹא יָכְלוּ לְהִתְמַהְמֵהַּ וְגַם־צֵדָה לֹא־עָשׂוּ לָהֶם:
מ וּמוֹשַׁב בְּנֵי יִשְׂרָאֵל אֲשֶׁר יָשְׁבוּ בְּמִצְרָיִם שְׁלֹשִׁים שָׁנָה וְאַרְבַּע מֵאוֹת
מא שָׁנָה: וַיְהִי מִקֵּץ שְׁלֹשִׁים שָׁנָה וְאַרְבַּע מֵאוֹת שָׁנָה וַיְהִי בְּעֶצֶם הַיּוֹם
מב הַזֶּה יָצְאוּ כׇּל־צִבְאוֹת יהוה מֵאֶרֶץ מִצְרָיִם: לֵיל שִׁמֻּרִים הוּא לַיהוה
לְהוֹצִיאָם מֵאֶרֶץ מִצְרָיִם הוּא־הַלַּיְלָה הַזֶּה לַיהוה שִׁמֻּרִים לְכׇל־בְּנֵי
יִשְׂרָאֵל לְדֹרֹתָם:
מג וַיֹּאמֶר יהוה אֶל־מֹשֶׁה וְאַהֲרֹן זֹאת חֻקַּת הַפָּסַח כׇּל־בֶּן־נֵכָר לֹא־יֹאכַל
מד מה בּוֹ: וְכׇל־עֶבֶד אִישׁ מִקְנַת־כָּסֶף וּמַלְתָּה אֹתוֹ אָז יֹאכַל בּוֹ: תּוֹשָׁב
מו וְשָׂכִיר לֹא־יֹאכַל בּוֹ: בְּבַיִת אֶחָד יֵאָכֵל לֹא־תוֹצִיא מִן־הַבַּיִת מִן־
מז הַבָּשָׂר חוּצָה וְעֶצֶם לֹא תִשְׁבְּרוּ־בוֹ: כׇּל־עֲדַת יִשְׂרָאֵל יַעֲשׂוּ אֹתוֹ:
מח וְכִי־יָגוּר אִתְּךָ גֵּר וְעָשָׂה פֶסַח לַיהוה הִמּוֹל לוֹ כׇל־זָכָר וְאָז יִקְרַב
מט לַעֲשֹׂתוֹ וְהָיָה כְּאֶזְרַח הָאָרֶץ וְכׇל־עָרֵל לֹא־יֹאכַל בּוֹ: תּוֹרָה אַחַת
נ יִהְיֶה לָאֶזְרָח וְלַגֵּר הַגָּר בְּתוֹכְכֶם: וַיַּעֲשׂוּ כׇּל־בְּנֵי יִשְׂרָאֵל כַּאֲשֶׁר צִוָּה
נא יהוה אֶת־מֹשֶׁה וְאֶת־אַהֲרֹן כֵּן עָשׂוּ: וַיְהִי בְּעֶצֶם הַיּוֹם הַזֶּה
הוֹצִיא יהוה אֶת־בְּנֵי יִשְׂרָאֵל מֵאֶרֶץ מִצְרַיִם עַל־צִבְאֹתָם:
יג א ב וַיְדַבֵּר יהוה אֶל־מֹשֶׁה לֵּאמֹר: קַדֶּשׁ־לִי כׇל־בְּכוֹר פֶּטֶר כׇּל־רֶחֶם שביעי
ג בִּבְנֵי יִשְׂרָאֵל בָּאָדָם וּבַבְּהֵמָה לִי הוּא: וַיֹּאמֶר מֹשֶׁה אֶל־הָעָם זָכוֹר
אֶת־הַיּוֹם הַזֶּה אֲשֶׁר יְצָאתֶם מִמִּצְרַיִם מִבֵּית עֲבָדִים כִּי בְּחֹזֶק יָד
ד הוֹצִיא יהוה אֶתְכֶם מִזֶּה וְלֹא יֵאָכֵל חָמֵץ: הַיּוֹם אַתֶּם יֹצְאִים בְּחֹדֶשׁ
ה הָאָבִיב: וְהָיָה כִי־יְבִיאֲךָ יהוה אֶל־אֶרֶץ הַכְּנַעֲנִי וְהַחִתִּי וְהָאֱמֹרִי
וְהַחִוִּי וְהַיְבוּסִי אֲשֶׁר נִשְׁבַּע לַאֲבֹתֶיךָ לָתֶת לָךְ אֶרֶץ זָבַת חָלָב וּדְבָשׁ
ו וְעָבַדְתָּ אֶת־הָעֲבֹדָה הַזֹּאת בַּחֹדֶשׁ הַזֶּה: שִׁבְעַת יָמִים תֹּאכַל מַצֹּת
ז וּבַיּוֹם הַשְּׁבִיעִי חַג לַיהוה: מַצּוֹת יֵאָכֵל אֵת שִׁבְעַת הַיָּמִים וְלֹא־יֵרָאֶה
ח לְךָ חָמֵץ וְלֹא־יֵרָאֶה לְךָ שְׂאֹר בְּכׇל־גְּבֻלֶךָ: וְהִגַּדְתָּ לְבִנְךָ בַּיּוֹם הַהוּא
ט לֵאמֹר בַּעֲבוּר זֶה עָשָׂה יהוה לִי בְּצֵאתִי מִמִּצְרָיִם: וְהָיָה לְךָ לְאוֹת
עַל־יָדְךָ וּלְזִכָּרוֹן בֵּין עֵינֶיךָ לְמַעַן תִּהְיֶה תּוֹרַת יהוה בְּפִיךָ כִּי בְּיָד
י חֲזָקָה הוֹצִאֲךָ יהוה מִמִּצְרָיִם: וְשָׁמַרְתָּ אֶת־הַחֻקָּה הַזֹּאת לְמוֹעֲדָהּ
מִיָּמִים יָמִימָה:

11 When the Lord brings you to the land of the Canaanites, as He promised
12 you and your ancestors, and He gives it to you, you shall give over to the Lord
the first to emerge from every womb. Every male firstborn of your animals
13 shall be His. You shall redeem every firstborn donkey with a lamb; otherwise,
you must break the donkey's neck. You must redeem every firstborn among
14 your sons. And in the future, when your children ask, 'What is this?' you
shall answer, 'With a mighty hand the Lord brought us out of Egypt, the
15 house of slaves. And when Pharaoh was obstinate and refused to set us free,
the Lord killed all the firstborn sons in Egypt, man and beast alike. That is
why I sacrifice every male firstborn animal to the Lord, and redeem all my
16 firstborn sons.' It shall be a sign on your arm and an emblem between your
17 eyes – with a mighty hand the Lord rescued us from Egypt." When BESHALAḤ
Pharaoh let the people go, God did not lead them through the land of the
Philistines, though it was the shorter way. "If the people face war," thought
18 God, "they will change their minds and go back to Egypt." So He led them
on a roundabout course, by way of the wilderness, to the Sea of Reeds.[29] The
19 Israelites left Egypt armed for battle. And Moshe took with him the remains
of Yosef, who had bound the Israelites by oath: "When God comes to your
20 aid, bring my remains with you out of here." They set out from Sukkot and
21 camped at Etam, at the edge of the desert. The Lord went ahead of them by
day in a column of cloud to guide them, and at night in a column of fire to
22 give them light, so that they might travel day and night. Neither the column
of cloud by day nor that of fire by night once departed from the people.
14 1 2 Then the Lord said to Moshe, "Speak to the Israelites and tell them to turn
back and camp in front of Pi HaḤirot, between Migdol and the sea, before
3 Baal Tzefon. Encamp facing it, by the sea. Pharaoh will think that the Israelites
4 are lost across the land, that they are trapped in the desert. I will toughen
Pharaoh's heart, and he will pursue them. I will be glorified over Pharaoh
and all his force, and the Egyptians will know that I am the Lord." And so
5 they did. When the king of Egypt was told that the Israelites had escaped, he
and his officials changed their minds about the people: "What have we done,
6 releasing the Israelites from serving us?" So the king harnessed his chariot
7 and brought out his army. He took six hundred elite chariots and all the
8 other chariots of Egypt, with officers over them all. The Lord strengthened
the heart of Pharaoh, king of Egypt, and he pursued the Israelites, who were
9 leaving in defiance of them. The Egyptians, with all the king's horses and
chariots, cavalry and infantry, chased and caught up with them as they were
10 encamped by the sea near Pi HaḤirot, before Baal Tzefon. Pharaoh drew
near – the Israelites looked up: there were the Egyptians thundering after
11 them. They were terrified and cried to the Lord for help. "Were there no

29 | See note on 10:19.

יא והיה כי־יבאך יהוה אל־ארץ הכנעני כאשר נשבע לך ולאבתיך
יב ונתנה לך: והעברת כל־פטר־רחם ליהוה וכל־פטר ׀ שגר בהמה
יג אשר יהיה לך הזכרים ליהוה: וכל־פטר חמר תפדה בשה ואם־
יד לא תפדה וערפתו וכל בכור אדם בבניך תפדה: והיה כי־ישאלך מפטיר
בנך מחר לאמר מה־זאת ואמרת אליו בחזק יד הוציאנו יהוה
טו ממצרים מבית עבדים: ויהי כי־הקשה פרעה לשלחנו ויהרג
יהוה כל־בכור בארץ מצרים מבכר אדם ועד־בכור בהמה על־
כן אני זבח ליהוה כל־פטר רחם הזכרים וכל־בכור בני אפדה:
טז והיה לאות על־ידכה ולטוטפת בין עיניך כי בחזק יד הוציאנו
יז יהוה ממצרים: ויהי בשלח פרעה את־העם ולא־ בשלח
נחם אלהים דרך ארץ פלשתים כי קרוב הוא כי ׀ אמר אלהים
יח פן־ינחם העם בראתם מלחמה ושבו מצרימה: ויסב אלהים ׀
את־העם דרך המדבר ים־סוף וחמשים עלו בני־ישראל מארץ
יט מצרים: ויקח משה את־עצמות יוסף עמו כי השבע השביע את־
בני ישראל לאמר פקד יפקד אלהים אתכם והעליתם את־עצמתי
כ כא מזה אתכם: ויסעו מסכת ויחנו באתם בקצה המדבר: ויהוה הלך
לפניהם יומם בעמוד ענן לנחתם הדרך ולילה בעמוד אש להאיר
כב להם ללכת יומם ולילה: לא־ימיש עמוד הענן יומם ועמוד האש
לילה לפני העם:

יד א ב וידבר יהוה אל־משה לאמר: דבר אל־בני ישראל וישבו ויחנו לפני
פי החירת בין מגדל ובין הים לפני בעל צפן נכחו תחנו על־הים:
ג ואמר פרעה לבני ישראל נבכים הם בארץ סגר עליהם המדבר:
ד וחזקתי את־לב־פרעה ורדף אחריהם ואכבדה בפרעה ובכל־חילו
ה וידעו מצרים כי־אני יהוה ויעשו־כן: ויגד למלך מצרים כי ברח
העם ויהפך לבב פרעה ועבדיו אל־העם ויאמרו מה־זאת עשינו
ו כי־שלחנו את־ישראל מעבדנו: ויאסר את־רכבו ואת־עמו לקח
ז עמו: ויקח שש־מאות רכב בחור וכל רכב מצרים ושלשם על־כלו:
ח ויחזק יהוה את־לב פרעה מלך מצרים וירדף אחרי בני ישראל ובני
ט ישראל יצאים ביד רמה: וירדפו מצרים אחריהם וישיגו אותם חנים שני
על־הים כל־סוס רכב פרעה ופרשיו וחילו על־פי החירת לפני בעל
י צפן: ופרעה הקריב וישאו בני־ישראל את־עיניהם והנה מצרים ׀
יא נסע אחריהם וייראו מאד ויצעקו בני־ישראל אל־יהוה: ויאמרו

graves in Egypt?" they asked Moshe. "Is that why you brought us here to die
12 in the desert? What have you done to us, bringing us out of Egypt? Did we
not tell you in Egypt: Leave us alone – let us serve the Egyptians. Better a life
13 in servitude to Egypt than death in the desert." But Moshe told the people,
"Fear not. Stand firm and see the deliverance the LORD will bring you today.
14 The Egyptians you see today, you shall never see again. The LORD will fight
for you. You stay silent."
15 The LORD said to Moshe, "Why are you crying out to Me? Speak to the
16 Israelites; have them move forward. Raise your staff, stretch out your hand
over the sea and divide it, and the Israelites will walk through the sea on dry
17 land. I will strengthen the Egyptians' hearts and they will go after them. Then
will My glory bear down hard upon Pharaoh and his entire army, his chariots
18 and cavalry. And when My glory bears down upon Pharaoh, his chariots and
19 cavalry, the Egyptians will know that I am the LORD." Then the angel of God
who had been traveling ahead of the Israelite camp moved and went behind
20 them, and the column of cloud moved from in front of them to their rear. It
came between the Egyptian and Israelite camps, as cloud and darkness for
21 one, but lighting the night for the other, keeping the two apart all night. Then
Moshe stretched out his hand over the sea, and the LORD drove the sea back
by a strong east wind all night, turning it to dry land and dividing the waters.
22 So the Israelites walked through the sea on dry land. To their right and left, the
23 water was like a wall. The Egyptians chased after them. All Pharaoh's horses,
24 chariots, and cavalry followed them into the sea. During the last watch of
the night,[30] the LORD looked down at the Egyptian army from a column of
25 fire and cloud and threw them into a panic, clogging their chariot wheels so
that it was hard for them to move. The Egyptians said, "Let us flee from the
Israelites. The LORD is fighting for them against Egypt."
26 Then the LORD said to Moshe, "Stretch out your hand over the sea. The waters
27 will flow back over the Egyptians and their chariots and cavalry." Moshe
stretched out his hand over the sea, and at daybreak the water came back in
full force. The Egyptians fled at its approach but the LORD swept them into
28 the sea. The waters returned, covering the chariots, the cavalry, and the whole
Egyptian army that had followed the Israelites into the sea. Not one of them
29 remained. But the Israelites had walked through the sea on dry land, with a
30 wall of water to their right and left. That day, the LORD saved the Israelites
from the Egyptians. And when the Israelites saw the Egyptians dead on
31 the seashore, and witnessed the wondrous power the LORD had unleashed
against the Egyptians, the people were in awe of the LORD, and they believed
in Him and in Moshe His servant.

---

30 | The night was divided into three sections, each one called a watch.

אֶל־מֹשֶׁה הֲֽמִבְּלִי אֵין־קְבָרִים בְּמִצְרַיִם לְקַחְתָּנוּ לָמוּת בַּמִּדְבָּר מַה־
יב זֹּאת עָשִׂיתָ לָּנוּ לְהוֹצִיאָנוּ מִמִּצְרָיִם׃ הֲלֹא־זֶה הַדָּבָר אֲשֶׁר דִּבַּרְנוּ
אֵלֶיךָ בְמִצְרַיִם לֵאמֹר חֲדַל מִמֶּנּוּ וְנַעַבְדָה אֶת־מִצְרָיִם כִּי טוֹב לָנוּ
יג עֲבֹד אֶת־מִצְרַיִם מִמֻּתֵנוּ בַּמִּדְבָּר׃ וַיֹּאמֶר מֹשֶׁה אֶל־הָעָם אַל־תִּירָאוּ
הִֽתְיַצְּבוּ וּרְאוּ אֶת־יְשׁוּעַת יהוה אֲשֶׁר־יַעֲשֶׂה לָכֶם הַיּוֹם כִּי אֲשֶׁר
יד רְאִיתֶם אֶת־מִצְרַיִם הַיּוֹם לֹא תֹסִפוּ לִרְאֹתָם עוֹד עַד־עוֹלָם׃ יהוה
יִלָּחֵם לָכֶם וְאַתֶּם תַּחֲרִשׁוּן׃
טו וַיֹּאמֶר יהוה אֶל־מֹשֶׁה מַה־תִּצְעַק אֵלָי דַּבֵּר אֶל־בְּנֵי־יִשְׂרָאֵל וְיִסָּעוּ׃ יא שלישי
טז וְאַתָּה הָרֵם אֶת־מַטְּךָ וּנְטֵה אֶת־יָדְךָ עַל־הַיָּם וּבְקָעֵהוּ וְיָבֹאוּ בְנֵי־
יז יִשְׂרָאֵל בְּתוֹךְ הַיָּם בַּיַּבָּשָׁה׃ וַאֲנִי הִנְנִי מְחַזֵּק אֶת־לֵב מִצְרַיִם וְיָבֹאוּ
יח אַחֲרֵיהֶם וְאִכָּבְדָה בְּפַרְעֹה וּבְכָל־חֵילוֹ בְּרִכְבּוֹ וּבְפָרָשָׁיו׃ וְיָדְעוּ
יט מִצְרַיִם כִּי־אֲנִי יהוה בְּהִכָּבְדִי בְּפַרְעֹה בְּרִכְבּוֹ וּבְפָרָשָׁיו׃ וַיִּסַּע מַלְאַךְ
הָאֱלֹהִים הַהֹלֵךְ לִפְנֵי מַחֲנֵה יִשְׂרָאֵל וַיֵּלֶךְ מֵאַחֲרֵיהֶם וַיִּסַּע עַמּוּד
כ הֶעָנָן מִפְּנֵיהֶם וַיַּעֲמֹד מֵאַחֲרֵיהֶם׃ וַיָּבֹא בֵּין ׀ מַחֲנֵה מִצְרַיִם וּבֵין
מַחֲנֵה יִשְׂרָאֵל וַיְהִי הֶעָנָן וְהַחֹשֶׁךְ וַיָּאֶר אֶת־הַלָּיְלָה וְלֹא־קָרַב זֶה
כא אֶל־זֶה כָּל־הַלָּיְלָה׃ וַיֵּט מֹשֶׁה אֶת־יָדוֹ עַל־הַיָּם וַיּוֹלֶךְ יהוה ׀ אֶת־
הַיָּם בְּרוּחַ קָדִים עַזָּה כָּל־הַלַּיְלָה וַיָּשֶׂם אֶת־הַיָּם לֶחָרָבָה וַיִּבָּקְעוּ
כב הַמָּיִם׃ וַיָּבֹאוּ בְנֵי־יִשְׂרָאֵל בְּתוֹךְ הַיָּם בַּיַּבָּשָׁה וְהַמַּיִם לָהֶם חוֹמָה
כג מִימִינָם וּמִשְּׂמֹאלָם׃ וַיִּרְדְּפוּ מִצְרַיִם וַיָּבֹאוּ אַחֲרֵיהֶם כֹּל סוּס פַּרְעֹה
כד רִכְבּוֹ וּפָרָשָׁיו אֶל־תּוֹךְ הַיָּם׃ וַיְהִי בְּאַשְׁמֹרֶת הַבֹּקֶר וַיַּשְׁקֵף יהוה אֶל־
כה מַחֲנֵה מִצְרַיִם בְּעַמּוּד אֵשׁ וְעָנָן וַיָּהָם אֵת מַחֲנֵה מִצְרָיִם׃ וַיָּסַר אֵת
אֹפַן מַרְכְּבֹתָיו וַיְנַהֲגֵהוּ בִּכְבֵדֻת וַיֹּאמֶר מִצְרַיִם אָנוּסָה מִפְּנֵי יִשְׂרָאֵל
כִּי יהוה נִלְחָם לָהֶם בְּמִצְרָיִם׃
כו וַיֹּאמֶר יהוה אֶל־מֹשֶׁה נְטֵה אֶת־יָדְךָ עַל־הַיָּם וְיָשֻׁבוּ הַמַּיִם עַל־ רביעי
כז מִצְרַיִם עַל־רִכְבּוֹ וְעַל־פָּרָשָׁיו׃ וַיֵּט מֹשֶׁה אֶת־יָדוֹ עַל־הַיָּם וַיָּשָׁב הַיָּם
לִפְנוֹת בֹּקֶר לְאֵיתָנוֹ וּמִצְרַיִם נָסִים לִקְרָאתוֹ וַיְנַעֵר יהוה אֶת־מִצְרַיִם
כח בְּתוֹךְ הַיָּם׃ וַיָּשֻׁבוּ הַמַּיִם וַיְכַסּוּ אֶת־הָרֶכֶב וְאֶת־הַפָּרָשִׁים לְכֹל חֵיל
כט פַּרְעֹה הַבָּאִים אַחֲרֵיהֶם בַּיָּם לֹא־נִשְׁאַר בָּהֶם עַד־אֶחָד׃ וּבְנֵי יִשְׂרָאֵל
הָלְכוּ בַיַּבָּשָׁה בְּתוֹךְ הַיָּם וְהַמַּיִם לָהֶם חֹמָה מִימִינָם וּמִשְּׂמֹאלָם׃
ל וַיּוֹשַׁע יהוה בַּיּוֹם הַהוּא אֶת־יִשְׂרָאֵל מִיַּד מִצְרָיִם וַיַּרְא יִשְׂרָאֵל אֶת־
לא מִצְרַיִם מֵת עַל־שְׂפַת הַיָּם׃ וַיַּרְא יִשְׂרָאֵל אֶת־הַיָּד הַגְּדֹלָה אֲשֶׁר עָשָׂה
יהוה בְּמִצְרַיִם וַיִּירְאוּ הָעָם אֶת־יהוה וַיַּאֲמִינוּ בַּיהוה וּבְמֹשֶׁה עַבְדּוֹ׃

15 1 And then, Moshe and the Israelites sang this song to the LORD: I will sing to
the LORD, for He has triumphed in glory; / horse and horseman He hurled
2 into the sea. / The LORD is my strength and song – / and now my salvation. /
3 This is my God, I will glorify Him, / my father's God, I will exalt Him. / The
4 LORD is a Master of war; / the LORD is His name. / Pharaoh's chariots and
army / He hurled into the sea; / the best of his officers / drowned in the Sea
5 of Reeds. / The deep waters covered them; / they sank to the depths like a
6 stone. / Your right hand, LORD, majestic in power, / Your right hand, LORD,
7 shatters the enemy. / In the greatness of Your majesty, You overthrew those
who rose against You. / You sent forth Your rage; it consumed them like
8 stubble. / By the blast of Your nostrils the waters heaped; / the surge stood
9 upright as a wall; / the deeps congealed at the heart of the sea. / The enemy
said, "I will give chase, will overtake, / I will divide the spoils. / My desire shall
gorge its fill of them. / I will draw my sword, / and my hand destroy them." /
10 You blew with Your wind; the sea covered over them. / They sank like lead
11 in mighty waters. / Who is like You, LORD, among the mighty? / Who is
12 like You – majestic in holiness, / awesome in glory, working wonders? / You
13 reached out Your right hand – / the earth swallowed them up. / In Your love,
You guided out the people You redeemed. / In Your strength, You led them
14 to Your holy abode. / Nations heard and they trembled; / terror seized the
15 Philistines. / The chiefs of Edom were dismayed, then, / Moav's leaders were
16 seized with trembling, / the people of Canaan melted away. / Dread, terror
fell upon them; / by Your arm's power they were stilled as stone – / until Your
17 people crossed, LORD, / until the people You acquired crossed over. / You
will bring them, You will plant them on the mountain, Your heritage – / the
place, LORD, that You made for Your dwelling, / the Sanctuary, LORD, that
18 19 Your hands established. / The LORD will reign for ever and all time. // This
they sang when Pharaoh's horses, chariots, and cavalry had gone into the sea /
and the LORD had brought the waters of the sea back over them / while the
Israelites had walked on dry land through the sea.

טו א אָז יָשִׁיר־מֹשֶׁה וּבְנֵי יִשְׂרָאֵל אֶת־הַשִּׁירָה הַזֹּאת לַיהוָה וַיֹּאמְרוּ
לֵאמֹר   אָשִׁירָה לַיהוָה כִּי־גָאֹה גָּאָה   סוּס
ב וְרֹכְבוֹ רָמָה בַיָּם: עָזִּי וְזִמְרָת יָהּ וַיְהִי־לִי
לִישׁוּעָה   זֶה אֵלִי וְאַנְוֵהוּ   אֱלֹהֵי
ג אָבִי וַאֲרֹמְמֶנְהוּ:   יְהוָה אִישׁ מִלְחָמָה יְהוָה
ד שְׁמוֹ:   מַרְכְּבֹת פַּרְעֹה וְחֵילוֹ יָרָה בַיָּם   וּמִבְחַר
ה שָׁלִשָׁיו טֻבְּעוּ בְיַם־סוּף: תְּהֹמֹת יְכַסְיֻמוּ יָרְדוּ בִמְצוֹלֹת
ו כְּמוֹ־אָבֶן: יְמִינְךָ יְהוָה נֶאְדָּרִי בַּכֹּחַ   יְמִינְךָ
ז יְהוָה תִּרְעַץ אוֹיֵב: וּבְרֹב גְּאוֹנְךָ תַּהֲרֹס
ח קָמֶיךָ   תְּשַׁלַּח חֲרֹנְךָ יֹאכְלֵמוֹ כַּקַּשׁ:   וּבְרוּחַ
אַפֶּיךָ נֶעֶרְמוּ מַיִם   נִצְּבוּ כְמוֹ־נֵד
ט נֹזְלִים   קָפְאוּ תְהֹמֹת בְּלֶב־יָם: אָמַר
אוֹיֵב אֶרְדֹּף אַשִּׂיג   אֲחַלֵּק שָׁלָל תִּמְלָאֵמוֹ
י נַפְשִׁי   אָרִיק חַרְבִּי תּוֹרִישֵׁמוֹ יָדִי: נָשַׁפְתָּ
בְרוּחֲךָ כִּסָּמוֹ יָם   צָלְלוּ כַּעוֹפֶרֶת בְּמַיִם
יא אַדִּירִים: מִי־כָמֹכָה בָּאֵלִם יְהוָה   מִי
כָּמֹכָה נֶאְדָּר בַּקֹּדֶשׁ   נוֹרָא תְהִלֹּת עֹשֵׂה
יב יג פֶלֶא: נָטִיתָ יְמִינְךָ תִּבְלָעֵמוֹ אָרֶץ: נָחִיתָ
בְחַסְדְּךָ עַם־זוּ גָּאָלְתָּ   נֵהַלְתָּ בְעָזְּךָ אֶל־נְוֵה
יד קָדְשֶׁךָ:   שָׁמְעוּ עַמִּים יִרְגָּזוּן   חִיל
טו אָחַז יֹשְׁבֵי פְּלָשֶׁת: אָז נִבְהֲלוּ אַלּוּפֵי
אֱדוֹם   אֵילֵי מוֹאָב יֹאחֲזֵמוֹ רָעַד   נָמֹגוּ
טז כֹּל יֹשְׁבֵי כְנָעַן: תִּפֹּל עֲלֵיהֶם אֵימָתָה
וָפַחַד   בִּגְדֹל זְרוֹעֲךָ יִדְּמוּ כָּאָבֶן   עַד־
יַעֲבֹר עַמְּךָ יְהוָה   עַד־יַעֲבֹר עַם־זוּ
יז קָנִיתָ:   תְּבִאֵמוֹ וְתִטָּעֵמוֹ בְּהַר נַחֲלָתְךָ   מָכוֹן
לְשִׁבְתְּךָ פָּעַלְתָּ יְהוָה   מִקְּדָשׁ אֲדֹנָי כּוֹנְנוּ
יח יט יָדֶיךָ:   יְהוָה יִמְלֹךְ לְעֹלָם וָעֶד: כִּי
בָא סוּס פַּרְעֹה בְּרִכְבּוֹ וּבְפָרָשָׁיו בַּיָּם   וַיָּשֶׁב יְהוָה עֲלֵהֶם אֶת־מֵי
הַיָּם   וּבְנֵי יִשְׂרָאֵל הָלְכוּ בַיַּבָּשָׁה בְּתוֹךְ   הַיָּם:

20 Then Miriam, the prophetess, sister of Aharon, took a tambourine in her
21 hand, and all the women followed her with tambourines and dance. And
Miriam led them in song: Sing to the LORD, for He has triumphed in glory; /
22 horse and horseman He hurled into the sea. Moshe then led the
Israelites from the Sea of Reeds out into the desert of Shur. For three days,
23 they journeyed across the desert without finding water. Eventually they
came to Mara, but they could not drink the water there because it was bitter;
24 because of this it was named Mara.[31] The people railed against Moshe – "What
25 are we to drink?" Moshe cried out to the LORD. And the LORD showed him a
piece of wood, which he threw into the water – and the water became sweet.
It was there that the LORD gave His people decree and law; it was there that
26 He put them to the test.[32] He said, "If you listen faithfully to the voice of the
LORD your God, doing what is right in His eyes, heeding His commands and
keeping His decrees, I will not bring on you any of the sicknesses I brought
27 on the Egyptians, for I am the LORD – your Healer." And then they
arrived at Eilim, where there were twelve springs and seventy date palms.
16 1 They encamped there by the water. They set out from Eilim, and on the
fifteenth day of the second month after leaving Egypt, the congregation of
2 Israel all arrived at the desert of Sin, between Eilim and Sinai. In the desert,
3 all the community started railing against Moshe and Aharon. The Israelites
said to them, "If only we had died by the LORD's hand in Egypt, when we sat
by the fleshpots and ate our fill of bread. Instead, you have brought us out
4 into this desert to kill the entire assembly by starvation." Then the
LORD said to Moshe, "I am going to rain down bread from heaven. Let the
people go out and gather enough for each day; I will test them to see whether
5 they will follow My law or not. On the sixth day, they will have to prepare
what they bring in. It will be twice as much as they gather on all other days."
6 So Moshe and Aharon told all the Israelites, "At evening you will know that it
7 was the LORD who brought you out of Egypt, and by morning you shall see
the LORD's glory, for He has heard you railing against Him. As for us, what are
8 we that you rail against us?" Then Moshe said, "In the evening, the LORD will
give you meat to eat, and in the morning bread to fill you, for He has heard
you railing against Him. We – what are we? It is not us you rail against, but the
9 LORD." Then Moshe said to Aharon, "Tell all the community of Israel to come
10 before the LORD, because He has heard your railing." As soon as Aharon had
spoken to the whole community of Israel, they looked toward the desert – and
the glory of the LORD appeared in the midst of cloud.
11 12 The LORD spoke to Moshe and said, "I have heard the Israelites' railing. Tell
them: At twilight you shall eat meat, and in the morning your fill of bread.
13 Then you will know that I am the LORD your God." That evening a flock of
quail flew in and covered the camp; next morning a layer of dew surrounded

---

31 | *Mara* means "bitter."

32 | This "test" apparently refers to the challenge that follows. Opinions vary regarding the "decree and law" – a phrase that the text does not clarify.

כ וַתִּקַּח מִרְיָם הַנְּבִיאָה אֲחוֹת אַהֲרֹן אֶת־הַתֹּף בְּיָדָהּ וַתֵּצֶאןָ כָל־
כא הַנָּשִׁים אַחֲרֶיהָ בְּתֻפִּים וּבִמְחֹלֹת׃ וַתַּעַן לָהֶם מִרְיָם שִׁירוּ לַיהוה כִּי־
כב גָאֹה גָּאָה סוּס וְרֹכְבוֹ רָמָה בַיָּם׃ וַיַּסַּע מֹשֶׁה אֶת־יִשְׂרָאֵל
מִיַּם־סוּף וַיֵּצְאוּ אֶל־מִדְבַּר־שׁוּר וַיֵּלְכוּ שְׁלֹשֶׁת־יָמִים בַּמִּדְבָּר וְלֹא־
כג מָצְאוּ מָיִם׃ וַיָּבֹאוּ מָרָתָה וְלֹא יָכְלוּ לִשְׁתֹּת מַיִם מִמָּרָה כִּי מָרִים הֵם
כד עַל־כֵּן קָרָא־שְׁמָהּ מָרָה׃ וַיִּלֹּנוּ הָעָם עַל־מֹשֶׁה לֵּאמֹר מַה־נִּשְׁתֶּה׃
כה וַיִּצְעַק אֶל־יהוה וַיּוֹרֵהוּ יהוה עֵץ וַיַּשְׁלֵךְ אֶל־הַמַּיִם וַיִּמְתְּקוּ הַמָּיִם
כו שָׁם שָׂם לוֹ חֹק וּמִשְׁפָּט וְשָׁם נִסָּהוּ׃ וַיֹּאמֶר אִם־שָׁמוֹעַ תִּשְׁמַע לְקוֹל ׀
יהוה אֱלֹהֶיךָ וְהַיָּשָׁר בְּעֵינָיו תַּעֲשֶׂה וְהַאֲזַנְתָּ לְמִצְוֺתָיו וְשָׁמַרְתָּ כָּל־
חֻקָּיו כָּל־הַמַּחֲלָה אֲשֶׁר־שַׂמְתִּי בְמִצְרַיִם לֹא־אָשִׂים עָלֶיךָ כִּי אֲנִי
כז יהוה רֹפְאֶךָ׃ וַיָּבֹאוּ אֵילִמָה וְשָׁם שְׁתֵּים עֶשְׂרֵה עֵינֹת מַיִם חמישי
טז א וְשִׁבְעִים תְּמָרִים וַיַּחֲנוּ־שָׁם עַל־הַמָּיִם׃ וַיִּסְעוּ מֵאֵילִם וַיָּבֹאוּ כָּל־עֲדַת
בְּנֵי־יִשְׂרָאֵל אֶל־מִדְבַּר־סִין אֲשֶׁר בֵּין־אֵילִם וּבֵין סִינָי בַּחֲמִשָּׁה עָשָׂר
ב יוֹם לַחֹדֶשׁ הַשֵּׁנִי לְצֵאתָם מֵאֶרֶץ מִצְרָיִם׃ וילינו כָּל־עֲדַת בְּנֵי־יִשְׂרָאֵל וַיִּלּוֹנוּ
ג עַל־מֹשֶׁה וְעַל־אַהֲרֹן בַּמִּדְבָּר׃ וַיֹּאמְרוּ אֲלֵהֶם בְּנֵי יִשְׂרָאֵל מִי־יִתֵּן
מוּתֵנוּ בְיַד־יהוה בְּאֶרֶץ מִצְרַיִם בְּשִׁבְתֵּנוּ עַל־סִיר הַבָּשָׂר בְּאָכְלֵנוּ
לֶחֶם לָשֹׂבַע כִּי־הוֹצֵאתֶם אֹתָנוּ אֶל־הַמִּדְבָּר הַזֶּה לְהָמִית אֶת־כָּל־
ד הַקָּהָל הַזֶּה בָּרָעָב׃ וַיֹּאמֶר יהוה אֶל־מֹשֶׁה הִנְנִי מַמְטִיר יב
לָכֶם לֶחֶם מִן־הַשָּׁמָיִם וְיָצָא הָעָם וְלָקְטוּ דְּבַר־יוֹם בְּיוֹמוֹ לְמַעַן אֲנַסֶּנּוּ
ה הֲיֵלֵךְ בְּתוֹרָתִי אִם־לֹא׃ וְהָיָה בַּיּוֹם הַשִּׁשִּׁי וְהֵכִינוּ אֵת אֲשֶׁר־יָבִיאוּ
ו וְהָיָה מִשְׁנֶה עַל אֲשֶׁר־יִלְקְטוּ יוֹם ׀ יוֹם׃ וַיֹּאמֶר מֹשֶׁה וְאַהֲרֹן אֶל־כָּל־
ז בְּנֵי יִשְׂרָאֵל עֶרֶב וִידַעְתֶּם כִּי יהוה הוֹצִיא אֶתְכֶם מֵאֶרֶץ מִצְרָיִם׃ וּבֹקֶר
וּרְאִיתֶם אֶת־כְּבוֹד יהוה בְּשָׁמְעוֹ אֶת־תְּלֻנֹּתֵיכֶם עַל־יהוה וְנַחְנוּ מָה
ח כִּי תלונו עָלֵינוּ׃ וַיֹּאמֶר מֹשֶׁה בְּתֵת יהוה לָכֶם בָּעֶרֶב בָּשָׂר לֶאֱכֹל תַלִּינוּ
וְלֶחֶם בַּבֹּקֶר לִשְׂבֹּעַ בִּשְׁמֹעַ יהוה אֶת־תְּלֻנֹּתֵיכֶם אֲשֶׁר־אַתֶּם מַלִּינִם
ט עָלָיו וְנַחְנוּ מָה לֹא־עָלֵינוּ תְלֻנֹּתֵיכֶם כִּי עַל־יהוה׃ וַיֹּאמֶר מֹשֶׁה אֶל־
אַהֲרֹן אֱמֹר אֶל־כָּל־עֲדַת בְּנֵי יִשְׂרָאֵל קִרְבוּ לִפְנֵי יהוה כִּי שָׁמַע אֵת
י תְּלֻנֹּתֵיכֶם׃ וַיְהִי כְּדַבֵּר אַהֲרֹן אֶל־כָּל־עֲדַת בְּנֵי־יִשְׂרָאֵל וַיִּפְנוּ אֶל־
הַמִּדְבָּר וְהִנֵּה כְּבוֹד יהוה נִרְאָה בֶּעָנָן׃
יא יב וַיְדַבֵּר יהוה אֶל־מֹשֶׁה לֵּאמֹר׃ שָׁמַעְתִּי אֶת־תְּלוּנֹּת בְּנֵי יִשְׂרָאֵל ששי
דַּבֵּר אֲלֵהֶם לֵאמֹר בֵּין הָעַרְבַּיִם תֹּאכְלוּ בָשָׂר וּבַבֹּקֶר תִּשְׂבְּעוּ־לָחֶם
יג וִידַעְתֶּם כִּי אֲנִי יהוה אֱלֹהֵיכֶם׃ וַיְהִי בָעֶרֶב וַתַּעַל הַשְּׂלָו וַתְּכַס אֶת־

14 the camp. When the dew covering lifted, fine flakes covered the floor of
15 the desert like fine frost on the ground. When the Israelites saw it, they
asked one another, "What[33] is it?" for they did not recognize it. Moshe said
16 to them, "This is the bread the LORD has given you to eat. This is what the
LORD has instructed: Each of you gather as much as you need, an omer[34] for
17 every person; each take enough for all the people in your tent." The people
18 of Israel did so. Some gathered more, others less. But when they measured it
with an omer measure, those who had gathered much had none left over, and
those who gathered but little did not fall short. All had gathered as much as
19 20 they could eat. "Let no one leave any over for the morning," said Moshe; but
they did not listen to Moshe. Some of them left part of it till morning, and
21 it became worm infested and stank. Moshe was enraged with them. Every
morning they gathered it, all as much as they could eat, and when the sun
22 grew hot, it melted away. When the sixth day came, they gathered a double
portion, two omer each. All the leaders of the community came and reported
23 this to Moshe. "This," he told them, "is what the LORD has said: Tomorrow
is a day of rest, a holy Sabbath to the LORD. Bake now what you need to bake
and cook what you need to cook. Whatever is left, keep carefully aside for the
24 morning." So they put it aside until the morning, as Moshe had instructed
25 them, and it did not stink, nor did worms infest it. And Moshe said, "Today,
eat this, for today is a Sabbath to the LORD; today you will not find it on the
26 ground. Six days shall you gather it, but on the seventh day, the Sabbath, it
27 will not be there." Some people did go out to gather it on the seventh day; but
28 they found none. Then the LORD said to Moshe, "How long will you
29 refuse to keep My commandments and laws? Understand that the LORD has
given you a Sabbath – that is why He gave you two days' bread on the sixth
day. You shall each rest where you are: let no man depart from where he is on
30 31 the seventh day." So the people rested on the seventh day. The House of Israel
named it manna.[35] It looked like white coriander seeds, and tasted like wafers
32 made with honey. Moshe said, "This is what the LORD commands: Let an
omer of it be kept carefully aside for your descendants, that they may see the
33 bread I fed you in the desert when I brought you out of Egypt." Moshe said
to Aharon, "Take an urn, put an omer of manna in it, and place it before the
34 LORD to be kept for future generations." As the LORD commanded Moshe,
35 so Aharon placed it before the Ark of Testimony[36] to be kept with care. The
Israelites ate manna for forty years, until they came to the land where they
could settle down. They ate the manna until they came to the border of
36 Canaan. An omer is a tenth of an ephah.[37]

---

33 | Hebrew *man*; cf. verse 31: "The House of Israel named it *man* (manna)."

34 | A solid measure somewhat larger than the equivalent of two liters or half a gallon.

35 | See note on verse 15.

36 | Literally "before the Testimony." See 25:22, 32:15. It would seem that Aharon performed this action only after the construction of the Ark.

37 | See note on verse 16.

יד הַמַּחֲנֶה וּבַבֹּקֶר הָיְתָה שִׁכְבַת הַטַּל סָבִיב לַמַּחֲנֶה: וַתַּעַל שִׁכְבַת הַטָּל
טו וְהִנֵּה עַל־פְּנֵי הַמִּדְבָּר דַּק מְחֻסְפָּס דַּק כַּכְּפֹר עַל־הָאָרֶץ: וַיִּרְאוּ בְנֵי־
יִשְׂרָאֵל וַיֹּאמְרוּ אִישׁ אֶל־אָחִיו מָן הוּא כִּי לֹא יָדְעוּ מַה־הוּא וַיֹּאמֶר
טז מֹשֶׁה אֲלֵהֶם הוּא הַלֶּחֶם אֲשֶׁר נָתַן יהוה לָכֶם לְאָכְלָה: זֶה הַדָּבָר
אֲשֶׁר צִוָּה יהוה לִקְטוּ מִמֶּנּוּ אִישׁ לְפִי אָכְלוֹ עֹמֶר לַגֻּלְגֹּלֶת מִסְפַּר
יז נַפְשֹׁתֵיכֶם אִישׁ לַאֲשֶׁר בְּאָהֳלוֹ תִּקָּחוּ: וַיַּעֲשׂוּ־כֵן בְּנֵי יִשְׂרָאֵל וַיִּלְקְטוּ
יח הַמַּרְבֶּה וְהַמַּמְעִיט: וַיָּמֹדּוּ בָעֹמֶר וְלֹא הֶעְדִּיף הַמַּרְבֶּה וְהַמַּמְעִיט לֹא
יט הֶחְסִיר אִישׁ לְפִי־אָכְלוֹ לָקָטוּ: וַיֹּאמֶר מֹשֶׁה אֲלֵהֶם אִישׁ אַל־יוֹתֵר
כ מִמֶּנּוּ עַד־בֹּקֶר: וְלֹא־שָׁמְעוּ אֶל־מֹשֶׁה וַיּוֹתִרוּ אֲנָשִׁים מִמֶּנּוּ עַד־בֹּקֶר
כא וַיָּרֻם תּוֹלָעִים וַיִּבְאַשׁ וַיִּקְצֹף עֲלֵהֶם מֹשֶׁה: וַיִּלְקְטוּ אֹתוֹ בַּבֹּקֶר בַּבֹּקֶר
כב אִישׁ כְּפִי אָכְלוֹ וְחַם הַשֶּׁמֶשׁ וְנָמָס: וַיְהִי ׀ בַּיּוֹם הַשִּׁשִּׁי לָקְטוּ לֶחֶם
מִשְׁנֶה שְׁנֵי הָעֹמֶר לָאֶחָד וַיָּבֹאוּ כָּל־נְשִׂיאֵי הָעֵדָה וַיַּגִּידוּ לְמֹשֶׁה:
כג וַיֹּאמֶר אֲלֵהֶם הוּא אֲשֶׁר דִּבֶּר יהוה שַׁבָּתוֹן שַׁבַּת־קֹדֶשׁ לַיהוה מָחָר
אֵת אֲשֶׁר־תֹּאפוּ אֵפוּ וְאֵת אֲשֶׁר־תְּבַשְּׁלוּ בַּשֵּׁלוּ וְאֵת כָּל־הָעֹדֵף הַנִּיחוּ
כד לָכֶם לְמִשְׁמֶרֶת עַד־הַבֹּקֶר: וַיַּנִּיחוּ אֹתוֹ עַד־הַבֹּקֶר כַּאֲשֶׁר צִוָּה מֹשֶׁה
כה וְלֹא הִבְאִישׁ וְרִמָּה לֹא־הָיְתָה־בּוֹ: וַיֹּאמֶר מֹשֶׁה אִכְלֻהוּ הַיּוֹם כִּי־שַׁבָּת
כו הַיּוֹם לַיהוה הַיּוֹם לֹא תִמְצָאֻהוּ בַּשָּׂדֶה: שֵׁשֶׁת יָמִים תִּלְקְטֻהוּ וּבַיּוֹם
כז הַשְּׁבִיעִי שַׁבָּת לֹא יִהְיֶה־בּוֹ: וַיְהִי בַּיּוֹם הַשְּׁבִיעִי יָצְאוּ מִן־הָעָם לִלְקֹט
כח וְלֹא מָצָאוּ: וַיֹּאמֶר יהוה אֶל־מֹשֶׁה עַד־אָנָה מֵאַנְתֶּם יג
כט לִשְׁמֹר מִצְוֹתַי וְתוֹרֹתָי: רְאוּ כִּי־יהוה נָתַן לָכֶם הַשַּׁבָּת עַל־כֵּן הוּא
נֹתֵן לָכֶם בַּיּוֹם הַשִּׁשִּׁי לֶחֶם יוֹמָיִם שְׁבוּ ׀ אִישׁ תַּחְתָּיו אַל־יֵצֵא אִישׁ
ל לא מִמְּקֹמוֹ בַּיּוֹם הַשְּׁבִיעִי: וַיִּשְׁבְּתוּ הָעָם בַּיּוֹם הַשְּׁבִעִי: וַיִּקְרְאוּ בֵית־
יִשְׂרָאֵל אֶת־שְׁמוֹ מָן וְהוּא כְּזֶרַע גַּד לָבָן וְטַעְמוֹ כְּצַפִּיחִת בִּדְבָשׁ:
לב וַיֹּאמֶר מֹשֶׁה זֶה הַדָּבָר אֲשֶׁר צִוָּה יהוה מְלֹא הָעֹמֶר מִמֶּנּוּ לְמִשְׁמֶרֶת
לְדֹרֹתֵיכֶם לְמַעַן ׀ יִרְאוּ אֶת־הַלֶּחֶם אֲשֶׁר הֶאֱכַלְתִּי אֶתְכֶם בַּמִּדְבָּר
לג בְּהוֹצִיאִי אֶתְכֶם מֵאֶרֶץ מִצְרָיִם: וַיֹּאמֶר מֹשֶׁה אֶל־אַהֲרֹן קַח צִנְצֶנֶת
אַחַת וְתֶן־שָׁמָּה מְלֹא־הָעֹמֶר מָן וְהַנַּח אֹתוֹ לִפְנֵי יהוה לְמִשְׁמֶרֶת
לד לְדֹרֹתֵיכֶם: כַּאֲשֶׁר צִוָּה יהוה אֶל־מֹשֶׁה וַיַּנִּיחֵהוּ אַהֲרֹן לִפְנֵי הָעֵדֻת
לה לְמִשְׁמָרֶת: וּבְנֵי יִשְׂרָאֵל אָכְלוּ אֶת־הַמָּן אַרְבָּעִים שָׁנָה עַד־בֹּאָם אֶל־
לו אֶרֶץ נוֹשָׁבֶת אֶת־הַמָּן אָכְלוּ עַד־בֹּאָם אֶל־קְצֵה אֶרֶץ כְּנָעַן: וְהָעֹמֶר
עֲשִׂרִית הָאֵיפָה הוּא:

17 1 All the community of Israel moved on after that from the desert of Sin,
traveling from place to place as the LORD guided them, and they camped at
2 Refidim, but there was no water there for the people to drink. The people
started to wrangle with Moshe. "Give us water to drink," they raged. "Why do
3 you wrangle with me?" asked Moshe. "Why are you testing the LORD?" But
the people were thirsty for water. They railed against Moshe, "Why did you
bring us out of Egypt? Was it to kill me, my children, and all my livestock by
4 thirst?" "What shall I do with this people?" Moshe cried to the LORD. "Another
5 moment and they will stone me." The LORD answered Moshe, "Walk out to
face the people taking some of the elders of Israel with you. Take the staff with
6 which you struck the Nile in your hand, and go. I will be there before you by
the rock at Ḥorev. Strike the rock; water will come out of it and the people will
7 drink." And that is what Moshe did, before the eyes of the elders of Israel. He
named the place Masa and Meriva, because the people had quarreled[38] and
had tested[39] the LORD, demanding, "Is the LORD among us or not?"
8 9 Then, at Refidim, Amalek came and attacked Israel. Moshe said to Yehoshua,
"Choose men for us, and go out and do battle against Amalek. Tomorrow
10 I will stand on top of the hill with the staff of God in my hand." Yehoshua
fought the Amalekites as Moshe had directed him, while Moshe, Aharon,
11 and Ḥur climbed to the top of the hill. Whenever Moshe held his hand high,
the Israelites prevailed, but whenever he let his hand drop, the Amalekites
12 prevailed. But Moshe's hands grew heavy. So they took a stone and placed it
under him and he sat, while Aharon and Ḥur held up his hands, one on each
13 side, so that his hands held true until sunset. And Yehoshua overcame Amalek
and his people by the sword.
14 Then the LORD said to Moshe, "Write this as a memorial on a scroll, and
commit it to Yehoshua's ears: I will erase the memory of Amalek, utterly,
15 from under the heavens." Moshe built an altar and named it "The LORD Is
16 My Banner," saying, "There is a hand on the LORD's throne.[40] The LORD will
be at war with Amalek throughout the ages."
18 1 Moshe's father-in-law Yitro, priest of Midyan, heard about all that God had YITRO
done for Moshe and for His people Israel when the LORD brought Israel out
2 of Egypt. Yitro had received Moshe's wife Tzipora after he had sent her home,
3 together with her two sons. One was named Gershom, for Moshe had said, "I
4 have been a stranger in a foreign land,"[41] and the other, Eliezer, for he had said,
5 "My father's God has helped me, saving me from Pharaoh's sword."[42] And now
Moshe's father-in-law Yitro came to Moshe in the desert, bringing his sons
6 and his wife, to where he was encamped by the mountain of God. Yitro sent
word to Moshe, "I am coming to you – your father-in-law Yitro – together

---

38 | *Meriva* means "quarrel."
39 | *Masa* means "test."
40 | Interpretations of this proclamation vary. Many commentaries understand the image of a raised hand as symbolizing an oath; cf. Genesis 24:2; Deuteronomy 32:40.
41 | See note on 2:22.
42 | *Eliezer* literally means "God has helped."

יז א וַיִּסְעוּ כָּל־עֲדַת בְּנֵי־יִשְׂרָאֵל מִמִּדְבַּר־סִין לְמַסְעֵיהֶם עַל־פִּי יְהוָה שביעי
ב וַיַּחֲנוּ בִּרְפִידִים וְאֵין מַיִם לִשְׁתֹּת הָעָם׃ וַיָּרֶב הָעָם עִם־מֹשֶׁה וַיֹּאמְרוּ
תְּנוּ־לָנוּ מַיִם וְנִשְׁתֶּה וַיֹּאמֶר לָהֶם מֹשֶׁה מַה־תְּרִיבוּן עִמָּדִי מַה־תְּנַסּוּן
ג אֶת־יְהוָה׃ וַיִּצְמָא שָׁם הָעָם לַמַּיִם וַיָּלֶן הָעָם עַל־מֹשֶׁה וַיֹּאמֶר לָמָּה זֶּה
ד הֶעֱלִיתָנוּ מִמִּצְרַיִם לְהָמִית אֹתִי וְאֶת־בָּנַי וְאֶת־מִקְנַי בַּצָּמָא׃ וַיִּצְעַק
מֹשֶׁה אֶל־יְהוָה לֵאמֹר מָה אֶעֱשֶׂה לָעָם הַזֶּה עוֹד מְעַט וּסְקָלֻנִי׃
ה וַיֹּאמֶר יְהוָה אֶל־מֹשֶׁה עֲבֹר לִפְנֵי הָעָם וְקַח אִתְּךָ מִזִּקְנֵי יִשְׂרָאֵל
ו וּמַטְּךָ אֲשֶׁר הִכִּיתָ בּוֹ אֶת־הַיְאֹר קַח בְּיָדְךָ וְהָלָכְתָּ׃ הִנְנִי עֹמֵד לְפָנֶיךָ
שָּׁם ׀ עַל־הַצּוּר בְּחֹרֵב וְהִכִּיתָ בַצּוּר וְיָצְאוּ מִמֶּנּוּ מַיִם וְשָׁתָה הָעָם
ז וַיַּעַשׂ כֵּן מֹשֶׁה לְעֵינֵי זִקְנֵי יִשְׂרָאֵל׃ וַיִּקְרָא שֵׁם הַמָּקוֹם מַסָּה וּמְרִיבָה
עַל־רִיב ׀ בְּנֵי יִשְׂרָאֵל וְעַל נַסֹּתָם אֶת־יְהוָה לֵאמֹר הֲיֵשׁ יְהוָה בְּקִרְבֵּנוּ
אִם־אָיִן׃

ח ט וַיָּבֹא עֲמָלֵק וַיִּלָּחֶם עִם־יִשְׂרָאֵל בִּרְפִידִם׃ וַיֹּאמֶר מֹשֶׁה אֶל־יְהוֹשֻׁעַ
בְּחַר־לָנוּ אֲנָשִׁים וְצֵא הִלָּחֵם בַּעֲמָלֵק מָחָר אָנֹכִי נִצָּב עַל־רֹאשׁ
י הַגִּבְעָה וּמַטֵּה הָאֱלֹהִים בְּיָדִי׃ וַיַּעַשׂ יְהוֹשֻׁעַ כַּאֲשֶׁר אָמַר־לוֹ מֹשֶׁה
יא לְהִלָּחֵם בַּעֲמָלֵק וּמֹשֶׁה אַהֲרֹן וְחוּר עָלוּ רֹאשׁ הַגִּבְעָה׃ וְהָיָה כַּאֲשֶׁר
יב יָרִים מֹשֶׁה יָדוֹ וְגָבַר יִשְׂרָאֵל וְכַאֲשֶׁר יָנִיחַ יָדוֹ וְגָבַר עֲמָלֵק׃ וִידֵי מֹשֶׁה
כְּבֵדִים וַיִּקְחוּ־אֶבֶן וַיָּשִׂימוּ תַחְתָּיו וַיֵּשֶׁב עָלֶיהָ וְאַהֲרֹן וְחוּר תָּמְכוּ
יג בְיָדָיו מִזֶּה אֶחָד וּמִזֶּה אֶחָד וַיְהִי יָדָיו אֱמוּנָה עַד־בֹּא הַשָּׁמֶשׁ׃ וַיַּחֲלֹשׁ
יְהוֹשֻׁעַ אֶת־עֲמָלֵק וְאֶת־עַמּוֹ לְפִי־חָרֶב׃

יד וַיֹּאמֶר יְהוָה אֶל־מֹשֶׁה כְּתֹב זֹאת זִכָּרוֹן בַּסֵּפֶר וְשִׂים בְּאָזְנֵי יְהוֹשֻׁעַ מפטיר
טו כִּי־מָחֹה אֶמְחֶה אֶת־זֵכֶר עֲמָלֵק מִתַּחַת הַשָּׁמָיִם׃ וַיִּבֶן מֹשֶׁה מִזְבֵּחַ
טז וַיִּקְרָא שְׁמוֹ יְהוָה ׀ נִסִּי׃ וַיֹּאמֶר כִּי־יָד עַל־כֵּס יָהּ מִלְחָמָה לַיהוָה
בַּעֲמָלֵק מִדֹּר דֹּר׃

יח א וַיִּשְׁמַע יִתְרוֹ כֹהֵן מִדְיָן חֹתֵן מֹשֶׁה אֵת כָּל־אֲשֶׁר עָשָׂה אֱלֹהִים לְמֹשֶׁה יד יתרו
ב וּלְיִשְׂרָאֵל עַמּוֹ כִּי־הוֹצִיא יְהוָה אֶת־יִשְׂרָאֵל מִמִּצְרָיִם׃ וַיִּקַּח יִתְרוֹ חֹתֵן
ג מֹשֶׁה אֶת־צִפֹּרָה אֵשֶׁת מֹשֶׁה אַחַר שִׁלּוּחֶיהָ׃ וְאֵת שְׁנֵי בָנֶיהָ אֲשֶׁר שֵׁם
ד הָאֶחָד גֵּרְשֹׁם כִּי אָמַר גֵּר הָיִיתִי בְּאֶרֶץ נָכְרִיָּה׃ וְשֵׁם הָאֶחָד אֱלִיעֶזֶר
ה כִּי־אֱלֹהֵי אָבִי בְּעֶזְרִי וַיַּצִּלֵנִי מֵחֶרֶב פַּרְעֹה׃ וַיָּבֹא יִתְרוֹ חֹתֵן מֹשֶׁה וּבָנָיו
וְאִשְׁתּוֹ אֶל־מֹשֶׁה אֶל־הַמִּדְבָּר אֲשֶׁר־הוּא חֹנֶה שָׁם הַר הָאֱלֹהִים׃
ו וַיֹּאמֶר אֶל־מֹשֶׁה אֲנִי חֹתֶנְךָ יִתְרוֹ בָּא אֵלֶיךָ וְאִשְׁתְּךָ וּשְׁנֵי בָנֶיהָ עִמָּהּ׃

7 with your wife and both of your sons." Moshe went out to greet his father-in-
law and bowed down and kissed him. Each asked after the other's welfare, and
8 they went inside the tent. And Moshe told his father-in-law all that the LORD
had done to Pharaoh and the Egyptians, for Israel's sake, all the hardship they
9 had encountered along the way, and how the LORD had rescued them. Yitro
delighted in all the good that the LORD had done for Israel, in His liberating
10 them from the Egyptians, and said, "Blessed be the LORD who has rescued
you from Egypt and Pharaoh and liberated the people from the Egyptians'
11 hands. Now I know that the LORD is greater than all gods – for He brought
12 upon them what they schemed against others." Then Yitro brought a burnt
offering and sacrifices to God. And Aharon and all the elders of Israel came
13 to break bread with Moshe's father-in-law before God. The next day Moshe
sat to serve the people as judge. From morning to evening the people stood
14 before him. When Moshe's father-in-law saw everything Moshe did for the
people, he asked, "What is this that you do for the people? Why do you sit
15 alone while all the people stand over you from morning to evening?" "The
16 people come to me to inquire of God," Moshe replied. "When they have a
dispute, they come to me and I judge between one neighbor and another,
17 and I make God's laws and teachings known." Moshe's father-in-law said
18 to him, "What you are doing is not good. You will be worn away, and this
people along with you. It is too heavy a burden for you. You cannot carry it
19 alone. Now listen to me, let me advise you; and may God be with you. You
20 speak for the people before God, and bring their concerns to Him. And
you must acquaint them with His precepts and laws, and make known to
21 them the path they are to walk and the way they must act. You, as well, must
seek out among the people capable men – God-fearing, trustworthy men,
who despise corruption; and appoint them over the people as leaders of
22 thousands, hundreds, fifties, and tens. Have them serve as daily judges for
the people; let them bring the major cases to you, but judge the minor ones
themselves. In this way they will lighten your load, and bear it together with
23 you. If you do this, and God so commands, then you will endure, and all these
24 people will be able to go home in peace." Moshe listened to his father-in-law
25 and did all that he said. Moshe chose capable men from all Israel and made
them chiefs over the people, leaders of thousands, hundreds, fifties, and tens.
26 They judged the people every day. Any major case they brought to Moshe,
27 but they decided every minor matter themselves. Then Moshe parted from
his father-in-law, and the latter went forth, back to his own land.

ז וַיֵּצֵא מֹשֶׁה לִקְרַאת חֹתְנוֹ וַיִּשְׁתַּחוּ וַיִּשַּׁק־לוֹ וַיִּשְׁאֲלוּ אִישׁ־לְרֵעֵהוּ
ח לְשָׁלוֹם וַיָּבֹאוּ הָאֹהֱלָה: וַיְסַפֵּר מֹשֶׁה לְחֹתְנוֹ אֵת כׇּל־אֲשֶׁר עָשָׂה יהוה
לְפַרְעֹה וּלְמִצְרַיִם עַל אוֹדֹת יִשְׂרָאֵל אֵת כׇּל־הַתְּלָאָה אֲשֶׁר מְצָאָתַם
ט בַּדֶּרֶךְ וַיַּצִּלֵם יהוה: וַיִּחַדְּ יִתְרוֹ עַל כׇּל־הַטּוֹבָה אֲשֶׁר־עָשָׂה יהוה
י לְיִשְׂרָאֵל אֲשֶׁר הִצִּילוֹ מִיַּד מִצְרָיִם: וַיֹּאמֶר יִתְרוֹ בָּרוּךְ יהוה אֲשֶׁר
הִצִּיל אֶתְכֶם מִיַּד מִצְרַיִם וּמִיַּד פַּרְעֹה אֲשֶׁר הִצִּיל אֶת־הָעָם מִתַּחַת
יא יַד־מִצְרָיִם: עַתָּה יָדַעְתִּי כִּי־גָדוֹל יהוה מִכׇּל־הָאֱלֹהִים כִּי בַדָּבָר אֲשֶׁר
יב זָדוּ עֲלֵיהֶם: וַיִּקַּח יִתְרוֹ חֹתֵן מֹשֶׁה עֹלָה וּזְבָחִים לֵאלֹהִים וַיָּבֹא אַהֲרֹן
יג וְכֹל ׀ זִקְנֵי יִשְׂרָאֵל לֶאֱכׇל־לֶחֶם עִם־חֹתֵן מֹשֶׁה לִפְנֵי הָאֱלֹהִים: וַיְהִי שני
מִמׇּחֳרָת וַיֵּשֶׁב מֹשֶׁה לִשְׁפֹּט אֶת־הָעָם וַיַּעֲמֹד הָעָם עַל־מֹשֶׁה מִן־
יד הַבֹּקֶר עַד־הָעָרֶב: וַיַּרְא חֹתֵן מֹשֶׁה אֵת כׇּל־אֲשֶׁר־הוּא עֹשֶׂה לָעָם
וַיֹּאמֶר מָה־הַדָּבָר הַזֶּה אֲשֶׁר אַתָּה עֹשֶׂה לָעָם מַדּוּעַ אַתָּה יוֹשֵׁב לְבַדֶּךָ
טו וְכׇל־הָעָם נִצָּב עָלֶיךָ מִן־בֹּקֶר עַד־עָרֶב: וַיֹּאמֶר מֹשֶׁה לְחֹתְנוֹ כִּי־יָבֹא
טז אֵלַי הָעָם לִדְרֹשׁ אֱלֹהִים: כִּי־יִהְיֶה לָהֶם דָּבָר בָּא אֵלַי וְשָׁפַטְתִּי בֵּין
יז אִישׁ וּבֵין רֵעֵהוּ וְהוֹדַעְתִּי אֶת־חֻקֵּי הָאֱלֹהִים וְאֶת־תּוֹרֹתָיו: וַיֹּאמֶר
יח חֹתֵן מֹשֶׁה אֵלָיו לֹא־טוֹב הַדָּבָר אֲשֶׁר אַתָּה עֹשֶׂה: נָבֹל תִּבֹּל גַּם־
אַתָּה גַּם־הָעָם הַזֶּה אֲשֶׁר עִמָּךְ כִּי־כָבֵד מִמְּךָ הַדָּבָר לֹא־תוּכַל עֲשֹׂהוּ
יט לְבַדֶּךָ: עַתָּה שְׁמַע בְּקֹלִי אִיעָצְךָ וִיהִי אֱלֹהִים עִמָּךְ הֱיֵה אַתָּה לָעָם
כ מוּל הָאֱלֹהִים וְהֵבֵאתָ אַתָּה אֶת־הַדְּבָרִים אֶל־הָאֱלֹהִים: וְהִזְהַרְתָּה
אֶתְהֶם אֶת־הַחֻקִּים וְאֶת־הַתּוֹרֹת וְהוֹדַעְתָּ לָהֶם אֶת־הַדֶּרֶךְ יֵלְכוּ
כא בָהּ וְאֶת־הַמַּעֲשֶׂה אֲשֶׁר יַעֲשׂוּן: וְאַתָּה תֶחֱזֶה מִכׇּל־הָעָם אַנְשֵׁי־חַיִל
יִרְאֵי אֱלֹהִים אַנְשֵׁי אֱמֶת שֹׂנְאֵי בָצַע וְשַׂמְתָּ עֲלֵהֶם שָׂרֵי אֲלָפִים שָׂרֵי
כב מֵאוֹת שָׂרֵי חֲמִשִּׁים וְשָׂרֵי עֲשָׂרֹת: וְשָׁפְטוּ אֶת־הָעָם בְּכׇל־עֵת וְהָיָה
כׇּל־הַדָּבָר הַגָּדֹל יָבִיאוּ אֵלֶיךָ וְכׇל־הַדָּבָר הַקָּטֹן יִשְׁפְּטוּ־הֵם וְהָקֵל
כג מֵעָלֶיךָ וְנָשְׂאוּ אִתָּךְ: אִם אֶת־הַדָּבָר הַזֶּה תַּעֲשֶׂה וְצִוְּךָ אֱלֹהִים וְיָכׇלְתָּ
כד עֲמֹד וְגַם כׇּל־הָעָם הַזֶּה עַל־מְקֹמוֹ יָבֹא בְשָׁלוֹם: וַיִּשְׁמַע מֹשֶׁה לְקוֹל שלישי
כה חֹתְנוֹ וַיַּעַשׂ כֹּל אֲשֶׁר אָמָר: וַיִּבְחַר מֹשֶׁה אַנְשֵׁי־חַיִל מִכׇּל־יִשְׂרָאֵל
וַיִּתֵּן אֹתָם רָאשִׁים עַל־הָעָם שָׂרֵי אֲלָפִים שָׂרֵי מֵאוֹת שָׂרֵי חֲמִשִּׁים
כו וְשָׂרֵי עֲשָׂרֹת: וְשָׁפְטוּ אֶת־הָעָם בְּכׇל־עֵת אֶת־הַדָּבָר הַקָּשֶׁה יְבִיאוּן
כז אֶל־מֹשֶׁה וְכׇל־הַדָּבָר הַקָּטֹן יִשְׁפּוּטוּ הֵם: וַיְשַׁלַּח מֹשֶׁה אֶת־חֹתְנוֹ
וַיֵּלֶךְ לוֹ אֶל־אַרְצוֹ:

19 1 On the first day of the third month after the Israelites had left Egypt they
2 came to the Sinai Desert. Setting out from Refidim they had arrived at the
Sinai Desert, encamping in the wilderness, and there Israel camped, facing
3 the mountain, while Moshe went up to God. And the Lord called to him
from the mountain: "This is what you shall say to the House of Yaakov, what
4 you shall tell the people of Israel: You yourselves have seen what I did to the
5 Egyptians: how I lifted you up on eagles' wings and brought you to Me. Now,
if you faithfully heed My voice and keep My covenant, you will be My treasure
6 among all the peoples, although the whole earth is Mine. A kingdom of priests
and a holy nation you shall be to Me. These are the words you must speak
7 to the Israelites." So Moshe came and summoned the elders of the people,
8 and set before them all that the Lord had commanded him. And the people
answered as one – "All that the Lord has spoken we will do." Moshe brought
9 their answer back to the Lord. Then the Lord said to Moshe, "I will come to
you in a dense cloud, that the people may hear Me speaking to you. They will
then believe you forever." When Moshe reported the words of the people to
10 the Lord, the Lord said to Moshe, "Go to the people and consecrate them
11 today and tomorrow; let them wash their clothes and be ready for the third
day, for on that third day the Lord will descend on Mount Sinai before all the
12 peoples' eyes. Set a boundary for the people around the mountain; tell them
to take care not to ascend to it, not even touch its edge. Anyone who touches
13 the mountain must be put to death. No hand shall touch him: he shall be
stoned or shot with arrows; beast or man, he shall not live. When the ram's
14 horn sounds a long blast – only then may they go up on the mountain." So
Moshe came down from the mountain to the people; he consecrated them
15 and they cleansed their clothes. "Be ready for the third day," he told them,
16 "and do not draw close to your wives." The third day came; and that morning
there was thunder and lightning and a dense cloud on the mountain and the
sound of a ram's horn, intensely loud, and all the people in the camp shook.
17 Then Moshe led the people out of the camp to meet God, and they stood
18 at the foot of the mountain. Mount Sinai was enveloped in smoke because
the Lord had descended on it in fire. Smoke billowed up from it as if from a
19 furnace, and the mountain shook violently as one. As the sound of the ram's
horn grew louder and louder, Moshe spoke and God answered him aloud.
20 And the Lord descended on Mount Sinai, to the top of the mountain,
21 and called Moshe to the mountaintop, and Moshe ascended. The Lord told
Moshe, "Go back down – warn the people not to force their way through
22 to look at the Lord, or many will die. Even priests who come near to the
Lord must first consecrate themselves, or the Lord will break out against
23 them." Moshe replied to the Lord, "The people cannot climb Mount Sinai.
You Yourself warned us to set a boundary around the mountain and
24 consecrate it." The Lord said to him, "Go down, and come back
together with Aharon. But do not let the priests or people force their way
through to come up to the Lord, or He will break out against them."

יט א בַּחֹדֶשׁ הַשְּׁלִישִׁי לְצֵאת בְּנֵי־יִשְׂרָאֵל מֵאֶרֶץ מִצְרָיִם בַּיּוֹם הַזֶּה בָּאוּ רביעי
ב מִדְבַּר סִינָי׃ וַיִּסְעוּ מֵרְפִידִים וַיָּבֹאוּ מִדְבַּר סִינַי וַיַּחֲנוּ בַּמִּדְבָּר וַיִּחַן־שָׁם
ג יִשְׂרָאֵל נֶגֶד הָהָר׃ וּמֹשֶׁה עָלָה אֶל־הָאֱלֹהִים וַיִּקְרָא אֵלָיו יְהוָה מִן־
ד הָהָר לֵאמֹר כֹּה תֹאמַר לְבֵית יַעֲקֹב וְתַגֵּיד לִבְנֵי יִשְׂרָאֵל׃ אַתֶּם רְאִיתֶם
אֲשֶׁר עָשִׂיתִי לְמִצְרָיִם וָאֶשָּׂא אֶתְכֶם עַל־כַּנְפֵי נְשָׁרִים וָאָבִא אֶתְכֶם
ה אֵלָי׃ וְעַתָּה אִם־שָׁמוֹעַ תִּשְׁמְעוּ בְּקֹלִי וּשְׁמַרְתֶּם אֶת־בְּרִיתִי וִהְיִיתֶם לִי
ו סְגֻלָּה מִכָּל־הָעַמִּים כִּי־לִי כָּל־הָאָרֶץ׃ וְאַתֶּם תִּהְיוּ־לִי מַמְלֶכֶת כֹּהֲנִים טו
ז וְגוֹי קָדוֹשׁ אֵלֶּה הַדְּבָרִים אֲשֶׁר תְּדַבֵּר אֶל־בְּנֵי יִשְׂרָאֵל׃ וַיָּבֹא מֹשֶׁה חמישי
וַיִּקְרָא לְזִקְנֵי הָעָם וַיָּשֶׂם לִפְנֵיהֶם אֵת כָּל־הַדְּבָרִים הָאֵלֶּה אֲשֶׁר צִוָּהוּ
ח יְהוָה׃ וַיַּעֲנוּ כָל־הָעָם יַחְדָּו וַיֹּאמְרוּ כֹּל אֲשֶׁר־דִּבֶּר יְהוָה נַעֲשֶׂה וַיָּשֶׁב
ט מֹשֶׁה אֶת־דִּבְרֵי הָעָם אֶל־יְהוָה׃ וַיֹּאמֶר יְהוָה אֶל־מֹשֶׁה הִנֵּה אָנֹכִי
בָּא אֵלֶיךָ בְּעַב הֶעָנָן בַּעֲבוּר יִשְׁמַע הָעָם בְּדַבְּרִי עִמָּךְ וְגַם־בְּךָ יַאֲמִינוּ
י לְעוֹלָם וַיַּגֵּד מֹשֶׁה אֶת־דִּבְרֵי הָעָם אֶל־יְהוָה׃ וַיֹּאמֶר יְהוָה אֶל־מֹשֶׁה
יא לֵךְ אֶל־הָעָם וְקִדַּשְׁתָּם הַיּוֹם וּמָחָר וְכִבְּסוּ שִׂמְלֹתָם׃ וְהָיוּ נְכֹנִים לַיּוֹם
הַשְּׁלִישִׁי כִּי ׀ בַּיּוֹם הַשְּׁלִשִׁי יֵרֵד יְהוָה לְעֵינֵי כָל־הָעָם עַל־הַר סִינָי׃
יב וְהִגְבַּלְתָּ אֶת־הָעָם סָבִיב לֵאמֹר הִשָּׁמְרוּ לָכֶם עֲלוֹת בָּהָר וּנְגֹעַ בְּקָצֵהוּ
יג כָּל־הַנֹּגֵעַ בָּהָר מוֹת יוּמָת׃ לֹא־תִגַּע בּוֹ יָד כִּי־סָקוֹל יִסָּקֵל אוֹ־יָרֹה יִיָּרֶה
יד אִם־בְּהֵמָה אִם־אִישׁ לֹא יִחְיֶה בִּמְשֹׁךְ הַיֹּבֵל הֵמָּה יַעֲלוּ בָהָר׃ וַיֵּרֶד
טו מֹשֶׁה מִן־הָהָר אֶל־הָעָם וַיְקַדֵּשׁ אֶת־הָעָם וַיְכַבְּסוּ שִׂמְלֹתָם׃ וַיֹּאמֶר
טז אֶל־הָעָם הֱיוּ נְכֹנִים לִשְׁלֹשֶׁת יָמִים אַל־תִּגְּשׁוּ אֶל־אִשָּׁה׃ וַיְהִי בַיּוֹם
הַשְּׁלִישִׁי בִּהְיֹת הַבֹּקֶר וַיְהִי קֹלֹת וּבְרָקִים וְעָנָן כָּבֵד עַל־הָהָר וְקֹל
יז שֹׁפָר חָזָק מְאֹד וַיֶּחֱרַד כָּל־הָעָם אֲשֶׁר בַּמַּחֲנֶה׃ וַיּוֹצֵא מֹשֶׁה אֶת־הָעָם
יח לִקְרַאת הָאֱלֹהִים מִן־הַמַּחֲנֶה וַיִּתְיַצְּבוּ בְּתַחְתִּית הָהָר׃ וְהַר סִינַי
עָשַׁן כֻּלּוֹ מִפְּנֵי אֲשֶׁר יָרַד עָלָיו יְהוָה בָּאֵשׁ וַיַּעַל עֲשָׁנוֹ כְּעֶשֶׁן הַכִּבְשָׁן
יט וַיֶּחֱרַד כָּל־הָהָר מְאֹד׃ וַיְהִי קוֹל הַשֹּׁפָר הוֹלֵךְ וְחָזֵק מְאֹד מֹשֶׁה יְדַבֵּר
כ וְהָאֱלֹהִים יַעֲנֶנּוּ בְקוֹל׃ וַיֵּרֶד יְהוָה עַל־הַר סִינַי אֶל־רֹאשׁ הָהָר וַיִּקְרָא ששי
כא יְהוָה לְמֹשֶׁה אֶל־רֹאשׁ הָהָר וַיַּעַל מֹשֶׁה׃ וַיֹּאמֶר יְהוָה אֶל־מֹשֶׁה רֵד
כב הָעֵד בָּעָם פֶּן־יֶהֶרְסוּ אֶל־יְהוָה לִרְאוֹת וְנָפַל מִמֶּנּוּ רָב׃ וְגַם הַכֹּהֲנִים
כג הַנִּגָּשִׁים אֶל־יְהוָה יִתְקַדָּשׁוּ פֶּן־יִפְרֹץ בָּהֶם יְהוָה׃ וַיֹּאמֶר מֹשֶׁה אֶל־
יְהוָה לֹא־יוּכַל הָעָם לַעֲלֹת אֶל־הַר סִינָי כִּי־אַתָּה הַעֵדֹתָה בָּנוּ לֵאמֹר
כד הַגְבֵּל אֶת־הָהָר וְקִדַּשְׁתּוֹ׃ וַיֹּאמֶר אֵלָיו יְהוָה לֶךְ־רֵד וְעָלִיתָ אַתָּה
וְאַהֲרֹן עִמָּךְ וְהַכֹּהֲנִים וְהָעָם אַל־יֶהֶרְסוּ לַעֲלֹת אֶל־יְהוָה פֶּן־יִפְרָץ־

25 So Moshe went down to the people and told them. Then God spoke
20 1
2 all these words: "I am the LORD your God who brought you out
3 of the land of Egypt, out of the house of slaves. Have no other gods than
4 Me. Do not make for yourself any carved image or likeness of any creature
in the heavens above or the earth beneath or the water beneath the earth.
5 Do not bow down to them or worship them, for I the LORD your God
demand absolute loyalty. For those who hate Me, I hold the descendants
6 to account for the sins of the fathers to the third and fourth generation, but
to those who love Me and keep My commands – I shall act with faithful
7 love for thousands. Do not speak the name of the LORD your
God in vain, for the LORD will not hold guiltless those who speak His name
in vain.
8
9 Remember the Sabbath to keep it holy. Six days you shall work, and
10 carry out all your labors, but the seventh is a Sabbath to the LORD your
God. On it, do no work – neither you, nor your son or daughter, your
male or female servant, your livestock, or the migrant within your gates.
11 For in six days the LORD made heaven and earth, the sea, and all that
they contain, and He rested on the seventh day. And so the LORD blessed
12 the Sabbath day and made it holy. Honor your father and
mother. Then you will live long in the land that the LORD your God is
13 giving you. Do not murder. Do not
commit adultery. Do not steal. Do not
14 bear false witness against your neighbor. Do not
crave your neighbor's house. Do not
crave your neighbor's wife, his male or female servant, his ox, his donkey, or
anything else that is your neighbor's."
15 Every one of the people witnessed the thunder and lightning and the sound
of the ram's horn and the smoke-covered mountain; they saw and they
16 shook – and they stood at a distance, and said to Moshe, "Speak to us yourself
17 and we will listen, but let not God say any more to us, or we will die." "Do
not be afraid," said Moshe to the people, "God has come to lift you up, so
18 that the awe of Him will be with you always, keeping you from sin." But the
people remained at a distance while Moshe approached the thick darkness
19 where God was. Then the LORD said to Moshe, "This is what you
shall tell the Israelites: You yourselves have seen that I, from the heavens,
20 have spoken to you. Have no others alongside Me; make yourselves no silver
21 gods, no golden gods. Make for Me an altar of earth and on that sacrifice your
burnt offerings and peace offerings, your sheep and your cattle. Wherever I

כה כ א בם: וירד משה אל־העם ויאמר אלהם: וידבר אלהים
ב את כל־הדברים האלה לאמר: אנכי יהוה אלהיך אשר
ג הוצאתיך מארץ מצרים מבית עבדים: לא־יהיה לך אלהים אחרים
ד על־פני: לא־תעשה לך פסל וכל־תמונה אשר בשמים ממעל ואשר
ה בארץ מתחת ואשר במים מתחת לארץ: לא־תשתחוה להם ולא
תעבדם כי אנכי יהוה אלהיך אל קנא פקד עון אבת על־בנים על־
ו שלשים ועל־רבעים לשנאי: ועשה חסד לאלפים לאהבי ולשמרי
ז מצותי: לא תשא את־שם־יהוה אלהיך לשוא כי לא
ינקה יהוה את אשר־ישא את־שמו לשוא:
ח ט זכור את־יום השבת לקדשו: ששת ימים תעבד ועשית כל־
י מלאכתך: ויום השביעי שבת ליהוה אלהיך לא־תעשה כל־
מלאכה אתה ׀ ובנך ובתך עבדך ואמתך ובהמתך וגרך אשר
יא בשעריך: כי ששת־ימים עשה יהוה את־השמים ואת־הארץ
את־הים ואת־כל־אשר־בם וינח ביום השביעי על־כן ברך
יב יהוה את־יום השבת ויקדשהו: כבד את־אביך
ואת־אמך למען יארכון ימיך על האדמה אשר־יהוה אלהיך
יג נתן לך: לא תרצח לא
תנאף לא תגנב לא־
יד תענה ברעך עד שקר: לא
תחמד בית רעך לא־
תחמד אשת רעך ועבדו ואמתו ושורו וחמרו וכל אשר
לרעך:
טו וכל־העם ראים את־הקולת ואת־הלפידם ואת קול השפר ואת־ שביעי
טז ההר עשן וירא העם וינעו ויעמדו מרחק: ויאמרו אל־משה דבר־
יז אתה עמנו ונשמעה ואל־ידבר עמנו אלהים פן־נמות: ויאמר משה
אל־העם אל־תיראו כי לבעבור נסות אתכם בא האלהים ובעבור
יח תהיה יראתו על־פניכם לבלתי תחטאו: ויעמד העם מרחק ומשה
יט נגש אל־הערפל אשר־שם האלהים: ויאמר יהוה אל־ מפטיר
משה כה תאמר אל־בני ישראל אתם ראיתם כי מן־השמים דברתי
כ עמכם: לא תעשון אתי אלהי כסף ואלהי זהב לא תעשו לכם:
כא מזבח אדמה תעשה־לי וזבחת עליו את־עלתיך ואת־שלמיך את־
צאנך ואת־בקרך בכל־המקום אשר אזכיר את־שמי אבוא אליך

22 cause My name to be invoked, I will come to you and I will bless you. If you
make Me an altar of stones, do not build it of hewn stone, for in wielding a
23 sword upon it, you profane it. Do not ascend to My altar with steps, for your
nakedness must not be exposed on it.[43]

21 1 And these are the laws that you shall set before them. If you buy a Hebrew MISHPATIM
2 slave, he shall serve for six years, but in the seventh he shall go forth free,
3 without paying anything. If he came alone, he shall leave alone. But if he
4 was a married man, his wife shall leave with him. If his master gave him a
wife and she bore him sons or daughters, the woman and her children shall
5 remain her master's, while he shall leave alone. But if the slave declares, 'I
6 love my master, my wife, and my children; I do not want to go free,' then his
master shall bring him before the judges. He shall take him to the door or to
the doorpost and pierce his ear with an awl; after that he shall then remain
7 his slave forever. If a man sells his daughter as a maidservant, she
8 does not go free in the usual way of slaves. If her master, who intended to wed
her, finds that he dislikes her, he must let her be redeemed. He has no right
9 to sell her to foreigners, because he has broken faith with her. If he intends
10 her for his son, he shall grant her all the rights of a daughter. If he marries
another woman alongside her, he shall not reduce her food, her clothing, or
11 marital rights. If he fails her in any of these three things, she shall go forth
12 free without paying anything. One person who strikes another so
13 that he dies shall be put to death. If he did not lie in wait to harm him, but it
came about by an act of God – I am setting apart a place where he may find
14 refuge.[44] But if someone schemes against another and kills him by
15 stealth, you shall take him even from My altar[45] and he shall die. One
16 who wounds his father or mother shall be put to death. One who
kidnaps a person shall be put to death, whether the victim has been sold or
17 found in his possession. One who curses his father or mother shall
18 be put to death. If two people fight and one strikes another with a
19 stone or with his fist – if the victim does not die but is confined to bed, and
afterward he gets up and walks outdoors even leaning on a cane, the assailant
is absolved, but he must pay for the victim's loss of time and provide for his
20 cure. If a man strikes his slave, male or female, with a rod and the
21 slave dies there and then, the death shall be avenged. But if the slave survives
a day, two days – since the money lost is the master's, the death shall not be
22 avenged. If two men fight and one of them hits a pregnant woman,
and she miscarries but suffers no irreparable injury herself, the offender must
23 be fined, as the woman's husband demands and as the judges rule. But if she
24 suffers an irreparable injury, he must compensate life for life, eye for eye,
25 tooth for tooth, hand for hand, foot for foot, burn for burn, wound for wound,
26 bruise for bruise.[46] If a man should strike the eye of his slave, male

43 | Most Israelites wore only loose clothing, and spreading the feet apart could expose one's genitalia.

44 | That is, from a vengeful relative of the victim.

45 | The altar was considered a place of sanctuary; cf. I Kings 1:51, 2:28.

46 | According to rabbinic interpretation (Bava Kamma 83b), the punishments in verses 24–25 are monetary.

כב וּבֵרַכְתִּיךָ: וְאִם־מִזְבַּח אֲבָנִים תַּעֲשֶׂה־לִּי לֹא־תִבְנֶה אֶתְהֶן גָּזִית כִּי
כג חַרְבְּךָ הֵנַפְתָּ עָלֶיהָ וַתְּחַלְלֶהָ: וְלֹא־תַעֲלֶה בְמַעֲלֹת עַל־מִזְבְּחִי אֲשֶׁר
לֹא־תִגָּלֶה עֶרְוָתְךָ עָלָיו:
כא א ב וְאֵלֶּה הַמִּשְׁפָּטִים אֲשֶׁר תָּשִׂים לִפְנֵיהֶם: כִּי תִקְנֶה עֶבֶד עִבְרִי שֵׁשׁ טז משפטים
ג שָׁנִים יַעֲבֹד וּבַשְּׁבִעִת יֵצֵא לַחָפְשִׁי חִנָּם: אִם־בְּגַפּוֹ יָבֹא בְּגַפּוֹ יֵצֵא
ד אִם־בַּעַל אִשָּׁה הוּא וְיָצְאָה אִשְׁתּוֹ עִמּוֹ: אִם־אֲדֹנָיו יִתֶּן־לוֹ אִשָּׁה
וְיָלְדָה־לוֹ בָנִים אוֹ בָנוֹת הָאִשָּׁה וִילָדֶיהָ תִּהְיֶה לַאדֹנֶיהָ וְהוּא
ה יֵצֵא בְגַפּוֹ: וְאִם־אָמֹר יֹאמַר הָעֶבֶד אָהַבְתִּי אֶת־אֲדֹנִי אֶת־אִשְׁתִּי
ו וְאֶת־בָּנָי לֹא אֵצֵא חָפְשִׁי: וְהִגִּישׁוֹ אֲדֹנָיו אֶל־הָאֱלֹהִים וְהִגִּישׁוֹ
אֶל־הַדֶּלֶת אוֹ אֶל־הַמְּזוּזָה וְרָצַע אֲדֹנָיו אֶת־אָזְנוֹ בַּמַּרְצֵעַ וַעֲבָדוֹ
ז לְעֹלָם: וְכִי־יִמְכֹּר אִישׁ אֶת־בִּתּוֹ לְאָמָה לֹא תֵצֵא כְּצֵאת
ח הָעֲבָדִים: אִם־רָעָה בְּעֵינֵי אֲדֹנֶיהָ אֲשֶׁר־לֹא יְעָדָהּ וְהֶפְדָּהּ לְעַם לו
ט נָכְרִי לֹא־יִמְשֹׁל לְמָכְרָהּ בְּבִגְדוֹ־בָהּ: וְאִם־לִבְנוֹ יִיעָדֶנָּה כְּמִשְׁפַּט
י הַבָּנוֹת יַעֲשֶׂה־לָּהּ: אִם־אַחֶרֶת יִקַּח־לוֹ שְׁאֵרָהּ כְּסוּתָהּ וְעֹנָתָהּ
יא לֹא יִגְרָע: וְאִם־שְׁלָשׁ־אֵלֶּה לֹא יַעֲשֶׂה לָהּ וְיָצְאָה חִנָּם אֵין
יב יג כָּסֶף: מַכֵּה אִישׁ וָמֵת מוֹת יוּמָת: וַאֲשֶׁר לֹא צָדָה וְהָאֱלֹהִים
יד אִנָּה לְיָדוֹ וְשַׂמְתִּי לְךָ מָקוֹם אֲשֶׁר יָנוּס שָׁמָּה: וְכִי־
יָזִד אִישׁ עַל־רֵעֵהוּ לְהָרְגוֹ בְעָרְמָה מֵעִם מִזְבְּחִי תִּקָּחֶנּוּ
טו טז לָמוּת: וּמַכֵּה אָבִיו וְאִמּוֹ מוֹת יוּמָת: וְגֹנֵב אִישׁ
יז וּמְכָרוֹ וְנִמְצָא בְיָדוֹ מוֹת יוּמָת: וּמְקַלֵּל אָבִיו וְאִמּוֹ
יח מוֹת יוּמָת: וְכִי־יְרִיבֻן אֲנָשִׁים וְהִכָּה־אִישׁ אֶת־רֵעֵהוּ
יט בְּאֶבֶן אוֹ בְאֶגְרֹף וְלֹא יָמוּת וְנָפַל לְמִשְׁכָּב: אִם־יָקוּם וְהִתְהַלֵּךְ בַּחוּץ
כ עַל־מִשְׁעַנְתּוֹ וְנִקָּה הַמַּכֶּה רַק שִׁבְתּוֹ יִתֵּן וְרַפֹּא יְרַפֵּא: וְכִי־ שני
יַכֶּה אִישׁ אֶת־עַבְדּוֹ אוֹ אֶת־אֲמָתוֹ בַּשֵּׁבֶט וּמֵת תַּחַת יָדוֹ נָקֹם יִנָּקֵם:
כא כב אַךְ אִם־יוֹם אוֹ יוֹמַיִם יַעֲמֹד לֹא יֻקַּם כִּי כַסְפּוֹ הוּא: וְכִי־
יִנָּצוּ אֲנָשִׁים וְנָגְפוּ אִשָּׁה הָרָה וְיָצְאוּ יְלָדֶיהָ וְלֹא יִהְיֶה אָסוֹן עָנוֹשׁ
כג יֵעָנֵשׁ כַּאֲשֶׁר יָשִׁית עָלָיו בַּעַל הָאִשָּׁה וְנָתַן בִּפְלִלִים: וְאִם־אָסוֹן
כד יִהְיֶה וְנָתַתָּה נֶפֶשׁ תַּחַת נָפֶשׁ: עַיִן תַּחַת עַיִן שֵׁן תַּחַת שֵׁן יָד תַּחַת
כה יָד רֶגֶל תַּחַת רָגֶל: כְּוִיָּה תַּחַת כְּוִיָּה פֶּצַע תַּחַת פָּצַע חַבּוּרָה תַּחַת
כו חַבּוּרָה: וְכִי־יַכֶּה אִישׁ אֶת־עֵין עַבְדּוֹ אוֹ־אֶת־עֵין אֲמָתוֹ

or female, and maim it, he must send the slave out free on account of his eye.
27 If he knocks out the tooth of his slave, male or female, he must send the slave
out free on account of his tooth.
28 If an ox gores a man or a woman to death, the ox shall be stoned, and its flesh
29 not eaten, but the owner of the ox shall not be liable. But if the ox has already
gored in the past, and its owner was warned but failed to guard it, and it kills
a man or a woman, the ox shall be stoned, and its owner also shall be put to
30 death. If a ransom is imposed on his life, then he shall pay whatever is imposed
31 on him and redeem his life. This rule also applies if the ox gores a minor son
32 or daughter, but if the ox gores a slave, male or female, the owner shall give
33 thirty shekels of silver to the master, and the ox must be stoned. If a
man uncovers a hole or digs one and fails to cover it, and an ox or a donkey
34 falls into it, the one responsible for the pit shall make restitution. He shall
35 give its owner its full value, and the dead animal shall be his. If one
man's ox injures another's so that it dies, they shall sell the live ox and share
36 the money. The dead animal they shall also share. If, however, it is known that
the ox had gored in the past, and still the owner failed to guard it, he shall pay
37 an ox for an ox, and the dead animal shall be his. If a man steals an ox
or a sheep and kills it or sells it, he shall pay five oxen for an ox, four sheep for
22 1 a sheep. If a burglar is caught tunneling in, and is struck and killed, there is no
2 bloodguilt on his account.[47] But if the sun has risen on him, there is bloodguilt
on his account. A thief must make restitution; if he lacks the means, he shall
3 be sold as a slave to repay his debt. If what he stole – an ox, ass, or sheep – is
4 found alive in his possession, he shall pay double. If a person lets
a field or vineyard be damaged, either by letting his livestock loose or by
letting them graze in someone else's field, he must repay the best of his field
5 or vineyard. If a fire is started and spreads to thorns, so that grain is
destroyed, stacked or standing or growing in the field, the person who started
6 the fire must redress the damage. If one person entrusts another with
money or goods, and they are stolen from his house, then if the thief is found
7 he must pay double. If the thief is not found, then the owner of the house
must swear before the court that he has not laid hands on his neighbor's goods
8 himself. In every case of betrayal of trust, whether concerning an ox, donkey
or sheep, clothing, or any loss that one can point to and say, 'This is it,' – both
parties' claims shall be brought to the court. The one the court finds guilty
9 shall pay the other double. If one person entrusts another with a
donkey, ox, sheep, or any animal, for safekeeping, and it dies or is injured or
10 is carried away unseen, an oath before the LORD shall settle between them;
if the second man swears that he did not lay his hands on his charge, then the
11 owner must accept this, and no restitution need be made. But if the charge
12 was stolen from him, he must make restitution to the owner. If it was torn by
a wild animal and the second man brings the remains as evidence, he need
not make good the loss.

---

47 | That is, one who kills him is not culpable for murder, because the thief poses a mortal threat.

כו וְשִׁחֲתָהּ לַחָפְשִׁי יְשַׁלְּחֶנּוּ תַּחַת עֵינוֹ: וְאִם־שֵׁן עַבְדּוֹ אוֹ־שֵׁן אֲמָתוֹ
יַפִּיל לַחָפְשִׁי יְשַׁלְּחֶנּוּ תַּחַת שִׁנּוֹ:
כח וְכִי־יִגַּח שׁוֹר אֶת־אִישׁ אוֹ אֶת־אִשָּׁה וָמֵת סָקוֹל יִסָּקֵל הַשּׁוֹר וְלֹא
כט יֵאָכֵל אֶת־בְּשָׂרוֹ וּבַעַל הַשּׁוֹר נָקִי: וְאִם שׁוֹר נַגָּח הוּא מִתְּמֹל שִׁלְשֹׁם
וְהוּעַד בִּבְעָלָיו וְלֹא יִשְׁמְרֶנּוּ וְהֵמִית אִישׁ אוֹ אִשָּׁה הַשּׁוֹר יִסָּקֵל
ל וְגַם־בְּעָלָיו יוּמָת: אִם־כֹּפֶר יוּשַׁת עָלָיו וְנָתַן פִּדְיֹן נַפְשׁוֹ כְּכֹל אֲשֶׁר־
לא לב יוּשַׁת עָלָיו: אוֹ־בֵן יִגָּח אוֹ־בַת יִגָּח כַּמִּשְׁפָּט הַזֶּה יֵעָשֶׂה לּוֹ: אִם־
עֶבֶד יִגַּח הַשּׁוֹר אוֹ אָמָה כֶּסֶף ׀ שְׁלֹשִׁים שְׁקָלִים יִתֵּן לַאדֹנָיו וְהַשּׁוֹר
לג יִסָּקֵל: וְכִי־יִפְתַּח אִישׁ בּוֹר אוֹ כִּי־יִכְרֶה אִישׁ בֹּר וְלֹא
לד יְכַסֶּנּוּ וְנָפַל־שָׁמָּה שּׁוֹר אוֹ חֲמוֹר: בַּעַל הַבּוֹר יְשַׁלֵּם כֶּסֶף יָשִׁיב לִבְעָלָיו
לה וְהַמֵּת יִהְיֶה־לּוֹ: וְכִי־יִגֹּף שׁוֹר־אִישׁ אֶת־שׁוֹר רֵעֵהוּ וָמֵת
לו וּמָכְרוּ אֶת־הַשּׁוֹר הַחַי וְחָצוּ אֶת־כַּסְפּוֹ וְגַם אֶת־הַמֵּת יֶחֱצוּן: אוֹ נוֹדַע
כִּי שׁוֹר נַגָּח הוּא מִתְּמוֹל שִׁלְשֹׁם וְלֹא יִשְׁמְרֶנּוּ בְּעָלָיו שַׁלֵּם יְשַׁלֵּם
לז שׁוֹר תַּחַת הַשּׁוֹר וְהַמֵּת יִהְיֶה־לּוֹ: כִּי יִגְנֹב־אִישׁ שׁוֹר
אוֹ־שֶׂה וּטְבָחוֹ אוֹ מְכָרוֹ חֲמִשָּׁה בָקָר יְשַׁלֵּם תַּחַת הַשּׁוֹר וְאַרְבַּע־צֹאן
כב א תַּחַת הַשֶּׂה: אִם־בַּמַּחְתֶּרֶת יִמָּצֵא הַגַּנָּב וְהֻכָּה וָמֵת אֵין לוֹ דָּמִים:
ב אִם־זָרְחָה הַשֶּׁמֶשׁ עָלָיו דָּמִים לוֹ שַׁלֵּם יְשַׁלֵּם אִם־אֵין לוֹ וְנִמְכַּר
ג בִּגְנֵבָתוֹ: אִם־הִמָּצֵא תִמָּצֵא בְיָדוֹ הַגְּנֵבָה מִשּׁוֹר עַד־חֲמוֹר עַד־
ד שֶׂה חַיִּים שְׁנַיִם יְשַׁלֵּם: כִּי יַבְעֶר־אִישׁ שָׂדֶה אוֹ־כֶרֶם שלישי
וְשִׁלַּח אֶת־בְּעִירֹה וּבִעֵר בִּשְׂדֵה אַחֵר מֵיטַב שָׂדֵהוּ וּמֵיטַב כַּרְמוֹ
ה יְשַׁלֵּם: כִּי־תֵצֵא אֵשׁ וּמָצְאָה קֹצִים וְנֶאֱכַל גָּדִישׁ אוֹ הַקָּמָה
ו אוֹ הַשָּׂדֶה שַׁלֵּם יְשַׁלֵּם הַמַּבְעִר אֶת־הַבְּעֵרָה: כִּי־יִתֵּן אִישׁ
אֶל־רֵעֵהוּ כֶּסֶף אוֹ־כֵלִים לִשְׁמֹר וְגֻנַּב מִבֵּית הָאִישׁ אִם־יִמָּצֵא הַגַּנָּב
ז יְשַׁלֵּם שְׁנָיִם: אִם־לֹא יִמָּצֵא הַגַּנָּב וְנִקְרַב בַּעַל־הַבַּיִת אֶל־הָאֱלֹהִים
ח אִם־לֹא שָׁלַח יָדוֹ בִּמְלֶאכֶת רֵעֵהוּ: עַל־כָּל־דְּבַר־פֶּשַׁע עַל־שׁוֹר עַל־
חֲמוֹר עַל־שֶׂה עַל־שַׂלְמָה עַל־כָּל־אֲבֵדָה אֲשֶׁר יֹאמַר כִּי־הוּא זֶה
עַד הָאֱלֹהִים יָבֹא דְּבַר־שְׁנֵיהֶם אֲשֶׁר יַרְשִׁיעֻן אֱלֹהִים יְשַׁלֵּם שְׁנַיִם
ט לְרֵעֵהוּ: כִּי־יִתֵּן אִישׁ אֶל־רֵעֵהוּ חֲמוֹר אוֹ־שׁוֹר אוֹ־שֶׂה
י וְכָל־בְּהֵמָה לִשְׁמֹר וּמֵת אוֹ־נִשְׁבַּר אוֹ־נִשְׁבָּה אֵין רֹאֶה: שְׁבֻעַת יְהוָה
תִּהְיֶה בֵּין שְׁנֵיהֶם אִם־לֹא שָׁלַח יָדוֹ בִּמְלֶאכֶת רֵעֵהוּ וְלָקַח בְּעָלָיו וְלֹא
יא יב יְשַׁלֵּם: וְאִם־גָּנֹב יִגָּנֵב מֵעִמּוֹ יְשַׁלֵּם לִבְעָלָיו: אִם־טָרֹף יִטָּרֵף יְבִאֵהוּ
עֵד הַטְּרֵפָה לֹא יְשַׁלֵּם:

13 If one person borrows a creature from his neighbor, and it is injured or dies
14 while the owner is not there, he must make restitution. But if the owner
was present, he need not make restitution; if the animal was hired, only the
15 hiring fee is due. If a man seduces a virgin who is not betrothed,
16 and lies with her, he must pay her bride price and marry her. If her father
refuses to let him marry her, he must still pay out the full bride price for
17 18 virgins. Do not allow a witch to live. And any person who lies with
19 an animal shall be put to death. Whoever sacrifices to any other deity
20 shall be utterly destroyed. Do not oppress a stranger or exploit him, for you
21 yourselves were strangers in the land of Egypt. Do not abuse a widow or an
22 orphan. For if you do abuse them, if they cry out to Me, I will unquestionably
23 heed their cry. My anger will flare and I will kill you by the sword – and then
your wives will be widows and your children orphans.
24 If you lend money to one of My people who is poor, do not act with him as
25 a harsh creditor, and do not charge him interest. If you take your neighbor's
26 garment as collateral, return it to him before the sun sets, because it is his only
clothing, the sole covering for his skin. What else does he have in which to
27 sleep? And if he cries out to Me, I will be listening: I am gracious. Do
28 not curse a judge, and do not deride a leader of your people. Do not delay
offerings from your harvest of grain or wine. The firstborn of your sons
29 you must give to Me.[48] Likewise with your oxen and sheep; let them stay
30 with their mothers for seven days, and on the eighth, give them over to Me.
You are to be My holy people. Do not eat flesh torn by beasts in the wild.
23 1 Throw it to the dogs. Do not accept a false report. Do not join with
2 an unscrupulous person to bear corrupt witness. Do not follow the crowd
to do evil. When you give testimony in a lawsuit, do not pervert justice
3 by siding with the crowd. Do not show favoritism even to a poor man in
4 a dispute. If you come across your enemy's ox or donkey going
5 astray – bring it back to him. If you see the donkey of someone who
hates you, fallen under its load, resist the impulse to leave it there. Help him to
6 release it. Do not subvert the rights of the needy when they come to
7 court. Keep far from a false charge. Do not bring death on the innocent and
8 righteous, for I will not acquit the wrongdoer. Take no bribe, for bribes blind
9 the sighted and subvert the cause of the just. Do not oppress a stranger. You
know what it is to be a stranger, for you yourselves were strangers in the land
10 11 of Egypt. For six years, sow your land and gather its crops, but in the seventh
let it rest and lie fallow. Let the needy of your people eat from it, and what
they leave, let the wild animals eat. Do the same with your vineyards and olive
12 groves. For six days carry out your work, but on the seventh you must cease,
so that your ox and donkey may rest, and even the children of maidservants
13 and strangers be revived. Take care in all that I have said to you. Never invoke
14 the names of other gods; let them never pass your lips. Three times a year,
15 celebrate a festival for Me. Keep the Festival of Unleavened Bread. For seven

48 | Meaning redeem them from the priest; see 13:13.

יג וְכִֽי־יִשְׁאַל אִישׁ מֵעִם רֵעֵהוּ וְנִשְׁבַּר אוֹ־מֵת בְּעָלָיו אֵין־עִמּוֹ
יד שַׁלֵּם יְשַׁלֵּם: אִם־בְּעָלָיו עִמּוֹ לֹא יְשַׁלֵּם אִם־שָׂכִיר הוּא בָּא
טו בִּשְׂכָרוֹ: וְכִֽי־יְפַתֶּה אִישׁ בְּתוּלָה אֲשֶׁר לֹא־אֹרָשָׂה וְשָׁכַב
טז עִמָּהּ מָהֹר יִמְהָרֶנָּה לּוֹ לְאִשָּׁה: אִם־מָאֵן יְמָאֵן אָבִיהָ לְתִתָּהּ לוֹ כֶּסֶף
יז יח יִשְׁקֹל כְּמֹהַר הַבְּתוּלֹת: מְכַשֵּׁפָה לֹא תְחַיֶּה: כָּל־שֹׁכֵב
יט עִם־בְּהֵמָה מוֹת יוּמָת: זֹבֵחַ לָאֱלֹהִים יָחֳרָם בִּלְתִּי לַיהוָה
כ לְבַדּוֹ: וְגֵר לֹא־תוֹנֶה וְלֹא תִלְחָצֶנּוּ כִּי־גֵרִים הֱיִיתֶם בְּאֶרֶץ מִצְרָיִם:
כא כב כָּל־אַלְמָנָה וְיָתוֹם לֹא תְעַנּוּן: אִם־עַנֵּה תְעַנֶּה אֹתוֹ כִּי אִם־צָעֹק יִצְעַק
כג אֵלַי שָׁמֹעַ אֶשְׁמַע צַעֲקָתוֹ: וְחָרָה אַפִּי וְהָרַגְתִּי אֶתְכֶם בֶּחָרֶב וְהָיוּ
נְשֵׁיכֶם אַלְמָנוֹת וּבְנֵיכֶם יְתֹמִים:
כד אִם־כֶּסֶף ׀ תַּלְוֶה אֶת־עַמִּי אֶת־הֶעָנִי עִמָּךְ לֹא־תִהְיֶה לוֹ כְּנֹשֶׁה לֹא־ יז
כה תְשִׂימוּן עָלָיו נֶשֶׁךְ: אִם־חָבֹל תַּחְבֹּל שַׂלְמַת רֵעֶךָ עַד־בֹּא הַשֶּׁמֶשׁ
כו תְּשִׁיבֶנּוּ לוֹ: כִּי הִוא כְסוּתֹה לְבַדָּהּ הִוא שִׂמְלָתוֹ לְעֹרוֹ בַּמֶּה יִשְׁכָּב
כז וְהָיָה כִּי־יִצְעַק אֵלַי וְשָׁמַעְתִּי כִּי־חַנּוּן אָנִי: אֱלֹהִים לֹא רביעי
כח תְקַלֵּל וְנָשִׂיא בְעַמְּךָ לֹא תָאֹר: מְלֵאָתְךָ וְדִמְעֲךָ לֹא תְאַחֵר בְּכוֹר
כט בָּנֶיךָ תִּתֶּן־לִּי: כֵּן־תַּעֲשֶׂה לְשֹׁרְךָ לְצֹאנֶךָ שִׁבְעַת יָמִים יִהְיֶה עִם־אִמּוֹ
ל בַּיּוֹם הַשְּׁמִינִי תִּתְּנוֹ־לִי: וְאַנְשֵׁי־קֹדֶשׁ תִּהְיוּן לִי וּבָשָׂר בַּשָּׂדֶה טְרֵפָה
כג א לֹא תֹאכֵלוּ לַכֶּלֶב תַּשְׁלִכוּן אֹתוֹ: לֹא תִשָּׂא שֵׁמַע שָׁוְא
ב אַל־תָּשֶׁת יָדְךָ עִם־רָשָׁע לִהְיֹת עֵד חָמָס: לֹא־תִהְיֶה אַחֲרֵי־רַבִּים
ג לְרָעֹת וְלֹא־תַעֲנֶה עַל־רִב לִנְטֹת אַחֲרֵי רַבִּים לְהַטֹּת: וְדָל לֹא תֶהְדַּר
ד בְּרִיבוֹ: כִּי תִפְגַּע שׁוֹר אֹיִבְךָ אוֹ חֲמֹרוֹ תֹּעֶה הָשֵׁב תְּשִׁיבֶנּוּ
ה לוֹ: כִּי־תִרְאֶה חֲמוֹר שֹׂנַאֲךָ רֹבֵץ תַּחַת מַשָּׂאוֹ וְחָדַלְתָּ
ו מֵעֲזֹב לוֹ עָזֹב תַּעֲזֹב עִמּוֹ: לֹא תַטֶּה מִשְׁפַּט אֶבְיֹנְךָ בְּרִיבוֹ: חמישי
ז מִדְּבַר־שֶׁקֶר תִּרְחָק וְנָקִי וְצַדִּיק אַל־תַּהֲרֹג כִּי לֹא־אַצְדִּיק רָשָׁע:
ח ט וְשֹׁחַד לֹא תִקָּח כִּי הַשֹּׁחַד יְעַוֵּר פִּקְחִים וִיסַלֵּף דִּבְרֵי צַדִּיקִים: וְגֵר לֹא
תִלְחָץ וְאַתֶּם יְדַעְתֶּם אֶת־נֶפֶשׁ הַגֵּר כִּי־גֵרִים הֱיִיתֶם בְּאֶרֶץ מִצְרָיִם:
י יא וְשֵׁשׁ שָׁנִים תִּזְרַע אֶת־אַרְצֶךָ וְאָסַפְתָּ אֶת־תְּבוּאָתָהּ: וְהַשְּׁבִיעִת
תִּשְׁמְטֶנָּה וּנְטַשְׁתָּהּ וְאָכְלוּ אֶבְיֹנֵי עַמֶּךָ וְיִתְרָם תֹּאכַל חַיַּת הַשָּׂדֶה
יב כֵּן־תַּעֲשֶׂה לְכַרְמְךָ לְזֵיתֶךָ: שֵׁשֶׁת יָמִים תַּעֲשֶׂה מַעֲשֶׂיךָ וּבַיּוֹם הַשְּׁבִיעִי
יג תִּשְׁבֹּת לְמַעַן יָנוּחַ שׁוֹרְךָ וַחֲמֹרֶךָ וְיִנָּפֵשׁ בֶּן־אֲמָתְךָ וְהַגֵּר: וּבְכֹל
אֲשֶׁר־אָמַרְתִּי אֲלֵיכֶם תִּשָּׁמֵרוּ וְשֵׁם אֱלֹהִים אֲחֵרִים לֹא תַזְכִּירוּ לֹא
יד טו יִשָּׁמַע עַל־פִּיךָ: שָׁלֹשׁ רְגָלִים תָּחֹג לִי בַּשָּׁנָה: אֶת־חַג הַמַּצּוֹת תִּשְׁמֹר

days, eat unleavened bread as I commanded you, at the time appointed, in
the month of Aviv,[49] for at that time you left Egypt. Do not appear before Me
16 empty-handed. Likewise, keep the Festival of the Harvest, of the first fruits of
the produce that you sowed in the field.[50] Keep the Festival of Ingathering at
the end of the year, when you gather in the fruit of your labor from the field.[51]
17 Three times a year, all the males among you shall appear before the Master,
18 the LORD. Do not offer the blood of My sacrifice together with anything
19 leavened. Do not let the fat of My festive offering remain until morning. Bring
the best first fruits of your land to the House of the LORD your God. Do not
boil a kid in the milk of its mother.
20 I am sending a messenger ahead of you to guard you on the way and to bring
21 you to the place that I have prepared. Heed his presence and listen to his
voice. Do not rebel against him, for he will not let your transgression pass,
22 because My name is with him. But if you listen carefully to him and do all that
23 I tell you, then I will be an enemy to your enemies, a foe to your foes. When
My messenger goes ahead of you and brings you to the Amorites, Hittites,
24 Perizzites, Canaanites, Hivites, and Jebusites, and I wipe them out, do not
bow down to their gods or worship them, and do not do as they do. Demolish
25 their gods and shatter their worship pillars. Serve the LORD your God, and
He will bless your bread, your water. I will banish all sickness from your
26 midst. No woman in your land will suffer miscarriage or barrenness.
27 I will fill out the full measure of your years. I will send My terror before you,
throwing into panic all the people you come upon. All you will see of your
28 enemies will be their fleeing backs. I will send hornets ahead of you, and they
29 will drive the Hivites, Canaanites, and Hittites out before you. I will not drive
them out in a single year, lest the land become desolate and the wild animals
30 too numerous for you. No – little by little I will drive them out before you, as
31 you burgeon and come to take possession of the land. I will set your borders
from the Sea of Reeds to the Sea of the Philistines, and from the wilderness
to the Euphrates, for I will deliver the inhabitants of the land into your hands:
32 you will drive them out before you. Make no covenant with them and their
33 gods. They must not stay in your land, for they would make you sin against
Me. If you worship their gods, it will be a trap for you."
24 1 Then He said to Moshe, "Ascend to the LORD, you and Aharon, Nadav and
2 Avihu, and seventy of Israel's elders and bow down from afar. Moshe alone
shall approach the LORD. The others must not come close, nor shall the
3 people come up with him." Moshe came and told the people all the LORD's
words and laws, and the people all responded with one voice, "All that the
4 LORD has spoken we shall do." Then Moshe wrote down all the LORD's words.
Early the next morning he rose and built an altar at the base of the mountain,
5 and also twelve pillars for the twelve tribes of Israel. Then he sent young men
of Israel, and they sacrificed bulls as burnt offerings and peace offerings to

49 | See note on 13:4.
50 | The Festival of Shavuot; cf. 34:22.
51 | The Festival of Sukkot; cf. Leviticus 23:33–43.

שִׁבְעַת יָמִים תֹּאכַל מַצּוֹת כַּאֲשֶׁר צִוִּיתִךָ לְמוֹעֵד חֹדֶשׁ הָאָבִיב כִּי־
טז בוֹ יָצָאתָ מִמִּצְרָיִם וְלֹא־יֵרָאוּ פָנַי רֵיקָם׃ וְחַג הַקָּצִיר בִּכּוּרֵי מַעֲשֶׂיךָ
אֲשֶׁר תִּזְרַע בַּשָּׂדֶה וְחַג הָאָסִף בְּצֵאת הַשָּׁנָה בְּאָסְפְּךָ אֶת־מַעֲשֶׂיךָ
יז מִן־הַשָּׂדֶה׃ שָׁלֹשׁ פְּעָמִים בַּשָּׁנָה יֵרָאֶה כָּל־זְכוּרְךָ אֶל־פְּנֵי הָאָדֹן ׀
יח יְהוָה׃ לֹא־תִזְבַּח עַל־חָמֵץ דַּם־זִבְחִי וְלֹא־יָלִין חֵלֶב־חַגִּי עַד־בֹּקֶר׃
יט רֵאשִׁית בִּכּוּרֵי אַדְמָתְךָ תָּבִיא בֵּית יְהוָה אֱלֹהֶיךָ לֹא־תְבַשֵּׁל גְּדִי
בַּחֲלֵב אִמּוֹ׃
כ הִנֵּה אָנֹכִי שֹׁלֵחַ מַלְאָךְ לְפָנֶיךָ לִשְׁמָרְךָ בַּדָּרֶךְ וְלַהֲבִיאֲךָ אֶל־הַמָּקוֹם ששי
כא אֲשֶׁר הֲכִנֹתִי׃ הִשָּׁמֶר מִפָּנָיו וּשְׁמַע בְּקֹלוֹ אַל־תַּמֵּר בּוֹ כִּי לֹא יִשָּׂא
כב לְפִשְׁעֲכֶם כִּי שְׁמִי בְּקִרְבּוֹ׃ כִּי אִם־שָׁמוֹעַ תִּשְׁמַע בְּקֹלוֹ וְעָשִׂיתָ כֹּל
כג אֲשֶׁר אֲדַבֵּר וְאָיַבְתִּי אֶת־אֹיְבֶיךָ וְצַרְתִּי אֶת־צֹרְרֶיךָ׃ כִּי־יֵלֵךְ מַלְאָכִי
לְפָנֶיךָ וֶהֱבִיאֲךָ אֶל־הָאֱמֹרִי וְהַחִתִּי וְהַפְּרִזִּי וְהַכְּנַעֲנִי הַחִוִּי וְהַיְבוּסִי
כד וְהִכְחַדְתִּיו׃ לֹא־תִשְׁתַּחֲוֶה לֵאלֹהֵיהֶם וְלֹא תָעָבְדֵם וְלֹא תַעֲשֶׂה
כה כְּמַעֲשֵׂיהֶם כִּי הָרֵס תְּהָרְסֵם וְשַׁבֵּר תְּשַׁבֵּר מַצֵּבֹתֵיהֶם׃ וַעֲבַדְתֶּם
אֵת יְהוָה אֱלֹהֵיכֶם וּבֵרַךְ אֶת־לַחְמְךָ וְאֶת־מֵימֶיךָ וַהֲסִרֹתִי מַחֲלָה
כו מִקִּרְבֶּךָ׃ לֹא תִהְיֶה מְשַׁכֵּלָה וַעֲקָרָה בְּאַרְצֶךָ אֶת־מִסְפַּר שביעי
כז יָמֶיךָ אֲמַלֵּא׃ אֶת־אֵימָתִי אֲשַׁלַּח לְפָנֶיךָ וְהַמֹּתִי אֶת־כָּל־הָעָם אֲשֶׁר
כח תָּבֹא בָּהֶם וְנָתַתִּי אֶת־כָּל־אֹיְבֶיךָ אֵלֶיךָ עֹרֶף׃ וְשָׁלַחְתִּי אֶת־הַצִּרְעָה
כט לְפָנֶיךָ וְגֵרְשָׁה אֶת־הַחִוִּי אֶת־הַכְּנַעֲנִי וְאֶת־הַחִתִּי מִלְּפָנֶיךָ׃ לֹא
אֲגָרְשֶׁנּוּ מִפָּנֶיךָ בְּשָׁנָה אֶחָת פֶּן־תִּהְיֶה הָאָרֶץ שְׁמָמָה וְרַבָּה עָלֶיךָ
ל חַיַּת הַשָּׂדֶה׃ מְעַט מְעַט אֲגָרְשֶׁנּוּ מִפָּנֶיךָ עַד אֲשֶׁר תִּפְרֶה וְנָחַלְתָּ
לא אֶת־הָאָרֶץ׃ וְשַׁתִּי אֶת־גְּבֻלְךָ מִיַּם־סוּף וְעַד־יָם פְּלִשְׁתִּים וּמִמִּדְבָּר
לב עַד־הַנָּהָר כִּי ׀ אֶתֵּן בְּיֶדְכֶם אֵת יֹשְׁבֵי הָאָרֶץ וְגֵרַשְׁתָּמוֹ מִפָּנֶיךָ׃ לֹא־
לג תִכְרֹת לָהֶם וְלֵאלֹהֵיהֶם בְּרִית׃ לֹא יֵשְׁבוּ בְּאַרְצְךָ פֶּן־יַחֲטִיאוּ אֹתְךָ
לִי כִּי תַעֲבֹד אֶת־אֱלֹהֵיהֶם כִּי־יִהְיֶה לְךָ לְמוֹקֵשׁ׃
כד א וְאֶל־מֹשֶׁה אָמַר עֲלֵה אֶל־יְהוָה אַתָּה וְאַהֲרֹן נָדָב וַאֲבִיהוּא וְשִׁבְעִים
ב מִזִּקְנֵי יִשְׂרָאֵל וְהִשְׁתַּחֲוִיתֶם מֵרָחֹק׃ וְנִגַּשׁ מֹשֶׁה לְבַדּוֹ אֶל־יְהוָה וְהֵם
ג לֹא יִגָּשׁוּ וְהָעָם לֹא יַעֲלוּ עִמּוֹ׃ וַיָּבֹא מֹשֶׁה וַיְסַפֵּר לָעָם אֵת כָּל־דִּבְרֵי
יְהוָה וְאֵת כָּל־הַמִּשְׁפָּטִים וַיַּעַן כָּל־הָעָם קוֹל אֶחָד וַיֹּאמְרוּ כָּל־
ד הַדְּבָרִים אֲשֶׁר־דִּבֶּר יְהוָה נַעֲשֶׂה׃ וַיִּכְתֹּב מֹשֶׁה אֵת כָּל־דִּבְרֵי יְהוָה
וַיַּשְׁכֵּם בַּבֹּקֶר וַיִּבֶן מִזְבֵּחַ תַּחַת הָהָר וּשְׁתֵּים עֶשְׂרֵה מַצֵּבָה לִשְׁנֵים
ה עָשָׂר שִׁבְטֵי יִשְׂרָאֵל׃ וַיִּשְׁלַח אֶת־נַעֲרֵי בְּנֵי יִשְׂרָאֵל וַיַּעֲלוּ עֹלֹת וַיִּזְבְּחוּ

6 the LORD. Moshe took half the blood and put it in bowls. The other half he
7 sprinkled on the altar. Then he took the book of the covenant and read it
aloud to the people. They replied, "All that the LORD has spoken we shall do
8 and we shall heed." Then Moshe took the blood, sprinkled it on the people,
and said, "This is the blood of the covenant that the LORD is making with
9 you regarding all these words." Then Moshe went up with Aharon, Nadav,
10 Avihu, and seventy of Israel's elders. They saw a vision of the God of Israel,
and beneath His feet what looked like a lapis lazuli pavement as clear as the
11 sky itself. And He did the leaders of Israel no harm – and they looked upon
12 God and they ate and they drank. The LORD said to Moshe, "Ascend
to Me on the mountain, and as you stand there I will give you the stone
tablets with the teaching and commandments that I have written to instruct
13 the people." So Moshe set out with Yehoshua, his disciple, and ascended the
14 mountain of God. He told the elders, "Wait for us here until we return to you.
Aharon and Ḥur will stay here with you; whoever has a dispute shall go to
15 16 them." As Moshe climbed the mountain, it was covered in a cloud. The glory
of the LORD rested on Mount Sinai, and the cloud covered it for six days. On
17 the seventh, He called to Moshe from within the cloud. To the Israelites the
appearance of the LORD's glory on the mountaintop was like consuming fire.
18 Moshe entered the cloud and climbed the mountain, and he stayed there for
forty days and forty nights.

25 1 2 The LORD spoke to Moshe, saying, "Tell the Israelites to take an offering for TERUMA
3 Me; take My offering from all whose heart moves them to give. These are
4 the offerings you shall receive from them: gold, silver and bronze; sky-blue,
5 purple, and scarlet wool; linen and goats' hair; rams' hides dyed red and fine
6 leather;[52] acacia wood; oil for the lamps; spices for the anointing oil and the
7 fragrant incense; and rock crystal together with other precious stones for the
8 ephod[53] and breast piece. They shall make Me a Sanctuary and I will dwell in
9 their midst. Form the Tabernacle and form all of its furnishings following the
10 patterns that I show you. Make an Ark of acacia wood, two and a half
11 cubits long, a cubit and a half wide, and a cubit and a half high. Overlay it with
12 pure gold, inside and out, and around it make a gold rim. Cast four gold rings
for it and place them on its four corners, two rings on one side and two on the
13 14 other. Make staves of acacia wood and overlay them with gold; place these
15 staves in the rings on the sides of the Ark so that the Ark may be carried. The
16 staves must stay in the rings of the Ark; they must not be removed. Inside the
17 Ark, place the tablets of the Covenant that I will give you. Make an Ark cover

52 | Literally "*taḥash* hides." The term has been interpreted as referring to some sort of rare animal.
53 | An apron-like garment.

ו זְבָחִים שְׁלָמִים לַיהוָה פָּרִים: וַיִּקַּח מֹשֶׁה חֲצִי הַדָּם וַיָּשֶׂם בָּאַגָּנֹת
ז וַחֲצִי הַדָּם זָרַק עַל־הַמִּזְבֵּחַ: וַיִּקַּח סֵפֶר הַבְּרִית וַיִּקְרָא בְּאָזְנֵי הָעָם
ח וַיֹּאמְרוּ כֹּל אֲשֶׁר־דִּבֶּר יְהוָה נַעֲשֶׂה וְנִשְׁמָע: וַיִּקַּח מֹשֶׁה אֶת־הַדָּם
וַיִּזְרֹק עַל־הָעָם וַיֹּאמֶר הִנֵּה דַם־הַבְּרִית אֲשֶׁר כָּרַת יְהוָה עִמָּכֶם עַל
ט כָּל־הַדְּבָרִים הָאֵלֶּה: וַיַּעַל מֹשֶׁה וְאַהֲרֹן נָדָב וַאֲבִיהוּא וְשִׁבְעִים מִזִּקְנֵי
י יִשְׂרָאֵל: וַיִּרְאוּ אֵת אֱלֹהֵי יִשְׂרָאֵל וְתַחַת רַגְלָיו כְּמַעֲשֵׂה לִבְנַת הַסַּפִּיר
יא וּכְעֶצֶם הַשָּׁמַיִם לָטֹהַר: וְאֶל־אֲצִילֵי בְּנֵי יִשְׂרָאֵל לֹא שָׁלַח יָדוֹ וַיֶּחֱזוּ
יב אֶת־הָאֱלֹהִים וַיֹּאכְלוּ וַיִּשְׁתּוּ: וַיֹּאמֶר יְהוָה אֶל־מֹשֶׁה
עֲלֵה אֵלַי הָהָרָה וֶהְיֵה־שָׁם וְאֶתְּנָה לְךָ אֶת־לֻחֹת הָאֶבֶן וְהַתּוֹרָה
יג וְהַמִּצְוָה אֲשֶׁר כָּתַבְתִּי לְהוֹרֹתָם: וַיָּקָם מֹשֶׁה וִיהוֹשֻׁעַ מְשָׁרְתוֹ וַיַּעַל
יד מֹשֶׁה אֶל־הַר הָאֱלֹהִים: וְאֶל־הַזְּקֵנִים אָמַר שְׁבוּ־לָנוּ בָזֶה עַד אֲשֶׁר־
נָשׁוּב אֲלֵיכֶם וְהִנֵּה אַהֲרֹן וְחוּר עִמָּכֶם מִי־בַעַל דְּבָרִים יִגַּשׁ אֲלֵהֶם:
טו טז וַיַּעַל מֹשֶׁה אֶל־הָהָר וַיְכַס הֶעָנָן אֶת־הָהָר: וַיִּשְׁכֹּן כְּבוֹד־יְהוָה עַל־ מפטיר
הַר סִינַי וַיְכַסֵּהוּ הֶעָנָן שֵׁשֶׁת יָמִים וַיִּקְרָא אֶל־מֹשֶׁה בַּיּוֹם הַשְּׁבִיעִי
יז מִתּוֹךְ הֶעָנָן: וּמַרְאֵה כְּבוֹד יְהוָה כְּאֵשׁ אֹכֶלֶת בְּרֹאשׁ הָהָר לְעֵינֵי
יח בְּנֵי יִשְׂרָאֵל: וַיָּבֹא מֹשֶׁה בְּתוֹךְ הֶעָנָן וַיַּעַל אֶל־הָהָר וַיְהִי מֹשֶׁה בָּהָר
אַרְבָּעִים יוֹם וְאַרְבָּעִים לָיְלָה:

כה א ב וַיְדַבֵּר יְהוָה אֶל־מֹשֶׁה לֵּאמֹר: דַּבֵּר אֶל־בְּנֵי יִשְׂרָאֵל וְיִקְחוּ־לִי תְּרוּמָה יח תרומה
ג מֵאֵת כָּל־אִישׁ אֲשֶׁר יִדְּבֶנּוּ לִבּוֹ תִּקְחוּ אֶת־תְּרוּמָתִי: וְזֹאת הַתְּרוּמָה
ד אֲשֶׁר תִּקְחוּ מֵאִתָּם זָהָב וָכֶסֶף וּנְחֹשֶׁת: וּתְכֵלֶת וְאַרְגָּמָן וְתוֹלַעַת
ה שָׁנִי וְשֵׁשׁ וְעִזִּים: וְעֹרֹת אֵילִם מְאָדָּמִים וְעֹרֹת תְּחָשִׁים וַעֲצֵי שִׁטִּים:
ו ז שֶׁמֶן לַמָּאֹר בְּשָׂמִים לְשֶׁמֶן הַמִּשְׁחָה וְלִקְטֹרֶת הַסַּמִּים: אַבְנֵי־שֹׁהַם
ח ט וְאַבְנֵי מִלֻּאִים לָאֵפֹד וְלַחֹשֶׁן: וְעָשׂוּ לִי מִקְדָּשׁ וְשָׁכַנְתִּי בְּתוֹכָם: כְּכֹל
אֲשֶׁר אֲנִי מַרְאֶה אוֹתְךָ אֵת תַּבְנִית הַמִּשְׁכָּן וְאֵת תַּבְנִית כָּל־כֵּלָיו
י וְכֵן תַּעֲשׂוּ: וְעָשׂוּ אֲרוֹן עֲצֵי שִׁטִּים אַמָּתַיִם וָחֵצִי אָרְכּוֹ
יא וְאַמָּה וָחֵצִי רָחְבּוֹ וְאַמָּה וָחֵצִי קֹמָתוֹ: וְצִפִּיתָ אֹתוֹ זָהָב טָהוֹר מִבַּיִת
יב וּמִחוּץ תְּצַפֶּנּוּ וְעָשִׂיתָ עָלָיו זֵר זָהָב סָבִיב: וְיָצַקְתָּ לּוֹ אַרְבַּע טַבְּעֹת
זָהָב וְנָתַתָּה עַל אַרְבַּע פַּעֲמֹתָיו וּשְׁתֵּי טַבָּעֹת עַל־צַלְעוֹ הָאֶחָת וּשְׁתֵּי
יג טַבָּעֹת עַל־צַלְעוֹ הַשֵּׁנִית: וְעָשִׂיתָ בַדֵּי עֲצֵי שִׁטִּים וְצִפִּיתָ אֹתָם זָהָב:
יד וְהֵבֵאתָ אֶת־הַבַּדִּים בַּטַּבָּעֹת עַל צַלְעֹת הָאָרֹן לָשֵׂאת אֶת־הָאָרֹן
טו טז בָּהֶם: בְּטַבְּעֹת הָאָרֹן יִהְיוּ הַבַּדִּים לֹא יָסֻרוּ מִמֶּנּוּ: וְנָתַתָּ אֶל־הָאָרֹן
יז אֵת הָעֵדֻת אֲשֶׁר אֶתֵּן אֵלֶיךָ: וְעָשִׂיתָ כַפֹּרֶת זָהָב טָהוֹר אַמָּתַיִם וָחֵצִי שני

18 of pure gold, two and a half cubits long and a cubit and a half wide. Make
two cherubim[54] of beaten gold and place them at the two ends of the cover:
19 one cherub at one end and one at the other; the cherubim shall be made of
20 one piece with the cover. These cherubim should have wings spread upward,
sheltering the cover. They should face one another, and look toward the cover.
21 Place the cover on top of the Ark, and inside the Ark place the tablets of the
22 Covenant that I will give you. There, from above the cover, between the two
cherubim, above the Ark of the Testimony, I will meet with you and speak
with you, and give you all My commands to the Israelites.
23 Make a table of acacia wood, two cubits long, a cubit wide, and a cubit and
24 25 a half high. Overlay it with pure gold and around it make a gold rim. Make a
frame a handbreadth wide all around, and around the frame also make a gold
26 rim. Make for it four gold rings, and place the rings on the four corners where
27 the four legs are. The rings should be attached next to the frame as holders
28 for staves to carry the table. Make the staves of acacia wood and overlay them
29 with gold; by these the table shall be carried. You must also make, out of pure
30 gold, its bowls, spoons, pitchers, and jars for pouring libations. On this table
the showbread must be placed before Me at all times.
31 Make a candelabrum of pure gold. Its base and shaft, cups, knobs, and flowers
32 shall be hammered from a single piece. Six branches shall extend from its
33 sides, three on one side, three on the other. On each branch there shall be
three finely crafted cups, each with a knob and a flower. All six branches
34 extending from the candelabrum shall be like this. The shaft of the
candelabrum shall have four finely crafted cups, each with a knob and a
35 flower. For the six branches that extend from the candelabrum, there must
36 be a knob at the base of each pair of branches. The knobs and their branches
shall be of one piece with it, the whole of it a single, hammered piece of pure
37 gold. Make its seven lamps and mount them so that they light the space in
38 39 front of it. Make its tongs and pans of pure gold. All these items shall be
40 made from a talent of pure gold.[55] Take care to make them according to that
26 1 design that is shown to you on the mountain. As for the Tabernacle
itself, make it with ten sheets of finely spun linen and sky-blue, purple, and
2 scarlet wool, with a design of cherubim worked into them. Each sheet shall

54 | Opinions differ as to the appearance of the cherubim, which had a human or animal likeness.

55 | A talent in this context equals three thousand shekels; see note on 30:13.

יח אַרְכָּהּ וְאַמָּה וָחֵצִי רָחְבָּהּ׃ וְעָשִׂיתָ שְׁנַיִם כְּרֻבִים זָהָב מִקְשָׁה תַּעֲשֶׂה
יט אֹתָם מִשְּׁנֵי קְצוֹת הַכַּפֹּרֶת׃ וַעֲשֵׂה כְּרוּב אֶחָד מִקָּצָה מִזֶּה וּכְרוּב־
אֶחָד מִקָּצָה מִזֶּה מִן־הַכַּפֹּרֶת תַּעֲשׂוּ אֶת־הַכְּרֻבִים עַל־שְׁנֵי קְצוֹתָיו׃
כ וְהָיוּ הַכְּרֻבִים פֹּרְשֵׂי כְנָפַיִם לְמַעְלָה סֹכְכִים בְּכַנְפֵיהֶם עַל־הַכַּפֹּרֶת
כא וּפְנֵיהֶם אִישׁ אֶל־אָחִיו אֶל־הַכַּפֹּרֶת יִהְיוּ פְּנֵי הַכְּרֻבִים׃ וְנָתַתָּ
אֶת־הַכַּפֹּרֶת עַל־הָאָרֹן מִלְמָעְלָה וְאֶל־הָאָרֹן תִּתֵּן אֶת־הָעֵדֻת אֲשֶׁר
כב אֶתֵּן אֵלֶיךָ׃ וְנוֹעַדְתִּי לְךָ שָׁם וְדִבַּרְתִּי אִתְּךָ מֵעַל הַכַּפֹּרֶת מִבֵּין
שְׁנֵי הַכְּרֻבִים אֲשֶׁר עַל־אֲרוֹן הָעֵדֻת אֵת כָּל־אֲשֶׁר אֲצַוֶּה אוֹתְךָ אֶל־
בְּנֵי יִשְׂרָאֵל׃
כג וְעָשִׂיתָ שֻׁלְחָן עֲצֵי שִׁטִּים אַמָּתַיִם אָרְכּוֹ וְאַמָּה רָחְבּוֹ וְאַמָּה וָחֵצִי
כד כה קֹמָתוֹ׃ וְצִפִּיתָ אֹתוֹ זָהָב טָהוֹר וְעָשִׂיתָ לּוֹ זֵר זָהָב סָבִיב׃ וְעָשִׂיתָ לּוֹ
כו מִסְגֶּרֶת טֹפַח סָבִיב וְעָשִׂיתָ זֵר־זָהָב לְמִסְגַּרְתּוֹ סָבִיב׃ וְעָשִׂיתָ לּוֹ אַרְבַּע
טַבְּעֹת זָהָב וְנָתַתָּ אֶת־הַטַּבָּעֹת עַל אַרְבַּע הַפֵּאֹת אֲשֶׁר לְאַרְבַּע
כז רַגְלָיו׃ לְעֻמַּת הַמִּסְגֶּרֶת תִּהְיֶיןָ הַטַּבָּעֹת לְבָתִּים לְבַדִּים לָשֵׂאת אֶת־
כח הַשֻּׁלְחָן׃ וְעָשִׂיתָ אֶת־הַבַּדִּים עֲצֵי שִׁטִּים וְצִפִּיתָ אֹתָם זָהָב וְנִשָּׂא־
כט בָם אֶת־הַשֻּׁלְחָן׃ וְעָשִׂיתָ קְּעָרֹתָיו וְכַפֹּתָיו וּקְשׂוֹתָיו וּמְנַקִּיֹּתָיו אֲשֶׁר
ל יֻסַּךְ בָּהֵן זָהָב טָהוֹר תַּעֲשֶׂה אֹתָם׃ וְנָתַתָּ עַל־הַשֻּׁלְחָן לֶחֶם פָּנִים
לְפָנַי תָּמִיד׃
לא וְעָשִׂיתָ מְנֹרַת זָהָב טָהוֹר מִקְשָׁה תֵּיעָשֶׂה הַמְּנוֹרָה יְרֵכָהּ וְקָנָהּ גְּבִיעֶיהָ
לב כַּפְתֹּרֶיהָ וּפְרָחֶיהָ מִמֶּנָּה יִהְיוּ׃ וְשִׁשָּׁה קָנִים יֹצְאִים מִצִּדֶּיהָ שְׁלֹשָׁה ׀
לג קְנֵי מְנֹרָה מִצִּדָּהּ הָאֶחָד וּשְׁלֹשָׁה קְנֵי מְנֹרָה מִצִּדָּהּ הַשֵּׁנִי׃ שְׁלֹשָׁה
גְבִעִים מְשֻׁקָּדִים בַּקָּנֶה הָאֶחָד כַּפְתֹּר וָפֶרַח וּשְׁלֹשָׁה גְבִעִים מְשֻׁקָּדִים
בַּקָּנֶה הָאֶחָד כַּפְתֹּר וָפָרַח כֵּן לְשֵׁשֶׁת הַקָּנִים הַיֹּצְאִים מִן־הַמְּנֹרָה׃
לד לה וּבַמְּנֹרָה אַרְבָּעָה גְבִעִים מְשֻׁקָּדִים כַּפְתֹּרֶיהָ וּפְרָחֶיהָ׃ וְכַפְתֹּר תַּחַת
שְׁנֵי הַקָּנִים מִמֶּנָּה וְכַפְתֹּר תַּחַת שְׁנֵי הַקָּנִים מִמֶּנָּה וְכַפְתֹּר תַּחַת־שְׁנֵי
לו הַקָּנִים מִמֶּנָּה לְשֵׁשֶׁת הַקָּנִים הַיֹּצְאִים מִן־הַמְּנֹרָה׃ כַּפְתֹּרֵיהֶם וּקְנֹתָם
לז מִמֶּנָּה יִהְיוּ כֻּלָּהּ מִקְשָׁה אַחַת זָהָב טָהוֹר׃ וְעָשִׂיתָ אֶת־נֵרֹתֶיהָ שִׁבְעָה
לח וְהֶעֱלָה אֶת־נֵרֹתֶיהָ וְהֵאִיר עַל־עֵבֶר פָּנֶיהָ׃ וּמַלְקָחֶיהָ וּמַחְתֹּתֶיהָ
לט זָהָב טָהוֹר׃ כִּכָּר זָהָב טָהוֹר יַעֲשֶׂה אֹתָהּ אֵת כָּל־הַכֵּלִים הָאֵלֶּה׃
מ כו א וּרְאֵה וַעֲשֵׂה בְּתַבְנִיתָם אֲשֶׁר־אַתָּה מָרְאֶה בָּהָר׃ וְאֶת־ יט שלישי
הַמִּשְׁכָּן תַּעֲשֶׂה עֶשֶׂר יְרִיעֹת שֵׁשׁ מָשְׁזָר וּתְכֵלֶת וְאַרְגָּמָן וְתֹלַעַת שָׁנִי
ב כְּרֻבִים מַעֲשֵׂה חֹשֵׁב תַּעֲשֶׂה אֹתָם׃ אֹרֶךְ ׀ הַיְרִיעָה הָאַחַת שְׁמֹנֶה

be twenty-eight cubits long and four cubits wide; all the sheets should be the
3 same size. Five of the sheets should be sewn together; the other five likewise.
4 Make loops of sky-blue wool on the upper edge of the end sheet in the first
set, and likewise on the upper edge of the outermost sheet in the second set.
5 Make fifty loops on each sheet on one side and fifty on the upper edge of the
corresponding sheets in the other set, with the loops opposite one another.
6 And make fifty gold clasps. With the clasps, join the sheets together so that the
7 Tabernacle becomes one whole. Make sheets of goats' hair as a tent over the
8 Tabernacle; make eleven of these sheets. Each sheet shall be thirty cubits long
9 and four cubits wide, all eleven sheets the same size. Join five of the sheets
by themselves, and the other six by themselves. Fold the sixth sheet over the
10 front of the Tent. Make fifty loops on the edge of the end sheet of one set, and
11 fifty on the edge of the end sheet of the other. Make, also, fifty bronze clasps.
Put the clasps through the loops, joining the tent together so that it becomes
12 one whole. As for the additional length of the tent sheets, the extra half sheet
13 is to hang down at the rear of the Tabernacle. The extra cubit at either end of
each of the tent sheets should hang over the sides of the Tabernacle to cover it
14 on both sides. Make a covering for the tent from rams' hides dyed red. Above
it make a covering of fine leather.
15 16 Make the upright boards for the Tabernacle of acacia wood. Each board shall
17 be ten cubits long and one and a half cubits wide. Each board should have
two matching tenons; all the Tabernacle's boards should be made in this way.
18 19 Make twenty boards for the southern side of the Tabernacle, and forty silver
sockets under the twenty boards, two sockets under the first board for its two
20 tenons, and two under the next. For the second side of the Tabernacle, the
21 northern side, there should be twenty boards, along with their forty silver
22 sockets, two under the first board and two under each of the others. Make
23 six boards for the west side of the Tabernacle, and two additional boards for
24 the Tabernacle's rear corners. These should adjoin each other at the bottom,
and be joined together at the top by a ring. So it should be for both sides;
25 they shall form the two corners. So there should be eight boards and sixteen

וְעֶשְׂרִים בָּאַמָּה וְרֹחַב אַרְבַּע בָּאַמָּה הַיְרִיעָה הָאֶחָת מִדָּה אַחַת
ג לְכָל־הַיְרִיעֹת: חֲמֵשׁ הַיְרִיעֹת תִּהְיֶיןָ חֹבְרֹת אִשָּׁה אֶל־אֲחֹתָהּ וְחָמֵשׁ
ד יְרִיעֹת חֹבְרֹת אִשָּׁה אֶל־אֲחֹתָהּ: וְעָשִׂיתָ לֻלְאֹת תְּכֵלֶת עַל שְׂפַת
הַיְרִיעָה הָאֶחָת מִקָּצָה בַּחֹבָרֶת וְכֵן תַּעֲשֶׂה בִּשְׂפַת הַיְרִיעָה הַקִּיצוֹנָה
ה בַּמַּחְבֶּרֶת הַשֵּׁנִית: חֲמִשִּׁים לֻלָאֹת תַּעֲשֶׂה בַּיְרִיעָה הָאֶחָת וַחֲמִשִּׁים
לֻלָאֹת תַּעֲשֶׂה בִּקְצֵה הַיְרִיעָה אֲשֶׁר בַּמַּחְבֶּרֶת הַשֵּׁנִית מַקְבִּילֹת
ו הַלֻּלָאֹת אִשָּׁה אֶל־אֲחֹתָהּ: וְעָשִׂיתָ חֲמִשִּׁים קַרְסֵי זָהָב וְחִבַּרְתָּ אֶת־
ז הַיְרִיעֹת אִשָּׁה אֶל־אֲחֹתָהּ בַּקְּרָסִים וְהָיָה הַמִּשְׁכָּן אֶחָד: וְעָשִׂיתָ
יְרִיעֹת עִזִּים לְאֹהֶל עַל־הַמִּשְׁכָּן עַשְׁתֵּי־עֶשְׂרֵה יְרִיעֹת תַּעֲשֶׂה אֹתָם:
ח אֹרֶךְ ׀ הַיְרִיעָה הָאַחַת שְׁלֹשִׁים בָּאַמָּה וְרֹחַב אַרְבַּע בָּאַמָּה הַיְרִיעָה
ט הָאֶחָת מִדָּה אַחַת לְעַשְׁתֵּי עֶשְׂרֵה יְרִיעֹת: וְחִבַּרְתָּ אֶת־חֲמֵשׁ הַיְרִיעֹת
לְבָד וְאֶת־שֵׁשׁ הַיְרִיעֹת לְבָד וְכָפַלְתָּ אֶת־הַיְרִיעָה הַשִּׁשִּׁית אֶל־
י מוּל פְּנֵי הָאֹהֶל: וְעָשִׂיתָ חֲמִשִּׁים לֻלָאֹת עַל שְׂפַת הַיְרִיעָה הָאֶחָת
הַקִּיצֹנָה בַּחֹבָרֶת וַחֲמִשִּׁים לֻלָאֹת עַל שְׂפַת הַיְרִיעָה הַחֹבֶרֶת הַשֵּׁנִית:
יא וְעָשִׂיתָ קַרְסֵי נְחֹשֶׁת חֲמִשִּׁים וְהֵבֵאתָ אֶת־הַקְּרָסִים בַּלֻּלָאֹת וְחִבַּרְתָּ
יב אֶת־הָאֹהֶל וְהָיָה אֶחָד: וְסֶרַח הָעֹדֵף בִּירִיעֹת הָאֹהֶל חֲצִי הַיְרִיעָה
יג הָעֹדֶפֶת תִּסְרַח עַל אֲחֹרֵי הַמִּשְׁכָּן: וְהָאַמָּה מִזֶּה וְהָאַמָּה מִזֶּה
בָּעֹדֵף בְּאֹרֶךְ יְרִיעֹת הָאֹהֶל יִהְיֶה סָרוּחַ עַל־צִדֵּי הַמִּשְׁכָּן מִזֶּה וּמִזֶּה
יד לְכַסֹּתוֹ: וְעָשִׂיתָ מִכְסֶה לָאֹהֶל עֹרֹת אֵילִם מְאָדָּמִים וּמִכְסֵה עֹרֹת
תְּחָשִׁים מִלְמָעְלָה:
טו טז וְעָשִׂיתָ אֶת־הַקְּרָשִׁים לַמִּשְׁכָּן עֲצֵי שִׁטִּים עֹמְדִים: עֶשֶׂר אַמּוֹת אֹרֶךְ רביעי
יז הַקָּרֶשׁ וְאַמָּה וַחֲצִי הָאַמָּה רֹחַב הַקֶּרֶשׁ הָאֶחָד: שְׁתֵּי יָדוֹת לַקֶּרֶשׁ
הָאֶחָד מְשֻׁלָּבֹת אִשָּׁה אֶל־אֲחֹתָהּ כֵּן תַּעֲשֶׂה לְכֹל קַרְשֵׁי הַמִּשְׁכָּן:
יח וְעָשִׂיתָ אֶת־הַקְּרָשִׁים לַמִּשְׁכָּן עֶשְׂרִים קֶרֶשׁ לִפְאַת נֶגְבָּה תֵימָנָה:
יט וְאַרְבָּעִים אַדְנֵי־כֶסֶף תַּעֲשֶׂה תַּחַת עֶשְׂרִים הַקָּרֶשׁ שְׁנֵי אֲדָנִים תַּחַת־
הַקֶּרֶשׁ הָאֶחָד לִשְׁתֵּי יְדֹתָיו וּשְׁנֵי אֲדָנִים תַּחַת־הַקֶּרֶשׁ הָאֶחָד לִשְׁתֵּי
כ כא יְדֹתָיו: וּלְצֶלַע הַמִּשְׁכָּן הַשֵּׁנִית לִפְאַת צָפוֹן עֶשְׂרִים קָרֶשׁ: וְאַרְבָּעִים
אַדְנֵיהֶם כָּסֶף שְׁנֵי אֲדָנִים תַּחַת הַקֶּרֶשׁ הָאֶחָד וּשְׁנֵי אֲדָנִים תַּחַת
כב כג הַקֶּרֶשׁ הָאֶחָד: וּלְיַרְכְּתֵי הַמִּשְׁכָּן יָמָּה תַּעֲשֶׂה שִׁשָּׁה קְרָשִׁים: וּשְׁנֵי
כד קְרָשִׁים תַּעֲשֶׂה לִמְקֻצְעֹת הַמִּשְׁכָּן בַּיַּרְכָתָיִם: וְיִהְיוּ תֹאֲמִם מִלְּמַטָּה
וְיַחְדָּו יִהְיוּ תַמִּים עַל־רֹאשׁוֹ אֶל־הַטַּבַּעַת הָאֶחָת כֵּן יִהְיֶה לִשְׁנֵיהֶם
כה לִשְׁנֵי הַמִּקְצֹעֹת יִהְיוּ: וְהָיוּ שְׁמֹנָה קְרָשִׁים וְאַדְנֵיהֶם כֶּסֶף שִׁשָּׁה

26 silver sockets, two sockets under each board. Make crossbars, too, of acacia
27 wood, five for the boards of the first side of the Tabernacle, five for the boards
of the second side of the Tabernacle, and five for the boards of the western
28 side of the Tabernacle at the rear. The central crossbar should go through the
29 middle of the boards from one end to the other. Overlay the boards with gold,
and make gold rings for the crossbars. The crossbars too should be overlaid
30 with gold. So shall you set up the Tabernacle, according to the plan you were
31 shown on the mountain. Make a curtain of sky-blue, purple, and
scarlet wool, and finely spun linen with a design of cherubim worked into
32 it. Hang it on four gold-covered posts of acacia wood with gold hooks, set
33 on four sockets of silver. Hang the curtain under the clasps and bring the
Ark of the Testimony behind it, so that the curtain separates the holy place
34 from the Holy of Holies. Put the cover on the Ark of the Testimony in the
35 Holy of Holies. The table shall be placed on the north side of the Tabernacle
outside the curtain, and the candelabrum on the south side, opposite the
36 table. Make a screen for the entrance to the Tent, embroidered with sky-
37 blue, purple, and scarlet wool and finely spun linen. Make five posts of acacia
wood for the screen and overlay them with gold; their hooks, also, shall be of
27 1 gold. Cast for them, too, five sockets of bronze. Make the altar from
acacia wood. It should be square, five cubits long, five cubits wide, and three
2 cubits high. Make horns for it on its four corners, the horns being of one
3 piece with it, and overlay it with bronze. Make pots for removing its ashes,
together with shovels, basins, forks, and pans. Make all of these of bronze.
4 Make a grate of bronze mesh for it, and on the mesh make four bronze
5 rings at its four corners. The grate should be set below, under the ledge of
6 the altar, so that the mesh reaches the middle of the altar. And make staves
7 of acacia wood for the altar, and overlay them with bronze. Place the poles
in the rings, so that the poles will be on the two sides of the altar when it is
8 carried. Make it hollow, with planks; make it as it was shown to you on the
9 mountain. Make the courtyard of the Tabernacle thus: on the south
side there should be hangings a hundred cubits long of finely spun linen, all
10 the length of the courtyard on that side, with twenty posts and their twenty
11 bronze sockets. The hooks and bands of the posts shall be of silver. Likewise
on the north side; the hangings shall be a hundred cubits long, with twenty
posts and their twenty corresponding bronze sockets, with hooks and bands
12 of silver. The width of the hangings at the western end of the courtyard shall
be fifty cubits, and it should have ten posts and their ten corresponding

עֶשֶׂר אֲדָנִים שְׁנֵי אֲדָנִים תַּחַת הַקֶּרֶשׁ הָאֶחָד וּשְׁנֵי אֲדָנִים תַּחַת
כו הַקֶּרֶשׁ הָאֶחָד: וְעָשִׂיתָ בְרִיחִם עֲצֵי שִׁטִּים חֲמִשָּׁה לְקַרְשֵׁי צֶלַע־
כז הַמִּשְׁכָּן הָאֶחָד: וַחֲמִשָּׁה בְרִיחִם לְקַרְשֵׁי צֶלַע־הַמִּשְׁכָּן הַשֵּׁנִית
כח וַחֲמִשָּׁה בְרִיחִם לְקַרְשֵׁי צֶלַע הַמִּשְׁכָּן לַיַּרְכָתַיִם יָמָּה: וְהַבְּרִיחַ הַתִּיכֹן
כט בְּתוֹךְ הַקְּרָשִׁים מַבְרִחַ מִן־הַקָּצֶה אֶל־הַקָּצֶה: וְאֶת־הַקְּרָשִׁים תְּצַפֶּה
זָהָב וְאֶת־טַבְּעֹתֵיהֶם תַּעֲשֶׂה זָהָב בָּתִּים לַבְּרִיחִם וְצִפִּיתָ אֶת־
ל הַבְּרִיחִם זָהָב: וַהֲקֵמֹתָ אֶת־הַמִּשְׁכָּן כְּמִשְׁפָּטוֹ אֲשֶׁר הָרְאֵיתָ
לא בָּהָר: וְעָשִׂיתָ פָרֹכֶת תְּכֵלֶת וְאַרְגָּמָן וְתוֹלַעַת שָׁנִי וְשֵׁשׁ כ חמישי
לב מָשְׁזָר מַעֲשֵׂה חֹשֵׁב יַעֲשֶׂה אֹתָהּ כְּרֻבִים: וְנָתַתָּה אֹתָהּ עַל־אַרְבָּעָה
לג עַמּוּדֵי שִׁטִּים מְצֻפִּים זָהָב וָוֵיהֶם זָהָב עַל־אַרְבָּעָה אַדְנֵי־כָסֶף: וְנָתַתָּה
אֶת־הַפָּרֹכֶת תַּחַת הַקְּרָסִים וְהֵבֵאתָ שָׁמָּה מִבֵּית לַפָּרֹכֶת אֵת אֲרוֹן
לד הָעֵדוּת וְהִבְדִּילָה הַפָּרֹכֶת לָכֶם בֵּין הַקֹּדֶשׁ וּבֵין קֹדֶשׁ הַקֳּדָשִׁים: וְנָתַתָּ
לה אֶת־הַכַּפֹּרֶת עַל אֲרוֹן הָעֵדֻת בְּקֹדֶשׁ הַקֳּדָשִׁים: וְשַׂמְתָּ אֶת־הַשֻּׁלְחָן
מִחוּץ לַפָּרֹכֶת וְאֶת־הַמְּנֹרָה נֹכַח הַשֻּׁלְחָן עַל צֶלַע הַמִּשְׁכָּן תֵּימָנָה
לו וְהַשֻּׁלְחָן תִּתֵּן עַל־צֶלַע צָפוֹן: וְעָשִׂיתָ מָסָךְ לְפֶתַח הָאֹהֶל תְּכֵלֶת
לז וְאַרְגָּמָן וְתוֹלַעַת שָׁנִי וְשֵׁשׁ מָשְׁזָר מַעֲשֵׂה רֹקֵם: וְעָשִׂיתָ לַמָּסָךְ חֲמִשָּׁה
עַמּוּדֵי שִׁטִּים וְצִפִּיתָ אֹתָם זָהָב וָוֵיהֶם זָהָב וְיָצַקְתָּ לָהֶם חֲמִשָּׁה אַדְנֵי
כז א נְחֹשֶׁת: וְעָשִׂיתָ אֶת־הַמִּזְבֵּחַ עֲצֵי שִׁטִּים חָמֵשׁ אַמּוֹת אֹרֶךְ ששי
ב וְחָמֵשׁ אַמּוֹת רֹחַב רָבוּעַ יִהְיֶה הַמִּזְבֵּחַ וְשָׁלֹשׁ אַמּוֹת קֹמָתוֹ: וְעָשִׂיתָ
קַרְנֹתָיו עַל אַרְבַּע פִּנֹּתָיו מִמֶּנּוּ תִּהְיֶיןָ קַרְנֹתָיו וְצִפִּיתָ אֹתוֹ נְחֹשֶׁת:
ג וְעָשִׂיתָ סִּירֹתָיו לְדַשְּׁנוֹ וְיָעָיו וּמִזְרְקֹתָיו וּמִזְלְגֹתָיו וּמַחְתֹּתָיו לְכָל־
ד כֵּלָיו תַּעֲשֶׂה נְחֹשֶׁת: וְעָשִׂיתָ לּוֹ מִכְבָּר מַעֲשֵׂה רֶשֶׁת נְחֹשֶׁת וְעָשִׂיתָ
ה עַל־הָרֶשֶׁת אַרְבַּע טַבְּעֹת נְחֹשֶׁת עַל אַרְבַּע קְצוֹתָיו: וְנָתַתָּה אֹתָהּ
ו תַּחַת כַּרְכֹּב הַמִּזְבֵּחַ מִלְּמָטָּה וְהָיְתָה הָרֶשֶׁת עַד חֲצִי הַמִּזְבֵּחַ: וְעָשִׂיתָ
ז בַדִּים לַמִּזְבֵּחַ בַּדֵּי עֲצֵי שִׁטִּים וְצִפִּיתָ אֹתָם נְחֹשֶׁת: וְהוּבָא אֶת־בַּדָּיו
ח בַּטַּבָּעֹת וְהָיוּ הַבַּדִּים עַל־שְׁתֵּי צַלְעֹת הַמִּזְבֵּחַ בִּשְׂאֵת אֹתוֹ: נְבוּב לֻחֹת
ט תַּעֲשֶׂה אֹתוֹ כַּאֲשֶׁר הֶרְאָה אֹתְךָ בָּהָר כֵּן יַעֲשׂוּ: וְעָשִׂיתָ שביעי
אֵת חֲצַר הַמִּשְׁכָּן לִפְאַת נֶגֶב־תֵּימָנָה קְלָעִים לֶחָצֵר שֵׁשׁ מָשְׁזָר מֵאָה
י בָאַמָּה אֹרֶךְ לַפֵּאָה הָאֶחָת: וְעַמֻּדָיו עֶשְׂרִים וְאַדְנֵיהֶם עֶשְׂרִים נְחֹשֶׁת
יא וָוֵי הָעַמֻּדִים וַחֲשֻׁקֵיהֶם כָּסֶף: וְכֵן לִפְאַת צָפוֹן בָּאֹרֶךְ קְלָעִים מֵאָה
אֹרֶךְ וְעַמֻּדָו עֶשְׂרִים וְאַדְנֵיהֶם עֶשְׂרִים נְחֹשֶׁת וָוֵי הָעַמֻּדִים וַחֲשֻׁקֵיהֶם
יב כָּסֶף: וְרֹחַב הֶחָצֵר לִפְאַת־יָם קְלָעִים חֲמִשִּׁים אַמָּה עַמֻּדֵיהֶם עֲשָׂרָה

13 sockets. The width of the courtyard at the front, facing east, shall be fifty
14 cubits: fifteen cubits of hangings with three posts and three sockets on one
15 side, and fifteen cubits of hangings with three posts and three sockets on the
16 other, and for the gate of the courtyard there shall be an embroidered screen
of twenty cubits of sky-blue, purple, and scarlet wool and finely spun linen,
17 with four posts and four sockets. All the posts around the courtyard should
be banded with silver. Their hooks shall be of silver, and their sockets of
18 bronze. The courtyard shall be a hundred cubits long, fifty cubits wide, and
19 five cubits high, with hangings of finely spun linen and sockets of bronze. All
the Tabernacle utensils, for every use, as well as all its tent pegs and the tent
20 pegs of the courtyard, shall be of bronze. Command the Israelites TETZAVEH
to bring you pure oil from crushed olives for light, to kindle the lamp, every
21 night. From evening to morning, before the LORD, Aharon and his sons
shall set it up to burn in the Tent of Meeting,[56] outside the curtain that veils
the Ark of the Testimony. This shall be a rule for all time for the Israelites,
28 1 throughout their generations. From among the Israelites, draw your
brother Aharon and his sons close to you to serve Me as priests – Aharon and
2 his sons Nadav and Avihu, Elazar and Itamar. Make sacred vestments for your
3 brother Aharon, for glory and for splendor. Speak to all the skilled craftsmen
whom I have endowed with a spirit of wisdom, and have them make Aharon's
4 vestments; these will consecrate him to serve Me as priest. These are the
garments they shall make: a breast piece, an ephod,[57] a robe, a quilted tunic,
a miter and a sash; sacred vestments shall they make, for your brother Aharon
5 and his sons to serve Me in. They should use gold, and sky-blue, purple, and
scarlet wool, and fine linen.
6 They are to make the ephod of finely spun linen embroidered with gold, and
7 sky-blue, purple, and scarlet wool. It should have two shoulder pieces attached
8 to its two edges so that it can be joined together. The decorated waistband on
it shall be like it and of one piece with it, made of gold, of sky-blue, purple,
9 and scarlet wool and finely spun linen. Take two rock crystal stones and
10 engrave on them the names of Yisrael's sons: six names on one stone and the
11 remaining six names on the other, in the order of their birth. Engrave the two
stones with the names of Yisrael's sons as a gem cutter engraves a seal, then
12 mount them in gold filigree settings. Place the two stones on the shoulder
pieces of the ephod as remembrance stones for the sons of Yisrael. Thus will
Aharon carry their names on his shoulders as a remembrance before the
13 14 LORD. Make gold filigree settings and two sets of pure
gold chains braided into cords, and attach the cords of chains to the
15 settings. Make a breast piece for judgment. Make it with the

56 | That is, the Tabernacle, the locus of divine communication; cf. 25:22, 29:43.

57 | See note on 25:7.

יג וְאַדְנֵיהֶם עֲשָׂרָה: וְרֹחַב הֶחָצֵר לִפְאַת קֵדְמָה מִזְרָחָה חֲמִשִּׁים אַמָּה:
יד וַחֲמֵשׁ עֶשְׂרֵה אַמָּה קְלָעִים לַכָּתֵף עַמֻּדֵיהֶם שְׁלֹשָׁה וְאַדְנֵיהֶם שְׁלֹשָׁה:
טו וְלַכָּתֵף הַשֵּׁנִית חֲמֵשׁ עֶשְׂרֵה קְלָעִים עַמֻּדֵיהֶם שְׁלֹשָׁה וְאַדְנֵיהֶם
טז שְׁלֹשָׁה: וּלְשַׁעַר הֶחָצֵר מָסָךְ ׀ עֶשְׂרִים אַמָּה תְּכֵלֶת וְאַרְגָּמָן וְתוֹלַעַת
שְׁנִי וְשֵׁשׁ מָשְׁזָר מַעֲשֵׂה רֹקֵם עַמֻּדֵיהֶם אַרְבָּעָה וְאַדְנֵיהֶם אַרְבָּעָה:
יז כָּל־עַמּוּדֵי הֶחָצֵר סָבִיב מְחֻשָּׁקִים כֶּסֶף וָוֵיהֶם כָּסֶף וְאַדְנֵיהֶם נְחֹשֶׁת: מפטיר
יח אֹרֶךְ הֶחָצֵר מֵאָה בָאַמָּה וְרֹחַב ׀ חֲמִשִּׁים בַּחֲמִשִּׁים וְקֹמָה חָמֵשׁ
יט אַמּוֹת שֵׁשׁ מָשְׁזָר וְאַדְנֵיהֶם נְחֹשֶׁת: לְכֹל כְּלֵי הַמִּשְׁכָּן בְּכֹל עֲבֹדָתוֹ
כ וְכָל־יְתֵדֹתָיו וְכָל־יִתְדֹת הֶחָצֵר נְחֹשֶׁת: וְאַתָּה תְּצַוֶּה ׀ כא תצוה
אֶת־בְּנֵי יִשְׂרָאֵל וְיִקְחוּ אֵלֶיךָ שֶׁמֶן זַיִת זָךְ כָּתִית לַמָּאוֹר לְהַעֲלֹת נֵר
כא תָּמִיד: בְּאֹהֶל מוֹעֵד מִחוּץ לַפָּרֹכֶת אֲשֶׁר עַל־הָעֵדֻת יַעֲרֹךְ אֹתוֹ
אַהֲרֹן וּבָנָיו מֵעֶרֶב עַד־בֹּקֶר לִפְנֵי יְהוָה חֻקַּת עוֹלָם לְדֹרֹתָם מֵאֵת בְּנֵי
כח א יִשְׂרָאֵל: וְאַתָּה הַקְרֵב אֵלֶיךָ אֶת־אַהֲרֹן אָחִיךָ וְאֶת־בָּנָיו
אִתּוֹ מִתּוֹךְ בְּנֵי יִשְׂרָאֵל לְכַהֲנוֹ־לִי אַהֲרֹן נָדָב וַאֲבִיהוּא אֶלְעָזָר וְאִיתָמָר
ב ג בְּנֵי אַהֲרֹן: וְעָשִׂיתָ בִגְדֵי־קֹדֶשׁ לְאַהֲרֹן אָחִיךָ לְכָבוֹד וּלְתִפְאָרֶת: וְאַתָּה
תְּדַבֵּר אֶל־כָּל־חַכְמֵי־לֵב אֲשֶׁר מִלֵּאתִיו רוּחַ חָכְמָה וְעָשׂוּ אֶת־בִּגְדֵי
ד אַהֲרֹן לְקַדְּשׁוֹ לְכַהֲנוֹ־לִי: וְאֵלֶּה הַבְּגָדִים אֲשֶׁר יַעֲשׂוּ חֹשֶׁן וְאֵפוֹד
וּמְעִיל וּכְתֹנֶת תַּשְׁבֵּץ מִצְנֶפֶת וְאַבְנֵט וְעָשׂוּ בִגְדֵי־קֹדֶשׁ לְאַהֲרֹן אָחִיךָ
ה וּלְבָנָיו לְכַהֲנוֹ־לִי: וְהֵם יִקְחוּ אֶת־הַזָּהָב וְאֶת־הַתְּכֵלֶת וְאֶת־הָאַרְגָּמָן
וְאֶת־תּוֹלַעַת הַשָּׁנִי וְאֶת־הַשֵּׁשׁ:
ו וְעָשׂוּ אֶת־הָאֵפֹד זָהָב תְּכֵלֶת וְאַרְגָּמָן תּוֹלַעַת שָׁנִי וְשֵׁשׁ מָשְׁזָר מַעֲשֵׂה
ז ח חֹשֵׁב: שְׁתֵּי כְתֵפֹת חֹבְרֹת יִהְיֶה־לּוֹ אֶל־שְׁנֵי קְצוֹתָיו וְחֻבָּר: וְחֵשֶׁב
אֲפֻדָּתוֹ אֲשֶׁר עָלָיו כְּמַעֲשֵׂהוּ מִמֶּנּוּ יִהְיֶה זָהָב תְּכֵלֶת וְאַרְגָּמָן וְתוֹלַעַת
ט שָׁנִי וְשֵׁשׁ מָשְׁזָר: וְלָקַחְתָּ אֶת־שְׁתֵּי אַבְנֵי־שֹׁהַם וּפִתַּחְתָּ עֲלֵיהֶם שְׁמוֹת
י בְּנֵי יִשְׂרָאֵל: שִׁשָּׁה מִשְּׁמֹתָם עַל הָאֶבֶן הָאֶחָת וְאֶת־שְׁמוֹת הַשִּׁשָּׁה
יא הַנּוֹתָרִים עַל־הָאֶבֶן הַשֵּׁנִית כְּתוֹלְדֹתָם: מַעֲשֵׂה חָרַשׁ אֶבֶן פִּתּוּחֵי
חֹתָם תְּפַתַּח אֶת־שְׁתֵּי הָאֲבָנִים עַל־שְׁמֹת בְּנֵי יִשְׂרָאֵל מֻסַבֹּת
יב מִשְׁבְּצוֹת זָהָב תַּעֲשֶׂה אֹתָם: וְשַׂמְתָּ אֶת־שְׁתֵּי הָאֲבָנִים עַל כִּתְפֹת
הָאֵפֹד אַבְנֵי זִכָּרֹן לִבְנֵי יִשְׂרָאֵל וְנָשָׂא אַהֲרֹן אֶת־שְׁמוֹתָם לִפְנֵי יְהוָה
יג יד עַל־שְׁתֵּי כְתֵפָיו לְזִכָּרֹן: וְעָשִׂיתָ מִשְׁבְּצֹת זָהָב: וּשְׁתֵּי שני
שַׁרְשְׁרֹת זָהָב טָהוֹר מִגְבָּלֹת תַּעֲשֶׂה אֹתָם מַעֲשֵׂה עֲבֹת וְנָתַתָּה אֶת־
טו שַׁרְשְׁרֹת הָעֲבֹתֹת עַל־הַמִּשְׁבְּצֹת: וְעָשִׂיתָ חֹשֶׁן מִשְׁפָּט

same skilled craftsmanship as the ephod: of gold, of sky-blue, purple, and
16 scarlet wool, and of finely spun linen. It shall be square and folded double, a
17 span long and a span wide. Mount four rows of precious stones onto it: the
18 first row a carnelian,[58] an olivine, and a garnet; the second row an emerald, a
19 lapis lazuli, and a green quartz; the third row an amber, a jet, and a sardonyx;
20 and the fourth an aquamarine, a rock crystal, and a jasper or opal. Mount
21 them in gold filigree settings. The stones shall correspond to the names of
Yisrael's sons. Each stone should be engraved like a seal, with one of the names
22 of the twelve tribes. Make chains of pure gold, braided into cords, for the
23 breast piece. Make the breast piece two gold rings and attach them to its two
24 corners. Then fasten the two gold chains to the two gold rings at the corners
25 of the breast piece. Attach the other ends of the chains to the two settings.
26 They will thus be joined to the ephod's shoulder pieces at the front. Make
two gold rings and place them at the two other corners of the breast piece on
27 the edge, inside, next to the ephod. Make two more gold rings and attach
them to the bottom of the ephod's two shoulder pieces facing its front, close
28 to its seam and above the ephod's woven waistband. The breast piece shall be
held in place by a cord of sky blue from its rings to the rings of the ephod, so
that the breast piece remains secured above the ephod's waistband, and does
29 not come loose from the ephod. Thus will Aharon carry the names of Yisrael's
sons on the breast piece of judgment at his heart whenever he enters the
30 Sanctuary, as a remembrance before the Lord at all times. Place the Urim
and Tumim[59] in the breast piece of judgment so that they too will be at
Aharon's heart when he comes before the Lord. Aharon will then
always be carrying at his heart Israel's means of judgment, before the
31 Lord.
32 Make the robe of the ephod entirely of sky-blue wool. It
should have an opening for the head in the middle with a woven border
33 around it like the neck of a coat of mail, so that it does not tear. Around the
hem of the robe make pomegranates of sky-blue, purple, and scarlet wool,
34 and between them put gold bells, so that gold bells and pomegranates
35 alternate around the hem of the robe. Aharon shall wear this robe whenever
he ministers, and its sound will be heard when he enters the Sanctuary before
36 the Lord and when he leaves, so that he will not die. Make a
headplate of pure gold and engrave on it, as on a seal: Holy to the Lord.
37 Attach a cord of sky blue to it, so that it can be fixed to the miter, affixed to
38 the miter's front. It shall remain on Aharon's forehead, that Aharon may bear
away all guilt that arises from the holy offerings the Israelites consecrate, from
all their sacred gifts;[60] it shall be on his forehead always, that they may find
39 favor in the Lord's sight. Quilt the tunic of fine linen. Make a miter out of

---

58 | Identifications of these stones vary.

59 | Explanations of the nature of this item vary. Numbers 27:21 makes clear that it is a conduit for divine communication.

60 | As generally understood, this means that the diadem atones for certain deviations from the rules that govern offerings.

מַעֲשֵׂה חֹשֵׁב כְּמַעֲשֵׂה אֵפֹד תַּעֲשֶׂנּוּ זָהָב תְּכֵלֶת וְאַרְגָּמָן וְתוֹלַעַת שָׁנִי
טז וְשֵׁשׁ מָשְׁזָר תַּעֲשֶׂה אֹתוֹ׃ רָבוּעַ יִהְיֶה כָּפוּל זֶרֶת אָרְכּוֹ וְזֶרֶת רָחְבּוֹ׃
יז וּמִלֵּאתָ בוֹ מִלֻּאַת אֶבֶן אַרְבָּעָה טוּרִים אָבֶן טוּר אֹדֶם פִּטְדָה וּבָרֶקֶת
יח יט הַטּוּר הָאֶחָד׃ וְהַטּוּר הַשֵּׁנִי נֹפֶךְ סַפִּיר וְיָהֲלֹם׃ וְהַטּוּר הַשְּׁלִישִׁי לֶשֶׁם
כ שְׁבוֹ וְאַחְלָמָה׃ וְהַטּוּר הָרְבִיעִי תַּרְשִׁישׁ וְשֹׁהַם וְיָשְׁפֵה מְשֻׁבָּצִים זָהָב
כא יִהְיוּ בְּמִלּוּאֹתָם׃ וְהָאֲבָנִים תִּהְיֶיןָ עַל־שְׁמֹת בְּנֵי־יִשְׂרָאֵל שְׁתֵּים עֶשְׂרֵה
עַל־שְׁמֹתָם פִּתּוּחֵי חוֹתָם אִישׁ עַל־שְׁמוֹ תִּהְיֶיןָ לִשְׁנֵי עָשָׂר שָׁבֶט׃
כב כג וְעָשִׂיתָ עַל־הַחֹשֶׁן שַׁרְשֹׁת גַּבְלֻת מַעֲשֵׂה עֲבֹת זָהָב טָהוֹר׃ וְעָשִׂיתָ
עַל־הַחֹשֶׁן שְׁתֵּי טַבְּעוֹת זָהָב וְנָתַתָּ אֶת־שְׁתֵּי הַטַּבָּעוֹת עַל־שְׁנֵי קְצוֹת
כד הַחֹשֶׁן׃ וְנָתַתָּה אֶת־שְׁתֵּי עֲבֹתֹת הַזָּהָב עַל־שְׁתֵּי הַטַּבָּעֹת אֶל־קְצוֹת
כה הַחֹשֶׁן׃ וְאֵת שְׁתֵּי קְצוֹת שְׁתֵּי הָעֲבֹתֹת תִּתֵּן עַל־שְׁתֵּי הַמִּשְׁבְּצוֹת
כו וְנָתַתָּה עַל־כִּתְפוֹת הָאֵפֹד אֶל־מוּל פָּנָיו׃ וְעָשִׂיתָ שְׁתֵּי טַבְּעוֹת זָהָב
וְשַׂמְתָּ אֹתָם עַל־שְׁנֵי קְצוֹת הַחֹשֶׁן עַל־שְׂפָתוֹ אֲשֶׁר אֶל־עֵבֶר הָאֵפוֹד
כז בָּיְתָה׃ וְעָשִׂיתָ שְׁתֵּי טַבְּעוֹת זָהָב וְנָתַתָּה אֹתָם עַל־שְׁתֵּי כִתְפוֹת
הָאֵפוֹד מִלְּמַטָּה מִמּוּל פָּנָיו לְעֻמַּת מַחְבַּרְתּוֹ מִמַּעַל לְחֵשֶׁב הָאֵפוֹד׃
כח וְיִרְכְּסוּ אֶת־הַחֹשֶׁן מִטַּבְּעֹתָו אֶל־טַבְּעֹת הָאֵפוֹד בִּפְתִיל תְּכֵלֶת לִהְיוֹת
כט עַל־חֵשֶׁב הָאֵפוֹד וְלֹא־יִזַּח הַחֹשֶׁן מֵעַל הָאֵפוֹד׃ וְנָשָׂא אַהֲרֹן אֶת־
שְׁמוֹת בְּנֵי־יִשְׂרָאֵל בְּחֹשֶׁן הַמִּשְׁפָּט עַל־לִבּוֹ בְּבֹאוֹ אֶל־הַקֹּדֶשׁ
ל לְזִכָּרֹן לִפְנֵי־יְהוָה תָּמִיד׃ וְנָתַתָּ אֶל־חֹשֶׁן הַמִּשְׁפָּט אֶת־הָאוּרִים וְאֶת־
הַתֻּמִּים וְהָיוּ עַל־לֵב אַהֲרֹן בְּבֹאוֹ לִפְנֵי יְהוָה וְנָשָׂא אַהֲרֹן אֶת־מִשְׁפַּט
לא בְּנֵי־יִשְׂרָאֵל עַל־לִבּוֹ לִפְנֵי יְהוָה תָּמִיד׃ וְעָשִׂיתָ אֶת־מְעִיל שלישי
לב הָאֵפוֹד כְּלִיל תְּכֵלֶת׃ וְהָיָה פִי־רֹאשׁוֹ בְּתוֹכוֹ שָׂפָה יִהְיֶה לְפִיו סָבִיב
לג מַעֲשֵׂה אֹרֵג כְּפִי תַחְרָא יִהְיֶה־לּוֹ לֹא יִקָּרֵעַ׃ וְעָשִׂיתָ עַל־שׁוּלָיו רִמֹּנֵי
תְּכֵלֶת וְאַרְגָּמָן וְתוֹלַעַת שָׁנִי עַל־שׁוּלָיו סָבִיב וּפַעֲמֹנֵי זָהָב בְּתוֹכָם
לד סָבִיב׃ פַּעֲמֹן זָהָב וְרִמּוֹן פַּעֲמֹן זָהָב וְרִמּוֹן עַל־שׁוּלֵי הַמְּעִיל סָבִיב׃
לה וְהָיָה עַל־אַהֲרֹן לְשָׁרֵת וְנִשְׁמַע קוֹלוֹ בְּבֹאוֹ אֶל־הַקֹּדֶשׁ לִפְנֵי יְהוָה
לו וּבְצֵאתוֹ וְלֹא יָמוּת׃ וְעָשִׂיתָ צִּיץ זָהָב טָהוֹר וּפִתַּחְתָּ
לז עָלָיו פִּתּוּחֵי חֹתָם קֹדֶשׁ לַיהוָה׃ וְשַׂמְתָּ אֹתוֹ עַל־פְּתִיל תְּכֵלֶת וְהָיָה
לח עַל־הַמִּצְנֶפֶת אֶל־מוּל פְּנֵי־הַמִּצְנֶפֶת יִהְיֶה׃ וְהָיָה עַל־מֵצַח אַהֲרֹן
וְנָשָׂא אַהֲרֹן אֶת־עֲוֹן הַקֳּדָשִׁים אֲשֶׁר יַקְדִּישׁוּ בְּנֵי יִשְׂרָאֵל לְכָל־מַתְּנֹת
לט קָדְשֵׁיהֶם וְהָיָה עַל־מִצְחוֹ תָּמִיד לְרָצוֹן לָהֶם לִפְנֵי יְהוָה׃ וְשִׁבַּצְתָּ
הַכְּתֹנֶת שֵׁשׁ וְעָשִׂיתָ מִצְנֶפֶת שֵׁשׁ וְאַבְנֵט תַּעֲשֶׂה מַעֲשֵׂה רֹקֵם׃

40 fine linen, and an embroidered sash. Make tunics, sashes, and caps for
41 Aharon's sons, for glory and for splendor. Put these on your brother Aharon
and his sons; then anoint, ordain, and consecrate them to serve Me as priests.
42 Make them linen trousers to cover their nakedness, reaching from waist to
43 thigh. They must be worn by Aharon and his sons whenever they enter the
Tent of Meeting or approach the altar to minister in the Sanctuary so that
they do not incur guilt and die. This shall be a law for Aharon and his
29 1 descendants for all time. This is what you must do to consecrate
2 them to serve Me as priests. Take a young bull, two unblemished rams, and
unleavened bread, unleavened loaves mixed with oil, and unleavened wafers
3 brushed with oil – all made of fine wheat flour. Place these in a basket and
4 bring them in the basket together with the young bull and two rams. Bring
Aharon and his sons to the entrance of the Tent of Meeting, and you shall
5 wash them with water. Then take the vestments and dress Aharon in the tunic,
the robe of the ephod, the ephod itself, and the breast piece. Fasten the ephod
6 on him by its woven waistband. Put the miter on his head and on the miter
7 place the sacred diadem. Take the anointing oil, pour it on his head, and
8 9 anoint him. Then bring his sons forward and dress them with the tunics. Gird
Aharon and his sons with the sashes and fasten their headdresses. The
priesthood shall be theirs as a law for all time. Thus you shall ordain Aharon
10 and his sons. Then bring the young bull in front of the Tent of Meeting, and
11 have Aharon and his sons lay their hands on its head. Slaughter the bull before
12 the Lord at the entrance of the Tent of Meeting. Take some of the bull's
blood and put it on the horns of the altar with your finger. Pour out the rest
13 of the blood at the base of the altar. Take all the fat that covers the entrails,
the diaphragm of the liver, and the two kidneys with the fat around them, and
14 burn them on the altar. Burn the bull's flesh, its hide, and its waste outside the
15 camp; it is a purification offering. Then take one of the rams and have Aharon
16 and his sons lay their hands upon its head, then slaughter it; let them take its
17 blood and sprinkle it on all the sides of the altar. Cut the ram into pieces, wash
18 its entrails and legs, and put them with its pieces and its head. Burn the entire
ram on the altar. It is a burnt offering to the Lord, a pleasing aroma, a fire
19 offering to the Lord. Then take the second ram, and have Aharon and his
20 sons lay their hands on its head. Slaughter the ram, take some of its blood and
put it on the ridges of the right ears of Aharon and his sons, and on the thumbs
of their right hands and on the big toes of their right feet. Sprinkle the rest of
21 the blood on the sides of the altar. Collect some of the blood on the altar and

מ וְלִבְנֵי אַהֲרֹן תַּעֲשֶׂה כֻתֳּנֹת וְעָשִׂיתָ לָהֶם אַבְנֵטִים וּמִגְבָּעוֹת תַּעֲשֶׂה
מא לָהֶם לְכָבוֹד וּלְתִפְאָרֶת׃ וְהִלְבַּשְׁתָּ אֹתָם אֶת־אַהֲרֹן אָחִיךָ וְאֶת־בָּנָיו
מב אִתּוֹ וּמָשַׁחְתָּ אֹתָם וּמִלֵּאתָ אֶת־יָדָם וְקִדַּשְׁתָּ אֹתָם וְכִהֲנוּ־לִי׃ וַעֲשֵׂה
מג לָהֶם מִכְנְסֵי־בָד לְכַסּוֹת בְּשַׂר עֶרְוָה מִמָּתְנַיִם וְעַד־יְרֵכַיִם יִהְיוּ׃ וְהָיוּ
עַל־אַהֲרֹן וְעַל־בָּנָיו בְּבֹאָם ׀ אֶל־אֹהֶל מוֹעֵד אוֹ בְגִשְׁתָּם אֶל־הַמִּזְבֵּחַ
לְשָׁרֵת בַּקֹּדֶשׁ וְלֹא־יִשְׂאוּ עָוֺן וָמֵתוּ חֻקַּת עוֹלָם לוֹ וּלְזַרְעוֹ
כט א אַחֲרָיו׃ וְזֶה הַדָּבָר אֲשֶׁר תַּעֲשֶׂה לָהֶם לְקַדֵּשׁ אֹתָם לְכַהֵן כב רביעי
ב לִי לְקַח פַּר אֶחָד בֶּן־בָּקָר וְאֵילִם שְׁנַיִם תְּמִימִם׃ וְלֶחֶם מַצּוֹת וְחַלֹּת
מַצֹּת בְּלוּלֹת בַּשֶּׁמֶן וּרְקִיקֵי מַצּוֹת מְשֻׁחִים בַּשָּׁמֶן סֹלֶת חִטִּים תַּעֲשֶׂה
ג אֹתָם׃ וְנָתַתָּ אוֹתָם עַל־סַל אֶחָד וְהִקְרַבְתָּ אֹתָם בַּסָּל וְאֶת־הַפָּר וְאֵת
ד שְׁנֵי הָאֵילִם׃ וְאֶת־אַהֲרֹן וְאֶת־בָּנָיו תַּקְרִיב אֶל־פֶּתַח אֹהֶל מוֹעֵד
ה וְרָחַצְתָּ אֹתָם בַּמָּיִם׃ וְלָקַחְתָּ אֶת־הַבְּגָדִים וְהִלְבַּשְׁתָּ אֶת־אַהֲרֹן אֶת־
הַכֻּתֹּנֶת וְאֵת מְעִיל הָאֵפֹד וְאֶת־הָאֵפֹד וְאֶת־הַחֹשֶׁן וְאָפַדְתָּ לוֹ בְּחֵשֶׁב
ו הָאֵפֹד׃ וְשַׂמְתָּ הַמִּצְנֶפֶת עַל־רֹאשׁוֹ וְנָתַתָּ אֶת־נֵזֶר הַקֹּדֶשׁ עַל־
ז הַמִּצְנָפֶת׃ וְלָקַחְתָּ אֶת־שֶׁמֶן הַמִּשְׁחָה וְיָצַקְתָּ עַל־רֹאשׁוֹ וּמָשַׁחְתָּ
ח ט אֹתוֹ׃ וְאֶת־בָּנָיו תַּקְרִיב וְהִלְבַּשְׁתָּם כֻּתֳּנֹת׃ וְחָגַרְתָּ אֹתָם אַבְנֵט אַהֲרֹן
וּבָנָיו וְחָבַשְׁתָּ לָהֶם מִגְבָּעֹת וְהָיְתָה לָהֶם כְּהֻנָּה לְחֻקַּת עוֹלָם וּמִלֵּאתָ
י יַד־אַהֲרֹן וְיַד־בָּנָיו׃ וְהִקְרַבְתָּ אֶת־הַפָּר לִפְנֵי אֹהֶל מוֹעֵד וְסָמַךְ אַהֲרֹן
יא וּבָנָיו אֶת־יְדֵיהֶם עַל־רֹאשׁ הַפָּר׃ וְשָׁחַטְתָּ אֶת־הַפָּר לִפְנֵי יְהוָה פֶּתַח
יב אֹהֶל מוֹעֵד׃ וְלָקַחְתָּ מִדַּם הַפָּר וְנָתַתָּה עַל־קַרְנֹת הַמִּזְבֵּחַ בְּאֶצְבָּעֶךָ
יג וְאֶת־כָּל־הַדָּם תִּשְׁפֹּךְ אֶל־יְסוֹד הַמִּזְבֵּחַ׃ וְלָקַחְתָּ אֶת־כָּל־הַחֵלֶב
הַמְכַסֶּה אֶת־הַקֶּרֶב וְאֵת הַיֹּתֶרֶת עַל־הַכָּבֵד וְאֵת שְׁתֵּי הַכְּלָיֹת וְאֶת־
יד הַחֵלֶב אֲשֶׁר עֲלֵיהֶן וְהִקְטַרְתָּ הַמִּזְבֵּחָה׃ וְאֶת־בְּשַׂר הַפָּר וְאֶת־עֹרוֹ
טו וְאֶת־פִּרְשׁוֹ תִּשְׂרֹף בָּאֵשׁ מִחוּץ לַמַּחֲנֶה חַטָּאת הוּא׃ וְאֶת־הָאַיִל
טז הָאֶחָד תִּקָּח וְסָמְכוּ אַהֲרֹן וּבָנָיו אֶת־יְדֵיהֶם עַל־רֹאשׁ הָאָיִל׃ וְשָׁחַטְתָּ
יז אֶת־הָאָיִל וְלָקַחְתָּ אֶת־דָּמוֹ וְזָרַקְתָּ עַל־הַמִּזְבֵּחַ סָבִיב׃ וְאֶת־הָאַיִל
תְּנַתֵּחַ לִנְתָחָיו וְרָחַצְתָּ קִרְבּוֹ וּכְרָעָיו וְנָתַתָּ עַל־נְתָחָיו וְעַל־רֹאשׁוֹ׃
יח וְהִקְטַרְתָּ אֶת־כָּל־הָאַיִל הַמִּזְבֵּחָה עֹלָה הוּא לַיהוָה רֵיחַ נִיחוֹחַ אִשֶּׁה
יט לַיהוָה הוּא׃ וְלָקַחְתָּ אֵת הָאַיִל הַשֵּׁנִי וְסָמַךְ אַהֲרֹן וּבָנָיו אֶת־יְדֵיהֶם חמישי
כ עַל־רֹאשׁ הָאָיִל׃ וְשָׁחַטְתָּ אֶת־הָאַיִל וְלָקַחְתָּ מִדָּמוֹ וְנָתַתָּה עַל־תְּנוּךְ
אֹזֶן אַהֲרֹן וְעַל־תְּנוּךְ אֹזֶן בָּנָיו הַיְמָנִית וְעַל־בֹּהֶן יָדָם הַיְמָנִית וְעַל־בֹּהֶן
כא רַגְלָם הַיְמָנִית וְזָרַקְתָּ אֶת־הַדָּם עַל־הַמִּזְבֵּחַ סָבִיב׃ וְלָקַחְתָּ מִן־הַדָּם

some of the anointing oil and sprinkle it on Aharon and his vestments, and
on his sons and his sons' vestments. Then he, and his sons with him, and their
22 vestments, will be consecrated. From the ram take its fat parts – the broad
tail, the fat that covers the entrails, the diaphragm of the liver, and the two
kidneys with the fat on them – and the right thigh, for this is the ram of
23 ordination. From the basket of unleavened bread before the LORD, take one
24 loaf of bread, one loaf of oil bread, and one wafer. Place all of these on the
palms of Aharon and his sons, and have them wave them as a wave offering
25 before the LORD. Then take them from their hands and burn them on the
altar with the burnt offering, for a pleasing aroma before the LORD. It is a fire
26 offering to the LORD. Take the breast of Aharon's ram of ordination and wave
27 it as a wave offering before the LORD; it shall be your portion. From Aharon
and his sons' ram of ordination, consecrate the breast, the wave offering and
28 the thigh, the upraised gift. These parts shall be the Israelites' due to Aharon
and his sons for all time. They are the Israelites' gift from their peace offerings,
29 their gift to the LORD. Aharon's sacred vestments shall pass on to his sons
30 after him. In them they shall be anointed and ordained. The son who succeeds
him as priest, entering the Tent of Meeting to minister in the Sanctuary, shall
31 wear them for seven days. Take the ram of ordination and, in the sacred
32 precinct, cook its flesh. Aharon and his sons shall eat the meat of the ram, and
33 the bread in the basket, near the entrance of the Tent of Meeting. They shall
eat these things, through which atonement will be made, to be ordained and
34 consecrated. Because they are consecrated no layman may eat of them. If any
of the meat of the ordination ram or any of the bread is left over until morning,
you shall burn what remains with fire. It must not be eaten, for it is consecrated.
35 This is what you must do for Aharon and his sons, just as I have commanded
36 you. Their ordination shall take seven days. Each day, offer a bull as a
purification offering for atonement. Purify the altar by making atonement for
37 it, and consecrate it by anointing it. For seven days, make atonement for the
altar and consecrate it, so that the altar becomes holy of holies – and anything
38 that touches it will become holy. This is what you shall offer on the
39 altar: two yearling lambs each day, with constancy. Offer one lamb in the
40 morning, and the other in the afternoon. With the first lamb offer a tenth
measure of fine flour mixed with a quarter of a hin[61] of beaten oil, and a
41 quarter of a hin of wine as a libation. Offer the other lamb in the afternoon
together with a grain offering and libation as in the morning, as a pleasing
42 aroma, a fire offering to the LORD. This shall be the regular burnt offering
throughout your generations at the entrance of the Tent of Meeting before
43 the LORD. There I will meet with you, there I will speak to you, and there I
44 will meet with the Israelites. It will be sanctified by My glory. I will consecrate

61 | A liquid measure, equivalent to approximately 4 liters or 1 gallon.

אשר על־המזבח ומשמן המשחה והזית על־אהרן ועל־בגדיו ועל־
בניו ועל־בגדי בניו אתו וקדש הוא ובגדיו ובניו ובגדי בניו אתו:
כב ולקחת מן־האיל החלב והאליה ואת־החלב ׀ המכסה את־הקרב
ואת יתרת הכבד ואת ׀ שתי הכלית ואת־החלב אשר עליהן ואת
כג שוק הימין כי איל מלאים הוא: וככר לחם אחת וחלת לחם שמן
כד אחת ורקיק אחד מסל המצות אשר לפני יהוה: ושמת הכל על
כה כפי אהרן ועל כפי בניו והנפת אתם תנופה לפני יהוה: ולקחת
אתם מידם והקטרת המזבחה על־העלה לריח ניחוח לפני יהוה
כו אשה הוא ליהוה: ולקחת את־החזה מאיל המלאים אשר לאהרן
כז והנפת אתו תנופה לפני יהוה והיה לך למנה: וקדשת את ׀ חזה
התנופה ואת שוק התרומה אשר הונף ואשר הורם מאיל המלאים
כח מאשר לאהרן ומאשר לבניו: והיה לאהרן ולבניו לחק־עולם מאת
בני ישראל כי תרומה הוא ותרומה יהיה מאת בני־ישראל מזבחי
כט שלמיהם תרומתם ליהוה: ובגדי הקדש אשר לאהרן יהיו לבניו
ל אחריו למשחה בהם ולמלא־בם את־ידם: שבעת ימים ילבשם
לא הכהן תחתיו מבניו אשר יבא אל־אהל מועד לשרת בקדש: ואת
לב איל המלאים תקח ובשלת את־בשרו במקם קדש: ואכל אהרן
לג ובניו את־בשר האיל ואת־הלחם אשר בסל פתח אהל מועד: ואכלו
אתם אשר כפר בהם למלא את־ידם לקדש אתם וזר לא־יאכל
לד כי־קדש הם: ואם־יותר מבשר המלאים ומן־הלחם עד־הבקר
לה ושרפת את־הנותר באש לא יאכל כי־קדש הוא: ועשית לאהרן
לו ולבניו ככה ככל אשר־צויתי אתכה שבעת ימים תמלא ידם: ופר
חטאת תעשה ליום על־הכפרים וחטאת על־המזבח בכפרך עליו
לז ומשחת אתו לקדשו: שבעת ימים תכפר על־המזבח וקדשת אתו
לח והיה המזבח קדש קדשים כל־הנגע במזבח יקדש: וזה ששי
לט אשר תעשה על־המזבח כבשים בני־שנה שנים ליום תמיד: את־
הכבש האחד תעשה בבקר ואת הכבש השני תעשה בין הערבים:
מ ועשרן סלת בלול בשמן כתית רבע ההין ונסך רביעת ההין יין
מא לכבש האחד: ואת הכבש השני תעשה בין הערבים כמנחת
מב הבקר וכנסכה תעשה־לה לריח ניחח אשה ליהוה: עלת תמיד
לדרתיכם פתח אהל־מועד לפני יהוה אשר אועד לכם שמה לדבר
מג מד אליך שם: ונעדתי שמה לבני ישראל ונקדש בכבדי: וקדשתי את־

the Tent of Meeting and the altar. I will also consecrate Aharon and his
45 sons to serve Me as priests. I will have My Presence dwell among the Israelites
46 and I shall be their God. Then they will know that I am the LORD their God,
who brought them out of Egypt to dwell among them. I am the LORD
their God.
30 1 2 Make an altar on which to burn incense; make it of acacia wood. It shall be
square, a cubit long, a cubit wide, and two cubits high, its horns of one piece
3 with it. Overlay it with pure gold on its top, all around its sides, and on its
4 horns, and around it make a gold molding. Make two gold rings for it under
5 its molding on both sides to hold the staves used to carry it. Make the staves
6 of acacia wood and overlay them with gold. Put it in front of the screen that
veils the Ark of the Testimony, in front of the cover above the Ark, where I
7 will meet with you. Aharon should burn incense on it every morning when
8 he tends the lamps, and before evening when he lights the lamps. It shall be
a perpetual incense offering before the LORD throughout your generations.
9 Offer no unauthorized incense on it, or any burnt offering, grain offering,
10 or libation. Once a year Aharon shall make atonement on its horns; once
a year, with the blood of the purification offering of atonement, he shall
make atonement on it, throughout your generations. It is holy of holies to
the LORD."

KI TISA

11 12 The LORD said to Moshe, "When you take the census of the Israelites, as you
count, each must give ransom for his life to the LORD, so that no plague strikes
13 them when you count them.[62] Everyone numbered in the census shall give
half a shekel according to the Sanctuary weight,[63] where the shekel is twenty
14 gerah.[64] This half shekel is an offering to the LORD. Every male over twenty
15 is to be included in the census and must give the LORD's offering. The rich
shall not give more, and the poor shall not give less, than this half shekel.
16 It is an offering to the LORD to redeem your lives. Take this redemption
money from the Israelites and assign it for the service of the Tent of
Meeting. It shall be a remembrance for the Israelites before the LORD, to
redeem your lives."
17 18 The LORD said to Moshe, "Make a bronze laver with a bronze base for
washing. Place it between the Tent of Meeting and the altar, and put water in
19 20 it, for Aharon and his sons to wash their hands and feet. When they enter the
Tent of Meeting or approach the altar to minister by presenting a food offering
21 to the LORD, they must wash with water, so that they do not die. They must
wash their hands and feet so that they do not die; it shall be an eternal law for
them, for Aharon and his offspring, throughout the generations."

---

62 | Taking a census posed the threat of a plague; cf. II Samuel, chapter 24.

63 | Sanctuary weights differed from standard weights.

64 | The gerah and the shekel are units of weight and currency. A shekel is close to 20 grams or three-quarters of an ounce.

אֹהֶל מוֹעֵד וְאֶת־הַמִּזְבֵּחַ וְאֶת־אַהֲרֹן וְאֶת־בָּנָיו אֲקַדֵּשׁ לְכַהֵן לִי:
מה מו וְשָׁכַנְתִּי בְּתוֹךְ בְּנֵי יִשְׂרָאֵל וְהָיִיתִי לָהֶם לֵאלֹהִים: וְיָדְעוּ כִּי אֲנִי
יהוה אֱלֹהֵיהֶם אֲשֶׁר הוֹצֵאתִי אֹתָם מֵאֶרֶץ מִצְרַיִם לְשָׁכְנִי בְתוֹכָם
אֲנִי יהוה אֱלֹהֵיהֶם:

ל א ב וְעָשִׂיתָ מִזְבֵּחַ מִקְטַר קְטֹרֶת עֲצֵי שִׁטִּים תַּעֲשֶׂה אֹתוֹ: אַמָּה אָרְכּוֹ כג שביעי
ג וְאַמָּה רָחְבּוֹ רָבוּעַ יִהְיֶה וְאַמָּתַיִם קֹמָתוֹ מִמֶּנּוּ קַרְנֹתָיו: וְצִפִּיתָ אֹתוֹ
זָהָב טָהוֹר אֶת־גַּגּוֹ וְאֶת־קִירֹתָיו סָבִיב וְאֶת־קַרְנֹתָיו וְעָשִׂיתָ לּוֹ זֵר זָהָב
ד סָבִיב: וּשְׁתֵּי טַבְּעֹת זָהָב תַּעֲשֶׂה־לּוֹ | מִתַּחַת לְזֵרוֹ עַל שְׁתֵּי צַלְעֹתָיו
ה תַּעֲשֶׂה עַל־שְׁנֵי צִדָּיו וְהָיָה לְבָתִּים לְבַדִּים לָשֵׂאת אֹתוֹ בָּהֵמָּה: וְעָשִׂיתָ
ו אֶת־הַבַּדִּים עֲצֵי שִׁטִּים וְצִפִּיתָ אֹתָם זָהָב: וְנָתַתָּה אֹתוֹ לִפְנֵי הַפָּרֹכֶת
אֲשֶׁר עַל־אֲרֹן הָעֵדֻת לִפְנֵי הַכַּפֹּרֶת אֲשֶׁר עַל־הָעֵדֻת אֲשֶׁר אִוָּעֵד לְךָ
ז שָׁמָּה: וְהִקְטִיר עָלָיו אַהֲרֹן קְטֹרֶת סַמִּים בַּבֹּקֶר בַּבֹּקֶר בְּהֵיטִיבוֹ אֶת־
ח הַנֵּרֹת יַקְטִירֶנָּה: וּבְהַעֲלֹת אַהֲרֹן אֶת־הַנֵּרֹת בֵּין הָעַרְבַּיִם יַקְטִירֶנָּה מפטיר
ט קְטֹרֶת תָּמִיד לִפְנֵי יהוה לְדֹרֹתֵיכֶם: לֹא־תַעֲלוּ עָלָיו קְטֹרֶת זָרָה וְעֹלָה
י וּמִנְחָה וְנֶסֶךְ לֹא תִסְּכוּ עָלָיו: וְכִפֶּר אַהֲרֹן עַל־קַרְנֹתָיו אַחַת בַּשָּׁנָה
מִדַּם חַטַּאת הַכִּפֻּרִים אַחַת בַּשָּׁנָה יְכַפֵּר עָלָיו לְדֹרֹתֵיכֶם קֹדֶשׁ־
קָדָשִׁים הוּא לַיהוה:
יא יב וַיְדַבֵּר יהוה אֶל־מֹשֶׁה לֵּאמֹר: כִּי תִשָּׂא אֶת־רֹאשׁ בְּנֵי־יִשְׂרָאֵל כי תשא
לִפְקֻדֵיהֶם וְנָתְנוּ אִישׁ כֹּפֶר נַפְשׁוֹ לַיהוה בִּפְקֹד אֹתָם וְלֹא־יִהְיֶה בָהֶם
יג נֶגֶף בִּפְקֹד אֹתָם: זֶה | יִתְּנוּ כָּל־הָעֹבֵר עַל־הַפְּקֻדִים מַחֲצִית הַשֶּׁקֶל
בְּשֶׁקֶל הַקֹּדֶשׁ עֶשְׂרִים גֵּרָה הַשֶּׁקֶל מַחֲצִית הַשֶּׁקֶל תְּרוּמָה לַיהוה:
יד כֹּל הָעֹבֵר עַל־הַפְּקֻדִים מִבֶּן עֶשְׂרִים שָׁנָה וָמָעְלָה יִתֵּן תְּרוּמַת יהוה:
טו הֶעָשִׁיר לֹא־יַרְבֶּה וְהַדַּל לֹא יַמְעִיט מִמַּחֲצִית הַשָּׁקֶל לָתֵת אֶת־
טז תְּרוּמַת יהוה לְכַפֵּר עַל־נַפְשֹׁתֵיכֶם: וְלָקַחְתָּ אֶת־כֶּסֶף הַכִּפֻּרִים מֵאֵת
בְּנֵי יִשְׂרָאֵל וְנָתַתָּ אֹתוֹ עַל־עֲבֹדַת אֹהֶל מוֹעֵד וְהָיָה לִבְנֵי יִשְׂרָאֵל
לְזִכָּרוֹן לִפְנֵי יהוה לְכַפֵּר עַל־נַפְשֹׁתֵיכֶם:
יז יח וַיְדַבֵּר יהוה אֶל־מֹשֶׁה לֵּאמֹר: וְעָשִׂיתָ כִּיּוֹר נְחֹשֶׁת וְכַנּוֹ נְחֹשֶׁת לְרָחְצָה
יט וְנָתַתָּ אֹתוֹ בֵּין־אֹהֶל מוֹעֵד וּבֵין הַמִּזְבֵּחַ וְנָתַתָּ שָׁמָּה מָיִם: וְרָחֲצוּ
כ אַהֲרֹן וּבָנָיו מִמֶּנּוּ אֶת־יְדֵיהֶם וְאֶת־רַגְלֵיהֶם: בְּבֹאָם אֶל־אֹהֶל מוֹעֵד
יִרְחֲצוּ־מַיִם וְלֹא יָמֻתוּ אוֹ בְגִשְׁתָּם אֶל־הַמִּזְבֵּחַ לְשָׁרֵת לְהַקְטִיר אִשֶּׁה
כא לַיהוה: וְרָחֲצוּ יְדֵיהֶם וְרַגְלֵיהֶם וְלֹא יָמֻתוּ וְהָיְתָה לָהֶם חָק־עוֹלָם לוֹ
וּלְזַרְעוֹ לְדֹרֹתָם:

22 23 Then the LORD said to Moshe, "Take the finest spices: five hundred shekel
of liquid myrrh, and half as much, two hundred fifty, of fragrant cinnamon,
24 as well as two hundred fifty of aromatic cane, and five hundred shekel of
25 cassia – all according to the Sanctuary weight – and a hin of olive oil. Make
from these a sacred anointing oil, blended as by a perfumer; it shall be a
26 sacred anointing oil. With it, anoint the Tent of Meeting and the Ark of the
27 Testimony, the table and all its utensils, the candelabrum and its utensils,
28 the incense altar, the sacrificial altar with all its utensils, and the laver and
29 its base. You shall consecrate them and they will become holy of holies,
30 and whatever touches them will become holy. You shall anoint Aharon and
31 his sons and consecrate them to serve Me as priests. And you shall tell the
Israelites: This shall be My sacred anointing oil throughout the generations.
32 Do not pour it on anyone else's body, and do not make any other oil with
33 the same formula. It is sacred, and shall remain sacred to you. Whoever
makes perfume like it or applies it to a layperson shall be severed from his
34 people." The LORD said to Moshe, "Take sweet spices, equal parts
35 of stacte, onycha, galbanum, and pure frankincense and make them into
36 incense, blended as by a perfumer, salted, pure and sacred. Beat some of it into
powder and put part of it before the covenant in the Tent of Meeting where I
37 will meet with you. It shall be holy of holies to you. Do not make any incense
with this formula for yourselves. It must, for you, remain sacred to the LORD.
38 The person who makes any incense like it to use as perfume shall be severed
31 1 2 from his people." The LORD said to Moshe, "See, I have called by
3 name Betzalel, son of Uri, son of Ḥur from the tribe of Yehuda, and I have
filled him with a divine spirit, with wisdom, understanding, and knowledge
4 5 in every craft. He will fashion works of art in gold, silver, and bronze. He will
6 cut stones for setting, carve wood, and work in every craft. I have assigned to
him Oholiav, son of Aḥisamakh from the tribe of Dan. I have also put wisdom
into the heart of all the wise-hearted, so that they will be able to make all I
7 have commanded you: the Tent of Meeting, the Ark of the Testimony and
8 its cover, and all other furnishings of the Tent; the table and its utensils, the
9 pure candelabrum and all its utensils, the incense altar, the sacrificial altar
10 with all its utensils, the laver and its base, the service vestments, the sacred
vestments for Aharon the priest and the vestments for his sons for when they
11 serve as priests, the anointing oil and the fragrant incense for the Sanctuary;
they shall make them exactly as I have commanded you."
12 13 Then the LORD said to Moshe, "Speak to the Israelites and say: Nevertheless,
you shall keep My Sabbaths. It is a sign between Me and you throughout
the generations, that you may know that I, the LORD, make you holy.

כב כג וַיְדַבֵּר יְהוָה אֶל־מֹשֶׁה לֵּאמֹר: וְאַתָּה קַח־לְךָ בְּשָׂמִים רֹאשׁ מָר־
דְּרוֹר חֲמֵשׁ מֵאוֹת וְקִנְּמָן־בֶּשֶׂם מַחֲצִיתוֹ חֲמִשִּׁים וּמָאתָיִם וּקְנֵה־
כד בֹשֶׂם חֲמִשִּׁים וּמָאתָיִם: וְקִדָּה חֲמֵשׁ מֵאוֹת בְּשֶׁקֶל הַקֹּדֶשׁ וְשֶׁמֶן
כה זַיִת הִין: וְעָשִׂיתָ אֹתוֹ שֶׁמֶן מִשְׁחַת־קֹדֶשׁ רֹקַח מִרְקַחַת מַעֲשֵׂה
כו רֹקֵחַ שֶׁמֶן מִשְׁחַת־קֹדֶשׁ יִהְיֶה: וּמָשַׁחְתָּ בוֹ אֶת־אֹהֶל מוֹעֵד וְאֵת
כז אֲרוֹן הָעֵדֻת: וְאֶת־הַשֻּׁלְחָן וְאֶת־כָּל־כֵּלָיו וְאֶת־הַמְּנֹרָה וְאֶת־כֵּלֶיהָ
כח וְאֵת מִזְבַּח הַקְּטֹרֶת: וְאֶת־מִזְבַּח הָעֹלָה וְאֶת־כָּל־כֵּלָיו וְאֶת־הַכִּיֹּר
כט וְאֶת־כַּנּוֹ: וְקִדַּשְׁתָּ אֹתָם וְהָיוּ קֹדֶשׁ קָדָשִׁים כָּל־הַנֹּגֵעַ בָּהֶם יִקְדָּשׁ:
ל לא וְאֶת־אַהֲרֹן וְאֶת־בָּנָיו תִּמְשָׁח וְקִדַּשְׁתָּ אֹתָם לְכַהֵן לִי: וְאֶל־בְּנֵי
יִשְׂרָאֵל תְּדַבֵּר לֵאמֹר שֶׁמֶן מִשְׁחַת־קֹדֶשׁ יִהְיֶה זֶה לִי לְדֹרֹתֵיכֶם:
לב עַל־בְּשַׂר אָדָם לֹא יִיסָךְ וּבְמַתְכֻּנְתּוֹ לֹא תַעֲשׂוּ כָּמֹהוּ קֹדֶשׁ הוּא
לג קֹדֶשׁ יִהְיֶה לָכֶם: אִישׁ אֲשֶׁר יִרְקַח כָּמֹהוּ וַאֲשֶׁר יִתֵּן מִמֶּנּוּ עַל־זָר
לד וְנִכְרַת מֵעַמָּיו: וַיֹּאמֶר יְהוָה אֶל־מֹשֶׁה קַח־לְךָ סַמִּים
לה נָטָף ׀ וּשְׁחֵלֶת וְחֶלְבְּנָה סַמִּים וּלְבֹנָה זַכָּה בַּד בְּבַד יִהְיֶה: וְעָשִׂיתָ אֹתָהּ
לו קְטֹרֶת רֹקַח מַעֲשֵׂה רוֹקֵחַ מְמֻלָּח טָהוֹר קֹדֶשׁ: וְשָׁחַקְתָּ מִמֶּנָּה הָדֵק
וְנָתַתָּה מִמֶּנָּה לִפְנֵי הָעֵדֻת בְּאֹהֶל מוֹעֵד אֲשֶׁר אִוָּעֵד לְךָ שָׁמָּה קֹדֶשׁ
לז קָדָשִׁים תִּהְיֶה לָכֶם: וְהַקְּטֹרֶת אֲשֶׁר תַּעֲשֶׂה בְּמַתְכֻּנְתָּהּ לֹא תַעֲשׂוּ
לח לָכֶם קֹדֶשׁ תִּהְיֶה לְךָ לַיהוָה: אִישׁ אֲשֶׁר־יַעֲשֶׂה כָמוֹהָ לְהָרִיחַ בָּהּ
לא א ב וְנִכְרַת מֵעַמָּיו: וַיְדַבֵּר יְהוָה אֶל־מֹשֶׁה לֵּאמֹר: רְאֵה קָרָאתִי כד
ג בְשֵׁם בְּצַלְאֵל בֶּן־אוּרִי בֶן־חוּר לְמַטֵּה יְהוּדָה: וָאֲמַלֵּא אֹתוֹ רוּחַ
ד אֱלֹהִים בְּחָכְמָה וּבִתְבוּנָה וּבְדַעַת וּבְכָל־מְלָאכָה: לַחְשֹׁב מַחֲשָׁבֹת
ה לַעֲשׂוֹת בַּזָּהָב וּבַכֶּסֶף וּבַנְּחֹשֶׁת: וּבַחֲרֹשֶׁת אֶבֶן לְמַלֹּאת וּבַחֲרֹשֶׁת
ו עֵץ לַעֲשׂוֹת בְּכָל־מְלָאכָה: וַאֲנִי הִנֵּה נָתַתִּי אִתּוֹ אֵת אָהֳלִיאָב בֶּן־
אֲחִיסָמָךְ לְמַטֵּה־דָן וּבְלֵב כָּל־חֲכַם־לֵב נָתַתִּי חָכְמָה וְעָשׂוּ אֵת כָּל־
ז אֲשֶׁר צִוִּיתִךָ: אֵת ׀ אֹהֶל מוֹעֵד וְאֶת־הָאָרֹן לָעֵדֻת וְאֶת־הַכַּפֹּרֶת אֲשֶׁר
ח עָלָיו וְאֵת כָּל־כְּלֵי הָאֹהֶל: וְאֶת־הַשֻּׁלְחָן וְאֶת־כֵּלָיו וְאֶת־הַמְּנֹרָה
ט הַטְּהֹרָה וְאֶת־כָּל־כֵּלֶיהָ וְאֵת מִזְבַּח הַקְּטֹרֶת: וְאֶת־מִזְבַּח הָעֹלָה וְאֶת־
י כָּל־כֵּלָיו וְאֶת־הַכִּיּוֹר וְאֶת־כַּנּוֹ: וְאֵת בִּגְדֵי הַשְּׂרָד וְאֶת־בִּגְדֵי הַקֹּדֶשׁ
יא לְאַהֲרֹן הַכֹּהֵן וְאֶת־בִּגְדֵי בָנָיו לְכַהֵן: וְאֵת שֶׁמֶן הַמִּשְׁחָה וְאֶת־קְטֹרֶת
הַסַּמִּים לַקֹּדֶשׁ כְּכֹל אֲשֶׁר־צִוִּיתִךָ יַעֲשׂוּ:
יב יג וַיֹּאמֶר יְהוָה אֶל־מֹשֶׁה לֵּאמֹר: וְאַתָּה דַּבֵּר אֶל־בְּנֵי יִשְׂרָאֵל לֵאמֹר
אַךְ אֶת־שַׁבְּתֹתַי תִּשְׁמֹרוּ כִּי אוֹת הִוא בֵּינִי וּבֵינֵיכֶם לְדֹרֹתֵיכֶם לָדַעַת

14 Keep the Sabbath, for it is holy to you. Whoever profanes it shall be put to
15 death. Whoever does work on it shall be severed from his people. Six days
shall work be done, but the seventh day is a Sabbath of complete rest, sacred
to the Lord. Whoever does any work on the Sabbath shall be put to death.
16 The Israelites shall keep the Sabbath, making it a day of rest throughout their
17 generations as a covenant forever. It is an eternal sign between Me and the
Israelites that in six days the Lord made heaven and earth, and on the seventh
18 day He ceased and was revived." When He had finished speaking to
Moshe on Mount Sinai, He gave him the two tablets of the covenant, stone
32 1 tablets, inscribed by the finger of God. When the people saw that Moshe was
long delayed in coming down the mountain, they gathered around Aharon
and said to him, "Get up, make us gods to go before us. This man Moshe
who brought us out of Egypt – we have no idea what has become of him."
2 So Aharon said to them, "Remove the gold rings from the ears of your wives,
3 your sons and your daughters and bring them to me." So all the people took
4 the gold rings from their ears and brought them to Aharon. He took the gold
from them and, fashioning it with a chisel, made a molten calf. And they
5 said, "These, Israel, are your gods who brought you out of Egypt!" Seeing
this, Aharon built an altar in front of it and announced, "Tomorrow will be
6 a festival to the Lord." The next day, they rose early and sacrificed burnt
offerings and brought peace offerings. The people sat down to eat and drink
and then stood up to engage in revelry.
7 The Lord said to Moshe, "Quick – go down. Your people, whom you brought
8 out of Egypt, are acting ruinously. They have deviated swiftly from the way I
commanded them; they have made themselves a molten calf and are bowing
down and sacrificing to it, saying, 'These, Israel, are your gods who brought
9 you out of Egypt!'" Then the Lord said to Moshe, "I have seen this people;
10 it is a stiff-necked people. So do not try to stop Me when My anger burns
11 against them. I will put an end to them and make of you a great nation." Moshe
implored the Lord his God, "Why, O Lord, unleash Your anger against Your
people, whom You brought out of Egypt with such vast power and mighty
12 force? Why should the Egyptians be able to say that You brought them out
with evil intent, to kill them in the mountains and purge them from the face
of the earth? Turn from Your fierce anger and relent from doing evil to Your
13 people. Remember Avraham, Yitzḥak, and Yisrael, Your servants, to whom
You swore by Your very Self, telling them, 'I will make your descendants as
many as the stars of the heavens, and give them this land of which I spoke,
14 to inherit forever.'" Then the Lord relented from the evil He had spoken of
doing to His people.
15 Then Moshe turned and came down the mountain with the two tablets of

יד כִּי אֲנִי יהוה מְקַדִּשְׁכֶם: וּשְׁמַרְתֶּם אֶת־הַשַּׁבָּת כִּי קֹדֶשׁ הִוא לָכֶם
מְחַלְלֶיהָ מוֹת יוּמָת כִּי כָּל־הָעֹשֶׂה בָהּ מְלָאכָה וְנִכְרְתָה הַנֶּפֶשׁ הַהִוא
טו מִקֶּרֶב עַמֶּיהָ: שֵׁשֶׁת יָמִים יֵעָשֶׂה מְלָאכָה וּבַיּוֹם הַשְּׁבִיעִי שַׁבַּת
שַׁבָּתוֹן קֹדֶשׁ לַיהוה כָּל־הָעֹשֶׂה מְלָאכָה בְּיוֹם הַשַּׁבָּת מוֹת יוּמָת:
טז וְשָׁמְרוּ בְנֵי־יִשְׂרָאֵל אֶת־הַשַּׁבָּת לַעֲשׂוֹת אֶת־הַשַּׁבָּת לְדֹרֹתָם
יז בְּרִית עוֹלָם: בֵּינִי וּבֵין בְּנֵי יִשְׂרָאֵל אוֹת הִוא לְעֹלָם כִּי־שֵׁשֶׁת
יָמִים עָשָׂה יהוה אֶת־הַשָּׁמַיִם וְאֶת־הָאָרֶץ וּבַיּוֹם הַשְּׁבִיעִי שָׁבַת
יח וַיִּנָּפַשׁ: וַיִּתֵּן אֶל־מֹשֶׁה כְּכַלֹּתוֹ לְדַבֵּר אִתּוֹ בְּהַר סִינַי שְׁנֵי שני
לב א לֻחֹת הָעֵדֻת לֻחֹת אֶבֶן כְּתֻבִים בְּאֶצְבַּע אֱלֹהִים: וַיַּרְא הָעָם כִּי־בֹשֵׁשׁ
מֹשֶׁה לָרֶדֶת מִן־הָהָר וַיִּקָּהֵל הָעָם עַל־אַהֲרֹן וַיֹּאמְרוּ אֵלָיו קוּם ׀
עֲשֵׂה־לָנוּ אֱלֹהִים אֲשֶׁר יֵלְכוּ לְפָנֵינוּ כִּי־זֶה ׀ מֹשֶׁה הָאִישׁ אֲשֶׁר הֶעֱלָנוּ
ב מֵאֶרֶץ מִצְרַיִם לֹא יָדַעְנוּ מֶה־הָיָה לוֹ: וַיֹּאמֶר אֲלֵהֶם אַהֲרֹן פָּרְקוּ נִזְמֵי
ג הַזָּהָב אֲשֶׁר בְּאָזְנֵי נְשֵׁיכֶם בְּנֵיכֶם וּבְנֹתֵיכֶם וְהָבִיאוּ אֵלָי: וַיִּתְפָּרְקוּ
ד כָּל־הָעָם אֶת־נִזְמֵי הַזָּהָב אֲשֶׁר בְּאָזְנֵיהֶם וַיָּבִיאוּ אֶל־אַהֲרֹן: וַיִּקַּח
מִיָּדָם וַיָּצַר אֹתוֹ בַּחֶרֶט וַיַּעֲשֵׂהוּ עֵגֶל מַסֵּכָה וַיֹּאמְרוּ אֵלֶּה אֱלֹהֶיךָ
ה יִשְׂרָאֵל אֲשֶׁר הֶעֱלוּךָ מֵאֶרֶץ מִצְרָיִם: וַיַּרְא אַהֲרֹן וַיִּבֶן מִזְבֵּחַ לְפָנָיו
ו וַיִּקְרָא אַהֲרֹן וַיֹּאמַר חַג לַיהוה מָחָר: וַיַּשְׁכִּימוּ מִמָּחֳרָת וַיַּעֲלוּ עֹלֹת
וַיַּגִּשׁוּ שְׁלָמִים וַיֵּשֶׁב הָעָם לֶאֱכֹל וְשָׁתוֹ וַיָּקֻמוּ לְצַחֵק:
ז וַיְדַבֵּר יהוה אֶל־מֹשֶׁה לֶךְ־רֵד כִּי שִׁחֵת עַמְּךָ אֲשֶׁר הֶעֱלֵיתָ מֵאֶרֶץ
ח מִצְרָיִם: סָרוּ מַהֵר מִן־הַדֶּרֶךְ אֲשֶׁר צִוִּיתִם עָשׂוּ לָהֶם עֵגֶל מַסֵּכָה
וַיִּשְׁתַּחֲווּ־לוֹ וַיִּזְבְּחוּ־לוֹ וַיֹּאמְרוּ אֵלֶּה אֱלֹהֶיךָ יִשְׂרָאֵל אֲשֶׁר הֶעֱלוּךָ
ט מֵאֶרֶץ מִצְרָיִם: וַיֹּאמֶר יהוה אֶל־מֹשֶׁה רָאִיתִי אֶת־הָעָם הַזֶּה וְהִנֵּה
י עַם־קְשֵׁה־עֹרֶף הוּא: וְעַתָּה הַנִּיחָה לִּי וְיִחַר־אַפִּי בָהֶם וַאֲכַלֵּם וְאֶעֱשֶׂה
יא אוֹתְךָ לְגוֹי גָּדוֹל: וַיְחַל מֹשֶׁה אֶת־פְּנֵי יהוה אֱלֹהָיו וַיֹּאמֶר לָמָה יהוה
יֶחֱרֶה אַפְּךָ בְּעַמֶּךָ אֲשֶׁר הוֹצֵאתָ מֵאֶרֶץ מִצְרַיִם בְּכֹחַ גָּדוֹל וּבְיָד
יב חֲזָקָה: לָמָּה יֹאמְרוּ מִצְרַיִם לֵאמֹר בְּרָעָה הוֹצִיאָם לַהֲרֹג אֹתָם בֶּהָרִים
וּלְכַלֹּתָם מֵעַל פְּנֵי הָאֲדָמָה שׁוּב מֵחֲרוֹן אַפֶּךָ וְהִנָּחֵם עַל־הָרָעָה
יג לְעַמֶּךָ: זְכֹר לְאַבְרָהָם לְיִצְחָק וּלְיִשְׂרָאֵל עֲבָדֶיךָ אֲשֶׁר נִשְׁבַּעְתָּ לָהֶם
בָּךְ וַתְּדַבֵּר אֲלֵהֶם אַרְבֶּה אֶת־זַרְעֲכֶם כְּכוֹכְבֵי הַשָּׁמָיִם וְכָל־הָאָרֶץ
יד הַזֹּאת אֲשֶׁר אָמַרְתִּי אֶתֵּן לְזַרְעֲכֶם וְנָחֲלוּ לְעֹלָם: וַיִּנָּחֶם יהוה עַל־
הָרָעָה אֲשֶׁר דִּבֶּר לַעֲשׂוֹת לְעַמּוֹ:
טו וַיִּפֶן וַיֵּרֶד מֹשֶׁה מִן־הָהָר וּשְׁנֵי לֻחֹת הָעֵדֻת בְּיָדוֹ לֻחֹת כְּתֻבִים מִשְּׁנֵי כה

16 testimony in his hand, inscribed on both sides, front and back. The tablets
were the work of God, and the writing was God's writing, engraved on the
17 tablets. When Yehoshua heard the noise of the people shouting, he said to
18 Moshe, "The sound of war is coming from the camp." But Moshe said, "It
is neither the sound of triumph nor the wailing of defeat. What I hear is
19 the sound of revelry." As he approached the camp and saw the calf and the
dancing, Moshe's anger blazed, and he flung the tablets from his hands and
20 smashed them at the foot of the mountain. Then he took the calf that they
had made, burned it with fire, ground it to fine powder, scattered it on the
21 water, and made the Israelites drink it. "What did this people do to you,"
said Moshe to Aharon, "that you should have brought so great a sin upon
22 it?" Aharon replied, "Do not be angry with me. You know that the people are
23 set on evil. They said to me, 'Make us gods to go before us. This man Moshe
24 who brought us out of Egypt – we have no idea what has become of him.' So
I told them, 'Who has gold? Take it off.' They gave it to me, I threw it into the
25 fire – and out came this calf." Moshe saw that the people were running wild,
for Aharon had let them run beyond control and become a laughingstock to
26 their enemies. So Moshe stood at the gate of the camp and said, "Who is for
27 the LORD? Come to me." All the Levites rallied round him. He said to them,
"This is what the LORD God of Israel says: Let each of you put sword on
thigh and go back and forth from gate to gate throughout the camp – slaying
28 brother, neighbor, kinsman." The Levites did as Moshe had ordered. Some
29 three thousand people fell that day. Moshe said, "Dedicate yourselves to the
LORD today. You have been willing to act even against your son or brother.
30 May He bestow a blessing on you this day." On the following day, Moshe
said to the people, "You have committed a grievous sin. Now I must go back
31 up to the LORD. Perhaps I can secure atonement for your sin." So Moshe
went back to the LORD and said, "I beg of You. This people has committed
32 a grievous sin. They made gods of gold for themselves. But now, if only You
would forgive their sin – but if not, please blot me out of the book You have
33 written." The LORD said to Moshe, "I will blot out of My book those who have
34 sinned against Me. Now go and lead the people to the place about which I
have spoken to you. My messenger shall go before you. But when the time
35 comes for Me to punish, I will punish them for their sin." Thus the LORD
struck the people with a plague for what they had done with the calf Aharon
33 1 had made. The LORD said to Moshe, "Go. Set out from here – you
and the people you brought out of Egypt – to the land I promised to Avraham,
2 Yitzḥak, and Yaakov, saying, 'I will give this to your descendants.' I will send
a messenger ahead of you and drive out the Canaanites and Amorites, the
3 Hittites and the Perizzites, the Hivites, and the Jebusites. You will come to
a land flowing with milk and honey, but I will not go among you, because

טו עֹבְרֵיהֶם מִזֶּה וּמִזֶּה הֵם כְּתֻבִים׃ וְהַלֻּחֹת מַעֲשֵׂה אֱלֹהִים הֵמָּה
יז וְהַמִּכְתָּב מִכְתַּב אֱלֹהִים הוּא חָרוּת עַל־הַלֻּחֹת׃ וַיִּשְׁמַע יְהוֹשֻׁעַ
יח אֶת־קוֹל הָעָם בְּרֵעֹה וַיֹּאמֶר אֶל־מֹשֶׁה קוֹל מִלְחָמָה בַּמַּחֲנֶה׃ וַיֹּאמֶר
אֵין קוֹל עֲנוֹת גְּבוּרָה וְאֵין קוֹל עֲנוֹת חֲלוּשָׁה קוֹל עַנּוֹת אָנֹכִי שֹׁמֵעַ׃
יט וַיְהִי כַּאֲשֶׁר קָרַב אֶל־הַמַּחֲנֶה וַיַּרְא אֶת־הָעֵגֶל וּמְחֹלֹת וַיִּחַר־אַף מֹשֶׁה
כ וַיַּשְׁלֵךְ מִיָּדָו אֶת־הַלֻּחֹת וַיְשַׁבֵּר אֹתָם תַּחַת הָהָר׃ וַיִּקַּח אֶת־הָעֵגֶל
אֲשֶׁר עָשׂוּ וַיִּשְׂרֹף בָּאֵשׁ וַיִּטְחַן עַד אֲשֶׁר־דָּק וַיִּזֶר עַל־פְּנֵי הַמַּיִם וַיַּשְׁקְ
כא אֶת־בְּנֵי יִשְׂרָאֵל׃ וַיֹּאמֶר מֹשֶׁה אֶל־אַהֲרֹן מֶה־עָשָׂה לְךָ הָעָם הַזֶּה
כב כִּי־הֵבֵאתָ עָלָיו חֲטָאָה גְדֹלָה׃ וַיֹּאמֶר אַהֲרֹן אַל־יִחַר אַף אֲדֹנִי אַתָּה
כג יָדַעְתָּ אֶת־הָעָם כִּי בְרָע הוּא׃ וַיֹּאמְרוּ לִי עֲשֵׂה־לָנוּ אֱלֹהִים אֲשֶׁר
יֵלְכוּ לְפָנֵינוּ כִּי־זֶה ׀ מֹשֶׁה הָאִישׁ אֲשֶׁר הֶעֱלָנוּ מֵאֶרֶץ מִצְרַיִם לֹא
כד יָדַעְנוּ מֶה־הָיָה לוֹ׃ וָאֹמַר לָהֶם לְמִי זָהָב הִתְפָּרָקוּ וַיִּתְּנוּ־לִי וָאַשְׁלִכֵהוּ
כה בָאֵשׁ וַיֵּצֵא הָעֵגֶל הַזֶּה׃ וַיַּרְא מֹשֶׁה אֶת־הָעָם כִּי פָרֻעַ הוּא כִּי־פְרָעֹה
כו אַהֲרֹן לְשִׁמְצָה בְּקָמֵיהֶם׃ וַיַּעֲמֹד מֹשֶׁה בְּשַׁעַר הַמַּחֲנֶה וַיֹּאמֶר מִי
כז לַיהוה אֵלָי וַיֵּאָסְפוּ אֵלָיו כָּל־בְּנֵי לֵוִי׃ וַיֹּאמֶר לָהֶם כֹּה־אָמַר יהוה
אֱלֹהֵי יִשְׂרָאֵל שִׂימוּ אִישׁ־חַרְבּוֹ עַל־יְרֵכוֹ עִבְרוּ וָשׁוּבוּ מִשַּׁעַר לָשַׁעַר
בַּמַּחֲנֶה וְהִרְגוּ אִישׁ־אֶת־אָחִיו וְאִישׁ אֶת־רֵעֵהוּ וְאִישׁ אֶת־קְרֹבוֹ׃
כח וַיַּעֲשׂוּ בְנֵי־לֵוִי כִּדְבַר מֹשֶׁה וַיִּפֹּל מִן־הָעָם בַּיּוֹם הַהוּא כִּשְׁלֹשֶׁת אַלְפֵי
כט אִישׁ׃ וַיֹּאמֶר מֹשֶׁה מִלְאוּ יֶדְכֶם הַיּוֹם לַיהוה כִּי אִישׁ בִּבְנוֹ וּבְאָחִיו
ל וְלָתֵת עֲלֵיכֶם הַיּוֹם בְּרָכָה׃ וַיְהִי מִמָּחֳרָת וַיֹּאמֶר מֹשֶׁה אֶל־הָעָם
אַתֶּם חֲטָאתֶם חֲטָאָה גְדֹלָה וְעַתָּה אֶעֱלֶה אֶל־יהוה אוּלַי אֲכַפְּרָה
לא בְּעַד חַטַּאתְכֶם׃ וַיָּשָׁב מֹשֶׁה אֶל־יהוה וַיֹּאמַר אָנָּא חָטָא הָעָם הַזֶּה
לב חֲטָאָה גְדֹלָה וַיַּעֲשׂוּ לָהֶם אֱלֹהֵי זָהָב׃ וְעַתָּה אִם־תִּשָּׂא חַטָּאתָם וְאִם־
לג אַיִן מְחֵנִי נָא מִסִּפְרְךָ אֲשֶׁר כָּתָבְתָּ׃ וַיֹּאמֶר יהוה אֶל־מֹשֶׁה מִי אֲשֶׁר
לד חָטָא־לִי אֶמְחֶנּוּ מִסִּפְרִי׃ וְעַתָּה לֵךְ ׀ נְחֵה אֶת־הָעָם אֶל אֲשֶׁר־דִּבַּרְתִּי
לָךְ הִנֵּה מַלְאָכִי יֵלֵךְ לְפָנֶיךָ וּבְיוֹם פָּקְדִי וּפָקַדְתִּי עֲלֵהֶם חַטָּאתָם׃
לה וַיִּגֹּף יהוה אֶת־הָעָם עַל אֲשֶׁר עָשׂוּ אֶת־הָעֵגֶל אֲשֶׁר עָשָׂה
לג א אַהֲרֹן׃ וַיְדַבֵּר יהוה אֶל־מֹשֶׁה לֵךְ עֲלֵה מִזֶּה אַתָּה וְהָעָם
אֲשֶׁר הֶעֱלִיתָ מֵאֶרֶץ מִצְרָיִם אֶל־הָאָרֶץ אֲשֶׁר נִשְׁבַּעְתִּי לְאַבְרָהָם
ב לְיִצְחָק וּלְיַעֲקֹב לֵאמֹר לְזַרְעֲךָ אֶתְּנֶנָּה׃ וְשָׁלַחְתִּי לְפָנֶיךָ מַלְאָךְ
ג וְגֵרַשְׁתִּי אֶת־הַכְּנַעֲנִי הָאֱמֹרִי וְהַחִתִּי וְהַפְּרִזִּי הַחִוִּי וְהַיְבוּסִי׃ אֶל־אֶרֶץ
זָבַת חָלָב וּדְבָשׁ כִּי לֹא אֶעֱלֶה בְּקִרְבְּךָ כִּי עַם־קְשֵׁה־עֹרֶף אַתָּה פֶּן־

4 you are a stiff-necked people; I might destroy you on the way." When the
people heard this distressing news, they were grief-stricken. None put on
5 their finery; for the LORD had said to Moshe, "Tell the Israelites: You are
a stiff-necked people. If for one moment I were to go among you, I might
destroy you. So now take off your finery; and I will consider what to do
6 with you." So the Israelites stripped themselves of their finery from Mount
7 Ḥorev onward. Moshe took the tent and pitched it at a distance outside the
camp, calling it the Tent of Meeting. Whoever sought the LORD would go
8 to the Tent of Meeting, outside the camp. And when Moshe went out to the
Tent, all the people would rise, standing at the openings of their tents, and
9 watch Moshe until he had entered the Tent. When Moshe entered the Tent,
the pillar of cloud would descend and stand at the Tent's opening while He
10 spoke with Moshe. When the people saw the pillar of cloud standing at the
Tent's opening, all the people would rise and bow down, each at the opening
11 of his own tent. The LORD would speak to Moshe face-to-face, as one person
speaks to his friend. And then Moshe would return to the camp, but his young
disciple, Yehoshua son of Nun, did not leave the Tent.
12 Moshe said to the LORD, "You told me to lead this people forth, but You
have not let me know whom You will send with me. And You said, 'I have
13 known you by name, and you have found favor in My sight.' So now, if I have
found favor in Your sight, please show me Your ways, so that I may know
You and continue to find favor in Your sight. And look upon this nation: it is
14 Your people." "My Presence," He replied, "will go with you, and I will grant
15 you rest."[65] Then Moshe said to Him, "If Your Presence does not go with us,
16 do not make us leave this place. For unless You go with us, how shall it be
known that I and Your people have found favor in Your sight? That is how
I and Your people are distinguished from every other people on the face of
the earth."
17 Then the LORD said to Moshe, "In this too I will do what you ask, for you
18 have found favor in My sight; for I know you by name." Then Moshe said,
19 "Show me, please, Your glory." And He said, "I will cause all My goodness to
pass before you and in your presence I will proclaim My name: The LORD.
But I will be gracious to whom I choose to be gracious, and will show mercy
20 to whom I decide to show mercy. Nor," He said, "can you see My face. For
21 no one can see Me and live." Then the LORD said, "Look, there is a place by
22 Me where you may stand on the rock, and while My glory passes by I will
put you in a cleft of the rock, and I will shield you with My hand until I have
23 passed. Then I will take My hand away, and you will see My back, but My
face may not be seen."
34 1 The LORD said to Moshe, "Carve two tablets of stone like the first, and I
will inscribe on them the words that were on the first tablets that you broke.
2 Be ready in the morning. Climb Mount Sinai in the morning and present

65 | "Rest" here is subject to varying interpretations, such as peace of mind or military success.

ד אֹכֶלְךָ בַּדָּרֶךְ: וַיִּשְׁמַע הָעָם אֶת־הַדָּבָר הָרָע הַזֶּה וַיִּתְאַבָּלוּ וְלֹא־שָׁתוּ
ה אִישׁ עֶדְיוֹ עָלָיו: וַיֹּאמֶר יהוה אֶל־מֹשֶׁה אֱמֹר אֶל־בְּנֵי־יִשְׂרָאֵל אַתֶּם
עַם־קְשֵׁה־עֹרֶף רֶגַע אֶחָד אֶעֱלֶה בְקִרְבְּךָ וְכִלִּיתִיךָ וְעַתָּה הוֹרֵד עֶדְיְךָ
ו מֵעָלֶיךָ וְאֵדְעָה מָה אֶעֱשֶׂה־לָּךְ: וַיִּתְנַצְּלוּ בְנֵי־יִשְׂרָאֵל אֶת־עֶדְיָם מֵהַר
ז חוֹרֵב: וּמֹשֶׁה יִקַּח אֶת־הָאֹהֶל וְנָטָה־לוֹ ׀ מִחוּץ לַמַּחֲנֶה הַרְחֵק מִן־
הַמַּחֲנֶה וְקָרָא לוֹ אֹהֶל מוֹעֵד וְהָיָה כָּל־מְבַקֵּשׁ יהוה יֵצֵא אֶל־אֹהֶל
ח מוֹעֵד אֲשֶׁר מִחוּץ לַמַּחֲנֶה: וְהָיָה כְּצֵאת מֹשֶׁה אֶל־הָאֹהֶל יָקוּמוּ כָּל־
הָעָם וְנִצְּבוּ אִישׁ פֶּתַח אָהֳלוֹ וְהִבִּיטוּ אַחֲרֵי מֹשֶׁה עַד־בֹּאוֹ הָאֹהֱלָה:
ט וְהָיָה כְּבֹא מֹשֶׁה הָאֹהֱלָה יֵרֵד עַמּוּד הֶעָנָן וְעָמַד פֶּתַח הָאֹהֶל וְדִבֶּר
י עִם־מֹשֶׁה: וְרָאָה כָל־הָעָם אֶת־עַמּוּד הֶעָנָן עֹמֵד פֶּתַח הָאֹהֶל וְקָם
יא כָּל־הָעָם וְהִשְׁתַּחֲווּ אִישׁ פֶּתַח אָהֳלוֹ: וְדִבֶּר יהוה אֶל־מֹשֶׁה פָּנִים
אֶל־פָּנִים כַּאֲשֶׁר יְדַבֵּר אִישׁ אֶל־רֵעֵהוּ וְשָׁב אֶל־הַמַּחֲנֶה וּמְשָׁרְתוֹ
יְהוֹשֻׁעַ בִּן־נוּן נַעַר לֹא יָמִישׁ מִתּוֹךְ הָאֹהֶל:
יב וַיֹּאמֶר מֹשֶׁה אֶל־יהוה רְאֵה אַתָּה אֹמֵר אֵלַי הַעַל אֶת־הָעָם הַזֶּה שלישי
וְאַתָּה לֹא הוֹדַעְתַּנִי אֵת אֲשֶׁר־תִּשְׁלַח עִמִּי וְאַתָּה אָמַרְתָּ יְדַעְתִּיךָ
יג בְשֵׁם וְגַם־מָצָאתָ חֵן בְּעֵינָי: וְעַתָּה אִם־נָא מָצָאתִי חֵן בְּעֵינֶיךָ הוֹדִעֵנִי
נָא אֶת־דְּרָכֶךָ וְאֵדָעֲךָ לְמַעַן אֶמְצָא־חֵן בְּעֵינֶיךָ וּרְאֵה כִּי עַמְּךָ הַגּוֹי
יד טו הַזֶּה: וַיֹּאמַר פָּנַי יֵלֵכוּ וַהֲנִחֹתִי לָךְ: וַיֹּאמֶר אֵלָיו אִם־אֵין פָּנֶיךָ הֹלְכִים
טז אַל־תַּעֲלֵנוּ מִזֶּה: וּבַמֶּה ׀ יִוָּדַע אֵפוֹא כִּי־מָצָאתִי חֵן בְּעֵינֶיךָ אֲנִי וְעַמֶּךָ
הֲלוֹא בְּלֶכְתְּךָ עִמָּנוּ וְנִפְלֵינוּ אֲנִי וְעַמְּךָ מִכָּל־הָעָם אֲשֶׁר עַל־פְּנֵי
הָאֲדָמָה:
יז וַיֹּאמֶר יהוה אֶל־מֹשֶׁה גַּם אֶת־הַדָּבָר הַזֶּה אֲשֶׁר דִּבַּרְתָּ אֶעֱשֶׂה רביעי
יח כִּי־מָצָאתָ חֵן בְּעֵינַי וָאֵדָעֲךָ בְּשֵׁם: וַיֹּאמַר הַרְאֵנִי נָא אֶת־כְּבֹדֶךָ:
יט וַיֹּאמֶר אֲנִי אַעֲבִיר כָּל־טוּבִי עַל־פָּנֶיךָ וְקָרָאתִי בְשֵׁם יהוה לְפָנֶיךָ
כ וְחַנֹּתִי אֶת־אֲשֶׁר אָחֹן וְרִחַמְתִּי אֶת־אֲשֶׁר אֲרַחֵם: וַיֹּאמֶר לֹא תוּכַל
כא לִרְאֹת אֶת־פָּנָי כִּי לֹא־יִרְאַנִי הָאָדָם וָחָי: וַיֹּאמֶר יהוה הִנֵּה מָקוֹם
כב אִתִּי וְנִצַּבְתָּ עַל־הַצּוּר: וְהָיָה בַּעֲבֹר כְּבֹדִי וְשַׂמְתִּיךָ בְּנִקְרַת הַצּוּר
כג וְשַׂכֹּתִי כַפִּי עָלֶיךָ עַד־עָבְרִי: וַהֲסִרֹתִי אֶת־כַּפִּי וְרָאִיתָ אֶת־אֲחֹרָי
וּפָנַי לֹא יֵרָאוּ:
לד א וַיֹּאמֶר יהוה אֶל־מֹשֶׁה פְּסָל־לְךָ שְׁנֵי־לֻחֹת אֲבָנִים כָּרִאשֹׁנִים וְכָתַבְתִּי חמישי
עַל־הַלֻּחֹת אֶת־הַדְּבָרִים אֲשֶׁר הָיוּ עַל־הַלֻּחֹת הָרִאשֹׁנִים אֲשֶׁר
ב שִׁבַּרְתָּ: וֶהְיֵה נָכוֹן לַבֹּקֶר וְעָלִיתָ בַבֹּקֶר אֶל־הַר סִינַי וְנִצַּבְתָּ לִי שָׁם

3 yourself to Me there on the mountaintop. Let no one come up with you.
No one else should be seen anywhere on the mountain, nor may flocks or
4 herds graze near the mountain." So Moshe carved two stone tablets like the
first. He rose early in the morning and climbed Mount Sinai, as the LORD
5 had commanded him. In his hand he took the two tablets of stone. The
LORD descended in a cloud and stood with him there, and proclaimed the
6 name: The LORD. And the LORD passed before him, and proclaimed, "The
LORD, the LORD, God compassionate and gracious, slow to anger, abounding
7 in kindness and truth, extending kindness for thousands of generations,
forgiving sin, rebellion, and error, but who does not acquit the guilty, holding
descendants to account for the sins of the fathers, children and grandchildren
8 to the third and fourth generation." Moshe quickly bowed and prostrated
9 himself, and he said, "If now I have found favor in Your sight, O LORD, please,
let my LORD go among us. Though this is a stiff-necked people, pardon our
10 sins and errors, and keep us as Your own." The LORD said, "Now am I hereby
making a covenant. Before your entire people I will perform such wonders as
never have been performed anywhere on earth, for any nation. All the peoples
you live among shall see: how awe-inspiring are the deeds that I the LORD will
11 do for you. Be vigilant in what I am commanding you this day. I am going to
drive out before you the Amorites, Canaanites, Hittites, Perizzites, Hivites,
12 and Jebusites. Take care not to make a treaty with the inhabitants of the land
13 you are going to; for they would become a dangerous trap to you. Tear down
their altars, smash their worship pillars, and cut down their sacred trees,
14 for you must worship no other god. The LORD, known to demand absolute
15 loyalty, is your God who demands it indeed. You must not make a treaty with
the inhabitants of the land, for they will lust after their gods and sacrifice to
16 them; they will invite you to join them and you will eat of their sacrifice, and
you will take their daughters as wives for your sons, and their daughters will
17 lust after their gods and cause your sons to do as they do. Make for yourselves
18 no molten gods. Keep the Festival of Unleavened Bread. For seven days, eat
unleavened bread as I commanded you, at the time appointed, in the month
19 of Aviv,[66] because in that month you left Egypt. The first to emerge from
every womb is Mine; among all your livestock, firstborn cattle, and sheep.
20 Redeem each firstborn donkey with a sheep; if you do not redeem it, you
must break its neck. Also redeem all your firstborn sons. Do not appear before
21 Me empty-handed. Six days you shall work, but on the seventh day you shall
22 rest, ceasing from labor even at plowing time and harvest time. Observe the
Festival of Weeks, of the first fruits of wheat harvest, as well as the Festival of
23 Ingathering[67] at the close of the year. Three times a year all the males among
24 you shall appear before the Master, the LORD, God of Israel. For I will banish
nations before you and enlarge your territory. No one will covet your land
25 when you go up, three times a year, to appear before the LORD your God. Do
not offer the blood of My sacrifice with anything leavened. Do not let any

---

66 | See note on 13:4.
67 | See notes on 23:16.

ג עַל־רֹאשׁ הָהָר׃ וְאִישׁ לֹא־יַעֲלֶה עִמָּךְ וְגַם־אִישׁ אַל־יֵרָא בְּכָל־הָהָר
ד גַּם־הַצֹּאן וְהַבָּקָר אַל־יִרְעוּ אֶל־מוּל הָהָר הַהוּא׃ וַיִּפְסֹל שְׁנֵי־לֻחֹת
אֲבָנִים כָּרִאשֹׁנִים וַיַּשְׁכֵּם מֹשֶׁה בַבֹּקֶר וַיַּעַל אֶל־הַר סִינַי כַּאֲשֶׁר צִוָּה
ה יְהוָה אֹתוֹ וַיִּקַּח בְּיָדוֹ שְׁנֵי לֻחֹת אֲבָנִים׃ וַיֵּרֶד יְהוָה בֶּעָנָן וַיִּתְיַצֵּב עִמּוֹ
ו שָׁם וַיִּקְרָא בְשֵׁם יְהוָה׃ וַיַּעֲבֹר יְהוָה ׀ עַל־פָּנָיו וַיִּקְרָא יְהוָה ׀ יְהוָה אֵל
ז רַחוּם וְחַנּוּן אֶרֶךְ אַפַּיִם וְרַב־חֶסֶד וֶאֱמֶת׃ נֹצֵר חֶסֶד לָאֲלָפִים נֹשֵׂא
עָוֺן וָפֶשַׁע וְחַטָּאָה וְנַקֵּה לֹא יְנַקֶּה פֹּקֵד ׀ עֲוֺן אָבוֹת עַל־בָּנִים וְעַל־בְּנֵי
ח בָנִים עַל־שִׁלֵּשִׁים וְעַל־רִבֵּעִים׃ וַיְמַהֵר מֹשֶׁה וַיִּקֹּד אַרְצָה וַיִּשְׁתָּחוּ׃
ט וַיֹּאמֶר אִם־נָא מָצָאתִי חֵן בְּעֵינֶיךָ אֲדֹנָי יֵלֶךְ־נָא אֲדֹנָי בְּקִרְבֵּנוּ כִּי עַם־
י קְשֵׁה־עֹרֶף הוּא וְסָלַחְתָּ לַעֲוֺנֵנוּ וּלְחַטָּאתֵנוּ וּנְחַלְתָּנוּ׃ וַיֹּאמֶר הִנֵּה ששי
אָנֹכִי כֹּרֵת בְּרִית נֶגֶד כָּל־עַמְּךָ אֶעֱשֶׂה נִפְלָאֹת אֲשֶׁר לֹא־נִבְרְאוּ בְכָל־
הָאָרֶץ וּבְכָל־הַגּוֹיִם וְרָאָה כָל־הָעָם אֲשֶׁר־אַתָּה בְקִרְבּוֹ אֶת־מַעֲשֵׂה
יא יְהוָה כִּי־נוֹרָא הוּא אֲשֶׁר אֲנִי עֹשֶׂה עִמָּךְ׃ שְׁמָר־לְךָ אֵת אֲשֶׁר אָנֹכִי
מְצַוְּךָ הַיּוֹם הִנְנִי גֹרֵשׁ מִפָּנֶיךָ אֶת־הָאֱמֹרִי וְהַכְּנַעֲנִי וְהַחִתִּי וְהַפְּרִזִּי
יב וְהַחִוִּי וְהַיְבוּסִי׃ הִשָּׁמֶר לְךָ פֶּן־תִּכְרֹת בְּרִית לְיוֹשֵׁב הָאָרֶץ אֲשֶׁר
יג אַתָּה בָּא עָלֶיהָ פֶּן־יִהְיֶה לְמוֹקֵשׁ בְּקִרְבֶּךָ׃ כִּי אֶת־מִזְבְּחֹתָם תִּתֹּצוּן
יד וְאֶת־מַצֵּבֹתָם תְּשַׁבֵּרוּן וְאֶת־אֲשֵׁרָיו תִּכְרֹתוּן׃ כִּי לֹא תִשְׁתַּחֲוֶה לְאֵל
טו אַחֵר כִּי יְהוָה קַנָּא שְׁמוֹ אֵל קַנָּא הוּא׃ פֶּן־תִּכְרֹת בְּרִית לְיוֹשֵׁב הָאָרֶץ
וְזָנוּ ׀ אַחֲרֵי אֱלֹהֵיהֶם וְזָבְחוּ לֵאלֹהֵיהֶם וְקָרָא לְךָ וְאָכַלְתָּ מִזִּבְחוֹ׃
טז וְלָקַחְתָּ מִבְּנֹתָיו לְבָנֶיךָ וְזָנוּ בְנֹתָיו אַחֲרֵי אֱלֹהֵיהֶן וְהִזְנוּ אֶת־בָּנֶיךָ
יז יח אַחֲרֵי אֱלֹהֵיהֶן׃ אֱלֹהֵי מַסֵּכָה לֹא תַעֲשֶׂה־לָּךְ׃ אֶת־חַג הַמַּצּוֹת תִּשְׁמֹר
שִׁבְעַת יָמִים תֹּאכַל מַצּוֹת אֲשֶׁר צִוִּיתִךָ לְמוֹעֵד חֹדֶשׁ הָאָבִיב כִּי
יט בְּחֹדֶשׁ הָאָבִיב יָצָאתָ מִמִּצְרָיִם׃ כָּל־פֶּטֶר רֶחֶם לִי וְכָל־מִקְנְךָ תִּזָּכָר
כ פֶּטֶר שׁוֹר וָשֶׂה׃ וּפֶטֶר חֲמוֹר תִּפְדֶּה בְשֶׂה וְאִם־לֹא תִפְדֶּה וַעֲרַפְתּוֹ
כא כֹּל בְּכוֹר בָּנֶיךָ תִּפְדֶּה וְלֹא־יֵרָאוּ פָנַי רֵיקָם׃ שֵׁשֶׁת יָמִים תַּעֲבֹד וּבַיּוֹם
כב הַשְּׁבִיעִי תִּשְׁבֹּת בֶּחָרִישׁ וּבַקָּצִיר תִּשְׁבֹּת׃ וְחַג שָׁבֻעֹת תַּעֲשֶׂה לְךָ
כג בִּכּוּרֵי קְצִיר חִטִּים וְחַג הָאָסִיף תְּקוּפַת הַשָּׁנָה׃ שָׁלֹשׁ פְּעָמִים בַּשָּׁנָה
כד יֵרָאֶה כָּל־זְכוּרְךָ אֶת־פְּנֵי הָאָדֹן ׀ יְהוָה אֱלֹהֵי יִשְׂרָאֵל׃ כִּי־אוֹרִישׁ
גּוֹיִם מִפָּנֶיךָ וְהִרְחַבְתִּי אֶת־גְּבֻלֶךָ וְלֹא־יַחְמֹד אִישׁ אֶת־אַרְצְךָ בַּעֲלֹתְךָ
כה לֵרָאוֹת אֶת־פְּנֵי יְהוָה אֱלֹהֶיךָ שָׁלֹשׁ פְּעָמִים בַּשָּׁנָה׃ לֹא־תִשְׁחַט עַל־

26 of the Passover festival sacrifice remain until morning. Bring the best first
fruits of your land to the House of the LORD your God. Do not cook a kid in
the milk of its mother."
27 Then the LORD said to Moshe, "Write down these words, for in accordance
28 with these words I have made a covenant with you and with Israel." He stayed
there with the LORD for forty days and forty nights, eating no bread and
drinking no water. And on the tablets, He wrote the words of the covenant,
29 the Ten Commandments. When Moshe came down from Mount Sinai with
the two tablets of testimony in his hand, he was unaware that the skin of his
30 face shone with light, because he had been speaking with God. When Aharon
and all the Israelites saw the light that shone from the skin of Moshe's face,
31 they were afraid to come close to him. But Moshe called them, and Aharon
32 and all the community leaders came back to him, and Moshe spoke. After
that, all the Israelites approached, and he instructed them in all that the LORD
33 had spoken to him on Mount Sinai. And when Moshe had finished speaking
34 to them, he veiled his face. Whenever Moshe came before the LORD to speak
with Him, he would remove the veil until he came out. When he came out
35 and told the Israelites what he had been commanded, the Israelites would
see how the skin of Moshe's face shone wi th light, and he would veil his face
35 1 again until he went back in to speak with Him. Moshe assembled VAYAK'HEL
all the community of Israel and said to them, "These are the things the LORD
2 has commanded you to do. For six days, let work be done, but the seventh
must be sacred to you. It is a Sabbath of complete rest dedicated to the LORD.
3 Whoever does work on it shall be put to death. Do not light a fire in any of
your dwellings on the Sabbath day."
4 Then Moshe said to all the community of Israel, "This is what the LORD has
5 commanded. Bring of what is yours an offering to the LORD. Let everyone
whose heart moves him bring an offering to the LORD: gold, silver, and bronze;
6 7 sky-blue, purple, and scarlet wool; linen and goats' hair; rams' hides dyed red
8 and fine leather; acacia wood; oil for the lamp; spices for the anointing oil
9 and the fragrant incense; and rock crystal together with other precious stones
10 for the ephod and breast piece. And let all among you who are skilled come
11 and make the things that the LORD has commanded: the Tabernacle, its tent
12 and covering, its hooks and frames, its bars, posts, and sockets; the Ark and
13 its staves, the cover and the curtain for the screen; the table, its staves and
14 all its utensils, and the showbread; the candelabrum for light, together with
15 its utensils, lamps, and the oil for lighting; the incense altar with its staves,
the anointing oil and the fragrant incense, and the entrance screen for the
16 entrance of the Tabernacle; the sacrificial altar, its bronze grate, its staves

כו חֲמֵץ דַּם־זִבְחִי וְלֹא־יָלִין לַבֹּקֶר זֶבַח חַג הַפָּסַח׃ רֵאשִׁית בִּכּוּרֵי אַדְמָתְךָ
תָּבִיא בֵּית יהוה אֱלֹהֶיךָ לֹא־תְבַשֵּׁל גְּדִי בַּחֲלֵב אִמּוֹ׃
כז וַיֹּאמֶר יהוה אֶל־מֹשֶׁה כְּתָב־לְךָ אֶת־הַדְּבָרִים הָאֵלֶּה כִּי עַל־פִּי | כו שביעי
כח הַדְּבָרִים הָאֵלֶּה כָּרַתִּי אִתְּךָ בְּרִית וְאֶת־יִשְׂרָאֵל׃ וַיְהִי־שָׁם עִם־יהוה
אַרְבָּעִים יוֹם וְאַרְבָּעִים לַיְלָה לֶחֶם לֹא אָכַל וּמַיִם לֹא שָׁתָה וַיִּכְתֹּב
כט עַל־הַלֻּחֹת אֵת דִּבְרֵי הַבְּרִית עֲשֶׂרֶת הַדְּבָרִים׃ וַיְהִי בְּרֶדֶת מֹשֶׁה מֵהַר
סִינַי וּשְׁנֵי לֻחֹת הָעֵדֻת בְּיַד־מֹשֶׁה בְּרִדְתּוֹ מִן־הָהָר וּמֹשֶׁה לֹא־יָדַע
ל כִּי קָרַן עוֹר פָּנָיו בְּדַבְּרוֹ אִתּוֹ׃ וַיַּרְא אַהֲרֹן וְכָל־בְּנֵי יִשְׂרָאֵל אֶת־מֹשֶׁה
לא וְהִנֵּה קָרַן עוֹר פָּנָיו וַיִּירְאוּ מִגֶּשֶׁת אֵלָיו׃ וַיִּקְרָא אֲלֵהֶם מֹשֶׁה וַיָּשֻׁבוּ
לב אֵלָיו אַהֲרֹן וְכָל־הַנְּשִׂאִים בָּעֵדָה וַיְדַבֵּר מֹשֶׁה אֲלֵהֶם׃ וְאַחֲרֵי־כֵן נִגְּשׁוּ
לג כָּל־בְּנֵי יִשְׂרָאֵל וַיְצַוֵּם אֵת כָּל־אֲשֶׁר דִּבֶּר יהוה אִתּוֹ בְּהַר סִינָי׃ וַיְכַל מפטיר
לד מֹשֶׁה מִדַּבֵּר אִתָּם וַיִּתֵּן עַל־פָּנָיו מַסְוֶה׃ וּבְבֹא מֹשֶׁה לִפְנֵי יהוה לְדַבֵּר
אִתּוֹ יָסִיר אֶת־הַמַּסְוֶה עַד־צֵאתוֹ וְיָצָא וְדִבֶּר אֶל־בְּנֵי יִשְׂרָאֵל אֵת אֲשֶׁר
לה יְצֻוֶּה׃ וְרָאוּ בְנֵי־יִשְׂרָאֵל אֶת־פְּנֵי מֹשֶׁה כִּי קָרַן עוֹר פְּנֵי מֹשֶׁה וְהֵשִׁיב
לה א מֹשֶׁה אֶת־הַמַּסְוֶה עַל־פָּנָיו עַד־בֹּאוֹ לְדַבֵּר אִתּוֹ׃ וַיַּקְהֵל ויקהל
מֹשֶׁה אֶת־כָּל־עֲדַת בְּנֵי יִשְׂרָאֵל וַיֹּאמֶר אֲלֵהֶם אֵלֶּה הַדְּבָרִים אֲשֶׁר־
ב צִוָּה יהוה לַעֲשֹׂת אֹתָם׃ שֵׁשֶׁת יָמִים תֵּעָשֶׂה מְלָאכָה וּבַיּוֹם הַשְּׁבִיעִי
יִהְיֶה לָכֶם קֹדֶשׁ שַׁבַּת שַׁבָּתוֹן לַיהוה כָּל־הָעֹשֶׂה בוֹ מְלָאכָה יוּמָת׃
ג לֹא־תְבַעֲרוּ אֵשׁ בְּכֹל מֹשְׁבֹתֵיכֶם בְּיוֹם הַשַּׁבָּת׃
ד וַיֹּאמֶר מֹשֶׁה אֶל־כָּל־עֲדַת בְּנֵי־יִשְׂרָאֵל לֵאמֹר זֶה הַדָּבָר אֲשֶׁר־צִוָּה
ה יהוה לֵאמֹר׃ קְחוּ מֵאִתְּכֶם תְּרוּמָה לַיהוה כֹּל נְדִיב לִבּוֹ יְבִיאֶהָ אֵת
ו תְּרוּמַת יהוה זָהָב וָכֶסֶף וּנְחֹשֶׁת׃ וּתְכֵלֶת וְאַרְגָּמָן וְתוֹלַעַת שָׁנִי וְשֵׁשׁ
ז ח וְעִזִּים׃ וְעֹרֹת אֵילִם מְאָדָּמִים וְעֹרֹת תְּחָשִׁים וַעֲצֵי שִׁטִּים׃ וְשֶׁמֶן
ט לַמָּאוֹר וּבְשָׂמִים לְשֶׁמֶן הַמִּשְׁחָה וְלִקְטֹרֶת הַסַּמִּים׃ וְאַבְנֵי־שֹׁהַם
י וְאַבְנֵי מִלֻּאִים לָאֵפוֹד וְלַחֹשֶׁן׃ וְכָל־חֲכַם־לֵב בָּכֶם יָבֹאוּ וְיַעֲשׂוּ אֵת
יא כָּל־אֲשֶׁר צִוָּה יהוה׃ אֶת־הַמִּשְׁכָּן אֶת־אָהֳלוֹ וְאֶת־מִכְסֵהוּ אֶת־קְרָסָיו
יב וְאֶת־קְרָשָׁיו אֶת־בְּרִיחָו אֶת־עַמֻּדָיו וְאֶת־אֲדָנָיו׃ אֶת־הָאָרֹן וְאֶת־בַּדָּיו
יג אֶת־הַכַּפֹּרֶת וְאֵת פָּרֹכֶת הַמָּסָךְ׃ אֶת־הַשֻּׁלְחָן וְאֶת־בַּדָּיו וְאֶת־כָּל־
יד כֵּלָיו וְאֵת לֶחֶם הַפָּנִים׃ וְאֶת־מְנֹרַת הַמָּאוֹר וְאֶת־כֵּלֶיהָ וְאֶת־נֵרֹתֶיהָ
טו וְאֵת שֶׁמֶן הַמָּאוֹר׃ וְאֶת־מִזְבַּח הַקְּטֹרֶת וְאֶת־בַּדָּיו וְאֵת שֶׁמֶן הַמִּשְׁחָה
טז וְאֵת קְטֹרֶת הַסַּמִּים וְאֶת־מָסַךְ הַפֶּתַח לְפֶתַח הַמִּשְׁכָּן׃ אֵת | מִזְבַּח
הָעֹלָה וְאֶת־מִכְבַּר הַנְּחֹשֶׁת אֲשֶׁר־לוֹ אֶת־בַּדָּיו וְאֶת־כָּל־כֵּלָיו אֶת־

17 and all its utensils, the laver and its base; the hangings of the courtyard, its
18 posts and its sockets, and the screen for the gate of the court; the tent pegs
19 of the Tabernacle and of the courtyard and their ropes; the vestments for
ministering in the Sanctuary, and the sacred vestments for Aharon the priest
20 and for his sons for their priestly service." So all the community of Israel left
21 Moshe's presence. And they came, everyone whose heart inspired him and
whose spirit moved him, and brought an offering for the LORD, to be used for
22 the Tent of Meeting and all its service, and for the sacred vestments. All whose
hearts moved them – the men with the women – brought brooches, earrings,
signet rings and pendants, all kinds of gold ornaments, together with all those
23 who gave gold as a wave offering to the LORD. Everyone who had sky-blue,
purple, or scarlet wool, linen or goats' hair, rams' hides dyed red or fine leather
24 brought them. Whoever could make an offering of silver or bronze brought it
as an offering to the LORD, as did everyone who had acacia wood that could
25 be used for the work. Every skilled woman spun with her own hands, and
brought what she had spun: sky-blue, purple, and scarlet wool and fine linen.
26 All the women whose hearts inspired them used their skill to spin the goats'
27 hair. The leaders brought rock crystal stones and other precious stones for
28 setting in the ephod and the breast piece, together with spices and oil for
29 the light, the anointing oil and the fragrant incense. So the Israelites – all the
men and women whose hearts moved them to bring anything for the work
that the LORD, through Moshe, had commanded – brought it as a freewill
offering to the LORD.

30 Then Moshe said to the Israelites, "Know that the LORD has summoned by
31 name Betzalel, son of Uri, son of Ḥur, of the tribe of Yehuda, and has filled
him with a divine spirit of wisdom, understanding, and knowledge in every
32 33 craft, to devise designs, working in gold, silver, and bronze, as well as cutting
34 stones for setting, carving wood, and working in every other craft. He has also
given him the ability to teach others, together with Oholiav, son of Aḥisamakh
35 of the tribe of Dan. He has filled them with the skill to do all kinds of work,
as engravers, designers, embroiderers in sky-blue, purple, or scarlet wool or
fine linen, and as weavers. They will be able to carry out all the necessary
36 1 work and design. And so Betzalel and Oholiav shall carry out everything
the LORD has commanded, together with all the skilled people to whom the
LORD has granted expertise and acumen to do all the work necessary for the
2 service of the Sanctuary." Then Moshe summoned Betzalel and Oholiav and
all the skilled craftsmen to whom God had given expertise and who were
3 inspired to dedicate themselves and come to carry out the work. From Moshe
they received all the offerings the Israelites had brought for the work of the

יז הַכִּיֹּר וְאֶת־כַּנּוֹ: אֵת קַלְעֵי הֶחָצֵר אֶת־עַמֻּדָיו וְאֶת־אֲדָנֶיהָ וְאֵת מָסַךְ
יח שַׁעַר הֶחָצֵר: אֶת־יִתְדֹת הַמִּשְׁכָּן וְאֶת־יִתְדֹת הֶחָצֵר וְאֶת־מֵיתְרֵיהֶם:
יט אֶת־בִּגְדֵי הַשְּׂרָד לְשָׁרֵת בַּקֹּדֶשׁ אֶת־בִּגְדֵי הַקֹּדֶשׁ לְאַהֲרֹן הַכֹּהֵן וְאֶת־
כ כא בִּגְדֵי בָנָיו לְכַהֵן: וַיֵּצְאוּ כָּל־עֲדַת בְּנֵי־יִשְׂרָאֵל מִלִּפְנֵי מֹשֶׁה: וַיָּבֹאוּ שני
כָּל־אִישׁ אֲשֶׁר־נְשָׂאוֹ לִבּוֹ וְכֹל אֲשֶׁר נָדְבָה רוּחוֹ אֹתוֹ הֵבִיאוּ אֶת־
תְּרוּמַת יהוה לִמְלֶאכֶת אֹהֶל מוֹעֵד וּלְכָל־עֲבֹדָתוֹ וּלְבִגְדֵי הַקֹּדֶשׁ:
כב וַיָּבֹאוּ הָאֲנָשִׁים עַל־הַנָּשִׁים כֹּל ׀ נְדִיב לֵב הֵבִיאוּ חָח וָנֶזֶם וְטַבַּעַת
כג וְכוּמָז כָּל־כְּלִי זָהָב וְכָל־אִישׁ אֲשֶׁר הֵנִיף תְּנוּפַת זָהָב לַיהוה: וְכָל־
אִישׁ אֲשֶׁר־נִמְצָא אִתּוֹ תְּכֵלֶת וְאַרְגָּמָן וְתוֹלַעַת שָׁנִי וְשֵׁשׁ וְעִזִּים
כד וְעֹרֹת אֵילִם מְאָדָּמִים וְעֹרֹת תְּחָשִׁים הֵבִיאוּ: כָּל־מֵרִים תְּרוּמַת
כֶּסֶף וּנְחֹשֶׁת הֵבִיאוּ אֵת תְּרוּמַת יהוה וְכֹל אֲשֶׁר נִמְצָא אִתּוֹ עֲצֵי
כה שִׁטִּים לְכָל־מְלֶאכֶת הָעֲבֹדָה הֵבִיאוּ: וְכָל־אִשָּׁה חַכְמַת־לֵב בְּיָדֶיהָ
טָווּ וַיָּבִיאוּ מַטְוֶה אֶת־הַתְּכֵלֶת וְאֶת־הָאַרְגָּמָן אֶת־תּוֹלַעַת הַשָּׁנִי
כו וְאֶת־הַשֵּׁשׁ: וְכָל־הַנָּשִׁים אֲשֶׁר נָשָׂא לִבָּן אֹתָנָה בְּחָכְמָה טָווּ אֶת־
כז הָעִזִּים: וְהַנְּשִׂאִם הֵבִיאוּ אֵת אַבְנֵי הַשֹּׁהַם וְאֵת אַבְנֵי הַמִּלֻּאִים
כח לָאֵפוֹד וְלַחֹשֶׁן: וְאֶת־הַבֹּשֶׂם וְאֶת־הַשָּׁמֶן לְמָאוֹר וּלְשֶׁמֶן הַמִּשְׁחָה
כט וְלִקְטֹרֶת הַסַּמִּים: כָּל־אִישׁ וְאִשָּׁה אֲשֶׁר נָדַב לִבָּם אֹתָם לְהָבִיא לְכָל־
הַמְּלָאכָה אֲשֶׁר צִוָּה יהוה לַעֲשׂוֹת בְּיַד־מֹשֶׁה הֵבִיאוּ בְנֵי־יִשְׂרָאֵל
נְדָבָה לַיהוה:

ל וַיֹּאמֶר מֹשֶׁה אֶל־בְּנֵי יִשְׂרָאֵל רְאוּ קָרָא יהוה בְּשֵׁם בְּצַלְאֵל בֶּן־אוּרִי שלישי /שני/
לא בֶן־חוּר לְמַטֵּה יְהוּדָה: וַיְמַלֵּא אֹתוֹ רוּחַ אֱלֹהִים בְּחָכְמָה בִּתְבוּנָה
לב וּבְדַעַת וּבְכָל־מְלָאכָה: וְלַחְשֹׁב מַחֲשָׁבֹת לַעֲשֹׂת בַּזָּהָב וּבַכֶּסֶף
לג וּבַנְּחֹשֶׁת: וּבַחֲרֹשֶׁת אֶבֶן לְמַלֹּאת וּבַחֲרֹשֶׁת עֵץ לַעֲשׂוֹת בְּכָל־מְלֶאכֶת
לד מַחֲשָׁבֶת: וּלְהוֹרֹת נָתַן בְּלִבּוֹ הוּא וְאָהֳלִיאָב בֶּן־אֲחִיסָמָךְ לְמַטֵּה־
לה דָן: מִלֵּא אֹתָם חָכְמַת־לֵב לַעֲשׂוֹת כָּל־מְלֶאכֶת חָרָשׁ ׀ וְחֹשֵׁב וְרֹקֵם
בַּתְּכֵלֶת וּבָאַרְגָּמָן בְּתוֹלַעַת הַשָּׁנִי וּבַשֵּׁשׁ וְאֹרֵג עֹשֵׂי כָּל־מְלָאכָה
לו א וְחֹשְׁבֵי מַחֲשָׁבֹת: וְעָשָׂה בְצַלְאֵל וְאָהֳלִיאָב וְכֹל ׀ אִישׁ חֲכַם־לֵב אֲשֶׁר
נָתַן יהוה חָכְמָה וּתְבוּנָה בָּהֵמָּה לָדַעַת לַעֲשֹׂת אֶת־כָּל־מְלֶאכֶת
ב עֲבֹדַת הַקֹּדֶשׁ לְכֹל אֲשֶׁר־צִוָּה יהוה: וַיִּקְרָא מֹשֶׁה אֶל־בְּצַלְאֵל וְאֶל־
אָהֳלִיאָב וְאֶל כָּל־אִישׁ חֲכַם־לֵב אֲשֶׁר נָתַן יהוה חָכְמָה בְּלִבּוֹ כֹּל
ג אֲשֶׁר נְשָׂאוֹ לִבּוֹ לְקָרְבָה אֶל־הַמְּלָאכָה לַעֲשֹׂת אֹתָהּ: וַיִּקְחוּ מִלִּפְנֵי
מֹשֶׁה אֵת כָּל־הַתְּרוּמָה אֲשֶׁר הֵבִיאוּ בְּנֵי יִשְׂרָאֵל לִמְלֶאכֶת עֲבֹדַת

Sanctuary. And the people kept bringing him additional gifts every morning.
4 So all the craftsmen engaged in the work of the Sanctuary left what they were
5 doing, and said to Moshe, "The people are bringing more than is necessary for
6 the work God has commanded us to do." Moshe ordered an announcement
to be made throughout the camp: "Let no man or woman make anything
7 more as an offering for the Sanctuary." So the people brought no more; for
what they already had was more than enough for all the work that was to be
8 done. All the skilled craftsmen among those engaged in the work
made the Tabernacle with ten sheets of fine linen and sky-blue, purple, and
9 scarlet wool, with a woven design of cherubim. All the sheets were of the same
10 size: twenty-eight cubits long and four cubits wide. Five sheets were sown
11 together, and likewise the second five. He made loops of sky-blue wool on
the edge of the outermost sheet of the first set and likewise on the outermost
12 sheet of the second set: fifty loops on the first sheet and fifty on the edge of
13 the end sheet of the other set, so that the loops were opposite one another. He
made fifty gold clasps and used them to fasten the two sets of sheets together
so that the Tabernacle was all of one piece.
14 He made sheets of goats' hair for a tent over the Tabernacle. There were
15 eleven such sheets. All eleven were the same size: thirty cubits long and four
16 17 cubits wide. He joined five of the sheets into one set and six into another. He
made fifty loops on the edge of the outermost sheet of the first set, and fifty
18 loops on the edge of the second set. He made fifty bronze clasps to join the
19 tent together into a single piece. And for the tent he made a covering of rams'
20 skins dyed red, with a covering of fine leather above. Then he made
21 the upright boards for the Tabernacle from acacia wood. Each was ten cubits
22 long and a cubit and a half wide. Each board had two matching tenons; all
23 the Tabernacle's boards were made in this way. He made twenty boards for
24 the south side, and forty silver sockets to go under them, two sockets under
25 each board, one under each tenon. For the second side of the Tabernacle,
26 the north side, he made twenty boards and their forty silver sockets, two

ד הַקֹּדֶשׁ לַעֲשֹׂת אֹתָהּ וְהֵם הֵבִיאוּ אֵלָיו עוֹד נְדָבָה בַּבֹּקֶר בַּבֹּקֶר: וַיָּבֹאוּ
כָּל־הַחֲכָמִים הָעֹשִׂים אֵת כָּל־מְלֶאכֶת הַקֹּדֶשׁ אִישׁ אִישׁ מִמְּלַאכְתּוֹ
ה אֲשֶׁר־הֵמָּה עֹשִׂים: וַיֹּאמְרוּ אֶל־מֹשֶׁה לֵּאמֹר מַרְבִּים הָעָם לְהָבִיא
ו מִדֵּי הָעֲבֹדָה לַמְּלָאכָה אֲשֶׁר־צִוָּה יהוה לַעֲשֹׂת אֹתָהּ: וַיְצַו מֹשֶׁה
וַיַּעֲבִירוּ קוֹל בַּמַּחֲנֶה לֵאמֹר אִישׁ וְאִשָּׁה אַל־יַעֲשׂוּ־עוֹד מְלָאכָה
ז לִתְרוּמַת הַקֹּדֶשׁ וַיִּכָּלֵא הָעָם מֵהָבִיא: וְהַמְּלָאכָה הָיְתָה דַיָּם לְכָל־
ח הַמְּלָאכָה לַעֲשׂוֹת אֹתָהּ וְהוֹתֵר: וַיַּעֲשׂוּ כָל־חֲכַם־לֵב רביעי
בְּעֹשֵׂי הַמְּלָאכָה אֶת־הַמִּשְׁכָּן עֶשֶׂר יְרִיעֹת שֵׁשׁ מָשְׁזָר וּתְכֵלֶת וְאַרְגָּמָן
ט וְתוֹלַעַת שָׁנִי כְּרֻבִים מַעֲשֵׂה חֹשֵׁב עָשָׂה אֹתָם: אֹרֶךְ הַיְרִיעָה הָאַחַת
שְׁמֹנֶה וְעֶשְׂרִים בָּאַמָּה וְרֹחַב אַרְבַּע בָּאַמָּה הַיְרִיעָה הָאֶחָת מִדָּה
י אַחַת לְכָל־הַיְרִיעֹת: וַיְחַבֵּר אֶת־חֲמֵשׁ הַיְרִיעֹת אַחַת אֶל־אֶחָת וְחָמֵשׁ
יא יְרִיעֹת חִבַּר אַחַת אֶל־אֶחָת: וַיַּעַשׂ לֻלְאֹת תְּכֵלֶת עַל שְׂפַת הַיְרִיעָה
הָאֶחָת מִקָּצָה בַּמַּחְבָּרֶת כֵּן עָשָׂה בִּשְׂפַת הַיְרִיעָה הַקִּיצוֹנָה בַּמַּחְבֶּרֶת
יב הַשֵּׁנִית: חֲמִשִּׁים לֻלָאֹת עָשָׂה בַּיְרִיעָה הָאֶחָת וַחֲמִשִּׁים לֻלָאֹת עָשָׂה
בִּקְצֵה הַיְרִיעָה אֲשֶׁר בַּמַּחְבֶּרֶת הַשֵּׁנִית מַקְבִּילֹת הַלֻּלָאֹת אַחַת אֶל־
יג אֶחָת: וַיַּעַשׂ חֲמִשִּׁים קַרְסֵי זָהָב וַיְחַבֵּר אֶת־הַיְרִיעֹת אַחַת אֶל־אַחַת
בַּקְּרָסִים וַיְהִי הַמִּשְׁכָּן אֶחָד:
יד וַיַּעַשׂ יְרִיעֹת עִזִּים לְאֹהֶל עַל־הַמִּשְׁכָּן עַשְׁתֵּי־עֶשְׂרֵה יְרִיעֹת עָשָׂה
טו אֹתָם: אֹרֶךְ הַיְרִיעָה הָאַחַת שְׁלֹשִׁים בָּאַמָּה וְאַרְבַּע אַמּוֹת רֹחַב
טז הַיְרִיעָה הָאֶחָת מִדָּה אַחַת לְעַשְׁתֵּי עֶשְׂרֵה יְרִיעֹת: וַיְחַבֵּר אֶת־חֲמֵשׁ
יז הַיְרִיעֹת לְבָד וְאֶת־שֵׁשׁ הַיְרִיעֹת לְבָד: וַיַּעַשׂ לֻלָאֹת חֲמִשִּׁים עַל שְׂפַת
הַיְרִיעָה הַקִּיצֹנָה בַּמַּחְבָּרֶת וַחֲמִשִּׁים לֻלָאֹת עָשָׂה עַל־שְׂפַת הַיְרִיעָה
יח הַחֹבֶרֶת הַשֵּׁנִית: וַיַּעַשׂ קַרְסֵי נְחֹשֶׁת חֲמִשִּׁים לְחַבֵּר אֶת־הָאֹהֶל
יט לִהְיֹת אֶחָד: וַיַּעַשׂ מִכְסֶה לָאֹהֶל עֹרֹת אֵילִם מְאָדָּמִים וּמִכְסֵה עֹרֹת
כ תְּחָשִׁים מִלְמָעְלָה: וַיַּעַשׂ אֶת־הַקְּרָשִׁים לַמִּשְׁכָּן עֲצֵי חמישי
כא שִׁטִּים עֹמְדִים: עֶשֶׂר אַמֹּת אֹרֶךְ הַקָּרֶשׁ וְאַמָּה וַחֲצִי הָאַמָּה רֹחַב
כב הַקֶּרֶשׁ הָאֶחָד: שְׁתֵּי יָדֹת לַקֶּרֶשׁ הָאֶחָד מְשֻׁלָּבֹת אַחַת אֶל־אֶחָת
כג כֵּן עָשָׂה לְכֹל קַרְשֵׁי הַמִּשְׁכָּן: וַיַּעַשׂ אֶת־הַקְּרָשִׁים לַמִּשְׁכָּן עֶשְׂרִים
כד קְרָשִׁים לִפְאַת נֶגֶב תֵּימָנָה: וְאַרְבָּעִים אַדְנֵי־כֶסֶף עָשָׂה תַּחַת עֶשְׂרִים
הַקְּרָשִׁים שְׁנֵי אֲדָנִים תַּחַת־הַקֶּרֶשׁ הָאֶחָד לִשְׁתֵּי יְדֹתָיו וּשְׁנֵי אֲדָנִים
כה תַּחַת־הַקֶּרֶשׁ הָאֶחָד לִשְׁתֵּי יְדֹתָיו: וּלְצֶלַע הַמִּשְׁכָּן הַשֵּׁנִית לִפְאַת
כו צָפוֹן עָשָׂה עֶשְׂרִים קְרָשִׁים: וְאַרְבָּעִים אַדְנֵיהֶם כֶּסֶף שְׁנֵי אֲדָנִים

27 under each board. For the rear of the Tabernacle on the west side he made six
28 boards, along with two boards for each of the rear corners of the Tabernacle.
29 They were even at the bottom, and joined at the top by a ring. This was so for
30 the other corner also. So there were eight boards and sixteen silver sockets,
31 two under each board. He made crossbars of acacia wood, five for the boards
32 of the first side of the Tabernacle, five for the boards of the second, and five
33 for those of the rear of the Tabernacle on the west side. He made the central
crossbar to go across the middles of the boards from one end to the other.
34 He overlaid the boards with gold, and made gold rings to hold the crossbars;
35 he overlaid the crossbars themselves with gold. He made the curtain of sky-
blue, purple, and scarlet wool and finely spun linen, with a design of cherubim
36 worked into it. He also made four posts of acacia wood for it and overlaid
them with gold. Their hooks were of gold, and he cast for them four sockets
37 of silver. He made an embroidered screen for the entrance of the Tent, of
38 sky-blue, purple, and scarlet wool and finely spun linen, as well as five posts
with their hooks. He overlaid their tops and bands with gold, but their five
sockets were of bronze.

37 1 Betzalel made the Ark of acacia wood, two and a half cubits long, a cubit and
2 a half wide, and a cubit and a half high. He overlaid it with pure gold inside
3 and out, and encircled it around with a gold rim. He cast four gold rings for
4 its four corners, two rings on one side and two on the other. He made staves
5 of acacia wood and overlaid them with gold. He then placed the staves in the
6 rings on the Ark's sides so that it could be carried. He made a cover of pure
7 gold, two and a half cubits long and a cubit and a half wide. He made two
8 cherubim of beaten gold for the two ends of the cover, one cherub at one
9 end and one at the other. He made them of one piece with the cover, and the
wings of the cherubim were spread upward, sheltering the cover. They faced
each other, their faces toward the cover.

10 He made a table of acacia wood, two cubits long, a cubit wide, and a cubit
11 and a half high. He overlaid it with pure gold and around it made a gold rim.
12 He also made a frame a handbreadth wide around it and made a gold rim for
13 the frame. He cast four gold rings and placed the rings on the corners of its
14 four legs. The rings were close to the frame to hold the staves used to carry

כז תַּחַת הַקֶּרֶשׁ הָאֶחָד וּשְׁנֵי אֲדָנִים תַּחַת הַקֶּרֶשׁ הָאֶחָד׃ וּלְיַרְכְּתֵי
כח הַמִּשְׁכָּן יָמָּה עָשָׂה שִׁשָּׁה קְרָשִׁים׃ וּשְׁנֵי קְרָשִׁים עָשָׂה לִמְקֻצְעֹת
כט הַמִּשְׁכָּן בַּיַּרְכָתָיִם׃ וְהָיוּ תוֹאֲמִם מִלְּמַטָּה וְיַחְדָּו יִהְיוּ תַמִּים אֶל־
ל רֹאשׁוֹ אֶל־הַטַּבַּעַת הָאֶחָת כֵּן עָשָׂה לִשְׁנֵיהֶם לִשְׁנֵי הַמִּקְצֹעֹת׃ וְהָיוּ
שְׁמֹנָה קְרָשִׁים וְאַדְנֵיהֶם כֶּסֶף שִׁשָּׁה עָשָׂר אֲדָנִים שְׁנֵי אֲדָנִים שְׁנֵי
לא אֲדָנִים תַּחַת הַקֶּרֶשׁ הָאֶחָד׃ וַיַּעַשׂ בְּרִיחֵי עֲצֵי שִׁטִּים חֲמִשָּׁה לְקַרְשֵׁי
לב צֶלַע־הַמִּשְׁכָּן הָאֶחָת׃ וַחֲמִשָּׁה בְרִיחִם לְקַרְשֵׁי צֶלַע־הַמִּשְׁכָּן הַשֵּׁנִית
לג וַחֲמִשָּׁה בְרִיחִם לְקַרְשֵׁי הַמִּשְׁכָּן לַיַּרְכָתַיִם יָמָּה׃ וַיַּעַשׂ אֶת־הַבְּרִיחַ
לד הַתִּיכֹן לִבְרֹחַ בְּתוֹךְ הַקְּרָשִׁים מִן־הַקָּצֶה אֶל־הַקָּצֶה׃ וְאֶת־הַקְּרָשִׁים
צִפָּה זָהָב וְאֶת־טַבְּעֹתָם עָשָׂה זָהָב בָּתִּים לַבְּרִיחִם וַיְצַף אֶת־הַבְּרִיחִם
לה זָהָב׃ וַיַּעַשׂ אֶת־הַפָּרֹכֶת תְּכֵלֶת וְאַרְגָּמָן וְתוֹלַעַת שָׁנִי וְשֵׁשׁ מָשְׁזָר
לו מַעֲשֵׂה חֹשֵׁב עָשָׂה אֹתָהּ כְּרֻבִים׃ וַיַּעַשׂ לָהּ אַרְבָּעָה עַמּוּדֵי שִׁטִּים
לז וַיְצַפֵּם זָהָב וָוֵיהֶם זָהָב וַיִּצֹק לָהֶם אַרְבָּעָה אַדְנֵי־כָסֶף׃ וַיַּעַשׂ מָסָךְ
לְפֶתַח הָאֹהֶל תְּכֵלֶת וְאַרְגָּמָן וְתוֹלַעַת שָׁנִי וְשֵׁשׁ מָשְׁזָר מַעֲשֵׂה רֹקֵם׃
לח וְאֶת־עַמּוּדָיו חֲמִשָּׁה וְאֶת־וָוֵיהֶם וְצִפָּה רָאשֵׁיהֶם וַחֲשֻׁקֵיהֶם זָהָב
וְאַדְנֵיהֶם חֲמִשָּׁה נְחֹשֶׁת׃

לז א וַיַּעַשׂ בְּצַלְאֵל אֶת־הָאָרֹן עֲצֵי שִׁטִּים אַמָּתַיִם וָחֵצִי אָרְכּוֹ וְאַמָּה וָחֵצִי כז
ב רָחְבּוֹ וְאַמָּה וָחֵצִי קֹמָתוֹ׃ וַיְצַפֵּהוּ זָהָב טָהוֹר מִבַּיִת וּמִחוּץ וַיַּעַשׂ לוֹ
ג זֵר זָהָב סָבִיב׃ וַיִּצֹק לוֹ אַרְבַּע טַבְּעֹת זָהָב עַל אַרְבַּע פַּעֲמֹתָיו וּשְׁתֵּי
ד טַבָּעֹת עַל־צַלְעוֹ הָאֶחָת וּשְׁתֵּי טַבָּעֹת עַל־צַלְעוֹ הַשֵּׁנִית׃ וַיַּעַשׂ בַּדֵּי
ה עֲצֵי שִׁטִּים וַיְצַף אֹתָם זָהָב׃ וַיָּבֵא אֶת־הַבַּדִּים בַּטַּבָּעֹת עַל צַלְעֹת
ו הָאָרֹן לָשֵׂאת אֶת־הָאָרֹן׃ וַיַּעַשׂ כַּפֹּרֶת זָהָב טָהוֹר אַמָּתַיִם וָחֵצִי אָרְכָּהּ
ז וְאַמָּה וָחֵצִי רָחְבָּהּ׃ וַיַּעַשׂ שְׁנֵי כְרֻבִים זָהָב מִקְשָׁה עָשָׂה אֹתָם מִשְּׁנֵי
ח קְצוֹת הַכַּפֹּרֶת׃ כְּרוּב־אֶחָד מִקָּצָה מִזֶּה וּכְרוּב־אֶחָד מִקָּצָה מִזֶּה
ט מִן־הַכַּפֹּרֶת עָשָׂה אֶת־הַכְּרֻבִים מִשְּׁנֵי קצוותו׃ וַיִּהְיוּ הַכְּרֻבִים פֹּרְשֵׂי קְצוֹתָיו
כְנָפַיִם לְמַעְלָה סֹכְכִים בְּכַנְפֵיהֶם עַל־הַכַּפֹּרֶת וּפְנֵיהֶם אִישׁ אֶל־אָחִיו
אֶל־הַכַּפֹּרֶת הָיוּ פְּנֵי הַכְּרֻבִים׃

י וַיַּעַשׂ אֶת־הַשֻּׁלְחָן עֲצֵי שִׁטִּים אַמָּתַיִם אָרְכּוֹ וְאַמָּה רָחְבּוֹ וְאַמָּה
יא יב וָחֵצִי קֹמָתוֹ׃ וַיְצַף אֹתוֹ זָהָב טָהוֹר וַיַּעַשׂ לוֹ זֵר זָהָב סָבִיב׃ וַיַּעַשׂ לוֹ
יג מִסְגֶּרֶת טֹפַח סָבִיב וַיַּעַשׂ זֵר־זָהָב לְמִסְגַּרְתּוֹ סָבִיב׃ וַיִּצֹק לוֹ אַרְבַּע
טַבְּעֹת זָהָב וַיִּתֵּן אֶת־הַטַּבָּעֹת עַל אַרְבַּע הַפֵּאֹת אֲשֶׁר לְאַרְבַּע רַגְלָיו׃
יד לְעֻמַּת הַמִּסְגֶּרֶת הָיוּ הַטַּבָּעֹת בָּתִּים לַבַּדִּים לָשֵׂאת אֶת־הַשֻּׁלְחָן׃

15 the table. He made the staves for carrying the table of acacia wood overlaid
16 with gold. The articles for the table – the bowls, spoons, jars, and pitchers for
pouring libations – he made of pure gold.
17 He made the candelabrum of pure beaten gold. Its base and shaft, cups, knobs,
18 and flowers were hammered from a single piece. Six branches extended from
19 its sides, three on one side, three on the other. On each of the six branches
extending from the candelabrum were three finely crafted cups, each with a
20 knob and a flower. On the candelabrum itself there were four finely crafted
21 cups, each, also, with a knob and a flower. At the base of each of the three
pairs of branches extending from the candelabrum there was a knob of one
22 piece with it; their knobs and branches were of one piece with it, so that
23 the whole of it was a single piece of pure beaten gold. Its seven lamps and
24 its tongs and pans were of pure gold; it and all its utensils were made from a
talent of pure gold.[68]
25 He made the incense altar of acacia wood, square, a cubit long, a cubit wide,
26 and two cubits high, with horns of one piece with it. He overlaid its top, its
sides all around, and its horns with pure gold and around it he made a gold
27 molding. Under the molding he made two gold rings on the two sides, to
28 hold the staves by which it was carried. The staves themselves were made of
29 acacia wood, overlaid with gold. As well as this, with the skill of a perfumer,
38 1 he prepared the sacred anointing oil and the fragrant incense. He
made the sacrificial altar of acacia wood, square, five cubits long, five cubits
2 wide, and three cubits high. He made horns on its four corners, of one piece
3 with it, and then overlaid it with bronze. He made all the altar's utensils: pots,
4 shovels, basins, forks, and pans, out of bronze. He made a grate of bronze
5 mesh beneath the ledge, extending downward to the middle of the altar. Four
rings were cast for the four corners of the bronze mesh, to hold the staves,
6 7 which were made of acacia wood and overlaid with bronze. He placed the
staves in the rings on the sides of the altar so that it could be carried. The altar
8 itself was hollow, made of planks. He made the bronze laver and
its bronze base from the mirrors of the women who served at the entrance
9 of the Tent of Meeting. On the south side, the hangings were of
10 finely spun linen, a hundred cubits long, with twenty posts and their twenty

68 | See note on 25:39.

טו וַיַּעַשׂ אֶת־הַבַּדִּים עֲצֵי שִׁטִּים וַיְצַף אֹתָם זָהָב לָשֵׂאת אֶת־הַשֻּׁלְחָן׃
טז וַיַּעַשׂ אֶת־הַכֵּלִים ׀ אֲשֶׁר עַל־הַשֻּׁלְחָן אֶת־קְעָרֹתָיו וְאֶת־כַּפֹּתָיו וְאֵת
מְנַקִּיֹּתָיו וְאֶת־הַקְּשָׂוֺת אֲשֶׁר יֻסַּךְ בָּהֵן זָהָב טָהוֹר׃
יז וַיַּעַשׂ אֶת־הַמְּנֹרָה זָהָב טָהוֹר מִקְשָׁה עָשָׂה אֶת־הַמְּנֹרָה יְרֵכָהּ וְקָנָהּ ששי /שלישי/
יח גְּבִיעֶיהָ כַּפְתֹּרֶיהָ וּפְרָחֶיהָ מִמֶּנָּה הָיוּ׃ וְשִׁשָּׁה קָנִים יֹצְאִים מִצִּדֶּיהָ
שְׁלֹשָׁה ׀ קְנֵי מְנֹרָה מִצִּדָּהּ הָאֶחָד וּשְׁלֹשָׁה קְנֵי מְנֹרָה מִצִּדָּהּ הַשֵּׁנִי׃
יט שְׁלֹשָׁה גְבִעִים מְשֻׁקָּדִים בַּקָּנֶה הָאֶחָד כַּפְתֹּר וָפֶרַח וּשְׁלֹשָׁה גְבִעִים
מְשֻׁקָּדִים בְּקָנֶה אֶחָד כַּפְתֹּר וָפָרַח כֵּן לְשֵׁשֶׁת הַקָּנִים הַיֹּצְאִים
כ מִן־הַמְּנֹרָה׃ וּבַמְּנֹרָה אַרְבָּעָה גְבִעִים מְשֻׁקָּדִים כַּפְתֹּרֶיהָ וּפְרָחֶיהָ׃
כא וְכַפְתֹּר תַּחַת שְׁנֵי הַקָּנִים מִמֶּנָּה וְכַפְתֹּר תַּחַת שְׁנֵי הַקָּנִים מִמֶּנָּה
וְכַפְתֹּר תַּחַת־שְׁנֵי הַקָּנִים מִמֶּנָּה לְשֵׁשֶׁת הַקָּנִים הַיֹּצְאִים מִמֶּנָּה׃
כב כג כַּפְתֹּרֵיהֶם וּקְנֹתָם מִמֶּנָּה הָיוּ כֻּלָּהּ מִקְשָׁה אַחַת זָהָב טָהוֹר׃ וַיַּעַשׂ
כד אֶת־נֵרֹתֶיהָ שִׁבְעָה וּמַלְקָחֶיהָ וּמַחְתֹּתֶיהָ זָהָב טָהוֹר׃ כִּכָּר זָהָב טָהוֹר
עָשָׂה אֹתָהּ וְאֵת כָּל־כֵּלֶיהָ׃
כה וַיַּעַשׂ אֶת־מִזְבַּח הַקְּטֹרֶת עֲצֵי שִׁטִּים אַמָּה אָרְכּוֹ וְאַמָּה רָחְבּוֹ רָבוּעַ
כו וְאַמָּתַיִם קֹמָתוֹ מִמֶּנּוּ הָיוּ קַרְנֹתָיו׃ וַיְצַף אֹתוֹ זָהָב טָהוֹר אֶת־גַּגּוֹ וְאֶת־
כז קִירֹתָיו סָבִיב וְאֶת־קַרְנֹתָיו וַיַּעַשׂ לוֹ זֵר זָהָב סָבִיב׃ וּשְׁתֵּי טַבְּעֹת זָהָב
עָשָׂה־לוֹ ׀ מִתַּחַת לְזֵרוֹ עַל שְׁתֵּי צַלְעֹתָיו עַל שְׁנֵי צִדָּיו לְבָתִּים לְבַדִּים
כח לָשֵׂאת אֹתוֹ בָּהֶם׃ וַיַּעַשׂ אֶת־הַבַּדִּים עֲצֵי שִׁטִּים וַיְצַף אֹתָם זָהָב׃
כט וַיַּעַשׂ אֶת־שֶׁמֶן הַמִּשְׁחָה קֹדֶשׁ וְאֶת־קְטֹרֶת הַסַּמִּים טָהוֹר מַעֲשֵׂה
לח א רֹקֵחַ׃ וַיַּעַשׂ אֶת־מִזְבַּח הָעֹלָה עֲצֵי שִׁטִּים חָמֵשׁ אַמּוֹת שביעי /רביעי/
ב אָרְכּוֹ וְחָמֵשׁ־אַמּוֹת רָחְבּוֹ רָבוּעַ וְשָׁלֹשׁ אַמּוֹת קֹמָתוֹ׃ וַיַּעַשׂ קַרְנֹתָיו
ג עַל אַרְבַּע פִּנֹּתָיו מִמֶּנּוּ הָיוּ קַרְנֹתָיו וַיְצַף אֹתוֹ נְחֹשֶׁת׃ וַיַּעַשׂ אֶת־כָּל־
כְּלֵי הַמִּזְבֵּחַ אֶת־הַסִּירֹת וְאֶת־הַיָּעִים וְאֶת־הַמִּזְרָקֹת אֶת־הַמִּזְלָגֹת
ד וְאֶת־הַמַּחְתֹּת כָּל־כֵּלָיו עָשָׂה נְחֹשֶׁת׃ וַיַּעַשׂ לַמִּזְבֵּחַ מִכְבָּר מַעֲשֵׂה
ה רֶשֶׁת נְחֹשֶׁת תַּחַת כַּרְכֻּבּוֹ מִלְּמַטָּה עַד־חֶצְיוֹ׃ וַיִּצֹק אַרְבַּע טַבָּעֹת
ו בְּאַרְבַּע הַקְּצָוֺת לְמִכְבַּר הַנְּחֹשֶׁת בָּתִּים לַבַּדִּים׃ וַיַּעַשׂ אֶת־הַבַּדִּים
ז עֲצֵי שִׁטִּים וַיְצַף אֹתָם נְחֹשֶׁת׃ וַיָּבֵא אֶת־הַבַּדִּים בַּטַּבָּעֹת עַל צַלְעֹת
ח הַמִּזְבֵּחַ לָשֵׂאת אֹתוֹ בָּהֶם נְבוּב לֻחֹת עָשָׂה אֹתוֹ׃ וַיַּעַשׂ אֵת
הַכִּיּוֹר נְחֹשֶׁת וְאֵת כַּנּוֹ נְחֹשֶׁת בְּמַרְאֹת הַצֹּבְאֹת אֲשֶׁר צָבְאוּ פֶּתַח
ט אֹהֶל מוֹעֵד׃ וַיַּעַשׂ אֶת־הֶחָצֵר לִפְאַת ׀ נֶגֶב תֵּימָנָה קַלְעֵי
י הֶחָצֵר שֵׁשׁ מָשְׁזָר מֵאָה בָּאַמָּה׃ עַמּוּדֵיהֶם עֶשְׂרִים וְאַדְנֵיהֶם עֶשְׂרִים

11 bronze sockets. The posts' hooks and bands were of silver. Likewise on the
north side: the hangings were a hundred cubits long, with twenty pillars and
12 their bronze sockets, and hooks and bands of silver. On the west side the
hangings were fifty cubits long, with ten posts and ten sockets, and hooks
13 14 and bands of silver. The east side was also fifty cubits long: fifteen cubits of
15 hangings with three posts and three sockets on one side, and fifteen cubits
16 of hangings with three posts and three sockets on the other. All the hangings
17 of the courtyard were of finely spun linen. The sockets for the posts were of
bronze, the posts' hooks and bands were of silver, and their tops were overlaid
18 with silver; all the posts had silver bands. At the entrance of the courtyard
there was an embroidered screen of sky-blue, purple, and scarlet wool and
finely spun linen, twenty cubits long and five cubits wide, like the hangings
19 of the courtyard. It had four posts with four bronze sockets and with hooks
20 and bands of silver; their tops were overlaid with silver. All the tent pegs for
21 the Tabernacle and the surrounding courtyard were of bronze. These PEKUDEI
are the accounts of the Tabernacle, the Tabernacle of testimony, recorded at
Moshe's command by the Levites under Itamar, son of Aharon the priest.
22 Betzalel, son of Uri, son of Ḥur, from the tribe of Yehuda, made everything
23 that the Lord had commanded Moshe. He was assisted by Oholiav, son of
Aḥisamakh, from the tribe of Dan, an engraver, designer, and embroiderer
24 in sky-blue, purple, and scarlet wool and fine linen. All the gold
used in all the sacred work, donated as wave offerings, came to twenty-nine
25 talents and 730 shekels according to the Sanctuary weight. The silver of those
recorded in the census came to a hundred talents and 1,775 shekels, according
26 to the Sanctuary weight. One beka – half a shekel according to the Sanctuary
weight – was given by each of the 603,550 men aged twenty or over included
27 in the census. A hundred talents of silver were used for casting the sockets of
the Sanctuary and the curtain, one talent for each socket: a hundred talents
28 for the hundred sockets. Of 1,775 shekels he made the hooks and bands of
29 the posts and their silver-plated tops. The bronze given as an offering came
30 to seventy talents and 2,400 shekels. With this were made the sockets for the
entrance of the Tent of Meeting, the bronze altar with its bronze mesh, and all
31 the utensils of the altar, the sockets around the courtyard, the sockets at the
courtyard gate, and all the tent pegs for the Tabernacle and the surrounding
39 1 courtyard. From the sky-blue, purple, and scarlet wool they made woven

יא נְחֹשֶׁת וָוֵי הָעַמּוּדִים וַחֲשֻׁקֵיהֶם כָּסֶף׃ וְלִפְאַת צָפוֹן מֵאָה בָאַמָּה
עַמּוּדֵיהֶם עֶשְׂרִים וְאַדְנֵיהֶם עֶשְׂרִים נְחֹשֶׁת וָוֵי הָעַמּוּדִים וַחֲשֻׁקֵיהֶם
יב כָּסֶף׃ וְלִפְאַת־יָם קְלָעִים חֲמִשִּׁים בָּאַמָּה עַמּוּדֵיהֶם עֲשָׂרָה וְאַדְנֵיהֶם
יג עֲשָׂרָה וָוֵי הָעַמֻּדִים וַחֲשׁוּקֵיהֶם כָּסֶף׃ וְלִפְאַת קֵדְמָה מִזְרָחָה חֲמִשִּׁים
יד אַמָּה׃ קְלָעִים חֲמֵשׁ־עֶשְׂרֵה אַמָּה אֶל־הַכָּתֵף עַמּוּדֵיהֶם שְׁלֹשָׁה
טו וְאַדְנֵיהֶם שְׁלֹשָׁה׃ וְלַכָּתֵף הַשֵּׁנִית מִזֶּה וּמִזֶּה לְשַׁעַר הֶחָצֵר קְלָעִים
טז חֲמֵשׁ עֶשְׂרֵה אַמָּה עַמֻּדֵיהֶם שְׁלֹשָׁה וְאַדְנֵיהֶם שְׁלֹשָׁה׃ כָּל־קַלְעֵי
יז הֶחָצֵר סָבִיב שֵׁשׁ מָשְׁזָר׃ וְהָאֲדָנִים לָעַמֻּדִים נְחֹשֶׁת וָוֵי הָעַמּוּדִים
וַחֲשׁוּקֵיהֶם כֶּסֶף וְצִפּוּי רָאשֵׁיהֶם כָּסֶף וְהֵם מְחֻשָּׁקִים כֶּסֶף כֹּל עַמֻּדֵי
יח הֶחָצֵר׃ וּמָסַךְ שַׁעַר הֶחָצֵר מַעֲשֵׂה רֹקֵם תְּכֵלֶת וְאַרְגָּמָן וְתוֹלַעַת שָׁנִי מפטיר
וְשֵׁשׁ מָשְׁזָר וְעֶשְׂרִים אַמָּה אֹרֶךְ וְקוֹמָה בְרֹחַב חָמֵשׁ אַמּוֹת לְעֻמַּת
יט קַלְעֵי הֶחָצֵר׃ וְעַמֻּדֵיהֶם אַרְבָּעָה וְאַדְנֵיהֶם אַרְבָּעָה נְחֹשֶׁת וָוֵיהֶם
כ כֶּסֶף וְצִפּוּי רָאשֵׁיהֶם וַחֲשֻׁקֵיהֶם כָּסֶף׃ וְכָל־הַיְתֵדֹת לַמִּשְׁכָּן וְלֶחָצֵר
כא סָבִיב נְחֹשֶׁת׃ אֵלֶּה פְקוּדֵי הַמִּשְׁכָּן מִשְׁכַּן הָעֵדֻת כח פקודי
אֲשֶׁר פֻּקַּד עַל־פִּי מֹשֶׁה עֲבֹדַת הַלְוִיִּם בְּיַד אִיתָמָר בֶּן־אַהֲרֹן הַכֹּהֵן׃
כב וּבְצַלְאֵל בֶּן־אוּרִי בֶן־חוּר לְמַטֵּה יְהוּדָה עָשָׂה אֵת כָּל־אֲשֶׁר־צִוָּה
כג יהוה אֶת־מֹשֶׁה׃ וְאִתּוֹ אָהֳלִיאָב בֶּן־אֲחִיסָמָךְ לְמַטֵּה־דָן חָרָשׁ וְחֹשֵׁב
כד וְרֹקֵם בַּתְּכֵלֶת וּבָאַרְגָּמָן וּבְתוֹלַעַת הַשָּׁנִי וּבַשֵּׁשׁ׃ כָּל־
הַזָּהָב הֶעָשׂוּי לַמְּלָאכָה בְּכֹל מְלֶאכֶת הַקֹּדֶשׁ וַיְהִי ׀ זְהַב הַתְּנוּפָה
תֵּשַׁע וְעֶשְׂרִים כִּכָּר וּשְׁבַע מֵאוֹת וּשְׁלֹשִׁים שֶׁקֶל בְּשֶׁקֶל הַקֹּדֶשׁ׃
כה וְכֶסֶף פְּקוּדֵי הָעֵדָה מְאַת כִּכָּר וְאֶלֶף וּשְׁבַע מֵאוֹת וַחֲמִשָּׁה וְשִׁבְעִים
כו שֶׁקֶל בְּשֶׁקֶל הַקֹּדֶשׁ׃ בֶּקַע לַגֻּלְגֹּלֶת מַחֲצִית הַשֶּׁקֶל בְּשֶׁקֶל הַקֹּדֶשׁ
לְכֹל הָעֹבֵר עַל־הַפְּקֻדִים מִבֶּן עֶשְׂרִים שָׁנָה וָמַעְלָה לְשֵׁשׁ־מֵאוֹת
כז אֶלֶף וּשְׁלֹשֶׁת אֲלָפִים וַחֲמֵשׁ מֵאוֹת וַחֲמִשִּׁים׃ וַיְהִי מְאַת כִּכַּר הַכֶּסֶף
לָצֶקֶת אֵת אַדְנֵי הַקֹּדֶשׁ וְאֵת אַדְנֵי הַפָּרֹכֶת מְאַת אֲדָנִים לִמְאַת
כח הַכִּכָּר כִּכָּר לָאָדֶן׃ וְאֶת־הָאֶלֶף וּשְׁבַע הַמֵּאוֹת וַחֲמִשָּׁה וְשִׁבְעִים
כט עָשָׂה וָוִים לָעַמּוּדִים וְצִפָּה רָאשֵׁיהֶם וְחִשַּׁק אֹתָם׃ וּנְחֹשֶׁת הַתְּנוּפָה
ל שִׁבְעִים כִּכָּר וְאַלְפַּיִם וְאַרְבַּע־מֵאוֹת שָׁקֶל׃ וַיַּעַשׂ בָּהּ אֶת־אַדְנֵי פֶּתַח
אֹהֶל מוֹעֵד וְאֵת מִזְבַּח הַנְּחֹשֶׁת וְאֶת־מִכְבַּר הַנְּחֹשֶׁת אֲשֶׁר־לוֹ וְאֵת
לא כָּל־כְּלֵי הַמִּזְבֵּחַ׃ וְאֶת־אַדְנֵי הֶחָצֵר סָבִיב וְאֶת־אַדְנֵי שַׁעַר הֶחָצֵר
לט א וְאֵת כָּל־יִתְדֹת הַמִּשְׁכָּן וְאֶת־כָּל־יִתְדֹת הֶחָצֵר סָבִיב׃ וּמִן־הַתְּכֵלֶת
וְהָאַרְגָּמָן וְתוֹלַעַת הַשָּׁנִי עָשׂוּ בִגְדֵי־שְׂרָד לְשָׁרֵת בַּקֹּדֶשׁ וַיַּעֲשׂוּ אֶת־

garments for ministering in the Sanctuary. They also made sacred vestments
for Aharon, as the LORD commanded Moshe.
2 He made the ephod of gold, with sky-blue, purple, and scarlet wool and
3 finely spun linen. They hammered out thin sheets of gold and cut strands to
be worked into the sky-blue, purple, and scarlet wool and fine linen – highly
4 skilled work. They made fixed shoulder pieces for the ephod; these were
5 affixed to its two ends. Its decorated waistband was like it and of one piece
with the ephod, made with gold, with sky-blue, purple, and scarlet wool and
6 finely spun linen, as the LORD commanded Moshe. They mounted
the rock crystal stones in gold filigree settings and engraved them as a seal
7 with the names of Yisrael's sons. He fastened them on the shoulder pieces of
the ephod as remembrance stones for Yisrael's sons, as the LORD commanded
Moshe.
8 He made the breast piece with the same skilled craftsmanship as the ephod:
9 of gold, of sky-blue, purple, and scarlet wool, and of finely spun linen. It was
10 square and folded double, a span long and a span wide. Then they mounted
four rows of precious stones on it. The first row was a carnelian, an olivine,
11 and a garnet; the second row was an emerald, a lapis lazuli, and a green
12 13 quartz; the third row was an amber, a jet, and a sardonyx; and the fourth
was an aquamarine, a rock crystal, and a jasper or opal. They were mounted
14 in gold filigree settings. There were twelve stones, one for each of the names
of Yisrael's sons. Each was engraved like a seal with the name of one of the
15 twelve tribes. For the breast piece they made chains of pure gold, braided like
16 cords. They made two gold filigree settings and two gold rings, and attached
17 the rings to two of the corners of the breast piece. They fastened the two gold
18 chains to the rings at the corners of the breast piece, and the other ends of the
chains to the two settings, attaching them to the ephod's shoulder pieces at the
19 front. They made two gold rings and placed them at the two other corners of
20 the breast piece on the edge, inside, next to the ephod. Then they made two
more gold rings and attached them to the bottom of the ephod's two shoulder
pieces facing the priest's front, close to the seam and above the ephod's
21 woven waistband. They tied the rings of the breast piece to the rings of
the ephod with a sky-blue cord, connecting it to the waistband so that the
breast piece would remain secured to the ephod, as the LORD had commanded Moshe.
22 23 They made the robe of the ephod woven entirely of sky-blue wool, with an
opening in the center like the neck of a coat of mail, with a woven border
24 around it so that it would not tear. They made pomegranates of sky-blue,
purple, and scarlet wool and finely spun linen around the hem of the robe.
25 And they made bells of pure gold and attached them around the hem

בִּגְדֵי הַקֹּדֶשׁ אֲשֶׁר לְאַהֲרֹן כַּאֲשֶׁר צִוָּה יְהוָה אֶת־מֹשֶׁה׃
ב וַיַּעַשׂ אֶת־הָאֵפֹד זָהָב תְּכֵלֶת וְאַרְגָּמָן וְתוֹלַעַת שָׁנִי וְשֵׁשׁ מָשְׁזָר׃ שני /חמישי/
ג וַיְרַקְּעוּ אֶת־פַּחֵי הַזָּהָב וְקִצֵּץ פְּתִילִם לַעֲשׂוֹת בְּתוֹךְ הַתְּכֵלֶת וּבְתוֹךְ
ד הָאַרְגָּמָן וּבְתוֹךְ תּוֹלַעַת הַשָּׁנִי וּבְתוֹךְ הַשֵּׁשׁ מַעֲשֵׂה חֹשֵׁב׃ כְּתֵפֹת
ה עָשׂוּ־לוֹ חֹבְרֹת עַל־שְׁנֵי קצוותו חֻבָּר׃ וְחֵשֶׁב אֲפֻדָּתוֹ אֲשֶׁר עָלָיו קְצוֹתָיו
מִמֶּנּוּ הוּא כְּמַעֲשֵׂהוּ זָהָב תְּכֵלֶת וְאַרְגָּמָן וְתוֹלַעַת שָׁנִי וְשֵׁשׁ מָשְׁזָר
ו כַּאֲשֶׁר צִוָּה יְהוָה אֶת־מֹשֶׁה׃ וַיַּעֲשׂוּ אֶת־אַבְנֵי הַשֹּׁהַם
מֻסַבֹּת מִשְׁבְּצֹת זָהָב מְפֻתָּחֹת פִּתּוּחֵי חוֹתָם עַל־שְׁמוֹת בְּנֵי יִשְׂרָאֵל׃
ז וַיָּשֶׂם אֹתָם עַל כִּתְפֹת הָאֵפֹד אַבְנֵי זִכָּרוֹן לִבְנֵי יִשְׂרָאֵל כַּאֲשֶׁר צִוָּה
יְהוָה אֶת־מֹשֶׁה׃

ח וַיַּעַשׂ אֶת־הַחֹשֶׁן מַעֲשֵׂה חֹשֵׁב כְּמַעֲשֵׂה אֵפֹד זָהָב תְּכֵלֶת וְאַרְגָּמָן
ט וְתוֹלַעַת שָׁנִי וְשֵׁשׁ מָשְׁזָר׃ רָבוּעַ הָיָה כָּפוּל עָשׂוּ אֶת־הַחֹשֶׁן זֶרֶת
י אָרְכּוֹ וְזֶרֶת רָחְבּוֹ כָּפוּל׃ וַיְמַלְאוּ־בוֹ אַרְבָּעָה טוּרֵי אָבֶן טוּר אֹדֶם
יא יב פִּטְדָה וּבָרֶקֶת הַטּוּר הָאֶחָד׃ וְהַטּוּר הַשֵּׁנִי נֹפֶךְ סַפִּיר וְיָהֲלֹם׃ וְהַטּוּר
יג הַשְּׁלִישִׁי לֶשֶׁם שְׁבוֹ וְאַחְלָמָה׃ וְהַטּוּר הָרְבִיעִי תַּרְשִׁישׁ שֹׁהַם וְיָשְׁפֵה
יד מוּסַבֹּת מִשְׁבְּצוֹת זָהָב בְּמִלֻּאֹתָם׃ וְהָאֲבָנִים עַל־שְׁמֹת בְּנֵי־יִשְׂרָאֵל
הֵנָּה שְׁתֵּים עֶשְׂרֵה עַל־שְׁמֹתָם פִּתּוּחֵי חֹתָם אִישׁ עַל־שְׁמוֹ לִשְׁנֵים
טו עָשָׂר שָׁבֶט׃ וַיַּעֲשׂוּ עַל־הַחֹשֶׁן שַׁרְשְׁרֹת גַּבְלֻת מַעֲשֵׂה עֲבֹת זָהָב
טז טָהוֹר׃ וַיַּעֲשׂוּ שְׁתֵּי מִשְׁבְּצֹת זָהָב וּשְׁתֵּי טַבְּעֹת זָהָב וַיִּתְּנוּ אֶת־שְׁתֵּי
יז הַטַּבָּעֹת עַל־שְׁנֵי קְצוֹת הַחֹשֶׁן׃ וַיִּתְּנוּ שְׁתֵּי הָעֲבֹתֹת הַזָּהָב עַל־שְׁתֵּי
יח הַטַּבָּעֹת עַל־קְצוֹת הַחֹשֶׁן׃ וְאֵת שְׁתֵּי קְצוֹת שְׁתֵּי הָעֲבֹתֹת נָתְנוּ
יט עַל־שְׁתֵּי הַמִּשְׁבְּצֹת וַיִּתְּנֻם עַל־כִּתְפֹת הָאֵפֹד אֶל־מוּל פָּנָיו׃ וַיַּעֲשׂוּ
שְׁתֵּי טַבְּעֹת זָהָב וַיָּשִׂימוּ עַל־שְׁנֵי קְצוֹת הַחֹשֶׁן עַל־שְׂפָתוֹ אֲשֶׁר
כ אֶל־עֵבֶר הָאֵפֹד בָּיְתָה׃ וַיַּעֲשׂוּ שְׁתֵּי טַבְּעֹת זָהָב וַיִּתְּנֻם עַל־שְׁתֵּי
כִּתְפֹת הָאֵפֹד מִלְּמַטָּה מִמּוּל פָּנָיו לְעֻמַּת מַחְבַּרְתּוֹ מִמַּעַל לְחֵשֶׁב
כא הָאֵפֹד׃ וַיִּרְכְּסוּ אֶת־הַחֹשֶׁן מִטַּבְּעֹתָיו אֶל־טַבְּעֹת הָאֵפֹד בִּפְתִיל
תְּכֵלֶת לִהְיֹת עַל־חֵשֶׁב הָאֵפֹד וְלֹא־יִזַּח הַחֹשֶׁן מֵעַל הָאֵפֹד כַּאֲשֶׁר
צִוָּה יְהוָה אֶת־מֹשֶׁה׃

כב כג וַיַּעַשׂ אֶת־מְעִיל הָאֵפֹד מַעֲשֵׂה אֹרֵג כְּלִיל תְּכֵלֶת׃ וּפִי־הַמְּעִיל שלישי /ששי/
כד בְּתוֹכוֹ כְּפִי תַחְרָא שָׂפָה לְפִיו סָבִיב לֹא יִקָּרֵעַ׃ וַיַּעֲשׂוּ עַל־שׁוּלֵי
כה הַמְּעִיל רִמּוֹנֵי תְּכֵלֶת וְאַרְגָּמָן וְתוֹלַעַת שָׁנִי מָשְׁזָר׃ וַיַּעֲשׂוּ פַעֲמֹנֵי
זָהָב טָהוֹר וַיִּתְּנוּ אֶת־הַפַּעֲמֹנִים בְּתוֹךְ הָרִמֹּנִים עַל־שׁוּלֵי הַמְּעִיל

26 between the pomegranates. The bells and pomegranates alternated around
the hem of the robe worn for ministering, as the LORD commanded
27 Moshe. For Aharon and his sons, they made tunics woven from
28 fine linen, together with a linen miter, linen headdresses, and trousers of finely
29 spun linen. The sash was embroidered out of finely spun linen and sky-blue,
30 purple, and scarlet wool, as the LORD commanded Moshe. They
made the headplate, the holy diadem, of pure gold and engraved on it, as on
31 a seal: Holy to the LORD. Then they attached a sky-blue cord to it to affix it to
32 the miter, as the LORD had commanded Moshe. Thus all the work
on the Tabernacle, the Tent of Meeting, was completed. The Israelites did
everything exactly as the LORD had commanded Moshe.
33 They brought the Tabernacle to Moshe: the Tent and all its furnishings, its
34 clasps, frames, crossbars, posts, and sockets; the covering of reddened rams'
hides and the covering of fine leather and the curtain that covered the screen;
35 36 the Ark of the Testimony and its carrying staves; the Ark cover; the table with
37 all its utensils; the showbread; the pure gold candelabrum with its row of
38 lamps and all its accessories, together with the oil for lighting; the gold altar,
the anointing oil, the fragrant incense, and the curtain for the entrance to the
39 Tent; the bronze altar with its bronze mesh, its staves, and all its utensils; the
40 laver with its base; the hangings for the courtyard, its posts and sockets, and
the screen for the courtyard gate; the ropes and tent pegs for the courtyard;
all the furnishings for the service of the Tabernacle, the Tent of Meeting;
41 and the woven garments for ministering in the Sanctuary, both the sacred
vestments for Aharon the priest and the vestments for his sons to wear when
42 serving as priests. The Israelites had completed all the work exactly as the
43 LORD commanded Moshe. Moshe saw that all the work had been done just
as the LORD had commanded – and Moshe blessed them.
40 1 2 Then the LORD spoke to Moshe, saying, "On the first day of the first month
3 you shall set up the Tabernacle of the Tent of Meeting. Put in it the Ark of the
4 Testimony, and screen the Ark with the curtain. Bring in the table and set it.
5 Bring in the candelabrum and light its lamps. Put the golden incense altar in
front of the Ark of the Testimony, and hang the screen for the Tabernacle's
6 entrance. Put the sacrificial altar in front of the entrance of the Tabernacle
7 of the Tent of Meeting. Place the laver between the Tent of Meeting and
8 the altar, and put water in it. Arrange the courtyard all around, and put in
9 place the screen for the courtyard gate. Take the anointing oil and anoint the
Tabernacle and everything in it. Consecrate it and all its furnishings so that

כו סָבִיב בְּתוֹךְ הָרִמֹּנִים: פַּעֲמֹן וְרִמֹּן פַּעֲמֹן וְרִמֹּן עַל־שׁוּלֵי הַמְּעִיל
כז סָבִיב לְשָׁרֵת כַּאֲשֶׁר צִוָּה יהוה אֶת־מֹשֶׁה: וַיַּעֲשׂוּ
כח אֶת־הַכָּתְנֹת שֵׁשׁ מַעֲשֵׂה אֹרֵג לְאַהֲרֹן וּלְבָנָיו: וְאֵת הַמִּצְנֶפֶת שֵׁשׁ
כט וְאֶת־פַּאֲרֵי הַמִּגְבָּעֹת שֵׁשׁ וְאֶת־מִכְנְסֵי הַבָּד שֵׁשׁ מָשְׁזָר: וְאֶת־
הָאַבְנֵט שֵׁשׁ מָשְׁזָר וּתְכֵלֶת וְאַרְגָּמָן וְתוֹלַעַת שָׁנִי מַעֲשֵׂה רֹקֵם כַּאֲשֶׁר
ל צִוָּה יהוה אֶת־מֹשֶׁה: וַיַּעֲשׂוּ אֶת־צִיץ נֵזֶר־הַקֹּדֶשׁ זָהָב
לא טָהוֹר וַיִּכְתְּבוּ עָלָיו מִכְתַּב פִּתּוּחֵי חוֹתָם קֹדֶשׁ לַיהוה: וַיִּתְּנוּ עָלָיו
פְּתִיל תְּכֵלֶת לָתֵת עַל־הַמִּצְנֶפֶת מִלְמָעְלָה כַּאֲשֶׁר צִוָּה יהוה אֶת־
לב מֹשֶׁה: וַתֵּכֶל כָּל־עֲבֹדַת מִשְׁכַּן אֹהֶל מוֹעֵד וַיַּעֲשׂוּ בְּנֵי
יִשְׂרָאֵל כְּכֹל אֲשֶׁר צִוָּה יהוה אֶת־מֹשֶׁה כֵּן עָשׂוּ:
לג וַיָּבִיאוּ אֶת־הַמִּשְׁכָּן אֶל־מֹשֶׁה אֶת־הָאֹהֶל וְאֶת־כָּל־כֵּלָיו קְרָסָיו קְרָשָׁיו כט רביעי
לד בְּרִיחָו וְעַמֻּדָיו וַאֲדָנָיו: וְאֶת־מִכְסֵה עוֹרֹת הָאֵילִם הַמְאָדָּמִים וְאֶת־
לה מִכְסֵה עֹרֹת הַתְּחָשִׁים וְאֵת פָּרֹכֶת הַמָּסָךְ: אֶת־אֲרוֹן הָעֵדֻת וְאֶת־
לו בַּדָּיו וְאֵת הַכַּפֹּרֶת: אֶת־הַשֻּׁלְחָן אֶת־כָּל־כֵּלָיו וְאֵת לֶחֶם הַפָּנִים:
לז אֶת־הַמְּנֹרָה הַטְּהֹרָה אֶת־נֵרֹתֶיהָ נֵרֹת הַמַּעֲרָכָה וְאֶת־כָּל־כֵּלֶיהָ וְאֵת
לח שֶׁמֶן הַמָּאוֹר: וְאֵת מִזְבַּח הַזָּהָב וְאֵת שֶׁמֶן הַמִּשְׁחָה וְאֵת קְטֹרֶת
לט הַסַּמִּים וְאֵת מָסַךְ פֶּתַח הָאֹהֶל: אֵת ׀ מִזְבַּח הַנְּחֹשֶׁת וְאֶת־מִכְבַּר
מ הַנְּחֹשֶׁת אֲשֶׁר־לוֹ אֶת־בַּדָּיו וְאֶת־כָּל־כֵּלָיו אֶת־הַכִּיֹּר וְאֶת־כַּנּוֹ: אֵת
קַלְעֵי הֶחָצֵר אֶת־עַמֻּדֶיהָ וְאֶת־אֲדָנֶיהָ וְאֶת־הַמָּסָךְ לְשַׁעַר הֶחָצֵר
אֶת־מֵיתָרָיו וִיתֵדֹתֶיהָ וְאֵת כָּל־כְּלֵי עֲבֹדַת הַמִּשְׁכָּן לְאֹהֶל מוֹעֵד:
מא אֶת־בִּגְדֵי הַשְּׂרָד לְשָׁרֵת בַּקֹּדֶשׁ אֶת־בִּגְדֵי הַקֹּדֶשׁ לְאַהֲרֹן הַכֹּהֵן
מב וְאֶת־בִּגְדֵי בָנָיו לְכַהֵן: כְּכֹל אֲשֶׁר־צִוָּה יהוה אֶת־מֹשֶׁה כֵּן עָשׂוּ בְּנֵי
מג יִשְׂרָאֵל אֵת כָּל־הָעֲבֹדָה: וַיַּרְא מֹשֶׁה אֶת־כָּל־הַמְּלָאכָה וְהִנֵּה עָשׂוּ
אֹתָהּ כַּאֲשֶׁר צִוָּה יהוה כֵּן עָשׂוּ וַיְבָרֶךְ אֹתָם מֹשֶׁה:
מ א ב וַיְדַבֵּר יהוה אֶל־מֹשֶׁה לֵּאמֹר: בְּיוֹם־הַחֹדֶשׁ הָרִאשׁוֹן בְּאֶחָד לַחֹדֶשׁ חמישי /שביעי/
ג תָּקִים אֶת־מִשְׁכַּן אֹהֶל מוֹעֵד: וְשַׂמְתָּ שָׁם אֵת אֲרוֹן הָעֵדוּת וְסַכֹּתָ
ד עַל־הָאָרֹן אֶת־הַפָּרֹכֶת: וְהֵבֵאתָ אֶת־הַשֻּׁלְחָן וְעָרַכְתָּ אֶת־עֶרְכּוֹ
ה וְהֵבֵאתָ אֶת־הַמְּנֹרָה וְהַעֲלֵיתָ אֶת־נֵרֹתֶיהָ: וְנָתַתָּה אֶת־מִזְבַּח הַזָּהָב
ו לִקְטֹרֶת לִפְנֵי אֲרוֹן הָעֵדֻת וְשַׂמְתָּ אֶת־מָסַךְ הַפֶּתַח לַמִּשְׁכָּן: וְנָתַתָּה
ז אֵת מִזְבַּח הָעֹלָה לִפְנֵי פֶּתַח מִשְׁכַּן אֹהֶל־מוֹעֵד: וְנָתַתָּ אֶת־הַכִּיֹּר
ח בֵּין־אֹהֶל מוֹעֵד וּבֵין הַמִּזְבֵּחַ וְנָתַתָּ שָׁם מָיִם: וְשַׂמְתָּ אֶת־הֶחָצֵר סָבִיב
ט וְנָתַתָּ אֶת־מָסַךְ שַׁעַר הֶחָצֵר: וְלָקַחְתָּ אֶת־שֶׁמֶן הַמִּשְׁחָה וּמָשַׁחְתָּ

10 it becomes holy. Anoint the sacrificial altar and all its utensils, consecrating
11 it so that it becomes holy of holies. Anoint the laver with its base, making it
12 holy. Then bring Aharon and his sons to the entrance of the Tent of Meeting,
13 and cleanse them with water. Robe Aharon with the sacred vestments and
14 anoint him, that he may serve Me as priest. Then bring his sons forward,
15 robe them with tunics, and anoint them as you anointed their father, that
they may serve Me as priests. Through this anointing, theirs will become an
16 everlasting priesthood throughout the generations." Moshe did exactly as the
17 LORD had commanded him. On the first day of the first month of
18 the second year[69] the Tabernacle was set up. Moshe set up the Tabernacle,
placed its sockets, erected its frames, inserted its bars, and put up its posts.
19 He spread the tent over the Tabernacle and placed the covering over the
20 tent, as the LORD had commanded him. He took the covenant and
put it in the Ark. He inserted the carrying staves into the Ark and placed
21 the cover on top of it. He brought the Ark into the Tabernacle and hung
the cloth curtain, screening off the Ark of the Testimony, as the LORD had
22 commanded him. He put the table in the Tent of Meeting, outside
23 the curtain on the north side of the Tabernacle, and arranged the bread on it
24 before the LORD, as the LORD had commanded him. He placed the
candelabrum in the Tent of Meeting, opposite the table, on the Tabernacle's
25 south side, and lit the lamps before the LORD, as the LORD had commanded
26 him. He placed the golden altar in the Tent of Meeting, in front of the
27 curtain, and on it he burned fragrant incense, as the LORD had commanded
28 him. He hung the curtain at the entrance of the Tabernacle. He put
29 the sacrificial altar at the entrance of the Tabernacle of the Tent of Meeting,
and on it sacrificed a burnt offering and a grain offering, as the LORD had
30 commanded him. He placed the laver between the Tent of Meeting
31 and the altar, and in it he put water for washing. Moshe, Aharon, and his sons
32 would wash their hands and feet there, for they washed themselves whenever
they went into the Tent of Meeting or approached the altar, as the LORD
33 had commanded Moshe. Then he set up the courtyard around the
Tabernacle and the altar, and hung the curtain for the courtyard gate. And so
Moshe completed the work.
34 Then the cloud covered the Tent of Meeting, and the glory of the LORD
35 filled the Tabernacle. Moshe could not now enter the Tent of Meeting,
because the cloud had settled on it, and the glory of the LORD filled the
36 Tabernacle. In all the journeys of the Israelites, when the cloud rose from the

69 | Since the exodus from Egypt.

אֶת־הַמִּשְׁכָּן וְאֶת־כָּל־אֲשֶׁר־בּוֹ וְקִדַּשְׁתָּ אֹתוֹ וְאֶת־כָּל־כֵּלָיו וְהָיָה
י קֹדֶשׁ׃ וּמָשַׁחְתָּ אֶת־מִזְבַּח הָעֹלָה וְאֶת־כָּל־כֵּלָיו וְקִדַּשְׁתָּ אֶת־הַמִּזְבֵּחַ
יא וְהָיָה הַמִּזְבֵּחַ קֹדֶשׁ קָדָשִׁים׃ וּמָשַׁחְתָּ אֶת־הַכִּיֹּר וְאֶת־כַּנּוֹ וְקִדַּשְׁתָּ
יב אֹתוֹ׃ וְהִקְרַבְתָּ אֶת־אַהֲרֹן וְאֶת־בָּנָיו אֶל־פֶּתַח אֹהֶל מוֹעֵד וְרָחַצְתָּ
יג אֹתָם בַּמָּיִם׃ וְהִלְבַּשְׁתָּ אֶת־אַהֲרֹן אֵת בִּגְדֵי הַקֹּדֶשׁ וּמָשַׁחְתָּ אֹתוֹ
יד וְקִדַּשְׁתָּ אֹתוֹ וְכִהֵן לִי׃ וְאֶת־בָּנָיו תַּקְרִיב וְהִלְבַּשְׁתָּ אֹתָם כֻּתֳּנֹת׃
טו וּמָשַׁחְתָּ אֹתָם כַּאֲשֶׁר מָשַׁחְתָּ אֶת־אֲבִיהֶם וְכִהֲנוּ לִי וְהָיְתָה לִהְיֹת
טז לָהֶם מָשְׁחָתָם לִכְהֻנַּת עוֹלָם לְדֹרֹתָם׃ וַיַּעַשׂ מֹשֶׁה כְּכֹל אֲשֶׁר צִוָּה
יז יְהוָה אֹתוֹ כֵּן עָשָׂה׃ וַיְהִי בַּחֹדֶשׁ הָרִאשׁוֹן בַּשָּׁנָה הַשֵּׁנִית ששי
יח בְּאֶחָד לַחֹדֶשׁ הוּקַם הַמִּשְׁכָּן׃ וַיָּקֶם מֹשֶׁה אֶת־הַמִּשְׁכָּן וַיִּתֵּן אֶת־אֲדָנָיו
יט וַיָּשֶׂם אֶת־קְרָשָׁיו וַיִּתֵּן אֶת־בְּרִיחָיו וַיָּקֶם אֶת־עַמּוּדָיו׃ וַיִּפְרֹשׂ אֶת־
הָאֹהֶל עַל־הַמִּשְׁכָּן וַיָּשֶׂם אֶת־מִכְסֵה הָאֹהֶל עָלָיו מִלְמָעְלָה כַּאֲשֶׁר
כ צִוָּה יְהוָה אֶת־מֹשֶׁה׃ וַיִּקַּח וַיִּתֵּן אֶת־הָעֵדֻת אֶל־הָאָרֹן
וַיָּשֶׂם אֶת־הַבַּדִּים עַל־הָאָרֹן וַיִּתֵּן אֶת־הַכַּפֹּרֶת עַל־הָאָרֹן מִלְמָעְלָה׃
כא וַיָּבֵא אֶת־הָאָרֹן אֶל־הַמִּשְׁכָּן וַיָּשֶׂם אֵת פָּרֹכֶת הַמָּסָךְ וַיָּסֶךְ עַל אֲרוֹן
כב הָעֵדוּת כַּאֲשֶׁר צִוָּה יְהוָה אֶת־מֹשֶׁה׃ וַיִּתֵּן אֶת־הַשֻּׁלְחָן
כג בְּאֹהֶל מוֹעֵד עַל יֶרֶךְ הַמִּשְׁכָּן צָפֹנָה מִחוּץ לַפָּרֹכֶת׃ וַיַּעֲרֹךְ עָלָיו עֵרֶךְ
כד לֶחֶם לִפְנֵי יְהוָה כַּאֲשֶׁר צִוָּה יְהוָה אֶת־מֹשֶׁה׃ וַיָּשֶׂם אֶת־
כה הַמְּנֹרָה בְּאֹהֶל מוֹעֵד נֹכַח הַשֻּׁלְחָן עַל יֶרֶךְ הַמִּשְׁכָּן נֶגְבָּה׃ וַיַּעַל הַנֵּרֹת
כו לִפְנֵי יְהוָה כַּאֲשֶׁר צִוָּה יְהוָה אֶת־מֹשֶׁה׃ וַיָּשֶׂם אֶת־מִזְבַּח
כז הַזָּהָב בְּאֹהֶל מוֹעֵד לִפְנֵי הַפָּרֹכֶת׃ וַיַּקְטֵר עָלָיו קְטֹרֶת סַמִּים כַּאֲשֶׁר
כח צִוָּה יְהוָה אֶת־מֹשֶׁה׃ וַיָּשֶׂם אֶת־מָסַךְ הַפֶּתַח לַמִּשְׁכָּן׃ שביעי
כט וְאֵת מִזְבַּח הָעֹלָה שָׂם פֶּתַח מִשְׁכַּן אֹהֶל־מוֹעֵד וַיַּעַל עָלָיו אֶת־הָעֹלָה
ל וְאֶת־הַמִּנְחָה כַּאֲשֶׁר צִוָּה יְהוָה אֶת־מֹשֶׁה׃ וַיָּשֶׂם אֶת־
לא הַכִּיֹּר בֵּין־אֹהֶל מוֹעֵד וּבֵין הַמִּזְבֵּחַ וַיִּתֵּן שָׁמָּה מַיִם לְרָחְצָה׃ וְרָחֲצוּ
לב מִמֶּנּוּ מֹשֶׁה וְאַהֲרֹן וּבָנָיו אֶת־יְדֵיהֶם וְאֶת־רַגְלֵיהֶם׃ בְּבֹאָם אֶל־
אֹהֶל מוֹעֵד וּבְקָרְבָתָם אֶל־הַמִּזְבֵּחַ יִרְחָצוּ כַּאֲשֶׁר צִוָּה יְהוָה אֶת־
לג מֹשֶׁה׃ וַיָּקֶם אֶת־הֶחָצֵר סָבִיב לַמִּשְׁכָּן וְלַמִּזְבֵּחַ וַיִּתֵּן אֶת־
מָסַךְ שַׁעַר הֶחָצֵר וַיְכַל מֹשֶׁה אֶת־הַמְּלָאכָה׃
לד לה וַיְכַס הֶעָנָן אֶת־אֹהֶל מוֹעֵד וּכְבוֹד יְהוָה מָלֵא אֶת־הַמִּשְׁכָּן׃ וְלֹא־יָכֹל מפטיר
מֹשֶׁה לָבוֹא אֶל־אֹהֶל מוֹעֵד כִּי־שָׁכַן עָלָיו הֶעָנָן וּכְבוֹד יְהוָה מָלֵא
לו אֶת־הַמִּשְׁכָּן׃ וּבְהֵעָלוֹת הֶעָנָן מֵעַל הַמִּשְׁכָּן יִסְעוּ בְּנֵי יִשְׂרָאֵל בְּכֹל

37 Tabernacle, they would set out. But if the cloud did not lift, they did not move
38 on; they waited until it had lifted. The LORD's cloud was over the Tabernacle
by day, and fire was in it at night, in view of all the House of Israel through
all their journeys.

לז לח מַסְעֵיהֶם׃ וְאִם־לֹא יֵעָלֶה הֶעָנָן וְלֹא יִסְעוּ עַד־יוֹם הֵעָלֹתוֹ׃ כִּי עֲנַן
יְהוָה עַל־הַמִּשְׁכָּן יוֹמָם וְאֵשׁ תִּהְיֶה לַיְלָה בּוֹ לְעֵינֵי כָל־בֵּית־יִשְׂרָאֵל
בְּכָל־מַסְעֵיהֶם׃

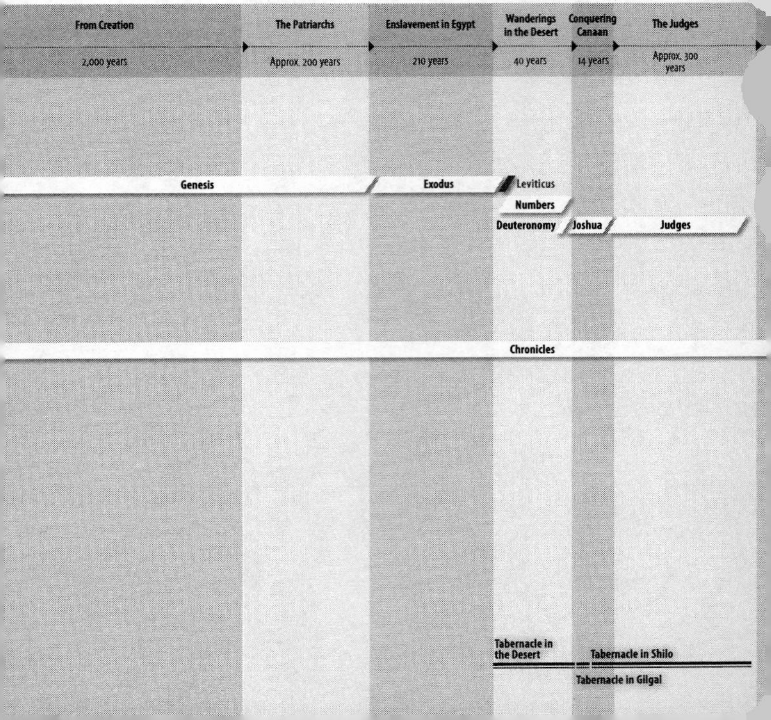
From Creation
2,000 years
The Patriarchs
Approx. 200 years
Enslavement in Egypt
210 years
Wanderings in the Desert
40 years
Conquering Canaan
14 years
The Judges
Approx. 300 years
Genesis
Exodus
Leviticus
Numbers
Deuteronomy
Joshua
Judges
Chronicles
Tabernacle in the Desert
Tabernacle in Shilo
Tabernacle in Gilgal

ויקרא
VAYIKRA/LEVITICUS

LEVITICUS	Offerings	Initiation of the priests and their service	Ritual purity and impurity	Laws of sanctity
	Chs. 1–7	8–10	11–16	17–27
	Approx. 1 month			

1 1 The LORD called to Moshe. From the Tent of Meeting He spoke to him and VAYIKRA
2 said, "Speak to the Israelites. Say: When one of you brings an animal offering
3 to the LORD, you may bring it either from the herd or from the flock. If the
offering is a burnt offering from the herd, one must offer a male animal
without blemish. The one making the offering shall bring it to the entrance
4 to the Tent of Meeting to be accepted on his behalf before the LORD; and,
that it be accepted on his behalf, to make his atonement, he shall lay his hand
5 on the head of the burnt offering and shall have the bull slaughtered before
the LORD. And Aharon's sons the priests shall present the blood, dashing
6 it against each side of the altar at the entrance to the Tent of Meeting. The
7 burnt offering shall then be skinned and cut into pieces. The sons of Aharon
the priest shall arrange wood on the fire they will have placed upon the altar.
8 Then Aharon's sons the priests shall arrange the pieces of the sacrifice, with
9 the head and the fat, upon the wood on the altar fire; the inner organs and legs
shall first be washed with water. The priest shall then burn it all on the altar as
10 a burnt offering, an offering of fire, a pleasing aroma to the LORD. If
the offering is a burnt offering from the flock, whether a sheep or a goat, one
11 must offer a male without blemish. The one making the sacrifice shall have
it slaughtered on the north side of the altar before the LORD, and Aharon's
12 sons the priests shall dash its blood against each side of the altar. The sacrifice
shall be cut into pieces, including the head and the fat, and the priest shall
13 arrange these upon the wood on the altar fire, the inner organs and legs
having been washed with water. The priest shall then offer it all, sending it
up in smoke upon the altar as a burnt offering, an offering of fire, a pleasing
aroma to the LORD.
14 If the offering for the LORD is to be a burnt offering of fowl, one may offer
15 doves or pigeons. The priest shall bring the offering to the altar, sever its neck,
16 and burn it on the altar; its blood shall be drained against the altar wall: the
priest shall remove the crop with its feathers and throw that to the east side
17 of the altar, to the place where the ashes are gathered. Then he shall tear the
bird open by its wings, without dividing it completely. The priest shall then
send it up in smoke upon the altar, on the wood of the altar fire. It is a burnt
2 1 offering, an offering of fire, a pleasing aroma to the LORD. When one
brings a grain offering to the LORD, it shall be of fine flour. The one who brings
2 the sacrifice shall pour oil over it, then place incense upon it, and bring it to
Aharon's sons, the priests. From this, the priest shall scoop out a handful of
its fine flour and oil, together with all its incense, and send this remembrance[1]
up in smoke upon the altar as an offering of fire, a pleasing aroma to the LORD.
3 What remains of the grain offering shall belong to Aharon and his sons; it
4 is holy of holies among the fire offerings to the LORD.[2] When you
bring a grain offering baked in an oven, it shall be of fine flour: unleavened

---

1 | A part of the offering sent up in smoke, prompting the Lord to "remember" the individual in a favorable way.

2 | Offerings in the category of "holy of holies" bear greater restrictions and may be eaten only by the priests.

א

א ב וַיִּקְרָא אֶל־מֹשֶׁה וַיְדַבֵּר יהוה אֵלָיו מֵאֹהֶל מוֹעֵד לֵאמֹר: דַּבֵּר אֶל־בְּנֵי
יִשְׂרָאֵל וְאָמַרְתָּ אֲלֵהֶם אָדָם כִּי־יַקְרִיב מִכֶּם קָרְבָּן לַיהוה מִן־הַבְּהֵמָה
ג מִן־הַבָּקָר וּמִן־הַצֹּאן תַּקְרִיבוּ אֶת־קָרְבַּנְכֶם: אִם־עֹלָה קָרְבָּנוֹ מִן־
הַבָּקָר זָכָר תָּמִים יַקְרִיבֶנּוּ אֶל־פֶּתַח אֹהֶל מוֹעֵד יַקְרִיב אֹתוֹ לִרְצֹנוֹ
ד ה לִפְנֵי יהוה: וְסָמַךְ יָדוֹ עַל רֹאשׁ הָעֹלָה וְנִרְצָה לוֹ לְכַפֵּר עָלָיו: וְשָׁחַט
אֶת־בֶּן הַבָּקָר לִפְנֵי יהוה וְהִקְרִיבוּ בְּנֵי אַהֲרֹן הַכֹּהֲנִים אֶת־הַדָּם וְזָרְקוּ
ו אֶת־הַדָּם עַל־הַמִּזְבֵּחַ סָבִיב אֲשֶׁר־פֶּתַח אֹהֶל מוֹעֵד: וְהִפְשִׁיט אֶת־
ז הָעֹלָה וְנִתַּח אֹתָהּ לִנְתָחֶיהָ: וְנָתְנוּ בְּנֵי אַהֲרֹן הַכֹּהֵן אֵשׁ עַל־הַמִּזְבֵּחַ
ח וְעָרְכוּ עֵצִים עַל־הָאֵשׁ: וְעָרְכוּ בְּנֵי אַהֲרֹן הַכֹּהֲנִים אֵת הַנְּתָחִים אֶת־
הָרֹאשׁ וְאֶת־הַפָּדֶר עַל־הָעֵצִים אֲשֶׁר עַל־הָאֵשׁ אֲשֶׁר עַל־הַמִּזְבֵּחַ:
ט וְקִרְבּוֹ וּכְרָעָיו יִרְחַץ בַּמָּיִם וְהִקְטִיר הַכֹּהֵן אֶת־הַכֹּל הַמִּזְבֵּחָה עֹלָה
י אִשֵּׁה רֵיחַ־נִיחוֹחַ לַיהוה: וְאִם־מִן־הַצֹּאן קָרְבָּנוֹ מִן־
יא הַכְּשָׂבִים אוֹ מִן־הָעִזִּים לְעֹלָה זָכָר תָּמִים יַקְרִיבֶנּוּ: וְשָׁחַט אֹתוֹ עַל
יֶרֶךְ הַמִּזְבֵּחַ צָפֹנָה לִפְנֵי יהוה וְזָרְקוּ בְּנֵי אַהֲרֹן הַכֹּהֲנִים אֶת־דָּמוֹ
יב עַל־הַמִּזְבֵּחַ סָבִיב: וְנִתַּח אֹתוֹ לִנְתָחָיו וְאֶת־רֹאשׁוֹ וְאֶת־פִּדְרוֹ וְעָרַךְ
יג הַכֹּהֵן אֹתָם עַל־הָעֵצִים אֲשֶׁר עַל־הָאֵשׁ אֲשֶׁר עַל־הַמִּזְבֵּחַ: וְהַקֶּרֶב
וְהַכְּרָעַיִם יִרְחַץ בַּמָּיִם וְהִקְרִיב הַכֹּהֵן אֶת־הַכֹּל וְהִקְטִיר הַמִּזְבֵּחָה
עֹלָה הוּא אִשֵּׁה רֵיחַ נִיחֹחַ לַיהוה:
יד וְאִם מִן־הָעוֹף עֹלָה קָרְבָּנוֹ לַיהוה וְהִקְרִיב מִן־הַתֹּרִים אוֹ מִן־בְּנֵי שני
טו הַיּוֹנָה אֶת־קָרְבָּנוֹ: וְהִקְרִיבוֹ הַכֹּהֵן אֶל־הַמִּזְבֵּחַ וּמָלַק אֶת־רֹאשׁוֹ
טז וְהִקְטִיר הַמִּזְבֵּחָה וְנִמְצָה דָמוֹ עַל קִיר הַמִּזְבֵּחַ: וְהֵסִיר אֶת־מֻרְאָתוֹ
יז בְּנֹצָתָהּ וְהִשְׁלִיךְ אֹתָהּ אֵצֶל הַמִּזְבֵּחַ קֵדְמָה אֶל־מְקוֹם הַדָּשֶׁן: וְשִׁסַּע
אֹתוֹ בִכְנָפָיו לֹא יַבְדִּיל וְהִקְטִיר אֹתוֹ הַכֹּהֵן הַמִּזְבֵּחָה עַל־הָעֵצִים
ב א אֲשֶׁר עַל־הָאֵשׁ עֹלָה הוּא אִשֵּׁה רֵיחַ נִיחֹחַ לַיהוה: וְנֶפֶשׁ
כִּי־תַקְרִיב קָרְבַּן מִנְחָה לַיהוה סֹלֶת יִהְיֶה קָרְבָּנוֹ וְיָצַק עָלֶיהָ שֶׁמֶן
ב וְנָתַן עָלֶיהָ לְבֹנָה: וֶהֱבִיאָהּ אֶל־בְּנֵי אַהֲרֹן הַכֹּהֲנִים וְקָמַץ מִשָּׁם מְלֹא
קֻמְצוֹ מִסָּלְתָּהּ וּמִשַּׁמְנָהּ עַל כָּל־לְבֹנָתָהּ וְהִקְטִיר הַכֹּהֵן אֶת־אַזְכָּרָתָהּ
ג הַמִּזְבֵּחָה אִשֵּׁה רֵיחַ נִיחֹחַ לַיהוה: וְהַנּוֹתֶרֶת מִן־הַמִּנְחָה לְאַהֲרֹן
ד וּלְבָנָיו קֹדֶשׁ קָדָשִׁים מֵאִשֵּׁי יהוה: וְכִי תַקְרִב קָרְבַּן
מִנְחָה מַאֲפֵה תַנּוּר סֹלֶת חַלּוֹת מַצֹּת בְּלוּלֹת בַּשֶּׁמֶן וּרְקִיקֵי מַצּוֹת

5 loaves mixed with oil or unleavened wafers spread with oil. If your
offering is grain prepared on a griddle, it shall be of fine flour mixed with oil,
6 and unleavened. Crumble it into pieces and pour oil over it; this is a grain
7 offering. If your offering is grain prepared in a pan, it shall be of fine
8 flour in oil. You shall bring the grain offering made in one of these ways to the
9 Lord, presenting it to the priest, who will bring it to the altar. The priest shall
lift a remembrance from the grain offering and send it up in smoke upon the
10 altar as an offering of fire, a pleasing aroma to the Lord. What is left of this
grain offering shall belong to Aharon and his sons; it is holy of holies among
11 the fire offerings to the Lord. No grain offering that you bring to the Lord
shall be made with leaven, for no leaven or honey may be used in a fire offering
12 to the Lord, sent up in smoke. You may bring them as offerings of first
produce to the Lord, but they may not be offered on the altar as a pleasing
13 aroma.[3] You shall season all your grain offerings with salt; do not omit from
your grain offering the salt of your covenant with God. You shall offer salt
14 with all your offerings. If you bring a grain offering of first produce
to the Lord, it shall be brought as soon as it ripens on the stalk. Roasted in
fire, crushed from fresh kernels; thus shall you bring the grain offering of first
15 16 produce. You shall put oil and incense on it; it is a grain offering. The priest
shall send its remembrance up in smoke – some of the crushed new grain and
oil together with all of the incense – as a fire offering to the Lord.

3 1 If one's sacrifice is a peace offering, and brought from the herd, whether
male or female, the animal one offers before the Lord must be without
2 blemish. The one bringing the offering shall lay his hand on its head and have
it slaughtered at the entrance to the Tent of Meeting. Aharon's sons the priests
3 shall dash the blood against each side of the altar. A priest shall present of
the peace offering a fire offering to the Lord: the fat that covers the entrails
4 and all the fat surrounding them; the two kidneys and the fat that is on them
at the loins; and the diaphragm of the liver, which should be removed with
5 the kidneys. Aharon's sons shall send all these up in smoke upon the altar,
along with the burnt offering[4] on the wood on the altar fire – a fire offering,
a pleasing aroma to the Lord.

6 If one's offering is a peace offering from the flock, whether male or female, it
7 must be without blemish. If one brings a sheep as his offering, he shall present
8 it before the Lord. He shall lay his hand on the head of the offering and have
it slaughtered at the entrance to the Tent of Meeting. Aharon's sons the priests
9 shall dash the blood against each side of the altar. The priest shall present the
fat from the peace offering as a fire offering to the Lord: the whole broad tail,
removed close to the backbone; the fat that covers the entrails and all the fat
10 surrounding them; the two kidneys and the fat that is on them at the loins;
and the diaphragm of the liver, which should be removed with the kidneys.
11 The priest shall send these up in smoke upon the altar: foodstuffs – a fire
offering to the Lord.

---

3 | See, for example, Deuteronomy 26:2.

4 | Apparently the burnt offering that was brought every morning (see Ex. 29:38–42).

ה מְשֻׁחִים בַּשָּׁמֶן: וְאִם־מִנְחָה עַל־הַמַּחֲבַת קָרְבָּנֶךָ
ו סֹלֶת בְּלוּלָה בַשֶּׁמֶן מַצָּה תִהְיֶה: פָּתוֹת אֹתָהּ פִּתִּים וְיָצַקְתָּ עָלֶיהָ
ז שָׁמֶן מִנְחָה הִוא: וְאִם־מִנְחַת מַרְחֶשֶׁת קָרְבָּנֶךָ שלישי
ח סֹלֶת בַּשֶּׁמֶן תֵּעָשֶׂה: וְהֵבֵאתָ אֶת־הַמִּנְחָה אֲשֶׁר יֵעָשֶׂה מֵאֵלֶּה לַיהוָה
ט וְהִקְרִיבָהּ אֶל־הַכֹּהֵן וְהִגִּישָׁהּ אֶל־הַמִּזְבֵּחַ: וְהֵרִים הַכֹּהֵן מִן־הַמִּנְחָה
י אֶת־אַזְכָּרָתָהּ וְהִקְטִיר הַמִּזְבֵּחָה אִשֵּׁה רֵיחַ נִיחֹחַ לַיהוָה: וְהַנּוֹתֶרֶת
יא מִן־הַמִּנְחָה לְאַהֲרֹן וּלְבָנָיו קֹדֶשׁ קָדָשִׁים מֵאִשֵּׁי יְהוָה: כָּל־הַמִּנְחָה
אֲשֶׁר תַּקְרִיבוּ לַיהוָה לֹא תֵעָשֶׂה חָמֵץ כִּי כָל־שְׂאֹר וְכָל־דְּבַשׁ לֹא־
יב תַקְטִירוּ מִמֶּנּוּ אִשֶּׁה לַיהוָה: קָרְבַּן רֵאשִׁית תַּקְרִיבוּ אֹתָם לַיהוָה
יג וְאֶל־הַמִּזְבֵּחַ לֹא־יַעֲלוּ לְרֵיחַ נִיחֹחַ: וְכָל־קָרְבַּן מִנְחָתְךָ בַּמֶּלַח תִּמְלָח
וְלֹא תַשְׁבִּית מֶלַח בְּרִית אֱלֹהֶיךָ מֵעַל מִנְחָתֶךָ עַל כָּל־קָרְבָּנְךָ תַּקְרִיב
יד מֶלַח: וְאִם־תַּקְרִיב מִנְחַת בִּכּוּרִים לַיהוָה אָבִיב
טו קָלוּי בָּאֵשׁ גֶּרֶשׂ כַּרְמֶל תַּקְרִיב אֵת מִנְחַת בִּכּוּרֶיךָ: וְנָתַתָּ עָלֶיהָ
טז שֶׁמֶן וְשַׂמְתָּ עָלֶיהָ לְבֹנָה מִנְחָה הִוא: וְהִקְטִיר הַכֹּהֵן אֶת־אַזְכָּרָתָהּ
מִגִּרְשָׂהּ וּמִשַּׁמְנָהּ עַל כָּל־לְבֹנָתָהּ אִשֶּׁה לַיהוָה:

ג א וְאִם־זֶבַח שְׁלָמִים קָרְבָּנוֹ אִם מִן־הַבָּקָר הוּא מַקְרִיב אִם־זָכָר אִם־ רביעי
ב נְקֵבָה תָּמִים יַקְרִיבֶנּוּ לִפְנֵי יְהוָה: וְסָמַךְ יָדוֹ עַל־רֹאשׁ קָרְבָּנוֹ וּשְׁחָטוֹ
פֶּתַח אֹהֶל מוֹעֵד וְזָרְקוּ בְּנֵי אַהֲרֹן הַכֹּהֲנִים אֶת־הַדָּם עַל־הַמִּזְבֵּחַ
ג סָבִיב: וְהִקְרִיב מִזֶּבַח הַשְּׁלָמִים אִשֶּׁה לַיהוָה אֶת־הַחֵלֶב הַמְכַסֶּה
ד אֶת־הַקֶּרֶב וְאֵת כָּל־הַחֵלֶב אֲשֶׁר עַל־הַקֶּרֶב: וְאֵת שְׁתֵּי הַכְּלָיֹת
וְאֶת־הַחֵלֶב אֲשֶׁר עֲלֵהֶן אֲשֶׁר עַל־הַכְּסָלִים וְאֶת־הַיֹּתֶרֶת עַל־הַכָּבֵד
ה עַל־הַכְּלָיוֹת יְסִירֶנָּה: וְהִקְטִירוּ אֹתוֹ בְנֵי־אַהֲרֹן הַמִּזְבֵּחָה עַל־הָעֹלָה
אֲשֶׁר עַל־הָעֵצִים אֲשֶׁר עַל־הָאֵשׁ אִשֵּׁה רֵיחַ נִיחֹחַ לַיהוָה:

ו וְאִם־מִן־הַצֹּאן קָרְבָּנוֹ לְזֶבַח שְׁלָמִים לַיהוָה זָכָר אוֹ נְקֵבָה תָּמִים
ז יַקְרִיבֶנּוּ: אִם־כֶּשֶׂב הוּא־מַקְרִיב אֶת־קָרְבָּנוֹ וְהִקְרִיב אֹתוֹ לִפְנֵי יְהוָה:
ח וְסָמַךְ אֶת־יָדוֹ עַל־רֹאשׁ קָרְבָּנוֹ וְשָׁחַט אֹתוֹ לִפְנֵי אֹהֶל מוֹעֵד וְזָרְקוּ
ט בְּנֵי אַהֲרֹן אֶת־דָּמוֹ עַל־הַמִּזְבֵּחַ סָבִיב: וְהִקְרִיב מִזֶּבַח הַשְּׁלָמִים אִשֶּׁה
לַיהוָה חֶלְבּוֹ הָאַלְיָה תְמִימָה לְעֻמַּת הֶעָצֶה יְסִירֶנָּה וְאֶת־הַחֵלֶב
י הַמְכַסֶּה אֶת־הַקֶּרֶב וְאֵת כָּל־הַחֵלֶב אֲשֶׁר עַל־הַקֶּרֶב: וְאֵת שְׁתֵּי
הַכְּלָיֹת וְאֶת־הַחֵלֶב אֲשֶׁר עֲלֵהֶן אֲשֶׁר עַל־הַכְּסָלִים וְאֶת־הַיֹּתֶרֶת
יא עַל־הַכָּבֵד עַל־הַכְּלָיֹת יְסִירֶנָּה: וְהִקְטִירוֹ הַכֹּהֵן הַמִּזְבֵּחָה לֶחֶם אִשֶּׁה
לַיהוָה:

12 If the sacrifice is a goat, the one bringing it shall present it before the LORD.
13 He shall lay his hand on the head of the offering and have it slaughtered at
the entrance to the Tent of Meeting. Aharon's sons the priests shall dash the
14 blood against each side of the altar. The priest shall present of the offering
a fire offering to the LORD: the fat that covers the entrails and all the fat
15 surrounding them; the two kidneys and the fat that is on them at the loins;
and the diaphragm of the liver, which should be removed with the kidneys.
16 The priest shall send these up in smoke upon the altar: foodstuffs – a fire
17 offering to the LORD. All the fatty parts belong to the LORD: this is an
everlasting statute throughout your generations in all your dwellings: you
shall not eat either that fat or blood."

4 1 2 The LORD spoke to Moshe: "Tell the Israelites: If a person sins unintentionally
with regard to any of the LORD's commands, doing what should not be
3 done; any transgression – if it is the anointed priest who sins, bringing guilt
upon his people, he shall bring an unblemished young bull to the LORD as
4 a purification offering for the sin he has committed. He shall bring the bull
before the LORD at the entrance to the Tent of Meeting, lay his hand upon
5 the bull's head, and slaughter the bull before the LORD. The anointed priest
6 shall take some of the bull's blood and bring it into the Tent of Meeting. The
priest shall dip his finger into the blood and sprinkle of it seven times before
7 the LORD in front of the Sanctuary's inner curtain. Then the priest shall
apply some of the blood to the horns of the altar of fragrant incense, which
is in the Tent of Meeting before the LORD.[5] The rest of the bull's blood he
shall pour out at the base of the altar of burnt offerings, at the entrance to the
8 Tent of Meeting.[6] He shall remove all the fat from the bull of the purification
9 offering: the fat that covers the entrails and all the fat surrounding them; the
two kidneys and the fat that is on them at the loins; and the diaphragm of the
10 liver, which should be removed with the kidneys, just as it is removed from
the ox of the peace offering.[7] The priest shall send these up in smoke upon
11 the altar of burnt offerings. But the bull's skin and all its flesh, together with
12 its head, legs, entrails, and dung – all the rest of the bull – he shall take to a
ritually pure place outside the camp, to the ash heap, and burn upon a wood
fire; at the ash heap it shall be burned.

13 If it is the entire community of Israel that commits an unintentional sin, the
congregation unwittingly violating one of the LORD's commands, doing what
14 must not be done, when the sin that they committed becomes known, the
community shall bring a young bull as a purification offering, presenting
15 it before the Tent of Meeting. The community elders shall lay their hands
on the bull's head before the LORD and, before the LORD, the bull shall be
16 slaughtered. The anointed priest shall take some of the bull's blood into the
17 Tent of Meeting. The priest shall dip his finger into the blood and sprinkle
18 it seven times before the LORD in front of the curtain. Then he shall apply

5 | See Exodus 30:1–10.
6 | See Exodus 27:1–7.
7 | See 3:3–4.

יב יג וְאִם עֵז קָרְבָּנוֹ וְהִקְרִיבוֹ לִפְנֵי יְהוָה: וְסָמַךְ אֶת־יָדוֹ עַל־רֹאשׁוֹ וְשָׁחַט
אֹתוֹ לִפְנֵי אֹהֶל מוֹעֵד וְזָרְקוּ בְּנֵי אַהֲרֹן אֶת־דָּמוֹ עַל־הַמִּזְבֵּחַ סָבִיב:
יד וְהִקְרִיב מִמֶּנּוּ קָרְבָּנוֹ אִשֶּׁה לַיהוָה אֶת־הַחֵלֶב הַמְכַסֶּה אֶת־הַקֶּרֶב
טו וְאֵת כָּל־הַחֵלֶב אֲשֶׁר עַל־הַקֶּרֶב: וְאֵת שְׁתֵּי הַכְּלָיֹת וְאֶת־הַחֵלֶב
אֲשֶׁר עֲלֵהֶן אֲשֶׁר עַל־הַכְּסָלִים וְאֶת־הַיֹּתֶרֶת עַל־הַכָּבֵד עַל־הַכְּלָיֹת
טז יְסִירֶנָּה: וְהִקְטִירָם הַכֹּהֵן הַמִּזְבֵּחָה לֶחֶם אִשֶּׁה לְרֵיחַ נִיחֹחַ כָּל־חֵלֶב
יז לַיהוָה: חֻקַּת עוֹלָם לְדֹרֹתֵיכֶם בְּכֹל מוֹשְׁבֹתֵיכֶם כָּל־חֵלֶב וְכָל־דָּם
לֹא תֹאכֵלוּ:

ד א ב וַיְדַבֵּר יְהוָה אֶל־מֹשֶׁה לֵּאמֹר: דַּבֵּר אֶל־בְּנֵי יִשְׂרָאֵל לֵאמֹר נֶפֶשׁ כִּי־ ב חמישי
תֶחֱטָא בִשְׁגָגָה מִכֹּל מִצְוֺת יְהוָה אֲשֶׁר לֹא תֵעָשֶׂינָה וְעָשָׂה מֵאַחַת
ג מֵהֵנָּה: אִם הַכֹּהֵן הַמָּשִׁיחַ יֶחֱטָא לְאַשְׁמַת הָעָם וְהִקְרִיב עַל חַטָּאתוֹ
ד אֲשֶׁר חָטָא פַּר בֶּן־בָּקָר תָּמִים לַיהוָה לְחַטָּאת: וְהֵבִיא אֶת־הַפָּר
אֶל־פֶּתַח אֹהֶל מוֹעֵד לִפְנֵי יְהוָה וְסָמַךְ אֶת־יָדוֹ עַל־רֹאשׁ הַפָּר וְשָׁחַט
ה אֶת־הַפָּר לִפְנֵי יְהוָה: וְלָקַח הַכֹּהֵן הַמָּשִׁיחַ מִדַּם הַפָּר וְהֵבִיא אֹתוֹ אֶל־
ו אֹהֶל מוֹעֵד: וְטָבַל הַכֹּהֵן אֶת־אֶצְבָּעוֹ בַּדָּם וְהִזָּה מִן־הַדָּם שֶׁבַע פְּעָמִים
ז לִפְנֵי יְהוָה אֶת־פְּנֵי פָּרֹכֶת הַקֹּדֶשׁ: וְנָתַן הַכֹּהֵן מִן־הַדָּם עַל־קַרְנוֹת
מִזְבַּח קְטֹרֶת הַסַּמִּים לִפְנֵי יְהוָה אֲשֶׁר בְּאֹהֶל מוֹעֵד וְאֵת ׀ כָּל־דַּם הַפָּר
ח יִשְׁפֹּךְ אֶל־יְסוֹד מִזְבַּח הָעֹלָה אֲשֶׁר־פֶּתַח אֹהֶל מוֹעֵד: וְאֶת־כָּל־חֵלֶב
ט פַּר הַחַטָּאת יָרִים מִמֶּנּוּ אֶת־הַחֵלֶב הַמְכַסֶּה עַל־הַקֶּרֶב וְאֵת כָּל־
הַחֵלֶב אֲשֶׁר עַל־הַקֶּרֶב: וְאֵת שְׁתֵּי הַכְּלָיֹת וְאֶת־הַחֵלֶב אֲשֶׁר עֲלֵיהֶן
אֲשֶׁר עַל־הַכְּסָלִים וְאֶת־הַיֹּתֶרֶת עַל־הַכָּבֵד עַל־הַכְּלָיוֹת יְסִירֶנָּה:
י כַּאֲשֶׁר יוּרַם מִשּׁוֹר זֶבַח הַשְּׁלָמִים וְהִקְטִירָם הַכֹּהֵן עַל מִזְבַּח הָעֹלָה:
יא וְאֶת־עוֹר הַפָּר וְאֶת־כָּל־בְּשָׂרוֹ עַל־רֹאשׁוֹ וְעַל־כְּרָעָיו וְקִרְבּוֹ וּפִרְשׁוֹ:
יב וְהוֹצִיא אֶת־כָּל־הַפָּר אֶל־מִחוּץ לַמַּחֲנֶה אֶל־מָקוֹם טָהוֹר אֶל־שֶׁפֶךְ
הַדֶּשֶׁן וְשָׂרַף אֹתוֹ עַל־עֵצִים בָּאֵשׁ עַל־שֶׁפֶךְ הַדֶּשֶׁן יִשָּׂרֵף:
יג וְאִם כָּל־עֲדַת יִשְׂרָאֵל יִשְׁגּוּ וְנֶעְלַם דָּבָר מֵעֵינֵי הַקָּהָל וְעָשׂוּ אַחַת
יד מִכָּל־מִצְוֺת יְהוָה אֲשֶׁר לֹא־תֵעָשֶׂינָה וְאָשֵׁמוּ: וְנוֹדְעָה הַחַטָּאת אֲשֶׁר
חָטְאוּ עָלֶיהָ וְהִקְרִיבוּ הַקָּהָל פַּר בֶּן־בָּקָר לְחַטָּאת וְהֵבִיאוּ אֹתוֹ
טו לִפְנֵי אֹהֶל מוֹעֵד: וְסָמְכוּ זִקְנֵי הָעֵדָה אֶת־יְדֵיהֶם עַל־רֹאשׁ הַפָּר לִפְנֵי
טז יְהוָה וְשָׁחַט אֶת־הַפָּר לִפְנֵי יְהוָה: וְהֵבִיא הַכֹּהֵן הַמָּשִׁיחַ מִדַּם הַפָּר
יז אֶל־אֹהֶל מוֹעֵד: וְטָבַל הַכֹּהֵן אֶצְבָּעוֹ מִן־הַדָּם וְהִזָּה שֶׁבַע פְּעָמִים
יח לִפְנֵי יְהוָה אֶת־פְּנֵי הַפָּרֹכֶת: וּמִן־הַדָּם יִתֵּן ׀ עַל־קַרְנֹת הַמִּזְבֵּחַ אֲשֶׁר

some of the blood to the horns of the altar before the LORD in the Tent of
Meeting, and pour out all the rest at the base of the altar of burnt offerings,
19 at the entrance to the Tent of Meeting. Then he shall remove all its fat and
20 send it up in smoke upon the altar. He shall do the same with this bull as he
does with the bull of his purification offering;[8] he shall do the same with this.
So shall the priest make atonement for the people, and they shall be forgiven.
21 The priest shall then take the bull outside the camp and burn it just as he
burns the first bull.[9] This is the community's purification offering.
22 When a leader sins unintentionally with regard to any of the LORD's commands,
23 doing what must not be done and thus incurring guilt, when the sin that he
has committed is made known to him, he shall bring an unblemished male
24 goat as his offering. He shall lay his hand upon the goat's head, and it shall
be slaughtered in the place where burnt offerings are slaughtered before the
25 LORD. It is a purification offering. The priest shall take some of the blood
from the purification offering with his finger, and apply it to the horns of the
altar of burnt offerings. The rest of the blood he shall pour out at the base
26 of the altar of burnt offerings. He shall send up all its fat in smoke upon the
altar, like the fat of the peace offerings.[10] So shall the priest make atonement
for that leader for his sin, and he will be forgiven.
27 If an individual among the people sins unintentionally with regard to any of
the LORD's commands, doing what should not be done and thus incurring
28 guilt, when the sin he has committed is made known to him, he shall bring an
unblemished female goat as his offering to atone for the sin that he committed.
29 He shall lay his hand on the head of the purification offering, and it shall be
30 slaughtered in the same place as the burnt offerings. The priest shall take
some of its blood with his finger, and apply it to the horns of the altar of burnt
31 offerings. The rest of the blood he shall pour out at the base of the altar. The
priest shall remove all its fat, just as the fat is removed from a peace offering,
and send it up in smoke upon the altar as a pleasing aroma to the LORD. So
shall the priest make atonement for that person, and he will be forgiven.
32 If one brings a sheep as a purification offering,[11] it shall be an unblemished
33 female. One shall lay one's hand upon the head of the purification offering,
and it shall be slaughtered in the place where burnt offerings are slaughtered.
34 The priest shall take some of its blood with his finger, and apply it to the horns
of the altar of burnt offering. The rest of the blood he shall pour out at the base
35 of the altar. He shall remove all its fat, as the fat of a sheep is removed from
a peace offering. The priest shall send it up in smoke upon the altar with the
other fire offerings to the LORD. So shall the priest make atonement for that
person for the sin that he committed, and he will be forgiven.
5 1 If a person sins by failing to testify after hearing a public adjuration to do so:
if he knows or has seen something, yet does not speak up, and thus bears his

8 | Above, verses 5–10.
9 | Above, verses 11–12.
10 | See 3:3–5.
11 | Meaning as an alternative to the goat mentioned in verse 28.

לִפְנֵי יְהוָה אֲשֶׁר בְּאֹהֶל מוֹעֵד וְאֵת כׇּל־הַדָּם יִשְׁפֹּךְ אֶל־יְסוֹד מִזְבַּח
יט הָעֹלָה אֲשֶׁר־פֶּתַח אֹהֶל מוֹעֵד׃ וְאֵת כׇּל־חֶלְבּוֹ יָרִים מִמֶּנּוּ וְהִקְטִיר
כ הַמִּזְבֵּחָה׃ וְעָשָׂה לַפָּר כַּאֲשֶׁר עָשָׂה לְפַר הַחַטָּאת כֵּן יַעֲשֶׂה־לּוֹ וְכִפֶּר
כא עֲלֵהֶם הַכֹּהֵן וְנִסְלַח לָהֶם׃ וְהוֹצִיא אֶת־הַפָּר אֶל־מִחוּץ לַמַּחֲנֶה וְשָׂרַף
אֹתוֹ כַּאֲשֶׁר שָׂרַף אֵת הַפָּר הָרִאשׁוֹן חַטַּאת הַקָּהָל הוּא׃
כב אֲשֶׁר נָשִׂיא יֶחֱטָא וְעָשָׂה אַחַת מִכׇּל־מִצְוֺת יְהוָה אֱלֹהָיו אֲשֶׁר לֹא־
כג תֵעָשֶׂינָה בִּשְׁגָגָה וְאָשֵׁם׃ אוֹ־הוֹדַע אֵלָיו חַטָּאתוֹ אֲשֶׁר חָטָא בָּהּ
כד וְהֵבִיא אֶת־קׇרְבָּנוֹ שְׂעִיר עִזִּים זָכָר תָּמִים׃ וְסָמַךְ יָדוֹ עַל־רֹאשׁ הַשָּׂעִיר
וְשָׁחַט אֹתוֹ בִּמְקוֹם אֲשֶׁר־יִשְׁחַט אֶת־הָעֹלָה לִפְנֵי יְהוָה חַטָּאת
כה הוּא׃ וְלָקַח הַכֹּהֵן מִדַּם הַחַטָּאת בְּאֶצְבָּעוֹ וְנָתַן עַל־קַרְנֹת מִזְבַּח
כו הָעֹלָה וְאֶת־דָּמוֹ יִשְׁפֹּךְ אֶל־יְסוֹד מִזְבַּח הָעֹלָה׃ וְאֶת־כׇּל־חֶלְבּוֹ יַקְטִיר
הַמִּזְבֵּחָה כְּחֵלֶב זֶבַח הַשְּׁלָמִים וְכִפֶּר עָלָיו הַכֹּהֵן מֵחַטָּאתוֹ וְנִסְלַח
לוֹ׃
כז וְאִם־נֶפֶשׁ אַחַת תֶּחֱטָא בִשְׁגָגָה מֵעַם הָאָרֶץ בַּעֲשֹׂתָהּ אַחַת מִמִּצְוֺת ששי
כח יְהוָה אֲשֶׁר לֹא־תֵעָשֶׂינָה וְאָשֵׁם׃ אוֹ הוֹדַע אֵלָיו חַטָּאתוֹ אֲשֶׁר חָטָא
וְהֵבִיא קׇרְבָּנוֹ שְׂעִירַת עִזִּים תְּמִימָה נְקֵבָה עַל־חַטָּאתוֹ אֲשֶׁר חָטָא׃
כט וְסָמַךְ אֶת־יָדוֹ עַל רֹאשׁ הַחַטָּאת וְשָׁחַט אֶת־הַחַטָּאת בִּמְקוֹם
ל הָעֹלָה׃ וְלָקַח הַכֹּהֵן מִדָּמָהּ בְּאֶצְבָּעוֹ וְנָתַן עַל־קַרְנֹת מִזְבַּח הָעֹלָה
לא וְאֶת־כׇּל־דָּמָהּ יִשְׁפֹּךְ אֶל־יְסוֹד הַמִּזְבֵּחַ׃ וְאֶת־כׇּל־חֶלְבָּהּ יָסִיר כַּאֲשֶׁר
הוּסַר חֵלֶב מֵעַל זֶבַח הַשְּׁלָמִים וְהִקְטִיר הַכֹּהֵן הַמִּזְבֵּחָה לְרֵיחַ נִיחֹחַ
לַיהוָה וְכִפֶּר עָלָיו הַכֹּהֵן וְנִסְלַח לוֹ׃
לב לג וְאִם־כֶּבֶשׂ יָבִיא קׇרְבָּנוֹ לְחַטָּאת נְקֵבָה תְמִימָה יְבִיאֶנָּה׃ וְסָמַךְ אֶת־
יָדוֹ עַל רֹאשׁ הַחַטָּאת וְשָׁחַט אֹתָהּ לְחַטָּאת בִּמְקוֹם אֲשֶׁר יִשְׁחַט
לד אֶת־הָעֹלָה׃ וְלָקַח הַכֹּהֵן מִדַּם הַחַטָּאת בְּאֶצְבָּעוֹ וְנָתַן עַל־קַרְנֹת
לה מִזְבַּח הָעֹלָה וְאֶת־כׇּל־דָּמָהּ יִשְׁפֹּךְ אֶל־יְסוֹד הַמִּזְבֵּחַ׃ וְאֶת־כׇּל־חֶלְבָּהּ
יָסִיר כַּאֲשֶׁר יוּסַר חֵלֶב־הַכֶּשֶׂב מִזֶּבַח הַשְּׁלָמִים וְהִקְטִיר הַכֹּהֵן אֹתָם
הַמִּזְבֵּחָה עַל אִשֵּׁי יְהוָה וְכִפֶּר עָלָיו הַכֹּהֵן עַל־חַטָּאתוֹ אֲשֶׁר־חָטָא
וְנִסְלַח לוֹ׃
ה א וְנֶפֶשׁ כִּי־תֶחֱטָא וְשָׁמְעָה קוֹל אָלָה וְהוּא עֵד אוֹ רָאָה אוֹ יָדָע אִם־

2 guilt; or sins through touching an impure thing – the carcass of an impure
beast, or a carcass of impure livestock, or the carcass of an impure creeping
3 creature – and it escapes his notice, and while impure, he incurs guilt;[12] or
sins by touching human impurity of any kind that makes him impure, and it
4 escapes his notice, but later he realizes his guilt; or sins by making a verbal oath
to do something, bad or good – whatever one might carelessly swear – and it
escapes his attention, but later he realizes his guilt;[13] in any one of these ways –
5 when he realizes the guilt he has incurred in any of these ways, he shall confess
6 the sin he has committed, and bring the amends of his guilt to the LORD for
the sin he has committed: a female sheep or goat as a purification offering. So
7 shall the priest make atonement for that person for his sin. If he cannot afford
a sheep,[14] he shall bring two doves or two pigeons as his guilt offering to the
8 LORD, one as a purification offering and the other as a burnt offering. He
shall bring them to the priest, who will offer the first as a purification offering,
9 severing its neck at the back without detaching the head. Then he shall sprinkle
some of the blood of the purification offering against the side of the altar; the
rest of the blood shall be drained out at its base. This is the purification offering.
10 He shall then offer the second bird as a burnt offering in the prescribed way. So
shall the priest make atonement for that person for the sin he has committed,
11 and he will be forgiven. If he cannot afford two doves or two pigeons,
he shall bring the purification offering of a tenth of an ephah of fine flour as the
sacrifice for his sin. He shall not put any oil on it, nor place on it any incense,
12 for it is a purification offering. He shall bring it to the priest, and the priest shall
lift a handful from it – its remembrance – and send it up in smoke upon the
13 altar with the LORD's fire offerings. It is a purification offering. Thus shall the
priest make atonement for that person for whichever one of these sins he has
committed, and he will be forgiven. The rest of the offering, as in the case of
14 a grain offering,[15] shall belong to the priest." And the LORD spoke to
15 Moshe: "If a person commits a trespass, sinning unintentionally with respect
to any of the LORD's sacred objects, he shall bring an unblemished ram from
the flock, valued in silver shekel by the Sanctuary weight,[16] as his guilt offering
16 to the LORD; it is a guilt offering. He shall make restitution for his trespass
against the sacred object, adding one-fifth to its value and giving it to the
priest. The priest shall make his atonement with the ram of the guilt offering,
and he will be forgiven.
17 If a person sins without realizing it, doing any of the things that the LORD
18 commanded not to be done, he incurs guilt and is subject to punishment. He
shall bring an unblemished ram from the flock, of the appropriate value, as a
guilt offering to the priest. The priest shall atone for him for that unintentional
19 sin, committed unknowingly, and he will be forgiven. This is a guilt offering,
for he had incurred guilt before the LORD."

12 | For example, by entering the Sanctuary while impure.

13 | In that he has violated his oath.

14 | The word *seh*, here translated "sheep," can denote either a sheep or a goat; see verse 6.

15 | See 2:3.

16 | Sanctuary weights differed from standard weights.

ב לוֹא יַגִּיד וְנָשָׂא עֲוֺנוֹ: אוֹ נֶפֶשׁ אֲשֶׁר תִּגַּע בְּכָל־דָּבָר טָמֵא אוֹ בְנִבְלַת
חַיָּה טְמֵאָה אוֹ בְּנִבְלַת בְּהֵמָה טְמֵאָה אוֹ בְּנִבְלַת שֶׁרֶץ טָמֵא וְנֶעְלַם
ג מִמֶּנּוּ וְהוּא טָמֵא וְאָשֵׁם: אוֹ כִי יִגַּע בְּטֻמְאַת אָדָם לְכֹל טֻמְאָתוֹ אֲשֶׁר
ד יִטְמָא בָּהּ וְנֶעְלַם מִמֶּנּוּ וְהוּא יָדַע וְאָשֵׁם: אוֹ נֶפֶשׁ כִּי תִשָּׁבַע לְבַטֵּא
בִשְׂפָתַיִם לְהָרַע ׀ אוֹ לְהֵיטִיב לְכֹל אֲשֶׁר יְבַטֵּא הָאָדָם בִּשְׁבֻעָה וְנֶעְלַם
ה מִמֶּנּוּ וְהוּא־יָדַע וְאָשֵׁם לְאַחַת מֵאֵלֶּה: וְהָיָה כִי־יֶאְשַׁם לְאַחַת מֵאֵלֶּה
ו וְהִתְוַדָּה אֲשֶׁר חָטָא עָלֶיהָ: וְהֵבִיא אֶת־אֲשָׁמוֹ לַיהוה עַל חַטָּאתוֹ
אֲשֶׁר חָטָא נְקֵבָה מִן־הַצֹּאן כִּשְׂבָּה אוֹ־שְׂעִירַת עִזִּים לְחַטָּאת וְכִפֶּר
ז עָלָיו הַכֹּהֵן מֵחַטָּאתוֹ: וְאִם־לֹא תַגִּיעַ יָדוֹ דֵּי שֶׂה וְהֵבִיא אֶת־אֲשָׁמוֹ
אֲשֶׁר חָטָא שְׁתֵּי תֹרִים אוֹ־שְׁנֵי בְנֵי־יוֹנָה לַיהוה אֶחָד לְחַטָּאת וְאֶחָד
ח לְעֹלָה: וְהֵבִיא אֹתָם אֶל־הַכֹּהֵן וְהִקְרִיב אֶת־אֲשֶׁר לַחַטָּאת רִאשׁוֹנָה
ט וּמָלַק אֶת־רֹאשׁוֹ מִמּוּל עָרְפּוֹ וְלֹא יַבְדִּיל: וְהִזָּה מִדַּם הַחַטָּאת עַל־
קִיר הַמִּזְבֵּחַ וְהַנִּשְׁאָר בַּדָּם יִמָּצֵה אֶל־יְסוֹד הַמִּזְבֵּחַ חַטָּאת הוּא:
י וְאֶת־הַשֵּׁנִי יַעֲשֶׂה עֹלָה כַּמִּשְׁפָּט וְכִפֶּר עָלָיו הַכֹּהֵן מֵחַטָּאתוֹ אֲשֶׁר־
יא חָטָא וְנִסְלַח לוֹ: וְאִם־לֹא תַשִּׂיג יָדוֹ לִשְׁתֵּי תֹרִים אוֹ שביעי
לִשְׁנֵי בְנֵי־יוֹנָה וְהֵבִיא אֶת־קָרְבָּנוֹ אֲשֶׁר חָטָא עֲשִׂירִת הָאֵפָה סֹלֶת
לְחַטָּאת לֹא־יָשִׂים עָלֶיהָ שֶׁמֶן וְלֹא־יִתֵּן עָלֶיהָ לְבֹנָה כִּי חַטָּאת הִוא:
יב וֶהֱבִיאָהּ אֶל־הַכֹּהֵן וְקָמַץ הַכֹּהֵן ׀ מִמֶּנָּה מְלוֹא קֻמְצוֹ אֶת־אַזְכָּרָתָהּ
יג וְהִקְטִיר הַמִּזְבֵּחָה עַל אִשֵּׁי יהוה חַטָּאת הִוא: וְכִפֶּר עָלָיו הַכֹּהֵן
עַל־חַטָּאתוֹ אֲשֶׁר־חָטָא מֵאַחַת מֵאֵלֶּה וְנִסְלַח לוֹ וְהָיְתָה לַכֹּהֵן
יד טו כַּמִּנְחָה: וַיְדַבֵּר יהוה אֶל־מֹשֶׁה לֵּאמֹר: נֶפֶשׁ כִּי־תִמְעֹל
מַעַל וְחָטְאָה בִּשְׁגָגָה מִקָּדְשֵׁי יהוה וְהֵבִיא אֶת־אֲשָׁמוֹ לַיהוה אַיִל
טז תָּמִים מִן־הַצֹּאן בְּעֶרְכְּךָ כֶּסֶף־שְׁקָלִים בְּשֶׁקֶל־הַקֹּדֶשׁ לְאָשָׁם: וְאֵת
אֲשֶׁר חָטָא מִן־הַקֹּדֶשׁ יְשַׁלֵּם וְאֶת־חֲמִישִׁתוֹ יוֹסֵף עָלָיו וְנָתַן אֹתוֹ
לַכֹּהֵן וְהַכֹּהֵן יְכַפֵּר עָלָיו בְּאֵיל הָאָשָׁם וְנִסְלַח לוֹ:
יז וְאִם־נֶפֶשׁ כִּי תֶחֱטָא וְעָשְׂתָה אַחַת מִכָּל־מִצְוֺת יהוה אֲשֶׁר לֹא
יח תֵעָשֶׂינָה וְלֹא־יָדַע וְאָשֵׁם וְנָשָׂא עֲוֺנוֹ: וְהֵבִיא אַיִל תָּמִים מִן־הַצֹּאן
בְּעֶרְכְּךָ לְאָשָׁם אֶל־הַכֹּהֵן וְכִפֶּר עָלָיו הַכֹּהֵן עַל שִׁגְגָתוֹ אֲשֶׁר־שָׁגָג
יט וְהוּא לֹא־יָדַע וְנִסְלַח לוֹ: אָשָׁם הוּא אָשֹׁם אָשַׁם לַיהוה:

20 21 The Lord spoke to Moshe: "If a person sins, committing a trespass against
the Lord by lying to his neighbor about a deposit or pledge, or by robbery,
22 or by defrauding his neighbor, or by finding lost property and lying about
it; if he swears falsely about anything he does in any of the ways a person
23 sins, afterward acknowledging guilt for the sin, he shall return what he took
by robbery or fraud, or the deposit left with him for safekeeping, or the lost
24 property that he found, or anything else about which he swore falsely. He
shall repay its value and add to that a fifth; he shall pay this to its owner on
25 the day he presents his guilt offering. And as his guilt offering to the Lord he
shall bring the priest an unblemished ram from the flock of the appropriate
26 value. The priest shall make his atonement before the Lord, and he will be
forgiven for whatever he did to incur this guilt."

6 1 2 The Lord spoke to Moshe: "Instruct Aharon and his sons: This is the law TZAV
of the burnt offering.[17] The burnt offering shall remain on the altar hearth all
3 night until the morning, and the altar fire shall be kept alight upon it. The
priest shall dress in his linen vestments, with linen undergarments against his
skin. He shall lift the ashes of the burnt offering that the fire consumed on the
4 altar, and place them by the altar's side. Then he shall take off his vestments,
put on other garments, and take the ashes to a ritually pure place outside the
5 camp. The altar fire shall be kept alight; it shall not go out. Every morning
the priest shall add wood to it, lay out the burnt offering upon it, and send
6 the fat parts of the peace offering up in smoke upon it. A daily fire shall be
7 kept alight on the altar; it shall not go out. This is the law of the grain
offering. Aharon's sons shall bring these before the Lord in front of the altar.
8 The priest shall lift a handful of the fine flour and oil from the grain offering,
and all the incense on it, and send this remembrance up in smoke upon the
9 altar as a pleasing aroma to the Lord. Aharon and his sons shall eat what is
left of it. It shall be eaten as unleavened bread in a holy place; in the courtyard
10 of the Tent of Meeting shall they eat it. It shall not be baked with any leaven.
I have given it as their portion of My fire offerings; it is holy of holies, like
11 the purification offering and the guilt offering. Any male among Aharon's
descendants may eat it as their eternal share of the Lord's fire offerings
throughout their generations; anything that touches it is sanctified."

12 13 The Lord spoke to Moshe: "This is the offering of Aharon and his sons that
each shall present to the Lord on the day when he is anointed: one-tenth of
an ephah of fine flour as a continual grain offering, half in the morning and
14 half in the evening. It shall be made on a griddle with oil. You shall bring it
well mixed, and offer it in pieces like a crumbled grain offering, as a pleasing
15 aroma to the Lord. The priest among Aharon's sons who is anointed to
succeed him shall prepare it; it is the Lord's perpetual share, to be sent up in
16 smoke in its entirety. Any grain offering from a priest shall be wholly burned;
it shall not be eaten."

17 | The passages that follow concentrate on the responsibilities of the priests with regard to each type of offering.

כ כא וַיְדַבֵּר יְהוָה אֶל־מֹשֶׁה לֵּאמֹר: נֶפֶשׁ כִּי תֶחֱטָא וּמָעֲלָה מַעַל בַּיהוָה
וְכִחֵשׁ בַּעֲמִיתוֹ בְּפִקָּדוֹן אוֹ־בִתְשׂוּמֶת יָד אוֹ בְגָזֵל אוֹ עָשַׁק אֶת־
כב עֲמִיתוֹ: אוֹ־מָצָא אֲבֵדָה וְכִחֶשׁ בָּהּ וְנִשְׁבַּע עַל־שָׁקֶר עַל־אַחַת מִכֹּל
כג אֲשֶׁר־יַעֲשֶׂה הָאָדָם לַחֲטֹא בָהֵנָּה: וְהָיָה כִּי־יֶחֱטָא וְאָשֵׁם וְהֵשִׁיב
אֶת־הַגְּזֵלָה אֲשֶׁר גָּזָל אוֹ אֶת־הָעֹשֶׁק אֲשֶׁר עָשָׁק אוֹ אֶת־הַפִּקָּדוֹן
כד אֲשֶׁר הָפְקַד אִתּוֹ אוֹ אֶת־הָאֲבֵדָה אֲשֶׁר מָצָא: אוֹ מִכֹּל אֲשֶׁר־יִשָּׁבַע מפטיר
עָלָיו לַשֶּׁקֶר וְשִׁלַּם אֹתוֹ בְּרֹאשׁוֹ וַחֲמִשִׁתָיו יֹסֵף עָלָיו לַאֲשֶׁר הוּא לוֹ
כה יִתְּנֶנּוּ בְּיוֹם אַשְׁמָתוֹ: וְאֶת־אֲשָׁמוֹ יָבִיא לַיהוָה אַיִל תָּמִים מִן־הַצֹּאן
כו בְּעֶרְכְּךָ לְאָשָׁם אֶל־הַכֹּהֵן: וְכִפֶּר עָלָיו הַכֹּהֵן לִפְנֵי יְהוָה וְנִסְלַח לוֹ
עַל־אַחַת מִכֹּל אֲשֶׁר־יַעֲשֶׂה לְאַשְׁמָה בָהּ:
ו א ב וַיְדַבֵּר יְהוָה אֶל־מֹשֶׁה לֵּאמֹר: צַו אֶת־אַהֲרֹן וְאֶת־בָּנָיו לֵאמֹר זֹאת צו
תּוֹרַת הָעֹלָה הִוא הָעֹלָה עַל מוֹקְדָה עַל־הַמִּזְבֵּחַ כָּל־הַלַּיְלָה עַד־
ג הַבֹּקֶר וְאֵשׁ הַמִּזְבֵּחַ תּוּקַד בּוֹ: וְלָבַשׁ הַכֹּהֵן מִדּוֹ בַד וּמִכְנְסֵי־בַד יִלְבַּשׁ
עַל־בְּשָׂרוֹ וְהֵרִים אֶת־הַדֶּשֶׁן אֲשֶׁר תֹּאכַל הָאֵשׁ אֶת־הָעֹלָה עַל־
ד הַמִּזְבֵּחַ וְשָׂמוֹ אֵצֶל הַמִּזְבֵּחַ: וּפָשַׁט אֶת־בְּגָדָיו וְלָבַשׁ בְּגָדִים אֲחֵרִים
ה וְהוֹצִיא אֶת־הַדֶּשֶׁן אֶל־מִחוּץ לַמַּחֲנֶה אֶל־מָקוֹם טָהוֹר: וְהָאֵשׁ עַל־
הַמִּזְבֵּחַ תּוּקַד־בּוֹ לֹא תִכְבֶּה וּבִעֵר עָלֶיהָ הַכֹּהֵן עֵצִים בַּבֹּקֶר בַּבֹּקֶר
ו וְעָרַךְ עָלֶיהָ הָעֹלָה וְהִקְטִיר עָלֶיהָ חֶלְבֵי הַשְּׁלָמִים: אֵשׁ תָּמִיד תּוּקַד
ז עַל־הַמִּזְבֵּחַ לֹא תִכְבֶּה: וְזֹאת תּוֹרַת הַמִּנְחָה הַקְרֵב
ח אֹתָהּ בְּנֵי־אַהֲרֹן לִפְנֵי יְהוָה אֶל־פְּנֵי הַמִּזְבֵּחַ: וְהֵרִים מִמֶּנּוּ בְּקֻמְצוֹ
מִסֹּלֶת הַמִּנְחָה וּמִשַּׁמְנָהּ וְאֵת כָּל־הַלְּבֹנָה אֲשֶׁר עַל־הַמִּנְחָה וְהִקְטִיר
ט הַמִּזְבֵּחַ רֵיחַ נִיחֹחַ אַזְכָּרָתָהּ לַיהוָה: וְהַנּוֹתֶרֶת מִמֶּנָּה יֹאכְלוּ אַהֲרֹן
י וּבָנָיו מַצּוֹת תֵּאָכֵל בְּמָקוֹם קָדֹשׁ בַּחֲצַר אֹהֶל־מוֹעֵד יֹאכְלוּהָ: לֹא
תֵאָפֶה חָמֵץ חֶלְקָם נָתַתִּי אֹתָהּ מֵאִשָּׁי קֹדֶשׁ קָדָשִׁים הִוא כַּחַטָּאת
יא וְכָאָשָׁם: כָּל־זָכָר בִּבְנֵי אַהֲרֹן יֹאכְלֶנָּה חָק־עוֹלָם לְדֹרֹתֵיכֶם מֵאִשֵּׁי
יְהוָה כֹּל אֲשֶׁר־יִגַּע בָּהֶם יִקְדָּשׁ:
יב יג וַיְדַבֵּר יְהוָה אֶל־מֹשֶׁה לֵּאמֹר: זֶה קָרְבַּן אַהֲרֹן וּבָנָיו אֲשֶׁר־יַקְרִיבוּ ג שני
לַיהוָה בְּיוֹם הִמָּשַׁח אֹתוֹ עֲשִׂירִת הָאֵפָה סֹלֶת מִנְחָה תָּמִיד מַחֲצִיתָהּ
יד בַּבֹּקֶר וּמַחֲצִיתָהּ בָּעָרֶב: עַל־מַחֲבַת בַּשֶּׁמֶן תֵּעָשֶׂה מֻרְבֶּכֶת תְּבִיאֶנָּה
טו תֻּפִינֵי מִנְחַת פִּתִּים תַּקְרִיב רֵיחַ־נִיחֹחַ לַיהוָה: וְהַכֹּהֵן הַמָּשִׁיחַ תַּחְתָּיו
טז מִבָּנָיו יַעֲשֶׂה אֹתָהּ חָק־עוֹלָם לַיהוָה כָּלִיל תָּקְטָר: וְכָל־מִנְחַת כֹּהֵן
כָּלִיל תִּהְיֶה לֹא תֵאָכֵל:

17 18 The LORD spoke to Moshe: "Tell Aharon and his sons: This is the law of the
purification offering. The purification offering shall be slaughtered before the
LORD at the place where burnt offerings are slaughtered; it is holy of holies.
19 The priest who offers it as a purification offering shall eat of it. It shall be
20 eaten in a holy place, in the courtyard of the Tent of Meeting. Anything that
touches its flesh is sanctified; if any of its blood splashes on a garment, you
21 shall wash that part in a holy place. An earthen vessel in which it was cooked
shall be broken, but if it was cooked in a bronze vessel, that shall be scoured
22 and rinsed with water. Any male among the priests may eat of it; it is holy of
23 holies. But no purification offering shall be eaten from which blood is brought
inside the Tent of Meeting to make atonement within the Sanctuary;[18] that
shall be burned with fire.

7 1 2 And this is the law of the guilt offering; it is holy of holies. The guilt offering
shall be slaughtered at the place where burnt offerings are slaughtered, and
3 its blood dashed against each side of the altar. All its fat shall be offered: the
4 broad tail, the fat covering the entrails, the two kidneys and the fat around
them at the loins, and the diaphragm of the liver, which shall be removed
5 with the kidneys. The priest shall turn these into smoke on the altar as a fire
6 offering for the LORD; it is a guilt offering. Any male priest may eat of it and
7 it shall be eaten in a holy place; it is holy of holies. The guilt offering follows
the same law as the purification offering: it belongs to the priest who makes
8 atonement with it. The priest who offers any person's burnt offering shall keep
9 the skin of the burnt offering that he has offered. Any grain offering baked in
an oven or prepared in a pan or griddle also belongs to the priest who offers it,
10 while every other grain offering, whether mixed with oil or dry, shall belong
equally to all of Aharon's sons.

11 12 This is the law of the peace sacrifice that one may offer to the LORD: If it is
offered for thanksgiving, one offers unleavened loaves mixed with oil with
the thanksgiving sacrifice, and unleavened wafers spread with oil, and loaves
13 of fine flour mixed with oil. This offering, together with loaves of leavened
14 bread, he shall present with the peace sacrifice of thanksgiving. Of these he
shall offer one of each kind as a gift raised up to the LORD. This shall belong to
15 the priest who dashed the blood of the peace offering. The flesh of the peace
sacrifice of thanksgiving shall be eaten on the day it is offered; you may not
16 leave any of it to the morning. If the sacrifice is to fulfill a vow, however, or is
a freewill offering, it shall be eaten on the day when one offers the sacrifice,
17 while what is left over may be eaten the next day. Whatever of the flesh of the
18 sacrifice is left over on the third day shall be burned with fire. If any of the flesh
of the peace sacrifice is eaten on the third day, it shall not be accepted, nor
shall it be credited to the one who offered it. It is offensive, and anyone who
19 eats of it is liable to punishment. Flesh that touches any impure thing shall
not be eaten; it shall be burned with fire. As for other flesh, any ritually pure
20 person may eat it, but one who eats the flesh of a peace sacrifice to the LORD

18 | See, e.g., 4:3–21.

יז יח וַיְדַבֵּר יְהוָה אֶל־מֹשֶׁה לֵּאמֹר: דַּבֵּר אֶל־אַהֲרֹן וְאֶל־בָּנָיו לֵאמֹר זֹאת
תּוֹרַת הַחַטָּאת בִּמְקוֹם אֲשֶׁר תִּשָּׁחֵט הָעֹלָה תִּשָּׁחֵט הַחַטָּאת לִפְנֵי
יט יְהוָה קֹדֶשׁ קָדָשִׁים הִוא: הַכֹּהֵן הַמְחַטֵּא אֹתָהּ יֹאכְלֶנָּה בְּמָקוֹם
כ קָדֹשׁ תֵּאָכֵל בַּחֲצַר אֹהֶל מוֹעֵד: כֹּל אֲשֶׁר־יִגַּע בִּבְשָׂרָהּ יִקְדָּשׁ וַאֲשֶׁר
כא יִזֶּה מִדָּמָהּ עַל־הַבֶּגֶד אֲשֶׁר יִזֶּה עָלֶיהָ תְּכַבֵּס בְּמָקוֹם קָדֹשׁ: וּכְלִי־
חֶרֶשׂ אֲשֶׁר תְּבֻשַּׁל־בּוֹ יִשָּׁבֵר וְאִם־בִּכְלִי נְחֹשֶׁת בֻּשָּׁלָה וּמֹרַק וְשֻׁטַּף
כב כג בַּמָּיִם: כָּל־זָכָר בַּכֹּהֲנִים יֹאכַל אֹתָהּ קֹדֶשׁ קָדָשִׁים הִוא: וְכָל־חַטָּאת
אֲשֶׁר יוּבָא מִדָּמָהּ אֶל־אֹהֶל מוֹעֵד לְכַפֵּר בַּקֹּדֶשׁ לֹא תֵאָכֵל בָּאֵשׁ
תִּשָּׂרֵף:
ז א ב וְזֹאת תּוֹרַת הָאָשָׁם קֹדֶשׁ קָדָשִׁים הוּא: בִּמְקוֹם אֲשֶׁר יִשְׁחֲטוּ אֶת־
ג הָעֹלָה יִשְׁחֲטוּ אֶת־הָאָשָׁם וְאֶת־דָּמוֹ יִזְרֹק עַל־הַמִּזְבֵּחַ סָבִיב: וְאֵת־
כָּל־חֶלְבּוֹ יַקְרִיב מִמֶּנּוּ אֵת הָאַלְיָה וְאֶת־הַחֵלֶב הַמְכַסֶּה אֶת־הַקֶּרֶב:
ד וְאֵת שְׁתֵּי הַכְּלָיֹת וְאֶת־הַחֵלֶב אֲשֶׁר עֲלֵיהֶן אֲשֶׁר עַל־הַכְּסָלִים וְאֶת־
ה הַיֹּתֶרֶת עַל־הַכָּבֵד עַל־הַכְּלָיֹת יְסִירֶנָּה: וְהִקְטִיר אֹתָם הַכֹּהֵן הַמִּזְבֵּחָה
ו אִשֶּׁה לַיהוָה אָשָׁם הוּא: כָּל־זָכָר בַּכֹּהֲנִים יֹאכְלֶנּוּ בְּמָקוֹם קָדוֹשׁ יֵאָכֵל
ז קֹדֶשׁ קָדָשִׁים הוּא: כַּחַטָּאת כָּאָשָׁם תּוֹרָה אַחַת לָהֶם הַכֹּהֵן אֲשֶׁר
ח יְכַפֶּר־בּוֹ לוֹ יִהְיֶה: וְהַכֹּהֵן הַמַּקְרִיב אֶת־עֹלַת אִישׁ עוֹר הָעֹלָה אֲשֶׁר
ט הִקְרִיב לַכֹּהֵן לוֹ יִהְיֶה: וְכָל־מִנְחָה אֲשֶׁר תֵּאָפֶה בַּתַּנּוּר וְכָל־נַעֲשָׂה
י בַמַּרְחֶשֶׁת וְעַל־מַחֲבַת לַכֹּהֵן הַמַּקְרִיב אֹתָהּ לוֹ תִהְיֶה: וְכָל־מִנְחָה
בְלוּלָה־בַשֶּׁמֶן וַחֲרֵבָה לְכָל־בְּנֵי אַהֲרֹן תִּהְיֶה אִישׁ כְּאָחִיו:
יא יב וְזֹאת תּוֹרַת זֶבַח הַשְּׁלָמִים אֲשֶׁר יַקְרִיב לַיהוָה: אִם עַל־תּוֹדָה יַקְרִיבֶנּוּ שלישי
וְהִקְרִיב ׀ עַל־זֶבַח הַתּוֹדָה חַלּוֹת מַצּוֹת בְּלוּלֹת בַּשֶּׁמֶן וּרְקִיקֵי מַצּוֹת
יג מְשֻׁחִים בַּשָּׁמֶן וְסֹלֶת מֻרְבֶּכֶת חַלֹּת בְּלוּלֹת בַּשָּׁמֶן: עַל־חַלֹּת לֶחֶם
יד חָמֵץ יַקְרִיב קָרְבָּנוֹ עַל־זֶבַח תּוֹדַת שְׁלָמָיו: וְהִקְרִיב מִמֶּנּוּ אֶחָד מִכָּל־
טו קָרְבָּן תְּרוּמָה לַיהוָה לַכֹּהֵן הַזֹּרֵק אֶת־דַּם הַשְּׁלָמִים לוֹ יִהְיֶה: וּבְשַׂר
טז זֶבַח תּוֹדַת שְׁלָמָיו בְּיוֹם קָרְבָּנוֹ יֵאָכֵל לֹא־יַנִּיחַ מִמֶּנּוּ עַד־בֹּקֶר: וְאִם־
נֶדֶר ׀ אוֹ נְדָבָה זֶבַח קָרְבָּנוֹ בְּיוֹם הַקְרִיבוֹ אֶת־זִבְחוֹ יֵאָכֵל וּמִמָּחֳרָת
יז וְהַנּוֹתָר מִמֶּנּוּ יֵאָכֵל: וְהַנּוֹתָר מִבְּשַׂר הַזָּבַח בַּיּוֹם הַשְּׁלִישִׁי בָּאֵשׁ
יח יִשָּׂרֵף: וְאִם הֵאָכֹל יֵאָכֵל מִבְּשַׂר־זֶבַח שְׁלָמָיו בַּיּוֹם הַשְּׁלִישִׁי לֹא יֵרָצֶה
הַמַּקְרִיב אֹתוֹ לֹא יֵחָשֵׁב לוֹ פִּגּוּל יִהְיֶה וְהַנֶּפֶשׁ הָאֹכֶלֶת מִמֶּנּוּ עֲוֺנָהּ
יט תִּשָּׂא: וְהַבָּשָׂר אֲשֶׁר־יִגַּע בְּכָל־טָמֵא לֹא יֵאָכֵל בָּאֵשׁ יִשָּׂרֵף וְהַבָּשָׂר
כ כָּל־טָהוֹר יֹאכַל בָּשָׂר: וְהַנֶּפֶשׁ אֲשֶׁר־תֹּאכַל בָּשָׂר מִזֶּבַח הַשְּׁלָמִים

21 in a state of impurity shall be severed from his people. When anyone touches
any impure thing – human impurity, or an impure animal, or any impure,
detested creature – and then eats flesh from the LORD's peace sacrifice, that
22 23 person shall be severed from his people." The LORD spoke to Moshe: "Tell
24 the Israelites: Do not eat the fat of an ox, sheep, or goat. The fat of one of these
that died naturally or was killed by another animal may be put to other use,
25 but you may not eat it. For anyone who eats the fat of an animal of which a fire
26 offering could be offered to the LORD – he is severed from his people. Do not
27 eat any blood, whether that of a bird or of an animal, in any of your dwellings.
Anyone who eats any blood shall be cut off from his people."
28 29 And the LORD spoke to Moshe: "Tell the Israelites: One who brings a peace
sacrifice to the LORD is to bring the offering of his peace sacrifice before the
30 LORD himself; with his own hands he shall present the LORD's fire offerings.
He shall bring the animal's fat and breast so that the breast can be displayed,
31 this way and that, as a wave offering before the LORD. The priest shall send
the fat up in smoke upon the altar, but the breast shall go to Aharon and his
32 sons. The right thigh of your peace offering you shall give as an upraised gift
33 to the priest.[19] The one among the sons of Aharon who offers the blood and
34 fat of the peace offering shall receive the right thigh as his portion. For I have
taken from the peace sacrifices of the Israelites the breast of the wave offering
and the thigh of the upraised gift, and given them to Aharon the priest and
35 to his sons as their perpetual share from the Israelites. This is the anointed
right of Aharon and his sons from the LORD's fire offerings from the day
36 they are presented to serve the LORD as priests; when the LORD anointed
them as priests He commanded that these be given them by the Israelites
37 as their perpetual share throughout the generations." This, then, is the law
for the burnt offering, the grain offering, the purification offering, the guilt
38 offering, the ordination offering,[20] and the peace offering, which the LORD
commanded Moshe at Mount Sinai when he commanded the Israelites to
bring their offerings to the LORD, in the Wilderness of Sinai.
8 1 2 The LORD said to Moshe:[21] "Take Aharon, and his sons with him, the
vestments, the anointing oil, a bull for the purification offering, two rams, and
3 a basket of unleavened bread, and assemble the whole community at the
4 entrance to the Tent of Meeting." Moshe did as the LORD commanded him;
and the community was assembled at the entrance to the Tent of Meeting.
5 And Moshe told the community, "This is what the LORD has commanded us
6 to do." Then Moshe brought Aharon and his sons close, and he washed them
7 with water. He put the tunic on Aharon, tied the sash around him, clothed
him in the robe, and placed the ephod on him. He bound the ephod's
8 decorated belt about him, securing the ephod to him.[22] Then he put the breast
9 piece on him, and inside the breast piece he placed the Urim and Tumim. On

19 | The term *teruma* – here translated "upraised gift" – commonly denotes a sanctified gift.

20 | See Exodus, chapter 29.

21 | This passage recounts the performance of the priestly ordination ritual.

22 | See Exodus, chapter 28, for descriptions of the priestly vestments.

כא אֲשֶׁר לַיהוָה וְטֻמְאָתוֹ עָלָיו וְנִכְרְתָה הַנֶּפֶשׁ הַהִוא מֵעַמֶּיהָ׃ וְנֶפֶשׁ כִּי־
תִגַּע בְּכָל־טָמֵא בְּטֻמְאַת אָדָם אוֹ ׀ בִּבְהֵמָה טְמֵאָה אוֹ בְּכָל־שֶׁקֶץ
טָמֵא וְאָכַל מִבְּשַׂר־זֶבַח הַשְּׁלָמִים אֲשֶׁר לַיהוָה וְנִכְרְתָה הַנֶּפֶשׁ הַהִוא
כב כג מֵעַמֶּיהָ׃ וַיְדַבֵּר יְהוָה אֶל־מֹשֶׁה לֵּאמֹר׃ דַּבֵּר אֶל־בְּנֵי יִשְׂרָאֵל לֵאמֹר
כד כָּל־חֵלֶב שׁוֹר וְכֶשֶׂב וָעֵז לֹא תֹאכֵלוּ׃ וְחֵלֶב נְבֵלָה וְחֵלֶב טְרֵפָה יֵעָשֶׂה
כה לְכָל־מְלָאכָה וְאָכֹל לֹא תֹאכְלֻהוּ׃ כִּי כָּל־אֹכֵל חֵלֶב מִן־הַבְּהֵמָה אֲשֶׁר
כו יַקְרִיב מִמֶּנָּה אִשֶּׁה לַיהוָה וְנִכְרְתָה הַנֶּפֶשׁ הָאֹכֶלֶת מֵעַמֶּיהָ׃ וְכָל־דָּם
כז לֹא תֹאכְלוּ בְּכֹל מוֹשְׁבֹתֵיכֶם לָעוֹף וְלַבְּהֵמָה׃ כָּל־נֶפֶשׁ אֲשֶׁר־תֹּאכַל
כָּל־דָּם וְנִכְרְתָה הַנֶּפֶשׁ הַהִוא מֵעַמֶּיהָ׃

כח כט וַיְדַבֵּר יְהוָה אֶל־מֹשֶׁה לֵּאמֹר׃ דַּבֵּר אֶל־בְּנֵי יִשְׂרָאֵל לֵאמֹר הַמַּקְרִיב
ל אֶת־זֶבַח שְׁלָמָיו לַיהוָה יָבִיא אֶת־קָרְבָּנוֹ לַיהוָה מִזֶּבַח שְׁלָמָיו׃ יָדָיו
תְּבִיאֶינָה אֵת אִשֵּׁי יְהוָה אֶת־הַחֵלֶב עַל־הֶחָזֶה יְבִיאֶנּוּ אֵת הֶחָזֶה
לא לְהָנִיף אֹתוֹ תְּנוּפָה לִפְנֵי יְהוָה׃ וְהִקְטִיר הַכֹּהֵן אֶת־הַחֵלֶב הַמִּזְבֵּחָה
לב וְהָיָה הֶחָזֶה לְאַהֲרֹן וּלְבָנָיו׃ וְאֵת שׁוֹק הַיָּמִין תִּתְּנוּ תְרוּמָה לַכֹּהֵן
לג מִזִּבְחֵי שַׁלְמֵיכֶם׃ הַמַּקְרִיב אֶת־דַּם הַשְּׁלָמִים וְאֶת־הַחֵלֶב מִבְּנֵי אַהֲרֹן
לד לוֹ תִהְיֶה שׁוֹק הַיָּמִין לְמָנָה׃ כִּי אֶת־חֲזֵה הַתְּנוּפָה וְאֵת ׀ שׁוֹק הַתְּרוּמָה
לָקַחְתִּי מֵאֵת בְּנֵי־יִשְׂרָאֵל מִזִּבְחֵי שַׁלְמֵיהֶם וָאֶתֵּן אֹתָם לְאַהֲרֹן הַכֹּהֵן
לה וּלְבָנָיו לְחָק־עוֹלָם מֵאֵת בְּנֵי יִשְׂרָאֵל׃ זֹאת מִשְׁחַת אַהֲרֹן וּמִשְׁחַת
לו בָּנָיו מֵאִשֵּׁי יְהוָה בְּיוֹם הִקְרִיב אֹתָם לְכַהֵן לַיהוָה׃ אֲשֶׁר צִוָּה יְהוָה
לָתֵת לָהֶם בְּיוֹם מָשְׁחוֹ אֹתָם מֵאֵת בְּנֵי יִשְׂרָאֵל חֻקַּת עוֹלָם לְדֹרֹתָם׃
לז זֹאת הַתּוֹרָה לָעֹלָה לַמִּנְחָה וְלַחַטָּאת וְלָאָשָׁם וְלַמִּלּוּאִים וּלְזֶבַח
לח הַשְּׁלָמִים׃ אֲשֶׁר צִוָּה יְהוָה אֶת־מֹשֶׁה בְּהַר סִינָי בְּיוֹם צַוֺּתוֹ אֶת־בְּנֵי
יִשְׂרָאֵל לְהַקְרִיב אֶת־קָרְבְּנֵיהֶם לַיהוָה בְּמִדְבַּר סִינָי׃

ח א ב וַיְדַבֵּר יְהוָה אֶל־מֹשֶׁה לֵּאמֹר׃ קַח אֶת־אַהֲרֹן וְאֶת־בָּנָיו אִתּוֹ וְאֵת ד רביעי
הַבְּגָדִים וְאֵת שֶׁמֶן הַמִּשְׁחָה וְאֵת ׀ פַּר הַחַטָּאת וְאֵת שְׁנֵי הָאֵילִים
ג ד וְאֵת סַל הַמַּצּוֹת׃ וְאֵת כָּל־הָעֵדָה הַקְהֵל אֶל־פֶּתַח אֹהֶל מוֹעֵד׃ וַיַּעַשׂ
מֹשֶׁה כַּאֲשֶׁר צִוָּה יְהוָה אֹתוֹ וַתִּקָּהֵל הָעֵדָה אֶל־פֶּתַח אֹהֶל מוֹעֵד׃
ה ו וַיֹּאמֶר מֹשֶׁה אֶל־הָעֵדָה זֶה הַדָּבָר אֲשֶׁר־צִוָּה יְהוָה לַעֲשׂוֹת׃ וַיַּקְרֵב
ז מֹשֶׁה אֶת־אַהֲרֹן וְאֶת־בָּנָיו וַיִּרְחַץ אֹתָם בַּמָּיִם׃ וַיִּתֵּן עָלָיו אֶת־הַכֻּתֹּנֶת
וַיַּחְגֹּר אֹתוֹ בָּאַבְנֵט וַיַּלְבֵּשׁ אֹתוֹ אֶת־הַמְּעִיל וַיִּתֵּן עָלָיו אֶת־הָאֵפֹד
ח וַיַּחְגֹּר אֹתוֹ בְּחֵשֶׁב הָאֵפֹד וַיֶּאְפֹּד לוֹ בּוֹ׃ וַיָּשֶׂם עָלָיו אֶת־הַחֹשֶׁן וַיִּתֵּן
ט אֶל־הַחֹשֶׁן אֶת־הָאוּרִים וְאֶת־הַתֻּמִּים׃ וַיָּשֶׂם אֶת־הַמִּצְנֶפֶת עַל־רֹאשׁוֹ

his head he placed the miter, and on the miter in front, he placed the golden
10 head plate, the holy diadem, as the LORD had commanded him. Then Moshe
took the anointing oil and anointed the Tabernacle and everything in it; thus
11 he consecrated them. He sprinkled some of the oil on the altar seven times.
He anointed the altar and all its vessels, and the laver and its base, thus
12 consecrating them. Some of the anointing oil he poured on Aharon's head,
13 anointing him, consecrating him. Then Moshe brought close Aharon's sons,
dressed them in their tunics, bound sashes about them, and placed their
14 headdresses on them, just as the LORD had commanded him. Moshe drew
close the bull for the purification offering, and Aharon and his sons laid their
15 hands on its head. It was slaughtered, and Moshe took the blood and applied
it with his finger to all the altar's horns, purifying the altar. The rest of the
blood he poured out at the altar's base. Thus he consecrated it so that, upon
16 it, atonement could be made. Moshe removed all the fat around the entrails,
the diaphragm of the liver, the two kidneys and their fat, and sent them up in
17 smoke upon the altar. But the rest of the bull, its skin, its flesh, and its dung,
he burned with fire outside the camp as the LORD had commanded him.
18 Then Moshe drew close the ram for the burnt offering, and Aharon and his
19 sons laid their hands on its head. Moshe slaughtered it and dashed the blood
20 against each side of the altar. He cut the ram into pieces and sent the head,
21 pieces, and suet up in smoke. After washing the entrails and legs with water,
Moshe sent the entire ram up in smoke upon the altar. It was a burnt offering
for a pleasing aroma: a fire offering to the LORD, as the LORD had commanded
22 Moshe. Moshe then drew close the second ram, the ram of ordination.
23 Aharon and his sons laid their hands upon its head. It was slaughtered; and
Moshe took some of its blood and applied it to the ridge of Aharon's right ear,
24 to his right thumb, and to his right big toe. He drew Aharon's sons close and
put some of the blood on the ridges of their right ears, on their right thumbs,
and on their right big toes. Moshe dashed the rest of the blood against each
25 of the altar's sides. Then he took the fat, the broad tail, all the fat around the
entrails, the diaphragm of the liver, and the two kidneys with their fat, as well
26 as the right thigh. He took a loaf of unleavened bread from the basket, before
the LORD, and also one loaf of oil bread, and one wafer, and placed them on
27 the fat and on the right thigh. All of this he placed on the palms of Aharon
and of his sons, and displayed them this way and that as a wave offering before
28 the LORD. Then Moshe took them from their hands and burnt them upon
the altar with the burnt offering. This was the ordination offering, a pleasing
29 aroma, a fire offering to the LORD. Moshe then took the breast and waved it
as a wave offering before the LORD. This was Moshe's portion of the ordination
30 ram, as the LORD had commanded him. Moshe took some of the anointing

וַיָּשֶׂם עַל־הַמִּצְנֶפֶת אֶל־מוּל פָּנָיו אֵת צִיץ הַזָּהָב נֵזֶר הַקֹּדֶשׁ כַּאֲשֶׁר
י צִוָּה יהוה אֶת־מֹשֶׁה: וַיִּקַּח מֹשֶׁה אֶת־שֶׁמֶן הַמִּשְׁחָה וַיִּמְשַׁח אֶת־
יא הַמִּשְׁכָּן וְאֶת־כָּל־אֲשֶׁר־בּוֹ וַיְקַדֵּשׁ אֹתָם: וַיַּז מִמֶּנּוּ עַל־הַמִּזְבֵּחַ שֶׁבַע
פְּעָמִים וַיִּמְשַׁח אֶת־הַמִּזְבֵּחַ וְאֶת־כָּל־כֵּלָיו וְאֶת־הַכִּיֹּר וְאֶת־כַּנּוֹ
יב לְקַדְּשָׁם: וַיִּצֹק מִשֶּׁמֶן הַמִּשְׁחָה עַל רֹאשׁ אַהֲרֹן וַיִּמְשַׁח אֹתוֹ לְקַדְּשׁוֹ:
יג וַיַּקְרֵב מֹשֶׁה אֶת־בְּנֵי אַהֲרֹן וַיַּלְבִּשֵׁם כֻּתֳּנֹת וַיַּחְגֹּר אֹתָם אַבְנֵט וַיַּחֲבֹשׁ
יד לָהֶם מִגְבָּעוֹת כַּאֲשֶׁר צִוָּה יהוה אֶת־מֹשֶׁה: וַיַּגֵּשׁ אֵת פַּר הַחַטָּאת חמישי
טו וַיִּסְמֹךְ אַהֲרֹן וּבָנָיו אֶת־יְדֵיהֶם עַל־רֹאשׁ פַּר הַחַטָּאת: וַיִּשְׁחָט וַיִּקַּח
מֹשֶׁה אֶת־הַדָּם וַיִּתֵּן עַל־קַרְנוֹת הַמִּזְבֵּחַ סָבִיב בְּאֶצְבָּעוֹ וַיְחַטֵּא אֶת־
טז הַמִּזְבֵּחַ וְאֶת־הַדָּם יָצַק אֶל־יְסוֹד הַמִּזְבֵּחַ וַיְקַדְּשֵׁהוּ לְכַפֵּר עָלָיו: וַיִּקַּח
אֶת־כָּל־הַחֵלֶב אֲשֶׁר עַל־הַקֶּרֶב וְאֵת יֹתֶרֶת הַכָּבֵד וְאֶת־שְׁתֵּי הַכְּלָיֹת
יז וְאֶת־חֶלְבְּהֶן וַיַּקְטֵר מֹשֶׁה הַמִּזְבֵּחָה: וְאֶת־הַפָּר וְאֶת־עֹרוֹ וְאֶת־בְּשָׂרוֹ
וְאֶת־פִּרְשׁוֹ שָׂרַף בָּאֵשׁ מִחוּץ לַמַּחֲנֶה כַּאֲשֶׁר צִוָּה יהוה אֶת־מֹשֶׁה:
יח וַיַּקְרֵב אֵת אֵיל הָעֹלָה וַיִּסְמְכוּ אַהֲרֹן וּבָנָיו אֶת־יְדֵיהֶם עַל־רֹאשׁ הָאָיִל:
יט כ וַיִּשְׁחָט וַיִּזְרֹק מֹשֶׁה אֶת־הַדָּם עַל־הַמִּזְבֵּחַ סָבִיב: וְאֶת־הָאַיִל נִתַּח
כא לִנְתָחָיו וַיַּקְטֵר מֹשֶׁה אֶת־הָרֹאשׁ וְאֶת־הַנְּתָחִים וְאֶת־הַפָּדֶר: וְאֶת־
הַקֶּרֶב וְאֶת־הַכְּרָעַיִם רָחַץ בַּמָּיִם וַיַּקְטֵר מֹשֶׁה אֶת־כָּל־הָאַיִל הַמִּזְבֵּחָה
עֹלָה הוּא לְרֵיחַ־נִיחֹחַ אִשֶּׁה הוּא לַיהוה כַּאֲשֶׁר צִוָּה יהוה אֶת־מֹשֶׁה:
כב וַיַּקְרֵב אֶת־הָאַיִל הַשֵּׁנִי אֵיל הַמִּלֻּאִים וַיִּסְמְכוּ אַהֲרֹן וּבָנָיו אֶת־יְדֵיהֶם ששי
כג עַל־רֹאשׁ הָאָיִל: וַיִּשְׁחָט ׀ וַיִּקַּח מֹשֶׁה מִדָּמוֹ וַיִּתֵּן עַל־תְּנוּךְ אֹזֶן־אַהֲרֹן
כד הַיְמָנִית וְעַל־בֹּהֶן יָדוֹ הַיְמָנִית וְעַל־בֹּהֶן רַגְלוֹ הַיְמָנִית: וַיַּקְרֵב אֶת־בְּנֵי
אַהֲרֹן וַיִּתֵּן מֹשֶׁה מִן־הַדָּם עַל־תְּנוּךְ אָזְנָם הַיְמָנִית וְעַל־בֹּהֶן יָדָם
הַיְמָנִית וְעַל־בֹּהֶן רַגְלָם הַיְמָנִית וַיִּזְרֹק מֹשֶׁה אֶת־הַדָּם עַל־הַמִּזְבֵּחַ
כה סָבִיב: וַיִּקַּח אֶת־הַחֵלֶב וְאֶת־הָאַלְיָה וְאֶת־כָּל־הַחֵלֶב אֲשֶׁר עַל־הַקֶּרֶב
וְאֵת יֹתֶרֶת הַכָּבֵד וְאֶת־שְׁתֵּי הַכְּלָיֹת וְאֶת־חֶלְבְּהֶן וְאֵת שׁוֹק הַיָּמִין:
כו וּמִסַּל הַמַּצּוֹת אֲשֶׁר ׀ לִפְנֵי יהוה לָקַח חַלַּת מַצָּה אַחַת וְחַלַּת לֶחֶם
כז שֶׁמֶן אַחַת וְרָקִיק אֶחָד וַיָּשֶׂם עַל־הַחֲלָבִים וְעַל שׁוֹק הַיָּמִין: וַיִּתֵּן
אֶת־הַכֹּל עַל כַּפֵּי אַהֲרֹן וְעַל כַּפֵּי בָנָיו וַיָּנֶף אֹתָם תְּנוּפָה לִפְנֵי יהוה:
כח וַיִּקַּח מֹשֶׁה אֹתָם מֵעַל כַּפֵּיהֶם וַיַּקְטֵר הַמִּזְבֵּחָה עַל־הָעֹלָה מִלֻּאִים
כט הֵם לְרֵיחַ נִיחֹחַ אִשֶּׁה הוּא לַיהוה: וַיִּקַּח מֹשֶׁה אֶת־הֶחָזֶה וַיְנִיפֵהוּ
תְנוּפָה לִפְנֵי יהוה מֵאֵיל הַמִּלֻּאִים לְמֹשֶׁה הָיָה לְמָנָה כַּאֲשֶׁר צִוָּה
ל יהוה אֶת־מֹשֶׁה: וַיִּקַּח מֹשֶׁה מִשֶּׁמֶן הַמִּשְׁחָה וּמִן־הַדָּם אֲשֶׁר עַל־ שביעי

oil and some of the blood from the altar and sprinkled it on Aharon and on
his vestments, and on his sons and theirs. Thus Moshe consecrated Aharon
31 and his vestments, and his sons and their vestments. Then Moshe said to
Aharon and his sons: "Cook the meat at the entrance to the Tent of Meeting
and eat it there together with the bread in the basket of the ordination offering,
32 as I have charged you: Aharon and his sons shall eat it. Whatever is left over
33 of the meat and the bread, burn with fire. Do not leave the entrance to the
Tent of Meeting for seven days, until the days of your ordination are complete,
34 for your ordination will take seven days, each like today. This is what the
35 LORD has commanded to be done to make your atonement. Stay, then, at the
entrance to the Tent of Meeting for seven days, day and night, keeping the
LORD's charge – and you will not die. This is what I have been commanded."
36 And Aharon and his sons did everything that the LORD had commanded
9 1 through Moshe. On the eighth day, Moshe called to Aharon and his SHEMINI
2 sons, and to the elders of Israel. "Take a bull calf for yourself as a purification
offering," he told Aharon, "and a ram for a burnt offering, both without
3 blemish, and offer them up before the LORD. Then tell the Israelites: Take a
goat for a purification offering, and a calf and a lamb, both yearlings without
4 blemish, for a burnt offering, a bull and a ram for a peace offering to offer up
before the LORD, and a grain offering mixed with oil – for on this day the
5 LORD will be revealed to you." They brought what Moshe had commanded
to the space before the Tent of Meeting, and all the community drew
6 near and stood before the LORD. Moshe said, "This is what the LORD has
7 commanded you to do so that the LORD's glory be revealed to you." Moshe
said to Aharon, "Approach the altar, prepare your purification offering
and burnt offering, and make atonement for you and for the people. Then
prepare the people's offering to make atonement for them, as the LORD has
8 commanded." Aharon drew close to the altar and slaughtered the calf of his
9 purification offering. Aharon's sons presented him with the blood, and he
dipped his finger into it and applied the blood to the horns of the altar; the
10 rest of the blood he poured out at the altar's base. Then he sent the fat, the
kidneys, and the diaphragm of the liver from the purification offering up in
11 smoke upon the altar as the LORD had commanded Moshe, and he burned
12 the flesh and skin with fire outside the camp. Then he slaughtered the burnt
offering. Aharon's sons presented him with the blood, and he dashed it on
13 each side of the altar. Then they presented him with the burnt offering in its
14 pieces, with its head, and he sent them up in smoke upon the altar. Having
washed the entrails and legs, he sent them up in smoke upon the altar with
15 the burnt offering. Then he brought close the people's offering. He took the
goat of the people's purification offering, slaughtered it, and prepared it as
16 a purification offering like the first. He presented the burnt offering and
17 sacrificed it in the prescribed way. He then presented the grain offering,
took a handful from it, and sent this portion up in smoke upon the altar, with
18 the morning's burnt offering. He slaughtered the ox and the ram: the people's
peace sacrifice. Aharon's sons presented him with the blood, and he dashed

הַמִּזְבֵּחַ וַיַּז עַל־אַהֲרֹן עַל־בְּגָדָיו וְעַל־בָּנָיו וְעַל־בִּגְדֵי בָנָיו אִתּוֹ וַיְקַדֵּשׁ
לא אֶת־אַהֲרֹן אֶת־בְּגָדָיו וְאֶת־בָּנָיו וְאֶת־בִּגְדֵי בָנָיו אִתּוֹ: וַיֹּאמֶר מֹשֶׁה
אֶל־אַהֲרֹן וְאֶל־בָּנָיו בַּשְּׁלוּ אֶת־הַבָּשָׂר פֶּתַח אֹהֶל מוֹעֵד וְשָׁם תֹּאכְלוּ
אֹתוֹ וְאֶת־הַלֶּחֶם אֲשֶׁר בְּסַל הַמִּלֻּאִים כַּאֲשֶׁר צִוֵּיתִי לֵאמֹר אַהֲרֹן
לב לג וּבָנָיו יֹאכְלֻהוּ: וְהַנּוֹתָר בַּבָּשָׂר וּבַלָּחֶם בָּאֵשׁ תִּשְׂרֹפוּ: וּמִפֶּתַח אֹהֶל מפטיר
מוֹעֵד לֹא תֵצְאוּ שִׁבְעַת יָמִים עַד יוֹם מְלֹאת יְמֵי מִלֻּאֵיכֶם כִּי שִׁבְעַת
לד יָמִים יְמַלֵּא אֶת־יֶדְכֶם: כַּאֲשֶׁר עָשָׂה בַּיּוֹם הַזֶּה צִוָּה יהוה לַעֲשֹׂת
לה לְכַפֵּר עֲלֵיכֶם: וּפֶתַח אֹהֶל מוֹעֵד תֵּשְׁבוּ יוֹמָם וָלַיְלָה שִׁבְעַת יָמִים
לו וּשְׁמַרְתֶּם אֶת־מִשְׁמֶרֶת יהוה וְלֹא תָמוּתוּ כִּי־כֵן צֻוֵּיתִי: וַיַּעַשׂ אַהֲרֹן
ט א וּבָנָיו אֵת כָּל־הַדְּבָרִים אֲשֶׁר־צִוָּה יהוה בְּיַד־מֹשֶׁה: וַיְהִי שמיני
ב בַּיּוֹם הַשְּׁמִינִי קָרָא מֹשֶׁה לְאַהֲרֹן וּלְבָנָיו וּלְזִקְנֵי יִשְׂרָאֵל: וַיֹּאמֶר אֶל־
אַהֲרֹן קַח־לְךָ עֵגֶל בֶּן־בָּקָר לְחַטָּאת וְאַיִל לְעֹלָה תְּמִימִם וְהַקְרֵב
ג לִפְנֵי יהוה: וְאֶל־בְּנֵי יִשְׂרָאֵל תְּדַבֵּר לֵאמֹר קְחוּ שְׂעִיר־עִזִּים לְחַטָּאת
ד וְעֵגֶל וָכֶבֶשׂ בְּנֵי־שָׁנָה תְּמִימִם לְעֹלָה: וְשׁוֹר וָאַיִל לִשְׁלָמִים לִזְבֹּחַ
ה לִפְנֵי יהוה וּמִנְחָה בְּלוּלָה בַשָּׁמֶן כִּי הַיּוֹם יהוה נִרְאָה אֲלֵיכֶם: וַיִּקְחוּ
אֵת אֲשֶׁר צִוָּה מֹשֶׁה אֶל־פְּנֵי אֹהֶל מוֹעֵד וַיִּקְרְבוּ כָּל־הָעֵדָה וַיַּעַמְדוּ
ו לִפְנֵי יהוה: וַיֹּאמֶר מֹשֶׁה זֶה הַדָּבָר אֲשֶׁר־צִוָּה יהוה תַּעֲשׂוּ וְיֵרָא
ז אֲלֵיכֶם כְּבוֹד יהוה: וַיֹּאמֶר מֹשֶׁה אֶל־אַהֲרֹן קְרַב אֶל־הַמִּזְבֵּחַ וַעֲשֵׂה
אֶת־חַטָּאתְךָ וְאֶת־עֹלָתֶךָ וְכַפֵּר בַּעַדְךָ וּבְעַד הָעָם וַעֲשֵׂה אֶת־קָרְבַּן
ח הָעָם וְכַפֵּר בַּעֲדָם כַּאֲשֶׁר צִוָּה יהוה: וַיִּקְרַב אַהֲרֹן אֶל־הַמִּזְבֵּחַ וַיִּשְׁחַט
ט אֶת־עֵגֶל הַחַטָּאת אֲשֶׁר־לוֹ: וַיַּקְרִבוּ בְּנֵי אַהֲרֹן אֶת־הַדָּם אֵלָיו וַיִּטְבֹּל
אֶצְבָּעוֹ בַּדָּם וַיִּתֵּן עַל־קַרְנוֹת הַמִּזְבֵּחַ וְאֶת־הַדָּם יָצַק אֶל־יְסוֹד
י הַמִּזְבֵּחַ: וְאֶת־הַחֵלֶב וְאֶת־הַכְּלָיֹת וְאֶת־הַיֹּתֶרֶת מִן־הַכָּבֵד מִן־
יא הַחַטָּאת הִקְטִיר הַמִּזְבֵּחָה כַּאֲשֶׁר צִוָּה יהוה אֶת־מֹשֶׁה: וְאֶת־הַבָּשָׂר
יב וְאֶת־הָעוֹר שָׂרַף בָּאֵשׁ מִחוּץ לַמַּחֲנֶה: וַיִּשְׁחַט אֶת־הָעֹלָה וַיַּמְצִאוּ
יג בְּנֵי אַהֲרֹן אֵלָיו אֶת־הַדָּם וַיִּזְרְקֵהוּ עַל־הַמִּזְבֵּחַ סָבִיב: וְאֶת־הָעֹלָה
יד הִמְצִיאוּ אֵלָיו לִנְתָחֶיהָ וְאֶת־הָרֹאשׁ וַיַּקְטֵר עַל־הַמִּזְבֵּחַ: וַיִּרְחַץ
טו אֶת־הַקֶּרֶב וְאֶת־הַכְּרָעָיִם וַיַּקְטֵר עַל־הָעֹלָה הַמִּזְבֵּחָה: וַיַּקְרֵב אֵת
קָרְבַּן הָעָם וַיִּקַּח אֶת־שְׂעִיר הַחַטָּאת אֲשֶׁר לָעָם וַיִּשְׁחָטֵהוּ וַיְחַטְּאֵהוּ
טז יז כָּרִאשׁוֹן: וַיַּקְרֵב אֶת־הָעֹלָה וַיַּעֲשֶׂהָ כַּמִּשְׁפָּט: וַיַּקְרֵב אֶת־הַמִּנְחָה שני
יח וַיְמַלֵּא כַפּוֹ מִמֶּנָּה וַיַּקְטֵר עַל־הַמִּזְבֵּחַ מִלְּבַד עֹלַת הַבֹּקֶר: וַיִּשְׁחַט
אֶת־הַשּׁוֹר וְאֶת־הָאַיִל זֶבַח הַשְּׁלָמִים אֲשֶׁר לָעָם וַיַּמְצִאוּ בְּנֵי אַהֲרֹן

19 it against each side of the altar, and the fat parts of the ox and ram:[23] the broad
20 tail, the covering fat, the kidneys, and the diaphragm of the liver. They laid
the fat parts over the breasts, and he sent them up in smoke upon the altar.
21 But the breasts and right thigh Aharon displayed, this way and that, as a
22 wave offering before the LORD, as Moshe had commanded. Then Aharon
raised his hands to the people and blessed them. And, having presented the
purification offering, the burnt offering, and the peace sacrifice, he stepped
23 down. Moshe and Aharon entered the Tent of Meeting; when they came out,
they blessed the people, and the glory of the LORD was revealed to all the
24 people. And from before the LORD, fire came forth. It consumed the burnt
offering and the fat pieces on the altar; and all the people saw it, and cried out
10 1 for joy, and threw themselves facedown upon the ground. Aharon's sons
Nadav and Avihu took their fire pans, put fire in them, and placed incense
upon it, and they offered unauthorized fire before the LORD: fire He had not
2 commanded. And fire came forth from before the LORD and consumed them.
3 They died before the LORD. Moshe said to Aharon, "Of this the LORD spoke
when He said: I will be sanctified through those close to Me, and before all
4 the people I will be honored."[24] And Aharon was silent. Moshe called to
Mishael and Eltzafan, sons of Uziel, Aharon's uncle; "Draw near," he said,
"carry your kinsmen from the Sanctuary and take them outside the camp."
5 They approached and, as Moshe had instructed them, they carried Nadav and
6 Avihu out by their tunics to a place outside the camp. Moshe said to Aharon
and to Elazar and Itamar his sons, "Do not dishevel your hair or tear your
clothes[25] or you will die and bring fury down upon the whole community.
Your brothers, the whole House of Israel, may mourn the burning that the
7 LORD has brought about. But you must not leave the entrance to the Tent of
Meeting or you will die, for the LORD's anointing oil is upon you." They did
as Moshe had told them.
8 9 And the LORD spoke to Aharon: "You and your sons must not drink wine
or strong drink when you enter the Tent of Meeting, so that you do not die.
10 This is an everlasting statute throughout your generations, to enable you
to distinguish between sacred and profane, and between impure and pure,
11 and to teach the Israelites all the statutes that the LORD has spoken to them
through Moshe."
12 Moshe told Aharon, and Elazar and Itamar, the two sons left to him, "Take
the grain offering left over after the fire offerings to the LORD and eat it
13 unleavened beside the altar, for it is holy of holies. You must eat it in a
holy place because it is your share, and that of your sons, from the LORD's
14 fire offerings, for so I have been commanded. But you and your sons and
daughters may eat the breast of the wave offering and the thigh of the upraised
gift in any ritually pure place, for these have been given to you from the peace
15 sacrifices of Israel as your portion and the portion of your children. The thigh

---

23 | In addition to the blood, Aharon's sons also presented him with the fat.

24 | Explanations of this statement and when it was uttered vary.

25 | Acts that a mourner would typically have performed.

יט אֶת־הַדָּם אֵלָיו וַיִּזְרְקֵהוּ עַל־הַמִּזְבֵּחַ סָבִיב: וְאֶת־הַחֲלָבִים מִן־הַשּׁוֹר
כ וּמִן־הָאַיִל הָאַלְיָה וְהַמְכַסֶּה וְהַכְּלָיֹת וְיֹתֶרֶת הַכָּבֵד: וַיָּשִׂימוּ אֶת־
כא הַחֲלָבִים עַל־הֶחָזוֹת וַיַּקְטֵר הַחֲלָבִים הַמִּזְבֵּחָה: וְאֵת הֶחָזוֹת וְאֵת
כב שׁוֹק הַיָּמִין הֵנִיף אַהֲרֹן תְּנוּפָה לִפְנֵי יהוה כַּאֲשֶׁר צִוָּה מֹשֶׁה: וַיִּשָּׂא
אַהֲרֹן אֶת־יָדָו אֶל־הָעָם וַיְבָרְכֵם וַיֵּרֶד מֵעֲשֹׂת הַחַטָּאת וְהָעֹלָה
כג וְהַשְּׁלָמִים: וַיָּבֹא מֹשֶׁה וְאַהֲרֹן אֶל־אֹהֶל מוֹעֵד וַיֵּצְאוּ וַיְבָרְכוּ אֶת־הָעָם
כד וַיֵּרָא כְבוֹד־יהוה אֶל־כָּל־הָעָם: וַתֵּצֵא אֵשׁ מִלִּפְנֵי יהוה וַתֹּאכַל עַל־ שלישי
הַמִּזְבֵּחַ אֶת־הָעֹלָה וְאֶת־הַחֲלָבִים וַיַּרְא כָּל־הָעָם וַיָּרֹנּוּ וַיִּפְּלוּ עַל־
י א פְּנֵיהֶם: וַיִּקְחוּ בְנֵי־אַהֲרֹן נָדָב וַאֲבִיהוּא אִישׁ מַחְתָּתוֹ וַיִּתְּנוּ בָהֵן אֵשׁ
וַיָּשִׂימוּ עָלֶיהָ קְטֹרֶת וַיַּקְרִיבוּ לִפְנֵי יהוה אֵשׁ זָרָה אֲשֶׁר לֹא צִוָּה
ב ג אֹתָם: וַתֵּצֵא אֵשׁ מִלִּפְנֵי יהוה וַתֹּאכַל אוֹתָם וַיָּמֻתוּ לִפְנֵי יהוה: וַיֹּאמֶר
מֹשֶׁה אֶל־אַהֲרֹן הוּא אֲשֶׁר־דִּבֶּר יהוה ׀ לֵאמֹר בִּקְרֹבַי אֶקָּדֵשׁ וְעַל־
ד פְּנֵי כָל־הָעָם אֶכָּבֵד וַיִּדֹּם אַהֲרֹן: וַיִּקְרָא מֹשֶׁה אֶל־מִישָׁאֵל וְאֶל
אֶלְצָפָן בְּנֵי עֻזִּיאֵל דֹּד אַהֲרֹן וַיֹּאמֶר אֲלֵהֶם קִרְבוּ שְׂאוּ אֶת־אֲחֵיכֶם
ה מֵאֵת פְּנֵי־הַקֹּדֶשׁ אֶל־מִחוּץ לַמַּחֲנֶה: וַיִּקְרְבוּ וַיִּשָּׂאֻם בְּכֻתֳּנֹתָם אֶל־
ו מִחוּץ לַמַּחֲנֶה כַּאֲשֶׁר דִּבֶּר מֹשֶׁה: וַיֹּאמֶר מֹשֶׁה אֶל־אַהֲרֹן וּלְאֶלְעָזָר
וּלְאִיתָמָר ׀ בָּנָיו רָאשֵׁיכֶם אַל־תִּפְרָעוּ ׀ וּבִגְדֵיכֶם לֹא־תִפְרֹמוּ וְלֹא
תָמֻתוּ וְעַל כָּל־הָעֵדָה יִקְצֹף וַאֲחֵיכֶם כָּל־בֵּית יִשְׂרָאֵל יִבְכּוּ אֶת־
ז הַשְּׂרֵפָה אֲשֶׁר שָׂרַף יהוה: וּמִפֶּתַח אֹהֶל מוֹעֵד לֹא תֵצְאוּ פֶּן־תָּמֻתוּ
כִּי־שֶׁמֶן מִשְׁחַת יהוה עֲלֵיכֶם וַיַּעֲשׂוּ כִּדְבַר מֹשֶׁה:
ח ט וַיְדַבֵּר יהוה אֶל־אַהֲרֹן לֵאמֹר: יַיִן וְשֵׁכָר אַל־תֵּשְׁתְּ ׀ אַתָּה ׀ וּבָנֶיךָ ה
אִתָּךְ בְּבֹאֲכֶם אֶל־אֹהֶל מוֹעֵד וְלֹא תָמֻתוּ חֻקַּת עוֹלָם לְדֹרֹתֵיכֶם:
י יא וּלְהַבְדִּיל בֵּין הַקֹּדֶשׁ וּבֵין הַחֹל וּבֵין הַטָּמֵא וּבֵין הַטָּהוֹר: וּלְהוֹרֹת
אֶת־בְּנֵי יִשְׂרָאֵל אֵת כָּל־הַחֻקִּים אֲשֶׁר דִּבֶּר יהוה אֲלֵיהֶם בְּיַד־
מֹשֶׁה:
יב וַיְדַבֵּר מֹשֶׁה אֶל־אַהֲרֹן וְאֶל אֶלְעָזָר וְאֶל־אִיתָמָר ׀ בָּנָיו הַנּוֹתָרִים קְחוּ רביעי
אֶת־הַמִּנְחָה הַנּוֹתֶרֶת מֵאִשֵּׁי יהוה וְאִכְלוּהָ מַצּוֹת אֵצֶל הַמִּזְבֵּחַ כִּי
יג קֹדֶשׁ קָדָשִׁים הִוא: וַאֲכַלְתֶּם אֹתָהּ בְּמָקוֹם קָדוֹשׁ כִּי חָקְךָ וְחָק־בָּנֶיךָ
יד הִוא מֵאִשֵּׁי יהוה כִּי־כֵן צֻוֵּיתִי: וְאֵת חֲזֵה הַתְּנוּפָה וְאֵת ׀ שׁוֹק הַתְּרוּמָה
תֹּאכְלוּ בְּמָקוֹם טָהוֹר אַתָּה וּבָנֶיךָ וּבְנֹתֶיךָ אִתָּךְ כִּי־חָקְךָ וְחָק־בָּנֶיךָ
טו נִתְּנוּ מִזִּבְחֵי שַׁלְמֵי בְּנֵי יִשְׂרָאֵל: שׁוֹק הַתְּרוּמָה וַחֲזֵה הַתְּנוּפָה עַל

for the upraised gift and the breast for the wave offering are to be brought,
with the fat of the fire offering, to be waved as a wave offering before the
LORD. These are to be your share and that of your children forever, as the
16 LORD has commanded." Moshe inquired about the goat for the purification
offering, and discovered that it had been burned. He was furious with Elazar
17 and Itamar, the two sons left to Aharon. "Why did you not eat the purification
offering in the holy area?" he asked. "It is holy of holies, and it has been given
to you to remove the guilt of the community and atone for them before the
18 LORD. Because its blood was not to be brought into the inner Sanctuary, you
19 should have eaten it in the Sanctuary, as I commanded."[26] It was Aharon who
replied to Moshe, "They offered their purification offering and their burnt
offerings before the LORD today – but such things have happened to me.
Would it really have been right in the LORD's eyes if I had eaten a purification
20 offering today?" Moshe listened; and it was right in his eyes.
11 1 2 The LORD spoke to Moshe and Aharon, saying to them: "Tell the Israelites:
3 These are the creatures that you may eat among the land mammals: You may
4 eat any animal that has divided hoofs, fully split, and chews the cud. Among
those that chew the cud or have divided hoofs you must not eat the following:
the camel, because though it chews the cud, it does not have divided hoofs,
5 and so it is impure for you; the hyrax, though it chews the cud, does not have
6 divided hoofs and so it is impure for you; the hare, though it chews the cud,
7 does not have divided hoofs and so it is impure for you; the pig, though it
has fully divided hoofs, does not chew the cud and so it is impure for you.
8 You may not eat the flesh of these animals or touch their carcasses; they
9 are impure for you. These you may eat among the creatures of the water:
anything in the water, whether in sea or in stream, that has fins and scales
10 may be eaten, whereas anything in the sea or the stream that does not have
fins and scales, whether one of the swarming creatures of the water or any
11 other of living creature there, is detestable to you and will remain so. You
12 may not eat their flesh, and you shall detest their carcasses. Anything in the
13 water that does not have fins or scales is detestable to you. Among the birds,
the following you shall regard as detestable – being detested they shall not
be eaten:[27] the griffon vulture, the bearded vulture, the lappet-faced vulture,
14, 15, 16 the kite, any kind of buzzard, any kind of raven, the ostrich, the swift, the
17 gull, any kind of sparrow hawk, the little owl, the fish owl, the short-eared
18, 19 owl, the barn owl, the pelican, the vulture, the stork, any kind of heron, the
20 hoopoe, and the bat. All swarming, flying creatures that crawl on fours are
21 detestable to you, but you may eat those swarming, flying creatures that crawl
on four legs, with legs jointed above their feet with which they hop on the
22 ground. Of these you may eat the following: any kind of locust, bald locust,

---

26 | See 6:23.

27 | The identities of many of these birds are subject to debate.

אִשֵּׁי הַחֲלָבִים יָבִיאוּ לְהָנִיף תְּנוּפָה לִפְנֵי יהוה וְהָיָה לְךָ וּלְבָנֶיךָ אִתְּךָ
טז לְחָק־עוֹלָם כַּאֲשֶׁר צִוָּה יהוה: וְאֵת | שְׂעִיר הַחַטָּאת דָּרֹשׁ דָּרַשׁ מֹשֶׁה חמישי
וְהִנֵּה שֹׂרָף וַיִּקְצֹף עַל־אֶלְעָזָר וְעַל־אִיתָמָר בְּנֵי אַהֲרֹן הַנּוֹתָרִם לֵאמֹר:
יז מַדּוּעַ לֹא־אֲכַלְתֶּם אֶת־הַחַטָּאת בִּמְקוֹם הַקֹּדֶשׁ כִּי קֹדֶשׁ קָדָשִׁים הִוא
יח וְאֹתָהּ | נָתַן לָכֶם לָשֵׂאת אֶת־עֲוֹן הָעֵדָה לְכַפֵּר עֲלֵיהֶם לִפְנֵי יהוה: הֵן
לֹא־הוּבָא אֶת־דָּמָהּ אֶל־הַקֹּדֶשׁ פְּנִימָה אָכוֹל תֹּאכְלוּ אֹתָהּ בַּקֹּדֶשׁ
יט כַּאֲשֶׁר צִוֵּיתִי: וַיְדַבֵּר אַהֲרֹן אֶל־מֹשֶׁה הֵן הַיּוֹם הִקְרִיבוּ אֶת־חַטָּאתָם
וְאֶת־עֹלָתָם לִפְנֵי יהוה וַתִּקְרֶאנָה אֹתִי כָּאֵלֶּה וְאָכַלְתִּי חַטָּאת הַיּוֹם
כ הַיִּיטַב בְּעֵינֵי יהוה: וַיִּשְׁמַע מֹשֶׁה וַיִּיטַב בְּעֵינָיו:
יא א ב וַיְדַבֵּר יהוה אֶל־מֹשֶׁה וְאֶל־אַהֲרֹן לֵאמֹר אֲלֵהֶם: דַּבְּרוּ אֶל־בְּנֵי ו ששי
יִשְׂרָאֵל לֵאמֹר זֹאת הַחַיָּה אֲשֶׁר תֹּאכְלוּ מִכָּל־הַבְּהֵמָה אֲשֶׁר עַל־
ג הָאָרֶץ: כֹּל | מַפְרֶסֶת פַּרְסָה וְשֹׁסַעַת שֶׁסַע פְּרָסֹת מַעֲלַת גֵּרָה בַּבְּהֵמָה
ד אֹתָהּ תֹּאכֵלוּ: אַךְ אֶת־זֶה לֹא תֹאכְלוּ מִמַּעֲלֵי הַגֵּרָה וּמִמַּפְרִסֵי הַפַּרְסָה
אֶת־הַגָּמָל כִּי־מַעֲלֵה גֵרָה הוּא וּפַרְסָה אֵינֶנּוּ מַפְרִיס טָמֵא הוּא לָכֶם:
ה וְאֶת־הַשָּׁפָן כִּי־מַעֲלֵה גֵרָה הוּא וּפַרְסָה לֹא יַפְרִיס טָמֵא הוּא לָכֶם:
ו וְאֶת־הָאַרְנֶבֶת כִּי־מַעֲלַת גֵּרָה הִוא וּפַרְסָה לֹא הִפְרִיסָה טְמֵאָה הִוא
ז לָכֶם: וְאֶת־הַחֲזִיר כִּי־מַפְרִיס פַּרְסָה הוּא וְשֹׁסַע שֶׁסַע פַּרְסָה וְהוּא
ח גֵּרָה לֹא־יִגָּר טָמֵא הוּא לָכֶם: מִבְּשָׂרָם לֹא תֹאכֵלוּ וּבְנִבְלָתָם לֹא
ט תִגָּעוּ טְמֵאִים הֵם לָכֶם: אֶת־זֶה תֹּאכְלוּ מִכֹּל אֲשֶׁר בַּמָּיִם כֹּל אֲשֶׁר־
י לוֹ סְנַפִּיר וְקַשְׂקֶשֶׂת בַּמַּיִם בַּיַּמִּים וּבַנְּחָלִים אֹתָם תֹּאכֵלוּ: וְכֹל אֲשֶׁר
אֵין־לוֹ סְנַפִּיר וְקַשְׂקֶשֶׂת בַּיַּמִּים וּבַנְּחָלִים מִכֹּל שֶׁרֶץ הַמַּיִם וּמִכֹּל
יא נֶפֶשׁ הַחַיָּה אֲשֶׁר בַּמָּיִם שֶׁקֶץ הֵם לָכֶם: וְשֶׁקֶץ יִהְיוּ לָכֶם מִבְּשָׂרָם
יב לֹא תֹאכֵלוּ וְאֶת־נִבְלָתָם תְּשַׁקֵּצוּ: כֹּל אֲשֶׁר אֵין־לוֹ סְנַפִּיר וְקַשְׂקֶשֶׂת
יג בַּמָּיִם שֶׁקֶץ הוּא לָכֶם: וְאֶת־אֵלֶּה תְּשַׁקְּצוּ מִן־הָעוֹף לֹא יֵאָכְלוּ שֶׁקֶץ
יד הֵם אֶת־הַנֶּשֶׁר וְאֶת־הַפֶּרֶס וְאֵת הָעָזְנִיָּה: וְאֶת־הַדָּאָה וְאֶת־הָאַיָּה
טו טז לְמִינָהּ: אֵת כָּל־עֹרֵב לְמִינוֹ: וְאֵת בַּת הַיַּעֲנָה וְאֶת־הַתַּחְמָס וְאֶת־
יז הַשָּׁחַף וְאֶת־הַנֵּץ לְמִינֵהוּ: וְאֶת־הַכּוֹס וְאֶת־הַשָּׁלָךְ וְאֶת־הַיַּנְשׁוּף:
יח יט וְאֶת־הַתִּנְשֶׁמֶת וְאֶת־הַקָּאָת וְאֶת־הָרָחָם: וְאֵת הַחֲסִידָה הָאֲנָפָה
כ לְמִינָהּ וְאֶת־הַדּוּכִיפַת וְאֶת־הָעֲטַלֵּף: כֹּל שֶׁרֶץ הָעוֹף הַהֹלֵךְ עַל־
כא אַרְבַּע שֶׁקֶץ הוּא לָכֶם: אַךְ אֶת־זֶה תֹּאכְלוּ מִכֹּל שֶׁרֶץ הָעוֹף הַהֹלֵךְ
עַל־אַרְבַּע אֲשֶׁר־לא כְרָעַיִם מִמַּעַל לְרַגְלָיו לְנַתֵּר בָּהֵן עַל־הָאָרֶץ: לוֹ
כב אֶת־אֵלֶּה מֵהֶם תֹּאכֵלוּ אֶת־הָאַרְבֶּה לְמִינוֹ וְאֶת־הַסָּלְעָם לְמִינֵהוּ

23 cricket, or grasshopper. Every other swarming, flying, crawling creature
24 on fours is detestable to you. You become impure through these: whoever
25 touches their carcasses shall be impure until evening, and whoever moves
26 their carcasses shall immerse his clothes and be impure until evening. All
livestock with divided hoofs that are not completely split, or that do not
chew the cud, are impure for you; whoever touches them becomes impure.
27 Among four-footed animals, all those that walk on their paws are impure for
28 you; anyone touching their carcasses shall be impure until evening. One who
moves their carcasses shall immerse his clothes and be impure until evening;
29 these animals are impure for you. Among the creatures that creep
along the ground, the following are impure for you:[28] the marten, the mouse,
30 every kind of spiny-tailed lizard, the legless lizard, the chameleon, the lizard,
31 the skink, and the mole rat. Of all the creatures that creep along the ground,
these are impure for you; whoever touches them when they are dead shall
32 be impure until evening. And if any of these dies and falls on something – a
wooden vessel, clothing, leather goods or sackcloth, any utensil with which
work is done – it renders it impure. The article must be immersed in water and
33 then remains impure until evening, when it will become pure again. If any of
these falls into a pottery jar, everything inside it becomes impure; you must
34 smash the pot. Edible food becomes impure in such a jar if water has been
35 poured over; any drinkable beverage in such a jar becomes impure. Anything
on which a part of one of their dead bodies falls becomes impure. If it is an
oven or stove, it must be broken into pieces; it is impure for you and will
36 remain so. A spring or cistern holding water remains pure, but anyone who
37 touches one of their dead bodies in it becomes impure. If any part of their
38 dead bodies falls on seed that has been planted, the seed remains pure. But
if water has been poured over the seed and afterward any part of their dead
39 bodies falls upon it, it is rendered impure for you. If an animal of a
kind that you are allowed to eat dies naturally, one who touches its carcass
40 shall be impure until evening. Anyone who eats of its carcass must immerse
his clothes, and he remains impure until evening. Anyone who moves the
41 carcass must immerse his clothes, and he remains impure until evening. All
42 creatures that swarm on the earth are detested; they shall not be eaten. Of
these swarming things you shall not eat any, those that move on their bellies
43 or crawl on all fours or on many feet – for they are all detestable. Do not make
yourselves detestable by contact with any of these swarming creatures. Do not
44 defile yourselves with them or be defiled by them. I am the Lord your God.
Consecrate yourselves and be holy, for I am holy. Do not defile yourselves
45 with any swarming creature that crawls on the ground. I am the Lord, who
46 brought you up out of Egypt to be your God. Be holy, for I am holy." This is
the law concerning animals, birds, all creatures that live in water and all that
47 swarm on the earth, to distinguish between the impure and the pure and
between creatures that may be eaten and those that may not.

---

28 | The identities of these animals are debated.

כג וְאֶת־הַחַרְגֹּל לְמִינֵהוּ וְאֶת־הֶחָגָב לְמִינֵהוּ׃ וְכֹל שֶׁרֶץ הָעוֹף אֲשֶׁר־
כד לוֹ אַרְבַּע רַגְלָיִם שֶׁקֶץ הוּא לָכֶם׃ וּלְאֵלֶּה תִּטַּמָּאוּ כָּל־הַנֹּגֵעַ בְּנִבְלָתָם
כה יִטְמָא עַד־הָעָרֶב׃ וְכָל־הַנֹּשֵׂא מִנִּבְלָתָם יְכַבֵּס בְּגָדָיו וְטָמֵא עַד־
כו הָעָרֶב׃ לְכָל־הַבְּהֵמָה אֲשֶׁר הִוא מַפְרֶסֶת פַּרְסָה וְשֶׁסַע ׀ אֵינֶנָּה
שֹׁסַעַת וְגֵרָה אֵינֶנָּה מַעֲלָה טְמֵאִים הֵם לָכֶם כָּל־הַנֹּגֵעַ בָּהֶם יִטְמָא׃
כז וְכֹל ׀ הוֹלֵךְ עַל־כַּפָּיו בְּכָל־הַחַיָּה הַהֹלֶכֶת עַל־אַרְבַּע טְמֵאִים הֵם לָכֶם
כח כָּל־הַנֹּגֵעַ בְּנִבְלָתָם יִטְמָא עַד־הָעָרֶב׃ וְהַנֹּשֵׂא אֶת־נִבְלָתָם יְכַבֵּס
כט בְּגָדָיו וְטָמֵא עַד־הָעָרֶב טְמֵאִים הֵמָּה לָכֶם׃ וְזֶה לָכֶם
הַטָּמֵא בַּשֶּׁרֶץ הַשֹּׁרֵץ עַל־הָאָרֶץ הַחֹלֶד וְהָעַכְבָּר וְהַצָּב לְמִינֵהוּ׃
ל לא וְהָאֲנָקָה וְהַכֹּחַ וְהַלְּטָאָה וְהַחֹמֶט וְהַתִּנְשָׁמֶת׃ אֵלֶּה הַטְּמֵאִים לָכֶם
לב בְּכָל־הַשָּׁרֶץ כָּל־הַנֹּגֵעַ בָּהֶם בְּמֹתָם יִטְמָא עַד־הָעָרֶב׃ וְכֹל אֲשֶׁר־יִפֹּל
עָלָיו מֵהֶם ׀ בְּמֹתָם יִטְמָא מִכָּל־כְּלִי־עֵץ אוֹ בֶגֶד אוֹ־עוֹר אוֹ שָׂק כָּל־
כְּלִי אֲשֶׁר־יֵעָשֶׂה מְלָאכָה בָּהֶם בַּמַּיִם יוּבָא וְטָמֵא עַד־הָעֶרֶב וְטָהֵר׃
לג וְכָל־כְּלִי־חֶרֶשׂ אֲשֶׁר־יִפֹּל מֵהֶם אֶל־תּוֹכוֹ כֹּל אֲשֶׁר בְּתוֹכוֹ יִטְמָא וְאֹתוֹ שביעי
לד תִשְׁבֹּרוּ׃ מִכָּל־הָאֹכֶל אֲשֶׁר יֵאָכֵל אֲשֶׁר יָבוֹא עָלָיו מַיִם יִטְמָא וְכָל־
לה מַשְׁקֶה אֲשֶׁר יִשָּׁתֶה בְּכָל־כְּלִי יִטְמָא׃ וְכֹל אֲשֶׁר־יִפֹּל מִנִּבְלָתָם ׀ עָלָיו
לו יִטְמָא תַּנּוּר וְכִירַיִם יֻתָּץ טְמֵאִים הֵם וּטְמֵאִים יִהְיוּ לָכֶם׃ אַךְ מַעְיָן
לז וּבוֹר מִקְוֵה־מַיִם יִהְיֶה טָהוֹר וְנֹגֵעַ בְּנִבְלָתָם יִטְמָא׃ וְכִי יִפֹּל מִנִּבְלָתָם
לח עַל־כָּל־זֶרַע זֵרוּעַ אֲשֶׁר יִזָּרֵעַ טָהוֹר הוּא׃ וְכִי יֻתַּן־מַיִם עַל־זֶרַע וְנָפַל
לט מִנִּבְלָתָם עָלָיו טָמֵא הוּא לָכֶם׃ וְכִי יָמוּת מִן־הַבְּהֵמָה
מ אֲשֶׁר־הִיא לָכֶם לְאָכְלָה הַנֹּגֵעַ בְּנִבְלָתָהּ יִטְמָא עַד־הָעָרֶב׃ וְהָאֹכֵל
מִנִּבְלָתָהּ יְכַבֵּס בְּגָדָיו וְטָמֵא עַד־הָעָרֶב וְהַנֹּשֵׂא אֶת־נִבְלָתָהּ יְכַבֵּס
מא בְּגָדָיו וְטָמֵא עַד־הָעָרֶב׃ וְכָל־הַשֶּׁרֶץ הַשֹּׁרֵץ עַל־הָאָרֶץ שֶׁקֶץ הוּא לֹא
מב יֵאָכֵל׃ כֹּל הוֹלֵךְ עַל־גָּחוֹן וְכֹל ׀ הוֹלֵךְ עַל־אַרְבַּע עַד כָּל־מַרְבֵּה רַגְלַיִם
מג לְכָל־הַשֶּׁרֶץ הַשֹּׁרֵץ עַל־הָאָרֶץ לֹא תֹאכְלוּם כִּי־שֶׁקֶץ הֵם׃ אַל־תְּשַׁקְּצוּ
אֶת־נַפְשֹׁתֵיכֶם בְּכָל־הַשֶּׁרֶץ הַשֹּׁרֵץ וְלֹא תִטַּמְּאוּ בָּהֶם וְנִטְמֵתֶם בָּם׃
מד כִּי אֲנִי יהוה אֱלֹהֵיכֶם וְהִתְקַדִּשְׁתֶּם וִהְיִיתֶם קְדֹשִׁים כִּי קָדוֹשׁ אָנִי וְלֹא
מה תְטַמְּאוּ אֶת־נַפְשֹׁתֵיכֶם בְּכָל־הַשֶּׁרֶץ הָרֹמֵשׂ עַל־הָאָרֶץ׃ כִּי ׀ אֲנִי יהוה מפטיר
הַמַּעֲלֶה אֶתְכֶם מֵאֶרֶץ מִצְרַיִם לִהְיֹת לָכֶם לֵאלֹהִים וִהְיִיתֶם קְדֹשִׁים
מו כִּי קָדוֹשׁ אָנִי׃ זֹאת תּוֹרַת הַבְּהֵמָה וְהָעוֹף וְכֹל נֶפֶשׁ הַחַיָּה הָרֹמֶשֶׂת
מז בַּמָּיִם וּלְכָל־נֶפֶשׁ הַשֹּׁרֶצֶת עַל־הָאָרֶץ׃ לְהַבְדִּיל בֵּין הַטָּמֵא וּבֵין
הַטָּהֹר וּבֵין הַחַיָּה הַנֶּאֱכֶלֶת וּבֵין הַחַיָּה אֲשֶׁר לֹא תֵאָכֵל׃

12 1 2 The LORD spoke to Moshe: "Tell the Israelites: If a woman conceives and TAZRIA
gives birth to a son, she shall be impure for seven days, as she is during her
3 menstrual period. On the eighth day, the child's foreskin shall be circumcised.
4 For thirty-three days she shall wait, bleeding pure blood, but until her time
of purification is completed, she must not touch anything holy or enter the
5 Sanctuary. If she gives birth to a daughter, she shall be impure – as she is
during her menstrual period – for two weeks, and bleeds in purity for sixty-
6 six days. When the days of her purification are complete, whether for a son
or a daughter, she shall bring a yearling sheep to the priest at the entrance to
the Tent of Meeting as a burnt offering and a pigeon or dove as a purification
7 offering. The priest shall present it before the LORD and make atonement
for her; so shall she be purified of her source of blood." This is the law for a
8 woman who bears a child, male or female. "But if she cannot afford a sheep,
she may bring two doves or two pigeons – one for the burnt offering and the
other for the purification offering. The priest will then make atonement for
her, and she shall be pure."

13 1 2 The LORD spoke to Moshe and Aharon: "When a person has a swelling, a rash,
or a bright patch on his skin, and it develops on his skin into what seems to be
an impure blight, he shall be brought to the priests, to Aharon or one of his
3 sons. The priest shall examine the disease on his skin. If hair in the diseased
part has turned white and the disease appears to be deeper than the skin,
then it is the disease of an impure blight. When the priest sees this, he shall
4 declare the person impure. But if the bright patch on the skin is white but
does not appear to be deeper than the skin and the hair in it has not turned
5 white, the priest shall quarantine the patient for seven days. On the seventh
day the priest shall examine him again. If the disease has remained the same
in appearance and not spread on the patient's skin, the priest shall quarantine
6 him for another seven days. On the seventh day the priest shall examine it
again. If the diseased area has receded and not spread over the skin, the priest
shall declare the patient pure; it was only a rash. He shall immerse his clothes,
7 and he shall be pure. But if the rash does spread over the skin after he has
appeared before the priest for purification, he must appear before the priest
8 again. If the priest sees that the rash has indeed spread over the skin, he shall
declare the person impure; it is a blight.

9 10 When a person has a blight-like disease, he shall be brought to the priest, and
the priest shall look. If there is a white swelling in the skin that has turned the
11 hair white, and within the swelling there is healthy flesh, it is a chronic blight
on the skin of his body, and the priest shall pronounce the patient impure; he
12 need not quarantine him, for he is definitely impure. If, however, the blight
has spread over the skin, so that it covers all of the patient's skin from head
13 to foot, wherever the priest can see, the priest shall make an examination,
and if the blight has covered all his body, he shall pronounce him pure of the
14 disease; if he has turned completely white, he is pure. But as soon as healthy
15 flesh appears, the patient is impure. The priest shall examine the healthy flesh
and pronounce him impure; the healthy flesh is impure, for it indicates a

יב א ב וַיְדַבֵּר יְהוָה אֶל־מֹשֶׁה לֵּאמֹר׃ דַּבֵּר אֶל־בְּנֵי יִשְׂרָאֵל לֵאמֹר אִשָּׁה כִּי ז תזריע
תַזְרִיעַ וְיָלְדָה זָכָר וְטָמְאָה שִׁבְעַת יָמִים כִּימֵי נִדַּת דְּוֺתָהּ תִּטְמָא׃
ג ד וּבַיּוֹם הַשְּׁמִינִי יִמּוֹל בְּשַׂר עָרְלָתוֹ׃ וּשְׁלֹשִׁים יוֹם וּשְׁלֹשֶׁת יָמִים תֵּשֵׁב
בִּדְמֵי טָהֳרָה בְּכָל־קֹדֶשׁ לֹא־תִגָּע וְאֶל־הַמִּקְדָּשׁ לֹא תָבֹא עַד־מְלֹאת
ה יְמֵי טָהֳרָהּ׃ וְאִם־נְקֵבָה תֵלֵד וְטָמְאָה שְׁבֻעַיִם כְּנִדָּתָהּ וְשִׁשִּׁים יוֹם
ו וְשֵׁשֶׁת יָמִים תֵּשֵׁב עַל־דְּמֵי טָהֳרָה׃ וּבִמְלֹאת ׀ יְמֵי טָהֳרָהּ לְבֵן אוֹ
לְבַת תָּבִיא כֶּבֶשׂ בֶּן־שְׁנָתוֹ לְעֹלָה וּבֶן־יוֹנָה אוֹ־תֹר לְחַטָּאת אֶל־
ז פֶּתַח אֹהֶל־מוֹעֵד אֶל־הַכֹּהֵן׃ וְהִקְרִיבוֹ לִפְנֵי יְהוָה וְכִפֶּר עָלֶיהָ וְטָהֲרָה
ח מִמְּקֹר דָּמֶיהָ זֹאת תּוֹרַת הַיֹּלֶדֶת לַזָּכָר אוֹ לַנְּקֵבָה׃ וְאִם־לֹא תִמְצָא
יָדָהּ דֵּי שֶׂה וְלָקְחָה שְׁתֵּי־תֹרִים אוֹ שְׁנֵי בְּנֵי יוֹנָה אֶחָד לְעֹלָה וְאֶחָד
לְחַטָּאת וְכִפֶּר עָלֶיהָ הַכֹּהֵן וְטָהֵרָה׃
יג א ב וַיְדַבֵּר יְהוָה אֶל־מֹשֶׁה וְאֶל־אַהֲרֹן לֵאמֹר׃ אָדָם כִּי־יִהְיֶה בְעוֹר־בְּשָׂרוֹ
שְׂאֵת אוֹ־סַפַּחַת אוֹ בַהֶרֶת וְהָיָה בְעוֹר־בְּשָׂרוֹ לְנֶגַע צָרָעַת וְהוּבָא
ג אֶל־אַהֲרֹן הַכֹּהֵן אוֹ אֶל־אַחַד מִבָּנָיו הַכֹּהֲנִים׃ וְרָאָה הַכֹּהֵן אֶת־הַנֶּגַע
בְּעוֹר־הַבָּשָׂר וְשֵׂעָר בַּנֶּגַע הָפַךְ ׀ לָבָן וּמַרְאֵה הַנֶּגַע עָמֹק מֵעוֹר
ד בְּשָׂרוֹ נֶגַע צָרַעַת הוּא וְרָאָהוּ הַכֹּהֵן וְטִמֵּא אֹתוֹ׃ וְאִם־בַּהֶרֶת לְבָנָה
הִוא בְּעוֹר בְּשָׂרוֹ וְעָמֹק אֵין־מַרְאֶהָ מִן־הָעוֹר וּשְׂעָרָה לֹא־הָפַךְ לָבָן
ה וְהִסְגִּיר הַכֹּהֵן אֶת־הַנֶּגַע שִׁבְעַת יָמִים׃ וְרָאָהוּ הַכֹּהֵן בַּיּוֹם הַשְּׁבִיעִי
וְהִנֵּה הַנֶּגַע עָמַד בְּעֵינָיו לֹא־פָשָׂה הַנֶּגַע בָּעוֹר וְהִסְגִּירוֹ הַכֹּהֵן שִׁבְעַת
ו יָמִים שֵׁנִית׃ וְרָאָה הַכֹּהֵן אֹתוֹ בַּיּוֹם הַשְּׁבִיעִי שֵׁנִית וְהִנֵּה כֵּהָה הַנֶּגַע שני
וְלֹא־פָשָׂה הַנֶּגַע בָּעוֹר וְטִהֲרוֹ הַכֹּהֵן מִסְפַּחַת הִוא וְכִבֶּס בְּגָדָיו וְטָהֵר׃
ז וְאִם־פָּשֹׂה תִפְשֶׂה הַמִּסְפַּחַת בָּעוֹר אַחֲרֵי הֵרָאֹתוֹ אֶל־הַכֹּהֵן לְטָהֳרָתוֹ
ח וְנִרְאָה שֵׁנִית אֶל־הַכֹּהֵן׃ וְרָאָה הַכֹּהֵן וְהִנֵּה פָּשְׂתָה הַמִּסְפַּחַת בָּעוֹר
וְטִמְּאוֹ הַכֹּהֵן צָרַעַת הִוא׃
ט י נֶגַע צָרַעַת כִּי תִהְיֶה בְּאָדָם וְהוּבָא אֶל־הַכֹּהֵן׃ וְרָאָה הַכֹּהֵן וְהִנֵּה
שְׂאֵת־לְבָנָה בָּעוֹר וְהִיא הָפְכָה שֵׂעָר לָבָן וּמִחְיַת בָּשָׂר חַי בַּשְׂאֵת׃
יא צָרַעַת נוֹשֶׁנֶת הִוא בְּעוֹר בְּשָׂרוֹ וְטִמְּאוֹ הַכֹּהֵן לֹא יַסְגִּרֶנּוּ כִּי טָמֵא
יב הוּא׃ וְאִם־פָּרוֹחַ תִּפְרַח הַצָּרַעַת בָּעוֹר וְכִסְּתָה הַצָּרַעַת אֵת כָּל־עוֹר
יג הַנֶּגַע מֵרֹאשׁוֹ וְעַד־רַגְלָיו לְכָל־מַרְאֵה עֵינֵי הַכֹּהֵן׃ וְרָאָה הַכֹּהֵן וְהִנֵּה
כִסְּתָה הַצָּרַעַת אֶת־כָּל־בְּשָׂרוֹ וְטִהַר אֶת־הַנָּגַע כֻּלּוֹ הָפַךְ לָבָן טָהוֹר
יד טו הוּא׃ וּבְיוֹם הֵרָאוֹת בּוֹ בָּשָׂר חַי יִטְמָא׃ וְרָאָה הַכֹּהֵן אֶת־הַבָּשָׂר הַחַי

16 blight.[29] But if the healthy flesh turns white again, the patient shall come
17 back to the priest. The priest shall examine him, and if the disease has
indeed whitened, the priest shall pronounce the patient pure, and he shall
be pure.
18
19 When one has a boil on his skin and it heals, and in the place of the boil there
comes a white swelling or a bright patch of white and reddish color, this shall
20 be shown to the priest. The priest shall then make an examination, and if the
area appears lower than the rest of the skin and its hair has turned white, the
priest shall declare the patient impure: it is a case of blight that has broken
21 out in the boil. But if the priest examines it and there is no white hair in it
and it does not appear lower than the skin, but it has not receded, then the
22 priest shall quarantine the patient for seven days. If it spreads in the skin, the
23 priest shall declare him impure; it is a blight. But if the bright patch remains
in one place and does not spread, it is scar tissue from the boil, and the priest
24 shall declare the patient pure. When one has a burn on his skin and
the raw flesh of the burn becomes a bright patch, either white and reddish or
25 only white, the priest shall examine it, and if the hair in the bright patch has
turned white and it appears to be deeper than the skin, then it is a blight. It has
broken out in the burn, and the priest shall pronounce the patient impure: it
26 is a blight. But if the priest examines it and there is no white hair in the spot
and it appears no deeper than the skin, but it has not receded, the priest shall
27 quarantine him for seven days. The priest shall examine him on the seventh
day. If the disease is spreading on the skin, then the priest shall declare him
28 impure; it is a blight. But if the spot remains in its place and has not spread on
the skin, but has receded, then it was a swelling from the burn, and the priest
shall pronounce him pure; it is merely scar tissue from the burn.
29
30 When a man or woman has a disease on the scalp or beard,[30] and the priest
examines the disease and finds that it appears to be deeper than the skin,
and has fine blond hairs in it, the priest shall declare the person impure. It
31 is a scaling eruption, a blight of the head or beard. If the priest examines
the scaling and it appears no deeper than the skin but there is no black hair
in it, then the priest shall quarantine the person with the scaling eruption
32 for seven days, and on the seventh day the priest shall examine the disease.
If the scaling has not spread, and there is no blond hair among it, and the
33 scaling appears to be no deeper than the skin, then the patient shall shave
himself, but shall not shave the scaled part; and the priest shall quarantine
34 the person with the scaling eruption for a further seven days. On the seventh
day the priest shall examine the scaling, and if it has not spread in the skin
and it appears to be no deeper than the skin, then the priest shall pronounce
35 the patient pure; he shall immerse his clothes and be pure. But if the scaling
36 spreads in the skin after he is declared pure, and when the priest examines
him, if the scaling has spread in the skin, the priest need not seek the blond
37 hair; he is impure. But if it appears to him that the scaling is unchanged and if

29 | In conjunction with the surrounding blight, the healthy flesh renders the individual impure.

30 | Meaning on the area where a beard grows.

טז וטמאו הבשר החי טמא הוא צרעת הוא: או כי ישוב הבשר החי
יז ונהפך ללבן ובא אל־הכהן: וראהו הכהן והנה נהפך הנגע ללבן
וטהר הכהן את־הנגע טהור הוא:
יח יט ובשר כי־יהיה בו־בערו שחין ונרפא: והיה במקום השחין שאת שלישי
כ לבנה או בהרת לבנה אדמדמת ונראה אל־הכהן: וראה הכהן והנה
מראה שפל מן־העור ושערה הפך לבן וטמאו הכהן נגע־צרעת
כא הוא בשחין פרחה: ואם ׀ יראנה הכהן והנה אין־בה שער לבן
כב ושפלה איננה מן־העור והיא כהה והסגירו הכהן שבעת ימים: ואם־
כג פשה תפשה בעור וטמא הכהן אתו נגע הוא: ואם־תחתיה תעמד
כד הבהרת לא פשתה צרבת השחין הוא וטהרו הכהן: או רביעי /שני/
בשר כי־יהיה בערו מכות־אש והיתה מחית המכוה בהרת לבנה
כה אדמדמת או לבנה: וראה אתה הכהן והנה נהפך שער לבן בבהרת
ומראה עמק מן־העור צרעת הוא במכוה פרחה וטמא אתו הכהן
כו נגע צרעת הוא: ואם ׀ יראנה הכהן והנה אין־בבהרת שער לבן
ושפלה איננה מן־העור והוא כהה והסגירו הכהן שבעת ימים:
כז וראהו הכהן ביום השביעי אם־פשה תפשה בעור וטמא הכהן
כח אתו נגע צרעת הוא: ואם־תחתיה תעמד הבהרת לא־פשתה
בעור והוא כהה שאת המכוה הוא וטהרו הכהן כי־צרבת המכוה
הוא:
כט ל ואיש או אשה כי־יהיה בו נגע בראש או בזקן: וראה הכהן את־ ח חמישי
הנגע והנה מראהו עמק מן־העור ובו שער צהב דק וטמא אתו
לא הכהן נתק הוא צרעת הראש או הזקן הוא: וכי־יראה הכהן את־נגע
הנתק והנה אין־מראהו עמק מן־העור ושער שחר אין בו והסגיר
לב הכהן את־נגע הנתק שבעת ימים: וראה הכהן את־הנגע ביום
השביעי והנה לא־פשה הנתק ולא־היה בו שער צהב ומראה הנתק
לג אין עמק מן־העור: והתגלח ואת־הנתק לא יגלח והסגיר הכהן את־
לד הנתק שבעת ימים שנית: וראה הכהן את־הנתק ביום השביעי והנה
לא־פשה הנתק בעור ומראהו איננו עמק מן־העור וטהר אתו הכהן
לה וכבס בגדיו וטהר: ואם־פשה יפשה הנתק בעור אחרי טהרתו:
לו וראהו הכהן והנה פשה הנתק בעור לא־יבקר הכהן לשער הצהב
לז טמא הוא: ואם־בעיניו עמד הנתק ושער שחר צמח־בו נרפא הנתק

black hair has grown in among it, the eruption is healed and is pure, and the
38 priest shall declare the person pure. When a man or a woman has
39 white patches on the skin of his or her body, the priest shall examine them,
and if the patches on the skin are dull white, it is merely a rash breaking out
40 on the skin; the person is pure. If a man loses the hair on his head,
41 it is merely baldness; he is pure. If he loses the hair from his forehead, it is
42 merely a receding hairline; he is pure. But if there is a white and reddish
diseased area on his bald spot or receding hairline, it is a blight erupting in
43 his bald spot or at his receding hairline. The priest shall examine him, and if
the diseased swelling is a white and reddish area on his bald spot or receding
44 hairline, resembling a blight in the skin of the body, he is a blighted person;
he is impure. The priest shall declare him impure; he has a blight on his scalp.
45 And a blighted person, one bearing the disease – his clothes shall be torn and
the hair of his head disarrayed. And he shall cover his upper lip as he cries
46 out, 'Impure, impure.' He shall be in a state of impurity for as long as he has
the disease; he is impure. He shall live apart; outside the camp shall be his
47 dwelling. When a blight appears in a garment, whether the garment
48 is of wool or of linen, or in the warp or in the weft of the linen or wool cloth,
49 in leather or anything made of leather, if the infection shows as green or red
in the garment, the leather, the warp or the weft, or the article of leather, it is
50 a case of the impure blight and shall be shown to the priest. And the priest
shall examine the disease and quarantine the diseased article for seven days.
51 He shall examine the disease on the seventh day. If the disease has spread
in the garment, the warp or the weft, or the leather, whatever the leather is
52 used for, the infection is a malignant disease blight; it is impure. The garment
shall be burned – or the warp or weft, wool or linen, or any article of leather
that is infected – for it is a malignant disease blight; it must be burned in
53 fire. If, however, the priest examines it and the disease has not spread in the
54 garment, the warp or the weft, or the article of leather, then the priest shall
command the article in which the disease appears to be washed, and he
55 shall quarantine it for another seven days. After this washing the priest shall
once more examine the diseased article. If the diseased area has not changed
color, though the disease has not spread, it is impure. You shall burn it in fire,
56 whether the mark of decay is on the inside or on the outside. But if the priest
examines it and the diseased area has faded after washing, he shall tear it out
57 of the garment or the leather or the warp or the weft. If it appears again in the
garment, in the warp or weft, or in the leather article, it is erupting. Whatever
58 has the disease, you shall burn with fire. But the garment, or the warp or weft,
or the leather article from which the disease departs after you have washed it
59 shall be washed a second time and then be pure." This is the law concerning
the disease blight in a garment of wool or of linen, in warp or in weft, or in any
article made of leather, to determine whether it is pure or impure.
14 1 The Lord spoke to Moshe: "This shall be the law of the person with an METZORA
2 impure blight on the day he is to be purified. He shall be brought to see the

לח טָהוֹר הוּא וְטִהֲרוֹ הַכֹּהֵן: וְאִישׁ אוֹ־אִשָּׁה כִּי־יִהְיֶה בְעוֹר־
לט בְּשָׂרָם בֶּהָרֹת בֶּהָרֹת לְבָנֹת: וְרָאָה הַכֹּהֵן וְהִנֵּה בְעוֹר־בְּשָׂרָם בֶּהָרֹת
מ כֵּהוֹת לְבָנֹת בֹּהַק הוּא פָּרַח בָּעוֹר טָהוֹר הוּא: וְאִישׁ כִּי ששי /שלישי/
מא יִמָּרֵט רֹאשׁוֹ קֵרֵחַ הוּא טָהוֹר הוּא: וְאִם מִפְּאַת פָּנָיו יִמָּרֵט רֹאשׁוֹ
מב גִּבֵּחַ הוּא טָהוֹר הוּא: וְכִי־יִהְיֶה בַקָּרַחַת אוֹ בַגַּבַּחַת נֶגַע לָבָן אֲדַמְדָּם
מג צָרַעַת פֹּרַחַת הִוא בְּקָרַחְתּוֹ אוֹ בְגַבַּחְתּוֹ: וְרָאָה אֹתוֹ הַכֹּהֵן וְהִנֵּה
שְׂאֵת־הַנֶּגַע לְבָנָה אֲדַמְדֶּמֶת בְּקָרַחְתּוֹ אוֹ בְגַבַּחְתּוֹ כְּמַרְאֵה צָרַעַת
מד עוֹר בָּשָׂר: אִישׁ־צָרוּעַ הוּא טָמֵא הוּא טַמֵּא יְטַמְּאֶנּוּ הַכֹּהֵן בְּרֹאשׁוֹ
מה נִגְעוֹ: וְהַצָּרוּעַ אֲשֶׁר־בּוֹ הַנֶּגַע בְּגָדָיו יִהְיוּ פְרֻמִים וְרֹאשׁוֹ יִהְיֶה פָרוּעַ
מו וְעַל־שָׂפָם יַעְטֶה וְטָמֵא | טָמֵא יִקְרָא: כָּל־יְמֵי אֲשֶׁר הַנֶּגַע בּוֹ יִטְמָא
מז טָמֵא הוּא בָּדָד יֵשֵׁב מִחוּץ לַמַּחֲנֶה מוֹשָׁבוֹ: וְהַבֶּגֶד כִּי־
מח יִהְיֶה בוֹ נֶגַע צָרָעַת בְּבֶגֶד צֶמֶר אוֹ בְּבֶגֶד פִּשְׁתִּים: אוֹ בִשְׁתִי אוֹ בְעֵרֶב
מט לַפִּשְׁתִּים וְלַצָּמֶר אוֹ בְעוֹר אוֹ בְּכָל־מְלֶאכֶת עוֹר: וְהָיָה הַנֶּגַע יְרַקְרַק |
אוֹ אֲדַמְדָּם בַּבֶּגֶד אוֹ בָעוֹר אוֹ־בַשְּׁתִי אוֹ־בָעֵרֶב אוֹ בְכָל־כְּלִי־עוֹר נֶגַע
נ צָרַעַת הוּא וְהָרְאָה אֶת־הַכֹּהֵן: וְרָאָה הַכֹּהֵן אֶת־הַנָּגַע וְהִסְגִּיר אֶת־
נא הַנֶּגַע שִׁבְעַת יָמִים: וְרָאָה אֶת־הַנֶּגַע בַּיּוֹם הַשְּׁבִיעִי כִּי־פָשָׂה הַנֶּגַע
בַּבֶּגֶד אוֹ־בַשְּׁתִי אוֹ־בָעֵרֶב אוֹ בָעוֹר לְכֹל אֲשֶׁר־יֵעָשֶׂה הָעוֹר לִמְלָאכָה
נב צָרַעַת מַמְאֶרֶת הַנֶּגַע טָמֵא הוּא: וְשָׂרַף אֶת־הַבֶּגֶד אוֹ אֶת־הַשְּׁתִי |
אוֹ אֶת־הָעֵרֶב בַּצֶּמֶר אוֹ בַפִּשְׁתִּים אוֹ אֶת־כָּל־כְּלִי הָעוֹר אֲשֶׁר־יִהְיֶה
נג בוֹ הַנָּגַע כִּי־צָרַעַת מַמְאֶרֶת הִוא בָּאֵשׁ תִּשָּׂרֵף: וְאִם יִרְאֶה הַכֹּהֵן
וְהִנֵּה לֹא־פָשָׂה הַנֶּגַע בַּבֶּגֶד אוֹ בַשְּׁתִי אוֹ בָעֵרֶב אוֹ בְּכָל־כְּלִי־עוֹר:
נד וְצִוָּה הַכֹּהֵן וְכִבְּסוּ אֵת אֲשֶׁר־בּוֹ הַנָּגַע וְהִסְגִּירוֹ שִׁבְעַת־יָמִים שֵׁנִית:
נה וְרָאָה הַכֹּהֵן אַחֲרֵי | הֻכַּבֵּס אֶת־הַנֶּגַע וְהִנֵּה לֹא־הָפַךְ הַנֶּגַע אֶת־עֵינוֹ שביעי /רביעי/
וְהַנֶּגַע לֹא־פָשָׂה טָמֵא הוּא בָּאֵשׁ תִּשְׂרְפֶנּוּ פְּחֶתֶת הִוא בְּקָרַחְתּוֹ אוֹ
נו בְגַבַּחְתּוֹ: וְאִם רָאָה הַכֹּהֵן וְהִנֵּה כֵּהָה הַנֶּגַע אַחֲרֵי הֻכַּבֵּס אֹתוֹ וְקָרַע
נז אֹתוֹ מִן־הַבֶּגֶד אוֹ מִן־הָעוֹר אוֹ מִן־הַשְּׁתִי אוֹ מִן־הָעֵרֶב: וְאִם־תֵּרָאֶה מפטיר
עוֹד בַּבֶּגֶד אוֹ־בַשְּׁתִי אוֹ־בָעֵרֶב אוֹ בְכָל־כְּלִי־עוֹר פֹּרַחַת הִוא בָּאֵשׁ
נח תִּשְׂרְפֶנּוּ אֵת אֲשֶׁר־בּוֹ הַנָּגַע: וְהַבֶּגֶד אוֹ־הַשְּׁתִי אוֹ־הָעֵרֶב אוֹ־כָל־כְּלִי
נט הָעוֹר אֲשֶׁר תְּכַבֵּס וְסָר מֵהֶם הַנָּגַע וְכֻבַּס שֵׁנִית וְטָהֵר: זֹאת תּוֹרַת
נֶגַע־צָרַעַת בֶּגֶד הַצֶּמֶר | אוֹ הַפִּשְׁתִּים אוֹ הַשְּׁתִי אוֹ הָעֵרֶב אוֹ כָּל־
כְּלִי־עוֹר לְטַהֲרוֹ אוֹ לְטַמְּאוֹ:

יד א ב וַיְדַבֵּר יְהוָה אֶל־מֹשֶׁה לֵּאמֹר: זֹאת תִּהְיֶה תּוֹרַת הַמְּצֹרָע בְּיוֹם ט מצרע

3 priest, and the priest shall go out of the camp to examine him. If the disease
4 is healed in the blighted person, the priest shall command two living ritually
pure birds, and cedarwood, scarlet wool, and hyssop to be brought for the
5 one who is to be purified. The priest shall command one of the birds to be
6 slaughtered into an earthen vessel, over living water.[31] Then he shall take the
living bird, together with the cedarwood, the scarlet wool, and the hyssop,
and dip them and the living bird in the blood of the bird that was killed over
7 living water. With these he shall sprinkle seven times over the one who is to
be purified of the blight to purify him; and he shall set the living bird free
8 into the open field. The one who is to be purified shall then wash his clothes,
shave off all his hair, and immerse himself in water; then he shall be purified.
After that he may come into the camp, but he shall dwell outside his tent for
9 seven days. On the seventh day he shall shave all the hair from his head, his
beard, and his eyebrows. When he has shaved off all his hair, he shall wash his
10 clothes and immerse his body in water, and he shall be pure. On the eighth
day he shall take two unblemished male lambs and one unblemished ewe
lamb in its first year, with three-tenths of an ephah of fine flour mixed with
11 oil as a grain offering, and one *log* of oil. The priest who purifies shall present
the one to be purified, together with these, to the LORD at the entrance to the
12 Tent of Meeting. The priest shall take one of the male lambs and offer it as a
guilt offering, along with the *log* of oil; he shall display these, this way and that,
13 as a wave offering before the LORD. He shall slaughter the lamb in the place
where purification offerings and burnt offerings are slaughtered within the
holy place. For the guilt offering, like the purification offering, belongs to the
14 priest and is holy of holies. The priest shall take some of the blood of the guilt
offering and apply it to the ridge of the right ear, to the right thumb, and to the
15 right big toe of the one who is to be purified. The priest shall pour some of the
16 *log* of oil into his own left palm, dip his right finger into the oil in his left hand,
17 and sprinkle of the oil with his finger seven times before the LORD. The priest
shall apply some of the remaining oil in his hand to the ridge of the right ear,
to the right thumb, and to the right big toe of the one who is to be purified,
18 over the guilt offering blood. What remains of the oil in his hand the priest
shall pour on the head of the one to be purified. Thus shall the priest make
19 his atonement before the LORD. Then the priest shall offer the purification
offering to make atonement for the one to be purified of his defilement. Then
20 he shall slaughter the burnt offering.[32] The priest shall offer the burnt offering
and the grain offering on the altar.[33] Thus shall the priest make his atonement,
21 and he shall be purified. If, however, the person is poor and cannot
afford so much, he shall take one male lamb as a guilt offering to be made
a wave offering[34] to make his atonement, and one-tenth of an ephah of fine

31 | Water that is taken from a flowing source.

32 | Verse 10 refers to three animals, which are used for a guilt offering, a purification offering, and a burnt offering.

33 | Most parts of the other offerings, by contrast, are eaten by the priests.

34 | The Torah clarifies this procedure in the next passage.

ג טָהֳרָתוֹ וְהוּבָא אֶל־הַכֹּהֵן: וְיָצָא הַכֹּהֵן אֶל־מִחוּץ לַמַּחֲנֶה וְרָאָה הַכֹּהֵן
ד וְהִנֵּה נִרְפָּא נֶגַע־הַצָּרַעַת מִן־הַצָּרוּעַ: וְצִוָּה הַכֹּהֵן וְלָקַח לַמִּטַּהֵר
ה שְׁתֵּי־צִפֳּרִים חַיּוֹת טְהֹרוֹת וְעֵץ אֶרֶז וּשְׁנִי תוֹלַעַת וְאֵזֹב: וְצִוָּה הַכֹּהֵן
ו וְשָׁחַט אֶת־הַצִּפּוֹר הָאֶחָת אֶל־כְּלִי־חֶרֶשׂ עַל־מַיִם חַיִּים: אֶת־הַצִּפֹּר
הַחַיָּה יִקַּח אֹתָהּ וְאֶת־עֵץ הָאֶרֶז וְאֶת־שְׁנִי הַתּוֹלַעַת וְאֶת־הָאֵזֹב וְטָבַל
אוֹתָם וְאֵת ׀ הַצִּפֹּר הַחַיָּה בְּדַם הַצִּפֹּר הַשְּׁחֻטָה עַל הַמַּיִם הַחַיִּים:
ז וְהִזָּה עַל הַמִּטַּהֵר מִן־הַצָּרַעַת שֶׁבַע פְּעָמִים וְטִהֲרוֹ וְשִׁלַּח אֶת־
ח הַצִּפֹּר הַחַיָּה עַל־פְּנֵי הַשָּׂדֶה: וְכִבֶּס הַמִּטַּהֵר אֶת־בְּגָדָיו וְגִלַּח אֶת־
כָּל־שְׂעָרוֹ וְרָחַץ בַּמַּיִם וְטָהֵר וְאַחַר יָבוֹא אֶל־הַמַּחֲנֶה וְיָשַׁב מִחוּץ
ט לְאָהֳלוֹ שִׁבְעַת יָמִים: וְהָיָה בַיּוֹם הַשְּׁבִיעִי יְגַלַּח אֶת־כָּל־שְׂעָרוֹ אֶת־
רֹאשׁוֹ וְאֶת־זְקָנוֹ וְאֵת גַּבֹּת עֵינָיו וְאֶת־כָּל־שְׂעָרוֹ יְגַלֵּחַ וְכִבֶּס אֶת־
י בְּגָדָיו וְרָחַץ אֶת־בְּשָׂרוֹ בַּמַּיִם וְטָהֵר: וּבַיּוֹם הַשְּׁמִינִי יִקַּח שְׁנֵי־כְבָשִׂים
תְּמִימִם וְכַבְשָׂה אַחַת בַּת־שְׁנָתָהּ תְּמִימָה וּשְׁלֹשָׁה עֶשְׂרֹנִים סֹלֶת
יא מִנְחָה בְּלוּלָה בַשֶּׁמֶן וְלֹג אֶחָד שָׁמֶן: וְהֶעֱמִיד הַכֹּהֵן הַמְטַהֵר אֵת
יב הָאִישׁ הַמִּטַּהֵר וְאֹתָם לִפְנֵי יהוה פֶּתַח אֹהֶל מוֹעֵד: וְלָקַח הַכֹּהֵן
אֶת־הַכֶּבֶשׂ הָאֶחָד וְהִקְרִיב אֹתוֹ לְאָשָׁם וְאֶת־לֹג הַשָּׁמֶן וְהֵנִיף אֹתָם
יג תְּנוּפָה לִפְנֵי יהוה: וְשָׁחַט אֶת־הַכֶּבֶשׂ בִּמְקוֹם אֲשֶׁר יִשְׁחַט אֶת־ שני
הַחַטָּאת וְאֶת־הָעֹלָה בִּמְקוֹם הַקֹּדֶשׁ כִּי כַּחַטָּאת הָאָשָׁם הוּא לַכֹּהֵן
יד קֹדֶשׁ קָדָשִׁים הוּא: וְלָקַח הַכֹּהֵן מִדַּם הָאָשָׁם וְנָתַן הַכֹּהֵן עַל־תְּנוּךְ
אֹזֶן הַמִּטַּהֵר הַיְמָנִית וְעַל־בֹּהֶן יָדוֹ הַיְמָנִית וְעַל־בֹּהֶן רַגְלוֹ הַיְמָנִית:
טו טז וְלָקַח הַכֹּהֵן מִלֹּג הַשָּׁמֶן וְיָצַק עַל־כַּף הַכֹּהֵן הַשְּׂמָאלִית: וְטָבַל הַכֹּהֵן
אֶת־אֶצְבָּעוֹ הַיְמָנִית מִן־הַשֶּׁמֶן אֲשֶׁר עַל־כַּפּוֹ הַשְּׂמָאלִית וְהִזָּה מִן־
יז הַשֶּׁמֶן בְּאֶצְבָּעוֹ שֶׁבַע פְּעָמִים לִפְנֵי יהוה: וּמִיֶּתֶר הַשֶּׁמֶן אֲשֶׁר עַל־
כַּפּוֹ יִתֵּן הַכֹּהֵן עַל־תְּנוּךְ אֹזֶן הַמִּטַּהֵר הַיְמָנִית וְעַל־בֹּהֶן יָדוֹ הַיְמָנִית
יח וְעַל־בֹּהֶן רַגְלוֹ הַיְמָנִית עַל דַּם הָאָשָׁם: וְהַנּוֹתָר בַּשֶּׁמֶן אֲשֶׁר עַל־כַּף
יט הַכֹּהֵן יִתֵּן עַל־רֹאשׁ הַמִּטַּהֵר וְכִפֶּר עָלָיו הַכֹּהֵן לִפְנֵי יהוה: וְעָשָׂה הַכֹּהֵן
אֶת־הַחַטָּאת וְכִפֶּר עַל־הַמִּטַּהֵר מִטֻּמְאָתוֹ וְאַחַר יִשְׁחַט אֶת־הָעֹלָה:
כ וְהֶעֱלָה הַכֹּהֵן אֶת־הָעֹלָה וְאֶת־הַמִּנְחָה הַמִּזְבֵּחָה וְכִפֶּר עָלָיו הַכֹּהֵן
כא וְטָהֵר: וְאִם־דַּל הוּא וְאֵין יָדוֹ מַשֶּׂגֶת וְלָקַח כֶּבֶשׂ אֶחָד שלישי /חמישי/
אָשָׁם לִתְנוּפָה לְכַפֵּר עָלָיו וְעִשָּׂרוֹן סֹלֶת אֶחָד בָּלוּל בַּשֶּׁמֶן לְמִנְחָה

22 flour mixed with oil as a grain offering, and a *log* of oil, and two doves or two
pigeons, such as he can afford; one shall be a purification offering and the
23 other a burnt offering. On the eighth day of his purification, he shall bring
them to the priest at the entrance to the Tent of Meeting before the LORD.
24 The priest shall take the lamb of the guilt offering, together with the *log* of oil,
25 and move them this way and that as a wave offering before the LORD. Then he
shall slaughter the guilt offering lamb. The priest shall take some of the blood
of the guilt offering and apply it to the ridge of the right ear, to the right thumb,
26 and to the right big toe of the one who is to be purified. The priest shall then
27 pour some of the oil into his own left palm, and, using his right finger, shall
28 sprinkle of the oil that is in his left hand seven times before the LORD. He
shall apply some of the oil remaining in his hand to the ridge of the right ear,
to the right thumb, and to the right big toe of the person to be purified, over
29 the guilt offering blood. What remains of the oil in his hand the priest shall
pour on the head of the one to be purified, to make his atonement before the
30 LORD. He shall then offer up one of the doves or pigeons the person could
31 afford; whatever he can afford, one as a purification offering, and the other
as a burnt offering, together with the grain offering; and thus shall the priest
32 make atonement for the person who is to be purified before the LORD." This
is the law for a person who has an impure blight and cannot afford the regular
offerings for his purification.

33 34 The LORD spoke to Moshe and to Aharon: "When you enter the land of
Canaan that I am giving you as a possession, and I afflict a house in the land
35 you possess with an impure blight, the owner of the house shall come and
36 tell the priest, 'It looks to me as if there were some disease in the house.' The
priest shall instruct them to empty the house before he goes to examine the
disease, to prevent everything in the house from becoming impure. After that,
37 the priest shall go to examine the house. He shall look at the disease. If the
disease is in the walls of the house with greenish or reddish spots that appear
38 to go deep into the wall, the priest shall go out to the door of the house and
39 shut the house up for seven days. On the seventh day, the priest shall return;
40 he shall examine the disease and, if it has spread in the walls of the house, the
priest shall order the stones in which the disease appears to be removed and
41 thrown into a ritually impure place outside the town. He shall have the inside
of the house scraped all around, and the plaster that they scrape off shall be
42 poured out in an impure place outside the city. They shall take other stones
and put them in the place of those stones, and take new plaster and replaster
43 the house. If the disease breaks out again in the house after the stones have
44 been removed and the house has been scraped and plastered, the priest shall
come back and examine it. If the disease has spread, then there is malignant
45 blight in the house; it is impure. He shall have the house torn down, its stones,
timber, and all the plaster from the house, and have them all taken outside the
46 town to an impure place. Anyone who entered the house while it was shut up

כב וְלֹג שָׁמֶן: וּשְׁתֵּי תֹרִים אוֹ שְׁנֵי בְּנֵי יוֹנָה אֲשֶׁר תַּשִּׂיג יָדוֹ וְהָיָה אֶחָד
כג חַטָּאת וְהָאֶחָד עֹלָה: וְהֵבִיא אֹתָם בַּיּוֹם הַשְּׁמִינִי לְטׇהֳרָתוֹ אֶל־הַכֹּהֵן
כד אֶל־פֶּתַח אֹהֶל־מוֹעֵד לִפְנֵי יהוה: וְלָקַח הַכֹּהֵן אֶת־כֶּבֶשׂ הָאָשָׁם
כה וְאֶת־לֹג הַשָּׁמֶן וְהֵנִיף אֹתָם הַכֹּהֵן תְּנוּפָה לִפְנֵי יהוה: וְשָׁחַט אֶת־כֶּבֶשׂ
הָאָשָׁם וְלָקַח הַכֹּהֵן מִדַּם הָאָשָׁם וְנָתַן עַל־תְּנוּךְ אֹזֶן־הַמִּטַּהֵר הַיְמָנִית
כו וְעַל־בֹּהֶן יָדוֹ הַיְמָנִית וְעַל־בֹּהֶן רַגְלוֹ הַיְמָנִית: וּמִן־הַשֶּׁמֶן יִצֹק הַכֹּהֵן
כז עַל־כַּף הַכֹּהֵן הַשְּׂמָאלִית: וְהִזָּה הַכֹּהֵן בְּאֶצְבָּעוֹ הַיְמָנִית מִן־הַשֶּׁמֶן
כח אֲשֶׁר עַל־כַּפּוֹ הַשְּׂמָאלִית שֶׁבַע פְּעָמִים לִפְנֵי יהוה: וְנָתַן הַכֹּהֵן מִן־
הַשֶּׁמֶן ׀ אֲשֶׁר עַל־כַּפּוֹ עַל־תְּנוּךְ אֹזֶן הַמִּטַּהֵר הַיְמָנִית וְעַל־בֹּהֶן יָדוֹ
כט הַיְמָנִית וְעַל־בֹּהֶן רַגְלוֹ הַיְמָנִית עַל־מְקוֹם דַּם הָאָשָׁם: וְהַנּוֹתָר מִן־
הַשֶּׁמֶן אֲשֶׁר עַל־כַּף הַכֹּהֵן יִתֵּן עַל־רֹאשׁ הַמִּטַּהֵר לְכַפֵּר עָלָיו לִפְנֵי
ל יהוה: וְעָשָׂה אֶת־הָאֶחָד מִן־הַתֹּרִים אוֹ מִן־בְּנֵי הַיּוֹנָה מֵאֲשֶׁר תַּשִּׂיג
לא יָדוֹ: אֵת אֲשֶׁר־תַּשִּׂיג יָדוֹ אֶת־הָאֶחָד חַטָּאת וְאֶת־הָאֶחָד עֹלָה עַל־
לב הַמִּנְחָה וְכִפֶּר הַכֹּהֵן עַל הַמִּטַּהֵר לִפְנֵי יהוה: זֹאת תּוֹרַת אֲשֶׁר־בּוֹ
נֶגַע צָרָעַת אֲשֶׁר לֹא־תַשִּׂיג יָדוֹ בְּטׇהֳרָתוֹ:
לג לד י וַיְדַבֵּר יהוה אֶל־מֹשֶׁה וְאֶל־אַהֲרֹן לֵאמֹר: כִּי תָבֹאוּ אֶל־אֶרֶץ כְּנַעַן רביעי /ששי/
אֲשֶׁר אֲנִי נֹתֵן לָכֶם לַאֲחֻזָּה וְנָתַתִּי נֶגַע צָרַעַת בְּבֵית אֶרֶץ אֲחֻזַּתְכֶם:
לה לו וּבָא אֲשֶׁר־לוֹ הַבַּיִת וְהִגִּיד לַכֹּהֵן לֵאמֹר כְּנֶגַע נִרְאָה לִי בַּבָּיִת: וְצִוָּה
הַכֹּהֵן וּפִנּוּ אֶת־הַבַּיִת בְּטֶרֶם יָבֹא הַכֹּהֵן לִרְאוֹת אֶת־הַנֶּגַע וְלֹא יִטְמָא
לז כׇּל־אֲשֶׁר בַּבָּיִת וְאַחַר כֵּן יָבֹא הַכֹּהֵן לִרְאוֹת אֶת־הַבָּיִת: וְרָאָה אֶת־
הַנֶּגַע וְהִנֵּה הַנֶּגַע בְּקִירֹת הַבַּיִת שְׁקַעֲרוּרֹת יְרַקְרַקֹּת אוֹ אֲדַמְדַּמֹּת
לח וּמַרְאֵיהֶן שָׁפָל מִן־הַקִּיר: וְיָצָא הַכֹּהֵן מִן־הַבַּיִת אֶל־פֶּתַח הַבָּיִת
לט וְהִסְגִּיר אֶת־הַבַּיִת שִׁבְעַת יָמִים: וְשָׁב הַכֹּהֵן בַּיּוֹם הַשְּׁבִיעִי וְרָאָה וְהִנֵּה
מ פָּשָׂה הַנֶּגַע בְּקִירֹת הַבָּיִת: וְצִוָּה הַכֹּהֵן וְחִלְּצוּ אֶת־הָאֲבָנִים אֲשֶׁר בָּהֵן
מא הַנָּגַע וְהִשְׁלִיכוּ אֶתְהֶן אֶל־מִחוּץ לָעִיר אֶל־מָקוֹם טָמֵא: וְאֶת־הַבַּיִת
יַקְצִעַ מִבַּיִת סָבִיב וְשָׁפְכוּ אֶת־הֶעָפָר אֲשֶׁר הִקְצוּ אֶל־מִחוּץ לָעִיר
מב אֶל־מָקוֹם טָמֵא: וְלָקְחוּ אֲבָנִים אֲחֵרוֹת וְהֵבִיאוּ אֶל־תַּחַת הָאֲבָנִים
מג וְעָפָר אַחֵר יִקַּח וְטָח אֶת־הַבָּיִת: וְאִם־יָשׁוּב הַנֶּגַע וּפָרַח בַּבַּיִת אַחַר
מד חִלֵּץ אֶת־הָאֲבָנִים וְאַחֲרֵי הִקְצוֹת אֶת־הַבַּיִת וְאַחֲרֵי הִטּוֹחַ: וּבָא
הַכֹּהֵן וְרָאָה וְהִנֵּה פָּשָׂה הַנֶּגַע בַּבָּיִת צָרַעַת מַמְאֶרֶת הִוא בַּבַּיִת
מה טָמֵא הוּא: וְנָתַץ אֶת־הַבַּיִת אֶת־אֲבָנָיו וְאֶת־עֵצָיו וְאֵת כׇּל־עֲפַר
מו הַבָּיִת וְהוֹצִיא אֶל־מִחוּץ לָעִיר אֶל־מָקוֹם טָמֵא: וְהַבָּא אֶל־הַבַּיִת

47 shall be impure until the evening. Anyone who slept in the house shall wash
48 his clothes; anyone who ate in the house shall wash his clothes. If, however,
the priest comes and examines it and the disease has not spread in the house
after its plastering, then the priest shall pronounce the house pure; the disease
49 is healed. He shall take two birds, and cedarwood, scarlet wool, and hyssop to
50 purify the house. He shall slaughter one of the birds in an earthen vessel over
51 living water. He shall take the cedarwood, the hyssop, the scarlet wool, and
the living bird and dip them in the blood of the slaughtered bird, in the living
52 water, and sprinkle the house seven times. He shall purify the house with the
blood of the bird and the living water, with the living bird, the cedarwood,
53 the hyssop, and the scarlet wool. And he shall send the living bird forth free
outside the city, into the open field. Thus shall he make atonement for the
54 house,[35] and it shall be purified." This is the law for every impure blight of
55 56 disease, for a scaling eruption, for blight of a garment or a house, and for
57 swellings, eruptions, and bright patches on the skin, to determine when they
are impure and when they are pure. This is the law of the blight.
15 1 2 The Lord spoke to Moshe and Aharon: "Speak to the Israelites. Say: When
3 any man has a genital discharge,[36] he is rendered impure. This is the impurity
brought about by his discharge: whether his member allows the discharge
4 to flow or whether it blocks it, the discharge renders him impure, so that any
5 bed he lies upon and any object he sits upon becomes impure. Anyone who
touches his bed shall wash his clothes, immerse in water, and remain impure
6 until evening. Anyone who sits on something he has sat upon shall wash
7 his clothes, immerse in water, and remain impure until evening. Anyone
who touches his body shall wash his clothes, immerse in water, and remain
8 impure until evening. If the man with the discharge spits on a person who
is pure, that person shall wash his clothes, immerse in water, and remain
9 impure until evening. Any saddle on which the man with the discharge rides
10 becomes impure. Anyone who touches anything that was underneath him
shall be impure until evening. Anyone who moves[37] such an item shall wash
11 his clothes, immerse in water, and be impure until evening. If the man with
the discharge touches someone without first washing his hands with water,
that person shall wash his clothes, immerse in water, and remain impure
12 until evening. Any earthen vessel that the man with the discharge touches
13 shall be broken, any wooden vessel immersed in water. When the man with
the discharge is purified of it, he shall count seven days for his purification.
Then he shall wash his clothes and immerse his body in flowing water; then
14 he is pure. On the eighth day he shall take two doves or two pigeons before
the Lord to the entrance of the Tent of Meeting and give them to the priest.
15 The priest shall offer them, one as a purification offering, the other as a burnt

35 | Perhaps for the sins of the house's owner. Others render the formulation in the sense of "purification" instead of "atonement"; cf. 12:7.

36 | Generally identified as gonorrhea. Verses 16–17 assign a different law to the emission of semen.

37 | Literally "carries." In rabbinic law, however, this rule applies to one who moves the object even without lifting it.

מז כל־ימי הסגיר אתו יטמא עד־הערב: והשכב בבית יכבס את־בגדיו
מח והאכל בבית יכבס את־בגדיו: ואם־בא יבא הכהן וראה והנה לא־
פשה הנגע בבית אחרי הטח את־הבית וטהר הכהן את־הבית כי
מט נרפא הנגע: ולקח לחטא את־הבית שתי צפרים ועץ ארז ושני
נ תולעת ואזב: ושחט את־הצפר האחת אל־כלי־חרש על־מים
נא חיים: ולקח את־עץ־הארז ואת־האזב ואת | שני התולעת ואת
הצפר החיה וטבל אתם בדם הצפר השחוטה ובמים החיים והזה
נב אל־הבית שבע פעמים: וחטא את־הבית בדם הצפור ובמים החיים
נג ובצפר החיה ובעץ הארז ובאזב ובשני התולעת: ושלח את־הצפר
נד החיה אל־מחוץ לעיר אל־פני השדה וכפר על־הבית וטהר: זאת חמישי
נה נו התורה לכל־נגע הצרעת ולנתק: ולצרעת הבגד ולבית: ולשאת
נז ולספחת ולבהרת: להורת ביום הטמא וביום הטהר זאת תורת
הצרעת:

טו א ב וידבר יהוה אל־משה ואל־אהרן לאמר: דברו אל־בני ישראל יא
ג ואמרתם אלהם איש איש כי יהיה זב מבשרו זובו טמא הוא: וזאת
תהיה טמאתו בזובו רר בשרו את־זובו או־החתים בשרו מזובו
ד טמאתו הוא: כל־המשכב אשר ישכב עליו הזב יטמא וכל־הכלי
ה אשר־ישב עליו יטמא: ואיש אשר יגע במשכבו יכבס בגדיו ורחץ
ו במים וטמא עד־הערב: והישב על־הכלי אשר־ישב עליו הזב יכבס
ז בגדיו ורחץ במים וטמא עד־הערב: והנגע בבשר הזב יכבס בגדיו
ח ורחץ במים וטמא עד־הערב: וכי־ירק הזב בטהור וכבס בגדיו ורחץ
ט במים וטמא עד־הערב: וכל־המרכב אשר ירכב עליו הזב יטמא:
י וכל־הנגע בכל אשר יהיה תחתיו יטמא עד־הערב והנושא אותם
יא יכבס בגדיו ורחץ במים וטמא עד־הערב: וכל אשר יגע־בו הזב
וידיו לא־שטף במים וכבס בגדיו ורחץ במים וטמא עד־הערב:
יב יג וכלי־חרש אשר־יגע־בו הזב ישבר וכל־כלי־עץ ישטף במים: וכי־
יטהר הזב מזובו וספר לו שבעת ימים לטהרתו וכבס בגדיו ורחץ
יד בשרו במים חיים וטהר: וביום השמיני יקח־לו שתי תרים או שני
בני יונה ובא | לפני יהוה אל־פתח אהל מועד ונתנם אל־הכהן:
טו ועשה אתם הכהן אחד חטאת והאחד עלה וכפר עליו הכהן לפני

offering. Thus shall the priest make the man's atonement before the Lord
16 after his discharge. If a man has an emission of semen, he shall
17 immerse his entire body in water, and he remains impure until evening. Any
clothing or leather on which there is an emission of semen shall be washed
18 in water and shall be impure until evening. And any woman with whom a
man lies carnally – both partners shall immerse in water and remain impure
until evening.
19 When a woman has a discharge of blood that is her usual bodily discharge,
she retains her menstrual status for seven days. Any person who touches her
20 then shall be impure until evening. Anything on which she lies or sits during
21 her menstrual time becomes impure. Whoever touches her bed shall wash
22 his clothes, immerse in water, and remain impure until evening. Whoever
touches any object she has sat upon shall wash his clothes, immerse in water,
23 and remain impure until evening. Whether it be a bed or any object she
24 sits upon, when one touches it he shall be impure until evening. If a man
has sexual relations with her, her menstrual status is extended to him; he
too shall be impure for seven days, and any bed he lies upon is rendered
25 impure. Whenever a woman has a discharge of blood for many days
at a time other than her menstrual period, or if she has a discharge beyond
her menstrual period, she shall be impure as long as she has the discharge,
26 as she is in her menstrual time. Any bed she lies upon while she has this
discharge shall be treated like the bed she uses during her menstruation,
and any object she sits upon becomes impure, as during her menstrual time.
27 Whoever touches these things is rendered impure; he shall wash his clothes,
28 immerse in water, and remain impure until evening. When the woman's
discharge ends,[38] she shall count seven days; after that, she will be purified.
29 On the eighth day she shall take two doves or two pigeons and bring them
30 to the priest at the entrance to the Tent of Meeting. The priest shall prepare
one as a purification offering and the other as a burnt offering. Thus shall the
priest make her atonement before the Lord following her impure discharge.
31 You must separate the Israelites from their own impurity so that they do not
32 die in their impurity by making My Tabernacle impure in their midst." This is
the law concerning the man who is impure because of a discharge or seminal
33 emission, the woman during her menstrual period, the man or woman who
has a discharge, and the man who has sexual relations with a woman who is
impure.

AHAREI MOT

16 1 After the deaths of Aharon's two sons – when they came close to the Lord
2 and died – the Lord spoke to Moshe. "Tell your brother Aharon," said the
Lord to Moshe, "that he may not come at any time[39] into the holy place inside
the inner curtain in front of the cover on the Ark, or he will die – for in a cloud
3 above the cover I appear. This is how Aharon is to enter the holy place: with
4 a young bull as a purification offering and a ram as a burnt offering; he shall
put on the sacred linen tunic with linen undergarments covering his body.

---

38 | Referring to the extended, unnatural discharge mentioned in verse 25.

39 | Meaning except under the circumstances described below. Alternatively, "any time he wants."

טז יְהוָה מִזּוֹבוֹ׃ וְאִישׁ כִּי־תֵצֵא מִמֶּנּוּ שִׁכְבַת־זָרַע וְרָחַץ בַּמַּיִם ששי /שביעי/
יז אֶת־כָּל־בְּשָׂרוֹ וְטָמֵא עַד־הָעָרֶב׃ וְכָל־בֶּגֶד וְכָל־עוֹר אֲשֶׁר־יִהְיֶה עָלָיו
יח שִׁכְבַת־זָרַע וְכֻבַּס בַּמַּיִם וְטָמֵא עַד־הָעָרֶב׃ וְאִשָּׁה אֲשֶׁר יִשְׁכַּב אִישׁ
אֹתָהּ שִׁכְבַת־זָרַע וְרָחֲצוּ בַמַּיִם וְטָמְאוּ עַד־הָעָרֶב׃
יט וְאִשָּׁה כִּי־תִהְיֶה זָבָה דָּם יִהְיֶה זֹבָהּ בִּבְשָׂרָהּ שִׁבְעַת יָמִים תִּהְיֶה
כ בְנִדָּתָהּ וְכָל־הַנֹּגֵעַ בָּהּ יִטְמָא עַד־הָעָרֶב׃ וְכֹל אֲשֶׁר תִּשְׁכַּב עָלָיו
כא בְּנִדָּתָהּ יִטְמָא וְכֹל אֲשֶׁר־תֵּשֵׁב עָלָיו יִטְמָא׃ וְכָל־הַנֹּגֵעַ בְּמִשְׁכָּבָהּ
כב יְכַבֵּס בְּגָדָיו וְרָחַץ בַּמַּיִם וְטָמֵא עַד־הָעָרֶב׃ וְכָל־הַנֹּגֵעַ בְּכָל־כְּלִי
כג אֲשֶׁר־תֵּשֵׁב עָלָיו יְכַבֵּס בְּגָדָיו וְרָחַץ בַּמַּיִם וְטָמֵא עַד־הָעָרֶב׃ וְאִם
עַל־הַמִּשְׁכָּב הוּא אוֹ עַל־הַכְּלִי אֲשֶׁר־הִוא יֹשֶׁבֶת־עָלָיו בְּנָגְעוֹ־בוֹ
כד יִטְמָא עַד־הָעָרֶב׃ וְאִם שָׁכֹב יִשְׁכַּב אִישׁ אֹתָהּ וּתְהִי נִדָּתָהּ עָלָיו וְטָמֵא
כה שִׁבְעַת יָמִים וְכָל־הַמִּשְׁכָּב אֲשֶׁר־יִשְׁכַּב עָלָיו יִטְמָא׃ וְאִשָּׁה יב
כִּי־יָזוּב זוֹב דָּמָהּ יָמִים רַבִּים בְּלֹא עֶת־נִדָּתָהּ אוֹ כִי־תָזוּב עַל־נִדָּתָהּ
כו כָּל־יְמֵי זוֹב טֻמְאָתָהּ כִּימֵי נִדָּתָהּ תִּהְיֶה טְמֵאָה הִוא׃ כָּל־הַמִּשְׁכָּב
אֲשֶׁר־תִּשְׁכַּב עָלָיו כָּל־יְמֵי זוֹבָהּ כְּמִשְׁכַּב נִדָּתָהּ יִהְיֶה־לָּהּ וְכָל־הַכְּלִי
כז אֲשֶׁר תֵּשֵׁב עָלָיו טָמֵא יִהְיֶה כְּטֻמְאַת נִדָּתָהּ׃ וְכָל־הַנּוֹגֵעַ בָּם יִטְמָא
כח וְכִבֶּס בְּגָדָיו וְרָחַץ בַּמַּיִם וְטָמֵא עַד־הָעָרֶב׃ וְאִם־טָהֲרָה מִזּוֹבָהּ
כט וְסָפְרָה לָּהּ שִׁבְעַת יָמִים וְאַחַר תִּטְהָר׃ וּבַיּוֹם הַשְּׁמִינִי תִּקַּח־לָהּ שביעי
שְׁתֵּי תֹרִים אוֹ שְׁנֵי בְּנֵי יוֹנָה וְהֵבִיאָה אוֹתָם אֶל־הַכֹּהֵן אֶל־פֶּתַח אֹהֶל
ל מוֹעֵד׃ וְעָשָׂה הַכֹּהֵן אֶת־הָאֶחָד חַטָּאת וְאֶת־הָאֶחָד עֹלָה וְכִפֶּר עָלֶיהָ
לא הַכֹּהֵן לִפְנֵי יְהוָה מִזּוֹב טֻמְאָתָהּ׃ וְהִזַּרְתֶּם אֶת־בְּנֵי־יִשְׂרָאֵל מִטֻּמְאָתָם מפטיר
לב וְלֹא יָמֻתוּ בְּטֻמְאָתָם בְּטַמְּאָם אֶת־מִשְׁכָּנִי אֲשֶׁר בְּתוֹכָם׃ זֹאת תּוֹרַת
לג הַזָּב וַאֲשֶׁר תֵּצֵא מִמֶּנּוּ שִׁכְבַת־זֶרַע לְטָמְאָה־בָהּ׃ וְהַדָּוָה בְּנִדָּתָהּ וְהַזָּב
אֶת־זוֹבוֹ לַזָּכָר וְלַנְּקֵבָה וּלְאִישׁ אֲשֶׁר יִשְׁכַּב עִם־טְמֵאָה׃
טז א וַיְדַבֵּר יְהוָה אֶל־מֹשֶׁה אַחֲרֵי מוֹת שְׁנֵי בְּנֵי אַהֲרֹן בְּקָרְבָתָם לִפְנֵי־ אחרי מות
ב יְהוָה וַיָּמֻתוּ׃ וַיֹּאמֶר יְהוָה אֶל־מֹשֶׁה דַּבֵּר אֶל־אַהֲרֹן אָחִיךָ וְאַל־יָבֹא
בְכָל־עֵת אֶל־הַקֹּדֶשׁ מִבֵּית לַפָּרֹכֶת אֶל־פְּנֵי הַכַּפֹּרֶת אֲשֶׁר עַל־הָאָרֹן
ג וְלֹא יָמוּת כִּי בֶּעָנָן אֵרָאֶה עַל־הַכַּפֹּרֶת׃ בְּזֹאת יָבֹא אַהֲרֹן אֶל־הַקֹּדֶשׁ
ד בְּפַר בֶּן־בָּקָר לְחַטָּאת וְאַיִל לְעֹלָה׃ כְּתֹנֶת־בַּד קֹדֶשׁ יִלְבָּשׁ וּמִכְנְסֵי־
בַד יִהְיוּ עַל־בְּשָׂרוֹ וּבְאַבְנֵט בַּד יַחְגֹּר וּבְמִצְנֶפֶת בַּד יִצְנֹף בִּגְדֵי־

He shall bind the linen sash around himself and wrap a linen turban about
his head. These are sacred vestments; he shall immerse himself in water and
5 only then put them on. From the community of Israel he shall take two male
6 goats for a purification offering and a ram for a burnt offering. And Aharon
shall bring close the bull for his purification offering, to make atonement for
7 him and for his family. He shall take the two goats and set them before the
8 Lord at the entrance to the Tent of Meeting. Aharon shall cast lots over the
9 two goats, one lot marked 'For the Lord,' the other 'For Azazel.'[40] The goat
on which the lot for the Lord fell, Aharon should bring close and offer up
10 as a purification offering. But the goat on which the lot fell for Azazel shall
be presented alive before the Lord; atonement shall be made over it; it shall
11 be sent forth, away into the wilderness to Azazel. Aharon shall bring close
the bull for his purification offering to make atonement for him and for his
12 family; he shall slaughter the bull as his purification offering. He shall then
take a pan full of burning coals from the altar, from before the Lord, and two
handfuls of finely ground fragrant incense, and bring them inside the inner
13 curtain. He shall place the incense on the fire before the Lord so that the
cloud of incense conceals the cover on top of the Ark of the Testimony, so that
14 he does not die.[41] He shall take some of the bull's blood and sprinkle it with
his finger on the cover on the east side. Then, in front of the cover, he shall
15 sprinkle some of the blood with his finger seven times. He shall then slaughter
the goat for the people's purification offering, bring its blood inside the inner
curtain, and do with it as he did with the blood of the bull, sprinkling it on
16 the cover and before the cover. In this way, he shall make atonement for the
Sanctuary – from the impurity of the Israelites, from their rebellions and all
their sins. And he shall do the same for the Tent of Meeting, which is with
17 them in the midst of their impurity. No one shall be in the Tent of Meeting
from the time Aharon enters to make atonement in the Sanctuary until he
comes out. Thus he shall make atonement for himself, for his house, and for
18 the whole assembly of Israel. He shall then go out to the altar that is before
the Lord and make its atonement. He shall take some of the bull's blood
19 and some of the goat's blood and apply it to each of the altar's horns. He shall
sprinkle some of the blood upon it with his finger seven times, to purify it and
20 sanctify it from the impurity of the Israelites. When he has finished making
atonement for the Sanctuary, the Tent of Meeting and the altar, he shall bring
21 close the live goat. Aharon shall lay both his hands on the head of the live
goat and confess over it all the Israelites' iniquities and rebellions, all of their
sins, putting them on the head of the goat and then sending it away into the
22 wilderness with the person designated for the task. The goat shall carry all
their iniquities upon itself to a desolate place, and then the goat shall be sent
23 forth into the wilderness. Then Aharon shall enter the Tent of Meeting, take
off the linen vestments he was wearing when he entered the Sanctuary, and
24 leave them there. He shall immerse his body in water in a holy place and put

40 | The word "Azazel" and the purpose of this ritual are subject to varying interpretations.

41 | As punishment for looking at the Divine Presence. See, e.g., verse 2; Exodus 25:22.

ה קֹדֶשׁ הֵם וְרָחַץ בַּמַּיִם אֶת־בְּשָׂרוֹ וּלְבֵשָׁם: וּמֵאֵת עֲדַת בְּנֵי יִשְׂרָאֵל
ו יִקַּח שְׁנֵי־שְׂעִירֵי עִזִּים לְחַטָּאת וְאַיִל אֶחָד לְעֹלָה: וְהִקְרִיב אַהֲרֹן
ז אֶת־פַּר הַחַטָּאת אֲשֶׁר־לוֹ וְכִפֶּר בַּעֲדוֹ וּבְעַד בֵּיתוֹ: וְלָקַח אֶת־שְׁנֵי
ח הַשְּׂעִירִם וְהֶעֱמִיד אֹתָם לִפְנֵי יהוה פֶּתַח אֹהֶל מוֹעֵד: וְנָתַן אַהֲרֹן
עַל־שְׁנֵי הַשְּׂעִירִם גֹּרָלוֹת גּוֹרָל אֶחָד לַיהוה וְגוֹרָל אֶחָד לַעֲזָאזֵל:
ט וְהִקְרִיב אַהֲרֹן אֶת־הַשָּׂעִיר אֲשֶׁר עָלָה עָלָיו הַגּוֹרָל לַיהוה וְעָשָׂהוּ
י חַטָּאת: וְהַשָּׂעִיר אֲשֶׁר עָלָה עָלָיו הַגּוֹרָל לַעֲזָאזֵל יָעֳמַד־חַי לִפְנֵי יהוה
יא לְכַפֵּר עָלָיו לְשַׁלַּח אֹתוֹ לַעֲזָאזֵל הַמִּדְבָּרָה: וְהִקְרִיב אַהֲרֹן אֶת־פַּר
הַחַטָּאת אֲשֶׁר־לוֹ וְכִפֶּר בַּעֲדוֹ וּבְעַד בֵּיתוֹ וְשָׁחַט אֶת־פַּר הַחַטָּאת
יב אֲשֶׁר־לוֹ: וְלָקַח מְלֹא־הַמַּחְתָּה גַּחֲלֵי־אֵשׁ מֵעַל הַמִּזְבֵּחַ מִלִּפְנֵי יהוה
יג וּמְלֹא חָפְנָיו קְטֹרֶת סַמִּים דַּקָּה וְהֵבִיא מִבֵּית לַפָּרֹכֶת: וְנָתַן אֶת־
הַקְּטֹרֶת עַל־הָאֵשׁ לִפְנֵי יהוה וְכִסָּה ׀ עֲנַן הַקְּטֹרֶת אֶת־הַכַּפֹּרֶת
יד אֲשֶׁר עַל־הָעֵדוּת וְלֹא יָמוּת: וְלָקַח מִדַּם הַפָּר וְהִזָּה בְאֶצְבָּעוֹ עַל־פְּנֵי
הַכַּפֹּרֶת קֵדְמָה וְלִפְנֵי הַכַּפֹּרֶת יַזֶּה שֶׁבַע־פְּעָמִים מִן־הַדָּם בְּאֶצְבָּעוֹ:
טו וְשָׁחַט אֶת־שְׂעִיר הַחַטָּאת אֲשֶׁר לָעָם וְהֵבִיא אֶת־דָּמוֹ אֶל־מִבֵּית
לַפָּרֹכֶת וְעָשָׂה אֶת־דָּמוֹ כַּאֲשֶׁר עָשָׂה לְדַם הַפָּר וְהִזָּה אֹתוֹ עַל־
טז הַכַּפֹּרֶת וְלִפְנֵי הַכַּפֹּרֶת: וְכִפֶּר עַל־הַקֹּדֶשׁ מִטֻּמְאֹת בְּנֵי יִשְׂרָאֵל
וּמִפִּשְׁעֵיהֶם לְכָל־חַטֹּאתָם וְכֵן יַעֲשֶׂה לְאֹהֶל מוֹעֵד הַשֹּׁכֵן אִתָּם בְּתוֹךְ
יז טֻמְאֹתָם: וְכָל־אָדָם לֹא־יִהְיֶה ׀ בְּאֹהֶל מוֹעֵד בְּבֹאוֹ לְכַפֵּר בַּקֹּדֶשׁ
יח עַד־צֵאתוֹ וְכִפֶּר בַּעֲדוֹ וּבְעַד בֵּיתוֹ וּבְעַד כָּל־קְהַל יִשְׂרָאֵל: וְיָצָא אֶל־ שני
הַמִּזְבֵּחַ אֲשֶׁר לִפְנֵי־יהוה וְכִפֶּר עָלָיו וְלָקַח מִדַּם הַפָּר וּמִדַּם הַשָּׂעִיר
יט וְנָתַן עַל־קַרְנוֹת הַמִּזְבֵּחַ סָבִיב: וְהִזָּה עָלָיו מִן־הַדָּם בְּאֶצְבָּעוֹ שֶׁבַע
כ פְּעָמִים וְטִהֲרוֹ וְקִדְּשׁוֹ מִטֻּמְאֹת בְּנֵי יִשְׂרָאֵל: וְכִלָּה מִכַּפֵּר אֶת־הַקֹּדֶשׁ
כא וְאֶת־אֹהֶל מוֹעֵד וְאֶת־הַמִּזְבֵּחַ וְהִקְרִיב אֶת־הַשָּׂעִיר הֶחָי: וְסָמַךְ אַהֲרֹן
אֶת־שְׁתֵּי יָדָו עַל־רֹאשׁ הַשָּׂעִיר הַחַי וְהִתְוַדָּה עָלָיו אֶת־כָּל־עֲוֹנֹת
בְּנֵי יִשְׂרָאֵל וְאֶת־כָּל־פִּשְׁעֵיהֶם לְכָל־חַטֹּאתָם וְנָתַן אֹתָם עַל־רֹאשׁ
כב הַשָּׂעִיר וְשִׁלַּח בְּיַד־אִישׁ עִתִּי הַמִּדְבָּרָה: וְנָשָׂא הַשָּׂעִיר עָלָיו אֶת־
כג כָּל־עֲוֹנֹתָם אֶל־אֶרֶץ גְּזֵרָה וְשִׁלַּח אֶת־הַשָּׂעִיר בַּמִּדְבָּר: וּבָא אַהֲרֹן
אֶל־אֹהֶל מוֹעֵד וּפָשַׁט אֶת־בִּגְדֵי הַבָּד אֲשֶׁר לָבַשׁ בְּבֹאוֹ אֶל־הַקֹּדֶשׁ
כד וְהִנִּיחָם שָׁם: וְרָחַץ אֶת־בְּשָׂרוֹ בַמַּיִם בְּמָקוֹם קָדוֹשׁ וְלָבַשׁ אֶת־בְּגָדָיו

on his vestments. Then he shall come out and offer his burnt offering and
the burnt offering of the people, to make atonement for himself and for the
25 people. And he shall send the fat of the purification offering up in smoke upon
26 the altar. The man who sent forth the goat for Azazel shall wash his clothes
27 and immerse his body in water; after that he may return to the camp. The
purification offering bull and the purification offering goat, whose blood was
brought in to make atonement in the inner Sanctuary, shall be removed from
28 the camp. Their skin, flesh, and dung shall be burned with fire. The one who
burns them shall wash his clothes and immerse his body in water. After that,
29 he too may return to the camp. This shall be an everlasting statute for you:
on the tenth day of the seventh month, you must afflict yourselves. You shall
perform no work at all – neither the native born nor the migrant living among
30 you. On this day, atonement shall be made for you to purify you; of all your
31 sins you shall be purified before the LORD. It shall be a Sabbath of complete
rest for you, and on it you shall afflict yourselves. This is an everlasting statute.
32 The priest who is anointed and ordained to succeed his father and serve as
33 priest[42] shall perform the atonement, wearing the sacred linen vestments. He
shall make atonement for the innermost Sanctuary, for the Tent of Meeting,
and for the altar. He shall make atonement for the priests and for all the
34 people of the community. This shall be an everlasting statute for you, making
atonement for the Israelites once a year for all their sins." And as the LORD
commanded Moshe, so it was done.
17 1 The LORD spoke to Moshe: "Speak to Aharon, his sons, and all the Israelites.
2
3 Say: This is what the LORD has commanded: Any Israelite who slaughters
4 an ox, sheep, or goat inside or outside the camp without then bringing it to
the entrance of the Tent of Meeting to bring close an offering to the LORD
before the LORD's Tabernacle will be considered guilty of bloodshed. He
5 has shed blood; he shall be severed from his people. For the Israelites must
bring the sacrifices they have been offering in the open fields – to the LORD,
to the priest at the entrance of the Tent of Meeting, and offer them as peace
6 sacrifices to the LORD. The priest shall dash the blood against the LORD's
altar at the entrance to the Tent of Meeting and send the fat up in smoke
7 as a pleasing aroma to the LORD; and no more may they offer sacrifices
to the goat demons to whom they prostitute themselves. This shall be an
8 everlasting statute for them throughout their generations. And you shall
tell them: Anyone of the House of Israel or any migrant living among you
9 who offers up a burnt offering or other sacrifice and does not bring it to the
entrance of the Tent of Meeting to offer it to the LORD shall be severed from
10 his people. Anyone of the House of Israel, or any migrant living among you,
who eats blood – I will set My face against that person who eats blood and will
11 sever him from his people, for the life of a creature is in its blood. I have given
it to you to make atonement for your lives on the altar, for blood, which is

42 | That is, the High Priest.

וְיָצָא וְעָשָׂה אֶת־עֹלָתוֹ וְאֶת־עֹלַת הָעָם וְכִפֶּר בַּעֲדוֹ וּבְעַד הָעָם׃
כה כו וְאֵת חֵלֶב הַחַטָּאת יַקְטִיר הַמִּזְבֵּחָה׃ וְהַמְשַׁלֵּחַ אֶת־הַשָּׂעִיר לַעֲזָאזֵל שלישי /שני/
יְכַבֵּס בְּגָדָיו וְרָחַץ אֶת־בְּשָׂרוֹ בַּמָּיִם וְאַחֲרֵי־כֵן יָבוֹא אֶל־הַמַּחֲנֶה׃
כז וְאֵת פַּר הַחַטָּאת וְאֵת ׀ שְׂעִיר הַחַטָּאת אֲשֶׁר הוּבָא אֶת־דָּמָם לְכַפֵּר
בַּקֹּדֶשׁ יוֹצִיא אֶל־מִחוּץ לַמַּחֲנֶה וְשָׂרְפוּ בָאֵשׁ אֶת־עֹרֹתָם וְאֶת־
כח בְּשָׂרָם וְאֶת־פִּרְשָׁם׃ וְהַשֹּׂרֵף אֹתָם יְכַבֵּס בְּגָדָיו וְרָחַץ אֶת־בְּשָׂרוֹ
כט בַּמָּיִם וְאַחֲרֵי־כֵן יָבוֹא אֶל־הַמַּחֲנֶה׃ וְהָיְתָה לָכֶם לְחֻקַּת עוֹלָם בַּחֹדֶשׁ
הַשְּׁבִיעִי בֶּעָשׂוֹר לַחֹדֶשׁ תְּעַנּוּ אֶת־נַפְשֹׁתֵיכֶם וְכָל־מְלָאכָה לֹא תַעֲשׂוּ
ל הָאֶזְרָח וְהַגֵּר הַגָּר בְּתוֹכְכֶם׃ כִּי־בַיּוֹם הַזֶּה יְכַפֵּר עֲלֵיכֶם לְטַהֵר אֶתְכֶם
לא מִכֹּל חַטֹּאתֵיכֶם לִפְנֵי יהוה תִּטְהָרוּ׃ שַׁבַּת שַׁבָּתוֹן הִיא לָכֶם וְעִנִּיתֶם
לב אֶת־נַפְשֹׁתֵיכֶם חֻקַּת עוֹלָם׃ וְכִפֶּר הַכֹּהֵן אֲשֶׁר־יִמְשַׁח אֹתוֹ וַאֲשֶׁר
יְמַלֵּא אֶת־יָדוֹ לְכַהֵן תַּחַת אָבִיו וְלָבַשׁ אֶת־בִּגְדֵי הַבָּד בִּגְדֵי הַקֹּדֶשׁ׃
לג וְכִפֶּר אֶת־מִקְדַּשׁ הַקֹּדֶשׁ וְאֶת־אֹהֶל מוֹעֵד וְאֶת־הַמִּזְבֵּחַ יְכַפֵּר וְעַל
לד הַכֹּהֲנִים וְעַל־כָּל־עַם הַקָּהָל יְכַפֵּר׃ וְהָיְתָה־זֹּאת לָכֶם לְחֻקַּת עוֹלָם
לְכַפֵּר עַל־בְּנֵי יִשְׂרָאֵל מִכָּל־חַטֹּאתָם אַחַת בַּשָּׁנָה וַיַּעַשׂ כַּאֲשֶׁר צִוָּה
יהוה אֶת־מֹשֶׁה׃
יז א ב וַיְדַבֵּר יהוה אֶל־מֹשֶׁה לֵּאמֹר׃ דַּבֵּר אֶל־אַהֲרֹן וְאֶל־בָּנָיו וְאֶל כָּל־בְּנֵי יג רביעי
ג יִשְׂרָאֵל וְאָמַרְתָּ אֲלֵיהֶם זֶה הַדָּבָר אֲשֶׁר־צִוָּה יהוה לֵאמֹר׃ אִישׁ אִישׁ
מִבֵּית יִשְׂרָאֵל אֲשֶׁר יִשְׁחַט שׁוֹר אוֹ־כֶשֶׂב אוֹ־עֵז בַּמַּחֲנֶה אוֹ אֲשֶׁר
ד יִשְׁחַט מִחוּץ לַמַּחֲנֶה׃ וְאֶל־פֶּתַח אֹהֶל מוֹעֵד לֹא הֱבִיאוֹ לְהַקְרִיב
קָרְבָּן לַיהוה לִפְנֵי מִשְׁכַּן יהוה דָּם יֵחָשֵׁב לָאִישׁ הַהוּא דָּם שָׁפָךְ וְנִכְרַת
ה הָאִישׁ הַהוּא מִקֶּרֶב עַמּוֹ׃ לְמַעַן אֲשֶׁר יָבִיאוּ בְּנֵי יִשְׂרָאֵל אֶת־זִבְחֵיהֶם
אֲשֶׁר הֵם זֹבְחִים עַל־פְּנֵי הַשָּׂדֶה וֶהֱבִיאֻם לַיהוה אֶל־פֶּתַח אֹהֶל
ו מוֹעֵד אֶל־הַכֹּהֵן וְזָבְחוּ זִבְחֵי שְׁלָמִים לַיהוה אוֹתָם׃ וְזָרַק הַכֹּהֵן אֶת־
הַדָּם עַל־מִזְבַּח יהוה פֶּתַח אֹהֶל מוֹעֵד וְהִקְטִיר הַחֵלֶב לְרֵיחַ נִיחֹחַ
ז לַיהוה׃ וְלֹא־יִזְבְּחוּ עוֹד אֶת־זִבְחֵיהֶם לַשְּׂעִירִם אֲשֶׁר הֵם זֹנִים אַחֲרֵיהֶם
ח חֻקַּת עוֹלָם תִּהְיֶה־זֹּאת לָהֶם לְדֹרֹתָם׃ וַאֲלֵהֶם תֹּאמַר אִישׁ אִישׁ חמישי /שלישי/
מִבֵּית יִשְׂרָאֵל וּמִן־הַגֵּר אֲשֶׁר־יָגוּר בְּתוֹכָם אֲשֶׁר־יַעֲלֶה עֹלָה אוֹ־
ט זָבַח׃ וְאֶל־פֶּתַח אֹהֶל מוֹעֵד לֹא יְבִיאֶנּוּ לַעֲשׂוֹת אֹתוֹ לַיהוה וְנִכְרַת
י הָאִישׁ הַהוּא מֵעַמָּיו׃ וְאִישׁ אִישׁ מִבֵּית יִשְׂרָאֵל וּמִן־הַגֵּר הַגָּר בְּתוֹכָם
אֲשֶׁר יֹאכַל כָּל־דָּם וְנָתַתִּי פָנַי בַּנֶּפֶשׁ הָאֹכֶלֶת אֶת־הַדָּם וְהִכְרַתִּי אֹתָהּ
יא מִקֶּרֶב עַמָּהּ׃ כִּי־נֶפֶשׁ הַבָּשָׂר בַּדָּם הִוא וַאֲנִי נְתַתִּיו לָכֶם עַל־הַמִּזְבֵּחַ

12 bound up with life, atones. That is why I have told the Israelites: None of you
13 may eat blood, nor may any migrant living among you eat blood. Any Israelite
or migrant living among you who hunts an animal or bird that may be eaten
14 shall pour out its blood and cover it with earth, for the life of all flesh – its
blood is its life. That is why I have said to the Israelites: You must not eat any
creature's blood, because the life of every creature is bound up with its blood.
15 All who eat it will be severed. Anyone, native born or migrant, who eats an
animal that has died of itself or been torn by beasts shall wash his clothes,
immerse in water, and remain impure until evening; then he shall be purified.
16 If he does not wash or immerse his body, he shall bear his guilt."
18 1 2 The LORD spoke to Moshe: "Speak to the Israelites. Say: I am the LORD your
3 God. You shall not do as they do in the land of Egypt where you lived. Nor
shall you do as they do in the land of Canaan where I am bringing you; do not
4 follow their practices. Observe My laws, keep My statutes and follow them;
5 I am the LORD your God. Keep My statutes and laws, for by them a person
6 shall live; I am the LORD. No one among you shall draw close to
7 any near relative to expose their nakedness;[43] I am the LORD. You
shall not expose your father's and mother's nakedness. She is your mother;
8 you shall not expose her nakedness. You shall not expose the
9 nakedness of your father's wife; it is your father's nakedness. You
shall not expose the nakedness of your sister – whether she is your father's
daughter or your mother's, whether born into the household or outside, you
10 shall not expose her nakedness. You shall not expose the
nakedness of your son's daughter or your daughter's daughter; it is your own
11 nakedness.[44] The nakedness of your father's wife's daughter, born to
12 your father[45] – she is your sister; do not expose her nakedness. You
shall not expose the nakedness of your father's sister; she is of your father's
13 flesh. You shall not expose the nakedness of your mother's
14 sister, for she is of your mother's flesh. You shall not expose the
nakedness of your father's brother – do not draw close to his wife; she is
15 your aunt. You shall not expose the nakedness of your daughter-
16 in-law: she is your son's wife; do not expose her nakedness. You
shall not expose the nakedness of your brother's wife; it is your brother's
17 nakedness. You shall not expose the nakedness of a woman
and her daughter, nor shall you marry her son's daughter or her daughter's
daughter, exposing her nakedness; they are of the same flesh; it would be
18 depravity. Do not marry a woman to be a rival to her sister,[46] exposing her
19 nakedness while her sister is alive. Do not draw close to a woman to expose
20 her nakedness while she bears the impurity of her menstruation. Do not have

43 | This expression is a euphemism for sexual relations.

44 | Meaning they are your own blood relatives.

45 | This verse seems to repeat a case already mentioned in verse 9. Interpretations vary.

46 | Meaning to be a rival wife to her sister, to whom you are already married.

יב לְכַפֵּר עַל־נַפְשֹׁתֵיכֶם כִּי־הַדָּם הוּא בַּנֶּפֶשׁ יְכַפֵּר: עַל־כֵּן אָמַרְתִּי לִבְנֵי
יִשְׂרָאֵל כָּל־נֶפֶשׁ מִכֶּם לֹא־תֹאכַל דָּם וְהַגֵּר הַגָּר בְּתוֹכְכֶם לֹא־יֹאכַל
יג דָּם: וְאִישׁ אִישׁ מִבְּנֵי יִשְׂרָאֵל וּמִן־הַגֵּר הַגָּר בְּתוֹכָם אֲשֶׁר יָצוּד צֵיד
יד חַיָּה אוֹ־עוֹף אֲשֶׁר יֵאָכֵל וְשָׁפַךְ אֶת־דָּמוֹ וְכִסָּהוּ בֶּעָפָר: כִּי־נֶפֶשׁ כָּל־
בָּשָׂר דָּמוֹ בְנַפְשׁוֹ הוּא וָאֹמַר לִבְנֵי יִשְׂרָאֵל דַּם כָּל־בָּשָׂר לֹא תֹאכֵלוּ
טו כִּי נֶפֶשׁ כָּל־בָּשָׂר דָּמוֹ הִוא כָּל־אֹכְלָיו יִכָּרֵת: וְכָל־נֶפֶשׁ אֲשֶׁר תֹּאכַל
נְבֵלָה וּטְרֵפָה בָּאֶזְרָח וּבַגֵּר וְכִבֶּס בְּגָדָיו וְרָחַץ בַּמַּיִם וְטָמֵא עַד־הָעֶרֶב
טז וְטָהֵר: וְאִם לֹא יְכַבֵּס וּבְשָׂרוֹ לֹא יִרְחָץ וְנָשָׂא עֲוֺנוֹ:
יח א ב וַיְדַבֵּר יְהוָה אֶל־מֹשֶׁה לֵּאמֹר: דַּבֵּר אֶל־בְּנֵי יִשְׂרָאֵל וְאָמַרְתָּ אֲלֵהֶם יד
ג אֲנִי יְהוָה אֱלֹהֵיכֶם: כְּמַעֲשֵׂה אֶרֶץ־מִצְרַיִם אֲשֶׁר יְשַׁבְתֶּם־בָּהּ לֹא
תַעֲשׂוּ וּכְמַעֲשֵׂה אֶרֶץ־כְּנַעַן אֲשֶׁר אֲנִי מֵבִיא אֶתְכֶם שָׁמָּה לֹא תַעֲשׂוּ
ד וּבְחֻקֹּתֵיהֶם לֹא תֵלֵכוּ: אֶת־מִשְׁפָּטַי תַּעֲשׂוּ וְאֶת־חֻקֹּתַי תִּשְׁמְרוּ לָלֶכֶת
ה בָּהֶם אֲנִי יְהוָה אֱלֹהֵיכֶם: וּשְׁמַרְתֶּם אֶת־חֻקֹּתַי וְאֶת־מִשְׁפָּטַי אֲשֶׁר
ו יַעֲשֶׂה אֹתָם הָאָדָם וָחַי בָּהֶם אֲנִי יְהוָה: אִישׁ אִישׁ אֶל־כָּל־ ששי
ז שְׁאֵר בְּשָׂרוֹ לֹא תִקְרְבוּ לְגַלּוֹת עֶרְוָה אֲנִי יְהוָה: עֶרְוַת אָבִיךָ
ח וְעֶרְוַת אִמְּךָ לֹא תְגַלֵּה אִמְּךָ הִוא לֹא תְגַלֶּה עֶרְוָתָהּ: עֶרְוַת
ט אֵשֶׁת־אָבִיךָ לֹא תְגַלֵּה עֶרְוַת אָבִיךָ הִוא: עֶרְוַת אֲחוֹתְךָ
בַת־אָבִיךָ אוֹ בַת־אִמֶּךָ מוֹלֶדֶת בַּיִת אוֹ מוֹלֶדֶת חוּץ לֹא תְגַלֶּה
י עֶרְוָתָן: עֶרְוַת בַּת־בִּנְךָ אוֹ בַת־בִּתְּךָ לֹא תְגַלֶּה עֶרְוָתָן
יא כִּי עֶרְוָתְךָ הֵנָּה: עֶרְוַת בַּת־אֵשֶׁת אָבִיךָ מוֹלֶדֶת אָבִיךָ
יב אֲחוֹתְךָ הִוא לֹא תְגַלֶּה עֶרְוָתָהּ: עֶרְוַת אֲחוֹת־אָבִיךָ
יג לֹא תְגַלֵּה שְׁאֵר אָבִיךָ הִוא: עֶרְוַת אֲחוֹת־אִמְּךָ לֹא
יד תְגַלֵּה כִּי־שְׁאֵר אִמְּךָ הִוא: עֶרְוַת אֲחִי־אָבִיךָ לֹא תְגַלֵּה
טו אֶל־אִשְׁתּוֹ לֹא תִקְרָב דֹּדָתְךָ הִוא: עֶרְוַת כַּלָּתְךָ לֹא
טז תְגַלֵּה אֵשֶׁת בִּנְךָ הִוא לֹא תְגַלֶּה עֶרְוָתָהּ: עֶרְוַת אֵשֶׁת־
יז אָחִיךָ לֹא תְגַלֵּה עֶרְוַת אָחִיךָ הִוא: עֶרְוַת אִשָּׁה וּבִתָּהּ
לֹא תְגַלֵּה אֶת־בַּת־בְּנָהּ וְאֶת־בַּת־בִּתָּהּ לֹא תִקַּח לְגַלּוֹת עֶרְוָתָהּ
יח שַׁאֲרָה הֵנָּה זִמָּה הִוא: וְאִשָּׁה אֶל־אֲחֹתָהּ לֹא תִקָּח לִצְרֹר לְגַלּוֹת
יט עֶרְוָתָהּ עָלֶיהָ בְּחַיֶּיהָ: וְאֶל־אִשָּׁה בְּנִדַּת טֻמְאָתָהּ לֹא תִקְרַב לְגַלּוֹת
כ עֶרְוָתָהּ: וְאֶל־אֵשֶׁת עֲמִיתְךָ לֹא־תִתֵּן שְׁכָבְתְּךָ לְזָרַע לְטָמְאָה־בָהּ:

21 carnal relations with your neighbor's wife, becoming impure through her. Do
not give any of your children over to be sacrificed to Molekh,[47] profaning the
22 name of your God; I am the LORD. Do not lie with a male as with a woman;
23 this is an abhorrent act. Do not have carnal relations with any animal, through
it making yourself impure; nor may a woman give herself to an animal to mate
24 with it – this is perversion. Do not make yourselves impure in any of these
ways, for it is by all these that the nations I am casting out before you made
25 themselves impure. And so the land itself became impure, and I held it to
26 account for its sins, and the land vomited out its inhabitants. But you shall
keep My statutes and My laws and do none of these abhorrent acts, neither
27 the native born nor the migrant living among you. The people who lived in
the land before you committed all these abhorrent acts and the land became
28 impure. Let the land not vomit you out for making it impure, as it vomited out
29 the nation there before you, for anyone who performs any of these abhorrent
30 acts shall be severed from his people. Keep My charge and do not follow any
of these abhorrent practices that were followed before you; do not by them
make yourselves impure; I am the LORD your God."

KEDOSHIM

19 1 2 The LORD spoke to Moshe: "Speak to all the community of Israel. Say: Be
3 holy, for I am holy; I, the LORD your God. Each one of you, revere your
4 mother and father and keep My Sabbaths; I am the LORD your God. Do
5 not turn to idols or cast yourselves gods; I am the LORD your God. When
you offer a peace sacrifice to the LORD, offer it in such a way that it may
6 be accepted for you. It shall be eaten on the day you sacrifice it or on the
7 following day; what is left on the third day shall be burned with fire. If any of
8 it is eaten on the third day, it is repugnant; it will not be accepted. Anyone
who eats it shall bear his guilt, for he has desecrated what is holy to the LORD;
9 he shall be severed from his people. When you reap the harvest of your land,
do not reap all the way to the edge of your field or gather the gleanings[48] of
10 your harvest. Do not harvest your vineyard bare or gather the grapes that have
fallen there. Leave them for the poor and for the migrant; I am the LORD your
11 12 God. Do not steal; do not deceive; do not lie to one another. Do not swear
13 falsely by My name, desecrating the name of your God; I am the LORD. Do
not defraud or rob[49] your neighbor. Do not hold back the wages of a hired
14 worker until the morning. Do not curse the deaf or put a stumbling-block
15 before the blind. Fear your God; I am the LORD. Do not pervert justice: do
not show partiality to the poor or deference to the great; judge your fellow
16 man fairly. Do not go around as a gossipmonger among your people. Do not
17 stand by while your neighbor's life is in danger; I am the LORD. Do not hate
your brother in your heart. Admonish your fellow and do not bear guilt on
18 his account. Do not take revenge or bear a grudge against any one among
19 your people, but love your neighbor as your own self; I am the LORD. Keep
My decrees. Do not crossbreed different kinds of animal, do not plant your

47 | A Canaanite ritual (see, e.g., Jer. 32:35).

48 | Individual stalks that fall from the bundle.

49 | Whereas "stealing" (*geneva*, v. 11) denotes taking by stealth, "robbery" (*gezela*) denotes taking by force.

כא וּמִזַּרְעֲךָ לֹא־תִתֵּן לְהַעֲבִיר לַמֹּלֶךְ וְלֹא תְחַלֵּל אֶת־שֵׁם אֱלֹהֶיךָ אֲנִי
כב כג יְהוָה: וְאֶת־זָכָר לֹא תִשְׁכַּב מִשְׁכְּבֵי אִשָּׁה תּוֹעֵבָה הִוא: וּבְכָל־בְּהֵמָה שביעי
לֹא־תִתֵּן שְׁכָבְתְּךָ לְטָמְאָה־בָהּ וְאִשָּׁה לֹא־תַעֲמֹד לִפְנֵי בְהֵמָה לְרִבְעָהּ /רביעי/
כד תֶּבֶל הוּא: אַל־תִּטַּמְּאוּ בְּכָל־אֵלֶּה כִּי בְכָל־אֵלֶּה נִטְמְאוּ הַגּוֹיִם
כה אֲשֶׁר־אֲנִי מְשַׁלֵּחַ מִפְּנֵיכֶם: וַתִּטְמָא הָאָרֶץ וָאֶפְקֹד עֲוֺנָהּ עָלֶיהָ וַתָּקִא
כו הָאָרֶץ אֶת־יֹשְׁבֶיהָ: וּשְׁמַרְתֶּם אַתֶּם אֶת־חֻקֹּתַי וְאֶת־מִשְׁפָּטַי וְלֹא
כז תַעֲשׂוּ מִכֹּל הַתּוֹעֵבֹת הָאֵלֶּה הָאֶזְרָח וְהַגֵּר הַגָּר בְּתוֹכְכֶם: כִּי אֶת־
כָּל־הַתּוֹעֵבֹת הָאֵל עָשׂוּ אַנְשֵׁי־הָאָרֶץ אֲשֶׁר לִפְנֵיכֶם וַתִּטְמָא הָאָרֶץ:
כח וְלֹא־תָקִיא הָאָרֶץ אֶתְכֶם בְּטַמַּאֲכֶם אֹתָהּ כַּאֲשֶׁר קָאָה אֶת־הַגּוֹי מפטיר
כט אֲשֶׁר לִפְנֵיכֶם: כִּי כָּל־אֲשֶׁר יַעֲשֶׂה מִכֹּל הַתּוֹעֵבֹת הָאֵלֶּה וְנִכְרְתוּ
ל הַנְּפָשׁוֹת הָעֹשֹׂת מִקֶּרֶב עַמָּם: וּשְׁמַרְתֶּם אֶת־מִשְׁמַרְתִּי לְבִלְתִּי עֲשׂוֹת
מֵחֻקּוֹת הַתּוֹעֵבֹת אֲשֶׁר נַעֲשׂוּ לִפְנֵיכֶם וְלֹא תִטַּמְּאוּ בָּהֶם אֲנִי יְהוָה
אֱלֹהֵיכֶם:

יט א ב וַיְדַבֵּר יְהוָה אֶל־מֹשֶׁה לֵּאמֹר: דַּבֵּר אֶל־כָּל־עֲדַת בְּנֵי־יִשְׂרָאֵל וְאָמַרְתָּ טו קדשים
ג אֲלֵהֶם קְדֹשִׁים תִּהְיוּ כִּי קָדוֹשׁ אֲנִי יְהוָה אֱלֹהֵיכֶם: אִישׁ אִמּוֹ וְאָבִיו
ד תִּירָאוּ וְאֶת־שַׁבְּתֹתַי תִּשְׁמֹרוּ אֲנִי יְהוָה אֱלֹהֵיכֶם: אַל־תִּפְנוּ אֶל־
ה הָאֱלִילִם וֵאלֹהֵי מַסֵּכָה לֹא תַעֲשׂוּ לָכֶם אֲנִי יְהוָה אֱלֹהֵיכֶם: וְכִי תִזְבְּחוּ
ו זֶבַח שְׁלָמִים לַיהוָה לִרְצֹנְכֶם תִּזְבָּחֻהוּ: בְּיוֹם זִבְחֲכֶם יֵאָכֵל וּמִמָּחֳרָת
ז וְהַנּוֹתָר עַד־יוֹם הַשְּׁלִישִׁי בָּאֵשׁ יִשָּׂרֵף: וְאִם הֵאָכֹל יֵאָכֵל בַּיּוֹם
ח הַשְּׁלִישִׁי פִּגּוּל הוּא לֹא יֵרָצֶה: וְאֹכְלָיו עֲוֺנוֹ יִשָּׂא כִּי־אֶת־קֹדֶשׁ יְהוָה
ט חִלֵּל וְנִכְרְתָה הַנֶּפֶשׁ הַהִוא מֵעַמֶּיהָ: וּבְקֻצְרְכֶם אֶת־קְצִיר אַרְצְכֶם לֹא
י תְכַלֶּה פְּאַת שָׂדְךָ לִקְצֹר וְלֶקֶט קְצִירְךָ לֹא תְלַקֵּט: וְכַרְמְךָ לֹא תְעוֹלֵל
וּפֶרֶט כַּרְמְךָ לֹא תְלַקֵּט לֶעָנִי וְלַגֵּר תַּעֲזֹב אֹתָם אֲנִי יְהוָה אֱלֹהֵיכֶם:
יא יב לֹא תִּגְנֹבוּ וְלֹא־תְכַחֲשׁוּ וְלֹא־תְשַׁקְּרוּ אִישׁ בַּעֲמִיתוֹ: וְלֹא־תִשָּׁבְעוּ
יג בִשְׁמִי לַשָּׁקֶר וְחִלַּלְתָּ אֶת־שֵׁם אֱלֹהֶיךָ אֲנִי יְהוָה: לֹא־תַעֲשֹׁק אֶת־רֵעֲךָ
יד וְלֹא תִגְזֹל לֹא־תָלִין פְּעֻלַּת שָׂכִיר אִתְּךָ עַד־בֹּקֶר: לֹא־תְקַלֵּל חֵרֵשׁ שני
טו וְלִפְנֵי עִוֵּר לֹא תִתֵּן מִכְשֹׁל וְיָרֵאתָ מֵּאֱלֹהֶיךָ אֲנִי יְהוָה: לֹא־תַעֲשׂוּ /חמישי/
עָוֶל בַּמִּשְׁפָּט לֹא־תִשָּׂא פְנֵי־דָל וְלֹא תֶהְדַּר פְּנֵי גָדוֹל בְּצֶדֶק תִּשְׁפֹּט
טז עֲמִיתֶךָ: לֹא־תֵלֵךְ רָכִיל בְּעַמֶּיךָ לֹא תַעֲמֹד עַל־דַּם רֵעֶךָ אֲנִי יְהוָה:
יז לֹא־תִשְׂנָא אֶת־אָחִיךָ בִּלְבָבֶךָ הוֹכֵחַ תּוֹכִיחַ אֶת־עֲמִיתֶךָ וְלֹא־תִשָּׂא
יח עָלָיו חֵטְא: לֹא־תִקֹּם וְלֹא־תִטֹּר אֶת־בְּנֵי עַמֶּךָ וְאָהַבְתָּ לְרֵעֲךָ כָּמוֹךָ
יט אֲנִי יְהוָה: אֶת־חֻקֹּתַי תִּשְׁמֹרוּ בְּהֶמְתְּךָ לֹא־תַרְבִּיעַ כִּלְאַיִם שָׂדְךָ

field with two kinds of seed intermixed, and do not wear clothing made from
20 two materials combined. If a man has carnal relations with a woman who is a
slave designated for another man, and who has not been redeemed or given
her freedom, there shall be punishment but they shall not be put to death
21 since she has not been freed. The man shall bring his guilt offering to the
22 LORD at the entrance of the Tent of Meeting: a ram for a guilt offering. The
priest shall make his atonement before the LORD with the ram of the guilt
offering for the sin that he committed, and the sin he committed shall be
forgiven.
23 When you enter the land and plant any tree for food, you shall regard its fruit
as forbidden. For three years it shall be forbidden to you; it must not be eaten.
24 25 In the fourth year, all its fruit shall be holy, to give praise to the LORD. In the
fifth year you may eat its fruit – and so shall its yield proliferate for you; I am
26 the LORD your God. Do not eat any creature with its blood. Do not practice
27 divination or seek omens. Do not cut off the hair on the sides of your head or
28 destroy the edges of your beard. Do not gash your body for the dead or put
29 tattoo marks on yourself; I am the LORD. Do not profane your daughter by
making her a prostitute, that the land shall not be prostituted, the land filled
30 with depravity. Keep My Sabbaths, revere My Sanctuary; I am the LORD.
31 Do not turn to ghosts or inquire of spirits, rendering yourself impure; I am
32 the LORD your God. Stand up in the presence of the white-haired and show
33 respect to the elderly; revere your God; I am the LORD. When a
34 stranger lives with you in your land, do not wrong him. The stranger living
with you shall be like one of your native born to you: love him as your own self,
for you yourselves were strangers in the land of Egypt; I am the LORD your
35 God. Do not falsify measures – not of length, nor of weight, nor of volume.
36 You shall have honest scales, honest weights, an honest ephah, and an honest
hin.[50] I am the LORD your God, who brought you out of the land of Egypt.
37 Keep all My decrees and laws and fulfill them; I am the LORD."
20 1 2 The LORD spoke to Moshe: "Tell the Israelites: Any person – any Israelite
or any migrant residing among Israel – who sacrifices any of his children to
3 Molekh[51] shall be put to death. The people of the land shall stone him, and I
Myself will set My face against that person; I will sever him from his people
because, in sacrificing his children to Molekh, he defiles My Sanctuary; he
4 desecrates My holy name. If the people of the land close their eyes to a man
5 as he sacrifices his children to Molekh – if they do not put him to death – I
Myself will set My face against him and his family; I will sever him from his
6 people, and with him all who follow him in going astray after Molekh. And
anyone who turns to ghosts or spirits, going astray after them – I will set My

50 | An ephah is a solid measure, and a hin is a liquid measure.
51 | See note on 18:21.

כ לֹא־תִזְרַע כִּלְאָיִם וּבֶגֶד כִּלְאַיִם שַׁעַטְנֵז לֹא יַעֲלֶה עָלֶיךָ: וְאִישׁ כִּי־
יִשְׁכַּב אֶת־אִשָּׁה שִׁכְבַת־זֶרַע וְהִוא שִׁפְחָה נֶחֱרֶפֶת לְאִישׁ וְהׇפְדֵּה
לֹא נִפְדָּתָה אוֹ חֻפְשָׁה לֹא נִתַּן־לָהּ בִּקֹּרֶת תִּהְיֶה לֹא יוּמְתוּ כִּי־לֹא
כא חֻפָּשָׁה: וְהֵבִיא אֶת־אֲשָׁמוֹ לַיהוה אֶל־פֶּתַח אֹהֶל מוֹעֵד אֵיל אָשָׁם:
כב וְכִפֶּר עָלָיו הַכֹּהֵן בְּאֵיל הָאָשָׁם לִפְנֵי יהוה עַל־חַטָּאתוֹ אֲשֶׁר חָטָא
וְנִסְלַח לוֹ מֵחַטָּאתוֹ אֲשֶׁר חָטָא:
כג וְכִי־תָבֹאוּ אֶל־הָאָרֶץ וּנְטַעְתֶּם כׇּל־עֵץ מַאֲכָל וַעֲרַלְתֶּם עׇרְלָתוֹ אֶת־ טז שלישי
כד פִּרְיוֹ שָׁלֹשׁ שָׁנִים יִהְיֶה לָכֶם עֲרֵלִים לֹא יֵאָכֵל: וּבַשָּׁנָה הָרְבִיעִת יִהְיֶה
כה כׇּל־פִּרְיוֹ קֹדֶשׁ הִלּוּלִים לַיהוה: וּבַשָּׁנָה הַחֲמִישִׁת תֹּאכְלוּ אֶת־פִּרְיוֹ
כו לְהוֹסִיף לָכֶם תְּבוּאָתוֹ אֲנִי יהוה אֱלֹהֵיכֶם: לֹא תֹאכְלוּ עַל־הַדָּם לֹא
כז תְנַחֲשׁוּ וְלֹא תְעוֹנֵנוּ: לֹא תַקִּפוּ פְּאַת רֹאשְׁכֶם וְלֹא תַשְׁחִית אֵת פְּאַת
כח זְקָנֶךָ: וְשֶׂרֶט לָנֶפֶשׁ לֹא תִתְּנוּ בִּבְשַׂרְכֶם וּכְתֹבֶת קַעֲקַע לֹא תִתְּנוּ
כט בָּכֶם אֲנִי יהוה: אַל־תְּחַלֵּל אֶת־בִּתְּךָ לְהַזְנוֹתָהּ וְלֹא־תִזְנֶה הָאָרֶץ
ל וּמָלְאָה הָאָרֶץ זִמָּה: אֶת־שַׁבְּתֹתַי תִּשְׁמֹרוּ וּמִקְדָּשִׁי תִּירָאוּ אֲנִי יהוה:
לא אַל־תִּפְנוּ אֶל־הָאֹבֹת וְאֶל־הַיִּדְּעֹנִים אַל־תְּבַקְשׁוּ לְטׇמְאָה בָהֶם אֲנִי
לב יהוה אֱלֹהֵיכֶם: מִפְּנֵי שֵׂיבָה תָּקוּם וְהָדַרְתָּ פְּנֵי זָקֵן וְיָרֵאתָ מֵּאֱלֹהֶיךָ
לג אֲנִי יהוה: וְכִי־יָגוּר אִתְּךָ גֵּר בְּאַרְצְכֶם לֹא תוֹנוּ אֹתוֹ: רביעי /ששי/
לד כְּאֶזְרָח מִכֶּם יִהְיֶה לָכֶם הַגֵּר ׀ הַגָּר אִתְּכֶם וְאָהַבְתָּ לוֹ כָּמוֹךָ כִּי־גֵרִים
לה הֱיִיתֶם בְּאֶרֶץ מִצְרָיִם אֲנִי יהוה אֱלֹהֵיכֶם: לֹא־תַעֲשׂוּ עָוֶל בַּמִּשְׁפָּט
לו בַּמִּדָּה בַּמִּשְׁקָל וּבַמְּשׂוּרָה: מֹאזְנֵי צֶדֶק אַבְנֵי־צֶדֶק אֵיפַת צֶדֶק וְהִין
צֶדֶק יִהְיֶה לָכֶם אֲנִי יהוה אֱלֹהֵיכֶם אֲשֶׁר־הוֹצֵאתִי אֶתְכֶם מֵאֶרֶץ
לז מִצְרָיִם: וּשְׁמַרְתֶּם אֶת־כׇּל־חֻקֹּתַי וְאֶת־כׇּל־מִשְׁפָּטַי וַעֲשִׂיתֶם אֹתָם
אֲנִי יהוה:
כ א ב וַיְדַבֵּר יהוה אֶל־מֹשֶׁה לֵּאמֹר: וְאֶל־בְּנֵי יִשְׂרָאֵל תֹּאמַר אִישׁ אִישׁ חמישי
מִבְּנֵי יִשְׂרָאֵל וּמִן־הַגֵּר ׀ הַגָּר בְּיִשְׂרָאֵל אֲשֶׁר יִתֵּן מִזַּרְעוֹ לַמֹּלֶךְ מוֹת
ג יוּמָת עַם הָאָרֶץ יִרְגְּמֻהוּ בָאָבֶן: וַאֲנִי אֶתֵּן אֶת־פָּנַי בָּאִישׁ הַהוּא
וְהִכְרַתִּי אֹתוֹ מִקֶּרֶב עַמּוֹ כִּי מִזַּרְעוֹ נָתַן לַמֹּלֶךְ לְמַעַן טַמֵּא אֶת־
ד מִקְדָּשִׁי וּלְחַלֵּל אֶת־שֵׁם קׇדְשִׁי: וְאִם הַעְלֵם יַעְלִימוּ עַם הָאָרֶץ
אֶת־עֵינֵיהֶם מִן־הָאִישׁ הַהוּא בְּתִתּוֹ מִזַּרְעוֹ לַמֹּלֶךְ לְבִלְתִּי הָמִית
ה אֹתוֹ: וְשַׂמְתִּי אֲנִי אֶת־פָּנַי בָּאִישׁ הַהוּא וּבְמִשְׁפַּחְתּוֹ וְהִכְרַתִּי אֹתוֹ
ו וְאֵת ׀ כׇּל־הַזֹּנִים אַחֲרָיו לִזְנוֹת אַחֲרֵי הַמֹּלֶךְ מִקֶּרֶב עַמָּם: וְהַנֶּפֶשׁ אֲשֶׁר
תִּפְנֶה אֶל־הָאֹבֹת וְאֶל־הַיִּדְּעֹנִים לִזְנֹת אַחֲרֵיהֶם וְנָתַתִּי אֶת־פָּנַי בַּנֶּפֶשׁ

7 face against him and sever him from his people. Consecrate yourselves and
8 be holy, for I am the LORD your God. Keep My decrees and fulfill them; I am
9 the LORD, who makes you holy. One who curses his father or mother shall
be put to death. Since he has cursed his father or mother, his bloodguilt is
10 upon him. If a man commits adultery with a married woman, another man's
11 wife, both the adulterer and the adulteress shall be put to death. If a man lies
with his father's wife, he has exposed his father's nakedness;[52] both of them[53]
12 shall be put to death; their bloodguilt is upon them. If a man lies with his
daughter-in-law, both of them shall be put to death. They have committed
13 perversion; their bloodguilt is upon them. If a man lies with a male as he
would with a woman, both have performed an abhorrent act; they shall be put
14 to death; their bloodguilt is upon them. If a man marries a woman and also
her mother, it is depravity. He and they shall be burned by fire; there must be
15 no depravity among you. If a man lies with an animal, he shall be put to death
16 and you shall kill the animal. If a woman approaches an animal to mate with
it, you shall kill the woman and the animal; they shall both be put to death;
17 their bloodguilt is upon them. If a man takes his sister – his father's daughter
or his mother's daughter – and they see one another's nakedness, it is a deep
disgrace; they shall be severed in the sight of their people. He has exposed
18 his sister's nakedness; he shall bear his guilt. If a man lies with a menstruating
woman and exposes her nakedness, he has laid her hidden source bare; she
has exposed the source of her blood; both of them shall be severed from their
19 people. Do not expose the nakedness of your mother's sister or your father's
sister, because that is to lay bare your own near relative; both shall bear their
20 guilt. If a man lies with his aunt, he has exposed his uncle's nakedness. Both
21 parties shall bear their guilt; they shall die childless. For a man to marry his
brother's wife – that is taboo. He has exposed his brother's nakedness; both
22 parties shall be childless. Keep all My decrees and all My laws and fulfill
them, so that the land to which I am bringing you to settle will not vomit
23 you out. Do not follow the practices of the nation I am driving out before
24 you, for they did all these things and I was disgusted with them. I have told
you: You shall possess their land; I am giving it to you to possess. It is a land
that flows with milk and with honey. I am the LORD your God, who has set
25 you apart from all other peoples. You, then, shall set pure apart from impure
animals, pure from impure birds. Do not make yourselves detestable by an
animal or bird or anything that creeps upon the ground that I have set apart
26 from you to regard as impure.[54] Be holy to Me, for I the LORD am holy, and
27 I have set you apart from all other peoples to be My own. A man or woman
who seeks ghosts or spirits shall be put to death. They shall be stoned; their
bloodguilt is on them."
21 1 The LORD said to Moshe, "Speak to the priests, Aharon's sons. Say: No one of EMOR

52 | See 18:6–8.
53 | Both participants in the act.
54 | See chapter 11.

ז הַהוּא וְהִכְרַתִּי אֹתוֹ מִקֶּרֶב עַמּוֹ: וְהִתְקַדִּשְׁתֶּם וִהְיִיתֶם קְדֹשִׁים כִּי
ח אֲנִי יהוה אֱלֹהֵיכֶם: וּשְׁמַרְתֶּם אֶת־חֻקֹּתַי וַעֲשִׂיתֶם אֹתָם אֲנִי יהוה ששי /שביעי/
ט מְקַדִּשְׁכֶם: כִּי־אִישׁ אִישׁ אֲשֶׁר יְקַלֵּל אֶת־אָבִיו וְאֶת־אִמּוֹ מוֹת יוּמָת
י אָבִיו וְאִמּוֹ קִלֵּל דָּמָיו בּוֹ: וְאִישׁ אֲשֶׁר יִנְאַף אֶת־אֵשֶׁת אִישׁ אֲשֶׁר
יא יִנְאַף אֶת־אֵשֶׁת רֵעֵהוּ מוֹת־יוּמַת הַנֹּאֵף וְהַנֹּאָפֶת: וְאִישׁ אֲשֶׁר יִשְׁכַּב
אֶת־אֵשֶׁת אָבִיו עֶרְוַת אָבִיו גִּלָּה מוֹת־יוּמְתוּ שְׁנֵיהֶם דְּמֵיהֶם בָּם:
יב וְאִישׁ אֲשֶׁר יִשְׁכַּב אֶת־כַּלָּתוֹ מוֹת יוּמְתוּ שְׁנֵיהֶם תֶּבֶל עָשׂוּ דְּמֵיהֶם
יג בָּם: וְאִישׁ אֲשֶׁר יִשְׁכַּב אֶת־זָכָר מִשְׁכְּבֵי אִשָּׁה תּוֹעֵבָה עָשׂוּ שְׁנֵיהֶם
יד מוֹת יוּמָתוּ דְּמֵיהֶם בָּם: וְאִישׁ אֲשֶׁר יִקַּח אֶת־אִשָּׁה וְאֶת־אִמָּהּ זִמָּה
טו הִוא בָּאֵשׁ יִשְׂרְפוּ אֹתוֹ וְאֶתְהֶן וְלֹא־תִהְיֶה זִמָּה בְּתוֹכְכֶם: וְאִישׁ אֲשֶׁר
טז יִתֵּן שְׁכָבְתּוֹ בִּבְהֵמָה מוֹת יוּמָת וְאֶת־הַבְּהֵמָה תַּהֲרֹגוּ: וְאִשָּׁה אֲשֶׁר
תִּקְרַב אֶל־כָּל־בְּהֵמָה לְרִבְעָה אֹתָהּ וְהָרַגְתָּ אֶת־הָאִשָּׁה וְאֶת־הַבְּהֵמָה
יז מוֹת יוּמָתוּ דְּמֵיהֶם בָּם: וְאִישׁ אֲשֶׁר־יִקַּח אֶת־אֲחֹתוֹ בַּת־אָבִיו אוֹ
בַת־אִמּוֹ וְרָאָה אֶת־עֶרְוָתָהּ וְהִיא תִרְאֶה אֶת־עֶרְוָתוֹ חֶסֶד הוּא
יח וְנִכְרְתוּ לְעֵינֵי בְּנֵי עַמָּם עֶרְוַת אֲחֹתוֹ גִּלָּה עֲוֹנוֹ יִשָּׂא: וְאִישׁ אֲשֶׁר־
יִשְׁכַּב אֶת־אִשָּׁה דָּוָה וְגִלָּה אֶת־עֶרְוָתָהּ אֶת־מְקֹרָהּ הֶעֱרָה וְהִוא
יט גִּלְּתָה אֶת־מְקוֹר דָּמֶיהָ וְנִכְרְתוּ שְׁנֵיהֶם מִקֶּרֶב עַמָּם: וְעֶרְוַת אֲחוֹת
כ אִמְּךָ וַאֲחוֹת אָבִיךָ לֹא תְגַלֵּה כִּי אֶת־שְׁאֵרוֹ הֶעֱרָה עֲוֹנָם יִשָּׂאוּ: וְאִישׁ
אֲשֶׁר יִשְׁכַּב אֶת־דֹּדָתוֹ עֶרְוַת דֹּדוֹ גִּלָּה חֶטְאָם יִשָּׂאוּ עֲרִירִים יָמֻתוּ:
כא וְאִישׁ אֲשֶׁר יִקַּח אֶת־אֵשֶׁת אָחִיו נִדָּה הִוא עֶרְוַת אָחִיו גִּלָּה עֲרִירִים
כב יִהְיוּ: וּשְׁמַרְתֶּם אֶת־כָּל־חֻקֹּתַי וְאֶת־כָּל־מִשְׁפָּטַי וַעֲשִׂיתֶם אֹתָם וְלֹא־
כג תָקִיא אֶתְכֶם הָאָרֶץ אֲשֶׁר אֲנִי מֵבִיא אֶתְכֶם שָׁמָּה לָשֶׁבֶת בָּהּ: וְלֹא שביעי
תֵלְכוּ בְּחֻקֹּת הַגּוֹי אֲשֶׁר־אֲנִי מְשַׁלֵּחַ מִפְּנֵיכֶם כִּי אֶת־כָּל־אֵלֶּה עָשׂוּ
כד וָאָקֻץ בָּם: וָאֹמַר לָכֶם אַתֶּם תִּירְשׁוּ אֶת־אַדְמָתָם וַאֲנִי אֶתְּנֶנָּה לָכֶם
לָרֶשֶׁת אֹתָהּ אֶרֶץ זָבַת חָלָב וּדְבָשׁ אֲנִי יהוה אֱלֹהֵיכֶם אֲשֶׁר־הִבְדַּלְתִּי
כה אֶתְכֶם מִן־הָעַמִּים: וְהִבְדַּלְתֶּם בֵּין־הַבְּהֵמָה הַטְּהֹרָה לַטְּמֵאָה וּבֵין־ מפטיר
הָעוֹף הַטָּמֵא לַטָּהֹר וְלֹא־תְשַׁקְּצוּ אֶת־נַפְשֹׁתֵיכֶם בַּבְּהֵמָה וּבָעוֹף
כו וּבְכֹל אֲשֶׁר תִּרְמֹשׂ הָאֲדָמָה אֲשֶׁר־הִבְדַּלְתִּי לָכֶם לְטַמֵּא: וִהְיִיתֶם
לִי קְדֹשִׁים כִּי קָדוֹשׁ אֲנִי יהוה וָאַבְדִּל אֶתְכֶם מִן־הָעַמִּים לִהְיוֹת לִי:
כז וְאִישׁ אוֹ־אִשָּׁה כִּי־יִהְיֶה בָהֶם אוֹב אוֹ יִדְּעֹנִי מוֹת יוּמָתוּ בָּאֶבֶן יִרְגְּמוּ
אֹתָם דְּמֵיהֶם בָּם:

כא א וַיֹּאמֶר יהוה אֶל־מֹשֶׁה אֱמֹר אֶל־הַכֹּהֲנִים בְּנֵי אַהֲרֹן וְאָמַרְתָּ אֲלֵהֶם יז אמר

2 you shall render himself impure for any dead person among his people except
3 for his nearest relatives: his mother, father, son, daughter, or brother; or his
virgin sister who has remained close to him because she has not married –
4 for her, he may render himself impure. But he shall not become impure for
5 those he is related to by marriage, and so become profane. Priests shall not
make bald patches on their heads, or shave off the edges of their beards, or
6 gash wounds into their flesh. They shall be holy to their God and not profane
God's name, for they bring close the LORD's fire offerings, foodstuff offerings
7 to their God; therefore they shall be holy. They may not marry a woman
made profane by immorality,[55] nor may they marry a woman divorced from
8 her husband, for they are holy to their God. You shall treat a priest as holy, for
he brings close the offerings of foodstuffs to your God. And he shall be holy
9 to you, because I, the LORD, am holy and make you holy. If the daughter of a
priest profanes herself by immorality, she profanes her father also; she shall
10 be burned with fire. The priest, the highest among his brothers, on
whose head the anointing oil has been poured and who has been ordained
11 to wear the vestments, shall not dishevel his hair or tear his clothes. He shall
not go near the dead; even for his father or mother he shall not render himself
12 impure. He shall not leave the Sanctuary, profaning his God's Sanctuary, for
13 the crown of his God's anointing oil rests upon him; I am the LORD. He may
14 marry a woman only in her virginity. He may not marry a widow, a divorcée,
or one profaned by immorality. He may marry only a virgin from his own
15 people, so that he will not profane his children among his people, for I, the
16 17 LORD, sanctify him." The LORD spoke to Moshe: "Tell Aharon: Any
of your future descendants who has a physical blemish may not draw close to
18 present foodstuff offerings to his God. No one with a blemish shall approach:
19 this includes one who is blind, lame, disfigured, or deformed; or who has a
20 broken foot or hand; or who is a hunchback or a dwarf, or who has a growth
21 in his eye, a severe rash, scabs, or crushed testicles. No descendant of Aharon
the priest who has a physical blemish shall draw near to present the LORD's
fire offerings; because of his blemish, he shall not approach to present an
22 offering of foodstuffs to his God. He may eat the foodstuff offerings of his
23 God, the holy of holies as well as the holy.[56] But he may not come close to
the inner curtain or approach the altar, because of his blemish; he shall not
24 profane My Sanctuary; I am the LORD who makes them holy." Moshe told
this to Aharon, his sons, and all the Israelites.

22 1 2 The LORD spoke to Moshe: "Tell Aharon and his sons to take great care with
the sacred offerings that the Israelites consecrate to Me, so that they do not
3 profane My holy name: I am the LORD. Tell them: If any descendant of yours
throughout the generations comes near the sacred offerings that the Israelites
have consecrated to the LORD while in an impure state, he shall be severed
4 from My presence; I am the LORD. Any descendant of Aharon who has a

---

55 | Referring to forbidden sexual relations.

56 | Offerings designated as "holy of holies" are eaten exclusively by the priests and bear other restrictions. See, e.g., 6:10–11, 22, 24:9.

ב לְנֶפֶשׁ לֹא־יִטַּמָּא בְּעַמָּיו׃ כִּי אִם־לִשְׁאֵרוֹ הַקָּרֹב אֵלָיו לְאִמּוֹ וּלְאָבִיו
ג וְלִבְנוֹ וּלְבִתּוֹ וּלְאָחִיו׃ וְלַאֲחֹתוֹ הַבְּתוּלָה הַקְּרוֹבָה אֵלָיו אֲשֶׁר לֹא־
ד ה הָיְתָה לְאִישׁ לָהּ יִטַּמָּא׃ לֹא יִטַּמָּא בַּעַל בְּעַמָּיו לְהֵחַלּוֹ׃ לֹא־יקרחה יִקְרְחוּ
קָרְחָה בְּרֹאשָׁם וּפְאַת זְקָנָם לֹא יְגַלֵּחוּ וּבִבְשָׂרָם לֹא יִשְׂרְטוּ שָׂרָטֶת׃
ו קְדֹשִׁים יִהְיוּ לֵאלֹהֵיהֶם וְלֹא יְחַלְּלוּ שֵׁם אֱלֹהֵיהֶם כִּי אֶת־אִשֵּׁי יְהוָה
ז לֶחֶם אֱלֹהֵיהֶם הֵם מַקְרִיבִם וְהָיוּ קֹדֶשׁ׃ אִשָּׁה זֹנָה וַחֲלָלָה לֹא יִקָּחוּ
ח וְאִשָּׁה גְּרוּשָׁה מֵאִישָׁהּ לֹא יִקָּחוּ כִּי־קָדֹשׁ הוּא לֵאלֹהָיו׃ וְקִדַּשְׁתּוֹ
כִּי־אֶת־לֶחֶם אֱלֹהֶיךָ הוּא מַקְרִיב קָדֹשׁ יִהְיֶה־לָּךְ כִּי קָדוֹשׁ אֲנִי יְהוָה
ט מְקַדִּשְׁכֶם׃ וּבַת אִישׁ כֹּהֵן כִּי תֵחֵל לִזְנוֹת אֶת־אָבִיהָ הִיא מְחַלֶּלֶת
י בָּאֵשׁ תִּשָּׂרֵף׃ וְהַכֹּהֵן הַגָּדוֹל מֵאֶחָיו אֲשֶׁר־יוּצַק עַל־רֹאשׁוֹ ׀
שֶׁמֶן הַמִּשְׁחָה וּמִלֵּא אֶת־יָדוֹ לִלְבֹּשׁ אֶת־הַבְּגָדִים אֶת־רֹאשׁוֹ לֹא יִפְרָע
יא וּבְגָדָיו לֹא יִפְרֹם׃ וְעַל כָּל־נַפְשֹׁת מֵת לֹא יָבֹא לְאָבִיו וּלְאִמּוֹ לֹא יִטַּמָּא׃
יב וּמִן־הַמִּקְדָּשׁ לֹא יֵצֵא וְלֹא יְחַלֵּל אֵת מִקְדַּשׁ אֱלֹהָיו כִּי נֵזֶר שֶׁמֶן
יג יד מִשְׁחַת אֱלֹהָיו עָלָיו אֲנִי יְהוָה׃ וְהוּא אִשָּׁה בִבְתוּלֶיהָ יִקָּח׃ אַלְמָנָה
וּגְרוּשָׁה וַחֲלָלָה זֹנָה אֶת־אֵלֶּה לֹא יִקָּח כִּי אִם־בְּתוּלָה מֵעַמָּיו יִקַּח
טו טז אִשָּׁה׃ וְלֹא־יְחַלֵּל זַרְעוֹ בְּעַמָּיו כִּי אֲנִי יְהוָה מְקַדְּשׁוֹ׃ וַיְדַבֵּר שני
יז יְהוָה אֶל־מֹשֶׁה לֵּאמֹר׃ דַּבֵּר אֶל־אַהֲרֹן לֵאמֹר אִישׁ מִזַּרְעֲךָ לְדֹרֹתָם
יח אֲשֶׁר יִהְיֶה בוֹ מוּם לֹא יִקְרַב לְהַקְרִיב לֶחֶם אֱלֹהָיו׃ כִּי כָל־אִישׁ
יט אֲשֶׁר־בּוֹ מוּם לֹא יִקְרָב אִישׁ עִוֵּר אוֹ פִסֵּחַ אוֹ חָרֻם אוֹ שָׂרוּעַ׃ אוֹ אִישׁ
כ אֲשֶׁר־יִהְיֶה בוֹ שֶׁבֶר רָגֶל אוֹ שֶׁבֶר יָד׃ אוֹ־גִבֵּן אוֹ־דַק אוֹ תְּבַלֻּל בְּעֵינוֹ
כא אוֹ גָרָב אוֹ יַלֶּפֶת אוֹ מְרוֹחַ אָשֶׁךְ׃ כָּל־אִישׁ אֲשֶׁר־בּוֹ מוּם מִזֶּרַע אַהֲרֹן
הַכֹּהֵן לֹא יִגַּשׁ לְהַקְרִיב אֶת־אִשֵּׁי יְהוָה מוּם בּוֹ אֵת לֶחֶם אֱלֹהָיו לֹא
כב יִגַּשׁ לְהַקְרִיב׃ לֶחֶם אֱלֹהָיו מִקָּדְשֵׁי הַקֳּדָשִׁים וּמִן־הַקֳּדָשִׁים יֹאכֵל׃
כג אַךְ אֶל־הַפָּרֹכֶת לֹא יָבֹא וְאֶל־הַמִּזְבֵּחַ לֹא יִגַּשׁ כִּי־מוּם בּוֹ וְלֹא יְחַלֵּל
כד אֶת־מִקְדָּשַׁי כִּי אֲנִי יְהוָה מְקַדְּשָׁם׃ וַיְדַבֵּר מֹשֶׁה אֶל־אַהֲרֹן וְאֶל־בָּנָיו
וְאֶל־כָּל־בְּנֵי יִשְׂרָאֵל׃

כב א ב וַיְדַבֵּר יְהוָה אֶל־מֹשֶׁה לֵּאמֹר׃ דַּבֵּר אֶל־אַהֲרֹן וְאֶל־בָּנָיו וְיִנָּזְרוּ מִקָּדְשֵׁי
בְנֵי־יִשְׂרָאֵל וְלֹא יְחַלְּלוּ אֶת־שֵׁם קָדְשִׁי אֲשֶׁר הֵם מַקְדִּשִׁים לִי אֲנִי
ג יְהוָה׃ אֱמֹר אֲלֵהֶם לְדֹרֹתֵיכֶם כָּל־אִישׁ ׀ אֲשֶׁר־יִקְרַב מִכָּל־זַרְעֲכֶם אֶל־
הַקֳּדָשִׁים אֲשֶׁר יַקְדִּישׁוּ בְנֵי־יִשְׂרָאֵל לַיהוָה וְטֻמְאָתוֹ עָלָיו וְנִכְרְתָה
ד הַנֶּפֶשׁ הַהִוא מִלְּפָנַי אֲנִי יְהוָה׃ אִישׁ אִישׁ מִזֶּרַע אַהֲרֹן וְהוּא צָרוּעַ

defiling blight of the skin or a discharge may not eat of the sacred offerings
until he becomes pure. One who touches anything made impure by contact
5 with the dead, or who has had a seminal emission, or who has touched
any swarming thing or any person who renders him impure – whatever
6 his impurity – the one who touches these things shall be impure until the
evening, and shall not eat of the sacred offerings until he has washed his body
7 in water. When the sun sets, he shall become pure again and may eat of the
8 sacred offerings, for they are his food. He may not eat an animal found dead
or one that was torn by wild animals, becoming impure by doing so; I am
9 the LORD. They shall keep My charge and not bear guilt and die through it,
10 having profaned it. I am the LORD, who makes them holy. No layman may eat
of the sacred offerings,[57] nor may a priest's visitor or hired laborer eat of them.
11 But if a priest acquires a slave for money, the slave may eat of them, and those
12 born into his household also may eat his food. If a priest's daughter marries
13 a layman, she may no longer eat of the sacred gifts. If a priest's daughter is a
widow or a divorcée, has no children, and returns to live in her father's house
as when she was young, she may eat her father's food again; but no layperson
14 may do so. If someone eats of the sacred gift unintentionally, he shall make
15 restitution to the priest, adding an extra fifth to its value. The people must
16 not profane the sacred meats that Israelites bring as offerings to the LORD or
incur the penalty of iniquity by eating their sacred offerings; for I, the LORD,
make them holy."

17 18 The LORD spoke to Moshe: "Speak to Aharon, his sons, and all the Israelites.
Say: When anyone of the House of Israel or of the migrants living in Israel
presents an offering to the LORD as a burnt offering – whether in fulfillment
19 of a vow or as a freewill offering – to be acceptable on your behalf, it must
20 be an unblemished male from the herd, or of the sheep or goats. Do not
offer anything that has a blemish, for it will not be accepted on your behalf.
21 When someone presents a peace sacrifice to the LORD from the herd or
flock – whether because of a spoken vow or as a freewill offering – it must be
22 unblemished to be acceptable; there shall be no blemish on it. Do not present
to the LORD anything blind, injured, or maimed, or with warts, a severe rash,
or scabs. Do not place any of these on the altar as a fire offering to the LORD.
23 You may offer as a freewill offering an ox or sheep with a limb deformed or
24 uncloven, but they will not be accepted in fulfillment of a vow. Do not offer
to the LORD an animal whose testicles are bruised, crushed, torn, or cut off;
25 and do not do such things in your land. Do not accept such animals from a
migrant as an offering of foodstuffs to your God. Because they are mutilated
26 and blemished, they will not be accepted on your behalf." The
27 LORD spoke to Moshe: "When an ox or sheep or goat is born, it shall remain
with its mother for seven days. From the eighth day it is acceptable as a
28 sacrifice, a fire offering to the LORD, but do not slaughter an ox or sheep
29 and its young on the same day. When you sacrifice a thanksgiving offering
30 for the LORD, sacrifice it so that it will be acceptable on your behalf. It shall

57 | The sacred gifts designated for the priests.

אוֹ זָב בַּקֳּדָשִׁים לֹא יֹאכַל עַד אֲשֶׁר יִטְהָר וְהַנֹּגֵעַ בְּכָל־טְמֵא־נֶפֶשׁ
ה אוֹ אִישׁ אֲשֶׁר־תֵּצֵא מִמֶּנּוּ שִׁכְבַת־זָרַע׃ אוֹ־אִישׁ אֲשֶׁר יִגַּע בְּכָל־
ו שֶׁרֶץ אֲשֶׁר יִטְמָא־לוֹ אוֹ בְאָדָם אֲשֶׁר יִטְמָא־לוֹ לְכֹל טֻמְאָתוֹ׃ נֶפֶשׁ
אֲשֶׁר תִּגַּע־בּוֹ וְטָמְאָה עַד־הָעָרֶב וְלֹא יֹאכַל מִן־הַקֳּדָשִׁים כִּי אִם־
ז רָחַץ בְּשָׂרוֹ בַּמָּיִם׃ וּבָא הַשֶּׁמֶשׁ וְטָהֵר וְאַחַר יֹאכַל מִן־הַקֳּדָשִׁים כִּי
ח ט לַחְמוֹ הוּא׃ נְבֵלָה וּטְרֵפָה לֹא יֹאכַל לְטָמְאָה־בָהּ אֲנִי יְהוָה׃ וְשָׁמְרוּ
אֶת־מִשְׁמַרְתִּי וְלֹא־יִשְׂאוּ עָלָיו חֵטְא וּמֵתוּ בוֹ כִּי יְחַלְּלֻהוּ אֲנִי יְהוָה
י מְקַדְּשָׁם׃ וְכָל־זָר לֹא־יֹאכַל קֹדֶשׁ תּוֹשַׁב כֹּהֵן וְשָׂכִיר לֹא־יֹאכַל קֹדֶשׁ׃
יא וְכֹהֵן כִּי־יִקְנֶה נֶפֶשׁ קִנְיַן כַּסְפּוֹ הוּא יֹאכַל בּוֹ וִילִיד בֵּיתוֹ הֵם יֹאכְלוּ
יב בְלַחְמוֹ׃ וּבַת־כֹּהֵן כִּי תִהְיֶה לְאִישׁ זָר הִוא בִּתְרוּמַת הַקֳּדָשִׁים לֹא
יג תֹאכֵל׃ וּבַת־כֹּהֵן כִּי תִהְיֶה אַלְמָנָה וּגְרוּשָׁה וְזֶרַע אֵין לָהּ וְשָׁבָה
אֶל־בֵּית אָבִיהָ כִּנְעוּרֶיהָ מִלֶּחֶם אָבִיהָ תֹּאכֵל וְכָל־זָר לֹא־יֹאכַל
יד בּוֹ׃ וְאִישׁ כִּי־יֹאכַל קֹדֶשׁ בִּשְׁגָגָה וְיָסַף חֲמִשִׁיתוֹ עָלָיו וְנָתַן לַכֹּהֵן
טו אֶת־הַקֹּדֶשׁ׃ וְלֹא יְחַלְּלוּ אֶת־קָדְשֵׁי בְּנֵי יִשְׂרָאֵל אֵת אֲשֶׁר־יָרִימוּ
טז לַיהוָה׃ וְהִשִּׂיאוּ אוֹתָם עֲוֺן אַשְׁמָה בְּאָכְלָם אֶת־קָדְשֵׁיהֶם כִּי אֲנִי יְהוָה
מְקַדְּשָׁם׃
יז יח וַיְדַבֵּר יְהוָה אֶל־מֹשֶׁה לֵּאמֹר׃ דַּבֵּר אֶל־אַהֲרֹן וְאֶל־בָּנָיו וְאֶל כָּל־בְּנֵי יח שלישי
יִשְׂרָאֵל וְאָמַרְתָּ אֲלֵהֶם אִישׁ אִישׁ מִבֵּית יִשְׂרָאֵל וּמִן־הַגֵּר בְּיִשְׂרָאֵל
אֲשֶׁר יַקְרִיב קָרְבָּנוֹ לְכָל־נִדְרֵיהֶם וּלְכָל־נִדְבוֹתָם אֲשֶׁר־יַקְרִיבוּ לַיהוָה
יט כ לְעֹלָה׃ לִרְצֹנְכֶם תָּמִים זָכָר בַּבָּקָר בַּכְּשָׂבִים וּבָעִזִּים׃ כֹּל אֲשֶׁר־בּוֹ
כא מוּם לֹא תַקְרִיבוּ כִּי־לֹא לְרָצוֹן יִהְיֶה לָכֶם׃ וְאִישׁ כִּי־יַקְרִיב זֶבַח־
שְׁלָמִים לַיהוָה לְפַלֵּא־נֶדֶר אוֹ לִנְדָבָה בַּבָּקָר אוֹ בַצֹּאן תָּמִים יִהְיֶה
כב לְרָצוֹן כָּל־מוּם לֹא יִהְיֶה־בּוֹ׃ עַוֶּרֶת אוֹ שָׁבוּר אוֹ־חָרוּץ אוֹ־יַבֶּלֶת אוֹ
גָרָב אוֹ יַלֶּפֶת לֹא־תַקְרִיבוּ אֵלֶּה לַיהוָה וְאִשֶּׁה לֹא־תִתְּנוּ מֵהֶם עַל־
כג הַמִּזְבֵּחַ לַיהוָה׃ וְשׁוֹר וָשֶׂה שָׂרוּעַ וְקָלוּט נְדָבָה תַּעֲשֶׂה אֹתוֹ וּלְנֵדֶר לֹא
כד יֵרָצֶה׃ וּמָעוּךְ וְכָתוּת וְנָתוּק וְכָרוּת לֹא תַקְרִיבוּ לַיהוָה וּבְאַרְצְכֶם לֹא
כה תַעֲשׂוּ׃ וּמִיַּד בֶּן־נֵכָר לֹא תַקְרִיבוּ אֶת־לֶחֶם אֱלֹהֵיכֶם מִכָּל־אֵלֶּה כִּי
כו מָשְׁחָתָם בָּהֶם מוּם בָּם לֹא יֵרָצוּ לָכֶם׃ וַיְדַבֵּר יְהוָה אֶל־
כז מֹשֶׁה לֵּאמֹר׃ שׁוֹר אוֹ־כֶשֶׂב אוֹ־עֵז כִּי יִוָּלֵד וְהָיָה שִׁבְעַת יָמִים תַּחַת
כח אִמּוֹ וּמִיּוֹם הַשְּׁמִינִי וָהָלְאָה יֵרָצֶה לְקָרְבַּן אִשֶּׁה לַיהוָה׃ וְשׁוֹר אוֹ־שֶׂה
כט אֹתוֹ וְאֶת־בְּנוֹ לֹא תִשְׁחֲטוּ בְּיוֹם אֶחָד׃ וְכִי־תִזְבְּחוּ זֶבַח־תּוֹדָה לַיהוָה
ל לִרְצֹנְכֶם תִּזְבָּחוּ׃ בַּיּוֹם הַהוּא יֵאָכֵל לֹא־תוֹתִירוּ מִמֶּנּוּ עַד־בֹּקֶר אֲנִי

be eaten on the same day – leave none of it to the morning; I am the LORD.
31 32 Keep My commands and fulfill them; I am the LORD. Do not profane My
holy name – that I may be sanctified in the midst of the Israelites. I am the
33 LORD, who makes you holy, who brought you out of Egypt to be your God:
I am the LORD."
23 1 2 The LORD spoke to Moshe: "Speak to the Israelites. Say: These are the LORD's
appointed times that you shall proclaim as sacred assemblies; these are My
3 appointed times. Work shall be done through six days, but the seventh day
shall be a Sabbath of complete rest, a sacred assembly. You shall perform no
work at all; it shall be a Sabbath for the LORD in all your dwellings.
4 These are the LORD's appointed times, sacred assemblies, which you shall
5 proclaim at their appointed times. In the first month, the fourteenth of the
month in the afternoon is the time for the Passover sacrifice to the LORD.
6 The fifteenth day of this month is the LORD's Festival of Unleavened Bread;
7 for seven days you shall eat unleavened bread. The first day shall be a sacred
8 assembly for you; you shall perform no laborious work. And you shall present
a fire offering for the LORD for seven days; on the seventh day there shall be
a sacred assembly; you shall perform no laborious work."
9 10 The LORD spoke to Moshe: "Speak to the Israelites. Say: When you come
to the land that I am giving you and reap its harvest, bring the first sheaf of
11 your harvest to the priest. He shall display the sheaf this way and that before
the LORD for your acceptance; on the day after the day of rest the priest shall
12 display it. On the day you display the sheaf this way and that, you shall offer
13 a yearling sheep without blemish as a burnt offering to the LORD. Its grain
offering shall be two-tenths of an ephah of fine flour mixed with oil, a fire
offering for the LORD, a pleasing aroma; and its libation shall be a quarter of
14 a hin of wine. Until that day, until you bring this sacrifice to your God, you
shall eat no bread or roasted grain or ripe grain. This is an everlasting statute
15 throughout your generations, in all your dwellings. And from
the day you bring the sheaf of the wave offering, the day after the day of rest,
16 you shall count for yourselves seven complete weeks. To the day after the
seventh week, you shall count fifty days; and then you shall present a new
17 grain offering to the LORD. You shall bring two loaves of bread from your
dwellings made with two-tenths of an ephah of fine flour baked with leaven,
18 as a wave offering: first produce to the LORD. Together with the bread, you
shall present seven unblemished yearling male lambs, one young bull, and
two rams – these shall be a burnt offering for the LORD with their grain
offering and their libations, a fire offering, a pleasing aroma to the LORD.
19 And you shall offer one he-goat as a purification offering and two yearling
20 male sheep as peace sacrifices. The priest shall display them this way and
that with the bread of the first produce as a wave offering before the LORD
together with the two sheep; they shall be holy to the LORD and belong to
21 the priest. On that day you shall make a proclamation; it shall be a sacred
assembly for you; you shall perform no laborious work. This is an everlasting
22 statute throughout your generations in all your dwellings. And when you

לא לב יְהוָה: וּשְׁמַרְתֶּם מִצְוֹתַי וַעֲשִׂיתֶם אֹתָם אֲנִי יְהוָה: וְלֹא תְחַלְּלוּ אֶת־
לג שֵׁם קָדְשִׁי וְנִקְדַּשְׁתִּי בְּתוֹךְ בְּנֵי יִשְׂרָאֵל אֲנִי יְהוָה מְקַדִּשְׁכֶם: הַמּוֹצִיא
אֶתְכֶם מֵאֶרֶץ מִצְרַיִם לִהְיוֹת לָכֶם לֵאלֹהִים אֲנִי יְהוָה:
כג א ב וַיְדַבֵּר יְהוָה אֶל־מֹשֶׁה לֵּאמֹר: דַּבֵּר אֶל־בְּנֵי יִשְׂרָאֵל וְאָמַרְתָּ אֲלֵהֶם רביעי
ג מוֹעֲדֵי יְהוָה אֲשֶׁר־תִּקְרְאוּ אֹתָם מִקְרָאֵי קֹדֶשׁ אֵלֶּה הֵם מוֹעֲדָי: שֵׁשֶׁת
יָמִים תֵּעָשֶׂה מְלָאכָה וּבַיּוֹם הַשְּׁבִיעִי שַׁבַּת שַׁבָּתוֹן מִקְרָא־קֹדֶשׁ כָּל־
מְלָאכָה לֹא תַעֲשׂוּ שַׁבָּת הִוא לַיהוָה בְּכֹל מוֹשְׁבֹתֵיכֶם:
ד ה אֵלֶּה מוֹעֲדֵי יְהוָה מִקְרָאֵי קֹדֶשׁ אֲשֶׁר־תִּקְרְאוּ אֹתָם בְּמוֹעֲדָם: בַּחֹדֶשׁ
ו הָרִאשׁוֹן בְּאַרְבָּעָה עָשָׂר לַחֹדֶשׁ בֵּין הָעַרְבָּיִם פֶּסַח לַיהוָה: וּבַחֲמִשָּׁה
עָשָׂר יוֹם לַחֹדֶשׁ הַזֶּה חַג הַמַּצּוֹת לַיהוָה שִׁבְעַת יָמִים מַצּוֹת תֹּאכֵלוּ:
ז בַּיּוֹם הָרִאשׁוֹן מִקְרָא־קֹדֶשׁ יִהְיֶה לָכֶם כָּל־מְלֶאכֶת עֲבֹדָה לֹא תַעֲשׂוּ:
ח וְהִקְרַבְתֶּם אִשֶּׁה לַיהוָה שִׁבְעַת יָמִים בַּיּוֹם הַשְּׁבִיעִי מִקְרָא־קֹדֶשׁ
כָּל־מְלֶאכֶת עֲבֹדָה לֹא תַעֲשׂוּ:
ט י וַיְדַבֵּר יְהוָה אֶל־מֹשֶׁה לֵּאמֹר: דַּבֵּר אֶל־בְּנֵי יִשְׂרָאֵל וְאָמַרְתָּ אֲלֵהֶם
כִּי־תָבֹאוּ אֶל־הָאָרֶץ אֲשֶׁר אֲנִי נֹתֵן לָכֶם וּקְצַרְתֶּם אֶת־קְצִירָהּ וַהֲבֵאתֶם
יא אֶת־עֹמֶר רֵאשִׁית קְצִירְכֶם אֶל־הַכֹּהֵן: וְהֵנִיף אֶת־הָעֹמֶר לִפְנֵי יְהוָה
יב לִרְצֹנְכֶם מִמָּחֳרַת הַשַּׁבָּת יְנִיפֶנּוּ הַכֹּהֵן: וַעֲשִׂיתֶם בְּיוֹם הֲנִיפְכֶם אֶת־
יג הָעֹמֶר כֶּבֶשׂ תָּמִים בֶּן־שְׁנָתוֹ לְעֹלָה לַיהוָה: וּמִנְחָתוֹ שְׁנֵי עֶשְׂרֹנִים סֹלֶת
יד בְּלוּלָה בַשֶּׁמֶן אִשֶּׁה לַיהוָה רֵיחַ נִיחֹחַ וְנִסְכֹּה יַיִן רְבִיעִת הַהִין: וְלֶחֶם
וְקָלִי וְכַרְמֶל לֹא תֹאכְלוּ עַד־עֶצֶם הַיּוֹם הַזֶּה עַד הֲבִיאֲכֶם אֶת־קָרְבַּן
טו אֱלֹהֵיכֶם חֻקַּת עוֹלָם לְדֹרֹתֵיכֶם בְּכֹל מֹשְׁבֹתֵיכֶם: וּסְפַרְתֶּם יט
לָכֶם מִמָּחֳרַת הַשַּׁבָּת מִיּוֹם הֲבִיאֲכֶם אֶת־עֹמֶר הַתְּנוּפָה שֶׁבַע שַׁבָּתוֹת
טז תְּמִימֹת תִּהְיֶינָה: עַד מִמָּחֳרַת הַשַּׁבָּת הַשְּׁבִיעִת תִּסְפְּרוּ חֲמִשִּׁים יוֹם
יז וְהִקְרַבְתֶּם מִנְחָה חֲדָשָׁה לַיהוָה: מִמּוֹשְׁבֹתֵיכֶם תָּבִיאוּ ׀ לֶחֶם תְּנוּפָה
שְׁתַּיִם שְׁנֵי עֶשְׂרֹנִים סֹלֶת תִּהְיֶינָה חָמֵץ תֵּאָפֶינָה בִּכּוּרִים לַיהוָה:
יח וְהִקְרַבְתֶּם עַל־הַלֶּחֶם שִׁבְעַת כְּבָשִׂים תְּמִימִם בְּנֵי שָׁנָה וּפַר בֶּן־בָּקָר
אֶחָד וְאֵילִם שְׁנָיִם יִהְיוּ עֹלָה לַיהוָה וּמִנְחָתָם וְנִסְכֵּיהֶם אִשֵּׁה רֵיחַ־
יט נִיחֹחַ לַיהוָה: וַעֲשִׂיתֶם שְׂעִיר־עִזִּים אֶחָד לְחַטָּאת וּשְׁנֵי כְבָשִׂים בְּנֵי
כ שָׁנָה לְזֶבַח שְׁלָמִים: וְהֵנִיף הַכֹּהֵן ׀ אֹתָם עַל לֶחֶם הַבִּכֻּרִים תְּנוּפָה
כא לִפְנֵי יְהוָה עַל־שְׁנֵי כְּבָשִׂים קֹדֶשׁ יִהְיוּ לַיהוָה לַכֹּהֵן: וּקְרָאתֶם בְּעֶצֶם ׀
הַיּוֹם הַזֶּה מִקְרָא־קֹדֶשׁ יִהְיֶה לָכֶם כָּל־מְלֶאכֶת עֲבֹדָה לֹא תַעֲשׂוּ חֻקַּת
כב עוֹלָם בְּכָל־מוֹשְׁבֹתֵיכֶם לְדֹרֹתֵיכֶם: וּבְקֻצְרְכֶם אֶת־קְצִיר אַרְצְכֶם לֹא־

reap the harvest of your land, do not reap to the edge of your field or gather
the gleanings of your harvest. Leave them for the poor and for the migrant;
I am the Lord your God."
23 Then the Lord spoke to Moshe: "Tell the Israelites: On the first day of the
24 seventh month, you shall observe a day of rest, a commemoration with the
25 sounding of the ram's horn, a sacred assembly. You shall perform no laborious
26 work, and you shall bring close a fire offering to the Lord." The
27 Lord spoke to Moshe: "Hear: the tenth day of this seventh month is the
Day of Atonement. It shall be a sacred assembly for you, and you shall afflict
28 yourselves and bring a fire offering to the Lord. You shall perform no work
at all during this entire day, for it is the Day of Atonement, there to make
29 atonement for you before the Lord your God. Anyone who does not afflict
30 himself for this whole day shall be severed from his people, and if anyone
performs any work during this whole day, I will annihilate that person from
31 among his people. No work at all may you perform; this is an everlasting
32 statute throughout your generations in all your dwellings. It is a Sabbath of
complete rest for you, and you shall afflict yourselves from the evening of
the ninth day of the month: from evening to evening shall you observe your
Sabbath."
33 The Lord spoke to Moshe: "Tell the Israelites: From the fifteenth day of
34 this seventh month, for seven days shall be the Festival of Tabernacles to
35 the Lord. The first day shall be a sacred assembly; on it, you shall perform
36 no laborious work. For seven days you must bring close a fire offering to
the Lord. The eighth day shall be a sacred assembly for you, and you shall
present a fire offering to the Lord. It is an assembly; you shall perform no
37 laborious work. These are the Lord's festivals, which you shall proclaim,
sacred assemblies to present a fire offering to the Lord: burnt offering, grain
38 offering, sacrifice, and libations, each on its appointed day; in addition to the
Lord's Sabbaths,[58] and in addition to your gifts and all your offerings in the
fulfillment of vows and all the freewill offerings that you give to the Lord.
39 Hear: on the fifteenth day of the seventh month, when you have harvested
the land's produce, you shall celebrate a festival to the Lord for seven days.
40 The first day shall be a day of rest; the eighth day shall be a day of rest. On
the first day you shall take for yourselves fruit of the majestic tree, branches
of palm trees, boughs of the leafy tree, and willows of the brook, and rejoice
41 before the Lord your God for seven days. You shall celebrate it as a festival
to the Lord for seven days in the year. It shall be an everlasting statute
42 throughout your generations; celebrate this in the seventh month. For seven
43 days you shall live in huts. All those native born in Israel must live in huts, so
that future generations may know that I had the Israelites live in huts when
44 I brought them out of the land of Egypt; I am the Lord your God." Thus
Moshe announced the Lord's appointed times to the Israelites.
24 1
2 The Lord spoke to Moshe: "Command the Israelites to bring you pure

58 | Meaning the special Sabbath offerings.

תְּכַלֶּה פְּאַת שָׂדְךָ בְּקֻצְרֶךָ וְלֶקֶט קְצִירְךָ לֹא תְלַקֵּט לֶעָנִי וְלַגֵּר תַּעֲזֹב
אֹתָם אֲנִי יהוה אֱלֹהֵיכֶם׃
כג כד וַיְדַבֵּר יהוה אֶל־מֹשֶׁה לֵּאמֹר׃ דַּבֵּר אֶל־בְּנֵי יִשְׂרָאֵל לֵאמֹר בַּחֹדֶשׁ חמישי
הַשְּׁבִיעִי בְּאֶחָד לַחֹדֶשׁ יִהְיֶה לָכֶם שַׁבָּתוֹן זִכְרוֹן תְּרוּעָה מִקְרָא־קֹדֶשׁ׃
כה כו כָּל־מְלֶאכֶת עֲבֹדָה לֹא תַעֲשׂוּ וְהִקְרַבְתֶּם אִשֶּׁה לַיהוה׃ וַיְדַבֵּר
כז יהוה אֶל־מֹשֶׁה לֵּאמֹר׃ אַךְ בֶּעָשׂוֹר לַחֹדֶשׁ הַשְּׁבִיעִי הַזֶּה יוֹם הַכִּפֻּרִים
הוּא מִקְרָא־קֹדֶשׁ יִהְיֶה לָכֶם וְעִנִּיתֶם אֶת־נַפְשֹׁתֵיכֶם וְהִקְרַבְתֶּם אִשֶּׁה
כח לַיהוה׃ וְכָל־מְלָאכָה לֹא תַעֲשׂוּ בְּעֶצֶם הַיּוֹם הַזֶּה כִּי יוֹם כִּפֻּרִים הוּא
כט לְכַפֵּר עֲלֵיכֶם לִפְנֵי יהוה אֱלֹהֵיכֶם׃ כִּי כָל־הַנֶּפֶשׁ אֲשֶׁר לֹא־תְעֻנֶּה
ל בְּעֶצֶם הַיּוֹם הַזֶּה וְנִכְרְתָה מֵעַמֶּיהָ׃ וְכָל־הַנֶּפֶשׁ אֲשֶׁר תַּעֲשֶׂה כָּל־
מְלָאכָה בְּעֶצֶם הַיּוֹם הַזֶּה וְהַאֲבַדְתִּי אֶת־הַנֶּפֶשׁ הַהִוא מִקֶּרֶב עַמָּהּ׃
לא לב כָּל־מְלָאכָה לֹא תַעֲשׂוּ חֻקַּת עוֹלָם לְדֹרֹתֵיכֶם בְּכֹל מֹשְׁבֹתֵיכֶם׃ שַׁבַּת
שַׁבָּתוֹן הוּא לָכֶם וְעִנִּיתֶם אֶת־נַפְשֹׁתֵיכֶם בְּתִשְׁעָה לַחֹדֶשׁ בָּעֶרֶב
מֵעֶרֶב עַד־עֶרֶב תִּשְׁבְּתוּ שַׁבַּתְּכֶם׃
לג לד וַיְדַבֵּר יהוה אֶל־מֹשֶׁה לֵּאמֹר׃ דַּבֵּר אֶל־בְּנֵי יִשְׂרָאֵל לֵאמֹר בַּחֲמִשָּׁה ששי
לה עָשָׂר יוֹם לַחֹדֶשׁ הַשְּׁבִיעִי הַזֶּה חַג הַסֻּכּוֹת שִׁבְעַת יָמִים לַיהוה׃ בַּיּוֹם
לו הָרִאשׁוֹן מִקְרָא־קֹדֶשׁ כָּל־מְלֶאכֶת עֲבֹדָה לֹא תַעֲשׂוּ׃ שִׁבְעַת יָמִים
תַּקְרִיבוּ אִשֶּׁה לַיהוה בַּיּוֹם הַשְּׁמִינִי מִקְרָא־קֹדֶשׁ יִהְיֶה לָכֶם וְהִקְרַבְתֶּם
לז אִשֶּׁה לַיהוה עֲצֶרֶת הִוא כָּל־מְלֶאכֶת עֲבֹדָה לֹא תַעֲשׂוּ׃ אֵלֶּה מוֹעֲדֵי
יהוה אֲשֶׁר־תִּקְרְאוּ אֹתָם מִקְרָאֵי קֹדֶשׁ לְהַקְרִיב אִשֶּׁה לַיהוה עֹלָה
לח וּמִנְחָה זֶבַח וּנְסָכִים דְּבַר־יוֹם בְּיוֹמוֹ׃ מִלְּבַד שַׁבְּתֹת יהוה וּמִלְּבַד
מַתְּנוֹתֵיכֶם וּמִלְּבַד כָּל־נִדְרֵיכֶם וּמִלְּבַד כָּל־נִדְבֹתֵיכֶם אֲשֶׁר תִּתְּנוּ
לט לַיהוה׃ אַךְ בַּחֲמִשָּׁה עָשָׂר יוֹם לַחֹדֶשׁ הַשְּׁבִיעִי בְּאָסְפְּכֶם אֶת־תְּבוּאַת
הָאָרֶץ תָּחֹגּוּ אֶת־חַג־יהוה שִׁבְעַת יָמִים בַּיּוֹם הָרִאשׁוֹן שַׁבָּתוֹן וּבַיּוֹם
מ הַשְּׁמִינִי שַׁבָּתוֹן׃ וּלְקַחְתֶּם לָכֶם בַּיּוֹם הָרִאשׁוֹן פְּרִי עֵץ הָדָר כַּפֹּת
תְּמָרִים וַעֲנַף עֵץ־עָבֹת וְעַרְבֵי־נָחַל וּשְׂמַחְתֶּם לִפְנֵי יהוה אֱלֹהֵיכֶם
מא שִׁבְעַת יָמִים׃ וְחַגֹּתֶם אֹתוֹ חַג לַיהוה שִׁבְעַת יָמִים בַּשָּׁנָה חֻקַּת עוֹלָם
מב לְדֹרֹתֵיכֶם בַּחֹדֶשׁ הַשְּׁבִיעִי תָּחֹגּוּ אֹתוֹ׃ בַּסֻּכֹּת תֵּשְׁבוּ שִׁבְעַת יָמִים
מג כָּל־הָאֶזְרָח בְּיִשְׂרָאֵל יֵשְׁבוּ בַּסֻּכֹּת׃ לְמַעַן יֵדְעוּ דֹרֹתֵיכֶם כִּי בַסֻּכּוֹת
הוֹשַׁבְתִּי אֶת־בְּנֵי יִשְׂרָאֵל בְּהוֹצִיאִי אוֹתָם מֵאֶרֶץ מִצְרָיִם אֲנִי יהוה
מד אֱלֹהֵיכֶם׃ וַיְדַבֵּר מֹשֶׁה אֶת־מֹעֲדֵי יהוה אֶל־בְּנֵי יִשְׂרָאֵל׃
כד א ב וַיְדַבֵּר יהוה אֶל־מֹשֶׁה לֵּאמֹר׃ צַו אֶת־בְּנֵי יִשְׂרָאֵל וְיִקְחוּ אֵלֶיךָ שֶׁמֶן שביעי

3 oil from crushed olives for the light, to kindle the lamp, every night. From
evening to morning, before the LORD, Aharon shall set it up outside the
curtain of the testimony in the Tent of Meeting to burn each night. This shall
4 be a rule for all time, throughout your generations. Aharon shall set out the
lamps on the pure candelabrum each day before the LORD.
5 And you shall take fine flour and bake twelve loaves, two-tenths of an ephah
6 for each loaf. You shall place them in two columns, six to each column,
7 on the pure table[59] before the LORD. Lay pure incense on each stack, as a
8 remembrance[60] for the bread, as a fire offering to the LORD. Every Sabbath
he shall set it out, always, before the LORD on behalf of the Israelites: an
9 everlasting covenant. It shall belong to Aharon and his sons. They shall eat
it in a holy place because it is holy of holies among the LORD's fire offerings,
10 their perpetual share." A man went out among the Israelites, the
son of an Israelite woman and an Egyptian man. And a fight broke out in
11 the camp between this son of an Israelite woman, and an Israelite man. The
Israelite woman's son blasphemed the Name and cursed – his mother's name
was Shlomit, daughter of Divri, of the tribe of Dan – and they brought him
12 before Moshe. They placed the man in custody until the LORD's verdict would
be pronounced to them.
13 And the LORD spoke to Moshe: "Take the one who cursed outside the camp.
14 All the people who heard him shall lay their hands on his head – and then the
15 whole community shall stone him. Tell the Israelites: Anyone who curses his
16 God shall bear the sin, and anyone who blasphemes the LORD's name shall
be put to death: the whole community shall stone him. Migrant and native
17 born alike: one who blasphemes the LORD's name shall be put to death. One
18 who takes the life of any human being shall be put to death. One who takes
19 the life of an animal shall make restitution for it: life for life. One who injures
20 his fellow man shall be penalized in proportion to the injury inflicted:[61] the
cost of[62] a broken bone for a broken bone, of an eye for an eye, of a tooth for a
tooth. Just as he inflicted injury on another human being, so shall he suffer the
21 loss.[63] One who kills an animal shall make restitution for it; but one who kills a
22 human being shall be put to death. There shall be one law for you, for migrant
23 and for native born alike, for I am the LORD your God." Moshe told this to the
Israelites, and so they took the blasphemer outside the camp and stoned him.
Thus the Israelites did as the LORD had commanded Moshe.
25 1 On Mount Sinai the LORD spoke to Moshe: "Speak to the Israelites. Say: BEHAR
2 When you enter the land that I am giving you, the land shall keep a Sabbath
3 to the LORD. For six years you may plant your fields, prune your vineyards,
4 and harvest their crops. But the seventh year shall be to the land a Sabbath of

59 | That is, of pure gold, referring to the overlay (see Ex. 25:24).

60 | See note on 2:2. This incense, unlike the bread, was burned on the altar.

61 | Literally "shall have done to him the same thing that he did." The translation follows the rabbinic interpretation.

62 | This phrase is not explicit in the Hebrew; see previous note.

63 | Literally "so shall it be inflicted on him."

ג זֵית זָךְ כָּתִית לַמָּאוֹר לְהַעֲלֹת נֵר תָּמִיד: מִחוּץ לְפָרֹכֶת הָעֵדֻת
בְּאֹהֶל מוֹעֵד יַעֲרֹךְ אֹתוֹ אַהֲרֹן מֵעֶרֶב עַד־בֹּקֶר לִפְנֵי יהוה תָּמִיד
ד חֻקַּת עוֹלָם לְדֹרֹתֵיכֶם: עַל הַמְּנֹרָה הַטְּהֹרָה יַעֲרֹךְ אֶת־הַנֵּרוֹת לִפְנֵי
יהוה תָּמִיד:
ה וְלָקַחְתָּ סֹלֶת וְאָפִיתָ אֹתָהּ שְׁתֵּים עֶשְׂרֵה חַלּוֹת שְׁנֵי עֶשְׂרֹנִים יִהְיֶה
ו הַחַלָּה הָאֶחָת: וְשַׂמְתָּ אוֹתָם שְׁתַּיִם מַעֲרָכוֹת שֵׁשׁ הַמַּעֲרָכֶת עַל
ז הַשֻּׁלְחָן הַטָּהֹר לִפְנֵי יהוה: וְנָתַתָּ עַל־הַמַּעֲרֶכֶת לְבֹנָה זַכָּה וְהָיְתָה
ח לַלֶּחֶם לְאַזְכָּרָה אִשֶּׁה לַיהוה: בְּיוֹם הַשַּׁבָּת בְּיוֹם הַשַּׁבָּת יַעַרְכֶנּוּ לִפְנֵי
ט יהוה תָּמִיד מֵאֵת בְּנֵי־יִשְׂרָאֵל בְּרִית עוֹלָם: וְהָיְתָה לְאַהֲרֹן וּלְבָנָיו
וַאֲכָלֻהוּ בְּמָקוֹם קָדֹשׁ כִּי קֹדֶשׁ קָדָשִׁים הוּא לוֹ מֵאִשֵּׁי יהוה חָק־
י עוֹלָם: וַיֵּצֵא בֶּן־אִשָּׁה יִשְׂרְאֵלִית וְהוּא בֶּן־אִישׁ מִצְרִי
בְּתוֹךְ בְּנֵי יִשְׂרָאֵל וַיִּנָּצוּ בַּמַּחֲנֶה בֶּן הַיִּשְׂרְאֵלִית וְאִישׁ הַיִּשְׂרְאֵלִי:
יא וַיִּקֹּב בֶּן־הָאִשָּׁה הַיִּשְׂרְאֵלִית אֶת־הַשֵּׁם וַיְקַלֵּל וַיָּבִיאוּ אֹתוֹ אֶל־מֹשֶׁה
יב וְשֵׁם אִמּוֹ שְׁלֹמִית בַּת־דִּבְרִי לְמַטֵּה־דָן: וַיַּנִּיחֻהוּ בַּמִּשְׁמָר לִפְרֹשׁ
לָהֶם עַל־פִּי יהוה:
יג יד וַיְדַבֵּר יהוה אֶל־מֹשֶׁה לֵּאמֹר: הוֹצֵא אֶת־הַמְקַלֵּל אֶל־מִחוּץ לַמַּחֲנֶה
וְסָמְכוּ כָל־הַשֹּׁמְעִים אֶת־יְדֵיהֶם עַל־רֹאשׁוֹ וְרָגְמוּ אֹתוֹ כָּל־הָעֵדָה:
טו וְאֶל־בְּנֵי יִשְׂרָאֵל תְּדַבֵּר לֵאמֹר אִישׁ אִישׁ כִּי־יְקַלֵּל אֱלֹהָיו וְנָשָׂא
טז חֶטְאוֹ: וְנֹקֵב שֵׁם־יהוה מוֹת יוּמָת רָגוֹם יִרְגְּמוּ־בוֹ כָּל־הָעֵדָה כַּגֵּר
יז כָּאֶזְרָח בְּנָקְבוֹ־שֵׁם יוּמָת: וְאִישׁ כִּי יַכֶּה כָּל־נֶפֶשׁ אָדָם מוֹת יוּמָת:
יח יט וּמַכֵּה נֶפֶשׁ־בְּהֵמָה יְשַׁלְּמֶנָּה נֶפֶשׁ תַּחַת נָפֶשׁ: וְאִישׁ כִּי־יִתֵּן מוּם
כ בַּעֲמִיתוֹ כַּאֲשֶׁר עָשָׂה כֵּן יֵעָשֶׂה לּוֹ: שֶׁבֶר תַּחַת שֶׁבֶר עַיִן תַּחַת עַיִן שֵׁן
כא תַּחַת שֵׁן כַּאֲשֶׁר יִתֵּן מוּם בָּאָדָם כֵּן יִנָּתֶן בּוֹ: וּמַכֵּה בְהֵמָה יְשַׁלְּמֶנָּה מפטיר
כב וּמַכֵּה אָדָם יוּמָת: מִשְׁפַּט אֶחָד יִהְיֶה לָכֶם כַּגֵּר כָּאֶזְרָח יִהְיֶה כִּי אֲנִי
כג יהוה אֱלֹהֵיכֶם: וַיְדַבֵּר מֹשֶׁה אֶל־בְּנֵי יִשְׂרָאֵל וַיּוֹצִיאוּ אֶת־הַמְקַלֵּל
אֶל־מִחוּץ לַמַּחֲנֶה וַיִּרְגְּמוּ אֹתוֹ אָבֶן וּבְנֵי־יִשְׂרָאֵל עָשׂוּ כַּאֲשֶׁר צִוָּה
יהוה אֶת־מֹשֶׁה:
כה א ב וַיְדַבֵּר יהוה אֶל־מֹשֶׁה בְּהַר סִינַי לֵאמֹר: דַּבֵּר אֶל־בְּנֵי יִשְׂרָאֵל וְאָמַרְתָּ בהר
אֲלֵהֶם כִּי תָבֹאוּ אֶל־הָאָרֶץ אֲשֶׁר אֲנִי נֹתֵן לָכֶם וְשָׁבְתָה הָאָרֶץ שַׁבָּת
ג לַיהוה: שֵׁשׁ שָׁנִים תִּזְרַע שָׂדֶךָ וְשֵׁשׁ שָׁנִים תִּזְמֹר כַּרְמֶךָ וְאָסַפְתָּ
ד אֶת־תְּבוּאָתָהּ: וּבַשָּׁנָה הַשְּׁבִיעִת שַׁבַּת שַׁבָּתוֹן יִהְיֶה לָאָרֶץ שַׁבָּת

complete rest, a Sabbath to the LORD. You shall not sow your fields or prune
5 your vineyards; you shall not harvest what grows of itself or gather the grapes
6 of your unpruned vine; it is a year of rest for the land. You may eat the land's
Sabbath yield: you, your male and female servants, and the hired worker and
7 resident worker who live with you, your livestock and the wild animals in your
8 land – whatever the land produces is there to be eaten. And you shall
count off seven Sabbaths of years – seven times seven years – so that the seven
9 Sabbath cycles total forty-nine years. Then you shall sound the ram's horn.
On the tenth day of the seventh month, on the Day of Atonement, you shall
10 sound the horn all across your land. You shall consecrate the fiftieth year and
proclaim liberty throughout the land to all its inhabitants. This shall be your
Jubilee; each person shall return to his hereditary home, each to his family.
11 The fiftieth year shall be a Jubilee for you. Do not sow, or reap what grows
12 of itself, or harvest the unpruned vines, for it is a Jubilee; it shall be holy to
13 you. You shall eat only directly from the field. And in this Jubilee year, each
14 person shall return to his hereditary home. But when you sell land to your
15 fellow or buy it from him, brother must not cheat brother: you shall buy from
your neighbor by the number of years since the Jubilee; he shall sell to you
16 by the number of years left for harvesting. You shall increase the price if the
remaining years are many, and lower it if they are few; what is being sold to
17 you is the number of harvests. You shall not cheat one another; you shall hold
18 your God in awe; I am the LORD your God. You shall fulfill My statutes, and
keep and act in accordance with My laws – then you will live securely on the
19 land. The land will yield its fruit and you will eat your fill and live securely
20 there. If you should ask, 'What shall we eat in the seventh year? We may not
21 sow and may not harvest our crops' – I will send My blessing over you in the
22 sixth year and it will yield three years' harvest. As you sow in the eighth year,
you will eat of the old harvest; you will be still be eating of the old when the
23 crop of the ninth year comes. And the land shall not be sold in perpetuity, for
24 the land is Mine. You are merely migrants and visitors to Me. Throughout
25 the land that you possess, you must allow land to be redeemed. If
your brother grows poor and sells part of his hereditary land, his closest
26 redeeming relative shall come and redeem what his kinsman has sold. If the
person lacks a relative to redeem it, but later prospers and can afford to buy
27 it back, he shall calculate the years since its sale and refund the balance to
28 the one to whom he sold it, and return to his hereditary home. If he cannot
afford to recover it, what was sold shall remain in the possession of the buyer
until the Jubilee year; but at the Jubilee it shall be released, and he shall return
29 to his possession. One who sells a house in a walled city retains the
right to redeem it until a year after its sale. This is the period of redemption.

ה לַיהוָה שָׂדְךָ לֹא תִזְרָע וְכַרְמְךָ לֹא תִזְמֹר: אֵת סְפִיחַ קְצִירְךָ לֹא
ו תִקְצוֹר וְאֶת־עִנְּבֵי נְזִירֶךָ לֹא תִבְצֹר שְׁנַת שַׁבָּתוֹן יִהְיֶה לָאָרֶץ: וְהָיְתָה
שַׁבַּת הָאָרֶץ לָכֶם לְאָכְלָה לְךָ וּלְעַבְדְּךָ וְלַאֲמָתֶךָ וְלִשְׂכִירְךָ וּלְתוֹשָׁבְךָ
ז הַגָּרִים עִמָּךְ: וְלִבְהֶמְתְּךָ וְלַחַיָּה אֲשֶׁר בְּאַרְצֶךָ תִּהְיֶה כָל־תְּבוּאָתָהּ
ח לֶאֱכֹל: וְסָפַרְתָּ לְךָ שֶׁבַע שַׁבְּתֹת שָׁנִים שֶׁבַע שָׁנִים
שֶׁבַע פְּעָמִים וְהָיוּ לְךָ יְמֵי שֶׁבַע שַׁבְּתֹת הַשָּׁנִים תֵּשַׁע וְאַרְבָּעִים שָׁנָה:
ט וְהַעֲבַרְתָּ שׁוֹפַר תְּרוּעָה בַּחֹדֶשׁ הַשְּׁבִעִי בֶּעָשׂוֹר לַחֹדֶשׁ בְּיוֹם הַכִּפֻּרִים
י תַּעֲבִירוּ שׁוֹפָר בְּכָל־אַרְצְכֶם: וְקִדַּשְׁתֶּם אֵת שְׁנַת הַחֲמִשִּׁים שָׁנָה
וּקְרָאתֶם דְּרוֹר בָּאָרֶץ לְכָל־יֹשְׁבֶיהָ יוֹבֵל הִוא תִּהְיֶה לָכֶם וְשַׁבְתֶּם אִישׁ
יא אֶל־אֲחֻזָּתוֹ וְאִישׁ אֶל־מִשְׁפַּחְתּוֹ תָּשֻׁבוּ: יוֹבֵל הִוא שְׁנַת הַחֲמִשִּׁים
שָׁנָה תִּהְיֶה לָכֶם לֹא תִזְרָעוּ וְלֹא תִקְצְרוּ אֶת־סְפִיחֶיהָ וְלֹא תִבְצְרוּ
יב אֶת־נְזִרֶיהָ: כִּי יוֹבֵל הִוא קֹדֶשׁ תִּהְיֶה לָכֶם מִן־הַשָּׂדֶה תֹּאכְלוּ אֶת־
יג יד תְּבוּאָתָהּ: בִּשְׁנַת הַיּוֹבֵל הַזֹּאת תָּשֻׁבוּ אִישׁ אֶל־אֲחֻזָּתוֹ: וְכִי־תִמְכְּרוּ ב שני
מִמְכָּר לַעֲמִיתֶךָ אוֹ קָנֹה מִיַּד עֲמִיתֶךָ אַל־תּוֹנוּ אִישׁ אֶת־אָחִיו:
טו בְּמִסְפַּר שָׁנִים אַחַר הַיּוֹבֵל תִּקְנֶה מֵאֵת עֲמִיתֶךָ בְּמִסְפַּר שְׁנֵי־תְבוּאֹת
טז יִמְכָּר־לָךְ: לְפִי ׀ רֹב הַשָּׁנִים תַּרְבֶּה מִקְנָתוֹ וּלְפִי מְעֹט הַשָּׁנִים תַּמְעִיט
יז מִקְנָתוֹ כִּי מִסְפַּר תְּבוּאֹת הוּא מֹכֵר לָךְ: וְלֹא תוֹנוּ אִישׁ אֶת־עֲמִיתוֹ
יח וְיָרֵאתָ מֵּאֱלֹהֶיךָ כִּי אֲנִי יְהוָה אֱלֹהֵיכֶם: וַעֲשִׂיתֶם אֶת־חֻקֹּתַי וְאֶת־ שלישי
יט מִשְׁפָּטַי תִּשְׁמְרוּ וַעֲשִׂיתֶם אֹתָם וִישַׁבְתֶּם עַל־הָאָרֶץ לָבֶטַח: וְנָתְנָה /שני/
כ הָאָרֶץ פִּרְיָהּ וַאֲכַלְתֶּם לָשֹׂבַע וִישַׁבְתֶּם לָבֶטַח עָלֶיהָ: וְכִי תֹאמְרוּ
מַה־נֹּאכַל בַּשָּׁנָה הַשְּׁבִיעִת הֵן לֹא נִזְרָע וְלֹא נֶאֱסֹף אֶת־תְּבוּאָתֵנוּ:
כא וְצִוִּיתִי אֶת־בִּרְכָתִי לָכֶם בַּשָּׁנָה הַשִּׁשִּׁית וְעָשָׂת אֶת־הַתְּבוּאָה לִשְׁלֹשׁ
כב הַשָּׁנִים: וּזְרַעְתֶּם אֵת הַשָּׁנָה הַשְּׁמִינִת וַאֲכַלְתֶּם מִן־הַתְּבוּאָה יָשָׁן עַד ׀
כג הַשָּׁנָה הַתְּשִׁיעִת עַד־בּוֹא תְּבוּאָתָהּ תֹּאכְלוּ יָשָׁן: וְהָאָרֶץ לֹא תִמָּכֵר
כד לִצְמִתֻת כִּי־לִי הָאָרֶץ כִּי־גֵרִים וְתוֹשָׁבִים אַתֶּם עִמָּדִי: וּבְכֹל אֶרֶץ
כה אֲחֻזַּתְכֶם גְּאֻלָּה תִּתְּנוּ לָאָרֶץ: כִּי־יָמוּךְ אָחִיךָ וּמָכַר רביעי
כו מֵאֲחֻזָּתוֹ וּבָא גֹאֲלוֹ הַקָּרֹב אֵלָיו וְגָאַל אֵת מִמְכַּר אָחִיו: וְאִישׁ כִּי לֹא
כז יִהְיֶה־לּוֹ גֹּאֵל וְהִשִּׂיגָה יָדוֹ וּמָצָא כְּדֵי גְאֻלָּתוֹ: וְחִשַּׁב אֶת־שְׁנֵי מִמְכָּרוֹ
כח וְהֵשִׁיב אֶת־הָעֹדֵף לָאִישׁ אֲשֶׁר מָכַר־לוֹ וְשָׁב לַאֲחֻזָּתוֹ: וְאִם לֹא־
מָצְאָה יָדוֹ דֵּי הָשִׁיב לוֹ וְהָיָה מִמְכָּרוֹ בְּיַד הַקֹּנֶה אֹתוֹ עַד שְׁנַת הַיּוֹבֵל
כט וְיָצָא בַּיֹּבֵל וְשָׁב לַאֲחֻזָּתוֹ: וְאִישׁ כִּי־יִמְכֹּר בֵּית־מוֹשַׁב חמישי /שלישי/
עִיר חוֹמָה וְהָיְתָה גְּאֻלָּתוֹ עַד־תֹּם שְׁנַת מִמְכָּרוֹ יָמִים תִּהְיֶה גְאֻלָּתוֹ:

30 If it is not redeemed before a full year has passed, the house in the walled city
shall belong permanently to the buyer and his descendants forever; it is not
31 released at the Jubilee. Houses in villages without surrounding walls, however,
are considered as if they were open country. They may be redeemed, and they
32 are released at the Jubilee. In the Levitical towns – Levites always retain the
33 right to redeem houses in their ancestral towns. Levite property that can be
redeemed – houses sold in towns belonging to them – shall be released at the
Jubilee, because the houses in Levitical towns are their ancestral possession
34 among the Israelites. But the pastureland around their towns can never be
35 sold, because that is their permanent possession. If your brother
becomes poor and is struggling, extend him support – a migrant or visitor
36 also – that he may live among you. Do not take advance or accrued interest
37 from him; fear your God so that your brother can live with you. Do not lend
38 him your money at interest or provide him with food at a profit. I am the
Lord your God, who brought you out of the land of Egypt to give the land
39 of Canaan to you, to be your God. If your brother becomes poor
40 and sells himself to you, do not work him as a slave. He shall abide with you
like a hired worker or a resident worker and work for you until the Jubilee
41 year. Then he and his children shall be free to leave you and return to their
42 family and their ancestral land. For they are My servants whom I brought
43 out from Egypt: they cannot be sold as slaves. Do not rule them harshly with
44 backbreaking labor; fear your God. As for male or female slaves that you may
have: from the nations around you, you may acquire a male or female slave.
45 You may also acquire them from among the migrants residing with you and
from their families among you who were born in your land; they may be yours,
46 in your possession. They become hereditary property that you can bequeath
to your children; they may be your slaves, but over your brother Israelites you
47 may not rule so harshly. If a migrant or temporary resident prospers
among you, and your fellow Israelite becomes poor and is sold to a migrant
48 residing among you or to a branch of a foreign family, the Israelite has the
right, subsequent to the sale, to be redeemed; one of his relatives may redeem
49 him. His uncle or cousin or any other blood relative may redeem him, or if
50 he can afford to do so, he may redeem himself. Together with his owner, he
shall calculate the time from the year he was sold until the Jubilee year. The
price of his release shall be based on that number of years, as if he had been
51 there as a hired laborer. If many years remain, he shall pay that proportion
52 of his purchase price for his redemption. If only a few years remain until the
Jubilee year, he shall calculate that and pay for the redemption accordingly.
53 He shall be with him like a worker hired year by year; and never shall he be
54 oppressed in his labors while you look on. And if he is not redeemed in any of
55 these ways, he and his children shall be released in the Jubilee year. For it is to
Me that the Israelites are servants. They are My servants whom I brought out
26 1 of the land of Egypt; I am the Lord your God. You shall make no idols, nor
may you erect any divine image or worship pillar.[64] Do not set up any carved

64 | Pillars were a feature of certain forms of ancient worship (see also Ex. 23:24).

ל וְאִם לֹא־יִגָּאֵל עַד־מְלֹאת לוֹ שָׁנָה תְמִימָה וְקָם הַבַּיִת אֲשֶׁר־בָּעִיר
לא אֲשֶׁר־לֹא חֹמָה לַצְּמִיתֻת לַקֹּנֶה אֹתוֹ לְדֹרֹתָיו לֹא יֵצֵא בַּיֹּבֵל׃ וּבָתֵּי לוֹ
הַחֲצֵרִים אֲשֶׁר אֵין־לָהֶם חֹמָה סָבִיב עַל־שְׂדֵה הָאָרֶץ יֵחָשֵׁב גְּאֻלָּה
לב תִּהְיֶה־לּוֹ וּבַיֹּבֵל יֵצֵא׃ וְעָרֵי הַלְוִיִּם בָּתֵּי עָרֵי אֲחֻזָּתָם גְּאֻלַּת עוֹלָם
לג תִּהְיֶה לַלְוִיִּם׃ וַאֲשֶׁר יִגְאַל מִן־הַלְוִיִּם וְיָצָא מִמְכַּר־בַּיִת וְעִיר אֲחֻזָּתוֹ
לד בַּיֹּבֵל כִּי בָתֵּי עָרֵי הַלְוִיִּם הִוא אֲחֻזָּתָם בְּתוֹךְ בְּנֵי יִשְׂרָאֵל׃ וּשְׂדֵה מִגְרַשׁ
לה עָרֵיהֶם לֹא יִמָּכֵר כִּי־אֲחֻזַּת עוֹלָם הוּא לָהֶם׃   וְכִי־יָמוּךְ כא
לו אָחִיךָ וּמָטָה יָדוֹ עִמָּךְ וְהֶחֱזַקְתָּ בּוֹ גֵּר וְתוֹשָׁב וָחַי עִמָּךְ׃ אַל־תִּקַּח
לז מֵאִתּוֹ נֶשֶׁךְ וְתַרְבִּית וְיָרֵאתָ מֵאֱלֹהֶיךָ וְחֵי אָחִיךָ עִמָּךְ׃ אֶת־כַּסְפְּךָ לֹא־
לח תִתֵּן לוֹ בְּנֶשֶׁךְ וּבְמַרְבִּית לֹא־תִתֵּן אָכְלֶךָ׃ אֲנִי יהוה אֱלֹהֵיכֶם אֲשֶׁר־
הוֹצֵאתִי אֶתְכֶם מֵאֶרֶץ מִצְרָיִם לָתֵת לָכֶם אֶת־אֶרֶץ כְּנַעַן לִהְיוֹת לָכֶם
לט לֵאלֹהִים׃   וְכִי־יָמוּךְ אָחִיךָ עִמָּךְ וְנִמְכַּר־לָךְ לֹא־תַעֲבֹד ששי /רביעי/
מ בּוֹ עֲבֹדַת עָבֶד׃ כְּשָׂכִיר כְּתוֹשָׁב יִהְיֶה עִמָּךְ עַד־שְׁנַת הַיֹּבֵל יַעֲבֹד
מא עִמָּךְ׃ וְיָצָא מֵעִמָּךְ הוּא וּבָנָיו עִמּוֹ וְשָׁב אֶל־מִשְׁפַּחְתּוֹ וְאֶל־אֲחֻזַּת
מב אֲבֹתָיו יָשׁוּב׃ כִּי־עֲבָדַי הֵם אֲשֶׁר־הוֹצֵאתִי אֹתָם מֵאֶרֶץ מִצְרָיִם לֹא
מג מד יִמָּכְרוּ מִמְכֶּרֶת עָבֶד׃ לֹא־תִרְדֶּה בוֹ בְּפָרֶךְ וְיָרֵאתָ מֵאֱלֹהֶיךָ׃ וְעַבְדְּךָ
וַאֲמָתְךָ אֲשֶׁר יִהְיוּ־לָךְ מֵאֵת הַגּוֹיִם אֲשֶׁר סְבִיבֹתֵיכֶם מֵהֶם תִּקְנוּ עֶבֶד
מה וְאָמָה׃ וְגַם מִבְּנֵי הַתּוֹשָׁבִים הַגָּרִים עִמָּכֶם מֵהֶם תִּקְנוּ וּמִמִּשְׁפַּחְתָּם
מו אֲשֶׁר עִמָּכֶם אֲשֶׁר הוֹלִידוּ בְּאַרְצְכֶם וְהָיוּ לָכֶם לַאֲחֻזָּה׃ וְהִתְנַחַלְתֶּם
אֹתָם לִבְנֵיכֶם אַחֲרֵיכֶם לָרֶשֶׁת אֲחֻזָּה לְעֹלָם בָּהֶם תַּעֲבֹדוּ וּבְאַחֵיכֶם
מז בְּנֵי־יִשְׂרָאֵל אִישׁ בְּאָחִיו לֹא־תִרְדֶּה בוֹ בְּפָרֶךְ׃   וְכִי תַשִּׂיג שביעי
יַד גֵּר וְתוֹשָׁב עִמָּךְ וּמָךְ אָחִיךָ עִמּוֹ וְנִמְכַּר לְגֵר תּוֹשָׁב עִמָּךְ אוֹ לְעֵקֶר
מח מִשְׁפַּחַת גֵּר׃ אַחֲרֵי נִמְכַּר גְּאֻלָּה תִּהְיֶה־לּוֹ אֶחָד מֵאֶחָיו יִגְאָלֶנּוּ׃
מט אוֹ־דֹדוֹ אוֹ בֶן־דֹּדוֹ יִגְאָלֶנּוּ אוֹ־מִשְּׁאֵר בְּשָׂרוֹ מִמִּשְׁפַּחְתּוֹ יִגְאָלֶנּוּ
נ אוֹ־הִשִּׂיגָה יָדוֹ וְנִגְאָל׃ וְחִשַּׁב עִם־קֹנֵהוּ מִשְּׁנַת הִמָּכְרוֹ לוֹ עַד שְׁנַת
נא הַיֹּבֵל וְהָיָה כֶּסֶף מִמְכָּרוֹ בְּמִסְפַּר שָׁנִים כִּימֵי שָׂכִיר יִהְיֶה עִמּוֹ׃ אִם־
נב עוֹד רַבּוֹת בַּשָּׁנִים לְפִיהֶן יָשִׁיב גְּאֻלָּתוֹ מִכֶּסֶף מִקְנָתוֹ׃ וְאִם־מְעַט
נִשְׁאַר בַּשָּׁנִים עַד־שְׁנַת הַיֹּבֵל וְחִשַּׁב־לוֹ כְּפִי שָׁנָיו יָשִׁיב אֶת־גְּאֻלָּתוֹ׃
נג נד כִּשְׂכִיר שָׁנָה בְּשָׁנָה יִהְיֶה עִמּוֹ לֹא־יִרְדֶּנּוּ בְּפֶרֶךְ לְעֵינֶיךָ׃ וְאִם־לֹא יִגָּאֵל
נה בְּאֵלֶּה וְיָצָא בִּשְׁנַת הַיֹּבֵל הוּא וּבָנָיו עִמּוֹ׃ כִּי־לִי בְנֵי־יִשְׂרָאֵל עֲבָדִים מפטיר
עֲבָדַי הֵם אֲשֶׁר־הוֹצֵאתִי אוֹתָם מֵאֶרֶץ מִצְרָיִם אֲנִי יהוה אֱלֹהֵיכֶם׃
כו א לֹא־תַעֲשׂוּ לָכֶם אֱלִילִם וּפֶסֶל וּמַצֵּבָה לֹא־תָקִימוּ לָכֶם וְאֶבֶן מַשְׂכִּית

2 stone in your land and bow down to it, for I am the LORD your God. Keep
My Sabbaths, revere My Sanctuary; I am the LORD.

BEḤUKOTAI

3 4 If you follow My decrees, keep My commands, and fulfill them, then I shall
give you rain in its due time. The land shall yield its crops and the trees of
5 the field shall yield their fruit. Your threshing season shall last until the grape
harvest; the grape harvest shall last until sowing time. You shall eat your
6 bread to the full and live securely in your land. And I will grant peace in the
land; when you lie down, no one will make you afraid. I will cause dangerous
7 animals to cease in the land, and through that land no sword shall pass. You
8 shall chase your enemies, and they shall fall before you by the sword. Five of
you shall chase away a hundred, and a hundred of you shall put ten thousand
9 to flight; your enemies shall fall before you by the sword. I will turn to you
and make you fruitful, make you numerous, and I will uphold My covenant
10 with you. You shall eat the grain of long ago and take the old grain out to
11 make space for all the new. I shall set My dwelling among you, and I shall not
12 despise you; I shall walk among you. I shall be your God, and you shall be
13 My people. I am the LORD your God, who brought you out of Egypt, to be
their slaves no more. I broke the bars of your yoke and led you to walk with
your heads held high.

14 15 But if you do not listen to Me and do not carry out all these commands – if
you spurn My decrees and despise My laws, not keeping all My commands;
16 violating My covenant – then I will do this to you: I will appoint over you
terror, consumption, and fever, which make your eyes fail and your spirit
languish. In vain shall you sow your seed, for your enemies will eat its yield.
17 I shall set My face against you. You will be struck down before your enemies.
Those who hate you will rule over you; you will flee, though no one chases
18 you. And if, in spite of all this, you still will not listen to Me, I shall punish you
19 seven times over for your sins. I will break down the majesty of your power. I
20 will make your sky like iron, your land like brass. Your strength will be spent
in vain. Your land will not yield its produce, nor the trees of the land their
21 fruit. If you still walk contrary to Me and refuse to listen to Me, I will strike
22 you seven times over for your sins: I will send wild animals against you. They
will bereave you of your children and annihilate your cattle. They will make
23 you few in number and your roads will be deserted. If, despite all this, you
24 still do not accept My discipline and still you walk contrary to Me, then I too
25 will walk contrary to you and strike you seven times over for your sins. I will
bring a sword against you to avenge the broken covenant. If you retreat into
your cities, I shall send pestilence against you, and you will be delivered up
26 into your enemy's hand. When I cut off your supply of bread, ten women shall
bake bread in a single oven. They will ration it out by weight, and you will eat

ב לֹא תִתְּנוּ בְּאַרְצְכֶם לְהִשְׁתַּחֲוֺת עָלֶיהָ כִּי אֲנִי יהוה אֱלֹהֵיכֶם: אֶת־
שַׁבְּתֹתַי תִּשְׁמֹרוּ וּמִקְדָּשִׁי תִּירָאוּ אֲנִי יהוה:
ג ד אִם־בְּחֻקֹּתַי תֵּלֵכוּ וְאֶת־מִצְוֺתַי תִּשְׁמְרוּ וַעֲשִׂיתֶם אֹתָם: וְנָתַתִּי כב בחקתי
ה גִשְׁמֵיכֶם בְּעִתָּם וְנָתְנָה הָאָרֶץ יְבוּלָהּ וְעֵץ הַשָּׂדֶה יִתֵּן פִּרְיוֹ: וְהִשִּׂיג
לָכֶם דַּיִשׁ אֶת־בָּצִיר וּבָצִיר יַשִּׂיג אֶת־זָרַע וַאֲכַלְתֶּם לַחְמְכֶם לָשֹׂבַע
ו וִישַׁבְתֶּם לָבֶטַח בְּאַרְצְכֶם: וְנָתַתִּי שָׁלוֹם בָּאָרֶץ וּשְׁכַבְתֶּם וְאֵין מַחֲרִיד שני
ז וְהִשְׁבַּתִּי חַיָּה רָעָה מִן־הָאָרֶץ וְחֶרֶב לֹא־תַעֲבֹר בְּאַרְצְכֶם: וּרְדַפְתֶּם
ח אֶת־אֹיְבֵיכֶם וְנָפְלוּ לִפְנֵיכֶם לֶחָרֶב: וְרָדְפוּ מִכֶּם חֲמִשָּׁה מֵאָה וּמֵאָה
ט מִכֶּם רְבָבָה יִרְדֹּפוּ וְנָפְלוּ אֹיְבֵיכֶם לִפְנֵיכֶם לֶחָרֶב: וּפָנִיתִי אֲלֵיכֶם
וְהִפְרֵיתִי אֶתְכֶם וְהִרְבֵּיתִי אֶתְכֶם וַהֲקִימֹתִי אֶת־בְּרִיתִי אִתְּכֶם:
י יא וַאֲכַלְתֶּם יָשָׁן נוֹשָׁן וְיָשָׁן מִפְּנֵי חָדָשׁ תּוֹצִיאוּ: וְנָתַתִּי מִשְׁכָּנִי בְּתוֹכְכֶם שלישי /חמישי/
יב וְלֹא־תִגְעַל נַפְשִׁי אֶתְכֶם: וְהִתְהַלַּכְתִּי בְּתוֹכְכֶם וְהָיִיתִי לָכֶם לֵאלֹהִים
יג וְאַתֶּם תִּהְיוּ־לִי לְעָם: אֲנִי יהוה אֱלֹהֵיכֶם אֲשֶׁר הוֹצֵאתִי אֶתְכֶם
מֵאֶרֶץ מִצְרַיִם מִהְיֹת לָהֶם עֲבָדִים וָאֶשְׁבֹּר מֹטֹת עֻלְּכֶם וָאוֹלֵךְ אֶתְכֶם
קוֹמְמִיּוּת:
יד טו וְאִם־לֹא תִשְׁמְעוּ לִי וְלֹא תַעֲשׂוּ אֵת כָּל־הַמִּצְוֺת הָאֵלֶּה: וְאִם־בְּחֻקֹּתַי
תִּמְאָסוּ וְאִם אֶת־מִשְׁפָּטַי תִּגְעַל נַפְשְׁכֶם לְבִלְתִּי עֲשׂוֹת אֶת־כָּל־
טז מִצְוֺתַי לְהַפְרְכֶם אֶת־בְּרִיתִי: אַף־אֲנִי אֶעֱשֶׂה־זֹּאת לָכֶם וְהִפְקַדְתִּי
עֲלֵיכֶם בֶּהָלָה אֶת־הַשַּׁחֶפֶת וְאֶת־הַקַּדַּחַת מְכַלּוֹת עֵינַיִם וּמְדִיבֹת
יז נָפֶשׁ וּזְרַעְתֶּם לָרִיק זַרְעֲכֶם וַאֲכָלֻהוּ אֹיְבֵיכֶם: וְנָתַתִּי פָנַי בָּכֶם וְנִגַּפְתֶּם
יח לִפְנֵי אֹיְבֵיכֶם וְרָדוּ בָכֶם שֹׂנְאֵיכֶם וְנַסְתֶּם וְאֵין־רֹדֵף אֶתְכֶם: וְאִם־עַד־
אֵלֶּה לֹא תִשְׁמְעוּ לִי וְיָסַפְתִּי לְיַסְּרָה אֶתְכֶם שֶׁבַע עַל־חַטֹּאתֵיכֶם:
יט וְשָׁבַרְתִּי אֶת־גְּאוֹן עֻזְּכֶם וְנָתַתִּי אֶת־שְׁמֵיכֶם כַּבַּרְזֶל וְאֶת־אַרְצְכֶם
כ כַּנְּחֻשָׁה: וְתַם לָרִיק כֹּחֲכֶם וְלֹא־תִתֵּן אַרְצְכֶם אֶת־יְבוּלָהּ וְעֵץ הָאָרֶץ
כא לֹא יִתֵּן פִּרְיוֹ: וְאִם־תֵּלְכוּ עִמִּי קֶרִי וְלֹא תֹאבוּ לִשְׁמֹעַ לִי וְיָסַפְתִּי
כב עֲלֵיכֶם מַכָּה שֶׁבַע כְּחַטֹּאתֵיכֶם: וְהִשְׁלַחְתִּי בָכֶם אֶת־חַיַּת הַשָּׂדֶה
וְשִׁכְּלָה אֶתְכֶם וְהִכְרִיתָה אֶת־בְּהֶמְתְּכֶם וְהִמְעִיטָה אֶתְכֶם וְנָשַׁמּוּ
כג כד דַּרְכֵיכֶם: וְאִם־בְּאֵלֶּה לֹא תִוָּסְרוּ לִי וַהֲלַכְתֶּם עִמִּי קֶרִי: וְהָלַכְתִּי
אַף־אֲנִי עִמָּכֶם בְּקֶרִי וְהִכֵּיתִי אֶתְכֶם גַּם־אָנִי שֶׁבַע עַל־חַטֹּאתֵיכֶם:
כה וְהֵבֵאתִי עֲלֵיכֶם חֶרֶב נֹקֶמֶת נְקַם־בְּרִית וְנֶאֱסַפְתֶּם אֶל־עָרֵיכֶם
כו וְשִׁלַּחְתִּי דֶבֶר בְּתוֹכְכֶם וְנִתַּתֶּם בְּיַד־אוֹיֵב: בְּשִׁבְרִי לָכֶם מַטֵּה־לֶחֶם
וְאָפוּ עֶשֶׂר נָשִׁים לַחְמְכֶם בְּתַנּוּר אֶחָד וְהֵשִׁיבוּ לַחְמְכֶם בַּמִּשְׁקָל

27 but not be full. If, despite all this, you still do not listen to Me – if
28 still you walk contrary to Me – then I, in My fury, will walk contrary to you.
29 I will punish you seven times more for your sins: you shall eat the flesh of
30 your own sons; the flesh of your own daughters you shall eat. I will destroy
your high shrines, cut down your incense altars, and heap your corpses on
31 the corpses of your idols. I shall despise you. I will turn your cities into ruins
32 and make your sanctuaries desolate. I will not savor your pleasing aromas. I
Myself will devastate the land, so that your enemies who settle there will be
33 appalled. I shall scatter you among the nations; I will draw My sword against
34 you. Your land will be desolate; your cities, ruins. Then shall the land make
appeasement for its Sabbaths[65] for as long as it lies desolate and you are in
your enemies' lands. Then the land will rest and make appeasement for its
35 Sabbaths. In its desolation, the land will have the rest it did not have during
36 the Sabbaths when you were dwelling there. As for the survivors, I will bring
such insecurity into their hearts in their enemies' lands that the sound of a
windblown leaf will make them run as if they fled the sword; and they will
37 fall, though no one is chasing them. They will stumble over one another as
if fleeing the sword, when no one chases them. You will have no power to
38 stand before your enemies. You will perish among the nations; your enemies'
39 lands will devour you. Those of you who survive will waste away in their
enemies' lands because of their sins – for their ancestors' sins also, they will
40 waste away. But if they confess their sins and those of their ancestors – their
41 trespass against Me and their walking contrary to Me, which made Me walk
contrary to them, bringing them into their enemies' lands – if their obstinate[66]
42 hearts are humbled and they atone for their sin, then I will remember My
covenant with Yaakov; and My covenant with Yitzḥak and My covenant with
43 Avraham I will also remember, and I will remember the land. The land will be
deserted, making appeasement for its Sabbaths, lying desolate of them, while
they will be making appeasement for their sins, because they rejected My laws,
44 because they despised My statutes. Yet even then, when they are in the land
of their enemies, I will not reject them nor despise them and annihilate them,
45 will not break My covenant with them, for I am the Lord their God. I will
remember for them the covenant with their ancestors whom I brought out
46 of Egypt in the sight of the nations, to be their God; I am the Lord." These
are the statutes, laws, and instructions that the Lord established between
Himself and the Israelites, through Moshe, on Mount Sinai.
27 1 The Lord spoke to Moshe: "Speak to the Israelites. Say: When a person
2 makes a spoken vow to the Lord to give the equivalent of the value of a
3 person – if it is a male from twenty to sixty years old, his equivalent is fifty
4 silver shekel by the Sanctuary weight. If it is a female, the equivalent is thirty
5 shekel. If the person's age is between five and twenty years, the equivalent

65 | Referring to those described in 25:1–24. If the Israelites do not observe these Sabbaths, they will be banished and the land will finally be allowed to lie fallow in their absence.

66 | Literally "uncircumcised."

כז וַאֲכַלְתֶּם וְלֹא תִשְׂבָּעוּ: וְאִם־בְּזֹאת לֹא תִשְׁמְעוּ לִי וַהֲלַכְתֶּם
כח עִמִּי בְּקֶרִי: וְהָלַכְתִּי עִמָּכֶם בַּחֲמַת־קֶרִי וְיִסַּרְתִּי אֶתְכֶם אַף־אָנִי
כט שֶׁבַע עַל־חַטֹּאתֵיכֶם: וַאֲכַלְתֶּם בְּשַׂר בְּנֵיכֶם וּבְשַׂר בְּנֹתֵיכֶם תֹּאכֵלוּ:
ל וְהִשְׁמַדְתִּי אֶת־בָּמֹתֵיכֶם וְהִכְרַתִּי אֶת־חַמָּנֵיכֶם וְנָתַתִּי אֶת־פִּגְרֵיכֶם
לא עַל־פִּגְרֵי גִּלּוּלֵיכֶם וְגָעֲלָה נַפְשִׁי אֶתְכֶם: וְנָתַתִּי אֶת־עָרֵיכֶם חָרְבָּה
לב וַהֲשִׁמּוֹתִי אֶת־מִקְדְּשֵׁיכֶם וְלֹא אָרִיחַ בְּרֵיחַ נִיחֹחֲכֶם: וַהֲשִׁמֹּתִי אֲנִי
לג אֶת־הָאָרֶץ וְשָׁמְמוּ עָלֶיהָ אֹיְבֵיכֶם הַיֹּשְׁבִים בָּהּ: וְאֶתְכֶם אֱזָרֶה בַגּוֹיִם
וַהֲרִיקֹתִי אַחֲרֵיכֶם חָרֶב וְהָיְתָה אַרְצְכֶם שְׁמָמָה וְעָרֵיכֶם יִהְיוּ חָרְבָּה:
לד אָז תִּרְצֶה הָאָרֶץ אֶת־שַׁבְּתֹתֶיהָ כֹּל יְמֵי הָשַּׁמָּה וְאַתֶּם בְּאֶרֶץ אֹיְבֵיכֶם
לה אָז תִּשְׁבַּת הָאָרֶץ וְהִרְצָת אֶת־שַׁבְּתֹתֶיהָ: כָּל־יְמֵי הָשַּׁמָּה תִּשְׁבֹּת אֵת
לו אֲשֶׁר לֹא־שָׁבְתָה בְּשַׁבְּתֹתֵיכֶם בְּשִׁבְתְּכֶם עָלֶיהָ: וְהַנִּשְׁאָרִים בָּכֶם
וְהֵבֵאתִי מֹרֶךְ בִּלְבָבָם בְּאַרְצֹת אֹיְבֵיהֶם וְרָדַף אֹתָם קוֹל עָלֶה נִדָּף
לז וְנָסוּ מְנֻסַת־חֶרֶב וְנָפְלוּ וְאֵין רֹדֵף: וְכָשְׁלוּ אִישׁ־בְּאָחִיו כְּמִפְּנֵי־חֶרֶב
לח וְרֹדֵף אָיִן וְלֹא־תִהְיֶה לָכֶם תְּקוּמָה לִפְנֵי אֹיְבֵיכֶם: וַאֲבַדְתֶּם בַּגּוֹיִם
לט וְאָכְלָה אֶתְכֶם אֶרֶץ אֹיְבֵיכֶם: וְהַנִּשְׁאָרִים בָּכֶם יִמַּקּוּ בַּעֲוֺנָם בְּאַרְצֹת
מ אֹיְבֵיכֶם וְאַף בַּעֲוֺנֹת אֲבֹתָם אִתָּם יִמָּקּוּ: וְהִתְוַדּוּ אֶת־עֲוֺנָם וְאֶת־עֲוֺן
מא אֲבֹתָם בְּמַעֲלָם אֲשֶׁר מָעֲלוּ־בִי וְאַף אֲשֶׁר־הָלְכוּ עִמִּי בְּקֶרִי: אַף־אֲנִי
אֵלֵךְ עִמָּם בְּקֶרִי וְהֵבֵאתִי אֹתָם בְּאֶרֶץ אֹיְבֵיהֶם אוֹ־אָז יִכָּנַע לְבָבָם
מב הֶעָרֵל וְאָז יִרְצוּ אֶת־עֲוֺנָם: וְזָכַרְתִּי אֶת־בְּרִיתִי יַעֲקוֹב וְאַף אֶת־
מג בְּרִיתִי יִצְחָק וְאַף אֶת־בְּרִיתִי אַבְרָהָם אֶזְכֹּר וְהָאָרֶץ אֶזְכֹּר: וְהָאָרֶץ
תֵּעָזֵב מֵהֶם וְתִרֶץ אֶת־שַׁבְּתֹתֶיהָ בָּהְשַׁמָּה מֵהֶם וְהֵם יִרְצוּ אֶת־עֲוֺנָם
מד יַעַן וּבְיַעַן בְּמִשְׁפָּטַי מָאָסוּ וְאֶת־חֻקֹּתַי גָּעֲלָה נַפְשָׁם: וְאַף גַּם־זֹאת
בִּהְיוֹתָם בְּאֶרֶץ אֹיְבֵיהֶם לֹא־מְאַסְתִּים וְלֹא־גְעַלְתִּים לְכַלֹּתָם לְהָפֵר
מה בְּרִיתִי אִתָּם כִּי אֲנִי יהוה אֱלֹהֵיהֶם: וְזָכַרְתִּי לָהֶם בְּרִית רִאשֹׁנִים אֲשֶׁר
הוֹצֵאתִי־אֹתָם מֵאֶרֶץ מִצְרַיִם לְעֵינֵי הַגּוֹיִם לִהְיוֹת לָהֶם לֵאלֹהִים אֲנִי
מו יהוה: אֵלֶּה הַחֻקִּים וְהַמִּשְׁפָּטִים וְהַתּוֹרֹת אֲשֶׁר נָתַן יהוה בֵּינוֹ וּבֵין
בְּנֵי יִשְׂרָאֵל בְּהַר סִינַי בְּיַד־מֹשֶׁה:

כז א ב וַיְדַבֵּר יהוה אֶל־מֹשֶׁה לֵּאמֹר: דַּבֵּר אֶל־בְּנֵי יִשְׂרָאֵל וְאָמַרְתָּ אֲלֵהֶם כג רביעי /ששי/
ג אִישׁ כִּי יַפְלִא נֶדֶר בְּעֶרְכְּךָ נְפָשֹׁת לַיהוה: וְהָיָה עֶרְכְּךָ הַזָּכָר מִבֶּן
עֶשְׂרִים שָׁנָה וְעַד בֶּן־שִׁשִּׁים שָׁנָה וְהָיָה עֶרְכְּךָ חֲמִשִּׁים שֶׁקֶל כֶּסֶף
ד ה בְּשֶׁקֶל הַקֹּדֶשׁ: וְאִם־נְקֵבָה הִוא וְהָיָה עֶרְכְּךָ שְׁלֹשִׁים שָׁקֶל: וְאִם מִבֶּן־
חָמֵשׁ שָׁנִים וְעַד בֶּן־עֶשְׂרִים שָׁנָה וְהָיָה עֶרְכְּךָ הַזָּכָר עֶשְׂרִים שְׁקָלִים

6 for a male is twenty shekel, and for a female, ten shekel. If the age is between
one month and five years, the equivalent for a male is five silver shekel; for
7 a female, three silver shekel. If the age is sixty years or more, the equivalent
8 for a male is fifteen shekel, and for a female, ten shekel. But if the person is
too poor to pay the full amount, he shall be presented to the priest, who will
assess him. The priest shall assess him with reference to the means of the
9 person making the vow. If the vow concerns an animal of a type that
may be offered to the LORD, any such animal given to the LORD becomes
10 sacred. One may not exchange it or offer a substitute for it, either better for
worse or worse for better; and if one animal is substituted for another, both
11 it and the substitute become holy. If the vow involves any type of impure
animal, which cannot be offered to the LORD, the animal shall be brought
12 to stand before the priest. The priest shall assess it, whether good or bad,
13 and its value shall accord to the priest's assessment. If the donor wishes to
14 redeem it, a fifth shall be added to its valuation. When someone consecrates
his house to be sacred to the LORD, the priest shall assess it, whether good
15 or bad, and its value shall accord to the priest's assessment. If the donor
wishes to redeem it, he shall add a fifth to its valuation, and it shall be his
16 again. If someone consecrates part of his hereditary land to the LORD, its
value shall be set in relation to the seed needed to sow it: fifty silver shekel
17 for each omer[67] of barley seed. If the person consecrates his field from the
18 Jubilee year, the value that has been set stands.[68] But if the person consecrates
the field after the Jubilee, the priest shall calculate its value in relation to
the number of years left until the next Jubilee year, and the valuation shall
19 be reduced accordingly. If the person who consecrated the field wishes to
20 redeem it, he shall add a fifth to its valuation, and it shall be his again. But
if he does not redeem the field, or if it has been sold to someone else, it can
21 no longer be redeemed. When the field is released in the Jubilee, it shall be
22 holy to the LORD like devoted land; it comes into the priest's possession. If
the person consecrates to the LORD a field he has purchased – not part of his
23 hereditary land – the priest shall calculate its proportionate value until the
Jubilee year, and the donor shall pay its valuation on that day,[69] as a sacred
24 donation to the LORD. In the Jubilee year the field shall return to the person
25 from whom it was bought, whose hereditary land it was. All assessments
26 shall follow the Sanctuary standard, by which a shekel is twenty gerah. A
person cannot consecrate a firstborn animal, whether ox or sheep, because,
27 being a firstling, it already belongs to the LORD. If it is an impure animal, it
may be redeemed for its valuation with a fifth added. If it is not redeemed, it
28 shall be sold at its assessed value.[70] Nothing that a person owns that has been
devoted to the LORD – be it a person, an animal, or inherited land – may be

---

67 | An omer is a solid measure equivalent to roughly 2.5 liters.

68 | That is, if he consecrates it at the onset of the Jubilee cycle and wishes to redeem it immediately, he pays a full fifty shekel per omer of barley seed.

69 | Meaning the proportionate value calculated as of that day.

70 | That is, with no fifth added.

ו וְלַנְּקֵבָה עֲשֶׂרֶת שְׁקָלִים׃ וְאִם מִבֶּן־חֹדֶשׁ וְעַד בֶּן־חָמֵשׁ שָׁנִים וְהָיָה
עֶרְכְּךָ הַזָּכָר חֲמִשָּׁה שְׁקָלִים כָּסֶף וְלַנְּקֵבָה עֶרְכְּךָ שְׁלֹשֶׁת שְׁקָלִים
ז כָּסֶף׃ וְאִם מִבֶּן־שִׁשִּׁים שָׁנָה וָמַעְלָה אִם־זָכָר וְהָיָה עֶרְכְּךָ חֲמִשָּׁה
ח עָשָׂר שָׁקֶל וְלַנְּקֵבָה עֲשָׂרָה שְׁקָלִים׃ וְאִם־מָךְ הוּא מֵעֶרְכֶּךָ וְהֶעֱמִידוֹ
לִפְנֵי הַכֹּהֵן וְהֶעֱרִיךְ אֹתוֹ הַכֹּהֵן עַל־פִּי אֲשֶׁר תַּשִּׂיג יַד הַנֹּדֵר יַעֲרִיכֶנּוּ
ט הַכֹּהֵן׃ וְאִם־בְּהֵמָה אֲשֶׁר יַקְרִיבוּ מִמֶּנָּה קָרְבָּן לַיהוָה
י כֹּל אֲשֶׁר יִתֵּן מִמֶּנּוּ לַיהוָה יִהְיֶה־קֹּדֶשׁ׃ לֹא יַחֲלִיפֶנּוּ וְלֹא־יָמִיר אֹתוֹ
טוֹב בְּרָע אוֹ־רַע בְּטוֹב וְאִם־הָמֵר יָמִיר בְּהֵמָה בִּבְהֵמָה וְהָיָה־הוּא
יא וּתְמוּרָתוֹ יִהְיֶה־קֹּדֶשׁ׃ וְאִם כָּל־בְּהֵמָה טְמֵאָה אֲשֶׁר לֹא־יַקְרִיבוּ
יב מִמֶּנָּה קָרְבָּן לַיהוָה וְהֶעֱמִיד אֶת־הַבְּהֵמָה לִפְנֵי הַכֹּהֵן׃ וְהֶעֱרִיךְ הַכֹּהֵן
יג אֹתָהּ בֵּין טוֹב וּבֵין רָע כְּעֶרְכְּךָ הַכֹּהֵן כֵּן יִהְיֶה׃ וְאִם־גָּאֹל יִגְאָלֶנָּה
יד וְיָסַף חֲמִישִׁתוֹ עַל־עֶרְכֶּךָ׃ וְאִישׁ כִּי־יַקְדִּשׁ אֶת־בֵּיתוֹ קֹדֶשׁ לַיהוָה
וְהֶעֱרִיכוֹ הַכֹּהֵן בֵּין טוֹב וּבֵין רָע כַּאֲשֶׁר יַעֲרִיךְ אֹתוֹ הַכֹּהֵן כֵּן יָקוּם׃
טו וְאִם־הַמַּקְדִּישׁ יִגְאַל אֶת־בֵּיתוֹ וְיָסַף חֲמִישִׁית כֶּסֶף־עֶרְכְּךָ עָלָיו וְהָיָה
טז לוֹ׃ וְאִם ׀ מִשְּׂדֵה אֲחֻזָּתוֹ יַקְדִּישׁ אִישׁ לַיהוָה וְהָיָה עֶרְכְּךָ לְפִי זַרְעוֹ חמישי /שביעי/
יז זֶרַע חֹמֶר שְׂעֹרִים בַּחֲמִשִּׁים שֶׁקֶל כָּסֶף׃ אִם־מִשְּׁנַת הַיֹּבֵל יַקְדִּישׁ
יח שָׂדֵהוּ כְּעֶרְכְּךָ יָקוּם׃ וְאִם־אַחַר הַיֹּבֵל יַקְדִּישׁ שָׂדֵהוּ וְחִשַּׁב־לוֹ הַכֹּהֵן
אֶת־הַכֶּסֶף עַל־פִּי הַשָּׁנִים הַנּוֹתָרֹת עַד שְׁנַת הַיֹּבֵל וְנִגְרַע מֵעֶרְכֶּךָ׃
יט וְאִם־גָּאֹל יִגְאַל אֶת־הַשָּׂדֶה הַמַּקְדִּישׁ אֹתוֹ וְיָסַף חֲמִשִׁית כֶּסֶף־עֶרְכְּךָ
כ עָלָיו וְקָם לוֹ׃ וְאִם־לֹא יִגְאַל אֶת־הַשָּׂדֶה וְאִם־מָכַר אֶת־הַשָּׂדֶה לְאִישׁ
כא אַחֵר לֹא־יִגָּאֵל עוֹד׃ וְהָיָה הַשָּׂדֶה בְּצֵאתוֹ בַיֹּבֵל קֹדֶשׁ לַיהוָה כִּשְׂדֵה
כב הַחֵרֶם לַכֹּהֵן תִּהְיֶה אֲחֻזָּתוֹ׃ וְאִם אֶת־שְׂדֵה מִקְנָתוֹ אֲשֶׁר לֹא מִשְּׂדֵה ששי
כג אֲחֻזָּתוֹ יַקְדִּישׁ לַיהוָה׃ וְחִשַּׁב־לוֹ הַכֹּהֵן אֵת מִכְסַת הָעֶרְכְּךָ עַד שְׁנַת
כד הַיֹּבֵל וְנָתַן אֶת־הָעֶרְכְּךָ בַּיּוֹם הַהוּא קֹדֶשׁ לַיהוָה׃ בִּשְׁנַת הַיּוֹבֵל
כה יָשׁוּב הַשָּׂדֶה לַאֲשֶׁר קָנָהוּ מֵאִתּוֹ לַאֲשֶׁר־לוֹ אֲחֻזַּת הָאָרֶץ׃ וְכָל־
כו עֶרְכְּךָ יִהְיֶה בְּשֶׁקֶל הַקֹּדֶשׁ עֶשְׂרִים גֵּרָה יִהְיֶה הַשָּׁקֶל׃ אַךְ־בְּכוֹר
אֲשֶׁר יְבֻכַּר לַיהוָה בִּבְהֵמָה לֹא־יַקְדִּישׁ אִישׁ אֹתוֹ אִם־שׁוֹר אִם־שֶׂה
כז לַיהוָה הוּא׃ וְאִם בַּבְּהֵמָה הַטְּמֵאָה וּפָדָה בְעֶרְכֶּךָ וְיָסַף חֲמִשִׁתוֹ
כח עָלָיו וְאִם־לֹא יִגָּאֵל וְנִמְכַּר בְּעֶרְכֶּךָ׃ אַךְ כָּל־חֵרֶם אֲשֶׁר יַחֲרִם אִישׁ
לַיהוָה מִכָּל־אֲשֶׁר־לוֹ מֵאָדָם וּבְהֵמָה וּמִשְּׂדֵה אֲחֻזָּתוֹ לֹא יִמָּכֵר וְלֹא

29 sold or redeemed. Every devoted thing is holy of holies to the LORD.[71] And
no person condemned to utter destruction may be ransomed; he must be
30 put to death. All tithes from the land, whether seed from the ground or fruit
31 of the tree, belong to the LORD; they are sacred to the LORD. If a person
32 wishes to redeem part of his tithe, he shall add a fifth to its value. All tithes
from the herd or flock – every tenth animal that passes under the shepherd's
33 staff – shall be sacred to the LORD. One should not pick out the good from
the bad or make any substitution. But if a substitution is made, both the item
34 and its substitute shall be sacred; they cannot be redeemed." These are the
commands that the LORD gave Moshe, on Mount Sinai, for the people of Israel.

---

71 | This verse introduces a new type of consecrated entity called *ḥerem* (devoted thing), which is not subject to redemption.

כט יִגָּאֵל כׇּל־חֵרֶם קֹדֶשׁ־קׇדָשִׁים הוּא לַיהוָה: כׇּל־חֵרֶם אֲשֶׁר יׇחֳרַם שביעי
ל מִן־הָאָדָם לֹא יִפָּדֶה מוֹת יוּמָת: וְכׇל־מַעְשַׂר הָאָרֶץ מִזֶּרַע הָאָרֶץ
לא מִפְּרִי הָעֵץ לַיהוָה הוּא קֹדֶשׁ לַיהוָה: וְאִם־גָּאֹל יִגְאַל אִישׁ מִמַּעַשְׂרוֹ
לב חֲמִשִׁיתוֹ יֹסֵף עָלָיו: וְכׇל־מַעְשַׂר בָּקָר וָצֹאן כֹּל אֲשֶׁר־יַעֲבֹר תַּחַת מפטיר
לג הַשָּׁבֶט הָעֲשִׂירִי יִהְיֶה־קֹּדֶשׁ לַיהוָה: לֹא יְבַקֵּר בֵּין־טוֹב לָרַע וְלֹא
יְמִירֶנּוּ וְאִם־הָמֵר יְמִירֶנּוּ וְהָיָה־הוּא וּתְמוּרָתוֹ יִהְיֶה־קֹּדֶשׁ לֹא יִגָּאֵל:
לד אֵלֶּה הַמִּצְוֺת אֲשֶׁר צִוָּה יהוה אֶת־מֹשֶׁה אֶל־בְּנֵי יִשְׂרָאֵל בְּהַר סִינָי:

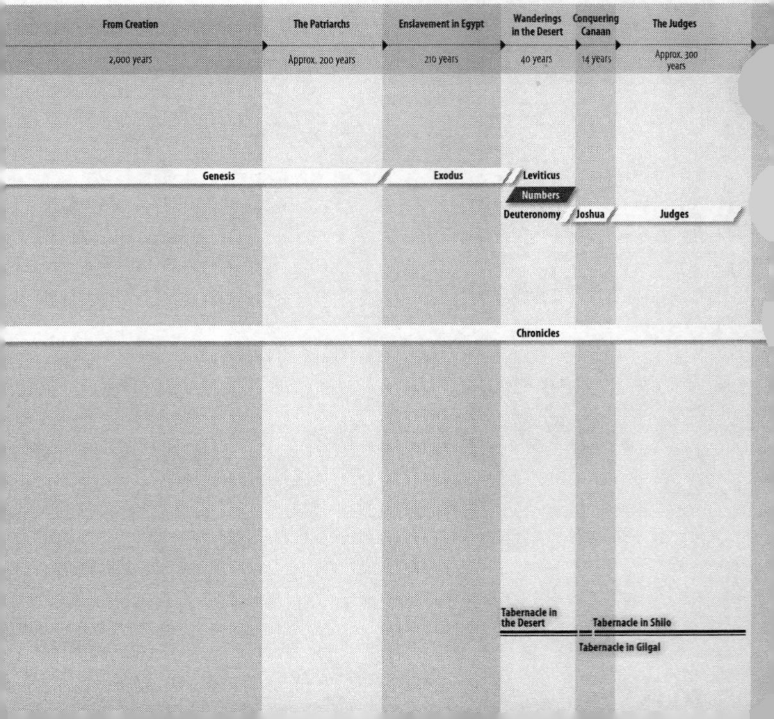
From Creation
2,000 years
The Patriarchs
Approx. 200 years
Enslavement in Egypt
210 years
Wanderings in the Desert
40 years
Conquering Canaan
14 years
The Judges
Approx. 300 years
Genesis
Exodus
Leviticus
Numbers
Deuteronomy
Joshua
Judges
Chronicles
Tabernacle in the Desert
Tabernacle in Shilo
Tabernacle in Gilgal

במדבר
BEMIDBAR/NUMBERS

NUMBERS	Preparations for the journey to the land of Israel	Crises during the second year of the journey	Events of the fortieth year of the journey	Preparations for entering the land
	Chs. 1–10	11–19	20–25	26–36
		38 years and 9 months		

BEMIDBAR

1 1 The LORD spoke to Moshe in the Sinai Desert, in the Tent of Meeting, on the
first of the second month, in the second year since their coming out from the
2 land of Egypt. He said: "Take a census of the entire community of Israel by
their clans and their ancestral houses, listing every male by name individually,
3 twenty years of age and upward: everyone in Israel who is capable of active
4 service. You and Aharon shall number them by their divisions.[1] And one
man from each tribe shall join you in the task, each the head of his ancestral
5 house. These are the names of the men who will assist you: from Reuven,
6 7 Elitzur son of Shedeiur; from Shimon, Shelumiel son of Tzurishadai; from
8 Yehuda, Naḥshon son of Aminadav; from Yissakhar, Netanel son of Tzuar;
9 10 from Zevulun, Eliav son of Ḥelon. For the sons of Yosef: from Efrayim,
11 Elishama son of Amihud; from Menashe, Gamliel son of Pedatzur. From
12 Binyamin, Avidan son of Gidoni; from Dan, Aḥiezer son of Amishadai;
13, 14, 15 from Asher, Pagiel son of Okhran; from Gad, Elyasaf son of Deuel; and from
16 Naftali, Aḥira son of Einan." These were the ones chosen from the community,
17 princes of their ancestral tribes; they are the heads of Israel's clans. Moshe
18 and Aharon took these men, those who had been marked out by name, and
they convened the entire community on the first day of the second month.
And the people declared themselves by their clans and their ancestral houses.
19 All those over twenty years old were counted individually by name, as the
LORD had commanded Moshe; so it was that he counted them in the Sinai
20 Desert. The children of Reuven, Yisrael's firstborn – his descendants
by their clans and their ancestral families – the tally of their names, each
male aged twenty years and above: everyone capable of active service, all
21 counted individually – those counted from the tribe of Reuven numbered
46,500.
22 Of the children of Shimon – his descendants by their clans and their ancestral
families – the tally of their names, each male aged twenty years and above:
23 everyone capable of active service, all counted individually – those counted
from the tribe of Shimon numbered 59,300.
24 Of the children of Gad – his descendants by their clans and their ancestral
families – the tally of their names, each male aged twenty years and above:
25 everyone capable of active service, all counted individually – those counted
from the tribe of Gad numbered 45,650.
26 Of the children of Yehuda – his descendants by their clans and their ancestral
families – the tally of their names, each male aged twenty years and above:
27 everyone capable of active service, all counted individually – those counted
from the tribe of Yehuda numbered 74,600.
28 Of the children of Yissakhar – his descendants by their clans and their ancestral families – the tally of their names, each male aged twenty years and above:
29 everyone capable of active service, all counted individually – those counted
from the tribe of Yissakhar numbered 54,400.
30 Of the children of Zevulun – his descendants by their clans and their ancestral

1 | That is, military divisions. Chapter 2 assigns a division to each tribe.

א א וַיְדַבֵּר יְהוָה אֶל־מֹשֶׁה בְּמִדְבַּר סִינַי בְּאֹהֶל מוֹעֵד בְּאֶחָד לַחֹדֶשׁ הַשֵּׁנִי א
ב בַּשָּׁנָה הַשֵּׁנִית לְצֵאתָם מֵאֶרֶץ מִצְרַיִם לֵאמֹר: שְׂאוּ אֶת־רֹאשׁ כָּל־
עֲדַת בְּנֵי־יִשְׂרָאֵל לְמִשְׁפְּחֹתָם לְבֵית אֲבֹתָם בְּמִסְפַּר שֵׁמוֹת כָּל־זָכָר
ג לְגֻלְגְּלֹתָם: מִבֶּן עֶשְׂרִים שָׁנָה וָמַעְלָה כָּל־יֹצֵא צָבָא בְּיִשְׂרָאֵל תִּפְקְדוּ
ד אֹתָם לְצִבְאֹתָם אַתָּה וְאַהֲרֹן: וְאִתְּכֶם יִהְיוּ אִישׁ אִישׁ לַמַּטֶּה אִישׁ רֹאשׁ
ה לְבֵית־אֲבֹתָיו הוּא: וְאֵלֶּה שְׁמוֹת הָאֲנָשִׁים אֲשֶׁר יַעַמְדוּ אִתְּכֶם לִרְאוּבֵן
ו ז אֱלִיצוּר בֶּן־שְׁדֵיאוּר: לְשִׁמְעוֹן שְׁלֻמִיאֵל בֶּן־צוּרִישַׁדָּי: לִיהוּדָה נַחְשׁוֹן
ח ט בֶּן־עַמִּינָדָב: לְיִשָּׂשכָר נְתַנְאֵל בֶּן־צוּעָר: לִזְבוּלֻן אֱלִיאָב בֶּן־חֵלֹן:
י לִבְנֵי יוֹסֵף לְאֶפְרַיִם אֱלִישָׁמָע בֶּן־עַמִּיהוּד לִמְנַשֶּׁה גַּמְלִיאֵל בֶּן־
יא יב יג פְּדָהצוּר: לְבִנְיָמִן אֲבִידָן בֶּן־גִּדְעֹנִי: לְדָן אֲחִיעֶזֶר בֶּן־עַמִּישַׁדָּי: לְאָשֵׁר
יד טו פַּגְעִיאֵל בֶּן־עָכְרָן: לְגָד אֶלְיָסָף בֶּן־דְּעוּאֵל: לְנַפְתָּלִי אֲחִירַע בֶּן־עֵינָן:
טז אֵלֶּה קְרִיאֵי הָעֵדָה נְשִׂיאֵי מַטּוֹת אֲבוֹתָם רָאשֵׁי אַלְפֵי יִשְׂרָאֵל הֵם: קְרוּאֵי
יז יח וַיִּקַּח מֹשֶׁה וְאַהֲרֹן אֵת הָאֲנָשִׁים הָאֵלֶּה אֲשֶׁר נִקְּבוּ בְּשֵׁמוֹת: וְאֵת
כָּל־הָעֵדָה הִקְהִילוּ בְּאֶחָד לַחֹדֶשׁ הַשֵּׁנִי וַיִּתְיַלְדוּ עַל־מִשְׁפְּחֹתָם לְבֵית
יט אֲבֹתָם בְּמִסְפַּר שֵׁמוֹת מִבֶּן עֶשְׂרִים שָׁנָה וָמַעְלָה לְגֻלְגְּלֹתָם: כַּאֲשֶׁר
כ צִוָּה יְהוָה אֶת־מֹשֶׁה וַיִּפְקְדֵם בְּמִדְבַּר סִינָי: וַיִּהְיוּ בְנֵי־ שני
רְאוּבֵן בְּכֹר יִשְׂרָאֵל תּוֹלְדֹתָם לְמִשְׁפְּחֹתָם לְבֵית אֲבֹתָם בְּמִסְפַּר שֵׁמוֹת
כא לְגֻלְגְּלֹתָם כָּל־זָכָר מִבֶּן עֶשְׂרִים שָׁנָה וָמַעְלָה כֹּל יֹצֵא צָבָא: פְּקֻדֵיהֶם
לְמַטֵּה רְאוּבֵן שִׁשָּׁה וְאַרְבָּעִים אֶלֶף וַחֲמֵשׁ מֵאוֹת:
כב לִבְנֵי שִׁמְעוֹן תּוֹלְדֹתָם לְמִשְׁפְּחֹתָם לְבֵית אֲבֹתָם פְּקֻדָיו בְּמִסְפַּר שֵׁמוֹת
כג לְגֻלְגְּלֹתָם כָּל־זָכָר מִבֶּן עֶשְׂרִים שָׁנָה וָמַעְלָה כֹּל יֹצֵא צָבָא: פְּקֻדֵיהֶם
לְמַטֵּה שִׁמְעוֹן תִּשְׁעָה וַחֲמִשִּׁים אֶלֶף וּשְׁלֹשׁ מֵאוֹת:
כד לִבְנֵי גָד תּוֹלְדֹתָם לְמִשְׁפְּחֹתָם לְבֵית אֲבֹתָם בְּמִסְפַּר שֵׁמוֹת מִבֶּן
כה עֶשְׂרִים שָׁנָה וָמַעְלָה כֹּל יֹצֵא צָבָא: פְּקֻדֵיהֶם לְמַטֵּה גָד חֲמִשָּׁה
וְאַרְבָּעִים אֶלֶף וְשֵׁשׁ מֵאוֹת וַחֲמִשִּׁים:
כו לִבְנֵי יְהוּדָה תּוֹלְדֹתָם לְמִשְׁפְּחֹתָם לְבֵית אֲבֹתָם בְּמִסְפַּר שֵׁמֹת מִבֶּן
כז עֶשְׂרִים שָׁנָה וָמַעְלָה כֹּל יֹצֵא צָבָא: פְּקֻדֵיהֶם לְמַטֵּה יְהוּדָה אַרְבָּעָה
וְשִׁבְעִים אֶלֶף וְשֵׁשׁ מֵאוֹת:
כח לִבְנֵי יִשָּׂשכָר תּוֹלְדֹתָם לְמִשְׁפְּחֹתָם לְבֵית אֲבֹתָם בְּמִסְפַּר שֵׁמֹת מִבֶּן
כט עֶשְׂרִים שָׁנָה וָמַעְלָה כֹּל יֹצֵא צָבָא: פְּקֻדֵיהֶם לְמַטֵּה יִשָּׂשכָר אַרְבָּעָה
וַחֲמִשִּׁים אֶלֶף וְאַרְבַּע מֵאוֹת:
ל לִבְנֵי זְבוּלֻן תּוֹלְדֹתָם לְמִשְׁפְּחֹתָם לְבֵית אֲבֹתָם בְּמִסְפַּר שֵׁמֹת מִבֶּן

families – the tally of their names, each male aged twenty years and above:
31 everyone capable of active service, all counted individually – those counted
from the tribe of Zevulun numbered 57,400.
32 Of the children of Yosef: of the children of Efrayim – his descendants
by their clans and their ancestral families – the tally of their names, each
male aged twenty years and above: everyone capable of active service, all
33 counted individually – those counted from the tribe of Efrayim numbered
40,500.
34 Of the children of Menashe – his descendants by their clans and their ancestral families – the tally of their names, each male aged twenty years and above:
35 everyone capable of active service, all counted individually – those counted
from the tribe of Menashe numbered 32,200.
36 Of the children of Binyamin – his descendants by their clans and their ancestral families – the tally of their names, each male aged twenty years and above:
37 everyone capable of active service, all counted individually – those counted
from the tribe of Binyamin numbered 35,400.
38 Of the children of Dan – his descendants by their clans and their ancestral
families – the tally of their names, each male aged twenty years and above:
39 everyone capable of active service, all counted individually – those counted
from the tribe of Dan numbered 62,700.
40 Of the children of Asher – his descendants by their clans and their ancestral
families – the tally of their names, each male aged twenty years and above:
41 everyone capable of active service, all counted individually – those counted
from the tribe of Asher numbered 41,500.
42 The children of Naftali – his descendants by their clans and their ancestral
families – the tally of their names, each male aged twenty years and above:
43 everyone capable of active service, all counted individually – those counted
from the tribe of Naftali numbered 53,400.
44 These were the ones counted by Moshe, Aharon, and the twelve princes of
45 Israel, one from each ancestral house. Thus the total number of the Israelites
counted, by their ancestral houses, aged twenty years and above – everyone
46 47 in Israel capable of active service – was 603,550. The ancestral house of the
Levites, however, was not counted among them.
48 49 For the LORD had spoken to Moshe and said, "You shall not count the tribe
50 of Levi, nor take a census of them among the Israelites. Instead, you shall
appoint the Levites over the Tabernacle of the Testimony, over all its utensils and all that belongs to it. For they are to carry the Tabernacle and all its
utensils; they are to tend to it, and around the Tabernacle they shall encamp.
51 When the Tabernacle is to move onward, the Levites shall take it down, and
when the Tabernacle is to encamp, the Levites shall erect it. Any outsider
52 who draws close to it shall be put to death. The Israelites shall encamp in their
53 respective camps, each by his own banner, in his division. But the Levites shall
encamp around the Tabernacle of the Testimony, so that fury does not engulf
the community of the Israelites; the Levites shall keep watch faithfully over

לא עֶשְׂרִים שָׁנָה וָמַעְלָה כֹּל יֹצֵא צָבָא׃ פְּקֻדֵיהֶם לְמַטֵּה זְבוּלֻן שִׁבְעָה
וַחֲמִשִּׁים אֶלֶף וְאַרְבַּע מֵאוֹת׃
לב לִבְנֵי יוֹסֵף לִבְנֵי אֶפְרַיִם תּוֹלְדֹתָם לְמִשְׁפְּחֹתָם לְבֵית אֲבֹתָם בְּמִסְפַּר
לג שֵׁמֹת מִבֶּן עֶשְׂרִים שָׁנָה וָמַעְלָה כֹּל יֹצֵא צָבָא׃ פְּקֻדֵיהֶם לְמַטֵּה
אֶפְרָיִם אַרְבָּעִים אֶלֶף וַחֲמֵשׁ מֵאוֹת׃
לד לִבְנֵי מְנַשֶּׁה תּוֹלְדֹתָם לְמִשְׁפְּחֹתָם לְבֵית אֲבֹתָם בְּמִסְפַּר שֵׁמוֹת מִבֶּן
לה עֶשְׂרִים שָׁנָה וָמַעְלָה כֹּל יֹצֵא צָבָא׃ פְּקֻדֵיהֶם לְמַטֵּה מְנַשֶּׁה שְׁנַיִם
וּשְׁלֹשִׁים אֶלֶף וּמָאתָיִם׃
לו לִבְנֵי בִנְיָמִן תּוֹלְדֹתָם לְמִשְׁפְּחֹתָם לְבֵית אֲבֹתָם בְּמִסְפַּר שֵׁמֹת מִבֶּן
לז עֶשְׂרִים שָׁנָה וָמַעְלָה כֹּל יֹצֵא צָבָא׃ פְּקֻדֵיהֶם לְמַטֵּה בִנְיָמִן חֲמִשָּׁה
וּשְׁלֹשִׁים אֶלֶף וְאַרְבַּע מֵאוֹת׃
לח לִבְנֵי דָן תּוֹלְדֹתָם לְמִשְׁפְּחֹתָם לְבֵית אֲבֹתָם בְּמִסְפַּר שֵׁמֹת מִבֶּן
לט עֶשְׂרִים שָׁנָה וָמַעְלָה כֹּל יֹצֵא צָבָא׃ פְּקֻדֵיהֶם לְמַטֵּה דָן שְׁנַיִם וְשִׁשִּׁים
אֶלֶף וּשְׁבַע מֵאוֹת׃
מ לִבְנֵי אָשֵׁר תּוֹלְדֹתָם לְמִשְׁפְּחֹתָם לְבֵית אֲבֹתָם בְּמִסְפַּר שֵׁמֹת מִבֶּן
מא עֶשְׂרִים שָׁנָה וָמַעְלָה כֹּל יֹצֵא צָבָא׃ פְּקֻדֵיהֶם לְמַטֵּה אָשֵׁר אֶחָד
וְאַרְבָּעִים אֶלֶף וַחֲמֵשׁ מֵאוֹת׃
מב בְּנֵי נַפְתָּלִי תּוֹלְדֹתָם לְמִשְׁפְּחֹתָם לְבֵית אֲבֹתָם בְּמִסְפַּר שֵׁמֹת מִבֶּן
מג עֶשְׂרִים שָׁנָה וָמַעְלָה כֹּל יֹצֵא צָבָא׃ פְּקֻדֵיהֶם לְמַטֵּה נַפְתָּלִי שְׁלֹשָׁה
וַחֲמִשִּׁים אֶלֶף וְאַרְבַּע מֵאוֹת׃
מד אֵלֶּה הַפְּקֻדִים אֲשֶׁר פָּקַד מֹשֶׁה וְאַהֲרֹן וּנְשִׂיאֵי יִשְׂרָאֵל שְׁנֵים עָשָׂר
מה אִישׁ אִישׁ־אֶחָד לְבֵית־אֲבֹתָיו הָיוּ׃ וַיִּהְיוּ כׇּל־פְּקוּדֵי בְנֵי־יִשְׂרָאֵל לְבֵית
מו אֲבֹתָם מִבֶּן עֶשְׂרִים שָׁנָה וָמַעְלָה כׇּל־יֹצֵא צָבָא בְּיִשְׂרָאֵל׃ וַיִּהְיוּ כׇּל־
הַפְּקֻדִים שֵׁשׁ־מֵאוֹת אֶלֶף וּשְׁלֹשֶׁת אֲלָפִים וַחֲמֵשׁ מֵאוֹת וַחֲמִשִּׁים׃
מז וְהַלְוִיִּם לְמַטֵּה אֲבֹתָם לֹא הׇתְפָּקְדוּ בְּתוֹכָם׃
מח מט וַיְדַבֵּר יְהוָה אֶל־מֹשֶׁה לֵּאמֹר׃ אַךְ אֶת־מַטֵּה לֵוִי לֹא תִפְקֹד וְאֶת־
נ רֹאשָׁם לֹא תִשָּׂא בְּתוֹךְ בְּנֵי יִשְׂרָאֵל׃ וְאַתָּה הַפְקֵד אֶת־הַלְוִיִּם עַל־
מִשְׁכַּן הָעֵדֻת וְעַל כׇּל־כֵּלָיו וְעַל כׇּל־אֲשֶׁר־לוֹ הֵמָּה יִשְׂאוּ אֶת־הַמִּשְׁכָּן
נא וְאֶת־כׇּל־כֵּלָיו וְהֵם יְשָׁרְתֻהוּ וְסָבִיב לַמִּשְׁכָּן יַחֲנוּ׃ וּבִנְסֹעַ הַמִּשְׁכָּן
יוֹרִידוּ אֹתוֹ הַלְוִיִּם וּבַחֲנֹת הַמִּשְׁכָּן יָקִימוּ אֹתוֹ הַלְוִיִּם וְהַזָּר הַקָּרֵב
נב יוּמָת׃ וְחָנוּ בְּנֵי יִשְׂרָאֵל אִישׁ עַל־מַחֲנֵהוּ וְאִישׁ עַל־דִּגְלוֹ לְצִבְאֹתָם׃
נג וְהַלְוִיִּם יַחֲנוּ סָבִיב לְמִשְׁכַּן הָעֵדֻת וְלֹא־יִהְיֶה קֶצֶף עַל־עֲדַת בְּנֵי

54 the Tabernacle of the Testimony."[2] The Israelites did so; all that the LORD had
commanded Moshe, they fulfilled.
2 1 2 The LORD spoke to Moshe and Aharon: "The Israelites shall camp, each by
his banner, the ensign of his ancestral house, positioned around the Tent of
3 Meeting at a distance. Camping to the east, toward the sunrise, shall be the
divisions under the banner of Yehuda. The leader of Yehuda's descendants is
4 5 Naḥshon son of Aminadav. And his division numbers 74,600. Camping next
to them shall be the tribe of Yissakhar. The leader of Yissakhar's descendants
6 7 is Netanel son of Tzuar. And his division numbers 54,400. Then the tribe of
8 Zevulun. The leader of Zevulun's descendants is Eliav son of Ḥelon. His divi-
9 sion numbers 57,400. The total number in Yehuda's camp, in their divisions,
10 is 186,400. They shall be the first to set out. The divisions under
the banner of Reuven's camp shall be to the south. The leader of Reuven's
11 descendants is Elitzur son of Shedeiur. And his division numbers 46,500.
12 Camping next to them shall be the tribe of Shimon. The leader of Shimon's
13 descendants is Shelumiel son of Tzurishadai. His division numbers 59,300.
14 Then the tribe of Gad: the leader of Gad's descendants is Elyasaf son of Reuel.
15 16 And his division numbers 45,650. The total number in Reuven's camp, in
17 their divisions, is 186,400. They shall set out second. And the Tent of
Meeting and the Levite camp shall set out in the midst of the camps. All shall
18 set out as they encamp, each in his own place under his banner. The
divisions under the banner of Efrayim shall be to the west. The leader of
19 Efrayim's descendants is Elishama son of Amihud. And his division numbers
20 40,500. Next to them shall be the tribe of Menashe. The leader of Menashe's
21 descendants is Gamliel son of Pedatzur. His division numbers 32,200.
22 Then the tribe of Binyamin: the leader of Binyamin's descendants is
23 24 Avidan son of Gidoni. His division numbers 35,400. The total number of men in Efrayim's camp, in their divisions, is 108,100. They shall set
25 out third. The divisions under the banner of Dan shall be to the
26 north. The leader of Dan's descendants is Aḥiezer son of Amishadai. His
27 division numbers 62,700. Camping next to them shall be the tribe of Asher.
28 The leader of Asher's descendants is Pagiel son of Okhran. His division
29 numbers 41,500. Then the tribe of Naftali: the leader of Naftali's descen-
30 31 dants is Aḥira son of Einan. His division numbers 53,400. The total number

2 | The verse implies that unauthorized entry into the Tabernacle may provoke God's wrath.

נג יִשְׂרָאֵל וְשָׁמְרוּ הַלְוִיִּם אֶת־מִשְׁמֶרֶת מִשְׁכַּן הָעֵדוּת: וַיַּעֲשׂוּ בְּנֵי
יִשְׂרָאֵל כְּכֹל אֲשֶׁר צִוָּה יְהוָה אֶת־מֹשֶׁה כֵּן עָשׂוּ:
ב א ב וַיְדַבֵּר יְהוָה אֶל־מֹשֶׁה וְאֶל־אַהֲרֹן לֵאמֹר: אִישׁ עַל־דִּגְלוֹ בְאֹתֹת ב שלישי
ג לְבֵית אֲבֹתָם יַחֲנוּ בְּנֵי יִשְׂרָאֵל מִנֶּגֶד סָבִיב לְאֹהֶל־מוֹעֵד יַחֲנוּ: וְהַחֹנִים
קֵדְמָה מִזְרָחָה דֶּגֶל מַחֲנֵה יְהוּדָה לְצִבְאֹתָם וְנָשִׂיא לִבְנֵי יְהוּדָה
ד נַחְשׁוֹן בֶּן־עַמִּינָדָב: וּצְבָאוֹ וּפְקֻדֵיהֶם אַרְבָּעָה וְשִׁבְעִים אֶלֶף וְשֵׁשׁ
ה מֵאוֹת: וְהַחֹנִים עָלָיו מַטֵּה יִשָּׂשכָר וְנָשִׂיא לִבְנֵי יִשָּׂשכָר נְתַנְאֵל בֶּן־
ו ז צוּעָר: וּצְבָאוֹ וּפְקֻדָיו אַרְבָּעָה וַחֲמִשִּׁים אֶלֶף וְאַרְבַּע מֵאוֹת: מַטֵּה
ח זְבוּלֻן וְנָשִׂיא לִבְנֵי זְבוּלֻן אֱלִיאָב בֶּן־חֵלֹן: וּצְבָאוֹ וּפְקֻדָיו שִׁבְעָה
ט וַחֲמִשִּׁים אֶלֶף וְאַרְבַּע מֵאוֹת: כָּל־הַפְּקֻדִים לְמַחֲנֵה יְהוּדָה מְאַת
אֶלֶף וּשְׁמֹנִים אֶלֶף וְשֵׁשֶׁת־אֲלָפִים וְאַרְבַּע־מֵאוֹת לְצִבְאֹתָם רִאשֹׁנָה
י יִסָּעוּ: דֶּגֶל מַחֲנֵה רְאוּבֵן תֵּימָנָה לְצִבְאֹתָם וְנָשִׂיא לִבְנֵי
יא רְאוּבֵן אֱלִיצוּר בֶּן־שְׁדֵיאוּר: וּצְבָאוֹ וּפְקֻדָיו שִׁשָּׁה וְאַרְבָּעִים אֶלֶף
יב וַחֲמֵשׁ מֵאוֹת: וְהַחוֹנִם עָלָיו מַטֵּה שִׁמְעוֹן וְנָשִׂיא לִבְנֵי שִׁמְעוֹן שְׁלֻמִיאֵל
יג בֶּן־צוּרִישַׁדָּי: וּצְבָאוֹ וּפְקֻדֵיהֶם תִּשְׁעָה וַחֲמִשִּׁים אֶלֶף וּשְׁלֹשׁ מֵאוֹת:
יד טו וּמַטֵּה גָּד וְנָשִׂיא לִבְנֵי גָד אֶלְיָסָף בֶּן־רְעוּאֵל: וּצְבָאוֹ וּפְקֻדֵיהֶם חֲמִשָּׁה
טז וְאַרְבָּעִים אֶלֶף וְשֵׁשׁ מֵאוֹת וַחֲמִשִּׁים: כָּל־הַפְּקֻדִים לְמַחֲנֵה רְאוּבֵן
מְאַת אֶלֶף וְאֶחָד וַחֲמִשִּׁים אֶלֶף וְאַרְבַּע־מֵאוֹת וַחֲמִשִּׁים לְצִבְאֹתָם
יז וּשְׁנִיִּם יִסָּעוּ: וְנָסַע אֹהֶל־מוֹעֵד מַחֲנֵה הַלְוִיִּם בְּתוֹךְ הַמַּחֲנֹת
יח כַּאֲשֶׁר יַחֲנוּ כֵּן יִסָּעוּ אִישׁ עַל־יָדוֹ לְדִגְלֵיהֶם: דֶּגֶל מַחֲנֵה
אֶפְרַיִם לְצִבְאֹתָם יָמָּה וְנָשִׂיא לִבְנֵי אֶפְרַיִם אֱלִישָׁמָע בֶּן־עַמִּיהוּד:
יט כ וּצְבָאוֹ וּפְקֻדֵיהֶם אַרְבָּעִים אֶלֶף וַחֲמֵשׁ מֵאוֹת: וְעָלָיו מַטֵּה מְנַשֶּׁה
כא וּנְשִׂיא לִבְנֵי מְנַשֶּׁה גַּמְלִיאֵל בֶּן־פְּדָהצוּר: וּצְבָאוֹ וּפְקֻדֵיהֶם שְׁנַיִם
כב וּשְׁלֹשִׁים אֶלֶף וּמָאתָיִם: וּמַטֵּה בִּנְיָמִן וְנָשִׂיא לִבְנֵי בִנְיָמִן אֲבִידָן
כג בֶּן־גִּדְעֹנִי: וּצְבָאוֹ וּפְקֻדֵיהֶם חֲמִשָּׁה וּשְׁלֹשִׁים אֶלֶף וְאַרְבַּע מֵאוֹת:
כד כָּל־הַפְּקֻדִים לְמַחֲנֵה אֶפְרַיִם מְאַת אֶלֶף וּשְׁמֹנַת־אֲלָפִים וּמֵאָה
כה לְצִבְאֹתָם וּשְׁלִשִׁים יִסָּעוּ: דֶּגֶל מַחֲנֵה דָן צָפֹנָה לְצִבְאֹתָם
כו וְנָשִׂיא לִבְנֵי דָן אֲחִיעֶזֶר בֶּן־עַמִּישַׁדָּי: וּצְבָאוֹ וּפְקֻדֵיהֶם שְׁנַיִם וְשִׁשִּׁים
כז אֶלֶף וּשְׁבַע מֵאוֹת: וְהַחֹנִים עָלָיו מַטֵּה אָשֵׁר וְנָשִׂיא לִבְנֵי אָשֵׁר
כח פַּגְעִיאֵל בֶּן־עָכְרָן: וּצְבָאוֹ וּפְקֻדֵיהֶם אֶחָד וְאַרְבָּעִים אֶלֶף וַחֲמֵשׁ
כט ל מֵאוֹת: וּמַטֵּה נַפְתָּלִי וְנָשִׂיא לִבְנֵי נַפְתָּלִי אֲחִירַע בֶּן־עֵינָן: וּצְבָאוֹ
לא וּפְקֻדֵיהֶם שְׁלֹשָׁה וַחֲמִשִּׁים אֶלֶף וְאַרְבַּע מֵאוֹת: כָּל־הַפְּקֻדִים לְמַחֲנֵה

in Dan's camp, in their divisions, is 157,600. They shall set out last, by their
banners."
32 These were the numbers of the Israelites by their ancestral houses. The total
33 number in the camps by their divisions was 603,550. As the LORD had commanded Moshe, the Levites were not counted among the other Israelites.
34 And so the Israelites did all that the LORD had commanded Moshe. Thus
they camped by their banners, and thus they set out, each amid his clan and
his ancestral house.
3 1 These were the descendants of Aharon and Moshe at the time when the LORD
2 spoke to Moshe at Mount Sinai. The names of Aharon's sons were Nadav, the
3 firstborn, Avihu, Elazar, and Itamar. These were the names of Aharon's sons,
4 the anointed priests, ordained for priestly service. But Nadav and Avihu died
before the LORD when, before the LORD, they offered unauthorized fire in the
Wilderness of Sinai;[3] they had had no sons. And Elazar and Itamar served as
priests while their father Aharon lived.[4]
5 6 The LORD said to Moshe, "Bring close the tribe of Levi and set them before
7 Aharon the priest to assist him. They shall keep his charge and that of the
whole community at the Tent of Meeting, carrying out the service of the
8 Tabernacle. Theirs shall be the charge of all the utensils of the Tent of
Meeting, and they shall keep, too, the charge of the Israelites by performing
9 the service of the Tabernacle. Give the Levites over to Aharon and his sons;
10 they among the Israelites are to be dedicated wholly to him. Appoint Aharon
and his sons to attend to the priestly duties; any outsider who draws close[5]
will die."
11 12 And the LORD spoke to Moshe: "In place of the firstborn, the first to emerge
from every womb among the Israelites, I have taken the Levites from among
13 the Israelites; the Levites shall be Mine, for all the firstborn are Mine. On
the day I struck down all the firstborn in Egypt, I consecrated every firstborn in Israel to Myself, man and animal. They are to be Mine; I am the
LORD."
14 15 Then the LORD spoke to Moshe in the Sinai Desert: "Count the Levites
by their ancestral houses and their clans. Count every male a month old or
16 more." So Moshe counted them at the LORD's word as he was commanded.
17 18 These were the names of Levi's sons: Gershon, Kehat, and Merari. These
19 were the names of Gershon's sons with their clans: Livni and Shimi. Kehat's
20 sons with their clans: Amram, Yitzhar, Ḥevron, and Uziel. Merari's sons with
their clans: Maḥli and Mushi. These were the Levite clans by their ancestral
21 houses. Gershon encompassed the clans of Livni and Shimi; these were the
22 Gershonite clans. Their total number of males a month old and upward was

3 | See Leviticus 10:1–2.

4 | In other words, only these two remaining sons served during Aharon's lifetime.

5 | See note on 1:53.

דָּן מְאַת אֶלֶף וְשִׁבְעָה וַחֲמִשִּׁים אֶלֶף וְשֵׁשׁ מֵאוֹת לָאַחֲרֹנָה יִסְעוּ
לְדִגְלֵיהֶם׃
לב אֵלֶּה פְּקוּדֵי בְנֵי־יִשְׂרָאֵל לְבֵית אֲבֹתָם כָּל־פְּקוּדֵי הַמַּחֲנֹת לְצִבְאֹתָם
לג שֵׁשׁ־מֵאוֹת אֶלֶף וּשְׁלֹשֶׁת אֲלָפִים וַחֲמֵשׁ מֵאוֹת וַחֲמִשִּׁים׃ וְהַלְוִיִּם לֹא
לד הָתְפָּקְדוּ בְּתוֹךְ בְּנֵי יִשְׂרָאֵל כַּאֲשֶׁר צִוָּה יְהוָה אֶת־מֹשֶׁה׃ וַיַּעֲשׂוּ בְּנֵי
יִשְׂרָאֵל כְּכֹל אֲשֶׁר־צִוָּה יְהוָה אֶת־מֹשֶׁה כֵּן־חָנוּ לְדִגְלֵיהֶם וְכֵן נָסָעוּ
אִישׁ לְמִשְׁפְּחֹתָיו עַל־בֵּית אֲבֹתָיו׃
ג א וְאֵלֶּה תּוֹלְדֹת אַהֲרֹן וּמֹשֶׁה בְּיוֹם דִּבֶּר יְהוָה אֶת־מֹשֶׁה בְּהַר סִינָי׃ ג רביעי
ב וְאֵלֶּה שְׁמוֹת בְּנֵי־אַהֲרֹן הַבְּכֹר ׀ נָדָב וַאֲבִיהוּא אֶלְעָזָר וְאִיתָמָר׃
ג אֵלֶּה שְׁמוֹת בְּנֵי אַהֲרֹן הַכֹּהֲנִים הַמְּשֻׁחִים אֲשֶׁר־מִלֵּא יָדָם לְכַהֵן׃
ד וַיָּמָת נָדָב וַאֲבִיהוּא לִפְנֵי יְהוָה בְּהַקְרִבָם אֵשׁ זָרָה לִפְנֵי יְהוָה בְּמִדְבַּר
סִינַי וּבָנִים לֹא־הָיוּ לָהֶם וַיְכַהֵן אֶלְעָזָר וְאִיתָמָר עַל־פְּנֵי אַהֲרֹן
אֲבִיהֶם׃
ה ו וַיְדַבֵּר יְהוָה אֶל־מֹשֶׁה לֵּאמֹר׃ הַקְרֵב אֶת־מַטֵּה לֵוִי וְהַעֲמַדְתָּ אֹתוֹ
ז לִפְנֵי אַהֲרֹן הַכֹּהֵן וְשֵׁרְתוּ אֹתוֹ׃ וְשָׁמְרוּ אֶת־מִשְׁמַרְתּוֹ וְאֶת־מִשְׁמֶרֶת
ח כָּל־הָעֵדָה לִפְנֵי אֹהֶל מוֹעֵד לַעֲבֹד אֶת־עֲבֹדַת הַמִּשְׁכָּן׃ וְשָׁמְרוּ אֶת־
כָּל־כְּלֵי אֹהֶל מוֹעֵד וְאֶת־מִשְׁמֶרֶת בְּנֵי יִשְׂרָאֵל לַעֲבֹד אֶת־עֲבֹדַת
ט הַמִּשְׁכָּן׃ וְנָתַתָּה אֶת־הַלְוִיִּם לְאַהֲרֹן וּלְבָנָיו נְתוּנִם נְתוּנִם הֵמָּה לוֹ
י מֵאֵת בְּנֵי יִשְׂרָאֵל׃ וְאֶת־אַהֲרֹן וְאֶת־בָּנָיו תִּפְקֹד וְשָׁמְרוּ אֶת־כְּהֻנָּתָם
וְהַזָּר הַקָּרֵב יוּמָת׃
יא יב וַיְדַבֵּר יְהוָה אֶל־מֹשֶׁה לֵּאמֹר׃ וַאֲנִי הִנֵּה לָקַחְתִּי אֶת־הַלְוִיִּם מִתּוֹךְ
בְּנֵי יִשְׂרָאֵל תַּחַת כָּל־בְּכוֹר פֶּטֶר רֶחֶם מִבְּנֵי יִשְׂרָאֵל וְהָיוּ לִי הַלְוִיִּם׃
יג כִּי לִי כָּל־בְּכוֹר בְּיוֹם הַכֹּתִי כָל־בְּכוֹר בְּאֶרֶץ מִצְרַיִם הִקְדַּשְׁתִּי לִי כָל־
בְּכוֹר בְּיִשְׂרָאֵל מֵאָדָם עַד־בְּהֵמָה לִי יִהְיוּ אֲנִי יְהוָה׃
יד טו וַיְדַבֵּר יְהוָה אֶל־מֹשֶׁה בְּמִדְבַּר סִינַי לֵאמֹר׃ פְּקֹד אֶת־בְּנֵי לֵוִי לְבֵית חמישי
טז אֲבֹתָם לְמִשְׁפְּחֹתָם כָּל־זָכָר מִבֶּן־חֹדֶשׁ וָמַעְלָה תִּפְקְדֵם׃ וַיִּפְקֹד אֹתָם
יז מֹשֶׁה עַל־פִּי יְהוָה כַּאֲשֶׁר צֻוָּה׃ וַיִּהְיוּ־אֵלֶּה בְנֵי־לֵוִי בִּשְׁמֹתָם גֵּרְשׁוֹן
יח יט וּקְהָת וּמְרָרִי׃ וְאֵלֶּה שְׁמוֹת בְּנֵי־גֵרְשׁוֹן לְמִשְׁפְּחֹתָם לִבְנִי וְשִׁמְעִי׃ וּבְנֵי
כ קְהָת לְמִשְׁפְּחֹתָם עַמְרָם וְיִצְהָר חֶבְרוֹן וְעֻזִּיאֵל׃ וּבְנֵי מְרָרִי לְמִשְׁפְּחֹתָם
כא מַחְלִי וּמוּשִׁי אֵלֶּה הֵם מִשְׁפְּחֹת הַלֵּוִי לְבֵית אֲבֹתָם׃ לְגֵרְשׁוֹן מִשְׁפַּחַת
כב הַלִּבְנִי וּמִשְׁפַּחַת הַשִּׁמְעִי אֵלֶּה הֵם מִשְׁפְּחֹת הַגֵּרְשֻׁנִּי׃ פְּקֻדֵיהֶם
בְּמִסְפַּר כָּל־זָכָר מִבֶּן־חֹדֶשׁ וָמַעְלָה פְּקֻדֵיהֶם שִׁבְעַת אֲלָפִים וַחֲמֵשׁ

23 7,500. The Gershonite families were to camp behind the Tabernacle to the
24 25 west. And the leader of the Gershonite families was Elyasaf son of Lael. The
charge of the sons of Gershon at the Tent of Meeting was the Tabernacle
and the tent, its covering,[6] the screen at the entrance to the Tent of Meeting,
26 the curtains of the courtyard, the screen at the entrance to the courtyard
surrounding the Tabernacle and altar, and its ropes – and all the service
27 related to these. Kehat encompassed the clans of Amram, Yitzhar,
28 Ḥevron, and Uziel; these were the Kohatite clans. Their total number of males
a month old and upward was 8,600; these kept the charge of the Sanctuary.
29 The Kohatite families were to camp on the south side of the Tabernacle.
30 The leader of the ancestral house of the Kohatite families was Elitzafan son
31 of Uziel. Their charge was the Ark, the table, the candelabrum, the altars,
and the sacred utensils used in their service, and the screen and everything
32 pertaining to it. Chief of the leaders of the Levites was Elazar son of Aharon
the priest; he was appointed over those responsible for keeping charge of
33 the Sanctuary. Merari encompassed the clans of Maḥli and Mushi; these
34 were the Merarite families. The total number of their males a month old and
35 upward was 6,200. The leader of the ancestral house of the Merarite families
was Tzuriel son of Aviḥayil; and they were to camp on the north side of the
36 Tabernacle. The Merarites were appointed to take care of the frames, bars,
37 posts, and bases of the Tabernacle, all its utensils and accessories, as well as
the posts of the surrounding courtyard with their bases, pegs, and ropes.
38 Those who were to camp to the east of the Tabernacle in front of the Tent of
Meeting toward the sunrise were Moshe, Aharon, and his sons. They were
charged, on the Israelites' behalf, to keep faithful watch over the Sanctuary.
39 Any outsider who drew close would die. The total number of Levites counted
by Moshe and Aharon at the LORD's command, by their clans, all the males a
40 month old and upward, was 22,000. Then the LORD said to Moshe,
"Count all the firstborn Israelite males a month of age and upward, taking a
41 census of their names. Take the Levites for Me – I am the LORD – in place
of all the firstborn of the Israelites, and the livestock of the Levites in place
42 of all the firstborn of the Israelites' livestock." So Moshe counted all the first-
43 born of the Israelites, as the LORD had commanded him. The total number
of firstborn males a month of age and upward, the full tally of their names,
was 22,273.
44 45 Then the LORD spoke to Moshe: "Take the Levites in place of all the firstborn of Israel, and the livestock of the Levites in place of their livestock.
46 The Levites shall be Mine; I am the LORD. As for the redemption of the 273
47 firstborn Israelites who exceed the number of the Levites, collect five shekel
for each, according to the Sanctuary weight – a shekel being twenty gerah.[7]
48 Give the money to Aharon and his sons as a redemption for the additional

---

6 | The Tabernacle, the tent, and the covering represent different layers of the structure; see Exodus 26:1–14. For components of the Tabernacle generally, see Exodus, chapters 25–27.

7 | The gerah and the shekel are units of weight and currency, of which Sanctuary weights differed from the standard measure. A shekel was close to 20 grams or three-quarters of an ounce.

כג כד מֵאוֹת: מִשְׁפְּחֹת הַגֵּרְשֻׁנִּי אַחֲרֵי הַמִּשְׁכָּן יַחֲנוּ יָמָּה: וּנְשִׂיא בֵית־אָב
כה לַגֵּרְשֻׁנִּי אֶלְיָסָף בֶּן־לָאֵל: וּמִשְׁמֶרֶת בְּנֵי־גֵרְשׁוֹן בְּאֹהֶל מוֹעֵד הַמִּשְׁכָּן
כו וְהָאֹהֶל מִכְסֵהוּ וּמָסַךְ פֶּתַח אֹהֶל מוֹעֵד: וְקַלְעֵי הֶחָצֵר וְאֶת־מָסַךְ
פֶּתַח הֶחָצֵר אֲשֶׁר עַל־הַמִּשְׁכָּן וְעַל־הַמִּזְבֵּחַ סָבִיב וְאֵת מֵיתָרָיו לְכֹל
כז עֲבֹדָתוֹ: וְלִקְהָת מִשְׁפַּחַת הָעַמְרָמִי וּמִשְׁפַּחַת הַיִּצְהָרִי
וּמִשְׁפַּחַת הַחֶבְרֹנִי וּמִשְׁפַּחַת הָעָזִּיאֵלִי אֵלֶּה הֵם מִשְׁפְּחֹת הַקְּהָתִי:
כח בְּמִסְפַּר כָּל־זָכָר מִבֶּן־חֹדֶשׁ וָמָעְלָה שְׁמֹנַת אֲלָפִים וְשֵׁשׁ מֵאוֹת שֹׁמְרֵי
כט מִשְׁמֶרֶת הַקֹּדֶשׁ: מִשְׁפְּחֹת בְּנֵי־קְהָת יַחֲנוּ עַל יֶרֶךְ הַמִּשְׁכָּן תֵּימָנָה:
ל לא וּנְשִׂיא בֵית־אָב לְמִשְׁפְּחֹת הַקְּהָתִי אֱלִיצָפָן בֶּן־עֻזִּיאֵל: וּמִשְׁמַרְתָּם
הָאָרֹן וְהַשֻּׁלְחָן וְהַמְּנֹרָה וְהַמִּזְבְּחֹת וּכְלֵי הַקֹּדֶשׁ אֲשֶׁר יְשָׁרְתוּ בָּהֶם
לב וְהַמָּסָךְ וְכֹל עֲבֹדָתוֹ: וּנְשִׂיא נְשִׂיאֵי הַלֵּוִי אֶלְעָזָר בֶּן־אַהֲרֹן הַכֹּהֵן
לג פְּקֻדַּת שֹׁמְרֵי מִשְׁמֶרֶת הַקֹּדֶשׁ: לִמְרָרִי מִשְׁפַּחַת הַמַּחְלִי וּמִשְׁפַּחַת
לד הַמּוּשִׁי אֵלֶּה הֵם מִשְׁפְּחֹת מְרָרִי: וּפְקֻדֵיהֶם בְּמִסְפַּר כָּל־זָכָר מִבֶּן־
לה חֹדֶשׁ וָמָעְלָה שֵׁשֶׁת אֲלָפִים וּמָאתָיִם: וּנְשִׂיא בֵית־אָב לְמִשְׁפְּחֹת מְרָרִי
לו צוּרִיאֵל בֶּן־אֲבִיחָיִל עַל יֶרֶךְ הַמִּשְׁכָּן יַחֲנוּ צָפֹנָה: וּפְקֻדַּת מִשְׁמֶרֶת בְּנֵי
מְרָרִי קַרְשֵׁי הַמִּשְׁכָּן וּבְרִיחָיו וְעַמֻּדָיו וַאֲדָנָיו וְכָל־כֵּלָיו וְכֹל עֲבֹדָתוֹ:
לז לח וְעַמֻּדֵי הֶחָצֵר סָבִיב וְאַדְנֵיהֶם וִיתֵדֹתָם וּמֵיתְרֵיהֶם: וְהַחֹנִים לִפְנֵי
הַמִּשְׁכָּן קֵדְמָה לִפְנֵי אֹהֶל־מוֹעֵד ׀ מִזְרָחָה מֹשֶׁה ׀ וְאַהֲרֹן וּבָנָיו שֹׁמְרִים
לט מִשְׁמֶרֶת הַמִּקְדָּשׁ לְמִשְׁמֶרֶת בְּנֵי יִשְׂרָאֵל וְהַזָּר הַקָּרֵב יוּמָת: כָּל־
פְּקוּדֵי הַלְוִיִּם אֲשֶׁר פָּקַד מֹשֶׁה וְאַהֲרֹן עַל־פִּי יְהוָה לְמִשְׁפְּחֹתָם כָּל־
מ זָכָר מִבֶּן־חֹדֶשׁ וָמַעְלָה שְׁנַיִם וְעֶשְׂרִים אָלֶף: וַיֹּאמֶר יְהוָה ששי
אֶל־מֹשֶׁה פְּקֹד כָּל־בְּכֹר זָכָר לִבְנֵי יִשְׂרָאֵל מִבֶּן־חֹדֶשׁ וָמָעְלָה וְשָׂא
מא אֵת מִסְפַּר שְׁמֹתָם: וְלָקַחְתָּ אֶת־הַלְוִיִּם לִי אֲנִי יְהוָה תַּחַת כָּל־בְּכֹר
בִּבְנֵי יִשְׂרָאֵל וְאֵת בֶּהֱמַת הַלְוִיִּם תַּחַת כָּל־בְּכוֹר בְּבֶהֱמַת בְּנֵי יִשְׂרָאֵל:
מב וַיִּפְקֹד מֹשֶׁה כַּאֲשֶׁר צִוָּה יְהוָה אֹתוֹ אֶת־כָּל־בְּכוֹר בִּבְנֵי יִשְׂרָאֵל:
מג וַיְהִי כָל־בְּכוֹר זָכָר בְּמִסְפַּר שֵׁמֹת מִבֶּן־חֹדֶשׁ וָמַעְלָה לִפְקֻדֵיהֶם שְׁנַיִם
וְעֶשְׂרִים אֶלֶף שְׁלֹשָׁה וְשִׁבְעִים וּמָאתָיִם:
מד מה וַיְדַבֵּר יְהוָה אֶל־מֹשֶׁה לֵּאמֹר: קַח אֶת־הַלְוִיִּם תַּחַת כָּל־בְּכוֹר בִּבְנֵי
יִשְׂרָאֵל וְאֶת־בֶּהֱמַת הַלְוִיִּם תַּחַת בְּהֶמְתָּם וְהָיוּ־לִי הַלְוִיִּם אֲנִי יְהוָה:
מו וְאֵת פְּדוּיֵי הַשְּׁלֹשָׁה וְהַשִּׁבְעִים וְהַמָּאתָיִם הָעֹדְפִים עַל־הַלְוִיִּם
מז מִבְּכוֹר בְּנֵי יִשְׂרָאֵל: וְלָקַחְתָּ חֲמֵשֶׁת חֲמֵשֶׁת שְׁקָלִים לַגֻּלְגֹּלֶת בְּשֶׁקֶל
מח הַקֹּדֶשׁ תִּקָּח עֶשְׂרִים גֵּרָה הַשָּׁקֶל: וְנָתַתָּה הַכֶּסֶף לְאַהֲרֹן וּלְבָנָיו פְּדוּיֵ

49 Israelites." Moshe took the redemption money from those who were over and
50 above those redeemed by the Levites; from the firstborn of the Israelites he
51 took silver weighing 1,365 shekel by the Sanctuary weight. Moshe gave the
redemption money to Aharon and his sons, at the Lord's word, as the Lord
had commanded Moshe.
4 1 2 The Lord spoke to Moshe and Aharon: "Take a census of the Kohatites
3 among the Levites, by their families and their ancestral houses, from thirty to
fifty years old: all those able to go into service to perform the work of the Tent
4 of Meeting. This will be the service of the Kohatites in the Tent of Meeting:
5 the most sacred objects; when the camp is about to set out, Aharon and his
sons shall come and take down the screening curtain and cover the Ark of
6 the Testimony with it. Then they shall put over it a covering of fine leather,
7 and over that a cloth of pure blue, and then they shall insert its poles. On
the table of the showbread they shall spread a blue cloth, and on it place the
bowls, spoons, jars, and the libation pitchers; and the bread of the Presence
8 shall be on it constantly. They shall spread over them a scarlet cloth, and then
cover it with a covering of fine leather; and then they shall insert its poles.
9 They shall take a blue cloth and cover the candelabrum and its lamps, tongs,
10 pans, and all the oil vessels used in its service. Then they must put it and all
its utensils into a covering of fine leather, and place them on a carrying frame.
11 They shall spread a blue cloth on the golden altar, and cover it with a covering
12 of fine leather; and then they shall insert its poles. Then they shall take all the
service utensils, with which they serve in the Sanctuary, put them into a blue
cloth, cover them with a covering of fine leather, and place them on a carrying
13 frame. They shall remove the ashes from the altar and spread a purple cloth
14 over it. Then they shall place upon it all the special implements with which
they serve there – the pans, the forks, the shovels, the basins, and all the altar's
utensils – and spread over it all a covering of fine leather, and then insert its
15 poles. When Aharon and his sons have finished covering the Sanctuary and
all the furnishings of the Sanctuary, when the camp is ready to set out, then
the Kohatites shall come to carry them; but they must not touch the sacred
objects lest they die. These are what the Kohatites must carry for the Tent
16 of Meeting. The responsibility of Elazar son of Aharon the priest is for the
lighting oil, the fragrant incense, the daily grain offering, and the anointing
oil. He is also responsible for the whole Tabernacle and all that is in it, for the
Sanctuary and all its utensils."
17 18 Again the Lord spoke to Moshe and Aharon: "Do not let the tribe of the
19 clans of Kehat be cut off from among the Levites. So that they may live and
not die when they come close to the most sacred things, they must do this: let
Aharon and his sons go in and assign each man his duties and what he must
20 carry; but they themselves must not go in and watch while the holy things
are being covered, for they would die."

מט הָעֹדְפִים בָּהֶם: וַיִּקַּח מֹשֶׁה אֵת כֶּסֶף הַפִּדְיוֹם מֵאֵת הָעֹדְפִים עַל פְּדוּיֵי
נ הַלְוִיִּם: מֵאֵת בְּכוֹר בְּנֵי יִשְׂרָאֵל לָקַח אֶת־הַכָּסֶף חֲמִשָּׁה וְשִׁשִּׁים
נא וּשְׁלֹשׁ מֵאוֹת וָאֶלֶף בְּשֶׁקֶל הַקֹּדֶשׁ: וַיִּתֵּן מֹשֶׁה אֶת־כֶּסֶף הַפְּדֻיִם
לְאַהֲרֹן וּלְבָנָיו עַל־פִּי יהוה כַּאֲשֶׁר צִוָּה יהוה אֶת־מֹשֶׁה:
ד א ב וַיְדַבֵּר יהוה אֶל־מֹשֶׁה וְאֶל־אַהֲרֹן לֵאמֹר: נָשֹׂא אֶת־רֹאשׁ בְּנֵי קְהָת שביעי
ג מִתּוֹךְ בְּנֵי לֵוִי לְמִשְׁפְּחֹתָם לְבֵית אֲבֹתָם: מִבֶּן שְׁלֹשִׁים שָׁנָה וָמַעְלָה
וְעַד בֶּן־חֲמִשִּׁים שָׁנָה כָּל־בָּא לַצָּבָא לַעֲשׂוֹת מְלָאכָה בְּאֹהֶל מוֹעֵד:
ד ה זֹאת עֲבֹדַת בְּנֵי־קְהָת בְּאֹהֶל מוֹעֵד קֹדֶשׁ הַקֳּדָשִׁים: וּבָא אַהֲרֹן וּבָנָיו
בִּנְסֹעַ הַמַּחֲנֶה וְהוֹרִדוּ אֵת פָּרֹכֶת הַמָּסָךְ וְכִסּוּ־בָהּ אֵת אֲרֹן הָעֵדֻת:
ו וְנָתְנוּ עָלָיו כְּסוּי עוֹר תַּחַשׁ וּפָרְשׂוּ בֶגֶד־כְּלִיל תְּכֵלֶת מִלְמָעְלָה וְשָׂמוּ
ז בַּדָּיו: וְעַל | שֻׁלְחַן הַפָּנִים יִפְרְשׂוּ בֶּגֶד תְּכֵלֶת וְנָתְנוּ עָלָיו אֶת־הַקְּעָרֹת
וְאֶת־הַכַּפֹּת וְאֶת־הַמְּנַקִּיֹּת וְאֵת קְשׂוֹת הַנָּסֶךְ וְלֶחֶם הַתָּמִיד עָלָיו
ח יִהְיֶה: וּפָרְשׂוּ עֲלֵיהֶם בֶּגֶד תּוֹלַעַת שָׁנִי וְכִסּוּ אֹתוֹ בְּמִכְסֵה עוֹר תָּחַשׁ
ט וְשָׂמוּ אֶת־בַּדָּיו: וְלָקְחוּ | בֶּגֶד תְּכֵלֶת וְכִסּוּ אֶת־מְנֹרַת הַמָּאוֹר וְאֶת־
נֵרֹתֶיהָ וְאֶת־מַלְקָחֶיהָ וְאֶת־מַחְתֹּתֶיהָ וְאֵת כָּל־כְּלֵי שַׁמְנָהּ אֲשֶׁר
י יְשָׁרְתוּ־לָהּ בָּהֶם: וְנָתְנוּ אֹתָהּ וְאֶת־כָּל־כֵּלֶיהָ אֶל־מִכְסֵה עוֹר תָּחַשׁ
יא וְנָתְנוּ עַל־הַמּוֹט: וְעַל | מִזְבַּח הַזָּהָב יִפְרְשׂוּ בֶּגֶד תְּכֵלֶת וְכִסּוּ אֹתוֹ
יב בְּמִכְסֵה עוֹר תָּחַשׁ וְשָׂמוּ אֶת־בַּדָּיו: וְלָקְחוּ אֶת־כָּל־כְּלֵי הַשָּׁרֵת אֲשֶׁר
יְשָׁרְתוּ־בָם בַּקֹּדֶשׁ וְנָתְנוּ אֶל־בֶּגֶד תְּכֵלֶת וְכִסּוּ אוֹתָם בְּמִכְסֵה עוֹר
יג תָּחַשׁ וְנָתְנוּ עַל־הַמּוֹט: וְדִשְּׁנוּ אֶת־הַמִּזְבֵּחַ וּפָרְשׂוּ עָלָיו בֶּגֶד אַרְגָּמָן:
יד וְנָתְנוּ עָלָיו אֶת־כָּל־כֵּלָיו אֲשֶׁר יְשָׁרְתוּ עָלָיו בָּהֶם אֶת־הַמַּחְתֹּת אֶת־
הַמִּזְלָגֹת וְאֶת־הַיָּעִים וְאֶת־הַמִּזְרָקֹת כֹּל כְּלֵי הַמִּזְבֵּחַ וּפָרְשׂוּ עָלָיו כְּסוּי
טו עוֹר תַּחַשׁ וְשָׂמוּ בַדָּיו: וְכִלָּה אַהֲרֹן־וּבָנָיו לְכַסֹּת אֶת־הַקֹּדֶשׁ וְאֶת־כָּל־
כְּלֵי הַקֹּדֶשׁ בִּנְסֹעַ הַמַּחֲנֶה וְאַחֲרֵי־כֵן יָבֹאוּ בְנֵי־קְהָת לָשֵׂאת וְלֹא־יִגְּעוּ
טז אֶל־הַקֹּדֶשׁ וָמֵתוּ אֵלֶּה מַשָּׂא בְנֵי־קְהָת בְּאֹהֶל מוֹעֵד: וּפְקֻדַּת אֶלְעָזָר |
בֶּן־אַהֲרֹן הַכֹּהֵן שֶׁמֶן הַמָּאוֹר וּקְטֹרֶת הַסַּמִּים וּמִנְחַת הַתָּמִיד וְשֶׁמֶן
הַמִּשְׁחָה פְּקֻדַּת כָּל־הַמִּשְׁכָּן וְכָל־אֲשֶׁר־בּוֹ בְּקֹדֶשׁ וּבְכֵלָיו:
יז יח וַיְדַבֵּר יהוה אֶל־מֹשֶׁה וְאֶל־אַהֲרֹן לֵאמֹר: אַל־תַּכְרִיתוּ אֶת־שֵׁבֶט ד מפטיר
יט מִשְׁפְּחֹת הַקְּהָתִי מִתּוֹךְ הַלְוִיִּם: וְזֹאת | עֲשׂוּ לָהֶם וְחָיוּ וְלֹא יָמֻתוּ
בְּגִשְׁתָּם אֶת־קֹדֶשׁ הַקֳּדָשִׁים אַהֲרֹן וּבָנָיו יָבֹאוּ וְשָׂמוּ אוֹתָם אִישׁ
כ אִישׁ עַל־עֲבֹדָתוֹ וְאֶל־מַשָּׂאוֹ: וְלֹא־יָבֹאוּ לִרְאוֹת כְּבַלַּע אֶת־הַקֹּדֶשׁ
וָמֵתוּ:

NASO

21 22 Then the LORD spoke to Moshe: "Take a census too of the Gershonites, by
23 their clans and their ancestral houses, from thirty years old to fifty: all who
24 go into service to carry out the work of the Tent of Meeting. This will be the
25 service of the clans of Gershon, serving and carrying: they shall carry the
curtains of the Tabernacle and the Tent of Meeting, its covering, the covering
of fine leather that is over it, the screen at the entrance to the Tent of Meeting,
26 the hangings for the courtyard, the curtain for the entrance of the gate to the
courtyard around the Tabernacle and the altar, and their ropes, together with
all the utensils for their service and everything made for them; and they will
27 serve. All the carrying and service of the Gershonites shall be performed at
Aharon and his sons' command; you shall assign to their charge all that they
28 are to carry. This is the service of the families of the Gershonites for the Tent
of Meeting. Their charge will be under the authority of Itamar son of Aharon
29 the priest. As for the sons of Merari, you shall number them by their
30 clans and ancestral houses, from thirty years old to fifty, all who go into service
31 to carry out the work of the Tent of Meeting. This is what they are charged
to carry as the whole of their service in the Tent of Meeting: the boards
32 of the Tabernacle, its crossbars, its posts, its sockets; and the posts of the
surrounding courtyard with their sockets, pegs, and ropes, together with all
their furnishings and everything for their service. You shall assign each object
33 by name to the man charged with carrying it. This is the service of the families
of the Merarites, the whole of their service for the Tent of Meeting, under
34 the authority of Itamar son of Aharon the priest." So Moshe and Aharon and
the leaders of the community counted the Kohatites by their clans and their
35 ancestral houses, from thirty years old to fifty, all who went into the service
36 37 of the Tent of Meeting; and those numbered by their clans were 2,750. These
were the ones numbered from the clans of Kehat, all who served in the Tent
of Meeting, whom Moshe and Aharon numbered at the LORD's command
38 through Moshe. Those numbered of the Gershonites, by their
39 families and ancestral houses, from thirty years old to fifty: all who went
40 into the service of the Tent of Meeting – those numbered by their clans and
41 ancestral houses were 2,630. These were the ones numbered from the families
of the Gershonites, all who served in the Tent of Meeting, whom Moshe and
42 Aharon numbered at the command of the LORD. Those numbered from the
43 clans of the Merarites, by their clans and ancestral houses, from thirty years
44 old to fifty, all who went into the service of the Tent of Meeting – those
45 numbered by their clans were 3,200. These were the ones numbered from the
clans of the Merarites, whom Moshe and Aharon numbered at the LORD's
46 command through Moshe. All the Levites, whom Moshe, Aharon, and the

כא כב וידבר יהוה אל־משה לאמר: נשא את־ראש בני גרשון גם־הם לבית נשא
כג אבתם למשפחתם: מבן שלשים שנה ומעלה עד בן־חמשים שנה
כד תפקד אותם כל־הבא לצבא צבא לעבד עבדה באהל מועד: זאת
כה עבדת משפחת הגרשני לעבד ולמשא: ונשאו את־יריעת המשכן
ואת־אהל מועד מכסהו ומכסה התחש אשר־עליו מלמעלה ואת־
כו מסך פתח אהל מועד: ואת קלעי החצר ואת־מסך | פתח | שער
החצר אשר על־המשכן ועל־המזבח סביב ואת מיתריהם ואת־כל־
כז כלי עבדתם ואת כל־אשר יעשה להם ועבדו: על־פי אהרן ובניו
תהיה כל־עבדת בני הגרשני לכל־משאם ולכל עבדתם ופקדתם
כח עלהם במשמרת את כל־משאם: זאת עבדת משפחת בני הגרשני
כט באהל מועד ומשמרתם ביד איתמר בן־אהרן הכהן: בני
ל מררי למשפחתם לבית־אבתם תפקד אתם: מבן שלשים שנה
ומעלה ועד בן־חמשים שנה תפקדם כל־הבא לצבא לעבד את־
לא עבדת אהל מועד: וזאת משמרת משאם לכל־עבדתם באהל
לב מועד קרשי המשכן ובריחיו ועמודיו ואדניו: ועמודי החצר סביב
ואדניהם ויתדתם ומיתריהם לכל־כליהם ולכל עבדתם ובשמת
לג תפקדו את־כלי משמרת משאם: זאת עבדת משפחת בני מררי
לד לכל־עבדתם באהל מועד ביד איתמר בן־אהרן הכהן: ויפקד משה
ואהרן ונשיאי העדה את־בני הקהתי למשפחתם ולבית אבתם:
לה מבן שלשים שנה ומעלה ועד בן־חמשים שנה כל־הבא לצבא
לו לעבדה באהל מועד: ויהיו פקדיהם למשפחתם אלפים שבע מאות
לז וחמשים: אלה פקודי משפחת הקהתי כל־העבד באהל מועד
לח אשר פקד משה ואהרן על־פי יהוה ביד־משה: ופקודי שני
לט בני גרשון למשפחותם ולבית אבתם: מבן שלשים שנה ומעלה
מ ועד בן־חמשים שנה כל־הבא לצבא לעבדה באהל מועד: ויהיו
פקדיהם למשפחתם לבית אבתם אלפים ושש מאות ושלשים:
מא אלה פקודי משפחת בני גרשון כל־העבד באהל מועד אשר פקד
מב משה ואהרן על־פי יהוה: ופקודי משפחת בני מררי למשפחתם
מג לבית אבתם: מבן שלשים שנה ומעלה ועד בן־חמשים שנה
מד כל־הבא לצבא לעבדה באהל מועד: ויהיו פקדיהם למשפחתם
מה שלשת אלפים ומאתים: אלה פקודי משפחת בני מררי אשר פקד
מו משה ואהרן על־פי יהוה ביד־משה: כל־הפקדים אשר פקד משה

47 leaders of Israel numbered by their clans and ancestral houses, from thirty
years old to fifty: all who entered to do the work of service and the work of
48 49 carrying relating to the Tent of Meeting – those numbered were 8,580. At
the command of the LORD they were listed, and by the authority of Moshe,
each according to his service and to what he was to carry; thus was each one
numbered as the LORD had commanded Moshe.
5 1 2 Then the LORD spoke to Moshe: "Command the Israelites to send away
from the camp anyone who has an impure blight,[8] or has had a discharge,[9] or
3 anyone made impure by contact with the dead. Male or female, you must send
them away – send them away outside the camp, so that they do not defile their
4 camps, in the midst of which I dwell." The Israelites did so: outside the camp
they sent them. As the LORD spoke to Moshe, so the Israelites did.
5 6 And the LORD spoke to Moshe: "Tell the Israelites: When one man or woman
commits any sin against another, breaking faith with the LORD and incurring
7 guilt, then he or she shall confess the sin committed and make restitution,
adding a fifth to its value, and giving it all to the one whom he has wronged.[10]
8 But if there is no relative to whom restitution can be made for the wrong,[11]
the restitution for that wrong shall go to the LORD, to the priest, in addition
9 to the ram of atonement by which atonement is made on his behalf. All gifts
10 the Israelites present to the priest as sacred offerings shall be his. Each priest's
sacred offerings will be his; whatever anyone gives him shall be his."
11 12 The LORD spoke to Moshe: "Speak to the Israelites and tell them: If any man's
13 wife goes astray and is unfaithful to him; if another man has sexual relations
with her, and this happens without the husband's knowledge because she
defiled herself in secret, there were no witness against her, and she was not
14 caught in the act – if a fit of jealousy overcomes him, making him jealous
over his wife who has defiled herself, or a fit of jealousy overcomes him,
15 making him jealous over his wife who has not defiled herself[12] – then the
man shall bring his wife to the priest together with the prescribed offering
for her, one-tenth of an ephah[13] of barley flour. He shall not pour oil on it or
place frankincense upon it, for it is a grain offering of jealousy, a grain offer-
16 ing of remembrance, calling attention to a wrong. The priest shall bring the
17 woman close and have her stand before the LORD. He shall then take sacred
water in an earthenware vessel, and pick up some earth from the floor of the
18 Tabernacle and place it in the water. He shall have the woman stand before
the LORD, and loosen the hair of the woman's head, placing on her palms the
grain offering of remembrance, the grain offering of jealousy. His hand shall
19 hold the bitter water that gives rise to a curse. And the priest shall administer

8 | See Leviticus, chapter 13.

9 | See Leviticus, chapter 15.

10 | Cf. Leviticus 5:20–26; one who takes a false oath denying theft or embezzlement must add a fifth when making restoration.

11 | According to the traditional understanding, this means that the victim is a since-deceased convert, who has no Israelite heirs.

12 | In other words, the husband does not know for sure whether his wife has "defiled herself."

13 | An ephah is a solid measure equivalent to approximately 25 liters.

מו וְאַהֲרֹן וּנְשִׂיאֵי יִשְׂרָאֵל אֶת־הַלְוִיִּם לְמִשְׁפְּחֹתָם וּלְבֵית אֲבֹתָם: מִבֶּן
שְׁלֹשִׁים שָׁנָה וָמַעְלָה וְעַד בֶּן־חֲמִשִּׁים שָׁנָה כָּל־הַבָּא לַעֲבֹד עֲבֹדַת
מח עֲבֹדָה וַעֲבֹדַת מַשָּׂא בְּאֹהֶל מוֹעֵד: וַיִּהְיוּ פְּקֻדֵיהֶם שְׁמֹנַת אֲלָפִים
מט וַחֲמֵשׁ מֵאוֹת וּשְׁמֹנִים: עַל־פִּי יְהוָה פָּקַד אוֹתָם בְּיַד־מֹשֶׁה אִישׁ אִישׁ
עַל־עֲבֹדָתוֹ וְעַל־מַשָּׂאוֹ וּפְקֻדָיו אֲשֶׁר־צִוָּה יְהוָה אֶת־מֹשֶׁה:

ה א ב וַיְדַבֵּר יְהוָה אֶל־מֹשֶׁה לֵּאמֹר: צַו אֶת־בְּנֵי יִשְׂרָאֵל וִישַׁלְּחוּ מִן־הַמַּחֲנֶה שלישי
ג כָּל־צָרוּעַ וְכָל־זָב וְכֹל טָמֵא לָנָפֶשׁ: מִזָּכָר עַד־נְקֵבָה תְּשַׁלֵּחוּ אֶל־
מִחוּץ לַמַּחֲנֶה תְּשַׁלְּחוּם וְלֹא יְטַמְּאוּ אֶת־מַחֲנֵיהֶם אֲשֶׁר אֲנִי שֹׁכֵן
ד בְּתוֹכָם: וַיַּעֲשׂוּ־כֵן בְּנֵי יִשְׂרָאֵל וַיְשַׁלְּחוּ אוֹתָם אֶל־מִחוּץ לַמַּחֲנֶה
כַּאֲשֶׁר דִּבֶּר יְהוָה אֶל־מֹשֶׁה כֵּן עָשׂוּ בְּנֵי יִשְׂרָאֵל:

ה ו וַיְדַבֵּר יְהוָה אֶל־מֹשֶׁה לֵּאמֹר: דַּבֵּר אֶל־בְּנֵי יִשְׂרָאֵל אִישׁ אוֹ־אִשָּׁה
כִּי יַעֲשׂוּ מִכָּל־חַטֹּאת הָאָדָם לִמְעֹל מַעַל בַּיהוָה וְאָשְׁמָה הַנֶּפֶשׁ
ז הַהִוא: וְהִתְוַדּוּ אֶת־חַטָּאתָם אֲשֶׁר עָשׂוּ וְהֵשִׁיב אֶת־אֲשָׁמוֹ בְּרֹאשׁוֹ
ח וַחֲמִישִׁתוֹ יֹסֵף עָלָיו וְנָתַן לַאֲשֶׁר אָשַׁם לוֹ: וְאִם־אֵין לָאִישׁ גֹּאֵל לְהָשִׁיב
הָאָשָׁם אֵלָיו הָאָשָׁם הַמּוּשָׁב לַיהוָה לַכֹּהֵן מִלְּבַד אֵיל הַכִּפֻּרִים אֲשֶׁר
ט יְכַפֶּר־בּוֹ עָלָיו: וְכָל־תְּרוּמָה לְכָל־קָדְשֵׁי בְנֵי־יִשְׂרָאֵל אֲשֶׁר־יַקְרִיבוּ
י לַכֹּהֵן לוֹ יִהְיֶה: וְאִישׁ אֶת־קֳדָשָׁיו לוֹ יִהְיוּ אִישׁ אֲשֶׁר־יִתֵּן לַכֹּהֵן לוֹ
יִהְיֶה:

יא יב וַיְדַבֵּר יְהוָה אֶל־מֹשֶׁה לֵּאמֹר: דַּבֵּר אֶל־בְּנֵי יִשְׂרָאֵל וְאָמַרְתָּ אֲלֵהֶם ה רביעי
יג אִישׁ אִישׁ כִּי־תִשְׂטֶה אִשְׁתּוֹ וּמָעֲלָה בוֹ מָעַל: וְשָׁכַב אִישׁ אֹתָהּ
שִׁכְבַת־זֶרַע וְנֶעְלַם מֵעֵינֵי אִישָׁהּ וְנִסְתְּרָה וְהִיא נִטְמָאָה וְעֵד אֵין
יד בָּהּ וְהִוא לֹא נִתְפָּשָׂה: וְעָבַר עָלָיו רוּחַ־קִנְאָה וְקִנֵּא אֶת־אִשְׁתּוֹ
וְהִוא נִטְמָאָה אוֹ־עָבַר עָלָיו רוּחַ־קִנְאָה וְקִנֵּא אֶת־אִשְׁתּוֹ וְהִיא לֹא
טו נִטְמָאָה: וְהֵבִיא הָאִישׁ אֶת־אִשְׁתּוֹ אֶל־הַכֹּהֵן וְהֵבִיא אֶת־קָרְבָּנָהּ
עָלֶיהָ עֲשִׂירִת הָאֵיפָה קֶמַח שְׂעֹרִים לֹא־יִצֹק עָלָיו שֶׁמֶן וְלֹא־יִתֵּן עָלָיו
טז לְבֹנָה כִּי־מִנְחַת קְנָאֹת הוּא מִנְחַת זִכָּרוֹן מַזְכֶּרֶת עָוֹן: וְהִקְרִיב אֹתָהּ
יז הַכֹּהֵן וְהֶעֱמִדָהּ לִפְנֵי יְהוָה: וְלָקַח הַכֹּהֵן מַיִם קְדֹשִׁים בִּכְלִי־חָרֶשׂ
וּמִן־הֶעָפָר אֲשֶׁר יִהְיֶה בְּקַרְקַע הַמִּשְׁכָּן יִקַּח הַכֹּהֵן וְנָתַן אֶל־הַמָּיִם:
יח וְהֶעֱמִיד הַכֹּהֵן אֶת־הָאִשָּׁה לִפְנֵי יְהוָה וּפָרַע אֶת־רֹאשׁ הָאִשָּׁה וְנָתַן
עַל־כַּפֶּיהָ אֵת מִנְחַת הַזִּכָּרוֹן מִנְחַת קְנָאֹת הִוא וּבְיַד הַכֹּהֵן יִהְיוּ מֵי
יט הַמָּרִים הַמְאָרְרִים: וְהִשְׁבִּיעַ אֹתָהּ הַכֹּהֵן וְאָמַר אֶל־הָאִשָּׁה אִם־לֹא

an oath to her, saying to the woman, 'If no man has had sexual relations with
you, and if you have not gone astray, letting yourself be defiled while married
to your husband, may your innocence be established by this bitter, cursing
20 water. But if you have gone astray while married to your husband, and if
you have let yourself be defiled and a man other than your husband has had
21 relations with you' – the priest shall here put the woman under the oath of the
curse, and say to her – 'the LORD make you a curse and an oath among your
22 people, when the LORD makes your thigh sag and your belly swell;[14] may this
curse-causing water enter your intestines and make your belly swell and your
23 thigh sag.' And the woman shall say, 'Amen, Amen.' Then the priest shall write
24 these curses on a scroll and wash them off into the bitter water. He shall make
the woman drink the bitter water that causes a curse, and the curse-causing
25 water will enter into her and turn bitter. The priest shall take the grain offering
of jealousy from the woman's hand, wave the grain offering before the LORD,
26 and bring it close to the altar. Then the priest shall take a handful of the grain
offering as a token, and burn it on the altar, after which he shall make the
27 woman drink the water. He having given her the water to drink, then, if she
has let herself be defiled and behaved unfaithfully toward her husband, the
curse-causing water will turn bitter, her belly will swell, her thigh will sag,
28 and the woman will become a curse among her people. But if the woman
has not let herself be defiled and is pure, then she shall be cleared and will
29 conceive children." This is the law for cases of jealousy, when a woman goes
30 astray with someone in place of her husband and becomes defiled, or when a
fit of jealousy overcomes a man and he grows jealous over his wife.[15] He shall
have the woman stand before the LORD, and the priest will deal with her as
31 all this law prescribes. No guilt will attach to the husband,[16] but the woman
in question will bear the punishment of her offense.
6 1 Then the LORD spoke to Moshe: "Speak to the Israelites. Say: When a man
2 or a woman takes a special vow, the vow of a nazirite,[17] to separate him or
3 herself to the LORD, he must separate himself from wine and strong drink.
He must drink neither vinegar made from wine nor vinegar made from any
other strong drink, nor may he drink any juice made with grapes, nor eat fresh
4 grapes or raisins. All the days of his separation he must not eat anything that
5 comes from the grapevine, from seed to skin. All the days of his separation
vow, no razor shall touch his head. Until the completion of the time for which
he separated himself to the LORD, he shall be holy, and must let the locks of his
6 hair grow long. All the days of his separation to the LORD, he must not come
7 near a dead body. Even for his father or mother or brother or sister, if they
die, he must not defile himself, for his vow of separation to his God is on his

---

14 | Opinions vary regarding the precise nature and implications of this physical reaction.

15 | That is, even though she in fact did not defile herself.

16 | According to rabbinic interpretation, the husband may initiate the process only if there is testimony that his wife, despite being warned, secluded herself with a particular man. The husband therefore does not bear responsibility for subjecting her to the procedure without cause.

17 | Literally "one who is separated." *Nezer* can also mean "crown"; see verse 7 below.

שָׁכַב אִישׁ אֹתָךְ וְאִם־לֹא שָׂטִית טֻמְאָה תַּחַת אִישֵׁךְ הִנָּקִי מִמֵּי
כ הַמָּרִים הַמְאָרְרִים הָאֵלֶּה: וְאַתְּ כִּי שָׂטִית תַּחַת אִישֵׁךְ וְכִי נִטְמֵאת
כא וַיִּתֵּן אִישׁ בָּךְ אֶת־שְׁכָבְתּוֹ מִבַּלְעֲדֵי אִישֵׁךְ: וְהִשְׁבִּיעַ הַכֹּהֵן אֶת־
הָאִשָּׁה בִּשְׁבֻעַת הָאָלָה וְאָמַר הַכֹּהֵן לָאִשָּׁה יִתֵּן יהוה אוֹתָךְ לְאָלָה
וְלִשְׁבֻעָה בְּתוֹךְ עַמֵּךְ בְּתֵת יהוה אֶת־יְרֵכֵךְ נֹפֶלֶת וְאֶת־בִּטְנֵךְ צָבָה:
כב וּבָאוּ הַמַּיִם הַמְאָרְרִים הָאֵלֶּה בְּמֵעַיִךְ לַצְבּוֹת בֶּטֶן וְלַנְפִּל יָרֵךְ וְאָמְרָה
כג הָאִשָּׁה אָמֵן ׀ אָמֵן: וְכָתַב אֶת־הָאָלֹת הָאֵלֶּה הַכֹּהֵן בַּסֵּפֶר וּמָחָה
כד אֶל־מֵי הַמָּרִים: וְהִשְׁקָה אֶת־הָאִשָּׁה אֶת־מֵי הַמָּרִים הַמְאָרְרִים וּבָאוּ
כה בָהּ הַמַּיִם הַמְאָרְרִים לְמָרִים: וְלָקַח הַכֹּהֵן מִיַּד הָאִשָּׁה אֵת מִנְחַת
הַקְּנָאֹת וְהֵנִיף אֶת־הַמִּנְחָה לִפְנֵי יהוה וְהִקְרִיב אֹתָהּ אֶל־הַמִּזְבֵּחַ:
כו וְקָמַץ הַכֹּהֵן מִן־הַמִּנְחָה אֶת־אַזְכָּרָתָהּ וְהִקְטִיר הַמִּזְבֵּחָה וְאַחַר
כז יַשְׁקֶה אֶת־הָאִשָּׁה אֶת־הַמָּיִם: וְהִשְׁקָהּ אֶת־הַמַּיִם וְהָיְתָה אִם־
נִטְמְאָה וַתִּמְעֹל מַעַל בְּאִישָׁהּ וּבָאוּ בָהּ הַמַּיִם הַמְאָרְרִים לְמָרִים
כח וְצָבְתָה בִטְנָהּ וְנָפְלָה יְרֵכָהּ וְהָיְתָה הָאִשָּׁה לְאָלָה בְּקֶרֶב עַמָּהּ: וְאִם־
כט לֹא נִטְמְאָה הָאִשָּׁה וּטְהֹרָה הִוא וְנִקְּתָה וְנִזְרְעָה זָרַע: זֹאת תּוֹרַת
ל הַקְּנָאֹת אֲשֶׁר תִּשְׂטֶה אִשָּׁה תַּחַת אִישָׁהּ וְנִטְמָאָה: אוֹ אִישׁ אֲשֶׁר
תַּעֲבֹר עָלָיו רוּחַ קִנְאָה וְקִנֵּא אֶת־אִשְׁתּוֹ וְהֶעֱמִיד אֶת־הָאִשָּׁה לִפְנֵי
לא יהוה וְעָשָׂה לָהּ הַכֹּהֵן אֵת כָּל־הַתּוֹרָה הַזֹּאת: וְנִקָּה הָאִישׁ מֵעָוֺן
וְהָאִשָּׁה הַהִוא תִּשָּׂא אֶת־עֲוֺנָהּ:
ו א ב וַיְדַבֵּר יהוה אֶל־מֹשֶׁה לֵּאמֹר: דַּבֵּר אֶל־בְּנֵי יִשְׂרָאֵל וְאָמַרְתָּ אֲלֵהֶם
ג אִישׁ אוֹ־אִשָּׁה כִּי יַפְלִא לִנְדֹּר נֶדֶר נָזִיר לְהַזִּיר לַיהוה: מִיַּיִן וְשֵׁכָר
יַזִּיר חֹמֶץ יַיִן וְחֹמֶץ שֵׁכָר לֹא יִשְׁתֶּה וְכָל־מִשְׁרַת עֲנָבִים לֹא יִשְׁתֶּה
ד וַעֲנָבִים לַחִים וִיבֵשִׁים לֹא יֹאכֵל: כֹּל יְמֵי נִזְרוֹ מִכֹּל אֲשֶׁר יֵעָשֶׂה מִגֶּפֶן
ה הַיַּיִן מֵחַרְצַנִּים וְעַד־זָג לֹא יֹאכֵל: כָּל־יְמֵי נֶדֶר נִזְרוֹ תַּעַר לֹא־יַעֲבֹר
עַל־רֹאשׁוֹ עַד־מְלֹאת הַיָּמִם אֲשֶׁר־יַזִּיר לַיהוה קָדֹשׁ יִהְיֶה גַּדֵּל פֶּרַע
ו ז שְׂעַר רֹאשׁוֹ: כָּל־יְמֵי הַזִּירוֹ לַיהוה עַל־נֶפֶשׁ מֵת לֹא יָבֹא: לְאָבִיו וּלְאִמּוֹ
לְאָחִיו וּלְאַחֹתוֹ לֹא־יִטַּמָּא לָהֶם בְּמֹתָם כִּי נֵזֶר אֱלֹהָיו עַל־רֹאשׁוֹ:

8 9 head.[18] All the days of his separation he is holy to the Lord. If someone dies
suddenly beside him, defiling his consecrated head, he shall shave his head
10 on the day of his purification; on the seventh day he shall shave it. Then, on
the eighth day, he shall bring two turtledoves or two young pigeons to the
11 priest, to the entrance of the Tent of Meeting. The priest will offer one as a
purification offering and the other as a burnt offering, and make atonement
for him for the guilt he incurred through contact with the dead body. He
12 shall consecrate his head anew on that day. He must rededicate himself to the
Lord for the full term of his vow, and bring a yearling lamb as a guilt offering.
13 The former days are discounted because his separation was defiled. This is the
law of the nazirite: On the day that the term of his nazirite vow is completed,
14 he shall be brought to the entrance to the Tent of Meeting. He shall present
his offering to the Lord: one male yearling lamb without blemish for a burnt
offering, one yearling ewe lamb without blemish for a purification offering,
15 one ram without blemish for a peace offering, and a basket of unleavened
bread, loaves of fine flour mixed with olive oil, and unleavened wafers smeared
16 with olive oil, along with their grain offering and libations. The priest shall
present these before the Lord and offer up his purification offering and his
17 burnt offering. He shall then offer the ram as a sacrifice, a peace offering to the
Lord, together with the basket of unleavened bread. The priest shall also offer
18 his grain offering and his libation. The nazirite shall shave his consecrated hair
at the entrance to the Tent of Meeting and take the hair of his consecrated
19 head and place it on the fire beneath the peace offering. The priest shall take
the boiled foreleg of the ram, one unleavened loaf from the basket, and one
unleavened wafer, and place them on the hands of the nazirite after he has
20 shaved his consecrated head. The priest shall wave them as a wave offering
before the Lord. It is a sacred gift for the priest, together with the breast of the
wave offering and the thigh of the upraised gift.[19] After this the nazirite may
21 drink wine." This is the law of the nazirite who vows offerings to the Lord as
a nazirite. Whatever he can afford further and vows to give, beyond what the
law of the nazirite obliges him to, that too shall he fulfill.
22 23 The Lord spoke to Moshe: "Tell Aharon and his sons: This is how you are
24 to bless the Israelites. Say to them: 'May the Lord bless you and
25 watch over you. May the Lord make His face shine upon you and
26 be gracious to you. May the Lord raise His face toward you and
27 grant you peace.' They shall set My name upon the Israelites,[20] and
7 1 I will bless them." On the day when Moshe finished establishing the
Tabernacle, he anointed it and consecrated it. He anointed and consecrated
2 the altar, too, and all its utensils. And the princes of Israel, leaders of their
ancestral houses, drew close. They were the princes of the tribes, the ones
3 who had directed the census. And they brought their offerings before the

---

18 | The phrase can simultaneously be understood to mean: "the crown (*nezer*) of his God is on his head."

19 | See Leviticus 7:28–34.

20 | By invoking God's name during the blessing.

ח ט כֹּל יְמֵי נִזְרוֹ קָדֹשׁ הוּא לַיהוה: וְכִי־יָמוּת מֵת עָלָיו בְּפֶתַע פִּתְאֹם
וְטִמֵּא רֹאשׁ נִזְרוֹ וְגִלַּח רֹאשׁוֹ בְּיוֹם טָהֳרָתוֹ בַּיּוֹם הַשְּׁבִיעִי יְגַלְּחֶנּוּ:
י וּבַיּוֹם הַשְּׁמִינִי יָבִא שְׁתֵּי תֹרִים אוֹ שְׁנֵי בְּנֵי יוֹנָה אֶל־הַכֹּהֵן אֶל־פֶּתַח
יא אֹהֶל מוֹעֵד: וְעָשָׂה הַכֹּהֵן אֶחָד לְחַטָּאת וְאֶחָד לְעֹלָה וְכִפֶּר עָלָיו
יב מֵאֲשֶׁר חָטָא עַל־הַנָּפֶשׁ וְקִדַּשׁ אֶת־רֹאשׁוֹ בַּיּוֹם הַהוּא: וְהִזִּיר לַיהוה
אֶת־יְמֵי נִזְרוֹ וְהֵבִיא כֶּבֶשׂ בֶּן־שְׁנָתוֹ לְאָשָׁם וְהַיָּמִים הָרִאשֹׁנִים יִפְּלוּ
יג כִּי טָמֵא נִזְרוֹ: וְזֹאת תּוֹרַת הַנָּזִיר בְּיוֹם מְלֹאת יְמֵי נִזְרוֹ יָבִיא אֹתוֹ אֶל־
יד פֶּתַח אֹהֶל מוֹעֵד: וְהִקְרִיב אֶת־קָרְבָּנוֹ לַיהוה כֶּבֶשׂ בֶּן־שְׁנָתוֹ תָמִים
אֶחָד לְעֹלָה וְכַבְשָׂה אַחַת בַּת־שְׁנָתָהּ תְּמִימָה לְחַטָּאת וְאַיִל־אֶחָד
טו תָּמִים לִשְׁלָמִים: וְסַל מַצּוֹת סֹלֶת חַלֹּת בְּלוּלֹת בַּשֶּׁמֶן וּרְקִיקֵי מַצּוֹת
טז מְשֻׁחִים בַּשָּׁמֶן וּמִנְחָתָם וְנִסְכֵּיהֶם: וְהִקְרִיב הַכֹּהֵן לִפְנֵי יהוה וְעָשָׂה
יז אֶת־חַטָּאתוֹ וְאֶת־עֹלָתוֹ: וְאֶת־הָאַיִל יַעֲשֶׂה זֶבַח שְׁלָמִים לַיהוה עַל
יח סַל הַמַּצּוֹת וְעָשָׂה הַכֹּהֵן אֶת־מִנְחָתוֹ וְאֶת־נִסְכּוֹ: וְגִלַּח הַנָּזִיר פֶּתַח
אֹהֶל מוֹעֵד אֶת־רֹאשׁ נִזְרוֹ וְלָקַח אֶת־שְׂעַר רֹאשׁ נִזְרוֹ וְנָתַן עַל־הָאֵשׁ
יט אֲשֶׁר־תַּחַת זֶבַח הַשְּׁלָמִים: וְלָקַח הַכֹּהֵן אֶת־הַזְּרֹעַ בְּשֵׁלָה מִן־הָאַיִל
וְחַלַּת מַצָּה אַחַת מִן־הַסַּל וּרְקִיק מַצָּה אֶחָד וְנָתַן עַל־כַּפֵּי הַנָּזִיר אַחַר
כ הִתְגַּלְּחוֹ אֶת־נִזְרוֹ: וְהֵנִיף אוֹתָם הַכֹּהֵן ׀ תְּנוּפָה לִפְנֵי יהוה קֹדֶשׁ הוּא
לַכֹּהֵן עַל חֲזֵה הַתְּנוּפָה וְעַל שׁוֹק הַתְּרוּמָה וְאַחַר יִשְׁתֶּה הַנָּזִיר יָיִן:
כא זֹאת תּוֹרַת הַנָּזִיר אֲשֶׁר יִדֹּר קָרְבָּנוֹ לַיהוה עַל־נִזְרוֹ מִלְּבַד אֲשֶׁר־תַּשִּׂיג
יָדוֹ כְּפִי נִדְרוֹ אֲשֶׁר יִדֹּר כֵּן יַעֲשֶׂה עַל תּוֹרַת נִזְרוֹ:
כב כג ו וַיְדַבֵּר יהוה אֶל־מֹשֶׁה לֵּאמֹר: דַּבֵּר אֶל־אַהֲרֹן וְאֶל־בָּנָיו לֵאמֹר
כד כֹּה תְבָרְכוּ אֶת־בְּנֵי יִשְׂרָאֵל אָמוֹר לָהֶם: יְבָרֶכְךָ יהוה
כה כו וְיִשְׁמְרֶךָ: יָאֵר יהוה ׀ פָּנָיו אֵלֶיךָ וִיחֻנֶּךָּ: יִשָּׂא
כז יהוה ׀ פָּנָיו אֵלֶיךָ וְיָשֵׂם לְךָ שָׁלוֹם: וְשָׂמוּ אֶת־שְׁמִי עַל־
ז א בְּנֵי יִשְׂרָאֵל וַאֲנִי אֲבָרְכֵם: וַיְהִי בְּיוֹם כַּלּוֹת מֹשֶׁה לְהָקִים חמישי
אֶת־הַמִּשְׁכָּן וַיִּמְשַׁח אֹתוֹ וַיְקַדֵּשׁ אֹתוֹ וְאֶת־כָּל־כֵּלָיו וְאֶת־הַמִּזְבֵּחַ
ב וְאֶת־כָּל־כֵּלָיו וַיִּמְשָׁחֵם וַיְקַדֵּשׁ אֹתָם: וַיַּקְרִיבוּ נְשִׂיאֵי יִשְׂרָאֵל רָאשֵׁי
ג בֵּית אֲבֹתָם הֵם נְשִׂיאֵי הַמַּטֹּת הֵם הָעֹמְדִים עַל־הַפְּקֻדִים: וַיָּבִיאוּ
אֶת־קָרְבָּנָם לִפְנֵי יהוה שֵׁשׁ־עֶגְלֹת צָב וּשְׁנֵי־עָשָׂר בָּקָר עֲגָלָה עַל־

Lord: six covered wagons and twelve oxen – a wagon for every two leaders,
4 and for each one an ox. They presented them before the Tabernacle. The
5 Lord said to Moshe, "Accept these from them and use them for service in the
Tent of Meeting. Give them to the Levites, to each according to his service."
6 7 Moshe took the wagons and the oxen, and he gave them to the Levites. He
gave two wagons and four oxen to the Gershonites as their service required.
8 He gave four wagons and eight oxen to the Merarites for their service under
9 the supervision of Itamar son of Aharon the priest. But to the Kohatites he
gave none, for their responsibility was for the sacred articles that had to be
10 carried on their shoulders. The princes presented their dedication offering
for the altar at the time when it was anointed. The princes brought their
11 offerings before the altar. The Lord said to Moshe, "Each day one prince is to
12 bring close his offering for the dedication of the altar." The one who
presented his offering on the first day was Naḥshon son of Aminadav, from
13 the tribe of Yehuda. His offering was one silver bowl weighing one hundred
and thirty shekel and one silver basin weighing seventy shekel according to
the Sanctuary weight, both filled with fine flour mixed with oil for a grain
14 15 offering; one golden spoon weighing ten shekel, full of incense; one young
16 bull, one ram, and one yearling sheep for a burnt offering; one goat for a
17 purification offering; and for the peace sacrifice two oxen, five rams, five
male goats, and five yearling sheep. This was the offering of Naḥshon son of
Aminadav.
18 On the second day Netanel son of Tzuar, prince of Yissakhar, presented his
19 offering. He presented as his offering one silver bowl weighing one hundred
and thirty shekel and one silver basin weighing seventy shekel according to
the Sanctuary weight, both filled with fine flour mixed with oil for a grain
20 21 offering; one golden spoon weighing ten shekel, full of incense; one young
22 bull, one ram, and one yearling sheep for a burnt offering; one goat for a
23 purification offering; and for the peace sacrifice two oxen, five rams, five
male goats, and five yearling sheep. This was the offering of Netanel son of
Tzuar.
24 25 On the third day came Eliav son of Ḥelon, prince of the Zebulunites: His
offering was one silver bowl weighing one hundred and thirty shekel and one
silver basin weighing seventy shekel according to the Sanctuary weight, both
26 filled with fine flour mixed with oil for a grain offering; one golden spoon
27 weighing ten shekel, full of incense; one young bull, one ram, and one yearling
28 29 sheep for a burnt offering; one goat for a purification offering; and for the
peace sacrifice two oxen, five rams, five male goats, and five yearling sheep.
This was the offering of Eliav son of Ḥelon.

ד שְׁנֵי הַנְּשִׂאִים וְשׁוֹר לְאֶחָד וַיַּקְרִיבוּ אוֹתָם לִפְנֵי הַמִּשְׁכָּן: וַיֹּאמֶר
ה יְהוָה אֶל־מֹשֶׁה לֵּאמֹר: קַח מֵאִתָּם וְהָיוּ לַעֲבֹד אֶת־עֲבֹדַת אֹהֶל
ו מוֹעֵד וְנָתַתָּה אוֹתָם אֶל־הַלְוִיִּם אִישׁ כְּפִי עֲבֹדָתוֹ: וַיִּקַּח מֹשֶׁה אֶת־
ז הָעֲגָלֹת וְאֶת־הַבָּקָר וַיִּתֵּן אוֹתָם אֶל־הַלְוִיִּם: אֵת ׀ שְׁתֵּי הָעֲגָלוֹת
ח וְאֵת אַרְבַּעַת הַבָּקָר נָתַן לִבְנֵי גֵרְשׁוֹן כְּפִי עֲבֹדָתָם: וְאֵת ׀ אַרְבַּע
הָעֲגָלֹת וְאֵת שְׁמֹנַת הַבָּקָר נָתַן לִבְנֵי מְרָרִי כְּפִי עֲבֹדָתָם בְּיַד אִיתָמָר
ט בֶּן־אַהֲרֹן הַכֹּהֵן: וְלִבְנֵי קְהָת לֹא נָתָן כִּי־עֲבֹדַת הַקֹּדֶשׁ עֲלֵהֶם
י בַּכָּתֵף יִשָּׂאוּ: וַיַּקְרִיבוּ הַנְּשִׂאִים אֵת חֲנֻכַּת הַמִּזְבֵּחַ בְּיוֹם הִמָּשַׁח
יא אֹתוֹ וַיַּקְרִיבוּ הַנְּשִׂיאִם אֶת־קָרְבָּנָם לִפְנֵי הַמִּזְבֵּחַ: וַיֹּאמֶר יְהוָה אֶל־
מֹשֶׁה נָשִׂיא אֶחָד לַיּוֹם נָשִׂיא אֶחָד לַיּוֹם יַקְרִיבוּ אֶת־קָרְבָּנָם לַחֲנֻכַּת
יב הַמִּזְבֵּחַ: וַיְהִי הַמַּקְרִיב בַּיּוֹם הָרִאשׁוֹן אֶת־קָרְבָּנוֹ נַחְשׁוֹן
יג בֶּן־עַמִּינָדָב לְמַטֵּה יְהוּדָה: וְקָרְבָּנוֹ קַעֲרַת־כֶּסֶף אַחַת שְׁלֹשִׁים וּמֵאָה
מִשְׁקָלָהּ מִזְרָק אֶחָד כֶּסֶף שִׁבְעִים שֶׁקֶל בְּשֶׁקֶל הַקֹּדֶשׁ שְׁנֵיהֶם ׀
יד מְלֵאִים סֹלֶת בְּלוּלָה בַשֶּׁמֶן לְמִנְחָה: כַּף אַחַת עֲשָׂרָה זָהָב מְלֵאָה
טו קְטֹרֶת: פַּר אֶחָד בֶּן־בָּקָר אַיִל אֶחָד כֶּבֶשׂ־אֶחָד בֶּן־שְׁנָתוֹ לְעֹלָה:
טז יז שְׂעִיר־עִזִּים אֶחָד לְחַטָּאת: וּלְזֶבַח הַשְּׁלָמִים בָּקָר שְׁנַיִם אֵילִם
חֲמִשָּׁה עַתּוּדִים חֲמִשָּׁה כְּבָשִׂים בְּנֵי־שָׁנָה חֲמִשָּׁה זֶה קָרְבַּן נַחְשׁוֹן בֶּן־
עַמִּינָדָב:
יח יט בַּיּוֹם הַשֵּׁנִי הִקְרִיב נְתַנְאֵל בֶּן־צוּעָר נְשִׂיא יִשָּׂשכָר: הִקְרִב אֶת־קָרְבָּנוֹ
קַעֲרַת־כֶּסֶף אַחַת שְׁלֹשִׁים וּמֵאָה מִשְׁקָלָהּ מִזְרָק אֶחָד כֶּסֶף שִׁבְעִים
שֶׁקֶל בְּשֶׁקֶל הַקֹּדֶשׁ שְׁנֵיהֶם ׀ מְלֵאִים סֹלֶת בְּלוּלָה בַשֶּׁמֶן לְמִנְחָה:
כ כא כַּף אַחַת עֲשָׂרָה זָהָב מְלֵאָה קְטֹרֶת: פַּר אֶחָד בֶּן־בָּקָר אַיִל אֶחָד
כב כג כֶּבֶשׂ־אֶחָד בֶּן־שְׁנָתוֹ לְעֹלָה: שְׂעִיר־עִזִּים אֶחָד לְחַטָּאת: וּלְזֶבַח
הַשְּׁלָמִים בָּקָר שְׁנַיִם אֵילִם חֲמִשָּׁה עַתֻּדִים חֲמִשָּׁה כְּבָשִׂים בְּנֵי־שָׁנָה
חֲמִשָּׁה זֶה קָרְבַּן נְתַנְאֵל בֶּן־צוּעָר:
כד כה בַּיּוֹם הַשְּׁלִישִׁי נָשִׂיא לִבְנֵי זְבוּלֻן אֱלִיאָב בֶּן־חֵלֹן: קָרְבָּנוֹ קַעֲרַת־
כֶּסֶף אַחַת שְׁלֹשִׁים וּמֵאָה מִשְׁקָלָהּ מִזְרָק אֶחָד כֶּסֶף שִׁבְעִים שֶׁקֶל
כו בְּשֶׁקֶל הַקֹּדֶשׁ שְׁנֵיהֶם ׀ מְלֵאִים סֹלֶת בְּלוּלָה בַשֶּׁמֶן לְמִנְחָה: כַּף אַחַת
כז עֲשָׂרָה זָהָב מְלֵאָה קְטֹרֶת: פַּר אֶחָד בֶּן־בָּקָר אַיִל אֶחָד כֶּבֶשׂ־אֶחָד
כח כט בֶּן־שְׁנָתוֹ לְעֹלָה: שְׂעִיר־עִזִּים אֶחָד לְחַטָּאת: וּלְזֶבַח הַשְּׁלָמִים בָּקָר
שְׁנַיִם אֵילִם חֲמִשָּׁה עַתֻּדִים חֲמִשָּׁה כְּבָשִׂים בְּנֵי־שָׁנָה חֲמִשָּׁה זֶה קָרְבַּן
אֱלִיאָב בֶּן־חֵלֹן:

30 On the fourth day came Elitzur son of Shedeiur, prince of the Reubenites:
31 His offering was one silver bowl weighing one hundred and thirty shekel and
one silver basin weighing seventy shekel according to the Sanctuary weight,
32 both filled with fine flour mixed with oil for a grain offering; one golden
33 spoon weighing ten shekel, full of incense; one young bull, one ram, and one
34 35 yearling sheep for a burnt offering; one goat for a purification offering; and
for the peace sacrifice two oxen, five rams, five male goats, and five yearling
sheep. This was the offering of Elitzur son of Shedeiur.
36 On the fifth day came Shelumiel son of Tzurishadai, prince of the Simeonites:
37 His offering was one silver bowl weighing one hundred and thirty shekel and
one silver basin weighing seventy shekel according to the Sanctuary weight,
38 both filled with fine flour mixed with oil for a grain offering; one golden
39 spoon weighing ten shekel, full of incense; one young bull, one ram, and one
40 41 yearling sheep for a burnt offering; one goat for a purification offering; and
for the peace sacrifice two oxen, five rams, five male goats, and five yearling
sheep. This was the offering of Shelumiel son of Tzurishadai.
42 43 On the sixth day came Elyasaf son of Deuel, prince of the Gadites: His
offering was one silver bowl weighing one hundred and thirty shekel and
one silver basin weighing seventy shekel according to the Sanctuary weight,
44 both filled with fine flour mixed with oil for a grain offering; one golden
45 spoon weighing ten shekel, full of incense; one young bull, one ram, and one
46 47 yearling sheep for a burnt offering; one goat for a purification offering; and
for the peace sacrifice two oxen, five rams, five male goats, and five yearling
sheep. This was the offering of Elyasaf son of Deuel.
48 On the seventh day came Elishama son of Amihud, prince of the Efraimites:
49 His offering was one silver bowl weighing one hundred and thirty shekel and
one silver basin weighing seventy shekel according to the Sanctuary weight,
50 both filled with fine flour mixed with oil for a grain offering; one golden
51 spoon weighing ten shekel, full of incense; one young bull, one ram, and one
52 53 yearling sheep for a burnt offering; one goat for a purification offering; and
for the peace sacrifice two oxen, five rams, five male goats, and five yearling
sheep. This was the offering of Elishama son of Amihud.
54 On the eighth day came Gamliel son of Pedahtzur, prince of the Manassites:
55 His offering was one silver bowl weighing one hundred and thirty shekel and
one silver basin weighing seventy shekel according to the Sanctuary weight,
56 both filled with fine flour mixed with oil for a grain offering; one golden
57 spoon weighing ten shekel, full of incense; one young bull, one ram, and one

ל לא בְּיוֹם֙ הָֽרְבִיעִ֔י נָשִׂ֖יא לִבְנֵ֣י רְאוּבֵ֑ן אֱלִיצ֖וּר בֶּן־שְׁדֵיאֽוּר׃ קָרְבָּנ֞וֹ קַעֲרַת־
כֶּ֣סֶף אַחַ֗ת שְׁלֹשִׁ֣ים וּמֵאָה֮ מִשְׁקָלָהּ֒ מִזְרָ֣ק אֶחָ֔ד כֶּ֕סֶף שִׁבְעִ֥ים שֶׁ֖קֶל
לב בְּשֶׁ֣קֶל הַקֹּ֑דֶשׁ שְׁנֵיהֶ֣ם ׀ מְלֵאִ֗ים סֹ֛לֶת בְּלוּלָ֥ה בַשֶּׁ֖מֶן לְמִנְחָֽה׃ כַּ֥ף אַחַ֛ת
לג עֲשָׂרָ֥ה זָהָ֖ב מְלֵאָ֥ה קְטֹֽרֶת׃ פַּ֣ר אֶחָ֞ד בֶּן־בָּקָ֗ר אַ֧יִל אֶחָ֛ד כֶּֽבֶשׂ־אֶחָ֥ד
לד לה בֶּן־שְׁנָת֖וֹ לְעֹלָֽה׃ שְׂעִיר־עִזִּ֥ים אֶחָ֖ד לְחַטָּֽאת׃ וּלְזֶ֣בַח הַשְּׁלָמִים֮ בָּקָ֣ר
שְׁנַ֒יִם֒ אֵילִ֤ם חֲמִשָּׁה֙ עַתֻּדִ֣ים חֲמִשָּׁ֔ה כְּבָשִׂ֥ים בְּנֵי־שָׁנָ֖ה חֲמִשָּׁ֑ה זֶ֛ה קָרְבַּ֥ן
אֱלִיצ֖וּר בֶּן־שְׁדֵיאֽוּר׃
לו לז בַּיּוֹם֙ הַחֲמִישִׁ֔י נָשִׂ֖יא לִבְנֵ֣י שִׁמְע֑וֹן שְׁלֻמִיאֵ֖ל בֶּן־צוּרִֽישַׁדָּֽי׃ קָרְבָּנ֞וֹ
קַעֲרַת־כֶּ֣סֶף אַחַ֗ת שְׁלֹשִׁ֣ים וּמֵאָה֮ מִשְׁקָלָהּ֒ מִזְרָ֣ק אֶחָ֔ד כֶּ֕סֶף שִׁבְעִ֥ים
שֶׁ֖קֶל בְּשֶׁ֣קֶל הַקֹּ֑דֶשׁ שְׁנֵיהֶ֣ם ׀ מְלֵאִ֗ים סֹ֛לֶת בְּלוּלָ֥ה בַשֶּׁ֖מֶן לְמִנְחָֽה׃
לח לט כַּ֥ף אַחַ֛ת עֲשָׂרָ֥ה זָהָ֖ב מְלֵאָ֥ה קְטֹֽרֶת׃ פַּ֣ר אֶחָ֞ד בֶּן־בָּקָ֗ר אַ֧יִל אֶחָ֛ד
מ מא כֶּֽבֶשׂ־אֶחָ֥ד בֶּן־שְׁנָת֖וֹ לְעֹלָֽה׃ שְׂעִיר־עִזִּ֥ים אֶחָ֖ד לְחַטָּֽאת׃ וּלְזֶ֣בַח
הַשְּׁלָמִים֮ בָּקָ֣ר שְׁנַ֒יִם֒ אֵילִ֤ם חֲמִשָּׁה֙ עַתֻּדִ֣ים חֲמִשָּׁ֔ה כְּבָשִׂ֥ים בְּנֵי־שָׁנָ֖ה
חֲמִשָּׁ֑ה זֶ֛ה קָרְבַּ֥ן שְׁלֻמִיאֵ֖ל בֶּן־צוּרִֽישַׁדָּֽי׃
מב מג בַּיּוֹם֙ הַשִּׁשִּׁ֔י נָשִׂ֖יא לִבְנֵ֣י גָ֑ד אֶלְיָסָ֖ף בֶּן־דְּעוּאֵֽל׃ קָרְבָּנ֞וֹ קַֽעֲרַת־כֶּ֣סֶף ששי
אַחַ֗ת שְׁלֹשִׁ֣ים וּמֵאָה֮ מִשְׁקָלָהּ֒ מִזְרָ֣ק אֶחָ֔ד כֶּ֕סֶף שִׁבְעִ֥ים שֶׁ֖קֶל בְּשֶׁ֣קֶל
מד הַקֹּ֑דֶשׁ שְׁנֵיהֶ֣ם ׀ מְלֵאִ֗ים סֹ֛לֶת בְּלוּלָ֥ה בַשֶּׁ֖מֶן לְמִנְחָֽה׃ כַּ֥ף אַחַ֛ת עֲשָׂרָ֥ה
מה זָהָ֖ב מְלֵאָ֥ה קְטֹֽרֶת׃ פַּ֣ר אֶחָ֞ד בֶּן־בָּקָ֗ר אַ֧יִל אֶחָ֛ד כֶּֽבֶשׂ־אֶחָ֥ד בֶּן־שְׁנָת֖וֹ
מו מז לְעֹלָֽה׃ שְׂעִיר־עִזִּ֥ים אֶחָ֖ד לְחַטָּֽאת׃ וּלְזֶ֣בַח הַשְּׁלָמִים֮ בָּקָ֣ר שְׁנַ֒יִם֒
אֵילִ֤ם חֲמִשָּׁה֙ עַתֻּדִ֣ים חֲמִשָּׁ֔ה כְּבָשִׂ֥ים בְּנֵי־שָׁנָ֖ה חֲמִשָּׁ֑ה זֶ֛ה קָרְבַּ֥ן
אֶלְיָסָ֖ף בֶּן־דְּעוּאֵֽל׃
מח מט בַּיּוֹם֙ הַשְּׁבִיעִ֔י נָשִׂ֖יא לִבְנֵ֣י אֶפְרָ֑יִם אֱלִישָׁמָ֖ע בֶּן־עַמִּיהֽוּד׃ קָרְבָּנ֞וֹ ז
קַעֲרַת־כֶּ֣סֶף אַחַ֗ת שְׁלֹשִׁ֣ים וּמֵאָה֮ מִשְׁקָלָהּ֒ מִזְרָ֣ק אֶחָ֔ד כֶּ֕סֶף שִׁבְעִ֥ים
שֶׁ֖קֶל בְּשֶׁ֣קֶל הַקֹּ֑דֶשׁ שְׁנֵיהֶ֣ם ׀ מְלֵאִ֗ים סֹ֛לֶת בְּלוּלָ֥ה בַשֶּׁ֖מֶן לְמִנְחָֽה׃
נ נא כַּ֥ף אַחַ֛ת עֲשָׂרָ֥ה זָהָ֖ב מְלֵאָ֥ה קְטֹֽרֶת׃ פַּ֣ר אֶחָ֞ד בֶּן־בָּקָ֗ר אַ֧יִל אֶחָ֛ד
נב נג כֶּֽבֶשׂ־אֶחָ֥ד בֶּן־שְׁנָת֖וֹ לְעֹלָֽה׃ שְׂעִיר־עִזִּ֥ים אֶחָ֖ד לְחַטָּֽאת׃ וּלְזֶ֣בַח
הַשְּׁלָמִים֮ בָּקָ֣ר שְׁנַ֒יִם֒ אֵילִ֤ם חֲמִשָּׁה֙ עַתֻּדִ֣ים חֲמִשָּׁ֔ה כְּבָשִׂ֥ים בְּנֵי־שָׁנָ֖ה
חֲמִשָּׁ֑ה זֶ֛ה קָרְבַּ֥ן אֱלִישָׁמָ֖ע בֶּן־עַמִּיהֽוּד׃
נד נה בַּיּוֹם֙ הַשְּׁמִינִ֔י נָשִׂ֖יא לִבְנֵ֣י מְנַשֶּׁ֑ה גַּמְלִיאֵ֖ל בֶּן־פְּדָהצֽוּר׃ קָרְבָּנ֞וֹ קַעֲרַת־
כֶּ֣סֶף אַחַ֗ת שְׁלֹשִׁ֣ים וּמֵאָה֮ מִשְׁקָלָהּ֒ מִזְרָ֣ק אֶחָ֔ד כֶּ֕סֶף שִׁבְעִ֥ים שֶׁ֖קֶל
נו בְּשֶׁ֣קֶל הַקֹּ֑דֶשׁ שְׁנֵיהֶ֣ם ׀ מְלֵאִ֗ים סֹ֛לֶת בְּלוּלָ֥ה בַשֶּׁ֖מֶן לְמִנְחָֽה׃ כַּ֥ף אַחַ֛ת
נז עֲשָׂרָ֥ה זָהָ֖ב מְלֵאָ֥ה קְטֹֽרֶת׃ פַּ֣ר אֶחָ֞ד בֶּן־בָּקָ֗ר אַ֧יִל אֶחָ֛ד כֶּֽבֶשׂ־אֶחָ֥ד

58 59 yearling sheep for a burnt offering; one goat for a purification offering; and
for the peace sacrifice two oxen, five rams, five male goats, and five yearling
sheep. This was the offering of Gamliel son of Pedahtzur.
60 61 On the ninth day came Avidan son of Gidoni, prince of the Benjaminites: His
offering was one silver bowl weighing one hundred and thirty shekel and one
silver basin weighing seventy shekel according to the Sanctuary weight, both
62 filled with fine flour mixed with oil for a grain offering; one golden spoon
63 weighing ten shekel, full of incense; one young bull, one ram, and one yearling
64 65 sheep for a burnt offering; one goat for a purification offering; and for the
peace sacrifice two oxen, five rams, five male goats, and five yearling sheep.
This was the offering of Avidan son of Gidoni.
66 67 On the tenth day came Aḥiezer son of Amishadai, prince of the Danites: His
offering was one silver bowl weighing one hundred and thirty shekel and
one silver basin weighing seventy shekel according to the Sanctuary weight,
68 both filled with fine flour mixed with oil for a grain offering; one golden
69 spoon weighing ten shekel, full of incense; one young bull, one ram, and one
70 71 yearling sheep for a burnt offering; one goat for a purification offering; and
for the peace sacrifice two oxen, five rams, five male goats, and five yearling
sheep. This was the offering of Aḥiezer son of Amishadai.
72 73 On the eleventh day came Pagiel son of Okhran, prince of the Asherites: His
offering was one silver bowl weighing one hundred and thirty shekel and
one silver basin weighing seventy shekel according to the Sanctuary weight,
74 both filled with fine flour mixed with oil for a grain offering; one golden
75 spoon weighing ten shekel, full of incense; one young bull, one ram, and one
76 77 yearling sheep for a burnt offering; one goat for a purification offering; and
for the peace sacrifice two oxen, five rams, five male goats, and five yearling
sheep. This was the offering of Pagiel son of Okhran.
78 79 On the twelfth day came Aḥira son of Einan, prince of the Naftalites: His
offering was one silver bowl weighing one hundred and thirty shekel and one
silver basin weighing seventy shekel according to the Sanctuary weight, both
80 filled with fine flour mixed with oil for a grain offering; one golden spoon
81 weighing ten shekel, full of incense; one young bull, one ram, and one yearling
82 83 sheep for a burnt offering; one goat for a purification offering; and for the
peace sacrifice two oxen, five rams, five male goats, and five yearling sheep.
This was the offering of Aḥira son of Einan.
84 All this was the dedication offering from the princes of Israel for the altar at
the time it was anointed: There were twelve silver bowls, twelve silver basins,

נח נט בֶּן־שְׁנָתוֹ לְעֹלָה: שְׂעִיר־עִזִּים אֶחָד לְחַטָּאת: וּלְזֶבַח הַשְּׁלָמִים בָּקָר
שְׁנַיִם אֵילִם חֲמִשָּׁה עַתֻּדִים חֲמִשָּׁה כְּבָשִׂים בְּנֵי־שָׁנָה חֲמִשָּׁה זֶה קָרְבַּן
גַּמְלִיאֵל בֶּן־פְּדָהצוּר:
ס סא בַּיּוֹם הַתְּשִׁיעִי נָשִׂיא לִבְנֵי בִנְיָמִן אֲבִידָן בֶּן־גִּדְעֹנִי: קָרְבָּנוֹ קַעֲרַת־
כֶּסֶף אַחַת שְׁלֹשִׁים וּמֵאָה מִשְׁקָלָהּ מִזְרָק אֶחָד כֶּסֶף שִׁבְעִים שֶׁקֶל
סב בְּשֶׁקֶל הַקֹּדֶשׁ שְׁנֵיהֶם ׀ מְלֵאִים סֹלֶת בְּלוּלָה בַשֶּׁמֶן לְמִנְחָה: כַּף אַחַת
סג עֲשָׂרָה זָהָב מְלֵאָה קְטֹרֶת: פַּר אֶחָד בֶּן־בָּקָר אַיִל אֶחָד כֶּבֶשׂ־אֶחָד
סד סה בֶּן־שְׁנָתוֹ לְעֹלָה: שְׂעִיר־עִזִּים אֶחָד לְחַטָּאת: וּלְזֶבַח הַשְּׁלָמִים בָּקָר
שְׁנַיִם אֵילִם חֲמִשָּׁה עַתֻּדִים חֲמִשָּׁה כְּבָשִׂים בְּנֵי־שָׁנָה חֲמִשָּׁה זֶה קָרְבַּן
אֲבִידָן בֶּן־גִּדְעֹנִי:
סו סז בַּיּוֹם הָעֲשִׂירִי נָשִׂיא לִבְנֵי דָן אֲחִיעֶזֶר בֶּן־עַמִּישַׁדָּי: קָרְבָּנוֹ קַעֲרַת־
כֶּסֶף אַחַת שְׁלֹשִׁים וּמֵאָה מִשְׁקָלָהּ מִזְרָק אֶחָד כֶּסֶף שִׁבְעִים שֶׁקֶל
סח בְּשֶׁקֶל הַקֹּדֶשׁ שְׁנֵיהֶם ׀ מְלֵאִים סֹלֶת בְּלוּלָה בַשֶּׁמֶן לְמִנְחָה: כַּף אַחַת
סט עֲשָׂרָה זָהָב מְלֵאָה קְטֹרֶת: פַּר אֶחָד בֶּן־בָּקָר אַיִל אֶחָד כֶּבֶשׂ־אֶחָד
ע עא בֶּן־שְׁנָתוֹ לְעֹלָה: שְׂעִיר־עִזִּים אֶחָד לְחַטָּאת: וּלְזֶבַח הַשְּׁלָמִים בָּקָר
שְׁנַיִם אֵילִם חֲמִשָּׁה עַתֻּדִים חֲמִשָּׁה כְּבָשִׂים בְּנֵי־שָׁנָה חֲמִשָּׁה זֶה קָרְבַּן
אֲחִיעֶזֶר בֶּן־עַמִּישַׁדָּי:
עב עג בְּיוֹם עַשְׁתֵּי עָשָׂר יוֹם נָשִׂיא לִבְנֵי אָשֵׁר פַּגְעִיאֵל בֶּן־עָכְרָן: קָרְבָּנוֹ שביעי
קַעֲרַת־כֶּסֶף אַחַת שְׁלֹשִׁים וּמֵאָה מִשְׁקָלָהּ מִזְרָק אֶחָד כֶּסֶף שִׁבְעִים
שֶׁקֶל בְּשֶׁקֶל הַקֹּדֶשׁ שְׁנֵיהֶם ׀ מְלֵאִים סֹלֶת בְּלוּלָה בַשֶּׁמֶן לְמִנְחָה:
עד עה כַּף אַחַת עֲשָׂרָה זָהָב מְלֵאָה קְטֹרֶת: פַּר אֶחָד בֶּן־בָּקָר אַיִל אֶחָד
עו עז כֶּבֶשׂ־אֶחָד בֶּן־שְׁנָתוֹ לְעֹלָה: שְׂעִיר־עִזִּים אֶחָד לְחַטָּאת: וּלְזֶבַח
הַשְּׁלָמִים בָּקָר שְׁנַיִם אֵילִם חֲמִשָּׁה עַתֻּדִים חֲמִשָּׁה כְּבָשִׂים בְּנֵי־שָׁנָה
חֲמִשָּׁה זֶה קָרְבַּן פַּגְעִיאֵל בֶּן־עָכְרָן:
עח עט בְּיוֹם שְׁנֵים עָשָׂר יוֹם נָשִׂיא לִבְנֵי נַפְתָּלִי אֲחִירַע בֶּן־עֵינָן: קָרְבָּנוֹ
קַעֲרַת־כֶּסֶף אַחַת שְׁלֹשִׁים וּמֵאָה מִשְׁקָלָהּ מִזְרָק אֶחָד כֶּסֶף שִׁבְעִים
שֶׁקֶל בְּשֶׁקֶל הַקֹּדֶשׁ שְׁנֵיהֶם ׀ מְלֵאִים סֹלֶת בְּלוּלָה בַשֶּׁמֶן לְמִנְחָה:
פ פא כַּף אַחַת עֲשָׂרָה זָהָב מְלֵאָה קְטֹרֶת: פַּר אֶחָד בֶּן־בָּקָר אַיִל אֶחָד
פב פג כֶּבֶשׂ־אֶחָד בֶּן־שְׁנָתוֹ לְעֹלָה: שְׂעִיר־עִזִּים אֶחָד לְחַטָּאת: וּלְזֶבַח
הַשְּׁלָמִים בָּקָר שְׁנַיִם אֵילִם חֲמִשָּׁה עַתֻּדִים חֲמִשָּׁה כְּבָשִׂים בְּנֵי־שָׁנָה
חֲמִשָּׁה זֶה קָרְבַּן אֲחִירַע בֶּן־עֵינָן:
פד זֹאת ׀ חֲנֻכַּת הַמִּזְבֵּחַ בְּיוֹם הִמָּשַׁח אֹתוֹ מֵאֵת נְשִׂיאֵי יִשְׂרָאֵל קַעֲרֹת

85 and twelve golden spoons, each silver bowl weighing one hundred and thirty
shekel and each basin seventy shekel – so all the silver in the utensils weighed
86 two thousand four hundred shekel according to the Sanctuary weight. There
were twelve gold spoons full of incense weighing ten shekel each according
to the Sanctuary weight – so all the gold of the spoons weighed one hundred
87 and twenty shekel. The total number of the animals for the burnt offerings
was twelve bulls, twelve rams, and twelve yearling sheep, along with their
grain offerings. There were also twelve goats for the purification offerings.
88 The total number of all the animals for the peace sacrifices was twenty-four
bulls, sixty rams, sixty goats, and sixty yearling sheep. This was the dedication
89 offering for the altar after it was anointed. When Moshe entered the Tent of
Meeting to speak with the LORD, he would hear the Voice speaking to him
from above the cover over the Ark of the Covenant, from between the two
cherubim. Thus did He speak to him.

BEHAALOTEKHA

8 1 2 And the LORD spoke to Moshe: "Speak to Aharon; say to him: When you
raise up the lamps, the seven lamps shall light the space in front of the
3 candelabrum."[21] Aharon did so; he mounted the lamps toward the front
4 of the candelabrum as the LORD had commanded Moshe. This is how the
lampstand was made: of hammered gold, hammered from its base to its
flowers. According to the vision that the LORD had shown Moshe, so was
the lampstand made.
5 6 The LORD spoke to Moshe: "Take the Levites from among the Israelites and
7 purify them. This is what you shall do to them to purify them: Sprinkle upon
them the water of purification,[22] and have them shave their whole bodies and
8 wash their clothes; then they will be purified. They shall take a young bull
with its grain offering of fine flour mixed with oil. You, meanwhile, shall take
9 a second young bull for a purification offering. You shall bring the Levites
10 before the Tent of Meeting and assemble all the community of Israel. Then
you shall bring the Levites forward before the LORD, and the Israelites shall
11 lay their hands upon the Levites. Aharon shall then present the Levites before
the LORD like a wave offering from the Israelites, so that they may perform
12 the LORD's service. The Levites shall then lay their hands upon the heads of
the bulls, and Aharon shall offer one as a purification offering and the other
13 as a burnt offering to the LORD, to make atonement for the Levites. You shall
have the Levites stand before Aharon and his sons, and then present them like
14 a wave offering to the LORD. Thus you shall separate the Levites from among
15 the other Israelites; the Levites shall become Mine. After that, the Levites
shall enter to perform the service of the Tent of Meeting, once you have
16 purified them and presented them as a wave offering. They are wholly given
over to Me from among the Israelites. I have taken them for Myself in place of
17 the first to emerge from every womb, the firstborn of all the Israelites. For all
the firstborn among the Israelites, man and beast alike, are Mine; on the day
18 that I struck down the firstborn in Egypt, I consecrated them to Myself. But

21 | Concerning the candelabrum, see Exodus 25:31–40.
22 | Cf. the ritual described in chapter 19.

כֶּסֶף שְׁתַּיִם עֶשְׂרֵה מִזְרְקֵי־כֶסֶף שְׁנֵים עָשָׂר כַּפּוֹת זָהָב שְׁתֵּים עֶשְׂרֵה׃
פה שְׁלֹשִׁים וּמֵאָה הַקְּעָרָה הָאַחַת כֶּסֶף וְשִׁבְעִים הַמִּזְרָק הָאֶחָד כֹּל כֶּסֶף
פו הַכֵּלִים אַלְפַּיִם וְאַרְבַּע־מֵאוֹת בְּשֶׁקֶל הַקֹּדֶשׁ׃ כַּפּוֹת זָהָב שְׁתֵּים־
עֶשְׂרֵה מְלֵאֹת קְטֹרֶת עֲשָׂרָה עֲשָׂרָה הַכַּף בְּשֶׁקֶל הַקֹּדֶשׁ כָּל־זְהַב
פז הַכַּפּוֹת עֶשְׂרִים וּמֵאָה׃ כָּל־הַבָּקָר לָעֹלָה שְׁנֵים עָשָׂר פָּרִים אֵילִם מפטיר
שְׁנֵים־עָשָׂר כְּבָשִׂים בְּנֵי־שָׁנָה שְׁנֵים עָשָׂר וּמִנְחָתָם וּשְׂעִירֵי עִזִּים שְׁנֵים
פח עָשָׂר לְחַטָּאת׃ וְכֹל בְּקַר ׀ זֶבַח הַשְּׁלָמִים עֶשְׂרִים וְאַרְבָּעָה פָּרִים אֵילִם
שִׁשִּׁים עַתֻּדִים שִׁשִּׁים כְּבָשִׂים בְּנֵי־שָׁנָה שִׁשִּׁים זֹאת חֲנֻכַּת הַמִּזְבֵּחַ
פט אַחֲרֵי הִמָּשַׁח אֹתוֹ׃ וּבְבֹא מֹשֶׁה אֶל־אֹהֶל מוֹעֵד לְדַבֵּר אִתּוֹ וַיִּשְׁמַע
אֶת־הַקּוֹל מִדַּבֵּר אֵלָיו מֵעַל הַכַּפֹּרֶת אֲשֶׁר עַל־אֲרֹן הָעֵדֻת מִבֵּין שְׁנֵי
הַכְּרֻבִים וַיְדַבֵּר אֵלָיו׃
ח א ב וַיְדַבֵּר יהוה אֶל־מֹשֶׁה לֵּאמֹר׃ דַּבֵּר אֶל־אַהֲרֹן וְאָמַרְתָּ אֵלָיו בְּהַעֲלֹתְךָ ח בהעלתך
ג אֶת־הַנֵּרֹת אֶל־מוּל פְּנֵי הַמְּנוֹרָה יָאִירוּ שִׁבְעַת הַנֵּרוֹת׃ וַיַּעַשׂ כֵּן אַהֲרֹן
אֶל־מוּל פְּנֵי הַמְּנוֹרָה הֶעֱלָה נֵרֹתֶיהָ כַּאֲשֶׁר צִוָּה יהוה אֶת־מֹשֶׁה׃
ד וְזֶה מַעֲשֵׂה הַמְּנֹרָה מִקְשָׁה זָהָב עַד־יְרֵכָהּ עַד־פִּרְחָהּ מִקְשָׁה הִוא
כַּמַּרְאֶה אֲשֶׁר הֶרְאָה יהוה אֶת־מֹשֶׁה כֵּן עָשָׂה אֶת־הַמְּנֹרָה׃
ה ו וַיְדַבֵּר יהוה אֶל־מֹשֶׁה לֵּאמֹר׃ קַח אֶת־הַלְוִיִּם מִתּוֹךְ בְּנֵי יִשְׂרָאֵל
ז וְטִהַרְתָּ אֹתָם׃ וְכֹה־תַעֲשֶׂה לָהֶם לְטַהֲרָם הַזֵּה עֲלֵיהֶם מֵי חַטָּאת
ח וְהֶעֱבִירוּ תַעַר עַל־כָּל־בְּשָׂרָם וְכִבְּסוּ בִגְדֵיהֶם וְהִטֶּהָרוּ׃ וְלָקְחוּ פַּר בֶּן־
בָּקָר וּמִנְחָתוֹ סֹלֶת בְּלוּלָה בַשָּׁמֶן וּפַר־שֵׁנִי בֶן־בָּקָר תִּקַּח לְחַטָּאת׃
ט וְהִקְרַבְתָּ אֶת־הַלְוִיִּם לִפְנֵי אֹהֶל מוֹעֵד וְהִקְהַלְתָּ אֶת־כָּל־עֲדַת בְּנֵי
י יִשְׂרָאֵל׃ וְהִקְרַבְתָּ אֶת־הַלְוִיִּם לִפְנֵי יהוה וְסָמְכוּ בְנֵי־יִשְׂרָאֵל אֶת־
יא יְדֵיהֶם עַל־הַלְוִיִּם׃ וְהֵנִיף אַהֲרֹן אֶת־הַלְוִיִּם תְּנוּפָה לִפְנֵי יהוה מֵאֵת
יב בְּנֵי יִשְׂרָאֵל וְהָיוּ לַעֲבֹד אֶת־עֲבֹדַת יהוה׃ וְהַלְוִיִּם יִסְמְכוּ אֶת־יְדֵיהֶם
עַל רֹאשׁ הַפָּרִים וַעֲשֵׂה אֶת־הָאֶחָד חַטָּאת וְאֶת־הָאֶחָד עֹלָה לַיהוה
יג לְכַפֵּר עַל־הַלְוִיִּם׃ וְהַעֲמַדְתָּ אֶת־הַלְוִיִּם לִפְנֵי אַהֲרֹן וְלִפְנֵי בָנָיו וְהֵנַפְתָּ
יד אֹתָם תְּנוּפָה לַיהוה׃ וְהִבְדַּלְתָּ אֶת־הַלְוִיִּם מִתּוֹךְ בְּנֵי יִשְׂרָאֵל וְהָיוּ לִי
טו הַלְוִיִּם׃ וְאַחֲרֵי־כֵן יָבֹאוּ הַלְוִיִּם לַעֲבֹד אֶת־אֹהֶל מוֹעֵד וְטִהַרְתָּ אֹתָם שני
טז וְהֵנַפְתָּ אֹתָם תְּנוּפָה׃ כִּי נְתֻנִים נְתֻנִים הֵמָּה לִי מִתּוֹךְ בְּנֵי יִשְׂרָאֵל
תַּחַת פִּטְרַת כָּל־רֶחֶם בְּכוֹר כֹּל מִבְּנֵי יִשְׂרָאֵל לָקַחְתִּי אֹתָם לִי׃
יז כִּי לִי כָל־בְּכוֹר בִּבְנֵי יִשְׂרָאֵל בָּאָדָם וּבַבְּהֵמָה בְּיוֹם הַכֹּתִי כָל־בְּכוֹר
יח בְּאֶרֶץ מִצְרַיִם הִקְדַּשְׁתִּי אֹתָם לִי׃ וָאֶקַּח אֶת־הַלְוִיִּם תַּחַת כָּל־בְּכוֹר

19 I have now taken the Levites in place of all the firstborn among the Israelites,
and I have given the Levites to Aharon and his sons from among the Israelites,
to perform the service of the Israelites in the Tent of Meeting and to make
atonement for the Israelites, so that no plague will come among the Israelites
20 for drawing too close to the Sanctuary." Moshe, Aharon, and all the community of Israel did this for the Levites; all that the LORD commanded
21 Moshe with regard to the Levites, so the Israelites did. The Levites purified
themselves and washed their clothes. Aharon presented them as a wave
offering before the LORD, and made atonement for them in order to purify
22 them. And after that, the Levites went in to perform their service in the
Tent of Meeting before Aharon and his sons. As the LORD had commanded
23 Moshe regarding the Levites, so they did for them. And the LORD
24 spoke to Moshe: "The Levites: From twenty-five years upward they shall
25 go into the service of the Tent of Meeting. At fifty years old they shall retire
26 from the service and serve no longer. They may assist their fellow Levites in
carrying out their duties in the Tent of Meeting, but shall not perform the
service itself. This is how you shall conduct the Levites with regard to their
duties."

9 1 The LORD spoke to Moshe in the Sinai Desert in the first month of the second
2 year after they had left Egypt: "Let the Israelites offer the Passover sacrifice at
3 its appointed time. On the fourteenth day of this month in the afternoon you
shall offer it at its appointed time. Bring it in accordance with all its decrees
4 and laws."[23] And so Moshe instructed the Israelites to offer the Passover
5 sacrifice. On the afternoon of the fourteenth day of the first month they
offered the Passover sacrifice in the Sinai Desert. Just as the LORD com-
6 manded Moshe, so the Israelites did. But there were people who were impure
because of contact with the dead, and they were unable to offer the Passover
7 sacrifice on that day. That very day they approached Moshe and Aharon: "We
have become impure because of contact with the dead," these people said
to him, "but must we be debarred from presenting the LORD's offering at its
8 appointed time among all the Israelites?" "Wait," Moshe replied, "and let me
hear what the LORD commands concerning you."
9 10 And the LORD spoke to Moshe: "Tell the Israelites: When any of you or your
future descendants are impure because of contact with the dead, or away on
11 a journey, they may still offer a Passover sacrifice to the LORD. They shall
offer it in the afternoon of the fourteenth day of the second month; then
12 shall they eat it with unleavened bread and bitter herbs. They shall not leave
any of it over until morning, nor shall they break any of its bones. They shall
13 offer it in compliance with all the rules of the Passover sacrifice. But anyone
who is ritually pure and not on a journey, but still fails to offer the Passover
sacrifice, that person shall be severed from his people, because he did not offer
14 the LORD's sacrifice at its appointed time; he will bear his guilt. If there is a
migrant living among you and he offers a Passover sacrifice to the LORD, he
shall do so in compliance with all its rules and laws. You shall have one law

23 | See Exodus, chapter 12.

יט בִּבְנֵי יִשְׂרָאֵל: וָאֶתְּנָה אֶת־הַלְוִיִּם נְתֻנִים ׀ לְאַהֲרֹן וּלְבָנָיו מִתּוֹךְ בְּנֵי
יִשְׂרָאֵל לַעֲבֹד אֶת־עֲבֹדַת בְּנֵי־יִשְׂרָאֵל בְּאֹהֶל מוֹעֵד וּלְכַפֵּר עַל־בְּנֵי
יִשְׂרָאֵל וְלֹא יִהְיֶה בִּבְנֵי יִשְׂרָאֵל נֶגֶף בְּגֶשֶׁת בְּנֵי־יִשְׂרָאֵל אֶל־הַקֹּדֶשׁ:
כ וַיַּעַשׂ מֹשֶׁה וְאַהֲרֹן וְכָל־עֲדַת בְּנֵי־יִשְׂרָאֵל לַלְוִיִּם כְּכֹל אֲשֶׁר־צִוָּה
כא יהוה אֶת־מֹשֶׁה לַלְוִיִּם כֵּן־עָשׂוּ לָהֶם בְּנֵי יִשְׂרָאֵל: וַיִּתְחַטְּאוּ הַלְוִיִּם
וַיְכַבְּסוּ בִּגְדֵיהֶם וַיָּנֶף אַהֲרֹן אֹתָם תְּנוּפָה לִפְנֵי יהוה וַיְכַפֵּר עֲלֵיהֶם
כב אַהֲרֹן לְטַהֲרָם: וְאַחֲרֵי־כֵן בָּאוּ הַלְוִיִּם לַעֲבֹד אֶת־עֲבֹדָתָם בְּאֹהֶל
מוֹעֵד לִפְנֵי אַהֲרֹן וְלִפְנֵי בָנָיו כַּאֲשֶׁר צִוָּה יהוה אֶת־מֹשֶׁה עַל־הַלְוִיִּם
כג כד כֵּן עָשׂוּ לָהֶם: וַיְדַבֵּר יהוה אֶל־מֹשֶׁה לֵּאמֹר: זֹאת אֲשֶׁר
לַלְוִיִּם מִבֶּן חָמֵשׁ וְעֶשְׂרִים שָׁנָה וָמַעְלָה יָבוֹא לִצְבֹא צָבָא בַּעֲבֹדַת
כה אֹהֶל מוֹעֵד: וּמִבֶּן חֲמִשִּׁים שָׁנָה יָשׁוּב מִצְּבָא הָעֲבֹדָה וְלֹא יַעֲבֹד עוֹד:
כו וְשֵׁרֵת אֶת־אֶחָיו בְּאֹהֶל מוֹעֵד לִשְׁמֹר מִשְׁמֶרֶת וַעֲבֹדָה לֹא יַעֲבֹד כָּכָה
תַּעֲשֶׂה לַלְוִיִּם בְּמִשְׁמְרֹתָם:
ט א וַיְדַבֵּר יהוה אֶל־מֹשֶׁה בְמִדְבַּר־סִינַי בַּשָּׁנָה הַשֵּׁנִית לְצֵאתָם מֵאֶרֶץ שלישי
ב מִצְרַיִם בַּחֹדֶשׁ הָרִאשׁוֹן לֵאמֹר: וְיַעֲשׂוּ בְנֵי־יִשְׂרָאֵל אֶת־הַפָּסַח
ג בְּמוֹעֲדוֹ: בְּאַרְבָּעָה עָשָׂר־יוֹם בַּחֹדֶשׁ הַזֶּה בֵּין הָעַרְבַּיִם תַּעֲשׂוּ אֹתוֹ
ד בְּמֹעֲדוֹ כְּכָל־חֻקֹּתָיו וּכְכָל־מִשְׁפָּטָיו תַּעֲשׂוּ אֹתוֹ: וַיְדַבֵּר מֹשֶׁה אֶל־בְּנֵי
ה יִשְׂרָאֵל לַעֲשֹׂת הַפָּסַח: וַיַּעֲשׂוּ אֶת־הַפֶּסַח בָּרִאשׁוֹן בְּאַרְבָּעָה עָשָׂר
יוֹם לַחֹדֶשׁ בֵּין הָעַרְבַּיִם בְּמִדְבַּר סִינָי כְּכֹל אֲשֶׁר צִוָּה יהוה אֶת־מֹשֶׁה
ו כֵּן עָשׂוּ בְּנֵי יִשְׂרָאֵל: וַיְהִי אֲנָשִׁים אֲשֶׁר הָיוּ טְמֵאִים לְנֶפֶשׁ אָדָם וְלֹא־
יָכְלוּ לַעֲשֹׂת־הַפֶּסַח בַּיּוֹם הַהוּא וַיִּקְרְבוּ לִפְנֵי מֹשֶׁה וְלִפְנֵי אַהֲרֹן בַּיּוֹם
ז הַהוּא: וַיֹּאמְרוּ הָאֲנָשִׁים הָהֵמָּה אֵלָיו אֲנַחְנוּ טְמֵאִים לְנֶפֶשׁ אָדָם
לָמָּה נִגָּרַע לְבִלְתִּי הַקְרִב אֶת־קָרְבַּן יהוה בְּמֹעֲדוֹ בְּתוֹךְ בְּנֵי יִשְׂרָאֵל:
ח וַיֹּאמֶר אֲלֵהֶם מֹשֶׁה עִמְדוּ וְאֶשְׁמְעָה מַה־יְצַוֶּה יהוה לָכֶם:
ט וַיְדַבֵּר יהוה אֶל־מֹשֶׁה לֵּאמֹר: דַּבֵּר אֶל־בְּנֵי יִשְׂרָאֵל לֵאמֹר אִישׁ אִישׁ
י כִּי־יִהְיֶה טָמֵא ׀ לָנֶפֶשׁ אוֹ בְדֶרֶךְ רְחֹקָה לָכֶם אוֹ לְדֹרֹתֵיכֶם וְעָשָׂה
יא פֶסַח לַיהוה: בַּחֹדֶשׁ הַשֵּׁנִי בְּאַרְבָּעָה עָשָׂר יוֹם בֵּין הָעַרְבַּיִם יַעֲשׂוּ
יב אֹתוֹ עַל־מַצּוֹת וּמְרֹרִים יֹאכְלֻהוּ: לֹא־יַשְׁאִירוּ מִמֶּנּוּ עַד־בֹּקֶר וְעֶצֶם
יג לֹא יִשְׁבְּרוּ־בוֹ כְּכָל־חֻקַּת הַפֶּסַח יַעֲשׂוּ אֹתוֹ: וְהָאִישׁ אֲשֶׁר־הוּא
טָהוֹר וּבְדֶרֶךְ לֹא־הָיָה וְחָדַל לַעֲשׂוֹת הַפֶּסַח וְנִכְרְתָה הַנֶּפֶשׁ הַהִוא
מֵעַמֶּיהָ כִּי ׀ קָרְבַּן יהוה לֹא הִקְרִיב בְּמֹעֲדוֹ חֶטְאוֹ יִשָּׂא הָאִישׁ הַהוּא:
יד וְכִי־יָגוּר אִתְּכֶם גֵּר וְעָשָׂה פֶסַח לַיהוה כְּחֻקַּת הַפֶּסַח וּכְמִשְׁפָּטוֹ כֵּן

15 for migrant and native born alike." On the day when the Tabernacle
was erected, the cloud covered the Tabernacle, the Tent of the Testimony, and
from evening until morning it hung over the Tabernacle with the appearance
16 of fire. It was always there; the cloud covered the Tent, appearing at night as
17 fire. Whenever the cloud rose above the Tent, the Israelites would set out,
18 and wherever the cloud settled, the Israelites would encamp. At the Lord's
command, the Israelites set out, and at the Lord's command they would
encamp; for as long as the cloud rested on the Tabernacle, they continued
19 to camp there. Even when the cloud lingered over the Tabernacle for many
20 days, the Israelites kept the Lord's charge and did not journey on. Sometimes
the cloud would be over the Tabernacle for just a few days; at the Lord's
command they would camp, and at the Lord's command they would set
21 out. Sometimes the cloud stayed only from evening to morning, and in the
morning it rose, and they set out. Day or night, they would set out when the
22 cloud rose. Whether it was two days, or a month, or for many days together,
the Israelites would camp as long as the cloud rested over the Tabernacle, and
23 would not move on. They journeyed only when the cloud rose. At the Lord's
command they camped, and at the Lord's command they set out. And they
kept the Lord's charge, the Lord's word through Moshe.
10 1 2 The Lord spoke to Moshe: "Make two silver trumpets; make them of hammered metal. Use them for summoning the community and for having the
3 camps set out. When both are blown with a long note, the entire community
4 shall assemble before you at the entrance to the Tent of Meeting. If only
one is blown, the princes, leaders of Israel's divisions, shall assemble before
5 you. When you blow a series of short blasts, the camps on the east side
6 shall march, and when you blow a second series of short blasts, the camps
on the south side will march; thus shall a series of short blasts signal them
7 to move on. To assemble the community, blow a long blast, not a series of
8 short blasts. Aharon's sons the priests shall blow the trumpets. This shall be
9 for you an everlasting decree throughout your generations. When you go to
war against an enemy who is attacking you in your land, you shall blow short
blasts on the trumpets to be remembered before the Lord your God, to be
10 delivered from your enemies. And on your days of rejoicing, your festivals
and New Moons, you shall blow the trumpets over your burnt offerings and
your peace offerings. They will be a reminder of you before your God. I am
the Lord your God."
11 On the twentieth day of the second month in the second year, the cloud
12 rose above the Tabernacle of the Covenant. The Israelites set out on their
journey from the Sinai Desert, and the cloud came to rest in the Wilderness
13 of Paran. For the first time, at the Lord's command through Moshe, they
14 set out. The divisions of Yehuda's camp set out first, under their banner.
15 Leading that division was Naḥshon son of Aminadav. Netanel son of Tzuar
16 was in charge of the division of the tribe of Yissakhar. Eliav son of Ḥelon
17 was in charge of the division of the tribe of Zevulun. The Tabernacle was
taken down, and the Gershonites and the Merarites, who carried it, set out.

טו יעשה חקה אחת יהיה לכם ולגר ולאזרח הארץ: וביום רביעי
הקים את־המשכן כסה הענן את־המשכן לאהל העדת ובערב
טז יהיה על־המשכן כמראה־אש עד־בקר: כן יהיה תמיד הענן יכסנו
יז ומראה־אש לילה: ולפי העלות הענן מעל האהל ואחרי כן יסעו
בני ישראל ובמקום אשר ישכן־שם הענן שם יחנו בני ישראל:
יח על־פי יהוה יסעו בני ישראל ועל־פי יהוה יחנו כל־ימי אשר ישכן
יט הענן על־המשכן יחנו: ובהאריך הענן על־המשכן ימים רבים
כ ושמרו בני־ישראל את־משמרת יהוה ולא יסעו: ויש אשר יהיה
הענן ימים מספר על־המשכן על־פי יהוה יחנו ועל־פי יהוה יסעו:
כא ויש אשר יהיה הענן מערב עד־בקר ונעלה הענן בבקר ונסעו או
כב יומם ולילה ונעלה הענן ונסעו: או־ימים או־חדש או־ימים בהאריך
הענן על־המשכן לשכן עליו יחנו בני־ישראל ולא יסעו ובהעלתו
כג יסעו: על־פי יהוה יחנו ועל־פי יהוה יסעו את־משמרת יהוה שמרו
על־פי יהוה ביד־משה:

י א ב וידבר יהוה אל־משה לאמר: עשה לך שתי חצוצרת כסף מקשה ט
ג תעשה אתם והיו לך למקרא העדה ולמסע את־המחנות: ותקעו
ד בהן ונועדו אליך כל־העדה אל־פתח אהל מועד: ואם־באחת
ה יתקעו ונועדו אליך הנשיאים ראשי אלפי ישראל: ותקעתם תרועה
ו ונסעו המחנות החנים קדמה: ותקעתם תרועה שנית ונסעו המחנות
ז החנים תימנה תרועה יתקעו למסעיהם: ובהקהיל את־הקהל
ח תתקעו ולא תריעו: ובני אהרן הכהנים יתקעו בחצצרות והיו לכם
ט לחקת עולם לדרתיכם: וכי־תבאו מלחמה בארצכם על־הצר הצרר
אתכם והרעתם בחצצרת ונזכרתם לפני יהוה אלהיכם ונושעתם
י מאיביכם: וביום שמחתכם ובמועדיכם ובראשי חדשיכם ותקעתם
בחצצרת על עלתיכם ועל זבחי שלמיכם והיו לכם לזכרון לפני
אלהיכם אני יהוה אלהיכם:

יא ויהי בשנה השנית בחדש השני בעשרים בחדש נעלה הענן מעל חמישי
יב משכן העדת: ויסעו בני־ישראל למסעיהם ממדבר סיני וישכן הענן
יג יד במדבר פארן: ויסעו בראשנה על־פי יהוה ביד־משה: ויסע דגל
מחנה בני־יהודה בראשנה לצבאתם ועל־צבאו נחשון בן־עמינדב:
טו טז ועל־צבא מטה בני יששכר נתנאל בן־צוער: ועל־צבא מטה בני
יז זבולן אליאב בן־חלן: והורד המשכן ונסעו בני־גרשון ובני מררי

18 The divisions of the camp of Reuven set out next, under their banner. Leading
19 that division was Elitzur son of Shedeiur. Shelumiel son of Tzurishadai was
20 in charge of the division of the tribe of Shimon. Elyasaf son of Deuel was in
21 charge of the division of the tribe of Gad. Then the Kohatites, who carried
the sacred objects, set out. By the time they arrived, the Tabernacle would
22 have been erected. The divisions of the camp of Efrayim set out next, under
23 their banner. Leading that division was Elishama son of Amihud. Gamliel son
24 of Pedahtzur was in charge of the division of the tribe of Menashe. Avidan
25 son of Gidoni was in charge of the division of the tribe of Binyamin. Then,
at the rear of the whole camp, the divisions of the camp of Dan set out under
26 their banner. Leading that division was Aḥiezer son of Amishadai. Pagiel
27 son of Okhran was in charge of the division of the tribe of Asher. Aḥira son
28 of Einan was in charge of the division of the tribe of Naftali. This was the
29 order in which the Israelites set out in their divisions. Moshe said
to Ḥovav son of Reuel the Midianite, Moshe's father-in-law,[24] "We are setting
out to the place that the Lord said He would give us. Come with us and we
30 will be good to you, for the Lord has promised good things to Israel." But he
replied, "I will not come; I must go back to my own land and my own people."
31 "Please do not leave us," said Moshe, "for you know where we should camp in
32 the wilderness; you would be our eyes. If you come with us, whatever good
33 the Lord does for us, we will do for you." They journeyed from the Lord's
mountain for three days; and the Ark of the Lord's Covenant went ahead of
34 them for those three days to find a resting place for them. The Lord's cloud
35 was over them by day as they journeyed from the camp. When the
Ark set out, Moshe would say, "Arise, Lord; let Your enemies be scattered,
36 and Your foes flee before You." When it came to rest, he would say, "Bring
back, O Lord, the myriad thousands of Israel."[25]
11 1 The people began to rail bitterly in the Lord's presence. And the Lord heard
and was incensed; fire from the Lord blazed against them, consuming at
2 the edge of the camp. The people cried out to Moshe – Moshe prayed to the
3 Lord – and the fire subsided. And so that place was named Tavera,[26] because
4 the Lord's fire had blazed against them. The rabble in their midst began to
have strong cravings, and once again the Israelites began to weep, saying,
5 "Who will give us meat to eat? We remember the fish we ate in Egypt at no
cost, the cucumbers, and the melons, and the leeks, and the onions, and the
6 garlic. But now our throats are dry. There is nothing at all but this manna
7 to look at." The manna was like coriander seed, and like bdellium in color.[27]
8 The people went around gathering it. Then they would grind it in a mill or
crush it in a mortar. They cooked it in a pot and they made cakes from it; it
9 tasted like cakes made with oil. When the dew fell over the camp at night,

---

24 | Cf. Exodus 2:18; Judges 4:11.

25 | Perhaps referring to Israelite fighters. According to this approach, these verses invoke the military function of the Ark, which represented God's presence in battle.

26 | Literally "burning."

27 | That is, of exquisite taste and beauty.

יח נֹשְׂאֵי הַמִּשְׁכָּן: וְנָסַע דֶּגֶל מַחֲנֵה רְאוּבֵן לְצִבְאֹתָם וְעַל־צְבָאוֹ אֱלִיצוּר
יט בֶּן־שְׁדֵיאוּר: וְעַל־צְבָא מַטֵּה בְּנֵי שִׁמְעוֹן שְׁלֻמִיאֵל בֶּן־צוּרִישַׁדָּי:
כ כא וְעַל־צְבָא מַטֵּה בְנֵי־גָד אֶלְיָסָף בֶּן־דְּעוּאֵל: וְנָסְעוּ הַקְּהָתִים נֹשְׂאֵי
כב הַמִּקְדָּשׁ וְהֵקִימוּ אֶת־הַמִּשְׁכָּן עַד־בֹּאָם: וְנָסַע דֶּגֶל מַחֲנֵה בְנֵי־אֶפְרַיִם
כג לְצִבְאֹתָם וְעַל־צְבָאוֹ אֱלִישָׁמָע בֶּן־עַמִּיהוּד: וְעַל־צְבָא מַטֵּה בְּנֵי
כד מְנַשֶּׁה גַּמְלִיאֵל בֶּן־פְּדָהצוּר: וְעַל־צְבָא מַטֵּה בְּנֵי בִנְיָמִן אֲבִידָן בֶּן־
כה גִּדְעוֹנִי: וְנָסַע דֶּגֶל מַחֲנֵה בְנֵי־דָן מְאַסֵּף לְכָל־הַמַּחֲנֹת לְצִבְאֹתָם
כו וְעַל־צְבָאוֹ אֲחִיעֶזֶר בֶּן־עַמִּישַׁדָּי: וְעַל־צְבָא מַטֵּה בְּנֵי אָשֵׁר פַּגְעִיאֵל
כז כח בֶּן־עָכְרָן: וְעַל־צְבָא מַטֵּה בְּנֵי נַפְתָּלִי אֲחִירַע בֶּן־עֵינָן: אֵלֶּה מַסְעֵי
כט בְנֵי־יִשְׂרָאֵל לְצִבְאֹתָם וַיִּסָּעוּ: וַיֹּאמֶר מֹשֶׁה לְחֹבָב בֶּן־
רְעוּאֵל הַמִּדְיָנִי חֹתֵן מֹשֶׁה נֹסְעִים | אֲנַחְנוּ אֶל־הַמָּקוֹם אֲשֶׁר אָמַר
יְהוָה אֹתוֹ אֶתֵּן לָכֶם לְכָה אִתָּנוּ וְהֵטַבְנוּ לָךְ כִּי־יְהוָה דִּבֶּר־טוֹב עַל־
ל יִשְׂרָאֵל: וַיֹּאמֶר אֵלָיו לֹא אֵלֵךְ כִּי אִם־אֶל־אַרְצִי וְאֶל־מוֹלַדְתִּי אֵלֵךְ:
לא וַיֹּאמֶר אַל־נָא תַּעֲזֹב אֹתָנוּ כִּי | עַל־כֵּן יָדַעְתָּ חֲנֹתֵנוּ בַּמִּדְבָּר וְהָיִיתָ
לב לָּנוּ לְעֵינָיִם: וְהָיָה כִּי־תֵלֵךְ עִמָּנוּ וְהָיָה | הַטּוֹב הַהוּא אֲשֶׁר יֵיטִיב
לג יְהוָה עִמָּנוּ וְהֵטַבְנוּ לָךְ: וַיִּסְעוּ מֵהַר יְהוָה דֶּרֶךְ שְׁלֹשֶׁת יָמִים וַאֲרוֹן
בְּרִית־יְהוָה נֹסֵעַ לִפְנֵיהֶם דֶּרֶךְ שְׁלֹשֶׁת יָמִים לָתוּר לָהֶם מְנוּחָה:
לד לה וַעֲנַן יְהוָה עֲלֵיהֶם יוֹמָם בְּנָסְעָם מִן־הַמַּחֲנֶה: ׆ וַיְהִי בִּנְסֹעַ ששי
הָאָרֹן וַיֹּאמֶר מֹשֶׁה קוּמָה | יְהוָה וְיָפֻצוּ אֹיְבֶיךָ וְיָנֻסוּ מְשַׂנְאֶיךָ מִפָּנֶיךָ:
לו וּבְנֻחֹה יֹאמַר שׁוּבָה יְהוָה רִבְבוֹת אַלְפֵי יִשְׂרָאֵל: ׆
יא א וַיְהִי הָעָם כְּמִתְאֹנְנִים רַע בְּאָזְנֵי יְהוָה וַיִּשְׁמַע יְהוָה וַיִּחַר אַפּוֹ וַתִּבְעַר־
ב בָּם אֵשׁ יְהוָה וַתֹּאכַל בִּקְצֵה הַמַּחֲנֶה: וַיִּצְעַק הָעָם אֶל־מֹשֶׁה וַיִּתְפַּלֵּל
ג מֹשֶׁה אֶל־יְהוָה וַתִּשְׁקַע הָאֵשׁ: וַיִּקְרָא שֵׁם־הַמָּקוֹם הַהוּא תַּבְעֵרָה
ד כִּי־בָעֲרָה בָם אֵשׁ יְהוָה: וְהָאסַפְסֻף אֲשֶׁר בְּקִרְבּוֹ הִתְאַוּוּ תַּאֲוָה וַיָּשֻׁבוּ
ה וַיִּבְכּוּ גַּם בְּנֵי יִשְׂרָאֵל וַיֹּאמְרוּ מִי יַאֲכִלֵנוּ בָּשָׂר: זָכַרְנוּ אֶת־הַדָּגָה אֲשֶׁר־
נֹאכַל בְּמִצְרַיִם חִנָּם אֵת הַקִּשֻּׁאִים וְאֵת הָאֲבַטִּחִים וְאֶת־הֶחָצִיר וְאֶת־
ו הַבְּצָלִים וְאֶת־הַשּׁוּמִים: וְעַתָּה נַפְשֵׁנוּ יְבֵשָׁה אֵין כֹּל בִּלְתִּי אֶל־הַמָּן
ז ח עֵינֵינוּ: וְהַמָּן כִּזְרַע־גַּד הוּא וְעֵינוֹ כְּעֵין הַבְּדֹלַח: שָׁטוּ הָעָם וְלָקְטוּ
וְטָחֲנוּ בָרֵחַיִם אוֹ דָכוּ בַּמְּדֹכָה וּבִשְּׁלוּ בַּפָּרוּר וְעָשׂוּ אֹתוֹ עֻגוֹת וְהָיָה
ט טַעְמוֹ כְּטַעַם לְשַׁד הַשָּׁמֶן: וּבְרֶדֶת הַטַּל עַל־הַמַּחֲנֶה לָיְלָה יֵרֵד הַמָּן

10 the manna would fall upon that. Moshe heard the people weeping clan by
clan, each one at his tent's opening. The LORD's anger blazed intensely, and
11 Moshe was distressed. "Why have You treated Your servant so badly?" asked
Moshe of the LORD. "Why have I found so little favor in Your sight that
12 You lay all the burden of this people upon me? Was it I who conceived all
this people? Was it I who gave birth to them all, that You should say to me,
'Carry them in your bosom, as a nursemaid carries a baby,' to the land that
13 You swore to their fathers? Where am I to get meat to give all this people
14 when they come wailing to me, 'Give us meat to eat'? I cannot bear all this
15 people alone; the burden is too heavy for me. If this is how You treat me,
kill me now, if I find any favor in Your sight, and let me not see my own
misery."
16 Then the LORD said to Moshe, "Gather for Me seventy of Israel's elders,
whom you know to be the people's elders and officers, and bring them to the
17 Tent of Meeting. Let them stand there with you. I will come down and speak
with you there, and I will take some of the spirit that is on you and place it
upon them; they will share the burden of the people with you, and you will
18 not have to bear it alone. And say to the people: Consecrate yourselves for
tomorrow; you will then have meat to eat, for you have been wailing in the
presence of the LORD, 'Who will give us meat to eat? It was better for us in
19 Egypt.' The LORD will give you meat, and you will eat. You will eat it not
20 just for one day, or two days, or five, or ten, or twenty days, but for a whole
month, until it comes out at your nostrils and becomes nauseating to you;
for you have rejected the LORD who is among you and have come wailing
21 in His presence, 'Why ever did we leave Egypt?'" But Moshe said, "Here I
am among six hundred thousand men on foot, and You say, 'I will give them
22 meat to eat for a whole month'! If whole flocks and herds were slaughtered for
them, would there be enough? If all the fish of the sea were caught for them,
would there be enough?!"
23 The LORD said to Moshe, "Does the LORD's hand fall short? Soon you shall
24 see whether what I say comes true or not." Moshe went out and told the
people what the LORD had said. He gathered seventy of the people's elders
25 and had them stand surrounding the Tent. Then the LORD came down in
the cloud and spoke to him, and took some of the spirit that was upon him
and placed it on the seventy elders. When the spirit rested upon them, they
26 prophesied – but they did not do so again.[28] Two men, one named Eldad and
the other Meidad, had remained in the camp, yet the spirit rested upon them.
Though they were among those listed, they had not gone out to the Tent – and
27 they spoke prophecy in the camp. A young man ran and told Moshe, "Eldad
28 and Meidad are speaking prophecy in the camp!" Yehoshua son of Nun, who
had been Moshe's disciple since his youth, said, "My lord Moshe, stop them!"
29 But Moshe replied, "Are you jealous for me? Would that all the LORD's people

---

28 | That is, sustained prophetic capacity was not essential to these elders' leadership function.

י עָלָיו: וַיִּשְׁמַע מֹשֶׁה אֶת־הָעָם בֹּכֶה לְמִשְׁפְּחֹתָיו אִישׁ לְפֶתַח אָהֳלוֹ
יא וַיִּחַר־אַף יְהוָה מְאֹד וּבְעֵינֵי מֹשֶׁה רָע: וַיֹּאמֶר מֹשֶׁה אֶל־יְהוָה לָמָה
הֲרֵעֹתָ לְעַבְדֶּךָ וְלָמָּה לֹא־מָצָתִי חֵן בְּעֵינֶיךָ לָשׂוּם אֶת־מַשָּׂא כָּל־הָעָם
יב הַזֶּה עָלָי: הֶאָנֹכִי הָרִיתִי אֵת כָּל־הָעָם הַזֶּה אִם־אָנֹכִי יְלִדְתִּיהוּ כִּי־
תֹאמַר אֵלַי שָׂאֵהוּ בְחֵיקֶךָ כַּאֲשֶׁר יִשָּׂא הָאֹמֵן אֶת־הַיֹּנֵק עַל הָאֲדָמָה
יג אֲשֶׁר נִשְׁבַּעְתָּ לַאֲבֹתָיו: מֵאַיִן לִי בָּשָׂר לָתֵת לְכָל־הָעָם הַזֶּה כִּי־יִבְכּוּ
יד עָלַי לֵאמֹר תְּנָה־לָּנוּ בָשָׂר וְנֹאכֵלָה: לֹא־אוּכַל אָנֹכִי לְבַדִּי לָשֵׂאת
טו אֶת־כָּל־הָעָם הַזֶּה כִּי כָבֵד מִמֶּנִּי: וְאִם־כָּכָה ׀ אַתְּ־עֹשֶׂה לִּי הָרְגֵנִי נָא
הָרֹג אִם־מָצָאתִי חֵן בְּעֵינֶיךָ וְאַל־אֶרְאֶה בְּרָעָתִי:
טז וַיֹּאמֶר יְהוָה אֶל־מֹשֶׁה אֶסְפָה־לִּי שִׁבְעִים אִישׁ מִזִּקְנֵי יִשְׂרָאֵל אֲשֶׁר י
יָדַעְתָּ כִּי־הֵם זִקְנֵי הָעָם וְשֹׁטְרָיו וְלָקַחְתָּ אֹתָם אֶל־אֹהֶל מוֹעֵד וְהִתְיַצְּבוּ
יז שָׁם עִמָּךְ: וְיָרַדְתִּי וְדִבַּרְתִּי עִמְּךָ שָׁם וְאָצַלְתִּי מִן־הָרוּחַ אֲשֶׁר עָלֶיךָ
וְשַׂמְתִּי עֲלֵיהֶם וְנָשְׂאוּ אִתְּךָ בְּמַשָּׂא הָעָם וְלֹא־תִשָּׂא אַתָּה לְבַדֶּךָ:
יח וְאֶל־הָעָם תֹּאמַר הִתְקַדְּשׁוּ לְמָחָר וַאֲכַלְתֶּם בָּשָׂר כִּי בְּכִיתֶם בְּאָזְנֵי
יְהוָה לֵאמֹר מִי יַאֲכִלֵנוּ בָּשָׂר כִּי־טוֹב לָנוּ בְּמִצְרָיִם וְנָתַן יְהוָה לָכֶם
יט בָּשָׂר וַאֲכַלְתֶּם: לֹא יוֹם אֶחָד תֹּאכְלוּן וְלֹא יוֹמָיִם וְלֹא ׀ חֲמִשָּׁה יָמִים
כ וְלֹא עֲשָׂרָה יָמִים וְלֹא עֶשְׂרִים יוֹם: עַד ׀ חֹדֶשׁ יָמִים עַד אֲשֶׁר־יֵצֵא
מֵאַפְּכֶם וְהָיָה לָכֶם לְזָרָא יַעַן כִּי־מְאַסְתֶּם אֶת־יְהוָה אֲשֶׁר בְּקִרְבְּכֶם
כא וַתִּבְכּוּ לְפָנָיו לֵאמֹר לָמָּה זֶּה יָצָאנוּ מִמִּצְרָיִם: וַיֹּאמֶר מֹשֶׁה שֵׁשׁ־
מֵאוֹת אֶלֶף רַגְלִי הָעָם אֲשֶׁר אָנֹכִי בְּקִרְבּוֹ וְאַתָּה אָמַרְתָּ בָּשָׂר אֶתֵּן
כב לָהֶם וְאָכְלוּ חֹדֶשׁ יָמִים: הֲצֹאן וּבָקָר יִשָּׁחֵט לָהֶם וּמָצָא לָהֶם אִם
אֶת־כָּל־דְּגֵי הַיָּם יֵאָסֵף לָהֶם וּמָצָא לָהֶם:
כג וַיֹּאמֶר יְהוָה אֶל־מֹשֶׁה הֲיַד יְהוָה תִּקְצָר עַתָּה תִרְאֶה הֲיִקְרְךָ דְבָרִי יא
כד אִם־לֹא: וַיֵּצֵא מֹשֶׁה וַיְדַבֵּר אֶל־הָעָם אֵת דִּבְרֵי יְהוָה וַיֶּאֱסֹף שִׁבְעִים
כה אִישׁ מִזִּקְנֵי הָעָם וַיַּעֲמֵד אֹתָם סְבִיבֹת הָאֹהֶל: וַיֵּרֶד יְהוָה ׀ בֶּעָנָן וַיְדַבֵּר
אֵלָיו וַיָּאצֶל מִן־הָרוּחַ אֲשֶׁר עָלָיו וַיִּתֵּן עַל־שִׁבְעִים אִישׁ הַזְּקֵנִים
כו וַיְהִי כְּנוֹחַ עֲלֵיהֶם הָרוּחַ וַיִּתְנַבְּאוּ וְלֹא יָסָפוּ: וַיִּשָּׁאֲרוּ שְׁנֵי־אֲנָשִׁים ׀
בַּמַּחֲנֶה שֵׁם הָאֶחָד ׀ אֶלְדָּד וְשֵׁם הַשֵּׁנִי מֵידָד וַתָּנַח עֲלֵהֶם הָרוּחַ
כז וְהֵמָּה בַּכְּתֻבִים וְלֹא יָצְאוּ הָאֹהֱלָה וַיִּתְנַבְּאוּ בַּמַּחֲנֶה: וַיָּרָץ הַנַּעַר
כח וַיַּגֵּד לְמֹשֶׁה וַיֹּאמַר אֶלְדָּד וּמֵידָד מִתְנַבְּאִים בַּמַּחֲנֶה: וַיַּעַן יְהוֹשֻׁעַ
כט בִּן־נוּן מְשָׁרֵת מֹשֶׁה מִבְּחֻרָיו וַיֹּאמַר אֲדֹנִי מֹשֶׁה כְּלָאֵם: וַיֹּאמֶר לוֹ
מֹשֶׁה הַמְקַנֵּא אַתָּה לִי וּמִי יִתֵּן כָּל־עַם יְהוָה נְבִיאִים כִּי־יִתֵּן יְהוָה

30 were prophets, that the LORD would put His spirit upon them all!" And
31 Moshe returned to the camp together with the elders of Israel. Then a wind
from the LORD sprang up, sweeping quail in from the sea and letting them fall
near the camp, about a day's journey on one side and a day's journey on the
32 other, around the camp and piled up two cubits above the ground. All that day,
all night, and all the next day, the people went out and gathered quail. Even
those who gathered least gathered ten omer,[29] and they spread them out all
33 around the camp. While the meat was still between their teeth, before it was
eaten, the LORD's anger blazed against the people, and the LORD struck the
34 people with a very great plague. The place was named Kivrot HaTaava, because
35 there they buried the people who had craved.[30] And from Kivrot HaTaava the
people journeyed to Ḥatzerot, and at Ḥatzerot they stayed.
12 1 Once, Miriam and Aharon spoke against Moshe because of his Kushite wife;
2 he had married a Kushite woman. "Has the LORD spoken only through
Moshe?" they said. "Has He not spoken through us also?" The LORD heard
3 this. Now the man Moshe was very humble, more so than any other man
4 on earth. And suddenly the LORD said to Moshe and Aharon and
Miriam: "All three of you, come out to the Tent of Meeting." So the three of
5 them went. The LORD came down in a column of cloud, and, standing at the
entrance to the Tent, called, "Aharon and Miriam." The two of them came
6 forward. The LORD said: "Now listen to My words: When there is a prophet
among you, I make Myself known to him in a vision, I speak to him in a
7 8 dream. Not so with Moshe My servant: he is trusted in all My House: With
him I speak mouth to mouth, clearly, never in riddles. He sees the LORD's
9 form. Why, then, are you not afraid to speak against My servant Moshe?" The
10 LORD's anger flared against them; and He departed. When the cloud withdrew from the Tent, Miriam had been struck with an impure blight, white as
11 snow. Aharon turned toward Miriam and saw that she was blighted. Aharon
said to Moshe, "Please, my lord, do not hold against us the sin that we have
12 foolishly committed! Let her not be like a stillborn child emerging from its
13 mother's womb with half its flesh eaten away!"[31] And Moshe cried out to the
LORD, "Please, God, heal her now!"
14 But the LORD said to Moshe: "If her father had spat in her face, would she
not be shamed for seven days? Let her be shut out of the camp for seven days;
15 after that, she may be brought back." So Miriam was shut out of the camp for
seven days, and the people did not move on until Miriam was brought back.
16 After that, the people set out from Ḥatzerot and encamped in the Wilderness
of Paran.
13 1 2 Then the LORD spoke to Moshe: "Send out men to scout the land of Canaan, SHELAḤ
which I am going to give to the Israelites, one man from each of their ances-
3 tral tribes, each a leader among them." So Moshe sent them at the LORD's
command from the Wilderness of Paran. They were all leading men among

29 | An omer is a solid measure equal to one-tenth of an ephah; see 5:15 and note.
30 | The name literally means "graves of craving."
31 | Apparently a description of the disease that afflicted Miriam.

ל לא אֶת־רוּחוֹ עֲלֵיהֶם׃ וַיֵּאָסֵף מֹשֶׁה אֶל־הַמַּחֲנֶה הוּא וְזִקְנֵי יִשְׂרָאֵל׃ וְרוּחַ שביעי
נָסַע ׀ מֵאֵת יהוה וַיָּגָז שַׂלְוִים מִן־הַיָּם וַיִּטֹּשׁ עַל־הַמַּחֲנֶה כְּדֶרֶךְ יוֹם
לב כֹּה וּכְדֶרֶךְ יוֹם כֹּה סְבִיבוֹת הַמַּחֲנֶה וּכְאַמָּתַיִם עַל־פְּנֵי הָאָרֶץ׃ וַיָּקָם
הָעָם כָּל־הַיּוֹם הַהוּא וְכָל־הַלַּיְלָה וְכֹל ׀ יוֹם הַמָּחֳרָת וַיַּאַסְפוּ אֶת־
הַשְּׂלָו הַמַּמְעִיט אָסַף עֲשָׂרָה חֳמָרִים וַיִּשְׁטְחוּ לָהֶם שָׁטוֹחַ סְבִיבוֹת
לג הַמַּחֲנֶה׃ הַבָּשָׂר עוֹדֶנּוּ בֵּין שִׁנֵּיהֶם טֶרֶם יִכָּרֵת וְאַף יהוה חָרָה בָעָם וַיַּךְ
לד יהוה בָּעָם מַכָּה רַבָּה מְאֹד׃ וַיִּקְרָא אֶת־שֵׁם־הַמָּקוֹם הַהוּא קִבְרוֹת
לה הַתַּאֲוָה כִּי־שָׁם קָבְרוּ אֶת־הָעָם הַמִּתְאַוִּים׃ מִקִּבְרוֹת הַתַּאֲוָה נָסְעוּ
הָעָם חֲצֵרוֹת וַיִּהְיוּ בַּחֲצֵרוֹת׃
יב א וַתְּדַבֵּר מִרְיָם וְאַהֲרֹן בְּמֹשֶׁה עַל־אֹדוֹת הָאִשָּׁה הַכֻּשִׁית אֲשֶׁר לָקָח
ב כִּי־אִשָּׁה כֻשִׁית לָקָח׃ וַיֹּאמְרוּ הֲרַק אַךְ־בְּמֹשֶׁה דִּבֶּר יהוה הֲלֹא גַּם־
ג בָּנוּ דִבֵּר וַיִּשְׁמַע יהוה׃ וְהָאִישׁ מֹשֶׁה עָנָו מְאֹד מִכֹּל הָאָדָם אֲשֶׁר
ד עַל־פְּנֵי הָאֲדָמָה׃ וַיֹּאמֶר יהוה פִּתְאֹם אֶל־מֹשֶׁה וְאֶל־
אַהֲרֹן וְאֶל־מִרְיָם צְאוּ שְׁלָשְׁתְּכֶם אֶל־אֹהֶל מוֹעֵד וַיֵּצְאוּ שְׁלָשְׁתָּם׃
ה וַיֵּרֶד יהוה בְּעַמּוּד עָנָן וַיַּעֲמֹד פֶּתַח הָאֹהֶל וַיִּקְרָא אַהֲרֹן וּמִרְיָם וַיֵּצְאוּ
ו שְׁנֵיהֶם׃ וַיֹּאמֶר שִׁמְעוּ־נָא דְבָרָי אִם־יִהְיֶה נְבִיאֲכֶם יהוה בַּמַּרְאָה
ז אֵלָיו אֶתְוַדָּע בַּחֲלוֹם אֲדַבֶּר־בּוֹ׃ לֹא־כֵן עַבְדִּי מֹשֶׁה בְּכָל־בֵּיתִי נֶאֱמָן
ח הוּא׃ פֶּה אֶל־פֶּה אֲדַבֶּר־בּוֹ וּמַרְאֶה וְלֹא בְחִידֹת וּתְמֻנַת יהוה יַבִּיט
ט וּמַדּוּעַ לֹא יְרֵאתֶם לְדַבֵּר בְּעַבְדִּי בְמֹשֶׁה׃ וַיִּחַר־אַף יהוה בָּם וַיֵּלַךְ׃
י וְהֶעָנָן סָר מֵעַל הָאֹהֶל וְהִנֵּה מִרְיָם מְצֹרַעַת כַּשָּׁלֶג וַיִּפֶן אַהֲרֹן אֶל־
יא מִרְיָם וְהִנֵּה מְצֹרָעַת׃ וַיֹּאמֶר אַהֲרֹן אֶל־מֹשֶׁה בִּי אֲדֹנִי אַל־נָא תָשֵׁת
יב עָלֵינוּ חַטָּאת אֲשֶׁר נוֹאַלְנוּ וַאֲשֶׁר חָטָאנוּ׃ אַל־נָא תְהִי כַּמֵּת אֲשֶׁר
יג בְּצֵאתוֹ מֵרֶחֶם אִמּוֹ וַיֵּאָכֵל חֲצִי בְשָׂרוֹ׃ וַיִּצְעַק מֹשֶׁה אֶל־יהוה לֵאמֹר
אֵל נָא רְפָא נָא לָהּ׃
יד וַיֹּאמֶר יהוה אֶל־מֹשֶׁה וְאָבִיהָ יָרֹק יָרַק בְּפָנֶיהָ הֲלֹא תִכָּלֵם שִׁבְעַת מפטיר
טו יָמִים תִּסָּגֵר שִׁבְעַת יָמִים מִחוּץ לַמַּחֲנֶה וְאַחַר תֵּאָסֵף׃ וַתִּסָּגֵר מִרְיָם
טז מִחוּץ לַמַּחֲנֶה שִׁבְעַת יָמִים וְהָעָם לֹא נָסַע עַד הֵאָסֵף מִרְיָם׃ וְאַחַר
נָסְעוּ הָעָם מֵחֲצֵרוֹת וַיַּחֲנוּ בְּמִדְבַּר פָּארָן׃
יג א ב וַיְדַבֵּר יהוה אֶל־מֹשֶׁה לֵּאמֹר׃ שְׁלַח־לְךָ אֲנָשִׁים וְיָתֻרוּ אֶת־אֶרֶץ יב שלח
כְּנַעַן אֲשֶׁר־אֲנִי נֹתֵן לִבְנֵי יִשְׂרָאֵל אִישׁ אֶחָד אִישׁ אֶחָד לְמַטֵּה אֲבֹתָיו
ג תִּשְׁלָחוּ כֹּל נָשִׂיא בָהֶם׃ וַיִּשְׁלַח אֹתָם מֹשֶׁה מִמִּדְבַּר פָּארָן עַל־פִּי

4 the Israelites. These were their names: from the tribe of Reuven, Shamua
5 6 son of Zakur; from the tribe of Shimon, Shafat son of Ḥori; from the tribe of
7 8 Yehuda, Kalev son of Yefuneh; from the tribe of Yissakhar, Yigal son of Yosef;
9 from the tribe of Efrayim, Hoshe'a son of Nun; from the tribe of Binyamin,
10 11 Palti son of Rafu; from the tribe of Zevulun, Gadiel son of Sodi; from the
12 tribe of Yosef, from the tribe of Menashe, Gadi son of Susi; from the tribe
13 of Dan, Amiel son of Gemali; from the tribe of Asher, Setur son of Mikhael;
14 15 from the tribe of Naftali, Naḥbi son of Vofsi; from the tribe of Gad, Geuel son
16 of Makhi. These were the names of the men Moshe sent to scout the land.
17 And Moshe named Hoshe'a son of Nun Yehoshua. When Moshe sent them
to scout the land of Canaan, he told them, "Ascend there into the Negev;
18 then go up into the hill country. See what the land is like. Are the people
19 who live there strong or weak, few or many? Is the land in which they live a
20 good place or bad? Are the cities in which they live open or fortified? Is the
soil rich or poor? Are there trees in it or not? Take courage and bring back
21 some of the fruit of the land" – it was the season of the first ripe grapes. So
they went up and scouted the land from the Wilderness of Tzin to Reḥov,
22 near Levo Ḥamat.[32] They went up through the Negev and came to Ḥevron,
where Aḥiman, Sheshai, and Talmai, descendants of Anak, were dwelling.
23 Ḥevron had been built seven years before the Egyptian city of Tzoan. Then
they came to the Eshkol Ravine and there they cut down a vine branch, and
on it one cluster of grapes, which they carried on a pole between two men.
24 They also took some pomegranates and figs. That place was named the Eshkol
25 Ravine, because of the cluster that the Israelites cut there.[33] They returned
26 from scouting the land when forty days had passed. As soon as they arrived
they came to Moshe and Aharon and to all the community of Israel at Kadesh
in the Wilderness of Paran, and brought their report to them and to all the
27 community, and showed them the fruit of the land. They told Moshe, "We
came to the land you sent us to, and it is indeed flowing with milk and with
28 honey, and this is its fruit. But the people who live in the land are fierce, and
the cities are fortified and very large indeed. We even saw the descendants of
29 Anak there.[34] In the Negev region, Amalek lives; the Hittites, Jebusites, and
Amorites live in the hill country, and the Canaanites live by the sea and by
30 the Jordan." But Kalev silenced the people around Moshe and said, "Let us
31 go up at once and take possession of it, for certainly we are able." The men
who had gone up with him said, "We cannot go up against those people, for
32 they are stronger than us." So they gave the Israelites an adverse report of
the land that they had scouted: "The land which we have journeyed through
and scouted is a land that consumes its inhabitants; the people we saw in it
33 were tall and broad to a man. There we saw the Nefilim – the descendants of
Anak are from the Nefilim.[35] We looked to our own eyes like grasshoppers,

32 | The southern and northern reaches of Canaan, respectively; cf. chapter 34.

33 | *Eshkol* denotes a cluster of fruit.

34 | The Anakites were of giant stature; see verse 33.

35 | See Genesis 6:4.

ד יהוה כֻּלָּם אֲנָשִׁים רָאשֵׁי בְנֵי־יִשְׂרָאֵל הֵמָּה: וְאֵלֶּה שְׁמוֹתָם לְמַטֵּה
ה ו רְאוּבֵן שַׁמּוּעַ בֶּן־זַכּוּר: לְמַטֵּה שִׁמְעוֹן שָׁפָט בֶּן־חוֹרִי: לְמַטֵּה יְהוּדָה
ז ח כָּלֵב בֶּן־יְפֻנֶּה: לְמַטֵּה יִשָּׂשכָר יִגְאָל בֶּן־יוֹסֵף: לְמַטֵּה אֶפְרָיִם הוֹשֵׁעַ
ט י בִּן־נוּן: לְמַטֵּה בִנְיָמִן פַּלְטִי בֶּן־רָפוּא: לְמַטֵּה זְבוּלֻן גַּדִּיאֵל בֶּן־סוֹדִי:
יא יב לְמַטֵּה יוֹסֵף לְמַטֵּה מְנַשֶּׁה גַּדִּי בֶּן־סוּסִי: לְמַטֵּה דָן עַמִּיאֵל בֶּן־גְּמַלִּי:
יג יד טו לְמַטֵּה אָשֵׁר סְתוּר בֶּן־מִיכָאֵל: לְמַטֵּה נַפְתָּלִי נַחְבִּי בֶּן־וָפְסִי: לְמַטֵּה
טז גָד גְּאוּאֵל בֶּן־מָכִי: אֵלֶּה שְׁמוֹת הָאֲנָשִׁים אֲשֶׁר־שָׁלַח מֹשֶׁה לָתוּר
יז אֶת־הָאָרֶץ וַיִּקְרָא מֹשֶׁה לְהוֹשֵׁעַ בִּן־נוּן יְהוֹשֻׁעַ: וַיִּשְׁלַח אֹתָם מֹשֶׁה
לָתוּר אֶת־אֶרֶץ כְּנָעַן וַיֹּאמֶר אֲלֵהֶם עֲלוּ זֶה בַּנֶּגֶב וַעֲלִיתֶם אֶת־הָהָר:
יח וּרְאִיתֶם אֶת־הָאָרֶץ מַה־הִוא וְאֶת־הָעָם הַיֹּשֵׁב עָלֶיהָ הֶחָזָק הוּא
יט הֲרָפֶה הַמְעַט הוּא אִם־רָב: וּמָה הָאָרֶץ אֲשֶׁר־הוּא יֹשֵׁב בָּהּ הֲטוֹבָה
הִוא אִם־רָעָה וּמָה הֶעָרִים אֲשֶׁר־הוּא יוֹשֵׁב בָּהֵנָּה הַבְּמַחֲנִים אִם
כ בְּמִבְצָרִים: וּמָה הָאָרֶץ הַשְּׁמֵנָה הִוא אִם־רָזָה הֲיֵשׁ־בָּהּ עֵץ אִם־אַיִן
כא וְהִתְחַזַּקְתֶּם וּלְקַחְתֶּם מִפְּרִי הָאָרֶץ וְהַיָּמִים יְמֵי בִּכּוּרֵי עֲנָבִים: וַיַּעֲלוּ שני
כב וַיָּתֻרוּ אֶת־הָאָרֶץ מִמִּדְבַּר־צִן עַד־רְחֹב לְבֹא חֲמָת: וַיַּעֲלוּ בַנֶּגֶב
וַיָּבֹא עַד־חֶבְרוֹן וְשָׁם אֲחִימַן שֵׁשַׁי וְתַלְמַי יְלִידֵי הָעֲנָק וְחֶבְרוֹן שֶׁבַע
כג שָׁנִים נִבְנְתָה לִפְנֵי צֹעַן מִצְרָיִם: וַיָּבֹאוּ עַד־נַחַל אֶשְׁכֹּל וַיִּכְרְתוּ מִשָּׁם
זְמוֹרָה וְאֶשְׁכּוֹל עֲנָבִים אֶחָד וַיִּשָּׂאֻהוּ בַמּוֹט בִּשְׁנָיִם וּמִן־הָרִמֹּנִים
כד וּמִן־הַתְּאֵנִים: לַמָּקוֹם הַהוּא קָרָא נַחַל אֶשְׁכּוֹל עַל אֹדוֹת הָאֶשְׁכּוֹל
כה אֲשֶׁר־כָּרְתוּ מִשָּׁם בְּנֵי יִשְׂרָאֵל: וַיָּשֻׁבוּ מִתּוּר הָאָרֶץ מִקֵּץ אַרְבָּעִים
כו יוֹם: וַיֵּלְכוּ וַיָּבֹאוּ אֶל־מֹשֶׁה וְאֶל־אַהֲרֹן וְאֶל־כָּל־עֲדַת בְּנֵי־יִשְׂרָאֵל
אֶל־מִדְבַּר פָּארָן קָדֵשָׁה וַיָּשִׁיבוּ אֹתָם דָּבָר וְאֶת־כָּל־הָעֵדָה וַיַּרְאוּם
כז אֶת־פְּרִי הָאָרֶץ: וַיְסַפְּרוּ־לוֹ וַיֹּאמְרוּ בָּאנוּ אֶל־הָאָרֶץ אֲשֶׁר שְׁלַחְתָּנוּ
כח וְגַם זָבַת חָלָב וּדְבַשׁ הִוא וְזֶה־פִּרְיָהּ: אֶפֶס כִּי־עַז הָעָם הַיֹּשֵׁב בָּאָרֶץ
כט וְהֶעָרִים בְּצֻרוֹת גְּדֹלֹת מְאֹד וְגַם־יְלִדֵי הָעֲנָק רָאִינוּ שָׁם: עֲמָלֵק יוֹשֵׁב
בְּאֶרֶץ הַנֶּגֶב וְהַחִתִּי וְהַיְבוּסִי וְהָאֱמֹרִי יוֹשֵׁב בָּהָר וְהַכְּנַעֲנִי יֹשֵׁב עַל־
ל הַיָּם וְעַל יַד הַיַּרְדֵּן: וַיַּהַס כָּלֵב אֶת־הָעָם אֶל־מֹשֶׁה וַיֹּאמֶר עָלֹה נַעֲלֶה
לא וְיָרַשְׁנוּ אֹתָהּ כִּי־יָכוֹל נוּכַל לָהּ: וְהָאֲנָשִׁים אֲשֶׁר עָלוּ עִמּוֹ אָמְרוּ לֹא
לב נוּכַל לַעֲלוֹת אֶל־הָעָם כִּי־חָזָק הוּא מִמֶּנּוּ: וַיֹּצִיאוּ דִּבַּת הָאָרֶץ אֲשֶׁר
תָּרוּ אֹתָהּ אֶל־בְּנֵי יִשְׂרָאֵל לֵאמֹר הָאָרֶץ אֲשֶׁר עָבַרְנוּ בָהּ לָתוּר אֹתָהּ
אֶרֶץ אֹכֶלֶת יוֹשְׁבֶיהָ הִוא וְכָל־הָעָם אֲשֶׁר־רָאִינוּ בְתוֹכָהּ אַנְשֵׁי מִדּוֹת:
לג וְשָׁם רָאִינוּ אֶת־הַנְּפִילִים בְּנֵי עֲנָק מִן־הַנְּפִלִים וַנְּהִי בְעֵינֵינוּ כַּחֲגָבִים

14 1 and so we were in theirs." All the community lifted their heads and cried
2 out – that night the people wept. And all the Israelites railed against Moshe
and Aharon; all the community said to them, "If only we had died in Egypt,
3 if only we had died in this wilderness! Why is the LORD bringing us as far
as this land only to fall by the sword? Our wives and children will be made
4 plunder. Would it not be better for us to go back to Egypt?" So they said to
5 one another, "Let us appoint a leader and go back to Egypt." Moshe and
6 Aharon fell facedown before all the assembled community of Israel. Yehoshua
son of Nun and Kalev son of Yefuneh, who were among those who scouted
7 the land, tore their clothes and said before the entire community of Israel:
8 "The land we journeyed through and scouted is a very, very good land. If the
LORD favors us, He will bring us into this land, a land flowing with milk and
9 with honey, and He will give it to us. Do not rebel against the LORD, and
do not be afraid of the people of the land, for they are no more than bread
for us. They have been stripped of their protection and the LORD is with us.
10 Do not be afraid of them!" The community, all, threatened to stone them to
death – but then the LORD's glory was revealed to all the Israelites at the Tent
of Meeting.
11 The LORD said to Moshe, "How long will these people provoke Me? How
long will they fail to have faith in Me in spite of all the signs I have performed
12 among them? I will strike them with a plague now and disinherit them, and
13 make you into a nation greater and mightier than they." But Moshe said to the
LORD, "The Egyptians will hear about it, for by Your power You brought this
14 people up from among them, and they will tell the inhabitants of this land.
They have heard that You, LORD, are among these people, that You, LORD,
are seen face-to-face, that Your cloud stands over them, that You go before
15 them in a pillar of cloud by day and in a pillar of fire by night. If You kill this
16 people like a single man, the nations that have heard of Your fame will say, 'It
was because the LORD was unable to bring this people into the land He swore
17 to them; that is why He slaughtered them in the wilderness.' So now, let my
18 LORD's power be great, as You declared when You said:[36] 'The LORD is slow
to anger and abounding in kindness, forgiving sin and rebellion, though He
does not acquit the guilty, but holds the descendants to account for the sins
of the fathers; children and grandchildren to the third and fourth generation.'
19 Please – pardon the sin of this people in Your great kindness, as You have
20 forgiven this people from the time of Egypt until now." And the LORD said,
21 "I have forgiven them at your word. Yet as surely as I live and as the LORD's
22 glory fills the whole earth, none of those who have seen My glory and the
signs I performed in Egypt and in the wilderness, and have tested Me these
23 ten times and not obeyed Me, shall see the land I swore to their fathers. None
24 of those who have provoked Me will see it. But My servant Kalev, because
he was filled with a different spirit and has followed Me wholeheartedly –
him I will bring into the land he came to, and his descendants will inherit it.

36 | See Exodus 34:6–7.

יד א וְכֵן הָיִינוּ בְּעֵינֵיהֶם: וַתִּשָּׂא כׇּל־הָעֵדָה וַיִּתְּנוּ אֶת־קוֹלָם וַיִּבְכּוּ הָעָם
ב בַּלַּיְלָה הַהוּא: וַיִּלֹּנוּ עַל־מֹשֶׁה וְעַל־אַהֲרֹן כֹּל בְּנֵי יִשְׂרָאֵל וַיֹּאמְרוּ
אֲלֵהֶם כׇּל־הָעֵדָה לוּ־מַתְנוּ בְּאֶרֶץ מִצְרַיִם אוֹ בַּמִּדְבָּר הַזֶּה לוּ־מָתְנוּ:
ג וְלָמָה יְהוָה מֵבִיא אֹתָנוּ אֶל־הָאָרֶץ הַזֹּאת לִנְפֹּל בַּחֶרֶב נָשֵׁינוּ וְטַפֵּנוּ
ד יִהְיוּ לָבַז הֲלוֹא טוֹב לָנוּ שׁוּב מִצְרָיְמָה: וַיֹּאמְרוּ אִישׁ אֶל־אָחִיו נִתְּנָה
ה רֹאשׁ וְנָשׁוּבָה מִצְרָיְמָה: וַיִּפֹּל מֹשֶׁה וְאַהֲרֹן עַל־פְּנֵיהֶם לִפְנֵי כׇּל־קְהַל
ו עֲדַת בְּנֵי יִשְׂרָאֵל: וִיהוֹשֻׁעַ בִּן־נוּן וְכָלֵב בֶּן־יְפֻנֶּה מִן־הַתָּרִים אֶת־
ז הָאָרֶץ קָרְעוּ בִּגְדֵיהֶם: וַיֹּאמְרוּ אֶל־כׇּל־עֲדַת בְּנֵי־יִשְׂרָאֵל לֵאמֹר
ח הָאָרֶץ אֲשֶׁר עָבַרְנוּ בָהּ לָתוּר אֹתָהּ טוֹבָה הָאָרֶץ מְאֹד מְאֹד: אִם־ שלישי
חָפֵץ בָּנוּ יְהוָה וְהֵבִיא אֹתָנוּ אֶל־הָאָרֶץ הַזֹּאת וּנְתָנָהּ לָנוּ אֶרֶץ אֲשֶׁר־
ט הִוא זָבַת חָלָב וּדְבָשׁ: אַךְ בַּיהוָה אַל־תִּמְרֹדוּ וְאַתֶּם אַל־תִּירְאוּ אֶת־
עַם הָאָרֶץ כִּי לַחְמֵנוּ הֵם סָר צִלָּם מֵעֲלֵיהֶם וַיהוָה אִתָּנוּ אַל־תִּירָאֻם:
י וַיֹּאמְרוּ כׇּל־הָעֵדָה לִרְגּוֹם אֹתָם בָּאֲבָנִים וּכְבוֹד יְהוָה נִרְאָה בְּאֹהֶל
מוֹעֵד אֶל־כׇּל־בְּנֵי יִשְׂרָאֵל:

יא וַיֹּאמֶר יְהוָה אֶל־מֹשֶׁה עַד־אָנָה יְנַאֲצֻנִי הָעָם הַזֶּה וְעַד־אָנָה לֹא־ יג
יב יַאֲמִינוּ בִי בְּכֹל הָאֹתוֹת אֲשֶׁר עָשִׂיתִי בְּקִרְבּוֹ: אַכֶּנּוּ בַדֶּבֶר וְאוֹרִשֶׁנּוּ
יג וְאֶעֱשֶׂה אֹתְךָ לְגוֹי־גָּדוֹל וְעָצוּם מִמֶּנּוּ: וַיֹּאמֶר מֹשֶׁה אֶל־יְהוָה וְשָׁמְעוּ
יד מִצְרַיִם כִּי־הֶעֱלִיתָ בְכֹחֲךָ אֶת־הָעָם הַזֶּה מִקִּרְבּוֹ: וְאָמְרוּ אֶל־יוֹשֵׁב
הָאָרֶץ הַזֹּאת שָׁמְעוּ כִּי־אַתָּה יְהוָה בְּקֶרֶב הָעָם הַזֶּה אֲשֶׁר־עַיִן בְּעַיִן
נִרְאָה ׀ אַתָּה יְהוָה וַעֲנָנְךָ עֹמֵד עֲלֵהֶם וּבְעַמֻּד עָנָן אַתָּה הֹלֵךְ לִפְנֵיהֶם
טו יוֹמָם וּבְעַמּוּד אֵשׁ לָיְלָה: וְהֵמַתָּה אֶת־הָעָם הַזֶּה כְּאִישׁ אֶחָד וְאָמְרוּ
טז הַגּוֹיִם אֲשֶׁר־שָׁמְעוּ אֶת־שִׁמְעֲךָ לֵאמֹר: מִבִּלְתִּי יְכֹלֶת יְהוָה לְהָבִיא
יז אֶת־הָעָם הַזֶּה אֶל־הָאָרֶץ אֲשֶׁר־נִשְׁבַּע לָהֶם וַיִּשְׁחָטֵם בַּמִּדְבָּר: וְעַתָּה
יח יִגְדַּל־נָא כֹּחַ אֲדֹנָי כַּאֲשֶׁר דִּבַּרְתָּ לֵאמֹר: יְהוָה אֶרֶךְ אַפַּיִם וְרַב־חֶסֶד
נֹשֵׂא עָוֺן וָפָשַׁע וְנַקֵּה לֹא יְנַקֶּה פֹּקֵד עֲוֺן אָבוֹת עַל־בָּנִים עַל־שִׁלֵּשִׁים
יט וְעַל־רִבֵּעִים: סְלַח־נָא לַעֲוֺן הָעָם הַזֶּה כְּגֹדֶל חַסְדֶּךָ וְכַאֲשֶׁר נָשָׂאתָה
כ כא לָעָם הַזֶּה מִמִּצְרַיִם וְעַד־הֵנָּה: וַיֹּאמֶר יְהוָה סָלַחְתִּי כִּדְבָרֶךָ: וְאוּלָם
כב חַי־אָנִי וְיִמָּלֵא כְבוֹד־יְהוָה אֶת־כׇּל־הָאָרֶץ: כִּי כׇל־הָאֲנָשִׁים הָרֹאִים
אֶת־כְּבֹדִי וְאֶת־אֹתֹתַי אֲשֶׁר־עָשִׂיתִי בְמִצְרַיִם וּבַמִּדְבָּר וַיְנַסּוּ אֹתִי
כג זֶה עֶשֶׂר פְּעָמִים וְלֹא שָׁמְעוּ בְּקוֹלִי: אִם־יִרְאוּ אֶת־הָאָרֶץ אֲשֶׁר
כד נִשְׁבַּעְתִּי לַאֲבֹתָם וְכׇל־מְנַאֲצַי לֹא יִרְאוּהָ: וְעַבְדִּי כָלֵב עֵקֶב הָיְתָה
רוּחַ אַחֶרֶת עִמּוֹ וַיְמַלֵּא אַחֲרָי וַהֲבִיאֹתִיו אֶל־הָאָרֶץ אֲשֶׁר־בָּא שָׁמָּה

25 The Amalekites and Canaanites are living in the valleys; so turn tomorrow
and head for the wilderness by way of the Sea of Reeds."[37]
26 27 Then the LORD spoke to Moshe and Aharon: "How long shall this wicked
community keep railing against Me? I have heard the Israelites' complaints
28 with which they rail against Me. Tell them: 'As surely as I live,' says the LORD,
29 'I will do to you the very thing I heard you say. In this wilderness your corpses
will fall, all of your number, all those listed in the census, from twenty years
30 old and upward: all those who have railed against Me. None of you will enter
the land that I promised to settle you in, except for Kalev son of Yefuneh and
31 Yehoshua son of Nun. I will bring in Your children, whom you said would
32 be taken captive, and they will know the land you rejected. But as for you,
33 your corpses will fall in this wilderness. Your children will shepherd in the
wilderness for forty years, suffering for your faithlessness until the last of your
34 corpses lies here in the wilderness. For the number of the days in which you
scouted the land, forty days, you shall bear your sins – for every day a year:
35 forty years. You will know what it is to oppose Me. I, the LORD, have spoken.'
This will I do to this entire wicked community that has gathered together
against Me. In this wilderness they shall come to their end, and there they
36 shall die." So the men Moshe sent to scout the land, and who came back and
caused all the community to rail against him by giving an adverse report
37 of the land – those men who gave the adverse report of the land died by a
38 plague before the LORD. And only Yehoshua son of Nun and Kalev son of
39 Yefuneh remained alive of all those men who went to scout the land. When
Moshe reported these words to all the Israelites, the people were overcome
40 with grief. They rose early the next morning and climbed up to the heights
of the hill country, saying, "We are ready to go up to the place that the LORD
41 spoke of; we were wrong." But Moshe said, "Why are you transgressing the
42 LORD's command? It will not work. Do not go up; the LORD is not with you.
43 Do not be struck down by your enemies. Ahead of you are the Amalekites
and Canaanites, and you will fall by the sword. Because you have turned
44 away from following the LORD, the LORD will not be with you." Defiantly,
they went up to the heights of the hill country. Neither the Ark of the LORD's
45 Covenant nor Moshe left the camp. And the Amalekites and Canaanites who
lived in that hill country came down, and fought them, and crushed them,
all the way to Ḥorma.[38]
15 1 2 The LORD spoke to Moshe: "Speak to the Israelites. Say: When you come to
3 the land that I am giving you to live in, and you present a fire offering from the
herd or from the flock for a pleasing aroma to the LORD – whether it be a burnt
offering or a sacrifice to fulfill a spoken vow, or brought as a freewill offering,
4 or a festival offering – the one who brings this offering to the LORD shall bring
with it a grain offering of a tenth of a measure[39] of fine flour mixed with a quar-

37 | That is, toward the southwest, away from the land of Israel and its hostile peoples.
38 | The name of this place literally means "destruction."
39 | That is, of an ephah. This measure is identical to an omer; see notes on 5:15 and 11:32.

כה וְהָעֲמָלֵקִי וְהַכְּנַעֲנִי יוֹשֵׁב בָּעֵמֶק מָחָר פְּנוּ וּסְעוּ לָכֶם
הַמִּדְבָּר דֶּרֶךְ יַם־סוּף:
כו כז וַיְדַבֵּר יְהוָה אֶל־מֹשֶׁה וְאֶל־אַהֲרֹן לֵאמֹר: עַד־מָתַי לָעֵדָה הָרָעָה רביעי
הַזֹּאת אֲשֶׁר הֵמָּה מַלִּינִים עָלָי אֶת־תְּלֻנּוֹת בְּנֵי יִשְׂרָאֵל אֲשֶׁר הֵמָּה
כח מַלִּינִים עָלַי שָׁמָעְתִּי: אֱמֹר אֲלֵהֶם חַי־אָנִי נְאֻם־יְהוָה אִם־לֹא כַּאֲשֶׁר
כט דִּבַּרְתֶּם בְּאָזְנָי כֵּן אֶעֱשֶׂה לָכֶם: בַּמִּדְבָּר הַזֶּה יִפְּלוּ פִגְרֵיכֶם וְכָל־
פְּקֻדֵיכֶם לְכָל־מִסְפַּרְכֶם מִבֶּן עֶשְׂרִים שָׁנָה וָמָעְלָה אֲשֶׁר הֲלִינֹתֶם עָלָי:
ל אִם־אַתֶּם תָּבֹאוּ אֶל־הָאָרֶץ אֲשֶׁר נָשָׂאתִי אֶת־יָדִי לְשַׁכֵּן אֶתְכֶם בָּהּ
לא כִּי אִם־כָּלֵב בֶּן־יְפֻנֶּה וִיהוֹשֻׁעַ בִּן־נוּן: וְטַפְּכֶם אֲשֶׁר אֲמַרְתֶּם לָבַז יִהְיֶה
לב וְהֵבֵיאתִי אֹתָם וְיָדְעוּ אֶת־הָאָרֶץ אֲשֶׁר מְאַסְתֶּם בָּהּ: וּפִגְרֵיכֶם אַתֶּם
לג יִפְּלוּ בַּמִּדְבָּר הַזֶּה: וּבְנֵיכֶם יִהְיוּ רֹעִים בַּמִּדְבָּר אַרְבָּעִים שָׁנָה וְנָשְׂאוּ
לד אֶת־זְנוּתֵיכֶם עַד־תֹּם פִּגְרֵיכֶם בַּמִּדְבָּר: בְּמִסְפַּר הַיָּמִים אֲשֶׁר־תַּרְתֶּם
אֶת־הָאָרֶץ אַרְבָּעִים יוֹם יוֹם לַשָּׁנָה יוֹם לַשָּׁנָה תִּשְׂאוּ אֶת־עֲוֹנֹתֵיכֶם
לה אַרְבָּעִים שָׁנָה וִידַעְתֶּם אֶת־תְּנוּאָתִי: אֲנִי יְהוָה דִּבַּרְתִּי אִם־לֹא ׀ זֹאת
אֶעֱשֶׂה לְכָל־הָעֵדָה הָרָעָה הַזֹּאת הַנּוֹעָדִים עָלָי בַּמִּדְבָּר הַזֶּה יִתַּמּוּ
לו וְשָׁם יָמֻתוּ: וְהָאֲנָשִׁים אֲשֶׁר־שָׁלַח מֹשֶׁה לָתוּר אֶת־הָאָרֶץ וַיָּשֻׁבוּ
לז וילונו עָלָיו אֶת־כָּל־הָעֵדָה לְהוֹצִיא דִבָּה עַל־הָאָרֶץ: וַיָּמֻתוּ הָאֲנָשִׁים וַיַּלִּינוּ
לח מוֹצִאֵי דִבַּת־הָאָרֶץ רָעָה בַּמַּגֵּפָה לִפְנֵי יְהוָה: וִיהוֹשֻׁעַ בִּן־נוּן וְכָלֵב
לט בֶּן־יְפֻנֶּה חָיוּ מִן־הָאֲנָשִׁים הָהֵם הַהֹלְכִים לָתוּר אֶת־הָאָרֶץ: וַיְדַבֵּר
מֹשֶׁה אֶת־הַדְּבָרִים הָאֵלֶּה אֶל־כָּל־בְּנֵי יִשְׂרָאֵל וַיִּתְאַבְּלוּ הָעָם מְאֹד:
מ וַיַּשְׁכִּמוּ בַבֹּקֶר וַיַּעֲלוּ אֶל־רֹאשׁ־הָהָר לֵאמֹר הִנֶּנּוּ וְעָלִינוּ אֶל־הַמָּקוֹם
מא אֲשֶׁר־אָמַר יְהוָה כִּי חָטָאנוּ: וַיֹּאמֶר מֹשֶׁה לָמָּה זֶּה אַתֶּם עֹבְרִים
מב אֶת־פִּי יְהוָה וְהִוא לֹא תִצְלָח: אַל־תַּעֲלוּ כִּי אֵין יְהוָה בְּקִרְבְּכֶם וְלֹא
מג תִּנָּגְפוּ לִפְנֵי אֹיְבֵיכֶם: כִּי הָעֲמָלֵקִי וְהַכְּנַעֲנִי שָׁם לִפְנֵיכֶם וּנְפַלְתֶּם
מד בֶּחָרֶב כִּי־עַל־כֵּן שַׁבְתֶּם מֵאַחֲרֵי יְהוָה וְלֹא־יִהְיֶה יְהוָה עִמָּכֶם: וַיַּעְפִּלוּ
לַעֲלוֹת אֶל־רֹאשׁ הָהָר וַאֲרוֹן בְּרִית־יְהוָה וּמֹשֶׁה לֹא־מָשׁוּ מִקֶּרֶב
מה הַמַּחֲנֶה: וַיֵּרֶד הָעֲמָלֵקִי וְהַכְּנַעֲנִי הַיֹּשֵׁב בָּהָר הַהוּא וַיַּכּוּם וַיַּכְּתוּם עַד־
הַחָרְמָה:
טו א ב וַיְדַבֵּר יְהוָה אֶל־מֹשֶׁה לֵּאמֹר: דַּבֵּר אֶל־בְּנֵי יִשְׂרָאֵל וְאָמַרְתָּ אֲלֵהֶם יד
ג כִּי תָבֹאוּ אֶל־אֶרֶץ מוֹשְׁבֹתֵיכֶם אֲשֶׁר אֲנִי נֹתֵן לָכֶם: וַעֲשִׂיתֶם אִשֶּׁה
לַיהוָה עֹלָה אוֹ־זֶבַח לְפַלֵּא־נֶדֶר אוֹ בִנְדָבָה אוֹ בְּמֹעֲדֵיכֶם לַעֲשׂוֹת
ד רֵיחַ נִיחֹחַ לַיהוָה מִן־הַבָּקָר אוֹ מִן־הַצֹּאן: וְהִקְרִיב הַמַּקְרִיב קָרְבָּנוֹ

5 ter of a hin[40] of oil, and with the burnt offering or the sacrifice, a quarter of a
6 hin of wine as a libation for every lamb. In the case of a ram, you shall bring a
grain offering of two-tenths of a measure of fine flour mixed with a third of a
7 hin of oil. You shall also offer a third of a hin of wine as a libation, for a pleasing
8 aroma to the LORD. If, however, you offer an animal from the herd as a burnt
offering or as a sacrifice to fulfill a spoken vow, or as a peace offering to the
9 LORD, then you shall bring with each animal a grain offering of three-tenths
10 of a measure of fine flour mixed with half a hin of oil. You shall also offer half a
11 hin of wine as a libation; it is a fire offering, a pleasing aroma to the LORD. So
12 shall it be with each ox, each ram, and with any sheep or goat. However many
13 you offer, you shall do the same for each. Every native-born person, presenting
a fire offering as a pleasing aroma to the LORD, shall perform them in this way.
14 And whensoever, through the generations, a migrant joins you or lives among
you, and he too prepares a fire offering for a pleasing aroma to the LORD, he
15 shall do just as you do. There shall be one law for the congregation: as for you,
so for any migrant. It shall be an eternal decree throughout the generations:
16 you and the migrant shall be the same before the LORD. One law and one rule
for you and for the migrant who lives among you."
17 18 The LORD spoke to Moshe: "Speak to the Israelites. Say: When you come to
19 the land to which I am bringing you, and eat the bread of the land, you shall set
20 some aside as an offering to the LORD. As the first portion of your kneading,
you shall set aside a loaf as an offering, like the offering you present from the
21 threshing floor. You shall present to the LORD an offering from the first of your
22 kneading throughout your generations. If, without intention, you
fail to perform any of these commandments that the LORD gave to Moshe,
23 anything that the LORD has commanded you through Moshe from the day
24 the LORD commanded it and onward – in all generations to come – if it is
done unintentionally by the community, the entire community must offer
one bull from the herd as a burnt offering, a pleasing aroma to the LORD,
with its prescribed grain offering and libation, and one goat as a purification
25 offering. The priest shall then make atonement for all the community of Israel
and they will be forgiven, because it was an accidental failing, and because
they brought their sacrifice, a fire offering to the LORD and the purification
26 offering for their error before the LORD. The community of Israel and the
migrants living among them will all be forgiven, because all the people acted
27 in error. If it is an individual who sins inadvertently, he shall offer a
28 year-old female goat as a purification offering. The priest shall make atonement before the LORD for the person who sinned inadvertently, to atone for
29 his sin, and he will be forgiven. There shall be one law for one who inadvertently commits a sin, whether he is a native-born Israelite or a migrant living
30 among them. However, if a person commits a sin high-handedly, whether
he is native born or a migrant, he reviles the LORD and shall be severed from
31 the people. Because he despises the LORD's word and violates His commandments, he will be severed utterly and must bear his guilt."

40 | A hin is a liquid measure equal to approximately 4 liters.

ה לַֽיהוָה מִנְחָה סֹלֶת עִשָּׂרוֹן בָּלוּל בִּרְבִעִית הַהִין שָׁמֶן: וְיַיִן לַנֶּסֶךְ
ו רְבִיעִית הַהִין תַּעֲשֶׂה עַל־הָעֹלָה אוֹ לַזָּבַח לַכֶּבֶשׂ הָאֶחָד: אוֹ לָאַיִל
ז תַּעֲשֶׂה מִנְחָה סֹלֶת שְׁנֵי עֶשְׂרֹנִים בְּלוּלָה בַשֶּׁמֶן שְׁלִשִׁית הַהִין: וְיַיִן
ח לַנֶּסֶךְ שְׁלִשִׁית הַהִין תַּקְרִיב רֵיחַ־נִיחֹחַ לַיהוָה: וְכִי־תַעֲשֶׂה בֶן־בָּקָר חמישי
ט עֹלָה אוֹ־זָבַח לְפַלֵּא־נֶדֶר אוֹ־שְׁלָמִים לַיהוָה: וְהִקְרִיב עַל־בֶּן־הַבָּקָר
י מִנְחָה סֹלֶת שְׁלֹשָׁה עֶשְׂרֹנִים בָּלוּל בַּשֶּׁמֶן חֲצִי הַהִין: וְיַיִן תַּקְרִיב לַנֶּסֶךְ
יא חֲצִי הַהִין אִשֵּׁה רֵיחַ־נִיחֹחַ לַיהוָה: כָּכָה יֵעָשֶׂה לַשּׁוֹר הָאֶחָד אוֹ לָאַיִל
יב הָאֶחָד אוֹ־לַשֶּׂה בַכְּבָשִׂים אוֹ בָעִזִּים: כַּמִּסְפָּר אֲשֶׁר תַּעֲשׂוּ כָּכָה תַּעֲשׂוּ
יג לָאֶחָד כְּמִסְפָּרָם: כָּל־הָאֶזְרָח יַעֲשֶׂה־כָּכָה אֶת־אֵלֶּה לְהַקְרִיב אִשֵּׁה
יד רֵיחַ־נִיחֹחַ לַיהוָה: וְכִי־יָגוּר אִתְּכֶם גֵּר אוֹ אֲשֶׁר־בְּתוֹכְכֶם לְדֹרֹתֵיכֶם
טו וְעָשָׂה אִשֵּׁה רֵיחַ־נִיחֹחַ לַיהוָה כַּאֲשֶׁר תַּעֲשׂוּ כֵּן יַעֲשֶׂה: הַקָּהָל חֻקָּה
אַחַת לָכֶם וְלַגֵּר הַגָּר חֻקַּת עוֹלָם לְדֹרֹתֵיכֶם כָּכֶם כַּגֵּר יִהְיֶה לִפְנֵי יְהוָה:
טז תּוֹרָה אַחַת וּמִשְׁפָּט אֶחָד יִהְיֶה לָכֶם וְלַגֵּר הַגָּר אִתְּכֶם:
יז יח וַיְדַבֵּר יְהוָה אֶל־מֹשֶׁה לֵּאמֹר: דַּבֵּר אֶל־בְּנֵי יִשְׂרָאֵל וְאָמַרְתָּ אֲלֵהֶם ששי
יט בְּבֹאֲכֶם אֶל־הָאָרֶץ אֲשֶׁר אֲנִי מֵבִיא אֶתְכֶם שָׁמָּה: וְהָיָה בַּאֲכָלְכֶם
כ מִלֶּחֶם הָאָרֶץ תָּרִימוּ תְרוּמָה לַיהוָה: רֵאשִׁית עֲרִסֹתֵכֶם חַלָּה תָּרִימוּ
כא תְרוּמָה כִּתְרוּמַת גֹּרֶן כֵּן תָּרִימוּ אֹתָהּ: מֵרֵאשִׁית עֲרִסֹתֵיכֶם תִּתְּנוּ
כב לַיהוָה תְּרוּמָה לְדֹרֹתֵיכֶם: וְכִי תִשְׁגּוּ וְלֹא תַעֲשׂוּ אֵת כָּל־
כג הַמִּצְוֹת הָאֵלֶּה אֲשֶׁר־דִּבֶּר יְהוָה אֶל־מֹשֶׁה: אֵת כָּל־אֲשֶׁר צִוָּה יְהוָה
כד אֲלֵיכֶם בְּיַד־מֹשֶׁה מִן־הַיּוֹם אֲשֶׁר צִוָּה יְהוָה וָהָלְאָה לְדֹרֹתֵיכֶם: וְהָיָה
אִם מֵעֵינֵי הָעֵדָה נֶעֶשְׂתָה לִשְׁגָגָה וְעָשׂוּ כָל־הָעֵדָה פַּר בֶּן־בָּקָר אֶחָד
לְעֹלָה לְרֵיחַ נִיחֹחַ לַיהוָה וּמִנְחָתוֹ וְנִסְכּוֹ כַּמִּשְׁפָּט וּשְׂעִיר־עִזִּים אֶחָד
כה לְחַטָּת: וְכִפֶּר הַכֹּהֵן עַל־כָּל־עֲדַת בְּנֵי יִשְׂרָאֵל וְנִסְלַח לָהֶם כִּי־שְׁגָגָה
הִוא וְהֵם הֵבִיאוּ אֶת־קָרְבָּנָם אִשֶּׁה לַיהוָה וְחַטָּאתָם לִפְנֵי יְהוָה עַל־
כו שִׁגְגָתָם: וְנִסְלַח לְכָל־עֲדַת בְּנֵי יִשְׂרָאֵל וְלַגֵּר הַגָּר בְּתוֹכָם כִּי לְכָל־
כז הָעָם בִּשְׁגָגָה: וְאִם־נֶפֶשׁ אַחַת תֶּחֱטָא בִשְׁגָגָה וְהִקְרִיבָה שביעי
כח עֵז בַּת־שְׁנָתָהּ לְחַטָּאת: וְכִפֶּר הַכֹּהֵן עַל־הַנֶּפֶשׁ הַשֹּׁגֶגֶת בְּחֶטְאָה
כט בִשְׁגָגָה לִפְנֵי יְהוָה לְכַפֵּר עָלָיו וְנִסְלַח לוֹ: הָאֶזְרָח בִּבְנֵי יִשְׂרָאֵל
ל וְלַגֵּר הַגָּר בְּתוֹכָם תּוֹרָה אַחַת יִהְיֶה לָכֶם לָעֹשֶׂה בִּשְׁגָגָה: וְהַנֶּפֶשׁ
אֲשֶׁר־תַּעֲשֶׂה ׀ בְּיָד רָמָה מִן־הָאֶזְרָח וּמִן־הַגֵּר אֶת־יְהוָה הוּא מְגַדֵּף
לא וְנִכְרְתָה הַנֶּפֶשׁ הַהִוא מִקֶּרֶב עַמָּהּ: כִּי דְבַר־יְהוָה בָּזָה וְאֶת־מִצְוָתוֹ
הֵפַר הִכָּרֵת ׀ תִּכָּרֵת הַנֶּפֶשׁ הַהִוא עֲוֺנָה בָהּ:

32 When the Israelites were in the wilderness, they encountered a man gathering
33 wood on the Sabbath. Those who found him gathering wood brought him
34 before Moshe and Aharon, and before the whole community, and he was
placed in custody, because it had not been specified what should be done to
35 him. And the Lord said to Moshe, "The man shall be put to death.
36 The whole community must stone him outside the camp." And so, as the
Lord had commanded Moshe, the whole community took him outside the
camp and stoned him to death.
37 38 The Lord said to Moshe: "Speak to the Israelites; tell them to make fringes
on the corners of their garments throughout the generations. To the fringe
39 on each corner they should attach a blue cord. And this shall be your fringe:
seeing it, you shall remember all the Lord's commands and keep them. You
40 will not then go astray, following the lusts of your heart or of your eyes. This
41 is to remind you to keep all My commands, to remain holy to your God. I
am the Lord your God, who brought you out of Egypt to be your God. I am
the Lord your God."

16 1 Koraḥ, son of Yitzhar son of Kehat son of Levi, together with Datan and KORAḤ
Aviram sons of Eliav and On son of Pelet – descendants of Reuven – took
2 two hundred fifty Israelite men, leaders of the community, chosen from the
3 assembly, men of repute, and confronted Moshe and Aharon together. They
said to them, "You have gone too far. All the community is holy, every one of
them, and the Lord is in their midst. Why then do you set yourselves above
4 5 the Lord's people?" When Moshe heard this, he fell upon his face. Then he
spoke to Koraḥ and all his company. "In the morning," he said, "the Lord will
make known who is His and who is holy, and will bring that one close to Him.
6 The one He chooses will be the one He will allow to come close. Do this: Let
7 Koraḥ and his company take censers. Tomorrow light fire in them and place
incense upon them before the Lord. The man whom the Lord chooses – he
8 is holy. It is you, sons of Levi, who have gone too far!" Moshe said to Koraḥ,
9 "Listen now, you sons of Levi. Is it not enough for you that the God of Israel
has separated you from the Israelite community, enabling you to come close
to Him, to serve in the Lord's Tabernacle, and stand in the presence of the
10 community to minister to them? He has brought you, and with you all your
11 fellow Levites, to be close to Him, and yet you seek the priesthood also? And
so you and all your company have assembled to defy the Lord. Aharon – who
12 is he that you should have grievances against him?" After this, Moshe sent
13 for Datan and Aviram, sons of Eliav. But they said, "We will not come up. Is
it not enough that you have brought us out of a land flowing with milk and
14 with honey to kill us in the desert, that you insist on lording it over us? And
more: you have not brought us to a land flowing with milk and with honey,
nor have you given us an inheritance of cropland and vineyard. Would you

לב וַיִּהְיוּ בְנֵי־יִשְׂרָאֵל בַּמִּדְבָּר וַיִּמְצְאוּ אִישׁ מְקֹשֵׁשׁ עֵצִים בְּיוֹם הַשַּׁבָּת׃
לג וַיַּקְרִיבוּ אֹתוֹ הַמֹּצְאִים אֹתוֹ מְקֹשֵׁשׁ עֵצִים אֶל־מֹשֶׁה וְאֶל־אַהֲרֹן
לד וְאֶל כָּל־הָעֵדָה׃ וַיַּנִּיחוּ אֹתוֹ בַּמִּשְׁמָר כִּי לֹא פֹרַשׁ מַה־יֵּעָשֶׂה
לה לוֹ׃ וַיֹּאמֶר יהוה אֶל־מֹשֶׁה מוֹת יוּמַת הָאִישׁ רָגוֹם אֹתוֹ
לו בָאֲבָנִים כָּל־הָעֵדָה מִחוּץ לַמַּחֲנֶה׃ וַיֹּצִיאוּ אֹתוֹ כָּל־הָעֵדָה אֶל־
מִחוּץ לַמַּחֲנֶה וַיִּרְגְּמוּ אֹתוֹ בָּאֲבָנִים וַיָּמֹת כַּאֲשֶׁר צִוָּה יהוה אֶת־
מֹשֶׁה׃
לז לח וַיֹּאמֶר יהוה אֶל־מֹשֶׁה לֵּאמֹר׃ דַּבֵּר אֶל־בְּנֵי יִשְׂרָאֵל וְאָמַרְתָּ אֲלֵהֶם מפטיר
וְעָשׂוּ לָהֶם צִיצִת עַל־כַּנְפֵי בִגְדֵיהֶם לְדֹרֹתָם וְנָתְנוּ עַל־צִיצִת הַכָּנָף
לט פְּתִיל תְּכֵלֶת׃ וְהָיָה לָכֶם לְצִיצִת וּרְאִיתֶם אֹתוֹ וּזְכַרְתֶּם אֶת־כָּל־מִצְוֹת
יהוה וַעֲשִׂיתֶם אֹתָם וְלֹא תָתֻרוּ אַחֲרֵי לְבַבְכֶם וְאַחֲרֵי עֵינֵיכֶם אֲשֶׁר־
מ אַתֶּם זֹנִים אַחֲרֵיהֶם׃ לְמַעַן תִּזְכְּרוּ וַעֲשִׂיתֶם אֶת־כָּל־מִצְוֹתָי וִהְיִיתֶם
מא קְדֹשִׁים לֵאלֹהֵיכֶם׃ אֲנִי יהוה אֱלֹהֵיכֶם אֲשֶׁר הוֹצֵאתִי אֶתְכֶם מֵאֶרֶץ
מִצְרַיִם לִהְיוֹת לָכֶם לֵאלֹהִים אֲנִי יהוה אֱלֹהֵיכֶם׃

טז א וַיִּקַּח קֹרַח בֶּן־יִצְהָר בֶּן־קְהָת בֶּן־לֵוִי וְדָתָן וַאֲבִירָם בְּנֵי אֱלִיאָב וְאוֹן טו קרח
ב בֶּן־פֶּלֶת בְּנֵי רְאוּבֵן׃ וַיָּקֻמוּ לִפְנֵי מֹשֶׁה וַאֲנָשִׁים מִבְּנֵי־יִשְׂרָאֵל חֲמִשִּׁים
ג וּמָאתָיִם נְשִׂיאֵי עֵדָה קְרִאֵי מוֹעֵד אַנְשֵׁי־שֵׁם׃ וַיִּקָּהֲלוּ עַל־מֹשֶׁה וְעַל־
אַהֲרֹן וַיֹּאמְרוּ אֲלֵהֶם רַב־לָכֶם כִּי כָל־הָעֵדָה כֻּלָּם קְדֹשִׁים וּבְתוֹכָם
ד יהוה וּמַדּוּעַ תִּתְנַשְּׂאוּ עַל־קְהַל יהוה׃ וַיִּשְׁמַע מֹשֶׁה וַיִּפֹּל עַל־פָּנָיו׃
ה וַיְדַבֵּר אֶל־קֹרַח וְאֶל־כָּל־עֲדָתוֹ לֵאמֹר בֹּקֶר וְיֹדַע יהוה אֶת־אֲשֶׁר־לוֹ
ו וְאֶת־הַקָּדוֹשׁ וְהִקְרִיב אֵלָיו וְאֵת אֲשֶׁר יִבְחַר־בּוֹ יַקְרִיב אֵלָיו׃ זֹאת עֲשׂוּ
ז קְחוּ־לָכֶם מַחְתּוֹת קֹרַח וְכָל־עֲדָתוֹ׃ וּתְנוּ־בָהֵן ׀ אֵשׁ וְשִׂימוּ עֲלֵיהֶן ׀
קְטֹרֶת לִפְנֵי יהוה מָחָר וְהָיָה הָאִישׁ אֲשֶׁר־יִבְחַר יהוה הוּא הַקָּדוֹשׁ
ח ט רַב־לָכֶם בְּנֵי לֵוִי׃ וַיֹּאמֶר מֹשֶׁה אֶל־קֹרַח שִׁמְעוּ־נָא בְּנֵי לֵוִי׃ הַמְעַט
מִכֶּם כִּי־הִבְדִּיל אֱלֹהֵי יִשְׂרָאֵל אֶתְכֶם מֵעֲדַת יִשְׂרָאֵל לְהַקְרִיב אֶתְכֶם
אֵלָיו לַעֲבֹד אֶת־עֲבֹדַת מִשְׁכַּן יהוה וְלַעֲמֹד לִפְנֵי הָעֵדָה לְשָׁרְתָם׃
י יא וַיַּקְרֵב אֹתְךָ וְאֶת־כָּל־אַחֶיךָ בְנֵי־לֵוִי אִתָּךְ וּבִקַּשְׁתֶּם גַּם־כְּהֻנָּה׃ לָכֵן
אַתָּה וְכָל־עֲדָתְךָ הַנֹּעָדִים עַל־יהוה וְאַהֲרֹן מַה־הוּא כִּי תלונו עָלָיו׃ תַּלִּינוּ
יב וַיִּשְׁלַח מֹשֶׁה לִקְרֹא לְדָתָן וְלַאֲבִירָם בְּנֵי אֱלִיאָב וַיֹּאמְרוּ לֹא נַעֲלֶה׃
יג הַמְעַט כִּי הֶעֱלִיתָנוּ מֵאֶרֶץ זָבַת חָלָב וּדְבַשׁ לַהֲמִיתֵנוּ בַּמִּדְבָּר כִּי־
יד תִשְׂתָּרֵר עָלֵינוּ גַּם־הִשְׂתָּרֵר׃ אַף לֹא אֶל־אֶרֶץ זָבַת חָלָב וּדְבַשׁ שני
הֲבִיאֹתָנוּ וַתִּתֶּן־לָנוּ נַחֲלַת שָׂדֶה וָכָרֶם הַעֵינֵי הָאֲנָשִׁים הָהֵם תְּנַקֵּר

15 pull out these people's eyes?! We will not come up!" Moshe became very
angry and said to the LORD, "Pay no attention to their offering. I have not
taken a single donkey from them, nor have I wronged any one of them."
16 Moshe said to Koraḥ, "You and your entire company shall appear before the
17 LORD tomorrow: you, they, and Aharon. Each one shall take his censer, place
incense upon it, and present it before the LORD, each holding his censer, two
18 hundred fifty censers in all, and you and Aharon likewise with yours." Each
took his censer, placed fire in it, put incense upon it, and stood at the entrance
19 to the Tent of Meeting, as did Moshe and Aharon. Koraḥ gathered all his
company against them to the entrance to the Tent of Meeting. Then the glory
20 of the LORD was revealed to the entire community. The LORD spoke
21 to Moshe and Aharon: "Separate yourselves from this community and let
22 Me consume them in a moment." They fell on their faces and said, "God, the
God of the spirit of all flesh, if one man sins, will You rage against the entire
23 24 community?" The LORD spoke to Moshe: "Tell the community to
25 move away from the dwellings of Koraḥ, Datan, and Aviram." Moshe rose
26 and went to Datan and Aviram. Israel's elders followed him. He spoke to the
community, saying: "Turn away now from the tents of these wicked men. Do
27 not touch anything of theirs, lest you be swept away for all their sins." So they
moved away from around the dwellings of Koraḥ, Datan, and Aviram. Datan
and Aviram came out and stood at the openings of their tents with their wives,
28 children, and infants. Moshe said, "By this you will know that the LORD sent
29 me to do these deeds; it was not my idea. If all these men die as others do,
and share the common fate of all humanity, then the LORD has not sent me.
30 But if the LORD creates something entirely new, so that the ground opens
its mouth and swallows them and all they have, and they go down alive to
31 Sheol,[41] then you will know that these men have provoked the LORD." As soon
as he had finished speaking these words, the ground beneath them split open.
32 The earth opened its mouth and swallowed them and their households, with
33 all the people who pertained to Koraḥ and all their possessions – they and all
that was theirs descended alive to Sheol – the earth closed over them – and
34 they perished from the midst of the assembly. At their cry, all the Israelites
35 around them fled, for they said, "The earth could swallow us." And fire came
forth from the LORD and consumed the two hundred fifty men who were
17 1 2 offering incense. Then the LORD spoke to Moshe: "Tell Elazar son
of Aharon the priest to remove the censers from the fire, for they have become
3 holy. Scatter the burning coals far and wide. And the censers of those who
committed a mortal sin – make them into hammered plates as a covering
for the altar. Having been offered before the LORD, they have become holy.

41 | The netherworld.

טו לֹא נַעֲלֶה: וַיִּחַר לְמֹשֶׁה מְאֹד וַיֹּאמֶר אֶל־יהוה אַל־תֵּפֶן אֶל־מִנְחָתָם
טז לֹא חֲמוֹר אֶחָד מֵהֶם נָשָׂאתִי וְלֹא הֲרֵעֹתִי אֶת־אַחַד מֵהֶם: וַיֹּאמֶר
מֹשֶׁה אֶל־קֹרַח אַתָּה וְכָל־עֲדָתְךָ הֱיוּ לִפְנֵי יהוה אַתָּה וָהֵם וְאַהֲרֹן
יז מָחָר: וּקְחוּ ׀ אִישׁ מַחְתָּתוֹ וּנְתַתֶּם עֲלֵיהֶם קְטֹרֶת וְהִקְרַבְתֶּם לִפְנֵי
יהוה אִישׁ מַחְתָּתוֹ חֲמִשִּׁים וּמָאתַיִם מַחְתֹּת וְאַתָּה וְאַהֲרֹן אִישׁ
יח מַחְתָּתוֹ: וַיִּקְחוּ אִישׁ מַחְתָּתוֹ וַיִּתְּנוּ עֲלֵיהֶם אֵשׁ וַיָּשִׂימוּ עֲלֵיהֶם
יט קְטֹרֶת וַיַּעַמְדוּ פֶּתַח אֹהֶל מוֹעֵד וּמֹשֶׁה וְאַהֲרֹן: וַיַּקְהֵל עֲלֵיהֶם קֹרַח
אֶת־כָּל־הָעֵדָה אֶל־פֶּתַח אֹהֶל מוֹעֵד וַיֵּרָא כְבוֹד־יהוה אֶל־כָּל־
כ כא הָעֵדָה: וַיְדַבֵּר יהוה אֶל־מֹשֶׁה וְאֶל־אַהֲרֹן לֵאמֹר: הִבָּדְלוּ שלישי
כב מִתּוֹךְ הָעֵדָה הַזֹּאת וַאֲכַלֶּה אֹתָם כְּרָגַע: וַיִּפְּלוּ עַל־פְּנֵיהֶם וַיֹּאמְרוּ
אֵל אֱלֹהֵי הָרוּחֹת לְכָל־בָּשָׂר הָאִישׁ אֶחָד יֶחֱטָא וְעַל כָּל־הָעֵדָה
כג כד תִּקְצֹף: וַיְדַבֵּר יהוה אֶל־מֹשֶׁה לֵּאמֹר: דַּבֵּר אֶל־הָעֵדָה
כה לֵאמֹר הֵעָלוּ מִסָּבִיב לְמִשְׁכַּן־קֹרַח דָּתָן וַאֲבִירָם: וַיָּקָם מֹשֶׁה וַיֵּלֶךְ
כו אֶל־דָּתָן וַאֲבִירָם וַיֵּלְכוּ אַחֲרָיו זִקְנֵי יִשְׂרָאֵל: וַיְדַבֵּר אֶל־הָעֵדָה לֵאמֹר
סוּרוּ נָא מֵעַל אָהֳלֵי הָאֲנָשִׁים הָרְשָׁעִים הָאֵלֶּה וְאַל־תִּגְּעוּ בְּכָל־
כז אֲשֶׁר לָהֶם פֶּן־תִּסָּפוּ בְּכָל־חַטֹּאתָם: וַיֵּעָלוּ מֵעַל מִשְׁכַּן־קֹרַח דָּתָן
וַאֲבִירָם מִסָּבִיב וְדָתָן וַאֲבִירָם יָצְאוּ נִצָּבִים פֶּתַח אָהֳלֵיהֶם וּנְשֵׁיהֶם
כח וּבְנֵיהֶם וְטַפָּם: וַיֹּאמֶר מֹשֶׁה בְּזֹאת תֵּדְעוּן כִּי־יהוה שְׁלָחַנִי לַעֲשׂוֹת
כט אֵת כָּל־הַמַּעֲשִׂים הָאֵלֶּה כִּי־לֹא מִלִּבִּי: אִם־כְּמוֹת כָּל־הָאָדָם יְמֻתוּן
ל אֵלֶּה וּפְקֻדַּת כָּל־הָאָדָם יִפָּקֵד עֲלֵיהֶם לֹא יהוה שְׁלָחָנִי: וְאִם־בְּרִיאָה
יִבְרָא יהוה וּפָצְתָה הָאֲדָמָה אֶת־פִּיהָ וּבָלְעָה אֹתָם וְאֶת־כָּל־אֲשֶׁר
לָהֶם וְיָרְדוּ חַיִּים שְׁאֹלָה וִידַעְתֶּם כִּי נִאֲצוּ הָאֲנָשִׁים הָאֵלֶּה אֶת־
לא יהוה: וַיְהִי כְּכַלֹּתוֹ לְדַבֵּר אֵת כָּל־הַדְּבָרִים הָאֵלֶּה וַתִּבָּקַע הָאֲדָמָה
לב אֲשֶׁר תַּחְתֵּיהֶם: וַתִּפְתַּח הָאָרֶץ אֶת־פִּיהָ וַתִּבְלַע אֹתָם וְאֶת־בָּתֵּיהֶם
לג וְאֵת כָּל־הָאָדָם אֲשֶׁר לְקֹרַח וְאֵת כָּל־הָרְכוּשׁ: וַיֵּרְדוּ הֵם וְכָל־אֲשֶׁר
לד לָהֶם חַיִּים שְׁאֹלָה וַתְּכַס עֲלֵיהֶם הָאָרֶץ וַיֹּאבְדוּ מִתּוֹךְ הַקָּהָל: וְכָל־
יִשְׂרָאֵל אֲשֶׁר סְבִיבֹתֵיהֶם נָסוּ לְקֹלָם כִּי אָמְרוּ פֶּן־תִּבְלָעֵנוּ הָאָרֶץ:
לה וְאֵשׁ יָצְאָה מֵאֵת יהוה וַתֹּאכַל אֵת הַחֲמִשִּׁים וּמָאתַיִם אִישׁ מַקְרִיבֵי
יז א ב הַקְּטֹרֶת: וַיְדַבֵּר יהוה אֶל־מֹשֶׁה לֵּאמֹר: אֱמֹר אֶל־אֶלְעָזָר
בֶּן־אַהֲרֹן הַכֹּהֵן וְיָרֵם אֶת־הַמַּחְתֹּת מִבֵּין הַשְּׂרֵפָה וְאֶת־הָאֵשׁ זְרֵה־
ג הָלְאָה כִּי קָדֵשׁוּ: אֵת מַחְתּוֹת הַחַטָּאִים הָאֵלֶּה בְּנַפְשֹׁתָם וְעָשׂוּ אֹתָם
רִקֻּעֵי פַחִים צִפּוּי לַמִּזְבֵּחַ כִּי־הִקְרִיבֻם לִפְנֵי־יהוה וַיִּקְדָּשׁוּ וְיִהְיוּ לְאוֹת

4 And they will be a sign for the Israelites." Elazar the priest took the bronze
censers that the men consumed by fire had presented, and hammered them
5 into a covering for the altar, as the Lord had said to him through Moshe –
a reminder for the Israelites that no outsider, no one not descended from
Aharon, should offer incense before the Lord, and become like Koraḥ and his
company.
6 The next day the entire Israelite community complained to Moshe and
7 Aharon, "You have killed the Lord's people!" As the community assembled
against Moshe and Aharon, they turned toward the Tent of Meeting. A cloud
8 was covering it, and the glory of the Lord appeared. Moshe and Aharon
9 came to the front of the Tent of Meeting. And the Lord spoke
10 to Moshe: "Get away from this community; let Me consume them in an
11 instant." They fell on their faces, and Moshe said to Aharon, "Take the censer,
put fire from the altar into it, place incense upon it, and go quickly to the
community and make atonement for them. Fury has come forth from the
12 Lord; the plague has begun." Aharon took it as Moshe said and ran into the
midst of the assembly, for the plague had already begun among the people.
13 He offered incense and made atonement for the people; he stood between
14 the dead and the living, and the plague was halted; 14,700 died from that
15 plague, in addition to those who died on account of Koraḥ. And Aharon
returned to Moshe at the entrance to the Tent of Meeting – for the plague had
stopped.
16 17 Then the Lord spoke to Moshe: "Speak to the Israelites and take from
them twelve staffs, one for each ancestral house, from all the leaders of their
18 ancestral houses. Write each man's name on his staff, and on Levi's staff write
Aharon's name, for there shall be one staff for the head of each ancestral house.
19 Place them in the Tent of Meeting in front of the Ark of the Covenant, where
20 I meet with you. The staff of the man I choose – that will give flower. Thus I
21 will rid myself of the incessant railings of the Israelites against you." Moshe
spoke to the Israelites, and each of their leaders gave him a staff, one for each
leader, according to their ancestral houses, twelve staffs with Aharon's staff
22 among them. Moshe placed the staffs before the Lord in the Tent of the
23 Testimony. And the following day Moshe entered the Tent of the Testimony,
and Aharon's staff, representing the House of Levi, had given flower. It had
24 budded, produced blossoms, and was now bearing almonds. Moshe brought
out all the staffs from before the Lord to all the Israelites. They saw. And each
man took back his staff.
25 Then the Lord said to Moshe, "Put back Aharon's staff in front of the Ark
of the Covenant to serve as a sign to rebels so that their railings against Me
26 end, and they will not die." Moshe did so. As the Lord commanded him,
so he did.

ד לִבְנֵי יִשְׂרָאֵל: וַיִּקַּח אֶלְעָזָר הַכֹּהֵן אֵת מַחְתּוֹת הַנְּחֹשֶׁת אֲשֶׁר הִקְרִיבוּ
ה הַשְּׂרֻפִים וַיְרַקְּעוּם צִפּוּי לַמִּזְבֵּחַ: זִכָּרוֹן לִבְנֵי יִשְׂרָאֵל לְמַעַן אֲשֶׁר לֹא־
יִקְרַב אִישׁ זָר אֲשֶׁר לֹא מִזֶּרַע אַהֲרֹן הוּא לְהַקְטִיר קְטֹרֶת לִפְנֵי יְהוָה
וְלֹא־יִהְיֶה כְקֹרַח וְכַעֲדָתוֹ כַּאֲשֶׁר דִּבֶּר יְהוָה בְּיַד־מֹשֶׁה לוֹ:
ו וַיִּלֹּנוּ כָּל־עֲדַת בְּנֵי־יִשְׂרָאֵל מִמָּחֳרָת עַל־מֹשֶׁה וְעַל־אַהֲרֹן לֵאמֹר
ז אַתֶּם הֲמִתֶּם אֶת־עַם יְהוָה: וַיְהִי בְּהִקָּהֵל הָעֵדָה עַל־מֹשֶׁה וְעַל־אַהֲרֹן
ח וַיִּפְנוּ אֶל־אֹהֶל מוֹעֵד וְהִנֵּה כִסָּהוּ הֶעָנָן וַיֵּרָא כְּבוֹד יְהוָה: וַיָּבֹא מֹשֶׁה
ט וְאַהֲרֹן אֶל־פְּנֵי אֹהֶל מוֹעֵד: וַיְדַבֵּר יְהוָה אֶל־מֹשֶׁה לֵּאמֹר: רביעי
י הֵרֹמּוּ מִתּוֹךְ הָעֵדָה הַזֹּאת וַאֲכַלֶּה אֹתָם כְּרָגַע וַיִּפְּלוּ עַל־פְּנֵיהֶם:
יא וַיֹּאמֶר מֹשֶׁה אֶל־אַהֲרֹן קַח אֶת־הַמַּחְתָּה וְתֶן־עָלֶיהָ אֵשׁ מֵעַל הַמִּזְבֵּחַ
וְשִׂים קְטֹרֶת וְהוֹלֵךְ מְהֵרָה אֶל־הָעֵדָה וְכַפֵּר עֲלֵיהֶם כִּי־יָצָא הַקֶּצֶף
יב מִלִּפְנֵי יְהוָה הֵחֵל הַנָּגֶף: וַיִּקַּח אַהֲרֹן כַּאֲשֶׁר ׀ דִּבֶּר מֹשֶׁה וַיָּרָץ אֶל־
תּוֹךְ הַקָּהָל וְהִנֵּה הֵחֵל הַנֶּגֶף בָּעָם וַיִּתֵּן אֶת־הַקְּטֹרֶת וַיְכַפֵּר עַל־הָעָם:
יג יד וַיַּעֲמֹד בֵּין־הַמֵּתִים וּבֵין הַחַיִּים וַתֵּעָצַר הַמַּגֵּפָה: וַיִּהְיוּ הַמֵּתִים בַּמַּגֵּפָה
טו אַרְבָּעָה עָשָׂר אֶלֶף וּשְׁבַע מֵאוֹת מִלְּבַד הַמֵּתִים עַל־דְּבַר־קֹרַח: וַיָּשָׁב
אַהֲרֹן אֶל־מֹשֶׁה אֶל־פֶּתַח אֹהֶל מוֹעֵד וְהַמַּגֵּפָה נֶעֱצָרָה:
טז יז וַיְדַבֵּר יְהוָה אֶל־מֹשֶׁה לֵּאמֹר: דַּבֵּר ׀ אֶל־בְּנֵי יִשְׂרָאֵל וְקַח מֵאִתָּם טז חמישי
מַטֶּה מַטֶּה לְבֵית אָב מֵאֵת כָּל־נְשִׂיאֵהֶם לְבֵית אֲבֹתָם שְׁנֵים עָשָׂר
יח מַטּוֹת אִישׁ אֶת־שְׁמוֹ תִּכְתֹּב עַל־מַטֵּהוּ: וְאֵת שֵׁם אַהֲרֹן תִּכְתֹּב עַל־
יט מַטֵּה לֵוִי כִּי מַטֶּה אֶחָד לְרֹאשׁ בֵּית אֲבוֹתָם: וְהִנַּחְתָּם בְּאֹהֶל מוֹעֵד
כ לִפְנֵי הָעֵדוּת אֲשֶׁר אִוָּעֵד לָכֶם שָׁמָּה: וְהָיָה הָאִישׁ אֲשֶׁר אֶבְחַר־בּוֹ
מַטֵּהוּ יִפְרָח וַהֲשִׁכֹּתִי מֵעָלַי אֶת־תְּלֻנּוֹת בְּנֵי יִשְׂרָאֵל אֲשֶׁר הֵם מַלִּינִם
כא עֲלֵיכֶם: וַיְדַבֵּר מֹשֶׁה אֶל־בְּנֵי יִשְׂרָאֵל וַיִּתְּנוּ אֵלָיו ׀ כָּל־נְשִׂיאֵיהֶם מַטֶּה
לְנָשִׂיא אֶחָד מַטֶּה לְנָשִׂיא אֶחָד לְבֵית אֲבֹתָם שְׁנֵים עָשָׂר מַטּוֹת
כב וּמַטֵּה אַהֲרֹן בְּתוֹךְ מַטּוֹתָם: וַיַּנַּח מֹשֶׁה אֶת־הַמַּטֹּת לִפְנֵי יְהוָה
כג בְּאֹהֶל הָעֵדֻת: וַיְהִי מִמָּחֳרָת וַיָּבֹא מֹשֶׁה אֶל־אֹהֶל הָעֵדוּת וְהִנֵּה פָּרַח
כד מַטֵּה־אַהֲרֹן לְבֵית לֵוִי וַיֹּצֵא פֶרַח וַיָּצֵץ צִיץ וַיִּגְמֹל שְׁקֵדִים: וַיֹּצֵא מֹשֶׁה
אֶת־כָּל־הַמַּטֹּת מִלִּפְנֵי יְהוָה אֶל־כָּל־בְּנֵי יִשְׂרָאֵל וַיִּרְאוּ וַיִּקְחוּ אִישׁ
מַטֵּהוּ:
כה וַיֹּאמֶר יְהוָה אֶל־מֹשֶׁה הָשֵׁב אֶת־מַטֵּה אַהֲרֹן לִפְנֵי הָעֵדוּת לְמִשְׁמֶרֶת ששי
כו לְאוֹת לִבְנֵי־מֶרִי וּתְכַל תְּלוּנֹּתָם מֵעָלַי וְלֹא יָמֻתוּ: וַיַּעַשׂ מֹשֶׁה כַּאֲשֶׁר
צִוָּה יְהוָה אֹתוֹ כֵּן עָשָׂה:

27 The Israelites said to Moshe, "We are going to die. We are lost; all of us are
28 lost. Whoever approaches the LORD's Tabernacle is to die. Will we die out
18 1 completely?" The LORD said to Aharon: "You, your sons, and your
ancestral house shall bear any guilt connected with the Sanctuary, and you
2 and your sons will bear any guilt connected with your priesthood. Bring with
you also your brothers from the tribe of Levi, your father's tribe. Let them
join you and minister to you and your sons before the Tent of the Testimony.
3 They shall discharge their duties to you and to the Tent as a whole, but they
must not draw close to the utensils of the Sanctuary or the altar, or both they
4 and you will die. They will join you in discharging the duties of the Tent of
5 Meeting for all the service of the Tent; no outsider shall draw near you. You
shall discharge the duties of the Sanctuary and the altar, so that fury may never
6 again fall upon the Israelites. I have singled out your brothers, the Levites,
from among the Israelites as a gift to you, dedicated to the LORD to perform
7 the service of the Tent of Meeting. You and your sons shall take care to
perform the duties of your priesthood in all matters pertaining to the altar
and inside the curtain. I give you your priestly service as a gift, but any outsider who draws close will die."
8 The LORD spoke to Aharon: "I place in your charge the offerings made to
Me, all the sacred gifts of the Israelites. I give them to you and your sons
9 as an anointed right; this is an everlasting decree. This is what belongs to
you among the holiest offerings, from the fire: all their offerings, their grain
offerings, their purification offerings, and their guilt offerings. The holiest
10 offerings that they bring to Me will be yours and your sons'. You shall eat them
in the way of the holiest things. All your males may eat it; it is holy to you.
11 This too will be yours: as an everlasting statute I give the upraised gifts of all
the Israelites' wave offerings to you,[42] together with your sons and daughters.
12 Anyone who is ritually pure in your household may eat of them. All the best
of the oil, wine, and grain, the choice produce that they give to the LORD,
13 I give to you. The first fruits of all that is in their land that they bring to the
14 LORD will be yours. Anyone who is pure in your household may eat it. Every-
15 thing that is set aside in Israel shall be yours. All the first to emerge from the
womb of any creature, human or animal, that is offered to the LORD shall be
yours. You must, however, redeem firstborn boys and the firstborn of impure
16 animals.[43] Their redemption price from the age of one month shall be set
at five shekel of silver according to the Sanctuary weight: twenty gerah per
17 shekel. You must not redeem the firstborn of an ox, sheep, or goat; they
are sacred. You must dash their blood on the altar and send their fat up in
18 smoke for a pleasing aroma to the LORD. But their meat is yours. It shall
19 be yours like the breast of the wave offering and the right thigh. All the
sacred gifts that the Israelites raise up to the LORD I give to you, your sons,
and your daughters as an everlasting statute. It is an everlasting covenant

---

42 | That is, the priests shall receive portions from offerings whose procedures include elevating and waving.

43 | The Israelites must redeem them with the priests' involvement, as the passage proceeds to clarify.

כז וַיֹּאמְרוּ בְּנֵי יִשְׂרָאֵל אֶל־מֹשֶׁה לֵאמֹר הֵן גָּוַעְנוּ אָבַדְנוּ כֻּלָּנוּ
כח אָבָדְנוּ: כֹּל הַקָּרֵב ׀ הַקָּרֵב אֶל־מִשְׁכַּן יהוה יָמוּת הַאִם תַּמְנוּ
יח א לִגְוֹעַ: וַיֹּאמֶר יהוה אֶל־אַהֲרֹן אַתָּה וּבָנֶיךָ וּבֵית־אָבִיךָ
אִתָּךְ תִּשְׂאוּ אֶת־עֲוֹן הַמִּקְדָּשׁ וְאַתָּה וּבָנֶיךָ אִתָּךְ תִּשְׂאוּ אֶת־עֲוֹן
ב כְּהֻנַּתְכֶם: וְגַם אֶת־אַחֶיךָ מַטֵּה לֵוִי שֵׁבֶט אָבִיךָ הַקְרֵב אִתָּךְ וְיִלָּווּ עָלֶיךָ
ג וִישָׁרְתוּךָ וְאַתָּה וּבָנֶיךָ אִתָּךְ לִפְנֵי אֹהֶל הָעֵדֻת: וְשָׁמְרוּ מִשְׁמַרְתְּךָ
וּמִשְׁמֶרֶת כָּל־הָאֹהֶל אַךְ אֶל־כְּלֵי הַקֹּדֶשׁ וְאֶל־הַמִּזְבֵּחַ לֹא יִקְרָבוּ
ד וְלֹא־יָמֻתוּ גַם־הֵם גַּם־אַתֶּם: וְנִלְווּ עָלֶיךָ וְשָׁמְרוּ אֶת־מִשְׁמֶרֶת אֹהֶל
ה מוֹעֵד לְכֹל עֲבֹדַת הָאֹהֶל וְזָר לֹא־יִקְרַב אֲלֵיכֶם: וּשְׁמַרְתֶּם אֵת
מִשְׁמֶרֶת הַקֹּדֶשׁ וְאֵת מִשְׁמֶרֶת הַמִּזְבֵּחַ וְלֹא־יִהְיֶה עוֹד קֶצֶף עַל־בְּנֵי
ו יִשְׂרָאֵל: וַאֲנִי הִנֵּה לָקַחְתִּי אֶת־אֲחֵיכֶם הַלְוִיִּם מִתּוֹךְ בְּנֵי יִשְׂרָאֵל לָכֶם
ז מַתָּנָה נְתֻנִים לַיהוה לַעֲבֹד אֶת־עֲבֹדַת אֹהֶל מוֹעֵד: וְאַתָּה וּבָנֶיךָ אִתְּךָ
תִּשְׁמְרוּ אֶת־כְּהֻנַּתְכֶם לְכָל־דְּבַר הַמִּזְבֵּחַ וּלְמִבֵּית לַפָּרֹכֶת וַעֲבַדְתֶּם
עֲבֹדַת מַתָּנָה אֶתֵּן אֶת־כְּהֻנַּתְכֶם וְהַזָּר הַקָּרֵב יוּמָת:
ח וַיְדַבֵּר יהוה אֶל־אַהֲרֹן וַאֲנִי הִנֵּה נָתַתִּי לְךָ אֶת־מִשְׁמֶרֶת תְּרוּמֹתָי
לְכָל־קָדְשֵׁי בְנֵי־יִשְׂרָאֵל לְךָ נְתַתִּים לְמָשְׁחָה וּלְבָנֶיךָ לְחָק־עוֹלָם:
ט זֶה־יִהְיֶה לְךָ מִקֹּדֶשׁ הַקֳּדָשִׁים מִן־הָאֵשׁ כָּל־קָרְבָּנָם לְכָל־מִנְחָתָם
וּלְכָל־חַטָּאתָם וּלְכָל־אֲשָׁמָם אֲשֶׁר יָשִׁיבוּ לִי קֹדֶשׁ קָדָשִׁים לְךָ הוּא
י וּלְבָנֶיךָ: בְּקֹדֶשׁ הַקֳּדָשִׁים תֹּאכְלֶנּוּ כָּל־זָכָר יֹאכַל אֹתוֹ קֹדֶשׁ יִהְיֶה־
יא לָּךְ: וְזֶה־לְּךָ תְּרוּמַת מַתָּנָם לְכָל־תְּנוּפֹת בְּנֵי יִשְׂרָאֵל לְךָ נְתַתִּים
וּלְבָנֶיךָ וְלִבְנֹתֶיךָ אִתְּךָ לְחָק־עוֹלָם כָּל־טָהוֹר בְּבֵיתְךָ יֹאכַל אֹתוֹ:
יב כֹּל חֵלֶב יִצְהָר וְכָל־חֵלֶב תִּירוֹשׁ וְדָגָן רֵאשִׁיתָם אֲשֶׁר־יִתְּנוּ לַיהוה
יג לְךָ נְתַתִּים: בִּכּוּרֵי כָּל־אֲשֶׁר בְּאַרְצָם אֲשֶׁר־יָבִיאוּ לַיהוה לְךָ יִהְיֶה
יד טו כָּל־טָהוֹר בְּבֵיתְךָ יֹאכְלֶנּוּ: כָּל־חֵרֶם בְּיִשְׂרָאֵל לְךָ יִהְיֶה: כָּל־פֶּטֶר
רֶחֶם לְכָל־בָּשָׂר אֲשֶׁר־יַקְרִיבוּ לַיהוה בָּאָדָם וּבַבְּהֵמָה יִהְיֶה־לָּךְ אַךְ ׀
פָּדֹה תִפְדֶּה אֵת בְּכוֹר הָאָדָם וְאֵת בְּכוֹר־הַבְּהֵמָה הַטְּמֵאָה תִּפְדֶּה:
טז וּפְדוּיָו מִבֶּן־חֹדֶשׁ תִּפְדֶּה בְּעֶרְכְּךָ כֶּסֶף חֲמֵשֶׁת שְׁקָלִים בְּשֶׁקֶל הַקֹּדֶשׁ
יז עֶשְׂרִים גֵּרָה הוּא: אַךְ בְּכוֹר־שׁוֹר אוֹ־בְכוֹר כֶּשֶׂב אוֹ־בְכוֹר עֵז לֹא
תִפְדֶּה קֹדֶשׁ הֵם אֶת־דָּמָם תִּזְרֹק עַל־הַמִּזְבֵּחַ וְאֶת־חֶלְבָּם תַּקְטִיר
יח אִשֶּׁה לְרֵיחַ נִיחֹחַ לַיהוה: וּבְשָׂרָם יִהְיֶה־לָּךְ כַּחֲזֵה הַתְּנוּפָה וּכְשׁוֹק
יט הַיָּמִין לְךָ יִהְיֶה: כֹּל ׀ תְּרוּמֹת הַקֳּדָשִׁים אֲשֶׁר יָרִימוּ בְנֵי־יִשְׂרָאֵל
לַיהוה נָתַתִּי לְךָ וּלְבָנֶיךָ וְלִבְנֹתֶיךָ אִתְּךָ לְחָק־עוֹלָם בְּרִית מֶלַח עוֹלָם

20 of salt[44] before the LORD, for you and for your descendants." The LORD said
to Aharon: "You will have no inheritance in their land, nor shall you have
any share among them. I am your share, your inheritance, among the Israel-
21 ites. And I give to the Levites all tithes in Israel as an inheritance in
22 return for the service they perform, the service in the Tent of Meeting. From
now the Israelites shall no longer come close to the Tent of Meeting, or they
23 will incur guilt and die. Instead, the Levites will perform the service of the
Tent of Meeting, and they will bear responsibility for their own sins; this is
an everlasting decree through all your generations. But among the Israelites
24 they will not inherit land, because I have given as an inheritance to the Levites
the tithe of the Israelites which they have lifted up to the LORD as an upraised
gift. That is why I have said of them that they shall have no land inheritance
among the Israelites."
25 26 The LORD spoke to Moshe: "Speak to the Levites and say to them: When
you receive from the Israelites the tithe that I have given you from them as
your inheritance, you shall lift up a tenth of it as an offering to the LORD, a
27 tithe of the tithe. It will be considered your own upraised gift, like the grain of
28 the threshing floor or the flow from the winepress.[45] So shall you set aside an
offering to the LORD from all the tithes that you take from the Israelites, and
29 you shall give it as an upraised gift to the LORD for Aharon the priest. From
all your gifts, you shall set aside an offering to the LORD; of each the finest
30 portion shall be consecrated. Say to the Levites: When you have presented
the best portion of it, it will be reckoned to you as the yield of the threshing
31 floor and the winepress.[46] You and your household may eat of it anywhere,
32 because this is your payment for your service in the Tent of Meeting. You
will not bear guilt for it once you have separated out the finest portion; then
you will not be profaning the sacred offerings of the Israelites, and will not
die."

19 1 2 The LORD spoke to Moshe and Aharon: "This is the decree of the Law that — ḤUKAT
the LORD commands. Tell the Israelites to bring you a cow, completely red,
3 without blemish, on which no yoke has been laid. Give this to Elazar the
priest; it shall be taken outside the camp and slaughtered in his presence.
4 Elazar the priest shall take some of its blood with his finger and sprinkle it
5 seven times toward the front of the Tent of Meeting. The cow shall then be
burned in front of him; its skin, flesh, and blood shall be burned, together
6 with its dung. The priest shall take cedarwood, hyssop, and scarlet cloth and
7 throw them into the fire where the cow is burning. Then the priest shall wash
his clothes and bathe his body in water. Afterward he may enter the camp,
8 but he will remain impure until that evening. The one who burned it shall
wash his clothes in water and bathe his body in water, but he too will remain
9 impure until evening. Meanwhile, one who is pure shall gather up the ashes
of the cow and place them outside the camp in a pure place. And they shall be

---

44 | Salt, which is used for preservation, signifies Israel's enduring covenant with God.

45 | Meaning this tithe is comparable to the tithe taken by a landowner from his produce.

46 | Meaning the Levites may then partake of what remains as though it is their own produce.

כ הוּא לִפְנֵי יְהוָה לְךָ וּלְזַרְעֲךָ אִתָּךְ: וַיֹּאמֶר יְהוָה אֶל־אַהֲרֹן בְּאַרְצָם
לֹא תִנְחָל וְחֵלֶק לֹא־יִהְיֶה לְךָ בְּתוֹכָם אֲנִי חֶלְקְךָ וְנַחֲלָתְךָ בְּתוֹךְ
כא בְּנֵי יִשְׂרָאֵל: וְלִבְנֵי לֵוִי הִנֵּה נָתַתִּי כָּל־מַעֲשֵׂר בְּיִשְׂרָאֵל שביעי
לְנַחֲלָה חֵלֶף עֲבֹדָתָם אֲשֶׁר־הֵם עֹבְדִים אֶת־עֲבֹדַת אֹהֶל מוֹעֵד:
כב וְלֹא־יִקְרְבוּ עוֹד בְּנֵי יִשְׂרָאֵל אֶל־אֹהֶל מוֹעֵד לָשֵׂאת חֵטְא לָמוּת:
כג וְעָבַד הַלֵּוִי הוּא אֶת־עֲבֹדַת אֹהֶל מוֹעֵד וְהֵם יִשְׂאוּ עֲוֺנָם חֻקַּת
כד עוֹלָם לְדֹרֹתֵיכֶם וּבְתוֹךְ בְּנֵי יִשְׂרָאֵל לֹא יִנְחֲלוּ נַחֲלָה: כִּי אֶת־מַעְשַׂר
בְּנֵי־יִשְׂרָאֵל אֲשֶׁר יָרִימוּ לַיהוָה תְּרוּמָה נָתַתִּי לַלְוִיִּם לְנַחֲלָה עַל־כֵּן
אָמַרְתִּי לָהֶם בְּתוֹךְ בְּנֵי יִשְׂרָאֵל לֹא יִנְחֲלוּ נַחֲלָה:
כה כו וַיְדַבֵּר יְהוָה אֶל־מֹשֶׁה לֵּאמֹר: וְאֶל־הַלְוִיִּם תְּדַבֵּר וְאָמַרְתָּ אֲלֵהֶם יז
כִּי־תִקְחוּ מֵאֵת בְּנֵי־יִשְׂרָאֵל אֶת־הַמַּעֲשֵׂר אֲשֶׁר נָתַתִּי לָכֶם מֵאִתָּם
כז בְּנַחֲלַתְכֶם וַהֲרֵמֹתֶם מִמֶּנּוּ תְּרוּמַת יְהוָה מַעֲשֵׂר מִן־הַמַּעֲשֵׂר: וְנֶחְשַׁב
כח לָכֶם תְּרוּמַתְכֶם כַּדָּגָן מִן־הַגֹּרֶן וְכַמְלֵאָה מִן־הַיָּקֶב: כֵּן תָּרִימוּ גַם־
אַתֶּם תְּרוּמַת יְהוָה מִכֹּל מַעְשְׂרֹתֵיכֶם אֲשֶׁר תִּקְחוּ מֵאֵת בְּנֵי יִשְׂרָאֵל
כט וּנְתַתֶּם מִמֶּנּוּ אֶת־תְּרוּמַת יְהוָה לְאַהֲרֹן הַכֹּהֵן: מִכֹּל מַתְּנֹתֵיכֶם תָּרִימוּ
ל אֵת כָּל־תְּרוּמַת יְהוָה מִכָּל־חֶלְבּוֹ אֶת־מִקְדְּשׁוֹ מִמֶּנּוּ: וְאָמַרְתָּ אֲלֵהֶם מפטיר
בַּהֲרִימְכֶם אֶת־חֶלְבּוֹ מִמֶּנּוּ וְנֶחְשַׁב לַלְוִיִּם כִּתְבוּאַת גֹּרֶן וְכִתְבוּאַת
לא יָקֶב: וַאֲכַלְתֶּם אֹתוֹ בְּכָל־מָקוֹם אַתֶּם וּבֵיתְכֶם כִּי־שָׂכָר הוּא לָכֶם חֵלֶף
לב עֲבֹדַתְכֶם בְּאֹהֶל מוֹעֵד: וְלֹא־תִשְׂאוּ עָלָיו חֵטְא בַּהֲרִימְכֶם אֶת־חֶלְבּוֹ
מִמֶּנּוּ וְאֶת־קָדְשֵׁי בְנֵי־יִשְׂרָאֵל לֹא תְחַלְּלוּ וְלֹא תָמוּתוּ:
יט א ב וַיְדַבֵּר יְהוָה אֶל־מֹשֶׁה וְאֶל־אַהֲרֹן לֵאמֹר: זֹאת חֻקַּת הַתּוֹרָה אֲשֶׁר־ חקת
צִוָּה יְהוָה לֵאמֹר דַּבֵּר ׀ אֶל־בְּנֵי יִשְׂרָאֵל וְיִקְחוּ אֵלֶיךָ פָרָה אֲדֻמָּה
ג תְּמִימָה אֲשֶׁר אֵין־בָּהּ מוּם אֲשֶׁר לֹא־עָלָה עָלֶיהָ עֹל: וּנְתַתֶּם אֹתָהּ
אֶל־אֶלְעָזָר הַכֹּהֵן וְהוֹצִיא אֹתָהּ אֶל־מִחוּץ לַמַּחֲנֶה וְשָׁחַט אֹתָהּ
ד לְפָנָיו: וְלָקַח אֶלְעָזָר הַכֹּהֵן מִדָּמָהּ בְּאֶצְבָּעוֹ וְהִזָּה אֶל־נֹכַח פְּנֵי אֹהֶל־
ה מוֹעֵד מִדָּמָהּ שֶׁבַע פְּעָמִים: וְשָׂרַף אֶת־הַפָּרָה לְעֵינָיו אֶת־עֹרָהּ וְאֶת־
ו בְּשָׂרָהּ וְאֶת־דָּמָהּ עַל־פִּרְשָׁהּ יִשְׂרֹף: וְלָקַח הַכֹּהֵן עֵץ אֶרֶז וְאֵזוֹב וּשְׁנִי
ז תוֹלָעַת וְהִשְׁלִיךְ אֶל־תּוֹךְ שְׂרֵפַת הַפָּרָה: וְכִבֶּס בְּגָדָיו הַכֹּהֵן וְרָחַץ
ח בְּשָׂרוֹ בַּמַּיִם וְאַחַר יָבֹא אֶל־הַמַּחֲנֶה וְטָמֵא הַכֹּהֵן עַד־הָעָרֶב: וְהַשֹּׂרֵף
ט אֹתָהּ יְכַבֵּס בְּגָדָיו בַּמַּיִם וְרָחַץ בְּשָׂרוֹ בַּמָּיִם וְטָמֵא עַד־הָעָרֶב: וְאָסַף ׀
אִישׁ טָהוֹר אֵת אֵפֶר הַפָּרָה וְהִנִּיחַ מִחוּץ לַמַּחֲנֶה בְּמָקוֹם טָהוֹר וְהָיְתָה

kept by the Israelite community for the water of lustration, as a purification
10 offering. The one who gathers the ashes of the cow shall likewise wash his
clothes but remains impure until evening. This shall be an everlasting decree
11 for the Israelites and for any migrant living among them. Whoever touches
12 the dead body of any person shall be impure for seven days. He must purify
himself with the water on the third and seventh days to become pure. If he
does not purify himself on the third and seventh days, he will not be pure.
13 Whoever touches a corpse of a person who has died, and fails to purify himself, defiles the LORD's Tabernacle. He shall be severed from Israel because,
since the water of lustration was not sprinkled on him, he remains impure;
14 his impurity is still with him. This is the law: when a person dies in a tent,
whoever enters that tent and whoever is in it shall remain impure for seven
15 16 days. Any open vessel not sealed with a cover shall be impure. Anyone in the
open field who touches a person killed by the sword, or who died naturally,
17 or a human bone or a grave, shall be impure for seven days. For this impure
person they shall take some of the ashes of the burnt purification offering,
18 and place living water[47] along with it into a vessel. A person who is pure shall
then take hyssop, dip it into the water, and sprinkle it on the tent, on all the
vessels, on the people who were there, and on anyone who touched the bone,
19 the slain person, or any other corpse, or a grave. On the third day and seventh
day the person who is pure shall sprinkle it on the one who is impure, thus
purifying him on the seventh day. He shall then wash his clothes and immerse
20 in water, and at evening he will be pure. Anyone who becomes impure and
fails to purify himself shall be severed from the assembly, for he has defiled
the LORD's Sanctuary. Since water of lustration was not sprinkled on him,
21 he is impure. This is an everlasting decree for them. The one who sprinkles
the water of lustration shall wash his own clothes. Anyone who had contact
22 with the water of lustration shall remain impure until evening. Anything the
impure person touches is rendered impure, and one who touches him remains
impure until evening."

20 1 The Israelites, all the community, arrived at the Wilderness of Tzin in the first
month, and the people stayed at Kadesh. There Miriam died and was buried.
2 And there was no water for the community, and together they confronted
3 Moshe and Aharon. The people contended with Moshe: "If only we had died
4 when our brothers died before the LORD! Why have you brought the LORD's
5 assembly into this wilderness only for us and our livestock to die here? Why
did you take us up out of Egypt to bring us to this dreadful place with no grain,
6 no figs, no vines or pomegranates – there is no water to drink!" Moshe and
Aharon went away from the assembly to the entrance of the Tent of Meeting.
They fell on their faces, and the LORD's glory was revealed to them.
7 8 And the LORD spoke to Moshe: "Take the staff, you and your brother Aharon,
and assemble the community. Speak to the rock before their eyes and it will
give forth water. You shall bring forth water for them from the rock, giving
9 the community and their animals to drink." Moshe took the staff from before

47 | Water taken from a flowing source.

י לעדת בני־ישראל למשמרת למי נדה חטאת הוא: וכבס האסף
את־אפר הפרה את־בגדיו וטמא עד־הערב והיתה לבני ישראל
יא ולגר הגר בתוכם לחקת עולם: הנגע במת לכל־נפש אדם וטמא
יב שבעת ימים: הוא יתחטא־בו ביום השלישי וביום השביעי יטהר
יג ואם־לא יתחטא ביום השלישי וביום השביעי לא יטהר: כל־הנגע
במת בנפש האדם אשר־ימות ולא יתחטא את־משכן יהוה טמא
ונכרתה הנפש ההוא מישראל כי מי נדה לא־זרק עליו טמא יהיה
יד עוד טמאתו בו: זאת התורה אדם כי־ימות באהל כל־הבא אל־
טו האהל וכל־אשר באהל יטמא שבעת ימים: וכל כלי פתוח אשר
טז אין־צמיד פתיל עליו טמא הוא: וכל אשר־יגע על־פני השדה
בחלל־חרב או במת או־בעצם אדם או בקבר יטמא שבעת ימים:
יז ולקחו לטמא מעפר שרפת החטאת ונתן עליו מים חיים אל־כלי:
שני יח ולקח אזוב וטבל במים איש טהור והזה על־האהל ועל־כל־הכלים
ועל־הנפשות אשר היו־שם ועל־הנגע בעצם או בחלל או במת
יט או בקבר: והזה הטהר על־הטמא ביום השלישי וביום השביעי
כ וחטאו ביום השביעי וכבס בגדיו ורחץ במים וטהר בערב: ואיש
אשר־יטמא ולא יתחטא ונכרתה הנפש ההוא מתוך הקהל כי
כא את־מקדש יהוה טמא מי נדה לא־זרק עליו טמא הוא: והיתה
להם לחקת עולם ומזה מי־הנדה יכבס בגדיו והנגע במי הנדה
כב יטמא עד־הערב: וכל אשר־יגע־בו הטמא יטמא והנפש הנגעת
תטמא עד־הערב:
כ א ויבאו בני־ישראל כל־העדה מדבר־צן בחדש הראשון וישב העם
ב בקדש ותמת שם מרים ותקבר שם: ולא־היה מים לעדה ויקהלו
ג על־משה ועל־אהרן: וירב העם עם־משה ויאמרו לאמר ולו גוענו
ד בגוע אחינו לפני יהוה: ולמה הבאתם את־קהל יהוה אל־המדבר
ה הזה למות שם אנחנו ובעירנו: ולמה העליתנו ממצרים להביא
אתנו אל־המקום הרע הזה לא | מקום זרע ותאנה וגפן ורמון ומים
ו אין לשתות: ויבא משה ואהרן מפני הקהל אל־פתח אהל מועד
ויפלו על־פניהם וירא כבוד־יהוה אליהם:
שלישי /שני/ ז ח וידבר יהוה אל־משה לאמר: קח את־המטה והקהל את־העדה
אתה ואהרן אחיך ודברתם אל־הסלע לעיניהם ונתן מימיו והוצאת
ט להם מים מן־הסלע והשקית את־העדה ואת־בעירם: ויקח משה

10 the LORD, as He had commanded him. And Moshe and Aharon gathered the
assembly together before the rock. He said to them, "Listen now, rebels! Shall
11 we produce water for you from this rock?" Then Moshe raised his hand and
struck the rock twice with his staff. Water gushed out, and the community
12 and their animals drank. But the LORD said to Moshe and Aharon,
"Because you did not put your trust in Me to demonstrate My holiness in the
Israelites' eyes, you shall not bring this assembly into the land that I am giving
13 them." These were the waters of Meriva,[48] where the Israelites quarreled with
14 the LORD and where He showed them His holiness.[49] Moshe sent
messengers from Kadesh to the king of Edom: "This is what your brother
15 Israel says: 'You know all the hardship we have encountered, how our ancestors went down to Egypt and lived in Egypt for a long time. And the Egyptians
16 oppressed us and our forebears, and we cried out to the LORD. He heard our
voice, sent a messenger, and He brought us out of Egypt. Now here we are
17 in Kadesh, a town adjoining your border. Please, let us pass through your
land. We will not pass through any field or vineyard, nor will we drink water
from any well. We will go along the King's Highway and not turn from it to
18 the right or the left until we have passed through your territory.'" But Edom
said to him, "You shall not pass through, or I will come out against you with
19 the sword." The Israelites said, "We will keep to the beaten track. If we or our
livestock drink any of your water, we will pay for it. It is such a small matter; we
20 only want to pass through on foot." But they said, "You will not pass through."
And Edom came out against them with a large fighting force, heavily armed.
21 Edom refused to let Israel pass through their territory, and Israel turned
away.
22 They set out from Kadesh, and all the Israelite community arrived at Mount
23 Hor. There at Mount Hor, by the border of the land of Edom, the LORD said
24 to Moshe and Aharon, "Aharon is to be gathered to his people. He shall not
enter the land that I have given to the Israelites, because you disobeyed My
25 command at the waters of Meriva. Take Aharon and his son Elazar, and bring
26 them up onto Mount Hor. Strip Aharon of his vestments and put them on
27 his son Elazar. There will Aharon be gathered in and he will die." Moshe did
as the LORD commanded. They ascended Mount Hor in the sight of all the
28 community. Moshe stripped Aharon of his vestments and put them on his
son Elazar. And there, Aharon died, at the top of the mountain; and Moshe
29 and Elazar came down from the mountain. When all the community saw that
Aharon had perished, the whole House of Israel wept for Aharon for thirty
21 1 days. When the Canaanite king of Arad, dwelling in the Negev,
heard that the Israelites were coming by the way of Atarim, he attacked the
2 Israelites and took captives. And the Israelites vowed to the LORD: "If You
3 give this people over into our hands, we will utterly destroy[50] their towns." The

48 | Literally "quarrel."

49 | "He showed them His holiness," Hebrew *vayikadesh,* resonates with the place-name Kadesh.

50 | The Israelites employ the root *ḥ-r-m* (ח־ר־ם), indicating devotion of the towns to God. The present translation adopts the view that the devotion of these towns implies their destruction.

י אֶת־הַמַּטֶּה מִלִּפְנֵי יהוה כַּאֲשֶׁר צִוָּהוּ׃ וַיַּקְהִלוּ מֹשֶׁה וְאַהֲרֹן אֶת־
הַקָּהָל אֶל־פְּנֵי הַסָּלַע וַיֹּאמֶר לָהֶם שִׁמְעוּ־נָא הַמֹּרִים הֲמִן־הַסֶּלַע
יא הַזֶּה נוֹצִיא לָכֶם מָיִם׃ וַיָּרֶם מֹשֶׁה אֶת־יָדוֹ וַיַּךְ אֶת־הַסֶּלַע בְּמַטֵּהוּ
יב פַּעֲמָיִם וַיֵּצְאוּ מַיִם רַבִּים וַתֵּשְׁתְּ הָעֵדָה וּבְעִירָם׃ וַיֹּאמֶר
יהוה אֶל־מֹשֶׁה וְאֶל־אַהֲרֹן יַעַן לֹא־הֶאֱמַנְתֶּם בִּי לְהַקְדִּישֵׁנִי לְעֵינֵי
בְּנֵי יִשְׂרָאֵל לָכֵן לֹא תָבִיאוּ אֶת־הַקָּהָל הַזֶּה אֶל־הָאָרֶץ אֲשֶׁר־נָתַתִּי
יג לָהֶם׃ הֵמָּה מֵי מְרִיבָה אֲשֶׁר־רָבוּ בְנֵי־יִשְׂרָאֵל אֶת־יהוה וַיִּקָּדֵשׁ
יד בָּם׃ וַיִּשְׁלַח מֹשֶׁה מַלְאָכִים מִקָּדֵשׁ אֶל־מֶלֶךְ אֱדוֹם כֹּה יח רביעי
אָמַר אָחִיךָ יִשְׂרָאֵל אַתָּה יָדַעְתָּ אֵת כָּל־הַתְּלָאָה אֲשֶׁר מְצָאָתְנוּ׃
טו וַיֵּרְדוּ אֲבֹתֵינוּ מִצְרַיְמָה וַנֵּשֶׁב בְּמִצְרַיִם יָמִים רַבִּים וַיָּרֵעוּ לָנוּ מִצְרַיִם
טז וְלַאֲבֹתֵינוּ׃ וַנִּצְעַק אֶל־יהוה וַיִּשְׁמַע קֹלֵנוּ וַיִּשְׁלַח מַלְאָךְ וַיֹּצִאֵנוּ
יז מִמִּצְרָיִם וְהִנֵּה אֲנַחְנוּ בְקָדֵשׁ עִיר קְצֵה גְבוּלֶךָ׃ נַעְבְּרָה־נָּא בְאַרְצֶךָ
לֹא נַעֲבֹר בְּשָׂדֶה וּבְכֶרֶם וְלֹא נִשְׁתֶּה מֵי בְאֵר דֶּרֶךְ הַמֶּלֶךְ נֵלֵךְ לֹא נִטֶּה
יח יָמִין וּשְׂמֹאול עַד אֲשֶׁר־נַעֲבֹר גְּבֻלֶךָ׃ וַיֹּאמֶר אֵלָיו אֱדוֹם לֹא תַעֲבֹר
יט בִּי פֶּן־בַּחֶרֶב אֵצֵא לִקְרָאתֶךָ׃ וַיֹּאמְרוּ אֵלָיו בְּנֵי־יִשְׂרָאֵל בַּמְסִלָּה
נַעֲלֶה וְאִם־מֵימֶיךָ נִשְׁתֶּה אֲנִי וּמִקְנַי וְנָתַתִּי מִכְרָם רַק אֵין־דָּבָר
כ בְּרַגְלַי אֶעֱבֹרָה׃ וַיֹּאמֶר לֹא תַעֲבֹר וַיֵּצֵא אֱדוֹם לִקְרָאתוֹ בְּעַם כָּבֵד
כא וּבְיָד חֲזָקָה׃ וַיְמָאֵן ׀ אֱדוֹם נְתֹן אֶת־יִשְׂרָאֵל עֲבֹר בִּגְבֻלוֹ וַיֵּט יִשְׂרָאֵל
מֵעָלָיו׃

כב כג וַיִּסְעוּ מִקָּדֵשׁ וַיָּבֹאוּ בְנֵי־יִשְׂרָאֵל כָּל־הָעֵדָה הֹר הָהָר׃ וַיֹּאמֶר יהוה חמישי /שלישי/
כד אֶל־מֹשֶׁה וְאֶל־אַהֲרֹן בְּהֹר הָהָר עַל־גְּבוּל אֶרֶץ־אֱדוֹם לֵאמֹר׃ יֵאָסֵף
אַהֲרֹן אֶל־עַמָּיו כִּי לֹא יָבֹא אֶל־הָאָרֶץ אֲשֶׁר נָתַתִּי לִבְנֵי יִשְׂרָאֵל
כה עַל אֲשֶׁר־מְרִיתֶם אֶת־פִּי לְמֵי מְרִיבָה׃ קַח אֶת־אַהֲרֹן וְאֶת־אֶלְעָזָר
כו בְּנוֹ וְהַעַל אֹתָם הֹר הָהָר׃ וְהַפְשֵׁט אֶת־אַהֲרֹן אֶת־בְּגָדָיו וְהִלְבַּשְׁתָּם
כז אֶת־אֶלְעָזָר בְּנוֹ וְאַהֲרֹן יֵאָסֵף וּמֵת שָׁם׃ וַיַּעַשׂ מֹשֶׁה כַּאֲשֶׁר צִוָּה יהוה
כח וַיַּעֲלוּ אֶל־הֹר הָהָר לְעֵינֵי כָּל־הָעֵדָה׃ וַיַּפְשֵׁט מֹשֶׁה אֶת־אַהֲרֹן אֶת־
בְּגָדָיו וַיַּלְבֵּשׁ אֹתָם אֶת־אֶלְעָזָר בְּנוֹ וַיָּמָת אַהֲרֹן שָׁם בְּרֹאשׁ הָהָר
כט וַיֵּרֶד מֹשֶׁה וְאֶלְעָזָר מִן־הָהָר׃ וַיִּרְאוּ כָּל־הָעֵדָה כִּי גָוַע אַהֲרֹן וַיִּבְכּוּ
כא א אֶת־אַהֲרֹן שְׁלֹשִׁים יוֹם כֹּל בֵּית יִשְׂרָאֵל׃ וַיִּשְׁמַע הַכְּנַעֲנִי
מֶלֶךְ־עֲרָד יֹשֵׁב הַנֶּגֶב כִּי בָּא יִשְׂרָאֵל דֶּרֶךְ הָאֲתָרִים וַיִּלָּחֶם בְּיִשְׂרָאֵל
ב וַיִּשְׁבְּ ׀ מִמֶּנּוּ שֶׁבִי׃ וַיִּדַּר יִשְׂרָאֵל נֶדֶר לַיהוה וַיֹּאמַר אִם־נָתֹן תִּתֵּן אֶת־
ג הָעָם הַזֶּה בְּיָדִי וְהַחֲרַמְתִּי אֶת־עָרֵיהֶם׃ וַיִּשְׁמַע יהוה בְּקוֹל יִשְׂרָאֵל

Lord listened to Israel's plea and gave over the Canaanites. They completely
destroyed them and their cities; and so the place was named Ḥorma.[51]
4 They set out from Mount Hor by the way to the Reed Sea, going around
5 the land of Edom. But the people became restive along the way. The people
spoke out against God and Moshe: "Why did you bring us up from Egypt
to die in the desert? There is no bread, there is no water; we detest this
6 miserable food!" The Lord sent venomous snakes among the people; they
7 bit the people, and many Israelites died. The people came to Moshe and said,
"We sinned when we spoke against the Lord and you. Pray to the Lord
8 to take the snakes away from us." Moshe prayed for the people. The Lord
then said to Moshe, "Fashion a snake and place it on a pole. Anyone who
9 is bitten shall look at that and live." Moshe fashioned a bronze snake and
placed it on a pole. When anyone was bitten by a snake, he would look at the
10 11 bronze snake and live. The Israelites moved on and camped at Ovot. Then
they moved on from Ovot, and camped at Iyei HaAvarim in the wilderness
12 bordering Moav to the east. From there they moved on and camped at the
13 Zered Stream. From there they moved on and camped beyond the Arnon, in
the wilderness that extends from the border of the Amorites, for the Arnon
14 marks the border of Moav, between Moav and the Amorites. That is why the
Book of the Wars of the Lord[52] records: "Vahev in Sufa and the wadis, Arnon
15 and the wadi slopes that lead to the settlement of Ar and lie along the border
16 of Moav." And from there to Be'er, the well where the Lord said to Moshe,
17 "Gather the people, and I will give them water."[53] Then the Israelites
18 sang this song: "Spring up, well – sing to her – that the nobles of the people
carved out with their scepter and their staffs." They went from the desert
19 20 to Matana, from Matana to Naḥaliel, from Naḥaliel to Bamot, and from
Bamot to the valley in the fields of Moav, to the top of Pisga, overlooking the
wasteland.
21 22 Then the Israelites sent messengers to Siḥon, king of the Amorites: "Let us
pass through your land. We will not turn aside into any field or vineyard,
nor will we drink water from any well. We will walk on the king's highway
23 until we have passed through your territory." But Siḥon would not allow the
Israelites to pass through his territory. He gathered all his people and went
out to confront the Israelites in the wilderness. When he arrived at Yahatz,
24 he launched an attack on the Israelites. The Israelites struck him down with
their swords and took possession of his land from the Arnon to the Yabok,
25 as far as the Amonites, for the border of the Amonites was strong. The
Israelites took all these cities, and they settled in all the cities of the Amorites,
26 in Ḥeshbon and all its surrounding settlements. Ḥeshbon was the city of
Siḥon, king of the Amorites, who had fought against the former king of
27 Moav and had taken all his land from him as far as the Arnon. That is why
the ballad singers sing: "Come to Ḥeshbon, build and refound the town

---

51 | Literally "destruction" or "devotion"; see previous note.

52 | The book in question has not survived.

53 | *Be'er* means "well."

וַיִּתֵּן אֶת־הַכְּנַעֲנִי וַיַּחֲרֵם אֶתְהֶם וְאֶת־עָרֵיהֶם וַיִּקְרָא שֵׁם־הַמָּקוֹם
חׇרְמָה׃
ד וַיִּסְעוּ מֵהֹר הָהָר דֶּרֶךְ יַם־סוּף לִסְבֹב אֶת־אֶרֶץ אֱדוֹם וַתִּקְצַר נֶפֶשׁ־
ה הָעָם בַּדָּרֶךְ׃ וַיְדַבֵּר הָעָם בֵּאלֹהִים וּבְמֹשֶׁה לָמָה הֶעֱלִיתֻנוּ מִמִּצְרַיִם
לָמוּת בַּמִּדְבָּר כִּי אֵין לֶחֶם וְאֵין מַיִם וְנַפְשֵׁנוּ קָצָה בַּלֶּחֶם הַקְּלֹקֵל׃
ו וַיְשַׁלַּח יהוה בָּעָם אֵת הַנְּחָשִׁים הַשְּׂרָפִים וַיְנַשְּׁכוּ אֶת־הָעָם וַיָּמׇת
ז עַם־רָב מִיִּשְׂרָאֵל׃ וַיָּבֹא הָעָם אֶל־מֹשֶׁה וַיֹּאמְרוּ חָטָאנוּ כִּי־דִבַּרְנוּ
בַיהוה וָבָךְ הִתְפַּלֵּל אֶל־יהוה וְיָסֵר מֵעָלֵינוּ אֶת־הַנָּחָשׁ וַיִּתְפַּלֵּל
ח מֹשֶׁה בְּעַד הָעָם׃ וַיֹּאמֶר יהוה אֶל־מֹשֶׁה עֲשֵׂה לְךָ שָׂרָף וְשִׂים אֹתוֹ
ט עַל־נֵס וְהָיָה כׇּל־הַנָּשׁוּךְ וְרָאָה אֹתוֹ וָחָי׃ וַיַּעַשׂ מֹשֶׁה נְחַשׁ נְחֹשֶׁת
וַיְשִׂמֵהוּ עַל־הַנֵּס וְהָיָה אִם־נָשַׁךְ הַנָּחָשׁ אֶת־אִישׁ וְהִבִּיט אֶל־נְחַשׁ
י יא הַנְּחֹשֶׁת וָחָי׃ וַיִּסְעוּ בְּנֵי יִשְׂרָאֵל וַיַּחֲנוּ בְּאֹבֹת׃ וַיִּסְעוּ מֵאֹבֹת וַיַּחֲנוּ ששי
יב בְּעִיֵּי הָעֲבָרִים בַּמִּדְבָּר אֲשֶׁר עַל־פְּנֵי מוֹאָב מִמִּזְרַח הַשָּׁמֶשׁ׃ מִשָּׁם
יג נָסָעוּ וַיַּחֲנוּ בְּנַחַל זָרֶד׃ מִשָּׁם נָסָעוּ וַיַּחֲנוּ מֵעֵבֶר אַרְנוֹן אֲשֶׁר בַּמִּדְבָּר
הַיֹּצֵא מִגְּבֻל הָאֱמֹרִי כִּי אַרְנוֹן גְּבוּל מוֹאָב בֵּין מוֹאָב וּבֵין הָאֱמֹרִי׃
יד עַל־כֵּן יֵאָמַר בְּסֵפֶר מִלְחֲמֹת יהוה אֶת־וָהֵב בְּסוּפָה וְאֶת־הַנְּחָלִים
טו אַרְנוֹן׃ וְאֶשֶׁד הַנְּחָלִים אֲשֶׁר נָטָה לְשֶׁבֶת עָר וְנִשְׁעַן לִגְבוּל מוֹאָב׃
טז וּמִשָּׁם בְּאֵרָה הִוא הַבְּאֵר אֲשֶׁר אָמַר יהוה לְמֹשֶׁה אֱסֹף אֶת־הָעָם
יז וְאֶתְּנָה לָהֶם מָיִם׃ אָז יָשִׁיר יִשְׂרָאֵל אֶת־הַשִּׁירָה הַזֹּאת
יח עֲלִי בְאֵר עֱנוּ־לָהּ׃ בְּאֵר חֲפָרוּהָ שָׂרִים כָּרוּהָ נְדִיבֵי הָעָם בִּמְחֹקֵק
יט בְּמִשְׁעֲנֹתָם וּמִמִּדְבָּר מַתָּנָה׃ וּמִמַּתָּנָה נַחֲלִיאֵל וּמִנַּחֲלִיאֵל בָּמוֹת׃
כ וּמִבָּמוֹת הַגַּיְא אֲשֶׁר בִּשְׂדֵה מוֹאָב רֹאשׁ הַפִּסְגָּה וְנִשְׁקָפָה עַל־פְּנֵי
הַיְשִׁימֹן׃
כא כב וַיִּשְׁלַח יִשְׂרָאֵל מַלְאָכִים אֶל־סִיחֹן מֶלֶךְ־הָאֱמֹרִי לֵאמֹר׃ אֶעְבְּרָה שביעי /רביעי/
בְאַרְצֶךָ לֹא נִטֶּה בְּשָׂדֶה וּבְכֶרֶם לֹא נִשְׁתֶּה מֵי בְאֵר בְּדֶרֶךְ הַמֶּלֶךְ
כג נֵלֵךְ עַד אֲשֶׁר־נַעֲבֹר גְּבֻלֶךָ׃ וְלֹא־נָתַן סִיחֹן אֶת־יִשְׂרָאֵל עֲבֹר בִּגְבֻלוֹ
וַיֶּאֱסֹף סִיחֹן אֶת־כׇּל־עַמּוֹ וַיֵּצֵא לִקְרַאת יִשְׂרָאֵל הַמִּדְבָּרָה וַיָּבֹא יָהְצָה
כד וַיִּלָּחֶם בְּיִשְׂרָאֵל׃ וַיַּכֵּהוּ יִשְׂרָאֵל לְפִי־חָרֶב וַיִּירַשׁ אֶת־אַרְצוֹ מֵאַרְנֹן
כה עַד־יַבֹּק עַד־בְּנֵי עַמּוֹן כִּי עַז גְּבוּל בְּנֵי עַמּוֹן׃ וַיִּקַּח יִשְׂרָאֵל אֵת כׇּל־
הֶעָרִים הָאֵלֶּה וַיֵּשֶׁב יִשְׂרָאֵל בְּכׇל־עָרֵי הָאֱמֹרִי בְּחֶשְׁבּוֹן וּבְכׇל־בְּנֹתֶיהָ׃
כו כִּי חֶשְׁבּוֹן עִיר סִיחֹן מֶלֶךְ הָאֱמֹרִי הִוא וְהוּא נִלְחַם בְּמֶלֶךְ מוֹאָב
כז הָרִאשׁוֹן וַיִּקַּח אֶת־כׇּל־אַרְצוֹ מִיָּדוֹ עַד־אַרְנֹן׃ עַל־כֵּן יֹאמְרוּ הַמֹּשְׁלִים

28 of Siḥon. For fire had gone forth from Ḥeshbon, a flame from the town of
29 Siḥon. It consumed Ar of Moav the masters of Arnon's high shrines. Woe for
you, Moav! You are destroyed, men of Kemosh![54] He made his sons fugitives,
30 his daughters fugitives, to Siḥon the Amorite king. Yet we – we threw them
wholly down, from Ḥeshbon to Divon, laid waste as far as Nofaḥ, as far as
31 32 Meideva." So Israel settled in the land of the Amorites. And Moshe sent spies
to Yazer. And Israel captured its surrounding settlements and dispossessed
33 the Amorites who were there. Then they turned and journeyed along the
road toward Bashan. Og, king of Bashan, with all his people came out to Edrei
34 to engage them in battle. But the LORD said to Moshe: "Do not be afraid of
him, for I have given him into your hand, with all his people and his land. Do
35 to him what you did to Siḥon, king of the Amorites, who lived in Ḥeshbon."
So they struck him down, together with his sons and all his people until
22 1 there were no survivors, and they took possession of his land. The Israelites
moved on and encamped in the plains of Moav across the Jordan from
2 Yeriḥo. And Balak son of Tzipor had seen all that the Israelites had BALAK
3 done to the Amorites. The Moabites were in deep dread of the people because
4 they were so numerous. Fearful of the Israelites, the Moabites said to the
elders of Midyan, "This horde will now lick up everything around us, as an
ox licks up grass in the field." Balak son of Tzipor was king of Moav at that
5 time. He sent messengers to summon Bilam son of Beor who was at Petor
near the River[55] in his native land: "A people has come out of Egypt, and now
they cover the face of the land – and they have settled down alongside me.
6 Please, come now and curse this people for me, for they are stronger than I.
Perhaps then I will be able to defeat them and drive them from the land, for
I know that whomsoever you bless is blessed and whomsoever you curse is
7 cursed." So the elders of Moav and Midyan went, carrying with them payment
8 for divination. They came to Bilam and repeated Balak's words to him. "Spend
the night here," he said, "and I will give you your reply the LORD speaks to
9 me." So the princes of Moav stayed the night with Bilam. God came to Bilam
10 and said, "Who are these men with you?" And Bilam replied to God, "Balak
11 son of Tzipor, king of Moav, has sent me a message: 'A people has come out
of Egypt and covers the face of the land. Now come and curse them for me.
12 Perhaps I will be able to fight against them and drive them away.'" "Do not
go with them," said God to Bilam. "Do not curse this people, for they are
13 blessed." Then Bilam arose in the morning and said to Balak's princes, "Go
14 back to your land, because the LORD has refused to let me go with you." The
15 princes of Moav rose and went to Balak and said, "Bilam refuses to go with
16 us." Balak then sent other princes, yet more numerous and eminent than the
first. They came to Bilam and said to him, "This is what Balak son of Tzipor
17 says: 'Do not let anything prevent you from coming to me, for I will do you
great honor, and whatever else you ask of me. Please – come and curse this

---

54 | Kemosh was the Moabite deity.

55 | Referring to the Euphrates.

כח בֹּאוּ חֶשְׁבּוֹן תִּבָּנֶה וְתִכּוֹנֵן עִיר סִיחוֹן: כִּי־אֵשׁ יָצְאָה מֵחֶשְׁבּוֹן לֶהָבָה
כט מִקִּרְיַת סִיחֹן אָכְלָה עָר מוֹאָב בַּעֲלֵי בָּמוֹת אַרְנֹן: אוֹי־לְךָ מוֹאָב
אָבַדְתָּ עַם־כְּמוֹשׁ נָתַן בָּנָיו פְּלֵיטִם וּבְנֹתָיו בַּשְּׁבִית לְמֶלֶךְ אֱמֹרִי סִיחוֹן:
ל לא וַנִּירָם אָבַד חֶשְׁבּוֹן עַד־דִּיבֹן וַנַּשִּׁים עַד־נֹפַח אֲשֶׁר עַד־מֵידְבָא: וַיֵּשֶׁב
לב יִשְׂרָאֵל בְּאֶרֶץ הָאֱמֹרִי: וַיִּשְׁלַח מֹשֶׁה לְרַגֵּל אֶת־יַעְזֵר וַיִּלְכְּדוּ בְּנֹתֶיהָ
לג ויירש אֶת־הָאֱמֹרִי אֲשֶׁר־שָׁם: וַיִּפְנוּ וַיַּעֲלוּ דֶּרֶךְ הַבָּשָׁן וַיֵּצֵא עוֹג מֶלֶךְ־ וַיּוֹרֶשׁ
לד הַבָּשָׁן לִקְרָאתָם הוּא וְכָל־עַמּוֹ לַמִּלְחָמָה אֶדְרֶעִי: וַיֹּאמֶר יהוה אֶל־ מפטיר
מֹשֶׁה אַל־תִּירָא אֹתוֹ כִּי בְיָדְךָ נָתַתִּי אֹתוֹ וְאֶת־כָּל־עַמּוֹ וְאֶת־אַרְצוֹ
וְעָשִׂיתָ לּוֹ כַּאֲשֶׁר עָשִׂיתָ לְסִיחֹן מֶלֶךְ הָאֱמֹרִי אֲשֶׁר יוֹשֵׁב בְּחֶשְׁבּוֹן:
לה וַיַּכּוּ אֹתוֹ וְאֶת־בָּנָיו וְאֶת־כָּל־עַמּוֹ עַד־בִּלְתִּי הִשְׁאִיר־לוֹ שָׂרִיד וַיִּירְשׁוּ
כב א אֶת־אַרְצוֹ: וַיִּסְעוּ בְּנֵי יִשְׂרָאֵל וַיַּחֲנוּ בְּעַרְבוֹת מוֹאָב מֵעֵבֶר לְיַרְדֵּן
ב יְרֵחוֹ: וַיַּרְא בָּלָק בֶּן־צִפּוֹר אֵת כָּל־אֲשֶׁר־עָשָׂה יִשְׂרָאֵל יט בלק
ג לָאֱמֹרִי: וַיָּגָר מוֹאָב מִפְּנֵי הָעָם מְאֹד כִּי רַב־הוּא וַיָּקָץ מוֹאָב מִפְּנֵי
ד בְּנֵי יִשְׂרָאֵל: וַיֹּאמֶר מוֹאָב אֶל־זִקְנֵי מִדְיָן עַתָּה יְלַחֲכוּ הַקָּהָל אֶת־
כָּל־סְבִיבֹתֵינוּ כִּלְחֹךְ הַשּׁוֹר אֵת יֶרֶק הַשָּׂדֶה וּבָלָק בֶּן־צִפּוֹר מֶלֶךְ
ה לְמוֹאָב בָּעֵת הַהִוא: וַיִּשְׁלַח מַלְאָכִים אֶל־בִּלְעָם בֶּן־בְּעֹר פְּתוֹרָה
אֲשֶׁר עַל־הַנָּהָר אֶרֶץ בְּנֵי־עַמּוֹ לִקְרֹא־לוֹ לֵאמֹר הִנֵּה עַם יָצָא מִמִּצְרַיִם
ו הִנֵּה כִסָּה אֶת־עֵין הָאָרֶץ וְהוּא יֹשֵׁב מִמֻּלִי: וְעַתָּה לְכָה־נָּא אָרָה־לִּי
אֶת־הָעָם הַזֶּה כִּי־עָצוּם הוּא מִמֶּנִּי אוּלַי אוּכַל נַכֶּה־בּוֹ וַאֲגָרְשֶׁנּוּ מִן־
ז הָאָרֶץ כִּי יָדַעְתִּי אֵת אֲשֶׁר־תְּבָרֵךְ מְבֹרָךְ וַאֲשֶׁר תָּאֹר יוּאָר: וַיֵּלְכוּ
זִקְנֵי מוֹאָב וְזִקְנֵי מִדְיָן וּקְסָמִים בְּיָדָם וַיָּבֹאוּ אֶל־בִּלְעָם וַיְדַבְּרוּ אֵלָיו
ח דִּבְרֵי בָלָק: וַיֹּאמֶר אֲלֵיהֶם לִינוּ פֹה הַלַּיְלָה וַהֲשִׁבֹתִי אֶתְכֶם דָּבָר
ט כַּאֲשֶׁר יְדַבֵּר יהוה אֵלָי וַיֵּשְׁבוּ שָׂרֵי־מוֹאָב עִם־בִּלְעָם: וַיָּבֹא אֱלֹהִים
י אֶל־בִּלְעָם וַיֹּאמֶר מִי הָאֲנָשִׁים הָאֵלֶּה עִמָּךְ: וַיֹּאמֶר בִּלְעָם אֶל־
יא הָאֱלֹהִים בָּלָק בֶּן־צִפֹּר מֶלֶךְ מוֹאָב שָׁלַח אֵלָי: הִנֵּה הָעָם הַיֹּצֵא
מִמִּצְרַיִם וַיְכַס אֶת־עֵין הָאָרֶץ עַתָּה לְכָה קָבָה־לִּי אֹתוֹ אוּלַי אוּכַל
יב לְהִלָּחֶם בּוֹ וְגֵרַשְׁתִּיו: וַיֹּאמֶר אֱלֹהִים אֶל־בִּלְעָם לֹא תֵלֵךְ עִמָּהֶם לֹא
יג תָאֹר אֶת־הָעָם כִּי בָרוּךְ הוּא: וַיָּקָם בִּלְעָם בַּבֹּקֶר וַיֹּאמֶר אֶל־שָׂרֵי שני /חמישי/
יד בָלָק לְכוּ אֶל־אַרְצְכֶם כִּי מֵאֵן יהוה לְתִתִּי לַהֲלֹךְ עִמָּכֶם: וַיָּקוּמוּ שָׂרֵי
טו מוֹאָב וַיָּבֹאוּ אֶל־בָּלָק וַיֹּאמְרוּ מֵאֵן בִּלְעָם הֲלֹךְ עִמָּנוּ: וַיֹּסֶף עוֹד בָּלָק
טז שְׁלֹחַ שָׂרִים רַבִּים וְנִכְבָּדִים מֵאֵלֶּה: וַיָּבֹאוּ אֶל־בִּלְעָם וַיֹּאמְרוּ לוֹ כֹּה
יז אָמַר בָּלָק בֶּן־צִפּוֹר אַל־נָא תִמָּנַע מֵהֲלֹךְ אֵלָי: כִּי־כַבֵּד אֲכַבֶּדְךָ מְאֹד

18 people for me.'" Bilam replied to Balak's servants, "Even if Balak were to give
me his palace full of silver and gold, I could not do anything, small or great,
19 to transgress the word of the LORD my God. But now, you too remain here
20 tonight so that I may know what else the LORD may tell me." God came to
Bilam that night and said to him, "If the men have come to summon you, you
21 may get up and go with them; but do only what I tell you to do." So Bilam
22 rose in the morning, saddled his donkey, and went along with the princes of
Moav. God was furious at his going, and an angel of the LORD stood in the
23 road to oppose him as he was riding on his donkey, his two servants with him.
The donkey saw the angel of the LORD standing in the road, drawn sword in
hand, and she swerved from the road into a field. And Bilam beat the donkey
24 to urge her back onto the road. Then the angel of the LORD was standing in a
25 narrow path between vineyards with a wall on either side. When the donkey
saw the angel of the LORD, she pressed against the wall, crushing Bilam's foot
26 against it. He beat her once again. And the angel of the LORD went ahead
27 and stood in a narrow place where there was no room at all to turn right or
left. When the donkey saw the angel of the LORD, she lay down under Bilam.
28 Bilam was furious and beat the donkey with his stick. Then the LORD opened
the donkey's mouth and – "What have I done to you," she said to Bilam, "that
29 you have struck me these three times?" "You are playing games with me," said
Bilam to the donkey. "If only I had a sword in my hand, I would kill you here
30 and now." But the donkey said to Bilam, "Am I not your donkey on whom
you have always ridden to this day? Have I been in the habit of doing this to
31 you?" "No," he replied. Then the LORD uncovered Bilam's eyes, and he saw
the angel of the LORD standing in the road, drawn sword in hand. He bowed
32 and prostrated himself facedown. The angel of the LORD said to him, "Why
have you beaten your donkey these three times? It was I who came out here
33 to oppose you, because your way is perverse to me. The donkey saw me and
turned away from me these three times. If she had not turned away from me,
34 I would certainly have killed you by now and let her live." Bilam said to the
angel of the LORD, "I have sinned, for I did not know that you were standing
35 against me in the road. Now, if you consider it wrong, I will go back." The
angel of the LORD said to Bilam, "Go with the men, but say nothing except
36 what I tell you." So Bilam continued on with Balak's princes. When Balak
heard that Bilam was coming, he went out to meet him at the city of Moav, at
37 the Arnon border on the edge of his territory. Balak said to Bilam, "Did I not
send to summon you? Why did you not come to me? Am I really not able to
38 offer you any honor?" Bilam replied to Balak, "Well, I have come to you now.
But can I speak any words I choose? I can only say the word God puts into

יח וְכֹל אֲשֶׁר־תֹּאמַר אֵלַי אֶעֱשֶׂה וּלְכָה־נָּא קָבָה־לִּי אֵת הָעָם הַזֶּה: וַיַּעַן
בִּלְעָם וַיֹּאמֶר אֶל־עַבְדֵי בָלָק אִם־יִתֶּן־לִי בָלָק מְלֹא בֵיתוֹ כֶּסֶף וְזָהָב
יט לֹא אוּכַל לַעֲבֹר אֶת־פִּי יהוה אֱלֹהָי לַעֲשׂוֹת קְטַנָּה אוֹ גְדוֹלָה: וְעַתָּה
כ שְׁבוּ נָא בָזֶה גַּם־אַתֶּם הַלָּיְלָה וְאֵדְעָה מַה־יֹּסֵף יהוה דַּבֵּר עִמִּי: וַיָּבֹא
אֱלֹהִים | אֶל־בִּלְעָם לַיְלָה וַיֹּאמֶר לוֹ אִם־לִקְרֹא לְךָ בָּאוּ הָאֲנָשִׁים
כא קוּם לֵךְ אִתָּם וְאַךְ אֶת־הַדָּבָר אֲשֶׁר־אֲדַבֵּר אֵלֶיךָ אֹתוֹ תַעֲשֶׂה: וַיָּקָם שלישי
כב בִּלְעָם בַּבֹּקֶר וַיַּחֲבֹשׁ אֶת־אֲתֹנוֹ וַיֵּלֶךְ עִם־שָׂרֵי מוֹאָב: וַיִּחַר־אַף
אֱלֹהִים כִּי־הוֹלֵךְ הוּא וַיִּתְיַצֵּב מַלְאַךְ יהוה בַּדֶּרֶךְ לְשָׂטָן לוֹ וְהוּא רֹכֵב
כג עַל־אֲתֹנוֹ וּשְׁנֵי נְעָרָיו עִמּוֹ: וַתֵּרֶא הָאָתוֹן אֶת־מַלְאַךְ יהוה נִצָּב בַּדֶּרֶךְ
וְחַרְבּוֹ שְׁלוּפָה בְּיָדוֹ וַתֵּט הָאָתוֹן מִן־הַדֶּרֶךְ וַתֵּלֶךְ בַּשָּׂדֶה וַיַּךְ בִּלְעָם
כד אֶת־הָאָתוֹן לְהַטֹּתָהּ הַדָּרֶךְ: וַיַּעֲמֹד מַלְאַךְ יהוה בְּמִשְׁעוֹל הַכְּרָמִים
כה גָּדֵר מִזֶּה וְגָדֵר מִזֶּה: וַתֵּרֶא הָאָתוֹן אֶת־מַלְאַךְ יהוה וַתִּלָּחֵץ אֶל־הַקִּיר
כו וַתִּלְחַץ אֶת־רֶגֶל בִּלְעָם אֶל־הַקִּיר וַיֹּסֶף לְהַכֹּתָהּ: וַיּוֹסֶף מַלְאַךְ־יהוה
כז עֲבוֹר וַיַּעֲמֹד בְּמָקוֹם צָר אֲשֶׁר אֵין־דֶּרֶךְ לִנְטוֹת יָמִין וּשְׂמֹאול: וַתֵּרֶא
הָאָתוֹן אֶת־מַלְאַךְ יהוה וַתִּרְבַּץ תַּחַת בִּלְעָם וַיִּחַר־אַף בִּלְעָם וַיַּךְ
כח אֶת־הָאָתוֹן בַּמַּקֵּל: וַיִּפְתַּח יהוה אֶת־פִּי הָאָתוֹן וַתֹּאמֶר לְבִלְעָם
כט מֶה־עָשִׂיתִי לְךָ כִּי הִכִּיתַנִי זֶה שָׁלֹשׁ רְגָלִים: וַיֹּאמֶר בִּלְעָם לָאָתוֹן כִּי
ל הִתְעַלַּלְתְּ בִּי לוּ יֶשׁ־חֶרֶב בְּיָדִי כִּי עַתָּה הֲרַגְתִּיךְ: וַתֹּאמֶר הָאָתוֹן
אֶל־בִּלְעָם הֲלוֹא אָנֹכִי אֲתֹנְךָ אֲשֶׁר־רָכַבְתָּ עָלַי מֵעוֹדְךָ עַד־הַיּוֹם הַזֶּה
לא הַהַסְכֵּן הִסְכַּנְתִּי לַעֲשׂוֹת לְךָ כֹּה וַיֹּאמֶר לֹא: וַיְגַל יהוה אֶת־עֵינֵי בִלְעָם
וַיַּרְא אֶת־מַלְאַךְ יהוה נִצָּב בַּדֶּרֶךְ וְחַרְבּוֹ שְׁלֻפָה בְּיָדוֹ וַיִּקֹּד וַיִּשְׁתַּחוּ
לב לְאַפָּיו: וַיֹּאמֶר אֵלָיו מַלְאַךְ יהוה עַל־מָה הִכִּיתָ אֶת־אֲתֹנְךָ זֶה שָׁלוֹשׁ
לג רְגָלִים הִנֵּה אָנֹכִי יָצָאתִי לְשָׂטָן כִּי־יָרַט הַדֶּרֶךְ לְנֶגְדִּי: וַתִּרְאַנִי הָאָתוֹן
וַתֵּט לְפָנַי זֶה שָׁלֹשׁ רְגָלִים אוּלַי נָטְתָה מִפָּנַי כִּי עַתָּה גַּם־אֹתְכָה
לד הָרַגְתִּי וְאוֹתָהּ הֶחֱיֵיתִי: וַיֹּאמֶר בִּלְעָם אֶל־מַלְאַךְ יהוה חָטָאתִי כִּי
לֹא יָדַעְתִּי כִּי אַתָּה נִצָּב לִקְרָאתִי בַּדָּרֶךְ וְעַתָּה אִם־רַע בְּעֵינֶיךָ אָשׁוּבָה
לה לִּי: וַיֹּאמֶר מַלְאַךְ יהוה אֶל־בִּלְעָם לֵךְ עִם־הָאֲנָשִׁים וְאֶפֶס אֶת־הַדָּבָר
לו אֲשֶׁר־אֲדַבֵּר אֵלֶיךָ אֹתוֹ תְדַבֵּר וַיֵּלֶךְ בִּלְעָם עִם־שָׂרֵי בָלָק: וַיִּשְׁמַע
בָלָק כִּי־בָא בִלְעָם וַיֵּצֵא לִקְרָאתוֹ אֶל־עִיר מוֹאָב אֲשֶׁר עַל־גְּבוּל
לז אַרְנֹן אֲשֶׁר בִּקְצֵה הַגְּבוּל: וַיֹּאמֶר בָּלָק אֶל־בִּלְעָם הֲלֹא שָׁלֹחַ שָׁלַחְתִּי
אֵלֶיךָ לִקְרֹא־לָךְ לָמָּה לֹא־הָלַכְתָּ אֵלָי הַאֻמְנָם לֹא אוּכַל כַּבְּדֶךָ:
לח וַיֹּאמֶר בִּלְעָם אֶל־בָּלָק הִנֵּה־בָאתִי אֵלֶיךָ עַתָּה הֲיָכֹל אוּכַל דַּבֵּר

39 my mouth." Then Bilam went with Balak and they came to Kiryat Ḥutzot.
40 Balak sacrificed oxen and sheep and sent them to Bilam and the princes who
41 were with him. In the morning Balak took Bilam up to Bamot Baal, where
23 1 he could see part of the people. Bilam said to Balak, "Build me seven altars
2 here and prepare for me seven bulls and seven rams." Balak did as Bilam said,
3 and Balak and Bilam offered a bull and a ram on each altar. Then Bilam said
to Balak, "Stand by your offerings and I will go; perhaps the LORD will come
4 to meet me. Whatever He shows me, I will tell you." And he went off alone.
God met Bilam, who said to Him, "I have prepared seven altars; on each altar
5 I have offered a bull and a ram." And the LORD put a word in Bilam's mouth,
6 "Go back to Balak and say this." He went back to him, and found him standing
7 by his offering together with all the princes of Moav. And Bilam took up his
oracle and said: "Balak brought me from Aram, the king of Moav from the
8 eastern hills. 'Go: curse Yaakov for me; go: denounce Israel.' How can I curse
whom God has not cursed? How can I denounce whom the LORD has not
9 denounced? From the tops of crags I see him; from the hills I gaze down: a
10 people that dwells alone; not reckoning itself among nations. Who can number the dust of Yaakov, count even a fourth of Israel? Let me die the death of
11 the upright, and let my end be like his." And Balak said to Bilam, "What have
you done to me? I brought you to curse my enemies, and you have blessed
12 them." He answered, "Am I not obliged to speak strictly the words the LORD
13 puts in my mouth?" Then Balak said to him, "Come with me to another place
where you will see them. You will see only part of them; you will not see them
14 all. Curse them for me from there." He took him to the field of Tzofim, to the
top of Pisga. He built seven altars and on each altar offered a bull and a ram.
15 Then Bilam said to Balak, "Stand here beside your offering, while I seek
16 a meeting there." The LORD met Bilam and put a word in his mouth. "Go
17 back to Balak," He said, "and tell him this." He came to him and found him
standing by his offering together with the princes of Moav. Balak asked him,
18 "What did the LORD say?" So he took up his oracle and said: "Stand up,
19 Balak, listen; pay attention, son of Tzipor. Not man is God, to lie; no mortal,
20 to change His mind. Would He speak and not fulfill, would He promise and
21 not keep? I received an order to bless. He has blessed; I cannot revoke it. He
has glimpsed no wrong in Yaakov, He has seen no sin in Israel. The LORD
22 their God is with them, in them the King's horn blasts sounds. God, who
23 freed them from Egypt, is like the oryx's proud horn for them. There is no
divination over Yaakov, no spell against Israel can hold. It will now[56] be said of
24 Yaakov, of Israel, 'See what God has done.' A people – see – rises like a lioness,
lifts itself up like a lion. It will not lie down until it eats its meat and drinks the
25 26 blood of the slain." Balak said to Bilam, "Do not curse or bless them." But
Bilam answered, "Did I not tell you, 'I must do whatever the LORD says'?"

---

56 | That is, after God's salvation of Israel.

לט מְאוּמָה הַדָּבָר אֲשֶׁר יָשִׂים אֱלֹהִים בְּפִי אֹתוֹ אֲדַבֵּר: וַיֵּלֶךְ בִּלְעָם עִם־ רביעי /ששי/
מ בָּלָק וַיָּבֹאוּ קִרְיַת חֻצוֹת: וַיִּזְבַּח בָּלָק בָּקָר וָצֹאן וַיְשַׁלַּח לְבִלְעָם
מא וְלַשָּׂרִים אֲשֶׁר אִתּוֹ: וַיְהִי בַבֹּקֶר וַיִּקַּח בָּלָק אֶת־בִּלְעָם וַיַּעֲלֵהוּ בָּמוֹת
כג א בָּעַל וַיַּרְא מִשָּׁם קְצֵה הָעָם: וַיֹּאמֶר בִּלְעָם אֶל־בָּלָק בְּנֵה־לִי בָזֶה
ב שִׁבְעָה מִזְבְּחֹת וְהָכֵן לִי בָּזֶה שִׁבְעָה פָרִים וְשִׁבְעָה אֵילִים: וַיַּעַשׂ בָּלָק
ג כַּאֲשֶׁר דִּבֶּר בִּלְעָם וַיַּעַל בָּלָק וּבִלְעָם פַּר וָאַיִל בַּמִּזְבֵּחַ: וַיֹּאמֶר בִּלְעָם
לְבָלָק הִתְיַצֵּב עַל־עֹלָתֶךָ וְאֵלְכָה אוּלַי יִקָּרֵה יְהוָה לִקְרָאתִי וּדְבַר
ד מַה־יַּרְאֵנִי וְהִגַּדְתִּי לָךְ וַיֵּלֶךְ שֶׁפִי: וַיִּקָּר אֱלֹהִים אֶל־בִּלְעָם וַיֹּאמֶר
ה אֵלָיו אֶת־שִׁבְעַת הַמִּזְבְּחֹת עָרַכְתִּי וָאַעַל פַּר וָאַיִל בַּמִּזְבֵּחַ: וַיָּשֶׂם
ו יְהוָה דָּבָר בְּפִי בִלְעָם וַיֹּאמֶר שׁוּב אֶל־בָּלָק וְכֹה תְדַבֵּר: וַיָּשָׁב אֵלָיו
ז וְהִנֵּה נִצָּב עַל־עֹלָתוֹ הוּא וְכָל־שָׂרֵי מוֹאָב: וַיִּשָּׂא מְשָׁלוֹ וַיֹּאמַר מִן־
אֲרָם יַנְחֵנִי בָלָק מֶלֶךְ־מוֹאָב מֵהַרְרֵי־קֶדֶם לְכָה אָרָה־לִּי יַעֲקֹב וּלְכָה
ח זֹעֲמָה יִשְׂרָאֵל: מָה אֶקֹּב לֹא קַבֹּה אֵל וּמָה אֶזְעֹם לֹא זָעַם יְהוָה:
ט כִּי־מֵרֹאשׁ צֻרִים אֶרְאֶנּוּ וּמִגְּבָעוֹת אֲשׁוּרֶנּוּ הֶן־עָם לְבָדָד יִשְׁכֹּן וּבַגּוֹיִם
י לֹא יִתְחַשָּׁב: מִי מָנָה עֲפַר יַעֲקֹב וּמִסְפָּר אֶת־רֹבַע יִשְׂרָאֵל תָּמֹת נַפְשִׁי כ
יא מוֹת יְשָׁרִים וּתְהִי אַחֲרִיתִי כָּמֹהוּ: וַיֹּאמֶר בָּלָק אֶל־בִּלְעָם מֶה עָשִׂיתָ
יב לִי לָקֹב אֹיְבַי לְקַחְתִּיךָ וְהִנֵּה בֵּרַכְתָּ בָרֵךְ: וַיַּעַן וַיֹּאמַר הֲלֹא אֵת אֲשֶׁר
יג יָשִׂים יְהוָה בְּפִי אֹתוֹ אֶשְׁמֹר לְדַבֵּר: וַיֹּאמֶר אֵלָיו בָּלָק לְךָ־נָּא אִתִּי חמישי
אֶל־מָקוֹם אַחֵר אֲשֶׁר תִּרְאֶנּוּ מִשָּׁם אֶפֶס קָצֵהוּ תִרְאֶה וְכֻלּוֹ לֹא תִרְאֶה
יד וְקָבְנוֹ־לִי מִשָּׁם: וַיִּקָּחֵהוּ שְׂדֵה צֹפִים אֶל־רֹאשׁ הַפִּסְגָּה וַיִּבֶן שִׁבְעָה
טו מִזְבְּחֹת וַיַּעַל פַּר וָאַיִל בַּמִּזְבֵּחַ: וַיֹּאמֶר אֶל־בָּלָק הִתְיַצֵּב כֹּה עַל־עֹלָתֶךָ
טז וְאָנֹכִי אִקָּרֶה כֹּה: וַיִּקָּר יְהוָה אֶל־בִּלְעָם וַיָּשֶׂם דָּבָר בְּפִיו וַיֹּאמֶר שׁוּב
יז אֶל־בָּלָק וְכֹה תְדַבֵּר: וַיָּבֹא אֵלָיו וְהִנּוֹ נִצָּב עַל־עֹלָתוֹ וְשָׂרֵי מוֹאָב
יח אִתּוֹ וַיֹּאמֶר לוֹ בָּלָק מַה־דִּבֶּר יְהוָה: וַיִּשָּׂא מְשָׁלוֹ וַיֹּאמַר קוּם בָּלָק
יט וּשְׁמָע הַאֲזִינָה עָדַי בְּנוֹ צִפֹּר: לֹא אִישׁ אֵל וִיכַזֵּב וּבֶן־אָדָם וְיִתְנֶחָם
כ הַהוּא אָמַר וְלֹא יַעֲשֶׂה וְדִבֶּר וְלֹא יְקִימֶנָּה: הִנֵּה בָרֵךְ לָקָחְתִּי וּבֵרֵךְ
כא וְלֹא אֲשִׁיבֶנָּה: לֹא־הִבִּיט אָוֶן בְּיַעֲקֹב וְלֹא־רָאָה עָמָל בְּיִשְׂרָאֵל יְהוָה
כב אֱלֹהָיו עִמּוֹ וּתְרוּעַת מֶלֶךְ בּוֹ: אֵל מוֹצִיאָם מִמִּצְרָיִם כְּתוֹעֲפֹת רְאֵם
כג לוֹ: כִּי לֹא־נַחַשׁ בְּיַעֲקֹב וְלֹא־קֶסֶם בְּיִשְׂרָאֵל כָּעֵת יֵאָמֵר לְיַעֲקֹב
כד וּלְיִשְׂרָאֵל מַה־פָּעַל אֵל: הֶן־עָם כְּלָבִיא יָקוּם וְכַאֲרִי יִתְנַשָּׂא לֹא יִשְׁכַּב
כה עַד־יֹאכַל טֶרֶף וְדַם־חֲלָלִים יִשְׁתֶּה: וַיֹּאמֶר בָּלָק אֶל־בִּלְעָם גַּם־קֹב
כו לֹא תִקֳּבֶנּוּ גַּם־בָּרֵךְ לֹא תְבָרְכֶנּוּ: וַיַּעַן בִּלְעָם וַיֹּאמֶר אֶל־בָּלָק הֲלֹא

27 Then Balak said to Bilam, "Come now and I will take you to another place.
28 Perhaps God will deem it right to let you curse them for me there." So Balak
29 took Bilam to the top of Peor, overlooking the wasteland. Bilam said to Balak,
"Build me seven altars here and prepare for me seven bulls and seven rams."
30 Balak did as Bilam had said, and offered a bull and a ram on each altar. When
24 1 Bilam saw that it pleased the LORD to bless the Israelites, he did not go as at
2 other times to seek omens. Instead, he turned toward the wilderness. And
Bilam raised his eyes and saw Israel encamped there tribe by tribe, and God's
3 spirit came upon him. He took up his oracle and said: "The word of Bilam,
4 son of Beor; the word of the man whose eye is opened. The word of one
who hears God's speech, who sees a vision of Shaddai, who falls, but with
5 6 eyes unveiled.[57] How good are your tents, Yaakov, your homes, O Israel. Like
palm groves stretching forth, like gardens by the river, like aloes the LORD
7 planted, like cedars by the waters. Water will drip from his branches; his seed
has abundant water; his king will be higher than Agag,[58] his kingdom exalted.
8 God, who freed him from Egypt, is the oryx's proud horn to him. He will
9 devour enemy nations, break their bones, pierce them with arrows. Like a lion
he crouches, lies down, like a lioness; who dares to rouse him? Blessing on all
10 who bless you, on those who curse you, curse." Balak was furious with Bilam.
He struck his hands together. Balak said to Bilam, "I summoned you to curse
11 my enemies. Instead you have blessed them these three times over. Now get
away from here and go home. I said that I would honor you, but the LORD has
12 denied you all honor." Bilam replied to Balak, "Did I not tell the messengers
13 whom you sent to me, 'Even if Balak were to give me his palace full of silver
and gold, I could not do anything to transgress the word of the LORD, doing
either good or bad of my own accord. What the LORD says is what I must say.'
14 So now that I am going back to my people, let me advise you what this people
15 will do to your people in days to come." He took up his oracle, saying: "The
16 word of Bilam son of Beor, the word of a man whose eye is opened. The word
of one who hears God's speech, and has knowledge from the Most High, who
17 sees a vision of Shaddai, who falls, but with eyes unveiled. I see him,[59] but not
now; I gaze upon him, though not near: A star will shoot forth from Yaakov;
a scepter will arise from Israel, and smash the brow of Moav, and devastate
18 all children of Shet. Edom will become a possession, Se'ir the possession of
19 its foes. But Israel will act valiantly. From Yaakov will come forth a ruler and
20 empty the city[60] of survivors." He looked at Amalek; he took up his oracle and
21 said: "Amalek is first among nations,[61] but its end will be death forever." He
looked at the Kenites; he took up his oracle and said: "Invincible your dwell-
22 ing, your nest set in the rock. Yet Kayin is destined for burning, when Assyria
23 seizes you captive." And he took up his oracle and said, "Alas! Who will live

57 | Perhaps this line describes Bilam prophesying in a fallen position; cf., for example, Genesis 17:3.

58 | Agag was an Amalekite king; see I Samuel, chapter 15.

59 | This apparently refers to a future king of Israel.

60 | Perhaps an unspecified Edomite city, or the region of Edom generally.

61 | Amalek was the first group to attack Israel after the exodus from Egypt; see Exodus 17:8.

כז דִּבַּרְתִּי אֵלֶיךָ לֵאמֹר כֹּל אֲשֶׁר־יְדַבֵּר יְהוָה אֹתוֹ אֶעֱשֶׂה׃ וַיֹּאמֶר בָּלָק ששי /שביעי/
אֶל־בִּלְעָם לְכָה־נָּא אֶקָּחֲךָ אֶל־מָקוֹם אַחֵר אוּלַי יִישַׁר בְּעֵינֵי הָאֱלֹהִים
כח וְקַבֹּתוֹ לִי מִשָּׁם׃ וַיִּקַּח בָּלָק אֶת־בִּלְעָם רֹאשׁ הַפְּעוֹר הַנִּשְׁקָף עַל־פְּנֵי
כט הַיְשִׁימֹן׃ וַיֹּאמֶר בִּלְעָם אֶל־בָּלָק בְּנֵה־לִי בָזֶה שִׁבְעָה מִזְבְּחֹת וְהָכֵן
ל לִי בָּזֶה שִׁבְעָה פָרִים וְשִׁבְעָה אֵילִים׃ וַיַּעַשׂ בָּלָק כַּאֲשֶׁר אָמַר בִּלְעָם
כד א וַיַּעַל פָּר וָאַיִל בַּמִּזְבֵּחַ׃ וַיַּרְא בִּלְעָם כִּי טוֹב בְּעֵינֵי יְהוָה לְבָרֵךְ אֶת־
יִשְׂרָאֵל וְלֹא־הָלַךְ כְּפַעַם־בְּפַעַם לִקְרַאת נְחָשִׁים וַיָּשֶׁת אֶל־הַמִּדְבָּר
ב פָּנָיו׃ וַיִּשָּׂא בִלְעָם אֶת־עֵינָיו וַיַּרְא אֶת־יִשְׂרָאֵל שֹׁכֵן לִשְׁבָטָיו וַתְּהִי
ג עָלָיו רוּחַ אֱלֹהִים׃ וַיִּשָּׂא מְשָׁלוֹ וַיֹּאמַר נְאֻם בִּלְעָם בְּנוֹ בְעֹר וּנְאֻם
ד הַגֶּבֶר שְׁתֻם הָעָיִן׃ נְאֻם שֹׁמֵעַ אִמְרֵי־אֵל אֲשֶׁר מַחֲזֵה שַׁדַּי יֶחֱזֶה נֹפֵל
ה ו וּגְלוּי עֵינָיִם׃ מַה־טֹּבוּ אֹהָלֶיךָ יַעֲקֹב מִשְׁכְּנֹתֶיךָ יִשְׂרָאֵל׃ כִּנְחָלִים נִטָּיוּ
ז כְּגַנֹּת עֲלֵי נָהָר כַּאֲהָלִים נָטַע יְהוָה כַּאֲרָזִים עֲלֵי־מָיִם׃ יִזַּל־מַיִם מִדָּלְיָו
ח וְזַרְעוֹ בְּמַיִם רַבִּים וְיָרֹם מֵאֲגַג מַלְכּוֹ וְתִנַּשֵּׂא מַלְכֻתוֹ׃ אֵל מוֹצִיאוֹ
מִמִּצְרַיִם כְּתוֹעֲפֹת רְאֵם לוֹ יֹאכַל גּוֹיִם צָרָיו וְעַצְמֹתֵיהֶם יְגָרֵם וְחִצָּיו
ט יִמְחָץ׃ כָּרַע שָׁכַב כַּאֲרִי וּכְלָבִיא מִי יְקִימֶנּוּ מְבָרְכֶיךָ בָרוּךְ וְאֹרְרֶיךָ
י אָרוּר׃ וַיִּחַר־אַף בָּלָק אֶל־בִּלְעָם וַיִּסְפֹּק אֶת־כַּפָּיו וַיֹּאמֶר בָּלָק אֶל־
יא בִּלְעָם לָקֹב אֹיְבַי קְרָאתִיךָ וְהִנֵּה בֵּרַכְתָּ בָרֵךְ זֶה שָׁלֹשׁ פְּעָמִים׃ וְעַתָּה
בְּרַח־לְךָ אֶל־מְקוֹמֶךָ אָמַרְתִּי כַּבֵּד אֲכַבֶּדְךָ וְהִנֵּה מְנָעֲךָ יְהוָה מִכָּבוֹד׃
יב וַיֹּאמֶר בִּלְעָם אֶל־בָּלָק הֲלֹא גַּם אֶל־מַלְאָכֶיךָ אֲשֶׁר־שָׁלַחְתָּ אֵלַי
יג דִּבַּרְתִּי לֵאמֹר׃ אִם־יִתֶּן־לִי בָלָק מְלֹא בֵיתוֹ כֶּסֶף וְזָהָב לֹא אוּכַל
לַעֲבֹר אֶת־פִּי יְהוָה לַעֲשׂוֹת טוֹבָה אוֹ רָעָה מִלִּבִּי אֲשֶׁר־יְדַבֵּר יְהוָה
יד אֹתוֹ אֲדַבֵּר׃ וְעַתָּה הִנְנִי הוֹלֵךְ לְעַמִּי לְכָה אִיעָצְךָ אֲשֶׁר יַעֲשֶׂה הָעָם שביעי
טו הַזֶּה לְעַמְּךָ בְּאַחֲרִית הַיָּמִים׃ וַיִּשָּׂא מְשָׁלוֹ וַיֹּאמַר נְאֻם בִּלְעָם בְּנוֹ
טז בְעֹר וּנְאֻם הַגֶּבֶר שְׁתֻם הָעָיִן׃ נְאֻם שֹׁמֵעַ אִמְרֵי־אֵל וְיֹדֵעַ דַּעַת עֶלְיוֹן
יז מַחֲזֵה שַׁדַּי יֶחֱזֶה נֹפֵל וּגְלוּי עֵינָיִם׃ אֶרְאֶנּוּ וְלֹא עַתָּה אֲשׁוּרֶנּוּ וְלֹא
קָרוֹב דָּרַךְ כּוֹכָב מִיַּעֲקֹב וְקָם שֵׁבֶט מִיִּשְׂרָאֵל וּמָחַץ פַּאֲתֵי מוֹאָב
יח וְקַרְקַר כָּל־בְּנֵי־שֵׁת׃ וְהָיָה אֱדוֹם יְרֵשָׁה וְהָיָה יְרֵשָׁה שֵׂעִיר אֹיְבָיו
יט כ וְיִשְׂרָאֵל עֹשֶׂה חָיִל׃ וְיֵרְדְּ מִיַּעֲקֹב וְהֶאֱבִיד שָׂרִיד מֵעִיר׃ וַיַּרְא אֶת־
עֲמָלֵק וַיִּשָּׂא מְשָׁלוֹ וַיֹּאמַר רֵאשִׁית גּוֹיִם עֲמָלֵק וְאַחֲרִיתוֹ עֲדֵי אֹבֵד׃
כא וַיַּרְא אֶת־הַקֵּינִי וַיִּשָּׂא מְשָׁלוֹ וַיֹּאמַר אֵיתָן מוֹשָׁבֶךָ וְשִׂים בַּסֶּלַע
כב כג קִנֶּךָ׃ כִּי אִם־יִהְיֶה לְבָעֵר קָיִן עַד־מָה אַשּׁוּר תִּשְׁבֶּךָּ׃ וַיִּשָּׂא מְשָׁלוֹ

24 when God does this? Ships from the coast of Kitim will afflict Assyria, afflict
25 Ever; they too will perish for all time." Then Bilam rose and returned home,
and Balak also set off upon his way.
25 1 Israel was dwelling at Shitim. And the men began to consort with Moabite
2 women, who invited the people to join the sacrifices to their god; the men
3 ate, and then they worshipped the women's god. Israel allied itself with Baal
4 Peor,[62] and the LORD was filled with fury against Israel. "Take all the people's
leaders," said the LORD to Moshe, "and have them impaled before the LORD
5 in broad daylight, so that the LORD's fury with Israel may be allayed." Moshe
said to Israel's judges, "Each of you kill those of your men who have allied
6 themselves with Baal Peor." At that moment, an Israelite man brought a Midianite woman to his friends before the eyes of Moshe and the entire Israelite
7 community, who were weeping at the entrance to the Tent of Meeting. When
Pinḥas son of Elazar son of Aharon the priest saw this, he rose from the midst
8 of the community, took a spear in his hand, went after the Israelite man into
the tent, and stabbed both of them, the Israelite man and the woman, through
9 the stomach – and the plague among the Israelites ended. Those who had died
by the plague numbered twenty-four thousand.

PINḤAS

10 11 The LORD spoke to Moshe: "Pinḥas son of Elazar son of Aharon the priest has
allayed My rage against the Israelites. Because he was passionate on My behalf
12 among you, I did not destroy the Israelites in My own passion. Therefore, say
13 this: I grant him My covenant of peace. For him and for his descendants, it
shall be a covenant of everlasting priesthood, because he was passionate for
14 his God and made atonement on the part of the Israelites." The name of the
slain Israelite man who was killed with the Midianite woman was Zimri son
15 of Salu, leader of the ancestral House of Shimon. The name of the Midianite
woman who was killed was Kozbi, daughter of Tzur the tribal leader of a
Midianite ancestral house.
16 17 And the LORD spoke to Moshe: "Attack the Midianites and defeat them,
18 for they attacked you by the deception they practiced against you in the
Peor affair, and in the affair of their sister Kozbi, daughter of a Midianite
26 1 leader, who was killed on the day of the plague in the Peor affair."[63] After the
plague –
2 the LORD said to Moshe and Elazar son of Aharon the priest: "Take a census
of the entire Israelite community, from twenty years of age and upward, by
3 their ancestral houses: everyone in Israel capable of active service." Moshe
and Elazar the priest spoke to them in the plains of Moav by the Jordan
4 opposite Yeriḥo: "Take a census of those twenty years of age and upward just
as the LORD commanded Moshe and the Israelites who came out of Egypt."

---

62 | A local deity.

63 | The account of the attack itself appears in chapter 31.

כד וַיֹּאמַר אוֹי מִי יִחְיֶה מִשֻּׂמוֹ אֵל: וְצִים מִיַּד כִּתִּים וְעִנּוּ אַשּׁוּר וְעִנּוּ־עֵבֶר
כה וְגַם־הוּא עֲדֵי אֹבֵד: וַיָּקָם בִּלְעָם וַיֵּלֶךְ וַיָּשָׁב לִמְקֹמוֹ וְגַם־בָּלָק הָלַךְ
לְדַרְכּוֹ:
כה א ב וַיֵּשֶׁב יִשְׂרָאֵל בַּשִּׁטִּים וַיָּחֶל הָעָם לִזְנוֹת אֶל־בְּנוֹת מוֹאָב: וַתִּקְרֶאןָ כא
ג לָעָם לְזִבְחֵי אֱלֹהֵיהֶן וַיֹּאכַל הָעָם וַיִּשְׁתַּחֲווּ לֵאלֹהֵיהֶן: וַיִּצָּמֶד יִשְׂרָאֵל
ד לְבַעַל פְּעוֹר וַיִּחַר־אַף יהוה בְּיִשְׂרָאֵל: וַיֹּאמֶר יהוה אֶל־מֹשֶׁה קַח
אֶת־כָּל־רָאשֵׁי הָעָם וְהוֹקַע אוֹתָם לַיהוה נֶגֶד הַשָּׁמֶשׁ וְיָשֹׁב חֲרוֹן אַף־
ה יהוה מִיִּשְׂרָאֵל: וַיֹּאמֶר מֹשֶׁה אֶל־שֹׁפְטֵי יִשְׂרָאֵל הִרְגוּ אִישׁ אֲנָשָׁיו
ו הַנִּצְמָדִים לְבַעַל פְּעוֹר: וְהִנֵּה אִישׁ מִבְּנֵי יִשְׂרָאֵל בָּא וַיַּקְרֵב אֶל־אֶחָיו
אֶת־הַמִּדְיָנִית לְעֵינֵי מֹשֶׁה וּלְעֵינֵי כָּל־עֲדַת בְּנֵי־יִשְׂרָאֵל וְהֵמָּה בֹכִים
ז פֶּתַח אֹהֶל מוֹעֵד: וַיַּרְא פִּינְחָס בֶּן־אֶלְעָזָר בֶּן־אַהֲרֹן הַכֹּהֵן וַיָּקָם מפטיר
ח מִתּוֹךְ הָעֵדָה וַיִּקַּח רֹמַח בְּיָדוֹ: וַיָּבֹא אַחַר אִישׁ־יִשְׂרָאֵל אֶל־הַקֻּבָּה
וַיִּדְקֹר אֶת־שְׁנֵיהֶם אֵת אִישׁ יִשְׂרָאֵל וְאֶת־הָאִשָּׁה אֶל־קֳבָתָהּ וַתֵּעָצַר
ט הַמַּגֵּפָה מֵעַל בְּנֵי יִשְׂרָאֵל: וַיִּהְיוּ הַמֵּתִים בַּמַּגֵּפָה אַרְבָּעָה וְעֶשְׂרִים
אָלֶף:
י יא וַיְדַבֵּר יהוה אֶל־מֹשֶׁה לֵּאמֹר: פִּינְחָס בֶּן־אֶלְעָזָר בֶּן־אַהֲרֹן הַכֹּהֵן כב פינחס
הֵשִׁיב אֶת־חֲמָתִי מֵעַל בְּנֵי־יִשְׂרָאֵל בְּקַנְאוֹ אֶת־קִנְאָתִי בְּתוֹכָם וְלֹא־
יב כִלִּיתִי אֶת־בְּנֵי־יִשְׂרָאֵל בְּקִנְאָתִי: לָכֵן אֱמֹר הִנְנִי נֹתֵן לוֹ אֶת־בְּרִיתִי
יג שָׁלוֹם: וְהָיְתָה לּוֹ וּלְזַרְעוֹ אַחֲרָיו בְּרִית כְּהֻנַּת עוֹלָם תַּחַת אֲשֶׁר קִנֵּא
יד לֵאלֹהָיו וַיְכַפֵּר עַל־בְּנֵי יִשְׂרָאֵל: וְשֵׁם אִישׁ יִשְׂרָאֵל הַמֻּכֶּה אֲשֶׁר
טו הֻכָּה אֶת־הַמִּדְיָנִית זִמְרִי בֶּן־סָלוּא נְשִׂיא בֵית־אָב לַשִּׁמְעֹנִי: וְשֵׁם
הָאִשָּׁה הַמֻּכָּה הַמִּדְיָנִית כָּזְבִּי בַת־צוּר רֹאשׁ אֻמּוֹת בֵּית־אָב בְּמִדְיָן
הוּא:
טז יז וַיְדַבֵּר יהוה אֶל־מֹשֶׁה לֵּאמֹר: צָרוֹר אֶת־הַמִּדְיָנִים וְהִכִּיתֶם אוֹתָם:
יח כִּי־צֹרְרִים הֵם לָכֶם בְּנִכְלֵיהֶם אֲשֶׁר־נִכְּלוּ לָכֶם עַל־דְּבַר פְּעוֹר וְעַל־
דְּבַר כָּזְבִּי בַת־נְשִׂיא מִדְיָן אֲחֹתָם הַמֻּכָּה בְיוֹם־הַמַּגֵּפָה עַל־דְּבַר
כו א פְּעוֹר: וַיְהִי אַחֲרֵי הַמַּגֵּפָה
ב וַיֹּאמֶר יהוה אֶל־מֹשֶׁה וְאֶל אֶלְעָזָר בֶּן־אַהֲרֹן הַכֹּהֵן לֵאמֹר: שְׂאוּ
אֶת־רֹאשׁ ׀ כָּל־עֲדַת בְּנֵי־יִשְׂרָאֵל מִבֶּן עֶשְׂרִים שָׁנָה וָמַעְלָה לְבֵית
ג אֲבֹתָם כָּל־יֹצֵא צָבָא בְּיִשְׂרָאֵל: וַיְדַבֵּר מֹשֶׁה וְאֶלְעָזָר הַכֹּהֵן אֹתָם
ד בְּעַרְבֹת מוֹאָב עַל־יַרְדֵּן יְרֵחוֹ לֵאמֹר: מִבֶּן עֶשְׂרִים שָׁנָה וָמָעְלָה
כַּאֲשֶׁר צִוָּה יהוה אֶת־מֹשֶׁה וּבְנֵי יִשְׂרָאֵל הַיֹּצְאִים מֵאֶרֶץ מִצְרָיִם:

5 Reuven was Yisrael's firstborn. Reuven's descendants: of Ḥanokh, the clan of
6 Ḥanokh; of Palu, the clan of Palu; of Ḥetzron, the clan of Ḥetzron; of Karmi,
7 the clan of Karmi. These are the Reubenite clans. Their tally was 43,730.
8 9 Palu's descendants: Eliav. Eliav's descendants: Nemuel, Datan, and Aviram. These were the same Datan and Aviram, elect of the community, who
rebelled against Moshe and Aharon in the company of Koraḥ, when they
10 rebelled against the Lord.[64] The earth opened its mouth and swallowed
them, along with Koraḥ, when the company died and fire consumed the
11 two hundred fifty men; and they became a sign. But the sons of Koraḥ did
12 not die. Shimon's descendants by their clans: of Nemuel, the clan of
13 Nemuel; of Yamin, the clan of Yamin; of Yakhin, the clan of Yakhin; of Zeraḥ,
14 the clan of Zeraḥ; of Sha'ul, the clan of Sha'ul. These are the Simeonite clans:
15 22,200. Gad's descendants by their clans: of Tzefon, the clan of
16 Tzefon; of Ḥagi, the clan of Ḥagi; of Shuni, the clan of Shuni; of Ozni, the
17 clan of Ozni; of Eri, the clan of Eri; of Arod, the clan of Arod; of Areli, the clan
18 19 of Areli. These are the Gadite clans. Their tally was 40,500. Among
Yehuda's sons were Er and Onan; Er and Onan died in the land of Canaan.[65]
20 Yehuda's descendants by their clans: of Shela, the clan of Shela; of Peretz, the
21 clan of Peretz; of Zeraḥ, the clan of Zeraḥ. Peretz's descendants: of Ḥetzron,
22 the clan of Ḥetzron; of Ḥamul, the clan of Ḥamul. These are the clans of
23 Yehuda. Their tally was 76,500. Yissakhar's descendants by their
24 clans: of Tola, the clan of Tola; of Puva, the clan of Puva; of Yashuv, the clan
25 of Yashuv; of Shimron, the clan of Shimron. These are the clans of Yissakhar.
26 Their tally was 64,300. Zevulun's descendants by their clans: of Sered,
the clan of Sered; of Elon, the clan of Elon; of Yaḥle'el, the clan of Yaḥle'el.
27 28 These are the Zebulunite clans. Their tally was 60,500. Yosef's
29 descendants by their clans: Menashe and Efrayim – Menashe's descendants: of Makhir, the clan of Makhir. Makhir had a son Gilad. Of Gilad, the
30 clan of Gilad. These are Gilad's descendants: of I'ezer, the clan of I'ezer; of
31 Ḥelek, the clan of Ḥelek; of Asriel, the clan of Asriel; of Shekhem, the clan of
32 Shekhem; of Shemida, the clan of Shemida; and of Ḥefer, the clan of Ḥefer.
33 But Tzelofḥad son of Ḥefer had no sons, only daughters. The names of
34 Tzelofḥad's daughters were Maḥla, Noa, Ḥogla, Milka, and Tirtza.[66] These
35 are the clans of Menashe. Their tally was 52,700. These are Efrayim's

64 | See chapter 16.

65 | See Genesis, chapter 38.

66 | See 27:1–11.

ה רְאוּבֵן בְּכוֹר יִשְׂרָאֵל בְּנֵי רְאוּבֵן חֲנוֹךְ מִשְׁפַּחַת הַחֲנֹכִי לְפַלּוּא מִשְׁפַּחַת שני
ו ז הַפַּלֻּאִי׃ לְחֶצְרֹן מִשְׁפַּחַת הַחֶצְרוֹנִי לְכַרְמִי מִשְׁפַּחַת הַכַּרְמִי׃ אֵלֶּה
מִשְׁפְּחֹת הָרְאוּבֵנִי וַיִּהְיוּ פְקֻדֵיהֶם שְׁלֹשָׁה וְאַרְבָּעִים אֶלֶף וּשְׁבַע מֵאוֹת
ח ט וּשְׁלֹשִׁים׃ וּבְנֵי פַלּוּא אֱלִיאָב׃ וּבְנֵי אֱלִיאָב נְמוּאֵל וְדָתָן וַאֲבִירָם
הוּא־דָתָן וַאֲבִירָם קרואי הָעֵדָה אֲשֶׁר הִצּוּ עַל־מֹשֶׁה וְעַל־אַהֲרֹן קְרִיאֵי
י בַּעֲדַת־קֹרַח בְּהַצֹּתָם עַל־יְהוָה׃ וַתִּפְתַּח הָאָרֶץ אֶת־פִּיהָ וַתִּבְלַע
אֹתָם וְאֶת־קֹרַח בְּמוֹת הָעֵדָה בַּאֲכֹל הָאֵשׁ אֵת חֲמִשִּׁים וּמָאתַיִם אִישׁ
יא יב וַיִּהְיוּ לְנֵס׃ וּבְנֵי־קֹרַח לֹא־מֵתוּ׃ בְּנֵי שִׁמְעוֹן לְמִשְׁפְּחֹתָם
לִנְמוּאֵל מִשְׁפַּחַת הַנְּמוּאֵלִי לְיָמִין מִשְׁפַּחַת הַיָּמִינִי לְיָכִין מִשְׁפַּחַת
יג יד הַיָּכִינִי׃ לְזֶרַח מִשְׁפַּחַת הַזַּרְחִי לְשָׁאוּל מִשְׁפַּחַת הַשָּׁאוּלִי׃ אֵלֶּה
טו מִשְׁפְּחֹת הַשִּׁמְעֹנִי שְׁנַיִם וְעֶשְׂרִים אֶלֶף וּמָאתָיִם׃ בְּנֵי גָד
לְמִשְׁפְּחֹתָם לִצְפוֹן מִשְׁפַּחַת הַצְּפוֹנִי לְחַגִּי מִשְׁפַּחַת הַחַגִּי לְשׁוּנִי
טז יז מִשְׁפַּחַת הַשּׁוּנִי׃ לְאָזְנִי מִשְׁפַּחַת הָאָזְנִי לְעֵרִי מִשְׁפַּחַת הָעֵרִי׃ לַאֲרוֹד
יח מִשְׁפַּחַת הָאֲרוֹדִי לְאַרְאֵלִי מִשְׁפַּחַת הָאַרְאֵלִי׃ אֵלֶּה מִשְׁפְּחֹת בְּנֵי־
יט גָד לִפְקֻדֵיהֶם אַרְבָּעִים אֶלֶף וַחֲמֵשׁ מֵאוֹת׃ בְּנֵי יְהוּדָה
כ עֵר וְאוֹנָן וַיָּמָת עֵר וְאוֹנָן בְּאֶרֶץ כְּנָעַן׃ וַיִּהְיוּ בְנֵי־יְהוּדָה לְמִשְׁפְּחֹתָם
לְשֵׁלָה מִשְׁפַּחַת הַשֵּׁלָנִי לְפֶרֶץ מִשְׁפַּחַת הַפַּרְצִי לְזֶרַח מִשְׁפַּחַת
כא הַזַּרְחִי׃ וַיִּהְיוּ בְנֵי־פֶרֶץ לְחֶצְרֹן מִשְׁפַּחַת הַחֶצְרֹנִי לְחָמוּל מִשְׁפַּחַת
כב הֶחָמוּלִי׃ אֵלֶּה מִשְׁפְּחֹת יְהוּדָה לִפְקֻדֵיהֶם שִׁשָּׁה וְשִׁבְעִים אֶלֶף וַחֲמֵשׁ
כג מֵאוֹת׃ בְּנֵי יִשָּׂשכָר לְמִשְׁפְּחֹתָם תּוֹלָע מִשְׁפַּחַת הַתּוֹלָעִי
כד לְפֻוָּה מִשְׁפַּחַת הַפּוּנִי׃ לְיָשׁוּב מִשְׁפַּחַת הַיָּשֻׁבִי לְשִׁמְרֹן מִשְׁפַּחַת
כה הַשִּׁמְרֹנִי׃ אֵלֶּה מִשְׁפְּחֹת יִשָּׂשכָר לִפְקֻדֵיהֶם אַרְבָּעָה וְשִׁשִּׁים אֶלֶף
כו וּשְׁלֹשׁ מֵאוֹת׃ בְּנֵי זְבוּלֻן לְמִשְׁפְּחֹתָם לְסֶרֶד מִשְׁפַּחַת
כז הַסַּרְדִּי לְאֵלוֹן מִשְׁפַּחַת הָאֵלֹנִי לְיַחְלְאֵל מִשְׁפַּחַת הַיַּחְלְאֵלִי׃ אֵלֶּה
כח מִשְׁפְּחֹת הַזְּבוּלֹנִי לִפְקֻדֵיהֶם שִׁשִּׁים אֶלֶף וַחֲמֵשׁ מֵאוֹת׃ בְּנֵי
כט יוֹסֵף לְמִשְׁפְּחֹתָם מְנַשֶּׁה וְאֶפְרָיִם׃ בְּנֵי מְנַשֶּׁה לְמָכִיר מִשְׁפַּחַת הַמָּכִירִי
ל וּמָכִיר הוֹלִיד אֶת־גִּלְעָד לְגִלְעָד מִשְׁפַּחַת הַגִּלְעָדִי׃ אֵלֶּה בְּנֵי גִלְעָד
לא אִיעֶזֶר מִשְׁפַּחַת הָאִיעֶזְרִי לְחֵלֶק מִשְׁפַּחַת הַחֶלְקִי׃ וְאַשְׂרִיאֵל מִשְׁפַּחַת
לב הָאַשְׂרִאֵלִי וְשֶׁכֶם מִשְׁפַּחַת הַשִּׁכְמִי׃ וּשְׁמִידָע מִשְׁפַּחַת הַשְּׁמִידָעִי
לג וְחֵפֶר מִשְׁפַּחַת הַחֶפְרִי׃ וּצְלָפְחָד בֶּן־חֵפֶר לֹא־הָיוּ לוֹ בָּנִים כִּי אִם־בָּנוֹת
לד וְשֵׁם בְּנוֹת צְלָפְחָד מַחְלָה וְנֹעָה חָגְלָה מִלְכָּה וְתִרְצָה׃ אֵלֶּה מִשְׁפְּחֹת
לה מְנַשֶּׁה וּפְקֻדֵיהֶם שְׁנַיִם וַחֲמִשִּׁים אֶלֶף וּשְׁבַע מֵאוֹת׃ אֵלֶּה

descendants by their clans: of Shutelaḥ, the clan of Shutelaḥ; of Bekher, the
36 clan of Bekher; of Taḥan, the clan of Taḥan. These are Shutelaḥ's descendants:
37 of Eran, the clan of Eran. These are the clans of Efrayim. Their tally was 32,500.
38 All these are Yosef's descendants by their clans. Binyamin's descendants by their clans: of Bela, the clan of Bela; of Ashbel, the clan of Ashbel;
39 of Aḥiram, the clan of Aḥiram; of Shefufam, the clan of Shefufam; of Ḥufam,
40 the clan of Ḥufam. Bela's descendants were Ard and Naaman: the clan of Ard;
41 of Naaman, the clan of Naaman. These are the clans of Binyamin. Their tally
42 was 45,600. These are Dan's descendants by their clans: of Shuham,
43 the clan of Shuham. These are the clans of Dan; all the Shuhamite clans
44 according to their tally were 64,400. Asher's descendants by their
clans: of Yimna, the clan of Yimna; of Yishvi, the clan of Yishvi; of Beria, the
45 clan of Beria. Of Beria's descendants: of Ḥever, the clan of Ḥever; of Malkiel,
46 47 the clan of Malkiel. The name of Asher's daughter was Seraḥ. These are the
48 clans of Asher; their tally was 53,400. Naftali's descendants by their
49 clans: of Yaḥtze'el, the clan of Yaḥtze'el; of Guni, the clan of Guni; of Yetzer,
50 the clan of Yetzer; of Shilem, the clan of Shilem. These are all the clans of
51 Naftali. Their tally was 45,400. The total number of those Israelite men was
601,730.
52 53 The Lord spoke to Moshe: "The land shall be apportioned to them for
54 inheritance by the tally of their names. To those who are many, give a large
inheritance; to those who are few, a small inheritance. Let each be given its
55 inheritance in keeping with its number. The land must be apportioned by
56 lot. By the names of their ancestral tribes they shall inherit. Whether large
57 or small, each tribe will inherit by means of the lot." These are the
numbers of the Levites by their clans: of Gershon, the clan of Gershon;
58 of Kehat, the clan of Kehat; of Merari, the clan of Merari. These are the
Levite clans: the clan of Livna, the clan of Ḥevron, the clan of Maḥli, the
59 clan of Mushi, and the clan of Koraḥ. Kehat had a son Amram. The name
of Amram's wife was Yokheved daughter of Levi; she had been born to Levi
60 in Egypt. She bore to Amram Aharon, Moshe, and their sister Miriam. To
61 Aharon were born Nadav, Avihu, Elazar, and Itamar. Nadav and Avihu died
62 when they offered unauthorized fire before the Lord.[67] Their number was
23,000, this including every male one month of age and upward. They were

67 | See Leviticus 10:1–2.

בְּנֵי־אֶפְרַיִם לְמִשְׁפְּחֹתָם לְשׁוּתֶלַח מִשְׁפַּחַת הַשֻּׁתַלְחִי לְבֶכֶר מִשְׁפַּחַת
לו הַבַּכְרִי לְתַחַן מִשְׁפַּחַת הַתַּחֲנִי׃ וְאֵלֶּה בְּנֵי שׁוּתָלַח לְעֵרָן מִשְׁפַּחַת
לז הָעֵרָנִי׃ אֵלֶּה מִשְׁפְּחֹת בְּנֵי־אֶפְרַיִם לִפְקֻדֵיהֶם שְׁנַיִם וּשְׁלֹשִׁים אֶלֶף
לח וַחֲמֵשׁ מֵאוֹת אֵלֶּה בְנֵי־יוֹסֵף לְמִשְׁפְּחֹתָם׃ בְּנֵי בִנְיָמִן
לְמִשְׁפְּחֹתָם לְבֶלַע מִשְׁפַּחַת הַבַּלְעִי לְאַשְׁבֵּל מִשְׁפַּחַת הָאַשְׁבֵּלִי
לט לַאֲחִירָם מִשְׁפַּחַת הָאֲחִירָמִי׃ לִשְׁפוּפָם מִשְׁפַּחַת הַשּׁוּפָמִי לְחוּפָם
מ מִשְׁפַּחַת הַחוּפָמִי׃ וַיִּהְיוּ בְנֵי־בֶלַע אַרְדְּ וְנַעֲמָן מִשְׁפַּחַת הָאַרְדִּי
מא לְנַעֲמָן מִשְׁפַּחַת הַנַּעֲמִי׃ אֵלֶּה בְנֵי־בִנְיָמִן לְמִשְׁפְּחֹתָם וּפְקֻדֵיהֶם
מב חֲמִשָּׁה וְאַרְבָּעִים אֶלֶף וְשֵׁשׁ מֵאוֹת׃ אֵלֶּה בְנֵי־דָן
לְמִשְׁפְּחֹתָם לְשׁוּחָם מִשְׁפַּחַת הַשּׁוּחָמִי אֵלֶּה מִשְׁפְּחֹת דָּן לְמִשְׁפְּחֹתָם׃
מג כָּל־מִשְׁפְּחֹת הַשּׁוּחָמִי לִפְקֻדֵיהֶם אַרְבָּעָה וְשִׁשִּׁים אֶלֶף וְאַרְבַּע
מד מֵאוֹת׃ בְּנֵי אָשֵׁר לְמִשְׁפְּחֹתָם לְיִמְנָה מִשְׁפַּחַת הַיִּמְנָה
מה לְיִשְׁוִי מִשְׁפַּחַת הַיִּשְׁוִי לִבְרִיעָה מִשְׁפַּחַת הַבְּרִיעִי׃ לִבְנֵי בְרִיעָה
מו לְחֶבֶר מִשְׁפַּחַת הַחֶבְרִי לְמַלְכִּיאֵל מִשְׁפַּחַת הַמַּלְכִּיאֵלִי׃ וְשֵׁם בַּת־
מז אָשֵׁר שָׂרַח׃ אֵלֶּה מִשְׁפְּחֹת בְּנֵי־אָשֵׁר לִפְקֻדֵיהֶם שְׁלֹשָׁה וַחֲמִשִּׁים
מח אֶלֶף וְאַרְבַּע מֵאוֹת׃ בְּנֵי נַפְתָּלִי לְמִשְׁפְּחֹתָם לְיַחְצְאֵל
מט מִשְׁפַּחַת הַיַּחְצְאֵלִי לְגוּנִי מִשְׁפַּחַת הַגּוּנִי׃ לְיֵצֶר מִשְׁפַּחַת הַיִּצְרִי
נ לְשִׁלֵּם מִשְׁפַּחַת הַשִּׁלֵּמִי׃ אֵלֶּה מִשְׁפְּחֹת נַפְתָּלִי לְמִשְׁפְּחֹתָם וּפְקֻדֵיהֶם
נא חֲמִשָּׁה וְאַרְבָּעִים אֶלֶף וְאַרְבַּע מֵאוֹת׃ אֵלֶּה פְּקוּדֵי בְּנֵי יִשְׂרָאֵל
שֵׁשׁ־מֵאוֹת אֶלֶף וָאָלֶף שְׁבַע מֵאוֹת וּשְׁלֹשִׁים׃
נב נג וַיְדַבֵּר יהוה אֶל־מֹשֶׁה לֵּאמֹר׃ לָאֵלֶּה תֵּחָלֵק הָאָרֶץ בְּנַחֲלָה בְּמִסְפַּר כג שלישי
נד שֵׁמוֹת׃ לָרַב תַּרְבֶּה נַחֲלָתוֹ וְלַמְעַט תַּמְעִיט נַחֲלָתוֹ אִישׁ לְפִי פְקֻדָיו
נה יֻתַּן נַחֲלָתוֹ׃ אַךְ־בְּגוֹרָל יֵחָלֵק אֶת־הָאָרֶץ לִשְׁמוֹת מַטּוֹת־אֲבֹתָם
נו נז יִנְחָלוּ׃ עַל־פִּי הַגּוֹרָל תֵּחָלֵק נַחֲלָתוֹ בֵּין רַב לִמְעָט׃ וְאֵלֶּה
פְקוּדֵי הַלֵּוִי לְמִשְׁפְּחֹתָם לְגֵרְשׁוֹן מִשְׁפַּחַת הַגֵּרְשֻׁנִּי לִקְהָת מִשְׁפַּחַת
נח הַקְּהָתִי לִמְרָרִי מִשְׁפַּחַת הַמְּרָרִי׃ אֵלֶּה ׀ מִשְׁפְּחֹת לֵוִי מִשְׁפַּחַת
הַלִּבְנִי מִשְׁפַּחַת הַחֶבְרֹנִי מִשְׁפַּחַת הַמַּחְלִי מִשְׁפַּחַת הַמּוּשִׁי מִשְׁפַּחַת
נט הַקָּרְחִי וּקְהָת הוֹלִד אֶת־עַמְרָם׃ וְשֵׁם ׀ אֵשֶׁת עַמְרָם יוֹכֶבֶד בַּת־לֵוִי
אֲשֶׁר יָלְדָה אֹתָהּ לְלֵוִי בְּמִצְרָיִם וַתֵּלֶד לְעַמְרָם אֶת־אַהֲרֹן וְאֶת־מֹשֶׁה
ס וְאֵת מִרְיָם אֲחֹתָם׃ וַיִּוָּלֵד לְאַהֲרֹן אֶת־נָדָב וְאֶת־אֲבִיהוּא אֶת־אֶלְעָזָר
סא וְאֶת־אִיתָמָר׃ וַיָּמָת נָדָב וַאֲבִיהוּא בְּהַקְרִיבָם אֵשׁ־זָרָה לִפְנֵי יהוה׃
סב וַיִּהְיוּ פְקֻדֵיהֶם שְׁלֹשָׁה וְעֶשְׂרִים אֶלֶף כָּל־זָכָר מִבֶּן־חֹדֶשׁ וָמָעְלָה

not numbered along with the Israelites because no land inheritance was
63 given to them in the Israelites' midst. This was the census that Moshe and
Elazar the priest took of the Israelites on the plains of Moav by the Jordan
64 opposite Yeriḥo. It contained not one man who had been counted by Moshe
and Aharon the priest when they took the census of the Israelites in the Sinai
65 Desert. For the LORD had said of those, "They shall die in the wilderness."
Not one of them was left now except for Kalev son of Yefuneh and Yehoshua
27 1 son of Nun.[68] Then the daughters of Tzelofḥad son of Ḥefer son of
Gilad son of Makhir son of Menashe, of the clans of Menashe son of Yosef,
came forward; the daughters' names were Maḥla, Noa, Ḥogla, Milka, and
2 Tirtza. And they stood before Moshe, Elazar the priest, the princes, and
3 all the community at the entrance to the Tent of Meeting, and said, "Our
father died in the wilderness. He was not among the company of those who
gathered together against the LORD in the company of Koraḥ; he died in his
4 own sin, and had no sons. Why should our father's name be lost to his family
only because he had no son? Give us a portion of land along with our father's
5 brothers." Moshe brought their case before the LORD.
6 7 And the LORD said to Moshe: "What Tzelofḥad's daughters say is right. You
must certainly give them a heritable portion of land along with their father's
8 kin. Transfer their father's portion to them. Speak to the Israelites; tell them:
If a man dies and has no son, you shall transfer his property to his daughters.
9 10 If he does not have a daughter, you shall give his property to his brothers. If
11 he has no brothers, you shall give his property to his father's brothers. If his
father had no brothers, give his property to the closest relative in his clan, and
that person shall inherit it." This shall be a decree of law for the Israelites, as
the LORD commanded Moshe.
12 The LORD said to Moshe, "Ascend this mountain of Avarim, and gaze upon
13 the land that I have given to the Israelites. After you have seen it, you too
14 will be gathered to your people, like Aharon your brother, because when the
community rebelled in the Wilderness of Tzin, you disobeyed Me, failing to
affirm My sanctity in their eyes through the water." These were the waters of
15 Merivat Kadesh in the Wilderness of Tzin.[69] Moshe spoke to the
16 LORD: "Let the LORD, God of the spirit of all flesh, appoint a man over the
17 community who will go out before them and come in before them, who will
lead them out and bring them home. Let not the LORD's community be like
18 sheep without a shepherd." The LORD said to Moshe, "Take Yehoshua son
19 of Nun, a man infused with My spirit, and lay your hand upon him. Have
him stand before Elazar the priest and the entire community, and in their
20 sight, give him this charge. Give over to him some of your majesty, so that
21 the entire Israelite community will obey him. Let him stand before Elazar
the priest, who shall seek the decision of the Urim before the LORD on his
behalf. By this word they will go out and by this word they will return, he and

68 | See 14:30.

69 | See above, 20:1–13.

כִּי ׀ לֹא הָתְפָּקְדוּ בְּתוֹךְ בְּנֵי יִשְׂרָאֵל כִּי לֹא־נִתַּן לָהֶם נַחֲלָה בְּתוֹךְ
סג בְּנֵי יִשְׂרָאֵל: אֵלֶּה פְּקוּדֵי מֹשֶׁה וְאֶלְעָזָר הַכֹּהֵן אֲשֶׁר פָּקְדוּ אֶת־בְּנֵי
סד יִשְׂרָאֵל בְּעַרְבֹת מוֹאָב עַל יַרְדֵּן יְרֵחוֹ: וּבְאֵלֶּה לֹא־הָיָה אִישׁ מִפְּקוּדֵי
סה מֹשֶׁה וְאַהֲרֹן הַכֹּהֵן אֲשֶׁר פָּקְדוּ אֶת־בְּנֵי יִשְׂרָאֵל בְּמִדְבַּר סִינָי: כִּי־אָמַר
יהוה לָהֶם מוֹת יָמֻתוּ בַּמִּדְבָּר וְלֹא־נוֹתַר מֵהֶם אִישׁ כִּי אִם־כָּלֵב בֶּן־
כז א יְפֻנֶּה וִיהוֹשֻׁעַ בִּן־נוּן: וַתִּקְרַבְנָה בְּנוֹת צְלָפְחָד בֶּן־חֵפֶר
בֶּן־גִּלְעָד בֶּן־מָכִיר בֶּן־מְנַשֶּׁה לְמִשְׁפְּחֹת מְנַשֶּׁה בֶן־יוֹסֵף וְאֵלֶּה שְׁמוֹת
ב בְּנֹתָיו מַחְלָה נֹעָה וְחָגְלָה וּמִלְכָּה וְתִרְצָה: וַתַּעֲמֹדְנָה לִפְנֵי מֹשֶׁה וְלִפְנֵי
אֶלְעָזָר הַכֹּהֵן וְלִפְנֵי הַנְּשִׂיאִם וְכָל־הָעֵדָה פֶּתַח אֹהֶל־מוֹעֵד לֵאמֹר:
ג אָבִינוּ מֵת בַּמִּדְבָּר וְהוּא לֹא־הָיָה בְּתוֹךְ הָעֵדָה הַנּוֹעָדִים עַל־יהוה
ד בַּעֲדַת־קֹרַח כִּי־בְחֶטְאוֹ מֵת וּבָנִים לֹא־הָיוּ לוֹ: לָמָּה יִגָּרַע שֵׁם־אָבִינוּ
מִתּוֹךְ מִשְׁפַּחְתּוֹ כִּי אֵין לוֹ בֵּן תְּנָה־לָּנוּ אֲחֻזָּה בְּתוֹךְ אֲחֵי אָבִינוּ:
ה וַיַּקְרֵב מֹשֶׁה אֶת־מִשְׁפָּטָן לִפְנֵי יהוה:
ו ז וַיֹּאמֶר יהוה אֶל־מֹשֶׁה לֵּאמֹר: כֵּן בְּנוֹת צְלָפְחָד דֹּבְרֹת נָתֹן תִּתֵּן לָהֶם רביעי
אֲחֻזַּת נַחֲלָה בְּתוֹךְ אֲחֵי אֲבִיהֶם וְהַעֲבַרְתָּ אֶת־נַחֲלַת אֲבִיהֶן לָהֶן:
ח וְאֶל־בְּנֵי יִשְׂרָאֵל תְּדַבֵּר לֵאמֹר אִישׁ כִּי־יָמוּת וּבֵן אֵין לוֹ וְהַעֲבַרְתֶּם
ט אֶת־נַחֲלָתוֹ לְבִתּוֹ: וְאִם־אֵין לוֹ בַּת וּנְתַתֶּם אֶת־נַחֲלָתוֹ לְאֶחָיו: וְאִם־
יא אֵין לוֹ אַחִים וּנְתַתֶּם אֶת־נַחֲלָתוֹ לַאֲחֵי אָבִיו: וְאִם־אֵין אַחִים לְאָבִיו
וּנְתַתֶּם אֶת־נַחֲלָתוֹ לִשְׁאֵרוֹ הַקָּרֹב אֵלָיו מִמִּשְׁפַּחְתּוֹ וְיָרַשׁ אֹתָהּ וְהָיְתָה
לִבְנֵי יִשְׂרָאֵל לְחֻקַּת מִשְׁפָּט כַּאֲשֶׁר צִוָּה יהוה אֶת־מֹשֶׁה:
יב וַיֹּאמֶר יהוה אֶל־מֹשֶׁה עֲלֵה אֶל־הַר הָעֲבָרִים הַזֶּה וּרְאֵה אֶת־הָאָרֶץ
יג אֲשֶׁר נָתַתִּי לִבְנֵי יִשְׂרָאֵל: וְרָאִיתָה אֹתָהּ וְנֶאֱסַפְתָּ אֶל־עַמֶּיךָ גַּם־אָתָּה
יד כַּאֲשֶׁר נֶאֱסַף אַהֲרֹן אָחִיךָ: כַּאֲשֶׁר מְרִיתֶם פִּי בְּמִדְבַּר־צִן בִּמְרִיבַת
הָעֵדָה לְהַקְדִּישֵׁנִי בַמַּיִם לְעֵינֵיהֶם הֵם מֵי־מְרִיבַת קָדֵשׁ מִדְבַּר־
טו טז צִן: וַיְדַבֵּר מֹשֶׁה אֶל־יהוה לֵאמֹר: יִפְקֹד יהוה אֱלֹהֵי הָרוּחֹת כד
יז לְכָל־בָּשָׂר אִישׁ עַל־הָעֵדָה: אֲשֶׁר־יֵצֵא לִפְנֵיהֶם וַאֲשֶׁר יָבֹא לִפְנֵיהֶם
וַאֲשֶׁר יוֹצִיאֵם וַאֲשֶׁר יְבִיאֵם וְלֹא תִהְיֶה עֲדַת יהוה כַּצֹּאן אֲשֶׁר אֵין־
יח לָהֶם רֹעֶה: וַיֹּאמֶר יהוה אֶל־מֹשֶׁה קַח־לְךָ אֶת־יְהוֹשֻׁעַ בִּן־נוּן אִישׁ
יט אֲשֶׁר־רוּחַ בּוֹ וְסָמַכְתָּ אֶת־יָדְךָ עָלָיו: וְהַעֲמַדְתָּ אֹתוֹ לִפְנֵי אֶלְעָזָר
כ הַכֹּהֵן וְלִפְנֵי כָּל־הָעֵדָה וְצִוִּיתָה אֹתוֹ לְעֵינֵיהֶם: וְנָתַתָּה מֵהוֹדְךָ עָלָיו
כא לְמַעַן יִשְׁמְעוּ כָּל־עֲדַת בְּנֵי יִשְׂרָאֵל: וְלִפְנֵי אֶלְעָזָר הַכֹּהֵן יַעֲמֹד וְשָׁאַל
לוֹ בְּמִשְׁפַּט הָאוּרִים לִפְנֵי יהוה עַל־פִּיו יֵצְאוּ וְעַל־פִּיו יָבֹאוּ הוּא וְכָל־

22 all Israel, the entire community." Moshe did as the LORD commanded him.
He took Yehoshua and had him stand before Elazar the priest and the entire
23 community. And he laid his hands upon him and commissioned him, as the
LORD had spoken through Moshe.
28 1 2 The LORD spoke to Moshe: "Command the Israelites; say to them: Take care
to present My offering of foodstuffs – fire offerings of pleasing aroma to Me –
3 at its appointed times. Say to them: This is the fire offering you must present
to the LORD: two yearling lambs without blemish as a regular burnt offering
4 each day. Offer one lamb in the morning and the second in the afternoon,
5 with a tenth of an ephah of fine flour as a grain offering mixed with a quarter
6 of a hin of beaten oil. This is the regular burnt offering instituted at Mount
7 Sinai, as a pleasing aroma, a fire offering to the LORD. Its libation shall be a
quarter of a hin for each lamb, to be poured out in the Sanctuary as a libation
8 of fermented drink to the LORD. Offer the other lamb in the afternoon
together with a grain offering and libation as in the morning; a fire offering,
a pleasing aroma to the LORD.
9 On the Sabbath day: two yearling lambs without blemish and two-tenths
of a measure of fine flour as a grain offering, mixed with oil, and its libation.
10 This is the burnt offering for every Sabbath, to be brought in addition to the
regular daily burnt offering and its libation.
11 On your New Moons you shall present a burnt offering to the LORD: two
12 young bulls, one ram, and seven yearling lambs, all without blemish. There
shall be a grain offering of three-tenths of a measure of fine flour mixed with
oil for each bull, a grain offering of two-tenths of fine flour mixed with oil
13 for each ram, and a grain offering of one-tenth of fine flour mixed with oil
for each lamb. This shall be a burnt offering of pleasing aroma, a fire offering
14 to the LORD. Their libations shall be half a hin of wine for a bull, a third of
a hin of wine for a ram, and a quarter of a hin of wine for a lamb. This is the
15 monthly burnt offering for each New Moon of the year. One male goat shall
be brought as a purification offering to the LORD, in addition to the regular
16 burnt offering and its libation. On the fourteenth day of the first
17 month, a Passover sacrifice shall be brought to the LORD. And the fifteenth
day of this month will be a festival. For seven days unleavened bread shall be
18 eaten. The first day shall be a sacred assembly; you shall perform no laborious
19 work. You shall offer a burnt fire offering to the LORD: two young bulls, one
20 ram, and seven yearling lambs, all unblemished. Their grain offering shall be
fine flour mixed with oil: three-tenths of a measure for each bull, two-tenths
21 22 for the ram, and one-tenth for each of the seven lambs, together with one
23 male goat as a purification offering to make your atonement. These you shall
offer in addition to the morning burnt offering, the regular daily offering.
24 In the same way you shall offer daily for seven days the foodstuffs of a fire
offering, a pleasing aroma to the LORD. It shall be offered in addition to the
25 regular burnt offering and its libation. The seventh day shall be for you a

כב בְּנֵי־יִשְׂרָאֵל אִתּוֹ וְכָל־הָעֵדָה: וַיַּעַשׂ מֹשֶׁה כַּאֲשֶׁר צִוָּה יְהוָה אֹתוֹ וַיִּקַּח
כג אֶת־יְהוֹשֻׁעַ וַיַּעֲמִדֵהוּ לִפְנֵי אֶלְעָזָר הַכֹּהֵן וְלִפְנֵי כָּל־הָעֵדָה: וַיִּסְמֹךְ
אֶת־יָדָיו עָלָיו וַיְצַוֵּהוּ כַּאֲשֶׁר דִּבֶּר יְהוָה בְּיַד־מֹשֶׁה:
כח א ב וַיְדַבֵּר יְהוָה אֶל־מֹשֶׁה לֵּאמֹר: צַו אֶת־בְּנֵי יִשְׂרָאֵל וְאָמַרְתָּ אֲלֵהֶם אֶת־ חמישי
ג קָרְבָּנִי לַחְמִי לְאִשַּׁי רֵיחַ נִיחֹחִי תִּשְׁמְרוּ לְהַקְרִיב לִי בְּמוֹעֲדוֹ: וְאָמַרְתָּ
לָהֶם זֶה הָאִשֶּׁה אֲשֶׁר תַּקְרִיבוּ לַיהוָה כְּבָשִׂים בְּנֵי־שָׁנָה תְמִימִם שְׁנַיִם
ד לַיּוֹם עֹלָה תָמִיד: אֶת־הַכֶּבֶשׂ אֶחָד תַּעֲשֶׂה בַבֹּקֶר וְאֵת הַכֶּבֶשׂ הַשֵּׁנִי
ה תַּעֲשֶׂה בֵּין הָעַרְבָּיִם: וַעֲשִׂירִית הָאֵיפָה סֹלֶת לְמִנְחָה בְּלוּלָה בְּשֶׁמֶן
ו כָּתִית רְבִיעִת הַהִין: עֹלַת תָּמִיד הָעֲשֻׂיָה בְּהַר סִינַי לְרֵיחַ נִיחֹחַ אִשֶּׁה
ז לַיהוָה: וְנִסְכּוֹ רְבִיעִת הַהִין לַכֶּבֶשׂ הָאֶחָד בַּקֹּדֶשׁ הַסֵּךְ נֶסֶךְ שֵׁכָר
ח לַיהוָה: וְאֵת הַכֶּבֶשׂ הַשֵּׁנִי תַּעֲשֶׂה בֵּין הָעַרְבָּיִם כְּמִנְחַת הַבֹּקֶר וּכְנִסְכּוֹ
תַּעֲשֶׂה אִשֵּׁה רֵיחַ נִיחֹחַ לַיהוָה:
ט וּבְיוֹם הַשַּׁבָּת שְׁנֵי־כְבָשִׂים בְּנֵי־שָׁנָה תְּמִימִם וּשְׁנֵי עֶשְׂרֹנִים סֹלֶת
י מִנְחָה בְּלוּלָה בַשֶּׁמֶן וְנִסְכּוֹ: עֹלַת שַׁבַּת בְּשַׁבַּתּוֹ עַל־עֹלַת הַתָּמִיד
וְנִסְכָּהּ:
יא וּבְרָאשֵׁי חָדְשֵׁיכֶם תַּקְרִיבוּ עֹלָה לַיהוָה פָּרִים בְּנֵי־בָקָר שְׁנַיִם וְאַיִל
יב אֶחָד כְּבָשִׂים בְּנֵי־שָׁנָה שִׁבְעָה תְּמִימִם: וּשְׁלֹשָׁה עֶשְׂרֹנִים סֹלֶת מִנְחָה
בְּלוּלָה בַשֶּׁמֶן לַפָּר הָאֶחָד וּשְׁנֵי עֶשְׂרֹנִים סֹלֶת מִנְחָה בְּלוּלָה בַשֶּׁמֶן
יג לָאַיִל הָאֶחָד: וְעִשָּׂרֹן עִשָּׂרוֹן סֹלֶת מִנְחָה בְּלוּלָה בַשֶּׁמֶן לַכֶּבֶשׂ הָאֶחָד
יד עֹלָה רֵיחַ נִיחֹחַ אִשֶּׁה לַיהוָה: וְנִסְכֵּיהֶם חֲצִי הַהִין יִהְיֶה לַפָּר וּשְׁלִישִׁת
הַהִין לָאַיִל וּרְבִיעִת הַהִין לַכֶּבֶשׂ יָיִן זֹאת עֹלַת חֹדֶשׁ בְּחָדְשׁוֹ לְחָדְשֵׁי
טו הַשָּׁנָה: וּשְׂעִיר עִזִּים אֶחָד לְחַטָּאת לַיהוָה עַל־עֹלַת הַתָּמִיד יֵעָשֶׂה
טז וְנִסְכּוֹ: וּבַחֹדֶשׁ הָרִאשׁוֹן בְּאַרְבָּעָה עָשָׂר יוֹם לַחֹדֶשׁ פֶּסַח ששי
יז לַיהוָה: וּבַחֲמִשָּׁה עָשָׂר יוֹם לַחֹדֶשׁ הַזֶּה חָג שִׁבְעַת יָמִים מַצּוֹת יֵאָכֵל:
יח יט בַּיּוֹם הָרִאשׁוֹן מִקְרָא־קֹדֶשׁ כָּל־מְלֶאכֶת עֲבֹדָה לֹא תַעֲשׂוּ: וְהִקְרַבְתֶּם
אִשֶּׁה עֹלָה לַיהוָה פָּרִים בְּנֵי־בָקָר שְׁנַיִם וְאַיִל אֶחָד וְשִׁבְעָה כְבָשִׂים בְּנֵי
כ שָׁנָה תְּמִימִם יִהְיוּ לָכֶם: וּמִנְחָתָם סֹלֶת בְּלוּלָה בַשָּׁמֶן שְׁלֹשָׁה עֶשְׂרֹנִים
כא לַפָּר וּשְׁנֵי עֶשְׂרֹנִים לָאַיִל תַּעֲשׂוּ: עִשָּׂרוֹן עִשָּׂרוֹן תַּעֲשֶׂה לַכֶּבֶשׂ הָאֶחָד
כב כג לְשִׁבְעַת הַכְּבָשִׂים: וּשְׂעִיר חַטָּאת אֶחָד לְכַפֵּר עֲלֵיכֶם: מִלְּבַד עֹלַת
כד הַבֹּקֶר אֲשֶׁר לְעֹלַת הַתָּמִיד תַּעֲשׂוּ אֶת־אֵלֶּה: כָּאֵלֶּה תַּעֲשׂוּ לַיּוֹם
שִׁבְעַת יָמִים לֶחֶם אִשֵּׁה רֵיחַ־נִיחֹחַ לַיהוָה עַל־עוֹלַת הַתָּמִיד יֵעָשֶׂה
כה וְנִסְכּוֹ: וּבַיּוֹם הַשְּׁבִיעִי מִקְרָא־קֹדֶשׁ יִהְיֶה לָכֶם כָּל־מְלֶאכֶת עֲבֹדָה

26 sacred assembly; you shall perform no laborious work. The day of
first produce, when you bring an offering of new grain[70] to the LORD on your
Festival of Weeks, shall be a sacred assembly for you. On it you shall perform
27 no laborious work. You shall present a burnt offering as a pleasing aroma to
28 the LORD: two young bulls, one ram, and seven yearling lambs. Their grain
offering shall be fine flour mixed with oil: three-tenths of a measure for each
29 bull, two-tenths for the one ram, and one-tenth for each of the seven lambs.
30 31 Offer one male goat to atone for you. These you shall offer in addition to the
regular burnt offering, its grain offering and libations. They shall be without
blemish.
29 1 The first day of the seventh month shall be a sacred assembly for you; you
shall perform no laborious work on it. It shall be for you a day of the horn's
2 sounding. You shall present a burnt offering as a pleasing aroma to the LORD:
3 one young bull, one ram, and seven yearling lambs, all without blemish. Their
grain offering shall be fine flour mixed with oil, three-tenths of a measure for
4 the bull, two-tenths for the ram, and one-tenth for each of the seven lambs;
5 and there shall be one male goat as a purification offering to atone for you.
6 This will be in addition to the monthly burnt offering with its grain offering,
and the regular burnt offering with its grain offering and libations as pre-
7 scribed. It shall be a pleasing aroma, a fire offering to the LORD. The
tenth day of this seventh month shall be a sacred assembly for you; you shall
8 afflict yourselves on it and perform no work at all.[71] You shall present a burnt
offering to the LORD for a pleasing aroma: one young bull, one ram, and
9 seven yearling lambs, all without blemish. Their grain offering shall be fine
flour mixed with oil, three-tenths of a measure for the bull, two-tenths for the
10 11 single ram, and one-tenth for each of the seven sheep. There shall be one male
goat as a purification offering, in addition to the special purification offering of atonement and the regular burnt offering with its grain offering and
12 libations. The fifteenth day of the seventh month shall be a sacred
assembly for you; you shall perform no laborious work on it; you shall cel-
13 ebrate a festival to the LORD for seven days.[72] And you shall present a burnt
offering, a fire offering, for a pleasing aroma to the LORD: thirteen young
14 bulls, two rams, and fourteen yearling lambs, all without blemish. Their grain
offering shall be fine flour mixed with oil: three-tenths of a measure for each
15 of the thirteen bulls, two-tenths for each of the two rams, and one-tenth for
16 each of the fourteen lambs. There shall be one male goat as a purification
offering, in addition to the regular burnt offering with its grain offering and
17 libation. On the second day: twelve young bulls, two rams, and
18 fourteen yearling lambs, all without blemish. The grain offering and libations
19 for the bulls, rams, and sheep shall be as prescribed for their number. There
shall be one male goat as a purification offering, in addition to the regular
20 burnt offering with its grain offering and libations. On the third

70 | See Leviticus 23:16.
71 | Cf. Leviticus 23:26–32.
72 | Cf. Leviticus 23:33–43

כו לֹא תַעֲשׂוּ׃ וּבְיוֹם הַבִּכּוּרִים בְּהַקְרִיבְכֶם מִנְחָה חֲדָשָׁה כה
לַיהוָה בְּשָׁבֻעֹתֵיכֶם מִקְרָא־קֹדֶשׁ יִהְיֶה לָכֶם כָּל־מְלֶאכֶת עֲבֹדָה לֹא
כז תַעֲשׂוּ׃ וְהִקְרַבְתֶּם עוֹלָה לְרֵיחַ נִיחֹחַ לַיהוָה פָּרִים בְּנֵי־בָקָר שְׁנַיִם אַיִל
כח אֶחָד שִׁבְעָה כְבָשִׂים בְּנֵי שָׁנָה׃ וּמִנְחָתָם סֹלֶת בְּלוּלָה בַשָּׁמֶן שְׁלֹשָׁה
כט עֶשְׂרֹנִים לַפָּר הָאֶחָד שְׁנֵי עֶשְׂרֹנִים לָאַיִל הָאֶחָד׃ עִשָּׂרוֹן עִשָּׂרוֹן לַכֶּבֶשׂ
ל לא הָאֶחָד לְשִׁבְעַת הַכְּבָשִׂים׃ שְׂעִיר עִזִּים אֶחָד לְכַפֵּר עֲלֵיכֶם׃ מִלְּבַד
עֹלַת הַתָּמִיד וּמִנְחָתוֹ תַּעֲשׂוּ תְּמִימִם יִהְיוּ־לָכֶם וְנִסְכֵּיהֶם׃

כט א וּבַחֹדֶשׁ הַשְּׁבִיעִי בְּאֶחָד לַחֹדֶשׁ מִקְרָא־קֹדֶשׁ יִהְיֶה לָכֶם כָּל־מְלֶאכֶת
ב עֲבֹדָה לֹא תַעֲשׂוּ יוֹם תְּרוּעָה יִהְיֶה לָכֶם׃ וַעֲשִׂיתֶם עֹלָה לְרֵיחַ נִיחֹחַ
לַיהוָה פַּר בֶּן־בָּקָר אֶחָד אַיִל אֶחָד כְּבָשִׂים בְּנֵי־שָׁנָה שִׁבְעָה תְּמִימִם׃
ג וּמִנְחָתָם סֹלֶת בְּלוּלָה בַשָּׁמֶן שְׁלֹשָׁה עֶשְׂרֹנִים לַפָּר שְׁנֵי עֶשְׂרֹנִים
ד ה לָאָיִל׃ וְעִשָּׂרוֹן אֶחָד לַכֶּבֶשׂ הָאֶחָד לְשִׁבְעַת הַכְּבָשִׂים׃ וּשְׂעִיר־
ו עִזִּים אֶחָד חַטָּאת לְכַפֵּר עֲלֵיכֶם׃ מִלְּבַד עֹלַת הַחֹדֶשׁ וּמִנְחָתָהּ
וְעֹלַת הַתָּמִיד וּמִנְחָתָהּ וְנִסְכֵּיהֶם כְּמִשְׁפָּטָם לְרֵיחַ נִיחֹחַ אִשֶּׁה
ז לַיהוָה׃ וּבֶעָשׂוֹר לַחֹדֶשׁ הַשְּׁבִיעִי הַזֶּה מִקְרָא־קֹדֶשׁ יִהְיֶה
ח לָכֶם וְעִנִּיתֶם אֶת־נַפְשֹׁתֵיכֶם כָּל־מְלָאכָה לֹא תַעֲשׂוּ׃ וְהִקְרַבְתֶּם
עֹלָה לַיהוָה רֵיחַ נִיחֹחַ פַּר בֶּן־בָּקָר אֶחָד אַיִל אֶחָד כְּבָשִׂים בְּנֵי־
ט שָׁנָה שִׁבְעָה תְּמִימִם יִהְיוּ לָכֶם׃ וּמִנְחָתָם סֹלֶת בְּלוּלָה בַשָּׁמֶן שְׁלֹשָׁה
י עֶשְׂרֹנִים לַפָּר שְׁנֵי עֶשְׂרֹנִים לָאַיִל הָאֶחָד׃ עִשָּׂרוֹן עִשָּׂרוֹן לַכֶּבֶשׂ
יא הָאֶחָד לְשִׁבְעַת הַכְּבָשִׂים׃ שְׂעִיר־עִזִּים אֶחָד חַטָּאת מִלְּבַד חַטַּאת
יב הַכִּפֻּרִים וְעֹלַת הַתָּמִיד וּמִנְחָתָהּ וְנִסְכֵּיהֶם׃ וּבַחֲמִשָּׁה שביעי
עָשָׂר יוֹם לַחֹדֶשׁ הַשְּׁבִיעִי מִקְרָא־קֹדֶשׁ יִהְיֶה לָכֶם כָּל־מְלֶאכֶת עֲבֹדָה
יג לֹא תַעֲשׂוּ וְחַגֹּתֶם חַג לַיהוָה שִׁבְעַת יָמִים׃ וְהִקְרַבְתֶּם עֹלָה אִשֵּׁה
רֵיחַ נִיחֹחַ לַיהוָה פָּרִים בְּנֵי־בָקָר שְׁלֹשָׁה עָשָׂר אֵילִם שְׁנָיִם כְּבָשִׂים
יד בְּנֵי־שָׁנָה אַרְבָּעָה עָשָׂר תְּמִימִם יִהְיוּ׃ וּמִנְחָתָם סֹלֶת בְּלוּלָה בַשָּׁמֶן
שְׁלֹשָׁה עֶשְׂרֹנִים לַפָּר הָאֶחָד לִשְׁלֹשָׁה עָשָׂר פָּרִים שְׁנֵי עֶשְׂרֹנִים לָאַיִל
טו הָאֶחָד לִשְׁנֵי הָאֵילִם׃ וְעִשָּׂרוֹן עִשָּׂרוֹן לַכֶּבֶשׂ הָאֶחָד לְאַרְבָּעָה עָשָׂר
טז כְּבָשִׂים׃ וּשְׂעִיר־עִזִּים אֶחָד חַטָּאת מִלְּבַד עֹלַת הַתָּמִיד מִנְחָתָהּ
יז וְנִסְכָּהּ׃ וּבַיּוֹם הַשֵּׁנִי פָּרִים בְּנֵי־בָקָר שְׁנֵים עָשָׂר אֵילִם
יח שְׁנָיִם כְּבָשִׂים בְּנֵי־שָׁנָה אַרְבָּעָה עָשָׂר תְּמִימִם׃ וּמִנְחָתָם וְנִסְכֵּיהֶם
יט לַפָּרִים לָאֵילִם וְלַכְּבָשִׂים בְּמִסְפָּרָם כַּמִּשְׁפָּט׃ וּשְׂעִיר־עִזִּים אֶחָד
כ חַטָּאת מִלְּבַד עֹלַת הַתָּמִיד וּמִנְחָתָהּ וְנִסְכֵּיהֶם׃ וּבַיּוֹם

day: eleven bulls, two rams, and fourteen yearling lambs, all without blem-
21 ish. The grain offering and libations for the bulls, rams, and lambs shall be
22 as prescribed for their number. There shall be one male goat as a purification offering, in addition to the regular burnt offering with its grain offering
23 and libation. On the fourth day: ten bulls, two rams, and fourteen
24 yearling lambs, all without blemish. The grain offering and libations for the
25 bulls, rams, and sheep shall be as prescribed for their number. And there shall
be one male goat as a purification offering, in addition to the regular burnt
26 offering with its grain offering and libation. On the fifth day: nine
27 bulls, two rams, and fourteen yearling lambs, all without blemish. The grain
offering and libations for the bulls, rams, and lambs shall be as prescribed
28 for their number. And there shall be one male goat as a purification offering,
in addition to the regular burnt offering with its grain offering and liba-
29 tion. On the sixth day: eight bulls, two rams, and fourteen yearling
30 lambs, all without blemish. The grain offering and libations for the bulls, rams,
31 and lambs shall be as prescribed for their number. And there shall be one male
goat as a purification offering, in addition to the regular burnt offering with
32 its grain offering and libations. On the seventh day: seven bulls, two
33 rams, and fourteen yearling lambs, all without blemish. The grain offering and
libation for the bulls, rams, and lambs shall be as prescribed for their number.
34 And there shall be one male goat as a purification offering, in addition to
35 the regular burnt offering with its grain offering and libation. On
the eighth day you shall hold an assembly; you shall perform no laborious
36 work on it. You shall present a burnt offering, a fire offering, for a pleasing
aroma to the LORD: one bull, one ram, and seven yearling lambs, all without
37 blemish. The grain offering and libations for the bull, ram, and lambs shall be
38 as prescribed for their number. And there shall be one male goat as a purification offering, in addition to the regular burnt offering with its grain offering
39 and libation. These you shall offer to the LORD on your festivals, in addition
to your vows and freewill offerings: your burnt offerings, grain offerings,
30 1 libations, and peace offerings." And Moshe told the Israelites all that the LORD
had commanded him.

MATTOT

2 Moshe spoke to the tribal heads of the Israelites: This is what the LORD has
3 commanded: When a man makes a vow to the LORD or takes an oath binding
himself to an obligation, he must not break his word; whatever he speaks, that
4 he must fulfill. When a woman makes a vow to the LORD or takes an oath
5 binding herself to an obligation while still a girl in her father's house, and her
father hears of her vow or self-imposed obligation and remains silent, then
6 all her vows and self-imposed obligations stand. But if her father restrains
her[73] on the day he hears her, none of her vows or self-imposed obligations shall stand. The LORD will forgo them for her, because her father has
7 restrained her. If she marries, having made vows or verbally bound herself,

---

73 | That is, he nullifies the vow or oath.

הַשְּׁלִישִׁי פָּרִים עַשְׁתֵּי־עָשָׂר אֵילִם שְׁנָיִם כְּבָשִׂים בְּנֵי־שָׁנָה אַרְבָּעָה
כא עָשָׂר תְּמִימִם׃ וּמִנְחָתָם וְנִסְכֵּיהֶם לַפָּרִים לָאֵילִם וְלַכְּבָשִׂים בְּמִסְפָּרָם
כב כַּמִּשְׁפָּט׃ וּשְׂעִיר חַטָּאת אֶחָד מִלְּבַד עֹלַת הַתָּמִיד וּמִנְחָתָהּ
כג וְנִסְכָּהּ׃ וּבַיּוֹם הָרְבִיעִי פָּרִים עֲשָׂרָה אֵילִם שְׁנָיִם כְּבָשִׂים
כד בְּנֵי־שָׁנָה אַרְבָּעָה עָשָׂר תְּמִימִם׃ מִנְחָתָם וְנִסְכֵּיהֶם לַפָּרִים לָאֵילִם
כה וְלַכְּבָשִׂים בְּמִסְפָּרָם כַּמִּשְׁפָּט׃ וּשְׂעִיר־עִזִּים אֶחָד חַטָּאת מִלְּבַד עֹלַת
כו הַתָּמִיד מִנְחָתָהּ וְנִסְכָּהּ׃ וּבַיּוֹם הַחֲמִישִׁי פָּרִים תִּשְׁעָה אֵילִם
כז שְׁנָיִם כְּבָשִׂים בְּנֵי־שָׁנָה אַרְבָּעָה עָשָׂר תְּמִימִם׃ וּמִנְחָתָם וְנִסְכֵּיהֶם
כח לַפָּרִים לָאֵילִם וְלַכְּבָשִׂים בְּמִסְפָּרָם כַּמִּשְׁפָּט׃ וּשְׂעִיר חַטָּאת אֶחָד
כט מִלְּבַד עֹלַת הַתָּמִיד וּמִנְחָתָהּ וְנִסְכָּהּ׃ וּבַיּוֹם הַשִּׁשִּׁי פָּרִים
ל שְׁמֹנָה אֵילִם שְׁנָיִם כְּבָשִׂים בְּנֵי־שָׁנָה אַרְבָּעָה עָשָׂר תְּמִימִם׃ וּמִנְחָתָם
לא וְנִסְכֵּיהֶם לַפָּרִים לָאֵילִם וְלַכְּבָשִׂים בְּמִסְפָּרָם כַּמִּשְׁפָּט׃ וּשְׂעִיר
לב חַטָּאת אֶחָד מִלְּבַד עֹלַת הַתָּמִיד מִנְחָתָהּ וּנְסָכֶיהָ׃ וּבַיּוֹם
הַשְּׁבִיעִי פָּרִים שִׁבְעָה אֵילִם שְׁנָיִם כְּבָשִׂים בְּנֵי־שָׁנָה אַרְבָּעָה עָשָׂר
לג תְּמִימִם׃ וּמִנְחָתָם וְנִסְכֵּהֶם לַפָּרִים לָאֵילִם וְלַכְּבָשִׂים בְּמִסְפָּרָם
לד כְּמִשְׁפָּטָם׃ וּשְׂעִיר חַטָּאת אֶחָד מִלְּבַד עֹלַת הַתָּמִיד מִנְחָתָהּ
לה וְנִסְכָּהּ׃ בַּיּוֹם הַשְּׁמִינִי עֲצֶרֶת תִּהְיֶה לָכֶם כָּל־מְלֶאכֶת מפטיר
לו עֲבֹדָה לֹא תַעֲשׂוּ׃ וְהִקְרַבְתֶּם עֹלָה אִשֵּׁה רֵיחַ נִיחֹחַ לַיהוה פַּר אֶחָד
לז אַיִל אֶחָד כְּבָשִׂים בְּנֵי־שָׁנָה שִׁבְעָה תְּמִימִם׃ מִנְחָתָם וְנִסְכֵּיהֶם לַפָּר
לח לָאַיִל וְלַכְּבָשִׂים בְּמִסְפָּרָם כַּמִּשְׁפָּט׃ וּשְׂעִיר חַטָּאת אֶחָד מִלְּבַד
לט עֹלַת הַתָּמִיד וּמִנְחָתָהּ וְנִסְכָּהּ׃ אֵלֶּה תַּעֲשׂוּ לַיהוה בְּמוֹעֲדֵיכֶם
לְבַד מִנִּדְרֵיכֶם וְנִדְבֹתֵיכֶם לְעֹלֹתֵיכֶם וּלְמִנְחֹתֵיכֶם וּלְנִסְכֵּיכֶם
ל א וּלְשַׁלְמֵיכֶם׃ וַיֹּאמֶר מֹשֶׁה אֶל־בְּנֵי יִשְׂרָאֵל כְּכֹל אֲשֶׁר־צִוָּה יהוה אֶת־
מֹשֶׁה׃

ב וַיְדַבֵּר מֹשֶׁה אֶל־רָאשֵׁי הַמַּטּוֹת לִבְנֵי יִשְׂרָאֵל לֵאמֹר זֶה הַדָּבָר אֲשֶׁר כו מטות
ג צִוָּה יהוה׃ אִישׁ כִּי־יִדֹּר נֶדֶר לַיהוה אוֹ־הִשָּׁבַע שְׁבֻעָה לֶאְסֹר אִסָּר
ד עַל־נַפְשׁוֹ לֹא יַחֵל דְּבָרוֹ כְּכָל־הַיֹּצֵא מִפִּיו יַעֲשֶׂה׃ וְאִשָּׁה כִּי־תִדֹּר נֶדֶר
ה לַיהוה וְאָסְרָה אִסָּר בְּבֵית אָבִיהָ בִּנְעֻרֶיהָ׃ וְשָׁמַע אָבִיהָ אֶת־נִדְרָהּ
וֶאֱסָרָהּ אֲשֶׁר אָסְרָה עַל־נַפְשָׁהּ וְהֶחֱרִישׁ לָהּ אָבִיהָ וְקָמוּ כָּל־נְדָרֶיהָ
ו וְכָל־אִסָּר אֲשֶׁר־אָסְרָה עַל־נַפְשָׁהּ יָקוּם׃ וְאִם־הֵנִיא אָבִיהָ אֹתָהּ בְּיוֹם
שָׁמְעוֹ כָּל־נְדָרֶיהָ וֶאֱסָרֶיהָ אֲשֶׁר־אָסְרָה עַל־נַפְשָׁהּ לֹא יָקוּם וַיהוה
ז יִסְלַח־לָהּ כִּי־הֵנִיא אָבִיהָ אֹתָהּ׃ וְאִם־הָיוֹ תִהְיֶה לְאִישׁ וּנְדָרֶיהָ עָלֶיהָ

8 and her husband hears of it and on the day he does so keeps silent, then her
9 vow or any pledge by which she has bound herself shall stand. But if, on the
day that her husband hears of it, he restrains her, he can annul her vow or the
pledge by which she has bound herself, and the Lord will forgo them for her.
10 11 The vow of a widow or a divorcée – whatever she binds herself by – stands. If,
while in her husband's house, a woman makes a vow or takes an oath binding
12 herself to an obligation and her husband hears and keeps silent, and does not
restrain her, then all her vows and the obligations by which she binds herself
13 shall stand. But if her husband annuls them on the day when he hears them,
then the words she spoke as a vow or the obligation by which she bound herself will not stand. Her husband has annulled them, and the Lord will forgo
14 them for her. Every vow or binding by oath may be upheld by her husband or
15 else annulled by her husband. But if her husband keeps silent from that day
to the next, then he has upheld all her vows and the obligations by which she
has bound herself. He has upheld them by remaining silent on the day when
16 he heard them. If he nullifies them some time after he has heard of them, he
17 shall bear her guilt."[74] These are the decrees that the Lord issued to Moshe,
between a husband and his wife and between a father and his daughter while
she is a girl in her father's home.
31 1 2 The Lord spoke to Moshe: "Take revenge for the Israelites against the
3 Midianites;[75] after that you will be gathered in to your people." Moshe spoke
to the people: "Equip men from among you for active service, to go out
4 against Midyan, to execute the Lord's vengeance against Midyan. For this
5 service, call up one thousand from each of Israel's tribes." And so, of the
thousands of Israel, one thousand men were selected from each tribe, twelve
6 thousand in all, all armed for battle. Moshe sent them, a thousand from each
tribe, into service, together with Pinḥas son of Elazar the priest, who was in
7 charge of the sacred utensils and the trumpets for sounding the blast. And
they did battle against Midyan as the Lord had commanded Moshe, and
8 killed every male. And, among the slain, they killed the kings of Midyan: Evi,
Rekem, Tzur, Ḥur, and Reva – all five kings of Midyan. At the sword's edge
9 they also killed Bilam son of Beor. The Israelites took captive the Midianite
women and children, and took as booty all their cattle, flocks, and wealth.
10 11 They burned all the towns where they lived and their encampments. They
12 gathered all the spoil and plunder, people and animals, and they brought the
captives and the plunder and spoil to Moshe, Elazar the priest, and the Israelite community, at the camp on the plains of Moav by the Jordan across from
13 Yeriḥo. Moshe, Elazar the priest, and all the community princes
14 went to meet them outside the camp. And Moshe grew furious with the
commanders of the forces, the officers of thousands and of hundreds, now

74 | In other words, if she violates her obligation because she thinks that he successfully nullified it, it is he who bears responsibility.

75 | See above, chapter 25.

ח אוֹ מִבְטָא שְׂפָתֶיהָ אֲשֶׁר אָסְרָה עַל־נַפְשָׁהּ׃ וְשָׁמַע אִישָׁהּ בְּיוֹם שָׁמְעוֹ
וְהֶחֱרִישׁ לָהּ וְקָמוּ נְדָרֶיהָ וֶאֱסָרֶהָ אֲשֶׁר־אָסְרָה עַל־נַפְשָׁהּ יָקֻמוּ׃
ט וְאִם בְּיוֹם שְׁמֹעַ אִישָׁהּ יָנִיא אוֹתָהּ וְהֵפֵר אֶת־נִדְרָהּ אֲשֶׁר עָלֶיהָ וְאֵת
י מִבְטָא שְׂפָתֶיהָ אֲשֶׁר אָסְרָה עַל־נַפְשָׁהּ וַיהוָה יִסְלַח־לָהּ׃ וְנֵדֶר אַלְמָנָה
יא וּגְרוּשָׁה כֹּל אֲשֶׁר־אָסְרָה עַל־נַפְשָׁהּ יָקוּם עָלֶיהָ׃ וְאִם־בֵּית אִישָׁהּ
יב נָדָרָה אוֹ־אָסְרָה אִסָּר עַל־נַפְשָׁהּ בִּשְׁבֻעָה׃ וְשָׁמַע אִישָׁהּ וְהֶחֱרִשׁ לָהּ
לֹא הֵנִיא אֹתָהּ וְקָמוּ כָּל־נְדָרֶיהָ וְכָל־אִסָּר אֲשֶׁר־אָסְרָה עַל־נַפְשָׁהּ
יג יָקוּם׃ וְאִם־הָפֵר יָפֵר אֹתָם ׀ אִישָׁהּ בְּיוֹם שָׁמְעוֹ כָּל־מוֹצָא שְׂפָתֶיהָ
לִנְדָרֶיהָ וּלְאִסַּר נַפְשָׁהּ לֹא יָקוּם אִישָׁהּ הֲפֵרָם וַיהוָה יִסְלַח־לָהּ׃
יד כָּל־נֵדֶר וְכָל־שְׁבֻעַת אִסָּר לְעַנֹּת נָפֶשׁ אִישָׁהּ יְקִימֶנּוּ וְאִישָׁהּ יְפֵרֶנּוּ׃
טו וְאִם־הַחֲרֵשׁ יַחֲרִישׁ לָהּ אִישָׁהּ מִיּוֹם אֶל־יוֹם וְהֵקִים אֶת־כָּל־נְדָרֶיהָ
אוֹ אֶת־כָּל־אֱסָרֶיהָ אֲשֶׁר עָלֶיהָ הֵקִים אֹתָם כִּי־הֶחֱרִשׁ לָהּ בְּיוֹם
טז יז שָׁמְעוֹ׃ וְאִם־הָפֵר יָפֵר אֹתָם אַחֲרֵי שָׁמְעוֹ וְנָשָׂא אֶת־עֲוֺנָהּ׃ אֵלֶּה
הַחֻקִּים אֲשֶׁר צִוָּה יְהוָה אֶת־מֹשֶׁה בֵּין אִישׁ לְאִשְׁתּוֹ בֵּין־אָב לְבִתּוֹ
בִּנְעֻרֶיהָ בֵּית אָבִיהָ׃

לא א ב וַיְדַבֵּר יְהוָה אֶל־מֹשֶׁה לֵּאמֹר׃ נְקֹם נִקְמַת בְּנֵי יִשְׂרָאֵל מֵאֵת הַמִּדְיָנִים כז שני
ג אַחַר תֵּאָסֵף אֶל־עַמֶּיךָ׃ וַיְדַבֵּר מֹשֶׁה אֶל־הָעָם לֵאמֹר הֵחָלְצוּ מֵאִתְּכֶם
ד אֲנָשִׁים לַצָּבָא וְיִהְיוּ עַל־מִדְיָן לָתֵת נִקְמַת־יְהוָה בְּמִדְיָן׃ אֶלֶף לַמַּטֶּה
ה אֶלֶף לַמַּטֶּה לְכֹל מַטּוֹת יִשְׂרָאֵל תִּשְׁלְחוּ לַצָּבָא׃ וַיִּמָּסְרוּ מֵאַלְפֵי
ו יִשְׂרָאֵל אֶלֶף לַמַּטֶּה שְׁנֵים־עָשָׂר אֶלֶף חֲלוּצֵי צָבָא׃ וַיִּשְׁלַח אֹתָם
מֹשֶׁה אֶלֶף לַמַּטֶּה לַצָּבָא אֹתָם וְאֶת־פִּינְחָס בֶּן־אֶלְעָזָר הַכֹּהֵן לַצָּבָא
ז וּכְלֵי הַקֹּדֶשׁ וַחֲצֹצְרוֹת הַתְּרוּעָה בְּיָדוֹ׃ וַיִּצְבְּאוּ עַל־מִדְיָן כַּאֲשֶׁר
ח צִוָּה יְהוָה אֶת־מֹשֶׁה וַיַּהַרְגוּ כָּל־זָכָר׃ וְאֶת־מַלְכֵי מִדְיָן הָרְגוּ עַל־
חַלְלֵיהֶם אֶת־אֱוִי וְאֶת־רֶקֶם וְאֶת־צוּר וְאֶת־חוּר וְאֶת־רֶבַע חֲמֵשֶׁת
ט מַלְכֵי מִדְיָן וְאֵת בִּלְעָם בֶּן־בְּעוֹר הָרְגוּ בֶּחָרֶב׃ וַיִּשְׁבּוּ בְנֵי־יִשְׂרָאֵל
אֶת־נְשֵׁי מִדְיָן וְאֶת־טַפָּם וְאֵת כָּל־בְּהֶמְתָּם וְאֶת־כָּל־מִקְנֵהֶם וְאֶת־
י כָּל־חֵילָם בָּזָזוּ׃ וְאֵת כָּל־עָרֵיהֶם בְּמוֹשְׁבֹתָם וְאֵת כָּל־טִירֹתָם שָׂרְפוּ
יא בָּאֵשׁ׃ וַיִּקְחוּ אֶת־כָּל־הַשָּׁלָל וְאֵת כָּל־הַמַּלְקוֹחַ בָּאָדָם וּבַבְּהֵמָה׃
יב וַיָּבִאוּ אֶל־מֹשֶׁה וְאֶל־אֶלְעָזָר הַכֹּהֵן וְאֶל־עֲדַת בְּנֵי־יִשְׂרָאֵל אֶת־
הַשְּׁבִי וְאֶת־הַמַּלְקוֹחַ וְאֶת־הַשָּׁלָל אֶל־הַמַּחֲנֶה אֶל־עַרְבֹת מוֹאָב
יג אֲשֶׁר עַל־יַרְדֵּן יְרֵחוֹ׃ וַיֵּצְאוּ מֹשֶׁה וְאֶלְעָזָר הַכֹּהֵן וְכָל־ שלישי /שני/
יד נְשִׂיאֵי הָעֵדָה לִקְרָאתָם אֶל־מִחוּץ לַמַּחֲנֶה׃ וַיִּקְצֹף מֹשֶׁה עַל פְּקוּדֵי

15 returned from the service of war. "Have you left all the women alive?" Moshe
16 demanded. "These were the very ones who, on Bilam's advice, induced the
Israelites to betray the Lord during the Peor affair, so that a plague struck
17 down the Lord's community. Now, therefore, kill every male child and kill
18 every woman who has had relations with a man. All the young girls who
19 have not had relations with any man – them you may spare alive. You must
stay outside the camp for seven days. Every one among you or your captives
who has killed a person or touched a corpse must purify himself or herself
20 on the third and seventh days. You must also purify every garment, as well
21 as every article of leather, goats' hair, or wood." Elazar the priest
said to the soldiers returning from war, "This is the Law's decree that the
22 23 Lord commanded Moshe: Gold, silver, bronze, iron, tin, and lead – anything that can withstand fire – you shall pass through the fire and it will
be purified, though it must also be purified with the water of lustration.
24 Anything that cannot withstand fire, you must immerse in water. You shall
wash your clothes on the seventh day and you will then be pure, and may
25 26 enter the camp." The Lord said to Moshe: "Together with Elazar
the priest and the family heads of the community, you must make an inven-
27 tory of the plunder that was taken, people and animals, giving half to the
28 soldiers who went into battle and half to the rest of the community. Levy
a tribute to the Lord. From the soldiers who took part in the battle, take
one part of every five hundred, be it of people, oxen, donkeys, or flocks.
29 Take this from their half and give it to Elazar the priest as an upraised gift
30 to the Lord. From the Israelites' half, take one out of every fifty, be it of
people, cattle, donkeys, or flock – all the animals – and give them to the
31 Levites who carry out the duties of the Lord's Tabernacle." Moshe and
32 Elazar the priest did as the Lord commanded Moshe. The plunder, aside
33, 34 from the spoil the troops had taken, was 675,000 sheep, 72,000 oxen, 61,000
35, 36 donkeys, and 32,000 women who had not had relations with a man. The half
37 share of those who had served in battle was 337,500 sheep, of which the Lord's
38 tribute was 675. The cattle were 36,000, of which the Lord's tribute was 72.
39, 40 The donkeys were 30,500, of which the Lord's tribute was 61. There were
41 16,000 people, of which the Lord's tribute was 32 persons. Moshe gave the
tribute, an upraised gift for the Lord, to Elazar the priest, as the Lord had

טו הֶחָיִל שָׂרֵי הָאֲלָפִים וְשָׂרֵי הַמֵּאוֹת הַבָּאִים מִצְּבָא הַמִּלְחָמָה: וַיֹּאמֶר
טז אֲלֵיהֶם מֹשֶׁה הַחִיִּיתֶם כָּל־נְקֵבָה: הֵן הֵנָּה הָיוּ לִבְנֵי יִשְׂרָאֵל בִּדְבַר
בִּלְעָם לִמְסָר־מַעַל בַּיהוָה עַל־דְּבַר פְּעוֹר וַתְּהִי הַמַּגֵּפָה בַּעֲדַת יְהוָה:
יז וְעַתָּה הִרְגוּ כָל־זָכָר בַּטָּף וְכָל־אִשָּׁה יֹדַעַת אִישׁ לְמִשְׁכַּב זָכָר הֲרֹגוּ:
יח יט וְכֹל הַטַּף בַּנָּשִׁים אֲשֶׁר לֹא־יָדְעוּ מִשְׁכַּב זָכָר הַחֲיוּ לָכֶם: וְאַתֶּם חֲנוּ
מִחוּץ לַמַּחֲנֶה שִׁבְעַת יָמִים כֹּל הֹרֵג נֶפֶשׁ וְכֹל ׀ נֹגֵעַ בֶּחָלָל תִּתְחַטְּאוּ
כ בַּיּוֹם הַשְּׁלִישִׁי וּבַיּוֹם הַשְּׁבִיעִי אַתֶּם וּשְׁבִיכֶם: וְכָל־בֶּגֶד וְכָל־כְּלִי־עוֹר
כא וְכָל־מַעֲשֵׂה עִזִּים וְכָל־כְּלִי־עֵץ תִּתְחַטָּאוּ: וַיֹּאמֶר אֶלְעָזָר
הַכֹּהֵן אֶל־אַנְשֵׁי הַצָּבָא הַבָּאִים לַמִּלְחָמָה זֹאת חֻקַּת הַתּוֹרָה אֲשֶׁר־
כב צִוָּה יְהוָה אֶת־מֹשֶׁה: אַךְ אֶת־הַזָּהָב וְאֶת־הַכָּסֶף אֶת־הַנְּחֹשֶׁת אֶת־
כג הַבַּרְזֶל אֶת־הַבְּדִיל וְאֶת־הָעֹפָרֶת: כָּל־דָּבָר אֲשֶׁר־יָבֹא בָאֵשׁ תַּעֲבִירוּ
בָאֵשׁ וְטָהֵר אַךְ בְּמֵי נִדָּה יִתְחַטָּא וְכֹל אֲשֶׁר לֹא־יָבֹא בָּאֵשׁ תַּעֲבִירוּ
כד בַּמָּיִם: וְכִבַּסְתֶּם בִּגְדֵיכֶם בַּיּוֹם הַשְּׁבִיעִי וּטְהַרְתֶּם וְאַחַר תָּבֹאוּ אֶל־
כה כו הַמַּחֲנֶה: וַיֹּאמֶר יְהוָה אֶל־מֹשֶׁה לֵּאמֹר: שָׂא אֵת רֹאשׁ כח רביעי
מַלְקוֹחַ הַשְּׁבִי בָּאָדָם וּבַבְּהֵמָה אַתָּה וְאֶלְעָזָר הַכֹּהֵן וְרָאשֵׁי אֲבוֹת
כז הָעֵדָה: וְחָצִיתָ אֶת־הַמַּלְקוֹחַ בֵּין תֹּפְשֵׂי הַמִּלְחָמָה הַיֹּצְאִים לַצָּבָא
כח וּבֵין כָּל־הָעֵדָה: וַהֲרֵמֹתָ מֶכֶס לַיהוָה מֵאֵת אַנְשֵׁי הַמִּלְחָמָה הַיֹּצְאִים
לַצָּבָא אֶחָד נֶפֶשׁ מֵחֲמֵשׁ הַמֵּאוֹת מִן־הָאָדָם וּמִן־הַבָּקָר וּמִן־הַחֲמֹרִים
כט וּמִן־הַצֹּאן: מִמַּחֲצִיתָם תִּקָּחוּ וְנָתַתָּה לְאֶלְעָזָר הַכֹּהֵן תְּרוּמַת יְהוָה:
ל וּמִמַּחֲצִת בְּנֵי־יִשְׂרָאֵל תִּקַּח ׀ אֶחָד ׀ אָחֻז מִן־הַחֲמִשִּׁים מִן־הָאָדָם
מִן־הַבָּקָר מִן־הַחֲמֹרִים וּמִן־הַצֹּאן מִכָּל־הַבְּהֵמָה וְנָתַתָּה אֹתָם לַלְוִיִּם
לא שֹׁמְרֵי מִשְׁמֶרֶת מִשְׁכַּן יְהוָה: וַיַּעַשׂ מֹשֶׁה וְאֶלְעָזָר הַכֹּהֵן כַּאֲשֶׁר צִוָּה
לב יְהוָה אֶת־מֹשֶׁה: וַיְהִי הַמַּלְקוֹחַ יֶתֶר הַבָּז אֲשֶׁר בָּזְזוּ עַם הַצָּבָא צֹאן
לג שֵׁשׁ־מֵאוֹת אֶלֶף וְשִׁבְעִים אֶלֶף וַחֲמֵשֶׁת אֲלָפִים: וּבָקָר שְׁנַיִם וְשִׁבְעִים
לד לה אָלֶף: וַחֲמֹרִים אֶחָד וְשִׁשִּׁים אָלֶף: וְנֶפֶשׁ אָדָם מִן־הַנָּשִׁים אֲשֶׁר לֹא־
לו יָדְעוּ מִשְׁכַּב זָכָר כָּל־נֶפֶשׁ שְׁנַיִם וּשְׁלֹשִׁים אָלֶף: וַתְּהִי הַמֶּחֱצָה חֵלֶק
הַיֹּצְאִים בַּצָּבָא מִסְפַּר הַצֹּאן שְׁלֹשׁ־מֵאוֹת אֶלֶף וּשְׁלֹשִׁים אֶלֶף וְשִׁבְעַת
לז אֲלָפִים וַחֲמֵשׁ מֵאוֹת: וַיְהִי הַמֶּכֶס לַיהוָה מִן־הַצֹּאן שֵׁשׁ מֵאוֹת חָמֵשׁ
לח וְשִׁבְעִים: וְהַבָּקָר שִׁשָּׁה וּשְׁלֹשִׁים אָלֶף וּמִכְסָם לַיהוָה שְׁנַיִם וְשִׁבְעִים:
לט וַחֲמֹרִים שְׁלֹשִׁים אֶלֶף וַחֲמֵשׁ מֵאוֹת וּמִכְסָם לַיהוָה אֶחָד וְשִׁשִּׁים:
מ וְנֶפֶשׁ אָדָם שִׁשָּׁה עָשָׂר אָלֶף וּמִכְסָם לַיהוָה שְׁנַיִם וּשְׁלֹשִׁים נָפֶשׁ:
מא וַיִּתֵּן מֹשֶׁה אֶת־מֶכֶס תְּרוּמַת יְהוָה לְאֶלְעָזָר הַכֹּהֵן כַּאֲשֶׁר צִוָּה יְהוָה

42 commanded Moshe. The half share that Moshe took for the Israelites from
43 those who had served in battle as the community's half consisted of 337,500
44, 45 46, 47 sheep, 36,000 heads of cattle, 30,500 donkeys, and 16,000 people. Moshe
took from the Israelites' half one out of every 50 humans and animals. These
he gave to the Levites who keep the charge of the LORD's Tabernacle, as the
48 LORD had commanded Moshe. The commanders over the thousands of the
warriors – officers over thousands and officers over hundreds – approached
49 Moshe and said to him, "Your servants have counted the warriors in our
50 charge; not one of us is missing. And so we make an offering to the LORD
of the gold articles each man found – anklets, bracelets, signet rings, ear-
51 rings, and pendants – to make our atonement before the LORD." Moshe
52 and Elazar the priest took all the gold from them, all the crafted objects. All
the gold for the upraised gift presented to the LORD by the officers of thou-
53 sands and the officers of hundreds was worth 16,750 shekel. Yet the men of
54 the army each kept plunder for themselves.[76] Moshe and Elazar the priest
took the gold from the officers of thousands and of hundreds, and brought
it to the Tent of Meeting as a remembrance for the Israelites before the
LORD.

32 1 The people of Reuven and Gad had much cattle – in this they were very rich.
And seeing the lands of Yazer and Gilad they noticed that this was cattle
2 country. So the people of Gad and Reuven came to Moshe, Elazar the priest,
3 and the princes of the community and said: "Atarot, Divon, Yazer, Nimra,
4 Ḥeshbon, Elaleh, Sevam, Nevo, and Beon, the land that the LORD struck
down before the community of Israel, is good cattle country, and your ser-
5 vants keep cattle."[77] They said, "If we have found favor with you, let
this land be given to your servants as our possession. Do not make us cross
6 the Jordan." But Moshe asked the Gadites and Reubenites, "Are your brothers
7 to go to war while you stay here? Why would you discourage the Israelites
8 from crossing into the land the LORD has given them? That is what your
9 fathers did when I sent them from Kadesh Barne'a to see the land.[78] They
went as far as the Eshkol Ravine and saw the land, but they discouraged the
10 Israelites from entering the land the LORD had given them, and on that day
11 the LORD's rage burned, and He swore: None of the men twenty years of
age or above who left Egypt will see the land that I swore to give Avraham,
12 Yitzḥak, and Yaakov, because they did not follow Me wholeheartedly – none
except Kalev son of Yefuneh the Kenizzite and Yehoshua son of Nun, because
13 they wholeheartedly followed the LORD. The LORD was incensed at Israel,
and He made them wander in the wilderness for forty years until the whole

76 | That is, only the commanders offered their plunder to the LORD.

77 | Although this request appears after the Midianite war, the areas in question include those conquered earlier; see chapter 21.

78 | See chapter 13.

מב אֶת־מֹשֶׁה: וּמִמַּחֲצִית בְּנֵי יִשְׂרָאֵל אֲשֶׁר חָצָה מֹשֶׁה מִן־הָאֲנָשִׁים חמישי
מג הַצֹּבְאִים: וַתְּהִי מֶחֱצַת הָעֵדָה מִן־הַצֹּאן שְׁלֹשׁ־מֵאוֹת אֶלֶף וּשְׁלֹשִׁים
מד אֶלֶף שִׁבְעַת אֲלָפִים וַחֲמֵשׁ מֵאוֹת: וּבָקָר שִׁשָּׁה וּשְׁלֹשִׁים אָלֶף:
מה מו וַחֲמֹרִים שְׁלֹשִׁים אֶלֶף וַחֲמֵשׁ מֵאוֹת: וְנֶפֶשׁ אָדָם שִׁשָּׁה עָשָׂר אָלֶף:
מז וַיִּקַּח מֹשֶׁה מִמַּחֲצִת בְּנֵי־יִשְׂרָאֵל אֶת־הָאָחֻז אֶחָד מִן־הַחֲמִשִּׁים מִן־
הָאָדָם וּמִן־הַבְּהֵמָה וַיִּתֵּן אֹתָם לַלְוִיִּם שֹׁמְרֵי מִשְׁמֶרֶת מִשְׁכַּן יְהוָה
מח כַּאֲשֶׁר צִוָּה יְהוָה אֶת־מֹשֶׁה: וַיִּקְרְבוּ אֶל־מֹשֶׁה הַפְּקֻדִים אֲשֶׁר לְאַלְפֵי
מט הַצָּבָא שָׂרֵי הָאֲלָפִים וְשָׂרֵי הַמֵּאוֹת: וַיֹּאמְרוּ אֶל־מֹשֶׁה עֲבָדֶיךָ נָשְׂאוּ
נ אֶת־רֹאשׁ אַנְשֵׁי הַמִּלְחָמָה אֲשֶׁר בְּיָדֵנוּ וְלֹא־נִפְקַד מִמֶּנּוּ אִישׁ: וַנַּקְרֵב
אֶת־קָרְבַּן יְהוָה אִישׁ אֲשֶׁר מָצָא כְלִי־זָהָב אֶצְעָדָה וְצָמִיד טַבַּעַת
נא עָגִיל וְכוּמָז לְכַפֵּר עַל־נַפְשֹׁתֵינוּ לִפְנֵי יְהוָה: וַיִּקַּח מֹשֶׁה וְאֶלְעָזָר הַכֹּהֵן
נב אֶת־הַזָּהָב מֵאִתָּם כֹּל כְּלִי מַעֲשֶׂה: וַיְהִי ׀ כָּל־זְהַב הַתְּרוּמָה אֲשֶׁר
הֵרִימוּ לַיהוָה שִׁשָּׁה עָשָׂר אֶלֶף שְׁבַע־מֵאוֹת וַחֲמִשִּׁים שָׁקֶל מֵאֵת
נג נד שָׂרֵי הָאֲלָפִים וּמֵאֵת שָׂרֵי הַמֵּאוֹת: אַנְשֵׁי הַצָּבָא בָּזְזוּ אִישׁ לוֹ: וַיִּקַּח
מֹשֶׁה וְאֶלְעָזָר הַכֹּהֵן אֶת־הַזָּהָב מֵאֵת שָׂרֵי הָאֲלָפִים וְהַמֵּאוֹת וַיָּבִאוּ
אֹתוֹ אֶל־אֹהֶל מוֹעֵד זִכָּרוֹן לִבְנֵי־יִשְׂרָאֵל לִפְנֵי יְהוָה:

לב א וּמִקְנֶה ׀ רַב הָיָה לִבְנֵי רְאוּבֵן וְלִבְנֵי־גָד עָצוּם מְאֹד וַיִּרְאוּ אֶת־אֶרֶץ כט ששי /שלישי/
ב יַעְזֵר וְאֶת־אֶרֶץ גִּלְעָד וְהִנֵּה הַמָּקוֹם מְקוֹם מִקְנֶה: וַיָּבֹאוּ בְנֵי־גָד
וּבְנֵי רְאוּבֵן וַיֹּאמְרוּ אֶל־מֹשֶׁה וְאֶל־אֶלְעָזָר הַכֹּהֵן וְאֶל־נְשִׂיאֵי הָעֵדָה
ג לֵאמֹר: עֲטָרוֹת וְדִיבֹן וְיַעְזֵר וְנִמְרָה וְחֶשְׁבּוֹן וְאֶלְעָלֵה וּשְׂבָם וּנְבוֹ
ד וּבְעֹן: הָאָרֶץ אֲשֶׁר הִכָּה יְהוָה לִפְנֵי עֲדַת יִשְׂרָאֵל אֶרֶץ מִקְנֶה הִוא
ה וְלַעֲבָדֶיךָ מִקְנֶה: וַיֹּאמְרוּ אִם־מָצָאנוּ חֵן בְּעֵינֶיךָ יֻתַּן אֶת־
ו הָאָרֶץ הַזֹּאת לַעֲבָדֶיךָ לַאֲחֻזָּה אַל־תַּעֲבִרֵנוּ אֶת־הַיַּרְדֵּן: וַיֹּאמֶר מֹשֶׁה
לִבְנֵי־גָד וְלִבְנֵי רְאוּבֵן הַאַחֵיכֶם יָבֹאוּ לַמִּלְחָמָה וְאַתֶּם תֵּשְׁבוּ פֹה:
ז וְלָמָּה תנואון אֶת־לֵב בְּנֵי יִשְׂרָאֵל מֵעֲבֹר אֶל־הָאָרֶץ אֲשֶׁר־נָתַן לָהֶם תְּנִיאוּן
ח יְהוָה: כֹּה עָשׂוּ אֲבֹתֵיכֶם בְּשָׁלְחִי אֹתָם מִקָּדֵשׁ בַּרְנֵעַ לִרְאוֹת אֶת־
ט הָאָרֶץ: וַיַּעֲלוּ עַד־נַחַל אֶשְׁכּוֹל וַיִּרְאוּ אֶת־הָאָרֶץ וַיָּנִיאוּ אֶת־לֵב בְּנֵי
י יִשְׂרָאֵל לְבִלְתִּי־בֹא אֶל־הָאָרֶץ אֲשֶׁר־נָתַן לָהֶם יְהוָה: וַיִּחַר־אַף יְהוָה
יא בַּיּוֹם הַהוּא וַיִּשָּׁבַע לֵאמֹר: אִם־יִרְאוּ הָאֲנָשִׁים הָעֹלִים מִמִּצְרַיִם מִבֶּן
עֶשְׂרִים שָׁנָה וָמַעְלָה אֵת הָאֲדָמָה אֲשֶׁר נִשְׁבַּעְתִּי לְאַבְרָהָם לְיִצְחָק
יב וּלְיַעֲקֹב כִּי לֹא־מִלְאוּ אַחֲרָי: בִּלְתִּי כָּלֵב בֶּן־יְפֻנֶּה הַקְּנִזִּי וִיהוֹשֻׁעַ
יג בִּן־נוּן כִּי מִלְאוּ אַחֲרֵי יְהוָה: וַיִּחַר־אַף יְהוָה בְּיִשְׂרָאֵל וַיְנִעֵם בַּמִּדְבָּר

14 generation that had done evil in the LORD's sight was gone. And here you
are, a brood of sinners, taking your fathers' places and bringing yet more of
15 the LORD's burning rage down upon Israel. If you turn back from following
Him, He will once again leave them in the wilderness, and you will destroy
16 this entire people." Then they set forward and said to him, "Let us
17 build sheep pens here for our livestock and towns for our children. But we
will arm ourselves and go ahead of the Israelites until we have seen them safely
to their place. Meanwhile, our children will remain in the fortified towns,
18 protected from the inhabitants of the land. We will not return to our homes
19 until every one of the Israelites has taken possession of his inheritance. We,
however, will not take possession with them on the far side of the Jordan, for
our inheritance will be on the east side of the Jordan."
20 Moshe replied to them, "If you do this – if you arm yourselves for battle
21 before the LORD, and each of your armed men crosses the Jordan before the
22 LORD until He has driven out His enemies before Him, and the land has
been subdued before the LORD – then you may return and be clear before
the LORD and before Israel, and this land will be yours as a possession before
23 the LORD. But if you do not do this, you will have sinned against the LORD,
24 and know that your sin will find you. Build towns for your children and pens
25 for your flocks, but do what you have promised." The people of Gad and
Reuven replied to Moshe, "Your servants will do just as my lord charges us.
26 Our children, wives, livestock, and all our animals will remain here in the
27 towns of Gilad, but your servants, all equipped for war, will cross over to do
28 battle before the LORD, as my lord has said." Moshe gave instructions concerning them to Elazar the priest, Yehoshua son of Nun, and the family heads
29 of the Israelite tribes. Moshe said to them, "If the men of Gad and Reuven
cross the Jordan with you, each equipped for battle before the LORD, and
the land is subdued before you, then you shall give them the land of Gilad as
30 a possession. But if they do not cross with you, equipped for war, then they
31 must have their possession with you in the land of Canaan." The Gadites and
the Reubenites answered, "What the LORD has spoken to your servants,
32 we will do. We will cross into the land of Canaan equipped for war before
33 the LORD, and we shall then have our hereditary land across the Jordan." So
Moshe gave to them – the people of Gad and Reuven, and half the tribe of
Menashe son of Yosef – the kingdom of Siḥon, king of the Amorites, and the
kingdom of Og, king of Bashan, the land along with its towns and the territory
34 of the surrounding towns. The Gadites rebuilt Divon, Atarot, Aroer, Atrot
35
36 Shofan, Yazer, Yogbeha, Beit Nimra, and Beit Haran, as fortified towns and
37 enclosures for flocks. The Reubenites built Ḥeshbon, Elaleh, Kiryatayim,
38 Nevo and Baal Meon – the names of which were changed – and Sivma.

יד אַרְבָּעִים שָׁנָה עַד־תֹּם כׇּל־הַדּוֹר הָעֹשֶׂה הָרַע בְּעֵינֵי יְהוָה׃ וְהִנֵּה
קַמְתֶּם תַּחַת אֲבֹתֵיכֶם תַּרְבּוּת אֲנָשִׁים חַטָּאִים לִסְפּוֹת עוֹד עַל חֲרוֹן
טו אַף־יְהוָה אֶל־יִשְׂרָאֵל׃ כִּי תְשׁוּבֻן מֵאַחֲרָיו וְיָסַף עוֹד לְהַנִּיחוֹ בַּמִּדְבָּר
טז וְשִׁחַתֶּם לְכׇל־הָעָם הַזֶּה׃ וַיִּגְּשׁוּ אֵלָיו וַיֹּאמְרוּ גִּדְרֹת צֹאן
יז נִבְנֶה לְמִקְנֵנוּ פֹּה וְעָרִים לְטַפֵּנוּ׃ וַאֲנַחְנוּ נֵחָלֵץ חֻשִׁים לִפְנֵי בְּנֵי
יִשְׂרָאֵל עַד אֲשֶׁר אִם־הֲבִיאֹנֻם אֶל־מְקוֹמָם וְיָשַׁב טַפֵּנוּ בְּעָרֵי הַמִּבְצָר
יח מִפְּנֵי יֹשְׁבֵי הָאָרֶץ׃ לֹא נָשׁוּב אֶל־בָּתֵּינוּ עַד הִתְנַחֵל בְּנֵי יִשְׂרָאֵל אִישׁ
יט נַחֲלָתוֹ׃ כִּי לֹא נִנְחַל אִתָּם מֵעֵבֶר לַיַּרְדֵּן וָהָלְאָה כִּי בָאָה נַחֲלָתֵנוּ
אֵלֵינוּ מֵעֵבֶר הַיַּרְדֵּן מִזְרָחָה׃
כ וַיֹּאמֶר אֲלֵיהֶם מֹשֶׁה אִם־תַּעֲשׂוּן אֶת־הַדָּבָר הַזֶּה אִם־תֵּחָלְצוּ לִפְנֵי שביעי /רביעי/
כא יְהוָה לַמִּלְחָמָה׃ וְעָבַר לָכֶם כׇּל־חָלוּץ אֶת־הַיַּרְדֵּן לִפְנֵי יְהוָה עַד
כב הוֹרִישׁוֹ אֶת־אֹיְבָיו מִפָּנָיו׃ וְנִכְבְּשָׁה הָאָרֶץ לִפְנֵי יְהוָה וְאַחַר תָּשֻׁבוּ
וִהְיִיתֶם נְקִיִּם מֵיְהוָה וּמִיִּשְׂרָאֵל וְהָיְתָה הָאָרֶץ הַזֹּאת לָכֶם לַאֲחֻזָּה
כג לִפְנֵי יְהוָה׃ וְאִם־לֹא תַעֲשׂוּן כֵּן הִנֵּה חֲטָאתֶם לַיהוָה וּדְעוּ חַטַּאתְכֶם
כד אֲשֶׁר תִּמְצָא אֶתְכֶם׃ בְּנוּ־לָכֶם עָרִים לְטַפְּכֶם וּגְדֵרֹת לְצֹנַאֲכֶם וְהַיֹּצֵא
כה מִפִּיכֶם תַּעֲשׂוּ׃ וַיֹּאמֶר בְּנֵי־גָד וּבְנֵי רְאוּבֵן אֶל־מֹשֶׁה לֵאמֹר עֲבָדֶיךָ
כו יַעֲשׂוּ כַּאֲשֶׁר אֲדֹנִי מְצַוֶּה׃ טַפֵּנוּ נָשֵׁינוּ מִקְנֵנוּ וְכׇל־בְּהֶמְתֵּנוּ יִהְיוּ־שָׁם
כז בְּעָרֵי הַגִּלְעָד׃ וַעֲבָדֶיךָ יַעַבְרוּ כׇּל־חֲלוּץ צָבָא לִפְנֵי יְהוָה לַמִּלְחָמָה
כח כַּאֲשֶׁר אֲדֹנִי דֹּבֵר׃ וַיְצַו לָהֶם מֹשֶׁה אֵת אֶלְעָזָר הַכֹּהֵן וְאֵת יְהוֹשֻׁעַ
כט בִּן־נוּן וְאֶת־רָאשֵׁי אֲבוֹת הַמַּטּוֹת לִבְנֵי יִשְׂרָאֵל׃ וַיֹּאמֶר מֹשֶׁה אֲלֵהֶם
אִם־יַעַבְרוּ בְנֵי־גָד וּבְנֵי־רְאוּבֵן ׀ אִתְּכֶם אֶת־הַיַּרְדֵּן כׇּל־חָלוּץ לַמִּלְחָמָה
לִפְנֵי יְהוָה וְנִכְבְּשָׁה הָאָרֶץ לִפְנֵיכֶם וּנְתַתֶּם לָהֶם אֶת־אֶרֶץ הַגִּלְעָד
ל לַאֲחֻזָּה׃ וְאִם־לֹא יַעַבְרוּ חֲלוּצִים אִתְּכֶם וְנֹאחֲזוּ בְתֹכְכֶם בְּאֶרֶץ כְּנָעַן׃
לא וַיַּעֲנוּ בְנֵי־גָד וּבְנֵי רְאוּבֵן לֵאמֹר אֵת אֲשֶׁר דִּבֶּר יְהוָה אֶל־עֲבָדֶיךָ
לב כֵּן נַעֲשֶׂה׃ נַחְנוּ נַעֲבֹר חֲלוּצִים לִפְנֵי יְהוָה אֶרֶץ כְּנָעַן וְאִתָּנוּ אֲחֻזַּת
לג נַחֲלָתֵנוּ מֵעֵבֶר לַיַּרְדֵּן׃ וַיִּתֵּן לָהֶם ׀ מֹשֶׁה לִבְנֵי־גָד וְלִבְנֵי רְאוּבֵן וְלַחֲצִי ׀
שֵׁבֶט ׀ מְנַשֶּׁה בֶן־יוֹסֵף אֶת־מַמְלֶכֶת סִיחֹן מֶלֶךְ הָאֱמֹרִי וְאֶת־מַמְלֶכֶת
לד עוֹג מֶלֶךְ הַבָּשָׁן הָאָרֶץ לְעָרֶיהָ בִּגְבֻלֹת עָרֵי הָאָרֶץ סָבִיב׃ וַיִּבְנוּ בְנֵי־
לה גָד אֶת־דִּיבֹן וְאֶת־עֲטָרֹת וְאֵת עֲרֹעֵר׃ וְאֶת־עַטְרֹת שׁוֹפָן וְאֶת־יַעְזֵר
לו וְיׇגְבְּהָה׃ וְאֶת־בֵּית נִמְרָה וְאֶת־בֵּית הָרָן עָרֵי מִבְצָר וְגִדְרֹת צֹאן׃
לז לח וּבְנֵי רְאוּבֵן בָּנוּ אֶת־חֶשְׁבּוֹן וְאֶת־אֶלְעָלֵא וְאֵת קִרְיָתָיִם׃ וְאֶת־נְבוֹ
וְאֶת־בַּעַל מְעוֹן מוּסַבֹּת שֵׁם וְאֶת־שִׂבְמָה וַיִּקְרְאוּ בְשֵׁמֹת אֶת־שְׁמוֹת

39 They named the cities that they built up. The descendants of Makhir son of
Menashe went to Gilad and captured it, driving out the Amorites who were
40 there. So Moshe gave Gilad to Makhir son of Menashe, and he settled there.
41 Yair son of Menashe went and captured their villages, naming them Hamlets
42 of Yair. Novaḥ went and captured Kenat and its surrounding villages, renaming it Novaḥ after himself.

33 1 These were the journeys of the Israelites when they left Egypt by their divi- MASEI
2 sions under the leadership of Moshe and Aharon. Moshe recorded the places
of their setting out on every journey at the Lord's command. These are their
3 journeys, by the places from which they set out. They set out from Ramesses
on the fifteenth day of the first month. On the day after the Passover the Isra-
4 elites went out defiantly, before all the Egyptians' eyes, while the Egyptians
were burying their firstborns, whom the Lord had struck down, every one.
5 The Lord had executed judgments even against their gods. The Israelites
6 set out from Ramesses and camped at Sukkot. They set out from Sukkot
7 and camped at Etam on the edge of the wilderness. They set out from Etam
and turned back to Pi HaḤirot, which faces Baal Tzefon, and camped before
8 Migdol. They set out from Pi HaḤirot and passed through the sea into the
wilderness – and they made a three-day journey through the Wilderness of
9 Etam and camped at Mara. They set out from Mara and came to Eilim. At
Eilim there were twelve springs and seventy date palms, and they encamped
10 11 there. They set out from Eilim and camped by the Sea of Reeds. They set out
12 from the Sea of Reeds and camped in the Wilderness of Sin. They set out
13 from the wilderness of Sin and camped at Dofka. They set out from Dofka
14 and camped at Alush. They set out from Alush and camped at Refidim, where
15 there was no water for the people to drink. They set out from Refidim and
16 camped in the Sinai Desert. They set out from the Sinai Desert and camped at
17 Kivrot HaTaava. They set out from Kivrot HaTaava and camped at Ḥatzerot.
18 19 They set out from Ḥatzerot and camped at Ritma. They set out from Ritma
20 and camped at Rimon Peretz. They set out from Rimon Peretz and camped
21 22 at Livna. They set out from Livna and camped at Risa. They set out from Risa
23 and camped at Kehelata. They set out from Kehelata and camped at Mount
24 25 Shefer. They set out from Mount Shefer and camped at Ḥarada. They set out
26 from Ḥarada and camped at Mak'helot. They set out from Mak'helot and
27 28 camped at Taḥat. They set out from Taḥat and camped at Teraḥ. They set
29 out from Teraḥ and camped at Mitka. They set out from Mitka and camped
30 31 at Ḥashmona. They set out from Ḥashmona and camped at Moserot. They
32 set out from Moserot and camped at Benei Yaakan. They set out from Benei
33 Yaakan and camped at Ḥor HaGidgad. They set out from Ḥor HaGidgad and
34 35 camped at Yotvata. They set out from Yotvata and camped at Avrona. They
36 set out from Avrona and camped at Etzyon Gever. They set out from Etzyon
37 Gever and camped in the Wilderness of Tzin, that is, Kadesh. They set out
38 from Kadesh and camped at Mount Hor, at the edge of the land of Edom. And

לט הֶעָרִים אֲשֶׁר בָּנוּ: וַיֵּלְכוּ בְּנֵי מָכִיר בֶּן־מְנַשֶּׁה גִּלְעָדָה וַיִּלְכְּדֻהָ וַיּוֹרֶשׁ
מ אֶת־הָאֱמֹרִי אֲשֶׁר־בָּהּ: וַיִּתֵּן מֹשֶׁה אֶת־הַגִּלְעָד לְמָכִיר בֶּן־מְנַשֶּׁה מפטיר
מא וַיֵּשֶׁב בָּהּ: וְיָאִיר בֶּן־מְנַשֶּׁה הָלַךְ וַיִּלְכֹּד אֶת־חַוֺּתֵיהֶם וַיִּקְרָא אֶתְהֶן
מב חַוֺּת יָאִיר: וְנֹבַח הָלַךְ וַיִּלְכֹּד אֶת־קְנָת וְאֶת־בְּנֹתֶיהָ וַיִּקְרָא לָה נֹבַח
בִשְׁמוֹ:

לג א אֵלֶּה מַסְעֵי בְנֵי־יִשְׂרָאֵל אֲשֶׁר יָצְאוּ מֵאֶרֶץ מִצְרַיִם לְצִבְאֹתָם בְּיַד־ ל מסעי
ב מֹשֶׁה וְאַהֲרֹן: וַיִּכְתֹּב מֹשֶׁה אֶת־מוֹצָאֵיהֶם לְמַסְעֵיהֶם עַל־פִּי יְהוָה
ג וְאֵלֶּה מַסְעֵיהֶם לְמוֹצָאֵיהֶם: וַיִּסְעוּ מֵרַעְמְסֵס בַּחֹדֶשׁ הָרִאשׁוֹן
בַּחֲמִשָּׁה עָשָׂר יוֹם לַחֹדֶשׁ הָרִאשׁוֹן מִמָּחֳרַת הַפֶּסַח יָצְאוּ בְנֵי־יִשְׂרָאֵל
ד בְּיָד רָמָה לְעֵינֵי כָּל־מִצְרָיִם: וּמִצְרַיִם מְקַבְּרִים אֵת אֲשֶׁר הִכָּה יְהוָה
ה בָּהֶם כָּל־בְּכוֹר וּבֵאלֹהֵיהֶם עָשָׂה יְהוָה שְׁפָטִים: וַיִּסְעוּ בְנֵי־יִשְׂרָאֵל
ו מֵרַעְמְסֵס וַיַּחֲנוּ בְּסֻכֹּת: וַיִּסְעוּ מִסֻּכֹּת וַיַּחֲנוּ בְאֵתָם אֲשֶׁר בִּקְצֵה
ז הַמִּדְבָּר: וַיִּסְעוּ מֵאֵתָם וַיָּשָׁב עַל־פִּי הַחִירֹת אֲשֶׁר עַל־פְּנֵי בַּעַל צְפוֹן
ח וַיַּחֲנוּ לִפְנֵי מִגְדֹּל: וַיִּסְעוּ מִפְּנֵי הַחִירֹת וַיַּעַבְרוּ בְתוֹךְ־הַיָּם הַמִּדְבָּרָה
ט וַיֵּלְכוּ דֶּרֶךְ שְׁלֹשֶׁת יָמִים בְּמִדְבַּר אֵתָם וַיַּחֲנוּ בְּמָרָה: וַיִּסְעוּ מִמָּרָה
וַיָּבֹאוּ אֵילִמָה וּבְאֵילִם שְׁתֵּים עֶשְׂרֵה עֵינֹת מַיִם וְשִׁבְעִים תְּמָרִים
י יא וַיַּחֲנוּ־שָׁם: וַיִּסְעוּ מֵאֵילִם וַיַּחֲנוּ עַל־יַם־סוּף: וַיִּסְעוּ מִיַּם־סוּף וַיַּחֲנוּ שני
יב יג בְּמִדְבַּר־סִין: וַיִּסְעוּ מִמִּדְבַּר־סִין וַיַּחֲנוּ בְּדָפְקָה: וַיִּסְעוּ מִדָּפְקָה
יד וַיַּחֲנוּ בְּאָלוּשׁ: וַיִּסְעוּ מֵאָלוּשׁ וַיַּחֲנוּ בִּרְפִידִם וְלֹא־הָיָה שָׁם מַיִם
טו טז לָעָם לִשְׁתּוֹת: וַיִּסְעוּ מֵרְפִידִם וַיַּחֲנוּ בְּמִדְבַּר סִינָי: וַיִּסְעוּ מִמִּדְבַּר
יז סִינָי וַיַּחֲנוּ בְּקִבְרֹת הַתַּאֲוָה: וַיִּסְעוּ מִקִּבְרֹת הַתַּאֲוָה וַיַּחֲנוּ בַּחֲצֵרֹת:
יח יט כ וַיִּסְעוּ מֵחֲצֵרֹת וַיַּחֲנוּ בְּרִתְמָה: וַיִּסְעוּ מֵרִתְמָה וַיַּחֲנוּ בְּרִמֹּן פָּרֶץ:
כא כב וַיִּסְעוּ מֵרִמֹּן פָּרֶץ וַיַּחֲנוּ בְּלִבְנָה: וַיִּסְעוּ מִלִּבְנָה וַיַּחֲנוּ בְּרִסָּה: וַיִּסְעוּ
כג כד מֵרִסָּה וַיַּחֲנוּ בִּקְהֵלָתָה: וַיִּסְעוּ מִקְּהֵלָתָה וַיַּחֲנוּ בְּהַר־שָׁפֶר: וַיִּסְעוּ
כה כו מֵהַר־שָׁפֶר וַיַּחֲנוּ בַּחֲרָדָה: וַיִּסְעוּ מֵחֲרָדָה וַיַּחֲנוּ בְּמַקְהֵלֹת: וַיִּסְעוּ
כז כח מִמַּקְהֵלֹת וַיַּחֲנוּ בְּתָחַת: וַיִּסְעוּ מִתָּחַת וַיַּחֲנוּ בְּתָרַח: וַיִּסְעוּ מִתָּרַח
כט ל וַיַּחֲנוּ בְּמִתְקָה: וַיִּסְעוּ מִמִּתְקָה וַיַּחֲנוּ בְּחַשְׁמֹנָה: וַיִּסְעוּ מֵחַשְׁמֹנָה
לא לב וַיַּחֲנוּ בְּמֹסֵרוֹת: וַיִּסְעוּ מִמֹּסֵרוֹת וַיַּחֲנוּ בִּבְנֵי יַעֲקָן: וַיִּסְעוּ מִבְּנֵי
לג לד יַעֲקָן וַיַּחֲנוּ בְּחֹר הַגִּדְגָּד: וַיִּסְעוּ מֵחֹר הַגִּדְגָּד וַיַּחֲנוּ בְּיָטְבָתָה: וַיִּסְעוּ
לה לו מִיָּטְבָתָה וַיַּחֲנוּ בְּעַבְרֹנָה: וַיִּסְעוּ מֵעַבְרֹנָה וַיַּחֲנוּ בְּעֶצְיֹן גָּבֶר: וַיִּסְעוּ
לז מֵעֶצְיֹן גָּבֶר וַיַּחֲנוּ בְמִדְבַּר־צִן הִוא קָדֵשׁ: וַיִּסְעוּ מִקָּדֵשׁ וַיַּחֲנוּ בְּהֹר
לח הָהָר בִּקְצֵה אֶרֶץ אֱדוֹם: וַיַּעַל אַהֲרֹן הַכֹּהֵן אֶל־הֹר הָהָר עַל־פִּי

Aharon the priest ascended Mount Hor at the Lord's command, and he died
there in the fortieth year, on the first day of the fifth month after the Israelites
39 left Egypt. Aharon was one hundred and twenty-three years old when he died
40 on Mount Hor. And the Canaanite king of Arad, who lived in the
41 Negev in the land of Canaan, heard that the Israelites were coming.[79] They set
42 out from Mount Hor and camped at Tzalmona. They set out from Tzalmona
43 44 and camped at Punon. They set out from Punon and camped at Ovot. They
set out from Ovot and camped at Iyei HaAvarim in the territory of Moav.
45 46 They set out from Iyim and camped at Divon Gad. They set out from Divon
47 Gad and camped at Almon Divlatayma. They set out from Almon Divlatayma
48 and camped in the Mountains of Avarim, before Nevo. They set out from the
Mountains of Avarim and camped in the plains of Moav by the Jordan across
49 from Yeriḥo. And they camped by the Jordan from Beit HaYeshimot to Avel
50 HaShitim in the plains of Moav. And the Lord spoke to Moshe on
51 the plains of Moav by the Jordan across from Yeriḥo: "Speak to the Israelites.
52 Say: When you cross the Jordan into the land of Canaan, you shall drive out
all the inhabitants of the land before you. You shall destroy all their carved
53 images and all their molten idols and demolish all their high shrines. You shall
take possession of the land and settle there, for I have given you the land to
54 possess. You shall divide up the land by lot among your clans: to a large clan
give a large inheritance, and to a small one a small inheritance. Whatever
falls to them by lot will be theirs. According to your ancestral tribes you shall
55 inherit. But if you do not drive the inhabitants out of the land before you, then
those you allow to remain will be barbs in your eyes and thorns in your sides.
56 They will harass you in the land where you settle. Then, what I intended to
do to them, I will do instead to you."

34 1 2 The Lord said to Moshe: "Command the Israelites. Say to them: As you
enter the land of Canaan – this is the land that will become your posses-
3 sion, the land of Canaan with its borders: Your southern sector shall extend
from the Wilderness of Tzin alongside Edom; your southern border to the
4 east begins at the end of the Dead Sea. The border shall then turn south of
Scorpion Ascent and cross toward Tzin. Its outer limit shall be south of
5 Kadesh Barne'a, extending to Ḥatzar Adar and continuing toward Atzmon.
The border shall then turn from Atzmon to the Ravine of Egypt and end
6 at the sea. Your western border will be the Great Sea and its coast; this
7 shall be your western border. This shall be your northern border: from the
8 Great Sea, mark a line to Mount Hor. From Mount Hor mark a line to Levo
9 Ḥamat. The outer limit of the border shall be at Tzedad; the border shall then
extend to Zifron, and its outer limit shall be Ḥatzar Einan. This shall be your
10 northern border. Mark your eastern border from Ḥatzar Einan to Shefam.
11 The border will run down from Shefam to Rivla on the east side of Ayin.

79 | See 21:1–3.

יְהוָה וַיָּמָת שָׁם בִּשְׁנַת הָאַרְבָּעִים לְצֵאת בְּנֵי־יִשְׂרָאֵל מֵאֶרֶץ מִצְרַיִם
לט בַּחֹדֶשׁ הַחֲמִישִׁי בְּאֶחָד לַחֹדֶשׁ: וְאַהֲרֹן בֶּן־שָׁלֹשׁ וְעֶשְׂרִים וּמְאַת
מ שָׁנָה בְּמֹתוֹ בְּהֹר הָהָר: וַיִּשְׁמַע הַכְּנַעֲנִי מֶלֶךְ עֲרָד וְהוּא־
מא יֹשֵׁב בַּנֶּגֶב בְּאֶרֶץ כְּנָעַן בְּבֹא בְּנֵי יִשְׂרָאֵל: וַיִּסְעוּ מֵהֹר הָהָר וַיַּחֲנוּ
מב מג בְּצַלְמֹנָה: וַיִּסְעוּ מִצַּלְמֹנָה וַיַּחֲנוּ בְּפוּנֹן: וַיִּסְעוּ מִפּוּנֹן וַיַּחֲנוּ בְּאֹבֹת:
מד מה וַיִּסְעוּ מֵאֹבֹת וַיַּחֲנוּ בְּעִיֵּי הָעֲבָרִים בִּגְבוּל מוֹאָב: וַיִּסְעוּ מֵעִיִּים וַיַּחֲנוּ
מו מז בְּדִיבֹן גָּד: וַיִּסְעוּ מִדִּיבֹן גָּד וַיַּחֲנוּ בְּעַלְמֹן דִּבְלָתָיְמָה: וַיִּסְעוּ מֵעַלְמֹן
מח דִּבְלָתָיְמָה וַיַּחֲנוּ בְּהָרֵי הָעֲבָרִים לִפְנֵי נְבוֹ: וַיִּסְעוּ מֵהָרֵי הָעֲבָרִים
מט וַיַּחֲנוּ בְּעַרְבֹת מוֹאָב עַל יַרְדֵּן יְרֵחוֹ: וַיַּחֲנוּ עַל־הַיַּרְדֵּן מִבֵּית הַיְשִׁמֹת
נ עַד אָבֵל הַשִּׁטִּים בְּעַרְבֹת מוֹאָב: וַיְדַבֵּר יְהוָה אֶל־מֹשֶׁה שלישי /חמישי/
נא בְּעַרְבֹת מוֹאָב עַל־יַרְדֵּן יְרֵחוֹ לֵאמֹר: דַּבֵּר אֶל־בְּנֵי יִשְׂרָאֵל וְאָמַרְתָּ
נב אֲלֵהֶם כִּי אַתֶּם עֹבְרִים אֶת־הַיַּרְדֵּן אֶל־אֶרֶץ כְּנָעַן: וְהוֹרַשְׁתֶּם אֶת־
כָּל־יֹשְׁבֵי הָאָרֶץ מִפְּנֵיכֶם וְאִבַּדְתֶּם אֵת כָּל־מַשְׂכִּיֹּתָם וְאֵת כָּל־צַלְמֵי
נג מַסֵּכֹתָם תְּאַבֵּדוּ וְאֵת כָּל־בָּמוֹתָם תַּשְׁמִידוּ: וְהוֹרַשְׁתֶּם אֶת־הָאָרֶץ
נד וִישַׁבְתֶּם־בָּהּ כִּי לָכֶם נָתַתִּי אֶת־הָאָרֶץ לָרֶשֶׁת אֹתָהּ: וְהִתְנַחַלְתֶּם
אֶת־הָאָרֶץ בְּגוֹרָל לְמִשְׁפְּחֹתֵיכֶם לָרַב תַּרְבּוּ אֶת־נַחֲלָתוֹ וְלַמְעַט
תַּמְעִיט אֶת־נַחֲלָתוֹ אֶל אֲשֶׁר־יֵצֵא לוֹ שָׁמָּה הַגּוֹרָל לוֹ יִהְיֶה לְמַטּוֹת
נה אֲבֹתֵיכֶם תִּתְנֶחָלוּ: וְאִם־לֹא תוֹרִישׁוּ אֶת־יֹשְׁבֵי הָאָרֶץ מִפְּנֵיכֶם וְהָיָה
אֲשֶׁר תּוֹתִירוּ מֵהֶם לְשִׂכִּים בְּעֵינֵיכֶם וְלִצְנִינִם בְּצִדֵּיכֶם וְצָרְרוּ אֶתְכֶם
נו עַל־הָאָרֶץ אֲשֶׁר אַתֶּם יֹשְׁבִים בָּהּ: וְהָיָה כַּאֲשֶׁר דִּמִּיתִי לַעֲשׂוֹת לָהֶם
אֶעֱשֶׂה לָכֶם:
לד א ב וַיְדַבֵּר יְהוָה אֶל־מֹשֶׁה לֵּאמֹר: צַו אֶת־בְּנֵי יִשְׂרָאֵל וְאָמַרְתָּ אֲלֵהֶם לא
כִּי־אַתֶּם בָּאִים אֶל־הָאָרֶץ כְּנָעַן זֹאת הָאָרֶץ אֲשֶׁר תִּפֹּל לָכֶם בְּנַחֲלָה
ג אֶרֶץ כְּנַעַן לִגְבֻלֹתֶיהָ: וְהָיָה לָכֶם פְּאַת־נֶגֶב מִמִּדְבַּר־צִן עַל־יְדֵי אֱדוֹם
ד וְהָיָה לָכֶם גְּבוּל נֶגֶב מִקְצֵה יָם־הַמֶּלַח קֵדְמָה: וְנָסַב לָכֶם הַגְּבוּל מִנֶּגֶב
לְמַעֲלֵה עַקְרַבִּים וְעָבַר צִנָה והיה תּוֹצְאֹתָיו מִנֶּגֶב לְקָדֵשׁ בַּרְנֵעַ וְיָצָא וְהָיוּ
ה חֲצַר־אַדָּר וְעָבַר עַצְמֹנָה: וְנָסַב הַגְּבוּל מֵעַצְמוֹן נַחְלָה מִצְרָיִם וְהָיוּ
ו תוֹצְאֹתָיו הַיָּמָּה: וּגְבוּל יָם וְהָיָה לָכֶם הַיָּם הַגָּדוֹל וּגְבוּל זֶה־יִהְיֶה
ז לָכֶם גְּבוּל יָם: וְזֶה־יִהְיֶה לָכֶם גְּבוּל צָפוֹן מִן־הַיָּם הַגָּדֹל תְּתָאוּ לָכֶם
ח הֹר הָהָר: מֵהֹר הָהָר תְּתָאוּ לְבֹא חֲמָת וְהָיוּ תּוֹצְאֹת הַגְּבֻל צְדָדָה:
ט וְיָצָא הַגְּבֻל זִפְרֹנָה וְהָיוּ תוֹצְאֹתָיו חֲצַר עֵינָן זֶה־יִהְיֶה לָכֶם גְּבוּל צָפוֹן:
י יא וְהִתְאַוִּיתֶם לָכֶם לִגְבוּל קֵדְמָה מֵחֲצַר עֵינָן שְׁפָמָה: וְיָרַד הַגְּבֻל מִשְּׁפָם

It will then continue down to reach the eastern slope of the Sea of Galilee.
12 From there the border will run down along the Jordan, ending at the Dead
13 Sea. This is to be your land with its borders on all sides." Moshe commanded
the Israelites: "This is the land of which you take possession by lot, which the
14 LORD has commanded to give to the nine and a half tribes – for the tribe of
Reuven by its ancestral houses, and the tribe of Gad by its ancestral houses,
15 and half the tribe of Menashe have taken their possession. The two and a half
tribes have taken their possession across the Jordan from Yeriḥo to the east
as the sun rises."
16 17 And the LORD spoke to Moshe: "These are the names of the men who shall
apportion the land to you for possession: Elazar the priest and Yehoshua son
18 of Nun. And you shall also take one leader from each tribe to apportion the
19 land. These are the names of the men: for the tribe of Yehuda, Kalev son of
20 21 Yefuneh; for the tribe of the Simeonites, Shmuel son of Amihud; for the tribe
22 of Binyamin, Elidad son of Kislon; for the tribe of the Danites, a leader, Buki
23 son of Yogli. For the descendants of Yosef: for the tribe of the Manassites a
24 leader, Ḥaniel son of Efod; for the tribe of the Efraimites a leader, Kemuel
25 son of Shiftan. For the tribe of the Zebulunites a leader, Elitzafan son of
26 27 Parnakh. For the tribe of the Issacharites a leader, Paltiel son of Azan. For
28 the tribe of the Asherites a leader, Aḥihud son of Shelomi. For the tribe of
29 the Naftalites a leader, Pedahel son of Amihud." These were the ones whom
the LORD commanded to apportion the possession for the Israelites in the
land of Canaan.
35 1 The LORD spoke to Moshe in the plains of Moav by the Jordan across from
2 Yeriḥo: "Command the Israelites to grant the Levites towns to live in, among
the inheritance they will possess. Grant them also pasturelands around the
3 towns. The towns shall be theirs to live in, and the pasturelands shall be
4 for their cattle, all that they own, and all their animals. The pasturelands of
the towns that you shall give to the Levites shall extend from the town wall
5 outward for a thousand cubits in all directions; you shall measure out from
the town, two thousand cubits on the east side, two thousand cubits on the
south side, two thousand cubits on the west side, and two thousand cubits on
the north side, with the town in the middle, and this shall belong to them as
6 pastureland for their towns. Six of the towns that you give to the Levites shall
be towns of refuge, which you will designate as places to which a manslayer
7 may flee. In addition to these, you shall give them forty-two more towns. Thus
the total number of towns you shall give to the Levites shall be forty-eight,
8 along with their pastureland. As for the towns that you give from the possession of the Israelites, take more from the larger tribes and fewer from the
smaller so that each grants towns to the Levites in proportion to its own
inheritance."
9 10 The LORD spoke to Moshe: "Speak to the Israelites. Tell them: When you
11 cross the Jordan into the land of Canaan, select towns to be your refuge cities,

הָרִבְלָה מִקֶּדֶם לָעָיִן וְיָרַד הַגְּבֻל וּמָחָה עַל־כֶּתֶף יָם־כִּנֶּרֶת קֵדְמָה׃
יב וְיָרַד הַגְּבוּל הַיַּרְדֵּנָה וְהָיוּ תוֹצְאֹתָיו יָם הַמֶּלַח זֹאת תִּהְיֶה לָכֶם הָאָרֶץ
יג לִגְבֻלֹתֶיהָ סָבִיב׃ וַיְצַו מֹשֶׁה אֶת־בְּנֵי יִשְׂרָאֵל לֵאמֹר זֹאת הָאָרֶץ אֲשֶׁר
תִּתְנַחֲלוּ אֹתָהּ בְּגוֹרָל אֲשֶׁר צִוָּה יְהוָה לָתֵת לְתִשְׁעַת הַמַּטּוֹת וַחֲצִי
יד הַמַּטֶּה׃ כִּי לָקְחוּ מַטֵּה בְנֵי הָראוּבֵנִי לְבֵית אֲבֹתָם וּמַטֵּה בְנֵי־הַגָּדִי
טו לְבֵית אֲבֹתָם וַחֲצִי מַטֵּה מְנַשֶּׁה לָקְחוּ נַחֲלָתָם׃ שְׁנֵי הַמַּטּוֹת וַחֲצִי
הַמַּטֶּה לָקְחוּ נַחֲלָתָם מֵעֵבֶר לְיַרְדֵּן יְרֵחוֹ קֵדְמָה מִזְרָחָה׃
טז יז וַיְדַבֵּר יְהוָה אֶל־מֹשֶׁה לֵּאמֹר׃ אֵלֶּה שְׁמוֹת הָאֲנָשִׁים אֲשֶׁר־יִנְחֲלוּ רביעי /ששי/
יח לָכֶם אֶת־הָאָרֶץ אֶלְעָזָר הַכֹּהֵן וִיהוֹשֻׁעַ בִּן־נוּן׃ וְנָשִׂיא אֶחָד נָשִׂיא
יט אֶחָד מִמַּטֶּה תִּקְחוּ לִנְחֹל אֶת־הָאָרֶץ׃ וְאֵלֶּה שְׁמוֹת הָאֲנָשִׁים לְמַטֵּה
כ כא יְהוּדָה כָּלֵב בֶּן־יְפֻנֶּה׃ וּלְמַטֵּה בְּנֵי שִׁמְעוֹן שְׁמוּאֵל בֶּן־עַמִּיהוּד׃ לְמַטֵּה
כב כג בִנְיָמִן אֱלִידָד בֶּן־כִּסְלוֹן׃ וּלְמַטֵּה בְנֵי־דָן נָשִׂיא בֻּקִּי בֶּן־יָגְלִי׃ לִבְנֵי
כד יוֹסֵף לְמַטֵּה בְנֵי־מְנַשֶּׁה נָשִׂיא חַנִּיאֵל בֶּן־אֵפֹד׃ וּלְמַטֵּה בְנֵי־אֶפְרַיִם
כה נָשִׂיא קְמוּאֵל בֶּן־שִׁפְטָן׃ וּלְמַטֵּה בְנֵי־זְבוּלֻן נָשִׂיא אֱלִיצָפָן בֶּן־פַּרְנָךְ׃
כו כז וּלְמַטֵּה בְנֵי־יִשָּׂשכָר נָשִׂיא פַּלְטִיאֵל בֶּן־עַזָּן׃ וּלְמַטֵּה בְנֵי־אָשֵׁר נָשִׂיא
כח אֲחִיהוּד בֶּן־שְׁלֹמִי׃ וּלְמַטֵּה בְנֵי־נַפְתָּלִי נָשִׂיא פְּדַהְאֵל בֶּן־עַמִּיהוּד׃
כט אֵלֶּה אֲשֶׁר צִוָּה יְהוָה לְנַחֵל אֶת־בְּנֵי־יִשְׂרָאֵל בְּאֶרֶץ כְּנָעַן׃
לה א ב וַיְדַבֵּר יְהוָה אֶל־מֹשֶׁה בְּעַרְבֹת מוֹאָב עַל־יַרְדֵּן יְרֵחוֹ לֵאמֹר׃ צַו אֶת־ חמישי
בְּנֵי יִשְׂרָאֵל וְנָתְנוּ לַלְוִיִּם מִנַּחֲלַת אֲחֻזָּתָם עָרִים לָשָׁבֶת וּמִגְרָשׁ לֶעָרִים
ג סְבִיבֹתֵיהֶם תִּתְּנוּ לַלְוִיִּם׃ וְהָיוּ הֶעָרִים לָהֶם לָשָׁבֶת וּמִגְרְשֵׁיהֶם יִהְיוּ
ד לִבְהֶמְתָּם וְלִרְכֻשָׁם וּלְכֹל חַיָּתָם׃ וּמִגְרְשֵׁי הֶעָרִים אֲשֶׁר תִּתְּנוּ לַלְוִיִּם
ה מִקִּיר הָעִיר וָחוּצָה אֶלֶף אַמָּה סָבִיב׃ וּמַדֹּתֶם מִחוּץ לָעִיר אֶת־פְּאַת־
קֵדְמָה אַלְפַּיִם בָּאַמָּה וְאֶת־פְּאַת־נֶגֶב אַלְפַּיִם בָּאַמָּה וְאֶת־פְּאַת־יָם ׀
אַלְפַּיִם בָּאַמָּה וְאֵת פְּאַת צָפוֹן אַלְפַּיִם בָּאַמָּה וְהָעִיר בַּתָּוֶךְ זֶה יִהְיֶה
ו לָהֶם מִגְרְשֵׁי הֶעָרִים׃ וְאֵת הֶעָרִים אֲשֶׁר תִּתְּנוּ לַלְוִיִּם אֵת שֵׁשׁ־עָרֵי
הַמִּקְלָט אֲשֶׁר תִּתְּנוּ לָנֻס שָׁמָּה הָרֹצֵחַ וַעֲלֵיהֶם תִּתְּנוּ אַרְבָּעִים וּשְׁתַּיִם
ז עִיר׃ כָּל־הֶעָרִים אֲשֶׁר תִּתְּנוּ לַלְוִיִּם אַרְבָּעִים וּשְׁמֹנֶה עִיר אֶתְהֶן
ח וְאֶת־מִגְרְשֵׁיהֶן׃ וְהֶעָרִים אֲשֶׁר תִּתְּנוּ מֵאֲחֻזַּת בְּנֵי־יִשְׂרָאֵל מֵאֵת
הָרַב תַּרְבּוּ וּמֵאֵת הַמְעַט תַּמְעִיטוּ אִישׁ כְּפִי נַחֲלָתוֹ אֲשֶׁר יִנְחָלוּ יִתֵּן
מֵעָרָיו לַלְוִיִּם׃
לב ט י וַיְדַבֵּר יְהוָה אֶל־מֹשֶׁה לֵּאמֹר׃ דַּבֵּר אֶל־בְּנֵי יִשְׂרָאֵל וְאָמַרְתָּ אֲלֵהֶם ששי /שביעי/
יא כִּי אַתֶּם עֹבְרִים אֶת־הַיַּרְדֵּן אַרְצָה כְּנָעַן׃ וְהִקְרִיתֶם לָכֶם עָרִים עָרֵי

12 to which a person who kills another unintentionally may flee. The cities shall
be a refuge for you from avengers,[80] so that no person who has killed another
13 may die without standing trial before the community. The towns that you
14 designate shall be six cities of refuge for you; you shall designate three towns
15 across the Jordan and three in the land of Canaan as cities of refuge. These
six towns shall be a place of refuge for Israelites, migrants, and temporary
residents alike, so that anyone who kills a person unintentionally may flee
16 there. If a person strikes another with an iron object,[81] however, and he dies,
17 that person is a murderer; the murderer must be put to death. If he strikes
him with a hand held stone that could cause death and he dies, that person
18 is a murderer; the murderer must be put to death. Likewise, if he strikes him
with a wooden tool that could cause death and he dies, that person is a mur-
19 derer; the murderer must be put to death. The blood avenger shall put the
20 murderer to death; whenever he meets him, he may put him to death. So too
if one person pushes another in hate, or throws something at him with prior
21 intent, he shall be put to death. If in enmity someone strikes a person with
his hand and he dies, the one who struck the blow is a murderer and shall be
put to death. The blood avenger shall put the murderer to death whenever
22 they meet. If, however, one person pushes another suddenly, without enmity,
23 or throws an object at him unintentionally, or drops a fatal stone on him
without seeing him and he dies – they were not enemies, he intended him
24 no harm – then the community must judge between the killer and the blood
25 avenger in accordance with these laws.[82] And the community must protect
the manslayer from the avenger of blood and return him to the refuge city to
which he fled. There he shall live until the death of the High Priest anointed
26 with the sacred oil. But if the manslayer ever goes outside the limits of the city
27 of refuge to which he fled and the blood avenger finds him outside the limits
28 of his city of refuge and kills him, the avenger is not liable for murder; the
manslayer must stay in his city of refuge until the High Priest dies. After the
death of the High Priest the manslayer may return to his own hereditary land.
29 These shall be a decree of law for you throughout your generations, wherever
30 you should live. If anyone kills a human being, the murderer shall be put to
death on the evidence of eyewitnesses. No one shall be put to death on the
31 testimony of one witness alone. You may not accept a ransom for the life of
32 a murderer found guilty of a capital crime; he must be put to death. Nor may
you accept a ransom for someone who has fled to his city of refuge, to allow
33 him to return and live on his land before the priest dies. You shall not pollute
the land in which you live; blood pollutes the land. And the land can have no
atonement for the blood that is shed in it – except through the blood of the
34 one who shed it. Do not defile the land in which you live, and in the midst of
which I dwell – for I the LORD dwell in the midst of Israel."
36 1 The heads of the ancestral houses of the descendants of Gilad son of Makhir

---

80 | Referring to the victim's next of kin.

81 | An iron object is considered a deadly weapon.

82 | In other words, they must carefully determine that the killing was in fact unintentional.

יב מִקְלָט תִּהְיֶינָה לָכֶם וְנָס שָׁמָּה רֹצֵחַ מַכֵּה־נֶפֶשׁ בִּשְׁגָגָה: וְהָיוּ לָכֶם
הֶעָרִים לְמִקְלָט מִגֹּאֵל וְלֹא יָמוּת הָרֹצֵחַ עַד־עָמְדוֹ לִפְנֵי הָעֵדָה
יג יד לַמִּשְׁפָּט: וְהֶעָרִים אֲשֶׁר תִּתֵּנוּ שֵׁשׁ־עָרֵי מִקְלָט תִּהְיֶינָה לָכֶם: אֵת ׀
שְׁלֹשׁ הֶעָרִים תִּתְּנוּ מֵעֵבֶר לַיַּרְדֵּן וְאֵת שְׁלֹשׁ הֶעָרִים תִּתְּנוּ בְּאֶרֶץ
טו כְּנָעַן עָרֵי מִקְלָט תִּהְיֶינָה: לִבְנֵי יִשְׂרָאֵל וְלַגֵּר וְלַתּוֹשָׁב בְּתוֹכָם תִּהְיֶינָה
טז שֵׁשׁ־הֶעָרִים הָאֵלֶּה לְמִקְלָט לָנוּס שָׁמָּה כָּל־מַכֵּה־נֶפֶשׁ בִּשְׁגָגָה: וְאִם־
יז בִּכְלִי בַרְזֶל ׀ הִכָּהוּ וַיָּמֹת רֹצֵחַ הוּא מוֹת יוּמַת הָרֹצֵחַ: וְאִם בְּאֶבֶן יָד
יח אֲשֶׁר־יָמוּת בָּהּ הִכָּהוּ וַיָּמֹת רֹצֵחַ הוּא מוֹת יוּמַת הָרֹצֵחַ: אוֹ בִּכְלִי
יט עֵץ־יָד אֲשֶׁר־יָמוּת בּוֹ הִכָּהוּ וַיָּמֹת רֹצֵחַ הוּא מוֹת יוּמַת הָרֹצֵחַ: גֹּאֵל
כ הַדָּם הוּא יָמִית אֶת־הָרֹצֵחַ בְּפִגְעוֹ־בוֹ הוּא יְמִתֶנּוּ: וְאִם־בְּשִׂנְאָה
כא יֶהְדָּפֶנּוּ אוֹ־הִשְׁלִיךְ עָלָיו בִּצְדִיָּה וַיָּמֹת: אוֹ בְאֵיבָה הִכָּהוּ בְיָדוֹ וַיָּמֹת
מוֹת־יוּמַת הַמַּכֶּה רֹצֵחַ הוּא גֹּאֵל הַדָּם יָמִית אֶת־הָרֹצֵחַ בְּפִגְעוֹ־בוֹ:
כב כג וְאִם־בְּפֶתַע בְּלֹא־אֵיבָה הֲדָפוֹ אוֹ־הִשְׁלִיךְ עָלָיו כָּל־כְּלִי בְּלֹא צְדִיָּה: אוֹ
בְכָל־אֶבֶן אֲשֶׁר־יָמוּת בָּהּ בְּלֹא רְאוֹת וַיַּפֵּל עָלָיו וַיָּמֹת וְהוּא לֹא־אוֹיֵב
כד לוֹ וְלֹא מְבַקֵּשׁ רָעָתוֹ: וְשָׁפְטוּ הָעֵדָה בֵּין הַמַּכֶּה וּבֵין גֹּאֵל הַדָּם עַל
כה הַמִּשְׁפָּטִים הָאֵלֶּה: וְהִצִּילוּ הָעֵדָה אֶת־הָרֹצֵחַ מִיַּד גֹּאֵל הַדָּם וְהֵשִׁיבוּ
אֹתוֹ הָעֵדָה אֶל־עִיר מִקְלָטוֹ אֲשֶׁר־נָס שָׁמָּה וְיָשַׁב בָּהּ עַד־מוֹת הַכֹּהֵן
כו הַגָּדֹל אֲשֶׁר־מָשַׁח אֹתוֹ בְּשֶׁמֶן הַקֹּדֶשׁ: וְאִם־יָצֹא יֵצֵא הָרֹצֵחַ אֶת־גְּבוּל
כז עִיר מִקְלָטוֹ אֲשֶׁר יָנוּס שָׁמָּה: וּמָצָא אֹתוֹ גֹּאֵל הַדָּם מִחוּץ לִגְבוּל עִיר
כח מִקְלָטוֹ וְרָצַח גֹּאֵל הַדָּם אֶת־הָרֹצֵחַ אֵין לוֹ דָּם: כִּי בְעִיר מִקְלָטוֹ יֵשֵׁב
עַד־מוֹת הַכֹּהֵן הַגָּדֹל וְאַחֲרֵי־מוֹת הַכֹּהֵן הַגָּדֹל יָשׁוּב הָרֹצֵחַ אֶל־אֶרֶץ
כט אֲחֻזָּתוֹ: וְהָיוּ אֵלֶּה לָכֶם לְחֻקַּת מִשְׁפָּט לְדֹרֹתֵיכֶם בְּכֹל מוֹשְׁבֹתֵיכֶם:
ל כָּל־מַכֵּה־נֶפֶשׁ לְפִי עֵדִים יִרְצַח אֶת־הָרֹצֵחַ וְעֵד אֶחָד לֹא־יַעֲנֶה בְנֶפֶשׁ
לא לָמוּת: וְלֹא־תִקְחוּ כֹפֶר לְנֶפֶשׁ רֹצֵחַ אֲשֶׁר־הוּא רָשָׁע לָמוּת כִּי־מוֹת
לב יוּמָת: וְלֹא־תִקְחוּ כֹפֶר לָנוּס אֶל־עִיר מִקְלָטוֹ לָשׁוּב לָשֶׁבֶת בָּאָרֶץ
לג עַד־מוֹת הַכֹּהֵן: וְלֹא־תַחֲנִיפוּ אֶת־הָאָרֶץ אֲשֶׁר אַתֶּם בָּהּ כִּי הַדָּם הוּא
יַחֲנִיף אֶת־הָאָרֶץ וְלָאָרֶץ לֹא־יְכֻפַּר לַדָּם אֲשֶׁר שֻׁפַּךְ־בָּהּ כִּי־אִם בְּדַם
לד שֹׁפְכוֹ: וְלֹא תְטַמֵּא אֶת־הָאָרֶץ אֲשֶׁר אַתֶּם יֹשְׁבִים בָּהּ אֲשֶׁר אֲנִי שֹׁכֵן
בְּתוֹכָהּ כִּי אֲנִי יְהוָה שֹׁכֵן בְּתוֹךְ בְּנֵי יִשְׂרָאֵל:

לו א וַיִּקְרְבוּ רָאשֵׁי הָאָבוֹת לְמִשְׁפַּחַת בְּנֵי־גִלְעָד בֶּן־מָכִיר בֶּן־מְנַשֶּׁה שביעי

son of Menashe, one of the families of Yosef's sons, came forward and spoke
before Moshe and the leaders, the heads of the ancestral houses of the
2 Israelites. "The LORD," they said, "commanded my lord to give the land as an
inheritance to the Israelites by lot. But my lord was also commanded by the
3 LORD to give the inheritance of our brother Tzelofḥad to his daughters. If
they marry men from another Israelite tribe, their share will be taken away
from our ancestral inheritance and given to the tribe into which they marry.
4 It will be taken away from the allotted portion of our inheritance. When the
Israelites observe the Jubilee, their inheritance will be added to that of the
tribe into which they married; their inheritance will be taken away from the
5 inheritance of our forefathers' tribe."[83] Then Moshe, at the LORD's word, com-
6 manded the Israelites: "What the tribe of Yosef's descendants say is right. This
is the word that the LORD has commanded to Tzelofḥad's daughters: They
may marry whomever they wish as long as they marry within a clan of their
7 father's tribe, so that the Israelites' inheritance does not pass from one tribe to
another. Thus the Israelites will each stay attached to the inheritance of their
8 ancestral tribes. Every daughter among the Israelite tribes who inherits land
must marry a member of her father's tribe, so that the Israelites may possess
9 the inheritance of their ancestors. No inheritance may pass from one tribe
to another; each Israelite tribe shall remain attached to its own inheritance."
10 11 Tzelofḥad's daughters did as the LORD commanded Moshe. Maḥla, Tirtza,
Ḥogla, Milka, and Noa, Tzelofḥad's daughters, were each married to men
12 who were their cousins. They thus married into the families of Menashe son
of Yosef, and their inheritance remained within the tribe of their father's clan.
13 All these are the commandments and laws that the LORD gave through Moshe
to the Israelites on the plains of Moav, by the Jordan, across from Yeriḥo.

83 | At the Jubilee year, land goes back to its original owner (see Lev. 25:7–13), and each tribe thereby ought to retain its allotment. But if these women were to marry men from other tribes, the land inherited from Tzelofḥad would enter the possession of those men permanently.

מִמִּשְׁפְּחֹת בְּנֵי יוֹסֵף וַיְדַבְּרוּ לִפְנֵי מֹשֶׁה וְלִפְנֵי הַנְּשִׂאִים רָאשֵׁי אָבוֹת
ב לִבְנֵי יִשְׂרָאֵל: וַיֹּאמְרוּ אֶת־אֲדֹנִי צִוָּה יהוה לָתֵת אֶת־הָאָרֶץ בְּנַחֲלָה
בְּגוֹרָל לִבְנֵי יִשְׂרָאֵל וַאדֹנִי צֻוָּה בַיהוה לָתֵת אֶת־נַחֲלַת צְלָפְחָד אָחִינוּ
ג לִבְנֹתָיו: וְהָיוּ לְאֶחָד מִבְּנֵי שִׁבְטֵי בְנֵי־יִשְׂרָאֵל לְנָשִׁים וְנִגְרְעָה נַחֲלָתָן
מִנַּחֲלַת אֲבֹתֵינוּ וְנוֹסַף עַל נַחֲלַת הַמַּטֶּה אֲשֶׁר תִּהְיֶינָה לָהֶם וּמִגֹּרַל
ד נַחֲלָתֵנוּ יִגָּרֵעַ: וְאִם־יִהְיֶה הַיֹּבֵל לִבְנֵי יִשְׂרָאֵל וְנוֹסְפָה נַחֲלָתָן עַל נַחֲלַת
ה הַמַּטֶּה אֲשֶׁר תִּהְיֶינָה לָהֶם וּמִנַּחֲלַת מַטֵּה אֲבֹתֵינוּ יִגָּרַע נַחֲלָתָן: וַיְצַו
מֹשֶׁה אֶת־בְּנֵי יִשְׂרָאֵל עַל־פִּי יהוה לֵאמֹר כֵּן מַטֵּה בְנֵי־יוֹסֵף דֹּבְרִים:
ו זֶה הַדָּבָר אֲשֶׁר־צִוָּה יהוה לִבְנוֹת צְלָפְחָד לֵאמֹר לַטּוֹב בְּעֵינֵיהֶם
ז תִּהְיֶינָה לְנָשִׁים אַךְ לְמִשְׁפַּחַת מַטֵּה אֲבִיהֶם תִּהְיֶינָה לְנָשִׁים: וְלֹא־תִסֹּב
נַחֲלָה לִבְנֵי יִשְׂרָאֵל מִמַּטֶּה אֶל־מַטֶּה כִּי אִישׁ בְּנַחֲלַת מַטֵּה אֲבֹתָיו
ח יִדְבְּקוּ בְּנֵי יִשְׂרָאֵל: וְכָל־בַּת יֹרֶשֶׁת נַחֲלָה מִמַּטּוֹת בְּנֵי יִשְׂרָאֵל לְאֶחָד
מִמִּשְׁפַּחַת מַטֵּה אָבִיהָ תִּהְיֶה לְאִשָּׁה לְמַעַן יִירְשׁוּ בְּנֵי יִשְׂרָאֵל אִישׁ
ט נַחֲלַת אֲבֹתָיו: וְלֹא־תִסֹּב נַחֲלָה מִמַּטֶּה לְמַטֶּה אַחֵר כִּי־אִישׁ בְּנַחֲלָתוֹ
י יִדְבְּקוּ מַטּוֹת בְּנֵי יִשְׂרָאֵל: כַּאֲשֶׁר צִוָּה יהוה אֶת־מֹשֶׁה כֵּן עָשׂוּ בְּנוֹת
יא צְלָפְחָד: וַתִּהְיֶינָה מַחְלָה תִרְצָה וְחָגְלָה וּמִלְכָּה וְנֹעָה בְּנוֹת צְלָפְחָד מפטיר
יב לִבְנֵי דֹדֵיהֶן לְנָשִׁים: מִמִּשְׁפְּחֹת בְּנֵי־מְנַשֶּׁה בֶן־יוֹסֵף הָיוּ לְנָשִׁים וַתְּהִי
יג נַחֲלָתָן עַל־מַטֵּה מִשְׁפַּחַת אֲבִיהֶן: אֵלֶּה הַמִּצְוֹת וְהַמִּשְׁפָּטִים אֲשֶׁר
צִוָּה יהוה בְּיַד־מֹשֶׁה אֶל־בְּנֵי יִשְׂרָאֵל בְּעַרְבֹת מוֹאָב עַל יַרְדֵּן יְרֵחוֹ:

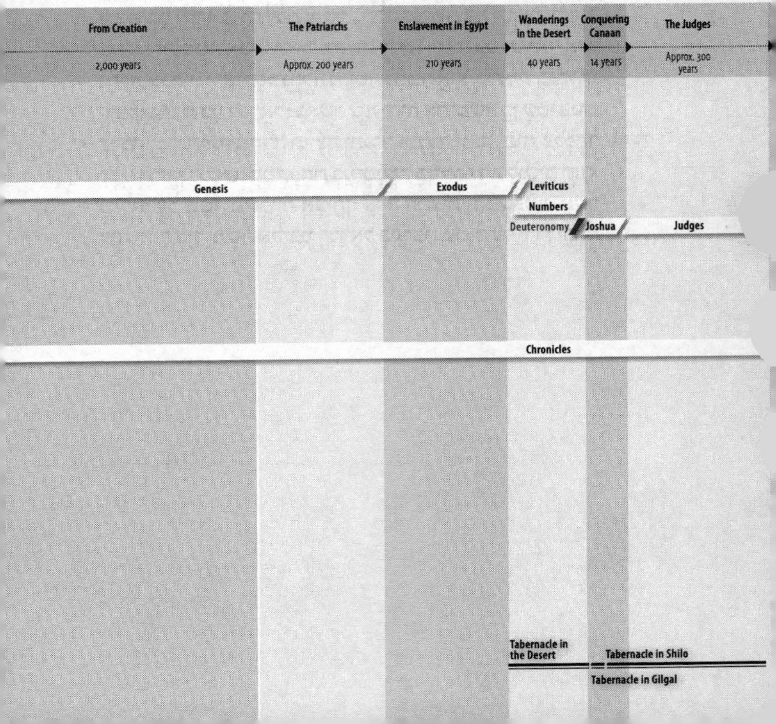
From Creation
2,000 years
The Patriarchs
Approx. 200 years
Enslavement in Egypt
210 years
Wanderings in the Desert
40 years
Conquering Canaan
14 years
The Judges
Approx. 300 years
Genesis
Exodus
Leviticus
Numbers
Deuteronomy
Joshua
Judges
Chronicles
Tabernacle in the Desert
Tabernacle in Shilo
Tabernacle in Gilgal

דברים
DEVARIM/DEUTERONOMY

DEUTERONOMY	The historical address	The address about the commandments	The covenantal address	Moshe's departure
	Chs. 1–4	5–26	27–30	31–34

DEVARIM

1 1 These are the words that Moshe spoke to all Israel east of the Jordan, in the
wilderness; in the Arava across from Suf, between Paran and Tofel, Lavan,
2 Ḥatzerot, and Di Zahav. By way of Mount Se'ir, it takes eleven days to cross
3 from Ḥorev to Kadesh Barnea.[1] In the fortieth year,[2] on the first day of the
eleventh month, Moshe spoke to the Israelites exactly as the LORD had com-
4 manded him regarding them, after he had defeated Siḥon, king of the Amorites,
who lived in Ḥeshbon, and Og, king of Bashan, who lived in Ashtarot and in
5 Edre'i.[3] On the east bank of the Jordan, in the land of Moav, Moshe began to
6 expound this Law:[4] "The LORD our God spoke to us at Ḥorev; He said: You
7 have settled long enough at this mountain. Start out and advance into the hill
country of the Amorites and all the neighboring regions – the Arava, the hill
country, the lowlands, the Negev, and the seacoast – the land of the Canaanites
8 and the Lebanon, as far as the Euphrates River. See: I have set the land before
you. Go in and take possession of the land that the LORD swore He would give
to your ancestors – to Avraham, Yitzḥak, and Yaakov – and to their descendants
9 after them. At that time[5] I said to you, 'I cannot bear the burden of you alone.
10 The LORD your God has increased your numbers: today you are as numerous
11 as the stars of the heavens. May the LORD, God of your ancestors, multiply you
12 again a thousandfold and bless you, as He has promised. But how can I bear
13 alone all your problems, your burdens, your disputes? Choose for yourselves
men who are wise, discerning, and known to your tribes, and I will appoint
14 them as your leaders.' You answered me, 'The plan you propose is a good one.'
15 So I took the leaders of your tribes, wise men and well known, and appointed
them to be leaders over you, chiefs of thousands, chiefs of hundreds, chiefs of
16 fifties, chiefs of tens, and officials, for your tribes. I charged your judges at that
time: 'Hear the disputes among your people and judge fairly, between one
17 person and another, whether Israelite or migrant. Do not show partiality in
judgment: listen equally to the small and the great. Do not be intimidated by
any man, for judgment belongs to God. Any case that is too difficult for you,
18 bring to me, and I will hear it.' I charged you at that time, with all the things
19 you are to do. Then we set out from Ḥorev and journeyed through all that vast
and fearful wilderness that you have seen, toward the hill country of the Amorites, as the LORD our God had commanded us, until we reached Kadesh Bar-
20 nea. I said to you, 'You have reached the hill country of the Amorites, which
21 the LORD our God is giving us. See, the LORD your God has laid the land out
before you. Go up, take possession, as the LORD, God of your ancestors, has
22 promised. Do not fear and do not be dismayed.' Then all of you drew close to
me and said, 'Let us send men ahead of us to explore the land and bring back

---

1 | Ḥorev is the same as Sinai. These two verses seem to convey that much of the contents of the following orations (from v. 5), delivered in Moav, were originally communicated to the people earlier in the wilderness, in the area that extends from Sinai to Kadesh Barnea south of Canaan.

2 | After the exodus from Egypt.

3 | See Numbers 21:21–35.

4 | The legal portions of Moshe's presentation appear later, beginning in chapter 12.

5 | This probably refers to the episode recounted in Exodus 18:13–26.

א א אֵלֶּה הַדְּבָרִים אֲשֶׁר דִּבֶּר מֹשֶׁה אֶל־כָּל־יִשְׂרָאֵל בְּעֵבֶר הַיַּרְדֵּן בַּמִּדְבָּר א
ב בָּעֲרָבָה מוֹל סוּף בֵּין־פָּארָן וּבֵין־תֹּפֶל וְלָבָן וַחֲצֵרֹת וְדִי זָהָב׃ אַחַד
ג עָשָׂר יוֹם מֵחֹרֵב דֶּרֶךְ הַר־שֵׂעִיר עַד קָדֵשׁ בַּרְנֵעַ׃ וַיְהִי בְּאַרְבָּעִים
שָׁנָה בְּעַשְׁתֵּי־עָשָׂר חֹדֶשׁ בְּאֶחָד לַחֹדֶשׁ דִּבֶּר מֹשֶׁה אֶל־בְּנֵי יִשְׂרָאֵל
ד כְּכֹל אֲשֶׁר צִוָּה יְהוָה אֹתוֹ אֲלֵהֶם׃ אַחֲרֵי הַכֹּתוֹ אֵת סִיחֹן מֶלֶךְ הָאֱמֹרִי
אֲשֶׁר יוֹשֵׁב בְּחֶשְׁבּוֹן וְאֵת עוֹג מֶלֶךְ הַבָּשָׁן אֲשֶׁר־יוֹשֵׁב בְּעַשְׁתָּרֹת
ה בְּאֶדְרֶעִי׃ בְּעֵבֶר הַיַּרְדֵּן בְּאֶרֶץ מוֹאָב הוֹאִיל מֹשֶׁה בֵּאֵר אֶת־הַתּוֹרָה
ו הַזֹּאת לֵאמֹר׃ יְהוָה אֱלֹהֵינוּ דִּבֶּר אֵלֵינוּ בְּחֹרֵב לֵאמֹר רַב־לָכֶם שֶׁבֶת
ז בָּהָר הַזֶּה׃ פְּנוּ ׀ וּסְעוּ לָכֶם וּבֹאוּ הַר הָאֱמֹרִי וְאֶל־כָּל־שְׁכֵנָיו בָּעֲרָבָה
בָהָר וּבַשְּׁפֵלָה וּבַנֶּגֶב וּבְחוֹף הַיָּם אֶרֶץ הַכְּנַעֲנִי וְהַלְּבָנוֹן עַד־הַנָּהָר
ח הַגָּדֹל נְהַר־פְּרָת׃ רְאֵה נָתַתִּי לִפְנֵיכֶם אֶת־הָאָרֶץ בֹּאוּ וּרְשׁוּ אֶת־
הָאָרֶץ אֲשֶׁר נִשְׁבַּע יְהוָה לַאֲבֹתֵיכֶם לְאַבְרָהָם לְיִצְחָק וּלְיַעֲקֹב לָתֵת
ט לָהֶם וּלְזַרְעָם אַחֲרֵיהֶם׃ וָאֹמַר אֲלֵכֶם בָּעֵת הַהִוא לֵאמֹר לֹא־אוּכַל
י לְבַדִּי שְׂאֵת אֶתְכֶם׃ יְהוָה אֱלֹהֵיכֶם הִרְבָּה אֶתְכֶם וְהִנְּכֶם הַיּוֹם כְּכוֹכְבֵי
יא הַשָּׁמַיִם לָרֹב׃ יְהוָה אֱלֹהֵי אֲבוֹתֵכֶם יֹסֵף עֲלֵיכֶם כָּכֶם אֶלֶף פְּעָמִים שני
יב וִיבָרֵךְ אֶתְכֶם כַּאֲשֶׁר דִּבֶּר לָכֶם׃ אֵיכָה אֶשָּׂא לְבַדִּי טָרְחֲכֶם וּמַשַּׂאֲכֶם
יג וְרִיבְכֶם׃ הָבוּ לָכֶם אֲנָשִׁים חֲכָמִים וּנְבֹנִים וִידֻעִים לְשִׁבְטֵיכֶם וַאֲשִׂימֵם
יד בְּרָאשֵׁיכֶם׃ וַתַּעֲנוּ אֹתִי וַתֹּאמְרוּ טוֹב־הַדָּבָר אֲשֶׁר־דִּבַּרְתָּ לַעֲשׂוֹת׃
טו וָאֶקַּח אֶת־רָאשֵׁי שִׁבְטֵיכֶם אֲנָשִׁים חֲכָמִים וִידֻעִים וָאֶתֵּן אֹתָם
רָאשִׁים עֲלֵיכֶם שָׂרֵי אֲלָפִים וְשָׂרֵי מֵאוֹת וְשָׂרֵי חֲמִשִּׁים וְשָׂרֵי עֲשָׂרֹת
טז וְשֹׁטְרִים לְשִׁבְטֵיכֶם׃ וָאֲצַוֶּה אֶת־שֹׁפְטֵיכֶם בָּעֵת הַהִוא לֵאמֹר שָׁמֹעַ
יז בֵּין־אֲחֵיכֶם וּשְׁפַטְתֶּם צֶדֶק בֵּין־אִישׁ וּבֵין־אָחִיו וּבֵין גֵּרוֹ׃ לֹא־תַכִּירוּ
פָנִים בַּמִּשְׁפָּט כַּקָּטֹן כַּגָּדֹל תִּשְׁמָעוּן לֹא תָגוּרוּ מִפְּנֵי־אִישׁ כִּי הַמִּשְׁפָּט
לֵאלֹהִים הוּא וְהַדָּבָר אֲשֶׁר יִקְשֶׁה מִכֶּם תַּקְרִבוּן אֵלַי וּשְׁמַעְתִּיו׃
יח יט וָאֲצַוֶּה אֶתְכֶם בָּעֵת הַהִוא אֵת כָּל־הַדְּבָרִים אֲשֶׁר תַּעֲשׂוּן׃ וַנִּסַּע מֵחֹרֵב
וַנֵּלֶךְ אֵת כָּל־הַמִּדְבָּר הַגָּדוֹל וְהַנּוֹרָא הַהוּא אֲשֶׁר רְאִיתֶם דֶּרֶךְ הַר
כ הָאֱמֹרִי כַּאֲשֶׁר צִוָּה יְהוָה אֱלֹהֵינוּ אֹתָנוּ וַנָּבֹא עַד קָדֵשׁ בַּרְנֵעַ׃ וָאֹמַר
כא אֲלֵכֶם בָּאתֶם עַד־הַר הָאֱמֹרִי אֲשֶׁר־יְהוָה אֱלֹהֵינוּ נֹתֵן לָנוּ׃ רְאֵה נָתַן
יְהוָה אֱלֹהֶיךָ לְפָנֶיךָ אֶת־הָאָרֶץ עֲלֵה רֵשׁ כַּאֲשֶׁר דִּבֶּר יְהוָה אֱלֹהֵי
כב אֲבֹתֶיךָ לָךְ אַל־תִּירָא וְאַל־תֵּחָת׃ וַתִּקְרְבוּן אֵלַי כֻּלְּכֶם וַתֹּאמְרוּ שלישי
נִשְׁלְחָה אֲנָשִׁים לְפָנֵינוּ וְיַחְפְּרוּ־לָנוּ אֶת־הָאָרֶץ וְיָשִׁבוּ אֹתָנוּ דָּבָר

a report to us about the route by which we should go up and the towns we will
23 come to.'[6] The plan seemed good to me, so I selected twelve of you, one man
24 from each tribe. They set out and went up into the hill country. And, arriving
25 at the Eshkol Ravine, they spied it out. They took some of the fruit of the land,
which they brought down to us, and they brought us back a report: 'The land
26 that the LORD our God is giving us is good.' But you were unwilling to go up,
27 and you rebelled against the word of the LORD your God. You grumbled in
your tents and said, 'It is because the LORD hates us that He has brought us
28 out of the land of Egypt, to hand us over to the Amorites to destroy us. Where
can we go? Our brothers have melted all the bravado from our hearts by telling
us, "The people are stronger and taller than we are. The cities are large and
29 walled to the sky; we even saw the Anakites there."'[7] And I said to you, 'Do not
30 be terrified and have no fear of them. The LORD your God, who is going before
31 you, He will fight for you, just as He did for you in Egypt before your eyes, and
in the wilderness, where you saw the LORD your God carry you as a man
carries his child, all along the way you traveled until you reached this place.
32 33 And yet despite all this, you show no faith in the LORD your God, who goes
ahead of you on your journey – in fire by night, and cloud by day – to seek out
34 a place for you to camp and show you the way you should go.' Hearing your
35 words, the LORD became furious and swore an oath: 'Not one man of this evil
36 generation shall see the good land that I swore to give your ancestors, except
for Kalev son of Yefuneh. He will see it, and to him and his descendants I will
give the land on which he set foot, because he followed the LORD wholeheart-
37 edly.'[8] And because of you, the LORD was enraged even with me, and said, 'You
38 also shall not enter it. Yehoshua son of Nun, who stands before you – he shall
39 enter there. Encourage him, for he will give Israel their possession. As for your
little ones, whom you thought would be taken captive, and your children who
do not yet know good from bad, they shall enter, and I will give it to them, and
40 they will take possession of it. But you – turn around and set out into the
41 wilderness by way of the Sea of Reeds.' And you answered me: 'We have sinned
against the LORD! We will go up and fight, as the LORD our God commanded
us.' So each of you strapped on your weapons thinking that it would be easy to
42 go up into the hill country. The LORD said to me, 'Tell them, "Do not go up
and do not fight, for I will not be with you. Do not be struck down by your
43 enemies."' And I told you, but you would not listen. You rebelled against the
44 word of the LORD and willfully went up into the hill country. The Amorites
who lived in those hills came out against you and chased you like a swarm of
45 bees. In Se'ir they struck you down, as far as Ḥorma.[9] You came back and wept
before the LORD, but the LORD would not listen to you, nor pay you any heed.

---

6 | Cf. Numbers, chapters 13–14.

7 | The Anakites were of giant stature; see Numbers 13:33.

8 | Kalev, although one of the spies, did not participate in the discouraging report. The same is true of Yehoshua son of Nun who, as verse 38 affirms, not only would enter the land but also would succeed Moshe as Israel's leader.

9 | *Ḥorma* literally means "destruction."

כג אֶת־הַדֶּרֶךְ אֲשֶׁר נַעֲלֶה־בָּהּ וְאֵת הֶעָרִים אֲשֶׁר נָבֹא אֲלֵיהֶן׃ וַיִּיטַב
כד בְּעֵינַי הַדָּבָר וָאֶקַּח מִכֶּם שְׁנֵים עָשָׂר אֲנָשִׁים אִישׁ אֶחָד לַשָּׁבֶט׃ וַיִּפְנוּ
כה וַיַּעֲלוּ הָהָרָה וַיָּבֹאוּ עַד־נַחַל אֶשְׁכֹּל וַיְרַגְּלוּ אֹתָהּ׃ וַיִּקְחוּ בְיָדָם מִפְּרִי
הָאָרֶץ וַיּוֹרִדוּ אֵלֵינוּ וַיָּשִׁבוּ אֹתָנוּ דָבָר וַיֹּאמְרוּ טוֹבָה הָאָרֶץ אֲשֶׁר־
כו יהוה אֱלֹהֵינוּ נֹתֵן לָנוּ׃ וְלֹא אֲבִיתֶם לַעֲלֹת וַתַּמְרוּ אֶת־פִּי יהוה
כז אֱלֹהֵיכֶם׃ וַתֵּרָגְנוּ בְאָהֳלֵיכֶם וַתֹּאמְרוּ בְּשִׂנְאַת יהוה אֹתָנוּ הוֹצִיאָנוּ
כח מֵאֶרֶץ מִצְרָיִם לָתֵת אֹתָנוּ בְּיַד הָאֱמֹרִי לְהַשְׁמִידֵנוּ׃ אָנָה ׀ אֲנַחְנוּ
עֹלִים אַחֵינוּ הֵמַסּוּ אֶת־לְבָבֵנוּ לֵאמֹר עַם גָּדוֹל וָרָם מִמֶּנּוּ עָרִים גְּדֹלֹת
כט וּבְצוּרֹת בַּשָּׁמָיִם וְגַם־בְּנֵי עֲנָקִים רָאִינוּ שָׁם׃ וָאֹמַר אֲלֵכֶם לֹא־תַעַרְצוּן
ל וְלֹא־תִירְאוּן מֵהֶם׃ יהוה אֱלֹהֵיכֶם הַהֹלֵךְ לִפְנֵיכֶם הוּא יִלָּחֵם לָכֶם
לא כְּכֹל אֲשֶׁר עָשָׂה אִתְּכֶם בְּמִצְרַיִם לְעֵינֵיכֶם׃ וּבַמִּדְבָּר אֲשֶׁר רָאִיתָ
אֲשֶׁר נְשָׂאֲךָ יהוה אֱלֹהֶיךָ כַּאֲשֶׁר יִשָּׂא־אִישׁ אֶת־בְּנוֹ בְּכָל־הַדֶּרֶךְ
לב אֲשֶׁר הֲלַכְתֶּם עַד־בֹּאֲכֶם עַד־הַמָּקוֹם הַזֶּה׃ וּבַדָּבָר הַזֶּה אֵינְכֶם
לג מַאֲמִינִם בַּיהוה אֱלֹהֵיכֶם׃ הַהֹלֵךְ לִפְנֵיכֶם בַּדֶּרֶךְ לָתוּר לָכֶם מָקוֹם
לַחֲנֹתְכֶם בָּאֵשׁ ׀ לַיְלָה לַרְאֹתְכֶם בַּדֶּרֶךְ אֲשֶׁר תֵּלְכוּ־בָהּ וּבֶעָנָן יוֹמָם׃
לד לה וַיִּשְׁמַע יהוה אֶת־קוֹל דִּבְרֵיכֶם וַיִּקְצֹף וַיִּשָּׁבַע לֵאמֹר׃ אִם־יִרְאֶה אִישׁ
בָּאֲנָשִׁים הָאֵלֶּה הַדּוֹר הָרָע הַזֶּה אֵת הָאָרֶץ הַטּוֹבָה אֲשֶׁר נִשְׁבַּעְתִּי
לו לָתֵת לַאֲבֹתֵיכֶם׃ זוּלָתִי כָּלֵב בֶּן־יְפֻנֶּה הוּא יִרְאֶנָּה וְלוֹ־אֶתֵּן אֶת־הָאָרֶץ
לז אֲשֶׁר דָּרַךְ־בָּהּ וּלְבָנָיו יַעַן אֲשֶׁר מִלֵּא אַחֲרֵי יהוה׃ גַּם־בִּי הִתְאַנַּף
לח יהוה בִּגְלַלְכֶם לֵאמֹר גַּם־אַתָּה לֹא־תָבֹא שָׁם׃ יְהוֹשֻׁעַ בִּן־נוּן הָעֹמֵד
לט לְפָנֶיךָ הוּא יָבֹא שָׁמָּה אֹתוֹ חַזֵּק כִּי־הוּא יַנְחִלֶנָּה אֶת־יִשְׂרָאֵל׃ וְטַפְּכֶם רביעי
אֲשֶׁר אֲמַרְתֶּם לָבַז יִהְיֶה וּבְנֵיכֶם אֲשֶׁר לֹא־יָדְעוּ הַיּוֹם טוֹב וָרָע הֵמָּה
מ יָבֹאוּ שָׁמָּה וְלָהֶם אֶתְּנֶנָּה וְהֵם יִירָשׁוּהָ׃ וְאַתֶּם פְּנוּ לָכֶם וּסְעוּ הַמִּדְבָּרָה
מא דֶּרֶךְ יַם־סוּף׃ וַתַּעֲנוּ ׀ וַתֹּאמְרוּ אֵלַי חָטָאנוּ לַיהוה אֲנַחְנוּ נַעֲלֶה
וְנִלְחַמְנוּ כְּכֹל אֲשֶׁר־צִוָּנוּ יהוה אֱלֹהֵינוּ וַתַּחְגְּרוּ אִישׁ אֶת־כְּלֵי מִלְחַמְתּוֹ
מב וַתָּהִינוּ לַעֲלֹת הָהָרָה׃ וַיֹּאמֶר יהוה אֵלַי אֱמֹר לָהֶם לֹא תַעֲלוּ וְלֹא
מג תִלָּחֲמוּ כִּי אֵינֶנִּי בְּקִרְבְּכֶם וְלֹא תִּנָּגְפוּ לִפְנֵי אֹיְבֵיכֶם׃ וָאֲדַבֵּר אֲלֵיכֶם
מד וְלֹא שְׁמַעְתֶּם וַתַּמְרוּ אֶת־פִּי יהוה וַתָּזִדוּ וַתַּעֲלוּ הָהָרָה׃ וַיֵּצֵא הָאֱמֹרִי
הַיֹּשֵׁב בָּהָר הַהוּא לִקְרַאתְכֶם וַיִּרְדְּפוּ אֶתְכֶם כַּאֲשֶׁר תַּעֲשֶׂינָה הַדְּבֹרִים
מה וַיַּכְּתוּ אֶתְכֶם בְּשֵׂעִיר עַד־חׇרְמָה׃ וַתָּשֻׁבוּ וַתִּבְכּוּ לִפְנֵי יהוה וְלֹא־שָׁמַע

46 And so you remained at Kadesh for a long time – all that time that you were
2 1 there. Then we turned and journeyed back into the wilderness, by way of the
Sea of Reeds, as the LORD had told me and, for a long time, made our way
2 around Mount Se'ir.
3 Then the LORD said to me: 'You have circled
4 about this hill country long enough now. Turn to the north. And give the
people these orders: You are about to pass through the territory of your kinsmen, the descendants of Esav, who live in Se'ir. They will be afraid of you, but
5 be very careful. Do not provoke them, for I will not give you even a foot of their
6 land; I have given Mount Se'ir to Esav as his possession. You shall pay them in
silver for the food you eat, pay them silver for the water that you buy from them
7 and drink. For the LORD your God has blessed you in all the work of your
hands. He has watched over your wanderings through this vast wilderness.
These forty years the LORD your God has been with you: you have lacked for
8 nothing.' So we passed by, away from our kinsmen, the descendants of Esav
who live in Se'ir. We turned from the route of the Arava, away from Eilat and
Etzyon Gever, and journeyed in the direction of the Wilderness of
9 Moav. Then the LORD said to me: 'Do not mistreat the Moabites or provoke
them to war, for I will not give you any of their land as a possession: I have
10 given Ar to the descendants of Lot for a possession.'"[10] The Emim lived there
11 originally – a strong and numerous people, as tall as the Anakites. Like the
12 Anakites, they are considered Refaim, but the Moabites call them Emim.
Horites used to live in Se'ir, but the descendants of Esav dispossessed them,
destroying them and settling in their place, as Israel did in the land that the
13 LORD gave them as a possession. "'Now, get up and cross the Zered Stream.'
14 So we crossed the Zered Stream. From the time we left Kadesh Barnea to the
time we crossed the Zered Stream was thirty-eight years – until the entire
generation of warriors had perished from the camp – as the LORD had sworn
15 to them. And the LORD's hand was against them to trouble them from the
16 camp until they had all perished. When all those warriors among the people
17 had died,
18 the LORD spoke to me: 'Today you are going to cross the
19 border of Moav at Ar. When you come to the Amonites, do not harass them
or provoke them to war, for I will not give you any of the land of the Amonites
20 as a possession: I have given it as a possession to the descendants of Lot.'" This
too was considered a land of Refaim. Refaim lived there originally, although
21 the Amonites call them Zamzumim – a strong and numerous people, as tall as
the Anakites. The LORD destroyed them so that the Amonites could dispossess
22 them and settle in their place, just as He did for the descendants of Esav, who
live in Se'ir, by destroying the Horites before them so that they could dispossess them and settle in their place to this day, where they still remain; likewise
23 the Avim, who had lived in villages as far as Aza – the Caftorites, emerging
24 from Caftor, destroyed them and settled in their place. "'Set out and cross
the Arnon Stream. I have given over Siḥon, the Amorite king of Ḥeshbon,

---

10 | Ar is the equivalent of Moav; see, e.g., Numbers 21:28. The Moabites and the Amonites descended from Lot; see Genesis 19:36–38.

מו יהוה בקלכם ולא האזין אליכם: ותשבו בקדש ימים רבים כימים
ב א אשר ישבתם: ונפן ונסע המדברה דרך ים־סוף כאשר דבר יהוה
ב אלי ונסב את־הר־שעיר ימים רבים: ויאמר יהוה אלי ב חמישי
ג ד לאמר: רב־לכם סב את־ההר הזה פנו לכם צפנה: ואת־העם צו
לאמר אתם עברים בגבול אחיכם בני־עשו הישבים בשעיר וייראו
ה מכם ונשמרתם מאד: אל־תתגרו בם כי לא־אתן לכם מארצם
ו עד מדרך כף־רגל כי־ירשה לעשו נתתי את־הר שעיר: אכל תשברו
ז מאתם בכסף ואכלתם וגם־מים תכרו מאתם בכסף ושתיתם: כי
יהוה אלהיך ברכך בכל מעשה ידך ידע לכתך את־המדבר הגדל
ח הזה זה ׀ ארבעים שנה יהוה אלהיך עמך לא חסרת דבר: ונעבר
מאת אחינו בני־עשו הישבים בשעיר מדרך הערבה מאילת
ט ומעצין גבר ונפן ונעבר דרך מדבר מואב: ויאמר יהוה
אלי אל־תצר את־מואב ואל־תתגר בם מלחמה כי לא־אתן לך
י מארצו ירשה כי לבני־לוט נתתי את־ער ירשה: האמים לפנים ישבו
יא בה עם גדול ורב ורם כענקים: רפאים יחשבו אף־הם כענקים
יב והמאבים יקראו להם אמים: ובשעיר ישבו החרים לפנים ובני עשו
יירשום וישמידום מפניהם וישבו תחתם כאשר עשה ישראל לארץ
יג ירשתו אשר־נתן יהוה להם: עתה קמו ועברו לכם את־נחל זרד
יד ונעבר את־נחל זרד: והימים אשר־הלכנו ׀ מקדש ברנע עד אשר־
עברנו את־נחל זרד שלשים ושמנה שנה עד־תם כל־הדור אנשי
טו המלחמה מקרב המחנה כאשר נשבע יהוה להם: וגם יד־יהוה
טז היתה בם להמם מקרב המחנה עד תמם: ויהי כאשר־תמו כל־אנשי
יז המלחמה למות מקרב העם: וידבר יהוה אלי לאמר:
יח יט אתה עבר היום את־גבול מואב את־ער: וקרבת מול בני עמון
אל־תצרם ואל־תתגר בם כי לא־אתן מארץ בני־עמון לך ירשה
כ כי לבני־לוט נתתיה ירשה: ארץ־רפאים תחשב אף־הוא רפאים
כא ישבו־בה לפנים והעמנים יקראו להם זמזמים: עם גדול ורב ורם
כב כענקים וישמידם יהוה מפניהם ויירשם וישבו תחתם: כאשר עשה
לבני עשו הישבים בשעיר אשר השמיד את־החרי מפניהם ויירשם
כג וישבו תחתם עד היום הזה: והעוים הישבים בחצרים עד־עזה
כד כפתרים היצאים מכפתור השמידם וישבו תחתם: קומו סעו ועברו
את־נחל ארנן ראה נתתי בידך את־סיחן מלך־חשבון האמרי

with his land, into your hands. Begin to take possession of it; enter into battle
25 with him.[11] This day I am beginning to put the terror and fear of you upon the
peoples everywhere under the skies. When they hear reports of you, they will
26 tremble in dread of you.' So I sent messengers from the Kedemot wilderness
27 to Siḥon, king of Ḥeshbon, with an offer of peace: 'Let us pass through your
land. We will stay on the main road, turning aside neither to the right nor to
28 the left. Provide us with food and we will pay for it in silver and eat; give us
water and we will pay for it in silver and drink. Only let us pass through on
29 foot – just as the descendants of Esav living in Se'ir and the Moabites living
in Ar did for us – until we cross the Jordan into the land that the LORD our
30 God is giving us.' But Siḥon, king of Ḥeshbon, refused to let us pass through,
for the LORD your God had hardened his spirit and made his heart defiant
31 in order to give him over into your hands, as He has now done. The
LORD said to me, 'I have begun to give Siḥon and his land over to you. Go:
32 begin to conquer and possess his land.' Then Siḥon and all his people came
33 out to meet us in battle at Yahatz. The LORD our God gave him over to us,
34 and we struck him down, together with his sons and all his people. At that
time we captured all his towns and completely destroyed them, men, women,
35 and children alike, leaving not a single survivor. Only the livestock and the
36 spoil of the cities we captured did we keep as booty for ourselves. From Aroer
on the banks of the Arnon Stream, including the town in the ravine, as far as
Gilad, not one city was unattainable to us. The LORD our God gave us all of
37 them. But you did not touch the land of the Amonites, not the land around
the Yabok Stream, nor the towns of the hill country that the LORD our God
3 1 commanded us to leave. After this, we turned and journeyed along the road
toward Bashan. Og, king of Bashan, with all his people came out to Edre'i to
2 engage us in battle. But the LORD said to me, 'Do not be afraid of him, for
I have given him into you hand, with all his people and his land. Do to him
3 what you did to Siḥon, king of the Amorites, who lived in Ḥeshbon.' So the
LORD our God also gave over to us Og, king of Bashan, and all his people.
4 We struck him down until not a single survivor remained. We captured all
his towns at that time; there was not a single town we did not take from
5 them – sixty towns, the entire region of Argov, Og's kingdom in Bashan. And
these were all fortress towns with high walls, gates, and bars – there were a
6 great many unwalled towns besides. And we utterly destroyed them, as we
had done to Siḥon, king of Ḥeshbon, in each town utterly destroying them:
7 men, women, and children. All the livestock and the spoil of the towns we
8 kept as booty for ourselves. At that time, then, we took from the two kings of
the Amorites the land beyond the Jordan, from the Arnon Stream to Mount
9 Ḥermon" – the Sidonians call Ḥermon Siryon, and the Amorites call it Senir –
10 "all the towns of the plateau, the whole of Gilad, and the whole of Bashan, as
11 far as Salkha and Edre'i, towns of Og's kingdom in Bashan." Only Og, king of

---

11 | Concerning the battles with Siḥon and Og recounted in this passage, cf. Numbers 21:21–35.

כה וְאֶת־אַרְצ֑וֹ הָחֵ֣ל רָ֔שׁ וְהִתְגָּ֥ר בּ֖וֹ מִלְחָמָֽה׃ הַיּ֣וֹם הַזֶּ֗ה אָחֵל֙ תֵּ֤ת פַּחְדְּךָ֙
וְיִרְאָ֣תְךָ֔ עַל־פְּנֵי֙ הָֽעַמִּ֔ים תַּ֖חַת כָּל־הַשָּׁמָ֑יִם אֲשֶׁר֙ יִשְׁמְעוּן֙ שִׁמְעֲךָ֔
כו וְרָגְז֥וּ וְחָל֖וּ מִפָּנֶֽיךָ׃ וָאֶשְׁלַ֤ח מַלְאָכִים֙ מִמִּדְבַּ֣ר קְדֵמ֔וֹת אֶל־סִיח֖וֹן מֶ֣לֶךְ
כז חֶשְׁבּ֑וֹן דִּבְרֵ֥י שָׁל֖וֹם לֵאמֹֽר׃ אֶעְבְּרָ֣ה בְאַרְצֶ֔ךָ בַּדֶּ֥רֶךְ בַּדֶּ֖רֶךְ אֵלֵ֑ךְ לֹ֥א
כח אָס֖וּר יָמִ֥ין וּשְׂמֹֽאול׃ אֹ֣כֶל בַּכֶּ֤סֶף תַּשְׁבִּרֵ֙נִי֙ וְאָכַ֔לְתִּי וּמַ֛יִם בַּכֶּ֥סֶף תִּתֶּן־
כט לִ֖י וְשָׁתִ֑יתִי רַ֖ק אֶעְבְּרָ֥ה בְרַגְלָֽי׃ כַּאֲשֶׁ֨ר עָֽשׂוּ־לִ֜י בְּנֵ֣י עֵשָׂ֗ו הַיֹּֽשְׁבִים֙
בְּשֵׂעִ֔יר וְהַמּ֣וֹאָבִ֔ים הַיֹּֽשְׁבִ֖ים בְּעָ֑ר עַ֤ד אֲשֶׁר־אֶֽעֱבֹר֙ אֶת־הַיַּרְדֵּ֔ן אֶל־
ל הָאָ֕רֶץ אֲשֶׁר־יְהוָ֥ה אֱלֹהֵ֖ינוּ נֹתֵ֥ן לָֽנוּ׃ וְלֹ֣א אָבָ֗ה סִיחֹן֙ מֶ֣לֶךְ חֶשְׁבּ֔וֹן
הַעֲבִרֵ֖נוּ בּ֑וֹ כִּֽי־הִקְשָׁה֩ יְהוָ֨ה אֱלֹהֶ֜יךָ אֶת־רוּח֗וֹ וְאִמֵּץ֙ אֶת־לְבָב֔וֹ לְמַ֛עַן
לא תִּתּ֥וֹ בְיָדְךָ֖ כַּיּ֥וֹם הַזֶּֽה׃ וַיֹּ֤אמֶר יְהוָה֙ אֵלַ֔י רְאֵ֗ה הַחִלֹּ֙תִי֙ תֵּ֣ת ג ששי
לב לְפָנֶ֔יךָ אֶת־סִיחֹ֖ן וְאֶת־אַרְצ֑וֹ הָחֵ֣ל רָ֔שׁ לָרֶ֖שֶׁת אֶת־אַרְצֽוֹ׃ וַיֵּצֵ֨א סִיחֹ֜ן
לג לִקְרָאתֵ֗נוּ ה֛וּא וְכָל־עַמּ֖וֹ לַמִּלְחָמָ֥ה יָֽהְצָה׃ וַֽיִּתְּנֵ֛הוּ יְהוָ֥ה אֱלֹהֵ֖ינוּ
לד לְפָנֵ֑ינוּ וַנַּ֥ךְ אֹת֛וֹ וְאֶת־בָּנָ֖ו וְאֶת־כָּל־עַמּֽוֹ׃ וַנִּלְכֹּ֤ד אֶת־כָּל־עָרָיו֙ בָּעֵ֣ת
הַהִ֔וא וַֽנַּחֲרֵם֙ אֶת־כָּל־עִ֣יר מְתִ֔ם וְהַנָּשִׁ֖ים וְהַטָּ֑ף לֹ֥א הִשְׁאַ֖רְנוּ שָׂרִֽיד׃
לה לו רַ֥ק הַבְּהֵמָ֖ה בָּזַ֣זְנוּ לָ֑נוּ וּשְׁלַ֥ל הֶעָרִ֖ים אֲשֶׁ֥ר לָכָֽדְנוּ׃ מֵעֲרֹעֵ֡ר אֲשֶׁר֩
עַל־שְׂפַת־נַ֨חַל אַרְנֹ֜ן וְהָעִ֨יר אֲשֶׁ֤ר בַּנַּ֙חַל֙ וְעַד־הַגִּלְעָ֔ד לֹ֤א הָֽיְתָה֙ קִרְיָ֔ה
לז אֲשֶׁ֥ר שָׂגְבָ֖ה מִמֶּ֑נּוּ אֶת־הַכֹּ֕ל נָתַ֛ן יְהוָ֥ה אֱלֹהֵ֖ינוּ לְפָנֵֽינוּ׃ רַ֛ק אֶל־אֶ֥רֶץ
בְּנֵי־עַמּ֖וֹן לֹ֣א קָרָ֑בְתָּ כָּל־יַ֞ד נַ֤חַל יַבֹּק֙ וְעָרֵ֣י הָהָ֔ר וְכֹ֥ל אֲשֶׁר־צִוָּ֖ה יְהוָ֥ה
ג א אֱלֹהֵֽינוּ׃ וַנֵּ֣פֶן וַנַּ֔עַל דֶּ֖רֶךְ הַבָּשָׁ֑ן וַיֵּצֵ֣א עוֹג֩ מֶלֶךְ־הַבָּשָׁ֨ן לִקְרָאתֵ֜נוּ ה֧וּא
ב וְכָל־עַמּ֛וֹ לַמִּלְחָמָ֖ה אֶדְרֶֽעִי׃ וַיֹּ֨אמֶר יְהוָ֤ה אֵלַי֙ אַל־תִּירָ֣א אֹת֔וֹ כִּ֣י בְיָדְךָ֞
נָתַ֧תִּי אֹת֛וֹ וְאֶת־כָּל־עַמּ֖וֹ וְאֶת־אַרְצ֑וֹ וְעָשִׂ֣יתָ לּ֔וֹ כַּאֲשֶׁ֣ר עָשִׂ֗יתָ לְסִיחֹן֙
ג מֶ֣לֶךְ הָֽאֱמֹרִ֔י אֲשֶׁ֥ר יוֹשֵׁ֖ב בְּחֶשְׁבּֽוֹן׃ וַיִּתֵּן֩ יְהוָ֨ה אֱלֹהֵ֜ינוּ בְּיָדֵ֗נוּ גַּ֛ם אֶת־
ע֥וֹג מֶֽלֶךְ־הַבָּשָׁ֖ן וְאֶת־כָּל־עַמּ֑וֹ וַנַּכֵּ֕הוּ עַד־בִּלְתִּ֥י הִשְׁאִֽיר־ל֖וֹ שָׂרִֽיד׃
ד וַנִּלְכֹּ֤ד אֶת־כָּל־עָרָיו֙ בָּעֵ֣ת הַהִ֔וא לֹ֤א הָֽיְתָה֙ קִרְיָ֔ה אֲשֶׁ֥ר לֹא־לָקַ֖חְנוּ
ה מֵאִתָּ֑ם שִׁשִּׁ֥ים עִיר֙ כָּל־חֶ֣בֶל אַרְגֹּ֔ב מַמְלֶ֥כֶת ע֖וֹג בַּבָּשָֽׁן׃ כָּל־אֵ֜לֶּה
עָרִ֧ים בְּצֻר֛וֹת חוֹמָ֥ה גְבֹהָ֖ה דְּלָתַ֣יִם וּבְרִ֑יחַ לְבַ֛ד מֵעָרֵ֥י הַפְּרָזִ֖י הַרְבֵּ֥ה
ו מְאֹֽד׃ וַנַּחֲרֵ֣ם אוֹתָ֔ם כַּאֲשֶׁ֣ר עָשִׂ֔ינוּ לְסִיחֹ֖ן מֶ֣לֶךְ חֶשְׁבּ֑וֹן הַחֲרֵם֙ כָּל־
ז עִ֣יר מְתִ֔ם הַנָּשִׁ֖ים וְהַטָּֽף׃ וְכָל־הַבְּהֵמָ֛ה וּשְׁלַ֥ל הֶעָרִ֖ים בַּזּ֥וֹנוּ לָֽנוּ׃
ח וַנִּקַּ֞ח בָּעֵ֤ת הַהִוא֙ אֶת־הָאָ֔רֶץ מִיַּ֗ד שְׁנֵי֙ מַלְכֵ֣י הָֽאֱמֹרִ֔י אֲשֶׁ֖ר בְּעֵ֣בֶר
ט הַיַּרְדֵּ֑ן מִנַּ֥חַל אַרְנֹ֖ן עַד־הַ֥ר חֶרְמֽוֹן׃ צִידֹנִ֖ים יִקְרְא֣וּ לְחֶרְמ֣וֹן שִׂרְיֹ֑ן
י וְהָ֣אֱמֹרִ֔י יִקְרְאוּ־ל֖וֹ שְׂנִֽיר׃ כֹּ֣ל ׀ עָרֵ֣י הַמִּישֹׁ֗ר וְכָל־הַגִּלְעָד֙ וְכָל־הַבָּשָׁ֔ן
יא עַד־סַלְכָ֖ה וְאֶדְרֶ֑עִי עָרֵ֖י מַמְלֶ֥כֶת ע֖וֹג בַּבָּשָֽׁן׃ כִּ֣י רַק־ע֞וֹג מֶ֣לֶךְ הַבָּשָׁ֗ן

Bashan, was left then of the remaining Refaim. His bed, made of iron, is still
there, in Raba of the Amonites: it is nine cubits long and four cubits wide,
12 as measured by a man's forearm. "Of the land that we took possession of at
that time, I gave to the Reubenites and Gadites the territory from Aroer on
the edge of the Arnon Stream, as well as half the hill country of Gilad with
13 its towns.[12] To the half tribe of Menashe I gave the rest of Gilad and all of
Bashan, Og's kingdom – the whole region of Argov: all that portion of Bashan
14 that used to be known as the land of the Refaim." Yair of Menashe took the
whole region of Argov – that is, Bashan – as far as the border of the people
of Geshur and of Maakha – and named it after himself, hamlets of Yair, as it
15 16 is called to this day. "To Makhir I gave Gilad, and to the Reubenites and
the Gadites I gave the territory from Gilad as far as the Arnon Stream, with
the middle of the ravine as a border, and up to the Yabok Stream and the
17 Amonites' border. It included also the Arava, with the Jordan and its banks,
from the Sea of Galilee down to the Arava Sea, the Dead Sea, with the lower
18 slopes of Pisga on the east. At that time, I charged you:[13] 'The LORD your God
has given you this land to possess, but all your troops must cross over armed
19 before your fellow Israelites. Only your wives, children, and cattle – I know
that you have much cattle – shall stay behind in the towns I have given you,
20 until the LORD gives rest to your fellows as to you, and they too have taken
possession of the land that the LORD your God is giving them beyond the
Jordan. Then you may each return to the land that I have given to you.' And
21 I charged Yehoshua also at that time: 'Your own eyes have seen all that the
LORD your God has done to these two kings; so will the LORD do to all the
22 kingdoms into which you are about to cross. Do not fear them, for it is the
23 LORD your God who is fighting for you.' At that time, I pleaded with VAETḤANAN
24 the LORD: 'O Lord GOD, You have begun to show Your servant Your greatness
and Your mighty hand; what force in heaven or earth can do deeds and mighty
25 acts like Yours! Please let me cross over and see the good land beyond the
26 Jordan, that good hill country and the Lebanon.' But the LORD was enraged
with me because of you,[14] and would not listen to me. 'It is enough!' the LORD
27 said to me. 'Never speak to Me about this again! Go up to the top of Pisga and
gaze around you to the west, to the north, to the south, and to the east. See it
28 with your eyes, for you will not cross this Jordan. But charge Yehoshua, make
him strong and determined, for he will be the one to cross over at the head
of this people and who will secure their possession of the land that you may
29 only see.' And we came to rest in the valley beside Beit Peor.
4 1 And now, Israel, listen to the decrees and laws that I am teaching you to keep,
so that you may live to enter and take possession of the land that the LORD,
2 God of your ancestors, is giving to you. Do not add anything to that which

---

12 | Cf. Numbers, chapter 32.

13 | "You" refers to the Reubenites and Gadites.

14 | See 1:37.

נִשְׁאַר מִיֶּתֶר הָרְפָאִים הִנֵּה עַרְשׂוֹ עֶרֶשׂ בַּרְזֶל הֲלֹה הִוא בְּרַבַּת בְּנֵי
יב עַמּוֹן תֵּשַׁע אַמּוֹת אָרְכָּהּ וְאַרְבַּע אַמּוֹת רָחְבָּהּ בְּאַמַּת־אִישׁ: וְאֶת־
הָאָרֶץ הַזֹּאת יָרַשְׁנוּ בָּעֵת הַהִוא מֵעֲרֹעֵר אֲשֶׁר־עַל־נַחַל אַרְנֹן וַחֲצִי
יג הַר־הַגִּלְעָד וְעָרָיו נָתַתִּי לָראוּבֵנִי וְלַגָּדִי: וְיֶתֶר הַגִּלְעָד וְכָל־הַבָּשָׁן
מַמְלֶכֶת עוֹג נָתַתִּי לַחֲצִי שֵׁבֶט הַמְנַשֶּׁה כֹּל חֶבֶל הָאַרְגֹּב לְכָל־הַבָּשָׁן
יד הַהוּא יִקָּרֵא אֶרֶץ רְפָאִים: יָאִיר בֶּן־מְנַשֶּׁה לָקַח אֶת־כָּל־חֶבֶל אַרְגֹּב
עַד־גְּבוּל הַגְּשׁוּרִי וְהַמַּעֲכָתִי וַיִּקְרָא אֹתָם עַל־שְׁמוֹ אֶת־הַבָּשָׁן חַוֹּת
טו טז שביעי יָאִיר עַד הַיּוֹם הַזֶּה: וּלְמָכִיר נָתַתִּי אֶת־הַגִּלְעָד: וְלָראוּבֵנִי וְלַגָּדִי נָתַתִּי
מִן־הַגִּלְעָד וְעַד־נַחַל אַרְנֹן תּוֹךְ הַנַּחַל וּגְבֻל וְעַד יַבֹּק הַנַּחַל גְּבוּל בְּנֵי
יז עַמּוֹן: וְהָעֲרָבָה וְהַיַּרְדֵּן וּגְבֻל מִכִּנֶּרֶת וְעַד יָם הָעֲרָבָה יָם הַמֶּלַח תַּחַת
יח אַשְׁדֹּת הַפִּסְגָּה מִזְרָחָה: וָאֲצַו אֶתְכֶם בָּעֵת הַהִוא לֵאמֹר יְהוָה
אֱלֹהֵיכֶם נָתַן לָכֶם אֶת־הָאָרֶץ הַזֹּאת לְרִשְׁתָּהּ חֲלוּצִים תַּעַבְרוּ לִפְנֵי
יט אֲחֵיכֶם בְּנֵי־יִשְׂרָאֵל כָּל־בְּנֵי־חָיִל: רַק נְשֵׁיכֶם וְטַפְּכֶם וּמִקְנֵכֶם יָדַעְתִּי
כ מפטיר כִּי־מִקְנֶה רַב לָכֶם יֵשְׁבוּ בְּעָרֵיכֶם אֲשֶׁר נָתַתִּי לָכֶם: עַד אֲשֶׁר־יָנִיחַ
יְהוָה ׀ לַאֲחֵיכֶם כָּכֶם וְיָרְשׁוּ גַם־הֵם אֶת־הָאָרֶץ אֲשֶׁר יְהוָה אֱלֹהֵיכֶם
נֹתֵן לָהֶם בְּעֵבֶר הַיַּרְדֵּן וְשַׁבְתֶּם אִישׁ לִירֻשָּׁתוֹ אֲשֶׁר נָתַתִּי לָכֶם:
כא וְאֶת־יְהוֹשׁוּעַ צִוֵּיתִי בָּעֵת הַהִוא לֵאמֹר עֵינֶיךָ הָרֹאֹת אֵת כָּל־אֲשֶׁר
עָשָׂה יְהוָה אֱלֹהֵיכֶם לִשְׁנֵי הַמְּלָכִים הָאֵלֶּה כֵּן־יַעֲשֶׂה יְהוָה לְכָל־
כב הַמַּמְלָכוֹת אֲשֶׁר אַתָּה עֹבֵר שָׁמָּה: לֹא תִּירָאוּם כִּי יְהוָה אֱלֹהֵיכֶם
כג ד ואתחנן הוּא הַנִּלְחָם לָכֶם: וָאֶתְחַנַּן אֶל־יְהוָה בָּעֵת הַהִוא לֵאמֹר:
כד אֲדֹנָי יְהוִה אַתָּה הַחִלּוֹתָ לְהַרְאוֹת אֶת־עַבְדְּךָ אֶת־גָּדְלְךָ וְאֶת־יָדְךָ
הַחֲזָקָה אֲשֶׁר מִי־אֵל בַּשָּׁמַיִם וּבָאָרֶץ אֲשֶׁר־יַעֲשֶׂה כְמַעֲשֶׂיךָ
כה וְכִגְבוּרֹתֶךָ: אֶעְבְּרָה־נָּא וְאֶרְאֶה אֶת־הָאָרֶץ הַטּוֹבָה אֲשֶׁר בְּעֵבֶר
כו הַיַּרְדֵּן הָהָר הַטּוֹב הַזֶּה וְהַלְּבָנֹן: וַיִּתְעַבֵּר יְהוָה בִּי לְמַעַנְכֶם וְלֹא שָׁמַע
אֵלָי וַיֹּאמֶר יְהוָה אֵלַי רַב־לָךְ אַל־תּוֹסֶף דַּבֵּר אֵלַי עוֹד בַּדָּבָר הַזֶּה:
כז עֲלֵה ׀ רֹאשׁ הַפִּסְגָּה וְשָׂא עֵינֶיךָ יָמָּה וְצָפֹנָה וְתֵימָנָה וּמִזְרָחָה וּרְאֵה
כח בְעֵינֶיךָ כִּי־לֹא תַעֲבֹר אֶת־הַיַּרְדֵּן הַזֶּה: וְצַו אֶת־יְהוֹשֻׁעַ וְחַזְּקֵהוּ
וְאַמְּצֵהוּ כִּי־הוּא יַעֲבֹר לִפְנֵי הָעָם הַזֶּה וְהוּא יַנְחִיל אוֹתָם אֶת־הָאָרֶץ
כט אֲשֶׁר תִּרְאֶה: וַנֵּשֶׁב בַּגָּיְא מוּל בֵּית פְּעוֹר:

ד א וְעַתָּה יִשְׂרָאֵל שְׁמַע אֶל־הַחֻקִּים וְאֶל־הַמִּשְׁפָּטִים אֲשֶׁר אָנֹכִי מְלַמֵּד
אֶתְכֶם לַעֲשׂוֹת לְמַעַן תִּחְיוּ וּבָאתֶם וִירִשְׁתֶּם אֶת־הָאָרֶץ אֲשֶׁר יְהוָה
ב אֱלֹהֵי אֲבֹתֵיכֶם נֹתֵן לָכֶם: לֹא תֹסִפוּ עַל־הַדָּבָר אֲשֶׁר אָנֹכִי מְצַוֶּה

I command you, or subtract from it; keep the commandments of the LORD
3 your God with which I am charging you. You saw with your own eyes what
the LORD did in the affair of Baal Peor[15] – how the LORD your God wiped
4 out from among you everyone who followed Baal Peor, while you, who held
5 firmly to the LORD your God, are all here living today. See: I have taught you
decrees and laws as the LORD my God commanded me, for you to keep in
6 the land that you are about to enter and possess. Take care to keep them, for
this will be your wisdom and understanding in the eyes of the peoples: when
they hear all these decrees they will say, 'Surely this great nation is a wise and
7 understanding people!' For what other great nation has God so close to it as
8 the LORD our God is to us whenever we call out to Him? And what other great
nation has decrees and laws as just as this entire Torah that I am setting before
9 you today? But take care and be very vigilant not to forget the things that your
eyes have seen, nor to let them fade from your mind, as long as you live. Make
10 known to your children and your children's children, how you once stood
before the LORD your God at Ḥorev,[16] when the LORD said to me, 'Assemble
the people for Me, and I will let them hear My words so that they may learn to
be in awe of Me as long as they live on earth, and teach their children likewise.'
11 And you came close and stood at the foot of the mountain while the mountain
12 was ablaze to high heaven and shrouded in dark clouds. Then the LORD spoke
to you out of the fire. You heard the sound of words but saw no image; there
13 was only a voice. He announced to you His covenant, which He charged you
to keep – the Ten Commandments – and He wrote them on two tablets of
14 stone. And the LORD charged me at that time to teach you decrees and laws
15 for you to keep in the land that you are about to cross into and possess. You
saw no image when the LORD spoke to you at Ḥorev out of the fire, and so take
16 great care for your own sake not to act in self-destruction, making yourselves
17 any idol, an image of any shape, any form of man or of woman, or in the form
18 of any animal of the land, or any winged bird that flies in the sky, or in the form
of anything that crawls on the ground, or of any fish in the waters below the
19 earth. And when you raise your eyes to the heavens and see the sun, moon,
and stars, all the heavenly array, do not be led astray to bow down to them
and worship them; the LORD your God has allotted them to all the other
20 peoples beneath the sky. But you, the LORD took, and He brought you out
of the iron crucible that was Egypt, to become the people of His heritage, as
21 you are on this day. The LORD was incensed with me because of your words,
and He vowed that I would not cross the Jordan nor enter the good land that
22 the LORD your God is giving you as a heritage. I will die in this land without

15 | See Numbers, chapter 25.
16 | Sinai; see Exodus, chapters 19–20.

אֶתְכֶם וְלֹא תִגְרְעוּ מִמֶּנּוּ לִשְׁמֹר אֶת־מִצְוֺת יהוה אֱלֹהֵיכֶם אֲשֶׁר אָנֹכִי
ג מְצַוֶּה אֶתְכֶם: עֵינֵיכֶם הָרֹאוֹת אֵת אֲשֶׁר־עָשָׂה יהוה בְּבַעַל פְּעוֹר
כִּי כָל־הָאִישׁ אֲשֶׁר הָלַךְ אַחֲרֵי בַעַל־פְּעוֹר הִשְׁמִידוֹ יהוה אֱלֹהֶיךָ
ד ה מִקִּרְבֶּךָ: וְאַתֶּם הַדְּבֵקִים בַּיהוה אֱלֹהֵיכֶם חַיִּים כֻּלְּכֶם הַיּוֹם: רְאֵה | שני
לִמַּדְתִּי אֶתְכֶם חֻקִּים וּמִשְׁפָּטִים כַּאֲשֶׁר צִוַּנִי יהוה אֱלֹהָי לַעֲשׂוֹת כֵּן
ו בְּקֶרֶב הָאָרֶץ אֲשֶׁר אַתֶּם בָּאִים שָׁמָּה לְרִשְׁתָּהּ: וּשְׁמַרְתֶּם וַעֲשִׂיתֶם
כִּי הִוא חָכְמַתְכֶם וּבִינַתְכֶם לְעֵינֵי הָעַמִּים אֲשֶׁר יִשְׁמְעוּן אֵת כָּל־
ז הַחֻקִּים הָאֵלֶּה וְאָמְרוּ רַק עַם־חָכָם וְנָבוֹן הַגּוֹי הַגָּדוֹל הַזֶּה: כִּי מִי־
גוֹי גָדוֹל אֲשֶׁר־לוֹ אֱלֹהִים קְרֹבִים אֵלָיו כַּיהוה אֱלֹהֵינוּ בְּכָל־קָרְאֵנוּ
ח אֵלָיו: וּמִי גּוֹי גָּדוֹל אֲשֶׁר־לוֹ חֻקִּים וּמִשְׁפָּטִים צַדִּיקִם כְּכֹל הַתּוֹרָה
ט הַזֹּאת אֲשֶׁר אָנֹכִי נֹתֵן לִפְנֵיכֶם הַיּוֹם: רַק הִשָּׁמֶר לְךָ וּשְׁמֹר נַפְשְׁךָ
מְאֹד פֶּן־תִּשְׁכַּח אֶת־הַדְּבָרִים אֲשֶׁר־רָאוּ עֵינֶיךָ וּפֶן־יָסוּרוּ מִלְּבָבְךָ
י כֹּל יְמֵי חַיֶּיךָ וְהוֹדַעְתָּם לְבָנֶיךָ וְלִבְנֵי בָנֶיךָ: יוֹם אֲשֶׁר עָמַדְתָּ לִפְנֵי
יהוה אֱלֹהֶיךָ בְּחֹרֵב בֶּאֱמֹר יהוה אֵלַי הַקְהֶל־לִי אֶת־הָעָם וְאַשְׁמִעֵם
אֶת־דְּבָרָי אֲשֶׁר יִלְמְדוּן לְיִרְאָה אֹתִי כָּל־הַיָּמִים אֲשֶׁר הֵם חַיִּים עַל־
יא הָאֲדָמָה וְאֶת־בְּנֵיהֶם יְלַמֵּדוּן: וַתִּקְרְבוּן וַתַּעַמְדוּן תַּחַת הָהָר וְהָהָר
יב בֹּעֵר בָּאֵשׁ עַד־לֵב הַשָּׁמַיִם חֹשֶׁךְ עָנָן וַעֲרָפֶל: וַיְדַבֵּר יהוה אֲלֵיכֶם
מִתּוֹךְ הָאֵשׁ קוֹל דְּבָרִים אַתֶּם שֹׁמְעִים וּתְמוּנָה אֵינְכֶם רֹאִים זוּלָתִי
יג קוֹל: וַיַּגֵּד לָכֶם אֶת־בְּרִיתוֹ אֲשֶׁר צִוָּה אֶתְכֶם לַעֲשׂוֹת עֲשֶׂרֶת הַדְּבָרִים
יד וַיִּכְתְּבֵם עַל־שְׁנֵי לֻחוֹת אֲבָנִים: וְאֹתִי צִוָּה יהוה בָּעֵת הַהִוא לְלַמֵּד
אֶתְכֶם חֻקִּים וּמִשְׁפָּטִים לַעֲשֹׂתְכֶם אֹתָם בָּאָרֶץ אֲשֶׁר אַתֶּם עֹבְרִים
טו שָׁמָּה לְרִשְׁתָּהּ: וְנִשְׁמַרְתֶּם מְאֹד לְנַפְשֹׁתֵיכֶם כִּי לֹא רְאִיתֶם כָּל־תְּמוּנָה
טז בְּיוֹם דִּבֶּר יהוה אֲלֵיכֶם בְּחֹרֵב מִתּוֹךְ הָאֵשׁ: פֶּן־תַּשְׁחִתוּן וַעֲשִׂיתֶם
יז לָכֶם פֶּסֶל תְּמוּנַת כָּל־סָמֶל תַּבְנִית זָכָר אוֹ נְקֵבָה: תַּבְנִית כָּל־בְּהֵמָה
יח אֲשֶׁר בָּאָרֶץ תַּבְנִית כָּל־צִפּוֹר כָּנָף אֲשֶׁר תָּעוּף בַּשָּׁמָיִם: תַּבְנִית כָּל־
יט רֹמֵשׂ בָּאֲדָמָה תַּבְנִית כָּל־דָּגָה אֲשֶׁר־בַּמַּיִם מִתַּחַת לָאָרֶץ: וּפֶן־תִּשָּׂא
עֵינֶיךָ הַשָּׁמַיְמָה וְרָאִיתָ אֶת־הַשֶּׁמֶשׁ וְאֶת־הַיָּרֵחַ וְאֶת־הַכּוֹכָבִים כֹּל
צְבָא הַשָּׁמַיִם וְנִדַּחְתָּ וְהִשְׁתַּחֲוִיתָ לָהֶם וַעֲבַדְתָּם אֲשֶׁר חָלַק יהוה
כ אֱלֹהֶיךָ אֹתָם לְכֹל הָעַמִּים תַּחַת כָּל־הַשָּׁמָיִם: וְאֶתְכֶם לָקַח יהוה
וַיּוֹצִא אֶתְכֶם מִכּוּר הַבַּרְזֶל מִמִּצְרָיִם לִהְיוֹת לוֹ לְעַם נַחֲלָה כַּיּוֹם
כא הַזֶּה: וַיהוה הִתְאַנַּף־בִּי עַל־דִּבְרֵיכֶם וַיִּשָּׁבַע לְבִלְתִּי עָבְרִי אֶת־הַיַּרְדֵּן
כב וּלְבִלְתִּי־בֹא אֶל־הָאָרֶץ הַטּוֹבָה אֲשֶׁר יהוה אֱלֹהֶיךָ נֹתֵן לְךָ נַחֲלָה: כִּי

crossing the Jordan – but you will cross over and take possession of that good
23 land. Take care not to forget the covenant that the Lord your God has forged
with you. Do not make yourselves an idol in any form: the Lord your God
24 has forbidden it. For the Lord your God is a consuming fire, an impassioned
God.
25 When you have had children and grandchildren, and have lived long in the
land, if you act destructively, forming an idol in any image, wreaking evil in
26 the sight of the Lord your God and provoking Him to anger, I call heaven
and earth to witness against you today – to bear witness that you will quickly
perish from the land that you are crossing the Jordan to take possession of.
27 You will not live long there; you will be utterly destroyed. The Lord will
scatter you among the peoples. Only a few of you will remain among the
28 nations that the Lord will drive you away to. There you will worship man-
made gods of wood and of stone, ones that do not see, do not hear, do not
29 eat or smell. Yet there, if you seek the Lord your God, you will find Him: if
30 you search after Him with all your heart and all your soul. In your distress,
when all these things have happened to you, in the days to come, you will
31 finally return to the Lord your God and heed His voice. For the Lord your
God is a merciful God. He will not forsake or destroy you. He will not forget
32 the covenant that He forged on oath with your ancestors. For ask now about
earliest times, times long before your own, from the day God created humans
on the earth; ask from one end of heaven to the other: Has anything as great
33 as this ever happened before? Has anyone heard of anything like this? Has
any people ever heard the voice of God speaking out of fire, as you have, and
34 lived? Has God ever taken one nation to Himself, by miracles, from the midst
of another, by trials, signs, wonders, and war, with a mighty hand and an arm
stretched forth and terrifying displays of power, as the Lord your God did
35 for you in Egypt before your eyes? To you this was shown – so that you may
36 know that the Lord is God; besides Him, there is no other. From heaven He
let you hear His voice to discipline you. On earth He showed you His great
37 fire, and from within the fire you heard His words. And because He loved
your ancestors and chose their descendants after them He brought you out
38 of Egypt with His own presence and by His great power, driving out from
before you nations greater and mightier than you, to bring you in and give
39 you their land as a possession, as it is on this day. Know today and take to
heart that the Lord is God in heaven above and on the earth beneath; there
40 is no other. Keep His decrees and commandments, with which I am charging
you today, so that it may be well for you and your children after you, and
that you may live long in the land that the Lord your God is giving you for
all time."
41 42 Then Moshe designated three cities to the east side of the Jordan to which a
manslayer could flee, someone who had killed a fellow human being without

אָנֹכִי מֵת בָּאָרֶץ הַזֹּאת אֵינֶנִּי עֹבֵר אֶת־הַיַּרְדֵּן וְאַתֶּם עֹבְרִים וִירִשְׁתֶּם
כג אֶת־הָאָרֶץ הַטּוֹבָה הַזֹּאת: הִשָּׁמְרוּ לָכֶם פֶּן־תִּשְׁכְּחוּ אֶת־בְּרִית יְהוָה
אֱלֹהֵיכֶם אֲשֶׁר כָּרַת עִמָּכֶם וַעֲשִׂיתֶם לָכֶם פֶּסֶל תְּמוּנַת כֹּל אֲשֶׁר צִוְּךָ
כד יְהוָה אֱלֹהֶיךָ: כִּי יְהוָה אֱלֹהֶיךָ אֵשׁ אֹכְלָה הוּא אֵל קַנָּא:
כה כִּי־תוֹלִיד בָּנִים וּבְנֵי בָנִים וְנוֹשַׁנְתֶּם בָּאָרֶץ וְהִשְׁחַתֶּם וַעֲשִׂיתֶם פֶּסֶל
כו תְּמוּנַת כֹּל וַעֲשִׂיתֶם הָרַע בְּעֵינֵי־יְהוָה אֱלֹהֶיךָ לְהַכְעִיסוֹ: הַעִידֹתִי
בָכֶם הַיּוֹם אֶת־הַשָּׁמַיִם וְאֶת־הָאָרֶץ כִּי־אָבֹד תֹּאבֵדוּן מַהֵר מֵעַל
הָאָרֶץ אֲשֶׁר אַתֶּם עֹבְרִים אֶת־הַיַּרְדֵּן שָׁמָּה לְרִשְׁתָּהּ לֹא־תַאֲרִיכֻן
כז יָמִים עָלֶיהָ כִּי הִשָּׁמֵד תִּשָּׁמֵדוּן: וְהֵפִיץ יְהוָה אֶתְכֶם בָּעַמִּים וְנִשְׁאַרְתֶּם
כח מְתֵי מִסְפָּר בַּגּוֹיִם אֲשֶׁר יְנַהֵג יְהוָה אֶתְכֶם שָׁמָּה: וַעֲבַדְתֶּם־שָׁם
אֱלֹהִים מַעֲשֵׂה יְדֵי אָדָם עֵץ וָאֶבֶן אֲשֶׁר לֹא־יִרְאוּן וְלֹא יִשְׁמְעוּן וְלֹא
כט יֹאכְלוּן וְלֹא יְרִיחֻן: וּבִקַּשְׁתֶּם מִשָּׁם אֶת־יְהוָה אֱלֹהֶיךָ וּמָצָאתָ כִּי
ל תִדְרְשֶׁנּוּ בְּכָל־לְבָבְךָ וּבְכָל־נַפְשֶׁךָ: בַּצַּר לְךָ וּמְצָאוּךָ כֹּל הַדְּבָרִים
לא הָאֵלֶּה בְּאַחֲרִית הַיָּמִים וְשַׁבְתָּ עַד־יְהוָה אֱלֹהֶיךָ וְשָׁמַעְתָּ בְּקֹלוֹ: כִּי
אֵל רַחוּם יְהוָה אֱלֹהֶיךָ לֹא יַרְפְּךָ וְלֹא יַשְׁחִיתֶךָ וְלֹא יִשְׁכַּח אֶת־בְּרִית
לב אֲבֹתֶיךָ אֲשֶׁר נִשְׁבַּע לָהֶם: כִּי שְׁאַל־נָא לְיָמִים רִאשֹׁנִים אֲשֶׁר־הָיוּ
לְפָנֶיךָ לְמִן־הַיּוֹם אֲשֶׁר בָּרָא אֱלֹהִים ׀ אָדָם עַל־הָאָרֶץ וּלְמִקְצֵה
הַשָּׁמַיִם וְעַד־קְצֵה הַשָּׁמָיִם הֲנִהְיָה כַּדָּבָר הַגָּדוֹל הַזֶּה אוֹ הֲנִשְׁמַע
לג כָּמֹהוּ: הֲשָׁמַע עָם קוֹל אֱלֹהִים מְדַבֵּר מִתּוֹךְ־הָאֵשׁ כַּאֲשֶׁר־שָׁמַעְתָּ
לד אַתָּה וַיֶּחִי: אוֹ ׀ הֲנִסָּה אֱלֹהִים לָבוֹא לָקַחַת לוֹ גוֹי מִקֶּרֶב גּוֹי בְּמַסֹּת
בְּאֹתֹת וּבְמוֹפְתִים וּבְמִלְחָמָה וּבְיָד חֲזָקָה וּבִזְרוֹעַ נְטוּיָה וּבְמוֹרָאִים
לה גְּדֹלִים כְּכֹל אֲשֶׁר־עָשָׂה לָכֶם יְהוָה אֱלֹהֵיכֶם בְּמִצְרַיִם לְעֵינֶיךָ: אַתָּה
לו הָרְאֵתָ לָדַעַת כִּי יְהוָה הוּא הָאֱלֹהִים אֵין עוֹד מִלְּבַדּוֹ: מִן־הַשָּׁמַיִם
הִשְׁמִיעֲךָ אֶת־קֹלוֹ לְיַסְּרֶךָּ וְעַל־הָאָרֶץ הֶרְאֲךָ אֶת־אִשּׁוֹ הַגְּדוֹלָה
לז וּדְבָרָיו שָׁמַעְתָּ מִתּוֹךְ הָאֵשׁ: וְתַחַת כִּי אָהַב אֶת־אֲבֹתֶיךָ וַיִּבְחַר
לח בְּזַרְעוֹ אַחֲרָיו וַיּוֹצִאֲךָ בְּפָנָיו בְּכֹחוֹ הַגָּדֹל מִמִּצְרָיִם: לְהוֹרִישׁ גּוֹיִם
גְּדֹלִים וַעֲצֻמִים מִמְּךָ מִפָּנֶיךָ לַהֲבִיאֲךָ לָתֶת־לְךָ אֶת־אַרְצָם נַחֲלָה כַּיּוֹם
לט הַזֶּה: וְיָדַעְתָּ הַיּוֹם וַהֲשֵׁבֹתָ אֶל־לְבָבֶךָ כִּי יְהוָה הוּא הָאֱלֹהִים בַּשָּׁמַיִם
מ מִמַּעַל וְעַל־הָאָרֶץ מִתָּחַת אֵין עוֹד: וְשָׁמַרְתָּ אֶת־חֻקָּיו וְאֶת־מִצְוֺתָיו
אֲשֶׁר אָנֹכִי מְצַוְּךָ הַיּוֹם אֲשֶׁר יִיטַב לְךָ וּלְבָנֶיךָ אַחֲרֶיךָ וּלְמַעַן תַּאֲרִיךְ
יָמִים עַל־הָאֲדָמָה אֲשֶׁר יְהוָה אֱלֹהֶיךָ נֹתֵן לְךָ כָּל־הַיָּמִים:
מא מב אָז יַבְדִּיל מֹשֶׁה שָׁלֹשׁ עָרִים בְּעֵבֶר הַיַּרְדֵּן מִזְרְחָה שָׁמֶשׁ: לָנֻס שָׁמָּה ה שלישי

43 intent or prior enmity.[17] He could flee to one of these cities and live: Betzer
in the wilderness plateau for the people of Reuven, Ramot in Gilad for the
44 people of Gad, and Golan in Bashan for the people of Menashe. This is the
45 Law that Moshe set before the people of Israel. These are the testimonies,
decrees, and laws that Moshe spoke to the Israelites when they had come
46 out of Egypt and were beyond the Jordan in the valley opposite Beit Peor,
in the land of Siḥon, king of the Amorites, who reigned at Ḥeshbon, whom
47 Moshe and the Israelites defeated when they came out of Egypt. They had
taken possession of his land and the land of Og, king of Bashan, the two
48 Amorite kings east of the Jordan: from Aroer on the edge of the Arnon
49 Stream, as far as Mount Siyon – that is, Ḥermon – together with all the Arava
on the east bank of the Jordan as far as the Arava Sea, below the slopes of
Pisga.

5 1 Moshe summoned all Israel, and said to them: "Listen, Israel, to the decrees
and laws that I shall declare in your hearing today; learn them and carefully
2 observe them. The LORD our God forged a covenant with us at Ḥorev. Not
3 with our ancestors did the LORD forge this covenant,[18] but with us who are
4 here today, all of us, alive. Face-to-face from amid the fire the LORD spoke to
5 you at the mountain.I was standing between the LORD and you at that time
to tell you the word of the LORD, because you were afraid of the fire and did
6 not go up the mountain. He said: I am the LORD your God, who
7 brought you out of the land of Egypt, out of the house of slaves. Have no
8 other gods than Me. Do not make for yourself a carved image or likeness of
any creature in the heavens above or the earth beneath or the water beneath
9 the earth. Do not bow down to them or worship them, for I the LORD your
God demand absolute loyalty. For those who hate Me, I hold the descendants
10 to account for the sins of the fathers to the third and fourth generation, but
to those who love Me and keep My commands – I shall act with faithful
11 love for thousands. Do not speak the name of the LORD your God
in vain, for the LORD will not hold guiltless those who speak His name in
12 vain. Guard the Sabbath to keep it holy, as the LORD your God has
13 commanded you. Six days you shall work and carry out all your labors, but
14 the seventh is a Sabbath to the LORD your God. On it, do no work at all –
neither you, nor your son or daughter, your male or female servant, your ox,
your donkey, nor any of your livestock, or the migrant within your gates,
15 so that your male and female servants may rest as you do. Remember that
you were slaves in Egypt, and the LORD your God brought you out of there
with a mighty hand and an arm stretched forth. That is why the LORD your
16 God has commanded you to keep the Sabbath day. Honor your
father and mother, as the LORD your God has commanded you, so that you

---

17 | See Numbers 35:10–15.

18 | That is, not with our ancestors exclusively.

רֹצֵחַ אֲשֶׁר יִרְצַח אֶת־רֵעֵהוּ בִּבְלִי־דַעַת וְהוּא לֹא־שֹׂנֵא לוֹ מִתְּמֹל
מג שִׁלְשֹׁם וְנָס אֶל־אַחַת מִן־הֶעָרִים הָאֵל וָחָי: אֶת־בֶּצֶר בַּמִּדְבָּר בְּאֶרֶץ
הַמִּישֹׁר לָראוּבֵנִי וְאֶת־רָאמֹת בַּגִּלְעָד לַגָּדִי וְאֶת־גּוֹלָן בַּבָּשָׁן לַמְנַשִּׁי:
מד מה וְזֹאת הַתּוֹרָה אֲשֶׁר־שָׂם מֹשֶׁה לִפְנֵי בְּנֵי יִשְׂרָאֵל: אֵלֶּה הָעֵדֹת וְהַחֻקִּים
וְהַמִּשְׁפָּטִים אֲשֶׁר דִּבֶּר מֹשֶׁה אֶל־בְּנֵי יִשְׂרָאֵל בְּצֵאתָם מִמִּצְרָיִם:
מו בְּעֵבֶר הַיַּרְדֵּן בַּגַּיְא מוּל בֵּית פְּעוֹר בְּאֶרֶץ סִיחֹן מֶלֶךְ הָאֱמֹרִי אֲשֶׁר
יוֹשֵׁב בְּחֶשְׁבּוֹן אֲשֶׁר הִכָּה מֹשֶׁה וּבְנֵי יִשְׂרָאֵל בְּצֵאתָם מִמִּצְרָיִם:
מז וַיִּירְשׁוּ אֶת־אַרְצוֹ וְאֶת־אֶרֶץ | עוֹג מֶלֶךְ־הַבָּשָׁן שְׁנֵי מַלְכֵי הָאֱמֹרִי
מח אֲשֶׁר בְּעֵבֶר הַיַּרְדֵּן מִזְרַח שָׁמֶשׁ: מֵעֲרֹעֵר אֲשֶׁר עַל־שְׂפַת־נַחַל אַרְנֹן
מט וְעַד־הַר שִׂיאֹן הוּא חֶרְמוֹן: וְכָל־הָעֲרָבָה עֵבֶר הַיַּרְדֵּן מִזְרָחָה וְעַד יָם
הָעֲרָבָה תַּחַת אַשְׁדֹּת הַפִּסְגָּה:
ה א וַיִּקְרָא מֹשֶׁה אֶל־כָּל־יִשְׂרָאֵל וַיֹּאמֶר אֲלֵהֶם שְׁמַע יִשְׂרָאֵל אֶת־הַחֻקִּים רביעי
וְאֶת־הַמִּשְׁפָּטִים אֲשֶׁר אָנֹכִי דֹּבֵר בְּאָזְנֵיכֶם הַיּוֹם וּלְמַדְתֶּם אֹתָם
ב ג וּשְׁמַרְתֶּם לַעֲשֹׂתָם: יהוה אֱלֹהֵינוּ כָּרַת עִמָּנוּ בְּרִית בְּחֹרֵב: לֹא אֶת־
אֲבֹתֵינוּ כָּרַת יהוה אֶת־הַבְּרִית הַזֹּאת כִּי אִתָּנוּ אֲנַחְנוּ אֵלֶּה פֹה הַיּוֹם
ד ה כֻּלָּנוּ חַיִּים: פָּנִים | בְּפָנִים דִּבֶּר יהוה עִמָּכֶם בָּהָר מִתּוֹךְ הָאֵשׁ: אָנֹכִי
עֹמֵד בֵּין־יהוה וּבֵינֵיכֶם בָּעֵת הַהִוא לְהַגִּיד לָכֶם אֶת־דְּבַר יהוה כִּי
ו יְרֵאתֶם מִפְּנֵי הָאֵשׁ וְלֹא־עֲלִיתֶם בָּהָר לֵאמֹר: אָנֹכִי יהוה
ז אֱלֹהֶיךָ אֲשֶׁר הוֹצֵאתִיךָ מֵאֶרֶץ מִצְרַיִם מִבֵּית עֲבָדִים: לֹא־יִהְיֶה לְךָ
ח אֱלֹהִים אֲחֵרִים עַל־פָּנָי: לֹא־תַעֲשֶׂה לְךָ פֶסֶל כָּל־תְּמוּנָה אֲשֶׁר בַּשָּׁמַיִם
ט מִמַּעַל וַאֲשֶׁר בָּאָרֶץ מִתָּחַת וַאֲשֶׁר בַּמַּיִם מִתַּחַת לָאָרֶץ: לֹא־תִשְׁתַּחֲוֶה
לָהֶם וְלֹא תָעָבְדֵם כִּי אָנֹכִי יהוה אֱלֹהֶיךָ אֵל קַנָּא פֹּקֵד עֲוֺן אָבוֹת עַל־
י בָּנִים וְעַל־שִׁלֵּשִׁים וְעַל־רִבֵּעִים לְשֹׂנְאָי: וְעֹשֶׂה חֶסֶד לַאֲלָפִים לְאֹהֲבַי
יא וּלְשֹׁמְרֵי מִצְוֺתָו: לֹא תִשָּׂא אֶת־שֵׁם־יהוה אֱלֹהֶיךָ לַשָּׁוְא מִצְוֺתָי
יב כִּי לֹא יְנַקֶּה יהוה אֵת אֲשֶׁר־יִשָּׂא אֶת־שְׁמוֹ לַשָּׁוְא: שָׁמוֹר
יג אֶת־יוֹם הַשַּׁבָּת לְקַדְּשׁוֹ כַּאֲשֶׁר צִוְּךָ יהוה אֱלֹהֶיךָ: שֵׁשֶׁת יָמִים
יד תַּעֲבֹד וְעָשִׂיתָ כָּל־מְלַאכְתֶּךָ: וְיוֹם הַשְּׁבִיעִי שַׁבָּת לַיהוה
אֱלֹהֶיךָ לֹא־תַעֲשֶׂה כָל־מְלָאכָה אַתָּה | וּבִנְךָ־וּבִתֶּךָ וְעַבְדְּךָ־
וַאֲמָתֶךָ וְשׁוֹרְךָ וַחֲמֹרְךָ וְכָל־בְּהֶמְתֶּךָ וְגֵרְךָ אֲשֶׁר בִּשְׁעָרֶיךָ
טו לְמַעַן יָנוּחַ עַבְדְּךָ וַאֲמָתְךָ כָּמוֹךָ: וְזָכַרְתָּ כִּי עֶבֶד הָיִיתָ בְּאֶרֶץ
מִצְרַיִם וַיֹּצִאֲךָ יהוה אֱלֹהֶיךָ מִשָּׁם בְּיָד חֲזָקָה וּבִזְרֹעַ נְטוּיָה עַל־
טז כֵּן צִוְּךָ יהוה אֱלֹהֶיךָ לַעֲשׂוֹת אֶת־יוֹם הַשַּׁבָּת: כַּבֵּד

may live long and that it may be well for you in the land that the Lord your
17 God is giving you. Do not murder. Do not
commit adultery. Do not steal. Do not
bear false witness against your neighbor. Do not
18 crave your neighbor's wife. Do not
set your desire on your neighbor's house, or field, or male or female servant,
19 his ox, his donkey, or anything else that is your neighbor's. The
Lord spoke these words with a loud voice to your whole assembly at the
mountain from amid the fire, cloud, and thick darkness, and He added no
20 more. And He wrote them on two stone tablets, and gave them to me. When
you heard the voice out of the darkness, while the mountain was ablaze with
21 fire, your tribal leaders and elders came to me; they said, 'The Lord our God
has shown us His glory and greatness – we have heard His voice from within
the fire. Today we have seen that God may speak to a person and that person
22 still live. But now, must we die? For this great fire will consume us. If we hear
23 the voice of the Lord our God for any longer, we will die. For what mortal
has heard the voice of the Living God speaking from within the fire, as we
24 have, and yet lived? You go near and listen to all that the Lord our God says.
Then tell us all that the Lord our God tells you, and we will heed and do
25 it.' The Lord heard your words when you spoke to me, and to me the Lord
said: 'I have heard the words this people have spoken to you; they did well to
26 speak as they did. If only they would have such a mind as this always, to hold
Me in awe and to keep all My commandments, so that it might be well for
27 them and for their children forever! Go, tell them to go back to their tents.
28 But you stay here by Me, and I will tell you all the commandments, decrees,
and laws that you shall teach them, so that they may keep them in the land
29 that I am giving them to possess.' Take care to do as the Lord your God
has commanded you; do not turn aside – neither to the right nor to the left.
30 Follow only the path that the Lord your God has commanded you, so that
you may live and it may be well for you, and your years may be long in the
6 1 land you are to possess. This is the command – the decrees and the laws – that
the Lord your God charged me to teach you to keep in the land that you are
2 about to cross over into and take possession of, so that you and your children
and grandchildren may remain in awe of the Lord your God as long as you
live, keeping all His decrees and commandments that I am commanding
3 you and so that your years may be long. Listen, Israel, and take care to keep
them, so that it may be well for you, and so that you may be abundantly fertile

אֶת־אָבִיךָ וְאֶת־אִמֶּךָ כַּאֲשֶׁר צִוְּךָ יהוה אֱלֹהֶיךָ לְמַעַן ׀ יַאֲרִיכֻן
יָמֶיךָ וּלְמַעַן יִיטַב לָךְ עַל הָאֲדָמָה אֲשֶׁר־יהוה אֱלֹהֶיךָ נֹתֵן
יז לָךְ׃ לֹא תִרְצָח וְלֹא
תִנְאָף וְלֹא תִגְנֹב וְלֹא־
יח תַעֲנֶה בְרֵעֲךָ עֵד שָׁוְא׃ וְלֹא
תַחְמֹד אֵשֶׁת רֵעֶךָ וְלֹא
תִתְאַוֶּה בֵּית רֵעֶךָ שָׂדֵהוּ וְעַבְדּוֹ וַאֲמָתוֹ שׁוֹרוֹ וַחֲמֹרוֹ וְכֹל אֲשֶׁר
יט לְרֵעֶךָ׃ אֶת־הַדְּבָרִים הָאֵלֶּה דִּבֶּר יהוה אֶל־כָּל־קְהַלְכֶם חמישי
בָּהָר מִתּוֹךְ הָאֵשׁ הֶעָנָן וְהָעֲרָפֶל קוֹל גָּדוֹל וְלֹא יָסָף וַיִּכְתְּבֵם עַל־
כ שְׁנֵי לֻחֹת אֲבָנִים וַיִּתְּנֵם אֵלָי׃ וַיְהִי כְּשָׁמְעֲכֶם אֶת־הַקּוֹל מִתּוֹךְ
הַחֹשֶׁךְ וְהָהָר בֹּעֵר בָּאֵשׁ וַתִּקְרְבוּן אֵלַי כָּל־רָאשֵׁי שִׁבְטֵיכֶם וְזִקְנֵיכֶם׃
כא וַתֹּאמְרוּ הֵן הֶרְאָנוּ יהוה אֱלֹהֵינוּ אֶת־כְּבֹדוֹ וְאֶת־גָּדְלוֹ וְאֶת־קֹלוֹ
שָׁמַעְנוּ מִתּוֹךְ הָאֵשׁ הַיּוֹם הַזֶּה רָאִינוּ כִּי־יְדַבֵּר אֱלֹהִים אֶת־הָאָדָם
כב וָחָי׃ וְעַתָּה לָמָּה נָמוּת כִּי תֹאכְלֵנוּ הָאֵשׁ הַגְּדֹלָה הַזֹּאת אִם־יֹסְפִים ׀
כג אֲנַחְנוּ לִשְׁמֹעַ אֶת־קוֹל יהוה אֱלֹהֵינוּ עוֹד וָמָתְנוּ׃ כִּי מִי כָל־בָּשָׂר
כד אֲשֶׁר שָׁמַע קוֹל אֱלֹהִים חַיִּים מְדַבֵּר מִתּוֹךְ־הָאֵשׁ כָּמֹנוּ וַיֶּחִי׃ קְרַב
אַתָּה וּשְׁמָע אֵת כָּל־אֲשֶׁר יֹאמַר יהוה אֱלֹהֵינוּ וְאַתְּ ׀ תְּדַבֵּר אֵלֵינוּ אֵת
כה כָּל־אֲשֶׁר יְדַבֵּר יהוה אֱלֹהֵינוּ אֵלֶיךָ וְשָׁמַעְנוּ וְעָשִׂינוּ׃ וַיִּשְׁמַע יהוה
אֶת־קוֹל דִּבְרֵיכֶם בְּדַבֶּרְכֶם אֵלָי וַיֹּאמֶר יהוה אֵלַי שָׁמַעְתִּי אֶת־
קוֹל דִּבְרֵי הָעָם הַזֶּה אֲשֶׁר דִּבְּרוּ אֵלֶיךָ הֵיטִיבוּ כָּל־אֲשֶׁר דִּבֵּרוּ׃
כו מִי־יִתֵּן וְהָיָה לְבָבָם זֶה לָהֶם לְיִרְאָה אֹתִי וְלִשְׁמֹר אֶת־כָּל־מִצְוֹתַי
כז כָּל־הַיָּמִים לְמַעַן יִיטַב לָהֶם וְלִבְנֵיהֶם לְעֹלָם׃ לֵךְ אֱמֹר לָהֶם שׁוּבוּ
כח לָכֶם לְאָהֳלֵיכֶם׃ וְאַתָּה פֹּה עֲמֹד עִמָּדִי וַאֲדַבְּרָה אֵלֶיךָ אֵת כָּל־
הַמִּצְוָה וְהַחֻקִּים וְהַמִּשְׁפָּטִים אֲשֶׁר תְּלַמְּדֵם וְעָשׂוּ בָאָרֶץ אֲשֶׁר אָנֹכִי
כט נֹתֵן לָהֶם לְרִשְׁתָּהּ׃ וּשְׁמַרְתֶּם לַעֲשׂוֹת כַּאֲשֶׁר צִוָּה יהוה אֱלֹהֵיכֶם
ל אֶתְכֶם לֹא תָסֻרוּ יָמִין וּשְׂמֹאל׃ בְּכָל־הַדֶּרֶךְ אֲשֶׁר צִוָּה יהוה אֱלֹהֵיכֶם
אֶתְכֶם תֵּלֵכוּ לְמַעַן תִּחְיוּן וְטוֹב לָכֶם וְהַאֲרַכְתֶּם יָמִים בָּאָרֶץ אֲשֶׁר
ו א תִּירָשׁוּן׃ וְזֹאת הַמִּצְוָה הַחֻקִּים וְהַמִּשְׁפָּטִים אֲשֶׁר צִוָּה יהוה אֱלֹהֵיכֶם
לְלַמֵּד אֶתְכֶם לַעֲשׂוֹת בָּאָרֶץ אֲשֶׁר אַתֶּם עֹבְרִים שָׁמָּה לְרִשְׁתָּהּ׃
ב לְמַעַן תִּירָא אֶת־יהוה אֱלֹהֶיךָ לִשְׁמֹר אֶת־כָּל־חֻקֹּתָיו וּמִצְוֹתָיו
אֲשֶׁר אָנֹכִי מְצַוֶּךָּ אַתָּה וּבִנְךָ וּבֶן־בִּנְךָ כֹּל יְמֵי חַיֶּיךָ וּלְמַעַן יַאֲרִכֻן
ג יָמֶיךָ׃ וְשָׁמַעְתָּ יִשְׂרָאֵל וְשָׁמַרְתָּ לַעֲשׂוֹת אֲשֶׁר יִיטַב לְךָ וַאֲשֶׁר

in a land flowing with milk and with honey, as the LORD, the God of your
ancestors, promised you.
4 5 Listen, Israel: the LORD our God – the LORD is one.[19] You shall love the
LORD your God with all your heart, with all your soul, and with all your
6 might. Let these words that I charge you with today remain impressed upon
7 your heart. Teach them to your children, speaking of them when you sit at
home and when you travel on the way, when you lie down and when you
8 rise. Bind them as a sign upon your hand, and have them as an emblem
9 between your eyes. Write them on the doorposts of your houses and on your
10 gates. When the LORD your God brings you into the land that he
swore to your ancestors Avraham, Yitzḥak, and Yaakov that He would give
11 to you, a land with great and goodly towns you did not build, houses full
of all good things that you did not provide, hewn cisterns you did not hew,
and vineyards and olive groves that you did not plant – and you eat and are
12 satisfied, take care that you do not forget the LORD who brought you out of
13 Egypt, out of the house of slaves. It is the LORD your God you must revere,
14 Him you must serve, and only by His name that you must swear. Do not
15 walk after other gods, after gods of the peoples around you, for the LORD
your God in your midst demands absolute loyalty. The anger of the LORD
your God would burn against you and He would annihilate you from the face
16 of the earth. Do not test the LORD your God as you tested Him at
17 Masa.[20] Be very vigilant to keep the commandments of the LORD your God,
18 and the testimonies and decrees with which He has charged you. Do what
is right and what is good in the LORD's eyes, so that it may go well with you,
and you may go in and take possession of the good land that the LORD swore
19 to your ancestors to give you, driving out all your enemies before you, as the
20 LORD promised. And in the future, when your child asks you, 'What
is the meaning of the testimonies, decrees, and laws that the LORD our God
21 has commanded you?' tell him, 'We were slaves to Pharaoh in Egypt, but the
22 LORD brought us out of Egypt with a mighty hand. Before our eyes the LORD
sent great and awesome signs and wonders against Egypt and Pharaoh and
23 his whole household. And He freed us from there, to bring us in and give us
24 the land that He promised on oath to our ancestors. The LORD commanded
us to keep all these decrees, to revere the LORD our God, so that we might
25 always prosper; to keep us alive, as we are today. And if we carefully keep all
this command before the LORD our God, as He has charged us, this will be
7 1 our righteousness.' When the LORD your God brings you into the
land that you are about to enter and possess, when you drive out many nations
before you – the Hittites, Girgashites, Amorites, Canaanites, Perizzites, Hivites,
and Jebusites, seven nations larger and stronger than you – and the LORD
2 your God gives them over to you and you defeat them, you must utterly
destroy them. Make no covenant with them and grant them no mercy. Do not

19 | There is only one God. The Hebrew could equally be translated "Listen, Israel, the LORD is our God, the LORD alone," stressing Israel's exclusive loyalty to God.

20 | See Exodus 17:1–7.

תִּרְבּוּן מְאֹד כַּאֲשֶׁר דִּבֶּר יְהוָה אֱלֹהֵי אֲבֹתֶיךָ לָךְ אֶרֶץ זָבַת חָלָב
וּדְבָשׁ׃
ד ה שְׁמַע יִשְׂרָאֵל יְהוָה אֱלֹהֵינוּ יְהוָה ׀ אֶחָד׃ וְאָהַבְתָּ אֵת יְהוָה ו ששי
ו אֱלֹהֶיךָ בְּכָל־לְבָבְךָ וּבְכָל־נַפְשְׁךָ וּבְכָל־מְאֹדֶךָ׃ וְהָיוּ הַדְּבָרִים
ז הָאֵלֶּה אֲשֶׁר אָנֹכִי מְצַוְּךָ הַיּוֹם עַל־לְבָבֶךָ׃ וְשִׁנַּנְתָּם לְבָנֶיךָ וְדִבַּרְתָּ
ח בָּם בְּשִׁבְתְּךָ בְּבֵיתֶךָ וּבְלֶכְתְּךָ בַדֶּרֶךְ וּבְשָׁכְבְּךָ וּבְקוּמֶךָ׃ וּקְשַׁרְתָּם
ט לְאוֹת עַל־יָדֶךָ וְהָיוּ לְטֹטָפֹת בֵּין עֵינֶיךָ׃ וּכְתַבְתָּם עַל־מְזֻזוֹת בֵּיתֶךָ
י וּבִשְׁעָרֶיךָ׃ וְהָיָה כִּי־יְבִיאֲךָ ׀ יְהוָה אֱלֹהֶיךָ אֶל־הָאָרֶץ אֲשֶׁר
נִשְׁבַּע לַאֲבֹתֶיךָ לְאַבְרָהָם לְיִצְחָק וּלְיַעֲקֹב לָתֶת לָךְ עָרִים גְּדֹלֹת
יא וְטֹבֹת אֲשֶׁר לֹא־בָנִיתָ׃ וּבָתִּים מְלֵאִים כָּל־טוּב אֲשֶׁר לֹא־מִלֵּאתָ וּבֹרֹת
חֲצוּבִים אֲשֶׁר לֹא־חָצַבְתָּ כְּרָמִים וְזֵיתִים אֲשֶׁר לֹא־נָטָעְתָּ וְאָכַלְתָּ
יב וְשָׂבָעְתָּ׃ הִשָּׁמֶר לְךָ פֶּן־תִּשְׁכַּח אֶת־יְהוָה אֲשֶׁר הוֹצִיאֲךָ מֵאֶרֶץ מִצְרַיִם
יג מִבֵּית עֲבָדִים׃ אֶת־יְהוָה אֱלֹהֶיךָ תִּירָא וְאֹתוֹ תַעֲבֹד וּבִשְׁמוֹ תִּשָּׁבֵעַ׃
יד לֹא תֵלְכוּן אַחֲרֵי אֱלֹהִים אֲחֵרִים מֵאֱלֹהֵי הָעַמִּים אֲשֶׁר סְבִיבוֹתֵיכֶם׃
טו כִּי אֵל קַנָּא יְהוָה אֱלֹהֶיךָ בְּקִרְבֶּךָ פֶּן־יֶחֱרֶה אַף־יְהוָה אֱלֹהֶיךָ בָּךְ
טז וְהִשְׁמִידְךָ מֵעַל פְּנֵי הָאֲדָמָה׃ לֹא תְנַסּוּ אֶת־יְהוָה אֱלֹהֵיכֶם
יז כַּאֲשֶׁר נִסִּיתֶם בַּמַּסָּה׃ שָׁמוֹר תִּשְׁמְרוּן אֶת־מִצְוֺת יְהוָה אֱלֹהֵיכֶם
יח וְעֵדֹתָיו וְחֻקָּיו אֲשֶׁר צִוָּךְ׃ וְעָשִׂיתָ הַיָּשָׁר וְהַטּוֹב בְּעֵינֵי יְהוָה לְמַעַן
יִיטַב לָךְ וּבָאתָ וְיָרַשְׁתָּ אֶת־הָאָרֶץ הַטֹּבָה אֲשֶׁר־נִשְׁבַּע יְהוָה לַאֲבֹתֶיךָ׃
יט כ לַהֲדֹף אֶת־כָּל־אֹיְבֶיךָ מִפָּנֶיךָ כַּאֲשֶׁר דִּבֶּר יְהוָה׃ כִּי־יִשְׁאָלְךָ
בִנְךָ מָחָר לֵאמֹר מָה הָעֵדֹת וְהַחֻקִּים וְהַמִּשְׁפָּטִים אֲשֶׁר צִוָּה יְהוָה
כא אֱלֹהֵינוּ אֶתְכֶם׃ וְאָמַרְתָּ לְבִנְךָ עֲבָדִים הָיִינוּ לְפַרְעֹה בְּמִצְרָיִם וַיֹּצִיאֵנוּ
כב יְהוָה מִמִּצְרַיִם בְּיָד חֲזָקָה׃ וַיִּתֵּן יְהוָה אוֹתֹת וּמֹפְתִים גְּדֹלִים וְרָעִים ׀
כג בְּמִצְרַיִם בְּפַרְעֹה וּבְכָל־בֵּיתוֹ לְעֵינֵינוּ׃ וְאוֹתָנוּ הוֹצִיא מִשָּׁם לְמַעַן
כד הָבִיא אֹתָנוּ לָתֶת לָנוּ אֶת־הָאָרֶץ אֲשֶׁר נִשְׁבַּע לַאֲבֹתֵינוּ׃ וַיְצַוֵּנוּ יְהוָה
לַעֲשׂוֹת אֶת־כָּל־הַחֻקִּים הָאֵלֶּה לְיִרְאָה אֶת־יְהוָה אֱלֹהֵינוּ לְטוֹב לָנוּ
כה כָּל־הַיָּמִים לְחַיֹּתֵנוּ כְּהַיּוֹם הַזֶּה׃ וּצְדָקָה תִּהְיֶה־לָּנוּ כִּי־נִשְׁמֹר לַעֲשׂוֹת
ז א אֶת־כָּל־הַמִּצְוָה הַזֹּאת לִפְנֵי יְהוָה אֱלֹהֵינוּ כַּאֲשֶׁר צִוָּנוּ׃ כִּי שביעי
יְבִיאֲךָ יְהוָה אֱלֹהֶיךָ אֶל־הָאָרֶץ אֲשֶׁר־אַתָּה בָא־שָׁמָּה לְרִשְׁתָּהּ וְנָשַׁל
גּוֹיִם־רַבִּים ׀ מִפָּנֶיךָ הַחִתִּי וְהַגִּרְגָּשִׁי וְהָאֱמֹרִי וְהַכְּנַעֲנִי וְהַפְּרִזִּי וְהַחִוִּי
ב וְהַיְבוּסִי שִׁבְעָה גוֹיִם רַבִּים וַעֲצוּמִים מִמֶּךָּ׃ וּנְתָנָם יְהוָה אֱלֹהֶיךָ
לְפָנֶיךָ וְהִכִּיתָם הַחֲרֵם תַּחֲרִים אֹתָם לֹא־תִכְרֹת לָהֶם בְּרִית וְלֹא

3 intermarry with them; do not give your daughters to their sons in marriage or
4 take their daughters for your sons. For they will turn your children away from
walking after Me, and bring them to serve other gods. The LORD's anger will
5 burn against you, and He will quickly destroy you. Instead, this is what you
must do to them: tear down their altars, smash their worship pillars, cut down
6 their sacred trees,[21] and burn their idols with fire. For you are a holy people to
the LORD your God. The LORD your God has chosen you, of all the peoples
7 on earth, to be His treasured people. It is not because you were more numerous than other peoples that the LORD desired you and chose you, for you are
8 the smallest of all peoples. It was because of the love the LORD had for you,
because of the oath He kept, that He swore to your ancestors, that the LORD
freed you with a mighty hand, and redeemed you from the house of slaves,
9 from the grip of Pharaoh, king of Egypt. Know therefore that only the LORD
your God is God, the faithful God who keeps His covenant and the love to a
thousand generations of those who love Him and keep His commandments,
10 and who instantly repays with destruction those who reject Him, requiting
11 them in a moment. Therefore, carefully keep the command – the decrees and
the laws – that I am charging you with today.
12 If, indeed, you heed these laws, always vigilant to keep them, the LORD your EKEV
God will keep with you the covenant and the love He forged on oath with your
13 ancestors. He will love you, bless you, and multiply you. He will bless the fruit
of your womb and the fruit of your land, your grain and wine and oil, the calves
of your herds and the lambs of your flock, in the land that He swore to your
14 ancestors to give you. You shall be blessed above all other peoples, and no male
15 or female among you or your livestock will be barren or childless. The LORD
will keep you free from all sickness. All the terrible diseases of Egypt that you
knew, He will not inflict upon you, but He will lay them upon all those who
16 hate you. You shall devour all the peoples that the LORD your God is giving
over to you. Do not show them pity, and do not worship their gods – for that
17 would be a snare to you. You might say to yourself, 'These nations are
18 more numerous than I. How can I possibly dispossess them?' Do not be afraid
of them. Remember well what the LORD your God did to Pharaoh and to all
19 Egypt. Your own eyes saw the great trials, the signs and wonders, the mighty
hand and the arm stretched forth, with which the LORD your God brought you
20 out. The LORD your God will do the same to all the peoples you fear. The LORD
your God will send the hornet,[22] too, against them until even the survivors who
21 hide from you are destroyed. Do not be terrified of them, for the LORD your
22 God, a great and awesome God, is in your midst. The LORD your God will drive
out these nations before you, little by little. You may not put an end to them at
23 once, or the wild beasts would become too numerous for you.[23] But the LORD
your God will give them over to you, throwing them into great panic until

---

21 | Literally "Asheras": trees, wooden posts, or images representing the Canaanite fertility goddess Ashera.

22 | This may refer to actual hornets or to a different means of destruction.

23 | That is, the desolation would allow a proliferation of wild animals.

ג תְחָנֵּם: וְלֹא תִתְחַתֵּן בָּם בִּתְּךָ לֹא־תִתֵּן לִבְנוֹ וּבִתּוֹ לֹא־תִקַּח לִבְנֶךָ:
ד כִּי־יָסִיר אֶת־בִּנְךָ מֵאַחֲרַי וְעָבְדוּ אֱלֹהִים אֲחֵרִים וְחָרָה אַף־יהוה
ה בָּכֶם וְהִשְׁמִידְךָ מַהֵר: כִּי אִם־כֹּה תַעֲשׂוּ לָהֶם מִזְבְּחֹתֵיהֶם תִּתֹּצוּ
וּמַצֵּבֹתָם תְּשַׁבֵּרוּ וַאֲשֵׁירֵהֶם תְּגַדֵּעוּן וּפְסִילֵיהֶם תִּשְׂרְפוּן בָּאֵשׁ:
ו כִּי עַם קָדוֹשׁ אַתָּה לַיהוה אֱלֹהֶיךָ בְּךָ בָּחַר ׀ יהוה אֱלֹהֶיךָ לִהְיוֹת
ז לוֹ לְעַם סְגֻלָּה מִכֹּל הָעַמִּים אֲשֶׁר עַל־פְּנֵי הָאֲדָמָה: לֹא מֵרֻבְּכֶם
מִכָּל־הָעַמִּים חָשַׁק יהוה בָּכֶם וַיִּבְחַר בָּכֶם כִּי־אַתֶּם הַמְעַט מִכָּל־
ח הָעַמִּים: כִּי מֵאַהֲבַת יהוה אֶתְכֶם וּמִשָּׁמְרוֹ אֶת־הַשְּׁבֻעָה אֲשֶׁר נִשְׁבַּע
לַאֲבֹתֵיכֶם הוֹצִיא יהוה אֶתְכֶם בְּיָד חֲזָקָה וַיִּפְדְּךָ מִבֵּית עֲבָדִים מִיַּד
ט פַּרְעֹה מֶלֶךְ־מִצְרָיִם: וְיָדַעְתָּ כִּי־יהוה אֱלֹהֶיךָ הוּא הָאֱלֹהִים הָאֵל מפטיר
הַנֶּאֱמָן שֹׁמֵר הַבְּרִית וְהַחֶסֶד לְאֹהֲבָיו וּלְשֹׁמְרֵי מִצְוֺתָו לְאֶלֶף דּוֹר:
י וּמְשַׁלֵּם לְשֹׂנְאָיו אֶל־פָּנָיו לְהַאֲבִידוֹ לֹא יְאַחֵר לְשֹׂנְאוֹ אֶל־פָּנָיו יְשַׁלֶּם־
יא לוֹ: וְשָׁמַרְתָּ אֶת־הַמִּצְוָה וְאֶת־הַחֻקִּים וְאֶת־הַמִּשְׁפָּטִים אֲשֶׁר אָנֹכִי
מְצַוְּךָ הַיּוֹם לַעֲשׂוֹתָם:
יב וְהָיָה ׀ עֵקֶב תִּשְׁמְעוּן אֵת הַמִּשְׁפָּטִים הָאֵלֶּה וּשְׁמַרְתֶּם וַעֲשִׂיתֶם ז עקב
אֹתָם וְשָׁמַר יהוה אֱלֹהֶיךָ לְךָ אֶת־הַבְּרִית וְאֶת־הַחֶסֶד אֲשֶׁר נִשְׁבַּע
יג לַאֲבֹתֶיךָ: וַאֲהֵבְךָ וּבֵרַכְךָ וְהִרְבֶּךָ וּבֵרַךְ פְּרִי־בִטְנְךָ וּפְרִי־אַדְמָתֶךָ
דְּגָנְךָ וְתִירֹשְׁךָ וְיִצְהָרֶךָ שְׁגַר־אֲלָפֶיךָ וְעַשְׁתְּרֹת צֹאנֶךָ עַל הָאֲדָמָה
יד אֲשֶׁר־נִשְׁבַּע לַאֲבֹתֶיךָ לָתֶת לָךְ: בָּרוּךְ תִּהְיֶה מִכָּל־הָעַמִּים לֹא־יִהְיֶה
טו בְךָ עָקָר וַעֲקָרָה וּבִבְהֶמְתֶּךָ: וְהֵסִיר יהוה מִמְּךָ כָּל־חֹלִי וְכָל־מַדְוֵי
מִצְרַיִם הָרָעִים אֲשֶׁר יָדַעְתָּ לֹא יְשִׂימָם בָּךְ וּנְתָנָם בְּכָל־שֹׂנְאֶיךָ:
טז וְאָכַלְתָּ אֶת־כָּל־הָעַמִּים אֲשֶׁר יהוה אֱלֹהֶיךָ נֹתֵן לָךְ לֹא־תָחוֹס עֵינְךָ
יז עֲלֵיהֶם וְלֹא תַעֲבֹד אֶת־אֱלֹהֵיהֶם כִּי־מוֹקֵשׁ הוּא לָךְ: כִּי
יח תֹאמַר בִּלְבָבְךָ רַבִּים הַגּוֹיִם הָאֵלֶּה מִמֶּנִּי אֵיכָה אוּכַל לְהוֹרִישָׁם: לֹא
תִירָא מֵהֶם זָכֹר תִּזְכֹּר אֵת אֲשֶׁר־עָשָׂה יהוה אֱלֹהֶיךָ לְפַרְעֹה וּלְכָל־
יט מִצְרָיִם: הַמַּסֹּת הַגְּדֹלֹת אֲשֶׁר־רָאוּ עֵינֶיךָ וְהָאֹתֹת וְהַמֹּפְתִים וְהַיָּד
הַחֲזָקָה וְהַזְּרֹעַ הַנְּטוּיָה אֲשֶׁר הוֹצִאֲךָ יהוה אֱלֹהֶיךָ כֵּן־יַעֲשֶׂה יהוה
כ אֱלֹהֶיךָ לְכָל־הָעַמִּים אֲשֶׁר־אַתָּה יָרֵא מִפְּנֵיהֶם: וְגַם אֶת־הַצִּרְעָה
כא יְשַׁלַּח יהוה אֱלֹהֶיךָ בָּם עַד־אֲבֹד הַנִּשְׁאָרִים וְהַנִּסְתָּרִים מִפָּנֶיךָ: לֹא
כב תַעֲרֹץ מִפְּנֵיהֶם כִּי־יהוה אֱלֹהֶיךָ בְּקִרְבֶּךָ אֵל גָּדוֹל וְנוֹרָא: וְנָשַׁל יהוה
אֱלֹהֶיךָ אֶת־הַגּוֹיִם הָאֵל מִפָּנֶיךָ מְעַט מְעָט לֹא תוּכַל כַּלֹּתָם מַהֵר פֶּן־
כג תִּרְבֶּה עָלֶיךָ חַיַּת הַשָּׂדֶה: וּנְתָנָם יהוה אֱלֹהֶיךָ לְפָנֶיךָ וְהָמָם מְהוּמָה

24 they are destroyed. He will give their kings over to your hands and you shall
wipe out their name from under heaven. No one will be able to stand against
25 you, until you have destroyed them. You shall burn the images of their gods
with fire. Do not covet the silver or gold on them and take it for yourself,
because you would be ensnared by it, for it is abhorrent to the LORD your
26 God. Do not bring any abhorrent thing into your house, or you, like it, will
be set apart for utter destruction. Detest and abhor it utterly, for it is set apart
for utter destruction.
8 1 Take care to keep every command that I am charging you with on this day,
so that you may survive and thrive, go in, and take possession of the land that
2 the LORD swore He would give to your ancestors. Remember that the LORD
your God has led you through all this journey of forty years in the wilderness,
to humble you and to test you, and to know what was in your heart: to know
whether you would keep His commandments or whether you would fail to.
3 He humbled you by leaving you hungry, then feeding you manna, which neither you nor your ancestors had ever known – to teach you that one does not
live by bread alone, but by all that comes forth from the mouth of the LORD.
4 5 Your clothes did not wear out, nor did your feet swell these forty years. Know
then in your heart that just as a parent disciplines his child, so the LORD your
6 God disciplines you. And so keep the commandments of the LORD your God,
7 walking in His ways and revering Him. For the LORD your God is bringing
you into a good land, a land of streams and springs and deep waters gushing
8 out to the valleys and the hills, a land of wheat and barley, vines, fig trees and
9 pomegranates, a land of olive oil and honey, a land where bread will not be
scarce, where you will lack nothing, a land where the rocks are iron and where
10 you can hew bronze from her hills. And when you eat and are satisfied, you
11 shall bless the LORD your God for the good land that He has given you. Take
care not to forget the LORD your God, failing to keep His commandments,
12 laws, and decrees, with which I am charging you this day. Otherwise, when
you have eaten and been satisfied, and have built fine houses and lived in
13 them, when your herds and flocks have grown abundant, and your silver and
14 gold is abundant, and all that you have has grown abundant, your heart may
become proud, forgetting the LORD your God who brought you out of Egypt,
15 the house of slaves, who led you through the vast and terrifying wilderness,
an arid wasteland with venomous snakes and scorpions, who brought forth
16 water from flint rock for you, and fed you manna in the wilderness, something your ancestors did not know, to humble and to test you – so that in the
17 end it would be well for you. You might be tempted to say to yourself, 'My
18 power, the strength of my own hand, have brought me this great wealth.' But
remember the LORD your God, for it is He who gives you the power to do
great things, upholding the covenant that He swore to your ancestors, as He
is doing on this day.
19 If you do forget the LORD your God and follow other gods, serving and worshipping them, I solemnly warn you today that you will be altogether lost.

כד גְּדֹלָה עַד הִשָּׁמְדָם: וְנָתַן מַלְכֵיהֶם בְּיָדֶךָ וְהַאֲבַדְתָּ אֶת־שְׁמָם מִתַּחַת
כה הַשָּׁמָיִם לֹא־יִתְיַצֵּב אִישׁ בְּפָנֶיךָ עַד הִשְׁמִדְךָ אֹתָם: פְּסִילֵי אֱלֹהֵיהֶם
תִּשְׂרְפוּן בָּאֵשׁ לֹא־תַחְמֹד כֶּסֶף וְזָהָב עֲלֵיהֶם וְלָקַחְתָּ לָךְ פֶּן תִּוָּקֵשׁ בּוֹ
כו כִּי תוֹעֲבַת יהוה אֱלֹהֶיךָ הוּא: וְלֹא־תָבִיא תוֹעֵבָה אֶל־בֵּיתֶךָ וְהָיִיתָ
חֵרֶם כָּמֹהוּ שַׁקֵּץ | תְּשַׁקְּצֶנּוּ וְתַעֵב | תְּתַעֲבֶנּוּ כִּי־חֵרֶם הוּא:

ח א כָּל־הַמִּצְוָה אֲשֶׁר אָנֹכִי מְצַוְּךָ הַיּוֹם תִּשְׁמְרוּן לַעֲשׂוֹת לְמַעַן תִּחְיוּן
וּרְבִיתֶם וּבָאתֶם וִירִשְׁתֶּם אֶת־הָאָרֶץ אֲשֶׁר־נִשְׁבַּע יהוה לַאֲבֹתֵיכֶם:
ב וְזָכַרְתָּ אֶת־כָּל־הַדֶּרֶךְ אֲשֶׁר הוֹלִיכְךָ יהוה אֱלֹהֶיךָ זֶה אַרְבָּעִים שָׁנָה
בַּמִּדְבָּר לְמַעַן עַנֹּתְךָ לְנַסֹּתְךָ לָדַעַת אֶת־אֲשֶׁר בִּלְבָבְךָ הֲתִשְׁמֹר מִצְוֺתָו
ג אִם־לֹא: וַיְעַנְּךָ וַיַּרְעִבֶךָ וַיַּאֲכִלְךָ אֶת־הַמָּן אֲשֶׁר לֹא־יָדַעְתָּ וְלֹא יָדְעוּן
אֲבֹתֶיךָ לְמַעַן הוֹדִיעֲךָ כִּי לֹא עַל־הַלֶּחֶם לְבַדּוֹ יִחְיֶה הָאָדָם כִּי עַל־
ד כָּל־מוֹצָא פִי־יהוה יִחְיֶה הָאָדָם: שִׂמְלָתְךָ לֹא בָלְתָה מֵעָלֶיךָ וְרַגְלְךָ
ה לֹא בָצֵקָה זֶה אַרְבָּעִים שָׁנָה: וְיָדַעְתָּ עִם־לְבָבֶךָ כִּי כַּאֲשֶׁר יְיַסֵּר אִישׁ
ו אֶת־בְּנוֹ יהוה אֱלֹהֶיךָ מְיַסְּרֶךָּ: וְשָׁמַרְתָּ אֶת־מִצְוֺת יהוה אֱלֹהֶיךָ לָלֶכֶת
ז בִּדְרָכָיו וּלְיִרְאָה אֹתוֹ: כִּי יהוה אֱלֹהֶיךָ מְבִיאֲךָ אֶל־אֶרֶץ טוֹבָה אֶרֶץ
ח נַחֲלֵי מָיִם עֲיָנֹת וּתְהֹמֹת יֹצְאִים בַּבִּקְעָה וּבָהָר: אֶרֶץ חִטָּה וּשְׂעֹרָה
ט וְגֶפֶן וּתְאֵנָה וְרִמּוֹן אֶרֶץ־זֵית שֶׁמֶן וּדְבָשׁ: אֶרֶץ אֲשֶׁר לֹא בְמִסְכֵּנֻת
תֹּאכַל־בָּהּ לֶחֶם לֹא־תֶחְסַר כֹּל בָּהּ אֶרֶץ אֲשֶׁר אֲבָנֶיהָ בַרְזֶל וּמֵהֲרָרֶיהָ
י תַּחְצֹב נְחֹשֶׁת: וְאָכַלְתָּ וְשָׂבָעְתָּ וּבֵרַכְתָּ אֶת־יהוה אֱלֹהֶיךָ עַל־הָאָרֶץ
יא הַטֹּבָה אֲשֶׁר נָתַן־לָךְ: הִשָּׁמֶר לְךָ פֶּן־תִּשְׁכַּח אֶת־יהוה אֱלֹהֶיךָ לְבִלְתִּי שני
יב שְׁמֹר מִצְוֺתָיו וּמִשְׁפָּטָיו וְחֻקֹּתָיו אֲשֶׁר אָנֹכִי מְצַוְּךָ הַיּוֹם: פֶּן־תֹּאכַל
יג וְשָׂבָעְתָּ וּבָתִּים טֹבִים תִּבְנֶה וְיָשָׁבְתָּ: וּבְקָרְךָ וְצֹאנְךָ יִרְבְּיֻן וְכֶסֶף וְזָהָב
יד יִרְבֶּה־לָּךְ וְכֹל אֲשֶׁר־לְךָ יִרְבֶּה: וְרָם לְבָבֶךָ וְשָׁכַחְתָּ אֶת־יהוה אֱלֹהֶיךָ
טו הַמּוֹצִיאֲךָ מֵאֶרֶץ מִצְרַיִם מִבֵּית עֲבָדִים: הַמּוֹלִיכְךָ בַּמִּדְבָּר | הַגָּדֹל
וְהַנּוֹרָא נָחָשׁ | שָׂרָף וְעַקְרָב וְצִמָּאוֹן אֲשֶׁר אֵין־מָיִם הַמּוֹצִיא לְךָ מַיִם
טז מִצּוּר הַחַלָּמִישׁ: הַמַּאֲכִלְךָ מָן בַּמִּדְבָּר אֲשֶׁר לֹא־יָדְעוּן אֲבֹתֶיךָ לְמַעַן
יז עַנֹּתְךָ וּלְמַעַן נַסֹּתֶךָ לְהֵיטִבְךָ בְּאַחֲרִיתֶךָ: וְאָמַרְתָּ בִּלְבָבֶךָ כֹּחִי וְעֹצֶם
יח יָדִי עָשָׂה לִי אֶת־הַחַיִל הַזֶּה: וְזָכַרְתָּ אֶת־יהוה אֱלֹהֶיךָ כִּי הוּא הַנֹּתֵן
לְךָ כֹּחַ לַעֲשׂוֹת חָיִל לְמַעַן הָקִים אֶת־בְּרִיתוֹ אֲשֶׁר־נִשְׁבַּע לַאֲבֹתֶיךָ
כַּיּוֹם הַזֶּה:

יט וְהָיָה אִם־שָׁכֹחַ תִּשְׁכַּח אֶת־יהוה אֱלֹהֶיךָ וְהָלַכְתָּ אַחֲרֵי אֱלֹהִים
אֲחֵרִים וַעֲבַדְתָּם וְהִשְׁתַּחֲוִיתָ לָהֶם הַעִדֹתִי בָכֶם הַיּוֹם כִּי אָבֹד

20 Like the nations that the LORD will cause to die before you, so shall you be
lost, because you would not listen to the voice of the LORD your God.
9 1 Listen, Israel! You are now about to cross the Jordan, to go in and dispossess
nations larger and mightier than you, with great cities, fortified to high heaven.
2 The people are strong and lofty – Anakites. You know of them; you have heard
3 it said of them, 'Who can stand up against the descendants of Anak?' Know
then today that it is the LORD your God, who is crossing over before you like
a consuming fire: He will wipe them out, subduing them before you, so that
you may rapidly dispossess and destroy them, as the LORD promised you.
4 When the LORD your God drives them out before you, do not say to yourself,
'It is because of my righteousness that the LORD has brought me in to take
possession of this land.' The LORD is dispossessing these nations before you
5 because of their own wickedness. Not for your righteousness or rectitude are
you coming to take possession of their land; it is for these nations' wickedness that the LORD your God is driving them out before you and to fulfill the
promise that the LORD made on oath to your ancestors, Avraham, Yitzḥak,
6 and Yaakov. Know, then, that it is not for your righteousness that the LORD
your God is giving you this good land to possess, for you are a stiff-necked
7 people. Remember and never forget how you provoked the LORD your God
to fury in the wilderness. From the day you left Egypt until you arrived here,
8 you have always been rebellious against the LORD. At Ḥorev you provoked
the LORD to fury:[24] so incensed was the LORD that He was ready to destroy
9 you. I had ascended the mountain to receive the stone tablets, the tablets of
the Covenant the LORD made with you. I remained on the mountain forty
10 days and forty nights; I ate no bread and I drank no water. The LORD gave
me two stone tablets inscribed by the finger of God. And upon them were all
the words that the LORD had spoken to you at the mountain out of the fire,
11 on the day of that assembly. And when the forty days and forty nights were at
an end, the LORD gave me the two stone tablets, the tablets of the Covenant.
12 And then the LORD said to me, 'Get up; go down from here immediately,
because your people whom you brought from Egypt have acted disastrously;
how rapidly they strayed from the path that I commanded them to follow –
13 they have made a molten image for themselves.' The LORD said to me, 'I have
14 seen this people, and they are a stiff-necked people. Stand back from Me and
I will destroy them and erase their name from under the heavens, and I will
15 make of you a nation mightier and more numerous than they.' I turned and
went down from the mountain while it was still ablaze with fire, and the two
16 tablets of the Covenant were in my two hands. When I looked, I saw that you
had indeed sinned against the LORD your God. You had made for yourselves
a molten calf; you had strayed rapidly indeed from the path that the LORD
17 had commanded you to follow. So I took hold of the two tablets and flung
18 them from my hands, smashing them to pieces before your eyes. Then I threw
myself down before the LORD as before, for forty days and forty nights; I ate

24 | See Exodus, chapter 32.

כ תֹּאבֵדוּן: כַּגּוֹיִם אֲשֶׁר יְהוָה מַאֲבִיד מִפְּנֵיכֶם כֵּן תֹּאבֵדוּן עֵקֶב לֹא
תִשְׁמְעוּן בְּקוֹל יְהוָה אֱלֹהֵיכֶם:
ט א שְׁמַע יִשְׂרָאֵל אַתָּה עֹבֵר הַיּוֹם אֶת־הַיַּרְדֵּן לָבֹא לָרֶשֶׁת גּוֹיִם גְּדֹלִים ח
ב וַעֲצֻמִים מִמֶּךָּ עָרִים גְּדֹלֹת וּבְצֻרֹת בַּשָּׁמָיִם: עַם־גָּדוֹל וָרָם בְּנֵי עֲנָקִים
ג אֲשֶׁר אַתָּה יָדַעְתָּ וְאַתָּה שָׁמַעְתָּ מִי יִתְיַצֵּב לִפְנֵי בְּנֵי עֲנָק: וְיָדַעְתָּ הַיּוֹם
כִּי יְהוָה אֱלֹהֶיךָ הוּא־הָעֹבֵר לְפָנֶיךָ אֵשׁ אֹכְלָה הוּא יַשְׁמִידֵם וְהוּא
ד יַכְנִיעֵם לְפָנֶיךָ וְהוֹרַשְׁתָּם וְהַאֲבַדְתָּם מַהֵר כַּאֲשֶׁר דִּבֶּר יְהוָה לָךְ: אַל־ שלישי
תֹּאמַר בִּלְבָבְךָ בַּהֲדֹף יְהוָה אֱלֹהֶיךָ אֹתָם | מִלְּפָנֶיךָ לֵאמֹר בְּצִדְקָתִי
הֱבִיאַנִי יְהוָה לָרֶשֶׁת אֶת־הָאָרֶץ הַזֹּאת וּבְרִשְׁעַת הַגּוֹיִם הָאֵלֶּה
ה יְהוָה מוֹרִישָׁם מִפָּנֶיךָ: לֹא בְצִדְקָתְךָ וּבְיֹשֶׁר לְבָבְךָ אַתָּה בָא לָרֶשֶׁת
אֶת־אַרְצָם כִּי בְּרִשְׁעַת | הַגּוֹיִם הָאֵלֶּה יְהוָה אֱלֹהֶיךָ מוֹרִישָׁם מִפָּנֶיךָ
וּלְמַעַן הָקִים אֶת־הַדָּבָר אֲשֶׁר נִשְׁבַּע יְהוָה לַאֲבֹתֶיךָ לְאַבְרָהָם לְיִצְחָק
ו וּלְיַעֲקֹב: וְיָדַעְתָּ כִּי לֹא בְצִדְקָתְךָ יְהוָה אֱלֹהֶיךָ נֹתֵן לְךָ אֶת־הָאָרֶץ
ז הַטּוֹבָה הַזֹּאת לְרִשְׁתָּהּ כִּי עַם־קְשֵׁה־עֹרֶף אָתָּה: זְכֹר אַל־תִּשְׁכַּח אֵת
אֲשֶׁר־הִקְצַפְתָּ אֶת־יְהוָה אֱלֹהֶיךָ בַּמִּדְבָּר לְמִן־הַיּוֹם אֲשֶׁר־יָצָאתָ |
מֵאֶרֶץ מִצְרַיִם עַד־בֹּאֲכֶם עַד־הַמָּקוֹם הַזֶּה מַמְרִים הֱיִיתֶם עִם־יְהוָה:
ח וּבְחֹרֵב הִקְצַפְתֶּם אֶת־יְהוָה וַיִּתְאַנַּף יְהוָה בָּכֶם לְהַשְׁמִיד אֶתְכֶם:
ט בַּעֲלֹתִי הָהָרָה לָקַחַת לוּחֹת הָאֲבָנִים לוּחֹת הַבְּרִית אֲשֶׁר־כָּרַת יְהוָה
עִמָּכֶם וָאֵשֵׁב בָּהָר אַרְבָּעִים יוֹם וְאַרְבָּעִים לַיְלָה לֶחֶם לֹא אָכַלְתִּי
י וּמַיִם לֹא שָׁתִיתִי: וַיִּתֵּן יְהוָה אֵלַי אֶת־שְׁנֵי לוּחֹת הָאֲבָנִים כְּתֻבִים
בְּאֶצְבַּע אֱלֹהִים וַעֲלֵיהֶם כְּכָל־הַדְּבָרִים אֲשֶׁר דִּבֶּר יְהוָה עִמָּכֶם בָּהָר
יא מִתּוֹךְ הָאֵשׁ בְּיוֹם הַקָּהָל: וַיְהִי מִקֵּץ אַרְבָּעִים יוֹם וְאַרְבָּעִים לַיְלָה
יב נָתַן יְהוָה אֵלַי אֶת־שְׁנֵי לֻחֹת הָאֲבָנִים לֻחוֹת הַבְּרִית: וַיֹּאמֶר יְהוָה
אֵלַי קוּם רֵד מַהֵר מִזֶּה כִּי שִׁחֵת עַמְּךָ אֲשֶׁר הוֹצֵאתָ מִמִּצְרָיִם סָרוּ
יג מַהֵר מִן־הַדֶּרֶךְ אֲשֶׁר צִוִּיתִם עָשׂוּ לָהֶם מַסֵּכָה: וַיֹּאמֶר יְהוָה אֵלַי
יד לֵאמֹר רָאִיתִי אֶת־הָעָם הַזֶּה וְהִנֵּה עַם־קְשֵׁה־עֹרֶף הוּא: הֶרֶף מִמֶּנִּי
וְאַשְׁמִידֵם וְאֶמְחֶה אֶת־שְׁמָם מִתַּחַת הַשָּׁמָיִם וְאֶעֱשֶׂה אוֹתְךָ לְגוֹי־
טו עָצוּם וָרָב מִמֶּנּוּ: וָאֵפֶן וָאֵרֵד מִן־הָהָר וְהָהָר בֹּעֵר בָּאֵשׁ וּשְׁנֵי לוּחֹת
טז הַבְּרִית עַל שְׁתֵּי יָדָי: וָאֵרֶא וְהִנֵּה חֲטָאתֶם לַיהוָה אֱלֹהֵיכֶם עֲשִׂיתֶם
לָכֶם עֵגֶל מַסֵּכָה סַרְתֶּם מַהֵר מִן־הַדֶּרֶךְ אֲשֶׁר־צִוָּה יְהוָה אֶתְכֶם:
יז וָאֶתְפֹּשׂ בִּשְׁנֵי הַלֻּחֹת וָאַשְׁלִכֵם מֵעַל שְׁתֵּי יָדָי וָאֲשַׁבְּרֵם לְעֵינֵיכֶם:
יח וָאֶתְנַפַּל לִפְנֵי יְהוָה כָּרִאשֹׁנָה אַרְבָּעִים יוֹם וְאַרְבָּעִים לַיְלָה לֶחֶם

no bread and I drank no water, because of the great sin you had committed,
19 angering the LORD by doing what was evil in His eyes. I was terrified of
the LORD's blazing fury and rage against you, ready to destroy you. But the
20 LORD listened to me that time also. The LORD was so enraged with Aharon
that He was ready to destroy him, but I prayed for Aharon also at that time.
21 Then I took that thing of sin you had made, the calf, and burned it in fire. I
crushed it and ground it thoroughly, until it was as fine as dust, and I threw
22 the dust into a stream running down the mountain. At Tavera also,[25] and at
23 Masa[26] and Kivrot HaTaava,[27] you provoked the LORD. And when the LORD
sent you from Kadesh Barnea, saying, 'Go up and take possession of the
land that I have given you,' you rebelled against the command of the LORD
24 your God.[28] You did not have faith in Him and did not obey Him. You have
25 rebelled against the LORD as long as I have known you. I threw myself down
before the LORD, and as I lay prostrate those forty days and forty nights, when
26 the LORD had said He would destroy you, I prayed to the LORD – 'Lord GOD,'
I said, 'do not destroy the people, Your heritage, those whom You redeemed
in Your greatness and brought out of Egypt with a mighty hand. Remember
27 Your servants Avraham, Yitzḥak, and Yaakov; do not attend to the stubborn-
28 ness of this people, to their wickedness or sinfulness; otherwise the nation
from which You brought us will say, "It was because the LORD was unable
to bring them into the land that He promised them, and because He hated
29 them, that He took them out to kill them in the wilderness." But they are Your
people, Your possession, whom You freed by Your great power and Your arm
stretched forth.'

10 1 And then the LORD said to me, 'Carve two tablets of stone like the first, and
2 come up to Me on the mountain. Make, as well, a wooden ark. I will inscribe
upon these tablets the words that were on the first, which you smashed, and
3 you shall place them in the ark.' So I made an ark of acacia wood and carved
two tablets of stone like the first. I ascended the mountain with these two tab-
4 lets in my hand. And He inscribed on the tablets the same words as before, the
Ten Commandments that the LORD had proclaimed to you on the mountain
5 out of the fire on the day of the assembly; and the LORD gave them to me. I
turned, came down from the mountain, and put the tablets in the ark that I
6 had made. And there they have remained, as the LORD commanded me. And
the Israelites journeyed from Be'erot Benei Yaakan to Mosera. There Aharon
7 died and was buried. Elazar, his son, succeeded him as priest. From there
they journeyed to Gudgod, and from Gudgod to Yotvat, a region of flowing
8 streams. At that time the LORD set the tribe of Levi apart to carry the Ark
of the LORD's Covenant, to stand before the LORD to minister to Him, and
9 to give blessing in His name, as they do to this day. This is why the Levites
have no share or inheritance among their fellow Israelites. The LORD is their

---

25 | See Numbers 11:1–3.
26 | See Exodus 17:1–7.
27 | See Numbers 11:4–34.
28 | See above, 1:19–46.

לֹא אָכַלְתִּי וּמַיִם לֹא שָׁתִיתִי עַל כָּל־חַטַּאתְכֶם אֲשֶׁר חֲטָאתֶם לַעֲשׂוֹת
יט הָרַע בְּעֵינֵי יהוה לְהַכְעִיסוֹ: כִּי יָגֹרְתִּי מִפְּנֵי הָאַף וְהַחֵמָה אֲשֶׁר קָצַף
יהוה עֲלֵיכֶם לְהַשְׁמִיד אֶתְכֶם וַיִּשְׁמַע יהוה אֵלַי גַּם בַּפַּעַם הַהִוא:
כ וּבְאַהֲרֹן הִתְאַנַּף יהוה מְאֹד לְהַשְׁמִידוֹ וָאֶתְפַּלֵּל גַּם־בְּעַד אַהֲרֹן בָּעֵת
כא הַהִוא: וְאֶת־חַטַּאתְכֶם אֲשֶׁר־עֲשִׂיתֶם אֶת־הָעֵגֶל לָקַחְתִּי וָאֶשְׂרֹף
אֹתוֹ ׀ בָּאֵשׁ וָאֶכֹּת אֹתוֹ טָחוֹן הֵיטֵב עַד אֲשֶׁר־דַּק לְעָפָר וָאַשְׁלִךְ
כב אֶת־עֲפָרוֹ אֶל־הַנַּחַל הַיֹּרֵד מִן־הָהָר: וּבְתַבְעֵרָה וּבְמַסָּה וּבְקִבְרֹת
כג הַתַּאֲוָה מַקְצִפִים הֱיִיתֶם אֶת־יהוה: וּבִשְׁלֹחַ יהוה אֶתְכֶם מִקָּדֵשׁ
בַּרְנֵעַ לֵאמֹר עֲלוּ וּרְשׁוּ אֶת־הָאָרֶץ אֲשֶׁר נָתַתִּי לָכֶם וַתַּמְרוּ אֶת־
כד פִּי יהוה אֱלֹהֵיכֶם וְלֹא הֶאֱמַנְתֶּם לוֹ וְלֹא שְׁמַעְתֶּם בְּקֹלוֹ: מַמְרִים
כה הֱיִיתֶם עִם־יהוה מִיּוֹם דַּעְתִּי אֶתְכֶם: וָאֶתְנַפַּל לִפְנֵי יהוה אֵת־
אַרְבָּעִים הַיּוֹם וְאֶת־אַרְבָּעִים הַלַּיְלָה אֲשֶׁר הִתְנַפָּלְתִּי כִּי־אָמַר יהוה
כו לְהַשְׁמִיד אֶתְכֶם: וָאֶתְפַּלֵּל אֶל־יהוה וָאֹמַר אֲדֹנָי יֱהוִה אַל־תַּשְׁחֵת
עַמְּךָ וְנַחֲלָתְךָ אֲשֶׁר פָּדִיתָ בְּגָדְלֶךָ אֲשֶׁר־הוֹצֵאתָ מִמִּצְרַיִם בְּיָד חֲזָקָה:
כז זְכֹר לַעֲבָדֶיךָ לְאַבְרָהָם לְיִצְחָק וּלְיַעֲקֹב אַל־תֵּפֶן אֶל־קְשִׁי הָעָם הַזֶּה
כח וְאֶל־רִשְׁעוֹ וְאֶל־חַטָּאתוֹ: פֶּן־יֹאמְרוּ הָאָרֶץ אֲשֶׁר הוֹצֵאתָנוּ מִשָּׁם
מִבְּלִי יְכֹלֶת יהוה לַהֲבִיאָם אֶל־הָאָרֶץ אֲשֶׁר־דִּבֶּר לָהֶם וּמִשִּׂנְאָתוֹ
כט אוֹתָם הוֹצִיאָם לַהֲמִתָם בַּמִּדְבָּר: וְהֵם עַמְּךָ וְנַחֲלָתֶךָ אֲשֶׁר הוֹצֵאתָ
בְּכֹחֲךָ הַגָּדֹל וּבִזְרֹעֲךָ הַנְּטוּיָה:
י א בָּעֵת הַהִוא אָמַר יהוה אֵלַי פְּסָל־לְךָ שְׁנֵי־לוּחֹת אֲבָנִים כָּרִאשֹׁנִים ט רביעי
ב וַעֲלֵה אֵלַי הָהָרָה וְעָשִׂיתָ לְּךָ אֲרוֹן עֵץ: וְאֶכְתֹּב עַל־הַלֻּחֹת אֶת־
הַדְּבָרִים אֲשֶׁר הָיוּ עַל־הַלֻּחֹת הָרִאשֹׁנִים אֲשֶׁר שִׁבַּרְתָּ וְשַׂמְתָּם בָּאָרוֹן:
ג וָאַעַשׂ אֲרוֹן עֲצֵי שִׁטִּים וָאֶפְסֹל שְׁנֵי־לֻחֹת אֲבָנִים כָּרִאשֹׁנִים וָאַעַל
ד הָהָרָה וּשְׁנֵי הַלֻּחֹת בְּיָדִי: וַיִּכְתֹּב עַל־הַלֻּחֹת כַּמִּכְתָּב הָרִאשׁוֹן אֵת
עֲשֶׂרֶת הַדְּבָרִים אֲשֶׁר דִּבֶּר יהוה אֲלֵיכֶם בָּהָר מִתּוֹךְ הָאֵשׁ בְּיוֹם
ה הַקָּהָל וַיִּתְּנֵם יהוה אֵלָי: וָאֵפֶן וָאֵרֵד מִן־הָהָר וָאָשִׂם אֶת־הַלֻּחֹת
ו בָּאָרוֹן אֲשֶׁר עָשִׂיתִי וַיִּהְיוּ שָׁם כַּאֲשֶׁר צִוַּנִי יהוה: וּבְנֵי יִשְׂרָאֵל נָסְעוּ
מִבְּאֵרֹת בְּנֵי־יַעֲקָן מוֹסֵרָה שָׁם מֵת אַהֲרֹן וַיִּקָּבֵר שָׁם וַיְכַהֵן אֶלְעָזָר בְּנוֹ
ז תַּחְתָּיו: מִשָּׁם נָסְעוּ הַגֻּדְגֹּדָה וּמִן־הַגֻּדְגֹּדָה יָטְבָתָה אֶרֶץ נַחֲלֵי־מָיִם:
ח בָּעֵת הַהִוא הִבְדִּיל יהוה אֶת־שֵׁבֶט הַלֵּוִי לָשֵׂאת אֶת־אֲרוֹן בְּרִית־
ט יהוה לַעֲמֹד לִפְנֵי יהוה לְשָׁרְתוֹ וּלְבָרֵךְ בִּשְׁמוֹ עַד הַיּוֹם הַזֶּה: עַל־כֵּן
לֹא־הָיָה לְלֵוִי חֵלֶק וְנַחֲלָה עִם־אֶחָיו יהוה הוּא נַחֲלָתוֹ כַּאֲשֶׁר דִּבֶּר

10 inheritance, as the LORD your God promised them. I stayed on the mountain
forty days and forty nights, as I had the first time. And this time too, the LORD
11 listened to me; the LORD did not choose to destroy you. Then the LORD said
to me, 'Rise and resume your journey at the head of the people, so that they
may go in and take possession of the land that I swore to their ancestors to
give to them.'
12 So now, Israel, what does the LORD your God ask of you? Only this: to
revere the LORD your God, to walk in all His ways and love Him; to serve
13 the LORD your God with all your heart and all your soul, and to keep the
commandments and decrees of the LORD your God that I am commanding
14 you today, for your own good. Look: the heavens, even the highest heavens,
15 belong to the LORD your God, with the earth and all it contains. Yet it was
on your ancestors alone that the LORD set His heart in love, and it was you,
their descendants after them, that He chose among all the peoples, as He does
16 to this day. And so remove the hardness[29] of your heart, and be stiff-necked
17 no longer. For the LORD your God is God of gods and Lord of lords, the
great, mighty, and awesome God, who shows no partiality and accepts no
18 bribe, who executes justice for the orphan and the widow, and who loves the
19 stranger, giving him food and clothing. You too must love the stranger, for
20 you yourselves were strangers in the land of Egypt. Revere the LORD your
21 God and worship Him. Hold fast to Him and swear by His name. He is your
praise;[30] He is your God, who has done these great and awesome things for
22 you that your own eyes have seen. When your ancestors went down to Egypt,
they were but seventy souls. Now the LORD your God has made you as many
11 1 as the stars of the heavens. And so – love the LORD your God and keep His
charge: His decrees, His laws, and His commands through all your days.
2 Know today that it was not your children who knew or saw the LORD your
God's lesson – His greatness, His mighty hand, and His arm stretched forth,
3 the signs and the acts that He performed in Egypt against Pharaoh, Egypt's
4 king, and all his land; what He did to the Egyptian fighting force, their horses
and their chariots, how He made the Reed Sea's water flood over them as
5 they pursued you, so that the LORD destroyed them forever; what He did for
6 you in the wilderness until you came to this place; and what he did to Datan
and Aviram, sons of Eliav son of Reuven, in the midst of all Israel, how the
earth opened its mouth and swallowed them, their families, tents, and every
7 living thing in their households: it is your own eyes that have seen all these
8 immense acts, all that the LORD did. And so – keep all of this command with
which I charge you on this day, so that you may be empowered to go in and
9 take possession of the land that you are crossing over to possess, and so that
your years may be long in the land that the LORD swore to your ancestors to
give to them and their descendants, a land flowing with milk and with
10 honey. For the land that you are about to go into and take possession

---

29 | Literally "circumcise the foreskin."

30 | In other words, the proper object of your praise, or the source of your pride.

י יְהוָה אֱלֹהֶיךָ לוֹ: וְאָנֹכִי עָמַדְתִּי בָהָר כַּיָּמִים הָרִאשֹׁנִים אַרְבָּעִים יוֹם
וְאַרְבָּעִים לָיְלָה וַיִּשְׁמַע יְהוָה אֵלַי גַּם בַּפַּעַם הַהִוא לֹא־אָבָה יְהוָה
יא הַשְׁחִיתֶךָ: וַיֹּאמֶר יְהוָה אֵלַי קוּם לֵךְ לְמַסַּע לִפְנֵי הָעָם וְיָבֹאוּ וְיִירְשׁוּ
אֶת־הָאָרֶץ אֲשֶׁר־נִשְׁבַּעְתִּי לַאֲבֹתָם לָתֵת לָהֶם:
יב וְעַתָּה יִשְׂרָאֵל מָה יְהוָה אֱלֹהֶיךָ שֹׁאֵל מֵעִמָּךְ כִּי אִם־לְיִרְאָה אֶת־יְהוָה חמישי
אֱלֹהֶיךָ לָלֶכֶת בְּכָל־דְּרָכָיו וּלְאַהֲבָה אֹתוֹ וְלַעֲבֹד אֶת־יְהוָה אֱלֹהֶיךָ
יג בְּכָל־לְבָבְךָ וּבְכָל־נַפְשֶׁךָ: לִשְׁמֹר אֶת־מִצְוֺת יְהוָה וְאֶת־חֻקֹּתָיו
יד אֲשֶׁר אָנֹכִי מְצַוְּךָ הַיּוֹם לְטוֹב לָךְ: הֵן לַיהוָה אֱלֹהֶיךָ הַשָּׁמַיִם וּשְׁמֵי
טו הַשָּׁמָיִם הָאָרֶץ וְכָל־אֲשֶׁר־בָּהּ: רַק בַּאֲבֹתֶיךָ חָשַׁק יְהוָה לְאַהֲבָה
טז אוֹתָם וַיִּבְחַר בְּזַרְעָם אַחֲרֵיהֶם בָּכֶם מִכָּל־הָעַמִּים כַּיּוֹם הַזֶּה: וּמַלְתֶּם
יז אֵת עָרְלַת לְבַבְכֶם וְעָרְפְּכֶם לֹא תַקְשׁוּ עוֹד: כִּי יְהוָה אֱלֹהֵיכֶם הוּא
אֱלֹהֵי הָאֱלֹהִים וַאֲדֹנֵי הָאֲדֹנִים הָאֵל הַגָּדֹל הַגִּבֹּר וְהַנּוֹרָא אֲשֶׁר לֹא־
יח יִשָּׂא פָנִים וְלֹא יִקַּח שֹׁחַד: עֹשֶׂה מִשְׁפַּט יָתוֹם וְאַלְמָנָה וְאֹהֵב גֵּר לָתֶת
יט לוֹ לֶחֶם וְשִׂמְלָה: וַאֲהַבְתֶּם אֶת־הַגֵּר כִּי־גֵרִים הֱיִיתֶם בְּאֶרֶץ מִצְרָיִם:
כ כא אֶת־יְהוָה אֱלֹהֶיךָ תִּירָא אֹתוֹ תַעֲבֹד וּבוֹ תִדְבָּק וּבִשְׁמוֹ תִּשָּׁבֵעַ: הוּא
תְהִלָּתְךָ וְהוּא אֱלֹהֶיךָ אֲשֶׁר־עָשָׂה אִתְּךָ אֶת־הַגְּדֹלֹת וְאֶת־הַנּוֹרָאֹת
כב הָאֵלֶּה אֲשֶׁר רָאוּ עֵינֶיךָ: בְּשִׁבְעִים נֶפֶשׁ יָרְדוּ אֲבֹתֶיךָ מִצְרָיְמָה וְעַתָּה
יא א שָׂמְךָ יְהוָה אֱלֹהֶיךָ כְּכוֹכְבֵי הַשָּׁמַיִם לָרֹב: וְאָהַבְתָּ אֵת יְהוָה אֱלֹהֶיךָ
ב וְשָׁמַרְתָּ מִשְׁמַרְתּוֹ וְחֻקֹּתָיו וּמִשְׁפָּטָיו וּמִצְוֺתָיו כָּל־הַיָּמִים: וִידַעְתֶּם
הַיּוֹם כִּי ׀ לֹא אֶת־בְּנֵיכֶם אֲשֶׁר לֹא־יָדְעוּ וַאֲשֶׁר לֹא־רָאוּ אֶת־מוּסַר
ג יְהוָה אֱלֹהֵיכֶם אֶת־גָּדְלוֹ אֶת־יָדוֹ הַחֲזָקָה וּזְרֹעוֹ הַנְּטוּיָה: וְאֶת־אֹתֹתָיו
וְאֶת־מַעֲשָׂיו אֲשֶׁר עָשָׂה בְּתוֹךְ מִצְרָיִם לְפַרְעֹה מֶלֶךְ־מִצְרַיִם וּלְכָל־
ד אַרְצוֹ: וַאֲשֶׁר עָשָׂה לְחֵיל מִצְרַיִם לְסוּסָיו וּלְרִכְבּוֹ אֲשֶׁר הֵצִיף אֶת־
מֵי יַם־סוּף עַל־פְּנֵיהֶם בְּרָדְפָם אַחֲרֵיכֶם וַיְאַבְּדֵם יְהוָה עַד הַיּוֹם הַזֶּה:
ה ו וַאֲשֶׁר עָשָׂה לָכֶם בַּמִּדְבָּר עַד־בֹּאֲכֶם עַד־הַמָּקוֹם הַזֶּה: וַאֲשֶׁר עָשָׂה
לְדָתָן וְלַאֲבִירָם בְּנֵי אֱלִיאָב בֶּן־רְאוּבֵן אֲשֶׁר פָּצְתָה הָאָרֶץ אֶת־פִּיהָ
וַתִּבְלָעֵם וְאֶת־בָּתֵּיהֶם וְאֶת־אָהֳלֵיהֶם וְאֵת כָּל־הַיְקוּם אֲשֶׁר בְּרַגְלֵיהֶם
ז בְּקֶרֶב כָּל־יִשְׂרָאֵל: כִּי עֵינֵיכֶם הָרֹאֹת אֶת־כָּל־מַעֲשֵׂה יְהוָה הַגָּדֹל
ח אֲשֶׁר עָשָׂה: וּשְׁמַרְתֶּם אֶת־כָּל־הַמִּצְוָה אֲשֶׁר אָנֹכִי מְצַוְּךָ הַיּוֹם לְמַעַן
תֶּחֶזְקוּ וּבָאתֶם וִירִשְׁתֶּם אֶת־הָאָרֶץ אֲשֶׁר אַתֶּם עֹבְרִים שָׁמָּה
ט לְרִשְׁתָּהּ: וּלְמַעַן תַּאֲרִיכוּ יָמִים עַל־הָאֲדָמָה אֲשֶׁר נִשְׁבַּע יְהוָה
י לַאֲבֹתֵיכֶם לָתֵת לָהֶם וּלְזַרְעָם אֶרֶץ זָבַת חָלָב וּדְבָשׁ: כִּי י ששי

of is not like the land of Egypt you left behind, where you could sow your
11 seed and irrigate by foot as in a vegetable garden. The land that you are
crossing over to possess is a land of hills and valleys; it is watered by the sky's
12 rains. It is a land the LORD your God watches over; the eyes of the LORD your
13 God are always upon it, from the year's opening to its end. And if
you heed My commands, with which I charge you on this day, to love the
LORD your God and to serve Him with all your heart and with all your soul,
14 I will grants your land's rain in its season, the early and the late rain; you
15 shall gather in your grain, your wine, your oil. I will grant your fields grass
16 for your cattle, and you will eat and be satisfied. Be vigilant lest your heart
17 be seduced and you go astray and serve other gods and worship them. Then
the LORD's rage will blaze against you, and He will close the skies; there will
be no rain. The land will not yield its crops, and you will swiftly perish from
18 the good land that the LORD is giving you. Therefore set these words of
Mine upon your heart and upon your soul. Bind them as a sign upon your
19 hand, and have them as an emblem between your eyes. Teach them to your
children, speaking of them when you sit at home and when you travel on the
20 way, when you lie down and when you rise. Write them on the doorposts of
21 your house and on your gates, so that you and your children may live long
years in the land that the LORD swore to your ancestors to give to them for
22 as long as the sky endures above the land. If you carefully keep all
of this command with which I am charging you, loving the LORD your God,
23 walking in all His ways, and holding fast to Him, then the LORD will drive
all these nations out before you, and you will dispossess nations larger and
24 mightier than you. Every place where you set foot shall be yours. Your territory shall stretch from the wilderness to the Lebanon, from the Euphrates
25 River to the Western Sea.[31] No one will be able to stand against you. The
LORD your God will put the fear and dread of you over all the land you set
26 foot upon, just as He promised you. See this: I am setting before RE'EH
27 you on this day a blessing and a curse: the blessing, if you obey the com-
28 mandments of the LORD your God that I am commanding you today; and
the curse, if you do not obey the commandments of the LORD your God,
and instead stray from the way I am commanding you this day to follow, to
29 walk after other gods that you have not known. When the LORD
your God has brought you into the land that you are entering to possess,
you shall proclaim the blessing on Mount Gerizim and the curse on Mount
30 Eival.[32] They are across the Jordan, westward toward the setting sun, near the
Oaks of Moreh, in the territory of the Canaanites who live in the Arava, near

---

31 | The Mediterranean.

32 | See below, 27:11–26; Joshua 8:30–35.

הָאָרֶץ אֲשֶׁר אַתָּה בָא־שָׁמָּה לְרִשְׁתָּהּ לֹא כְאֶרֶץ מִצְרַיִם הִוא
אֲשֶׁר יְצָאתֶם מִשָּׁם אֲשֶׁר תִּזְרַע אֶת־זַרְעֲךָ וְהִשְׁקִיתָ בְרַגְלְךָ כְּגַן
יא הַיָּרָק׃ וְהָאָרֶץ אֲשֶׁר אַתֶּם עֹבְרִים שָׁמָּה לְרִשְׁתָּהּ אֶרֶץ הָרִים
יב וּבְקָעֹת לִמְטַר הַשָּׁמַיִם תִּשְׁתֶּה־מָּיִם׃ אֶרֶץ אֲשֶׁר־יְהוָה אֱלֹהֶיךָ דֹּרֵשׁ
אֹתָהּ תָּמִיד עֵינֵי יְהוָה אֱלֹהֶיךָ בָּהּ מֵרֵשִׁית הַשָּׁנָה וְעַד אַחֲרִית
יג שָׁנָה׃ וְהָיָה אִם־שָׁמֹעַ תִּשְׁמְעוּ אֶל־מִצְוֺתַי אֲשֶׁר אָנֹכִי
מְצַוֶּה אֶתְכֶם הַיּוֹם לְאַהֲבָה אֶת־יְהוָה אֱלֹהֵיכֶם וּלְעָבְדוֹ בְּכָל־לְבַבְכֶם
יד וּבְכָל־נַפְשְׁכֶם׃ וְנָתַתִּי מְטַר־אַרְצְכֶם בְּעִתּוֹ יוֹרֶה וּמַלְקוֹשׁ וְאָסַפְתָּ
טו דְגָנֶךָ וְתִירֹשְׁךָ וְיִצְהָרֶךָ׃ וְנָתַתִּי עֵשֶׂב בְּשָׂדְךָ לִבְהֶמְתֶּךָ וְאָכַלְתָּ וְשָׂבָעְתָּ׃
טז הִשָּׁמְרוּ לָכֶם פֶּן־יִפְתֶּה לְבַבְכֶם וְסַרְתֶּם וַעֲבַדְתֶּם אֱלֹהִים אֲחֵרִים
יז וְהִשְׁתַּחֲוִיתֶם לָהֶם׃ וְחָרָה אַף־יְהוָה בָּכֶם וְעָצַר אֶת־הַשָּׁמַיִם וְלֹא־
יִהְיֶה מָטָר וְהָאֲדָמָה לֹא תִתֵּן אֶת־יְבוּלָהּ וַאֲבַדְתֶּם מְהֵרָה מֵעַל הָאָרֶץ
יח הַטֹּבָה אֲשֶׁר יְהוָה נֹתֵן לָכֶם׃ וְשַׂמְתֶּם אֶת־דְּבָרַי אֵלֶּה עַל־לְבַבְכֶם
וְעַל־נַפְשְׁכֶם וּקְשַׁרְתֶּם אֹתָם לְאוֹת עַל־יֶדְכֶם וְהָיוּ לְטוֹטָפֹת בֵּין
יט עֵינֵיכֶם׃ וְלִמַּדְתֶּם אֹתָם אֶת־בְּנֵיכֶם לְדַבֵּר בָּם בְּשִׁבְתְּךָ בְּבֵיתֶךָ וּבְלֶכְתְּךָ
כ בַדֶּרֶךְ וּבְשָׁכְבְּךָ וּבְקוּמֶךָ׃ וּכְתַבְתָּם עַל־מְזוּזוֹת בֵּיתֶךָ וּבִשְׁעָרֶיךָ׃
כא לְמַעַן יִרְבּוּ יְמֵיכֶם וִימֵי בְנֵיכֶם עַל הָאֲדָמָה אֲשֶׁר נִשְׁבַּע יְהוָה לַאֲבֹתֵיכֶם
כב לָתֵת לָהֶם כִּימֵי הַשָּׁמַיִם עַל־הָאָרֶץ׃ כִּי אִם־שָׁמֹר תִּשְׁמְרוּן שביעי ומפטיר
אֶת־כָּל־הַמִּצְוָה הַזֹּאת אֲשֶׁר אָנֹכִי מְצַוֶּה אֶתְכֶם לַעֲשֹׂתָהּ לְאַהֲבָה
כג אֶת־יְהוָה אֱלֹהֵיכֶם לָלֶכֶת בְּכָל־דְּרָכָיו וּלְדָבְקָה־בוֹ׃ וְהוֹרִישׁ יְהוָה
אֶת־כָּל־הַגּוֹיִם הָאֵלֶּה מִלִּפְנֵיכֶם וִירִשְׁתֶּם גּוֹיִם גְּדֹלִים וַעֲצֻמִים מִכֶּם׃
כד כָּל־הַמָּקוֹם אֲשֶׁר תִּדְרֹךְ כַּף־רַגְלְכֶם בּוֹ לָכֶם יִהְיֶה מִן־הַמִּדְבָּר וְהַלְּבָנוֹן
כה מִן־הַנָּהָר נְהַר־פְּרָת וְעַד הַיָּם הָאַחֲרוֹן יִהְיֶה גְּבֻלְכֶם׃ לֹא־יִתְיַצֵּב אִישׁ
בִּפְנֵיכֶם פַּחְדְּכֶם וּמוֹרַאֲכֶם יִתֵּן ׀ יְהוָה אֱלֹהֵיכֶם עַל־פְּנֵי כָל־הָאָרֶץ
כו אֲשֶׁר תִּדְרְכוּ־בָהּ כַּאֲשֶׁר דִּבֶּר לָכֶם׃ רְאֵה אָנֹכִי נֹתֵן לִפְנֵיכֶם ראה
כז הַיּוֹם בְּרָכָה וּקְלָלָה׃ אֶת־הַבְּרָכָה אֲשֶׁר תִּשְׁמְעוּ אֶל־מִצְוֺת יְהוָה
כח אֱלֹהֵיכֶם אֲשֶׁר אָנֹכִי מְצַוֶּה אֶתְכֶם הַיּוֹם׃ וְהַקְּלָלָה אִם־לֹא תִשְׁמְעוּ
אֶל־מִצְוֺת יְהוָה אֱלֹהֵיכֶם וְסַרְתֶּם מִן־הַדֶּרֶךְ אֲשֶׁר אָנֹכִי מְצַוֶּה אֶתְכֶם
כט הַיּוֹם לָלֶכֶת אַחֲרֵי אֱלֹהִים אֲחֵרִים אֲשֶׁר לֹא־יְדַעְתֶּם׃ וְהָיָה
כִּי יְבִיאֲךָ יְהוָה אֱלֹהֶיךָ אֶל־הָאָרֶץ אֲשֶׁר־אַתָּה בָא־שָׁמָּה לְרִשְׁתָּהּ
וְנָתַתָּה אֶת־הַבְּרָכָה עַל־הַר גְּרִזִים וְאֶת־הַקְּלָלָה עַל־הַר עֵיבָל׃
ל הֲלֹא־הֵמָּה בְּעֵבֶר הַיַּרְדֵּן אַחֲרֵי דֶּרֶךְ מְבוֹא הַשֶּׁמֶשׁ בְּאֶרֶץ הַכְּנַעֲנִי

31 Gilgal. You are about to cross the Jordan, to go into and take possession of
the land that the Lord your God is giving you. When you have possession
32 of it and live there, you must be vigilant to keep all the decrees and laws that
12 1 I am setting before you on this day. These are the decrees and laws that you
must take care to keep in the land that the Lord, God of your ancestors, has
2 given you to possess for as long as you live on this earth. Demolish completely all the shrines where the nations you are about to dispossess served
their gods: on the high mountains, on the hills, and under every leafy tree.
3 Tear down their altars, smash their worship pillars, burn their sacred trees
with fire, and cut down the statues of their gods, obliterating their names
4 5 from that place. Do not make such things for the Lord your God; instead,
seek the place that the Lord your God will choose from among all your
6 tribes to set His name there, to be His dwelling. Go there, bringing your
burnt offerings and peace offerings, your tithes and your offerings, your
gifts in fulfillment of vows and your freewill offerings, and the firstborns of
7 your herds and flocks. There you and your families shall eat in the presence
of the Lord your God, rejoicing in all your endeavors in which the Lord
8 your God has granted blessing. Do not behave as we have been behaving
9 here, now, everyone doing what is right in his own eyes. For you have not
yet reached the resting place and inheritance that the Lord your God is
10 giving you. But you will cross the Jordan and live in the land that the Lord
your God is giving you as an inheritance. When He gives you rest from all
11 the enemies around you so that you are living in safety, then you shall bring
everything that I command you to the place that the Lord your God will
choose as a dwelling for His name: your burnt offerings and peace offerings,
your tithes and your offerings, and all the choice gifts that you commit by
12 vow to the Lord. And you shall rejoice before the Lord your God, along
with your sons and daughters, your male and female servants, and the Levites
13 living in your towns, for they have no share or inheritance with you. Take
14 care not to offer your burnt offerings in any place you may see. Only in the
place that the Lord will choose of one of your tribes – there you shall offer
15 your burnt offerings and there do all that I command you. Whenever you
desire, you may slaughter and eat meat in any of your towns, according to
the blessing that the Lord your God gives you. People both impure and
16 pure may eat of it, as they would of gazelle or of deer.[33] The blood, however,
17 you must not eat. Pour it out on the ground like water. You may not eat the
tithe of your grain, wine, and oil within your towns, or the firstlings of your
herds and flocks, or any of the gifts that you commit by vow, your freewill
18 offerings, or your gifts.[34] These you must eat in the presence of the Lord
your God at the place that the Lord your God will choose, along with your

33 | Wild animals not used for sacrifices at all.

34 | Various types of consecrated food and offerings. According to rabbinic tradition, this last term refers to first fruits.

לא הַיֹּשֵׁב בָּעֲרָבָה מוּל הַגִּלְגָּל אֵצֶל אֵלוֹנֵי מֹרֶה: כִּי אַתֶּם עֹבְרִים אֶת־
הַיַּרְדֵּן לָבֹא לָרֶשֶׁת אֶת־הָאָרֶץ אֲשֶׁר־יְהוָה אֱלֹהֵיכֶם נֹתֵן לָכֶם וִירִשְׁתֶּם
לב אֹתָהּ וִישַׁבְתֶּם־בָּהּ: וּשְׁמַרְתֶּם לַעֲשׂוֹת אֵת כָּל־הַחֻקִּים וְאֶת־
יב א הַמִּשְׁפָּטִים אֲשֶׁר אָנֹכִי נֹתֵן לִפְנֵיכֶם הַיּוֹם: אֵלֶּה הַחֻקִּים וְהַמִּשְׁפָּטִים
אֲשֶׁר תִּשְׁמְרוּן לַעֲשׂוֹת בָּאָרֶץ אֲשֶׁר נָתַן יְהוָה אֱלֹהֵי אֲבֹתֶיךָ לְךָ
ב לְרִשְׁתָּהּ כָּל־הַיָּמִים אֲשֶׁר־אַתֶּם חַיִּים עַל־הָאֲדָמָה: אַבֵּד תְּאַבְּדוּן
אֶת־כָּל־הַמְּקֹמוֹת אֲשֶׁר עָבְדוּ־שָׁם הַגּוֹיִם אֲשֶׁר אַתֶּם יֹרְשִׁים אֹתָם
אֶת־אֱלֹהֵיהֶם עַל־הֶהָרִים הָרָמִים וְעַל־הַגְּבָעוֹת וְתַחַת כָּל־עֵץ רַעֲנָן:
ג וְנִתַּצְתֶּם אֶת־מִזְבְּחֹתָם וְשִׁבַּרְתֶּם אֶת־מַצֵּבֹתָם וַאֲשֵׁרֵיהֶם תִּשְׂרְפוּן
בָּאֵשׁ וּפְסִילֵי אֱלֹהֵיהֶם תְּגַדֵּעוּן וְאִבַּדְתֶּם אֶת־שְׁמָם מִן־הַמָּקוֹם הַהוּא:
ד ה לֹא־תַעֲשׂוּן כֵּן לַיהוָה אֱלֹהֵיכֶם: כִּי אִם־אֶל־הַמָּקוֹם אֲשֶׁר־יִבְחַר יְהוָה
אֱלֹהֵיכֶם מִכָּל־שִׁבְטֵיכֶם לָשׂוּם אֶת־שְׁמוֹ שָׁם לְשִׁכְנוֹ תִדְרְשׁוּ וּבָאתָ
ו שָׁמָּה: וַהֲבֵאתֶם שָׁמָּה עֹלֹתֵיכֶם וְזִבְחֵיכֶם וְאֵת מַעְשְׂרֹתֵיכֶם וְאֵת
ז תְּרוּמַת יֶדְכֶם וְנִדְרֵיכֶם וְנִדְבֹתֵיכֶם וּבְכֹרֹת בְּקַרְכֶם וְצֹאנְכֶם: וַאֲכַלְתֶּם־
שָׁם לִפְנֵי יְהוָה אֱלֹהֵיכֶם וּשְׂמַחְתֶּם בְּכֹל מִשְׁלַח יֶדְכֶם אַתֶּם וּבָתֵּיכֶם
ח אֲשֶׁר בֵּרַכְךָ יְהוָה אֱלֹהֶיךָ: לֹא תַעֲשׂוּן כְּכֹל אֲשֶׁר אֲנַחְנוּ עֹשִׂים פֹּה
ט הַיּוֹם אִישׁ כָּל־הַיָּשָׁר בְּעֵינָיו: כִּי לֹא־בָאתֶם עַד־עָתָּה אֶל־הַמְּנוּחָה
י וְאֶל־הַנַּחֲלָה אֲשֶׁר־יְהוָה אֱלֹהֶיךָ נֹתֵן לָךְ: וַעֲבַרְתֶּם אֶת־הַיַּרְדֵּן
וִישַׁבְתֶּם בָּאָרֶץ אֲשֶׁר־יְהוָה אֱלֹהֵיכֶם מַנְחִיל אֶתְכֶם וְהֵנִיחַ לָכֶם מִכָּל־
יא אֹיְבֵיכֶם מִסָּבִיב וִישַׁבְתֶּם־בֶּטַח: וְהָיָה הַמָּקוֹם אֲשֶׁר־יִבְחַר יְהוָה שני
אֱלֹהֵיכֶם בּוֹ לְשַׁכֵּן שְׁמוֹ שָׁם שָׁמָּה תָבִיאוּ אֵת כָּל־אֲשֶׁר אָנֹכִי מְצַוֶּה
אֶתְכֶם עוֹלֹתֵיכֶם וְזִבְחֵיכֶם מַעְשְׂרֹתֵיכֶם וּתְרֻמַת יֶדְכֶם וְכֹל מִבְחַר
יב נִדְרֵיכֶם אֲשֶׁר תִּדְּרוּ לַיהוָה: וּשְׂמַחְתֶּם לִפְנֵי יְהוָה אֱלֹהֵיכֶם אַתֶּם
וּבְנֵיכֶם וּבְנֹתֵיכֶם וְעַבְדֵיכֶם וְאַמְהֹתֵיכֶם וְהַלֵּוִי אֲשֶׁר בְּשַׁעֲרֵיכֶם כִּי אֵין
יג לוֹ חֵלֶק וְנַחֲלָה אִתְּכֶם: הִשָּׁמֶר לְךָ פֶּן־תַּעֲלֶה עֹלֹתֶיךָ בְּכָל־מָקוֹם
יד אֲשֶׁר תִּרְאֶה: כִּי אִם־בַּמָּקוֹם אֲשֶׁר־יִבְחַר יְהוָה בְּאַחַד שְׁבָטֶיךָ שָׁם
טו תַּעֲלֶה עֹלֹתֶיךָ וְשָׁם תַּעֲשֶׂה כֹּל אֲשֶׁר אָנֹכִי מְצַוֶּךָּ: רַק בְּכָל־אַוַּת נַפְשְׁךָ
תִּזְבַּח ׀ וְאָכַלְתָּ בָשָׂר כְּבִרְכַּת יְהוָה אֱלֹהֶיךָ אֲשֶׁר נָתַן־לְךָ בְּכָל־שְׁעָרֶיךָ
טז הַטָּמֵא וְהַטָּהוֹר יֹאכְלֶנּוּ כַּצְּבִי וְכָאַיָּל: רַק הַדָּם לֹא תֹאכֵלוּ עַל־הָאָרֶץ
יז תִּשְׁפְּכֶנּוּ כַּמָּיִם: לֹא־תוּכַל לֶאֱכֹל בִּשְׁעָרֶיךָ מַעְשַׂר דְּגָנְךָ וְתִירֹשְׁךָ
וְיִצְהָרֶךָ וּבְכֹרֹת בְּקָרְךָ וְצֹאנֶךָ וְכָל־נְדָרֶיךָ אֲשֶׁר תִּדֹּר וְנִדְבֹתֶיךָ וּתְרוּמַת
יח יָדֶךָ: כִּי אִם־לִפְנֵי יְהוָה אֱלֹהֶיךָ תֹּאכְלֶנּוּ בַּמָּקוֹם אֲשֶׁר יִבְחַר יְהוָה

sons and daughters, your male and female servants, and the Levites living
in your towns, rejoicing in all your endeavors in the presence of the Lord
19 your God. Take care not to neglect the Levite in all your years living in your
20 land. When the Lord your God has enlarged your territory as He
has promised, and you say, 'I shall eat some meat,' because you have the urge
21 to eat it, you may eat meat whenever you desire it. If the place where the
Lord your God chooses to place His name is too distant from you, you may
slaughter animals from the herds and flocks the Lord has given you, as I have
commanded you. These you may eat within your towns whenever you wish.
22 Eat them as you would eat gazelle or a deer;[35] the impure may eat together
23 with the pure. But make sure that you do not eat the blood, for blood is life,
24 and you must not eat the life with the meat. Do not eat it; pour it out onto
25 the ground like water; do not eat it, so that all may be well for you and your
26 children after you, because you do what is right in the Lord's eyes. But your
sacred offerings and the gifts you commit by vow you must bring to the place
27 that the Lord will choose. Present your burnt offerings – the meat and the
blood – on the altar of the Lord your God. Of your other sacrifices, the blood
shall be poured out on the altar of the Lord your God, but you may eat the
28 meat. Take care to heed all these words that I command you today, so that it
may be well for you and for your children after you forever, because you will
29 be doing what is good and right in the Lord your God's eyes. When
the Lord your God has cut down before you the nations that you are about
to come to and dispossess, after you have dispossessed them and live in their
30 land, beware being tempted into their ways after they have been destroyed
before you. Do not inquire about their gods, saying, 'How did these nations
31 worship their gods? Let me do the same.' You must not worship the Lord
your God in their way, because they have done for their gods every abhorrent
thing that the Lord hates. They even offer their sons and daughters up in fire
13 1 to their gods. Take care: fulfill all that I command you. Neither add to it nor
subtract from it.
2 If a prophet rises up among you, or one who divines by dreams, and he tells
3 you of some sign or omen, and the sign or omen of which he spoke is realized – and he had said, 'Let us walk after other gods and worship them' – gods
4 you have not known – do not listen to the words of that prophet or dream
diviner. The Lord your God will be testing you, to know whether you really
5 love the Lord your God with all your heart and with all your soul. Follow
the Lord your God, revere Him, keep His commandments, and listen to His
6 voice. Worship Him; stay close to Him. And that prophet or dream diviner –
he shall be put to death for inciting rebellion against the Lord your God
who brought you out of Egypt and redeemed you from the house of slaves,

---

35 | See note on verse 15.

אֱלֹהֶיךָ בּוֹ אַתָּה וּבִנְךָ וּבִתֶּךָ וְעַבְדְּךָ וַאֲמָתֶךָ וְהַלֵּוִי אֲשֶׁר בִּשְׁעָרֶיךָ
יט וְשָׂמַחְתָּ לִפְנֵי יהוה אֱלֹהֶיךָ בְּכֹל מִשְׁלַח יָדֶךָ: הִשָּׁמֶר לְךָ פֶּן־תַּעֲזֹב
כ אֶת־הַלֵּוִי כָּל־יָמֶיךָ עַל־אַדְמָתֶךָ: כִּי־יַרְחִיב יהוה אֱלֹהֶיךָ יא
אֶת־גְּבֻלְךָ כַּאֲשֶׁר דִּבֶּר־לָךְ וְאָמַרְתָּ אֹכְלָה בָשָׂר כִּי־תְאַוֶּה נַפְשְׁךָ
כא לֶאֱכֹל בָּשָׂר בְּכָל־אַוַּת נַפְשְׁךָ תֹּאכַל בָּשָׂר: כִּי־יִרְחַק מִמְּךָ הַמָּקוֹם
אֲשֶׁר יִבְחַר יהוה אֱלֹהֶיךָ לָשׂוּם שְׁמוֹ שָׁם וְזָבַחְתָּ מִבְּקָרְךָ וּמִצֹּאנְךָ
אֲשֶׁר נָתַן יהוה לְךָ כַּאֲשֶׁר צִוִּיתִךָ וְאָכַלְתָּ בִּשְׁעָרֶיךָ בְּכֹל אַוַּת נַפְשֶׁךָ:
כב אַךְ כַּאֲשֶׁר יֵאָכֵל אֶת־הַצְּבִי וְאֶת־הָאַיָּל כֵּן תֹּאכְלֶנּוּ הַטָּמֵא וְהַטָּהוֹר
כג יַחְדָּו יֹאכְלֶנּוּ: רַק חֲזַק לְבִלְתִּי אֲכֹל הַדָּם כִּי הַדָּם הוּא הַנָּפֶשׁ וְלֹא־
כד תֹאכַל הַנֶּפֶשׁ עִם־הַבָּשָׂר: לֹא תֹּאכְלֶנּוּ עַל־הָאָרֶץ תִּשְׁפְּכֶנּוּ כַּמָּיִם:
כה לֹא תֹּאכְלֶנּוּ לְמַעַן יִיטַב לְךָ וּלְבָנֶיךָ אַחֲרֶיךָ כִּי־תַעֲשֶׂה הַיָּשָׁר בְּעֵינֵי
כו יהוה: רַק קָדָשֶׁיךָ אֲשֶׁר־יִהְיוּ לְךָ וּנְדָרֶיךָ תִּשָּׂא וּבָאתָ אֶל־הַמָּקוֹם
כז אֲשֶׁר־יִבְחַר יהוה: וְעָשִׂיתָ עֹלֹתֶיךָ הַבָּשָׂר וְהַדָּם עַל־מִזְבַּח יהוה אֱלֹהֶיךָ
כח וְדַם־זְבָחֶיךָ יִשָּׁפֵךְ עַל־מִזְבַּח יהוה אֱלֹהֶיךָ וְהַבָּשָׂר תֹּאכֵל: שְׁמֹר
וְשָׁמַעְתָּ אֵת כָּל־הַדְּבָרִים הָאֵלֶּה אֲשֶׁר אָנֹכִי מְצַוֶּךָּ לְמַעַן יִיטַב לְךָ
וּלְבָנֶיךָ אַחֲרֶיךָ עַד־עוֹלָם כִּי תַעֲשֶׂה הַטּוֹב וְהַיָּשָׁר בְּעֵינֵי יהוה
כט אֱלֹהֶיךָ: כִּי־יַכְרִית יהוה אֱלֹהֶיךָ אֶת־הַגּוֹיִם אֲשֶׁר אַתָּה שלישי
ל בָא־שָׁמָּה לָרֶשֶׁת אוֹתָם מִפָּנֶיךָ וְיָרַשְׁתָּ אֹתָם וְיָשַׁבְתָּ בְּאַרְצָם: הִשָּׁמֶר
לְךָ פֶּן־תִּנָּקֵשׁ אַחֲרֵיהֶם אַחֲרֵי הִשָּׁמְדָם מִפָּנֶיךָ וּפֶן־תִּדְרֹשׁ לֵאלֹהֵיהֶם
לֵאמֹר אֵיכָה יַעַבְדוּ הַגּוֹיִם הָאֵלֶּה אֶת־אֱלֹהֵיהֶם וְאֶעֱשֶׂה־כֵּן גַּם־אָנִי:
לא לֹא־תַעֲשֶׂה כֵן לַיהוה אֱלֹהֶיךָ כִּי כָל־תּוֹעֲבַת יהוה אֲשֶׁר שָׂנֵא עָשׂוּ
לֵאלֹהֵיהֶם כִּי גַם אֶת־בְּנֵיהֶם וְאֶת־בְּנֹתֵיהֶם יִשְׂרְפוּ בָאֵשׁ לֵאלֹהֵיהֶם:
יג א אֵת כָּל־הַדָּבָר אֲשֶׁר אָנֹכִי מְצַוֶּה אֶתְכֶם אֹתוֹ תִשְׁמְרוּ לַעֲשׂוֹת לֹא־
תֹסֵף עָלָיו וְלֹא תִגְרַע מִמֶּנּוּ:
ב ג כִּי־יָקוּם בְּקִרְבְּךָ נָבִיא אוֹ חֹלֵם חֲלוֹם וְנָתַן אֵלֶיךָ אוֹת אוֹ מוֹפֵת: וּבָא
הָאוֹת וְהַמּוֹפֵת אֲשֶׁר־דִּבֶּר אֵלֶיךָ לֵאמֹר נֵלְכָה אַחֲרֵי אֱלֹהִים אֲחֵרִים
ד אֲשֶׁר לֹא־יְדַעְתָּם וְנָעָבְדֵם: לֹא תִשְׁמַע אֶל־דִּבְרֵי הַנָּבִיא הַהוּא אוֹ
אֶל־חוֹלֵם הַחֲלוֹם הַהוּא כִּי מְנַסֶּה יהוה אֱלֹהֵיכֶם אֶתְכֶם לָדַעַת
הֲיִשְׁכֶם אֹהֲבִים אֶת־יהוה אֱלֹהֵיכֶם בְּכָל־לְבַבְכֶם וּבְכָל־נַפְשְׁכֶם:
ה אַחֲרֵי יהוה אֱלֹהֵיכֶם תֵּלֵכוּ וְאֹתוֹ תִירָאוּ וְאֶת־מִצְוֹתָיו תִּשְׁמֹרוּ וּבְקֹלוֹ
ו תִשְׁמָעוּ וְאֹתוֹ תַעֲבֹדוּ וּבוֹ תִדְבָּקוּן: וְהַנָּבִיא הַהוּא אוֹ חֹלֵם הַחֲלוֹם
הַהוּא יוּמָת כִּי דִבֶּר־סָרָה עַל־יהוה אֱלֹהֵיכֶם הַמּוֹצִיא אֶתְכֶם ׀ מֵאֶרֶץ

seeking to make you stray from the path the LORD your God commanded
7 you to walk. You must purge the evil from your midst. If anyone,
even your brother, your mother's son, or your own son or daughter, the
wife of your embrace, or the friend who is like your own self to you, secretly
tempts you: 'Let us go and worship other gods' – whom neither you nor your
8 ancestors have known, gods of the peoples around you, near or far, end to
9 end of the earth – do not acquiesce, do not listen to him, do not show him
10 pity or compassion, or cover up for him. You must put him to death. Your
own hand shall be first against him to kill him, and after yours, the hand of all
11 the people. Stone him to death for seeking to make you abandon the LORD
12 your God who brought you out of Egypt, the house of slaves. And all Israel
13 shall hear, and fear, and never commit such an evil again. If you hear
it said about one of the towns that the LORD your God is giving you to live
14 in that depraved men among you have gone out and led the people of the
town astray, saying, 'Let us go and worship other gods' – gods you have not
15 known – you shall seek the truth, investigate, and inquire thoroughly abroad.
If it is true and is confirmed that this abhorrent thing has been done among
16 you, you shall put the inhabitants of that town to the sword, destroying it and
17 everything in it; put even its animals to the sword. Gather all its spoil into
its public square, then burn with fire the town and all its spoil, in its entirety,
18 to the LORD your God. It shall be an eternal ruin, never to be rebuilt. Let
nothing that has been banned remain in your hands, so that the LORD may
turn away from His flaming rage, show you compassion, and in His compas-
19 sion increase your numbers, as He swore to your ancestors, for you will have
heeded the voice of the LORD your God, keeping all His commandments
that I am giving you today and doing what is right in the LORD your God's
14 1 eyes. You are children of the LORD your God. Do not lacerate your-
2 selves or make bald patches in the middle of your heads for the dead. For you
are a people sacred to the LORD your God. The LORD has chosen you of all
3 the peoples on earth to be to Him a treasured people. Do not eat
4 any abhorrent thing. These are the animals you may eat: the ox, the sheep,
5 the goat, the deer, the gazelle, the hartebeest, the ibex, the white antelope, the
6 wild ox, and the giraffe. You may eat any animal that has divided hoofs, fully
7 split in two, and chews the cud. Of those that chew the cud or that have a cleft
hoof, these you shall not eat: the camel, the hare, and the hyrax, because they
8 chew the cud but do not have a divided hoof – they are impure for you; and
the pig, because it has a divided hoof but does not chew the cud – it is impure
9 for you. You may not eat their flesh or touch their carcasses. These

מִצְרַיִם וְהַפֹּדְךָ מִבֵּית עֲבָדִים לְהַדִּיחֲךָ מִן־הַדֶּרֶךְ אֲשֶׁר צִוְּךָ יהוה
ז אֱלֹהֶיךָ לָלֶכֶת בָּהּ וּבִעַרְתָּ הָרָע מִקִּרְבֶּךָ: כִּי יְסִיתְךָ אָחִיךָ
בֶן־אִמֶּךָ אוֹ־בִנְךָ אוֹ־בִתְּךָ אוֹ ׀ אֵשֶׁת חֵיקֶךָ אוֹ רֵעֲךָ אֲשֶׁר כְּנַפְשְׁךָ
בַּסֵּתֶר לֵאמֹר נֵלְכָה וְנַעַבְדָה אֱלֹהִים אֲחֵרִים אֲשֶׁר לֹא יָדַעְתָּ אַתָּה
ח וַאֲבֹתֶיךָ: מֵאֱלֹהֵי הָעַמִּים אֲשֶׁר סְבִיבֹתֵיכֶם הַקְּרֹבִים אֵלֶיךָ אוֹ הָרְחֹקִים
ט מִמֶּךָּ מִקְצֵה הָאָרֶץ וְעַד־קְצֵה הָאָרֶץ: לֹא־תֹאבֶה לוֹ וְלֹא תִשְׁמַע אֵלָיו
י וְלֹא־תָחוֹס עֵינְךָ עָלָיו וְלֹא־תַחְמֹל וְלֹא־תְכַסֶּה עָלָיו: כִּי הָרֹג תַּהַרְגֶנּוּ
יא יָדְךָ תִּהְיֶה־בּוֹ בָרִאשׁוֹנָה לַהֲמִיתוֹ וְיַד כָּל־הָעָם בָּאַחֲרֹנָה: וּסְקַלְתּוֹ
בָאֲבָנִים וָמֵת כִּי בִקֵּשׁ לְהַדִּיחֲךָ מֵעַל יהוה אֱלֹהֶיךָ הַמּוֹצִיאֲךָ מֵאֶרֶץ
יב מִצְרַיִם מִבֵּית עֲבָדִים: וְכָל־יִשְׂרָאֵל יִשְׁמְעוּ וְיִרָאוּן וְלֹא־יוֹסִפוּ לַעֲשׂוֹת
יג כַּדָּבָר הָרָע הַזֶּה בְּקִרְבֶּךָ: כִּי־תִשְׁמַע בְּאַחַת עָרֶיךָ אֲשֶׁר
יד יהוה אֱלֹהֶיךָ נֹתֵן לְךָ לָשֶׁבֶת שָׁם לֵאמֹר: יָצְאוּ אֲנָשִׁים בְּנֵי־בְלִיַּעַל
מִקִּרְבֶּךָ וַיַּדִּיחוּ אֶת־יֹשְׁבֵי עִירָם לֵאמֹר נֵלְכָה וְנַעַבְדָה אֱלֹהִים אֲחֵרִים
טו אֲשֶׁר לֹא־יְדַעְתֶּם: וְדָרַשְׁתָּ וְחָקַרְתָּ וְשָׁאַלְתָּ הֵיטֵב וְהִנֵּה אֱמֶת נָכוֹן
טז הַדָּבָר נֶעֶשְׂתָה הַתּוֹעֵבָה הַזֹּאת בְּקִרְבֶּךָ: הַכֵּה תַכֶּה אֶת־יֹשְׁבֵי הָעִיר
הַהִוא לְפִי־חָרֶב הַחֲרֵם אֹתָהּ וְאֶת־כָּל־אֲשֶׁר־בָּהּ וְאֶת־בְּהֶמְתָּהּ לְפִי־
יז חָרֶב: וְאֶת־כָּל־שְׁלָלָהּ תִּקְבֹּץ אֶל־תּוֹךְ רְחֹבָהּ וְשָׂרַפְתָּ בָאֵשׁ אֶת־הָעִיר
וְאֶת־כָּל־שְׁלָלָהּ כָּלִיל לַיהוה אֱלֹהֶיךָ וְהָיְתָה תֵּל עוֹלָם לֹא תִבָּנֶה עוֹד:
יח וְלֹא־יִדְבַּק בְּיָדְךָ מְאוּמָה מִן־הַחֵרֶם לְמַעַן יָשׁוּב יהוה מֵחֲרוֹן אַפּוֹ
יט וְנָתַן־לְךָ רַחֲמִים וְרִחַמְךָ וְהִרְבֶּךָ כַּאֲשֶׁר נִשְׁבַּע לַאֲבֹתֶיךָ: כִּי תִשְׁמַע
בְּקוֹל יהוה אֱלֹהֶיךָ לִשְׁמֹר אֶת־כָּל־מִצְוֹתָיו אֲשֶׁר אָנֹכִי מְצַוְּךָ הַיּוֹם
יד א לַעֲשׂוֹת הַיָּשָׁר בְּעֵינֵי יהוה אֱלֹהֶיךָ: בָּנִים אַתֶּם לַיהוה יב רביעי
ב אֱלֹהֵיכֶם לֹא תִתְגֹּדְדוּ וְלֹא־תָשִׂימוּ קָרְחָה בֵּין עֵינֵיכֶם לָמֵת: כִּי עַם
קָדוֹשׁ אַתָּה לַיהוה אֱלֹהֶיךָ וּבְךָ בָּחַר יהוה לִהְיוֹת לוֹ לְעַם סְגֻלָּה מִכֹּל
ג הָעַמִּים אֲשֶׁר עַל־פְּנֵי הָאֲדָמָה: לֹא תֹאכַל כָּל־תּוֹעֵבָה:
ד ה זֹאת הַבְּהֵמָה אֲשֶׁר תֹּאכֵלוּ שׁוֹר שֵׂה כְשָׂבִים וְשֵׂה עִזִּים: אַיָּל וּצְבִי
ו וְיַחְמוּר וְאַקּוֹ וְדִישֹׁן וּתְאוֹ וָזָמֶר: וְכָל־בְּהֵמָה מַפְרֶסֶת פַּרְסָה וְשֹׁסַעַת
ז שֶׁסַע שְׁתֵּי פְרָסוֹת מַעֲלַת גֵּרָה בַּבְּהֵמָה אֹתָהּ תֹּאכֵלוּ: אַךְ אֶת־זֶה לֹא
תֹאכְלוּ מִמַּעֲלֵי הַגֵּרָה וּמִמַּפְרִיסֵי הַפַּרְסָה הַשְּׁסוּעָה אֶת־הַגָּמָל וְאֶת־
הָאַרְנֶבֶת וְאֶת־הַשָּׁפָן כִּי־מַעֲלֵה גֵרָה הֵמָּה וּפַרְסָה לֹא הִפְרִיסוּ טְמֵאִים
ח הֵם לָכֶם: וְאֶת־הַחֲזִיר כִּי־מַפְרִיס פַּרְסָה הוּא וְלֹא גֵרָה טָמֵא הוּא לָכֶם
ט מִבְּשָׂרָם לֹא תֹאכֵלוּ וּבְנִבְלָתָם לֹא תִגָּעוּ: אֶת־זֶה תֹּאכְלוּ

you may eat among the creatures of the water: anything that has fins and
10 scales. Whatever does not have fins and scales you may not eat; it is impure
11 12 for you. You may eat any pure species of bird. These you may not
13 eat:[36] the griffon vulture, the bearded vulture, the lappet-faced vulture, the
14 15 glede, the buzzard, the kite of any kind, any kind of raven, the ostrich, the
16 swift, the gull, any kind of sparrow hawk, the little owl, the short-eared owl,
17 18 the barn owl, the pelican, the vulture, the fish owl, the stork, any kind of
19 heron, the hoopoe, and the bat. All swarming, flying creatures are impure for
20 you; they may not be eaten. You may, however, eat any pure flying creature.
21 Do not eat any creature that has died of itself. Give it to the migrant in your
town to eat, or you may sell it to a foreigner. For you are a people holy to the
Lord your God.
22 Do not boil a kid in the milk of its mother. Each year, set aside a tenth of the
23 yield of all you have sown in the field. You shall eat the tithe of your grain,
wine, and oil, as well as the firstborn of your herds and flocks in the presence
of the Lord your God in the place that He will choose as a dwelling for His
24 name, so that you may learn to hold the Lord your God in awe always. But
if the distance is too great for you to carry them, because the place where the
Lord your God chooses to set His name is far from you and because the
25 Lord your God has blessed you, then you may exchange the tithe for money.
Wrap up the money in your hand, go to the place that the Lord your God will
26 choose, and spend the money on whatever you choose: cattle, sheep, wine,
strong drink, or whatever else you like. There you shall eat it in the presence
27 of the Lord your God, and rejoice together with your household. As for the
Levites living in your towns, do not neglect them, because they have no share
28 or inheritance as you do. At the end of every third year, bring out
29 the full tithe of your produce for that year, and leave it within your towns, so
that the Levites, who have no share or inheritance as you have, together with
the migrants, orphans, and widows in your towns, may come and eat and be
satisfied, so that the Lord your God will grant you blessing in all the work
15 1 of your hands. At the end of every seventh year, you shall grant a
2 remission of debts. This is how the remission is carried out: every creditor
shall relinquish any debt owed by his fellow. He shall not exact it from his
3 brother, his fellow, because the Lord's remission has been proclaimed. You
may require payment from a foreigner, but you must remit any debt owed to
4 you by a brother. There should be no poor among you, because the Lord will
bless you in the land that the Lord your God is giving you to possess as your
5 inheritance, if only you obey the Lord your God, staying vigilant to keep
6 all the command with which I am charging you this day. For the Lord your
God will bless you as He has promised you. You will lend to many nations,
but will not borrow. You will rule over many nations, and they will not rule
7 over you. If there be a poor person among your kinsfolk in any of

---

36 | The identities of many of these birds are subject to debate.

י מִכֹּל אֲשֶׁר בַּמָּיִם כֹּל אֲשֶׁר־לוֹ סְנַפִּיר וְקַשְׂקֶשֶׂת תֹּאכֵלוּ׃ וְכֹל אֲשֶׁר
יא אֵין־לוֹ סְנַפִּיר וְקַשְׂקֶשֶׂת לֹא תֹאכֵלוּ טָמֵא הוּא לָכֶם׃ כָּל־
יב צִפּוֹר טְהֹרָה תֹּאכֵלוּ׃ וְזֶה אֲשֶׁר לֹא־תֹאכְלוּ מֵהֶם הַנֶּשֶׁר וְהַפֶּרֶס
יג יד וְהָעָזְנִיָּה׃ וְהָרָאָה וְאֶת־הָאַיָּה וְהַדַּיָּה לְמִינָהּ׃ וְאֵת כָּל־עֹרֵב לְמִינוֹ׃
טו טז וְאֵת בַּת הַיַּעֲנָה וְאֶת־הַתַּחְמָס וְאֶת־הַשָּׁחַף וְאֶת־הַנֵּץ לְמִינֵהוּ׃ אֶת־
יז הַכּוֹס וְאֶת־הַיַּנְשׁוּף וְהַתִּנְשָׁמֶת׃ וְהַקָּאָת וְאֶת־הָרָחָמָה וְאֶת־הַשָּׁלָךְ׃
יח יט וְהַחֲסִידָה וְהָאֲנָפָה לְמִינָהּ וְהַדּוּכִיפַת וְהָעֲטַלֵּף׃ וְכֹל שֶׁרֶץ הָעוֹף טָמֵא
כ כא הוּא לָכֶם לֹא יֵאָכֵלוּ׃ כָּל־עוֹף טָהוֹר תֹּאכֵלוּ׃ לֹא־תֹאכְלוּ כָל־נְבֵלָה
לַגֵּר אֲשֶׁר־בִּשְׁעָרֶיךָ תִּתְּנֶנָּה וַאֲכָלָהּ אוֹ מָכֹר לְנָכְרִי כִּי עַם קָדוֹשׁ
אַתָּה לַיהוָה אֱלֹהֶיךָ לֹא־תְבַשֵּׁל גְּדִי בַּחֲלֵב אִמּוֹ׃
כב כג עַשֵּׂר תְּעַשֵּׂר אֵת כָּל־תְּבוּאַת זַרְעֶךָ הַיֹּצֵא הַשָּׂדֶה שָׁנָה שָׁנָה׃ וְאָכַלְתָּ חמישי
לִפְנֵי ׀ יְהוָה אֱלֹהֶיךָ בַּמָּקוֹם אֲשֶׁר־יִבְחַר לְשַׁכֵּן שְׁמוֹ שָׁם מַעְשַׂר דְּגָנְךָ
תִּירֹשְׁךָ וְיִצְהָרֶךָ וּבְכֹרֹת בְּקָרְךָ וְצֹאנֶךָ לְמַעַן תִּלְמַד לְיִרְאָה אֶת־יְהוָה
כד אֱלֹהֶיךָ כָּל־הַיָּמִים׃ וְכִי־יִרְבֶּה מִמְּךָ הַדֶּרֶךְ כִּי לֹא תוּכַל שְׂאֵתוֹ כִּי־
יִרְחַק מִמְּךָ הַמָּקוֹם אֲשֶׁר יִבְחַר יְהוָה אֱלֹהֶיךָ לָשׂוּם שְׁמוֹ שָׁם כִּי יְבָרֶכְךָ
כה יְהוָה אֱלֹהֶיךָ׃ וְנָתַתָּה בַּכָּסֶף וְצַרְתָּ הַכֶּסֶף בְּיָדְךָ וְהָלַכְתָּ אֶל־הַמָּקוֹם
כו אֲשֶׁר יִבְחַר יְהוָה אֱלֹהֶיךָ בּוֹ׃ וְנָתַתָּה הַכֶּסֶף בְּכֹל אֲשֶׁר־תְּאַוֶּה נַפְשְׁךָ
בַּבָּקָר וּבַצֹּאן וּבַיַּיִן וּבַשֵּׁכָר וּבְכֹל אֲשֶׁר תִּשְׁאָלְךָ נַפְשֶׁךָ וְאָכַלְתָּ שָּׁם
כז לִפְנֵי יְהוָה אֱלֹהֶיךָ וְשָׂמַחְתָּ אַתָּה וּבֵיתֶךָ׃ וְהַלֵּוִי אֲשֶׁר־בִּשְׁעָרֶיךָ לֹא
כח תַעַזְבֶנּוּ כִּי אֵין לוֹ חֵלֶק וְנַחֲלָה עִמָּךְ׃ מִקְצֵה ׀ שָׁלֹשׁ
שָׁנִים תּוֹצִיא אֶת־כָּל־מַעְשַׂר תְּבוּאָתְךָ בַּשָּׁנָה הַהִוא וְהִנַּחְתָּ בִּשְׁעָרֶיךָ׃
כט וּבָא הַלֵּוִי כִּי אֵין־לוֹ חֵלֶק וְנַחֲלָה עִמָּךְ וְהַגֵּר וְהַיָּתוֹם וְהָאַלְמָנָה אֲשֶׁר
בִּשְׁעָרֶיךָ וְאָכְלוּ וְשָׂבֵעוּ לְמַעַן יְבָרֶכְךָ יְהוָה אֱלֹהֶיךָ בְּכָל־מַעֲשֵׂה יָדְךָ
טו א ב אֲשֶׁר תַּעֲשֶׂה׃ מִקֵּץ שֶׁבַע־שָׁנִים תַּעֲשֶׂה שְׁמִטָּה׃ וְזֶה דְּבַר ששי
הַשְּׁמִטָּה שָׁמוֹט כָּל־בַּעַל מַשֵּׁה יָדוֹ אֲשֶׁר יַשֶּׁה בְּרֵעֵהוּ לֹא־יִגֹּשׂ אֶת־
ג רֵעֵהוּ וְאֶת־אָחִיו כִּי־קָרָא שְׁמִטָּה לַיהוָה׃ אֶת־הַנָּכְרִי תִּגֹּשׂ וַאֲשֶׁר
ד יִהְיֶה לְךָ אֶת־אָחִיךָ תַּשְׁמֵט יָדֶךָ׃ אֶפֶס כִּי לֹא יִהְיֶה־בְּךָ אֶבְיוֹן כִּי־בָרֵךְ
יְבָרֶכְךָ יְהוָה בָּאָרֶץ אֲשֶׁר יְהוָה אֱלֹהֶיךָ נֹתֵן־לְךָ נַחֲלָה לְרִשְׁתָּהּ׃
ה רַק אִם־שָׁמוֹעַ תִּשְׁמַע בְּקוֹל יְהוָה אֱלֹהֶיךָ לִשְׁמֹר לַעֲשׂוֹת אֶת־כָּל־
ו הַמִּצְוָה הַזֹּאת אֲשֶׁר אָנֹכִי מְצַוְּךָ הַיּוֹם׃ כִּי־יְהוָה אֱלֹהֶיךָ בֵּרַכְךָ כַּאֲשֶׁר
דִּבֶּר־לָךְ וְהַעֲבַטְתָּ גּוֹיִם רַבִּים וְאַתָּה לֹא תַעֲבֹט וּמָשַׁלְתָּ בְּגוֹיִם רַבִּים
ז וּבְךָ לֹא יִמְשֹׁלוּ׃ כִּי־יִהְיֶה בְךָ אֶבְיוֹן מֵאַחַד אַחֶיךָ בְּאַחַד יג

your towns in the land that the LORD your God is giving you, do not harden
8 your heart or close your hand toward your brother in need. Open your hand
9 generously and freely lend him enough to answer all his needs. Be vigilant:
let your heart not whisper a depraved thought: 'The seventh year, the year of
remission, is close,' making you miserly toward your brother in need, giving
him nothing. He will cry out to the LORD about you, and you will be held
10 guilty. Give to him generously, and do not let your heart begrudge it, for by
merit of this the LORD your God will grant you blessing in all your work and
11 all your hands' endeavors. There will never cease to be poor people in the
land. And so I command you: open your hand generously to your kinsmen,
12 your poor and needy, who share your land. If a fellow Hebrew, man
or woman, is sold to you, he or she shall work for you for six years; in the
13 seventh year you shall send him or her forth free. And when you send one
14 forth free, do not send him empty-handed. Provide for him liberally from
your flock, your threshing floor, and your winepress, giving him a share in the
15 things with which the LORD your God has blessed you. Remember: you were
a slave in Egypt and the LORD your God redeemed you; and so I give you this
16 command today. But if he says to you, 'I do not want to leave you' – because
17 he loves you and your household and he fares well with you, then take an awl
and put it through his ear into the door, and he will be your slave for all time;
18 you shall do the same with a female slave. Do not consider it a hardship when
you set him free, because for six years he has given you twice the service of a
hired laborer; and the LORD your God will bless you in all your work.
19 Every firstborn male among your herd and flock you shall consecrate to
the LORD your God. Do not work your firstborn ox or shear your firstborn
20 sheep. You and your household shall eat them year by year in the presence
21 of the LORD your God in the place that the LORD will choose. If the animal has a blemish, a serious blemish such as lameness or blindness, you
22 shall not sacrifice it to the LORD your God. The impure as well as the pure
23 among you shall eat it within your towns, as you would a gazelle or a deer. Its
blood, however, you must not eat. You must pour it out onto the ground like
water.

16 1 Observe the month of Aviv[37] by offering a Passover sacrifice to the LORD
your God; for in the month of Aviv the LORD your God brought you out of
2 Egypt by night.[38] You shall offer up the Passover sacrifice to the LORD your
God, from the flock and the herd, at the place that the LORD will choose as a
3 dwelling for His name. You must not eat anything leavened with it. For seven
days, eat unleavened bread – the bread of affliction – because you left Egypt in
haste. This is for you to remember the day you left Egypt all the days of your
4 life. For seven days no leaven shall be found with you in all your land. And
do not let any of the meat that you sacrificed on the evening of the first day
5 remain until morning. You may not slaughter the Passover sacrifice in any of

---

37 | See note on Exodus 13:14.

38 | According to Exodus 12:29–42, the Israelites began to leave Egypt at night.

שְׁעָרֶיךָ בְּאַרְצְךָ אֲשֶׁר־יְהוָה אֱלֹהֶיךָ נֹתֵן לָךְ לֹא תְאַמֵּץ אֶת־לְבָבְךָ
ח וְלֹא תִקְפֹּץ אֶת־יָדְךָ מֵאָחִיךָ הָאֶבְיוֹן׃ כִּי־פָתֹחַ תִּפְתַּח אֶת־יָדְךָ לוֹ
ט וְהַעֲבֵט תַּעֲבִיטֶנּוּ דֵּי מַחְסֹרוֹ אֲשֶׁר יֶחְסַר לוֹ׃ הִשָּׁמֶר לְךָ פֶּן־יִהְיֶה
דָבָר עִם־לְבָבְךָ בְלִיַּעַל לֵאמֹר קָרְבָה שְׁנַת־הַשֶּׁבַע שְׁנַת הַשְּׁמִטָּה
וְרָעָה עֵינְךָ בְּאָחִיךָ הָאֶבְיוֹן וְלֹא תִתֵּן לוֹ וְקָרָא עָלֶיךָ אֶל־יְהוָה וְהָיָה
י בְךָ חֵטְא׃ נָתוֹן תִּתֵּן לוֹ וְלֹא־יֵרַע לְבָבְךָ בְּתִתְּךָ לוֹ כִּי בִּגְלַל ׀ הַדָּבָר
יא הַזֶּה יְבָרֶכְךָ יְהוָה אֱלֹהֶיךָ בְּכָל־מַעֲשֶׂךָ וּבְכֹל מִשְׁלַח יָדֶךָ׃ כִּי לֹא־
יֶחְדַּל אֶבְיוֹן מִקֶּרֶב הָאָרֶץ עַל־כֵּן אָנֹכִי מְצַוְּךָ לֵאמֹר פָּתֹחַ תִּפְתַּח
יב אֶת־יָדְךָ לְאָחִיךָ לַעֲנִיֶּךָ וּלְאֶבְיֹנְךָ בְּאַרְצֶךָ׃ כִּי־יִמָּכֵר לְךָ
אָחִיךָ הָעִבְרִי אוֹ הָעִבְרִיָּה וַעֲבָדְךָ שֵׁשׁ שָׁנִים וּבַשָּׁנָה הַשְּׁבִיעִת
יג תְּשַׁלְּחֶנּוּ חָפְשִׁי מֵעִמָּךְ׃ וְכִי־תְשַׁלְּחֶנּוּ חָפְשִׁי מֵעִמָּךְ לֹא תְשַׁלְּחֶנּוּ
יד רֵיקָם׃ הַעֲנֵיק תַּעֲנִיק לוֹ מִצֹּאנְךָ וּמִגָּרְנְךָ וּמִיִּקְבֶךָ אֲשֶׁר בֵּרַכְךָ יְהוָה
טו אֱלֹהֶיךָ תִּתֶּן־לוֹ׃ וְזָכַרְתָּ כִּי עֶבֶד הָיִיתָ בְּאֶרֶץ מִצְרַיִם וַיִּפְדְּךָ יְהוָה
טז אֱלֹהֶיךָ עַל־כֵּן אָנֹכִי מְצַוְּךָ אֶת־הַדָּבָר הַזֶּה הַיּוֹם׃ וְהָיָה כִּי־יֹאמַר
אֵלֶיךָ לֹא אֵצֵא מֵעִמָּךְ כִּי אֲהֵבְךָ וְאֶת־בֵּיתֶךָ כִּי־טוֹב לוֹ עִמָּךְ׃
יז וְלָקַחְתָּ אֶת־הַמַּרְצֵעַ וְנָתַתָּה בְאָזְנוֹ וּבַדֶּלֶת וְהָיָה לְךָ עֶבֶד עוֹלָם
יח וְאַף לַאֲמָתְךָ תַּעֲשֶׂה־כֵּן׃ לֹא־יִקְשֶׁה בְעֵינֶךָ בְּשַׁלֵּחֲךָ אֹתוֹ חָפְשִׁי
מֵעִמָּךְ כִּי מִשְׁנֶה שְׂכַר שָׂכִיר עֲבָדְךָ שֵׁשׁ שָׁנִים וּבֵרַכְךָ יְהוָה אֱלֹהֶיךָ
בְּכֹל אֲשֶׁר תַּעֲשֶׂה׃
יט כָּל־הַבְּכוֹר אֲשֶׁר יִוָּלֵד בִּבְקָרְךָ וּבְצֹאנְךָ הַזָּכָר תַּקְדִּישׁ לַיהוָה אֱלֹהֶיךָ שביעי
כ לֹא תַעֲבֹד בִּבְכֹר שׁוֹרֶךָ וְלֹא תָגֹז בְּכוֹר צֹאנֶךָ׃ לִפְנֵי יְהוָה אֱלֹהֶיךָ
כא תֹאכְלֶנּוּ שָׁנָה בְשָׁנָה בַּמָּקוֹם אֲשֶׁר־יִבְחַר יְהוָה אַתָּה וּבֵיתֶךָ׃ וְכִי־
יִהְיֶה בוֹ מוּם פִּסֵּחַ אוֹ עִוֵּר כֹּל מוּם רָע לֹא תִזְבָּחֶנּוּ לַיהוָה אֱלֹהֶיךָ׃
כב כג בִּשְׁעָרֶיךָ תֹּאכְלֶנּוּ הַטָּמֵא וְהַטָּהוֹר יַחְדָּו כַּצְּבִי וְכָאַיָּל׃ רַק אֶת־דָּמוֹ
לֹא תֹאכֵל עַל־הָאָרֶץ תִּשְׁפְּכֶנּוּ כַּמָּיִם׃
טז א שָׁמוֹר אֶת־חֹדֶשׁ הָאָבִיב וְעָשִׂיתָ פֶּסַח לַיהוָה אֱלֹהֶיךָ כִּי בְּחֹדֶשׁ
ב הָאָבִיב הוֹצִיאֲךָ יְהוָה אֱלֹהֶיךָ מִמִּצְרַיִם לָיְלָה׃ וְזָבַחְתָּ פֶּסַח לַיהוָה
ג אֱלֹהֶיךָ צֹאן וּבָקָר בַּמָּקוֹם אֲשֶׁר יִבְחַר יְהוָה לְשַׁכֵּן שְׁמוֹ שָׁם׃ לֹא־
תֹאכַל עָלָיו חָמֵץ שִׁבְעַת יָמִים תֹּאכַל־עָלָיו מַצּוֹת לֶחֶם עֹנִי כִּי בְחִפָּזוֹן
יָצָאתָ מֵאֶרֶץ מִצְרַיִם לְמַעַן תִּזְכֹּר אֶת־יוֹם צֵאתְךָ מֵאֶרֶץ מִצְרַיִם כֹּל
ד יְמֵי חַיֶּיךָ׃ וְלֹא־יֵרָאֶה לְךָ שְׂאֹר בְּכָל־גְּבֻלְךָ שִׁבְעַת יָמִים וְלֹא־יָלִין
ה מִן־הַבָּשָׂר אֲשֶׁר תִּזְבַּח בָּעֶרֶב בַּיּוֹם הָרִאשׁוֹן לַבֹּקֶר׃ לֹא תוּכַל לִזְבֹּחַ

6 the towns that the LORD your God is giving you. Only at the place that the
LORD your God chooses as a dwelling for His name, there shall you slaughter
the Passover sacrifice in the evening; [39] at sunset,[40] at the time appointed to
7 leave Egypt, you shall cook and eat it at the place that the LORD your God will
8 choose, and on the following morning you may set out to your tents. For six
days you shall eat unleavened bread and, on the seventh day, you shall hold
9 an assembly for the LORD your God and perform no work. You shall
count seven weeks. At the time when you first put sickle to standing grain,
10 begin your count of seven weeks. And then celebrate the Festival of Weeks to
the LORD your God, bringing a freewill offering, tribute proportionate to the
11 blessing the LORD your God has granted you. And rejoice before the LORD
your God – you and your sons and daughters, your male and female slaves,
and the Levites living in your towns, together with the migrants, orphans,
and widows among you – at the place that the LORD your God will choose
12 as a dwelling for His name. Remember that you were a slave in Egypt, and so
take care to fulfill these decrees.
13 You shall keep the Festival of Tabernacles for seven days, after you have gath-
14 ered the produce from your threshing floor and winepress. Rejoice in your
festival, you and your sons and daughters; your male and female servants;
15 the Levites; and the migrants, orphans, and widows living in your towns. For
seven days, celebrate before the LORD your God at the place that the LORD
will choose, for the LORD your God will grant you blessing in all your harvest
16 and in all the work of your hands, and you shall be wholly joyful. Three times
a year, all the males among you shall appear before the LORD your God in the
place that He will choose: on the Festival of Unleavened Bread, the Festival
of Weeks, and the Festival of Tabernacles. They shall not appear before the
17 LORD empty-handed; each shall bring a gift, in keeping with the blessing that
18 the LORD your God has given you. Appoint judges and officials for SHOFETIM
your tribes in all the towns that the LORD your God is giving you, to govern
19 the people with equitable justice. Do not pervert justice or show partiality.
Do not take bribes, for bribes blind the eyes of the wise and subvert the cause
20 of the just. Pursue justice, only justice, so that you may live and possess the
21 land that the LORD your God is giving you. Do not plant a sacred
22 tree of any kind beside the altar that you make for the LORD your God, and
do not erect a worship pillar, for these are things that the LORD your God
17 1 hates.[41] Do not sacrifice an ox or a sheep that has any blemish, any
serious defect, to the LORD your God, for that to the LORD your God would
2 be abhorrent. If a man or woman living among you in one of the
towns the LORD your God is giving you is found doing what is evil in the
3 LORD your God's eyes, breaking His covenant by going off to serve or bow
to other gods – the sun or moon or any of the heavenly host, which I have

39 | See Exodus 12:33–34.

40 | As traditionally understood, the sacrifice is slaughtered before sunset and consumed after sunset; cf. Exodus 12:6–8.

41 | See 7:5 and the note there.

ו אֶת־הַפָּסַח בְּאַחַד שְׁעָרֶיךָ אֲשֶׁר־יהוה אֱלֹהֶיךָ נֹתֵן לָךְ: כִּי אִם־אֶל־
הַמָּקוֹם אֲשֶׁר־יִבְחַר יהוה אֱלֹהֶיךָ לְשַׁכֵּן שְׁמוֹ שָׁם תִּזְבַּח אֶת־הַפֶּסַח
ז בָּעָרֶב כְּבוֹא הַשֶּׁמֶשׁ מוֹעֵד צֵאתְךָ מִמִּצְרָיִם: וּבִשַּׁלְתָּ וְאָכַלְתָּ בַּמָּקוֹם
ח אֲשֶׁר יִבְחַר יהוה אֱלֹהֶיךָ בּוֹ וּפָנִיתָ בַבֹּקֶר וְהָלַכְתָּ לְאֹהָלֶיךָ: שֵׁשֶׁת
יָמִים תֹּאכַל מַצּוֹת וּבַיּוֹם הַשְּׁבִיעִי עֲצֶרֶת לַיהוה אֱלֹהֶיךָ לֹא תַעֲשֶׂה
ט מְלָאכָה: שִׁבְעָה שָׁבֻעֹת תִּסְפָּר־לָךְ מֵהָחֵל חֶרְמֵשׁ בַּקָּמָה
י תָּחֵל לִסְפֹּר שִׁבְעָה שָׁבֻעוֹת: וְעָשִׂיתָ חַג שָׁבֻעוֹת לַיהוה אֱלֹהֶיךָ
יא מִסַּת נִדְבַת יָדְךָ אֲשֶׁר תִּתֵּן כַּאֲשֶׁר יְבָרֶכְךָ יהוה אֱלֹהֶיךָ: וְשָׂמַחְתָּ
לִפְנֵי ׀ יהוה אֱלֹהֶיךָ אַתָּה וּבִנְךָ וּבִתֶּךָ וְעַבְדְּךָ וַאֲמָתֶךָ וְהַלֵּוִי אֲשֶׁר
בִּשְׁעָרֶיךָ וְהַגֵּר וְהַיָּתוֹם וְהָאַלְמָנָה אֲשֶׁר בְּקִרְבֶּךָ בַּמָּקוֹם אֲשֶׁר יִבְחַר
יב יהוה אֱלֹהֶיךָ לְשַׁכֵּן שְׁמוֹ שָׁם: וְזָכַרְתָּ כִּי־עֶבֶד הָיִיתָ בְּמִצְרָיִם וְשָׁמַרְתָּ
וְעָשִׂיתָ אֶת־הַחֻקִּים הָאֵלֶּה:
יג יד חַג הַסֻּכֹּת תַּעֲשֶׂה לְךָ שִׁבְעַת יָמִים בְּאָסְפְּךָ מִגָּרְנְךָ וּמִיִּקְבֶךָ: וְשָׂמַחְתָּ מפטיר
בְּחַגֶּךָ אַתָּה וּבִנְךָ וּבִתֶּךָ וְעַבְדְּךָ וַאֲמָתֶךָ וְהַלֵּוִי וְהַגֵּר וְהַיָּתוֹם וְהָאַלְמָנָה
טו אֲשֶׁר בִּשְׁעָרֶיךָ: שִׁבְעַת יָמִים תָּחֹג לַיהוה אֱלֹהֶיךָ בַּמָּקוֹם אֲשֶׁר־
יִבְחַר יהוה כִּי יְבָרֶכְךָ יהוה אֱלֹהֶיךָ בְּכֹל תְּבוּאָתְךָ וּבְכֹל מַעֲשֵׂה יָדֶיךָ
טז וְהָיִיתָ אַךְ שָׂמֵחַ: שָׁלוֹשׁ פְּעָמִים ׀ בַּשָּׁנָה יֵרָאֶה כָל־זְכוּרְךָ אֶת־פְּנֵי ׀
יהוה אֱלֹהֶיךָ בַּמָּקוֹם אֲשֶׁר יִבְחָר בְּחַג הַמַּצּוֹת וּבְחַג הַשָּׁבֻעוֹת וּבְחַג
יז הַסֻּכּוֹת וְלֹא יֵרָאֶה אֶת־פְּנֵי יהוה רֵיקָם: אִישׁ כְּמַתְּנַת יָדוֹ כְּבִרְכַּת
יח יהוה אֱלֹהֶיךָ אֲשֶׁר נָתַן־לָךְ: שֹׁפְטִים וְשֹׁטְרִים תִּתֶּן־לְךָ יד שפטים
בְּכָל־שְׁעָרֶיךָ אֲשֶׁר יהוה אֱלֹהֶיךָ נֹתֵן לְךָ לִשְׁבָטֶיךָ וְשָׁפְטוּ אֶת־הָעָם
יט מִשְׁפַּט־צֶדֶק: לֹא־תַטֶּה מִשְׁפָּט לֹא תַכִּיר פָּנִים וְלֹא־תִקַּח שֹׁחַד כִּי
כ הַשֹּׁחַד יְעַוֵּר עֵינֵי חֲכָמִים וִיסַלֵּף דִּבְרֵי צַדִּיקִם: צֶדֶק צֶדֶק תִּרְדֹּף לְמַעַן
כא תִּחְיֶה וְיָרַשְׁתָּ אֶת־הָאָרֶץ אֲשֶׁר־יהוה אֱלֹהֶיךָ נֹתֵן לָךְ: לֹא־
תִטַּע לְךָ אֲשֵׁרָה כָּל־עֵץ אֵצֶל מִזְבַּח יהוה אֱלֹהֶיךָ אֲשֶׁר תַּעֲשֶׂה־לָּךְ:
כב יז א וְלֹא־תָקִים לְךָ מַצֵּבָה אֲשֶׁר שָׂנֵא יהוה אֱלֹהֶיךָ: לֹא־תִזְבַּח
לַיהוה אֱלֹהֶיךָ שׁוֹר וָשֶׂה אֲשֶׁר יִהְיֶה בוֹ מוּם כֹּל דָּבָר רָע כִּי תוֹעֲבַת
ב יהוה אֱלֹהֶיךָ הוּא: כִּי־יִמָּצֵא בְקִרְבְּךָ בְּאַחַד שְׁעָרֶיךָ
אֲשֶׁר־יהוה אֱלֹהֶיךָ נֹתֵן לָךְ אִישׁ אוֹ־אִשָּׁה אֲשֶׁר יַעֲשֶׂה אֶת־הָרַע
ג בְּעֵינֵי יהוה־אֱלֹהֶיךָ לַעֲבֹר בְּרִיתוֹ: וַיֵּלֶךְ וַיַּעֲבֹד אֱלֹהִים אֲחֵרִים
וַיִּשְׁתַּחוּ לָהֶם וְלַשֶּׁמֶשׁ ׀ אוֹ לַיָּרֵחַ אוֹ לְכָל־צְבָא הַשָּׁמַיִם אֲשֶׁר לֹא־

4 forbidden – if you have been told of this or have heard about it, then you
must make thorough inquiry. If it is true and is confirmed that this abhorrent
5 deed has been done in Israel, then you shall take the man or woman who has
done this evil act out to the town gates and stone that man or that woman
6 to death. The accused shall be put to death only on the testimony of two or
three witnesses; no one shall be put to death on the evidence of one witness
7 alone. The hand of the witnesses shall be the first against him to kill him, and
after theirs, the hand of all the people. You must purge the evil from your
midst.
8 If a case is beyond your judgment, be it a conflict over bloodshed, over civil
claims or over injury – any dispute in your town courts – then you shall go up
9 to the place that the LORD your God will choose. There you shall approach
the Levitical priests or the judge who is in office at that time. Inquire of them
10 and they will give you the verdict. You must act in accordance with the ruling they give you from the place that the LORD will choose, taking care to
11 do exactly as they instruct you. You shall act in accord with the Law as they
interpret it for you and the judgment as they tell you, not deviating from their
12 declaration to the right or to the left. Should anyone act in wickedness, refusing to listen to the priest appointed to minister there to the LORD your God,
or the judge, that person shall be put to death. You must purge the evil from
13 Israel. All the people will hear and fear and will not act in such wickedness
14 again. When you enter the land that the LORD your God is giving
you, and have taken possession of it and settled in it, should you say, 'I will
15 set a king over me, like all the surrounding nations,' set over you a king whom
the LORD your God chooses. The king you set over you must be one of your
own people. You may not set a foreigner over you, who is not your brother.
16 Further, he must not acquire many horses for himself, he must not make the
people return to Egypt to acquire more horses, since the LORD has told you:
17 You must not go back that way again. He must not accumulate wives and let
his heart be led astray, nor should he amass large amounts of silver and gold.
18 As he presides upon his royal throne, he must inscribe a copy of this Law for
19 himself upon a scroll in the presence of the Levitical priests. It must always
be with him, and he shall read from it all the days of his life, so that he may
learn to revere the LORD his God, taking care to keep all the words of this
20 commandment and these decrees, not considering himself superior to his
people, or straying from the commandments to the right or to the left. Then
18 1 he and his descendants will reign long in the midst of Israel. The
Levitical priests, the whole tribe of Levi, will have no share or inheritance
2 with Israel. They will eat the LORD's fire offerings as their inheritance, but
will have no inheritance among their kinsfolk. The LORD is their inheritance,
3 as He has promised them. This shall be the priests' due from the

ד צִוִּיתִי: וְהֻגַּד־לְךָ וְשָׁמָעְתָּ וְדָרַשְׁתָּ הֵיטֵב וְהִנֵּה אֱמֶת נָכוֹן הַדָּבָר
ה נֶעֶשְׂתָה הַתּוֹעֵבָה הַזֹּאת בְּיִשְׂרָאֵל: וְהוֹצֵאתָ אֶת־הָאִישׁ הַהוּא אוֹ
אֶת־הָאִשָּׁה הַהִוא אֲשֶׁר עָשׂוּ אֶת־הַדָּבָר הָרָע הַזֶּה אֶל־שְׁעָרֶיךָ
ו אֶת־הָאִישׁ אוֹ אֶת־הָאִשָּׁה וּסְקַלְתָּם בָּאֲבָנִים וָמֵתוּ: עַל־פִּי | שְׁנַיִם
ז עֵדִים אוֹ שְׁלֹשָׁה עֵדִים יוּמַת הַמֵּת לֹא יוּמַת עַל־פִּי עֵד אֶחָד: יַד
הָעֵדִים תִּהְיֶה־בּוֹ בָרִאשֹׁנָה לַהֲמִיתוֹ וְיַד כָּל־הָעָם בָּאַחֲרֹנָה וּבִעַרְתָּ
הָרָע מִקִּרְבֶּךָ:
ח כִּי יִפָּלֵא מִמְּךָ דָבָר לַמִּשְׁפָּט בֵּין־דָּם | לְדָם בֵּין־דִּין לְדִין וּבֵין נֶגַע לָנֶגַע
דִּבְרֵי רִיבֹת בִּשְׁעָרֶיךָ וְקַמְתָּ וְעָלִיתָ אֶל־הַמָּקוֹם אֲשֶׁר יִבְחַר יהוה
ט אֱלֹהֶיךָ בּוֹ: וּבָאתָ אֶל־הַכֹּהֲנִים הַלְוִיִּם וְאֶל־הַשֹּׁפֵט אֲשֶׁר יִהְיֶה בַּיָּמִים
י הָהֵם וְדָרַשְׁתָּ וְהִגִּידוּ לְךָ אֵת דְּבַר הַמִּשְׁפָּט: וְעָשִׂיתָ עַל־פִּי הַדָּבָר
אֲשֶׁר יַגִּידוּ לְךָ מִן־הַמָּקוֹם הַהוּא אֲשֶׁר יִבְחַר יהוה וְשָׁמַרְתָּ לַעֲשׂוֹת
יא כְּכֹל אֲשֶׁר יוֹרוּךָ: עַל־פִּי הַתּוֹרָה אֲשֶׁר יוֹרוּךָ וְעַל־הַמִּשְׁפָּט אֲשֶׁר־
יֹאמְרוּ לְךָ תַּעֲשֶׂה לֹא תָסוּר מִן־הַדָּבָר אֲשֶׁר־יַגִּידוּ לְךָ יָמִין וּשְׂמֹאל:
יב וְהָאִישׁ אֲשֶׁר־יַעֲשֶׂה בְזָדוֹן לְבִלְתִּי שְׁמֹעַ אֶל־הַכֹּהֵן הָעֹמֵד לְשָׁרֶת
שָׁם אֶת־יהוה אֱלֹהֶיךָ אוֹ אֶל־הַשֹּׁפֵט וּמֵת הָאִישׁ הַהוּא וּבִעַרְתָּ הָרָע
יג יד מִיִּשְׂרָאֵל: וְכָל־הָעָם יִשְׁמְעוּ וְיִרָאוּ וְלֹא יְזִידוּן עוֹד: כִּי־ טו שני
תָבֹא אֶל־הָאָרֶץ אֲשֶׁר יהוה אֱלֹהֶיךָ נֹתֵן לָךְ וִירִשְׁתָּהּ וְיָשַׁבְתָּה בָּהּ
טו וְאָמַרְתָּ אָשִׂימָה עָלַי מֶלֶךְ כְּכָל־הַגּוֹיִם אֲשֶׁר סְבִיבֹתָי: שׂוֹם תָּשִׂים
עָלֶיךָ מֶלֶךְ אֲשֶׁר יִבְחַר יהוה אֱלֹהֶיךָ בּוֹ מִקֶּרֶב אַחֶיךָ תָּשִׂים עָלֶיךָ
טז מֶלֶךְ לֹא תוּכַל לָתֵת עָלֶיךָ אִישׁ נָכְרִי אֲשֶׁר לֹא־אָחִיךָ הוּא: רַק לֹא־
יַרְבֶּה־לּוֹ סוּסִים וְלֹא־יָשִׁיב אֶת־הָעָם מִצְרַיְמָה לְמַעַן הַרְבּוֹת סוּס
יז וַיהוה אָמַר לָכֶם לֹא תֹסִפוּן לָשׁוּב בַּדֶּרֶךְ הַזֶּה עוֹד: וְלֹא יַרְבֶּה־לּוֹ
יח נָשִׁים וְלֹא יָסוּר לְבָבוֹ וְכֶסֶף וְזָהָב לֹא יַרְבֶּה־לּוֹ מְאֹד: וְהָיָה כְשִׁבְתּוֹ
עַל כִּסֵּא מַמְלַכְתּוֹ וְכָתַב לוֹ אֶת־מִשְׁנֵה הַתּוֹרָה הַזֹּאת עַל־סֵפֶר
יט מִלִּפְנֵי הַכֹּהֲנִים הַלְוִיִּם: וְהָיְתָה עִמּוֹ וְקָרָא בוֹ כָּל־יְמֵי חַיָּיו לְמַעַן
יִלְמַד לְיִרְאָה אֶת־יהוה אֱלֹהָיו לִשְׁמֹר אֶת־כָּל־דִּבְרֵי הַתּוֹרָה הַזֹּאת
כ וְאֶת־הַחֻקִּים הָאֵלֶּה לַעֲשֹׂתָם: לְבִלְתִּי רוּם־לְבָבוֹ מֵאֶחָיו וּלְבִלְתִּי
סוּר מִן־הַמִּצְוָה יָמִין וּשְׂמֹאול לְמַעַן יַאֲרִיךְ יָמִים עַל־מַמְלַכְתּוֹ הוּא
יח א וּבָנָיו בְּקֶרֶב יִשְׂרָאֵל: לֹא־יִהְיֶה לַכֹּהֲנִים הַלְוִיִּם כָּל־שֵׁבֶט שלישי
ב לֵוִי חֵלֶק וְנַחֲלָה עִם־יִשְׂרָאֵל אִשֵּׁי יהוה וְנַחֲלָתוֹ יֹאכֵלוּן: וְנַחֲלָה לֹא־
ג יִהְיֶה־לּוֹ בְּקֶרֶב אֶחָיו יהוה הוּא נַחֲלָתוֹ כַּאֲשֶׁר דִּבֶּר־לוֹ: וְזֶה

people: those offering a sacrifice – an ox or a sheep – shall give to the priest
4 the shoulder, the cheeks, and the stomach. You shall give him the first yield of
5 your grain, wine, and oil, and the first wool from the shearing of your sheep.
For the LORD your God has chosen him out of all your tribes to stand and
6 minister in the name of the LORD – him and his sons for all time. If
a Levite leaves any of your towns throughout Israel where he has been living,
and comes to the place that the LORD will choose – he may do so whenever
7 he wishes – then he may minister in the name of the LORD his God, along-
8 side any of his brother Levites who serve there before the LORD. They shall
have equal portions to eat, regardless of income they may have from the sale
9 of family possessions. When you come into the land that the LORD
your God is giving you, do not learn to partake in the abhorrent practices
10 those nations carry out. Let no one be found among you who makes a son
or daughter pass through fire,[42] or who casts spells, or is an augur or diviner
11 or soothsayer, or who practices sorcery, or consults ghosts or spirits, or
12 seeks oracles from the dead. For anyone who does these things is abhorrent
to the LORD; it is because of such abhorrent acts that the LORD your God
13 is driving them out before you. You must be wholly loyal to the LORD your
14 God. The nations that you are driving out listen to augurs and to those who
cast spells. But as for you – the LORD your God does not permit you these.
15 The LORD your God will raise up another prophet like me from among your
16 own people. To him you must listen. For this is what you asked of the LORD
your God at Ḥorev on the day of the assembly when you said: 'If I hear the
voice of the LORD my God any more, or continue to see this great fire, I will
17 18 die.' The LORD said to me: They have spoken well. I will raise up for them a
prophet like you from among their own people. I will put My words in the
19 prophet's mouth and he will tell them all that I command. Anyone who does
not listen to My words that he speaks in My name, I Myself will call him to
20 account. But a prophet who acts in wickedness, speaking anything I have
not commanded in My name, or speaking in the name of other gods – that
21 prophet shall die. You may say to yourself, 'How can we recognize a message
22 that the LORD has not spoken?' If what a prophet proclaims in the name of
the LORD does not take place or come true, that is a message that the LORD
has not spoken. The prophet has proclaimed it in wickedness. Do not be afraid
19 1 of him. When the LORD your God has cut down the nations whose
land the LORD your God is giving you, and you have driven them out and
2 are living in their towns and in their houses, you shall set aside three cities
3 in that land that the LORD your God gives you to possess. Determine the
distances and divide the land that the LORD your God is giving you as a heritage into three equal parts – so that any manslayer will be able to flee to one
4 of these cities.[43] This is the rule for a manslayer who may flee to one of these
and live: it is one who has killed another person unintentionally, without
5 prior hatred. For instance, a man may go into the forest with a neighbor to

42 | This is traditionally equated with Molekh worship; see Leviticus 18:21 and the note there.
43 | Three parallel cities east of the Jordan had already been designated by Moshe in 4:41–43.

יִהְיֶה מִשְׁפַּט הַכֹּהֲנִים מֵאֵת הָעָם מֵאֵת זֹבְחֵי הַזֶּבַח אִם־שׁוֹר אִם־שֶׂה
ד וְנָתַן לַכֹּהֵן הַזְּרֹעַ וְהַלְּחָיַיִם וְהַקֵּבָה: רֵאשִׁית דְּגָנְךָ תִּירֹשְׁךָ וְיִצְהָרֶךָ
ה וְרֵאשִׁית גֵּז צֹאנְךָ תִּתֶּן־לּוֹ: כִּי בוֹ בָּחַר יהוה אֱלֹהֶיךָ מִכָּל־שְׁבָטֶיךָ
ו לַעֲמֹד לְשָׁרֵת בְּשֵׁם־יהוה הוּא וּבָנָיו כָּל־הַיָּמִים: וְכִי־יָבֹא רביעי
הַלֵּוִי מֵאַחַד שְׁעָרֶיךָ מִכָּל־יִשְׂרָאֵל אֲשֶׁר־הוּא גָּר שָׁם וּבָא בְּכָל־
ז אַוַּת נַפְשׁוֹ אֶל־הַמָּקוֹם אֲשֶׁר־יִבְחַר יהוה: וְשֵׁרֵת בְּשֵׁם יהוה אֱלֹהָיו
ח כְּכָל־אֶחָיו הַלְוִיִּם הָעֹמְדִים שָׁם לִפְנֵי יהוה: חֵלֶק כְּחֵלֶק יֹאכֵלוּ לְבַד
ט מִמְכָּרָיו עַל־הָאָבוֹת: כִּי אַתָּה בָּא אֶל־הָאָרֶץ אֲשֶׁר־יהוה
י אֱלֹהֶיךָ נֹתֵן לָךְ לֹא־תִלְמַד לַעֲשׂוֹת כְּתוֹעֲבֹת הַגּוֹיִם הָהֵם: לֹא־יִמָּצֵא
בְךָ מַעֲבִיר בְּנוֹ־וּבִתּוֹ בָּאֵשׁ קֹסֵם קְסָמִים מְעוֹנֵן וּמְנַחֵשׁ וּמְכַשֵּׁף:
יא יב וְחֹבֵר חָבֶר וְשֹׁאֵל אוֹב וְיִדְּעֹנִי וְדֹרֵשׁ אֶל־הַמֵּתִים: כִּי־תוֹעֲבַת יהוה
כָּל־עֹשֵׂה אֵלֶּה וּבִגְלַל הַתּוֹעֵבֹת הָאֵלֶּה יהוה אֱלֹהֶיךָ מוֹרִישׁ אוֹתָם
יג יד מִפָּנֶיךָ: תָּמִים תִּהְיֶה עִם יהוה אֱלֹהֶיךָ: כִּי ׀ הַגּוֹיִם הָאֵלֶּה אֲשֶׁר אַתָּה חמישי
יוֹרֵשׁ אוֹתָם אֶל־מְעֹנְנִים וְאֶל־קֹסְמִים יִשְׁמָעוּ וְאַתָּה לֹא כֵן נָתַן
טו לְךָ יהוה אֱלֹהֶיךָ: נָבִיא מִקִּרְבְּךָ מֵאַחֶיךָ כָּמֹנִי יָקִים לְךָ יהוה אֱלֹהֶיךָ
טז אֵלָיו תִּשְׁמָעוּן: כְּכֹל אֲשֶׁר־שָׁאַלְתָּ מֵעִם יהוה אֱלֹהֶיךָ בְּחֹרֵב בְּיוֹם
הַקָּהָל לֵאמֹר לֹא אֹסֵף לִשְׁמֹעַ אֶת־קוֹל יהוה אֱלֹהָי וְאֶת־הָאֵשׁ הַגְּדֹלָה
יז הַזֹּאת לֹא־אֶרְאֶה עוֹד וְלֹא אָמוּת: וַיֹּאמֶר יהוה אֵלָי הֵיטִיבוּ אֲשֶׁר
יח דִּבֵּרוּ: נָבִיא אָקִים לָהֶם מִקֶּרֶב אֲחֵיהֶם כָּמוֹךָ וְנָתַתִּי דְבָרַי בְּפִיו וְדִבֶּר
יט אֲלֵיהֶם אֵת כָּל־אֲשֶׁר אֲצַוֶּנּוּ: וְהָיָה הָאִישׁ אֲשֶׁר לֹא־יִשְׁמַע אֶל־דְּבָרַי
כ אֲשֶׁר יְדַבֵּר בִּשְׁמִי אָנֹכִי אֶדְרֹשׁ מֵעִמּוֹ: אַךְ הַנָּבִיא אֲשֶׁר יָזִיד לְדַבֵּר
דָּבָר בִּשְׁמִי אֵת אֲשֶׁר לֹא־צִוִּיתִיו לְדַבֵּר וַאֲשֶׁר יְדַבֵּר בְּשֵׁם אֱלֹהִים
כא אֲחֵרִים וּמֵת הַנָּבִיא הַהוּא: וְכִי תֹאמַר בִּלְבָבֶךָ אֵיכָה נֵדַע אֶת־הַדָּבָר
כב אֲשֶׁר לֹא־דִבְּרוֹ יהוה: אֲשֶׁר יְדַבֵּר הַנָּבִיא בְּשֵׁם יהוה וְלֹא־יִהְיֶה הַדָּבָר
וְלֹא יָבֹא הוּא הַדָּבָר אֲשֶׁר לֹא־דִבְּרוֹ יהוה בְּזָדוֹן דִּבְּרוֹ הַנָּבִיא לֹא
יט א תָגוּר מִמֶּנּוּ: כִּי־יַכְרִית יהוה אֱלֹהֶיךָ אֶת־הַגּוֹיִם אֲשֶׁר
יהוה אֱלֹהֶיךָ נֹתֵן לְךָ אֶת־אַרְצָם וִירִשְׁתָּם וְיָשַׁבְתָּ בְעָרֵיהֶם וּבְבָתֵּיהֶם:
ב שָׁלוֹשׁ עָרִים תַּבְדִּיל לָךְ בְּתוֹךְ אַרְצְךָ אֲשֶׁר יהוה אֱלֹהֶיךָ נֹתֵן לְךָ
ג לְרִשְׁתָּהּ: תָּכִין לְךָ הַדֶּרֶךְ וְשִׁלַּשְׁתָּ אֶת־גְּבוּל אַרְצְךָ אֲשֶׁר יַנְחִילְךָ
ד יהוה אֱלֹהֶיךָ וְהָיָה לָנוּס שָׁמָּה כָּל־רֹצֵחַ: וְזֶה דְּבַר הָרֹצֵחַ אֲשֶׁר־יָנוּס
שָׁמָּה וָחָי אֲשֶׁר יַכֶּה אֶת־רֵעֵהוּ בִּבְלִי־דַעַת וְהוּא לֹא־שֹׂנֵא לוֹ מִתְּמֹל
ה שִׁלְשֹׁם: וַאֲשֶׁר יָבֹא אֶת־רֵעֵהוּ בַיַּעַר לַחְטֹב עֵצִים וְנִדְּחָה יָדוֹ בַגַּרְזֶן

cut wood, and as he swings the ax to cut down a tree, the ax-head may fly off
the handle and strike the neighbor and kill him; that man may flee to one of
6 these cities and live. Should the distance be too great, the avenger of blood[44]
might pursue him in hot anger, overtake, and kill him even though he did
7 not deserve to die, there having been no prior enmity between the two. That
8 is why I charge you thus: three cities must you set aside. If the LORD your
God enlarges your territory, as He swore to your ancestors, and gives you
9 all of that land that He promised to give your ancestors,[45] if you vigilantly
observe all of this commandment with which I charge you today, loving the
LORD your God and walking in all His ways, then you shall add to these three,
10 three cities more so that innocent blood is not shed, bringing bloodguilt
upon you, in the land that the LORD your God is giving you as a possession.
11 But if one person hates his fellow, lies in wait for him, and attacks and kills
12 him, and then flees to one of these cities, the elders of his town shall have
him brought back from there and handed over to the avenger of blood to die.
13 Show him no pity. You must purge the guilt of innocent blood from Israel,
14 so that it may be well for you. Do not move back your neighbor's
boundary marker, set up by those long ago in the allotted land that the LORD
15 your God is giving you to possess. One witness alone is not enough
to convict a person of any crime or wrongdoing. A case is to be established
16 only on the evidence of two or three witnesses. If a corrupt witness comes
17 forward to accuse someone of wrongdoing, both parties to the dispute shall
appear before the LORD, before the priests and judges in office in that time.
18 The judges shall make a thorough investigation. If the man who testified
19 proves to be a false witness, having testified falsely against his fellow, then
inflict upon the false witness what the false witness had intended to inflict
20 upon his fellow; you must purge the evil from your midst. Others will hear
21 and fear, and such an evil will not be committed again in your midst. Show
no pity: life for life, eye for eye, tooth for tooth, hand for hand, foot for
20 1 foot.[46] When you go out to battle your enemies, and see horses and
chariots, an army greater than yours, do not be afraid of them; for the LORD
2 your God, who brought you out of Egypt, He will be with you. Before you
3 engage in battle, the priest shall come forward and address the men. 'Listen,
Israel,' he shall say to them, 'this day you are going into battle against your
4 enemies. Do not lose heart or be afraid, do not panic or dread them; for it
is the LORD your God who goes with you, to fight against your enemies for
5 you, to bring you victory.' Then the officers shall address the men: 'Is there
a man here who has built a new house but not yet dedicated it? Let him go
6 back home, or he may die in battle and someone else will dedicate it. Is there
a man here who has planted a vineyard but not yet harvested it? Let him go

---

44| That is, the victim's vengeful relative.

45 | See the expansive borders promised to Avraham in Genesis 15:18.

46| See notes on Exodus 21:23 and Leviticus 24:19–20.

לִכְרֹת הָעֵץ וְנָשַׁל הַבַּרְזֶל מִן־הָעֵץ וּמָצָא אֶת־רֵעֵהוּ וָמֵת הוּא יָנוּס
ו אֶל־אַחַת הֶעָרִים־הָאֵלֶּה וָחָי׃ פֶּן־יִרְדֹּף גֹּאֵל הַדָּם אַחֲרֵי הָרֹצֵחַ כִּי
יֵחַם לְבָבוֹ וְהִשִּׂיגוֹ כִּי־יִרְבֶּה הַדֶּרֶךְ וְהִכָּהוּ נָפֶשׁ וְלוֹ אֵין מִשְׁפַּט־מָוֶת
ז כִּי לֹא־שֹׂנֵא הוּא לוֹ מִתְּמוֹל שִׁלְשׁוֹם׃ עַל־כֵּן אָנֹכִי מְצַוְּךָ לֵאמֹר
ח שָׁלֹשׁ עָרִים תַּבְדִּיל לָךְ׃ וְאִם־יַרְחִיב יְהוָה אֱלֹהֶיךָ אֶת־גְּבֻלְךָ כַּאֲשֶׁר
נִשְׁבַּע לַאֲבֹתֶיךָ וְנָתַן לְךָ אֶת־כָּל־הָאָרֶץ אֲשֶׁר דִּבֶּר לָתֵת לַאֲבֹתֶיךָ׃
ט כִּי־תִשְׁמֹר אֶת־כָּל־הַמִּצְוָה הַזֹּאת לַעֲשֹׂתָהּ אֲשֶׁר אָנֹכִי מְצַוְּךָ הַיּוֹם
לְאַהֲבָה אֶת־יְהוָה אֱלֹהֶיךָ וְלָלֶכֶת בִּדְרָכָיו כָּל־הַיָּמִים וְיָסַפְתָּ לְךָ עוֹד
י שָׁלֹשׁ עָרִים עַל הַשָּׁלֹשׁ הָאֵלֶּה׃ וְלֹא יִשָּׁפֵךְ דָּם נָקִי בְּקֶרֶב אַרְצְךָ אֲשֶׁר
יְהוָה אֱלֹהֶיךָ נֹתֵן לְךָ נַחֲלָה וְהָיָה עָלֶיךָ דָּמִים׃
יא וְכִי־יִהְיֶה אִישׁ שֹׂנֵא לְרֵעֵהוּ וְאָרַב לוֹ וְקָם עָלָיו וְהִכָּהוּ נֶפֶשׁ וָמֵת וְנָס
יב אֶל־אַחַת הֶעָרִים הָאֵל׃ וְשָׁלְחוּ זִקְנֵי עִירוֹ וְלָקְחוּ אֹתוֹ מִשָּׁם וְנָתְנוּ
יג אֹתוֹ בְּיַד גֹּאֵל הַדָּם וָמֵת׃ לֹא־תָחוֹס עֵינְךָ עָלָיו וּבִעַרְתָּ דַם־הַנָּקִי
יד מִיִּשְׂרָאֵל וְטוֹב לָךְ׃ לֹא תַסִּיג גְּבוּל רֵעֲךָ אֲשֶׁר גָּבְלוּ ששי
רִאשֹׁנִים בְּנַחֲלָתְךָ אֲשֶׁר תִּנְחַל בָּאָרֶץ אֲשֶׁר יְהוָה אֱלֹהֶיךָ נֹתֵן לְךָ
טו לְרִשְׁתָּהּ׃ לֹא־יָקוּם עֵד אֶחָד בְּאִישׁ לְכָל־עָוֺן וּלְכָל־חַטָּאת
בְּכָל־חֵטְא אֲשֶׁר יֶחֱטָא עַל־פִּי ׀ שְׁנֵי עֵדִים אוֹ עַל־פִּי שְׁלֹשָׁה־עֵדִים
טז יז יָקוּם דָּבָר׃ כִּי־יָקוּם עֵד־חָמָס בְּאִישׁ לַעֲנוֹת בּוֹ סָרָה׃ וְעָמְדוּ שְׁנֵי־
הָאֲנָשִׁים אֲשֶׁר־לָהֶם הָרִיב לִפְנֵי יְהוָה לִפְנֵי הַכֹּהֲנִים וְהַשֹּׁפְטִים אֲשֶׁר
יח יִהְיוּ בַּיָּמִים הָהֵם׃ וְדָרְשׁוּ הַשֹּׁפְטִים הֵיטֵב וְהִנֵּה עֵד־שֶׁקֶר הָעֵד שֶׁקֶר
יט עָנָה בְאָחִיו׃ וַעֲשִׂיתֶם לוֹ כַּאֲשֶׁר זָמַם לַעֲשׂוֹת לְאָחִיו וּבִעַרְתָּ הָרָע
כ מִקִּרְבֶּךָ׃ וְהַנִּשְׁאָרִים יִשְׁמְעוּ וְיִרָאוּ וְלֹא־יֹסִפוּ לַעֲשׂוֹת עוֹד כַּדָּבָר הָרָע
כא הַזֶּה בְּקִרְבֶּךָ׃ וְלֹא תָחוֹס עֵינֶךָ נֶפֶשׁ בְּנֶפֶשׁ עַיִן בְּעַיִן שֵׁן בְּשֵׁן יָד בְּיָד
כ א רֶגֶל בְּרָגֶל׃ כִּי־תֵצֵא לַמִּלְחָמָה עַל־אֹיְבֶךָ וְרָאִיתָ סוּס וָרֶכֶב
עַם רַב מִמְּךָ לֹא תִירָא מֵהֶם כִּי־יְהוָה אֱלֹהֶיךָ עִמָּךְ הַמַּעַלְךָ מֵאֶרֶץ
ב מִצְרָיִם׃ וְהָיָה כְּקָרָבְכֶם אֶל־הַמִּלְחָמָה וְנִגַּשׁ הַכֹּהֵן וְדִבֶּר אֶל־הָעָם׃
ג וְאָמַר אֲלֵהֶם שְׁמַע יִשְׂרָאֵל אַתֶּם קְרֵבִים הַיּוֹם לַמִּלְחָמָה עַל־אֹיְבֵיכֶם
ד אַל־יֵרַךְ לְבַבְכֶם אַל־תִּירְאוּ וְאַל־תַּחְפְּזוּ וְאַל־תַּעַרְצוּ מִפְּנֵיהֶם׃ כִּי
יְהוָה אֱלֹהֵיכֶם הַהֹלֵךְ עִמָּכֶם לְהִלָּחֵם לָכֶם עִם־אֹיְבֵיכֶם לְהוֹשִׁיעַ
ה אֶתְכֶם׃ וְדִבְּרוּ הַשֹּׁטְרִים אֶל־הָעָם לֵאמֹר מִי־הָאִישׁ אֲשֶׁר בָּנָה בַיִת־
חָדָשׁ וְלֹא חֲנָכוֹ יֵלֵךְ וְיָשֹׁב לְבֵיתוֹ פֶּן־יָמוּת בַּמִּלְחָמָה וְאִישׁ אַחֵר
ו יַחְנְכֶנּוּ׃ וּמִי־הָאִישׁ אֲשֶׁר נָטַע כֶּרֶם וְלֹא חִלְּלוֹ יֵלֵךְ וְיָשֹׁב לְבֵיתוֹ פֶּן־

7 back home, or he may die in the battle and someone else will harvest it. Is
there a man here who has betrothed a woman but not yet married her? Let
him go back home, or he may die in battle and someone else will marry her.'
8 And further, 'Is there a man here,' the officers shall say to the men, 'who is afraid
or fainthearted? Let him go back home so that his comrades do not become
9 fainthearted along with him.' When the officers have finished addressing the
10 men, they shall appoint the commanders to lead them. When you
11 approach a town to fight against it, first offer it peace. If it accepts your terms
of peace and lets you in, all the people found there shall serve you a tribute
12 of forced labor. If it rejects your peace offer and wages war against you, you
13 shall lay siege. When the LORD your God gives it over into your hands, you
14 shall put all its males to the sword. You may, however, take as your plunder the
women, children, livestock, and all else in the town, all its spoil; you may use
15 the spoil of your enemies, which the LORD your God has given you. This is
how you are to treat all the towns that are distant from you and do not belong
16 to the nations nearby. However, in the towns of the nations that the LORD
your God is giving you as an inheritance, let nothing that breathes remain
17 alive. These, the Hittites and Amorites, Canaanites and Perizzites, Hivites and
Jebusites, you must utterly destroy as the LORD your God has commanded
18 you, so that they cannot teach you to do all the abhorrent things that they do
19 for their gods, causing you to sin against your God, the LORD. When
you lay siege to a town and wage war against it for a long time to capture it,
do not destroy its trees; do not wield an ax against them. You may eat from
them; you must not cut them down. Are trees of the field human beings that
20 you should besiege them too? Only trees that you know do not produce food
may you cut down for use building siege works until the town that has made
war against you falls.

21 1 If a person is found lying slain in a field on the land that the LORD your God
2 is giving you to possess, and it is not known who killed him, your elders and
judges must go out and measure the distances from the slain person to each
3 of the surrounding towns. The elders of the town nearest the body shall take
4 a female calf that has never been worked or drawn a load with a yoke, and
lead it to a valley with a flowing stream that has not been plowed or planted,
5 and there in the valley the elders of that town shall break the calf's neck. The
priests, sons of Levi, shall step forward, for it is them the LORD your God
has chosen to minister to Him, to give blessing in the LORD's name, and to
6 decide all cases of dispute and assault. Then all the elders of the town nearest
the slain person shall wash their hands over the calf whose neck was broken
7 in the valley and declare: 'Our hands did not shed this blood[47] and our eyes
8 did not witness it. Absolve Your people Israel, whom You redeemed, LORD,
and do not leave the guilt of innocent blood among Your people Israel.'

47 | Meaning the blood of the slain individual.

ז יָמוּת בַּמִּלְחָמָה וְאִישׁ אַחֵר יְחַלְּלֶנּוּ: וּמִי־הָאִישׁ אֲשֶׁר אֵרַשׂ אִשָּׁה וְלֹא
ח לְקָחָהּ יֵלֵךְ וְיָשֹׁב לְבֵיתוֹ פֶּן־יָמוּת בַּמִּלְחָמָה וְאִישׁ אַחֵר יִקָּחֶנָּה: וְיָסְפוּ
הַשֹּׁטְרִים לְדַבֵּר אֶל־הָעָם וְאָמְרוּ מִי־הָאִישׁ הַיָּרֵא וְרַךְ הַלֵּבָב יֵלֵךְ
ט וְיָשֹׁב לְבֵיתוֹ וְלֹא יִמַּס אֶת־לְבַב אֶחָיו כִּלְבָבוֹ: וְהָיָה כְּכַלֹּת הַשֹּׁטְרִים
י לְדַבֵּר אֶל־הָעָם וּפָקְדוּ שָׂרֵי צְבָאוֹת בְּרֹאשׁ הָעָם: כִּי־ טז שביעי
יא תִקְרַב אֶל־עִיר לְהִלָּחֵם עָלֶיהָ וְקָרָאתָ אֵלֶיהָ לְשָׁלוֹם: וְהָיָה אִם־
שָׁלוֹם תַּעַנְךָ וּפָתְחָה לָךְ וְהָיָה כָּל־הָעָם הַנִּמְצָא־בָהּ יִהְיוּ לְךָ לָמַס
יב וַעֲבָדוּךָ: וְאִם־לֹא תַשְׁלִים עִמָּךְ וְעָשְׂתָה עִמְּךָ מִלְחָמָה וְצַרְתָּ עָלֶיהָ:
יג יד וּנְתָנָהּ יְהוָה אֱלֹהֶיךָ בְּיָדֶךָ וְהִכִּיתָ אֶת־כָּל־זְכוּרָהּ לְפִי־חָרֶב: רַק
הַנָּשִׁים וְהַטַּף וְהַבְּהֵמָה וְכֹל אֲשֶׁר יִהְיֶה בָעִיר כָּל־שְׁלָלָהּ תָּבֹז לָךְ
טו וְאָכַלְתָּ אֶת־שְׁלַל אֹיְבֶיךָ אֲשֶׁר נָתַן יְהוָה אֱלֹהֶיךָ לָךְ: כֵּן תַּעֲשֶׂה
לְכָל־הֶעָרִים הָרְחֹקֹת מִמְּךָ מְאֹד אֲשֶׁר לֹא־מֵעָרֵי הַגּוֹיִם־הָאֵלֶּה
טז הֵנָּה: רַק מֵעָרֵי הָעַמִּים הָאֵלֶּה אֲשֶׁר יְהוָה אֱלֹהֶיךָ נֹתֵן לְךָ נַחֲלָה
יז לֹא תְחַיֶּה כָּל־נְשָׁמָה: כִּי־הַחֲרֵם תַּחֲרִימֵם הַחִתִּי וְהָאֱמֹרִי הַכְּנַעֲנִי
יח וְהַפְּרִזִּי הַחִוִּי וְהַיְבוּסִי כַּאֲשֶׁר צִוְּךָ יְהוָה אֱלֹהֶיךָ: לְמַעַן אֲשֶׁר לֹא־
יְלַמְּדוּ אֶתְכֶם לַעֲשׂוֹת כְּכֹל תּוֹעֲבֹתָם אֲשֶׁר עָשׂוּ לֵאלֹהֵיהֶם וַחֲטָאתֶם
יט לַיהוָה אֱלֹהֵיכֶם: כִּי־תָצוּר אֶל־עִיר יָמִים רַבִּים לְהִלָּחֵם
עָלֶיהָ לְתָפְשָׂהּ לֹא־תַשְׁחִית אֶת־עֵצָהּ לִנְדֹּחַ עָלָיו גַּרְזֶן כִּי מִמֶּנּוּ תֹאכֵל
כ וְאֹתוֹ לֹא תִכְרֹת כִּי הָאָדָם עֵץ הַשָּׂדֶה לָבֹא מִפָּנֶיךָ בַּמָּצוֹר: רַק עֵץ
אֲשֶׁר־תֵּדַע כִּי לֹא־עֵץ מַאֲכָל הוּא אֹתוֹ תַשְׁחִית וְכָרָתָּ וּבָנִיתָ מָצוֹר
עַל־הָעִיר אֲשֶׁר־הִוא עֹשָׂה עִמְּךָ מִלְחָמָה עַד רִדְתָּהּ:
א כִּי־יִמָּצֵא חָלָל בָּאֲדָמָה אֲשֶׁר יְהוָה אֱלֹהֶיךָ נֹתֵן לְךָ לְרִשְׁתָּהּ נֹפֵל כא
ב בַּשָּׂדֶה לֹא נוֹדַע מִי הִכָּהוּ: וְיָצְאוּ זְקֵנֶיךָ וְשֹׁפְטֶיךָ וּמָדְדוּ אֶל־הֶעָרִים
ג אֲשֶׁר סְבִיבֹת הֶחָלָל: וְהָיָה הָעִיר הַקְּרֹבָה אֶל־הֶחָלָל וְלָקְחוּ זִקְנֵי
הָעִיר הַהִוא עֶגְלַת בָּקָר אֲשֶׁר לֹא־עֻבַּד בָּהּ אֲשֶׁר לֹא־מָשְׁכָה בְּעֹל:
ד וְהוֹרִדוּ זִקְנֵי הָעִיר הַהִוא אֶת־הָעֶגְלָה אֶל־נַחַל אֵיתָן אֲשֶׁר לֹא־
ה יֵעָבֵד בּוֹ וְלֹא יִזָּרֵעַ וְעָרְפוּ־שָׁם אֶת־הָעֶגְלָה בַּנָּחַל: וְנִגְּשׁוּ הַכֹּהֲנִים
בְּנֵי לֵוִי כִּי בָם בָּחַר יְהוָה אֱלֹהֶיךָ לְשָׁרְתוֹ וּלְבָרֵךְ בְּשֵׁם יְהוָה וְעַל־
ו פִּיהֶם יִהְיֶה כָּל־רִיב וְכָל־נָגַע: וְכֹל זִקְנֵי הָעִיר הַהִוא הַקְּרֹבִים אֶל־
ז הֶחָלָל יִרְחֲצוּ אֶת־יְדֵיהֶם עַל־הָעֶגְלָה הָעֲרוּפָה בַנָּחַל: וְעָנוּ וְאָמְרוּ מפטיר
ח יָדֵינוּ לֹא שפכה אֶת־הַדָּם הַזֶּה וְעֵינֵינוּ לֹא רָאוּ: כַּפֵּר לְעַמְּךָ יִשְׂרָאֵל שָׁפְכוּ
אֲשֶׁר־פָּדִיתָ יְהוָה וְאַל־תִּתֵּן דָּם נָקִי בְּקֶרֶב עַמְּךָ יִשְׂרָאֵל וְנִכַּפֵּר לָהֶם

9 So shall atonement be made for the bloodshed, and so will you purge the
guilt of innocent blood from yourselves, by doing what is right in the Lord's
10 eyes. When you wage war against your enemies, and the Lord your KI TETZEH
11 God gives them into your hand and you take captives, if you see a beautiful
12 woman among the captives, and you desire her and wish to marry her, bring
13 her to your house. Have her shave her head, pare her nails, and remove her
captive's garb. She shall sit in your house mourning for her father and mother
for a full month. Only after that may you go in to her and be her husband,
14 and she shall be your wife. But if you no longer desire her, you must let her
go free. You may not sell her for money or treat her as a slave, since you have
15 dishonored her. If a man has two wives, and loves one but not the
other, and if both the loved and unloved bear him sons, but the firstborn is
16 the son of the one unloved, then on the day he bequeaths his possessions to
his sons, he may not give the rights of the firstborn to the son of the loved in
17 preference to the son of the unloved, the true firstborn. He must acknowledge
the son of his unloved wife as the firstborn, giving him a double portion of
all that he has. He is the first fruit of his manhood; the right of the firstborn
18 belongs to him. If a man has a wayward and rebellious son who does
not listen to his father and mother and, though they discipline him, still will
19 not listen, his father and his mother shall take hold of him and bring him
20 out to the elders at the town gate. They shall say to the town elders, 'This
son of ours is wayward and rebellious. He does not listen to us. He is a glut-
21 ton and a drunkard.' Then all the men of the town shall stone him to death.
Thus you shall purge the evil from your midst, and all Israel will hear, and
22 be afraid.[48] When someone is convicted of a capital crime and is
23 executed and you hang him from a post, do not let his corpse remain all night
upon that post. You must bury him that same day, because a man left hanging
is a slur upon God, and you must not defile the land that the Lord your God
22 1 is giving you as your possession. If you see your kinsman's ox or
2 sheep straying away, do not ignore it; you must return it to its owner. If the
owner does not live nearby or you do not know who the owner is, you must
bring it home with you and keep it until the owner claims it; then you must
3 return it. You must do the same with his donkey, the same with his garment,
the same with anything your kinsman loses and you find. You cannot ignore
4 it. You shall not see your kinsman's donkey or ox fallen on the road
5 and ignore it. Help him to lift it. Men's clothing shall not be seen on
a woman, nor shall a man wear women's dress. Whoever does such things is
abhorrent to the Lord your God.
6 If you come across a bird's nest containing fledglings or eggs by the roadside, in a tree, or on the ground, and the mother is sitting on the fledglings

48| As with other death sentences in the Torah, the Sages listed numerous qualifications, leading to the opinion that this case and the one above in 13:13–19 "never happened and never will" (Sanhedrin 71a).

ט הַדָּם: וְאַתָּה תְּבַעֵר הַדָּם הַנָּקִי מִקִּרְבֶּךָ כִּי־תַעֲשֶׂה הַיָּשָׁר בְּעֵינֵי
י יהוה: כִּי־תֵצֵא לַמִּלְחָמָה עַל־אֹיְבֶיךָ וּנְתָנוֹ יהוה אֱלֹהֶיךָ כי תצא
יא בְּיָדֶךָ וְשָׁבִיתָ שִׁבְיוֹ: וְרָאִיתָ בַּשִּׁבְיָה אֵשֶׁת יְפַת־תֹּאַר וְחָשַׁקְתָּ בָהּ
יב וְלָקַחְתָּ לְךָ לְאִשָּׁה: וַהֲבֵאתָהּ אֶל־תּוֹךְ בֵּיתֶךָ וְגִלְּחָה אֶת־רֹאשָׁהּ
יג וְעָשְׂתָה אֶת־צִפָּרְנֶיהָ: וְהֵסִירָה אֶת־שִׂמְלַת שִׁבְיָהּ מֵעָלֶיהָ וְיָשְׁבָה
בְּבֵיתֶךָ וּבָכְתָה אֶת־אָבִיהָ וְאֶת־אִמָּהּ יֶרַח יָמִים וְאַחַר כֵּן תָּבוֹא אֵלֶיהָ
יד וּבְעַלְתָּהּ וְהָיְתָה לְךָ לְאִשָּׁה: וְהָיָה אִם־לֹא חָפַצְתָּ בָּהּ וְשִׁלַּחְתָּהּ
לְנַפְשָׁהּ וּמָכֹר לֹא־תִמְכְּרֶנָּה בַּכָּסֶף לֹא־תִתְעַמֵּר בָּהּ תַּחַת אֲשֶׁר
טו עִנִּיתָהּ: כִּי־תִהְיֶיןָ לְאִישׁ שְׁתֵּי נָשִׁים הָאַחַת אֲהוּבָה
וְהָאַחַת שְׂנוּאָה וְיָלְדוּ־לוֹ בָנִים הָאֲהוּבָה וְהַשְּׂנוּאָה וְהָיָה הַבֵּן הַבְּכֹר
טז לַשְּׂנִיאָה: וְהָיָה בְּיוֹם הַנְחִילוֹ אֶת־בָּנָיו אֵת אֲשֶׁר־יִהְיֶה לוֹ לֹא יוּכַל
יז לְבַכֵּר אֶת־בֶּן־הָאֲהוּבָה עַל־פְּנֵי בֶן־הַשְּׂנוּאָה הַבְּכֹר: כִּי אֶת־הַבְּכֹר
בֶּן־הַשְּׂנוּאָה יַכִּיר לָתֶת לוֹ פִּי שְׁנַיִם בְּכֹל אֲשֶׁר־יִמָּצֵא לוֹ כִּי־הוּא
יח רֵאשִׁית אֹנוֹ לוֹ מִשְׁפַּט הַבְּכֹרָה: כִּי־יִהְיֶה לְאִישׁ בֵּן סוֹרֵר
וּמוֹרֶה אֵינֶנּוּ שֹׁמֵעַ בְּקוֹל אָבִיו וּבְקוֹל אִמּוֹ וְיִסְּרוּ אֹתוֹ וְלֹא יִשְׁמַע
יט אֲלֵיהֶם: וְתָפְשׂוּ בוֹ אָבִיו וְאִמּוֹ וְהוֹצִיאוּ אֹתוֹ אֶל־זִקְנֵי עִירוֹ וְאֶל־
כ שַׁעַר מְקֹמוֹ: וְאָמְרוּ אֶל־זִקְנֵי עִירוֹ בְּנֵנוּ זֶה סוֹרֵר וּמֹרֶה אֵינֶנּוּ שֹׁמֵעַ
כא בְּקֹלֵנוּ זוֹלֵל וְסֹבֵא: וּרְגָמֻהוּ כָּל־אַנְשֵׁי עִירוֹ בָאֲבָנִים וָמֵת וּבִעַרְתָּ הָרָע
כב מִקִּרְבֶּךָ וְכָל־יִשְׂרָאֵל יִשְׁמְעוּ וְיִרָאוּ: וְכִי־יִהְיֶה בְאִישׁ חֵטְא שני
כג מִשְׁפַּט־מָוֶת וְהוּמָת וְתָלִיתָ אֹתוֹ עַל־עֵץ: לֹא־תָלִין נִבְלָתוֹ עַל־הָעֵץ
כִּי־קָבוֹר תִּקְבְּרֶנּוּ בַּיּוֹם הַהוּא כִּי־קִלְלַת אֱלֹהִים תָּלוּי וְלֹא תְטַמֵּא
כב א אֶת־אַדְמָתְךָ אֲשֶׁר יהוה אֱלֹהֶיךָ נֹתֵן לְךָ נַחֲלָה: לֹא־
תִרְאֶה אֶת־שׁוֹר אָחִיךָ אוֹ אֶת־שֵׂיוֹ נִדָּחִים וְהִתְעַלַּמְתָּ מֵהֶם הָשֵׁב
ב תְּשִׁיבֵם לְאָחִיךָ: וְאִם־לֹא קָרוֹב אָחִיךָ אֵלֶיךָ וְלֹא יְדַעְתּוֹ וַאֲסַפְתּוֹ
ג אֶל־תּוֹךְ בֵּיתֶךָ וְהָיָה עִמְּךָ עַד דְּרֹשׁ אָחִיךָ אֹתוֹ וַהֲשֵׁבֹתוֹ לוֹ: וְכֵן
תַּעֲשֶׂה לַחֲמֹרוֹ וְכֵן תַּעֲשֶׂה לְשִׂמְלָתוֹ וְכֵן תַּעֲשֶׂה לְכָל־אֲבֵדַת אָחִיךָ
ד אֲשֶׁר־תֹּאבַד מִמֶּנּוּ וּמְצָאתָהּ לֹא תוּכַל לְהִתְעַלֵּם: לֹא־
תִרְאֶה אֶת־חֲמוֹר אָחִיךָ אוֹ שׁוֹרוֹ נֹפְלִים בַּדֶּרֶךְ וְהִתְעַלַּמְתָּ מֵהֶם הָקֵם
ה תָּקִים עִמּוֹ: לֹא־יִהְיֶה כְלִי־גֶבֶר עַל־אִשָּׁה וְלֹא־יִלְבַּשׁ גֶּבֶר
שִׂמְלַת אִשָּׁה כִּי תוֹעֲבַת יהוה אֱלֹהֶיךָ כָּל־עֹשֵׂה אֵלֶּה:
ו כִּי יִקָּרֵא קַן־צִפּוֹר ׀ לְפָנֶיךָ בַּדֶּרֶךְ בְּכָל־עֵץ ׀ אוֹ עַל־הָאָרֶץ אֶפְרֹחִים יז
אוֹ בֵיצִים וְהָאֵם רֹבֶצֶת עַל־הָאֶפְרֹחִים אוֹ עַל־הַבֵּיצִים לֹא־תִקַּח הָאֵם

7 or the eggs, do not take the mother with the young. Let the mother go;
only then may you take the young, so that it may be well for you and you
8 may live long. When you build a new house, erect a parapet for
your roof. Otherwise you may bring bloodguilt on your house should any-
9 one fall from it. Do not sow your vineyard with a second kind of seed,[49]
or the whole yield – both the crop you have sown and the yield of the
10 11 vineyard – will have to be forfeited. Do not plow with an ox and a
12 donkey yoked together. Do not wear clothes made of wool and linen woven
together. Make tassels on the four corners of the garment with which
13 you cover yourself. If a man takes a wife and, after sleeping with
14 her, he dislikes her, and he makes up charges against her, sullying her name,
15 saying, 'I married this woman, but when I lay with her, I did not find her to be
a virgin,' the girl's father and mother shall produce the evidence of the girl's
16 virginity before the town elders at the gate. The girl's father shall say to the
17 elders: 'I gave my daughter in marriage to this man but he dislikes her. Now he
has made up charges against her, saying, "I did not find your daughter to be a
virgin." But here is the evidence of my daughter's virginity.' They shall spread
18 out the cloth before the town elders.[50] And then the town elders shall take
19 the man and flog him. They shall fine him one hundred shekel of silver, and
give it to the girl's father, because he has sullied the name of an Israelite virgin.
She shall remain his wife; he does not have the choice to divorce her as long
20 as he lives. If, however, the charge is true, no evidence being found
21 that the girl was a virgin, then the girl shall be brought to the entrance of her
father's house and the men of her town shall stone her to death, for she committed an outrage in Israel by acting immorally while in her father's house.
22 You shall purge the evil from your midst. If a man is caught lying
with the wife of another, both shall die, the man and the woman with whom
23 he lay. You shall purge the evil from Israel. If a virgin is betrothed
24 to be married, and a man encounters her within a town and lies with her,
you shall bring them both to the town gate and stone them to death, the girl
because she did not cry for help in the town, and the man because he violated
25 the wife of his fellow. You shall purge the evil from your midst. But
if the man encounters the betrothed woman in the open country, forces her
26 and lies with her, only the man who did this shall die. You shall do nothing
to the girl; she did not commit the capital offense. Just as one man at times
27 attacks and murders his fellow man, so too here; he came upon her in open
country. The betrothed woman may have cried out for help, but no one
28 was there to rescue her. If a man encounters a virgin who is not
29 betrothed and rapes her, and they are caught in the act, the man who lay
with her shall pay the girl's father fifty shekel of silver, and she shall become
his wife. Because he violated her he does not have the choice to divorce her
23 1 as long as he lives. A man cannot marry his father's wife; he must

49 | That is, apart from the grape seed.

50 | Tradition assigns a metaphorical meaning to this formulation.

ז עַל־הַבָּנִים: שַׁלֵּחַ תְּשַׁלַּח אֶת־הָאֵם וְאֶת־הַבָּנִים תִּקַּח־לָךְ לְמַעַן יִיטַב
ח לָךְ וְהַאֲרַכְתָּ יָמִים: כִּי תִבְנֶה בַּיִת חָדָשׁ וְעָשִׂיתָ מַעֲקֶה שלישי
ט לְגַגֶּךָ וְלֹא־תָשִׂים דָּמִים בְּבֵיתֶךָ כִּי־יִפֹּל הַנֹּפֵל מִמֶּנּוּ: לֹא־תִזְרַע כַּרְמְךָ
כִּלְאָיִם פֶּן־תִּקְדַּשׁ הַמְלֵאָה הַזֶּרַע אֲשֶׁר תִּזְרָע וּתְבוּאַת
י יא הַכָּרֶם: לֹא־תַחֲרֹשׁ בְּשׁוֹר־וּבַחֲמֹר יַחְדָּו: לֹא תִלְבַּשׁ שַׁעַטְנֵז
יב צֶמֶר וּפִשְׁתִּים יַחְדָּו: גְּדִלִים תַּעֲשֶׂה־לָּךְ עַל־אַרְבַּע כַּנְפוֹת
יג כְּסוּתְךָ אֲשֶׁר תְּכַסֶּה־בָּהּ: כִּי־יִקַּח אִישׁ אִשָּׁה וּבָא אֵלֶיהָ
יד וּשְׂנֵאָהּ: וְשָׂם לָהּ עֲלִילֹת דְּבָרִים וְהוֹצִא עָלֶיהָ שֵׁם רָע וְאָמַר אֶת־
טו הָאִשָּׁה הַזֹּאת לָקַחְתִּי וָאֶקְרַב אֵלֶיהָ וְלֹא־מָצָאתִי לָהּ בְּתוּלִים: וְלָקַח
אֲבִי הַנַּעֲרָ וְאִמָּהּ וְהוֹצִיאוּ אֶת־בְּתוּלֵי הַנַּעֲרָ אֶל־זִקְנֵי הָעִיר הַשָּׁעְרָה:
טז וְאָמַר אֲבִי הַנַּעֲרָ אֶל־הַזְּקֵנִים אֶת־בִּתִּי נָתַתִּי לָאִישׁ הַזֶּה לְאִשָּׁה
יז וַיִּשְׂנָאֶהָ: וְהִנֵּה־הוּא שָׂם עֲלִילֹת דְּבָרִים לֵאמֹר לֹא־מָצָאתִי לְבִתְּךָ
יח בְּתוּלִים וְאֵלֶּה בְּתוּלֵי בִתִּי וּפָרְשׂוּ הַשִּׂמְלָה לִפְנֵי זִקְנֵי הָעִיר: וְלָקְחוּ
יט זִקְנֵי הָעִיר־הַהִוא אֶת־הָאִישׁ וְיִסְּרוּ אֹתוֹ: וְעָנְשׁוּ אֹתוֹ מֵאָה כֶסֶף וְנָתְנוּ
לַאֲבִי הַנַּעֲרָה כִּי הוֹצִיא שֵׁם רָע עַל בְּתוּלַת יִשְׂרָאֵל וְלוֹ־תִהְיֶה לְאִשָּׁה
כ לֹא־יוּכַל לְשַׁלְּחָהּ כָּל־יָמָיו: וְאִם־אֱמֶת הָיָה הַדָּבָר הַזֶּה
כא לֹא־נִמְצְאוּ בְתוּלִים לַנַּעֲרָ: וְהוֹצִיאוּ אֶת־הַנַּעֲרָ אֶל־פֶּתַח בֵּית־אָבִיהָ
וּסְקָלוּהָ אַנְשֵׁי עִירָהּ בָּאֲבָנִים וָמֵתָה כִּי־עָשְׂתָה נְבָלָה בְּיִשְׂרָאֵל לִזְנוֹת
כב בֵּית אָבִיהָ וּבִעַרְתָּ הָרָע מִקִּרְבֶּךָ: כִּי־יִמָּצֵא אִישׁ שֹׁכֵב ׀
עִם־אִשָּׁה בְעֻלַת־בַּעַל וּמֵתוּ גַּם־שְׁנֵיהֶם הָאִישׁ הַשֹּׁכֵב עִם־הָאִשָּׁה
כג וְהָאִשָּׁה וּבִעַרְתָּ הָרָע מִיִּשְׂרָאֵל: כִּי יִהְיֶה נַעֲרָ בְתוּלָה
כד מְאֹרָשָׂה לְאִישׁ וּמְצָאָהּ אִישׁ בָּעִיר וְשָׁכַב עִמָּהּ: וְהוֹצֵאתֶם אֶת־שְׁנֵיהֶם
אֶל־שַׁעַר ׀ הָעִיר הַהִוא וּסְקַלְתֶּם אֹתָם בָּאֲבָנִים וָמֵתוּ אֶת־הַנַּעֲרָ עַל־
דְּבַר אֲשֶׁר לֹא־צָעֲקָה בָעִיר וְאֶת־הָאִישׁ עַל־דְּבַר אֲשֶׁר־עִנָּה אֶת־אֵשֶׁת
כה רֵעֵהוּ וּבִעַרְתָּ הָרָע מִקִּרְבֶּךָ: וְאִם־בַּשָּׂדֶה יִמְצָא הָאִישׁ
אֶת־הַנַּעֲרָ הַמְאֹרָשָׂה וְהֶחֱזִיק־בָּהּ הָאִישׁ וְשָׁכַב עִמָּהּ וּמֵת הָאִישׁ
כו אֲשֶׁר־שָׁכַב עִמָּהּ לְבַדּוֹ: וְלַנַּעֲרָ לֹא־תַעֲשֶׂה דָבָר אֵין לַנַּעֲרָ חֵטְא מָוֶת
כז כִּי כַּאֲשֶׁר יָקוּם אִישׁ עַל־רֵעֵהוּ וּרְצָחוֹ נֶפֶשׁ כֵּן הַדָּבָר הַזֶּה: כִּי בַשָּׂדֶה
כח מְצָאָהּ צָעֲקָה הַנַּעֲרָ הַמְאֹרָשָׂה וְאֵין מוֹשִׁיעַ לָהּ: כִּי־יִמְצָא
אִישׁ נַעֲרָ בְתוּלָה אֲשֶׁר לֹא־אֹרָשָׂה וּתְפָשָׂהּ וְשָׁכַב עִמָּהּ וְנִמְצָאוּ:
כט וְנָתַן הָאִישׁ הַשֹּׁכֵב עִמָּהּ לַאֲבִי הַנַּעֲרָ חֲמִשִּׁים כָּסֶף וְלוֹ־תִהְיֶה לְאִשָּׁה
כג א תַּחַת אֲשֶׁר עִנָּהּ לֹא־יוּכַל שַׁלְּחָהּ כָּל־יָמָיו: לֹא־יִקַּח אִישׁ

2 not dishonor his father's bed. No one whose testicles have been
crushed or whose member is severed shall be admitted to the congregation
3 of the LORD.[51] No one born of an illicit union[52] shall be admitted to
the congregation of the LORD; even to the tenth generation, no descendant of
4 such a union may be admitted to the congregation of the LORD. No
Amonite or Moabite shall be admitted to the congregation of the LORD;
even to the tenth generation, none of their descendants shall be admitted to
5 the congregation of the LORD, for they would not greet you with food and
water on your way when you came out of Egypt; and in hostility against you
6 they hired Bilam son of Beor from Petor of Aram Naharayim to curse you.[53]
But the LORD your God chose not to listen to Bilam; the LORD your God
7 turned the curse into a blessing for you, because the LORD your God loves
8 you. Do not seek their ease or welfare as long as you live. Do not
despise an Edomite, for he is your kin. Do not despise an Egyptian, for you
9 lived as a stranger in his land. Children born to them may be admitted, in the
10 third generation, to the congregation of the LORD. When you are
11 encamped against your enemies, guard against any impropriety. If one of the
men becomes impure because of a nocturnal emission, he shall go outside
12 the camp and not reenter it. As evening approaches, he shall bathe in water,
13 and at sunset he may reenter the camp. You must designate an area outside
14 the camp where you may relieve yourself. Among your gear you shall have
a trowel. When you relieve yourself outside, you shall dig a hole with it and
15 cover up your excrement. The LORD your God travels with your camp, to
protect you and to deliver your enemies to you. Therefore your camp must
16 be holy; He must not find any indecent thing among you and turn away from
you. If a slaves seeks refuge with you from his master, do not hand
17 him back to his master. He shall live with you in the place he chooses, in which-
18 ever of your towns he likes. Do not ill-treat him. No woman of Israel
19 shall be a cult prostitute;[54] no man of Israel shall be a male cult prostitute. Do
not bring wages of prostitution or the payment for a dog[55] into the house of the
LORD your God in fulfillment of any vow, for both are abhorrent to the LORD
20 your God. Do not charge interest on loans to your kinsmen, whether
21 on money or food or anything that could earn interest. You may charge interest
on loans to a foreigner, but on loans to your kinsmen do not charge, so that
the LORD your God may bless you in all your endeavors in the land you are
22 entering to possess. When you make a vow to the LORD your God,
do not delay in fulfilling it, for the LORD your God will certainly require it of
23 you; you will incur guilt. But if you refrain from vowing you will not incur guilt.
24 Whatever your lips utter, take care to do, since you have voluntarily vowed to
25 the LORD your God, with your own mouth. When you enter your

51 | That is, such people may not marry an Israelite.
52 | According to tradition, an adulterous or incestuous relationship.
53 | See Numbers, chapters 22–24.
54 | Referring to a prostitute at a place of worship.
55 | "Dog" may refer to a male prostitute.

ב אֶת־אֵשֶׁת אָבִיו וְלֹא יְגַלֶּה כְּנַף אָבִיו׃ לֹא־יָבֹא פְצוּעַ־דַּכָּה
ג וּכְרוּת שָׁפְכָה בִּקְהַל יהוה׃ לֹא־יָבֹא מַמְזֵר בִּקְהַל יהוה
ד גַּם דּוֹר עֲשִׂירִי לֹא־יָבֹא לוֹ בִּקְהַל יהוה׃ לֹא־יָבֹא עַמּוֹנִי
וּמוֹאָבִי בִּקְהַל יהוה גַּם דּוֹר עֲשִׂירִי לֹא־יָבֹא לָהֶם בִּקְהַל יהוה עַד־
ה עוֹלָם׃ עַל־דְּבַר אֲשֶׁר לֹא־קִדְּמוּ אֶתְכֶם בַּלֶּחֶם וּבַמַּיִם בַּדֶּרֶךְ בְּצֵאתְכֶם
מִמִּצְרָיִם וַאֲשֶׁר שָׂכַר עָלֶיךָ אֶת־בִּלְעָם בֶּן־בְּעוֹר מִפְּתוֹר אֲרַם נַהֲרַיִם
ו לְקַלְלֶךָּ׃ וְלֹא־אָבָה יהוה אֱלֹהֶיךָ לִשְׁמֹעַ אֶל־בִּלְעָם וַיַּהֲפֹךְ יהוה
ז אֱלֹהֶיךָ לְּךָ אֶת־הַקְּלָלָה לִבְרָכָה כִּי אֲהֵבְךָ יהוה אֱלֹהֶיךָ׃ לֹא־תִדְרֹשׁ
ח שְׁלֹמָם וְטֹבָתָם כָּל־יָמֶיךָ לְעוֹלָם׃ לֹא־תְתַעֵב אֲדֹמִי כִּי רביעי
ט אָחִיךָ הוּא לֹא־תְתַעֵב מִצְרִי כִּי־גֵר הָיִיתָ בְאַרְצוֹ׃ בָּנִים אֲשֶׁר־יִוָּלְדוּ
י לָהֶם דּוֹר שְׁלִישִׁי יָבֹא לָהֶם בִּקְהַל יהוה׃ כִּי־תֵצֵא מַחֲנֶה יח
יא עַל־אֹיְבֶיךָ וְנִשְׁמַרְתָּ מִכֹּל דָּבָר רָע׃ כִּי־יִהְיֶה בְךָ אִישׁ אֲשֶׁר לֹא־
יִהְיֶה טָהוֹר מִקְּרֵה־לָיְלָה וְיָצָא אֶל־מִחוּץ לַמַּחֲנֶה לֹא יָבֹא אֶל־תּוֹךְ
יב הַמַּחֲנֶה׃ וְהָיָה לִפְנוֹת־עֶרֶב יִרְחַץ בַּמָּיִם וּכְבֹא הַשֶּׁמֶשׁ יָבֹא אֶל־תּוֹךְ
יג יד הַמַּחֲנֶה׃ וְיָד תִּהְיֶה לְךָ מִחוּץ לַמַּחֲנֶה וְיָצָאתָ שָׁמָּה חוּץ׃ וְיָתֵד תִּהְיֶה
לְךָ עַל־אֲזֵנֶךָ וְהָיָה בְּשִׁבְתְּךָ חוּץ וְחָפַרְתָּה בָהּ וְשַׁבְתָּ וְכִסִּיתָ אֶת־
טו צֵאָתֶךָ׃ כִּי יהוה אֱלֹהֶיךָ מִתְהַלֵּךְ ׀ בְּקֶרֶב מַחֲנֶךָ לְהַצִּילְךָ וְלָתֵת
אֹיְבֶיךָ לְפָנֶיךָ וְהָיָה מַחֲנֶיךָ קָדוֹשׁ וְלֹא־יִרְאֶה בְךָ עֶרְוַת דָּבָר וְשָׁב
טז מֵאַחֲרֶיךָ׃ לֹא־תַסְגִּיר עֶבֶד אֶל־אֲדֹנָיו אֲשֶׁר־יִנָּצֵל
יז אֵלֶיךָ מֵעִם אֲדֹנָיו׃ עִמְּךָ יֵשֵׁב בְּקִרְבְּךָ בַּמָּקוֹם אֲשֶׁר־יִבְחַר בְּאַחַד
יח שְׁעָרֶיךָ בַּטּוֹב לוֹ לֹא תּוֹנֶנּוּ׃ לֹא־תִהְיֶה קְדֵשָׁה מִבְּנוֹת
יט יִשְׂרָאֵל וְלֹא־יִהְיֶה קָדֵשׁ מִבְּנֵי יִשְׂרָאֵל׃ לֹא־תָבִיא אֶתְנַן זוֹנָה וּמְחִיר
כֶּלֶב בֵּית יהוה אֱלֹהֶיךָ לְכָל־נֶדֶר כִּי תוֹעֲבַת יהוה אֱלֹהֶיךָ גַּם־
כ שְׁנֵיהֶם׃ לֹא־תַשִּׁיךְ לְאָחִיךָ נֶשֶׁךְ כֶּסֶף נֶשֶׁךְ אֹכֶל נֶשֶׁךְ
כא כָּל־דָּבָר אֲשֶׁר יִשָּׁךְ׃ לַנָּכְרִי תַשִּׁיךְ וּלְאָחִיךָ לֹא תַשִּׁיךְ לְמַעַן יְבָרֶכְךָ
יהוה אֱלֹהֶיךָ בְּכֹל מִשְׁלַח יָדֶךָ עַל־הָאָרֶץ אֲשֶׁר־אַתָּה בָא־שָׁמָּה
כב לְרִשְׁתָּהּ׃ כִּי־תִדֹּר נֶדֶר לַיהוה אֱלֹהֶיךָ לֹא תְאַחֵר לְשַׁלְּמוֹ יט
כג כִּי־דָרֹשׁ יִדְרְשֶׁנּוּ יהוה אֱלֹהֶיךָ מֵעִמָּךְ וְהָיָה בְךָ חֵטְא׃ וְכִי תֶחְדַּל
כד לִנְדֹּר לֹא־יִהְיֶה בְךָ חֵטְא׃ מוֹצָא שְׂפָתֶיךָ תִּשְׁמֹר וְעָשִׂיתָ כַּאֲשֶׁר
כה נָדַרְתָּ לַיהוה אֱלֹהֶיךָ נְדָבָה אֲשֶׁר דִּבַּרְתָּ בְּפִיךָ׃ כִּי חמישי

neighbor's vineyard,[56] you may eat as many grapes as you wish; eat your fill,
26 but do not put any in a container. When you enter your neighbor's
field of standing grain, you may pluck ears with your hand, but you may
24 1 not put a sickle to your neighbor's grain. If a man takes a wife and
becomes her husband, but begins to dislike her because he finds something
indecent in her if he writes her a bill of divorce, puts it in her hand, and sends
2 her from his house, she may leave his house and become another man's wife.
3 However, if the second husband rejects her, writes her a bill of divorce, puts
it in her hand, and sends her from his house, or the second husband dies, her
4 first husband, who sent her away, is not permitted to take her again to be his
wife after she has been defiled,[57] for that would be abhorrent to the Lord, and
you must not bring sin into the land that the Lord your God is giving you
5 for your possession. When a man is newly married, he shall not go
out with the army or have any related duty laid on him. He shall be exempt
for one year, to be with his home and bring happiness to the woman he has
6 married. Do not take an upper or lower millstone as security for a debt, for that
7 would be taking a person's livelihood as security. If someone is found
to have kidnapped another Israelite, enslaving or selling him, the kidnapper
8 shall die. You must purge the evil from your midst. Take great care
in cases of impure blight. Carefully do whatever the Levitical priests instruct
9 you, as I have commanded them. Remember what the Lord your God did
10 to Miriam on your way when you left Egypt.[58] When you make
your neighbor a loan of any kind, do not go into his house to take his pledge.
11 Wait outside while the person to whom you are making the loan brings the
12 pledge out to you. If the person is poor, do not go to sleep with the pledge in
13 your possession. You must return his pledge by sunset, so that he may sleep
in his cloak[59] and bless you. This will be accounted to you as a righteous act
14 before the Lord your God. Do not take advantage of a poor and
destitute laborer, whether he is a kinsman or a migrant living in one of the
15 towns in your land. Pay him his wages on the same day, before sunset, because
he is poor and his livelihood depends on it. Otherwise he will cry out to the
16 Lord against you, and you will bear your guilt. Parents shall not
be put to death for their children, nor shall children be put to death for their
17 parents. A person shall be put to death only for his own sin. Do not
deprive a migrant or an orphan of justice. Do not take a widow's garment as
18 a pledge. Remember that you were a slave in Egypt and the Lord your God
19 redeemed you from there. And so I command you in this. When you
reap the harvest in your field and forget a sheaf in the field, do not go back to
get it. Leave it for the migrant, the orphan, and the widow, so that the Lord
20 your God may grant you blessing in all the work of your hands. When

---

56 | According to tradition, this refers to a laborer employed in the field.

57 | That is, the second relationship makes a return to her first husband improper. The word "defiled" does not imply any indecency inherent in the second marriage.

58 | See Numbers, chapter 12.

59 | The pledge in question is evidently a garment worn at night; cf. Exodus 22:24–26.

תָבֹא בְּכֶרֶם רֵעֶךָ וְאָכַלְתָּ עֲנָבִים כְּנַפְשְׁךָ שָׂבְעֶךָ וְאֶל־כֶּלְיְךָ לֹא
כו תִתֵּן׃ כִּי תָבֹא בְּקָמַת רֵעֶךָ וְקָטַפְתָּ מְלִילֹת בְּיָדֶךָ
כד א וְחֶרְמֵשׁ לֹא תָנִיף עַל קָמַת רֵעֶךָ׃ כִּי־יִקַּח אִישׁ אִשָּׁה
וּבְעָלָהּ וְהָיָה אִם־לֹא תִמְצָא־חֵן בְּעֵינָיו כִּי־מָצָא בָהּ עֶרְוַת דָּבָר
ב וְכָתַב לָהּ סֵפֶר כְּרִיתֻת וְנָתַן בְּיָדָהּ וְשִׁלְּחָהּ מִבֵּיתוֹ׃ וְיָצְאָה מִבֵּיתוֹ
ג וְהָלְכָה וְהָיְתָה לְאִישׁ־אַחֵר׃ וּשְׂנֵאָהּ הָאִישׁ הָאַחֲרוֹן וְכָתַב לָהּ סֵפֶר
כְּרִיתֻת וְנָתַן בְּיָדָהּ וְשִׁלְּחָהּ מִבֵּיתוֹ אוֹ כִי יָמוּת הָאִישׁ הָאַחֲרוֹן אֲשֶׁר־
ד לְקָחָהּ לוֹ לְאִשָּׁה׃ לֹא־יוּכַל בַּעְלָהּ הָרִאשׁוֹן אֲשֶׁר־שִׁלְּחָהּ לָשׁוּב
לְקַחְתָּהּ לִהְיוֹת לוֹ לְאִשָּׁה אַחֲרֵי אֲשֶׁר הֻטַּמָּאָה כִּי־תוֹעֵבָה הִוא
לִפְנֵי יְהוָה וְלֹא תַחֲטִיא אֶת־הָאָרֶץ אֲשֶׁר יְהוָה אֱלֹהֶיךָ נֹתֵן לְךָ
ה נַחֲלָה׃ כִּי־יִקַּח אִישׁ אִשָּׁה חֲדָשָׁה לֹא יֵצֵא בַּצָּבָא וְלֹא־ ששי
יַעֲבֹר עָלָיו לְכָל־דָּבָר נָקִי יִהְיֶה לְבֵיתוֹ שָׁנָה אֶחָת וְשִׂמַּח אֶת־אִשְׁתּוֹ
ו ז אֲשֶׁר־לָקָח׃ לֹא־יַחֲבֹל רֵחַיִם וָרָכֶב כִּי־נֶפֶשׁ הוּא חֹבֵל׃ כִּי־
יִמָּצֵא אִישׁ גֹּנֵב נֶפֶשׁ מֵאֶחָיו מִבְּנֵי יִשְׂרָאֵל וְהִתְעַמֶּר־בּוֹ וּמְכָרוֹ
ח וּמֵת הַגַּנָּב הַהוּא וּבִעַרְתָּ הָרָע מִקִּרְבֶּךָ׃ הִשָּׁמֶר בְּנֶגַע־
הַצָּרַעַת לִשְׁמֹר מְאֹד וְלַעֲשׂוֹת כְּכֹל אֲשֶׁר־יוֹרוּ אֶתְכֶם הַכֹּהֲנִים
ט הַלְוִיִּם כַּאֲשֶׁר צִוִּיתִם תִּשְׁמְרוּ לַעֲשׂוֹת׃ זָכוֹר אֵת אֲשֶׁר־עָשָׂה יְהוָה
י אֱלֹהֶיךָ לְמִרְיָם בַּדָּרֶךְ בְּצֵאתְכֶם מִמִּצְרָיִם׃ כִּי־תַשֶּׁה בְרֵעֲךָ
יא מַשַּׁאת מְאוּמָה לֹא־תָבֹא אֶל־בֵּיתוֹ לַעֲבֹט עֲבֹטוֹ׃ בַּחוּץ תַּעֲמֹד
יב וְהָאִישׁ אֲשֶׁר אַתָּה נֹשֶׁה בוֹ יוֹצִיא אֵלֶיךָ אֶת־הַעֲבוֹט הַחוּצָה׃ וְאִם־
יג אִישׁ עָנִי הוּא לֹא תִשְׁכַּב בַּעֲבֹטוֹ׃ הָשֵׁב תָּשִׁיב לוֹ אֶת־הַעֲבוֹט כְּבוֹא
הַשֶּׁמֶשׁ וְשָׁכַב בְּשַׂלְמָתוֹ וּבֵרְכֶךָּ וּלְךָ תִּהְיֶה צְדָקָה לִפְנֵי יְהוָה
יד אֱלֹהֶיךָ׃ לֹא־תַעֲשֹׁק שָׂכִיר עָנִי וְאֶבְיוֹן מֵאַחֶיךָ אוֹ מִגֵּרְךָ שביעי
טו אֲשֶׁר בְּאַרְצְךָ בִּשְׁעָרֶיךָ׃ בְּיוֹמוֹ תִתֵּן שְׂכָרוֹ וְלֹא־תָבוֹא עָלָיו הַשֶּׁמֶשׁ
כִּי עָנִי הוּא וְאֵלָיו הוּא נֹשֵׂא אֶת־נַפְשׁוֹ וְלֹא־יִקְרָא עָלֶיךָ אֶל־יְהוָה
טז וְהָיָה בְךָ חֵטְא׃ לֹא־יוּמְתוּ אָבוֹת עַל־בָּנִים וּבָנִים לֹא־
יז יוּמְתוּ עַל־אָבוֹת אִישׁ בְּחֶטְאוֹ יוּמָתוּ׃ לֹא תַטֶּה מִשְׁפַּט
יח גֵּר יָתוֹם וְלֹא תַחֲבֹל בֶּגֶד אַלְמָנָה׃ וְזָכַרְתָּ כִּי עֶבֶד הָיִיתָ בְּמִצְרַיִם
וַיִּפְדְּךָ יְהוָה אֱלֹהֶיךָ מִשָּׁם עַל־כֵּן אָנֹכִי מְצַוְּךָ לַעֲשׂוֹת אֶת־הַדָּבָר
יט הַזֶּה׃ כִּי תִקְצֹר קְצִירְךָ בְשָׂדֶךָ וְשָׁכַחְתָּ עֹמֶר בַּשָּׂדֶה לֹא כ
תָשׁוּב לְקַחְתּוֹ לַגֵּר לַיָּתוֹם וְלָאַלְמָנָה יִהְיֶה לְמַעַן יְבָרֶכְךָ יְהוָה
כ אֱלֹהֶיךָ בְּכֹל מַעֲשֵׂה יָדֶיךָ׃ כִּי תַחְבֹּט זֵיתְךָ לֹא תְפַאֵר

you beat the fruit from your olive trees, do not go over them again. Leave what
21 remains for the migrant, the orphan, and the widow. When you gather the
grapes of your vineyard, do not go over the vines again. Leave what remains
22 for the migrant, the orphan, and the widow. Remember that you were a slave
25 1 in the land of Egypt. And so I command you in this. When two
people have a dispute they shall go to the court of justice and the judges shall
2 decide between them, acquitting the innocent and condemning the guilty. If
the guilty person is to be flogged, the judge shall make him lie down and have
3 him flogged there in his presence with the requisite number of lashes. He may
be given as many as forty lashes but no more; if he is given more lashes than
4 this, an excessive flogging, your kinsman will be degraded in your eyes. Do
5 not muzzle an ox while it is treading out the grain. When brothers
live together, and one of them dies without a son, his widow shall not be
married to a stranger outside the family. Her husband's brother shall come
6 to her and take her in marriage, fulfilling the duty of a brother-in-law. The
firstborn son whom she bears will perpetuate the name of the dead brother,
7 so that his name is not erased from Israel. But if the man does not wish to
marry his brother's widow, she shall go up to the elders at the gate and say,
'My husband's brother refuses to perpetuate his brother's name in Israel. He
8 does not care to perform the duty of a brother-in-law for me.' The elders of
the town shall summon him and they must talk to him. If he persists in saying,
9 'I have no desire to marry her,' then his brother's widow shall go up to him
in the presence of the elders, pull the sandal from his foot, spit in his face,
and say, 'This is what is done to the man who will not build up his brother's
10 house.' Throughout Israel his family shall be known as 'the house of the one
11 whose sandal was pulled off.' If two men fight, and the wife of one
comes to defend her husband from the one who does him harm by reaching
12 out and seizing the man's genitals, you shall cut off her hand: show no
13 pity.[60] Do not have two different weights in your bag, one large and
14 the other small. Do not have in your house two different measures, one large
15 and other small. You must have a full and honest weight and a full and honest
measure, so that your days may be long on the land that the LORD your God is
16 giving you. Whoever does such things, whoever acts dishonestly, is abhorrent
to the LORD your God.
17 18 Remember what Amalek did to you on your way as you left Egypt,[61] how he
attacked you on the way, when you were tired and exhausted, striking down
19 all the stragglers in your rear, with no fear of God. And so, when the LORD
your God gives you rest from all the enemies around you in the land that the
LORD your God is giving you as an inheritance to possess, you shall blot out
the memory of Amalek from beneath the sky. Do not forget.
26 1 "When you have come into the land that the LORD your God is giving you as KI TAVO
2 a possession, and have taken possession and settled in it, you shall take some
of every first fruit of the soil, which you harvest from the land that the LORD

60 | According to rabbinic interpretation, the actual punishment is monetary.
61 | See Exodus 17:8–16.

כא אחריך לגר ליתום ולאלמנה יהיה: כי תבצר כרמך לא תעולל
כב אחריך לגר ליתום ולאלמנה יהיה: וזכרת כי־עבד היית בארץ
כה א מצרים על־כן אנכי מצוך לעשות את־הדבר הזה: כי־
יהיה ריב בין אנשים ונגשו אל־המשפט ושפטום והצדיקו את־
ב הצדיק והרשיעו את־הרשע: והיה אם־בן הכות הרשע והפילו
ג השפט והכהו לפניו כדי רשעתו במספר: ארבעים יכנו לא יסיף
ד פן־יסיף להכתו על־אלה מכה רבה ונקלה אחיך לעיניך: לא־תחסם
ה שור בדישו: כי־ישבו אחים יחדו ומת אחד מהם ובן
אין־לו לא־תהיה אשת־המת החוצה לאיש זר יבמה יבא עליה
ו ולקחה לו לאשה ויבמה: והיה הבכור אשר תלד יקום על־שם אחיו
ז המת ולא־ימחה שמו מישראל: ואם־לא יחפץ האיש לקחת את־
יבמתו ועלתה יבמתו השערה אל־הזקנים ואמרה מאן יבמי להקים
ח לאחיו שם בישראל לא אבה יבמי: וקראו־לו זקני־עירו ודברו אליו
ט ועמד ואמר לא חפצתי לקחתה: ונגשה יבמתו אליו לעיני הזקנים
וחלצה נעלו מעל רגלו וירקה בפניו וענתה ואמרה ככה יעשה
י לאיש אשר לא־יבנה את־בית אחיו: ונקרא שמו בישראל בית
יא חלוץ הנעל: כי־ינצו אנשים יחדו איש ואחיו וקרבה
אשת האחד להציל את־אישה מיד מכהו ושלחה ידה והחזיקה
יב יג במבשיו: וקצתה את־כפה לא תחוס עינך: לא־יהיה לך
יד בכיסך אבן ואבן גדולה וקטנה: לא־יהיה לך בביתך איפה ואיפה
טו גדולה וקטנה: אבן שלמה וצדק יהיה־לך איפה שלמה וצדק יהיה־
טז לך למען יאריכו ימיך על האדמה אשר־יהוה אלהיך נתן לך: כי
תועבת יהוה אלהיך כל־עשה אלה כל עשה עול:
יז יח זכור את אשר־עשה לך עמלק בדרך בצאתכם ממצרים: אשר מפטיר
קרך בדרך ויזנב בך כל־הנחשלים אחריך ואתה עיף ויגע ולא
יט ירא אלהים: והיה בהניח יהוה אלהיך ׀ לך מכל־איביך מסביב
בארץ אשר־יהוה אלהיך נתן לך נחלה לרשתה תמחה את־זכר
עמלק מתחת השמים לא תשכח: כא
כו א והיה כי־תבוא אל־הארץ אשר יהוה אלהיך נתן לך נחלה וירשתה כי תבוא
ב וישבת בה: ולקחת מראשית ׀ כל־פרי האדמה אשר תביא מארצך
אשר יהוה אלהיך נתן לך ושמת בטנא והלכת אל־המקום אשר

your God is giving you. Put it in a basket and go to the place that the LORD
3 your God will choose as a dwelling for His name. You shall go to the priest
officiating at that time and say to him, 'I declare today to the LORD your God
that I have come into the land that the LORD swore to our ancestors to give
4 us.' The priest shall take the basket from your hand and set it down before the
5 altar of the LORD your God. You shall then make this declaration before the
LORD your God: 'My ancestor was a wandering Aramean.[62] He went down
into Egypt and lived there as a stranger, just a handful of souls, and there he
6 became a nation – large, mighty, and great. And the Egyptians dealt cruelly
7 with us and oppressed us, subjecting us to harsh labor. We cried out to the
LORD, God of our ancestors. And the LORD heard our voice and He saw our
8 oppression, our toil, and our enslavement. The LORD brought us out of Egypt
with a mighty hand and His arm stretched forth, with terrifying power, with
9 signs, and with wonders. He brought us into this place and He gave us this
10 land, a land flowing with milk and with honey. And now I am bringing the
first fruit of the land that You, O LORD, have given me.' Set the basket down
before the LORD your God, and then bow down low before the LORD your
11 God. Then you, with the Levites and the migrants who live among you, shall
rejoice in all the good that the LORD your God has bestowed on you and on
12 your household. When you have finished setting aside a tenth of all
your produce in the third year, the year of the tithe,[63] and have given it to the
Levites, the migrants, the orphans, and the widows, so that they may eat in
13 your towns and be satisfied, you shall declare before the LORD your God: 'I
have removed the consecrated portion from my house, and I have given it to
the Levites and the migrants, the orphans, and the widows, just as You commanded me. I have not transgressed or forgotten any of Your commandments.
14 I have not eaten of it while in mourning. I have not removed any of it while
impure. I have not offered any of it to the dead. I have obeyed the LORD my
15 God, doing just as You commanded me. Look down from Your holy habi-
tation, from heaven, and bless Your people Israel and the land that You have
given us, as You swore to our ancestors – a land flowing with milk and with
16 honey.' The LORD your God is commanding you this day to keep
these decrees and laws. Take care to keep them with all your heart and with all
17 your soul. Today you have proclaimed the LORD to be your God, and that you
will walk in His ways, keep His decrees, commandments, and laws, and listen
18 to His voice. And today the LORD has proclaimed you to be, as He promised
19 you, His treasured people who guard His commands; He will set you high
above all the nations He has made, in praise, fame, and honor. You will be a
people holy to the LORD your God, just as He has promised."
27 1 Then Moshe and the elders of Israel charged the people: "Keep all of the
2 command that I charge you with this day. On the day that you cross the Jordan
to the land that the LORD your God is giving you, set up large boulders, and

---

62 | Apparently a reference to Yaakov, whose mother Rivka was Aramean and who lived for a time in Aram (Gen. 27:41–28:5).

63 | See 14:28–29.

ג יִבְחַר יְהוָה אֱלֹהֶיךָ לְשַׁכֵּן שְׁמוֹ שָׁם: וּבָאתָ אֶל־הַכֹּהֵן אֲשֶׁר יִהְיֶה
בַּיָּמִים הָהֵם וְאָמַרְתָּ אֵלָיו הִגַּדְתִּי הַיּוֹם לַיהוָה אֱלֹהֶיךָ כִּי־בָאתִי אֶל־
ד הָאָרֶץ אֲשֶׁר נִשְׁבַּע יְהוָה לַאֲבֹתֵינוּ לָתֶת לָנוּ: וְלָקַח הַכֹּהֵן הַטֶּנֶא
ה מִיָּדֶךָ וְהִנִּיחוֹ לִפְנֵי מִזְבַּח יְהוָה אֱלֹהֶיךָ: וְעָנִיתָ וְאָמַרְתָּ לִפְנֵי ׀ יְהוָה
אֱלֹהֶיךָ אֲרַמִּי אֹבֵד אָבִי וַיֵּרֶד מִצְרַיְמָה וַיָּגָר שָׁם בִּמְתֵי מְעָט וַיְהִי־
ו שָׁם לְגוֹי גָּדוֹל עָצוּם וָרָב: וַיָּרֵעוּ אֹתָנוּ הַמִּצְרִים וַיְעַנּוּנוּ וַיִּתְּנוּ עָלֵינוּ
ז עֲבֹדָה קָשָׁה: וַנִּצְעַק אֶל־יְהוָה אֱלֹהֵי אֲבֹתֵינוּ וַיִּשְׁמַע יְהוָה אֶת־קֹלֵנוּ
ח וַיַּרְא אֶת־עָנְיֵנוּ וְאֶת־עֲמָלֵנוּ וְאֶת־לַחֲצֵנוּ: וַיּוֹצִאֵנוּ יְהוָה מִמִּצְרַיִם
ט בְּיָד חֲזָקָה וּבִזְרֹעַ נְטוּיָה וּבְמֹרָא גָּדֹל וּבְאֹתוֹת וּבְמֹפְתִים: וַיְבִאֵנוּ
אֶל־הַמָּקוֹם הַזֶּה וַיִּתֶּן־לָנוּ אֶת־הָאָרֶץ הַזֹּאת אֶרֶץ זָבַת חָלָב וּדְבָשׁ:
י וְעַתָּה הִנֵּה הֵבֵאתִי אֶת־רֵאשִׁית פְּרִי הָאֲדָמָה אֲשֶׁר־נָתַתָּה לִּי יְהוָה
יא וְהִנַּחְתּוֹ לִפְנֵי יְהוָה אֱלֹהֶיךָ וְהִשְׁתַּחֲוִיתָ לִפְנֵי יְהוָה אֱלֹהֶיךָ: וְשָׂמַחְתָּ
בְכָל־הַטּוֹב אֲשֶׁר נָתַן־לְךָ יְהוָה אֱלֹהֶיךָ וּלְבֵיתֶךָ אַתָּה וְהַלֵּוִי וְהַגֵּר
יב אֲשֶׁר בְּקִרְבֶּךָ: כִּי תְכַלֶּה לַעְשֵׂר אֶת־כָּל־מַעְשַׂר תְּבוּאָתְךָ שני
בַּשָּׁנָה הַשְּׁלִישִׁת שְׁנַת הַמַּעֲשֵׂר וְנָתַתָּה לַלֵּוִי לַגֵּר לַיָּתוֹם וְלָאַלְמָנָה
יג וְאָכְלוּ בִשְׁעָרֶיךָ וְשָׂבֵעוּ: וְאָמַרְתָּ לִפְנֵי יְהוָה אֱלֹהֶיךָ בִּעַרְתִּי הַקֹּדֶשׁ
מִן־הַבַּיִת וְגַם נְתַתִּיו לַלֵּוִי וְלַגֵּר לַיָּתוֹם וְלָאַלְמָנָה כְּכָל־מִצְוָתְךָ אֲשֶׁר
יד צִוִּיתָנִי לֹא־עָבַרְתִּי מִמִּצְוֺתֶיךָ וְלֹא שָׁכָחְתִּי: לֹא־אָכַלְתִּי בְאֹנִי מִמֶּנּוּ
וְלֹא־בִעַרְתִּי מִמֶּנּוּ בְּטָמֵא וְלֹא־נָתַתִּי מִמֶּנּוּ לְמֵת שָׁמַעְתִּי בְּקוֹל יְהוָה
טו אֱלֹהָי עָשִׂיתִי כְּכֹל אֲשֶׁר צִוִּיתָנִי: הַשְׁקִיפָה מִמְּעוֹן קָדְשְׁךָ מִן־הַשָּׁמַיִם
וּבָרֵךְ אֶת־עַמְּךָ אֶת־יִשְׂרָאֵל וְאֵת הָאֲדָמָה אֲשֶׁר נָתַתָּה לָנוּ כַּאֲשֶׁר
טז נִשְׁבַּעְתָּ לַאֲבֹתֵינוּ אֶרֶץ זָבַת חָלָב וּדְבָשׁ: הַיּוֹם הַזֶּה יְהוָה שלישי
אֱלֹהֶיךָ מְצַוְּךָ לַעֲשׂוֹת אֶת־הַחֻקִּים הָאֵלֶּה וְאֶת־הַמִּשְׁפָּטִים וְשָׁמַרְתָּ
יז וְעָשִׂיתָ אוֹתָם בְּכָל־לְבָבְךָ וּבְכָל־נַפְשֶׁךָ: אֶת־יְהוָה הֶאֱמַרְתָּ הַיּוֹם
לִהְיוֹת לְךָ לֵאלֹהִים וְלָלֶכֶת בִּדְרָכָיו וְלִשְׁמֹר חֻקָּיו וּמִצְוֺתָיו וּמִשְׁפָּטָיו
יח וְלִשְׁמֹעַ בְּקֹלוֹ: וַיהוָה הֶאֱמִירְךָ הַיּוֹם לִהְיוֹת לוֹ לְעַם סְגֻלָּה כַּאֲשֶׁר
יט דִּבֶּר־לָךְ וְלִשְׁמֹר כָּל־מִצְוֺתָיו: וּלְתִתְּךָ עֶלְיוֹן עַל כָּל־הַגּוֹיִם אֲשֶׁר
עָשָׂה לִתְהִלָּה וּלְשֵׁם וּלְתִפְאָרֶת וְלִהְיֹתְךָ עַם־קָדֹשׁ לַיהוָה אֱלֹהֶיךָ
כַּאֲשֶׁר דִּבֵּר:
כז א וַיְצַו מֹשֶׁה וְזִקְנֵי יִשְׂרָאֵל אֶת־הָעָם לֵאמֹר שָׁמֹר אֶת־כָּל־הַמִּצְוָה רביעי
ב אֲשֶׁר אָנֹכִי מְצַוֶּה אֶתְכֶם הַיּוֹם: וְהָיָה בַּיּוֹם אֲשֶׁר תַּעַבְרוּ אֶת־הַיַּרְדֵּן
אֶל־הָאָרֶץ אֲשֶׁר־יְהוָה אֱלֹהֶיךָ נֹתֵן לָךְ וַהֲקֵמֹתָ לְךָ אֲבָנִים גְּדֹלוֹת

3 coat them with plaster, and write on them all the words of this Law when you
cross over, that you may enter the land that the Lord your God is giving you,
a land flowing with milk and with honey, as the Lord, God of your ancestors,
4 promised you. When you cross the Jordan, set up these stones, as I command
5 you today, on Mount Eival,[64] and coat them with plaster. And there, build an
altar to the Lord your God, an altar of stones. Do not take any iron tool to
6 them: of uncut stones[65] you shall build the altar of the Lord your God. On
7 it, offer burnt offerings to the Lord your God. You shall also sacrifice peace
8 offerings and eat them there, rejoicing before the Lord your God. On the
9 boulders you shall write very clearly all the words of this Law." Then
Moshe and the Levitical priests spoke to all Israel: "Be still and listen, Israel.
10 Today you have become the people of the Lord your God. Therefore listen
to the Lord your God, keeping His commandments and decrees, with which
11 I charge you on this day." On that day Moshe charged the people:
12 "When you have crossed the Jordan, these shall stand on Mount Gerizim
to bless the people: Shimon, Levi, Yehuda, Yissakhar, Yosef, and Binyamin.
13 And these shall stand on Mount Eival for the curse: Reuven, Gad, Asher,
14 Zevulun, Dan, and Naftali. The Levites shall then recite to all the Israelites
15 in a loud voice: 'Cursed be one who makes a graven or molten
image, abhorrent to the Lord, the work of a craftsman, and secretly sets
16 it up.' And all the people shall respond and say, 'Amen!' 'Cursed
be one who degrades his father or mother.' And all the people shall say,
17 'Amen!' 'Cursed be one who moves back his neighbor's bound-
18 ary marker.' And all the people shall say, 'Amen!' 'Cursed be one
who leads a blind person astray along his way.' And all the people shall say,
19 'Amen!' 'Cursed be one who deprives the migrant, orphan, or widow
20 of justice.' And all the people shall say, 'Amen!' 'Cursed be one who lies with
his father's wife, dishonoring his father's bed.' And all the people shall say,
21 'Amen!' 'Cursed be one who lies with any animal.' And all the people
22 shall say, 'Amen!' 'Cursed be anyone who lies with his sister, whether
she is the daughter of his father or of his mother.' And all the people shall
23 say, 'Amen!' 'Cursed be one who lies with his mother-in-law.' And
24 all the people shall say, 'Amen!' 'Cursed be one who strikes down
25 his fellow in secret.' And all the people shall say, 'Amen!' 'Cursed
be one who accepts a bribe to execute an innocent man.' And all the people
26 shall say, 'Amen!' 'Cursed be one who does not uphold the words
of this Law by keeping them.' And all the people shall say, 'Amen!'
28 1 If you listen faithfully to the Lord your God, taking care to keep all His
commandments, which I am commanding you today, the Lord your God

---

64 | See Joshua 8:30–35.
65 | Cf. Exodus 20:22.

ג וְשַׂדְתָּ אֹתָם בַּשִּׂיד׃ וְכָתַבְתָּ עֲלֵיהֶן אֶת־כָּל־דִּבְרֵי הַתּוֹרָה הַזֹּאת
בְּעָבְרֶךָ לְמַעַן אֲשֶׁר תָּבֹא אֶל־הָאָרֶץ אֲשֶׁר־יהוה אֱלֹהֶיךָ ׀ נֹתֵן
לְךָ אֶרֶץ זָבַת חָלָב וּדְבַשׁ כַּאֲשֶׁר דִּבֶּר יהוה אֱלֹהֵי־אֲבֹתֶיךָ לָךְ׃
ד וְהָיָה בְּעָבְרְכֶם אֶת־הַיַּרְדֵּן תָּקִימוּ אֶת־הָאֲבָנִים הָאֵלֶּה אֲשֶׁר
ה אָנֹכִי מְצַוֶּה אֶתְכֶם הַיּוֹם בְּהַר עֵיבָל וְשַׂדְתָּ אוֹתָם בַּשִּׂיד׃ וּבָנִיתָ
שָּׁם מִזְבֵּחַ לַיהוה אֱלֹהֶיךָ מִזְבַּח אֲבָנִים לֹא־תָנִיף עֲלֵיהֶם בַּרְזֶל׃
ו אֲבָנִים שְׁלֵמוֹת תִּבְנֶה אֶת־מִזְבַּח יהוה אֱלֹהֶיךָ וְהַעֲלִיתָ עָלָיו עוֹלֹת
ז לַיהוה אֱלֹהֶיךָ׃ וְזָבַחְתָּ שְׁלָמִים וְאָכַלְתָּ שָּׁם וְשָׂמַחְתָּ לִפְנֵי יהוה
ח אֱלֹהֶיךָ׃ וְכָתַבְתָּ עַל־הָאֲבָנִים אֶת־כָּל־דִּבְרֵי הַתּוֹרָה הַזֹּאת בַּאֵר
ט הֵיטֵב׃ וַיְדַבֵּר מֹשֶׁה וְהַכֹּהֲנִים הַלְוִיִּם אֶל־כָּל־יִשְׂרָאֵל
לֵאמֹר הַסְכֵּת ׀ וּשְׁמַע יִשְׂרָאֵל הַיּוֹם הַזֶּה נִהְיֵיתָ לְעָם לַיהוה אֱלֹהֶיךָ׃
י וְשָׁמַעְתָּ בְּקוֹל יהוה אֱלֹהֶיךָ וְעָשִׂיתָ אֶת־מִצְוֺתָו וְאֶת־חֻקָּיו אֲשֶׁר
יא אָנֹכִי מְצַוְּךָ הַיּוֹם׃ וַיְצַו מֹשֶׁה אֶת־הָעָם בַּיּוֹם הַהוּא חמישי
יב לֵאמֹר׃ אֵלֶּה יַעַמְדוּ לְבָרֵךְ אֶת־הָעָם עַל־הַר גְּרִזִּים בְּעָבְרְכֶם אֶת־
יג הַיַּרְדֵּן שִׁמְעוֹן וְלֵוִי וִיהוּדָה וְיִשָּׂשכָר וְיוֹסֵף וּבִנְיָמִן׃ וְאֵלֶּה יַעַמְדוּ
יד עַל־הַקְּלָלָה בְּהַר עֵיבָל רְאוּבֵן גָּד וְאָשֵׁר וּזְבוּלֻן דָּן וְנַפְתָּלִי׃ וְעָנוּ
טו הַלְוִיִּם וְאָמְרוּ אֶל־כָּל־אִישׁ יִשְׂרָאֵל קוֹל רָם׃ אָרוּר
הָאִישׁ אֲשֶׁר יַעֲשֶׂה פֶסֶל וּמַסֵּכָה תּוֹעֲבַת יהוה מַעֲשֵׂה יְדֵי חָרָשׁ
טז וְשָׂם בַּסָּתֶר וְעָנוּ כָל־הָעָם וְאָמְרוּ אָמֵן׃ אָרוּר מַקְלֶה
יז אָבִיו וְאִמּוֹ וְאָמַר כָּל־הָעָם אָמֵן׃ אָרוּר מַסִּיג גְּבוּל רֵעֵהוּ
יח וְאָמַר כָּל־הָעָם אָמֵן׃ אָרוּר מַשְׁגֶּה עִוֵּר בַּדָּרֶךְ וְאָמַר
יט כָּל־הָעָם אָמֵן׃ אָרוּר מַטֶּה מִשְׁפַּט גֵּר־יָתוֹם וְאַלְמָנָה
כ וְאָמַר כָּל־הָעָם אָמֵן׃ אָרוּר שֹׁכֵב עִם־אֵשֶׁת אָבִיו כִּי גִלָּה כְּנַף אָבִיו
כא וְאָמַר כָּל־הָעָם אָמֵן׃ אָרוּר שֹׁכֵב עִם־כָּל־בְּהֵמָה וְאָמַר
כב כָּל־הָעָם אָמֵן׃ אָרוּר שֹׁכֵב עִם־אֲחֹתוֹ בַּת־אָבִיו אוֹ בַת־
כג אִמּוֹ וְאָמַר כָּל־הָעָם אָמֵן׃ אָרוּר שֹׁכֵב עִם־חֹתַנְתּוֹ וְאָמַר
כד כָּל־הָעָם אָמֵן׃ אָרוּר מַכֵּה רֵעֵהוּ בַּסָּתֶר וְאָמַר כָּל־
כה הָעָם אָמֵן׃ אָרוּר לֹקֵחַ שֹׁחַד לְהַכּוֹת נֶפֶשׁ דַּם נָקִי וְאָמַר
כו כָּל־הָעָם אָמֵן׃ אָרוּר אֲשֶׁר לֹא־יָקִים אֶת־דִּבְרֵי הַתּוֹרָה־
הַזֹּאת לַעֲשׂוֹת אוֹתָם וְאָמַר כָּל־הָעָם אָמֵן׃
כח א וְהָיָה אִם־שָׁמוֹעַ תִּשְׁמַע בְּקוֹל יהוה אֱלֹהֶיךָ לִשְׁמֹר לַעֲשׂוֹת אֶת־ כב
כָּל־מִצְוֺתָיו אֲשֶׁר אָנֹכִי מְצַוְּךָ הַיּוֹם וּנְתָנְךָ יהוה אֱלֹהֶיךָ עֶלְיוֹן עַל

2 will set you above all the nations of this earth. All these blessings will come
upon you – overtake you – if you listen to the voice of the LORD your God:
3 4 Blessed shall you be in the town, and blessed shall you be in the field. Blessed
shall be the fruit of your womb, the fruit of your land, and the fruit of your
5 cattle, the calves of your herd, the lambs of your flock. Blessed shall be your
6 basket and your kneading pan. Blessed shall you be when you enter, and
7 blessed shall you be when you leave. The LORD will cause your enemies who
rise against you to be vanquished before you. They will come at you from one
8 direction, but flee from you in seven. The LORD will send you blessing in your
barns and in all your endeavors. He will bless you in the land that the LORD
9 your God is giving you. The LORD will establish you as His holy people, just
as He has sworn to you, if you keep the LORD your God's commandments
10 and walk in His ways. All the peoples of earth shall see that you are called by
11 the LORD's name, and they shall hold you in awe. The LORD will make you
abound in prosperity, in the fruit of your womb, the fruit of your cattle, and
the fruit of your soil in the land that the LORD swore to your ancestors to give
12 you. The LORD will open for you His treasury of good, the heavens, to give
your land rain in its season, to bless all the work of your hands. You will lend
13 to many nations, and borrow from none. The LORD will make you the head,
never the tail. You shall be always above, and never beneath – if you obey the
commandments of the LORD your God that I am charging you with on this
14 day, taking care to keep them, and if you do not stray from any of the words
that I am commanding you today, either to the right or to the left, to follow
other gods and serve them.

15 But if you do not listen to the voice of the LORD your God, taking care to
keep all His commandments and decrees that I am charging you with on this
16 day, all these curses will come upon you and overtake you: Cursed shall you
17 be in the town, and cursed shall you be in the field. Cursed shall be your
18 basket and your kneading pan. Cursed shall be the fruit of your womb, the
19 fruit of your land, the calves of your herd, the lambs of your flock. Cursed
20 shall you be when you enter, and cursed shall you be when you leave. The
LORD will send upon you curse, panic, and thwarting in every endeavor you
undertake, until you are destroyed and come to sudden ruin because of the
21 evil you have done in forsaking Me. The LORD will make disease cling to you
22 until it consumes you entirely in the land you are coming into to possess. The
LORD will afflict you with consumption, fever, inflammation, scorching heat
23 and drought, blight and mildew. They will pursue you until you die. The sky
24 over your head will be like bronze, and the earth beneath you iron.[66] The
LORD will turn the rain of your land into powder and dust. It will descend
25 upon you from the sky until you are destroyed. The LORD will cause you to
be vanquished before your enemies. You will come at them from one direction but flee before them in seven. You will be an object of horror to all the
26 kingdoms on earth. Your corpses will be food for all the birds of the sky, for
27 the beasts of the earth; there will be no one to make them afraid. The LORD

66 | That is, the sky will not give rain, and the earth will not yield produce.

ב כׇּל־גּוֹיֵי הָאָרֶץ׃ וּבָאוּ עָלֶיךָ כׇּל־הַבְּרָכוֹת הָאֵלֶּה וְהִשִּׂיגֻךָ כִּי תִשְׁמַע
ג ד בְּקוֹל יהוה אֱלֹהֶיךָ׃ בָּרוּךְ אַתָּה בָּעִיר וּבָרוּךְ אַתָּה בַּשָּׂדֶה׃ בָּרוּךְ
פְּרִי־בִטְנְךָ וּפְרִי אַדְמָתְךָ וּפְרִי בְהֶמְתֶּךָ שְׁגַר אֲלָפֶיךָ וְעַשְׁתְּרוֹת צֹאנֶךָ׃
ה ו בָּרוּךְ טַנְאֲךָ וּמִשְׁאַרְתֶּךָ׃ בָּרוּךְ אַתָּה בְּבֹאֶךָ וּבָרוּךְ אַתָּה בְּצֵאתֶךָ׃
ז יִתֵּן יהוה אֶת־אֹיְבֶיךָ הַקָּמִים עָלֶיךָ נִגָּפִים לְפָנֶיךָ בְּדֶרֶךְ אֶחָד יֵצְאוּ ששי
ח אֵלֶיךָ וּבְשִׁבְעָה דְרָכִים יָנוּסוּ לְפָנֶיךָ׃ יְצַו יהוה אִתְּךָ אֶת־הַבְּרָכָה
בַּאֲסָמֶיךָ וּבְכֹל מִשְׁלַח יָדֶךָ וּבֵרַכְךָ בָּאָרֶץ אֲשֶׁר־יהוה אֱלֹהֶיךָ נֹתֵן לָךְ׃
ט יְקִימְךָ יהוה לוֹ לְעַם קָדוֹשׁ כַּאֲשֶׁר נִשְׁבַּע־לָךְ כִּי תִשְׁמֹר אֶת־מִצְוֺת
י יהוה אֱלֹהֶיךָ וְהָלַכְתָּ בִּדְרָכָיו׃ וְרָאוּ כׇּל־עַמֵּי הָאָרֶץ כִּי שֵׁם יהוה נִקְרָא
יא עָלֶיךָ וְיָרְאוּ מִמֶּךָּ׃ וְהוֹתִרְךָ יהוה לְטוֹבָה בִּפְרִי בִטְנְךָ וּבִפְרִי בְהֶמְתְּךָ
וּבִפְרִי אַדְמָתֶךָ עַל הָאֲדָמָה אֲשֶׁר נִשְׁבַּע יהוה לַאֲבֹתֶיךָ לָתֶת לָךְ׃
יב יִפְתַּח יהוה ׀ לְךָ אֶת־אוֹצָרוֹ הַטּוֹב אֶת־הַשָּׁמַיִם לָתֵת מְטַר־אַרְצְךָ
בְּעִתּוֹ וּלְבָרֵךְ אֵת כׇּל־מַעֲשֵׂה יָדֶךָ וְהִלְוִיתָ גּוֹיִם רַבִּים וְאַתָּה לֹא תִלְוֶה׃
יג וּנְתָנְךָ יהוה לְרֹאשׁ וְלֹא לְזָנָב וְהָיִיתָ רַק לְמַעְלָה וְלֹא תִהְיֶה לְמָטָּה
כִּי־תִשְׁמַע אֶל־מִצְוֺת ׀ יהוה אֱלֹהֶיךָ אֲשֶׁר אָנֹכִי מְצַוְּךָ הַיּוֹם לִשְׁמֹר
יד וְלַעֲשׂוֹת׃ וְלֹא תָסוּר מִכׇּל־הַדְּבָרִים אֲשֶׁר אָנֹכִי מְצַוֶּה אֶתְכֶם הַיּוֹם
יָמִין וּשְׂמֹאול לָלֶכֶת אַחֲרֵי אֱלֹהִים אֲחֵרִים לְעׇבְדָם׃
טו וְהָיָה אִם־לֹא תִשְׁמַע בְּקוֹל יהוה אֱלֹהֶיךָ לִשְׁמֹר לַעֲשׂוֹת אֶת־כׇּל־
מִצְוֺתָיו וְחֻקֹּתָיו אֲשֶׁר אָנֹכִי מְצַוְּךָ הַיּוֹם וּבָאוּ עָלֶיךָ כׇּל־הַקְּלָלוֹת
טז יז הָאֵלֶּה וְהִשִּׂיגוּךָ׃ אָרוּר אַתָּה בָּעִיר וְאָרוּר אַתָּה בַּשָּׂדֶה׃ אָרוּר טַנְאֲךָ
יח וּמִשְׁאַרְתֶּךָ׃ אָרוּר פְּרִי־בִטְנְךָ וּפְרִי אַדְמָתֶךָ שְׁגַר אֲלָפֶיךָ וְעַשְׁתְּרֹת
יט כ צֹאנֶךָ׃ אָרוּר אַתָּה בְּבֹאֶךָ וְאָרוּר אַתָּה בְּצֵאתֶךָ׃ יְשַׁלַּח יהוה ׀ בְּךָ
אֶת־הַמְּאֵרָה אֶת־הַמְּהוּמָה וְאֶת־הַמִּגְעֶרֶת בְּכׇל־מִשְׁלַח יָדְךָ אֲשֶׁר
תַּעֲשֶׂה עַד הִשָּׁמֶדְךָ וְעַד־אֲבׇדְךָ מַהֵר מִפְּנֵי רֹעַ מַעֲלָלֶיךָ אֲשֶׁר עֲזַבְתָּנִי׃
כא יַדְבֵּק יהוה בְּךָ אֶת־הַדָּבֶר עַד כַּלֹּתוֹ אֹתְךָ מֵעַל הָאֲדָמָה אֲשֶׁר־אַתָּה
כב בָא־שָׁמָּה לְרִשְׁתָּהּ׃ יַכְּכָה יהוה בַּשַּׁחֶפֶת וּבַקַּדַּחַת וּבַדַּלֶּקֶת וּבַחַרְחֻר
כג וּבַחֶרֶב וּבַשִּׁדָּפוֹן וּבַיֵּרָקוֹן וּרְדָפוּךָ עַד אׇבְדֶךָ׃ וְהָיוּ שָׁמֶיךָ אֲשֶׁר עַל־
כד רֹאשְׁךָ נְחֹשֶׁת וְהָאָרֶץ אֲשֶׁר־תַּחְתֶּיךָ בַּרְזֶל׃ יִתֵּן יהוה אֶת־מְטַר אַרְצְךָ
כה אָבָק וְעָפָר מִן־הַשָּׁמַיִם יֵרֵד עָלֶיךָ עַד הִשָּׁמְדָךְ׃ יִתֶּנְךָ יהוה ׀ נִגָּף לִפְנֵי
אֹיְבֶיךָ בְּדֶרֶךְ אֶחָד תֵּצֵא אֵלָיו וּבְשִׁבְעָה דְרָכִים תָּנוּס לְפָנָיו וְהָיִיתָ
כו לְזַעֲוָה לְכֹל מַמְלְכוֹת הָאָרֶץ׃ וְהָיְתָה נִבְלָתְךָ לְמַאֲכָל לְכׇל־עוֹף
כז הַשָּׁמַיִם וּלְבֶהֱמַת הָאָרֶץ וְאֵין מַחֲרִיד׃ יַכְּכָה יהוה בִּשְׁחִין מִצְרַיִם

will afflict you with the boils of Egypt,[67] with hemorrhoids, rashes, and scabs,
28 from which you shall never recover. The LORD will afflict you with insanity,
29 blindness, confusion of mind. You will grope at noon as a blind man gropes
in darkness. Your way will not prosper. Day after day, you will be abused and
30 looted, and no one will be there to rescue you. You will betroth a woman and
some other man will lie with her. You will build a house, but will not live there.
31 You will plant a vineyard, but not harvest its fruit. Your ox will be slaughtered
before your eyes, but you will not eat of it. Your donkey will be stolen in front
of you, and never return. Your sheep will be given to your enemies, and no
32 one will be there to rescue you. Your sons and daughters will be given over
to another people. You will see it with your own eyes and pine for them all
33 through the day but have no power to act. A people that you do not know will
eat the fruit of your land and of your labor. You will be incessantly abused and
34 35 crushed. The sights you see will drive you to insanity. The LORD will strike
your knees and thighs with incurable infection, spreading from the sole of
36 your foot to the crown of your head. The LORD will bring you and the king
you set over you to a nation that neither you nor your ancestors have known.
37 There you will worship other gods, of wood and of stone. You will become
an object of horror, a proverb, and a byword among all the peoples into whose
38 midst the LORD will lead you. You will carry much seed into the field but
39 gather little, because locusts will eat it. You will plant vineyards and cultivate
them, but you will not drink the wine or gather the grapes, because worms
40 will devour them. You will have olive trees throughout your country, but you
41 will have no oil for anointing, because the olives will fall away. You will bear
sons and daughters, but they will not remain yours, for they will be taken into
42 captivity. Crickets will take over all your trees and the fruit of your land.
43 Strangers in your midst will rise ever higher above you, while you descend
44 ever further beneath. They will lend to you but you will be unable to lend to
45 them. They will be the head and you will be the tail. All these curses will come
upon you; they will pursue and overtake you, until you are destroyed –
because you did not listen to the voice of the LORD your God, keeping the
46 commandments and decrees with which He charged you. They will be a sign
47 and portent to you and your descendants forever. Because you did not serve
the LORD your God with joy and with a heart content in the abundance of
48 all things, you shall serve the enemies whom the LORD will send against you,
in hunger and thirst, in nakedness and the lack of all things. He will lay an iron
49 yoke upon your neck until He has destroyed you. The LORD will bring against
you a nation from afar, from the end of the earth, and it will dart down on you
50 like an eagle; a nation whose language you do not understand, a fierce-faced
51 nation with no respect for the old, no mercy for the young. They will eat the
fruit of your cattle and the fruit of your land until you are destroyed. They will
leave you no grain, wine, or oil, no calves of your herd or lambs of your flock,
52 until they have brought you to death. They will lay siege to you in all the towns
throughout your land until the high, fortified walls in which you placed your

67 | See Exodus 9:9–10.

כח וּבעפלים וּבַגָּרָב וּבֶחָרֶס אֲשֶׁר לֹא־תוּכַל לְהֵרָפֵא׃ יַכְּכָה יהוה בְּשִׁגָּעוֹן וּבַטְּחֹרִים
כט וּבְעִוָּרוֹן וּבְתִמְהוֹן לֵבָב׃ וְהָיִיתָ מְמַשֵּׁשׁ בַּצָּהֳרַיִם כַּאֲשֶׁר יְמַשֵּׁשׁ הָעִוֵּר
בָּאֲפֵלָה וְלֹא תַצְלִיחַ אֶת־דְּרָכֶיךָ וְהָיִיתָ אַךְ עָשׁוּק וְגָזוּל כָּל־הַיָּמִים
ל וְאֵין מוֹשִׁיעַ׃ אִשָּׁה תְאָרֵשׂ וְאִישׁ אַחֵר ישגלנה בַּיִת תִּבְנֶה וְלֹא־תֵשֵׁב יִשְׁכָּבֶנָּה
לא בּוֹ כֶּרֶם תִּטַּע וְלֹא תְחַלְּלֶנּוּ׃ שׁוֹרְךָ טָבוּחַ לְעֵינֶיךָ וְלֹא תֹאכַל מִמֶּנּוּ
חֲמֹרְךָ גָּזוּל מִלְּפָנֶיךָ וְלֹא יָשׁוּב לָךְ צֹאנְךָ נְתֻנוֹת לְאֹיְבֶיךָ וְאֵין לְךָ
לב מוֹשִׁיעַ׃ בָּנֶיךָ וּבְנֹתֶיךָ נְתֻנִים לְעַם אַחֵר וְעֵינֶיךָ רֹאוֹת וְכָלוֹת אֲלֵיהֶם
לג כָּל־הַיּוֹם וְאֵין לְאֵל יָדֶךָ׃ פְּרִי אַדְמָתְךָ וְכָל־יְגִיעֲךָ יֹאכַל עַם אֲשֶׁר
לד לֹא־יָדָעְתָּ וְהָיִיתָ רַק עָשׁוּק וְרָצוּץ כָּל־הַיָּמִים׃ וְהָיִיתָ מְשֻׁגָּע מִמַּרְאֵה
לה עֵינֶיךָ אֲשֶׁר תִּרְאֶה׃ יַכְּכָה יהוה בִּשְׁחִין רָע עַל־הַבִּרְכַּיִם וְעַל־הַשֹּׁקַיִם
לו אֲשֶׁר לֹא־תוּכַל לְהֵרָפֵא מִכַּף רַגְלְךָ וְעַד קָדְקֳדֶךָ׃ יוֹלֵךְ יהוה אֹתְךָ
וְאֶת־מַלְכְּךָ אֲשֶׁר תָּקִים עָלֶיךָ אֶל־גּוֹי אֲשֶׁר לֹא־יָדַעְתָּ אַתָּה וַאֲבֹתֶיךָ
לז וְעָבַדְתָּ שָּׁם אֱלֹהִים אֲחֵרִים עֵץ וָאָבֶן׃ וְהָיִיתָ לְשַׁמָּה לְמָשָׁל וְלִשְׁנִינָה
לח בְּכֹל הָעַמִּים אֲשֶׁר־יְנַהֶגְךָ יהוה שָׁמָּה׃ זֶרַע רַב תּוֹצִיא הַשָּׂדֶה וּמְעַט
לט תֶּאֱסֹף כִּי יַחְסְלֶנּוּ הָאַרְבֶּה׃ כְּרָמִים תִּטַּע וְעָבָדְתָּ וְיַיִן לֹא־תִשְׁתֶּה וְלֹא
מ תֶאֱגֹר כִּי תֹאכְלֶנּוּ הַתֹּלָעַת׃ זֵיתִים יִהְיוּ לְךָ בְּכָל־גְּבוּלֶךָ וְשֶׁמֶן לֹא
מא תָסוּךְ כִּי יִשַּׁל זֵיתֶךָ׃ בָּנִים וּבָנוֹת תּוֹלִיד וְלֹא־יִהְיוּ לָךְ כִּי יֵלְכוּ בַּשֶּׁבִי׃
מב מג כָּל־עֵצְךָ וּפְרִי אַדְמָתֶךָ יְיָרֵשׁ הַצְּלָצַל׃ הַגֵּר אֲשֶׁר בְּקִרְבְּךָ יַעֲלֶה עָלֶיךָ
מד מַעְלָה מָּעְלָה וְאַתָּה תֵרֵד מַטָּה מָּטָּה׃ הוּא יַלְוְךָ וְאַתָּה לֹא תַלְוֶנּוּ
מה הוּא יִהְיֶה לְרֹאשׁ וְאַתָּה תִּהְיֶה לְזָנָב׃ וּבָאוּ עָלֶיךָ כָּל־הַקְּלָלוֹת הָאֵלֶּה
וּרְדָפוּךָ וְהִשִּׂיגוּךָ עַד הִשָּׁמְדָךְ כִּי־לֹא שָׁמַעְתָּ בְּקוֹל יהוה אֱלֹהֶיךָ
מו לִשְׁמֹר מִצְוֺתָיו וְחֻקֹּתָיו אֲשֶׁר צִוָּךְ׃ וְהָיוּ בְךָ לְאוֹת וּלְמוֹפֵת וּבְזַרְעֲךָ
מז עַד־עוֹלָם׃ תַּחַת אֲשֶׁר לֹא־עָבַדְתָּ אֶת־יהוה אֱלֹהֶיךָ בְּשִׂמְחָה וּבְטוּב
מח לֵבָב מֵרֹב כֹּל׃ וְעָבַדְתָּ אֶת־אֹיְבֶיךָ אֲשֶׁר יְשַׁלְּחֶנּוּ יהוה בָּךְ בְּרָעָב
וּבְצָמָא וּבְעֵירֹם וּבְחֹסֶר כֹּל וְנָתַן עֹל בַּרְזֶל עַל־צַוָּארֶךָ עַד הִשְׁמִידוֹ
מט אֹתָךְ׃ יִשָּׂא יהוה עָלֶיךָ גּוֹי מֵרָחֹק מִקְצֵה הָאָרֶץ כַּאֲשֶׁר יִדְאֶה הַנָּשֶׁר
נ גּוֹי אֲשֶׁר לֹא־תִשְׁמַע לְשֹׁנוֹ׃ גּוֹי עַז פָּנִים אֲשֶׁר לֹא־יִשָּׂא פָנִים לְזָקֵן
נא וְנַעַר לֹא יָחֹן׃ וְאָכַל פְּרִי בְהֶמְתְּךָ וּפְרִי־אַדְמָתְךָ עַד הִשָּׁמְדָךְ אֲשֶׁר
לֹא־יַשְׁאִיר לְךָ דָּגָן תִּירוֹשׁ וְיִצְהָר שְׁגַר אֲלָפֶיךָ וְעַשְׁתְּרֹת צֹאנֶךָ עַד
נב הַאֲבִידוֹ אֹתָךְ׃ וְהֵצַר לְךָ בְּכָל־שְׁעָרֶיךָ עַד רֶדֶת חֹמֹתֶיךָ הַגְּבֹהֹת
וְהַבְּצֻרוֹת אֲשֶׁר אַתָּה בֹּטֵחַ בָּהֵן בְּכָל־אַרְצֶךָ וְהֵצַר לְךָ בְּכָל־שְׁעָרֶיךָ

trust have fallen. In all your towns throughout the land the LORD your God
53 has given you, they will lay siege to you. And you will eat the fruit of your
womb. When your enemies besiege you, so fiercely will they crush you that
you will eat the flesh of your own sons and daughters whom the LORD your
54 God has given you. Even the most gentle and sensitive of men among you
will begrudge food to his own brother, his beloved wife, those of his children
55 who survive, and give none of them any of the flesh of his own children when
he eats them, because he has nothing else left, so fiercely will the besieging
56 enemy crush you in all your towns. The most gentle and sensitive of women
among you, so sensitive and gentle that she would not venture to set the sole
of her foot on the ground, will begrudge food to the husband she loves, and
57 to her own son and daughter, the afterbirth from her womb and the children
she bears – she will eat them in secret for lack of anything else, so fiercely will
58 the besieging enemy crush you in your towns. If you do not take care to keep
all the words of this Law, written in this scroll, to revere this glorious, awesome
59 name, the LORD your God, then the LORD will overwhelm you and your
descendants with terrible and relentless plagues, and malignant and chronic
60 diseases. He will bring back on you all the diseases of Egypt that you dreaded,
61 and they will cling to you. Every other sickness and plague – even those not
recorded in this scroll of the Law – the LORD will inflict upon you until you
62 are destroyed. Though you were once as numerous as the stars in the sky, you
will be left but a handful of souls, because you did not listen to the LORD your
63 God. And as the LORD once delighted in making you prosperous and numerous, so will the LORD delight in bringing you to ruin and destruction. You
64 will be torn away from the land that you are now coming into to possess. The
LORD will scatter you among all nations, from one end of the earth to the
other, and there you will serve other gods, of wood and of stone, which nei-
65 ther you nor your ancestors have known. Yet even among those nations you
shall find no ease, no resting place for the sole of your foot. There the LORD
66 will give you a trembling heart, pining eyes, and a languishing spirit. Your life
will hang suspended before you; you will dread both night and day, never sure
67 you will survive. In the morning you will say, 'Would that it were evening!'
In the evening you will say, 'Would that it were morning!' – because of the
dread in your heart that you will dread, the scenes in your eyes that you will
68 see. The LORD will send you back in ships to Egypt, by a route that I told you
that you would never see again. You will offer yourselves to your enemies for
69 sale as male and female slaves, but none will buy you." These are the
words of the covenant that the LORD commanded Moshe to make with the
Israelites in the land of Moav, alongside the covenant that He had made with
them at Ḥorev.

29 1 Moshe summoned all Israel and said to them: "You have seen all that the
LORD did before your eyes in the land of Egypt, to Pharaoh, all his officials,
2 and all of his land. Your own eyes saw the great trials, the signs, and the great

נג בְּכָל־אַרְצְךָ אֲשֶׁר נָתַן יהוה אֱלֹהֶיךָ לָךְ: וְאָכַלְתָּ פְרִי־בִטְנְךָ בְּשַׂר
בָּנֶיךָ וּבְנֹתֶיךָ אֲשֶׁר נָתַן־לְךָ יהוה אֱלֹהֶיךָ בְּמָצוֹר וּבְמָצוֹק אֲשֶׁר־יָצִיק
נד לְךָ אֹיְבֶךָ: הָאִישׁ הָרַךְ בְּךָ וְהֶעָנֹג מְאֹד תֵּרַע עֵינוֹ בְאָחִיו וּבְאֵשֶׁת
נה חֵיקוֹ וּבְיֶתֶר בָּנָיו אֲשֶׁר יוֹתִיר: מִתֵּת ׀ לְאַחַד מֵהֶם מִבְּשַׂר בָּנָיו אֲשֶׁר
יֹאכֵל מִבְּלִי הִשְׁאִיר־לוֹ כֹּל בְּמָצוֹר וּבְמָצוֹק אֲשֶׁר יָצִיק לְךָ אֹיִבְךָ
נו בְּכָל־שְׁעָרֶיךָ: הָרַכָּה בְךָ וְהָעֲנֻגָּה אֲשֶׁר לֹא־נִסְּתָה כַף־רַגְלָהּ הַצֵּג
עַל־הָאָרֶץ מֵהִתְעַנֵּג וּמֵרֹךְ תֵּרַע עֵינָהּ בְּאִישׁ חֵיקָהּ וּבִבְנָהּ וּבְבִתָּהּ:
נז וּבְשִׁלְיָתָהּ הַיּוֹצֵת ׀ מִבֵּין רַגְלֶיהָ וּבְבָנֶיהָ אֲשֶׁר תֵּלֵד כִּי־תֹאכְלֵם בְּחֹסֶר־
נח כֹּל בַּסָּתֶר בְּמָצוֹר וּבְמָצוֹק אֲשֶׁר יָצִיק לְךָ אֹיִבְךָ בִּשְׁעָרֶיךָ: אִם־לֹא
תִשְׁמֹר לַעֲשׂוֹת אֶת־כָּל־דִּבְרֵי הַתּוֹרָה הַזֹּאת הַכְּתֻבִים בַּסֵּפֶר הַזֶּה
נט לְיִרְאָה אֶת־הַשֵּׁם הַנִּכְבָּד וְהַנּוֹרָא הַזֶּה אֵת יהוה אֱלֹהֶיךָ: וְהִפְלָא
יהוה אֶת־מַכֹּתְךָ וְאֵת מַכּוֹת זַרְעֶךָ מַכּוֹת גְּדֹלֹת וְנֶאֱמָנוֹת וָחֳלָיִם
ס רָעִים וְנֶאֱמָנִים: וְהֵשִׁיב בְּךָ אֵת כָּל־מַדְוֵה מִצְרַיִם אֲשֶׁר יָגֹרְתָּ מִפְּנֵיהֶם
סא וְדָבְקוּ בָּךְ: גַּם כָּל־חֳלִי וְכָל־מַכָּה אֲשֶׁר לֹא כָתוּב בְּסֵפֶר הַתּוֹרָה
סב הַזֹּאת יַעְלֵם יהוה עָלֶיךָ עַד הִשָּׁמְדָךְ: וְנִשְׁאַרְתֶּם בִּמְתֵי מְעָט תַּחַת
אֲשֶׁר הֱיִיתֶם כְּכוֹכְבֵי הַשָּׁמַיִם לָרֹב כִּי־לֹא שָׁמַעְתָּ בְּקוֹל יהוה אֱלֹהֶיךָ:
סג וְהָיָה כַּאֲשֶׁר־שָׂשׂ יהוה עֲלֵיכֶם לְהֵיטִיב אֶתְכֶם וּלְהַרְבּוֹת אֶתְכֶם כֵּן
יָשִׂישׂ יהוה עֲלֵיכֶם לְהַאֲבִיד אֶתְכֶם וּלְהַשְׁמִיד אֶתְכֶם וְנִסַּחְתֶּם מֵעַל
סד הָאֲדָמָה אֲשֶׁר־אַתָּה בָא־שָׁמָּה לְרִשְׁתָּהּ: וֶהֱפִיצְךָ יהוה בְּכָל־הָעַמִּים
מִקְצֵה הָאָרֶץ וְעַד־קְצֵה הָאָרֶץ וְעָבַדְתָּ שָּׁם אֱלֹהִים אֲחֵרִים אֲשֶׁר
סה לֹא־יָדַעְתָּ אַתָּה וַאֲבֹתֶיךָ עֵץ וָאָבֶן: וּבַגּוֹיִם הָהֵם לֹא תַרְגִּיעַ וְלֹא־יִהְיֶה
מָנוֹחַ לְכַף־רַגְלֶךָ וְנָתַן יהוה לְךָ שָׁם לֵב רַגָּז וְכִלְיוֹן עֵינַיִם וְדַאֲבוֹן נָפֶשׁ:
סו וְהָיוּ חַיֶּיךָ תְּלֻאִים לְךָ מִנֶּגֶד וּפָחַדְתָּ לַיְלָה וְיוֹמָם וְלֹא תַאֲמִין בְּחַיֶּיךָ:
סז בַּבֹּקֶר תֹּאמַר מִי־יִתֵּן עֶרֶב וּבָעֶרֶב תֹּאמַר מִי־יִתֵּן בֹּקֶר מִפַּחַד לְבָבְךָ
סח אֲשֶׁר תִּפְחָד וּמִמַּרְאֵה עֵינֶיךָ אֲשֶׁר תִּרְאֶה: וֶהֱשִׁיבְךָ יהוה ׀ מִצְרַיִם
בָּאֳנִיּוֹת בַּדֶּרֶךְ אֲשֶׁר אָמַרְתִּי לְךָ לֹא־תֹסִיף עוֹד לִרְאֹתָהּ וְהִתְמַכַּרְתֶּם
סט שָׁם לְאֹיְבֶיךָ לַעֲבָדִים וְלִשְׁפָחוֹת וְאֵין קֹנֶה: אֵלֶּה דִבְרֵי
הַבְּרִית אֲשֶׁר־צִוָּה יהוה אֶת־מֹשֶׁה לִכְרֹת אֶת־בְּנֵי יִשְׂרָאֵל בְּאֶרֶץ
מוֹאָב מִלְּבַד הַבְּרִית אֲשֶׁר־כָּרַת אִתָּם בְּחֹרֵב:
כט א וַיִּקְרָא מֹשֶׁה אֶל־כָּל־יִשְׂרָאֵל וַיֹּאמֶר אֲלֵהֶם אַתֶּם רְאִיתֶם אֵת כָּל־ שביעי
אֲשֶׁר עָשָׂה יהוה לְעֵינֵיכֶם בְּאֶרֶץ מִצְרַיִם לְפַרְעֹה וּלְכָל־עֲבָדָיו וּלְכָל־
ב אַרְצוֹ: הַמַּסּוֹת הַגְּדֹלֹת אֲשֶׁר רָאוּ עֵינֶיךָ הָאֹתֹת וְהַמֹּפְתִים הַגְּדֹלִים

3 wonders. But to this day the LORD has not given you a mind that understands,
4 or eyes that see, or ears that hear. For forty years I[68] brought you through the
wilderness. The clothes on your back did not wear out, nor the sandals on
5 your feet. You ate no bread and drank no wine or strong drink, so that you
6 might know that I am the LORD your God. When you came to this place,
Siḥon, king of Heshbon, and Og, king of Bashan, came out to meet us in
7 warfare, but we defeated them. We took their land and gave it as a heritage to
8 the Reubenites, the Gadites, and half the tribe of Menashe. Therefore take
great care to keep the words of this covenant, that you may succeed in all you
undertake.

NITZAVIM

9 All of you are standing today before the LORD your God – the leaders among
10 you, the tribes, the elders and officials, all the men of Israel, the children, the
11 women, the strangers in your camp, from woodcutter to water drawer – to
enter into the covenant of the LORD your God, and the oath the LORD your
12 God is making with you today, to establish you today as His people, that He
may be your God, as He promised you and swore to your ancestors, Avraham,
13 Yitzḥak, and Yaakov. Not with you alone am I making this covenant and oath;
14 with you who are standing here with us today before the LORD our God I
15 make it, and with those, too, who are not with us here today. You yourselves
know what it was like when we lived in Egypt, and when we passed through
16 the nations we encountered. You saw their detestable things, their abomina-
17 tions of wood and stone, of silver and gold. Let there be among you no man
or woman, family or tribe, whose heart turns away from the LORD our God
to serve the gods of those nations. Let there be among you no root whose
18 fruit is poison and wormwood. When such a person hears the words of this
oath, he may think himself immune, saying, 'I will be safe even if I go my
19 own stubborn way, sweeping away the moist and dry alike,'[69] but the LORD
will not be willing to pardon him. Instead, the LORD's anger and passion
will smolder against him; all the curses written in this scroll will fall on him,
20 and the LORD will erase his name from under the sky. The LORD will single
him out for disaster – from all the tribes of Israel – in line with all the curses
21 of the covenant written in this scroll of the Law. A future generation – your
descendants who rise after you, and foreigners from distant lands – will see
the land's devastation and the sicknesses with which the LORD has afflicted
22 it, all its soil a burning waste of sulfur and salt, nothing planted, nothing
sprouting, no vegetation growing on it, like the ruins of Sedom and Amora,
23 Adma and Tzevoyim, which the LORD overturned in His fierce rage.[70] All
the nations will ask, 'Why did the LORD do this to the land? Why this great,

68 | The voice now is that of God.

69 | This phrase is interpreted by traditional commentators to mean "sinning casually or lustfully."

70 | See Genesis 19:24–25.

ג הַהֵם: וְלֹא־נָתַן יְהוָה לָכֶם לֵב לָדַעַת וְעֵינַיִם לִרְאוֹת וְאָזְנַיִם לִשְׁמֹעַ עַד
ד הַיּוֹם הַזֶּה: וָאוֹלֵךְ אֶתְכֶם אַרְבָּעִים שָׁנָה בַּמִּדְבָּר לֹא־בָלוּ שַׂלְמֹתֵיכֶם
ה מֵעֲלֵיכֶם וְנַעַלְךָ לֹא־בָלְתָה מֵעַל רַגְלֶךָ: לֶחֶם לֹא אֲכַלְתֶּם וְיַיִן וְשֵׁכָר
ו לֹא שְׁתִיתֶם לְמַעַן תֵּדְעוּ כִּי אֲנִי יְהוָה אֱלֹהֵיכֶם: וַתָּבֹאוּ אֶל־הַמָּקוֹם מפטיר
הַזֶּה וַיֵּצֵא סִיחֹן מֶלֶךְ־חֶשְׁבּוֹן וְעוֹג מֶלֶךְ־הַבָּשָׁן לִקְרָאתֵנוּ לַמִּלְחָמָה
ז וַנַּכֵּם: וַנִּקַּח אֶת־אַרְצָם וַנִּתְּנָהּ לְנַחֲלָה לָראוּבֵנִי וְלַגָּדִי וְלַחֲצִי שֵׁבֶט
ח הַמְנַשִּׁי: וּשְׁמַרְתֶּם אֶת־דִּבְרֵי הַבְּרִית הַזֹּאת וַעֲשִׂיתֶם אֹתָם לְמַעַן
תַּשְׂכִּילוּ אֵת כָּל־אֲשֶׁר תַּעֲשׂוּן:

ט אַתֶּם נִצָּבִים הַיּוֹם כֻּלְּכֶם לִפְנֵי יְהוָה אֱלֹהֵיכֶם רָאשֵׁיכֶם שִׁבְטֵיכֶם כג נצבים
י זִקְנֵיכֶם וְשֹׁטְרֵיכֶם כֹּל אִישׁ יִשְׂרָאֵל: טַפְּכֶם נְשֵׁיכֶם וְגֵרְךָ אֲשֶׁר בְּקֶרֶב
יא מַחֲנֶיךָ מֵחֹטֵב עֵצֶיךָ עַד שֹׁאֵב מֵימֶיךָ: לְעָבְרְךָ בִּבְרִית יְהוָה אֱלֹהֶיךָ
יב וּבְאָלָתוֹ אֲשֶׁר יְהוָה אֱלֹהֶיךָ כֹּרֵת עִמְּךָ הַיּוֹם: לְמַעַן הָקִים־אֹתְךָ שני
הַיּוֹם ׀ לוֹ לְעָם וְהוּא יִהְיֶה־לְּךָ לֵאלֹהִים כַּאֲשֶׁר דִּבֶּר־לָךְ וְכַאֲשֶׁר
יג נִשְׁבַּע לַאֲבֹתֶיךָ לְאַבְרָהָם לְיִצְחָק וּלְיַעֲקֹב: וְלֹא אִתְּכֶם לְבַדְּכֶם
יד אָנֹכִי כֹּרֵת אֶת־הַבְּרִית הַזֹּאת וְאֶת־הָאָלָה הַזֹּאת: כִּי אֶת־אֲשֶׁר
יֶשְׁנוֹ פֹּה עִמָּנוּ עֹמֵד הַיּוֹם לִפְנֵי יְהוָה אֱלֹהֵינוּ וְאֵת אֲשֶׁר אֵינֶנּוּ פֹּה
טו עִמָּנוּ הַיּוֹם: כִּי־אַתֶּם יְדַעְתֶּם אֵת אֲשֶׁר־יָשַׁבְנוּ בְּאֶרֶץ מִצְרָיִם וְאֵת שלישי
טז אֲשֶׁר־עָבַרְנוּ בְּקֶרֶב הַגּוֹיִם אֲשֶׁר עֲבַרְתֶּם: וַתִּרְאוּ אֶת־שִׁקּוּצֵיהֶם
יז וְאֵת גִּלֻּלֵיהֶם עֵץ וָאֶבֶן כֶּסֶף וְזָהָב אֲשֶׁר עִמָּהֶם: פֶּן־יֵשׁ בָּכֶם אִישׁ
אוֹ־אִשָּׁה אוֹ מִשְׁפָּחָה אוֹ־שֵׁבֶט אֲשֶׁר לְבָבוֹ פֹנֶה הַיּוֹם מֵעִם יְהוָה
אֱלֹהֵינוּ לָלֶכֶת לַעֲבֹד אֶת־אֱלֹהֵי הַגּוֹיִם הָהֵם פֶּן־יֵשׁ בָּכֶם שֹׁרֶשׁ פֹּרֶה
יח רֹאשׁ וְלַעֲנָה: וְהָיָה בְּשָׁמְעוֹ אֶת־דִּבְרֵי הָאָלָה הַזֹּאת וְהִתְבָּרֵךְ בִּלְבָבוֹ
לֵאמֹר שָׁלוֹם יִהְיֶה־לִּי כִּי בִּשְׁרִרוּת לִבִּי אֵלֵךְ לְמַעַן סְפוֹת הָרָוָה אֶת־
יט הַצְּמֵאָה: לֹא־יֹאבֶה יְהוָה סְלֹחַ לוֹ כִּי אָז יֶעְשַׁן אַף־יְהוָה וְקִנְאָתוֹ
בָּאִישׁ הַהוּא וְרָבְצָה בּוֹ כָּל־הָאָלָה הַכְּתוּבָה בַּסֵּפֶר הַזֶּה וּמָחָה יְהוָה
כ אֶת־שְׁמוֹ מִתַּחַת הַשָּׁמָיִם: וְהִבְדִּילוֹ יְהוָה לְרָעָה מִכֹּל שִׁבְטֵי יִשְׂרָאֵל
כא כְּכֹל אָלוֹת הַבְּרִית הַכְּתוּבָה בְּסֵפֶר הַתּוֹרָה הַזֶּה: וְאָמַר הַדּוֹר הָאַחֲרוֹן
בְּנֵיכֶם אֲשֶׁר יָקוּמוּ מֵאַחֲרֵיכֶם וְהַנָּכְרִי אֲשֶׁר יָבֹא מֵאֶרֶץ רְחוֹקָה וְרָאוּ
כב אֶת־מַכּוֹת הָאָרֶץ הַהִוא וְאֶת־תַּחֲלֻאֶיהָ אֲשֶׁר־חִלָּה יְהוָה בָּהּ: גָּפְרִית
וָמֶלַח שְׂרֵפָה כָל־אַרְצָהּ לֹא תִזָּרַע וְלֹא תַצְמִחַ וְלֹא־יַעֲלֶה בָהּ כָּל־
עֵשֶׂב כְּמַהְפֵּכַת סְדֹם וַעֲמֹרָה אַדְמָה וּצְבוֹיִם אֲשֶׁר הָפַךְ יְהוָה בְּאַפּוֹ וּצְבוֹיִם
כג וּבַחֲמָתוֹ: וְאָמְרוּ כָּל־הַגּוֹיִם עַל־מֶה עָשָׂה יְהוָה כָּכָה לָאָרֶץ הַזֹּאת מָה

24 blazing anger?' They will say, 'It is because they abandoned the covenant
of the LORD, God of their ancestors, which He made with them when He
25 brought them out of Egypt. They went and served other gods and worshipped
26 them, gods they did not know and whom He had not allotted to them. So
the LORD's anger burned against that land, bringing on it every curse that
27 is written in this scroll. The LORD uprooted them from their land in anger,
rage, and great fury, and threw them into another land, as we now see them.'
28 Hidden things belong to the LORD our God, but as for overt acts – it is for us
30 1 and our children to eternity to keep all the words of this Law. When
all these things have come upon you, the blessings and the curses I have set
before you, and you – amidst all the nations where the LORD your God has
2 driven you – take them to heart, and return, you and your children, to the
LORD your God, obeying Him with all your heart and all your soul, just as I
3 am commanding you today, then the LORD your God will bring your captives
back and show you compassion. He will bring you back together from all the
4 nations among whom the LORD your God has scattered you. If you should
be expelled to the furthest of horizons, even from there the LORD your God
5 will gather you, from there He will take you back. The LORD your God will
bring you into the land that belonged to your ancestors, and you will possess
it. He will make you yet more prosperous and numerous than your ancestors
6 were. The LORD your God will circumcise your heart and the hearts of your
descendants,[71] so that you may love the LORD your God with all your heart,
7 with all your soul, that you may live. The LORD your God will inflict all these
8 curses on your enemies and on those who hate and persecute you. Then
you shall turn and heed the LORD's voice, keeping all His commandments
9 with which I am charging you this day, and the LORD your God will grant
you abundant prosperity in all the work of your hands, in the fruit of your
womb, the fruit of your cattle, and the fruit of your land. The LORD will again
10 delight in your well-being as He did in your ancestors', when you heed the
LORD your God, keeping His commandments and decrees that are written in
this book of the Law, and have returned to the LORD your God with all your
11 heart and with all your soul. For this commandment that I am giving
12 you today is not unattainable to you, neither is it distant. It is not in heaven,
that you should say, 'Who will go up to heaven for us and bring it to us that
13 we may hear it and keep it?' Nor is it beyond the sea, that you sheould say,
'Who will cross to the far side of the sea for us, and bring it to us that we may
14 hear it and keep it?' This word is very close to you. It is in your mouth and in
15 your heart for you to keep it. See: I have set before you today life and
16 goodness, and death and evil. For I charge you on this day to love the LORD
your God, walk in His ways, and keep His commandments, decrees, and laws.
Then you will survive and thrive and the LORD your God will bless you in the

71 | That is, He will soften their hearts, allowing them to devote themselves to Him.

כד חֳרִי הָאַף הַגָּדוֹל הַזֶּה: וְאָמְרוּ עַל אֲשֶׁר עָזְבוּ אֶת־בְּרִית יְהוָה אֱלֹהֵי
כה אֲבֹתָם אֲשֶׁר כָּרַת עִמָּם בְּהוֹצִיאוֹ אֹתָם מֵאֶרֶץ מִצְרָיִם: וַיֵּלְכוּ וַיַּעַבְדוּ
אֱלֹהִים אֲחֵרִים וַיִּשְׁתַּחֲווּ לָהֶם אֱלֹהִים אֲשֶׁר לֹא־יְדָעוּם וְלֹא חָלַק
כו לָהֶם: וַיִּחַר־אַף יְהוָה בָּאָרֶץ הַהִוא לְהָבִיא עָלֶיהָ אֶת־כָּל־הַקְּלָלָה
כז הַכְּתוּבָה בַּסֵּפֶר הַזֶּה: וַיִּתְּשֵׁם יְהוָה מֵעַל אַדְמָתָם בְּאַף וּבְחֵמָה
כח וּבְקֶצֶף גָּדוֹל וַיַּשְׁלִכֵם אֶל־אֶרֶץ אַחֶרֶת כַּיּוֹם הַזֶּה: הַנִּסְתָּרֹת לַיהוָה
אֱלֹהֵינוּ וְהַנִּגְלֹת לָנוּ וּלְבָנֵינוּ עַד־עוֹלָם לַעֲשׂוֹת אֶת־כָּל־דִּבְרֵי הַתּוֹרָה
ל א הַזֹּאת: וְהָיָה כִי־יָבֹאוּ עָלֶיךָ כָּל־הַדְּבָרִים הָאֵלֶּה הַבְּרָכָה רביעי /שני/
וְהַקְּלָלָה אֲשֶׁר נָתַתִּי לְפָנֶיךָ וַהֲשֵׁבֹתָ אֶל־לְבָבֶךָ בְּכָל־הַגּוֹיִם אֲשֶׁר
ב הִדִּיחֲךָ יְהוָה אֱלֹהֶיךָ שָׁמָּה: וְשַׁבְתָּ עַד־יְהוָה אֱלֹהֶיךָ וְשָׁמַעְתָּ בְקֹלוֹ
כְּכֹל אֲשֶׁר־אָנֹכִי מְצַוְּךָ הַיּוֹם אַתָּה וּבָנֶיךָ בְּכָל־לְבָבְךָ וּבְכָל־נַפְשֶׁךָ:
ג וְשָׁב יְהוָה אֱלֹהֶיךָ אֶת־שְׁבוּתְךָ וְרִחֲמֶךָ וְשָׁב וְקִבֶּצְךָ מִכָּל־הָעַמִּים
ד אֲשֶׁר הֱפִיצְךָ יְהוָה אֱלֹהֶיךָ שָׁמָּה: אִם־יִהְיֶה נִדַּחֲךָ בִּקְצֵה הַשָּׁמָיִם
ה מִשָּׁם יְקַבֶּצְךָ יְהוָה אֱלֹהֶיךָ וּמִשָּׁם יִקָּחֶךָ: וֶהֱבִיאֲךָ יְהוָה אֱלֹהֶיךָ
אֶל־הָאָרֶץ אֲשֶׁר־יָרְשׁוּ אֲבֹתֶיךָ וִירִשְׁתָּהּ וְהֵיטִבְךָ וְהִרְבְּךָ מֵאֲבֹתֶיךָ:
ו וּמָל יְהוָה אֱלֹהֶיךָ אֶת־לְבָבְךָ וְאֶת־לְבַב זַרְעֶךָ לְאַהֲבָה אֶת־יְהוָה
ז אֱלֹהֶיךָ בְּכָל־לְבָבְךָ וּבְכָל־נַפְשְׁךָ לְמַעַן חַיֶּיךָ: וְנָתַן יְהוָה אֱלֹהֶיךָ חמישי /שלישי/
ח אֵת כָּל־הָאָלוֹת הָאֵלֶּה עַל־אֹיְבֶיךָ וְעַל־שֹׂנְאֶיךָ אֲשֶׁר רְדָפוּךָ: וְאַתָּה
תָשׁוּב וְשָׁמַעְתָּ בְּקוֹל יְהוָה וְעָשִׂיתָ אֶת־כָּל־מִצְוֹתָיו אֲשֶׁר אָנֹכִי מְצַוְּךָ
ט הַיּוֹם: וְהוֹתִירְךָ יְהוָה אֱלֹהֶיךָ בְּכֹל | מַעֲשֵׂה יָדֶךָ בִּפְרִי בִטְנְךָ וּבִפְרִי
בְהֶמְתְּךָ וּבִפְרִי אַדְמָתְךָ לְטֹבָה כִּי | יָשׁוּב יְהוָה לָשׂוּשׂ עָלֶיךָ לְטוֹב
י כַּאֲשֶׁר־שָׂשׂ עַל־אֲבֹתֶיךָ: כִּי תִשְׁמַע בְּקוֹל יְהוָה אֱלֹהֶיךָ לִשְׁמֹר מִצְוֹתָיו
וְחֻקֹּתָיו הַכְּתוּבָה בְּסֵפֶר הַתּוֹרָה הַזֶּה כִּי תָשׁוּב אֶל־יְהוָה אֱלֹהֶיךָ
יא בְּכָל־לְבָבְךָ וּבְכָל־נַפְשֶׁךָ: כִּי הַמִּצְוָה הַזֹּאת אֲשֶׁר אָנֹכִי כד ששי
יב מְצַוְּךָ הַיּוֹם לֹא־נִפְלֵאת הִוא מִמְּךָ וְלֹא־רְחֹקָה הִוא: לֹא בַשָּׁמַיִם
הִוא לֵאמֹר מִי יַעֲלֶה־לָּנוּ הַשָּׁמַיְמָה וְיִקָּחֶהָ לָּנוּ וְיַשְׁמִעֵנוּ אֹתָהּ
יג וְנַעֲשֶׂנָּה: וְלֹא־מֵעֵבֶר לַיָּם הִוא לֵאמֹר מִי יַעֲבָר־לָנוּ אֶל־עֵבֶר הַיָּם
יד וְיִקָּחֶהָ לָּנוּ וְיַשְׁמִעֵנוּ אֹתָהּ וְנַעֲשֶׂנָּה: כִּי־קָרוֹב אֵלֶיךָ הַדָּבָר מְאֹד בְּפִיךָ
טו וּבִלְבָבְךָ לַעֲשֹׂתוֹ: רְאֵה נָתַתִּי לְפָנֶיךָ הַיּוֹם אֶת־הַחַיִּים שביעי ומפטיר /רביעי/
טז וְאֶת־הַטּוֹב וְאֶת־הַמָּוֶת וְאֶת־הָרָע: אֲשֶׁר אָנֹכִי מְצַוְּךָ הַיּוֹם לְאַהֲבָה
אֶת־יְהוָה אֱלֹהֶיךָ לָלֶכֶת בִּדְרָכָיו וְלִשְׁמֹר מִצְוֹתָיו וְחֻקֹּתָיו וּמִשְׁפָּטָיו
וְחָיִיתָ וְרָבִיתָ וּבֵרַכְךָ יְהוָה אֱלֹהֶיךָ בָּאָרֶץ אֲשֶׁר־אַתָּה בָא־שָׁמָּה

17 land you are coming into to possess. But if your heart turns away and you do
not listen and are led astray, and bow down to other gods and worship them,
18 then I declare to you today that you will certainly perish; you will not live
19 long in the land that you are crossing the Jordan to enter and possess. I call
heaven and earth as witnesses against you today: I have set before you life
and death, the blessing and the curse. Choose life – so that you and your
20 children may live, loving the LORD your God, heeding His voice and holding
fast to Him, for this is your life and the length of your days, living in the land
that the LORD swore to give to your ancestors, to Avraham, Yitzḥak, and
Yaakov."

31 1 2 Moshe went and spoke these words to all Israel. He told them, "I am a hun- VAYELEKH
dred and twenty years old now, and no longer able to enter and to leave. And
3 the LORD has told me, 'You shall not cross this Jordan.' The LORD your God
Himself will cross ahead of you. He will destroy these nations before you,
and you shall take possession in their place. It is Yehoshua who will lead
4 you across, as the LORD has spoken. The LORD will do to those nations as
He did to Siḥon and to Og, kings of the Amorites, and to their land, when
5 He destroyed them. The LORD will deliver them to you and you shall deal
6 with them just as I have commanded you. Be strong and be determined. Do
not fear or dread them, for the LORD your God is going with you. He will
7 not fail you or forsake you." Then Moshe summoned Yehoshua
and said to him in the sight of all Israel: "Be strong and be determined, for
it is you who will come with this people into the land that the LORD has
sworn to their ancestors to give them, and you will allocate it to them for an
8 inheritance. The LORD Himself will go before you. He will be with you. He
9 will not fail you or forsake you. Do not fear and do not be dismayed." Then
Moshe wrote down this Law and gave it to the priests, descendants of Levi,
who carried the Ark of the Covenant of the LORD, and to all the elders of
10 Israel. Moshe then commanded them: "At the end of every seventh year,
11 the year of remission,[72] during the Festival of Tabernacles, when all Israel
comes to appear before the LORD your God at the place that He will choose,
you shall read out this Law in the presence of all Israel, for them to hear.
12 Assemble the people – men, women, and children, including the migrants
living in your towns – so that they may listen and learn to fear the LORD
13 your God and carefully keep all the words of this Law, and so that their
children, who do not know it, may listen and learn to be in awe of the LORD
your God, as long as you live in the land that you are crossing the Jordan to
possess."
14 The LORD said to Moshe, "Your time to die draws near. Call Yehoshua and
come and stand in the Tent of Meeting, so that I may give him his charge."

---

72 | See 15:1–2.

יז לְרִשְׁתָּהּ: וְאִם־יִפְנֶה לְבָבְךָ וְלֹא תִשְׁמָע וְנִדַּחְתָּ וְהִשְׁתַּחֲוִיתָ לֵאלֹהִים
יח אֲחֵרִים וַעֲבַדְתָּם: הִגַּדְתִּי לָכֶם הַיּוֹם כִּי אָבֹד תֹּאבֵדוּן לֹא־תַאֲרִיכֻן
יָמִים עַל־הָאֲדָמָה אֲשֶׁר אַתָּה עֹבֵר אֶת־הַיַּרְדֵּן לָבוֹא שָׁמָּה לְרִשְׁתָּהּ:
יט הַעִדֹתִי בָכֶם הַיּוֹם אֶת־הַשָּׁמַיִם וְאֶת־הָאָרֶץ הַחַיִּים וְהַמָּוֶת נָתַתִּי
לְפָנֶיךָ הַבְּרָכָה וְהַקְּלָלָה וּבָחַרְתָּ בַּחַיִּים לְמַעַן תִּחְיֶה אַתָּה וְזַרְעֶךָ:
כ לְאַהֲבָה אֶת־יהוה אֱלֹהֶיךָ לִשְׁמֹעַ בְּקֹלוֹ וּלְדָבְקָה־בוֹ כִּי הוּא חַיֶּיךָ
וְאֹרֶךְ יָמֶיךָ לָשֶׁבֶת עַל־הָאֲדָמָה אֲשֶׁר נִשְׁבַּע יהוה לַאֲבֹתֶיךָ לְאַבְרָהָם
לְיִצְחָק וּלְיַעֲקֹב לָתֵת לָהֶם:
לא א ב וַיֵּלֶךְ מֹשֶׁה וַיְדַבֵּר אֶת־הַדְּבָרִים הָאֵלֶּה אֶל־כָּל־יִשְׂרָאֵל: וַיֹּאמֶר אֲלֵהֶם וילך
בֶּן־מֵאָה וְעֶשְׂרִים שָׁנָה אָנֹכִי הַיּוֹם לֹא־אוּכַל עוֹד לָצֵאת וְלָבוֹא
ג וַיהוָה אָמַר אֵלַי לֹא תַעֲבֹר אֶת־הַיַּרְדֵּן הַזֶּה: יהוה אֱלֹהֶיךָ הוּא ׀
עֹבֵר לְפָנֶיךָ הוּא־יַשְׁמִיד אֶת־הַגּוֹיִם הָאֵלֶּה מִלְּפָנֶיךָ וִירִשְׁתָּם יְהוֹשֻׁעַ
ד הוּא עֹבֵר לְפָנֶיךָ כַּאֲשֶׁר דִּבֶּר יהוה: וְעָשָׂה יהוה לָהֶם כַּאֲשֶׁר עָשָׂה שני
ה לְסִיחוֹן וּלְעוֹג מַלְכֵי הָאֱמֹרִי וּלְאַרְצָם אֲשֶׁר הִשְׁמִיד אֹתָם: וּנְתָנָם
ו יהוה לִפְנֵיכֶם וַעֲשִׂיתֶם לָהֶם כְּכָל־הַמִּצְוָה אֲשֶׁר צִוִּיתִי אֶתְכֶם: חִזְקוּ
וְאִמְצוּ אַל־תִּירְאוּ וְאַל־תַּעַרְצוּ מִפְּנֵיהֶם כִּי ׀ יהוה אֱלֹהֶיךָ הוּא הַהֹלֵךְ
ז עִמָּךְ לֹא יַרְפְּךָ וְלֹא יַעַזְבֶךָּ: וַיִּקְרָא מֹשֶׁה לִיהוֹשֻׁעַ וַיֹּאמֶר שלישי /חמישי/
אֵלָיו לְעֵינֵי כָל־יִשְׂרָאֵל חֲזַק וֶאֱמָץ כִּי אַתָּה תָּבוֹא אֶת־הָעָם הַזֶּה
אֶל־הָאָרֶץ אֲשֶׁר נִשְׁבַּע יהוה לַאֲבֹתָם לָתֵת לָהֶם וְאַתָּה תַּנְחִילֶנָּה
ח אוֹתָם: וַיהוָה הוּא ׀ הַהֹלֵךְ לְפָנֶיךָ הוּא יִהְיֶה עִמָּךְ לֹא יַרְפְּךָ וְלֹא יַעַזְבֶךָּ
ט לֹא תִירָא וְלֹא תֵחָת: וַיִּכְתֹּב מֹשֶׁה אֶת־הַתּוֹרָה הַזֹּאת וַיִּתְּנָהּ אֶל־
הַכֹּהֲנִים בְּנֵי לֵוִי הַנֹּשְׂאִים אֶת־אֲרוֹן בְּרִית יהוה וְאֶל־כָּל־זִקְנֵי יִשְׂרָאֵל:
י וַיְצַו מֹשֶׁה אוֹתָם לֵאמֹר מִקֵּץ ׀ שֶׁבַע שָׁנִים בְּמֹעֵד שְׁנַת הַשְּׁמִטָּה רביעי
יא בְּחַג הַסֻּכּוֹת: בְּבוֹא כָל־יִשְׂרָאֵל לֵרָאוֹת אֶת־פְּנֵי יהוה אֱלֹהֶיךָ בַּמָּקוֹם
אֲשֶׁר יִבְחָר תִּקְרָא אֶת־הַתּוֹרָה הַזֹּאת נֶגֶד כָּל־יִשְׂרָאֵל בְּאָזְנֵיהֶם:
יב הַקְהֵל אֶת־הָעָם הָאֲנָשִׁים וְהַנָּשִׁים וְהַטַּף וְגֵרְךָ אֲשֶׁר בִּשְׁעָרֶיךָ לְמַעַן
יִשְׁמְעוּ וּלְמַעַן יִלְמְדוּ וְיָרְאוּ אֶת־יהוה אֱלֹהֵיכֶם וְשָׁמְרוּ לַעֲשׂוֹת
יג אֶת־כָּל־דִּבְרֵי הַתּוֹרָה הַזֹּאת: וּבְנֵיהֶם אֲשֶׁר לֹא־יָדְעוּ יִשְׁמְעוּ וְלָמְדוּ
לְיִרְאָה אֶת־יהוה אֱלֹהֵיכֶם כָּל־הַיָּמִים אֲשֶׁר אַתֶּם חַיִּים עַל־הָאֲדָמָה
אֲשֶׁר אַתֶּם עֹבְרִים אֶת־הַיַּרְדֵּן שָׁמָּה לְרִשְׁתָּהּ:
יד כה וַיֹּאמֶר יהוה אֶל־מֹשֶׁה הֵן קָרְבוּ יָמֶיךָ לָמוּת קְרָא אֶת־יְהוֹשֻׁעַ וְהִתְיַצְּבוּ חמישי /ששי/
בְּאֹהֶל מוֹעֵד וַאֲצַוֶּנּוּ וַיֵּלֶךְ מֹשֶׁה וִיהוֹשֻׁעַ וַיִּתְיַצְּבוּ בְּאֹהֶל מוֹעֵד:

15 So Moshe and Yehoshua went and stood in the Tent of Meeting. The LORD
appeared in the Tent in a pillar of cloud; and the pillar of cloud stood at the
16 entrance to the Tent. Then the LORD said to Moshe, "Soon, you are going to
rest with your ancestors. And this people will begin to stray after the foreign
gods of the land into which they are going. They will forsake Me and break
17 the covenant I have made with them. My rage will flare against them at that
time. I will abandon them and hide My face from them. They will become
easy prey, and many evils and troubles will come upon them. On that day
they will ask, 'Have not these troubles come upon us because our God is not
18 in our midst?' And I – I will hide My face at that time because of all the evil
19 they have done by turning to other gods. So now write down this song and
teach it to the Israelites. Place it in their mouths, so that this song may be My
20 witness against them. When I have brought them into the land that flows with
milk and with honey, which I promised on oath to their ancestors, they will
eat their fill and grow fat, and they will turn to other gods and worship them,
21 rejecting Me and breaking My covenant. And when they are beset by many
evils and troubles, this song will testify as a witness against them, for it will
not be forgotten by their descendants. For I know what they are inclined to do
even now, before I have brought them into the land that I promised them on
22 oath." So, that day, Moshe wrote down this song and taught it to the Israelites.
23 And He charged Yehoshua son of Nun: "Be strong, be determined, because
you shall bring the Israelites into the land that I promised them – and I will be
24 with you." Moshe finished writing down in a scroll the words of this Law to
25 the very end; and then Moshe instructed the Levites who carried the Ark of
26 the Covenant of the LORD: "Take this scroll of the Law and place it beside the
Ark of the Covenant of the LORD your God. Let it remain there as a witness
27 to you. For I know how rebellious and stiff-necked you are. Even now, while
I am still living among you, you have been rebellious toward the LORD; how
28 much more so will you be after my death! Gather to me all the elders of your
tribes and your officials, so that I may proclaim these words in their hearing
29 and call heaven and earth to witness against them. For I know that after my
death you will act in self-destruction, turning away from the path that I have
commanded you. In the days to come evil will befall you, because you will
do evil in the sight of the LORD, angering Him with the work of your hands."
30 Then Moshe proclaimed the words of this song in the hearing of the entire
assembly of Israel, to the very end.

HAAZINU

32 1 "Listen, heavens, I will speak; / let the earth hear the words of my
2 mouth. / May my teaching pour down like rain, / let my speech fall
like the dew; / like gentle rain on tender plants, / like showers upon

טו וַיֵּרָא יְהוָה בָּאֹהֶל בְּעַמּוּד עָנָן וַיַּעֲמֹד עַמּוּד הֶעָנָן עַל־פֶּתַח הָאֹהֶל:
טז וַיֹּאמֶר יְהוָה אֶל־מֹשֶׁה הִנְּךָ שֹׁכֵב עִם־אֲבֹתֶיךָ וְקָם הָעָם הַזֶּה וְזָנָה ׀
אַחֲרֵי ׀ אֱלֹהֵי נֵכַר־הָאָרֶץ אֲשֶׁר הוּא בָא־שָׁמָּה בְּקִרְבּוֹ וַעֲזָבַנִי וְהֵפֵר
יז אֶת־בְּרִיתִי אֲשֶׁר כָּרַתִּי אִתּוֹ: וְחָרָה אַפִּי בוֹ בַיּוֹם־הַהוּא וַעֲזַבְתִּים
וְהִסְתַּרְתִּי פָנַי מֵהֶם וְהָיָה לֶאֱכֹל וּמְצָאֻהוּ רָעוֹת רַבּוֹת וְצָרוֹת וְאָמַר
בַּיּוֹם הַהוּא הֲלֹא עַל כִּי־אֵין אֱלֹהַי בְּקִרְבִּי מְצָאוּנִי הָרָעוֹת הָאֵלֶּה:
יח וְאָנֹכִי הַסְתֵּר אַסְתִּיר פָּנַי בַּיּוֹם הַהוּא עַל כָּל־הָרָעָה אֲשֶׁר עָשָׂה
יט כִּי פָנָה אֶל־אֱלֹהִים אֲחֵרִים: וְעַתָּה כִּתְבוּ לָכֶם אֶת־הַשִּׁירָה הַזֹּאת
וְלַמְּדָהּ אֶת־בְּנֵי־יִשְׂרָאֵל שִׂימָהּ בְּפִיהֶם לְמַעַן תִּהְיֶה־לִּי הַשִּׁירָה
כ הַזֹּאת לְעֵד בִּבְנֵי יִשְׂרָאֵל: כִּי־אֲבִיאֶנּוּ אֶל־הָאֲדָמָה ׀ אֲשֶׁר־נִשְׁבַּעְתִּי ששי /שביעי/
לַאֲבֹתָיו זָבַת חָלָב וּדְבַשׁ וְאָכַל וְשָׂבַע וְדָשֵׁן וּפָנָה אֶל־אֱלֹהִים אֲחֵרִים
כא וַעֲבָדוּם וְנִאֲצוּנִי וְהֵפֵר אֶת־בְּרִיתִי: וְהָיָה כִּי־תִמְצֶאןָ אֹתוֹ רָעוֹת רַבּוֹת
וְצָרוֹת וְעָנְתָה הַשִּׁירָה הַזֹּאת לְפָנָיו לְעֵד כִּי לֹא תִשָּׁכַח מִפִּי זַרְעוֹ כִּי
יָדַעְתִּי אֶת־יִצְרוֹ אֲשֶׁר הוּא עֹשֶׂה הַיּוֹם בְּטֶרֶם אֲבִיאֶנּוּ אֶל־הָאָרֶץ
כב אֲשֶׁר נִשְׁבָּעְתִּי: וַיִּכְתֹּב מֹשֶׁה אֶת־הַשִּׁירָה הַזֹּאת בַּיּוֹם הַהוּא וַיְלַמְּדָהּ
כג אֶת־בְּנֵי יִשְׂרָאֵל: וַיְצַו אֶת־יְהוֹשֻׁעַ בִּן־נוּן וַיֹּאמֶר חֲזַק וֶאֱמָץ כִּי אַתָּה
תָּבִיא אֶת־בְּנֵי יִשְׂרָאֵל אֶל־הָאָרֶץ אֲשֶׁר־נִשְׁבַּעְתִּי לָהֶם וְאָנֹכִי אֶהְיֶה
כד עִמָּךְ: וַיְהִי ׀ כְּכַלּוֹת מֹשֶׁה לִכְתֹּב אֶת־דִּבְרֵי הַתּוֹרָה־הַזֹּאת עַל־סֵפֶר
כה עַד תֻּמָּם: וַיְצַו מֹשֶׁה אֶת־הַלְוִיִּם נֹשְׂאֵי אֲרוֹן בְּרִית־יְהוָה לֵאמֹר: שביעי
כו לָקֹחַ אֵת סֵפֶר הַתּוֹרָה הַזֶּה וְשַׂמְתֶּם אֹתוֹ מִצַּד אֲרוֹן בְּרִית־יְהוָה
כז אֱלֹהֵיכֶם וְהָיָה־שָׁם בְּךָ לְעֵד: כִּי אָנֹכִי יָדַעְתִּי אֶת־מֶרְיְךָ וְאֶת־עָרְפְּךָ
הַקָּשֶׁה הֵן בְּעוֹדֶנִּי חַי עִמָּכֶם הַיּוֹם מַמְרִים הֱיִתֶם עִם־יְהוָה וְאַף כִּי־
כח אַחֲרֵי מוֹתִי: הַקְהִילוּ אֵלַי אֶת־כָּל־זִקְנֵי שִׁבְטֵיכֶם וְשֹׁטְרֵיכֶם וַאֲדַבְּרָה מפטיר
בְאָזְנֵיהֶם אֵת הַדְּבָרִים הָאֵלֶּה וְאָעִידָה בָּם אֶת־הַשָּׁמַיִם וְאֶת־הָאָרֶץ:
כט כִּי יָדַעְתִּי אַחֲרֵי מוֹתִי כִּי־הַשְׁחֵת תַּשְׁחִתוּן וְסַרְתֶּם מִן־הַדֶּרֶךְ אֲשֶׁר
צִוִּיתִי אֶתְכֶם וְקָרָאת אֶתְכֶם הָרָעָה בְּאַחֲרִית הַיָּמִים כִּי־תַעֲשׂוּ אֶת־
ל הָרַע בְּעֵינֵי יְהוָה לְהַכְעִיסוֹ בְּמַעֲשֵׂה יְדֵיכֶם: וַיְדַבֵּר מֹשֶׁה בְּאָזְנֵי כָּל־
קְהַל יִשְׂרָאֵל אֶת־דִּבְרֵי הַשִּׁירָה הַזֹּאת עַד תֻּמָּם:

לב א הַאֲזִינוּ הַשָּׁמַיִם וַאֲדַבֵּרָה   וְתִשְׁמַע הָאָרֶץ אִמְרֵי־פִי: כו האזינו
ב יַעֲרֹף כַּמָּטָר לִקְחִי   תִּזַּל כַּטַּל אִמְרָתִי
כִּשְׂעִירִם עֲלֵי־דֶשֶׁא   וְכִרְבִיבִים עֲלֵי־עֵשֶׂב:

3 the grasses. / As I call out the name of the LORD – / come, praise
4 the greatness of our God. / The Rock, His work is whole, / and all
His ways are justice. / A God of faith who does no wrong, / just
5 is He and upright. / Did He act ruinously? No, with His children lies the
6 fault, / a warped and twisted generation. / Is this how you repay
the LORD, / you foolish, unwise people? / Is not He your Father, your
7 Maker, / who formed you and set you on your feet? / Remember the
days of old, / consider the years of ages past; / ask your father, and he
8 will tell you; / your elders, and they will speak. / When the Highest
gave nations their heritage, / when He divided humankind, / He
fixed the boundaries of peoples / by the number of Israel's sons.[73] /
9 The LORD's own share is His people, / Yaakov His allotted place. /
10 He found him in a desert land, / in a barren, howling waste; / He
encircled him, watched over him, / guarded him close like the
11 apple of His eye. / As an eagle stirs up its nest, / and hovers over
its young; / as it spreads its plumes and takes them, / bearing them
12 aloft on its wings, / just so, the LORD alone led him – / no strange
13 god at His side – / He set him astride the heights of the earth, / and
fed him the bounty of meadows; / He nursed him with honey from the
14 crag, / and oil from flinty rock; / with curds from the herd, milk
from the flock, / and the fat of lambs and goats, / choice rams of
Bashan, / and the fattest buds of wheat – / you drank fine wine from
15 blood-red grapes. / Yeshurun[74] grew fat, and kicked;[75] / you grew fat,
grew gross, grew coarse. / They abandoned God who made them, /
16 rejected the Rock of their rescue. / They provoked Him with strange
17 gods, / and angered Him with abominations. / They sacrificed to
demons, no-gods, / to deities they never knew, / new ones, lately
18 arisen, / whom your forebears never feared. / You deserted the Rock
19 that bore you; / you forgot the God who gave you birth. / The LORD
saw this and He in turn rejected / the sons and daughters who angered Him
20 so. / He said: I will hide My face from them, / and see what their
end will be; / for they are a perverse generation, / children with
21 no faithfulness. / They incensed Me with a no-god, / they angered
Me with their vanities; / I will incense them with a no-people, /
22 enrage them with a fool nation. / For a fire My anger has kindled, /

---

73 | Explanations of this phrase vary, e.g., the seventy nations parallel the seventy descendants of Yaakov (Rashi), or Kenaan and his eleven descendants parallel the twelve sons of Israel (Bekhor Shor).

74 | A name for Israel, derived from a term denoting uprightness.

75 | Became ungrateful and rebellious.

ג כִּי שֵׁם יְהוָה אֶקְרָא   הָבוּ גֹדֶל לֵאלֹהֵינוּ:
ד הַצּוּר תָּמִים פָּעֳלוֹ   כִּי כָל־דְּרָכָיו מִשְׁפָּט
אֵל אֱמוּנָה וְאֵין עָוֶל   צַדִּיק וְיָשָׁר הוּא:
ה שִׁחֵת לוֹ לֹא בָּנָיו מוּמָם   דּוֹר עִקֵּשׁ וּפְתַלְתֹּל:
ו הֲ לַיהוָה תִּגְמְלוּ־זֹאת   עַם נָבָל וְלֹא חָכָם
הֲלוֹא־הוּא אָבִיךָ קָּנֶךָ   הוּא עָשְׂךָ וַיְכֹנְנֶךָ:
ז זְכֹר יְמוֹת עוֹלָם   בִּינוּ שְׁנוֹת דֹּר־וָדֹר   שני
שְׁאַל אָבִיךָ וְיַגֵּדְךָ   זְקֵנֶיךָ וְיֹאמְרוּ לָךְ:
ח בְּהַנְחֵל עֶלְיוֹן גּוֹיִם   בְּהַפְרִידוֹ בְּנֵי אָדָם
יַצֵּב גְּבֻלֹת עַמִּים   לְמִסְפַּר בְּנֵי יִשְׂרָאֵל:
ט כִּי חֵלֶק יְהוָה עַמּוֹ   יַעֲקֹב חֶבֶל נַחֲלָתוֹ:
י יִמְצָאֵהוּ בְּאֶרֶץ מִדְבָּר   וּבְתֹהוּ יְלֵל יְשִׁמֹן
יְסֹבְבֶנְהוּ יְבוֹנְנֵהוּ   יִצְּרֶנְהוּ כְּאִישׁוֹן עֵינוֹ:
יא כְּנֶשֶׁר יָעִיר קִנּוֹ   עַל־גּוֹזָלָיו יְרַחֵף
יִפְרֹשׂ כְּנָפָיו יִקָּחֵהוּ   יִשָּׂאֵהוּ עַל־אֶבְרָתוֹ:
יב יְהוָה בָּדָד יַנְחֶנּוּ   וְאֵין עִמּוֹ אֵל נֵכָר: שלישי
יג יַרְכִּבֵהוּ עַל־בָּמֳתֵי אָרֶץ   וַיֹּאכַל תְּנוּבֹת שָׂדָי   בָּמֳתֵי
וַיֵּנִקֵהוּ דְבַשׁ מִסֶּלַע   וְשֶׁמֶן מֵחַלְמִישׁ צוּר:
יד חֶמְאַת בָּקָר וַחֲלֵב צֹאן   עִם־חֵלֶב כָּרִים
וְאֵילִים בְּנֵי־בָשָׁן וְעַתּוּדִים   עִם־חֵלֶב כִּלְיוֹת חִטָּה
טו וְדַם־עֵנָב תִּשְׁתֶּה־חָמֶר: וַיִּשְׁמַן יְשֻׁרוּן וַיִּבְעָט
שָׁמַנְתָּ עָבִיתָ כָּשִׂיתָ   וַיִּטֹּשׁ אֱלוֹהַ עָשָׂהוּ
טז וַיְנַבֵּל צוּר יְשֻׁעָתוֹ:   יַקְנִאֻהוּ בְּזָרִים
יז בְּתוֹעֵבֹת יַכְעִיסֻהוּ:   יִזְבְּחוּ לַשֵּׁדִים לֹא אֱלֹהַ
אֱלֹהִים לֹא יְדָעוּם   חֲדָשִׁים מִקָּרֹב בָּאוּ
יח לֹא שְׂעָרוּם אֲבֹתֵיכֶם: צוּר יְלָדְךָ תֶּשִׁי
יט וַתִּשְׁכַּח אֵל מְחֹלְלֶךָ:   וַיַּרְא יְהוָה וַיִּנְאָץ   רביעי
כ מִכַּעַס בָּנָיו וּבְנֹתָיו: וַיֹּאמֶר אַסְתִּירָה פָנַי מֵהֶם
אֶרְאֶה מָה אַחֲרִיתָם   כִּי דוֹר תַּהְפֻּכֹת הֵמָּה
כא בָּנִים לֹא־אֵמֻן בָּם: הֵם קִנְאוּנִי בְלֹא־אֵל
כִּעֲסוּנִי בְּהַבְלֵיהֶם   וַאֲנִי אַקְנִיאֵם בְּלֹא־עָם
כב בְּגוֹי נָבָל אַכְעִיסֵם: כִּי־אֵשׁ קָדְחָה בְאַפִּי

it burns to the depths of Sheol,[76] / will devour the land and its
23 harvests, / and set fire to the hills' foundations. / I will heap evils
24 upon them, / exhaust My arrows on them: / consuming famine,
flaming fever, bitter plague, / and fanged beasts will I send against
25 them, / and venomous vipers crawling in the dust. / Sword outside
and terror within / will claim young men and women, / nursing
26 infants, and the gray-haired old. / I thought I would scatter them, /
27 erasing their memory from man, / were it not for fear of the enemy's
taunts, / lest their adversaries misunderstand / and say, 'Our hand
28 has triumphed; / it was not the LORD who did all this.' / They
29 are a nation devoid of sense;[77] / they have no understanding. / If
they were wise, they would contemplate this, / and know what their end
30 would be.[78] / How could one man pursue a thousand, / and two
put ten thousand to flight, / unless their Rock had sold them, /
31 the LORD had handed them over?[79] / For their rock[80] is not
32 like our Rock; / even in our enemies' judgment. / Their vine is
from Sedom, / from the vineyards of Amora;[81] / their grapes
33 are grapes of poison, / their clusters bitter; / their wine is ser-
34 pents' venom, / cruel poison of the viper. / Is this not kept in My
35 reserve, / sealed away in My treasury? / Vengeance is Mine; I will repay: /
in time, their foot will slip; / their day of disaster is near, / their
36 destiny hastens to meet them. / For the LORD will vindicate His
people, / bring solace to His servants, / when He sees their strength
37 has slipped away, / no one remains, no bond nor free. / He
will say: Where are these gods of theirs, / the rock they went to for
38 refuge, / that ate their sacrificial fat / and drank their wine of
libation? / Let those rise up and help you now, / let them be your
39 protection! / See now that I, I alone, am He; / there is no god
apart from Me. / I deal death and I bring life; / I wounded but will
40 heal; / and there is no rescue from My hand. / For I lift My hand sky-
41 ward and swear: / as sure as I live forever, / when I whet My flashing
sword, / and My hand grasps justice; / I will wreak vengeance on My
42 foes, / and repay those who hate Me.[82] / I will make My arrows drunk
with blood, / while My sword devours flesh, / the blood of the slain

---

76 | The netherworld.

77 | This refers to the enemy nation.

78 | That is, they would anticipate the consequences of oppressing Israel.

79 | In other words, a nation that defeats Israel ought to realize that it is God who enables such an outcome.

80 | Referring to the enemy's deity.

81 | Verses 32–33 describe the punishment that awaits the enemy, as the subsequent verses make clear.

82 | Referring to the enemies mentioned above.

וַתִּיקַד עַד־שְׁאוֹל תַּחְתִּית   וַתֹּאכַל אֶרֶץ וִיבֻלָהּ
כג וַתְּלַהֵט מוֹסְדֵי הָרִים׃   אַסְפֶּה עָלֵימוֹ רָעוֹת
כד חִצַּי אֲכַלֶּה־בָּם׃   מְזֵי רָעָב וּלְחֻמֵי רֶשֶׁף
וְקֶטֶב מְרִירִי   וְשֶׁן־בְּהֵמֹת אֲשַׁלַּח־בָּם
כה עִם־חֲמַת זֹחֲלֵי עָפָר׃   מִחוּץ תְּשַׁכֶּל־חֶרֶב
וּמֵחֲדָרִים אֵימָה   גַּם־בָּחוּר גַּם־בְּתוּלָה
כו יוֹנֵק עִם־אִישׁ שֵׂיבָה׃   אָמַרְתִּי אַפְאֵיהֶם
כז אַשְׁבִּיתָה מֵאֱנוֹשׁ זִכְרָם׃   לוּלֵי כַּעַס אוֹיֵב אָגוּר
פֶּן־יְנַכְּרוּ צָרֵימוֹ   פֶּן־יֹאמְרוּ יָדֵנוּ רָמָה
כח וְלֹא יְהוָה פָּעַל כָּל־זֹאת׃   כִּי־גוֹי אֹבַד עֵצוֹת הֵמָּה
כט וְאֵין בָּהֶם תְּבוּנָה׃   לוּ חָכְמוּ יַשְׂכִּילוּ זֹאת   חמישי
ל יָבִינוּ לְאַחֲרִיתָם׃   אֵיכָה יִרְדֹּף אֶחָד אֶלֶף
וּשְׁנַיִם יָנִיסוּ רְבָבָה   אִם־לֹא כִּי־צוּרָם מְכָרָם
לא וַיהוָה הִסְגִּירָם׃   כִּי לֹא כְצוּרֵנוּ צוּרָם
לב וְאֹיְבֵינוּ פְּלִילִים׃   כִּי־מִגֶּפֶן סְדֹם גַּפְנָם
וּמִשַּׁדְמֹת עֲמֹרָה   עֲנָבֵמוֹ עִנְּבֵי־רוֹשׁ
לג אַשְׁכְּלֹת מְרֹרֹת לָמוֹ׃   חֲמַת תַּנִּינִם יֵינָם
לד וְרֹאשׁ פְּתָנִים אַכְזָר׃   הֲלֹא־הוּא כָּמֻס עִמָּדִי
לה חָתוּם בְּאוֹצְרֹתָי׃   לִי נָקָם וְשִׁלֵּם
לְעֵת תָּמוּט רַגְלָם   כִּי קָרוֹב יוֹם אֵידָם
לו וְחָשׁ עֲתִדֹת לָמוֹ׃   כִּי־יָדִין יְהוָה עַמּוֹ
וְעַל־עֲבָדָיו יִתְנֶחָם   כִּי יִרְאֶה כִּי־אָזְלַת יָד
לז וְאֶפֶס עָצוּר וְעָזוּב׃   וְאָמַר אֵי אֱלֹהֵימוֹ
לח צוּר חָסָיוּ בוֹ׃   אֲשֶׁר חֵלֶב זְבָחֵימוֹ יֹאכֵלוּ
יִשְׁתּוּ יֵין נְסִיכָם   יָקוּמוּ וְיַעְזְרֻכֶם
לט יְהִי עֲלֵיכֶם סִתְרָה׃   רְאוּ ׀ עַתָּה כִּי אֲנִי אֲנִי הוּא
וְאֵין אֱלֹהִים עִמָּדִי   אֲנִי אָמִית וַאֲחַיֶּה
מָחַצְתִּי וַאֲנִי אֶרְפָּא   וְאֵין מִיָּדִי מַצִּיל׃
מ כִּי־אֶשָּׂא אֶל־שָׁמַיִם יָדִי   וְאָמַרְתִּי חַי אָנֹכִי לְעֹלָם׃   ששי
מא אִם־שַׁנּוֹתִי בְּרַק חַרְבִּי   וְתֹאחֵז בְּמִשְׁפָּט יָדִי
אָשִׁיב נָקָם לְצָרָי   וְלִמְשַׂנְאַי אֲשַׁלֵּם׃
מב אַשְׁכִּיר חִצַּי מִדָּם   וְחַרְבִּי תֹּאכַל בָּשָׂר

43 and the captives, / leaders of the long-haired foe. / O nations, sing
out of His people, / for He will avenge His servants' blood, / take
vengeance upon His foes, / and cleanse His land and His people."

44 Moshe came and proclaimed all the words of this song in the hearing of the
45 people, he and Hoshea son of Nun. When Moshe had finished speaking all
46 these words to all Israel, he said to them: "Take to heart all the words I testify
to you today, and charge your children with them, so that they may take care
47 to keep all the words of this Law. For these are not idle words for you; they are
your very life. By this word you may live long in the land that you are crossing
over the Jordan to possess."
48 49 On that very day the LORD spoke to Moshe: "Ascend this mountain of
Avarim, Mount Nevo, in the land of Moav, facing Yeriḥo, and gaze upon the
50 land of Canaan, which I am giving to the Israelites as a holding. There, on the
mountain that you ascend, you will die and be gathered to your people, as
your brother Aharon died on Mount Hor and was gathered to his people;[83]
51 because both of you broke faith with Me in the midst of the Israelites at the
waters of Merivat Kadesh in the Wilderness of Tzin, failing to affirm My
52 holiness among the Israelites.[84] You will see the land from afar, but you shall
not enter it – the land that I am giving to the people of Israel."

VEZOT HABERAKHA

33 1 This is the blessing with which Moshe, man of God, blessed the Israelites
2 before he died. Moshe said: "The LORD came from Sinai, He shone upon
them from Se'ir, He appeared over the crest of Paran and came among myr-
3 iads of holy ones:[85] at His right hand, darting fire. He is a lover of peoples,
all His holy ones are in Your hand;[86] they place themselves at Your feet,
4 upholding Your words. Moshe charged us with the Law, heritage of Yaakov's
5 assembly. He became king in Yeshurun,[87] when the heads of the people
6 gathered[88] – the tribes of Israel together. May Reuven live, and not die, even
7 though his men are few." And this he said of Yehuda: "Listen, LORD,
to Yehuda's voice, and bring him home to his people;[89] strengthen his hands,
be his support against his foes."
8 And of Levi he said: "Let Your Tumim and Urim[90] be with Your faithful, the
9 one You tested at Masa, and challenged at the Meriva waters;[91] who said of
his father and mother, 'I do not regard them,' ignored his brothers, and did
not acknowledge his children[92] – instead keeping Your word, and guarding

---

83 | See Numbers 20:22–29.
84 | See Numbers 20:1–12.
85 | Meaning angels.
86 | The varying second-person and third-person references to God are a feature of biblical poetry. The "holy ones" here are traditionally understood to refer to Israel.
87 | See note on 32:15.
88 | Perhaps a reference to the Revelation at Sinai.
89 | That is, from the battlefield.
90 | See note on Exodus 28:30.
91 | See Exodus 17:1–7.
92 | See Exodus 32:26–29.

מִדַּם חָלָל וְשִׁבְיָה   מֵרֹאשׁ פַּרְעוֹת אוֹיֵב׃
מג הַרְנִינוּ גוֹיִם עַמּוֹ   כִּי דַם־עֲבָדָיו יִקּוֹם
וְנָקָם יָשִׁיב לְצָרָיו   וְכִפֶּר אַדְמָתוֹ עַמּוֹ׃

מד וַיָּבֹא מֹשֶׁה וַיְדַבֵּר אֶת־כָּל־דִּבְרֵי הַשִּׁירָה־הַזֹּאת בְּאׇזְנֵי הָעָם הוּא שביעי
מה וְהוֹשֵׁעַ בִּן־נוּן׃ וַיְכַל מֹשֶׁה לְדַבֵּר אֶת־כָּל־הַדְּבָרִים הָאֵלֶּה אֶל־כׇּל־
מו יִשְׂרָאֵל׃ וַיֹּאמֶר אֲלֵהֶם שִׂימוּ לְבַבְכֶם לְכׇל־הַדְּבָרִים אֲשֶׁר אָנֹכִי מֵעִיד
בָּכֶם הַיּוֹם אֲשֶׁר תְּצַוֻּם אֶת־בְּנֵיכֶם לִשְׁמֹר לַעֲשׂוֹת אֶת־כׇּל־דִּבְרֵי
מז הַתּוֹרָה הַזֹּאת׃ כִּי לֹא־דָבָר רֵק הוּא מִכֶּם כִּי־הוּא חַיֵּיכֶם וּבַדָּבָר
הַזֶּה תַּאֲרִיכוּ יָמִים עַל־הָאֲדָמָה אֲשֶׁר אַתֶּם עֹבְרִים אֶת־הַיַּרְדֵּן שָׁמָּה
לְרִשְׁתָּהּ׃
מח מט וַיְדַבֵּר יהוה אֶל־מֹשֶׁה בְּעֶצֶם הַיּוֹם הַזֶּה לֵאמֹר׃ עֲלֵה אֶל־הַר הָעֲבָרִים מפטיר
הַזֶּה הַר־נְבוֹ אֲשֶׁר בְּאֶרֶץ מוֹאָב אֲשֶׁר עַל־פְּנֵי יְרֵחוֹ וּרְאֵה אֶת־אֶרֶץ
נ כְּנַעַן אֲשֶׁר אֲנִי נֹתֵן לִבְנֵי יִשְׂרָאֵל לַאֲחֻזָּה׃ וּמֻת בָּהָר אֲשֶׁר אַתָּה עֹלֶה
שָׁמָּה וְהֵאָסֵף אֶל־עַמֶּיךָ כַּאֲשֶׁר־מֵת אַהֲרֹן אָחִיךָ בְּהֹר הָהָר וַיֵּאָסֶף
נא אֶל־עַמָּיו׃ עַל אֲשֶׁר מְעַלְתֶּם בִּי בְּתוֹךְ בְּנֵי יִשְׂרָאֵל בְּמֵי־מְרִיבַת קָדֵשׁ
נב מִדְבַּר־צִן עַל אֲשֶׁר לֹא־קִדַּשְׁתֶּם אוֹתִי בְּתוֹךְ בְּנֵי יִשְׂרָאֵל׃ כִּי מִנֶּגֶד
תִּרְאֶה אֶת־הָאָרֶץ וְשָׁמָּה לֹא תָבוֹא אֶל־הָאָרֶץ אֲשֶׁר־אֲנִי נֹתֵן לִבְנֵי
יִשְׂרָאֵל׃ כז
לג א וְזֹאת הַבְּרָכָה אֲשֶׁר בֵּרַךְ מֹשֶׁה אִישׁ הָאֱלֹהִים אֶת־בְּנֵי יִשְׂרָאֵל לִפְנֵי וזאת הברכה
ב מוֹתוֹ׃ וַיֹּאמַר יהוה מִסִּינַי בָּא וְזָרַח מִשֵּׂעִיר לָמוֹ הוֹפִיעַ מֵהַר פָּארָן
ג וְאָתָה מֵרִבְבֹת קֹדֶשׁ מִימִינוֹ אשדת לָמוֹ׃ אַף חֹבֵב עַמִּים כׇּל־קְדֹשָׁיו אֵשׁ דָּת
ד בְּיָדֶךָ וְהֵם תֻּכּוּ לְרַגְלֶךָ יִשָּׂא מִדַּבְּרֹתֶיךָ׃ תּוֹרָה צִוָּה־לָנוּ מֹשֶׁה מוֹרָשָׁה
ה קְהִלַּת יַעֲקֹב׃ וַיְהִי בִישֻׁרוּן מֶלֶךְ בְּהִתְאַסֵּף רָאשֵׁי עָם יַחַד שִׁבְטֵי
ו ז יִשְׂרָאֵל׃ יְחִי רְאוּבֵן וְאַל־יָמֹת וִיהִי מְתָיו מִסְפָּר׃ וְזֹאת
לִיהוּדָה וַיֹּאמַר שְׁמַע יהוה קוֹל יְהוּדָה וְאֶל־עַמּוֹ תְּבִיאֶנּוּ יָדָיו רָב
לוֹ וְעֵזֶר מִצָּרָיו תִּהְיֶה׃
ח וּלְלֵוִי אָמַר תֻּמֶּיךָ וְאוּרֶיךָ לְאִישׁ חֲסִידֶךָ אֲשֶׁר נִסִּיתוֹ בְּמַסָּה תְּרִיבֵהוּ שני
ט עַל־מֵי מְרִיבָה׃ הָאֹמֵר לְאָבִיו וּלְאִמּוֹ לֹא רְאִיתִיו וְאֶת־אֶחָיו לֹא הִכִּיר

10 close Your covenant. They shall teach Your laws to Yaakov, and Your instruction to Israel; they shall place incense before You, and whole offerings on
11 Your altar. Bless, O LORD, his vigor, and accept the work of his hands; crush
12 the loins of his foes; let his enemies rise no more." Of Binyamin he
said: "Beloved of the LORD, may he dwell in safety with Him – He protects
13 him all day long as he rests between His shoulders."[93] And of Yosef
he said: "Blessed by the LORD be his land, with the bounty of heaven, with
14 dew, and the deep waters that lie below; with the bounty brought forth by
15 the sun, and the bounteous yield of the moon; with the best from the age-old
16 mountains, and the bounty of the everlasting hills; with the bounty of earth
and its fullness, and the will of Him who dwelt in the bush.[94] May these rest
17 on Yosef's head, on the brow of the prince among brothers. His glory is that of
a firstborn bull, his horns the grand horns of the wild ox; with them he gores
the peoples, all, to the ends of the earth. These are the myriads of Efrayim,
18 these the thousands of Menashe." And of Zevulun he said: "Rejoice,
19 Zevulun, as you set out; and Yissakhar, in your tents. They summon peoples
to the mountain;[95] there they offer righteous sacrifice; they will feast on the
20 plenty of oceans and the hidden, buried riches of the sands." And
of Gad he said: "Blessed be He who enlarges Gad! He lives like a lion, he
21 tears at arm and scalp.[96] He chose the first portion for himself,[97] for there
the lawgiver's portion is reserved,[98] where the heads of the people come. He
22 executed the LORD's justice, and His ordinances for Israel." And
23 of Dan he said: "Dan is a lion's whelp springing forth from Bashan." And of
Naftali he said: "Naftali, sated with favor, filled with the LORD's blessing, west
24 and south possess." And of Asher he said: "Most blessed of sons is
25 Asher; may he win his brothers' favor, and bathe his feet in oil. Your bars are
26 iron and bronze;[99] may your strength be equal to your days. There is none
like the God of Yeshurun, riding the skies to help you, the heavens, in His
27 grandeur. Your refuge the God of time immemorial, you rest in eternal arms.
28 Dispelling every enemy before you, He spoke: 'Destroy!' So Israel dwells in
safety; Yaakov takes refuge alone in a land of grain and wine, where the skies
29 drop their dew. Happy are you, Israel. Who is like you, a people rescued by
the LORD? He is your shield of help, your sword of triumph. Your enemies
34 1 will cower before you, and you shall tread their high places." Then
Moshe went up from the plains of Moav to Mount Nevo, to the summit
of Pisga, facing Yeriḥo. The LORD showed him all the land: from Gilad to

93 | Traditionally, this is understood to mean that the Sanctuary would ultimately stand in Benjaminite territory.

94 | See Exodus, chapter 3.

95 | Traditionally understood to mean Mount Zion, where the Temple eventually stood.

96 | In battle.

97 | The tribe of Gad settled east of the Jordan, in land that the Israelites conquered first; see Numbers, chapter 32.

98 | Often understood to refer to the burial place of Moshe.

99 | That is, you will live in security.

י וְאֶת־בָּנוֹ לֹא יָדָע כִּי שָׁמְרוּ אִמְרָתֶךָ וּבְרִיתְךָ יִנְצֹרוּ: יוֹרוּ מִשְׁפָּטֶיךָ
לְיַעֲקֹב וְתוֹרָתְךָ לְיִשְׂרָאֵל יָשִׂימוּ קְטוֹרָה בְּאַפֶּךָ וְכָלִיל עַל־מִזְבְּחֶךָ:
יא בָּרֵךְ יהוה חֵילוֹ וּפֹעַל יָדָיו תִּרְצֶה מְחַץ מָתְנַיִם קָמָיו וּמְשַׂנְאָיו
יב מִן־יְקוּמוּן: לְבִנְיָמִן אָמַר יְדִיד יהוה יִשְׁכֹּן לָבֶטַח עָלָיו
יג חֹפֵף עָלָיו כָּל־הַיּוֹם וּבֵין כְּתֵפָיו שָׁכֵן: וּלְיוֹסֵף אָמַר שלישי
מְבֹרֶכֶת יהוה אַרְצוֹ מִמֶּגֶד שָׁמַיִם מִטָּל וּמִתְּהוֹם רֹבֶצֶת תָּחַת:
יד טו וּמִמֶּגֶד תְּבוּאֹת שָׁמֶשׁ וּמִמֶּגֶד גֶּרֶשׁ יְרָחִים: וּמֵרֹאשׁ הַרְרֵי־קֶדֶם
טז וּמִמֶּגֶד גִּבְעוֹת עוֹלָם: וּמִמֶּגֶד אֶרֶץ וּמְלֹאָהּ וּרְצוֹן שֹׁכְנִי סְנֶה תָּבוֹאתָה
יז לְרֹאשׁ יוֹסֵף וּלְקָדְקֹד נְזִיר אֶחָיו: בְּכוֹר שׁוֹרוֹ הָדָר לוֹ וְקַרְנֵי רְאֵם
קַרְנָיו בָּהֶם עַמִּים יְנַגַּח יַחְדָּו אַפְסֵי־אָרֶץ וְהֵם רִבְבוֹת אֶפְרַיִם וְהֵם
יח אַלְפֵי מְנַשֶּׁה: וְלִזְבוּלֻן אָמַר שְׂמַח זְבוּלֻן בְּצֵאתֶךָ וְיִשָּׂשכָר רביעי
יט בְּאֹהָלֶיךָ: עַמִּים הַר־יִקְרָאוּ שָׁם יִזְבְּחוּ זִבְחֵי־צֶדֶק כִּי שֶׁפַע יַמִּים
כ יִינָקוּ וּשְׂפֻנֵי טְמוּנֵי חוֹל: וּלְגָד אָמַר בָּרוּךְ מַרְחִיב גָּד
כא כְּלָבִיא שָׁכֵן וְטָרַף זְרוֹעַ אַף־קָדְקֹד: וַיַּרְא רֵאשִׁית לוֹ כִּי־שָׁם חֶלְקַת
מְחֹקֵק סָפוּן וַיֵּתֵא רָאשֵׁי עָם צִדְקַת יהוה עָשָׂה וּמִשְׁפָּטָיו עִם־
כב יִשְׂרָאֵל: וּלְדָן אָמַר דָּן גּוּר אַרְיֵה יְזַנֵּק מִן־הַבָּשָׁן: חמישי
כג וּלְנַפְתָּלִי אָמַר נַפְתָּלִי שְׂבַע רָצוֹן וּמָלֵא בִּרְכַּת יהוה יָם וְדָרוֹם
כד יְרָשָׁה: וּלְאָשֵׁר אָמַר בָּרוּךְ מִבָּנִים אָשֵׁר יְהִי רְצוּי אֶחָיו
כה כו וְטֹבֵל בַּשֶּׁמֶן רַגְלוֹ: בַּרְזֶל וּנְחֹשֶׁת מִנְעָלֶךָ וּכְיָמֶיךָ דָּבְאֶךָ: אֵין כָּאֵל
כז יְשֻׁרוּן רֹכֵב שָׁמַיִם בְּעֶזְרֶךָ וּבְגַאֲוָתוֹ שְׁחָקִים: מְעֹנָה אֱלֹהֵי קֶדֶם וּמִתַּחַת חתן התורה
כח זְרֹעֹת עוֹלָם וַיְגָרֶשׁ מִפָּנֶיךָ אוֹיֵב וַיֹּאמֶר הַשְׁמֵד: וַיִּשְׁכֹּן יִשְׂרָאֵל בֶּטַח
כט בָּדָד עֵין יַעֲקֹב אֶל־אֶרֶץ דָּגָן וְתִירוֹשׁ אַף־שָׁמָיו יַעַרְפוּ־טָל: אַשְׁרֶיךָ
יִשְׂרָאֵל מִי כָמוֹךָ עַם נוֹשַׁע בַּיהוה מָגֵן עֶזְרֶךָ וַאֲשֶׁר־חֶרֶב גַּאֲוָתֶךָ
לד א וְיִכָּחֲשׁוּ אֹיְבֶיךָ לָךְ וְאַתָּה עַל־בָּמוֹתֵימוֹ תִדְרֹךְ: וַיַּעַל
מֹשֶׁה מֵעַרְבֹת מוֹאָב אֶל־הַר נְבוֹ רֹאשׁ הַפִּסְגָּה אֲשֶׁר עַל־פְּנֵי יְרֵחוֹ

2 Dan, all of Naftali, the land of Efrayim and Menashe, all the land of Yehuda
3 as far as the Westward Sea, the Negev, and the plain – the Valley of Yeriḥo,
4 city of palm trees – as far as Tzoar. The LORD said to him, "This is the land
I promised Avraham, Yitzḥak, and Yaakov, saying, 'I will give this to your
descendants'; I have let you see it with your eyes, but to that place you will
5 not cross over." Then Moshe, the LORD's own servant, died there in the land
6 of Moav, at the LORD's word. He buried him in Moav, in a valley opposite Beit
7 Peor, and to this day no one knows his burial place. Moshe was a hundred
and twenty years old when he died; his eyes had not grown dim, nor his vital-
8 ity fled. The Israelites wept for Moshe in the plains of Moav for thirty days,
9 until the time of weeping and mourning for him was over. Yehoshua son of
Nun was filled with the spirit of wisdom, for Moshe had laid his hands upon
him, and the Israelites listened to him, and did as the LORD had commanded
10 Moshe. There has never arisen a prophet in Israel like Moshe, whom the
11 LORD knew face-to-face, in all the signs and wonders the LORD sent him
to perform in Egypt, against Pharaoh, all his officials, and all of his land,
12 and in all the acts of a mighty hand and of terrifying power that Moshe performed before the eyes of all Israel.

ב וַיַּרְאֵ֨הוּ יְהוָ֜ה אֶת־כָּל־הָאָ֗רֶץ אֶת־הַגִּלְעָ֖ד עַד־דָּֽן׃ וְאֵת֙ כָּל־נַפְתָּלִ֔י
וְאֶת־אֶ֥רֶץ אֶפְרַ֖יִם וּמְנַשֶּׁ֑ה וְאֵ֙ת כָּל־אֶ֣רֶץ יְהוּדָ֔ה עַ֖ד הַיָּ֥ם הָאַחֲרֽוֹן׃
ג ד וְאֶת־הַנֶּ֗גֶב וְאֶת־הַכִּכָּ֞ר בִּקְעַ֧ת יְרֵח֛וֹ עִ֥יר הַתְּמָרִ֖ים עַד־צֹֽעַר׃ וַיֹּ֨אמֶר
יְהוָ֜ה אֵלָ֗יו זֹ֤את הָאָ֙רֶץ֙ אֲשֶׁ֣ר נִשְׁבַּ֡עְתִּי לְאַבְרָהָ֞ם לְיִצְחָ֤ק וּֽלְיַעֲקֹב֙
ה לֵאמֹ֔ר לְזַרְעֲךָ֖ אֶתְּנֶ֑נָּה הֶרְאִיתִ֣יךָ בְעֵינֶ֔יךָ וְשָׁ֖מָּה לֹ֥א תַעֲבֹֽר׃ וַיָּ֨מָת שָׁ֜ם
ו מֹשֶׁ֧ה עֶבֶד־יְהוָ֛ה בְּאֶ֥רֶץ מוֹאָ֖ב עַל־פִּ֥י יְהוָֽה׃ וַיִּקְבֹּ֨ר אֹת֤וֹ בַגַּי֙ בְּאֶ֣רֶץ
מוֹאָ֔ב מ֖וּל בֵּ֣ית פְּע֑וֹר וְלֹא־יָדַ֥ע אִישׁ֙ אֶת־קְבֻ֣רָת֔וֹ עַ֖ד הַיּ֥וֹם הַזֶּֽה׃
ז וּמֹשֶׁ֗ה בֶּן־מֵאָ֧ה וְעֶשְׂרִ֛ים שָׁנָ֖ה בְּמֹת֑וֹ לֹא־כָהֲתָ֥ה עֵינ֖וֹ וְלֹא־נָ֥ס לֵחֹֽה׃
ח וַ֠יִּבְכּוּ בְּנֵ֨י יִשְׂרָאֵ֧ל אֶת־מֹשֶׁ֛ה בְּעַרְבֹ֥ת מוֹאָ֖ב שְׁלֹשִׁ֣ים י֑וֹם וַיִּתְּמ֔וּ יְמֵ֥י
ט בְכִ֖י אֵ֥בֶל מֹשֶֽׁה׃ וִיהוֹשֻׁ֣עַ בִּן־נ֗וּן מָלֵא֙ ר֣וּחַ חָכְמָ֔ה כִּֽי־סָמַ֥ךְ מֹשֶׁ֛ה
אֶת־יָדָ֖יו עָלָ֑יו וַיִּשְׁמְע֨וּ אֵלָ֤יו בְּנֵֽי־יִשְׂרָאֵל֙ וַֽיַּעֲשׂ֔וּ כַּאֲשֶׁ֛ר צִוָּ֥ה יְהוָ֖ה
י אֶת־מֹשֶֽׁה׃ וְלֹֽא־קָ֨ם נָבִ֥יא ע֛וֹד בְּיִשְׂרָאֵ֖ל כְּמֹשֶׁ֑ה אֲשֶׁר֙ יְדָע֣וֹ יְהוָ֔ה
יא פָּנִ֖ים אֶל־פָּנִֽים׃ לְכָל־הָ֨אֹתֹ֜ת וְהַמּֽוֹפְתִ֗ים אֲשֶׁ֤ר שְׁלָחוֹ֙ יְהוָ֔ה לַעֲשׂ֖וֹת
יב בְּאֶ֣רֶץ מִצְרָ֑יִם לְפַרְעֹ֥ה וּלְכָל־עֲבָדָ֖יו וּלְכָל־אַרְצֽוֹ׃ וּלְכֹל֙ הַיָּ֣ד הַחֲזָקָ֔ה
וּלְכֹ֖ל הַמּוֹרָ֣א הַגָּד֑וֹל אֲשֶׁר֙ עָשָׂ֣ה מֹשֶׁ֔ה לְעֵינֵ֖י כָּל־יִשְׂרָאֵֽל׃

נביאים

NEVI'IM/PROPHETS

יהושע YEHOSHUA/JOSHUA

שופטים SHOFETIM/JUDGES

שמואל SHMUEL/SAMUEL

מלכים MELAKHIM/KINGS

ישעיה YESHAYA/ISAIAH

ירמיה YIRMEYA/JEREMIAH

יחזקאל YEḤEZKEL/EZEKIEL

שנים עשר SHENEIM ASAR/
THE TWELVE PROPHETS

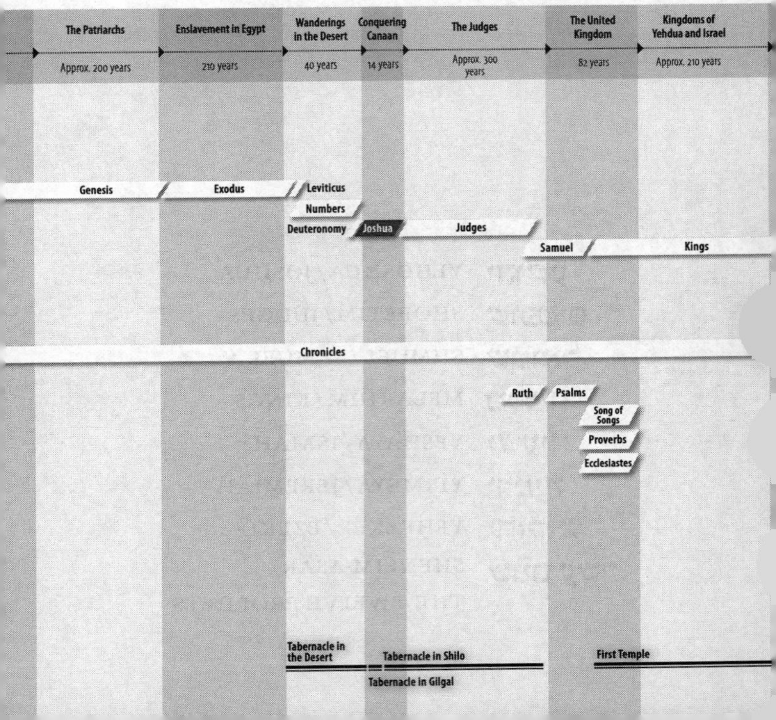

The Patriarchs
Approx. 200 years
Enslavement in Egypt
210 years
Wanderings in the Desert
40 years
Conquering Canaan
14 years
The Judges
Approx. 300 years
The United Kingdom
82 years
Kingdoms of Yehdua and Israel
Approx. 210 years
Genesis
Exodus
Leviticus
Numbers
Deuteronomy
Joshua
Judges
Samuel
Kings
Chronicles
Ruth
Psalms
Song of Songs
Proverbs
Ecclesiastes
Tabernacle in the Desert
Tabernacle in Shilo
Tabernacle in Gilgal
First Temple

יהושע
YEHOSHUA/JOSHUA

JOSHUA	From the Plains of Moav to the camp at Gilgal	Wars with the nations of Canaan	From the camp in Gilgal to the settlement of the land	The altar at the Jordan and Yehoshua's farewell speeches
	Chs. 1–5	6–12	13–21	22–24
	7 years		7 years	

1 1 After the death of Moshe, the LORD's servant, the LORD said to Moshe's
2 disciple, Yehoshua son of Nun: "Moshe, My servant, is dead; now arise, cross
the Jordan here – you and all this people – to the land that I am giving to the
3 Israelites. I have given you every place your foot will tread, just as I promised
4 Moshe. Your territory shall stretch from the wilderness and Lebanon here to
the Great River, the Euphrates River, and all the land of the Hittites, to the
5 Great Sea where the sun sets. No one will be able to stand against you for as
long as you live; just as I was with Moshe, I will be with you. I will never let
6 you go, and I will never leave you. Be strong and brave, for you will bring this
people into possession of the land I swore to their ancestors to give them.
7 But you must be strong and brave indeed to uphold faithfully all the Torah
that Moshe My servant commanded you; do not stray from it – neither
8 right nor left – so that you may triumph wherever you go. This book of
Torah must never leave your lips; contemplate it day and night, so that you
will faithfully uphold all that is written within it. For then your course will
9 succeed; then you will triumph. Hear now – I have charged you to be strong
and brave. Do not be frightened or dismayed, for the LORD your God is with
10 you wherever you go." Yehoshua commanded the officers of the
11 people: "Cross through the camp and instruct the people: 'Prepare provisions
for yourselves, for in three days' time you are to cross the Jordan here, to come
and take possession of the land that the LORD your God is giving you as your
12 own.'" Yehoshua then told the Reubenites, the Gadites, and half the
13 tribe of Menashe: "Remember what Moshe, the LORD's servant, commanded
14 you:[1] The LORD your God has granted you rest and given you this land. Your
wives and little ones and your cattle shall dwell in the land that Moshe gave
you across the Jordan, but all your warriors shall cross over armed to join
15 your brothers and assist them, until the LORD grants rest like yours to your
brothers and they too take possession of the land that the LORD your God
is giving them. Then you shall return to your own land, which Moshe, the
LORD's servant, gave you on the eastern side of the Jordan – and you shall take
16 possession of it." They answered Yehoshua, "As we obeyed Moshe, so we will
17 obey you as long as the LORD your God is with you, as He was with Moshe.
18 Whoever rebels against your word or disobeys anything you command shall
be put to death; only be strong and brave."
2 1 Yehoshua son of Nun had sent two men as spies from Shitim, in secret: "Go
forth and survey the land and the region of Yeriḥo." So the men had set out,
arriving at the house of a harlot named Raḥav, where they lay down for the

1 | See Numbers, chapter 32.

א א וַיְהִי אַחֲרֵי מוֹת מֹשֶׁה עֶבֶד יהוה וַיֹּאמֶר יהוה אֶל־יְהוֹשֻׁעַ בִּן־נוּן א
ב מְשָׁרֵת מֹשֶׁה לֵאמֹר: מֹשֶׁה עַבְדִּי מֵת וְעַתָּה קוּם עֲבֹר אֶת־הַיַּרְדֵּן
הַזֶּה אַתָּה וְכָל־הָעָם הַזֶּה אֶל־הָאָרֶץ אֲשֶׁר אָנֹכִי נֹתֵן לָהֶם לִבְנֵי
ג יִשְׂרָאֵל: כָּל־מָקוֹם אֲשֶׁר תִּדְרֹךְ כַּף־רַגְלְכֶם בּוֹ לָכֶם נְתַתִּיו כַּאֲשֶׁר
ד דִּבַּרְתִּי אֶל־מֹשֶׁה: מֵהַמִּדְבָּר וְהַלְּבָנוֹן הַזֶּה וְעַד־הַנָּהָר הַגָּדוֹל נְהַר־
פְּרָת כֹּל אֶרֶץ הַחִתִּים וְעַד־הַיָּם הַגָּדוֹל מְבוֹא הַשָּׁמֶשׁ יִהְיֶה גְּבוּלְכֶם:
ה לֹא־יִתְיַצֵּב אִישׁ לְפָנֶיךָ כֹּל יְמֵי חַיֶּיךָ כַּאֲשֶׁר הָיִיתִי עִם־מֹשֶׁה אֶהְיֶה
ו עִמָּךְ לֹא אַרְפְּךָ וְלֹא אֶעֶזְבֶךָּ: חֲזַק וֶאֱמָץ כִּי אַתָּה תַּנְחִיל אֶת־הָעָם
ז הַזֶּה אֶת־הָאָרֶץ אֲשֶׁר־נִשְׁבַּעְתִּי לַאֲבוֹתָם לָתֵת לָהֶם: רַק חֲזַק וֶאֱמַץ
מְאֹד לִשְׁמֹר לַעֲשׂוֹת כְּכָל־הַתּוֹרָה אֲשֶׁר צִוְּךָ מֹשֶׁה עַבְדִּי אַל־תָּסוּר
ח מִמֶּנּוּ יָמִין וּשְׂמֹאול לְמַעַן תַּשְׂכִּיל בְּכֹל אֲשֶׁר תֵּלֵךְ: לֹא־יָמוּשׁ סֵפֶר
הַתּוֹרָה הַזֶּה מִפִּיךָ וְהָגִיתָ בּוֹ יוֹמָם וָלַיְלָה לְמַעַן תִּשְׁמֹר לַעֲשׂוֹת
ט כְּכָל־הַכָּתוּב בּוֹ כִּי־אָז תַּצְלִיחַ אֶת־דְּרָכֶךָ וְאָז תַּשְׂכִּיל: הֲלוֹא צִוִּיתִיךָ
חֲזַק וֶאֱמָץ אַל־תַּעֲרֹץ וְאַל־תֵּחָת כִּי עִמְּךָ יהוה אֱלֹהֶיךָ בְּכֹל אֲשֶׁר
י יא תֵּלֵךְ: וַיְצַו יְהוֹשֻׁעַ אֶת־שֹׁטְרֵי הָעָם לֵאמֹר: עִבְרוּ ׀ בְּקֶרֶב
הַמַּחֲנֶה וְצַוּוּ אֶת־הָעָם לֵאמֹר הָכִינוּ לָכֶם צֵידָה כִּי בְּעוֹד ׀ שְׁלֹשֶׁת
יָמִים אַתֶּם עֹבְרִים אֶת־הַיַּרְדֵּן הַזֶּה לָבוֹא לָרֶשֶׁת אֶת־הָאָרֶץ אֲשֶׁר
יב יהוה אֱלֹהֵיכֶם נֹתֵן לָכֶם לְרִשְׁתָּהּ: וְלָרְאוּבֵנִי וְלַגָּדִי וְלַחֲצִי
יג שֵׁבֶט הַמְנַשֶּׁה אָמַר יְהוֹשֻׁעַ לֵאמֹר: זָכוֹר אֶת־הַדָּבָר אֲשֶׁר צִוָּה אֶתְכֶם
מֹשֶׁה עֶבֶד־יהוה לֵאמֹר יהוה אֱלֹהֵיכֶם מֵנִיחַ לָכֶם וְנָתַן לָכֶם אֶת־
יד הָאָרֶץ הַזֹּאת: נְשֵׁיכֶם טַפְּכֶם וּמִקְנֵיכֶם יֵשְׁבוּ בָּאָרֶץ אֲשֶׁר נָתַן לָכֶם
מֹשֶׁה בְּעֵבֶר הַיַּרְדֵּן וְאַתֶּם תַּעַבְרוּ חֲמֻשִׁים לִפְנֵי אֲחֵיכֶם כֹּל גִּבּוֹרֵי
טו הַחַיִל וַעֲזַרְתֶּם אוֹתָם: עַד אֲשֶׁר־יָנִיחַ יהוה ׀ לַאֲחֵיכֶם כָּכֶם וְיָרְשׁוּ
גַם־הֵמָּה אֶת־הָאָרֶץ אֲשֶׁר־יהוה אֱלֹהֵיכֶם נֹתֵן לָהֶם וְשַׁבְתֶּם לְאֶרֶץ
יְרֻשַּׁתְכֶם וִירִשְׁתֶּם אוֹתָהּ אֲשֶׁר ׀ נָתַן לָכֶם מֹשֶׁה עֶבֶד יהוה בְּעֵבֶר
טז הַיַּרְדֵּן מִזְרַח הַשָּׁמֶשׁ: וַיַּעֲנוּ אֶת־יְהוֹשֻׁעַ לֵאמֹר כֹּל אֲשֶׁר־צִוִּיתָנוּ
יז נַעֲשֶׂה וְאֶל־כָּל־אֲשֶׁר תִּשְׁלָחֵנוּ נֵלֵךְ: כְּכֹל אֲשֶׁר־שָׁמַעְנוּ אֶל־מֹשֶׁה
כֵּן נִשְׁמַע אֵלֶיךָ רַק יִהְיֶה יהוה אֱלֹהֶיךָ עִמָּךְ כַּאֲשֶׁר הָיָה עִם־מֹשֶׁה:
יח כָּל־אִישׁ אֲשֶׁר־יַמְרֶה אֶת־פִּיךָ וְלֹא־יִשְׁמַע אֶת־דְּבָרֶיךָ לְכֹל אֲשֶׁר־
תְּצַוֶּנּוּ יוּמָת רַק חֲזַק וֶאֱמָץ:
ב א וַיִּשְׁלַח יְהוֹשֻׁעַ בִּן־נוּן מִן־הַשִּׁטִּים שְׁנַיִם אֲנָשִׁים מְרַגְּלִים חֶרֶשׁ לֵאמֹר
לְכוּ רְאוּ אֶת־הָאָרֶץ וְאֶת־יְרִיחוֹ וַיֵּלְכוּ וַיָּבֹאוּ בֵּית אִשָּׁה זוֹנָה וּשְׁמָהּ

2 night. And word reached the king of Yeriḥo: "Listen, people have come here
3 tonight – Israelites – to probe the land." The king of Yeriḥo sent word to
Raḥav: "Bring out those men who came to you, who arrived at your house,
4 for they have come to probe the land." Now, the woman had taken the two
men and hidden them, and she replied, "Yes, men came to me, but I did not
5 know where they were from. Just as the gate was being closed at nightfall, the
men left, and I do not know where they went. Go after them quickly, for you
6 can overtake them." She had taken the spies up to the roof and hidden them
7 amongst the stalks of flax she had laid out on the roof. The king's men ran
after them toward the Jordan route, over the river fords; and the moment the
8 pursuers left, the gate was closed behind them. They were not yet asleep when
9 she went up to them on the roof. "I know that the LORD has given you the
land," she said to the men, "and that dread of you has fallen upon us; for all
10 the inhabitants of the land quake before you. For we have heard that the LORD
dried up the waters of the Sea of Reeds before you when you left Egypt, and
we have heard what you did to the two Amorite kings across the Jordan – how
11 you utterly destroyed Siḥon and Og. We heard it and our hearts dissolved;
no one has the spirit to face you, for the LORD your God is God of heaven
12 above and earth below. Now, please swear to me by the LORD – for I have
shown you loyalty – that you, too, will be loyal to my father's house. Give me
13 a true sign that you will spare my father and mother and my brothers and
14 sisters and all that is theirs. Please, save our souls from death!" The men
replied to her, "We pledge to die in your place, if you speak no word of this,
15 and when the LORD gives us the land, we will show you true loyalty." She let
them down by a rope through the window, for her house was built into the
16 city wall; she lived inside the wall. "Flee toward the hills," she said to them,
"lest the pursuers run into you. Hide there for three days until the pursuers
17 have returned; only then be on your way." They said to her, "We will be free
18 of this oath you have sworn us to unless, when we come back to the land, you
tie this scarlet thread in the window you let us down from. Bring your father,
your mother, your siblings, and all your father's household into your home.
19 If anyone ventures outside the doors of your house, his blood will be upon
his own head – we will be free of blame – while if a hand is laid on anyone
20 who remains in the house with you, his blood shall be upon ours. But if you
21 speak a word of this, we shall be free of the oath we swore to you." "As you
say, so be it," she said, and she sent them away. They left, and she tied the
22 scarlet thread in the window. They set out and arrived at the hills. They stayed
there for three days until the pursuers turned back, for the pursuers had

ב רָחָב וַיִּשְׁכְּבוּ־שָׁמָּה׃ וַיֵּאָמַר לְמֶלֶךְ יְרִיחוֹ לֵאמֹר הִנֵּה אֲנָשִׁים בָּאוּ
ג הֵנָּה הַלַּיְלָה מִבְּנֵי יִשְׂרָאֵל לַחְפֹּר אֶת־הָאָרֶץ׃ וַיִּשְׁלַח מֶלֶךְ יְרִיחוֹ
אֶל־רָחָב לֵאמֹר הוֹצִיאִי הָאֲנָשִׁים הַבָּאִים אֵלַיִךְ אֲשֶׁר־בָּאוּ לְבֵיתֵךְ
ד כִּי לַחְפֹּר אֶת־כָּל־הָאָרֶץ בָּאוּ׃ וַתִּקַּח הָאִשָּׁה אֶת־שְׁנֵי הָאֲנָשִׁים
ה וַתִּצְפְּנוֹ וַתֹּאמֶר כֵּן בָּאוּ אֵלַי הָאֲנָשִׁים וְלֹא יָדַעְתִּי מֵאַיִן הֵמָּה׃ וַיְהִי
הַשַּׁעַר לִסְגּוֹר בַּחֹשֶׁךְ וְהָאֲנָשִׁים יָצָאוּ לֹא יָדַעְתִּי אָנָה הָלְכוּ הָאֲנָשִׁים
ו רִדְפוּ מַהֵר אַחֲרֵיהֶם כִּי תַשִּׂיגוּם׃ וְהִיא הֶעֱלָתַם הַגָּגָה וַתִּטְמְנֵם בְּפִשְׁתֵּי
ז הָעֵץ הָעֲרֻכוֹת לָהּ עַל־הַגָּג׃ וְהָאֲנָשִׁים רָדְפוּ אַחֲרֵיהֶם דֶּרֶךְ הַיַּרְדֵּן
עַל הַמַּעְבְּרוֹת וְהַשַּׁעַר סָגָרוּ אַחֲרֵי כַּאֲשֶׁר יָצְאוּ הָרֹדְפִים אַחֲרֵיהֶם׃
ח ט וְהֵמָּה טֶרֶם יִשְׁכָּבוּן וְהִיא עָלְתָה עֲלֵיהֶם עַל־הַגָּג׃ וַתֹּאמֶר אֶל־
הָאֲנָשִׁים יָדַעְתִּי כִּי־נָתַן יְהוָה לָכֶם אֶת־הָאָרֶץ וְכִי־נָפְלָה אֵימַתְכֶם
י עָלֵינוּ וְכִי נָמֹגוּ כָּל־יֹשְׁבֵי הָאָרֶץ מִפְּנֵיכֶם׃ כִּי שָׁמַעְנוּ אֵת אֲשֶׁר־הוֹבִישׁ
יְהוָה אֶת־מֵי יַם־סוּף מִפְּנֵיכֶם בְּצֵאתְכֶם מִמִּצְרָיִם וַאֲשֶׁר עֲשִׂיתֶם
לִשְׁנֵי מַלְכֵי הָאֱמֹרִי אֲשֶׁר בְּעֵבֶר הַיַּרְדֵּן לְסִיחֹן וּלְעוֹג אֲשֶׁר הֶחֱרַמְתֶּם
יא אוֹתָם׃ וַנִּשְׁמַע וַיִּמַּס לְבָבֵנוּ וְלֹא־קָמָה עוֹד רוּחַ בְּאִישׁ מִפְּנֵיכֶם כִּי
יְהוָה אֱלֹהֵיכֶם הוּא אֱלֹהִים בַּשָּׁמַיִם מִמַּעַל וְעַל־הָאָרֶץ מִתָּחַת׃
יב וְעַתָּה הִשָּׁבְעוּ־נָא לִי בַּיהוָה כִּי־עָשִׂיתִי עִמָּכֶם חָסֶד וַעֲשִׂיתֶם גַּם־
יג אַתֶּם עִם־בֵּית אָבִי חֶסֶד וּנְתַתֶּם לִי אוֹת אֱמֶת׃ וְהַחֲיִתֶם אֶת־אָבִי
וְאֶת־אִמִּי וְאֶת־אַחַי וְאֶת־אחותי וְאֵת כָּל־אֲשֶׁר לָהֶם וְהִצַּלְתֶּם אֶת־ אַחְיוֹתַי
יד נַפְשֹׁתֵינוּ מִמָּוֶת׃ וַיֹּאמְרוּ לָהּ הָאֲנָשִׁים נַפְשֵׁנוּ תַחְתֵּיכֶם לָמוּת אִם לֹא
תַגִּידוּ אֶת־דְּבָרֵנוּ זֶה וְהָיָה בְּתֵת־יְהוָה לָנוּ אֶת־הָאָרֶץ וְעָשִׂינוּ עִמָּךְ
טו חֶסֶד וֶאֱמֶת׃ וַתּוֹרִדֵם בַּחֶבֶל בְּעַד הַחַלּוֹן כִּי בֵיתָהּ בְּקִיר הַחוֹמָה
טז וּבַחוֹמָה הִיא יוֹשָׁבֶת׃ וַתֹּאמֶר לָהֶם הָהָרָה לֵּכוּ פֶּן־יִפְגְּעוּ בָכֶם הָרֹדְפִים
וְנַחְבֵּתֶם שָׁמָּה שְׁלֹשֶׁת יָמִים עַד שׁוֹב הָרֹדְפִים וְאַחַר תֵּלְכוּ לְדַרְכְּכֶם׃
יז וַיֹּאמְרוּ אֵלֶיהָ הָאֲנָשִׁים נְקִיִּם אֲנַחְנוּ מִשְּׁבֻעָתֵךְ הַזֶּה אֲשֶׁר הִשְׁבַּעְתָּנוּ׃
יח הִנֵּה אֲנַחְנוּ בָאִים בָּאָרֶץ אֶת־תִּקְוַת חוּט הַשָּׁנִי הַזֶּה תִּקְשְׁרִי בַּחַלּוֹן
אֲשֶׁר הוֹרַדְתֵּנוּ בוֹ וְאֶת־אָבִיךְ וְאֶת־אִמֵּךְ וְאֶת־אַחַיִךְ וְאֵת כָּל־בֵּית
יט אָבִיךְ תַּאַסְפִי אֵלַיִךְ הַבָּיְתָה׃ וְהָיָה כֹּל אֲשֶׁר־יֵצֵא מִדַּלְתֵי בֵיתֵךְ ׀
הַחוּצָה דָּמוֹ בְרֹאשׁוֹ וַאֲנַחְנוּ נְקִיִּם וְכֹל אֲשֶׁר יִהְיֶה אִתָּךְ בַּבַּיִת דָּמוֹ
כ בְרֹאשֵׁנוּ אִם־יָד תִּהְיֶה־בּוֹ׃ וְאִם־תַּגִּידִי אֶת־דְּבָרֵנוּ זֶה וְהָיִינוּ נְקִיִּם
כא מִשְּׁבֻעָתֵךְ אֲשֶׁר הִשְׁבַּעְתָּנוּ׃ וַתֹּאמֶר כְּדִבְרֵיכֶם כֶּן־הוּא וַתְּשַׁלְּחֵם
כב וַיֵּלֵכוּ וַתִּקְשֹׁר אֶת־תִּקְוַת הַשָּׁנִי בַּחַלּוֹן׃ וַיֵּלְכוּ וַיָּבֹאוּ הָהָרָה וַיֵּשְׁבוּ

23 searched the entire route but failed to find them. The two men then went
back, descended the hills, and crossed over. They came to Yehoshua son of
24 Nun and reported all that had befallen them. "The LORD has delivered the
whole land into our hands," they said to Yehoshua, "and what is more, all the
3 1 people of the land quake before us." Early the next morning,
Yehoshua rose and journeyed on from Shitim together with all the people of
2 Israel. They arrived at the Jordan, where they stayed before crossing. Three
3 days had passed, and the officers crossed through the camp, commanding the
people, "When you see the Ark of the Covenant of the LORD your God, and
4 the Levite priests bearing it, set out from where you are and follow it. But
keep a distance between you and it, about two thousand cubits – do not come
any closer. You will then know the way to go, for you have never traveled this
5 way before." And Yehoshua told the people, "Sanctify yourselves, for
6 tomorrow the LORD will perform wonders in your midst." "Raise up the Ark
of the Covenant," said Yehoshua to the priests, "and cross before the people."
So they raised up the Ark of the Covenant and advanced to the front of the
7 people. And the LORD said to Yehoshua, "Today I shall begin to exalt
you in the eyes of all Israel so that they may know that I shall be with you as
8 I was with Moshe. Instruct the priests who bear the Ark of the Covenant:
when you reach the verge of the Jordan's waters, stand still there in the
9 Jordan." And Yehoshua called out to the Israelites, "Draw near to
10 hear the words of the LORD your God." "By this you shall know," Yehoshua
continued, "that the living God is in your midst, and that He will dispossess
the Canaanites, the Hittites and the Hivites, the Perizzites and the Girgashites,
11 the Amorites and the Jebusites, before you. Behold, the Ark of the Covenant
12 of the Master of all the earth is about to pass before you into the Jordan. Now,
13 take twelve men from the tribes of Israel, one from each tribe. As soon as the
feet of the priests who bear the Ark of the LORD, Master of all the earth, come
to rest in the waters of the Jordan, the waters of the Jordan will be cut off, and
14 the water flowing from upstream will stand still in one mound." When the
people set out from their tents to cross the Jordan, the priests bearing the Ark
15 of the Covenant went before them. When the bearers of the Ark reached the
Jordan, and the feet of the priests who bore the Ark dipped into the water's
edge – for the Jordan's banks had been overflowing throughout harvest
16 season – the waters flowing from upstream rose up in one mound far away
at Adam, the city beside Tzartan, while those flowing downstream toward
the Arava Sea – the Dead Sea – were cut off completely, and the people
17 crossed opposite Yeriḥo. The priests bearing the Ark of the LORD's Covenant
stood firmly on dry land in the midst of the Jordan until all the nation had

שָׁם שְׁלֹשֶׁת יָמִים עַד־שָׁבוּ הָרֹדְפִים וַיְבַקְשׁוּ הָרֹדְפִים בְּכָל־הַדֶּרֶךְ
כג וְלֹא מָצָאוּ׃ וַיָּשֻׁבוּ שְׁנֵי הָאֲנָשִׁים וַיֵּרְדוּ מֵהָהָר וַיַּעַבְרוּ וַיָּבֹאוּ אֶל־
כד יְהוֹשֻׁעַ בִּן־נוּן וַיְסַפְּרוּ־לוֹ אֵת כָּל־הַמֹּצְאוֹת אוֹתָם׃ וַיֹּאמְרוּ אֶל־
יְהוֹשֻׁעַ כִּי־נָתַן יהוה בְּיָדֵנוּ אֶת־כָּל־הָאָרֶץ וְגַם־נָמֹגוּ כָּל־יֹשְׁבֵי הָאָרֶץ
ג א מִפָּנֵינוּ׃ וַיַּשְׁכֵּם יְהוֹשֻׁעַ בַּבֹּקֶר וַיִּסְעוּ מֵהַשִּׁטִּים וַיָּבֹאוּ
ב עַד־הַיַּרְדֵּן הוּא וְכָל־בְּנֵי יִשְׂרָאֵל וַיָּלִנוּ שָׁם טֶרֶם יַעֲבֹרוּ׃ וַיְהִי מִקְצֵה
ג שְׁלֹשֶׁת יָמִים וַיַּעַבְרוּ הַשֹּׁטְרִים בְּקֶרֶב הַמַּחֲנֶה׃ וַיְצַוּוּ אֶת־הָעָם לֵאמֹר
כִּרְאֹתְכֶם אֵת אֲרוֹן בְּרִית־יהוה אֱלֹהֵיכֶם וְהַכֹּהֲנִים הַלְוִיִּם נֹשְׂאִים
ד אֹתוֹ וְאַתֶּם תִּסְעוּ מִמְּקוֹמְכֶם וַהֲלַכְתֶּם אַחֲרָיו׃ אַךְ ׀ רָחוֹק יִהְיֶה
בֵּינֵיכֶם וּבֵינָו כְּאַלְפַּיִם אַמָּה בַּמִּדָּה אַל־תִּקְרְבוּ אֵלָיו לְמַעַן אֲשֶׁר־
תֵּדְעוּ אֶת־הַדֶּרֶךְ אֲשֶׁר תֵּלְכוּ־בָהּ כִּי לֹא עֲבַרְתֶּם בַּדֶּרֶךְ מִתְּמוֹל
ה שִׁלְשׁוֹם׃ וַיֹּאמֶר יְהוֹשֻׁעַ אֶל־הָעָם הִתְקַדָּשׁוּ כִּי מָחָר יַעֲשֶׂה
ו יהוה בְּקִרְבְּכֶם נִפְלָאוֹת׃ וַיֹּאמֶר יְהוֹשֻׁעַ אֶל־הַכֹּהֲנִים לֵאמֹר שְׂאוּ
אֶת־אֲרוֹן הַבְּרִית וְעִבְרוּ לִפְנֵי הָעָם וַיִּשְׂאוּ אֶת־אֲרוֹן הַבְּרִית וַיֵּלְכוּ
ז לִפְנֵי הָעָם׃ וַיֹּאמֶר יהוה אֶל־יְהוֹשֻׁעַ הַיּוֹם הַזֶּה אָחֵל גַּדֶּלְךָ ב
בְּעֵינֵי כָּל־יִשְׂרָאֵל אֲשֶׁר יֵדְעוּן כִּי כַּאֲשֶׁר הָיִיתִי עִם־מֹשֶׁה אֶהְיֶה עִמָּךְ׃
ח וְאַתָּה תְּצַוֶּה אֶת־הַכֹּהֲנִים נֹשְׂאֵי אֲרוֹן־הַבְּרִית לֵאמֹר כְּבֹאֲכֶם עַד־
ט קְצֵה מֵי הַיַּרְדֵּן בַּיַּרְדֵּן תַּעֲמֹדוּ׃ וַיֹּאמֶר יְהוֹשֻׁעַ אֶל־בְּנֵי
י יִשְׂרָאֵל גֹּשׁוּ הֵנָּה וְשִׁמְעוּ אֶת־דִּבְרֵי יהוה אֱלֹהֵיכֶם׃ וַיֹּאמֶר יְהוֹשֻׁעַ
בְּזֹאת תֵּדְעוּן כִּי אֵל חַי בְּקִרְבְּכֶם וְהוֹרֵשׁ יוֹרִישׁ מִפְּנֵיכֶם אֶת־הַכְּנַעֲנִי
וְאֶת־הַחִתִּי וְאֶת־הַחִוִּי וְאֶת־הַפְּרִזִּי וְאֶת־הַגִּרְגָּשִׁי וְהָאֱמֹרִי וְהַיְבוּסִי׃
יא יב הִנֵּה אֲרוֹן הַבְּרִית אֲדוֹן כָּל־הָאָרֶץ עֹבֵר לִפְנֵיכֶם בַּיַּרְדֵּן׃ וְעַתָּה קְחוּ
לָכֶם שְׁנֵי עָשָׂר אִישׁ מִשִּׁבְטֵי יִשְׂרָאֵל אִישׁ־אֶחָד אִישׁ־אֶחָד לַשָּׁבֶט׃
יג וְהָיָה כְּנוֹחַ כַּפּוֹת רַגְלֵי הַכֹּהֲנִים נֹשְׂאֵי אֲרוֹן יהוה אֲדוֹן כָּל־הָאָרֶץ בְּמֵי
הַיַּרְדֵּן מֵי הַיַּרְדֵּן יִכָּרֵתוּן הַמַּיִם הַיֹּרְדִים מִלְמָעְלָה וְיַעַמְדוּ נֵד אֶחָד׃
יד וַיְהִי בִּנְסֹעַ הָעָם מֵאָהֳלֵיהֶם לַעֲבֹר אֶת־הַיַּרְדֵּן וְהַכֹּהֲנִים נֹשְׂאֵי הָאָרוֹן
טו הַבְּרִית לִפְנֵי הָעָם׃ וּכְבוֹא נֹשְׂאֵי הָאָרוֹן עַד־הַיַּרְדֵּן וְרַגְלֵי הַכֹּהֲנִים
נֹשְׂאֵי הָאָרוֹן נִטְבְּלוּ בִּקְצֵה הַמָּיִם וְהַיַּרְדֵּן מָלֵא עַל־כָּל־גְּדוֹתָיו כֹּל
טז יְמֵי קָצִיר׃ וַיַּעַמְדוּ הַמַּיִם הַיֹּרְדִים מִלְמַעְלָה קָמוּ נֵד־אֶחָד הַרְחֵק
מְאֹד באדם הָעִיר אֲשֶׁר מִצַּד צָרְתָן וְהַיֹּרְדִים עַל יָם הָעֲרָבָה יָם־ מֵאָדָם
יז הַמֶּלַח תַּמּוּ נִכְרָתוּ וְהָעָם עָבְרוּ נֶגֶד יְרִיחוֹ׃ וַיַּעַמְדוּ הַכֹּהֲנִים נֹשְׂאֵי
הָאָרוֹן בְּרִית־יהוה בֶּחָרָבָה בְּתוֹךְ הַיַּרְדֵּן הָכֵן וְכָל־יִשְׂרָאֵל עֹבְרִים

4 1 finished crossing the Jordan. And when all the nation had finished crossing
2 the Jordan, the LORD said to Yehoshua: "Select twelve men,
3 one from each tribe, and instruct them as follows: Lift twelve stones from
here, from the midst of the Jordan where the priests' feet stand firm. Carry
them with you and set them down at the campsite where you will stay
4 tonight." Yehoshua summoned the twelve men he had chosen
5 from the Israelites, one from each tribe. "Pass before the Ark of the LORD
your God," Yehoshua said to them, "into the Jordan, and let each one of you
lift one stone upon his shoulder, corresponding to the number of Israelite
6 tribes. This will be a sign among you. In the future, when your children ask
7 you, 'What do these stones mean to you?' you shall answer them that the
Jordan's waters were cut off before the Ark of the LORD's Covenant; when it
crossed the Jordan, the Jordan's waters were cut off, so that these stones shall
8 be a memorial for the Israelites forever." The Israelites did as Yehoshua
commanded and lifted twelve stones from the Jordan's midst – as the LORD
had bidden Yehoshua – corresponding to the number of the Israelite tribes.
They carried these with them to the campsite and set them down there.
9 Yehoshua then erected twelve stones within the Jordan where the feet of the
10 priests who bore the Ark had stood. There they remain to this day. The priests
who bore the Ark remained standing in the midst of the Jordan until the very
end of the message that the LORD had ordered Yehoshua to relate to the
people – in accordance with what Moshe had bidden Yehoshua – and the
11 people hastened across. When all the people had finished crossing, the Ark
12 of the LORD and the priests crossed to the front of the people. Ahead of the
Israelites, the Reubenites, the Gadites, and half the tribe of Menashe had
13 crossed, armed, as Moshe had instructed them. Around forty thousand
armed warriors crossed before the LORD to the plains of Yeriḥo, ready for
14 war. On that day, the LORD exalted Yehoshua in the eyes of all Israel,
and they revered him as they had revered Moshe all the days of his
15 16 life. The LORD said to Yehoshua, "Order the priests bearing the Ark
17 of Testimony to come up from the Jordan." And so Yehoshua ordered the
18 priests, "Come up from the Jordan." As the priests bearing the Ark of the
Covenant of the LORD came up from the Jordan – as soon as the soles of the
priests' feet stepped up onto dry land – the waters of the Jordan rushed back
19 to their place, overflowing its banks as before. The people came up from the
Jordan on the tenth of the first month, and they encamped at Gilgal, on the
20 eastern edge of Yeriḥo. As for the twelve stones they had taken from the

ד א בֶּחָרָבָה עַד אֲשֶׁר־תַּמּוּ כָּל־הַגּוֹי לַעֲבוֹר אֶת־הַיַּרְדֵּן׃ וַיְהִי כַּאֲשֶׁר־תַּמּוּ
כָל־הַגּוֹי לַעֲבוֹר אֶת־הַיַּרְדֵּן   וַיֹּאמֶר יְהוָה אֶל־יְהוֹשֻׁעַ
ב לֵאמֹר׃ קְחוּ לָכֶם מִן־הָעָם שְׁנֵים עָשָׂר אֲנָשִׁים אִישׁ־אֶחָד אִישׁ־אֶחָד
ג מִשָּׁבֶט׃ וְצַוּוּ אוֹתָם לֵאמֹר שְׂאוּ־לָכֶם מִזֶּה מִתּוֹךְ הַיַּרְדֵּן מִמַּצַּב רַגְלֵי
הַכֹּהֲנִים הָכִין שְׁתֵּים־עֶשְׂרֵה אֲבָנִים וְהַעֲבַרְתֶּם אוֹתָם עִמָּכֶם וְהִנַּחְתֶּם
ד אוֹתָם בַּמָּלוֹן אֲשֶׁר־תָּלִינוּ בוֹ הַלָּיְלָה׃   וַיִּקְרָא יְהוֹשֻׁעַ אֶל־
שְׁנֵים הֶעָשָׂר אִישׁ אֲשֶׁר הֵכִין מִבְּנֵי יִשְׂרָאֵל אִישׁ־אֶחָד אִישׁ־אֶחָד
ה מִשָּׁבֶט׃ וַיֹּאמֶר לָהֶם יְהוֹשֻׁעַ עִבְרוּ לִפְנֵי אֲרוֹן יְהוָה אֱלֹהֵיכֶם אֶל־תּוֹךְ
הַיַּרְדֵּן וְהָרִימוּ לָכֶם אִישׁ אֶבֶן אַחַת עַל־שִׁכְמוֹ לְמִסְפַּר שִׁבְטֵי בְנֵי־
ו יִשְׂרָאֵל׃ לְמַעַן תִּהְיֶה זֹאת אוֹת בְּקִרְבְּכֶם כִּי־יִשְׁאָלוּן בְּנֵיכֶם מָחָר
ז לֵאמֹר מָה הָאֲבָנִים הָאֵלֶּה לָכֶם׃ וַאֲמַרְתֶּם לָהֶם אֲשֶׁר נִכְרְתוּ מֵימֵי
הַיַּרְדֵּן מִפְּנֵי אֲרוֹן בְּרִית־יְהוָה בְּעָבְרוֹ בַּיַּרְדֵּן נִכְרְתוּ מֵי הַיַּרְדֵּן וְהָיוּ
ח הָאֲבָנִים הָאֵלֶּה לְזִכָּרוֹן לִבְנֵי יִשְׂרָאֵל עַד־עוֹלָם׃ וַיַּעֲשׂוּ־כֵן בְּנֵי־יִשְׂרָאֵל
כַּאֲשֶׁר צִוָּה יְהוֹשֻׁעַ וַיִּשְׂאוּ שְׁתֵּי־עֶשְׂרֵה אֲבָנִים מִתּוֹךְ הַיַּרְדֵּן כַּאֲשֶׁר
דִּבֶּר יְהוָה אֶל־יְהוֹשֻׁעַ לְמִסְפַּר שִׁבְטֵי בְנֵי־יִשְׂרָאֵל וַיַּעֲבִרוּם עִמָּם
ט אֶל־הַמָּלוֹן וַיַּנִּחוּם שָׁם׃ וּשְׁתֵּים עֶשְׂרֵה אֲבָנִים הֵקִים יְהוֹשֻׁעַ בְּתוֹךְ
הַיַּרְדֵּן תַּחַת מַצַּב רַגְלֵי הַכֹּהֲנִים נֹשְׂאֵי אֲרוֹן הַבְּרִית וַיִּהְיוּ שָׁם עַד
י הַיּוֹם הַזֶּה׃ וְהַכֹּהֲנִים נֹשְׂאֵי הָאָרוֹן עֹמְדִים בְּתוֹךְ הַיַּרְדֵּן עַד־תֹּם כָּל־
הַדָּבָר אֲשֶׁר־צִוָּה יְהוָה אֶת־יְהוֹשֻׁעַ לְדַבֵּר אֶל־הָעָם כְּכֹל אֲשֶׁר־צִוָּה
יא מֹשֶׁה אֶת־יְהוֹשֻׁעַ וַיְמַהֲרוּ הָעָם וַיַּעֲבֹרוּ׃ וַיְהִי כַּאֲשֶׁר־תַּם כָּל־הָעָם
יב לַעֲבוֹר וַיַּעֲבֹר אֲרוֹן־יְהוָה וְהַכֹּהֲנִים לִפְנֵי הָעָם׃ וַיַּעַבְרוּ בְּנֵי־רְאוּבֵן
וּבְנֵי־גָד וַחֲצִי שֵׁבֶט הַמְנַשֶּׁה חֲמֻשִׁים לִפְנֵי בְּנֵי יִשְׂרָאֵל כַּאֲשֶׁר דִּבֶּר
יג אֲלֵיהֶם מֹשֶׁה׃ כְּאַרְבָּעִים אֶלֶף חֲלוּצֵי הַצָּבָא עָבְרוּ לִפְנֵי יְהוָה
יד לַמִּלְחָמָה אֶל עַרְבוֹת יְרִיחוֹ׃   בַּיּוֹם הַהוּא גִּדַּל יְהוָה אֶת־
יְהוֹשֻׁעַ בְּעֵינֵי כָּל־יִשְׂרָאֵל וַיִּרְאוּ אֹתוֹ כַּאֲשֶׁר יָרְאוּ אֶת־מֹשֶׁה כָּל־יְמֵי
טו טז חַיָּיו׃   וַיֹּאמֶר יְהוָה אֶל־יְהוֹשֻׁעַ לֵאמֹר׃ צַוֵּה אֶת־הַכֹּהֲנִים
יז נֹשְׂאֵי אֲרוֹן הָעֵדוּת וְיַעֲלוּ מִן־הַיַּרְדֵּן׃ וַיְצַו יְהוֹשֻׁעַ אֶת־הַכֹּהֲנִים לֵאמֹר
יח עֲלוּ מִן־הַיַּרְדֵּן׃ וַיְהִי בעלות הַכֹּהֲנִים נֹשְׂאֵי אֲרוֹן בְּרִית־יְהוָה מִתּוֹךְ   כַּעֲלוֹת
הַיַּרְדֵּן נִתְּקוּ כַּפּוֹת רַגְלֵי הַכֹּהֲנִים אֶל הֶחָרָבָה וַיָּשֻׁבוּ מֵי־הַיַּרְדֵּן
יט לִמְקוֹמָם וַיֵּלְכוּ כִתְמוֹל־שִׁלְשׁוֹם עַל־כָּל־גְּדוֹתָיו׃ וְהָעָם עָלוּ מִן־הַיַּרְדֵּן
כ בֶּעָשׂוֹר לַחֹדֶשׁ הָרִאשׁוֹן וַיַּחֲנוּ בַּגִּלְגָּל בִּקְצֵה מִזְרַח יְרִיחוֹ׃ וְאֵת שְׁתֵּים
עֶשְׂרֵה הָאֲבָנִים הָאֵלֶּה אֲשֶׁר לָקְחוּ מִן־הַיַּרְדֵּן הֵקִים יְהוֹשֻׁעַ בַּגִּלְגָּל׃

21 Jordan, Yehoshua erected them at Gilgal and said to the Israelites, "In the
22 future, when your children ask their fathers, 'What are these stones?' make
23 sure your children know: 'On dry land Israel crossed this Jordan.[2] For the
Lord your God dried up before you the waters of the Jordan until you
crossed over, just as the Lord your God did to the Sea of Reeds, which He
24 dried up before us until we crossed. All the peoples of the land shall know
the might of the Lord's hand, and you shall revere the Lord your God
5 1 forever.'" When all the Amorite kings on the western side of the
Jordan and all the Canaanite kings by the sea heard how the Lord had dried
up the waters of the Jordan before the Israelites until they crossed over, their
2 hearts dissolved, and no spirit was left in them to face the Israelites. At
that time, the Lord said to Yehoshua, "Make yourselves knives of flint and
3 circumcise the Israelites a second time." So Yehoshua made knives of flint and
4 circumcised the Israelites at the Hill of Foreskins This is why Yehoshua
circumcised them: all the men who left Egypt – all the males fit for battle – had
died in the wilderness during the journey, as they came away from Egypt.
5 And while all the men who left there had been circumcised, all those who
were born in the wilderness during the journey away from Egypt had not
6 been circumcised. For forty years the Israelites had wandered in the
wilderness until those among the nation who had left Egypt fit for battle had
perished. They disobeyed the voice of the Lord, and the Lord swore not to
show them the land He had sworn to our ancestors that He would give us – a
7 land flowing with milk and honey. Yehoshua circumcised those children that
He raised in their stead, for they still had their foreskins, not having been
8 circumcised during the journey. When the whole nation's circumcision was
9 over, they remained in place in the camp until they recovered. The
Lord said to Yehoshua, "Today, I have rolled the shame of Egypt away from
10 you."[3] He has named that place Gilgal,[4] as it is known to this day. The Israelites
encamped at Gilgal and performed the Passover sacrifice on the fourteenth
11 day of the month at dusk on the plains of Yeriḥo. On the day after the Passover
sacrifice, they ate of the yield of the land – unleavened bread and roasted
12 grain – that very day. The manna stopped falling the day after they had eaten
from the yield of the land. The Israelites never had manna again; from that
13 year on they ate from the crops of the land of Canaan. When
Yehoshua was near Yeriḥo, he looked up and suddenly saw a man standing
opposite him, drawn sword in hand. Yehoshua approached him and asked,
14 "Are you for us or for our enemies?" He said, "No, for I am the commander of
the Lord's hosts. Now I have come!" Yehoshua flung his face to the ground
and prostrated himself, asking him, "What does my lord bid his servant?"
15 The commander of the Lord's hosts said to Yehoshua, "Remove the shoes

---

2 | See Numbers 32:20–22.

3 | Evoking the physical act of circumcision.

4 | Echoing the Hebrew *galloti*, "rolled away," in the previous verse.

כא וַיֹּאמֶר אֶל־בְּנֵי יִשְׂרָאֵל לֵאמֹר אֲשֶׁר יִשְׁאָלוּן בְּנֵיכֶם מָחָר אֶת־אֲבוֹתָם
כב לֵאמֹר מָה הָאֲבָנִים הָאֵלֶּה: וְהוֹדַעְתֶּם אֶת־בְּנֵיכֶם לֵאמֹר בַּיַּבָּשָׁה
כג עָבַר יִשְׂרָאֵל אֶת־הַיַּרְדֵּן הַזֶּה: אֲשֶׁר־הוֹבִישׁ יְהוָה אֱלֹהֵיכֶם אֶת־מֵי
הַיַּרְדֵּן מִפְּנֵיכֶם עַד־עָבְרְכֶם כַּאֲשֶׁר עָשָׂה יְהוָה אֱלֹהֵיכֶם לְיַם־סוּף
כד אֲשֶׁר־הוֹבִישׁ מִפָּנֵינוּ עַד־עָבְרֵנוּ: לְמַעַן דַּעַת כָּל־עַמֵּי הָאָרֶץ אֶת־ ג
יַד יְהוָה כִּי חֲזָקָה הִיא לְמַעַן יְרָאתֶם אֶת־יְהוָה אֱלֹהֵיכֶם כָּל־
ה א הַיָּמִים: וַיְהִי כִשְׁמֹעַ כָּל־מַלְכֵי הָאֱמֹרִי אֲשֶׁר בְּעֵבֶר הַיַּרְדֵּן
יָמָּה וְכָל־מַלְכֵי הַכְּנַעֲנִי אֲשֶׁר עַל־הַיָּם אֵת אֲשֶׁר־הוֹבִישׁ יְהוָה אֶת־מֵי
הַיַּרְדֵּן מִפְּנֵי בְנֵי־יִשְׂרָאֵל עַד־עברנו וַיִּמַּס לְבָבָם וְלֹא־הָיָה בָם עוֹד עָבְרָם
ב רוּחַ מִפְּנֵי בְּנֵי־יִשְׂרָאֵל: בָּעֵת הַהִיא אָמַר יְהוָה אֶל־יְהוֹשֻׁעַ
ג עֲשֵׂה לְךָ חַרְבוֹת צֻרִים וְשׁוּב מֹל אֶת־בְּנֵי־יִשְׂרָאֵל שֵׁנִית: וַיַּעַשׂ־לוֹ
ד יְהוֹשֻׁעַ חַרְבוֹת צֻרִים וַיָּמָל אֶת־בְּנֵי יִשְׂרָאֵל אֶל־גִּבְעַת הָעֲרָלוֹת: וְזֶה
הַדָּבָר אֲשֶׁר־מָל יְהוֹשֻׁעַ כָּל־הָעָם הַיֹּצֵא מִמִּצְרַיִם הַזְּכָרִים כֹּל ׀ אַנְשֵׁי
ה הַמִּלְחָמָה מֵתוּ בַמִּדְבָּר בַּדֶּרֶךְ בְּצֵאתָם מִמִּצְרָיִם: כִּי־מֻלִים הָיוּ כָּל־
הָעָם הַיֹּצְאִים וְכָל־הָעָם הַיִּלֹּדִים בַּמִּדְבָּר בַּדֶּרֶךְ בְּצֵאתָם מִמִּצְרַיִם
ו לֹא־מָלוּ: כִּי ׀ אַרְבָּעִים שָׁנָה הָלְכוּ בְנֵי־יִשְׂרָאֵל בַּמִּדְבָּר עַד־תֹּם כָּל־
הַגּוֹי אַנְשֵׁי הַמִּלְחָמָה הַיֹּצְאִים מִמִּצְרַיִם אֲשֶׁר לֹא־שָׁמְעוּ בְּקוֹל יְהוָה
אֲשֶׁר נִשְׁבַּע יְהוָה לָהֶם לְבִלְתִּי הַרְאוֹתָם אֶת־הָאָרֶץ אֲשֶׁר נִשְׁבַּע
ז יְהוָה לַאֲבוֹתָם לָתֶת לָנוּ אֶרֶץ זָבַת חָלָב וּדְבָשׁ: וְאֶת־בְּנֵיהֶם הֵקִים
תַּחְתָּם אֹתָם מָל יְהוֹשֻׁעַ כִּי־עֲרֵלִים הָיוּ כִּי לֹא־מָלוּ אוֹתָם בַּדָּרֶךְ:
ח וַיְהִי כַּאֲשֶׁר־תַּמּוּ כָל־הַגּוֹי לְהִמּוֹל וַיֵּשְׁבוּ תַחְתָּם בַּמַּחֲנֶה עַד
ט חֲיוֹתָם: וַיֹּאמֶר יְהוָה אֶל־יְהוֹשֻׁעַ הַיּוֹם גַּלּוֹתִי אֶת־חֶרְפַּת
י מִצְרַיִם מֵעֲלֵיכֶם וַיִּקְרָא שֵׁם הַמָּקוֹם הַהוּא גִּלְגָּל עַד הַיּוֹם הַזֶּה: וַיַּחֲנוּ
בְנֵי־יִשְׂרָאֵל בַּגִּלְגָּל וַיַּעֲשׂוּ אֶת־הַפֶּסַח בְּאַרְבָּעָה עָשָׂר יוֹם לַחֹדֶשׁ
יא בָּעֶרֶב בְּעַרְבוֹת יְרִיחוֹ: וַיֹּאכְלוּ מֵעֲבוּר הָאָרֶץ מִמָּחֳרַת הַפֶּסַח מַצּוֹת
יב וְקָלוּי בְּעֶצֶם הַיּוֹם הַזֶּה: וַיִּשְׁבֹּת הַמָּן מִמָּחֳרָת בְּאָכְלָם מֵעֲבוּר הָאָרֶץ
וְלֹא־הָיָה עוֹד לִבְנֵי יִשְׂרָאֵל מָן וַיֹּאכְלוּ מִתְּבוּאַת אֶרֶץ כְּנַעַן בַּשָּׁנָה
יג הַהִיא: וַיְהִי בִּהְיוֹת יְהוֹשֻׁעַ בִּירִיחוֹ וַיִּשָּׂא עֵינָיו וַיַּרְא וְהִנֵּה־
אִישׁ עֹמֵד לְנֶגְדּוֹ וְחַרְבּוֹ שְׁלוּפָה בְּיָדוֹ וַיֵּלֶךְ יְהוֹשֻׁעַ אֵלָיו וַיֹּאמֶר לוֹ
יד הֲלָנוּ אַתָּה אִם־לְצָרֵינוּ: וַיֹּאמֶר ׀ לֹא כִּי אֲנִי שַׂר־צְבָא־יְהוָה עַתָּה
בָאתִי וַיִּפֹּל יְהוֹשֻׁעַ אֶל־פָּנָיו אַרְצָה וַיִּשְׁתָּחוּ וַיֹּאמֶר לוֹ מָה אֲדֹנִי
טו מְדַבֵּר אֶל־עַבְדּוֹ: וַיֹּאמֶר שַׂר־צְבָא יְהוָה אֶל־יְהוֹשֻׁעַ שַׁל־נַעַלְךָ

from your feet, for the place where you stand is holy."[5] And Yehoshua did so.
6 1 Yeriḥo was barred and bolted against the Israelites; no one came out, and no
2 one went in. The LORD said to Yehoshua, "Behold, I have delivered
3 Yeriḥo and its king into your hands, though they are mighty warriors. March
around the city until all your fighting men have circled the city once. Do this
4 for six days while seven priests bear seven rams' horns before the Ark. And
on the seventh day, march around the city seven times as the priests blow on
5 the rams' horns. As the ram's horn resounds – when you hear the sound of
the ram's horn – all the people must give a mighty shout. Then the city wall
will come crashing down, and the people will rise up, each man charging
6 straight ahead." Yehoshua son of Nun summoned the priests. "Lift up the Ark
of the Covenant," he said to them, "and let seven priests bear seven rams'
7 horns before the Ark of the LORD." Then Yehoshua said to the people,
"Advance and march around the city, and let the vanguard pass before the Ark
8 of the LORD." As Yehoshua spoke to the people, seven priests bearing seven
rams' horns before the LORD advanced and sounded the rams' horns, with
9 the Ark of the LORD's Covenant following behind them. The vanguard
marched before the priests who blew the rams' horns, and the rearguard
10 marched behind the Ark, with the rams' horns blasting all the while. But
Yehoshua had instructed the people: "Do not shout; do not make a sound;
do not let a word out of your mouth – until the day when I tell you to shout.
11 Then you will shout!" The Ark of the LORD was marched around the city,
circling it once. Then they arrived back at the camp and spent the night
12 there. Yehoshua rose early in the morning, and the priests lifted up
13 the Ark of the LORD. The seven priests bearing the seven rams' horns marched
before the Ark of the LORD, sounding the rams' horns, with the vanguard
marching before them, the rearguard marching behind the Ark of the LORD,
14 and the rams' horns blasting all the while. They marched around the city once
15 on the second day and returned to the camp; this they did for six days. And
on the seventh day, they rose early, as dawn broke, and marched around the
city in this way seven times; only on that day did they circle it seven times.
16 And on the seventh circuit, as the priests blasted the rams' horns, Yehoshua
17 said to the people, "Shout out, for the LORD has given you the city! The city
and everything in it shall be placed under a ban and shall belong to the LORD;[6]
only Raḥav the harlot shall live, she and everyone in her home, for she hid
18 the messengers we sent. But beware of the ban lest you be subject to utter
destruction; if you take anything banned, you will subject the camp of Israel
19 to a scourge and to utter destruction.[7] All the silver and gold and all the
bronze and iron vessels are sacred to the LORD; to the LORD's treasury they

---

5 | Cf. Exodus 3:5.

6 | That is, the Israelites were prohibited from partaking of the spoils.

7 | Both "ban" and "utter destruction" correspond to the same Hebrew word: *ḥerem*. The verse thus describes a punishment in kind.

מֵעַל רַגְלֶךָ כִּי הַמָּקוֹם אֲשֶׁר אַתָּה עֹמֵד עָלָיו קֹדֶשׁ הוּא וַיַּעַשׂ יְהוֹשֻׁעַ
ו א כֵּן׃ וִירִיחוֹ סֹגֶרֶת וּמְסֻגֶּרֶת מִפְּנֵי בְּנֵי יִשְׂרָאֵל אֵין יוֹצֵא וְאֵין
ב בָּא׃ וַיֹּאמֶר יְהוָה אֶל־יְהוֹשֻׁעַ רְאֵה נָתַתִּי בְיָדְךָ אֶת־יְרִיחוֹ
ג וְאֶת־מַלְכָּהּ גִּבּוֹרֵי הֶחָיִל׃ וְסַבֹּתֶם אֶת־הָעִיר כֹּל אַנְשֵׁי הַמִּלְחָמָה
ד הַקֵּיף אֶת־הָעִיר פַּעַם אֶחָת כֹּה תַעֲשֶׂה שֵׁשֶׁת יָמִים׃ וְשִׁבְעָה כֹהֲנִים
יִשְׂאוּ שִׁבְעָה שׁוֹפְרוֹת הַיּוֹבְלִים לִפְנֵי הָאָרוֹן וּבַיּוֹם הַשְּׁבִיעִי תָּסֹבּוּ
ה אֶת־הָעִיר שֶׁבַע פְּעָמִים וְהַכֹּהֲנִים יִתְקְעוּ בַּשּׁוֹפָרוֹת׃ וְהָיָה בִּמְשֹׁךְ ׀
בְּקֶרֶן הַיּוֹבֵל בשמעכם אֶת־קוֹל הַשּׁוֹפָר יָרִיעוּ כָל־הָעָם תְּרוּעָה כְּשָׁמְעֲכֶם
ו גְדוֹלָה וְנָפְלָה חוֹמַת הָעִיר תַּחְתֶּיהָ וְעָלוּ הָעָם אִישׁ נֶגְדּוֹ׃ וַיִּקְרָא
יְהוֹשֻׁעַ בִּן־נוּן אֶל־הַכֹּהֲנִים וַיֹּאמֶר אֲלֵהֶם שְׂאוּ אֶת־אֲרוֹן הַבְּרִית
ז וְשִׁבְעָה כֹהֲנִים יִשְׂאוּ שִׁבְעָה שׁוֹפְרוֹת יוֹבְלִים לִפְנֵי אֲרוֹן יְהוָה׃ ויאמרו וַיֹּאמֶר
ח אֶל־הָעָם עִבְרוּ וְסֹבּוּ אֶת־הָעִיר וְהֶחָלוּץ יַעֲבֹר לִפְנֵי אֲרוֹן יְהוָה׃ וַיְהִי
כֶּאֱמֹר יְהוֹשֻׁעַ אֶל־הָעָם וְשִׁבְעָה הַכֹּהֲנִים נֹשְׂאִים שִׁבְעָה שׁוֹפְרוֹת
הַיּוֹבְלִים לִפְנֵי יְהוָה עָבְרוּ וְתָקְעוּ בַּשּׁוֹפָרוֹת וַאֲרוֹן בְּרִית יְהוָה הֹלֵךְ
ט אַחֲרֵיהֶם׃ וְהֶחָלוּץ הֹלֵךְ לִפְנֵי הַכֹּהֲנִים תקעו הַשּׁוֹפָרוֹת וְהַמְאַסֵּף תֹּקְעֵי
י הֹלֵךְ אַחֲרֵי הָאָרוֹן הָלוֹךְ וְתָקוֹעַ בַּשּׁוֹפָרוֹת׃ וְאֶת־הָעָם צִוָּה יְהוֹשֻׁעַ
לֵאמֹר לֹא תָרִיעוּ וְלֹא־תַשְׁמִיעוּ אֶת־קוֹלְכֶם וְלֹא־יֵצֵא מִפִּיכֶם דָּבָר
יא עַד יוֹם אָמְרִי אֲלֵיכֶם הָרִיעוּ וַהֲרֵיעֹתֶם׃ וַיַּסֵּב אֲרוֹן־יְהוָה אֶת־הָעִיר
יב הַקֵּף פַּעַם אֶחָת וַיָּבֹאוּ הַמַּחֲנֶה וַיָּלִינוּ בַּמַּחֲנֶה׃ וַיַּשְׁכֵּם
יג יְהוֹשֻׁעַ בַּבֹּקֶר וַיִּשְׂאוּ הַכֹּהֲנִים אֶת־אֲרוֹן יְהוָה׃ וְשִׁבְעָה הַכֹּהֲנִים נֹשְׂאִים
שִׁבְעָה שׁוֹפְרוֹת הַיֹּבְלִים לִפְנֵי אֲרוֹן יְהוָה הֹלְכִים הָלוֹךְ וְתָקְעוּ
בַּשּׁוֹפָרוֹת וְהֶחָלוּץ הֹלֵךְ לִפְנֵיהֶם וְהַמְאַסֵּף הֹלֵךְ אַחֲרֵי אֲרוֹן יְהוָה
יד הולך וְתָקוֹעַ בַּשּׁוֹפָרוֹת׃ וַיָּסֹבּוּ אֶת־הָעִיר בַּיּוֹם הַשֵּׁנִי פַּעַם אַחַת הָלוֹךְ
טו וַיָּשֻׁבוּ הַמַּחֲנֶה כֹּה עָשׂוּ שֵׁשֶׁת יָמִים׃ וַיְהִי ׀ בַּיּוֹם הַשְּׁבִיעִי וַיַּשְׁכִּמוּ
כַּעֲלוֹת הַשַּׁחַר וַיָּסֹבּוּ אֶת־הָעִיר כַּמִּשְׁפָּט הַזֶּה שֶׁבַע פְּעָמִים רַק בַּיּוֹם
טז הַהוּא סָבְבוּ אֶת־הָעִיר שֶׁבַע פְּעָמִים׃ וַיְהִי בַּפַּעַם הַשְּׁבִיעִית תָּקְעוּ
הַכֹּהֲנִים בַּשּׁוֹפָרוֹת וַיֹּאמֶר יְהוֹשֻׁעַ אֶל־הָעָם הָרִיעוּ כִּי־נָתַן יְהוָה לָכֶם
יז אֶת־הָעִיר׃ וְהָיְתָה הָעִיר חֵרֶם הִיא וְכָל־אֲשֶׁר־בָּהּ לַיהוָה רַק רָחָב
הַזּוֹנָה תִּחְיֶה הִיא וְכָל־אֲשֶׁר אִתָּהּ בַּבַּיִת כִּי הֶחְבְּאַתָה אֶת־הַמַּלְאָכִים
יח אֲשֶׁר שָׁלָחְנוּ׃ וְרַק־אַתֶּם שִׁמְרוּ מִן־הַחֵרֶם פֶּן־תַּחֲרִימוּ וּלְקַחְתֶּם
יט מִן־הַחֵרֶם וְשַׂמְתֶּם אֶת־מַחֲנֵה יִשְׂרָאֵל לְחֵרֶם וַעֲכַרְתֶּם אוֹתוֹ׃ וְכֹל ׀
כֶּסֶף וְזָהָב וּכְלֵי נְחֹשֶׁת וּבַרְזֶל קֹדֶשׁ הוּא לַיהוָה אוֹצַר יְהוָה יָבוֹא׃

20 shall be taken." The people shouted and blasted the rams' horns – and when
the people heard the sound of the ram's horn, they raised a mighty roar, and
the wall came crashing down. Then the people charged up to the city, each
21 man running straight ahead, and they captured the city. They destroyed
everything in the city with the sword: man and woman; young and old; ox,
22 lamb, and donkey. Yehoshua said to the two men who had scouted out the
land, "Go to the house of the harlot and rescue the woman and all that is hers,
23 as you swore to her that you would." So the young spies went and rescued
Raḥav, her father, her mother, her siblings, and all that was hers; they rescued
24 her entire family and set them down outside the Israelite camp. The city and
everything in it was burned with fire – only the silver and gold and the bronze
25 and iron vessels were delivered to the treasury of the LORD's House – but the
harlot Raḥav, her father's household, and all that was hers were spared by
Yehoshua; and she dwells among Israel to this day, for she hid the messengers
26 Yehoshua sent to scout out Yeriḥo. At that time, Yehoshua
pronounced this oath: "Cursed by the LORD is the man who attempts to
rebuild this city, Yeriḥo: He shall lay down his firstborn with its foundations;
27 with his youngest he will set its gates!" The LORD was with Yehoshua,
7 1 and his fame rang out across the land. But the Israelites broke the ban. It was
Akhan son of Karmi son of Zavdi son of Zeraḥ, of the tribe of Yehuda, who
took of what was banned; and the LORD's wrath raged against the
2 Israelites. Yehoshua sent men from Yeriḥo to Ai, which is near
Beit Aven, east of Beit El, bidding them, "Go up and spy out the land." The
3 men went up and spied on Ai. When they returned to Yehoshua, they said to
him: "All the people need not go up; let two thousand or three thousand men
go up to attack the Ai. Do not wear out all the fighters there, for the men of
4 Ai are few." So about three thousand fighters marched up there – but they fled
5 before the men of Ai. The men of Ai struck down about thirty-six of their
men, chasing them from the gate to the crags; they smote them at the descent,
6 and the people's hearts dissolved and turned to water. Yehoshua rent his
clothes and flung his face to the ground before the Ark of the LORD. Lying
prostrate until dusk, he and the elders of Israel smeared dust upon their heads.
7 "Alas, LORD God," Yehoshua said, "why did you bring this people across the
Jordan to give us over into Amorite hands to be destroyed? If we had only
8 been content to stay beyond the Jordan! Please, LORD, what have I left to say
9 now that Israel has turned tail before its enemies? The Canaanites and all the
inhabitants of the land will hear and turn on us and sever our very name from
10 the earth; what, then, will You do about Your great name?" The

כ וַיָּרַע הָעָם וַיִּתְקְעוּ בַּשֹּׁפָרוֹת וַיְהִי כִשְׁמֹעַ הָעָם אֶת־קוֹל הַשּׁוֹפָר
וַיָּרִיעוּ הָעָם תְּרוּעָה גְדוֹלָה וַתִּפֹּל הַחוֹמָה תַּחְתֶּיהָ וַיַּעַל הָעָם הָעִירָה
כא אִישׁ נֶגְדּוֹ וַיִּלְכְּדוּ אֶת־הָעִיר׃ וַיַּחֲרִימוּ אֶת־כָּל־אֲשֶׁר בָּעִיר מֵאִישׁ
כב וְעַד־אִשָּׁה מִנַּעַר וְעַד־זָקֵן וְעַד שׁוֹר וָשֶׂה וַחֲמוֹר לְפִי־חָרֶב׃ וְלִשְׁנַיִם
הָאֲנָשִׁים הַמְרַגְּלִים אֶת־הָאָרֶץ אָמַר יְהוֹשֻׁעַ בֹּאוּ בֵּית־הָאִשָּׁה הַזּוֹנָה
וְהוֹצִיאוּ מִשָּׁם אֶת־הָאִשָּׁה וְאֶת־כָּל־אֲשֶׁר־לָהּ כַּאֲשֶׁר נִשְׁבַּעְתֶּם לָהּ׃
כג וַיָּבֹאוּ הַנְּעָרִים הַמְרַגְּלִים וַיֹּצִיאוּ אֶת־רָחָב וְאֶת־אָבִיהָ וְאֶת־אִמָּהּ
וְאֶת־אַחֶיהָ וְאֶת־כָּל־אֲשֶׁר־לָהּ וְאֵת כָּל־מִשְׁפְּחוֹתֶיהָ הוֹצִיאוּ וַיַּנִּיחוּם
כד מִחוּץ לְמַחֲנֵה יִשְׂרָאֵל׃ וְהָעִיר שָׂרְפוּ בָאֵשׁ וְכָל־אֲשֶׁר־בָּהּ רַק ׀ הַכֶּסֶף
כה וְהַזָּהָב וּכְלֵי הַנְּחֹשֶׁת וְהַבַּרְזֶל נָתְנוּ אוֹצַר בֵּית־יְהוָה׃ וְאֶת־רָחָב הַזּוֹנָה
וְאֶת־בֵּית אָבִיהָ וְאֶת־כָּל־אֲשֶׁר־לָהּ הֶחֱיָה יְהוֹשֻׁעַ וַתֵּשֶׁב בְּקֶרֶב
יִשְׂרָאֵל עַד הַיּוֹם הַזֶּה כִּי הֶחְבִּיאָה אֶת־הַמַּלְאָכִים אֲשֶׁר־שָׁלַח יְהוֹשֻׁעַ
כו לְרַגֵּל אֶת־יְרִיחוֹ׃ וַיַּשְׁבַּע יְהוֹשֻׁעַ בָּעֵת הַהִיא לֵאמֹר אָרוּר
הָאִישׁ לִפְנֵי יְהוָה אֲשֶׁר יָקוּם וּבָנָה אֶת־הָעִיר הַזֹּאת אֶת־יְרִיחוֹ בִּבְכֹרוֹ
כז יְיַסְּדֶנָּה וּבִצְעִירוֹ יַצִּיב דְּלָתֶיהָ׃ וַיְהִי יְהוָה אֶת־יְהוֹשֻׁעַ ד
ז א וַיְהִי שָׁמְעוֹ בְּכָל־הָאָרֶץ׃ וַיִּמְעֲלוּ בְנֵי־יִשְׂרָאֵל מַעַל בַּחֵרֶם וַיִּקַּח עָכָן
בֶּן־כַּרְמִי בֶן־זַבְדִּי בֶן־זֶרַח לְמַטֵּה יְהוּדָה מִן־הַחֵרֶם וַיִּחַר־אַף יְהוָה
ב בִּבְנֵי יִשְׂרָאֵל׃ וַיִּשְׁלַח יְהוֹשֻׁעַ אֲנָשִׁים מִירִיחוֹ הָעַי אֲשֶׁר
עִם־בֵּית אָוֶן מִקֶּדֶם לְבֵית־אֵל וַיֹּאמֶר אֲלֵיהֶם לֵאמֹר עֲלוּ וְרַגְּלוּ אֶת־
ג הָאָרֶץ וַיַּעֲלוּ הָאֲנָשִׁים וַיְרַגְּלוּ אֶת־הָעָי׃ וַיָּשֻׁבוּ אֶל־יְהוֹשֻׁעַ וַיֹּאמְרוּ
אֵלָיו אַל־יַעַל כָּל־הָעָם כְּאַלְפַּיִם אִישׁ אוֹ כִּשְׁלֹשֶׁת אֲלָפִים אִישׁ יַעֲלוּ
ד וְיַכּוּ אֶת־הָעָי אַל־תְּיַגַּע שָׁמָּה אֶת־כָּל־הָעָם כִּי מְעַט הֵמָּה׃ וַיַּעֲלוּ
ה מִן־הָעָם שָׁמָּה כִּשְׁלֹשֶׁת אֲלָפִים אִישׁ וַיָּנֻסוּ לִפְנֵי אַנְשֵׁי הָעָי׃ וַיַּכּוּ מֵהֶם
אַנְשֵׁי הָעַי כִּשְׁלֹשִׁים וְשִׁשָּׁה אִישׁ וַיִּרְדְּפוּם לִפְנֵי הַשַּׁעַר עַד־הַשְּׁבָרִים
ו וַיַּכּוּם בַּמּוֹרָד וַיִּמַּס לְבַב־הָעָם וַיְהִי לְמָיִם׃ וַיִּקְרַע יְהוֹשֻׁעַ שִׂמְלֹתָיו
וַיִּפֹּל עַל־פָּנָיו אַרְצָה לִפְנֵי אֲרוֹן יְהוָה עַד־הָעֶרֶב הוּא וְזִקְנֵי יִשְׂרָאֵל
ז וַיַּעֲלוּ עָפָר עַל־רֹאשָׁם׃ וַיֹּאמֶר יְהוֹשֻׁעַ אֲהָהּ ׀ אֲדֹנָי יְהוִה לָמָה הֵעֲבַרְתָּ
הַעֲבִיר אֶת־הָעָם הַזֶּה אֶת־הַיַּרְדֵּן לָתֵת אֹתָנוּ בְּיַד הָאֱמֹרִי לְהַאֲבִידֵנוּ
ח וְלוּ הוֹאַלְנוּ וַנֵּשֶׁב בְּעֵבֶר הַיַּרְדֵּן׃ בִּי אֲדֹנָי מָה אֹמַר אַחֲרֵי אֲשֶׁר
ט הָפַךְ יִשְׂרָאֵל עֹרֶף לִפְנֵי אֹיְבָיו׃ וְיִשְׁמְעוּ הַכְּנַעֲנִי וְכֹל יֹשְׁבֵי הָאָרֶץ
וְנָסַבּוּ עָלֵינוּ וְהִכְרִיתוּ אֶת־שְׁמֵנוּ מִן־הָאָרֶץ וּמַה־תַּעֲשֵׂה לְשִׁמְךָ
י הַגָּדוֹל׃ וַיֹּאמֶר יְהוָה אֶל־יְהוֹשֻׁעַ קֻם לָךְ לָמָּה זֶּה אַתָּה

11 Lord said to Yehoshua, "Stand up! Why have you fallen on your face? Israel
has sinned; they have violated My covenant, which I charged them to obey.
They have taken from what was banned; they have stolen; they have deceived;
12 they have hidden it away among their vessels. The Israelites will not be able
to rise up before their enemies – they shall turn tail to their enemies – for
they have become subject to utter destruction.[8] I will no longer be with you
13 unless you purge from your midst what is banned. Arise; sanctify the people;
say, 'Sanctify yourselves for tomorrow, for thus says the Lord, God of Israel:
Something banned is among you, Israel; you shall not be able to rise up
against your enemies until you purge what has been banned from among you.
14 Come forward in the morning, grouped according to your tribes. The tribe
singled out by the Lord shall come forward grouped by clan; the family
singled out by the Lord shall come forward grouped by house; the house
15 singled out by the Lord shall come forward man by man. The one caught
with that which was banned shall be burned with fire, he and all that is his;
for he has violated the Lord's covenant – he has committed an outrage in
16 Israel.'" Early the next morning, Yehoshua rose and had Israel come forward
17 tribe by tribe; and the tribe of Yehuda was singled out. He had the clans of
Yehuda come forward, and he singled out the family of Zeraḥ; he had the
male heads of the family of Zeraḥ come forward, and Zavdi was singled out.
18 He then had the males of the house come forward – and Akhan son of Karmi
19 son of Zavdi son of Zeraḥ, of the tribe of Yehuda, was singled out. "My son,"
Yehoshua said to Akhan, "please – give glory to the Lord, God of Israel, and
make your confession to Him. Please: tell me what you did; do not hold back
20 from me." Akhan answered Yehoshua and said, "Truly, I have sinned against
21 the Lord, God of Israel. This is what I did: I saw among the spoils a fine
Shinar mantle and two hundred shekel of silver and a golden ingot weighing
fifty shekel. I coveted them and I took them. They are buried in the ground
22 inside my tent, with the silver underneath." Yehoshua sent messengers who
ran to the tent, and there it was, buried in his tent, with the silver underneath.
23 Taking them out of the tent, they brought them to Yehoshua and all the
24 Israelites and poured them out before the Lord. Then Yehoshua took Akhan
son of Zeraḥ, the silver, the mantle, the golden ingot, his sons and daughters,
his ox, his donkey, his tent, and all that was his – and brought them,
25 accompanied by all of Israel, up to the Valley of the Scourge.[9] Yehoshua said,
"A scourge have you been to us! Now, on this day, the Lord will bring a
scourge upon you." All of Israel pelted him with stones, burned them with
26 fire, and stoned them with stones, and erected a great heap of stones over
him – it endures there to this day. Then the raging wrath of the Lord subsided.
To this day that place is called the Valley of the Scourge.

8 1 The Lord said to Yehoshua, "Do not fear or hesitate; take all the fighting
men with you and march up against Ai. Behold: I have delivered the king of
2 Ai, his people, his city, and his land, all into your hands. You shall do to Ai

8 | Hebrew *ḥerem* (see note on 6:18).

9 | Hebrew *akhor*, resonating with the name Akhan.

יא נָפַל עַל־פָּנֶיךָ: חָטָא יִשְׂרָאֵל וְגַם עָבְרוּ אֶת־בְּרִיתִי אֲשֶׁר צִוִּיתִי אוֹתָם
יב וְגַם לָקְחוּ מִן־הַחֵרֶם וְגַם גָּנְבוּ וְגַם כִּחֲשׁוּ וְגַם שָׂמוּ בִכְלֵיהֶם: וְלֹא יֻכְלוּ
בְּנֵי יִשְׂרָאֵל לָקוּם לִפְנֵי אֹיְבֵיהֶם עֹרֶף יִפְנוּ לִפְנֵי אֹיְבֵיהֶם כִּי הָיוּ לְחֵרֶם
יג לֹא אוֹסִיף לִהְיוֹת עִמָּכֶם אִם־לֹא תַשְׁמִידוּ הַחֵרֶם מִקִּרְבְּכֶם: קֻם קַדֵּשׁ
אֶת־הָעָם וְאָמַרְתָּ הִתְקַדְּשׁוּ לְמָחָר כִּי כֹה אָמַר יהוה אֱלֹהֵי יִשְׂרָאֵל
חֵרֶם בְּקִרְבְּךָ יִשְׂרָאֵל לֹא תוּכַל לָקוּם לִפְנֵי אֹיְבֶיךָ עַד־הֲסִירְכֶם הַחֵרֶם
יד מִקִּרְבְּכֶם: וְנִקְרַבְתֶּם בַּבֹּקֶר לְשִׁבְטֵיכֶם וְהָיָה הַשֵּׁבֶט אֲשֶׁר־יִלְכְּדֶנּוּ
יהוה יִקְרַב לַמִּשְׁפָּחוֹת וְהַמִּשְׁפָּחָה אֲשֶׁר־יִלְכְּדֶנָּה יהוה תִּקְרַב לַבָּתִּים
טו וְהַבַּיִת אֲשֶׁר יִלְכְּדֶנּוּ יהוה יִקְרַב לַגְּבָרִים: וְהָיָה הַנִּלְכָּד בַּחֵרֶם יִשָּׂרֵף
בָּאֵשׁ אֹתוֹ וְאֶת־כָּל־אֲשֶׁר־לוֹ כִּי עָבַר אֶת־בְּרִית יהוה וְכִי־עָשָׂה נְבָלָה
טז בְּיִשְׂרָאֵל: וַיַּשְׁכֵּם יְהוֹשֻׁעַ בַּבֹּקֶר וַיַּקְרֵב אֶת־יִשְׂרָאֵל לִשְׁבָטָיו וַיִּלָּכֵד
יז שֵׁבֶט יְהוּדָה: וַיַּקְרֵב אֶת־מִשְׁפַּחַת יְהוּדָה וַיִּלְכֹּד אֵת מִשְׁפַּחַת הַזַּרְחִי
יח וַיַּקְרֵב אֶת־מִשְׁפַּחַת הַזַּרְחִי לַגְּבָרִים וַיִּלָּכֵד זַבְדִּי: וַיַּקְרֵב אֶת־בֵּיתוֹ
יט לַגְּבָרִים וַיִּלָּכֵד עָכָן בֶּן־כַּרְמִי בֶן־זַבְדִּי בֶּן־זֶרַח לְמַטֵּה יְהוּדָה: וַיֹּאמֶר
יְהוֹשֻׁעַ אֶל־עָכָן בְּנִי שִׂים־נָא כָבוֹד לַיהוה אֱלֹהֵי יִשְׂרָאֵל וְתֶן־לוֹ תוֹדָה
כ וְהַגֶּד־נָא לִי מֶה עָשִׂיתָ אַל־תְּכַחֵד מִמֶּנִּי: וַיַּעַן עָכָן אֶת־יְהוֹשֻׁעַ וַיֹּאמַר
אָמְנָה אָנֹכִי חָטָאתִי לַיהוה אֱלֹהֵי יִשְׂרָאֵל וְכָזֹאת וְכָזֹאת עָשִׂיתִי:
כא ואראה בַשָּׁלָל אַדֶּרֶת שִׁנְעָר אַחַת טוֹבָה וּמָאתַיִם שְׁקָלִים כֶּסֶף וּלְשׁוֹן וָאֵרֶא
זָהָב אֶחָד חֲמִשִּׁים שְׁקָלִים מִשְׁקָלוֹ וָאֶחְמְדֵם וָאֶקָּחֵם וְהִנָּם טְמוּנִים
כב בָּאָרֶץ בְּתוֹךְ הָאָהֳלִי וְהַכֶּסֶף תַּחְתֶּיהָ: וַיִּשְׁלַח יְהוֹשֻׁעַ מַלְאָכִים וַיָּרֻצוּ
כג הָאֹהֱלָה וְהִנֵּה טְמוּנָה בְּאָהֳלוֹ וְהַכֶּסֶף תַּחְתֶּיהָ: וַיִּקָּחוּם מִתּוֹךְ הָאֹהֶל
כד וַיְבִאוּם אֶל־יְהוֹשֻׁעַ וְאֶל כָּל־בְּנֵי יִשְׂרָאֵל וַיַּצִּקֻם לִפְנֵי יהוה: וַיִּקַּח
יְהוֹשֻׁעַ אֶת־עָכָן בֶּן־זֶרַח וְאֶת־הַכֶּסֶף וְאֶת־הָאַדֶּרֶת וְאֶת־לְשׁוֹן הַזָּהָב
וְאֶת־בָּנָיו וְאֶת־בְּנֹתָיו וְאֶת־שׁוֹרוֹ וְאֶת־חֲמֹרוֹ וְאֶת־צֹאנוֹ וְאֶת־אָהֳלוֹ
כה וְאֶת־כָּל־אֲשֶׁר־לוֹ וְכָל־יִשְׂרָאֵל עִמּוֹ וַיַּעֲלוּ אֹתָם עֵמֶק עָכוֹר: וַיֹּאמֶר
יְהוֹשֻׁעַ מֶה עֲכַרְתָּנוּ יַעְכָּרְךָ יהוה בַּיּוֹם הַזֶּה וַיִּרְגְּמוּ אֹתוֹ כָל־יִשְׂרָאֵל
כו אֶבֶן וַיִּשְׂרְפוּ אֹתָם בָּאֵשׁ וַיִּסְקְלוּ אֹתָם בָּאֲבָנִים: וַיָּקִימוּ עָלָיו גַּל־אֲבָנִים
גָּדוֹל עַד הַיּוֹם הַזֶּה וַיָּשָׁב יהוה מֵחֲרוֹן אַפּוֹ עַל־כֵּן קָרָא שֵׁם הַמָּקוֹם
הַהוּא עֵמֶק עָכוֹר עַד הַיּוֹם הַזֶּה:

ח א וַיֹּאמֶר יהוה אֶל־יְהוֹשֻׁעַ אַל־תִּירָא וְאַל־תֵּחָת קַח עִמְּךָ אֵת כָּל־עַם
הַמִּלְחָמָה וְקוּם עֲלֵה הָעָי רְאֵה ׀ נָתַתִּי בְיָדְךָ אֶת־מֶלֶךְ הָעַי וְאֶת־
ב עַמּוֹ וְאֶת־עִירוֹ וְאֶת־אַרְצוֹ: וְעָשִׂיתָ לָעַי וּלְמַלְכָּהּ כַּאֲשֶׁר עָשִׂיתָ

and to her king as you did to Yeriḥo and hers – but you may plunder her spoil
3 and livestock. Lay an ambush to the west of the city." Yehoshua and all the
fighting men marched up to Ai. Yehoshua selected thirty thousand warriors
4 and sent them off at night. "You are to lay an ambush west of the city," he
instructed them. "Do not stray too far from the city, and all of you – be at the
5 ready. I and all the men with me will approach the city. When they come out
6 toward us, as they did last time, we will flee. They will chase us until we have
lured them away from the city – for they will think, 'They are fleeing before
7 us as they did last time.' But as we flee them, you will rise up from ambush
8 and seize the city, and the LORD will deliver it into your hands. When you
capture the city, set it on fire; do what the LORD has said; I have commanded
9 you." Then Yehoshua sent them off; they proceeded to the ambush site, taking
up a position between Beit El and Ai to the west of Ai. Yehoshua spent that
10 night among the men. Early the next morning Yehoshua rose and mustered
the men, and he and the elders of Israel marched up toward Ai ahead of the
11 people. All the fighting men with him made their way up, advancing until they
faced the city. They laid their camp to the north of Ai, with the ravine dividing
12 them from Ai. Then he took about five thousand men and stationed them in
13 ambush between Beit El and Ai to the west of the city so that the main camp
of men was located to the north of the city while its rear guard stood to the
14 west. That night Yehoshua patrolled the valley. As soon as the king of Ai saw
the Israelites, the men of the city swiftly rose and charged out to meet Israel
in combat – he and all his men – on the spot they had planned for before the
15 plain; he did not know of the ambush lurking behind the city. Yehoshua and
16 all Israel feigned defeat and fled toward the wilderness. And all the people of
the city were alerted to pursue them; they went after Yehoshua and so
17 were lured away from the city. Not a man remained in Ai or Beit El who
did not go after Israel; they left the city open and ran in pursuit of the
18 Israelites. The LORD said to Yehoshua, "Stretch out the javelin in
your hand toward Ai, for I have delivered it into your hand," and Yehoshua
19 stretched the javelin in his hand toward the city. With the thrust of his hand,
the ambushers rose swiftly from their position and ran; they reached the city
20 and captured it, then swiftly set it alight. The men of Ai turned to look behind
them – all of a sudden, the smoke of the city rose skyward! Their hands were
tied – they had nowhere to flee – and the people fleeing from them desertward
21 had turned into their pursuers! When Yehoshua and all of Israel saw that the
ambush had captured the city, and that smoke rose from the city, they turned
22 around and attacked the men of Ai. Then the other Israelites came out of the
city toward them so that they were hemmed in on both sides by Israel, who
23 struck them down until neither survivor nor fugitive remained. But the king

לִירִיחוֹ וּלְמַלְכָּהּ רַק־שְׁלָלָהּ וּבְהֶמְתָּהּ תָּבֹזּוּ לָכֶם שִׂים־לְךָ אֹרֵב לָעִיר
ג מֵאַחֲרֶיהָ: וַיָּקָם יְהוֹשֻׁעַ וְכָל־עַם הַמִּלְחָמָה לַעֲלוֹת הָעָי וַיִּבְחַר יְהוֹשֻׁעַ
ד שְׁלֹשִׁים אֶלֶף אִישׁ גִּבּוֹרֵי הַחַיִל וַיִּשְׁלָחֵם לָיְלָה: וַיְצַו אֹתָם לֵאמֹר
רְאוּ אַתֶּם אֹרְבִים לָעִיר מֵאַחֲרֵי הָעִיר אַל־תַּרְחִיקוּ מִן־הָעִיר מְאֹד
ה וִהְיִיתֶם כֻּלְּכֶם נְכֹנִים: וַאֲנִי וְכָל־הָעָם אֲשֶׁר אִתִּי נִקְרַב אֶל־הָעִיר וְהָיָה
ו כִּי־יֵצְאוּ לִקְרָאתֵנוּ כַּאֲשֶׁר בָּרִאשֹׁנָה וְנַסְנוּ לִפְנֵיהֶם: וְיָצְאוּ אַחֲרֵינוּ עַד
הַתִּיקֵנוּ אוֹתָם מִן־הָעִיר כִּי יֹאמְרוּ נָסִים לְפָנֵינוּ כַּאֲשֶׁר בָּרִאשֹׁנָה וְנַסְנוּ
ז לִפְנֵיהֶם: וְאַתֶּם תָּקֻמוּ מֵהָאוֹרֵב וְהוֹרַשְׁתֶּם אֶת־הָעִיר וּנְתָנָהּ יְהוָה
ח אֱלֹהֵיכֶם בְּיֶדְכֶם: וְהָיָה כְּתָפְשְׂכֶם אֶת־הָעִיר תַּצִּיתוּ אֶת־הָעִיר בָּאֵשׁ
ט כִּדְבַר יְהוָה תַּעֲשׂוּ רְאוּ צִוִּיתִי אֶתְכֶם: וַיִּשְׁלָחֵם יְהוֹשֻׁעַ וַיֵּלְכוּ אֶל־
הַמַּאְרָב וַיֵּשְׁבוּ בֵּין בֵּית־אֵל וּבֵין הָעַי מִיָּם לָעָי וַיָּלֶן יְהוֹשֻׁעַ בַּלַּיְלָה
י הַהוּא בְּתוֹךְ הָעָם: וַיַּשְׁכֵּם יְהוֹשֻׁעַ בַּבֹּקֶר וַיִּפְקֹד אֶת־הָעָם וַיַּעַל
יא הוּא וְזִקְנֵי יִשְׂרָאֵל לִפְנֵי הָעָם הָעָי: וְכָל־הָעָם הַמִּלְחָמָה אֲשֶׁר אִתּוֹ
עָלוּ וַיִּגְּשׁוּ וַיָּבֹאוּ נֶגֶד הָעִיר וַיַּחֲנוּ מִצְּפוֹן לָעַי וְהַגַּי בֵּינָו וּבֵין הָעָי:
יב וַיִּקַּח כַּחֲמֵשֶׁת אֲלָפִים אִישׁ וַיָּשֶׂם אוֹתָם אֹרֵב בֵּין בֵּית־אֵל וּבֵין
יג הָעַי מִיָּם לָעִיר: וַיָּשִׂימוּ הָעָם אֶת־כָּל־הַמַּחֲנֶה אֲשֶׁר מִצְּפוֹן לָעִיר לָעָי
וְאֶת־עֲקֵבוֹ מִיָּם לָעִיר וַיֵּלֶךְ יְהוֹשֻׁעַ בַּלַּיְלָה הַהוּא בְּתוֹךְ הָעֵמֶק:
יד וַיְהִי כִּרְאוֹת מֶלֶךְ־הָעַי וַיְמַהֲרוּ וַיַּשְׁכִּימוּ וַיֵּצְאוּ אַנְשֵׁי־הָעִיר לִקְרַאת־
יִשְׂרָאֵל לַמִּלְחָמָה הוּא וְכָל־עַמּוֹ לַמּוֹעֵד לִפְנֵי הָעֲרָבָה וְהוּא לֹא יָדַע
טו כִּי־אֹרֵב לוֹ מֵאַחֲרֵי הָעִיר: וַיִּנָּגְעוּ יְהוֹשֻׁעַ וְכָל־יִשְׂרָאֵל לִפְנֵיהֶם וַיָּנֻסוּ
טז דֶּרֶךְ הַמִּדְבָּר: וַיִּזָּעֲקוּ כָּל־הָעָם אֲשֶׁר בָּעִיר לִרְדֹּף אַחֲרֵיהֶם וַיִּרְדְּפוּ בָּעַי
יז אַחֲרֵי יְהוֹשֻׁעַ וַיִּנָּתְקוּ מִן־הָעִיר: וְלֹא־נִשְׁאַר אִישׁ בָּעַי וּבֵית אֵל אֲשֶׁר
לֹא־יָצְאוּ אַחֲרֵי יִשְׂרָאֵל וַיַּעַזְבוּ אֶת־הָעִיר פְּתוּחָה וַיִּרְדְּפוּ אַחֲרֵי
יח יִשְׂרָאֵל: וַיֹּאמֶר יְהוָה אֶל־יְהוֹשֻׁעַ נְטֵה בַּכִּידוֹן אֲשֶׁר־בְּיָדְךָ
אֶל־הָעַי כִּי בְיָדְךָ אֶתְּנֶנָּה וַיֵּט יְהוֹשֻׁעַ בַּכִּידוֹן אֲשֶׁר־בְּיָדוֹ אֶל־הָעִיר:
יט וְהָאוֹרֵב קָם מְהֵרָה מִמְּקוֹמוֹ וַיָּרוּצוּ כִּנְטוֹת יָדוֹ וַיָּבֹאוּ הָעִיר וַיִּלְכְּדוּהָ
כ וַיְמַהֲרוּ וַיַּצִּיתוּ אֶת־הָעִיר בָּאֵשׁ: וַיִּפְנוּ אַנְשֵׁי הָעַי אַחֲרֵיהֶם וַיִּרְאוּ וְהִנֵּה
עָלָה עֲשַׁן הָעִיר הַשָּׁמַיְמָה וְלֹא־הָיָה בָהֶם יָדַיִם לָנוּס הֵנָּה וָהֵנָּה וְהָעָם
כא הַנָּס הַמִּדְבָּר נֶהְפַּךְ אֶל־הָרוֹדֵף: וִיהוֹשֻׁעַ וְכָל־יִשְׂרָאֵל רָאוּ כִּי־לָכַד
הָאֹרֵב אֶת־הָעִיר וְכִי עָלָה עֲשַׁן הָעִיר וַיָּשֻׁבוּ וַיַּכּוּ אֶת־אַנְשֵׁי הָעָי:
כב וְאֵלֶּה יָצְאוּ מִן־הָעִיר לִקְרָאתָם וַיִּהְיוּ לְיִשְׂרָאֵל בַּתָּוֶךְ אֵלֶּה מִזֶּה וְאֵלֶּה
כג מִזֶּה וַיַּכּוּ אוֹתָם עַד־בִּלְתִּי הִשְׁאִיר־לוֹ שָׂרִיד וּפָלִיט: וְאֶת־מֶלֶךְ הָעַי

24 of Ai they seized alive and brought forward to Yehoshua. When Israel had
finished killing all the inhabitants of Ai who had chased them toward the open
wilderness, and every last one of them had fallen by the sword, all of
25 Israel returned to Ai and put it to the sword. All the fallen on that day – man
26 and woman, Ai's entire population – numbered twelve thousand. Yehoshua
did not draw back the hand that stretched forth the javelin until he had utterly
27 destroyed all the people of Ai. And Israel plundered the livestock and spoil for
28 themselves, just as the LORD had commanded Yehoshua. Yehoshua burned
29 down Ai, rendering it an eternal ruin, a wasteland to this day. He hung the
king of Ai on a tree until evening time; when the sun set, Yehoshua gave
orders for the corpse to be lowered from the tree. They flung it outside the
gated entrance to the city and raised a great heap of stones on top; it endures
to this day.
30 31 Then Yehoshua built an altar to the LORD, God of Israel, on Mount Eival, as
Moshe, God's servant, had commanded the Israelites – as is written in the
book of Moshe's teaching: an altar of uncut stones upon which no iron tool
had been wielded.[10] They offered up burnt offerings to the LORD and
32 sacrificed peace offerings. And there, upon the stones, he inscribed a copy of
33 the teaching that Moshe had written before the Israelites. All Israel and its
elders, officers, and judges stood on either side of the Ark, opposite the
Levitical priests bearing the Ark of the LORD's Covenant. To bless the people
of Israel, half of the citizens and strangers alike faced Mount Gerizim and half
of them faced Mount Eival, just as Moshe, the LORD's servant, had originally
34 commanded. He then read out all the words of the Torah, blessing and curse,
35 exactly as written in the book of the Torah. There was not a single word
Moshe had commanded that Yehoshua failed to read before the whole
congregation of Israel, including the women, the children, and the strangers
9 1 who walked among them. When all the kings across the Jordan
heard – those in highlands and lowlands; those all along the coast of the Great
Sea facing Lebanon; the Hittites, Amorites, Perizzites, Hivites, and
2 Jebusites – they gathered together, of one accord, to fight against Yehoshua
3 and the Israelites. The inhabitants of Givon heard what Yehoshua
4 had done to Yeriḥo and Ai. So they, too, acted with guile; they went and
disguised themselves and took worn sackcloth for their donkeys; worn
5 wineskins, cracked and stitched; worn, patched shoes on their feet, and worn
clothes to wear; and all their bread provisions were dry and speckled with
6 mold. They went to Yehoshua at the camp at Gilgal. "We have come from a
distant land," they said to him and the men of Israel. "Please, form a pact with
7 us." "Perhaps you live among us," the men of Israel replied to the Hivites.[11]

---

10 | See Deuteronomy 27:5.
11 | See 11:19: "the Hivites who lived in Givon."

כד תַּפְשׂוּ חָי וַיַּקְרִבוּ אֹתוֹ אֶל־יְהוֹשֻׁעַ: וַיְהִי כְּכַלּוֹת יִשְׂרָאֵל לַהֲרֹג אֶת־
כָּל־יֹשְׁבֵי הָעַי בַּשָּׂדֶה בַּמִּדְבָּר אֲשֶׁר רְדָפוּם בּוֹ וַיִּפְּלוּ כֻלָּם לְפִי־חֶרֶב
עַד־תֻּמָּם   וַיָּשֻׁבוּ כָל־יִשְׂרָאֵל הָעַי וַיַּכּוּ אֹתָהּ לְפִי־חָרֶב:
כה וַיְהִי כָל־הַנֹּפְלִים בַּיּוֹם הַהוּא מֵאִישׁ וְעַד־אִשָּׁה שְׁנֵים עָשָׂר אָלֶף
כו כֹּל אַנְשֵׁי הָעָי: וִיהוֹשֻׁעַ לֹא־הֵשִׁיב יָדוֹ אֲשֶׁר נָטָה בַּכִּידוֹן עַד אֲשֶׁר
כז הֶחֱרִים אֵת כָּל־יֹשְׁבֵי הָעָי: רַק הַבְּהֵמָה וּשְׁלַל הָעִיר הַהִיא בָּזְזוּ לָהֶם
כח יִשְׂרָאֵל כִּדְבַר יְהוָה אֲשֶׁר צִוָּה אֶת־יְהוֹשֻׁעַ: וַיִּשְׂרֹף יְהוֹשֻׁעַ אֶת־הָעָי
כט וַיְשִׂימֶהָ תֵּל־עוֹלָם שְׁמָמָה עַד הַיּוֹם הַזֶּה: וְאֶת־מֶלֶךְ הָעַי תָּלָה עַל־
הָעֵץ עַד־עֵת הָעָרֶב וּכְבוֹא הַשֶּׁמֶשׁ צִוָּה יְהוֹשֻׁעַ וַיֹּרִידוּ אֶת־נִבְלָתוֹ
מִן־הָעֵץ וַיַּשְׁלִיכוּ אוֹתָהּ אֶל־פֶּתַח שַׁעַר הָעִיר וַיָּקִימוּ עָלָיו גַּל־אֲבָנִים
גָּדוֹל עַד הַיּוֹם הַזֶּה:
ל לא אָז יִבְנֶה יְהוֹשֻׁעַ מִזְבֵּחַ לַיהוָה אֱלֹהֵי יִשְׂרָאֵל בְּהַר עֵיבָל: כַּאֲשֶׁר צִוָּה
מֹשֶׁה עֶבֶד־יְהוָה אֶת־בְּנֵי יִשְׂרָאֵל כַּכָּתוּב בְּסֵפֶר תּוֹרַת מֹשֶׁה מִזְבַּח
אֲבָנִים שְׁלֵמוֹת אֲשֶׁר לֹא־הֵנִיף עֲלֵיהֶן בַּרְזֶל וַיַּעֲלוּ עָלָיו עֹלוֹת לַיהוָה
לב וַיִּזְבְּחוּ שְׁלָמִים: וַיִּכְתָּב־שָׁם עַל־הָאֲבָנִים אֵת מִשְׁנֵה תּוֹרַת מֹשֶׁה
לג אֲשֶׁר כָּתַב לִפְנֵי בְּנֵי יִשְׂרָאֵל: וְכָל־יִשְׂרָאֵל וּזְקֵנָיו וְשֹׁטְרִים | וְשֹׁפְטָיו ה
עֹמְדִים מִזֶּה | וּמִזֶּה | לָאָרוֹן נֶגֶד הַכֹּהֲנִים הַלְוִיִּם נֹשְׂאֵי | אֲרוֹן בְּרִית־
יְהוָה כַּגֵּר כָּאֶזְרָח חֶצְיוֹ אֶל־מוּל הַר־גְּרִזִים וְהַחֶצְיוֹ אֶל־מוּל הַר־עֵיבָל
כַּאֲשֶׁר צִוָּה מֹשֶׁה עֶבֶד־יְהוָה לְבָרֵךְ אֶת־הָעָם יִשְׂרָאֵל בָּרִאשֹׁנָה:
לד וְאַחֲרֵי־כֵן קָרָא אֶת־כָּל־דִּבְרֵי הַתּוֹרָה הַבְּרָכָה וְהַקְּלָלָה כְּכָל־הַכָּתוּב
לה בְּסֵפֶר הַתּוֹרָה: לֹא־הָיָה דָבָר מִכֹּל אֲשֶׁר־צִוָּה מֹשֶׁה אֲשֶׁר לֹא־
קָרָא יְהוֹשֻׁעַ נֶגֶד כָּל־קְהַל יִשְׂרָאֵל וְהַנָּשִׁים וְהַטַּף וְהַגֵּר הַהֹלֵךְ
ט א בְּקִרְבָּם: וַיְהִי כִשְׁמֹעַ כָּל־הַמְּלָכִים אֲשֶׁר בְּעֵבֶר הַיַּרְדֵּן בָּהָר
וּבַשְּׁפֵלָה וּבְכֹל חוֹף הַיָּם הַגָּדוֹל אֶל־מוּל הַלְּבָנוֹן הַחִתִּי וְהָאֱמֹרִי
ב הַכְּנַעֲנִי הַפְּרִזִּי הַחִוִּי וְהַיְבוּסִי: וַיִּתְקַבְּצוּ יַחְדָּו לְהִלָּחֵם עִם־יְהוֹשֻׁעַ
ג וְעִם־יִשְׂרָאֵל פֶּה אֶחָד: וְיֹשְׁבֵי גִבְעוֹן שָׁמְעוּ אֵת אֲשֶׁר
ד עָשָׂה יְהוֹשֻׁעַ לִירִיחוֹ וְלָעָי: וַיַּעֲשׂוּ גַם־הֵמָּה בְּעָרְמָה וַיֵּלְכוּ וַיִּצְטַיָּרוּ
וַיִּקְחוּ שַׂקִּים בָּלִים לַחֲמוֹרֵיהֶם וְנֹאדוֹת יַיִן בָּלִים וּמְבֻקָּעִים וּמְצֹרָרִים:
ה וּנְעָלוֹת בָּלוֹת וּמְטֻלָּאוֹת בְּרַגְלֵיהֶם וּשְׂלָמוֹת בָּלוֹת עֲלֵיהֶם וְכֹל לֶחֶם
ו צֵידָם יָבֵשׁ הָיָה נִקֻּדִים: וַיֵּלְכוּ אֶל־יְהוֹשֻׁעַ אֶל־הַמַּחֲנֶה הַגִּלְגָּל וַיֹּאמְרוּ
אֵלָיו וְאֶל־אִישׁ יִשְׂרָאֵל מֵאֶרֶץ רְחוֹקָה בָּאנוּ וְעַתָּה כִּרְתוּ־לָנוּ בְרִית:
ז וַיֹּאמְרוּ אִישׁ־יִשְׂרָאֵל אֶל־הַחִוִּי אוּלַי בְּקִרְבִּי אַתָּה יוֹשֵׁב וְאֵיךְ   וַיֹּאמֶר

8 "How, then, can we form a pact with you?"[12] "We are your servants," they
responded to Yehoshua. "Who are you?" Yehoshua said. "And where do you
9 come from?" "Your servants have come from a faraway land," they told him,
"because of the LORD your God's name, for we have heard of His fame and of
10 all He did in Egypt, and of all He did to the two Amorite kings on the other
side of the Jordan: to Siḥon, king of Ḥeshbon, and Og, king of Bashan, in
11 Ashtarot. Our elders and all the people of our land said to us, 'Take supplies
for the journey and go out to meet them; tell them, "We are your servants."'
12 Now, form a pact with us! This bread of ours – it was hot when we packed it
at home on the day we set out to meet you; now, look – it is dry and speckled
13 with mold! These wineskins were new when we filled them; now, look how
cracked they are! And these clothes and sandals of ours are worn out from
14 the sheer length of the journey." The men took of their supplies; they did not
15 seek the LORD's word. Yehoshua made peace with the Gibeonites and formed
a pact with them to spare their lives, and the leaders of the community gave
16 them their oath. Three days after they had formed a pact with them, they
17 heard that they were nearby, living among them. The Israelites set out and
arrived at their cities on the third day; their cities were Givon, Kefira, Be'erot,
18 and Kiryat Ye'arim. The Israelites did not attack them, for their community
leaders had sworn to them by the LORD, God of Israel, although the whole
19 community railed against the leaders. The leaders all answered the
community, "We swore to them by the LORD, God of Israel, and now we
20 cannot touch them. This we shall do for them: we will spare them, so that
21 there will not be wrath upon us for the oath we swore to them." The leaders
said to the people, "Let them live." They became woodcutters and water
22 drawers for the entire community, as the leaders decreed. But Yehoshua
summoned them and charged them: "Why did you deceive us, claiming, 'We
23 are so distant from you' when you live among us? Now you are cursed; you
shall never cease to be slaves, woodcutters, and water drawers for the House
24 of My God!" They countered Yehoshua, "We your servants were gravely
warned of what the LORD your God commanded Moshe His servant: to give
you the entire land and annihilate all the inhabitants of the land before you.
25 We feared greatly for our souls before you, and so we did this thing. Now we
26 are in your hands; do to us whatever seems good and fit in your eyes." So he
did; he saved them from the hands of the Israelites, who did not kill them.
27 On that day, Yehoshua designated them as woodcutters and water drawers
for the community and for the altar of the LORD – as they are to this day – in
10 1 the place He would choose. When Adoni Tzedek, king of Jerusalem,
heard that Yehoshua had captured Ai and utterly destroyed it – doing to Ai

12 | See Deuteronomy 7:2.

ח אכרות־לָךְ בְּרִית׃ וַיֹּאמְרוּ אֶל־יְהוֹשֻׁעַ עֲבָדֶיךָ אֲנָחְנוּ וַיֹּאמֶר אֲלֵיהֶם אַכְרָת־
ט יְהוֹשֻׁעַ מִי אַתֶּם וּמֵאַיִן תָּבֹאוּ׃ וַיֹּאמְרוּ אֵלָיו מֵאֶרֶץ רְחוֹקָה מְאֹד בָּאוּ
עֲבָדֶיךָ לְשֵׁם יְהוָה אֱלֹהֶיךָ כִּי־שָׁמַעְנוּ שָׁמְעוֹ וְאֵת כָּל־אֲשֶׁר עָשָׂה
י בְּמִצְרָיִם׃ וְאֵת ׀ כָּל־אֲשֶׁר עָשָׂה לִשְׁנֵי מַלְכֵי הָאֱמֹרִי אֲשֶׁר בְּעֵבֶר
הַיַּרְדֵּן לְסִיחוֹן מֶלֶךְ חֶשְׁבּוֹן וּלְעוֹג מֶלֶךְ־הַבָּשָׁן אֲשֶׁר בְּעַשְׁתָּרוֹת׃
יא וַיֹּאמְרוּ אֵלֵינוּ זְקֵינֵינוּ וְכָל־יֹשְׁבֵי אַרְצֵנוּ לֵאמֹר קְחוּ בְיֶדְכֶם צֵידָה
לַדֶּרֶךְ וּלְכוּ לִקְרָאתָם וַאֲמַרְתֶּם אֲלֵיהֶם עַבְדֵיכֶם אֲנַחְנוּ וְעַתָּה כִּרְתוּ־
יב לָנוּ בְרִית׃ זֶה ׀ לַחְמֵנוּ חָם הִצְטַיַּדְנוּ אֹתוֹ מִבָּתֵּינוּ בְּיוֹם צֵאתֵנוּ לָלֶכֶת
יג אֲלֵיכֶם וְעַתָּה הִנֵּה יָבֵשׁ וְהָיָה נִקֻּדִים׃ וְאֵלֶּה נֹאדוֹת הַיַּיִן אֲשֶׁר מִלֵּאנוּ
חֲדָשִׁים וְהִנֵּה הִתְבַּקָּעוּ וְאֵלֶּה שַׂלְמוֹתֵינוּ וּנְעָלֵינוּ בָּלוּ מֵרֹב הַדֶּרֶךְ
יד טו מְאֹד׃ וַיִּקְחוּ הָאֲנָשִׁים מִצֵּידָם וְאֶת־פִּי יְהוָה לֹא שָׁאָלוּ׃ וַיַּעַשׂ לָהֶם
יְהוֹשֻׁעַ שָׁלוֹם וַיִּכְרֹת לָהֶם בְּרִית לְחַיּוֹתָם וַיִּשָּׁבְעוּ לָהֶם נְשִׂיאֵי הָעֵדָה׃
טז וַיְהִי מִקְצֵה שְׁלֹשֶׁת יָמִים אַחֲרֵי אֲשֶׁר־כָּרְתוּ לָהֶם בְּרִית וַיִּשְׁמְעוּ
יז כִּי־קְרֹבִים הֵם אֵלָיו וּבְקִרְבּוֹ הֵם יֹשְׁבִים׃ וַיִּסְעוּ בְנֵי־יִשְׂרָאֵל וַיָּבֹאוּ
אֶל־עָרֵיהֶם בַּיּוֹם הַשְּׁלִישִׁי וְעָרֵיהֶם גִּבְעוֹן וְהַכְּפִירָה וּבְאֵרוֹת וְקִרְיַת
יח יְעָרִים׃ וְלֹא הִכּוּם בְּנֵי יִשְׂרָאֵל כִּי־נִשְׁבְּעוּ לָהֶם נְשִׂיאֵי הָעֵדָה בַּיהוָה
יט אֱלֹהֵי יִשְׂרָאֵל וַיִּלֹּנוּ כָל־הָעֵדָה עַל־הַנְּשִׂיאִים׃ וַיֹּאמְרוּ כָל־הַנְּשִׂיאִים
אֶל־כָּל־הָעֵדָה אֲנַחְנוּ נִשְׁבַּעְנוּ לָהֶם בַּיהוָה אֱלֹהֵי יִשְׂרָאֵל וְעַתָּה לֹא
כ נוּכַל לִנְגֹּעַ בָּהֶם׃ זֹאת נַעֲשֶׂה לָהֶם וְהַחֲיֵה אוֹתָם וְלֹא־יִהְיֶה עָלֵינוּ
כא קֶצֶף עַל־הַשְּׁבוּעָה אֲשֶׁר־נִשְׁבַּעְנוּ לָהֶם׃ וַיֹּאמְרוּ אֲלֵיהֶם הַנְּשִׂיאִים
יִחְיוּ וַיִּהְיוּ חֹטְבֵי עֵצִים וְשֹׁאֲבֵי־מַיִם לְכָל־הָעֵדָה כַּאֲשֶׁר דִּבְּרוּ לָהֶם
כב הַנְּשִׂיאִים׃ וַיִּקְרָא לָהֶם יְהוֹשֻׁעַ וַיְדַבֵּר אֲלֵיהֶם לֵאמֹר לָמָּה רִמִּיתֶם
כג אֹתָנוּ לֵאמֹר רְחוֹקִים אֲנַחְנוּ מִכֶּם מְאֹד וְאַתֶּם בְּקִרְבֵּנוּ יֹשְׁבִים׃ וְעַתָּה
אֲרוּרִים אַתֶּם וְלֹא־יִכָּרֵת מִכֶּם עֶבֶד וְחֹטְבֵי עֵצִים וְשֹׁאֲבֵי מַיִם לְבֵית
כד אֱלֹהָי׃ וַיַּעֲנוּ אֶת־יְהוֹשֻׁעַ וַיֹּאמְרוּ כִּי הֻגֵּד הֻגַּד לַעֲבָדֶיךָ אֵת אֲשֶׁר צִוָּה
יְהוָה אֱלֹהֶיךָ אֶת־מֹשֶׁה עַבְדּוֹ לָתֵת לָכֶם אֶת־כָּל־הָאָרֶץ וּלְהַשְׁמִיד
אֶת־כָּל־יֹשְׁבֵי הָאָרֶץ מִפְּנֵיכֶם וַנִּירָא מְאֹד לְנַפְשֹׁתֵינוּ מִפְּנֵיכֶם וַנַּעֲשֵׂה
כה אֶת־הַדָּבָר הַזֶּה׃ וְעַתָּה הִנְנוּ בְיָדֶךָ כַּטּוֹב וְכַיָּשָׁר בְּעֵינֶיךָ לַעֲשׂוֹת לָנוּ
כו כז עֲשֵׂה׃ וַיַּעַשׂ לָהֶם כֵּן וַיַּצֵּל אוֹתָם מִיַּד בְּנֵי־יִשְׂרָאֵל וְלֹא הֲרָגוּם׃ וַיִּתְּנֵם
יְהוֹשֻׁעַ בַּיּוֹם הַהוּא חֹטְבֵי עֵצִים וְשֹׁאֲבֵי מַיִם לָעֵדָה וּלְמִזְבַּח יְהוָה
י א עַד־הַיּוֹם הַזֶּה אֶל־הַמָּקוֹם אֲשֶׁר יִבְחָר׃ וַיְהִי כִשְׁמֹעַ אֲדֹנִי־
צֶדֶק מֶלֶךְ יְרוּשָׁלַםִ כִּי־לָכַד יְהוֹשֻׁעַ אֶת־הָעַי וַיַּחֲרִימָהּ כַּאֲשֶׁר עָשָׂה

what he had done to Yeriḥo and its king – and that the people of Givon had
2 made peace with Israel and dwelled among them, they were terrified. For
Givon was as mighty as any of the royal cities[13] – mightier than Ai – and all
3 its men were warriors. So Adoni Tzedek, king of Jerusalem, summoned
Hoham, king of Ḥevron; Piram, king of Yarmut; Yafia, king of Lakhish; and
4 Devir, king of Eglon, saying, "Come up and help me attack Givon, for they
5 have made peace with Yehoshua and the Israelites." The five Amorite
kings – the king of Jerusalem, the king of Ḥevron, the king of Yarmut, the
king of Lakhish, and the king of Eglon – assembled all their forces and
6 marched up together. They set up camp near Givon and attacked it. The
Gibeonites reached out to Yehoshua, to the camp at Gilgal: "Do not abandon
your servants; come up to us quickly! Deliver us and save us, for all the
7 Amorite kings of the highlands have gathered against us." Yehoshua marched
up from Gilgal together with all his fighting men – all his most valiant
8 warriors. The Lord said to Yehoshua, "Do not fear them, for I have
delivered them into your hands; not one of their men shall withstand you."
9 Yehoshua took them by surprise, having marched up from Gilgal all night.
10 The Lord threw them into a frenzy before Israel, and they dealt them a
mighty blow in Givon, chasing them along the Beit Ḥoron Ascent and striking
11 them up to Azeka and Makeda. As they fled before Israel along the Beit
Ḥoron Descent and up to Azeka, the Lord hurled great stones down from
the sky, and they died; more died from the hailstones than the Israelites slew
12 with the sword. Then Yehoshua spoke to the Lord on the day the
Lord delivered the Amorites to the Israelites, and said before the eyes of
13 Israel: "O Sun, halt in Givon, and Moon, in the Ayalon Valley!" And the sun
halted and the moon stood still until a nation had wreaked vengeance on its
foes. Is it not written in the Book of the Upright? How the sun stood still in
14 the midst of the sky, not rushing to set as in a natural day. Never before and
never again was there such a day when the Lord listened to the voice of a
15 man, for the Lord was fighting for Israel's sake. Yehoshua, and all
16 of Israel with him, returned to camp at Gilgal, and those five kings escaped
17 and hid in a cave. Yehoshua was informed, "The five kings have been found
18 hiding in a cave in Makeda." "Roll large stones over the mouth of the cave,"
19 Yehoshua said, "and post men by it to guard them. As for you, do not delay;
chase after your enemies and attack them from behind – do not let them reach
20 their cities, for the Lord has delivered them into your hand!" After Yehoshua
and the Israelites had defeated them in a deadly attack that finished them off,
21 only a few survivors reached the fortified cities. All the men made their way

13 | Cities where local kings resided, whose domain included the city and surrounding towns.

לירחו ולמלכה כן־עשה לעי ולמלכה וכי השלימו ישבי גבעון
ב את־ישראל ויהיו בקרבם: וייראו מאד כי עיר גדולה גבעון כאחת
ג ערי הממלכה וכי היא גדולה מן־העי וכל־אנשיה גברים: וישלח
אדני־צדק מלך ירושלם אל־הוהם מלך־חברון ואל־פראם מלך־
ד ירמות ואל־יפיע מלך־לכיש ואל־דביר מלך־עגלון לאמר: עלו־אלי
ועזרני ונכה את־גבעון כי־השלימה את־יהושע ואת־בני ישראל:
ה ויאספו ויעלו חמשת ׀ מלכי האמרי מלך ירושלם מלך־חברון
מלך־ירמות מלך־לכיש מלך־עגלון הם וכל־מחניהם ויחנו על־
ו גבעון וילחמו עליה: וישלחו אנשי גבעון אל־יהושע אל־המחנה
הגלגלה לאמר אל־תרף ידיך מעבדיך עלה אלינו מהרה והושיעה
ז לנו ועזרנו כי נקבצו אלינו כל־מלכי האמרי ישבי ההר: ויעל
יהושע מן־הגלגל הוא וכל־עם המלחמה עמו וכל גבורי
ח החיל: ויאמר יהוה אל־יהושע אל־תירא מהם כי בידך ו
ט נתתים לא־יעמד איש מהם בפניך: ויבא אליהם יהושע פתאם
י כל־הלילה עלה מן־הגלגל: ויהמם יהוה לפני ישראל ויכם מכה־
גדולה בגבעון וירדפם דרך מעלה בית־חורן ויכם עד־עזקה ועד־
יא מקדה: ויהי בנסם ׀ מפני ישראל הם במורד בית־חורן ויהוה השליך
עליהם אבנים גדלות מן־השמים עד־עזקה וימתו רבים אשר־מתו
יב באבני הברד מאשר הרגו בני ישראל בחרב: אז ידבר
יהושע ליהוה ביום תת יהוה את־האמרי לפני בני ישראל ויאמר ׀
יג לעיני ישראל שמש בגבעון דום וירח בעמק אילון: וידם השמש
וירח עמד עד־יקם גוי איביו הלא־היא כתובה על־ספר הישר
יד ויעמד השמש בחצי השמים ולא־אץ לבוא כיום תמים: ולא היה
כיום ההוא לפניו ואחריו לשמע יהוה בקול איש כי יהוה נלחם
טו לישראל: וישב יהושע וכל־ישראל עמו אל־המחנה
טז הגלגלה: וינסו חמשת המלכים האלה ויחבאו במערה במקדה:
יז ויגד ליהושע לאמר נמצאו חמשת המלכים נחבאים במערה
יח במקדה: ויאמר יהושע גלו אבנים גדלות אל־פי המערה והפקידו
יט עליה אנשים לשמרם: ואתם אל־תעמדו רדפו אחרי איביכם
וזנבתם אותם אל־תתנום לבוא אל־עריהם כי נתנם יהוה אלהיכם
כ בידכם: ויהי ככלות יהושע ובני ישראל להכתם מכה גדלה־מאד
כא עד־תמם והשרידים שרדו מהם ויבאו אל־ערי המבצר: וישבו

back to Yehoshua in the camp at Makeda in safety; no one even dared sneer
22 at the Israelites. Then Yehoshua said, "Open the mouth of the cave and bring
23 those five kings out of the cave to me." They obeyed and brought those five
kings out of the cave – the king of Jerusalem, the king of Ḥevron, the king of
24 Yarmut, the king of Lakhish, and the king of Eglon. As the kings were being
brought out to Yehoshua, he summoned all the men of Israel and said to the
captains of the fighting men who had marched with him, "Come forward and
place your feet upon these kings' necks." They came forward and placed their
25 feet upon their necks. "Do not fear or hesitate," Yehoshua said to them. "Be
strong and determined, for this is what the LORD shall do to all the enemies
26 you fight against." And Yehoshua struck them down, killed them, and hung
27 them on five trees; they hung from the trees until dusk. Toward sunset,
Yehoshua gave orders; they took them down from the trees and flung them
into the cave where they had hidden. Over the mouth of the cave they placed
28 the large stones, which remain there to this day. Yehoshua also
captured Makeda on that day and struck it down by sword; its king he
destroyed, together with every living soul there – leaving no survivor. He did
29 to the king of Makeda what he had done to the king of Yeriḥo. Then
Yehoshua and all of Israel with him proceeded from Makeda to Livna and
30 fought with Livna. The LORD delivered it, too, into the hand of Israel, along
with its king. He put it to the sword together with every living soul
there, leaving no survivor. He did to its king what he did to the king of
31 Yeriḥo. Then Yehoshua and all of Israel with him proceeded from
32 Livna to Lakhish; he encamped and fought against it, and the LORD delivered
Lakhish into Israel's hand. He conquered it on the second day and put it to
the sword together with every living soul there – just as he had done to
33 Livna. Then Horam, king of Gezer, marched up to assist Lakhish;
but Yehoshua struck him and his people down until no survivor was
34 left. Then Yehoshua and all of Israel with him proceeded from
35 Lakhish to Eglon; they encamped and fought against it. They captured it that
same day, putting it to the sword and destroying every living soul there – just
36 as he had done to Lakhish. Then Yehoshua and all of Israel with him
37 marched up from Eglon to Ḥevron and fought against it. He captured it and
put it to the sword, its king and all its towns and every living soul there, leaving
no survivor – just as he had done to Eglon. He utterly destroyed it, along with
38 every living soul there. Then Yehoshua and all of Israel with him

כָל־הָעָם אֶל־הַמַּחֲנֶה אֶל־יְהוֹשֻׁעַ מַקֵּדָה בְּשָׁלוֹם לֹא־חָרַץ לִבְנֵי
כב יִשְׂרָאֵל לְאִישׁ אֶת־לְשֹׁנוֹ׃ וַיֹּאמֶר יְהוֹשֻׁעַ פִּתְחוּ אֶת־פִּי הַמְּעָרָה
כג וְהוֹצִיאוּ אֵלַי אֶת־חֲמֵשֶׁת הַמְּלָכִים הָאֵלֶּה מִן־הַמְּעָרָה׃ וַיַּעֲשׂוּ כֵּן
וַיֹּצִיאוּ אֵלָיו אֶת־חֲמֵשֶׁת הַמְּלָכִים הָאֵלֶּה מִן־הַמְּעָרָה אֵת ׀ מֶלֶךְ
יְרוּשָׁלִַם אֶת־מֶלֶךְ חֶבְרוֹן אֶת־מֶלֶךְ יַרְמוּת אֶת־מֶלֶךְ לָכִישׁ אֶת־מֶלֶךְ
כד עֶגְלוֹן׃ וַיְהִי כְּהוֹצִיאָם אֶת־הַמְּלָכִים הָאֵלֶּה אֶל־יְהוֹשֻׁעַ וַיִּקְרָא יְהוֹשֻׁעַ
אֶל־כָּל־אִישׁ יִשְׂרָאֵל וַיֹּאמֶר אֶל־קְצִינֵי אַנְשֵׁי הַמִּלְחָמָה הֶהָלְכוּא
אִתּוֹ קִרְבוּ שִׂימוּ אֶת־רַגְלֵיכֶם עַל־צַוְּארֵי הַמְּלָכִים הָאֵלֶּה וַיִּקְרְבוּ
כה וַיָּשִׂימוּ אֶת־רַגְלֵיהֶם עַל־צַוְּארֵיהֶם׃ וַיֹּאמֶר אֲלֵיהֶם יְהוֹשֻׁעַ אַל־תִּירְאוּ
וְאַל־תֵּחָתּוּ חִזְקוּ וְאִמְצוּ כִּי כָכָה יַעֲשֶׂה יְהוָה לְכָל־אֹיְבֵיכֶם אֲשֶׁר
כו אַתֶּם נִלְחָמִים אוֹתָם׃ וַיַּכֵּם יְהוֹשֻׁעַ אַחֲרֵי־כֵן וַיְמִיתֵם וַיִּתְלֵם עַל
כז חֲמִשָּׁה עֵצִים וַיִּהְיוּ תְּלוּיִם עַל־הָעֵצִים עַד־הָעָרֶב׃ וַיְהִי לְעֵת ׀ בּוֹא
הַשֶּׁמֶשׁ צִוָּה יְהוֹשֻׁעַ וַיֹּרִידוּם מֵעַל הָעֵצִים וַיַּשְׁלִכֻם אֶל־הַמְּעָרָה אֲשֶׁר
נֶחְבְּאוּ־שָׁם וַיָּשִׂמוּ אֲבָנִים גְּדֹלוֹת עַל־פִּי הַמְּעָרָה עַד־עֶצֶם הַיּוֹם
כח הַזֶּה׃ וְאֶת־מַקֵּדָה לָכַד יְהוֹשֻׁעַ בַּיּוֹם הַהוּא וַיַּכֶּהָ לְפִי־חֶרֶב
וְאֶת־מַלְכָּהּ הֶחֱרִם אוֹתָם וְאֶת־כָּל־הַנֶּפֶשׁ אֲשֶׁר־בָּהּ לֹא הִשְׁאִיר שָׂרִיד
כט וַיַּעַשׂ לְמֶלֶךְ מַקֵּדָה כַּאֲשֶׁר עָשָׂה לְמֶלֶךְ יְרִיחוֹ׃ וַיַּעֲבֹר
ל יְהוֹשֻׁעַ וְכָל־יִשְׂרָאֵל עִמּוֹ מִמַּקֵּדָה לִבְנָה וַיִּלָּחֶם עִם־לִבְנָה׃ וַיִּתֵּן יְהוָה
גַּם־אוֹתָהּ בְּיַד יִשְׂרָאֵל וְאֶת־מַלְכָּהּ וַיַּכֶּהָ לְפִי־חֶרֶב וְאֶת־כָּל־הַנֶּפֶשׁ
אֲשֶׁר־בָּהּ לֹא־הִשְׁאִיר בָּהּ שָׂרִיד וַיַּעַשׂ לְמַלְכָּהּ כַּאֲשֶׁר עָשָׂה לְמֶלֶךְ
לא יְרִיחוֹ׃ וַיַּעֲבֹר יְהוֹשֻׁעַ וְכָל־יִשְׂרָאֵל עִמּוֹ מִלִּבְנָה לָכִישָׁה
לב וַיִּחַן עָלֶיהָ וַיִּלָּחֶם בָּהּ׃ וַיִּתֵּן יְהוָה אֶת־לָכִישׁ בְּיַד יִשְׂרָאֵל וַיִּלְכְּדָהּ
בַּיּוֹם הַשֵּׁנִי וַיַּכֶּהָ לְפִי־חֶרֶב וְאֶת־כָּל־הַנֶּפֶשׁ אֲשֶׁר־בָּהּ כְּכֹל אֲשֶׁר־עָשָׂה
לג לְלִבְנָה׃ אָז עָלָה הֹרָם מֶלֶךְ גֶּזֶר לַעְזֹר אֶת־לָכִישׁ וַיַּכֵּהוּ
לד יְהוֹשֻׁעַ וְאֶת־עַמּוֹ עַד־בִּלְתִּי הִשְׁאִיר־לוֹ שָׂרִיד׃ וַיַּעֲבֹר
יְהוֹשֻׁעַ וְכָל־יִשְׂרָאֵל עִמּוֹ מִלָּכִישׁ עֶגְלֹנָה וַיַּחֲנוּ עָלֶיהָ וַיִּלָּחֲמוּ עָלֶיהָ׃
לה וַיִּלְכְּדוּהָ בַּיּוֹם הַהוּא וַיַּכּוּהָ לְפִי־חֶרֶב וְאֵת כָּל־הַנֶּפֶשׁ אֲשֶׁר־בָּהּ בַּיּוֹם
לו הַהוּא הֶחֱרִים כְּכֹל אֲשֶׁר־עָשָׂה לְלָכִישׁ׃ וַיַּעַל יְהוֹשֻׁעַ
לז וְכָל־יִשְׂרָאֵל עִמּוֹ מֵעֶגְלוֹנָה חֶבְרוֹנָה וַיִּלָּחֲמוּ עָלֶיהָ׃ וַיִּלְכְּדוּהָ וַיַּכּוּהָ־
לְפִי־חֶרֶב וְאֶת־מַלְכָּהּ וְאֶת־כָּל־עָרֶיהָ וְאֶת־כָּל־הַנֶּפֶשׁ אֲשֶׁר־בָּהּ לֹא־
הִשְׁאִיר שָׂרִיד כְּכֹל אֲשֶׁר־עָשָׂה לְעֶגְלוֹן וַיַּחֲרֵם אוֹתָהּ וְאֶת־כָּל־הַנֶּפֶשׁ
לח אֲשֶׁר־בָּהּ׃ וַיָּשָׁב יְהוֹשֻׁעַ וְכָל־יִשְׂרָאֵל עִמּוֹ דְּבִרָה וַיִּלָּחֶם

39 turned back to Devir and fought against it. He captured its king and all its
towns and put them to the sword; they destroyed every living soul there,
leaving no survivor. They did to Devir and its king just as they had done to
40 Ḥevron and to Livna and its king. Thus Yehoshua conquered the entire
land – the hill country, the Negev, the lowlands, the slopes – and all their
kings; he left no survivor and destroyed everyone who drew breath, just as
41 the LORD, God of Israel, had commanded. Yehoshua defeated them from
42 Kadesh Barnea to Aza, and the entire land of Goshen up to Givon. Every one
of these kings and all their lands were captured by Yehoshua in a single
43 campaign, for the LORD, God of Israel, fought for Israel. Then Yehoshua and
11 1 all of Israel with him returned to the camp at Gilgal. When Yavin,
king of Ḥatzor, heard, he sent word to Yovav, king of Madon, to the king of
2 Shimron, to the king of Akhshaf; to the kings of the north in the hills, in the
plains south of Kinerot, in the lowlands, and in the district of Dor to the west;
3 to the Canaanites to the east and west; to the Amorites, Hittites, Perizzites,
and Jebusites in the hills; and to the Hivites at the foot of Ḥermon in the
4 Mitzpa region. Out they marched with all their forces, a horde of men as
5 boundless as the sand on the shore, with abundant horses and chariots. All
these kings convened; they arrived and set up camp together by the Merom
6 waters to wage war against Israel. The LORD said to Yehoshua,
"Do not fear them, for by this time tomorrow, I will have rendered them into
corpses before Israel. Maim their horses and burn their chariots with fire."
7 Yehoshua, with all his fighting men, caught them by surprise at the Merom
8 waters, swooping down upon them. The LORD delivered them into Israel's
hand; they attacked them and chased them to Greater Sidon, the Salt Pits,
and as far as the Mitzpeh Valley to the east, striking them down until no
9 survivor remained. Yehoshua did to them exactly what the LORD had
bidden him: he maimed their horses and burned their chariots with
10 fire. Then Yehoshua headed back and captured Ḥatzor. He put its
king to the sword, for until then, Ḥatzor had been the head of all those
11 kingdoms. They put every living soul there to the sword, utterly destroying
12 them – nothing breathing remained – and set Ḥatzor on fire. As for all those
royal cities and their kings, Yehoshua put them to the sword, utterly destroying
13 them as Moshe, the LORD's servant, had commanded. But Israel did not burn
all the cities mounted on their hilltops, only Ḥatzor alone, which Yehoshua
14 did burn. As for all the spoils and livestock of these cities, the Israelites
plundered them, but they put every person to the sword until they had
15 annihilated them; they left alive no one who drew breath. Just as the LORD
had commanded His servant Moshe, so Moshe had commanded Yehoshua,
and so Yehoshua did; he omitted nothing that the LORD had commanded

לט עָלֶ֑יהָ׃ וַֽיִּלְכְּדָ֞הּ וְאֶת־מַלְכָּ֤הּ וְאֶת־כָּל־עָרֶ֙יהָ֙ וַיַּכּ֣וּם לְפִי־חֶ֔רֶב וַיַּחֲרִ֙ימוּ֙
אֶת־כָּל־נֶ֔פֶשׁ אֲשֶׁר־בָּ֖הּ לֹ֣א הִשְׁאִ֣יר שָׂרִ֑יד כַּאֲשֶׁ֨ר עָשָׂ֜ה לְחֶבְר֗וֹן כֵּֽן־
מ עָשָׂ֤ה לִדְבִ֙רָה֙ וּלְמַלְכָּ֔הּ וְכַאֲשֶׁ֥ר עָשָׂ֛ה לְלִבְנָ֖ה וּלְמַלְכָּֽהּ׃ וַיַּכֶּ֣ה יְהוֹשֻׁ֣עַ
אֶת־כָּל־הָאָ֡רֶץ הָהָ֣ר וְהַנֶּגֶב֩ וְהַשְּׁפֵלָ֨ה וְהָאֲשֵׁד֜וֹת וְאֵ֤ת כָּל־מַלְכֵיהֶם֙
לֹ֥א הִשְׁאִ֖יר שָׂרִ֑יד וְאֵ֤ת כָּל־הַנְּשָׁמָה֙ הֶחֱרִ֔ים כַּאֲשֶׁ֣ר צִוָּ֔ה יְהוָ֖ה אֱלֹהֵ֥י
מא יִשְׂרָאֵֽל׃ וַיַּכֵּ֣ם יְהוֹשֻׁ֔עַ מִקָּדֵ֥שׁ בַּרְנֵ֖עַ וְעַד־עַזָּ֑ה וְאֵ֛ת כָּל־אֶ֥רֶץ גֹּ֖שֶׁן
מב וְעַד־גִּבְעֽוֹן׃ וְאֵ֨ת כָּל־הַמְּלָכִ֤ים הָאֵ֙לֶּה֙ וְאֶת־אַרְצָ֔ם לָכַ֥ד יְהוֹשֻׁ֖עַ פַּ֣עַם ז
מג אֶחָ֑ת כִּ֗י יְהוָה֙ אֱלֹהֵ֣י יִשְׂרָאֵ֔ל נִלְחָ֖ם לְיִשְׂרָאֵֽל׃ וַיָּ֤שָׁב יְהוֹשֻׁ֙עַ֙ וְכָל־
יא א יִשְׂרָאֵ֣ל עִמּ֔וֹ אֶל־הַֽמַּחֲנֶ֖ה הַגִּלְגָּֽלָה׃ וַיְהִ֕י כִּשְׁמֹ֖עַ יָבִ֣ין
מֶֽלֶךְ־חָצ֑וֹר וַיִּשְׁלַ֗ח אֶל־יוֹבָב֙ מֶ֣לֶךְ מָד֔וֹן וְאֶל־מֶ֥לֶךְ שִׁמְר֖וֹן וְאֶל־מֶ֥לֶךְ
ב אַכְשָֽׁף׃ וְאֶל־הַמְּלָכִ֞ים אֲשֶׁ֨ר מִצְּפ֥וֹן בָּהָ֛ר וּבָעֲרָבָ֖ה נֶ֣גֶב כִּנְר֑וֹת וּבַשְּׁפֵלָ֔ה
ג וּבְנָפ֥וֹת דּ֖וֹר מִיָּֽם׃ הַֽכְּנַעֲנִי֙ מִמִּזְרָ֣ח וּמִיָּ֔ם וְהָאֱמֹרִ֧י וְהַחִתִּ֛י וְהַפְּרִזִּ֥י
ד וְהַיְבוּסִ֖י בָּהָ֑ר וְהַֽחִוִּי֙ תַּ֣חַת חֶרְמ֔וֹן בְּאֶ֖רֶץ הַמִּצְפָּֽה׃ וַיֵּצְא֞וּ הֵ֤ם וְכָל־
מַֽחֲנֵיהֶם֙ עִמָּ֔ם עַם־רָ֕ב כַּח֛וֹל אֲשֶׁ֥ר עַל־שְׂפַת־הַיָּ֖ם לָרֹ֑ב וְס֥וּס וָרֶ֖כֶב
ה רַב־מְאֹֽד׃ וַיִּוָּ֣עֲד֔וּ כֹּ֖ל הַמְּלָכִ֣ים הָאֵ֑לֶּה וַיָּבֹ֜אוּ וַיַּחֲנ֤וּ יַחְדָּו֙ אֶל־מֵ֣י מֵר֔וֹם
ו לְהִלָּחֵ֖ם עִם־יִשְׂרָאֵֽל׃ וַיֹּ֨אמֶר יְהוָ֜ה אֶל־יְהוֹשֻׁ֗עַ אַל־תִּירָא֙
מִפְּנֵיהֶ֔ם כִּֽי מָחָ֞ר כָּעֵ֣ת הַזֹּ֗את אָֽנֹכִ֞י נֹתֵ֧ן אֶת־כֻּלָּ֛ם חֲלָלִ֖ים לִפְנֵ֣י יִשְׂרָאֵ֑ל
ז אֶת־סוּסֵיהֶ֣ם תְּעַקֵּ֔ר וְאֶת־מַרְכְּבֹתֵיהֶ֖ם תִּשְׂרֹ֥ף בָּאֵֽשׁ׃ וַיָּבֹא֩ יְהוֹשֻׁ֨עַ
וְכָל־עַ֧ם הַמִּלְחָמָ֛ה עִמּ֥וֹ עֲלֵיהֶ֛ם עַל־מֵ֥י מֵר֖וֹם פִּתְאֹ֑ם וַֽיִּפְּל֖וּ בָּהֶֽם׃
ח וַיִּתְּנֵ֨ם יְהוָ֥ה בְּיַד־יִשְׂרָאֵל֮ וַיַּכּוּם֒ וַֽיִּרְדְּפ֗וּם עַד־צִיד֤וֹן רַבָּה֙ וְעַד֙ מִשְׂרְפ֣וֹת
מַ֔יִם וְעַד־בִּקְעַ֥ת מִצְפֶּ֖ה מִזְרָ֑חָה וַיַּכֻּ֕ם עַד־בִּלְתִּ֥י הִשְׁאִֽיר־לָהֶ֖ם שָׂרִֽיד׃
ט וַיַּ֤עַשׂ לָהֶם֙ יְהוֹשֻׁ֔עַ כַּאֲשֶׁ֥ר אָֽמַר־ל֖וֹ יְהוָ֑ה אֶת־סוּסֵיהֶ֣ם עִקֵּ֔ר וְאֶת־
י מַרְכְּבֹתֵיהֶ֖ם שָׂרַ֥ף בָּאֵֽשׁ׃ וַיָּ֨שָׁב יְהוֹשֻׁ֜עַ בָּעֵ֤ת הַהִיא֙ וַיִּלְכֹּ֣ד
אֶת־חָצ֔וֹר וְאֶת־מַלְכָּ֖הּ הִכָּ֣ה בֶחָ֑רֶב כִּֽי־חָצ֣וֹר לְפָנִ֔ים הִ֕יא רֹ֖אשׁ כָּל־
יא הַמַּמְלָכ֥וֹת הָאֵֽלֶּה׃ וַ֠יַּכּוּ אֶת־כָּל־הַנֶּ֨פֶשׁ אֲשֶׁר־בָּ֤הּ לְפִי־חֶ֙רֶב֙ הַחֲרֵ֔ם
יב לֹ֥א נוֹתַ֖ר כָּל־נְשָׁמָ֑ה וְאֶת־חָצ֖וֹר שָׂרַ֥ף בָּאֵֽשׁ׃ וְאֶת־כָּל־עָרֵ֣י הַמְּלָכִֽים־
הָ֠אֵלֶּה וְאֶת־כָּל־מַלְכֵיהֶם֙ לָכַ֣ד יְהוֹשֻׁ֔עַ וַיַּכֵּ֖ם לְפִי־חָ֑רֶב הֶחֱרִ֣ים אוֹתָ֔ם
יג כַּאֲשֶׁ֣ר צִוָּ֔ה מֹשֶׁ֖ה עֶ֥בֶד יְהוָֽה׃ רַ֣ק כָּל־הֶעָרִ֗ים הָעֹֽמְדוֹת֙ עַל־תִּלָּ֔ם
יד לֹ֥א שְׂרָפָ֖ם יִשְׂרָאֵ֑ל זוּלָתִ֛י אֶת־חָצ֥וֹר לְבַדָּ֖הּ שָׂרַ֥ף יְהוֹשֻֽׁעַ׃ וְכֹ֨ל שְׁלַ֜ל
הֶעָרִ֣ים הָאֵ֗לֶּה וְהַבְּהֵמָ֔ה בָּזְז֥וּ לָהֶ֖ם בְּנֵ֣י יִשְׂרָאֵ֑ל רַ֣ק אֶֽת־כָּל־הָאָדָ֡ם
טו הִכּ֣וּ לְפִי־חֶ֗רֶב עַד־הִשְׁמִדָם֙ אוֹתָ֔ם לֹ֥א הִשְׁאִ֖ירוּ כָּל־נְשָׁמָֽה׃ כַּאֲשֶׁ֨ר
צִוָּ֤ה יְהוָה֙ אֶת־מֹשֶׁ֣ה עַבְדּ֔וֹ כֵּן־צִוָּ֥ה מֹשֶׁ֖ה אֶת־יְהוֹשֻׁ֑עַ וְכֵן֙ עָשָׂ֣ה יְהוֹשֻׁ֔עַ

16 Moshe. Yehoshua conquered this entire land: the hill country and all the
Negev and all the land of Goshen; the lowlands and the plain, the hill country
17 of Israel and its valleys; from the bare mountain rising up toward Se'ir as far
as Baal Gad in the Lebanon Valley at the foot of Mount Ḥermon. He captured
18 all their kings, struck them down, and put them to death. Yehoshua waged
19 war against all these kings for a long time. Except for the Hivites who lived
in Givon, no city made peace with the Israelites, who conquered all in battle.
20 For the LORD determined that their enemies' hearts would be obdurate
when waging war against Israel, so that Israel might destroy them without
mercy – so that they might annihilate them as the LORD had commanded
21 Moshe. At that time, Yehoshua went and obliterated Anakites
from the hill country, Ḥevron, Devir, Anav – all the hill country of Yehuda
and all the hill country of Israel. Yehoshua destroyed them together with their
22 cities. No Anakites were left in the land of the Israelites; they remained only
23 in Aza, Gat, and Ashdod. Yehoshua conquered the entire land, just as the
LORD had promised Moshe. Yehoshua assigned it to Israel as their inheritance,
allotted according to their tribal divisions. And the land rested from
12 1 war. These are the kings whom the Israelites defeated and the lands
that they took possession of on the eastern side of the Jordan, from the Arnon
2 Stream to Mount Hermon and the entire plain to the east: King Siḥon of the
Amorites, who resided at Ḥeshbon, ruling from Aroer on the banks of the
Arnon Stream and within the streambed and half of the Gilad to the Yabok
3 Stream, the Amonite border; and over the Arava up to east of the Sea of
Galilee and east of the Arava Sea, the Dead Sea, toward Beit HaYeshimot; and
4 his southern border was at the lower slopes of Pisga. And the region of Og,
5 king of Bashan, last of the Refaim, who resided at Ashtarot and Edre'i and
ruled over Mount Ḥermon and Salkha, the entire Bashan up to the Geshurite
and Maakhatite borders, and half of the Gilad to the border of Siḥon, king of
6 Ḥeshbon. Moshe, the LORD's servant, and the Israelites had defeated them,
and Moshe, the LORD's servant, had assigned the region as an inheritance to
7 the Reubenites, the Gadites, and half the tribe of Menashe. These
are the kings of the land whom Yehoshua and the Israelites defeated on the
western side of the Jordan, from Baal Gad in Lebanon Valley up to the bare
mountain rising up toward Se'ir. Yehoshua assigned it as an inheritance to the
8 tribes of Israel according to their divisions: the hill country and the lowlands,
the plains and the slopes, the wilderness and the Negev; that of the Hittite,
the Amorite, the Canaanite, the Perizzite, the Hivite, and the Jebusite:
9 The king of Yeriḥo one;
the king of Ai, near Beit El one;

טו לֹא־הֵסִיר דָּבָר מִכֹּל אֲשֶׁר־צִוָּה יְהוָה אֶת־מֹשֶׁה׃ וַיִּקַּח יְהוֹשֻׁעַ אֶת־
כָּל־הָאָרֶץ הַזֹּאת הָהָר וְאֶת־כָּל־הַנֶּגֶב וְאֵת כָּל־אֶרֶץ הַגֹּשֶׁן וְאֶת־
יז הַשְּׁפֵלָה וְאֶת־הָעֲרָבָה וְאֶת־הַר יִשְׂרָאֵל וּשְׁפֵלָתֹה׃ מִן־הָהָר הֶחָלָק
הָעוֹלֶה שֵׂעִיר וְעַד־בַּעַל גָּד בְּבִקְעַת הַלְּבָנוֹן תַּחַת הַר־חֶרְמוֹן וְאֵת
יח כָּל־מַלְכֵיהֶם לָכַד וַיַּכֵּם וַיְמִיתֵם׃ יָמִים רַבִּים עָשָׂה יְהוֹשֻׁעַ אֶת־כָּל־
יט הַמְּלָכִים הָאֵלֶּה מִלְחָמָה׃ לֹא־הָיְתָה עִיר אֲשֶׁר הִשְׁלִימָה אֶל־בְּנֵי
כ יִשְׂרָאֵל בִּלְתִּי הַחִוִּי יֹשְׁבֵי גִבְעוֹן אֶת־הַכֹּל לָקְחוּ בַמִּלְחָמָה׃ כִּי־מֵאֵת
יְהוָה ׀ הָיְתָה לְחַזֵּק אֶת־לִבָּם לִקְרַאת הַמִּלְחָמָה אֶת־יִשְׂרָאֵל לְמַעַן
הַחֲרִימָם לְבִלְתִּי הֱיוֹת־לָהֶם תְּחִנָּה כִּי לְמַעַן הַשְׁמִידָם כַּאֲשֶׁר צִוָּה
כא יְהוָה אֶת־מֹשֶׁה׃ וַיָּבֹא יְהוֹשֻׁעַ בָּעֵת הַהִיא וַיַּכְרֵת אֶת־
הָעֲנָקִים מִן־הָהָר מִן־חֶבְרוֹן מִן־דְּבִר מִן־עֲנָב וּמִכֹּל הַר יְהוּדָה וּמִכֹּל
כב הַר יִשְׂרָאֵל עִם־עָרֵיהֶם הֶחֱרִימָם יְהוֹשֻׁעַ׃ לֹא־נוֹתַר עֲנָקִים בְּאֶרֶץ
כג בְּנֵי יִשְׂרָאֵל רַק בְּעַזָּה בְּגַת וּבְאַשְׁדּוֹד נִשְׁאָרוּ׃ וַיִּקַּח יְהוֹשֻׁעַ אֶת־כָּל־
הָאָרֶץ כְּכֹל אֲשֶׁר דִּבֶּר יְהוָה אֶל־מֹשֶׁה וַיִּתְּנָהּ יְהוֹשֻׁעַ לְנַחֲלָה לְיִשְׂרָאֵל
יב א כְּמַחְלְקֹתָם לְשִׁבְטֵיהֶם וְהָאָרֶץ שָׁקְטָה מִמִּלְחָמָה׃ וְאֵלֶּה ׀
מַלְכֵי הָאָרֶץ אֲשֶׁר הִכּוּ בְנֵי־יִשְׂרָאֵל וַיִּרְשׁוּ אֶת־אַרְצָם בְּעֵבֶר הַיַּרְדֵּן
מִזְרְחָה הַשָּׁמֶשׁ מִנַּחַל אַרְנוֹן עַד־הַר חֶרְמוֹן וְכָל־הָעֲרָבָה מִזְרָחָה׃
ב סִיחוֹן מֶלֶךְ הָאֱמֹרִי הַיּוֹשֵׁב בְּחֶשְׁבּוֹן מֹשֵׁל מֵעֲרוֹעֵר אֲשֶׁר עַל־שְׂפַת־
נַחַל אַרְנוֹן וְתוֹךְ הַנַּחַל וַחֲצִי הַגִּלְעָד וְעַד יַבֹּק הַנַּחַל גְּבוּל בְּנֵי עַמּוֹן׃
ג וְהָעֲרָבָה עַד־יָם כִּנְרוֹת מִזְרָחָה וְעַד יָם הָעֲרָבָה יָם־הַמֶּלַח מִזְרָחָה
ד דֶּרֶךְ בֵּית הַיְשִׁמוֹת וּמִתֵּימָן תַּחַת אַשְׁדּוֹת הַפִּסְגָּה׃ וּגְבוּל עוֹג מֶלֶךְ
ה הַבָּשָׁן מִיֶּתֶר הָרְפָאִים הַיּוֹשֵׁב בְּעַשְׁתָּרוֹת וּבְאֶדְרֶעִי׃ וּמֹשֵׁל בְּהַר
חֶרְמוֹן וּבְסַלְכָה וּבְכָל־הַבָּשָׁן עַד־גְּבוּל הַגְּשׁוּרִי וְהַמַּעֲכָתִי וַחֲצִי
ו הַגִּלְעָד גְּבוּל סִיחוֹן מֶלֶךְ־חֶשְׁבּוֹן׃ מֹשֶׁה עֶבֶד־יְהוָה וּבְנֵי יִשְׂרָאֵל
הִכּוּם וַיִּתְּנָהּ מֹשֶׁה עֶבֶד־יְהוָה יְרֻשָּׁה לָרֻאוּבֵנִי וְלַגָּדִי וְלַחֲצִי שֵׁבֶט
ז הַמְנַשֶּׁה׃ וְאֵלֶּה מַלְכֵי הָאָרֶץ אֲשֶׁר הִכָּה יְהוֹשֻׁעַ
וּבְנֵי יִשְׂרָאֵל בְּעֵבֶר הַיַּרְדֵּן יָמָּה מִבַּעַל גָּד בְּבִקְעַת הַלְּבָנוֹן וְעַד־
הָהָר הֶחָלָק הָעֹלֶה שֵׂעִירָה וַיִּתְּנָהּ יְהוֹשֻׁעַ לְשִׁבְטֵי יִשְׂרָאֵל יְרֻשָּׁה
ח כְּמַחְלְקֹתָם׃ בָּהָר וּבַשְּׁפֵלָה וּבָעֲרָבָה וּבָאֲשֵׁדוֹת וּבַמִּדְבָּר וּבַנֶּגֶב הַחִתִּי
הָאֱמֹרִי וְהַכְּנַעֲנִי הַפְּרִזִּי הַחִוִּי וְהַיְבוּסִי׃
ט מֶלֶךְ יְרִיחוֹ אֶחָד
מֶלֶךְ הָעַי אֲשֶׁר־מִצַּד בֵּית־אֵל אֶחָד׃

10 the king of Jerusalem one;
the king of Ḥevron one;
11 the king of Yarmut one;
the king of Lakhish one;
12 the king of Eglon one;
the king of Gezer one;
13 the king of Devir one;
the king of Geder one;
14 the king of Ḥorma one;
the king of Arad one;
15 the king of Livna one;
the king of Adulam one;
16 the king of Makeda one;
the king of Beit El one;
17 the king of Tapuaḥ one;
the king of Ḥefer one;
18 the king of Afek one;
the king of Sharon one;
19 the king of Madon one;
the king of Ḥatzor one;
20 the king of Shimron Meron one;
the king of Akhshaf one;
21 the king of Tanakh one;
the king of Megiddo one;
22 the king of Kedesh one;
the king of Yokne'am of Carmel one;
23 the king of Dor of the district of Dor one;
the king of the Gilgal peoples one;
24 the king of Tirtza one;
thirty-one kings in all.

13 1 Now Yehoshua was old, advanced in years. "You have grown old," the Lord
said to him, "you have advanced in years, and so much of the land is yet to be
2 possessed. This is the land that remains: All the districts of the Philistines; all

י מֶלֶךְ יְרוּשָׁלִַם אֶחָד
מֶלֶךְ חֶבְרוֹן אֶחָד׃
יא מֶלֶךְ יַרְמוּת אֶחָד
מֶלֶךְ לָכִישׁ אֶחָד׃
יב מֶלֶךְ עֶגְלוֹן אֶחָד
מֶלֶךְ גֶּזֶר אֶחָד׃
יג מֶלֶךְ דְּבִר אֶחָד
מֶלֶךְ גֶּדֶר אֶחָד׃
יד מֶלֶךְ חָרְמָה אֶחָד
מֶלֶךְ עֲרָד אֶחָד׃
טו מֶלֶךְ לִבְנָה אֶחָד
מֶלֶךְ עֲדֻלָּם אֶחָד׃
טז מֶלֶךְ מַקֵּדָה אֶחָד
מֶלֶךְ בֵּית־אֵל אֶחָד׃
יז מֶלֶךְ תַּפּוּחַ אֶחָד
מֶלֶךְ חֵפֶר אֶחָד׃
יח מֶלֶךְ אֲפֵק אֶחָד
מֶלֶךְ לַשָּׁרוֹן אֶחָד׃
יט מֶלֶךְ מָדוֹן אֶחָד
מֶלֶךְ חָצוֹר אֶחָד׃
כ מֶלֶךְ שִׁמְרוֹן מְראוֹן אֶחָד
מֶלֶךְ אַכְשָׁף אֶחָד׃
כא מֶלֶךְ תַּעְנַךְ אֶחָד
מֶלֶךְ מְגִדּוֹ אֶחָד׃
כב מֶלֶךְ קֶדֶשׁ אֶחָד
מֶלֶךְ־יָקְנְעָם לַכַּרְמֶל אֶחָד׃
כג מֶלֶךְ דּוֹר לְנָפַת דּוֹר אֶחָד
מֶלֶךְ־גּוֹיִם לְגִלְגָּל אֶחָד׃
כד מֶלֶךְ תִּרְצָה אֶחָד
כָּל־מְלָכִים שְׁלֹשִׁים וְאֶחָד׃

יג א וִיהוֹשֻׁעַ זָקֵן בָּא בַּיָּמִים וַיֹּאמֶר יהוה אֵלָיו אַתָּה זָקַנְתָּה בָּאתָ בַיָּמִים ח
ב וְהָאָרֶץ נִשְׁאֲרָה הַרְבֵּה־מְאֹד לְרִשְׁתָּהּ׃ זֹאת הָאָרֶץ הַנִּשְׁאָרֶת כָּל־

3 of the Geshurites' from the Shiḥor, which is close to Egypt, to the border of
Ekron to the north, which are considered Canaanite; of the five chieftains of
the Philistines – the Gazite, the Ashdodite, the Ashkelonite, the Gittite, and
4 the Ekronite; of the Avite to the south; all the land of the Canaanites and
5 Sidonian Maara up to Afeka and the Amorite border; the land of the Giblite
and all Lebanon to the east of Baal Gad at the foot of Mount Ḥermon up to
6 Levo Ḥamat; all the people of the hills from Lebanon to the Salt Pits; all the
Sidonians – I Myself will dispossess them all before the Israelites. Now, allot
7 them to Israel as estates as I have commanded you; divide up this land into
8 estates for the nine tribes and half the tribe of Menashe." Now, the Reubenites
and Gadites had already received the estates that Moshe had assigned to them
on the eastern side of the Jordan, exactly as they were assigned by Moshe, the
9 LORD's servant: From Aroer on the banks of the Arnon Stream and the city
10 located within the streambed and all the Meideva Plains up to Divon; all the
cities of King Siḥon of the Amorites, who had ruled in Ḥeshbon, to the
11 Amonite border; the Gilad, the territory of the Geshurites and Maakhatites,
12 all of Mount Ḥermon, and all the Bashan up to Salkha. The entire kingdom
of Og of Bashan, who had ruled in Ashtarot and Edre'i – he was the last of
the remaining Refaim. Moshe had struck them down and dispossessed them.
13 The Israelites did not dispossess the Geshurites and the Maakhatites, and
14 Geshur and Maakhat dwell among Israel to this day. Only to the Levite tribe
he did not grant an estate; the fire offerings of the LORD, God of Israel, were
15 to be their share, as He had ordained for them. Moshe had assigned
16 the Reubenite tribe its estate according to its clans, granting them: the
territory from Aroer on the banks of the Arnon Stream and the city located
17 within the streambed and the entire plain of Meideva; Ḥeshbon and all its
18 towns on the plain; Dibon, Bamot, Baal, and Beit Baal Meon; Yahtza,
19 Kedemot, and Mefaat; Kiryatayim, Sivma, and Tzeret HaShaḥar in the hill
20 of the valley; Beit Peor, the Pisga slopes, and Beit HaYeshimot; all the cities
21 of the plain and the entire kingdom of Siḥon, king of the Amorites, who ruled
in Ḥeshbon, whom Moshe had defeated along with the princes of Midyan:
Evi, Rekem, Tzur, Ḥur, and Reva, who had resided in the land as princes of
22 Siḥon. As for the sorcerer Balaam son of Beor, Israel had put him to the sword
23 along with all the rest of their slain. The Reubenites' border was the Jordan;
this territory was the estate of the Reubenites by their clans – the cities with
24 their villages. Moshe had assigned an estate to the tribe of Gad
25 according to its clans, granting them: the territory of Yazer and all the cities
26 of Gilad; half the land of the Amonites up to Aroer, facing Raba; from
Ḥeshbon to the Heights of Mitzpeh and Betonim; from Maḥanayim to the
27 border of Lidvir; in the valley, Beit HaRam, Beit Nimra, Sukkot, and

ג גְּלִילוֹת הַפְּלִשְׁתִּים וְכׇל־הַגְּשׁוּרִי: מִן־הַשִּׁיחוֹר אֲשֶׁר ׀ עַל־פְּנֵי מִצְרַיִם
וְעַד גְּבוּל עֶקְרוֹן צָפוֹנָה לַכְּנַעֲנִי תֵּחָשֵׁב חֲמֵשֶׁת ׀ סַרְנֵי פְלִשְׁתִּים
ד הָעַזָּתִי וְהָאַשְׁדּוֹדִי הָאֶשְׁקְלוֹנִי הַגִּתִּי וְהָעֶקְרוֹנִי וְהָעַוִּים: מִתֵּימָן כׇּל־
אֶרֶץ הַכְּנַעֲנִי וּמְעָרָה אֲשֶׁר לַצִּידֹנִים עַד־אֲפֵקָה עַד גְּבוּל הָאֱמֹרִי:
ה וְהָאָרֶץ הַגִּבְלִי וְכׇל־הַלְּבָנוֹן מִזְרַח הַשֶּׁמֶשׁ מִבַּעַל גָּד תַּחַת הַר־חֶרְמוֹן
ו עַד לְבוֹא חֲמָת: כׇּל־יֹשְׁבֵי הָהָר מִן־הַלְּבָנוֹן עַד־מִשְׂרְפֹת מַיִם כׇּל־
צִידֹנִים אָנֹכִי אוֹרִישֵׁם מִפְּנֵי בְּנֵי יִשְׂרָאֵל רַק הַפִּלֶהָ לְיִשְׂרָאֵל בְּנַחֲלָה
ז כַּאֲשֶׁר צִוִּיתִךָ: וְעַתָּה חַלֵּק אֶת־הָאָרֶץ הַזֹּאת בְּנַחֲלָה לְתִשְׁעַת
ח הַשְּׁבָטִים וַחֲצִי הַשֵּׁבֶט הַמְנַשֶּׁה: עִמּוֹ הָראוּבֵנִי וְהַגָּדִי לָקְחוּ נַחֲלָתָם
אֲשֶׁר נָתַן לָהֶם מֹשֶׁה בְּעֵבֶר הַיַּרְדֵּן מִזְרָחָה כַּאֲשֶׁר נָתַן לָהֶם מֹשֶׁה
ט עֶבֶד יהוה: מֵעֲרוֹעֵר אֲשֶׁר עַל־שְׂפַת־נַחַל אַרְנוֹן וְהָעִיר אֲשֶׁר בְּתוֹךְ־
י הַנַּחַל וְכׇל־הַמִּישֹׁר מֵידְבָא עַד־דִּיבוֹן: וְכֹל עָרֵי סִיחוֹן מֶלֶךְ הָאֱמֹרִי
יא אֲשֶׁר מָלַךְ בְּחֶשְׁבּוֹן עַד־גְּבוּל בְּנֵי עַמּוֹן: וְהַגִּלְעָד וּגְבוּל הַגְּשׁוּרִי
יב וְהַמַּעֲכָתִי וְכֹל הַר חֶרְמוֹן וְכׇל־הַבָּשָׁן עַד־סַלְכָה: כׇּל־מַמְלְכוּת עוֹג
בַּבָּשָׁן אֲשֶׁר־מָלַךְ בְּעַשְׁתָּרוֹת וּבְאֶדְרֶעִי הוּא נִשְׁאַר מִיֶּתֶר הָרְפָאִים
יג וַיַּכֵּם מֹשֶׁה וַיֹּרִשֵׁם: וְלֹא הוֹרִישׁוּ בְּנֵי יִשְׂרָאֵל אֶת־הַגְּשׁוּרִי וְאֶת־
יד הַמַּעֲכָתִי וַיֵּשֶׁב גְּשׁוּר וּמַעֲכָת בְּקֶרֶב יִשְׂרָאֵל עַד הַיּוֹם הַזֶּה: רַק לְשֵׁבֶט
הַלֵּוִי לֹא נָתַן נַחֲלָה אִשֵּׁי יהוה אֱלֹהֵי יִשְׂרָאֵל הוּא נַחֲלָתוֹ כַּאֲשֶׁר
טו דִּבֶּר־לוֹ: וַיִּתֵּן מֹשֶׁה לְמַטֵּה בְנֵי־רְאוּבֵן לְמִשְׁפְּחֹתָם:
טז וַיְהִי לָהֶם הַגְּבוּל מֵעֲרוֹעֵר אֲשֶׁר עַל־שְׂפַת־נַחַל אַרְנוֹן וְהָעִיר אֲשֶׁר
יז בְּתוֹךְ־הַנַּחַל וְכׇל־הַמִּישֹׁר עַל־מֵידְבָא: חֶשְׁבּוֹן וְכׇל־עָרֶיהָ אֲשֶׁר
יח בַּמִּישֹׁר דִּיבוֹן וּבָמוֹת בַּעַל וּבֵית בַּעַל מְעוֹן: וְיַהְצָה וּקְדֵמֹת וּמֵפָעַת:
יט כ וְקִרְיָתַיִם וְשִׂבְמָה וְצֶרֶת הַשַּׁחַר בְּהַר הָעֵמֶק: וּבֵית פְּעוֹר וְאַשְׁדּוֹת
כא הַפִּסְגָּה וּבֵית הַיְשִׁמוֹת: וְכֹל עָרֵי הַמִּישֹׁר וְכׇל־מַמְלְכוּת סִיחוֹן מֶלֶךְ
הָאֱמֹרִי אֲשֶׁר מָלַךְ בְּחֶשְׁבּוֹן אֲשֶׁר הִכָּה מֹשֶׁה אֹתוֹ ׀ וְאֶת־נְשִׂיאֵי מִדְיָן
אֶת־אֱוִי וְאֶת־רֶקֶם וְאֶת־צוּר וְאֶת־חוּר וְאֶת־רֶבַע נְסִיכֵי סִיחוֹן יֹשְׁבֵי
כב הָאָרֶץ: וְאֶת־בִּלְעָם בֶּן־בְּעוֹר הַקּוֹסֵם הָרְגוּ בְנֵי־יִשְׂרָאֵל בַּחֶרֶב אֶל־
כג חַלְלֵיהֶם: וַיְהִי גְּבוּל בְּנֵי רְאוּבֵן הַיַּרְדֵּן וּגְבוּל זֹאת נַחֲלַת בְּנֵי־רְאוּבֵן
כד לְמִשְׁפְּחוֹתָם הֶעָרִים וְחַצְרֵיהֶן: וַיִּתֵּן מֹשֶׁה לְמַטֵּה־גָד לִבְנֵי־
כה גָד לְמִשְׁפְּחֹתָם: וַיְהִי לָהֶם הַגְּבוּל יַעְזֵר וְכׇל־עָרֵי הַגִּלְעָד וַחֲצִי אֶרֶץ
כו בְּנֵי עַמּוֹן עַד־עֲרוֹעֵר אֲשֶׁר עַל־פְּנֵי רַבָּה: וּמֵחֶשְׁבּוֹן עַד־רָמַת הַמִּצְפֶּה
כז וּבְטֹנִים וּמִמַּחֲנַיִם עַד־גְּבוּל לִדְבִר: וּבָעֵמֶק בֵּית הָרָם וּבֵית נִמְרָה

Tzafon – the rest of the kingdom of King Siḥon of Ḥeshbon; the Jordan and
its border to the edge of the Sea of Galilee on the eastern side of the Jordan.
28 This was the estate of the Gadites by their clans – the cities with their
29 villages. Moshe had assigned an estate to half the tribe of
30 Menashe – they were half of the tribe of Menashe by their clans: the territory
extending from Maḥanayim, the entire Bashan – the entire kingdom of King
31 Og of Bashan – and all the hamlets of Yair in the Bashan, sixty cities; half of
the Gilad; Ashtarot and Edrei, Og's royal cities in Bashan – he granted this
to the sons of Makhir son of Menashe, to half the clans of the Makhirites.
32 These had been allotted by Moshe in the plains of Moav, on the eastern side
33 of the Jordan by Yeriḥo. Moshe had not assigned an estate to the tribe of Levi;
14 1 the LORD, God of Israel, is their share, as He ordained for them. And this is
what the Israelites inherited in the land of Canaan, as allotted by the priest
2 Elazar, Yehoshua son of Nun, and the clan leaders of the Israelite tribes; the
estates by lot, as the LORD had commanded through Moshe, for the nine and
3 a half tribes. For Moshe had assigned estates to the two and a half tribes across
4 the Jordan, but he had assigned no estate to the Levites among them because
the sons of Yosef, Menashe and Efrayim, counted as two tribes. They gave no
share to the Levites in the land besides towns to live in and pasture for their
5 cattle and space for their possessions. The Israelites did as the LORD had
6 commanded Moshe and divided up the land. The Judahites
approached Yehoshua at Gilgal, and Kalev son of Yefuneh the Kenizzite said
to him, "You know what the LORD told Moshe, man of God, concerning me
7 and concerning you, in Kadesh Barnea. I was forty years old when Moshe,
the LORD's servant, sent me from Kadesh Barnea to scout out the land, and
8 I brought back an honest report. But my comrades who went up with me
dissolved the heart of the people, while I fulfilled the will of the LORD my
9 God. So that day, Moshe swore: 'The land upon which your foot trod shall
become yours and your children's estate forever, for you fulfilled the will of
10 the LORD my God.' Now look – the LORD has sustained me, as He promised,
for the past forty-five years, ever since the LORD spoke those words to Moshe
while Israel wandered the wilderness, and here I am today, eighty-five years
11 old. I am still as able as on the day Moshe sent me; my strength now is the
12 same as it was then to enter and to leave. Now give me this mountain, the one
the LORD spoke of on that day. You heard on that day of the Anakites and
great fortified cities there. Perhaps the LORD will be with me, and I shall
13 dispossess them as the LORD promised." Yehoshua blessed him and gave
14 Ḥevron to Kalev son of Yefuneh as an estate. Ḥevron has remained the estate
of Kalev son of Yefuneh the Kenizzite to this day, for he fulfilled the will of

וְסֻכּוֹת וְצָפוֹן יֶתֶר מַמְלְכוּת סִיחוֹן מֶלֶךְ חֶשְׁבּוֹן הַיַּרְדֵּן וּגְבֻל עַד־קְצֵה
כח יָם־כִּנֶּרֶת עֵבֶר הַיַּרְדֵּן מִזְרָחָה: זֹאת נַחֲלַת בְּנֵי־גָד לְמִשְׁפְּחֹתָם הֶעָרִים
כט וְחַצְרֵיהֶם: וַיִּתֵּן מֹשֶׁה לַחֲצִי שֵׁבֶט מְנַשֶּׁה וַיְהִי לַחֲצִי מַטֵּה
ל בְנֵי־מְנַשֶּׁה לְמִשְׁפְּחוֹתָם: וַיְהִי גְבוּלָם מִמַּחֲנַיִם כָּל־הַבָּשָׁן כָּל־מַמְלְכוּת ׀
לא עוֹג מֶלֶךְ־הַבָּשָׁן וְכָל־חַוֺּת יָאִיר אֲשֶׁר בַּבָּשָׁן שִׁשִּׁים עִיר: וַחֲצִי הַגִּלְעָד
וְעַשְׁתָּרוֹת וְאֶדְרֶעִי עָרֵי מַמְלְכוּת עוֹג בַּבָּשָׁן לִבְנֵי מָכִיר בֶּן־מְנַשֶּׁה
לב לַחֲצִי בְנֵי־מָכִיר לְמִשְׁפְּחוֹתָם: אֵלֶּה אֲשֶׁר־נִחַל מֹשֶׁה בְּעַרְבוֹת מוֹאָב
לג מֵעֵבֶר לְיַרְדֵּן יְרִיחוֹ מִזְרָחָה: וּלְשֵׁבֶט הַלֵּוִי לֹא־נָתַן מֹשֶׁה נַחֲלָה יְהוָה
יד א אֱלֹהֵי יִשְׂרָאֵל הוּא נַחֲלָתָם כַּאֲשֶׁר דִּבֶּר לָהֶם: וְאֵלֶּה אֲשֶׁר־נָחֲלוּ
בְנֵי־יִשְׂרָאֵל בְּאֶרֶץ כְּנָעַן אֲשֶׁר נִחֲלוּ אוֹתָם אֶלְעָזָר הַכֹּהֵן וִיהוֹשֻׁעַ
ב בִּן־נוּן וְרָאשֵׁי אֲבוֹת הַמַּטּוֹת לִבְנֵי יִשְׂרָאֵל: בְּגוֹרַל נַחֲלָתָם כַּאֲשֶׁר
ג צִוָּה יְהוָה בְּיַד־מֹשֶׁה לְתִשְׁעַת הַמַּטּוֹת וַחֲצִי הַמַּטֶּה: כִּי־נָתַן מֹשֶׁה
נַחֲלַת שְׁנֵי הַמַּטּוֹת וַחֲצִי הַמַּטֶּה מֵעֵבֶר לַיַּרְדֵּן וְלַלְוִיִּם לֹא־נָתַן נַחֲלָה
ד בְּתוֹכָם: כִּי־הָיוּ בְנֵי־יוֹסֵף שְׁנֵי מַטּוֹת מְנַשֶּׁה וְאֶפְרָיִם וְלֹא־נָתְנוּ חֵלֶק
לַלְוִיִּם בָּאָרֶץ כִּי אִם־עָרִים לָשֶׁבֶת וּמִגְרְשֵׁיהֶם לְמִקְנֵיהֶם וּלְקִנְיָנָם:
ה כַּאֲשֶׁר צִוָּה יְהוָה אֶת־מֹשֶׁה כֵּן עָשׂוּ בְּנֵי יִשְׂרָאֵל וַיַּחְלְקוּ אֶת־
ו הָאָרֶץ: וַיִּגְּשׁוּ בְנֵי־יְהוּדָה אֶל־יְהוֹשֻׁעַ בַּגִּלְגָּל וַיֹּאמֶר
אֵלָיו כָּלֵב בֶּן־יְפֻנֶּה הַקְּנִזִּי אַתָּה יָדַעְתָּ אֶת־הַדָּבָר אֲשֶׁר־דִּבֶּר יְהוָה
אֶל־מֹשֶׁה אִישׁ־הָאֱלֹהִים עַל אֹדוֹתַי וְעַל אֹדוֹתֶיךָ בְּקָדֵשׁ בַּרְנֵעַ:
ז בֶּן־אַרְבָּעִים שָׁנָה אָנֹכִי בִּשְׁלֹחַ מֹשֶׁה עֶבֶד־יְהוָה אֹתִי מִקָּדֵשׁ בַּרְנֵעַ
ח לְרַגֵּל אֶת־הָאָרֶץ וָאָשֵׁב אֹתוֹ דָּבָר כַּאֲשֶׁר עִם־לְבָבִי: וְאַחַי אֲשֶׁר עָלוּ
ט עִמִּי הִמְסִיו אֶת־לֵב הָעָם וְאָנֹכִי מִלֵּאתִי אַחֲרֵי יְהוָה אֱלֹהָי: וַיִּשָּׁבַע
מֹשֶׁה בַּיּוֹם הַהוּא לֵאמֹר אִם־לֹא הָאָרֶץ אֲשֶׁר דָּרְכָה רַגְלְךָ בָּהּ לְךָ
י תִהְיֶה לְנַחֲלָה וּלְבָנֶיךָ עַד־עוֹלָם כִּי מִלֵּאתָ אַחֲרֵי יְהוָה אֱלֹהָי: וְעַתָּה
הִנֵּה הֶחֱיָה יְהוָה ׀ אוֹתִי כַּאֲשֶׁר דִּבֵּר זֶה אַרְבָּעִים וְחָמֵשׁ שָׁנָה מֵאָז
דִּבֶּר יְהוָה אֶת־הַדָּבָר הַזֶּה אֶל־מֹשֶׁה אֲשֶׁר־הָלַךְ יִשְׂרָאֵל בַּמִּדְבָּר
יא וְעַתָּה הִנֵּה אָנֹכִי הַיּוֹם בֶּן־חָמֵשׁ וּשְׁמוֹנִים שָׁנָה: עוֹדֶנִּי הַיּוֹם חָזָק כַּאֲשֶׁר
בְּיוֹם שְׁלֹחַ אוֹתִי מֹשֶׁה כְּכֹחִי אָז וּכְכֹחִי עָתָּה לַמִּלְחָמָה וְלָצֵאת וְלָבוֹא:
יב וְעַתָּה תְּנָה־לִּי אֶת־הָהָר הַזֶּה אֲשֶׁר־דִּבֶּר יְהוָה בַּיּוֹם הַהוּא כִּי־אַתָּה
שָׁמַעְתָּ בַיּוֹם הַהוּא כִּי־עֲנָקִים שָׁם וְעָרִים גְּדֹלוֹת בְּצֻרוֹת אוּלַי יְהוָה
יג אוֹתִי וְהוֹרַשְׁתִּים כַּאֲשֶׁר דִּבֶּר יְהוָה: וַיְבָרְכֵהוּ יְהוֹשֻׁעַ וַיִּתֵּן אֶת־חֶבְרוֹן
יד לְכָלֵב בֶּן־יְפֻנֶּה לְנַחֲלָה: עַל־כֵּן הָיְתָה־חֶבְרוֹן לְכָלֵב בֶּן־יְפֻנֶּה הַקְּנִזִּי

15 the Lord, God of Israel. The name of Ḥevron was previously Kiryat Arba,
who was the mightiest of the Anakites. And the land rested from
15 1 war. The allotment of the Judahite tribe by their clans extended
southward to the border of Edom, to the wilderness of Tzin at the furthest
2 south. Their southern border ran from the end of the Dead Sea, from the
3 tongue projecting southward, and extended to the south of Scorpion Ascent,
continuing past Tzin and rising up to the south of Kadesh Barnea; then it
4 passed to Ḥetzron, rising up toward Adar and turning toward Karka; then it
passed through Atzmon, extended toward the Ravine of Egypt, and ended
5 at the sea; "that shall be your southern border." The eastern border was the
Dead Sea up to the mouth of the Jordan. The corner of the northern border
6 ran from the tongue of sea at the Jordan's mouth; the border rose up toward
Beit Ḥogla, passed north of Beit HaArava, then rose up to Even Bohan, son
7 of Reuven; the border then rose up toward Devir from the Valley of the
Scourge and turned north toward Gilgal, opposite the Ascent of Adumim,
south of the wadi; the border then continued to the waters of the Shemesh
8 Spring and ended at the Rogel Spring; the border then rose up to the Valley
of Ben Hinom to the southern slope of the Jebusites – that is, Jerusalem; then
the border rose up to the mountaintop overlooking the Valley of Ben Hinom
9 to the west, at the northern edge of the Refaim Valley; the border then curved
from the mountaintop toward the waters of the Fountainhead of Neftoaḥ and
extended toward the cities of Mount Efron; then the border curved toward
10 Baala – that is, Kiryat Ye'arim; the border turned west from Baala toward
Mount Se'ir, passing north of the slope of Mount Ye'arim – that is,
11 Kesalon – and descended toward Beit Shemesh and continued to Timna; the
border extended toward the northern slope of Ekron, then curved toward
Shikron, continuing toward Mount Baala and extending to Yavne'el; the
12 border ended at the sea. The western border was the Great Sea; this was the
13 border all around the territory of the Judahites, rendered by their clans. Kalev
son of Yefuneh was given a share among the Judahites because of the Lord's
word to Yehoshua: Kiryat Arba, who was father of the Anakites – that is,
14 Ḥevron. Kalev dispossessed the three sons of the giant from there: Sheshai,
15 Aḥiman, and Talmai, the descendants of Anak. From there he marched up
against the people of Devir,[14] the previous name of which was Kiryat Sefer.
16 Kalev declared: "Whoever defeats Kiryat Sefer and captures it – I shall give
17 him my daughter Akhsa for a wife." Otniel son of Kenaz, Kalev's kinsman,
18 captured it, and he gave him his daughter Akhsa for a wife. When she arrived,
having urged him to ask her father for the field, she dismounted rapidly from
19 the donkey. "What is the matter?" Kalev said to her. "Give me a blessing," she
replied, "for you have given me desert land, and you should give me springs of
20 water." So he gave her the upper springs and the lower springs. This
21 is the estate of the Judahite tribe by their clans: The cities at the edge of the
tribe of Yehuda, by the Edomite border in the Negev, were: Kavtze'el, Eder,

14 | Cf. Judges 1:11–15.

לְנַחֲלָה עַד הַיּוֹם הַזֶּה יַעַן אֲשֶׁר מִלֵּא אַחֲרֵי יהוה אֱלֹהֵי יִשְׂרָאֵל:
טו וְשֵׁם חֶבְרוֹן לְפָנִים קִרְיַת אַרְבַּע הָאָדָם הַגָּדוֹל בָּעֲנָקִים הוּא וְהָאָרֶץ ט
טו א שָׁקְטָה מִמִּלְחָמָה: וַיְהִי הַגּוֹרָל לְמַטֵּה בְּנֵי יְהוּדָה
ב לְמִשְׁפְּחֹתָם אֶל־גְּבוּל אֱדוֹם מִדְבַּר־צִן נֶגְבָּה מִקְצֵה תֵימָן: וַיְהִי לָהֶם
ג גְּבוּל נֶגֶב מִקְצֵה יָם הַמֶּלַח מִן־הַלָּשֹׁן הַפֹּנֶה נֶגְבָּה: וְיָצָא אֶל־מִנֶּגֶב
לְמַעֲלֵה עַקְרַבִּים וְעָבַר צִנָה וְעָלָה מִנֶּגֶב לְקָדֵשׁ בַּרְנֵעַ וְעָבַר חֶצְרוֹן
ד וְעָלָה אַדָּרָה וְנָסַב הַקַּרְקָעָה: וְעָבַר עַצְמוֹנָה וְיָצָא נַחַל מִצְרַיִם והיה וְהָיוּ
ה תֹּצְאוֹת הַגְּבוּל יָמָּה זֶה־יִהְיֶה לָכֶם גְּבוּל נֶגֶב: וּגְבוּל קֵדְמָה יָם הַמֶּלַח
עַד־קְצֵה הַיַּרְדֵּן וּגְבוּל לִפְאַת צָפוֹנָה מִלְּשׁוֹן הַיָּם מִקְצֵה הַיַּרְדֵּן:
ו וְעָלָה הַגְּבוּל בֵּית חָגְלָה וְעָבַר מִצְּפוֹן לְבֵית הָעֲרָבָה וְעָלָה הַגְּבוּל
ז אֶבֶן בֹּהַן בֶּן־רְאוּבֵן: וְעָלָה הַגְּבוּל ׀ דְּבִרָה מֵעֵמֶק עָכוֹר וְצָפוֹנָה פֹּנֶה
אֶל־הַגִּלְגָּל אֲשֶׁר־נֹכַח לְמַעֲלֵה אֲדֻמִּים אֲשֶׁר מִנֶּגֶב לַנָּחַל וְעָבַר
ח הַגְּבוּל אֶל־מֵי עֵין־שֶׁמֶשׁ וְהָיוּ תֹצְאֹתָיו אֶל־עֵין רֹגֵל: וְעָלָה הַגְּבוּל גֵּי
בֶן־הִנֹּם אֶל־כֶּתֶף הַיְבוּסִי מִנֶּגֶב הִיא יְרוּשָׁלִָם וְעָלָה הַגְּבוּל אֶל־רֹאשׁ
הָהָר אֲשֶׁר עַל־פְּנֵי גֵי־הִנֹּם יָמָּה אֲשֶׁר בִּקְצֵה עֵמֶק־רְפָאִים צָפֹנָה:
ט וְתָאַר הַגְּבוּל מֵרֹאשׁ הָהָר אֶל־מַעְיַן מֵי נֶפְתּוֹחַ וְיָצָא אֶל־עָרֵי הַר־
י עֶפְרוֹן וְתָאַר הַגְּבוּל בַּעֲלָה הִיא קִרְיַת יְעָרִים: וְנָסַב הַגְּבוּל מִבַּעֲלָה
יָמָּה אֶל־הַר שֵׂעִיר וְעָבַר אֶל־כֶּתֶף הַר־יְעָרִים מִצָּפוֹנָה הִיא כְסָלוֹן
יא וְיָרַד בֵּית־שֶׁמֶשׁ וְעָבַר תִּמְנָה: וְיָצָא הַגְּבוּל אֶל־כֶּתֶף עֶקְרוֹן צָפוֹנָה
וְתָאַר הַגְּבוּל שִׁכְּרוֹנָה וְעָבַר הַר־הַבַּעֲלָה וְיָצָא יַבְנְאֵל וְהָיוּ תֹּצְאוֹת
יב הַגְּבוּל יָמָּה: וּגְבוּל יָם הַיָּמָּה הַגָּדוֹל וּגְבוּל זֶה גְּבוּל בְּנֵי־יְהוּדָה סָבִיב
יג לְמִשְׁפְּחֹתָם: וּלְכָלֵב בֶּן־יְפֻנֶּה נָתַן חֵלֶק בְּתוֹךְ בְּנֵי־יְהוּדָה אֶל־פִּי יהוה
יד לִיהוֹשֻׁעַ אֶת־קִרְיַת אַרְבַּע אֲבִי הָעֲנָק הִיא חֶבְרוֹן: וַיֹּרֶשׁ מִשָּׁם כָּלֵב
אֶת־שְׁלוֹשָׁה בְּנֵי הָעֲנָק אֶת־שֵׁשַׁי וְאֶת־אֲחִימַן וְאֶת־תַּלְמַי יְלִידֵי
טו הָעֲנָק: וַיַּעַל מִשָּׁם אֶל־יֹשְׁבֵי דְּבִר וְשֵׁם־דְּבִר לְפָנִים קִרְיַת־סֵפֶר:
טז וַיֹּאמֶר כָּלֵב אֲשֶׁר־יַכֶּה אֶת־קִרְיַת־סֵפֶר וּלְכָדָהּ וְנָתַתִּי לוֹ אֶת־עַכְסָה
יז בִתִּי לְאִשָּׁה: וַיִּלְכְּדָהּ עָתְנִיאֵל בֶּן־קְנַז אֲחִי כָלֵב וַיִּתֶּן־לוֹ אֶת־עַכְסָה
יח בִתּוֹ לְאִשָּׁה: וַיְהִי בְּבוֹאָהּ וַתְּסִיתֵהוּ לִשְׁאוֹל מֵאֵת־אָבִיהָ שָׂדֶה וַתִּצְנַח
יט מֵעַל הַחֲמוֹר וַיֹּאמֶר־לָהּ כָּלֵב מַה־לָּךְ: וַתֹּאמֶר תְּנָה־לִּי בְרָכָה כִּי
אֶרֶץ הַנֶּגֶב נְתַתָּנִי וְנָתַתָּה לִי גֻּלֹּת מָיִם וַיִּתֶּן־לָהּ אֵת גֻּלֹּת עִלִּיּוֹת וְאֵת
כ גֻּלֹּת תַּחְתִּיּוֹת: זֹאת נַחֲלַת מַטֵּה בְנֵי־יְהוּדָה לְמִשְׁפְּחֹתָם:
כא וַיִּהְיוּ הֶעָרִים מִקְצֵה לְמַטֵּה בְנֵי־יְהוּדָה אֶל־גְּבוּל אֱדוֹם בַּנֶּגְבָּה

22, 23, 24 and Yagur, Kina, Dimona, and Adada, Kedesh, Ḥatzor, and Yitnan, Zif, Telem,
25, 26 and Be'alot, Ḥatzor Ḥadata, Keriyot, and Ḥetzron – that is, Ḥatzor, Amam,
27, 28 Shema, and Molada, Ḥatzar Gada, Ḥeshmon, and Beit Pelet, Ḥatzar Shual,
29, 30 Be'er Sheva, and Bizyotya, Baala, Iyim, and Etzem, Eltolad, Kesil, and Ḥorma,
31, 32 Tziklag, Madmana, and Sansana, Levaot, Shilḥim, Ayin, and Rimon; twenty-
33 nine cities in all, with their villages.[15] In the Shefela: Eshtaol, Tzora,
34, 35 and Ashna, Zanoaḥ, Ein Ganim, Tapuaḥ, and the Einam, Yarmut, Adulam,
36 Sokho, and Azeka, Shaarayim, Aditayim, the Gedera, and Gederotayim;
37 fourteen cities in all, with their villages. Tzenan, Ḥadasha, and
38, 39 Migdal Gad, Dilan, Mitzpeh, and Yokte'el, Lakhish, Botzkat, and Eglon,
40, 41 Kabon, Laḥmas, and Kitlish, Gederot, Beit Dagon, Naama, and Makeda;
42, 43 sixteen cities in all, with their villages. Livna, Eter, and Ashan, Yiftaḥ,
44 Ashna, and Netziv, Ke'ila, Akhziv, and Maresha; nine cities in all, with their
45, 46 villages. Ekron, with its dependencies and villages. From Ekron
47 westward, all that was near Ashdod, with their villages: Ashdod, its
dependencies and its villages; Aza, its dependencies and its villages, up
48 to the Ravine of Egypt – the Great Sea was its border. And in the hill
49, 50 country: Shamir, Yatir, and Sokho, Dana, Kiryat Sana – that is, Devir – Anav,
51 Eshtemoa, and Anim, Goshen, Ḥolon, and Gilo; eleven cities, with their
52, 53 villages. Arav, Duma, and Eshan, Yanum, Beit Tapuaḥ, and Afeka,
54 Ḥumta, Kiryat Arba – that is, Ḥevron – and Tzior; nine cities, with their
55, 56 villages. Maon, Carmel, Zif, and Yuta, Yizre'el, Yokde'am, and
57, 58 Zanoaḥ, Kain, Giva, and Timna; ten cities, with their villages. Ḥalḥul,
59 Beit Tzur, and Gedor, Maarat, Beit Anot, and Eltekon; six cities, with their
60 villages. Kiryat Baal – that is, Kiryat Ye'arim – and Rava; two cities,
61 with their villages. In the wilderness: Beit HaArava, Midin,
62 Sekhakha, Nivshan, City of Salt, and Ein Gedi; six cities, with their
63 villages. As for the Jebusites, the inhabitants of Jerusalem, the
Judahites, could not dispossess them; the Jebusites dwell with the Judahites
16 1 in Jerusalem to this day.[16] The allotment of the Josephites extended
from the Jordan at Yeriḥo eastward to the Yeriḥo waters, to the wilderness
2 rising from Yeriḥo, toward the hill country of Beit El; it extended from Beit
3 El to Luz and crossed through the territory of the Arkites at Atarot; descended
to the west into the territory of the Jafletites to Lower Beit Ḥoron, up to Gezer,
4 and ended at the Sea. The sons of Yosef, Menashe and Efrayim, received their
5 estates. This was the territory of the Efraimites by their clans: the eastern
6 border of their estate ran from Atarot Adar to Upper Beit Ḥoron; it extended

15 | Explanations vary as to why more than twenty-nine cities are listed here; either some of these cities were taken by the tribe of Shimon (19:2–7), or only twenty-nine are cities and the rest are villages.

16 | Cf. Judges 1:21.

כב כג קבצאל ועדר ויגור: וקינה ודימונה ועדעדה: וקדש וחצור ויתנן:
כד כה זיף וטלם ובעלות: וחצור חדתה וקריות חצרון היא חצור: אמם
כו כז כח ושמע ומולדה: וחצר גדה וחשמון ובית פלט: וחצר שועל ובאר
כט ל לא שבע ובזיותיה: בעלה ועיים ועצם: ואלתולד וכסיל וחרמה: וצקלג
לב ומדמנה וסנסנה: ולבאות ושלחים ועין ורמון כל־ערים עשרים
לג ותשע וחצריהן: בשפלה אשתאול וצרעה ואשנה:
לד לה וזנוח ועין גנים תפוח והעינם: ירמות ועדלם שוכה ועזקה:
לו ושערים ועדיתים והגדרה וגדרתים ערים ארבע־עשרה
לז לח וחצריהן: צנן וחדשה ומגדל־גד: ודלען והמצפה ויקתאל:
לט מ מא לכיש ובצקת ועגלון: וכבון ולחמס וכתליש: וגדרות בית־דגון
מב ונעמה ומקדה ערים שש־עשרה וחצריהן: לבנה ועתר
מג מד ועשן: ויפתח ואשנה ונציב: וקעילה ואכזיב ומראשה ערים תשע
מה מו וחצריהן: עקרון ובנתיה וחצריה: מעקרון וימה כל
מז אשר־על־יד אשדוד וחצריהן: אשדוד בנותיה וחצריה
מח עזה בנותיה וחצריה עד־נחל מצרים והים הגבול וגבול: ובהר הגדול
מט נ שמיר ויתיר ושוכה: ודנה וקרית־סנה היא דבר: וענב ואשתמה
נא נב וענים: וגשן וחלן וגלה ערים אחת־עשרה וחצריהן: ארב
נג נד ודומה ואשען: ויניס ובית־תפוח ואפקה: וחמטה וקרית ארבע וינום
נה היא חברון וציער ערים תשע וחצריהן: מעון כרמל
נו נז וזיף ויוטה: ויזרעאל ויקדעם וזנוח: הקין גבעה ותמנה ערים עשר
נח נט וחצריהן: חלחול בית־צור וגדור: ומערת ובית־ענות
ס ואלתקן ערים שש וחצריהן: קרית־בעל היא קרית
סא יערים והרבה ערים שתים וחצריהן: במדבר בית
סב הערבה מדין וסככה: והנבשן ועיר־המלח ועין גדי ערים שש
סג וחצריהן: ואת־היבוסי יושבי ירושלם לא־יוכלו יכלו
בני־יהודה להורישם וישב היבוסי את־בני יהודה בירושלם עד
טז א היום הזה: ויצא הגורל לבני יוסף מירדן יריחו למי יריחו
ב מזרחה המדבר עלה מיריחו בהר בית־אל: ויצא מבית־אל לוזה
ג ועבר אל־גבול הארכי עטרות: וירד ימה אל־גבול היפלטי עד־
ד גבול בית־חרון תחתון ועד־גזר והיו תצאתו ימה: וינחלו בני־יוסף
ה מנשה ואפרים: ויהי גבול בני־אפרים למשפחתם ויהי גבול נחלתם
ו מזרחה עטרות אדר עד־בית חרון עליון: ויצא הגבול הימה

westward toward Mikhmetat to the north, then it turned eastward to Taanat
7 Shilo, passed through it to the east of Yanoaḥ, descended from Yanoaḥ to
8 Atarot and Naarat, touched Yeriḥo, and extended to the Jordan; from Tapuaḥ,
the border ran westward to the Kana Ravine, ending at the Sea. This was the
9 Efraimites' estate by their clans, except for the cities reserved for the Efraimites
10 within the Manassites' estate, all the cities with their villages. But they did
not dispossess the Canaanites who live in Gezer; the Canaanites became
17 1 forced laborers and live among the Efraimites to this day. The tribe
of Menashe was allotted a territory, for he was Yosef's firstborn; as Makhir,
firstborn of Efrayim and ruler of Gilad, was a valiant warrior, the Gilad and
2 the Bashan became his. And Efrayim's remaining sons were assigned territory
by their clans: the sons of Aviezer, the sons of Ḥelek, the sons of Asriel, the
sons of Shekhem, the sons of Ḥefer, and the sons of Shemida – these are the
3 male descendants of Efrayim, son of Yosef, by their clans. Tzelofḥad son of
Ḥefer son of Gilad son of Makhir son of Efrayim had no sons, only daughters.
These are the names of his daughters: Maḥla, Noa, Ḥogla, Milka, and Tirtza.
4 They approached Elazar the priest, Yehoshua son of Nun, and the leaders,
saying, "The LORD instructed Moshe to grant us an estate among our
brothers."[17] In accordance with the LORD's word, he granted them an estate
5 among their father's brothers. Ten districts fell to Menashe besides the land
6 of Gilad and the Bashan beyond the Jordan, for the daughters of Efrayim
inherited an estate along with his sons, while the land of Gilad went to the
7 remaining sons of Efrayim. Manasseh's border ran from Asher to the
Mikhmetat, which is by Shekhem, then continued southward toward the
8 dwellers of Ein Tapuaḥ. The Tapuaḥ region belonged to Menashe, while
9 Tapuaḥ itself, on Menashe's border, belonged to the Efraimites. The border
then descended to the Kana Ravine. The cities south of the wadi there
belonged to Efrayim, enclaved among the cities of Menashe. Menashe's
10 border ran north of the wadi and ended at the Sea; the south belonged to
Efrayim and the north to Menashe, with the Sea their border; they touched
11 Asher on the north and Yissakhar on the east. Within Yissakhar and Asher,
Menashe possessed Beit She'an and its dependencies, Yivle'am and its
dependent towns, the people of Dor and its dependent towns, the people of
Ein Dor and its dependent towns, the people of Tanakh and its dependent
12 towns, the people of Megiddo and its dependent towns – three districts.[18] The
Manassites were unable to dispossess these cities, and the Canaanites were
13 determined to stay in that land. When the Israelites grew stronger, they
imposed tributes on the Canaanites, but they never dispossessed
14 them. The Josephites protested to Yehoshua, "Why have you given
me a single estate – a single district – when I am so vast a people, so blessed
15 by the LORD?" "If you are so vast a people," Yehoshua said to them, "then go
up to the forest and cut it down for yourselves there in the land of the

---

17 | See Numbers 27:1–7.

18 | Megiddo, Tanakh, and Yivle'am were located near each other in the eastern part of the Yizre'el Valley, and together probably constituted one district.

הַמִּכְמְתָת מִצָּפוֹן וְנָסַב הַגְּבוּל מִזְרָחָה תַּאֲנַת שִׁלֹה וְעָבַר אוֹתוֹ
ז מִמִּזְרַח יָנוֹחָה: וְיָרַד מִיָּנוֹחָה עֲטָרוֹת וְנַעֲרָתָה וּפָגַע בִּירִיחוֹ וְיָצָא
ח הַיַּרְדֵּן: מִתַּפּוּחַ יֵלֵךְ הַגְּבוּל יָמָּה נַחַל קָנָה וְהָיוּ תֹצְאֹתָיו הַיָּמָּה זֹאת
ט נַחֲלַת מַטֵּה בְנֵי־אֶפְרַיִם לְמִשְׁפְּחֹתָם: וְהֶעָרִים הַמִּבְדָּלוֹת לִבְנֵי אֶפְרַיִם
י בְּתוֹךְ נַחֲלַת בְּנֵי־מְנַשֶּׁה כָּל־הֶעָרִים וְחַצְרֵיהֶן: וְלֹא הוֹרִישׁוּ אֶת־
הַכְּנַעֲנִי הַיּוֹשֵׁב בְּגָזֶר וַיֵּשֶׁב הַכְּנַעֲנִי בְּקֶרֶב אֶפְרַיִם עַד־הַיּוֹם הַזֶּה וַיְהִי
יז א לְמַס־עֹבֵד: וַיְהִי הַגּוֹרָל לְמַטֵּה מְנַשֶּׁה כִּי־הוּא בְּכוֹר יוֹסֵף
לְמָכִיר בְּכוֹר מְנַשֶּׁה אֲבִי הַגִּלְעָד כִּי הוּא הָיָה אִישׁ מִלְחָמָה וַיְהִי־לוֹ
ב הַגִּלְעָד וְהַבָּשָׁן: וַיְהִי לִבְנֵי מְנַשֶּׁה הַנּוֹתָרִים לְמִשְׁפְּחֹתָם לִבְנֵי אֲבִיעֶזֶר
וְלִבְנֵי־חֵלֶק וְלִבְנֵי אַשְׂרִיאֵל וְלִבְנֵי־שֶׁכֶם וְלִבְנֵי־חֵפֶר וְלִבְנֵי שְׁמִידָע
ג אֵלֶּה בְּנֵי מְנַשֶּׁה בֶּן־יוֹסֵף הַזְּכָרִים לְמִשְׁפְּחֹתָם: וְלִצְלָפְחָד בֶּן־חֵפֶר
בֶּן־גִּלְעָד בֶּן־מָכִיר בֶּן־מְנַשֶּׁה לֹא־הָיוּ לוֹ בָּנִים כִּי אִם־בָּנוֹת וְאֵלֶּה
ד שְׁמוֹת בְּנֹתָיו מַחְלָה וְנֹעָה חָגְלָה מִלְכָּה וְתִרְצָה: וַתִּקְרַבְנָה לִפְנֵי י
אֶלְעָזָר הַכֹּהֵן וְלִפְנֵי יְהוֹשֻׁעַ בִּן־נוּן וְלִפְנֵי הַנְּשִׂיאִים לֵאמֹר יהוה צִוָּה
אֶת־מֹשֶׁה לָתֶת־לָנוּ נַחֲלָה בְּתוֹךְ אַחֵינוּ וַיִּתֵּן לָהֶם אֶל־פִּי יהוה נַחֲלָה
ה בְּתוֹךְ אֲחֵי אֲבִיהֶן: וַיִּפְּלוּ חַבְלֵי־מְנַשֶּׁה עֲשָׂרָה לְבַד מֵאֶרֶץ הַגִּלְעָד
ו וְהַבָּשָׁן אֲשֶׁר מֵעֵבֶר לַיַּרְדֵּן: כִּי בְּנוֹת מְנַשֶּׁה נָחֲלוּ נַחֲלָה בְּתוֹךְ בָּנָיו
ז וְאֶרֶץ הַגִּלְעָד הָיְתָה לִבְנֵי־מְנַשֶּׁה הַנּוֹתָרִים: וַיְהִי גְבוּל־מְנַשֶּׁה מֵאָשֵׁר
הַמִּכְמְתָת אֲשֶׁר עַל־פְּנֵי שְׁכֶם וְהָלַךְ הַגְּבוּל אֶל־הַיָּמִין אֶל־יֹשְׁבֵי עֵין
ח תַּפּוּחַ: לִמְנַשֶּׁה הָיְתָה אֶרֶץ תַּפּוּחַ וְתַפּוּחַ אֶל־גְּבוּל מְנַשֶּׁה לִבְנֵי
ט אֶפְרָיִם: וְיָרַד הַגְּבוּל נַחַל קָנָה נֶגְבָּה לַנַּחַל עָרִים הָאֵלֶּה לְאֶפְרַיִם
בְּתוֹךְ עָרֵי מְנַשֶּׁה וּגְבוּל מְנַשֶּׁה מִצְּפוֹן לַנַּחַל וַיְהִי תֹצְאֹתָיו הַיָּמָּה:
י נֶגְבָּה לְאֶפְרַיִם וְצָפוֹנָה לִמְנַשֶּׁה וַיְהִי הַיָּם גְּבוּלוֹ וּבְאָשֵׁר יִפְגְּעוּן מִצָּפוֹן
יא וּבְיִשָּׂשכָר מִמִּזְרָח: וַיְהִי לִמְנַשֶּׁה בְּיִשָּׂשכָר וּבְאָשֵׁר בֵּית־שְׁאָן וּבְנוֹתֶיהָ
וְיִבְלְעָם וּבְנוֹתֶיהָ וְאֶת־יֹשְׁבֵי דֹאר וּבְנוֹתֶיהָ וְיֹשְׁבֵי עֵין־דֹּר וּבְנֹתֶיהָ
יב וְיֹשְׁבֵי תַעְנַךְ וּבְנֹתֶיהָ וְיֹשְׁבֵי מְגִדּוֹ וּבְנוֹתֶיהָ שְׁלֹשֶׁת הַנָּפֶת: וְלֹא יָכְלוּ
בְּנֵי מְנַשֶּׁה לְהוֹרִישׁ אֶת־הֶעָרִים הָאֵלֶּה וַיּוֹאֶל הַכְּנַעֲנִי לָשֶׁבֶת בָּאָרֶץ
יג הַזֹּאת: וַיְהִי כִּי חָזְקוּ בְּנֵי יִשְׂרָאֵל וַיִּתְּנוּ אֶת־הַכְּנַעֲנִי לָמַס וְהוֹרֵשׁ לֹא
יד הוֹרִישׁוֹ: וַיְדַבְּרוּ בְּנֵי יוֹסֵף אֶת־יְהוֹשֻׁעַ לֵאמֹר מַדּוּעַ נָתַתָּה
לִּי נַחֲלָה גּוֹרָל אֶחָד וְחֶבֶל אֶחָד וַאֲנִי עַם רָב עַד אֲשֶׁר־עַד־כֹּה בֵּרְכַנִי
טו יהוה: וַיֹּאמֶר אֲלֵיהֶם יְהוֹשֻׁעַ אִם־עַם־רַב אַתָּה עֲלֵה לְךָ הַיַּעְרָה
וּבֵרֵאתָ לְךָ שָׁם בְּאֶרֶץ הַפְּרִזִּי וְהָרְפָאִים כִּי־אָץ לְךָ הַר־אֶפְרָיִם:

16 Perizzites and the Refaim, if the Efrayim hills are too confined for you." "The
hill country is not enough for us," replied the Josephites, "but all the
Canaanites living in the lowlands have iron chariots – both those in Beit
17 She'an and its dependencies and those in the Yizre'el Valley." Yehoshua said
to the House of Yosef, to Efrayim and Menashe, "You are a vast people, and
18 you have great power; you shall not have a single lot. The hill country shall
be yours; it may be forest, but you may cut it down and what comes out of it
shall be yours, and you shall dispossess the Canaanites despite their iron
18 1 chariots and despite their strength." The entire community of
Israelites assembled at Shilo, where they set up the Tent of Meeting, and the
2 land lay conquered before them. There remained seven Israelite tribes whose
3 estates had not yet been distributed. Yehoshua said to the Israelites, "How
long will you be slack about coming to inherit the land given to you by the
4 Lord, God of your forefathers? Provide three men from each tribe; I will
send them to travel around the land and map it out for apportionment; then
5 they will come back to me. Divide it up into seven parts, Yehuda retaining its
borders in the south and the House of Yosef retaining its borders in the north.
6 Map out the land into seven parts and bring it here to me; I shall then cast
7 lots for you here before the Lord our God. For there is to be no share among
you for the Levites since the Lord's priesthood is their estate, and Gad,
Reuven, and half the tribe of Menashe took their estates on the east side of
8 the Jordan – those that Moshe, the Lord's servant, had assigned to them." So
the men rose and set out, and Yehoshua commanded those who were
traveling to map out the land: "Go and travel the land and map it out, and
9 return to me; I will cast lots for you here before the Lord at Shilo." The men
set out and traveled across the land, mapping out its cities into seven parts
10 on a scroll. They came back to Yehoshua, to the camp at Shilo. Yehoshua cast
lots in Shilo before the Lord, and there Yehoshua divided the land for the
11 Israelites by their tribal divisions. The first lot fell to the tribe of
Binyamin by its clans. Their allotment lay between the Judahites and the
12 Josephites. The northern edge of their border began at the Jordan; then the
border rose to the northern slope of Yeriḥo, rose westward to the hills, and
13 reached the wilderness of Beit Aven; from there, the border continued toward
Luz, to the southern slope of Luz – that is, Beit El; the border then descended
14 to Aterot Adar on the hill south of Lower Beit Ḥoron. The border then curved,
turning to the west, southward from the hill facing Lower Beit Ḥoron, and
ended at Kiryat Baal – that is, Kiryat Ye'arim, a Judahite city. This was its
15 western edge. Its southern edge ran from the edge of Kiryat Ye'arim and
16 continued west, reaching the spring of the Fountainhead of Neftoaḥ; the
border then descended to the foot of the hill by the Valley of Ben Hinom at

טז וַיֹּאמְרוּ בְּנֵי יוֹסֵף לֹא־יִמָּצֵא לָנוּ הָהָר וְרֶכֶב בַּרְזֶל בְּכָל־הַכְּנַעֲנִי הַיֹּשֵׁב
בְּאֶרֶץ־הָעֵמֶק לַאֲשֶׁר בְּבֵית־שְׁאָן וּבְנוֹתֶיהָ וְלַאֲשֶׁר בְּעֵמֶק יִזְרְעֶאל:
יז וַיֹּאמֶר יְהוֹשֻׁעַ אֶל־בֵּית יוֹסֵף לְאֶפְרַיִם וְלִמְנַשֶּׁה לֵאמֹר עַם־רַב אַתָּה
יח וְכֹחַ גָּדוֹל לָךְ לֹא־יִהְיֶה לְךָ גּוֹרָל אֶחָד: כִּי הַר יִהְיֶה־לָּךְ כִּי־יַעַר הוּא
וּבֵרֵאתוֹ וְהָיָה לְךָ תֹּצְאֹתָיו כִּי־תוֹרִישׁ אֶת־הַכְּנַעֲנִי כִּי רֶכֶב בַּרְזֶל לוֹ
יח א כִּי חָזָק הוּא: וַיִּקָּהֲלוּ כָּל־עֲדַת בְּנֵי־יִשְׂרָאֵל שִׁלֹה וַיַּשְׁכִּינוּ
ב שָׁם אֶת־אֹהֶל מוֹעֵד וְהָאָרֶץ נִכְבְּשָׁה לִפְנֵיהֶם: וַיִּוָּתְרוּ בִּבְנֵי יִשְׂרָאֵל
ג אֲשֶׁר לֹא־חָלְקוּ אֶת־נַחֲלָתָם שִׁבְעָה שְׁבָטִים: וַיֹּאמֶר יְהוֹשֻׁעַ אֶל־בְּנֵי
יִשְׂרָאֵל עַד־אָנָה אַתֶּם מִתְרַפִּים לָבוֹא לָרֶשֶׁת אֶת־הָאָרֶץ אֲשֶׁר נָתַן
ד לָכֶם יְהוָה אֱלֹהֵי אֲבוֹתֵיכֶם: הָבוּ לָכֶם שְׁלֹשָׁה אֲנָשִׁים לַשָּׁבֶט וְאֶשְׁלָחֵם
וְיָקֻמוּ וְיִתְהַלְּכוּ בָאָרֶץ וְיִכְתְּבוּ אוֹתָהּ לְפִי נַחֲלָתָם וְיָבֹאוּ אֵלָי:
ה וְהִתְחַלְּקוּ אֹתָהּ לְשִׁבְעָה חֲלָקִים יְהוּדָה יַעֲמֹד עַל־גְּבוּלוֹ מִנֶּגֶב וּבֵית
ו יוֹסֵף יַעַמְדוּ עַל־גְּבוּלָם מִצָּפוֹן: וְאַתֶּם תִּכְתְּבוּ אֶת־הָאָרֶץ שִׁבְעָה
חֲלָקִים וַהֲבֵאתֶם אֵלַי הֵנָּה וְיָרִיתִי לָכֶם גּוֹרָל פֹּה לִפְנֵי יְהוָה אֱלֹהֵינוּ:
ז כִּי אֵין־חֵלֶק לַלְוִיִּם בְּקִרְבְּכֶם כִּי־כְהֻנַּת יְהוָה נַחֲלָתוֹ וְגָד וּרְאוּבֵן וַחֲצִי
שֵׁבֶט הַמְנַשֶּׁה לָקְחוּ נַחֲלָתָם מֵעֵבֶר לַיַּרְדֵּן מִזְרָחָה אֲשֶׁר נָתַן לָהֶם
ח מֹשֶׁה עֶבֶד יְהוָה: וַיָּקֻמוּ הָאֲנָשִׁים וַיֵּלֵכוּ וַיְצַו יְהוֹשֻׁעַ אֶת־הַהֹלְכִים
לִכְתֹּב אֶת־הָאָרֶץ לֵאמֹר לְכוּ וְהִתְהַלְּכוּ בָאָרֶץ וְכִתְבוּ אוֹתָהּ וְשׁוּבוּ
ט אֵלַי וּפֹה אַשְׁלִיךְ לָכֶם גּוֹרָל לִפְנֵי יְהוָה בְּשִׁלֹה: וַיֵּלְכוּ הָאֲנָשִׁים
וַיַּעַבְרוּ בָאָרֶץ וַיִּכְתְּבוּהָ לֶעָרִים לְשִׁבְעָה חֲלָקִים עַל־סֵפֶר וַיָּבֹאוּ
י אֶל־יְהוֹשֻׁעַ אֶל־הַמַּחֲנֶה שִׁלֹה: וַיַּשְׁלֵךְ לָהֶם יְהוֹשֻׁעַ גּוֹרָל בְּשִׁלֹה
לִפְנֵי יְהוָה וַיְחַלֶּק־שָׁם יְהוֹשֻׁעַ אֶת־הָאָרֶץ לִבְנֵי יִשְׂרָאֵל
יא כְּמַחְלְקֹתָם: וַיַּעַל גּוֹרַל מַטֵּה בְנֵי־בִנְיָמִן לְמִשְׁפְּחֹתָם וַיֵּצֵא
יב גְּבוּל גּוֹרָלָם בֵּין בְּנֵי יְהוּדָה וּבֵין בְּנֵי יוֹסֵף: וַיְהִי לָהֶם הַגְּבוּל לִפְאַת
צָפוֹנָה מִן־הַיַּרְדֵּן וְעָלָה הַגְּבוּל אֶל־כֶּתֶף יְרִיחוֹ מִצָּפוֹן וְעָלָה בָהָר
יג יָמָּה והיה תֹּצְאֹתָיו מִדְבַּרָה בֵּית אָוֶן: וְעָבַר מִשָּׁם הַגְּבוּל לוּזָה אֶל־ וְהָיוּ
כֶּתֶף לוּזָה נֶגְבָּה הִיא בֵּית־אֵל וְיָרַד הַגְּבוּל עַטְרוֹת אַדָּר עַל־הָהָר
יד אֲשֶׁר מִנֶּגֶב לְבֵית־חֹרוֹן תַּחְתּוֹן: וְתָאַר הַגְּבוּל וְנָסַב לִפְאַת־יָם נֶגְבָּה
מִן־הָהָר אֲשֶׁר עַל־פְּנֵי בֵית־חֹרוֹן נֶגְבָּה והיה תֹצְאֹתָיו אֶל־קִרְיַת־בַּעַל וְהָיוּ
טו הִיא קִרְיַת יְעָרִים עִיר בְּנֵי יְהוּדָה זֹאת פְּאַת־יָם: וּפְאַת־נֶגְבָּה מִקְצֵה
טז קִרְיַת יְעָרִים וְיָצָא הַגְּבוּל יָמָּה וְיָצָא אֶל־מַעְיַן מֵי נֶפְתּוֹחַ: וְיָרַד הַגְּבוּל
אֶל־קְצֵה הָהָר אֲשֶׁר עַל־פְּנֵי גֵּי בֶן־הִנֹּם אֲשֶׁר בְּעֵמֶק רְפָאִים צָפוֹנָה

the northern end of the Refaim Valley; it descended through the Hinom
Valley toward the Jebusite slope to the south, descending toward the Rogel
17 Spring; curving northward, it continued to the Shemesh Spring and then on
to Gelilot, by Maaleh Adumim, and descended to Even Bohan, son of Reuven;
18 continuing northward to the slope facing the Arava, it then descended to the
19 Arava; the border then continued northward to the Beit Ḥogla slope and
ended at the northern tongue of the Dead Sea, at the southern end of the
20 Jordan. This was its southern border. The Jordan bordered it on the eastern
edge. This was the Benjaminites' estate, defined by its borders all around,
21 divided according to its clans. The cities of the tribe of Benjamin by its clans
22 were: Yeriḥo, Beit Ḥogla, and Emek Ketzitz, Beit HaArava, Tzemarayim, and
23, 24 Beit El, Avim, Para, and Ofra, Kefar HaAmona, Ofni, and Geva; twelve cities
25, 26 with their villages. Givon, Rama, and Be'erot, Mitzpeh, Kefira, and Motza,
27, 28 Rekem, Yirpe'el, and Tarala, Tzela, Elef, and the Jebusite – that is,
Jerusalem – Givat, Kiryat; fourteen cities with their villages. This was the
19 1 estate of the Benjaminites by their clans. The second lot fell to
Shimon, to the tribe of the Simeonites by their clans. Their estate lay within
2 the Judahites' estate. Their estate included Be'er Sheva with Sheva, and
3, 4, 5 Molada, Ḥatzar Shual, Bala, and Etzem, Eltolad, Betul, and Ḥorma, Tziklag,
6 Beit HaMarkavot, and Ḥatzar Susa, Beit Levaot and Sharuḥen; thirteen cities
7 with their villages. Ayin, Rimon, Eter, and Ashan; four cities with their villages,
8 as well as all the villages surrounding these cities up to Baalat Be'er and Ramat
Negev – this was the tribe of Shimon's estate, divided according to its clans.
9 Simeon's estate was within Yehuda's district: because the Judahites' share was
10 too large for them, the Simeonites settled within Yehuda's estate. The
third lot fell to the Zebulunites by their clans; the borders of their estate ran
11 to Sarid. Their border rose up westward to Marala, touched Dabeshet, and
12 reached the wadi facing Yokne'am, then turned back from Sarid to the east,
where the sun rises, up to the border of Kislot Tavor, continuing on to Davrat
13 and rising up to Yafia; from there, it turned eastward to Gat Ḥefer and to Et
14 Katzin and reached Rimon, where it curved toward Ne'a; the border then
15 swung around north of Ḥanaton and ended in the Yiftaḥ El Valley. With Katat,
Nahalal, Shimron, Yidala, and Beit Leḥem, there were twelve cities with their
16 villages. This was the Zebulunites' estate, divided by their clans – these cities
17 with their villages. The fourth lot fell to Yissakhar, to the
18 Issacharites by their clans. Their territory comprised Yizre'el, Kesulot, and
19, 20, 21 Shunem, Ḥafarayim, Shion, and Anaḥarat, Rabit, Kishyon, and Evetz, Remet,
22 Ein Ganim, Ein Ḥada, and Beit Patzetz. Their border reached Tavor,
Shaḥatzima, and Beit Shemesh, and ended at the Jordan; sixteen cities with

יז וְיָרַד גֵּי הִנֹּם אֶל־כֶּתֶף הַיְבוּסִי נֶגְבָּה וְיָרַד עֵין רֹגֵל׃ וְתָאַר מִצָּפוֹן וְיָצָא
עֵין שֶׁמֶשׁ וְיָצָא אֶל־גְּלִילוֹת אֲשֶׁר־נֹכַח מַעֲלֵה אֲדֻמִּים וְיָרַד אֶבֶן בֹּהַן
יח בֶּן־רְאוּבֵן׃ וְעָבַר אֶל־כֶּתֶף מוּל־הָעֲרָבָה צָפוֹנָה וְיָרַד הָעֲרָבָתָה׃
יט וְעָבַר הַגְּבוּל אֶל־כֶּתֶף בֵּית־חָגְלָה צָפוֹנָה והיה ׀ תוצאותיו הַגְּבוּל וְהָיוּ | תּוֹצְאוֹת
אֶל־לְשׁוֹן יָם־הַמֶּלַח צָפוֹנָה אֶל־קְצֵה הַיַּרְדֵּן נֶגְבָּה זֶה גְּבוּל נֶגֶב׃
כ וְהַיַּרְדֵּן יִגְבֹּל־אֹתוֹ לִפְאַת־קֵדְמָה זֹאת נַחֲלַת בְּנֵי בִנְיָמִן לִגְבוּלֹתֶיהָ
כא סָבִיב לְמִשְׁפְּחֹתָם׃ וְהָיוּ הֶעָרִים לְמַטֵּה בְּנֵי בִנְיָמִן לְמִשְׁפְּחוֹתֵיהֶם
כב יְרִיחוֹ וּבֵית־חָגְלָה וְעֵמֶק קְצִיץ׃ וּבֵית הָעֲרָבָה וּצְמָרַיִם וּבֵית־אֵל׃
כג כד וְהָעַוִּים וְהַפָּרָה וְעָפְרָה׃ וּכְפַר העמוני וְהָעָפְנִי וָגָבַע עָרִים שְׁתֵּים־ הָעַמֹּנָה
כה כו עֶשְׂרֵה וְחַצְרֵיהֶן׃ גִּבְעוֹן וְהָרָמָה וּבְאֵרוֹת׃ וְהַמִּצְפֶּה וְהַכְּפִירָה וְהַמֹּצָה׃
כז כח וְרֶקֶם וְיִרְפְּאֵל וְתַרְאֲלָה׃ וְצֵלַע הָאֶלֶף וְהַיְבוּסִי הִיא יְרוּשָׁלַםִ גִּבְעַת יא
קִרְיַת עָרִים אַרְבַּע־עֶשְׂרֵה וְחַצְרֵיהֶן זֹאת נַחֲלַת בְּנֵי־בִנְיָמִן
יט א לְמִשְׁפְּחֹתָם׃ וַיֵּצֵא הַגּוֹרָל הַשֵּׁנִי לְשִׁמְעוֹן לְמַטֵּה בְנֵי־
ב שִׁמְעוֹן לְמִשְׁפְּחוֹתָם וַיְהִי נַחֲלָתָם בְּתוֹךְ נַחֲלַת בְּנֵי־יְהוּדָה׃ וַיְהִי לָהֶם
ג בְּנַחֲלָתָם בְּאֵר־שֶׁבַע וְשֶׁבַע וּמוֹלָדָה׃ וַחֲצַר שׁוּעָל וּבָלָה וָעָצֶם׃
ד ה ו וְאֶלְתּוֹלַד וּבְתוּל וְחָרְמָה׃ וְצִקְלַג וּבֵית־הַמַּרְכָּבוֹת וַחֲצַר סוּסָה׃ וּבֵית
ז לְבָאוֹת וְשָׁרוּחֶן עָרִים שְׁלֹשׁ־עֶשְׂרֵה וְחַצְרֵיהֶן׃ עַיִן רִמּוֹן וָעֶתֶר וְעָשָׁן
ח עָרִים אַרְבַּע וְחַצְרֵיהֶן׃ וְכָל־הַחֲצֵרִים אֲשֶׁר סְבִיבוֹת הֶעָרִים הָאֵלֶּה
עַד־בַּעֲלַת בְּאֵר רָאמַת נֶגֶב זֹאת נַחֲלַת מַטֵּה בְנֵי־שִׁמְעוֹן לְמִשְׁפְּחֹתָם׃
ט מֵחֶבֶל בְּנֵי יְהוּדָה נַחֲלַת בְּנֵי שִׁמְעוֹן כִּי־הָיָה חֵלֶק בְּנֵי־יְהוּדָה רַב
י מֵהֶם וַיִּנְחֲלוּ בְנֵי־שִׁמְעוֹן בְּתוֹךְ נַחֲלָתָם׃ וַיַּעַל הַגּוֹרָל
יא הַשְּׁלִישִׁי לִבְנֵי זְבוּלֻן לְמִשְׁפְּחֹתָם וַיְהִי גְּבוּל נַחֲלָתָם עַד־שָׂרִיד׃ וְעָלָה
גְבוּלָם ׀ לַיָּמָּה וּמַרְעֲלָה וּפָגַע בְּדַבָּשֶׁת וּפָגַע אֶל־הַנַּחַל אֲשֶׁר עַל־פְּנֵי
יב יָקְנְעָם׃ וְשָׁב מִשָּׂרִיד קֵדְמָה מִזְרַח הַשֶּׁמֶשׁ עַל־גְּבוּל כִּסְלֹת תָּבֹר
יג וְיָצָא אֶל־הַדָּבְרַת וְעָלָה יָפִיעַ׃ וּמִשָּׁם עָבַר קֵדְמָה מִזְרָחָה גִּתָּה חֵפֶר
יד עִתָּה קָצִין וְיָצָא רִמּוֹן הַמְּתֹאָר הַנֵּעָה׃ וְנָסַב אֹתוֹ הַגְּבוּל מִצְּפוֹן חַנָּתֹן
טו וְהָיוּ תֹּצְאֹתָיו גֵּי יִפְתַּח־אֵל׃ וְקַטָּת וְנַהֲלָל וְשִׁמְרוֹן וְיִדְאֲלָה וּבֵית
טז לָחֶם עָרִים שְׁתֵּים־עֶשְׂרֵה וְחַצְרֵיהֶן׃ זֹאת נַחֲלַת בְּנֵי־זְבוּלֻן לְמִשְׁפְּחוֹתָם
יז הֶעָרִים הָאֵלֶּה וְחַצְרֵיהֶן׃ לְיִשָּׂשכָר יָצָא הַגּוֹרָל הָרְבִיעִי
יח לִבְנֵי יִשָּׂשכָר לְמִשְׁפְּחוֹתָם׃ וַיְהִי גְּבוּלָם יִזְרְעֶאלָה וְהַכְּסוּלֹת וְשׁוּנֵם׃
יט כ כא וַחֲפָרַיִם וְשִׁיאֹן וַאֲנָחֲרַת׃ וְהָרַבִּית וְקִשְׁיוֹן וָאָבֶץ׃ וְרֶמֶת וְעֵין־גַּנִּים
כב וְעֵין חַדָּה וּבֵית פַּצֵּץ׃ וּפָגַע הַגְּבוּל בְּתָבוֹר ושחצומה וּבֵית שֶׁמֶשׁ וְשַׁחֲצִימָה

23 their villages. This was the tribe of Yissakhar's estate, divided by their
24 clans – the cities and their villages. The fifth lot fell to the tribe of
25 the Asherites by their clans. Their border encompassed Ḥelkat, Ḥali, Beten,
26 and Akhshaf, Alamelekh, Amad, and Mishal, then touched Carmel on the
27 west and Shiḥor Livnat; it turned back to the east toward Beit Dagon and
reached Zevulun and the Yiftaḥ El Valley to the north, Beit HaEmek and
28 Ne'iel, and continued on to Kabul on the north, Evron, Reḥov, Ḥamon, and
29 Kana, up to Greater Sidon; the border then turned back toward Rama to the
fortified city of Tyre; then the border turned back toward Ḥosa and ended
30 at the sea by the Akhziva district. With Uma, Afek, and Reḥov, there were
31 twenty-two cities with their villages. This was the tribe of Asher's estate,
32 divided by their clans; these cities and their villages. The sixth lot
33 fell to Naftali, to the tribe of the Naftalites by their clans. Their border ran
from Ḥelef, Elon in Tzaananim, Adami HaNekev, and Yavne'el, to Lakum,
34 and ended at the Jordan; the border then turned back westward to Aznot
Tavor and from there continued toward Ḥukok, reaching Zevulun at the
35 south, Asher at the west, and Yehuda at the Jordan to the east. Its fortified
36 cities were Tzidim, Tzer, Ḥamat, Rakat, and Kinneret, Adama, Rama, and
37 38 Ḥatzor, Kedesh, Edre'i, and Ein Ḥatzor, Yiron, Migdal El, Ḥorem, Beit Anat,
39 and Beit Shemesh: nineteen cities with their villages. This was the tribe of
Naftali's estate, divided according to its clans – the cities and their
40 41 villages. The seventh lot fell to the tribe of Dan by their clans. The
42 borders of their estate ran through Tzora, Eshta'ol, and Ir Shemesh, Shaalabin,
43 44 Ayalon, and Yitla, Eilon, Timna, and Ekron, Eltekeh, Gibeton, and Baalat,
45 46 Yehud, Benei Berak, and Gat Rimon, and the waters of the Yarkon and Rakon,
47 including the shoreline facing Jaffa. But the Danite territory was not sufficient
for them, so the Danites marched up to Leshem, captured it, and put it to the
sword. They took possession of it and settled it, renaming Leshem as Dan
48 after their ancestor Dan. This was the tribe of Dan's estate, divided by their
49 clans; these cities and their villages. When they had finished
allotting the land, with all its borders, the Israelites bestowed an estate on
50 Yehoshua son of Nun among them. At the Lord's word, they gave him the
city he requested: Timnat Seraḥ in the hill country of Efrayim. He built up
51 the city and settled it. These are the estates that the priest Elazar,
Yehoshua son of Nun, and the clan leaders allotted to the Israelite tribes at
Shilo, before the Lord, at the entrance to the Tent of Meeting. And so they
finished dividing up the land.
20 1 2 The Lord spoke to Yehoshua, saying, "Tell the Israelites: assign yourselves
3 the cities of refuge I bid you through Moshe,[19] so that an accidental, unwitting
killer – a manslaughterer – may flee there; they shall give him refuge from the

19 | See Numbers, chapter 35, and Deuteronomy 5:41–49.

כג וְהָיוּ תֹּצְאוֹת גְּבוּלָם הַיַּרְדֵּן עָרִים שֵׁשׁ־עֶשְׂרֵה וְחַצְרֵיהֶן: זֹאת נַחֲלַת
כד מַטֵּה בְנֵי־יִשָּׂשכָר לְמִשְׁפְּחֹתָם הֶעָרִים וְחַצְרֵיהֶן: וַיֵּצֵא
כה הַגּוֹרָל הַחֲמִישִׁי לְמַטֵּה בְנֵי־אָשֵׁר לְמִשְׁפְּחוֹתָם: וַיְהִי גְּבוּלָם חֶלְקַת
כו וַחֲלִי וָבֶטֶן וְאַכְשָׁף: וְאַלַּמֶּלֶךְ וְעַמְעָד וּמִשְׁאָל וּפָגַע בְּכַרְמֶל הַיָּמָּה
כז וּבְשִׁיחוֹר לִבְנָת: וְשָׁב מִזְרַח הַשֶּׁמֶשׁ בֵּית דָּגֹן וּפָגַע בִּזְבֻלוּן וּבְגֵי יִפְתַּח־
כח אֵל צָפוֹנָה בֵּית הָעֵמֶק וּנְעִיאֵל וְיָצָא אֶל־כָּבוּל מִשְּׂמֹאל: וְעֶבְרֹן וּרְחֹב
כט וְחַמּוֹן וְקָנָה עַד צִידוֹן רַבָּה: וְשָׁב הַגְּבוּל הָרָמָה וְעַד־עִיר מִבְצַר־צֹר
ל וְשָׁב הַגְּבוּל חֹסָה ויהיו תֹצְאֹתָיו הַיָּמָּה מֵחֶבֶל אַכְזִיבָה: וְעֻמָה וַאֲפֵק וְהָיוּ
לא וּרְחֹב עָרִים עֶשְׂרִים וּשְׁתַּיִם וְחַצְרֵיהֶן: זֹאת נַחֲלַת מַטֵּה בְנֵי־אָשֵׁר
לב לְמִשְׁפְּחֹתָם הֶעָרִים הָאֵלֶּה וְחַצְרֵיהֶן: לִבְנֵי נַפְתָּלִי יָצָא
לג הַגּוֹרָל הַשִּׁשִּׁי לִבְנֵי נַפְתָּלִי לְמִשְׁפְּחֹתָם: וַיְהִי גְבוּלָם מֵחֵלֶף מֵאֵלוֹן
לד בְּצַעֲנַנִּים וַאֲדָמִי הַנֶּקֶב וְיַבְנְאֵל עַד־לַקּוּם וַיְהִי תֹצְאֹתָיו הַיַּרְדֵּן: וְשָׁב
הַגְּבוּל יָמָּה אַזְנוֹת תָּבוֹר וְיָצָא מִשָּׁם חוּקֹקָה וּפָגַע בִּזְבֻלוּן מִנֶּגֶב
לה וּבְאָשֵׁר פָּגַע מִיָּם וּבִיהוּדָה הַיַּרְדֵּן מִזְרַח הַשָּׁמֶשׁ: וְעָרֵי מִבְצָר הַצִּדִּים
לו לז צֵר וְחַמַּת רַקַּת וְכִנָּרֶת: וַאֲדָמָה וְהָרָמָה וְחָצוֹר: וְקֶדֶשׁ וְאֶדְרֶעִי וְעֵין
לח חָצוֹר: וְיִרְאוֹן וּמִגְדַּל־אֵל חֳרֵם וּבֵית־עֲנָת וּבֵית שָׁמֶשׁ עָרִים תְּשַׁע־
לט עֶשְׂרֵה וְחַצְרֵיהֶן: זֹאת נַחֲלַת מַטֵּה בְנֵי־נַפְתָּלִי לְמִשְׁפְּחֹתָם הֶעָרִים
מ וְחַצְרֵיהֶן: לְמַטֵּה בְנֵי־דָן לְמִשְׁפְּחֹתָם יָצָא הַגּוֹרָל הַשְּׁבִיעִי:
מא מב וַיְהִי גְּבוּל נַחֲלָתָם צָרְעָה וְאֶשְׁתָּאוֹל וְעִיר שָׁמֶשׁ: וְשַׁעֲלַבִּין וְאַיָּלוֹן
מג מד מה וְיִתְלָה: וְאֵילוֹן וְתִמְנָתָה וְעֶקְרוֹן: וְאֶלְתְּקֵה וְגִבְּתוֹן וּבַעֲלָת: וִיהֻד
מו מז וּבְנֵי־בְרַק וְגַת־רִמּוֹן: וּמֵי הַיַּרְקוֹן וְהָרַקּוֹן עִם־הַגְּבוּל מוּל יָפוֹ: וַיֵּצֵא
גְּבוּל בְּנֵי־דָן מֵהֶם וַיַּעֲלוּ בְנֵי־דָן וַיִּלָּחֲמוּ עִם־לֶשֶׁם וַיִּלְכְּדוּ אוֹתָהּ ׀
וַיַּכּוּ אוֹתָהּ לְפִי־חֶרֶב וַיִּרְשׁוּ אוֹתָהּ וַיֵּשְׁבוּ בָהּ וַיִּקְרְאוּ לְלֶשֶׁם דָּן כְּשֵׁם
מח דָּן אֲבִיהֶם: זֹאת נַחֲלַת מַטֵּה בְנֵי־דָן לְמִשְׁפְּחֹתָם הֶעָרִים הָאֵלֶּה
מט וְחַצְרֵיהֶן: וַיְכַלּוּ לִנְחֹל אֶת־הָאָרֶץ לִגְבוּלֹתֶיהָ וַיִּתְּנוּ בְנֵי־
נ יִשְׂרָאֵל נַחֲלָה לִיהוֹשֻׁעַ בִּן־נוּן בְּתוֹכָם: עַל־פִּי יְהוָה נָתְנוּ לוֹ אֶת־
הָעִיר אֲשֶׁר שָׁאָל אֶת־תִּמְנַת־סֶרַח בְּהַר אֶפְרָיִם וַיִּבְנֶה אֶת־הָעִיר
נא וַיֵּשֶׁב בָּהּ: אֵלֶּה הַנְּחָלֹת אֲשֶׁר נִחֲלוּ אֶלְעָזָר הַכֹּהֵן ׀ יב
וִיהוֹשֻׁעַ בִּן־נוּן וְרָאשֵׁי הָאָבוֹת לְמַטּוֹת בְּנֵי־יִשְׂרָאֵל ׀ בְּגוֹרָל ׀ בְּשִׁלֹה
לִפְנֵי יְהוָה פֶּתַח אֹהֶל מוֹעֵד וַיְכַלּוּ מֵחַלֵּק אֶת־הָאָרֶץ:
כ א ב וַיְדַבֵּר יְהוָה אֶל־יְהוֹשֻׁעַ לֵאמֹר: דַּבֵּר אֶל־בְּנֵי יִשְׂרָאֵל לֵאמֹר תְּנוּ לָכֶם
ג אֶת־עָרֵי הַמִּקְלָט אֲשֶׁר־דִּבַּרְתִּי אֲלֵיכֶם בְּיַד־מֹשֶׁה: לָנוּס שָׁמָּה רוֹצֵחַ

4 blood avenger. When he flees to one of these cities, he shall stand by the
entrance of the city gate and plead his case before the city elders, and then
they will receive him into the city and give him a place to live among them.
5 If the blood avenger pursues him, they will not hand the killer over to him,
6 for he struck his fellow man unintentionally; he never hated him before. He
shall dwell in that city until he stands trial before the court. Upon the death
of the High Priest of that time, and only then, the killer may return to his
7 hometown and home, to the city from which he fled." So they dedicated
Kedesh in the Naftali hills in the Galilee, and Shekhem in the Efrayim hills,
8 and Kiryat Arba – that is, Ḥevron – in the Judean hills. Across the Jordan,
east of Yeriḥo, they assigned Betzer in the wilderness on the plain of the tribe
9 of Reuven, Ramot in Gadite Gilad, and Golan in the Manassite Bashan. In
any case of accidental manslaughter, any Israelite – or stranger staying
among them – could flee to any of these designated cities so that they would
not die at the hand of the blood avenger before standing trial before the
21 1 court. The ancestral heads of the Levites approached the priest
Elazar, Yehoshua son of Nun, and the ancestral heads of the tribes of Israel
2 and spoke to them at Shilo in the land of Canaan: "The LORD commanded,
through Moshe, that you give us cities to live in and pastureland for our
3 livestock." So, at the LORD's word, the Israelites gave the Levites these cities
4 and pasturelands from their own estates. The first lot fell to the
Kehatite clan, and the sons of Aharon the priest of the Levites received
thirteen cities, by lot, from the tribe of Yehuda, the tribe of Shimon, and the
5 tribe of Binyamin. The remaining Kehatites received ten cities by
lot from clans of the tribe of Efrayim, the tribe of Dan, and half of the tribe
6 of Menashe. The sons of Gershon received thirteen cities by lot from
the clans of the tribe of Yissakhar, the tribe of Asher, the tribe of Naftali, and
7 half the tribe of Menashe in the Bashan. The Merarites by their clans
received twelve cities from the tribe of Reuven, the tribe of Gad, and the
8 tribe of Zevulun. The Israelites gave these cities and their
pasturelands to the Levites by lot, as the LORD had commanded through
9 Moshe. The Judahite tribe and the Simeonite tribe gave these cities,
10 listed below by name, to the sons of Aharon, of the Levite Kehatites, for the
11 lot fell to them first. They gave them Kiryat Arba,[20] who was father of the
Anakites – that is, Ḥevron – in the Judean hills, and all the pastureland around
12 it; but the fields within the city and its villages were given to Kalev son of
13 Yefuneh as his property.[21] To the sons of the priest Aharon, they

20 | Meaning the City of Arba.

21 | The *migrash*, here translated "pastureland," refers to the band of land around the city and adjacent to its walls, used for sheep and goat pens and for other agricultural installations and equipment. The fields (*sadeh*) of the city were farther away, beyond the pasturelands.

מַכֵּה־נֶפֶשׁ בִּשְׁגָגָה בִּבְלִי־דָעַת וְהָיוּ לָכֶם לְמִקְלָט מִגֹּאֵל הַדָּם׃
ד וְנָס אֶל־אַחַת ׀ מֵהֶעָרִים הָאֵלֶּה וְעָמַד פֶּתַח שַׁעַר הָעִיר וְדִבֶּר בְּאָזְנֵי
זִקְנֵי הָעִיר־הַהִיא אֶת־דְּבָרָיו וְאָסְפוּ אֹתוֹ הָעִירָה אֲלֵיהֶם וְנָתְנוּ־לוֹ
ה מָקוֹם וְיָשַׁב עִמָּם׃ וְכִי יִרְדֹּף גֹּאֵל הַדָּם אַחֲרָיו וְלֹא־יַסְגִּרוּ אֶת־הָרֹצֵחַ
בְּיָדוֹ כִּי בִבְלִי־דַעַת הִכָּה אֶת־רֵעֵהוּ וְלֹא־שֹׂנֵא הוּא לוֹ מִתְּמוֹל
ו שִׁלְשׁוֹם׃ וְיָשַׁב ׀ בָּעִיר הַהִיא עַד־עָמְדוֹ לִפְנֵי הָעֵדָה לַמִּשְׁפָּט עַד־מוֹת
הַכֹּהֵן הַגָּדוֹל אֲשֶׁר יִהְיֶה בַּיָּמִים הָהֵם אָז ׀ יָשׁוּב הָרוֹצֵחַ וּבָא אֶל־עִירוֹ
ז וְאֶל־בֵּיתוֹ אֶל־הָעִיר אֲשֶׁר־נָס מִשָּׁם׃ וַיַּקְדִּשׁוּ אֶת־קֶדֶשׁ בַּגָּלִיל בְּהַר
נַפְתָּלִי וְאֶת־שְׁכֶם בְּהַר אֶפְרָיִם וְאֶת־קִרְיַת אַרְבַּע הִיא חֶבְרוֹן בְּהַר
ח יְהוּדָה׃ וּמֵעֵבֶר לְיַרְדֵּן יְרִיחוֹ מִזְרָחָה נָתְנוּ אֶת־בֶּצֶר בַּמִּדְבָּר בַּמִּישֹׁר
מִמַּטֵּה רְאוּבֵן וְאֶת־רָאמֹת בַּגִּלְעָד מִמַּטֵּה־גָד וְאֶת־גלון בַּבָּשָׁן מִמַּטֵּה גּוֹלָן
ט מְנַשֶּׁה׃ אֵלֶּה הָיוּ עָרֵי הַמּוּעָדָה לְכֹל ׀ בְּנֵי יִשְׂרָאֵל וְלַגֵּר הַגָּר בְּתוֹכָם
לָנוּס שָׁמָּה כָּל־מַכֵּה־נֶפֶשׁ בִּשְׁגָגָה וְלֹא יָמוּת בְּיַד גֹּאֵל הַדָּם עַד־עָמְדוֹ
כא א לִפְנֵי הָעֵדָה׃ וַיִּגְּשׁוּ רָאשֵׁי אֲבוֹת הַלְוִיִּם אֶל־אֶלְעָזָר הַכֹּהֵן
ב וְאֶל־יְהוֹשֻׁעַ בִּן־נוּן וְאֶל־רָאשֵׁי אֲבוֹת הַמַּטּוֹת לִבְנֵי יִשְׂרָאֵל׃ וַיְדַבְּרוּ
אֲלֵיהֶם בְּשִׁלֹה בְּאֶרֶץ כְּנַעַן לֵאמֹר יְהוָה צִוָּה בְיַד־מֹשֶׁה לָתֶת־לָנוּ עָרִים
ג לָשָׁבֶת וּמִגְרְשֵׁיהֶן לִבְהֶמְתֵּנוּ׃ וַיִּתְּנוּ בְנֵי־יִשְׂרָאֵל לַלְוִיִּם מִנַּחֲלָתָם
ד אֶל־פִּי יְהוָה אֶת־הֶעָרִים הָאֵלֶּה וְאֶת־מִגְרְשֵׁיהֶן׃ וַיֵּצֵא
הַגּוֹרָל לְמִשְׁפְּחֹת הַקְּהָתִי וַיְהִי לִבְנֵי אַהֲרֹן הַכֹּהֵן מִן־הַלְוִיִּם
מִמַּטֵּה יְהוּדָה וּמִמַּטֵּה הַשִּׁמְעֹנִי וּמִמַּטֵּה בִנְיָמִן בַּגּוֹרָל עָרִים שְׁלֹשׁ
ה עֶשְׂרֵה׃ וְלִבְנֵי קְהָת הַנּוֹתָרִים מִמִּשְׁפְּחֹת מַטֵּה־אֶפְרַיִם
ו וּמִמַּטֵּה־דָן וּמֵחֲצִי מַטֵּה מְנַשֶּׁה בַּגּוֹרָל עָרִים עָשֶׂר׃ וְלִבְנֵי
גֵרְשׁוֹן מִמִּשְׁפְּחוֹת מַטֵּה־יִשָּׂשכָר וּמִמַּטֵּה־אָשֵׁר וּמִמַּטֵּה נַפְתָּלִי וּמֵחֲצִי
ז מַטֵּה מְנַשֶּׁה בַבָּשָׁן בַּגּוֹרָל עָרִים שְׁלֹשׁ עֶשְׂרֵה׃ לִבְנֵי מְרָרִי
לְמִשְׁפְּחֹתָם מִמַּטֵּה רְאוּבֵן וּמִמַּטֵּה־גָד וּמִמַּטֵּה זְבוּלֻן עָרִים שְׁתֵּים
ח עֶשְׂרֵה׃ וַיִּתְּנוּ בְנֵי־יִשְׂרָאֵל לַלְוִיִּם אֶת־הֶעָרִים הָאֵלֶּה וְאֶת־
ט מִגְרְשֵׁיהֶן כַּאֲשֶׁר צִוָּה יְהוָה בְּיַד־מֹשֶׁה בַּגּוֹרָל׃ וַיִּתְּנוּ
מִמַּטֵּה בְּנֵי יְהוּדָה וּמִמַּטֵּה בְּנֵי שִׁמְעוֹן אֵת הֶעָרִים הָאֵלֶּה אֲשֶׁר־יִקְרָא
י אֶתְהֶן בְּשֵׁם׃ וַיְהִי לִבְנֵי אַהֲרֹן מִמִּשְׁפְּחוֹת הַקְּהָתִי מִבְּנֵי לֵוִי כִּי לָהֶם
יא הָיָה הַגּוֹרָל רִאישֹׁנָה׃ וַיִּתְּנוּ לָהֶם אֶת־קִרְיַת אַרְבַּע אֲבִי הָעֲנוֹק הִיא
יב חֶבְרוֹן בְּהַר יְהוּדָה וְאֶת־מִגְרָשֶׁהָ סְבִיבֹתֶיהָ׃ וְאֶת־שְׂדֵה הָעִיר וְאֶת־
יג חֲצֵרֶיהָ נָתְנוּ לְכָלֵב בֶּן־יְפֻנֶּה בַּאֲחֻזָּתוֹ׃ וְלִבְנֵי ׀ אַהֲרֹן הַכֹּהֵן

gave the killers' city of refuge – that is, Ḥevron – and its pasturelands, and
14 Livna and its pasturelands, Yatir and its pasturelands, Eshtemoa and its
15 16 pasturelands, Ḥolon and its pasturelands, Devir and its pasturelands, Ayin
and its pasturelands, Yuta and its pasturelands, and Beit Shemesh and its
17 pasturelands; nine cities from these two tribes. From the tribe
18 of Binyamin: Givon and its pasturelands, Geva and its pasturelands, Anatot
19 and its pasturelands, and Almon and its pasturelands; four cities. In
all, the cities of Aharon's sons numbered thirteen cities with their
20 pasturelands. As for the Levite Kehatite clans – the remaining
Kehatites – the cities that fell to them by lot were from the tribe of Efrayim.
21 They were given the killers' city of refuge Shekhem and its pasturelands in
22 the Efrayim hills, Gezer and its pasturelands, Kivtzayim and its pasturelands,
23 and Beit Ḥoron and its pasturelands – four cities. From the
tribe of Dan: Eltekeh and its pasturelands, Gibeton and its pasturelands,
24 Ayalon and its pasturelands, and Gat Rimon and its pasturelands – four
25 cities. From half the tribe of Menashe: Tanakh and its pasturelands
26 and Gat Rimon and its pasturelands – two cities. Ten cities in all and their
27 pasturelands for the remaining Kehatites. As for the Gershonite clan
of the Levites, from half the tribe of Menashe: the killers' city of refuge Golan
in Bashan and its pasturelands, and Be'eshtera and its pasturelands – two
28 cities. From the tribe of Yissakhar: Kishyon and its pasturelands,
29 Daverat and its pasturelands, Yarmut and its pasturelands, and Ein Ganim
30 and its pasturelands – four cities. From the tribe of Asher: Mishal
31 and its pasturelands, Avdon and its pasturelands, Ḥelkat and its pasturelands,
32 and Reḥov and its pasturelands – four cities. From the tribe of
Naftali: the killers' city of refuge Kedesh in Galilee and its pasturelands,
Ḥamot Dor and its pasturelands, and Kartan and its pasturelands – three
33 cities. In all, the cities of the Gershonite clan numbered thirteen cities with
34 their pasturelands. As for the Merarite clan, the remaining
Levites: from the tribe of Zevulun: Yokne'am and its pasturelands, Karta
35 and its pasturelands, Dimna and its pasturelands,[22] and Nahalal and its

---

22 | A parallel list of Levitical cities in 1 Chronicles, chapter 6, includes a description of cities from the tribe of Reuven, which can be seen in smaller font in the Hebrew text on the facing page. Mention of these cities in Joshua does not appear in most manuscripts, and our English translation does not include this description (cf. 1 Ch. 6:63–64), which reads as follows: "Beyond the Jordan at Yeriḥo, on the east side of the Jordan, from the tribe of Reuven: Betzer in the wilderness with its pasturelands, Yahtza with its pasturelands, Kedemot with its pasturelands, and Meifaat with its pasturelands."

נָתְנוּ אֶת־עִיר מִקְלַט הָרֹצֵחַ אֶת־חֶבְרוֹן וְאֶת־מִגְרָשֶׁהָ וְאֶת־לִבְנָה
יד וְאֶת־מִגְרָשֶׁהָ: וְאֶת־יַתִּר וְאֶת־מִגְרָשֶׁהָ וְאֶת־אֶשְׁתְּמוֹעַ וְאֶת־מִגְרָשֶׁהָ:
טו טז וְאֶת־חֹלֹן וְאֶת־מִגְרָשֶׁהָ וְאֶת־דְּבִר וְאֶת־מִגְרָשֶׁהָ: וְאֶת־עַיִן וְאֶת־
מִגְרָשֶׁהָ וְאֶת־יֻטָּה וְאֶת־מִגְרָשֶׁהָ אֶת־בֵּית שֶׁמֶשׁ וְאֶת־מִגְרָשֶׁהָ עָרִים
יז תֵּשַׁע מֵאֵת שְׁנֵי הַשְּׁבָטִים הָאֵלֶּה: וּמִמַּטֵּה בִנְיָמִן אֶת־
יח גִּבְעוֹן וְאֶת־מִגְרָשֶׁהָ אֶת־גֶּבַע וְאֶת־מִגְרָשֶׁהָ: אֶת־עֲנָתוֹת וְאֶת־
יט מִגְרָשֶׁהָ וְאֶת־עַלְמוֹן וְאֶת־מִגְרָשֶׁהָ עָרִים אַרְבַּע: כָּל־עָרֵי בְנֵי־אַהֲרֹן
כ הַכֹּהֲנִים שְׁלֹשׁ־עֶשְׂרֵה עָרִים וּמִגְרְשֵׁיהֶן: וּלְמִשְׁפְּחוֹת בְּנֵי־
קְהָת הַלְוִיִּם הַנּוֹתָרִים מִבְּנֵי קְהָת וַיְהִי עָרֵי גוֹרָלָם מִמַּטֵּה אֶפְרָיִם:
כא וַיִּתְּנוּ לָהֶם אֶת־עִיר מִקְלַט הָרֹצֵחַ אֶת־שְׁכֶם וְאֶת־מִגְרָשֶׁהָ בְּהַר
כב אֶפְרָיִם וְאֶת־גֶּזֶר וְאֶת־מִגְרָשֶׁהָ: וְאֶת־קִבְצַיִם וְאֶת־מִגְרָשֶׁהָ וְאֶת־בֵּית
כג חוֹרֹן וְאֶת־מִגְרָשֶׁהָ עָרִים אַרְבַּע: וּמִמַּטֵּה־דָן אֶת־אֶלְתְּקֵא
כד וְאֶת־מִגְרָשֶׁהָ אֶת־גִּבְּתוֹן וְאֶת־מִגְרָשֶׁהָ: אֶת־אַיָּלוֹן וְאֶת־מִגְרָשֶׁהָ
כה אֶת־גַּת־רִמּוֹן וְאֶת־מִגְרָשֶׁהָ עָרִים אַרְבַּע: וּמִמַּחֲצִית
מַטֵּה מְנַשֶּׁה אֶת־תַּעְנַךְ וְאֶת־מִגְרָשֶׁהָ וְאֶת־גַּת רִמּוֹן וְאֶת־מִגְרָשֶׁהָ
כו עָרִים שְׁתָּיִם: כָּל־עָרִים עֶשֶׂר וּמִגְרְשֵׁיהֶן לְמִשְׁפְּחוֹת בְּנֵי־קְהָת
כז הַנּוֹתָרִים: וְלִבְנֵי גֵרְשׁוֹן מִמִּשְׁפְּחֹת הַלְוִיִּם מֵחֲצִי מַטֵּה
מְנַשֶּׁה אֶת־עִיר מִקְלַט הָרֹצֵחַ אֶת־גלון בַּבָּשָׁן וְאֶת־מִגְרָשֶׁהָ וְאֶת־ גּוֹלָן
כח בְּעֶשְׁתְּרָה וְאֶת־מִגְרָשֶׁהָ עָרִים שְׁתָּיִם: וּמִמַּטֵּה יִשָּׂשכָר
כט אֶת־קִשְׁיוֹן וְאֶת־מִגְרָשֶׁהָ אֶת־דָּבְרַת וְאֶת־מִגְרָשֶׁהָ: אֶת־יַרְמוּת וְאֶת־
ל מִגְרָשֶׁהָ אֶת־עֵין גַּנִּים וְאֶת־מִגְרָשֶׁהָ עָרִים אַרְבַּע: וּמִמַּטֵּה
אָשֵׁר אֶת־מִשְׁאָל וְאֶת־מִגְרָשֶׁהָ אֶת־עַבְדּוֹן וְאֶת־מִגְרָשֶׁהָ:
לא אֶת־חֶלְקָת וְאֶת־מִגְרָשֶׁהָ וְאֶת־רְחֹב וְאֶת־מִגְרָשֶׁהָ עָרִים
לב אַרְבַּע: וּמִמַּטֵּה נַפְתָּלִי אֶת־עִיר ׀ מִקְלַט הָרֹצֵחַ אֶת־קֶדֶשׁ
בַּגָּלִיל וְאֶת־מִגְרָשֶׁהָ וְאֶת־חַמֹּת דֹּאר וְאֶת־מִגְרָשֶׁהָ וְאֶת־קַרְתָּן וְאֶת־
לג מִגְרָשֶׁהָ עָרִים שָׁלֹשׁ: כָּל־עָרֵי הַגֵּרְשֻׁנִּי לְמִשְׁפְּחֹתָם שְׁלֹשׁ־עֶשְׂרֵה
לד עִיר וּמִגְרְשֵׁיהֶן: וּלְמִשְׁפְּחוֹת בְּנֵי־מְרָרִי הַלְוִיִּם הַנּוֹתָרִים
מֵאֵת מַטֵּה זְבוּלֻן אֶת־יָקְנְעָם וְאֶת־מִגְרָשֶׁהָ אֶת־קַרְתָּה וְאֶת־
לה מִגְרָשֶׁהָ: אֶת־דִּמְנָה וְאֶת־מִגְרָשֶׁהָ אֶת־נַהֲלָל וְאֶת־מִגְרָשֶׁהָ עָרִים

בקצת ספרים אחר פסוק לה
וּמִמַּטֵּה רְאוּבֵן אֶת־בֶּצֶר וְאֶת־מִגְרָשֶׁהָ וְאֶת־יַהְצָה וְאֶת־מִגְרָשֶׁהָ: אֶת־קְדֵמוֹת
וְאֶת־מִגְרָשֶׁהָ וְאֶת־מֵיפַעַת וְאֶת־מִגְרָשֶׁהָ עָרִים אַרְבַּע:

36 pasturelands – four cities. From the tribe of Gad: the killers' city of
refuge Ramot in Gilad and its pasturelands, Maḥanayim and its pasturelands,
37 Ḥeshbon and its pasturelands, and Yazer and its pasturelands – four cities in
38 all. In all, the Merarite clans – the remaining Levites – were
39 allotted twelve cities. In all, the Levite cities in the midst of the Israelite
40 territories numbered forty-eight cities with their pasturelands. These were
the cities; each city was surrounded by its pasturelands, and so it was with
41 every one of these cities. The LORD gave Israel the entire land He
had sworn to give their ancestors; they took possession of it and settled in it.
42 The LORD granted them rest on all sides, just as He had sworn to their
ancestors. Not a single one of their enemies withstood them – the LORD
43 delivered all their enemies into their hands. Not one of the good things the
LORD had promised the House of Israel was wanting; everything came to
22 1 pass. Then Yehoshua summoned the Reubenites, the Gadites, and
2 half the tribe of Menashe and said to them, "You have performed everything
that Moshe, the LORD's servant, commanded you, and you have obeyed me
3 in all that I commanded you. You have not abandoned your brothers all this
time – to this very day – and you have fulfilled the charge of the LORD your
4 God's command. Now the LORD your God has granted rest to your brothers,
as He promised them, so turn now and make your way home to the lands of
your holding, which Moshe, the LORD's servant, assigned to you beyond the
5 Jordan. Only take great care to fulfill the laws and teachings that Moshe, the
LORD's servant, commanded you to follow, to love the LORD your God, to
walk in all His ways, to keep His commandments, to cling to Him, and to
6 serve Him with all your heart and all your soul." Yehoshua blessed them and
7 sent them off, and they made their way home. Moshe had
assigned the Bashan to half the tribe of Menashe, while to the other half
Yehoshua had assigned land with their brothers on the western side of the
8 Jordan. Yehoshua also sent them off and blessed them. "Go back home with
great wealth," he said to them, "with great wealth in cattle, silver and gold,
bronze and iron, and a great many garments. Share the spoils of your enemies
9 with your brothers." So the Reubenites, the Gadites, and half the
tribe of Menashe returned, setting out from the Israelites at Shilo in the land
of Canaan toward the land of the Gilad to the land of their holding, where
they had taken possession because of the LORD's word transmitted through
10 Moshe. They arrived at the Jordan region in the land of Canaan, and there
beside the Jordan, the Reubenites, the Gadites, and half the tribe of Menashe
11 built an altar – an altar mighty to behold. Word reached the Israelites: "The
Reubenites, the Gadites, and half the tribe of Menashe have built an altar

לו אַרְבַּע׃ וּמִמַּטֵּה־גָד אֶת־עִיר מִקְלַט הָרֹצֵחַ אֶת־רָמֹת
לז בַּגִּלְעָד וְאֶת־מִגְרָשֶׁהָ וְאֶת־מַחֲנַיִם וְאֶת־מִגְרָשֶׁהָ׃ אֶת־חֶשְׁבּוֹן וְאֶת־
לח מִגְרָשֶׁהָ אֶת־יַעְזֵר וְאֶת־מִגְרָשֶׁהָ כָּל־עָרִים אַרְבַּע׃ כָּל־
הֶעָרִים לִבְנֵי מְרָרִי לְמִשְׁפְּחֹתָם הַנּוֹתָרִים מִמִּשְׁפְּחוֹת הַלְוִיִּם וַיְהִי
לט גּוֹרָלָם עָרִים שְׁתֵּים עֶשְׂרֵה׃ כֹּל עָרֵי הַלְוִיִּם בְּתוֹךְ אֲחֻזַּת בְּנֵי־יִשְׂרָאֵל
מ עָרִים אַרְבָּעִים וּשְׁמֹנֶה וּמִגְרְשֵׁיהֶן׃ תִּהְיֶינָה הֶעָרִים הָאֵלֶּה עִיר עִיר
מא וּמִגְרָשֶׁיהָ סְבִיבֹתֶיהָ כֵּן לְכָל־הֶעָרִים הָאֵלֶּה׃ וַיִּתֵּן יְהוָה יג
לְיִשְׂרָאֵל אֶת־כָּל־הָאָרֶץ אֲשֶׁר נִשְׁבַּע לָתֵת לַאֲבוֹתָם וַיִּרָשׁוּהָ וַיֵּשְׁבוּ
מב בָהּ׃ וַיָּנַח יְהוָה לָהֶם מִסָּבִיב כְּכֹל אֲשֶׁר־נִשְׁבַּע לַאֲבוֹתָם וְלֹא־עָמַד
מג אִישׁ בִּפְנֵיהֶם מִכָּל־אֹיְבֵיהֶם אֵת כָּל־אֹיְבֵיהֶם נָתַן יְהוָה בְּיָדָם׃ לֹא־
נָפַל דָּבָר מִכֹּל הַדָּבָר הַטּוֹב אֲשֶׁר־דִּבֶּר יְהוָה אֶל־בֵּית יִשְׂרָאֵל הַכֹּל
כב א בָּא׃ אָז יִקְרָא יְהוֹשֻׁעַ לָראוּבֵנִי וְלַגָּדִי וְלַחֲצִי מַטֵּה מְנַשֶּׁה׃
ב וַיֹּאמֶר אֲלֵיהֶם אַתֶּם שְׁמַרְתֶּם אֵת כָּל־אֲשֶׁר צִוָּה אֶתְכֶם מֹשֶׁה עֶבֶד
ג יְהוָה וַתִּשְׁמְעוּ בְקוֹלִי לְכֹל אֲשֶׁר־צִוִּיתִי אֶתְכֶם׃ לֹא־עֲזַבְתֶּם אֶת־
אֲחֵיכֶם זֶה יָמִים רַבִּים עַד הַיּוֹם הַזֶּה וּשְׁמַרְתֶּם אֶת־מִשְׁמֶרֶת מִצְוַת
ד יְהוָה אֱלֹהֵיכֶם׃ וְעַתָּה הֵנִיחַ יְהוָה אֱלֹהֵיכֶם לַאֲחֵיכֶם כַּאֲשֶׁר דִּבֶּר
לָהֶם וְעַתָּה פְּנוּ וּלְכוּ לָכֶם לְאָהֳלֵיכֶם אֶל־אֶרֶץ אֲחֻזַּתְכֶם אֲשֶׁר ׀ נָתַן
ה לָכֶם מֹשֶׁה עֶבֶד יְהוָה בְּעֵבֶר הַיַּרְדֵּן׃ רַק ׀ שִׁמְרוּ מְאֹד לַעֲשׂוֹת אֶת־
הַמִּצְוָה וְאֶת־הַתּוֹרָה אֲשֶׁר צִוָּה אֶתְכֶם מֹשֶׁה עֶבֶד־יְהוָה לְאַהֲבָה
אֶת־יְהוָה אֱלֹהֵיכֶם וְלָלֶכֶת בְּכָל־דְּרָכָיו וְלִשְׁמֹר מִצְוֹתָיו וּלְדָבְקָה־
ו בוֹ וּלְעָבְדוֹ בְּכָל־לְבַבְכֶם וּבְכָל־נַפְשְׁכֶם׃ וַיְבָרְכֵם יְהוֹשֻׁעַ וַיְשַׁלְּחֵם
ז וַיֵּלְכוּ אֶל־אָהֳלֵיהֶם׃ וְלַחֲצִי ׀ שֵׁבֶט הַמְנַשֶּׁה נָתַן מֹשֶׁה
בַּבָּשָׁן וּלְחֶצְיוֹ נָתַן יְהוֹשֻׁעַ עִם־אֲחֵיהֶם מעבר הַיַּרְדֵּן יָמָּה וְגַם כִּי בְּעֵבֶר
ח שִׁלְּחָם יְהוֹשֻׁעַ אֶל־אָהֳלֵיהֶם וַיְבָרְכֵם׃ וַיֹּאמֶר אֲלֵיהֶם לֵאמֹר בִּנְכָסִים
רַבִּים שׁוּבוּ אֶל־אָהֳלֵיכֶם וּבְמִקְנֶה רַב־מְאֹד בְּכֶסֶף וּבְזָהָב
וּבִנְחֹשֶׁת וּבְבַרְזֶל וּבִשְׂלָמוֹת הַרְבֵּה מְאֹד חִלְקוּ שְׁלַל־אֹיְבֵיכֶם עִם־
ט אֲחֵיכֶם׃ וַיָּשֻׁבוּ וַיֵּלְכוּ בְּנֵי־רְאוּבֵן וּבְנֵי־גָד וַחֲצִי ׀ שֵׁבֶט
הַמְנַשֶּׁה מֵאֵת בְּנֵי יִשְׂרָאֵל מִשִּׁלֹה אֲשֶׁר בְּאֶרֶץ־כְּנָעַן לָלֶכֶת אֶל־אֶרֶץ
הַגִּלְעָד אֶל־אֶרֶץ אֲחֻזָּתָם אֲשֶׁר נֹאחֲזוּ־בָהּ עַל־פִּי יְהוָה בְּיַד־מֹשֶׁה׃
י וַיָּבֹאוּ אֶל־גְּלִילוֹת הַיַּרְדֵּן אֲשֶׁר בְּאֶרֶץ כְּנָעַן וַיִּבְנוּ בְנֵי־רְאוּבֵן וּבְנֵי־גָד
וַחֲצִי שֵׁבֶט הַמְנַשֶּׁה שָׁם מִזְבֵּחַ עַל־הַיַּרְדֵּן מִזְבֵּחַ גָּדוֹל לְמַרְאֶה׃
יא וַיִּשְׁמְעוּ בְנֵי־יִשְׂרָאֵל לֵאמֹר הִנֵּה־בָנוּ בְנֵי־רְאוּבֵן וּבְנֵי־גָד וַחֲצִי שֵׁבֶט

facing the land of Canaan in the Jordan region beyond the border of the
12 Israelites!" When the Israelites heard this, the entire Israelite assembly
13 gathered together at Shiloh to go to war against them. The Israelites
then sent Pinḥas, son of Elazar the priest, to the Reubenites, the Gadites, and
14 half the tribe of Menashe in the land of Gilad, along with ten leaders, one
head of an ancestral family for each of the Israelite tribes; each was the head
15 of his ancestral house of thousands of Israelites. They reached the Reubenites,
the Gadites, and half the tribe of Menashe in the land of Gilad and accused
16 them: "Thus says the entire community of the LORD: Why have you broken
faith with the God of Israel, turning away from the LORD today by building
17 yourselves an altar to rebel today against the LORD? Was the sin of Peor –
from which we have not yet purified ourselves to this day – not enough for
18 us, when the plague ravaged the LORD's community?[23] If you turn away
from the LORD today and rebel against the LORD today, tomorrow He shall
19 rage against the entire community of Israel! If the land of your holding is
unclean, then cross over to the land of the LORD's holding where the LORD's
Tabernacle dwells, and take possession among us. But do not rebel against
the LORD or rebel against us by building yourselves any altar besides an altar
20 for the LORD our God. When Akhan the Zeraḥite broke faith and broke the
ban, there was rage against the entire community of Israel – he was not the
21 only one who perished for his sin!"[24] The Reubenites, the Gadites,
and half the tribe of Menashe answered, speaking to the heads of Israel's
22 thousands: "O LORD, God of gods! O LORD, God of gods! He knows, and
Israel shall know. If we rebelled or broke faith with the LORD, do not save us
23 today! If we had built an altar to turn away from the LORD, to offer up burnt
offerings and grain offerings, or to offer up peace offerings – then the LORD
24 would seek us out. No – we were moved by concern that one day, your
children will say to our children, 'What have you to do with the LORD, God
25 of Israel? The LORD placed a boundary between you and us, Reubenites and
Gadites – the Jordan! You have no share in the LORD!' Your children will
26 prevent our children from fearing the LORD. So we said, let us now build an
27 altar – not for burnt offerings, and not for sacrifices, but as testimony between
us and you, and all future generations, that we remain entitled to perform
services to the LORD before Him with our burnt offerings and our sacrifices
and our peace offerings; so that your children will not say to our children
28 tomorrow, 'You have no share in the LORD!' We thought that if they say this
to us or to our future generations, we will reply, 'Look at this replica of the
LORD's altar that our ancestors made – not for burnt offerings or sacrifices
29 but as testimony between us and you.' Far be it from us to rebel against the

---

23 | See Numbers 25:1–9.

24 | See chapter 7.

הַמְנַשֶּׁה אֶת־הַמִּזְבֵּחַ אֶל־מוּל אֶרֶץ כְּנַעַן אֶל־גְּלִילוֹת הַיַּרְדֵּן אֶל־עֵבֶר
יב בְּנֵי יִשְׂרָאֵל׃ וַיִּשְׁמְעוּ בְּנֵי יִשְׂרָאֵל וַיִּקָּהֲלוּ כָּל־עֲדַת בְּנֵי־יִשְׂרָאֵל שִׁלֹה
יג לַעֲלוֹת עֲלֵיהֶם לַצָּבָא׃ וַיִּשְׁלְחוּ בְנֵי־יִשְׂרָאֵל אֶל־בְּנֵי־
רְאוּבֵן וְאֶל־בְּנֵי־גָד וְאֶל־חֲצִי שֵׁבֶט־מְנַשֶּׁה אֶל־אֶרֶץ הַגִּלְעָד אֶת־
יד פִּינְחָס בֶּן־אֶלְעָזָר הַכֹּהֵן׃ וַעֲשָׂרָה נְשִׂאִים עִמּוֹ נָשִׂיא אֶחָד נָשִׂיא אֶחָד
לְבֵית אָב לְכֹל מַטּוֹת יִשְׂרָאֵל וְאִישׁ רֹאשׁ בֵּית־אֲבוֹתָם הֵמָּה לְאַלְפֵי
טו יִשְׂרָאֵל׃ וַיָּבֹאוּ אֶל־בְּנֵי־רְאוּבֵן וְאֶל־בְּנֵי־גָד וְאֶל־חֲצִי שֵׁבֶט־מְנַשֶּׁה
טז אֶל־אֶרֶץ הַגִּלְעָד וַיְדַבְּרוּ אִתָּם לֵאמֹר׃ כֹּה אָמְרוּ כֹּל ׀ עֲדַת יְהוָה
מָה־הַמַּעַל הַזֶּה אֲשֶׁר מְעַלְתֶּם בֵּאלֹהֵי יִשְׂרָאֵל לָשׁוּב הַיּוֹם מֵאַחֲרֵי
יז יְהוָה בִּבְנוֹתְכֶם לָכֶם מִזְבֵּחַ לִמְרָדְכֶם הַיּוֹם בַּיהוָה׃ הַמְעַט־לָנוּ אֶת־
עֲוֺן פְּעוֹר אֲשֶׁר לֹא־הִטַּהַרְנוּ מִמֶּנּוּ עַד הַיּוֹם הַזֶּה וַיְהִי הַנֶּגֶף בַּעֲדַת
יח יְהוָה׃ וְאַתֶּם תָּשֻׁבוּ הַיּוֹם מֵאַחֲרֵי יְהוָה וְהָיָה אַתֶּם תִּמְרְדוּ הַיּוֹם
יט בַּיהוָה וּמָחָר אֶל־כָּל־עֲדַת יִשְׂרָאֵל יִקְצֹף׃ וְאַךְ אִם־טְמֵאָה אֶרֶץ
אֲחֻזַּתְכֶם עִבְרוּ לָכֶם אֶל־אֶרֶץ אֲחֻזַּת יְהוָה אֲשֶׁר שָׁכַן־שָׁם מִשְׁכַּן
יְהוָה וְהֵאָחֲזוּ בְּתוֹכֵנוּ וּבַיהוָה אַל־תִּמְרֹדוּ וְאֹתָנוּ אַל־תִּמְרֹדוּ
כ בִּבְנֹתְכֶם לָכֶם מִזְבֵּחַ מִבַּלְעֲדֵי מִזְבַּח יְהוָה אֱלֹהֵינוּ׃ הֲלוֹא ׀ עָכָן בֶּן־
זֶרַח מָעַל מַעַל בַּחֵרֶם וְעַל־כָּל־עֲדַת יִשְׂרָאֵל הָיָה קָצֶף וְהוּא אִישׁ
כא אֶחָד לֹא גָוַע בַּעֲוֺנוֹ׃ וַיַּעֲנוּ בְּנֵי־רְאוּבֵן וּבְנֵי־גָד וַחֲצִי שֵׁבֶט
כב הַמְנַשֶּׁה וַיְדַבְּרוּ אֶת־רָאשֵׁי אַלְפֵי יִשְׂרָאֵל׃ אֵל ׀ אֱלֹהִים ׀ יְהוָה אֵל ׀
אֱלֹהִים ׀ יְהוָה הוּא יֹדֵעַ וְיִשְׂרָאֵל הוּא יֵדָע אִם־בְּמֶרֶד וְאִם־בְּמַעַל
כג בַּיהוָה אַל־תּוֹשִׁיעֵנוּ הַיּוֹם הַזֶּה׃ לִבְנוֹת לָנוּ מִזְבֵּחַ לָשׁוּב מֵאַחֲרֵי
יְהוָה וְאִם־לְהַעֲלוֹת עָלָיו עוֹלָה וּמִנְחָה וְאִם־לַעֲשׂוֹת עָלָיו זִבְחֵי
כד שְׁלָמִים יְהוָה הוּא יְבַקֵּשׁ׃ וְאִם־לֹא מִדְּאָגָה מִדָּבָר עָשִׂינוּ אֶת־זֹאת
לֵאמֹר מָחָר יֹאמְרוּ בְנֵיכֶם לְבָנֵינוּ לֵאמֹר מַה־לָּכֶם וְלַיהוָה אֱלֹהֵי
כה יִשְׂרָאֵל׃ וּגְבוּל נָתַן־יְהוָה בֵּינֵנוּ וּבֵינֵיכֶם בְּנֵי־רְאוּבֵן וּבְנֵי־גָד אֶת־הַיַּרְדֵּן
אֵין־לָכֶם חֵלֶק בַּיהוָה וְהִשְׁבִּיתוּ בְנֵיכֶם אֶת־בָּנֵינוּ לְבִלְתִּי יְרֹא אֶת־
כו יְהוָה׃ וַנֹּאמֶר נַעֲשֶׂה־נָּא לָנוּ לִבְנוֹת אֶת־הַמִּזְבֵּחַ לֹא לְעוֹלָה וְלֹא
כז לְזָבַח׃ כִּי עֵד הוּא בֵּינֵינוּ וּבֵינֵיכֶם וּבֵין דֹּרוֹתֵינוּ אַחֲרֵינוּ לַעֲבֹד אֶת־
עֲבֹדַת יְהוָה לְפָנָיו בְּעֹלוֹתֵינוּ וּבִזְבָחֵינוּ וּבִשְׁלָמֵינוּ וְלֹא־יֹאמְרוּ בְנֵיכֶם
כח מָחָר לְבָנֵינוּ אֵין־לָכֶם חֵלֶק בַּיהוָה׃ וַנֹּאמֶר וְהָיָה כִּי־יֹאמְרוּ אֵלֵינוּ
וְאֶל־דֹּרֹתֵינוּ מָחָר וְאָמַרְנוּ רְאוּ אֶת־תַּבְנִית מִזְבַּח יְהוָה אֲשֶׁר־עָשׂוּ
כט אֲבוֹתֵינוּ לֹא לְעוֹלָה וְלֹא לְזֶבַח כִּי־עֵד הוּא בֵּינֵינוּ וּבֵינֵיכֶם׃ חָלִילָה

Lord and turn away from the Lord today by building an altar for burnt
offerings, grain offerings, or sacrifices other than the altar of the Lord our
30 God before His Tabernacle!" Pinḥas the priest, along with the
community leaders and the heads of Israel's thousands, heard the Reubenites,
31 Gadites', and Manassites' speech and approved. Pinḥas son of Elazar the priest
said to the Reubenites, Gadites, and Manassites, "Now we know that the
Lord is among us, for you have not broken faith with the Lord; you have
32 saved the Israelites from the Lord's hand!" Then Pinḥas son of Elazar the
priest and the leaders returned from the Reubenites and Gadites in the land
of Gilad to the Israelites in the land of Canaan and reported back to them.
33 The Israelites approved of the report and blessed God, and no longer spoke
of going to war against the Reubenites and Gadites in order to destroy the
34 land where they lived. The Reubenites and Gadites referred to the altar as
Witness,[25] "for it is a witness among us that the Lord is God."
23 1 Many years after the Lord had granted Israel rest from all their surrounding
2 enemies, when Yehoshua was old, advanced in years, he summoned all of
Israel – its elders, leaders, judges, and officers – and said to them, "I have
3 grown old, advanced in years. You have seen all that the Lord your God has
done to all these nations before you, for the Lord your God is the One who
4 has fought for you. Look – I have allotted to you the lands of the remaining
nations as estates by your tribes, along with those of all the nations that I
5 have cut off, from the Jordan to the Great Sea where the sun sets. The Lord
your God will drive them out before you and dispossess them, and you shall
6 inherit their land as the Lord your God promised you. But you must be
strong enough to keep faithfully all that is written in the book of Moshe's
7 Torah; not to stray from it, neither right nor left; not to mingle[26] with these
nations left among you – do not utter the names of their gods or swear by
8 them or worship them or bow down to them. Cling only to the Lord your
9 God, as you have done up to this day. The Lord has dispossessed great,
mighty nations from before you, and no one has withstood you to this day.
10 A single one of you shall put a thousand to flight, for the Lord your God
11 Himself is fighting for you, as He promised you. Take great care, though, for
12 your own sakes, to love the Lord your God. For if you regress and cling
to these remaining nations who live in your midst and marry among them,
13 mingling with them and they with you, know with certainty that the Lord
your God will not continue to dispossess these nations before you. They shall

25 | The name "Witness" (*Ed*) is not explicitly stated in the Hebrew but is implied. See also Genesis 31:48 for the name Galed (Gal-Ed), likely related to the area of Gilad, where both stories occur.

26 | See Deuteronomy 7:3.

לָנוּ מִמֶּנּוּ לִמְרֹד בַּיהוָה וְלָשׁוּב הַיּוֹם מֵאַחֲרֵי יְהוָה לִבְנוֹת מִזְבֵּחַ
לְעֹלָה לְמִנְחָה וּלְזָבַח מִלְּבַד מִזְבַּח יְהוָה אֱלֹהֵינוּ אֲשֶׁר לִפְנֵי
ל מִשְׁכָּנוֹ׃ וַיִּשְׁמַע פִּינְחָס הַכֹּהֵן וּנְשִׂיאֵי הָעֵדָה וְרָאשֵׁי אַלְפֵי
יִשְׂרָאֵל אֲשֶׁר אִתּוֹ אֶת־הַדְּבָרִים אֲשֶׁר דִּבְּרוּ בְנֵי־רְאוּבֵן וּבְנֵי־גָד וּבְנֵי
לא מְנַשֶּׁה וַיִּיטַב בְּעֵינֵיהֶם׃ וַיֹּאמֶר פִּינְחָס בֶּן־אֶלְעָזָר הַכֹּהֵן אֶל־בְּנֵי־רְאוּבֵן
וְאֶל־בְּנֵי־גָד וְאֶל־בְּנֵי מְנַשֶּׁה הַיּוֹם יָדַעְנוּ כִּי־בְתוֹכֵנוּ יְהוָה אֲשֶׁר לֹא־
מְעַלְתֶּם בַּיהוָה הַמַּעַל הַזֶּה אָז הִצַּלְתֶּם אֶת־בְּנֵי יִשְׂרָאֵל מִיַּד יְהוָה׃
לב וַיָּשָׁב פִּינְחָס בֶּן־אֶלְעָזָר הַכֹּהֵן ׀ וְהַנְּשִׂיאִים מֵאֵת בְּנֵי־רְאוּבֵן וּמֵאֵת
בְּנֵי־גָד מֵאֶרֶץ הַגִּלְעָד אֶל־אֶרֶץ כְּנַעַן אֶל־בְּנֵי יִשְׂרָאֵל וַיָּשִׁבוּ אוֹתָם
לג דָּבָר׃ וַיִּיטַב הַדָּבָר בְּעֵינֵי בְּנֵי יִשְׂרָאֵל וַיְבָרְכוּ אֱלֹהִים בְּנֵי יִשְׂרָאֵל וְלֹא
אָמְרוּ לַעֲלוֹת עֲלֵיהֶם לַצָּבָא לְשַׁחֵת אֶת־הָאָרֶץ אֲשֶׁר בְּנֵי־רְאוּבֵן
יד לד וּבְנֵי־גָד יֹשְׁבִים בָּהּ׃ וַיִּקְרְאוּ בְּנֵי־רְאוּבֵן וּבְנֵי־גָד לַמִּזְבֵּחַ כִּי־עֵד הוּא
בֵּינֹתֵינוּ כִּי יְהוָה הָאֱלֹהִים׃
כג א וַיְהִי מִיָּמִים רַבִּים אַחֲרֵי אֲשֶׁר־הֵנִיחַ יְהוָה לְיִשְׂרָאֵל מִכָּל־אֹיְבֵיהֶם
ב מִסָּבִיב וִיהוֹשֻׁעַ זָקֵן בָּא בַּיָּמִים׃ וַיִּקְרָא יְהוֹשֻׁעַ לְכָל־יִשְׂרָאֵל לִזְקֵנָיו
וּלְרָאשָׁיו וּלְשֹׁפְטָיו וּלְשֹׁטְרָיו וַיֹּאמֶר אֲלֵהֶם אֲנִי זָקַנְתִּי בָּאתִי בַּיָּמִים׃
ג וְאַתֶּם רְאִיתֶם אֵת כָּל־אֲשֶׁר עָשָׂה יְהוָה אֱלֹהֵיכֶם לְכָל־הַגּוֹיִם הָאֵלֶּה
ד מִפְּנֵיכֶם כִּי יְהוָה אֱלֹהֵיכֶם הוּא הַנִּלְחָם לָכֶם׃ רְאוּ הִפַּלְתִּי לָכֶם אֶת־
הַגּוֹיִם הַנִּשְׁאָרִים הָאֵלֶּה בְּנַחֲלָה לְשִׁבְטֵיכֶם מִן־הַיַּרְדֵּן וְכָל־הַגּוֹיִם
ה אֲשֶׁר הִכְרַתִּי וְהַיָּם הַגָּדוֹל מְבוֹא הַשָּׁמֶשׁ׃ וַיהוָה אֱלֹהֵיכֶם הוּא יֶהְדֳּפֵם
מִפְּנֵיכֶם וְהוֹרִישׁ אֹתָם מִלִּפְנֵיכֶם וִירִשְׁתֶּם אֶת־אַרְצָם כַּאֲשֶׁר דִּבֶּר
ו יְהוָה אֱלֹהֵיכֶם לָכֶם׃ וַחֲזַקְתֶּם מְאֹד לִשְׁמֹר וְלַעֲשׂוֹת אֵת כָּל־הַכָּתוּב
ז בְּסֵפֶר תּוֹרַת מֹשֶׁה לְבִלְתִּי סוּר־מִמֶּנּוּ יָמִין וּשְׂמֹאול׃ לְבִלְתִּי־בוֹא
בַּגּוֹיִם הָאֵלֶּה הַנִּשְׁאָרִים הָאֵלֶּה אִתְּכֶם וּבְשֵׁם אֱלֹהֵיהֶם לֹא־תַזְכִּירוּ
ח וְלֹא תַשְׁבִּיעוּ וְלֹא תַעַבְדוּם וְלֹא תִשְׁתַּחֲווּ לָהֶם׃ כִּי אִם־בַּיהוָה
ט אֱלֹהֵיכֶם תִּדְבָּקוּ כַּאֲשֶׁר עֲשִׂיתֶם עַד הַיּוֹם הַזֶּה׃ וַיּוֹרֶשׁ יְהוָה מִפְּנֵיכֶם
גּוֹיִם גְּדֹלִים וַעֲצוּמִים וְאַתֶּם לֹא־עָמַד אִישׁ בִּפְנֵיכֶם עַד הַיּוֹם הַזֶּה׃
י אִישׁ־אֶחָד מִכֶּם יִרְדָּף־אָלֶף כִּי ׀ יְהוָה אֱלֹהֵיכֶם הוּא הַנִּלְחָם לָכֶם
יא כַּאֲשֶׁר דִּבֶּר לָכֶם׃ וְנִשְׁמַרְתֶּם מְאֹד לְנַפְשֹׁתֵיכֶם לְאַהֲבָה אֶת־יְהוָה
יב אֱלֹהֵיכֶם׃ כִּי ׀ אִם־שׁוֹב תָּשׁוּבוּ וּדְבַקְתֶּם בְּיֶתֶר הַגּוֹיִם הָאֵלֶּה הַנִּשְׁאָרִים
יג הָאֵלֶּה אִתְּכֶם וְהִתְחַתַּנְתֶּם בָּהֶם וּבָאתֶם בָּהֶם וְהֵם בָּכֶם׃ יָדוֹעַ תֵּדְעוּ
כִּי לֹא יוֹסִיף יְהוָה אֱלֹהֵיכֶם לְהוֹרִישׁ אֶת־הַגּוֹיִם הָאֵלֶּה מִלִּפְנֵיכֶם וְהָיוּ

become a snare and an obstacle for you, a whip for your sides and thorns in
your eyes[27] until you perish from this good land that the LORD your God has
14 granted you. Today I am going the way of all the earth. Know with all your
heart and all your soul that not a single thing is wanting among all the good
things the LORD your God promised you – everything has been fulfilled
15 for you; no, not a single thing is wanting. But just as all the good things the
LORD your God promised have come, the LORD can bring all the evils, too,
until He has eliminated you from this good land that the LORD your God
16 granted you. If you violate the covenant of the LORD your God that He
commanded you, and if you follow and worship other gods and bow down
to them, then the LORD's wrath will rage against you, and you will swiftly
perish from the good land He has granted you."

24 1 Yehoshua gathered
all the tribes of Israel at Shekhem. He summoned the elders of Israel, its
leaders, judges, and officers, and they presented themselves before God.
2 Yehoshua said to the entire people: "Thus says the LORD, God of Israel:
From time immemorial, your ancestors – Teraḥ, the father of Avraham and
3 the father of Naḥor – dwelled across the river and worshipped other gods. I
took your forefather Avraham from across the river, and I led him all about
4 the land of Canaan and multiplied his seed and granted him Yitzḥak. To
Yitzḥak I granted Yaakov and Esav. I granted Mount Se'ir as the inheritance
5 to Esav, while Yaakov and his sons went down to Egypt. I sent Moshe and
Aharon and devastated Egypt with plagues in its midst; then I took you out.
6 I took your ancestors out of Egypt, and you came to the sea; the Egyptians
7 chased your ancestors with chariots and cavalry to the Sea of Reeds. They
cried out to the LORD, and He put a veil of darkness between you and the
Egyptians, and He brought the sea upon them, entombing them. Your own
eyes have seen what I did in Egypt. You dwelled in the wilderness for many
8 years, then I brought you to the land of the Amorite, who live on the banks of
the Jordan. They fought with you, and I delivered them into your hand; you
9 inherited their land, and I annihilated them before you. Then Balak son of
Tzipor, king of Moav, rose up to fight against Israel. He sent for Bilam son of
10 Beor and directed him to curse you,[28] but I was not willing to listen to Bilam,
11 and he was compelled to bless you – I saved you from his hand. You crossed
the Jordan and arrived at Yeriḥo. The citizens of Yeriḥo fought against you,
and the Amorites, Perizzites, Canaanites, Hittites, Girgashites, Hivites, and
12 Jebusites; and I delivered them into your hand. I sent the plague of hornets
ahead of you,[29] and it drove out the two Amorite kings before you – it was
13 not by your sword or your bow. I granted you a land that you did not toil for

27 | Cf. Deuteronomy 33:55.
28 | See Numbers, chapters 22–24.
29 | Cf. Exodus 23:28.

לָכֶם לְפַח וּלְמוֹקֵשׁ וּלְשֹׁטֵט בְּצִדֵּיכֶם וְלִצְנִנִים בְּעֵינֵיכֶם עַד אֲבָדְכֶם
יד מֵעַל הָאֲדָמָה הַטּוֹבָה הַזֹּאת אֲשֶׁר נָתַן לָכֶם יהוה אֱלֹהֵיכֶם: וְהִנֵּה
אָנֹכִי הוֹלֵךְ הַיּוֹם בְּדֶרֶךְ כָּל־הָאָרֶץ וִידַעְתֶּם בְּכָל־לְבַבְכֶם וּבְכָל־
נַפְשְׁכֶם כִּי לֹא־נָפַל דָּבָר אֶחָד מִכֹּל ׀ הַדְּבָרִים הַטּוֹבִים אֲשֶׁר דִּבֶּר
טו יהוה אֱלֹהֵיכֶם עֲלֵיכֶם הַכֹּל בָּאוּ לָכֶם לֹא־נָפַל מִמֶּנּוּ דָּבָר אֶחָד: וְהָיָה
כַּאֲשֶׁר־בָּא עֲלֵיכֶם כָּל־הַדָּבָר הַטּוֹב אֲשֶׁר דִּבֶּר יהוה אֱלֹהֵיכֶם אֲלֵיכֶם
כֵּן יָבִיא יהוה עֲלֵיכֶם אֵת כָּל־הַדָּבָר הָרָע עַד־הַשְׁמִידוֹ אוֹתְכֶם מֵעַל
טז הָאֲדָמָה הַטּוֹבָה הַזֹּאת אֲשֶׁר נָתַן לָכֶם יהוה אֱלֹהֵיכֶם: בְּעָבְרְכֶם
אֶת־בְּרִית יהוה אֱלֹהֵיכֶם אֲשֶׁר צִוָּה אֶתְכֶם וַהֲלַכְתֶּם וַעֲבַדְתֶּם אֱלֹהִים
אֲחֵרִים וְהִשְׁתַּחֲוִיתֶם לָהֶם וְחָרָה אַף־יהוה בָּכֶם וַאֲבַדְתֶּם מְהֵרָה
כד א מֵעַל הָאָרֶץ הַטּוֹבָה אֲשֶׁר נָתַן לָכֶם: וַיֶּאֱסֹף יְהוֹשֻׁעַ אֶת־
כָּל־שִׁבְטֵי יִשְׂרָאֵל שְׁכֶמָה וַיִּקְרָא לְזִקְנֵי יִשְׂרָאֵל וּלְרָאשָׁיו וּלְשֹׁפְטָיו
ב וּלְשֹׁטְרָיו וַיִּתְיַצְּבוּ לִפְנֵי הָאֱלֹהִים: וַיֹּאמֶר יְהוֹשֻׁעַ אֶל־כָּל־הָעָם כֹּה־
אָמַר יהוה אֱלֹהֵי יִשְׂרָאֵל בְּעֵבֶר הַנָּהָר יָשְׁבוּ אֲבוֹתֵיכֶם מֵעוֹלָם תֶּרַח
ג אֲבִי אַבְרָהָם וַאֲבִי נָחוֹר וַיַּעַבְדוּ אֱלֹהִים אֲחֵרִים: וָאֶקַּח אֶת־אֲבִיכֶם
אֶת־אַבְרָהָם מֵעֵבֶר הַנָּהָר וָאוֹלֵךְ אוֹתוֹ בְּכָל־אֶרֶץ כְּנָעַן וָאַרְבֶּה אֶת־
ד זַרְעוֹ וָאֶתֶּן־לוֹ אֶת־יִצְחָק: וָאֶתֵּן לְיִצְחָק אֶת־יַעֲקֹב וְאֶת־עֵשָׂו וָאֶתֵּן
ה לְעֵשָׂו אֶת־הַר שֵׂעִיר לָרֶשֶׁת אוֹתוֹ וְיַעֲקֹב וּבָנָיו יָרְדוּ מִצְרָיִם: וָאֶשְׁלַח
אֶת־מֹשֶׁה וְאֶת־אַהֲרֹן וָאֶגֹּף אֶת־מִצְרַיִם כַּאֲשֶׁר עָשִׂיתִי בְּקִרְבּוֹ וְאַחַר
ו הוֹצֵאתִי אֶתְכֶם: וָאוֹצִיא אֶת־אֲבוֹתֵיכֶם מִמִּצְרַיִם וַתָּבֹאוּ הַיָּמָּה
ז וַיִּרְדְּפוּ מִצְרַיִם אַחֲרֵי אֲבוֹתֵיכֶם בְּרֶכֶב וּבְפָרָשִׁים יַם־סוּף: וַיִּצְעֲקוּ
אֶל־יהוה וַיָּשֶׂם מַאֲפֵל בֵּינֵיכֶם ׀ וּבֵין הַמִּצְרִים וַיָּבֵא עָלָיו אֶת־הַיָּם
וַיְכַסֵּהוּ וַתִּרְאֶינָה עֵינֵיכֶם אֵת אֲשֶׁר־עָשִׂיתִי בְּמִצְרָיִם וַתֵּשְׁבוּ בַמִּדְבָּר
ח יָמִים רַבִּים: ואביאה אֶתְכֶם אֶל־אֶרֶץ הָאֱמֹרִי הַיּוֹשֵׁב בְּעֵבֶר הַיַּרְדֵּן וָאָבִיא
וַיִּלָּחֲמוּ אִתְּכֶם וָאֶתֵּן אוֹתָם בְּיֶדְכֶם וַתִּירְשׁוּ אֶת־אַרְצָם וָאַשְׁמִידֵם
ט מִפְּנֵיכֶם: וַיָּקָם בָּלָק בֶּן־צִפּוֹר מֶלֶךְ מוֹאָב וַיִּלָּחֶם בְּיִשְׂרָאֵל וַיִּשְׁלַח
י וַיִּקְרָא לְבִלְעָם בֶּן־בְּעוֹר לְקַלֵּל אֶתְכֶם: וְלֹא אָבִיתִי לִשְׁמֹעַ לְבִלְעָם
יא וַיְבָרֶךְ בָּרוֹךְ אֶתְכֶם וָאַצִּל אֶתְכֶם מִיָּדוֹ: וַתַּעַבְרוּ אֶת־הַיַּרְדֵּן וַתָּבֹאוּ
אֶל־יְרִיחוֹ וַיִּלָּחֲמוּ בָכֶם בַּעֲלֵי־יְרִיחוֹ הָאֱמֹרִי וְהַפְּרִזִּי וְהַכְּנַעֲנִי וְהַחִתִּי
יב וְהַגִּרְגָּשִׁי הַחִוִּי וְהַיְבוּסִי וָאֶתֵּן אוֹתָם בְּיֶדְכֶם: וָאֶשְׁלַח לִפְנֵיכֶם אֶת־
הַצִּרְעָה וַתְּגָרֶשׁ אוֹתָם מִפְּנֵיכֶם שְׁנֵי מַלְכֵי הָאֱמֹרִי לֹא בְחַרְבְּךָ וְלֹא
יג בְקַשְׁתֶּךָ: וָאֶתֵּן לָכֶם אֶרֶץ ׀ אֲשֶׁר לֹא־יָגַעְתָּ בָּהּ וְעָרִים אֲשֶׁר לֹא־בְנִיתֶם

and cities that you did not build, to live in; you eat from vineyards and olive
14 groves that you did not plant. Now fear the LORD and serve Him fully and
truly. Remove the gods your ancestors served across the river and in Egypt,
15 and worship the LORD! If serving the LORD seems evil in your eyes, then
choose whom to worship today: the gods your ancestors served across the
river or the gods of the Amorites whose land you live in. But as for me and my
16 household – we shall serve the LORD!" "Far be it from us to abandon
17 the LORD and serve other gods!" the people answered. "For the LORD our
God is the One who brought us and our ancestors up from the land of Egypt,
from the house of slavery; who performed these great wonders before our
eyes; who watched over us all along the way we traveled and amidst all the
18 peoples through whom we passed. The LORD drove out all the peoples – even
the Amorites, dwellers of the land – before us. We too shall serve the LORD,
19 for He is our God!" "You cannot serve the LORD," said Yehoshua to
the people, "for He is a holy God, a jealous God – He will not tolerate your
20 crimes and your sins. If you abandon the LORD and serve alien gods, He will
turn on you, harm you, and cause you to perish after dealing so kindly with
21 22 you." "No," the people said to Yehoshua, "we will serve the LORD!" Yehoshua
said to the people, "You are your own witnesses that you, yourselves, have
23 chosen the LORD, to serve Him," and they confirmed, "Witnesses!" "Now,
purge the alien gods from your midst and direct your hearts toward the LORD,
24 God of Israel!" The people said to Yehoshua, "The LORD our God we shall
25 serve, and His voice we shall obey!" Yehoshua formed a covenant with the
26 people on that day and instituted law and order in Shekhem. Yehoshua then
inscribed these words in the book of God's Torah; he took a large stone and
27 erected it there under the terebinth by the LORD's Sanctuary. Then
Yehoshua said to the entire people, "Behold, this stone shall be our witness,
for it has heard all the LORD's words that He spoke to us; it shall be a witness
28 against you lest you deny your God." And Yehoshua sent the people away,
29 each to his estate. After these events, Yehoshua son of Nun, the
30 LORD's servant, died at the age of one hundred and ten.[30] They buried him at
the border of his estate at Timnat Seraḥ in the hill country of Efrayim, north
31 of Mount Gaash. Israel served the LORD all the days of Yehoshua and all
the days of the elders who lived on after Yehoshua and who knew of all the
32 deeds the LORD had done for Israel. As for Yosef's bones, which the Israelites

30 | Cf. Judges 2:7–9.

יד וַתֵּשְׁבוּ בָּהֶם כְּרָמִים וְזֵיתִים אֲשֶׁר לֹא־נְטַעְתֶּם אַתֶּם אֹכְלִים: וְעַתָּה
יְראוּ אֶת־יְהוָה וְעִבְדוּ אֹתוֹ בְּתָמִים וּבֶאֱמֶת וְהָסִירוּ אֶת־אֱלֹהִים אֲשֶׁר
טו עָבְדוּ אֲבוֹתֵיכֶם בְּעֵבֶר הַנָּהָר וּבְמִצְרַיִם וְעִבְדוּ אֶת־יְהוָה: וְאִם רַע
בְּעֵינֵיכֶם לַעֲבֹד אֶת־יְהוָה בַּחֲרוּ לָכֶם הַיּוֹם אֶת־מִי תַעֲבֹדוּן אִם אֶת־
אֱלֹהִים אֲשֶׁר־עָבְדוּ אֲבוֹתֵיכֶם אֲשֶׁר בעבר הַנָּהָר וְאִם אֶת־ מֵעֵבֶר
אֱלֹהֵי הָאֱמֹרִי אֲשֶׁר אַתֶּם יֹשְׁבִים בְּאַרְצָם וְאָנֹכִי וּבֵיתִי נַעֲבֹד אֶת־
טז יְהוָה: וַיַּעַן הָעָם וַיֹּאמֶר חָלִילָה לָּנוּ מֵעֲזֹב אֶת־יְהוָה
יז לַעֲבֹד אֱלֹהִים אֲחֵרִים: כִּי יְהוָה אֱלֹהֵינוּ הוּא הַמַּעֲלֶה אֹתָנוּ וְאֶת־
אֲבוֹתֵינוּ מֵאֶרֶץ מִצְרַיִם מִבֵּית עֲבָדִים וַאֲשֶׁר עָשָׂה לְעֵינֵינוּ אֶת־
הָאֹתוֹת הַגְּדֹלוֹת הָאֵלֶּה וַיִּשְׁמְרֵנוּ בְּכָל־הַדֶּרֶךְ אֲשֶׁר הָלַכְנוּ בָהּ וּבְכֹל
יח הָעַמִּים אֲשֶׁר עָבַרְנוּ בְּקִרְבָּם: וַיְגָרֶשׁ יְהוָה אֶת־כָּל־הָעַמִּים וְאֶת־
הָאֱמֹרִי יֹשֵׁב הָאָרֶץ מִפָּנֵינוּ גַּם־אֲנַחְנוּ נַעֲבֹד אֶת־יְהוָה כִּי־הוּא
יט אֱלֹהֵינוּ: וַיֹּאמֶר יְהוֹשֻׁעַ אֶל־הָעָם לֹא תוּכְלוּ לַעֲבֹד אֶת־
יְהוָה כִּי־אֱלֹהִים קְדֹשִׁים הוּא אֵל־קַנּוֹא הוּא לֹא־יִשָּׂא לְפִשְׁעֲכֶם
כ וּלְחַטֹּאותֵיכֶם: כִּי תַעַזְבוּ אֶת־יְהוָה וַעֲבַדְתֶּם אֱלֹהֵי נֵכָר וְשָׁב וְהֵרַע
כא לָכֶם וְכִלָּה אֶתְכֶם אַחֲרֵי אֲשֶׁר־הֵיטִיב לָכֶם: וַיֹּאמֶר הָעָם אֶל־יְהוֹשֻׁעַ
כב לֹא כִּי אֶת־יְהוָה נַעֲבֹד: וַיֹּאמֶר יְהוֹשֻׁעַ אֶל־הָעָם עֵדִים אַתֶּם בָּכֶם
כג כִּי־אַתֶּם בְּחַרְתֶּם לָכֶם אֶת־יְהוָה לַעֲבֹד אוֹתוֹ וַיֹּאמְרוּ עֵדִים: וְעַתָּה
הָסִירוּ אֶת־אֱלֹהֵי הַנֵּכָר אֲשֶׁר בְּקִרְבְּכֶם וְהַטּוּ אֶת־לְבַבְכֶם אֶל־יְהוָה
כד אֱלֹהֵי יִשְׂרָאֵל: וַיֹּאמְרוּ הָעָם אֶל־יְהוֹשֻׁעַ אֶת־יְהוָה אֱלֹהֵינוּ נַעֲבֹד
כה וּבְקוֹלוֹ נִשְׁמָע: וַיִּכְרֹת יְהוֹשֻׁעַ בְּרִית לָעָם בַּיּוֹם הַהוּא וַיָּשֶׂם לוֹ חֹק
כו וּמִשְׁפָּט בִּשְׁכֶם: וַיִּכְתֹּב יְהוֹשֻׁעַ אֶת־הַדְּבָרִים הָאֵלֶּה בְּסֵפֶר תּוֹרַת
אֱלֹהִים וַיִּקַּח אֶבֶן גְּדוֹלָה וַיְקִימֶהָ שָּׁם תַּחַת הָאַלָּה אֲשֶׁר בְּמִקְדַּשׁ
כז יְהוָה: וַיֹּאמֶר יְהוֹשֻׁעַ אֶל־כָּל־הָעָם הִנֵּה הָאֶבֶן הַזֹּאת
תִּהְיֶה־בָּנוּ לְעֵדָה כִּי־הִיא שָׁמְעָה אֵת כָּל־אִמְרֵי יְהוָה אֲשֶׁר דִּבֶּר
כח עִמָּנוּ וְהָיְתָה בָכֶם לְעֵדָה פֶּן־תְּכַחֲשׁוּן בֵּאלֹהֵיכֶם: וַיְשַׁלַּח יְהוֹשֻׁעַ
כט אֶת־הָעָם אִישׁ לְנַחֲלָתוֹ: וַיְהִי אַחֲרֵי הַדְּבָרִים הָאֵלֶּה
ל וַיָּמָת יְהוֹשֻׁעַ בִּן־נוּן עֶבֶד יְהוָה בֶּן־מֵאָה וָעֶשֶׂר שָׁנִים: וַיִּקְבְּרוּ אוֹתוֹ
בִּגְבוּל נַחֲלָתוֹ בְּתִמְנַת־סֶרַח אֲשֶׁר בְּהַר־אֶפְרָיִם מִצְּפוֹן לְהַר־גָּעַשׁ:
לא וַיַּעֲבֹד יִשְׂרָאֵל אֶת־יְהוָה כֹּל יְמֵי יְהוֹשֻׁעַ וְכֹל ׀ יְמֵי הַזְּקֵנִים אֲשֶׁר
הֶאֱרִיכוּ יָמִים אַחֲרֵי יְהוֹשֻׁעַ וַאֲשֶׁר יָדְעוּ אֵת כָּל־מַעֲשֵׂה יְהוָה
לב אֲשֶׁר עָשָׂה לְיִשְׂרָאֵל: וְאֶת־עַצְמוֹת יוֹסֵף אֲשֶׁר־הֶעֱלוּ בְנֵי־יִשְׂרָאֵל ׀

brought up from Egypt,[31] they were buried at Shekhem in the field which
Yaakov had purchased from the sons of Ḥamor, the father of Shekhem, for one
33 hundred *kesita*,[32] and they became the Josephites' heritage. And when Elazar
son of Aharon died, they buried him on the hill of his son Pinḥas, which had
been given to him in the hill country of Efrayim.

31 | See Exodus 13:19.
32 | See Genesis 33:19.

מִמִּצְרַ֗יִם קָבְר֤וּ בִשְׁכֶם֙ בְּחֶלְקַ֣ת הַשָּׂדֶ֔ה אֲשֶׁ֨ר קָנָ֧ה יַעֲקֹ֛ב מֵאֵ֛ת בְּנֵֽי־
לג חֲמ֥וֹר אֲבִֽי־שְׁכֶ֖ם בְּמֵאָ֣ה קְשִׂיטָ֑ה וַיִּהְי֥וּ לִבְנֵֽי־יוֹסֵ֖ף לְנַחֲלָֽה׃ וְאֶלְעָזָ֤ר
בֶּֽן־אַהֲרֹן֙ מֵ֔ת וַיִּקְבְּר֣וּ אֹת֗וֹ בְּגִבְעַת֙ פִּֽינְחָ֣ס בְּנ֔וֹ אֲשֶׁ֥ר נִתַּן־ל֖וֹ בְּהַ֥ר
אֶפְרָֽיִם׃

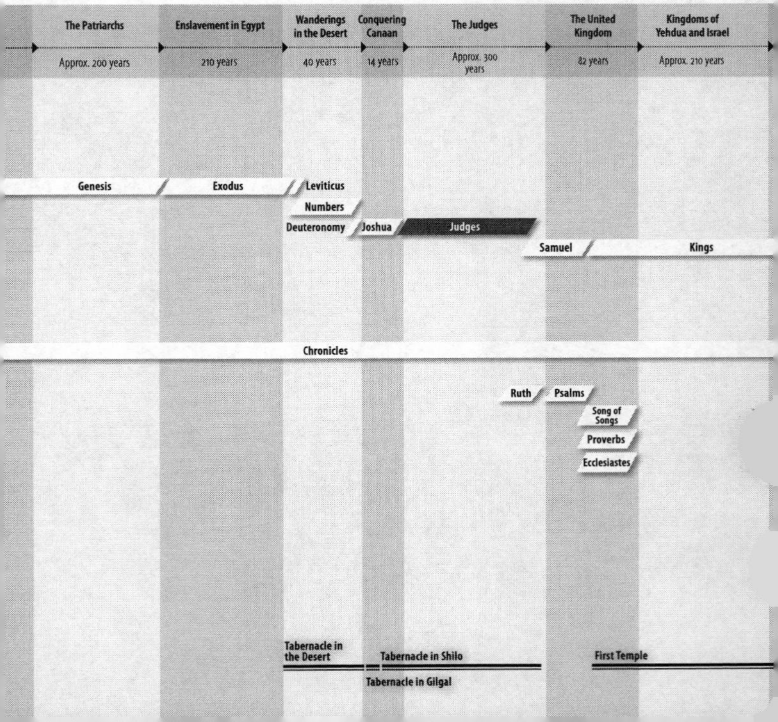

The Patriarchs
Approx. 200 years
Enslavement in Egypt
210 years
Wanderings in the Desert
40 years
Conquering Canaan
14 years
The Judges
Approx. 300 years
The United Kingdom
82 years
Kingdoms of Yehdua and Israel
Approx. 210 years
Genesis
Exodus
Leviticus
Numbers
Deuteronomy
Joshua
Judges
Samuel
Kings
Chronicles
Ruth
Psalms
Song of Songs
Proverbs
Ecclesiastes
Tabernacle in the Desert
Tabernacle in Shilo
Tabernacle in Gilgal
First Temple

שופטים
SHOFETIM/JUDGES

JUDGES	Tribal inheritances and relations with neighbors and Canaanites	Judges, saviors, and their actions	Mikha's idol and the migration of the tribe of Dan	The concubine at Giva and the wars of Israel and Binyamin
	Chs. 1:1–3:6	3:7–16:31	17–18	19–21
	Approx. 300 years			

1 1 After the death of Yehoshua, the Israelites inquired of the LORD, asking,
"Who should be the first to go up against the Canaanites and fight them?"
2 "Yehuda shall go up," said the LORD. "Behold, I will now deliver the land
3 into their hands." "Advance with us to our allotment," Yehuda said to their
brother-tribe, Shimon, "and we will fight the Canaanites together. Then we
4 will accompany you to your allotment." So Shimon joined them. Yehuda
went up, and the LORD delivered the Canaanites and the Perizzites into their
5 hands; they struck down ten thousand men in Bezek. They found Adoni
Bezek in Bezek and fought against him and defeated the Canaanites and the
6 Perizzites. Adoni Bezek fled, but they chased after him; they seized him and
7 severed his thumbs and big toes. "Seventy kings with severed thumbs and
big toes have gathered the scraps under my table," said Adoni Bezek. "As I
have done, so God has requited me." They brought him to Jerusalem, and
there he died.
8 The Judahites attacked Jerusalem and captured it, then they put it to the
9 sword and set the city alight. After that, the Judahites went down to attack
the Canaanites who lived in the hill country, the Negev, and the lowlands.
10 Yehuda marched against the Canaanites of Ḥevron – its previous name was
11 Kiryat Arba – and they struck down Sheshai, Aḥiman, and Talmai. From there,
they set out against the people of Dvir, the previous name of which was Kiryat
12 Sefer. Kalev declared: "Whoever defeats Kiryat Sefer and captures it – I shall
13 give him my daughter Akhsa for a wife." Otniel son of Kenaz, Kalev's younger
14 brother, captured it, and he gave him his daughter Akhsa for a wife. When
she arrived, having urged him to ask her father for the field, she dismounted
15 rapidly from the donkey. "What is the matter?" Kalev said to her. "Grant me
blessing," she replied, "for you have given me desert land, and you should
give me springs of water." So he gave her the upper springs and the lower
16 springs.[1] Now, the descendants of the Kenite, Moshe's father-in-law,
ascended from the City of Palms with the Judahites to the Wilderness of
Yehuda in the Negev region near Arad; they came and settled among the
17 people. Yehuda joined its brother-tribe Shimon, and they attacked the
Canaanites of Tzefat; they laid it to waste and renamed the city Ḥorma.[2]
18 Yehuda captured Aza and its surroundings, Ashkelon and its surroundings,
19 and Ekron and its surroundings. The LORD was with Yehuda, and they seized
the hills, but they did not dispossess the people of the valley, for they had
20 iron chariots. As Moses had promised, they gave Ḥevron to Kalev, who
21 dispossessed from there the three sons of Anak. As for the Jebusites, the
inhabitants of Jerusalem, the Benjaminites did not dispossess them; the
22 Jebusites dwell with the Benjaminites in Jerusalem to this day.[3] The
23 House of Yosef also advanced to Beit El, and the LORD was with them. As
24 they scouted out Beit El – previously called Luz – the sentries saw a man
leaving the city. "Show us the way into the city," they said to him, "and we will

1 | Cf. Joshua 15:13–19.
2 | Literally "waste" or "destruction."
3 | Cf. Joshua 15:63.

א א וַיְהִי אַחֲרֵי מוֹת יְהוֹשֻׁעַ וַיִּשְׁאֲלוּ בְּנֵי יִשְׂרָאֵל בַּיהוָה לֵאמֹר מִי יַעֲלֶה־ א
ב לָּנוּ אֶל־הַכְּנַעֲנִי בַּתְּחִלָּה לְהִלָּחֶם בּוֹ: וַיֹּאמֶר יְהוָה יְהוּדָה יַעֲלֶה הִנֵּה
ג נָתַתִּי אֶת־הָאָרֶץ בְּיָדוֹ: וַיֹּאמֶר יְהוּדָה לְשִׁמְעוֹן אָחִיו עֲלֵה אִתִּי
בְגוֹרָלִי וְנִלָּחֲמָה בַּכְּנַעֲנִי וְהָלַכְתִּי גַם־אֲנִי אִתְּךָ בְּגוֹרָלֶךָ וַיֵּלֶךְ אִתּוֹ
ד שִׁמְעוֹן: וַיַּעַל יְהוּדָה וַיִּתֵּן יְהוָה אֶת־הַכְּנַעֲנִי וְהַפְּרִזִּי בְּיָדָם וַיַּכּוּם בְּבֶזֶק
ה עֲשֶׂרֶת אֲלָפִים אִישׁ: וַיִּמְצְאוּ אֶת־אֲדֹנִי בֶזֶק בְּבֶזֶק וַיִּלָּחֲמוּ בּוֹ וַיַּכּוּ
ו אֶת־הַכְּנַעֲנִי וְאֶת־הַפְּרִזִּי: וַיָּנָס אֲדֹנִי בֶזֶק וַיִּרְדְּפוּ אַחֲרָיו וַיֹּאחֲזוּ אוֹתוֹ
ז וַיְקַצְּצוּ אֶת־בְּהֹנוֹת יָדָיו וְרַגְלָיו: וַיֹּאמֶר אֲדֹנִי־בֶזֶק שִׁבְעִים ׀ מְלָכִים
בְּהֹנוֹת יְדֵיהֶם וְרַגְלֵיהֶם מְקֻצָּצִים הָיוּ מְלַקְּטִים תַּחַת שֻׁלְחָנִי כַּאֲשֶׁר
עָשִׂיתִי כֵּן שִׁלַּם־לִי אֱלֹהִים וַיְבִיאֻהוּ יְרוּשָׁלִַם וַיָּמָת שָׁם:
ח וַיִּלָּחֲמוּ בְנֵי־יְהוּדָה בִּירוּשָׁלִַם וַיִּלְכְּדוּ אוֹתָהּ וַיַּכּוּהָ לְפִי־חָרֶב וְאֶת־
ט הָעִיר שִׁלְּחוּ בָאֵשׁ: וְאַחַר יָרְדוּ בְּנֵי יְהוּדָה לְהִלָּחֵם בַּכְּנַעֲנִי יוֹשֵׁב הָהָר
י וְהַנֶּגֶב וְהַשְּׁפֵלָה: וַיֵּלֶךְ יְהוּדָה אֶל־הַכְּנַעֲנִי הַיּוֹשֵׁב בְּחֶבְרוֹן וְשֵׁם־חֶבְרוֹן
יא לְפָנִים קִרְיַת אַרְבַּע וַיַּכּוּ אֶת־שֵׁשַׁי וְאֶת־אֲחִימַן וְאֶת־תַּלְמָי: וַיֵּלֶךְ
יב מִשָּׁם אֶל־יוֹשְׁבֵי דְּבִיר וְשֵׁם־דְּבִיר לְפָנִים קִרְיַת־סֵפֶר: וַיֹּאמֶר כָּלֵב
אֲשֶׁר־יַכֶּה אֶת־קִרְיַת־סֵפֶר וּלְכָדָהּ וְנָתַתִּי לוֹ אֶת־עַכְסָה בִתִּי לְאִשָּׁה:
יג וַיִּלְכְּדָהּ עָתְנִיאֵל בֶּן־קְנַז אֲחִי כָלֵב הַקָּטֹן מִמֶּנּוּ וַיִּתֶּן־לוֹ אֶת־עַכְסָה
יד בִתּוֹ לְאִשָּׁה: וַיְהִי בְּבוֹאָהּ וַתְּסִיתֵהוּ לִשְׁאוֹל מֵאֵת־אָבִיהָ הַשָּׂדֶה
טו וַתִּצְנַח מֵעַל הַחֲמוֹר וַיֹּאמֶר־לָהּ כָּלֵב מַה־לָּךְ: וַתֹּאמֶר לוֹ הָבָה־לִּי
בְרָכָה כִּי אֶרֶץ הַנֶּגֶב נְתַתָּנִי וְנָתַתָּה לִי גֻּלֹּת מָיִם וַיִּתֶּן־לָהּ כָּלֵב אֵת
טז גֻּלֹּת עִלִּית וְאֵת גֻּלֹּת תַּחְתִּית: וּבְנֵי קֵינִי חֹתֵן מֹשֶׁה עָלוּ
מֵעִיר הַתְּמָרִים אֶת־בְּנֵי יְהוּדָה מִדְבַּר יְהוּדָה אֲשֶׁר בְּנֶגֶב עֲרָד וַיֵּלֶךְ
יז וַיֵּשֶׁב אֶת־הָעָם: וַיֵּלֶךְ יְהוּדָה אֶת־שִׁמְעוֹן אָחִיו וַיַּכּוּ אֶת־הַכְּנַעֲנִי
יח יוֹשֵׁב צְפַת וַיַּחֲרִימוּ אוֹתָהּ וַיִּקְרָא אֶת־שֵׁם־הָעִיר חָרְמָה: וַיִּלְכֹּד יְהוּדָה
אֶת־עַזָּה וְאֶת־גְּבוּלָהּ וְאֶת־אַשְׁקְלוֹן וְאֶת־גְּבוּלָהּ וְאֶת־עֶקְרוֹן וְאֶת־
יט גְּבוּלָהּ: וַיְהִי יְהוָה אֶת־יְהוּדָה וַיֹּרֶשׁ אֶת־הָהָר כִּי לֹא לְהוֹרִישׁ אֶת־
כ יֹשְׁבֵי הָעֵמֶק כִּי־רֶכֶב בַּרְזֶל לָהֶם: וַיִּתְּנוּ לְכָלֵב אֶת־חֶבְרוֹן כַּאֲשֶׁר
כא דִּבֶּר מֹשֶׁה וַיּוֹרֶשׁ מִשָּׁם אֶת־שְׁלֹשָׁה בְּנֵי הָעֲנָק: וְאֶת־הַיְבוּסִי יֹשֵׁב
יְרוּשָׁלִַם לֹא הוֹרִישׁוּ בְּנֵי בִנְיָמִן וַיֵּשֶׁב הַיְבוּסִי אֶת־בְּנֵי בִנְיָמִן בִּירוּשָׁלִַם
כב עַד הַיּוֹם הַזֶּה: וַיַּעֲלוּ בֵית־יוֹסֵף גַּם־הֵם בֵּית־אֵל וַיהוָה
כג כד עִמָּם: וַיָּתִירוּ בֵית־יוֹסֵף בְּבֵית־אֵל וְשֵׁם־הָעִיר לְפָנִים לוּז: וַיִּרְאוּ
הַשֹּׁמְרִים אִישׁ יוֹצֵא מִן־הָעִיר וַיֹּאמְרוּ לוֹ הַרְאֵנוּ נָא אֶת־מְבוֹא הָעִיר

25 show you loyalty." He showed them the way into the city, and they attacked
26 the city by sword, but they let the man and all his family go. The man made
his way to the Hittite country. He built a city and named it Luz, which is its
27 name to this day. Menashe did not dispossess Beit She'an and its
dependencies, Tanakh and its dependencies, the people of Dor and its
dependencies, Yivle'am and its dependencies, or Megiddo and its
28 dependencies; the Canaanites were determined to stay in that land. When
Israel grew strong, they taxed the Canaanites with forced labor, but they never
29 dispossessed them. Efrayim did not dispossess the Canaanites who
30 lived in Gezer, and the Canaanites lived among them in Gezer. Zevulun
did not dispossess the people of Kitron or the people of Nahalol, and the
31 Canaanites lived among them and were taxed with forced labor. Asher
did not dispossess the people of Akko, nor the people of Sidon, Aḥlav, Akhziv,
32 Ḥelba, Afik, and Reḥov. The Asherites lived among the Canaanite inhabitants
33 of the land, for they did not dispossess them. Naftali did not
dispossess the people of Beit Shemesh or the people of Beit Anat; they lived
among the Canaanites, the inhabitants of the land, and the people of Beit
34 Shemesh and Beit Anat became forced laborers for them. The Amorites
forced the people of Dan into the hills; they would not allow them to descend
35 into the valley. The Amorites were determined to stay in Mount Ḥeres, Ayalon,
and Shaalvim, but the hand of the House of Yosef weighed heavily upon them
36 and taxed them with forced labor. The Amorite border extended from
2 1 Scorpion Ascent, upward from the Rock. Once, an angel of the
Lord ascended from Gilgal to Bokhim and declared: "I raised you
up out of Egypt and brought you to the land that I promised your forefathers,
2 saying, 'I will never break My Covenant with you, and you must never form
a covenant with the inhabitants of this land – you must smash their altars,'
3 but you have not obeyed Me. What have you done? Therefore, I said, 'I shall
not drive them out from your midst; they will be thorns in your sides, their
4 gods will be a snare for you.'" As the angel of the Lord uttered these words
5 to all the Israelites, the people raised their voices and wept. They named that
6 place Bokhim,[4] and they sacrificed there to the Lord. Then
Yehoshua sent the people away, and each of the Israelites went to his estate,
7 taking possession of the land. And the people served the Lord all the days
of Yehoshua and all the days of the elders who lived on after Yehoshua and
who had seen all the mighty deeds that the Lord had done for Israel.
8 Yehoshua son of Nun, the Lord's servant, died at the age of one hundred and
9 ten.[5] They buried him at the border of his estate, at Timnat Ḥeres in the
10 Efrayim hills, north of Mount Gaash. And when all of that generation, too,
were gathered to their fathers, a new generation arose after them, who did

---

4 | Meaning "weepers."
5 | Cf. Joshua 24:29–30.

כה וְעָשִׂינוּ עִמְּךָ חָסֶד׃ וַיַּרְאֵם אֶת־מְבוֹא הָעִיר וַיַּכּוּ אֶת־הָעִיר לְפִי־חָרֶב
כו וְאֶת־הָאִישׁ וְאֶת־כָּל־מִשְׁפַּחְתּוֹ שִׁלֵּחוּ׃ וַיֵּלֶךְ הָאִישׁ אֶרֶץ הַחִתִּים וַיִּבֶן
כז עִיר וַיִּקְרָא שְׁמָהּ לוּז הוּא שְׁמָהּ עַד הַיּוֹם הַזֶּה׃ וְלֹא־הוֹרִישׁ
מְנַשֶּׁה אֶת־בֵּית־שְׁאָן וְאֶת־בְּנוֹתֶיהָ וְאֶת־תַּעְנַךְ וְאֶת־בְּנֹתֶיהָ וְאֶת־יֹשֵׁב
דּוֹר וְאֶת־בְּנוֹתֶיהָ וְאֶת־יוֹשְׁבֵי יִבְלְעָם וְאֶת־בְּנֹתֶיהָ וְאֶת־יוֹשְׁבֵי מְגִדּוֹ
כח וְאֶת־בְּנוֹתֶיהָ וַיּוֹאֶל הַכְּנַעֲנִי לָשֶׁבֶת בָּאָרֶץ הַזֹּאת׃ וַיְהִי כִּי־חָזַק יִשְׂרָאֵל
כט וַיָּשֶׂם אֶת־הַכְּנַעֲנִי לָמַס וְהוֹרֵישׁ לֹא הוֹרִישׁוֹ׃ וְאֶפְרַיִם
לֹא הוֹרִישׁ אֶת־הַכְּנַעֲנִי הַיּוֹשֵׁב בְּגָזֶר וַיֵּשֶׁב הַכְּנַעֲנִי בְּקִרְבּוֹ
ל בְּגָזֶר׃ זְבוּלֻן לֹא הוֹרִישׁ אֶת־יוֹשְׁבֵי קִטְרוֹן וְאֶת־יוֹשְׁבֵי
לא נַהֲלֹל וַיֵּשֶׁב הַכְּנַעֲנִי בְּקִרְבּוֹ וַיִּהְיוּ לָמַס׃ אָשֵׁר לֹא הוֹרִישׁ
אֶת־יֹשְׁבֵי עַכּוֹ וְאֶת־יוֹשְׁבֵי צִידוֹן וְאֶת־אַחְלָב וְאֶת־אַכְזִיב וְאֶת־חֶלְבָּה
לב וְאֶת־אֲפִיק וְאֶת־רְחֹב׃ וַיֵּשֶׁב הָאָשֵׁרִי בְּקֶרֶב הַכְּנַעֲנִי יֹשְׁבֵי הָאָרֶץ כִּי
לג לֹא הוֹרִישׁוֹ׃ נַפְתָּלִי לֹא־הוֹרִישׁ אֶת־יֹשְׁבֵי בֵית־שֶׁמֶשׁ
וְאֶת־יֹשְׁבֵי בֵית־עֲנָת וַיֵּשֶׁב בְּקֶרֶב הַכְּנַעֲנִי יֹשְׁבֵי הָאָרֶץ וְיֹשְׁבֵי בֵית־
לד שֶׁמֶשׁ וּבֵית עֲנָת הָיוּ לָהֶם לָמַס׃ וַיִּלְחֲצוּ הָאֱמֹרִי אֶת־בְּנֵי־דָן הָהָרָה
לה כִּי־לֹא נְתָנוֹ לָרֶדֶת לָעֵמֶק׃ וַיּוֹאֶל הָאֱמֹרִי לָשֶׁבֶת בְּהַר־חֶרֶס בְּאַיָּלוֹן
לו וּבְשַׁעַלְבִים וַתִּכְבַּד יַד בֵּית־יוֹסֵף וַיִּהְיוּ לָמַס׃ וּגְבוּל הָאֱמֹרִי מִמַּעֲלֵה
ב א עַקְרַבִּים מֵהַסֶּלַע וָמָעְלָה׃ וַיַּעַל מַלְאַךְ־יְהוָה מִן־הַגִּלְגָּל
אֶל־הַבֹּכִים וַיֹּאמֶר אַעֲלֶה אֶתְכֶם מִמִּצְרַיִם וָאָבִיא
אֶתְכֶם אֶל־הָאָרֶץ אֲשֶׁר נִשְׁבַּעְתִּי לַאֲבֹתֵיכֶם וָאֹמַר לֹא־אָפֵר בְּרִיתִי
ב אִתְּכֶם לְעוֹלָם׃ וְאַתֶּם לֹא־תִכְרְתוּ בְרִית לְיוֹשְׁבֵי הָאָרֶץ הַזֹּאת
ג מִזְבְּחוֹתֵיהֶם תִּתֹּצוּן וְלֹא־שְׁמַעְתֶּם בְּקֹלִי מַה־זֹּאת עֲשִׂיתֶם׃ וְגַם
אָמַרְתִּי לֹא־אֲגָרֵשׁ אוֹתָם מִפְּנֵיכֶם וְהָיוּ לָכֶם לְצִדִּים וֵאלֹהֵיהֶם יִהְיוּ
ד לָכֶם לְמוֹקֵשׁ׃ וַיְהִי כְּדַבֵּר מַלְאַךְ יְהוָה אֶת־הַדְּבָרִים הָאֵלֶּה אֶל־כָּל־
ה בְּנֵי יִשְׂרָאֵל וַיִּשְׂאוּ הָעָם אֶת־קוֹלָם וַיִּבְכּוּ׃ וַיִּקְרְאוּ שֵׁם־הַמָּקוֹם הַהוּא
ו בֹּכִים וַיִּזְבְּחוּ־שָׁם לַיהוָה׃ וַיְשַׁלַּח יְהוֹשֻׁעַ אֶת־
ב ז הָעָם וַיֵּלְכוּ בְנֵי־יִשְׂרָאֵל אִישׁ לְנַחֲלָתוֹ לָרֶשֶׁת אֶת־הָאָרֶץ׃ וַיַּעַבְדוּ
הָעָם אֶת־יְהוָה כֹּל יְמֵי יְהוֹשֻׁעַ וְכֹל ׀ יְמֵי הַזְּקֵנִים אֲשֶׁר הֶאֱרִיכוּ יָמִים
אַחֲרֵי יְהוֹשׁוּעַ אֲשֶׁר רָאוּ אֵת כָּל־מַעֲשֵׂה יְהוָה הַגָּדוֹל אֲשֶׁר עָשָׂה
ח לְיִשְׂרָאֵל׃ וַיָּמָת יְהוֹשֻׁעַ בִּן־נוּן עֶבֶד יְהוָה בֶּן־מֵאָה וָעֶשֶׂר שָׁנִים׃
ט וַיִּקְבְּרוּ אוֹתוֹ בִּגְבוּל נַחֲלָתוֹ בְּתִמְנַת־חֶרֶס בְּהַר אֶפְרָיִם מִצְּפוֹן
י לְהַר־גָּעַשׁ׃ וְגַם כָּל־הַדּוֹר הַהוּא נֶאֶסְפוּ אֶל־אֲבוֹתָיו וַיָּקָם דּוֹר אַחֵר

11 not know the Lord or the deeds He had done for Israel. Then the
Israelites did what was evil in the eyes of the Lord, and they worshipped the
12 Be'alim. They abandoned the Lord, the God of their ancestors who had taken
them out of the land of Egypt, and embraced other gods – gods of the peoples
13 around them – and bowed to them, angering the Lord. They abandoned the
14 Lord and served Baal and Ashtarot. The Lord's wrath raged against Israel,
and He abandoned them to the hands of marauders who oppressed them. He
handed them over to the foes that surrounded them – no longer could they
15 withstand their foes. Wherever they went, the Lord's hand moved to harm
them, as the Lord had warned them and as the Lord had sworn to them,
16 and they suffered terribly. So the Lord appointed judges who saved them
17 from the hands of their oppressors. But they did not obey their judges either,
for they strayed after other gods and worshipped them. They swiftly slipped
away from the path that their ancestors had followed in order to obey the
18 Lord's command; they did not do what was right. Yet when the Lord
appointed a judge for them, the Lord would side with that judge. He would
save them from their enemies' hands throughout the judge's life, for the Lord
19 was moved by their moaning under their oppressors and tormentors. But
with the judge's death, they would relapse into worse corruption than their
fathers, following other gods, serving and bowing down to them, and they
20 would not relinquish their practices or their harsh ways. So the Lord's wrath
raged against Israel, and He said, "This nation has violated the Covenant with
21 which I charged their ancestors, and has not obeyed Me; I will no longer
dispossess before them any of the nations that Yehoshua left upon his death
22 in order to test whether or not Israel will keep following the path of the Lord
23 as their ancestors did." The Lord had let these nations be rather than swiftly
dispossessing them, and He did not give them over into Yehoshua's
3 1 hands. These are the nations that the Lord left behind to test Israel –
2 all those who had not experienced the Canaanite wars – for the Israelite
generations to gain experience of warfare, which they had not known before.
3 The five Philistine chieftains,[6] and all the Canaanites, Sidonians, and Hivites
living in the Lebanon Mountains, from Mount Baal Ḥermon to Levo Ḥamat –
4 they served to test Israel, to determine whether or not they would obey the
Lord's commandments which He had transmitted to their ancestors through
5 Moses. The Israelites lived among the Canaanites, the Hittites, the Amorites,
6 the Perizzites, the Hivites, and the Jebusites. They took their daughters
as wives, gave their own daughters to their sons, and worshipped their
7 gods. Israel did what was evil in the eyes of the Lord; they
8 forgot the Lord their God and worshipped the Be'alim and the Asherot. The
Lord's wrath raged against Israel, and He handed them over to King Kushan

6 | As in Joshua 13:1 and I Samuel 6, these are the leaders of Aza, Ashkelon, Ashdod, Ekron, and Philistine Gat.

אַחֲרֵיהֶם אֲשֶׁר לֹא־יָדְעוּ אֶת־יהוה וְגַם אֶת־הַמַּעֲשֶׂה אֲשֶׁר עָשָׂה
יא לְיִשְׂרָאֵל: וַיַּעֲשׂוּ בְנֵי־יִשְׂרָאֵל אֶת־הָרַע בְּעֵינֵי יהוה
יב וַיַּעַבְדוּ אֶת־הַבְּעָלִים: וַיַּעַזְבוּ אֶת־יהוה ׀ אֱלֹהֵי אֲבוֹתָם הַמּוֹצִיא
אוֹתָם מֵאֶרֶץ מִצְרַיִם וַיֵּלְכוּ אַחֲרֵי ׀ אֱלֹהִים אֲחֵרִים מֵאֱלֹהֵי הָעַמִּים
יג אֲשֶׁר סְבִיבוֹתֵיהֶם וַיִּשְׁתַּחֲווּ לָהֶם וַיַּכְעִסוּ אֶת־יהוה: וַיַּעַזְבוּ אֶת־יהוה
יד וַיַּעַבְדוּ לַבַּעַל וְלָעַשְׁתָּרוֹת: וַיִּחַר־אַף יהוה בְּיִשְׂרָאֵל וַיִּתְּנֵם בְּיַד
שֹׁסִים וַיָּשֹׁסּוּ אוֹתָם וַיִּמְכְּרֵם בְּיַד אוֹיְבֵיהֶם מִסָּבִיב וְלֹא־יָכְלוּ עוֹד
טו לַעֲמֹד לִפְנֵי אוֹיְבֵיהֶם: בְּכֹל ׀ אֲשֶׁר יָצְאוּ יַד־יהוה הָיְתָה־בָּם לְרָעָה
טז כַּאֲשֶׁר דִּבֶּר יהוה וְכַאֲשֶׁר נִשְׁבַּע יהוה לָהֶם וַיֵּצֶר לָהֶם מְאֹד: וַיָּקֶם
יז יהוה שֹׁפְטִים וַיּוֹשִׁיעוּם מִיַּד שֹׁסֵיהֶם: וְגַם אֶל־שֹׁפְטֵיהֶם לֹא שָׁמֵעוּ
כִּי זָנוּ אַחֲרֵי אֱלֹהִים אֲחֵרִים וַיִּשְׁתַּחֲווּ לָהֶם סָרוּ מַהֵר מִן־הַדֶּרֶךְ אֲשֶׁר
יח הָלְכוּ אֲבוֹתָם לִשְׁמֹעַ מִצְוֹת־יהוה לֹא־עָשׂוּ כֵן: וְכִי־הֵקִים יהוה ׀
לָהֶם שֹׁפְטִים וְהָיָה יהוה עִם־הַשֹּׁפֵט וְהוֹשִׁיעָם מִיַּד אֹיְבֵיהֶם כֹּל יְמֵי
יט הַשּׁוֹפֵט כִּי־יִנָּחֵם יהוה מִנַּאֲקָתָם מִפְּנֵי לֹחֲצֵיהֶם וְדֹחֲקֵיהֶם: וְהָיָה ׀
בְּמוֹת הַשּׁוֹפֵט יָשֻׁבוּ וְהִשְׁחִיתוּ מֵאֲבוֹתָם לָלֶכֶת אַחֲרֵי אֱלֹהִים אֲחֵרִים
לְעָבְדָם וּלְהִשְׁתַּחֲוֹת לָהֶם לֹא הִפִּילוּ מִמַּעַלְלֵיהֶם וּמִדַּרְכָּם הַקָּשָׁה:
כ וַיִּחַר־אַף יהוה בְּיִשְׂרָאֵל וַיֹּאמֶר יַעַן אֲשֶׁר עָבְרוּ הַגּוֹי הַזֶּה אֶת־
כא בְּרִיתִי אֲשֶׁר צִוִּיתִי אֶת־אֲבוֹתָם וְלֹא שָׁמְעוּ לְקוֹלִי: גַּם־אֲנִי לֹא אוֹסִיף
כב לְהוֹרִישׁ אִישׁ מִפְּנֵיהֶם מִן־הַגּוֹיִם אֲשֶׁר־עָזַב יְהוֹשֻׁעַ וַיָּמֹת: לְמַעַן
נַסּוֹת בָּם אֶת־יִשְׂרָאֵל הֲשֹׁמְרִים הֵם אֶת־דֶּרֶךְ יהוה לָלֶכֶת בָּם כַּאֲשֶׁר
כג שָׁמְרוּ אֲבוֹתָם אִם־לֹא: וַיַּנַּח יהוה אֶת־הַגּוֹיִם הָאֵלֶּה לְבִלְתִּי הוֹרִישָׁם
ג א מַהֵר וְלֹא נְתָנָם בְּיַד־יְהוֹשֻׁעַ: וְאֵלֶּה הַגּוֹיִם אֲשֶׁר הִנִּיחַ
יהוה לְנַסּוֹת בָּם אֶת־יִשְׂרָאֵל אֵת כָּל־אֲשֶׁר לֹא־יָדְעוּ אֵת כָּל־מִלְחֲמוֹת
ב כְּנָעַן: רַק לְמַעַן דַּעַת דֹּרוֹת בְּנֵי־יִשְׂרָאֵל לְלַמְּדָם מִלְחָמָה רַק אֲשֶׁר־
ג לְפָנִים לֹא יְדָעוּם: חֲמֵשֶׁת ׀ סַרְנֵי פְלִשְׁתִּים וְכָל־הַכְּנַעֲנִי וְהַצִּידֹנִי וְהַחִוִּי
ד יֹשֵׁב הַר הַלְּבָנוֹן מֵהַר בַּעַל חֶרְמוֹן עַד לְבוֹא חֲמָת: וַיִּהְיוּ לְנַסּוֹת בָּם
אֶת־יִשְׂרָאֵל לָדַעַת הֲיִשְׁמְעוּ אֶת־מִצְוֹת יהוה אֲשֶׁר־צִוָּה אֶת־אֲבוֹתָם
ה בְּיַד־מֹשֶׁה: וּבְנֵי יִשְׂרָאֵל יָשְׁבוּ בְּקֶרֶב הַכְּנַעֲנִי הַחִתִּי וְהָאֱמֹרִי וְהַפְּרִזִּי
ו וְהַחִוִּי וְהַיְבוּסִי: וַיִּקְחוּ אֶת־בְּנוֹתֵיהֶם לָהֶם לְנָשִׁים וְאֶת־בְּנוֹתֵיהֶם
ז נָתְנוּ לִבְנֵיהֶם וַיַּעַבְדוּ אֶת־אֱלֹהֵיהֶם: וַיַּעֲשׂוּ בְנֵי־יִשְׂרָאֵל
אֶת־הָרַע בְּעֵינֵי יהוה וַיִּשְׁכְּחוּ אֶת־יהוה אֱלֹהֵיהֶם וַיַּעַבְדוּ אֶת־הַבְּעָלִים
ח וְאֶת־הָאֲשֵׁרוֹת: וַיִּחַר־אַף יהוה בְּיִשְׂרָאֵל וַיִּמְכְּרֵם בְּיַד כּוּשַׁן רִשְׁעָתַיִם

Rishatayim of Aram Naharayim. The Israelites served Kushan Rishatayim for
9 eight years. Then the Israelites cried out to the LORD, and the LORD appointed
10 a savior to rescue them: Otniel son of Kenaz, Kalev's younger brother. The
spirit of the LORD was upon him, and he judged Israel. He went out to war,
and the LORD delivered Kushan Rishatayim, king of Aram, into his hand;
11 against Kushan Rishatayim his hand prevailed. And the land was quiet for
12 forty years; then Otniel son of Kenaz died. Then the Israelites
resumed doing what was evil in the eyes of the LORD, and the LORD inspired
Eglon, king of Moav, to overcome Israel, for they had done evil in the eyes of
13 the LORD. He rallied the Amonites and Amalek to him, and they launched an
14 attack on Israel and seized the City of Palms. The Israelites served Eglon, king
15 of Moav, for eighteen years. Then the Israelites cried out to the LORD, and the
LORD appointed a savior for them: Ehud son of Gera the Benjaminite, a left-
handed man. When the Israelites sent tribute to Eglon, king of Moav, through
16 him, Ehud made himself a two-edged dagger a cubit long and fastened it
17 under his uniform onto his right thigh. He presented the tribute to Eglon,
18 king of Moav, an exceedingly portly man. When Ehud had finished presenting
19 the tribute, he sent the men who had carried it on their way, but he himself
doubled back from the carved images near Gilgal and said, "I have a secret
message for you, O king." "Silence!" said the king, and all his attendants left
20 him. Ehud drew near him – he was lounging alone in his private cooling
chamber. "I have a message for you from God," said Ehud. The king heaved
21 himself up from the throne. Ehud thrust out his left hand, seized the sword
22 from his right thigh, and drove it into Eglon's belly. The hilt was sucked in
after the blade, and the fat closed over the blade, for he did not withdraw the
23 dagger from his belly – and the filth oozed out. Ehud slipped out to the
24 corridor, closed the chamber doors behind him, and locked them. As he left,
the servants came back and saw that the chamber doors were locked. "He
25 must be relieving himself in the cooling chamber," they thought. They waited
until it grew late, but he had still not opened the chamber doors, so they took
the key and opened them up – and there, sprawled on the floor, lay their
26 master, dead. Ehud had escaped while they tarried; he passed by the carved
27 images and fled toward Se'ira. As soon as he arrived, he blasted the ram's horn
on Mount Efrayim, and the Israelites marched with him down the hills; he
28 took the lead. "Follow me," he said to them, "for the LORD has delivered your
enemies – Moav – into your hands!" They marched down after him, captured
29 the Jordan fords bordering on Moav, and let no one cross. They defeated
Moav on that day – about ten thousand men, each one robust and valiant,

מֶלֶךְ אֲרַם נַהֲרָיִם וַיַּעַבְדוּ בְנֵי־יִשְׂרָאֵל אֶת־כּוּשַׁן רִשְׁעָתַיִם שְׁמֹנֶה
ט שָׁנִים: וַיִּזְעֲקוּ בְנֵי־יִשְׂרָאֵל אֶל־יהוה וַיָּקֶם יהוה מוֹשִׁיעַ לִבְנֵי יִשְׂרָאֵל
י וַיּוֹשִׁיעֵם אֵת עָתְנִיאֵל בֶּן־קְנַז אֲחִי כָלֵב הַקָּטֹן מִמֶּנּוּ: וַתְּהִי עָלָיו
רוּחַ־יהוה וַיִּשְׁפֹּט אֶת־יִשְׂרָאֵל וַיֵּצֵא לַמִּלְחָמָה וַיִּתֵּן יהוה בְּיָדוֹ אֶת־
יא כּוּשַׁן רִשְׁעָתַיִם מֶלֶךְ אֲרָם וַתָּעָז יָדוֹ עַל כּוּשַׁן רִשְׁעָתָיִם: וַתִּשְׁקֹט
יב הָאָרֶץ אַרְבָּעִים שָׁנָה וַיָּמָת עָתְנִיאֵל בֶּן־קְנַז: וַיֹּסִפוּ בְּנֵי
יִשְׂרָאֵל לַעֲשׂוֹת הָרַע בְּעֵינֵי יהוה וַיְחַזֵּק יהוה אֶת־עֶגְלוֹן מֶלֶךְ־מוֹאָב
יג עַל־יִשְׂרָאֵל עַל כִּי־עָשׂוּ אֶת־הָרַע בְּעֵינֵי יהוה: וַיֶּאֱסֹף אֵלָיו אֶת־בְּנֵי
יד עַמּוֹן וַעֲמָלֵק וַיֵּלֶךְ וַיַּךְ אֶת־יִשְׂרָאֵל וַיִּירְשׁוּ אֶת־עִיר הַתְּמָרִים: וַיַּעַבְדוּ
טו בְנֵי־יִשְׂרָאֵל אֶת־עֶגְלוֹן מֶלֶךְ־מוֹאָב שְׁמוֹנֶה עֶשְׂרֵה שָׁנָה: וַיִּזְעֲקוּ
בְנֵי־יִשְׂרָאֵל אֶל־יהוה וַיָּקֶם יהוה לָהֶם מוֹשִׁיעַ אֶת־אֵהוּד בֶּן־גֵּרָא
בֶּן־הַיְמִינִי אִישׁ אִטֵּר יַד־יְמִינוֹ וַיִּשְׁלְחוּ בְנֵי־יִשְׂרָאֵל בְּיָדוֹ מִנְחָה
טז לְעֶגְלוֹן מֶלֶךְ מוֹאָב: וַיַּעַשׂ לוֹ אֵהוּד חֶרֶב וְלָהּ שְׁנֵי פֵיוֹת גֹּמֶד אָרְכָּהּ
יז וַיַּחְגֹּר אוֹתָהּ מִתַּחַת לְמַדָּיו עַל יֶרֶךְ יְמִינוֹ: וַיַּקְרֵב אֶת־הַמִּנְחָה לְעֶגְלוֹן
יח מֶלֶךְ מוֹאָב וְעֶגְלוֹן אִישׁ בָּרִיא מְאֹד: וַיְהִי כַּאֲשֶׁר כִּלָּה לְהַקְרִיב אֶת־
יט הַמִּנְחָה וַיְשַׁלַּח אֶת־הָעָם נֹשְׂאֵי הַמִּנְחָה: וְהוּא שָׁב מִן־הַפְּסִילִים
אֲשֶׁר אֶת־הַגִּלְגָּל וַיֹּאמֶר דְּבַר־סֵתֶר לִי אֵלֶיךָ הַמֶּלֶךְ וַיֹּאמֶר הָס
כ וַיֵּצְאוּ מֵעָלָיו כָּל־הָעֹמְדִים עָלָיו: וְאֵהוּד ׀ בָּא אֵלָיו וְהוּא יֹשֵׁב בַּעֲלִיַּת
הַמְּקֵרָה אֲשֶׁר־לוֹ לְבַדּוֹ וַיֹּאמֶר אֵהוּד דְּבַר־אֱלֹהִים לִי אֵלֶיךָ וַיָּקָם
כא מֵעַל הַכִּסֵּא: וַיִּשְׁלַח אֵהוּד אֶת־יַד שְׂמֹאלוֹ וַיִּקַּח אֶת־הַחֶרֶב מֵעַל
כב יֶרֶךְ יְמִינוֹ וַיִּתְקָעֶהָ בְּבִטְנוֹ: וַיָּבֹא גַם־הַנִּצָּב אַחַר הַלַּהַב וַיִּסְגֹּר הַחֵלֶב
כג בְּעַד הַלַּהַב כִּי לֹא שָׁלַף הַחֶרֶב מִבִּטְנוֹ וַיֵּצֵא הַפַּרְשְׁדֹנָה: וַיֵּצֵא אֵהוּד
כד הַמִּסְדְּרוֹנָה וַיִּסְגֹּר דַּלְתוֹת הָעֲלִיָּה בַּעֲדוֹ וְנָעָל: וְהוּא יָצָא וַעֲבָדָיו בָּאוּ
וַיִּרְאוּ וְהִנֵּה דַּלְתוֹת הָעֲלִיָּה נְעֻלוֹת וַיֹּאמְרוּ אַךְ מֵסִיךְ הוּא אֶת־רַגְלָיו
כה בַּחֲדַר הַמְּקֵרָה: וַיָּחִילוּ עַד־בּוֹשׁ וְהִנֵּה אֵינֶנּוּ פֹתֵחַ דַּלְתוֹת הָעֲלִיָּה
כו וַיִּקְחוּ אֶת־הַמַּפְתֵּחַ וַיִּפְתָּחוּ וְהִנֵּה אֲדֹנֵיהֶם נֹפֵל אַרְצָה מֵת: וְאֵהוּד
נִמְלַט עַד הִתְמַהְמְהָם וְהוּא עָבַר אֶת־הַפְּסִילִים וַיִּמָּלֵט הַשְּׂעִירָתָה:
כז וַיְהִי בְּבוֹאוֹ וַיִּתְקַע בַּשּׁוֹפָר בְּהַר אֶפְרָיִם וַיֵּרְדוּ עִמּוֹ בְנֵי־יִשְׂרָאֵל
כח מִן־הָהָר וְהוּא לִפְנֵיהֶם: וַיֹּאמֶר אֲלֵהֶם רִדְפוּ אַחֲרַי כִּי־נָתַן יהוה
אֶת־אֹיְבֵיכֶם אֶת־מוֹאָב בְּיֶדְכֶם וַיֵּרְדוּ אַחֲרָיו וַיִּלְכְּדוּ אֶת־מַעְבְּרוֹת
כט הַיַּרְדֵּן לְמוֹאָב וְלֹא־נָתְנוּ אִישׁ לַעֲבֹר: וַיַּכּוּ אֶת־מוֹאָב בָּעֵת הַהִיא
כַּעֲשֶׂרֶת אֲלָפִים אִישׁ כָּל־שָׁמֵן וְכָל־אִישׁ חָיִל וְלֹא נִמְלַט אִישׁ:

30 and not a man escaped. On that day, Moav surrendered to Israel's hand. And
31 the land was quiet for eighty years. After him came Shamgar son of
Anat, who defeated six hundred Philistines with an ox-goad; he, too, rescued
4 1 Israel. The Israelites resumed doing what was evil in the eyes of the
2 LORD once Ehud had died. So the LORD handed them over to Yavin, king of
Canaan, who reigned in Ḥatzor; his general was Sisera, who ruled at Ḥaroshet
3 HaGoyim. The Israelites cried out to the LORD, for he had nine hundred iron
chariots, and he oppressed Israel fiercely for twenty years.
4 Devora was a prophetess, the wife of Lapidot; she was judging Israel at that
5 time. She sat beneath Devora's palm between Rama and Beit El in the Efrayim
6 hills; the Israelites would go up to her for judgment. One day, she summoned
Barak son of Avinoam from Kedesh Naftali and said to him, "The LORD, God
of Israel, has commanded: Go, take ten thousand men of the people of Naftali
7 and Zevulun and lead them to Mount Tavor. And at the Kishon Stream I
shall lead to you to Sisera, Yavin's general, along with his chariots and his
8 hordes, and deliver him into your hands." Barak said to her, "If you go with
9 me, I will go; if not, I will not." "Then I shall go with you," she said, "but you
will find no glory on the path you are taking, for the LORD will deliver Sisera
into the hands of a woman." So Devora arose and accompanied Barak to
10 Kedesh. Barak mustered Zevulun and Naftali at Kedesh and advanced with
11 ten thousand men behind him, and Devora went up with him. Ḥever the
Kenite had parted ways from the Kenites, who were descended from Ḥovav,
Moshe's father-in-law. He had pitched his tent at Elon BeTzaananim, which
12 was by Kedesh. Sisera was informed that Barak son of Avinoam had advanced
13 to Mount Tavor. And Sisera mustered all his chariots – nine hundred iron
chariots – and all his warriors from Ḥaroshet HaGoyim to Kishon Stream.
14 "Rise up!" Devora said to Barak. "For on this day, the LORD will deliver
Sisera into your hands – the LORD marches before you!" Barak charged down
15 Mount Tavor with ten thousand men behind him. And the LORD threw Sisera,
all his chariots, and his entire force into panic before Barak's swords. Sisera
16 dismounted from his chariot and fled on foot. Barak chased the chariots and
warriors to Ḥaroshet HaGoyim, and all of Sisera's army fell by the sword; not
17 a single man survived. Now Sisera had fled on foot to the tent of Yael, the
wife of Ḥever the Kenite, for there was peace between Yavin, king of Ḥatzor,
18 and Ḥever's family. Yael went out to meet Sisera. "Turn aside, my lord," she
said to him, "turn aside to me – do not fear." He turned aside into her tent,

ל וַתִּכָּנַע מוֹאָב בַּיּוֹם הַהוּא תַּחַת יַד יִשְׂרָאֵל וַתִּשְׁקֹט הָאָרֶץ שְׁמוֹנִים
לא שָׁנָה׃ וְאַחֲרָיו הָיָה שַׁמְגַּר בֶּן־עֲנָת וַיַּךְ אֶת־ ג
פְּלִשְׁתִּים שֵׁשׁ־מֵאוֹת אִישׁ בְּמַלְמַד הַבָּקָר וַיּוֹשַׁע גַּם־הוּא אֶת־
ד א יִשְׂרָאֵל׃ וַיֹּסִפוּ בְּנֵי יִשְׂרָאֵל לַעֲשׂוֹת הָרַע בְּעֵינֵי יְהוָה
ב וְאֵהוּד מֵת׃ וַיִּמְכְּרֵם יְהוָה בְּיַד יָבִין מֶלֶךְ־כְּנַעַן אֲשֶׁר מָלַךְ בְּחָצוֹר
ג וְשַׂר־צְבָאוֹ סִיסְרָא וְהוּא יוֹשֵׁב בַּחֲרֹשֶׁת הַגּוֹיִם׃ וַיִּצְעֲקוּ בְנֵי־יִשְׂרָאֵל
אֶל־יְהוָה כִּי תְּשַׁע מֵאוֹת רֶכֶב־בַּרְזֶל לוֹ וְהוּא לָחַץ אֶת־בְּנֵי יִשְׂרָאֵל
בְּחָזְקָה עֶשְׂרִים שָׁנָה׃
ד וּדְבוֹרָה אִשָּׁה נְבִיאָה אֵשֶׁת לַפִּידוֹת הִיא שֹׁפְטָה אֶת־יִשְׂרָאֵל בָּעֵת
ה הַהִיא׃ וְהִיא יוֹשֶׁבֶת תַּחַת־תֹּמֶר דְּבוֹרָה בֵּין הָרָמָה וּבֵין בֵּית־אֵל בְּהַר
ו אֶפְרָיִם וַיַּעֲלוּ אֵלֶיהָ בְּנֵי יִשְׂרָאֵל לַמִּשְׁפָּט׃ וַתִּשְׁלַח וַתִּקְרָא לְבָרָק
בֶּן־אֲבִינֹעַם מִקֶּדֶשׁ נַפְתָּלִי וַתֹּאמֶר אֵלָיו הֲלֹא־צִוָּה ׀ יְהוָה אֱלֹהֵי־
יִשְׂרָאֵל לֵךְ וּמָשַׁכְתָּ בְּהַר תָּבוֹר וְלָקַחְתָּ עִמְּךָ עֲשֶׂרֶת אֲלָפִים אִישׁ
ז מִבְּנֵי נַפְתָּלִי וּמִבְּנֵי זְבֻלוּן׃ וּמָשַׁכְתִּי אֵלֶיךָ אֶל־נַחַל קִישׁוֹן אֶת־סִיסְרָא
ח שַׂר־צְבָא יָבִין וְאֶת־רִכְבּוֹ וְאֶת־הֲמוֹנוֹ וּנְתַתִּיהוּ בְּיָדֶךָ׃ וַיֹּאמֶר אֵלֶיהָ
ט בָּרָק אִם־תֵּלְכִי עִמִּי וְהָלָכְתִּי וְאִם־לֹא תֵלְכִי עִמִּי לֹא אֵלֵךְ׃ וַתֹּאמֶר
הָלֹךְ אֵלֵךְ עִמָּךְ אֶפֶס כִּי לֹא תִהְיֶה תִּפְאַרְתְּךָ עַל־הַדֶּרֶךְ אֲשֶׁר אַתָּה
הוֹלֵךְ כִּי בְיַד־אִשָּׁה יִמְכֹּר יְהוָה אֶת־סִיסְרָא וַתָּקָם דְּבוֹרָה וַתֵּלֶךְ
י עִם־בָּרָק קֶדְשָׁה׃ וַיַּזְעֵק בָּרָק אֶת־זְבוּלֻן וְאֶת־נַפְתָּלִי קֶדְשָׁה וַיַּעַל
יא בְּרַגְלָיו עֲשֶׂרֶת אַלְפֵי אִישׁ וַתַּעַל עִמּוֹ דְּבוֹרָה׃ וְחֶבֶר הַקֵּינִי נִפְרָד מִקַּיִן
מִבְּנֵי חֹבָב חֹתֵן מֹשֶׁה וַיֵּט אָהֳלוֹ עַד־אֵלוֹן בצענים אֲשֶׁר אֶת־קֶדֶשׁ׃ בְּצַעֲנַנִּים
יב יג וַיַּגִּדוּ לְסִיסְרָא כִּי עָלָה בָּרָק בֶּן־אֲבִינֹעַם הַר־תָּבוֹר׃ וַיַּזְעֵק סִיסְרָא
אֶת־כָּל־רִכְבּוֹ תְּשַׁע מֵאוֹת רֶכֶב בַּרְזֶל וְאֶת־כָּל־הָעָם אֲשֶׁר אִתּוֹ
יד מֵחֲרֹשֶׁת הַגּוֹיִם אֶל־נַחַל קִישׁוֹן׃ וַתֹּאמֶר דְּבֹרָה אֶל־בָּרָק קוּם כִּי זֶה
הַיּוֹם אֲשֶׁר נָתַן יְהוָה אֶת־סִיסְרָא בְּיָדֶךָ הֲלֹא יְהוָה יָצָא לְפָנֶיךָ וַיֵּרֶד
טו בָּרָק מֵהַר תָּבוֹר וַעֲשֶׂרֶת אֲלָפִים אִישׁ אַחֲרָיו׃ וַיָּהָם יְהוָה אֶת־סִיסְרָא
וְאֶת־כָּל־הָרֶכֶב וְאֶת־כָּל־הַמַּחֲנֶה לְפִי־חֶרֶב לִפְנֵי בָרָק וַיֵּרֶד סִיסְרָא
טז מֵעַל הַמֶּרְכָּבָה וַיָּנָס בְּרַגְלָיו׃ וּבָרָק רָדַף אַחֲרֵי הָרֶכֶב וְאַחֲרֵי הַמַּחֲנֶה
עַד חֲרֹשֶׁת הַגּוֹיִם וַיִּפֹּל כָּל־מַחֲנֵה סִיסְרָא לְפִי־חֶרֶב לֹא נִשְׁאַר עַד־
יז אֶחָד׃ וְסִיסְרָא נָס בְּרַגְלָיו אֶל־אֹהֶל יָעֵל אֵשֶׁת חֶבֶר הַקֵּינִי כִּי שָׁלוֹם
יח בֵּין יָבִין מֶלֶךְ־חָצוֹר וּבֵין בֵּית חֶבֶר הַקֵּינִי׃ וַתֵּצֵא יָעֵל לִקְרַאת סִיסְרָא
וַתֹּאמֶר אֵלָיו סוּרָה אֲדֹנִי סוּרָה אֵלַי אַל־תִּירָא וַיָּסַר אֵלֶיהָ הָאֹהֱלָה

19 and she covered him with a blanket. "Give me a little water, please," he asked
her, "for I am thirsty." She opened a skin of milk, gave him some to drink, and
20 covered him once again. "Stand at the entrance to the tent," he told her, "and
21 if anyone comes and asks you if someone is here, say, 'No.'" Then Yael, wife
of Ḥever, picked up a tent peg, grasped a mallet, crept up to him – he had
fallen asleep, exhausted – and hammered the tent peg through his temple
22 until it sunk into the ground and he died. Now Barak was chasing Sisera,
and Yael went out to meet him. "Come," she said to him, "I will show you
the man you seek." He came to her, and there was Sisera, sprawled out dead,
23 with the tent peg through his temple. On that day, God subdued Yavin, king
24 of Canaan, before the Israelites. And the hand of the Israelites grew harsher
and harsher against Yavin, king of Canaan, until they had destroyed him.

5 1 2 And Devora sang – and Barak son of Avinoam with her – on that day: / When
chaos was loosed in Israel, / when people offered themselves willingly[7] – /
3 bless the LORD! / Hear, O kings, / give ear, O rulers, / I – to the LORD I will
4 sing, / I will chant to the LORD, God of Israel. / O LORD, when You left Se'ir, /
when You marched from the fields of Edom, / the earth shook, / the heavens
5 poured – / rain poured from the clouds, / the mountains melted before the
6 LORD, / Sinai itself before the LORD, God of Israel! / In the days of Shamgar
son of Anat, / in the days of Yael, / there were no caravans; / wayfarers walked
7 roundabout paths. / There were no unwalled cities in Israel, / none – / until
8 you arose, Devora, / until you arose, a mother in Israel! / When they chose
new gods, / there was war at the gates – / but no shield or spear was seen /
9 amid forty thousand of Israel! / My heart is with Israel's leaders, / the people
10 who offer themselves willingly – / bless the LORD! / O riders of white she-
11 donkeys, / mounted on fine saddles, / O wayfarers: / speak out – / louder
than the sound of archers / by the watering places; / there they shall recount
the LORD's graces, / how He graced the unwalled cities in Israel; / then, down

7 | Devora praises the volunteering spirit of the Israelite warriors.

יט וַתְּכַסֵּ֖הוּ בַּשְּׂמִיכָֽה׃ וַיֹּ֧אמֶר אֵלֶ֛יהָ הַשְׁקִֽינִי־נָ֥א מְעַט־מַ֖יִם כִּ֣י צָמֵ֑תִי
כ וַתִּפְתַּ֞ח אֶת־נֹ֧אוד הֶחָלָ֛ב וַתַּשְׁקֵ֖הוּ וַתְּכַסֵּֽהוּ׃ וַיֹּ֣אמֶר אֵלֶ֔יהָ עֲמֹ֖ד פֶּ֣תַח
הָאֹ֑הֶל וְהָיָ֡ה אִם־אִ֨ישׁ יָב֜וֹא וּשְׁאֵלֵ֗ךְ וְאָמַ֛ר הֲיֵשׁ־פֹּ֥ה אִ֖ישׁ וְאָמַ֥רְתְּ אָֽיִן׃
כא וַתִּקַּ֣ח יָעֵ֣ל אֵֽשֶׁת־חֶ֠בֶר אֶת־יְתַ֨ד הָאֹ֜הֶל וַתָּ֧שֶׂם אֶת־הַמַּקֶּ֣בֶת בְּיָדָ֗הּ
וַתָּב֤וֹא אֵלָיו֙ בַּלָּ֔אט וַתִּתְקַ֤ע אֶת־הַיָּתֵד֙ בְּרַקָּת֔וֹ וַתִּצְנַ֖ח בָּאָ֑רֶץ וְהֽוּא־
כב נִרְדָּ֥ם וַיָּ֖עַף וַיָּמֹֽת׃ וְהִנֵּ֣ה בָרָק֮ רֹדֵ֣ף אֶת־סִֽיסְרָא֒ וַתֵּצֵ֧א יָעֵ֣ל לִקְרָאת֗וֹ
וַתֹּ֤אמֶר לוֹ֙ לֵ֣ךְ וְאַרְאֶ֔ךָּ אֶת־הָאִ֖ישׁ אֲשֶׁר־אַתָּ֣ה מְבַקֵּ֑שׁ וַיָּבֹ֣א אֵלֶ֔יהָ
כג וְהִנֵּ֤ה סִֽיסְרָא֙ נֹפֵ֣ל מֵ֔ת וְהַיָּתֵ֖ד בְּרַקָּתֽוֹ׃ וַיַּכְנַ֤ע אֱלֹהִים֙ בַּיּ֣וֹם הַה֔וּא
כד אֵ֖ת יָבִ֣ין מֶלֶךְ־כְּנָ֑עַן לִפְנֵ֖י בְּנֵ֥י יִשְׂרָאֵֽל׃ וַתֵּ֨לֶךְ יַ֤ד בְּנֵֽי־יִשְׂרָאֵל֙ הָל֣וֹךְ
וְקָשָׁ֔ה עַ֖ל יָבִ֣ין מֶלֶךְ־כְּנָ֑עַן עַ֚ד אֲשֶׁ֣ר הִכְרִ֔יתוּ אֵ֖ת יָבִ֥ין מֶֽלֶךְ־כְּנָֽעַן׃

ה א וַתָּ֣שַׁר דְּבוֹרָ֔ה וּבָרָ֖ק בֶּן־אֲבִינֹ֑עַם בַּיּ֥וֹם הַה֖וּא
ב לֵאמֹֽר׃ בִּפְרֹ֤עַ פְּרָעוֹת֙ בְּיִשְׂרָאֵ֔ל בְּהִתְנַדֵּ֖ב
ג עָ֑ם בָּרֲכ֖וּ יְהוָֽה׃ שִׁמְע֣וּ מְלָכִ֔ים הַאֲזִ֖ינוּ
רֹזְנִ֑ים אָנֹכִ֗י לַֽיהוָה֙ אָנֹכִ֣י אָשִׁ֔ירָה אֲזַמֵּ֕ר
ד לַֽיהוָ֖ה אֱלֹהֵ֥י יִשְׂרָאֵֽל׃ יְהוָ֗ה בְּצֵאתְךָ֤
מִשֵּׂעִיר֙ בְּצַעְדְּךָ֙ מִשְּׂדֵ֣ה אֱד֔וֹם אֶ֣רֶץ
רָעָ֔שָׁה גַּם־שָׁמַ֖יִם נָטָ֑פוּ גַּם־עָבִ֖ים נָ֥טְפוּ
ה מָֽיִם׃ הָרִ֥ים נָזְל֖וּ מִפְּנֵ֣י יְהוָ֑ה זֶ֣ה
ו סִינַ֔י מִפְּנֵ֕י יְהוָ֖ה אֱלֹהֵ֥י יִשְׂרָאֵֽל׃ בִּימֵ֞י שַׁמְגַּ֤ר בֶּן־
עֲנָת֙ בִּימֵ֣י יָעֵ֔ל חָדְל֖וּ אֳרָח֑וֹת וְהֹלְכֵ֣י
ז נְתִיב֔וֹת יֵלְכ֕וּ אֳרָח֖וֹת עֲקַלְקַלּֽוֹת׃ חָדְל֧וּ פְרָז֛וֹן בְּיִשְׂרָאֵ֖ל
חָדֵ֑לּוּ עַ֤ד שַׁקַּ֙מְתִּי֙ דְּבוֹרָ֔ה שַׁקַּ֖מְתִּי
ח אֵ֥ם בְּיִשְׂרָאֵֽל׃ יִבְחַר֙ אֱלֹהִ֣ים
חֲדָשִׁ֔ים אָ֖ז לָחֶ֣ם שְׁעָרִ֑ים מָגֵ֤ן
אִם־יֵרָאֶה֙ וָרֹ֔מַח בְּאַרְבָּעִ֥ים אֶ֖לֶף
ט בְּיִשְׂרָאֵֽל׃ לִבִּי֙ לְחוֹקְקֵ֣י יִשְׂרָאֵ֔ל הַמִּֽתְנַדְּבִ֖ים
י בָּעָ֑ם בָּרֲכ֖וּ יְהוָֽה׃ רֹכְבֵ֞י אֲתֹנ֗וֹת
צְחֹר֔וֹת יֹשְׁבֵ֖י עַל־מִדִּ֑ין וְהֹלְכֵ֥י
יא עַל־דֶּ֖רֶךְ שִֽׂיחוּ׃ מִקּ֣וֹל מְחַצְצִ֗ים בֵּ֚ין
מַשְׁאַבִּ֔ים שָׁ֤ם יְתַנּוּ֙ צִדְק֣וֹת יְהוָ֔ה צִדְקֹ֥ת
פִּרְזֹנ֖וֹ בְּיִשְׂרָאֵ֑ל אָ֛ז יָרְד֥וּ לַשְּׁעָרִ֖ים עַם־

12 to the gates / marched the people of the LORD! / Awake, awake, Devora – /
awake, awake, burst into song! / Arise, Barak – / seize your captives, son
13 of Avinoam; / then the remnant ruled over the mighty people, / the LORD
14 ruled over the warriors for me! / From Efrayim, rooted in Amalek: / "After
you, Binyamin, with your people!" / From Makhir marched down leaders, /
15 from Zevulun, wielders of the scribal staff.[8] / Yissakhar chiefs were with
Devora, / Yissakhar, like Barak, charged into the valley, / while amongst the
16 clans of Reuven / was great soul-searching. / Why did you linger among
the sheepfolds / to hear the whistling for the flocks? / Amongst the clans
17 of Reuven / was great soul-searching. / Gilad stayed put across the Jordan, /
and why did Dan stay by the ships? / Asher lingered by the seashore, / staying
18 put by its harbors. / Zevulun, a people who risked their lives for death /
19 with Naftali on the open heights; / then came the kings to do battle, / then
Canaan's kings did battle / at Tanakh, by the waters of Megiddo – / but they
20 took no spoil of silver! / From the heavens they fought; / the stars from
21 their courses fought against Sisera! / Kishon Stream swept them away, /
the ancient stream, the Kishon Stream – / march on, my soul, with might! /
22 The hooves of horses hammered / with the gallop, the gallop of the steeds! /
23 "Curse Meroz," said the LORD's angel, / "curse its people harshly, / for they
did not come to the aid of the LORD, / to the aid of the LORD amidst the
24 warriors." / Blessed beyond women be Yael, / wife of Ḥever the Kenite, /
25 blessed beyond women in tents! / Water he asked for, milk she gave; / in
26 a princely bowl she offered cream. / Her hand shot out for the tent peg, /
her right hand for the workman's hammer, / and hammered Sisera / and
27 crushed his head / and smashed and pierced his temple! / Between her legs

8 | This and the following verses alternately praise the Israelite tribes that came to war and castigate those who did not.

יב יְהֹוָה: עוּרִי עוּרִי דְּבוֹרָה עוּרִי
עוּרִי דַּבְּרִי־שִׁיר קוּם בָּרָק וּשְׁבֵה שֶׁבְיְךָ בֶּן־
יג אֲבִינֹעַם: אָז יְרַד שָׂרִיד לְאַדִּירִים עָם יְהֹוָה
יד יְרַד־לִי בַּגִּבּוֹרִים: מִנִּי אֶפְרַיִם שָׁרְשָׁם
בַּעֲמָלֵק אַחֲרֶיךָ בִנְיָמִין בַּעֲמָמֶיךָ מִנִּי
מָכִיר יָרְדוּ מְחֹקְקִים וּמִזְּבוּלֻן מֹשְׁכִים בְּשֵׁבֶט
טו סֹפֵר: וְשָׂרַי בְּיִשָּׂשכָר עִם־דְּבֹרָה וְיִשָּׂשכָר
כֵּן בָּרָק בָּעֵמֶק שֻׁלַּח
בְּרַגְלָיו בִּפְלַגּוֹת רְאוּבֵן גְּדֹלִים
טז חִקְקֵי־לֵב: לָמָּה יָשַׁבְתָּ בֵּין
הַמִּשְׁפְּתַיִם לִשְׁמֹעַ שְׁרִקוֹת עֲדָרִים לִפְלַגּוֹת
יז רְאוּבֵן גְּדוֹלִים חִקְרֵי־לֵב: גִּלְעָד בְּעֵבֶר הַיַּרְדֵּן
שָׁכֵן וְדָן לָמָּה יָגוּר אֳנִיּוֹת אָשֵׁר
יָשַׁב לְחוֹף יַמִּים וְעַל מִפְרָצָיו
יח יִשְׁכּוֹן: זְבֻלוּן עַם חֵרֵף נַפְשׁוֹ לָמוּת וְנַפְתָּלִי
יט עַל מְרוֹמֵי שָׂדֶה: בָּאוּ מְלָכִים
נִלְחָמוּ אָז נִלְחֲמוּ מַלְכֵי כְנַעַן בְּתַעְנַךְ
עַל־מֵי מְגִדּוֹ בֶּצַע כֶּסֶף לֹא
כ לָקָחוּ: מִן־שָׁמַיִם נִלְחָמוּ הַכּוֹכָבִים
כא מִמְּסִלּוֹתָם נִלְחֲמוּ עִם סִיסְרָא: נַחַל קִישׁוֹן
גְּרָפָם נַחַל קְדוּמִים נַחַל קִישׁוֹן תִּדְרְכִי
כב נַפְשִׁי עֹז: אָז הָלְמוּ עִקְּבֵי־
כג סוּס מִדַּהֲרוֹת דַּהֲרוֹת אַבִּירָיו: אוֹרוּ
מֵרוֹז אָמַר מַלְאַךְ יְהֹוָה אֹרוּ אָרוֹר
יֹשְׁבֶיהָ כִּי לֹא־בָאוּ לְעֶזְרַת יְהֹוָה לְעֶזְרַת
כד יְהֹוָה בַּגִּבּוֹרִים: תְּבֹרַךְ מִנָּשִׁים
יָעֵל אֵשֶׁת חֶבֶר הַקֵּינִי מִנָּשִׁים
כה בָּאֹהֶל תְּבֹרָךְ: מַיִם שָׁאַל חָלָב
כו נָתָנָה בְּסֵפֶל אַדִּירִים הִקְרִיבָה חֶמְאָה: יָדָהּ
לַיָּתֵד תִּשְׁלַחְנָה וִימִינָהּ לְהַלְמוּת
עֲמֵלִים וְהָלְמָה סִיסְרָא מָחֲקָה רֹאשׁוֹ וּמָחֲצָה
כז וְחָלְפָה רַקָּתוֹ: בֵּין רַגְלֶיהָ כָּרַע נָפַל

he lay slumped, sprawled, / between her legs he slumped, sprawled, / where
28 he slumped, there he sprawled, slain! / Through the window she peered, /
Sisera's mother wailed through the lattice, / "Why does his chariot tarry so? /
29 Why so late, the clank of his chariots?" / The wisest of her ladies reply – /
30 she even answers herself – / "Why, they are dividing up the spoil they
found, / a womb or two for every man, / a haul of colors for Sisera, / a
haul of colors of embroidery, / colored embroidery, two apiece, for the
31 spoilers' throats." / Thus may all Your enemies perish, O LORD, / and may
His friends be like the risen sun! / And the land was quiet for forty years.

6 1 The Israelites did what was evil in the eyes of the LORD, so the LORD handed
2 them over to Midyan for seven years. And Midyan's hand grew harsh against
Israel; because of Midyan, the Israelites made themselves the tunnels that are
3 in the mountains, and the caves, and the mountain strongholds. Whenever
Israel would sow, Midyan, Amalek, and the peoples of the East would come
4 up and raid them. They attacked them and destroyed the land's produce all
the way to Aza; they left no sustenance in Israel, no sheep, no ox, no donkey.
5 For they would ascend with their cattle and tents like a swarm of locusts; they
and their camels were innumerable, and they raided the land to ravage it.
6 Israel was reduced to destitution by Midyan, and the Israelites cried out to
7 8 the LORD. When the Israelites cried out to the LORD because of Midyan, the
LORD sent a prophet to the Israelites. He said to them, "Thus says the LORD,
God of Israel: I brought you out of Egypt and freed you from the house of
9 bondage. I delivered you from Egypt's hand and from the hands of all your
10 oppressors; I drove them out before you and gave you their land. I said to
you, 'I am the LORD your God; you shall not revere the gods of the Amorites
11 whose land you live in' – but you did not listen to My voice." An
angel of the LORD came and sat beneath the terebinth in Ofra of Yoash the
Aviezrite.[9] His son Gidon was threshing wheat in the winepress to hide it from
12 Midyan. The LORD's angel appeared to him and said to him: "The LORD is
13 with you, valiant warrior!" "If you please, my lord," Gidon said to him, "if the
LORD is with us, then why has all this befallen us? Where are all the wonders
our ancestors have told us about, saying, 'The LORD brought us out of Egypt'?
But now the LORD has forsaken us and given us over to the clutches of
14 Midyan." The LORD turned to Gidon and said, "Go with this power of yours

9 | Aviezer was one of the clans of Menashe (presumably identical with I'ezer in Num. 26:30).

שָׁכָב בֵּין רַגְלֶיהָ כָּרַע נָפָל בַּאֲשֶׁר
כח כָּרַע שָׁם נָפַל שָׁדוּד: בְּעַד הַחַלּוֹן נִשְׁקְפָה
וַתְּיַבֵּב אֵם סִיסְרָא בְּעַד הָאֶשְׁנָב מַדּוּעַ
בֹּשֵׁשׁ רִכְבּוֹ לָבוֹא מַדּוּעַ אֶחֱרוּ פַּעֲמֵי
כט מַרְכְּבוֹתָיו: חַכְמוֹת שָׂרוֹתֶיהָ תַּעֲנֶינָּה אַף־
ל הִיא תָּשִׁיב אֲמָרֶיהָ לָהּ: הֲלֹא יִמְצְאוּ יְחַלְּקוּ
שָׁלָל רַחַם רַחֲמָתַיִם לְרֹאשׁ גֶּבֶר שְׁלַל
צְבָעִים לְסִיסְרָא שְׁלַל צְבָעִים
לא רִקְמָה צֶבַע רִקְמָתַיִם לְצַוְּארֵי שָׁלָל: כֵּן ד
יֹאבְדוּ כָל־אוֹיְבֶיךָ יְהוָה וְאֹהֲבָיו כְּצֵאת הַשֶּׁמֶשׁ
בִּגְבֻרָתוֹ וַתִּשְׁקֹט הָאָרֶץ אַרְבָּעִים שָׁנָה:

ו א וַיַּעֲשׂוּ בְנֵי־יִשְׂרָאֵל הָרַע בְּעֵינֵי יְהוָה וַיִּתְּנֵם יְהוָה בְּיַד־מִדְיָן שֶׁבַע
ב שָׁנִים: וַתָּעָז יַד־מִדְיָן עַל־יִשְׂרָאֵל מִפְּנֵי מִדְיָן עָשׂוּ לָהֶם ׀ בְּנֵי יִשְׂרָאֵל
ג אֶת־הַמִּנְהָרוֹת אֲשֶׁר בֶּהָרִים וְאֶת־הַמְּעָרוֹת וְאֶת־הַמְּצָדוֹת: וְהָיָה
ד אִם־זָרַע יִשְׂרָאֵל וְעָלָה מִדְיָן וַעֲמָלֵק וּבְנֵי־קֶדֶם וְעָלוּ עָלָיו: וַיַּחֲנוּ
עֲלֵיהֶם וַיַּשְׁחִיתוּ אֶת־יְבוּל הָאָרֶץ עַד־בּוֹאֲךָ עַזָּה וְלֹא־יַשְׁאִירוּ
ה מִחְיָה בְּיִשְׂרָאֵל וְשֶׂה וָשׁוֹר וַחֲמוֹר: כִּי הֵם וּמִקְנֵיהֶם יַעֲלוּ וְאָהֳלֵיהֶם
יָבֹאוּ כְדֵי־אַרְבֶּה לָרֹב וְלָהֶם וְלִגְמַלֵּיהֶם אֵין מִסְפָּר וַיָּבֹאוּ בָאָרֶץ וּבָאוּ
ו לְשַׁחֲתָהּ: וַיִּדַּל יִשְׂרָאֵל מְאֹד מִפְּנֵי מִדְיָן וַיִּזְעֲקוּ בְנֵי־יִשְׂרָאֵל אֶל־יְהוָה:
ז ח וַיְהִי כִּי־זָעֲקוּ בְנֵי־יִשְׂרָאֵל אֶל־יְהוָה עַל אֹדוֹת מִדְיָן: וַיִּשְׁלַח יְהוָה
אִישׁ נָבִיא אֶל־בְּנֵי יִשְׂרָאֵל וַיֹּאמֶר לָהֶם כֹּה־אָמַר יְהוָה ׀ אֱלֹהֵי יִשְׂרָאֵל
אָנֹכִי הֶעֱלֵיתִי אֶתְכֶם מִמִּצְרַיִם וָאֹצִיא אֶתְכֶם מִבֵּית עֲבָדִים:
ט וָאַצִּל אֶתְכֶם מִיַּד מִצְרַיִם וּמִיַּד כָּל־לֹחֲצֵיכֶם וָאֲגָרֵשׁ אוֹתָם מִפְּנֵיכֶם
י וָאֶתְּנָה לָכֶם אֶת־אַרְצָם: וָאֹמְרָה לָכֶם אֲנִי יְהוָה אֱלֹהֵיכֶם לֹא תִירְאוּ
אֶת־אֱלֹהֵי הָאֱמֹרִי אֲשֶׁר אַתֶּם יוֹשְׁבִים בְּאַרְצָם וְלֹא שְׁמַעְתֶּם
יא בְּקוֹלִי: וַיָּבֹא מַלְאַךְ יְהוָה וַיֵּשֶׁב תַּחַת הָאֵלָה אֲשֶׁר בְּעָפְרָה
אֲשֶׁר לְיוֹאָשׁ אֲבִי הָעֶזְרִי וְגִדְעוֹן בְּנוֹ חֹבֵט חִטִּים בַּגַּת לְהָנִיס מִפְּנֵי
יב מִדְיָן: וַיֵּרָא אֵלָיו מַלְאַךְ יְהוָה וַיֹּאמֶר אֵלָיו יְהוָה עִמְּךָ גִּבּוֹר הֶחָיִל:
יג וַיֹּאמֶר אֵלָיו גִּדְעוֹן בִּי אֲדֹנִי וְיֵשׁ יְהוָה עִמָּנוּ וְלָמָּה מְצָאַתְנוּ כָּל־זֹאת
וְאַיֵּה כָל־נִפְלְאֹתָיו אֲשֶׁר סִפְּרוּ־לָנוּ אֲבוֹתֵינוּ לֵאמֹר הֲלֹא מִמִּצְרַיִם
יד הֶעֱלָנוּ יְהוָה וְעַתָּה נְטָשָׁנוּ יְהוָה וַיִּתְּנֵנוּ בְּכַף־מִדְיָן: וַיִּפֶן אֵלָיו יְהוָה

15 and save Israel from Midyan's hand: I hereby send you." "Please, my Lord,"
Gidon replied to Him, "how am I to save Israel? Look, my clan is the poorest
16 among Menashe, and I am the youngest of my father's household." "Because
I shall be with you," the Lord said to him, "and you shall strike Midyan down
17 as if they were a single man." "Please," he said to Him, "if I have found favor
18 in Your eyes, give me a sign that You are indeed speaking to me. Please do
not move from here until I come back to You, produce my offering, and set
19 it down before You." He replied, "I will remain here until your return." Gidon
went in and prepared a young goat and unleavened bread from an ephah of
flour. He placed the meat in a basket and poured the broth into a pot. He
20 brought it out to Him under the terebinth and served it. The angel
of God said to him, "Take the meat and the unleavened bread; place them on
21 that crag over there, and pour out the broth," and he did so. The angel of the
Lord extended the tip of the staff in his hand and touched the meat and
unleavened bread; fire flared up from the rock and consumed the meat and
the unleavened bread, and the angel of the Lord vanished before his eyes.
22 Gidon realized that he was indeed an angel of the Lord. "Alas, O Lord God,"
23 said Gidon, "I have seen an angel of the Lord face-to-face!" "All is well with
24 you," the Lord said to him. "Fear not; you will not die." Gidon built an altar
there for the Lord and called it Adonai Shalom. To this day, it is still in Ofra
25 of the Aviezrites. That night, the Lord said to him, "Take your
father's special bull and the second one, the seven-year-old bull. Destroy the
altar of Baal which belongs to your father, and cut down the Ashera over it.
26 Then build an altar to the Lord your God on the level surface on top of this
stronghold. Take the second bull and offer it up as a burnt offering, using the
27 wood of the Ashera that you cut down." So Gidon took ten of his servants
and did as the Lord had told him. Since he was afraid to act during the day
because of his father's household and the townspeople, he acted at night.
28 Early the next morning, the townspeople rose to see that the altar of Baal had
been shattered, the Ashera over it cut down, and the second bull offered up
29 on the newly built altar! "Who did this deed?" they asked one another, and
inquired and investigated until they determined that Gidon son of Yoash
30 had done this deed. "Bring out your son," the townspeople said to Yoash, "he
must die, for he has smashed the altar of Baal and cut down the Ashera over
31 it." Yoash replied to all those who confronted him, "Why should you contend
for Baal? Do you have to save him? Whoever contends for him shall be put
to death by morning. If he is a god, let him contend for himself if someone
32 smashes his altar." On that day, Yoash called Gidon "Yerubaal" – "let Baal
33 contend with him" – for he had smashed his altar. All of Midyan,
Amalek, and the peoples of the East gathered together, crossing over and

וַיֹּאמֶר לֵךְ בְּכֹחֲךָ זֶה וְהוֹשַׁעְתָּ אֶת־יִשְׂרָאֵל מִכַּף מִדְיָן הֲלֹא שְׁלַחְתִּיךָ׃
טו וַיֹּאמֶר אֵלָיו בִּי אֲדֹנָי בַּמָּה אוֹשִׁיעַ אֶת־יִשְׂרָאֵל הִנֵּה אַלְפִּי הַדַּל
טז בִּמְנַשֶּׁה וְאָנֹכִי הַצָּעִיר בְּבֵית אָבִי׃ וַיֹּאמֶר אֵלָיו יְהוָה כִּי אֶהְיֶה עִמָּךְ
יז וְהִכִּיתָ אֶת־מִדְיָן כְּאִישׁ אֶחָד׃ וַיֹּאמֶר אֵלָיו אִם־נָא מָצָאתִי חֵן בְּעֵינֶיךָ
יח וְעָשִׂיתָ לִּי אוֹת שָׁאַתָּה מְדַבֵּר עִמִּי׃ אַל־נָא תָמֻשׁ מִזֶּה עַד־בֹּאִי
אֵלֶיךָ וְהֹצֵאתִי אֶת־מִנְחָתִי וְהִנַּחְתִּי לְפָנֶיךָ וַיֹּאמַר אָנֹכִי אֵשֵׁב
יט עַד שׁוּבֶךָ׃ וְגִדְעוֹן בָּא וַיַּעַשׂ גְּדִי־עִזִּים וְאֵיפַת־קֶמַח מַצּוֹת הַבָּשָׂר
שָׂם בַּסַּל וְהַמָּרַק שָׂם בַּפָּרוּר וַיּוֹצֵא אֵלָיו אֶל־תַּחַת הָאֵלָה
כ וַיַּגַּשׁ׃ וַיֹּאמֶר אֵלָיו מַלְאַךְ הָאֱלֹהִים קַח אֶת־הַבָּשָׂר
כא וְאֶת־הַמַּצּוֹת וְהַנַּח אֶל־הַסֶּלַע הַלָּז וְאֶת־הַמָּרַק שְׁפוֹךְ וַיַּעַשׂ כֵּן׃ וַיִּשְׁלַח
מַלְאַךְ יְהוָה אֶת־קְצֵה הַמִּשְׁעֶנֶת אֲשֶׁר בְּיָדוֹ וַיִּגַּע בַּבָּשָׂר וּבַמַּצּוֹת
וַתַּעַל הָאֵשׁ מִן־הַצּוּר וַתֹּאכַל אֶת־הַבָּשָׂר וְאֶת־הַמַּצּוֹת וּמַלְאַךְ יְהוָה
כב הָלַךְ מֵעֵינָיו׃ וַיַּרְא גִּדְעוֹן כִּי־מַלְאַךְ יְהוָה הוּא וַיֹּאמֶר גִּדְעוֹן אֲהָהּ
כג אֲדֹנָי יְהוִה כִּי־עַל־כֵּן רָאִיתִי מַלְאַךְ יְהוָה פָּנִים אֶל־פָּנִים׃ וַיֹּאמֶר
כד לוֹ יְהוָה שָׁלוֹם לְךָ אַל־תִּירָא לֹא תָּמוּת׃ וַיִּבֶן שָׁם גִּדְעוֹן מִזְבֵּחַ
לַיהוָה וַיִּקְרָא־לוֹ יְהוָה ׀ שָׁלוֹם עַד הַיּוֹם הַזֶּה עוֹדֶנּוּ בְּעָפְרַת אֲבִי
כה הָעֶזְרִי׃ וַיְהִי בַּלַּיְלָה הַהוּא וַיֹּאמֶר לוֹ יְהוָה קַח אֶת־פַּר־
הַשּׁוֹר אֲשֶׁר לְאָבִיךָ וּפַר הַשֵּׁנִי שֶׁבַע שָׁנִים וְהָרַסְתָּ אֶת־מִזְבַּח הַבַּעַל
כו אֲשֶׁר לְאָבִיךָ וְאֶת־הָאֲשֵׁרָה אֲשֶׁר־עָלָיו תִּכְרֹת׃ וּבָנִיתָ מִזְבֵּחַ לַיהוָה
אֱלֹהֶיךָ עַל רֹאשׁ הַמָּעוֹז הַזֶּה בַּמַּעֲרָכָה וְלָקַחְתָּ אֶת־הַפָּר הַשֵּׁנִי
כז וְהַעֲלִיתָ עוֹלָה בַּעֲצֵי הָאֲשֵׁרָה אֲשֶׁר תִּכְרֹת׃ וַיִּקַּח גִּדְעוֹן עֲשָׂרָה אֲנָשִׁים
מֵעֲבָדָיו וַיַּעַשׂ כַּאֲשֶׁר דִּבֶּר אֵלָיו יְהוָה וַיְהִי כַּאֲשֶׁר יָרֵא אֶת־בֵּית אָבִיו
כח וְאֶת־אַנְשֵׁי הָעִיר מֵעֲשׂוֹת יוֹמָם וַיַּעַשׂ לָיְלָה׃ וַיַּשְׁכִּימוּ אַנְשֵׁי הָעִיר
בַּבֹּקֶר וְהִנֵּה נֻתַּץ מִזְבַּח הַבַּעַל וְהָאֲשֵׁרָה אֲשֶׁר־עָלָיו כֹּרָתָה וְאֵת הַפָּר
כט הַשֵּׁנִי הֹעֲלָה עַל־הַמִּזְבֵּחַ הַבָּנוּי׃ וַיֹּאמְרוּ אִישׁ אֶל־רֵעֵהוּ מִי עָשָׂה
הַדָּבָר הַזֶּה וַיִּדְרְשׁוּ וַיְבַקְשׁוּ וַיֹּאמְרוּ גִּדְעוֹן בֶּן־יוֹאָשׁ עָשָׂה הַדָּבָר הַזֶּה׃
ל וַיֹּאמְרוּ אַנְשֵׁי הָעִיר אֶל־יוֹאָשׁ הוֹצֵא אֶת־בִּנְךָ וְיָמֹת כִּי נָתַץ אֶת־
לא מִזְבַּח הַבַּעַל וְכִי כָרַת הָאֲשֵׁרָה אֲשֶׁר־עָלָיו׃ וַיֹּאמֶר יוֹאָשׁ לְכֹל אֲשֶׁר־
עָמְדוּ עָלָיו הַאַתֶּם ׀ תְּרִיבוּן לַבַּעַל אִם־אַתֶּם תּוֹשִׁיעוּן אוֹתוֹ אֲשֶׁר
יָרִיב לוֹ יוּמַת עַד־הַבֹּקֶר אִם־אֱלֹהִים הוּא יָרֶב לוֹ כִּי נָתַץ אֶת־מִזְבְּחוֹ׃
לב וַיִּקְרָא־לוֹ בַיּוֹם־הַהוּא יְרֻבַּעַל לֵאמֹר יָרֶב בּוֹ הַבַּעַל כִּי נָתַץ אֶת־
לג מִזְבְּחוֹ׃ וְכָל־מִדְיָן וַעֲמָלֵק וּבְנֵי־קֶדֶם נֶאֶסְפוּ יַחְדָּו

34 encamping at Yizre'el Valley. The spirit of the LORD swathed Gidon, and he
35 blasted the ram's horn, rallying Aviezer next to him. He sent messengers
throughout Menashe to rally them as well; he sent messengers to Asher,
36 Zevulun, and Naftali, and they marched up to meet them. Then Gidon said
37 to God, "If You indeed wish to deliver Israel through me, as You said – here,
I have placed a woolen fleece on the threshing floor. If there will be dew on
the fleece alone, while the surrounding ground is dry, then I shall know that
38 You will save Israel through me, as You said." So it was; he rose early the next
day, wrung out the fleece, and squeezed dew from the fleece – a whole bowlful
39 of water. Then Gidon said to God, "Do not be angry with me – let me speak
just once more. Please, let me test the fleece just once more: let the fleece
40 alone remain dry, but let there be dew all over the ground." That night God
made it so: the fleece alone remained dry, while there was dew all over the
7 1 ground. Early the next morning, Yerubaal – that is, Gidon – rose, along with
all his men. They encamped by Ḥarod Spring. The Midianite camp was to
2 their north, in the valley by the Heights of Moreh. The LORD said
to Gidon, "There are too many men with you for Me to deliver Midyan
into their hands – Israel might glorify themselves instead of Me, thinking,
3 'My own hands saved me.' Now, call out in the people's hearing, 'If any of
you are fearful or anxious, let them go back and take flight from the hill
country of Gilad.'" Twenty-two thousand troops returned, and ten thousand
4 remained. "There are still too many men," the LORD said to Gidon.
"Take them down to the water; I will select them for you there. Whoever I tell
5 you shall go, shall go. Whoever I tell you shall not go, shall not go." He brought
the people down to the water, and the LORD said to Gidon, "Separate all those
who lap at the water with their tongues, as a dog laps, from all those who kneel
6 down to drink water."[10] The number of men who lapped from their hands into
their mouths came to three hundred, while all the rest of the men kneeled
7 down to drink water. The LORD said to Gidon, "With these three
hundred men who lapped, I will save you and deliver Midyan into your hand;
8 let all the other men return home." Keeping hold of the men's provisions as
well as their rams' horns, he sent all the rest of the men of Israel back to their
tents, retaining only the three hundred men. The Midianite camp was below
9 them in the valley. That night the LORD said to him, "Get up and
10 head down to the camp, for I have delivered it into your hand. If you are afraid
11 to march down, then go down to the camp with your lad Pura. When you
hear what they speak of, you will be encouraged – then you will march down
to the camp." So he and his lad Pura went down to the outposts of the camp,

10 | Kneeling down to drink like a dog was degrading and may have had idolatrous connotations. God selected only those who raised the water to their mouths with their hands like dignified human beings, without kneeling and bending over.

לד וַיַּעַבְרוּ וַיַּחֲנוּ בְּעֵמֶק יִזְרְעֶאל: וְרוּחַ יְהוָה לָבְשָׁה אֶת־גִּדְעוֹן וַיִּתְקַע
לה בַּשּׁוֹפָר וַיִּזָּעֵק אֲבִיעֶזֶר אַחֲרָיו: וּמַלְאָכִים שָׁלַח בְּכָל־מְנַשֶּׁה וַיִּזָּעֵק
גַּם־הוּא אַחֲרָיו וּמַלְאָכִים שָׁלַח בְּאָשֵׁר וּבִזְבֻלוּן וּבְנַפְתָּלִי וַיַּעֲלוּ
לו לִקְרָאתָם: וַיֹּאמֶר גִּדְעוֹן אֶל־הָאֱלֹהִים אִם־יֶשְׁךָ מוֹשִׁיעַ בְּיָדִי אֶת־
לז יִשְׂרָאֵל כַּאֲשֶׁר דִּבַּרְתָּ: הִנֵּה אָנֹכִי מַצִּיג אֶת־גִּזַּת הַצֶּמֶר בַּגֹּרֶן אִם טַל
יִהְיֶה עַל־הַגִּזָּה לְבַדָּהּ וְעַל־כָּל־הָאָרֶץ חֹרֶב וְיָדַעְתִּי כִּי־תוֹשִׁיעַ בְּיָדִי
לח אֶת־יִשְׂרָאֵל כַּאֲשֶׁר דִּבַּרְתָּ: וַיְהִי־כֵן וַיַּשְׁכֵּם מִמָּחֳרָת וַיָּזַר אֶת־הַגִּזָּה
לט וַיִּמֶץ טַל מִן־הַגִּזָּה מְלוֹא הַסֵּפֶל מָיִם: וַיֹּאמֶר גִּדְעוֹן אֶל־הָאֱלֹהִים
אַל־יִחַר אַפְּךָ בִּי וַאֲדַבְּרָה אַךְ הַפָּעַם אֲנַסֶּה נָּא־רַק־הַפַּעַם בַּגִּזָּה
מ יְהִי־נָא חֹרֶב אֶל־הַגִּזָּה לְבַדָּהּ וְעַל־כָּל־הָאָרֶץ יִהְיֶה־טָּל: וַיַּעַשׂ ה
אֱלֹהִים כֵּן בַּלַּיְלָה הַהוּא וַיְהִי־חֹרֶב אֶל־הַגִּזָּה לְבַדָּהּ וְעַל־כָּל־
ז א הָאָרֶץ הָיָה טָל: וַיַּשְׁכֵּם יְרֻבַּעַל הוּא גִדְעוֹן וְכָל־הָעָם אֲשֶׁר אִתּוֹ
וַיַּחֲנוּ עַל־עֵין חֲרֹד וּמַחֲנֵה מִדְיָן הָיָה־לוֹ מִצָּפוֹן מִגִּבְעַת הַמּוֹרֶה
ב בָּעֵמֶק: וַיֹּאמֶר יְהוָה אֶל־גִּדְעוֹן רַב הָעָם אֲשֶׁר
אִתָּךְ מִתִּתִּי אֶת־מִדְיָן בְּיָדָם פֶּן־יִתְפָּאֵר עָלַי יִשְׂרָאֵל לֵאמֹר יָדִי
ג הוֹשִׁיעָה לִּי: וְעַתָּה קְרָא נָא בְּאָזְנֵי הָעָם לֵאמֹר מִי־יָרֵא וְחָרֵד יָשֹׁב
וְיִצְפֹּר מֵהַר הַגִּלְעָד וַיָּשָׁב מִן־הָעָם עֶשְׂרִים וּשְׁנַיִם אֶלֶף וַעֲשֶׂרֶת אֲלָפִים
ד נִשְׁאָרוּ: וַיֹּאמֶר יְהוָה אֶל־גִּדְעוֹן עוֹד הָעָם רָב הוֹרֵד
אוֹתָם אֶל־הַמַּיִם וְאֶצְרְפֶנּוּ לְךָ שָׁם וְהָיָה אֲשֶׁר אֹמַר אֵלֶיךָ זֶה ׀ יֵלֵךְ
אִתָּךְ הוּא יֵלֵךְ אִתָּךְ וְכֹל אֲשֶׁר־אֹמַר אֵלֶיךָ זֶה לֹא־יֵלֵךְ עִמָּךְ הוּא
ה לֹא יֵלֵךְ: וַיּוֹרֶד אֶת־הָעָם אֶל־הַמָּיִם וַיֹּאמֶר יְהוָה אֶל־גִּדְעוֹן כֹּל אֲשֶׁר־
יָלֹק בִּלְשׁוֹנוֹ מִן־הַמַּיִם כַּאֲשֶׁר יָלֹק הַכֶּלֶב תַּצִּיג אוֹתוֹ לְבָד וְכֹל
ו אֲשֶׁר־יִכְרַע עַל־בִּרְכָּיו לִשְׁתּוֹת: וַיְהִי מִסְפַּר הַמְלַקְקִים בְּיָדָם אֶל־
פִּיהֶם שְׁלֹשׁ מֵאוֹת אִישׁ וְכֹל יֶתֶר הָעָם כָּרְעוּ עַל־בִּרְכֵיהֶם לִשְׁתּוֹת
ז מָיִם: וַיֹּאמֶר יְהוָה אֶל־גִּדְעוֹן בִּשְׁלֹשׁ מֵאוֹת הָאִישׁ
הַמְלַקְקִים אוֹשִׁיעַ אֶתְכֶם וְנָתַתִּי אֶת־מִדְיָן בְּיָדֶךָ וְכָל־הָעָם יֵלְכוּ אִישׁ
ח לִמְקֹמוֹ: וַיִּקְחוּ אֶת־צֵדָה הָעָם בְּיָדָם וְאֵת שׁוֹפְרֹתֵיהֶם וְאֵת כָּל־אִישׁ
יִשְׂרָאֵל שִׁלַּח אִישׁ לְאֹהָלָיו וּבִשְׁלֹשׁ־מֵאוֹת הָאִישׁ הֶחֱזִיק וּמַחֲנֵה
ט מִדְיָן הָיָה לוֹ מִתַּחַת בָּעֵמֶק: וַיְהִי בַּלַּיְלָה הַהוּא וַיֹּאמֶר
י אֵלָיו יְהוָה קוּם רֵד בַּמַּחֲנֶה כִּי נְתַתִּיו בְּיָדֶךָ: וְאִם־יָרֵא אַתָּה לָרֶדֶת
יא רֵד אַתָּה וּפֻרָה נַעַרְךָ אֶל־הַמַּחֲנֶה: וְשָׁמַעְתָּ מַה־יְדַבֵּרוּ וְאַחַר תֶּחֱזַקְנָה
יָדֶיךָ וְיָרַדְתָּ בַּמַּחֲנֶה וַיֵּרֶד הוּא וּפֻרָה נַעֲרוֹ אֶל־קְצֵה הַחֲמֻשִׁים אֲשֶׁר

12 where the armed sentries were. Midyan, Amalek, and all the people of the
East sprawled throughout the valley, swarming like locusts; their camels were
13 without number, as boundless as the sand of the seashore. Gidon arrived just
as a man was recounting a dream to another. "I dreamed a dream," he said. "A
loaf of barley bread came rolling through the Midianite camp – it came up to
a tent, struck it, knocked it down, turned it upside down – and the tent
14 collapsed." His friend answered, "That can only be the sword of Gidon son
of Yoash the Israelite – God has delivered Midyan and all its forces into his
15 hand." When Gidon heard the tale of the dream and its interpretation,
he bowed down low and went back to the Israelite camp. "Get up," he
announced, "for the LORD has delivered the Midianite camp into your hands!"
16 He split the three hundred men into three groups and gave each of them rams'
17 horns and empty jars, with torches inside the jars. "Watch me and do as I do,"
18 he said to them. "As soon as I reach the edge of the camp, do as I do. When I
blast the ram's horn – along with all those who are with me – you too will
blast the ram's horn all around the camp and cry, 'For the LORD and for
19 Gidon!'" Gidon and the hundred men with him reached the edge
of the camp as the middle watch began, just after the sentries had been posted.
20 They blasted the rams' horns and smashed the jars in their hands. Then all
three groups blasted the rams' horns and broke the jars, holding the torches
in their left hands and the rams' horns in their right to blast, and called out,
21 "A sword for the LORD and for Gidon!" Each one stood in position all around
22 the camp, and the whole camp ran off, shrieking as they fled. As the three
hundred rams' horns blasted, the LORD set everyone's swords against each
other all across the camp. The forces fled toward Beit HaShita, in the direction
23 of Tzerera, and farther toward Avel Meḥola, which is by Tabat.[11] The men of
Israel were alerted – Naftali, Asher, and all of Menashe, who chased after
24 Midyan. Gidon sent messengers throughout the Efrayim hills, bidding them,
"March down toward Midyan and seize control of the water sources from
them as far as Beit Bara and the Jordan." Every man in Efrayim was rallied,
and they seized control of the water sources as far as Beit Bara and the Jordan.
25 They captured two Midianite leaders, Orev and Ze'ev. They killed Orev at the
Rock of Orev and Ze'ev at the Winepress of Ze'ev, and they chased Midyan
away. They brought the heads of Orev and Ze'ev across the Jordan to Gidon.
8 1 The men of Efrayim said to him, "Why have you done this to us, not calling
us when you went to fight against Midyan?" They contended with him fiercely.
2 "Why, what have I done compared to you?" he said to them. "Efrayim's
3 gleanings are better than Aviezer's finest vintage! It was into your hand that

---

11 | These are apparently two different locations at which it was possible to ford the Jordan River.

יב בַּמַּחֲנֶה: וּמִדְיָן וַעֲמָלֵק וְכָל־בְּנֵי־קֶדֶם נֹפְלִים בָּעֵמֶק כָּאַרְבֶּה לָרֹב
יג וְלִגְמַלֵּיהֶם אֵין מִסְפָּר כַּחוֹל שֶׁעַל־שְׂפַת הַיָּם לָרֹב: וַיָּבֹא גִדְעוֹן וְהִנֵּה־
אִישׁ מְסַפֵּר לְרֵעֵהוּ חֲלוֹם וַיֹּאמֶר הִנֵּה חֲלוֹם חָלַמְתִּי וְהִנֵּה צלול לֶחֶם צְלִיל
שְׂעֹרִים מִתְהַפֵּךְ בְּמַחֲנֵה מִדְיָן וַיָּבֹא עַד־הָאֹהֶל וַיַּכֵּהוּ וַיִּפֹּל וַיַּהַפְכֵהוּ
יד לְמַעְלָה וְנָפַל הָאֹהֶל: וַיַּעַן רֵעֵהוּ וַיֹּאמֶר אֵין זֹאת בִּלְתִּי אִם־חֶרֶב
גִּדְעוֹן בֶּן־יוֹאָשׁ אִישׁ יִשְׂרָאֵל נָתַן הָאֱלֹהִים בְּיָדוֹ אֶת־מִדְיָן וְאֶת־כָּל־
טו הַמַּחֲנֶה: וַיְהִי כִשְׁמֹעַ גִּדְעוֹן אֶת־מִסְפַּר הַחֲלוֹם וְאֶת־
שִׁבְרוֹ וַיִּשְׁתָּחוּ וַיָּשָׁב אֶל־מַחֲנֵה יִשְׂרָאֵל וַיֹּאמֶר קוּמוּ כִּי־נָתַן יְהוָה
טז בְּיֶדְכֶם אֶת־מַחֲנֵה מִדְיָן: וַיַּחַץ אֶת־שְׁלֹשׁ־מֵאוֹת הָאִישׁ שְׁלֹשָׁה
רָאשִׁים וַיִּתֵּן שׁוֹפָרוֹת בְּיַד־כֻּלָּם וְכַדִּים רֵקִים וְלַפִּדִים בְּתוֹךְ הַכַּדִּים:
יז וַיֹּאמֶר אֲלֵיהֶם מִמֶּנִּי תִרְאוּ וְכֵן תַּעֲשׂוּ וְהִנֵּה אָנֹכִי בָא בִּקְצֵה הַמַּחֲנֶה
יח וְהָיָה כַאֲשֶׁר אֶעֱשֶׂה כֵּן תַּעֲשׂוּן: וְתָקַעְתִּי בַּשּׁוֹפָר אָנֹכִי וְכָל־אֲשֶׁר אִתִּי
וּתְקַעְתֶּם בַּשּׁוֹפָרוֹת גַּם־אַתֶּם סְבִיבוֹת כָּל־הַמַּחֲנֶה וַאֲמַרְתֶּם לַיהוָה
יט וּלְגִדְעוֹן: וַיָּבֹא גִדְעוֹן וּמֵאָה־אִישׁ אֲשֶׁר־אִתּוֹ בִּקְצֵה
הַמַּחֲנֶה רֹאשׁ הָאַשְׁמֹרֶת הַתִּיכוֹנָה אַךְ הָקֵם הֵקִימוּ אֶת־הַשֹּׁמְרִים
כ וַיִּתְקְעוּ בַּשּׁוֹפָרוֹת וְנָפוֹץ הַכַּדִּים אֲשֶׁר בְּיָדָם: וַיִּתְקְעוּ שְׁלֹשֶׁת הָרָאשִׁים
בַּשּׁוֹפָרוֹת וַיִּשְׁבְּרוּ הַכַּדִּים וַיַּחֲזִיקוּ בְיַד־שְׂמֹאולָם בַּלַּפִּדִים וּבְיַד־יְמִינָם
כא הַשּׁוֹפָרוֹת לִתְקוֹעַ וַיִּקְרְאוּ חֶרֶב לַיהוָה וּלְגִדְעוֹן: וַיַּעַמְדוּ אִישׁ תַּחְתָּיו
כב סָבִיב לַמַּחֲנֶה וַיָּרָץ כָּל־הַמַּחֲנֶה וַיָּרִיעוּ ויניסו: וַיִּתְקְעוּ שְׁלֹשׁ־מֵאוֹת וַיָּנוּסוּ
הַשּׁוֹפָרוֹת וַיָּשֶׂם יְהוָה אֵת חֶרֶב אִישׁ בְּרֵעֵהוּ וּבְכָל־הַמַּחֲנֶה וַיָּנָס
הַמַּחֲנֶה עַד־בֵּית הַשִּׁטָּה צְרֵרָתָה עַד שְׂפַת־אָבֵל מְחוֹלָה עַל־טַבָּת:
כג וַיִּצָּעֵק אִישׁ־יִשְׂרָאֵל מִנַּפְתָּלִי וּמִן־אָשֵׁר וּמִן־כָּל־מְנַשֶּׁה וַיִּרְדְּפוּ אַחֲרֵי
כד מִדְיָן: וּמַלְאָכִים שָׁלַח גִּדְעוֹן בְּכָל־הַר אֶפְרַיִם לֵאמֹר רְדוּ לִקְרַאת
מִדְיָן וְלִכְדוּ לָהֶם אֶת־הַמַּיִם עַד בֵּית בָּרָה וְאֶת־הַיַּרְדֵּן וַיִּצָּעֵק כָּל־
כה אִישׁ אֶפְרַיִם וַיִּלְכְּדוּ אֶת־הַמַּיִם עַד בֵּית בָּרָה וְאֶת־הַיַּרְדֵּן: וַיִּלְכְּדוּ
שְׁנֵי־שָׂרֵי מִדְיָן אֶת־עֹרֵב וְאֶת־זְאֵב וַיַּהַרְגוּ אֶת־עוֹרֵב בְּצוּר־עוֹרֵב
וְאֶת־זְאֵב הָרְגוּ בְיֶקֶב־זְאֵב וַיִּרְדְּפוּ אֶל־מִדְיָן וְרֹאשׁ־עֹרֵב וּזְאֵב הֵבִיאוּ
ח א אֶל־גִּדְעוֹן מֵעֵבֶר לַיַּרְדֵּן: וַיֹּאמְרוּ אֵלָיו אִישׁ אֶפְרַיִם מָה־הַדָּבָר הַזֶּה
עָשִׂיתָ לָּנוּ לְבִלְתִּי קְרֹאות לָנוּ כִּי הָלַכְתָּ לְהִלָּחֵם בְּמִדְיָן וַיְרִיבוּן אִתּוֹ
ב בְּחָזְקָה: וַיֹּאמֶר אֲלֵיהֶם מֶה־עָשִׂיתִי עַתָּה כָּכֶם הֲלֹא טוֹב עֹלְלוֹת
ג אֶפְרַיִם מִבְצִיר אֲבִיעֶזֶר: בְּיֶדְכֶם נָתַן אֱלֹהִים אֶת־שָׂרֵי מִדְיָן אֶת־ ו

God delivered the leaders of Midyan, Orev and Ze'ev – what could I have
done compared to you?" As he spoke to them in this way, their rage against
4 him abated. Gidon reached the Jordan and crossed over, but the three
5 hundred men with him were weary from the chase. He said to the people of
Sukkot, "Please, provide loaves of bread for the men following me, for they
6 are weary and I am pursuing Zevaḥ and Tzalmuna, the kings of Midyan." "Are
Zevaḥ or Tzalmuna already in your hands," the leaders of Sukkot replied, "that
7 we should supply bread for your army?" "If not," Gidon said, "when the Lord
does deliver Zevaḥ and Tzalmuna into my hands, I shall thresh your flesh
8 against the desert thorns and briars." From there he marched up to Penuel
and asked them the same, but the people of Penuel answered him as the
9 people of Sukkot had answered him. So he retorted to the people of Penuel,
10 saying, "Upon my safe return, I shall smash down this tower." Zevaḥ
and Tzalmuna were in Karkor with their forces – about fifteen thousand were
all that remained of the camp of the peoples of the East; one hundred twenty
11 thousand swordsmen had fallen. Gidon marched up through the tent dwellers'
route, east of Novaḥ and Yogbeha, and attacked the camp – which was
12 unsecured. When Zevaḥ and Tzalmuna fled, he chased after them; he captured
the two Midianite kings, Zevaḥ and Tzalmuna, and terrified their entire army.
13 Gidon son of Yoash returned from the battle via the Ascent of Ḥeres. He
14 captured a boy from among the people of Sukkot and interrogated him; he
had him dictate a list of the leaders of Sukkot and its elders, who numbered
15 seventy-seven men. When he came to the people of Sukkot, he said, "Here
are Zevaḥ and Tzalmuna, about whom you taunted me! You said, 'Are Zevaḥ
and Tzalmuna already in your hands, that we should give bread to your weary
16 men?'" He seized the elders of the city along with desert thorns and briars and
17 taught the people of Sukkot a lesson. As for the Tower of Penuel, he smashed
18 it down and killed the townspeople. He then said to Zevaḥ and Tzalmuna,
"What kind of men did you kill at Tavor?" "They were just like you," they replied.
19 "Each had the bearing of a king's son." "They were my brothers," he said, "my
mother's sons! As the Lord lives, if you had let them live, I would not have
20 killed you." He then said to Yeter, his firstborn, "Get up; kill them!" But the
21 boy did not draw his sword; he was frightened, for he was still a boy. "You get
up!" said Zevaḥ and Tzalmuna. "You strike us down, for strength comes with
manhood." So Gidon got up and killed Zevaḥ and Tzalmuna and took the
22 crescents from their camels' necks. The men of Israel said to
Gidon, "Rule over us, you and your son and the son of your son – for you have
23 saved us from Midyan's hand!" "I shall not rule over you," Gidon said to them,
24 "nor shall my son rule over you – the Lord shall rule over you." Gidon then
said to them, "Let me make a request of you – let each man give me an earring
25 from his spoil." They had gold earrings, for they were Ishmaelites. "Of course

עֹרֵב וְאֶת־זְאֵב וּמַה־יָּכֹלְתִּי עֲשׂוֹת כָּכֶם אָז רָפְתָה רוּחָם מֵעָלָיו בְּדַבְּרוֹ
ד הַדָּבָר הַזֶּה: וַיָּבֹא גִדְעוֹן הַיַּרְדֵּנָה עֹבֵר הוּא וּשְׁלֹשׁ־מֵאוֹת הָאִישׁ אֲשֶׁר
ה אִתּוֹ עֲיֵפִים וְרֹדְפִים: וַיֹּאמֶר לְאַנְשֵׁי סֻכּוֹת תְּנוּ־נָא כִּכְּרוֹת לֶחֶם לָעָם
אֲשֶׁר בְּרַגְלָי כִּי־עֲיֵפִים הֵם וְאָנֹכִי רֹדֵף אַחֲרֵי זֶבַח וְצַלְמֻנָּע מַלְכֵי מִדְיָן:
ו וַיֹּאמֶר שָׂרֵי סֻכּוֹת הֲכַף זֶבַח וְצַלְמֻנָּע עַתָּה בְּיָדֶךָ כִּי־נִתֵּן לִצְבָאֲךָ
ז לָחֶם: וַיֹּאמֶר גִּדְעוֹן לָכֵן בְּתֵת יְהוָה אֶת־זֶבַח וְאֶת־צַלְמֻנָּע בְּיָדִי וְדַשְׁתִּי
ח אֶת־בְּשַׂרְכֶם אֶת־קוֹצֵי הַמִּדְבָּר וְאֶת־הַבַּרְקֳנִים: וַיַּעַל מִשָּׁם פְּנוּאֵל
וַיְדַבֵּר אֲלֵיהֶם כָּזֹאת וַיַּעֲנוּ אוֹתוֹ אַנְשֵׁי פְנוּאֵל כַּאֲשֶׁר עָנוּ אַנְשֵׁי סֻכּוֹת:
ט וַיֹּאמֶר גַּם־לְאַנְשֵׁי פְנוּאֵל לֵאמֹר בְּשׁוּבִי בְשָׁלוֹם אֶתֹּץ אֶת־הַמִּגְדָּל
י הַזֶּה: וְזֶבַח וְצַלְמֻנָּע בַּקַּרְקֹר וּמַחֲנֵיהֶם עִמָּם
כַּחֲמֵשֶׁת עָשָׂר אֶלֶף כֹּל הַנּוֹתָרִים מִכֹּל מַחֲנֵה בְנֵי־קֶדֶם וְהַנֹּפְלִים
יא מֵאָה וְעֶשְׂרִים אֶלֶף אִישׁ שֹׁלֵף חָרֶב: וַיַּעַל גִּדְעוֹן דֶּרֶךְ הַשְּׁכוּנֵי בָאֳהָלִים
יב מִקֶּדֶם לְנֹבַח וְיָגְבְּהָה וַיַּךְ אֶת־הַמַּחֲנֶה וְהַמַּחֲנֶה הָיָה בֶטַח: וַיָּנוּסוּ זֶבַח
וְצַלְמֻנָּע וַיִּרְדֹּף אַחֲרֵיהֶם וַיִּלְכֹּד אֶת־שְׁנֵי ׀ מַלְכֵי מִדְיָן אֶת־זֶבַח וְאֶת־
יג צַלְמֻנָּע וְכָל־הַמַּחֲנֶה הֶחֱרִיד: וַיָּשָׁב גִּדְעוֹן בֶּן־יוֹאָשׁ מִן־הַמִּלְחָמָה
יד מִלְמַעֲלֵה הֶחָרֶס: וַיִּלְכָּד־נַעַר מֵאַנְשֵׁי סֻכּוֹת וַיִּשְׁאָלֵהוּ וַיִּכְתֹּב אֵלָיו
טו אֶת־שָׂרֵי סֻכּוֹת וְאֶת־זְקֵנֶיהָ שִׁבְעִים וְשִׁבְעָה אִישׁ: וַיָּבֹא אֶל־אַנְשֵׁי
סֻכּוֹת וַיֹּאמֶר הִנֵּה זֶבַח וְצַלְמֻנָּע אֲשֶׁר חֵרַפְתֶּם אוֹתִי לֵאמֹר הֲכַף זֶבַח
טז וְצַלְמֻנָּע עַתָּה בְּיָדֶךָ כִּי נִתֵּן לַאֲנָשֶׁיךָ הַיְּעֵפִים לָחֶם: וַיִּקַּח אֶת־זִקְנֵי
הָעִיר וְאֶת־קוֹצֵי הַמִּדְבָּר וְאֶת־הַבַּרְקֳנִים וַיֹּדַע בָּהֶם אֵת אַנְשֵׁי סֻכּוֹת:
יז יח וְאֶת־מִגְדַּל פְּנוּאֵל נָתָץ וַיַּהֲרֹג אֶת־אַנְשֵׁי הָעִיר: וַיֹּאמֶר אֶל־זֶבַח
וְאֶל־צַלְמֻנָּע אֵיפֹה הָאֲנָשִׁים אֲשֶׁר הֲרַגְתֶּם בְּתָבוֹר וַיֹּאמְרוּ כָּמוֹךָ
יט כְמוֹהֶם אֶחָד כְּתֹאַר בְּנֵי הַמֶּלֶךְ: וַיֹּאמַר אַחַי בְּנֵי־אִמִּי הֵם חַי־
כ יְהוָה לוּ הַחֲיִתֶם אוֹתָם לֹא הָרַגְתִּי אֶתְכֶם: וַיֹּאמֶר לְיֶתֶר בְּכוֹרוֹ קוּם
כא הֲרֹג אוֹתָם וְלֹא־שָׁלַף הַנַּעַר חַרְבּוֹ כִּי יָרֵא כִּי עוֹדֶנּוּ נָעַר: וַיֹּאמֶר
זֶבַח וְצַלְמֻנָּע קוּם אַתָּה וּפְגַע־בָּנוּ כִּי כָאִישׁ גְּבוּרָתוֹ וַיָּקָם גִּדְעוֹן
וַיַּהֲרֹג אֶת־זֶבַח וְאֶת־צַלְמֻנָּע וַיִּקַּח אֶת־הַשַּׂהֲרֹנִים אֲשֶׁר בְּצַוְּארֵי
כב גְמַלֵּיהֶם: וַיֹּאמְרוּ אִישׁ־יִשְׂרָאֵל אֶל־גִּדְעוֹן מְשָׁל־בָּנוּ
כג גַּם־אַתָּה גַּם־בִּנְךָ גַּם בֶּן־בְּנֶךָ כִּי הוֹשַׁעְתָּנוּ מִיַּד מִדְיָן: וַיֹּאמֶר אֲלֵהֶם
גִּדְעוֹן לֹא־אֶמְשֹׁל אֲנִי בָּכֶם וְלֹא־יִמְשֹׁל בְּנִי בָּכֶם יְהוָה יִמְשֹׁל בָּכֶם:
כד וַיֹּאמֶר אֲלֵהֶם גִּדְעוֹן אֶשְׁאֲלָה מִכֶּם שְׁאֵלָה וּתְנוּ־לִי אִישׁ נֶזֶם שְׁלָלוֹ
כה כִּי־נִזְמֵי זָהָב לָהֶם כִּי יִשְׁמְעֵאלִים הֵם: וַיֹּאמְרוּ נָתוֹן נִתֵּן וַיִּפְרְשׂוּ אֶת־

we will," they said, and spread out a garment where each man tossed an
26 earring from his spoil. The mass of the golden earrings he had asked for came
to one thousand seven hundred in gold – besides the crescents, pendants, and
purple robes of the Midianite kings, and besides the collars on their camels'
27 necks. Gidon made it into an ephod[12] and mounted it in his own city, in
Ofra. All of Israel lusted after it there, and it became a snare for Gidon and
28 his household. Midyan submitted to the Israelites and did not rear their
heads again. And the land was quiet for forty years, throughout the days of
29 Gidon. Yerubaal son of Yoash went home and settled down. Gidon
30
31 had seventy sons of his own issue, for he had many wives. His concubine in
Shekhem also bore him a son, and he established his name as Avimelekh.
32 Gidon son of Yoash died at a ripe old age and was buried in the tomb of his
33 father Yoash, in Ofra of the Aviezrites. After Gidon died, the Israelites
relapsed and strayed after the Be'alim; they established Baal Brit as their own
34 god. No longer did the Israelites remember the Lord their God, who had
35 saved them from all their surrounding enemies. And they showed no loyalty
to the house of Yerubaal-Gidon in return for all the good he had done for
9 1 Israel. Avimelekh son of Yerubaal went to Shekhem, to his mother's
kinsmen, and addressed them along with the whole clan of his mother's father.
2 "Speak up now to all the citizens of Shekhem: What is better for you? For
seventy men to rule over you – all the sons of Yerubaal – or for a single man
3 to rule over you? Remember that I am your own bones and flesh!" His
mother's brothers repeated all this on his behalf to all the citizens of Shekhem,
and they were won over by Avimelekh, for they thought: "He is our brother."
4 They gave him seventy pieces of silver from the temple of Baal Brit, which
5 Avimelekh used to hire worthless, reckless men to follow him. He arrived at
his father's house in Ofra and killed his brothers, the sons of Yerubaal – seventy
men upon a single stone. Only Yotam, Yerubaal's youngest son, was left, for
6 he had hidden. All the citizens of Shekhem and Beit Milo assembled
7 and proclaimed Avimelekh king at the Monumental Oak at Shekhem. When
they informed Yotam, he went and stood at the top of Mount Gerizim. He
raised his voice and cried out, "Listen to me, citizens of Shekhem, so that God
8 may listen to you. Once, the trees set out to anoint themselves a king. They
9 said to the olive tree, 'Rule over us!' But the olive tree replied, 'Have I ceased
10 to yield my oil, which honors God and men, to go waving over the trees?' So
11 the trees said to the fig tree, 'Come, rule over us!' But the fig tree replied, 'Have
I ceased to yield my sweetness, my good fruit, to go waving over the trees?'
12 So the trees said to the grapevine, 'Come, rule over us!' But the grapevine
13

12 | An outer garment worn by the priests (see Ex. 28).

כו הַשִּׂמְלָה וַיַּשְׁלִיכוּ שָׁמָּה אִישׁ נֶזֶם שְׁלָלוֹ: וַיְהִי מִשְׁקַל נִזְמֵי הַזָּהָב אֲשֶׁר
שָׁאָל אֶלֶף וּשְׁבַע־מֵאוֹת זָהָב לְבַד מִן־הַשַּׂהֲרֹנִים וְהַנְּטִפוֹת וּבִגְדֵי
הָאַרְגָּמָן שֶׁעַל מַלְכֵי מִדְיָן וּלְבַד מִן־הָעֲנָקוֹת אֲשֶׁר בְּצַוְּארֵי גְמַלֵּיהֶם:
כז וַיַּעַשׂ אוֹתוֹ גִדְעוֹן לְאֵפוֹד וַיַּצֵּג אוֹתוֹ בְעִירוֹ בְּעָפְרָה וַיִּזְנוּ כָל־יִשְׂרָאֵל
כח אַחֲרָיו שָׁם וַיְהִי לְגִדְעוֹן וּלְבֵיתוֹ לְמוֹקֵשׁ: וַיִּכָּנַע מִדְיָן לִפְנֵי בְּנֵי
יִשְׂרָאֵל וְלֹא יָסְפוּ לָשֵׂאת רֹאשָׁם וַתִּשְׁקֹט הָאָרֶץ אַרְבָּעִים שָׁנָה בִּימֵי
כט ל גִדְעוֹן: וַיֵּלֶךְ יְרֻבַּעַל בֶּן־יוֹאָשׁ וַיֵּשֶׁב בְּבֵיתוֹ: וּלְגִדְעוֹן
לא הָיוּ שִׁבְעִים בָּנִים יֹצְאֵי יְרֵכוֹ כִּי־נָשִׁים רַבּוֹת הָיוּ לוֹ: וּפִילַגְשׁוֹ אֲשֶׁר
לב בִּשְׁכֶם יָלְדָה־לּוֹ גַם־הִיא בֵּן וַיָּשֶׂם אֶת־שְׁמוֹ אֲבִימֶלֶךְ: וַיָּמָת גִּדְעוֹן
בֶּן־יוֹאָשׁ בְּשֵׂיבָה טוֹבָה וַיִּקָּבֵר בְּקֶבֶר יוֹאָשׁ אָבִיו בְּעָפְרָה אֲבִי
לג הָעֶזְרִי: וַיְהִי כַּאֲשֶׁר מֵת גִּדְעוֹן וַיָּשׁוּבוּ בְּנֵי יִשְׂרָאֵל
לד וַיִּזְנוּ אַחֲרֵי הַבְּעָלִים וַיָּשִׂימוּ לָהֶם בַּעַל בְּרִית לֵאלֹהִים: וְלֹא זָכְרוּ בְּנֵי
יִשְׂרָאֵל אֶת־יְהוָה אֱלֹהֵיהֶם הַמַּצִּיל אוֹתָם מִיַּד כָּל־אֹיְבֵיהֶם מִסָּבִיב:
לה וְלֹא־עָשׂוּ חֶסֶד עִם־בֵּית יְרֻבַּעַל גִּדְעוֹן כְּכָל־הַטּוֹבָה אֲשֶׁר עָשָׂה עִם־
ט א יִשְׂרָאֵל: וַיֵּלֶךְ אֲבִימֶלֶךְ בֶּן־יְרֻבַּעַל שְׁכֶמָה אֶל־אֲחֵי
ב אִמּוֹ וַיְדַבֵּר אֲלֵיהֶם וְאֶל־כָּל־מִשְׁפַּחַת בֵּית־אֲבִי אִמּוֹ לֵאמֹר: דַּבְּרוּ־
נָא בְּאָזְנֵי כָל־בַּעֲלֵי שְׁכֶם מַה־טּוֹב לָכֶם הַמְשֹׁל בָּכֶם שִׁבְעִים אִישׁ
כֹּל בְּנֵי יְרֻבַּעַל אִם־מְשֹׁל בָּכֶם אִישׁ אֶחָד וּזְכַרְתֶּם כִּי־עַצְמְכֶם וּבְשַׂרְכֶם
ג אָנִי: וַיְדַבְּרוּ אֲחֵי־אִמּוֹ עָלָיו בְּאָזְנֵי כָּל־בַּעֲלֵי שְׁכֶם אֵת כָּל־הַדְּבָרִים
ד הָאֵלֶּה וַיֵּט לִבָּם אַחֲרֵי אֲבִימֶלֶךְ כִּי אָמְרוּ אָחִינוּ הוּא: וַיִּתְּנוּ־לוֹ
שִׁבְעִים כֶּסֶף מִבֵּית בַּעַל בְּרִית וַיִּשְׂכֹּר בָּהֶם אֲבִימֶלֶךְ אֲנָשִׁים רֵיקִים
ה וּפֹחֲזִים וַיֵּלְכוּ אַחֲרָיו: וַיָּבֹא בֵית־אָבִיו עָפְרָתָה וַיַּהֲרֹג אֶת־אֶחָיו בְּנֵי־
יְרֻבַּעַל שִׁבְעִים אִישׁ עַל־אֶבֶן אֶחָת וַיִּוָּתֵר יוֹתָם בֶּן־יְרֻבַּעַל הַקָּטֹן כִּי
ו נֶחְבָּא: וַיֵּאָסְפוּ כָּל־בַּעֲלֵי שְׁכֶם וְכָל־בֵּית מִלּוֹא וַיֵּלְכוּ
ז וַיַּמְלִיכוּ אֶת־אֲבִימֶלֶךְ לְמֶלֶךְ עִם־אֵלוֹן מֻצָּב אֲשֶׁר בִּשְׁכֶם: וַיַּגִּדוּ ז
לְיוֹתָם וַיֵּלֶךְ וַיַּעֲמֹד בְּרֹאשׁ הַר־גְּרִזִים וַיִּשָּׂא קוֹלוֹ וַיִּקְרָא וַיֹּאמֶר לָהֶם
ח שִׁמְעוּ אֵלַי בַּעֲלֵי שְׁכֶם וְיִשְׁמַע אֲלֵיכֶם אֱלֹהִים: הָלוֹךְ הָלְכוּ הָעֵצִים
ט לִמְשֹׁחַ עֲלֵיהֶם מֶלֶךְ וַיֹּאמְרוּ לַזַּיִת מלוכה עָלֵינוּ: וַיֹּאמֶר לָהֶם הַזַּיִת מָלְכָה
הֶחֳדַלְתִּי אֶת־דִּשְׁנִי אֲשֶׁר־בִּי יְכַבְּדוּ אֱלֹהִים וַאֲנָשִׁים וְהָלַכְתִּי לָנוּעַ
י יא עַל־הָעֵצִים: וַיֹּאמְרוּ הָעֵצִים לַתְּאֵנָה לְכִי־אַתְּ מָלְכִי עָלֵינוּ: וַתֹּאמֶר
לָהֶם הַתְּאֵנָה הֶחֳדַלְתִּי אֶת־מָתְקִי וְאֶת־תְּנוּבָתִי הַטּוֹבָה וְהָלַכְתִּי
יב יג לָנוּעַ עַל־הָעֵצִים: וַיֹּאמְרוּ הָעֵצִים לַגֶּפֶן לְכִי־אַתְּ מלוכי עָלֵינוּ: וַתֹּאמֶר מָלְכִי

replied, 'Have I ceased to yield my wine, which cheers God and men, to go
14 waving over the trees?' So all the trees said to the thornbush, 'Come, rule over
15 us!' The thornbush replied to the trees, 'If you are truly anointing me as king
over you, then come, take shelter in my shade. But if not, then may fire flare
16 from the thornbush and consume the cedars of Lebanon!' If you have acted
truly and sincerely in appointing Avimelekh as king; if you have treated
17 Yerubaal and his household well; if you have treated him as he deserves – for
my father fought for you, risking his life to save you from the hand of Midyan,
18 yet today you have risen against my father's house and killed his sons, seventy
men upon a single stone, and appointed Avimelekh, the son of his handmaiden,
19 king over the citizens of Shekhem, just because he is your kin! – if you have
dealt truly and sincerely with Yerubaal and his house today, then rejoice in
20 Avimelekh, and may he, too, rejoice in you. But if not, may fire flare from
Avimelekh and consume the citizens of Shekhem and Beit Milo, and may fire
flare from the citizens of Shekhem and Beit Milo and consume Avimelekh!"
21 With that, Yotam fled, escaping toward Be'er, where he stayed because of his
22 brother Avimelekh. Avimelekh ruled over Shekhem for three years.
23 Then God stirred up an ill wind between Avimelekh and the citizens of
24 Shekhem, and the citizens of Shekhem betrayed Avimelekh. This was in order
to turn the violence against and the blood of the seventy sons of Yerubaal
toward their brother Avimelekh, who killed them, and toward the citizens of
25 Shekhem, who empowered him to kill his brothers. The citizens of Shekhem
lay ambushes against him on the hilltops and robbed everyone who passed
26 by them on the road, but Avimelekh was informed of this. Gaal son
of Eved and his brothers passed through Shekhem, and the citizens of
27 Shekhem placed their confidence in him. They went out to the fields,
harvested and trampled the vintage of their vineyards, and held celebrations;
they went to the temple of their gods and feasted, drank, and cursed
28 Avimelekh. "Who is this Avimelekh compared to Shekhem, that we need
serve him?" said Gaal son of Eved. "He is but the son of Yerubaal, and Zevul
is but his deputy. We should serve the descendants of Ḥamor, Shekhem's
29 father – why should we be serving him? If only this people were in my hands –
I would get rid of Avimelekh!" And he addressed Avimelekh, "Muster your
30 full forces and come forth!" Zevul, the city governor, heard Gaal's speech and
31 grew furious. He sent a secret message to Avimelekh: "Beware – Gaal son of
Eved and his brothers have arrived in Shekhem, and they are inciting the city
32 against you. Take action tonight, you and the men on your side, and lay
33 ambush in the field. Early in the morning, at daybreak, raid the city – he and
the troops on his side will charge at you, and you will do to him what you
34 find in your power." So Avimelekh and all the men on his side rose at night:

לָהֶם הֶחֳדַלְתִּי אֶת־תִּירוֹשִׁי הַמְשַׂמֵּחַ אֱלֹהִים וַאֲנָשִׁים וְהָלַכְתִּי
יד לָנוּעַ עַל־הָעֵצִים: וַיֹּאמְרוּ כָל־הָעֵצִים אֶל־הָאָטָד לֵךְ אַתָּה מְלָךְ־
טו עָלֵינוּ: וַיֹּאמֶר הָאָטָד אֶל־הָעֵצִים אִם בֶּאֱמֶת אַתֶּם מֹשְׁחִים אֹתִי
לְמֶלֶךְ עֲלֵיכֶם בֹּאוּ חֲסוּ בְצִלִּי וְאִם־אַיִן תֵּצֵא אֵשׁ מִן־הָאָטָד וְתֹאכַל
טז אֶת־אַרְזֵי הַלְּבָנוֹן: וְעַתָּה אִם־בֶּאֱמֶת וּבְתָמִים עֲשִׂיתֶם וַתַּמְלִיכוּ
אֶת־אֲבִימֶלֶךְ וְאִם־טוֹבָה עֲשִׂיתֶם עִם־יְרֻבַּעַל וְעִם־בֵּיתוֹ וְאִם־כִּגְמוּל
יז יָדָיו עֲשִׂיתֶם לוֹ: אֲשֶׁר־נִלְחַם אָבִי עֲלֵיכֶם וַיַּשְׁלֵךְ אֶת־נַפְשׁוֹ מִנֶּגֶד
יח וַיַּצֵּל אֶתְכֶם מִיַּד מִדְיָן: וְאַתֶּם קַמְתֶּם עַל־בֵּית אָבִי הַיּוֹם וַתַּהַרְגוּ
אֶת־בָּנָיו שִׁבְעִים אִישׁ עַל־אֶבֶן אֶחָת וַתַּמְלִיכוּ אֶת־אֲבִימֶלֶךְ בֶּן־
יט אֲמָתוֹ עַל־בַּעֲלֵי שְׁכֶם כִּי אֲחִיכֶם הוּא: וְאִם־בֶּאֱמֶת וּבְתָמִים עֲשִׂיתֶם
עִם־יְרֻבַּעַל וְעִם־בֵּיתוֹ הַיּוֹם הַזֶּה שִׂמְחוּ בַּאֲבִימֶלֶךְ וְיִשְׂמַח גַּם־
כ הוּא בָּכֶם: וְאִם־אַיִן תֵּצֵא אֵשׁ מֵאֲבִימֶלֶךְ וְתֹאכַל אֶת־בַּעֲלֵי שְׁכֶם
וְאֶת־בֵּית מִלּוֹא וְתֵצֵא אֵשׁ מִבַּעֲלֵי שְׁכֶם וּמִבֵּית מִלּוֹא וְתֹאכַל אֶת־
כא אֲבִימֶלֶךְ: וַיָּנָס יוֹתָם וַיִּבְרַח וַיֵּלֶךְ בְּאֵרָה וַיֵּשֶׁב שָׁם מִפְּנֵי אֲבִימֶלֶךְ
כב כג אָחִיו: וַיָּשַׂר אֲבִימֶלֶךְ עַל־יִשְׂרָאֵל שָׁלֹשׁ שָׁנִים: וַיִּשְׁלַח
אֱלֹהִים רוּחַ רָעָה בֵּין אֲבִימֶלֶךְ וּבֵין בַּעֲלֵי שְׁכֶם וַיִּבְגְּדוּ בַעֲלֵי־שְׁכֶם
כד בַּאֲבִימֶלֶךְ: לָבוֹא חֲמַס שִׁבְעִים בְּנֵי־יְרֻבָּעַל וְדָמָם לָשׂוּם עַל־אֲבִימֶלֶךְ
אֲחִיהֶם אֲשֶׁר הָרַג אוֹתָם וְעַל בַּעֲלֵי שְׁכֶם אֲשֶׁר־חִזְּקוּ אֶת־יָדָיו לַהֲרֹג
כה אֶת־אֶחָיו: וַיָּשִׂימוּ לוֹ בַעֲלֵי שְׁכֶם מְאָרְבִים עַל רָאשֵׁי הֶהָרִים וַיִּגְזְלוּ
כו אֵת כָּל־אֲשֶׁר־יַעֲבֹר עֲלֵיהֶם בַּדָּרֶךְ וַיֻּגַּד לַאֲבִימֶלֶךְ: וַיָּבֹא
כז גַּעַל בֶּן־עֶבֶד וְאֶחָיו וַיַּעַבְרוּ בִּשְׁכֶם וַיִּבְטְחוּ־בוֹ בַּעֲלֵי שְׁכֶם: וַיֵּצְאוּ
הַשָּׂדֶה וַיִּבְצְרוּ אֶת־כַּרְמֵיהֶם וַיִּדְרְכוּ וַיַּעֲשׂוּ הִלּוּלִים וַיָּבֹאוּ בֵּית אֱלֹהֵיהֶם
כח וַיֹּאכְלוּ וַיִּשְׁתּוּ וַיְקַלְלוּ אֶת־אֲבִימֶלֶךְ: וַיֹּאמֶר ׀ גַּעַל בֶּן־עֶבֶד מִי־אֲבִימֶלֶךְ
וּמִי־שְׁכֶם כִּי נַעַבְדֶנּוּ הֲלֹא בֶן־יְרֻבַּעַל וּזְבֻל פְּקִידוֹ עִבְדוּ אֶת־אַנְשֵׁי
כט חֲמוֹר אֲבִי שְׁכֶם וּמַדּוּעַ נַעַבְדֶנּוּ אֲנָחְנוּ: וּמִי יִתֵּן אֶת־הָעָם הַזֶּה בְּיָדִי
ל וְאָסִירָה אֶת־אֲבִימֶלֶךְ וַיֹּאמֶר לַאֲבִימֶלֶךְ רַבֶּה צְבָאֲךָ וָצֵאָה: וַיִּשְׁמַע
לא זְבֻל שַׂר הָעִיר אֶת־דִּבְרֵי גַּעַל בֶּן־עָבֶד וַיִּחַר אַפּוֹ: וַיִּשְׁלַח מַלְאָכִים
אֶל־אֲבִימֶלֶךְ בְּתָרְמָה לֵאמֹר הִנֵּה גַעַל בֶּן־עֶבֶד וְאֶחָיו בָּאִים שְׁכֶמָה
לב וְהִנָּם צָרִים אֶת־הָעִיר עָלֶיךָ: וְעַתָּה קוּם לַיְלָה אַתָּה וְהָעָם אֲשֶׁר־
לג אִתָּךְ וֶאֱרֹב בַּשָּׂדֶה: וְהָיָה בַבֹּקֶר כִּזְרֹחַ הַשֶּׁמֶשׁ תַּשְׁכִּים וּפָשַׁטְתָּ עַל־
הָעִיר וְהִנֵּה־הוּא וְהָעָם אֲשֶׁר־אִתּוֹ יֹצְאִים אֵלֶיךָ וְעָשִׂיתָ לּוֹ כַּאֲשֶׁר
לד תִּמְצָא יָדֶךָ: וַיָּקָם אֲבִימֶלֶךְ וְכָל־הָעָם אֲשֶׁר־עִמּוֹ לַיְלָה וַיֶּאֶרְבוּ

35 they set up four large groups in ambush against Shekhem. When Gaal son of
Eved went out and stood by the entrance to the city gate, Avimelekh and his
36 men rose from ambush. Gaal saw the men and said to Zevul, "Look – men
are coming down from the mountaintops!" Zevul replied, "The shadows of
37 the mountains look like people to you." But Gaal spoke up again. "Look," he
said, "men are coming down from the uplands, and another large group is
38 coming from the Augurs' Oak Road." Zevul said to him, "Where, then, is that
bold mouth of yours, boasting, 'Who is Avimelekh, that we should serve him?'
39 Aren't those the men you scorned? Go on, now – go fight him!" So Gaal went
40 out before the citizens of Shekhem and fought with Avimelekh. Avimelekh
pursued him, and Gaal fled before him. Many fell slain all the way up to the
41 entrance gate. Avimelekh remained in Aruma while Zevul drove Gaal and
42 his kinsmen away and kept them out of Shekhem. The next day, the
43 men marched out to the field, and Avimelekh was informed. He took his men,
split them into three large groups, and lay an ambush in the field. When he
saw the men marching out of the city, he pounced on them and attacked them.
44 Avimelekh and the group with him rushed ahead and stationed themselves
by the entrance gate of the city while the other two companies charged
45 against everyone in the field and struck them down. Avimelekh fought in the
city that entire day and captured the city; he slew everyone in it, razed the
46 city, and sowed it with salt. All the citizens of Tower of Shekhem
47 heard, and they made for the stronghold of the El Brit temple. When
Avimelekh was informed that all the citizens of Tower of Shekhem had
48 gathered, he marched up Mount Tzalmon together with all his men. Taking
hold of an ax, Avimelekh chopped off a branch, lifted it up, and placed it on
his shoulder. He told the troops, "What you saw me do – quickly, do as I did!"
49 So each of the men chopped off a branch and followed Avimelekh; they
placed them against the walls and used them to set the stronghold on fire.
And all the people of Tower of Shekhem died, around a thousand men and
50 women. Avimelekh then marched to Tevetz; he set up camp at
51 Tevetz and captured it. There was a stronghold in the town where all the
town's citizens, men and women, had fled; they locked themselves in and
52 went up to the roof of the tower. Avimelekh reached the tower and attacked
53 it. Just as he was approaching the entrance of the tower to set it alight, a
woman dropped an upper millstone on Avimelekh's head and shattered his
54 skull. He called urgently to the boy who bore his arms. "Draw your sword
and put me to death," he said to him, "lest they say of me, 'A woman killed
55 him.'" So his boy stabbed him, and he died. When the people of Israel
56 saw that Avimelekh had died, they all went back to their own places. Thus
God requited the evil Avimelekh had done to his father by murdering
57 his seventy brothers. As for the evil of the people of Shekhem, God requited

לה עַל־שְׁכֶם אַרְבָּעָה רָאשִׁים: וַיֵּצֵא גַּעַל בֶּן־עֶבֶד וַיַּעֲמֹד פֶּתַח שַׁעַר
לו הָעִיר וַיָּקָם אֲבִימֶלֶךְ וְהָעָם אֲשֶׁר־אִתּוֹ מִן־הַמַּאְרָב: וַיַּרְא־גַעַל אֶת־
הָעָם וַיֹּאמֶר אֶל־זְבֻל הִנֵּה־עָם יוֹרֵד מֵרָאשֵׁי הֶהָרִים וַיֹּאמֶר אֵלָיו זְבֻל
לז אֵת צֵל הֶהָרִים אַתָּה רֹאֶה כָּאֲנָשִׁים: וַיֹּסֶף עוֹד גַּעַל לְדַבֵּר וַיֹּאמֶר
הִנֵּה־עָם יוֹרְדִים מֵעִם טַבּוּר הָאָרֶץ וְרֹאשׁ־אֶחָד בָּא מִדֶּרֶךְ אֵלוֹן
לח מְעוֹנְנִים: וַיֹּאמֶר אֵלָיו זְבֻל אַיֵּה אֵפוֹא פִיךָ אֲשֶׁר תֹּאמַר מִי אֲבִימֶלֶךְ
כִּי נַעַבְדֶנּוּ הֲלֹא זֶה הָעָם אֲשֶׁר מָאַסְתָּה בּוֹ צֵא־נָא עַתָּה וְהִלָּחֶם בּוֹ:
לט מ וַיֵּצֵא גַעַל לִפְנֵי בַּעֲלֵי שְׁכֶם וַיִּלָּחֶם בַּאֲבִימֶלֶךְ: וַיִּרְדְּפֵהוּ אֲבִימֶלֶךְ וַיָּנָס
מא מִפָּנָיו וַיִּפְּלוּ חֲלָלִים רַבִּים עַד־פֶּתַח הַשָּׁעַר: וַיֵּשֶׁב אֲבִימֶלֶךְ בָּארוּמָה
מב וַיְגָרֶשׁ זְבֻל אֶת־גַּעַל וְאֶת־אֶחָיו מִשֶּׁבֶת בִּשְׁכֶם: וַיְהִי
מג מִמָּחֳרָת וַיֵּצֵא הָעָם הַשָּׂדֶה וַיַּגִּדוּ לַאֲבִימֶלֶךְ: וַיִּקַּח אֶת־הָעָם וַיֶּחֱצֵם
לִשְׁלֹשָׁה רָאשִׁים וַיֶּאֱרֹב בַּשָּׂדֶה וַיַּרְא וְהִנֵּה הָעָם יֹצֵא מִן־הָעִיר
מד וַיָּקָם עֲלֵיהֶם וַיַּכֵּם: וַאֲבִימֶלֶךְ וְהָרָאשִׁים אֲשֶׁר עִמּוֹ פָּשְׁטוּ וַיַּעַמְדוּ
פֶּתַח שַׁעַר הָעִיר וּשְׁנֵי הָרָאשִׁים פָּשְׁטוּ עַל־כָּל־אֲשֶׁר בַּשָּׂדֶה וַיַּכּוּם:
מה וַאֲבִימֶלֶךְ נִלְחָם בָּעִיר כֹּל הַיּוֹם הַהוּא וַיִּלְכֹּד אֶת־הָעִיר וְאֶת־הָעָם
מו אֲשֶׁר־בָּהּ הָרָג וַיִּתֹּץ אֶת־הָעִיר וַיִּזְרָעֶהָ מֶלַח: וַיִּשְׁמְעוּ
מז כָּל־בַּעֲלֵי מִגְדַּל־שְׁכֶם וַיָּבֹאוּ אֶל־צְרִיחַ בֵּית אֵל בְּרִית: וַיֻּגַּד לַאֲבִימֶלֶךְ
מח כִּי הִתְקַבְּצוּ כָּל־בַּעֲלֵי מִגְדַּל־שְׁכֶם: וַיַּעַל אֲבִימֶלֶךְ הַר־צַלְמוֹן
הוּא וְכָל־הָעָם אֲשֶׁר־אִתּוֹ וַיִּקַּח אֲבִימֶלֶךְ אֶת־הַקַּרְדֻּמּוֹת בְּיָדוֹ
וַיִּכְרֹת שׂוֹכַת עֵצִים וַיִּשָּׂאֶהָ וַיָּשֶׂם עַל־שִׁכְמוֹ וַיֹּאמֶר אֶל־הָעָם
מט אֲשֶׁר־עִמּוֹ מָה רְאִיתֶם עָשִׂיתִי מַהֲרוּ עֲשׂוּ כָמוֹנִי: וַיִּכְרְתוּ גַם־כָּל־
הָעָם אִישׁ שׂוֹכֹה וַיֵּלְכוּ אַחֲרֵי אֲבִימֶלֶךְ וַיָּשִׂימוּ עַל־הַצְּרִיחַ וַיַּצִּיתוּ
עֲלֵיהֶם אֶת־הַצְּרִיחַ בָּאֵשׁ וַיָּמֻתוּ גַּם כָּל־אַנְשֵׁי מִגְדַּל־שְׁכֶם כְּאֶלֶף אִישׁ
נ וְאִשָּׁה: וַיֵּלֶךְ אֲבִימֶלֶךְ אֶל־תֵּבֵץ וַיִּחַן בְּתֵבֵץ וַיִּלְכְּדָהּ:
נא וּמִגְדַּל־עֹז הָיָה בְתוֹךְ־הָעִיר וַיָּנֻסוּ שָׁמָּה כָּל־הָאֲנָשִׁים וְהַנָּשִׁים וְכֹל
נב בַּעֲלֵי הָעִיר וַיִּסְגְּרוּ בַּעֲדָם וַיַּעֲלוּ עַל־גַּג הַמִּגְדָּל: וַיָּבֹא אֲבִימֶלֶךְ עַד־
נג הַמִּגְדָּל וַיִּלָּחֶם בּוֹ וַיִּגַּשׁ עַד־פֶּתַח הַמִּגְדָּל לְשָׂרְפוֹ בָאֵשׁ: וַתַּשְׁלֵךְ אִשָּׁה
נד אַחַת פֶּלַח רֶכֶב עַל־רֹאשׁ אֲבִימֶלֶךְ וַתָּרִץ אֶת־גֻּלְגָּלְתּוֹ: וַיִּקְרָא מְהֵרָה
אֶל־הַנַּעַר ׀ נֹשֵׂא כֵלָיו וַיֹּאמֶר לוֹ שְׁלֹף חַרְבְּךָ וּמוֹתְתֵנִי פֶּן־יֹאמְרוּ לִי
נה אִשָּׁה הֲרָגָתְהוּ וַיִּדְקְרֵהוּ נַעֲרוֹ וַיָּמֹת: וַיִּרְאוּ אִישׁ־יִשְׂרָאֵל כִּי־מֵת
נו אֲבִימֶלֶךְ וַיֵּלְכוּ אִישׁ לִמְקֹמוֹ: וַיָּשֶׁב אֱלֹהִים אֵת רָעַת אֲבִימֶלֶךְ
נז אֲשֶׁר עָשָׂה לְאָבִיו לַהֲרֹג אֶת־שִׁבְעִים אֶחָיו: וְאֵת כָּל־רָעַת אַנְשֵׁי

it upon their own heads; the curse of Yotam son of Yerubaal overcame
10 1 them. After Avimelekh, Tola son of Puah son of Dodo, a man
2 of Yissakhar, arose to rescue Israel. He lived in Shamir in the Efrayim hills.
He judged Israel for twenty-three years. He died and was buried in
3 Shamir. After him, Yair the Gileadite arose; he judged Israel for
4 twenty-two years. He had thirty sons who rode on thirty donkeys and owned
thirty villages;[13] they are called the Hamlets of Yair[14] to this day in the land of
5 the Gilad. Yair died and was buried in Kamon.
6 The Israelites resumed doing evil in the eyes of the LORD; they worshipped the
Be'alim, the Ashtarot, the gods of Aram, the gods of Sidon, the gods of Moav,
the gods of the Amonites, and the gods of the Philistines. They abandoned
7 the LORD and did not worship Him. The LORD's wrath raged against Israel,
8 and He handed them over to the Philistines and the Amonites. They harassed
and suppressed the Israelites that year and for the next eighteen years – all
the Israelites across the Jordan in the land of the Amorites in the Gilad region.
9 Then the Amonites crossed the Jordan to attack Yehuda, Binyamin, and the
10 House of Efrayim as well; Israel was in desperate straits. The Israelites cried
out to the LORD, wailing, "We have sinned against You, for we abandoned
11 You our God and served the Be'alim." The LORD said to the Israelites,
12 "Indeed, Egypt and the Amorites and the Amonites and the Philistines and
the Sidonites and Amalek and Maon oppressed you; then you cried out to Me,
13 and I saved you from their hands. But you abandoned Me and worshipped
14 other gods – I will save you no longer. Go and cry out to the other gods you
15 chose – let them save you in your times of trouble." "We have sinned," the
Israelites said to the LORD. "Do to us as You see fit – but please, save us this very
16 day." They purged the alien gods from their midst and worshipped the LORD,
17 and He could not bear Israel's misery any longer. The Amonites
mustered and encamped in Gilad, and Israel gathered and encamped at
18 Mitzpa. The leaders of the men of Gilad said among themselves, "Whoever
launches the first attack against the Amonites shall become the head of all the
11 1 people of Gilad." Yiftaḥ the Gileadite was a valiant warrior. He was
2 the son of a harlot; Gilad sired Yiftaḥ, but Gilad's wife bore him sons as well.
When the wife's sons grew up, they drove Yiftaḥ away, telling him, "You shall
have no share in our father's estate, for you are the son of another woman."
3 So Yiftaḥ fled from his brothers; he settled in the land of Tov. Worthless men
4 were drawn to him and went out raiding with him. Time passed, and

13 | "Donkeys," *ayarim*, and "villages," *ayarim*, are homonyms in Hebrew.
14 | Cf. Numbers 32:41.

שְׁכֶם הֵשִׁיב אֱלֹהִים בְּרֹאשָׁם וַתָּבֹא אֲלֵיהֶם קִלְלַת יוֹתָם בֶּן־
י א יְרֻבָּעַל׃ וַיָּקָם אַחֲרֵי אֲבִימֶלֶךְ לְהוֹשִׁיעַ אֶת־ ח
יִשְׂרָאֵל תּוֹלָע בֶּן־פּוּאָה בֶּן־דּוֹדוֹ אִישׁ יִשָּׂשכָר וְהוּא־יֹשֵׁב בְּשָׁמִיר
ב בְּהַר אֶפְרָיִם׃ וַיִּשְׁפֹּט אֶת־יִשְׂרָאֵל עֶשְׂרִים וְשָׁלֹשׁ שָׁנָה וַיָּמָת וַיִּקָּבֵר
ג בְּשָׁמִיר׃ וַיָּקָם אַחֲרָיו יָאִיר הַגִּלְעָדִי וַיִּשְׁפֹּט אֶת־יִשְׂרָאֵל
ד עֶשְׂרִים וּשְׁתַּיִם שָׁנָה׃ וַיְהִי־לוֹ שְׁלֹשִׁים בָּנִים רֹכְבִים עַל־שְׁלֹשִׁים
עֲיָרִים וּשְׁלֹשִׁים עֲיָרִים לָהֶם לָהֶם יִקְרְאוּ ׀ חַוֺּת יָאִיר עַד הַיּוֹם הַזֶּה
ה אֲשֶׁר בְּאֶרֶץ הַגִּלְעָד׃ וַיָּמָת יָאִיר וַיִּקָּבֵר בְּקָמוֹן׃
ו וַיֹּסִפוּ ׀ בְּנֵי יִשְׂרָאֵל לַעֲשׂוֹת הָרַע בְּעֵינֵי יְהוָה וַיַּעַבְדוּ אֶת־הַבְּעָלִים וְאֶת־
הָעַשְׁתָּרוֹת וְאֶת־אֱלֹהֵי אֲרָם וְאֶת־אֱלֹהֵי צִידוֹן וְאֵת ׀ אֱלֹהֵי מוֹאָב וְאֵת
אֱלֹהֵי בְנֵי־עַמּוֹן וְאֵת אֱלֹהֵי פְלִשְׁתִּים וַיַּעַזְבוּ אֶת־יְהוָה וְלֹא עֲבָדוּהוּ׃
ז ח וַיִּחַר־אַף יְהוָה בְּיִשְׂרָאֵל וַיִּמְכְּרֵם בְּיַד־פְּלִשְׁתִּים וּבְיַד בְּנֵי עַמּוֹן׃ וַיִּרְעֲצוּ
וַיְרֹצְצוּ אֶת־בְּנֵי יִשְׂרָאֵל בַּשָּׁנָה הַהִיא שְׁמֹנֶה עֶשְׂרֵה שָׁנָה אֶת־כָּל־
ט בְּנֵי יִשְׂרָאֵל אֲשֶׁר בְּעֵבֶר הַיַּרְדֵּן בְּאֶרֶץ הָאֱמֹרִי אֲשֶׁר בַּגִּלְעָד׃ וַיַּעַבְרוּ
בְנֵי־עַמּוֹן אֶת־הַיַּרְדֵּן לְהִלָּחֵם גַּם־בִּיהוּדָה וּבְבִנְיָמִין וּבְבֵית אֶפְרָיִם
י וַתֵּצֶר לְיִשְׂרָאֵל מְאֹד׃ וַיִּזְעֲקוּ בְּנֵי יִשְׂרָאֵל אֶל־יְהוָה לֵאמֹר חָטָאנוּ
יא לָךְ וְכִי עָזַבְנוּ אֶת־אֱלֹהֵינוּ וַנַּעֲבֹד אֶת־הַבְּעָלִים׃ וַיֹּאמֶר
יְהוָה אֶל־בְּנֵי יִשְׂרָאֵל הֲלֹא מִמִּצְרַיִם וּמִן־הָאֱמֹרִי וּמִן־בְּנֵי עַמּוֹן
יב וּמִן־פְּלִשְׁתִּים׃ וְצִידוֹנִים וַעֲמָלֵק וּמָעוֹן לָחֲצוּ אֶתְכֶם וַתִּצְעֲקוּ אֵלַי
יג וָאוֹשִׁיעָה אֶתְכֶם מִיָּדָם׃ וְאַתֶּם עֲזַבְתֶּם אוֹתִי וַתַּעַבְדוּ אֱלֹהִים אֲחֵרִים
יד לָכֵן לֹא־אוֹסִיף לְהוֹשִׁיעַ אֶתְכֶם׃ לְכוּ וְזַעֲקוּ אֶל־הָאֱלֹהִים אֲשֶׁר
טו בְּחַרְתֶּם בָּם הֵמָּה יוֹשִׁיעוּ לָכֶם בְּעֵת צָרַתְכֶם׃ וַיֹּאמְרוּ בְנֵי־יִשְׂרָאֵל
אֶל־יְהוָה חָטָאנוּ עֲשֵׂה־אַתָּה לָנוּ כְּכָל־הַטּוֹב בְּעֵינֶיךָ אַךְ הַצִּילֵנוּ נָא
טז הַיּוֹם הַזֶּה׃ וַיָּסִירוּ אֶת־אֱלֹהֵי הַנֵּכָר מִקִּרְבָּם וַיַּעַבְדוּ אֶת־יְהוָה וַתִּקְצַר
יז נַפְשׁוֹ בַּעֲמַל יִשְׂרָאֵל׃ וַיִּצָּעֲקוּ בְּנֵי עַמּוֹן וַיַּחֲנוּ בַּגִּלְעָד
יח וַיֵּאָסְפוּ בְּנֵי יִשְׂרָאֵל וַיַּחֲנוּ בַּמִּצְפָּה׃ וַיֹּאמְרוּ הָעָם שָׂרֵי גִלְעָד אִישׁ
אֶל־רֵעֵהוּ מִי הָאִישׁ אֲשֶׁר יָחֵל לְהִלָּחֵם בִּבְנֵי עַמּוֹן יִהְיֶה לְרֹאשׁ לְכֹל
יא א יֹשְׁבֵי גִלְעָד׃ וְיִפְתָּח הַגִּלְעָדִי הָיָה גִּבּוֹר חַיִל וְהוּא בֶּן־
ב אִשָּׁה זוֹנָה וַיּוֹלֶד גִּלְעָד אֶת־יִפְתָּח׃ וַתֵּלֶד אֵשֶׁת־גִּלְעָד לוֹ בָּנִים וַיִּגְדְּלוּ
בְנֵי־הָאִשָּׁה וַיְגָרְשׁוּ אֶת־יִפְתָּח וַיֹּאמְרוּ לוֹ לֹא־תִנְחַל בְּבֵית־אָבִינוּ כִּי
ג בֶּן־אִשָּׁה אַחֶרֶת אָתָּה׃ וַיִּבְרַח יִפְתָּח מִפְּנֵי אֶחָיו וַיֵּשֶׁב בְּאֶרֶץ טוֹב
ד וַיִּתְלַקְּטוּ אֶל־יִפְתָּח אֲנָשִׁים רֵיקִים וַיֵּצְאוּ עִמּוֹ׃ וַיְהִי

5 the Amonites waged war upon Israel. When the Amonites attacked Israel, the
6 elders of Gilad set out to bring Yiftaḥ back from the land of Tov. "Come with
us," they said to Yiftaḥ, "and be our commander, so that we can fight against
7 the Amonites." "But you despised me," Yiftaḥ said to the elders of Gilad, "and
drove me away from my father's house. Why do you come to me now, when
8 you are in trouble?" "For that reason we ourselves have come back to you
now," the elders of Gilad said to Yiftaḥ. "You shall march out with us and
9 fight the Amonites, and you shall be the leader of all the people of Gilad." "If
you bring me back to fight against the Amonites," Yiftaḥ replied to the elders
of Gilad, "and the LORD delivers them to me, then I shall be your leader."
10 The elders of Gilad said to Yiftaḥ, "The LORD shall bear witness between
11 us if we do not comply with your words." So Yiftaḥ went with the elders of
Gilad, and the people made him their head and commander. Yiftaḥ repeated
12 all his terms before the LORD at Mitzpa. Yiftaḥ sent messengers to
the king of the Amonites: "What do you have against us, that you came to
13 attack our land?" The king of the Amonites replied to Yiftaḥ's messengers,
"Israel seized my lands when they came out of Egypt – from the Arnon to the
14 Yabok and up to the Jordan. Now hand them back peacefully." Once again
15 Yiftaḥ sent messengers to the king of the Amonites. "Thus says Yiftaḥ," they
16 said. "Israel did not seize the land of Moav nor the land of the Amonites. For
when they came out of Egypt, Israel trekked through the wilderness to the
17 Sea of Reeds, then they arrived at Kadesh. And Israel sent messengers to the
king of Edom, saying, 'Please let us pass through your land,' but the king of
Edom would not listen; they also reached out to the king of Moav, but he
18 would not comply. So Israel remained in Kadesh. They trekked through the
wilderness, making their way around the land of Edom and the land of Moav
until they reached the eastern side of the land of Moav, where they encamped
across the Arnon. They did not enter Moabite territory, for the Arnon is the
19 Moabite border. Then Israel sent messengers to Siḥon, king of the Amorites,
the king of Ḥeshbon. Israel said to him, 'Please, let us pass through your land
20 to our own place.' But Siḥon did not trust Israel to pass through his territory.
And Siḥon assembled all his troops, encamped at Yahtza, and attacked Israel.
21 The LORD, God of Israel, delivered Siḥon and all of his people into Israel's
hands; they defeated them, and the Israelites took possession of the entire
22 land of the Amorites, who lived in that land. They took possession of all the
Amorite territory from Arnon to the Yabok, and from the wilderness to the
23 Jordan. Now, the LORD, God of Israel, dispossessed the Amorites before
24 His people, Israel – why should you possess it? You take possession of what
Kemosh, your god, grants you, and we will take possession of everything the
25 LORD, our God, grants us. Now, are you any better than Balak son of Tzipor,
king of Moav? Did he pick a quarrel with Israel? Did he wage war against

ה מִיָּמִים וַיִּלָּחֲמוּ בְנֵי־עַמּוֹן עִם־יִשְׂרָאֵל׃ וַיְהִי כַּאֲשֶׁר נִלְחֲמוּ בְנֵי־עַמּוֹן
ו עִם־יִשְׂרָאֵל וַיֵּלְכוּ זִקְנֵי גִלְעָד לָקַחַת אֶת־יִפְתָּח מֵאֶרֶץ טוֹב׃ וַיֹּאמְרוּ
ז לְיִפְתָּח לְכָה וְהָיִיתָה לָּנוּ לְקָצִין וְנִלָּחֲמָה בִּבְנֵי עַמּוֹן׃ וַיֹּאמֶר יִפְתָּח
לְזִקְנֵי גִלְעָד הֲלֹא אַתֶּם שְׂנֵאתֶם אוֹתִי וַתְּגָרְשׁוּנִי מִבֵּית אָבִי וּמַדּוּעַ
ח בָּאתֶם אֵלַי עַתָּה כַּאֲשֶׁר צַר לָכֶם׃ וַיֹּאמְרוּ זִקְנֵי גִלְעָד אֶל־יִפְתָּח לָכֵן
עַתָּה שַׁבְנוּ אֵלֶיךָ וְהָלַכְתָּ עִמָּנוּ וְנִלְחַמְתָּ בִּבְנֵי עַמּוֹן וְהָיִיתָ לָּנוּ לְרֹאשׁ
ט לְכֹל יֹשְׁבֵי גִלְעָד׃ וַיֹּאמֶר יִפְתָּח אֶל־זִקְנֵי גִלְעָד אִם־מְשִׁיבִים אַתֶּם
אוֹתִי לְהִלָּחֵם בִּבְנֵי עַמּוֹן וְנָתַן יְהוָה אוֹתָם לְפָנָי אָנֹכִי אֶהְיֶה לָכֶם
י לְרֹאשׁ׃ וַיֹּאמְרוּ זִקְנֵי־גִלְעָד אֶל־יִפְתָּח יְהוָה יִהְיֶה שֹׁמֵעַ בֵּינוֹתֵינוּ
יא אִם־לֹא כִדְבָרְךָ כֵּן נַעֲשֶׂה׃ וַיֵּלֶךְ יִפְתָּח עִם־זִקְנֵי גִלְעָד וַיָּשִׂימוּ הָעָם
אוֹתוֹ עֲלֵיהֶם לְרֹאשׁ וּלְקָצִין וַיְדַבֵּר יִפְתָּח אֶת־כָּל־דְּבָרָיו לִפְנֵי יְהוָה
יב בַּמִּצְפָּה׃ וַיִּשְׁלַח יִפְתָּח מַלְאָכִים אֶל־מֶלֶךְ בְּנֵי־עַמּוֹן
יג לֵאמֹר מַה־לִּי וָלָךְ כִּי־בָאתָ אֵלַי לְהִלָּחֵם בְּאַרְצִי׃ וַיֹּאמֶר מֶלֶךְ בְּנֵי־
עַמּוֹן אֶל־מַלְאֲכֵי יִפְתָּח כִּי־לָקַח יִשְׂרָאֵל אֶת־אַרְצִי בַּעֲלוֹתוֹ מִמִּצְרַיִם
יד מֵאַרְנוֹן וְעַד־הַיַּבֹּק וְעַד־הַיַּרְדֵּן וְעַתָּה הָשִׁיבָה אֶתְהֶן בְּשָׁלוֹם׃ וַיּוֹסֶף
טו עוֹד יִפְתָּח וַיִּשְׁלַח מַלְאָכִים אֶל־מֶלֶךְ בְּנֵי עַמּוֹן׃ וַיֹּאמֶר לוֹ כֹּה אָמַר
טז יִפְתָּח לֹא־לָקַח יִשְׂרָאֵל אֶת־אֶרֶץ מוֹאָב וְאֶת־אֶרֶץ בְּנֵי עַמּוֹן׃ כִּי
בַּעֲלוֹתָם מִמִּצְרָיִם וַיֵּלֶךְ יִשְׂרָאֵל בַּמִּדְבָּר עַד־יַם־סוּף וַיָּבֹא קָדֵשָׁה׃
יז וַיִּשְׁלַח יִשְׂרָאֵל מַלְאָכִים ׀ אֶל־מֶלֶךְ אֱדוֹם לֵאמֹר אֶעְבְּרָה־נָּא בְאַרְצֶךָ
וְלֹא שָׁמַע מֶלֶךְ אֱדוֹם וְגַם אֶל־מֶלֶךְ מוֹאָב שָׁלַח וְלֹא אָבָה וַיֵּשֶׁב
יח יִשְׂרָאֵל בְּקָדֵשׁ׃ וַיֵּלֶךְ בַּמִּדְבָּר וַיָּסָב אֶת־אֶרֶץ אֱדוֹם וְאֶת־אֶרֶץ מוֹאָב
וַיָּבֹא מִמִּזְרַח־שֶׁמֶשׁ לְאֶרֶץ מוֹאָב וַיַּחֲנוּן בְּעֵבֶר אַרְנוֹן וְלֹא־בָאוּ בִּגְבוּל
יט מוֹאָב כִּי אַרְנוֹן גְּבוּל מוֹאָב׃ וַיִּשְׁלַח יִשְׂרָאֵל מַלְאָכִים אֶל־סִיחוֹן
מֶלֶךְ־הָאֱמֹרִי מֶלֶךְ חֶשְׁבּוֹן וַיֹּאמֶר לוֹ יִשְׂרָאֵל נַעְבְּרָה־נָּא בְאַרְצְךָ
כ עַד־מְקוֹמִי׃ וְלֹא־הֶאֱמִין סִיחוֹן אֶת־יִשְׂרָאֵל עֲבֹר בִּגְבֻלוֹ וַיֶּאֱסֹף סִיחוֹן
כא אֶת־כָּל־עַמּוֹ וַיַּחֲנוּ בְּיָהְצָה וַיִּלָּחֶם עִם־יִשְׂרָאֵל׃ וַיִּתֵּן יְהוָה אֱלֹהֵי־
יִשְׂרָאֵל אֶת־סִיחוֹן וְאֶת־כָּל־עַמּוֹ בְּיַד יִשְׂרָאֵל וַיַּכּוּם וַיִּירַשׁ יִשְׂרָאֵל
כב אֵת כָּל־אֶרֶץ הָאֱמֹרִי יוֹשֵׁב הָאָרֶץ הַהִיא׃ וַיִּירְשׁוּ אֵת כָּל־גְּבוּל הָאֱמֹרִי
כג מֵאַרְנוֹן וְעַד־הַיַּבֹּק וּמִן־הַמִּדְבָּר וְעַד־הַיַּרְדֵּן׃ וְעַתָּה יְהוָה ׀ אֱלֹהֵי
כד יִשְׂרָאֵל הוֹרִישׁ אֶת־הָאֱמֹרִי מִפְּנֵי עַמּוֹ יִשְׂרָאֵל וְאַתָּה תִּירָשֶׁנּוּ׃ הֲלֹא
אֵת אֲשֶׁר יוֹרִישְׁךָ כְּמוֹשׁ אֱלֹהֶיךָ אוֹתוֹ תִירָשׁ וְאֵת כָּל־אֲשֶׁר הוֹרִישׁ
כה יְהוָה אֱלֹהֵינוּ מִפָּנֵינוּ אוֹתוֹ נִירָשׁ׃ וְעַתָּה הֲטוֹב טוֹב אַתָּה מִבָּלָק בֶּן־

26 them? Israel has been dwelling in Ḥeshbon and its boroughs, Aroer and its
boroughs, and in all the towns near Arnon, for three hundred years – why
27 have you not reclaimed them all this time? I have never offended you, yet
you do me wrong by fighting against me. May the Lord, who judges, judge
28 between the Israelites and the Amonites today." But the king of the Amonites
29 did not listen to the words Yiftaḥ delivered to him. The spirit of
the Lord settled upon Yiftaḥ, and he crossed through Gilad and Menashe;
he crossed Mitzpeh Gilad; and from Mitzpeh Gilad he crossed over to the
30 Amonites. Then Yiftaḥ swore a vow to the Lord. He said, "If You deliver the
31 Amonites into my hand, then whatever comes out of the doors of my home
to meet me when I return safely from the Amonites shall be for the Lord,
and I shall offer it up as a burnt offering."
32 Yiftaḥ crossed over to the Amonites and attacked them, and the Lord
33 delivered them into his hand. He defeated them from Aroer to Minit, twenty
towns, all the way to Avel Keramim – a crushing defeat – and the Amonites
34 were conquered by the Israelites. Yiftaḥ arrived home in Mitzpa –
and there was his daughter, coming out to meet him, drumming and dancing!
35 She was his one and only – he had no son or daughter besides her. When he
saw her, he rent his clothes. "O, O, my daughter," he said, "you have brought
me down low – you have become my scourge! I have gone and opened up
36 my mouth to the Lord, and I cannot go back." "O, Father," she said to him,
"If you opened your mouth up to the Lord, do to me whatever it was that
came out of your mouth – after what the Lord has done for you, defeating
37 your enemies the Amonites. Only grant me this one thing," she said to her
father. "Let me go for two months so that I may roam the hills and weep for
38 my maidenhood, my friends and I." "Go," he said to her, and sent her off for
two months; she and her friends went and wept for her maidenhood upon
39 the hills. At the end of two months, she returned to her father. He did to her
what he had vowed to do. She never knew a man.[15] It became a custom in
40 Israel: every year, the daughters of Israel would go and lament the daughter
12 1 of Yiftaḥ the Gileadite for four days a year. The men of Efrayim
mustered and crossed over, moving northward. They said to Yiftaḥ, "Why
did you cross over to attack the Amonites without calling us to march with
2 you? We will burn down your house around you!" "My troops and I were
in fierce combat with the Amonites," Yiftaḥ said to them. "I summoned you,
3 but you did not rescue me from their hands. I saw that you were not coming
to my aid, so I took my life in my hands and crossed over to the Amonites,
and the Lord delivered them into my hands. Why have you come up to
4 fight me now?" Yiftaḥ assembled all the men of Gilad and attacked Efrayim.
The men of Gilad struck Efrayim down for saying, "You are merely fugitives

15 | Commentators are divided over whether Yiftaḥ made his daughter live a solitary life or actually sacrificed her.

כו צִפּוֹר מֶלֶךְ מוֹאָב הֲרוֹב רָב עִם־יִשְׂרָאֵל אִם־נִלְחֹם נִלְחַם בָּם: בְּשֶׁבֶת
יִשְׂרָאֵל בְּחֶשְׁבּוֹן וּבִבְנוֹתֶיהָ וּבְעַרְעוֹר וּבִבְנוֹתֶיהָ וּבְכָל־הֶעָרִים אֲשֶׁר
עַל־יְדֵי אַרְנוֹן שְׁלֹשׁ מֵאוֹת שָׁנָה וּמַדּוּעַ לֹא־הִצַּלְתֶּם בָּעֵת הַהִיא:
כז וְאָנֹכִי לֹא־חָטָאתִי לָךְ וְאַתָּה עֹשֶׂה אִתִּי רָעָה לְהִלָּחֶם בִּי יִשְׁפֹּט יהוה
כח הַשֹּׁפֵט הַיּוֹם בֵּין בְּנֵי יִשְׂרָאֵל וּבֵין בְּנֵי עַמּוֹן: וְלֹא שָׁמַע מֶלֶךְ בְּנֵי עַמּוֹן
כט אֶל־דִּבְרֵי יִפְתָּח אֲשֶׁר שָׁלַח אֵלָיו: וַתְּהִי עַל־יִפְתָּח רוּחַ
יהוה וַיַּעֲבֹר אֶת־הַגִּלְעָד וְאֶת־מְנַשֶּׁה וַיַּעֲבֹר אֶת־מִצְפֵּה גִלְעָד וּמִמִּצְפֵּה
ל גִלְעָד עָבַר בְּנֵי עַמּוֹן: וַיִּדַּר יִפְתָּח נֶדֶר לַיהוה וַיֹּאמַר אִם־נָתוֹן תִּתֵּן
לא אֶת־בְּנֵי עַמּוֹן בְּיָדִי: וְהָיָה הַיּוֹצֵא אֲשֶׁר יֵצֵא מִדַּלְתֵי בֵיתִי לִקְרָאתִי
בְּשׁוּבִי בְשָׁלוֹם מִבְּנֵי עַמּוֹן וְהָיָה לַיהוה וְהַעֲלִיתִהוּ עוֹלָה:
לב לג וַיַּעֲבֹר יִפְתָּח אֶל־בְּנֵי עַמּוֹן לְהִלָּחֶם בָּם וַיִּתְּנֵם יהוה בְּיָדוֹ: וַיַּכֵּם ט
מֵעֲרוֹעֵר וְעַד־בּוֹאֲךָ מִנִּית עֶשְׂרִים עִיר וְעַד אָבֵל כְּרָמִים מַכָּה גְּדוֹלָה
לד מְאֹד וַיִּכָּנְעוּ בְּנֵי עַמּוֹן מִפְּנֵי בְּנֵי יִשְׂרָאֵל: וַיָּבֹא יִפְתָּח
הַמִּצְפָּה אֶל־בֵּיתוֹ וְהִנֵּה בִתּוֹ יֹצֵאת לִקְרָאתוֹ בְּתֻפִּים וּבִמְחֹלוֹת וְרַק
לה הִיא יְחִידָה אֵין־לוֹ מִמֶּנּוּ בֵּן אוֹ־בַת: וַיְהִי כִרְאוֹתוֹ אוֹתָהּ וַיִּקְרַע אֶת־
בְּגָדָיו וַיֹּאמֶר אֲהָהּ בִּתִּי הַכְרֵעַ הִכְרַעְתִּנִי וְאַתְּ הָיִית בְּעֹכְרָי וְאָנֹכִי
לו פָּצִיתִי פִי אֶל־יהוה וְלֹא אוּכַל לָשׁוּב: וַתֹּאמֶר אֵלָיו אָבִי פָּצִיתָה אֶת־
פִּיךָ אֶל־יהוה עֲשֵׂה לִי כַּאֲשֶׁר יָצָא מִפִּיךָ אַחֲרֵי אֲשֶׁר עָשָׂה לְךָ יהוה
לז נְקָמוֹת מֵאֹיְבֶיךָ מִבְּנֵי עַמּוֹן: וַתֹּאמֶר אֶל־אָבִיהָ יֵעָשֶׂה לִּי הַדָּבָר הַזֶּה
הַרְפֵּה מִמֶּנִּי שְׁנַיִם חֳדָשִׁים וְאֵלְכָה וְיָרַדְתִּי עַל־הֶהָרִים וְאֶבְכֶּה עַל־
לח בְּתוּלַי אָנֹכִי ורעיתי: וַיֹּאמֶר לֵכִי וַיִּשְׁלַח אוֹתָהּ שְׁנֵי חֳדָשִׁים וַתֵּלֶךְ הִיא וְרֵעוֹתָי
לט וְרֵעוֹתֶיהָ וַתֵּבְךְּ עַל־בְּתוּלֶיהָ עַל־הֶהָרִים: וַיְהִי מִקֵּץ ׀ שְׁנַיִם חֳדָשִׁים
וַתָּשָׁב אֶל־אָבִיהָ וַיַּעַשׂ לָהּ אֶת־נִדְרוֹ אֲשֶׁר נָדָר וְהִיא לֹא־יָדְעָה אִישׁ
מ וַתְּהִי־חֹק בְּיִשְׂרָאֵל: מִיָּמִים ׀ יָמִימָה תֵּלַכְנָה בְּנוֹת יִשְׂרָאֵל לְתַנּוֹת
יב א לְבַת־יִפְתָּח הַגִּלְעָדִי אַרְבַּעַת יָמִים בַּשָּׁנָה: וַיִּצָּעֵק
אִישׁ אֶפְרַיִם וַיַּעֲבֹר צָפוֹנָה וַיֹּאמְרוּ לְיִפְתָּח מַדּוּעַ ׀ עָבַרְתָּ ׀ לְהִלָּחֵם
בִּבְנֵי־עַמּוֹן וְלָנוּ לֹא קָרָאתָ לָלֶכֶת עִמָּךְ בֵּיתְךָ נִשְׂרֹף עָלֶיךָ בָּאֵשׁ:
ב וַיֹּאמֶר יִפְתָּח אֲלֵיהֶם אִישׁ רִיב הָיִיתִי אֲנִי וְעַמִּי וּבְנֵי־עַמּוֹן מְאֹד
ג וָאֶזְעַק אֶתְכֶם וְלֹא־הוֹשַׁעְתֶּם אוֹתִי מִיָּדָם: וָאֶרְאֶה כִּי־אֵינְךָ מוֹשִׁיעַ
וָאָשִׂימָה נַפְשִׁי בְכַפִּי וָאֶעְבְּרָה אֶל־בְּנֵי עַמּוֹן וַיִּתְּנֵם יהוה בְּיָדִי וְלָמָּה
ד עֲלִיתֶם אֵלַי הַיּוֹם הַזֶּה לְהִלָּחֶם בִּי: וַיִּקְבֹּץ יִפְתָּח אֶת־כָּל־אַנְשֵׁי גִלְעָד
וַיִּלָּחֶם אֶת־אֶפְרָיִם וַיַּכּוּ אַנְשֵׁי גִלְעָד אֶת־אֶפְרַיִם כִּי אָמְרוּ פְּלִיטֵי

5 within Efrayim – Gilad is within Efrayim and within Menashe!"[16] Gilad
captured the Jordan fords that belonged to Efrayim. When a fugitive from
Efrayim would say, "Let me pass," the men of Gilad would say to him, "Are
6 you an Efraimite?" If he denied it, they would order him, "Say Shibolet," and
he would instead say "Sibolet," unable to pronounce the word properly.[17]
Then they would seize him and slay him by the Jordan fords. Forty-two
7 thousand from Efrayim fell victim during that time. Yiftaḥ judged Israel
for six years. Yiftaḥ the Gileadite then died, and he was buried in the Gilad
8 9 region. After him, Ivtzan of Beit Leḥem judged Israel. He had thirty
sons, he married off thirty daughters, and he had thirty young women brought
10 in for his sons from outside. He judged Israel for seven years. Then Ivtzan
11 died and was buried in Beit Leḥem. After him, Eilon the Zebulunite
12 judged Israel; he judged Israel for ten years. Eilon the Zebulunite died and
13 was buried in Ayalon, in the land of Zevulun. After him, Avdon son
14 of Hillel the Piratonite judged Israel. He had forty sons and thirty grandsons
15 who rode on seventy donkeys; he judged Israel for eight years. Then Avdon
son of Hillel the Piratonite died and was buried in Piraton, in the Amalekite
13 1 hills in the land of Efrayim. The Israelites resumed doing evil in the
eyes of the LORD, and the LORD handed them over to the Philistines for forty
2 years. There was a man of Tzora whose name was Manoaḥ, from the
3 family of Dan. His wife was barren and had never given birth. An angel of
the LORD appeared to the woman and said to her: "Look! Though you have
been barren and have never given birth, you shall conceive and bear a son.
4 5 Take care: drink neither wine nor strong drink, and eat nothing unclean. For
indeed, you shall be with child; you shall bear a son. Let no razor touch his
head, for the boy shall be a nazirite to God from the womb.[18] He will begin
6 to save Israel from the hands of the Philistines." The woman went and told
her husband, "A man of God came to me; he looked like an angel of God –
dazzling, awe-inspiring. I did not ask him where he was from, and he did not
7 tell me his name. He said to me, 'You shall be with child, and you shall bear
a son; drink neither wine nor strong drink and eat nothing unclean, for the
boy will be a nazirite to the Lord from the womb until his dying day.'"
8 Then Manoaḥ appealed to the LORD. "Please, my Lord," he said, "let the man
of God whom You sent come to us again and teach us what to do with the
9 boy who will be born." God heard Manoaḥ's voice, and God's angel came to
the woman once more. She was sitting in the field, her husband Manoaḥ not
10 with her. The woman rushed to tell her husband. "Look!" she said to him.
11 "The man who came to visit me that day has appeared!" Manoaḥ rose and
followed his wife. When he reached the man, he said to him, "Are you the

16 | Apparently, a taunt denying Gilad's status within these tribes.

17 | Due to the difference in pronunciation between the dialect of the Gileadites and that of the Israelites of the west bank of the Jordan.

18 | See Numbers, chapter 6.

ה אפרים אתם גלעד בתוך אפרים בתוך מנשה: וילכד גלעד את־
מעברות הירדן לאפרים והיה כי יאמרו פליטי אפרים אעברה
ו ויאמרו לו אנשי־גלעד האפרתי אתה ויאמר | לא: ויאמרו לו אמר־
נא שבלת ויאמר סבלת ולא יכין לדבר כן ויאחזו אותו וישחטוהו
אל־מעברות הירדן ויפל בעת ההיא מאפרים ארבעים ושנים אלף:
ז וישפט יפתח את־ישראל שש שנים וימת יפתח הגלעדי ויקבר
ח בערי גלעד: וישפט אחריו את־ישראל אבצן מבית
ט לחם: ויהי־לו שלשים בנים ושלשים בנות שלח החוצה ושלשים
י בנות הביא לבניו מן־החוץ וישפט את־ישראל שבע שנים: וימת
יא אבצן ויקבר בבית לחם: וישפט אחריו את־ישראל
יב אילון הזבולני וישפט את־ישראל עשר שנים: וימת אילון הזבולני
יג ויקבר באילון בארץ זבולן: וישפט אחריו את־ישראל
יד עבדון בן־הלל הפרעתוני: ויהי־לו ארבעים בנים ושלשים בני בנים
טו רכבים על־שבעים עירם וישפט את־ישראל שמנה שנים: וימת
עבדון בן־הלל הפרעתוני ויקבר בפרעתון בארץ אפרים בהר
יג א העמלקי: ויספו בני ישראל לעשות הרע בעיני
ב יהוה ויתנם יהוה ביד־פלשתים ארבעים שנה: ויהי
איש אחד מצרעה ממשפחת הדני ושמו מנוח ואשתו עקרה ולא
ג ילדה: וירא מלאך־יהוה אל־האשה ויאמר אליה הנה־נא את־עקרה
ד ולא ילדת והרית וילדת בן: ועתה השמרי נא ואל־תשתי יין ושכר
ה ואל־תאכלי כל־טמא: כי הנך הרה וילדת בן ומורה לא־יעלה
על־ראשו כי־נזיר אלהים יהיה הנער מן־הבטן והוא יחל להושיע
ו את־ישראל מיד פלשתים: ותבא האשה ותאמר לאישה לאמר
איש האלהים בא אלי ומראהו כמראה מלאך האלהים נורא מאד
ז ולא שאלתיהו אי־מזה הוא ואת־שמו לא־הגיד לי: ויאמר לי הנך
הרה וילדת בן ועתה אל־תשתי | יין ושכר ואל־תאכלי כל־טמאה
כי־נזיר אלהים יהיה הנער מן־הבטן עד־יום מותו:
ח ויעתר מנוח אל־יהוה ויאמר בי אדוני איש האלהים אשר שלחת
ט יבוא־נא עוד אלינו ויורנו מה־נעשה לנער היולד: וישמע האלהים
בקול מנוח ויבא מלאך האלהים עוד אל־האשה והיא יושבת
י בשדה ומנוח אישה אין עמה: ותמהר האשה ותרץ ותגד לאישה
יא ותאמר אליו הנה נראה אלי האיש אשר־בא ביום אלי: ויקם וילך

12 man who spoke to this woman?" "I am," he said. "Now," said Manoaḥ, "may
13 your words come to pass. How should the boy be properly dealt with?" The
LORD's angel replied to Manoaḥ, "The woman must be kept from all that I
14 said to her. She must eat nothing derived from the grapevine, drink neither
wine nor strong drink, and eat nothing unclean; she must follow all my
15 instructions." Manoaḥ said to the LORD's angel, "Please let us detain you, and
16 we will prepare a young goat for you." "Even if you detain me, I will not eat
your food," the LORD's angel said to Manoaḥ, "but if you prepare a burnt
offering, offer it to the LORD." For Manoaḥ did not realize that he was an angel
17 of the LORD. "What is your name," Manoaḥ asked the LORD's angel, "so that
18 when your words come to pass, we may honor you?" "Why should you ask
19 my name?" the LORD's angel replied to him. "For it is wondrous." Manoaḥ
took the young goat and the grain offering and offered them up on the rock
to the LORD. As Manoaḥ and his wife were watching, He performed wonders:
20 as the flames flared up from the altar to the heavens, the LORD's angel
ascended in the altar's flames while Manoaḥ and his wife were watching. They
21 threw themselves down with their faces to the ground. When the LORD's
angel did not appear again to Manoaḥ and his wife, Manoaḥ realized that he
22 had been an angel of the LORD. "We will surely die!" Manoaḥ said to his wife,
23 "for it was God we saw!" "Had the LORD wanted to kill us," his wife said to
him, "He would not have accepted burnt offerings or grain offerings from us.
And He would not have shown us all that we saw or made this announcement."
24 The woman bore a son and named him Shimshon. The boy grew up and
25 the LORD blessed him. The spirit of the LORD first stirred him in the Dan
14 1 encampment between Tzora and Eshtaol. Shimshon went down to
Timna and noticed a woman in Timna among the daughters of the Philistines.
2 He went up and told his father and mother. "I noticed a woman in Timna
3 among the Philistines," he said. "Now, acquire her as a wife for me." His father
and mother replied, "Are there no women among your kin or among all my
people that you must go and take a wife from the uncircumcised Philistines?"
"Take her for me," Shimshon said to his father, "for in my eyes, she is the right
4 one." His father and mother did not know that this was from the LORD, for
He was seeking a pretext against the Philistines. At that time, the Philistines
5 were ruling over Israel. Shimshon and his father and mother went down to
Timna, and when they reached the vineyards of Timna, a young lion suddenly
6 came roaring toward him. The spirit of the LORD seized him, and he ripped
the lion apart with his bare hands as if ripping apart a kid. But he did not tell
7 his father or mother what he had done. He went down and spoke with the
8 woman, and in Shimshon's eyes, she seemed right. Some time later, he
returned to marry her. He made a detour to see the fallen lion – and there, in
9 the lion's carcass, was a swarm of bees – with honey! He scooped the honey
up in his hands and continued on, eating as he walked. He went to his father
and mother and gave them some, and they ate, but he did not tell them that

מָנוֹחַ אַחֲרֵי אִשְׁתּוֹ וַיָּבֹא אֶל־הָאִישׁ וַיֹּאמֶר לוֹ הַאַתָּה הָאִישׁ אֲשֶׁר־
יב דִּבַּרְתָּ אֶל־הָאִשָּׁה וַיֹּאמֶר אָנִי׃ וַיֹּאמֶר מָנוֹחַ עַתָּה יָבֹא דְבָרֶיךָ מַה־
יג יִהְיֶה מִשְׁפַּט־הַנַּעַר וּמַעֲשֵׂהוּ׃ וַיֹּאמֶר מַלְאַךְ יְהוָה אֶל־מָנוֹחַ מִכֹּל
יד אֲשֶׁר־אָמַרְתִּי אֶל־הָאִשָּׁה תִּשָּׁמֵר׃ מִכֹּל אֲשֶׁר־יֵצֵא מִגֶּפֶן הַיַּיִן לֹא
תֹאכַל וְיַיִן וְשֵׁכָר אַל־תֵּשְׁתְּ וְכָל־טֻמְאָה אַל־תֹּאכַל כֹּל אֲשֶׁר־צִוִּיתִיהָ
טו תִּשְׁמֹר׃ וַיֹּאמֶר מָנוֹחַ אֶל־מַלְאַךְ יְהוָה נַעְצְרָה־נָּא אוֹתָךְ וְנַעֲשֶׂה
טז לְפָנֶיךָ גְּדִי עִזִּים׃ וַיֹּאמֶר מַלְאַךְ יְהוָה אֶל־מָנוֹחַ אִם־תַּעְצְרֵנִי לֹא־אֹכַל
בְּלַחְמֶךָ וְאִם־תַּעֲשֶׂה עֹלָה לַיהוָה תַּעֲלֶנָּה כִּי לֹא־יָדַע מָנוֹחַ כִּי־מַלְאַךְ
יז יְהוָה הוּא׃ וַיֹּאמֶר מָנוֹחַ אֶל־מַלְאַךְ יְהוָה מִי שְׁמֶךָ כִּי־יָבֹא דבריך דְבָרְךָ
יח וְכִבַּדְנוּךָ׃ וַיֹּאמֶר לוֹ מַלְאַךְ יְהוָה לָמָּה זֶּה תִּשְׁאַל לִשְׁמִי וְהוּא־פֶלִאי׃
יט וַיִּקַּח מָנוֹחַ אֶת־גְּדִי הָעִזִּים וְאֶת־הַמִּנְחָה וַיַּעַל עַל־הַצּוּר לַיהוָה
כ וּמַפְלִא לַעֲשׂוֹת וּמָנוֹחַ וְאִשְׁתּוֹ רֹאִים׃ וַיְהִי בַעֲלוֹת הַלַּהַב מֵעַל הַמִּזְבֵּחַ
הַשָּׁמַיְמָה וַיַּעַל מַלְאַךְ־יְהוָה בְּלַהַב הַמִּזְבֵּחַ וּמָנוֹחַ וְאִשְׁתּוֹ רֹאִים
כא וַיִּפְּלוּ עַל־פְּנֵיהֶם אָרְצָה׃ וְלֹא־יָסַף עוֹד מַלְאַךְ יְהוָה לְהֵרָאֹה אֶל־מָנוֹחַ
כב וְאֶל־אִשְׁתּוֹ אָז יָדַע מָנוֹחַ כִּי־מַלְאַךְ יְהוָה הוּא׃ וַיֹּאמֶר מָנוֹחַ אֶל־
כג אִשְׁתּוֹ מוֹת נָמוּת כִּי אֱלֹהִים רָאִינוּ׃ וַתֹּאמֶר לוֹ אִשְׁתּוֹ לוּ חָפֵץ יְהוָה
לַהֲמִיתֵנוּ לֹא־לָקַח מִיָּדֵנוּ עֹלָה וּמִנְחָה וְלֹא הֶרְאָנוּ אֶת־כָּל־אֵלֶּה
כד וְכָעֵת לֹא הִשְׁמִיעָנוּ כָּזֹאת׃ וַתֵּלֶד הָאִשָּׁה בֵּן וַתִּקְרָא אֶת־שְׁמוֹ שִׁמְשׁוֹן
כה וַיִּגְדַּל הַנַּעַר וַיְבָרְכֵהוּ יְהוָה׃ וַתָּחֶל רוּחַ יְהוָה לְפַעֲמוֹ בְּמַחֲנֵה־דָן בֵּין
יד א צָרְעָה וּבֵין אֶשְׁתָּאֹל׃ וַיֵּרֶד שִׁמְשׁוֹן תִּמְנָתָה וַיַּרְא
ב אִשָּׁה בְּתִמְנָתָה מִבְּנוֹת פְּלִשְׁתִּים׃ וַיַּעַל וַיַּגֵּד לְאָבִיו וּלְאִמּוֹ וַיֹּאמֶר
אִשָּׁה רָאִיתִי בְתִמְנָתָה מִבְּנוֹת פְּלִשְׁתִּים וְעַתָּה קְחוּ־אוֹתָהּ לִי לְאִשָּׁה׃
ג וַיֹּאמֶר לוֹ אָבִיו וְאִמּוֹ הַאֵין בִּבְנוֹת אַחֶיךָ וּבְכָל־עַמִּי אִשָּׁה כִּי־אַתָּה
הוֹלֵךְ לָקַחַת אִשָּׁה מִפְּלִשְׁתִּים הָעֲרֵלִים וַיֹּאמֶר שִׁמְשׁוֹן אֶל־אָבִיו
ד אוֹתָהּ קַח־לִי כִּי־הִיא יָשְׁרָה בְעֵינָי׃ וְאָבִיו וְאִמּוֹ לֹא יָדְעוּ כִּי מֵיְהוָה
הִיא כִּי־תֹאֲנָה הוּא־מְבַקֵּשׁ מִפְּלִשְׁתִּים וּבָעֵת הַהִיא פְּלִשְׁתִּים מֹשְׁלִים
ה בְּיִשְׂרָאֵל׃ וַיֵּרֶד שִׁמְשׁוֹן וְאָבִיו וְאִמּוֹ תִּמְנָתָה וַיָּבֹאוּ עַד־כַּרְמֵי תִמְנָתָה
ו וְהִנֵּה כְּפִיר אֲרָיוֹת שֹׁאֵג לִקְרָאתוֹ׃ וַתִּצְלַח עָלָיו רוּחַ יְהוָה וַיְשַׁסְּעֵהוּ
כְּשַׁסַּע הַגְּדִי וּמְאוּמָה אֵין בְּיָדוֹ וְלֹא הִגִּיד לְאָבִיו וּלְאִמּוֹ אֵת אֲשֶׁר
ז ח עָשָׂה׃ וַיֵּרֶד וַיְדַבֵּר לָאִשָּׁה וַתִּישַׁר בְּעֵינֵי שִׁמְשׁוֹן׃ וַיָּשָׁב מִיָּמִים לְקַחְתָּהּ
וַיָּסַר לִרְאוֹת אֵת מַפֶּלֶת הָאַרְיֵה וְהִנֵּה עֲדַת דְּבוֹרִים בִּגְוִיַּת הָאַרְיֵה
ט וּדְבָשׁ׃ וַיִּרְדֵּהוּ אֶל־כַּפָּיו וַיֵּלֶךְ הָלוֹךְ וְאָכֹל וַיֵּלֶךְ אֶל־אָבִיו וְאֶל־אִמּוֹ

10 he had scooped the honey out of a lion's carcass. His father went down to the
11 woman, and Shimshon made a feast there as the young men used to do. When
12 they saw him, they assigned thirty companions to be with him. "Let me riddle
you a riddle," Shimshon said to them. "If you can answer correctly during the
seven days of the feast, then I will give you thirty blankets and thirty sets of
13 clothing. But if you cannot tell me, then you must give me thirty blankets and
thirty sets of clothing." "Riddle us your riddle," they said to him. "Let us hear
14 it." And he said to them, "From the predator came meat; from the fierce came
15 something sweet." They could not solve the riddle for three days. On the
seventh day[19] they said to Shimshon's wife, "Lure your husband into telling
us the answer, or we will set you and your father's house on fire. Did you invite
16 us here to ruin us?" So Shimshon's wife whined to him: "You only hate me,"
she said. "You never loved me. You told my countrymen a riddle, but you
never told me the answer." "Look," he said to her, "I have not even told my
17 father and mother – why should I tell you?" She whined at him for the rest
of the seven days of the feast they had; on the seventh day he told her, for
18 she had nagged him so, and she told the answer to her countrymen. The
townspeople said to him on the seventh day before sundown, "Honey: What
more sweet? Lion: What terror more complete?" He said to them, "Had you
not plowed with my young cow, You would not have guessed my riddle now!"
19 Then the spirit of the LORD seized him; he marched down to Ashkelon,
struck down thirty of their men, stripped their robes, and gave the garments
20 to the riddle solvers. Furiously, he went up to his father's house. And
Shimshon's wife was given to the groomsman who had been assigned as his
15 1 companion. It was some time later, during the time of the wheat
harvest, that Shimshon visited his wife with a young goat. He said, "Let me
2 enter my wife's chamber," but her father would not let him in. "I was sure that
you hated her," her father said, "so I gave her to your companion. But her
younger sister is better than she is, is she not? Let her be yours instead now."
3 "This time," Shimshon told them, "the Philistines cannot hold me accountable
4 for the harm I am about to do them." Shimshon went and snared three
hundred foxes. Turning them tail to tail, he took torches and placed a torch
5 between each pair of tails. He set the torches alight and let them loose into
the Philistines' standing grain, setting fire to the stacked sheaves, the standing
6 grain, and even the olive groves. "Who did this?" said the Philistines, and
they were told, "Shimshon, the son-in-law of the Timnite who took his wife
away and gave her to his companion." The Philistines stormed up and burned
7 her and her father with fire. "Now that you have done that," Shimshon told
8 them, "I will not back down until I have taken revenge upon you!" With a
fierce beating, he brought them to their knees; then he made his way down
9 and stayed in a cave of the rock at Eitam. The Philistines marched

19 | Perhaps the Sabbath, which was the fourth of the seven feast days (Radak).

וַיִּתֵּן לָהֶם וַיֹּאכֵלוּ וְלֹא־הִגִּיד לָהֶם כִּי מִגְּוִיַּת הָאַרְיֵה רָדָה הַדְּבָשׁ:
י וַיֵּרֶד אָבִיהוּ אֶל־הָאִשָּׁה וַיַּעַשׂ שָׁם שִׁמְשׁוֹן מִשְׁתֶּה כִּי כֵּן יַעֲשׂוּ
יא הַבַּחוּרִים: וַיְהִי כִּרְאוֹתָם אוֹתוֹ וַיִּקְחוּ שְׁלֹשִׁים מֵרֵעִים וַיִּהְיוּ אִתּוֹ:
יב וַיֹּאמֶר לָהֶם שִׁמְשׁוֹן אָחוּדָה־נָּא לָכֶם חִידָה אִם־הַגֵּד תַּגִּידוּ אוֹתָהּ
לִי שִׁבְעַת יְמֵי הַמִּשְׁתֶּה וּמְצָאתֶם וְנָתַתִּי לָכֶם שְׁלֹשִׁים סְדִינִים וּשְׁלֹשִׁים
יג חֲלִפֹת בְּגָדִים: וְאִם־לֹא תוּכְלוּ לְהַגִּיד לִי וּנְתַתֶּם אַתֶּם לִי שְׁלֹשִׁים
סְדִינִים וּשְׁלֹשִׁים חֲלִיפוֹת בְּגָדִים וַיֹּאמְרוּ לוֹ חוּדָה חִידָתְךָ וְנִשְׁמָעֶנָּה:
יד וַיֹּאמֶר לָהֶם מֵהָאֹכֵל יָצָא מַאֲכָל וּמֵעַז יָצָא מָתוֹק וְלֹא יָכְלוּ לְהַגִּיד
טו הַחִידָה שְׁלֹשֶׁת יָמִים: וַיְהִי | בַּיּוֹם הַשְּׁבִיעִי וַיֹּאמְרוּ לְאֵשֶׁת־שִׁמְשׁוֹן
פַּתִּי אֶת־אִישֵׁךְ וְיַגֶּד־לָנוּ אֶת־הַחִידָה פֶּן־נִשְׂרֹף אוֹתָךְ וְאֶת־בֵּית אָבִיךְ
טז בָּאֵשׁ הַלְיָרְשֵׁנוּ קְרָאתֶם לָנוּ הֲלֹא: וַתֵּבְךְּ אֵשֶׁת שִׁמְשׁוֹן עָלָיו וַתֹּאמֶר
רַק־שְׂנֵאתַנִי וְלֹא אֲהַבְתָּנִי הַחִידָה חַדְתָּ לִבְנֵי עַמִּי וְלִי לֹא הִגַּדְתָּה
יז וַיֹּאמֶר לָהּ הִנֵּה לְאָבִי וּלְאִמִּי לֹא הִגַּדְתִּי וְלָךְ אַגִּיד: וַתֵּבְךְּ עָלָיו שִׁבְעַת
הַיָּמִים אֲשֶׁר־הָיָה לָהֶם הַמִּשְׁתֶּה וַיְהִי | בַּיּוֹם הַשְּׁבִיעִי וַיַּגֶּד־לָהּ כִּי
יח הֱצִיקַתְהוּ וַתַּגֵּד הַחִידָה לִבְנֵי עַמָּהּ: וַיֹּאמְרוּ לוֹ אַנְשֵׁי הָעִיר בַּיּוֹם
הַשְּׁבִיעִי בְּטֶרֶם יָבֹא הַחַרְסָה מַה־מָּתוֹק מִדְּבַשׁ וּמֶה עַז מֵאֲרִי וַיֹּאמֶר
יט לָהֶם לוּלֵא חֲרַשְׁתֶּם בְּעֶגְלָתִי לֹא מְצָאתֶם חִידָתִי: וַתִּצְלַח עָלָיו רוּחַ
יהוה וַיֵּרֶד אַשְׁקְלוֹן וַיַּךְ מֵהֶם | שְׁלֹשִׁים אִישׁ וַיִּקַּח אֶת־חֲלִיצוֹתָם וַיִּתֵּן
כ הַחֲלִיפוֹת לְמַגִּידֵי הַחִידָה וַיִּחַר אַפּוֹ וַיַּעַל בֵּית אָבִיהוּ: וַתְּהִי אֵשֶׁת
טו א שִׁמְשׁוֹן לְמֵרֵעֵהוּ אֲשֶׁר רֵעָה לוֹ: וַיְהִי מִיָּמִים בִּימֵי קְצִיר־
חִטִּים וַיִּפְקֹד שִׁמְשׁוֹן אֶת־אִשְׁתּוֹ בִּגְדִי עִזִּים וַיֹּאמֶר אָבֹאָה אֶל־אִשְׁתִּי
ב הֶחָדְרָה וְלֹא־נְתָנוֹ אָבִיהָ לָבוֹא: וַיֹּאמֶר אָבִיהָ אָמֹר אָמַרְתִּי כִּי־שָׂנֹא
שְׂנֵאתָהּ וָאֶתְּנֶנָּה לְמֵרֵעֶךָ הֲלֹא אֲחוֹתָהּ הַקְּטַנָּה טוֹבָה מִמֶּנָּה תְּהִי־
ג נָא לְךָ תַּחְתֶּיהָ: וַיֹּאמֶר לָהֶם שִׁמְשׁוֹן נִקֵּיתִי הַפַּעַם מִפְּלִשְׁתִּים כִּי־
ד עֹשֶׂה אֲנִי עִמָּם רָעָה: וַיֵּלֶךְ שִׁמְשׁוֹן וַיִּלְכֹּד שְׁלֹשׁ־מֵאוֹת שׁוּעָלִים
וַיִּקַּח לַפִּדִים וַיֶּפֶן זָנָב אֶל־זָנָב וַיָּשֶׂם לַפִּיד אֶחָד בֵּין־שְׁנֵי הַזְּנָבוֹת
ה בַּתָּוֶךְ: וַיַּבְעֶר־אֵשׁ בַּלַּפִּידִים וַיְשַׁלַּח בְּקָמוֹת פְּלִשְׁתִּים וַיַּבְעֵר מִגָּדִישׁ
ו וְעַד־קָמָה וְעַד־כֶּרֶם זָיִת: וַיֹּאמְרוּ פְלִשְׁתִּים מִי עָשָׂה זֹאת וַיֹּאמְרוּ
שִׁמְשׁוֹן חֲתַן הַתִּמְנִי כִּי לָקַח אֶת־אִשְׁתּוֹ וַיִּתְּנָהּ לְמֵרֵעֵהוּ וַיַּעֲלוּ
ז פְלִשְׁתִּים וַיִּשְׂרְפוּ אוֹתָהּ וְאֶת־אָבִיהָ בָּאֵשׁ: וַיֹּאמֶר לָהֶם שִׁמְשׁוֹן אִם־
ח תַּעֲשׂוּן כָּזֹאת כִּי אִם־נִקַּמְתִּי בָכֶם וְאַחַר אֶחְדָּל: וַיַּךְ אוֹתָם שׁוֹק עַל־
ט יָרֵךְ מַכָּה גְדוֹלָה וַיֵּרֶד וַיֵּשֶׁב בִּסְעִיף סֶלַע עֵיטָם: וַיַּעֲלוּ

10 up and encamped at Yehuda, deploying at Leḥi.[20] "Why have you marched
up against us?" said the men of Yehuda. "We have marched up to bind
11 Shimshon," they replied, "to do to him as he did to us." Three thousand men
of Yehuda went down to the cave of the rock at Eitam. "You know the
Philistines rule over us," they said to Shimshon. "What have you done to us?"
12 He said to them, "I did to them as they did to me." "We came down to bind
you," they told him, "to give you over to the Philistines." And Shimshon said
13 to them, "Swear to me that you will not harm me yourselves." "We will not,"
they said. "We will only bind you and hand you over to them; we will certainly
not kill you." They bound him with two new cords and brought him up from
14 the rock. When he reached Leḥi, the Philistines shouted out to him, and the
spirit of the LORD seized him. The cords around his arms became like flax
15 singed by fire; his bonds melted off his hands. He spotted the fresh jawbone
of a donkey and shot out his hand to seize it; with it, he then struck down a
16 thousand men. Shimshon declared: "With a donkey's jaw – a mound and still
17 more – with a donkey's jaw, I brought down a thousand men." As he finished
speaking, he tossed the jawbone from his hand. And he called that place
18 Heights of Leḥi.[21] But he grew desperately thirsty and called out to the LORD:
"You granted this great victory to Your servant's hand," he said, "but shall
19 I now die from thirst and fall into heathen hands?" So God split the crater
at Leḥi and water flowed forth. He drank and his spirit was restored; he
revived. Therefore, he called it Spring of the Caller at Leḥi,[22] and that has been
20 its name to this day. And he judged Israel during the Philistine era for twenty
16 1 years. Shimshon went to Aza. He noticed a harlot woman there and
2 slept with her. When the people of Aza were told, "Shimshon has come here,"
they surrounded the city gate and lay in wait for him all night long. And all
3 night long, they remained silent, thinking, "We will kill him at dawn." But
Shimshon slept only until midnight. He rose at midnight, grasped the doors
of the city gate and both its gateposts, and pried them loose – bolt and all. He
hoisted them onto his shoulders and carried them off to the top of the hill
4 facing Ḥevron. Afterward it happened that he fell in love with a
5 woman from Sorek Stream whose name was Delila. The Philistine chieftains
approached her. "Lure him," they said to her, "and find out why he is so strong,
and how we can overcome him and bind him in order to subdue him. Then
6 each of us will give you eleven hundred pieces of silver." So Delila said to
Shimshon, "Tell me now, how are you so strong, and what might be used to
7 bind you in order to subdue you?" "If they bind me up with seven fresh
bowstrings that have not yet dried," Shimshon replied to her, "I would become
8 as frail as any other man." So the Philistine chieftains supplied her with seven
9 fresh bowstrings that had not yet dried, and she bound him up with them. As
the ambush lay in wait in her chamber, she said to him, "The Philistines are

20 | *Leḥi* means jawbone; the name is given based on the subsequent story.
21 | Literally "heights of the jawbone."
22 | Literally "spring of the caller at jawbone."

י פְּלִשְׁתִּים וַיַּחֲנוּ בִּיהוּדָה וַיִּנָּטְשׁוּ בַּלֶּחִי: וַיֹּאמְרוּ אִישׁ יְהוּדָה לָמָה
עֲלִיתֶם עָלֵינוּ וַיֹּאמְרוּ לֶאֱסוֹר אֶת־שִׁמְשׁוֹן עָלִינוּ לַעֲשׂוֹת לוֹ כַּאֲשֶׁר
יא עָשָׂה לָנוּ: וַיֵּרְדוּ שְׁלֹשֶׁת אֲלָפִים אִישׁ מִיהוּדָה אֶל־סְעִיף סֶלַע עֵיטָם
וַיֹּאמְרוּ לְשִׁמְשׁוֹן הֲלֹא יָדַעְתָּ כִּי־מֹשְׁלִים בָּנוּ פְּלִשְׁתִּים וּמַה־זֹּאת
יב עָשִׂיתָ לָּנוּ וַיֹּאמֶר לָהֶם כַּאֲשֶׁר עָשׂוּ לִי כֵּן עָשִׂיתִי לָהֶם: וַיֹּאמְרוּ לוֹ
לֶאֱסָרְךָ יָרַדְנוּ לְתִתְּךָ בְּיַד־פְּלִשְׁתִּים וַיֹּאמֶר לָהֶם שִׁמְשׁוֹן הִשָּׁבְעוּ לִי
יג פֶּן־תִּפְגְּעוּן בִּי אַתֶּם: וַיֹּאמְרוּ לוֹ לֵאמֹר לֹא כִּי־אָסֹר נֶאֱסָרְךָ וּנְתַנּוּךָ
בְיָדָם וְהָמֵת לֹא נְמִיתֶךָ וַיַּאַסְרֻהוּ בִּשְׁנַיִם עֲבֹתִים חֲדָשִׁים וַיַּעֲלוּהוּ
יד מִן־הַסָּלַע: הוּא־בָא עַד־לֶחִי וּפְלִשְׁתִּים הֵרִיעוּ לִקְרָאתוֹ וַתִּצְלַח עָלָיו
רוּחַ יהוה וַתִּהְיֶינָה הָעֲבֹתִים אֲשֶׁר־עַל־זְרוֹעוֹתָיו כַּפִּשְׁתִּים אֲשֶׁר בָּעֲרוּ
טו בָאֵשׁ וַיִּמַּסּוּ אֱסוּרָיו מֵעַל יָדָיו: וַיִּמְצָא לְחִי־חֲמוֹר טְרִיָּה וַיִּשְׁלַח יָדוֹ
טז וַיִּקָּחֶהָ וַיַּךְ־בָּהּ אֶלֶף אִישׁ: וַיֹּאמֶר שִׁמְשׁוֹן בִּלְחִי הַחֲמוֹר חֲמוֹר
יז חֲמֹרָתָיִם בִּלְחִי הַחֲמוֹר הִכֵּיתִי אֶלֶף אִישׁ: וַיְהִי כְּכַלֹּתוֹ לְדַבֵּר וַיַּשְׁלֵךְ
יח הַלְּחִי מִיָּדוֹ וַיִּקְרָא לַמָּקוֹם הַהוּא רָמַת לֶחִי: וַיִּצְמָא מְאֹד וַיִּקְרָא
אֶל־יהוה וַיֹּאמַר אַתָּה נָתַתָּ בְיַד־עַבְדְּךָ אֶת־הַתְּשׁוּעָה הַגְּדֹלָה הַזֹּאת
יט וְעַתָּה אָמוּת בַּצָּמָא וְנָפַלְתִּי בְּיַד הָעֲרֵלִים: וַיִּבְקַע אֱלֹהִים אֶת־
הַמַּכְתֵּשׁ אֲשֶׁר־בַּלֶּחִי וַיֵּצְאוּ מִמֶּנּוּ מַיִם וַיֵּשְׁתְּ וַתָּשָׁב רוּחוֹ וַיֶּחִי עַל־כֵּן ׀
כ קָרָא שְׁמָהּ עֵין הַקּוֹרֵא אֲשֶׁר בַּלֶּחִי עַד הַיּוֹם הַזֶּה: וַיִּשְׁפֹּט אֶת־יִשְׂרָאֵל
טז א בִּימֵי פְלִשְׁתִּים עֶשְׂרִים שָׁנָה: וַיֵּלֶךְ שִׁמְשׁוֹן עַזָּתָה וַיַּרְא־
ב שָׁם אִשָּׁה זוֹנָה וַיָּבֹא אֵלֶיהָ: לָעַזָּתִים ׀ לֵאמֹר בָּא שִׁמְשׁוֹן הֵנָּה וַיָּסֹבּוּ
וַיֶּאֶרְבוּ־לוֹ כָל־הַלַּיְלָה בְּשַׁעַר הָעִיר וַיִּתְחָרְשׁוּ כָל־הַלַּיְלָה לֵאמֹר
ג עַד־אוֹר הַבֹּקֶר וַהֲרַגְנֻהוּ: וַיִּשְׁכַּב שִׁמְשׁוֹן עַד־חֲצִי הַלַּיְלָה וַיָּקָם ׀ יא
בַּחֲצִי הַלַּיְלָה וַיֶּאֱחֹז בְּדַלְתוֹת שַׁעַר־הָעִיר וּבִשְׁתֵּי הַמְּזֻזוֹת וַיִּסָּעֵם
עִם־הַבְּרִיחַ וַיָּשֶׂם עַל־כְּתֵפָיו וַיַּעֲלֵם אֶל־רֹאשׁ הָהָר אֲשֶׁר עַל־פְּנֵי
ד חֶבְרוֹן: וַיְהִי אַחֲרֵי־כֵן וַיֶּאֱהַב אִשָּׁה בְּנַחַל שֹׂרֵק וּשְׁמָהּ
ה דְּלִילָה: וַיַּעֲלוּ אֵלֶיהָ סַרְנֵי פְלִשְׁתִּים וַיֹּאמְרוּ לָהּ פַּתִּי אוֹתוֹ וּרְאִי
בַּמֶּה כֹּחוֹ גָדוֹל וּבַמֶּה נוּכַל לוֹ וַאֲסַרְנֻהוּ לְעַנֹּתוֹ וַאֲנַחְנוּ נִתַּן־לָךְ
ו אִישׁ אֶלֶף וּמֵאָה כָּסֶף: וַתֹּאמֶר דְּלִילָה אֶל־שִׁמְשׁוֹן הַגִּידָה־נָּא לִי
ז בַּמֶּה כֹּחֲךָ גָדוֹל וּבַמֶּה תֵאָסֵר לְעַנּוֹתֶךָ: וַיֹּאמֶר אֵלֶיהָ שִׁמְשׁוֹן אִם־
יַאַסְרֻנִי בְּשִׁבְעָה יְתָרִים לַחִים אֲשֶׁר לֹא־חֹרָבוּ וְחָלִיתִי וְהָיִיתִי כְּאַחַד
ח הָאָדָם: וַיַּעֲלוּ־לָהּ סַרְנֵי פְלִשְׁתִּים שִׁבְעָה יְתָרִים לַחִים אֲשֶׁר לֹא־חֹרָבוּ
ט וַתַּאַסְרֵהוּ בָּהֶם: וְהָאֹרֵב יֹשֵׁב לָהּ בַּחֶדֶר וַתֹּאמֶר אֵלָיו פְּלִשְׁתִּים עָלֶיךָ

upon you, Shimshon!" He snapped the bowstrings the way a thread of tow
10 snaps near fire; the secret of his strength was not revealed. "Oh, you have
mocked me and told me lies!" Delila said to Shimshon. "Now tell me, with
11 what can you be bound?" "If they bind me with new cords that have never
been used," he said to her, "then I would become as frail as any other man."
12 So Delila took new cords and bound him with them. She said to him, "The
Philistines are upon you, Shimshon!" – for the ambush lay in wait in the
13 chamber – and he snapped them off his arms like thread. Delila said to
Shimshon, "Until now you have mocked me and told me lies. Tell me how
you can be bound!" He replied to her, "Weave the seven locks of my hair into
14 the web." Fastening it around the shuttle, she said to him, "The Philistines are
upon you, Shimshon." He stirred from his sleep and pried loose the shuttle,
15 loom, and web. "How can you say you love me when your heart is not with
me?" she said to him. "You have mocked me three times now, but you have
16 not told me how you are so strong." She nagged him and pestered him with
17 her talk day after day until he longed to die. Then he poured out his heart to
her. "No razor has ever touched my head," he told her, "for I have been a
nazirite to God from my mother's womb. If I were to be shaved, my strength
would slip away from me, and I would become as frail as any other man."
18 Delila realized that he had poured out his heart to her, and she summoned
the Philistine chieftains, saying, "Come up, for this time he has poured out
his heart to me." The Philistine chieftains went up to her, bringing the money
19 in hand. She soothed him to sleep on her lap, called to the man, and had him
shave the seven locks of his hair. As she began to subdue him, his strength
20 slipped away from him. She said, "The Philistines are upon you, Shimshon!"
and he stirred from his sleep, thinking, "I will break free and shake myself
21 loose as before," not knowing that the LORD had turned away from him. The
Philistines seized him and gouged out his eyes. They brought him down
to Aza and bound him in bronze shackles, and he became a grinder in the
22 prison. But the hair on his head began to grow back as soon as it had been
23 shaved. The Philistine chieftains gathered to offer great sacrifices to
their god Dagon and to celebrate. They declared, "Our god has delivered
24 Shimshon, our enemy, into our hands." The people saw him and praised their
gods, declaring, "Our gods delivered into our hands our foe, destroyer of our
25 lands, who left so many dead." As their hearts grew merry, they said, "Call for
Shimshon and let him amuse us!" They summoned Shimshon from prison,
and he performed before them. They positioned him between the pillars.
26 "Leave me," Shimshon said to the boy who held his hand, "but help me
27 feel out the pillars the temple rests upon, so I can lean on them." The temple
was full of men and women, and all the Philistine chieftains were there,
and from the roof about three thousand men and women were watching

שִׁמְשׁוֹן וַיְנַתֵּק אֶת־הַיְתָרִים כַּאֲשֶׁר יִנָּתֵק פְּתִיל־הַנְּעֹרֶת בַּהֲרִיחוֹ אֵשׁ
י וְלֹא נוֹדַע כֹּחוֹ: וַתֹּאמֶר דְּלִילָה אֶל־שִׁמְשׁוֹן הִנֵּה הֵתַלְתָּ בִּי וַתְּדַבֵּר
יא אֵלַי כְּזָבִים עַתָּה הַגִּידָה־נָּא לִי בַּמֶּה תֵּאָסֵר: וַיֹּאמֶר אֵלֶיהָ אִם־אָסוֹר
יַאַסְרוּנִי בַּעֲבֹתִים חֲדָשִׁים אֲשֶׁר לֹא־נַעֲשָׂה בָהֶם מְלָאכָה וְחָלִיתִי
יב וְהָיִיתִי כְּאַחַד הָאָדָם: וַתִּקַּח דְּלִילָה עֲבֹתִים חֲדָשִׁים וַתַּאַסְרֵהוּ בָהֶם
וַתֹּאמֶר אֵלָיו פְּלִשְׁתִּים עָלֶיךָ שִׁמְשׁוֹן וְהָאֹרֵב יֹשֵׁב בֶּחָדֶר וַיְנַתְּקֵם
יג מֵעַל זְרֹעֹתָיו כַּחוּט: וַתֹּאמֶר דְּלִילָה אֶל־שִׁמְשׁוֹן עַד־הֵנָּה הֵתַלְתָּ בִּי
וַתְּדַבֵּר אֵלַי כְּזָבִים הַגִּידָה לִּי בַּמֶּה תֵּאָסֵר וַיֹּאמֶר אֵלֶיהָ אִם־תַּאַרְגִי
יד אֶת־שֶׁבַע מַחְלְפוֹת רֹאשִׁי עִם־הַמַּסָּכֶת: וַתִּתְקַע בַּיָּתֵד וַתֹּאמֶר אֵלָיו
פְּלִשְׁתִּים עָלֶיךָ שִׁמְשׁוֹן וַיִּיקַץ מִשְּׁנָתוֹ וַיִּסַּע אֶת־הַיְתַד הָאֶרֶג וְאֶת־
טו הַמַּסָּכֶת: וַתֹּאמֶר אֵלָיו אֵיךְ תֹּאמַר אֲהַבְתִּיךְ וְלִבְּךָ אֵין אִתִּי זֶה שָׁלֹשׁ
טז פְּעָמִים הֵתַלְתָּ בִּי וְלֹא־הִגַּדְתָּ לִּי בַּמֶּה כֹּחֲךָ גָדוֹל: וַיְהִי כִּי־הֵצִיקָה
יז לּוֹ בִדְבָרֶיהָ כָּל־הַיָּמִים וַתְּאַלְצֵהוּ וַתִּקְצַר נַפְשׁוֹ לָמוּת: וַיַּגֶּד־לָהּ
אֶת־כָּל־לִבּוֹ וַיֹּאמֶר לָהּ מוֹרָה לֹא־עָלָה עַל־רֹאשִׁי כִּי־נְזִיר אֱלֹהִים
אֲנִי מִבֶּטֶן אִמִּי אִם־גֻּלַּחְתִּי וְסָר מִמֶּנִּי כֹחִי וְחָלִיתִי וְהָיִיתִי כְּכָל־
יח הָאָדָם: וַתֵּרֶא דְלִילָה כִּי־הִגִּיד לָהּ אֶת־כָּל־לִבּוֹ וַתִּשְׁלַח וַתִּקְרָא
לְסַרְנֵי פְלִשְׁתִּים לֵאמֹר עֲלוּ הַפַּעַם כִּי־הִגִּיד לה אֶת־כָּל־לִבּוֹ וְעָלוּ לִי
יט אֵלֶיהָ סַרְנֵי פְלִשְׁתִּים וַיַּעֲלוּ הַכֶּסֶף בְּיָדָם: וַתְּיַשְּׁנֵהוּ עַל־בִּרְכֶּיהָ וַתִּקְרָא
לָאִישׁ וַתְּגַלַּח אֶת־שֶׁבַע מַחְלְפוֹת רֹאשׁוֹ וַתָּחֶל לְעַנּוֹתוֹ וַיָּסַר כֹּחוֹ
כ מֵעָלָיו: וַתֹּאמֶר פְּלִשְׁתִּים עָלֶיךָ שִׁמְשׁוֹן וַיִּקַץ מִשְּׁנָתוֹ וַיֹּאמֶר אֵצֵא
כא כְּפַעַם בְּפַעַם וְאִנָּעֵר וְהוּא לֹא יָדַע כִּי יְהוָה סָר מֵעָלָיו: וַיֹּאחֲזוּהוּ
פְלִשְׁתִּים וַיְנַקְּרוּ אֶת־עֵינָיו וַיּוֹרִידוּ אוֹתוֹ עַזָּתָה וַיַּאַסְרוּהוּ בַּנְחֻשְׁתַּיִם
כב וַיְהִי טוֹחֵן בְּבֵית האסירים: וַיָּחֶל שְׂעַר־רֹאשׁוֹ לְצַמֵּחַ כַּאֲשֶׁר הָאֲסוּרִים
כג גֻּלָּח: וְסַרְנֵי פְלִשְׁתִּים נֶאֶסְפוּ לִזְבֹּחַ זֶבַח־גָּדוֹל לְדָגוֹן אֱלֹהֵיהֶם
כד וּלְשִׂמְחָה וַיֹּאמְרוּ נָתַן אֱלֹהֵינוּ בְּיָדֵנוּ אֵת שִׁמְשׁוֹן אוֹיְבֵנוּ: וַיִּרְאוּ
אֹתוֹ הָעָם וַיְהַלְלוּ אֶת־אֱלֹהֵיהֶם כִּי אָמְרוּ נָתַן אֱלֹהֵינוּ בְיָדֵנוּ אֶת־
כה אוֹיְבֵנוּ וְאֵת מַחֲרִיב אַרְצֵנוּ וַאֲשֶׁר הִרְבָּה אֶת־חֲלָלֵינוּ: וַיְהִי כי טוב כְּטוֹב
לִבָּם וַיֹּאמְרוּ קִרְאוּ לְשִׁמְשׁוֹן וִישַׂחֶק־לָנוּ וַיִּקְרְאוּ לְשִׁמְשׁוֹן מִבֵּית
כו האסירים וַיְצַחֵק לִפְנֵיהֶם וַיַּעֲמִידוּ אוֹתוֹ בֵּין הָעַמּוּדִים: וַיֹּאמֶר שִׁמְשׁוֹן הָאֲסוּרִים
אֶל־הַנַּעַר הַמַּחֲזִיק בְּיָדוֹ הַנִּיחָה אוֹתִי והימשני אֶת־הָעַמֻּדִים אֲשֶׁר וַהֲמִשֵׁנִי
כז הַבַּיִת נָכוֹן עֲלֵיהֶם וְאֶשָּׁעֵן עֲלֵיהֶם: וְהַבַּיִת מָלֵא הָאֲנָשִׁים וְהַנָּשִׁים
וְשָׁמָּה כֹּל סַרְנֵי פְלִשְׁתִּים וְעַל־הַגָּג כִּשְׁלֹשֶׁת אֲלָפִים אִישׁ וְאִשָּׁה

28 Shimshon perform. Shimshon called out to the Lord: "O Lord God," he
said, "remember me – please – and strengthen me – please! Just this once,
God, let me take revenge against the Philistines – just one act of vengeance
29 for both of my eyes!" Shimshon gripped the two central pillars that the
temple rested upon and leaned against them, one with his right arm and
30 one with his left. And Shimshon cried, "Let me die with the Philistines!"
He thrust with all his might, and the temple collapsed on the chieftains and
all the people inside. The dead he killed as he died outnumbered those
31 he had killed throughout his life. His brothers and all his father's house
went down and carried him back up. They buried him between Tzora and
Eshtaol in the tomb of his father Manoaḥ. He had judged Israel for twenty
17 1 years. There was a man from the Efrayim hills by the name of
2 Mikhayehu. He said to his mother, "About the eleven hundred pieces of silver
that were taken from you, about which you uttered a curse[23] and echoed it in
my hearing – look, I have the silver. I took it." His mother replied, "Blessed is
3 my son to the Lord!" As he returned the eleven hundred pieces of silver to
his mother, his mother said, "I hereby devote the silver to the Lord from my
own hand for the sake of my son, to make a statue and a cast image; let me
4 return it to you." But he returned the silver to his mother, and his mother took
two hundred pieces of silver and gave them to the silversmith, who made
them into a statue and a cast image. They remained in Mikhayehu's house.
5 That man, Mikha, owned a temple. He had made an ephod[24] and household
6 idols and had appointed one of his sons to become a priest for him. In those
days, there was no king in Israel; each one did what was right in his own
7 eyes. There was a young man from Beit Leḥem of Yehuda, which
8 belonged to a clan of Yehuda; he was a Levite who was staying there. The man
had traveled from the city, from Beit Leḥem of Yehuda, to settle wherever he
could; as he made his way through the Efrayim hills, he reached the house of
9 Mikha. "Where are you from?" Mikha said to him. "I am a Levite from Beit
Leḥem of Yehuda," he said to him, "and I am traveling to settle wherever I can."
10 "Stay with me," Mikha said to him. "Be my father and priest, and I will give
you ten pieces of silver a year, a clothing allowance, and board." The Levite
11 went along with this; he agreed to stay with him, and the young man became
12 like one of his own sons to him. Mikha ordained the Levite, and the young
13 man became his priest and stayed in the house of Mikha. Mikha thought,
"Now I know that the Lord will be good to me, for the Levite has become a
18 1 priest for me." In those days, there was no king in Israel; in those days, the
Danite tribe sought out territory to live in, for before that day, no estate had
2 fallen to them among the tribes of Israel. Out of their clan, the
Danites sent five of their number, valiant warriors from Tzora and Eshtaol, to
scout out the land and explore it. "Go," they said to them, "explore the land."
They traveled as far as the house of Mikha in the Efrayim hills, and there they
3 spent the night. While they were passing the house of Mikha, they recognized

23 | Either on the thief, or on anyone who withheld its whereabouts from you (cf. Lev. 5:1).
24 | See note on 8:27.

כח הָרֹאִים בִּשְׂחוֹק שִׁמְשׁוֹן׃ וַיִּקְרָא שִׁמְשׁוֹן אֶל־יְהוָה וַיֹּאמַר אֲדֹנָי יְהוִה
זָכְרֵנִי נָא וְחַזְּקֵנִי נָא אַךְ הַפַּעַם הַזֶּה הָאֱלֹהִים וְאִנָּקְמָה נְקַם־אַחַת
כט מִשְּׁתֵי עֵינַי מִפְּלִשְׁתִּים׃ וַיִּלְפֹּת שִׁמְשׁוֹן אֶת־שְׁנֵי ׀ עַמּוּדֵי הַתָּוֶךְ אֲשֶׁר
הַבַּיִת נָכוֹן עֲלֵיהֶם וַיִּסָּמֵךְ עֲלֵיהֶם אֶחָד בִּימִינוֹ וְאֶחָד בִּשְׂמֹאלוֹ׃
ל וַיֹּאמֶר שִׁמְשׁוֹן תָּמוֹת נַפְשִׁי עִם־פְּלִשְׁתִּים וַיֵּט בְּכֹחַ וַיִּפֹּל הַבַּיִת עַל־
הַסְּרָנִים וְעַל־כָּל־הָעָם אֲשֶׁר־בּוֹ וַיִּהְיוּ הַמֵּתִים אֲשֶׁר הֵמִית בְּמוֹתוֹ
לא רַבִּים מֵאֲשֶׁר הֵמִית בְּחַיָּיו׃ וַיֵּרְדוּ אֶחָיו וְכָל־בֵּית אָבִיהוּ וַיִּשְׂאוּ אֹתוֹ
וַיַּעֲלוּ ׀ וַיִּקְבְּרוּ אוֹתוֹ בֵּין צָרְעָה וּבֵין אֶשְׁתָּאֹל בְּקֶבֶר מָנוֹחַ אָבִיו
יז א וְהוּא שָׁפַט אֶת־יִשְׂרָאֵל עֶשְׂרִים שָׁנָה׃ וַיְהִי־אִישׁ
ב מֵהַר־אֶפְרָיִם וּשְׁמוֹ מִיכָיְהוּ׃ וַיֹּאמֶר לְאִמּוֹ אֶלֶף וּמֵאָה הַכֶּסֶף אֲשֶׁר
לֻקַּח־לָךְ וְאַתִּי אָלִית וְגַם אָמַרְתְּ בְּאָזְנַי הִנֵּה־הַכֶּסֶף אִתִּי אֲנִי לְקַחְתִּיו וְאַתְּ
ג וַתֹּאמֶר אִמּוֹ בָּרוּךְ בְּנִי לַיהוָה׃ וַיָּשֶׁב אֶת־אֶלֶף־וּמֵאָה הַכֶּסֶף לְאִמּוֹ
וַתֹּאמֶר אִמּוֹ הַקְדֵּשׁ הִקְדַּשְׁתִּי אֶת־הַכֶּסֶף לַיהוָה מִיָּדִי לִבְנִי לַעֲשׂוֹת
ד פֶּסֶל וּמַסֵּכָה וְעַתָּה אֲשִׁיבֶנּוּ לָךְ׃ וַיָּשֶׁב אֶת־הַכֶּסֶף לְאִמּוֹ וַתִּקַּח אִמּוֹ
מָאתַיִם כֶּסֶף וַתִּתְּנֵהוּ לַצּוֹרֵף וַיַּעֲשֵׂהוּ פֶּסֶל וּמַסֵּכָה וַיְהִי בְּבֵית מִיכָיְהוּ׃
ה וְהָאִישׁ מִיכָה לוֹ בֵּית אֱלֹהִים וַיַּעַשׂ אֵפוֹד וּתְרָפִים וַיְמַלֵּא אֶת־יַד
ו אַחַד מִבָּנָיו וַיְהִי־לוֹ לְכֹהֵן׃ בַּיָּמִים הָהֵם אֵין מֶלֶךְ בְּיִשְׂרָאֵל אִישׁ הַיָּשָׁר
ז בְּעֵינָיו יַעֲשֶׂה׃ וַיְהִי־נַעַר מִבֵּית לֶחֶם יְהוּדָה
ח מִמִּשְׁפַּחַת יְהוּדָה וְהוּא לֵוִי וְהוּא גָר־שָׁם׃ וַיֵּלֶךְ הָאִישׁ מֵהָעִיר מִבֵּית
לֶחֶם יְהוּדָה לָגוּר בַּאֲשֶׁר יִמְצָא וַיָּבֹא הַר־אֶפְרַיִם עַד־בֵּית מִיכָה
ט לַעֲשׂוֹת דַּרְכּוֹ׃ וַיֹּאמֶר־לוֹ מִיכָה מֵאַיִן תָּבוֹא וַיֹּאמֶר אֵלָיו לֵוִי אָנֹכִי
י מִבֵּית לֶחֶם יְהוּדָה וְאָנֹכִי הֹלֵךְ לָגוּר בַּאֲשֶׁר אֶמְצָא׃ וַיֹּאמֶר לוֹ מִיכָה
שְׁבָה עִמָּדִי וֶהְיֵה־לִי לְאָב וּלְכֹהֵן וְאָנֹכִי אֶתֶּן־לְךָ עֲשֶׂרֶת כֶּסֶף לַיָּמִים
יא וְעֵרֶךְ בְּגָדִים וּמִחְיָתֶךָ וַיֵּלֶךְ הַלֵּוִי׃ וַיּוֹאֶל הַלֵּוִי לָשֶׁבֶת אֶת־הָאִישׁ וַיְהִי
יב הַנַּעַר לוֹ כְּאַחַד מִבָּנָיו׃ וַיְמַלֵּא מִיכָה אֶת־יַד הַלֵּוִי וַיְהִי־לוֹ הַנַּעַר
יג לְכֹהֵן וַיְהִי בְּבֵית מִיכָה׃ וַיֹּאמֶר מִיכָה עַתָּה יָדַעְתִּי כִּי־יֵיטִיב יְהוָה לִי
יח א כִּי הָיָה־לִי הַלֵּוִי לְכֹהֵן׃ בַּיָּמִים הָהֵם אֵין מֶלֶךְ בְּיִשְׂרָאֵל וּבַיָּמִים הָהֵם
שֵׁבֶט הַדָּנִי מְבַקֶּשׁ־לוֹ נַחֲלָה לָשֶׁבֶת כִּי לֹא־נָפְלָה לּוֹ עַד־הַיּוֹם הַהוּא
ב בְּתוֹךְ־שִׁבְטֵי יִשְׂרָאֵל בְּנַחֲלָה׃ וַיִּשְׁלְחוּ בְנֵי־דָן ׀
מִמִּשְׁפַּחְתָּם חֲמִשָּׁה אֲנָשִׁים מִקְצוֹתָם אֲנָשִׁים בְּנֵי־חַיִל מִצָּרְעָה
וּמֵאֶשְׁתָּאֹל לְרַגֵּל אֶת־הָאָרֶץ וּלְחָקְרָהּ וַיֹּאמְרוּ אֲלֵהֶם לְכוּ חִקְרוּ
ג אֶת־הָאָרֶץ וַיָּבֹאוּ הַר־אֶפְרַיִם עַד־בֵּית מִיכָה וַיָּלִינוּ שָׁם׃ הֵמָּה עִם־

the voice of the Levite boy, so they made a detour and said to him, "Who
brought you here? What have you been doing here, and what is your business
4 here?" "This is what Mikha has done for me," he told them, "and he hired me,
5 and I have become his priest." They said to him, "Please inquire of God –
6 we want to know whether the path we are taking will be successful." "Go in
peace," the priest said to them. "The Lord is watching the path that you are
7 following." The five men moved on and arrived in Layish. They saw
the people there dwelling in security as the Sidonians do, tranquil and
unsuspecting, with no one troubling them in the area and no heir to the
throne. They were far removed from the Sidonians and had nothing to do
8 with anyone. They came back to their kinsmen at Tzora and Eshtaol. "How
9 did you fare?" their kinsmen said to them. "Rise up, and let us attack them,"
they said. "We saw the land, and look – it is very good, yet you do nothing!
10 Do not delay; go and attack and seize possession of the land. When you arrive,
you will meet an unsuspecting people. The land is spacious, for God has given
11 it into your hands – a place where nothing on earth is lacking." They set out
from there, from the Danite clan of Tzora and Eshtaol, six hundred men
12 armed with battle gear. They marched up and encamped at Kiryat Ye'arim in
Yehuda; hence that place, west of Kiryat Ye'arim, has been called Camp Dan
13 to this day. From there, they passed onward to the Efrayim hills and reached
14 the house of Mikha. The five men who had gone to scout the land of Layish
observed to their kinsmen, "Did you know that there are an ephod, household
idols, a statue, and a cast image in these buildings? Now, you know what to
15 do!" They turned off there, and when they reached the quarters of the Levite
16 boy in the house of Mikha, they greeted him. The Danites – six hundred men,
17 armed with their battle gear – stood at the entrance gate, while the five men
who went up to scout the land went inside to seize the statue, the ephod, the
household idols, and the cast image. The priest stood at the entrance gate by
18 the six hundred men armed with battle gear. As they entered Mikha's temple
and seized the statue, the ephod, the household idols, and the cast image, the
19 priest asked them, "What are you doing?" "Be quiet!" they said to him. "Put
your hand over your mouth, come with us, and be our father and priest.
Would you rather be the priest of one man's household or the priest of a whole
20 tribal clan in Israel?" The priest was very pleased; he took the ephod,
21 household idols, and statue and joined the people. They turned and left,
22 placing the little ones, the cattle, and the goods in front of them. They had
already distanced themselves from the house of Mikha when the people in
the homes near Mikha's house mustered and caught up with the Danites.
23 They called out to the Danites, who turned their heads and said to Mikha,

בֵּית מִיכָה וְהֵמָּה הִכִּירוּ אֶת־קוֹל הַנַּעַר הַלֵּוִי וַיָּסוּרוּ שָׁם וַיֹּאמְרוּ לוֹ
ד מִי־הֱבִיאֲךָ הֲלֹם וּמָה־אַתָּה עֹשֶׂה בָּזֶה וּמַה־לְּךָ פֹה: וַיֹּאמֶר אֲלֵהֶם
ה כָּזֶה וְכָזֶה עָשָׂה לִי מִיכָה וַיִּשְׂכְּרֵנִי וָאֱהִי־לוֹ לְכֹהֵן: וַיֹּאמְרוּ לוֹ שְׁאַל־
נָא בֵאלֹהִים וְנֵדְעָה הֲתַצְלִחַ דַּרְכֵּנוּ אֲשֶׁר אֲנַחְנוּ הֹלְכִים עָלֶיהָ:
ו וַיֹּאמֶר לָהֶם הַכֹּהֵן לְכוּ לְשָׁלוֹם נֹכַח יהוה דַּרְכְּכֶם אֲשֶׁר תֵּלְכוּ־ יב
ז בָהּ: וַיֵּלְכוּ חֲמֵשֶׁת הָאֲנָשִׁים וַיָּבֹאוּ לָיְשָׁה וַיִּרְאוּ אֶת־
הָעָם אֲשֶׁר־בְּקִרְבָּהּ יוֹשֶׁבֶת לָבֶטַח כְּמִשְׁפַּט צִדֹנִים שֹׁקֵט ׀ וּבֹטֵחַ
וְאֵין־מַכְלִים דָּבָר בָּאָרֶץ יוֹרֵשׁ עֶצֶר וּרְחֹקִים הֵמָּה מִצִּדֹנִים וְדָבָר
ח אֵין־לָהֶם עִם־אָדָם: וַיָּבֹאוּ אֶל־אֲחֵיהֶם צָרְעָה וְאֶשְׁתָּאֹל וַיֹּאמְרוּ לָהֶם
ט אֲחֵיהֶם מָה אַתֶּם: וַיֹּאמְרוּ קוּמָה וְנַעֲלֶה עֲלֵיהֶם כִּי רָאִינוּ אֶת־הָאָרֶץ
וְהִנֵּה טוֹבָה מְאֹד וְאַתֶּם מַחְשִׁים אַל־תֵּעָצְלוּ לָלֶכֶת לָבֹא לָרֶשֶׁת
י אֶת־הָאָרֶץ: כְּבֹאֲכֶם תָּבֹאוּ ׀ אֶל־עַם בֹּטֵחַ וְהָאָרֶץ רַחֲבַת יָדַיִם כִּי־
נְתָנָהּ אֱלֹהִים בְּיֶדְכֶם מְקוֹם אֲשֶׁר אֵין־שָׁם מַחְסוֹר כָּל־דָּבָר אֲשֶׁר
יא בָּאָרֶץ: וַיִּסְעוּ מִשָּׁם מִמִּשְׁפַּחַת הַדָּנִי מִצָּרְעָה וּמֵאֶשְׁתָּאֹל שֵׁשׁ־מֵאוֹת
יב אִישׁ חָגוּר כְּלֵי מִלְחָמָה: וַיַּעֲלוּ וַיַּחֲנוּ בְּקִרְיַת יְעָרִים בִּיהוּדָה עַל־כֵּן
קָרְאוּ לַמָּקוֹם הַהוּא מַחֲנֵה־דָן עַד הַיּוֹם הַזֶּה הִנֵּה אַחֲרֵי קִרְיַת יְעָרִים:
יג יד וַיַּעַבְרוּ מִשָּׁם הַר־אֶפְרָיִם וַיָּבֹאוּ עַד־בֵּית מִיכָה: וַיַּעֲנוּ חֲמֵשֶׁת הָאֲנָשִׁים
הַהֹלְכִים לְרַגֵּל אֶת־הָאָרֶץ לַיִשׁ וַיֹּאמְרוּ אֶל־אֲחֵיהֶם הַיְדַעְתֶּם כִּי
יֵשׁ בַּבָּתִּים הָאֵלֶּה אֵפוֹד וּתְרָפִים וּפֶסֶל וּמַסֵּכָה וְעַתָּה דְּעוּ מַה־
טו תַּעֲשׂוּ: וַיָּסוּרוּ שָׁמָּה וַיָּבֹאוּ אֶל־בֵּית־הַנַּעַר הַלֵּוִי בֵּית מִיכָה וַיִּשְׁאֲלוּ־
טז לוֹ לְשָׁלוֹם: וְשֵׁשׁ־מֵאוֹת אִישׁ חֲגוּרִים כְּלֵי מִלְחַמְתָּם נִצָּבִים פֶּתַח
יז הַשָּׁעַר אֲשֶׁר מִבְּנֵי־דָן: וַיַּעֲלוּ חֲמֵשֶׁת הָאֲנָשִׁים הַהֹלְכִים לְרַגֵּל אֶת־
הָאָרֶץ בָּאוּ שָׁמָּה לָקְחוּ אֶת־הַפֶּסֶל וְאֶת־הָאֵפוֹד וְאֶת־הַתְּרָפִים
וְאֶת־הַמַּסֵּכָה וְהַכֹּהֵן נִצָּב פֶּתַח הַשַּׁעַר וְשֵׁשׁ־מֵאוֹת הָאִישׁ הֶחָגוּר
יח כְּלֵי הַמִּלְחָמָה: וְאֵלֶּה בָּאוּ בֵּית מִיכָה וַיִּקְחוּ אֶת־פֶּסֶל הָאֵפוֹד וְאֶת־
יט הַתְּרָפִים וְאֶת־הַמַּסֵּכָה וַיֹּאמֶר אֲלֵיהֶם הַכֹּהֵן מָה אַתֶּם עֹשִׂים: וַיֹּאמְרוּ
לוֹ הַחֲרֵשׁ שִׂים־יָדְךָ עַל־פִּיךָ וְלֵךְ עִמָּנוּ וֶהְיֵה־לָנוּ לְאָב וּלְכֹהֵן הֲטוֹב ׀
הֱיוֹתְךָ כֹהֵן לְבֵית אִישׁ אֶחָד אוֹ הֱיוֹתְךָ כֹהֵן לְשֵׁבֶט וּלְמִשְׁפָּחָה בְּיִשְׂרָאֵל:
כ וַיִּיטַב לֵב הַכֹּהֵן וַיִּקַּח אֶת־הָאֵפוֹד וְאֶת־הַתְּרָפִים וְאֶת־הַפָּסֶל וַיָּבֹא
כא בְּקֶרֶב הָעָם: וַיִּפְנוּ וַיֵּלֵכוּ וַיָּשִׂימוּ אֶת־הַטַּף וְאֶת־הַמִּקְנֶה וְאֶת־הַכְּבוּדָּה
כב לִפְנֵיהֶם: הֵמָּה הִרְחִיקוּ מִבֵּית מִיכָה וְהָאֲנָשִׁים אֲשֶׁר בַּבָּתִּים אֲשֶׁר
כג עִם־בֵּית מִיכָה נִזְעֲקוּ וַיַּדְבִּיקוּ אֶת־בְּנֵי־דָן: וַיִּקְרְאוּ אֶל־בְּנֵי־דָן וַיַּסֵּבּוּ

24 "What happened to you that caused you to muster?" "My gods," he said, "the
ones I made – you took them, along with the priest, and left! What else do I
25 have? How can you ask me, 'What happened to you?'" "Do not raise your
voice at us," the Danites said to him, "or bitter-souled men might attack you,
26 and you will squander your own lives and the lives of your household." The
Danites continued on their way. When Mikha realized that they were stronger
27 than he, he turned and went back to his house. Having seized what Mikha
had made along with the priest that had been his, they reached Layish, a
tranquil and unsuspecting people. They put them to the sword and set the
28 city on fire. No one came to the rescue, for they were far away from Sidon
and had nothing to do with anyone, situated as they were in the valley by Beit
29 Reḥov. The Danites built up the city and settled in it. They named the city
Dan after their ancestor Dan who was born to the man Yisrael – whereas
30 Layish was the city's former name. The Danites set up the statue as their own,
and Yehonatan son of Gershom son of Menashe,[25] along with his sons, served
31 as priests of the Danite tribe until the day of their exile from the land. They
maintained the statue that Mikha had made as their own throughout the time
19 1 that God's House remained at Shilo. Back then, when there was no
king in Israel, a Levite man who lived on the outskirts of the Efrayim hills
2 took for himself a concubine from Beit Leḥem of Yehuda. His concubine
betrayed him and left him for her father's house in Beit Leḥem of Yehuda. She
3 stayed there for a while – for four months. Then her husband got up and
followed her to implore her to return; his servant boy was with him, along
with a pair of donkeys. She brought him into her father's house, and the girl's
4 father was glad to see him. His father-in-law, the girl's father, pressured him
into staying with him for three days, and they feasted, drank, and slept there.
5 On the fourth day, they rose early in the morning and got up to leave, but the
6 girl's father said to his son-in-law, "Eat your fill of bread before you go." So the
two of them sat down to eat together, and then they drank. "Please," the girl's
7 father said to the man, "stay for the night! Enjoy yourself!" The man got up
to leave, but when his father-in-law urged him, he turned back and spent the
8 night there. On the fifth day, he rose early in the morning to leave, but the
girl's father said to him, "Please, just eat your fill." But they lingered past noon,
9 with the two of them eating. The man then got up to leave – he and his
concubine and his servant boy. "Look now, the day is dwindling to evening,"
his father-in-law, the girl's father, said to him. "Stay over today; stay here and
10 enjoy yourself. Then be on your way early tomorrow and go home." But the
man would not agree to stay; he got up and left and reached the vicinity of
Yebus – that is, Jerusalem – with his pair of loaded donkeys and his concubine.
11 They were near Yebus, and the day was fading fast. The servant boy said to
his master, "Come now – let us turn off to this Jebusite city and spend the
12 night there." But his master said, "We will not turn off to a foreign city where

25 | The *nun* of Menashe is written suspended in the Masoretic Text. Without this *nun*, the word "Menashe" could be read as "Moshe."

כד פְּנֵיהֶם וַיֹּאמְרוּ לְמִיכָה מַה־לְּךָ כִּי נִזְעָקְתָּ: וַיֹּאמֶר אֶת־אֱלֹהַי אֲשֶׁר־
עָשִׂיתִי לְקַחְתֶּם וְאֶת־הַכֹּהֵן וַתֵּלְכוּ וּמַה־לִּי עוֹד וּמַה־זֶּה תֹּאמְרוּ אֵלַי
כה מַה־לָּךְ: וַיֹּאמְרוּ אֵלָיו בְּנֵי־דָן אַל־תַּשְׁמַע קוֹלְךָ עִמָּנוּ פֶּן־יִפְגְּעוּ בָכֶם
כו אֲנָשִׁים מָרֵי נֶפֶשׁ וְאָסַפְתָּה נַפְשְׁךָ וְנֶפֶשׁ בֵּיתֶךָ: וַיֵּלְכוּ בְנֵי־דָן לְדַרְכָּם
כז וַיַּרְא מִיכָה כִּי־חֲזָקִים הֵמָּה מִמֶּנּוּ וַיִּפֶן וַיָּשָׁב אֶל־בֵּיתוֹ: וְהֵמָּה לָקְחוּ
אֵת אֲשֶׁר־עָשָׂה מִיכָה וְאֶת־הַכֹּהֵן אֲשֶׁר הָיָה־לוֹ וַיָּבֹאוּ עַל־לַיִשׁ עַל־
כח עַם שֹׁקֵט וּבֹטֵחַ וַיַּכּוּ אוֹתָם לְפִי־חָרֶב וְאֶת־הָעִיר שָׂרְפוּ בָאֵשׁ: וְאֵין
מַצִּיל כִּי רְחוֹקָה־הִיא מִצִּידוֹן וְדָבָר אֵין־לָהֶם עִם־אָדָם וְהִיא בָּעֵמֶק
כט אֲשֶׁר לְבֵית־רְחוֹב וַיִּבְנוּ אֶת־הָעִיר וַיֵּשְׁבוּ בָהּ: וַיִּקְרְאוּ שֵׁם־הָעִיר
דָּן בְּשֵׁם דָּן אֲבִיהֶם אֲשֶׁר יוּלַּד לְיִשְׂרָאֵל וְאוּלָם לַיִשׁ שֵׁם־הָעִיר
ל לָרִאשֹׁנָה: וַיָּקִימוּ לָהֶם בְּנֵי־דָן אֶת־הַפָּסֶל וִיהוֹנָתָן בֶּן־גֵּרְשֹׁם בֶּן־
לא מְנַשֶּׁה הוּא וּבָנָיו הָיוּ כֹהֲנִים לְשֵׁבֶט הַדָּנִי עַד־יוֹם גְּלוֹת הָאָרֶץ: וַיָּשִׂימוּ
לָהֶם אֶת־פֶּסֶל מִיכָה אֲשֶׁר עָשָׂה כָּל־יְמֵי הֱיוֹת בֵּית־הָאֱלֹהִים
יט א בְּשִׁלֹה: וַיְהִי בַּיָּמִים הָהֵם וּמֶלֶךְ אֵין בְּיִשְׂרָאֵל וַיְהִי ׀
אִישׁ לֵוִי גָּר בְּיַרְכְּתֵי הַר־אֶפְרַיִם וַיִּקַּח־לוֹ אִשָּׁה פִילֶגֶשׁ מִבֵּית לֶחֶם
ב יְהוּדָה: וַתִּזְנֶה עָלָיו פִּילַגְשׁוֹ וַתֵּלֶךְ מֵאִתּוֹ אֶל־בֵּית אָבִיהָ אֶל־בֵּית
ג לֶחֶם יְהוּדָה וַתְּהִי־שָׁם יָמִים אַרְבָּעָה חֳדָשִׁים: וַיָּקָם אִישָׁהּ וַיֵּלֶךְ
אַחֲרֶיהָ לְדַבֵּר עַל־לִבָּהּ להשיבו וְנַעֲרוֹ עִמּוֹ וְצֶמֶד חֲמֹרִים וַתְּבִיאֵהוּ לַהֲשִׁיבָהּ
ד בֵּית אָבִיהָ וַיִּרְאֵהוּ אֲבִי הַנַּעֲרָה וַיִּשְׂמַח לִקְרָאתוֹ: וַיֶּחֱזַק־בּוֹ חֹתְנוֹ
ה אֲבִי הַנַּעֲרָה וַיֵּשֶׁב אִתּוֹ שְׁלֹשֶׁת יָמִים וַיֹּאכְלוּ וַיִּשְׁתּוּ וַיָּלִינוּ שָׁם: וַיְהִי
בַּיּוֹם הָרְבִיעִי וַיַּשְׁכִּימוּ בַבֹּקֶר וַיָּקָם לָלֶכֶת וַיֹּאמֶר אֲבִי הַנַּעֲרָה אֶל־
ו חֲתָנוֹ סְעָד לִבְּךָ פַּת־לֶחֶם וְאַחַר תֵּלֵכוּ: וַיֵּשְׁבוּ וַיֹּאכְלוּ שְׁנֵיהֶם יַחְדָּו
וַיִּשְׁתּוּ וַיֹּאמֶר אֲבִי הַנַּעֲרָה אֶל־הָאִישׁ הוֹאֶל־נָא וְלִין וְיִטַב לִבֶּךָ:
ז ח וַיָּקָם הָאִישׁ לָלֶכֶת וַיִּפְצַר־בּוֹ חֹתְנוֹ וַיָּשָׁב וַיָּלֶן שָׁם: וַיַּשְׁכֵּם בַּבֹּקֶר
בַּיּוֹם הַחֲמִישִׁי לָלֶכֶת וַיֹּאמֶר ׀ אֲבִי הַנַּעֲרָה סְעָד־נָא לְבָבְךָ וְהִתְמַהְמְהוּ
ט עַד־נְטוֹת הַיּוֹם וַיֹּאכְלוּ שְׁנֵיהֶם: וַיָּקָם הָאִישׁ לָלֶכֶת הוּא וּפִילַגְשׁוֹ
וְנַעֲרוֹ וַיֹּאמֶר לוֹ חֹתְנוֹ אֲבִי הַנַּעֲרָה הִנֵּה נָא רָפָה הַיּוֹם לַעֲרֹב לִינוּ־
נָא הִנֵּה חֲנוֹת הַיּוֹם לִין פֹּה וְיִיטַב לְבָבֶךָ וְהִשְׁכַּמְתֶּם מָחָר לְדַרְכְּכֶם
י וְהָלַכְתָּ לְאֹהָלֶךָ: וְלֹא־אָבָה הָאִישׁ לָלוּן וַיָּקָם וַיֵּלֶךְ וַיָּבֹא עַד־נֹכַח
יא יְבוּס הִיא יְרוּשָׁלִָם וְעִמּוֹ צֶמֶד חֲמוֹרִים חֲבוּשִׁים וּפִילַגְשׁוֹ עִמּוֹ: הֵם
עִם־יְבוּס וְהַיּוֹם רַד מְאֹד וַיֹּאמֶר הַנַּעַר אֶל־אֲדֹנָיו לְכָה־נָּא וְנָסוּרָה
יב אֶל־עִיר־הַיְבוּסִי הַזֹּאת וְנָלִין בָּהּ: וַיֹּאמֶר אֵלָיו אֲדֹנָיו לֹא נָסוּר אֶל־

13 there are no Israelites. We will continue toward Giva." "Come," he said to his
servant boy, "let us move closer to one of the places, and we will spend the
14 night in Giva or Rama." They kept going, but the sun went down on them by
15 Giva of Binyamin. So they turned off there and sought to spend the night in
Giva. He reached the town square and stopped, but no one was taking them
16 in to spend the night. Just then, an old man was coming back from his work
in the field in the evening – the man was from the Efrayim hills, but he was
17 living in Giva; the locals were Benjaminites – and he looked up and noticed
the traveler in the town square. "Where are you going?" asked the old man.
18 "And where are you from?" He said to him, "We are passing through from Beit
Leḥem of Yehuda to the outskirts of the Efrayim hills – I am from there. I
have journeyed from Beit Leḥem of Yehuda, and I am going to the House of
19 the Lord, but no one has taken me in. We have straw and fodder for our
donkeys as well as food and wine for myself, your handmaiden, and your
20 servant's boy; nothing at all is lacking." "Welcome," said the old man,
21 "everything you lack is on me – just don't spend the night in the square." He
brought him into his home and mixed fodder for the donkeys; they washed
22 their feet and ate and drank. As they were enjoying themselves, some
townspeople – depraved men – suddenly surrounded the house, pounding
on the door. They said to the elderly host, "Bring out the man who came to
23 your house so that we can get to know him intimately." The host went out to
them and said to them, "No, my brothers, please do no harm since this man
24 has entered my home – do not commit such an outrage. Look, here are my
virgin daughter and his concubine. I will bring them out now; torment them
and do to them as you please, but do not commit such an outrage with this
25 man." But the men would not listen to him, so the man seized his concubine
and forced her out to them. They raped her and abused her all night long,
26 until dawn approached, and sent her off at daybreak. As dawn rose, the
woman came back to the entrance of the man's house where her master was,
27 and she collapsed there as it grew light. Her master got up in the morning
and opened the doors of the house to set out and continue on his way – and
there was his concubine, sprawled at the entrance of the house with her hand
28 upon the threshold. "Get up, let's go," he said to her, but there was no answer.
Having lifted her onto the donkey, the man mounted and proceeded to his
29 destination. When he reached his house, he took a knife, seized hold of his
concubine and hacked her up, limb by limb, into twelve pieces, and he sent
30 one to each and every region of Israel. And all who saw said, "Nothing like
this has ever happened or been witnessed from the day the Israelites came
out of Egypt until this very day; bear this in mind, take counsel, and speak
20 1 out!" All the Israelites marched forth. From Dan to Be'er Sheva
and the Gilad region, the entire gathering assembled before the Lord at

יג עִיר נָכְרִי אֲשֶׁר לֹא־מִבְּנֵי יִשְׂרָאֵל הֵנָּה וְעָבַרְנוּ עַד־גִּבְעָה: וַיֹּאמֶר
יד לְנַעֲרוֹ לְךָ וְנִקְרְבָה בְּאַחַד הַמְּקֹמוֹת וְלַנּוּ בַגִּבְעָה אוֹ בָרָמָה: וַיַּעַבְרוּ
טו וַיֵּלֵכוּ וַתָּבֹא לָהֶם הַשֶּׁמֶשׁ אֵצֶל הַגִּבְעָה אֲשֶׁר לְבִנְיָמִן: וַיָּסֻרוּ שָׁם
לָבוֹא לָלוּן בַּגִּבְעָה וַיָּבֹא וַיֵּשֶׁב בִּרְחוֹב הָעִיר וְאֵין אִישׁ מְאַסֵּף־אוֹתָם
טז הַבַּיְתָה לָלוּן: וְהִנֵּה ׀ אִישׁ זָקֵן בָּא מִן־מַעֲשֵׂהוּ מִן־הַשָּׂדֶה בָּעֶרֶב
יז וְהָאִישׁ מֵהַר אֶפְרַיִם וְהוּא־גָר בַּגִּבְעָה וְאַנְשֵׁי הַמָּקוֹם בְּנֵי יְמִינִי: וַיִּשָּׂא
עֵינָיו וַיַּרְא אֶת־הָאִישׁ הָאֹרֵחַ בִּרְחוֹב הָעִיר וַיֹּאמֶר הָאִישׁ הַזָּקֵן אָנָה
יח תֵלֵךְ וּמֵאַיִן תָּבוֹא: וַיֹּאמֶר אֵלָיו עֹבְרִים אֲנַחְנוּ מִבֵּית־לֶחֶם יְהוּדָה
עַד־יַרְכְּתֵי הַר־אֶפְרַיִם מִשָּׁם אָנֹכִי וָאֵלֵךְ עַד־בֵּית לֶחֶם יְהוּדָה וְאֶת־
יט בֵּית יְהוָה אֲנִי הֹלֵךְ וְאֵין אִישׁ מְאַסֵּף אוֹתִי הַבָּיְתָה: וְגַם־תֶּבֶן גַּם־
מִסְפּוֹא יֵשׁ לַחֲמוֹרֵינוּ וְגַם לֶחֶם וָיַיִן יֶשׁ־לִי וְלַאֲמָתֶךָ וְלַנַּעַר עִם־עֲבָדֶיךָ
כ אֵין מַחְסוֹר כָּל־דָּבָר: וַיֹּאמֶר הָאִישׁ הַזָּקֵן שָׁלוֹם לָךְ רַק כָּל־מַחְסוֹרְךָ יג
כא עָלָי רַק בָּרְחוֹב אַל־תָּלַן: וַיְבִיאֵהוּ לְבֵיתוֹ ויבול לַחֲמוֹרִים וַיִּרְחֲצוּ וַיָּבָל
כב רַגְלֵיהֶם וַיֹּאכְלוּ וַיִּשְׁתּוּ: הֵמָּה מֵיטִיבִים אֶת־לִבָּם וְהִנֵּה אַנְשֵׁי הָעִיר
אַנְשֵׁי בְנֵי־בְלִיַּעַל נָסַבּוּ אֶת־הַבַּיִת מִתְדַּפְּקִים עַל־הַדָּלֶת וַיֹּאמְרוּ
אֶל־הָאִישׁ בַּעַל הַבַּיִת הַזָּקֵן לֵאמֹר הוֹצֵא אֶת־הָאִישׁ אֲשֶׁר־בָּא אֶל־
כג בֵּיתְךָ וְנֵדָעֶנּוּ: וַיֵּצֵא אֲלֵיהֶם הָאִישׁ בַּעַל הַבַּיִת וַיֹּאמֶר אֲלֵהֶם אַל־אַחַי
אַל־תָּרֵעוּ נָא אַחֲרֵי אֲשֶׁר־בָּא הָאִישׁ הַזֶּה אֶל־בֵּיתִי אַל־תַּעֲשׂוּ אֶת־
כד הַנְּבָלָה הַזֹּאת: הִנֵּה בִתִּי הַבְּתוּלָה וּפִילַגְשֵׁהוּ אוֹצִיאָה־נָּא אוֹתָם
וְעַנּוּ אוֹתָם וַעֲשׂוּ לָהֶם הַטּוֹב בְּעֵינֵיכֶם וְלָאִישׁ הַזֶּה לֹא תַעֲשׂוּ דְּבַר
כה הַנְּבָלָה הַזֹּאת: וְלֹא־אָבוּ הָאֲנָשִׁים לִשְׁמֹעַ לוֹ וַיַּחֲזֵק הָאִישׁ בְּפִילַגְשׁוֹ
וַיֹּצֵא אֲלֵיהֶם הַחוּץ וַיֵּדְעוּ אוֹתָהּ וַיִּתְעַלְּלוּ־בָהּ כָּל־הַלַּיְלָה עַד־הַבֹּקֶר
כו וַיְשַׁלְּחוּהָ בעלות הַשָּׁחַר: וַתָּבֹא הָאִשָּׁה לִפְנוֹת הַבֹּקֶר וַתִּפֹּל פֶּתַח כַּעֲלוֹת
כז בֵּית־הָאִישׁ אֲשֶׁר־אֲדוֹנֶיהָ שָּׁם עַד־הָאוֹר: וַיָּקָם אֲדֹנֶיהָ בַּבֹּקֶר וַיִּפְתַּח
דַּלְתוֹת הַבַּיִת וַיֵּצֵא לָלֶכֶת לְדַרְכּוֹ וְהִנֵּה הָאִשָּׁה פִילַגְשׁוֹ נֹפֶלֶת פֶּתַח
כח הַבַּיִת וְיָדֶיהָ עַל־הַסַּף: וַיֹּאמֶר אֵלֶיהָ קוּמִי וְנֵלֵכָה וְאֵין עֹנֶה וַיִּקָּחֶהָ
כט עַל־הַחֲמוֹר וַיָּקָם הָאִישׁ וַיֵּלֶךְ לִמְקֹמוֹ: וַיָּבֹא אֶל־בֵּיתוֹ וַיִּקַּח אֶת־
הַמַּאֲכֶלֶת וַיַּחֲזֵק בְּפִילַגְשׁוֹ וַיְנַתְּחֶהָ לַעֲצָמֶיהָ לִשְׁנַיִם עָשָׂר נְתָחִים
ל וַיְשַׁלְּחֶהָ בְּכֹל גְּבוּל יִשְׂרָאֵל: וְהָיָה כָל־הָרֹאֶה וְאָמַר לֹא־נִהְיְתָה
וְלֹא־נִרְאֲתָה כָּזֹאת לְמִיּוֹם עֲלוֹת בְּנֵי־יִשְׂרָאֵל מֵאֶרֶץ מִצְרַיִם עַד הַיּוֹם
כ א הַזֶּה שִׂימוּ־לָכֶם עָלֶיהָ עֻצוּ וְדַבֵּרוּ: וַיֵּצְאוּ
כָּל־בְּנֵי יִשְׂרָאֵל וַתִּקָּהֵל הָעֵדָה כְּאִישׁ אֶחָד לְמִדָּן וְעַד־בְּאֵר שֶׁבַע

2 Mitzpa. All the leaders of the people, of all the tribes of Israel, presented
themselves at the assembly of God's people: four hundred thousand
3 swordsmen. And the Benjaminites heard that the Israelites had
marched up to Mitzpa. "Speak up," said the Israelites. "How did this evil come
4 to pass?" The Levite man, husband of the murdered woman, answered. "To
5 Giva of Binyamin," he said, "my concubine and I came to stay. The citizens of
Giva attacked me and surrounded the house at night; me they meant to kill,
6 and as for my concubine – they tortured her to death. So I seized hold of my
concubine, cut her in pieces, and sent them out to each and every estate in
7 Israel, for they committed a foul, outrageous thing in Israel. Now look, all you
8 Israelites – devise a plan of action, here and now!" The entire people rose as
one, saying, "We will not go back to our tents, and we will not turn back home.
9 Now, this is what we will do to Giva. We will draw lots; we will take ten out
10 of every hundred men from all the tribes of Israel; a hundred out of every
thousand; a thousand out of every ten thousand, to collect supplies for the
fighters in preparation for their arrival at Geva of Binyamin – because of the
11 outrage they committed in Israel." Every single man in Israel gathered near
12 the city, united as one. The tribes of Israel sent men to all the tribal
13 clans of Binyamin, saying, "Why has such evil transpired among you? Hand
over those depraved men from Giva. We will put them to death and purge
evil from Israel." But Binyamin would not comply with their Israelite brothers.
14 So the Benjaminites gathered from their towns at Giva to wage war against
15 the Israelites. On that day, the Benjaminites mustered twenty-six thousand
swordsmen from the towns, besides the people of Giva, who mustered
16 seven hundred elite warriors. Out of all these men, seven hundred elite
warriors were left-handed; each one could sling a stone at a hair without
17 missing. The men of Israel mustered; without Binyamin, their
troops were four hundred thousand swordsmen, all of them ready for battle.
18 They set out and marched up to Beit El, where they consulted God. The
Israelites asked, "Who of us should lead the attack against the Benjaminites?"
19 The Lord responded, "Yehuda should lead." So the Israelites set out in the
20 morning and set up camp at Giva. The Israelite troops set out for battle against
21 Binyamin, and the Israelite troops took up positions at Giva. The Benjaminites
charged out of Giva and struck down twenty-two thousand Israelite troops
22 that day. Then the Israelite troops rallied and set out for battle once more
23 where they had fought the first day. The Israelites had gone up to weep before
the Lord until dusk; they had inquired of the Lord, asking, "Shall we once

ב וארץ הגלעד אל־יהוה המצפה: ויתיצבו פנות כל־העם כל שבטי
ישראל בקהל עם האלהים ארבע מאות אלף איש רגלי שלף
ג חרב: וישמעו בני בנימן כי־עלו בני־ישראל המצפה
ד ויאמרו בני ישראל דברו איכה נהיתה הרעה הזאת: ויען האיש
הלוי איש האשה הנרצחה ויאמר הגבעתה אשר לבנימן באתי
ה אני ופילגשי ללון: ויקמו עלי בעלי הגבעה ויסבו עלי את־הבית
ו לילה אותי דמו להרג ואת־פילגשי ענו ותמת: ואחז בפילגשי
ואנתחה ואשלחה בכל־שדה נחלת ישראל כי עשו זמה ונבלה
ז ח בישראל: הנה כלכם בני ישראל הבו לכם דבר ועצה הלם: ויקם
כל־העם כאיש אחד לאמר לא נלך איש לאהלו ולא נסור איש
ט י לביתו: ועתה זה הדבר אשר נעשה לגבעה עליה בגורל: ולקחנו
עשרה אנשים למאה לכל | שבטי ישראל ומאה לאלף ואלף לרבבה
לקחת צדה לעם לעשות לבואם לגבע בנימן ככל־הנבלה אשר
יא עשה בישראל: ויאסף כל־איש ישראל אל־העיר כאיש אחד
יב חברים: וישלחו שבטי ישראל אנשים בכל־שבטי
יג בנימן לאמר מה הרעה הזאת אשר נהיתה בכם: ועתה תנו את־
האנשים בני־בליעל אשר בגבעה ונמיתם ונבערה רעה מישראל
יד ולא אבו בנימן לשמע בקול אחיהם בני־ישראל: ויאספו בני־ בני
בנימן מן־הערים הגבעתה לצאת למלחמה עם־בני ישראל:
טו ויתפקדו בני בנימן ביום ההוא מהערים עשרים וששה אלף איש
שלף חרב לבד מישבי הגבעה התפקדו שבע מאות איש בחור:
טז מכל | העם הזה שבע מאות איש בחור אטר יד־ימינו כל־זה
יז קלע באבן אל־השערה ולא יחטא: ואיש ישראל
התפקדו לבד מבנימן ארבע מאות אלף איש שלף חרב כל־זה איש
יח מלחמה: ויקמו ויעלו בית־אל וישאלו באלהים ויאמרו בני ישראל
מי יעלה־לנו בתחלה למלחמה עם־בני בנימן ויאמר יהוה יהודה
יט כ בתחלה: ויקומו בני־ישראל בבקר ויחנו על־הגבעה: ויצא איש
ישראל למלחמה עם־בנימן ויערכו אתם איש־ישראל מלחמה
כא אל־הגבעה: ויצאו בני־בנימן מן־הגבעה וישחיתו בישראל ביום
כב ההוא שנים ועשרים אלף איש ארצה: ויתחזק העם איש ישראל
כג ויספו לערך מלחמה במקום אשר־ערכו שם ביום הראשון: ויעלו
בני־ישראל ויבכו לפני־יהוה עד־הערב וישאלו ביהוה לאמר

again meet our brothers, the Benjaminites, in battle?" And the LORD had said,
24 "March up against them." The Israelites advanced toward the
25 Benjaminites on the second day. Binyamin charged out toward them from
Giva on the second day and laid waste to another eighteen thousand Israelite
26 troops, every one of them a swordsman. Then all the Israelites and all their
men went up and arrived at Beit El, and weeping, they sat there before the
LORD. On that day, they fasted until dusk and offered burnt offerings and
27 peace offerings before the LORD. Then the Israelites inquired of the LORD,
28 for the Ark of God's Covenant was there in those days; in those days, Pinḥas
son of Elazar son of Aharon was stationed before it. "Shall we persevere in
battle with the Benjaminites, our brothers, or shall we withdraw?" The LORD
29 said, "March up, for tomorrow I shall deliver them into your hands." Israel
30 set up ambushes around Giva. The Israelites advanced toward the
31 Benjaminites on the third day and took up positions at Giva, as before. The
Benjaminites, having been lured away from the city, charged out toward the
men and began striking them down as before on the highways, one leading
to Beit El and the other in the field toward Giva; there were about thirty
32 Israelite casualties. The Benjaminites thought: "They are being routed by us
as they were last time" – but the Israelites had made plans: "We will flee and
33 lure them away from the city to the highways." All the main Israelite forces
rose from their positions and regrouped at Baal Tamar; the Israelite ambush
34 burst out from its position by the Plain of Geva.[26] In the thick of battle, ten
thousand elite Israelite troops arrived across from Giva, and before Binyamin
35 realized that disaster had befallen them, the LORD routed them
before Israel. On that day, the Israelites slaughtered 25,100 from Binyamin,
36 everyone a swordsman, and the Benjaminites realized that they had been
routed. Now, the Israelite men had given ground to Binyamin, for they were
37 relying on the ambush they had set up at Giva. The ambushers swiftly spread
38 out toward Giva, advanced, and put the entire city to the sword. The main
Israelite army and the ambushers had agreed on a signal: when they sent up
39 a great column of smoke from the city, the Israelite men would turn around
and attack. Binyamin had begun striking at the Israelite men – inflicting about
thirty casualties – leading them to think: "They are being routed by us again,
40 as in the previous battles." When the pillar of smoke began to rise from the
city, Binyamin turned around – the entire city had suddenly flared up to the
41 heavens! The Israelite troops then turned on them, and the Benjaminite
42 troops panicked, for they realized that disaster had befallen them. They
retreated before Israel along the wilderness route, but the battle caught up
with them at the same time that those in the cities were massacring them
43 from within. They surrounded Binyamin, hunted them down, and easily

26 | This likely refers to Giva (cf. v. 10).

הַאוֹסִיף לָגֶשֶׁת לַמִּלְחָמָה עִם־בְּנֵי בִּנְיָמִן אָחִי וַיֹּאמֶר יְהוָה עֲלוּ
כד אֵלָיו׃ וַיִּקְרְבוּ בְנֵי־יִשְׂרָאֵל אֶל־בְּנֵי בִנְיָמִן
כה בַּיּוֹם הַשֵּׁנִי׃ וַיֵּצֵא בִנְיָמִן ׀ לִקְרָאתָם ׀ מִן־הַגִּבְעָה בַּיּוֹם הַשֵּׁנִי וַיַּשְׁחִיתוּ
בִבְנֵי יִשְׂרָאֵל עוֹד שְׁמֹנַת עָשָׂר אֶלֶף אִישׁ אַרְצָה כָּל־אֵלֶּה שֹׁלְפֵי חָרֶב׃
כו וַיַּעֲלוּ כָל־בְּנֵי יִשְׂרָאֵל וְכָל־הָעָם וַיָּבֹאוּ בֵית־אֵל וַיִּבְכּוּ וַיֵּשְׁבוּ שָׁם
לִפְנֵי יְהוָה וַיָּצוּמוּ בַיּוֹם־הַהוּא עַד־הָעָרֶב וַיַּעֲלוּ עֹלוֹת וּשְׁלָמִים לִפְנֵי
כז יְהוָה׃ וַיִּשְׁאֲלוּ בְנֵי־יִשְׂרָאֵל בַּיהוָה וְשָׁם אֲרוֹן בְּרִית הָאֱלֹהִים בַּיָּמִים יד
כח הָהֵם׃ וּפִינְחָס בֶּן־אֶלְעָזָר בֶּן־אַהֲרֹן עֹמֵד ׀ לְפָנָיו בַּיָּמִים הָהֵם לֵאמֹר
הַאוֹסִף עוֹד לָצֵאת לַמִּלְחָמָה עִם־בְּנֵי־בִנְיָמִן אָחִי אִם־אֶחְדָּל וַיֹּאמֶר
כט יְהוָה עֲלוּ כִּי מָחָר אֶתְּנֶנּוּ בְיָדֶךָ׃ וַיָּשֶׂם יִשְׂרָאֵל אֹרְבִים אֶל־הַגִּבְעָה
ל סָבִיב׃ וַיַּעֲלוּ בְנֵי־יִשְׂרָאֵל אֶל־בְּנֵי בִנְיָמִן בַּיּוֹם הַשְּׁלִישִׁי
לא וַיַּעַרְכוּ אֶל־הַגִּבְעָה כְּפַעַם בְּפָעַם׃ וַיֵּצְאוּ בְנֵי־בִנְיָמִן לִקְרַאת הָעָם
הָנְתְּקוּ מִן־הָעִיר וַיָּחֵלּוּ לְהַכּוֹת מֵהָעָם חֲלָלִים כְּפַעַם ׀ בְּפַעַם בַּמְסִלּוֹת
אֲשֶׁר אַחַת עֹלָה בֵית־אֵל וְאַחַת גִּבְעָתָה בַּשָּׂדֶה כִּשְׁלֹשִׁים אִישׁ
לב בְּיִשְׂרָאֵל׃ וַיֹּאמְרוּ בְּנֵי בִנְיָמִן נִגָּפִים הֵם לְפָנֵינוּ כְּבָרִאשֹׁנָה וּבְנֵי יִשְׂרָאֵל
לג אָמְרוּ נָנוּסָה וּנְתַקְּנֻהוּ מִן־הָעִיר אֶל־הַמְסִלּוֹת׃ וְכֹל ׀ אִישׁ יִשְׂרָאֵל
קָמוּ מִמְּקוֹמוֹ וַיַּעַרְכוּ בְּבַעַל תָּמָר וְאֹרֵב יִשְׂרָאֵל מֵגִיחַ מִמְּקֹמוֹ
לד מִמַּעֲרֵה־גָבַע׃ וַיָּבֹאוּ מִנֶּגֶד לַגִּבְעָה עֲשֶׂרֶת אֲלָפִים אִישׁ בָּחוּר
מִכָּל־יִשְׂרָאֵל וְהַמִּלְחָמָה כָּבֵדָה וְהֵם לֹא יָדְעוּ כִּי־נֹגַעַת עֲלֵיהֶם
לה הָרָעָה׃ וַיִּגֹּף יְהוָה ׀ אֶת־בִּנְיָמִן לִפְנֵי יִשְׂרָאֵל וַיַּשְׁחִיתוּ
בְנֵי יִשְׂרָאֵל בְּבִנְיָמִן בַּיּוֹם הַהוּא עֶשְׂרִים וַחֲמִשָּׁה אֶלֶף וּמֵאָה אִישׁ
לו כָּל־אֵלֶּה שֹׁלֵף חָרֶב׃ וַיִּרְאוּ בְנֵי־בִנְיָמִן כִּי נִגָּפוּ וַיִּתְּנוּ אִישׁ־יִשְׂרָאֵל
לז מָקוֹם לְבִנְיָמִן כִּי בָטְחוּ אֶל־הָאֹרֵב אֲשֶׁר שָׂמוּ אֶל־הַגִּבְעָה׃ וְהָאֹרֵב
הֵחִישׁוּ וַיִּפְשְׁטוּ אֶל־הַגִּבְעָה וַיִּמְשֹׁךְ הָאֹרֵב וַיַּךְ אֶת־כָּל־הָעִיר לְפִי־
לח חָרֶב׃ וְהַמּוֹעֵד הָיָה לְאִישׁ יִשְׂרָאֵל עִם־הָאֹרֵב הֶרֶב לְהַעֲלוֹתָם מַשְׂאַת
לט הֶעָשָׁן מִן־הָעִיר׃ וַיַּהֲפֹךְ אִישׁ־יִשְׂרָאֵל בַּמִּלְחָמָה וּבִנְיָמִן הֵחֵל לְהַכּוֹת
חֲלָלִים בְּאִישׁ־יִשְׂרָאֵל כִּשְׁלֹשִׁים אִישׁ כִּי אָמְרוּ אַךְ נִגּוֹף נִגָּף הוּא
מ לְפָנֵינוּ כַּמִּלְחָמָה הָרִאשֹׁנָה׃ וְהַמַּשְׂאֵת הֵחֵלָּה לַעֲלוֹת מִן־הָעִיר עַמּוּד
מא עָשָׁן וַיִּפֶן בִּנְיָמִן אַחֲרָיו וְהִנֵּה עָלָה כְלִיל־הָעִיר הַשָּׁמָיְמָה׃ וְאִישׁ
מב יִשְׂרָאֵל הָפַךְ וַיִּבָּהֵל אִישׁ בִּנְיָמִן כִּי רָאָה כִּי־נָגְעָה עָלָיו הָרָעָה׃ וַיִּפְנוּ
לִפְנֵי אִישׁ יִשְׂרָאֵל אֶל־דֶּרֶךְ הַמִּדְבָּר וְהַמִּלְחָמָה הִדְבִּיקָתְהוּ וַאֲשֶׁר
מג מֵהֶעָרִים מַשְׁחִיתִים אוֹתוֹ בְּתוֹכוֹ׃ כִּתְּרוּ אֶת־בִּנְיָמִן הִרְדִיפֻהוּ מְנוּחָה

44 crushed them at Menuḥa, by the eastern front of Giva. Eighteen thousand
45 fell among Binyamin, all of them valiant warriors. They retreated and fled to
the wilderness, to Pomegranate Rock, but the Israelites picked off five
thousand men along the highway; they caught up with them at Gidom and
46 struck down two thousand more men. In all, Binyamin's casualties on that
47 day totaled twenty-five thousand swordsmen, all of them valiant warriors. Six
hundred men who had retreated and fled toward the wilderness hid out at
48 Pomegranate Rock for four months. As for the Israelite men, they headed
back to the Benjaminites and put them to the sword – town, man, beast –
21 1 everything in sight; they set fire to every city that remained. Now,
the Israelites had pronounced this oath at Mitzpa: "Not one of us shall give
2 his daughter as a wife to Binyamin." But when the people arrived at Beit El,
they sat there before God until dusk and raised their voices, weeping bitterly.
3 "Why, O Lord, God of Israel," they said, "did this happen in Israel? Now one
4 tribe from Israel is missing." The next morning, the people rose early, built
5 an altar there, and offered up burnt offerings and peace offerings. Then
the Israelites said, "Who among all the tribes of Israel did not go up to the
assembly before the Lord?" For a solemn oath had been pronounced against
6 anyone who did not go up to the Lord at Mitzpa: "He is doomed to die." But
the Israelites felt remorse toward their brother Binyamin and said, "Today, a
7 tribe has been severed from Israel. How can we provide wives for those who
are left when we have sworn by the Lord not to give them our daughters as
8 wives?" So they said, "Was there anyone among the tribes of Israel who did
not go up to the Lord at Mitzpa?" Now, no one from Yavesh Gilad had come
9 to the camp and to the assembly, and when the men were counted, not a man
10 from the people of Yavesh Gilad was there. The assembly dispatched twelve
thousand warriors, instructing them, "Go and put the people of Yavesh Gilad
11 to the sword – including women and children. This is the course of action
you should take: every male and every woman who has lain with a man –
12 utterly destroy them." Out of the people of Yavesh Gilad, they found four
hundred maidens who had never lain with a man, and they brought them to
13 the Shilo camp in the land of Canaan. The whole congregation sent
word to the Benjaminites at Pomegranate Rock, declaring peace with them.
14 The Benjaminites immediately returned, and they gave them as wives the
women they had spared from the women of Yavesh Gilad, but there were not
15 enough of them. And the people felt remorse toward Binyamin, for the Lord
16 had caused a rift in the tribes of Israel. The community elders asked, "How
can we provide wives for those who are left when the women of Binyamin
17 have been annihilated? There must be a surviving remnant for Binyamin,"
18 they continued, "so that a tribe of Israel will not be wiped out. But we cannot

מד הִדְרִיכֻהוּ עַד נֹכַח הַגִּבְעָה מִמִּזְרַח־שָׁמֶשׁ׃ וַיִּפְּלוּ מִבִּנְיָמִן שְׁמֹנָה־עָשָׂר
מה אֶלֶף אִישׁ אֶת־כָּל־אֵלֶּה אַנְשֵׁי־חָיִל׃ וַיִּפְנוּ וַיָּנֻסוּ הַמִּדְבָּרָה אֶל־סֶלַע
הָרִמּוֹן וַיְעֹלְלֻהוּ בַּמְסִלּוֹת חֲמֵשֶׁת אֲלָפִים אִישׁ וַיַּדְבִּיקוּ אַחֲרָיו עַד־
מו גִּדְעֹם וַיַּכּוּ מִמֶּנּוּ אַלְפַּיִם אִישׁ׃ וַיְהִי כָל־הַנֹּפְלִים מִבִּנְיָמִן עֶשְׂרִים
וַחֲמִשָּׁה אֶלֶף אִישׁ שֹׁלֵף חֶרֶב בַּיּוֹם הַהוּא אֶת־כָּל־אֵלֶּה אַנְשֵׁי־חָיִל׃
מז וַיִּפְנוּ וַיָּנֻסוּ הַמִּדְבָּרָה אֶל־סֶלַע הָרִמּוֹן שֵׁשׁ מֵאוֹת אִישׁ וַיֵּשְׁבוּ בְּסֶלַע
מח רִמּוֹן אַרְבָּעָה חֳדָשִׁים׃ וְאִישׁ יִשְׂרָאֵל שָׁבוּ אֶל־בְּנֵי בִנְיָמִן וַיַּכּוּם לְפִי־
חֶרֶב מֵעִיר מְתֹם עַד־בְּהֵמָה עַד כָּל־הַנִּמְצָא גַּם כָּל־הֶעָרִים הַנִּמְצָאוֹת
כא א שִׁלְּחוּ בָאֵשׁ׃ וְאִישׁ יִשְׂרָאֵל נִשְׁבַּע בַּמִּצְפָּה לֵאמֹר אִישׁ
ב מִמֶּנּוּ לֹא־יִתֵּן בִּתּוֹ לְבִנְיָמִן לְאִשָּׁה׃ וַיָּבֹא הָעָם בֵּית־אֵל וַיֵּשְׁבוּ שָׁם
ג עַד־הָעֶרֶב לִפְנֵי הָאֱלֹהִים וַיִּשְׂאוּ קוֹלָם וַיִּבְכּוּ בְּכִי גָדוֹל׃ וַיֹּאמְרוּ לָמָה
יְהוָה אֱלֹהֵי יִשְׂרָאֵל הָיְתָה זֹּאת בְּיִשְׂרָאֵל לְהִפָּקֵד הַיּוֹם מִיִּשְׂרָאֵל
ד שֵׁבֶט אֶחָד׃ וַיְהִי מִמָּחֳרָת וַיַּשְׁכִּימוּ הָעָם וַיִּבְנוּ־שָׁם מִזְבֵּחַ וַיַּעֲלוּ עֹלוֹת
ה וּשְׁלָמִים׃ וַיֹּאמְרוּ בְּנֵי יִשְׂרָאֵל מִי אֲשֶׁר לֹא־עָלָה
בַקָּהָל מִכָּל־שִׁבְטֵי יִשְׂרָאֵל אֶל־יְהוָה כִּי הַשְּׁבוּעָה הַגְּדוֹלָה הָיְתָה
ו לַאֲשֶׁר לֹא־עָלָה אֶל־יְהוָה הַמִּצְפָּה לֵאמֹר מוֹת יוּמָת׃ וַיִּנָּחֲמוּ בְּנֵי
יִשְׂרָאֵל אֶל־בִּנְיָמִן אָחִיו וַיֹּאמְרוּ נִגְדַּע הַיּוֹם שֵׁבֶט אֶחָד מִיִּשְׂרָאֵל׃
ז מַה־נַּעֲשֶׂה לָהֶם לַנּוֹתָרִים לְנָשִׁים וַאֲנַחְנוּ נִשְׁבַּעְנוּ בַיהוָה לְבִלְתִּי
ח תֵּת־לָהֶם מִבְּנוֹתֵינוּ לְנָשִׁים׃ וַיֹּאמְרוּ מִי אֶחָד מִשִּׁבְטֵי יִשְׂרָאֵל אֲשֶׁר
לֹא־עָלָה אֶל־יְהוָה הַמִּצְפָּה וְהִנֵּה לֹא בָא־אִישׁ אֶל־הַמַּחֲנֶה מִיָּבֵישׁ
ט גִּלְעָד אֶל־הַקָּהָל׃ וַיִּתְפָּקֵד הָעָם וְהִנֵּה אֵין־שָׁם אִישׁ מִיּוֹשְׁבֵי יָבֵשׁ
י גִּלְעָד׃ וַיִּשְׁלְחוּ־שָׁם הָעֵדָה שְׁנֵים־עָשָׂר אֶלֶף אִישׁ מִבְּנֵי הֶחָיִל וַיְצַוּוּ
אוֹתָם לֵאמֹר לְכוּ וְהִכִּיתֶם אֶת־יוֹשְׁבֵי יָבֵשׁ גִּלְעָד לְפִי־חֶרֶב וְהַנָּשִׁים
יא וְהַטָּף׃ וְזֶה הַדָּבָר אֲשֶׁר תַּעֲשׂוּ כָּל־זָכָר וְכָל־אִשָּׁה יֹדַעַת מִשְׁכַּב־זָכָר
יב תַּחֲרִימוּ׃ וַיִּמְצְאוּ מִיּוֹשְׁבֵי ׀ יָבֵישׁ גִּלְעָד אַרְבַּע מֵאוֹת נַעֲרָה בְתוּלָה
אֲשֶׁר לֹא־יָדְעָה אִישׁ לְמִשְׁכַּב זָכָר וַיָּבִיאוּ אוֹתָם אֶל־הַמַּחֲנֶה שִׁלֹה
יג אֲשֶׁר בְּאֶרֶץ כְּנָעַן׃ וַיִּשְׁלְחוּ כָּל־הָעֵדָה וַיְדַבְּרוּ אֶל־בְּנֵי
יד בִנְיָמִן אֲשֶׁר בְּסֶלַע רִמּוֹן וַיִּקְרְאוּ לָהֶם שָׁלוֹם׃ וַיָּשָׁב בִּנְיָמִן בָּעֵת הַהִיא
וַיִּתְּנוּ לָהֶם הַנָּשִׁים אֲשֶׁר חִיּוּ מִנְּשֵׁי יָבֵשׁ גִּלְעָד וְלֹא־מָצְאוּ לָהֶם כֵּן׃
טו טז וְהָעָם נִחָם לְבִנְיָמִן כִּי־עָשָׂה יְהוָה פֶּרֶץ בְּשִׁבְטֵי יִשְׂרָאֵל׃ וַיֹּאמְרוּ זִקְנֵי
יז הָעֵדָה מַה־נַּעֲשֶׂה לַנּוֹתָרִים לְנָשִׁים כִּי־נִשְׁמְדָה מִבִּנְיָמִן אִשָּׁה׃ וַיֹּאמְרוּ
יח יְרֻשַּׁת פְּלֵיטָה לְבִנְיָמִן וְלֹא־יִמָּחֶה שֵׁבֶט מִיִּשְׂרָאֵל׃ וַאֲנַחְנוּ לֹא נוּכַל

give them wives from our daughters, for the Israelites have sworn, 'Cursed is
19 he who gives a wife to Binyamin.'" Then they said, "Look – the annual festival
to the LORD is now being held at Shilo," which is north of Beit El, east of the
20 highway leading from Beit El to Shekhem, and south of Levona. They
instructed the Benjaminites as follows: "Go and lie in wait in the vineyards.
21 When you see the girls of Shilo come out to dance, come out of the vineyards.
Each of you should snatch a wife for himself from the daughters of Shilo, then
22 head for the land of Binyamin. When their fathers or brothers arrive to
contend with us, we shall tell them, 'Be gracious to them, for we could not
provide each man with a wife through war; because you did not give your
23 daughters to them, now you will not be held guilty.'" So the Benjaminites did
so; they took as many women as they needed from the dancers they had
seized and headed back to their estate. They rebuilt their cities and settled in
24 them. Soon after, the Israelites went their own separate ways, each man back
to his own tribe and his own clan; from there, each man left for his own estate.
25 In those days, there was no king in Israel; everyone did what was right in his
own eyes.

לָתֵת־לָהֶם נָשִׁים מִבְּנוֹתֵינוּ כִּי־נִשְׁבְּעוּ בְנֵי־יִשְׂרָאֵל לֵאמֹר אָרוּר נֹתֵן
יט אִשָּׁה לְבִנְיָמִן׃ וַיֹּאמְרוּ הִנֵּה חַג־יהוה בְּשִׁלוֹ מִיָּמִים ׀ יָמִימָה אֲשֶׁר
מִצְּפוֹנָה לְבֵית־אֵל מִזְרְחָה הַשֶּׁמֶשׁ לִמְסִלָּה הָעֹלָה מִבֵּית־אֵל שְׁכֶמָה
כ וּמִנֶּגֶב לִלְבוֹנָה׃ וַיְצַו אֶת־בְּנֵי בִנְיָמִן לֵאמֹר לְכוּ וַאֲרַבְתֶּם בַּכְּרָמִים׃
כא וּרְאִיתֶם וְהִנֵּה אִם־יֵצְאוּ בְנוֹת־שִׁילוֹ לָחוּל בַּמְּחֹלוֹת וִיצָאתֶם מִן־
הַכְּרָמִים וַחֲטַפְתֶּם לָכֶם אִישׁ אִשְׁתּוֹ מִבְּנוֹת שִׁילוֹ וַהֲלַכְתֶּם אֶרֶץ
כב בִּנְיָמִן׃ וְהָיָה כִּי־יָבֹאוּ אֲבוֹתָם אוֹ אֲחֵיהֶם לרוב ׀ אֵלֵינוּ וְאָמַרְנוּ אֲלֵיהֶם לָרִיב
חָנּוּנוּ אוֹתָם כִּי לֹא לָקַחְנוּ אִישׁ אִשְׁתּוֹ בַּמִּלְחָמָה כִּי לֹא אַתֶּם נְתַתֶּם
כג לָהֶם כָּעֵת תֶּאְשָׁמוּ׃ וַיַּעֲשׂוּ־כֵן בְּנֵי בִנְיָמִן וַיִּשְׂאוּ נָשִׁים לְמִסְפָּרָם מִן־
הַמְּחֹלְלוֹת אֲשֶׁר גָּזָלוּ וַיֵּלְכוּ וַיָּשׁוּבוּ אֶל־נַחֲלָתָם וַיִּבְנוּ אֶת־הֶעָרִים
כד וַיֵּשְׁבוּ בָּהֶם׃ וַיִּתְהַלְּכוּ מִשָּׁם בְּנֵי־יִשְׂרָאֵל בָּעֵת הַהִיא אִישׁ לְשִׁבְטוֹ
כה וּלְמִשְׁפַּחְתּוֹ וַיֵּצְאוּ מִשָּׁם אִישׁ לְנַחֲלָתוֹ׃ בַּיָּמִים הָהֵם אֵין מֶלֶךְ בְּיִשְׂרָאֵל
אִישׁ הַיָּשָׁר בְּעֵינָיו יַעֲשֶׂה׃

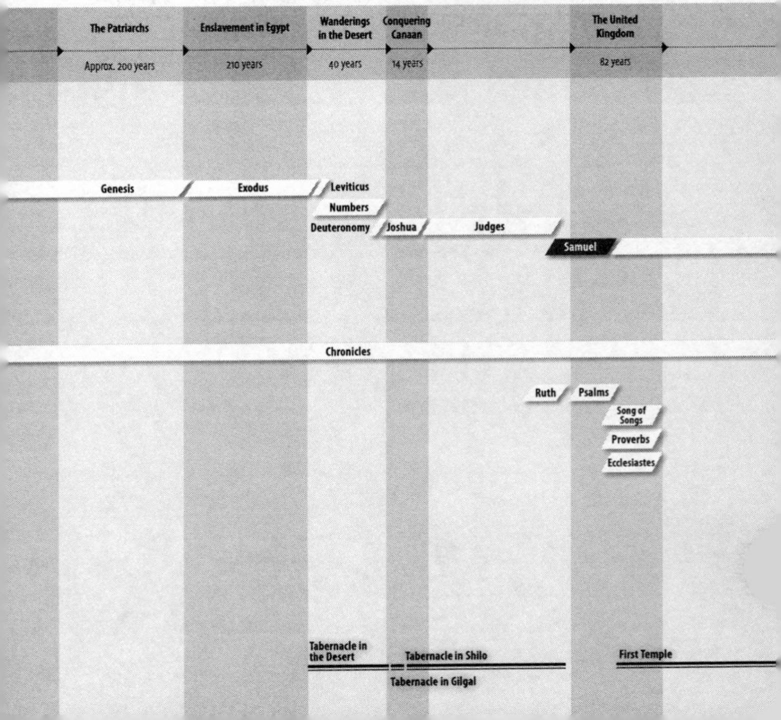

The Patriarchs
Approx. 200 years
Enslavement in Egypt
210 years
Wanderings in the Desert
40 years
Conquering Canaan
14 years
The United Kingdom
82 years
Genesis
Exodus
Leviticus
Numbers
Deuteronomy
Joshua
Judges
Samuel
Chronicles
Ruth
Psalms
Song of Songs
Proverbs
Ecclesiastes
Tabernacle in the Desert
Tabernacle in Shilo
Tabernacle in Gilgal
First Temple

שמואל
SHMUEL / SAMUEL

SAMUEL						
	Shmuel's life – from the period before his birth through his initiation as a prophet and judge	Laying the foundations of the monarchy in Israel, through Sha'ul's death and eulogy	David's reign in Ḥevron and the collapse of the house of Sha'ul	David's reign in Jerusalem	David's sin with Batsheva and its ramifications	The Gibeonites, David's warriors, David's song, the census, and the plague
	I Samuel Chs. 1–7	I Samuel 8– II Samuel 1	II Samuel 2–4	II Samuel 5–10	II Samuel 11–20	II Samuel 21–24
			7 years	Approx. 33 years		

1 1 There was once a man from Ramatayim, of the Zufite clan in the hill country
of Efrayim, whose name was Elkana son of Yeroḥam son of Elihu son of Toḥu
2 son of Zuf of Efrayim. He had two wives: the first was named Ḥana, and the
3 second Penina. Penina had children, but Ḥana had none. Year after year, that
man would make a pilgrimage from his town to worship and sacrifice to the
Lord of Hosts in Shilo, where the two sons of Eli, Ḥofni and Pinḥas, were
4 priests to the Lord. On the day of Elkana's sacrifice, he would give portions
5 to his wife Penina and all her sons and daughters. And to Ḥana he would
give a single portion, but choice, for it was Ḥana whom he loved, though the
6 Lord had closed her womb. Then her rival, to provoke her, would taunt her
7 fiercely, for the Lord had closed up her womb. The same thing would happen
year in, year out – whenever she went up to the Lord's House, Penina would
8 torment her, and she wept and would not eat. One year, her husband, Elkana,
said to her, "Ḥana, why do you weep? Why do you never eat, and why are you
9 so heartsore? Am I not better to you than ten sons?" Ḥana rose after the meal
at Shilo and after the drinking. Eli the priest sat stationed by the doorpost of
10 the Lord's Sanctuary. Wretched and bitter, she prayed to the Lord, weeping
11 all the while. She then swore a vow: "Lord of Hosts, if You look down with
sympathy on the misery of Your handmaid and recognize me; if You do not
forget Your handmaid and grant Your handmaid a son, I will then give him
to the Lord all the days of his life, and a razor will never pass over his head."
12 13 As she prayed on and on before the Lord, Eli was watching her mouth. Ḥana
was speaking in her heart; only her lips were moving, and her voice could not
14 be heard, so Eli thought her drunk. "How long will you act the drunkard?" he
15 said to her. "Deny yourself wine!" "No, sir," Ḥana answered, "I am a woman
of troubled spirit. Neither wine nor beer have I drunk, but I have poured out
16 my soul before the Lord. Do not think your handmaid depraved, for it was
my overwhelming worry and my torment that moved me to pray just now."
17 "Go in peace," Eli answered, "and may the God of Israel grant what you seek
18 of Him." "May I, your servant, find favor in your eyes," she said. And the
19 woman went on her way, and ate, and was downcast no longer. They rose
early in the morning and bowed down before the Lord, then headed back
and arrived home in Rama. Elkana was intimate with his wife Ḥana, and the
20 Lord remembered her. At the turn of the year, Ḥana conceived and bore a
21 son, and she named him Shmuel,[1] "for I sought him from the Lord." The man
Elkana and all his household went up to offer the yearly sacrifice to the Lord
22 and fulfill his vow. But Ḥana did not go up, for she said to her husband, "When
the boy is weaned, I shall bring him; he will appear before the Lord, and he
23 will stay there forever." Her husband Elkana said to her, "Do what seems best
to you; stay behind until you wean him. May the Lord only keep His word."
24 And so she stayed behind and nursed her son until she weaned him. Once
she had weaned him, she brought him up with her, along with three bulls, an
ephah[2] of flour, and an amphora of wine, and presented him at the Lord's

1 | Evoking the Hebrew *sha'ul me'el* (sought from God).

2 | About 23 liters or, alternatively, 40 liters.

א א וַיְהִי אִישׁ אֶחָד מִן־הָרָמָתַיִם צוֹפִים מֵהַר אֶפְרָיִם וּשְׁמוֹ אֶלְקָנָה בֶּן־ א
ב יְרֹחָם בֶּן־אֱלִיהוּא בֶּן־תֹּחוּ בֶן־צוּף אֶפְרָתִי: וְלוֹ שְׁתֵּי נָשִׁים שֵׁם
אַחַת חַנָּה וְשֵׁם הַשֵּׁנִית פְּנִנָּה וַיְהִי לִפְנִנָּה יְלָדִים וּלְחַנָּה אֵין יְלָדִים:
ג וְעָלָה הָאִישׁ הַהוּא מֵעִירוֹ מִיָּמִים ׀ יָמִימָה לְהִשְׁתַּחֲוֺת וְלִזְבֹּחַ לַיהוָה
ד צְבָאוֹת בְּשִׁלֹה וְשָׁם שְׁנֵי בְנֵי־עֵלִי חָפְנִי וּפִנְחָס כֹּהֲנִים לַיהוָה: וַיְהִי
הַיּוֹם וַיִּזְבַּח אֶלְקָנָה וְנָתַן לִפְנִנָּה אִשְׁתּוֹ וּלְכָל־בָּנֶיהָ וּבְנוֹתֶיהָ מָנוֹת:
ה וּלְחַנָּה יִתֵּן מָנָה אַחַת אַפָּיִם כִּי אֶת־חַנָּה אָהֵב וַיהוָה סָגַר רַחְמָהּ:
ו וְכִעֲסַתָּה צָרָתָהּ גַּם־כַּעַס בַּעֲבוּר הַרְּעִמָהּ כִּי־סָגַר יְהוָה בְּעַד רַחְמָהּ:
ז וְכֵן יַעֲשֶׂה שָׁנָה בְשָׁנָה מִדֵּי עֲלֹתָהּ בְּבֵית יְהוָה כֵּן תַּכְעִסֶנָּה וַתִּבְכֶּה וְלֹא
ח תֹאכַל: וַיֹּאמֶר לָהּ אֶלְקָנָה אִישָׁהּ חַנָּה לָמֶה תִבְכִּי וְלָמֶה לֹא תֹאכְלִי
ט וְלָמֶה יֵרַע לְבָבֵךְ הֲלוֹא אָנֹכִי טוֹב לָךְ מֵעֲשָׂרָה בָּנִים: וַתָּקָם חַנָּה אַחֲרֵי
אָכְלָה בְשִׁלֹה וְאַחֲרֵי שָׁתֹה וְעֵלִי הַכֹּהֵן יֹשֵׁב עַל־הַכִּסֵּא עַל־מְזוּזַת
יא הֵיכַל יְהוָה: וְהִיא מָרַת נָפֶשׁ וַתִּתְפַּלֵּל עַל־יְהוָה וּבָכֹה תִבְכֶּה: וַתִּדֹּר
נֶדֶר וַתֹּאמַר יְהוָה צְבָאוֹת אִם־רָאֹה תִרְאֶה ׀ בָּעֳנִי אֲמָתֶךָ וּזְכַרְתַּנִי
וְלֹא־תִשְׁכַּח אֶת־אֲמָתֶךָ וְנָתַתָּה לַאֲמָתְךָ זֶרַע אֲנָשִׁים וּנְתַתִּיו לַיהוָה
יב כָּל־יְמֵי חַיָּיו וּמוֹרָה לֹא־יַעֲלֶה עַל־רֹאשׁוֹ: וְהָיָה כִּי הִרְבְּתָה לְהִתְפַּלֵּל
יג לִפְנֵי יְהוָה וְעֵלִי שֹׁמֵר אֶת־פִּיהָ: וְחַנָּה הִיא מְדַבֶּרֶת עַל־לִבָּהּ רַק
יד שְׂפָתֶיהָ נָּעוֹת וְקוֹלָהּ לֹא יִשָּׁמֵעַ וַיַּחְשְׁבֶהָ עֵלִי לְשִׁכֹּרָה: וַיֹּאמֶר אֵלֶיהָ
טו עֵלִי עַד־מָתַי תִּשְׁתַּכָּרִין הָסִירִי אֶת־יֵינֵךְ מֵעָלָיִךְ: וַתַּעַן חַנָּה וַתֹּאמֶר
לֹא אֲדֹנִי אִשָּׁה קְשַׁת־רוּחַ אָנֹכִי וְיַיִן וְשֵׁכָר לֹא שָׁתִיתִי וָאֶשְׁפֹּךְ אֶת־
טז נַפְשִׁי לִפְנֵי יְהוָה: אַל־תִּתֵּן אֶת־אֲמָתְךָ לִפְנֵי בַּת־בְּלִיָּעַל כִּי־מֵרֹב שִׂיחִי
יז וְכַעְסִי דִּבַּרְתִּי עַד־הֵנָּה: וַיַּעַן עֵלִי וַיֹּאמֶר לְכִי לְשָׁלוֹם וֵאלֹהֵי יִשְׂרָאֵל
יח יִתֵּן אֶת־שֵׁלָתֵךְ אֲשֶׁר שָׁאַלְתְּ מֵעִמּוֹ: וַתֹּאמֶר תִּמְצָא שִׁפְחָתְךָ חֵן
יט בְּעֵינֶיךָ וַתֵּלֶךְ הָאִשָּׁה לְדַרְכָּהּ וַתֹּאכַל וּפָנֶיהָ לֹא־הָיוּ־לָהּ עוֹד: וַיַּשְׁכִּמוּ
בַבֹּקֶר וַיִּשְׁתַּחֲווּ לִפְנֵי יְהוָה וַיָּשֻׁבוּ וַיָּבֹאוּ אֶל־בֵּיתָם הָרָמָתָה וַיֵּדַע
כ אֶלְקָנָה אֶת־חַנָּה אִשְׁתּוֹ וַיִּזְכְּרֶהָ יְהוָה: וַיְהִי לִתְקֻפוֹת הַיָּמִים וַתַּהַר
כא חַנָּה וַתֵּלֶד בֵּן וַתִּקְרָא אֶת־שְׁמוֹ שְׁמוּאֵל כִּי מֵיְהוָה שְׁאִלְתִּיו: וַיַּעַל
הָאִישׁ אֶלְקָנָה וְכָל־בֵּיתוֹ לִזְבֹּחַ לַיהוָה אֶת־זֶבַח הַיָּמִים וְאֶת־נִדְרוֹ:
כב וְחַנָּה לֹא עָלָתָה כִּי־אָמְרָה לְאִישָׁהּ עַד יִגָּמֵל הַנַּעַר וַהֲבִאֹתִיו וְנִרְאָה
כג אֶת־פְּנֵי יְהוָה וְיָשַׁב שָׁם עַד־עוֹלָם: וַיֹּאמֶר לָהּ אֶלְקָנָה אִישָׁהּ עֲשִׂי
הַטּוֹב בְּעֵינַיִךְ שְׁבִי עַד־גָּמְלֵךְ אֹתוֹ אַךְ יָקֵם יְהוָה אֶת־דְּבָרוֹ וַתֵּשֶׁב
כד הָאִשָּׁה וַתֵּינֶק אֶת־בְּנָהּ עַד־גָמְלָהּ אֹתוֹ: וַתַּעֲלֵהוּ עִמָּהּ כַּאֲשֶׁר גְּמָלַתּוּ

25 House at Shilo, though the boy was young. They slaughtered the bull and
26 presented the boy to Eli. She said, "If you please, my lord; as you live, my lord,
27 I am the woman who stood here beside you, praying to the LORD. This is the
28 boy I prayed for – the LORD gave me what I sought from Him. I, in turn, give
him over[3] to the LORD – he has been given over to the LORD for all his days."
2 1 And they bowed down there to the LORD. Then Ḥana prayed. She
said: "My heart exults in the LORD; my horn is raised up[4] by the LORD; my
2 mouth opens wide against my enemies, for I rejoice in Your salvation! There is
no holy being like the LORD, for there are none besides You, no Rock like our
3 God. Do not drone on in pride; let no insolence cross your lips, for the LORD
4 is an all-knowing God; by Him deeds are weighed. Heroes' bows are shattered
5 while the feeble are girded with power. Those once sated hire out for bread,
while those once hungry grow fat. By the time the barren has borne seven, the
6 mother of many has withered. The LORD deals out death and grants life, casts
7 down into Sheol[5] and lifts up. The LORD impoverishes and enriches, humbles
8 and exalts. He lifts the poor from the dust,[6] raises the needy from the refuse
heap and seats them beside nobility, bequeaths them the seat of honor. For
9 the pillars of the earth are the LORD's, and He set the world upon them. He
guards the steps of His faithful while the wicked perish in darkness, for man
10 does not prevail by power. The LORD's foes shall be shattered; He thunders
the heavens above them; the LORD shall judge to the ends of the earth. May
He grant might to His king and raise up the horn of His anointed!"
11 Elkana went home to Rama, while the boy became a servant of the LORD
12 under the priest Eli's supervision. Eli's sons were depraved men who would
13 not acknowledge the LORD. This was how the priests would deal with the
people: Whenever someone offered a sacrifice, the priest's boy would come
14 along as the meat was boiling, a three-pronged fork in his hand. He would stab
it into the cauldron, kettle, pot, or vat, and the priest would snatch whatever
came up on the fork. This was how they treated every Israelite who came there
15 to Shilo. Even before they burned off the fat, the priest's boy would come
and say to the person who was sacrificing, "Hand over some meat to roast
16 for the priest – he won't accept boiled meat from you, only raw." And if the
man would say to him, "Let them first burn off the fat, then take as much as
you want," he would reply, "No, hand it over at once – if not, I will take it by
17 force." The young men's offense was very grave before the LORD, for the men
18 showed contempt for the LORD's offerings. Now Shmuel was serving before
19 the LORD – a boy clad in a linen ephod[7] and a little robe that his mother made
for him; she brought one up for him year after year when she made pilgrimage
20 with her husband to offer the yearly sacrifice. And Eli would bless Elkana and

3 | The use of *hishil*, "to give over," mirrors that which Ḥana says she "sought" (*shaal*) from Him in the previous verse.
4 | Meaning "I am strengthened."
5 | The netherworld.
6 | Cf. Psalms 113:7–8.
7 | An outer garment worn by the priests (see Ex. ch. 28).

בְּפָרִים שְׁלֹשָׁה וְאֵיפָה אַחַת קֶמַח וְנֵבֶל יַיִן וַתְּבִאֵהוּ בֵית־יְהוָה שִׁלוֹ
כה כו וְהַנַּעַר נָעַר׃ וַיִּשְׁחֲטוּ אֶת־הַפָּר וַיָּבִאוּ אֶת־הַנַּעַר אֶל־עֵלִי׃ וַתֹּאמֶר
בִּי אֲדֹנִי חֵי נַפְשְׁךָ אֲדֹנִי אֲנִי הָאִשָּׁה הַנִּצֶּבֶת עִמְּכָה בָּזֶה לְהִתְפַּלֵּל
כז אֶל־יְהוָה׃ אֶל־הַנַּעַר הַזֶּה הִתְפַּלָּלְתִּי וַיִּתֵּן יְהוָה לִי אֶת־שְׁאֵלָתִי
כח אֲשֶׁר שָׁאַלְתִּי מֵעִמּוֹ׃ וְגַם אָנֹכִי הִשְׁאִלְתִּהוּ לַיהוָה כָּל־הַיָּמִים אֲשֶׁר
ב א הָיָה הוּא שָׁאוּל לַיהוָה וַיִּשְׁתַּחוּ שָׁם לַיהוָה׃ וַתִּתְפַּלֵּל
חַנָּה וַתֹּאמַר עָלַץ לִבִּי בַּיהוָה רָמָה קַרְנִי בַּיהוָה רָחַב פִּי עַל־אוֹיְבַי
ב כִּי שָׂמַחְתִּי בִּישׁוּעָתֶךָ׃ אֵין־קָדוֹשׁ כַּיהוָה כִּי־אֵין בִּלְתֶּךָ וְאֵין צוּר
ג כֵּאלֹהֵינוּ׃ אַל־תַּרְבּוּ תְדַבְּרוּ גְּבֹהָה גְבֹהָה יֵצֵא עָתָק מִפִּיכֶם כִּי אֵל
ד דֵּעוֹת יְהוָה וְלֹא נִתְכְּנוּ עֲלִלוֹת׃ קֶשֶׁת גִּבֹּרִים חַתִּים וְנִכְשָׁלִים אָזְרוּ וְלוֹ
ה חָיִל׃ שְׂבֵעִים בַּלֶּחֶם נִשְׂכָּרוּ וּרְעֵבִים חָדֵלּוּ עַד־עֲקָרָה יָלְדָה שִׁבְעָה
ו ז וְרַבַּת בָּנִים אֻמְלָלָה׃ יְהוָה מֵמִית וּמְחַיֶּה מוֹרִיד שְׁאוֹל וַיָּעַל׃ יְהוָה
ח מוֹרִישׁ וּמַעֲשִׁיר מַשְׁפִּיל אַף־מְרוֹמֵם׃ מֵקִים מֵעָפָר דָּל מֵאַשְׁפֹּת יָרִים
אֶבְיוֹן לְהוֹשִׁיב עִם־נְדִיבִים וְכִסֵּא כָבוֹד יַנְחִלֵם כִּי לַיהוָה מְצֻקֵי אֶרֶץ
ט וַיָּשֶׁת עֲלֵיהֶם תֵּבֵל׃ רַגְלֵי חֲסִידָו יִשְׁמֹר וּרְשָׁעִים בַּחֹשֶׁךְ יִדָּמּוּ כִּי־לֹא
י בְכֹחַ יִגְבַּר־אִישׁ׃ יְהוָה יֵחַתּוּ מְרִיבָו עָלָו בַּשָּׁמַיִם יַרְעֵם יְהוָה יָדִין ב
אַפְסֵי־אָרֶץ וְיִתֶּן־עֹז לְמַלְכּוֹ וְיָרֵם קֶרֶן מְשִׁיחוֹ׃
יא וַיֵּלֶךְ אֶלְקָנָה הָרָמָתָה עַל־בֵּיתוֹ וְהַנַּעַר הָיָה מְשָׁרֵת אֶת־יְהוָה אֶת־פְּנֵי
יב יג עֵלִי הַכֹּהֵן׃ וּבְנֵי עֵלִי בְּנֵי בְלִיָּעַל לֹא יָדְעוּ אֶת־יְהוָה׃ וּמִשְׁפַּט הַכֹּהֲנִים
אֶת־הָעָם כָּל־אִישׁ זֹבֵחַ זֶבַח וּבָא נַעַר הַכֹּהֵן כְּבַשֵּׁל הַבָּשָׂר וְהַמַּזְלֵג
יד שְׁלֹשׁ הַשִּׁנַּיִם בְּיָדוֹ׃ וְהִכָּה בַכִּיּוֹר אוֹ בַדּוּד אוֹ בַקַּלַּחַת אוֹ בַפָּרוּר כֹּל
אֲשֶׁר יַעֲלֶה הַמַּזְלֵג יִקַּח הַכֹּהֵן בּוֹ כָּכָה יַעֲשׂוּ לְכָל־יִשְׂרָאֵל הַבָּאִים שָׁם
טו בְּשִׁלֹה׃ גַּם בְּטֶרֶם יַקְטִרוּן אֶת־הַחֵלֶב וּבָא ׀ נַעַר הַכֹּהֵן וְאָמַר לָאִישׁ
הַזֹּבֵחַ תְּנָה בָשָׂר לִצְלוֹת לַכֹּהֵן וְלֹא־יִקַּח מִמְּךָ בָּשָׂר מְבֻשָּׁל כִּי אִם־חָי׃
טז וַיֹּאמֶר אֵלָיו הָאִישׁ קַטֵּר יַקְטִירוּן כַּיּוֹם הַחֵלֶב וְקַח־לְךָ כַּאֲשֶׁר תְּאַוֶּה
יז נַפְשֶׁךָ וְאָמַר ׀ לוֹ כִּי עַתָּה תִתֵּן וְאִם־לֹא לָקַחְתִּי בְחָזְקָה׃ וַתְּהִי חַטַּאת לֹא
הַנְּעָרִים גְּדוֹלָה מְאֹד אֶת־פְּנֵי יְהוָה כִּי נִאֲצוּ הָאֲנָשִׁים אֵת מִנְחַת
יח יט יְהוָה׃ וּשְׁמוּאֵל מְשָׁרֵת אֶת־פְּנֵי יְהוָה נַעַר חָגוּר אֵפוֹד בָּד׃ וּמְעִיל
קָטֹן תַּעֲשֶׂה־לּוֹ אִמּוֹ וְהַעַלְתָה לוֹ מִיָּמִים ׀ יָמִימָה בַּעֲלוֹתָהּ אֶת־אִישָׁהּ
כ לִזְבֹּחַ אֶת־זֶבַח הַיָּמִים׃ וּבֵרַךְ עֵלִי אֶת־אֶלְקָנָה וְאֶת־אִשְׁתּוֹ וְאָמַר יָשֵׂם
יְהוָה לְךָ זֶרַע מִן־הָאִשָּׁה הַזֹּאת תַּחַת הַשְּׁאֵלָה אֲשֶׁר שָׁאַל לַיהוָה

his wife and say, "May the LORD grant you seed from this woman in place of
21 the gift she has given to the LORD," and they would return home. As the LORD
took note of Ḥana, she conceived; she bore three sons and two daughters,
22 while young Shmuel grew up with the LORD. Now Eli was very old.
When he heard about all that his sons had done to all of Israel, and how they
23 lay with the women who served at the entrance of the Tent of Meeting, he
said to them, "How could you do such things? I hear of your terrible deeds
24 from so many people. No, my sons – the rumors I hear spreading among the
25 LORD's people are not good. If a man commits an offense against another
man, God might intercede for him, but if a man commits an offense against
the LORD – who will intercede for him?" But they would not heed their
26 father's voice, for the LORD wanted to put them to death. Meanwhile, young
Shmuel was growing in stature and favor with the LORD and with people
alike.
27 A man of God came to Eli. "Thus says the LORD," he said to him. "Did I not
reveal Myself to your ancestor when they were in Egypt, serving in Pharaoh's
28 house? Did I not choose him out of all the tribes of Israel as My priest – to
ascend My altar, to burn incense, to bear the ephod before Me? I granted your
29 ancestral house every one of the Israelites' fire offerings. Why, then, do you
spurn My sacrifices and My offerings, those I commanded at My dwelling?
You honor your sons more than Me, fattening yourselves from the first pick
30 of every offering of Israel – of My people! Therefore, declares the LORD, God
of Israel, I indeed said: Your house and your father's house shall walk before
Me forever. But now, declares the LORD, far be it from Me; I shall honor those
31 who honor Me, while those who scorn Me shall be slighted. Behold, a time
is coming when I shall sever your arm and the arm of your father's house;
32 there shall be no elder in your house. You shall gaze upon all the good your
rival for My dwelling will do for Israel, but never again will there be an elder
33 in your own house. I shall not cut off every one of you from My altar, but to
wear out your eyes and sadden your soul, all the children born to your family
34 will die in their prime. And this will be the sign for you that will befall your
35 two sons, Ḥofni and Pinḥas: the two of them will die in a single day. And I
shall appoint a faithful priest for Myself who will act according to My own
heart and soul; I shall build him a faithful house, and he will accompany My
36 anointed one for all time. But everyone left in your house will come and pay
homage before him for a pittance and a loaf of bread, pleading, 'Please, add
3 1 me to one of the priestly groups, just for a crust of bread to eat.'" Now
young Shmuel served the LORD under Eli's supervision. In those days, the
2 LORD's word was scarce; visions were far from common. On that fateful
day, Eli was lying in his usual place. His eyes had begun to grow dim, and he
3 could no longer see. The lamp of God had not yet gone out, and Shmuel was
4 lying in the LORD's Sanctuary where the Ark of God was when the
5 LORD called out to Shmuel, who said, "Here I am!" He ran to Eli and said,
"Here I am; you called me." "I did not call you," he said. "Go back to sleep."
6 So he went back in and lay back down. And the LORD called out to Shmuel

כא וְהָלְכוּ לִמְקֹמוֹ: כִּי־פָקַד יהוה אֶת־חַנָּה וַתַּהַר וַתֵּלֶד שְׁלֹשָׁה־בָנִים
כב וּשְׁתֵּי בָנוֹת וַיִּגְדַּל הַנַּעַר שְׁמוּאֵל עִם־יהוה: וְעֵלִי זָקֵן מְאֹד
וְשָׁמַע אֵת כָּל־אֲשֶׁר יַעֲשׂוּן בָּנָיו לְכָל־יִשְׂרָאֵל וְאֵת אֲשֶׁר־יִשְׁכְּבֻן אֶת־
כג הַנָּשִׁים הַצֹּבְאוֹת פֶּתַח אֹהֶל מוֹעֵד: וַיֹּאמֶר לָהֶם לָמָּה תַעֲשׂוּן כַּדְּבָרִים
הָאֵלֶּה אֲשֶׁר אָנֹכִי שֹׁמֵעַ אֶת־דִּבְרֵיכֶם רָעִים מֵאֵת כָּל־הָעָם אֵלֶּה:
כד אַל בָּנָי כִּי לוֹא־טוֹבָה הַשְּׁמֻעָה אֲשֶׁר אָנֹכִי שֹׁמֵעַ מַעֲבִרִים עַם־יהוה:
כה אִם־יֶחֱטָא אִישׁ לְאִישׁ וּפִלְלוֹ אֱלֹהִים וְאִם לַיהוה יֶחֱטָא־אִישׁ מִי
כו יִתְפַּלֶּל־לוֹ וְלֹא יִשְׁמְעוּ לְקוֹל אֲבִיהֶם כִּי־חָפֵץ יהוה לַהֲמִיתָם: וְהַנַּעַר
שְׁמוּאֵל הֹלֵךְ וְגָדֵל וָטוֹב גַּם עִם־יהוה וְגַם עִם־אֲנָשִׁים:
כז וַיָּבֹא אִישׁ־אֱלֹהִים אֶל־עֵלִי וַיֹּאמֶר אֵלָיו כֹּה אָמַר יהוה הֲנִגְלֹה נִגְלֵיתִי
כח אֶל־בֵּית אָבִיךָ בִּהְיוֹתָם בְּמִצְרַיִם לְבֵית פַּרְעֹה: וּבָחֹר אֹתוֹ מִכָּל־
שִׁבְטֵי יִשְׂרָאֵל לִי לְכֹהֵן לַעֲלוֹת עַל־מִזְבְּחִי לְהַקְטִיר קְטֹרֶת לָשֵׂאת
כט אֵפוֹד לְפָנָי וָאֶתְּנָה לְבֵית אָבִיךָ אֶת־כָּל־אִשֵּׁי בְּנֵי יִשְׂרָאֵל: לָמָּה
תִבְעֲטוּ בְּזִבְחִי וּבְמִנְחָתִי אֲשֶׁר צִוִּיתִי מָעוֹן וַתְּכַבֵּד אֶת־בָּנֶיךָ מִמֶּנִּי
ל לְהַבְרִיאֲכֶם מֵרֵאשִׁית כָּל־מִנְחַת יִשְׂרָאֵל לְעַמִּי: לָכֵן נְאֻם יהוה אֱלֹהֵי
יִשְׂרָאֵל אָמוֹר אָמַרְתִּי בֵּיתְךָ וּבֵית אָבִיךָ יִתְהַלְּכוּ לְפָנַי עַד־עוֹלָם
לא וְעַתָּה נְאֻם־יהוה חָלִילָה לִּי כִּי־מְכַבְּדַי אֲכַבֵּד וּבֹזַי יֵקָלּוּ: הִנֵּה יָמִים
בָּאִים וְגָדַעְתִּי אֶת־זְרֹעֲךָ וְאֶת־זְרֹעַ בֵּית אָבִיךָ מִהְיוֹת זָקֵן בְּבֵיתֶךָ:
לב וְהִבַּטְתָּ צַר מָעוֹן בְּכֹל אֲשֶׁר־יֵיטִיב אֶת־יִשְׂרָאֵל וְלֹא־יִהְיֶה זָקֵן בְּבֵיתְךָ
לג כָּל־הַיָּמִים: וְאִישׁ לֹא־אַכְרִית לְךָ מֵעִם מִזְבְּחִי לְכַלּוֹת אֶת־עֵינֶיךָ
לד וְלַאֲדִיב אֶת־נַפְשֶׁךָ וְכָל־מַרְבִּית בֵּיתְךָ יָמוּתוּ אֲנָשִׁים: וְזֶה־לְּךָ הָאוֹת
אֲשֶׁר יָבֹא אֶל־שְׁנֵי בָנֶיךָ אֶל־חָפְנִי וּפִינְחָס בְּיוֹם אֶחָד יָמוּתוּ שְׁנֵיהֶם:
לה וַהֲקִימֹתִי לִי כֹּהֵן נֶאֱמָן כַּאֲשֶׁר בִּלְבָבִי וּבְנַפְשִׁי יַעֲשֶׂה וּבָנִיתִי לוֹ בַּיִת
לו נֶאֱמָן וְהִתְהַלֵּךְ לִפְנֵי־מְשִׁיחִי כָּל־הַיָּמִים: וְהָיָה כָּל־הַנּוֹתָר בְּבֵיתְךָ
יָבוֹא לְהִשְׁתַּחֲוֺת לוֹ לַאֲגוֹרַת כֶּסֶף וְכִכַּר־לָחֶם וְאָמַר סְפָחֵנִי נָא אֶל־
ג א אַחַת הַכְּהֻנּוֹת לֶאֱכֹל פַּת־לָחֶם: וְהַנַּעַר שְׁמוּאֵל מְשָׁרֵת
אֶת־יהוה לִפְנֵי עֵלִי וּדְבַר יהוה הָיָה יָקָר בַּיָּמִים הָהֵם אֵין חָזוֹן נִפְרָץ:
ב וַיְהִי בַּיּוֹם הַהוּא וְעֵלִי שֹׁכֵב בִּמְקֹמוֹ וְעֵינָו הֵחֵלּוּ כֵהוֹת לֹא יוּכַל
ג לִרְאוֹת: וְנֵר אֱלֹהִים טֶרֶם יִכְבֶּה וּשְׁמוּאֵל שֹׁכֵב בְּהֵיכַל יהוה אֲשֶׁר־
ד שָׁם אֲרוֹן אֱלֹהִים: וַיִּקְרָא יהוה אֶל־שְׁמוּאֵל וַיֹּאמֶר הִנֵּנִי:
ה וַיָּרָץ אֶל־עֵלִי וַיֹּאמֶר הִנְנִי כִּי־קָרָאתָ לִּי וַיֹּאמֶר לֹא־קָרָאתִי שׁוּב שְׁכָב
ו וַיֵּלֶךְ וַיִּשְׁכָּב: וַיֹּסֶף יהוה קְרֹא עוֹד שְׁמוּאֵל וַיָּקָם שְׁמוּאֵל וַיֵּלֶךְ אֶל־

once more. Shmuel rose and went to Eli. "Here I am," he said, "for you called
7 me." "I did not call, my son," he said. "Go back to sleep." Shmuel did not yet
know the LORD; the word of the LORD had not yet been revealed to him.
8 And once again, the LORD called out to Shmuel – for the third time. He rose
and went to Eli. "Here I am," he said, "for you called me." And Eli realized
9 that the LORD was calling to the boy. "Go lie down," Eli said to Shmuel. "If
He calls out to you, say, 'Speak, O LORD, for Your servant is listening.'" So
10 Shmuel went and lay down in his place. The LORD came and stood there, and
called as before, "Shmuel, Shmuel." "Speak," Shmuel said, "for Your servant
11 is listening." The LORD said to Shmuel, "Now, whoever hears of the
12 deed I am about to do in Israel – why, both his ears will ring. On that day, I will
bring upon Eli all that I have warned of against his house, from beginning to
13 end. I shall tell him that I have sentenced his house forever, for he was aware
of a crime: his sons have been blasphemous, but he failed to rebuke them.
14 Therefore, I have sworn to the house of Eli that the crime of the house of Eli
15 shall never be expiated by sacrifice or offering." And Shmuel lay there until
morning, when he opened the doors of the LORD's house. Shmuel was afraid
16 to tell Eli about the vision, but Eli called Shmuel and said, "Shmuel, my son,"
17 and he replied, "Here I am." "Of what did He speak to you?" he asked. "Hide
nothing from me; so may God do to you – and more – if you hide any part of
18 all He told you." So Shmuel told him everything and hid nothing from him.
19 "He is the LORD," he said. "He will do as He sees fit." Shmuel grew up,
20 and the LORD was with him; He let none of his words go unfulfilled. And all
of Israel, from Dan until Be'er Sheva, knew that Shmuel was a faithful prophet
21 of the LORD. The LORD continued to appear at Shilo, for at Shilo the
4 1 LORD revealed the LORD's word to Shmuel. Shmuel's word became
the word of all Israel. Israel went out to war against the Philistines.
2 They encamped at Help Stone while the Philistines encamped at Afek. The
Philistines drew up their lines against Israel, and when battle erupted, Israel
was routed before the Philistines, who struck down about four thousand men
3 upon the battlefield. When the men reached the camp, the elders of Israel
said, "Why has the LORD routed us today before the Philistines? Let us take
the Ark of the LORD's Covenant with us from Shilo; when it comes among our
4 ranks, it will save us from the hands of our enemies." The men sent to Shilo
and carried out from there the Ark of the Covenant of the LORD of Hosts
Enthroned upon the Cherubim; from there the two sons of Eli, Ḥofni and
5 Pinḥas, accompanied the Ark of God's Covenant. When the Ark of the LORD's
Covenant arrived at the camp, all of Israel burst into a mighty roar, and the
6 earth resounded. The Philistines heard the roaring sound and said, "What is
that great roaring sound in the Hebrew camp?" When they learned that the

עֵלִי וַיֹּאמֶר הִנְנִי כִּי קָרָאתָ לִּי וַיֹּאמֶר לֹא־קָרָאתִי בְנִי שׁוּב שְׁכָב׃
ז ח וּשְׁמוּאֵל טֶרֶם יָדַע אֶת־יְהוָה וְטֶרֶם יִגָּלֶה אֵלָיו דְּבַר־יְהוָה׃ וַיֹּסֶף יְהוָה
קְרֹא־שְׁמוּאֵל בַּשְּׁלִשִׁית וַיָּקָם וַיֵּלֶךְ אֶל־עֵלִי וַיֹּאמֶר הִנְנִי כִּי קָרָאתָ
ט לִי וַיָּבֶן עֵלִי כִּי יְהוָה קֹרֵא לַנָּעַר׃ וַיֹּאמֶר עֵלִי לִשְׁמוּאֵל לֵךְ שְׁכָב וְהָיָה
אִם־יִקְרָא אֵלֶיךָ וְאָמַרְתָּ דַּבֵּר יְהוָה כִּי שֹׁמֵעַ עַבְדֶּךָ וַיֵּלֶךְ שְׁמוּאֵל
י וַיִּשְׁכַּב בִּמְקוֹמוֹ׃ וַיָּבֹא יְהוָה וַיִּתְיַצַּב וַיִּקְרָא כְפַעַם־בְּפַעַם שְׁמוּאֵל ׀
יא שְׁמוּאֵל וַיֹּאמֶר שְׁמוּאֵל דַּבֵּר כִּי שֹׁמֵעַ עַבְדֶּךָ׃ וַיֹּאמֶר
יְהוָה אֶל־שְׁמוּאֵל הִנֵּה אָנֹכִי עֹשֶׂה דָבָר בְּיִשְׂרָאֵל אֲשֶׁר כָּל־שֹׁמְעוֹ
יב תְּצִלֶּינָה שְׁתֵּי אָזְנָיו׃ בַּיּוֹם הַהוּא אָקִים אֶל־עֵלִי אֵת כָּל־אֲשֶׁר דִּבַּרְתִּי
יג אֶל־בֵּיתוֹ הָחֵל וְכַלֵּה׃ וְהִגַּדְתִּי לוֹ כִּי־שֹׁפֵט אֲנִי אֶת־בֵּיתוֹ עַד־עוֹלָם
יד בַּעֲוֹן אֲשֶׁר־יָדַע כִּי־מְקַלְלִים לָהֶם בָּנָיו וְלֹא כִהָה בָּם׃ וְלָכֵן נִשְׁבַּעְתִּי
טו לְבֵית עֵלִי אִם־יִתְכַּפֵּר עֲוֹן בֵּית־עֵלִי בְּזֶבַח וּבְמִנְחָה עַד־עוֹלָם׃ וַיִּשְׁכַּב
שְׁמוּאֵל עַד־הַבֹּקֶר וַיִּפְתַּח אֶת־דַּלְתוֹת בֵּית־יְהוָה וּשְׁמוּאֵל יָרֵא
טז מֵהַגִּיד אֶת־הַמַּרְאָה אֶל־עֵלִי׃ וַיִּקְרָא עֵלִי אֶת־שְׁמוּאֵל וַיֹּאמֶר שְׁמוּאֵל
יז בְּנִי וַיֹּאמֶר הִנֵּנִי׃ וַיֹּאמֶר מָה הַדָּבָר אֲשֶׁר דִּבֶּר אֵלֶיךָ אַל־נָא תְכַחֵד
מִמֶּנִּי כֹּה יַעֲשֶׂה־לְּךָ אֱלֹהִים וְכֹה יוֹסִיף אִם־תְּכַחֵד מִמֶּנִּי דָּבָר מִכָּל־
יח הַדָּבָר אֲשֶׁר־דִּבֶּר אֵלֶיךָ׃ וַיַּגֶּד־לוֹ שְׁמוּאֵל אֶת־כָּל־הַדְּבָרִים וְלֹא כִחֵד
יט מִמֶּנּוּ וַיֹּאמַר יְהוָה הוּא הַטּוֹב בְּעֵינָו יַעֲשֶׂה׃ וַיִּגְדַּל שְׁמוּאֵל
כ וַיהוָה הָיָה עִמּוֹ וְלֹא־הִפִּיל מִכָּל־דְּבָרָיו אָרְצָה׃ וַיֵּדַע כָּל־יִשְׂרָאֵל מִדָּן ג
כא וְעַד־בְּאֵר שָׁבַע כִּי נֶאֱמָן שְׁמוּאֵל לְנָבִיא לַיהוָה׃ וַיֹּסֶף
יְהוָה לְהֵרָאֹה בְשִׁלֹה כִּי־נִגְלָה יְהוָה אֶל־שְׁמוּאֵל בְּשִׁלוֹ בִּדְבַר
ד א יְהוָה׃ וַיְהִי דְבַר־שְׁמוּאֵל לְכָל־יִשְׂרָאֵל וַיֵּצֵא
יִשְׂרָאֵל לִקְרַאת פְּלִשְׁתִּים לַמִּלְחָמָה וַיַּחֲנוּ עַל־הָאֶבֶן הָעֵזֶר וּפְלִשְׁתִּים
ב חָנוּ בַאֲפֵק׃ וַיַּעַרְכוּ פְלִשְׁתִּים לִקְרַאת יִשְׂרָאֵל וַתִּטֹּשׁ הַמִּלְחָמָה וַיִּנָּגֶף
יִשְׂרָאֵל לִפְנֵי פְלִשְׁתִּים וַיַּכּוּ בַמַּעֲרָכָה בַּשָּׂדֶה כְּאַרְבַּעַת אֲלָפִים
ג אִישׁ׃ וַיָּבֹא הָעָם אֶל־הַמַּחֲנֶה וַיֹּאמְרוּ זִקְנֵי יִשְׂרָאֵל לָמָּה נְגָפָנוּ יְהוָה
הַיּוֹם לִפְנֵי פְלִשְׁתִּים נִקְחָה אֵלֵינוּ מִשִּׁלֹה אֶת־אֲרוֹן בְּרִית יְהוָה וְיָבֹא
ד בְקִרְבֵּנוּ וְיֹשִׁעֵנוּ מִכַּף אֹיְבֵינוּ׃ וַיִּשְׁלַח הָעָם שִׁלֹה וַיִּשְׂאוּ מִשָּׁם אֵת
אֲרוֹן בְּרִית־יְהוָה צְבָאוֹת יֹשֵׁב הַכְּרֻבִים וְשָׁם שְׁנֵי בְנֵי־עֵלִי עִם־אֲרוֹן
ה בְּרִית הָאֱלֹהִים חָפְנִי וּפִינְחָס׃ וַיְהִי כְּבוֹא אֲרוֹן בְּרִית־יְהוָה אֶל־
ו הַמַּחֲנֶה וַיָּרִעוּ כָל־יִשְׂרָאֵל תְּרוּעָה גְדוֹלָה וַתֵּהֹם הָאָרֶץ׃ וַיִּשְׁמְעוּ
פְלִשְׁתִּים אֶת־קוֹל הַתְּרוּעָה וַיֹּאמְרוּ מֶה קוֹל הַתְּרוּעָה הַגְּדוֹלָה

7 Ark of the Lord had come to the camp, the Philistines were frightened, for
they thought, "God has come to the camp." And they said, "Woe to us, for
8 this has never happened before! Woe to us! Who will save us from the hands
of these mighty gods – the very same gods who struck down Egypt with
9 every kind of plague in the wilderness! Muster your strength and be men,
Philistines, lest you become slaves to the Hebrews as they were slaves to you;
10 be men and fight!" And oh, the Philistines fought, and Israel was routed, and
11 every man fled back to his tent. The defeat was devastating; thirty thousand
foot soldiers of Israel fell. And the Ark of God was captured, and both of
12 Eli's sons died – Ḥofni and Pinḥas. A Benjaminite soldier ran from the battle
lines and reached Shilo that same day, his uniform torn and earth upon his
13 head.[8] He arrived and there was Eli, seated on a chair by the lookout road,
for his heart was trembling over the Ark of God. The man came to town to
14 announce the news, and the whole city cried out. When Eli heard the sound
of screaming, he asked, "What is that cacophony?" and the man rushed over
15 and broke the news to Eli. Eli was ninety-eight years old, and his eyes stared
16 out sightlessly. "I am the one who has come from the battle lines," the man said
to Eli. "I fled the battle lines just now." "What happened, my son?" he asked.
17 The news-bearer replied, "Israel has fled before the Philistines, and the men
were ravaged terribly. What is more, your two sons died – Ḥofni and Pinḥas –
18 and the Ark of God was taken." As soon as he mentioned the Ark of God, Eli
fell out of his chair backward by the gate post; his neck snapped and he died,
19 for the man was old and heavy. He had judged Israel for forty years. Now his
daughter-in-law, Pinḥas's wife, was about to give birth. When she heard the
news that God's Ark had been taken and that her father-in-law and husband
had died, she crouched down to give birth, for her birth pangs overwhelmed
20 her. As she lay dying, the women standing over her spoke to her. "Do not fear,
21 for you have given birth to a son." But she neither answered nor cared. And
she called the boy Ikhavod,[9] saying, "Glory is gone from Israel," referring to
22 the taking of the Ark of God, her father-in-law, and her husband. "Glory is
gone from Israel," she said, "for the Ark of God has been taken."
5 1 Meanwhile, the Philistines had taken the Ark of God and brought it from
2 Help Stone to Ashdod. The Philistines took hold of the Ark of God and
3 brought it into the temple of Dagon, placing it next to Dagon. But when the
men of Ashdod rose the next day, there lay Dagon, sprawled on the ground
before the Ark of the Lord. They took hold of Dagon and set him back in his
4 place. But when they rose the next morning, there lay Dagon, sprawled on
the ground before the Ark of the Lord – and Dagon's head and both his hands
5 had been chopped off on the threshold; only Dagon's torso was intact. That
is why to this day, the priests of Dagon or anyone who comes to Dagon's

8 | In mourning.
9 | Literally "no glory."

ז הַזֹּאת בְּמַחֲנֵה הָעִבְרִים וַיֵּדְעוּ כִּי אֲרוֹן יהוה בָּא אֶל־הַמַּחֲנֶה: וַיִּרְאוּ
הַפְּלִשְׁתִּים כִּי אָמְרוּ בָּא אֱלֹהִים אֶל־הַמַּחֲנֶה וַיֹּאמְרוּ אוֹי לָנוּ כִּי
ח לֹא הָיְתָה כָּזֹאת אֶתְמוֹל שִׁלְשֹׁם: אוֹי לָנוּ מִי יַצִּילֵנוּ מִיַּד הָאֱלֹהִים
הָאַדִּירִים הָאֵלֶּה אֵלֶּה הֵם הָאֱלֹהִים הַמַּכִּים אֶת־מִצְרַיִם בְּכָל־מַכָּה
ט בַּמִּדְבָּר: הִתְחַזְּקוּ וִהְיוּ לַאֲנָשִׁים פְּלִשְׁתִּים פֶּן תַּעַבְדוּ לָעִבְרִים כַּאֲשֶׁר
י עָבְדוּ לָכֶם וִהְיִיתֶם לַאֲנָשִׁים וְנִלְחַמְתֶּם: וַיִּלָּחֲמוּ פְלִשְׁתִּים וַיִּנָּגֶף
יִשְׂרָאֵל וַיָּנֻסוּ אִישׁ לְאֹהָלָיו וַתְּהִי הַמַּכָּה גְּדוֹלָה מְאֹד וַיִּפֹּל מִיִּשְׂרָאֵל
יא שְׁלֹשִׁים אֶלֶף רַגְלִי: וַאֲרוֹן אֱלֹהִים נִלְקָח וּשְׁנֵי בְנֵי־עֵלִי מֵתוּ חָפְנִי
יב וּפִינְחָס: וַיָּרָץ אִישׁ־בִּנְיָמִן מֵהַמַּעֲרָכָה וַיָּבֹא שִׁלֹה בַּיּוֹם הַהוּא וּמַדָּיו
יג קְרֻעִים וַאֲדָמָה עַל־רֹאשׁוֹ: וַיָּבוֹא וְהִנֵּה עֵלִי יֹשֵׁב עַל־הַכִּסֵּא יך דֶּרֶךְ יַד
מְצַפֶּה כִּי־הָיָה לִבּוֹ חָרֵד עַל אֲרוֹן הָאֱלֹהִים וְהָאִישׁ בָּא לְהַגִּיד בָּעִיר
יד וַתִּזְעַק כָּל־הָעִיר: וַיִּשְׁמַע עֵלִי אֶת־קוֹל הַצְּעָקָה וַיֹּאמֶר מֶה קוֹל
טו הֶהָמוֹן הַזֶּה וְהָאִישׁ מִהַר וַיָּבֹא וַיַּגֵּד לְעֵלִי: וְעֵלִי בֶּן־תִּשְׁעִים וּשְׁמֹנֶה
טז שָׁנָה וְעֵינָיו קָמָה וְלֹא יָכוֹל לִרְאוֹת: וַיֹּאמֶר הָאִישׁ אֶל־עֵלִי אָנֹכִי
הַבָּא מִן־הַמַּעֲרָכָה וַאֲנִי מִן־הַמַּעֲרָכָה נַסְתִּי הַיּוֹם וַיֹּאמֶר מֶה־הָיָה
יז הַדָּבָר בְּנִי: וַיַּעַן הַמְבַשֵּׂר וַיֹּאמֶר נָס יִשְׂרָאֵל לִפְנֵי פְלִשְׁתִּים וְגַם מַגֵּפָה
גְדוֹלָה הָיְתָה בָעָם וְגַם־שְׁנֵי בָנֶיךָ מֵתוּ חָפְנִי וּפִינְחָס וַאֲרוֹן הָאֱלֹהִים
יח נִלְקָחָה: וַיְהִי כְּהַזְכִּירוֹ ׀ אֶת־אֲרוֹן הָאֱלֹהִים וַיִּפֹּל מֵעַל־הַכִּסֵּא אֲחֹרַנִּית
בְּעַד ׀ יַד הַשַּׁעַר וַתִּשָּׁבֵר מַפְרַקְתּוֹ וַיָּמֹת כִּי־זָקֵן הָאִישׁ וְכָבֵד וְהוּא
יט שָׁפַט אֶת־יִשְׂרָאֵל אַרְבָּעִים שָׁנָה: וְכַלָּתוֹ אֵשֶׁת־פִּינְחָס הָרָה לָלַת
וַתִּשְׁמַע אֶת־הַשְּׁמֻעָה אֶל־הִלָּקַח אֲרוֹן הָאֱלֹהִים וּמֵת חָמִיהָ וְאִישָׁהּ
כ וַתִּכְרַע וַתֵּלֶד כִּי־נֶהֶפְכוּ עָלֶיהָ צִרֶיהָ: וּכְעֵת מוּתָהּ וַתְּדַבֵּרְנָה הַנִּצָּבוֹת
כא עָלֶיהָ אַל־תִּירְאִי כִּי־בֵן יָלָדְתְּ וְלֹא עָנְתָה וְלֹא־שָׁתָה לִבָּהּ: וַתִּקְרָא
לַנַּעַר אִי כָבוֹד לֵאמֹר גָּלָה כָבוֹד מִיִּשְׂרָאֵל אֶל־הִלָּקַח אֲרוֹן הָאֱלֹהִים
כב וְאֶל־חָמִיהָ וְאִישָׁהּ: וַתֹּאמֶר גָּלָה כָבוֹד מִיִּשְׂרָאֵל כִּי נִלְקַח אֲרוֹן
הָאֱלֹהִים:

ה א וּפְלִשְׁתִּים לָקְחוּ אֵת אֲרוֹן הָאֱלֹהִים וַיְבִאֻהוּ מֵאֶבֶן הָעֶזֶר אַשְׁדּוֹדָה:
ב וַיִּקְחוּ פְלִשְׁתִּים אֶת־אֲרוֹן הָאֱלֹהִים וַיָּבִיאוּ אֹתוֹ בֵּית דָּגוֹן וַיַּצִּיגוּ אֹתוֹ
ג אֵצֶל דָּגוֹן: וַיַּשְׁכִּמוּ אַשְׁדּוֹדִים מִמָּחֳרָת וְהִנֵּה דָגוֹן נֹפֵל לְפָנָיו אַרְצָה
ד לִפְנֵי אֲרוֹן יהוה וַיִּקְחוּ אֶת־דָּגוֹן וַיָּשִׁבוּ אֹתוֹ לִמְקוֹמוֹ: וַיַּשְׁכִּמוּ בַבֹּקֶר
מִמָּחֳרָת וְהִנֵּה דָגוֹן נֹפֵל לְפָנָיו אַרְצָה לִפְנֵי אֲרוֹן יהוה וְרֹאשׁ דָּגוֹן
ה וּשְׁתֵּי ׀ כַּפּוֹת יָדָיו כְּרֻתוֹת אֶל־הַמִּפְתָּן רַק דָּגוֹן נִשְׁאַר עָלָיו: עַל־כֵּן

6 temple will not tread upon the threshold of Dagon in Ashdod. The
hand of the LORD bore heavily against the Ashdodites, and He devastated
7 them, plaguing Ashdod and its territories with hemorrhoids. When the
people of Ashdod saw it was so, they said, "The Ark of Israel's God must not
remain among us, for His hand is harsh against us and against our god Dagon."
8 So they sent and summoned all the Philistine chieftains to them, asking,
"What shall we do about the Ark of Israel's God?" "Let the Ark of Israel's God
be removed to Gat," they determined. So they relocated the Ark of Israel's
9 God. Once they had removed it, the LORD's hand caused a mortifying panic
in the city, plaguing the people of the city – young and old – with hemorrhoids
10 bursting open on them. So they sent the Ark of God on to Ekron, but as soon
as the Ark of God reached Ekron, the Ekronites cried out in protest, "They
11 have removed the Ark of Israel's God to us to kill us and our people." And
they sent and summoned all the Philistine chieftains and said to them, "Send
the Ark of Israel's God back to its place so that it will not kill me and my
people." For a deadly panic had seized the city, God's hand bore down so
12 heavily there. The people who had not died were plagued with hemorrhoids,
6 1 and the shrieks of the city flared up to the heavens. The Ark of
2 the LORD had remained in Philistine territory for seven months when the
Philistines summoned the priests and diviners, asking them, "What shall we
do with the Ark of the LORD? Tell us, how should we send it back to its
3 place?" "If you are sending the Ark of Israel's God back," they said, "do not
send it empty-handed; be sure to recompense Him with a guilt offering. Only
then will you be cured – when you acknowledge why He would not turn His
4 hand away from you." "With what guilt offering shall we compensate him?"
they replied. "Five, according to the number of Philistine chieftains," they
said, "five golden hemorrhoids and five golden mice, for one plague befell all
5 of you and your chieftains. Make images of your hemorrhoids and those mice
of yours that are ravaging the land, and give honor to the God of Israel;
perhaps then He will lighten His hand from upon you, your gods, and your
6 land. Why should you harden your hearts, as Egypt and Pharaoh hardened
their hearts; after all, when He dealt harshly with them, did they not send
7 them off to go free? Now prepare a new cart and two nursing cows that have
never borne a yoke. Hitch the cows to the cart, but bring their calves back
8 inside behind them. Then take the Ark of the LORD, place it on the cart, and
put the gold objects that you are paying Him as compensation in a saddlebag
9 beside it. Send it off and let it go. Then watch: if it makes its way up to its own
territory, to Beit Shemesh, then it was He who inflicted this great evil upon
us; but if not, we shall know that it was not His hand that afflicted us; what
10 befell us was mere chance." And so the men did; they took two nursing cows,

לֹא־יִדְרְכוּ כֹהֲנֵי דָגוֹן וְכָל־הַבָּאִים בֵּית־דָּגוֹן עַל־מִפְתַּן דָּגוֹן בְּאַשְׁדּוֹד
ו עַד הַיּוֹם הַזֶּה: וַתִּכְבַּד יַד־יְהוָה אֶל־הָאַשְׁדּוֹדִים וַיְשִׁמֵּם וַיַּךְ
ז אֹתָם בעפלים אֶת־אַשְׁדּוֹד וְאֶת־גְּבוּלֶיהָ: וַיִּרְאוּ אַנְשֵׁי־אַשְׁדּוֹד כִּי־כֵן בַּטְּחֹרִים
וְאָמְרוּ לֹא־יֵשֵׁב אֲרוֹן אֱלֹהֵי יִשְׂרָאֵל עִמָּנוּ כִּי־קָשְׁתָה יָדוֹ עָלֵינוּ וְעַל
ח דָּגוֹן אֱלֹהֵינוּ: וַיִּשְׁלְחוּ וַיַּאַסְפוּ אֶת־כָּל־סַרְנֵי פְלִשְׁתִּים אֲלֵיהֶם וַיֹּאמְרוּ
מַה־נַּעֲשֶׂה לַאֲרוֹן אֱלֹהֵי יִשְׂרָאֵל וַיֹּאמְרוּ גַּת יִסֹּב אֲרוֹן אֱלֹהֵי יִשְׂרָאֵל
ט וַיַּסֵּבּוּ אֶת־אֲרוֹן אֱלֹהֵי יִשְׂרָאֵל: וַיְהִי אַחֲרֵי ׀ הֵסַבּוּ אֹתוֹ וַתְּהִי יַד־יְהוָה
בָּעִיר מְהוּמָה גְּדוֹלָה מְאֹד וַיַּךְ אֶת־אַנְשֵׁי הָעִיר מִקָּטֹן וְעַד־גָּדוֹל
י וַיִּשָּׂתְרוּ לָהֶם עפלים: וַיְשַׁלְּחוּ אֶת־אֲרוֹן הָאֱלֹהִים עֶקְרוֹן וַיְהִי כְּבוֹא טְחֹרִים
אֲרוֹן הָאֱלֹהִים עֶקְרוֹן וַיִּזְעֲקוּ הָעֶקְרֹנִים לֵאמֹר הֵסַבּוּ אֵלַי אֶת־אֲרוֹן
יא אֱלֹהֵי יִשְׂרָאֵל לַהֲמִיתֵנִי וְאֶת־עַמִּי: וַיִּשְׁלְחוּ וַיַּאַסְפוּ אֶת־כָּל־סַרְנֵי
פְלִשְׁתִּים וַיֹּאמְרוּ שַׁלְּחוּ אֶת־אֲרוֹן אֱלֹהֵי יִשְׂרָאֵל וְיָשֹׁב לִמְקֹמוֹ וְלֹא־
יָמִית אֹתִי וְאֶת־עַמִּי כִּי־הָיְתָה מְהוּמַת־מָוֶת בְּכָל־הָעִיר כָּבְדָה מְאֹד
יב יַד הָאֱלֹהִים שָׁם: וְהָאֲנָשִׁים אֲשֶׁר לֹא־מֵתוּ הֻכּוּ בעפלים וַתַּעַל שַׁוְעַת בַּטְּחֹרִים
ו א הָעִיר הַשָּׁמָיִם: וַיְהִי אֲרוֹן־יְהוָה בִּשְׂדֵה פְלִשְׁתִּים שִׁבְעָה
ב חֳדָשִׁים: וַיִּקְרְאוּ פְלִשְׁתִּים לַכֹּהֲנִים וְלַקֹּסְמִים לֵאמֹר מַה־נַּעֲשֶׂה לַאֲרוֹן
ג יְהוָה הוֹדִעֻנוּ בַּמֶּה נְשַׁלְּחֶנּוּ לִמְקוֹמוֹ: וַיֹּאמְרוּ אִם־מְשַׁלְּחִים אֶת־
אֲרוֹן אֱלֹהֵי יִשְׂרָאֵל אַל־תְּשַׁלְּחוּ אֹתוֹ רֵיקָם כִּי־הָשֵׁב תָּשִׁיבוּ לוֹ אָשָׁם
ד אָז תֵּרָפְאוּ וְנוֹדַע לָכֶם לָמָּה לֹא־תָסוּר יָדוֹ מִכֶּם: וַיֹּאמְרוּ מָה הָאָשָׁם
אֲשֶׁר נָשִׁיב לוֹ וַיֹּאמְרוּ מִסְפַּר סַרְנֵי פְלִשְׁתִּים חֲמִשָּׁה עפלי זָהָב טְחֹרֵי
ה וַחֲמִשָּׁה עַכְבְּרֵי זָהָב כִּי־מַגֵּפָה אַחַת לְכֻלָּם וּלְסַרְנֵיכֶם: וַעֲשִׂיתֶם צַלְמֵי
עפליכם וְצַלְמֵי עַכְבְּרֵיכֶם הַמַּשְׁחִיתִם אֶת־הָאָרֶץ וּנְתַתֶּם לֵאלֹהֵי טְחֹרֵיכֶם
יִשְׂרָאֵל כָּבוֹד אוּלַי יָקֵל אֶת־יָדוֹ מֵעֲלֵיכֶם וּמֵעַל אֱלֹהֵיכֶם וּמֵעַל
ו אַרְצְכֶם: וְלָמָּה תְכַבְּדוּ אֶת־לְבַבְכֶם כַּאֲשֶׁר כִּבְּדוּ מִצְרַיִם וּפַרְעֹה
ז אֶת־לִבָּם הֲלוֹא כַּאֲשֶׁר הִתְעַלֵּל בָּהֶם וַיְשַׁלְּחוּם וַיֵּלֵכוּ: וְעַתָּה קְחוּ
וַעֲשׂוּ עֲגָלָה חֲדָשָׁה אֶחָת וּשְׁתֵּי פָרוֹת עָלוֹת אֲשֶׁר לֹא־עָלָה עֲלֵיהֶם
עֹל וַאֲסַרְתֶּם אֶת־הַפָּרוֹת בָּעֲגָלָה וַהֲשֵׁיבֹתֶם בְּנֵיהֶם מֵאַחֲרֵיהֶם
ח הַבָּיְתָה: וּלְקַחְתֶּם אֶת־אֲרוֹן יְהוָה וּנְתַתֶּם אֹתוֹ אֶל־הָעֲגָלָה וְאֵת ׀
כְּלֵי הַזָּהָב אֲשֶׁר הֲשֵׁבֹתֶם לוֹ אָשָׁם תָּשִׂימוּ בָאַרְגַּז מִצִּדּוֹ וְשִׁלַּחְתֶּם
ט אֹתוֹ וְהָלָךְ: וּרְאִיתֶם אִם־דֶּרֶךְ גְּבוּלוֹ יַעֲלֶה בֵּית שֶׁמֶשׁ הוּא עָשָׂה
לָנוּ אֶת־הָרָעָה הַגְּדוֹלָה הַזֹּאת וְאִם־לֹא וְיָדַעְנוּ כִּי לֹא יָדוֹ נָגְעָה בָּנוּ
י מִקְרֶה הוּא הָיָה לָנוּ: וַיַּעֲשׂוּ הָאֲנָשִׁים כֵּן וַיִּקְחוּ שְׁתֵּי פָרוֹת עָלוֹת

11 hitched them to a cart, and shut their calves up indoors. Then they placed the
Ark of the LORD onto the cart, along with the saddlebag, the golden mice,
12 and the images of their hemorrhoids. The cows made their way straight to the
Beit Shemesh road and walked along that one highway; though they lowed
as they went, they veered neither right nor left, and the Philistine chieftains
13 followed them until the Beit Shemesh border. At Beit Shemesh, they were
reaping the wheat harvest in the valley. When they looked up and noticed the
14 Ark, they rejoiced at the sight. The cart reached the field of Yehoshua the Beit
Shemeshite and came to a halt there, where there was an enormous stone.
They split the wood of the cart to offer the cows as a burnt offering to the
15 LORD. The Levites had unloaded the Ark of the LORD and the
saddlebag containing the golden objects and placed them on the enormous
stone. Then the people of Beit Shemesh offered up burnt offerings and made
16 sacrifices to the LORD on that day. The five Philistine chieftains watched, then
17 returned to Ekron that same day. These are the golden hemorrhoids
that the Philistines paid as compensation to the LORD: one for Ashdod, one
18 for Aza, one for Ashkelon, one for Gat, and one for Ekron, while the
golden mice represented the number of all the Philistine towns belonging to
the chieftains, from the fortified cities to the open hamlets. And to this day,
the enormous stone where they placed the Ark of the LORD remains in the
19 field of Yehoshua the Beit Shemeshite. But He struck down the people of Beit
Shemesh, for they had looked upon the Ark of the LORD – He struck down
seventy as well as fifty thousand of the people. And the people mourned, for
20 the LORD had struck the people a grave blow. "Who can stand before the
LORD, this holy God," said the people of Beit Shemesh, "and to whom will it
21 depart from us?" They sent messengers to the inhabitants of Kiryat Ye'arim,
saying, "The Philistines have returned the Ark of the LORD; come down and
7 1 bring it up to you." So the men of Kiryat Ye'arim came and brought up the
Ark of the LORD. They conveyed it to the house of Avinadav on the hill and
2 appointed his son Elazar to guard the Ark of the LORD. From the
time the Ark came to dwell in Kiryat Ye'arim, the days slipped by into twenty
3 years, and all the House of Israel yearned for the LORD. Shmuel said
to all the House of Israel, "If you mean to return to the LORD with all your
heart, then remove the alien gods from among you, along with the Ashtarot,
and direct your hearts to the LORD, and serve Him alone; then He will save
4 you from the hand of the Philistines." So the Israelites removed the Baalim
5 and the Ashtarot and served the LORD alone. Then Shmuel said,
"Assemble all of Israel at Mitzpa, and I will pray to the LORD on your behalf."
6 They assembled at Mitzpa and drew water and poured it out before the LORD.
On that day they fasted, declaring there, "We have sinned against the LORD,"

יא וַיַּאַסְרוּם בָּעֲגָלָה וְאֶת־בְּנֵיהֶם כָּלוּ בַבָּיִת: וַיָּשִׂמוּ אֶת־אֲרוֹן יְהוָה אֶל־
יב הָעֲגָלָה וְאֵת הָאַרְגַּז וְאֵת עַכְבְּרֵי הַזָּהָב וְאֵת צַלְמֵי טְחֹרֵיהֶם: וַיִּשַּׁרְנָה
הַפָּרוֹת בַּדֶּרֶךְ עַל־דֶּרֶךְ בֵּית שֶׁמֶשׁ בִּמְסִלָּה אַחַת הָלְכוּ הָלֹךְ וְגָעוֹ
וְלֹא־סָרוּ יָמִין וּשְׂמֹאול וְסַרְנֵי פְלִשְׁתִּים הֹלְכִים אַחֲרֵיהֶם עַד־גְּבוּל
יג בֵּית שָׁמֶשׁ: וּבֵית שֶׁמֶשׁ קֹצְרִים קְצִיר־חִטִּים בָּעֵמֶק וַיִּשְׂאוּ אֶת־
יד עֵינֵיהֶם וַיִּרְאוּ אֶת־הָאָרוֹן וַיִּשְׂמְחוּ לִרְאוֹת: וְהָעֲגָלָה בָּאָה אֶל־שְׂדֵה ד
יְהוֹשֻׁעַ בֵּית־הַשִּׁמְשִׁי וַתַּעֲמֹד שָׁם וְשָׁם אֶבֶן גְּדוֹלָה וַיְבַקְּעוּ אֶת־עֲצֵי
טו הָעֲגָלָה וְאֶת־הַפָּרוֹת הֶעֱלוּ עֹלָה לַיהוָה: וְהַלְוִיִּם
הוֹרִידוּ | אֶת־אֲרוֹן יְהוָה וְאֶת־הָאַרְגַּז אֲשֶׁר־אִתּוֹ אֲשֶׁר־בּוֹ כְלֵי־זָהָב
וַיָּשִׂמוּ אֶל־הָאֶבֶן הַגְּדוֹלָה וְאַנְשֵׁי בֵית־שֶׁמֶשׁ הֶעֱלוּ עֹלוֹת וַיִּזְבְּחוּ
טז זְבָחִים בַּיּוֹם הַהוּא לַיהוָה: וַחֲמִשָּׁה סַרְנֵי־פְלִשְׁתִּים רָאוּ וַיָּשֻׁבוּ עֶקְרוֹן
יז בַּיּוֹם הַהוּא: וְאֵלֶּה טְחֹרֵי הַזָּהָב אֲשֶׁר הֵשִׁיבוּ פְלִשְׁתִּים אָשָׁם
לַיהוָה לְאַשְׁדּוֹד אֶחָד לְעַזָּה אֶחָד לְאַשְׁקְלוֹן אֶחָד לְגַת אֶחָד לְעֶקְרוֹן
יח אֶחָד: וְעַכְבְּרֵי הַזָּהָב מִסְפַּר כָּל־עָרֵי פְלִשְׁתִּים לַחֲמֵשֶׁת
הַסְּרָנִים מֵעִיר מִבְצָר וְעַד כֹּפֶר הַפְּרָזִי וְעַד | אָבֵל הַגְּדוֹלָה אֲשֶׁר הִנִּיחוּ
יט עָלֶיהָ אֵת אֲרוֹן יְהוָה עַד הַיּוֹם הַזֶּה בִּשְׂדֵה יְהוֹשֻׁעַ בֵּית־הַשִּׁמְשִׁי: וַיַּךְ
בְּאַנְשֵׁי בֵית־שֶׁמֶשׁ כִּי רָאוּ בַּאֲרוֹן יְהוָה וַיַּךְ בָּעָם שִׁבְעִים אִישׁ חֲמִשִּׁים
כ אֶלֶף אִישׁ וַיִּתְאַבְּלוּ הָעָם כִּי־הִכָּה יְהוָה בָּעָם מַכָּה גְדוֹלָה: וַיֹּאמְרוּ
אַנְשֵׁי בֵית־שֶׁמֶשׁ מִי יוּכַל לַעֲמֹד לִפְנֵי יְהוָה הָאֱלֹהִים הַקָּדוֹשׁ הַזֶּה
כא וְאֶל־מִי יַעֲלֶה מֵעָלֵינוּ: וַיִּשְׁלְחוּ מַלְאָכִים אֶל־יוֹשְׁבֵי קִרְיַת־יְעָרִים
ז א לֵאמֹר הֵשִׁבוּ פְלִשְׁתִּים אֶת־אֲרוֹן יְהוָה רְדוּ הַעֲלוּ אֹתוֹ אֲלֵיכֶם: וַיָּבֹאוּ
אַנְשֵׁי | קִרְיַת יְעָרִים וַיַּעֲלוּ אֶת־אֲרוֹן יְהוָה וַיָּבִאוּ אֹתוֹ אֶל־בֵּית אֲבִינָדָב
ב בַּגִּבְעָה וְאֶת־אֶלְעָזָר בְּנוֹ קִדְּשׁוּ לִשְׁמֹר אֶת־אֲרוֹן יְהוָה: וַיְהִי
מִיּוֹם שֶׁבֶת הָאָרוֹן בְּקִרְיַת יְעָרִים וַיִּרְבּוּ הַיָּמִים וַיִּהְיוּ עֶשְׂרִים שָׁנָה
ג וַיִּנָּהוּ כָּל־בֵּית יִשְׂרָאֵל אַחֲרֵי יְהוָה: וַיֹּאמֶר שְׁמוּאֵל אֶל־כָּל־
בֵּית יִשְׂרָאֵל לֵאמֹר אִם־בְּכָל־לְבַבְכֶם אַתֶּם שָׁבִים אֶל־יְהוָה הָסִירוּ
אֶת־אֱלֹהֵי הַנֵּכָר מִתּוֹכְכֶם וְהָעַשְׁתָּרוֹת וְהָכִינוּ לְבַבְכֶם אֶל־יְהוָה
ד וְעִבְדֻהוּ לְבַדּוֹ וְיַצֵּל אֶתְכֶם מִיַּד פְּלִשְׁתִּים: וַיָּסִירוּ בְּנֵי יִשְׂרָאֵל אֶת־
ה הַבְּעָלִים וְאֶת־הָעַשְׁתָּרֹת וַיַּעַבְדוּ אֶת־יְהוָה לְבַדּוֹ: וַיֹּאמֶר
שְׁמוּאֵל קִבְצוּ אֶת־כָּל־יִשְׂרָאֵל הַמִּצְפָּתָה וְאֶתְפַּלֵּל בַּעַדְכֶם אֶל־יְהוָה:
ו וַיִּקָּבְצוּ הַמִּצְפָּתָה וַיִּשְׁאֲבוּ־מַיִם וַיִּשְׁפְּכוּ | לִפְנֵי יְהוָה וַיָּצוּמוּ בַּיּוֹם
הַהוּא וַיֹּאמְרוּ שָׁם חָטָאנוּ לַיהוָה וַיִּשְׁפֹּט שְׁמוּאֵל אֶת־בְּנֵי יִשְׂרָאֵל

7 and Shmuel judged the Israelites at Mitzpa. When the Philistines heard that
the Israelites had gathered at Mitzpa, the Philistine chieftains marched up
toward Israel. And when the Israelites heard, they were frightened of the
8 Philistines, and the Israelites said to Shmuel, "Do not be deaf and dumb to
us, not crying out to the LORD our God – let Him save us from the hand of
9 the Philistines!" Shmuel took a suckling lamb and offered it up as a whole
burnt offering to the LORD. And Shmuel cried out to the LORD for Israel's
10 sake, and the LORD answered him. For just as Shmuel was offering up the
burnt offering, and the Philistines advanced to attack Israel, the LORD
thundered with a mighty voice against the Philistines at that moment,
11 throwing them into a panic, and they were routed before Israel. The men of
Israel charged out of Mitzpa and chased the Philistines, striking them down
12 as far as below Beit Kar. And Shmuel took a single stone and placed it between
Mitzpa and Shen, naming it Help Stone: "For thus far," he said, "the LORD
13 has helped us." The Philistines were crushed and no longer ventured into
Israel's territory, and the LORD's hand bore down against the Philistines for
14 the rest of Shmuel's life. And the cities that the Philistines had seized from
Israel, from Ekron to Gat, were restored to Israel; Israel recovered their
territory from Philistine control, and there was peace between Israel and the
15 16 Amorites. Shmuel judged Israel all the days of his life. Year after year, he would
make his rounds from Beit El to Gilgal to Mitzpa, judging Israel in all those
17 places before returning to Rama; for there was his home, and there he judged
Israel, and there he built an altar to the LORD.
8 1 2 When Shmuel grew old, he appointed his sons to be Israel's judges. The name
of his elder son was Yoel, and the name of his second was Aviya; they were
3 judges in Be'er Sheva. But his sons did not follow his path; they were bent on
4 gain, and they took bribes, and they bent justice. All the elders of
5 Israel gathered and came to Shmuel at Rama. "Look, you have grown old,"
they said to him, "and your sons have not followed in your path. Now appoint
6 a king for us to govern us like any other nation." When they said, "Give us a
king to govern us," the idea displeased Shmuel, and Shmuel prayed to the
7 LORD. The LORD said to Shmuel, "Heed the voice of the people in
all they say to you. For it is not you they have rejected – it is Me they have
8 rejected, from reigning over them. All the deeds they have done since the day
I brought them up from Egypt to this day – forsaking Me and serving other
9 gods – they are doing to you as well. So now, heed their voice; but you must
solemnly warn them, informing them of the royal rights of the king who will
10 reign over them." Shmuel relayed all the words of the LORD to the
11 people who were asking him for a king. "These will be the royal

ז בַּמִּצְפָּה: וַיִּשְׁמְעוּ פְלִשְׁתִּים כִּי־הִתְקַבְּצוּ בְנֵי־יִשְׂרָאֵל הַמִּצְפָּתָה וַיַּעֲלוּ
סַרְנֵי־פְלִשְׁתִּים אֶל־יִשְׂרָאֵל וַיִּשְׁמְעוּ בְּנֵי יִשְׂרָאֵל וַיִּרְאוּ מִפְּנֵי פְּלִשְׁתִּים:
ח וַיֹּאמְרוּ בְנֵי־יִשְׂרָאֵל אֶל־שְׁמוּאֵל אַל־תַּחֲרֵשׁ מִמֶּנּוּ מִזְּעֹק אֶל־יְהוָה
ט אֱלֹהֵינוּ וְיֹשִׁעֵנוּ מִיַּד פְּלִשְׁתִּים: וַיִּקַּח שְׁמוּאֵל טְלֵה חָלָב אֶחָד וַיַּעֲלֵה
עוֹלָה כָּלִיל לַיהוָה וַיִּזְעַק שְׁמוּאֵל אֶל־יְהוָה בְּעַד יִשְׂרָאֵל וַיַּעֲנֵהוּ
י יְהוָה: וַיְהִי שְׁמוּאֵל מַעֲלֶה הָעוֹלָה וּפְלִשְׁתִּים נִגְּשׁוּ לַמִּלְחָמָה בְּיִשְׂרָאֵל
וַיַּרְעֵם יְהוָה ׀ בְּקוֹל־גָּדוֹל בַּיּוֹם הַהוּא עַל־פְּלִשְׁתִּים וַיְהֻמֵּם וַיִּנָּגְפוּ
יא לִפְנֵי יִשְׂרָאֵל: וַיֵּצְאוּ אַנְשֵׁי יִשְׂרָאֵל מִן־הַמִּצְפָּה וַיִּרְדְּפוּ אֶת־פְּלִשְׁתִּים
יב וַיַּכּוּם עַד־מִתַּחַת לְבֵית כָּר: וַיִּקַּח שְׁמוּאֵל אֶבֶן אַחַת וַיָּשֶׂם בֵּין־
הַמִּצְפָּה וּבֵין הַשֵּׁן וַיִּקְרָא אֶת־שְׁמָהּ אֶבֶן הָעָזֶר וַיֹּאמַר עַד־הֵנָּה עֲזָרָנוּ
יג יְהוָה: וַיִּכָּנְעוּ הַפְּלִשְׁתִּים וְלֹא־יָסְפוּ עוֹד לָבוֹא בִּגְבוּל יִשְׂרָאֵל וַתְּהִי
יד יַד־יְהוָה בַּפְּלִשְׁתִּים כֹּל יְמֵי שְׁמוּאֵל: וַתָּשֹׁבְנָה הֶעָרִים אֲשֶׁר לָקְחוּ־
פְלִשְׁתִּים מֵאֵת יִשְׂרָאֵל ׀ לְיִשְׂרָאֵל מֵעֶקְרוֹן וְעַד־גַּת וְאֶת־גְּבוּלָן הִצִּיל
טו יִשְׂרָאֵל מִיַּד פְּלִשְׁתִּים וַיְהִי שָׁלוֹם בֵּין יִשְׂרָאֵל וּבֵין הָאֱמֹרִי: וַיִּשְׁפֹּט
טז שְׁמוּאֵל אֶת־יִשְׂרָאֵל כֹּל יְמֵי חַיָּיו: וְהָלַךְ מִדֵּי שָׁנָה בְּשָׁנָה וְסָבַב בֵּית־
אֵל וְהַגִּלְגָּל וְהַמִּצְפָּה וְשָׁפַט אֶת־יִשְׂרָאֵל אֵת כָּל־הַמְּקוֹמוֹת הָאֵלֶּה:
יז וּתְשֻׁבָתוֹ הָרָמָתָה כִּי־שָׁם בֵּיתוֹ וְשָׁם שָׁפָט אֶת־יִשְׂרָאֵל וַיִּבֶן־שָׁם
מִזְבֵּחַ לַיהוָה:
ח א ב וַיְהִי כַּאֲשֶׁר זָקֵן שְׁמוּאֵל וַיָּשֶׂם אֶת־בָּנָיו שֹׁפְטִים לְיִשְׂרָאֵל: וַיְהִי
שֶׁם־בְּנוֹ הַבְּכוֹר יוֹאֵל וְשֵׁם מִשְׁנֵהוּ אֲבִיָּה שֹׁפְטִים בִּבְאֵר שָׁבַע:
ג וְלֹא־הָלְכוּ בָנָיו בִּדְרָכָו וַיִּטּוּ אַחֲרֵי הַבָּצַע וַיִּקְחוּ־שֹׁחַד וַיַּטּוּ
ד מִשְׁפָּט: וַיִּתְקַבְּצוּ כֹּל זִקְנֵי יִשְׂרָאֵל וַיָּבֹאוּ אֶל־שְׁמוּאֵל
ה הָרָמָתָה: וַיֹּאמְרוּ אֵלָיו הִנֵּה אַתָּה זָקַנְתָּ וּבָנֶיךָ לֹא הָלְכוּ בִּדְרָכֶיךָ
ו עַתָּה שִׂימָה־לָּנוּ מֶלֶךְ לְשָׁפְטֵנוּ כְּכָל־הַגּוֹיִם: וַיֵּרַע הַדָּבָר בְּעֵינֵי
שְׁמוּאֵל כַּאֲשֶׁר אָמְרוּ תְּנָה־לָּנוּ מֶלֶךְ לְשָׁפְטֵנוּ וַיִּתְפַּלֵּל שְׁמוּאֵל אֶל־
ז יְהוָה: וַיֹּאמֶר יְהוָה אֶל־שְׁמוּאֵל שְׁמַע בְּקוֹל הָעָם לְכֹל
אֲשֶׁר־יֹאמְרוּ אֵלֶיךָ כִּי לֹא אֹתְךָ מָאָסוּ כִּי־אֹתִי מָאֲסוּ מִמְּלֹךְ עֲלֵיהֶם:
ח כְּכָל־הַמַּעֲשִׂים אֲשֶׁר־עָשׂוּ מִיּוֹם הַעֲלֹתִי אֹתָם מִמִּצְרַיִם וְעַד־הַיּוֹם
ט הַזֶּה וַיַּעַזְבֻנִי וַיַּעַבְדוּ אֱלֹהִים אֲחֵרִים כֵּן הֵמָּה עֹשִׂים גַּם־לָךְ: וְעַתָּה
שְׁמַע בְּקוֹלָם אַךְ כִּי־הָעֵד תָּעִיד בָּהֶם וְהִגַּדְתָּ לָהֶם מִשְׁפַּט הַמֶּלֶךְ
י אֲשֶׁר יִמְלֹךְ עֲלֵיהֶם: וַיֹּאמֶר שְׁמוּאֵל אֵת כָּל־דִּבְרֵי יְהוָה
יא אֶל־הָעָם הַשֹּׁאֲלִים מֵאִתּוֹ מֶלֶךְ: וַיֹּאמֶר זֶה יִהְיֶה מִשְׁפַּט

rights of the king who will reign over you," he said. "He will seize your sons
12 and assign them as his charioteers and riders to run before his chariot; and
assign them as his officers of thousands and his officers of fifty, and to till his
soil, and reap his harvest, and to manufacture his weapons and his chariots.
13 14 He will seize your daughters as perfumers and cooks and bakers. He will seize
15 your best fields, vineyards, and olive groves and give them to his servants. He
will tithe your seeds and vineyards and give them to his officials and his staff.
16 He will seize your best servants, maidservants, and young workers, and your
17 donkeys, and he will use them for his own work. He will tithe your flocks,
18 and you yourselves shall become his slaves. And on that day, you will cry out
because of your own king, whom you yourselves chose, but the LORD will
19 not answer you on that day." But the people refused to heed the voice of
20 Shmuel. "No," they declared, "we must have a king over us, so we, too, will be
like all the other nations. Our king shall govern us and go out before us and
21 fight our battles." So Shmuel heeded all the words of the people and repeated
22 them before the LORD. And the LORD replied to Shmuel, "Heed
their voice and appoint a king over them." Shmuel then said to the men of
9 1 Israel, "Go back, each to his own town." There was a man of Binyamin
whose name was Kish son of Aviel son of Tzeror son of Bekhorat son of Afiaḥ;
2 a Benjaminite, he was a powerful man. He had a son whose name was Sha'ul.
He was a fine young man, and no one in Israel was finer than he; he was head
3 and shoulders above everyone else. Once, some donkeys belonging to Kish,
Sha'ul's father, went missing, and Kish said to Sha'ul, his son, "Now, take one
4 of the stewards and go out to search for the donkeys." So he traveled through
the Efrayim hills and crossed through the Shalisha region, but they did not
find them; they crossed through the Shaalim region, but nothing; and they
5 crossed through the territory of Binyamin, but they did not find them. As
they reached the Zuf region, Sha'ul said to the steward with him, "Come, let
us go back, or my father might give up on the donkeys and begin to worry
6 about us." "Look now," he said to him, "there is a man of God in this town,
and the man is highly esteemed – whatever he says comes to pass. Let us go
there now – perhaps he will advise us about the journey we have undertaken."
7 "If we do go," Sha'ul said to his steward, "then what can we bring for the man?
The bread in our packs is finished, and there is no gift to present to the man
8 of God – what do we have?" "Here," replied the steward to Sha'ul again, "I
find I have a quarter shekel of silver with me. If I give it to the man of God, he
9 might advise us about our journey" – formerly in Israel, when someone went
to inquire of God, he would say, "Let us go to the seer," for today's prophet
10 was then referred to as a "seer." "Well said," Sha'ul said to his steward. "Come,
let us go." And they made their way to the town where the man of God was.
11 As they were traveling up the ascent to the town, they met some girls going

הַמֶּלֶךְ אֲשֶׁר יִמְלֹךְ עֲלֵיכֶם אֶת־בְּנֵיכֶם יִקָּח וְשָׂם לוֹ בְּמֶרְכַּבְתּוֹ וּבְפָרָשָׁיו
יב וְרָצוּ לִפְנֵי מֶרְכַּבְתּוֹ: וְלָשׂוּם לוֹ שָׂרֵי אֲלָפִים וְשָׂרֵי חֲמִשִּׁים וְלַחֲרֹשׁ
יג חֲרִישׁוֹ וְלִקְצֹר קְצִירוֹ וְלַעֲשׂוֹת כְּלֵי־מִלְחַמְתּוֹ וּכְלֵי רִכְבּוֹ: וְאֶת־
יד בְּנוֹתֵיכֶם יִקָּח לְרַקָּחוֹת וּלְטַבָּחוֹת וּלְאֹפוֹת: וְאֶת־שְׂדוֹתֵיכֶם וְאֶת־
טו כַּרְמֵיכֶם וְזֵיתֵיכֶם הַטּוֹבִים יִקָּח וְנָתַן לַעֲבָדָיו: וְזַרְעֵיכֶם וְכַרְמֵיכֶם
טז יַעְשֹׂר וְנָתַן לְסָרִיסָיו וְלַעֲבָדָיו: וְאֶת־עַבְדֵיכֶם וְאֶת־שִׁפְחוֹתֵיכֶם וְאֶת־
יז בַּחוּרֵיכֶם הַטּוֹבִים וְאֶת־חֲמוֹרֵיכֶם יִקָּח וְעָשָׂה לִמְלַאכְתּוֹ: צֹאנְכֶם
יח יַעְשֹׂר וְאַתֶּם תִּהְיוּ־לוֹ לַעֲבָדִים: וּזְעַקְתֶּם בַּיּוֹם הַהוּא מִלִּפְנֵי מַלְכְּכֶם
יט אֲשֶׁר בְּחַרְתֶּם לָכֶם וְלֹא־יַעֲנֶה יְהוָה אֶתְכֶם בַּיּוֹם הַהוּא: וַיְמָאֲנוּ
הָעָם לִשְׁמֹעַ בְּקוֹל שְׁמוּאֵל וַיֹּאמְרוּ לֹּא כִּי אִם־מֶלֶךְ יִהְיֶה עָלֵינוּ:
כ וְהָיִינוּ גַם־אֲנַחְנוּ כְּכָל־הַגּוֹיִם וּשְׁפָטָנוּ מַלְכֵּנוּ וְיָצָא לְפָנֵינוּ וְנִלְחַם
כא אֶת־מִלְחֲמֹתֵנוּ: וַיִּשְׁמַע שְׁמוּאֵל אֵת כָּל־דִּבְרֵי הָעָם וַיְדַבְּרֵם בְּאָזְנֵי
כב יְהוָה: וַיֹּאמֶר יְהוָה אֶל־שְׁמוּאֵל שְׁמַע בְּקוֹלָם וְהִמְלַכְתָּ לָהֶם
ט א מֶלֶךְ וַיֹּאמֶר שְׁמוּאֵל אֶל־אַנְשֵׁי יִשְׂרָאֵל לְכוּ אִישׁ לְעִירוֹ: וַיְהִי־
אִישׁ מבן ימין וּשְׁמוֹ קִישׁ בֶּן־אֲבִיאֵל בֶּן־צְרוֹר בֶּן־בְּכוֹרַת בֶּן־אֲפִיחַ (מִבִּנְיָמִין)
ב בֶּן־אִישׁ יְמִינִי גִּבּוֹר חָיִל: וְלוֹ־הָיָה בֵן וּשְׁמוֹ שָׁאוּל בָּחוּר וָטוֹב וְאֵין ה
אִישׁ מִבְּנֵי יִשְׂרָאֵל טוֹב מִמֶּנּוּ מִשִּׁכְמוֹ וָמַעְלָה גָּבֹהַּ מִכָּל־הָעָם:
ג וַתֹּאבַדְנָה הָאֲתֹנוֹת לְקִישׁ אֲבִי שָׁאוּל וַיֹּאמֶר קִישׁ אֶל־שָׁאוּל בְּנוֹ
ד קַח־נָא אִתְּךָ אֶת־אַחַד מֵהַנְּעָרִים וְקוּם לֵךְ בַּקֵּשׁ אֶת־הָאֲתֹנֹת: וַיַּעֲבֹר
בְּהַר־אֶפְרַיִם וַיַּעֲבֹר בְּאֶרֶץ־שָׁלִשָׁה וְלֹא מָצָאוּ וַיַּעַבְרוּ בְאֶרֶץ־שַׁעֲלִים
ה וָאַיִן וַיַּעֲבֹר בְּאֶרֶץ־יְמִינִי וְלֹא מָצָאוּ: הֵמָּה בָּאוּ בְּאֶרֶץ צוּף וְשָׁאוּל
אָמַר לְנַעֲרוֹ אֲשֶׁר־עִמּוֹ לְכָה וְנָשׁוּבָה פֶּן־יֶחְדַּל אָבִי מִן־הָאֲתֹנוֹת
ו וְדָאַג לָנוּ: וַיֹּאמֶר לוֹ הִנֵּה־נָא אִישׁ־אֱלֹהִים בָּעִיר הַזֹּאת וְהָאִישׁ נִכְבָּד
כֹּל אֲשֶׁר־יְדַבֵּר בּוֹא יָבוֹא עַתָּה נֵלְכָה שָּׁם אוּלַי יַגִּיד לָנוּ אֶת־דַּרְכֵּנוּ
ז אֲשֶׁר־הָלַכְנוּ עָלֶיהָ: וַיֹּאמֶר שָׁאוּל לְנַעֲרוֹ וְהִנֵּה נֵלֵךְ וּמַה־נָּבִיא לָאִישׁ
כִּי הַלֶּחֶם אָזַל מִכֵּלֵינוּ וּתְשׁוּרָה אֵין־לְהָבִיא לְאִישׁ הָאֱלֹהִים מָה
ח אִתָּנוּ: וַיֹּסֶף הַנַּעַר לַעֲנוֹת אֶת־שָׁאוּל וַיֹּאמֶר הִנֵּה נִמְצָא בְיָדִי רֶבַע
ט שֶׁקֶל כָּסֶף וְנָתַתִּי לְאִישׁ הָאֱלֹהִים וְהִגִּיד לָנוּ אֶת־דַּרְכֵּנוּ: לְפָנִים ׀
בְּיִשְׂרָאֵל כֹּה־אָמַר הָאִישׁ בְּלֶכְתּוֹ לִדְרוֹשׁ אֱלֹהִים לְכוּ וְנֵלְכָה עַד־
י הָרֹאֶה כִּי לַנָּבִיא הַיּוֹם יִקָּרֵא לְפָנִים הָרֹאֶה: וַיֹּאמֶר שָׁאוּל לְנַעֲרוֹ טוֹב
יא דְּבָרְךָ לְכָה ׀ נֵלֵכָה וַיֵּלְכוּ אֶל־הָעִיר אֲשֶׁר־שָׁם אִישׁ הָאֱלֹהִים: הֵמָּה
עֹלִים בְּמַעֲלֵה הָעִיר וְהֵמָּה מָצְאוּ נְעָרוֹת יֹצְאוֹת לִשְׁאֹב מָיִם וַיֹּאמְרוּ

12 out to draw water and asked them, "Is the seer here?" "Oh yes, he is," they
answered him, and added, "Look – he is just ahead of you. Hurry, now – he
just came to town today, for the people have a sacrifice today at the high
13 shrine. When you reach the town, you will find him about to go up to the high
shrine to eat – for the people will not eat until he arrives; he must bless the
sacrifice, and only then will the guests eat. Now go up, for this is the right
14 moment to find him." So they went up to the town, and just as they entered
the city, there was Shmuel coming out toward them, going up to the high
15 shrine. Now, the LORD had revealed the following to Shmuel on the
16 day before Sha'ul's arrival: "At this time tomorrow, I will send a man from the
land of Binyamin to you, and you shall anoint him as ruler over My people,
Israel. He shall rescue My people from the hand of the Philistines, for I have
17 taken notice of My people – their cries have reached Me." As Shmuel noticed
Sha'ul, the LORD answered him, "Here is the man I told you about – the one
18 who will rule over My people." Then Sha'ul approached Shmuel inside the
19 gate. "Please tell me," he asked, "where is the house of the seer?" "I am the
seer," Shmuel answered Sha'ul. "Go up to the high shrine before me – you
shall eat with me today. I will send you off in the morning when I have told
20 you about whatever is on your mind. As for the donkeys lost to you these
three days – do not be concerned about them, for they have been found, while
21 whom do all of Israel long for but you and all your father's house?" "But
I am a Benjaminite," Sha'ul answered, "of the smallest of Israel's tribes. And
my family is the most junior of all the clans of the tribe of Binyamin. Why do
22 you speak to me in this way?" But Shmuel took Sha'ul and his steward
and brought them to the hall. He gave them places among the guests of honor,
23 who numbered about thirty. Shmuel said to the carver, "Fetch the portion I
24 gave you – the one I told you to set aside." When the carver had served up the
thigh and the fat around it and set it before Sha'ul, he said, "Here, what was
reserved has been set before you. Eat, for it was kept for you for this occasion
when I said I had invited the people." So Sha'ul ate with Shmuel on that day.
25 They descended from the high shrine to the town, and he spoke with Sha'ul
26 on the roof. They awoke early; when dawn rose Shmuel called Sha'ul to the
roof. "Arise," he said, "and I will send you off." Sha'ul arose and the two of
27 them – he and Shmuel – went outside. As they made their way down to the
edge of the city, Shmuel said to Sha'ul, "Tell the steward to go on ahead of us,"
and he went on ahead. "As for you, stay here for a moment, and I will let you
10 1 hear the word of God." And Shmuel took the juglet of oil and poured
it over his head and kissed him. And he said, "The LORD hereby anoints you
2 as ruler over His estate. Now, when you leave me today, you will meet two
men near Raḥel's tomb on the border of Binyamin, in Tzeltzaḥ. They will tell
you, 'The donkeys you set out to search for have been found – by now, your

יב לָהֶן הֲיֵשׁ בָּזֶה הָרֹאֶה: וַתַּעֲנֶינָה אוֹתָם וַתֹּאמַרְנָה יֵּשׁ הִנֵּה לְפָנֶיךָ
יג מַהֵר ׀ עַתָּה כִּי הַיּוֹם בָּא לָעִיר כִּי זֶבַח הַיּוֹם לָעָם בַּבָּמָה: כְּבֹאֲכֶם
הָעִיר כֵּן תִּמְצְאוּן אֹתוֹ בְּטֶרֶם יַעֲלֶה הַבָּמָתָה לֶאֱכֹל כִּי לֹא־יֹאכַל
הָעָם עַד־בֹּאוֹ כִּי־הוּא יְבָרֵךְ הַזֶּבַח אַחֲרֵי־כֵן יֹאכְלוּ הַקְּרֻאִים וְעַתָּה
יד עֲלוּ כִּי־אֹתוֹ כְהַיּוֹם תִּמְצְאוּן אֹתוֹ: וַיַּעֲלוּ הָעִיר הֵמָּה בָּאִים בְּתוֹךְ
טו הָעִיר וְהִנֵּה שְׁמוּאֵל יֹצֵא לִקְרָאתָם לַעֲלוֹת הַבָּמָה: וַיהוָה
טז גָּלָה אֶת־אֹזֶן שְׁמוּאֵל יוֹם אֶחָד לִפְנֵי בוֹא־שָׁאוּל לֵאמֹר: כָּעֵת ׀ מָחָר
אֶשְׁלַח אֵלֶיךָ אִישׁ מֵאֶרֶץ בִּנְיָמִן וּמְשַׁחְתּוֹ לְנָגִיד עַל־עַמִּי יִשְׂרָאֵל
וְהוֹשִׁיעַ אֶת־עַמִּי מִיַּד פְּלִשְׁתִּים כִּי רָאִיתִי אֶת־עַמִּי כִּי בָּאָה צַעֲקָתוֹ
יז אֵלָי: וּשְׁמוּאֵל רָאָה אֶת־שָׁאוּל וַיהוָה עָנָהוּ הִנֵּה הָאִישׁ אֲשֶׁר אָמַרְתִּי
יח אֵלֶיךָ זֶה יַעְצֹר בְּעַמִּי: וַיִּגַּשׁ שָׁאוּל אֶת־שְׁמוּאֵל בְּתוֹךְ הַשָּׁעַר וַיֹּאמֶר
יט הַגִּידָה־נָּא לִי אֵי־זֶה בֵּית הָרֹאֶה: וַיַּעַן שְׁמוּאֵל אֶת־שָׁאוּל וַיֹּאמֶר
אָנֹכִי הָרֹאֶה עֲלֵה לְפָנַי הַבָּמָה וַאֲכַלְתֶּם עִמִּי הַיּוֹם וְשִׁלַּחְתִּיךָ בַבֹּקֶר
כ וְכֹל אֲשֶׁר בִּלְבָבְךָ אַגִּיד לָךְ: וְלָאֲתֹנוֹת הָאֹבְדוֹת לְךָ הַיּוֹם שְׁלֹשֶׁת
הַיָּמִים אַל־תָּשֶׂם אֶת־לִבְּךָ לָהֶם כִּי נִמְצָאוּ וּלְמִי כָּל־חֶמְדַּת יִשְׂרָאֵל
כא הֲלוֹא לְךָ וּלְכֹל בֵּית אָבִיךָ: וַיַּעַן שָׁאוּל וַיֹּאמֶר הֲלוֹא
בֶן־יְמִינִי אָנֹכִי מִקַּטַנֵּי שִׁבְטֵי יִשְׂרָאֵל וּמִשְׁפַּחְתִּי הַצְּעִרָה מִכָּל־
כב מִשְׁפְּחוֹת שִׁבְטֵי בִנְיָמִן וְלָמָּה דִּבַּרְתָּ אֵלַי כַּדָּבָר הַזֶּה: וַיִּקַּח
שְׁמוּאֵל אֶת־שָׁאוּל וְאֶת־נַעֲרוֹ וַיְבִיאֵם לִשְׁכָּתָה וַיִּתֵּן לָהֶם מָקוֹם
כג בְּרֹאשׁ הַקְּרוּאִים וְהֵמָּה כִּשְׁלֹשִׁים אִישׁ: וַיֹּאמֶר שְׁמוּאֵל לַטַּבָּח תְּנָה
כד אֶת־הַמָּנָה אֲשֶׁר נָתַתִּי לָךְ אֲשֶׁר אָמַרְתִּי אֵלֶיךָ שִׂים אֹתָהּ עִמָּךְ: וַיָּרֶם
הַטַּבָּח אֶת־הַשּׁוֹק וְהֶעָלֶיהָ וַיָּשֶׂם ׀ לִפְנֵי שָׁאוּל וַיֹּאמֶר הִנֵּה הַנִּשְׁאָר
שִׂים־לְפָנֶיךָ אֱכֹל כִּי לַמּוֹעֵד שָׁמוּר־לְךָ לֵאמֹר הָעָם קָרָאתִי וַיֹּאכַל
כה שָׁאוּל עִם־שְׁמוּאֵל בַּיּוֹם הַהוּא: וַיֵּרְדוּ מֵהַבָּמָה הָעִיר וַיְדַבֵּר עִם־
כו שָׁאוּל עַל־הַגָּג: וַיַּשְׁכִּמוּ וַיְהִי כַּעֲלוֹת הַשַּׁחַר וַיִּקְרָא שְׁמוּאֵל אֶל־שָׁאוּל
הַגָּג לֵאמֹר קוּמָה וַאֲשַׁלְּחֶךָּ וַיָּקָם שָׁאוּל וַיֵּצְאוּ שְׁנֵיהֶם הוּא וּשְׁמוּאֵל
כז הַחוּצָה: הֵמָּה יוֹרְדִים בִּקְצֵה הָעִיר וּשְׁמוּאֵל אָמַר אֶל־שָׁאוּל אֱמֹר
לַנַּעַר וְיַעֲבֹר לְפָנֵינוּ וַיַּעֲבֹר וְאַתָּה עֲמֹד כַּיּוֹם וְאַשְׁמִיעֲךָ אֶת־דְּבַר
י א אֱלֹהִים: וַיִּקַּח שְׁמוּאֵל אֶת־פַּךְ הַשֶּׁמֶן וַיִּצֹק עַל־רֹאשׁוֹ
ב וַיִּשָּׁקֵהוּ וַיֹּאמֶר הֲלוֹא כִּי־מְשָׁחֲךָ יְהוָה עַל־נַחֲלָתוֹ לְנָגִיד: בְּלֶכְתְּךָ
הַיּוֹם מֵעִמָּדִי וּמָצָאתָ שְׁנֵי אֲנָשִׁים עִם־קְבֻרַת רָחֵל בִּגְבוּל בִּנְיָמִן
בְּצֶלְצַח וְאָמְרוּ אֵלֶיךָ נִמְצְאוּ הָאֲתֹנוֹת אֲשֶׁר הָלַכְתָּ לְבַקֵּשׁ וְהִנֵּה

father has dropped the matter of the donkeys and is worried about you,
3 saying, "What shall I do about my son?"' Pass on swiftly from there until you
reach the Oak of Tavor. There, three men making pilgrimage to God at Beit
El will find you: one bearing three kid goats, one bearing three loaves of bread,
4 and one bearing an amphora of wine. They will greet you and give you two
5 loaves of bread; you shall accept them from their hands. After that, you will
come to Givat HaElohim where the Philistine garrisons are. When you reach
the city, you will walk right into a band of prophets coming down from the
high shrine, with harp and drum and flute and lyre before them, caught up in
6 prophetic frenzy. And the spirit of the LORD will seize you, and you will be
caught up in their prophetic frenzy, and you will be transformed into a
7 different person. Then, once all these signs have come to pass for you, do what
8 you find in your power to do, for God is with you. You shall go down before
me to Gilgal – I will soon come down to you to offer up burnt offerings and
to sacrifice peace offerings. Wait for seven days until I come to you; then I
9 will inform you what you are to do." And just as he turned away to leave
Shmuel, God transformed his heart, and all these signs came to pass that very
10 day. When they arrived there at Giva, there was the band of prophets
coming toward him – and the spirit of God seized him, and he was caught up
11 in their prophetic frenzy. And when all those who knew him from before saw
him – there he was, in a prophetic frenzy along with the prophets – the
people asked one another, "What happened to the son of Kish? Is Sha'ul, too,
12 among the prophets?" Then one man from there retorted, "Well, who is their
father?" Thus the saying came about: "Is Sha'ul, too, among the prophets?"
13 14 When the prophetic frenzy had worn off, he arrived at the high shrine. Sha'ul's
uncle said to him and his steward, "Where have you been?" "To search for
the donkeys," he said, "but when we saw they were nowhere to be found, we
15 came to Shmuel." "Tell me, now," said Sha'ul's uncle, "what did Shmuel say to
16 you?" "Sure enough, he told us that the donkeys had been found," Sha'ul said
to his uncle, but he told him nothing of the matter of kingship that Shmuel
17 had mentioned. Shmuel summoned the people to the LORD at
18 Mitzpa. "Thus says the LORD, God of Israel," he proclaimed to the Israelites,
"I have brought Israel out of Egypt, and I have delivered you from the hand
19 of Egypt and from the hands of all the kingdoms who oppress you. But today
you have rejected Your God, who is your Savior from all your troubles and all
your crises; you have said to Him, 'Set a king over us.' Now, present yourselves
20 before the LORD by your tribes and by your clans." And Shmuel had all the
tribes of Israel come forward, and the tribe of Binyamin was singled out by
21 lot. Then he had the tribe of Binyamin come forward, clan by clan, and the
Matrite clan was singled out; then Sha'ul son of Kish was singled out. And
22 they searched for him, but he was nowhere to be found. So they inquired of
the LORD again, "Is the man even here?" And the LORD said, "There
23 he is – hiding among the baggage." They ran and took him from there, and
when he presented himself among the people, he towered head and shoulders

נָטַשׁ אָבִיךָ אֶת־דִּבְרֵי הָאֲתֹנוֹת וְדָאַג לָכֶם לֵאמֹר מָה אֶעֱשֶׂה לִבְנִי׃
ג וְחָלַפְתָּ מִשָּׁם וָהָלְאָה וּבָאתָ עַד־אֵלוֹן תָּבוֹר וּמְצָאוּךָ שָּׁם שְׁלֹשָׁה
אֲנָשִׁים עֹלִים אֶל־הָאֱלֹהִים בֵּית־אֵל אֶחָד נֹשֵׂא ׀ שְׁלֹשָׁה גְדָיִים וְאֶחָד
ד נֹשֵׂא שְׁלֹשֶׁת כִּכְּרוֹת לֶחֶם וְאֶחָד נֹשֵׂא נֵבֶל־יָיִן׃ וְשָׁאֲלוּ לְךָ לְשָׁלוֹם
ה וְנָתְנוּ לְךָ שְׁתֵּי־לֶחֶם וְלָקַחְתָּ מִיָּדָם׃ אַחַר כֵּן תָּבוֹא גִּבְעַת הָאֱלֹהִים
אֲשֶׁר־שָׁם נְצִבֵי פְלִשְׁתִּים וִיהִי כְבֹאֲךָ שָׁם הָעִיר וּפָגַעְתָּ חֶבֶל נְבִאִים
יֹרְדִים מֵהַבָּמָה וְלִפְנֵיהֶם נֵבֶל וְתֹף וְחָלִיל וְכִנּוֹר וְהֵמָּה מִתְנַבְּאִים׃
ו ז וְצָלְחָה עָלֶיךָ רוּחַ יהוה וְהִתְנַבִּיתָ עִמָּם וְנֶהְפַּכְתָּ לְאִישׁ אַחֵר׃ וְהָיָה
כִּי תבאינה הָאֹתוֹת הָאֵלֶּה לָךְ עֲשֵׂה לְךָ אֲשֶׁר תִּמְצָא יָדֶךָ כִּי הָאֱלֹהִים תָּבֹאנָה
ח עִמָּךְ׃ וְיָרַדְתָּ לְפָנַי הַגִּלְגָּל וְהִנֵּה אָנֹכִי יֹרֵד אֵלֶיךָ לְהַעֲלוֹת עֹלוֹת לִזְבֹּחַ
זִבְחֵי שְׁלָמִים שִׁבְעַת יָמִים תּוֹחֵל עַד־בּוֹאִי אֵלֶיךָ וְהוֹדַעְתִּי לְךָ אֵת
ט אֲשֶׁר תַּעֲשֶׂה׃ וְהָיָה כְּהַפְנֹתוֹ שִׁכְמוֹ לָלֶכֶת מֵעִם שְׁמוּאֵל וַיַּהֲפָךְ־לוֹ
י אֱלֹהִים לֵב אַחֵר וַיָּבֹאוּ כָּל־הָאֹתוֹת הָאֵלֶּה בַּיּוֹם הַהוּא׃ וַיָּבֹאוּ
שָׁם הַגִּבְעָתָה וְהִנֵּה חֶבֶל־נְבִאִים לִקְרָאתוֹ וַתִּצְלַח עָלָיו רוּחַ אֱלֹהִים
יא וַיִּתְנַבֵּא בְּתוֹכָם׃ וַיְהִי כָּל־יוֹדְעוֹ מֵאִתְּמוֹל שִׁלְשֹׁם וַיִּרְאוּ וְהִנֵּה עִם־
נְבִאִים נִבָּא וַיֹּאמֶר הָעָם אִישׁ אֶל־רֵעֵהוּ מַה־זֶּה הָיָה
יב לְבֶן־קִישׁ הֲגַם שָׁאוּל בַּנְּבִיאִם׃ וַיַּעַן אִישׁ מִשָּׁם וַיֹּאמֶר וּמִי אֲבִיהֶם
יג עַל־כֵּן הָיְתָה לְמָשָׁל הֲגַם שָׁאוּל בַּנְּבִאִים׃ וַיְכַל מֵהִתְנַבּוֹת וַיָּבֹא
יד הַבָּמָה׃ וַיֹּאמֶר דּוֹד שָׁאוּל אֵלָיו וְאֶל־נַעֲרוֹ אָן הֲלַכְתֶּם וַיֹּאמֶר לְבַקֵּשׁ
טו אֶת־הָאֲתֹנוֹת וַנִּרְאֶה כִי־אַיִן וַנָּבוֹא אֶל־שְׁמוּאֵל׃ וַיֹּאמֶר דּוֹד שָׁאוּל
טז הַגִּידָה־נָּא לִי מָה־אָמַר לָכֶם שְׁמוּאֵל׃ וַיֹּאמֶר שָׁאוּל אֶל־דּוֹדוֹ הַגֵּד
הִגִּיד לָנוּ כִּי נִמְצְאוּ הָאֲתֹנוֹת וְאֶת־דְּבַר הַמְּלוּכָה לֹא־הִגִּיד לוֹ אֲשֶׁר
יז אָמַר שְׁמוּאֵל׃ וַיַּצְעֵק שְׁמוּאֵל אֶת־הָעָם אֶל־יהוה הַמִּצְפָּה׃
יח וַיֹּאמֶר ׀ אֶל־בְּנֵי יִשְׂרָאֵל כֹּה־אָמַר יהוה אֱלֹהֵי יִשְׂרָאֵל אָנֹכִי הֶעֱלֵיתִי
אֶת־יִשְׂרָאֵל מִמִּצְרָיִם וָאַצִּיל אֶתְכֶם מִיַּד מִצְרַיִם וּמִיַּד כָּל־הַמַּמְלָכוֹת
יט הַלֹּחֲצִים אֶתְכֶם׃ וְאַתֶּם הַיּוֹם מְאַסְתֶּם אֶת־אֱלֹהֵיכֶם אֲשֶׁר־הוּא
מוֹשִׁיעַ לָכֶם מִכָּל־רָעוֹתֵיכֶם וְצָרֹתֵיכֶם וַתֹּאמְרוּ לוֹ כִּי־מֶלֶךְ תָּשִׂים
כ עָלֵינוּ וְעַתָּה הִתְיַצְּבוּ לִפְנֵי יהוה לְשִׁבְטֵיכֶם וּלְאַלְפֵיכֶם׃ וַיַּקְרֵב שְׁמוּאֵל
כא אֵת כָּל־שִׁבְטֵי יִשְׂרָאֵל וַיִּלָּכֵד שֵׁבֶט בִּנְיָמִן׃ וַיַּקְרֵב אֶת־שֵׁבֶט בִּנְיָמִן
לְמִשְׁפְּחֹתָו וַתִּלָּכֵד מִשְׁפַּחַת הַמַּטְרִי וַיִּלָּכֵד שָׁאוּל בֶּן־קִישׁ וַיְבַקְשֻׁהוּ
כב וְלֹא נִמְצָא׃ וַיִּשְׁאֲלוּ־עוֹד בַּיהוה הֲבָא עוֹד הֲלֹם אִישׁ וַיֹּאמֶר
כג יהוה הִנֵּה־הוּא נֶחְבָּא אֶל־הַכֵּלִים׃ וַיָּרֻצוּ וַיִּקָּחֻהוּ מִשָּׁם וַיִּתְיַצֵּב בְּתוֹךְ

24 above everyone else. And Shmuel said to all the nation, "Have you seen whom
the LORD has chosen – for there is none like him among all the people!" And
25 all the people cheered and shouted, "Long live the king!" Shmuel
announced the royal rights to the people and recorded them in a scroll that
he placed before the LORD. Then Shmuel sent everyone back, each to his own
26 home. And Sha'ul, too, went back home to Giva, escorted by the throngs
27 whose heart had been touched by God. But some depraved men said, "How
is that one going to save us?" They scorned him and did not bring him any
11 1 gifts, but he feigned indifference. Now, Naḥash the Amonite advanced
and set up camp against Yavesh Gilad. All the men of Yavesh said to Naḥash,
2 "Form a pact with us, and we will serve you." But Naḥash the Amonite replied
to them, "This is how I will a form a pact with you: by gouging out every one
3 of your right eyes, thus casting disgrace upon all of Israel." "Grant us seven
days' respite," the elders of Yavesh said to him, "and we will send messengers
throughout all of Israel's borders. If no one comes to our rescue, then we shall
4 come out to you." The messengers arrived at Givat Sha'ul and conveyed the
message in the people's hearing, and all the people lifted their voices and wept.
5 Just then, Sha'ul came in after the oxen from the field. "What happened, that
the people weep so?" Sha'ul asked, and they told him the message of the men
6 of Yavesh. The spirit of God rushed upon Sha'ul as he heard these words, and
7 his wrath flared up fiercely. And he took a pair of oxen and hacked them up
and sent them out to every border of Israel with the messengers, saying,
"Whoever does not follow after Sha'ul and after Shmuel – this will be done
to his oxen!" And the fear of the LORD fell upon the people, and they charged
8 out as one man. He marshaled them at Bezek; the Israelites totaled three
9 hundred thousand, and the men of Yehuda were thirty thousand. He told the
messengers who had just arrived, "This is what you should say to the men of
Yavesh Gilad: tomorrow, victory will be yours as the sun grows hot." When
10 the messengers arrived and told the men of Yavesh, they rejoiced. Then the
men of Yavesh said, "Tomorrow we will come out to you; do to us whatever
11 is best in your eyes." The next day, Sha'ul arranged the men into three
companies, and they infiltrated the camp during the morning watch. They
struck at Amon until the heat of the day; by then, all those who were left had
12 scattered; no two remained together. And the people said to Shmuel, "Who
was it that said, 'Should Sha'ul reign over us?' Hand the men over, and we will
13 put them to death." But Sha'ul said, "No one will be put to death on this day,
14 for today, the LORD has granted victory in Israel." And Shmuel said
to the people, "Come, let us go to Gilgal, and we will renew the kingship
15 there." All the people went to Gilgal, and they crowned Sha'ul king there at
Gilgal before the LORD. They sacrificed peace offerings before the LORD, and
12 1 Sha'ul rejoiced greatly along with all the men of Israel. Then Shmuel
addressed all of Israel. "Now, I have heeded your voices in all you said to me,

כד הָעָם וַיִּגְבַּהּ מִכָּל־הָעָם מִשִּׁכְמוֹ וָמָעְלָה: וַיֹּאמֶר שְׁמוּאֵל אֶל־כָּל־הָעָם ו
הַרְּאִיתֶם אֲשֶׁר בָּחַר־בּוֹ יְהוָה כִּי אֵין כָּמֹהוּ בְּכָל־הָעָם וַיָּרִעוּ כָל־הָעָם
כה וַיֹּאמְרוּ יְחִי הַמֶּלֶךְ: וַיְדַבֵּר שְׁמוּאֵל אֶל־הָעָם אֵת מִשְׁפַּט
הַמְּלֻכָה וַיִּכְתֹּב בַּסֵּפֶר וַיַּנַּח לִפְנֵי יְהוָה וַיְשַׁלַּח שְׁמוּאֵל אֶת־כָּל־הָעָם
כו אִישׁ לְבֵיתוֹ: וְגַם־שָׁאוּל הָלַךְ לְבֵיתוֹ גִּבְעָתָה וַיֵּלְכוּ עִמּוֹ הַחַיִל אֲשֶׁר־
כז נָגַע אֱלֹהִים בְּלִבָּם: וּבְנֵי בְלִיַּעַל אָמְרוּ מַה־יֹּשִׁעֵנוּ זֶה וַיִּבְזֻהוּ וְלֹא־
יא א הֵבִיאוּ לוֹ מִנְחָה וַיְהִי כְּמַחֲרִישׁ: וַיַּעַל נָחָשׁ הָעַמּוֹנִי וַיִּחַן
עַל־יָבֵישׁ גִּלְעָד וַיֹּאמְרוּ כָּל־אַנְשֵׁי יָבֵישׁ אֶל־נָחָשׁ כְּרָת־לָנוּ בְרִית
ב וְנַעַבְדֶךָּ: וַיֹּאמֶר אֲלֵיהֶם נָחָשׁ הָעַמּוֹנִי בְּזֹאת אֶכְרֹת לָכֶם בִּנְקוֹר לָכֶם
ג כָּל־עֵין יָמִין וְשַׂמְתִּיהָ חֶרְפָּה עַל־כָּל־יִשְׂרָאֵל: וַיֹּאמְרוּ אֵלָיו זִקְנֵי יָבֵישׁ
הֶרֶף לָנוּ שִׁבְעַת יָמִים וְנִשְׁלְחָה מַלְאָכִים בְּכֹל גְּבוּל יִשְׂרָאֵל וְאִם־אֵין
ד מוֹשִׁיעַ אֹתָנוּ וְיָצָאנוּ אֵלֶיךָ: וַיָּבֹאוּ הַמַּלְאָכִים גִּבְעַת שָׁאוּל וַיְדַבְּרוּ
ה הַדְּבָרִים בְּאָזְנֵי הָעָם וַיִּשְׂאוּ כָל־הָעָם אֶת־קוֹלָם וַיִּבְכּוּ: וְהִנֵּה שָׁאוּל
בָּא אַחֲרֵי הַבָּקָר מִן־הַשָּׂדֶה וַיֹּאמֶר שָׁאוּל מַה־לָּעָם כִּי יִבְכּוּ וַיְסַפְּרוּ־
ו לוֹ אֶת־דִּבְרֵי אַנְשֵׁי יָבֵישׁ: וַתִּצְלַח רוּחַ־אֱלֹהִים עַל־שָׁאוּל בשמעו כְּשָׁמְעוֹ
ז אֶת־הַדְּבָרִים הָאֵלֶּה וַיִּחַר אַפּוֹ מְאֹד: וַיִּקַּח צֶמֶד בָּקָר וַיְנַתְּחֵהוּ וַיְשַׁלַּח
בְּכָל־גְּבוּל יִשְׂרָאֵל בְּיַד הַמַּלְאָכִים ׀ לֵאמֹר אֲשֶׁר אֵינֶנּוּ יֹצֵא אַחֲרֵי
שָׁאוּל וְאַחַר שְׁמוּאֵל כֹּה יֵעָשֶׂה לִבְקָרוֹ וַיִּפֹּל פַּחַד־יְהוָה עַל־הָעָם
ח וַיֵּצְאוּ כְּאִישׁ אֶחָד: וַיִּפְקְדֵם בְּבָזֶק וַיִּהְיוּ בְנֵי־יִשְׂרָאֵל שְׁלֹשׁ מֵאוֹת
ט אֶלֶף וְאִישׁ יְהוּדָה שְׁלֹשִׁים אָלֶף: וַיֹּאמְרוּ לַמַּלְאָכִים הַבָּאִים כֹּה
תֹאמְרוּן לְאִישׁ יָבֵישׁ גִּלְעָד מָחָר תִּהְיֶה־לָכֶם תְּשׁוּעָה בחם הַשָּׁמֶשׁ כְּחֹם
י וַיָּבֹאוּ הַמַּלְאָכִים וַיַּגִּידוּ לְאַנְשֵׁי יָבֵישׁ וַיִּשְׂמָחוּ: וַיֹּאמְרוּ אַנְשֵׁי יָבֵישׁ
יא מָחָר נֵצֵא אֲלֵיכֶם וַעֲשִׂיתֶם לָּנוּ כְּכָל־הַטּוֹב בְּעֵינֵיכֶם: וַיְהִי
מִמָּחֳרָת וַיָּשֶׂם שָׁאוּל אֶת־הָעָם שְׁלֹשָׁה רָאשִׁים וַיָּבֹאוּ בְתוֹךְ־הַמַּחֲנֶה
בְּאַשְׁמֹרֶת הַבֹּקֶר וַיַּכּוּ אֶת־עַמּוֹן עַד־חֹם הַיּוֹם וַיְהִי הַנִּשְׁאָרִים וַיָּפֻצוּ
יב וְלֹא נִשְׁאֲרוּ־בָם שְׁנַיִם יָחַד: וַיֹּאמֶר הָעָם אֶל־שְׁמוּאֵל מִי הָאֹמֵר שָׁאוּל
יג יִמְלֹךְ עָלֵינוּ תְּנוּ הָאֲנָשִׁים וּנְמִיתֵם: וַיֹּאמֶר שָׁאוּל לֹא־יוּמַת אִישׁ בַּיּוֹם
יד הַזֶּה כִּי הַיּוֹם עָשָׂה־יְהוָה תְּשׁוּעָה בְּיִשְׂרָאֵל: וַיֹּאמֶר
טו שְׁמוּאֵל אֶל־הָעָם לְכוּ וְנֵלְכָה הַגִּלְגָּל וּנְחַדֵּשׁ שָׁם הַמְּלוּכָה: וַיֵּלְכוּ
כָל־הָעָם הַגִּלְגָּל וַיַּמְלִכוּ שָׁם אֶת־שָׁאוּל לִפְנֵי יְהוָה בַּגִּלְגָּל וַיִּזְבְּחוּ־שָׁם
זְבָחִים שְׁלָמִים לִפְנֵי יְהוָה וַיִּשְׂמַח שָׁם שָׁאוּל וְכָל־אַנְשֵׁי יִשְׂרָאֵל עַד־
יב א מְאֹד: וַיֹּאמֶר שְׁמוּאֵל אֶל־כָּל־יִשְׂרָאֵל הִנֵּה שָׁמַעְתִּי

2 and I have crowned a king over you – and now, here is the king, walking before
you. I have grown old and grey, but my sons are here with you; I have been
3 walking before you from my youth until this day. Here I am – testify against
me in front of the LORD and in front of His anointed – whose ox have I seized,
and whose donkey have I seized? Whom have I cheated, and whom have
I oppressed, and from whose hand have I taken a bribe and averted my eyes
4 from him? Let me repay you." And they said, "You have not cheated us,
5 nor oppressed us, nor taken anything from anyone." "The LORD is witness
against you," he said to them, "and His anointed is witness on this day, that
you have found nothing in my possession." And it was declared, "The witness
6 is… the LORD," Shmuel said to the people, "who appointed Moshe
7 and Aharon and brought your ancestors out of the land of Egypt. Now take
your stand, and I will plead my case with you before the LORD: all the LORD's
8 acts of loyalty that He has done for you and your ancestors. When Yaakov
arrived in Egypt and your ancestors cried out to the LORD, the LORD sent
Moshe and Aharon to take them out of Egypt, and they settled them in this
9 place. But they forgot the LORD their God, and He sold them into the hands
of Sisera, the general of Ḥatzor, and into the hands of the Philistines, and into
10 the hands of the king of Moav, who attacked them. Then they cried out to the
LORD. 'We have sinned,' they said, 'for we left the LORD and served the Baalim
and the Ashterot – oh, save us from the hands of our enemies, and we will
11 serve You.' So the LORD sent Yerubaal and Bedan and Yiftaḥ and Shmuel and
saved you from the hands of the enemies around you, and you dwelled in
12 safety. But when you saw that King Naḥash of the Amonites came upon you,
you told me, 'No, we must have a king to reign over us,' though the LORD your
13 God is your King. And now, here is the king that you yourselves have chosen –
14 that you yourselves demanded – here, the LORD has set a king over you! If
you fear the LORD, then serve him and heed his voice, and do not spurn the
word of GOD; both you and the king who reigns over you must follow the
15 LORD your God. But if you do not heed the LORD's voice and rebel against
the LORD's word, then the LORD's hand shall bear down against you and your
16 ancestral houses. And now, stand by and see what a tremendous feat the LORD
17 is about to perform before your very eyes: Is it not the wheat harvest today?
I will call out to the LORD, and He will unleash thunder and rain. Then you
will know, and then you will see, how great an evil you have committed in the
18 eyes of the LORD by asking for a king for yourselves." Then Shmuel
called out to the LORD, and the LORD unleashed thunder and rain on that
day. All the people were struck with terror of the LORD, and of Shmuel as well.
19 And all the people said to Shmuel, "Pray on your servants' behalf to the LORD
your God so that we will not die; for we have added yet another evil to all our
20 offenses by asking for a king for ourselves." "Do not fear, though you
have done all this evil," Shmuel said to the people, "so long as you do not turn

ב בְּקֹלְכֶם לְכֹל אֲשֶׁר־אֲמַרְתֶּם לִי וָאַמְלִיךְ עֲלֵיכֶם מֶלֶךְ: וְעַתָּה הִנֵּה
הַמֶּלֶךְ ׀ מִתְהַלֵּךְ לִפְנֵיכֶם וַאֲנִי זָקַנְתִּי וָשַׂבְתִּי וּבָנַי הִנָּם אִתְּכֶם וַאֲנִי
ג הִתְהַלַּכְתִּי לִפְנֵיכֶם מִנְּעֻרַי עַד־הַיּוֹם הַזֶּה: הִנְנִי עֲנוּ בִי נֶגֶד יְהוָה וְנֶגֶד
מְשִׁיחוֹ אֶת־שׁוֹר ׀ מִי לָקַחְתִּי וַחֲמוֹר מִי לָקַחְתִּי וְאֶת־מִי עָשַׁקְתִּי
אֶת־מִי רַצּוֹתִי וּמִיַּד־מִי לָקַחְתִּי כֹפֶר וְאַעְלִים עֵינַי בּוֹ וְאָשִׁיב לָכֶם:
ד וַיֹּאמְרוּ לֹא עֲשַׁקְתָּנוּ וְלֹא רַצּוֹתָנוּ וְלֹא־לָקַחְתָּ מִיַּד־אִישׁ מְאוּמָה:
ה וַיֹּאמֶר אֲלֵיהֶם עֵד יְהוָה בָּכֶם וְעֵד מְשִׁיחוֹ הַיּוֹם הַזֶּה כִּי לֹא מְצָאתֶם
ו בְּיָדִי מְאוּמָה וַיֹּאמֶר עֵד: וַיֹּאמֶר שְׁמוּאֵל אֶל־הָעָם יְהוָה
אֲשֶׁר עָשָׂה אֶת־מֹשֶׁה וְאֶת־אַהֲרֹן וַאֲשֶׁר הֶעֱלָה אֶת־אֲבֹתֵיכֶם מֵאֶרֶץ
ז מִצְרָיִם: וְעַתָּה הִתְיַצְּבוּ וְאִשָּׁפְטָה אִתְּכֶם לִפְנֵי יְהוָה אֵת כָּל־צִדְקוֹת
ח יְהוָה אֲשֶׁר־עָשָׂה אִתְּכֶם וְאֶת־אֲבוֹתֵיכֶם: כַּאֲשֶׁר־בָּא יַעֲקֹב מִצְרָיִם
וַיִּזְעֲקוּ אֲבֹתֵיכֶם אֶל־יְהוָה וַיִּשְׁלַח יְהוָה אֶת־מֹשֶׁה וְאֶת־אַהֲרֹן וַיּוֹצִיאוּ
ט אֶת־אֲבֹתֵיכֶם מִמִּצְרַיִם וַיֹּשִׁבוּם בַּמָּקוֹם הַזֶּה: וַיִּשְׁכְּחוּ אֶת־יְהוָה
אֱלֹהֵיהֶם וַיִּמְכֹּר אֹתָם בְּיַד סִיסְרָא שַׂר־צְבָא חָצוֹר וּבְיַד־פְּלִשְׁתִּים
י וּבְיַד מֶלֶךְ מוֹאָב וַיִּלָּחֲמוּ בָּם: וַיִּזְעֲקוּ אֶל־יְהוָה וַיֹּאמֶר חָטָאנוּ כִּי
עָזַבְנוּ אֶת־יְהוָה וַנַּעֲבֹד אֶת־הַבְּעָלִים וְאֶת־הָעַשְׁתָּרוֹת וְעַתָּה הַצִּילֵנוּ
יא מִיַּד אֹיְבֵינוּ וְנַעַבְדֶךָּ: וַיִּשְׁלַח יְהוָה אֶת־יְרֻבַּעַל וְאֶת־בְּדָן וְאֶת־יִפְתָּח
יב וְאֶת־שְׁמוּאֵל וַיַּצֵּל אֶתְכֶם מִיַּד אֹיְבֵיכֶם מִסָּבִיב וַתֵּשְׁבוּ בֶּטַח: וַתִּרְאוּ
כִּי נָחָשׁ מֶלֶךְ בְּנֵי־עַמּוֹן בָּא עֲלֵיכֶם וַתֹּאמְרוּ לִי לֹא כִּי־מֶלֶךְ יִמְלֹךְ
יג עָלֵינוּ וַיהוָה אֱלֹהֵיכֶם מַלְכְּכֶם: וְעַתָּה הִנֵּה הַמֶּלֶךְ אֲשֶׁר בְּחַרְתֶּם אֲשֶׁר
יד שְׁאֶלְתֶּם וְהִנֵּה נָתַן יְהוָה עֲלֵיכֶם מֶלֶךְ: אִם־תִּירְאוּ אֶת־יְהוָה וַעֲבַדְתֶּם
אֹתוֹ וּשְׁמַעְתֶּם בְּקֹלוֹ וְלֹא תַמְרוּ אֶת־פִּי יְהוָה וִהְיִתֶם גַּם־אַתֶּם וְגַם־
טו הַמֶּלֶךְ אֲשֶׁר מָלַךְ עֲלֵיכֶם אַחַר יְהוָה אֱלֹהֵיכֶם: וְאִם־לֹא תִשְׁמְעוּ
בְּקוֹל יְהוָה וּמְרִיתֶם אֶת־פִּי יְהוָה וְהָיְתָה יַד־יְהוָה בָּכֶם וּבַאֲבֹתֵיכֶם:
טז גַּם־עַתָּה הִתְיַצְּבוּ וּרְאוּ אֶת־הַדָּבָר הַגָּדוֹל הַזֶּה אֲשֶׁר יְהוָה עֹשֶׂה
יז לְעֵינֵיכֶם: הֲלוֹא קְצִיר־חִטִּים הַיּוֹם אֶקְרָא אֶל־יְהוָה וְיִתֵּן קֹלוֹת וּמָטָר
וּדְעוּ וּרְאוּ כִּי־רָעַתְכֶם רַבָּה אֲשֶׁר עֲשִׂיתֶם בְּעֵינֵי יְהוָה לִשְׁאוֹל לָכֶם
יח מֶלֶךְ: וַיִּקְרָא שְׁמוּאֵל אֶל־יְהוָה וַיִּתֵּן יְהוָה קֹלֹת וּמָטָר בַּיּוֹם
יט הַהוּא וַיִּירָא כָל־הָעָם מְאֹד אֶת־יְהוָה וְאֶת־שְׁמוּאֵל: וַיֹּאמְרוּ כָל־הָעָם
אֶל־שְׁמוּאֵל הִתְפַּלֵּל בְּעַד־עֲבָדֶיךָ אֶל־יְהוָה אֱלֹהֶיךָ וְאַל־נָמוּת כִּי־
כ יָסַפְנוּ עַל־כָּל־חַטֹּאתֵינוּ רָעָה לִשְׁאֹל לָנוּ מֶלֶךְ: וַיֹּאמֶר
שְׁמוּאֵל אֶל־הָעָם אַל־תִּירָאוּ אַתֶּם עֲשִׂיתֶם אֵת כָּל־הָרָעָה הַזֹּאת

21 away from the LORD; serve the LORD with all your heart. But do not turn
22 away to follow futilities that neither help nor save, for they are futile. For the
LORD will not desert His people for the sake of His great name, because the
23 LORD has undertaken to make you His people. As for me – far be it from me
to sin against the LORD by ceasing to pray on your behalf; I will teach you the
24 good and the straight path. But you must revere the LORD and serve Him
25 truly with all your heart – just look at how well He has treated you. But if you
lapse into evil, then both you and your king shall be swept away."
13 1 A year passed before Sha'ul became king, and he had been reigning over
2 Israel for two years when he selected three thousand men from Israel. Two
thousand were with Sha'ul at Mikhmas in the hills of Beit El, and a thousand
were with Yonatan at Giva of Binyamin. As for the rest of the men, he sent
3 them back to their tents. Yonatan struck down the Philistine governor at
Geva, and the Philistines heard. And Sha'ul blasted the ram's horn throughout
4 the land, declaring, "Let the Hebrews hear." When all of Israel heard how
Sha'ul had struck down the Philistine governor, and how Israel had become
5 odious to the Philistines, the people rallied to Sha'ul at Gilgal. But then the
Philistines gathered to fight with Israel – thirty thousand chariots and six
thousand riders and men as innumerable as the sand on the shore – and they
6 advanced and set up camp at Mikhmas, east of Beit Aven. When the men of
Israel saw that they were in dire straits, for the men were hard-pressed, the
people hid in caves, and among the crevices and the rocks, and in tunnels and
7 pits. And some Hebrews crossed the Jordan to the land of Gad and the Gilad,
8 while Sha'ul remained at Gilgal with all the men trembling behind him. He
waited seven days until Shmuel's appointed time, but Shmuel did not arrive
9 at Gilgal, and the men began to disperse. So Sha'ul said, "Bring the burnt
10 offering and peace offerings to me," and he offered up the burnt offering. Just
as he finished offering up the burnt offering, Shmuel suddenly arrived, and
11 Sha'ul went out toward him to greet him. "What have you done?" said Shmuel.
"When I saw that the men were beginning to disperse from me," Sha'ul said,
"but you had not come on the designated day, though the Philistines were
12 gathering at Mikhmas, I thought, 'Now the Philistines will swoop down on
me at Gilgal, but I have not yet invoked the LORD's presence.' So I spurred
13 myself to offer up the burnt offering." "You have acted foolishly,"
Shmuel said to Sha'ul. "You have not kept the commandment that the LORD,
your God, commanded you. Though the LORD would have established
14 your dynasty over Israel forever, now your dynasty will not endure. The LORD
will seek out a man after His own heart, and the LORD will charge him as
ruler over His people, for you have not done what the LORD commanded
15 you." And Shmuel arose and made his way up from Gilgal to Giva
of Binyamin while Sha'ul mustered the men who were with him, around six
16 hundred men. Sha'ul, his son Yonatan, and the men with them were stationed

כא אך אל־תסורו מאחרי יהוה ועבדתם את־יהוה בכל־לבבכם: ולא
תסורו כי ׀ אחרי התהו אשר לא־יועילו ולא יצילו כי־תהו המה:
כב כי לא־יטש יהוה את־עמו בעבור שמו הגדול כי הואיל יהוה לעשות ז
כג אתכם לו לעם: גם אנכי חלילה לי מחטא ליהוה מחדל להתפלל
כד בעדכם והוריתי אתכם בדרך הטובה והישרה: אך ׀ יראו את־יהוה
ועבדתם אתו באמת בכל־לבבכם כי ראו את אשר־הגדל עמכם:
כה ואם־הרע תרעו גם־אתם גם־מלככם תספו:
יג א ב בן־שנה שאול במלכו ושתי שנים מלך על־ישראל: ויבחר־לו שאול
שלשת אלפים מישראל ויהיו עם־שאול אלפים במכמש ובהר
בית־אל ואלף היו עם־יונתן בגבעת בנימין ויתר העם שלח איש
ג לאהליו: ויך יונתן את נציב פלשתים אשר בגבע וישמעו פלשתים
ד ושאול תקע בשופר בכל־הארץ לאמר ישמעו העברים: וכל־
ישראל שמעו לאמר הכה שאול את־נציב פלשתים וגם־נבאש
ה ישראל בפלשתים ויצעקו העם אחרי שאול הגלגל: ופלשתים
נאספו ׀ להלחם עם־ישראל שלשים אלף רכב וששת אלפים
פרשים ועם כחול אשר על־שפת־הים לרב ויעלו ויחנו במכמש
ו קדמת בית און: ואיש ישראל ראו כי צר־לו כי נגש העם ויתחבאו
ז העם במערות ובחוחים ובסלעים ובצרחים ובברות: ועברים עברו
את־הירדן ארץ גד וגלעד ושאול עודנו בגלגל וכל־העם חרדו
ח אחריו: וייחל ׀ שבעת ימים למועד אשר שמואל ולא־בא שמואל ויוחל
ט הגלגל ויפץ העם מעליו: ויאמר שאול הגשו אלי העלה והשלמים
י ויעל העלה: ויהי ככלתו להעלות העלה והנה שמואל בא ויצא
יא שאול לקראתו לברכו: ויאמר שמואל מה עשית ויאמר שאול
כי־ראיתי כי־נפץ העם מעלי ואתה לא־באת למועד הימים ופלשתים
יב נאספים מכמש: ואמר עתה ירדו פלשתים אלי הגלגל ופני יהוה
יג לא חליתי ואתאפק ואעלה העלה: ויאמר שמואל אל־
שאול נסכלת לא שמרת את־מצות יהוה אלהיך אשר צוך כי עתה
יד הכין יהוה את־ממלכתך אל־ישראל עד־עולם: ועתה ממלכתך
לא־תקום בקש יהוה לו איש כלבבו ויצוהו יהוה לנגיד על־עמו כי
טו לא שמרת את אשר־צוך יהוה: ויקם שמואל ויעל
מן־הגלגל גבעת בנימן ויפקד שאול את־העם הנמצאים עמו כשש
טז מאות איש: ושאול ויונתן בנו והעם הנמצא עמם ישבים בגבע

17 at Giva of Binyamin while the Philistines camped at Mikhmas. And the sortie
marched out of the Philistine camp in three divisions; one division headed
18 for the Ofra road that led to the land of Shual; one division headed for the
Beit Ḥoron road; and one division headed for the frontier road overlooking
19 the Valley of the Hyenas, toward the wilderness. There was no smith
to be found anywhere in the land of Israel, for the Philistines were concerned
20 that the Hebrews would make swords or spears. All of Israel needed to go
down to the Philistines to sharpen their plowshares, mattocks, axes, and
21 sickles. The sharpening fee was a *pim*[10] for plowshares, mattocks, three-
22 pronged pitchforks, axes, or setting the goad. So on the day of battle, neither
sword nor spear was to be found among Sha'ul and Yonatan's men; they could
23 be found only for Sha'ul and Yonatan his son. Meanwhile, the Philistine
14 1 garrison had set out toward the Mikhmas pass. Soon after, Yonatan
son of Sha'ul said to his armor-bearer, "Come, let us cross over to the Philistine
2 garrison on the other side." But he did not tell his father. Now Sha'ul was
stationed on the outskirts of Giva, under the pomegranate tree in Migron,
3 and the men with him numbered around six hundred. Aḥiya son of Aḥituv,
the brother of Ikhavod, who was the son of Pinḥas son of Eli, the LORD's priest
at Shilo, bore the ephod.[11] The men did not know that Yonatan had gone.
4 Between the passes through which Yonatan planned to reach the Philistine
garrison, there was a rocky crag on one side and a rocky crag on the other;
5 one was called Botzetz and the other was called Seneh. One crag rose to a
crest on the north, facing Mikhmas, while the other was south, facing
6 Geva. Yehonatan said to his armor-bearer, "Come – let us cross over
to the garrison of these heathens; perhaps the LORD will act on our behalf,
for nothing can stop the LORD from achieving victory through many or few."
7 "Do whatever your heart tells you," his armor-bearer said to him. "Lead on; I
8 am with you wholeheartedly." "Look," said Yehonatan, "we will cross
9 over to the men and show ourselves to them. If they say to us, 'Halt until we
10 reach you,' we will stay where we are and not go up to them, and if they say
to us, 'Come up to us,' then let us go up, for the LORD has delivered them into
11 our hands – that will be the sign." And the two of them showed themselves
to the Philistine garrison. "Look!" said the Philistines. "Hebrews have come
12 crawling out of the holes where they were hiding." The garrison men called
out to Yonatan and his armor-bearer. "Come up to us!" they said, "and we will
teach you a thing or two." "Come up after me," Yonatan said to his
13 arms-bearer, "for the LORD has delivered them into Israel's hands." Yonatan
made his way up on his hands and knees, with his arms-bearer right behind
him; they fell before Yonatan while his arms-bearer finished them off behind
14 him. The first attack launched by Yonatan and his arms-bearer was against
15 about twenty men over about half a furrow of an acre of land. And terror

10 | Two-thirds of a shekel, about 10 grams of silver.
11 | See note on 2:18.

יז בִנְיָמִן וּפְלִשְׁתִּים חָנוּ בְמִכְמָשׂ: וַיֵּצֵא הַמַּשְׁחִית מִמַּחֲנֵה פְלִשְׁתִּים
שְׁלֹשָׁה רָאשִׁים הָרֹאשׁ אֶחָד יִפְנֶה אֶל־דֶּרֶךְ עָפְרָה אֶל־אֶרֶץ שׁוּעָל:
יח וְהָרֹאשׁ אֶחָד יִפְנֶה דֶּרֶךְ בֵּית חֹרוֹן וְהָרֹאשׁ אֶחָד יִפְנֶה דֶּרֶךְ הַגְּבוּל
יט הַנִּשְׁקָף עַל־גֵּי הַצְּבֹעִים הַמִּדְבָּרָה: וְחָרָשׁ לֹא יִמָּצֵא בְּכֹל
אֶרֶץ יִשְׂרָאֵל כִּי־אָמַר פְּלִשְׁתִּים פֶּן יַעֲשׂוּ הָעִבְרִים חֶרֶב אוֹ חֲנִית:
כ וַיֵּרְדוּ כָל־יִשְׂרָאֵל הַפְּלִשְׁתִּים לִלְטוֹשׁ אִישׁ אֶת־מַחֲרַשְׁתּוֹ וְאֶת־
כא אֵתוֹ וְאֶת־קַרְדֻּמּוֹ וְאֵת מַחֲרֵשָׁתוֹ: וְהָיְתָה הַפְּצִירָה פִים לַמַּחֲרֵשֹׁת
כב וְלָאֵתִים וְלִשְׁלֹשׁ קִלְּשׁוֹן וּלְהַקַּרְדֻּמִּים וּלְהַצִּיב הַדָּרְבָן: וְהָיָה בְּיוֹם
מִלְחֶמֶת וְלֹא נִמְצָא חֶרֶב וַחֲנִית בְּיַד כָּל־הָעָם אֲשֶׁר אֶת־שָׁאוּל וְאֶת־
כג יוֹנָתָן וַתִּמָּצֵא לְשָׁאוּל וּלְיוֹנָתָן בְּנוֹ: וַיֵּצֵא מַצַּב פְּלִשְׁתִּים אֶל־מַעֲבַר
יד א מִכְמָשׂ: וַיְהִי הַיּוֹם וַיֹּאמֶר יוֹנָתָן בֶּן־שָׁאוּל אֶל־הַנַּעַר נֹשֵׂא
כֵלָיו לְכָה וְנַעְבְּרָה אֶל־מַצַּב פְּלִשְׁתִּים אֲשֶׁר מֵעֵבֶר הַלָּז וּלְאָבִיו לֹא
ב הִגִּיד: וְשָׁאוּל יוֹשֵׁב בִּקְצֵה הַגִּבְעָה תַּחַת הָרִמּוֹן אֲשֶׁר בְּמִגְרוֹן וְהָעָם
ג אֲשֶׁר עִמּוֹ כְּשֵׁשׁ מֵאוֹת אִישׁ: וַאֲחִיָּה בֶן־אֲחִטוּב אֲחִי אִיכָבוֹד | בֶּן־
פִּינְחָס בֶּן־עֵלִי כֹּהֵן | יהוה בְּשִׁלוֹ נֹשֵׂא אֵפוֹד וְהָעָם לֹא יָדַע כִּי הָלַךְ
ד יוֹנָתָן: וּבֵין הַמַּעְבְּרוֹת אֲשֶׁר בִּקֵּשׁ יוֹנָתָן לַעֲבֹר עַל־מַצַּב פְּלִשְׁתִּים
שֵׁן־הַסֶּלַע מֵהָעֵבֶר מִזֶּה וְשֵׁן־הַסֶּלַע מֵהָעֵבֶר מִזֶּה וְשֵׁם הָאֶחָד בּוֹצֵץ
ה וְשֵׁם הָאֶחָד סֶנֶּה: הַשֵּׁן הָאֶחָד מָצוּק מִצָּפוֹן מוּל מִכְמָשׂ וְהָאֶחָד מִנֶּגֶב
ו מוּל גָּבַע: וַיֹּאמֶר יְהוֹנָתָן אֶל־הַנַּעַר | נֹשֵׂא כֵלָיו לְכָה
וְנַעְבְּרָה אֶל־מַצַּב הָעֲרֵלִים הָאֵלֶּה אוּלַי יַעֲשֶׂה יהוה לָנוּ כִּי אֵין לַיהוה
ז מַעְצוֹר לְהוֹשִׁיעַ בְּרַב אוֹ בִמְעָט: וַיֹּאמֶר לוֹ נֹשֵׂא כֵלָיו עֲשֵׂה כָּל־אֲשֶׁר
ח בִּלְבָבֶךָ נְטֵה לָךְ הִנְנִי עִמְּךָ כִּלְבָבֶךָ: וַיֹּאמֶר יְהוֹנָתָן הִנֵּה
ט אֲנַחְנוּ עֹבְרִים אֶל־הָאֲנָשִׁים וְנִגְלֵינוּ אֲלֵיהֶם: אִם־כֹּה יֹאמְרוּ אֵלֵינוּ
י דֹּמּוּ עַד־הַגִּיעֵנוּ אֲלֵיכֶם וְעָמַדְנוּ תַחְתֵּינוּ וְלֹא נַעֲלֶה אֲלֵיהֶם: וְאִם־כֹּה
יא יֹאמְרוּ עֲלוּ עָלֵינוּ וְעָלִינוּ כִּי־נְתָנָם יהוה בְּיָדֵנוּ וְזֶה־לָּנוּ הָאוֹת: וַיִּגָּלוּ
שְׁנֵיהֶם אֶל־מַצַּב פְּלִשְׁתִּים וַיֹּאמְרוּ פְלִשְׁתִּים הִנֵּה עִבְרִים יֹצְאִים מִן־
יב הַחֹרִים אֲשֶׁר הִתְחַבְּאוּ־שָׁם: וַיַּעֲנוּ אַנְשֵׁי הַמַּצָּבָה אֶת־יוֹנָתָן | וְאֶת־
נֹשֵׂא כֵלָיו וַיֹּאמְרוּ עֲלוּ אֵלֵינוּ וְנוֹדִיעָה אֶתְכֶם דָּבָר וַיֹּאמֶר
יג יוֹנָתָן אֶל־נֹשֵׂא כֵלָיו עֲלֵה אַחֲרַי כִּי־נְתָנָם יהוה בְּיַד יִשְׂרָאֵל: וַיַּעַל
יוֹנָתָן עַל־יָדָיו וְעַל־רַגְלָיו וְנֹשֵׂא כֵלָיו אַחֲרָיו וַיִּפְּלוּ לִפְנֵי יוֹנָתָן וְנֹשֵׂא
יד כֵלָיו מְמוֹתֵת אַחֲרָיו: וַתְּהִי הַמַּכָּה הָרִאשֹׁנָה אֲשֶׁר הִכָּה יוֹנָתָן וְנֹשֵׂא
טו כֵלָיו כְּעֶשְׂרִים אִישׁ כְּבַחֲצִי מַעֲנָה צֶמֶד שָׂדֶה: וַתְּהִי חֲרָדָה בַמַּחֲנֶה

seized the camp in the field and all the men – the garrison and the raiders
16 trembled too – and the very earth shuddered in holy terror. The lookouts for
Sha'ul, who was in Giva of Binyamin, saw that the horde was scattering,
17 rushing back and forth. Sha'ul said to the men with him, "Muster
now, and see who has left us"; they mustered and saw that Yonatan and his
18 arms-bearer were missing. And Sha'ul said to Aḥiya, "Bring the Ark of God
19 over," for the Ark was among the Israelites that day. But as Sha'ul was speaking
20 to the priest, the commotion in the Philistine camp kept rising, and
Sha'ul said to the priest, "Withdraw your hand." Sha'ul and the men with him
rallied and reached the battle – to find that each man's sword slashed his fellow
21 in utter pandemonium. And the Hebrews previously on the Philistines' side,
who had gone up with them to the camp, changed sides, and they too joined
22 the Israelites who were with Sha'ul and Yonatan. And when all the men of
Israel who had been hiding in the Efrayim hills heard that the Philistines had
23 fled, they too caught up with them in battle. And the LORD delivered Israel
24 on that day. But meanwhile, the battle spread past Beit Aven, and the men of
Israel were hard-pressed. For Sha'ul had placed the men under oath, saying,
"Cursed be the man who eats food until evening, when I have avenged myself
25 on my enemies," so none of the men had tasted food. Now, the whole area
26 had deepened to forest, where there was honey on the ground's surface.
The men reached the forest, and there was an oozing puddle of honey – but
27 no one dared touch his hand to his lips, for the men feared the oath. But
Yonatan had not heard that his father placed the men under oath, and
he extended the tip of the staff in his hand and dipped it in the honeycomb.
28 And when he brought his hand back to his mouth, his eyes brightened. One
of the men spoke up and said, "Your father placed the men under oath,
declaring, 'Cursed is the man who eats food today.' So the men are famished."
29 "My father has brought a scourge upon the land," said Yonatan. "Just look
30 how my eyes brightened when I tasted a bit of this honey. If only the men
had eaten from their enemies' spoil that they found – for so far, the
31 blow against the Philistines has not been great." On that day, they defeated
the Philistines from Mikhmas to Ayalon, and the men were utterly famished.
32 The men pounced upon the spoil; they seized sheep, cattle, and calves and
slaughtered them over the ground, and the men ate them with the blood.[12]
33 When they informed Sha'ul, saying, "Look – the men are sinning to the LORD
by eating with the blood," he said, "You have shown disloyalty. Roll a large
34 stone over to me now." Then Sha'ul said, "Spread out among the men, and
tell them, 'Each one of you – bring his ox and sheep to me, and slaughter them
on this; eat, but do not offend the LORD by eating with the blood.'" And
every one of the men brought forth the ox in his possession that night,
35 and slaughtered it there. And Sha'ul built an altar to the LORD; it was the
36 first altar he built to the LORD. Then Sha'ul said, "Let us descend

12 | Prohibited in Leviticus 19:26.

בַּשָּׂדֶה וּבְכָל־הָעָם הַמַּצָּב וְהַמַּשְׁחִית חָרְדוּ גַּם־הֵמָּה וַתִּרְגַּז הָאָרֶץ
טז וַתְּהִי לְחֶרְדַּת אֱלֹהִים: וַיִּרְאוּ הַצֹּפִים לְשָׁאוּל בְּגִבְעַת בִּנְיָמִן וְהִנֵּה
יז הֶהָמוֹן נָמוֹג וַיֵּלֶךְ וַהֲלֹם: וַיֹּאמֶר שָׁאוּל לָעָם אֲשֶׁר אִתּוֹ
פִּקְדוּ־נָא וּרְאוּ מִי הָלַךְ מֵעִמָּנוּ וַיִּפְקְדוּ וְהִנֵּה אֵין יוֹנָתָן וְנֹשֵׂא כֵלָיו:
יח וַיֹּאמֶר שָׁאוּל לַאֲחִיָּה הַגִּישָׁה אֲרוֹן הָאֱלֹהִים כִּי־הָיָה אֲרוֹן הָאֱלֹהִים
יט בַּיּוֹם הַהוּא וּבְנֵי יִשְׂרָאֵל: וַיְהִי עַד דִּבֶּר שָׁאוּל אֶל־הַכֹּהֵן וְהֶהָמוֹן
אֲשֶׁר בְּמַחֲנֵה פְלִשְׁתִּים וַיֵּלֶךְ הָלוֹךְ וָרָב וַיֹּאמֶר שָׁאוּל
כ אֶל־הַכֹּהֵן אֱסֹף יָדֶךָ: וַיִּזָּעֵק שָׁאוּל וְכָל־הָעָם אֲשֶׁר אִתּוֹ וַיָּבֹאוּ עַד־
הַמִּלְחָמָה וְהִנֵּה הָיְתָה חֶרֶב אִישׁ בְּרֵעֵהוּ מְהוּמָה גְּדוֹלָה מְאֹד:
כא וְהָעִבְרִים הָיוּ לַפְּלִשְׁתִּים כְּאֶתְמוֹל שִׁלְשׁוֹם אֲשֶׁר עָלוּ עִמָּם בַּמַּחֲנֶה
כב סָבִיב וְגַם־הֵמָּה לִהְיוֹת עִם־יִשְׂרָאֵל אֲשֶׁר עִם־שָׁאוּל וְיוֹנָתָן: וְכֹל אִישׁ
יִשְׂרָאֵל הַמִּתְחַבְּאִים בְּהַר־אֶפְרַיִם שָׁמְעוּ כִּי־נָסוּ פְּלִשְׁתִּים וַיַּדְבְּקוּ
כג גַם־הֵמָּה אַחֲרֵיהֶם בַּמִּלְחָמָה: וַיּוֹשַׁע יְהוָה בַּיּוֹם הַהוּא אֶת־יִשְׂרָאֵל ח
כד וְהַמִּלְחָמָה עָבְרָה אֶת־בֵּית אָוֶן: וְאִישׁ־יִשְׂרָאֵל נִגַּשׂ בַּיּוֹם הַהוּא וַיֹּאֶל
שָׁאוּל אֶת־הָעָם לֵאמֹר אָרוּר הָאִישׁ אֲשֶׁר־יֹאכַל לֶחֶם עַד־הָעֶרֶב
כה וְנִקַּמְתִּי מֵאֹיְבַי וְלֹא־טָעַם כָּל־הָעָם לָחֶם: וְכָל־הָאָרֶץ בָּאוּ בַיָּעַר וַיְהִי
כו דְבַשׁ עַל־פְּנֵי הַשָּׂדֶה: וַיָּבֹא הָעָם אֶל־הַיַּעַר וְהִנֵּה הֵלֶךְ דְּבָשׁ וְאֵין־
כז מַשִּׂיג יָדוֹ אֶל־פִּיו כִּי־יָרֵא הָעָם אֶת־הַשְּׁבֻעָה: וְיוֹנָתָן לֹא־שָׁמַע
בְּהַשְׁבִּיעַ אָבִיו אֶת־הָעָם וַיִּשְׁלַח אֶת־קְצֵה הַמַּטֶּה אֲשֶׁר בְּיָדוֹ וַיִּטְבֹּל
כח אוֹתָהּ בְּיַעְרַת הַדְּבָשׁ וַיָּשֶׁב יָדוֹ אֶל־פִּיו ותראנה עֵינָיו: וַיַּעַן אִישׁ וַתָּאֹרְנָה
מֵהָעָם וַיֹּאמֶר הַשְׁבֵּעַ הִשְׁבִּיעַ אָבִיךָ אֶת־הָעָם לֵאמֹר אָרוּר הָאִישׁ
כט אֲשֶׁר־יֹאכַל לֶחֶם הַיּוֹם וַיָּעַף הָעָם: וַיֹּאמֶר יוֹנָתָן עָכַר אָבִי אֶת־הָאָרֶץ
ל רְאוּ־נָא כִּי־אֹרוּ עֵינַי כִּי טָעַמְתִּי מְעַט דְּבַשׁ הַזֶּה: אַף כִּי לוּא אָכֹל
אָכַל הַיּוֹם הָעָם מִשְּׁלַל אֹיְבָיו אֲשֶׁר מָצָא כִּי עַתָּה לֹא־רָבְתָה מַכָּה
לא בַּפְּלִשְׁתִּים: וַיַּכּוּ בַּיּוֹם הַהוּא בַּפְּלִשְׁתִּים מִמִּכְמָשׂ אַיָּלֹנָה וַיָּעַף הָעָם
לב מְאֹד: ויעש הָעָם אֶל־שלל וַיִּקְחוּ צֹאן וּבָקָר וּבְנֵי בָקָר וַיִּשְׁחֲטוּ־אָרְצָה וַיַּעַט הַשָּׁלָל
לג וַיֹּאכַל הָעָם עַל־הַדָּם: וַיַּגִּידוּ לְשָׁאוּל לֵאמֹר הִנֵּה הָעָם חֹטְאִים לַיהוָה
לד לֶאֱכֹל עַל־הַדָּם וַיֹּאמֶר בְּגַדְתֶּם גֹּלּוּ־אֵלַי הַיּוֹם אֶבֶן גְּדוֹלָה: וַיֹּאמֶר
שָׁאוּל פֻּצוּ בָעָם וַאֲמַרְתֶּם לָהֶם הַגִּישׁוּ אֵלַי אִישׁ שׁוֹרוֹ וְאִישׁ שֵׂיֵהוּ
וּשְׁחַטְתֶּם בָּזֶה וַאֲכַלְתֶּם וְלֹא־תֶחֶטְאוּ לַיהוָה לֶאֱכֹל אֶל־הַדָּם וַיַּגִּשׁוּ
לה כָל־הָעָם אִישׁ שׁוֹרוֹ בְיָדוֹ הַלַּיְלָה וַיִּשְׁחֲטוּ־שָׁם: וַיִּבֶן שָׁאוּל מִזְבֵּחַ
לו לַיהוָה אֹתוֹ הֵחֵל לִבְנוֹת מִזְבֵּחַ לַיהוָה: וַיֹּאמֶר שָׁאוּל

upon the Philistines by night and ravage them until the light of morning – we
shall not leave a man among them," and they said, "Do whatever is best in
37 your eyes." But the priest said, "Let us approach God here." So Sha'ul
inquired of God, "Should I go down after the Philistines? Will You deliver
38 them into Israel's hand?" But He did not answer him on that day. "All troop
leaders, come forward," said Sha'ul, "and determine how such an offense
39 transpired today. For as the LORD lives – He who delivers Israel – even if it is
through Yonatan, my son, he will surely die." But none of the men would
40 answer him. So he addressed all of Israel, "Stay on one side, and I and Yonatan,
my son, will be on the other." "Do what is best in your eyes," the men said to
41 Sha'ul. "Produce the Tumim,"[13] Sha'ul said to the LORD, God of Israel;
42 Yonatan and Sha'ul were singled out, ruling out the men. "Cast the lots
between myself and my son Yonatan," Sha'ul said, and Yonatan was singled
43 out. "Tell me, what have you done?" Sha'ul said to Yonatan, and Yonatan told
him. "I indeed tasted a bit of honey from the very tip of the staff in my hand,"
44 he said. "I am ready to die." "So may God do – and more," Sha'ul said, "for you
45 will surely die, Yonatan!" But the men said to Sha'ul, "Shall Yonatan die – he
who brought this great victory to Israel? Never! As the LORD lives, not a hair
from his head shall fall to the ground – for he acted together with God on this
46 day." And the men came to Yonatan's rescue, and he did not die. And
Sha'ul went back up, desisting from the Philistines, and the Philistines
47 returned to their place. When Sha'ul won the kingship over Israel, he battled
against all his surrounding enemies: against Moav, the Amonites, Edom,
the kings of Tzova, and the Philistines; wherever he turned, he brought doom.
48 He valiantly struck down Amalek and saved Israel from the hands of their
49 oppressors. Sha'ul's sons were Yonatan, Yishvi, and Malki Shua, and
as for the names of his two daughters – the elder was named Merav and the
50 younger was named Mikhal. The name of Sha'ul's wife was Aḥinoam, daughter
of Aḥimaatz, and the commander of his army was named Aviner son of Ner,
51 Sha'ul's uncle; Kish, Sha'ul's father, and Ner, Avner's father, were sons of
52 Aviel. There was fierce war against the Philistines all the days
of Sha'ul, and whenever Sha'ul saw any strong man or valiant warrior, he
15 1 would recruit him. Shmuel said to Sha'ul, "It was I whom the
LORD sent to anoint you as king over His people, over Israel; now, heed the
2 words of the LORD. Thus says the LORD of Hosts: I have taken
note of what Amalek did to Israel; how they set upon them on the way as
3 they came out of Egypt. Now, go and strike down Amalek; you must utterly
destroy all that is theirs – spare nothing. You must slay man and woman; child
4 and infant; ox and sheep; camel and donkey." Sha'ul summoned the
men and mustered them at Telaim; two hundred thousand infantrymen and

13 | The oracle possessed by the high priest (see Ex. 28:30; Num. 27:21).

נרדה אחרי פלשתים לילה ונבזה בהם ׀ עד־אור הבקר ולא־נשאר
בהם איש ויאמרו כל־הטוב בעיניך עשה ויאמר הכהן
לז נקרבה הלם אל־האלהים: וישאל שאול באלהים הארד אחרי
לח פלשתים התתנם ביד ישראל ולא ענהו ביום ההוא: ויאמר שאול
גשו הלם כל פנות העם ודעו וראו במה היתה החטאת הזאת היום:
לט כי חי־יהוה המושיע את־ישראל כי אם־ישנו ביונתן בני כי מות
מ ימות ואין ענהו מכל־העם: ויאמר אל־כל־ישראל אתם תהיו לעבר
אחד ואני ויונתן בני נהיה לעבר אחד ויאמרו העם אל־שאול הטוב
מא בעיניך עשה: ויאמר שאול אל־יהוה אלהי ישראל הבה
מב תמים וילכד יונתן ושאול והעם יצאו: ויאמר שאול הפילו ביני
מג ובין יונתן בני וילכד יונתן: ויאמר שאול אל־יונתן הגידה לי מה
עשיתה ויגד־לו יונתן ויאמר טעם טעמתי בקצה המטה אשר־בידי
מד מעט דבש הנני אמות: ויאמר שאול כה־יעשה אלהים וכה יוסף
מה כי־מות תמות יונתן: ויאמר העם אל־שאול היונתן ימות אשר
עשה הישועה הגדולה הזאת בישראל חלילה חי־יהוה אם־יפל
משערת ראשו ארצה כי־עם־אלהים עשה היום הזה ויפדו העם
מו את־יונתן ולא־מת: ויעל שאול מאחרי פלשתים ופלשתים
מז הלכו למקומם: ושאול לכד המלוכה על־ישראל וילחם סביב ׀
בכל־איביו במואב ׀ ובבני־עמון ובאדום ובמלכי צובה ובפלשתים
מח ובכל אשר־יפנה ירשיע: ויעש חיל ויך את־עמלק ויצל את־ישראל
מט מיד שסהו: ויהיו בני שאול יונתן וישוי ומלכי־שוע ושם
נ שתי בנתיו שם הבכירה מרב ושם הקטנה מיכל: ושם אשת שאול
אחינעם בת־אחימעץ ושם שר־צבאו אבינר בן־נר דוד שאול:
נא נב וקיש אבי־שאול ונר אבי־אבנר בן־אביאל: ותהי המלחמה
חזקה על־פלשתים כל ימי שאול וראה שאול כל־איש גבור וכל־
טו א בן־חיל ויאספהו אליו: ויאמר שמואל אל־שאול אתי
שלח יהוה למשחך למלך על־עמו על־ישראל ועתה שמע לקול
ב דברי יהוה: כה אמר יהוה צבאות פקדתי את אשר־
ג עשה עמלק לישראל אשר־שם לו בדרך בעלתו ממצרים: עתה
לך והכיתה את־עמלק והחרמתם את־כל־אשר־לו ולא תחמל
עליו והמתה מאיש עד־אשה מעלל ועד־יונק משור ועד־שה מגמל
ד ועד־חמור: וישמע שאול את־העם ויפקדם בטלאים

5 ten thousand men from Yehuda. Sha'ul reached the city of Amalek and lay in
6 wait in the wadi. And Sha'ul said to the Kenites, "Leave; turn and withdraw
from among the Amalekites lest I destroy you together with them; you dealt
loyally with all the Israelites when they left Egypt," and the Kenites departed
7 from Amalek. Then Sha'ul struck down Amalek from Ḥavila up to Shur, which
8 is east of Egypt. He captured King Agag of Amalek alive and utterly destroyed
9 the entire people by the sword. But Sha'ul and the men spared Agag and the
best of the sheep, cattle, fat calves, and lambs – the very best of everything;
they were not willing to destroy them. As for all the spurned, worthless
10 property – that, they utterly destroyed. Then the word of the LORD
11 reached Shmuel: "I regret that I crowned Sha'ul as king, for he has turned
away from following Me and he has failed to fulfill My words." This enraged
12 Shmuel, and he cried out to the LORD all night long. And Shmuel set out early
in the morning toward Sha'ul, and Shmuel was told, "Sha'ul has gone to
Carmel, where he set up a monument for himself; then he turned off and
13 made his way down to Gilgal." When Shmuel reached Sha'ul, Sha'ul said to
14 him, "Blessed are you to the LORD! I have fulfilled the LORD's word." "Then
what is this bleating of sheep in my ears," said Shmuel, "and the lowing of
15 cattle that I hear?" "They brought them from the Amalekites," said Sha'ul, "for
the men spared the best of the sheep and cattle for sacrificing to the LORD,
16 your God – but we utterly destroyed the rest." "Stop," said Shmuel,
"and let me tell you what the LORD told me last night." "Speak," he said to
17 him. And Shmuel said, "Though you may seem small in your own
eyes, you are the head of the tribes of Israel, and the LORD anointed you as
18 king over Israel. The LORD sent you on a mission, bidding, 'Go and utterly
destroy the offenders – Amalek – and fight them until you have destroyed
19 them.' But why did you fail to heed the voice of the LORD, pouncing on the
20 spoil and doing evil in the eyes of the LORD?" "But I did heed the
voice of the LORD," Sha'ul said to Shmuel. "I set out on the mission the LORD
assigned me, and I brought Agag, king of Amalek, and utterly destroyed
21 Amalek. And the men took of the spoil – the choicest sheep and cattle from
22 what was banned – to sacrifice to the LORD, your God, at Gilgal." And
Shmuel said, "Does the LORD delight in burnt offerings and sacrifices as
much as obedience to the LORD's voice? Behold – obedience is better than
23 sacrifice, and compliance than the fat of rams. For rebellion is as bad as the
sin of divination, and presumption as corruption and idolatry. Because you
24 rejected the word of the LORD, He has rejected you as king." "I have
sinned," Sha'ul said to Shmuel, "for I violated the LORD's command and your
25 word, because I feared the people and heeded their voice. But now, please
26 forgive my sin and return with me, so I may worship before the LORD." "I will
not return with you," Shmuel said to Sha'ul, "for you have rejected the word

ה מָאתַיִם אֶלֶף רַגְלִי וַעֲשֶׂרֶת אֲלָפִים אֶת־אִישׁ יְהוּדָה: וַיָּבֹא שָׁאוּל
ו עַד־עִיר עֲמָלֵק וַיָּרֶב בַּנָּחַל: וַיֹּאמֶר שָׁאוּל אֶל־הַקֵּינִי לְכוּ סֻּרוּ רְדוּ
מִתּוֹךְ עֲמָלֵקִי פֶּן־אֹסִפְךָ עִמּוֹ וְאַתָּה עָשִׂיתָה חֶסֶד עִם־כָּל־בְּנֵי יִשְׂרָאֵל
ז בַּעֲלוֹתָם מִמִּצְרָיִם וַיָּסַר קֵינִי מִתּוֹךְ עֲמָלֵק: וַיַּךְ שָׁאוּל אֶת־עֲמָלֵק
ח מֵחֲוִילָה בּוֹאֲךָ שׁוּר אֲשֶׁר עַל־פְּנֵי מִצְרָיִם: וַיִּתְפֹּשׂ אֶת־אֲגַג מֶלֶךְ־
ט עֲמָלֵק חָי וְאֶת־כָּל־הָעָם הֶחֱרִים לְפִי־חָרֶב: וַיַּחְמֹל שָׁאוּל וְהָעָם
עַל־אֲגָג וְעַל־מֵיטַב הַצֹּאן וְהַבָּקָר וְהַמִּשְׁנִים וְעַל־הַכָּרִים וְעַל־
כָּל־הַטּוֹב וְלֹא אָבוּ הַחֲרִימָם וְכָל־הַמְּלָאכָה נְמִבְזָה וְנָמֵס אֹתָהּ
יא הֶחֱרִימוּ: וַיְהִי דְּבַר יהוה אֶל־שְׁמוּאֵל לֵאמֹר: נִחַמְתִּי
כִּי־הִמְלַכְתִּי אֶת־שָׁאוּל לְמֶלֶךְ כִּי־שָׁב מֵאַחֲרַי וְאֶת־דְּבָרַי לֹא הֵקִים
יב וַיִּחַר לִשְׁמוּאֵל וַיִּזְעַק אֶל־יהוה כָּל־הַלָּיְלָה: וַיַּשְׁכֵּם שְׁמוּאֵל לִקְרַאת
שָׁאוּל בַּבֹּקֶר וַיֻּגַּד לִשְׁמוּאֵל לֵאמֹר בָּא־שָׁאוּל הַכַּרְמֶלָה וְהִנֵּה מַצִּיב
יג לוֹ יָד וַיִּסֹּב וַיַּעֲבֹר וַיֵּרֶד הַגִּלְגָּל: וַיָּבֹא שְׁמוּאֵל אֶל־שָׁאוּל וַיֹּאמֶר
יד לוֹ שָׁאוּל בָּרוּךְ אַתָּה לַיהוה הֲקִימֹתִי אֶת־דְּבַר יהוה: וַיֹּאמֶר שְׁמוּאֵל
טו וּמֶה קוֹל־הַצֹּאן הַזֶּה בְּאָזְנָי וְקוֹל הַבָּקָר אֲשֶׁר אָנֹכִי שֹׁמֵעַ: וַיֹּאמֶר
שָׁאוּל מֵעֲמָלֵקִי הֱבִיאוּם אֲשֶׁר חָמַל הָעָם עַל־מֵיטַב הַצֹּאן וְהַבָּקָר
טז לְמַעַן זְבֹחַ לַיהוה אֱלֹהֶיךָ וְאֶת־הַיּוֹתֵר הֶחֱרַמְנוּ: וַיֹּאמֶר
שְׁמוּאֵל אֶל־שָׁאוּל הֶרֶף וְאַגִּידָה לְּךָ אֵת אֲשֶׁר דִּבֶּר יהוה אֵלַי
יז הַלָּיְלָה ויאמרו לוֹ דַּבֵּר: וַיֹּאמֶר שְׁמוּאֵל הֲלוֹא אִם־קָטֹן ט וַיֹּאמֶר
אַתָּה בְּעֵינֶיךָ רֹאשׁ שִׁבְטֵי יִשְׂרָאֵל אָתָּה וַיִּמְשָׁחֲךָ יהוה לְמֶלֶךְ עַל־
יח יִשְׂרָאֵל: וַיִּשְׁלָחֲךָ יהוה בְּדָרֶךְ וַיֹּאמֶר לֵךְ וְהַחֲרַמְתָּה אֶת־הַחַטָּאִים
יט אֶת־עֲמָלֵק וְנִלְחַמְתָּ בוֹ עַד־כַּלּוֹתָם אֹתָם: וְלָמָּה לֹא־שָׁמַעְתָּ בְּקוֹל
כ יהוה וַתַּעַט אֶל־הַשָּׁלָל וַתַּעַשׂ הָרַע בְּעֵינֵי יהוה: וַיֹּאמֶר
שָׁאוּל אֶל־שְׁמוּאֵל אֲשֶׁר שָׁמַעְתִּי בְּקוֹל יהוה וָאֵלֵךְ בַּדֶּרֶךְ אֲשֶׁר־
שְׁלָחַנִי יהוה וָאָבִיא אֶת־אֲגַג מֶלֶךְ עֲמָלֵק וְאֶת־עֲמָלֵק הֶחֱרַמְתִּי:
כא וַיִּקַּח הָעָם מֵהַשָּׁלָל צֹאן וּבָקָר רֵאשִׁית הַחֵרֶם לִזְבֹּחַ לַיהוה אֱלֹהֶיךָ
כב בַּגִּלְגָּל: וַיֹּאמֶר שְׁמוּאֵל הַחֵפֶץ לַיהוה בְּעֹלוֹת וּזְבָחִים
כִּשְׁמֹעַ בְּקוֹל יהוה הִנֵּה שְׁמֹעַ מִזֶּבַח טוֹב לְהַקְשִׁיב מֵחֵלֶב אֵילִים:
כג כִּי חַטַּאת־קֶסֶם מֶרִי וְאָוֶן וּתְרָפִים הַפְצַר יַעַן מָאַסְתָּ אֶת־דְּבַר יהוה
כד וַיִּמְאָסְךָ מִמֶּלֶךְ: וַיֹּאמֶר שָׁאוּל אֶל־שְׁמוּאֵל חָטָאתִי כִּי־
עָבַרְתִּי אֶת־פִּי־יהוה וְאֶת־דְּבָרֶיךָ כִּי יָרֵאתִי אֶת־הָעָם וָאֶשְׁמַע בְּקוֹלָם:
כה כו וְעַתָּה שָׂא נָא אֶת־חַטָּאתִי וְשׁוּב עִמִּי וְאֶשְׁתַּחֲוֶה לַיהוה: וַיֹּאמֶר

of the Lord – and the Lord has rejected you from being king over Israel."
27 And Shmuel turned to go, but Sha'ul grabbed the corner of his robe, and it
28 tore. "The Lord has torn the kingship of Israel away from you today," Shmuel
29 said to him, "and has granted it to your peer, who is better than you. What is
more, Israel's Eternal will not betray or waver, for He is not a mere wavering
30 human." "I have sinned," he said. "Now please honor me in front of the elders
of my people and in front of Israel; return with me and I will worship the
31 Lord your God." So Shmuel followed Sha'ul back, and Sha'ul worshipped
32 the Lord. Shmuel then gave the order, "Bring Agag, king of Amalek,
to me." Agag walked up to him with stately steps. "So," said Agag, "the
33 bitterness of death is upon me." And Shmuel said, "As your sword has made
women childless, so your mother shall be childless among women!" And
34 Shmuel hacked Agag to pieces before the Lord at Gilgal. Then
Shmuel went to Rama while Sha'ul made his way up to his home in Givat
35 Sha'ul. Shmuel never saw Sha'ul again to his dying day, yet Shmuel grieved
16 1 for Sha'ul, for the Lord regretted appointing Sha'ul over Israel. The
Lord said to Shmuel, "For how long will you grieve over Sha'ul when I have
rejected him from reigning over Israel? Fill your horn with oil and set off; I
am sending you to Yishai, the Bethlehemite, for I have seen a king for Me
2 among his sons." "How can I go?" said Shmuel. "If Sha'ul hears, he will kill
me!" The Lord said, "Take a heifer with you and say, 'I have come
3 to sacrifice to the Lord.' Then summon Yishai to the sacrifice, and I will let
4 you know what to do; you shall anoint for Me the one I reveal to you." Shmuel
did as the Lord bid and arrived in Beit Leḥem. The elders of the city came
5 trembling out to meet him and said, "Have you come in peace?" "Peace," he
replied. "I have come to sacrifice to the Lord. Sanctify yourselves and come
with me to the sacrifice." Then he sanctified Yishai and his sons and summoned
6 them to the sacrifice. When they arrived, he saw Eliav and thought, "Surely
7 the Lord's anointed is before Him." But the Lord said to Shmuel,
"Do not look upon his appearance or his tall bearing, for I have rejected him,
not seeing as man does; for man sees what the eyes see, but the Lord sees
8 into the heart." Then Yishai called to Avinadav and passed him before Shmuel,
9 who said, "The Lord has not chosen this one either." And when Yishai had
10 Shama pass, he said, "The Lord has not chosen this one either." Yishai had
his seven sons pass before Shmuel, but Shmuel said to Yishai, "The Lord has
11 not chosen any of these." Then Shmuel asked Yishai, "Are there no other
boys?" "There is still the youngest," he said. "Right now, he is shepherding the
flock." "Send out to fetch him," Shmuel said to Yishai, "for we will not move
12 on until he comes here." He sent out and brought him; he was ruddy, with
beautiful eyes, and handsome. And the Lord said, "Arise, anoint

שְׁמוּאֵל אֶל־שָׁאוּל לֹא אָשׁוּב עִמָּךְ כִּי מָאַסְתָּה אֶת־דְּבַר יְהוָה וַיִּמְאָסְךָ
כז יְהוָה מִהְיוֹת מֶלֶךְ עַל־יִשְׂרָאֵל: וַיִּסֹּב שְׁמוּאֵל לָלֶכֶת וַיַּחֲזֵק בִּכְנַף־
כח מְעִילוֹ וַיִּקָּרַע: וַיֹּאמֶר אֵלָיו שְׁמוּאֵל קָרַע יְהוָה אֶת־מַמְלְכוּת יִשְׂרָאֵל
כט מֵעָלֶיךָ הַיּוֹם וּנְתָנָהּ לְרֵעֲךָ הַטּוֹב מִמֶּךָּ: וְגַם נֵצַח יִשְׂרָאֵל לֹא יְשַׁקֵּר
ל וְלֹא יִנָּחֵם כִּי לֹא אָדָם הוּא לְהִנָּחֵם: וַיֹּאמֶר חָטָאתִי עַתָּה כַּבְּדֵנִי נָא
נֶגֶד זִקְנֵי־עַמִּי וְנֶגֶד יִשְׂרָאֵל וְשׁוּב עִמִּי וְהִשְׁתַּחֲוֵיתִי לַיהוָה אֱלֹהֶיךָ:
לא לב וַיָּשָׁב שְׁמוּאֵל אַחֲרֵי שָׁאוּל וַיִּשְׁתַּחוּ שָׁאוּל לַיהוָה: וַיֹּאמֶר
שְׁמוּאֵל הַגִּישׁוּ אֵלַי אֶת־אֲגַג מֶלֶךְ עֲמָלֵק וַיֵּלֶךְ אֵלָיו אֲגַג מַעֲדַנֹּת
לג וַיֹּאמֶר אֲגָג אָכֵן סָר מַר־הַמָּוֶת: וַיֹּאמֶר שְׁמוּאֵל כַּאֲשֶׁר שִׁכְּלָה נָשִׁים
חַרְבֶּךָ כֵּן־תִּשְׁכַּל מִנָּשִׁים אִמֶּךָ וַיְשַׁסֵּף שְׁמוּאֵל אֶת־אֲגָג לִפְנֵי יְהוָה
לד בַּגִּלְגָּל: וַיֵּלֶךְ שְׁמוּאֵל הָרָמָתָה וְשָׁאוּל עָלָה אֶל־בֵּיתוֹ
לה גִּבְעַת שָׁאוּל: וְלֹא־יָסַף שְׁמוּאֵל לִרְאוֹת אֶת־שָׁאוּל עַד־יוֹם מוֹתוֹ
כִּי־הִתְאַבֵּל שְׁמוּאֵל אֶל־שָׁאוּל וַיהוָה נִחָם כִּי־הִמְלִיךְ אֶת־שָׁאוּל
טז א עַל־יִשְׂרָאֵל: וַיֹּאמֶר יְהוָה אֶל־שְׁמוּאֵל עַד־מָתַי אַתָּה
מִתְאַבֵּל אֶל־שָׁאוּל וַאֲנִי מְאַסְתִּיו מִמְּלֹךְ עַל־יִשְׂרָאֵל מַלֵּא קַרְנְךָ
שֶׁמֶן וְלֵךְ אֶשְׁלָחֲךָ אֶל־יִשַׁי בֵּית־הַלַּחְמִי כִּי־רָאִיתִי בְּבָנָיו לִי מֶלֶךְ:
ב וַיֹּאמֶר שְׁמוּאֵל אֵיךְ אֵלֵךְ וְשָׁמַע שָׁאוּל וַהֲרָגָנִי וַיֹּאמֶר יְהוָה
ג עֶגְלַת בָּקָר תִּקַּח בְּיָדֶךָ וְאָמַרְתָּ לִזְבֹּחַ לַיהוָה בָּאתִי: וְקָרָאתָ לְיִשַׁי
בַּזָּבַח וְאָנֹכִי אוֹדִיעֲךָ אֵת אֲשֶׁר־תַּעֲשֶׂה וּמָשַׁחְתָּ לִי אֵת אֲשֶׁר־אֹמַר
ד אֵלֶיךָ: וַיַּעַשׂ שְׁמוּאֵל אֵת אֲשֶׁר דִּבֶּר יְהוָה וַיָּבֹא בֵּית לָחֶם וַיֶּחֶרְדוּ
ה זִקְנֵי הָעִיר לִקְרָאתוֹ וַיֹּאמֶר שָׁלֹם בּוֹאֶךָ: וַיֹּאמֶר ׀ שָׁלוֹם לִזְבֹּחַ לַיהוָה
בָּאתִי הִתְקַדְּשׁוּ וּבָאתֶם אִתִּי בַּזָּבַח וַיְקַדֵּשׁ אֶת־יִשַׁי וְאֶת־בָּנָיו וַיִּקְרָא
ו לָהֶם לַזָּבַח: וַיְהִי בְּבוֹאָם וַיַּרְא אֶת־אֱלִיאָב וַיֹּאמֶר אַךְ נֶגֶד יְהוָה
ז מְשִׁיחוֹ: וַיֹּאמֶר יְהוָה אֶל־שְׁמוּאֵל אַל־תַּבֵּט אֶל־מַרְאֵהוּ
וְאֶל־גְּבֹהַּ קוֹמָתוֹ כִּי מְאַסְתִּיהוּ כִּי ׀ לֹא אֲשֶׁר יִרְאֶה הָאָדָם כִּי הָאָדָם
ח יִרְאֶה לַעֵינַיִם וַיהוָה יִרְאֶה לַלֵּבָב: וַיִּקְרָא יִשַׁי אֶל־אֲבִינָדָב וַיַּעֲבִרֵהוּ
ט לִפְנֵי שְׁמוּאֵל וַיֹּאמֶר גַּם־בָּזֶה לֹא־בָחַר יְהוָה: וַיַּעֲבֵר יִשַׁי שַׁמָּה וַיֹּאמֶר
י גַּם־בָּזֶה לֹא־בָחַר יְהוָה: וַיַּעֲבֵר יִשַׁי שִׁבְעַת בָּנָיו לִפְנֵי שְׁמוּאֵל וַיֹּאמֶר
יא שְׁמוּאֵל אֶל־יִשַׁי לֹא־בָחַר יְהוָה בָּאֵלֶּה: וַיֹּאמֶר שְׁמוּאֵל אֶל־יִשַׁי
הֲתַמּוּ הַנְּעָרִים וַיֹּאמֶר עוֹד שָׁאַר הַקָּטָן וְהִנֵּה רֹעֶה בַּצֹּאן וַיֹּאמֶר
יב שְׁמוּאֵל אֶל־יִשַׁי שִׁלְחָה וְקָחֶנּוּ כִּי לֹא־נָסֹב עַד־בֹּאוֹ פֹה: וַיִּשְׁלַח
וַיְבִיאֵהוּ וְהוּא אַדְמוֹנִי עִם־יְפֵה עֵינַיִם וְטוֹב רֹאִי וַיֹּאמֶר יְהוָה

13 him – for he is the one." Shmuel took the horn of oil and anointed him in the
midst of his brothers, and the spirit of the LORD seized David from that day
14 onward. Then Shmuel rose and set out for Rama. Now the spirit of the LORD
had slipped away from Sha'ul, while a dark spirit from the LORD began to
15 haunt him. Sha'ul's servants said to him, "Look, a dark spirit from God is
16 haunting you. Perhaps our lord should bid the servants before you, 'Seek out
a man who knows how to play the lyre,' so that when the dark spirit from God
17 settles upon you, with the strumming of his fingers, you will feel well." And
Sha'ul said to his servants, "Seek out someone for me who plays well, and
18 bring him to me." One of the servant boys answered, "I have noticed that
Yishai the Bethlehemite has a son who knows how to play," he said. "He is a
powerful man, a seasoned warrior, wise of word and attractive – and the LORD
19 is with him." So Sha'ul sent messengers to Yishai, saying, "Send me your son
20 David, the one who is with the flock." Yishai loaded a donkey with bread, a
skin of wine, and a young goat, and sent it to Sha'ul along with his son David.
21 David came to Sha'ul and attended him; he loved him dearly, and he became
22 his armor-bearer. Sha'ul sent word to Yishai, "Let David attend me, for he has
23 found favor in my eyes." Whenever the spirit of God would settle upon Sha'ul,
David would take up his lyre and play; then Sha'ul would feel relieved and
well, and the dark spirit would leave him.
17 1 Now, the Philistines rallied
their forces for war; they rallied at Sokho of Yehuda; they set up camp
2 between Sokho and Azeka, at Efes Damim. And Sha'ul and the men of Israel
rallied and set up camp in the Valley of the Terebinth and arrayed for battle
3 against the Philistines. The Philistines were stationed on a hill on this side,
Israel were stationed on a hill on that side, and the valley lay between them.
4 Then the champion of the Philistine forces came forth; his name was Golyat,
5 of Gat, and he was six cubits and a span tall. A bronze helmet was on his head,
and he was clad in scale armor; the armor weighed five thousand shekel of
6 bronze. Bronze greaves were on his legs, and a bronze javelin was slung
7 between his shoulders. The shaft of his spear was like a weaver's beam, the
blade of his spear weighed six hundred shekel of iron, and a shield-bearer
8 marched before him. He stood and called out to the ranks of Israel. "Why
should you march out to wage battle?" he said to them. "I represent the
Philistines and you are Sha'ul's subjects; select a man, and let him come down
9 to me! If he beats me in combat and strikes me down, then we will become
your subjects; but if I beat him and strike him down, then you shall become
10 our subjects and serve us." And the Philistine concluded, "I challenge the
11 ranks of Israel today: give me a man, and let us duel!" When Sha'ul and all of
12 Israel heard the Philistine's speech, panic and terror seized them. Now
David was the son of a certain Efratite from Beit Leḥem of Yehuda; his name
was Yishai, and he had eight sons. By Sha'ul's time, the man had grown old,

יג קוּם מְשָׁחֵהוּ כִּי־זֶה הוּא: וַיִּקַּח שְׁמוּאֵל אֶת־קֶרֶן הַשֶּׁמֶן וַיִּמְשַׁח אֹתוֹ
בְּקֶרֶב אֶחָיו וַתִּצְלַח רוּחַ־יהוה אֶל־דָּוִד מֵהַיּוֹם הַהוּא וָמָעְלָה וַיָּקָם
יד שְׁמוּאֵל וַיֵּלֶךְ הָרָמָתָה: וְרוּחַ יהוה סָרָה מֵעִם שָׁאוּל וּבִעֲתַתּוּ רוּחַ־
טו רָעָה מֵאֵת יהוה: וַיֹּאמְרוּ עַבְדֵי־שָׁאוּל אֵלָיו הִנֵּה־נָא רוּחַ־אֱלֹהִים
טז רָעָה מְבַעִתֶּךָ: יֹאמַר־נָא אֲדֹנֵנוּ עֲבָדֶיךָ לְפָנֶיךָ יְבַקְשׁוּ אִישׁ יֹדֵעַ מְנַגֵּן
בַּכִּנּוֹר וְהָיָה בִּהְיוֹת עָלֶיךָ רוּחַ־אֱלֹהִים רָעָה וְנִגֵּן בְּיָדוֹ וְטוֹב לָךְ:
יז וַיֹּאמֶר שָׁאוּל אֶל־עֲבָדָיו רְאוּ־נָא לִי אִישׁ מֵיטִיב לְנַגֵּן וַהֲבִיאוֹתֶם
יח אֵלָי: וַיַּעַן אֶחָד מֵהַנְּעָרִים וַיֹּאמֶר הִנֵּה רָאִיתִי בֵּן לְיִשַׁי בֵּית הַלַּחְמִי י
יֹדֵעַ נַגֵּן וְגִבּוֹר חַיִל וְאִישׁ מִלְחָמָה וּנְבוֹן דָּבָר וְאִישׁ תֹּאַר וַיהוה עִמּוֹ:
יט וַיִּשְׁלַח שָׁאוּל מַלְאָכִים אֶל־יִשָׁי וַיֹּאמֶר שִׁלְחָה אֵלַי אֶת־דָּוִד בִּנְךָ
כ אֲשֶׁר בַּצֹּאן: וַיִּקַּח יִשַׁי חֲמוֹר לֶחֶם וְנֹאד יַיִן וּגְדִי עִזִּים אֶחָד וַיִּשְׁלַח
כא בְּיַד־דָּוִד בְּנוֹ אֶל־שָׁאוּל: וַיָּבֹא דָוִד אֶל־שָׁאוּל וַיַּעֲמֹד לְפָנָיו וַיֶּאֱהָבֵהוּ
כב מְאֹד וַיְהִי־לוֹ נֹשֵׂא כֵלִים: וַיִּשְׁלַח שָׁאוּל אֶל־יִשַׁי לֵאמֹר יַעֲמָד־נָא
כג דָוִד לְפָנַי כִּי־מָצָא חֵן בְּעֵינָי: וְהָיָה בִּהְיוֹת רוּחַ־אֱלֹהִים אֶל־שָׁאוּל
וְלָקַח דָּוִד אֶת־הַכִּנּוֹר וְנִגֵּן בְּיָדוֹ וְרָוַח לְשָׁאוּל וְטוֹב לוֹ וְסָרָה מֵעָלָיו
יז א רוּחַ הָרָעָה: וַיַּאַסְפוּ פְלִשְׁתִּים אֶת־מַחֲנֵיהֶם לַמִּלְחָמָה וַיֵּאָסְפוּ
ב שֹׂכֹה אֲשֶׁר לִיהוּדָה וַיַּחֲנוּ בֵּין־שׂוֹכֹה וּבֵין־עֲזֵקָה בְּאֶפֶס דַּמִּים: וְשָׁאוּל
וְאִישׁ־יִשְׂרָאֵל נֶאֶסְפוּ וַיַּחֲנוּ בְּעֵמֶק הָאֵלָה וַיַּעַרְכוּ מִלְחָמָה לִקְרַאת
ג פְלִשְׁתִּים: וּפְלִשְׁתִּים עֹמְדִים אֶל־הָהָר מִזֶּה וְיִשְׂרָאֵל עֹמְדִים אֶל־
ד הָהָר מִזֶּה וְהַגַּיְא בֵּינֵיהֶם: וַיֵּצֵא אִישׁ־הַבֵּנַיִם מִמַּחֲנוֹת פְּלִשְׁתִּים גָּלְיָת
ה שְׁמוֹ מִגַּת גָּבְהוֹ שֵׁשׁ אַמּוֹת וָזָרֶת: וְכוֹבַע נְחֹשֶׁת עַל־רֹאשׁוֹ וְשִׁרְיוֹן
קַשְׂקַשִּׂים הוּא לָבוּשׁ וּמִשְׁקַל הַשִּׁרְיוֹן חֲמֵשֶׁת־אֲלָפִים שְׁקָלִים נְחֹשֶׁת:
ו ז וּמִצְחַת נְחֹשֶׁת עַל־רַגְלָיו וְכִידוֹן נְחֹשֶׁת בֵּין כְּתֵפָיו: וְחֵץ חֲנִיתוֹ כִּמְנוֹר וְעֵץ
אֹרְגִים וְלַהֶבֶת חֲנִיתוֹ שֵׁשׁ־מֵאוֹת שְׁקָלִים בַּרְזֶל וְנֹשֵׂא הַצִּנָּה הֹלֵךְ
ח לְפָנָיו: וַיַּעֲמֹד וַיִּקְרָא אֶל־מַעַרְכֹת יִשְׂרָאֵל וַיֹּאמֶר לָהֶם לָמָּה תֵצְאוּ
לַעֲרֹךְ מִלְחָמָה הֲלוֹא אָנֹכִי הַפְּלִשְׁתִּי וְאַתֶּם עֲבָדִים לְשָׁאוּל בְּרוּ־
ט לָכֶם אִישׁ וְיֵרֵד אֵלָי: אִם־יוּכַל לְהִלָּחֵם אִתִּי וְהִכָּנִי וְהָיִינוּ לָכֶם לַעֲבָדִים
וְאִם־אֲנִי אוּכַל־לוֹ וְהִכִּיתִיו וִהְיִיתֶם לָנוּ לַעֲבָדִים וַעֲבַדְתֶּם אֹתָנוּ:
י וַיֹּאמֶר הַפְּלִשְׁתִּי אֲנִי חֵרַפְתִּי אֶת־מַעַרְכוֹת יִשְׂרָאֵל הַיּוֹם הַזֶּה תְּנוּ־
יא לִי אִישׁ וְנִלָּחֲמָה יָחַד: וַיִּשְׁמַע שָׁאוּל וְכָל־יִשְׂרָאֵל אֶת־דִּבְרֵי הַפְּלִשְׁתִּי
יב הָאֵלֶּה וַיֵּחַתּוּ וַיִּרְאוּ מְאֹד: וְדָוִד בֶּן־אִישׁ אֶפְרָתִי הַזֶּה
מִבֵּית לֶחֶם יְהוּדָה וּשְׁמוֹ יִשַׁי וְלוֹ שְׁמֹנָה בָנִים וְהָאִישׁ בִּימֵי שָׁאוּל זָקֵן

13 senior among men, so Yishai's three oldest sons had gone out to follow Sha'ul
in battle. The names of the three sons who had left for the war were Eliav, the
14 oldest; his second was Avinadav, and the third was Shama. David was the
15 youngest, while only the three oldest had left to follow Sha'ul; David was
going back and forth between Sha'ul and shepherding his father's flock in Beit
16 Leḥem. Meanwhile, the Philistine had been looming every morning and
17 evening, flaunting himself, for forty days. Yishai said to his son
David, "Please take an ephah of this toasted grain and ten loaves of this bread
18 for your brothers, and rush them over to your brothers in the camp. As for
these ten cheeses, bring them to the commander of the thousand. Take note
19 of your brothers' welfare, and bring some token from them. Sha'ul and they,
and all the men of Israel, are in the Valley of the Terebinth, at war with the
20 Philistines." David rose early in the morning, left the sheep with a
keeper, and set out, taking what Yishai had instructed him to. He arrived at
the entrenchment just as the force was marching out toward the battle lines
21 and sounding the war cry. And Israel and the Philistines deployed, line against
22 line. David left the baggage with him in the baggage-keeper's care, ran to
23 the battle line, and arrived and greeted his brothers. As he was speaking to
them, the champion came marching up from the Philistine ranks – Golyat
the Philistine was his name, from Gat – and gave his usual speech, and David
24 heard. When all the men of Israel saw the man, they retreated before him
25 in utter terror. And the men of Israel were saying, "Did you see that man,
the one marching up? To challenge Israel – that is why he marches up!
Whoever defeats him – the king will reward him with great riches and
give him his daughter, and his father's house will be granted exemption in
26 Israel." David said to the men who were standing with him, "What
will be done for the man who defeats that Philistine and clears Israel's
disgrace? For who is this heathen Philistine to dare to taunt the ranks of the
27 Living God?" And the people repeated to him what would be done for the
28 man who defeated him. When his older brother Eliav heard him speaking to
the men, he grew furious with David. "Why have you come down here," he
said, "and with whom did you leave that measly flock in the wilderness?
I know your presumption and your dark intentions – you just came down
29 to see the battle, did you not?" "What have I done now?" said David. "It was
30 only a question." But he turned away from him toward someone else and
31 asked the same thing, and the people gave the same answer as the first. And
the words David spoke were heard and reported to Sha'ul, and he took him
32 aside. David said to Sha'ul, "Let no one lose heart. Your servant will go and
33 fight with that Philistine." "You cannot go and fight against this Philistine,"
Sha'ul said to David, "for you are just a boy, while he has been a warrior
34 from his youth." "Your servant has been tending the sheep for

יג בָּא בַאֲנָשִׁים׃ וַיֵּלְכוּ שְׁלֹשֶׁת בְּנֵי־יִשַׁי הַגְּדֹלִים הָלְכוּ אַחֲרֵי־שָׁאוּל
לַמִּלְחָמָה וְשֵׁם ׀ שְׁלֹשֶׁת בָּנָיו אֲשֶׁר הָלְכוּ בַּמִּלְחָמָה אֱלִיאָב הַבְּכוֹר
יד וּמִשְׁנֵהוּ אֲבִינָדָב וְהַשְּׁלִשִׁי שַׁמָּה׃ וְדָוִד הוּא הַקָּטָן וּשְׁלֹשָׁה הַגְּדֹלִים
טו הָלְכוּ אַחֲרֵי שָׁאוּל׃ וְדָוִד הֹלֵךְ וָשָׁב מֵעַל שָׁאוּל לִרְעוֹת אֶת־צֹאן
טז אָבִיו בֵּית־לָחֶם׃ וַיִּגַּשׁ הַפְּלִשְׁתִּי הַשְׁכֵּם וְהַעֲרֵב וַיִּתְיַצֵּב אַרְבָּעִים
יז יוֹם׃ וַיֹּאמֶר יִשַׁי לְדָוִד בְּנוֹ קַח־נָא לְאַחֶיךָ אֵיפַת הַקָּלִיא
יח הַזֶּה וַעֲשָׂרָה לֶחֶם הַזֶּה וְהָרֵץ הַמַּחֲנֶה לְאַחֶיךָ׃ וְאֵת עֲשֶׂרֶת חֲרִיצֵי
הֶחָלָב הָאֵלֶּה תָּבִיא לְשַׂר־הָאָלֶף וְאֶת־אַחֶיךָ תִּפְקֹד לְשָׁלוֹם וְאֶת־
יט עֲרֻבָּתָם תִּקָּח׃ וְשָׁאוּל וְהֵמָּה וְכָל־אִישׁ יִשְׂרָאֵל בְּעֵמֶק הָאֵלָה נִלְחָמִים
כ עִם־פְּלִשְׁתִּים׃ וַיַּשְׁכֵּם דָּוִד בַּבֹּקֶר וַיִּטֹּשׁ אֶת־הַצֹּאן
עַל־שֹׁמֵר וַיִּשָּׂא וַיֵּלֶךְ כַּאֲשֶׁר צִוָּהוּ יִשָׁי וַיָּבֹא הַמַּעְגָּלָה וְהַחַיִל הַיֹּצֵא
כא אֶל־הַמַּעֲרָכָה וְהֵרֵעוּ בַּמִּלְחָמָה׃ וַתַּעֲרֹךְ יִשְׂרָאֵל וּפְלִשְׁתִּים מַעֲרָכָה
כב לִקְרַאת מַעֲרָכָה׃ וַיִּטֹּשׁ דָּוִד אֶת־הַכֵּלִים מֵעָלָיו עַל־יַד שׁוֹמֵר הַכֵּלִים
כג וַיָּרָץ הַמַּעֲרָכָה וַיָּבֹא וַיִּשְׁאַל לְאֶחָיו לְשָׁלוֹם׃ וְהוּא ׀ מְדַבֵּר עִמָּם וְהִנֵּה
אִישׁ הַבֵּנַיִם עוֹלֶה גָּלְיָת הַפְּלִשְׁתִּי שְׁמוֹ מִגַּת ממערות פְּלִשְׁתִּים וַיְדַבֵּר מִמַּעַרְכוֹת
כד כַּדְּבָרִים הָאֵלֶּה וַיִּשְׁמַע דָּוִד׃ וְכֹל אִישׁ יִשְׂרָאֵל בִּרְאוֹתָם אֶת־הָאִישׁ
כה וַיָּנֻסוּ מִפָּנָיו וַיִּירְאוּ מְאֹד׃ וַיֹּאמֶר ׀ אִישׁ יִשְׂרָאֵל הַרְּאִיתֶם הָאִישׁ הָעֹלֶה
הַזֶּה כִּי לְחָרֵף אֶת־יִשְׂרָאֵל עֹלֶה וְהָיָה הָאִישׁ אֲשֶׁר־יַכֶּנּוּ יַעְשְׁרֶנּוּ
הַמֶּלֶךְ ׀ עֹשֶׁר גָּדוֹל וְאֶת־בִּתּוֹ יִתֶּן־לוֹ וְאֵת בֵּית אָבִיו יַעֲשֶׂה חָפְשִׁי
כו בְּיִשְׂרָאֵל׃ וַיֹּאמֶר דָּוִד אֶל־הָאֲנָשִׁים הָעֹמְדִים עִמּוֹ לֵאמֹר
מַה־יֵּעָשֶׂה לָאִישׁ אֲשֶׁר יַכֶּה אֶת־הַפְּלִשְׁתִּי הַלָּז וְהֵסִיר חֶרְפָּה מֵעַל
יִשְׂרָאֵל כִּי מִי הַפְּלִשְׁתִּי הֶעָרֵל הַזֶּה כִּי חֵרֵף מַעַרְכוֹת אֱלֹהִים חַיִּים׃
כז כח וַיֹּאמֶר לוֹ הָעָם כַּדָּבָר הַזֶּה לֵאמֹר כֹּה יֵעָשֶׂה לָאִישׁ אֲשֶׁר יַכֶּנּוּ׃ וַיִּשְׁמַע
אֱלִיאָב אָחִיו הַגָּדוֹל בְּדַבְּרוֹ אֶל־הָאֲנָשִׁים וַיִּחַר־אַף אֱלִיאָב בְּדָוִד
וַיֹּאמֶר ׀ לָמָּה־זֶּה יָרַדְתָּ וְעַל־מִי נָטַשְׁתָּ מְעַט הַצֹּאן הָהֵנָּה בַּמִּדְבָּר
אֲנִי יָדַעְתִּי אֶת־זְדֹנְךָ וְאֵת רֹעַ לְבָבֶךָ כִּי לְמַעַן רְאוֹת הַמִּלְחָמָה יָרָדְתָּ׃
כט ל וַיֹּאמֶר דָּוִד מֶה עָשִׂיתִי עָתָּה הֲלוֹא דָּבָר הוּא׃ וַיִּסֹּב מֵאֶצְלוֹ אֶל־מוּל
לא אַחֵר וַיֹּאמֶר כַּדָּבָר הַזֶּה וַיְשִׁבֻהוּ הָעָם דָּבָר כַּדָּבָר הָרִאשׁוֹן׃ וַיִּשָּׁמְעוּ
לב הַדְּבָרִים אֲשֶׁר דִּבֶּר דָּוִד וַיַּגִּדוּ לִפְנֵי־שָׁאוּל וַיִּקָּחֵהוּ׃ וַיֹּאמֶר דָּוִד אֶל־
שָׁאוּל אַל־יִפֹּל לֵב־אָדָם עָלָיו עַבְדְּךָ יֵלֵךְ וְנִלְחַם עִם־הַפְּלִשְׁתִּי הַזֶּה׃
לג וַיֹּאמֶר שָׁאוּל אֶל־דָּוִד לֹא תוּכַל לָלֶכֶת אֶל־הַפְּלִשְׁתִּי הַזֶּה לְהִלָּחֵם
לד עִמּוֹ כִּי־נַעַר אַתָּה וְהוּא אִישׁ מִלְחָמָה מִנְּעֻרָיו׃ וַיֹּאמֶר

his father," David said to Sha'ul, "and whenever a lion or a bear came and
35 carried off a sheep off from the flock, I went after it, struck it down, and
rescued the sheep from its jaws. And if it charged at me, I seized its mane,
36 struck it down, and killed it. Your servant has defeated both lion and bear –
and this heathen Philistine is just like them, for he has taunted the ranks of
37 the Living God." And David continued, "The LORD who has rescued
me from the lion and the bear will rescue me from this Philistine." "Go,"
38 Sha'ul said to David, "and the LORD will be with you." And Sha'ul dressed
David in his own uniform, placed a bronze helmet on his head, and clad him
39 in armor. David girded himself with his sword over the uniform and tried to
walk, but he was not used to it. "I cannot walk in this," David said to Sha'ul,
40 "for I am not used to it," and David took them off. He took hold of his sling
stick and chose five smooth stones from the wadi bed, placing them in the
pouch of his shepherd's bag. Then, sling in hand, he approached the Philistine.
41 The Philistine was drawing closer and closer to David, with the man bearing
42 the shield before him, and when the Philistine looked down and saw David,
43 he scorned him, for he was young and ruddy with a handsome look. "Am I a
dog," the Philistine asked David, "that you come at me with sticks?" and the
44 Philistine cursed David by his gods. "Come here," the Philistine then said to
David, "and I will dole out your flesh to the birds of the sky and the beasts of
45 the field." And David replied to the Philistine, "You come at me with
sword and spear and javelin. But I come at you in the name of the LORD of
46 Hosts, the God of the ranks of Israel, whom you taunted. This very day, the
LORD will deliver you into my hands, and I will strike you down and sever
your head from your body. And I will dole out the corpses of the Philistine
camp for the birds of the sky and the beasts of the land, on this very day. Then
47 all the land will know that there is a God over Israel; and all this crowd will
know that the LORD does not grant victory by sword or by spear – for the
48 battle is the LORD's, and He will deliver you into our hands." And when the
Philistine rose up and drew closer to David, David rushed to the battle line
49 toward the Philistine. David thrust his hand into the bag, took out a stone,
slung, and hit the Philistine in his forehead; the stone sank into his forehead,
50 and he toppled face down to the ground. David overpowered the Philistine
with sling and stone; he struck the Philistine, and then he killed him. There
51 was no sword in David's hand, so he ran and stood over the Philistine; seized
his sword and drew it from its sheath, and killed him, cutting off his head.
52 When the Philistines saw that their hero was dead, they fled, but the men of
Israel and Yehuda rose up, sounding the battle cry, and chased the Philistines
to the valley, all the way up to the gates of Ekron; Philistine corpses littered
53 the way to Shaarayim as far as Gat and Ekron. Then the Israelites returned

דָּוִד אֶל־שָׁאוּל רֹעֶה הָיָה עַבְדְּךָ לְאָבִיו בַּצֹּאן וּבָא הָאֲרִי וְאֶת־הַדּוֹב
לה וְנָשָׂא שֶׂה מֵהָעֵדֶר׃ וְיָצָאתִי אַחֲרָיו וְהִכִּתִיו וְהִצַּלְתִּי מִפִּיו וַיָּקָם עָלַי
לו וְהֶחֱזַקְתִּי בִּזְקָנוֹ וְהִכִּתִיו וַהֲמִיתִּיו׃ גַּם אֶת־הָאֲרִי גַּם־הַדּוֹב הִכָּה עַבְדֶּךָ
וְהָיָה הַפְּלִשְׁתִּי הֶעָרֵל הַזֶּה כְּאַחַד מֵהֶם כִּי חֵרֵף מַעַרְכֹת אֱלֹהִים
לז חַיִּים׃ וַיֹּאמֶר דָּוִד יְהוָה אֲשֶׁר הִצִּלַנִי מִיַּד הָאֲרִי וּמִיַּד יא
הַדֹּב הוּא יַצִּילֵנִי מִיַּד הַפְּלִשְׁתִּי הַזֶּה וַיֹּאמֶר שָׁאוּל אֶל־
לח דָּוִד לֵךְ וַיהוָה יִהְיֶה עִמָּךְ׃ וַיַּלְבֵּשׁ שָׁאוּל אֶת־דָּוִד מַדָּיו וְנָתַן קוֹבַע
לט נְחֹשֶׁת עַל־רֹאשׁוֹ וַיַּלְבֵּשׁ אֹתוֹ שִׁרְיוֹן׃ וַיַּחְגֹּר דָּוִד אֶת־חַרְבּוֹ מֵעַל
לְמַדָּיו וַיֹּאֶל לָלֶכֶת כִּי לֹא־נִסָּה וַיֹּאמֶר דָּוִד אֶל־שָׁאוּל לֹא אוּכַל לָלֶכֶת
מ בָּאֵלֶּה כִּי לֹא נִסִּיתִי וַיְסִרֵם דָּוִד מֵעָלָיו׃ וַיִּקַּח מַקְלוֹ בְּיָדוֹ וַיִּבְחַר־לוֹ
חֲמִשָּׁה חַלֻּקֵי אֲבָנִים ׀ מִן־הַנַּחַל וַיָּשֶׂם אֹתָם בִּכְלִי הָרֹעִים אֲשֶׁר־לוֹ
מא וּבַיַּלְקוּט וְקַלְעוֹ בְיָדוֹ וַיִּגַּשׁ אֶל־הַפְּלִשְׁתִּי׃ וַיֵּלֶךְ הַפְּלִשְׁתִּי הֹלֵךְ וְקָרֵב
מב אֶל־דָּוִד וְהָאִישׁ נֹשֵׂא הַצִּנָּה לְפָנָיו׃ וַיַּבֵּט הַפְּלִשְׁתִּי וַיִּרְאֶה אֶת־דָּוִד
מג וַיִּבְזֵהוּ כִּי־הָיָה נַעַר וְאַדְמֹנִי עִם־יְפֵה מַרְאֶה׃ וַיֹּאמֶר הַפְּלִשְׁתִּי אֶל־
דָּוִד הֲכֶלֶב אָנֹכִי כִּי־אַתָּה בָא־אֵלַי בַּמַּקְלוֹת וַיְקַלֵּל הַפְּלִשְׁתִּי אֶת־דָּוִד
מד בֵּאלֹהָיו׃ וַיֹּאמֶר הַפְּלִשְׁתִּי אֶל־דָּוִד לְכָה אֵלַי וְאֶתְּנָה אֶת־בְּשָׂרְךָ
מה לְעוֹף הַשָּׁמַיִם וּלְבֶהֱמַת הַשָּׂדֶה׃ וַיֹּאמֶר דָּוִד אֶל־הַפְּלִשְׁתִּי
אַתָּה בָּא אֵלַי בְּחֶרֶב וּבַחֲנִית וּבְכִידוֹן וְאָנֹכִי בָא־אֵלֶיךָ בְּשֵׁם יְהוָה
מו צְבָאוֹת אֱלֹהֵי מַעַרְכוֹת יִשְׂרָאֵל אֲשֶׁר חֵרַפְתָּ׃ הַיּוֹם הַזֶּה יְסַגֶּרְךָ יְהוָה
בְּיָדִי וְהִכִּיתִךָ וַהֲסִרֹתִי אֶת־רֹאשְׁךָ מֵעָלֶיךָ וְנָתַתִּי פֶּגֶר מַחֲנֵה פְלִשְׁתִּים
הַיּוֹם הַזֶּה לְעוֹף הַשָּׁמַיִם וּלְחַיַּת הָאָרֶץ וְיֵדְעוּ כָּל־הָאָרֶץ כִּי יֵשׁ אֱלֹהִים
מז לְיִשְׂרָאֵל׃ וְיֵדְעוּ כָּל־הַקָּהָל הַזֶּה כִּי־לֹא בְּחֶרֶב וּבַחֲנִית יְהוֹשִׁיעַ יְהוָה
מח כִּי לַיהוָה הַמִּלְחָמָה וְנָתַן אֶתְכֶם בְּיָדֵנוּ׃ וְהָיָה כִּי־קָם הַפְּלִשְׁתִּי וַיֵּלֶךְ
וַיִּקְרַב לִקְרַאת דָּוִד וַיְמַהֵר דָּוִד וַיָּרָץ הַמַּעֲרָכָה לִקְרַאת הַפְּלִשְׁתִּי׃
מט וַיִּשְׁלַח דָּוִד אֶת־יָדוֹ אֶל־הַכֶּלִי וַיִּקַּח מִשָּׁם אֶבֶן וַיְקַלַּע וַיַּךְ אֶת־
הַפְּלִשְׁתִּי אֶל־מִצְחוֹ וַתִּטְבַּע הָאֶבֶן בְּמִצְחוֹ וַיִּפֹּל עַל־פָּנָיו אָרְצָה׃
נ וַיֶּחֱזַק דָּוִד מִן־הַפְּלִשְׁתִּי בַּקֶּלַע וּבָאֶבֶן וַיַּךְ אֶת־הַפְּלִשְׁתִּי וַיְמִיתֵהוּ
נא וְחֶרֶב אֵין בְּיַד־דָּוִד׃ וַיָּרָץ דָּוִד וַיַּעֲמֹד אֶל־הַפְּלִשְׁתִּי וַיִּקַּח אֶת־חַרְבּוֹ
וַיִּשְׁלְפָהּ מִתַּעְרָהּ וַיְמֹתְתֵהוּ וַיִּכְרָת־בָּהּ אֶת־רֹאשׁוֹ וַיִּרְאוּ הַפְּלִשְׁתִּים
נב כִּי־מֵת גִּבּוֹרָם וַיָּנֻסוּ׃ וַיָּקֻמוּ אַנְשֵׁי יִשְׂרָאֵל וִיהוּדָה וַיָּרִעוּ וַיִּרְדְּפוּ אֶת־
הַפְּלִשְׁתִּים עַד־בּוֹאֲךָ גַיְא וְעַד שַׁעֲרֵי עֶקְרוֹן וַיִּפְּלוּ חַלְלֵי פְלִשְׁתִּים
נג בְּדֶרֶךְ שַׁעֲרַיִם וְעַד־גַּת וְעַד־עֶקְרוֹן׃ וַיָּשֻׁבוּ בְּנֵי יִשְׂרָאֵל מִדְּלֹק אַחֲרֵי

54 from their hot pursuit of the Philistines and plundered their camp. And David
seized the Philistine's head and brought it to Jerusalem, but as for his weapons,
55 he placed them in his tent. As Sha'ul watched David charging out
toward the Philistine, he said to his army commander, Avner, "Whose son is
that boy again, Avner?" "By your life, O King," said Avner, "I do not know."
56 57 The king replied, "Find out whose son that youth is." So when
David returned from defeating the Philistine, Avner took him and brought
58 him before Sha'ul, with the head of the Philistine in his hand. "Whose son
are you, young man?" Sha'ul asked him, and David replied, "The son of your
18 1 servant, Yishai the Bethlehemite." By the time he had finished speaking to
Sha'ul, Yehonatan's very soul became bound up with David's, and Yehonatan
2 loved him as his own self. Sha'ul took him in on that day and did not allow
3 him to return to his father's house. And Yehonatan and David formed a pact;
4 because he loved him as himself, Yehonatan stripped off the robe he wore and
gave it to David, along with his uniform, his sword, his bow, and his belt.
5 When David set out, he was successful in every mission on which Sha'ul sent
him, so Sha'ul appointed him over the military force. This pleased all the men
6 and even Sha'ul's officials. Once, when they arrived after David
returned from defeating the Philistines, the women came out from all the
towns of Israel to sing, the dancers to meet Sha'ul the king, to the joyful
7 accompaniment of timbrels and lutes. The laughing women echoed each
other, chanting, "Sha'ul has struck down thousands, and David – myriads!"
8 This infuriated Sha'ul, and the affair seemed ominous to him. "They credited
myriads to David," he said, "and credited me with just thousands. Only the
9 kingship is yet to be his!" And Sha'ul kept a close eye on David from that day
10 onward. The next day, a dark spirit from God seized Sha'ul, and
he began to rave in the house. Now, David was strumming away as usual –
11 while the spear was in Sha'ul's hand. Sha'ul hurled the spear, thinking, "I will
12 pin David to the wall," but David turned away from him twice. And Sha'ul
became afraid of David, for the LORD was with him, while He had grown
13 distant from Sha'ul. So Sha'ul had him distanced from him; he appointed him
as a commander of a thousand, and he went out and came in at the head of
14 the people. David was successful in every way, and the LORD was
15 with him. When Sha'ul saw how successful he was, he shrank away from him,
16 but all of Israel and Yehuda loved David, for he went out and came in before
17 them. So Sha'ul said to David, "Here is my elder daughter, Merav;
her I shall give you for a wife on the condition that you be a valiant man for
me and fight the LORD's battles," for Sha'ul thought, "I need not deal with him
18 myself – let the Philistines deal with him." "Who am I," David said
to Sha'ul, "and how worthy is my father's kin in Israel, that I should become
19 son-in-law to the king?" So at the time that Merav, Sha'ul's daughter, was
supposed to be given to David, she was given to Adriel the Meholatite for a

נד פלשתים וישסו את־מחניהם: ויקח דוד את־ראש הפלשתי ויבאהו
נה ירושלם ואת־כליו שם באהלו: וכראות שאול את־
דוד יצא לקראת הפלשתי אמר אל־אבנר שר הצבא בן־מי־זה
נו הנער אבנר ויאמר אבנר חי־נפשך המלך אם־ידעתי: ויאמר המלך
נז שאל אתה בן־מי־זה העלם: וכשוב דוד מהכות את־
הפלשתי ויקח אתו אבנר ויבאהו לפני שאול וראש הפלשתי בידו:
נח ויאמר אליו שאול בן־מי אתה הנער ויאמר דוד בן־עבדך ישי בית
יח א הלחמי: ויהי ככלתו לדבר אל־שאול ונפש יהונתן נקשרה בנפש
ב דוד ויאהבו יהונתן כנפשו: ויקחהו שאול ביום ההוא ולא נתנו ויאהבהו
ג לשוב בית אביו: ויכרת יהונתן ודוד ברית באהבתו אתו כנפשו:
ד ויתפשט יהונתן את־המעיל אשר עליו ויתנהו לדוד ומדיו ועד־
ה חרבו ועד־קשתו ועד־חגרו: ויצא דוד בכל אשר ישלחנו שאול
ישכיל וישמהו שאול על אנשי המלחמה וייטב בעיני כל־העם וגם
ו בעיני עבדי שאול: ויהי בבואם בשוב דוד מהכות
את־הפלשתי ותצאנה הנשים מכל־ערי ישראל לשור והמחלות לשיר
ז לקראת שאול המלך בתפים בשמחה ובשלשים: ותענינה הנשים
ח המשחקות ותאמרן הכה שאול באלפו ודוד ברבבתיו: ויחר לשאול
מאד וירע בעיניו הדבר הזה ויאמר נתנו לדוד רבבות ולי נתנו
ט האלפים ועוד לו אך המלוכה: ויהי שאול עון את־דוד מהיום ההוא עוין
י והלאה: ויהי ממחרת ותצלח רוח אלהים ׀ רעה ׀
אל־שאול ויתנבא בתוך־הבית ודוד מנגן בידו כיום ׀ ביום והחנית
יא ביד־שאול: ויטל שאול את־החנית ויאמר אכה בדוד ובקיר ויסב
יב דוד מפניו פעמים: ויירא שאול מלפני דוד כי־היה יהוה עמו ומעם
יג שאול סר: ויסרהו שאול מעמו וישמהו לו שר־אלף ויצא ויבא לפני
יד טו העם: ויהי דוד לכל־דרכו משכיל ויהוה עמו: וירא שאול יב
טז אשר־הוא משכיל מאד ויגר מפניו: וכל־ישראל ויהודה אהב את־
יז דוד כי־הוא יוצא ובא לפניהם: ויאמר שאול אל־דוד
הנה בתי הגדולה מרב אתה אתן־לך לאשה אך היה־לי לבן־
חיל והלחם מלחמות יהוה ושאול אמר אל־תהי ידי בו ותהי־
יח בו יד־פלשתים: ויאמר דוד אל־שאול מי אנכי ומי
יט חיי משפחת אבי בישראל כי־אהיה חתן למלך: ויהי בעת תת
את־מרב בת־שאול לדוד והיא נתנה לעדריאל המחלתי לאשה:

20 wife. But Mikhal, Sha'ul's daughter, loved David, and when Sha'ul was told of
21 this, the matter pleased him. "If I give her to him," Sha'ul thought, "she will
be a distraction for him, and the Philistines will deal with him." So Sha'ul said
to David for the second time, "This time, you will become my son-in-law."
22 And Sha'ul commanded his servants, "Speak to David privately, saying, 'Now,
the king is delighted with you, and all his servants love you; now you should
23 become the king's son-in-law.'" Sha'ul's servants repeated these words in
David's hearing, and David said, "Is it a trivial matter in your eyes, to become
24 the king's son-in-law? I myself am but a poor, trivial man." When Sha'ul's
25 servants told him, "This was David's answer," Sha'ul said, "Tell
David the following: the only bride-price the king desires is a hundred
Philistine foreskins, to wreak vengeance upon the king's enemies," for Sha'ul
26 intended to have David fall into the hands of the Philistines. When Sha'ul's
servants repeated these words to David, the idea of becoming the king's son-
27 in-law pleased David. And before the set time was up, David rose and set out,
together with his men, and struck down two hundred Philistine men. David
brought their foreskins, fulfilling the king's conditions for becoming the king's
28 son-in-law, and Sha'ul gave him his daughter Mikhal for a wife. And Sha'ul
realized and acknowledged that the Lord was with David, and that Mikhal,
29 Sha'ul's daughter, loved him. Yet Sha'ul grew still more afraid of David,
30 and Sha'ul became David's lifelong enemy. The Philistine
officers launched attacks, and whenever they launched an attack, David was
the most successful of all of Sha'ul's servants. And his reputation soared
19 1 high. Sha'ul spoke to Yehonatan and to all his servants about having
2 David killed, but Yehonatan, the son of Sha'ul, stuck by David. So Yehonatan
told David, "Sha'ul, my father, seeks to kill you. Now be on your guard in the
3 morning – stay hidden in a secret place. I will go out and stand with my father
in the field where you are, and I will speak about you to my father. Then I will
4 see what there is to tell you." And Yehonatan spoke well of David to
Sha'ul, his father. "Do not let the king wrong his servant, David," he said to
him, "for he has not wronged you – in fact, his deeds are highly advantageous
5 for you. He took his life in his hands and defeated the Philistine, and the Lord
granted a great victory for Israel – when you saw it, you rejoiced. Why should
6 you sin by shedding innocent blood and kill David without cause?" Sha'ul
heeded Yehonatan's voice, and Sha'ul swore, "As the Lord lives, he shall not
7 be killed." Yehonatan called to David, and Yehonatan told him everything.
Then Yehonatan brought David to Sha'ul, and he remained in his presence as
8 before. War raged once more, and David charged out to fight against
9 the Philistines; he dealt them a mighty blow, and they fled before him. But a
dark spirit from the Lord settled on Sha'ul while he was sitting at home with
10 his spear in his hand as David strummed away. Sha'ul attempted to pin David

כ וַתֶּאֱהַב מִיכַל בַּת־שָׁאוּל אֶת־דָּוִד וַיַּגִּדוּ לְשָׁאוּל וַיִּשַׁר הַדָּבָר בְּעֵינָיו:
כא וַיֹּאמֶר שָׁאוּל אֶתְּנֶנָּה לּוֹ וּתְהִי־לוֹ לְמוֹקֵשׁ וּתְהִי־בוֹ יַד־פְּלִשְׁתִּים
כב וַיֹּאמֶר שָׁאוּל אֶל־דָּוִד בִּשְׁתַּיִם תִּתְחַתֵּן בִּי הַיּוֹם: וַיְצַו שָׁאוּל אֶת־
עֲבָדָו דַּבְּרוּ אֶל־דָּוִד בַּלָּט לֵאמֹר הִנֵּה חָפֵץ בְּךָ הַמֶּלֶךְ וְכָל־עֲבָדָיו
כג אֲהֵבוּךָ וְעַתָּה הִתְחַתֵּן בַּמֶּלֶךְ: וַיְדַבְּרוּ עַבְדֵי שָׁאוּל בְּאָזְנֵי דָוִד אֶת־
הַדְּבָרִים הָאֵלֶּה וַיֹּאמֶר דָּוִד הַנְקַלָּה בְעֵינֵיכֶם הִתְחַתֵּן בַּמֶּלֶךְ וְאָנֹכִי
כד אִישׁ־רָשׁ וְנִקְלֶה: וַיַּגִּדוּ עַבְדֵי שָׁאוּל לוֹ לֵאמֹר כַּדְּבָרִים הָאֵלֶּה דִּבֶּר
כה דָּוִד: וַיֹּאמֶר שָׁאוּל כֹּה־תֹאמְרוּ לְדָוִד אֵין־חֵפֶץ לַמֶּלֶךְ
בְּמֹהַר כִּי בְּמֵאָה עָרְלוֹת פְּלִשְׁתִּים לְהִנָּקֵם בְּאֹיְבֵי הַמֶּלֶךְ וְשָׁאוּל חָשַׁב
כו לְהַפִּיל אֶת־דָּוִד בְּיַד־פְּלִשְׁתִּים: וַיַּגִּדוּ עֲבָדָיו לְדָוִד אֶת־הַדְּבָרִים
הָאֵלֶּה וַיִּשַׁר הַדָּבָר בְּעֵינֵי דָוִד לְהִתְחַתֵּן בַּמֶּלֶךְ וְלֹא מָלְאוּ הַיָּמִים:
כז וַיָּקָם דָּוִד וַיֵּלֶךְ ׀ הוּא וַאֲנָשָׁיו וַיַּךְ בַּפְּלִשְׁתִּים מָאתַיִם אִישׁ וַיָּבֵא דָוִד
אֶת־עָרְלֹתֵיהֶם וַיְמַלְאוּם לַמֶּלֶךְ לְהִתְחַתֵּן בַּמֶּלֶךְ וַיִּתֶּן־לוֹ שָׁאוּל אֶת־
כח מִיכַל בִּתּוֹ לְאִשָּׁה: וַיַּרְא שָׁאוּל וַיֵּדַע כִּי יהוה עִם־דָּוִד וּמִיכַל בַּת־
כט שָׁאוּל אֲהֵבַתְהוּ: וַיֹּאסֶף שָׁאוּל לֵרֹא מִפְּנֵי דָוִד עוֹד וַיְהִי שָׁאוּל אֹיֵב
ל אֶת־דָּוִד כָּל־הַיָּמִים: וַיֵּצְאוּ שָׂרֵי פְלִשְׁתִּים וַיְהִי ׀ מִדֵּי
יט א צֵאתָם שָׂכַל דָּוִד מִכֹּל עַבְדֵי שָׁאוּל וַיִּיקַר שְׁמוֹ מְאֹד: וַיְדַבֵּר
שָׁאוּל אֶל־יוֹנָתָן בְּנוֹ וְאֶל־כָּל־עֲבָדָיו לְהָמִית אֶת־דָּוִד וִיהוֹנָתָן בֶּן־
ב שָׁאוּל חָפֵץ בְּדָוִד מְאֹד: וַיַּגֵּד יְהוֹנָתָן לְדָוִד לֵאמֹר מְבַקֵּשׁ שָׁאוּל
אָבִי לַהֲמִיתֶךָ וְעַתָּה הִשָּׁמֶר־נָא בַבֹּקֶר וְיָשַׁבְתָּ בַסֵּתֶר וְנַחְבֵּאתָ:
ג וַאֲנִי אֵצֵא וְעָמַדְתִּי לְיַד־אָבִי בַּשָּׂדֶה אֲשֶׁר אַתָּה שָׁם וַאֲנִי אֲדַבֵּר בְּךָ
ד אֶל־אָבִי וְרָאִיתִי מָה וְהִגַּדְתִּי לָךְ: וַיְדַבֵּר יְהוֹנָתָן בְּדָוִד טוֹב
אֶל־שָׁאוּל אָבִיו וַיֹּאמֶר אֵלָיו אַל־יֶחֱטָא הַמֶּלֶךְ בְּעַבְדּוֹ בְדָוִד כִּי לוֹא
ה חָטָא לָךְ וְכִי מַעֲשָׂיו טוֹב־לְךָ מְאֹד: וַיָּשֶׂם אֶת־נַפְשׁוֹ בְכַפּוֹ וַיַּךְ אֶת־
הַפְּלִשְׁתִּי וַיַּעַשׂ יהוה תְּשׁוּעָה גְדוֹלָה לְכָל־יִשְׂרָאֵל רָאִיתָ וַתִּשְׂמָח
ו וְלָמָּה תֶחֱטָא בְּדָם נָקִי לְהָמִית אֶת־דָּוִד חִנָּם: וַיִּשְׁמַע שָׁאוּל בְּקוֹל
ז יְהוֹנָתָן וַיִּשָּׁבַע שָׁאוּל חַי־יהוה אִם־יוּמָת: וַיִּקְרָא יְהוֹנָתָן לְדָוִד
וַיַּגֶּד־לוֹ יְהוֹנָתָן אֵת כָּל־הַדְּבָרִים הָאֵלֶּה וַיָּבֵא יְהוֹנָתָן אֶת־דָּוִד
ח אֶל־שָׁאוּל וַיְהִי לְפָנָיו כְּאֶתְמוֹל שִׁלְשׁוֹם: וַתּוֹסֶף
הַמִּלְחָמָה לִהְיוֹת וַיֵּצֵא דָוִד וַיִּלָּחֶם בַּפְּלִשְׁתִּים וַיַּךְ בָּהֶם מַכָּה גְדוֹלָה
ט וַיָּנֻסוּ מִפָּנָיו: וַתְּהִי רוּחַ יהוה ׀ רָעָה אֶל־שָׁאוּל וְהוּא בְּבֵיתוֹ יוֹשֵׁב
י וַחֲנִיתוֹ בְּיָדוֹ וְדָוִד מְנַגֵּן בְּיָד: וַיְבַקֵּשׁ שָׁאוּל לְהַכּוֹת בַּחֲנִית בְּדָוִד

to the wall with the spear, but he eluded Sha'ul, who rammed the spear into
11 the wall, and David bolted and escaped that very night. Sha'ul sent
messengers to David's house to keep watch over him so that they could kill
12 him in the morning. Mikhal, David's wife, told him, "If you do not run for
your life tonight, tomorrow you will be killed." Mikhal let David down
13 through the window; he managed to flee and escaped. Mikhal then took the
household gods and placed them on the bed, arranging a goat-hair quilt
14 around the head, and covering it with a sheet. When Sha'ul sent
15 messengers to arrest David, she said, "He is ill." But Sha'ul sent the
messengers to see David, insisting, "Bring him up to me in his bed to kill him!"
16 The messengers arrived, and there were the household gods upon the bed,
17 with the goat-hair rug at its head. "Why have you deceived me like
this," Sha'ul said to Mikhal, "letting my enemy escape?" Mikhal replied to
18 Sha'ul, "He said to me, 'Let me go – why should I have to kill you?'" David
fled, and escaped, and came to Shmuel in Rama. He told him all that Sha'ul
19 had done to him, then he and Shmuel left and stayed in Nayot. But Sha'ul was
20 informed, "Now David is in Nayot BaRama." When Sha'ul sent messengers
to arrest David, they saw a band of prophets in a prophetic frenzy, with
Shmuel standing over them. And the spirit of God settled on Sha'ul's
21 messengers, and they, too, were thrown into a prophetic frenzy. When they
informed Sha'ul, he sent other messengers, but they, too, were caught up in a
prophetic frenzy; Sha'ul sent messengers again, a third time, but they, too,
22 were caught up in a prophetic frenzy. So he himself made his way to Rama.
When he reached the great cistern by Sekhu, he asked, "Where are Shmuel
23 and David?" and someone said, "There – in Nayot BaRama." As he was
making his way there, to Nayot BaRama, the spirit of God settled on him as
24 well, and he went raving along until he reached Nayot BaRama. Then he, too,
stripped off his clothes, and he, too, was caught up in a prophetic frenzy before
Shmuel and sprawled naked all that day and all night long. And that is why
20 1 they say, "Is Sha'ul, too, among the prophets?" Meanwhile, David
had fled from Nayot BaRama, and he came to Yehonatan. "What have I
done?" he said. "How have I sinned or offended your father, that he seeks my
2 life?" "May it never come to pass," he said. "You shall not die. Look, my father
has never done anything, great or small, without revealing it to me; why
3 should my father hide this matter from me? It cannot be." But David swore
once more. "Your father surely knows that I have your favor,' he said, "so
he must think, 'Yehonatan must not know of this, lest he be grieved.' But
as the Lord lives, and as you live, there is but a step between me and death."
4 And Yehonatan said to David, "Whatever you have in mind, I will do for
5 you." "Now, tomorrow is the New Month," David said to Yehonatan,
"and I am supposed to sit with the king to feast. But let me go, and I will hide

וּבַקִּיר וַיִּפְטַר מִפְּנֵי שָׁאוּל וַיַּךְ אֶת־הַחֲנִית בַּקִּיר וְדָוִד נָס וַיִּמָּלֵט
יא בַּלַּיְלָה הוּא׃ וַיִּשְׁלַח שָׁאוּל מַלְאָכִים אֶל־בֵּית דָּוִד
לְשָׁמְרוֹ וְלַהֲמִיתוֹ בַּבֹּקֶר וַתַּגֵּד לְדָוִד מִיכַל אִשְׁתּוֹ לֵאמֹר אִם־
יב אֵינְךָ מְמַלֵּט אֶת־נַפְשְׁךָ הַלַּיְלָה מָחָר אַתָּה מוּמָת׃ וַתֹּרֶד מִיכַל
יג אֶת־דָּוִד בְּעַד הַחַלּוֹן וַיֵּלֶךְ וַיִּבְרַח וַיִּמָּלֵט׃ וַתִּקַּח מִיכַל אֶת־
הַתְּרָפִים וַתָּשֶׂם אֶל־הַמִּטָּה וְאֵת כְּבִיר הָעִזִּים שָׂמָה מְרַאֲשֹׁתָיו וַתְּכַס
יד בַּבָּגֶד׃ וַיִּשְׁלַח שָׁאוּל מַלְאָכִים לָקַחַת אֶת־דָּוִד וַתֹּאמֶר
טו חֹלֶה הוּא׃ וַיִּשְׁלַח שָׁאוּל אֶת־הַמַּלְאָכִים לִרְאוֹת אֶת־דָּוִד
טז לֵאמֹר הַעֲלוּ אֹתוֹ בַמִּטָּה אֵלַי לַהֲמִתוֹ׃ וַיָּבֹאוּ הַמַּלְאָכִים וְהִנֵּה
יז הַתְּרָפִים אֶל־הַמִּטָּה וּכְבִיר הָעִזִּים מְרַאֲשֹׁתָיו׃ וַיֹּאמֶר
שָׁאוּל אֶל־מִיכַל לָמָּה כָּכָה רִמִּיתִנִי וַתְּשַׁלְּחִי אֶת־אֹיְבִי וַיִּמָּלֵט וַתֹּאמֶר
יח מִיכַל אֶל־שָׁאוּל הוּא־אָמַר אֵלַי שַׁלְּחִנִי לָמָה אֲמִיתֵךְ׃ וְדָוִד בָּרַח
וַיִּמָּלֵט וַיָּבֹא אֶל־שְׁמוּאֵל הָרָמָתָה וַיַּגֶּד־לוֹ אֵת כָּל־אֲשֶׁר עָשָׂה־לוֹ
יט שָׁאוּל וַיֵּלֶךְ הוּא וּשְׁמוּאֵל וַיֵּשְׁבוּ בנוית׃ וַיֻּגַּד לְשָׁאוּל לֵאמֹר הִנֵּה בְּנָיוֹת
כ דָוִד בנוית בָּרָמָה׃ וַיִּשְׁלַח שָׁאוּל מַלְאָכִים לָקַחַת אֶת־דָּוִד וַיַּרְא בְּנָיוֹת
אֶת־לַהֲקַת הַנְּבִיאִים נִבְּאִים וּשְׁמוּאֵל עֹמֵד נִצָּב עֲלֵיהֶם וַתְּהִי עַל־
כא מַלְאֲכֵי שָׁאוּל רוּחַ אֱלֹהִים וַיִּתְנַבְּאוּ גַּם־הֵמָּה׃ וַיַּגִּדוּ לְשָׁאוּל וַיִּשְׁלַח
מַלְאָכִים אֲחֵרִים וַיִּתְנַבְּאוּ גַּם־הֵמָּה וַיֹּסֶף שָׁאוּל וַיִּשְׁלַח מַלְאָכִים
כב שְׁלִשִׁים וַיִּתְנַבְּאוּ גַּם־הֵמָּה׃ וַיֵּלֶךְ גַּם־הוּא הָרָמָתָה וַיָּבֹא עַד־בּוֹר
הַגָּדוֹל אֲשֶׁר בַּשֶּׂכוּ וַיִּשְׁאַל וַיֹּאמֶר אֵיפֹה שְׁמוּאֵל וְדָוִד וַיֹּאמֶר הִנֵּה
כג בנוית בָּרָמָה׃ וַיֵּלֶךְ שָׁם אֶל־נוית בָּרָמָה וַתְּהִי עָלָיו גַּם־הוּא רוּחַ בְּנָיוֹת נָיוֹת
כד אֱלֹהִים וַיֵּלֶךְ הָלוֹךְ וַיִּתְנַבֵּא עַד־בֹּאוֹ בנוית בָּרָמָה׃ וַיִּפְשַׁט גַּם־הוּא בְּנָיוֹת
בְּגָדָיו וַיִּתְנַבֵּא גַם־הוּא לִפְנֵי שְׁמוּאֵל וַיִּפֹּל עָרֹם כָּל־הַיּוֹם הַהוּא וְכָל־
כ א הַלָּיְלָה עַל־כֵּן יֹאמְרוּ הֲגַם שָׁאוּל בַּנְּבִיאִם׃ וַיִּבְרַח דָּוִד
מנוית בָּרָמָה וַיָּבֹא וַיֹּאמֶר ׀ לִפְנֵי יְהוֹנָתָן מֶה עָשִׂיתִי מֶה־עֲוֺנִי וּמֶה־ מִנָּיוֹת
ב חַטָּאתִי לִפְנֵי אָבִיךָ כִּי מְבַקֵּשׁ אֶת־נַפְשִׁי׃ וַיֹּאמֶר לוֹ חָלִילָה לֹא תָמוּת
הִנֵּה לו־עשה אָבִי דָּבָר גָּדוֹל אוֹ דָּבָר קָטֹן וְלֹא יִגְלֶה אֶת־אָזְנִי וּמַדּוּעַ לֹא־יַעֲשֶׂה
ג יַסְתִּיר אָבִי מִמֶּנִּי אֶת־הַדָּבָר הַזֶּה אֵין זֹאת׃ וַיִּשָּׁבַע עוֹד דָּוִד וַיֹּאמֶר
יָדֹעַ יָדַע אָבִיךָ כִּי־מָצָאתִי חֵן בְּעֵינֶיךָ וַיֹּאמֶר אַל־יֵדַע־זֹאת יְהוֹנָתָן
ד פֶּן־יֵעָצֵב וְאוּלָם חַי־יְהוָה וְחֵי נַפְשֶׁךָ כִּי כְפֶשַׂע בֵּינִי וּבֵין הַמָּוֶת׃ וַיֹּאמֶר יג
ה יְהוֹנָתָן אֶל־דָּוִד מַה־תֹּאמַר נַפְשְׁךָ וְאֶעֱשֶׂה־לָּךְ׃ וַיֹּאמֶר
דָּוִד אֶל־יְהוֹנָתָן הִנֵּה־חֹדֶשׁ מָחָר וְאָנֹכִי יָשֹׁב־אֵשֵׁב עִם־הַמֶּלֶךְ לֶאֱכוֹל

6 in the field until the third evening. If your father takes note of my absence,
then say, 'David asked an urgent favor of me: to run back to his hometown,
Beit Leḥem, as the yearly sacrificial feast for the entire clan is being held there.'
7 If he says, 'Fine,' then all is well with your servant, but if he becomes furious,
8 know that he has determined to do harm. Show loyalty to your servant, for
you have entered into a covenant of the LORD together with your servant. If
I am indeed at fault, then kill me yourself; but your father – why should you
9 hand me over to him?" "May it never happen to you," Yehonatan
said, "for if I indeed learn that my father is determined that harm will befall
10 you, would I not tell you?" "Who will tell me if your father answers
11 you harshly?" David asked Yehonatan. "Come, let us go out to the field," said
12 Yehonatan. And the two of them went out to the field. And Yehonatan
said to David, "By the LORD, God of Israel: by this time tomorrow or the next
day, I will determine whether my father is pleased with David. If not, then I
13 will send word to you and let you know. So may the LORD do to Yehonatan –
and more – if my father is pleased at the evil befalling you but I do not let you
know or let you go, and you do not go in peace. And may the LORD be with
14 you as He was once with my father. Now, if I remain alive, show me the LORD's
15 loyalty;[14] and if I die, never sever Your loyalty from my house – never – even
when the LORD has severed every one of David's enemies from the face of
16 the earth. Thus Yehonatan has sealed a pact with the house of David, and may
17 the LORD hold David's enemies[15] responsible." And Yehonatan made David
swear once more by his love for him, for he loved him as he loved his own
18 self. Yehonatan then said to David, "Tomorrow is the New Month,[16]
19 and you shall be missed, for your seat will be empty. Now wait three days,
then on the day people go back to work, make your way swiftly down to your
20 hiding place, and stay close to the Ezel Stone.[17] As for me – I will shoot three
21 arrows to its side, as though aiming at a target. Now, when I send the boy off
to find the arrows, if I say to him, 'Look, the arrows are just past you, come
take them,' then come, for all is well with you, and there is nothing wrong – as
22 the LORD lives. But if I say to the boy, 'Look, the arrows are far past you,' then
23 go, for the LORD has sent you away. As for the matter we spoke of, you and
24 I – the LORD is between me and you forever." David hid out in
the field. The New Month came around, and the king sat down at the feast to
25 eat. When the king sat in his usual seat by the wall, Yehonatan rose, and Avner
26 sat by Sha'ul's side while David's seat remained empty. Sha'ul did not mention
anything that day. "It must be by chance that he is not clean," he thought; "he
27 must be unclean." But the next day, on the second day of the New
Month, David's seat was still empty, and Sha'ul asked Yehonatan, his son,
"Why did the son of Yishai fail to come to the feast – both yesterday and
28 today?" "David urgently asked me for leave to Beit Leḥem," Yehonatan

---

14 | See verse 8 above; compare II Samuel 9:3.
15 | Possibly a euphemism for David himself.
16 | Observed with a feast at the beginning of every lunar month.
17 | Sometimes translated as "Traveler's Stone."

ו וְשִׁלַּחְתַּנִי וְנִסְתַּרְתִּי בַשָּׂדֶה עַד הָעֶרֶב הַשְּׁלִשִׁית: אִם־פָּקֹד יִפְקְדֵנִי
אָבִיךָ וְאָמַרְתָּ נִשְׁאֹל נִשְׁאַל מִמֶּנִּי דָוִד לָרוּץ בֵּית־לֶחֶם עִירוֹ כִּי זֶבַח
ז הַיָּמִים שָׁם לְכָל־הַמִּשְׁפָּחָה: אִם־כֹּה יֹאמַר טוֹב שָׁלוֹם לְעַבְדֶּךָ וְאִם־
ח חָרֹה יֶחֱרֶה לוֹ דַּע כִּי־כָלְתָה הָרָעָה מֵעִמּוֹ: וְעָשִׂיתָ חֶסֶד עַל־עַבְדֶּךָ
כִּי בִּבְרִית יהוה הֵבֵאתָ אֶת־עַבְדְּךָ עִמָּךְ וְאִם־יֶשׁ־בִּי עָוֺן הֲמִיתֵנִי
ט אַתָּה וְעַד־אָבִיךָ לָמָּה־זֶּה תְבִיאֵנִי: וַיֹּאמֶר יְהוֹנָתָן
חָלִילָה לָּךְ כִּי ׀ אִם־יָדֹעַ אֵדַע כִּי־כָלְתָה הָרָעָה מֵעִם אָבִי לָבוֹא עָלֶיךָ
י וְלֹא אֹתָהּ אַגִּיד לָךְ: וַיֹּאמֶר דָּוִד אֶל־יְהוֹנָתָן מִי יַגִּיד
יא לִי אוֹ מַה־יַּעַנְךָ אָבִיךָ קָשָׁה: וַיֹּאמֶר יְהוֹנָתָן אֶל־דָּוִד לְכָה וְנֵצֵא
יב הַשָּׂדֶה וַיֵּצְאוּ שְׁנֵיהֶם הַשָּׂדֶה: וַיֹּאמֶר יְהוֹנָתָן אֶל־דָּוִד
יהוה אֱלֹהֵי יִשְׂרָאֵל כִּי־אֶחְקֹר אֶת־אָבִי כָּעֵת ׀ מָחָר הַשְּׁלִשִׁית וְהִנֵּה־
יג טוֹב אֶל־דָּוִד וְלֹא־אָז אֶשְׁלַח אֵלֶיךָ וְגָלִיתִי אֶת־אָזְנֶךָ: כֹּה־יַעֲשֶׂה
יהוה לִיהוֹנָתָן וְכֹה יֹסִיף כִּי־יֵיטִב אֶל־אָבִי אֶת־הָרָעָה עָלֶיךָ וְגָלִיתִי
אֶת־אָזְנֶךָ וְשִׁלַּחְתִּיךָ וְהָלַכְתָּ לְשָׁלוֹם וִיהִי יהוה עִמָּךְ כַּאֲשֶׁר הָיָה
יד עִם־אָבִי: וְלֹא אִם־עוֹדֶנִּי חָי וְלֹא־תַעֲשֶׂה עִמָּדִי חֶסֶד יהוה וְלֹא אָמוּת:
טו וְלֹא־תַכְרִית אֶת־חַסְדְּךָ מֵעִם בֵּיתִי עַד־עוֹלָם וְלֹא בְּהַכְרִת יהוה
טז אֶת־אֹיְבֵי דָוִד אִישׁ מֵעַל פְּנֵי הָאֲדָמָה: וַיִּכְרֹת יְהוֹנָתָן עִם־בֵּית דָּוִד
יז וּבִקֵּשׁ יהוה מִיַּד אֹיְבֵי דָוִד: וַיּוֹסֶף יְהוֹנָתָן לְהַשְׁבִּיעַ אֶת־דָּוִד בְּאַהֲבָתוֹ
יח אֹתוֹ כִּי־אַהֲבַת נַפְשׁוֹ אֲהֵבוֹ: וַיֹּאמֶר־לוֹ יְהוֹנָתָן מָחָר חֹדֶשׁ
יט וְנִפְקַדְתָּ כִּי יִפָּקֵד מוֹשָׁבֶךָ: וְשִׁלַּשְׁתָּ תֵּרֵד מְאֹד וּבָאתָ אֶל־הַמָּקוֹם
כ אֲשֶׁר־נִסְתַּרְתָּ שָּׁם בְּיוֹם הַמַּעֲשֶׂה וְיָשַׁבְתָּ אֵצֶל הָאֶבֶן הָאָזֶל: וַאֲנִי
כא שְׁלֹשֶׁת הַחִצִּים צִדָּה אוֹרֶה לְשַׁלַּח־לִי לְמַטָּרָה: וְהִנֵּה אֶשְׁלַח אֶת־
הַנַּעַר לֵךְ מְצָא אֶת־הַחִצִּים אִם־אָמֹר אֹמַר לַנַּעַר הִנֵּה הַחִצִּים ׀ מִמְּךָ
כב וָהֵנָּה קָחֶנּוּ וָבֹאָה כִּי־שָׁלוֹם לְךָ וְאֵין דָּבָר חַי־יהוה: וְאִם־כֹּה אֹמַר
כג לָעֶלֶם הִנֵּה הַחִצִּים מִמְּךָ וָהָלְאָה לֵךְ כִּי שִׁלַּחֲךָ יהוה: וְהַדָּבָר אֲשֶׁר
כד דִּבַּרְנוּ אֲנִי וָאָתָּה הִנֵּה יהוה בֵּינִי וּבֵינְךָ עַד־עוֹלָם: וַיִּסָּתֵר
כה דָּוִד בַּשָּׂדֶה וַיְהִי הַחֹדֶשׁ וַיֵּשֶׁב הַמֶּלֶךְ על־הַלֶּחֶם לֶאֱכוֹל: וַיֵּשֶׁב הַמֶּלֶךְ אֶל־
עַל־מוֹשָׁבוֹ כְּפַעַם ׀ בְּפַעַם אֶל־מוֹשַׁב הַקִּיר וַיָּקָם יְהוֹנָתָן וַיֵּשֶׁב אַבְנֵר
כו מִצַּד שָׁאוּל וַיִּפָּקֵד מְקוֹם דָּוִד: וְלֹא־דִבֶּר שָׁאוּל מְאוּמָה בַּיּוֹם הַהוּא
כז כִּי אָמַר מִקְרֶה הוּא בִּלְתִּי טָהוֹר הוּא כִּי־לֹא טָהוֹר: וַיְהִי
מִמָּחֳרַת הַחֹדֶשׁ הַשֵּׁנִי וַיִּפָּקֵד מְקוֹם דָּוִד וַיֹּאמֶר שָׁאוּל אֶל־יְהוֹנָתָן
כח בְּנוֹ מַדּוּעַ לֹא־בָא בֶן־יִשַׁי גַּם־תְּמוֹל גַּם־הַיּוֹם אֶל־הַלָּחֶם: וַיַּעַן יְהוֹנָתָן

29 answered Sha'ul. "He said, 'Please let me go, for we have a family feast in the
city, and my brother has bid me – so now, if I have gained your favor, please
let me get away to see my brothers.' That is why he has not come to the king's
30 table." Sha'ul burst into a rage at Yehonatan. "Son of a perverse,
wayward woman!" he said. "Oh, I knew you would side with the son of
Yishai – to your own disgrace and the disgrace of your mother's nakedness!
31 But as long as the son of Yishai lives on this earth, you and your kingship will
32 not endure – so bring him to me now, for he is a dead man!" But
Yehonatan answered Sha'ul, his father. "Why should he be killed?" he said to
33 him. "What has he done?" And Sha'ul hurled the spear toward him to strike
him down, and Yehonatan realized that his father was determined to kill
34 David. Furious, Yehonatan rose up from the table; he ate no food on
the second day of the New Month out of anguish for David, for his father had
35 humiliated him. In the morning, Yehonatan went out to the field
for the rendezvous with David, a young boy with him. He said to his boy,
36 "Now, run and find the arrows I am about to shoot." The boy ran off, and he
37 shot the arrows past him. When the boy reached the place where Yehonatan's
arrows had fallen, Yehonatan called out after the boy, "Oh – the arrows are
far past you." Then Yehonatan called out after the boy, "Quick – hurry, do not
38 linger." When Yehonatan's boy gathered up the arrows and came back to his
39 master – the boy knew nothing; only Yehonatan and David knew about the
40 arrangement – Yehonatan gave his gear to his boy and said to him, "Go – bring
41 these back to town." When the boy had left, David emerged from the southern
side of the stone, flung his face to the ground, and bowed three times. And
they kissed each other and wept with each other until David's sobs reached a
42 crescendo. "Go in peace," Yehonatan said to David, "for the two of us have
sworn in the name of the LORD, 'May the LORD be between me and you, and
21 1 between my seed and your seed, forever.'" He got up and went on
2 his way while Yehonatan came back to town. And David came to Nov to the
priest Aḥimelekh. Aḥimelekh came trembling out toward David and asked
3 him, "Why are you alone, with no one with you?" "The king charged me with
a mission," David said to the priest Aḥimelekh, "and said to me, 'Let no one
know anything about the mission on which I have sent you, that I charged
4 you with.' So I dismissed the servants to a certain place. Now, what do you
5 have on hand? Provide me with five loaves of bread or whatever there is." The
priest answered David, "There is no ordinary bread on hand, but there is
sacred bread, as long as the young men have kept themselves away from
6 women." "Certainly – women have been kept from us, as always,"
David replied to the priest, "for whenever I set out, the men's vessels are
consecrated, even on an ordinary mission, so their vessels are certainly sacred

כט אֶת־שָׁאוּל נִשְׁאֹל נִשְׁאַל דָּוִד מֵעִמָּדִי עַד־בֵּית לָחֶם׃ וַיֹּאמֶר שַׁלְּחֵנִי
נָא כִּי זֶבַח מִשְׁפָּחָה לָנוּ בָּעִיר וְהוּא צִוָּה־לִי אָחִי וְעַתָּה אִם־מָצָאתִי
חֵן בְּעֵינֶיךָ אִמָּלְטָה נָּא וְאֶרְאֶה אֶת־אֶחָי עַל־כֵּן לֹא־בָא אֶל־שֻׁלְחַן
ל הַמֶּלֶךְ׃ וַיִּחַר־אַף שָׁאוּל בִּיהוֹנָתָן וַיֹּאמֶר לוֹ בֶּן־נַעֲוַת
הַמַּרְדּוּת הֲלוֹא יָדַעְתִּי כִּי־בֹחֵר אַתָּה לְבֶן־יִשַׁי לְבָשְׁתְּךָ וּלְבֹשֶׁת עֶרְוַת
לא אִמֶּךָ׃ כִּי כָל־הַיָּמִים אֲשֶׁר בֶּן־יִשַׁי חַי עַל־הָאֲדָמָה לֹא תִכּוֹן אַתָּה
לב וּמַלְכוּתֶךָ וְעַתָּה שְׁלַח וְקַח אֹתוֹ אֵלַי כִּי בֶן־מָוֶת הוּא׃ וַיַּעַן
לג יְהוֹנָתָן אֶת־שָׁאוּל אָבִיו וַיֹּאמֶר אֵלָיו לָמָּה יוּמַת מֶה עָשָׂה׃ וַיָּטֶל
שָׁאוּל אֶת־הַחֲנִית עָלָיו לְהַכֹּתוֹ וַיֵּדַע יְהוֹנָתָן כִּי־כָלָה הִיא מֵעִם
לד אָבִיו לְהָמִית אֶת־דָּוִד׃ וַיָּקָם יְהוֹנָתָן מֵעִם הַשֻּׁלְחָן בָּחֳרִי־
אָף וְלֹא־אָכַל בְּיוֹם־הַחֹדֶשׁ הַשֵּׁנִי לֶחֶם כִּי נֶעְצַב אֶל־דָּוִד כִּי הִכְלִמוֹ
לה אָבִיו׃ וַיְהִי בַבֹּקֶר וַיֵּצֵא יְהוֹנָתָן הַשָּׂדֶה לְמוֹעֵד דָּוִד וְנַעַר
לו קָטֹן עִמּוֹ׃ וַיֹּאמֶר לְנַעֲרוֹ רֻץ מְצָא־נָא אֶת־הַחִצִּים אֲשֶׁר אָנֹכִי מוֹרֶה
לז הַנַּעַר רָץ וְהוּא־יָרָה הַחֵצִי לְהַעֲבִרוֹ׃ וַיָּבֹא הַנַּעַר עַד־מְקוֹם הַחֵצִי
אֲשֶׁר יָרָה יְהוֹנָתָן וַיִּקְרָא יְהוֹנָתָן אַחֲרֵי הַנַּעַר וַיֹּאמֶר הֲלוֹא הַחֵצִי
לח מִמְּךָ וָהָלְאָה׃ וַיִּקְרָא יְהוֹנָתָן אַחֲרֵי הַנַּעַר מְהֵרָה חוּשָׁה אַל־תַּעֲמֹד
לט וַיְלַקֵּט נַעַר יְהוֹנָתָן אֶת־הַחִצִּי וַיָּבֹא אֶל־אֲדֹנָיו׃ וְהַנַּעַר לֹא־יָדַע מְאוּמָה הַחִצִּים
מ אַךְ יְהוֹנָתָן וְדָוִד יָדְעוּ אֶת־הַדָּבָר׃ וַיִּתֵּן יְהוֹנָתָן אֶת־כֵּלָיו אֶל־הַנַּעַר
מא אֲשֶׁר־לוֹ וַיֹּאמֶר לוֹ לֵךְ הָבֵיא הָעִיר׃ הַנַּעַר בָּא וְדָוִד קָם מֵאֵצֶל הַנֶּגֶב
וַיִּפֹּל לְאַפָּיו אַרְצָה וַיִּשְׁתַּחוּ שָׁלֹשׁ פְּעָמִים וַיִּשְּׁקוּ ׀ אִישׁ אֶת־רֵעֵהוּ
מב וַיִּבְכּוּ אִישׁ אֶת־רֵעֵהוּ עַד־דָּוִד הִגְדִּיל׃ וַיֹּאמֶר יְהוֹנָתָן לְדָוִד לֵךְ לְשָׁלוֹם יד
אֲשֶׁר נִשְׁבַּעְנוּ שְׁנֵינוּ אֲנַחְנוּ בְּשֵׁם יהוה לֵאמֹר יהוה יִהְיֶה ׀ בֵּינִי וּבֵינֶךָ
כא א וּבֵין זַרְעִי וּבֵין זַרְעֲךָ עַד־עוֹלָם׃ וַיָּקָם וַיֵּלַךְ וִיהוֹנָתָן בָּא הָעִיר׃
ב וַיָּבֹא דָוִד נֹבֶה אֶל־אֲחִימֶלֶךְ הַכֹּהֵן וַיֶּחֱרַד אֲחִימֶלֶךְ לִקְרַאת דָּוִד
ג וַיֹּאמֶר לוֹ מַדּוּעַ אַתָּה לְבַדֶּךָ וְאִישׁ אֵין אִתָּךְ׃ וַיֹּאמֶר דָּוִד לַאֲחִימֶלֶךְ
הַכֹּהֵן הַמֶּלֶךְ צִוַּנִי דָבָר וַיֹּאמֶר אֵלַי אִישׁ אַל־יֵדַע מְאוּמָה אֶת־הַדָּבָר
אֲשֶׁר־אָנֹכִי שֹׁלֵחֲךָ וַאֲשֶׁר צִוִּיתִךָ וְאֶת־הַנְּעָרִים יוֹדַעְתִּי אֶל־מְקוֹם
ד פְּלֹנִי אַלְמוֹנִי׃ וְעַתָּה מַה־יֵּשׁ תַּחַת־יָדְךָ חֲמִשָּׁה־לֶחֶם תְּנָה בְיָדִי אוֹ
ה הַנִּמְצָא׃ וַיַּעַן הַכֹּהֵן אֶת־דָּוִד וַיֹּאמֶר אֵין־לֶחֶם חֹל אֶל־תַּחַת יָדִי כִּי־
ו אִם־לֶחֶם קֹדֶשׁ יֵשׁ אִם־נִשְׁמְרוּ הַנְּעָרִים אַךְ מֵאִשָּׁה׃ וַיַּעַן
דָּוִד אֶת־הַכֹּהֵן וַיֹּאמֶר לוֹ כִּי אִם־אִשָּׁה עֲצֻרָה־לָנוּ כִּתְמוֹל שִׁלְשֹׁם
בְּצֵאתִי וַיִּהְיוּ כְלֵי־הַנְּעָרִים קֹדֶשׁ וְהוּא דֶּרֶךְ חֹל וְאַף כִּי הַיּוֹם יִקְדַּשׁ

7 today." So the priest gave him what was sacred, for there was no bread there
but the showbread that had been removed from the LORD's presence and
8 replaced with hot, fresh bread as soon as it was taken away. Meanwhile, one
of Sha'ul's servants had been detained there before the LORD; his name was
9 Doeg the Edomite, and he was the chief of Sha'ul's patrolmen. David then
said to Aḥimelekh, "Do you have any spear or sword on hand here? For I took
neither my sword nor any of my weapons with me due to the urgency of the
10 king's mission." "The sword of Golyat the Philistine, whom you
defeated in the Valley of the Terebinth," said the priest, "here it is, wrapped
in a cloth, behind the ephod.[18] If you wish to take it, then take it, for there is
11 nothing here besides it." "There is none like it," said David. "Give it
to me." And David set out and fled from Sha'ul on that very day and reached
12 Akhish, the king of Gat. But Akhish's servants said to him, "Isn't that David,
king of the land? Isn't that the one they sang and danced about, chanting,
13 'Sha'ul has struck down thousands, and David – myriads!'?" David took these
14 words to heart and became very wary of King Akhish of Gat. So he acted as
if he had lost his reason in their eyes; he ranted and raved at them and
15 scribbled on the doors of the gate and drooled into his beard. And
Akhish said to his servants, "Just look at that lunatic; why have you brought
16 him to me? Do I lack lunatics so that you brought this one here to play the
22 1 lunatic before me? Should this one be let into my house?" David
made his way out of there and escaped to the cave of Adulam. When his
brothers and all his father's household heard, they went down to him there.
2 And everyone who was distressed, and everyone in debt, and every wretched,
bitter soul gathered to him, and he became their leader; about four hundred
3 men were with him. From there, David went to Mitzpeh Moav. He said to
the king of Moav, "Please let my father and mother remain out here with
4 you until I know what God has in store for me." He led them before the
king of Moav, and they stayed with him for as long as David was in the
5 stronghold. When the prophet Gad said to David, "Do not remain
in the stronghold; set out for the land of Yehuda," David traveled until he
6 reached the Ḥeret Forest. When Sha'ul heard that David and his men
had been discovered, Sha'ul was stationed at Giva beneath the tamarisk at
7 Rama, with his spear at the ready and all his servants attending him. "Now
listen, Benjaminites," Sha'ul said to his officials, who were attending him, "will
the son of Yishai also give fields and vineyards to you? Will all of you be
8 appointed as captains of thousands and captains of hundreds? For you have
all conspired against me; no one let me know that my son formed a pact with
the son of Yishai. And not one of you felt sorry enough for me to let me know
9 that my son set my own servant as a trap against me this very day." And
Doeg the Edomite, who was standing by Sha'ul's servants, answered. "I saw
the son of Yishai – he came to Nov, to Aḥimelekh son of Aḥituv," he said,
10 "who made an inquiry of the LORD for him and gave him provisions – he even

18 | See note on 2:18.

ז בִּכְלִי: וַיִּתֶּן־לוֹ הַכֹּהֵן קֹדֶשׁ כִּי לֹא־הָיָה שָׁם לֶחֶם כִּי־אִם־לֶחֶם הַפָּנִים
ח הַמּוּסָרִים מִלִּפְנֵי יהוה לָשׂוּם לֶחֶם חֹם בְּיוֹם הִלָּקְחוֹ: וְשָׁם אִישׁ מֵעַבְדֵי
שָׁאוּל בַּיּוֹם הַהוּא נֶעְצָר לִפְנֵי יהוה וּשְׁמוֹ דֹּאֵג הָאֲדֹמִי אַבִּיר הָרֹעִים
ט אֲשֶׁר לְשָׁאוּל: וַיֹּאמֶר דָּוִד לַאֲחִימֶלֶךְ וְאִין יֶשׁ־פֹּה תַחַת־יָדְךָ חֲנִית
אוֹ־חָרֶב כִּי גַם־חַרְבִּי וְגַם־כֵּלַי לֹא־לָקַחְתִּי בְיָדִי כִּי־הָיָה דְבַר־הַמֶּלֶךְ
י נָחוּץ: וַיֹּאמֶר הַכֹּהֵן חֶרֶב גָּלְיָת הַפְּלִשְׁתִּי אֲשֶׁר־הִכִּיתָ ׀
בְּעֵמֶק הָאֵלָה הִנֵּה־הִיא לוּטָה בַשִּׂמְלָה אַחֲרֵי הָאֵפוֹד אִם־אֹתָהּ
תִּקַּח־לְךָ קָח כִּי אֵין אַחֶרֶת זוּלָתָהּ בָּזֶה וַיֹּאמֶר דָּוִד אֵין
יא כָּמוֹהָ תְּנֶנָּה לִּי: וַיָּקָם דָּוִד וַיִּבְרַח בַּיּוֹם־הַהוּא מִפְּנֵי שָׁאוּל וַיָּבֹא אֶל־
יב אָכִישׁ מֶלֶךְ גַּת: וַיֹּאמְרוּ עַבְדֵי אָכִישׁ אֵלָיו הֲלוֹא־זֶה דָוִד מֶלֶךְ הָאָרֶץ
הֲלוֹא לָזֶה יַעֲנוּ בַמְּחֹלוֹת לֵאמֹר הִכָּה שָׁאוּל בַּאֲלָפָו וְדָוִד בְּרִבְבֹתָו:
יג וַיָּשֶׂם דָּוִד אֶת־הַדְּבָרִים הָאֵלֶּה בִּלְבָבוֹ וַיִּרָא מְאֹד מִפְּנֵי אָכִישׁ מֶלֶךְ־
יד גַּת: וַיְשַׁנּוֹ אֶת־טַעְמוֹ בְּעֵינֵיהֶם וַיִּתְהֹלֵל בְּיָדָם וַיְתָו עַל־דַּלְתוֹת הַשַּׁעַר
טו וַיּוֹרֶד רִירוֹ אֶל־זְקָנוֹ: וַיֹּאמֶר אָכִישׁ אֶל־עֲבָדָיו הִנֵּה תִרְאוּ
טז אִישׁ מִשְׁתַּגֵּעַ לָמָּה תָּבִיאוּ אֹתוֹ אֵלָי: חֲסַר מְשֻׁגָּעִים אָנִי כִּי־הֲבֵאתֶם
כב א אֶת־זֶה לְהִשְׁתַּגֵּעַ עָלָי הֲזֶה יָבוֹא אֶל־בֵּיתִי: וַיֵּלֶךְ דָּוִד מִשָּׁם
וַיִּמָּלֵט אֶל־מְעָרַת עֲדֻלָּם וַיִּשְׁמְעוּ אֶחָיו וְכָל־בֵּית אָבִיו וַיֵּרְדוּ אֵלָיו
ב שָׁמָּה: וַיִּתְקַבְּצוּ אֵלָיו כָּל־אִישׁ מָצוֹק וְכָל־אִישׁ אֲשֶׁר־לוֹ נֹשֵׁא וְכָל־
ג אִישׁ מַר־נֶפֶשׁ וַיְהִי עֲלֵיהֶם לְשָׂר וַיִּהְיוּ עִמּוֹ כְּאַרְבַּע מֵאוֹת אִישׁ: וַיֵּלֶךְ
דָּוִד מִשָּׁם מִצְפֵּה מוֹאָב וַיֹּאמֶר ׀ אֶל־מֶלֶךְ מוֹאָב יֵצֵא־נָא אָבִי וְאִמִּי
ד אִתְּכֶם עַד אֲשֶׁר אֵדַע מַה־יַּעֲשֶׂה־לִּי אֱלֹהִים: וַיַּנְחֵם אֶת־פְּנֵי מֶלֶךְ
ה מוֹאָב וַיֵּשְׁבוּ עִמּוֹ כָּל־יְמֵי הֱיוֹת־דָּוִד בַּמְּצוּדָה: וַיֹּאמֶר
גָּד הַנָּבִיא אֶל־דָּוִד לֹא תֵשֵׁב בַּמְּצוּדָה לֵךְ וּבָאתָ־לְּךָ אֶרֶץ יְהוּדָה
ו וַיֵּלֶךְ דָּוִד וַיָּבֹא יַעַר חָרֶת: וַיִּשְׁמַע שָׁאוּל כִּי נוֹדַע דָּוִד
וַאֲנָשִׁים אֲשֶׁר אִתּוֹ וְשָׁאוּל יוֹשֵׁב בַּגִּבְעָה תַּחַת־הָאֶשֶׁל בָּרָמָה וַחֲנִיתוֹ
ז בְיָדוֹ וְכָל־עֲבָדָיו נִצָּבִים עָלָיו: וַיֹּאמֶר שָׁאוּל לַעֲבָדָיו הַנִּצָּבִים עָלָיו
שִׁמְעוּ־נָא בְּנֵי יְמִינִי גַּם־לְכֻלְּכֶם יִתֵּן בֶּן־יִשַׁי שָׂדוֹת וּכְרָמִים לְכֻלְּכֶם
ח יָשִׂים שָׂרֵי אֲלָפִים וְשָׂרֵי מֵאוֹת: כִּי קְשַׁרְתֶּם כֻּלְּכֶם עָלַי וְאֵין־גֹּלֶה
אֶת־אָזְנִי בִּכְרָת־בְּנִי עִם־בֶּן־יִשַׁי וְאֵין־חֹלֶה מִכֶּם עָלַי וְגֹלֶה אֶת־אָזְנִי
ט כִּי הֵקִים בְּנִי אֶת־עַבְדִּי עָלַי לְאֹרֵב כַּיּוֹם הַזֶּה: וַיַּעַן דֹּאֵג
הָאֲדֹמִי וְהוּא נִצָּב עַל־עַבְדֵי־שָׁאוּל וַיֹּאמַר רָאִיתִי אֶת־בֶּן־יִשַׁי בָּא
י נֹבֶה אֶל־אֲחִימֶלֶךְ בֶּן־אֲחִטוּב: וַיִּשְׁאַל־לוֹ בַּיהוה וְצֵידָה נָתַן לוֹ וְאֵת

11 gave him the sword of Golyat the Philistine." So the king summoned the priest
Aḥimelekh son of Aḥituv and all the priests of his father's house, who were
12 in Nov; and they all came to the king. Sha'ul said, "Now listen,
13 son of Aḥituv." "Here I am, my lord," he said. "Why did you conspire against
me, you and the son of Yishai," Sha'ul said to him, "by giving him bread and
a sword, and making an inquiry of God for him – that he may rise up against
14 me in ambush this very day?" "But out of all your servants, who
is as faithful as David?" Aḥimelekh answered the king. "The king's son-in-
15 law and captain of your bodyguard, so honored in your house? Have I begun
to make inquiries of God for him? Absolutely not! Let the king not accuse
his servant or any of my father's house of anything, for your servant knew
16 absolutely nothing of all this – not the slightest hint." But the king said, "You
17 will surely die, Aḥimelekh – you and all your father's house." And the king
said to the couriers attending him, "Go around and kill the priests of the
Lord, for they, too, side with David – they knew that he was fleeing, but
they did not let me know." But the servants of the king were not willing to
18 raise their hands to strike the priests of the Lord. So the king
said to Doeg, "You go around and strike down the priests." And Doeg the
Edomite went around and struck down the priests himself; that same day he
19 slaughtered eighty-five men who were clad in the linen ephod. And he put
Nov, the city of priests, to the sword – man and woman, child and infant, ox,
20 donkey, and sheep to the sword. A single son of Aḥimelekh son of Aḥituv
21 escaped; his name was Evyatar, and he ran away to David. Evyatar told David
22 that Sha'ul had murdered the priests of the Lord. "I knew on that day – when
Doeg was there – that he would surely inform Sha'ul," David said to Evyatar.
23 "I am responsible for all the lives of your father's household. Stay with me and
do not fear; though the one who seeks my life seeks your life, you are safe
23 1 with me." David was informed, "There are Philistines attacking Ke'ila, and
2 they are plundering the threshing floors." David asked the Lord, "Shall I go
and strike down these Philistines?" And the Lord said, "Go, strike
3 down the Philistines, and save Ke'ila." But David's men said to him, "Even
here in Yehuda we are afraid – must we really go to Ke'ila, to the ranks of the
4 Philistines?" So David asked the Lord once more, and the
Lord answered him. "Arise and go down to Ke'ila," He said, "for I shall deliver
5 the Philistines into your hand." David and his men marched on Ke'ila. They
fought against the Philistines, led away their cattle, and dealt them a great
6 blow; and David saved the people of Ke'ila. Now, when Evyatar son
of Aḥimelekh had fled to David in Ke'ila, he brought the ephod[19] down with
7 him. When Sha'ul was informed that David had come to Ke'ila, Sha'ul said,
"God has cast him away into my hands, for he has shut himself in by entering
8 a gated, bolted city." And Sha'ul rallied all the men for war, to march down to

---

19 | The ephod of the high priest held the Urim and Tumim. See note on 14:41.

יא חֶרֶב גָּלְיָת הַפְּלִשְׁתִּי נָתַן לוֹ: וַיִּשְׁלַח הַמֶּלֶךְ לִקְרֹא אֶת־אֲחִימֶלֶךְ בֶּן־
אֲחִיטוּב הַכֹּהֵן וְאֵת כָּל־בֵּית אָבִיו הַכֹּהֲנִים אֲשֶׁר בְּנֹב וַיָּבֹאוּ כֻלָּם
יב אֶל־הַמֶּלֶךְ: וַיֹּאמֶר שָׁאוּל שְׁמַע־נָא בֶּן־אֲחִיטוּב
יג וַיֹּאמֶר הִנְנִי אֲדֹנִי: וַיֹּאמֶר אֵלָו שָׁאוּל לָמָּה קְשַׁרְתֶּם עָלַי אַתָּה וּבֶן־
יִשָׁי בְּתִתְּךָ לוֹ לֶחֶם וְחֶרֶב וְשָׁאוֹל לוֹ בֵּאלֹהִים לָקוּם אֵלַי לְאֹרֵב כַּיּוֹם
יד הַזֶּה: וַיַּעַן אֲחִימֶלֶךְ אֶת־הַמֶּלֶךְ וַיֹּאמַר וּמִי בְכָל־עֲבָדֶיךָ
טו כְּדָוִד נֶאֱמָן וַחֲתַן הַמֶּלֶךְ וְסָר אֶל־מִשְׁמַעְתֶּךָ וְנִכְבָּד בְּבֵיתֶךָ: הַיּוֹם
הַחִלֹּתִי לשאול־לוֹ בֵאלֹהִים חָלִילָה לִּי אַל־יָשֵׂם הַמֶּלֶךְ בְּעַבְדּוֹ דָבָר לִשְׁאָל־
טז בְּכָל־בֵּית אָבִי כִּי לֹא־יָדַע עַבְדְּךָ בְּכָל־זֹאת דָּבָר קָטֹן אוֹ גָדוֹל: וַיֹּאמֶר
יז הַמֶּלֶךְ מוֹת תָּמוּת אֲחִימֶלֶךְ אַתָּה וְכָל־בֵּית אָבִיךָ: וַיֹּאמֶר הַמֶּלֶךְ
לָרָצִים הַנִּצָּבִים עָלָיו סֹבּוּ וְהָמִיתוּ ׀ כֹּהֲנֵי יְהוָה כִּי גַם־יָדָם עִם־דָּוִד
וְכִי יָדְעוּ כִּי־בֹרֵחַ הוּא וְלֹא גָלוּ אֶת־אזנו וְלֹא־אָבוּ עַבְדֵי הַמֶּלֶךְ לִשְׁלֹחַ אָזְנִי
יח אֶת־יָדָם לִפְגֹעַ בְּכֹהֲנֵי יְהוָה: וַיֹּאמֶר הַמֶּלֶךְ לדויג סֹב אַתָּה לְדוֹאֵג
וּפְגַע בַּכֹּהֲנִים וַיִּסֹּב דויג הָאֲדֹמִי וַיִּפְגַּע־הוּא בַּכֹּהֲנִים וַיָּמֶת ׀ בַּיּוֹם דּוֹאֵג
יט הַהוּא שְׁמֹנִים וַחֲמִשָּׁה אִישׁ נֹשֵׂא אֵפוֹד בָּד: וְאֵת נֹב עִיר־הַכֹּהֲנִים
הִכָּה לְפִי־חֶרֶב מֵאִישׁ וְעַד־אִשָּׁה מֵעוֹלֵל וְעַד־יוֹנֵק וְשׁוֹר וַחֲמוֹר וָשֶׂה
כ לְפִי־חָרֶב: וַיִּמָּלֵט בֵּן־אֶחָד לַאֲחִימֶלֶךְ בֶּן־אֲחִטוּב וּשְׁמוֹ אֶבְיָתָר
כא וַיִּבְרַח אַחֲרֵי דָוִד: וַיַּגֵּד אֶבְיָתָר לְדָוִד כִּי הָרַג שָׁאוּל אֵת כֹּהֲנֵי יְהוָה:
כב וַיֹּאמֶר דָּוִד לְאֶבְיָתָר יָדַעְתִּי בַּיּוֹם הַהוּא כִּי־שָׁם דויג הָאֲדֹמִי כִּי־הַגֵּד דּוֹאֵג
כג יַגִּיד לְשָׁאוּל אָנֹכִי סַבֹּתִי בְּכָל־נֶפֶשׁ בֵּית אָבִיךָ: שְׁבָה אִתִּי אַל־תִּירָא
כִּי אֲשֶׁר־יְבַקֵּשׁ אֶת־נַפְשִׁי יְבַקֵּשׁ אֶת־נַפְשֶׁךָ כִּי־מִשְׁמֶרֶת אַתָּה עִמָּדִי:
כג א וַיַּגִּדוּ לְדָוִד לֵאמֹר הִנֵּה פְלִשְׁתִּים נִלְחָמִים בִּקְעִילָה וְהֵמָּה שֹׁסִים
ב אֶת־הַגֳּרָנוֹת: וַיִּשְׁאַל דָּוִד בַּיהוָה לֵאמֹר הַאֵלֵךְ וְהִכֵּיתִי בַּפְּלִשְׁתִּים
הָאֵלֶּה וַיֹּאמֶר יְהוָה אֶל־דָּוִד לֵךְ וְהִכִּיתָ בַפְּלִשְׁתִּים וְהוֹשַׁעְתָּ
ג אֶת־קְעִילָה: וַיֹּאמְרוּ אַנְשֵׁי דָוִד אֵלָיו הִנֵּה אֲנַחְנוּ פֹה בִּיהוּדָה יְרֵאִים
ד וְאַף כִּי־נֵלֵךְ קְעִלָה אֶל־מַעַרְכוֹת פְּלִשְׁתִּים: וַיּוֹסֶף עוֹד טו
דָּוִד לִשְׁאוֹל בַּיהוָה וַיַּעֲנֵהוּ יְהוָה וַיֹּאמֶר קוּם רֵד קְעִילָה
ה כִּי־אֲנִי נֹתֵן אֶת־פְּלִשְׁתִּים בְּיָדֶךָ: וַיֵּלֶךְ דָּוִד וַאֲנָשָׁו קְעִילָה וַיִּלָּחֶם
בַּפְּלִשְׁתִּים וַיִּנְהַג אֶת־מִקְנֵיהֶם וַיַּךְ בָּהֶם מַכָּה גְדוֹלָה וַיֹּשַׁע דָּוִד אֵת
ו יֹשְׁבֵי קְעִילָה: וַיְהִי בִּבְרֹחַ אֶבְיָתָר בֶּן־אֲחִימֶלֶךְ אֶל־דָּוִד
ז קְעִילָה אֵפוֹד יָרַד בְּיָדוֹ: וַיֻּגַּד לְשָׁאוּל כִּי־בָא דָוִד קְעִילָה וַיֹּאמֶר שָׁאוּל
ח נִכַּר אֹתוֹ אֱלֹהִים בְּיָדִי כִּי נִסְגַּר לָבוֹא בְּעִיר דְּלָתַיִם וּבְרִיחַ: וַיְשַׁמַּע

9 Ke'ila and besiege David and his men. But David knew that Sha'ul was
scheming evil against him, and he said to Evyatar, the priest, "Bring the ephod
10 forth." David said, "O Lord, God of Israel, your servant has heard
11 that Sha'ul intends to come to Ke'ila to ravage the city because of me. Will the
citizens of Ke'ila hand me over to him? Will Sha'ul march down as your
servant has heard? O Lord, God of Israel, please tell your servant." And the
12 Lord said, "He will march down." And David asked, "Will the
citizens of Ke'ila hand me over to Sha'ul?" And the Lord said, "They will
13 hand you over." So David and his men arose, around six hundred
men; they made their way out of Ke'ila, and they wandered wherever they
could. When Sha'ul was informed that David has escaped from Ke'ila, he
14 abandoned the mission. David settled in the strongholds of the wilderness;
he settled in the hills of the Wilderness of Zif. Sha'ul constantly hunted for
15 him, but God did not let him fall into his hands. David learned that Sha'ul had
set out to hunt him down while David was in the Wilderness of Zif, at
16 Ḥoresh. Yehonatan, Sha'ul's son, rose and made his way to David at
17 Ḥoresh, to strengthen his commitment to God. "Do not fear," he said to him,
"for the hand of Sha'ul, my father, will not find you. You will be king over
Israel, and I will be your second in command – even Sha'ul, my father, knows
18 this is so." Then the two of them formed a pact before the Lord. And David
19 stayed in Ḥoresh while Yehonatan went back home. But the Zifites
went up to Sha'ul at Giva, saying, "David is hiding among us in the strongholds
20 of Ḥoresh, in the Heights of Ḥakhila south of Yeshimon. Now, if you so wish
to come down, O king, come down; and we shall be the ones to hand him
21 over to the king." "May the Lord bless you for taking pity on me," said Sha'ul.
22 "Now go and confirm once more; make sure you know every place where his
foot treads. Who has seen him there? For I have been told that he is very sly.
23 Make sure you know of all his possible hiding places; come back to me when
you are sure, and I shall set out with you. If he is in the area, I shall search for
24 him in all the clans of Yehuda." And they arose and went to Zif ahead of Sha'ul.
Meanwhile, David and his men were in the Wilderness of Maon, in the plains
25 south of Yeshimon. When Sha'ul and his men set out to search, David was
informed. He climbed down the rock and settled in the Wilderness of Maon.
26 When Sha'ul heard, he chased after David in the Wilderness of Maon. Sha'ul
made his way along one side of the mountain while David and his men were
on the other side; David was desperately running away from Sha'ul, but
27 Sha'ul and his men were closing in to trap David and his men. Just then, a
messenger came to Sha'ul and announced, "Hurry, go, for the Philistines have
28 invaded the land." Sha'ul turned back from chasing David and headed out
toward the Philistines. Therefore, they called that place Sela HaMaḥlekot.[20]
29 Then David climbed up from there and settled in the strongholds of Ein

20 | Literally "rock of the parting."

שָׁאוּל אֶת־כׇּל־הָעָם לַמִּלְחָמָה לָרֶדֶת קְעִילָה לָצוּר אֶל־דָּוִד וְאֶל־
ט אֲנָשָׁיו: וַיֵּדַע דָּוִד כִּי עָלָיו שָׁאוּל מַחֲרִישׁ הָרָעָה וַיֹּאמֶר אֶל־אֶבְיָתָר
י הַכֹּהֵן הַגִּישָׁה הָאֵפוֹד: וַיֹּאמֶר דָּוִד יְהוָה אֱלֹהֵי יִשְׂרָאֵל שָׁמֹעַ
שָׁמַע עַבְדְּךָ כִּי־מְבַקֵּשׁ שָׁאוּל לָבוֹא אֶל־קְעִילָה לְשַׁחֵת לָעִיר בַּעֲבוּרִי:
יא הֲיַסְגִּרֻנִי בַעֲלֵי קְעִילָה בְיָדוֹ הֲיֵרֵד שָׁאוּל כַּאֲשֶׁר שָׁמַע עַבְדְּךָ יְהוָה
יב אֱלֹהֵי יִשְׂרָאֵל הַגֶּד־נָא לְעַבְדֶּךָ וַיֹּאמֶר יְהוָה יֵרֵד: וַיֹּאמֶר
דָּוִד הֲיַסְגִּרוּ בַּעֲלֵי קְעִילָה אֹתִי וְאֶת־אֲנָשַׁי בְּיַד שָׁאוּל וַיֹּאמֶר יְהוָה
יג יַסְגִּירוּ: וַיָּקׇם דָּוִד וַאֲנָשָׁיו כְּשֵׁשׁ־מֵאוֹת אִישׁ וַיֵּצְאוּ מִקְּעִלָה
וַיִּתְהַלְּכוּ בַּאֲשֶׁר יִתְהַלָּכוּ וּלְשָׁאוּל הֻגַּד כִּי־נִמְלַט דָּוִד מִקְּעִילָה וַיֶּחְדַּל
יד לָצֵאת: וַיֵּשֶׁב דָּוִד בַּמִּדְבָּר בַּמְּצָדוֹת וַיֵּשֶׁב בָּהָר בְּמִדְבַּר־זִיף וַיְבַקְשֵׁהוּ
טו שָׁאוּל כׇּל־הַיָּמִים וְלֹא־נְתָנוֹ אֱלֹהִים בְּיָדוֹ: וַיַּרְא דָוִד כִּי־יָצָא שָׁאוּל
טז לְבַקֵּשׁ אֶת־נַפְשׁוֹ וְדָוִד בְּמִדְבַּר־זִיף בַּחֹרְשָׁה: וַיָּקׇם
יְהוֹנָתָן בֶּן־שָׁאוּל וַיֵּלֶךְ אֶל־דָּוִד חֹרְשָׁה וַיְחַזֵּק אֶת־יָדוֹ בֵּאלֹהִים:
יז וַיֹּאמֶר אֵלָיו אַל־תִּירָא כִּי לֹא תִמְצָאֲךָ יַד־שָׁאוּל אָבִי וְאַתָּה תִּמְלֹךְ
עַל־יִשְׂרָאֵל וְאָנֹכִי אֶהְיֶה־לְּךָ לְמִשְׁנֶה וְגַם־שָׁאוּל אָבִי יֹדֵעַ כֵּן:
יח וַיִּכְרְתוּ שְׁנֵיהֶם בְּרִית לִפְנֵי יְהוָה וַיֵּשֶׁב דָּוִד בַּחֹרְשָׁה וִיהוֹנָתָן הָלַךְ
יט לְבֵיתוֹ: וַיַּעֲלוּ זִפִים אֶל־שָׁאוּל הַגִּבְעָתָה לֵאמֹר הֲלוֹא דָוִד
מִסְתַּתֵּר עִמָּנוּ בַמְּצָדוֹת בַּחֹרְשָׁה בְּגִבְעַת הַחֲכִילָה אֲשֶׁר מִימִין
כ הַיְשִׁימוֹן: וְעַתָּה לְכׇל־אַוַּת נַפְשְׁךָ הַמֶּלֶךְ לָרֶדֶת רֵד וְלָנוּ הַסְגִּירוֹ
כא בְּיַד הַמֶּלֶךְ: וַיֹּאמֶר שָׁאוּל בְּרוּכִים אַתֶּם לַיהוָה כִּי חֲמַלְתֶּם עָלָי:
כב לְכוּ־נָא הָכִינוּ עוֹד וּדְעוּ וּרְאוּ אֶת־מְקוֹמוֹ אֲשֶׁר תִּהְיֶה רַגְלוֹ מִי רָאָהוּ
כג שָׁם כִּי אָמַר אֵלַי עָרוֹם יַעְרִם הוּא: וּרְאוּ וּדְעוּ מִכֹּל הַמַּחֲבֹאִים אֲשֶׁר
יִתְחַבֵּא שָׁם וְשַׁבְתֶּם אֵלַי אֶל־נָכוֹן וְהָלַכְתִּי אִתְּכֶם וְהָיָה אִם־יֶשְׁנוֹ
כד בָאָרֶץ וְחִפַּשְׂתִּי אֹתוֹ בְּכֹל אַלְפֵי יְהוּדָה: וַיָּקוּמוּ וַיֵּלְכוּ זִיפָה לִפְנֵי
כה שָׁאוּל וְדָוִד וַאֲנָשָׁיו בְּמִדְבַּר מָעוֹן בָּעֲרָבָה אֶל יְמִין הַיְשִׁימוֹן: וַיֵּלֶךְ
שָׁאוּל וַאֲנָשָׁיו לְבַקֵּשׁ וַיַּגִּדוּ לְדָוִד וַיֵּרֶד הַסֶּלַע וַיֵּשֶׁב בְּמִדְבַּר מָעוֹן
כו וַיִּשְׁמַע שָׁאוּל וַיִּרְדֹּף אַחֲרֵי־דָוִד מִדְבַּר מָעוֹן: וַיֵּלֶךְ שָׁאוּל מִצַּד הָהָר
מִזֶּה וְדָוִד וַאֲנָשָׁיו מִצַּד הָהָר מִזֶּה וַיְהִי דָוִד נֶחְפָּז לָלֶכֶת מִפְּנֵי שָׁאוּל
כז וְשָׁאוּל וַאֲנָשָׁיו עֹטְרִים אֶל־דָּוִד וְאֶל־אֲנָשָׁיו לְתׇפְשָׂם: וּמַלְאָךְ בָּא
אֶל־שָׁאוּל לֵאמֹר מַהֲרָה וְלֵכָה כִּי־פָשְׁטוּ פְלִשְׁתִּים עַל־הָאָרֶץ:
כח וַיָּשׇׁב שָׁאוּל מִרְדֹף אַחֲרֵי דָוִד וַיֵּלֶךְ לִקְרַאת פְּלִשְׁתִּים עַל־כֵּן קָרְאוּ
כט לַמָּקוֹם הַהוּא סֶלַע הַמַּחְלְקוֹת: וַיַּעַל דָּוִד מִשָּׁם וַיֵּשֶׁב בִּמְצָדוֹת עֵין־

24 1 Gedi. When Sha'ul returned from pursuing the Philistines, they
2 informed him, "David is now in the Wilderness of Ein Gedi." Sha'ul
took three thousand elite fighters from all of Israel and set out to search for
3 David and his men along the rocks of the wild goats. When they reached the
sheepfolds by the road, there was a cave there, and Sha'ul went inside to relieve
4 himself; David and his men were sitting in the depths of the cave. David's men
said to him, "Now is the very moment that the Lord spoke of to you: 'Now,
I am handing your enemies over to you.' Do to him as you see fit!" And David
5 got up and stealthily cut off the corner of Sha'ul's robe. Later on, though,
6 David's heart ached for having cut Sha'ul's hem. "Lord forbid that I should
do such a thing to my master – to the Lord's own anointed!" he said to his
7 men. "To raise my hand against him when he is the Lord's anointed?" David
restrained his men with words and did not allow them to rise against Sha'ul.
8 And Sha'ul rose out of the cave and went on his way. David then rose,
went out of the cave, and called after Sha'ul, "O my lord king!" Sha'ul looked
behind him, and David bowed down with his face to the ground in homage.
9 And David said to Sha'ul, "Why do you listen to the words of people who say,
10 'Look, David seeks to harm you?' Now, right now, see for yourself how the
Lord handed you over to me in the cave – though I was urged to kill you, I
showed you mercy. And I said, 'I will not raise my hand against my lord, for
11 he is the Lord's own anointed.' O my father, look – look closely at the corner
of your robe in my hand; when I cut off the corner of your robe, I did not kill
you. Realize that I have no intention of harm, or crime, or offending you – yet
12 you pursue my life to snatch it away. May the Lord judge between me and
you, and may the Lord avenge me on you – my own hand will never touch
13 you. As the ancient proverb says, 'Evil is as evil does' – my own hand will
14 never touch you. After whom, exactly, has the king of Israel set out? After
15 whom, exactly, are you chasing? After a dead dog! After a single flea! May the
Lord be Judge, and judge between me and you. May He witness and contend
16 on my behalf and defend me from you!" When David had finished
speaking these words to Sha'ul, Sha'ul said, "Is that your voice, my son David?"
17 And Sha'ul broke down and wept. "You are more just than I," he said to David,
18 "for you have shown me good while I have shown you evil. Now you have just
told me how you have acted toward me with good, for the Lord handed me
19 over to you, but you did not kill me. When a man finds his enemy, does he
send him away with good? May the Lord repay you with good for how you
20 acted toward me today. I now know that you will surely become king and that
21 the kingdom of Israel will be established through you. So now, swear to me
by the Lord that you will not cut off my seed after me, nor wipe out my name

כד א גְּדִי׃ וַיְהִי כַּאֲשֶׁר שָׁב שָׁאוּל מֵאַחֲרֵי פְּלִשְׁתִּים וַיַּגִּדוּ לוֹ
ב לֵאמֹר הִנֵּה דָוִד בְּמִדְבַּר עֵין גֶּדִי׃ וַיִּקַּח שָׁאוּל שְׁלֹשֶׁת
אֲלָפִים אִישׁ בָּחוּר מִכָּל־יִשְׂרָאֵל וַיֵּלֶךְ לְבַקֵּשׁ אֶת־דָּוִד וַאֲנָשָׁיו עַל־פְּנֵי
ג צוּרֵי הַיְּעֵלִים׃ וַיָּבֹא אֶל־גִּדְרוֹת הַצֹּאן עַל־הַדֶּרֶךְ וְשָׁם מְעָרָה וַיָּבֹא
ד שָׁאוּל לְהָסֵךְ אֶת־רַגְלָיו וְדָוִד וַאֲנָשָׁיו בְּיַרְכְּתֵי הַמְּעָרָה יֹשְׁבִים׃ וַיֹּאמְרוּ
אַנְשֵׁי דָוִד אֵלָיו הִנֵּה הַיּוֹם אֲשֶׁר־אָמַר יהוה אֵלֶיךָ הִנֵּה אָנֹכִי נֹתֵן
אֶת־איביך בְּיָדֶךָ וְעָשִׂיתָ לּוֹ כַּאֲשֶׁר יִטַב בְּעֵינֶיךָ וַיָּקָם דָּוִד וַיִּכְרֹת אֹיִבְךָ
ה אֶת־כְּנַף־הַמְּעִיל אֲשֶׁר־לְשָׁאוּל בַּלָּט׃ וַיְהִי אַחֲרֵי־כֵן וַיַּךְ לֵב־דָּוִד אֹתוֹ
ו עַל אֲשֶׁר כָּרַת אֶת־כָּנָף אֲשֶׁר לְשָׁאוּל׃ וַיֹּאמֶר לַאֲנָשָׁיו חָלִילָה לִּי
מֵיהוה אִם־אֶעֱשֶׂה אֶת־הַדָּבָר הַזֶּה לַאדֹנִי לִמְשִׁיחַ יהוה לִשְׁלֹחַ יָדִי
ז בּוֹ כִּי־מְשִׁיחַ יהוה הוּא׃ וַיְשַׁסַּע דָּוִד אֶת־אֲנָשָׁיו בַּדְּבָרִים וְלֹא נְתָנָם
ח לָקוּם אֶל־שָׁאוּל וְשָׁאוּל קָם מֵהַמְּעָרָה וַיֵּלֶךְ בַּדָּרֶךְ׃ וַיָּקָם
דָּוִד אַחֲרֵי־כֵן וַיֵּצֵא מן המערה וַיִּקְרָא אַחֲרֵי־שָׁאוּל לֵאמֹר אֲדֹנִי מֵהַמְּעָרָה
ט הַמֶּלֶךְ וַיַּבֵּט שָׁאוּל אַחֲרָיו וַיִּקֹּד דָּוִד אַפַּיִם אַרְצָה וַיִּשְׁתָּחוּ׃ וַיֹּאמֶר
דָּוִד לְשָׁאוּל לָמָּה תִשְׁמַע אֶת־דִּבְרֵי אָדָם לֵאמֹר הִנֵּה דָוִד מְבַקֵּשׁ
י רָעָתֶךָ׃ הִנֵּה הַיּוֹם הַזֶּה רָאוּ עֵינֶיךָ אֵת אֲשֶׁר־נְתָנְךָ יהוה | הַיּוֹם | בְּיָדִי
בַּמְּעָרָה וְאָמַר לַהֲרָגְךָ וַתָּחָס עָלֶיךָ וָאֹמַר לֹא־אֶשְׁלַח יָדִי בַּאדֹנִי כִּי־
יא מְשִׁיחַ יהוה הוּא׃ וְאָבִי רְאֵה גַּם רְאֵה אֶת־כְּנַף מְעִילְךָ בְּיָדִי כִּי בְּכָרְתִי
אֶת־כְּנַף מְעִילְךָ וְלֹא הֲרַגְתִּיךָ דַּע וּרְאֵה כִּי אֵין בְּיָדִי רָעָה וָפֶשַׁע
יב וְלֹא־חָטָאתִי לָךְ וְאַתָּה צֹדֶה אֶת־נַפְשִׁי לְקַחְתָּהּ׃ יִשְׁפֹּט יהוה בֵּינִי
יג וּבֵינֶךָ וּנְקָמַנִי יהוה מִמֶּךָּ וְיָדִי לֹא תִהְיֶה־בָּךְ׃ כַּאֲשֶׁר יֹאמַר מְשַׁל
יד הַקַּדְמֹנִי מֵרְשָׁעִים יֵצֵא רֶשַׁע וְיָדִי לֹא תִהְיֶה־בָּךְ׃ אַחֲרֵי מִי יָצָא
מֶלֶךְ יִשְׂרָאֵל אַחֲרֵי מִי אַתָּה רֹדֵף אַחֲרֵי כֶּלֶב מֵת אַחֲרֵי פַּרְעֹשׁ אֶחָד׃
טו וְהָיָה יהוה לְדַיָּן וְשָׁפַט בֵּינִי וּבֵינֶךָ וְיֵרֶא וְיָרֵב אֶת־רִיבִי וְיִשְׁפְּטֵנִי
טז מִיָּדֶךָ׃ וַיְהִי | כְּכַלּוֹת דָּוִד לְדַבֵּר אֶת־הַדְּבָרִים הָאֵלֶּה אֶל־
יז שָׁאוּל וַיֹּאמֶר שָׁאוּל הֲקֹלְךָ זֶה בְּנִי דָוִד וַיִּשָּׂא שָׁאוּל קֹלוֹ וַיֵּבְךְּ׃ וַיֹּאמֶר
אֶל־דָּוִד צַדִּיק אַתָּה מִמֶּנִּי כִּי אַתָּה גְּמַלְתַּנִי הַטּוֹבָה וַאֲנִי גְּמַלְתִּיךָ
יח הָרָעָה׃ וְאַתְּ הִגַּדְתָּ הַיּוֹם אֵת אֲשֶׁר־עָשִׂיתָה אִתִּי טוֹבָה אֵת אֲשֶׁר
יט סִגְּרַנִי יהוה בְּיָדְךָ וְלֹא הֲרַגְתָּנִי׃ וְכִי־יִמְצָא אִישׁ אֶת־אֹיְבוֹ וְשִׁלְּחוֹ
בְּדֶרֶךְ טוֹבָה וַיהוה יְשַׁלֶּמְךָ טוֹבָה תַּחַת הַיּוֹם הַזֶּה אֲשֶׁר עָשִׂיתָה לִי׃
כ וְעַתָּה הִנֵּה יָדַעְתִּי כִּי מָלֹךְ תִּמְלוֹךְ וְקָמָה בְּיָדְךָ מַמְלֶכֶת יִשְׂרָאֵל׃ טז
כא וְעַתָּה הִשָּׁבְעָה לִּי בַּיהוה אִם־תַּכְרִית אֶת־זַרְעִי אַחֲרָי וְאִם־תַּשְׁמִיד

22 from my father's house." And David swore to Sha'ul. And Sha'ul went back to
25 1 his house while David and his men ascended to the stronghold. Shmuel
died, and all of Israel gathered to mourn him. They buried him at his
home in Rama. Meanwhile, David had gone down to the Wilderness of
2 Paran. Now, there was a man in Maon whose business was in Carmel.
The man was very wealthy; he owned three thousand sheep and one thousand
3 goats. At the time, he was shearing his flock in Carmel. The man's name was
Naval, and his wife's name was Avigayil; the woman was intelligent and
4 beautiful, but the man, a Calebite, was coarse and vicious. When David, out
5 in the wilderness, heard that Naval was shearing his flock, David sent out ten
lads. "Go up to Carmel," David said to the lads, "and when you reach Naval,
6 ask about his welfare in my name. Say, 'To life! Peace unto you, and peace to
7 your household, and peace to all that is yours. I have heard that you are
presently holding your shearing. Now, the shepherds who belong to you have
been with us; we have not shamed them, nor did anything of theirs go missing
8 throughout the time they were in Carmel – ask your lads, and they will tell
you. May the lads find favor in your eyes, for we have come during a festive
time. Please give whatever you can to your servants and to your son, David.'"
9 So David's lads came and related all these words to Naval in David's name.
10 When they paused, Naval answered David's lads. "Who is David, and who is
the son of Yishai? Today, so many servants break away from their masters;
11 should I take my own bread and my own water and my own meat that I
slaughtered for my shearers and give it to people who come from I don't know
12 where?" So David's lads turned back around, and as soon as they arrived, they
13 reported everything to him. "Everyone, gird your swords!" David said to his
men, and each man girded his sword. David, too, girded his sword, and they
marched up after David, about four hundred men, while two hundred stayed
14 with the baggage. Meanwhile, one of the lads had told Avigayil, Naval's wife,
"David just sent messengers from the wilderness to greet our master, and he
15 shouted at them. But the men were very good to us; we were not shamed, and
we missed absolutely nothing throughout the time we went about with them
16 while we were in the field. They were a wall over us, both night and day, for
17 as long as we were with them tending the sheep. Now, consider what to do,
for harm has been determined for our master and all his household; and he
18 is too depraved to speak to." Avigayil quickly grabbed two hundred loaves of
bread, two amphorae of wine, five prepared lambs, five *se'a* of toasted grain,
one hundred cakes of raisins, and two hundred cakes of figs, and loaded them
19 onto the donkeys. "Go on before me," she said to her servants, "I am coming
20 right after you," but she did not tell Naval, her husband. As she was riding her
donkey down the shaded mountain trail, David and his men came down
21 toward her, and she met them. Now, David had been saying, "It was only in
vain that I guarded everything that belonged to this one; absolutely nothing

כב אֶת־שְׁמִי מִבֵּית אָבִי: וַיִּשָּׁבַע דָּוִד לְשָׁאוּל וַיֵּלֶךְ שָׁאוּל אֶל־בֵּיתוֹ וְדָוִד
כה א וַאֲנָשָׁיו עָלוּ עַל־הַמְּצוּדָה: וַיָּמָת שְׁמוּאֵל וַיִּקָּבְצוּ כָל־
יִשְׂרָאֵל וַיִּסְפְּדוּ־לוֹ וַיִּקְבְּרֻהוּ בְּבֵיתוֹ בָּרָמָה וַיָּקָם דָּוִד וַיֵּרֶד אֶל־מִדְבַּר
ב פָּארָן: וְאִישׁ בְּמָעוֹן וּמַעֲשֵׂהוּ בַכַּרְמֶל וְהָאִישׁ גָּדוֹל מְאֹד
וְלוֹ צֹאן שְׁלֹשֶׁת־אֲלָפִים וְאֶלֶף עִזִּים וַיְהִי בִּגְזֹז אֶת־צֹאנוֹ בַּכַּרְמֶל:
ג וְשֵׁם הָאִישׁ נָבָל וְשֵׁם אִשְׁתּוֹ אֲבִגָיִל וְהָאִשָּׁה טוֹבַת־שֶׂכֶל וִיפַת תֹּאַר
ד וְהָאִישׁ קָשֶׁה וְרַע מַעֲלָלִים וְהוּא כלבו: וַיִּשְׁמַע דָּוִד בַּמִּדְבָּר כִּי־גֹזֵז כָלִבִּי
ה נָבָל אֶת־צֹאנוֹ: וַיִּשְׁלַח דָּוִד עֲשָׂרָה נְעָרִים וַיֹּאמֶר דָּוִד לַנְּעָרִים עֲלוּ
ו כַרְמֶלָה וּבָאתֶם אֶל־נָבָל וּשְׁאֶלְתֶּם־לוֹ בִשְׁמִי לְשָׁלוֹם: וַאֲמַרְתֶּם כֹּה
ז לֶחָי וְאַתָּה שָׁלוֹם וּבֵיתְךָ שָׁלוֹם וְכֹל אֲשֶׁר־לְךָ שָׁלוֹם: וְעַתָּה שָׁמַעְתִּי
כִּי גֹזְזִים לָךְ עַתָּה הָרֹעִים אֲשֶׁר־לְךָ הָיוּ עִמָּנוּ לֹא הֶכְלַמְנוּם וְלֹא־נִפְקַד
ח לָהֶם מְאוּמָה כָּל־יְמֵי הֱיוֹתָם בַּכַּרְמֶל: שְׁאַל אֶת־נְעָרֶיךָ וְיַגִּידוּ לָךְ
וְיִמְצְאוּ הַנְּעָרִים חֵן בְּעֵינֶיךָ כִּי־עַל־יוֹם טוֹב באנו תְּנָה־נָּא אֵת אֲשֶׁר בָּאנוּ
ט תִּמְצָא יָדְךָ לַעֲבָדֶיךָ וּלְבִנְךָ לְדָוִד: וַיָּבֹאוּ נַעֲרֵי דָוִד וַיְדַבְּרוּ אֶל־נָבָל
י כְּכָל־הַדְּבָרִים הָאֵלֶּה בְּשֵׁם דָּוִד וַיָּנוּחוּ: וַיַּעַן נָבָל אֶת־עַבְדֵי דָוִד
וַיֹּאמֶר מִי דָוִד וּמִי בֶן־יִשָׁי הַיּוֹם רַבּוּ עֲבָדִים הַמִּתְפָּרְצִים אִישׁ מִפְּנֵי
יא אֲדֹנָיו: וְלָקַחְתִּי אֶת־לַחְמִי וְאֶת־מֵימַי וְאֵת טִבְחָתִי אֲשֶׁר טָבַחְתִּי
יב לְגֹזְזָי וְנָתַתִּי לַאֲנָשִׁים אֲשֶׁר לֹא יָדַעְתִּי אֵי מִזֶּה הֵמָּה: וַיַּהַפְכוּ נַעֲרֵי־
יג דָוִד לְדַרְכָּם וַיָּשֻׁבוּ וַיָּבֹאוּ וַיַּגִּדוּ לוֹ כְּכֹל הַדְּבָרִים הָאֵלֶּה: וַיֹּאמֶר דָּוִד
לַאֲנָשָׁיו חִגְרוּ ׀ אִישׁ אֶת־חַרְבּוֹ וַיַּחְגְּרוּ אִישׁ אֶת־חַרְבּוֹ וַיַּחְגֹּר גַּם־דָּוִד
אֶת־חַרְבּוֹ וַיַּעֲלוּ ׀ אַחֲרֵי דָוִד כְּאַרְבַּע מֵאוֹת אִישׁ וּמָאתַיִם יָשְׁבוּ עַל־
יד הַכֵּלִים: וְלַאֲבִיגַיִל אֵשֶׁת נָבָל הִגִּיד נַעַר־אֶחָד מֵהַנְּעָרִים לֵאמֹר הִנֵּה
טו שָׁלַח דָּוִד מַלְאָכִים ׀ מֵהַמִּדְבָּר לְבָרֵךְ אֶת־אֲדֹנֵינוּ וַיָּעַט בָּהֶם: וְהָאֲנָשִׁים
טֹבִים לָנוּ מְאֹד וְלֹא הָכְלַמְנוּ וְלֹא־פָקַדְנוּ מְאוּמָה כָּל־יְמֵי הִתְהַלַּכְנוּ
טז אִתָּם בִּהְיוֹתֵנוּ בַּשָּׂדֶה: חוֹמָה הָיוּ עָלֵינוּ גַּם־לַיְלָה גַּם־יוֹמָם כָּל־יְמֵי
יז הֱיוֹתֵנוּ עִמָּם רֹעִים הַצֹּאן: וְעַתָּה דְּעִי וּרְאִי מַה־תַּעֲשִׂי כִּי־כָלְתָה
יח הָרָעָה אֶל־אֲדֹנֵינוּ וְעַל־כָּל־בֵּיתוֹ וְהוּא בֶּן־בְּלִיַּעַל מִדַּבֵּר אֵלָיו: וַתְּמַהֵר
אבוגיל וַתִּקַּח מָאתַיִם לֶחֶם וּשְׁנַיִם נִבְלֵי־יַיִן וְחָמֵשׁ צֹאן עשוות וְחָמֵשׁ אֲבִיגַיִל עֲשׂוּיוֹת
סְאִים קָלִי וּמֵאָה צִמֻּקִים וּמָאתַיִם דְּבֵלִים וַתָּשֶׂם עַל־הַחֲמֹרִים:
יט וַתֹּאמֶר לִנְעָרֶיהָ עִבְרוּ לְפָנַי הִנְנִי אַחֲרֵיכֶם בָּאָה וּלְאִישָׁהּ נָבָל לֹא
כ הִגִּידָה: וְהָיָה הִיא ׀ רֹכֶבֶת עַל־הַחֲמוֹר וְיֹרֶדֶת בְּסֵתֶר הָהָר וְהִנֵּה דָוִד
כא וַאֲנָשָׁיו יֹרְדִים לִקְרָאתָהּ וַתִּפְגֹּשׁ אֹתָם: וְדָוִד אָמַר אַךְ לַשֶּׁקֶר שָׁמַרְתִּי

22 of his went missing, but he has paid me back with evil for good. So may
God do to David's enemies[21] – and more – if I leave a single male[22] of his
23 alive by the morning light." When Avigayil saw David, she swiftly alighted
from her donkey, flung herself face down before David, and bowed to the
24 ground. Then she flung herself at his feet. "It is my own fault, my lord," she
said. "Please let your handmaiden speak to you; listen to the words of your
25 handmaiden. Let my lord not take this depraved man, Naval, to heart, for he
is just like his name – 'fool' is his name, and a fool he is indeed; but I, your
26 handmaiden, never saw my lord's lads whom you sent. Now, my lord, as the
Lord lives, and as you yourself live, the Lord has prevented you from being
tainted by blood by taking matters into your own hands; and now may your
27 enemies and those who wish evil upon my lord be like Naval. As for this gift,
which your maidservant brought for my lord, let it be given to the lads who
28 accompany my lord. Please forgive your handmaiden's offense, for the Lord
will surely grant my lord an enduring house – as my lord fights the Lord's
29 battles – and no evil should be found in you all your days. If anyone should
arise to pursue you and seek your life, may the life of my lord be tucked
away in the pouch of life of the Lord your God as He slings away your
30 enemy's life as from the hollow of the sling. And when the Lord has fulfilled
for my lord all the good He has promised you and has appointed you
31 as ruler over Israel, my lord will have no qualms or pangs of conscience
for having spilled innocent blood through my lord's taking charge himself.
And when the Lord deals well with my lord, May you remember your
32 handmaiden." And David said to Avigayil, "Blessed is the Lord, God
33 of Israel, for having sent you to meet me today. And blessed is your sense of
reason, and blessed are you, who restrained me from being tainted with blood
34 and taking matters into my own hands. For as the Lord lives – the God of
Israel, who prevented me from harming you – had you not rushed out to meet
me, not a single male of Naval's would have been left by the morning light."
35 And David took what she had brought for him from her hands. "Go up to
your home in peace," he said to her. "See, I have heeded your voice and
36 granted your request." When Avigayil came to Naval, the feast he was holding
at his house was a feast fit for a king; he was in high spirits, enormously drunk.
37 So she told him nothing at all until the morning light, but in the morning,
when the wine had seeped out of Naval, his wife related these things to
38 him. And his heart died within him, and he stiffened like a stone. And
39 ten days later, the Lord struck Naval and he died. When David heard that
Naval had died, he said, "Blessed is the Lord, who has contended on my
behalf against Naval's insults; he kept His servant from evil and brought the
evil of Naval back down on his own head." Then David sent a proposal to
40 Avigayil to take her as a wife; David's servants came to Avigayil at Carmel and
spoke to her, saying, "David has sent us to you to take you for him as a wife."

---

21 | A euphemism for David himself, common in such oaths.
22 | Literally "one who urinates against a wall." The same phrase occurs in v. 34 below.

את־כל־אשר לזה במדבר ולא־נפקד מכל־אשר־לו מאומה וישב־לי
כב רעה תחת טובה: כה־יעשה אלהים לאיבי דוד וכה יסיף אם־אשאיר
כג מכל־אשר־לו עד־אור הבקר משתין בקיר: ותרא אביגיל את־דוד
ותמהר ותרד מעל החמור ותפל לאפי דוד על־פניה ותשתחו ארץ:
כד ותפל על־רגליו ותאמר בי־אני אדני העון ותדבר־נא אמתך באזניך
כה ושמע את דברי אמתך: אל־נא ישים אדני | את־לבו אל־איש
הבליעל הזה על־נבל כי כשמו כן־הוא נבל שמו ונבלה עמו ואני
כו אמתך לא ראיתי את־נערי אדני אשר שלחת: ועתה אדני חי־יהוה
וחי־נפשך אשר מנעך יהוה מבוא בדמים והושע ידך לך ועתה
כז יהיו כנבל איביך והמבקשים אל־אדני רעה: ועתה הברכה הזאת
אשר־הביא שפחתך לאדני ונתנה לנערים המתהלכים ברגלי אדני:
כח שא נא לפשע אמתך כי־עשה יעשה יהוה לאדני בית נאמן כי־
כט מלחמות יהוה אדני נלחם ורעה לא־תמצא בך מימיך: ויקם אדם
לרדפך ולבקש את־נפשך והיתה נפש אדני צרורה | בצרור החיים
ל את יהוה אלהיך ואת נפש איביך יקלענה בתוך כף הקלע: והיה
כי־יעשה יהוה לאדני ככל אשר־דבר את־הטובה עליך וצוך לנגיד
לא על־ישראל: ולא תהיה זאת | לך לפוקה ולמכשול לב לאדני
ולשפך־דם חנם ולהושיע אדני לו והיטב יהוה לאדני וזכרת את־
לב אמתך: ויאמר דוד לאביגל ברוך יהוה אלהי ישראל
לג אשר שלחך היום הזה לקראתי: וברוך טעמך וברוכה את אשר יז
לד כלתני היום הזה מבוא בדמים והשע ידי לי: ואולם חי־יהוה אלהי
ישראל אשר מנעני מהרע אתך כי | לולי מהרת ותבאתי לקראתי ותבאת
לה כי אם־נותר לנבל עד־אור הבקר משתין בקיר: ויקח דוד מידה
את אשר־הביאה לו ולה אמר עלי לשלום לביתך ראי שמעתי
לו בקולך ואשא פניך: ותבא אביגיל | אל־נבל והנה־לו משתה בביתו
כמשתה המלך ולב נבל טוב עליו והוא שכר עד־מאד ולא־הגידה
לז לו דבר קטן וגדול עד־אור הבקר: ויהי בבקר בצאת היין מנבל
ותגד־לו אשתו את־הדברים האלה וימת לבו בקרבו והוא היה
לח לט לאבן: ויהי כעשרת הימים ויגף יהוה את־נבל וימת: וישמע דוד
כי־מת נבל ויאמר ברוך יהוה אשר רב את־ריב חרפתי מיד
נבל ואת־עבדו חשך מרעה ואת רעת נבל השיב יהוה בראשו
מ וישלח דוד וידבר באביגיל לקחתה לו לאשה: ויבאו עבדי דוד

41 She rose, then bowed, face down, to the ground, and said, "Here is your
42 handmaiden as maidservant, to wash the feet of my lord's servants." Then
Avigayil swiftly rose and mounted her donkey, with her five maids following
43 at her heels; she followed David's messengers and became his wife. David
also took Aḥinoam from Yizre'el in marriage, and both of them became his
44 wives. Meanwhile, though, Sha'ul had given his daughter Mikhal,
26 1 David's wife, to Palti son of Layish, who was from Galim. Now the Zifites
came to Sha'ul at Giva, reporting, "David is hiding in the Heights of Ḥakhila
2 facing Yeshimon." And Sha'ul set out and went down to the Wilderness of Zif,
together with three thousand elite fighters of Israel, to track David down
3 in the Wilderness of Zif. Sha'ul set up camp by the road in the Heights of
Ḥakhila, facing Yeshimon; and David, who was staying in the wilderness,
4 realized that Sha'ul had followed him to the wilderness. So David sent out
5 spies, and confirmed that Sha'ul had indeed come. David rose and reached
the site where Sha'ul was encamped, and David could see exactly where Sha'ul
and Avner son of Ner, his army commander, were lying; Sha'ul lay within the
6 circle, while the men were encamped around him. David spoke up and asked
Aḥimelekh the Hittite and Avishai son of Tzeruya, Yoav's brother, "Who
will go down with me to Sha'ul, to the camp?" and Avishai said, "I will go
7 down with you." David and Avishai came to the camp at night, and there was
Sha'ul, lying asleep within the circle, with his spear thrust into the ground at
8 his head, and Avner and the men lying around him. "Today God has
delivered your enemy into your hands," Avishai said to David. "Now let me
pin him to the ground with a single thrust of the spear – I will not need to
9 strike him twice." But David said to Avishai, "Do no violence to him, for who
10 can strike against the anointed one of the Lord and be pardoned?" And
David continued, "As the Lord lives, only the Lord shall strike him – either
his time will come and he will die, or he will go down to battle and perish.
11 The Lord forbid that I raise my hand against the Lord's anointed. And now,
12 take the spear by his head and the water jar, and let us be off." And David took
the spear and the water jar from next to Sha'ul's head, and they made their
way out. No one saw, no one knew, and no one stirred, as all were fast asleep;
13 for a deep sleep from the Lord had fallen upon them. Then David crossed
over to the other side and stood upon a distant hilltop; vast space stretched
14 between them. And David called out to the men and to Avner son of Ner,
"Won't you answer, Avner?" And Avner answered, "Who are you, calling out
15 to the king?" "You are quite a man, Avner," David said to Avner. "Who is quite
like you in all of Israel? So why did you fail to guard your master the king,
16 when one of the people came to destroy the king your master? You have not
done your job well – as the Lord lives, you are dead men – for failing to guard
your master, the Lord's anointed. Now, look around: Where are the king's

אֶל־אֲבִיגַ֖יִל הַכַּרְמֶ֑לָה וַיְדַבְּר֤וּ אֵלֶ֙יהָ֙ לֵאמֹ֔ר דָּוִד֙ שְׁלָחָ֣נוּ אֵלַ֔יִךְ לְקַחְתֵּ֥ךְ
מא לֹ֖ו לְאִשָּֽׁה׃ וַתָּ֕קָם וַתִּשְׁתַּ֥חוּ אַפַּ֖יִם אָ֑רְצָה וַתֹּ֗אמֶר הִנֵּ֤ה אֲמָֽתְךָ֙ לְשִׁפְחָ֔ה
מב לִרְחֹ֕ץ רַגְלֵ֖י עַבְדֵ֥י אֲדֹנִֽי׃ וַתְּמַהֵ֞ר וַתָּ֣קָם אֲבִיגַ֗יִל וַתִּרְכַּב֙ עַֽל־הַחֲמ֔וֹר
וְחָמֵ֥שׁ נַעֲרֹתֶ֖יהָ הַהֹלְכ֣וֹת לְרַגְלָ֑הּ וַתֵּ֗לֶךְ אַֽחֲרֵי֙ מַלְאֲכֵ֣י דָוִ֔ד וַתְּהִי־ל֖וֹ
מג לְאִשָּֽׁה׃ וְאֶת־אֲחִינֹ֥עַם לָקַ֛ח דָּוִ֖ד מִיִּזְרְעֶ֑אל וַתִּהְיֶ֛יןָ גַּם־שְׁתֵּיהֶ֥ן ל֖וֹ
מד לְנָשִֽׁים׃ וְשָׁא֗וּל נָתַ֛ן אֶת־מִיכַ֥ל בִּתּ֖וֹ אֵ֣שֶׁת דָּוִ֑ד לְפַלְטִ֥י
כו א בֶן־לַ֖יִשׁ אֲשֶׁ֥ר מִגַּלִּֽים׃ וַיָּבֹ֤אוּ הַזִּפִים֙ אֶל־שָׁא֔וּל הַגִּבְעָ֖תָה לֵאמֹ֑ר הֲל֨וֹא
ב דָוִ֜ד מִסְתַּתֵּ֗ר בְּגִבְעַת֙ הַחֲכִילָ֔ה עַ֖ל פְּנֵ֥י הַיְשִׁימֹֽן׃ וַיָּ֣קָם שָׁא֗וּל וַיֵּ֙רֶד֙
אֶל־מִדְבַּר־זִ֔יף וְאִתּ֛וֹ שְׁלֹֽשֶׁת־אֲלָפִ֥ים אִ֖ישׁ בְּחוּרֵ֣י יִשְׂרָאֵ֑ל לְבַקֵּ֥שׁ
ג אֶת־דָּוִ֖ד בְּמִדְבַּר־זִֽיף׃ וַיִּ֨חַן שָׁא֜וּל בְּגִבְעַ֤ת הַֽחֲכִילָה֙ אֲשֶׁ֛ר עַל־פְּנֵ֥י
הַיְשִׁימֹ֖ן עַל־הַדָּ֑רֶךְ וְדָוִד֙ יֹשֵׁ֣ב בַּמִּדְבָּ֔ר וַיַּ֕רְא כִּ֣י בָ֥א שָׁא֛וּל אַחֲרָ֖יו
ד ה הַמִּדְבָּֽרָה׃ וַיִּשְׁלַ֥ח דָּוִ֖ד מְרַגְּלִ֑ים וַיֵּ֕דַע כִּֽי־בָ֥א שָׁא֖וּל אֶל־נָכֽוֹן׃ וַיָּ֣קָם
דָּוִ֗ד וַיָּבֹא֙ אֶל־הַמָּק֔וֹם אֲשֶׁ֥ר חָנָה־שָׁם֮ שָׁאוּל֒ וַיַּ֣רְא דָוִ֗ד אֶת־הַמָּקוֹם֙
אֲשֶׁ֧ר שָֽׁכַב־שָׁ֛ם שָׁא֖וּל וְאַבְנֵ֥ר בֶּן־נֵ֖ר שַׂר־צְבָא֑וֹ וְשָׁאוּל֙ שֹׁכֵ֣ב בַּמַּעְגָּ֔ל
ו וְהָעָ֖ם חֹנִ֥ים סְבִיבֹתָֽו׃ וַיַּ֣עַן דָּוִ֗ד וַיֹּ֣אמֶר ׀ אֶל־אֲחִימֶ֣לֶךְ הַחִתִּ֗י וְאֶל־
אֲבִישַׁ֨י בֶּן־צְרוּיָ֜ה אֲחִ֤י יוֹאָב֙ לֵאמֹ֔ר מִֽי־יֵרֵ֥ד אִתִּ֛י אֶל־שָׁא֖וּל אֶל־
ז הַֽמַּחֲנֶ֑ה וַיֹּ֣אמֶר אֲבִישַׁ֔י אֲנִ֖י אֵרֵ֥ד עִמָּֽךְ׃ וַיָּבֹא֩ דָוִ֨ד וַאֲבִישַׁ֥י ׀ אֶל־הָעָם֮
לַיְלָה֒ וְהִנֵּ֨ה שָׁא֜וּל שֹׁכֵ֤ב יָשֵׁן֙ בַּמַּעְגָּ֔ל וַחֲנִית֥וֹ מְעוּכָה־בָאָ֖רֶץ מְרַאֲשֹׁת֑וֹ
ח וְאַבְנֵר֙ וְהָעָ֔ם שֹׁכְבִ֖ים סְבִיבֹתָֽו׃ וַיֹּ֤אמֶר אֲבִישַׁי֙ אֶל־דָּוִ֔ד
סִגַּ֨ר אֱלֹהִ֥ים הַיּ֛וֹם אֶת־אֹיִבְךָ֖ בְּיָדֶ֑ךָ וְעַתָּה֩ אַכֶּ֨נּוּ נָ֜א בַּחֲנִ֤ית וּבָאָ֙רֶץ֙
ט פַּ֣עַם אַחַ֔ת וְלֹ֥א אֶשְׁנֶ֖ה לֽוֹ׃ וַיֹּ֥אמֶר דָּוִ֛ד אֶל־אֲבִישַׁ֖י אַל־תַּשְׁחִיתֵ֑הוּ כִּ֗י
י מִ֣י שָׁלַ֥ח יָד֛וֹ בִּמְשִׁ֥יחַ יְהוָ֖ה וְנִקָּֽה׃ וַיֹּ֣אמֶר דָּוִ֔ד חַי־יְהוָ֕ה כִּ֥י אִם־יְהוָ֖ה
יא יִגָּפֶ֑נּוּ אוֹ־יוֹמ֤וֹ יָבוֹא֙ וָמֵ֔ת א֧וֹ בַמִּלְחָמָ֛ה יֵרֵ֖ד וְנִסְפָּֽה׃ חָלִ֣ילָה לִּי֮ מֵֽיהוָה֒
מִשְּׁלֹ֥חַ יָדִ֖י בִּמְשִׁ֣יחַ יְהוָ֑ה וְעַתָּ֗ה קַח־נָ֤א אֶת־הַחֲנִית֙ אֲשֶׁ֣ר מְרַאֲשֹׁתָ֔ו
יב וְאֶת־צַפַּ֥חַת הַמַּ֖יִם וְנֵ֥לְכָה לָּֽנוּ׃ וַיִּקַּ֨ח דָּוִ֜ד אֶת־הַחֲנִ֗ית וְאֶת־צַפַּ֤חַת
הַמַּ֙יִם֙ מֵרַאֲשֹׁתֵ֣י שָׁא֔וּל וַיֵּלְכ֖וּ לָהֶ֑ם וְאֵ֣ין רֹאֶה֩ וְאֵ֨ין יוֹדֵ֜עַ וְאֵ֣ין מֵקִ֗יץ
יג כִּ֤י כֻלָּם֙ יְשֵׁנִ֔ים כִּ֚י תַּרְדֵּמַ֣ת יְהוָ֔ה נָפְלָ֖ה עֲלֵיהֶֽם׃ וַיַּעֲבֹ֤ר דָּוִד֙ הָעֵ֔בֶר
יד וַֽיַּעֲמֹ֥ד עַל־רֹאשׁ־הָהָ֖ר מֵרָחֹ֑ק רַ֥ב הַמָּק֖וֹם בֵּינֵיהֶֽם׃ וַיִּקְרָ֨א דָוִ֜ד אֶל־
הָעָ֗ם וְאֶל־אַבְנֵ֤ר בֶּן־נֵר֙ לֵאמֹ֔ר הֲל֥וֹא תַעֲנֶ֖ה אַבְנֵ֑ר וַיַּ֤עַן אַבְנֵר֙ וַיֹּ֔אמֶר
טו מִ֥י אַתָּ֖ה קָרָ֥אתָ אֶל־הַמֶּֽלֶךְ׃ וַיֹּ֨אמֶר דָּוִ֜ד אֶל־אַבְנֵ֗ר הֲלוֹא־אִ֙ישׁ֙ אַתָּ֔ה
וּמִ֣י כָמ֔וֹךָ בְּיִשְׂרָאֵ֔ל וְלָ֙מָּה֙ לֹ֣א שָׁמַ֔רְתָּ אֶל־אֲדֹנֶ֖יךָ הַמֶּ֑לֶךְ כִּי־בָא֙ אַחַ֣ד
טז הָעָ֔ם לְהַשְׁחִ֖ית אֶת־הַמֶּ֥לֶךְ אֲדֹנֶֽיךָ׃ לֹא־ט֞וֹב הַדָּבָ֤ר הַזֶּה֙ אֲשֶׁ֣ר עָשִׂ֔יתָ

17 spear and the water jar that were by his head?" And Sha'ul recognized David's
voice and said, "Is that your voice, my son David?" "It is my voice, my lord
18 the king," said David, and continued, "Why does my lord chase after his
19 servant so? What have I done; what guilt is on my hands? Now, may my lord
the king please listen to the words of his servant. If the Lord has incited you
against me, may He savor an offering, but if it was mere men, then may they
be cursed before the Lord, for they have driven me out today from sharing
20 in the Lord's estate, saying, 'Go serve other gods.' Now do not let my blood
spill to the ground far from the Lord's presence. For the king of Israel has set
out to hunt a single flea, just as he would chase after a partridge in the hills."
21 And Sha'ul said, "I have sinned. Come back, my son David, for I will never
harm you again, as my life was so precious in your eyes today. Oh, I have been
22 foolish and have strayed so far." "Here is the king's spear," answered David,
23 "let one of the lads come over and take it. May the Lord repay each man for
his virtue and faith; though the Lord handed you over to me today, I was not
24 willing to raise my hand against the anointed one of the Lord. Now, just as
I valued your life so highly today, may the Lord value my life and rescue me
25 from all danger." "Bless you, my son," said Sha'ul. "You will surely succeed in
whatever you do." And David went on his way while Sha'ul returned
27 1 home. Now David thought to himself, "One day soon, I might
perish at Sha'ul's hand; I have no better option than to escape to the land of
the Philistines. Then Sha'ul might despair of hunting me within the entire
2 border of Israel, and I shall escape his clutches." So David set out, together
with the six hundred men who were with him, and crossed over to Akhish
3 son of Maokh, king of Gat. And David stayed with Akhish in Gat, together
with his men, each with his own household and David with his two wives,
4 Aḥinoam the Jezreelite and Avigayil the Carmelite, the wife of Naval. When
Sha'ul was informed that David had fled to Gat, he never hunted him down
5 again. David said to Akhish, "If I have found favor in your sight, let
me be given a place in one of the rural towns, and I will live there; why should
6 your servant be living in the royal city together with you?" Soon after, Akhish
granted him Tziklag, therefore Tziklag has belonged to the kings of Yehuda
7 to this day. The amount of time David remained in the Philistine
8 country was a year and four months. David and his men would march up and
raid the Geshurites and the Gezerites and the Amalekites, for these were the
age-old inhabitants of the land leading from Shur up to the land of Egypt.
9 David would attack the land, never leaving man or woman alive, and he would
take sheep, cattle, donkeys, camels, and garments before returning and
10 coming back to Akhish. Akish would ask, "Where did you go raiding today?"
and David would answer, "The Negev of Yehuda" or "The Negev of the

חי־יהוה כי בני־מות אתם אשר לא־שמרתם על־אדניכם על־משיח
יהוה ועתה ׀ ראה אי־חנית המלך ואת־צפחת המים אשר מראשתו:
יז ויכר שאול את־קול דוד ויאמר הקולך זה בני דוד ויאמר דוד קולי
יח אדני המלך: ויאמר למה זה אדני רדף אחרי עבדו כי מה עשיתי
יט ומה־בידי רעה: ועתה ישמע־נא אדני המלך את דברי עבדו אם־
יהוה הסיתך בי ירח מנחה ואם ׀ בני האדם ארורים הם לפני יהוה
כי־גרשוני היום מהסתפח בנחלת יהוה לאמר לך עבד אלהים
כ אחרים: ועתה אל־יפל דמי ארצה מנגד פני יהוה כי־יצא מלך
כא ישראל לבקש את־פרעש אחד כאשר ירדף הקרא בהרים: ויאמר
שאול חטאתי שוב בני־דוד כי לא־ארע לך עוד תחת אשר יקרה
כב נפשי בעיניך היום הזה הנה הסכלתי ואשגה הרבה מאד: ויען דוד
כג ויאמר הנה החנית המלך ויעבר אחד מהנערים ויקחה: ויהוה ישיב חנית
לאיש את־צדקתו ואת־אמנתו אשר נתנך יהוה ׀ היום ביד ולא
כד אביתי לשלח ידי במשיח יהוה: והנה כאשר גדלה נפשך היום הזה
כה בעיני כן תגדל נפשי בעיני יהוה ויצלני מכל־צרה: ויאמר שאול יח
אל־דוד ברוך אתה בני דוד גם עשה תעשה וגם יכל תוכל וילך
דוד לדרכו ושאול שב למקומו:

כז א ויאמר דוד אל־לבו
עתה אספה יום־אחד ביד־שאול אין־לי טוב כי המלט אמלט ׀
אל־ארץ פלשתים ונואש ממני שאול לבקשני עוד בכל־גבול
ב ישראל ונמלטתי מידו: ויקם דוד ויעבר הוא ושש־מאות איש אשר
ג עמו אל־אכיש בן־מעוך מלך גת: וישב דוד עם־אכיש בגת הוא
ואנשיו איש וביתו דוד ושתי נשיו אחינעם היזרעאלת ואביגיל
ד אשת־נבל הכרמלית: ויגד לשאול כי־ברח דוד גת ולא־יוסף עוד יסף
ה לבקשו: ויאמר דוד אל־אכיש אם־נא מצאתי חן
בעיניך יתנו־לי מקום באחת ערי השדה ואשבה שם ולמה ישב
ו עבדך בעיר הממלכה עמך: ויתן־לו אכיש ביום ההוא את־צקלג
ז לכן היתה צקלג למלכי יהודה עד היום הזה: ויהי מספר
ח הימים אשר־ישב דוד בשדה פלשתים ימים וארבעה חדשים: ויעל
דוד ואנשיו ויפשטו אל־הגשורי והגרזי והעמלקי כי הנה ישבות והגזרי
ט הארץ אשר מעולם בואך שורה ועד־ארץ מצרים: והכה דוד את־
הארץ ולא יחיה איש ואשה ולקח צאן ובקר וחמרים וגמלים ובגדים
י וישב ויבא אל־אכיש: ויאמר אכיש אל־פשטתם היום ויאמר דוד

11 Jerahmeelites" or "The Negev of the Kenites."[23] David never left any men or
women alive to bring to Gat, for he thought, "They might inform on us,
saying, 'This is what David was doing.'" This was his practice throughout the
12 time he remained in the Philistine country. Akhish trusted David, saying, "He
must have become odious among his own people, Israel, so he has become
28 1 my vassal forever." It was around that time that the Philistines
gathered their forces for battle to fight against Israel. Akhish said to David,
"You know, of course, that you and your men are to march out to battle with
2 me." "Well," David said to Akhish, "then you must know just what your
servant will do." "Well," Akhish said to David, "then I shall appoint you as my
bodyguard forever."
3 Shmuel had died, and all of Israel had mourned him and buried him in his
hometown of Rama. And Sha'ul had already purged the necromancers and
4 mediums from the land. The Philistines gathered, and they came and set up
camp in Shunem, while Sha'ul gathered all of Israel and encamped at Gilboa.
5 6 When Sha'ul saw the Philistine camp, his heart shuddered with fear. And
Sha'ul inquired of the Lord, but the Lord did not answer him, neither in
7 dreams nor through the Urim[24] nor through prophets. So Sha'ul said to his
servants, "Seek out a necromancer for me, and I shall go to her and consult
through her." His servants replied to him, "There is a necromancer in Ein Dor."
8 So Sha'ul disguised himself and donned different clothing. Then he set
out with two of his servants, and they came to the woman by night. "Please
cast a spell for me by necromancy," he said, "and bring up for me the one I
9 bid you." "You must know what Sha'ul has done and how he cut off the
necromancers and the mediums from the land," the woman said to him, "so
10 why do you lay such a trap for me, to have me killed?" And Sha'ul swore to
her by the Lord. "As the Lord lives," he said, "no punishment will befall you
11 for this act." "Whom should I bring up for you?" said the woman. "Bring up
12 Shmuel for me," he said. When the woman saw Shmuel, she screamed out
13 loud. "Why have you deceived me?" she said to Sha'ul. "You are Sha'ul!" "Do
not be frightened," the king said to her, "but what have you seen?" And the
14 woman said to Sha'ul, "I saw divine beings rising up from the earth." "What
form does he have?" he asked her, and she replied, "An old man is rising up,
and he is cloaked in a robe." And Sha'ul knew that it was Shmuel, and he
15 bowed down with his face to the ground in homage. And Shmuel said
to Sha'ul, "Why have you disturbed me by bringing me up?" "I am in grave
danger," said Sha'ul. "The Philistines are fighting against me, but God has
turned away from me and no longer answers me, neither through prophets
16 nor in dreams – so I summoned you to tell me what to do." "Why should you
ask me," said Shmuel, "when the Lord has turned away from you and has
17 become your adversary? The Lord has executed what He spoke of through
me; the Lord has torn the kingship from your hands and given it to your

---

23 | Israelite localities.

24 | See note on 14:41.

יא על־נגב יהודה ועל־נגב הירחמאלי ואל־נגב הקיני: ואיש ואשה
לא־יחיה דוד להביא גת לאמר פן־יגדו עלינו לאמר כה־עשה
יב דוד וכה משפטו כל־הימים אשר ישב בשדה פלשתים: ויאמן
אכיש בדוד לאמר הבאש הבאיש בעמו בישראל והיה לי לעבד
כח א עולם: ויהי בימים ההם ויקבצו פלשתים את־מחניהם
לצבא להלחם בישראל ויאמר אכיש אל־דוד ידע תדע כי אתי
ב תצא במחנה אתה ואנשיך: ויאמר דוד אל־אכיש לכן אתה תדע
את אשר־יעשה עבדך ויאמר אכיש אל־דוד לכן שמר לראשי
אשימך כל־הימים:
ג ושמואל מת ויספדו־לו כל־ישראל ויקברהו ברמה ובעירו ושאול
ד הסיר האבות ואת־הידענים מהארץ: ויקבצו פלשתים ויבאו ויחנו
ה בשונם ויקבץ שאול את־כל־ישראל ויחנו בגלבע: וירא שאול
ו את־מחנה פלשתים וירא ויחרד לבו מאד: וישאל שאול ביהוה
ז ולא ענהו יהוה גם בחלמות גם באורים גם בנביאם: ויאמר שאול
לעבדיו בקשו־לי אשת בעלת־אוב ואלכה אליה ואדרשה־בה
ח ויאמרו עבדיו אליו הנה אשת בעלת־אוב בעין דור: ויתחפש שאול
וילבש בגדים אחרים וילך הוא ושני אנשים עמו ויבאו אל־האשה
לילה ויאמר קסומי־נא לי באוב והעלי לי את אשר־אמר אליך: קסמי־
ט ותאמר האשה אליו הנה אתה ידעת את אשר־עשה שאול אשר
הכרית את־האבות ואת־הידעני מן־הארץ ולמה אתה מתנקש
י בנפשי להמיתני: וישבע לה שאול ביהוה לאמר חי־יהוה אם־יקרך
יא עון בדבר הזה: ותאמר האשה את־מי אעלה־לך ויאמר את־שמואל
יב העלי־לי: ותרא האשה את־שמואל ותזעק בקול גדול ותאמר
יג האשה אל־שאול לאמר למה רמיתני ואתה שאול: ויאמר לה
המלך אל־תיראי כי מה ראית ותאמר האשה אל־שאול אלהים
יד ראיתי עלים מן־הארץ: ויאמר לה מה־תארו ותאמר איש זקן עלה
והוא עטה מעיל וידע שאול כי־שמואל הוא ויקד אפים ארצה
טו וישתחו: ויאמר שמואל אל־שאול למה הרגזתני
להעלות אתי ויאמר שאול צר־לי מאד ופלשתים | נלחמים בי
ואלהים סר מעלי ולא־ענני עוד גם ביד הנביאים גם בחלמות
טז ואקראה לך להודיעני מה אעשה: ויאמר שמואל ולמה תשאלני
יז ויהוה סר מעליך ויהי ערך: ויעש יהוה לו כאשר דבר בידי ויקרע

18 peer, to David. Because you failed to heed the voice of the LORD and failed
to execute His burning fury against Amalek, the LORD will therefore execute
19 this against you this very day: the LORD will deliver Israel, together with you,
into the hand of the Philistines. Tomorrow, you and your sons shall be with
me. And what is more, the LORD will deliver the forces of Israel into the hands
20 of the Philistines!" At once, Sha'ul fell to the ground from his full stately
height, terrified of Shmuel's words. Nor did he have any strength left in him,
21 for he had eaten nothing all day and all night. The woman came up to Sha'ul,
and seeing how aghast he was, said to him, "Look, your servant heeded your
voice, and I took my life in my hands and heeded the words that you spoke
22 to me. Now, please, you yourself should heed the voice of your servant. I will
set a morsel of food before you; eat it so that you will have the strength to go
23 on your way." And Sha'ul refused and said, "I will not eat," but when his
servants – along with the woman – urged him, he heeded their voice and got
24 up from the ground and sat on the bed. The woman had a fattened calf at
home, which she quickly slaughtered; she took flour, kneaded it, and baked
25 unleavened bread. Then she served Sha'ul and his servants, and they ate
29 1 before rising and setting out that same night. The Philistines
mustered all their forces to Afek, while Israel were encamped by the spring
2 at Yizre'el. The Philistine chieftains advanced in their hundreds and their
3 thousands while David and his men marched in the rear with Akhish. And
the Philistine chieftains said, "What are those Hebrews?" "Why, that is David,
the servant of King Sha'ul of Israel," Akhish said to the Philistine chieftains.
"He has been with me for a while – over a year now – and I have found nothing
4 wrong with him from the day he defected to this day." But the
Philistine officials were furious with him. "Send the man back, and let him go
back to the place you assigned him," the Philistine officials said to him. "He
must not march down to battle with us; he must not oppose us[25] in battle!
How can this one reconcile himself with his master? With the heads of these
5 men, of course – isn't this the David they sang and danced about, chanting,
6 'Sha'ul has struck down thousands, and David – myriads!'?" So
Akhish summoned David and said to him, "As the LORD lives, you are
certainly honest, and I approve of your marching in and out of battle with me,
for I have found no fault with you from the day you came to me until this very
7 day. But in the eyes of the chieftains, you are not acceptable. Now return, and
8 go in peace, so as not to offend the Philistine chieftains." "But what
have I done," David said to Akhish, "and of what did you disapprove in your
servant – from the day I entered your service to this day – that I should not
9 come and fight against the enemies of my lord, the king?" "I know that in my
eyes, you are as good as an angel of God," Akhish answered David, "but the
10 Philistine lords said, 'He must not march up with us in battle.' Now set out
early in the morning together with your lord's servants who came with you;

25 | Cf. Numbers 22:22, 32.

יח יהוה את־הממלכה מידך ויתנה לרעך לדוד: כאשר לא־שמעת
בקול יהוה ולא־עשית חרון־אפו בעמלק על־כן הדבר הזה עשה־
יט לך יהוה היום הזה: ויתן יהוה גם את־ישראל עמך ביד־פלשתים
ומחר אתה ובניך עמי גם את־מחנה ישראל יתן יהוה ביד־פלשתים:
כ וימהר שאול ויפל מלא־קומתו ארצה ויירא מאד מדברי שמואל
כא גם־כח לא־היה בו כי לא אכל לחם כל־היום וכל־הלילה: ותבוא
האשה אל־שאול ותרא כי־נבהל מאד ותאמר אליו הנה שמעה
שפחתך בקולך ואשים נפשי בכפי ואשמע את־דבריך אשר דברת
כב אלי: ועתה שמע־נא גם־אתה בקול שפחתך ואשמה לפניך פת־
כג לחם ואכול ויהי בך כח כי תלך בדרך: וימאן ויאמר לא אכל
ויפרצו־בו עבדיו וגם־האשה וישמע לקלם ויקם מהארץ וישב
כד אל־המטה: ולאשה עגל־מרבק בבית ותמהר ותזבחהו ותקח־ יט
כה קמח ותלש ותפהו מצות: ותגש לפני־שאול ולפני עבדיו ויאכלו
כט א ויקמו וילכו בלילה ההוא: ויקבצו פלשתים את־כל־
ב מחניהם אפקה וישראל חנים בעין אשר ביזרעאל: וסרני פלשתים
עברים למאות ולאלפים ודוד ואנשיו עברים באחרנה עם־אכיש:
ג ויאמרו שרי פלשתים מה העברים האלה ויאמר אכיש אל־שרי
פלשתים הלוא־זה דוד עבד | שאול מלך־ישראל אשר היה אתי
זה ימים או־זה שנים ולא־מצאתי בו מאומה מיום נפלו עד־היום
ד הזה: ויקצפו עליו שרי פלשתים ויאמרו לו שרי פלשתים
השב את־האיש וישב אל־מקומו אשר הפקדתו שם ולא־ירד עמנו
במלחמה ולא־יהיה־לנו לשטן במלחמה ובמה יתרצה זה אל־אדניו
ה הלוא בראשי האנשים ההם: הלוא־זה דוד אשר יענו־לו במחלות
ו לאמר הכה שאול באלפו ודוד ברבבתו: ויקרא אכיש
אל־דוד ויאמר אליו חי־יהוה כי־ישר אתה וטוב בעיני צאתך ובאך
אתי במחנה כי לא־מצאתי בך רעה מיום באך אלי עד־היום הזה
ז ובעיני הסרנים לא־טוב אתה: ועתה שוב ולך בשלום ולא־תעשה
ח רע בעיני סרני פלשתים: ויאמר דוד אל־אכיש כי מה
עשיתי ומה־מצאת בעבדך מיום אשר הייתי לפניך עד היום הזה
ט כי לא אבוא ונלחמתי באיבי אדני המלך: ויען אכיש ויאמר אל־
דוד ידעתי כי טוב אתה בעיני כמלאך אלהים אך שרי פלשתים
י אמרו לא־יעלה עמנו במלחמה: ועתה השכם בבקר ועבדי אדניך

11 rise early in the morning, and leave as soon as it is light." So David and his
men rose and set out early in the morning to return to the land of the
30 1 Philistines, while the Philistines advanced toward Yizre'el. But
by the time David and his men had reached Tziklag, on the third day, the
Amalekites had raided the Negev, including Tziklag; they had attacked Tziklag
2 and set it ablaze. They had taken the women there captive, from young to old,
though they had not killed anyone – they had led them off and gone on their
3 way. David and his men reached the town to find it burned down, with their
4 wives and sons and daughters taken captive. And David and the men with
him raised their voices and wept until they had no strength left to weep.
5 David's two wives, Aḥinoam the Jezreelite and Avigayil, the wife of Naval the
6 Carmelite, had been taken captive. And David was in grave danger, for the
men were all ready to stone him, wretched and bitter as every man was
about his sons and daughters; but David drew strength from the Lord, his
7 God. David said to the priest Evyatar son of Aḥimelekh, "Bring the
8 ephod[26] out to me," and Evyatar brought out the ephod to David. And David
inquired of the Lord, asking, "Shall I pursue this band? Can I overtake
them?" "Pursue," He said to him, "for you will surely overtake, and you will
9 surely rescue." David set out along with the six hundred men who were with
him. When they reached the Besor Stream, those who would stay behind
10 came to a halt. David led the chase with four hundred men, while two hundred
11 men who were too exhausted to cross the Besor Stream came to a halt. They
found an Egyptian man in the field and took him to David. They gave him
12 food, and he ate, and they gave him water to drink; they gave him a slice
of pressed figs and two cakes of raisins. When he had eaten, his spirits
revived, for he had not eaten food or drunk water for three days and three
13 nights. David then said to him, "To whom do you belong, and where
are you from?" "I am an Egyptian boy," he said, "a slave to an Amalekite man.
14 My master abandoned me when I fell ill three days ago; we were raiding the
south of the Keretites, next to Yehuda, and the south of Kalev, and as for
15 Tziklag, we set it alight." "Can you lead us down to this band?" David asked
him. "If you swear to me by God that you will not kill me or hand me over to
16 my master," he said, "then I will lead you down to this band." He led them
down, and there they were, all sprawled across the ground; feasting and
drinking and reveling in all the masses of spoil they had seized from the land
17 of the Philistines and the land of Yehuda. David attacked them the next day
from dawn until dusk, and not a man escaped, save four hundred young
18 fighters who fled on camelback. David rescued all that the Amalekites had
19 seized, and as for his own two wives, David rescued them. Nothing of theirs
was missing, from the youngest to the oldest; neither sons nor daughters nor
any of the spoil nor anything they had taken from them; David recovered
20 everything. Then David took all the sheep and cattle they were driving ahead

26 | See note on 23:6.

יא אֲשֶׁר־בָּאוּ אִתָּךְ וְהִשְׁכַּמְתֶּם בַּבֹּקֶר וְאוֹר לָכֶם וָלֵכוּ׃ וַיַּשְׁכֵּם דָּוִד
הוּא וַאֲנָשָׁיו לָלֶכֶת בַּבֹּקֶר לָשׁוּב אֶל־אֶרֶץ פְּלִשְׁתִּים וּפְלִשְׁתִּים עָלוּ
ל א יִזְרְעֶאל׃ וַיְהִי בְּבֹא דָוִד וַאֲנָשָׁיו צִקְלַג בַּיּוֹם הַשְּׁלִישִׁי
וַעֲמָלֵקִי פָשְׁטוּ אֶל־נֶגֶב וְאֶל־צִקְלַג וַיַּכּוּ אֶת־צִקְלַג וַיִּשְׂרְפוּ אֹתָהּ
ב בָּאֵשׁ׃ וַיִּשְׁבּוּ אֶת־הַנָּשִׁים אֲשֶׁר־בָּהּ מִקָּטֹן וְעַד־גָּדוֹל לֹא הֵמִיתוּ אִישׁ
ג וַיִּנְהֲגוּ וַיֵּלְכוּ לְדַרְכָּם׃ וַיָּבֹא דָוִד וַאֲנָשָׁיו אֶל־הָעִיר וְהִנֵּה שְׂרוּפָה בָּאֵשׁ
ד וּנְשֵׁיהֶם וּבְנֵיהֶם וּבְנֹתֵיהֶם נִשְׁבּוּ׃ וַיִּשָּׂא דָוִד וְהָעָם אֲשֶׁר־אִתּוֹ אֶת־
ה קוֹלָם וַיִּבְכּוּ עַד אֲשֶׁר אֵין־בָּהֶם כֹּחַ לִבְכּוֹת׃ וּשְׁתֵּי נְשֵׁי־דָוִד נִשְׁבּוּ
ו אֲחִינֹעַם הַיִּזְרְעֵלִית וַאֲבִיגַיִל אֵשֶׁת נָבָל הַכַּרְמְלִי׃ וַתֵּצֶר לְדָוִד מְאֹד
כִּי־אָמְרוּ הָעָם לְסָקְלוֹ כִּי־מָרָה נֶפֶשׁ כָּל־הָעָם אִישׁ עַל־בָּנָו וְעַל־בְּנֹתָיו
ז וַיִּתְחַזֵּק דָּוִד בַּיהוָה אֱלֹהָיו׃ וַיֹּאמֶר דָּוִד אֶל־אֶבְיָתָר
הַכֹּהֵן בֶּן־אֲחִימֶלֶךְ הַגִּישָׁה־נָּא לִי הָאֵפוֹד וַיַּגֵּשׁ אֶבְיָתָר אֶת־הָאֵפוֹד
ח אֶל־דָּוִד׃ וַיִּשְׁאַל דָּוִד בַּיהוָה לֵאמֹר אֶרְדֹּף אַחֲרֵי הַגְּדוּד־הַזֶּה הַאַשִּׂגֶנּוּ
ט וַיֹּאמֶר לוֹ רְדֹף כִּי־הַשֵּׂג תַּשִּׂיג וְהַצֵּל תַּצִּיל׃ וַיֵּלֶךְ דָּוִד הוּא וְשֵׁשׁ־מֵאוֹת
י אִישׁ אֲשֶׁר אִתּוֹ וַיָּבֹאוּ עַד־נַחַל הַבְּשׂוֹר וְהַנּוֹתָרִים עָמָדוּ׃ וַיִּרְדֹּף דָּוִד
הוּא וְאַרְבַּע־מֵאוֹת אִישׁ וַיַּעַמְדוּ מָאתַיִם אִישׁ אֲשֶׁר פִּגְּרוּ מֵעֲבֹר
יא אֶת־נַחַל הַבְּשׂוֹר׃ וַיִּמְצְאוּ אִישׁ־מִצְרִי בַּשָּׂדֶה וַיִּקְחוּ אֹתוֹ אֶל־דָּוִד
יב וַיִּתְּנוּ־לוֹ לֶחֶם וַיֹּאכַל וַיַּשְׁקֻהוּ מָיִם׃ וַיִּתְּנוּ־לוֹ פֶלַח דְּבֵלָה וּשְׁנֵי צִמֻּקִים
וַיֹּאכַל וַתָּשָׁב רוּחוֹ אֵלָיו כִּי לֹא־אָכַל לֶחֶם וְלֹא־שָׁתָה מַיִם שְׁלֹשָׁה
יג יָמִים וּשְׁלֹשָׁה לֵילוֹת׃ וַיֹּאמֶר לוֹ דָוִד לְמִי־אַתָּה וְאֵי מִזֶּה
אָתָּה וַיֹּאמֶר נַעַר מִצְרִי אָנֹכִי עֶבֶד לְאִישׁ עֲמָלֵקִי וַיַּעַזְבֵנִי אֲדֹנִי כִּי
יד חָלִיתִי הַיּוֹם שְׁלֹשָׁה׃ אֲנַחְנוּ פָּשַׁטְנוּ נֶגֶב הַכְּרֵתִי וְעַל־אֲשֶׁר לִיהוּדָה
טו וְעַל־נֶגֶב כָּלֵב וְאֶת־צִקְלַג שָׂרַפְנוּ בָאֵשׁ׃ וַיֹּאמֶר אֵלָיו דָּוִד הֲתוֹרִדֵנִי
אֶל־הַגְּדוּד הַזֶּה וַיֹּאמֶר הִשָּׁבְעָה לִּי בֵאלֹהִים אִם־תְּמִיתֵנִי וְאִם־
טז תַּסְגִּרֵנִי בְּיַד־אֲדֹנִי וְאוֹרִדְךָ אֶל־הַגְּדוּד הַזֶּה׃ וַיֹּרִדֵהוּ וְהִנֵּה נְטֻשִׁים
עַל־פְּנֵי כָל־הָאָרֶץ אֹכְלִים וְשֹׁתִים וְחֹגְגִים בְּכֹל הַשָּׁלָל הַגָּדוֹל אֲשֶׁר
יז לָקְחוּ מֵאֶרֶץ פְּלִשְׁתִּים וּמֵאֶרֶץ יְהוּדָה׃ וַיַּכֵּם דָּוִד מֵהַנֶּשֶׁף וְעַד־הָעֶרֶב
לְמָחֳרָתָם וְלֹא־נִמְלַט מֵהֶם אִישׁ כִּי אִם־אַרְבַּע מֵאוֹת אִישׁ־נַעַר
יח אֲשֶׁר־רָכְבוּ עַל־הַגְּמַלִּים וַיָּנֻסוּ׃ וַיַּצֵּל דָּוִד אֵת כָּל־אֲשֶׁר לָקְחוּ עֲמָלֵק
יט וְאֶת־שְׁתֵּי נָשָׁיו הִצִּיל דָּוִד׃ וְלֹא נֶעְדַּר־לָהֶם מִן־הַקָּטֹן וְעַד־הַגָּדוֹל
וְעַד־בָּנִים וּבָנוֹת וּמִשָּׁלָל וְעַד כָּל־אֲשֶׁר לָקְחוּ לָהֶם הַכֹּל הֵשִׁיב דָּוִד׃
כ וַיִּקַּח דָּוִד אֶת־כָּל־הַצֹּאן וְהַבָּקָר נָהֲגוּ לִפְנֵי הַמִּקְנֶה הַהוּא וַיֹּאמְרוּ

21 of the other livestock, and they declared, "This is David's spoil." When David
reached the two hundred men who had been too exhausted to follow him –
those who had been left in the Besor Stream – they went out toward David
and the men who were with him. David approached the men and greeted
22 them. But every spiteful, depraved man among the people who
had gone with David reacted. "Because they did not come with us," they said,
"we shall not give them any of the spoil we recovered except for each man's
23 wife and children – they can lead them away and be off." But
David said, "You shall not do so, my brothers, considering what the LORD has
given us and how He watched over us and handed over to us the band that
24 attacked us. Who would listen to you in this matter? For the share of those
who remain with the baggage should be the same as the share of those who
25 go down to battle; they will share together." And from that day
onward, he established it as law and order in Israel, which endures to this
26 day. When David reached Tziklag, he distributed some of the
spoil to the elders of Yehuda, his allies, saying, "Here is a gift for you from the
27 spoil of the enemies of the LORD": for those in Beit El, for those in Ramot
28 Negev, for those in Yatir, for those in Aroer, for those in Sifemot, for those in
29 Eshtemoa, for those in Rakhal, for those in the Jerahmeelite towns, for those
30 in the Kenite towns, for those in Ḥorma, for those in Bekhor Ashan, for those
31 in Atakh, for those in Ḥevron; for all the places where David and his men had
roamed.

31 1 Meanwhile, the Philistines were fighting against Israel; the men of Israel fled
2 before the Philistines and fell slain on Mount Gilboa.[27] And the Philistines
closed in on Sha'ul and his sons; the Philistines struck down Yehonatan and
3 Avinadav and Malki Shua, the sons of Sha'ul. And the battle weighed heavily
upon Sha'ul, and when the archer-men found him, he shook, terrified by the
4 archers. "Draw your sword and stab me with it," Sha'ul said to his arms-bearer,
"lest these heathens come and stab me and torture me," but his arms-bearer
was not willing because of his great reverence, so Sha'ul took the sword and
5 fell upon it. When his arms-bearer saw that Sha'ul was dead, he too fell upon
6 his sword and died along with him. Sha'ul, his three sons, and his arms-bearer
7 died on that day, together with all his men. When the men of Israel on the
other side of the valley, and on the other side of the Jordan, realized that the
men of Israel had fled and that Sha'ul and his sons were dead, they abandoned
8 the cities and fled. And Philistines came and settled in them. The
next day, when Philistines came to strip the corpses, they found Sha'ul and
9 his three sons fallen on Mount Gilboa. They cut off his head and stripped off
his armor and sent word throughout the land of the Philistines, bringing
10 tidings to the temples of their idols and to the people. They deposited his
armor in the temple of Ashtarot, and as for his corpse, they impaled it on the
11 wall of Beit Shan. Now when the inhabitants of Yavesh Gilad heard of it – what

27 | Cf. I Chronicles 10:1–12.

כא זֶה שְׁלַל דָּוִד: וַיָּבֹא דָוִד אֶל־מָאתַיִם הָאֲנָשִׁים אֲשֶׁר־פִּגְּרוּ ׀ מִלֶּכֶת ׀
אַחֲרֵי דָוִד וַיֹּשִׁבֻם בְּנַחַל הַבְּשׂוֹר וַיֵּצְאוּ לִקְרַאת דָּוִד וְלִקְרַאת הָעָם
כב אֲשֶׁר אִתּוֹ וַיִּגַּשׁ דָּוִד אֶת־הָעָם וַיִּשְׁאַל לָהֶם לְשָׁלוֹם: וַיַּעַן
כָּל־אִישׁ ׀ רָע וּבְלִיַּעַל מֵהָאֲנָשִׁים אֲשֶׁר הָלְכוּ עִם־דָּוִד וַיֹּאמְרוּ יַעַן
אֲשֶׁר לֹא־הָלְכוּ עִמִּי לֹא־נִתֵּן לָהֶם מֵהַשָּׁלָל אֲשֶׁר הִצַּלְנוּ כִּי אִם־אִישׁ
כג אֶת־אִשְׁתּוֹ וְאֶת־בָּנָיו וְיִנְהֲגוּ וְיֵלֵכוּ: וַיֹּאמֶר דָּוִד לֹא־תַעֲשׂוּ
כֵן אֶחָי אֵת אֲשֶׁר־נָתַן יהוה לָנוּ וַיִּשְׁמֹר אֹתָנוּ וַיִּתֵּן אֶת־הַגְּדוּד הַבָּא
כד עָלֵינוּ בְּיָדֵנוּ: וּמִי יִשְׁמַע לָכֶם לַדָּבָר הַזֶּה כִּי כְּחֵלֶק ׀ הורד בַּמִּלְחָמָה הַיֹּרֵד
כה וּכְחֵלֶק הַיֹּשֵׁב עַל־הַכֵּלִים יַחְדָּו יַחֲלֹקוּ: וַיְהִי מֵהַיּוֹם הַהוּא כ
כו וָמָעְלָה וַיְשִׂמֶהָ לְחֹק וּלְמִשְׁפָּט לְיִשְׂרָאֵל עַד הַיּוֹם הַזֶּה: וַיָּבֹא
דָוִד אֶל־צִקְלַג וַיְשַׁלַּח מֵהַשָּׁלָל לְזִקְנֵי יְהוּדָה לְרֵעֵהוּ לֵאמֹר הִנֵּה לָכֶם
כז בְּרָכָה מִשְּׁלַל אֹיְבֵי יהוה: לַאֲשֶׁר בְּבֵית־אֵל וְלַאֲשֶׁר בְּרָמוֹת־נֶגֶב
כח וְלַאֲשֶׁר בְּיַתִּר: וְלַאֲשֶׁר בַּעֲרֹעֵר וְלַאֲשֶׁר בְּשִׂפְמוֹת וְלַאֲשֶׁר בְּאֶשְׁתְּמֹעַ:
כט ל וְלַאֲשֶׁר בְּרָכָל וְלַאֲשֶׁר בְּעָרֵי הַיְּרַחְמְאֵלִי וְלַאֲשֶׁר בְּעָרֵי הַקֵּינִי: וְלַאֲשֶׁר
לא בְּחָרְמָה וְלַאֲשֶׁר בְּבוֹר־עָשָׁן וְלַאֲשֶׁר בַּעֲתָךְ: וְלַאֲשֶׁר בְּחֶבְרוֹן וּלְכָל־
הַמְּקֹמוֹת אֲשֶׁר־הִתְהַלֶּךְ־שָׁם דָּוִד הוּא וַאֲנָשָׁיו:

לא א וּפְלִשְׁתִּים נִלְחָמִים בְּיִשְׂרָאֵל וַיָּנֻסוּ אַנְשֵׁי יִשְׂרָאֵל מִפְּנֵי פְלִשְׁתִּים וַיִּפְּלוּ
ב חֲלָלִים בְּהַר הַגִּלְבֹּעַ: וַיַּדְבְּקוּ פְלִשְׁתִּים אֶת־שָׁאוּל וְאֶת־בָּנָיו וַיַּכּוּ
פְלִשְׁתִּים אֶת־יְהוֹנָתָן וְאֶת־אֲבִינָדָב וְאֶת־מַלְכִּי־שׁוּעַ בְּנֵי שָׁאוּל:
ג וַתִּכְבַּד הַמִּלְחָמָה אֶל־שָׁאוּל וַיִּמְצָאֻהוּ הַמּוֹרִים אֲנָשִׁים בַּקָּשֶׁת וַיָּחֶל
ד מְאֹד מֵהַמּוֹרִים: וַיֹּאמֶר שָׁאוּל לְנֹשֵׂא כֵלָיו שְׁלֹף חַרְבְּךָ ׀ וְדָקְרֵנִי בָהּ
פֶּן־יָבוֹאוּ הָעֲרֵלִים הָאֵלֶּה וּדְקָרֻנִי וְהִתְעַלְּלוּ־בִי וְלֹא אָבָה נֹשֵׂא כֵלָיו
ה כִּי יָרֵא מְאֹד וַיִּקַּח שָׁאוּל אֶת־הַחֶרֶב וַיִּפֹּל עָלֶיהָ: וַיַּרְא נֹשֵׂא־כֵלָיו
ו כִּי מֵת שָׁאוּל וַיִּפֹּל גַּם־הוּא עַל־חַרְבּוֹ וַיָּמָת עִמּוֹ: וַיָּמָת שָׁאוּל וּשְׁלֹשֶׁת
ז בָּנָיו וְנֹשֵׂא כֵלָיו גַּם כָּל־אֲנָשָׁיו בַּיּוֹם הַהוּא יַחְדָּו: וַיִּרְאוּ אַנְשֵׁי־יִשְׂרָאֵל
אֲשֶׁר־בְּעֵבֶר הָעֵמֶק וַאֲשֶׁר ׀ בְּעֵבֶר הַיַּרְדֵּן כִּי־נָסוּ אַנְשֵׁי יִשְׂרָאֵל וְכִי־
מֵתוּ שָׁאוּל וּבָנָיו וַיַּעַזְבוּ אֶת־הֶעָרִים וַיָּנֻסוּ וַיָּבֹאוּ פְלִשְׁתִּים וַיֵּשְׁבוּ
ח בָּהֶן: וַיְהִי מִמָּחֳרָת וַיָּבֹאוּ פְלִשְׁתִּים לְפַשֵּׁט אֶת־הַחֲלָלִים
ט וַיִּמְצְאוּ אֶת־שָׁאוּל וְאֶת־שְׁלֹשֶׁת בָּנָיו נֹפְלִים בְּהַר הַגִּלְבֹּעַ: וַיִּכְרְתוּ
אֶת־רֹאשׁוֹ וַיַּפְשִׁטוּ אֶת־כֵּלָיו וַיְשַׁלְּחוּ בְאֶרֶץ־פְּלִשְׁתִּים סָבִיב לְבַשֵּׂר
י בֵּית עֲצַבֵּיהֶם וְאֶת־הָעָם: וַיָּשִׂמוּ אֶת־כֵּלָיו בֵּית עַשְׁתָּרוֹת וְאֶת־גְּוִיָּתוֹ
יא תָּקְעוּ בְּחוֹמַת בֵּית שָׁן: וַיִּשְׁמְעוּ אֵלָיו יֹשְׁבֵי יָבֵישׁ גִּלְעָד אֵת אֲשֶׁר־

12 the Philistines had done to Sha'ul – all their boldest men set out and trekked
all night long. They took down Sha'ul's corpse and his sons' corpses from the
13 wall of Beit Shan and came back to Yavesh, where they burned them. Then
they took their bones and buried them under the tamarisk in Yavesh and
1 1 fasted for seven days. After the death of Sha'ul, David returned from II SAMUEL
defeating the Amalekites. David had been staying in Tziklag for two days
2 when, on the third day, a man suddenly came from Sha'ul's camp, his clothes
torn and earth on his head. When he came to David, he flung himself to the
3 ground and bowed down low. "Where have you come from?" David asked
4 him. "I have escaped from the camp of Israel," he said to him. "What has
happened?" David asked him. "Tell me now!" "The troops fled from the
battle," he said, "and so many of the troops fell and died; Sha'ul and his son
5 Yehonatan died as well." David asked the youth who was reporting to him,
6 "How do you know that Sha'ul and his son Yehonatan have died?" "I happened
to be on Mount Gilboa," said the youth who was reporting to him, "and there
was Sha'ul, leaning upon his spear, and there were the chariots and riders
7 closing in on him. He turned around, saw me, and called out to me, and I said,
8 9 'Here I am.' 'Who are you?' he asked me, and I said, 'I am an Amalekite.' Then
he said to me, 'Stand over me and finish me off, for I am wracked with
10 convulsions, but my life still lingers.' So I stood over him and finished him off,
for I knew that he would not live after his collapse. And I took the crown upon
11 his head and the armlet upon his arm and brought them here to my lord." And
David grasped hold of his clothes and rent them, and all the men with him
12 did as well. They grieved and wept and fasted until dusk; for Sha'ul, and for
his son Yehonatan, and for the men of the LORD, and for the House of Israel,
13 for they had fallen by the sword. Then David asked the youth who
was reporting to him, "Where are you from?" "I am the son of a sojourner,"
14 he said, "an Amalekite." And David said to him, "How did you dare raise your
15 hand to destroy the LORD's anointed?" David summoned one of the lads and
16 said, "Here! Fall upon him." He struck him and he died. "Your blood is on
your own head," David said to him, "for your own mouth testified against you,
17 declaring, 'I put the LORD's anointed to death.'" Then David
18 lamented over Sha'ul and over Yehonatan his son with this lament. He ordered
that the Judahites be instructed in archery, as is recorded in the Book of the
19 Upright. "The glory, O Israel, lies slain on your heights; oh, how heroes have
20 fallen! Say nothing in Gat, proclaim nothing in the streets of Ashkelon, lest
21 the daughters of Philistines rejoice, lest the daughters of heathens gloat.
O hills of Gilboa, let there be no dew nor rain nor bountiful fields upon you,
for there the shield of heroes was defiled – the shield of Sha'ul, unanointed
22 with oil. From the blood of the slain, from the fat of warriors, Yehonatan's
23 bow never retreated, and Sha'ul's sword never withdrew empty. Sha'ul and
Yehonatan, beloved and dear, never parted in life or in death! Swifter than

יב עָשׂוּ פְלִשְׁתִּים לְשָׁאוּל׃ וַיָּקוּמוּ כָּל־אִישׁ חַיִל וַיֵּלְכוּ כָל־הַלַּיְלָה וַיִּקְחוּ
אֶת־גְּוִיַּת שָׁאוּל וְאֵת גְּוִיֹּת בָּנָיו מֵחוֹמַת בֵּית שָׁן וַיָּבֹאוּ יָבֵשָׁה וַיִּשְׂרְפוּ
יג אֹתָם שָׁם׃ וַיִּקְחוּ אֶת־עַצְמֹתֵיהֶם וַיִּקְבְּרוּ תַחַת־הָאֶשֶׁל בְּיָבֵשָׁה וַיָּצֻמוּ
א א שִׁבְעַת יָמִים׃ וַיְהִי אַחֲרֵי מוֹת שָׁאוּל וְדָוִד שָׁב מֵהַכּוֹת שמואל ב
ב אֶת־הָעֲמָלֵק וַיֵּשֶׁב דָּוִד בְּצִקְלָג יָמִים שְׁנָיִם׃ וַיְהִי ׀ בַּיּוֹם הַשְּׁלִישִׁי
וְהִנֵּה אִישׁ בָּא מִן־הַמַּחֲנֶה מֵעִם שָׁאוּל וּבְגָדָיו קְרֻעִים וַאֲדָמָה עַל־
ג רֹאשׁוֹ וַיְהִי בְּבֹאוֹ אֶל־דָּוִד וַיִּפֹּל אַרְצָה וַיִּשְׁתָּחוּ׃ וַיֹּאמֶר לוֹ דָּוִד אֵי
ד מִזֶּה תָּבוֹא וַיֹּאמֶר אֵלָיו מִמַּחֲנֵה יִשְׂרָאֵל נִמְלָטְתִּי׃ וַיֹּאמֶר אֵלָיו דָּוִד
מֶה־הָיָה הַדָּבָר הַגֶּד־נָא לִי וַיֹּאמֶר אֲשֶׁר־נָס הָעָם מִן־הַמִּלְחָמָה וְגַם־
ה הַרְבֵּה נָפַל מִן־הָעָם וַיָּמֻתוּ וְגַם שָׁאוּל וִיהוֹנָתָן בְּנוֹ מֵתוּ׃ וַיֹּאמֶר דָּוִד
ו אֶל־הַנַּעַר הַמַּגִּיד לוֹ אֵיךְ יָדַעְתָּ כִּי־מֵת שָׁאוּל וִיהוֹנָתָן בְּנוֹ׃ וַיֹּאמֶר
הַנַּעַר ׀ הַמַּגִּיד לוֹ נִקְרֹא נִקְרֵיתִי בְּהַר הַגִּלְבֹּעַ וְהִנֵּה שָׁאוּל נִשְׁעָן עַל־
ז חֲנִיתוֹ וְהִנֵּה הָרֶכֶב וּבַעֲלֵי הַפָּרָשִׁים הִדְבִּקֻהוּ׃ וַיִּפֶן אַחֲרָיו וַיִּרְאֵנִי
ח וַיִּקְרָא אֵלָי וָאֹמַר הִנֵּנִי׃ וַיֹּאמֶר לִי מִי־אָתָּה ויאמר אֵלָיו עֲמָלֵקִי אָנֹכִי׃ וָאֹמַר
ט וַיֹּאמֶר אֵלַי עֲמָד־נָא עָלַי וּמֹתְתֵנִי כִּי אֲחָזַנִי הַשָּׁבָץ כִּי־כָל־עוֹד נַפְשִׁי
י בִּי׃ וָאֶעֱמֹד עָלָיו וַאֲמֹתְתֵהוּ כִּי יָדַעְתִּי כִּי לֹא יִחְיֶה אַחֲרֵי נִפְלוֹ וָאֶקַּח
הַנֵּזֶר ׀ אֲשֶׁר עַל־רֹאשׁוֹ וְאֶצְעָדָה אֲשֶׁר עַל־זְרֹעוֹ וָאֲבִיאֵם אֶל־אֲדֹנִי
יא יב הֵנָּה׃ וַיַּחֲזֵק דָּוִד בִּבְגָדוֹ וַיִּקְרָעֵם וְגַם כָּל־הָאֲנָשִׁים אֲשֶׁר אִתּוֹ׃ וַיִּסְפְּדוּ
וַיִּבְכּוּ וַיָּצֻמוּ עַד־הָעָרֶב עַל־שָׁאוּל וְעַל־יְהוֹנָתָן בְּנוֹ וְעַל־עַם יהוה
יג וְעַל־בֵּית יִשְׂרָאֵל כִּי נָפְלוּ בֶּחָרֶב׃ וַיֹּאמֶר דָּוִד אֶל־הַנַּעַר
יד הַמַּגִּיד לוֹ אֵי מִזֶּה אָתָּה וַיֹּאמֶר בֶּן־אִישׁ גֵּר עֲמָלֵקִי אָנֹכִי׃ וַיֹּאמֶר אֵלָיו
טו דָּוִד אֵיךְ לֹא יָרֵאתָ לִשְׁלֹחַ יָדְךָ לְשַׁחֵת אֶת־מְשִׁיחַ יהוה׃ וַיִּקְרָא דָוִד
טז לְאַחַד מֵהַנְּעָרִים וַיֹּאמֶר גַּשׁ פְּגַע־בּוֹ וַיַּכֵּהוּ וַיָּמֹת׃ וַיֹּאמֶר אֵלָיו דָּוִד
דמיך עַל־רֹאשֶׁךָ כִּי פִיךָ עָנָה בְךָ לֵאמֹר אָנֹכִי מֹתַתִּי אֶת־מְשִׁיחַ דָּמְךָ
יז יהוה׃ וַיְקֹנֵן דָּוִד אֶת־הַקִּינָה הַזֹּאת עַל־שָׁאוּל וְעַל־
יח יְהוֹנָתָן בְּנוֹ׃ וַיֹּאמֶר לְלַמֵּד בְּנֵי־יְהוּדָה קָשֶׁת הִנֵּה כְתוּבָה עַל־סֵפֶר
יט כ הַיָּשָׁר׃ הַצְּבִי יִשְׂרָאֵל עַל־בָּמוֹתֶיךָ חָלָל אֵיךְ נָפְלוּ גִבּוֹרִים׃ אַל־תַּגִּידוּ
בְגַת אַל־תְּבַשְּׂרוּ בְּחוּצֹת אַשְׁקְלוֹן פֶּן־תִּשְׂמַחְנָה בְּנוֹת פְּלִשְׁתִּים
כא פֶּן־תַּעֲלֹזְנָה בְּנוֹת הָעֲרֵלִים׃ הָרֵי בַגִּלְבֹּעַ אַל־טַל וְאַל־מָטָר עֲלֵיכֶם
וּשְׂדֵי תְרוּמֹת כִּי שָׁם נִגְעַל מָגֵן גִּבּוֹרִים מָגֵן שָׁאוּל בְּלִי מָשִׁיחַ בַּשָּׁמֶן׃
כב מִדַּם חֲלָלִים מֵחֵלֶב גִּבּוֹרִים קֶשֶׁת יְהוֹנָתָן לֹא נָשׂוֹג אָחוֹר וְחֶרֶב שָׁאוּל
כג לֹא תָשׁוּב רֵיקָם׃ שָׁאוּל וִיהוֹנָתָן הַנֶּאֱהָבִים וְהַנְּעִימִם בְּחַיֵּיהֶם וּבְמוֹתָם

24 eagles! Stronger than lions! O daughters of Israel, weep over Sha'ul, who
clothed you in scarlet, in finery; who draped golden jewelry over your dresses.
25 How heroes have fallen in the thick of battle! Yehonatan lies slain on your
26 heights – I ache for you, my brother, Yehonatan, you were so dear to me. More
27 wondrous was your love for me than the love of women. Oh, how heroes have
2 1 fallen, and the weapons of war are lost." Sometime later, David
inquired of the LORD, asking, "Shall I go up to one of the cities of Yehuda?"
And the LORD said to him, "Go up." "Where shall I go up?" asked David. "To
2 Ḥevron," He said. So David went up there, along with his two wives, Aḥinoam
3 the Jezreelite and Avigayil, wife of Naval the Carmelite. And David brought
up the men who were with him, each man with his household, and they
4 settled in the towns of Ḥevron. The people of Yehuda came, and there they
anointed David as king over the House of Yehuda. They informed David
5 about the men of Yavesh Gilad, who had buried Sha'ul. So David
sent messengers to the men of Yavesh Gilad, declaring to them, "Blessed are
you by the LORD for showing such loyalty to your lord, to Sha'ul, and burying
6 him. Now, may the LORD show you true loyalty; I too will reward you for
7 having done this deed. Now, be determined, valiant warriors, for your lord
Sha'ul is dead while the House of Yehuda has appointed me as king over
8 them." Meanwhile, Avner son of Ner, Sha'ul's army commander, had
9 taken Ish Boshet,[28] Sha'ul's son, and conveyed him to Maḥanayim. He
appointed him over the Gilad, the Ashurites, Yizre'el, Efrayim, and Binyamin –
10 over all of Israel. Ish Boshet, Sha'ul's son, was forty years old when
he reigned over Israel, and he reigned for two years, but the House of Yehuda
11 followed David. The length of time that David reigned in Ḥevron over the
12 House of Yehuda was seven years and six months. Avner son of Ner
and the men of Ish Boshet son of Sha'ul marched out from Maḥanayim
13 toward Givon. So Yoav son of Tzeruya and David's men marched out, and
they confronted each other at the pool of Givon; they positioned themselves
14 on one side of the pool, and they positioned themselves on the other. "Let
the lads get up and sport before us," Avner said to Yoav. "Let them," said Yoav.
15 They got up, crossed over, and counted off – twelve for Binyamin and Ish
16 Boshet son of Sha'ul and twelve of David's men. Each man grasped hold of
his opponent's head, with his sword in his opponent's side, and they fell
together. And that place was called Ḥelkat HaTzurim,[29] which is in Givon.
17 And the fighting grew brutally fierce that day, and Avner and the men of Israel
18 were routed before David's subjects. Now the three sons of Tzeruya were
there – Yoav, Avishai, and Asael; Asael was as swift-footed as a gazelle in the

---

28 | In 1 Chronicles 8:33, this character is called Eshbaal. *Boshet*, literally "shame," was a derogatory epithet commonly substituted for the name of the Canaanite god Baal. Cf. Jeremiah 11:13.

29 | Literally "field of the swords"; cf. *harvot tzurim* in Joshua 5:2.

כד לֹא נִפְרָדוּ מִנְּשָׁרִים קַלּוּ מֵאֲרָיוֹת גָּבֵרוּ׃ בְּנוֹת יִשְׂרָאֵל אֶל־שָׁאוּל
בְּכֶינָה הַמַּלְבִּשְׁכֶם שָׁנִי עִם־עֲדָנִים הַמַּעֲלֶה עֲדִי זָהָב עַל לְבוּשְׁכֶן׃
כה כו אֵיךְ נָפְלוּ גִבֹּרִים בְּתוֹךְ הַמִּלְחָמָה יְהוֹנָתָן עַל־בָּמוֹתֶיךָ חָלָל׃ צַר־לִי
עָלֶיךָ אָחִי יְהוֹנָתָן נָעַמְתָּ לִּי מְאֹד נִפְלְאַתָה אַהֲבָתְךָ לִי מֵאַהֲבַת
כז א נָשִׁים׃ אֵיךְ נָפְלוּ גִבּוֹרִים וַיֹּאבְדוּ כְּלֵי מִלְחָמָה׃ וַיְהִי אַחֲרֵי־ ב
כֵן וַיִּשְׁאַל דָּוִד בַּיהוָה ׀ לֵאמֹר הַאֶעֱלֶה בְּאַחַת עָרֵי יְהוּדָה וַיֹּאמֶר
ב יְהוָה אֵלָיו עֲלֵה וַיֹּאמֶר דָּוִד אָנָה אֶעֱלֶה וַיֹּאמֶר חֶבְרֹנָה׃ וַיַּעַל שָׁם
דָּוִד וְגַם שְׁתֵּי נָשָׁיו אֲחִינֹעַם הַיִּזְרְעֵלִית וַאֲבִיגַיִל אֵשֶׁת נָבָל הַכַּרְמְלִי׃
ג ד וַאֲנָשָׁיו אֲשֶׁר־עִמּוֹ הֶעֱלָה דָוִד אִישׁ וּבֵיתוֹ וַיֵּשְׁבוּ בְּעָרֵי חֶבְרוֹן׃ וַיָּבֹאוּ
אַנְשֵׁי יְהוּדָה וַיִּמְשְׁחוּ־שָׁם אֶת־דָּוִד לְמֶלֶךְ עַל־בֵּית יְהוּדָה וַיַּגִּדוּ לְדָוִד
ה לֵאמֹר אַנְשֵׁי יָבֵישׁ גִּלְעָד אֲשֶׁר קָבְרוּ אֶת־שָׁאוּל׃ וַיִּשְׁלַח
דָּוִד מַלְאָכִים אֶל־אַנְשֵׁי יָבֵישׁ גִּלְעָד וַיֹּאמֶר אֲלֵיהֶם בְּרֻכִים אַתֶּם
לַיהוָה אֲשֶׁר עֲשִׂיתֶם הַחֶסֶד הַזֶּה עִם־אֲדֹנֵיכֶם עִם־שָׁאוּל וַתִּקְבְּרוּ
ו אֹתוֹ׃ וְעַתָּה יַעַשׂ־יְהוָה עִמָּכֶם חֶסֶד וֶאֱמֶת וְגַם אָנֹכִי אֶעֱשֶׂה אִתְּכֶם
ז הַטּוֹבָה הַזֹּאת אֲשֶׁר עֲשִׂיתֶם הַדָּבָר הַזֶּה׃ וְעַתָּה ׀ תֶּחֱזַקְנָה יְדֵיכֶם כא
וִהְיוּ לִבְנֵי־חַיִל כִּי־מֵת אֲדֹנֵיכֶם שָׁאוּל וְגַם אֹתִי מָשְׁחוּ בֵית־יְהוּדָה
ח לְמֶלֶךְ עֲלֵיהֶם׃ וְאַבְנֵר בֶּן־נֵר שַׂר־צָבָא אֲשֶׁר לְשָׁאוּל
ט לָקַח אֶת־אִישׁ בֹּשֶׁת בֶּן־שָׁאוּל וַיַּעֲבִרֵהוּ מַחֲנָיִם׃ וַיַּמְלִכֵהוּ אֶל־הַגִּלְעָד
וְאֶל־הָאֲשׁוּרִי וְאֶל־יִזְרְעֶאל וְעַל־אֶפְרַיִם וְעַל־בִּנְיָמִן וְעַל־יִשְׂרָאֵל
י כֻּלֹּה׃ בֶּן־אַרְבָּעִים שָׁנָה אִישׁ־בֹּשֶׁת בֶּן־שָׁאוּל בְּמָלְכוֹ עַל־
יא יִשְׂרָאֵל וּשְׁתַּיִם שָׁנִים מָלָךְ אַךְ בֵּית יְהוּדָה הָיוּ אַחֲרֵי דָוִד׃ וַיְהִי מִסְפַּר
הַיָּמִים אֲשֶׁר הָיָה דָוִד מֶלֶךְ בְּחֶבְרוֹן עַל־בֵּית יְהוּדָה שֶׁבַע שָׁנִים
יב וְשִׁשָּׁה חֳדָשִׁים׃ וַיֵּצֵא אַבְנֵר בֶּן־נֵר וְעַבְדֵי אִישׁ־בֹּשֶׁת בֶּן־
יג שָׁאוּל מִמַּחֲנַיִם גִּבְעוֹנָה׃ וְיוֹאָב בֶּן־צְרוּיָה וְעַבְדֵי דָוִד יָצְאוּ וַיִּפְגְּשׁוּם
עַל־בְּרֵכַת גִּבְעוֹן יַחְדָּו וַיֵּשְׁבוּ אֵלֶּה עַל־הַבְּרֵכָה מִזֶּה וְאֵלֶּה עַל־
יד הַבְּרֵכָה מִזֶּה׃ וַיֹּאמֶר אַבְנֵר אֶל־יוֹאָב יָקוּמוּ נָא הַנְּעָרִים וִישַׂחֲקוּ
טו לְפָנֵינוּ וַיֹּאמֶר יוֹאָב יָקֻמוּ׃ וַיָּקֻמוּ וַיַּעַבְרוּ בְמִסְפָּר שְׁנֵים עָשָׂר לְבִנְיָמִן
טז וּלְאִישׁ בֹּשֶׁת בֶּן־שָׁאוּל וּשְׁנֵים עָשָׂר מֵעַבְדֵי דָוִד׃ וַיַּחֲזִקוּ אִישׁ ׀ בְּרֹאשׁ
רֵעֵהוּ וְחַרְבּוֹ בְּצַד רֵעֵהוּ וַיִּפְּלוּ יַחְדָּו וַיִּקְרָא לַמָּקוֹם הַהוּא חֶלְקַת
יז הַצֻּרִים אֲשֶׁר בְּגִבְעוֹן׃ וַתְּהִי הַמִּלְחָמָה קָשָׁה עַד־מְאֹד בַּיּוֹם הַהוּא
יח וַיִּנָּגֶף אַבְנֵר וְאַנְשֵׁי יִשְׂרָאֵל לִפְנֵי עַבְדֵי דָוִד׃ וַיִּהְיוּ שָׁם שְׁלֹשָׁה בְּנֵי
צְרוּיָה יוֹאָב וַאֲבִישַׁי וַעֲשָׂהאֵל וַעֲשָׂהאֵל קַל בְּרַגְלָיו כְּאַחַד הַצְּבָיִם

19 field. Asael chased after Avner, veering neither right nor left behind Avner.
20 21 Avner looked back and called, "Is that you, Asael?" "It is I," he said. "Veer to
your right or to your left," Avner said to him. "Grab hold of one of the lads
22 and seize his gear for yourself." But Asael would not turn away from him. So
Avner called out again to Asael, "Turn away from me – why should I strike
23 you to the ground? How will I look your brother Yoav in the face?" But he
refused to turn away, and Avner struck him in the stomach with the butt of
his spear; the spear burst out of his back, and he fell down and died on the
spot. And everyone who reached the place where Asael had fallen down and
24 died came to a halt there. But Yoav and Avishai chased after Avner. By the
time the sun was setting, they had gone as far as Heights of Ama overlooking
25 Giaḥ on the road to the Givon wilderness. And all the Benjaminites gathered
behind Avner, formed a single band, and positioned themselves on a single
26 hilltop. Then Avner called out to Yoav: "Must the sword consume forever?
You know how bitter the end will be – when will you order the troops to cease
27 pursuing their brothers?" "As God lives," said Yoav, "if you had not spoken –
why, since this morning the people would have moved on, each man away
28 from his brother." Yoav blasted the ram's horn, and all the troops came to a
29 halt; they left off their pursuit of Israel and did not continue fighting. Avner
and his men trudged through the plain all that night, crossed the Jordan, and
30 trudged all morning long until they reached Maḥanayim. And Yoav ceased
his pursuit of Avner and gathered all the troops. Nineteen men of David's
31 subjects – as well as Asael – were missing, while David's subjects had defeated
32 Binyamin and Avner's men; three hundred and sixty men were dead. They
carried Asael and buried him in his father's tomb, which was in Beit Leḥem;
then Yoav and his men marched all night, and light dawned on them at
3 1 Ḥevron. The war between the house of Sha'ul and the house of David proved
long and drawn out; David grew stronger while the house of Sha'ul grew
2 weaker. Sons were born to David at Ḥevron; his firstborn was
3 Amnon, by Aḥinoam the Jezreelite. His second born was Kilav, by Avigayil,
the wife of Naval the Carmelite, while his third was Avshalom, the son
4 of Maakha, who was the daughter of King Talmai of Geshur. The fourth
5 was Adoniya, son of Ḥagit, and the fifth was Shefatya, the son of Avital. The
sixth was Yitre'am, by Egla, the wife of David; these were born to David at
6 Ḥevron. As hostilities between the house of Sha'ul and the house of
7 David continued, Avner was gaining power within the house of Sha'ul. Now
Sha'ul had a concubine by the name of Ritzpa, daughter of Aya, and Avner
8 was accused: "Why have you slept with my father's concubine?" Ish Boshet's
words made Avner furious, and he said, "Am I but a dog's head of Yehuda? To
this day, I have shown loyalty to the house of your father, Sha'ul, and his
friends in not handing you over to David, yet you dare charge me with guilt

יט אֲשֶׁר בַּשָּׂדֶה: וַיִּרְדֹּף עֲשָׂהאֵל אַחֲרֵי אַבְנֵר וְלֹא־נָטָה לָלֶכֶת עַל־הַיָּמִין
כ וְעַל־הַשְּׂמֹאול מֵאַחֲרֵי אַבְנֵר: וַיִּפֶן אַבְנֵר אַחֲרָיו וַיֹּאמֶר הַאַתָּה זֶה
כא עֲשָׂהאֵל וַיֹּאמֶר אָנֹכִי: וַיֹּאמֶר לוֹ אַבְנֵר נְטֵה לְךָ עַל־יְמִינְךָ אוֹ עַל־
שְׂמֹאלֶךָ וֶאֱחֹז לְךָ אֶחָד מֵהַנְּעָרִים וְקַח־לְךָ אֶת־חֲלִצָתוֹ וְלֹא־אָבָה
כב עֲשָׂהאֵל לָסוּר מֵאַחֲרָיו: וַיֹּסֶף עוֹד אַבְנֵר לֵאמֹר אֶל־עֲשָׂהאֵל סוּר
כג לְךָ מֵאַחֲרָי לָמָּה אַכֶּכָּה אַרְצָה וְאֵיךְ אֶשָּׂא פָנַי אֶל־יוֹאָב אָחִיךָ: וַיְמָאֵן
לָסוּר וַיַּכֵּהוּ אַבְנֵר בְּאַחֲרֵי הַחֲנִית אֶל־הַחֹמֶשׁ וַתֵּצֵא הַחֲנִית מֵאַחֲרָיו
וַיִּפָּל־שָׁם וַיָּמָת תַּחְתָּו וַיְהִי כָּל־הַבָּא אֶל־הַמָּקוֹם אֲשֶׁר־נָפַל שָׁם
כד עֲשָׂהאֵל וַיָּמֹת וַיַּעֲמֹדוּ: וַיִּרְדְּפוּ יוֹאָב וַאֲבִישַׁי אַחֲרֵי אַבְנֵר וְהַשֶּׁמֶשׁ
בָּאָה וְהֵמָּה בָּאוּ עַד־גִּבְעַת אַמָּה אֲשֶׁר עַל־פְּנֵי־גִיחַ דֶּרֶךְ מִדְבַּר גִּבְעוֹן:
כה וַיִּתְקַבְּצוּ בְנֵי־בִנְיָמִן אַחֲרֵי אַבְנֵר וַיִּהְיוּ לַאֲגֻדָּה אֶחָת וַיַּעַמְדוּ עַל
כו רֹאשׁ־גִּבְעָה אֶחָת: וַיִּקְרָא אַבְנֵר אֶל־יוֹאָב וַיֹּאמֶר הֲלָנֶצַח תֹּאכַל
חֶרֶב הֲלוֹא יָדַעְתָּה כִּי־מָרָה תִהְיֶה בָּאַחֲרוֹנָה וְעַד־מָתַי לֹא־תֹאמַר
כז לָעָם לָשׁוּב מֵאַחֲרֵי אֲחֵיהֶם: וַיֹּאמֶר יוֹאָב חַי הָאֱלֹהִים כִּי לוּלֵא דִּבַּרְתָּ
כח כִּי אָז מֵהַבֹּקֶר נַעֲלָה הָעָם אִישׁ מֵאַחֲרֵי אָחִיו: וַיִּתְקַע יוֹאָב בַּשּׁוֹפָר
וַיַּעַמְדוּ כָּל־הָעָם וְלֹא־יִרְדְּפוּ עוֹד אַחֲרֵי יִשְׂרָאֵל וְלֹא־יָסְפוּ עוֹד
כט לְהִלָּחֵם: וְאַבְנֵר וַאֲנָשָׁיו הָלְכוּ בָּעֲרָבָה כֹּל הַלַּיְלָה הַהוּא וַיַּעַבְרוּ
ל אֶת־הַיַּרְדֵּן וַיֵּלְכוּ כָּל־הַבִּתְרוֹן וַיָּבֹאוּ מַחֲנָיִם: וְיוֹאָב שָׁב מֵאַחֲרֵי אַבְנֵר
וַיִּקְבֹּץ אֶת־כָּל־הָעָם וַיִּפָּקְדוּ מֵעַבְדֵי דָוִד תִּשְׁעָה־עָשָׂר אִישׁ וַעֲשָׂהאֵל:
לא וְעַבְדֵי דָוִד הִכּוּ מִבִּנְיָמִן וּבְאַנְשֵׁי אַבְנֵר שְׁלֹשׁ־מֵאוֹת וְשִׁשִּׁים אִישׁ
לב מֵתוּ: וַיִּשְׂאוּ אֶת־עֲשָׂהאֵל וַיִּקְבְּרֻהוּ בְּקֶבֶר אָבִיו אֲשֶׁר בֵּית לָחֶם וַיֵּלְכוּ
ג א כָל־הַלַּיְלָה יוֹאָב וַאֲנָשָׁיו וַיֵּאֹר לָהֶם בְּחֶבְרוֹן: וַתְּהִי הַמִּלְחָמָה אֲרֻכָּה
בֵּין בֵּית שָׁאוּל וּבֵין בֵּית דָּוִד וְדָוִד הֹלֵךְ וְחָזֵק וּבֵית שָׁאוּל הֹלְכִים
ב וְדַלִּים: וילדו לְדָוִד בָּנִים בְּחֶבְרוֹן וַיְהִי בְכוֹרוֹ אַמְנוֹן לַאֲחִינֹעַם וַיִּוָּלְדוּ
ג הַיִּזְרְעֵאלִת: וּמִשְׁנֵהוּ כִלְאָב לאביגל אֵשֶׁת נָבָל הַכַּרְמְלִי וְהַשְּׁלִשִׁי לַאֲבִיגַיִל
ד אַבְשָׁלוֹם בֶּן־מַעֲכָה בַּת־תַּלְמַי מֶלֶךְ גְּשׁוּר: וְהָרְבִיעִי אֲדֹנִיָּה בֶן־חַגִּית
ה וְהַחֲמִישִׁי שְׁפַטְיָה בֶן־אֲבִיטָל: וְהַשִּׁשִּׁי יִתְרְעָם לְעֶגְלָה אֵשֶׁת דָּוִד
ו אֵלֶּה יֻלְּדוּ לְדָוִד בְּחֶבְרוֹן: וַיְהִי בִּהְיוֹת הַמִּלְחָמָה בֵּין
ז בֵּית שָׁאוּל וּבֵין בֵּית דָּוִד וְאַבְנֵר הָיָה מִתְחַזֵּק בְּבֵית שָׁאוּל: וּלְשָׁאוּל
פִּלֶגֶשׁ וּשְׁמָהּ רִצְפָּה בַת־אַיָּה וַיֹּאמֶר אֶל־אַבְנֵר מַדּוּעַ בָּאתָה אֶל־
ח פִּילֶגֶשׁ אָבִי: וַיִּחַר לְאַבְנֵר מְאֹד עַל־דִּבְרֵי אִישׁ־בֹּשֶׁת וַיֹּאמֶר הֲרֹאשׁ
כֶּלֶב אָנֹכִי אֲשֶׁר לִיהוּדָה הַיּוֹם אֶעֱשֶׂה־חֶסֶד עִם־בֵּית ׀ שָׁאוּל אָבִיךָ

9 over this woman today? So may God do to Avner, and more, if I do not fulfill
10 for David what the Lord swore to him: to transfer the kingdom from the
house of Sha'ul and establish David's throne over Israel and Yehuda, from Dan
11 to Be'er Sheva." And he could not answer Avner back because of his fear of
12 him. Avner secretly sent messengers to David, saying, "To whom
does the land belong?" and further, "Form a pact with me, then my hand will
13 be with you, guiding all of Israel toward you." "Good," he replied, "I shall form
a pact with you – but I require one thing of you: you shall not be allowed in
my presence unless you bring Mikhal, Sha'ul's daughter, when you come to
14 see me." Then David sent messengers to Ish Boshet, son of Sha'ul,
declaring, "Give me my wife, Mikhal, for whom I paid a bride-price of a
15 hundred Philistine foreskins." So Ish Boshet sent and had her taken from her
16 husband, from Paltiel son of Layish. And her husband went with her, weeping
as he walked behind her, until Baḥurim. "Go back," Avner said to him, and he
17 went back. Now Avner had been conferring with the elders of Israel, saying,
18 "You have long sought out David as your king. Now take action, for the Lord
has said to David, 'Through the hand of My servant David, I will save My
people from the hand of the Philistines and the hands of all their enemies.'"
19 Avner made the same speech in Binyamin's hearing. Then Avner went to
David in Ḥevron to report all the decisions of Israel and the whole House of
20 Binyamin. Avner came to David in Ḥevron accompanied by twenty men, and
21 David held a feast for Avner and the men who had accompanied him. "I will
rise and set out to gather all of Israel to my lord, the king," Avner said to David.
"They will form a pact with you, and you shall rule over everything your heart
22 desires." David then dismissed Avner, who set out and departed in peace. Just
then, David's officials and Yoav arrived from a raid, bringing a wealth of spoil
with them. Avner was no longer with David in Ḥevron, for he had dismissed
23 him, and he had set out and departed in peace. Yoav and all the troops with
him arrived, and they informed Yoav: "Avner son of Ner came to the king,
24 and he dismissed him, and he set out and departed in peace." Then Yoav went
to the king. "What have you done?" he said. "Look, Avner came to you – why
25 did you just dismiss him, so that he went off? You know Avner son of Ner – he
26 came to lure you and learn of your maneuvers and learn of all you do." And
Yoav left David's presence and sent messengers after Avner, who brought him
27 back from the cistern of Sira without David's knowledge. When Avner came
back to Ḥevron, Yoav took him aside, within the gate, as if to talk with him
privately; but there he struck him in the stomach, and he died for the blood

אֶל־אֶחָיו וְאֶל־מֵרֵעֵהוּ וְלֹא הִמְצִיתִךָ בְּיַד דָּוִד וַתִּפְקֹד עָלַי עֲוֺן הָאִשָּׁה
ט הַיּוֹם: כֹּה־יַעֲשֶׂה אֱלֹהִים לְאַבְנֵר וְכֹה יֹסִיף לוֹ כִּי כַּאֲשֶׁר נִשְׁבַּע יהוה
י לְדָוִד כִּי־כֵן אֶעֱשֶׂה־לּוֹ: לְהַעֲבִיר הַמַּמְלָכָה מִבֵּית שָׁאוּל וּלְהָקִים
יא אֶת־כִּסֵּא דָוִד עַל־יִשְׂרָאֵל וְעַל־יְהוּדָה מִדָּן וְעַד־בְּאֵר שָׁבַע: וְלֹא־יָכֹל
יב עוֹד לְהָשִׁיב אֶת־אַבְנֵר דָּבָר מִיִּרְאָתוֹ אֹתוֹ: וַיִּשְׁלַח אַבְנֵר
מַלְאָכִים ׀ אֶל־דָּוִד תַּחְתָּו לֵאמֹר לְמִי־אָרֶץ לֵאמֹר כָּרְתָה בְרִיתְךָ
יג אִתִּי וְהִנֵּה יָדִי עִמָּךְ לְהָסֵב אֵלֶיךָ אֶת־כָּל־יִשְׂרָאֵל: וַיֹּאמֶר טוֹב אֲנִי
אֶכְרֹת אִתְּךָ בְּרִית אַךְ דָּבָר אֶחָד אָנֹכִי שֹׁאֵל מֵאִתְּךָ לֵאמֹר לֹא־
תִרְאֶה אֶת־פָּנַי כִּי ׀ אִם־לִפְנֵי הֲבִיאֲךָ אֵת מִיכַל בַּת־שָׁאוּל בְּבֹאֲךָ
יד לִרְאוֹת אֶת־פָּנָי: וַיִּשְׁלַח דָּוִד מַלְאָכִים אֶל־אִישׁ־בֹּשֶׁת בֶּן־
שָׁאוּל לֵאמֹר תְּנָה אֶת־אִשְׁתִּי אֶת־מִיכַל אֲשֶׁר אֵרַשְׂתִּי לִי בְּמֵאָה
טו עָרְלוֹת פְּלִשְׁתִּים: וַיִּשְׁלַח אִישׁ בֹּשֶׁת וַיִּקָּחֶהָ מֵעִם אִישׁ מֵעִם פַּלְטִיאֵל
טז בֶּן־לוּשׁ: וַיֵּלֶךְ אִתָּהּ אִישָׁהּ הָלוֹךְ וּבָכֹה אַחֲרֶיהָ עַד־בַּחֻרִים וַיֹּאמֶר לַיִשׁ
יז אֵלָיו אַבְנֵר לֵךְ שׁוּב וַיָּשֹׁב: וּדְבַר־אַבְנֵר הָיָה עִם־זִקְנֵי יִשְׂרָאֵל לֵאמֹר
יח גַּם־תְּמוֹל גַּם־שִׁלְשֹׁם הֱיִיתֶם מְבַקְשִׁים אֶת־דָּוִד לְמֶלֶךְ עֲלֵיכֶם: וְעַתָּה
עֲשׂוּ כִּי יהוה אָמַר אֶל־דָּוִד לֵאמֹר בְּיַד ׀ דָּוִד עַבְדִּי הוֹשִׁיעַ אֶת־עַמִּי
יט יִשְׂרָאֵל מִיַּד פְּלִשְׁתִּים וּמִיַּד כָּל־אֹיְבֵיהֶם: וַיְדַבֵּר גַּם־אַבְנֵר בְּאָזְנֵי
בִנְיָמִין וַיֵּלֶךְ גַּם־אַבְנֵר לְדַבֵּר בְּאָזְנֵי דָוִד בְּחֶבְרוֹן אֵת כָּל־אֲשֶׁר־טוֹב
כ בְּעֵינֵי יִשְׂרָאֵל וּבְעֵינֵי כָּל־בֵּית בִּנְיָמִן: וַיָּבֹא אַבְנֵר אֶל־דָּוִד חֶבְרוֹן
וְאִתּוֹ עֶשְׂרִים אֲנָשִׁים וַיַּעַשׂ דָּוִד לְאַבְנֵר וְלַאֲנָשִׁים אֲשֶׁר־אִתּוֹ מִשְׁתֶּה:
כא וַיֹּאמֶר אַבְנֵר אֶל־דָּוִד אָקוּמָה ׀ וְאֵלֵכָה וְאֶקְבְּצָה אֶל־אֲדֹנִי הַמֶּלֶךְ כב
אֶת־כָּל־יִשְׂרָאֵל וְיִכְרְתוּ אִתְּךָ בְּרִית וּמָלַכְתָּ בְּכֹל אֲשֶׁר־תְּאַוֶּה נַפְשֶׁךָ
כב וַיְשַׁלַּח דָּוִד אֶת־אַבְנֵר וַיֵּלֶךְ בְּשָׁלוֹם: וְהִנֵּה עַבְדֵי דָוִד וְיוֹאָב בָּא
מֵהַגְּדוּד וְשָׁלָל רָב עִמָּם הֵבִיאוּ וְאַבְנֵר אֵינֶנּוּ עִם־דָּוִד בְּחֶבְרוֹן כִּי
כג שִׁלְּחוֹ וַיֵּלֶךְ בְּשָׁלוֹם: וְיוֹאָב וְכָל־הַצָּבָא אֲשֶׁר־אִתּוֹ בָּאוּ וַיַּגִּדוּ לְיוֹאָב
כד לֵאמֹר בָּא־אַבְנֵר בֶּן־נֵר אֶל־הַמֶּלֶךְ וַיְשַׁלְּחֵהוּ וַיֵּלֶךְ בְּשָׁלוֹם: וַיָּבֹא
יוֹאָב אֶל־הַמֶּלֶךְ וַיֹּאמֶר מֶה עָשִׂיתָה הִנֵּה־בָא אַבְנֵר אֵלֶיךָ לָמָּה־זֶּה
כה שִׁלַּחְתּוֹ וַיֵּלֶךְ הָלוֹךְ: יָדַעְתָּ אֶת־אַבְנֵר בֶּן־נֵר כִּי לְפַתֹּתְךָ בָּא וְלָדַעַת
כו אֶת־מוֹצָאֲךָ וְאֶת־מבואך וְלָדַעַת אֵת כָּל־אֲשֶׁר אַתָּה עֹשֶׂה: וַיֵּצֵא מוֹבָאֶךָ
יוֹאָב מֵעִם דָּוִד וַיִּשְׁלַח מַלְאָכִים אַחֲרֵי אַבְנֵר וַיָּשִׁבוּ אֹתוֹ מִבּוֹר הַסִּרָה
כז וְדָוִד לֹא יָדָע: וַיָּשָׁב אַבְנֵר חֶבְרוֹן וַיַּטֵּהוּ יוֹאָב אֶל־תּוֹךְ הַשַּׁעַר לְדַבֵּר

28 of Asael, Yoav's brother. When David heard of this afterward, he declared: "I
and my kingdom are forever blameless before the LORD for the blood of
29 Avner son of Ner – may it fall upon the head of Yoav and all his family. May
Yoav's household never lack one who suffers from a discharge, or a leper, or
one who clings to a crutch, or a victim of the sword, or one who lacks bread."
30 Yoav and Avishai, his brother, had murdered Avner because he killed their
31 brother Asael during the battle at Givon. Now David said to Yoav
and to all the troops who were with him, "Tear your clothes, don sackcloth,
32 and wail before Avner," while King David himself walked after the bier. They
buried Avner in Ḥevron, and the king raised his voice and wept over Avner's
33 grave, as all the people wept. And the king lamented Avner and
34 uttered: "How could Avner have died such a lowly death? Your hands were
not bound, and your feet were not fettered; yet you fell as one falls before
35 violent men." And all the people continued to weep over him. When all the
troops came to serve David bread that same day, David swore, "So may God
36 do to me – and more – if I taste bread, or anything at all, before sunset." All
the troops acknowledged and approved of it, just as the troops approved of
37 everything else the king had done. And on that day all the troops – and all of
Israel – knew that it was not the king who had put Avner son of Ner to
38 death. Then the king announced to his subjects, "You certainly
39 know that a noble man, a great man, has fallen this day in Israel. And I am
mild and only just anointed king, while these men – the sons of Tzeruya –
are harsher than me; may the LORD repay the evildoer according to his
4 1 evil." When Sha'ul's son heard that Avner had died in Ḥevron, he lost
2 his grip, and all of Israel became anxious. Now the son of Sha'ul had two men,
leaders of raiding parties. One was called Baana and the other Rekhav; they
were sons of Rimon the Be'erotite, of the Benjaminites, for Be'erot was
3 considered part of Binyamin. The Be'erotites fled to Gitayim, and they live
4 there to this day. Yehonatan son of Sha'ul had a son who was lame.
He had been five years old when the news of Sha'ul and Yehonatan arrived
from Yizre'el. When his nurse picked him up and fled, in her rush to flee she
5 dropped him, and he became lame. His name was Mefivoshet.[30] The sons of
Rimon the Be'erotite – Rekhav and Baana – set out and reached the house of
Ish Boshet in the heat of the day, when he was lying down for his midday rest.
6 They entered the inner part of the house as though to fetch wheat and struck
7 him in the stomach; then Rekhav and Baana his brother escaped – when they
entered the house, he had been lying on his bed in his bedchamber, and they
had struck him, killed him, and cut off his head. They seized his head, and
8 then, all through the night, they made their way across the Arava. They
brought the head of Ish Boshet to David at Ḥevron. "Here is the head of Ish
Boshet, son of your enemy Sha'ul, who sought your life," they said to the king.
"On this day the LORD has granted vengeance to my lord the king against

30 | See note on 2:8 and cf. 1 Chronicles 8:34.

כח אֹתוֹ בַּשֶּׁלִי וַיַּכֵּהוּ שָׁם הַחֹמֶשׁ וַיָּמָת בְּדַם עֲשָׂהאֵל אָחִיו: וַיִּשְׁמַע דָּוִד
מֵאַחֲרֵי כֵן וַיֹּאמֶר נָקִי אָנֹכִי וּמַמְלַכְתִּי מֵעִם יהוה עַד־עוֹלָם מִדְּמֵי
כט אַבְנֵר בֶּן־נֵר: יָחֻלוּ עַל־רֹאשׁ יוֹאָב וְאֶל כָּל־בֵּית אָבִיו וְאַל־יִכָּרֵת
ל מִבֵּית יוֹאָב זָב וּמְצֹרָע וּמַחֲזִיק בַּפֶּלֶךְ וְנֹפֵל בַּחֶרֶב וַחֲסַר־לָחֶם: וְיוֹאָב
וַאֲבִישַׁי אָחִיו הָרְגוּ לְאַבְנֵר עַל אֲשֶׁר הֵמִית אֶת־עֲשָׂהאֵל אֲחִיהֶם
לא בְּגִבְעוֹן בַּמִּלְחָמָה: וַיֹּאמֶר דָּוִד אֶל־יוֹאָב וְאֶל־כָּל־הָעָם
אֲשֶׁר־אִתּוֹ קִרְעוּ בִגְדֵיכֶם וְחִגְרוּ שַׂקִּים וְסִפְדוּ לִפְנֵי אַבְנֵר וְהַמֶּלֶךְ
לב דָּוִד הֹלֵךְ אַחֲרֵי הַמִּטָּה: וַיִּקְבְּרוּ אֶת־אַבְנֵר בְּחֶבְרוֹן וַיִּשָּׂא הַמֶּלֶךְ
לג אֶת־קוֹלוֹ וַיֵּבְךְּ אֶל־קֶבֶר אַבְנֵר וַיִּבְכּוּ כָּל־הָעָם: וַיְקֹנֵן
לד הַמֶּלֶךְ אֶל־אַבְנֵר וַיֹּאמַר הַכְּמוֹת נָבָל יָמוּת אַבְנֵר: יָדֶךָ לֹא־אֲסֻרוֹת
וְרַגְלֶיךָ לֹא־לִנְחֻשְׁתַּיִם הֻגָּשׁוּ כִּנְפוֹל לִפְנֵי בְנֵי־עַוְלָה נָפָלְתָּ וַיֹּסִפוּ
לה כָל־הָעָם לִבְכּוֹת עָלָיו: וַיָּבֹא כָל־הָעָם לְהַבְרוֹת אֶת־דָּוִד לֶחֶם בְּעוֹד
הַיּוֹם וַיִּשָּׁבַע דָּוִד לֵאמֹר כֹּה יַעֲשֶׂה־לִּי אֱלֹהִים וְכֹה יֹסִיף כִּי אִם־לִפְנֵי
לו בוֹא־הַשֶּׁמֶשׁ אֶטְעַם־לֶחֶם אוֹ כָל־מְאוּמָה: וְכָל־הָעָם הִכִּירוּ וַיִּיטַב
לז בְּעֵינֵיהֶם כְּכֹל אֲשֶׁר עָשָׂה הַמֶּלֶךְ בְּעֵינֵי כָל־הָעָם טוֹב: וַיֵּדְעוּ כָל־
הָעָם וְכָל־יִשְׂרָאֵל בַּיּוֹם הַהוּא כִּי לֹא הָיְתָה מֵהַמֶּלֶךְ לְהָמִית אֶת־
לח אַבְנֵר בֶּן־נֵר: וַיֹּאמֶר הַמֶּלֶךְ אֶל־עֲבָדָיו הֲלוֹא תֵדְעוּ
לט כִּי־שַׂר וְגָדוֹל נָפַל הַיּוֹם הַזֶּה בְּיִשְׂרָאֵל: וְאָנֹכִי הַיּוֹם רַךְ וּמָשׁוּחַ מֶלֶךְ
וְהָאֲנָשִׁים הָאֵלֶּה בְּנֵי צְרוּיָה קָשִׁים מִמֶּנִּי יְשַׁלֵּם יהוה לְעֹשֵׂה הָרָעָה
ד א כְּרָעָתוֹ: וַיִּשְׁמַע בֶּן־שָׁאוּל כִּי מֵת אַבְנֵר בְּחֶבְרוֹן וַיִּרְפּוּ יָדָיו
ב וְכָל־יִשְׂרָאֵל נִבְהָלוּ: וּשְׁנֵי אֲנָשִׁים שָׂרֵי־גְדוּדִים הָיוּ בֶן־שָׁאוּל שֵׁם
הָאֶחָד בַּעֲנָה וְשֵׁם הַשֵּׁנִי רֵכָב בְּנֵי רִמּוֹן הַבְּאֵרֹתִי מִבְּנֵי בִנְיָמִן כִּי גַּם־
ג בְּאֵרוֹת תֵּחָשֵׁב עַל־בִּנְיָמִן: וַיִּבְרְחוּ הַבְּאֵרֹתִים גִּתָּיְמָה וַיִּהְיוּ־שָׁם גָּרִים
ד עַד הַיּוֹם הַזֶּה: וְלִיהוֹנָתָן בֶּן־שָׁאוּל בֵּן נְכֵה רַגְלָיִם בֶּן־
חָמֵשׁ שָׁנִים הָיָה בְּבֹא שְׁמֻעַת שָׁאוּל וִיהוֹנָתָן מִיִּזְרְעֶאל וַתִּשָּׂאֵהוּ
ה אֹמַנְתּוֹ וַתָּנֹס וַיְהִי בְּחָפְזָהּ לָנוּס וַיִּפֹּל וַיִּפָּסֵחַ וּשְׁמוֹ מְפִיבֹשֶׁת: וַיֵּלְכוּ
בְּנֵי־רִמּוֹן הַבְּאֵרֹתִי רֵכָב וּבַעֲנָה וַיָּבֹאוּ כְּחֹם הַיּוֹם אֶל־בֵּית אִישׁ בֹּשֶׁת
ו וְהוּא שֹׁכֵב אֵת מִשְׁכַּב הַצָּהֳרָיִם: וְהֵנָּה בָּאוּ עַד־תּוֹךְ הַבַּיִת לֹקְחֵי
ז חִטִּים וַיַּכֻּהוּ אֶל־הַחֹמֶשׁ וְרֵכָב וּבַעֲנָה אָחִיו נִמְלָטוּ: וַיָּבֹאוּ הַבַּיִת
וְהוּא־שֹׁכֵב עַל־מִטָּתוֹ בַּחֲדַר מִשְׁכָּבוֹ וַיַּכֻּהוּ וַיְמִתֻהוּ וַיָּסִירוּ אֶת־רֹאשׁוֹ
ח וַיִּקְחוּ אֶת־רֹאשׁוֹ וַיֵּלְכוּ דֶּרֶךְ הָעֲרָבָה כָּל־הַלָּיְלָה: וַיָּבִאוּ אֶת־רֹאשׁ
אִישׁ־בֹּשֶׁת אֶל־דָּוִד חֶבְרוֹן וַיֹּאמְרוּ אֶל־הַמֶּלֶךְ הִנֵּה־רֹאשׁ אִישׁ־בֹּשֶׁת

9 Sha'ul and his seed." But David retorted to Rekhav and Baana his brother, the
sons of Rimon the Be'erotite, "As the LORD lives – He who saved my life from
10 every danger," he said to them, "when the one who told me, 'look – Sha'ul is
dead,' thought he was bringing me good news, I seized hold of him and killed
11 him in Tziklag – that was his reward for the news. So when evil men have
murdered an innocent man in his own house in his own bed – now, will I not
12 demand his blood from your hands and purge you from the land?" David gave
the order to his lads; they killed them and severed their arms and legs and
hung them over the cistern in Ḥevron. As for the head of Ish Boshet, they
5 1 took it and buried it in Avner's grave in Ḥevron. Now all the tribes
of Israel came to David at Ḥevron. "Here we are, your own flesh and blood.
2 All along, even when Sha'ul was king over us, you were the one who led Israel
out and brought them back.[31] And the LORD said to you, 'You shall
3 shepherd My people Israel, and you shall be the ruler over Israel.'" All the
elders of Israel came to the king at Ḥevron. King David formed a covenant
with them at Ḥevron before the LORD, and they anointed David as king over
4 Israel. David was thirty years old when he became king, and he
5 reigned for forty years. In Ḥevron, he reigned over Yehuda for seven years
and six months, and in Jerusalem, he reigned over all of Israel and Yehuda for
6 thirty-three years. The king and his men set out for Jerusalem against the
Jebusites, who inhabited the land. David was told, "You shall not enter here;
surely even our blind and lame will repel you" – meaning, "David will not
7 enter here." But David captured the stronghold of Zion, that is, the City
8 of David. And David declared on that day, "Whoever attacks the Jebusites,
as well as their blind and lame, whom David despises with his very soul,
and reaches the water shaft ..."[32] – for this reason, they say, "The blind and
9 the lame may not enter the House." David settled in the stronghold and
named it "The City of David"; he then built up the surrounding area from the
10 Milo[33] inward. And David grew in greatness; the LORD, God of Hosts, was
11 with him. King Ḥiram of Tyre sent envoys to David with cedar logs,
12 and carpenters and stonemasons, who built a palace for David. And David
knew that the LORD had established him as the king over Israel and had
13 exalted his kingship for the sake of His people, Israel. David took
more concubines and wives from Jerusalem after his arrival from Ḥevron, and
14 more sons and daughters were born to David. These are the names of those
15 born to him in Jerusalem: Shamua, Shovav, Natan, and Shlomo; Yivḥar,
16 17 Elishua, Nefeg, and Yafia; Elishama, Elyada, and Elifelet. When
the Philistines heard that they had appointed David as king over Israel, all
the Philistines marched up to hunt David down. When David heard, he

31 | In battle; cf. I Samuel 8:20.

32 | See I Chronicles 11:6.

33 | Probably a terraced fortifying structure.

בֶּן־שָׁאוּל אֹיִבְךָ אֲשֶׁר בִּקֵּשׁ אֶת־נַפְשֶׁךָ וַיִּתֵּן יְהוָה לַאדֹנִי הַמֶּלֶךְ נְקָמוֹת
ט הַיּוֹם הַזֶּה מִשָּׁאוּל וּמִזַּרְעוֹ׃ וַיַּעַן דָּוִד אֶת־רֵכָב ׀ וְאֶת־בַּעֲנָה אָחִיו בְּנֵי
רִמּוֹן הַבְּאֵרֹתִי וַיֹּאמֶר לָהֶם חַי־יְהוָה אֲשֶׁר־פָּדָה אֶת־נַפְשִׁי מִכָּל־צָרָה׃
י כִּי הַמַּגִּיד לִי לֵאמֹר הִנֵּה־מֵת שָׁאוּל וְהוּא־הָיָה כִמְבַשֵּׂר בְּעֵינָיו וָאֹחֲזָה
יא בוֹ וָאֶהְרְגֵהוּ בְּצִקְלָג אֲשֶׁר לְתִתִּי־לוֹ בְּשֹׂרָה׃ אַף כִּי־אֲנָשִׁים רְשָׁעִים
הָרְגוּ אֶת־אִישׁ־צַדִּיק בְּבֵיתוֹ עַל־מִשְׁכָּבוֹ וְעַתָּה הֲלוֹא אֲבַקֵּשׁ אֶת־
יב דָּמוֹ מִיֶּדְכֶם וּבִעַרְתִּי אֶתְכֶם מִן־הָאָרֶץ׃ וַיְצַו דָּוִד אֶת־הַנְּעָרִים וַיַּהַרְגוּם
וַיְקַצְּצוּ אֶת־יְדֵיהֶם וְאֶת־רַגְלֵיהֶם וַיִּתְלוּ עַל־הַבְּרֵכָה בְּחֶבְרוֹן וְאֵת
ה א רֹאשׁ אִישׁ־בֹּשֶׁת לָקָחוּ וַיִּקְבְּרוּ בְקֶבֶר־אַבְנֵר בְּחֶבְרוֹן׃ וַיָּבֹאוּ
כָּל־שִׁבְטֵי יִשְׂרָאֵל אֶל־דָּוִד חֶבְרוֹנָה וַיֹּאמְרוּ לֵאמֹר הִנְנוּ עַצְמְךָ וּבְשָׂרְךָ
ב אֲנָחְנוּ׃ גַּם־אֶתְמוֹל גַּם־שִׁלְשׁוֹם בִּהְיוֹת שָׁאוּל מֶלֶךְ עָלֵינוּ אַתָּה
הָיִיתָה מוֹצִיא וְהַמֵּבִי אֶת־יִשְׂרָאֵל וַיֹּאמֶר יְהוָה לְךָ אַתָּה הַמּוֹצִיא
ג תִרְעֶה אֶת־עַמִּי אֶת־יִשְׂרָאֵל וְאַתָּה תִּהְיֶה לְנָגִיד עַל־יִשְׂרָאֵל׃ וַיָּבֹאוּ
כָּל־זִקְנֵי יִשְׂרָאֵל אֶל־הַמֶּלֶךְ חֶבְרוֹנָה וַיִּכְרֹת לָהֶם הַמֶּלֶךְ דָּוִד בְּרִית
ד בְּחֶבְרוֹן לִפְנֵי יְהוָה וַיִּמְשְׁחוּ אֶת־דָּוִד לְמֶלֶךְ עַל־יִשְׂרָאֵל׃ בֶּן־
ה שְׁלֹשִׁים שָׁנָה דָּוִד בְּמָלְכוֹ אַרְבָּעִים שָׁנָה מָלָךְ׃ בְּחֶבְרוֹן מָלַךְ עַל־
יְהוּדָה שֶׁבַע שָׁנִים וְשִׁשָּׁה חֳדָשִׁים וּבִירוּשָׁלַםִ מָלַךְ שְׁלֹשִׁים וְשָׁלֹשׁ
ו שָׁנָה עַל כָּל־יִשְׂרָאֵל וִיהוּדָה׃ וַיֵּלֶךְ הַמֶּלֶךְ וַאֲנָשָׁיו יְרוּשָׁלַםִ אֶל־הַיְבֻסִי
יוֹשֵׁב הָאָרֶץ וַיֹּאמֶר לְדָוִד לֵאמֹר לֹא־תָבוֹא הֵנָּה כִּי אִם־הֱסִירְךָ
ז הַעִוְרִים וְהַפִּסְחִים לֵאמֹר לֹא־יָבוֹא דָוִד הֵנָּה׃ וַיִּלְכֹּד דָּוִד אֵת מְצֻדַת
ח צִיּוֹן הִיא עִיר דָּוִד׃ וַיֹּאמֶר דָּוִד בַּיּוֹם הַהוּא כָּל־מַכֵּה יְבֻסִי וְיִגַּע בַּצִּנּוֹר
וְאֶת־הַפִּסְחִים וְאֶת־הַעִוְרִים שנאו נֶפֶשׁ דָּוִד עַל־כֵּן יֹאמְרוּ עִוֵּר וּפִסֵּחַ שְׂנֻאֵי
ט לֹא יָבוֹא אֶל־הַבָּיִת׃ וַיֵּשֶׁב דָּוִד בַּמְּצֻדָה וַיִּקְרָא־לָהּ עִיר דָּוִד וַיִּבֶן
י דָּוִד סָבִיב מִן־הַמִּלּוֹא וָבָיְתָה׃ וַיֵּלֶךְ דָּוִד הָלוֹךְ וְגָדוֹל וַיהוָה אֱלֹהֵי כג
יא צְבָאוֹת עִמּוֹ׃ וַיִּשְׁלַח חִירָם מֶלֶךְ־צֹר מַלְאָכִים אֶל־דָּוִד
יב וַעֲצֵי אֲרָזִים וְחָרָשֵׁי עֵץ וְחָרָשֵׁי אֶבֶן קִיר וַיִּבְנוּ־בַיִת לְדָוִד׃ וַיֵּדַע דָּוִד
כִּי־הֱכִינוֹ יְהוָה לְמֶלֶךְ עַל־יִשְׂרָאֵל וְכִי נִשֵּׂא מַמְלַכְתּוֹ בַּעֲבוּר עַמּוֹ
יג יִשְׂרָאֵל׃ וַיִּקַּח דָּוִד עוֹד פִּלַגְשִׁים וְנָשִׁים מִירוּשָׁלַםִ אַחֲרֵי
יד בֹּאוֹ מֵחֶבְרוֹן וַיִּוָּלְדוּ עוֹד לְדָוִד בָּנִים וּבָנוֹת׃ וְאֵלֶּה שְׁמוֹת הַיִּלֹּדִים
טו לוֹ בִּירוּשָׁלָםִ שַׁמּוּעַ וְשׁוֹבָב וְנָתָן וּשְׁלֹמֹה׃ וְיִבְחָר וֶאֱלִישׁוּעַ וְנֶפֶג וְיָפִיעַ׃
טז יז וֶאֱלִישָׁמָע וְאֶלְיָדָע וֶאֱלִיפָלֶט׃ וַיִּשְׁמְעוּ פְלִשְׁתִּים כִּי־
מָשְׁחוּ אֶת־דָּוִד לְמֶלֶךְ עַל־יִשְׂרָאֵל וַיַּעֲלוּ כָל־פְּלִשְׁתִּים לְבַקֵּשׁ אֶת־

18 descended into the stronghold. The Philistines came and spread out in the
19 Refaim Valley. David inquired of the Lord, "Shall I go up to the Philistines?
Will you deliver them into my hand?" "Go up," the Lord replied to
20 David, "for I will surely deliver the Philistines into your hands." David reached
Baal Peratzim, and there David defeated them. And he said, "The Lord has
blasted my enemies away before me like a blast of water." For that reason, he
21 named that place Baal Peratzim.[34] They abandoned their idols there, and
22 David and his men carried them off. But the Philistines marched up
23 once more and spread out in the Refaim Valley. David inquired of the Lord,
who said, "Do not go up; turn around to their rear, and advance upon them
24 opposite the baca trees. As soon as you hear the sound of marching echoing
across the tops of the baca trees, act swiftly, for then the Lord will go out
25 before you to strike down the Philistine force." And David did as the Lord
commanded him, and he defeated the Philistines from Geva all the way up
6 1 to Gezer. David mustered all of Israel's elite once more, thirty
2 thousand. Then David, along with all the troops with him, set out from Baalim
of Yehuda. From there they brought up the Ark of God, which is called by
a name: The Name of the Lord of Hosts Enthroned upon the Cherubim is
3 upon it. They mounted the Ark of God upon a new cart and conveyed it from
the house of Avinadav in Giva, with Uza and Aḥyo, the sons of Avinadav,
4 driving the new cart. They conveyed it from the house of Avinadav in Giva –
5 the Ark of God, Aḥyo walking before the Ark, and David and all the House
of Israel reveling before the Lord with all kinds of instruments of cypress
6 wood, lyres, harps, timbrels, sistra, and cymbals. When they reached the
threshing floor of Nakhon, Uza reached out toward the Ark of God and
7 grasped hold of it, for the oxen had stumbled. And the Lord's rage flared up
against Uza, and God struck him down on the spot for his impudence; he
8 died there with the Ark of God. David was enraged that the Lord had burst
9 out against Uza, and that place has been called Peretz Uza[35] to this day. David
feared the Lord on that day, and he said, "How will the Ark of the Lord
10 come to me?" And David was not willing to have the Ark of the Lord removed
to him in the City of David; David had it redirected to the house of Oved
11 Edom, the Gittite. The Ark of the Lord remained at the house of Oved Edom,
the Gittite, for three months, and the Lord blessed Oved Edom and his
12 whole household. When it was reported to King David that the Lord had
blessed Oved Edom's household and all that was his because of the Ark of
God, David went and brought up the Ark of God from the house of Oved
13 Edom to the City of David, with joy. When the bearers of the Ark of the Lord
14 had advanced six paces, he sacrificed an ox and a fatling. And David danced
15 with all his might before the Lord; David was clad in a linen ephod.[36] So
David and all the House of Israel led the Ark of the Lord up with joyous
16 shouting and the sound of the ram's horn. As the Ark of the Lord entered

---

34 | From the Hebrew *peretz*, meaning "blast."

35 | Literally "outburst [against] Uza."

36 | See note on 1 Samuel 2:18.

יח דָּוִד וַיִּשְׁמַע דָּוִד וַיֵּרֶד אֶל־הַמְּצוּדָה׃ וּפְלִשְׁתִּים בָּאוּ וַיִּנָּטְשׁוּ בְּעֵמֶק
יט רְפָאִים׃ וַיִּשְׁאַל דָּוִד בַּיהוָה לֵאמֹר הַאֶעֱלֶה אֶל־פְּלִשְׁתִּים הֲתִתְּנֵם
בְּיָדִי וַיֹּאמֶר יְהוָה אֶל־דָּוִד עֲלֵה כִּי־נָתֹן אֶתֵּן אֶת־הַפְּלִשְׁתִּים
כ בְּיָדֶךָ׃ וַיָּבֹא דָוִד בְּבַעַל־פְּרָצִים וַיַּכֵּם שָׁם דָּוִד וַיֹּאמֶר פָּרַץ יְהוָה אֶת־
אֹיְבַי לְפָנַי כְּפֶרֶץ מָיִם עַל־כֵּן קָרָא שֵׁם־הַמָּקוֹם הַהוּא בַּעַל פְּרָצִים׃
כא כב וַיַּעַזְבוּ־שָׁם אֶת־עֲצַבֵּיהֶם וַיִּשָּׂאֵם דָּוִד וַאֲנָשָׁיו׃ וַיֹּסִפוּ
כג עוֹד פְּלִשְׁתִּים לַעֲלוֹת וַיִּנָּטְשׁוּ בְּעֵמֶק רְפָאִים׃ וַיִּשְׁאַל דָּוִד בַּיהוָה
כד וַיֹּאמֶר לֹא תַעֲלֶה הָסֵב אֶל־אַחֲרֵיהֶם וּבָאתָ לָהֶם מִמּוּל בְּכָאִים׃ וִיהִי
בשמעך אֶת־קוֹל צְעָדָה בְּרָאשֵׁי הַבְּכָאִים אָז תֶּחֱרָץ כִּי אָז יָצָא יְהוָה כְּשָׁמְעֲךָ
כה לְפָנֶיךָ לְהַכּוֹת בְּמַחֲנֵה פְלִשְׁתִּים׃ וַיַּעַשׂ דָּוִד כֵּן כַּאֲשֶׁר צִוָּהוּ יְהוָה וַיַּךְ
ו א אֶת־פְּלִשְׁתִּים מִגֶּבַע עַד־בֹּאֲךָ גָזֶר׃ וַיֹּסֶף עוֹד דָּוִד
ב אֶת־כָּל־בָּחוּר בְּיִשְׂרָאֵל שְׁלֹשִׁים אָלֶף׃ וַיָּקָם ׀ וַיֵּלֶךְ דָּוִד וְכָל־הָעָם
אֲשֶׁר אִתּוֹ מִבַּעֲלֵי יְהוּדָה לְהַעֲלוֹת מִשָּׁם אֵת אֲרוֹן הָאֱלֹהִים אֲשֶׁר־
ג נִקְרָא שֵׁם שֵׁם יְהוָה צְבָאוֹת יֹשֵׁב הַכְּרֻבִים עָלָיו׃ וַיַּרְכִּבוּ אֶת־אֲרוֹן
הָאֱלֹהִים אֶל־עֲגָלָה חֲדָשָׁה וַיִּשָּׂאֻהוּ מִבֵּית אֲבִינָדָב אֲשֶׁר בַּגִּבְעָה
ד וְעֻזָּא וְאַחְיוֹ בְּנֵי אֲבִינָדָב נֹהֲגִים אֶת־הָעֲגָלָה חֲדָשָׁה׃ וַיִּשָּׂאֻהוּ מִבֵּית
אֲבִינָדָב אֲשֶׁר בַּגִּבְעָה עִם אֲרוֹן הָאֱלֹהִים וְאַחְיוֹ הֹלֵךְ לִפְנֵי הָאָרוֹן׃
ה וְדָוִד ׀ וְכָל־בֵּית יִשְׂרָאֵל מְשַׂחֲקִים לִפְנֵי יְהוָה בְּכֹל עֲצֵי בְרוֹשִׁים
ו וּבְכִנֹּרוֹת וּבִנְבָלִים וּבְתֻפִּים וּבִמְנַעַנְעִים וּבְצֶלְצֶלִים׃ וַיָּבֹאוּ עַד־גֹּרֶן
נָכוֹן וַיִּשְׁלַח עֻזָּא אֶל־אֲרוֹן הָאֱלֹהִים וַיֹּאחֶז בּוֹ כִּי שָׁמְטוּ הַבָּקָר׃
ז וַיִּחַר־אַף יְהוָה בְּעֻזָּה וַיַּכֵּהוּ שָׁם הָאֱלֹהִים עַל־הַשַּׁל וַיָּמָת שָׁם עִם
ח אֲרוֹן הָאֱלֹהִים׃ וַיִּחַר לְדָוִד עַל אֲשֶׁר פָּרַץ יְהוָה פֶּרֶץ בְּעֻזָּה וַיִּקְרָא
ט לַמָּקוֹם הַהוּא פֶּרֶץ עֻזָּה עַד הַיּוֹם הַזֶּה׃ וַיִּרָא דָוִד אֶת־יְהוָה בַּיּוֹם
י הַהוּא וַיֹּאמֶר אֵיךְ יָבוֹא אֵלַי אֲרוֹן יְהוָה׃ וְלֹא־אָבָה דָוִד לְהָסִיר אֵלָיו
יא אֶת־אֲרוֹן יְהוָה עַל־עִיר דָּוִד וַיַּטֵּהוּ דָוִד בֵּית עֹבֵד־אֱדֹם הַגִּתִּי׃ וַיֵּשֶׁב
אֲרוֹן יְהוָה בֵּית עֹבֵד אֱדֹם הַגִּתִּי שְׁלֹשָׁה חֳדָשִׁים וַיְבָרֶךְ יְהוָה אֶת־עֹבֵד
יב אֱדֹם וְאֶת־כָּל־בֵּיתוֹ׃ וַיֻּגַּד לַמֶּלֶךְ דָּוִד לֵאמֹר בֵּרַךְ יְהוָה אֶת־בֵּית עֹבֵד
אֱדֹם וְאֶת־כָּל־אֲשֶׁר־לוֹ בַּעֲבוּר אֲרוֹן הָאֱלֹהִים וַיֵּלֶךְ דָּוִד וַיַּעַל אֶת־
יג אֲרוֹן הָאֱלֹהִים מִבֵּית עֹבֵד אֱדֹם עִיר דָּוִד בְּשִׂמְחָה׃ וַיְהִי כִּי צָעֲדוּ
יד נֹשְׂאֵי אֲרוֹן־יְהוָה שִׁשָּׁה צְעָדִים וַיִּזְבַּח שׁוֹר וּמְרִיא׃ וְדָוִד מְכַרְכֵּר
טו בְּכָל־עֹז לִפְנֵי יְהוָה וְדָוִד חָגוּר אֵפוֹד בָּד׃ וְדָוִד וְכָל־בֵּית יִשְׂרָאֵל
טז מַעֲלִים אֶת־אֲרוֹן יְהוָה בִּתְרוּעָה וּבְקוֹל שׁוֹפָר׃ וְהָיָה אֲרוֹן יְהוָה

the City of David, Mikhal, Sha'ul's daughter, was watching through the
window; when she saw David – the king! – leaping and dancing before the
17 LORD, she felt a rush of contempt for him. They brought the Ark of the LORD
and set it in its place within the tent David had pitched for it, and David
18 offered burnt offerings and peace offerings before the LORD. When David
had finished offering the burnt offering and the peace offerings, he blessed
19 the people in the name of the LORD of Hosts. He then distributed a ring of
bread, a share of meat, and a cake of raisins to all the people – to all the
multitudes of Israel, every single man and woman. Then all the people, every
20 one, made their way home. When David returned to bless his own household,
Mikhal, Sha'ul's daughter, came out to meet him. "How dignified the king
of Israel was today," she said, "exposing himself before all the eyes of his
21 servants' slave girls just as one of the rabble might expose himself!" "It was
before the LORD, who chose me instead of your father and all his household
and appointed me as ruler over the LORD's people, Israel," David said to
22 Mikhal. "I danced before the LORD. And I would have lowered myself even
further and been humiliated in my own eyes – but to the slave girls you speak
23 of, I would still be dignified." And Mikhal, Sha'ul's daughter, never had a
7 1 child – to her dying day. Once the king had settled in his palace, and
2 the LORD had granted him repose from all his surrounding enemies, the king
said to the prophet Natan, "Look now – I am dwelling in a cedarwood palace
3 while the Ark of God is dwelling in a tent." "Go – do whatever you have in
4 mind," Natan said to the king, "for the LORD is with you." But that
5 same night, the word of the LORD came to Natan. "Go, and say to
My servant David: Thus says the LORD: Shall you be the one to build a house
6 for Me, for My abode? For I have not dwelt in a house from the day I brought
the Israelites out of Egypt to this day; I have roamed in tent and tabernacle.
7 But wherever I roamed, among all the Israelites, have I ever spoken a word to
any of the tribes of Israel whom I charged to shepherd My people Israel,
8 saying, 'Why have you not built Me a cedarwood palace?' Now you shall say
so to My servant David: Thus says the LORD of Hosts: I took you out of the
9 pastures, from following the sheep, to be ruler over My people Israel. I have
been with you wherever you went, and I have cut down all your enemies
before you. I will make your name great – one of the greatest names on earth.
10 I will set aside a place for My people Israel and let them take root and settle
down within it, and they will be disturbed no longer; violent men will no
11 longer oppress them as they once did in the days when I appointed judges
over My people Israel. To you I will grant repose from all your enemies;
moreover, the LORD declares that the LORD will establish a house for you.
12 For when your days are done and you lie with your ancestors, I will raise up
your own seed after you – the issue of your own loins – and I will establish
13 his kingdom. He will build a house in My name, and I will firmly establish his

בָּא עִיר דָּוִד וּמִיכַל בַּת־שָׁאוּל נִשְׁקְפָה ׀ בְּעַד הַחַלּוֹן וַתֵּרֶא אֶת־
יז הַמֶּלֶךְ דָּוִד מְפַזֵּז וּמְכַרְכֵּר לִפְנֵי יהוה וַתִּבֶז לוֹ בְּלִבָּהּ: וַיָּבִאוּ אֶת־אֲרוֹן
יהוה וַיַּצִּגוּ אֹתוֹ בִּמְקוֹמוֹ בְּתוֹךְ הָאֹהֶל אֲשֶׁר נָטָה־לוֹ דָּוִד וַיַּעַל דָּוִד
יח עֹלוֹת לִפְנֵי יהוה וּשְׁלָמִים: וַיְכַל דָּוִד מֵהַעֲלוֹת הָעוֹלָה וְהַשְּׁלָמִים
יט וַיְבָרֶךְ אֶת־הָעָם בְּשֵׁם יהוה צְבָאוֹת: וַיְחַלֵּק לְכָל־הָעָם לְכָל־הֲמוֹן
יִשְׂרָאֵל לְמֵאִישׁ וְעַד־אִשָּׁה לְאִישׁ חַלַּת לֶחֶם אַחַת וְאֶשְׁפָּר אֶחָד
כ וַאֲשִׁישָׁה אֶחָת וַיֵּלֶךְ כָּל־הָעָם אִישׁ לְבֵיתוֹ: וַיָּשָׁב דָּוִד לְבָרֵךְ אֶת־בֵּיתוֹ
וַתֵּצֵא מִיכַל בַּת־שָׁאוּל לִקְרַאת דָּוִד וַתֹּאמֶר מַה־נִּכְבַּד הַיּוֹם מֶלֶךְ
יִשְׂרָאֵל אֲשֶׁר נִגְלָה הַיּוֹם לְעֵינֵי אַמְהוֹת עֲבָדָיו כְּהִגָּלוֹת נִגְלוֹת אַחַד
כא הָרֵקִים: וַיֹּאמֶר דָּוִד אֶל־מִיכַל לִפְנֵי יהוה אֲשֶׁר בָּחַר־בִּי מֵאָבִיךְ
וּמִכָּל־בֵּיתוֹ לְצַוֹּת אֹתִי נָגִיד עַל־עַם יהוה עַל־יִשְׂרָאֵל וְשִׂחַקְתִּי לִפְנֵי
כב יהוה: וּנְקַלֹּתִי עוֹד מִזֹּאת וְהָיִיתִי שָׁפָל בְּעֵינָי וְעִם־הָאֲמָהוֹת אֲשֶׁר
כג אָמַרְתְּ עִמָּם אִכָּבֵדָה: וּלְמִיכַל בַּת־שָׁאוּל לֹא־הָיָה לָהּ יָלֶד עַד יוֹם
ז א מוֹתָהּ: וַיְהִי כִּי־יָשַׁב הַמֶּלֶךְ בְּבֵיתוֹ וַיהוה הֵנִיחַ־לוֹ מִסָּבִיב
ב מִכָּל־אֹיְבָיו: וַיֹּאמֶר הַמֶּלֶךְ אֶל־נָתָן הַנָּבִיא רְאֵה נָא אָנֹכִי יוֹשֵׁב בְּבֵית
ג אֲרָזִים וַאֲרוֹן הָאֱלֹהִים יֹשֵׁב בְּתוֹךְ הַיְרִיעָה: וַיֹּאמֶר נָתָן אֶל־הַמֶּלֶךְ
ד כֹּל אֲשֶׁר בִּלְבָבְךָ לֵךְ עֲשֵׂה כִּי יהוה עִמָּךְ: וַיְהִי בַּלַּיְלָה
ה הַהוּא וַיְהִי דְּבַר־יהוה אֶל־נָתָן לֵאמֹר: לֵךְ וְאָמַרְתָּ
אֶל־עַבְדִּי אֶל־דָּוִד כֹּה אָמַר יהוה הַאַתָּה תִּבְנֶה־לִּי בַיִת לְשִׁבְתִּי:
ו כִּי לֹא יָשַׁבְתִּי בְּבַיִת לְמִיּוֹם הַעֲלֹתִי אֶת־בְּנֵי יִשְׂרָאֵל מִמִּצְרַיִם וְעַד
ז הַיּוֹם הַזֶּה וָאֶהְיֶה מִתְהַלֵּךְ בְּאֹהֶל וּבְמִשְׁכָּן: בְּכֹל אֲשֶׁר־הִתְהַלַּכְתִּי
בְּכָל־בְּנֵי יִשְׂרָאֵל הֲדָבָר דִּבַּרְתִּי אֶת־אַחַד שִׁבְטֵי יִשְׂרָאֵל אֲשֶׁר צִוִּיתִי
לִרְעוֹת אֶת־עַמִּי אֶת־יִשְׂרָאֵל לֵאמֹר לָמָּה לֹא־בְנִיתֶם לִי בֵּית אֲרָזִים:
ח וְעַתָּה כֹּה־תֹאמַר לְעַבְדִּי לְדָוִד כֹּה אָמַר יהוה צְבָאוֹת אֲנִי לְקַחְתִּיךָ
ט מִן־הַנָּוֶה מֵאַחַר הַצֹּאן לִהְיוֹת נָגִיד עַל־עַמִּי עַל־יִשְׂרָאֵל: וָאֶהְיֶה
עִמְּךָ בְּכֹל אֲשֶׁר הָלַכְתָּ וָאַכְרִתָה אֶת־כָּל־אֹיְבֶיךָ מִפָּנֶיךָ וְעָשִׂתִי לְךָ
י שֵׁם גָּדוֹל כְּשֵׁם הַגְּדֹלִים אֲשֶׁר בָּאָרֶץ: וְשַׂמְתִּי מָקוֹם לְעַמִּי לְיִשְׂרָאֵל
וּנְטַעְתִּיו וְשָׁכַן תַּחְתָּיו וְלֹא יִרְגַּז עוֹד וְלֹא־יֹסִיפוּ בְנֵי־עַוְלָה לְעַנּוֹתוֹ
יא כַּאֲשֶׁר בָּרִאשׁוֹנָה: וּלְמִן־הַיּוֹם אֲשֶׁר צִוִּיתִי שֹׁפְטִים עַל־עַמִּי יִשְׂרָאֵל
וַהֲנִיחֹתִי לְךָ מִכָּל־אֹיְבֶיךָ וְהִגִּיד לְךָ יהוה כִּי־בַיִת יַעֲשֶׂה־לְּךָ יהוה:
יב כִּי ׀ יִמְלְאוּ יָמֶיךָ וְשָׁכַבְתָּ אֶת־אֲבֹתֶיךָ וַהֲקִימֹתִי אֶת־זַרְעֲךָ אַחֲרֶיךָ
יג אֲשֶׁר יֵצֵא מִמֵּעֶיךָ וַהֲכִינֹתִי אֶת־מַמְלַכְתּוֹ: הוּא יִבְנֶה־בַּיִת לִשְׁמִי

14 royal throne forever. I will be a father to him, and he will be a son to Me; and
should he do wrong, I will berate him with the rod of mortals and with human
15 afflictions. But My loyalties shall not move from him, as I removed them from
16 Sha'ul, whom I removed before you. And your house and your kingdom will
17 be ever steadfast before you, and your throne will be secure forever." Natan
related all these words and all this vision to David.
18 Now King David came and sat before the LORD. "Who am I, O Lord GOD,
19 and who is my house," he said, "that You have brought me so far? And yet
even this is small in Your eyes, O Lord GOD, as You also speak of Your servant's
house in the distant future – why, this is a revelation to humanity, O Lord
20 GOD. But what more can David say to You; You know Your servant, O Lord
21 GOD. It is for the sake of Your own word, and Your own will, that You brought
22 about this greatness and made it known to Your servant. How great You are,
O LORD God; there is no one like You, and no god besides You, as we have
23 heard all along. And who is like Your people Israel – the only nation on
earth God went to redeem as His own people, making a name for Himself
and performing great and wondrous deeds to the nations and gods in Your
24 land before the people You redeemed for Yourself from Egypt. You have
established Your people Israel as Your own people forever, and You, O LORD,
25 have become their God. Now, O LORD God, fulfill the promise You made
regarding Your servant, and regarding his house, forever; do as You have
26 promised. May Your name be exalted forever; let them say, 'The LORD of
Hosts is God of Israel,' and may the house of David be established before You.
27 As You, O LORD of Hosts, God of Israel, have revealed this to Your servant,
saying 'I will build a house for you,' Your servant has found the heart to
28 offer this prayer before You. And now, O Lord GOD – You are God, and Your
29 words are truth, and You have promised this favor to Your servant and now –
please bless Your servant's house to be before You forever, as You promised,
O Lord GOD, and by Your blessing, may Your servant's house be blessed
8 1 forever." Sometime later, David defeated the Philistines and
subjugated them; and David seized Meteg HaAma from the hand of the
2 Philistines. He defeated Moav and measured them out with a cord; he made
them lie on the ground and measured out two cord-lengths for execution,
and one full length to be kept alive. And Moav became David's tribute-bearing
3 vassals. David defeated Hadadezer son of Reḥov, the king of Tzova, who
4 had set out to extend his dominion to the Euphrates. David captured a
thousand seven hundred of his riders and twenty thousand infantrymen;
David hamstrung all the chariot horses, retaining one hundred chariot horses.
5 Aram of Damascus came to King Hadadezer of Tzova's aid, but David struck

יד וְכֹנַנְתִּי אֶת־כִּסֵּא מַמְלַכְתּוֹ עַד־עוֹלָם: אֲנִי אֶהְיֶה־לּוֹ לְאָב וְהוּא יִהְיֶה־
לִּי לְבֵן אֲשֶׁר בְּהַעֲוֺתוֹ וְהֹכַחְתִּיו בְּשֵׁבֶט אֲנָשִׁים וּבְנִגְעֵי בְּנֵי אָדָם:
טו וְחַסְדִּי לֹא־יָסוּר מִמֶּנּוּ כַּאֲשֶׁר הֲסִרֹתִי מֵעִם שָׁאוּל אֲשֶׁר הֲסִרֹתִי
טז מִלְּפָנֶיךָ: וְנֶאְמַן בֵּיתְךָ וּמַמְלַכְתְּךָ עַד־עוֹלָם לְפָנֶיךָ כִּסְאֲךָ יִהְיֶה נָכוֹן כד
יז עַד־עוֹלָם: כְּכֹל הַדְּבָרִים הָאֵלֶּה וּכְכֹל הַחִזָּיוֹן הַזֶּה כֵּן דִּבֶּר נָתָן אֶל־
דָּוִד:
יח וַיָּבֹא הַמֶּלֶךְ דָּוִד וַיֵּשֶׁב לִפְנֵי יְהוָה וַיֹּאמֶר מִי אָנֹכִי אֲדֹנָי יֱהֹוִה וּמִי
יט בֵיתִי כִּי הֲבִיאֹתַנִי עַד־הֲלֹם: וַתִּקְטַן עוֹד זֹאת בְּעֵינֶיךָ אֲדֹנָי יֱהֹוִה
וַתְּדַבֵּר גַּם אֶל־בֵּית־עַבְדְּךָ לְמֵרָחוֹק וְזֹאת תּוֹרַת הָאָדָם אֲדֹנָי יֱהֹוִה:
כ וּמַה־יּוֹסִיף דָּוִד עוֹד לְדַבֵּר אֵלֶיךָ וְאַתָּה יָדַעְתָּ אֶת־עַבְדְּךָ אֲדֹנָי יֱהֹוִה:
כא בַּעֲבוּר דְּבָרְךָ וּכְלִבְּךָ עָשִׂיתָ אֵת כָּל־הַגְּדוּלָּה הַזֹּאת לְהוֹדִיעַ אֶת־
כב עַבְדֶּךָ: עַל־כֵּן גָּדַלְתָּ יְהוָה אֱלֹהִים כִּי־אֵין כָּמוֹךָ וְאֵין אֱלֹהִים זוּלָתֶךָ
כג בְּכֹל אֲשֶׁר־שָׁמַעְנוּ בְּאָזְנֵינוּ: וּמִי כְעַמְּךָ כְּיִשְׂרָאֵל גּוֹי אֶחָד בָּאָרֶץ
אֲשֶׁר הָלְכוּ־אֱלֹהִים לִפְדּוֹת־לוֹ לְעָם וְלָשׂוּם לוֹ שֵׁם וְלַעֲשׂוֹת לָכֶם
הַגְּדוּלָּה וְנֹרָאוֹת לְאַרְצֶךָ מִפְּנֵי עַמְּךָ אֲשֶׁר פָּדִיתָ לְּךָ מִמִּצְרַיִם גּוֹיִם
כד וֵאלֹהָיו: וַתְּכוֹנֵן לְךָ אֶת־עַמְּךָ יִשְׂרָאֵל ׀ לְךָ לְעָם עַד־עוֹלָם וְאַתָּה
כה יְהוָה הָיִיתָ לָהֶם לֵאלֹהִים: וְעַתָּה יְהוָה אֱלֹהִים הַדָּבָר אֲשֶׁר דִּבַּרְתָּ
כו עַל־עַבְדְּךָ וְעַל־בֵּיתוֹ הָקֵם עַד־עוֹלָם וַעֲשֵׂה כַּאֲשֶׁר דִּבַּרְתָּ: וְיִגְדַּל
שִׁמְךָ עַד־עוֹלָם לֵאמֹר יְהוָה צְבָאוֹת אֱלֹהִים עַל־יִשְׂרָאֵל וּבֵית עַבְדְּךָ
כז דָוִד יִהְיֶה נָכוֹן לְפָנֶיךָ: כִּי־אַתָּה יְהוָה צְבָאוֹת אֱלֹהֵי יִשְׂרָאֵל גָּלִיתָה
אֶת־אֹזֶן עַבְדְּךָ לֵאמֹר בַּיִת אֶבְנֶה־לָּךְ עַל־כֵּן מָצָא עַבְדְּךָ אֶת־לִבּוֹ
כח לְהִתְפַּלֵּל אֵלֶיךָ אֶת־הַתְּפִלָּה הַזֹּאת: וְעַתָּה ׀ אֲדֹנָי יֱהֹוִה אַתָּה־הוּא
הָאֱלֹהִים וּדְבָרֶיךָ יִהְיוּ אֱמֶת וַתְּדַבֵּר אֶל־עַבְדְּךָ אֶת־הַטּוֹבָה הַזֹּאת:
כט וְעַתָּה הוֹאֵל וּבָרֵךְ אֶת־בֵּית עַבְדְּךָ לִהְיוֹת לְעוֹלָם לְפָנֶיךָ כִּי־אַתָּה
ח א אֲדֹנָי יֱהֹוִה דִּבַּרְתָּ וּמִבִּרְכָתְךָ יְבֹרַךְ בֵּית־עַבְדְּךָ לְעוֹלָם: וַיְהִי
אַחֲרֵי־כֵן וַיַּךְ דָּוִד אֶת־פְּלִשְׁתִּים וַיַּכְנִיעֵם וַיִּקַּח דָּוִד אֶת־מֶתֶג הָאַמָּה
ב מִיַּד פְּלִשְׁתִּים: וַיַּךְ אֶת־מוֹאָב וַיְמַדְּדֵם בַּחֶבֶל הַשְׁכֵּב אוֹתָם אַרְצָה
וַיְמַדֵּד שְׁנֵי־חֲבָלִים לְהָמִית וּמְלֹא הַחֶבֶל לְהַחֲיוֹת וַתְּהִי מוֹאָב לְדָוִד
ג לַעֲבָדִים נֹשְׂאֵי מִנְחָה: וַיַּךְ דָּוִד אֶת־הֲדַדְעֶזֶר בֶּן־רְחֹב מֶלֶךְ צוֹבָה
ד בְּלֶכְתּוֹ לְהָשִׁיב יָדוֹ בִּנְהַר־ : וַיִּלְכֹּד דָּוִד מִמֶּנּוּ אֶלֶף וּשְׁבַע־מֵאוֹת פְּרָת
פָּרָשִׁים וְעֶשְׂרִים אֶלֶף אִישׁ רַגְלִי וַיְעַקֵּר דָּוִד אֶת־כָּל־הָרֶכֶב וַיּוֹתֵר
ה מִמֶּנּוּ מֵאָה רָכֶב: וַתָּבֹא אֲרַם דַּמֶּשֶׂק לַעְזֹר לַהֲדַדְעֶזֶר מֶלֶךְ צוֹבָה

6 down twenty-two thousand of Aram's men. And David posted governors
in Aram of Damascus, and the Arameans became David's tribute-bearing
7 vassals. And the LORD granted David victory wherever he went. David took
the golden quivers that had belonged to Hadadezer's officials and brought
8 them to Jerusalem, and from Betaḥ and Berotai, Hadadezer's cities, David
9 confiscated a vast amount of bronze. When King To'i of Ḥamat
10 heard that David had defeated all of Hadadezer's forces, To'i sent his son
Yoram to King David to greet him and congratulate him for having conquered
Hadadezer in battle, for Hadadezer had been at war with To'i. He bore vessels
11 of silver, gold, and bronze. King David devoted those, too, to the LORD, in
addition to all the silver and gold he had devoted from all the nations he had
12 conquered; from Aram, Moav, the Amonites, the Philistines, Amalek, and the
13 spoil from Hadadezer son of Reḥov, King of Tzova. David made a name for
himself when he returned from defeating the Arameans in the Valley of Salt –
14 eighteen thousand of them.[37] He stationed governors in Edom – throughout
Edom, he stationed governors, and all of Edom became David's vassals. And
15 the LORD granted David victory wherever he went. David reigned over all of
16 Israel, and David upheld justice and righteousness for all his people. Yoav son
of Tzeruya was the commander of his army; Yehoshafat son of Aḥilud was
17 royal herald; Tzadok son of Aḥituv, and Aḥimelekh son of Evyatar, were
18 priests; Seraya was royal scribe; Benayahu son of Yehoyada commanded the
9 1 Keretites and Peletites; and David's sons were priests. Now David
said, "Is there anyone still left from the house of Sha'ul? I will show him
2 kindness for Yehonatan's sake." There was a servant of the house of Sha'ul
whose name was Tziva; they summoned him to David, and the king said to
3 him, "Are you Tziva?" "At your service," he said. "Is there anyone at all who is
still left from the house of Sha'ul?" said the king. "I will show him God's own
loyalty." "There is still a son of Yehonatan's, who is lame," Tziva said to the
4 king. "Where is he?" the king said to him, and Tziva replied to the king, "He
5 is there in the house of Makhir son of Amiel, in Lo Devar." King David sent
and had him brought from the house of Makhir son of Amiel, in Lo Devar.
6 And Mefivoshet son of Yehonatan son of Sha'ul came before David and flung
himself on his face in homage. "Mefivoshet," David said. "Here, at your
7 service," he replied. "Do not be afraid," David said to him, "for I will show you
nothing but kindness, for the sake of Yehonatan, your father. I will restore all
the fields of your grandfather Sha'ul to you, and as for you – you will always
8 dine at my table." He prostrated himself and said, "What is your servant, that
9 you should have turned to a dead dog like me?" The king summoned Tziva,
Sha'ul's lad, and said to him, "I have given all that belonged to Sha'ul and all
10 his household to the son of your master. Now, you shall work his land – you

37 | Cf. Psalms 60:2; 1 Chronicles 18:12.

ו וַיַּךְ דָּוִד בַּאֲרָם עֶשְׂרִים־וּשְׁנַיִם אֶלֶף אִישׁ: וַיָּשֶׂם דָּוִד נְצִבִים בַּאֲרַם
דַּמֶּשֶׂק וַתְּהִי אֲרָם לְדָוִד לַעֲבָדִים נוֹשְׂאֵי מִנְחָה וַיֹּשַׁע יהוה אֶת־
ז דָּוִד בְּכֹל אֲשֶׁר הָלָךְ: וַיִּקַּח דָּוִד אֵת שִׁלְטֵי הַזָּהָב אֲשֶׁר הָיוּ אֶל
ח עַבְדֵי הֲדַדְעָזֶר וַיְבִיאֵם יְרוּשָׁלָם: וּמִבֶּטַח וּמִבֵּרֹתַי עָרֵי הֲדַדְעָזֶר לָקַח
ט הַמֶּלֶךְ דָּוִד נְחֹשֶׁת הַרְבֵּה מְאֹד: וַיִּשְׁמַע תֹּעִי מֶלֶךְ חֲמָת
י כִּי הִכָּה דָוִד אֵת כָּל־חֵיל הֲדַדְעָזֶר: וַיִּשְׁלַח תֹּעִי אֶת־יוֹרָם־בְּנוֹ אֶל־
הַמֶּלֶךְ־דָּוִד לִשְׁאָל־לוֹ לְשָׁלוֹם וּלְבָרְכוֹ עַל אֲשֶׁר נִלְחַם בַּהֲדַדְעֶזֶר
וַיַּכֵּהוּ כִּי־אִישׁ מִלְחֲמוֹת תֹּעִי הָיָה הֲדַדְעָזֶר וּבְיָדוֹ הָיוּ כְּלֵי־כֶסֶף וּכְלֵי־
יא זָהָב וּכְלֵי נְחֹשֶׁת: גַּם־אֹתָם הִקְדִּישׁ הַמֶּלֶךְ דָּוִד לַיהוה עִם־הַכֶּסֶף
יב וְהַזָּהָב אֲשֶׁר הִקְדִּישׁ מִכָּל־הַגּוֹיִם אֲשֶׁר כִּבֵּשׁ: מֵאֲרָם וּמִמּוֹאָב וּמִבְּנֵי
עַמּוֹן וּמִפְּלִשְׁתִּים וּמֵעֲמָלֵק וּמִשְּׁלַל הֲדַדְעֶזֶר בֶּן־רְחֹב מֶלֶךְ צוֹבָה:
יג וַיַּעַשׂ דָּוִד שֵׁם בְּשֻׁבוֹ מֵהַכּוֹתוֹ אֶת־אֲרָם בְּגֵיא־מֶלַח שְׁמוֹנָה עָשָׂר
יד אָלֶף: וַיָּשֶׂם בֶּאֱדוֹם נְצִבִים בְּכָל־אֱדוֹם שָׂם נְצִבִים וַיְהִי כָל־אֱדוֹם
טו עֲבָדִים לְדָוִד וַיּוֹשַׁע יהוה אֶת־דָּוִד בְּכֹל אֲשֶׁר הָלָךְ: וַיִּמְלֹךְ דָּוִד עַל־
טז כָּל־יִשְׂרָאֵל וַיְהִי דָוִד עֹשֶׂה מִשְׁפָּט וּצְדָקָה לְכָל־עַמּוֹ: וְיוֹאָב בֶּן־צְרוּיָה
יז עַל־הַצָּבָא וִיהוֹשָׁפָט בֶּן־אֲחִילוּד מַזְכִּיר: וְצָדוֹק בֶּן־אֲחִיטוּב וַאֲחִימֶלֶךְ
יח בֶּן־אֶבְיָתָר כֹּהֲנִים וּשְׂרָיָה סוֹפֵר: וּבְנָיָהוּ בֶּן־יְהוֹיָדָע וְהַכְּרֵתִי וְהַפְּלֵתִי
ט א וּבְנֵי דָוִד כֹּהֲנִים הָיוּ: וַיֹּאמֶר דָּוִד הֲכִי יֶשׁ־עוֹד אֲשֶׁר נוֹתַר
ב לְבֵית שָׁאוּל וְאֶעֱשֶׂה עִמּוֹ חֶסֶד בַּעֲבוּר יְהוֹנָתָן: וּלְבֵית שָׁאוּל עֶבֶד
וּשְׁמוֹ צִיבָא וַיִּקְרְאוּ־לוֹ אֶל־דָּוִד וַיֹּאמֶר הַמֶּלֶךְ אֵלָיו הַאַתָּה צִיבָא
ג וַיֹּאמֶר עַבְדֶּךָ: וַיֹּאמֶר הַמֶּלֶךְ הַאֶפֶס עוֹד אִישׁ לְבֵית שָׁאוּל וְאֶעֱשֶׂה
עִמּוֹ חֶסֶד אֱלֹהִים וַיֹּאמֶר צִיבָא אֶל־הַמֶּלֶךְ עוֹד בֵּן לִיהוֹנָתָן נְכֵה
ד רַגְלָיִם: וַיֹּאמֶר־לוֹ הַמֶּלֶךְ אֵיפֹה הוּא וַיֹּאמֶר צִיבָא אֶל־הַמֶּלֶךְ הִנֵּה־
ה הוּא בֵּית מָכִיר בֶּן־עַמִּיאֵל בְּלוֹ דְבָר: וַיִּשְׁלַח הַמֶּלֶךְ דָּוִד וַיִּקָּחֵהוּ
ו מִבֵּית מָכִיר בֶּן־עַמִּיאֵל מִלּוֹ דְבָר: וַיָּבֹא מְפִיבֹשֶׁת בֶּן־יְהוֹנָתָן בֶּן־
שָׁאוּל אֶל־דָּוִד וַיִּפֹּל עַל־פָּנָיו וַיִּשְׁתָּחוּ וַיֹּאמֶר דָּוִד מְפִיבֹשֶׁת וַיֹּאמֶר
ז הִנֵּה עַבְדֶּךָ: וַיֹּאמֶר לוֹ דָוִד אַל־תִּירָא כִּי עָשֹׂה אֶעֱשֶׂה עִמְּךָ חֶסֶד
בַּעֲבוּר יְהוֹנָתָן אָבִיךָ וַהֲשִׁבֹתִי לְךָ אֶת־כָּל־שְׂדֵה שָׁאוּל אָבִיךָ וְאַתָּה
ח תֹּאכַל לֶחֶם עַל־שֻׁלְחָנִי תָּמִיד: וַיִּשְׁתַּחוּ וַיֹּאמֶר מֶה עַבְדֶּךָ כִּי פָנִיתָ
ט אֶל־הַכֶּלֶב הַמֵּת אֲשֶׁר כָּמוֹנִי: וַיִּקְרָא הַמֶּלֶךְ אֶל־צִיבָא נַעַר שָׁאוּל
וַיֹּאמֶר אֵלָיו כֹּל אֲשֶׁר הָיָה לְשָׁאוּל וּלְכָל־בֵּיתוֹ נָתַתִּי לְבֶן־אֲדֹנֶיךָ:
י וְעָבַדְתָּ לּוֹ אֶת־הָאֲדָמָה אַתָּה וּבָנֶיךָ וַעֲבָדֶיךָ וְהֵבֵאתָ וְהָיָה לְבֶן־אֲדֹנֶיךָ

and your sons and your slaves – and bring in food, so that the son of your
master will have sustenance; but Mefivoshet, son of your master, will always
11 dine at my table." Now Tziva had fifteen sons and twenty slaves. And Tziva
replied to the king, "Whatever the king commands his servant – so your
servant shall do." "Yes, Mefivoshet shall dine at my table, like one of the
12 king's sons." Mefivoshet had a small son whose name was Mikha; and all the
13 members of Tziva's household were Mefivoshet's servants. But Mefivoshet
lived in Jerusalem, for he always dined at the king's table. Both his feet were
10 1 crippled. Sometime later, the king of the Amonites died, and
2 Ḥanun, his son, reigned in his place. "I will show loyalty to Ḥanun son of
Naḥash," said David, "just as his father showed loyalty to me." David sent his
condolences for his father through his officials, and David's officials reached
3 the land of the Amonites. But the ministers of the Amonites said to their
master Ḥanun, "Do you really think that David honors your father because
he sent you condolences? No – David sent his officials to you to scout and
4 spy out the city to overthrow it." So Ḥanun had David's officials seized; he
shaved half their beards, cut off half of their uniforms – until their buttocks –
5 and sent them off. They reported this to David, and he sent word out to them,
for the men were utterly humiliated. "Remain in Jericho until your beards
6 grow," said the king, "and then return." When the Amonites realized that they
had become odious to David, the Amonites sent and hired twenty thousand
infantrymen from Aram of Beit Reḥov and Aram Tzova, a thousand men from
7 the king of Maakha, and twelve thousand men from Tov. When David heard,
8 he sent Yoav together with his entire military force. The Amonites advanced
and deployed for battle by the entrance of the gate, while the Arameans of
Tzova and Reḥov, the men of Tov, and Maakha were stationed separately, in
9 the open field. Yoav saw that he was faced with battle before him and behind
10 him, so he selected all of Israel's elite troops and deployed against Aram. He
handed command of the remaining troops to his brother Avshai and deployed
11 them against the Amonites. "If Aram overpowers me, come to my aid," he
12 said, "and if the Amonites overpower you, I will come to your aid. Let us be
strong and remain strong for the sake of our people and the cities of our
13 God – and may the Lord do as He sees fit." Then Yoav and all the troops with
14 him charged out to battle against Aram, who fled before them. When the
Amonites saw that Aram had fled, they fled before Avishai and entered the
15 city, so Yoav withdrew his attack on the Amonites and came to Jerusalem. But
when Aram saw that it had been defeated by Israel, they regrouped their
16 forces. Hadadezer sent and summoned Aram from across the Euphrates, and
their forces marched out with Shovakh, Hadadezer's army commander, at
17 their head. When this was reported to David, he mustered all of Israel and
crossed the Jordan; and when he reached Ḥelam, the Arameans charged out
18 toward David and fought against him. But Aram fled before Israel, and David
killed seven hundred charioteers and forty thousand riders of Aram, and as

לֶחֶם וַאֲכָלוֹ וּמְפִיבֹשֶׁת בֶּן־אֲדֹנֶיךָ יֹאכַל תָּמִיד לֶחֶם עַל־שֻׁלְחָנִי וּלְצִיבָא
יא חֲמִשָּׁה עָשָׂר בָּנִים וְעֶשְׂרִים עֲבָדִים׃ וַיֹּאמֶר צִיבָא אֶל־הַמֶּלֶךְ כְּכֹל
אֲשֶׁר יְצַוֶּה אֲדֹנִי הַמֶּלֶךְ אֶת־עַבְדּוֹ כֵּן יַעֲשֶׂה עַבְדֶּךָ וּמְפִיבֹשֶׁת אֹכֵל
יב עַל־שֻׁלְחָנִי כְּאַחַד מִבְּנֵי הַמֶּלֶךְ׃ וְלִמְפִיבֹשֶׁת בֵּן־קָטָן וּשְׁמוֹ מִיכָא וְכֹל
יג מוֹשַׁב בֵּית־צִיבָא עֲבָדִים לִמְפִיבֹשֶׁת׃ וּמְפִיבֹשֶׁת יֹשֵׁב בִּירוּשָׁלִַם כִּי
י א עַל־שֻׁלְחַן הַמֶּלֶךְ תָּמִיד הוּא אֹכֵל וְהוּא פִּסֵּחַ שְׁתֵּי רַגְלָיו׃ וַיְהִי
ב אַחֲרֵי־כֵן וַיָּמָת מֶלֶךְ בְּנֵי עַמּוֹן וַיִּמְלֹךְ חָנוּן בְּנוֹ תַּחְתָּיו׃ וַיֹּאמֶר דָּוִד
אֶעֱשֶׂה־חֶסֶד ׀ עִם־חָנוּן בֶּן־נָחָשׁ כַּאֲשֶׁר עָשָׂה אָבִיו עִמָּדִי חֶסֶד וַיִּשְׁלַח
דָּוִד לְנַחֲמוֹ בְּיַד־עֲבָדָיו אֶל־אָבִיו וַיָּבֹאוּ עַבְדֵי דָוִד אֶרֶץ בְּנֵי עַמּוֹן׃
ג וַיֹּאמְרוּ שָׂרֵי בְנֵי־עַמּוֹן אֶל־חָנוּן אֲדֹנֵיהֶם הַמְכַבֵּד דָּוִד אֶת־אָבִיךָ
בְּעֵינֶיךָ כִּי־שָׁלַח לְךָ מְנַחֲמִים הֲלוֹא בַּעֲבוּר חֲקֹר אֶת־הָעִיר וּלְרַגְּלָהּ
ד וּלְהָפְכָהּ שָׁלַח דָּוִד אֶת־עֲבָדָיו אֵלֶיךָ׃ וַיִּקַּח חָנוּן אֶת־עַבְדֵי דָוִד וַיְגַלַּח
אֶת־חֲצִי זְקָנָם וַיִּכְרֹת אֶת־מַדְוֵיהֶם בַּחֵצִי עַד־שְׁתוֹתֵיהֶם וַיְשַׁלְּחֵם׃
ה וַיַּגִּדוּ לְדָוִד וַיִּשְׁלַח לִקְרָאתָם כִּי־הָיוּ הָאֲנָשִׁים נִכְלָמִים מְאֹד וַיֹּאמֶר
ו הַמֶּלֶךְ שְׁבוּ בִירֵחוֹ עַד־יְצַמַּח זְקַנְכֶם וְשַׁבְתֶּם׃ וַיִּרְאוּ בְּנֵי עַמּוֹן כִּי
נִבְאֲשׁוּ בְּדָוִד וַיִּשְׁלְחוּ בְנֵי־עַמּוֹן וַיִּשְׂכְּרוּ אֶת־אֲרַם בֵּית־רְחוֹב וְאֶת־
אֲרַם צוֹבָא עֶשְׂרִים אֶלֶף רַגְלִי וְאֶת־מֶלֶךְ מַעֲכָה אֶלֶף אִישׁ וְאִישׁ טוֹב
ז שְׁנֵים־עָשָׂר אֶלֶף אִישׁ׃ וַיִּשְׁמַע דָּוִד וַיִּשְׁלַח אֶת־יוֹאָב וְאֵת כָּל־הַצָּבָא
ח הַגִּבֹּרִים׃ וַיֵּצְאוּ בְּנֵי עַמּוֹן וַיַּעַרְכוּ מִלְחָמָה פֶּתַח הַשָּׁעַר וַאֲרַם צוֹבָא
ט וּרְחוֹב וְאִישׁ־טוֹב וּמַעֲכָה לְבַדָּם בַּשָּׂדֶה׃ וַיַּרְא יוֹאָב כִּי־הָיְתָה אֵלָיו
פְּנֵי הַמִּלְחָמָה מִפָּנִים וּמֵאָחוֹר וַיִּבְחַר מִכֹּל בְּחוּרֵי בְּיִשְׂרָאֵל וַיַּעֲרֹךְ יִשְׂרָאֵל
י לִקְרַאת אֲרָם׃ וְאֵת יֶתֶר הָעָם נָתַן בְּיַד אַבְשַׁי אָחִיו וַיַּעֲרֹךְ לִקְרַאת
יא בְּנֵי עַמּוֹן׃ וַיֹּאמֶר אִם־תֶּחֱזַק אֲרָם מִמֶּנִּי וְהָיְתָה לִּי לִישׁוּעָה וְאִם־בְּנֵי
יב עַמּוֹן יֶחֶזְקוּ מִמְּךָ וְהָלַכְתִּי לְהוֹשִׁיעַ לָךְ׃ חֲזַק וְנִתְחַזַּק בְּעַד עַמֵּנוּ
יג וּבְעַד עָרֵי אֱלֹהֵינוּ וַיהוָה יַעֲשֶׂה הַטּוֹב בְּעֵינָיו׃ וַיִּגַּשׁ יוֹאָב וְהָעָם אֲשֶׁר כה
יד עִמּוֹ לַמִּלְחָמָה בַּאֲרָם וַיָּנֻסוּ מִפָּנָיו׃ וּבְנֵי עַמּוֹן ׀ רָאוּ כִּי־נָס אֲרָם וַיָּנֻסוּ
מִפְּנֵי אֲבִישַׁי וַיָּבֹאוּ הָעִיר וַיָּשָׁב יוֹאָב מֵעַל בְּנֵי עַמּוֹן וַיָּבֹא יְרוּשָׁלִָם׃
טו טז וַיַּרְא אֲרָם כִּי נִגַּף לִפְנֵי יִשְׂרָאֵל וַיֵּאָסְפוּ יָחַד׃ וַיִּשְׁלַח הֲדַדְעֶזֶר וַיֹּצֵא
אֶת־אֲרָם אֲשֶׁר מֵעֵבֶר הַנָּהָר וַיָּבֹאוּ חֵילָם וְשׁוֹבַךְ שַׂר־צְבָא הֲדַדְעֶזֶר
יז לִפְנֵיהֶם׃ וַיֻּגַּד לְדָוִד וַיֶּאֱסֹף אֶת־כָּל־יִשְׂרָאֵל וַיַּעֲבֹר אֶת־הַיַּרְדֵּן וַיָּבֹא
יח חֵלָאמָה וַיַּעַרְכוּ אֲרָם לִקְרַאת דָּוִד וַיִּלָּחֲמוּ עִמּוֹ׃ וַיָּנָס אֲרָם מִפְּנֵי
יִשְׂרָאֵל וַיַּהֲרֹג דָּוִד מֵאֲרָם שְׁבַע מֵאוֹת רֶכֶב וְאַרְבָּעִים אֶלֶף פָּרָשִׁים

for Shovakh, their army commander, he struck him down, and he died on
19 the spot. When all the kings who were subject to Hadadezer realized that
they had been routed before Israel, they surrendered to Israel and became
subject to them. And Aram was too frightened to come to the Amonites' aid
11 1 again. The next spring – when kings launch campaigns – David sent
out Yoav together with his officers and all of Israel. They ravaged the Amonites
2 and besieged Raba – while David remained in Jerusalem. As dusk
was falling, David rose from his bed and went for a stroll upon the roof of the
palace. And from the roof, he saw a woman bathing, and the woman was
3 absolutely beautiful. David sent and made inquiries about the woman and
4 was told, "She is Batsheva, daughter of Eliam, wife of Uriya the Hittite." David
sent messengers to fetch her. She came to him, and he lay with her – she had
5 just cleansed herself from her impurity. Then she returned home. The woman
6 conceived and sent word to David. "I am pregnant," she said. So David sent
a message to Yoav, "Send Uriya the Hittite to me," and Yoav sent Uriya to
7 David. When Uriya came to him, David asked how Yoav was faring, how the
8 troops were faring, and how the war was faring. "Go down to your home,"
David then said to Uriya, "and bathe your feet." When Uriya left the king's
9 palace, royal provisions were brought out after him. But Uriya lay at the
entrance of the king's palace along with all his lord's servants and did not go
10 down to his own home. When they told David, "Uriya has not gone down to
his home," David said to Uriya, "You have just come from a journey; why do
11 you not go down to your home?" "The Ark and Israel and Yehuda are dwelling
in huts," Uriya said to David, "and my lord Yoav and my lord's officers are
camping in the open field – how can I come to my own home, to eat and drink
and lie with my wife? By your life – by your very life – I will not do such a
12 thing." "Stay here today as well," David said to Uriya, "and tomorrow I will
13 send you off." And Uriya stayed in Jerusalem that day and the next. David
summoned him to eat and drink in his presence, and he got him drunk. But
he left in the evening to lie on his bed with his lord's servants – he did not go
14 down to his own home. In the morning, David wrote a letter to Yoav and sent
15 it by Uriya's hand. The letter he wrote said, "Position Uriya in the front line
where the battle is thickest, and then retreat, so he will be struck down and
16 killed." And when Yoav was keeping watch over the city, he assigned
17 Uriya a position where he knew the seasoned warriors would be. The men of
the city charged out and fought against Yoav, and some of the troops, David's
18 men, fell; Uriya the Hittite was among the dead. Yoav sent a message to David,
19 giving him a full report of the war. He instructed the messenger as follows:
20 "When you have finished giving the full report of the war to the king, if the
king's fury is roused, and he says to you, 'Why did you approach the city to

יט וְאֵת שׁוֹבַךְ שַׂר־צְבָאוֹ הִכָּה וַיָּמָת שָׁם׃ וַיִּרְאוּ כָל־הַמְּלָכִים עַבְדֵי
הֲדַדְעֶזֶר כִּי נִגְּפוּ לִפְנֵי יִשְׂרָאֵל וַיַּשְׁלִמוּ אֶת־יִשְׂרָאֵל וַיַּעַבְדוּם וַיִּרְאוּ
יא א אֲרָם לְהוֹשִׁיעַ עוֹד אֶת־בְּנֵי עַמּוֹן׃ וַיְהִי לִתְשׁוּבַת הַשָּׁנָה
לְעֵת | צֵאת הַמְּלָאכִים וַיִּשְׁלַח דָּוִד אֶת־יוֹאָב וְאֶת־עֲבָדָיו עִמּוֹ
וְאֶת־כָּל־יִשְׂרָאֵל וַיַּשְׁחִתוּ אֶת־בְּנֵי עַמּוֹן וַיָּצֻרוּ עַל־רַבָּה וְדָוִד יוֹשֵׁב
ב בִּירוּשָׁלָ‍ִם׃ וַיְהִי | לְעֵת הָעֶרֶב וַיָּקָם דָּוִד מֵעַל מִשְׁכָּבוֹ
וַיִּתְהַלֵּךְ עַל־גַּג בֵּית־הַמֶּלֶךְ וַיַּרְא אִשָּׁה רֹחֶצֶת מֵעַל הַגָּג וְהָאִשָּׁה
ג טוֹבַת מַרְאֶה מְאֹד׃ וַיִּשְׁלַח דָּוִד וַיִּדְרֹשׁ לָאִשָּׁה וַיֹּאמֶר הֲלוֹא־זֹאת
ד בַּת־שֶׁבַע בַּת־אֱלִיעָם אֵשֶׁת אוּרִיָּה הַחִתִּי׃ וַיִּשְׁלַח דָּוִד מַלְאָכִים
וַיִּקָּחֶהָ וַתָּבוֹא אֵלָיו וַיִּשְׁכַּב עִמָּהּ וְהִיא מִתְקַדֶּשֶׁת מִטֻּמְאָתָהּ וַתָּשָׁב
ה אֶל־בֵּיתָהּ׃ וַתַּהַר הָאִשָּׁה וַתִּשְׁלַח וַתַּגֵּד לְדָוִד וַתֹּאמֶר הָרָה אָנֹכִי׃
ו וַיִּשְׁלַח דָּוִד אֶל־יוֹאָב שְׁלַח אֵלַי אֶת־אוּרִיָּה הַחִתִּי וַיִּשְׁלַח יוֹאָב אֶת־
ז אוּרִיָּה אֶל־דָּוִד׃ וַיָּבֹא אוּרִיָּה אֵלָיו וַיִּשְׁאַל דָּוִד לִשְׁלוֹם יוֹאָב וְלִשְׁלוֹם
ח הָעָם וְלִשְׁלוֹם הַמִּלְחָמָה׃ וַיֹּאמֶר דָּוִד לְאוּרִיָּה רֵד לְבֵיתְךָ וּרְחַץ רַגְלֶיךָ
ט וַיֵּצֵא אוּרִיָּה מִבֵּית הַמֶּלֶךְ וַתֵּצֵא אַחֲרָיו מַשְׂאַת הַמֶּלֶךְ׃ וַיִּשְׁכַּב אוּרִיָּה
י פֶּתַח בֵּית הַמֶּלֶךְ אֵת כָּל־עַבְדֵי אֲדֹנָיו וְלֹא יָרַד אֶל־בֵּיתוֹ׃ וַיַּגִּדוּ לְדָוִד
לֵאמֹר לֹא־יָרַד אוּרִיָּה אֶל־בֵּיתוֹ וַיֹּאמֶר דָּוִד אֶל־אוּרִיָּה הֲלוֹא מִדֶּרֶךְ
יא אַתָּה בָא מַדּוּעַ לֹא־יָרַדְתָּ אֶל־בֵּיתֶךָ׃ וַיֹּאמֶר אוּרִיָּה אֶל־דָּוִד הָאָרוֹן
וְיִשְׂרָאֵל וִיהוּדָה יֹשְׁבִים בַּסֻּכּוֹת וַאדֹנִי יוֹאָב וְעַבְדֵי אֲדֹנִי עַל־פְּנֵי
הַשָּׂדֶה חֹנִים וַאֲנִי אָבוֹא אֶל־בֵּיתִי לֶאֱכֹל וְלִשְׁתּוֹת וְלִשְׁכַּב עִם־אִשְׁתִּי
יב חַיֶּךָ וְחֵי נַפְשֶׁךָ אִם־אֶעֱשֶׂה אֶת־הַדָּבָר הַזֶּה׃ וַיֹּאמֶר דָּוִד אֶל־אוּרִיָּה
שֵׁב בָּזֶה גַּם־הַיּוֹם וּמָחָר אֲשַׁלְּחֶךָּ וַיֵּשֶׁב אוּרִיָּה בִירוּשָׁלַ‍ִם בַּיּוֹם הַהוּא
יג וּמִמָּחֳרָת׃ וַיִּקְרָא־לוֹ דָוִד וַיֹּאכַל לְפָנָיו וַיֵּשְׁתְּ וַיְשַׁכְּרֵהוּ וַיֵּצֵא בָעֶרֶב
יד לִשְׁכַּב בְּמִשְׁכָּבוֹ עִם־עַבְדֵי אֲדֹנָיו וְאֶל־בֵּיתוֹ לֹא יָרָד׃ וַיְהִי בַבֹּקֶר
טו וַיִּכְתֹּב דָּוִד סֵפֶר אֶל־יוֹאָב וַיִּשְׁלַח בְּיַד אוּרִיָּה׃ וַיִּכְתֹּב בַּסֵּפֶר לֵאמֹר
הָבוּ אֶת־אוּרִיָּה אֶל־מוּל פְּנֵי הַמִּלְחָמָה הַחֲזָקָה וְשַׁבְתֶּם מֵאַחֲרָיו
טז וְנִכָּה וָמֵת׃ וַיְהִי בִּשְׁמוֹר יוֹאָב אֶל־הָעִיר וַיִּתֵּן אֶת־
יז אוּרִיָּה אֶל־הַמָּקוֹם אֲשֶׁר יָדַע כִּי אַנְשֵׁי־חַיִל שָׁם׃ וַיֵּצְאוּ אַנְשֵׁי הָעִיר
וַיִּלָּחֲמוּ אֶת־יוֹאָב וַיִּפֹּל מִן־הָעָם מֵעַבְדֵי דָוִד וַיָּמָת גַּם אוּרִיָּה הַחִתִּי׃
יח יט וַיִּשְׁלַח יוֹאָב וַיַּגֵּד לְדָוִד אֶת־כָּל־דִּבְרֵי הַמִּלְחָמָה׃ וַיְצַו אֶת־הַמַּלְאָךְ
כ לֵאמֹר כְּכַלּוֹתְךָ אֵת כָּל־דִּבְרֵי הַמִּלְחָמָה לְדַבֵּר אֶל־הַמֶּלֶךְ׃ וְהָיָה
אִם־תַּעֲלֶה חֲמַת הַמֶּלֶךְ וְאָמַר לְךָ מַדּוּעַ נִגַּשְׁתֶּם אֶל־הָעִיר לְהִלָּחֵם

21 fight – were you not aware that they would shoot over the wall? Who struck
down Avimelekh son of Yerubeshet?[38] It was a woman who hurled an upper
millstone over the wall, so that he died in Tevetz![39] Why did you approach
the wall?' – then say, 'Your servant, Uriya the Hittite, was among those who
22 died.'" The messenger set out and came to David, to deliver Yoav's full report.
23 "First the men were overpowering us, and they charged out at us toward the
open ground," the messenger said to David, "and then we drove them back
24 to the entrance of the gate. But then the archers shot at your servants from
the wall, and some of the king's servants were killed. Your servant, Uriya the
25 Hittite, was among the dead." "This is what you must say to Yoav,"
David told the messenger, "'Do not take this affair so gravely; the sword
consumes one way or another. Battle on against the city even more fiercely,
26 and destroy it!' Encourage him." Uriya's wife heard that her husband Uriya
27 was dead, and she mourned over her husband. When the mourning period
passed, David sent and had her brought to his palace. She became his wife,
and she bore him a son. But what David had done was grave in the eyes of the
12 1 LORD. The LORD sent the prophet Natan to David, and he came to
him. "There were two men in the same city," he said to him. "One was rich
2 3 and the other poor. The rich man had a great wealth of sheep and cattle, but
the poor man had nothing but one small lamb that he had bought. He
nurtured her, and she grew up together with him and his children; she would
eat from his own crusts of bread and drink from his own cup and sleep curled
4 up in his embrace – she was like his own daughter. But a traveler came to the
house of the rich man, and it seemed a pity to him to take from his own flock
and herd to prepare food for the guest who had come to him. So he took the
5 poor man's lamb and prepared it for the man who had come to him." David's
fury blazed hot against the man. "As the LORD lives," he said to Natan, "the
6 man who did this is a dead man. As for the lamb – he must pay for it four
7 times over for doing such a deed and for having no pity." "You are
the man!" Natan said to David. "Thus says the LORD, God of Israel: I anointed
8 you as king over Israel, and I saved you from the hand of Sha'ul. I gave you
your master's house and your master's wives into your embrace, and I gave
you the House of Israel and Yehuda, and if that would be too little, I would
9 give you even twice as much. Why, then, have you scorned the word of the
LORD, doing such evil in His eyes? You put Uriya the Hittite to the sword and
took his wife as your own wife; you killed him with the sword of the Amonites.
10 And now, the sword will never turn away from your house because you
11 scorned Me and took Uriya the Hittite's wife as your own wife. Thus
says the LORD: I am about to raise up evil against you from within your own
house; I will take your wives before your very eyes and give them to another
12 who will lie with your wives in broad daylight. You acted in secrecy, but I shall

38 | That is, Gidon, also called Yerubaal; see Judges 6:32. *Boshet* is a substitute for *baal*; see note on 2:8.
39 | See Judges 9:53.

כא הֲלוֹא יְדַעְתֶּם אֵת אֲשֶׁר־יֹרוּ מֵעַל הַחוֹמָה: מִֽי־הִכָּה אֶת־אֲבִימֶלֶךְ
בֶּן־יְרֻבֶּשֶׁת הֲלוֹא אִשָּׁה הִשְׁלִיכָה עָלָיו פֶּלַח רֶכֶב מֵעַל הַחוֹמָה וַיָּמָת
בְּתֵבֵץ לָמָּה נִגַּשְׁתֶּם אֶל־הַחוֹמָה וְאָמַרְתָּ גַּם עַבְדְּךָ אוּרִיָּה הַחִתִּי
כב כג מֵת: וַיֵּלֶךְ הַמַּלְאָךְ וַיָּבֹא וַיַּגֵּד לְדָוִד אֵת כָּל־אֲשֶׁר שְׁלָחוֹ יוֹאָב: וַיֹּאמֶר
הַמַּלְאָךְ אֶל־דָּוִד כִּי־גָבְרוּ עָלֵינוּ הָאֲנָשִׁים וַיֵּצְאוּ אֵלֵינוּ הַשָּׂדֶה וַנִּהְיֶה
כד עֲלֵיהֶם עַד־פֶּתַח הַשָּׁעַר: וַיֹּרְאוּ הַמּוֹרְאִים אֶל־עֲבָדֶיךָ מֵעַל הַחוֹמָה
כה וַיָּמוּתוּ מֵעַבְדֵי הַמֶּלֶךְ וְגַם עַבְדְּךָ אוּרִיָּה הַחִתִּי מֵת: וַיֹּאמֶר
דָּוִד אֶל־הַמַּלְאָךְ כֹּה־תֹאמַר אֶל־יוֹאָב אַל־יֵרַע בְּעֵינֶיךָ אֶת־הַדָּבָר
הַזֶּה כִּי־כָזֹה וְכָזֶה תֹּאכַל הֶחָרֶב הַחֲזֵק מִלְחַמְתְּךָ אֶל־הָעִיר וְהָרְסָהּ
כו וְחַזְּקֵהוּ: וַתִּשְׁמַע אֵשֶׁת אוּרִיָּה כִּי־מֵת אוּרִיָּה אִישָׁהּ וַתִּסְפֹּד עַל־
כז בַּעְלָהּ: וַיַּעֲבֹר הָאֵבֶל וַיִּשְׁלַח דָּוִד וַיַּאַסְפָהּ אֶל־בֵּיתוֹ וַתְּהִי־לוֹ לְאִשָּׁה
יב א וַתֵּלֶד לוֹ בֵּן וַיֵּרַע הַדָּבָר אֲשֶׁר־עָשָׂה דָוִד בְּעֵינֵי יְהוָה: וַיִּשְׁלַח
יְהוָה אֶת־נָתָן אֶל־דָּוִד וַיָּבֹא אֵלָיו וַיֹּאמֶר לוֹ שְׁנֵי אֲנָשִׁים הָיוּ בְּעִיר
ב אֶחָת אֶחָד עָשִׁיר וְאֶחָד רָאשׁ: לְעָשִׁיר הָיָה צֹאן וּבָקָר הַרְבֵּה מְאֹד:
ג וְלָרָשׁ אֵין־כֹּל כִּי אִם־כִּבְשָׂה אַחַת קְטַנָּה אֲשֶׁר קָנָה וַיְחַיֶּהָ וַתִּגְדַּל
עִמּוֹ וְעִם־בָּנָיו יַחְדָּו מִפִּתּוֹ תֹאכַל וּמִכֹּסוֹ תִשְׁתֶּה וּבְחֵיקוֹ תִשְׁכָּב
ד וַתְּהִי־לוֹ כְּבַת: וַיָּבֹא הֵלֶךְ לְאִישׁ הֶעָשִׁיר וַיַּחְמֹל לָקַחַת מִצֹּאנוֹ
וּמִבְּקָרוֹ לַעֲשׂוֹת לָאֹרֵחַ הַבָּא לוֹ וַיִּקַּח אֶת־כִּבְשַׂת הָאִישׁ הָרָאשׁ
ה וַיַּעֲשֶׂהָ לָאִישׁ הַבָּא אֵלָיו: וַיִּחַר־אַף דָּוִד בָּאִישׁ מְאֹד וַיֹּאמֶר אֶל־
ו נָתָן חַי־יְהוָה כִּי בֶן־מָוֶת הָאִישׁ הָעֹשֶׂה זֹאת: וְאֶת־הַכִּבְשָׂה
יְשַׁלֵּם אַרְבַּעְתָּיִם עֵקֶב אֲשֶׁר עָשָׂה אֶת־הַדָּבָר הַזֶּה וְעַל אֲשֶׁר לֹא־
ז חָמָל: וַיֹּאמֶר נָתָן אֶל־דָּוִד אַתָּה הָאִישׁ כֹּה־אָמַר יְהוָה
אֱלֹהֵי יִשְׂרָאֵל אָנֹכִי מְשַׁחְתִּיךָ לְמֶלֶךְ עַל־יִשְׂרָאֵל וְאָנֹכִי הִצַּלְתִּיךָ מִיַּד
ח שָׁאוּל: וָאֶתְּנָה לְךָ אֶת־בֵּית אֲדֹנֶיךָ וְאֶת־נְשֵׁי אֲדֹנֶיךָ בְּחֵיקֶךָ וָאֶתְּנָה
לְךָ אֶת־בֵּית יִשְׂרָאֵל וִיהוּדָה וְאִם־מְעָט וְאֹסִפָה לְּךָ כָּהֵנָּה וְכָהֵנָּה:
ט מַדּוּעַ בָּזִיתָ ׀ אֶת־דְּבַר יְהוָה לַעֲשׂוֹת הָרַע בעינו אֵת אוּרִיָּה הַחִתִּי בְּעֵינַי
הִכִּיתָ בַחֶרֶב וְאֶת־אִשְׁתּוֹ לָקַחְתָּ לְּךָ לְאִשָּׁה וְאֹתוֹ הָרַגְתָּ בְּחֶרֶב בְּנֵי
י עַמּוֹן: וְעַתָּה לֹא־תָסוּר חֶרֶב מִבֵּיתְךָ עַד־עוֹלָם עֵקֶב כִּי בְזִתָנִי וַתִּקַּח
יא אֶת־אֵשֶׁת אוּרִיָּה הַחִתִּי לִהְיוֹת לְךָ לְאִשָּׁה: כֹּה ׀ אָמַר
יְהוָה הִנְנִי מֵקִים עָלֶיךָ רָעָה מִבֵּיתֶךָ וְלָקַחְתִּי אֶת־נָשֶׁיךָ לְעֵינֶיךָ
יב וְנָתַתִּי לְרֵעֶיךָ וְשָׁכַב עִם־נָשֶׁיךָ לְעֵינֵי הַשֶּׁמֶשׁ הַזֹּאת: כִּי אַתָּה
עָשִׂיתָ בַסָּתֶר וַאֲנִי אֶעֱשֶׂה אֶת־הַדָּבָר הַזֶּה נֶגֶד כָּל־יִשְׂרָאֵל וְנֶגֶד

13 make this come to pass before all of Israel, in broad daylight." And
David said to Natan, "I have sinned against the LORD." "The LORD
14 has suspended your sin; you shall not die," Natan said to David. "However,
because through this affair you have scorned the enemies of the LORD,[40] the
15 son who has just been born to you will surely die." And with this, Natan went
home. The LORD struck the child that Uriya's wife had borne to David, and
16 he became mortally ill. David pleaded with God for the boy's sake; he fasted
17 and came in and spent the night lying on the ground. The elders of his house
stood over him and urged him to get up from the ground, but he would not
18 agree and would not eat with them. And on the seventh day, when the child
died, David's servants were afraid to tell him that the child was dead. "When
the child was alive, we spoke to him and he would not listen to us," they said,
"so how can we possibly tell him that the child has died? He might do harm."
19 But David saw that his servants were whispering among themselves, and
David understood that the child had died. "Is the child dead?" David asked
20 his servants. "He is dead," they said. David got up from the ground. When he
had washed, anointed himself, and changed his clothes, he came to the House
of the LORD to worship. Then he went back home; at his request they set food
21 before him, and he ate. His servants asked him, "Why have you acted in this
way? While the child was still alive, you fasted and wept, but now that the
22 child is dead, you get up and eat food." "While the child was still alive," he
said, "I fasted and wept, for I thought, 'Who knows; perhaps the LORD will
23 be gracious to me, and the child will live.' But now he is dead – why should I
fast? Will I be able to bring him back again? I shall go to him, but he will never
24 come back to me." And David comforted Batsheva, his wife; he came to her
and lay with her, and she bore a son. She named him Shlomo, and the LORD
25 loved him. And He sent a message through the prophet Natan, naming him
26 Yedidya,[41] for the LORD's sake. Meanwhile, Yoav was fighting against
27 Raba of the Amonites, and he captured the royal city. Yoav sent messengers
to David, reporting, "I have attacked Raba and seized control of the city's
28 water supply. Now muster the rest of the troops and encamp against the city
to capture it; otherwise I will capture the city myself, and my name will be
29 associated with it." So David mustered all the troops and set out for Raba; he
30 fought against it and captured it. And he took their king's crown from upon
his head – it weighed a talent of gold and was set with jewels – and it was
placed on David's head. And he brought out great masses of spoil from the
31 city. As for its people, he brought them out and set them to work with saws
and iron picks and iron axes and made them toil away at the kilns; so he
did for all the Amonite towns. Then David and all the troops returned to
13 1 Jerusalem. Sometime later, this came to pass: Avshalom, David's son,
had a beautiful sister whose name was Tamar, and Amnon, David's son, loved
2 her. Amnon grew obsessed to the point of sickness with his sister Tamar, for
she was a virgin, and it seemed impossible to Amnon that he would ever do

40 | A euphemism used to avoid blasphemy, meaning that he had scorned God Himself.
41 | Literally "the LORD's beloved."

יג הַשָּׁמֶשׁ׃ וַיֹּאמֶר דָּוִד אֶל־נָתָן חָטָאתִי לַיהוָה וַיֹּאמֶר כו
יד נָתָן אֶל־דָּוִד גַּם־יְהוָה הֶעֱבִיר חַטָּאתְךָ לֹא תָמוּת׃ אֶפֶס כִּי־נִאֵץ
טו נִאַצְתָּ אֶת־אֹיְבֵי יְהוָה בַּדָּבָר הַזֶּה גַּם הַבֵּן הַיִּלּוֹד לְךָ מוֹת יָמוּת׃ וַיֵּלֶךְ
נָתָן אֶל־בֵּיתוֹ וַיִּגֹּף יְהוָה אֶת־הַיֶּלֶד אֲשֶׁר יָלְדָה אֵשֶׁת־אוּרִיָּה לְדָוִד
טז וַיֵּאָנַשׁ׃ וַיְבַקֵּשׁ דָּוִד אֶת־הָאֱלֹהִים בְּעַד הַנָּעַר וַיָּצָם דָּוִד צוֹם וּבָא וְלָן
יז וְשָׁכַב אָרְצָה׃ וַיָּקֻמוּ זִקְנֵי בֵיתוֹ עָלָיו לַהֲקִימוֹ מִן־הָאָרֶץ וְלֹא אָבָה
יח וְלֹא־בָרָא אִתָּם לָחֶם׃ וַיְהִי בַּיּוֹם הַשְּׁבִיעִי וַיָּמָת הַיָּלֶד וַיִּרְאוּ עַבְדֵי
דָוִד לְהַגִּיד לוֹ ׀ כִּי־מֵת הַיֶּלֶד כִּי אָמְרוּ הִנֵּה בִהְיוֹת הַיֶּלֶד חַי דִּבַּרְנוּ
אֵלָיו וְלֹא־שָׁמַע בְּקוֹלֵנוּ וְאֵיךְ נֹאמַר אֵלָיו מֵת הַיֶּלֶד וְעָשָׂה רָעָה׃
יט וַיַּרְא דָּוִד כִּי עֲבָדָיו מִתְלַחֲשִׁים וַיָּבֶן דָּוִד כִּי מֵת הַיָּלֶד וַיֹּאמֶר דָּוִד
כ אֶל־עֲבָדָיו הֲמֵת הַיֶּלֶד וַיֹּאמְרוּ מֵת׃ וַיָּקָם דָּוִד מֵהָאָרֶץ וַיִּרְחַץ וַיָּסֶךְ
וַיְחַלֵּף שִׂמְלֹתָו וַיָּבֹא בֵית־יְהוָה וַיִּשְׁתָּחוּ וַיָּבֹא אֶל־בֵּיתוֹ וַיִּשְׁאַל וַיָּשִׂימוּ
כא לוֹ לֶחֶם וַיֹּאכַל׃ וַיֹּאמְרוּ עֲבָדָיו אֵלָיו מָה־הַדָּבָר הַזֶּה אֲשֶׁר עָשִׂיתָה
בַּעֲבוּר הַיֶּלֶד חַי צַמְתָּ וַתֵּבְךְּ וְכַאֲשֶׁר מֵת הַיֶּלֶד קַמְתָּ וַתֹּאכַל לָחֶם׃
כב וַיֹּאמֶר בְּעוֹד הַיֶּלֶד חַי צַמְתִּי וָאֶבְכֶּה כִּי אָמַרְתִּי מִי יוֹדֵעַ יחנני יְהוָה וְחַנַּנִי
כג וְחַי הַיָּלֶד׃ וְעַתָּה ׀ מֵת לָמָּה זֶּה אֲנִי צָם הַאוּכַל לַהֲשִׁיבוֹ עוֹד אֲנִי
כד הֹלֵךְ אֵלָיו וְהוּא לֹא־יָשׁוּב אֵלָי׃ וַיְנַחֵם דָּוִד אֵת בַּת־שֶׁבַע אִשְׁתּוֹ
וַיָּבֹא אֵלֶיהָ וַיִּשְׁכַּב עִמָּהּ וַתֵּלֶד בֵּן ויקרא אֶת־שְׁמוֹ שְׁלֹמֹה וַיהוָה וַתִּקְרָא
כה אֲהֵבוֹ׃ וַיִּשְׁלַח בְּיַד נָתָן הַנָּבִיא וַיִּקְרָא אֶת־שְׁמוֹ יְדִידְיָהּ בַּעֲבוּר
כו יְהוָה׃ וַיִּלָּחֶם יוֹאָב בְּרַבַּת בְּנֵי עַמּוֹן וַיִּלְכֹּד אֶת־עִיר הַמְּלוּכָה׃
כז וַיִּשְׁלַח יוֹאָב מַלְאָכִים אֶל־דָּוִד וַיֹּאמֶר נִלְחַמְתִּי בְרַבָּה גַּם־לָכַדְתִּי
כח אֶת־עִיר הַמָּיִם׃ וְעַתָּה אֱסֹף אֶת־יֶתֶר הָעָם וַחֲנֵה עַל־הָעִיר וְלָכְדָהּ
כט פֶּן־אֶלְכֹּד אֲנִי אֶת־הָעִיר וְנִקְרָא שְׁמִי עָלֶיהָ׃ וַיֶּאֱסֹף דָּוִד אֶת־כָּל־הָעָם
ל וַיֵּלֶךְ רַבָּתָה וַיִּלָּחֶם בָּהּ וַיִּלְכְּדָהּ׃ וַיִּקַּח אֶת־עֲטֶרֶת־מַלְכָּם מֵעַל רֹאשׁוֹ
וּמִשְׁקָלָהּ כִּכַּר זָהָב וְאֶבֶן יְקָרָה וַתְּהִי עַל־רֹאשׁ דָּוִד וּשְׁלַל הָעִיר
לא הוֹצִיא הַרְבֵּה מְאֹד׃ וְאֶת־הָעָם אֲשֶׁר־בָּהּ הוֹצִיא וַיָּשֶׂם בַּמְּגֵרָה וּבַחֲרִצֵי
הַבַּרְזֶל וּבְמַגְזְרֹת הַבַּרְזֶל וְהֶעֱבִיר אוֹתָם במלכן וְכֵן יַעֲשֶׂה לְכֹל עָרֵי בַּמַּלְבֵּן
יג א בְנֵי־עַמּוֹן וַיָּשָׁב דָּוִד וְכָל־הָעָם יְרוּשָׁלִָם׃ וַיְהִי אַחֲרֵי־כֵן
וּלְאַבְשָׁלוֹם בֶּן־דָּוִד אָחוֹת יָפָה וּשְׁמָהּ תָּמָר וַיֶּאֱהָבֶהָ אַמְנוֹן בֶּן־דָּוִד׃
ב וַיֵּצֶר לְאַמְנוֹן לְהִתְחַלּוֹת בַּעֲבוּר תָּמָר אֲחֹתוֹ כִּי בְתוּלָה הִיא וַיִּפָּלֵא

3 anything to her. Now, Amnon had a friend whose name was Yonadav son of
4 Shima, David's brother, and Yonadav was a very shrewd man. "Why do you
grow so haggard from morning to morning, O son of the king?" he asked him.
"Won't you tell me?" "It is Tamar, Avshalom's sister, whom I love," Amnon
5 said to him. "Lie on your bed and feign sickness," Yehonadav said to him, "and
when your father comes to see you, say to him, 'Let my sister Tamar come to
me and serve me food – let her prepare the fare before me, and I will eat
6 from her hand.'" So Amnon lay down and feigned sickness. When the king
came to see him, Amnon said to the king, "Let my sister Tamar come now
and form two heart-cakes before me, and I will take nourishment from her
7 hand." And David sent for Tamar at home, saying, "Now go to your brother
8 Amnon's house and prepare nourishment for him." Tamar went to her brother
Amnon's house; he was lying down. She took the dough and kneaded it and
9 formed it in his sight and cooked the heart-cakes. She took the pan and set it
before him, but he refused to eat. "Have everyone leave my presence!" Amnon
10 said, and everyone left his presence. "Bring the nourishment into the inner
chamber," Amnon said to Tamar, "and I will take nourishment from your
hand." So Tamar took the heart-cakes she had prepared and brought them to
11 Amnon, her brother, into the inner chamber. But when she served them to
him, to eat, he grasped hold of her and said to her, "Come, lie with me, my
12 sister." "No, my brother," she said to him, "do not violate me – such things are
13 not done in Israel. Do not commit such an outrage. As for me – where will I
drive my shame? While you – you will be considered a vile man in Israel!
14 Speak to the king now, for he will not hold me back from you." But he would
not heed her voice, and he overpowered her and violated her and lay with her.
15 Then Amnon hated her with a fierce hatred; his hatred for her was fiercer than
the love he had felt toward her. And Amnon said to her, "Get up! Be gone!"
16 "Don't!" she said to him. "This great wrong – to send me away – would be
17 even worse than what you did to me before." But he would not heed her. He
called his servant boy and said to him, "Send this away from me now, outside,
18 and lock the door behind her." She wore an ornate tunic, for the virgin
daughters of the king wore such robes. But when his servant boy put her
19 outside and locked the door behind her, Tamar put ashes on her head and
tore the ornate tunic that she wore; she put her hand to her head and went
20 off, screaming as she went. And Avshalom, her brother, said to her, "Has your
brother Amnon been with you? For now, my sister, be silent; he is your
brother. Do not take this affair to heart." And Tamar remained, forlorn, in the
21 house of her brother Avshalom. When King David heard all about this affair,
22 he was absolutely livid. And Avshalom would not speak a word to Amnon,
neither good nor bad, for Avshalom despised Amnon for having violated

ג בְּעֵינֵי אַמְנוֹן לַעֲשׂוֹת לָהּ מְאוּמָה: וּלְאַמְנוֹן רֵעַ וּשְׁמוֹ יוֹנָדָב בֶּן־שִׁמְעָה
ד אֲחִי דָוִד וְיוֹנָדָב אִישׁ חָכָם מְאֹד: וַיֹּאמֶר לוֹ מַדּוּעַ אַתָּה כָּכָה דַּל בֶּן־
הַמֶּלֶךְ בַּבֹּקֶר בַּבֹּקֶר הֲלוֹא תַּגִּיד לִי וַיֹּאמֶר לוֹ אַמְנוֹן אֶת־תָּמָר אֲחוֹת
ה אַבְשָׁלֹם אָחִי אֲנִי אֹהֵב: וַיֹּאמֶר לוֹ יְהוֹנָדָב שְׁכַב עַל־מִשְׁכָּבְךָ וְהִתְחָל
וּבָא אָבִיךָ לִרְאוֹתֶךָ וְאָמַרְתָּ אֵלָיו תָּבֹא נָא תָמָר אֲחוֹתִי וְתַבְרֵנִי לֶחֶם
ו וְעָשְׂתָה לְעֵינַי אֶת־הַבִּרְיָה לְמַעַן אֲשֶׁר אֶרְאֶה וְאָכַלְתִּי מִיָּדָהּ: וַיִּשְׁכַּב
אַמְנוֹן וַיִּתְחָל וַיָּבֹא הַמֶּלֶךְ לִרְאוֹתוֹ וַיֹּאמֶר אַמְנוֹן אֶל־הַמֶּלֶךְ תָּבוֹא־
ז נָא תָּמָר אֲחֹתִי וּתְלַבֵּב לְעֵינַי שְׁתֵּי לְבִבוֹת וְאֶבְרֶה מִיָּדָהּ: וַיִּשְׁלַח
דָּוִד אֶל־תָּמָר הַבַּיְתָה לֵאמֹר לְכִי נָא בֵּית אַמְנוֹן אָחִיךְ וַעֲשִׂי־לוֹ
ח הַבִּרְיָה: וַתֵּלֶךְ תָּמָר בֵּית אַמְנוֹן אָחִיהָ וְהוּא שֹׁכֵב וַתִּקַּח אֶת־הַבָּצֵק
ט ותלוש וַתְּלַבֵּב לְעֵינָיו וַתְּבַשֵּׁל אֶת־הַלְּבִבוֹת: וַתִּקַּח אֶת־הַמַּשְׂרֵת וַתָּלָשׁ
וַתִּצֹק לְפָנָיו וַיְמָאֵן לֶאֱכוֹל וַיֹּאמֶר אַמְנוֹן הוֹצִיאוּ כָל־אִישׁ מֵעָלַי וַיֵּצְאוּ
י כָל־אִישׁ מֵעָלָיו: וַיֹּאמֶר אַמְנוֹן אֶל־תָּמָר הָבִיאִי הַבִּרְיָה הַחֶדֶר וְאֶבְרֶה
מִיָּדֵךְ וַתִּקַּח תָּמָר אֶת־הַלְּבִבוֹת אֲשֶׁר עָשָׂתָה וַתָּבֵא לְאַמְנוֹן אָחִיהָ
יא הֶחָדְרָה: וַתַּגֵּשׁ אֵלָיו לֶאֱכֹל וַיַּחֲזֶק־בָּהּ וַיֹּאמֶר לָהּ בּוֹאִי שִׁכְבִי עִמִּי
יב אֲחוֹתִי: וַתֹּאמֶר לוֹ אַל־אָחִי אַל־תְּעַנֵּנִי כִּי לֹא־יֵעָשֶׂה כֵן בְּיִשְׂרָאֵל
יג אַל־תַּעֲשֵׂה אֶת־הַנְּבָלָה הַזֹּאת: וַאֲנִי אָנָה אוֹלִיךְ אֶת־חֶרְפָּתִי וְאַתָּה
תִּהְיֶה כְּאַחַד הַנְּבָלִים בְּיִשְׂרָאֵל וְעַתָּה דַּבֶּר־נָא אֶל־הַמֶּלֶךְ כִּי לֹא
יד יִמְנָעֵנִי מִמֶּךָּ: וְלֹא אָבָה לִשְׁמֹעַ בְּקוֹלָהּ וַיֶּחֱזַק מִמֶּנָּה וַיְעַנֶּהָ וַיִּשְׁכַּב
טו אֹתָהּ: וַיִּשְׂנָאֶהָ אַמְנוֹן שִׂנְאָה גְּדוֹלָה מְאֹד כִּי גְדוֹלָה הַשִּׂנְאָה אֲשֶׁר
טז שְׂנֵאָהּ מֵאַהֲבָה אֲשֶׁר אֲהֵבָהּ וַיֹּאמֶר־לָהּ אַמְנוֹן קוּמִי לֵכִי: וַתֹּאמֶר
לוֹ אַל־אוֹדֹת הָרָעָה הַגְּדוֹלָה הַזֹּאת מֵאַחֶרֶת אֲשֶׁר־עָשִׂיתָ עִמִּי
יז לְשַׁלְּחֵנִי וְלֹא אָבָה לִשְׁמֹעַ לָהּ: וַיִּקְרָא אֶת־נַעֲרוֹ מְשָׁרְתוֹ וַיֹּאמֶר
יח שִׁלְחוּ־נָא אֶת־זֹאת מֵעָלַי הַחוּצָה וּנְעֹל הַדֶּלֶת אַחֲרֶיהָ: וְעָלֶיהָ כְּתֹנֶת
פַּסִּים כִּי כֵן תִּלְבַּשְׁןָ בְנוֹת־הַמֶּלֶךְ הַבְּתוּלֹת מְעִילִים וַיֹּצֵא אוֹתָהּ
יט מְשָׁרְתוֹ הַחוּץ וְנָעַל הַדֶּלֶת אַחֲרֶיהָ: וַתִּקַּח תָּמָר אֵפֶר עַל־רֹאשָׁהּ
וּכְתֹנֶת הַפַּסִּים אֲשֶׁר עָלֶיהָ קָרָעָה וַתָּשֶׂם יָדָהּ עַל־רֹאשָׁהּ וַתֵּלֶךְ הָלוֹךְ
כ וְזָעָקָה: וַיֹּאמֶר אֵלֶיהָ אַבְשָׁלוֹם אָחִיהָ הַאֲמִינוֹן אָחִיךְ הָיָה עִמָּךְ וְעַתָּה
אֲחוֹתִי הַחֲרִישִׁי אָחִיךְ הוּא אַל־תָּשִׁיתִי אֶת־לִבֵּךְ לַדָּבָר הַזֶּה וַתֵּשֶׁב
כא תָּמָר וְשֹׁמֵמָה בֵּית אַבְשָׁלוֹם אָחִיהָ: וְהַמֶּלֶךְ דָּוִד שָׁמַע אֵת כָּל־
כב הַדְּבָרִים הָאֵלֶּה וַיִּחַר לוֹ מְאֹד: וְלֹא־דִבֶּר אַבְשָׁלוֹם עִם־אַמְנוֹן לְמֵרָע
וְעַד־טוֹב כִּי־שָׂנֵא אַבְשָׁלוֹם אֶת־אַמְנוֹן עַל־דְּבַר אֲשֶׁר עִנָּה אֵת תָּמָר

23 Tamar, his sister. But two years later, when Avshalom held a sheep-
24 shearing at Baal Hatzor in Efrayim, Avshalom invited all the king's sons. And
Avshalom came to the king and said, "Now, your servant is holding a sheep-
25 shearing. Let the king and his servants accompany your servant." "No, my
son," the king said to Avshalom, "we must not all come together, and impose
upon you." He pressed him, but he would not agree to go and bade Avshalom
26 farewell. "If not," said Avshalom, "let my brother Amnon accompany us."
27 "Why should he go with you?" asked the king. But Avshalom pressed him,
28 and he sent Amnon with him along with all the king's sons. Avshalom
then instructed his lads, saying, "Now look. When Amnon's heart is merry
with wine, and I say to you, 'Strike Amnon down,' then kill him; do not fear,
29 for I am the one giving you the order. Act boldly, like warriors." And when
Avshalom's lads did to Amnon just as Avshalom had instructed, all the king's
30 sons rose, mounted their mules, and fled. They were on their way when the
rumor reached David: "Avshalom has struck down all of the king's sons, and
31 not a single one is left." And the king got up and rent his clothes and
lay down on the ground, while all his servants stood around him with their
32 garments rent. But Yonadav son of Shima, David's brother, spoke
up. "My lord must not think that they have killed all of the young men,
the king's sons; for Amnon alone is dead – this has been determined by
33 Avshalom since the day he violated his sister Tamar. Now, my lord king must
not take the idea to heart that all the king's sons are dead, for Amnon alone
34 is dead." Meanwhile, Avshalom had fled. And the lookout boy raised
his eyes and suddenly saw a great crowd coming from the rear road by the
35 hillside. And Yonadav said to the king, "Look – the king's sons have come,
36 just as your servant said they would." And as he finished speaking, the king's
sons arrived and burst out weeping, and the king and all his servants wept
37 too, heaving with sobs. Now Avshalom had fled; he went to Talmai son
38 of Amihud, king of Geshur, while David mourned his son all the while.
39 Avshalom had fled and gone to Geshur and was there for three years. Then
David was no longer driven to march out against Avshalom, for he had grown
14 1 reconciled to Amnon's death. Now, Yoav son of Tzeruya knew
2 that the king's mind was on Avshalom. And Yoav sent to Tekoa and fetched a
wise woman from there. "Now pretend you are mourning," he said to her.
"Don mourning garb, do not anoint yourself with oil, and act like a woman
3 who has been mourning the dead for a long time. When you come to the king,
4 this is what you must say...," and Yoav put the words in her mouth. When
the Tekoite woman spoke to the king, she flung her face to the ground
5 and bowed down low. "Help, O king!" she said. "What is the matter?"
the king asked her. "I am but a widow woman," she said. "My husband

כג אֲחֹתוֹ: וַיְהִי לִשְׁנָתַיִם יָמִים וַיִּהְיוּ גֹזְזִים לְאַבְשָׁלוֹם בְּבַעַל
כד חָצוֹר אֲשֶׁר עִם־אֶפְרָיִם וַיִּקְרָא אַבְשָׁלוֹם לְכָל־בְּנֵי הַמֶּלֶךְ: וַיָּבֹא
אַבְשָׁלוֹם אֶל־הַמֶּלֶךְ וַיֹּאמֶר הִנֵּה־נָא גֹזְזִים לְעַבְדֶּךָ יֵלֶךְ־נָא הַמֶּלֶךְ
כה וַעֲבָדָיו עִם־עַבְדֶּךָ: וַיֹּאמֶר הַמֶּלֶךְ אֶל־אַבְשָׁלוֹם אַל־בְּנִי אַל־נָא כז
נֵלֵךְ כֻּלָּנוּ וְלֹא נִכְבַּד עָלֶיךָ וַיִּפְרָץ־בּוֹ וְלֹא־אָבָה לָלֶכֶת וַיְבָרְכֵהוּ:
כו וַיֹּאמֶר אַבְשָׁלֹם וָלֹא יֵלֶךְ־נָא אִתָּנוּ אַמְנוֹן אָחִי וַיֹּאמֶר לוֹ הַמֶּלֶךְ
כז לָמָּה יֵלֵךְ עִמָּךְ: וַיִּפְרָץ־בּוֹ אַבְשָׁלוֹם וַיִּשְׁלַח אִתּוֹ אֶת־אַמְנוֹן וְאֵת
כח כָּל־בְּנֵי הַמֶּלֶךְ: וַיְצַו אַבְשָׁלוֹם אֶת־נְעָרָיו לֵאמֹר רְאוּ־
נָא כְּטוֹב לֵב־אַמְנוֹן בַּיַּיִן וְאָמַרְתִּי אֲלֵיכֶם הַכּוּ אֶת־אַמְנוֹן וַהֲמִתֶּם
אֹתוֹ אַל־תִּירָאוּ הֲלוֹא כִּי אָנֹכִי צִוִּיתִי אֶתְכֶם חִזְקוּ וִהְיוּ לִבְנֵי־חָיִל:
כט וַיַּעֲשׂוּ נַעֲרֵי אַבְשָׁלוֹם לְאַמְנוֹן כַּאֲשֶׁר צִוָּה אַבְשָׁלֹם וַיָּקֻמוּ | כָּל־בְּנֵי
ל הַמֶּלֶךְ וַיִּרְכְּבוּ אִישׁ עַל־פִּרְדּוֹ וַיָּנֻסוּ: וַיְהִי הֵמָּה בַדֶּרֶךְ וְהַשְּׁמֻעָה בָאָה
אֶל־דָּוִד לֵאמֹר הִכָּה אַבְשָׁלוֹם אֶת־כָּל־בְּנֵי הַמֶּלֶךְ וְלֹא־נוֹתַר מֵהֶם
לא אֶחָד: וַיָּקָם הַמֶּלֶךְ וַיִּקְרַע אֶת־בְּגָדָיו וַיִּשְׁכַּב אָרְצָה וְכָל־עֲבָדָיו
לב נִצָּבִים קְרֻעֵי בְגָדִים: וַיַּעַן יוֹנָדָב | בֶּן־שִׁמְעָה אֲחִי־דָוִד
וַיֹּאמֶר אַל־יֹאמַר אֲדֹנִי אֵת כָּל־הַנְּעָרִים בְּנֵי־הַמֶּלֶךְ הֵמִיתוּ כִּי־אַמְנוֹן
לְבַדּוֹ מֵת כִּי־עַל־פִּי אַבְשָׁלוֹם הָיְתָה שִׂימָה מִיּוֹם עַנֹּתוֹ אֵת תָּמָר שׂוּמָה
לג אֲחֹתוֹ: וְעַתָּה אַל־יָשֵׂם אֲדֹנִי הַמֶּלֶךְ אֶל־לִבּוֹ דָּבָר לֵאמֹר כָּל־בְּנֵי
לד הַמֶּלֶךְ מֵתוּ כִּי־אִם אַמְנוֹן לְבַדּוֹ מֵת: וַיִּבְרַח אַבְשָׁלוֹם
וַיִּשָּׂא הַנַּעַר הַצֹּפֶה אֶת־עֵינָו וַיַּרְא וְהִנֵּה עַם־רַב הֹלְכִים מִדֶּרֶךְ אַחֲרָיו
לה מִצַּד הָהָר: וַיֹּאמֶר יוֹנָדָב אֶל־הַמֶּלֶךְ הִנֵּה בְנֵי־הַמֶּלֶךְ בָּאוּ כִּדְבַר עַבְדְּךָ
לו כֵּן הָיָה: וַיְהִי | כְּכַלֹּתוֹ לְדַבֵּר וְהִנֵּה בְנֵי־הַמֶּלֶךְ בָּאוּ וַיִּשְׂאוּ קוֹלָם וַיִּבְכּוּ
לז וְגַם־הַמֶּלֶךְ וְכָל־עֲבָדָיו בָּכוּ בְּכִי גָּדוֹל מְאֹד: וְאַבְשָׁלוֹם בָּרַח וַיֵּלֶךְ
אֶל־תַּלְמַי בֶּן־עַמִּיחוּר מֶלֶךְ גְּשׁוּר וַיִּתְאַבֵּל עַל־בְּנוֹ כָּל־הַיָּמִים: עַמִּיהוּד
לח לט וְאַבְשָׁלוֹם בָּרַח וַיֵּלֶךְ גְּשׁוּר וַיְהִי־שָׁם שָׁלֹשׁ שָׁנִים: וַתְּכַל דָּוִד הַמֶּלֶךְ
יד א לָצֵאת אֶל־אַבְשָׁלוֹם כִּי־נִחַם עַל־אַמְנוֹן כִּי־מֵת: וַיֵּדַע
ב יוֹאָב בֶּן־צְרֻיָה כִּי־לֵב הַמֶּלֶךְ עַל־אַבְשָׁלוֹם: וַיִּשְׁלַח יוֹאָב תְּקוֹעָה
וַיִּקַּח מִשָּׁם אִשָּׁה חֲכָמָה וַיֹּאמֶר אֵלֶיהָ הִתְאַבְּלִי־נָא וְלִבְשִׁי־נָא בִגְדֵי־
אֵבֶל וְאַל־תָּסוּכִי שֶׁמֶן וְהָיִית כְּאִשָּׁה זֶה יָמִים רַבִּים מִתְאַבֶּלֶת עַל־
ג מֵת: וּבָאת אֶל־הַמֶּלֶךְ וְדִבַּרְתְּ אֵלָיו כַּדָּבָר הַזֶּה וַיָּשֶׂם יוֹאָב אֶת־
ד הַדְּבָרִים בְּפִיהָ: וַתֹּאמֶר הָאִשָּׁה הַתְּקֹעִית אֶל־הַמֶּלֶךְ וַתִּפֹּל עַל־אַפֶּיהָ
ה אַרְצָה וַתִּשְׁתָּחוּ וַתֹּאמֶר הוֹשִׁעָה הַמֶּלֶךְ: וַיֹּאמֶר־לָהּ

6 died. Your servant had two sons, but they brawled in the field with no one
7 to come between them, and one struck the other and killed him. And now,
the whole family has risen against your servant, saying, 'Give over the one
who struck his brother, so we can put him to death for ending his brother's
life – we will destroy the heir as well.' They would extinguish my last remaining
ember, leaving my husband without name or remnant on the face of the
8 earth." "Go back home," the king said to the woman, "and I will issue
9 a command for you." "My lord the king," the Tekoite woman said to the king,
"may the guilt lie with me and my father's house; the king and his throne are
10 blameless." "If anyone speaks to you," said the king, "bring him to
11 me, and he shall harass you no longer." "Please," she said, "may the king keep
the LORD your God in mind and the blood avenger from too much corruption;
let them not destroy my son!" "As the LORD lives," he said, "not a hair of your
12 son shall fall to the ground." And the woman said, "Let your servant now
13 speak a word to my lord the king." "Speak," he said. "Why, then, have
you determined such a thing for God's people?" said the woman. "By making
this pronouncement, it is as if the king is guilty for not having brought back
14 the king's own banished one. For die we must, like water spilled to the earth
that cannot be gathered up, and God will not hold a soul accountable for
15 determining that none of his own shall be banished. Now I came to speak of
this to my lord the king because the people have frightened me, and your
servant thought, 'Let me speak to the king; perhaps the king will do as his
16 handmaid asks. For the king might pay heed and save his handmaid from the
hands of the man who would destroy both me and my son from God's
17 heritage.' And your servant thought, 'May the word of my lord the king grant
relief,' for my lord the king is like an angel of God, understanding good and
18 evil, and may the LORD your God be with you." And the king
responded. "Please," he said to the woman, "do not hide anything from me of
what I am about to ask you." "Please," said the woman, "let my lord the king
19 speak." "Does Yoav have a hand in all this along with you?" asked the king.
"As you live, my lord the king," the woman answered, "there is no turning right
or left from all the king has said! For indeed, your servant Yoav was the one
who gave me the orders, and he was the one who put all these words in the
20 mouth of your servant. Your servant Yoav arranged this scheme to turn
matters around, but my lord is as wise as an angel of God and is aware of all
21 that goes on in the land." Then the king said to Yoav, "Look, I will
22 fulfill this word: go, bring back the boy Avshalom." Yoav flung his face to the
ground and bowed down low and blessed the king. "Today," Yoav said, "I, your
servant, know that I have found favor in your sight, my lord the king, for the

ו הַמֶּלֶךְ מַה־לָּךְ וַתֹּאמֶר אֲבָל אִשָּׁה־אַלְמָנָה אָנִי וַיָּמָת אִישִׁי: וּלְשִׁפְחָתְךָ
שְׁנֵי בָנִים וַיִּנָּצוּ שְׁנֵיהֶם בַּשָּׂדֶה וְאֵין מַצִּיל בֵּינֵיהֶם וַיַּכּוֹ הָאֶחָד אֶת־
ז הָאֶחָד וַיָּמֶת אֹתוֹ: וְהִנֵּה קָמָה כָל־הַמִּשְׁפָּחָה עַל־שִׁפְחָתֶךָ וַיֹּאמְרוּ
תְּנִי ׀ אֶת־מַכֵּה אָחִיו וּנְמִתֵהוּ בְּנֶפֶשׁ אָחִיו אֲשֶׁר הָרָג וְנַשְׁמִידָה גַּם
אֶת־הַיּוֹרֵשׁ וְכִבּוּ אֶת־גַּחַלְתִּי אֲשֶׁר נִשְׁאָרָה לְבִלְתִּי שום־לְאִישִׁי   שִׂים־
ח שֵׁם וּשְׁאֵרִית עַל־פְּנֵי הָאֲדָמָה: וַיֹּאמֶר הַמֶּלֶךְ אֶל־
ט הָאִשָּׁה לְכִי לְבֵיתֵךְ וַאֲנִי אֲצַוֶּה עָלָיִךְ: וַתֹּאמֶר הָאִשָּׁה הַתְּקוֹעִית
אֶל־הַמֶּלֶךְ עָלַי אֲדֹנִי הַמֶּלֶךְ הֶעָוֺן וְעַל־בֵּית אָבִי וְהַמֶּלֶךְ וְכִסְאוֹ
י נָקִי: וַיֹּאמֶר הַמֶּלֶךְ הַמְדַבֵּר אֵלַיִךְ וַהֲבֵאתוֹ אֵלַי וְלֹא־
יא יֹסִיף עוֹד לָגַעַת בָּךְ: וַתֹּאמֶר יִזְכָּר־נָא הַמֶּלֶךְ אֶת־יְהוָה אֱלֹהֶיךָ
מהרבית גֹּאֵל הַדָּם לְשַׁחֵת וְלֹא יַשְׁמִידוּ אֶת־בְּנִי וַיֹּאמֶר חַי־יְהוָה   מֵהַרְבַּת
יב אִם־יִפֹּל מִשַּׂעֲרַת בְּנֵךְ אָרְצָה: וַתֹּאמֶר הָאִשָּׁה תְּדַבֶּר־נָא שִׁפְחָתְךָ
יג אֶל־אֲדֹנִי הַמֶּלֶךְ דָּבָר וַיֹּאמֶר דַּבֵּרִי: וַתֹּאמֶר הָאִשָּׁה
וְלָמָּה חָשַׁבְתָּה כָּזֹאת עַל־עַם אֱלֹהִים וּמִדַּבֵּר הַמֶּלֶךְ הַדָּבָר הַזֶּה
יד כְּאָשֵׁם לְבִלְתִּי הָשִׁיב הַמֶּלֶךְ אֶת־נִדְּחוֹ: כִּי־מוֹת נָמוּת וְכַמַּיִם הַנִּגָּרִים
אַרְצָה אֲשֶׁר לֹא יֵאָסֵפוּ וְלֹא־יִשָּׂא אֱלֹהִים נֶפֶשׁ וְחָשַׁב מַחֲשָׁבוֹת
טו לְבִלְתִּי יִדַּח מִמֶּנּוּ נִדָּח: וְעַתָּה אֲשֶׁר־בָּאתִי לְדַבֵּר אֶל־הַמֶּלֶךְ אֲדֹנִי
אֶת־הַדָּבָר הַזֶּה כִּי יֵרְאֻנִי הָעָם וַתֹּאמֶר שִׁפְחָתְךָ אֲדַבְּרָה־נָּא אֶל־
טז הַמֶּלֶךְ אוּלַי יַעֲשֶׂה הַמֶּלֶךְ אֶת־דְּבַר אֲמָתוֹ: כִּי יִשְׁמַע הַמֶּלֶךְ לְהַצִּיל
אֶת־אֲמָתוֹ מִכַּף הָאִישׁ לְהַשְׁמִיד אֹתִי וְאֶת־בְּנִי יַחַד מִנַּחֲלַת אֱלֹהִים:
יז וַתֹּאמֶר שִׁפְחָתְךָ יִהְיֶה־נָּא דְּבַר־אֲדֹנִי הַמֶּלֶךְ לִמְנוּחָה כִּי ׀ כְּמַלְאַךְ
הָאֱלֹהִים כֵּן אֲדֹנִי הַמֶּלֶךְ לִשְׁמֹעַ הַטּוֹב וְהָרָע וַיהוָה אֱלֹהֶיךָ יְהִי
יח עִמָּךְ: וַיַּעַן הַמֶּלֶךְ וַיֹּאמֶר אֶל־הָאִשָּׁה אַל־נָא תְכַחֲדִי
מִמֶּנִּי דָּבָר אֲשֶׁר אָנֹכִי שֹׁאֵל אֹתָךְ וַתֹּאמֶר הָאִשָּׁה יְדַבֶּר־נָא אֲדֹנִי
יט הַמֶּלֶךְ: וַיֹּאמֶר הַמֶּלֶךְ הֲיַד יוֹאָב אִתָּךְ בְּכָל־זֹאת וַתַּעַן הָאִשָּׁה וַתֹּאמֶר
חֵי־נַפְשְׁךָ אֲדֹנִי הַמֶּלֶךְ אִם־אִשׁ ׀ לְהֵמִין וּלְהַשְׂמִיל מִכֹּל אֲשֶׁר־דִּבֶּר
אֲדֹנִי הַמֶּלֶךְ כִּי־עַבְדְּךָ יוֹאָב הוּא צִוָּנִי וְהוּא שָׂם בְּפִי שִׁפְחָתְךָ אֵת
כ כָּל־הַדְּבָרִים הָאֵלֶּה: לְבַעֲבוּר סַבֵּב אֶת־פְּנֵי הַדָּבָר עָשָׂה עַבְדְּךָ יוֹאָב
אֶת־הַדָּבָר הַזֶּה וַאדֹנִי חָכָם כְּחָכְמַת מַלְאַךְ הָאֱלֹהִים לָדַעַת אֶת־
כא כָּל־אֲשֶׁר בָּאָרֶץ: וַיֹּאמֶר הַמֶּלֶךְ אֶל־יוֹאָב הִנֵּה־נָא עָשִׂיתִי
כב אֶת־הַדָּבָר הַזֶּה וְלֵךְ הָשֵׁב אֶת־הַנַּעַר אֶת־אַבְשָׁלוֹם: וַיִּפֹּל יוֹאָב אֶל־
פָּנָיו אַרְצָה וַיִּשְׁתַּחוּ וַיְבָרֶךְ אֶת־הַמֶּלֶךְ וַיֹּאמֶר יוֹאָב הַיּוֹם יָדַע עַבְדְּךָ

23 king has granted his servant's request." Yoav proceeded straight to Geshur and
24 brought Avshalom to Jerusalem. But the king said, "Let him turn off
to his house; he will not be admitted to my presence." So Avshalom turned
25 off to his house and was not admitted to the king's presence. Now
there was no one in all of Israel who was admired for his beauty as Avshalom
26 was; he was flawless from head to toe. When he cut his hair – he would
have it cut once a year when it grew too heavy for him – the hair of his head
27 weighed two hundred shekel by royal weight. Three sons were born to
Avshalom, and one daughter, whose name was Tamar; she became a beautiful
28 woman. Avshalom lived in Jerusalem for two years without being
29 admitted into the king's presence. And Avshalom sent for Yoav, to send him
to the king, but he would not come to him; he sent for him again, a second
30 time, but he would not come. So he said to his servants, "Do you see Yoav's
field over there, next to mine? He has barley there. Go and set it on fire." And
31 Avshalom's servants set the field on fire. Yoav went straight
to Avshalom's house. "Why have your servants set my field on fire?" he asked.
32 "Look," Avshalom said to Yoav, "I sent for you, asking you to come here so I
could send you to the king with the message, 'Why did I come back from
Geshur – had I stayed there, I would have been better off. Now admit me into
33 the king's presence; if I am guilty, then put me to death.'" So Yoav went to the
king and told him, and he summoned Avshalom. He came before the king
and bowed down low before the king with his face to the ground, and the
15 1 king kissed Avshalom. It was after this that Avshalom procured for
2 himself a chariot and horses and fifty men to run before him. Avshalom would
rise early and stand by the road to the main gate, and whenever anyone had
a dispute that was to come before the king in judgment, Avshalom would call
out to him. "Where are you from?" he would say, and when he replied, "Your
3 servant is from one of the tribes of Israel," Avshalom would answer, "Look,
your words are fair and frank – but there is no one from the king to hear you
4 out. If only someone would appoint me as judge in the land," Avshalom would
continue, "everyone with a legal dispute would come to me, and I would treat
5 him justly." And if someone approached him to bow to him, he would extend
6 his hand and take hold of him and kiss him. Avshalom acted in this way toward
all the Israelites who came to the king for justice, and Avshalom deceived the
7 people of Israel. At the end of forty years,[42] Avshalom said to the
king, "I will now go and fulfill the vow that I pledged to the LORD in Ḥevron.

42 | Aware of the chronological difficulties in this phrase, the major commentators, following talmudic sources, suggest that the reference here is to the forty years since the Israelites initially demanded a king of Samuel.

כִּי־מָצָאתִי חֵן בְּעֵינֶיךָ אֲדֹנִי הַמֶּלֶךְ אֲשֶׁר־עָשָׂה הַמֶּלֶךְ אֶת־דְּבַר עבדו: עַבְדֶּךָ
כג כד וַיָּקָם יוֹאָב וַיֵּלֶךְ גְּשׁוּרָה וַיָּבֵא אֶת־אַבְשָׁלוֹם יְרוּשָׁלָ‍ִם: וַיֹּאמֶר
הַמֶּלֶךְ יִסֹּב אֶל־בֵּיתוֹ וּפָנַי לֹא יִרְאֶה וַיִּסֹּב אַבְשָׁלוֹם אֶל־בֵּיתוֹ
כה וּפְנֵי הַמֶּלֶךְ לֹא רָאָה: וּכְאַבְשָׁלוֹם לֹא־הָיָה אִישׁ־יָפֶה
בְּכָל־יִשְׂרָאֵל לְהַלֵּל מְאֹד מִכַּף רַגְלוֹ וְעַד קָדְקֳדוֹ לֹא־הָיָה בוֹ מוּם:
כו וּבְגַלְּחוֹ אֶת־רֹאשׁוֹ וְהָיָה מִקֵּץ יָמִים | לַיָּמִים אֲשֶׁר יְגַלֵּחַ כִּי־כָבֵד עָלָיו
כז וְגִלְּחוֹ וְשָׁקַל אֶת־שְׂעַר רֹאשׁוֹ מָאתַיִם שְׁקָלִים בְּאֶבֶן הַמֶּלֶךְ: וַיִּוָּלְדוּ
לְאַבְשָׁלוֹם שְׁלוֹשָׁה בָנִים וּבַת אַחַת וּשְׁמָהּ תָּמָר הִיא הָיְתָה אִשָּׁה
כח יְפַת מַרְאֶה: וַיֵּשֶׁב אַבְשָׁלוֹם בִּירוּשָׁלַ‍ִם שְׁנָתַיִם יָמִים וּפְנֵי
כט הַמֶּלֶךְ לֹא רָאָה: וַיִּשְׁלַח אַבְשָׁלוֹם אֶל־יוֹאָב לִשְׁלֹחַ אֹתוֹ אֶל־הַמֶּלֶךְ
ל וְלֹא אָבָה לָבוֹא אֵלָיו וַיִּשְׁלַח עוֹד שֵׁנִית וְלֹא אָבָה לָבוֹא: וַיֹּאמֶר
אֶל־עֲבָדָיו רְאוּ חֶלְקַת יוֹאָב אֶל־יָדִי וְלוֹ־שָׁם שְׂעֹרִים לְכוּ והוצתיה וְהַצִּיתוּהָ
לא בָאֵשׁ וַיַּצִּתוּ עַבְדֵי אַבְשָׁלוֹם אֶת־הַחֶלְקָה בָּאֵשׁ: וַיָּקָם
יוֹאָב וַיָּבֹא אֶל־אַבְשָׁלוֹם הַבָּיְתָה וַיֹּאמֶר אֵלָיו לָמָּה הִצִּיתוּ עֲבָדֶיךָ
לב אֶת־הַחֶלְקָה אֲשֶׁר־לִי בָּאֵשׁ: וַיֹּאמֶר אַבְשָׁלוֹם אֶל־יוֹאָב הִנֵּה שָׁלַחְתִּי
אֵלֶיךָ | לֵאמֹר בֹּא הֵנָּה וְאֶשְׁלְחָה אֹתְךָ אֶל־הַמֶּלֶךְ לֵאמֹר לָמָּה בָּאתִי
מִגְּשׁוּר טוֹב לִי עֹד אֲנִי־שָׁם וְעַתָּה אֶרְאֶה פְּנֵי הַמֶּלֶךְ וְאִם־יֶשׁ־בִּי עָוֺן
לג וֶהֱמִתָנִי: וַיָּבֹא יוֹאָב אֶל־הַמֶּלֶךְ וַיַּגֶּד־לוֹ וַיִּקְרָא אֶל־אַבְשָׁלוֹם וַיָּבֹא כח
אֶל־הַמֶּלֶךְ וַיִּשְׁתַּחוּ לוֹ עַל־אַפָּיו אַרְצָה לִפְנֵי הַמֶּלֶךְ וַיִּשַּׁק הַמֶּלֶךְ
טו א לְאַבְשָׁלוֹם: וַיְהִי מֵאַחֲרֵי כֵן וַיַּעַשׂ לוֹ אַבְשָׁלוֹם מֶרְכָּבָה
ב וְסֻסִים וַחֲמִשִּׁים אִישׁ רָצִים לְפָנָיו: וְהִשְׁכִּים אַבְשָׁלוֹם וְעָמַד עַל־
יַד דֶּרֶךְ הַשָּׁעַר וַיְהִי כָּל־הָאִישׁ אֲשֶׁר־יִהְיֶה־לּוֹ רִיב לָבוֹא אֶל־
הַמֶּלֶךְ לַמִּשְׁפָּט וַיִּקְרָא אַבְשָׁלוֹם אֵלָיו וַיֹּאמֶר אֵי־מִזֶּה עִיר אַתָּה
ג וַיֹּאמֶר מֵאַחַד שִׁבְטֵי־יִשְׂרָאֵל עַבְדֶּךָ: וַיֹּאמֶר אֵלָיו אַבְשָׁלוֹם רְאֵה
ד דְבָרֶיךָ טוֹבִים וּנְכֹחִים וְשֹׁמֵעַ אֵין־לְךָ מֵאֵת הַמֶּלֶךְ: וַיֹּאמֶר אַבְשָׁלוֹם
מִי־יְשִׂמֵנִי שֹׁפֵט בָּאָרֶץ וְעָלַי יָבוֹא כָּל־אִישׁ אֲשֶׁר־יִהְיֶה־לּוֹ־רִיב
ה וּמִשְׁפָּט וְהִצְדַּקְתִּיו: וְהָיָה בִּקְרָב־אִישׁ לְהִשְׁתַּחֲוֺת לוֹ וְשָׁלַח אֶת־
ו יָדוֹ וְהֶחֱזִיק לוֹ וְנָשַׁק לוֹ: וַיַּעַשׂ אַבְשָׁלוֹם כַּדָּבָר הַזֶּה לְכָל־יִשְׂרָאֵל
אֲשֶׁר־יָבֹאוּ לַמִּשְׁפָּט אֶל־הַמֶּלֶךְ וַיְגַנֵּב אַבְשָׁלוֹם אֶת־לֵב אַנְשֵׁי
ז יִשְׂרָאֵל: וַיְהִי מִקֵּץ אַרְבָּעִים שָׁנָה וַיֹּאמֶר אַבְשָׁלוֹם אֶל־
הַמֶּלֶךְ אֵלְכָה נָּא וַאֲשַׁלֵּם אֶת־נִדְרִי אֲשֶׁר־נָדַרְתִּי לַיהוָה בְּחֶבְרוֹן:

8 For your servant pledged a vow when I was staying in Geshur of Aram, saying,
'If the LORD will bring me back to Jerusalem, then I will serve the LORD.'"
9 10 "Go in peace," said the king, and he arose and set out for Ḥevron. Then
Avshalom sent spies throughout every tribe of Israel, communicating: "When
you hear the sound of the ram's horn, announce, 'Avshalom has become king
11 in Ḥevron.'" Avshalom was accompanied by two hundred men of Jerusalem
who had been invited and went along with him, unsuspecting; they knew
12 nothing. And Avshalom sent Aḥitofel the Gilonite, David's advisor, from his
hometown of Gilo as he offered the sacrifices. The conspiracy gained power,
13 and the people's support for Avshalom increased. An informant came to
David reporting that the men of Israel's hearts were being drawn to Avshalom.
14 And David said to all the subjects who were with him in Jerusalem, "Rise – we
must flee, or none of us will escape from Avshalom. Hurry, leave, in case he
is faster and manages to overtake us, bringing ruin to us and putting the city
15 to the sword." And the king's subjects replied to the king, "Whatever our lord
16 the king decides – your servants are here." So the king set out on foot along
with all his household, save for ten concubines whom the king left to mind
17 the palace. The king set out with all the people at his heels, and they stopped
18 by the farthest house while all his subjects passed him, all the Keretites and
Peletites and all the Gittites – six hundred men who had followed him from
19 Gat passed ahead of the king. King David said to Itai the Gittite,
"Why should you, too, come with us? Go back; stay with the king, for you
20 are a foreigner as well as an exile from your own place. Just yesterday you
arrived; why should I make you wander about with us today while I myself
go wherever I can? Go back and take your brothers with you in true loyalty."
21 "As the LORD lives," Itai answered the king, "and by the life of my lord the
king, wherever my lord the king may be – for death or for life – there will be
22 your servant." "Go, pass ahead," David said to Itai, and Itai the Gittite passed
23 with all his men, and all the little ones who were with him. And all the land
wept aloud as all the troops passed by; the king crossed Kidron Valley, and
24 all the troops passed along the road to the wilderness. And now Tzadok and
all the Levites were with him as well, bearing the Ark of God's Covenant; they
set down the Ark of God until all the troops had passed over from the city
25 and Evyatar came up. Then the king said to Tzadok, "Bring the Ark
of God back to the city; if I find favor in the LORD's sight, He will bring me
26 back and let me see it and its abode. But if He says thus, 'I take no pleasure in
27 you,' I am ready; let Him do to me as He sees fit. Now, do you see?"
the king continued to the priest Tzadok. "Go back to the safety of the city,
along with both of your sons – your son Aḥimaatz, and Yehonatan son of

ח כִּי־נֵדֶר נָדַר עַבְדְּךָ בְּשִׁבְתִּי בִגְשׁוּר בַּאֲרָם לֵאמֹר אִם־יָשִׁיב יְשִׁיבֵנִי יָשׁוּב
ט יְהוָה יְרוּשָׁלַםִ וְעָבַדְתִּי אֶת־יְהוָה׃ וַיֹּאמֶר־לוֹ הַמֶּלֶךְ לֵךְ בְּשָׁלוֹם וַיָּקָם
י וַיֵּלֶךְ חֶבְרוֹנָה׃ וַיִּשְׁלַח אַבְשָׁלוֹם מְרַגְּלִים בְּכָל־שִׁבְטֵי
יִשְׂרָאֵל לֵאמֹר כְּשָׁמְעֲכֶם אֶת־קוֹל הַשֹּׁפָר וַאֲמַרְתֶּם מָלַךְ אַבְשָׁלוֹם
יא בְּחֶבְרוֹן׃ וְאֶת־אַבְשָׁלוֹם הָלְכוּ מָאתַיִם אִישׁ מִירוּשָׁלַםִ קְרֻאִים וְהֹלְכִים
יב לְתֻמָּם וְלֹא יָדְעוּ כָּל־דָּבָר׃ וַיִּשְׁלַח אַבְשָׁלוֹם אֶת־אֲחִיתֹפֶל הַגִּילֹנִי
יוֹעֵץ דָּוִד מֵעִירוֹ מִגִּלֹה בְּזָבְחוֹ אֶת־הַזְּבָחִים וַיְהִי הַקֶּשֶׁר אַמִּץ וְהָעָם
יג הוֹלֵךְ וָרָב אֶת־אַבְשָׁלוֹם׃ וַיָּבֹא הַמַּגִּיד אֶל־דָּוִד לֵאמֹר הָיָה לֶב־
יד אִישׁ יִשְׂרָאֵל אַחֲרֵי אַבְשָׁלוֹם׃ וַיֹּאמֶר דָּוִד לְכָל־עֲבָדָיו אֲשֶׁר־אִתּוֹ
בִירוּשָׁלַםִ קוּמוּ וְנִבְרָחָה כִּי לֹא־תִהְיֶה־לָּנוּ פְלֵיטָה מִפְּנֵי אַבְשָׁלֹם
מַהֲרוּ לָלֶכֶת פֶּן־יְמַהֵר וְהִשִּׂגֻנוּ וְהִדִּיחַ עָלֵינוּ אֶת־הָרָעָה וְהִכָּה הָעִיר
טו לְפִי־חָרֶב׃ וַיֹּאמְרוּ עַבְדֵי־הַמֶּלֶךְ אֶל־הַמֶּלֶךְ כְּכֹל אֲשֶׁר־יִבְחַר אֲדֹנִי
טז הַמֶּלֶךְ הִנֵּה עֲבָדֶיךָ׃ וַיֵּצֵא הַמֶּלֶךְ וְכָל־בֵּיתוֹ בְּרַגְלָיו וַיַּעֲזֹב הַמֶּלֶךְ אֵת
יז עֶשֶׂר נָשִׁים פִּלַגְשִׁים לִשְׁמֹר הַבָּיִת׃ וַיֵּצֵא הַמֶּלֶךְ וְכָל־הָעָם בְּרַגְלָיו
יח וַיַּעַמְדוּ בֵּית הַמֶּרְחָק׃ וְכָל־עֲבָדָיו עֹבְרִים עַל־יָדוֹ וְכָל־הַכְּרֵתִי וְכָל־
הַפְּלֵתִי וְכָל־הַגִּתִּים שֵׁשׁ־מֵאוֹת אִישׁ אֲשֶׁר־בָּאוּ בְרַגְלוֹ מִגַּת עֹבְרִים
יט עַל־פְּנֵי הַמֶּלֶךְ׃ וַיֹּאמֶר הַמֶּלֶךְ אֶל־אִתַּי הַגִּתִּי לָמָּה תֵלֵךְ
גַּם־אַתָּה אִתָּנוּ שׁוּב וְשֵׁב עִם־הַמֶּלֶךְ כִּי־נָכְרִי אַתָּה וְגַם־גֹּלֶה אַתָּה
כ לִמְקוֹמֶךָ׃ תְּמוֹל ׀ בּוֹאֶךָ וְהַיּוֹם אנועך עִמָּנוּ לָלֶכֶת וַאֲנִי הוֹלֵךְ עַל אֲנִיעֲךָ
כא אֲשֶׁר־אֲנִי הוֹלֵךְ שׁוּב וְהָשֵׁב אֶת־אַחֶיךָ עִמָּךְ חֶסֶד וֶאֱמֶת׃ וַיַּעַן אִתַּי
אֶת־הַמֶּלֶךְ וַיֹּאמַר חַי־יְהוָה וְחֵי אֲדֹנִי הַמֶּלֶךְ כִּי אִם בִּמְקוֹם אֲשֶׁר
יִהְיֶה־שָּׁם ׀ אֲדֹנִי הַמֶּלֶךְ אִם־לְמָוֶת אִם־לְחַיִּים כִּי־שָׁם יִהְיֶה עַבְדֶּךָ׃
כב וַיֹּאמֶר דָּוִד אֶל־אִתַּי לֵךְ וַעֲבֹר וַיַּעֲבֹר אִתַּי הַגִּתִּי וְכָל־אֲנָשָׁיו וְכָל־
כג הַטַּף אֲשֶׁר אִתּוֹ׃ וְכָל־הָאָרֶץ בּוֹכִים קוֹל גָּדוֹל וְכָל־הָעָם עֹבְרִים
וְהַמֶּלֶךְ עֹבֵר בְּנַחַל קִדְרוֹן וְכָל־הָעָם עֹבְרִים עַל־פְּנֵי־דֶרֶךְ אֶת־
כד הַמִּדְבָּר׃ וְהִנֵּה גַם־צָדוֹק וְכָל־הַלְוִיִּם אִתּוֹ נֹשְׂאִים אֶת־אֲרוֹן בְּרִית
הָאֱלֹהִים וַיַּצִּקוּ אֶת־אֲרוֹן הָאֱלֹהִים וַיַּעַל אֶבְיָתָר עַד־תֹּם כָּל־הָעָם
כה לַעֲבוֹר מִן־הָעִיר׃ וַיֹּאמֶר הַמֶּלֶךְ לְצָדוֹק הָשֵׁב אֶת־אֲרוֹן
הָאֱלֹהִים הָעִיר אִם־אֶמְצָא חֵן בְּעֵינֵי יְהוָה וֶהֱשִׁבַנִי וְהִרְאַנִי אֹתוֹ
כו וְאֶת־נָוֵהוּ׃ וְאִם כֹּה יֹאמַר לֹא חָפַצְתִּי בָּךְ הִנְנִי יַעֲשֶׂה־לִּי כַּאֲשֶׁר טוֹב
כז בְּעֵינָיו׃ וַיֹּאמֶר הַמֶּלֶךְ אֶל־צָדוֹק הַכֹּהֵן הֲרוֹאֶה אַתָּה
שֻׁבָה הָעִיר בְּשָׁלוֹם וַאֲחִימַעַץ בִּנְךָ וִיהוֹנָתָן בֶּן־אֶבְיָתָר שְׁנֵי בְנֵיכֶם

28 Evyatar. Look, I will linger in the wilderness steppes until your word reaches
29 me and informs me." So Tzadok and Evyatar brought the Ark of God back to
30 Jerusalem and stayed there. But David made his way up Maaleh HaZeitim,
weeping as he climbed; his head was covered, and he walked barefoot. And
all the troops with him each covered their heads and made their way up,
31 weeping as they climbed. When David was informed that Aḥitofel was part
of Avshalom's conspiracy, David said, "O Lord, make Aḥitofel's counsel
32 foolish." And as David reached the summit, where he was about to worship
before God, there was Ḥushai the Arkite coming toward him, his robe rent
33 and earth upon his head. "If you cross over with me, you will be a burden to
34 me," David said to him, "but if you go back to town and say to Avshalom, 'I
am your servant, O king – I was always your father's servant, but from now
on I am your servant,' then you will be able to thwart Aḥitofel's counsel for
35 me. The priests Tzadok and Evyatar will be there with you, so report anything
36 you hear in the palace to the priests Tzadok and Evyatar. Both their sons are
there with them – Tzadok's Aḥimaatz, and Evyatar's Yehonatan; send
37 anything you hear to me through them." So Ḥushai, David's friend, reached
16 1 the city just as Avshalom reached Jerusalem. David had passed only
a short distance from the summit when Tziva, Mefivoshet's servant, suddenly
approached him with a pair of saddled donkeys loaded with two hundred
loaves of bread, a hundred clusters of raisins, a hundred summer fruit, and an
2 amphora of wine. "Why have you brought all this?" the king asked Tziva. "The
donkeys are for the royalty to ride," said Tziva, "and the bread and summer
fruit are for the young men to eat, while the wine is for the weary to drink in
3 the wilderness." "And where is the son of your master?" asked the king. "Oh,
he is staying in Jerusalem," Tziva said to the king, "for he says, 'Today, the
4 House of Israel will restore my father's throne to me.'" "Now, all that belongs
to Mefivoshet belongs to you," the king said to Tziva. "I bow down low!" said
5 Tziva. "May I find favor in your sight, my lord the king." King David had
reached Baḥurim when a member of the house of Sha'ul, whose name was
6 Shimi son of Gera, suddenly charged out from there, cursing as he came. He
hurled stones at David and at all King David's subjects, and at all the troops
7 and warriors to his right and to his left. And this was the curse Shimi uttered:
8 "Get out, get out, you man of blood, you depraved man! The Lord has
brought all the blood of the house of Sha'ul back upon you for ruling in his
place, and the Lord has given the kingship over to Avshalom, your son! Now
9 you languish in your own evil, for you are a man of blood." Avishai son
of Tzeruya said to the king, "Why should this dead dog curse my lord the
10 king? Let me pass, please, and I will cut off his head." "What do
I have to do with you, sons of Tzeruya?" said the king. "Let him curse –
perhaps the Lord told him to curse David; who is to say, 'Why did you do

כח אִתְּכֶם: רְאוּ אָנֹכִי מִתְמַהְמֵהַּ בְּעַבְרוֹת הַמִּדְבָּר עַד בּוֹא דָבָר מֵעִמָּכֶם בְּעַרְבוֹת
כט לְהַגִּיד לִי: וַיָּשֶׁב צָדוֹק וְאֶבְיָתָר אֶת־אֲרוֹן הָאֱלֹהִים יְרוּשָׁלָ͏ִם וַיֵּשְׁבוּ
ל שָׁם: וְדָוִד עֹלֶה בְמַעֲלֵה הַזֵּיתִים עֹלֶה ׀ וּבוֹכֶה וְרֹאשׁ לוֹ חָפוּי וְהוּא
הֹלֵךְ יָחֵף וְכָל־הָעָם אֲשֶׁר־אִתּוֹ חָפוּ אִישׁ רֹאשׁוֹ וְעָלוּ עָלֹה וּבָכֹה:
לא וְדָוִד הִגִּיד לֵאמֹר אֲחִיתֹפֶל בַּקֹּשְׁרִים עִם־אַבְשָׁלוֹם וַיֹּאמֶר דָּוִד
לב סַכֶּל־נָא אֶת־עֲצַת אֲחִיתֹפֶל יְהוָה: וַיְהִי דָוִד בָּא עַד־הָרֹאשׁ אֲשֶׁר־
יִשְׁתַּחֲוֶה שָׁם לֵאלֹהִים וְהִנֵּה לִקְרָאתוֹ חוּשַׁי הָאַרְכִּי קָרוּעַ כֻּתָּנְתּוֹ
לג וַאֲדָמָה עַל־רֹאשׁוֹ: וַיֹּאמֶר לוֹ דָּוִד אִם עָבַרְתָּ אִתִּי וְהָיִתָ עָלַי לְמַשָּׂא:
לד וְאִם־הָעִיר תָּשׁוּב וְאָמַרְתָּ לְאַבְשָׁלוֹם עַבְדְּךָ אֲנִי הַמֶּלֶךְ אֶהְיֶה עֶבֶד
אָבִיךָ וַאֲנִי מֵאָז וְעַתָּה וַאֲנִי עַבְדֶּךָ וְהֵפַרְתָּה לִי אֵת עֲצַת אֲחִיתֹפֶל:
לה וַהֲלוֹא עִמְּךָ שָׁם צָדוֹק וְאֶבְיָתָר הַכֹּהֲנִים וְהָיָה כָּל־הַדָּבָר אֲשֶׁר תִּשְׁמַע
לו מִבֵּית הַמֶּלֶךְ תַּגִּיד לְצָדוֹק וּלְאֶבְיָתָר הַכֹּהֲנִים: הִנֵּה־שָׁם עִמָּם שְׁנֵי
בְנֵיהֶם אֲחִימַעַץ לְצָדוֹק וִיהוֹנָתָן לְאֶבְיָתָר וּשְׁלַחְתֶּם בְּיָדָם אֵלַי כָּל־
לז דָּבָר אֲשֶׁר תִּשְׁמָעוּ: וַיָּבֹא חוּשַׁי רֵעֶה דָוִד הָעִיר וְאַבְשָׁלֹם יָבוֹא כט
טז א יְרוּשָׁלָ͏ִם: וְדָוִד עָבַר מְעַט מֵהָרֹאשׁ וְהִנֵּה צִיבָא נַעַר
מְפִיבֹשֶׁת לִקְרָאתוֹ וְצֶמֶד חֲמֹרִים חֲבֻשִׁים וַעֲלֵיהֶם מָאתַיִם לֶחֶם וּמֵאָה
ב צִמּוּקִים וּמֵאָה קַיִץ וְנֵבֶל יָיִן: וַיֹּאמֶר הַמֶּלֶךְ אֶל־צִיבָא מָה־אֵלֶּה
לָּךְ וַיֹּאמֶר צִיבָא הַחֲמוֹרִים לְבֵית־הַמֶּלֶךְ לִרְכֹּב וּלְהַלֶּחֶם וְהַקַּיִץ וְהַלֶּחֶם
ג לֶאֱכוֹל הַנְּעָרִים וְהַיַּיִן לִשְׁתּוֹת הַיָּעֵף בַּמִּדְבָּר: וַיֹּאמֶר הַמֶּלֶךְ וְאַיֵּה
בֶּן־אֲדֹנֶיךָ וַיֹּאמֶר צִיבָא אֶל־הַמֶּלֶךְ הִנֵּה יוֹשֵׁב בִּירוּשָׁלַ͏ִם כִּי אָמַר
ד הַיּוֹם יָשִׁיבוּ לִי בֵּית יִשְׂרָאֵל אֵת מַמְלְכוּת אָבִי: וַיֹּאמֶר הַמֶּלֶךְ לְצִבָא
הִנֵּה לְךָ כֹּל אֲשֶׁר לִמְפִיבֹשֶׁת וַיֹּאמֶר צִיבָא הִשְׁתַּחֲוֵיתִי אֶמְצָא־חֵן
ה בְּעֵינֶיךָ אֲדֹנִי הַמֶּלֶךְ: וּבָא הַמֶּלֶךְ דָּוִד עַד־בַּחוּרִים וְהִנֵּה מִשָּׁם אִישׁ
יוֹצֵא מִמִּשְׁפַּחַת בֵּית־שָׁאוּל וּשְׁמוֹ שִׁמְעִי בֶן־גֵּרָא יֹצֵא יָצוֹא וּמְקַלֵּל:
ו וַיְסַקֵּל בָּאֲבָנִים אֶת־דָּוִד וְאֶת־כָּל־עַבְדֵי הַמֶּלֶךְ דָּוִד וְכָל־הָעָם
ז וְכָל־הַגִּבֹּרִים מִימִינוֹ וּמִשְּׂמֹאלוֹ: וְכֹה־אָמַר שִׁמְעִי בְּקַלְלוֹ צֵא צֵא
ח אִישׁ הַדָּמִים וְאִישׁ הַבְּלִיָּעַל: הֵשִׁיב עָלֶיךָ יְהוָה כֹּל ׀ דְּמֵי בֵית־שָׁאוּל
אֲשֶׁר מָלַכְתָּ תַּחְתָּו וַיִּתֵּן יְהוָה אֶת־הַמְּלוּכָה בְּיַד אַבְשָׁלוֹם בְּנֶךָ וְהִנְּךָ
ט בְּרָעָתֶךָ כִּי אִישׁ דָּמִים אָתָּה: וַיֹּאמֶר אֲבִישַׁי בֶן־צְרוּיָה אֶל־הַמֶּלֶךְ
לָמָּה יְקַלֵּל הַכֶּלֶב הַמֵּת הַזֶּה אֶת־אֲדֹנִי הַמֶּלֶךְ אֶעְבְּרָה־נָּא וְאָסִירָה
י אֶת־רֹאשׁוֹ: וַיֹּאמֶר הַמֶּלֶךְ מַה־לִּי וְלָכֶם בְּנֵי צְרֻיָה כִּי כֹּה
יְקַלֵּל וְכִי יְהוָה אָמַר לוֹ קַלֵּל אֶת־דָּוִד וּמִי יֹאמַר מַדּוּעַ עָשִׂיתָה כִּי

11 so?' Look, my own son, the issue of my own loins, seeks my life,"
David continued to Avishai and all his subjects, "and now the Benjaminite
does, all the more so. Let him be and let him curse, as the LORD bid him.
12 Perhaps the LORD will look upon my suffering and the LORD restore my favor
13 in place of his curses on this day." So David and his men went on
their way as Shimi walked along the opposite hillside, hurling curses and
14 stones toward them as he went, and flinging dust. The king and all
the troops with him were exhausted when they arrived, and there they paused
15 for breath. Meanwhile, Avshalom and all the people, the men of Israel, had
16 entered Jerusalem, and Aḥitofel with him. And when Ḥushai the Arkite,
David's friend, came to Avshalom, Ḥushai declared to Avshalom, "Long live
17 the king! Long live the king!" "Is this loyalty toward your friend?" Avshalom
18 asked Ḥushai. "Why haven't you followed your friend?" "No," Ḥushai said to
Avshalom. "Should I not be with the one whom the LORD and this people
19 and all the men of Israel have chosen? With him I shall remain. Besides,
whom shall I serve if not his son? As I was at your father's service, I am at
20 yours." Avshalom then said to Aḥitofel, "Let us have your counsel;
21 what shall we do?" "You should go to bed with your father's concubines, the
ones he left to mind the palace," Aḥitofel said to Avshalom, "and when all of
Israel hears that you have become odious to your father, the hand of all your
22 supporters will be strengthened." So they erected a tent for Avshalom on the
23 roof, and he bedded his father's concubines in full view of all Israel. In those
days, the counsel Aḥitofel gave was considered tantamount to the word
sought from God; that was how all of Aḥitofel's counsel was to David as well
17 1 as Avshalom. Now Aḥitofel said to Avshalom, "Let me select twelve
2 thousand men, and I will set out and pursue David this very night. I will come
upon him when he is weary and weak and throw him into a panic, and all the
3 troops with him will flee – then I will strike down just the king. And I will
bring all the troops back to you, and when all have come back but the man
4 you seek, all the people will have peace." This idea pleased Avshalom, and it
5 pleased all the elders of Israel. But Avshalom said, "Summon Ḥushai
6 the Arkite, and let us hear what he, too, has to say." Ḥushai came to Avshalom,
and Avshalom said to him, "This is what Aḥitofel said; shall we follow his
7 idea? If not, speak up." "This time," Ḥushai answered Avshalom, "the
8 counsel Aḥitofel has given you is not good. You know that your father and his
men are seasoned warriors," Ḥushai continued, "and they are as wretched and
bitter as a bereaved bear in the wild. Your father is a veteran of war; he will
9 not be spending the night with the troops – even now, he must be hiding in
some hollow or some other place. And as soon as any of them fall, rumor will
spread that there has been a massacre among the supporters of Avshalom,

יא כֵּן: וַיֹּאמֶר דָּוִד אֶל־אֲבִישַׁי וְאֶל־כָּל־עֲבָדָיו הִנֵּה בְנִי אֲשֶׁר־
יָצָא מִמֵּעַי מְבַקֵּשׁ אֶת־נַפְשִׁי וְאַף כִּי־עַתָּה בֶּן־הַיְמִינִי הַנִּחוּ לוֹ וִיקַלֵּל
יב כִּי־אָמַר־לוֹ יְהוָה: אוּלַי יִרְאֶה יְהוָה בעוני וְהֵשִׁיב יְהוָה לִי טוֹבָה בְּעֵינִי
יג תַּחַת קִלְלָתוֹ הַיּוֹם הַזֶּה: וַיֵּלֶךְ דָּוִד וַאֲנָשָׁיו בַּדָּרֶךְ וְשִׁמְעִי
הֹלֵךְ בְּצֵלַע הָהָר לְעֻמָּתוֹ הָלוֹךְ וַיְקַלֵּל וַיְסַקֵּל בָּאֲבָנִים לְעֻמָּתוֹ וְעִפַּר
יד בֶּעָפָר: וַיָּבֹא הַמֶּלֶךְ וְכָל־הָעָם אֲשֶׁר־אִתּוֹ עֲיֵפִים וַיִּנָּפֵשׁ
טו שָׁם: וְאַבְשָׁלוֹם וְכָל־הָעָם אִישׁ יִשְׂרָאֵל בָּאוּ יְרוּשָׁלָם וַאֲחִיתֹפֶל אִתּוֹ:
טז וַיְהִי כַּאֲשֶׁר־בָּא חוּשַׁי הָאַרְכִּי רֵעֶה דָוִד אֶל־אַבְשָׁלוֹם וַיֹּאמֶר חוּשַׁי
יז אֶל־אַבְשָׁלוֹם יְחִי הַמֶּלֶךְ יְחִי הַמֶּלֶךְ: וַיֹּאמֶר אַבְשָׁלוֹם אֶל־חוּשַׁי זֶה
יח חַסְדְּךָ אֶת־רֵעֶךָ לָמָּה לֹא־הָלַכְתָּ אֶת־רֵעֶךָ: וַיֹּאמֶר חוּשַׁי אֶל־אַבְשָׁלֹם
לא כִּי אֲשֶׁר בָּחַר יְהוָה וְהָעָם הַזֶּה וְכָל־אִישׁ יִשְׂרָאֵל לא אֶהְיֶה וְאִתּוֹ לוֹ
יט אֵשֵׁב: וְהַשֵּׁנִית לְמִי אֲנִי אֶעֱבֹד הֲלוֹא לִפְנֵי בְנוֹ כַּאֲשֶׁר עָבַדְתִּי לִפְנֵי
כ אָבִיךָ כֵּן אֶהְיֶה לְפָנֶיךָ: וַיֹּאמֶר אַבְשָׁלוֹם אֶל־אֲחִיתֹפֶל
כא הָבוּ לָכֶם עֵצָה מַה־נַּעֲשֶׂה: וַיֹּאמֶר אֲחִיתֹפֶל אֶל־אַבְשָׁלֹם בּוֹא אֶל־
פִּלַגְשֵׁי אָבִיךָ אֲשֶׁר הִנִּיחַ לִשְׁמוֹר הַבָּיִת וְשָׁמַע כָּל־יִשְׂרָאֵל כִּי־נִבְאַשְׁתָּ
כב אֶת־אָבִיךָ וְחָזְקוּ יְדֵי כָּל־אֲשֶׁר אִתָּךְ: וַיַּטּוּ לְאַבְשָׁלוֹם הָאֹהֶל עַל־הַגָּג
כג וַיָּבֹא אַבְשָׁלוֹם אֶל־פִּלַגְשֵׁי אָבִיו לְעֵינֵי כָּל־יִשְׂרָאֵל: וַעֲצַת אֲחִיתֹפֶל
אֲשֶׁר יָעַץ בַּיָּמִים הָהֵם כַּאֲשֶׁר יִשְׁאַל־ בִּדְבַר הָאֱלֹהִים כֵּן כָּל־עֲצַת אִישׁ
יז א אֲחִיתֹפֶל גַּם־לְדָוִד גַּם־לְאַבְשָׁלֹם: וַיֹּאמֶר אֲחִיתֹפֶל אֶל־
אַבְשָׁלֹם אֶבְחֲרָה־נָּא שְׁנֵים־עָשָׂר אֶלֶף אִישׁ וְאָקוּמָה וְאֶרְדְּפָה אַחֲרֵי־
ב דָוִד הַלָּיְלָה: וְאָבוֹא עָלָיו וְהוּא יָגֵעַ וּרְפֵה יָדַיִם וְהַחֲרַדְתִּי אֹתוֹ וְנָס
ג כָּל־הָעָם אֲשֶׁר־אִתּוֹ וְהִכֵּיתִי אֶת־הַמֶּלֶךְ לְבַדּוֹ: וְאָשִׁיבָה כָל־הָעָם
אֵלֶיךָ כְּשׁוּב הַכֹּל הָאִישׁ אֲשֶׁר אַתָּה מְבַקֵּשׁ כָּל־הָעָם יִהְיֶה שָׁלוֹם:
ד ה וַיִּישַׁר הַדָּבָר בְּעֵינֵי אַבְשָׁלֹם וּבְעֵינֵי כָּל־זִקְנֵי יִשְׂרָאֵל: וַיֹּאמֶר
אַבְשָׁלוֹם קְרָא נָא גַּם לְחוּשַׁי הָאַרְכִּי וְנִשְׁמְעָה מַה־בְּפִיו גַּם־הוּא:
ו וַיָּבֹא חוּשַׁי אֶל־אַבְשָׁלוֹם וַיֹּאמֶר אַבְשָׁלוֹם אֵלָיו לֵאמֹר כַּדָּבָר הַזֶּה
ז דִּבֶּר אֲחִיתֹפֶל הֲנַעֲשֶׂה אֶת־דְּבָרוֹ אִם־אַיִן אַתָּה דַבֵּר: וַיֹּאמֶר
חוּשַׁי אֶל־אַבְשָׁלוֹם לֹא־טוֹבָה הָעֵצָה אֲשֶׁר־יָעַץ אֲחִיתֹפֶל בַּפַּעַם
ח הַזֹּאת: וַיֹּאמֶר חוּשַׁי אַתָּה יָדַעְתָּ אֶת־אָבִיךָ וְאֶת־אֲנָשָׁיו כִּי גִבֹּרִים
הֵמָּה וּמָרֵי נֶפֶשׁ הֵמָּה כְּדֹב שַׁכּוּל בַּשָּׂדֶה וְאָבִיךָ אִישׁ מִלְחָמָה וְלֹא
ט יָלִין אֶת־הָעָם: הִנֵּה עַתָּה הוּא־נֶחְבָּא בְּאַחַת הַפְּחָתִים אוֹ בְּאַחַד
הַמְּקוֹמֹת וְהָיָה כִּנְפֹל בָּהֶם בַּתְּחִלָּה וְשָׁמַע הַשֹּׁמֵעַ וְאָמַר הָיְתָה מַגֵּפָה

10 and even the hearts of brave, lion-hearted men will surely melt, for all of Israel
knows that your father is a seasoned warrior, and that the men with him are
11 brave. And so I advise you: have all of Israel – from Dan to Be'er Sheva – gather
to you, as innumerable as the sand upon the seashore, and you yourself must
12 go forth in battle. When we come upon him – wherever he may be – we will
descend upon him as the dew settles on the earth, and not a single one will
13 be left of all the men who are with him. And should he withdraw into a city,
all of Israel will bring ropes to that city, and we will drag it away to the wadi
14 until not even a pebble remains." And Avshalom and all the men
of Israel declared, "The counsel of Ḥushai the Arkite is better than the counsel
of Aḥitofel." For the Lord had determined that Aḥitofel's
good counsel would be thwarted, in order for the Lord to bring evil upon
15 Avshalom. Then Ḥushai said to the priests Tzadok and Evyatar,
"This is what Aḥitofel advised Avshalom and the elders of Israel, and this is
16 what I advised. Now, send word quickly, informing David, 'Do not spend the
night on the wilderness steppes; cross over at once, or the king and everyone
17 with him will be engulfed.'" Now, Yehonatan and Aḥimaatz were stationed in
the Rogel Spring; a servant girl would go and inform them, and they would
go and inform King David, as they could not be seen coming into the city.
18 But when a boy saw them and informed Avshalom, the two of them left in a
hurry. They came to the house of a man in Baḥurim who had a well in his
19 courtyard, and they climbed down inside it. The man's wife then took a cloth,
stretched it over the mouth of the well, and spread groats over it, so nothing
20 was revealed. Avshalom's officials came to the woman's house and said,
"Where are Aḥimaatz and Yehonatan?" "They have crossed over the river
fords," the woman said to them. They searched but found nothing, and they
21 went back to Jerusalem. After they had left, they climbed out of the
well and went to inform King David. "Set out and cross over the water at
once," they said to David, "for this is how Aḥitofel advised to deal with you."
22 David set out at once along with all the troops who were with him, and they
crossed the Jordan; by the light of morning, every last one of them had
23 crossed the Jordan. When Aḥitofel saw that his counsel had not been taken,
he saddled his donkey and went straight to his home in his hometown. He
issued orders for his household, then he hanged himself. And he was buried
24 in his ancestral tomb. Meanwhile, David had reached Maḥanayim,
25 while Avshalom crossed the Jordan along with all the men of Israel. Avshalom
had appointed Amasa as army commander in Yoav's place. Amasa was the
son of a man named Yitra the Israelite, who had lain with Avigayil, the
26 daughter of Naḥash and the sister of Tzeruya, mother of Yoav. And Israel and
27 Avshalom set up camp in the land of Gilad. When David arrived in
Maḥanayim, Shovi son of Naḥash of Raba of the Amonites, Makhir son of

י בָּעָם אֲשֶׁר אַחֲרֵי אַבְשָׁלֹם: וְהוּא גַם־בֶּן־חַיִל אֲשֶׁר לִבּוֹ כְּלֵב הָאַרְיֵה
הִמֵּס יִמָּס כִּי־יֹדֵעַ כׇּל־יִשְׂרָאֵל כִּי־גִבּוֹר אָבִיךָ וּבְנֵי־חַיִל אֲשֶׁר אִתּוֹ:
יא כִּי יָעַצְתִּי הֵאָסֹף יֵאָסֵף עָלֶיךָ כׇל־יִשְׂרָאֵל מִדָּן וְעַד־בְּאֵר שֶׁבַע כַּחוֹל
יב אֲשֶׁר־עַל־הַיָּם לָרֹב וּפָנֶיךָ הֹלְכִים בַּקְרָב: וּבָאנוּ אֵלָיו באחת הַמְּקוֹמֹת בְּאַחַד
אֲשֶׁר נִמְצָא שָׁם וְנַחְנוּ עָלָיו כַּאֲשֶׁר יִפֹּל הַטַּל עַל־הָאֲדָמָה וְלֹא־נוֹתַר
יג בּוֹ וּבְכׇל־הָאֲנָשִׁים אֲשֶׁר־אִתּוֹ גַּם־אֶחָד: וְאִם־אֶל־עִיר יֵאָסֵף וְהִשִּׂיאוּ
כׇל־יִשְׂרָאֵל אֶל־הָעִיר הַהִיא חֲבָלִים וְסָחַבְנוּ אֹתוֹ עַד־הַנַּחַל עַד
יד אֲשֶׁר־לֹא־נִמְצָא שָׁם גַּם־צְרוֹר: וַיֹּאמֶר אַבְשָׁלוֹם וְכׇל־אִישׁ
יִשְׂרָאֵל טוֹבָה עֲצַת חוּשַׁי הָאַרְכִּי מֵעֲצַת אֲחִיתֹפֶל וַיהוָה
צִוָּה לְהָפֵר אֶת־עֲצַת אֲחִיתֹפֶל הַטּוֹבָה לְבַעֲבוּר הָבִיא יְהוָה אֶל־
טו אַבְשָׁלוֹם אֶת־הָרָעָה: וַיֹּאמֶר חוּשַׁי אֶל־צָדוֹק וְאֶל־אֶבְיָתָר
הַכֹּהֲנִים כָּזֹאת וְכָזֹאת יָעַץ אֲחִיתֹפֶל אֶת־אַבְשָׁלֹם וְאֵת זִקְנֵי יִשְׂרָאֵל
טז וְכָזֹאת וְכָזֹאת יָעַצְתִּי אָנִי: וְעַתָּה שִׁלְחוּ מְהֵרָה וְהַגִּידוּ לְדָוִד לֵאמֹר
אַל־תָּלֶן הַלַּיְלָה בְּעַרְבוֹת הַמִּדְבָּר וְגַם עָבוֹר תַּעֲבוֹר פֶּן יְבֻלַּע לַמֶּלֶךְ
יז וּלְכׇל־הָעָם אֲשֶׁר אִתּוֹ: וִיהוֹנָתָן וַאֲחִימַעַץ עֹמְדִים בְּעֵין־רֹגֵל וְהָלְכָה
הַשִּׁפְחָה וְהִגִּידָה לָהֶם וְהֵם יֵלְכוּ וְהִגִּידוּ לַמֶּלֶךְ דָּוִד כִּי לֹא יוּכְלוּ
יח לְהֵרָאוֹת לָבוֹא הָעִירָה: וַיַּרְא אֹתָם נַעַר וַיַּגֵּד לְאַבְשָׁלֹם וַיֵּלְכוּ שְׁנֵיהֶם
מְהֵרָה וַיָּבֹאוּ ׀ אֶל־בֵּית־אִישׁ בְּבַחוּרִים וְלוֹ בְאֵר בַּחֲצֵרוֹ וַיֵּרְדוּ שָׁם:
יט וַתִּקַּח הָאִשָּׁה וַתִּפְרֹשׂ אֶת־הַמָּסָךְ עַל־פְּנֵי הַבְּאֵר וַתִּשְׁטַח עָלָיו הָרִפוֹת
כ וְלֹא נוֹדַע דָּבָר: וַיָּבֹאוּ עַבְדֵי אַבְשָׁלוֹם אֶל־הָאִשָּׁה הַבַּיְתָה וַיֹּאמְרוּ ל
אַיֵּה אֲחִימַעַץ וִיהוֹנָתָן וַתֹּאמֶר לָהֶם הָאִשָּׁה עָבְרוּ מִיכַל הַמָּיִם
כא וַיְבַקְשׁוּ וְלֹא מָצָאוּ וַיָּשֻׁבוּ יְרוּשָׁלָם: וַיְהִי ׀ אַחֲרֵי לֶכְתָּם
וַיַּעֲלוּ מֵהַבְּאֵר וַיֵּלְכוּ וַיַּגִּדוּ לַמֶּלֶךְ דָּוִד וַיֹּאמְרוּ אֶל־דָּוִד קוּמוּ וְעִבְרוּ
כב מְהֵרָה אֶת־הַמַּיִם כִּי־כָכָה יָעַץ עֲלֵיכֶם אֲחִיתֹפֶל: וַיָּקׇם דָּוִד וְכׇל־הָעָם
אֲשֶׁר אִתּוֹ וַיַּעַבְרוּ אֶת־הַיַּרְדֵּן עַד־אוֹר הַבֹּקֶר עַד־אַחַד לֹא נֶעְדָּר
כג אֲשֶׁר לֹא־עָבַר אֶת־הַיַּרְדֵּן: וַאֲחִיתֹפֶל רָאָה כִּי לֹא נֶעֶשְׂתָה עֲצָתוֹ
וַיַּחֲבֹשׁ אֶת־הַחֲמוֹר וַיָּקׇם וַיֵּלֶךְ אֶל־בֵּיתוֹ אֶל־עִירוֹ וַיְצַו אֶל־בֵּיתוֹ
כד וַיֵּחָנַק וַיָּמׇת וַיִּקָּבֵר בְּקֶבֶר אָבִיו: וְדָוִד בָּא מַחֲנָיְמָה
כה וְאַבְשָׁלֹם עָבַר אֶת־הַיַּרְדֵּן הוּא וְכׇל־אִישׁ יִשְׂרָאֵל עִמּוֹ: וְאֶת־עֲמָשָׂא
שָׂם אַבְשָׁלֹם תַּחַת יוֹאָב עַל־הַצָּבָא וַעֲמָשָׂא בֶן־אִישׁ וּשְׁמוֹ יִתְרָא
הַיִּשְׂרְאֵלִי אֲשֶׁר־בָּא אֶל־אֲבִיגַל בַּת־נָחָשׁ אֲחוֹת צְרוּיָה אֵם יוֹאָב:
כו כז וַיִּחַן יִשְׂרָאֵל וְאַבְשָׁלֹם אֶרֶץ הַגִּלְעָד: וַיְהִי כְּבוֹא דָוִד

28 Amiel of Lo Devar, and Barzilai the Gileadite of Rogelim had set up couches
and basins and earthenware; wheat, barley, meal and toasted grain; beans and
29 roasted lentils and grain. They served honey and curds from the flock and
cheese from the herd for David and his troops to eat, for they thought, "The
18 1 troops must have grown hungry, weary, and thirsty in the wilderness." Now
David mustered the troops who were with him and appointed officers of
2 thousands and officers of hundreds over them. He sent a third of the troops
with Yoav, a third with Avishai son of Tzeruya, Yoav's brother, and a third with
Itai the Gittite. "And I, of course, will also march out with you," the
3 king proclaimed to the troops. But the troops said, "Do not march out, for if
we must retreat, they will pay us no heed; even if half of us die, they will pay
us no heed – for you are worth ten thousand of us. Right now, it is best if you
4 help us from the city." "Whatever seems best in your eyes, I will do,"
the king said to them. And the king stood by the gate as all the troops marched
5 out, in their hundreds and their thousands. The king then gave orders to Yoav,
Avishai, and Itai. "For my sake," he said, "deal gently with young Avshalom."
And the troops all heard the king's orders about Avshalom to all of his officials.
6 The troops marched out to the field toward Israel, and battle took place in the
7 forest of Efrayim. There, the Israelite troops were routed before David's men –
8 there was a devastating loss that day of twenty thousand. Battle broke out all
over the land, and on that day, the forest itself consumed more troops than
9 the sword. Meanwhile, Avshalom encountered David's men. Avshalom was
riding on his mule when the mule passed beneath the tangled branches of a
great oak; the hair of his head caught fast in the oak, and he was left dangling
10 between heaven and earth as the mule beneath him continued on. Someone
saw and reported this to Yoav. "Look!" he said. "I saw Avshalom hanging from
11 an oak." "What, you just saw that?" Yoav said to the man reporting to him.
"Why didn't you cut him down to the ground on the spot? I would have owed
12 you ten measures of silver and a belt." "Even if I felt the weight of a thousand
silver pieces in my hands, I would not dare make a move against the son of
the king," said the man to Yoav, "for we heard ourselves how the king charged
13 you, Avishai and Itai, 'Whoever it may be – watch over young Avshalom.' But
if I had betrayed myself – and nothing can be hidden from the king – why,
14 you would have stood aloof." "I'll wait for you no longer," said Yoav, and he
seized three darts and thrust them into the heart of Avshalom, who was still
15 alive in the heart of the oak. Ten of Yoav's arms-bearers closed in and struck
16 Avshalom to death. Then Yoav blasted the ram's horn and the troops ceased
17 their pursuit of Israel, for Yoav held back the troops. They took Avshalom and
flung him into a deep pit in the forest and set up a great heap of stones over

מַחֲנָיְמָה וְשֹׁבִי בֶן־נָחָשׁ מֵרַבַּת בְּנֵי־עַמּוֹן וּמָכִיר בֶּן־עַמִּיאֵל מִלֹּא דְבָר
כח וּבַרְזִלַּי הַגִּלְעָדִי מֵרֹגְלִים: מִשְׁכָּב וְסַפּוֹת וּכְלִי יוֹצֵר וְחִטִּים וּשְׂעֹרִים
כט וְקֶמַח וְקָלִי וּפוֹל וַעֲדָשִׁים וְקָלִי: וּדְבַשׁ וְחֶמְאָה וְצֹאן וּשְׁפוֹת בָּקָר
הִגִּישׁוּ לְדָוִד וְלָעָם אֲשֶׁר־אִתּוֹ לֶאֱכוֹל כִּי אָמְרוּ הָעָם רָעֵב וְעָיֵף
יח א וְצָמֵא בַּמִּדְבָּר: וַיִּפְקֹד דָּוִד אֶת־הָעָם אֲשֶׁר אִתּוֹ וַיָּשֶׂם עֲלֵיהֶם שָׂרֵי
ב אֲלָפִים וְשָׂרֵי מֵאוֹת: וַיְשַׁלַּח דָּוִד אֶת־הָעָם הַשְּׁלִשִׁית בְּיַד־יוֹאָב
וְהַשְּׁלִשִׁית בְּיַד אֲבִישַׁי בֶּן־צְרוּיָה אֲחִי יוֹאָב וְהַשְּׁלִשִׁת בְּיַד אִתַּי
הַגִּתִּי וַיֹּאמֶר הַמֶּלֶךְ אֶל־הָעָם יָצֹא אֵצֵא גַּם־אֲנִי עִמָּכֶם:
ג וַיֹּאמֶר הָעָם לֹא תֵצֵא כִּי אִם־נֹס נָנוּס לֹא־יָשִׂימוּ אֵלֵינוּ לֵב וְאִם־יָמֻתוּ
חֶצְיֵנוּ לֹא־יָשִׂימוּ אֵלֵינוּ לֵב כִּי־עַתָּה כָמֹנוּ עֲשָׂרָה אֲלָפִים וְעַתָּה
ד טוֹב כִּי־תִהְיֶה־לָּנוּ מֵעִיר לעזיר: וַיֹּאמֶר אֲלֵיהֶם הַמֶּלֶךְ לַעְזוֹר
אֲשֶׁר־יִיטַב בְּעֵינֵיכֶם אֶעֱשֶׂה וַיַּעֲמֹד הַמֶּלֶךְ אֶל־יַד הַשַּׁעַר וְכָל־הָעָם
ה יָצְאוּ לְמֵאוֹת וְלַאֲלָפִים: וַיְצַו הַמֶּלֶךְ אֶת־יוֹאָב וְאֶת־אֲבִישַׁי וְאֶת־אִתַּי
לֵאמֹר לְאַט־לִי לַנַּעַר לְאַבְשָׁלוֹם וְכָל־הָעָם שָׁמְעוּ בְּצַוֹּת הַמֶּלֶךְ אֶת־
ו כָּל־הַשָּׂרִים עַל־דְּבַר אַבְשָׁלוֹם: וַיֵּצֵא הָעָם הַשָּׂדֶה לִקְרַאת יִשְׂרָאֵל
ז וַתְּהִי הַמִּלְחָמָה בְּיַעַר אֶפְרָיִם: וַיִּנָּגְפוּ שָׁם עַם יִשְׂרָאֵל לִפְנֵי עַבְדֵי
ח דָוִד וַתְּהִי־שָׁם הַמַּגֵּפָה גְדוֹלָה בַּיּוֹם הַהוּא עֶשְׂרִים אָלֶף: וַתְּהִי־שָׁם
הַמִּלְחָמָה נפצות עַל־פְּנֵי כָל־הָאָרֶץ וַיֶּרֶב הַיַּעַר לֶאֱכֹל בָּעָם מֵאֲשֶׁר נָפֹצֶת
ט אָכְלָה הַחֶרֶב בַּיּוֹם הַהוּא: וַיִּקָּרֵא אַבְשָׁלוֹם לִפְנֵי עַבְדֵי דָוִד וְאַבְשָׁלוֹם
רֹכֵב עַל־הַפֶּרֶד וַיָּבֹא הַפֶּרֶד תַּחַת שׂוֹבֶךְ הָאֵלָה הַגְּדוֹלָה וַיֶּחֱזַק רֹאשׁוֹ
י בָאֵלָה וַיֻּתַּן בֵּין הַשָּׁמַיִם וּבֵין הָאָרֶץ וְהַפֶּרֶד אֲשֶׁר־תַּחְתָּיו עָבָר: וַיַּרְא
אִישׁ אֶחָד וַיַּגֵּד לְיוֹאָב וַיֹּאמֶר הִנֵּה רָאִיתִי אֶת־אַבְשָׁלֹם תָּלוּי בָּאֵלָה:
יא וַיֹּאמֶר יוֹאָב לָאִישׁ הַמַּגִּיד לוֹ וְהִנֵּה רָאִיתָ וּמַדּוּעַ לֹא־הִכִּיתוֹ שָׁם
יב אָרְצָה וְעָלַי לָתֶת לְךָ עֲשָׂרָה כֶסֶף וַחֲגֹרָה אֶחָת: וַיֹּאמֶר הָאִישׁ אֶל־
יוֹאָב ולא אָנֹכִי שֹׁקֵל עַל־כַּפַּי אֶלֶף כֶּסֶף לֹא־אֶשְׁלַח יָדִי אֶל־בֶּן־הַמֶּלֶךְ וְלוּ
כִּי בְאָזְנֵינוּ צִוָּה הַמֶּלֶךְ אֹתְךָ וְאֶת־אֲבִישַׁי וְאֶת־אִתַּי לֵאמֹר שִׁמְרוּ־
יג מִי בַּנַּעַר בְּאַבְשָׁלוֹם: אוֹ־עָשִׂיתִי בנפשו שֶׁקֶר וְכָל־דָּבָר לֹא־יִכָּחֵד בְנַפְשִׁי
יד מִן־הַמֶּלֶךְ וְאַתָּה תִּתְיַצֵּב מִנֶּגֶד: וַיֹּאמֶר יוֹאָב לֹא־כֵן אֹחִילָה לְפָנֶיךָ
וַיִּקַּח שְׁלֹשָׁה שְׁבָטִים בְּכַפּוֹ וַיִּתְקָעֵם בְּלֵב אַבְשָׁלוֹם עוֹדֶנּוּ חַי בְּלֵב
טו הָאֵלָה: וַיָּסֹבּוּ עֲשָׂרָה נְעָרִים נֹשְׂאֵי כְּלֵי יוֹאָב וַיַּכּוּ אֶת־אַבְשָׁלוֹם
טז וַיְמִתֻהוּ: וַיִּתְקַע יוֹאָב בַּשֹּׁפָר וַיָּשָׁב הָעָם מִרְדֹף אַחֲרֵי יִשְׂרָאֵל כִּי־חָשַׂךְ
יז יוֹאָב אֶת־הָעָם: וַיִּקְחוּ אֶת־אַבְשָׁלוֹם וַיַּשְׁלִכוּ אֹתוֹ בַיַּעַר אֶל־הַפַּחַת

18 him; meanwhile, all of Israel fled back to their tents. Now, during his lifetime,
Avshalom had taken over the monument in the Valley of the King and set it
up for himself, for he thought, "I have no son to commemorate my name,"
and he named the monument for himself, calling it Avshalom's Monument,
19 as it is called to this day. Aḥimaatz son of Tzadok then said, "I will
now run and bring news to the king, for the Lord has defended him from his
20 enemies' hands." "No, you will not be the bearer of news today," Yoav said to
him. "Perhaps another day you will bring news. But today you will not bring
21 news, for the king's son is dead." And Yoav said to the Kushite, "Go – report
22 what you have seen to the king." The Kushite bowed to Yoav and ran off. But
Aḥimaatz persisted and said to Yoav, "Come what may – let me run as well
after the Kushite." "Why should you run, my son," said Yoav, "when your news
23 will not be welcomed?" "Come what may, I will run." "So run," he said to him,
24 and Aḥimaatz ran by the way of the plain, and overtook the Kushite. Now
David was sitting between the two gates. The lookout had gone up to the roof
of the gate, to the wall, when he looked up and suddenly saw a man running
25 by himself. The lookout called out and reported to the king. "If he is alone,"
26 the king said, "he has news to tell," as he came closer. Then the lookout saw
another man running, and the lookout called out to the gate. "Look – a man
27 running by himself," he said. "He, too, has news," said the king. "It seems to
me that the first one runs like Aḥimaatz son of Tzadok," said the lookout.
"That one is a good man," said the king. "He must be coming with good news."
28 Aḥimaatz called out to the king, "All is well," and bowed to the king with his
face to the ground. "Blessed is the Lord your God," he said, "who has handed
29 over the men who raised their hands against my lord the king." "Is
all well with young Avshalom?" asked the king. "I saw a great crowd when the
king's servant, Yoav, was sending your servant off," said Aḥimaatz, "but I know
30 not what…" "Turn aside," said the king, "and stand by," and he turned aside
31 and stood by. Just then, the Kushite arrived. "Let it be known to my lord the
king," said the Kushite, "that today the Lord has defended you against all
32 those who rose against you." "But is all well with young Avshalom?"
the king said to the Kushite, and the Kushite replied, "May all my lord the
king's enemies, and all those who have risen against you to harm you, fare like
19 1 that young man." The king shuddered, made his way up to the chamber
above the gate, and wept. And this is what he cried as he went: "My son,
Avshalom! O my son, my son Avshalom! If only I had died instead of you, O
2 Avshalom, my son, my son!" Yoav was told, "Look, the king is weeping and
3 mourning for Avshalom." And that day's victory turned into mourning for all
the troops, for on that day, the troops heard that the king was grieving for his
4 son. And on that day, the troops stole into the city when they arrived, as

הַגָּדוֹל וַיַּצִּבוּ עָלָיו גַּל־אֲבָנִים גָּדוֹל מְאֹד וְכָל־יִשְׂרָאֵל נָסוּ אִישׁ לְאֹהָלָו׃
יח וְאַבְשָׁלֹם לָקַח וַיַּצֶּב־לוֹ בְחַיָּו אֶת־מַצֶּבֶת אֲשֶׁר בְּעֵמֶק־הַמֶּלֶךְ כִּי
אָמַר אֵין־לִי בֵן בַּעֲבוּר הַזְכִּיר שְׁמִי וַיִּקְרָא לַמַּצֶּבֶת עַל־שְׁמוֹ וַיִּקָּרֵא
יט לָהּ יַד אַבְשָׁלֹם עַד הַיּוֹם הַזֶּה׃ וַאֲחִימַעַץ בֶּן־צָדוֹק
אָמַר אָרוּצָה נָּא וַאֲבַשְּׂרָה אֶת־הַמֶּלֶךְ כִּי־שְׁפָטוֹ יְהוָה מִיַּד אֹיְבָיו׃
כ וַיֹּאמֶר לוֹ יוֹאָב לֹא אִישׁ בְּשֹׂרָה אַתָּה הַיּוֹם הַזֶּה וּבִשַּׂרְתָּ בְּיוֹם אַחֵר
כא וְהַיּוֹם הַזֶּה לֹא תְבַשֵּׂר כִּי עַל־ בֶּן־הַמֶּלֶךְ מֵת׃ וַיֹּאמֶר יוֹאָב לַכּוּשִׁי כֵּן
כב לֵךְ הַגֵּד לַמֶּלֶךְ אֲשֶׁר רָאִיתָה וַיִּשְׁתַּחוּ כוּשִׁי לְיוֹאָב וַיָּרֹץ׃ וַיֹּסֶף עוֹד
אֲחִימַעַץ בֶּן־צָדוֹק וַיֹּאמֶר אֶל־יוֹאָב וִיהִי מָה אָרֻצָה־נָּא גַם־אָנִי
אַחֲרֵי הַכּוּשִׁי וַיֹּאמֶר יוֹאָב לָמָּה־זֶּה אַתָּה רָץ בְּנִי וּלְכָה אֵין־בְּשׂוֹרָה
כג מֹצֵאת׃ וִיהִי־מָה אָרוּץ וַיֹּאמֶר לוֹ רוּץ וַיָּרָץ אֲחִימַעַץ דֶּרֶךְ הַכִּכָּר
כד וַיַּעֲבֹר אֶת־הַכּוּשִׁי׃ וְדָוִד יוֹשֵׁב בֵּין־שְׁנֵי הַשְּׁעָרִים וַיֵּלֶךְ הַצֹּפֶה אֶל־
גַּג הַשַּׁעַר אֶל־הַחוֹמָה וַיִּשָּׂא אֶת־עֵינָיו וַיַּרְא וְהִנֵּה־אִישׁ רָץ לְבַדּוֹ׃
כה וַיִּקְרָא הַצֹּפֶה וַיַּגֵּד לַמֶּלֶךְ וַיֹּאמֶר הַמֶּלֶךְ אִם־לְבַדּוֹ בְּשׂוֹרָה בְּפִיו וַיֵּלֶךְ
כו הָלוֹךְ וְקָרֵב׃ וַיַּרְא הַצֹּפֶה אִישׁ־אַחֵר רָץ וַיִּקְרָא הַצֹּפֶה אֶל־הַשֹּׁעֵר
כז וַיֹּאמֶר הִנֵּה־אִישׁ רָץ לְבַדּוֹ וַיֹּאמֶר הַמֶּלֶךְ גַּם־זֶה מְבַשֵּׂר׃ וַיֹּאמֶר לא
הַצֹּפֶה אֲנִי רֹאֶה אֶת־מְרוּצַת הָרִאשׁוֹן כִּמְרֻצַת אֲחִימַעַץ בֶּן־צָדוֹק
כח וַיֹּאמֶר הַמֶּלֶךְ אִישׁ־טוֹב זֶה וְאֶל־בְּשׂוֹרָה טוֹבָה יָבוֹא׃ וַיִּקְרָא אֲחִימַעַץ
וַיֹּאמֶר אֶל־הַמֶּלֶךְ שָׁלוֹם וַיִּשְׁתַּחוּ לַמֶּלֶךְ לְאַפָּיו אָרְצָה וַיֹּאמֶר בָּרוּךְ
יְהוָה אֱלֹהֶיךָ אֲשֶׁר סִגַּר אֶת־הָאֲנָשִׁים אֲשֶׁר־נָשְׂאוּ אֶת־יָדָם בַּאדֹנִי
כט הַמֶּלֶךְ׃ וַיֹּאמֶר הַמֶּלֶךְ שָׁלוֹם לַנַּעַר לְאַבְשָׁלוֹם וַיֹּאמֶר
אֲחִימַעַץ רָאִיתִי הֶהָמוֹן הַגָּדוֹל לִשְׁלֹחַ אֶת־עֶבֶד הַמֶּלֶךְ יוֹאָב וְאֶת־
ל עַבְדֶּךָ וְלֹא יָדַעְתִּי מָה׃ וַיֹּאמֶר הַמֶּלֶךְ סֹב הִתְיַצֵּב כֹּה וַיִּסֹּב וַיַּעֲמֹד׃
לא וְהִנֵּה הַכּוּשִׁי בָּא וַיֹּאמֶר הַכּוּשִׁי יִתְבַּשֵּׂר אֲדֹנִי הַמֶּלֶךְ כִּי־שְׁפָטְךָ יְהוָה
לב הַיּוֹם מִיַּד כָּל־הַקָּמִים עָלֶיךָ׃ וַיֹּאמֶר הַמֶּלֶךְ אֶל־הַכּוּשִׁי
הֲשָׁלוֹם לַנַּעַר לְאַבְשָׁלוֹם וַיֹּאמֶר הַכּוּשִׁי יִהְיוּ כַנַּעַר אֹיְבֵי אֲדֹנִי הַמֶּלֶךְ
יט א וְכֹל אֲשֶׁר־קָמוּ עָלֶיךָ לְרָעָה׃ וַיִּרְגַּז הַמֶּלֶךְ וַיַּעַל עַל־
עֲלִיַּת הַשַּׁעַר וַיֵּבְךְּ וְכֹה ׀ אָמַר בְּלֶכְתּוֹ בְּנִי אַבְשָׁלוֹם בְּנִי בְנִי אַבְשָׁלוֹם
ב מִי־יִתֵּן מוּתִי אֲנִי תַחְתֶּיךָ אַבְשָׁלוֹם בְּנִי בְנִי׃ וַיֻּגַּד לְיוֹאָב הִנֵּה הַמֶּלֶךְ
ג בֹּכֶה וַיִּתְאַבֵּל עַל־אַבְשָׁלֹם׃ וַתְּהִי הַתְּשֻׁעָה בַּיּוֹם הַהוּא לְאֵבֶל לְכָל־
ד הָעָם כִּי־שָׁמַע הָעָם בַּיּוֹם הַהוּא לֵאמֹר נֶעֱצַב הַמֶּלֶךְ עַל־בְּנוֹ׃ וַיִּתְגַּנֵּב
הָעָם בַּיּוֹם הַהוּא לָבוֹא הָעִיר כַּאֲשֶׁר יִתְגַּנֵּב הָעָם הַנִּכְלָמִים בְּנוּסָם

5 disgraced troops steal in when they flee from battle. And the king hid his
face, and cried out at the top of his voice, "My son, Avshalom! O Avshalom,
6 my son, my son!" But Yoav entered the king's quarters. "Today," he
said, "you have humiliated your own supporters, who saved your life – and
the lives of your sons and daughters, and the lives of your wives, and the lives
7 of your concubines – by showing love for those who hate you and hatred for
those who love you. Today, you have made it clear that your officers and
subjects are nothing to you. Today, I realize that were Avshalom alive and all
8 of us dead right now – why, then, you would be pleased. Now get up, and go
out, and make a heartfelt speech to your servants. For by the Lord, I swear
that if you do not go out, not a single man will be on your side by tonight, and
that would be a worse evil for you than all the evil that has befallen you from
9 your youth until now." And the king got up and sat by the gate.
All the troops were told, "The king is now sitting at the gate." And all the
troops came before the king. Meanwhile, the Israelites had fled back to their
10 homes. And all the people were arguing throughout the tribes of
Israel. "The king delivered us from the hands of our enemies," they said, "and
he saved us from the clutches of the Philistines, and now he has fled from
11 the land because of Avshalom. But Avshalom, whom we anointed over
us, died in battle. So now, why have you done nothing to bring the king
12 back?" King David sent to Tzadok and Evyatar the priests, saying,
"Speak to the elders of Yehuda, asking, 'Why should you be the last ones to
bring the king back to his palace? The word of all Israel has already reached
13 the king in his quarters. You are my brothers, my own flesh and blood – why
14 should you be the last ones to bring the king back?' And to Amasa, say, 'You
are of my own flesh and blood; so may God do to me – and more – if you will
15 not be the commander of my army in Yoav's place from now on.'" And he
drew the hearts of every man in Yehuda as if they were a single man, and they
16 sent a message to the king: "Come back, you and all your supporters." So the
king turned back, and when he reached the Jordan, the contingent from
Yehuda had come to Gilgal to meet the king and escort the king across the
17 Jordan. Shimi son of Gera, the Benjaminite from Baḥurim, hurried down
18 to meet David together with the men of Yehuda. A thousand men from
Binyamin accompanied him along with Tziva, the servant of the house of
Sha'ul, his fifteen sons, and twenty slaves. They rushed down to the Jordan
19 before the king, crossing back and forth to bring the royal household across,
to gain favor in his sight. And Shimi son of Gera flung himself before the king
20 as he was crossing the Jordan. "Let my lord not consider me guilty," he said
to the king, "and do not hark back to the crime your servant committed on
21 the day my lord the king left Jerusalem; let the king not take it to heart. For
your servant knows that I have sinned, and now I have come down here today,
22 the first of all the House of Yosef, to meet my lord the king." Avishai
son of Tzeruya spoke up. "Just for that, will Shimi be pardoned from death?"

ה בַּמִּלְחָמָה: וְהַמֶּלֶךְ לָאַט אֶת־פָּנָיו וַיִּזְעַק הַמֶּלֶךְ קוֹל גָּדוֹל בְּנִי אַבְשָׁלוֹם
ו אַבְשָׁלוֹם בְּנִי בְנִי: וַיָּבֹא יוֹאָב אֶל־הַמֶּלֶךְ הַבָּיִת וַיֹּאמַר
הֹבַשְׁתָּ הַיּוֹם אֶת־פְּנֵי כָל־עֲבָדֶיךָ הַמְמַלְּטִים אֶת־נַפְשְׁךָ הַיּוֹם וְאֵת
ז נֶפֶשׁ בָּנֶיךָ וּבְנֹתֶיךָ וְנֶפֶשׁ נָשֶׁיךָ וְנֶפֶשׁ פִּלַגְשֶׁיךָ: לְאַהֲבָה אֶת־שֹׂנְאֶיךָ
וְלִשְׂנֹא אֶת־אֹהֲבֶיךָ כִּי ׀ הִגַּדְתָּ הַיּוֹם כִּי אֵין לְךָ שָׂרִים וַעֲבָדִים כִּי ׀
יָדַעְתִּי הַיּוֹם כִּי לא אַבְשָׁלוֹם חַי וְכֻלָּנוּ הַיּוֹם מֵתִים כִּי־אָז יָשָׁר בְּעֵינֶיךָ: לו
ח וְעַתָּה קוּם צֵא וְדַבֵּר עַל־לֵב עֲבָדֶיךָ כִּי בַיהוה נִשְׁבַּעְתִּי כִּי־אֵינְךָ יוֹצֵא
אִם־יָלִין אִישׁ אִתְּךָ הַלַּיְלָה וְרָעָה לְךָ זֹאת מִכָּל־הָרָעָה אֲשֶׁר־בָּאָה
ט עָלֶיךָ מִנְּעֻרֶיךָ עַד־עָתָּה: וַיָּקָם הַמֶּלֶךְ וַיֵּשֶׁב בַּשָּׁעַר
וּלְכָל־הָעָם הִגִּידוּ לֵאמֹר הִנֵּה הַמֶּלֶךְ יוֹשֵׁב בַּשַּׁעַר וַיָּבֹא כָל־הָעָם
י לִפְנֵי הַמֶּלֶךְ וְיִשְׂרָאֵל נָס אִישׁ לְאֹהָלָיו: וַיְהִי כָּל־הָעָם נָדוֹן
בְּכָל־שִׁבְטֵי יִשְׂרָאֵל לֵאמֹר הַמֶּלֶךְ הִצִּילָנוּ ׀ מִכַּף אֹיְבֵינוּ וְהוּא מִלְּטָנוּ
יא מִכַּף פְּלִשְׁתִּים וְעַתָּה בָּרַח מִן־הָאָרֶץ מֵעַל אַבְשָׁלוֹם: וְאַבְשָׁלוֹם אֲשֶׁר
מָשַׁחְנוּ עָלֵינוּ מֵת בַּמִּלְחָמָה וְעַתָּה לָמָה אַתֶּם מַחֲרִשִׁים לְהָשִׁיב
יב אֶת־הַמֶּלֶךְ: וְהַמֶּלֶךְ דָּוִד שָׁלַח אֶל־צָדוֹק וְאֶל־אֶבְיָתָר
הַכֹּהֲנִים לֵאמֹר דַּבְּרוּ אֶל־זִקְנֵי יְהוּדָה לֵאמֹר לָמָּה תִהְיוּ אַחֲרֹנִים
לְהָשִׁיב אֶת־הַמֶּלֶךְ אֶל־בֵּיתוֹ וּדְבַר כָּל־יִשְׂרָאֵל בָּא אֶל־הַמֶּלֶךְ אֶל־
יג בֵּיתוֹ: אַחַי אַתֶּם עַצְמִי וּבְשָׂרִי אַתֶּם וְלָמָּה תִהְיוּ אַחֲרֹנִים לְהָשִׁיב
יד אֶת־הַמֶּלֶךְ: וְלַעֲמָשָׂא תֹּמְרוּ הֲלוֹא עַצְמִי וּבְשָׂרִי אַתָּה כֹּה יַעֲשֶׂה־לִּי
אֱלֹהִים וְכֹה יוֹסִיף אִם־לֹא שַׂר־צָבָא תִּהְיֶה לְפָנַי כָּל־הַיָּמִים תַּחַת
טו יוֹאָב: וַיַּט אֶת־לְבַב כָּל־אִישׁ־יְהוּדָה כְּאִישׁ אֶחָד וַיִּשְׁלְחוּ אֶל־הַמֶּלֶךְ
טז שׁוּב אַתָּה וְכָל־עֲבָדֶיךָ: וַיָּשָׁב הַמֶּלֶךְ וַיָּבֹא עַד־הַיַּרְדֵּן וִיהוּדָה בָּא
הַגִּלְגָּלָה לָלֶכֶת לִקְרַאת הַמֶּלֶךְ לְהַעֲבִיר אֶת־הַמֶּלֶךְ אֶת־הַיַּרְדֵּן:
יז וַיְמַהֵר שִׁמְעִי בֶן־גֵּרָא בֶּן־הַיְמִינִי אֲשֶׁר מִבַּחוּרִים וַיֵּרֶד עִם־אִישׁ יְהוּדָה
יח לִקְרַאת הַמֶּלֶךְ דָּוִד: וְאֶלֶף אִישׁ עִמּוֹ מִבִּנְיָמִן וְצִיבָא נַעַר בֵּית שָׁאוּל
וַחֲמֵשֶׁת עָשָׂר בָּנָיו וְעֶשְׂרִים עֲבָדָיו אִתּוֹ וְצָלְחוּ הַיַּרְדֵּן לִפְנֵי הַמֶּלֶךְ:
יט וְעָבְרָה הָעֲבָרָה לַעֲבִיר אֶת־בֵּית הַמֶּלֶךְ וְלַעֲשׂוֹת הַטּוֹב בְּעֵינָו וְשִׁמְעִי
כ בֶן־גֵּרָא נָפַל לִפְנֵי הַמֶּלֶךְ בְּעָבְרוֹ בַּיַּרְדֵּן: וַיֹּאמֶר אֶל־הַמֶּלֶךְ אַל־
יַחֲשָׁב־לִי אֲדֹנִי עָוֺן וְאַל־תִּזְכֹּר אֵת אֲשֶׁר הֶעֱוָה עַבְדְּךָ בַּיּוֹם אֲשֶׁר־יָצָא
כא אֲדֹנִי־הַמֶּלֶךְ מִירוּשָׁלִָם לָשׂוּם הַמֶּלֶךְ אֶל־לִבּוֹ: כִּי יָדַע עַבְדְּךָ כִּי אֲנִי
חָטָאתִי וְהִנֵּה־בָאתִי הַיּוֹם רִאשׁוֹן לְכָל־בֵּית יוֹסֵף לָרֶדֶת לִקְרַאת
כב אֲדֹנִי הַמֶּלֶךְ: וַיַּעַן אֲבִישַׁי בֶּן־צְרוּיָה וַיֹּאמֶר הֲתַחַת זֹאת

23 he asked. "He cursed the LORD's anointed one!" "What have I to do
with you, sons of Tzeruya, that you should oppose me today?" said David.
"Today, should any man of Israel be put to death? Today, am I not aware that
24 I am king of Israel? You shall not die," the king said to Shimi, and he gave him
25 his oath. And Mefivoshet, grandson of Sha'ul, had made his way
down to meet the king. He had not tended to his feet, trimmed his mustache,
or washed his clothes from the day of the king's departure to the day of
26 his safe return. When he arrived from Jerusalem to meet the king, the king
27 asked him, "Why did you fail to accompany me, Mefivoshet?" "My lord the
king," he said, "my servant deceived me, for your servant planned, 'I will
saddle a donkey for me to ride upon and accompany the king, as your servant
28 is lame.' But he slandered your servant to my lord the king. Now, my lord the
29 king is like an angel of God – do whatever is best in your eyes. For all of
my father's household was doomed to death by my lord the king, yet you set
your servant among those who dine at your table, so what further right do
30 I have to cry out to the king?" "Speak no further," the king said to
31 him. "I have decided that you and Tziva shall divide the land." "He can take
it all," Mefivoshet said to the king, "now that the king has come home
32 safely." And now Barzilai the Gileadite came down from Rogelim
and crossed over the Jordan with the king, to see him across the Jordan.
33 Barzilai was very old, eighty years old, yet he had provided the king with
34 sustenance upon his return to Maḥanayim, for he was a very great man. "Cross
over with me," the king said to Barzilai, "and I will provide for you in Jerusalem,
35 together with me." "How many years of my life are left that I should go up
36 to Jerusalem with the king?" Barzilai said to the king. "I am now eighty
years old; can I still tell the difference between good and bad when your
servant tastes food or drink or hears the voices of men and women singing?
37 Why, then, should your servant remain a burden to my lord the king? Your
servant barely managed to cross the Jordan with the king, so why should the
38 king repay me with this favor? Let your servant stay behind, and I will die in
my hometown where my mother and father are buried. But here – your
servant Kimham will cross over with my lord the king; treat him as you see
39 fit." "Kimham will cross over with me," said the king, "and I will treat
40 him as you see fit. Whatever you wish me to do, I will do for you." Then all
the troops crossed the Jordan, and the king crossed over. The king kissed
41 Barzilai and blessed him, and he went back home. Then the king
crossed over toward Gilgal, and Kimhan crossed over with him. All the men
42 of Yehuda crossed over with the king, as well as half of the men of Israel. And
now all the men of Israel reached the king, and they said to the king, "Why

כג לֹא יוּמַת שִׁמְעִי כִּי קִלֵּל אֶת־מְשִׁיחַ יְהוָה: וַיֹּאמֶר דָּוִד
מַה־לִּי וְלָכֶם בְּנֵי צְרוּיָה כִּי־תִהְיוּ־לִי הַיּוֹם לְשָׂטָן הַיּוֹם יוּמַת אִישׁ
כד בְּיִשְׂרָאֵל כִּי הֲלוֹא יָדַעְתִּי כִּי הַיּוֹם אֲנִי־מֶלֶךְ עַל־יִשְׂרָאֵל: וַיֹּאמֶר
כה הַמֶּלֶךְ אֶל־שִׁמְעִי לֹא תָמוּת וַיִּשָּׁבַע לוֹ הַמֶּלֶךְ: וּמְפִבֹשֶׁת
בֶּן־שָׁאוּל יָרַד לִקְרַאת הַמֶּלֶךְ וְלֹא־עָשָׂה רַגְלָיו וְלֹא־עָשָׂה שְׂפָמוֹ
וְאֶת־בְּגָדָיו לֹא כִבֵּס לְמִן־הַיּוֹם לֶכֶת הַמֶּלֶךְ עַד־הַיּוֹם אֲשֶׁר־בָּא
כו בְשָׁלוֹם: וַיְהִי כִּי־בָא יְרוּשָׁלַםִ לִקְרַאת הַמֶּלֶךְ וַיֹּאמֶר לוֹ הַמֶּלֶךְ לָמָּה
כז לֹא־הָלַכְתָּ עִמִּי מְפִיבֹשֶׁת: וַיֹּאמַר אֲדֹנִי הַמֶּלֶךְ עַבְדִּי רִמָּנִי כִּי־אָמַר
עַבְדְּךָ אֶחְבְּשָׁה־לִּי הַחֲמוֹר וְאֶרְכַּב עָלֶיהָ וְאֵלֵךְ אֶת־הַמֶּלֶךְ כִּי פִסֵּחַ
כח עַבְדֶּךָ: וַיְרַגֵּל בְּעַבְדְּךָ אֶל־אֲדֹנִי הַמֶּלֶךְ וַאדֹנִי הַמֶּלֶךְ כְּמַלְאַךְ הָאֱלֹהִים
כט וַעֲשֵׂה הַטּוֹב בְּעֵינֶיךָ: כִּי לֹא הָיָה כָּל־בֵּית אָבִי כִּי אִם־אַנְשֵׁי־מָוֶת
לַאדֹנִי הַמֶּלֶךְ וַתָּשֶׁת אֶת־עַבְדְּךָ בְּאֹכְלֵי שֻׁלְחָנֶךָ וּמַה־יֶּשׁ־לִי עוֹד
ל צְדָקָה וְלִזְעֹק עוֹד אֶל־הַמֶּלֶךְ: וַיֹּאמֶר לוֹ הַמֶּלֶךְ לָמָּה
לא תְּדַבֵּר עוֹד דְּבָרֶיךָ אָמַרְתִּי אַתָּה וְצִיבָא תַּחְלְקוּ אֶת־הַשָּׂדֶה: וַיֹּאמֶר
מְפִיבֹשֶׁת אֶל־הַמֶּלֶךְ גַּם אֶת־הַכֹּל יִקָּח אַחֲרֵי אֲשֶׁר־בָּא אֲדֹנִי הַמֶּלֶךְ
לב בְּשָׁלוֹם אֶל־בֵּיתוֹ: וּבַרְזִלַּי הַגִּלְעָדִי יָרַד מֵרֹגְלִים וַיַּעֲבֹר
לג אֶת־הַמֶּלֶךְ הַיַּרְדֵּן לְשַׁלְּחוֹ אֶת־בירדן: וּבַרְזִלַּי זָקֵן מְאֹד בֶּן־שְׁמֹנִים הַיַּרְדֵּן
שָׁנָה וְהוּא־כִלְכַּל אֶת־הַמֶּלֶךְ בְּשִׁיבָתוֹ בְמַחֲנַיִם כִּי־אִישׁ גָּדוֹל הוּא
לד מְאֹד: וַיֹּאמֶר הַמֶּלֶךְ אֶל־בַּרְזִלָּי אַתָּה עֲבֹר אִתִּי וְכִלְכַּלְתִּי אֹתְךָ עִמָּדִי
לה בִּירוּשָׁלָםִ: וַיֹּאמֶר בַּרְזִלַּי אֶל־הַמֶּלֶךְ כַּמָּה יְמֵי שְׁנֵי חַיַּי כִּי־אֶעֱלֶה
לו אֶת־הַמֶּלֶךְ יְרוּשָׁלָםִ: בֶּן־שְׁמֹנִים שָׁנָה אָנֹכִי הַיּוֹם הַאֵדַע ׀ בֵּין־טוֹב
לְרָע אִם־יִטְעַם עַבְדְּךָ אֶת־אֲשֶׁר אֹכַל וְאֶת־אֲשֶׁר אֶשְׁתֶּה אִם־אֶשְׁמַע
עוֹד בְּקוֹל שָׁרִים וְשָׁרוֹת וְלָמָּה יִהְיֶה עַבְדְּךָ עוֹד לְמַשָּׂא אֶל־אֲדֹנִי
לז הַמֶּלֶךְ: כִּמְעַט יַעֲבֹר עַבְדְּךָ אֶת־הַיַּרְדֵּן אֶת־הַמֶּלֶךְ וְלָמָּה יִגְמְלֵנִי
לח הַמֶּלֶךְ הַגְּמוּלָה הַזֹּאת: יָשָׁב־נָא עַבְדְּךָ וְאָמֻת בְּעִירִי עִם קֶבֶר אָבִי
וְאִמִּי וְהִנֵּה ׀ עַבְדְּךָ כִמְהָם יַעֲבֹר עִם־אֲדֹנִי הַמֶּלֶךְ וַעֲשֵׂה־לוֹ אֵת
לט אֲשֶׁר־טוֹב בְּעֵינֶיךָ: וַיֹּאמֶר הַמֶּלֶךְ אִתִּי יַעֲבֹר כִּמְהָם וַאֲנִי
אֶעֱשֶׂה־לּוֹ אֶת־הַטּוֹב בְּעֵינֶיךָ וְכֹל אֲשֶׁר־תִּבְחַר עָלַי אֶעֱשֶׂה־לָּךְ:
מ וַיַּעֲבֹר כָּל־הָעָם אֶת־הַיַּרְדֵּן וְהַמֶּלֶךְ עָבָר וַיִּשַּׁק הַמֶּלֶךְ לְבַרְזִלַּי וַיְבָרְכֵהוּ לב
מא וַיָּשָׁב לִמְקֹמוֹ: וַיַּעֲבֹר הַמֶּלֶךְ הַגִּלְגָּלָה וְכִמְהָן עָבַר עִמּוֹ
מב וְכָל־עַם יְהוּדָה ויעברו אֶת־הַמֶּלֶךְ וְגַם חֲצִי עַם יִשְׂרָאֵל: וְהִנֵּה כָל־ הֶעֱבִירוּ
אִישׁ יִשְׂרָאֵל בָּאִים אֶל־הַמֶּלֶךְ וַיֹּאמְרוּ אֶל־הַמֶּלֶךְ מַדּוּעַ גְּנָבוּךָ אַחֵינוּ

have our brothers, the men of Yehuda, stolen you away, bringing the king and
43 his household across the Jordan together with all of David's men?" "The
king is our kin," the men of Yehuda answered the men of Israel, "so why should
this matter infuriate you so? Have we eaten anything at the king's expense?
44 Have we been given any gifts?" "Why, we have ten shares in the king,
so we have more in David than you," the men of Israel retorted to the men of
Yehuda. "Why have you slighted us so when we first had the idea to bring our
king back?" But the men of Yehuda's word was harsher than the men of Israel's
20 1 word. Now a depraved man happened to be there; his name was Sheva son
of Bikhri, a Benjaminite. He blasted the ram's horn and declared, "We have
no portion in David and no share in the son of Yishai! Back to your tents, men
2 of Israel!" And all the men of Israel deserted David to follow Sheva son
of Bikhri, but the men of Yehuda stood by their king from the Jordan to
3 Jerusalem. David arrived at his palace in Jerusalem. The king took the ten
concubine women he had left to mind the palace and placed them in a house
under watch. He provided for them, but he did not come to bed with them,
4 and until their dying day, they were shut up in living widowhood. The
king then said to Amasa, "Rally the men of Yehuda within three days, then
5 stop off here." Amasa set out to rally Yehuda, but he missed the deadline that
6 had been set for him. "Now Sheva son of Bikhri will be worse for us
than Avshalom was," David said to Avishai. "Take your master's servants and
pursue him before he reaches the fortified cities and we lose sight of him."
7 Yoav's men set off along with the Keretites and Peletites and all the warriors,
8 and they left Jerusalem to pursue Sheva son of Bikhri. They were by the great
stone in Givon when Amasa came before them. Yoav was clad in his battle
garb with a sword strapped to his waist in its sheath; and as he came forward,
9 it slipped out. "Is all well with you, my brother?" Yoav asked Amasa
10 as Yoav took hold of Amasa's beard with his right hand, as if to kiss him. Amasa
was caught off guard by the sword in Yoav's hand. He struck him in the
stomach; his insides spilled out to the ground – he did not need to strike him
twice – and he died. As Yoav and his brother Avishai continued in
11 pursuit of Sheva son of Bikhri, one of Yoav's men stood by him and called out,
12 "Whoever favors Yoav, and whoever is for David – after Yoav!" Meanwhile,
Amasa lay wallowing in his blood in the middle of the road, and the man saw
that all the troops were coming to a halt. When he realized that everyone who
reached him came to a halt, he dragged Amasa off the road to the field and
13 flung a garment over him. Once he had been removed from the road, all the
troops marched ahead, following Yoav in his pursuit of Sheva son of Bikhri,
14 who had passed through all the tribes of Israel to Avel of Beit Maakha. All the
15 Berites[43] gathered to join him and followed him inside. All the troops who
were with Yoav came and besieged him within Avel of Beit Maakha; they

43 | Meaning of Hebrew uncertain.

אִ֣ישׁ יְהוּדָ֗ה וַיַּעֲבִ֙רוּ֙ אֶת־הַמֶּ֙לֶךְ֙ וְאֶת־בֵּית֜וֹ אֶת־הַיַּרְדֵּ֔ן וְכׇל־אַנְשֵׁ֥י דָוִ֖ד
מג עִמּֽוֹ׃ וַיַּ֜עַן כׇּל־אִ֣ישׁ יְהוּדָ֗ה עַל־אִ֣ישׁ יִשְׂרָאֵ֔ל כִּֽי־קָר֤וֹב
הַמֶּ֙לֶךְ֙ אֵלַ֔י וְלָ֤מָּה זֶּה֙ חָרָ֣ה לְךָ֔ עַל־הַדָּבָ֖ר הַזֶּ֑ה הֶאָכ֤וֹל אָכַ֙לְנוּ֙ מִן־
מד הַמֶּ֔לֶךְ אִם־נִשֵּׂ֥את נִשָּׂ֖א לָֽנוּ׃ וַיַּ֣עַן אִֽישׁ־יִשְׂרָאֵ֣ל אֶת־
אִ֣ישׁ יְהוּדָ֡ה וַיֹּאמֶר֩ עֶֽשֶׂר־יָד֨וֹת לִ֜י בַּמֶּ֗לֶךְ וְגַם־בְּדָוִד֙ אֲנִ֣י מִמְּךָ֔ וּמַדּ֖וּעַ
הֱקִלֹּתַ֑נִי וְלֹא־הָיָ֨ה דְבָרִ֥י רִאשׁ֛וֹן לִ֖י לְהָשִׁ֣יב אֶת־מַלְכִּ֑י וַיִּ֙קֶשׁ֙ דְּבַר־
כ א אִ֣ישׁ יְהוּדָ֔ה מִדְּבַ֖ר אִ֥ישׁ יִשְׂרָאֵֽל׃ וְשָׁ֨ם נִקְרָ֜א אִ֣ישׁ בְּלִיַּ֗עַל וּשְׁמ֛וֹ
שֶׁ֥בַע בֶּן־בִּכְרִ֖י אִ֣ישׁ יְמִינִ֑י וַיִּתְקַ֣ע בַּשֹּׁפָ֗ר וַיֹּ֙אמֶר֙ אֵֽין־לָ֨נוּ חֵ֜לֶק בְּדָוִ֗ד
ב וְלֹ֤א נַחֲלָה־לָ֙נוּ֙ בְּבֶן־יִשַׁ֔י אִ֥ישׁ לְאֹהָלָ֖יו יִשְׂרָאֵֽל׃ וַיַּ֜עַל כׇּל־אִ֤ישׁ יִשְׂרָאֵל֙
מֵאַחֲרֵ֣י דָוִ֔ד אַחֲרֵ֖י שֶׁ֣בַע בֶּן־בִּכְרִ֑י וְאִ֤ישׁ יְהוּדָה֙ דָּבְק֣וּ בְמַלְכָּ֔ם מִן־
ג הַיַּרְדֵּ֖ן וְעַד־יְרוּשָׁלָֽ͏ִם׃ וַיָּבֹ֨א דָוִ֣ד אֶל־בֵּיתוֹ֮ יְרוּשָׁלַ͏ִם֒ וַיִּקַּ֣ח הַמֶּ֡לֶךְ אֵ֣ת
עֶשֶׂר־נָשִׁ֣ים ׀ פִּלַגְשִׁ֡ים אֲשֶׁ֣ר הִנִּיחַ֩ לִשְׁמֹ֨ר הַבַּ֜יִת וַֽיִּתְּנֵ֤ם בֵּית־מִשְׁמֶ֙רֶת֙
וַֽיְכַלְכְּלֵ֔ם וַאֲלֵיהֶ֖ם לֹא־בָ֑א וַתִּהְיֶ֧ינָה צְרֻר֛וֹת עַד־י֥וֹם מֻתָ֖ן אַלְמְנ֥וּת
ד חַיּֽוּת׃ וַיֹּ֤אמֶר הַמֶּ֙לֶךְ֙ אֶל־עֲמָשָׂ֔א הַזְעֶק־לִ֥י אֶת־אִישׁ־יְהוּדָ֖ה
ה שְׁלֹ֣שֶׁת יָמִ֑ים וְאַתָּ֖ה פֹּ֥ה עֲמֹֽד׃ וַיֵּ֥לֶךְ עֲמָשָׂ֖א לְהַזְעִ֣יק אֶת־יְהוּדָ֑ה וייחר וַיּ֕וֹחֶר
ו מִן־הַמּוֹעֵ֖ד אֲשֶׁ֥ר יְעָדֽוֹ׃ וַיֹּ֤אמֶר דָּוִד֙ אֶל־אֲבִישַׁ֔י עַתָּ֗ה
יֵ֧רַע לָ֛נוּ שֶׁ֥בַע בֶּן־בִּכְרִ֖י מִן־אַבְשָׁל֑וֹם אַ֠תָּ֠ה קַ֞ח אֶת־עַבְדֵ֤י אֲדֹנֶ֙יךָ֙
ז וּרְדֹ֣ף אַחֲרָ֔יו פֶּן־מָ֥צָא ל֛וֹ עָרִ֥ים בְּצֻר֖וֹת וְהִצִּ֥יל עֵינֵֽנוּ׃ וַיֵּצְא֤וּ אַחֲרָיו֙
אַנְשֵׁ֣י יוֹאָ֔ב וְהַכְּרֵתִ֥י וְהַפְּלֵתִ֖י וְכׇל־הַגִּבֹּרִ֑ים וַיֵּֽצְאוּ֙ מִיר֣וּשָׁלַ֔͏ִם לִרְדֹּ֕ף
ח אַחֲרֵ֖י שֶׁ֥בַע בֶּן־בִּכְרִֽי׃ הֵ֗ם עִם־הָאֶ֤בֶן הַגְּדוֹלָה֙ אֲשֶׁ֣ר בְּגִבְע֔וֹן וַעֲמָשָׂ֖א
בָּ֣א לִפְנֵיהֶ֑ם וְיוֹאָ֞ב חָג֣וּר ׀ מִדּ֣וֹ לְבֻשׁ֗וֹ וְעָלָ֞ו חֲג֥וֹר חֶ֙רֶב֙ מְצֻמֶּ֤דֶת עַל־
ט מׇתְנָיו֙ בְּתַעְרָ֔הּ וְה֖וּא יָצָ֥א וַתִּפֹּֽל׃ וַיֹּ֤אמֶר יוֹאָב֙ לַעֲמָשָׂ֔א
הֲשָׁל֥וֹם אַתָּ֖ה אָחִ֑י וַתֹּ֜חֶז יַד־יְמִ֧ין יוֹאָ֛ב בִּזְקַ֥ן עֲמָשָׂ֖א לִנְשׇׁק־לֽוֹ׃
י וַעֲמָשָׂ֨א לֹא־נִשְׁמַ֜ר בַּחֶ֣רֶב ׀ אֲשֶׁ֣ר בְּיַד־יוֹאָ֗ב וַיַּכֵּ֨הוּ בָ֜הּ אֶל־הַחֹ֗מֶשׁ
וַיִּשְׁפֹּ֨ךְ מֵעָ֥יו אַ֛רְצָה וְלֹא־שָׁ֥נָה ל֖וֹ וַיָּמֹ֑ת וְיוֹאָב֙ וַאֲבִישַׁ֣י
יא אָחִ֔יו רָדַ֕ף אַחֲרֵ֖י שֶׁ֥בַע בֶּן־בִּכְרִֽי׃ וְאִ֗ישׁ עָמַ֤ד עָלָיו֙ מִנַּעֲרֵ֣י יוֹאָ֔ב וַיֹּ֕אמֶר
יב מִ֨י אֲשֶׁ֜ר חָפֵ֧ץ בְּיוֹאָ֛ב וּמִ֥י אֲשֶׁר־לְדָוִ֖ד אַחֲרֵ֥י יוֹאָֽב׃ וַעֲמָשָׂ֛א מִתְגֹּלֵ֥ל
בַּדָּ֖ם בְּת֣וֹךְ הַֽמְסִלָּ֑ה וַיַּ֨רְא הָאִ֜ישׁ כִּֽי־עָמַ֣ד כׇּל־הָעָ֗ם וַיַּסֵּ֨ב אֶת־עֲמָשָׂ֜א
מִן־הַֽמְסִלָּ֤ה הַשָּׂדֶה֙ וַיַּשְׁלֵ֤ךְ עָלָיו֙ בֶּ֔גֶד כַּאֲשֶׁ֣ר רָאָ֔ה כׇּל־הַבָּ֥א עָלָ֖יו
יג וְעָמָֽד׃ כַּאֲשֶׁ֥ר הֹגָ֖ה מִן־הַֽמְסִלָּ֑ה עָבַ֤ר כׇּל־אִישׁ֙ אַחֲרֵ֣י יוֹאָ֔ב לִרְדֹּ֕ף
יד אַחֲרֵ֖י שֶׁ֥בַע בֶּן־בִּכְרִֽי׃ וַיַּעֲבֹ֞ר בְּכׇל־שִׁבְטֵ֤י יִשְׂרָאֵל֙ אָבֵ֔לָה וּבֵ֥ית מַעֲכָ֖ה
טו וְכׇל־הַבֵּרִ֑ים ויקלהו וַיָּבֹ֖אוּ אַף־אַחֲרָֽיו׃ וַיָּבֹ֜אוּ וַיָּצֻ֣רוּ עָלָ֗יו בְּאָבֵ֙לָה֙ וַיִּקָּהֲל֔וּ

heaped up a mound against the city, and it stood against the rampart. As they
16 bombarded the wall to bring it down, a wise woman called out from the city,
"Listen! Listen! Please tell Yoav to come over here, and I will speak with him."
17 Yoav went over to her, and the woman asked, "Are you Yoav?" "I am," he said.
"Listen to the words of your handmaid," she said to him, and he said, "I am
18 listening." "There used to be a saying, 'Let them ask in Avel, and all will be
19 settled,'" she said. "I am a faithful peacekeeper of Israel. But you seek to kill a
20 mother city in Israel – why should you engulf the LORD's heritage?" "Far
21 be it! Far be it from me to engulf or destroy," answered Yoav. "That is not the
case, for a man from the hill country of Efrayim – Sheva son of Bikhri is his
name – has raised his hand against King David. If you hand him over – just
him – then I will leave the city alone." "Here!" said the woman. "His head is
22 about to be flung over the wall to you." The woman came to all the people
with her wise advice, and they cut off Sheva son of Bikhri's head and flung it
to Yoav. He blasted the ram's horn and the troops dispersed, each back to his
23 own tent, while Yoav headed back to the king in Jerusalem. Yoav was
in charge of all of Israel's army, while Benaya son of Yehoyada oversaw the
24 Keretites and Peletites. Adoram was in charge of taxation, and Yehoshafat son
25 of Aḥilud was royal herald. Sheva was a royal scribe, and Tzadok and Evyatar
26 were priests; Ira the Yairite was also priest to David. Now famine
21 1 struck in David's time for three years – year after year – and David sought the
presence of the LORD. And the LORD said, "It is on account
2 of Sha'ul and his house of bloodshed for having killed the Gibeonites." So
the king summoned the Gibeonites to speak to them. Now the Gibeonites
were not part of the Israelites; they were of the remaining Amorites. Though
the Israelites had given them their oath, Sha'ul had hunted them down in his
3 zeal for the people of Israel and Yehuda. David asked the Gibeonites, "What
shall I do for you, and how can I make amends so that you may bless the
4 LORD's heritage?" "We have no interest in the silver and gold of Sha'ul and
his house," the Gibeonites said to him, "or in killing any of the people of Israel."
5 "Whatever you say, I will do for you," he said. "There is a man who massacred
us and who plotted against us," they said to the king. "Why, we have been
6 wiped out from existence throughout Israel's borders. Let seven of his male
descendants be handed over to us, and we will impale them before the LORD
at Givat Sha'ul, the chosen one of the LORD." "I will hand them
7 over," said the king. The king took pity on Mefivoshet son of Yehonatan,
Sha'ul's son, because of the LORD's oath between them, between David and
8 Yehonatan, Sha'ul's son. So the king took the two sons that Ritzpa daughter
of Aya had borne to Sha'ul, Armoni and Mefivoshet, and the five sons that
Mikhal,[44] Sha'ul's daughter, had borne to Adriel son of Barzilai the Meholatite,

---

44 | Cf. I Samuel 18:19, which reads "Merav."

בֵּית הַמַּעֲכָה וַיִּשְׁפְּכוּ סֹלְלָה אֶל־הָעִיר וַתַּעֲמֹד בַּחֵל וְכָל־הָעָם אֲשֶׁר
טז אֶת־יוֹאָב מַשְׁחִיתִם לְהַפִּיל הַחוֹמָה: וַתִּקְרָא אִשָּׁה חֲכָמָה מִן־הָעִיר
שִׁמְעוּ שִׁמְעוּ אִמְרוּ־נָא אֶל־יוֹאָב קְרַב עַד־הֵנָּה וַאֲדַבְּרָה אֵלֶיךָ:
יז וַיִּקְרַב אֵלֶיהָ וַתֹּאמֶר הָאִשָּׁה הַאַתָּה יוֹאָב וַיֹּאמֶר אָנִי וַתֹּאמֶר לוֹ
יח שְׁמַע דִּבְרֵי אֲמָתֶךָ וַיֹּאמֶר שֹׁמֵעַ אָנֹכִי: וַתֹּאמֶר לֵאמֹר דַּבֵּר יְדַבְּרוּ
יט בָרִאשֹׁנָה לֵאמֹר שָׁאוֹל יְשָׁאֲלוּ בְּאָבֵל וְכֵן הֵתַמּוּ: אָנֹכִי שְׁלֻמֵי אֱמוּנֵי
יִשְׂרָאֵל אַתָּה מְבַקֵּשׁ לְהָמִית עִיר וְאֵם בְּיִשְׂרָאֵל לָמָּה תְבַלַּע נַחֲלַת
כ יהוה: וַיַּעַן יוֹאָב וַיֹּאמַר חָלִילָה חָלִילָה לִי אִם־אֲבַלַּע
כא וְאִם־אַשְׁחִית: לֹא־כֵן הַדָּבָר כִּי אִישׁ מֵהַר אֶפְרַיִם שֶׁבַע בֶּן־בִּכְרִי שְׁמוֹ
נָשָׂא יָדוֹ בַּמֶּלֶךְ בְּדָוִד תְּנוּ־אֹתוֹ לְבַדּוֹ וְאֵלְכָה מֵעַל הָעִיר וַתֹּאמֶר
כב הָאִשָּׁה אֶל־יוֹאָב הִנֵּה רֹאשׁוֹ מֻשְׁלָךְ אֵלֶיךָ בְּעַד הַחוֹמָה: וַתָּבוֹא
הָאִשָּׁה אֶל־כָּל־הָעָם בְּחָכְמָתָהּ וַיִּכְרְתוּ אֶת־רֹאשׁ שֶׁבַע בֶּן־בִּכְרִי
וַיַּשְׁלִכוּ אֶל־יוֹאָב וַיִּתְקַע בַּשֹּׁפָר וַיָּפֻצוּ מֵעַל־הָעִיר אִישׁ לְאֹהָלָיו וְיוֹאָב
כג שָׁב יְרוּשָׁלִַם אֶל־הַמֶּלֶךְ: וְיוֹאָב אֶל כָּל־הַצָּבָא יִשְׂרָאֵל
כד וּבְנָיָה בֶּן־יְהוֹיָדָע עַל־הכרי וְעַל־הַפְּלֵתִי: וַאֲדֹרָם עַל־הַמַּס וִיהוֹשָׁפָט הַכְּרֵתִי
כה כו בֶּן־אֲחִילוּד הַמַּזְכִּיר: ושיא סֹפֵר וְצָדוֹק וְאֶבְיָתָר כֹּהֲנִים: וְגַם עִירָא וּשְׁוָא
כא א הַיָּאִרִי הָיָה כֹהֵן לְדָוִד: וַיְהִי רָעָב בִּימֵי דָוִד שָׁלֹשׁ שָׁנִים
שָׁנָה אַחֲרֵי שָׁנָה וַיְבַקֵּשׁ דָּוִד אֶת־פְּנֵי יהוה וַיֹּאמֶר יהוה
ב אֶל־שָׁאוּל וְאֶל־בֵּית הַדָּמִים עַל אֲשֶׁר־הֵמִית אֶת־הַגִּבְעֹנִים: וַיִּקְרָא
הַמֶּלֶךְ לַגִּבְעֹנִים וַיֹּאמֶר אֲלֵיהֶם וְהַגִּבְעֹנִים לֹא מִבְּנֵי יִשְׂרָאֵל הֵמָּה כִּי
אִם־מִיֶּתֶר הָאֱמֹרִי וּבְנֵי יִשְׂרָאֵל נִשְׁבְּעוּ לָהֶם וַיְבַקֵּשׁ שָׁאוּל לְהַכֹּתָם
ג בְּקַנֹּאתוֹ לִבְנֵי־יִשְׂרָאֵל וִיהוּדָה: וַיֹּאמֶר דָּוִד אֶל־הַגִּבְעֹנִים מָה אֶעֱשֶׂה
ד לָכֶם וּבַמָּה אֲכַפֵּר וּבָרְכוּ אֶת־נַחֲלַת יהוה: וַיֹּאמְרוּ לוֹ הַגִּבְעֹנִים אֵין־
לי כֶּסֶף וְזָהָב עִם־שָׁאוּל וְעִם־בֵּיתוֹ וְאֵין־לָנוּ אִישׁ לְהָמִית בְּיִשְׂרָאֵל לָנוּ
ה וַיֹּאמֶר מָה־אַתֶּם אֹמְרִים אֶעֱשֶׂה לָכֶם: וַיֹּאמְרוּ אֶל־הַמֶּלֶךְ הָאִישׁ
אֲשֶׁר כִּלָּנוּ וַאֲשֶׁר דִּמָּה־לָנוּ נִשְׁמַדְנוּ מֵהִתְיַצֵּב בְּכָל־גְּבֻל יִשְׂרָאֵל:
ו ינתן־לָנוּ שִׁבְעָה אֲנָשִׁים מִבָּנָיו וְהוֹקַעֲנוּם לַיהוה בְּגִבְעַת שָׁאוּל בְּחִיר יֻתַּן־
ז יהוה וַיֹּאמֶר הַמֶּלֶךְ אֲנִי אֶתֵּן: וַיַּחְמֹל הַמֶּלֶךְ עַל־ לג
מְפִיבֹשֶׁת בֶּן־יְהוֹנָתָן בֶּן־שָׁאוּל עַל־שְׁבֻעַת יהוה אֲשֶׁר בֵּינֹתָם בֵּין
ח דָּוִד וּבֵין יְהוֹנָתָן בֶּן־שָׁאוּל: וַיִּקַּח הַמֶּלֶךְ אֶת־שְׁנֵי בְּנֵי רִצְפָּה בַת־
אַיָּה אֲשֶׁר יָלְדָה לְשָׁאוּל אֶת־אַרְמֹנִי וְאֶת־מְפִבֹשֶׁת וְאֶת־חֲמֵשֶׁת
בְּנֵי מִיכַל בַּת־שָׁאוּל אֲשֶׁר יָלְדָה לְעַדְרִיאֵל בֶּן־בַּרְזִלַּי הַמְּחֹלָתִי:

9 and handed them over to the Gibeonites. They impaled them on the hill
before the LORD, the seven of them in one fell swoop. They were put to death
during the first days of harvest time, at the beginning of the barley harvest.
10 Then Ritzpa daughter of Aya took sackcloth and stretched it out for herself
on a rock from the beginning of the harvest season until water poured down
on them from the sky. She would not let the birds of the sky settle on them
11 by day, nor the wild beasts by night. When David was told what Ritzpa
12 daughter of Aya, Sha'ul's concubine, had done, David went and took the bones
of Sha'ul, along with the bones of his son Yehonatan, from the citizens of
Yavesh Gilad. They had recaptured them from the Beit Shan square where
the Philistines had hung Sha'ul on the day the Philistines defeated Sha'ul
13 at Gilboa. He brought up Sha'ul's bones from there, along with the bones of
14 his son Yehonatan, and gathered up the bones of the impaled. They buried
the bones of Sha'ul and his son Yehonatan at Tzela in the Binyamin region,
in the tomb of his father Kish, and carried out all of the king's orders. And
15 after that, God responded to the plea of the land. War broke out
once again between the Philistines and Israel. David marched down with his
16 officials, and they fought against the Philistines, but David grew weary. And
Yishbi Benov, a descendant of the Rafa[45] – his spear weighed three hundred
weights of bronze, and he was clad in new armor – was determined to strike
17 David down. But Avishai son of Tzeruya came to his aid, struck down
the Philistine, and killed him. Right then, David's men swore to him: "You
will never go out to war with us again; you must not extinguish the lamp
18 of Israel!" Some time after that, another war broke out against the
Philistines, at Gov; this time, Sibekhai the Hushatite defeated Saf, a descendant
19 of the Rafa. Yet another war broke out against the Philistines, at
Gov, and Elḥanan son of Yaarei-Oregim[46] of Beit Leḥem defeated Golyat the
20 Gittite, whose spear shaft was like a weaver's beam. Yet another
war broke out, at Gat. There was a man of gigantic proportions who had six
fingers and six toes on his hands and feet, twenty-four in all; he, too, was
21 descended from the Rafa. When he taunted Israel, Yehonatan son of Shima,
22 David's brother, struck him down. All four of these were descendants of
the Rafa in Gat, and they fell at the hands of David and his subjects.

22 1 David uttered these words of song to the LORD on the day that the LORD
saved him from the hands of all his enemies and from the hand of Sha'ul.[47]
2 3 He said: The LORD is my Rock and my fortress, my own rescuer; // my God
is the Rock of my refuge / my shield, the horn of my salvation, my haven, /
4 my refuge, my savior who delivers me from violence. // Praise! When I call
5 on the LORD, / I am saved from my enemies. // For when waves of death

45 | A giant; see Deuteronomy 2:11.

46 | A compound family name, *oregim* meaning "weavers." Elḥanan was from a family of weavers located in Beit Leḥem. Cf. 1 Chronicles 20:5.

47 | Cf. Psalm 18.

ט וַיִּתְּנֵם בְּיַד הַגִּבְעֹנִים וַיֹּקִיעֻם בָּהָר לִפְנֵי יְהוָה וַיִּפְּלוּ שבעתים יָחַד שְׁבַעְתָּם
י והם הֻמְתוּ בִּימֵי קָצִיר בָּרִאשֹׁנִים תחלת קְצִיר שְׂעֹרִים: וַתִּקַּח רִצְפָּה וְהֵמָּה בִּתְחִלַּת
בַת־אַיָּה אֶת־הַשַּׂק וַתַּטֵּהוּ לָהּ אֶל־הַצּוּר מִתְּחִלַּת קָצִיר עַד נִתַּךְ־
מַיִם עֲלֵיהֶם מִן־הַשָּׁמָיִם וְלֹא־נָתְנָה עוֹף הַשָּׁמַיִם לָנוּחַ עֲלֵיהֶם יוֹמָם
יא וְאֶת־חַיַּת הַשָּׂדֶה לָיְלָה: וַיֻּגַּד לְדָוִד אֵת אֲשֶׁר־עָשְׂתָה רִצְפָּה בַת־
יב אַיָּה פִּלֶגֶשׁ שָׁאוּל: וַיֵּלֶךְ דָּוִד וַיִּקַּח אֶת־עַצְמוֹת שָׁאוּל וְאֶת־עַצְמוֹת
יְהוֹנָתָן בְּנוֹ מֵאֵת בַּעֲלֵי יָבֵישׁ גִּלְעָד אֲשֶׁר גָּנְבוּ אֹתָם מֵרְחֹב בֵּית־
שַׁן אֲשֶׁר תלום שם הפלשתים בְּיוֹם הַכּוֹת פְּלִשְׁתִּים אֶת־שָׁאוּל תְּלָאוּם שָׁמָּה פְּלִשְׁתִּים
יג בַּגִּלְבֹּעַ: וַיַּעַל מִשָּׁם אֶת־עַצְמוֹת שָׁאוּל וְאֶת־עַצְמוֹת יְהוֹנָתָן בְּנוֹ
יד וַיַּאַסְפוּ אֶת־עַצְמוֹת הַמּוּקָעִים: וַיִּקְבְּרוּ אֶת־עַצְמוֹת־שָׁאוּל וִיהוֹנָתָן
בְּנוֹ בְּאֶרֶץ בִּנְיָמִן בְּצֵלָע בְּקֶבֶר קִישׁ אָבִיו וַיַּעֲשׂוּ כֹּל אֲשֶׁר־צִוָּה הַמֶּלֶךְ
טו וַיֵּעָתֵר אֱלֹהִים לָאָרֶץ אַחֲרֵי־כֵן: וַתְּהִי־עוֹד מִלְחָמָה
לַפְּלִשְׁתִּים אֶת־יִשְׂרָאֵל וַיֵּרֶד דָּוִד וַעֲבָדָיו עִמּוֹ וַיִּלָּחֲמוּ אֶת־פְּלִשְׁתִּים
טז וַיָּעַף דָּוִד: וישבו בְּנֹב אֲשֶׁר | בִּילִידֵי הָרָפָה וּמִשְׁקַל קֵינוֹ שְׁלֹשׁ וְיִשְׁבִּי
מֵאוֹת מִשְׁקַל נְחֹשֶׁת וְהוּא חָגוּר חֲדָשָׁה וַיֹּאמֶר לְהַכּוֹת אֶת־דָּוִד:
יז וַיַּעֲזָר־לוֹ אֲבִישַׁי בֶּן־צְרוּיָה וַיַּךְ אֶת־הַפְּלִשְׁתִּי וַיְמִיתֵהוּ אָז נִשְׁבְּעוּ
אַנְשֵׁי־דָוִד לוֹ לֵאמֹר לֹא־תֵצֵא עוֹד אִתָּנוּ לַמִּלְחָמָה וְלֹא תְכַבֶּה
יח אֶת־נֵר יִשְׂרָאֵל: וַיְהִי אַחֲרֵי־כֵן וַתְּהִי־עוֹד הַמִּלְחָמָה
בְּגוֹב עִם־פְּלִשְׁתִּים אָז הִכָּה סִבְּכַי הַחֻשָׁתִי אֶת־סַף אֲשֶׁר בִּילִדֵי
יט הָרָפָה: וַתְּהִי־עוֹד הַמִּלְחָמָה בְּגוֹב עִם־פְּלִשְׁתִּים וַיַּךְ
אֶלְחָנָן בֶּן־יַעְרֵי אֹרְגִים בֵּית הַלַּחְמִי אֵת גָּלְיָת הַגִּתִּי וְעֵץ חֲנִיתוֹ כִּמְנוֹר
כ אֹרְגִים: וַתְּהִי־עוֹד מִלְחָמָה בְּגַת וַיְהִי | איש מדין וְאֶצְבְּעֹת מָדוֹן
יְדָיו וְאֶצְבְּעוֹת רַגְלָיו שֵׁשׁ וָשֵׁשׁ עֶשְׂרִים וְאַרְבַּע מִסְפָּר וְגַם־הוּא יֻלַּד
כא כב לְהָרָפָה: וַיְחָרֵף אֶת־יִשְׂרָאֵל וַיַּכֵּהוּ יְהוֹנָתָן בֶּן־שמעי אֲחִי דָוִד: אֶת־ שִׁמְעָה
אַרְבַּעַת אֵלֶּה יֻלְּדוּ לְהָרָפָה בְּגַת וַיִּפְּלוּ בְיַד־דָּוִד וּבְיַד עֲבָדָיו:

כב א וַיְדַבֵּר דָּוִד לַיהוָה אֶת־דִּבְרֵי הַשִּׁירָה הַזֹּאת בְּיוֹם
הִצִּיל יְהוָה אֹתוֹ מִכַּף כָּל־אֹיְבָיו וּמִכַּף שָׁאוּל:
ב ג וַיֹּאמַר יְהוָה סַלְעִי וּמְצֻדָתִי וּמְפַלְטִי־לִי: אֱלֹהֵי
צוּרִי אֶחֱסֶה־בּוֹ מָגִנִּי וְקֶרֶן יִשְׁעִי מִשְׂגַּבִּי
ד וּמְנוּסִי מֹשִׁעִי מֵחָמָס תֹּשִׁעֵנִי: מְהֻלָּל
ה אֶקְרָא יְהוָה וּמֵאֹיְבַי אִוָּשֵׁעַ: כִּי אֲפָפֻנִי מִשְׁבְּרֵי־

6 assailed me, / deadly torrents engulfed me, the cords of Sheol[48] entangled
7 me, / snares of death confronted me, // in my distress I called on the LORD; /
I called out to my God; / He heard my voice from His temple, / and my cry
8 rang in His ears. // Then the earth shook and shuddered; / the foundations
9 of heaven trembled; / they shuddered from His wrath. // Smoke issued from
His nostrils; / devouring flames flared from His mouth; / from Him gleaming
10 coals blazed forth. // He bent the heavens and descended, / dense cloud
11 beneath His feet; / He mounted a cherub and flew, / appearing on wings of
12 wind. // He surrounded Himself with a shelter of darkness, / of heavy storm
13 clouds dense with rain. // From the brilliant glow of His presence / blazed
14 fiery coals. // The LORD thundered from the heavens; / the Most High raised
15 His voice; / He shot arrows to scatter them, / lightning bolts to rout them. //
16 The ocean bed was exposed, / the foundations of the world laid bare / by
17 the onslaught of the LORD, / by the blast of His breath. // From on high
He reached down and took me; / He drew me out of the mighty waters. //
18 19 He saved me from my fierce enemy, / from foes too strong for me. // They
20 confronted me on my direst day, / but the LORD was my support. // He
brought me out to freedom; / He rescued me because He delighted in me. //
21 The LORD rewarded me as I deserved; / as my hands were clean, He repaid
22 23 me, / for I kept the ways of the LORD / and did not betray my God, / for
24 all His laws are before me; / I will not turn away from His statutes. / I am
25 blameless to Him / and keep myself from sin. / So the LORD repaid me as I
26 deserved / as I was pure in His sight. // You deal loyally with those who are
27 loyal, / to the blameless warrior You show Yourself blameless; / You are pure
28 with those who are pure, / but with the crooked, You are shrewd. / You bring
salvation to a humble people; / You cast Your eyes down on the haughty. //

48 | The grave or netherworld.

ו מָוֶת   נַחֲלֵי בְלִיַּעַל יְבַעֲתֻנִי: חֶבְלֵי
שְׁאוֹל סַבֻּנִי   קִדְּמֻנִי מֹקְשֵׁי־
ז מָוֶת: בַּצַּר־לִי אֶקְרָא יְהוָה   וְאֶל־
אֱלֹהַי אֶקְרָא   וַיִּשְׁמַע מֵהֵיכָלוֹ
ח קוֹלִי   וְשַׁוְעָתִי בְּאָזְנָיו: ותגעש   וַיִּתְגָּעַשׁ
וַתִּרְעַשׁ הָאָרֶץ   מוֹסְדוֹת הַשָּׁמַיִם
ט יִרְגָּזוּ   וַיִּתְגָּעֲשׁוּ כִּי־חָרָה לוֹ:   עָלָה
עָשָׁן בְּאַפּוֹ   וְאֵשׁ מִפִּיו
י תֹּאכֵל   גֶּחָלִים בָּעֲרוּ מִמֶּנּוּ:   וַיֵּט
שָׁמַיִם וַיֵּרַד   וַעֲרָפֶל תַּחַת
יא רַגְלָיו: וַיִּרְכַּב עַל־כְּרוּב וַיָּעֹף   וַיֵּרָא
יב עַל־כַּנְפֵי־רוּחַ:   וַיָּשֶׁת חֹשֶׁךְ סְבִיבֹתָיו
יג סֻכּוֹת   חַשְׁרַת־מַיִם עָבֵי שְׁחָקִים: מִנֹּגַהּ
יד נֶגְדּוֹ בָּעֲרוּ גַּחֲלֵי־אֵשׁ:   יַרְעֵם מִן־שָׁמַיִם
טו יְהוָה   וְעֶלְיוֹן יִתֵּן קוֹלוֹ:   וַיִּשְׁלַח
טז חִצִּים וַיְפִיצֵם בָּרָק ויהמם: וַיֵּרָאוּ אֲפִקֵי   וַיָּהֹם
יָם   יִגָּלוּ מֹסְדוֹת תֵּבֵל   בְּגַעֲרַת
יז יְהוָה מִנִּשְׁמַת רוּחַ אַפּוֹ:   יִשְׁלַח מִמָּרוֹם
יח יִקָּחֵנִי   יַמְשֵׁנִי מִמַּיִם רַבִּים: יַצִּילֵנִי
מֵאֹיְבִי עָז   מִשֹּׂנְאַי כִּי אָמְצוּ
יט מִמֶּנִּי: יְקַדְּמֻנִי בְּיוֹם אֵידִי   וַיְהִי
כ יְהוָה מִשְׁעָן לִי: וַיֹּצֵא לַמֶּרְחָב
כא אֹתִי   יְחַלְּצֵנִי כִּי־חָפֵץ בִּי: יִגְמְלֵנִי
יְהוָה כְּצִדְקָתִי   כְּבֹר יָדַי יָשִׁיב
כב לִי: כִּי שָׁמַרְתִּי דַּרְכֵי יְהוָה   וְלֹא
כג רָשַׁעְתִּי מֵאֱלֹהָי: כִּי כָל־מִשְׁפָּטָו
כד לְנֶגְדִּי   וְחֻקֹּתָיו לֹא־אָסוּר מִמֶּנָּה: וָאֶהְיֶה
כה תָמִים לוֹ וָאֶשְׁתַּמְּרָה מֵעֲוֺנִי: וַיָּשֶׁב יְהוָה לִי
כו כְּצִדְקָתִי   כְּבֹרִי לְנֶגֶד עֵינָיו: עִם־
חָסִיד תִּתְחַסָּד   עִם־גְּבוֹר תָּמִים
כז תִּתַּמָּם: עִם־נָבָר תִּתָּבָר   וְעִם־
כח עִקֵּשׁ תִּתַּפָּל: וְאֶת־עַם עָנִי

29 30 For You are my lamp, LORD; / the LORD lights up my darkness. / With You
31 I can rush a ridge; / with my God I can leap over a wall. // God's ways are
blameless; / the LORD's words are pure; / He is a shield to all who take refuge
32 in Him. // For who is a god besides the LORD; / who is a Rock besides our
33 God? / God is my powerful stronghold; / He frees my way so it is sound. /
34 35 He makes my legs like a deer's / and stands me on the heights. / He trains
36 my hands for battle / so that my arms can bend a bow of bronze. // You gave
37 me the shield of Your victory; / Your battle cry stirred me with power. / You
38 made my steps broad and firm; / my feet never faltered. / I pursued my enemy
39 to destroy them, / never turning back until they perished. / I cut them down
40 and crushed them, and they did not rise; / they fell beneath my feet. / You
girded me with power for battle / and sunk my adversaries far beneath me; /
41 42 You made my enemies turn tail before me; / my foes, too, I destroyed. / They
looked wildly about, but there was no savior – / called out to the LORD, but
43 He did not answer them – // while I ground them up like dust of the earth; /
44 I crushed and pounded them like street-mud. // You rescued me from civil
strife; / you kept me as the head of nations; / peoples I never knew of serve
45 me. / Foreign peoples come cringing before me; / they merely hear me and
46 obey; / foreign peoples lose heart / and come trembling out of their forts. //
47 The LORD lives! / Blessed is my Rock; / exalted is God, Rock of my rescue! /
48 49 God who grants vengeance to me, / who subjugates people under me, / my
redeemer from my enemies, / You raise me above those who rise against me; /
50 You save me from violent men. // So I praise You, LORD, among the nations, /
51 and sing to Your name. // He is a tower of victory for His king / and shows
loyalty to His anointed, / to David and his seed forever.

כט תּוֹשִׁיעַ וְעֵינֶיךָ עַל־רָמִים תַּשְׁפִּיל׃ כִּי־
אַתָּה נֵירִי יְהוָה וַיהוָה יַגִּיהַּ
ל חָשְׁכִּי׃ כִּי בְכָה אָרוּץ גְּדוּד בֵּאלֹהַי
לא אֲדַלֶּג־שׁוּר׃ הָאֵל תָּמִים
דַּרְכּוֹ אִמְרַת יְהוָה צְרוּפָה מָגֵן
לב הוּא לְכֹל הַחֹסִים בּוֹ׃ כִּי מִי־אֵל מִבַּלְעֲדֵי
לג יְהוָה וּמִי צוּר מִבַּלְעֲדֵי אֱלֹהֵינוּ׃ הָאֵל
מָעוּזִּי חָיִל וַיַּתֵּר תָּמִים
לד דרכו׃ מְשַׁוֶּה רגליו כָּאַיָּלוֹת וְעַל־ דַּרְכִּי רַגְלָי
לה בָּמוֹתַי יַעֲמִידֵנִי׃ מְלַמֵּד יָדַי
לו לַמִּלְחָמָה וְנִחַת קֶשֶׁת־נְחוּשָׁה זְרֹעֹתָי׃ וַתִּתֶּן־
לז לִי מָגֵן יִשְׁעֶךָ וַעֲנֹתְךָ תַּרְבֵּנִי׃ תַּרְחִיב צַעֲדִי
לח תַּחְתֵּנִי וְלֹא מָעֲדוּ קַרְסֻלָּי׃ אֶרְדְּפָה
אֹיְבַי וָאַשְׁמִידֵם וְלֹא אָשׁוּב עַד־
לט כַּלּוֹתָם׃ וָאֲכַלֵּם וָאֶמְחָצֵם וְלֹא יְקוּמוּן וַיִּפְּלוּ
מ תַּחַת רַגְלָי׃ וַתַּזְרֵנִי חַיִל
מא לַמִּלְחָמָה תַּכְרִיעַ קָמַי תַּחְתֵּנִי׃ וְאֹיְבַי
מב תַּתָּה לִּי עֹרֶף מְשַׂנְאַי וָאַצְמִיתֵם׃ יִשְׁעוּ וְאֵין
מג מֹשִׁיעַ אֶל־יְהוָה וְלֹא עָנָם׃ וְאֶשְׁחָקֵם
כַּעֲפַר־אָרֶץ כְּטִיט־חוּצוֹת אֲדִקֵּם
מד אֶרְקָעֵם׃ וַתְּפַלְּטֵנִי מֵרִיבֵי עַמִּי תִּשְׁמְרֵנִי
לְרֹאשׁ גּוֹיִם עַם לֹא־יָדַעְתִּי
מה יַעַבְדֻנִי׃ בְּנֵי נֵכָר יִתְכַּחֲשׁוּ־לִי לִשְׁמוֹעַ
מו אֹזֶן יִשָּׁמְעוּ לִי׃ בְּנֵי נֵכָר יִבֹּלוּ וְיַחְגְּרוּ
מז מִמִּסְגְּרוֹתָם׃ חַי־יְהוָה וּבָרוּךְ צוּרִי וְיָרֻם
מח אֱלֹהֵי צוּר יִשְׁעִי׃ הָאֵל הַנֹּתֵן נְקָמֹת
מט לִי וּמוֹרִיד עַמִּים תַּחְתֵּנִי׃ וּמוֹצִיאִי
מֵאֹיְבָי וּמִקָּמַי תְּרוֹמְמֵנִי מֵאִישׁ חֲמָסִים
נ תַּצִּילֵנִי׃ עַל־כֵּן אוֹדְךָ יְהוָה בַּגּוֹיִם וּלְשִׁמְךָ
נא אֲזַמֵּר׃ מגדיל יְשׁוּעוֹת לד מִגְדּוֹל
מַלְכּוֹ וְעֹשֶׂה־חֶסֶד לִמְשִׁיחוֹ
לְדָוִד וּלְזַרְעוֹ עַד־עוֹלָם׃

23 1 And these are the last words of David: "Thus spoke David, son of Yishai; /
thus spoke the man raised on high, / anointed of the God of Yaakov, / sweet
2 singer of Israel. / The spirit of the LORD has spoken through me; / His word
3 is on my tongue. / The God of Israel has declared, / the Rock of Israel has
4 said of me: / He who rules men justly, / he who rules in awe of God / is like
morning light at sunrise, / like a cloudless morning, / more radiant than the
5 gleam of rain / on the grass of the earth. / Is my house not so with God? /
For an eternal covenant He formed with me, / all in order, guaranteed. / Will
6 He not bring my every triumph, / my every desire, to bloom? / But as for the
depraved, / they will be thrust away like thorns; / they cannot be grasped
7 by hand; / whoever touches them / must be armed with iron and shaft of
spear – / or must burn them with fire on the spot."
8 These are the names of David's warriors: Yoshev Bashevet, a Tahkemonite,
head of the Three, he is Adino the Eznite – he wielded his spear[49] against eight
9 hundred victims at once. Next in rank was Elazar son of Dodo son
of Aḥoḥi, one of the three warriors with David who taunted the Philistines
10 gathered there for battle. The men of Israel retreated, but he stood his ground
and struck down the Philistines until his hand grew sore and his hand stuck
fast to his sword. The LORD granted a great victory on that day, and the
11 troops came back only to strip the slain. Next in rank was Shama son
of Ageh the Hararite. The Philistines had gathered into a pack where there
12 was a plot of land full of lentils, and the troops fled from the Philistines. But
he took his stand in the middle of the field and defended it, defeating the
13 Philistines, and the LORD granted a great victory. Once, during the
harvest, the chief three of the Thirty came to David in the cave of Adulam,
14 when a pack of Philistines was encamped in the Refaim Valley. At the time,
David was in the stronghold while the Philistines were then stationed at Beit
15 Leḥem. David was seized with a craving and said, "Oh, if only someone could
16 give me water to drink from the well of Beit Leḥem by the gate." So the three
warriors infiltrated the Philistine camp, drew water from the Beit Leḥem
well by the gate, and carried it back. But when they brought it to David, he
17 would not drink it and poured it out in a libation to the LORD. "The LORD
forbid that I do such a thing!" he said. "It is the blood of men who risked
their very lives by going." And he would not drink it. These were the feats
18 of the three warriors; Avishai, the brother of Yoav son of Tzeruya,
was the head of these three. He wielded his spear against three hundred
19 victims. He was famous among the Three and the most honored of these
three and so became their leader, though he never reached the rank of the
20 Three.[50] Benayahu son of Yehoyada, from Kavtze'el, was a powerful
man who achieved great feats. He defeated the two leonine warriors of Moav,
21 and he climbed down into a pit and overpowered a lion on a snowy day.
He defeated an Egyptian, a formidable man; the Egyptian held a spear, and
he charged down at him with a pole, snatched the spear from the Egyptian's

49 | This phrase is missing here but is present in the parallel verse in 1 Chronicles 11:6.
50 | Adino, Elazar, and Shama (v. 8–12).

כג א ואלה דברי דוד האחרנים נאם דוד בן־ישי ונאם הגבר הקם על
ב משיח אלהי יעקב ונעים זמרות ישראל: רוח יהוה דבר־בי ומלתו
ג על־לשוני: אמר אלהי ישראל לי דבר צור ישראל מושל באדם
ד צדיק מושל יראת אלהים: וכאור בקר יזרח־שמש בקר לא עבות
ה מנגה ממטר דשא מארץ: כי־לא־כן ביתי עם־אל כי ברית עולם
שם לי ערוכה בכל ושמרה כי־כל־ישעי וכל־חפץ כי־לא יצמיח:
ו ז ובליעל כקוץ מנד כלהם כי־לא ביד יקחו: ואיש יגע בהם ימלא
ברזל ועץ חנית ובאש שרוף ישרפו בשבת:
ח אלה שמות הגברים אשר לדוד ישב בשבת תחכמני | ראש השלשי
ט הוא עדינו העצנו על־שמנה מאות חלל בפעם אחד: ואחרו העצני אחת
אלעזר בן־דדי בן־אחחי בשלשה גברים עם־דוד בחרפם בפלשתים דדו הגברים
י נאספו־שם למלחמה ויעלו איש ישראל: הוא קם ויך בפלשתים
עד | כי־יגעה ידו ותדבק ידו אל־החרב ויעש יהוה תשועה גדולה
יא ביום ההוא והעם ישבו אחריו אך לפשט: ואחריו שמה
בן־אגא הררי ויאספו פלשתים לחיה ותהי־שם חלקת השדה
יב מלאה עדשים והעם נס מפני פלשתים: ויתיצב בתוך־החלקה
יג ויצילה ויך את־פלשתים ויעש יהוה תשועה גדולה: וירדו
שלשים מהשלשים ראש ויבאו אל־קציר אל־דוד אל־מערת עדלם שלשה
יד וחית פלשתים חנה בעמק רפאים: ודוד אז במצודה ומצב פלשתים
טו אז בית לחם: ויתאוה דוד ויאמר מי ישקני מים מבאר בית־לחם
טז אשר בשער: ויבקעו שלשת הגברים במחנה פלשתים וישאבו־
מים מבאר בית־לחם אשר בשער וישאו ויבאו אל־דוד ולא אבה
יז לשתותם ויסך אתם ליהוה: ויאמר חלילה לי יהוה מעשתי זאת
הדם האנשים ההלכים בנפשותם ולא אבה לשתותם אלה עשו
יח שלשת הגברים: ואבישי אחי | יואב בן־צרויה הוא
ראש השלשי והוא עורר את־חניתו על־שלש מאות חלל ולו־שם השלשה
יט בשלשה: מן־השלשה הכי נכבד ויהי להם לשר ועד־השלשה
כ לא־בא: ובניהו בן־יהוידע בן־איש־חי רב־פעלים חיל
מקבצאל הוא הכה את שני אראל מואב והוא ירד והכה את־האריה הארי
כא בתוך הבאר ביום השלג: והוא הכה את־איש מצרי אשר מראה איש
וביד המצרי חנית וירד אליו בשבט ויגזל את־החנית מיד המצרי

22 hand, and killed him with his own spear. These were the feats of Benayahu
23 son of Yehoyada, and he was famous among the three warriors. He was
among the most honored of the Thirty though he never reached the rank of
24 the Three, and David appointed him over his bodyguard. Among
the Thirty were: Asael, Yoav's brother, Elḥanan son of Dodo of Beit
25 26 Leḥem, Shama the Harodite, Elika the Harodite, Ḥeletz the
27 Paltite, Ira son of Ikesh the Tekoite, Aviezer the Anatotite,
28 Mevunai the Hushatite, Tzalmon the Ahohite, Mahrai the
29 Netofatite, Ḥelev son of Baana the Netofatite, Itai son of Rivai of Giva
30 of the Benjaminites, Benayahu the Piratonite, Hidai of Naḥalei
31 32 Gaash, Avi Alvon the Arbatite, Azmavet the Barhumite, Elyaḥba
33 the Shaalbonite, sons of Yashen, Yehonatan, Shama the Hararite,
34 Aḥiam son of Sharar the Ararite, Elifelet son of Aḥasbai, son of
35 the Maakhatite, Eliam son of Aḥitofel the Gilonite, Ḥezrai the
36 Carmelite, Paarai the Arbite, Yigal son of Natan of Tzova, Bani the
37 Gadite, Tzelek the Amonite, Naḥrai the Be'erotite, arms-bearer to
38 39 Yoav son of Tzeruya, Ira the Itrite, Garev the Itrite, Uriya
24 1 the Hittite – thirty-seven in all. The Lord's fury flared against Israel
once more, and He incited David against them, saying, "Go, count Israel and
2 Yehuda." The king said to Yoav, commander of his force, "Now make your way
around all the tribes of Israel, from Dan up to Be'er Sheva, and take a census of
3 the people to inform me of the number of the population." "May the
Lord your God increase the number of the people a hundred times over in
my lord the king's sight," Yoav said to the king, "but why does my lord the king
4 desire such a thing?" But the king's word prevailed over Yoav and the force
commanders, and Yoav and the force commanders left the king's presence
5 to take a census of the people, of Israel. They crossed the Jordan and camped
by Aroer to the south of the city, which is in the midst of the Gad Ravine,
6 and by Yazer. They came to Gilad and to the region of Taḥtim Ḥodshi, went
7 on to Dan Yaan, and made their way around to Sidon. They continued to
the fortress of Tyre and all the towns of the Hivites and Canaanites, and set
8 out for Be'er Sheva in southern Yehuda. They made their way all around the
9 land and reached Jerusalem at the end of nine months and twenty days. Yoav
delivered the census figures of the population to the king; Israel numbered
eight hundred thousand sword-wielding men of fighting age, and Yehuda
10 numbered five hundred thousand men. But afterward, David's heart ached
with remorse for having counted the people. "I have sinned gravely
by doing this," David said to the Lord. "Now, O Lord, please excuse Your
11 servant's offense, for I have been so foolish." By the time David rose in the
morning, the word of the Lord had reached the prophet Gad,
12 David's seer: "Go and tell David – thus says the Lord: I am holding three

כב וַיַּהַרְגֵהוּ בַּחֲנִיתוֹ: אֵלֶּה עָשָׂה בְּנָיָהוּ בֶּן־יְהוֹיָדָע וְלוֹ־שֵׁם בִּשְׁלֹשָׁה
כג הַגִּבֹּרִים: מִן־הַשְּׁלֹשִׁים נִכְבָּד וְאֶל־הַשְּׁלֹשָׁה לֹא־בָא וַיְשִׂמֵהוּ דָוִד
כד אֶל־מִשְׁמַעְתּוֹ: עֲשָׂהאֵל אֲחִי־יוֹאָב בַּשְּׁלֹשִׁים אֶלְחָנָן
כה כו בֶּן־דדי בֵּית לָחֶם: שַׁמָּה הַחֲרֹדִי אֱלִיקָא הַחֲרֹדִי: חֶלֶץ דּוֹדוֹ
כז הַפַּלְטִי עִירָא בֶן־עִקֵּשׁ הַתְּקוֹעִי: אֲבִיעֶזֶר הָעַנְּתֹתִי
כח כט מְבֻנַּי הַחֻשָׁתִי: צַלְמוֹן הָאֲחֹחִי מַהְרַי הַנְּטֹפָתִי: חֵלֶב בֶּן־
ל בַּעֲנָה הַנְּטֹפָתִי אִתַּי בֶּן־רִיבַי מִגִּבְעַת בְּנֵי בִנְיָמִן: בְּנָיָהוּ
לא פִּרְעָתֹנִי הִדַּי מִנַּחֲלֵי גָעַשׁ: אֲבִי־עַלְבוֹן הָעַרְבָתִי עַזְמָוֶת
לב לג הַבַּרְחֻמִי: אֶלְיַחְבָּא הַשַּׁעַלְבֹנִי בְּנֵי יָשֵׁן יְהוֹנָתָן: שַׁמָּה
לד הַהֲרָרִי אֲחִיאָם בֶּן־שָׁרָר הָאֲרָרִי: אֱלִיפֶלֶט בֶּן־אֲחַסְבַּי בֶּן־
לה הַמַּעֲכָתִי אֱלִיעָם בֶּן־אֲחִיתֹפֶל הַגִּלֹנִי: חצרו הַכַּרְמְלִי פַּעֲרַי חֶצְרַי
לו לז הָאַרְבִּי: יִגְאָל בֶּן־נָתָן מִצֹּבָה בָּנִי הַגָּדִי: צֶלֶק הָעַמֹּנִי
לח נַחְרַי הַבְּאֵרֹתִי נשאי כְּלֵי יוֹאָב בֶּן־צְרֻיָה: עִירָא הַיִּתְרִי גָּרֵב נֹשֵׂא
לט כד א הַיִּתְרִי: אוּרִיָּה הַחִתִּי כֹּל שְׁלֹשִׁים וְשִׁבְעָה: וַיֹּסֶף
אַף־יהוה לַחֲרוֹת בְּיִשְׂרָאֵל וַיָּסֶת אֶת־דָּוִד בָּהֶם לֵאמֹר לֵךְ מְנֵה אֶת־
ב יִשְׂרָאֵל וְאֶת־יְהוּדָה: וַיֹּאמֶר הַמֶּלֶךְ אֶל־יוֹאָב | שַׂר־הַחַיִל אֲשֶׁר־אִתּוֹ
שׁוּט־נָא בְּכָל־שִׁבְטֵי יִשְׂרָאֵל מִדָּן וְעַד־בְּאֵר שֶׁבַע וּפִקְדוּ אֶת־הָעָם
ג וְיָדַעְתִּי אֵת מִסְפַּר הָעָם: וַיֹּאמֶר יוֹאָב אֶל־הַמֶּלֶךְ וְיוֹסֵף
יהוה אֱלֹהֶיךָ אֶל־הָעָם כָּהֵם | וְכָהֵם מֵאָה פְעָמִים וְעֵינֵי אֲדֹנִי־הַמֶּלֶךְ
ד רֹאוֹת וַאדֹנִי הַמֶּלֶךְ לָמָּה חָפֵץ בַּדָּבָר הַזֶּה: וַיֶּחֱזַק דְּבַר־הַמֶּלֶךְ אֶל־
יוֹאָב וְעַל שָׂרֵי הֶחָיִל וַיֵּצֵא יוֹאָב וְשָׂרֵי הַחַיִל לִפְנֵי הַמֶּלֶךְ לִפְקֹד אֶת־
ה הָעָם אֶת־יִשְׂרָאֵל: וַיַּעַבְרוּ אֶת־הַיַּרְדֵּן וַיַּחֲנוּ בַעֲרוֹעֵר יְמִין הָעִיר אֲשֶׁר
ו בְּתוֹךְ־הַנַּחַל הַגָּד וְאֶל־יַעְזֵר: וַיָּבֹאוּ הַגִּלְעָדָה וְאֶל־אֶרֶץ תַּחְתִּים
ז חָדְשִׁי וַיָּבֹאוּ דָּנָה יַּעַן וְסָבִיב אֶל־צִידוֹן: וַיָּבֹאוּ מִבְצַר־צֹר וְכָל־עָרֵי
ח הַחִוִּי וְהַכְּנַעֲנִי וַיֵּצְאוּ אֶל־נֶגֶב יְהוּדָה בְּאֵר שָׁבַע: וַיָּשֻׁטוּ בְּכָל־הָאָרֶץ
ט וַיָּבֹאוּ מִקְצֵה תִשְׁעָה חֳדָשִׁים וְעֶשְׂרִים יוֹם יְרוּשָׁלָם: וַיִּתֵּן יוֹאָב אֶת־
מִסְפַּר מִפְקַד־הָעָם אֶל־הַמֶּלֶךְ וַתְּהִי יִשְׂרָאֵל שְׁמֹנֶה מֵאוֹת אֶלֶף
י אִישׁ־חַיִל שֹׁלֵף חֶרֶב וְאִישׁ יְהוּדָה חֲמֵשׁ־מֵאוֹת אֶלֶף אִישׁ: וַיַּךְ לֵב־
דָּוִד אֹתוֹ אַחֲרֵי־כֵן סָפַר אֶת־הָעָם וַיֹּאמֶר דָּוִד אֶל־יהוה
חָטָאתִי מְאֹד אֲשֶׁר עָשִׂיתִי וְעַתָּה יהוה הַעֲבֶר־נָא אֶת־עֲוֺן עַבְדְּךָ כִּי
יא נִסְכַּלְתִּי מְאֹד: וַיָּקָם דָּוִד בַּבֹּקֶר וּדְבַר־יהוה הָיָה אֶל־גָּד
יב הַנָּבִיא חֹזֵה דָוִד לֵאמֹר: הָלוֹךְ וְדִבַּרְתָּ אֶל־דָּוִד כֹּה אָמַר יהוה שָׁלֹשׁ

13 things over you; choose one of them, and I will bring it upon you." Gad came
to David and told him. "Will you suffer seven years of famine in your land,"
he said to him, "or will you flee before your foes for three months as they
pursue you, or will there be three days of sickness in your land? Now, consider
14 what reply I should bring back to Him who sent me." "I am in grave
torment," David said to Gad. "Let us fall into the Hand of the LORD, for His
15 mercy is great; do not let me fall into human hands." And the LORD sent a
sickness against Israel from morning until the set time, and from Dan up to
16 Be'er Sheva, seventy thousand of the people died. But as the angel raised his
hand to destroy Jerusalem, the LORD regretted the evil and said to the angel
who was wreaking destruction among the people, "Enough! Now, stay your
hand." The angel of the LORD was then by the threshing floor of Aravna the
17 Jebusite. When David saw the angel who was striking down the
people, he spoke to the LORD. "Look – I alone have sinned," he said, "and I
alone offended. But this flock – what have they done? Please, let Your hand
18 move against me and against my father's house." On that same day,
Gad came to David and said to him, "Go up; erect an altar to the LORD by the
19 threshing floor of Aravna the Jebusite." At Gad's word, David went up, just as
20 the LORD had charged. When Aravna looked out and saw the king and his
officials crossing over toward him, Aravna went out and bowed before the
21 king, his face to the ground. "Why has my lord the king come to his servant?"
asked Aravna. "To purchase your threshing floor from you to build an altar to
22 the LORD," said David, "so that the plague will cease among the people." "Let
my lord the king take and offer up as he sees fit," said Aravna. "Look, oxen
23 for a burnt offering and threshing boards and cattle gear for wood. O King,
Aravna has given it all to the king." And Aravna added to the king,
24 "May the LORD your God show you favor." "No, I insist on buying it from
you at a price," the king said to Aravna. "I will not offer up burnt offerings
to the LORD my God at no cost." And David bought the threshing floor and
25 the oxen for fifty shekel of silver. David built an altar there for the LORD and
offered up burnt offerings and peace offerings. And the LORD responded to
the plea of the land, and the plague ceased in Israel.

יג אָנֹכִי נוֹטֵל עָלֶיךָ בְּחַר־לְךָ אַחַת־מֵהֶם וְאֶעֱשֶׂה־לָּךְ׃ וַיָּבֹא־גָד אֶל־דָּוִד
וַיַּגֶּד־לוֹ וַיֹּאמֶר לוֹ הֲתָבוֹא לְךָ שֶׁבַע־שָׁנִים ׀ רָעָב ׀ בְּאַרְצֶךָ וְאִם־שְׁלֹשָׁה
חֳדָשִׁים נֻסְךָ לִפְנֵי־צָרֶיךָ וְהוּא רֹדְפֶךָ וְאִם־הֱיוֹת שְׁלֹשֶׁת יָמִים דֶּבֶר
יד בְּאַרְצֶךָ עַתָּה דַּע וּרְאֵה מָה־אָשִׁיב שֹׁלְחִי דָּבָר׃ וַיֹּאמֶר
דָּוִד אֶל־גָּד צַר־לִי מְאֹד נִפְּלָה־נָּא בְיַד־יהוה כִּי־רַבִּים רַחֲמָו וּבְיַד־
טו אָדָם אַל־אֶפֹּלָה׃ וַיִּתֵּן יהוה דֶּבֶר בְּיִשְׂרָאֵל מֵהַבֹּקֶר וְעַד־עֵת מוֹעֵד
טז וַיָּמָת מִן־הָעָם מִדָּן וְעַד־בְּאֵר שֶׁבַע שִׁבְעִים אֶלֶף אִישׁ׃ וַיִּשְׁלַח יָדוֹ
הַמַּלְאָךְ ׀ יְרוּשָׁלִַם לְשַׁחֲתָהּ וַיִּנָּחֶם יהוה אֶל־הָרָעָה וַיֹּאמֶר לַמַּלְאָךְ
הַמַּשְׁחִית בָּעָם רַב עַתָּה הֶרֶף יָדֶךָ וּמַלְאַךְ יהוה הָיָה עִם־גֹּרֶן האורנה הָאֲרַוְנָה
יז הַיְבֻסִי׃ וַיֹּאמֶר דָּוִד אֶל־יהוה בִּרְאֹתוֹ ׀ אֶת־הַמַּלְאָךְ ׀
הַמַּכֶּה בָעָם וַיֹּאמֶר הִנֵּה אָנֹכִי חָטָאתִי וְאָנֹכִי הֶעֱוֵיתִי וְאֵלֶּה הַצֹּאן
יח מֶה עָשׂוּ תְּהִי נָא יָדְךָ בִּי וּבְבֵית אָבִי׃ וַיָּבֹא־גָד אֶל־דָּוִד
בַּיּוֹם הַהוּא וַיֹּאמֶר לוֹ עֲלֵה הָקֵם לַיהוה מִזְבֵּחַ בְּגֹרֶן ארניה הַיְבֻסִי׃ אֲרַוְנָה
יט כ וַיַּעַל דָּוִד כִּדְבַר־גָּד כַּאֲשֶׁר צִוָּה יהוה׃ וַיַּשְׁקֵף אֲרַוְנָה וַיַּרְא אֶת־הַמֶּלֶךְ
וְאֶת־עֲבָדָיו עֹבְרִים עָלָיו וַיֵּצֵא אֲרַוְנָה וַיִּשְׁתַּחוּ לַמֶּלֶךְ אַפָּיו אָרְצָה׃
כא וַיֹּאמֶר אֲרַוְנָה מַדּוּעַ בָּא אֲדֹנִי־הַמֶּלֶךְ אֶל־עַבְדּוֹ וַיֹּאמֶר דָּוִד לִקְנוֹת
מֵעִמְּךָ אֶת־הַגֹּרֶן לִבְנוֹת מִזְבֵּחַ לַיהוה וְתֵעָצַר הַמַּגֵּפָה מֵעַל הָעָם׃
כב וַיֹּאמֶר אֲרַוְנָה אֶל־דָּוִד יִקַּח וְיַעַל אֲדֹנִי הַמֶּלֶךְ הַטּוֹב בְּעֵינָו רְאֵה
כג הַבָּקָר לָעֹלָה וְהַמֹּרִגִּים וּכְלֵי הַבָּקָר לָעֵצִים׃ הַכֹּל נָתַן אֲרַוְנָה הַמֶּלֶךְ
לַמֶּלֶךְ וַיֹּאמֶר אֲרַוְנָה אֶל־הַמֶּלֶךְ יהוה אֱלֹהֶיךָ יִרְצֶךָ׃
כד וַיֹּאמֶר הַמֶּלֶךְ אֶל־אֲרַוְנָה לֹא כִּי־קָנוֹ אֶקְנֶה מֵאוֹתְךָ בִּמְחִיר וְלֹא
אַעֲלֶה לַיהוה אֱלֹהַי עֹלוֹת חִנָּם וַיִּקֶן דָּוִד אֶת־הַגֹּרֶן וְאֶת־הַבָּקָר בְּכֶסֶף
כה שְׁקָלִים חֲמִשִּׁים׃ וַיִּבֶן שָׁם דָּוִד מִזְבֵּחַ לַיהוה וַיַּעַל עֹלוֹת וּשְׁלָמִים
וַיֵּעָתֵר יהוה לָאָרֶץ וַתֵּעָצַר הַמַּגֵּפָה מֵעַל יִשְׂרָאֵל׃

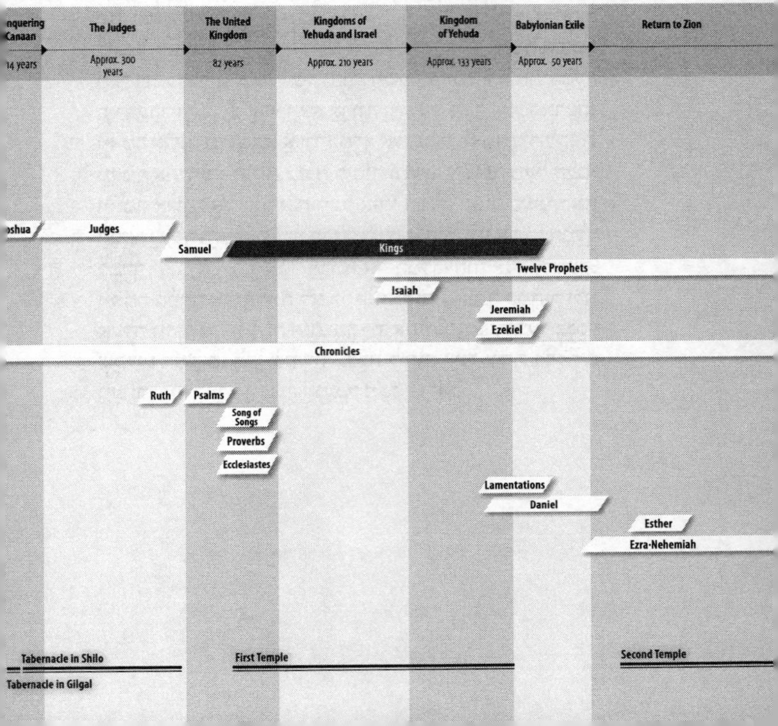
nquering Canaan
The Judges
The United Kingdom
Kingdoms of Yehuda and Israel
Kingdom of Yehuda
Babylonian Exile
Return to Zion
14 years
Approx. 300 years
82 years
Approx. 210 years
Approx. 133 years
Approx. 50 years
oshua
Judges
Samuel
Kings
Twelve Prophets
Isaiah
Jeremiah
Ezekiel
Chronicles
Ruth
Psalms
Song of Songs
Proverbs
Ecclesiastes
Lamentations
Daniel
Esther
Ezra-Nehemiah
Tabernacle in Shilo
First Temple
Second Temple
Tabernacle in Gilgal

מלכים
MELAKHIM / KINGS

KINGS

From David's reign to Shlomo's reign	Shlomo's reign	Kings of Yehuda and Israel – from the division of the monarchy through the final days of the house of Omri	Kings of Yehuda and Israel – from Yehu's rebellion through the destruction of the Kingdom of Israel	Kingdom of Yehuda – from the destruction of the Kingdom of Israel through the destruction of Jerusalem
I Kings Chs. 1–2	I Kings 3–11	I Kings 12 – II Kings 8	II Kings 9–17	II Kings 18–25
40 years		98 years	143 years	Approx. 135 years

1 1 King David was old, advanced in years, and though they covered him with
2 bedclothes, he never felt warm. His servants said to him, "Let a young virgin
be sought out for our lord the king, to wait upon the king and become his
companion; when she lies in your embrace, our lord the king will feel warm."
3 They searched throughout Israel's borders for a beautiful girl, found Avishag
4 the Shunamite, and brought her to the king. The girl was most beautiful, and
she became the king's companion and served him, but the king was not
5 intimate with her. Meanwhile, Adoniya son of Ḥagit promoted himself,
declaring, "I will become king," and he procured a chariot and riders and fifty
6 men to run before him. Now his father had never disciplined him, saying,
"Why have you acted like that?" He was born after Avshalom, and he too was
7 devastatingly handsome. He conspired with Yoav son of Tzeruya and Avyatar
8 the priest, and they lent their support to Adoniya. But Tzadok the priest,
Benayahu son of Yehoyada, Natan the prophet, Shimi and Rei, and David's
9 warriors were not on Adoniyahu's side. Adoniyahu sacrificed sheep, oxen, and
fatlings by the Zoḥelet Stone near the Rogel Spring, and he invited all his
brothers – the king's sons – and all the men of Yehuda, the king's subjects.
10 But he did not invite the prophet Natan or Benayahu or the warriors, or his
11 brother Shlomo. And Natan said to Batsheva, Shlomo's mother, "Have you
heard? Adoniyahu the son of Ḥagit has become king without our lord David's
12 knowledge. Come now, let me give you advice – to save your own life and
13 the life of your son Shlomo. Go to King David at once and say to him, 'My
lord the king, did you not swear to your handmaid, "Your son Shlomo will
rule after me, and he will sit on my throne"? Why, then, has Adoniyahu
14 become king?' And while you are still speaking there with the king, I will
15 come in after you and confirm your words." So Batsheva went to the king in
the inner chamber – the king had aged severely, and Avishag the Shunamite
16 was tending to him – and Batsheva bowed down low in homage to the king.
17 "What is the matter?" asked the king. "My lord," she said to him, "you swore
by the Lord your God to your handmaid, 'Your son Shlomo will rule after
18 me, and he will sit on my throne.' But now, look – Adoniya has become
19 king – and you, my lord the king, did not even know! He has sacrificed a
wealth of oxen and fatlings and sheep and invited all the king's sons, the priest
Avyatar, and the army commander Yoav, but he did not invite your servant
20 Shlomo. But all the eyes of Israel look to you, my lord the king, to tell them
21 who will succeed my lord the king on his throne. Otherwise, when my lord
the king lies with his ancestors, my son Shlomo and I will be considered
22 offenders." And as she was still speaking with the king, Natan the prophet
23 arrived. "Here is Natan the prophet," they announced to the king, and he
24 came before the king and bowed to him with his face to the ground. "My lord
the king," said Natan, "Did you yourself say, 'Adoniyahu will be king after me,

א א וְהַמֶּלֶךְ דָּוִד זָקֵן בָּא בַּיָּמִים וַיְכַסֻּהוּ בַּבְּגָדִים וְלֹא יִחַם לוֹ: וַיֹּאמְרוּ א
ב לוֹ עֲבָדָיו יְבַקְשׁוּ לַאדֹנִי הַמֶּלֶךְ נַעֲרָה בְתוּלָה וְעָמְדָה לִפְנֵי הַמֶּלֶךְ
ג וּתְהִי־לוֹ סֹכֶנֶת וְשָׁכְבָה בְחֵיקֶךָ וְחַם לַאדֹנִי הַמֶּלֶךְ: וַיְבַקְשׁוּ נַעֲרָה
יָפָה בְּכֹל גְּבוּל יִשְׂרָאֵל וַיִּמְצְאוּ אֶת־אֲבִישַׁג הַשּׁוּנַמִּית וַיָּבִאוּ אֹתָהּ
ד לַמֶּלֶךְ: וְהַנַּעֲרָה יָפָה עַד־מְאֹד וַתְּהִי לַמֶּלֶךְ סֹכֶנֶת וַתְּשָׁרְתֵהוּ וְהַמֶּלֶךְ
ה לֹא יְדָעָהּ: וַאֲדֹנִיָּה בֶן־חַגִּית מִתְנַשֵּׂא לֵאמֹר אֲנִי אֶמְלֹךְ וַיַּעַשׂ לוֹ
ו רֶכֶב וּפָרָשִׁים וַחֲמִשִּׁים אִישׁ רָצִים לְפָנָיו: וְלֹא־עֲצָבוֹ אָבִיו מִיָּמָיו
לֵאמֹר מַדּוּעַ כָּכָה עָשִׂיתָ וְגַם־הוּא טוֹב־תֹּאַר מְאֹד וְאֹתוֹ יָלְדָה
ז אַחֲרֵי אַבְשָׁלוֹם: וַיִּהְיוּ דְבָרָיו עִם יוֹאָב בֶּן־צְרוּיָה וְעִם אֶבְיָתָר הַכֹּהֵן
ח וַיַּעְזְרוּ אַחֲרֵי אֲדֹנִיָּה: וְצָדוֹק הַכֹּהֵן וּבְנָיָהוּ בֶן־יְהוֹיָדָע וְנָתָן הַנָּבִיא
ט וְשִׁמְעִי וְרֵעִי וְהַגִּבּוֹרִים אֲשֶׁר לְדָוִד לֹא הָיוּ עִם־אֲדֹנִיָּהוּ: וַיִּזְבַּח אֲדֹנִיָּהוּ
צֹאן וּבָקָר וּמְרִיא עִם אֶבֶן הַזֹּחֶלֶת אֲשֶׁר־אֵצֶל עֵין רֹגֵל וַיִּקְרָא אֶת־
י כָּל־אֶחָיו בְּנֵי הַמֶּלֶךְ וּלְכָל־אַנְשֵׁי יְהוּדָה עַבְדֵי הַמֶּלֶךְ: וְאֶת־נָתָן הַנָּבִיא
יא וּבְנָיָהוּ וְאֶת־הַגִּבּוֹרִים וְאֶת־שְׁלֹמֹה אָחִיו לֹא קָרָא: וַיֹּאמֶר נָתָן אֶל־
בַּת־שֶׁבַע אֵם־שְׁלֹמֹה לֵאמֹר הֲלוֹא שָׁמַעַתְּ כִּי מָלַךְ אֲדֹנִיָּהוּ בֶן־
יב חַגִּית וַאֲדֹנֵינוּ דָוִד לֹא יָדָע: וְעַתָּה לְכִי אִיעָצֵךְ נָא עֵצָה וּמַלְּטִי אֶת־
יג נַפְשֵׁךְ וְאֶת־נֶפֶשׁ בְּנֵךְ שְׁלֹמֹה: לְכִי וּבֹאִי ׀ אֶל־הַמֶּלֶךְ דָּוִד וְאָמַרְתְּ
אֵלָיו הֲלֹא־אַתָּה אֲדֹנִי הַמֶּלֶךְ נִשְׁבַּעְתָּ לַאֲמָתְךָ לֵאמֹר כִּי־שְׁלֹמֹה
יד בְנֵךְ יִמְלֹךְ אַחֲרַי וְהוּא יֵשֵׁב עַל־כִּסְאִי וּמַדּוּעַ מָלַךְ אֲדֹנִיָהוּ: הִנֵּה
עוֹדָךְ מְדַבֶּרֶת שָׁם עִם־הַמֶּלֶךְ וַאֲנִי אָבוֹא אַחֲרַיִךְ וּמִלֵּאתִי אֶת־
טו דְּבָרָיִךְ: וַתָּבֹא בַת־שֶׁבַע אֶל־הַמֶּלֶךְ הַחַדְרָה וְהַמֶּלֶךְ זָקֵן מְאֹד
טז וַאֲבִישַׁג הַשּׁוּנַמִּית מְשָׁרַת אֶת־הַמֶּלֶךְ: וַתִּקֹּד בַּת־שֶׁבַע וַתִּשְׁתַּחוּ
יז לַמֶּלֶךְ וַיֹּאמֶר הַמֶּלֶךְ מַה־לָּךְ: וַתֹּאמֶר לוֹ אֲדֹנִי אַתָּה נִשְׁבַּעְתָּ בַּיהוָה
אֱלֹהֶיךָ לַאֲמָתֶךָ כִּי־שְׁלֹמֹה בְנֵךְ יִמְלֹךְ אַחֲרָי וְהוּא יֵשֵׁב עַל־כִּסְאִי:
יח יט וְעַתָּה הִנֵּה אֲדֹנִיָּה מָלָךְ וְעַתָּה אֲדֹנִי הַמֶּלֶךְ לֹא יָדָעְתָּ: וַיִּזְבַּח שׁוֹר
וּמְרִיא־וְצֹאן לָרֹב וַיִּקְרָא לְכָל־בְּנֵי הַמֶּלֶךְ וּלְאֶבְיָתָר הַכֹּהֵן וּלְיֹאָב שַׂר
כ הַצָּבָא וְלִשְׁלֹמֹה עַבְדְּךָ לֹא קָרָא: וְאַתָּה אֲדֹנִי הַמֶּלֶךְ עֵינֵי כָל־יִשְׂרָאֵל
כא עָלֶיךָ לְהַגִּיד לָהֶם מִי יֵשֵׁב עַל־כִּסֵּא אֲדֹנִי־הַמֶּלֶךְ אַחֲרָיו: וְהָיָה כִּשְׁכַב
כב אֲדֹנִי־הַמֶּלֶךְ עִם־אֲבֹתָיו וְהָיִיתִי אֲנִי וּבְנִי שְׁלֹמֹה חַטָּאִים: וְהִנֵּה עוֹדֶנָּה
כג מְדַבֶּרֶת עִם־הַמֶּלֶךְ וְנָתָן הַנָּבִיא בָּא: וַיַּגִּידוּ לַמֶּלֶךְ לֵאמֹר הִנֵּה נָתָן
כד הַנָּבִיא וַיָּבֹא לִפְנֵי הַמֶּלֶךְ וַיִּשְׁתַּחוּ לַמֶּלֶךְ עַל־אַפָּיו אָרְצָה: וַיֹּאמֶר
נָתָן אֲדֹנִי הַמֶּלֶךְ אַתָּה אָמַרְתָּ אֲדֹנִיָּהוּ יִמְלֹךְ אַחֲרָי וְהוּא יֵשֵׁב עַל־

25 and he will sit on my throne'? For he went down today and sacrificed a wealth
of oxen, fatlings, and sheep and invited all the king's sons, the army officers,
and Avyatar the priest. And now they are feasting before him and toasting
26 him and declaring, 'Long live King Adoniyahu!' But he did not invite me,
your servant, or the priest Tzadok, or Benayahu son of Yehoyada, or your
27 servant Shlomo. Could it be that my lord the king has decided this without
informing your servant who will succeed my lord the king on his throne?"
28 "Summon Batsheva to me," King David said in response, and she came before
29 the king and stood in the king's presence. And the king swore an oath. "As
30 the Lord lives," he said, "who has rescued me from every danger, what I
swore to you by the Lord, God of Israel – that Shlomo your son will rule
after me, and that he will sit on my throne in my place – I shall fulfill this very
31 day." And Batsheva bowed her face to the ground in royal homage and
32 said, "May my lord, King David, live forever!" King David then
said, "Summon Tzadok the priest to me, along with Natan the prophet and
33 Benayahu son of Yehoyada," and they came before the king. "Take your lord's
servants with you," the king said to them, "and mount my son Shlomo upon
34 my own mule, and lead him down to Giḥon. There, the priest Tzadok and
the prophet Natan will anoint him as king over Israel; and you will sound the
35 ram's horn and declare, 'Long live King Shlomo!' Then you will go up after
him; he will enter and sit on my throne and reign in my place, for it is him
36 whom I have charged as ruler over Israel and Yehuda." "Amen," Benayahu son
of Yehoyada answered the king. "May the Lord, God of my lord the king,
37 deem it so. Just as the Lord has been with my lord the king, so may He be
with Shlomo, and may He make his throne even greater than the throne of
38 my lord, King David." So Tzadok the priest, the prophet Natan, and Benayahu
son of Yehoyada and the Keretites and Peletites[1] went down. They mounted
39 Shlomo on King David's mule and led him to Giḥon. Then Tzadok the priest
took the horn of oil from the Tent and anointed Shlomo. They sounded the
40 ram's horn, and all the people cried, "Long live King Shlomo!" And all the
people marched up after him, with the people piping away on pipes and
41 rejoicing with such great joy that the very earth split from the sound. As
Adoniyahu and all the guests who were with him finished eating, they heard.
When Yoav heard the sound of the ram's horn, he asked, "Why is there the
42 sound of commotion in the city?" And as he was still speaking, Yonatan, the
priest Avyatar's son, arrived. "Come in," said Adoniyahu, "for you are a worthy
43 man, and you surely bring good news." "Alas," Yonatan answered Adoniyahu,
44 "our lord, King David, has made Shlomo king. And with him, the king sent
Tzadok the priest, Natan the prophet, and Benayahu son of Yehoyada with
the Keretites and Peletites, and they mounted him on the king's own mule.
45 The priest Tzadok and the prophet Natan anointed him as king at Giḥon;

1 | Armed forces loyal to David, perhaps of foreign origin; see, e.g., II Samuel 8:18, 15:18, 20:23.

כה כִסְאִי: כִּי ׀ יָרַד הַיּוֹם וַיִּזְבַּח שׁוֹר וּמְרִיא־וְצֹאן לָרֹב וַיִּקְרָא לְכָל־בְּנֵי
הַמֶּלֶךְ וּלְשָׂרֵי הַצָּבָא וּלְאֶבְיָתָר הַכֹּהֵן וְהִנָּם אֹכְלִים וְשֹׁתִים לְפָנָיו
כו וַיֹּאמְרוּ יְחִי הַמֶּלֶךְ אֲדֹנִיָּהוּ: וְלִי אֲנִי־עַבְדֶּךָ וּלְצָדֹק הַכֹּהֵן וְלִבְנָיָהוּ
כז בֶן־יְהוֹיָדָע וְלִשְׁלֹמֹה עַבְדְּךָ לֹא קָרָא: אִם מֵאֵת אֲדֹנִי הַמֶּלֶךְ נִהְיָה
הַדָּבָר הַזֶּה וְלֹא הוֹדַעְתָּ אֶת־עַבְדיך מִי יֵשֵׁב עַל־כִּסֵּא אֲדֹנִי־הַמֶּלֶךְ עַבְדְּךָ
כח אַחֲרָיו: וַיַּעַן הַמֶּלֶךְ דָּוִד וַיֹּאמֶר קִרְאוּ־לִי לְבַת־שָׁבַע וַתָּבֹא לִפְנֵי
כט הַמֶּלֶךְ וַתַּעֲמֹד לִפְנֵי הַמֶּלֶךְ: וַיִּשָּׁבַע הַמֶּלֶךְ וַיֹּאמַר חַי־יְהוָה אֲשֶׁר־פָּדָה
ל אֶת־נַפְשִׁי מִכָּל־צָרָה: כִּי כַּאֲשֶׁר נִשְׁבַּעְתִּי לָךְ בַּיהוָה אֱלֹהֵי יִשְׂרָאֵל
לֵאמֹר כִּי־שְׁלֹמֹה בְנֵךְ יִמְלֹךְ אַחֲרַי וְהוּא יֵשֵׁב עַל־כִּסְאִי תַּחְתָּי כִּי כֵּן
לא אֶעֱשֶׂה הַיּוֹם הַזֶּה: וַתִּקֹּד בַּת־שֶׁבַע אַפַּיִם אֶרֶץ וַתִּשְׁתַּחוּ לַמֶּלֶךְ
לב וַתֹּאמֶר יְחִי אֲדֹנִי הַמֶּלֶךְ דָּוִד לְעֹלָם: וַיֹּאמֶר ׀ הַמֶּלֶךְ דָּוִד
קִרְאוּ־לִי לְצָדוֹק הַכֹּהֵן וּלְנָתָן הַנָּבִיא וְלִבְנָיָהוּ בֶּן־יְהוֹיָדָע וַיָּבֹאוּ לִפְנֵי
לג הַמֶּלֶךְ: וַיֹּאמֶר הַמֶּלֶךְ לָהֶם קְחוּ עִמָּכֶם אֶת־עַבְדֵי אֲדֹנֵיכֶם וְהִרְכַּבְתֶּם
אֶת־שְׁלֹמֹה בְנִי עַל־הַפִּרְדָּה אֲשֶׁר־לִי וְהוֹרַדְתֶּם אֹתוֹ אֶל־גִּחוֹן:
לד וּמָשַׁח אֹתוֹ שָׁם צָדוֹק הַכֹּהֵן וְנָתָן הַנָּבִיא לְמֶלֶךְ עַל־יִשְׂרָאֵל וּתְקַעְתֶּם
לה בַּשּׁוֹפָר וַאֲמַרְתֶּם יְחִי הַמֶּלֶךְ שְׁלֹמֹה: וַעֲלִיתֶם אַחֲרָיו וּבָא וְיָשַׁב
עַל־כִּסְאִי וְהוּא יִמְלֹךְ תַּחְתָּי וְאֹתוֹ צִוִּיתִי לִהְיוֹת נָגִיד עַל־יִשְׂרָאֵל
לו וְעַל־יְהוּדָה: וַיַּעַן בְּנָיָהוּ בֶן־יְהוֹיָדָע אֶת־הַמֶּלֶךְ וַיֹּאמֶר ׀ אָמֵן כֵּן יֹאמַר
לז יְהוָה אֱלֹהֵי אֲדֹנִי הַמֶּלֶךְ: כַּאֲשֶׁר הָיָה יְהוָה עִם־אֲדֹנִי הַמֶּלֶךְ כֵּן יְהִי
לח עִם־שְׁלֹמֹה וִיגַדֵּל אֶת־כִּסְאוֹ מִכִּסֵּא אֲדֹנִי הַמֶּלֶךְ דָּוִד: וַיֵּרֶד צָדוֹק
הַכֹּהֵן וְנָתָן הַנָּבִיא וּבְנָיָהוּ בֶן־יְהוֹיָדָע וְהַכְּרֵתִי וְהַפְּלֵתִי וַיַּרְכִּבוּ אֶת־
לט שְׁלֹמֹה עַל־פִּרְדַּת הַמֶּלֶךְ דָּוִד וַיֹּלִכוּ אֹתוֹ עַל־גִּחוֹן: וַיִּקַּח צָדוֹק
הַכֹּהֵן אֶת־קֶרֶן הַשֶּׁמֶן מִן־הָאֹהֶל וַיִּמְשַׁח אֶת־שְׁלֹמֹה וַיִּתְקְעוּ בַּשּׁוֹפָר
מ וַיֹּאמְרוּ כָּל־הָעָם יְחִי הַמֶּלֶךְ שְׁלֹמֹה: וַיַּעֲלוּ כָל־הָעָם אַחֲרָיו וְהָעָם
מְחַלְּלִים בַּחֲלִלִים וּשְׂמֵחִים שִׂמְחָה גְדוֹלָה וַתִּבָּקַע הָאָרֶץ בְּקוֹלָם:
מא וַיִּשְׁמַע אֲדֹנִיָּהוּ וְכָל־הַקְּרֻאִים אֲשֶׁר אִתּוֹ וְהֵם כִּלּוּ לֶאֱכֹל וַיִּשְׁמַע יוֹאָב
מב אֶת־קוֹל הַשּׁוֹפָר וַיֹּאמֶר מַדּוּעַ קוֹל־הַקִּרְיָה הוֹמָה: עוֹדֶנּוּ מְדַבֵּר וְהִנֵּה
יוֹנָתָן בֶּן־אֶבְיָתָר הַכֹּהֵן בָּא וַיֹּאמֶר אֲדֹנִיָּהוּ בֹּא כִּי אִישׁ חַיִל אַתָּה
מג וְטוֹב תְּבַשֵּׂר: וַיַּעַן יוֹנָתָן וַיֹּאמֶר לַאֲדֹנִיָּהוּ אֲבָל אֲדֹנֵינוּ הַמֶּלֶךְ־דָּוִד
מד הִמְלִיךְ אֶת־שְׁלֹמֹה: וַיִּשְׁלַח אִתּוֹ הַמֶּלֶךְ אֶת־צָדוֹק הַכֹּהֵן וְאֶת־נָתָן
הַנָּבִיא וּבְנָיָהוּ בֶּן־יְהוֹיָדָע וְהַכְּרֵתִי וְהַפְּלֵתִי וַיַּרְכִּבוּ אֹתוֹ עַל פִּרְדַּת
מה הַמֶּלֶךְ: וַיִּמְשְׁחוּ אֹתוֹ צָדוֹק הַכֹּהֵן וְנָתָן הַנָּבִיא ׀ לְמֶלֶךְ בְּגִחוֹן וַיַּעֲלוּ

they paraded up from there in celebration, and commotion swept the
46 city – that is the sound you heard. And what is more, Shlomo now sits on the
47 royal throne, and the king's subjects have come to bless our lord, King David,
saying, 'May God make Shlomo's name more famous than your own name,
and may He make his throne even greater than your own throne,' and the king
48 bowed down from his bed. And the king even said, 'Blessed is the LORD, God
of Israel, who has granted an heir to my throne today while my own eyes can
49 witness it.'" All of Adoniyahu's guests rose in alarm, and each went on his way,
50 while Adoniyahu, in fear of Shlomo, rose and made his way straight to the
51 horns of the altar and grasped hold of them. Shlomo was told, "Now, out of
fear of King Shlomo, Adoniyahu is clutching at the horns of the altar, saying,
'Let King Shlomo swear to me – right now – that he will not put his servant
52 to death by sword.'" "If he will prove to be a worthy man, not a hair of his
will fall to the ground," Shlomo said, "but if any fault will be found with him,
53 he is dead." And Shlomo sent and had him brought down from the altar, and
he came and bowed before King Shlomo. And Shlomo said to him, "Go
2 1 home." The time of David's death was drawing near, and he
2 gave instructions to his son Shlomo. "I am going the way of all the earth,"
3 he said. "You must be strong and prove yourself a man. You must keep the
charge of the LORD your God, following His ways and keeping His laws and
commandments, His rulings and decrees, as written in the teaching of Moshe.
4 For then you will succeed in whatever you do, wherever you turn. For then,
the LORD will fulfill the promise He made to me, saying: If your sons keep to
their path and walk before Me truly, with all their heart and all their soul, then
5 no one of your lineage will be cut off from the throne of Israel. Now you know
what Yoav son of Tzeruya did to me – how he dealt with the two commanders
of Israel's forces, Avner son of Ner and Amasa son of Yeter. By killing them, he
shed the blood of war in peacetime and tainted the belt around his waist and
6 the shoes upon his feet with the blood of war.[2] Use your wisdom – do not let
7 his gray-haired head go down to Sheol[3] in peace. As for the sons of
Barzilai the Gileadite, show them loyalty and let them dine at your table,[4] for
8 they befriended me when I was fleeing from Avshalom your brother.[5] Now,
look – though Shimi son of Gera the Benjaminite from Baḥurim is with you,
he cursed me with a vehement curse on the day I left Maḥanayim. When he
came down to meet me by the Jordan, I swore to him by the LORD that I would
9 not put him to death by sword[6] – but now, do not let him go free. You are a
wise man, and you will know how to deal with him – bring his gray-haired
10 head down in blood to Sheol." And David slept with his ancestors and was
11 buried in the City of David. The length of time that David had
reigned over Israel was forty years; he reigned in Ḥevron for seven years, and

---

2 | The murder of Avner is recounted in II Samuel 3:27 and the murder of Amasa in II Samuel 20:10.

3 | The netherworld.

4 | Provide for their maintenance.

5 | See II Samuel 19:32–40.

6 | See II Samuel 16:5–13, 19:16–24.

מו מִשָּׁם שְׂמֵחִים וַתֵּהֹם הַקִּרְיָה הוּא הַקּוֹל אֲשֶׁר שְׁמַעְתֶּם: וְגַם יָשַׁב
מז שְׁלֹמֹה עַל כִּסֵּא הַמְּלוּכָה: וְגַם־בָּאוּ עַבְדֵי הַמֶּלֶךְ לְבָרֵךְ אֶת־אֲדֹנֵינוּ
הַמֶּלֶךְ דָּוִד לֵאמֹר יֵיטֵב אלהיך אֶת־שֵׁם שְׁלֹמֹה מִשְּׁמֶךָ וִיגַדֵּל אֶת־ אֱלֹהִים
מח כִּסְאוֹ מִכִּסְאֶךָ וַיִּשְׁתַּחוּ הַמֶּלֶךְ עַל־הַמִּשְׁכָּב: וְגַם־כָּכָה אָמַר הַמֶּלֶךְ ב
בָּרוּךְ יְהוָה אֱלֹהֵי יִשְׂרָאֵל אֲשֶׁר נָתַן הַיּוֹם יֹשֵׁב עַל־כִּסְאִי וְעֵינַי רֹאוֹת:
מט וַיֶּחֶרְדוּ וַיָּקֻמוּ כָּל־הַקְּרֻאִים אֲשֶׁר לַאֲדֹנִיָּהוּ וַיֵּלְכוּ אִישׁ לְדַרְכּוֹ:
נ נא וַאֲדֹנִיָּהוּ יָרֵא מִפְּנֵי שְׁלֹמֹה וַיָּקָם וַיֵּלֶךְ וַיַּחֲזֵק בְּקַרְנוֹת הַמִּזְבֵּחַ: וַיֻּגַּד
לִשְׁלֹמֹה לֵאמֹר הִנֵּה אֲדֹנִיָּהוּ יָרֵא אֶת־הַמֶּלֶךְ שְׁלֹמֹה וְהִנֵּה אָחַז
בְּקַרְנוֹת הַמִּזְבֵּחַ לֵאמֹר יִשָּׁבַע־לִי כַיּוֹם הַמֶּלֶךְ שְׁלֹמֹה אִם־יָמִית אֶת־
נב עַבְדּוֹ בֶּחָרֶב: וַיֹּאמֶר שְׁלֹמֹה אִם יִהְיֶה לְבֶן־חַיִל לֹא־יִפֹּל מִשַּׂעֲרָתוֹ
נג אַרְצָה וְאִם־רָעָה תִמָּצֵא־בוֹ וָמֵת: וַיִּשְׁלַח הַמֶּלֶךְ שְׁלֹמֹה וַיֹּרִדֻהוּ
מֵעַל הַמִּזְבֵּחַ וַיָּבֹא וַיִּשְׁתַּחוּ לַמֶּלֶךְ שְׁלֹמֹה וַיֹּאמֶר־לוֹ שְׁלֹמֹה לֵךְ
ב א לְבֵיתֶךָ: וַיִּקְרְבוּ יְמֵי־דָוִד לָמוּת וַיְצַו אֶת־שְׁלֹמֹה בְנוֹ
ב ג לֵאמֹר: אָנֹכִי הֹלֵךְ בְּדֶרֶךְ כָּל־הָאָרֶץ וְחָזַקְתָּ וְהָיִיתָ לְאִישׁ: וְשָׁמַרְתָּ
אֶת־מִשְׁמֶרֶת ׀ יְהוָה אֱלֹהֶיךָ לָלֶכֶת בִּדְרָכָיו לִשְׁמֹר חֻקֹּתָיו מִצְוֹתָיו
וּמִשְׁפָּטָיו וְעֵדְוֹתָיו כַּכָּתוּב בְּתוֹרַת מֹשֶׁה לְמַעַן תַּשְׂכִּיל אֵת כָּל־
ד אֲשֶׁר תַּעֲשֶׂה וְאֵת כָּל־אֲשֶׁר תִּפְנֶה שָׁם: לְמַעַן יָקִים יְהוָה אֶת־דְּבָרוֹ
אֲשֶׁר דִּבֶּר עָלַי לֵאמֹר אִם־יִשְׁמְרוּ בָנֶיךָ אֶת־דַּרְכָּם לָלֶכֶת לְפָנַי
בֶּאֱמֶת בְּכָל־לְבָבָם וּבְכָל־נַפְשָׁם לֵאמֹר לֹא־יִכָּרֵת לְךָ אִישׁ מֵעַל כִּסֵּא
ה יִשְׂרָאֵל: וְגַם אַתָּה יָדַעְתָּ אֵת אֲשֶׁר־עָשָׂה לִי יוֹאָב בֶּן־צְרוּיָה אֲשֶׁר
עָשָׂה לִשְׁנֵי־שָׂרֵי צִבְאוֹת יִשְׂרָאֵל לְאַבְנֵר בֶּן־נֵר וְלַעֲמָשָׂא בֶן־יֶתֶר
וַיַּהַרְגֵם וַיָּשֶׂם דְּמֵי־מִלְחָמָה בְּשָׁלֹם וַיִּתֵּן דְּמֵי מִלְחָמָה בַּחֲגֹרָתוֹ אֲשֶׁר
ו בְּמָתְנָיו וּבְנַעֲלוֹ אֲשֶׁר בְּרַגְלָיו: וְעָשִׂיתָ כְּחָכְמָתֶךָ וְלֹא־תוֹרֵד שֵׂיבָתוֹ
ז בְּשָׁלֹם שְׁאֹל: וְלִבְנֵי בַרְזִלַּי הַגִּלְעָדִי תַּעֲשֶׂה־חֶסֶד וְהָיוּ
ח בְּאֹכְלֵי שֻׁלְחָנֶךָ כִּי־כֵן קָרְבוּ אֵלַי בְּבָרְחִי מִפְּנֵי אַבְשָׁלוֹם אָחִיךָ: וְהִנֵּה
עִמְּךָ שִׁמְעִי בֶן־גֵּרָא בֶן־הַיְמִינִי מִבַּחֻרִים וְהוּא קִלְלַנִי קְלָלָה נִמְרֶצֶת
בְּיוֹם לֶכְתִּי מַחֲנָיִם וְהוּא־יָרַד לִקְרָאתִי הַיַּרְדֵּן וָאֶשָּׁבַע לוֹ בַיהוָה לֵאמֹר
ט אִם־אֲמִיתְךָ בֶּחָרֶב: וְעַתָּה אַל־תְּנַקֵּהוּ כִּי אִישׁ חָכָם אָתָּה וְיָדַעְתָּ אֵת
י אֲשֶׁר תַּעֲשֶׂה־לּוֹ וְהוֹרַדְתָּ אֶת־שֵׂיבָתוֹ בְּדָם שְׁאוֹל: וַיִּשְׁכַּב דָּוִד עִם־
יא אֲבֹתָיו וַיִּקָּבֵר בְּעִיר דָּוִד: וְהַיָּמִים אֲשֶׁר מָלַךְ דָּוִד עַל־
יִשְׂרָאֵל אַרְבָּעִים שָׁנָה בְּחֶבְרוֹן מָלַךְ שֶׁבַע שָׁנִים וּבִירוּשָׁלִַם מָלַךְ

12 he reigned in Jerusalem for thirty-three years. Now Shlomo sat on his father
13 David's throne, and his kingdom was firmly established. Adoniya
son of Ḥagit came to Batsheva, Shlomo's mother. "Do you come in peace?"
14 she asked, and he said, "Yes, in peace. May I have a word with you?" he
15 continued, and she said, "Speak." "You know that the kingship was meant to
be mine," he said, "and that all of Israel expected me to reign. But the kingship
was transferred to my brother, for the Lord determined that it should be his.
16 Now I have but a single request of you – do not turn me away." "Speak," she
17 said to him. "Please ask King Shlomo," he said, "for he will not turn you away:
18 let him give me Avishag the Shunamite as a wife." "Very well," said Batsheva.
19 "I will speak to the king on your behalf." Batsheva came to King Shlomo to
speak to him on Adoniyahu's behalf. The king rose to greet her and bowed to
her before sitting down on his throne. He had a throne set out for the queen
20 mother, and she sat down on his right. "I have one small request of you," she
said. "Do not turn me away." "Make your request, Mother," the king said to
21 her, "for I will not turn you away." "Let Avishag the Shunamite be given to
22 your brother Adoniya as a wife," she said. "And why do you request Avishag
the Shunamite for Adoniyahu?" King Shlomo countered his mother. "You
might as well request the kingship for him – as he is my older brother – and
23 for Avyatar the priest, and for Yoav son of Tzeruya as well." And King
Shlomo swore by the Lord, "So may God do to me – and more," he said, "if
24 this affair has not cost Adoniyahu his life. And now, as the Lord lives – who
set me firmly on the throne of my father David, and who made a house for
25 me as He promised – on this very day, Adoniyahu will be put to death." And
King Shlomo sent orders to Benayahu son of Yehoyada, who struck him down,
26 and he died. As for Avyatar the priest, the king said, "Go to your
fields in Anatot. Though you deserve to die, I will not have you killed at this
time because you bore the Ark of the Lord God before my father David and
27 because you suffered along with my father throughout all his suffering." And
Shlomo dismissed Avyatar from the role of priest to the Lord, fulfilling what
28 the Lord had pronounced for the house of Eli at Shilo.[7] And the
news reached Yoav, and Yoav fled to the Tent of the Lord and grasped
hold of the horns of the altar, for Yoav had sided with Adoniya – though he
29 had not sided with Avshalom. When King Shlomo was informed that Yoav
had fled to the Tent of the Lord and that he was by the altar, Shlomo sent
30 Benayahu son of Yehoyada, ordering him, "Go, strike him down." When
Benayahu reached the Tent of the Lord, he said to him, "By order of the king,
come out!" "No!" he said. "I will die right here!" Benayahu reported back to
31 the king, saying, "This is what Yoav said to me in response." "Do as he says,"
the king said to him. "Strike him down and bury him and remove the innocent

7 | See 1 Samuel 2:27–36.

יב שְׁלֹשִׁים וְשָׁלֹשׁ שָׁנִים: וּשְׁלֹמֹה יָשַׁב עַל־כִּסֵּא דָּוִד אָבִיו וַתִּכֹּן מַלְכֻתוֹ
יג מְאֹד: וַיָּבֹא אֲדֹנִיָּהוּ בֶן־חַגִּית אֶל־בַּת־שֶׁבַע אֵם־
יד שְׁלֹמֹה וַתֹּאמֶר הֲשָׁלוֹם בֹּאֶךָ וַיֹּאמֶר שָׁלוֹם: וַיֹּאמֶר דָּבָר לִי אֵלָיִךְ
טו וַתֹּאמֶר דַּבֵּר: וַיֹּאמֶר אַתְּ יָדַעַתְּ כִּי־לִי הָיְתָה הַמְּלוּכָה וְעָלַי שָׂמוּ
כָל־יִשְׂרָאֵל פְּנֵיהֶם לִמְלֹךְ וַתִּסֹּב הַמְּלוּכָה וַתְּהִי לְאָחִי כִּי מֵיהוָה הָיְתָה
טז לּוֹ: וְעַתָּה שְׁאֵלָה אַחַת אָנֹכִי שֹׁאֵל מֵאִתָּךְ אַל־תָּשִׁבִי אֶת־פָּנָי וַתֹּאמֶר
יז אֵלָיו דַּבֵּר: וַיֹּאמֶר אִמְרִי־נָא לִשְׁלֹמֹה הַמֶּלֶךְ כִּי לֹא־יָשִׁיב אֶת־פָּנָיִךְ
יח וְיִתֶּן־לִי אֶת־אֲבִישַׁג הַשּׁוּנַמִּית לְאִשָּׁה: וַתֹּאמֶר בַּת־שֶׁבַע טוֹב אָנֹכִי
יט אֲדַבֵּר עָלֶיךָ אֶל־הַמֶּלֶךְ: וַתָּבֹא בַת־שֶׁבַע אֶל־הַמֶּלֶךְ שְׁלֹמֹה לְדַבֶּר־
לוֹ עַל־אֲדֹנִיָּהוּ וַיָּקָם הַמֶּלֶךְ לִקְרָאתָהּ וַיִּשְׁתַּחוּ לָהּ וַיֵּשֶׁב עַל־כִּסְאוֹ
כ וַיָּשֶׂם כִּסֵּא לְאֵם הַמֶּלֶךְ וַתֵּשֶׁב לִימִינוֹ: וַתֹּאמֶר שְׁאֵלָה אַחַת קְטַנָּה
אָנֹכִי שֹׁאֶלֶת מֵאִתָּךְ אַל־תָּשֶׁב אֶת־פָּנָי וַיֹּאמֶר־לָהּ הַמֶּלֶךְ שַׁאֲלִי אִמִּי
כא כִּי לֹא־אָשִׁיב אֶת־פָּנָיִךְ: וַתֹּאמֶר יֻתַּן אֶת־אֲבִישַׁג הַשֻּׁנַמִּית לַאֲדֹנִיָּהוּ
כב אָחִיךָ לְאִשָּׁה: וַיַּעַן הַמֶּלֶךְ שְׁלֹמֹה וַיֹּאמֶר לְאִמּוֹ וְלָמָה אַתְּ שֹׁאֶלֶת
אֶת־אֲבִישַׁג הַשֻּׁנַמִּית לַאֲדֹנִיָּהוּ וְשַׁאֲלִי־לוֹ אֶת־הַמְּלוּכָה כִּי הוּא אָחִי
כג הַגָּדוֹל מִמֶּנִּי וְלוֹ וּלְאֶבְיָתָר הַכֹּהֵן וּלְיוֹאָב בֶּן־צְרוּיָה: וַיִּשָּׁבַע
הַמֶּלֶךְ שְׁלֹמֹה בַּיהוָה לֵאמֹר כֹּה יַעֲשֶׂה־לִּי אֱלֹהִים וְכֹה יוֹסִיף כִּי בְנַפְשׁוֹ
כד דִּבֶּר אֲדֹנִיָּהוּ אֶת־הַדָּבָר הַזֶּה: וְעַתָּה חַי־יְהוָה אֲשֶׁר הֱכִינַנִי וויושיביני וַיּוֹשִׁיבַנִי
עַל־כִּסֵּא דָּוִד אָבִי וַאֲשֶׁר עָשָׂה־לִי בַּיִת כַּאֲשֶׁר דִּבֵּר כִּי הַיּוֹם יוּמַת
כה אֲדֹנִיָּהוּ: וַיִּשְׁלַח הַמֶּלֶךְ שְׁלֹמֹה בְּיַד בְּנָיָהוּ בֶן־יְהוֹיָדָע וַיִּפְגַּע־בּוֹ
כו וַיָּמֹת: וּלְאֶבְיָתָר הַכֹּהֵן אָמַר הַמֶּלֶךְ עֲנָתֹת לֵךְ עַל־שָׂדֶיךָ
כִּי אִישׁ מָוֶת אָתָּה וּבַיּוֹם הַזֶּה לֹא אֲמִיתֶךָ כִּי־נָשָׂאתָ אֶת־אֲרוֹן אֲדֹנָי
כז יְהוִה לִפְנֵי דָּוִד אָבִי וְכִי הִתְעַנִּיתָ בְּכֹל אֲשֶׁר־הִתְעַנָּה אָבִי: וַיְגָרֶשׁ
שְׁלֹמֹה אֶת־אֶבְיָתָר מִהְיוֹת כֹּהֵן לַיהוָה לְמַלֵּא אֶת־דְּבַר יְהוָה אֲשֶׁר
כח דִּבֶּר עַל־בֵּית עֵלִי בְּשִׁלֹה: וְהַשְּׁמֻעָה בָּאָה עַד־יוֹאָב כִּי
יוֹאָב נָטָה אַחֲרֵי אֲדֹנִיָּה וְאַחֲרֵי אַבְשָׁלוֹם לֹא נָטָה וַיָּנָס יוֹאָב אֶל־אֹהֶל
כט יְהוָה וַיַּחֲזֵק בְּקַרְנוֹת הַמִּזְבֵּחַ: וַיֻּגַּד לַמֶּלֶךְ שְׁלֹמֹה כִּי נָס יוֹאָב אֶל־אֹהֶל
יְהוָה וְהִנֵּה אֵצֶל הַמִּזְבֵּחַ וַיִּשְׁלַח שְׁלֹמֹה אֶת־בְּנָיָהוּ בֶן־יְהוֹיָדָע לֵאמֹר
ל לֵךְ פְּגַע־בּוֹ: וַיָּבֹא בְנָיָהוּ אֶל־אֹהֶל יְהוָה וַיֹּאמֶר אֵלָיו כֹּה־אָמַר הַמֶּלֶךְ
צֵא וַיֹּאמֶר ׀ לֹא כִּי פֹה אָמוּת וַיָּשֶׁב בְּנָיָהוּ אֶת־הַמֶּלֶךְ דָּבָר לֵאמֹר
לא כֹּה־דִבֶּר יוֹאָב וְכֹה עָנָנִי: וַיֹּאמֶר לוֹ הַמֶּלֶךְ עֲשֵׂה כַּאֲשֶׁר דִּבֶּר וּפְגַע־בּוֹ
וּקְבַרְתּוֹ וַהֲסִירֹתָ ׀ דְּמֵי חִנָּם אֲשֶׁר שָׁפַךְ יוֹאָב מֵעָלַי וּמֵעַל בֵּית אָבִי:

32 blood that Yoav spilled from upon me and my father's house. The LORD will
bring his bloodguilt back upon his own head for having struck down two
men who were more righteous and better than he – he put them to the
sword without my father David's knowledge – Avner son of Ner, the army
commander of Israel, and Amasa son of Yeter, the army commander of
33 Yehuda. May their bloodguilt be brought back upon Yoav's own head and
upon the head of his descendants forever; and may David and his descendants,
34 and his house and his throne, forever have peace from the LORD." And
Benayahu son of Yehoyada advanced and struck him down and put him to
35 death, and he was buried in his home in the wilderness. The king appointed
Benayahu son of Yehoyada in charge of the army in his place, and the king
36 appointed the priest Tzadok instead of Avyatar. Now the king sent for and
summoned Shimi. "Build yourself a house in Jerusalem and settle there," he
37 said to him, "but you must not leave there for anywhere else. For from the
very moment you leave, once you cross the Kidron Valley, know that you are
38 doomed to die, and your blood will be upon your own head." "Very well,"
Shimi said to the king. "Whatever my lord the king says, your servant will do."
39 Shimi remained in Jerusalem for a long time, but three years later,
two of Shimi's servants ran away to Akhish son of Maakha, the king of Gat.
40 When Shimi was told, "Look – your servants are in Gat," Shimi set out,
saddled his donkey, and went to Akhish in Gat to find his slaves; he went to
41 bring his slaves from Gat. When Shlomo was informed that Shimi
42 had gone from Jerusalem to Gat and back, the king sent and summoned
Shimi and said to him, "Did I not make you swear to the LORD and warn you
that from the moment you left and went anywhere else, you would know that
you would be doomed to death? And you said to me, 'Very well, I accept.'
43 Why did you fail to keep the LORD's oath and the command I charged you
44 with?" The king then continued to Shimi, "You are aware of all the evil you
harbored in your heart; of what you did to my father David. Now the LORD
45 has brought your own evil back on your own head. But King Shlomo will be
blessed, and the throne of David will be established before the LORD forever."
46 The king gave orders to Benayahu son of Yehoyada, and he set out and
struck him down, and he died. Thus the kingdom was secured in Shlomo's
3 1 hand. Shlomo formed a marriage alliance with King Pharaoh of
Egypt; he took Pharaoh's daughter in marriage and brought her to the City
of David until he had finished building his palace, the House of the LORD,
2 and the wall around Jerusalem. But the people were sacrificing at the high
shrines, for at that time a House for the LORD's name had not yet been
3 built. Shlomo loved the LORD and followed the laws of his father
4 David, but he still offered sacrifices and incense at the high shrines. And the
king went to Givon to sacrifice there, for it was the greatest of the high shrines,
5 and Shlomo offered up a thousand burnt offerings on that altar. At
Givon the LORD appeared to Shlomo in a dream. And God said, "Ask – what
6 shall I give you?" And Shlomo said, "You treated Your servant David, my

לב וְהֵשִׁיב יְהוָה אֶת־דָּמוֹ עַל־רֹאשׁוֹ אֲשֶׁר פָּגַע בִּשְׁנֵי־אֲנָשִׁים צַדִּקִים
וְטֹבִים מִמֶּנּוּ וַיַּהַרְגֵם בַּחֶרֶב וְאָבִי דָוִד לֹא יָדָע אֶת־אַבְנֵר בֶּן־נֵר שַׂר־
לג צְבָא יִשְׂרָאֵל וְאֶת־עֲמָשָׂא בֶן־יֶתֶר שַׂר־צְבָא יְהוּדָה׃ וְשָׁבוּ דְמֵיהֶם
בְּרֹאשׁ יוֹאָב וּבְרֹאשׁ זַרְעוֹ לְעֹלָם וּלְדָוִד וּלְזַרְעוֹ וּלְבֵיתוֹ וּלְכִסְאוֹ יִהְיֶה
לד שָׁלוֹם עַד־עוֹלָם מֵעִם יְהוָה׃ וַיַּעַל בְּנָיָהוּ בֶּן־יְהוֹיָדָע וַיִּפְגַּע־בּוֹ וַיְמִתֵהוּ
לה וַיִּקָּבֵר בְּבֵיתוֹ בַּמִּדְבָּר׃ וַיִּתֵּן הַמֶּלֶךְ אֶת־בְּנָיָהוּ בֶן־יְהוֹיָדָע תַּחְתָּיו
לו עַל־הַצָּבָא וְאֶת־צָדוֹק הַכֹּהֵן נָתַן הַמֶּלֶךְ תַּחַת אֶבְיָתָר׃ וַיִּשְׁלַח
הַמֶּלֶךְ וַיִּקְרָא לְשִׁמְעִי וַיֹּאמֶר לוֹ בְּנֵה־לְךָ בַיִת בִּירוּשָׁלִַם וְיָשַׁבְתָּ שָׁם
לז וְלֹא־תֵצֵא מִשָּׁם אָנֶה וָאָנָה׃ וְהָיָה ׀ בְּיוֹם צֵאתְךָ וְעָבַרְתָּ אֶת־נַחַל
לח קִדְרוֹן יָדֹעַ תֵּדַע כִּי מוֹת תָּמוּת דָּמְךָ יִהְיֶה בְרֹאשֶׁךָ׃ וַיֹּאמֶר שִׁמְעִי
לַמֶּלֶךְ טוֹב הַדָּבָר כַּאֲשֶׁר דִּבֶּר אֲדֹנִי הַמֶּלֶךְ כֵּן יַעֲשֶׂה עַבְדֶּךָ וַיֵּשֶׁב
לט שִׁמְעִי בִּירוּשָׁלִַם יָמִים רַבִּים׃ וַיְהִי מִקֵּץ שָׁלֹשׁ שָׁנִים
וַיִּבְרְחוּ שְׁנֵי־עֲבָדִים לְשִׁמְעִי אֶל־אָכִישׁ בֶּן־מַעֲכָה מֶלֶךְ גַּת וַיַּגִּידוּ
מ לְשִׁמְעִי לֵאמֹר הִנֵּה עֲבָדֶיךָ בְּגַת׃ וַיָּקָם שִׁמְעִי וַיַּחֲבֹשׁ אֶת־חֲמֹרוֹ וַיֵּלֶךְ
גַּתָה אֶל־אָכִישׁ לְבַקֵּשׁ אֶת־עֲבָדָיו וַיֵּלֶךְ שִׁמְעִי וַיָּבֵא אֶת־עֲבָדָיו
מא מִגַּת׃ וַיֻּגַּד לִשְׁלֹמֹה כִּי־הָלַךְ שִׁמְעִי מִירוּשָׁלִַם גַּת וַיָּשֹׁב׃
מב וַיִּשְׁלַח הַמֶּלֶךְ וַיִּקְרָא לְשִׁמְעִי וַיֹּאמֶר אֵלָיו הֲלוֹא הִשְׁבַּעְתִּיךָ בַיהוָה
וָאָעִד בְּךָ לֵאמֹר בְּיוֹם צֵאתְךָ וְהָלַכְתָּ אָנֶה וָאָנָה יָדֹעַ תֵּדַע כִּי מוֹת
מג תָּמוּת וַתֹּאמֶר אֵלַי טוֹב הַדָּבָר שָׁמָעְתִּי׃ וּמַדּוּעַ לֹא שָׁמַרְתָּ אֵת
מד שְׁבֻעַת יְהוָה וְאֶת־הַמִּצְוָה אֲשֶׁר־צִוִּיתִי עָלֶיךָ׃ וַיֹּאמֶר הַמֶּלֶךְ אֶל־
שִׁמְעִי אַתָּה יָדַעְתָּ אֵת כָּל־הָרָעָה אֲשֶׁר יָדַע לְבָבְךָ אֲשֶׁר עָשִׂיתָ לְדָוִד
מה אָבִי וְהֵשִׁיב יְהוָה אֶת־רָעָתְךָ בְּרֹאשֶׁךָ׃ וְהַמֶּלֶךְ שְׁלֹמֹה בָּרוּךְ וְכִסֵּא ג
מו דָּוִד יִהְיֶה נָכוֹן לִפְנֵי יְהוָה עַד־עוֹלָם׃ וַיְצַו הַמֶּלֶךְ אֶת־בְּנָיָהוּ בֶּן־יְהוֹיָדָע
ג א וַיֵּצֵא וַיִּפְגַּע־בּוֹ וַיָּמֹת וְהַמַּמְלָכָה נָכוֹנָה בְּיַד־שְׁלֹמֹה׃ וַיִּתְחַתֵּן
שְׁלֹמֹה אֶת־פַּרְעֹה מֶלֶךְ מִצְרָיִם וַיִּקַּח אֶת־בַּת־פַּרְעֹה וַיְבִיאֶהָ אֶל־עִיר
דָּוִד עַד כַּלֹּתוֹ לִבְנוֹת אֶת־בֵּיתוֹ וְאֶת־בֵּית יְהוָה וְאֶת־חוֹמַת יְרוּשָׁלִַם
ב סָבִיב׃ רַק הָעָם מְזַבְּחִים בַּבָּמוֹת כִּי לֹא־נִבְנָה בַיִת לְשֵׁם יְהוָה עַד
ג הַיָּמִים הָהֵם׃ וַיֶּאֱהַב שְׁלֹמֹה אֶת־יְהוָה לָלֶכֶת בְּחֻקּוֹת
ד דָּוִד אָבִיו רַק בַּבָּמוֹת הוּא מְזַבֵּחַ וּמַקְטִיר׃ וַיֵּלֶךְ הַמֶּלֶךְ גִּבְעֹנָה לִזְבֹּחַ
שָׁם כִּי־הִיא הַבָּמָה הַגְּדוֹלָה אֶלֶף עֹלוֹת יַעֲלֶה שְׁלֹמֹה עַל הַמִּזְבֵּחַ
ה הַהוּא׃ בְּגִבְעוֹן נִרְאָה יְהוָה אֶל־שְׁלֹמֹה בַּחֲלוֹם הַלָּיְלָה
ו וַיֹּאמֶר אֱלֹהִים שְׁאַל מָה אֶתֶּן־לָךְ׃ וַיֹּאמֶר שְׁלֹמֹה אַתָּה עָשִׂיתָ עִם־

father, with great kindness, for he walked before You in truth and in justice,
and with a sincere heart toward You. And You have maintained this great
kindness for him by granting him a son and heir to his throne, as is now the
7 case. And now, O LORD, my God, You made Your servant king in my father
8 David's place, but I am a young boy; I have no experience as a leader. Yet Your
servant is among Your own people, whom You have chosen, a people too vast
9 to be numbered or counted. Grant Your servant an understanding heart to
judge Your people, to distinguish between good and evil, for who can judge
10 this immense people of Yours?" And it pleased the LORD that Shlomo had
11 made this request, and God said to him, "Because this is the request you
made – you did not ask for long life, or for wealth, or for the lives of your
12 enemies, but you asked for wisdom to discern in judgment – I have fulfilled
your words. Here, I am granting you a wise, discerning heart – no one like
you has ever been before you, and no one like you will ever rise again after
13 you. But what is more, I am granting you what you did not ask for, both wealth
and honor – not a man among kings will compare to you for as long as you
14 live. And if you follow in My ways and keep My laws and commandments, as
15 your father David did, then I shall grant you long life." Then Shlomo
awoke – it had all been a dream! When he came to Jerusalem, he stood before
the Ark of the LORD's Covenant and offered up burnt offerings and presented
16 peace offerings, and he held a feast for all his servants. Then two
17 harlot women came before the king and stood before him. "If you please, my
lord," said the first woman, "this woman and I live in one house, and I gave
18 birth while she was in the house. On the third day after I gave birth, this
woman also gave birth. The two of us live together – there was no one else in
19 the house besides us, just the two of us in the house. The son of this woman
20 died in the night, for she lay on him. But she got up during the night and took
my own son from me while your handmaid was sleeping and lay down with
21 him in her embrace, and laid her own dead son in my embrace. I woke up in
the morning to nurse my son to find that he was dead! But when I looked at
him closely in the morning, why – it wasn't my own son, the one I had borne!"
22 "No!" said the other woman. "My son is the one who is alive, and your son
is the one who died!" "No," she said, "your son is dead, and my son is alive!"
23 and they continued arguing before the king. "This one says, 'This is my son,
who is alive, and your son is dead,'" said the king, "and this one says, 'No, your
24 son is dead, and my son is alive.'" And the king said, "Fetch me a
25 sword," and they brought a sword before the king. "Cut the living child into
26 two," the king declared, "and give half to one and half to the other." But the
woman whose son was alive spoke up, for she burned with compassion for
her son. "Please, my lord," she said, "give her the living child; do anything but
kill him!" while the other one said, "Neither of us will have him – cut him up."

עַבְדְּךָ דָוִד אָבִי חֶסֶד גָּדוֹל כַּאֲשֶׁר הָלַךְ לְפָנֶיךָ בֶּאֱמֶת וּבִצְדָקָה
וּבְיִשְׁרַת לֵבָב עִמָּךְ וַתִּשְׁמָר־לוֹ אֶת־הַחֶסֶד הַגָּדוֹל הַזֶּה וַתִּתֶּן־לוֹ בֵן
ז יֹשֵׁב עַל־כִּסְאוֹ כַּיּוֹם הַזֶּה: וְעַתָּה יהוה אֱלֹהָי אַתָּה הִמְלַכְתָּ אֶת־עַבְדְּךָ
ח תַּחַת דָּוִד אָבִי וְאָנֹכִי נַעַר קָטֹן לֹא אֵדַע צֵאת וָבֹא: וְעַבְדְּךָ בְּתוֹךְ
ט עַמְּךָ אֲשֶׁר בָּחָרְתָּ עַם־רָב אֲשֶׁר לֹא־יִמָּנֶה וְלֹא יִסָּפֵר מֵרֹב: וְנָתַתָּ
לְעַבְדְּךָ לֵב שֹׁמֵעַ לִשְׁפֹּט אֶת־עַמְּךָ לְהָבִין בֵּין־טוֹב לְרָע כִּי מִי יוּכַל
י לִשְׁפֹּט אֶת־עַמְּךָ הַכָּבֵד הַזֶּה: וַיִּיטַב הַדָּבָר בְּעֵינֵי אֲדֹנָי כִּי שָׁאַל
יא שְׁלֹמֹה אֶת־הַדָּבָר הַזֶּה: וַיֹּאמֶר אֱלֹהִים אֵלָיו יַעַן אֲשֶׁר שָׁאַלְתָּ אֶת־
הַדָּבָר הַזֶּה וְלֹא־שָׁאַלְתָּ לְּךָ יָמִים רַבִּים וְלֹא־שָׁאַלְתָּ לְּךָ עֹשֶׁר וְלֹא
יב שָׁאַלְתָּ נֶפֶשׁ אֹיְבֶיךָ וְשָׁאַלְתָּ לְּךָ הָבִין לִשְׁמֹעַ מִשְׁפָּט: הִנֵּה עָשִׂיתִי
כִּדְבָרֶיךָ הִנֵּה | נָתַתִּי לְךָ לֵב חָכָם וְנָבוֹן אֲשֶׁר כָּמוֹךָ לֹא־הָיָה לְפָנֶיךָ
יג וְאַחֲרֶיךָ לֹא־יָקוּם כָּמוֹךָ: וְגַם אֲשֶׁר לֹא־שָׁאַלְתָּ נָתַתִּי לָךְ גַּם־עֹשֶׁר
יד גַּם־כָּבוֹד אֲשֶׁר לֹא־הָיָה כָמוֹךָ אִישׁ בַּמְּלָכִים כָּל־יָמֶיךָ: וְאִם | תֵּלֵךְ
בִּדְרָכַי לִשְׁמֹר חֻקַּי וּמִצְוֺתַי כַּאֲשֶׁר הָלַךְ דָּוִיד אָבִיךָ וְהַאַרַכְתִּי אֶת־
טו יָמֶיךָ: וַיִּקַץ שְׁלֹמֹה וְהִנֵּה חֲלוֹם וַיָּבוֹא יְרוּשָׁלַם וַיַּעֲמֹד |
לִפְנֵי | אֲרוֹן בְּרִית־אֲדֹנָי וַיַּעַל עֹלוֹת וַיַּעַשׂ שְׁלָמִים וַיַּעַשׂ מִשְׁתֶּה
טז לְכָל־עֲבָדָיו: אָז תָּבֹאנָה שְׁתַּיִם נָשִׁים זֹנוֹת אֶל־הַמֶּלֶךְ
יז וַתַּעֲמֹדְנָה לְפָנָיו: וַתֹּאמֶר הָאִשָּׁה הָאַחַת בִּי אֲדֹנִי אֲנִי וְהָאִשָּׁה הַזֹּאת
יח יֹשְׁבֹת בְּבַיִת אֶחָד וָאֵלֵד עִמָּהּ בַּבָּיִת: וַיְהִי בַּיּוֹם הַשְּׁלִישִׁי לְלִדְתִּי
וַתֵּלֶד גַּם־הָאִשָּׁה הַזֹּאת וַאֲנַחְנוּ יַחְדָּו אֵין־זָר אִתָּנוּ בַּבַּיִת זוּלָתִי
יט שְׁתַּיִם־אֲנַחְנוּ בַּבָּיִת: וַיָּמָת בֶּן־הָאִשָּׁה הַזֹּאת לָיְלָה אֲשֶׁר שָׁכְבָה
כ עָלָיו: וַתָּקָם בְּתוֹךְ הַלַּיְלָה וַתִּקַּח אֶת־בְּנִי מֵאֶצְלִי וַאֲמָתְךָ יְשֵׁנָה
כא וַתַּשְׁכִּיבֵהוּ בְּחֵיקָהּ וְאֶת־בְּנָהּ הַמֵּת הִשְׁכִּיבָה בְחֵיקִי: וָאָקֻם בַּבֹּקֶר
לְהֵינִיק אֶת־בְּנִי וְהִנֵּה־מֵת וָאֶתְבּוֹנֵן אֵלָיו בַּבֹּקֶר וְהִנֵּה לֹא־הָיָה בְנִי
כב אֲשֶׁר יָלָדְתִּי: וַתֹּאמֶר הָאִשָּׁה הָאַחֶרֶת לֹא כִי בְּנִי הַחַי וּבְנֵךְ הַמֵּת
כג וְזֹאת אֹמֶרֶת לֹא כִי בְּנֵךְ הַמֵּת וּבְנִי הֶחָי וַתְּדַבֵּרְנָה לִפְנֵי הַמֶּלֶךְ: וַיֹּאמֶר
הַמֶּלֶךְ זֹאת אֹמֶרֶת זֶה־בְּנִי הַחַי וּבְנֵךְ הַמֵּת וְזֹאת אֹמֶרֶת לֹא כִי בְּנֵךְ
כד הַמֵּת וּבְנִי הֶחָי: וַיֹּאמֶר הַמֶּלֶךְ קְחוּ לִי־חָרֶב וַיָּבִאוּ הַחֶרֶב
כה לִפְנֵי הַמֶּלֶךְ: וַיֹּאמֶר הַמֶּלֶךְ גִּזְרוּ אֶת־הַיֶּלֶד הַחַי לִשְׁנָיִם וּתְנוּ אֶת־
כו הַחֲצִי לְאַחַת וְאֶת־הַחֲצִי לְאֶחָת: וַתֹּאמֶר הָאִשָּׁה אֲשֶׁר־בְּנָהּ הַחַי
אֶל־הַמֶּלֶךְ כִּי־נִכְמְרוּ רַחֲמֶיהָ עַל־בְּנָהּ וַתֹּאמֶר | בִּי אֲדֹנִי תְּנוּ־לָהּ
אֶת־הַיָּלוּד הַחַי וְהָמֵת אַל־תְּמִיתֻהוּ וְזֹאת אֹמֶרֶת גַּם־לִי גַם־לָךְ לֹא

27 And the king spoke up. "Give her the living child," he said, "and make no
28 move to kill him. She is his mother." When all of Israel heard about the
case that the king had judged, they held the king in awe, for they saw that
4 1 divine wisdom was within him to do justice. King Shlomo was king of all
2 Israel. These were the names of his officials: Azariya son of Tzadok
3 the priest. Eliḥoref and Aḥiya, sons of Shisha, scribes, Yehoshafat son of
4 Aḥilud, royal herald. Benayahu son of Yehoyada, in charge of the army, Tzadok
5 and Avyatar, priests. Azariya son of Natan, in charge of the prefects, Zavud
6 son of Natan the priest, the king's companion. Aḥishar, in charge of the palace,
7 Adoniram son of Avda, in charge of the forced labor. Shlomo had
twelve prefects over all of Israel who provided for the king and his household;
8 each one was responsible for provision for one month of the year. And these
9 are their names: Ben Ḥur in the Efrayim hills; Ben Deker in Makatz, Shaalvim,
10 Beit Shemesh, and Eilon Beit Ḥanan; Ben Ḥesed in Arubot – he oversaw
11 Sokho and all the region of Ḥefer; Ben Avinadav, all the region of Dor – Tafat,
12 Shlomo's daughter, was his wife; Baana son of Aḥilud in Ta'nakh,
Megiddo, and all of Beit She'an near Tzartan below Yizre'el, from Beit She'an
13 to Avel Meḥola to the other side of Yokme'am; Ben Gever
in Ramot Gilad – he oversaw the hamlets of Yair son of Menashe in the
Gilad and the Argov region in the Bashan – sixty great towns, walled,
14 with bolts of bronze; Aḥinadav son of Ido in
15 Maḥanayim; Aḥimaatz in Naftali – he, too, took a daughter
16 of Shlomo's in marriage, Basmat; Baana son
17 of Ḥushai in Asher and Be'alot; Yehoshafat son of Paruaḥ in
18 19 Yissakhar; Shimi son of Ela in Binyamin; Gever son of Uri
in the land of Gilad, the land of Siḥon, king of the Amorites, and Og, king of
20 the Bashan. And one prefect was in the land. Yehuda and Israel were as
boundless as the sand upon the seashore, eating and drinking and content.
5 1 Shlomo ruled over all the kingdoms from the River[8] to the land of the
Philistines, up to the border of Egypt. They offered tribute and served Shlomo
2 all his life. Shlomo's fare for a single day was thirty *kor*[9] of fine
3 flour, sixty *kor* of meal, ten fattened oxen, twenty pasture-raised oxen, and a
4 hundred sheep, besides deer, gazelle, antelope, and fattened geese. For he had
dominion over the whole region to the west of the River[10] – from Tifsaḥ up
to Aza – and over all the kings to the west of the River. He had peace on every
5 surrounding border; from Dan to Be'er Sheva, Yehuda and Israel dwelled
in safety, each person beneath his grapevine and fig tree, all the days of
6 Shlomo. Shlomo had forty thousand stalls for his cavalry horses and

8 | The Euphrates; cf. Genesis 15:18.
9 | A single *kor* is the equivalent of 60 gallons or 230 liters.
10 | Literally "the other side of the River," a widely used term referring to the part of the Fertile Crescent west and south of the Euphrates.

כז יִהְיֶה גְּזֹרוּ: וַיַּעַן הַמֶּלֶךְ וַיֹּאמֶר תְּנוּ־לָהּ אֶת־הַיָּלוּד הַחַי וְהָמֵת לֹא
כח תְמִיתֻהוּ הִיא אִמּוֹ: וַיִּשְׁמְעוּ כָל־יִשְׂרָאֵל אֶת־הַמִּשְׁפָּט אֲשֶׁר שָׁפַט
הַמֶּלֶךְ וַיִּרְאוּ מִפְּנֵי הַמֶּלֶךְ כִּי רָאוּ כִּי־חָכְמַת אֱלֹהִים בְּקִרְבּוֹ לַעֲשׂוֹת
ד א ב מִשְׁפָּט: וַיְהִי הַמֶּלֶךְ שְׁלֹמֹה מֶלֶךְ עַל־כָּל־יִשְׂרָאֵל: וְאֵלֶּה
ג הַשָּׂרִים אֲשֶׁר־לוֹ עֲזַרְיָהוּ בֶן־צָדוֹק הַכֹּהֵן: אֱלִיחֹרֶף וַאֲחִיָּה בְּנֵי שִׁישָׁא
ד סֹפְרִים יְהוֹשָׁפָט בֶּן־אֲחִילוּד הַמַּזְכִּיר: וּבְנָיָהוּ בֶן־יְהוֹיָדָע עַל־הַצָּבָא
ה וְצָדוֹק וְאֶבְיָתָר כֹּהֲנִים: וַעֲזַרְיָהוּ בֶן־נָתָן עַל־הַנִּצָּבִים וְזָבוּד בֶּן־נָתָן
ו כֹּהֵן רֵעֶה הַמֶּלֶךְ: וַאֲחִישָׁר עַל־הַבָּיִת וַאֲדֹנִירָם בֶּן־עַבְדָּא עַל־
ז הַמַּס: וְלִשְׁלֹמֹה שְׁנֵים־עָשָׂר נִצָּבִים עַל־כָּל־יִשְׂרָאֵל
וְכִלְכְּלוּ אֶת־הַמֶּלֶךְ וְאֶת־בֵּיתוֹ חֹדֶשׁ בַּשָּׁנָה יִהְיֶה עַל־אחד לְכַלְכֵּל: הָאֶחָד
ח ט וְאֵלֶּה שְׁמוֹתָם בֶּן־חוּר בְּהַר אֶפְרָיִם: בֶּן־דֶּקֶר בְּמָקַץ וּבְשַׁעַלְבִים
י וּבֵית שָׁמֶשׁ וְאֵילוֹן בֵּית חָנָן: בֶּן־חֶסֶד בָּאֲרֻבּוֹת לוֹ שֹׂכֹה וְכָל־
יא אֶרֶץ חֵפֶר: בֶּן־אֲבִינָדָב כָּל־נָפַת דֹּאר טָפַת בַּת־שְׁלֹמֹה הָיְתָה לּוֹ
יב לְאִשָּׁה: בַּעֲנָא בֶּן־אֲחִילוּד תַּעְנַךְ וּמְגִדּוֹ וְכָל־בֵּית שְׁאָן
אֲשֶׁר אֵצֶל צָרְתַנָה מִתַּחַת לְיִזְרְעֶאל מִבֵּית שְׁאָן עַד אָבֵל מְחוֹלָה
יג עַד מֵעֵבֶר לְיָקְמֳעָם: בֶּן־גֶּבֶר בְּרָמֹת גִּלְעָד לוֹ חַוֹּת
יָאִיר בֶּן־מְנַשֶּׁה אֲשֶׁר בַּגִּלְעָד לוֹ חֶבֶל אַרְגֹּב אֲשֶׁר בַּבָּשָׁן שִׁשִּׁים עָרִים
יד גְּדֹלוֹת חוֹמָה וּבְרִיחַ נְחֹשֶׁת: אֲחִינָדָב בֶּן־עִדֹּא
טו מַחֲנָיְמָה: אֲחִימַעַץ בְּנַפְתָּלִי גַּם־הוּא לָקַח אֶת־
טז בָּשְׂמַת בַּת־שְׁלֹמֹה לְאִשָּׁה: בַּעֲנָא בֶּן־חוּשַׁי בְּאָשֵׁר
יז יח וּבְעָלוֹת: יְהוֹשָׁפָט בֶּן־פָּרוּחַ בְּיִשָּׂשכָר: שִׁמְעִי
יט בֶן־אֵלָא בְּבִנְיָמִן: גֶּבֶר בֶּן־אֻרִי בְּאֶרֶץ גִּלְעָד אֶרֶץ
סִיחוֹן ׀ מֶלֶךְ הָאֱמֹרִי וְעֹג מֶלֶךְ הַבָּשָׁן וּנְצִיב אֶחָד אֲשֶׁר בָּאָרֶץ:
כ יְהוּדָה וְיִשְׂרָאֵל רַבִּים כַּחוֹל אֲשֶׁר־עַל־הַיָּם לָרֹב אֹכְלִים וְשֹׁתִים ד
ה א וּשְׂמֵחִים: וּשְׁלֹמֹה הָיָה מוֹשֵׁל בְּכָל־הַמַּמְלָכוֹת מִן־הַנָּהָר אֶרֶץ
פְּלִשְׁתִּים וְעַד גְּבוּל מִצְרָיִם מַגִּשִׁים מִנְחָה וְעֹבְדִים אֶת־שְׁלֹמֹה כָּל־
ב יְמֵי חַיָּיו: וַיְהִי לֶחֶם־שְׁלֹמֹה לְיוֹם אֶחָד שְׁלֹשִׁים כֹּר
ג סֹלֶת וְשִׁשִּׁים כֹּר קָמַח: עֲשָׂרָה בָקָר בְּרִאִים וְעֶשְׂרִים בָּקָר רְעִי וּמֵאָה
ד צֹאן לְבַד מֵאַיָּל וּצְבִי וְיַחְמוּר וּבַרְבֻּרִים אֲבוּסִים: כִּי־הוּא רֹדֶה ׀ בְּכָל־
עֵבֶר הַנָּהָר מִתִּפְסַח וְעַד־עַזָּה בְּכָל־מַלְכֵי עֵבֶר הַנָּהָר וְשָׁלוֹם הָיָה לוֹ
ה מִכָּל־עֲבָרָיו מִסָּבִיב: וַיֵּשֶׁב יְהוּדָה וְיִשְׂרָאֵל לָבֶטַח אִישׁ תַּחַת גַּפְנוֹ
ו וְתַחַת תְּאֵנָתוֹ מִדָּן וְעַד־בְּאֵר שָׁבַע כֹּל יְמֵי שְׁלֹמֹה: וַיְהִי

7 twelve thousand riders. During their assigned month, the aforementioned
prefects would provide for King Shlomo and all who were received at King
8 Shlomo's table, and they let nothing fall short. As for the barley and straw for
the horses and steeds, they would deliver it to the place where they were
9 stationed according to their schedule. God had granted wisdom to
Shlomo, and deep understanding, and a mind as broad as the sand upon
10 the seashore. Shlomo's wisdom surpassed the wisdom of all the peoples
11 of the East and all the wisdom of Egypt. He was wiser than any other
man – than Eitan the Ezrahite and Heiman, than Kalkol and Darda, the
12 sons of Maḥol – and he was famous among all the surrounding nations. He
composed three thousand proverbs, and his songs numbered a thousand
13 and five. And he spoke of the trees, from the cedar in Lebanon to the
hyssop that grows out of walls; and he spoke of the beasts and the birds and
14 the creeping creatures and the fish. People from all nations came to hear
Shlomo's wisdom on behalf of all the kings of the earth who had heard of his
15 wisdom. Ḥiram, king of Tyre, sent his officials to Shlomo when he
heard that he had been anointed king in his father's place, for Ḥiram had
16 always respected David. 17 And Shlomo sent a message to Ḥiram: "You
know that my father David was not able to build a house for the name of the
Lord his God, given how battle surrounded him, until the Lord brought
18 them to heel beneath him. But now, the Lord my God has granted me respite
19 all around; there is no adversary or misfortune. And so I intend to build a
House for the name of the Lord my God, just as the Lord promised my
father David, saying, 'Your son, whom I will enthrone in your stead, will be
20 the one to build the House for My name.'[11] And now, order them to cut down
cedars for me from Lebanon; my servants will work with your servants, and
I will provide whatever wages you demand for your servants, for as you know,
21 we have no one as skilled in cutting timber as the Sidonians." When
Ḥiram heard Shlomo's words, he was delighted and exclaimed, "Blessed is
the Lord today, for having given David such a wise son over this great people."
22 And Ḥiram sent word to Shlomo: "I have received your message; I will supply
23 all the cedarwood and cypress wood you require. My servants will bring them
down from Lebanon to the sea, and by the sea I will form them into rafts, to
go to whatever place you tell me. And there, I will dismantle them for you to
carry away. You, for your part, will supply the food I require for my household."
24 And so Ḥiram supplied Shlomo with all the cedarwood and cypress wood
25 he required, while Shlomo supplied Ḥiram with twenty thousand *kor* of
wheat as provision for his household, and twenty *kor* of fine-pressed oil; those
were the quantities Shlomo supplied to Ḥiram every year.

---

11 | See II Samuel 7:12–13.

לִשְׁלֹמֹה אַרְבָּעִים אֶלֶף אֻרְוֺת סוּסִים לְמֶרְכָּבוֹ וּשְׁנֵים־עָשָׂר אֶלֶף
ז פָּרָשִׁים: וְכִלְכְּלוּ הַנִּצָּבִים הָאֵלֶּה אֶת־הַמֶּלֶךְ שְׁלֹמֹה וְאֵת כָּל־הַקָּרֵב
ח אֶל־שֻׁלְחַן הַמֶּלֶךְ־שְׁלֹמֹה אִישׁ חָדְשׁוֹ לֹא יְעַדְּרוּ דָּבָר: וְהַשְּׂעֹרִים
וְהַתֶּבֶן לַסּוּסִים וְלָרֶכֶשׁ יָבִאוּ אֶל־הַמָּקוֹם אֲשֶׁר יִהְיֶה־שָּׁם אִישׁ
ט כְּמִשְׁפָּטוֹ: וַיִּתֵּן אֱלֹהִים חָכְמָה לִשְׁלֹמֹה וּתְבוּנָה הַרְבֵּה
י מְאֹד וְרֹחַב לֵב כַּחוֹל אֲשֶׁר עַל־שְׂפַת הַיָּם: וַתֵּרֶב חָכְמַת שְׁלֹמֹה
יא מֵחָכְמַת כָּל־בְּנֵי־קֶדֶם וּמִכֹּל חָכְמַת מִצְרָיִם: וַיֶּחְכַּם מִכָּל־הָאָדָם
מֵאֵיתָן הָאֶזְרָחִי וְהֵימָן וְכַלְכֹּל וְדַרְדַּע בְּנֵי מָחוֹל וַיְהִי־שְׁמוֹ בְכָל־
יב הַגּוֹיִם סָבִיב: וַיְדַבֵּר שְׁלֹשֶׁת אֲלָפִים מָשָׁל וַיְהִי שִׁירוֹ חֲמִשָּׁה וָאָלֶף:
יג וַיְדַבֵּר עַל־הָעֵצִים מִן־הָאֶרֶז אֲשֶׁר בַּלְּבָנוֹן וְעַד הָאֵזוֹב אֲשֶׁר יֹצֵא
יד בַּקִּיר וַיְדַבֵּר עַל־הַבְּהֵמָה וְעַל־הָעוֹף וְעַל־הָרֶמֶשׂ וְעַל־הַדָּגִים: וַיָּבֹאוּ
מִכָּל־הָעַמִּים לִשְׁמֹעַ אֵת חָכְמַת שְׁלֹמֹה מֵאֵת כָּל־מַלְכֵי הָאָרֶץ אֲשֶׁר
טו שָׁמְעוּ אֶת־חָכְמָתוֹ: וַיִּשְׁלַח חִירָם מֶלֶךְ־צוֹר אֶת־עֲבָדָיו
אֶל־שְׁלֹמֹה כִּי שָׁמַע כִּי אֹתוֹ מָשְׁחוּ לְמֶלֶךְ תַּחַת אָבִיהוּ כִּי אֹהֵב הָיָה
טז חִירָם לְדָוִד כָּל־הַיָּמִים: וַיִּשְׁלַח שְׁלֹמֹה אֶל־חִירָם לֵאמֹר:
יז אַתָּה יָדַעְתָּ אֶת־דָּוִד אָבִי כִּי לֹא יָכֹל לִבְנוֹת בַּיִת לְשֵׁם יהוה אֱלֹהָיו
מִפְּנֵי הַמִּלְחָמָה אֲשֶׁר סְבָבֻהוּ עַד תֵּת־יהוה אֹתָם תַּחַת כַּפּוֹת רגלו: רַגְלָי
יח יט וְעַתָּה הֵנִיחַ יהוה אֱלֹהַי לִי מִסָּבִיב אֵין שָׂטָן וְאֵין פֶּגַע רָע: וְהִנְנִי אֹמֵר
לִבְנוֹת בַּיִת לְשֵׁם יהוה אֱלֹהָי כַּאֲשֶׁר ׀ דִּבֶּר יהוה אֶל־דָּוִד אָבִי לֵאמֹר
כ בִּנְךָ אֲשֶׁר אֶתֵּן תַּחְתֶּיךָ עַל־כִּסְאֶךָ הוּא־יִבְנֶה הַבַּיִת לִשְׁמִי: וְעַתָּה
צַוֵּה וְיִכְרְתוּ־לִי אֲרָזִים מִן־הַלְּבָנוֹן וַעֲבָדַי יִהְיוּ עִם־עֲבָדֶיךָ וּשְׂכַר
עֲבָדֶיךָ אֶתֵּן לְךָ כְּכֹל אֲשֶׁר תֹּאמֵר כִּי ׀ אַתָּה יָדַעְתָּ כִּי אֵין בָּנוּ אִישׁ
כא יֹדֵעַ לִכְרָת־עֵצִים כַּצִּדֹנִים: וַיְהִי כִּשְׁמֹעַ חִירָם אֶת־דִּבְרֵי
שְׁלֹמֹה וַיִּשְׂמַח מְאֹד וַיֹּאמֶר בָּרוּךְ יהוה הַיּוֹם אֲשֶׁר נָתַן לְדָוִד בֵּן חָכָם
כב עַל־הָעָם הָרָב הַזֶּה: וַיִּשְׁלַח חִירָם אֶל־שְׁלֹמֹה לֵאמֹר שָׁמַעְתִּי אֵת
אֲשֶׁר־שָׁלַחְתָּ אֵלָי אֲנִי אֶעֱשֶׂה אֶת־כָּל־חֶפְצְךָ בַּעֲצֵי אֲרָזִים וּבַעֲצֵי
כג בְרוֹשִׁים: עֲבָדַי יֹרִדוּ מִן־הַלְּבָנוֹן יָמָּה וַאֲנִי אֲשִׂימֵם דֹּבְרוֹת בַּיָּם
עַד־הַמָּקוֹם אֲשֶׁר־תִּשְׁלַח אֵלַי וְנִפַּצְתִּים שָׁם וְאַתָּה תִשָּׂא וְאַתָּה
כד תַּעֲשֶׂה אֶת־חֶפְצִי לָתֵת לֶחֶם בֵּיתִי: וַיְהִי חִירוֹם נֹתֵן לִשְׁלֹמֹה עֲצֵי
כה אֲרָזִים וַעֲצֵי בְרוֹשִׁים כָּל־חֶפְצוֹ: וּשְׁלֹמֹה נָתַן לְחִירָם עֶשְׂרִים אֶלֶף כֹּר
חִטִּים מַכֹּלֶת לְבֵיתוֹ וְעֶשְׂרִים כֹּר שֶׁמֶן כָּתִית כֹּה־יִתֵּן שְׁלֹמֹה לְחִירָם
שָׁנָה בְשָׁנָה:

26 The LORD had endowed Shlomo with wisdom, as He had promised him.
There was peace between Ḥiram and Shlomo, and the two of them formed
27 an alliance. King Shlomo began to levy forced labor upon all of Israel; the
28 levy was thirty thousand men. He had ten thousand men sent to Lebanon
every month, in shifts; they would spend a month in Lebanon and two
29 months at home. Adoniram was in charge of the forced labor. And
Shlomo had seventy thousand porters and eight thousand quarriers in the
30 mountains, besides Shlomo's three thousand and three hundred prefect
officers in charge of the labor, who supervised the people who performed the
31 labor. At the king's command, they quarried enormous blocks of prime stone
so that the foundations of the House would be laid with hewn stone.
32 And Shlomo's builders, together with Ḥiram's builders and the Gevalites,[12]
carved the wood and the stone in preparation for the construction of the
6 1 House. In the four hundred and eightieth year after the Israelites left
Egypt, in the month of Ziv[13] – the second month – of the fourth year of
2 Shlomo's reign over Israel, he began to build the House for the LORD. The
House that King Shlomo built for the LORD was sixty cubits long, twenty
3 cubits wide, and thirty cubits high. The Hall leading up to the Sanctuary of
the House was twenty cubits long along the width of the House, and ten
4 cubits wide leading up to the House. He made recessed, paned windows for
5 the House. Around the outer wall of the House – the outer walls around the
Sanctuary and Inner Sanctuary[14] – he built a tiered structure and made side
6 chambers all around. The lowest tier was five cubits wide, the middle tier was
six cubits wide, and the third tier was seven cubits wide, as he had designed
recesses around the outside of the House to avoid making grooves in the walls
7 of the House. The House was entirely built of finished stones that had been
cut at the quarry; no hammer, ax, or iron tool was heard in the House during
8 its construction. There was an entrance through the central alcove on the
southern side of the House; a winding staircase led to the middle tier and
9 from the middle tier to the third one. When he finished building the House,
10 he paneled the House with beams and planks of cedar. He built the tiered
structure against the whole house, each story five cubits high, so that the
11 House was encased with cedarwood. And the word of the LORD
12 came to Shlomo: "Concerning this House that you are building: if you follow
My laws and uphold My rulings and keep all My commandments by following
them, then I will fulfill My promise through you, the promise that I made to
13 your father David. I will dwell in the midst of the Israelites, and I will never
14 abandon My people Israel." Shlomo completed the construction of
15 the House. He paneled the inside of the walls of the House with boards of
cedar – from the floor of the House to the ceiling, he overlaid the interior
with wood; and he overlaid the floor of the House with boards of cypress.
16 Twenty cubits from the end of the House, he built up boards of cedar from

12 | Skilled workers from the Phoenician port city of Byblos; cf. Ezekiel 27:9.
13 | The second month, known by Jews as Iyar after the Babylonian exile.
14 | Also called the Holy of Holies in verse 16 and elsewhere.

כו וַֽיהוָה נָתַן חׇכְמָה לִשְׁלֹמֹה כַּאֲשֶׁר דִּבֶּר־לוֹ וַיְהִי שָׁלֹם בֵּין חִירָם וּבֵין
כז שְׁלֹמֹה וַיִּכְרְתוּ בְרִית שְׁנֵיהֶם׃ וַיַּעַל הַמֶּלֶךְ שְׁלֹמֹה מַס מִכׇּל־יִשְׂרָאֵל
כח וַיְהִי הַמַּס שְׁלֹשִׁים אֶלֶף אִישׁ׃ וַיִּשְׁלָחֵם לְבָנוֹנָה עֲשֶׂרֶת אֲלָפִים
בַּחֹדֶשׁ חֲלִיפוֹת חֹדֶשׁ יִהְיוּ בַלְּבָנוֹן שְׁנַיִם חֳדָשִׁים בְּבֵיתוֹ וַאֲדֹנִירָם
כט עַל־הַמַּס׃ וַיְהִי לִשְׁלֹמֹה שִׁבְעִים אֶלֶף נֹשֵׂא סַבָּל וּשְׁמֹנִים
ל אֶלֶף חֹצֵב בָּהָר׃ לְבַד מִשָּׂרֵי הַנִּצָּבִים לִשְׁלֹמֹה אֲשֶׁר עַל־הַמְּלָאכָה
לא שְׁלֹשֶׁת אֲלָפִים וּשְׁלֹשׁ מֵאוֹת הָרֹדִים בָּעָם הָעֹשִׂים בַּמְּלָאכָה׃ וַיְצַו
הַמֶּלֶךְ וַיַּסִּעוּ אֲבָנִים גְּדֹלוֹת אֲבָנִים יְקָרוֹת לְיַסֵּד הַבָּיִת אַבְנֵי גָזִית׃
לב וַיִּפְסְלוּ בֹּנֵי שְׁלֹמֹה וּבֹנֵי חִירוֹם וְהַגִּבְלִים וַיָּכִינוּ הָעֵצִים וְהָאֲבָנִים
ו א לִבְנוֹת הַבָּיִת׃ וַיְהִי בִשְׁמוֹנִים שָׁנָה וְאַרְבַּע מֵאוֹת
שָׁנָה לְצֵאת בְּנֵי־יִשְׂרָאֵל מֵאֶרֶץ־מִצְרַיִם בַּשָּׁנָה הָרְבִיעִית בְּחֹדֶשׁ זִו
הוּא הַחֹדֶשׁ הַשֵּׁנִי לִמְלֹךְ שְׁלֹמֹה עַל־יִשְׂרָאֵל וַיִּבֶן הַבַּיִת לַיהוָה׃
ב וְהַבַּיִת אֲשֶׁר בָּנָה הַמֶּלֶךְ שְׁלֹמֹה לַיהוָה שִׁשִּׁים־אַמָּה אׇרְכּוֹ וְעֶשְׂרִים
ג רׇחְבּוֹ וּשְׁלֹשִׁים אַמָּה קוֹמָתוֹ׃ וְהָאוּלָם עַל־פְּנֵי הֵיכַל הַבַּיִת עֶשְׂרִים
אַמָּה אׇרְכּוֹ עַל־פְּנֵי רֹחַב הַבָּיִת עֶשֶׂר בָּאַמָּה רׇחְבּוֹ עַל־פְּנֵי הַבָּיִת׃
ד ה וַיַּעַשׂ לַבָּיִת חַלּוֹנֵי שְׁקֻפִים אֲטֻמִים׃ וַיִּבֶן עַל־קִיר הַבַּיִת יָצוּעַ סָבִיב יָצִיעַ
ו אֶת־קִירוֹת הַבַּיִת סָבִיב לַהֵיכָל וְלַדְּבִיר וַיַּעַשׂ צְלָעוֹת סָבִיב׃ הַיָּצוּעַ הַיָּצִיעַ
הַתַּחְתֹּנָה חָמֵשׁ בָּאַמָּה רׇחְבָּהּ וְהַתִּיכֹנָה שֵׁשׁ בָּאַמָּה רׇחְבָּהּ וְהַשְּׁלִישִׁית
שֶׁבַע בָּאַמָּה רׇחְבָּהּ כִּי מִגְרָעוֹת נָתַן לַבַּיִת סָבִיב חוּצָה לְבִלְתִּי אֲחֹז
ז בְּקִירוֹת הַבָּיִת׃ וְהַבַּיִת בְּהִבָּנֹתוֹ אֶבֶן־שְׁלֵמָה מַסָּע נִבְנָה וּמַקָּבוֹת
ח וְהַגַּרְזֶן כׇּל־כְּלִי בַרְזֶל לֹא־נִשְׁמַע בַּבַּיִת בְּהִבָּנֹתוֹ׃ פֶּתַח הַצֵּלָע הַתִּיכֹנָה
אֶל־כֶּתֶף הַבַּיִת הַיְמָנִית וּבְלוּלִּים יַעֲלוּ עַל־הַתִּיכֹנָה וּמִן־הַתִּיכֹנָה
ט אֶל־הַשְּׁלִשִׁים׃ וַיִּבֶן אֶת־הַבַּיִת וַיְכַלֵּהוּ וַיִּסְפֹּן אֶת־הַבַּיִת גֵּבִים וּשְׂדֵרֹת
י בָּאֲרָזִים׃ וַיִּבֶן אֶת־הַיָּצוּעַ עַל־כׇּל־הַבַּיִת חָמֵשׁ אַמּוֹת קוֹמָתוֹ וַיֶּאֱחֹז הַיָּצִיעַ
יא אֶת־הַבַּיִת בַּעֲצֵי אֲרָזִים׃ וַיְהִי דְּבַר־יְהוָה אֶל־שְׁלֹמֹה
יב לֵאמֹר׃ הַבַּיִת הַזֶּה אֲשֶׁר־אַתָּה בֹנֶה אִם־תֵּלֵךְ בְּחֻקֹּתַי וְאֶת־מִשְׁפָּטַי
תַּעֲשֶׂה וְשָׁמַרְתָּ אֶת־כׇּל־מִצְוֺתַי לָלֶכֶת בָּהֶם וַהֲקִמֹתִי אֶת־דְּבָרִי אִתָּךְ
יג אֲשֶׁר דִּבַּרְתִּי אֶל־דָּוִד אָבִיךָ׃ וְשָׁכַנְתִּי בְּתוֹךְ בְּנֵי יִשְׂרָאֵל וְלֹא אֶעֱזֹב ה
יד טו אֶת־עַמִּי יִשְׂרָאֵל׃ וַיִּבֶן שְׁלֹמֹה אֶת־הַבַּיִת וַיְכַלֵּהוּ׃ וַיִּבֶן
אֶת־קִירוֹת הַבַּיִת מִבַּיְתָה בְּצַלְעוֹת אֲרָזִים מִקַּרְקַע הַבַּיִת עַד־קִירוֹת
טז הַסִּפֻּן צִפָּה עֵץ מִבָּיִת וַיְצַף אֶת־קַרְקַע הַבַּיִת בְּצַלְעוֹת בְּרוֹשִׁים׃ וַיִּבֶן
אֶת־עֶשְׂרִים אַמָּה מִירְכּוֹתֵי הַבַּיִת בְּצַלְעוֹת אֲרָזִים מִן־הַקַּרְקַע עַד־ מִיַּרְכְּתֵי

the floor to the ceiling and built the Inner Sanctuary, the Holy of Holies, on
17 the inside. The front part of the House, the Sanctuary, measured forty cubits.
18 And cedar, the interior was all cedar, with carvings of bulbs and blossoming
19 flowers; there was no visible stone. In the innermost part of the House, he
20 furnished the Inner Sanctuary to place the Ark of the LORD's Covenant. The
interior of the Inner Sanctuary was twenty cubits long, twenty cubits wide,
and twenty cubits high; he overlaid it and overlaid the cedar altar with solid
21 gold. Shlomo overlaid the interior of the House with solid gold; he fastened
golden chains in front of the Inner Sanctuary, which he overlaid with gold.
22 He overlaid the whole House with gold, every last part of the House; and he
23 overlaid the whole altar within the Inner Sanctuary with gold. Within the
24 Inner Sanctuary, he formed two cherubim of olive wood, ten cubits high. One
cherub wing measured five cubits, and the second cherub wing measured five
25 cubits: ten cubits from wingtip to wingtip. The other cherub also measured
26 ten cubits, as the two cherubim were both of the same size and shape – one
27 cherub was ten cubits tall, and so was the second cherub. He placed the
cherubim within the innermost part of the House.[15] Their wings were spread
so that the tip of one cherub's wing touched one wall, and the tip of the other
cherub's wing touched the other wall; and their inner wings touched wing to
28 29 wing. And he overlaid the cherubim with gold. All over the walls, within and
without, he made carvings all around – carvings of cherubim and palms and
30 blossoming flowers. He overlaid the floor of the House with gold, within and
31 without. He made olive wood doors for the entrance to the Inner Sanctuary;
32 the lintel and doorposts were five-sided. The double doors were of olive wood,
and on them he carved cherubim and palms and blossoming flowers and
overlaid them with gold; he hammered the gold down over the cherubim
33 and the palms. For the entrance to the Sanctuary, too, he made olive wood
34 doorposts, which were four-sided. The double doors were of cypress wood,
with two folding leaves for one door and two folding leaves for the other door.
35 He carved cherubim and palms and blossoming flowers, and he overlaid the
36 reliefs evenly with gold. He built the inner courtyard with three rows of hewn
37 stone and a row of cut cedar beams. In the fourth year, in the month of Ziv,
38 the foundations for the House of the LORD were laid. And in the eleventh
year, in the month of Bul[16] – that is, the eighth month – the House was
finished down to every last detail and every last design. He had spent seven
7 1 years to complete it. Shlomo spent thirteen years building his own house,
2 until his house was completely finished. He built the House of the Lebanon
Forest[17] with four rows of cedar columns, with cut cedar beams on top of the
columns; it was a hundred cubits long, fifty cubits wide, and thirty cubits high.
3 It was paneled over in cedar, with boards atop the columns, forty-five in all;
4 fifteen in every row. There were three rows of frames, with three sets of

15 | The Inner Sanctuary, or Holy of Holies.

16 | The eighth month, known by Jews as Marḥeshvan after the Babylonian exile.

17 | This was apparently inspired by the large number of cedar columns and beams utilized in its construction.

יז הַקִּירוֹת וַיִּבֶן לוֹ מִבַּיִת לִדְבִיר לְקֹדֶשׁ הַקֳּדָשִׁים: וְאַרְבָּעִים בָּאַמָּה
יח הָיָה הַבָּיִת הוּא הַהֵיכָל לִפְנָי: וְאֶרֶז אֶל־הַבַּיִת פְּנִימָה מִקְלַעַת פְּקָעִים
יט וּפְטוּרֵי צִצִּים הַכֹּל אֶרֶז אֵין אֶבֶן נִרְאָה: וּדְבִיר בְּתוֹךְ־הַבַּיִת מִפְּנִימָה
כ הֵכִין לְתִתֵּן שָׁם אֶת־אֲרוֹן בְּרִית יהוה: וְלִפְנֵי הַדְּבִיר עֶשְׂרִים אַמָּה
אֹרֶךְ וְעֶשְׂרִים אַמָּה רֹחַב וְעֶשְׂרִים אַמָּה קוֹמָתוֹ וַיְצַפֵּהוּ זָהָב סָגוּר
כא וַיְצַף מִזְבֵּחַ אָרֶז: וַיְצַף שְׁלֹמֹה אֶת־הַבַּיִת מִפְּנִימָה זָהָב סָגוּר וַיְעַבֵּר
כב ברתיקות זָהָב לִפְנֵי הַדְּבִיר וַיְצַפֵּהוּ זָהָב: וְאֶת־כָּל־הַבַּיִת צִפָּה זָהָב בְּרַתּוּקוֹת
כג עַד־תֹּם כָּל־הַבָּיִת וְכָל־הַמִּזְבֵּחַ אֲשֶׁר־לַדְּבִיר צִפָּה זָהָב: וַיַּעַשׂ בַּדְּבִיר
כד שְׁנֵי כְרוּבִים עֲצֵי־שָׁמֶן עֶשֶׂר אַמּוֹת קוֹמָתוֹ: וְחָמֵשׁ אַמּוֹת כְּנַף הַכְּרוּב
הָאֶחָת וְחָמֵשׁ אַמּוֹת כְּנַף הַכְּרוּב הַשֵּׁנִית עֶשֶׂר אַמּוֹת מִקְצוֹת כְּנָפָיו
כה וְעַד־קְצוֹת כְּנָפָיו: וְעֶשֶׂר בָּאַמָּה הַכְּרוּב הַשֵּׁנִי מִדָּה אַחַת וְקֶצֶב אֶחָד
כו לִשְׁנֵי הַכְּרֻבִים: קוֹמַת הַכְּרוּב הָאֶחָד עֶשֶׂר בָּאַמָּה וְכֵן הַכְּרוּב הַשֵּׁנִי:
כז וַיִּתֵּן אֶת־הַכְּרוּבִים בְּתוֹךְ ׀ הַבַּיִת הַפְּנִימִי וַיִּפְרְשׂוּ אֶת־כַּנְפֵי הַכְּרֻבִים
וַתִּגַּע כְּנַף־הָאֶחָד בַּקִּיר וּכְנַף הַכְּרוּב הַשֵּׁנִי נֹגַעַת בַּקִּיר הַשֵּׁנִי וְכַנְפֵיהֶם
כח כט אֶל־תּוֹךְ הַבַּיִת נֹגְעֹת כָּנָף אֶל־כָּנָף: וַיְצַף אֶת־הַכְּרוּבִים זָהָב: וְאֵת
כָּל־קִירוֹת הַבַּיִת מֵסַב ׀ קָלַע פִּתּוּחֵי מִקְלְעוֹת כְּרוּבִים וְתִמֹרֹת וּפְטוּרֵי
ל צִצִּים מִלִּפְנִים וְלַחִיצוֹן: וְאֶת־קַרְקַע הַבַּיִת צִפָּה זָהָב לִפְנִימָה וְלַחִיצוֹן:
לא וְאֵת פֶּתַח הַדְּבִיר עָשָׂה דַּלְתוֹת עֲצֵי־שָׁמֶן הָאַיִל מְזוּזוֹת חֲמִשִׁית:
לב וּשְׁתֵּי דַּלְתוֹת עֲצֵי־שֶׁמֶן וְקָלַע עֲלֵיהֶם מִקְלְעוֹת כְּרוּבִים וְתִמֹרוֹת
וּפְטוּרֵי צִצִּים וְצִפָּה זָהָב וַיָּרֶד עַל־הַכְּרוּבִים וְעַל־הַתִּמֹרוֹת אֶת־הַזָּהָב:
לג לד וְכֵן עָשָׂה לְפֶתַח הַהֵיכָל מְזוּזוֹת עֲצֵי־שָׁמֶן מֵאֵת רְבִעִית: וּשְׁתֵּי דַלְתוֹת
עֲצֵי בְרוֹשִׁים שְׁנֵי צְלָעִים הַדֶּלֶת הָאַחַת גְּלִילִים וּשְׁנֵי קְלָעִים הַדֶּלֶת
לה הַשֵּׁנִית גְּלִילִים: וְקָלַע כְּרוּבִים וְתִמֹרוֹת וּפְטֻרֵי צִצִּים וְצִפָּה זָהָב מְיֻשָּׁר
לו עַל־הַמְּחֻקֶּה: וַיִּבֶן אֶת־הֶחָצֵר הַפְּנִימִית שְׁלֹשָׁה טוּרֵי גָזִית וְטוּר
לז לח כְּרֻתֹת אֲרָזִים: בַּשָּׁנָה הָרְבִיעִית יֻסַּד בֵּית יהוה בְּיֶרַח זִו: וּבַשָּׁנָה הָאַחַת
עֶשְׂרֵה בְּיֶרַח בּוּל הוּא הַחֹדֶשׁ הַשְּׁמִינִי כָּלָה הַבַּיִת לְכָל־דְּבָרָיו וּלְכָל־
ז א מִשְׁפָּטָו וַיִּבְנֵהוּ שֶׁבַע שָׁנִים: וְאֶת־בֵּיתוֹ בָּנָה שְׁלֹמֹה שְׁלֹשׁ עֶשְׂרֵה
ב שָׁנָה וַיְכַל אֶת־כָּל־בֵּיתוֹ: וַיִּבֶן אֶת־בֵּית ׀ יַעַר הַלְּבָנוֹן מֵאָה אַמָּה
אָרְכּוֹ וַחֲמִשִּׁים אַמָּה רָחְבּוֹ וּשְׁלֹשִׁים אַמָּה קוֹמָתוֹ עַל אַרְבָּעָה טוּרֵי
ג עַמּוּדֵי אֲרָזִים וּכְרֻתוֹת אֲרָזִים עַל־הָעַמּוּדִים: וְסָפֻן בָּאֶרֶז מִמַּעַל
עַל־הַצְּלָעֹת אֲשֶׁר עַל־הָעַמּוּדִים אַרְבָּעִים וַחֲמִשָּׁה חֲמִשָּׁה עָשָׂר
ד הַטּוּר: וּשְׁקֻפִים שְׁלֹשָׁה טוּרִים וּמֶחֱזָה אֶל־מֶחֱזָה שָׁלֹשׁ פְּעָמִים:

5 windows facing each other. All the entrances and doorframes had square
6 frames, with the three sets of windows facing each other. He made the hall
of columns fifty cubits long and thirty cubits wide; there was a hall in front
7 with columns and a canopy in front of them. He made the throne room
where he was to sit in judgment the Hall of Judgment and paneled its floor
8 with cedar from floor to floor. The house of his actual residence, in the rear
courtyard behind the Hall, was of similar design; and the house Shlomo made
9 for Pharaoh's daughter, whom he had married, was similar to that Hall. All
these were of prime stone – hewn to size and smoothed with a file on every
side – from foundation to coping, extending to the great courtyard on the
10 outside. The foundations were of prime stone, enormous stones – stones
11 measuring ten cubits and stones measuring eight cubits; and above were
12 prime stones hewn to size, and cedar. The surrounding great courtyard had
three rows of hewn stone and a row of cut cedar beams, the same as the inner
13 courtyard of the House of the Lord and the Hall of the House. King
14 Shlomo sent and had Ḥiram fetched from Tyre. He was the son of a widow
from the tribe of Naftali, and his father had been a Tyrian coppersmith. He
was brimming with the talent, expertise, and skill to craft any work in bronze;
15 he came to King Shlomo and crafted all his work. He formed the two pillars
of bronze; each pillar was eighteen cubits high, and the circumference of both
16 pillars was twelve cubits. He crafted two capitals, cast in bronze, to place atop
17 the pillars – the height of each capital was five cubits – as well as fronds of
meshwork and garlands of chainwork for the capitals atop the pillars, seven
18 for each of the two capitals. He crafted the pillars with two rows around one
mesh to cover the capitals that were above the pomegranates, and he did
19 the same with the second capital. The capitals atop the pillars in the Hall
20 were crafted in the form of a lily four cubits high; the capitals atop both
pillars bulged out through the meshwork over the rows of two hundred
21 pomegranates encircling both capitals. He erected the pillars by the Hall of
the Sanctuary; he set up the right pillar and named it Yakhin, and he set up
22 the left pillar and named it Boaz. Atop each pillar was the form of a lily; thus
23 the work of the pillars was complete. He made the Molten Sea,[18] ten
cubits across from rim to rim and perfectly round. It was five cubits high and
24 thirty cubits in circumference. There were bulb-shaped knobs beneath its
rim, encircling it all around, clustered around the Sea ten to a cubit; the two

18 | A large tank made of cast metal.

ה וְכָל־הַפְּתָחִים וְהַמְּזוּזוֹת רְבֻעִים שָׁקֶף וּמוּל מֶחֱזָה אֶל־מֶחֱזָה שָׁלֹשׁ
ו פְּעָמִים׃ וְאֵת אוּלָם הָעַמּוּדִים עָשָׂה חֲמִשִּׁים אַמָּה אָרְכּוֹ וּשְׁלֹשִׁים
ז אַמָּה רָחְבּוֹ וְאוּלָם עַל־פְּנֵיהֶם וְעַמֻּדִים וְעָב עַל־פְּנֵיהֶם׃ וְאוּלָם
הַכִּסֵּא אֲשֶׁר יִשְׁפָּט־שָׁם אֻלָם הַמִּשְׁפָּט עָשָׂה וְסָפוּן בָּאֶרֶז מֵהַקַּרְקַע
ח עַד־הַקַּרְקָע׃ וּבֵיתוֹ אֲשֶׁר־יֵשֶׁב שָׁם חָצֵר הָאַחֶרֶת מִבֵּית לָאוּלָם
כַּמַּעֲשֶׂה הַזֶּה הָיָה וּבַיִת יַעֲשֶׂה לְבַת־פַּרְעֹה אֲשֶׁר לָקַח שְׁלֹמֹה כָּאוּלָם
ט הַזֶּה׃ כָּל־אֵלֶּה אֲבָנִים יְקָרֹת כְּמִדֹּת גָּזִית מְגֹרָרוֹת בַּמְּגֵרָה מִבַּיִת
י וּמִחוּץ וּמִמַּסָּד עַד־הַטְּפָחוֹת וּמִחוּץ עַד־הֶחָצֵר הַגְּדוֹלָה׃ וּמְיֻסָּד
אֲבָנִים יְקָרוֹת אֲבָנִים גְּדֹלוֹת אַבְנֵי עֶשֶׂר אַמּוֹת וְאַבְנֵי שְׁמֹנֶה אַמּוֹת׃
יא יב וּמִלְמַעְלָה אֲבָנִים יְקָרוֹת כְּמִדּוֹת גָּזִית וָאָרֶז׃ וְחָצֵר הַגְּדוֹלָה סָבִיב
שְׁלֹשָׁה טוּרִים גָּזִית וְטוּר כְּרֻתֹת אֲרָזִים וְלַחֲצַר בֵּית־יהוה הַפְּנִימִית
יג וּלְאֻלָם הַבָּיִת׃ וַיִּשְׁלַח הַמֶּלֶךְ שְׁלֹמֹה וַיִּקַּח אֶת־חִירָם מִצֹּר׃
יד בֶּן־אִשָּׁה אַלְמָנָה הוּא מִמַּטֵּה נַפְתָּלִי וְאָבִיו אִישׁ־צֹרִי חֹרֵשׁ נְחֹשֶׁת
וַיִּמָּלֵא אֶת־הַחָכְמָה וְאֶת־הַתְּבוּנָה וְאֶת־הַדַּעַת לַעֲשׂוֹת כָּל־מְלָאכָה
טו בַּנְּחֹשֶׁת וַיָּבוֹא אֶל־הַמֶּלֶךְ שְׁלֹמֹה וַיַּעַשׂ אֶת־כָּל־מְלַאכְתּוֹ׃ וַיָּצַר
אֶת־שְׁנֵי הָעַמּוּדִים נְחֹשֶׁת שְׁמֹנֶה עֶשְׂרֵה אַמָּה קוֹמַת הָעַמּוּד הָאֶחָד
טז וְחוּט שְׁתֵּים־עֶשְׂרֵה אַמָּה יָסֹב אֶת־הָעַמּוּד הַשֵּׁנִי׃ וּשְׁתֵּי כֹתָרֹת עָשָׂה
לָתֵת עַל־רָאשֵׁי הָעַמּוּדִים מֻצַק נְחֹשֶׁת חָמֵשׁ אַמּוֹת קוֹמַת הַכֹּתֶרֶת
יז הָאֶחָת וְחָמֵשׁ אַמּוֹת קוֹמַת הַכֹּתֶרֶת הַשֵּׁנִית׃ שְׂבָכִים מַעֲשֵׂה שְׂבָכָה
גְּדִלִים מַעֲשֵׂה שַׁרְשְׁרוֹת לַכֹּתָרֹת אֲשֶׁר עַל־רֹאשׁ הָעַמּוּדִים שִׁבְעָה
יח לַכֹּתֶרֶת הָאֶחָת וְשִׁבְעָה לַכֹּתֶרֶת הַשֵּׁנִית׃ וַיַּעַשׂ אֶת־הָעַמּוּדִים וּשְׁנֵי
טוּרִים סָבִיב עַל־הַשְּׂבָכָה הָאֶחָת לְכַסּוֹת אֶת־הַכֹּתָרֹת אֲשֶׁר עַל־
יט רֹאשׁ הָרִמֹּנִים וְכֵן עָשָׂה לַכֹּתֶרֶת הַשֵּׁנִית׃ וְכֹתָרֹת אֲשֶׁר עַל־רֹאשׁ
כ הָעַמּוּדִים מַעֲשֵׂה שׁוּשַׁן בָּאוּלָם אַרְבַּע אַמּוֹת׃ וְכֹתָרֹת עַל־שְׁנֵי
הָעַמּוּדִים גַּם־מִמַּעַל מִלְּעֻמַּת הַבֶּטֶן אֲשֶׁר לְעֵבֶר שבכה וְהָרִמּוֹנִים הַשְּׂבָכָה
כא מָאתַיִם טֻרִים סָבִיב עַל הַכֹּתֶרֶת הַשֵּׁנִית׃ וַיָּקֶם אֶת־הָעַמֻּדִים לְאֻלָם ו
הַהֵיכָל וַיָּקֶם אֶת־הָעַמּוּד הַיְמָנִי וַיִּקְרָא אֶת־שְׁמוֹ יָכִין וַיָּקֶם אֶת־
כב הָעַמּוּד הַשְּׂמָאלִי וַיִּקְרָא אֶת־שְׁמוֹ בֹּעַז׃ וְעַל רֹאשׁ הָעַמּוּדִים מַעֲשֵׂה
כג שׁוֹשָׁן וַתִּתֹּם מְלֶאכֶת הָעַמּוּדִים׃ וַיַּעַשׂ אֶת־הַיָּם מוּצָק
עֶשֶׂר בָּאַמָּה מִשְּׂפָתוֹ עַד־שְׂפָתוֹ עָגֹל ׀ סָבִיב וְחָמֵשׁ בָּאַמָּה קוֹמָתוֹ
כד וקוה שְׁלֹשִׁים בָּאַמָּה יָסֹב אֹתוֹ סָבִיב׃ וּפְקָעִים מִתַּחַת לִשְׂפָתוֹ ׀ סָבִיב וְקָו
סֹבְבִים אֹתוֹ עֶשֶׂר בָּאַמָּה מַקִּפִים אֶת־הַיָּם סָבִיב שְׁנֵי טוּרִים הַפְּקָעִים

25 rows of bulbs were cast together with it. It stood upon twelve oxen, three
facing north, three facing west, three facing south, and three facing east; the
26 Sea was on top of them, and their haunches were all turned inward. It was a
handbreadth thick, and its rim was like the rim of a cup, like the petals of a
27 lily; its capacity was two thousand *bat*.[19] He made ten stands of
bronze; each stand was four cubits long, four cubits wide, and three cubits
28 high. This is how the stands were constructed: They consisted of panels; the
29 panels were joined by frames. On the panels in between the frames were lions,
oxen, and cherubim; there was a base above the frames, and hammered
30 spirals beneath the lions and oxen. There were four bronze wheels on
every stand, with bronze axles. Its four legs had brackets underneath the laver;
31 the brackets were cast with spirals on each side. Its spout rose a cubit above
the capital; the spout was shaped like a cylindrical base, a cubit and a half
across. On the spout, too, there were carvings; its panels were square, not
32 round. The four wheels were beneath the panels, with the wheel sockets
33 fixed into the stand; each wheel was a cubit and a half high. The wheels were
designed like chariot wheels; their sockets, rims, spokes, and hubs were
34 all of cast metal. The four brackets reached the four corners of each stand;
35 the brackets were part of the stand. A cylinder rose half a cubit above the top
36 of the stand; its handles and panels were part of the top of the stand. On
the surface of its handles, and on its panels, he engraved cherubim, lions,
37 and palms in the available space, with spirals all around. This was how
he crafted the ten stands: all of them were cast alike, of uniform size and
38 shape. And he made ten lavers of bronze, each laver with a capacity
of forty *bat*, each laver four cubits across; one laver for each of the ten stands.
39 He positioned five stands to the right side of the House, and five stands to
the left side of the House; and he positioned the Sea to the right side of the
40 House, in the southeast corner. Ḥiram crafted the lavers and the
shovels and the basins. And so Ḥiram completed all the work for the House
41 of the LORD as commissioned by King Shlomo: two pillars and two globe-
shaped capitals for the pillar tops; two pieces of meshwork to cover the two
42 globe-shaped capitals for the pillar tops; four hundred pomegranates for
the two pieces of meshwork – two rows of pomegranates for each piece of
meshwork, which covered the two globe-shaped capitals on top of the pillars;
43 44 ten stands and ten lavers for the stands; one Sea with twelve oxen beneath

19 | A single *bat* is the equivalent of 6 gallons or 23 liters.

כה יֹצָקִים בִּיצֻקָתוֹ: עֹמֵד עַל־שְׁנֵי עָשָׂר בָּקָר שְׁלֹשָׁה פֹנִים ׀ צָפוֹנָה וּשְׁלֹשָׁה
פֹנִים ׀ יָמָּה וּשְׁלֹשָׁה ׀ פֹּנִים נֶגְבָּה וּשְׁלֹשָׁה פֹּנִים מִזְרָחָה וְהַיָּם עֲלֵיהֶם
כו מִלְמָעְלָה וְכָל־אֲחֹרֵיהֶם בָּיְתָה: וְעָבְיוֹ טֶפַח וּשְׂפָתוֹ כְּמַעֲשֵׂה שְׂפַת־
כז כּוֹס פֶּרַח שׁוֹשָׁן אַלְפַּיִם בַּת יָכִיל: וַיַּעַשׂ אֶת־הַמְּכֹנוֹת
עֶשֶׂר נְחֹשֶׁת אַרְבַּע בָּאַמָּה אֹרֶךְ הַמְּכוֹנָה הָאֶחָת וְאַרְבַּע בָּאַמָּה
כח רָחְבָּהּ וְשָׁלֹשׁ בָּאַמָּה קוֹמָתָהּ: וְזֶה מַעֲשֵׂה הַמְּכוֹנָה מִסְגְּרֹת לָהֶם
כט וּמִסְגְּרֹת בֵּין הַשְׁלַבִּים: וְעַל־הַמִּסְגְּרוֹת אֲשֶׁר ׀ בֵּין הַשְׁלַבִּים אֲרָיוֹת ׀
בָּקָר וּכְרוּבִים וְעַל־הַשְׁלַבִּים כֵּן מִמָּעַל וּמִתַּחַת לַאֲרָיוֹת וְלַבָּקָר לֹיוֹת
ל מַעֲשֵׂה מוֹרָד: וְאַרְבָּעָה אוֹפַנֵּי נְחֹשֶׁת לַמְּכוֹנָה הָאַחַת וְסַרְנֵי נְחֹשֶׁת
וְאַרְבָּעָה פַעֲמֹתָיו כְּתֵפֹת לָהֶם מִתַּחַת לַכִּיֹּר הַכְּתֵפֹת יְצֻקוֹת מֵעֵבֶר
לא אִישׁ לֹיוֹת: וּפִיהוּ מִבֵּית לַכֹּתֶרֶת וָמַעְלָה בָּאַמָּה וּפִיהָ עָגֹל מַעֲשֵׂה־כֵן
אַמָּה וַחֲצִי הָאַמָּה וְגַם־עַל־פִּיהָ מִקְלָעוֹת וּמִסְגְּרֹתֵיהֶם מְרֻבָּעוֹת
לב לֹא עֲגֻלּוֹת: וְאַרְבַּעַת הָאוֹפַנִּים לְמִתַּחַת לַמִּסְגְּרוֹת וִידוֹת הָאוֹפַנִּים
לג בַּמְּכוֹנָה וְקוֹמַת הָאוֹפַן הָאֶחָד אַמָּה וַחֲצִי הָאַמָּה: וּמַעֲשֵׂה הָאוֹפַנִּים
כְּמַעֲשֵׂה אוֹפַן הַמֶּרְכָּבָה יְדוֹתָם וְגַבֵּיהֶם וְחִשֻּׁקֵיהֶם וְחִשֻּׁרֵיהֶם הַכֹּל
לד מוּצָק: וְאַרְבַּע כְּתֵפוֹת אֶל אַרְבַּע פִּנּוֹת הַמְּכֹנָה הָאֶחָת מִן־הַמְּכֹנָה
לה כְּתֵפֶיהָ: וּבְרֹאשׁ הַמְּכוֹנָה חֲצִי הָאַמָּה קוֹמָה עָגֹל ׀ סָבִיב וְעַל רֹאשׁ
לו הַמְּכֹנָה יְדֹתֶיהָ וּמִסְגְּרֹתֶיהָ מִמֶּנָּה: וַיְפַתַּח עַל־הַלֻּחֹת יְדֹתֶיהָ וְעַל
ומסגרתיה כְּרוּבִים אֲרָיוֹת וְתִמֹרֹת כְּמַעַר־אִישׁ וְלֹיוֹת סָבִיב: מִסְגְּרֹתֶיהָ
לז כָּזֹאת עָשָׂה אֵת עֶשֶׂר הַמְּכֹנוֹת מוּצָק אֶחָד מִדָּה אַחַת קֶצֶב אֶחָד
לח לְכֻלָּהְנָה: וַיַּעַשׂ עֲשָׂרָה כִיֹּרוֹת נְחֹשֶׁת אַרְבָּעִים בַּת יָכִיל ׀
הַכִּיּוֹר הָאֶחָד אַרְבַּע בָּאַמָּה הַכִּיּוֹר הָאֶחָד כִּיּוֹר אֶחָד עַל־הַמְּכוֹנָה
לט הָאַחַת לְעֶשֶׂר הַמְּכֹנוֹת: וַיִּתֵּן אֶת־הַמְּכֹנוֹת חָמֵשׁ עַל־כֶּתֶף הַבַּיִת
מִיָּמִין וְחָמֵשׁ עַל־כֶּתֶף הַבַּיִת מִשְּׂמֹאלוֹ וְאֶת־הַיָּם נָתַן מִכֶּתֶף הַבַּיִת
מ הַיְמָנִית קֵדְמָה מִמּוּל נֶגֶב: וַיַּעַשׂ חִירוֹם אֶת־הַכִּיֹּרוֹת
וְאֶת־הַיָּעִים וְאֶת־הַמִּזְרָקוֹת וַיְכַל חִירָם לַעֲשׂוֹת אֶת־כָּל־הַמְּלָאכָה
מא אֲשֶׁר עָשָׂה לַמֶּלֶךְ שְׁלֹמֹה בֵּית יהוה: עַמֻּדִים שְׁנַיִם וְגֻלֹּת הַכֹּתָרֹת
אֲשֶׁר־עַל־רֹאשׁ הָעַמֻּדִים שְׁתָּיִם וְהַשְּׂבָכוֹת שְׁתַּיִם לְכַסּוֹת אֶת־שְׁתֵּי
מב גֻּלּוֹת הַכֹּתָרֹת אֲשֶׁר עַל־רֹאשׁ הָעַמּוּדִים: וְאֶת־הָרִמֹּנִים אַרְבַּע מֵאוֹת
לִשְׁתֵּי הַשְּׂבָכוֹת שְׁנֵי־טוּרִים רִמֹּנִים לַשְּׂבָכָה הָאֶחָת לְכַסּוֹת אֶת־שְׁתֵּי
מג גֻּלֹּת הַכֹּתָרֹת אֲשֶׁר עַל־פְּנֵי הָעַמּוּדִים: וְאֶת־הַמְּכֹנוֹת עֶשֶׂר וְאֶת־
מד הַכִּיֹּרֹת עֲשָׂרָה עַל־הַמְּכֹנוֹת: וְאֶת־הַיָּם הָאֶחָד וְאֶת־הַבָּקָר שְׁנֵים־

45 the Sea; pots, shovels, and basins. All these vessels, which Ḥiram crafted for
46 King Shlomo, for the House of the LORD, were of burnished bronze. The king
had them cast in clay molds on the Jordan plain between Sukkot and Tzartan.
47 Due to their sheer abundance, Shlomo left all the vessels out of account; the
48 weight of the bronze was not determined. Shlomo made all the vessels for
the House of the LORD: the altar was of gold, and the table for the showbread
49 was of gold. The candelabra – five on the right and five on the left, in front of
the Inner Sanctuary – were of solid gold; the flowers, the lamps, and the tongs
50 were all of gold. The bowls, shears, basins, spoons, and firepans were of solid
gold. The hinges of the doors to the inner House, to the Holy of Holies, and
51 of the doors of the House to the Sanctuary, were of gold. When all
the work that King Shlomo did for the House of the LORD was finished,
Shlomo brought what David his father had dedicated – the silver, the gold,
and the vessels[20] – and placed them in the treasury of the House of the
8 1 LORD. Then Shlomo assembled the elders of Israel – all the heads
of the tribes, the ancestral leaders of the Israelites – before King Shlomo in
Jerusalem, to bring up the Ark of the LORD's Covenant from the City of David,
2 Zion. All the men of Israel assembled before King Shlomo in the month of
3 Etanim,[21] the seventh month, at the festival.[22] When all the elders of Israel had
4 arrived, the priests lifted up the Ark and brought up the Ark of the LORD, the
Tent of Meeting, and all the sacred vessels in the Tent. While the priests and
5 the Levites brought them up, King Shlomo and the whole community of
Israel, who had met him before the Ark, sacrificed sheep and oxen – far
6 too many to number or count. The priests brought the Ark of the LORD's
Covenant to its place – to the House's Inner Sanctuary, the Holy of Holies, to
7 under the shade of the wings of the cherubim. For the wings of the cherubim
were spread over the place of the Ark so that the cherubim sheltered the Ark
8 and its poles from above. The poles extended so that the ends of the poles
were visible from the Holy Place[23] in front of the Inner Sanctuary, but they
9 could not be seen from the outside, and they are there to this day. The Ark
contained nothing but the two stone tablets Moshe placed there at Ḥorev
when the LORD made a covenant with the Israelites as they left the land of
10 Egypt.[24] And as the priests left the Holy Place, a cloud filled the House of the
11 LORD; the priests could not stand and serve because of the cloud, for the
12 glory of the LORD had filled the House of the LORD. Then Shlomo
13 declared: "The LORD promised that He would dwell in deep mist; I have now
14 built You an exalted House, a permanent place for Your abode." And the king
turned his face and blessed the whole assembly of Israel, while the whole
15 assembly of Israel stood. "Blessed is the LORD, God of Israel," he said, "who
made a promise to my father David with His own mouth and has now

---

20 | See II Samuel 8:9–12.
21 | The seventh month, known by Jews as Tishrei after the Babylonian exile.
22 | The Festival of Tabernacles; cf. Leviticus 23:34.
23 | The main Sanctuary.
24 | See Deuteronomy 10:1–5.

מה עֶשֶׂר תַּחַת הַיָּם׃ וְאֶת־הַסִּירוֹת וְאֶת־הַיָּעִים וְאֶת־הַמִּזְרָקוֹת וְאֵת
כָּל־הַכֵּלִים הָאֹהֶל אֲשֶׁר עָשָׂה חִירָם לַמֶּלֶךְ שְׁלֹמֹה בֵּית יְהוָה נְחֹשֶׁת הָאֵלֶּה
מו מְמֹרָט׃ בְּכִכַּר הַיַּרְדֵּן יְצָקָם הַמֶּלֶךְ בְּמַעֲבֵה הָאֲדָמָה בֵּין סֻכּוֹת וּבֵין
מז צָרְתָן׃ וַיַּנַּח שְׁלֹמֹה אֶת־כָּל־הַכֵּלִים מֵרֹב מְאֹד מְאֹד לֹא נֶחְקַר מִשְׁקַל
מח הַנְּחֹשֶׁת׃ וַיַּעַשׂ שְׁלֹמֹה אֵת כָּל־הַכֵּלִים אֲשֶׁר בֵּית יְהוָה אֵת מִזְבַּח
מט הַזָּהָב וְאֶת־הַשֻּׁלְחָן אֲשֶׁר עָלָיו לֶחֶם הַפָּנִים זָהָב׃ וְאֶת־הַמְּנֹרוֹת
חָמֵשׁ מִיָּמִין וְחָמֵשׁ מִשְּׂמֹאל לִפְנֵי הַדְּבִיר זָהָב סָגוּר וְהַפֶּרַח וְהַנֵּרֹת
נ וְהַמֶּלְקָחַיִם זָהָב׃ וְהַסִּפּוֹת וְהַמְזַמְּרוֹת וְהַמִּזְרָקוֹת וְהַכַּפּוֹת וְהַמַּחְתּוֹת
זָהָב סָגוּר וְהַפֹּתוֹת לְדַלְתוֹת הַבַּיִת הַפְּנִימִי לְקֹדֶשׁ הַקֳּדָשִׁים לְדַלְתֵי
נא הַבַּיִת לְהֵיכָל זָהָב׃ וַתִּשְׁלַם כָּל־הַמְּלָאכָה אֲשֶׁר עָשָׂה
הַמֶּלֶךְ שְׁלֹמֹה בֵּית יְהוָה וַיָּבֵא שְׁלֹמֹה אֶת־קָדְשֵׁי ׀ דָּוִד אָבִיו אֶת־
ח א הַכֶּסֶף וְאֶת־הַזָּהָב וְאֶת־הַכֵּלִים נָתַן בְּאֹצְרוֹת בֵּית יְהוָה׃ אָז
יַקְהֵל שְׁלֹמֹה אֶת־זִקְנֵי יִשְׂרָאֵל אֶת־כָּל־רָאשֵׁי הַמַּטּוֹת נְשִׂיאֵי הָאָבוֹת
לִבְנֵי יִשְׂרָאֵל אֶל־הַמֶּלֶךְ שְׁלֹמֹה יְרוּשָׁלָםִ לְהַעֲלוֹת אֶת־אֲרוֹן בְּרִית־
ב יְהוָה מֵעִיר דָּוִד הִיא צִיּוֹן׃ וַיִּקָּהֲלוּ אֶל־הַמֶּלֶךְ שְׁלֹמֹה כָּל־אִישׁ יִשְׂרָאֵל
ג בְּיֶרַח הָאֵתָנִים בֶּחָג הוּא הַחֹדֶשׁ הַשְּׁבִיעִי׃ וַיָּבֹאוּ כֹּל זִקְנֵי יִשְׂרָאֵל
ד וַיִּשְׂאוּ הַכֹּהֲנִים אֶת־הָאָרוֹן׃ וַיַּעֲלוּ אֶת־אֲרוֹן יְהוָה וְאֶת־אֹהֶל מוֹעֵד
וְאֶת־כָּל־כְּלֵי הַקֹּדֶשׁ אֲשֶׁר בָּאֹהֶל וַיַּעֲלוּ אֹתָם הַכֹּהֲנִים וְהַלְוִיִּם׃
ה וְהַמֶּלֶךְ שְׁלֹמֹה וְכָל־עֲדַת יִשְׂרָאֵל הַנּוֹעָדִים עָלָיו אִתּוֹ לִפְנֵי הָאָרוֹן
ו מְזַבְּחִים צֹאן וּבָקָר אֲשֶׁר לֹא־יִסָּפְרוּ וְלֹא יִמָּנוּ מֵרֹב׃ וַיָּבִאוּ הַכֹּהֲנִים
אֶת־אֲרוֹן בְּרִית־יְהוָה אֶל־מְקוֹמוֹ אֶל־דְּבִיר הַבַּיִת אֶל־קֹדֶשׁ הַקֳּדָשִׁים
ז אֶל־תַּחַת כַּנְפֵי הַכְּרוּבִים׃ כִּי הַכְּרוּבִים פֹּרְשִׂים כְּנָפַיִם אֶל־מְקוֹם
ח הָאָרוֹן וַיָּסֹכּוּ הַכְּרֻבִים עַל־הָאָרוֹן וְעַל־בַּדָּיו מִלְמָעְלָה׃ וַיַּאֲרִכוּ הַבַּדִּים
וַיֵּרָאוּ רָאשֵׁי הַבַּדִּים מִן־הַקֹּדֶשׁ עַל־פְּנֵי הַדְּבִיר וְלֹא יֵרָאוּ הַחוּצָה
ט וַיִּהְיוּ שָׁם עַד הַיּוֹם הַזֶּה׃ אֵין בָּאָרוֹן רַק שְׁנֵי לֻחוֹת הָאֲבָנִים אֲשֶׁר
הִנִּחַ שָׁם מֹשֶׁה בְּחֹרֵב אֲשֶׁר כָּרַת יְהוָה עִם־בְּנֵי יִשְׂרָאֵל בְּצֵאתָם
י מֵאֶרֶץ מִצְרָיִם׃ וַיְהִי בְּצֵאת הַכֹּהֲנִים מִן־הַקֹּדֶשׁ וְהֶעָנָן מָלֵא אֶת־בֵּית
יא יְהוָה׃ וְלֹא־יָכְלוּ הַכֹּהֲנִים לַעֲמֹד לְשָׁרֵת מִפְּנֵי הֶעָנָן כִּי־מָלֵא כְבוֹד־ ז
יב יְהוָה אֶת־בֵּית יְהוָה׃ אָז אָמַר שְׁלֹמֹה יְהוָה אָמַר
יג יד לִשְׁכֹּן בָּעֲרָפֶל׃ בָּנֹה בָנִיתִי בֵּית זְבֻל לָךְ מָכוֹן לְשִׁבְתְּךָ עוֹלָמִים׃ וַיַּסֵּב
הַמֶּלֶךְ אֶת־פָּנָיו וַיְבָרֶךְ אֵת כָּל־קְהַל יִשְׂרָאֵל וְכָל־קְהַל יִשְׂרָאֵל עֹמֵד׃
טו וַיֹּאמֶר בָּרוּךְ יְהוָה אֱלֹהֵי יִשְׂרָאֵל אֲשֶׁר דִּבֶּר בְּפִיו אֵת דָּוִד אָבִי וּבְיָדוֹ

16 fulfilled it with His own hand, saying: From the day I brought My people,
Israel, out of Egypt, I never chose a city from among all the tribes of Israel, to
build a House where My name would be; but I chose David to be over My
17 people Israel.[25] My father David had his heart set on building a House for the
18 name of the LORD, God of Israel. But the LORD said to my father David:
Though you have set your heart on building a House for My name, and
19 though you have set your heart well, you will not be the one to build the
House. But your son, the issue of your own loins – he will be the one to build
20 the House for My name.[26] The LORD has fulfilled the promise He made; I
have risen in my father's stead, and I sit upon Israel's throne, as the LORD
promised. I have built the House for the name of the LORD, God of Israel.
21 And there I have set a place for the Ark, which contains the covenant that the
LORD made with our ancestors when He brought them out of the land of
22 Egypt." Shlomo stood before the Altar of the LORD, facing the whole
23 assembly of Israel, and he raised his palms heavenward. "O LORD, God of
Israel," he cried, "there is no God like You in the heavens above or the earth
below. O keeper of the covenant and the love for Your servants, who walk
24 before You with all their heart, You kept what You promised to my father
David; You made him a promise with Your own mouth, and You have fulfilled
25 it with Your own hand this very day. Now, O LORD, God of Israel, keep the
promise You made to Your servant David, my father, saying, 'No one of your
lineage shall be cut off from sitting on the throne of Israel before Me, but only
26 if your sons keep to their path before Me as you walked before Me.' Now, O
God of Israel, let the promise You made to Your servant David, my father, be
27 realized. For will God truly dwell on earth? If the heavens – the highest
28 heavens – cannot contain You, how will this House that I have built? Yet –
turn to the prayer of Your servant, O LORD my God, and to his plea; listen to
29 the cry and the prayer your servant offers before you today. Let Your eyes be
open to this House, night and day; to the place of which You said, 'There, My
30 name will be.' Listen to the prayer Your servant offers at this place. Listen to
the plea of Your servant; of Your people, Israel, who pray at this place; Listen
31 from Your heavenly abode; listen and forgive. Should a person wrong another
who then imposes an oath upon him and he thus becomes cursed, and he
32 comes before Your altar in this House with the curse – listen from
the heavens, take action, and judge Your servant. Condemn the wicked by
bringing his own ways upon his own head, and vindicate the righteous by
33 rewarding him as befits his righteousness. Should Your people Israel
be defeated by an enemy because they have sinned against You, and they
come back to You, acknowledging Your name in prayer and pleading to You
34 in this House – listen from the heavens, forgive the sin of Your people Israel,

25 | See II Samuel 7:6–7.
26 | See II Samuel 7:12–13.

טז מִלֵּא לֵאמֹר: מִן־הַיּוֹם אֲשֶׁר הוֹצֵאתִי אֶת־עַמִּי אֶת־יִשְׂרָאֵל מִמִּצְרַיִם
לֹא־בָחַרְתִּי בְעִיר מִכֹּל שִׁבְטֵי יִשְׂרָאֵל לִבְנוֹת בַּיִת לִהְיוֹת שְׁמִי שָׁם
יז וָאֶבְחַר בְּדָוִד לִהְיוֹת עַל־עַמִּי יִשְׂרָאֵל: וַיְהִי עִם־לְבַב דָּוִד אָבִי לִבְנוֹת
יח בַּיִת לְשֵׁם יהוה אֱלֹהֵי יִשְׂרָאֵל: וַיֹּאמֶר יהוה אֶל־דָּוִד אָבִי יַעַן אֲשֶׁר
יט הָיָה עִם־לְבָבְךָ לִבְנוֹת בַּיִת לִשְׁמִי הֱטִיבֹתָ כִּי הָיָה עִם־לְבָבֶךָ: רַק
אַתָּה לֹא תִבְנֶה הַבָּיִת כִּי אִם־בִּנְךָ הַיֹּצֵא מֵחֲלָצֶיךָ הוּא־יִבְנֶה הַבַּיִת
כ לִשְׁמִי: וַיָּקֶם יהוה אֶת־דְּבָרוֹ אֲשֶׁר דִּבֵּר וָאָקֻם תַּחַת דָּוִד אָבִי וָאֵשֵׁב ׀
עַל־כִּסֵּא יִשְׂרָאֵל כַּאֲשֶׁר דִּבֶּר יהוה וָאֶבְנֶה הַבַּיִת לְשֵׁם יהוה אֱלֹהֵי
כא יִשְׂרָאֵל: וָאָשִׂם שָׁם מָקוֹם לָאָרוֹן אֲשֶׁר־שָׁם בְּרִית יהוה אֲשֶׁר כָּרַת
כב עִם־אֲבֹתֵינוּ בְּהוֹצִיאוֹ אֹתָם מֵאֶרֶץ מִצְרָיִם: וַיַּעֲמֹד
שְׁלֹמֹה לִפְנֵי מִזְבַּח יהוה נֶגֶד כָּל־קְהַל יִשְׂרָאֵל וַיִּפְרֹשׂ כַּפָּיו הַשָּׁמָיִם:
כג וַיֹּאמַר יהוה אֱלֹהֵי יִשְׂרָאֵל אֵין־כָּמוֹךָ אֱלֹהִים בַּשָּׁמַיִם מִמַּעַל וְעַל־
הָאָרֶץ מִתָּחַת שֹׁמֵר הַבְּרִית וְהַחֶסֶד לַעֲבָדֶיךָ הַהֹלְכִים לְפָנֶיךָ בְּכָל־
כד לִבָּם: אֲשֶׁר שָׁמַרְתָּ לְעַבְדְּךָ דָּוִד אָבִי אֵת אֲשֶׁר־דִּבַּרְתָּ לוֹ וַתְּדַבֵּר בְּפִיךָ
כה וּבְיָדְךָ מִלֵּאתָ כַּיּוֹם הַזֶּה: וְעַתָּה יהוה ׀ אֱלֹהֵי יִשְׂרָאֵל שְׁמֹר לְעַבְדְּךָ
דָוִד אָבִי אֵת אֲשֶׁר דִּבַּרְתָּ לּוֹ לֵאמֹר לֹא־יִכָּרֵת לְךָ אִישׁ מִלְּפָנַי יֹשֵׁב
עַל־כִּסֵּא יִשְׂרָאֵל רַק אִם־יִשְׁמְרוּ בָנֶיךָ אֶת־דַּרְכָּם לָלֶכֶת לְפָנַי כַּאֲשֶׁר
כו הָלַכְתָּ לְפָנָי: וְעַתָּה אֱלֹהֵי יִשְׂרָאֵל יֵאָמֶן נָא דבריך אֲשֶׁר דִּבַּרְתָּ דְּבָרְךָ
כז לְעַבְדְּךָ דָּוִד אָבִי: כִּי הַאֻמְנָם יֵשֵׁב אֱלֹהִים עַל־הָאָרֶץ הִנֵּה הַשָּׁמַיִם
כח וּשְׁמֵי הַשָּׁמַיִם לֹא יְכַלְכְּלוּךָ אַף כִּי־הַבַּיִת הַזֶּה אֲשֶׁר בָּנִיתִי: וּפָנִיתָ
אֶל־תְּפִלַּת עַבְדְּךָ וְאֶל־תְּחִנָּתוֹ יהוה אֱלֹהָי לִשְׁמֹעַ אֶל־הָרִנָּה וְאֶל־
כט הַתְּפִלָּה אֲשֶׁר עַבְדְּךָ מִתְפַּלֵּל לְפָנֶיךָ הַיּוֹם: לִהְיוֹת עֵינֶךָ פְתֻחֹת
אֶל־הַבַּיִת הַזֶּה לַיְלָה וָיוֹם אֶל־הַמָּקוֹם אֲשֶׁר אָמַרְתָּ יִהְיֶה שְׁמִי שָׁם
ל לִשְׁמֹעַ אֶל־הַתְּפִלָּה אֲשֶׁר יִתְפַּלֵּל עַבְדְּךָ אֶל־הַמָּקוֹם הַזֶּה: וְשָׁמַעְתָּ
אֶל־תְּחִנַּת עַבְדְּךָ וְעַמְּךָ יִשְׂרָאֵל אֲשֶׁר יִתְפַּלְלוּ אֶל־הַמָּקוֹם הַזֶּה
לא וְאַתָּה תִּשְׁמַע אֶל־מְקוֹם שִׁבְתְּךָ אֶל־הַשָּׁמַיִם וְשָׁמַעְתָּ וְסָלָחְתָּ: אֵת
אֲשֶׁר יֶחֱטָא אִישׁ לְרֵעֵהוּ וְנָשָׁא־בוֹ אָלָה לְהַאֲלֹתוֹ וּבָא אָלָה לִפְנֵי
לב מִזְבַּחֲךָ בַּבַּיִת הַזֶּה: וְאַתָּה ׀ תִּשְׁמַע הַשָּׁמַיִם וְעָשִׂיתָ וְשָׁפַטְתָּ אֶת־
עֲבָדֶיךָ לְהַרְשִׁיעַ רָשָׁע לָתֵת דַּרְכּוֹ בְּרֹאשׁוֹ וּלְהַצְדִּיק צַדִּיק לָתֶת לוֹ
לג כְּצִדְקָתוֹ: בְּהִנָּגֵף עַמְּךָ יִשְׂרָאֵל לִפְנֵי אוֹיֵב אֲשֶׁר יֶחֶטְאוּ־
לָךְ וְשָׁבוּ אֵלֶיךָ וְהוֹדוּ אֶת־שְׁמֶךָ וְהִתְפַּלְלוּ וְהִתְחַנְּנוּ אֵלֶיךָ בַּבַּיִת הַזֶּה:
לד וְאַתָּה תִּשְׁמַע הַשָּׁמַיִם וְסָלַחְתָּ לְחַטַּאת עַמְּךָ יִשְׂרָאֵל וַהֲשֵׁבֹתָם

35 and bring them back to the land You gave to their ancestors. When
the heavens are stopped up and there is no rain because they have sinned
against You, and they pray at this place and acknowledge Your name, repenting
36 from their sins so that You will answer them – listen from the heavens and
forgive the sin of Your servants and Your people Israel, having taught them
the proper path to follow. Shower rain upon the land You gave to Your people
37 as their share. Should there be famine in the land; should there be
sickness; should there be blight, mildew, locust, or larvae; should the enemy
harass them in the land within their own gates – oh, any suffering, or any
38 disease! – and anyone from Your people, Israel, offers any prayer or any plea,
moved by the suffering of his own heart, and raises his palms toward this
39 House – listen from Your heavenly abode, forgive, and take action. Treat each
person according to his ways, for You know his heart – for You alone know
40 the hearts of all humanity – so that they will revere You for as long as they
41 live upon the soil that You gave to our ancestors. Should the
foreigner, too, not of Your people Israel, come from a distant land for the sake
42 of Your name, having heard of Your great name and Your mighty hand and
43 Your outstretched arm; should he come and pray at this House, listen from
Your heavenly abode and fulfill all that the foreigner calls out to You. For then
all the peoples of the land will know Your name and revere you as Your people
Israel does; for then they will know that it is Your name that is proclaimed
44 over this House. Should Your people go out to war against their
enemy, wherever You might send them, and they pray to the LORD toward
45 the city You have chosen and the House I built for Your name, listen from
46 the heavens to their prayer and plea, and uphold their cause. Should they sin
against You – for there is no person who does not sin – and You rage against
them and deliver them over to their enemy, who drags them off as captives
47 to the enemy's land, whether far or near, but they take it to heart in the land
where they are being held captive, and they repent and offer pleas to You in
the land of their captors, declaring, 'We have sinned and offended and done
48 evil,' and they come back to You with all their heart and all their soul in the
land of their enemy captors, and they pray to You, toward their own land
which You gave to their ancestors, to the city that You chose and the House
49 I built for Your name, listen from Your heavenly abode to their prayer and
50 their plea, and uphold their cause. Forgive Your people who sinned against
You, and all the transgressions they committed against You; grant them mercy
51 before their captors so that they will have mercy on them. For they are Your
people and Your share, whom You brought out from Egypt, from the midst
52 of the iron crucible.[27] Let Your eyes be open to the plea of Your servant and
the plea of Your people Israel; listen to them whenever they call out to You.
53 For You set them apart from all the other peoples of the land as Your own

27 | Cf. Deuteronomy 4:20; Jeremiah 11:4.

לה אֶל־הָאֲדָמָה אֲשֶׁר נָתַתָּ לַאֲבוֹתָם׃ בְּהֵעָצֵר שָׁמַיִם
וְלֹא־יִהְיֶה מָטָר כִּי יֶחֶטְאוּ־לָךְ וְהִתְפַּלְלוּ אֶל־הַמָּקוֹם הַזֶּה וְהוֹדוּ
לו אֶת־שְׁמֶךָ וּמֵחַטָּאתָם יְשׁוּבוּן כִּי תַעֲנֵם׃ וְאַתָּה ׀ תִּשְׁמַע הַשָּׁמַיִם
וְסָלַחְתָּ לְחַטַּאת עֲבָדֶיךָ וְעַמְּךָ יִשְׂרָאֵל כִּי תוֹרֵם אֶת־הַדֶּרֶךְ הַטּוֹבָה
אֲשֶׁר יֵלְכוּ־בָהּ וְנָתַתָּה מָטָר עַל־אַרְצְךָ אֲשֶׁר־נָתַתָּה לְעַמְּךָ
לז לְנַחֲלָה׃ רָעָב כִּי־יִהְיֶה בָאָרֶץ דֶּבֶר כִּי־יִהְיֶה שִׁדָּפוֹן יֵרָקוֹן
אַרְבֶּה חָסִיל כִּי יִהְיֶה כִּי יָצַר־לוֹ אֹיְבוֹ בְּאֶרֶץ שְׁעָרָיו כָּל־נֶגַע כָּל־
לח מַחֲלָה׃ כָּל־תְּפִלָּה כָל־תְּחִנָּה אֲשֶׁר תִהְיֶה לְכָל־הָאָדָם לְכֹל עַמְּךָ
לט יִשְׂרָאֵל אֲשֶׁר יֵדְעוּן אִישׁ נֶגַע לְבָבוֹ וּפָרַשׂ כַּפָּיו אֶל־הַבַּיִת הַזֶּה׃ וְאַתָּה
תִּשְׁמַע הַשָּׁמַיִם מְכוֹן שִׁבְתֶּךָ וְסָלַחְתָּ וְעָשִׂיתָ וְנָתַתָּ לָאִישׁ כְּכָל־דְּרָכָיו
אֲשֶׁר תֵּדַע אֶת־לְבָבוֹ כִּי־אַתָּה יָדַעְתָּ לְבַדְּךָ אֶת־לְבַב כָּל־בְּנֵי הָאָדָם׃
מ לְמַעַן יִרָאוּךָ כָּל־הַיָּמִים אֲשֶׁר־הֵם חַיִּים עַל־פְּנֵי הָאֲדָמָה אֲשֶׁר נָתַתָּה
מא לַאֲבֹתֵינוּ׃ וְגַם אֶל־הַנָּכְרִי אֲשֶׁר לֹא־מֵעַמְּךָ יִשְׂרָאֵל הוּא
מב וּבָא מֵאֶרֶץ רְחוֹקָה לְמַעַן שְׁמֶךָ׃ כִּי יִשְׁמְעוּן אֶת־שִׁמְךָ הַגָּדוֹל וְאֶת־
מג יָדְךָ הַחֲזָקָה וּזְרֹעֲךָ הַנְּטוּיָה וּבָא וְהִתְפַּלֵּל אֶל־הַבַּיִת הַזֶּה׃ אַתָּה
תִּשְׁמַע הַשָּׁמַיִם מְכוֹן שִׁבְתֶּךָ וְעָשִׂיתָ כְּכֹל אֲשֶׁר־יִקְרָא אֵלֶיךָ הַנָּכְרִי
לְמַעַן יֵדְעוּן כָּל־עַמֵּי הָאָרֶץ אֶת־שְׁמֶךָ לְיִרְאָה אֹתְךָ כְּעַמְּךָ יִשְׂרָאֵל
מד וְלָדַעַת כִּי־שִׁמְךָ נִקְרָא עַל־הַבַּיִת הַזֶּה אֲשֶׁר בָּנִיתִי׃ כִּי־
יֵצֵא עַמְּךָ לַמִּלְחָמָה עַל־אֹיְבוֹ בַּדֶּרֶךְ אֲשֶׁר תִּשְׁלָחֵם וְהִתְפַּלְלוּ אֶל־
מה יְהוָה דֶּרֶךְ הָעִיר אֲשֶׁר בָּחַרְתָּ בָּהּ וְהַבַּיִת אֲשֶׁר־בָּנִתִי לִשְׁמֶךָ׃ וְשָׁמַעְתָּ
מו הַשָּׁמַיִם אֶת־תְּפִלָּתָם וְאֶת־תְּחִנָּתָם וְעָשִׂיתָ מִשְׁפָּטָם׃ כִּי יֶחֶטְאוּ־לָךְ
כִּי אֵין אָדָם אֲשֶׁר לֹא־יֶחֱטָא וְאָנַפְתָּ בָם וּנְתַתָּם לִפְנֵי אוֹיֵב וְשָׁבוּם
מז שֹׁבֵיהֶם אֶל־אֶרֶץ הָאוֹיֵב רְחוֹקָה אוֹ קְרוֹבָה׃ וְהֵשִׁיבוּ אֶל־לִבָּם בָּאָרֶץ
אֲשֶׁר נִשְׁבּוּ־שָׁם וְשָׁבוּ ׀ וְהִתְחַנְּנוּ אֵלֶיךָ בְּאֶרֶץ שֹׁבֵיהֶם לֵאמֹר חָטָאנוּ
מח וְהֶעֱוִינוּ רָשָׁעְנוּ׃ וְשָׁבוּ אֵלֶיךָ בְּכָל־לְבָבָם וּבְכָל־נַפְשָׁם בְּאֶרֶץ אֹיְבֵיהֶם
אֲשֶׁר־שָׁבוּ אֹתָם וְהִתְפַּלְלוּ אֵלֶיךָ דֶּרֶךְ אַרְצָם אֲשֶׁר־נָתַתָּה לַאֲבוֹתָם
מט הָעִיר אֲשֶׁר בָּחַרְתָּ וְהַבַּיִת אֲשֶׁר־בָּנִיתִ לִשְׁמֶךָ׃ וְשָׁמַעְתָּ הַשָּׁמַיִם מְכוֹן
נ שִׁבְתְּךָ אֶת־תְּפִלָּתָם וְאֶת־תְּחִנָּתָם וְעָשִׂיתָ מִשְׁפָּטָם׃ וְסָלַחְתָּ לְעַמְּךָ
אֲשֶׁר חָטְאוּ־לָךְ וּלְכָל־פִּשְׁעֵיהֶם אֲשֶׁר פָּשְׁעוּ־בָךְ וּנְתַתָּם לְרַחֲמִים
נא לִפְנֵי שֹׁבֵיהֶם וְרִחֲמוּם׃ כִּי־עַמְּךָ וְנַחֲלָתְךָ הֵם אֲשֶׁר הוֹצֵאתָ מִמִּצְרַיִם
נב מִתּוֹךְ כּוּר הַבַּרְזֶל׃ לִהְיוֹת עֵינֶיךָ פְתֻחוֹת אֶל־תְּחִנַּת עַבְדְּךָ וְאֶל־
נג תְּחִנַּת עַמְּךָ יִשְׂרָאֵל לִשְׁמֹעַ אֲלֵיהֶם בְּכֹל קָרְאָם אֵלֶיךָ׃ כִּי־אַתָּה

share,[28] as You promised through Moshe, Your servant, when You brought
54 our ancestors out of Egypt, O LORD GOD." When Shlomo had
finished offering the whole of this prayer and plea to the LORD, he rose from
before the Altar of the LORD, where he had been kneeling on his knees with
55 his palms raised heavenward. And he stood and blessed the whole assembly
56 of Israel in a loud voice: "Blessed is the LORD, who has granted rest to His
people Israel, fulfilling all His promises," he said. "Not one thing is unfulfilled
57 from all the good promises He made through Moshe, His servant. May the
LORD our God be with us as He was with our ancestors; may He never
58 leave us or abandon us. May He sway our hearts toward Him so that we
follow in all His ways and keep His commandments, laws and rulings that He
59 commanded our ancestors. May these words of mine, which I have pleaded
before the LORD, stay close to the LORD our God day and night, to uphold
the cause of His servant and the cause of His people Israel as each day's needs
60 arise – so that all the peoples of the land will know that the LORD is God, and
61 there is no other. May your hearts be fully with the LORD our God, following
62 His laws and keeping His commandments, as today." And the king, together
63 with all of Israel, offered sacrifices before the LORD; Shlomo sacrificed the
peace sacrifices he offered to the LORD – twenty-two thousand cattle and one
hundred twenty thousand sheep – and thus the king and all of Israel
64 dedicated the House of the LORD. On that day, the king consecrated the
center of the courtyard in front of the House of the LORD, for it was there
that he prepared the burnt offering, the grain offering, and the fats of the
peace offerings. The bronze altar before the LORD was too small to contain
65 the burnt offering, the grain offering, and the fats of the peace offerings. At
that same time, Shlomo celebrated the festival[29] together with all of Israel;
they were a great assembly, from Levo Ḥamat to the Wadi of Egypt,[30] before
the LORD our God for seven days and seven days more – fourteen days in all.[31]
66 On the eighth day[32] he sent the people off, and they blessed the king; they
went back to their homes joyful and glad at heart for all the goodness the
9 1 LORD had shown to David, His servant, and Israel, His people. When
Shlomo had finished building the House of the LORD and the king's own
2 house, and fulfilled every desire he wished to fulfill, the LORD
3 appeared to Shlomo a second time as He had appeared to him at Givon.[33] And
the LORD said to him, "I have listened to the prayer and the plea that you
offered before Me. I have consecrated this House, which you built to set My
4 name there forever; My eyes and My heart will be there for all time. As for
you – if you walk before Me as your father David did, wholeheartedly and
sincerely fulfilling all I have commanded you, and if you keep My laws and

28 | Cf. Leviticus 20:24, 26.
29 | See note on verse 2.
30 | The northern and southern borders of the country.
31 | One week for the dedication of the altar and one week for the Festival of Tabernacles; cf. II Chronicles 7:9.
32 | Cf. II Chronicles 7:9–10.
33 | See 3:4–15.

הִבְדַּלְתָּם לְךָ לְנַחֲלָה מִכֹּל עַמֵּי הָאָרֶץ כַּאֲשֶׁר דִּבַּרְתָּ בְּיַד ׀ מֹשֶׁה
עַבְדֶּךָ בְּהוֹצִיאֲךָ אֶת־אֲבֹתֵינוּ מִמִּצְרַיִם אֲדֹנָי יְהוִה: וַיְהִי ׀ נד
כְּכַלּוֹת שְׁלֹמֹה לְהִתְפַּלֵּל אֶל־יְהוָה אֵת כָּל־הַתְּפִלָּה וְהַתְּחִנָּה הַזֹּאת
קָם מִלִּפְנֵי מִזְבַּח יְהוָה מִכְּרֹעַ עַל־בִּרְכָּיו וְכַפָּיו פְּרֻשׂוֹת הַשָּׁמָיִם: וַיַּעֲמֹד נה
וַיְבָרֶךְ אֵת כָּל־קְהַל יִשְׂרָאֵל קוֹל גָּדוֹל לֵאמֹר: בָּרוּךְ יְהוָה אֲשֶׁר נָתַן נו
מְנוּחָה לְעַמּוֹ יִשְׂרָאֵל כְּכֹל אֲשֶׁר דִּבֵּר לֹא־נָפַל דָּבָר אֶחָד מִכֹּל דְּבָרוֹ
הַטּוֹב אֲשֶׁר דִּבֶּר בְּיַד מֹשֶׁה עַבְדּוֹ: יְהִי יְהוָה אֱלֹהֵינוּ עִמָּנוּ כַּאֲשֶׁר נז
הָיָה עִם־אֲבֹתֵינוּ אַל־יַעַזְבֵנוּ וְאַל־יִטְּשֵׁנוּ: לְהַטּוֹת לְבָבֵנוּ אֵלָיו לָלֶכֶת נח ח
בְּכָל־דְּרָכָיו וְלִשְׁמֹר מִצְוֹתָיו וְחֻקָּיו וּמִשְׁפָּטָיו אֲשֶׁר צִוָּה אֶת־אֲבֹתֵינוּ:
וְיִהְיוּ דְבָרַי אֵלֶּה אֲשֶׁר הִתְחַנַּנְתִּי לִפְנֵי יְהוָה קְרֹבִים אֶל־יְהוָה אֱלֹהֵינוּ נט
יוֹמָם וָלָיְלָה לַעֲשׂוֹת ׀ מִשְׁפַּט עַבְדּוֹ וּמִשְׁפַּט עַמּוֹ יִשְׂרָאֵל דְּבַר־יוֹם
בְּיוֹמוֹ: לְמַעַן דַּעַת כָּל־עַמֵּי הָאָרֶץ כִּי יְהוָה הוּא הָאֱלֹהִים אֵין עוֹד: ס
וְהָיָה לְבַבְכֶם שָׁלֵם עִם יְהוָה אֱלֹהֵינוּ לָלֶכֶת בְּחֻקָּיו וְלִשְׁמֹר מִצְוֹתָיו סא
כַּיּוֹם הַזֶּה: וְהַמֶּלֶךְ וְכָל־יִשְׂרָאֵל עִמּוֹ זֹבְחִים זֶבַח לִפְנֵי יְהוָה: וַיִּזְבַּח סב סג
שְׁלֹמֹה אֵת זֶבַח הַשְּׁלָמִים אֲשֶׁר זָבַח לַיהוָה בָּקָר עֶשְׂרִים וּשְׁנַיִם
אֶלֶף וְצֹאן מֵאָה וְעֶשְׂרִים אָלֶף וַיַּחְנְכוּ אֶת־בֵּית יְהוָה הַמֶּלֶךְ וְכָל־בְּנֵי
יִשְׂרָאֵל: בַּיּוֹם הַהוּא קִדַּשׁ הַמֶּלֶךְ אֶת־תּוֹךְ הֶחָצֵר אֲשֶׁר לִפְנֵי בֵית־ סד
יְהוָה כִּי־עָשָׂה שָׁם אֶת־הָעֹלָה וְאֶת־הַמִּנְחָה וְאֵת חֶלְבֵי הַשְּׁלָמִים
כִּי־מִזְבַּח הַנְּחֹשֶׁת אֲשֶׁר לִפְנֵי יְהוָה קָטֹן מֵהָכִיל אֶת־הָעֹלָה וְאֶת־
הַמִּנְחָה וְאֵת חֶלְבֵי הַשְּׁלָמִים: וַיַּעַשׂ שְׁלֹמֹה בָעֵת־הַהִיא ׀ אֶת־הֶחָג סה
וְכָל־יִשְׂרָאֵל עִמּוֹ קָהָל גָּדוֹל מִלְּבוֹא חֲמָת ׀ עַד־נַחַל מִצְרַיִם לִפְנֵי
יְהוָה אֱלֹהֵינוּ שִׁבְעַת יָמִים וְשִׁבְעַת יָמִים אַרְבָּעָה עָשָׂר יוֹם: בַּיּוֹם סו
הַשְּׁמִינִי שִׁלַּח אֶת־הָעָם וַיְבָרְכוּ אֶת־הַמֶּלֶךְ וַיֵּלְכוּ לְאָהֳלֵיהֶם שְׂמֵחִים
וְטוֹבֵי לֵב עַל כָּל־הַטּוֹבָה אֲשֶׁר עָשָׂה יְהוָה לְדָוִד עַבְדּוֹ וּלְיִשְׂרָאֵל
עַמּוֹ: וַיְהִי כְּכַלּוֹת שְׁלֹמֹה לִבְנוֹת אֶת־בֵּית־יְהוָה וְאֶת־בֵּית ט א
הַמֶּלֶךְ וְאֵת כָּל־חֵשֶׁק שְׁלֹמֹה אֲשֶׁר חָפֵץ לַעֲשׂוֹת: וַיֵּרָא ב
יְהוָה אֶל־שְׁלֹמֹה שֵׁנִית כַּאֲשֶׁר נִרְאָה אֵלָיו בְּגִבְעוֹן: וַיֹּאמֶר יְהוָה ג
אֵלָיו שָׁמַעְתִּי אֶת־תְּפִלָּתְךָ וְאֶת־תְּחִנָּתְךָ אֲשֶׁר הִתְחַנַּנְתָּה לְפָנַי
הִקְדַּשְׁתִּי אֶת־הַבַּיִת הַזֶּה אֲשֶׁר בָּנִתָה לָשׂוּם־שְׁמִי שָׁם עַד־עוֹלָם
וְהָיוּ עֵינַי וְלִבִּי שָׁם כָּל־הַיָּמִים: וְאַתָּה אִם־תֵּלֵךְ לְפָנַי כַּאֲשֶׁר הָלַךְ דָּוִד ד
אָבִיךָ בְּתָם־לֵבָב וּבְיֹשֶׁר לַעֲשׂוֹת כְּכֹל אֲשֶׁר צִוִּיתִיךָ חֻקַּי וּמִשְׁפָּטַי

5 My rulings, then I will establish your royal throne over Israel forever, as I
promised your father David: No one of your lineage will be cut off from the
6 throne of Israel. But if you and your sons dare turn away from Me and do not
keep the commandments and laws I set before you, and serve other gods and
7 worship them, then I will cut Israel off from the face of the land that I gave
them, and I will cast away from My presence the House I have sanctified for
My name; and Israel will become but a proverb and a byword among all the
8 nations. And whoever passes by this once-exalted House will reel and hiss[34]
and say, 'Why did the LORD do such a thing to this land and this House?'
9 and they will answer, 'Because they left the LORD, their God, who brought
heir ancestors out of the land of Egypt, and they embraced other gods and
worshipped them and served them. For this the LORD brought all this evil
10 upon them.'" This came to pass at the end of the twenty years that
Shlomo had spent building the two houses, the House of the LORD and the
11 king's own house. Ḥiram, king of Tyre, had supplied Shlomo with all the
cedarwood, cypress wood, and gold that he required, and in return, King
12 Shlomo gave Ḥiram twenty towns in the region of Galil. But when Ḥiram
set out from Tyre to survey the towns that Shlomo had given him, they
13 did not please him. "What kind of towns have you given me, my brother?"
he asked, and named them the land of Kavul,[35] as they are called to this
14 day. Nonetheless, Ḥiram sent the king one hundred twenty talents
15 of gold.[36] For these purposes, King Shlomo imposed forced labor: to build
the House of the LORD and his own house, the Milo,[37] the wall of Jerusalem,
16 Ḥatzor, Megiddo, and Gezer. Pharaoh, king of Egypt, had marched up and
captured Gezer – he burned it with fire and killed the Canaanite inhabitants
of the city – and he gave it as a wedding gift to his daughter, Shlomo's wife.
17 18 Shlomo built Gezer, lower Beit Ḥoron, Baalat, and Tadmor in the wilderness
19 in the region, as well as all of Shlomo's store towns, chariot towns, and
cavalry towns – all that Shlomo desired to build in Jerusalem, Lebanon, and
20 throughout the land of his dominion. As for all the people who remained
among the Amorites, the Hittites, the Perizzites, the Hivites, and the Jebusites,
21 who were not of the Israelites – their remaining descendants in the land,
whom the Israelites had been unable to destroy – Shlomo drafted them for
22 forced labor to this day. Shlomo never reduced the Israelites to slavery, for
they were military men, his servants, ministers, officials, and the officers of
23 his chariots and cavalry. These were the ministers of prefects
in charge of Shlomo's work: five hundred fifty supervised the people who
24 executed the work. As soon as Pharaoh's daughter went up from the City of

---

34 | An expression of dismay.

35 | Perhaps deriving from the Phoenician, meaning "worthless."

36 | One talent is the equivalent of three thousand shekel and weighs about 34 kilograms.

37 | Apparently a fortification.

ה תִּשְׁמֹר׃ וַהֲקִמֹתִי אֶת־כִּסֵּא מַמְלַכְתְּךָ עַל־יִשְׂרָאֵל לְעֹלָם כַּאֲשֶׁר
דִּבַּרְתִּי עַל־דָּוִד אָבִיךָ לֵאמֹר לֹא־יִכָּרֵת לְךָ אִישׁ מֵעַל כִּסֵּא יִשְׂרָאֵל׃
ו אִם־שׁוֹב תְּשֻׁבוּן אַתֶּם וּבְנֵיכֶם מֵאַחֲרַי וְלֹא תִשְׁמְרוּ מִצְוֺתַי חֻקֹּתַי
אֲשֶׁר נָתַתִּי לִפְנֵיכֶם וַהֲלַכְתֶּם וַעֲבַדְתֶּם אֱלֹהִים אֲחֵרִים וְהִשְׁתַּחֲוִיתֶם
ז לָהֶם׃ וְהִכְרַתִּי אֶת־יִשְׂרָאֵל מֵעַל פְּנֵי הָאֲדָמָה אֲשֶׁר נָתַתִּי לָהֶם וְאֶת־
הַבַּיִת אֲשֶׁר הִקְדַּשְׁתִּי לִשְׁמִי אֲשַׁלַּח מֵעַל פָּנָי וְהָיָה יִשְׂרָאֵל לְמָשָׁל
ח וְלִשְׁנִינָה בְּכָל־הָעַמִּים׃ וְהַבַּיִת הַזֶּה יִהְיֶה עֶלְיוֹן כָּל־עֹבֵר עָלָיו יִשֹּׁם
וְשָׁרָק וְאָמְרוּ עַל־מֶה עָשָׂה יהוה כָּכָה לָאָרֶץ הַזֹּאת וְלַבַּיִת הַזֶּה׃
ט וְאָמְרוּ עַל אֲשֶׁר עָזְבוּ אֶת־יהוה אֱלֹהֵיהֶם אֲשֶׁר הוֹצִיא אֶת־אֲבֹתָם
מֵאֶרֶץ מִצְרַיִם וַיַּחֲזִקוּ בֵּאלֹהִים אֲחֵרִים וַיִּשְׁתַּחֲוּ לָהֶם וַיַּעַבְדֻם עַל־כֵּן
י הֵבִיא יהוה עֲלֵיהֶם אֵת כָּל־הָרָעָה הַזֹּאת׃ וַיְהִי מִקְצֵה
עֶשְׂרִים שָׁנָה אֲשֶׁר־בָּנָה שְׁלֹמֹה אֶת־שְׁנֵי הַבָּתִּים אֶת־בֵּית יהוה וְאֶת־
יא בֵּית הַמֶּלֶךְ׃ חִירָם מֶלֶךְ־צֹר נִשָּׂא אֶת־שְׁלֹמֹה בַּעֲצֵי אֲרָזִים וּבַעֲצֵי
בְרוֹשִׁים וּבַזָּהָב לְכָל־חֶפְצוֹ אָז יִתֵּן הַמֶּלֶךְ שְׁלֹמֹה לְחִירָם עֶשְׂרִים עִיר
יב בְּאֶרֶץ הַגָּלִיל׃ וַיֵּצֵא חִירָם מִצֹּר לִרְאוֹת אֶת־הֶעָרִים אֲשֶׁר נָתַן־לוֹ
יג שְׁלֹמֹה וְלֹא יָשְׁרוּ בְּעֵינָיו׃ וַיֹּאמֶר מָה הֶעָרִים הָאֵלֶּה אֲשֶׁר־נָתַתָּה לִּי
יד אָחִי וַיִּקְרָא לָהֶם אֶרֶץ כָּבוּל עַד הַיּוֹם הַזֶּה׃ וַיִּשְׁלַח
טו חִירָם לַמֶּלֶךְ מֵאָה וְעֶשְׂרִים כִּכַּר זָהָב׃ וְזֶה דְבַר־הַמַּס אֲשֶׁר־הֶעֱלָה ׀
הַמֶּלֶךְ שְׁלֹמֹה לִבְנוֹת אֶת־בֵּית יהוה וְאֶת־בֵּיתוֹ וְאֶת־הַמִּלּוֹא וְאֵת
טז חוֹמַת יְרוּשָׁלִָם וְאֶת־חָצֹר וְאֶת־מְגִדּוֹ וְאֶת־גָּזֶר׃ פַּרְעֹה מֶלֶךְ־מִצְרַיִם
עָלָה וַיִּלְכֹּד אֶת־גֶּזֶר וַיִּשְׂרְפָהּ בָּאֵשׁ וְאֶת־הַכְּנַעֲנִי הַיֹּשֵׁב בָּעִיר הָרָג
יז וַיִּתְּנָהּ שִׁלֻּחִים לְבִתּוֹ אֵשֶׁת שְׁלֹמֹה׃ וַיִּבֶן שְׁלֹמֹה אֶת־גֶּזֶר וְאֶת־בֵּית
יח יט חֹרֹן תַּחְתּוֹן׃ וְאֶת־בַּעֲלָת וְאֶת־תמר בַּמִּדְבָּר בָּאָרֶץ׃ וְאֵת כָּל־עָרֵי תַּדְמֹר
הַמִּסְכְּנוֹת אֲשֶׁר הָיוּ לִשְׁלֹמֹה וְאֵת עָרֵי הָרֶכֶב וְאֵת עָרֵי הַפָּרָשִׁים
וְאֵת ׀ חֵשֶׁק שְׁלֹמֹה אֲשֶׁר חָשַׁק לִבְנוֹת בִּירוּשָׁלִַם וּבַלְּבָנוֹן וּבְכֹל אֶרֶץ
כ מֶמְשַׁלְתּוֹ׃ כָּל־הָעָם הַנּוֹתָר מִן־הָאֱמֹרִי הַחִתִּי הַפְּרִזִּי הַחִוִּי וְהַיְבוּסִי
כא אֲשֶׁר לֹא־מִבְּנֵי יִשְׂרָאֵל הֵמָּה׃ בְּנֵיהֶם אֲשֶׁר נֹתְרוּ אַחֲרֵיהֶם בָּאָרֶץ
אֲשֶׁר לֹא־יָכְלוּ בְּנֵי יִשְׂרָאֵל לְהַחֲרִימָם וַיַּעֲלֵם שְׁלֹמֹה לְמַס־עֹבֵד עַד
כב הַיּוֹם הַזֶּה׃ וּמִבְּנֵי יִשְׂרָאֵל לֹא־נָתַן שְׁלֹמֹה עָבֶד כִּי־הֵם אַנְשֵׁי הַמִּלְחָמָה
כג וַעֲבָדָיו וְשָׂרָיו וְשָׁלִשָׁיו וְשָׂרֵי רִכְבּוֹ וּפָרָשָׁיו׃ אֵלֶּה ׀ שָׂרֵי
הַנִּצָּבִים אֲשֶׁר עַל־הַמְּלָאכָה לִשְׁלֹמֹה חֲמִשִּׁים וַחֲמֵשׁ מֵאוֹת הָרֹדִים
כד בָּעָם הָעֹשִׂים בַּמְּלָאכָה׃ אַךְ בַּת־פַּרְעֹה עָלְתָה מֵעִיר דָּוִד אֶל־בֵּיתָהּ

25 David to the palace he had built for her, he built the Milo.[38] Three times a
year, Shlomo would offer up burnt offerings and peace offerings on the altar
he had built for the LORD, and he would burn incense upon it before the
26 LORD; in this way he made the House complete. Shlomo built a fleet at
27 Etzyon Gever, which is by Elot[39] on the shore of the Red Sea, in the land of
Edom. Ḥiram sent his servants with the fleet, skilled seamen familiar with
28 the sea, to be with Shlomo's servants, and they traveled to Ofir.[40] There
they collected gold – four hundred twenty talents – and brought it to King
10 1 Shlomo. Now the Queen of Sheba[41] had been hearing of Shlomo's
fame through the name of the LORD, and she came to test him with riddles.
2 She came to Jerusalem with a vast entourage: with camels bearing spices, an
immense wealth of gold, and precious stones. She came to Shlomo and told
3 him all that she had in mind. Shlomo addressed all of her words; there was
nothing that remained hidden from the king, and there was nothing he failed
4 to address. When the Queen of Sheba saw all of Shlomo's wisdom and the
5 House he had built, and the fare of his table and how his subjects were seated
and his servants' attendance and attire, and his cupbearers and the burnt
offerings he offered up in the House of the LORD, she was left breathless.
6 "What I heard in my land about your deeds and your wisdom was true!" she
7 said to the king. "I never believed it until I came and saw it with my own
eyes – and I was not told even the half of it! Your wisdom and wealth far
8 exceeds the rumors I heard. How fortunate are your men – how fortunate
are these attendants of yours, who are always in your presence, hearing your
9 wisdom. Blessed be the LORD your God, who delighted in you and set you
upon the throne of Israel; because of the LORD's eternal love of Israel, He has
10 appointed you as king to uphold justice and righteousness." She gave the king
one hundred twenty talents of gold and a wealth of spices and precious
stones; never again has there been a wealth of spices as vast as the Queen of
11 Sheba's gift to King Shlomo – Ḥiram's fleet, which conveyed gold from Ofir,
12 also brought a vast wealth of sandalwood and precious stones. The king had
the sandalwood made into banisters for the House of the LORD and the royal
house, and harps and lyres for the singers; never again has such a wealth of
13 sandalwood arrived, or even been seen, to this day. He gave the Queen of
Sheba all that she desired, besides what he had already bestowed upon her
with the generous hand of King Shlomo. Then, together with her servants,
14 she took her leave and journeyed back to her own land. The weight
15 of gold that Shlomo received in a single year was 666 talents, beside what
came from traveling merchants and the business of traders, all the Arabian
16 kings, and the governors of the land. King Shlomo made two hundred shields
17 of beaten gold – six hundred pieces of gold went into each shield – and

38 | See note on verse 15.

39 | Eilat.

40 | An unknown location, sometimes identified with ports or regions in East Africa or the Arabian Peninsula.

41 | Sabea, in the southwestern Arabian Peninsula.

כה אֲשֶׁר בָּנָה־לָהּ אָז בָּנָה אֶת־הַמִּלּוֹא׃ וְהֶעֱלָה שְׁלֹמֹה שָׁלֹשׁ פְּעָמִים
בַּשָּׁנָה עֹלוֹת וּשְׁלָמִים עַל־הַמִּזְבֵּחַ אֲשֶׁר בָּנָה לַיהוָה וְהַקְטֵיר אִתּוֹ
כו אֲשֶׁר לִפְנֵי יְהוָה וְשִׁלַּם אֶת־הַבָּיִת׃ וָאֳנִי עָשָׂה הַמֶּלֶךְ שְׁלֹמֹה בְּעֶצְיוֹן־
כז גֶּבֶר אֲשֶׁר אֶת־אֵלוֹת עַל־שְׂפַת יַם־סוּף בְּאֶרֶץ אֱדוֹם׃ וַיִּשְׁלַח חִירָם
כח בָּאֳנִי אֶת־עֲבָדָיו אַנְשֵׁי אֳנִיּוֹת יֹדְעֵי הַיָּם עִם עַבְדֵי שְׁלֹמֹה׃ וַיָּבֹאוּ
אוֹפִירָה וַיִּקְחוּ מִשָּׁם זָהָב אַרְבַּע־מֵאוֹת וְעֶשְׂרִים כִּכָּר וַיָּבִאוּ אֶל־
י א הַמֶּלֶךְ שְׁלֹמֹה׃ וּמַלְכַּת־שְׁבָא שֹׁמַעַת אֶת־שֵׁמַע שְׁלֹמֹה
ב לְשֵׁם יְהוָה וַתָּבֹא לְנַסֹּתוֹ בְּחִידוֹת׃ וַתָּבֹא יְרוּשָׁלְַמָה בְּחַיִל כָּבֵד
מְאֹד גְּמַלִּים נֹשְׂאִים בְּשָׂמִים וְזָהָב רַב־מְאֹד וְאֶבֶן יְקָרָה וַתָּבֹא אֶל־
ג שְׁלֹמֹה וַתְּדַבֵּר אֵלָיו אֵת כָּל־אֲשֶׁר הָיָה עִם־לְבָבָהּ׃ וַיַּגֶּד־לָהּ שְׁלֹמֹה
אֶת־כָּל־דְּבָרֶיהָ לֹא־הָיָה דָּבָר נֶעְלָם מִן־הַמֶּלֶךְ אֲשֶׁר לֹא הִגִּיד לָהּ׃
ד ה וַתֵּרֶא מַלְכַּת־שְׁבָא אֵת כָּל־חָכְמַת שְׁלֹמֹה וְהַבַּיִת אֲשֶׁר בָּנָה׃ וּמַאֲכַל
שֻׁלְחָנוֹ וּמוֹשַׁב עֲבָדָיו וּמַעֲמַד מְשָׁרְתָו וּמַלְבֻּשֵׁיהֶם וּמַשְׁקָיו וְעֹלָתוֹ
ו אֲשֶׁר יַעֲלֶה בֵּית יְהוָה וְלֹא־הָיָה בָהּ עוֹד רוּחַ׃ וַתֹּאמֶר אֶל־הַמֶּלֶךְ
אֱמֶת הָיָה הַדָּבָר אֲשֶׁר שָׁמַעְתִּי בְּאַרְצִי עַל־דְּבָרֶיךָ וְעַל־חָכְמָתֶךָ׃
ז וְלֹא־הֶאֱמַנְתִּי לַדְּבָרִים עַד אֲשֶׁר־בָּאתִי וַתִּרְאֶינָה עֵינַי וְהִנֵּה לֹא־
הֻגַּד־לִי הַחֵצִי הוֹסַפְתָּ חָכְמָה וָטוֹב אֶל־הַשְּׁמוּעָה אֲשֶׁר שָׁמָעְתִּי׃
ח אַשְׁרֵי אֲנָשֶׁיךָ אַשְׁרֵי עֲבָדֶיךָ אֵלֶּה הָעֹמְדִים לְפָנֶיךָ תָּמִיד הַשֹּׁמְעִים
ט אֶת־חָכְמָתֶךָ׃ יְהִי יְהוָה אֱלֹהֶיךָ בָּרוּךְ אֲשֶׁר חָפֵץ בְּךָ לְתִתְּךָ עַל־כִּסֵּא ט
יִשְׂרָאֵל בְּאַהֲבַת יְהוָה אֶת־יִשְׂרָאֵל לְעֹלָם וַיְשִׂימְךָ לְמֶלֶךְ לַעֲשׂוֹת
י מִשְׁפָּט וּצְדָקָה׃ וַתִּתֵּן לַמֶּלֶךְ מֵאָה וְעֶשְׂרִים ׀ כִּכַּר זָהָב וּבְשָׂמִים הַרְבֵּה
מְאֹד וְאֶבֶן יְקָרָה לֹא בָא כַבֹּשֶׂם הַהוּא עוֹד לָרֹב אֲשֶׁר־נָתְנָה מַלְכַּת־
יא שְׁבָא לַמֶּלֶךְ שְׁלֹמֹה׃ וְגַם אֳנִי חִירָם אֲשֶׁר־נָשָׂא זָהָב מֵאוֹפִיר הֵבִיא
יב מֵאֹפִיר עֲצֵי אַלְמֻגִּים הַרְבֵּה מְאֹד וְאֶבֶן יְקָרָה׃ וַיַּעַשׂ הַמֶּלֶךְ אֶת־עֲצֵי
הָאַלְמֻגִּים מִסְעָד לְבֵית־יְהוָה וּלְבֵית הַמֶּלֶךְ וְכִנֹּרוֹת וּנְבָלִים לַשָּׁרִים
יג לֹא בָא־כֵן עֲצֵי אַלְמֻגִּים וְלֹא נִרְאָה עַד הַיּוֹם הַזֶּה׃ וְהַמֶּלֶךְ שְׁלֹמֹה
נָתַן לְמַלְכַּת־שְׁבָא אֶת־כָּל־חֶפְצָהּ אֲשֶׁר שָׁאָלָה מִלְּבַד אֲשֶׁר נָתַן־לָהּ
יד כְּיַד הַמֶּלֶךְ שְׁלֹמֹה וַתֵּפֶן וַתֵּלֶךְ לְאַרְצָהּ הִיא וַעֲבָדֶיהָ׃ וַיְהִי
מִשְׁקַל הַזָּהָב אֲשֶׁר־בָּא לִשְׁלֹמֹה בְּשָׁנָה אֶחָת שֵׁשׁ מֵאוֹת שִׁשִּׁים וָשֵׁשׁ
טו כִּכַּר זָהָב׃ לְבַד מֵאַנְשֵׁי הַתָּרִים וּמִסְחַר הָרֹכְלִים וְכָל־מַלְכֵי הָעֶרֶב
טז וּפַחוֹת הָאָרֶץ׃ וַיַּעַשׂ הַמֶּלֶךְ שְׁלֹמֹה מָאתַיִם צִנָּה זָהָב שָׁחוּט שֵׁשׁ־
יז מֵאוֹת זָהָב יַעֲלֶה עַל־הַצִּנָּה הָאֶחָת׃ וּשְׁלֹשׁ־מֵאוֹת מָגִנִּים זָהָב שָׁחוּט

three hundred bucklers of beaten gold – three mina[42] of gold went into
each buckler – and the king placed them in the House of the Lebanon
18 Forest.[43] The king made an enormous ivory throne and overlaid it
19 with the finest gold. Six steps led up to the throne; the back of the throne was
rounded at the top, and there were armrests on both sides of the seat. Two
20 lions were positioned by the armrests, and twelve lions stood there on the
six steps on either side. Nothing like it was ever made in any other kingdom.
21 All of the king's drinking vessels were of gold, and all the utensils of the
House of the Lebanon Forest were of solid gold. There was no silver; it
22 counted for nothing in the days of Shlomo. For the king had a Tarshish[44] fleet
at sea with Ḥiram's fleet; every three years, the Tarshish fleet would come
23 back loaded with gold and silver, ivory, monkeys, and peacocks. King Shlomo
24 surpassed all the kings of the earth in wealth and in wisdom; from all over
the world they sought audience with Shlomo to hear the wisdom that God
25 had granted him. And each one brought his tribute: vessels of silver and
vessels of gold, garments, weapons, spices, horses, and mules, according to
26 the yearly due. Shlomo amassed chariots and horsemen; he had
one thousand four hundred chariots and twelve thousand horsemen. He
27 stationed them in the chariot towns and with the king in Jerusalem. The king
made silver as common in Jerusalem as stones, while cedars were as common
28 as sycamores in the lowlands. Shlomo's horses were procured from Egypt
and Keveh; the king's traders would import them from Keveh at a set price.
29 The cost of importing a chariot from Egypt was six hundred pieces of silver,
while a horse was one hundred fifty; these, in turn, were exported to all the
11 1 kings of the Hittites and all the kings of Aram. King Shlomo loved
many foreign women besides the daughter of Pharaoh – Moabite women,
2 Amonite women, Edomite women, Sidonian women, Hittite women – from
the nations of which the LORD had warned the Israelites: "You must not join
with them, nor must they join with you, for they will turn your hearts astray
3 after their own gods."[45] Shlomo clung to these in love. He had seven hundred
wives of royal rank and three hundred concubines, and his wives turned his
4 heart astray.[46] By the time Shlomo grew old, his wives had turned his heart
to other gods, and his heart was not entirely with the LORD, his God, as his
5 father David's heart had been. Shlomo went after Ashtoret, the god of the
6 Sidonians, and after Milkom, the abomination of the Amonites. Shlomo did
what was evil in the LORD's sight and was not fully with the LORD, as his father
7 David was. It was then that Shlomo built a high shrine to Kemosh,
the abomination of Moav, on the hill overlooking Jerusalem,[47] and to Molekh,
8 the abomination of the Amonites. He did the same for all his foreign wives,

42 | One mina is the equivalent of fifty shekel and weighs 570 grams.
43 | See note on 7:2.
44 | Referring either to the destination of the fleet (perhaps Tarsus in Asia Minor), or to a type of ship.
45 | See Deuteronomy 7:3–4.
46 | Cf. Deuteronomy 17:17.
47 | The Mount of Olives.

שְׁלֹשֶׁת מָנִים זָהָב יַעֲלֶה עַל־הַמָּגֵן הָאֶחָת וַיִּתְּנֵם הַמֶּלֶךְ בֵּית יַעַר
יח הַלְּבָנוֹן: וַיַּעַשׂ הַמֶּלֶךְ כִּסֵּא־שֵׁן גָּדוֹל וַיְצַפֵּהוּ זָהָב מוּפָז:
יט שֵׁשׁ מַעֲלוֹת לַכִּסֵּה וְרֹאשׁ עָגֹל לַכִּסֵּה מֵאַחֲרָיו וְיָדֹת מִזֶּה וּמִזֶּה
כ אֶל־מְקוֹם הַשָּׁבֶת וּשְׁנַיִם אֲרָיוֹת עֹמְדִים אֵצֶל הַיָּדוֹת: וּשְׁנֵים עָשָׂר
אֲרָיִים עֹמְדִים שָׁם עַל־שֵׁשׁ הַמַּעֲלוֹת מִזֶּה וּמִזֶּה לֹא־נַעֲשָׂה כֵן לְכָל־
כא מַמְלָכוֹת: וְכֹל כְּלֵי מַשְׁקֵה הַמֶּלֶךְ שְׁלֹמֹה זָהָב וְכֹל כְּלֵי בֵּית־יַעַר
כב הַלְּבָנוֹן זָהָב סָגוּר אֵין כֶּסֶף לֹא נֶחְשָׁב בִּימֵי שְׁלֹמֹה לִמְאוּמָה: כִּי אֳנִי
תַרְשִׁישׁ לַמֶּלֶךְ בַּיָּם עִם אֳנִי חִירָם אַחַת לְשָׁלֹשׁ שָׁנִים תָּבוֹא ׀ אֳנִי
כג תַרְשִׁישׁ נֹשְׂאֵת זָהָב וָכֶסֶף שֶׁנְהַבִּים וְקֹפִים וְתֻכִּיִּים: וַיִּגְדַּל הַמֶּלֶךְ
כד שְׁלֹמֹה מִכֹּל מַלְכֵי הָאָרֶץ לְעֹשֶׁר וּלְחָכְמָה: וְכָל־הָאָרֶץ מְבַקְשִׁים
כה אֶת־פְּנֵי שְׁלֹמֹה לִשְׁמֹעַ אֶת־חָכְמָתוֹ אֲשֶׁר־נָתַן אֱלֹהִים בְּלִבּוֹ: וְהֵמָּה
מְבִאִים אִישׁ מִנְחָתוֹ כְּלֵי־כֶסֶף וּכְלֵי זָהָב וּשְׂלָמוֹת וְנֵשֶׁק וּבְשָׂמִים
כו סוּסִים וּפְרָדִים דְּבַר־שָׁנָה בְּשָׁנָה: וַיֶּאֱסֹף שְׁלֹמֹה רֶכֶב
וּפָרָשִׁים וַיְהִי־לוֹ אֶלֶף וְאַרְבַּע־מֵאוֹת רֶכֶב וּשְׁנֵים־עָשָׂר אֶלֶף פָּרָשִׁים
כז וַיַּנְחֵם בְּעָרֵי הָרֶכֶב וְעִם־הַמֶּלֶךְ בִּירוּשָׁלִָם: וַיִּתֵּן הַמֶּלֶךְ אֶת־הַכֶּסֶף
בִּירוּשָׁלִַם כָּאֲבָנִים וְאֵת הָאֲרָזִים נָתַן כַּשִּׁקְמִים אֲשֶׁר־בַּשְּׁפֵלָה לָרֹב:
כח וּמוֹצָא הַסּוּסִים אֲשֶׁר לִשְׁלֹמֹה מִמִּצְרָיִם וּמִקְוֵה סֹחֲרֵי הַמֶּלֶךְ יִקְחוּ
כט מִקְוֵה בִּמְחִיר: וַתַּעֲלֶה וַתֵּצֵא מֶרְכָּבָה מִמִּצְרַיִם בְּשֵׁשׁ מֵאוֹת כֶּסֶף
וְסוּס בַּחֲמִשִּׁים וּמֵאָה וְכֵן לְכָל־מַלְכֵי הַחִתִּים וּלְמַלְכֵי אֲרָם בְּיָדָם
יא א יֵצִאוּ: וְהַמֶּלֶךְ שְׁלֹמֹה אָהַב נָשִׁים נָכְרִיּוֹת רַבּוֹת וְאֶת־בַּת־
ב פַּרְעֹה מוֹאֲבִיּוֹת עַמֳּנִיּוֹת אֲדֹמִיֹּת צֵדְנִיֹּת חִתִּיֹּת: מִן־הַגּוֹיִם אֲשֶׁר
אָמַר־יְהוָה אֶל־בְּנֵי יִשְׂרָאֵל לֹא־תָבֹאוּ בָהֶם וְהֵם לֹא־יָבֹאוּ בָכֶם אָכֵן
ג יַטּוּ אֶת־לְבַבְכֶם אַחֲרֵי אֱלֹהֵיהֶם בָּהֶם דָּבַק שְׁלֹמֹה לְאַהֲבָה: וַיְהִי־לוֹ
נָשִׁים שָׂרוֹת שְׁבַע מֵאוֹת וּפִלַגְשִׁים שְׁלֹשׁ מֵאוֹת וַיַּטּוּ נָשָׁיו אֶת־לִבּוֹ:
ד וַיְהִי לְעֵת זִקְנַת שְׁלֹמֹה נָשָׁיו הִטּוּ אֶת־לְבָבוֹ אַחֲרֵי אֱלֹהִים אֲחֵרִים
ה וְלֹא־הָיָה לְבָבוֹ שָׁלֵם עִם־יְהוָה אֱלֹהָיו כִּלְבַב דָּוִיד אָבִיו: וַיֵּלֶךְ שְׁלֹמֹה
ו אַחֲרֵי עַשְׁתֹּרֶת אֱלֹהֵי צִדֹנִים וְאַחֲרֵי מִלְכֹּם שִׁקֻּץ עַמֹּנִים: וַיַּעַשׂ שְׁלֹמֹה
ז הָרַע בְּעֵינֵי יְהוָה וְלֹא מִלֵּא אַחֲרֵי יְהוָה כְּדָוִד אָבִיו: אָז
יִבְנֶה שְׁלֹמֹה בָּמָה לִכְמוֹשׁ שִׁקֻּץ מוֹאָב בָּהָר אֲשֶׁר עַל־פְּנֵי יְרוּשָׁלִָם
ח וּלְמֹלֶךְ שִׁקֻּץ בְּנֵי עַמּוֹן: וְכֵן עָשָׂה לְכָל־נָשָׁיו הַנָּכְרִיּוֹת מַקְטִירוֹת

9 who offered incense and sacrifices to their gods. Then the LORD raged
against Shlomo, for his heart had turned away from the LORD, God of Israel,
10 who had appeared to him twice[48] and commanded him about this very
matter – not to follow after other gods. But he failed to keep the LORD's
11 command. And the LORD said to Shlomo, "Because this has
been your will, and you failed to keep My covenant and My laws, which I
commanded you – I will surely tear the kingdom away from you, and I will
12 give it to your servant. But for the sake of your father David, I will not do this
13 in your own lifetime; I will tear it away from the hand of your son. And even
so, I will not tear the whole kingdom away; I will grant a single tribe to your
son for the sake of My servant David and for the sake of Jerusalem, which I
14 have chosen." The LORD raised up an adversary for Shlomo: Hadad
15 the Edomite, who was of the royal line of Edom. When David had been in
Edom, Yoav had gone up to bury the slain, for he had struck down every male
16 in Edom during the six months that Yoav and all of Israel had stayed there,
17 until they had wiped out every last male in Edom. But Hadad, together with
some Edomite men who were his father's servants, had fled toward Egypt;
18 Hadad had been a young boy. They left Midyan and reached Paran, taking
men with them from Paran, and when they reached Egypt, Pharaoh, king of
Egypt, provided him with a house, arranged for his provisions, and granted
19 him land. Hadad found great favor with Pharaoh, and he gave him his wife's
20 sister in marriage: the sister of Taḥpenes, the queen mother. The sister of
Taḥpenes bore him a son, Genuvat, and Taḥpenes weaned him in Pharaoh's
21 palace; Genuvat lived in Pharaoh's palace with Pharaoh's own sons. When
Hadad heard in Egypt that David slept with his ancestors, and that Yoav, the
army commander, had died, Hadad said to Pharaoh, "Give me leave, and I
22 will go to my own land." "But what do you lack here with me?" Pharaoh
asked him. "Why do you ask to go back to your own land?" "Nothing," he
23 said, "but please, permit me to leave." And God raised up Rezon son of Elyada
24 as his adversary. He had fled from King Hadadezer of Tzova, his master,
when David massacred them. He rallied men to him and became the troop
leader. They went to Damascus and settled there and established rule in
25 Damascus. He was an adversary to Israel all the days of Shlomo beyond
the trouble Hadad wrought; he was hostile toward Israel and reigned over
26 Aram. Yorovam son of Nevat was an Efraimite from Tzereda; his
mother was a widow by the name of Tzerua. He was a servant of Shlomo, but
27 he raised his hand against the king. This is how he came to raise his hand
against the king: Shlomo built the Milo[49] to repair a breach in the City of
28 David, his father. Yorovam was a capable man, and when Shlomo saw how
the young man performed his work, he appointed him over all the forced
29 labor of the House of Yosef. Around that time, Yorovam was leaving

48 | See 3:5, 9:2.
49 | See note on 9:15.

ט וּמְזַבְּחוֹת לֵאלֹהֵיהֶן׃ וַיִּתְאַנַּף יְהוָה בִּשְׁלֹמֹה כִּי־נָטָה לְבָבוֹ מֵעִם
י יְהוָה אֱלֹהֵי יִשְׂרָאֵל הַנִּרְאָה אֵלָיו פַּעֲמָיִם׃ וְצִוָּה אֵלָיו עַל־הַדָּבָר
הַזֶּה לְבִלְתִּי־לֶכֶת אַחֲרֵי אֱלֹהִים אֲחֵרִים וְלֹא שָׁמַר אֵת אֲשֶׁר־צִוָּה
יא יְהוָה׃ וַיֹּאמֶר יְהוָה לִשְׁלֹמֹה יַעַן אֲשֶׁר הָיְתָה־
זֹּאת עִמָּךְ וְלֹא שָׁמַרְתָּ בְּרִיתִי וְחֻקֹּתַי אֲשֶׁר צִוִּיתִי עָלֶיךָ קָרֹעַ אֶקְרַע
יב אֶת־הַמַּמְלָכָה מֵעָלֶיךָ וּנְתַתִּיהָ לְעַבְדֶּךָ׃ אַךְ־בְּיָמֶיךָ לֹא אֶעֱשֶׂנָּה
יג לְמַעַן דָּוִד אָבִיךָ מִיַּד בִּנְךָ אֶקְרָעֶנָּה׃ רַק אֶת־כָּל־הַמַּמְלָכָה לֹא
אֶקְרָע שֵׁבֶט אֶחָד אֶתֵּן לִבְנֶךָ לְמַעַן דָּוִד עַבְדִּי וּלְמַעַן יְרוּשָׁלַםִ אֲשֶׁר
יד בָּחָרְתִּי׃ וַיָּקֶם יְהוָה | שָׂטָן לִשְׁלֹמֹה אֵת הֲדַד הָאֲדֹמִי מִזֶּרַע
טו הַמֶּלֶךְ הוּא בֶּאֱדוֹם׃ וַיְהִי בִּהְיוֹת דָּוִד אֶת־אֱדוֹם בַּעֲלוֹת יוֹאָב שַׂר
טז הַצָּבָא לְקַבֵּר אֶת־הַחֲלָלִים וַיַּךְ כָּל־זָכָר בֶּאֱדוֹם׃ כִּי שֵׁשֶׁת חֳדָשִׁים
יז יָשַׁב־שָׁם יוֹאָב וְכָל־יִשְׂרָאֵל עַד־הִכְרִית כָּל־זָכָר בֶּאֱדוֹם׃ וַיִּבְרַח אֲדַד
הוּא וַאֲנָשִׁים אֲדֹמִיִּים מֵעַבְדֵי אָבִיו אִתּוֹ לָבוֹא מִצְרָיִם וַהֲדַד נַעַר
יח קָטָן׃ וַיָּקֻמוּ מִמִּדְיָן וַיָּבֹאוּ פָּארָן וַיִּקְחוּ אֲנָשִׁים עִמָּם מִפָּארָן וַיָּבֹאוּ
מִצְרַיִם אֶל־פַּרְעֹה מֶלֶךְ־מִצְרַיִם וַיִּתֶּן־לוֹ בַיִת וְלֶחֶם אָמַר לוֹ וְאֶרֶץ
יט נָתַן לוֹ׃ וַיִּמְצָא הֲדַד חֵן בְּעֵינֵי פַרְעֹה מְאֹד וַיִּתֶּן־לוֹ אִשָּׁה אֶת־אֲחוֹת
כ אִשְׁתּוֹ אֲחוֹת תַּחְפְּנֵיס הַגְּבִירָה׃ וַתֵּלֶד לוֹ אֲחוֹת תַּחְפְּנֵיס אֵת גְּנֻבַת
בְּנוֹ וַתִּגְמְלֵהוּ תַחְפְּנֵס בְּתוֹךְ בֵּית פַּרְעֹה וַיְהִי גְנֻבַת בֵּית פַּרְעֹה בְּתוֹךְ
כא בְּנֵי פַרְעֹה׃ וַהֲדַד שָׁמַע בְּמִצְרַיִם כִּי־שָׁכַב דָּוִד עִם־אֲבֹתָיו וְכִי־מֵת
יוֹאָב שַׂר־הַצָּבָא וַיֹּאמֶר הֲדַד אֶל־פַּרְעֹה שַׁלְּחֵנִי וְאֵלֵךְ אֶל־אַרְצִי׃
כב וַיֹּאמֶר לוֹ פַרְעֹה כִּי מָה־אַתָּה חָסֵר עִמִּי וְהִנְּךָ מְבַקֵּשׁ לָלֶכֶת אֶל־
כג אַרְצֶךָ וַיֹּאמֶר | לֹא כִּי שַׁלֵּחַ תְּשַׁלְּחֵנִי׃ וַיָּקֶם אֱלֹהִים לוֹ שָׂטָן אֶת־רְזוֹן
כד בֶּן־אֶלְיָדָע אֲשֶׁר בָּרַח מֵאֵת הֲדַדְעֶזֶר מֶלֶךְ־צוֹבָה אֲדֹנָיו׃ וַיִּקְבֹּץ עָלָיו
אֲנָשִׁים וַיְהִי שַׂר־גְּדוּד בַּהֲרֹג דָּוִד אֹתָם וַיֵּלְכוּ דַמֶּשֶׂק וַיֵּשְׁבוּ בָהּ וַיִּמְלְכוּ
כה בְּדַמָּשֶׂק׃ וַיְהִי שָׂטָן לְיִשְׂרָאֵל כָּל־יְמֵי שְׁלֹמֹה וְאֶת־הָרָעָה אֲשֶׁר
כו הֲדָד וַיָּקָץ בְּיִשְׂרָאֵל וַיִּמְלֹךְ עַל־אֲרָם׃ וְיָרָבְעָם בֶּן־נְבָט
אֶפְרָתִי מִן־הַצְּרֵדָה וְשֵׁם אִמּוֹ צְרוּעָה אִשָּׁה אַלְמָנָה עֶבֶד לִשְׁלֹמֹה
כז וַיָּרֶם יָד בַּמֶּלֶךְ׃ וְזֶה הַדָּבָר אֲשֶׁר־הֵרִים יָד בַּמֶּלֶךְ שְׁלֹמֹה בָּנָה אֶת־
כח הַמִּלּוֹא סָגַר אֶת־פֶּרֶץ עִיר דָּוִד אָבִיו׃ וְהָאִישׁ יָרָבְעָם גִּבּוֹר חָיִל וַיַּרְא
שְׁלֹמֹה אֶת־הַנַּעַר כִּי־עֹשֵׂה מְלָאכָה הוּא וַיַּפְקֵד אֹתוֹ לְכָל־סֵבֶל בֵּית
כט יוֹסֵף׃ וַיְהִי בָּעֵת הַהִיא וְיָרָבְעָם יָצָא מִירוּשָׁלָםִ וַיִּמְצָא אֹתוֹ
אֲחִיָּה הַשִּׁילֹנִי הַנָּבִיא בַּדֶּרֶךְ וְהוּא מִתְכַּסֶּה בְּשַׂלְמָה חֲדָשָׁה וּשְׁנֵיהֶם

Jerusalem when Aḥiya the Shilonite, the prophet, met him on the way. He
30 was dressed in a new robe, and the two of them were alone in the field. Aḥiya
31 grasped hold of the new robe he wore and tore it into twelve pieces. "Take
ten of the pieces," he said to Yorovam, "for thus says the LORD, God of Israel:
I am about to tear the kingdom from the hand of Shlomo, and I will give ten
32 tribes over to you. A single tribe will be his for the sake of my servant David
and for the sake of Jerusalem, the city I have chosen out of all the tribes of
33 Israel. For they have abandoned Me and bowed down to Ashtoret, god of
the Sidonians, and to Kemosh, god of Moav, and to Milkom, god of the
Amonites; they have failed to follow in My path, doing what is right in My
34 eyes, keeping My laws and My rulings like David, his father. But I will not
take the whole kingdom from his hands; I will let him remain as ruler for as
long as he lives, for the sake of My servant David, whom I chose – he kept
35 My commandments and laws. I will take the kingship from the hand of his
36 son and give it to you – over the ten tribes. I will give a single tribe to his son,
so there will always be a lamp for My servant David's sake before Me in
37 Jerusalem, the city where I chose to establish My name. But it is you that I
38 will take to reign over all you desire; you will become king over Israel. If you
obey all that I command you and follow in My path and do what is right in
My eyes, keeping My laws and My commandments as My servant David
did – then I will be with you, and I will build you a dynasty as lasting as I built
39 for My servant David, and I will give Israel over to you. And I will humble
40 David's descendants for this purpose, but not forever." Shlomo sought to put
Yorovam to death, but Yorovam fled straight to Egypt, to King Shishak of
41 Egypt, and he remained in Egypt until Shlomo's death. As for the rest of
Shlomo's history, and all his deeds, and his wisdom – they are recorded in the
42 book of the History of Shlomo. The length of Shlomo's reign in Jerusalem,
43 over all of Israel, was forty years. And Shlomo slept with his ancestors and
was buried in the City of David, his father. And his son Reḥavam reigned in
12 1 his place. Reḥavam went to Shekhem, for all of Israel had come to
2 Shekhem for his coronation. Yorovam son of Nevat heard this when he
was still in Egypt, for he had escaped from King Shlomo and settled in
3 Egypt. They sent for and summoned him, and Yorovam came with the whole
4 assembly of Israel, who made the following speech to Reḥavam: "Your father
made our yoke heavy – now, relieve the heavy workload and the harsh yoke
5 your father placed upon us, and we will serve you." "Leave for three days,"
6 he said to them, "and then come back to me," and the people left. King
Reḥavam consulted with the elders who had served his father Shlomo during
his lifetime. "How would you advise to answer this people's request?" he said.
7 "If you become this people's servant today," they told him, "and serve them

ל לְבַדָּם בַּשָּׂדֶה: וַיִּתְפֹּשׂ אֲחִיָּה בַּשַּׂלְמָה הַחֲדָשָׁה אֲשֶׁר עָלָיו וַיִּקְרָעֶהָ
לא שְׁנֵים עָשָׂר קְרָעִים: וַיֹּאמֶר לְיָרָבְעָם קַח־לְךָ עֲשָׂרָה קְרָעִים כִּי כֹה
אָמַר יְהוָה אֱלֹהֵי יִשְׂרָאֵל הִנְנִי קֹרֵעַ אֶת־הַמַּמְלָכָה מִיַּד שְׁלֹמֹה וְנָתַתִּי
לב לְךָ אֵת עֲשָׂרָה הַשְּׁבָטִים: וְהַשֵּׁבֶט הָאֶחָד יִהְיֶה־לּוֹ לְמַעַן ׀ עַבְדִּי דָוִד
לג וּלְמַעַן יְרוּשָׁלִַם הָעִיר אֲשֶׁר בָּחַרְתִּי בָהּ מִכֹּל שִׁבְטֵי יִשְׂרָאֵל: יַעַן ׀
אֲשֶׁר עֲזָבוּנִי וַיִּשְׁתַּחֲווּ לְעַשְׁתֹּרֶת אֱלֹהֵי צִדֹנִין לִכְמוֹשׁ אֱלֹהֵי מוֹאָב
וּלְמִלְכֹּם אֱלֹהֵי בְנֵי־עַמּוֹן וְלֹא־הָלְכוּ בִדְרָכַי לַעֲשׂוֹת הַיָּשָׁר בְּעֵינַי
לד וְחֻקֹּתַי וּמִשְׁפָּטַי כְּדָוִד אָבִיו: וְלֹא־אֶקַּח אֶת־כָּל־הַמַּמְלָכָה מִיָּדוֹ כִּי ׀
נָשִׂיא אֲשִׁתֶנּוּ כֹּל יְמֵי חַיָּיו לְמַעַן דָּוִד עַבְדִּי אֲשֶׁר בָּחַרְתִּי אֹתוֹ אֲשֶׁר
לה שָׁמַר מִצְוֺתַי וְחֻקֹּתָי: וְלָקַחְתִּי הַמְּלוּכָה מִיַּד בְּנוֹ וּנְתַתִּיהָ לְּךָ אֵת
לו עֲשֶׂרֶת הַשְּׁבָטִים: וְלִבְנוֹ אֶתֵּן שֵׁבֶט־אֶחָד לְמַעַן הֱיוֹת־נִיר לְדָוִיד־
עַבְדִּי כָּל־הַיָּמִים ׀ לְפָנַי בִּירוּשָׁלִַם הָעִיר אֲשֶׁר בָּחַרְתִּי לִי לָשׂוּם
לז שְׁמִי שָׁם: וְאֹתְךָ אֶקַּח וּמָלַכְתָּ בְּכֹל אֲשֶׁר־תְּאַוֶּה נַפְשֶׁךָ וְהָיִיתָ מֶּלֶךְ
לח עַל־יִשְׂרָאֵל: וְהָיָה אִם־תִּשְׁמַע אֶת־כָּל־אֲשֶׁר אֲצַוֶּךָ וְהָלַכְתָּ בִדְרָכַי
וְעָשִׂיתָ הַיָּשָׁר בְּעֵינַי לִשְׁמוֹר חֻקּוֹתַי וּמִצְוֺתַי כַּאֲשֶׁר עָשָׂה דָּוִד עַבְדִּי
וְהָיִיתִי עִמָּךְ וּבָנִיתִי לְךָ בַיִת־נֶאֱמָן כַּאֲשֶׁר בָּנִיתִי לְדָוִד וְנָתַתִּי לְךָ
לט אֶת־יִשְׂרָאֵל: וַאעַנֶּה אֶת־זֶרַע דָּוִד לְמַעַן זֹאת אַךְ לֹא כָל־הַיָּמִים:
מ וַיְבַקֵּשׁ שְׁלֹמֹה לְהָמִית אֶת־יָרָבְעָם וַיָּקָם יָרָבְעָם וַיִּבְרַח מִצְרַיִם אֶל־
מא שִׁישַׁק מֶלֶךְ־מִצְרַיִם וַיְהִי בְמִצְרַיִם עַד־מוֹת שְׁלֹמֹה: וְיֶתֶר דִּבְרֵי
שְׁלֹמֹה וְכָל־אֲשֶׁר עָשָׂה וְחָכְמָתוֹ הֲלוֹא־הֵם כְּתֻבִים עַל־סֵפֶר דִּבְרֵי
מב שְׁלֹמֹה: וְהַיָּמִים אֲשֶׁר מָלַךְ שְׁלֹמֹה בִירוּשָׁלִַם עַל־כָּל־יִשְׂרָאֵל אַרְבָּעִים
מג שָׁנָה: וַיִּשְׁכַּב שְׁלֹמֹה עִם־אֲבֹתָיו וַיִּקָּבֵר בְּעִיר דָּוִד אָבִיו וַיִּמְלֹךְ רְחַבְעָם
יב א בְּנוֹ תַּחְתָּיו: וַיֵּלֶךְ רְחַבְעָם שְׁכֶם כִּי שְׁכֶם בָּא כָל־
ב יִשְׂרָאֵל לְהַמְלִיךְ אֹתוֹ: וַיְהִי כִּשְׁמֹעַ ׀ יָרָבְעָם בֶּן־נְבָט וְהוּא עוֹדֶנּוּ
בְמִצְרַיִם אֲשֶׁר בָּרַח מִפְּנֵי הַמֶּלֶךְ שְׁלֹמֹה וַיֵּשֶׁב יָרָבְעָם בְּמִצְרָיִם:
ג וַיִּשְׁלְחוּ וַיִּקְרְאוּ־לוֹ ויבאו יָרָבְעָם וְכָל־קְהַל יִשְׂרָאֵל וַיְדַבְּרוּ אֶל־ וַיָּבֹא
ד רְחַבְעָם לֵאמֹר: אָבִיךָ הִקְשָׁה אֶת־עֻלֵּנוּ וְאַתָּה עַתָּה הָקֵל מֵעֲבֹדַת
ה אָבִיךָ הַקָּשָׁה וּמֵעֻלּוֹ הַכָּבֵד אֲשֶׁר־נָתַן עָלֵינוּ וְנַעַבְדֶךָּ: וַיֹּאמֶר אֲלֵיהֶם
ו לְכוּ־עֹד שְׁלֹשָׁה יָמִים וְשׁוּבוּ אֵלָי וַיֵּלְכוּ הָעָם: וַיִּוָּעַץ הַמֶּלֶךְ רְחַבְעָם
אֶת־הַזְּקֵנִים אֲשֶׁר־הָיוּ עֹמְדִים אֶת־פְּנֵי שְׁלֹמֹה אָבִיו בִּהְיֹתוֹ חַי לֵאמֹר
ז אֵיךְ אַתֶּם נוֹעָצִים לְהָשִׁיב אֶת־הָעָם־הַזֶּה דָּבָר: וַיְדַבֵּר אֵלָיו לֵאמֹר
אִם־הַיּוֹם תִּהְיֶה־עֶבֶד לָעָם הַזֶּה וַעֲבַדְתָּם וַעֲנִיתָם וְדִבַּרְתָּ אֲלֵיהֶם

and respond to them by speaking kind words, then they will become your
8 servants forever." But he rejected the advice that the elders gave him and
consulted with the youngsters who had grown up with him, who now
9 served him. "What do you advise?" he asked them. "How should we answer
this people's request? They told me, 'Relieve the yoke your father placed
10 upon us.'" The youngsters who had grown up with him said, "This is what
you should say to this people, who told you, 'Your father made our yoke
heavy – you should relieve us.' Tell them this: 'My little finger is thicker than
11 my father's loins. Now, my father burdened you with a heavy yoke, but I will
increase your yoke; my father flogged you with whips, but I will flog you with
12 scorpions.'" Yorovam and all the people came to Reḥavam on the third day,
just as the king had told them, saying, "Come back to me on the third day."
13 The king answered the people harshly, rejecting the advice that the elders had
14 given him. He answered them as the youngsters had advised, saying, "My
father burdened you with a heavy yoke, but I will increase your yoke. My
15 father flogged you with whips, but I will flog you with scorpions!" The king
would not listen to the people, for it was part of the Lord's plan to fulfill the
promise that the Lord had made to Yorovam son of Nevat through Aḥiya
16 the Shilonite. When all Israel saw that the king would not listen to them, the
people retorted to the king, "We have no part in David nor any share in the
son of Yishai! To your tents, O Israel! Now look to your own house, O David!"
17 And Israel went back to their tents. But as for the Israelites who lived in the
towns of Yehuda, Reḥavam ruled over them.
18 King Reḥavam sent out Adoram, who was in charge of the forced labor, but
all of Israel pelted him with stones, and he died. At that, Reḥavam forced
19 his way onto his chariot, to flee to Jerusalem. And the Israelites have rebelled
20 against the House of David ever since. When all of Israel heard
that Yorovam had returned, they sent and summoned him to the assembly
and made him king over all Israel. Only the tribe of Yehuda followed the
21 House of David. When Reḥavam reached Jerusalem, he assembled all the
House of Yehuda and the tribe of Binyamin – one hundred eighty thousand
elite fighters – to fight against the House of Israel, to restore the kingship to
22 Reḥavam son of Shlomo. But the word of God came to Shemaya,
23 man of God: "Say to Reḥavam son of Shlomo, king of Yehuda, and to all the
24 House of Yehuda and Binyamin and the rest of the people: Thus says the
Lord: Do not advance, and do not fight with your brothers, the Israelites. Let
every man go back home, for it is through Me that this has come about." And
they heeded the word of the Lord and turned back, following the Lord's
25 word. Yorovam built Shekhem in the Efrayim hills and settled there;

ח דְּבָרִים טוֹבִים וְהָיוּ לְךָ עֲבָדִים כָּל־הַיָּמִים: וַיַּעֲזֹב אֶת־עֲצַת הַזְּקֵנִים
אֲשֶׁר יְעָצֻהוּ וַיִּוָּעַץ אֶת־הַיְלָדִים אֲשֶׁר גָּדְלוּ אִתּוֹ אֲשֶׁר הָעֹמְדִים לְפָנָיו:
ט וַיֹּאמֶר אֲלֵיהֶם מָה אַתֶּם נוֹעָצִים וְנָשִׁיב דָּבָר אֶת־הָעָם הַזֶּה אֲשֶׁר
י דִּבְּרוּ אֵלַי לֵאמֹר הָקֵל מִן־הָעֹל אֲשֶׁר־נָתַן אָבִיךָ עָלֵינוּ: וַיְדַבְּרוּ אֵלָיו
הַיְלָדִים אֲשֶׁר גָּדְלוּ אִתּוֹ לֵאמֹר כֹּה־תֹאמַר לָעָם הַזֶּה אֲשֶׁר דִּבְּרוּ
אֵלֶיךָ לֵאמֹר אָבִיךָ הִכְבִּיד אֶת־עֻלֵּנוּ וְאַתָּה הָקֵל מֵעָלֵינוּ כֹּה תְּדַבֵּר
יא אֲלֵיהֶם קָטָנִּי עָבָה מִמָּתְנֵי אָבִי: וְעַתָּה אָבִי הֶעְמִיס עֲלֵיכֶם עֹל כָּבֵד
וַאֲנִי אֹסִיף עַל־עֻלְּכֶם אָבִי יִסַּר אֶתְכֶם בַּשּׁוֹטִים וַאֲנִי אֲיַסֵּר אֶתְכֶם
יב בָּעַקְרַבִּים: וַיָּבוֹ יָרָבְעָם וְכָל־הָעָם אֶל־רְחַבְעָם בַּיּוֹם הַשְּׁלִישִׁי כַּאֲשֶׁר
יג דִּבֶּר הַמֶּלֶךְ לֵאמֹר שׁוּבוּ אֵלַי בַּיּוֹם הַשְּׁלִישִׁי: וַיַּעַן הַמֶּלֶךְ אֶת־הָעָם
יד קָשָׁה וַיַּעֲזֹב אֶת־עֲצַת הַזְּקֵנִים אֲשֶׁר יְעָצֻהוּ: וַיְדַבֵּר אֲלֵיהֶם כַּעֲצַת
הַיְלָדִים לֵאמֹר אָבִי הִכְבִּיד אֶת־עֻלְּכֶם וַאֲנִי אֹסִיף עַל־עֻלְּכֶם אָבִי
טו יִסַּר אֶתְכֶם בַּשּׁוֹטִים וַאֲנִי אֲיַסֵּר אֶתְכֶם בָּעַקְרַבִּים: וְלֹא־שָׁמַע הַמֶּלֶךְ
אֶל־הָעָם כִּי־הָיְתָה סִבָּה מֵעִם יהוה לְמַעַן הָקִים אֶת־דְּבָרוֹ אֲשֶׁר
טז דִּבֶּר יהוה בְּיַד אֲחִיָּה הַשִּׁילֹנִי אֶל־יָרָבְעָם בֶּן־נְבָט: וַיַּרְא כָּל־יִשְׂרָאֵל
כִּי לֹא־שָׁמַע הַמֶּלֶךְ אֲלֵהֶם וַיָּשִׁבוּ הָעָם אֶת־הַמֶּלֶךְ ׀ דָּבָר ׀ לֵאמֹר
מַה־לָּנוּ חֵלֶק בְּדָוִד וְלֹא־נַחֲלָה בְּבֶן־יִשַׁי לְאֹהָלֶיךָ יִשְׂרָאֵל עַתָּה רְאֵה
יז בֵיתְךָ דָּוִד וַיֵּלֶךְ יִשְׂרָאֵל לְאֹהָלָיו: וּבְנֵי יִשְׂרָאֵל הַיֹּשְׁבִים בְּעָרֵי יְהוּדָה
וַיִּמְלֹךְ עֲלֵיהֶם רְחַבְעָם:
יח וַיִּשְׁלַח הַמֶּלֶךְ רְחַבְעָם אֶת־אֲדֹרָם אֲשֶׁר עַל־הַמַּס וַיִּרְגְּמוּ כָל־יִשְׂרָאֵל
בּוֹ אֶבֶן וַיָּמֹת וְהַמֶּלֶךְ רְחַבְעָם הִתְאַמֵּץ לַעֲלוֹת בַּמֶּרְכָּבָה לָנוּס
יט כ יְרוּשָׁלָםִ: וַיִּפְשְׁעוּ יִשְׂרָאֵל בְּבֵית דָּוִד עַד הַיּוֹם הַזֶּה: וַיְהִי
כִּשְׁמֹעַ כָּל־יִשְׂרָאֵל כִּי־שָׁב יָרָבְעָם וַיִּשְׁלְחוּ וַיִּקְרְאוּ אֹתוֹ אֶל־הָעֵדָה
וַיַּמְלִיכוּ אֹתוֹ עַל־כָּל־יִשְׂרָאֵל לֹא הָיָה אַחֲרֵי בֵית־דָּוִד זוּלָתִי שֵׁבֶט־
כא יְהוּדָה לְבַדּוֹ: ויבאו רְחַבְעָם יְרוּשָׁלַםִ וַיַּקְהֵל אֶת־כָּל־בֵּית יְהוּדָה וְאֶת־ וַיָּבֹא
שֵׁבֶט בִּנְיָמִן מֵאָה וּשְׁמֹנִים אֶלֶף בָּחוּר עֹשֵׂה מִלְחָמָה לְהִלָּחֵם עִם־בֵּית
כב יִשְׂרָאֵל לְהָשִׁיב אֶת־הַמְּלוּכָה לִרְחַבְעָם בֶּן־שְׁלֹמֹה: וַיְהִי
כג דְּבַר הָאֱלֹהִים אֶל־שְׁמַעְיָה אִישׁ־הָאֱלֹהִים לֵאמֹר: אֱמֹר אֶל־רְחַבְעָם
בֶּן־שְׁלֹמֹה מֶלֶךְ יְהוּדָה וְאֶל־כָּל־בֵּית יְהוּדָה וּבִנְיָמִין וְיֶתֶר הָעָם
כד לֵאמֹר: כֹּה אָמַר יהוה לֹא־תַעֲלוּ וְלֹא־תִלָּחֲמוּן עִם־אֲחֵיכֶם בְּנֵי־ יא
יִשְׂרָאֵל שׁוּבוּ אִישׁ לְבֵיתוֹ כִּי מֵאִתִּי נִהְיָה הַדָּבָר הַזֶּה וַיִּשְׁמְעוּ אֶת־
כה דְּבַר יהוה וַיָּשֻׁבוּ לָלֶכֶת כִּדְבַר יהוה: וַיִּבֶן יָרָבְעָם

26 later, he left there and built Penuel. "Now the kingdom will revert to the
27 House of David," Yorovam said to himself. "If this people makes pilgrimage
to offer sacrifices in the House of the LORD in Jerusalem, then the heart of
this people might turn back to their lord – to Reḥavam, king of Yehuda. They
28 might kill me and go back to Reḥavam, king of Yehuda." So the king took
counsel and made two calves of gold. "You have been making pilgrimage to
Jerusalem long enough," he said to them. "Here are your gods, O Israel, who
29 brought you up from the land of Egypt."[50] He placed one in Beit El and set
30 up the other in Dan.[51] This resulted in grave sin; the people went to worship
31 before the one or before the other in Dan. He made buildings for the high
32 shrines and made priests out of an array of people who were not Levites. And
Yorovam established a festival in the eighth month, on the fifteenth day of the
month, similar to the festival[52] in Yehuda, and he ascended the altar. The
sacrifice to the calves he had made took place in Beit El; he stationed at Beit
33 El the priests he had appointed in the shrines. He ascended the altar that he
had made in Beit El on the fifteenth day of the eighth month – on a date of
his own invention – to establish a festival for the Israelites. And he stepped
13 1 up to the altar to offer a sacrifice. Just then, a man of God from
Yehuda arrived at Beit El at the LORD's command; Yorovam was standing on
2 the altar about to offer a sacrifice when he called out against the altar with a
message from the LORD: "Altar, O altar," he said, "thus says the LORD: A son
will be born to the House of David, Yoshiyahu by name. Upon you, he will
slaughter the shrine priests who sacrifice upon you; upon you, human bones
3 will be burnt." And he gave a sign that same day, declaring, "This is the sign
the LORD has decreed: The altar will suddenly split apart, and the ashes upon
4 it will be spilled." When the king heard the message that the man of God
called out against the altar in Beit El, Yorovam thrust out his hand over the
altar, shouting, "Seize him!" but the hand he thrust against him froze, and he
5 could not draw it back again. And the altar split apart, and the ashes from the
altar spilled – the very sign that the man of God had given at the LORD's
6 command. "Please!" the king cried out to the man of God. "Entreat the LORD
your God and pray on my behalf that my hand will be restored to me." The
man of God entreated the LORD, and the king's hand was restored to its usual
7 state. "Come home with me and dine," the king told the man of God, "and I
8 will give you a gift." "Were you to give me half your house, I would not come
with you," the man of God said to the king. "I will not eat any food nor drink
9 any water in this place. For thus I was charged by the word of the LORD: Do
not eat any food, do not drink any water, and do not retrace the road you have
10 traveled." And he set out on a different road; he did not return by the road he

50 | Cf. Exodus 32:4.

51 | Respectively, the southern and northern limits of his realm.

52 | Referring to the Festival of Tabernacles, which took place one month earlier.

אֶת־שְׁכֶם בְּהַר אֶפְרַיִם וַיֵּשֶׁב בָּהּ וַיֵּצֵא מִשָּׁם וַיִּבֶן אֶת־פְּנוּאֵל׃
כו כז וַיֹּאמֶר יָרָבְעָם בְּלִבּוֹ עַתָּה תָּשׁוּב הַמַּמְלָכָה לְבֵית־דָּוִד׃ אִם־יַעֲלֶה ׀
הָעָם הַזֶּה לַעֲשׂוֹת זְבָחִים בְּבֵית־יהוה בִּירוּשָׁלַ͏ִם וְשָׁב לֵב הָעָם הַזֶּה
אֶל־אֲדֹנֵיהֶם אֶל־רְחַבְעָם מֶלֶךְ יְהוּדָה וַהֲרָגֻנִי וְשָׁבוּ אֶל־רְחַבְעָם
כח מֶלֶךְ־יְהוּדָה׃ וַיִּוָּעַץ הַמֶּלֶךְ וַיַּעַשׂ שְׁנֵי עֶגְלֵי זָהָב וַיֹּאמֶר אֲלֵהֶם רַב־
לָכֶם מֵעֲלוֹת יְרוּשָׁלַ͏ִם הִנֵּה אֱלֹהֶיךָ יִשְׂרָאֵל אֲשֶׁר הֶעֱלוּךָ מֵאֶרֶץ
כט ל מִצְרָיִם׃ וַיָּשֶׂם אֶת־הָאֶחָד בְּבֵית־אֵל וְאֶת־הָאֶחָד נָתַן בְּדָן׃ וַיְהִי
לא הַדָּבָר הַזֶּה לְחַטָּאת וַיֵּלְכוּ הָעָם לִפְנֵי הָאֶחָד עַד־דָּן׃ וַיַּעַשׂ אֶת־בֵּית
לב בָּמוֹת וַיַּעַשׂ כֹּהֲנִים מִקְצוֹת הָעָם אֲשֶׁר לֹא־הָיוּ מִבְּנֵי לֵוִי׃ וַיַּעַשׂ
יָרָבְעָם ׀ חָג בַּחֹדֶשׁ הַשְּׁמִינִי בַּחֲמִשָּׁה־עָשָׂר יוֹם ׀ לַחֹדֶשׁ כֶּחָג ׀ אֲשֶׁר
בִּיהוּדָה וַיַּעַל עַל־הַמִּזְבֵּחַ כֵּן עָשָׂה בְּבֵית־אֵל לְזַבֵּחַ לָעֲגָלִים אֲשֶׁר־
לג עָשָׂה וְהֶעֱמִיד בְּבֵית אֵל אֶת־כֹּהֲנֵי הַבָּמוֹת אֲשֶׁר עָשָׂה׃ וַיַּעַל עַל־
הַמִּזְבֵּחַ ׀ אֲשֶׁר־עָשָׂה בְּבֵית־אֵל בַּחֲמִשָּׁה עָשָׂר יוֹם בַּחֹדֶשׁ הַשְּׁמִינִי
בַּחֹדֶשׁ אֲשֶׁר־בָּדָא מלבד וַיַּעַשׂ חָג לִבְנֵי יִשְׂרָאֵל וַיַּעַל עַל־הַמִּזְבֵּחַ מִלִּבּוֹ
יג א לְהַקְטִיר׃ וְהִנֵּה ׀ אִישׁ אֱלֹהִים בָּא מִיהוּדָה בִּדְבַר יהוה
ב אֶל־בֵּית־אֵל וְיָרָבְעָם עֹמֵד עַל־הַמִּזְבֵּחַ לְהַקְטִיר׃ וַיִּקְרָא עַל־הַמִּזְבֵּחַ
בִּדְבַר יהוה וַיֹּאמֶר מִזְבֵּחַ מִזְבֵּחַ כֹּה אָמַר יהוה הִנֵּה־בֵן נוֹלָד לְבֵית־
דָּוִד יֹאשִׁיָּהוּ שְׁמוֹ וְזָבַח עָלֶיךָ אֶת־כֹּהֲנֵי הַבָּמוֹת הַמַּקְטִרִים עָלֶיךָ
ג וְעַצְמוֹת אָדָם יִשְׂרְפוּ עָלֶיךָ׃ וְנָתַן בַּיּוֹם הַהוּא מוֹפֵת לֵאמֹר זֶה הַמּוֹפֵת
ד אֲשֶׁר דִּבֶּר יהוה הִנֵּה הַמִּזְבֵּחַ נִקְרָע וְנִשְׁפַּךְ הַדֶּשֶׁן אֲשֶׁר־עָלָיו׃ וַיְהִי
כִשְׁמֹעַ הַמֶּלֶךְ אֶת־דְּבַר אִישׁ־הָאֱלֹהִים אֲשֶׁר קָרָא עַל־הַמִּזְבֵּחַ בְּבֵית־
אֵל וַיִּשְׁלַח יָרָבְעָם אֶת־יָדוֹ מֵעַל הַמִּזְבֵּחַ לֵאמֹר ׀ תִּפְשֻׂהוּ וַתִּיבַשׁ יָדוֹ
ה אֲשֶׁר שָׁלַח עָלָיו וְלֹא יָכֹל לַהֲשִׁיבָהּ אֵלָיו׃ וְהַמִּזְבֵּחַ נִקְרָע וַיִּשָּׁפֵךְ
ו הַדֶּשֶׁן מִן־הַמִּזְבֵּחַ כַּמּוֹפֵת אֲשֶׁר נָתַן אִישׁ הָאֱלֹהִים בִּדְבַר יהוה׃ וַיַּעַן
הַמֶּלֶךְ וַיֹּאמֶר ׀ אֶל־אִישׁ הָאֱלֹהִים חַל־נָא אֶת־פְּנֵי יהוה אֱלֹהֶיךָ
וְהִתְפַּלֵּל בַּעֲדִי וְתָשֹׁב יָדִי אֵלָי וַיְחַל אִישׁ־הָאֱלֹהִים אֶת־פְּנֵי יהוה
ז וַתָּשָׁב יַד־הַמֶּלֶךְ אֵלָיו וַתְּהִי כְּבָרִאשֹׁנָה׃ וַיְדַבֵּר הַמֶּלֶךְ אֶל־אִישׁ
ח הָאֱלֹהִים בֹּאָה־אִתִּי הַבַּיְתָה וּסְעָדָה וְאֶתְּנָה לְךָ מַתָּת׃ וַיֹּאמֶר אִישׁ־
הָאֱלֹהִים אֶל־הַמֶּלֶךְ אִם־תִּתֶּן־לִי אֶת־חֲצִי בֵיתֶךָ לֹא אָבֹא עִמָּךְ
ט וְלֹא־אֹכַל לֶחֶם וְלֹא אֶשְׁתֶּה־מַּיִם בַּמָּקוֹם הַזֶּה׃ כִּי־כֵן ׀ צִוָּה אֹתִי בִּדְבַר
יהוה לֵאמֹר לֹא־תֹאכַל לֶחֶם וְלֹא תִשְׁתֶּה־מָּיִם וְלֹא תָשׁוּב בַּדֶּרֶךְ
י אֲשֶׁר הָלָכְתָּ׃ וַיֵּלֶךְ בְּדֶרֶךְ אַחֵר וְלֹא־שָׁב בַּדֶּרֶךְ אֲשֶׁר בָּא בָהּ אֶל־

11 had taken to Beit El. There was an old prophet who lived in Beit El.
His sons came and told him all about the feats that the man of God had
performed that day in Beit El; they told their father all about the words
12 he had spoken to the king. "By which road did he leave?" their father asked
them, and his sons had noticed the road taken by the man of God who had
13 come from Yehuda. "Saddle the donkey for me," he said to his sons, and they
14 saddled the donkey for him. He mounted it and followed after the man of
God, and he found him sitting beneath a terebinth. "Are you the man of God
15 who came from Yehuda?" he asked him. "I am," he said. "Come home with
16 me and have some food," he said to him. "I cannot return with you and come
with you," he said, "I will not eat food or drink water with you in this place.
17 For I was told by the word of the LORD: Do not eat food or drink water there,
18 and do not retrace the road you have traveled." "I too am a prophet, just like
you," he said to him, "and an angel spoke to me with the word of the LORD,
saying: Bring him back with you to your home, and let him eat food and drink
19 water." But he was lying to him. He went back with him and ate food in his
20 house, and drank water. But as they sat at the table, the word of the
21 LORD came to the prophet who had brought the other back, and he called
out to the man of God who had come from Yehuda, "Thus says the LORD:
Because you have violated the word of the LORD and failed to keep the
22 instructions that the LORD your God charged you with – you came back
and ate food and drank water in the place where He told you: Do not eat
food, and do not drink water – your corpse will not reach the grave of your
23 ancestors." After he had eaten food, and drunk, he saddled the donkey for
24 him – for the prophet he had brought back. He set out, but a lion found him
on the road and killed him. His corpse was left flung down on the road while
25 the donkey stood close by; the lion, too, stood by the corpse. Just then some
people passed by, and they saw the corpse flung down on the road with the
lion standing by the corpse. They reached the town where the old prophet
26 lived and spread word about it. When the prophet who had brought him back
from the road heard about it, he said, "He is the man of God who violated
the word of the LORD. The LORD gave him over to the lion that mauled him
27 to death, fulfilling the word that the LORD spoke to him." And he told his
28 sons, "Saddle the donkey for me," and they saddled it. He set out and found
his corpse flung down on the road, with the donkey and the lion still standing
by the corpse; the lion had not eaten the corpse, nor had it mauled the donkey.
29 The prophet lifted the corpse of the man of God, placed it on the donkey, and
30 brought it back – it went to the old prophet's town for lament and burial. He
placed the corpse in its grave, and they lamented over it: "Alas, my brother!"
31 After he had buried him, he said to his sons, "When I die, bury me in the

יא בֵּית־אֵל: וְנָבִיא אֶחָד זָקֵן יֹשֵׁב בְּבֵית־אֵל וַיָּבוֹא בְנוֹ וַיְסַפֶּר־
לוֹ אֶת־כָּל־הַמַּעֲשֶׂה אֲשֶׁר־עָשָׂה אִישׁ־הָאֱלֹהִים ׀ הַיּוֹם בְּבֵית־אֵל
יב אֶת־הַדְּבָרִים אֲשֶׁר דִּבֶּר אֶל־הַמֶּלֶךְ וַיְסַפְּרוּם לַאֲבִיהֶם: וַיְדַבֵּר אֲלֵהֶם
אֲבִיהֶם אֵי־זֶה הַדֶּרֶךְ הָלָךְ וַיִּרְאוּ בָנָיו אֶת־הַדֶּרֶךְ אֲשֶׁר הָלַךְ אִישׁ
יג הָאֱלֹהִים אֲשֶׁר־בָּא מִיהוּדָה: וַיֹּאמֶר אֶל־בָּנָיו חִבְשׁוּ־לִי הַחֲמוֹר
יד וַיַּחְבְּשׁוּ־לוֹ הַחֲמוֹר וַיִּרְכַּב עָלָיו: וַיֵּלֶךְ אַחֲרֵי אִישׁ הָאֱלֹהִים וַיִּמְצָאֵהוּ
יֹשֵׁב תַּחַת הָאֵלָה וַיֹּאמֶר אֵלָיו הַאַתָּה אִישׁ־הָאֱלֹהִים אֲשֶׁר־בָּאתָ
טו טז מִיהוּדָה וַיֹּאמֶר אָנִי: וַיֹּאמֶר אֵלָיו לֵךְ אִתִּי הַבָּיְתָה וֶאֱכֹל לָחֶם: וַיֹּאמֶר
לֹא אוּכַל לָשׁוּב אִתָּךְ וְלָבוֹא אִתָּךְ וְלֹא־אֹכַל לֶחֶם וְלֹא־אֶשְׁתֶּה אִתְּךָ
יז מַיִם בַּמָּקוֹם הַזֶּה: כִּי־דָבָר אֵלַי בִּדְבַר יְהוָה לֹא־תֹאכַל לֶחֶם וְלֹא־
יח תִשְׁתֶּה שָׁם מָיִם לֹא־תָשׁוּב לָלֶכֶת בַּדֶּרֶךְ אֲשֶׁר־הָלַכְתָּ בָּהּ: וַיֹּאמֶר
לוֹ גַּם־אֲנִי נָבִיא כָּמוֹךָ וּמַלְאָךְ דִּבֶּר אֵלַי בִּדְבַר יְהוָה לֵאמֹר הֲשִׁבֵהוּ
יט אִתְּךָ אֶל־בֵּיתֶךָ וְיֹאכַל לֶחֶם וְיֵשְׁתְּ מָיִם כִּחֵשׁ לוֹ: וַיָּשָׁב אִתּוֹ וַיֹּאכַל
כ לֶחֶם בְּבֵיתוֹ וַיֵּשְׁתְּ מָיִם: וַיְהִי הֵם יֹשְׁבִים אֶל־הַשֻּׁלְחָן וַיְהִי
כא דְּבַר־יְהוָה אֶל־הַנָּבִיא אֲשֶׁר הֱשִׁיבוֹ: וַיִּקְרָא אֶל־אִישׁ הָאֱלֹהִים אֲשֶׁר־
בָּא מִיהוּדָה לֵאמֹר כֹּה אָמַר יְהוָה יַעַן כִּי מָרִיתָ פִּי יְהוָה וְלֹא שָׁמַרְתָּ
כב אֶת־הַמִּצְוָה אֲשֶׁר צִוְּךָ יְהוָה אֱלֹהֶיךָ: וַתָּשָׁב וַתֹּאכַל לֶחֶם וַתֵּשְׁתְּ מַיִם
בַּמָּקוֹם אֲשֶׁר דִּבֶּר אֵלֶיךָ אַל־תֹּאכַל לֶחֶם וְאַל־תֵּשְׁתְּ מָיִם לֹא־תָבוֹא
כג נִבְלָתְךָ אֶל־קֶבֶר אֲבֹתֶיךָ: וַיְהִי אַחֲרֵי אָכְלוֹ לֶחֶם וְאַחֲרֵי שְׁתוֹתוֹ
כד וַיַּחֲבָשׁ־לוֹ הַחֲמוֹר לַנָּבִיא אֲשֶׁר הֱשִׁיבוֹ: וַיֵּלֶךְ וַיִּמְצָאֵהוּ אַרְיֵה בַּדֶּרֶךְ
וַיְמִיתֵהוּ וַתְּהִי נִבְלָתוֹ מֻשְׁלֶכֶת בַּדֶּרֶךְ וְהַחֲמוֹר עֹמֵד אֶצְלָהּ וְהָאַרְיֵה
כה עֹמֵד אֵצֶל הַנְּבֵלָה: וְהִנֵּה אֲנָשִׁים עֹבְרִים וַיִּרְאוּ אֶת־הַנְּבֵלָה מֻשְׁלֶכֶת
בַּדֶּרֶךְ וְאֶת־הָאַרְיֵה עֹמֵד אֵצֶל הַנְּבֵלָה וַיָּבֹאוּ וַיְדַבְּרוּ בָעִיר אֲשֶׁר
כו הַנָּבִיא הַזָּקֵן יֹשֵׁב בָּהּ: וַיִּשְׁמַע הַנָּבִיא אֲשֶׁר הֱשִׁיבוֹ מִן־הַדֶּרֶךְ וַיֹּאמֶר
אִישׁ הָאֱלֹהִים הוּא אֲשֶׁר מָרָה אֶת־פִּי יְהוָה וַיִּתְּנֵהוּ יְהוָה לָאַרְיֵה
כז וַיִּשְׁבְּרֵהוּ וַיְמִתֵהוּ כִּדְבַר יְהוָה אֲשֶׁר דִּבֶּר־לוֹ: וַיְדַבֵּר אֶל־בָּנָיו לֵאמֹר
כח חִבְשׁוּ־לִי אֶת־הַחֲמוֹר וַיַּחֲבֹשׁוּ: וַיֵּלֶךְ וַיִּמְצָא אֶת־נִבְלָתוֹ מֻשְׁלֶכֶת
בַּדֶּרֶךְ וַחֲמוֹר וְהָאַרְיֵה עֹמְדִים אֵצֶל הַנְּבֵלָה לֹא־אָכַל הָאַרְיֵה אֶת־
כט הַנְּבֵלָה וְלֹא שָׁבַר אֶת־הַחֲמוֹר: וַיִּשָּׂא הַנָּבִיא אֶת־נִבְלַת אִישׁ־
הָאֱלֹהִים וַיַּנִּחֵהוּ אֶל־הַחֲמוֹר וַיְשִׁיבֵהוּ וַיָּבֹא אֶל־עִיר הַנָּבִיא הַזָּקֵן
ל לא לִסְפֹּד וּלְקָבְרוֹ: וַיַּנַּח אֶת־נִבְלָתוֹ בְּקִבְרוֹ וַיִּסְפְּדוּ עָלָיו הוֹי אָחִי: וַיְהִי יב
אַחֲרֵי קָבְרוֹ אֹתוֹ וַיֹּאמֶר אֶל־בָּנָיו לֵאמֹר בְּמוֹתִי וּקְבַרְתֶּם אֹתִי בַּקֶּבֶר

grave where the man of God is buried – lay my bones to rest next to his bones.
32 For the word of the LORD he pronounced against the altar in Beit El, and
against all the buildings of the high shrines in the towns of Shomron, will
33 surely come to pass." Even after this incident, Yorovam did not turn
back from his evil ways. He continued appointing an array of people as the
priests of the high shrines; he ordained anyone who so desired as a priest of
34 the high shrines. This counted as a grave sin for the house of Yorovam –
14 1 leading to their total obliteration from the face of the earth. Around
2 that time, Aviya, Yorovam's son, fell ill. Yorovam said to his wife, "Set out
now and disguise yourself so that no one will know that you are the wife of
Yorovam. Go to Shilo, where the prophet Aḥiya is; he was the one who
3 foretold I would be king over this people. Take ten loaves of bread, some cakes,
and a jar of honey with you, and go to him. He will tell you what will become
4 of the boy." Yorovam's wife did just that: she set out toward Shilo and reached
the house of Aḥiya. Aḥiyahu could no longer see, for his eyes had dimmed
5 with old age. But the LORD had said to Aḥiyahu, "The wife of
Yorovam will soon come to inquire about her son through you, for he is ill.
Thus and thus you shall speak to her. When she arrives, she will be in disguise."
6 When Aḥiyahu heard the sound of her footsteps approaching the door, he
said: "Come in, wife of Yorovam. Why are you in disguise? I have a harsh
7 message for you. Go and say to Yorovam, 'Thus says the LORD, God of Israel:
I raised you up from among the people and appointed you ruler over My
8 people Israel. But though I tore the kingdom away from the House of David
and gave it to you, you have not been like My servant David, who kept My
commandments and followed Me with all his heart, doing only what is right
9 in My eyes; you have acted worse than all those before you. You have made
yourself other gods – molten images – to anger Me, while as for Me – you
10 have cast Me behind your back. Therefore, I am about to bring evil to the
house of Yorovam. I will cut off every last male[53] of Yorovam in Israel, bond
and free, and I will burn up the house of Yorovam as a person burns every last
11 trace of dung. Those of Yorovam's who die in the city will be devoured by
dogs, and those who die in the field will be devoured by the birds of the sky,
12 for the LORD has spoken.' Now, go straight to your house; as soon as you set
13 foot in the city, the child will die. All of Israel will lament him and bury him,
and he alone of Yorovam will reach his grave, for the LORD, God of Israel,
14 has found good in him alone out of all the house of Yorovam. The LORD
will appoint a king for Himself over Israel, who will wipe out the house of
15 Yorovam this very day – yes, even now. And the LORD will strike Israel like a
reed that swishes in the water. He will uproot Israel from this good soil that
He gave to their ancestors, and He will scatter them beyond the Euphrates
16 because they have made their own sacred trees,[54] angering the LORD. He
will hand Israel over because of the sins that Yorovam committed, and

53 | Literally "one who urinates against a wall." This phrase appears also in 16:11, 21:21; II Kings 9:8; and I Samuel, chapter 25.

54 | Hebrew *asherim*: trees, wooden posts, or images representing the Canaanite fertility goddess Ashera.

אֲשֶׁר אִישׁ הָאֱלֹהִים קָבוּר בּוֹ אֵצֶל עַצְמֹתָיו הַנִּיחוּ אֶת־עַצְמֹתָי׃
לב כִּי הָיֹה יִהְיֶה הַדָּבָר אֲשֶׁר קָרָא בִּדְבַר יְהוָה עַל־הַמִּזְבֵּחַ אֲשֶׁר בְּבֵית־
לג אֵל וְעַל כָּל־בָּתֵּי הַבָּמוֹת אֲשֶׁר בְּעָרֵי שֹׁמְרוֹן׃ אַחַר הַדָּבָר
הַזֶּה לֹא־שָׁב יָרָבְעָם מִדַּרְכּוֹ הָרָעָה וַיָּשָׁב וַיַּעַשׂ מִקְצוֹת הָעָם כֹּהֲנֵי
לד בָמוֹת הֶחָפֵץ יְמַלֵּא אֶת־יָדוֹ וִיהִי כֹּהֲנֵי בָמוֹת׃ וַיְהִי בַּדָּבָר הַזֶּה לְחַטַּאת
יד א בֵּית יָרָבְעָם וּלְהַכְחִיד וּלְהַשְׁמִיד מֵעַל פְּנֵי הָאֲדָמָה׃ בָּעֵת
ב הַהִיא חָלָה אֲבִיָּה בֶן־יָרָבְעָם׃ וַיֹּאמֶר יָרָבְעָם לְאִשְׁתּוֹ קוּמִי נָא
וְהִשְׁתַּנִּית וְלֹא יֵדְעוּ כִּי־אתי אֵשֶׁת יָרָבְעָם וְהָלַכְתְּ שִׁלֹה הִנֵּה־שָׁם אַתְּ
ג אֲחִיָּה הַנָּבִיא הוּא־דִבֶּר עָלַי לְמֶלֶךְ עַל־הָעָם הַזֶּה׃ וְלָקַחַתְּ בְּיָדֵךְ
עֲשָׂרָה לֶחֶם וְנִקֻּדִים וּבַקְבֻּק דְּבַשׁ וּבָאת אֵלָיו הוּא יַגִּיד לָךְ מַה־יִּהְיֶה
ד לַנָּעַר׃ וַתַּעַשׂ כֵּן אֵשֶׁת יָרָבְעָם וַתָּקָם וַתֵּלֶךְ שִׁלֹה וַתָּבֹא בֵּית אֲחִיָּה
ה וַאֲחִיָּהוּ לֹא־יָכֹל לִרְאוֹת כִּי קָמוּ עֵינָיו מִשֵּׂיבוֹ׃ וַיהוָה
אָמַר אֶל־אֲחִיָּהוּ הִנֵּה אֵשֶׁת יָרָבְעָם בָּאָה לִדְרֹשׁ דָּבָר מֵעִמְּךָ אֶל־בְּנָהּ
ו כִּי־חֹלֶה הוּא כָּזֹה וְכָזֶה תְּדַבֵּר אֵלֶיהָ וִיהִי כְבֹאָהּ וְהִיא מִתְנַכֵּרָה׃ וַיְהִי
כִשְׁמֹעַ אֲחִיָּהוּ אֶת־קוֹל רַגְלֶיהָ בָּאָה בַפֶּתַח וַיֹּאמֶר בֹּאִי אֵשֶׁת יָרָבְעָם
ז לָמָּה זֶּה אַתְּ מִתְנַכֵּרָה וְאָנֹכִי שָׁלוּחַ אֵלַיִךְ קָשָׁה׃ לְכִי אִמְרִי לְיָרָבְעָם
כֹּה־אָמַר יְהוָה אֱלֹהֵי יִשְׂרָאֵל יַעַן אֲשֶׁר הֲרִימֹתִיךָ מִתּוֹךְ הָעָם וָאֶתֶּנְךָ
ח נָגִיד עַל עַמִּי יִשְׂרָאֵל׃ וָאֶקְרַע אֶת־הַמַּמְלָכָה מִבֵּית דָּוִד וָאֶתְּנֶהָ לָךְ
וְלֹא־הָיִיתָ כְּעַבְדִּי דָוִד אֲשֶׁר שָׁמַר מִצְוֺתַי וַאֲשֶׁר הָלַךְ אַחֲרַי בְּכָל־
ט לְבָבוֹ לַעֲשׂוֹת רַק הַיָּשָׁר בְּעֵינָי׃ וַתָּרַע לַעֲשׂוֹת מִכֹּל אֲשֶׁר־הָיוּ לְפָנֶיךָ
וַתֵּלֶךְ וַתַּעֲשֶׂה־לְּךָ אֱלֹהִים אֲחֵרִים וּמַסֵּכוֹת לְהַכְעִיסֵנִי וְאֹתִי הִשְׁלַכְתָּ
י אַחֲרֵי גַוֶּךָ׃ לָכֵן הִנְנִי מֵבִיא רָעָה אֶל־בֵּית יָרָבְעָם וְהִכְרַתִּי לְיָרָבְעָם
מַשְׁתִּין בְּקִיר עָצוּר וְעָזוּב בְּיִשְׂרָאֵל וּבִעַרְתִּי אַחֲרֵי בֵית־יָרָבְעָם כַּאֲשֶׁר
יא יְבַעֵר הַגָּלָל עַד־תֻּמּוֹ׃ הַמֵּת לְיָרָבְעָם בָּעִיר יֹאכְלוּ הַכְּלָבִים וְהַמֵּת
יב בַּשָּׂדֶה יֹאכְלוּ עוֹף הַשָּׁמָיִם כִּי יְהוָה דִּבֵּר׃ וְאַתְּ קוּמִי לְכִי לְבֵיתֵךְ
יג בְּבֹאָה רַגְלַיִךְ הָעִירָה וּמֵת הַיָּלֶד׃ וְסָפְדוּ־לוֹ כָל־יִשְׂרָאֵל וְקָבְרוּ אֹתוֹ
כִּי־זֶה לְבַדּוֹ יָבֹא לְיָרָבְעָם אֶל־קָבֶר יַעַן נִמְצָא־בוֹ דָּבָר טוֹב אֶל־יְהוָה
יד אֱלֹהֵי יִשְׂרָאֵל בְּבֵית יָרָבְעָם׃ וְהֵקִים יְהוָה לוֹ מֶלֶךְ עַל־יִשְׂרָאֵל אֲשֶׁר
טו יַכְרִית אֶת־בֵּית יָרָבְעָם זֶה הַיּוֹם וּמֶה גַּם־עָתָּה׃ וְהִכָּה יְהוָה אֶת־
יִשְׂרָאֵל כַּאֲשֶׁר יָנוּד הַקָּנֶה בַּמַּיִם וְנָתַשׁ אֶת־יִשְׂרָאֵל מֵעַל הָאֲדָמָה
הַטּוֹבָה הַזֹּאת אֲשֶׁר נָתַן לַאֲבוֹתֵיהֶם וְזֵרָם מֵעֵבֶר לַנָּהָר יַעַן אֲשֶׁר
טז עָשׂוּ אֶת־אֲשֵׁרֵיהֶם מַכְעִיסִים אֶת־יְהוָה׃ וְיִתֵּן אֶת־יִשְׂרָאֵל בִּגְלַל

17 because he led Israel to sin." Yorovam's wife set out immediately and came to
18 Tirtza. As soon as she reached the threshold of the house, the boy died. All
of Israel buried him and lamented him, just as the Lord had pronounced
19 through His servant, the prophet Aḥiyahu. As for the rest of Yorovam's
history – how he fought and how he reigned – it is recorded in the book of
20 the History of the Kings of Israel. The length of Yorovam's reign was twenty-
two years. And he slept with his ancestors, and his son Nadav reigned in his
21 place. Meanwhile, Reḥavam son of Shlomo reigned in Yehuda.
Reḥavam was forty-one years old when he became king, and for seventeen
years he reigned in Jerusalem, the city where the Lord had chosen to
establish His name out of all the tribes of Israel. His mother's name was
22 Naama the Amonite. Yehuda did what was evil in the eyes of the Lord; the
sins they committed enraged Him more than all that their ancestors had ever
23 done. They, too, built their own high shrines and worship pillars and sacred
24 trees on every high hill and under every shady tree; there were even male
ritual prostitutes in the land. They committed all the horrors of the nations
25 that the Lord had dispossessed before the Israelites. In the fifth year
of Reḥavam's reign, King Shishak of Egypt launched an attack on Jerusalem.
26 He seized the treasures of the House of the Lord and the treasures of the
royal palace; he seized everything. He even seized all the golden shields that
27 Shlomo had made.[55] King Reḥavam had bronze shields made in their place
and entrusted them to the chief sentry, who guarded the entrance of the
28 palace. Whenever the king went to the House of the Lord, the sentry would
29 carry them and then return them to the sentry armory. As for the rest of
Reḥavam's history and all his deeds – they are recorded in the book of the
30 History of the Kings of Yehuda. There was ongoing war between Reḥavam
31 and Yorovam. And Reḥavam slept with his ancestors and was buried with his
ancestors in the City of David. His mother's name was Naama the Amonite,
15 1 and his son Aviyam reigned in his place. In the eighteenth year of
2 King Yorovam son of Nevat, Aviyam became king over Yehuda. For three
years he reigned in Jerusalem, and his mother's name was Maakha daughter
3 of Avishalom. He followed in all the sinful ways his father had practiced
before him, and his heart was not fully with the Lord his God as his ancestor
4 David's heart had been. Yet for the sake of David, the Lord his God granted
him a lamp[56] in Jerusalem by establishing his son after him, and by upholding
5 Jerusalem. For David had done what was right in the eyes of the Lord
and never turned away from all He commanded him throughout his life –
6 except in the matter of Uriya the Hittite.[57] Hostility that had begun between
7 Reḥavam and Yorovam continued throughout his life. As for the rest of
Aviyam's history and all his deeds – they are recorded in the book of the
History of the Kings of Yehuda. Hostility continued between Aviyam and

---

55 | See 10:17.
56 | Cf. 11:36.
57 | See II Samuel 11:15–17.

יז חַטֹּאות יָרָבְעָם אֲשֶׁר חָטָא וַאֲשֶׁר הֶחֱטִיא אֶת־יִשְׂרָאֵל: וַתָּקָם אֵשֶׁת
יָרָבְעָם וַתֵּלֶךְ וַתָּבֹא תִרְצָתָה הִיא בָּאָה בְסַף־הַבַּיִת וְהַנַּעַר מֵת:
יח וַיִּקְבְּרוּ אֹתוֹ וַיִּסְפְּדוּ־לוֹ כָּל־יִשְׂרָאֵל כִּדְבַר יְהוָה אֲשֶׁר דִּבֶּר בְּיַד־
יט עַבְדּוֹ אֲחִיָּהוּ הַנָּבִיא: וְיֶתֶר דִּבְרֵי יָרָבְעָם אֲשֶׁר נִלְחַם וַאֲשֶׁר מָלָךְ
כ הִנָּם כְּתוּבִים עַל־סֵפֶר דִּבְרֵי הַיָּמִים לְמַלְכֵי יִשְׂרָאֵל: וְהַיָּמִים אֲשֶׁר
מָלַךְ יָרָבְעָם עֶשְׂרִים וּשְׁתַּיִם שָׁנָה וַיִּשְׁכַּב עִם־אֲבֹתָיו וַיִּמְלֹךְ נָדָב בְּנוֹ
כא תַּחְתָּיו: וּרְחַבְעָם בֶּן־שְׁלֹמֹה מָלַךְ בִּיהוּדָה בֶּן־אַרְבָּעִים
וְאַחַת שָׁנָה רְחַבְעָם בְּמָלְכוֹ וּשְׁבַע עֶשְׂרֵה שָׁנָה ׀ מָלַךְ בִּירוּשָׁלִַם הָעִיר
אֲשֶׁר־בָּחַר יְהוָה לָשׂוּם אֶת־שְׁמוֹ שָׁם מִכֹּל שִׁבְטֵי יִשְׂרָאֵל וְשֵׁם אִמּוֹ
כב נַעֲמָה הָעַמֹּנִית: וַיַּעַשׂ יְהוּדָה הָרַע בְּעֵינֵי יְהוָה וַיְקַנְאוּ אֹתוֹ מִכֹּל
כג אֲשֶׁר עָשׂוּ אֲבֹתָם בְּחַטֹּאתָם אֲשֶׁר חָטָאוּ: וַיִּבְנוּ גַם־הֵמָּה לָהֶם בָּמוֹת
כד וּמַצֵּבוֹת וַאֲשֵׁרִים עַל כָּל־גִּבְעָה גְבֹהָה וְתַחַת כָּל־עֵץ רַעֲנָן: וְגַם־קָדֵשׁ
הָיָה בָאָרֶץ עָשׂוּ כְּכֹל הַתּוֹעֲבֹת הַגּוֹיִם אֲשֶׁר הוֹרִישׁ יְהוָה מִפְּנֵי בְּנֵי
כה יִשְׂרָאֵל: וַיְהִי בַּשָּׁנָה הַחֲמִישִׁית לַמֶּלֶךְ רְחַבְעָם עָלָה שׁושַׁק שִׁישַׁק
כו מֶלֶךְ־מִצְרַיִם עַל־יְרוּשָׁלִָם: וַיִּקַּח אֶת־אֹצְרוֹת בֵּית־יְהוָה וְאֶת־אוֹצְרוֹת
בֵּית הַמֶּלֶךְ וְאֶת־הַכֹּל לָקָח וַיִּקַּח אֶת־כָּל־מָגִנֵּי הַזָּהָב אֲשֶׁר עָשָׂה
כז שְׁלֹמֹה: וַיַּעַשׂ הַמֶּלֶךְ רְחַבְעָם תַּחְתָּם מָגִנֵּי נְחֹשֶׁת וְהִפְקִיד עַל־יַד
כח שָׂרֵי הָרָצִים הַשֹּׁמְרִים פֶּתַח בֵּית הַמֶּלֶךְ: וַיְהִי מִדֵּי־בֹא הַמֶּלֶךְ בֵּית
כט יְהוָה יִשָּׂאוּם הָרָצִים וֶהֱשִׁיבוּם אֶל־תָּא הָרָצִים: וְיֶתֶר דִּבְרֵי רְחַבְעָם
וְכָל־אֲשֶׁר עָשָׂה הֲלֹא־הֵמָּה כְתוּבִים עַל־סֵפֶר דִּבְרֵי הַיָּמִים לְמַלְכֵי
ל לא יְהוּדָה: וּמִלְחָמָה הָיְתָה בֵין־רְחַבְעָם וּבֵין יָרָבְעָם כָּל־הַיָּמִים: וַיִּשְׁכַּב
רְחַבְעָם עִם־אֲבֹתָיו וַיִּקָּבֵר עִם־אֲבֹתָיו בְּעִיר דָּוִד וְשֵׁם אִמּוֹ נַעֲמָה
טו א הָעַמֹּנִית וַיִּמְלֹךְ אֲבִיָּם בְּנוֹ תַּחְתָּיו: וּבִשְׁנַת שְׁמֹנֶה
ב עֶשְׂרֵה לַמֶּלֶךְ יָרָבְעָם בֶּן־נְבָט מָלַךְ אֲבִיָּם עַל־יְהוּדָה: שָׁלֹשׁ שָׁנִים
ג מָלַךְ בִּירוּשָׁלִָם וְשֵׁם אִמּוֹ מַעֲכָה בַּת־אֲבִישָׁלוֹם: וַיֵּלֶךְ בְּכָל־חַטֹּאות
אָבִיו אֲשֶׁר־עָשָׂה לְפָנָיו וְלֹא־הָיָה לְבָבוֹ שָׁלֵם עִם־יְהוָה אֱלֹהָיו
ד כִּלְבַב דָּוִד אָבִיו: כִּי לְמַעַן דָּוִד נָתַן יְהוָה אֱלֹהָיו לוֹ נִיר בִּירוּשָׁלִָם
ה לְהָקִים אֶת־בְּנוֹ אַחֲרָיו וּלְהַעֲמִיד אֶת־יְרוּשָׁלִָם: אֲשֶׁר עָשָׂה דָוִד
אֶת־הַיָּשָׁר בְּעֵינֵי יְהוָה וְלֹא־סָר מִכֹּל ׀ אֲשֶׁר צִוָּהוּ כֹּל יְמֵי חַיָּיו רַק
ו בִּדְבַר אוּרִיָּה הַחִתִּי: וּמִלְחָמָה הָיְתָה בֵין־רְחַבְעָם וּבֵין יָרָבְעָם כָּל־יְמֵי
ז חַיָּיו: וְיֶתֶר דִּבְרֵי אֲבִיָּם וְכָל־אֲשֶׁר עָשָׂה הֲלוֹא־הֵם כְּתוּבִים עַל־סֵפֶר
דִּבְרֵי הַיָּמִים לְמַלְכֵי יְהוּדָה וּמִלְחָמָה הָיְתָה בֵּין אֲבִיָּם וּבֵין יָרָבְעָם:

8 Yorovam. And Aviyam slept with his ancestors and was buried in the City of
9 David. And his son Asa reigned in his place. In the twentieth year of
10 King Yorovam of Israel, Asa became king over Yehuda. For forty-one years
he reigned in Jerusalem, and his mother's name was Maakha daughter of
11 Avishalom. Asa did what was right in the eyes of the LORD like his ancestor
12 David. He banished the male ritual prostitutes from the land, and he removed
13 all the idols that his ancestors had made. He even deposed his mother Maakha
from the position of queen mother because she had made a monstrous image
for Ashera;[58] Asa cut down her monstrous image and burned it by the Kidron
14 Valley. Though the high shrines were not removed, Asa's heart was fully with
15 the LORD all the days of his life. He brought his father's sacred items and his
16 own[59] sacred items into the House of the LORD: silver, gold, and vessels. There
17 was ongoing war between Asa and Basha, king of Israel, all their days. Basha,
king of Israel, advanced against Yehuda and fortified Rama to prevent Asa,
18 king of Yehuda, from marching out into battle. So Asa took all the silver and
gold that remained in the treasury of the House of the LORD and the treasury
of the royal palace, and entrusted it to his officials. Then King Asa sent them
to Ben Hadad son of Tavrimon son of Ḥezyon, the king of Aram, who resided
19 in Damascus, with this message: "There is an alliance between me and you,
between my father and your father. Look, I have sent you an incentive of silver
and gold; go, break your alliance with Basha, king of Israel, so that he will
20 withdraw from me." Ben Hadad complied with King Asa and sent his military
officers against the towns of Israel; he attacked Iyon, Dan, Avel Beit Maakha,
21 all of Kinerot, and all the region of Naftali. When Basha heard, he ceased
22 construction in Rama and remained in Tirtza. Then King Asa rallied all of
Yehuda – no one was exempt – and they seized the stones and wood Basha
had been using to build up Rama, and with them, King Asa fortified Geva of
23 Binyamin and Mitzpa. As for the rest of Asa's history and all his exploits and
all his deeds and the towns he built – they are recorded in the book of the
History of the Kings of Yehuda. In his old age, however, he suffered from
24 a foot disease. And Asa slept with his ancestors and was buried with his
ancestors in the City of David his father. And his son Yehoshafat reigned in
25 his place. Meanwhile, Nadav son of Yorovam became king over
Israel in the second year of Asa, king of Yehuda. He reigned over Israel for
26 two years. He did what was evil in the eyes of the LORD and followed in his
27 father's ways; with his sin he led Israel to sin. Then Basha son of Aḥiya, of the
house of Yissakhar, formed a conspiracy against him; Basha struck him down
in Gibeton of the Philistines while Nadav and all of Israel were besieging
28 Gibeton. Basha killed him in the third year of King Asa of Yehuda, and he
29 reigned in his place. When he became king, he struck down all the house of
Yorovam – he left not a single soul to Yorovam – until he had destroyed it,
fulfilling the LORD's word that He had pronounced through His servant Aḥiya

58 | See note on 14:15.

59 | See II Chronicles 15:18, as well as Targum and Radak here.

יג ח וַיִּשְׁכַּב אֲבִיָּם עִם־אֲבֹתָיו וַיִּקְבְּרוּ אֹתוֹ בְּעִיר דָּוִד וַיִּמְלֹךְ אָסָא בְנוֹ
ט תַּחְתָּיו: וּבִשְׁנַת עֶשְׂרִים לְיָרָבְעָם מֶלֶךְ יִשְׂרָאֵל מָלַךְ אָסָא
י עַל־יְהוּדָה: וְאַרְבָּעִים וְאַחַת שָׁנָה מָלַךְ בִּירוּשָׁלִָם וְשֵׁם אִמּוֹ מַעֲכָה
יא יב בַּת־אֲבִישָׁלוֹם: וַיַּעַשׂ אָסָא הַיָּשָׁר בְּעֵינֵי יהוה כְּדָוִד אָבִיו: וַיַּעֲבֵר
יג הַקְּדֵשִׁים מִן־הָאָרֶץ וַיָּסַר אֶת־כָּל־הַגִּלֻּלִים אֲשֶׁר עָשׂוּ אֲבֹתָיו: וְגַם ׀
אֶת־מַעֲכָה אִמּוֹ וַיְסִרֶהָ מִגְּבִירָה אֲשֶׁר־עָשְׂתָה מִפְלֶצֶת לָאֲשֵׁרָה
יד וַיִּכְרֹת אָסָא אֶת־מִפְלַצְתָּהּ וַיִּשְׂרֹף בְּנַחַל קִדְרוֹן: וְהַבָּמוֹת לֹא־סָרוּ
טו רַק לְבַב־אָסָא הָיָה שָׁלֵם עִם־יהוה כָּל־יָמָיו: וַיָּבֵא אֶת־קָדְשֵׁי אָבִיו
טז וקדשו בֵּית יהוה כֶּסֶף וְזָהָב וְכֵלִים: וּמִלְחָמָה הָיְתָה בֵּין אָסָא וּבֵין וְקָדְשֵׁי
יז בַּעְשָׁא מֶלֶךְ־יִשְׂרָאֵל כָּל־יְמֵיהֶם: וַיַּעַל בַּעְשָׁא מֶלֶךְ־יִשְׂרָאֵל עַל־
יְהוּדָה וַיִּבֶן אֶת־הָרָמָה לְבִלְתִּי תֵּת יֹצֵא וָבָא לְאָסָא מֶלֶךְ יְהוּדָה:
יח וַיִּקַּח אָסָא אֶת־כָּל־הַכֶּסֶף וְהַזָּהָב הַנּוֹתָרִים ׀ בְּאוֹצְרוֹת בֵּית־יהוה
וְאֶת־אוֹצְרוֹת בֵּית מלך וַיִּתְּנֵם בְּיַד עֲבָדָיו וַיִּשְׁלָחֵם הַמֶּלֶךְ אָסָא הַמֶּלֶךְ
אֶל־בֶּן־הֲדַד בֶּן־טַבְרִמֹּן בֶּן־חֶזְיוֹן מֶלֶךְ אֲרָם הַיֹּשֵׁב בְּדַמֶּשֶׂק לֵאמֹר:
יט בְּרִית בֵּינִי וּבֵינֶךָ בֵּין אָבִי וּבֵין אָבִיךָ הִנֵּה שָׁלַחְתִּי לְךָ שֹׁחַד כֶּסֶף וְזָהָב
כ לֵךְ הָפֵרָה אֶת־בְּרִיתְךָ אֶת־בַּעְשָׁא מֶלֶךְ־יִשְׂרָאֵל וְיַעֲלֶה מֵעָלָי: וַיִּשְׁמַע
בֶּן־הֲדַד אֶל־הַמֶּלֶךְ אָסָא וַיִּשְׁלַח אֶת־שָׂרֵי הַחֲיָלִים אֲשֶׁר־לוֹ עַל־עָרֵי
יִשְׂרָאֵל וַיַּךְ אֶת־עִיּוֹן וְאֶת־דָּן וְאֵת אָבֵל בֵּית־מַעֲכָה וְאֵת כָּל־כִּנְרוֹת
כא עַל כָּל־אֶרֶץ נַפְתָּלִי: וַיְהִי כִּשְׁמֹעַ בַּעְשָׁא וַיֶּחְדַּל מִבְּנוֹת אֶת־הָרָמָה
כב וַיֵּשֶׁב בְּתִרְצָה: וְהַמֶּלֶךְ אָסָא הִשְׁמִיעַ אֶת־כָּל־יְהוּדָה אֵין נָקִי וַיִּשְׂאוּ
אֶת־אַבְנֵי הָרָמָה וְאֶת־עֵצֶיהָ אֲשֶׁר בָּנָה בַּעְשָׁא וַיִּבֶן בָּם הַמֶּלֶךְ אָסָא
כג אֶת־גֶּבַע בִּנְיָמִן וְאֶת־הַמִּצְפָּה: וְיֶתֶר כָּל־דִּבְרֵי אָסָא וְכָל־גְּבוּרָתוֹ
וְכָל־אֲשֶׁר עָשָׂה וְהֶעָרִים אֲשֶׁר בָּנָה הֲלֹא־הֵמָּה כְתוּבִים עַל־סֵפֶר
כד דִּבְרֵי הַיָּמִים לְמַלְכֵי יְהוּדָה רַק לְעֵת זִקְנָתוֹ חָלָה אֶת־רַגְלָיו: וַיִּשְׁכַּב
אָסָא עִם־אֲבֹתָיו וַיִּקָּבֵר עִם־אֲבֹתָיו בְּעִיר דָּוִד אָבִיו וַיִּמְלֹךְ יְהוֹשָׁפָט
כה בְּנוֹ תַּחְתָּיו: וְנָדָב בֶּן־יָרָבְעָם מָלַךְ עַל־יִשְׂרָאֵל בִּשְׁנַת
כו שְׁתַּיִם לְאָסָא מֶלֶךְ יְהוּדָה וַיִּמְלֹךְ עַל־יִשְׂרָאֵל שְׁנָתָיִם: וַיַּעַשׂ הָרַע
בְּעֵינֵי יהוה וַיֵּלֶךְ בְּדֶרֶךְ אָבִיו וּבְחַטָּאתוֹ אֲשֶׁר הֶחֱטִיא אֶת־יִשְׂרָאֵל:
כז וַיִּקְשֹׁר עָלָיו בַּעְשָׁא בֶן־אֲחִיָּה לְבֵית יִשָּׂשכָר וַיַּכֵּהוּ בַעְשָׁא בְּגִבְּתוֹן
כח אֲשֶׁר לַפְּלִשְׁתִּים וְנָדָב וְכָל־יִשְׂרָאֵל צָרִים עַל־גִּבְּתוֹן: וַיְמִתֵהוּ בַעְשָׁא
כט בִּשְׁנַת שָׁלֹשׁ לְאָסָא מֶלֶךְ יְהוּדָה וַיִּמְלֹךְ תַּחְתָּיו: וַיְהִי כְמָלְכוֹ הִכָּה
אֶת־כָּל־בֵּית יָרָבְעָם לֹא־הִשְׁאִיר כָּל־נְשָׁמָה לְיָרָבְעָם עַד־הִשְׁמִדוֹ

30 the Shilonite. This was on account of the sins that Yorovam had committed,
through which he led Israel to sin; he had provoked the LORD, God of
31 Israel, to anger. As for the rest of Nadav's history and all his deeds – they are
32 recorded in the book of the History of the Kings of Israel. There was ongoing
33 hostility between Asa and Basha, king of Israel, all their days. In the
third year of Asa, king of Yehuda, Basha son of Aḥiya became king over all
34 Israel in Tirtza for twenty-four years. He did what was evil in the eyes of the
LORD, and he followed in Yorovam's ways; through his sin he led Israel to
16 1 sin. The word of the LORD came to Yehu son of Ḥanani concerning
2 Basha: "Though I raised you up from the dust and appointed you ruler over
My people Israel, you followed in Yorovam's ways and led My people Israel
3 to sin, angering Me with their sins. Therefore I am about to burn up every
last trace of Basha and his house; I will make your house like the house of
4 Yorovam son of Nevat. Those of Basha who die in the city will be devoured
by dogs, and those of his who die in the field will be devoured by the birds of
5 the sky." As for the rest of Basha's history and his deeds and his exploits – they
6 are recorded in the book of the History of the Kings of Israel. And Basha slept
with his ancestors, and he was buried in Tirtza. And his son Ela reigned in
7 his place. But through the prophet Yehu son of Ḥanani, the word of the LORD
was against Basha and his house for all the evil he had done in the eyes of the
LORD, angering Him with his deeds: for striking down the house of Yorovam
8 but acting just like them. In the twenty-sixth year of Asa, king of
9 Yehuda, Ela son of Basha became king over Israel in Tirtza for two years. His
servant Zimri, commander of half the chariotry, formed a conspiracy against
him. While he was in Tirtza, drinking himself into a stupor in the house of
10 Artza, who was in charge of the palace at Tirtza, Zimri entered, struck him
down, and killed him. It was the twenty-seventh year of Asa, king of Yehuda,
11 when he became king in his place. As soon as he became king and took the
throne, he struck down all the house of Basha, not leaving a single male of
12 his kin or his friends. Zimri wiped out all the house of Basha, fulfilling the
13 LORD's word that He had promised to Basha through the prophet Yehu. This
was on account of all of Basha's sins and the sins of his son Ela; they sinned
and led Israel to sin, angering the LORD, God of Israel, with their worthless
14 idols. As for the rest of Ela's history and all his deeds – they are recorded in
15 the book of the History of the Kings of Israel. In the twenty-seventh
year of Asa, king of Yehuda, Zimri became king in Tirtza for seven days while
16 the troops were encamped at Gibeton of the Philistines. When the encamped
troops heard, "Zimri has formed a conspiracy and assassinated the king," all
of Israel made Omri, the army commander, king over Israel that very day in

ל כִּדְבַר יְהוָה אֲשֶׁר דִּבֶּר בְּיַד־עַבְדּוֹ אֲחִיָּה הַשִּׁילֹנִי׃ עַל־חַטֹּאות יָרָבְעָם
אֲשֶׁר חָטָא וַאֲשֶׁר הֶחֱטִיא אֶת־יִשְׂרָאֵל בְּכַעְסוֹ אֲשֶׁר הִכְעִיס אֶת־
לא יְהוָה אֱלֹהֵי יִשְׂרָאֵל׃ וְיֶתֶר דִּבְרֵי נָדָב וְכָל־אֲשֶׁר עָשָׂה הֲלֹא־הֵם
לב כְּתוּבִים עַל־סֵפֶר דִּבְרֵי הַיָּמִים לְמַלְכֵי יִשְׂרָאֵל׃ וּמִלְחָמָה הָיְתָה בֵּין
לג אָסָא וּבֵין בַּעְשָׁא מֶלֶךְ־יִשְׂרָאֵל כָּל־יְמֵיהֶם׃ בִּשְׁנַת שָׁלֹשׁ
לְאָסָא מֶלֶךְ יְהוּדָה מָלַךְ בַּעְשָׁא בֶן־אֲחִיָּה עַל־כָּל־יִשְׂרָאֵל בְּתִרְצָה
לד עֶשְׂרִים וְאַרְבַּע שָׁנָה׃ וַיַּעַשׂ הָרַע בְּעֵינֵי יְהוָה וַיֵּלֶךְ בְּדֶרֶךְ יָרָבְעָם
טז א וּבְחַטָּאתוֹ אֲשֶׁר הֶחֱטִיא אֶת־יִשְׂרָאֵל׃ וַיְהִי דְבַר־יְהוָה
ב אֶל־יֵהוּא בֶן־חֲנָנִי עַל־בַּעְשָׁא לֵאמֹר׃ יַעַן אֲשֶׁר הֲרִימֹתִיךָ מִן־
הֶעָפָר וָאֶתֶּנְךָ נָגִיד עַל עַמִּי יִשְׂרָאֵל וַתֵּלֶךְ ׀ בְּדֶרֶךְ יָרָבְעָם וַתַּחֲטִא
ג אֶת־עַמִּי יִשְׂרָאֵל לְהַכְעִיסֵנִי בְּחַטֹּאתָם׃ הִנְנִי מַבְעִיר אַחֲרֵי בַעְשָׁא
ד וְאַחֲרֵי בֵיתוֹ וְנָתַתִּי אֶת־בֵּיתְךָ כְּבֵית יָרָבְעָם בֶּן־נְבָט׃ הַמֵּת לְבַעְשָׁא
ה בָּעִיר יֹאכְלוּ הַכְּלָבִים וְהַמֵּת לוֹ בַּשָּׂדֶה יֹאכְלוּ עוֹף הַשָּׁמָיִם׃ וְיֶתֶר
דִּבְרֵי בַעְשָׁא וַאֲשֶׁר עָשָׂה וּגְבוּרָתוֹ הֲלֹא־הֵם כְּתוּבִים עַל־סֵפֶר דִּבְרֵי
ו הַיָּמִים לְמַלְכֵי יִשְׂרָאֵל׃ וַיִּשְׁכַּב בַּעְשָׁא עִם־אֲבֹתָיו וַיִּקָּבֵר בְּתִרְצָה
ז וַיִּמְלֹךְ אֵלָה בְנוֹ תַּחְתָּיו׃ וְגַם בְּיַד יֵהוּא בֶן־חֲנָנִי הַנָּבִיא דְּבַר־יְהוָה
הָיָה אֶל־בַּעְשָׁא וְאֶל־בֵּיתוֹ וְעַל כָּל־הָרָעָה ׀ אֲשֶׁר־עָשָׂה ׀ בְּעֵינֵי
יְהוָה לְהַכְעִיסוֹ בְּמַעֲשֵׂה יָדָיו לִהְיוֹת כְּבֵית יָרָבְעָם וְעַל אֲשֶׁר־הִכָּה
ח אֹתוֹ׃ בִּשְׁנַת עֶשְׂרִים וָשֵׁשׁ שָׁנָה לְאָסָא מֶלֶךְ יְהוּדָה מָלַךְ
ט אֵלָה בֶן־בַּעְשָׁא עַל־יִשְׂרָאֵל בְּתִרְצָה שְׁנָתָיִם׃ וַיִּקְשֹׁר עָלָיו עַבְדּוֹ
זִמְרִי שַׂר מַחֲצִית הָרָכֶב וְהוּא בְתִרְצָה שֹׁתֶה שִׁכּוֹר בֵּית אַרְצָא אֲשֶׁר
י עַל־הַבַּיִת בְּתִרְצָה׃ וַיָּבֹא זִמְרִי וַיַּכֵּהוּ וַיְמִיתֵהוּ בִּשְׁנַת עֶשְׂרִים וָשֶׁבַע
יא לְאָסָא מֶלֶךְ יְהוּדָה וַיִּמְלֹךְ תַּחְתָּיו׃ וַיְהִי בְמָלְכוֹ כְּשִׁבְתּוֹ עַל־כִּסְאוֹ
הִכָּה אֶת־כָּל־בֵּית בַּעְשָׁא לֹא־הִשְׁאִיר לוֹ מַשְׁתִּין בְּקִיר וְגֹאֲלָיו וְרֵעֵהוּ׃
יב וַיַּשְׁמֵד זִמְרִי אֵת כָּל־בֵּית בַּעְשָׁא כִּדְבַר יְהוָה אֲשֶׁר דִּבֶּר אֶל־בַּעְשָׁא
יג בְּיַד יֵהוּא הַנָּבִיא׃ אֶל כָּל־חַטֹּאות בַּעְשָׁא וְחַטֹּאות אֵלָה בְנוֹ אֲשֶׁר
חָטְאוּ וַאֲשֶׁר הֶחֱטִיאוּ אֶת־יִשְׂרָאֵל לְהַכְעִיס אֶת־יְהוָה אֱלֹהֵי יִשְׂרָאֵל
יד בְּהַבְלֵיהֶם׃ וְיֶתֶר דִּבְרֵי אֵלָה וְכָל־אֲשֶׁר עָשָׂה הֲלוֹא־הֵם כְּתוּבִים
טו עַל־סֵפֶר דִּבְרֵי הַיָּמִים לְמַלְכֵי יִשְׂרָאֵל׃ בִּשְׁנַת עֶשְׂרִים יד
וָשֶׁבַע שָׁנָה לְאָסָא מֶלֶךְ יְהוּדָה מָלַךְ זִמְרִי שִׁבְעַת יָמִים בְּתִרְצָה וְהָעָם
טז חֹנִים עַל־גִּבְּתוֹן אֲשֶׁר לַפְּלִשְׁתִּים׃ וַיִּשְׁמַע הָעָם הַחֹנִים לֵאמֹר קָשַׁר
זִמְרִי וְגַם הִכָּה אֶת־הַמֶּלֶךְ וַיַּמְלִכוּ כָל־יִשְׂרָאֵל אֶת־עָמְרִי שַׂר־צָבָא

17 the camp. Then Omri marched up from Gibeton, together with all Israel, and
18 besieged Tirtza. When Zimri saw that the city had been captured, he went
into the citadel of the royal palace, set the palace on fire over himself, and
19 died on account of the sins he had sinned, doing what was evil in the eyes of
the LORD. He followed in the ways of Yorovam and the sin he had committed,
20 which led Israel to sin. As for the rest of Zimri's history and the conspiracy
he formed – they are recorded in the book of the History of the Kings of
21 Israel. Then the people of Israel were divided into factions; half
the people supported Tivni son of Ginat, to make him king, while the other
22 half supported Omri. The people who supported Omri overpowered the
people who supported Tivni son of Ginat; Tivni died, and Omri became
king.
23 In the thirty-first year of King Asa of Yehuda, Omri became king over Israel
24 for twelve years; he reigned in Tirtza for six years. Then he purchased Mount
Shomron from Shemer for two talents of silver. He built up the hill and
25 named the city Shomron, after Shemer, the owner of the hill. Omri did what
was evil in the eyes of the LORD; he was worse than all who came before him.
26 He followed in all the ways of Yorovam son of Nevat and his sins, leading
27 Israel to sin, angering the LORD, God of Israel, with their worthless idols. As
for the rest of Omri's history, his deeds, and his exploits – they are recorded
28 in the book of the History of the Kings of Israel. And Omri slept with his
ancestors and was buried in Shomron. And his son Aḥav reigned in his
29 place. Aḥav son of Omri became king of Israel in the thirty-eighth
year of Asa, king of Yehuda. Aḥav son of Omri ruled over Israel in Shomron
30 for twenty-two years. Aḥav son of Omri did what was evil in the eyes of the
31 LORD, more than all who came before him. Following in the footsteps of
Yorovam son of Nevat was the slightest of his sins; he married Izevel, daughter
of King Etbaal of the Sidonians, and went and served Baal[60] and worshipped
32 him. He erected an altar for Baal in the temple of Baal he built in Shomron.
33 And Aḥav made a sacred tree; he did more to anger the LORD, God of Israel,
34 than any of the kings of Israel before him. In his time, Ḥiel of Beit El rebuilt
Yeriḥo; he lay down his firstborn, Aviram, with its foundations, and with
Seguv, his youngest, he set its gates, fulfilling the word of the LORD that
17 1 He had pronounced through Yehoshua son of Nun.[61] Eliyahu the
Tishbite, from the people of Gilad, said to Aḥav, "By the life of the LORD,
God of Israel, whom I serve – there will be no dew or rain these years,

60 | A Canaanite storm god.
61 | See Joshua 6:26.

יז עַל־יִשְׂרָאֵל בַּיּוֹם הַהוּא בַּמַּחֲנֶה: וַיַּעֲלֶה עָמְרִי וְכָל־יִשְׂרָאֵל עִמּוֹ
יח מִגִּבְּתוֹן וַיָּצֻרוּ עַל־תִּרְצָה: וַיְהִי כִּרְאוֹת זִמְרִי כִּי־נִלְכְּדָה הָעִיר וַיָּבֹא
אֶל־אַרְמוֹן בֵּית־הַמֶּלֶךְ וַיִּשְׂרֹף עָלָיו אֶת־בֵּית־מֶלֶךְ בָּאֵשׁ וַיָּמֹת:
יט עַל־חַטֹּאתָיו אֲשֶׁר חָטָא לַעֲשׂוֹת הָרַע בְּעֵינֵי יְהוָה לָלֶכֶת בְּדֶרֶךְ
כ יָרָבְעָם וּבְחַטָּאתוֹ אֲשֶׁר עָשָׂה לְהַחֲטִיא אֶת־יִשְׂרָאֵל: וְיֶתֶר דִּבְרֵי
זִמְרִי וְקִשְׁרוֹ אֲשֶׁר קָשָׁר הֲלֹא־הֵם כְּתוּבִים עַל־סֵפֶר דִּבְרֵי הַיָּמִים
כא לְמַלְכֵי יִשְׂרָאֵל: אָז יֵחָלֵק הָעָם יִשְׂרָאֵל לַחֵצִי חֲצִי הָעָם
כב הָיָה אַחֲרֵי תִבְנִי בֶן־גִּינַת לְהַמְלִיכוֹ וְהַחֵצִי אַחֲרֵי עָמְרִי: וַיֶּחֱזַק הָעָם
אֲשֶׁר אַחֲרֵי עָמְרִי אֶת־הָעָם אֲשֶׁר אַחֲרֵי תִּבְנִי בֶן־גִּינַת וַיָּמָת תִּבְנִי
וַיִּמְלֹךְ עָמְרִי:
כג בִּשְׁנַת שְׁלֹשִׁים וְאַחַת שָׁנָה לְאָסָא מֶלֶךְ יְהוּדָה מָלַךְ עָמְרִי עַל־
כד יִשְׂרָאֵל שְׁתֵּים עֶשְׂרֵה שָׁנָה בְּתִרְצָה מָלַךְ שֵׁשׁ־שָׁנִים: וַיִּקֶן אֶת־הָהָר
שֹׁמְרוֹן מֵאֶת שֶׁמֶר בְּכִכְּרַיִם כָּסֶף וַיִּבֶן אֶת־הָהָר וַיִּקְרָא אֶת־שֵׁם
כה הָעִיר אֲשֶׁר בָּנָה עַל שֶׁם־שֶׁמֶר אֲדֹנֵי הָהָר שֹׁמְרוֹן: וַיַּעֲשֶׂה עָמְרִי הָרַע
כו בְּעֵינֵי יְהוָה וַיָּרַע מִכֹּל אֲשֶׁר לְפָנָיו: וַיֵּלֶךְ בְּכָל־דֶּרֶךְ יָרָבְעָם בֶּן־נְבָט
ובחטאתיו אֲשֶׁר הֶחֱטִיא אֶת־יִשְׂרָאֵל לְהַכְעִיס אֶת־יְהוָה אֱלֹהֵי וּבְחַטָּאתוֹ
כז יִשְׂרָאֵל בְּהַבְלֵיהֶם: וְיֶתֶר דִּבְרֵי עָמְרִי אֲשֶׁר עָשָׂה וּגְבוּרָתוֹ אֲשֶׁר
עָשָׂה הֲלֹא־הֵם כְּתוּבִים עַל־סֵפֶר דִּבְרֵי הַיָּמִים לְמַלְכֵי יִשְׂרָאֵל:
כח וַיִּשְׁכַּב עָמְרִי עִם־אֲבֹתָיו וַיִּקָּבֵר בְּשֹׁמְרוֹן וַיִּמְלֹךְ אַחְאָב בְּנוֹ
כט תַּחְתָּיו: וְאַחְאָב בֶּן־עָמְרִי מָלַךְ עַל־יִשְׂרָאֵל בִּשְׁנַת
שְׁלֹשִׁים וּשְׁמֹנֶה שָׁנָה לְאָסָא מֶלֶךְ יְהוּדָה וַיִּמְלֹךְ אַחְאָב בֶּן־עָמְרִי
ל עַל־יִשְׂרָאֵל בְּשֹׁמְרוֹן עֶשְׂרִים וּשְׁתַּיִם שָׁנָה: וַיַּעַשׂ אַחְאָב בֶּן־עָמְרִי
לא הָרַע בְּעֵינֵי יְהוָה מִכֹּל אֲשֶׁר לְפָנָיו: וַיְהִי הֲנָקֵל לֶכְתּוֹ בְּחַטֹּאות יָרָבְעָם
בֶּן־נְבָט וַיִּקַּח אִשָּׁה אֶת־אִיזֶבֶל בַּת־אֶתְבַּעַל מֶלֶךְ צִידֹנִים וַיֵּלֶךְ
לב וַיַּעֲבֹד אֶת־הַבַּעַל וַיִּשְׁתַּחוּ לוֹ: וַיָּקֶם מִזְבֵּחַ לַבָּעַל בֵּית הַבַּעַל אֲשֶׁר
לג בָּנָה בְּשֹׁמְרוֹן: וַיַּעַשׂ אַחְאָב אֶת־הָאֲשֵׁרָה וַיּוֹסֶף אַחְאָב לַעֲשׂוֹת
לְהַכְעִיס אֶת־יְהוָה אֱלֹהֵי יִשְׂרָאֵל מִכֹּל מַלְכֵי יִשְׂרָאֵל אֲשֶׁר הָיוּ
לד לְפָנָיו: בְּיָמָיו בָּנָה חִיאֵל בֵּית הָאֱלִי אֶת־יְרִיחֹה בַּאֲבִירָם בְּכֹרוֹ יִסְּדָהּ
ובשגיב צְעִירוֹ הִצִּיב דְּלָתֶיהָ כִּדְבַר יְהוָה אֲשֶׁר דִּבֶּר בְּיַד יְהוֹשֻׁעַ בִּן־ וּבִשְׂגוּב
יז א נוּן: וַיֹּאמֶר אֵלִיָּהוּ הַתִּשְׁבִּי מִתֹּשָׁבֵי גִלְעָד אֶל־אַחְאָב
חַי־יְהוָה אֱלֹהֵי יִשְׂרָאֵל אֲשֶׁר עָמַדְתִּי לְפָנָיו אִם־יִהְיֶה הַשָּׁנִים הָאֵלֶּה

2 except by my word." Then the word of the LORD came to him:
3 "Get away from here; turn and make your way to the east and hide in the Kerit
4 Stream, which is east of the Jordan. You will be able to drink from the stream,
5 and I have bid the ravens to provide you with sustenance there." He went and
did as the LORD told him; he went and stayed in the Kerit Stream, which faces
6 the Jordan. The ravens brought him bread and meat each morning and bread
7 and meat each evening, and he drank from the stream. But after some time,
8 the stream dried up because no rain fell in the land. And the word
9 of the LORD came to him: "Go straight to Tzarfat of Sidon and stay there; I
10 have bid a certain widow to provide you with sustenance there." He went
straight to Tzarfat, and as he reached the entrance of the town, there was a
widow gathering wood, and he called out to her. "Please," he said, "fetch a
11 little water in a vessel for me to drink." As she was fetching it, he called to her
12 and added, "Please bring a piece of bread along for me." "By the life of the
LORD your God," she said, "I have nothing baked; just a handful of flour in
the jar and a little oil in the jug. Here I am, gathering a few sticks so I can go
13 and prepare it for my son and me; we will eat it, and then we will die." "Do
not fear," Eliyahu said to her. "Do as you say, but first make me a little cake
from it, and bring it out for me; prepare something for you and your son
14 afterward. For thus says the LORD, God of Israel: The jar of flour
will not run out, and the jug of oil will never be empty until the day that the
15 LORD sends rain upon the face of the earth." She went and did as Eliyahu told
16 her, and she, he, and her household had food for some time. The jar of flour
did not run out, and the jug of oil was never empty, fulfilling the word the
17 LORD had promised through Eliyahu. Some time later, the son of
the woman, the head of the household, fell ill; his illness was so severe that
18 he stopped breathing. "What have I to do with you, man of God?" she said
to Eliyahu. "Did you come to me just to draw attention to my sin and to kill
19 my son?" "Give me your son," he said to her, and he pried him from her
embrace and brought him up to the roof chamber where he was staying and
20 laid him out on his bed. And he called out to the LORD. "O LORD, my God,"
he cried, "must You even bring harm to the widow with whom I stay by killing
21 her son?" He stretched out over the child three times and called out to the
LORD. "O LORD, my God," he cried, "please – let this child's life stir again
22 within him!" And the LORD heeded Eliyahu's voice; the child's life stirred
23 again within him, and he revived. Eliyahu took the child, brought him down
from the roof chamber to the house, and gave him to his mother. "Look," said
24 Eliyahu, "your son is alive." "Now I know that you are a man of God," the
woman said to Eliyahu, "and that the word of the LORD is truly on your
18 1 lips." A long time passed. In the third year,[62] the word of the

62 | That is, since the drought began.

ב טַל וּמָטָר כִּי אִם־לְפִי דְבָרִי׃ וַיְהִי דְבַר־יְהוָה אֵלָיו לֵאמֹר׃
ג לֵךְ מִזֶּה וּפָנִיתָ לְּךָ קֵדְמָה וְנִסְתַּרְתָּ בְּנַחַל כְּרִית אֲשֶׁר עַל־פְּנֵי הַיַּרְדֵּן׃
ד ה וְהָיָה מֵהַנַּחַל תִּשְׁתֶּה וְאֶת־הָעֹרְבִים צִוִּיתִי לְכַלְכֶּלְךָ שָׁם׃ וַיֵּלֶךְ וַיַּעַשׂ
ו כִּדְבַר יְהוָה וַיֵּלֶךְ וַיֵּשֶׁב בְּנַחַל כְּרִית אֲשֶׁר עַל־פְּנֵי הַיַּרְדֵּן׃ וְהָעֹרְבִים
מְבִיאִים לוֹ לֶחֶם וּבָשָׂר בַּבֹּקֶר וְלֶחֶם וּבָשָׂר בָּעָרֶב וּמִן־הַנַּחַל יִשְׁתֶּה׃
ז ח וַיְהִי מִקֵּץ יָמִים וַיִּיבַשׁ הַנָּחַל כִּי לֹא־הָיָה גֶשֶׁם בָּאָרֶץ׃ וַיְהִי
ט דְבַר־יְהוָה אֵלָיו לֵאמֹר׃ קוּם לֵךְ צָרְפַתָה אֲשֶׁר לְצִידוֹן וְיָשַׁבְתָּ שָׁם
י הִנֵּה צִוִּיתִי שָׁם אִשָּׁה אַלְמָנָה לְכַלְכְּלֶךָ׃ וַיָּקָם ׀ וַיֵּלֶךְ צָרְפַתָה וַיָּבֹא
אֶל־פֶּתַח הָעִיר וְהִנֵּה־שָׁם אִשָּׁה אַלְמָנָה מְקֹשֶׁשֶׁת עֵצִים וַיִּקְרָא
יא אֵלֶיהָ וַיֹּאמַר קְחִי־נָא לִי מְעַט־מַיִם בַּכְּלִי וְאֶשְׁתֶּה׃ וַתֵּלֶךְ לָקַחַת
יב וַיִּקְרָא אֵלֶיהָ וַיֹּאמַר לִקְחִי־נָא לִי פַּת־לֶחֶם בְּיָדֵךְ׃ וַתֹּאמֶר חַי־יְהוָה
אֱלֹהֶיךָ אִם־יֶשׁ־לִי מָעוֹג כִּי אִם־מְלֹא כַף־קֶמַח בַּכַּד וּמְעַט־שֶׁמֶן
בַּצַּפָּחַת וְהִנְנִי מְקֹשֶׁשֶׁת שְׁנַיִם עֵצִים וּבָאתִי וַעֲשִׂיתִיהוּ לִי וְלִבְנִי
יג וַאֲכַלְנֻהוּ וָמָתְנוּ׃ וַיֹּאמֶר אֵלֶיהָ אֵלִיָּהוּ אַל־תִּירְאִי בֹּאִי עֲשִׂי כִדְבָרֵךְ
אַךְ עֲשִׂי־לִי מִשָּׁם עֻגָה קְטַנָּה בָרִאשֹׁנָה וְהוֹצֵאת לִי וְלָךְ וְלִבְנֵךְ תַּעֲשִׂי
יד בָּאַחֲרֹנָה׃ כִּי כֹה אָמַר יְהוָה אֱלֹהֵי יִשְׂרָאֵל כַּד הַקֶּמַח לֹא
תִכְלָה וְצַפַּחַת הַשֶּׁמֶן לֹא תֶחְסָר עַד יוֹם תתן־יְהוָה גֶּשֶׁם עַל־פְּנֵי תֵּת
טו הָאֲדָמָה׃ וַתֵּלֶךְ וַתַּעֲשֶׂה כִּדְבַר אֵלִיָּהוּ וַתֹּאכַל הוא־והיא וּבֵיתָהּ יָמִים׃ הִיא־וָהוּא
טז כַּד הַקֶּמַח לֹא כָלָתָה וְצַפַּחַת הַשֶּׁמֶן לֹא חָסֵר כִּדְבַר יְהוָה אֲשֶׁר דִּבֶּר
יז בְּיַד אֵלִיָּהוּ׃ וַיְהִי אַחַר הַדְּבָרִים הָאֵלֶּה חָלָה בֶּן־הָאִשָּׁה
בַּעֲלַת הַבָּיִת וַיְהִי חָלְיוֹ חָזָק מְאֹד עַד אֲשֶׁר לֹא־נוֹתְרָה־בּוֹ נְשָׁמָה׃
יח וַתֹּאמֶר אֶל־אֵלִיָּהוּ מַה־לִּי וָלָךְ אִישׁ הָאֱלֹהִים בָּאתָ אֵלַי לְהַזְכִּיר
יט אֶת־עֲוֺנִי וּלְהָמִית אֶת־בְּנִי׃ וַיֹּאמֶר אֵלֶיהָ תְּנִי־לִי אֶת־בְּנֵךְ וַיִּקָּחֵהוּ
מֵחֵיקָהּ וַיַּעֲלֵהוּ אֶל־הָעֲלִיָּה אֲשֶׁר־הוּא יֹשֵׁב שָׁם וַיַּשְׁכִּבֵהוּ עַל־
כ מִטָּתוֹ׃ וַיִּקְרָא אֶל־יְהוָה וַיֹּאמַר יְהוָה אֱלֹהָי הֲגַם עַל־הָאַלְמָנָה אֲשֶׁר־
כא אֲנִי מִתְגּוֹרֵר עִמָּהּ הֲרֵעוֹתָ לְהָמִית אֶת־בְּנָהּ׃ וַיִּתְמֹדֵד עַל־הַיֶּלֶד
שָׁלֹשׁ פְּעָמִים וַיִּקְרָא אֶל־יְהוָה וַיֹּאמַר יְהוָה אֱלֹהָי תָּשָׁב־נָא נֶפֶשׁ־
כב הַיֶּלֶד הַזֶּה עַל־קִרְבּוֹ׃ וַיִּשְׁמַע יְהוָה בְּקוֹל אֵלִיָּהוּ וַתָּשָׁב נֶפֶשׁ־הַיֶּלֶד
כג עַל־קִרְבּוֹ וַיֶּחִי׃ וַיִּקַּח אֵלִיָּהוּ אֶת־הַיֶּלֶד וַיֹּרִדֵהוּ מִן־הָעֲלִיָּה הַבַּיְתָה
כד וַיִּתְּנֵהוּ לְאִמּוֹ וַיֹּאמֶר אֵלִיָּהוּ רְאִי חַי בְּנֵךְ׃ וַתֹּאמֶר הָאִשָּׁה אֶל־ טו
אֵלִיָּהוּ עַתָּה זֶה יָדַעְתִּי כִּי אִישׁ אֱלֹהִים אָתָּה וּדְבַר־יְהוָה בְּפִיךָ
יח א אֱמֶת׃ וַיְהִי יָמִים רַבִּים וּדְבַר־יְהוָה הָיָה אֶל־אֵלִיָּהוּ

Lord came to Eliyahu: "Go, present yourself to Aḥav, and I will send down
2 rain on the face of the earth." So Eliyahu set out to present himself to Aḥav.
3 By then, famine was raging fiercely in Shomron. Aḥav summoned Ovadyahu,
who was in charge of the palace – Ovadyahu had deep reverence for the
4 Lord; when Izevel was annihilating the prophets of the Lord, Ovadyahu
had taken one hundred prophets and hidden them, fifty men to a cave, and
5 provided them with food and water. "Go about the land to every spring and
every wadi," Aḥav said to Ovadyahu. "Perhaps we will find some grass to keep
6 the horses and mules alive so that our animals will not be annihilated." They
divided up the land between them for exploration; Aḥav set out alone in one
7 direction, while Ovadyahu set out alone in another. As Ovadyahu was on the
road, he was suddenly met by Eliyahu. He recognized him at once and fell on
8 his face. "Is that you, my lord Eliyahu?" he said. "It is I," he said to him. "Go
9 and tell your lord: Eliyahu is here." "How have I offended you, that you hand
10 your servant over to Aḥav to be killed?" he said. "As the Lord your God
lives – is there a single nation or kingdom where my lord has not sent and
looked for you? And when they said, 'He is not here,' he had every kingdom
11 and every nation swear that you were nowhere to be found. Now you say, 'Go,
12 tell your lord that Eliyahu is here,' but as soon as I leave you, the spirit of the
Lord will carry you off – to where, I know not – and when I go to tell Aḥav
and he does not find you, he will kill me, though I, your servant, have revered
13 the Lord from my youth. Has my lord not been told what I did when Izevel
was killing the Lord's prophets, how I hid one hundred of the Lord's
14 prophets, fifty men to a cave, and provided them with food and water? Now
15 you say, 'Go, tell your lord that Eliyahu is here' – but he will kill me." "As the
Lord of Hosts lives, whom I serve," said Eliyahu, "Today I will present myself
16 to him." So Ovadyahu set out toward Aḥav and told him, and Aḥav went to
17 meet Eliyahu. When Aḥav saw Eliyahu, Aḥav said to him, "Is that you, O
18 scourge of Israel?" "I have not brought a scourge upon Israel," he said, "but
you and your father's house have by abandoning the Lord's commandments
19 and by following the Baalim.[63] Now summon all of Israel to gather to me at
Mount Carmel, together with the four hundred fifty prophets of Baal and the
20 four hundred prophets of Ashera, those who dine at Izevel's table."[64] Aḥav
summoned all the Israelites and gathered the prophets to Mount Carmel.
21 And Eliyahu drew close to all the people and said, "How long will you sway
from one side to another?[65] If the Lord is God, then follow Him, and if Baal,
22 follow him!" But the people had no reply. "I am the only prophet left to the
Lord," Eliyahu said to the people, "while the prophets of Baal are four
23 hundred fifty men. Let two bulls be given to us; let them choose one bull for

63 | The deity seems to have had multiple manifestations.

64 | See note on 2:7.

65 | Literally "hop between the two boughs."

בַּשָּׁנָה הַשְּׁלִישִׁית לֵאמֹר לֵךְ הֵרָאֵה אֶל־אַחְאָב וְאֶתְּנָה מָטָר עַל־פְּנֵי
ב הָאֲדָמָה: וַיֵּלֶךְ אֵלִיָּהוּ לְהֵרָאוֹת אֶל־אַחְאָב וְהָרָעָב חָזָק בְּשֹׁמְרוֹן:
ג וַיִּקְרָא אַחְאָב אֶל־עֹבַדְיָהוּ אֲשֶׁר עַל־הַבָּיִת וְעֹבַדְיָהוּ הָיָה יָרֵא אֶת־
ד יהוה מְאֹד: וַיְהִי בְּהַכְרִית אִיזֶבֶל אֵת נְבִיאֵי יהוה וַיִּקַּח עֹבַדְיָהוּ מֵאָה
ה נְבִאִים וַיַּחְבִּיאֵם חֲמִשִּׁים אִישׁ בַּמְּעָרָה וְכִלְכְּלָם לֶחֶם וָמָיִם: וַיֹּאמֶר
אַחְאָב אֶל־עֹבַדְיָהוּ לֵךְ בָּאָרֶץ אֶל־כָּל־מַעְיְנֵי הַמַּיִם וְאֶל כָּל־הַנְּחָלִים
ו אוּלַי ׀ נִמְצָא חָצִיר וּנְחַיֶּה סוּס וָפֶרֶד וְלוֹא נַכְרִית מֵהַבְּהֵמָה: וַיְחַלְּקוּ
לָהֶם אֶת־הָאָרֶץ לַעֲבָר־בָּהּ אַחְאָב הָלַךְ בְּדֶרֶךְ אֶחָד לְבַדּוֹ וְעֹבַדְיָהוּ
ז הָלַךְ בְּדֶרֶךְ־אֶחָד לְבַדּוֹ: וַיְהִי עֹבַדְיָהוּ בַּדֶּרֶךְ וְהִנֵּה אֵלִיָּהוּ לִקְרָאתוֹ
ח וַיַּכִּרֵהוּ וַיִּפֹּל עַל־פָּנָיו וַיֹּאמֶר הַאַתָּה זֶה אֲדֹנִי אֵלִיָּהוּ: וַיֹּאמֶר לוֹ אָנִי
ט לֵךְ אֱמֹר לַאדֹנֶיךָ הִנֵּה אֵלִיָּהוּ: וַיֹּאמֶר מֶה חָטָאתִי כִּי־אַתָּה נֹתֵן אֶת־
י עַבְדְּךָ בְּיַד־אַחְאָב לַהֲמִיתֵנִי: חַי ׀ יהוה אֱלֹהֶיךָ אִם־יֶשׁ־גּוֹי וּמַמְלָכָה
אֲשֶׁר לֹא־שָׁלַח אֲדֹנִי שָׁם לְבַקֶּשְׁךָ וְאָמְרוּ אָיִן וְהִשְׁבִּיעַ אֶת־הַמַּמְלָכָה
יא וְאֶת־הַגּוֹי כִּי לֹא יִמְצָאֶכָּה: וְעַתָּה אַתָּה אֹמֵר לֵךְ אֱמֹר לַאדֹנֶיךָ הִנֵּה
יב אֵלִיָּהוּ: וְהָיָה אֲנִי ׀ אֵלֵךְ מֵאִתָּךְ וְרוּחַ יהוה ׀ יִשָּׂאֲךָ עַל אֲשֶׁר לֹא־אֵדָע
וּבָאתִי לְהַגִּיד לְאַחְאָב וְלֹא יִמְצָאֲךָ וַהֲרָגָנִי וְעַבְדְּךָ יָרֵא אֶת־יהוה
יג מִנְּעֻרָי: הֲלֹא־הֻגַּד לַאדֹנִי אֵת אֲשֶׁר־עָשִׂיתִי בַּהֲרֹג אִיזֶבֶל אֵת נְבִיאֵי
יהוה וָאַחְבִּא מִנְּבִיאֵי יהוה מֵאָה אִישׁ חֲמִשִּׁים חֲמִשִּׁים אִישׁ בַּמְּעָרָה
יד וָאֲכַלְכְּלֵם לֶחֶם וָמָיִם: וְעַתָּה אַתָּה אֹמֵר לֵךְ אֱמֹר לַאדֹנֶיךָ הִנֵּה אֵלִיָּהוּ
טו וַהֲרָגָנִי: וַיֹּאמֶר אֵלִיָּהוּ חַי יהוה צְבָאוֹת אֲשֶׁר עָמַדְתִּי לְפָנָיו כִּי הַיּוֹם
טז אֵרָאֶה אֵלָיו: וַיֵּלֶךְ עֹבַדְיָהוּ לִקְרַאת אַחְאָב וַיַּגֶּד־לוֹ וַיֵּלֶךְ אַחְאָב
יז לִקְרַאת אֵלִיָּהוּ: וַיְהִי כִּרְאוֹת אַחְאָב אֶת־אֵלִיָּהוּ וַיֹּאמֶר אַחְאָב אֵלָיו
יח הַאַתָּה זֶה עֹכֵר יִשְׂרָאֵל: וַיֹּאמֶר לֹא עָכַרְתִּי אֶת־יִשְׂרָאֵל כִּי אִם־אַתָּה
יט וּבֵית אָבִיךָ בַּעֲזָבְכֶם אֶת־מִצְוֹת יהוה וַתֵּלֶךְ אַחֲרֵי הַבְּעָלִים: וְעַתָּה
שְׁלַח קְבֹץ אֵלַי אֶת־כָּל־יִשְׂרָאֵל אֶל־הַר הַכַּרְמֶל וְאֶת־נְבִיאֵי הַבַּעַל
אַרְבַּע מֵאוֹת וַחֲמִשִּׁים וּנְבִיאֵי הָאֲשֵׁרָה אַרְבַּע מֵאוֹת אֹכְלֵי שֻׁלְחַן
כ אִיזָבֶל: וַיִּשְׁלַח אַחְאָב בְּכָל־בְּנֵי יִשְׂרָאֵל וַיִּקְבֹּץ אֶת־הַנְּבִיאִים אֶל־הַר
כא הַכַּרְמֶל: וַיִּגַּשׁ אֵלִיָּהוּ אֶל־כָּל־הָעָם וַיֹּאמֶר עַד־מָתַי אַתֶּם פֹּסְחִים
עַל־שְׁתֵּי הַסְּעִפִּים אִם־יהוה הָאֱלֹהִים לְכוּ אַחֲרָיו וְאִם־הַבַּעַל לְכוּ
כב אַחֲרָיו וְלֹא־עָנוּ הָעָם אֹתוֹ דָּבָר: וַיֹּאמֶר אֵלִיָּהוּ אֶל־הָעָם אֲנִי נוֹתַרְתִּי
כג נָבִיא לַיהוה לְבַדִּי וּנְבִיאֵי הַבַּעַל אַרְבַּע־מֵאוֹת וַחֲמִשִּׁים אִישׁ: וְיִתְּנוּ־
לָנוּ שְׁנַיִם פָּרִים וְיִבְחֲרוּ לָהֶם הַפָּר הָאֶחָד וִינַתְּחֻהוּ וְיָשִׂימוּ עַל־הָעֵצִים

themselves, cut it up, and position it on the wood without setting it alight,
while I prepare the other bull and place it on the wood without setting it alight.
24 You will invoke your god by name, while I will invoke the LORD by name, and
the God who answers with fire – He is God." And all the people answered,
25 "We accept." "Choose one bull for yourselves, and go first," Eliyahu said to the
prophets of Baal, "for you are the majority. Do not set it alight yourselves;
26 invoke your god by name." They took the bull that was given to them and
prepared it, then invoked Baal by name from morning to noon, crying, "O
Baal, answer us," but there was no sound and no reply, and they swayed
27 around the altar that had been prepared. At noon, Eliyahu began to mock
them: "Shout louder," he said, "for he is a god – he may be in conversation, or
28 busy, or out traveling; he may be asleep – he might wake!" And they shouted
louder and gashed themselves with swords and spears, as was their custom,
29 until blood streamed down them. Noon passed by, and they raved until the
time of the grain offering, but there was no sound and no answer and no
30 response. Then Eliyahu said to all the people, "Draw close to me." All the
31 people drew close, and he began to repair the LORD's ruined altar. Eliyahu
took twelve stones, corresponding to the number of the tribes of the sons of
Yaakov, who received the word of the LORD: "Yisrael shall be your name."[66]
32 With the stones he built an altar for the name of the LORD and made a trench
33 large enough for two *se'a*[67] of seed all around the altar. He arranged the wood,
34 cut up the bull, and placed it on the wood. "Fill four jugs with water," he said,
"and pour it over the offering and the wood. Now do it a second time," he said,
and they did it a second time. "Do it a third time," he said, and they did it a
35 third time. The water flowed around the altar; he even filled the trench with
36 water. At the time of the grain offering, the prophet Eliyahu drew close and
said, "O LORD, God of Avraham, Yitzḥak, and Yisrael, let it be known today
that You are the God in Israel and that I am Your servant, and it was by Your
37 word that I have done all these things. Answer me, LORD, answer me, so that
this people will know that You, O LORD, are God; it was You who turned
38 their hearts backward." And fire from the LORD flared down and consumed
the offering, the wood, the stones, and the dirt, and licked up the water in the
39 trench. And all the people saw, and they fell on their faces and cried, "The
40 LORD – He is God! The LORD – He is God!" "Seize the prophets of Baal!"
Eliyahu said to them. "Let none of them escape!" They seized them, then
Eliyahu led them down to the Kishon Stream and slaughtered them there.
41 "Go up to eat and drink," Eliyahu then said to Aḥav, "for here comes the sound
42 of roaring rain." And Aḥav went up to eat and drink while Eliyahu went up
to the top of Mount Carmel. He crouched down on the ground and pressed
43 his face between his knees. "Go up now," he said to his boy, "and look out to
sea." He went up and looked out. "Nothing is there," he said. Seven times he
44 said, "Go back." The seventh time, he said, "A tiny cloud, the size of a man's

66 | See Genesis 35:10.
67 | A single *se'a* is the equivalent of 7.7 liters.

וְאֵשׁ לֹא יָשִׂימוּ וַאֲנִי אֶעֱשֶׂה ׀ אֶת־הַפָּר הָאֶחָד וְנָתַתִּי עַל־הָעֵצִים
כד וְאֵשׁ לֹא אָשִׂים׃ וּקְרָאתֶם בְּשֵׁם אֱלֹהֵיכֶם וַאֲנִי אֶקְרָא בְשֵׁם־יְהוָה
וְהָיָה הָאֱלֹהִים אֲשֶׁר־יַעֲנֶה בָאֵשׁ הוּא הָאֱלֹהִים וַיַּעַן כָּל־הָעָם וַיֹּאמְרוּ
כה טוֹב הַדָּבָר׃ וַיֹּאמֶר אֵלִיָּהוּ לִנְבִיאֵי הַבַּעַל בַּחֲרוּ לָכֶם הַפָּר הָאֶחָד
וַעֲשׂוּ רִאשֹׁנָה כִּי אַתֶּם הָרַבִּים וְקִרְאוּ בְּשֵׁם אֱלֹהֵיכֶם וְאֵשׁ לֹא
כו תָשִׂימוּ׃ וַיִּקְחוּ אֶת־הַפָּר אֲשֶׁר־נָתַן לָהֶם וַיַּעֲשׂוּ וַיִּקְרְאוּ בְשֵׁם־הַבַּעַל
מֵהַבֹּקֶר וְעַד־הַצָּהֳרַיִם לֵאמֹר הַבַּעַל עֲנֵנוּ וְאֵין קוֹל וְאֵין עֹנֶה וַיְפַסְּחוּ
כז עַל־הַמִּזְבֵּחַ אֲשֶׁר עָשָׂה׃ וַיְהִי בַצָּהֳרַיִם וַיְהַתֵּל בָּהֶם אֵלִיָּהוּ וַיֹּאמֶר
קִרְאוּ בְקוֹל־גָּדוֹל כִּי־אֱלֹהִים הוּא כִּי־שִׂיחַ וְכִי־שִׂיג לוֹ וְכִי־דֶרֶךְ לוֹ
כח אוּלַי יָשֵׁן הוּא וְיִקָץ׃ וַיִּקְרְאוּ בְּקוֹל גָּדוֹל וַיִּתְגֹּדְדוּ כְּמִשְׁפָּטָם בַּחֲרָבוֹת
כט וּבָרְמָחִים עַד־שְׁפָךְ־דָּם עֲלֵיהֶם׃ וַיְהִי כַּעֲבֹר הַצָּהֳרַיִם וַיִּתְנַבְּאוּ עַד
ל לַעֲלוֹת הַמִּנְחָה וְאֵין־קוֹל וְאֵין־עֹנֶה וְאֵין קָשֶׁב׃ וַיֹּאמֶר אֵלִיָּהוּ לְכָל־
הָעָם גְּשׁוּ אֵלַי וַיִּגְּשׁוּ כָל־הָעָם אֵלָיו וַיְרַפֵּא אֶת־מִזְבַּח יְהוָה הֶהָרוּס׃
לא וַיִּקַּח אֵלִיָּהוּ שְׁתֵּים עֶשְׂרֵה אֲבָנִים כְּמִסְפַּר שִׁבְטֵי בְנֵי־יַעֲקֹב אֲשֶׁר
לב הָיָה דְבַר־יְהוָה אֵלָיו לֵאמֹר יִשְׂרָאֵל יִהְיֶה שְׁמֶךָ׃ וַיִּבְנֶה אֶת־הָאֲבָנִים
מִזְבֵּחַ בְּשֵׁם יְהוָה וַיַּעַשׂ תְּעָלָה כְּבֵית סָאתַיִם זֶרַע סָבִיב לַמִּזְבֵּחַ׃
לג לד וַיַּעֲרֹךְ אֶת־הָעֵצִים וַיְנַתַּח אֶת־הַפָּר וַיָּשֶׂם עַל־הָעֵצִים׃ וַיֹּאמֶר מִלְאוּ
אַרְבָּעָה כַדִּים מַיִם וְיִצְקוּ עַל־הָעֹלָה וְעַל־הָעֵצִים וַיֹּאמֶר שְׁנוּ וַיִּשְׁנוּ
לה וַיֹּאמֶר שַׁלֵּשׁוּ וַיְשַׁלֵּשׁוּ׃ וַיֵּלְכוּ הַמַּיִם סָבִיב לַמִּזְבֵּחַ וְגַם אֶת־הַתְּעָלָה
לו מִלֵּא־מָיִם׃ וַיְהִי ׀ בַּעֲלוֹת הַמִּנְחָה וַיִּגַּשׁ אֵלִיָּהוּ הַנָּבִיא וַיֹּאמַר יְהוָה
אֱלֹהֵי אַבְרָהָם יִצְחָק וְיִשְׂרָאֵל הַיּוֹם יִוָּדַע כִּי־אַתָּה אֱלֹהִים בְּיִשְׂרָאֵל
לז וַאֲנִי עַבְדֶּךָ ובדבריך עָשִׂיתִי אֵת כָּל־הַדְּבָרִים הָאֵלֶּה׃ עֲנֵנִי יְהוָה עֲנֵנִי וּבִדְבָרְךָ
וְיֵדְעוּ הָעָם הַזֶּה כִּי־אַתָּה יְהוָה הָאֱלֹהִים וְאַתָּה הֲסִבֹּתָ אֶת־לִבָּם
לח אֲחֹרַנִּית׃ וַתִּפֹּל אֵשׁ־יְהוָה וַתֹּאכַל אֶת־הָעֹלָה וְאֶת־הָעֵצִים וְאֶת־
לט הָאֲבָנִים וְאֶת־הֶעָפָר וְאֶת־הַמַּיִם אֲשֶׁר־בַּתְּעָלָה לִחֵכָה׃ וַיַּרְא כָּל־הָעָם טז
וַיִּפְּלוּ עַל־פְּנֵיהֶם וַיֹּאמְרוּ יְהוָה הוּא הָאֱלֹהִים יְהוָה הוּא הָאֱלֹהִים׃
מ וַיֹּאמֶר אֵלִיָּהוּ לָהֶם תִּפְשׂוּ ׀ אֶת־נְבִיאֵי הַבַּעַל אִישׁ אַל־יִמָּלֵט מֵהֶם
מא וַיִּתְפְּשׂוּם וַיּוֹרִדֵם אֵלִיָּהוּ אֶל־נַחַל קִישׁוֹן וַיִּשְׁחָטֵם שָׁם׃ וַיֹּאמֶר אֵלִיָּהוּ
מב לְאַחְאָב עֲלֵה אֱכֹל וּשְׁתֵה כִּי־קוֹל הֲמוֹן הַגָּשֶׁם׃ וַיַּעֲלֶה אַחְאָב לֶאֱכֹל
וְלִשְׁתּוֹת וְאֵלִיָּהוּ עָלָה אֶל־רֹאשׁ הַכַּרְמֶל וַיִּגְהַר אַרְצָה וַיָּשֶׂם פָּנָיו בֵּין
מג בִּרְכָּו׃ וַיֹּאמֶר אֶל־נַעֲרוֹ עֲלֵה־נָא הַבֵּט דֶּרֶךְ־יָם וַיַּעַל וַיַּבֵּט וַיֹּאמֶר אֵין
מד מְאוּמָה וַיֹּאמֶר שֻׁב שֶׁבַע פְּעָמִים׃ וַיְהִי בַּשְּׁבִעִית וַיֹּאמֶר הִנֵּה־עָב

hand, is rising up from the sea." "Go up," he said, "and say to Aḥav, 'Harness
45 up and make your way down so that the rain will not hold you back.'" And
all the while, the skies grew dark with clouds and wind, and heavy rain began
46 to fall. Aḥav mounted his chariot and rode out to Yizre'el. The hand
of the Lord settled on Eliyahu, and he hitched up his tunic and ran before
19 1 Aḥav until he reached Yizre'el. When Aḥav told Izevel all that Eliyahu had
2 done and how he had put all the prophets to the sword, Izevel sent a messenger
to Eliyahu: "So may the gods do to me and more if by this time tomorrow, I
3 have not treated your life like one of theirs." Frightened, he understood
and fled for his life at once, and he reached Be'er Sheva of Yehuda and left
4 his servant boy there. But he continued a day's journey into the wilderness,
then came and sat under a certain broom tree and prayed that he might
die. "Enough!" he said. "O Lord, take my life now, for I am no better than
5 my ancestors." Then he lay down and fell asleep beneath that broom tree.
6 Suddenly, an angel was touching him, urging him, "Get up; eat." He looked
up and there, at his head, was a stone-baked cake and a flask of water. He ate
7 and drank and lay back down. The angel of the Lord came back a second
time and touched him. "Get up; eat," it said, "or the long journey will prove
8 too much for you." He got up and ate and drank, and by the strength of that
food, he walked forty days and forty nights to the mountain of God, Ḥorev.[68]
9 There he reached a cave, and there he spent the night. Suddenly, the word of
10 the Lord came to him and said to him, "Why are you here, Eliyahu?" "I acted
out of fervor, out of passion for the Lord, God of Hosts," he said, "for the
Israelites have abandoned Your covenant, destroyed Your altars, and put Your
prophets to the sword. I am the only one left, and they seek to take my life."
11 "Go out and stand on the mountain before the Lord," He said, "for the Lord
is about to pass by." And a great, powerful wind split mountains and shattered
rocks before the Lord – but the Lord was not in the wind. And after the
12 wind, an earthquake – but the Lord was not in the earthquake. And after the
earthquake, fire – but the Lord was not in the fire. And after the fire – a faint
13 sound of silence. And when Eliyahu heard, he wrapped his face in his cloak
and went out and stood by the entrance of the cave. And suddenly a voice
14 came to him and said, "Why are you here, Eliyahu?" "I acted out of fervor,
out of passion for the Lord, God of Hosts," he said, "for the Israelites have
abandoned Your covenant, destroyed Your altars, and put Your prophets to
15 the sword. I am the only one left, and they seek to take my life." And
the Lord answered him, "Set back out on your way to the Wilderness of
16 Damascus. When you arrive, anoint Ḥazael as king over Aram. As for Yehu
son of Nimshi, anoint him as king over Israel; and as for Elisha son of Shafat
17 of Avel Meḥola, anoint him as a prophet in your place. Whoever escapes the
sword of Ḥazael will be killed by Yehu, and whoever escapes the sword of
18 Yehu will be killed by Elisha. I will leave but seven thousand of Israel: every
knee that has not bowed to Baal and every mouth that has not kissed him."

68 | Mount Sinai.

קטנה ככף-איש עלה מים ויאמר עלה אמר אל-אחאב אסר ורד
מה ולא יעצרכה הגשם: ויהי | עד-כה ועד-כה והשמים התקדרו עבים
מו ורוח ויהי גשם גדול וירכב אחאב וילך יזרעאלה: ויד-
יהוה היתה אל-אליהו וישנס מתניו וירץ לפני אחאב עד-באכה
יט א יזרעאלה: ויגד אחאב לאיזבל את כל-אשר עשה אליהו ואת כל-
ב אשר הרג את-כל-הנביאים בחרב: ותשלח איזבל מלאך אל-אליהו
לאמר כה-יעשון אלהים וכה יוספון כי-כעת מחר אשים את-נפשך
ג כנפש אחד מהם: וירא ויקם וילך אל-נפשו ויבא באר שבע אשר
ד ליהודה וינח את-נערו שם: והוא-הלך במדבר דרך יום ויבא וישב
תחת רתם אחת [אחד] וישאל את-נפשו למות ויאמר | רב עתה יהוה קח
ה נפשי כי לא-טוב אנכי מאבתי: וישכב ויישן תחת רתם אחד והנה-
ו זה מלאך נגע בו ויאמר לו קום אכול: ויבט והנה מראשתיו עגת
ז רצפים וצפחת מים ויאכל וישת וישב וישכב: וישב מלאך יהוה |
ח שנית ויגע-בו ויאמר קום אכל כי רב ממך הדרך: ויקם ויאכל וישתה
וילך בכח | האכילה ההיא ארבעים יום וארבעים לילה עד הר
ט האלהים חרב: ויבא-שם אל-המערה וילן שם והנה דבר-יהוה
י אליו ויאמר לו מה-לך פה אליהו: ויאמר קנא קנאתי ליהוה | אלהי
צבאות כי-עזבו בריתך בני ישראל את-מזבחתיך הרסו ואת-נביאיך
יא הרגו בחרב ואותר אני לבדי ויבקשו את-נפשי לקחתה: ויאמר צא
ועמדת בהר לפני יהוה והנה יהוה עבר ורוח גדולה וחזק מפרק
הרים ומשבר סלעים לפני יהוה לא ברוח יהוה ואחר הרוח רעש
יב לא ברעש יהוה: ואחר הרעש אש לא באש יהוה ואחר האש קול
יג דממה דקה: ויהי | כשמע אליהו וילט פניו באדרתו ויצא ויעמד
יד פתח המערה והנה אליו קול ויאמר מה-לך פה אליהו: ויאמר קנא
קנאתי ליהוה | אלהי צבאות כי-עזבו בריתך בני ישראל את-
מזבחתיך הרסו ואת-נביאיך הרגו בחרב ואותר אני לבדי ויבקשו
טו את-נפשי לקחתה: ויאמר יהוה אליו לך שוב לדרכך
טז מדברה דמשק ובאת ומשחת את-חזאל למלך על-ארם: ואת
יהוא בן-נמשי תמשח למלך על-ישראל ואת-אלישע בן-שפט
יז מאבל מחולה תמשח לנביא תחתיך: והיה הנמלט מחרב חזאל
יח ימית יהוא והנמלט מחרב יהוא ימית אלישע: והשארתי בישראל
שבעת אלפים כל-הברכים אשר לא-כרעו לבעל וכל-הפה אשר

19 He set out from there and found Elisha son of Shafat. He was plowing
with twelve pairs of oxen before him, and he was with the twelfth. When
20 Eliyahu reached him, he tossed his cloak over him. He left the oxen and
went running after Eliyahu. "Let me just kiss my father and mother," he said,
"and I will follow you." "Go back, then," he said to him. "What have I done to
21 you?"[69] He turned back from him and took the pair of oxen; he slaughtered
them, and, using the oxen gear,[70] he boiled their meat and gave it out to
the people to eat. Then he set out and followed Eliyahu and became his
20 1 attendant. Ben Hadad, king of Aram, gathered all his forces;
thirty-two kings were with him, with horses and chariots. He advanced, laid
2 siege to Shomron, and launched an attack; he then sent messengers to Aḥav,
3 king of Israel, inside the city, saying, "Thus says Ben Hadad: 'Your silver and
4 gold are mine, and the finest of your women and children are mine.'" "As you
say, my lord the king," the king of Israel answered, "I and all I have are yours."
5 But the messengers returned, saying, "Thus says Ben Hadad: 'I have sent word
to you that you must hand over your silver, your gold, your women, and your
6 children to me. At this time tomorrow, I will send my servants to you; they
will search your house and the houses of your servants, and they will seize all
7 that you hold dear and carry it away.'" And the king of Israel summoned all
the elders of the land. "Be aware, now, and consider the evil this one seeks,"
he said. "He sent to me for my wives and my children, my silver and my gold,
8 and I have not refused him." And all the elders and all the people said, "Do
9 not listen, and do not consent!" So he said to Ben Hadad's messengers, "Say
to my lord the king, 'I will do all that you first demanded of your servant, but
this I cannot do.'" And the messengers went and brought the message back.
10 And Ben Hadad sent to him and said, "So may the gods do to me, and more,
if there is dust enough in Shomron for each of the troops at my heels to take
11 a handful." "Tell him," the king of Israel retorted, "that one who girds should
12 not boast like one who ungirds." He was drinking with the other kings at
Sukkot when he heard this message, and he ordered his servants, "Charge!"
13 And they charged against the city. Just then, a prophet came forward to Aḥav,
king of Israel. "Thus says the Lord," he said. "Have you seen all these great
hordes? I am about to hand them over to you today so that you will know
14 that I am the Lord." "Through whom?" asked Aḥav. "Thus says the Lord,"
he said. "Through the servants of the district officers." "Who will launch the
15 battle?" he asked. And he replied, "You." So he mustered the servants of
the district officers – they numbered 232 – and afterward, he mustered all
16 the troops; the Israelites numbered seven thousand in all. They marched
out at noon while Ben Hadad was drinking himself into a stupor in Sukkot
17 together with the kings – the thirty-two kings who had come to his aid. The
servants of the district officers marched out first. Ben Hadad had sent scouts,

69 | That is, I am not preventing you.
70 | To fuel the fire.

יט לֹא־נָשַׁק לוֹ: וַיֵּלֶךְ מִשָּׁם וַיִּמְצָא אֶת־אֱלִישָׁע בֶּן־שָׁפָט וְהוּא חֹרֵשׁ
שְׁנֵים־עָשָׂר צְמָדִים לְפָנָיו וְהוּא בִּשְׁנֵים הֶעָשָׂר וַיַּעֲבֹר אֵלִיָּהוּ אֵלָיו
כ וַיַּשְׁלֵךְ אַדַּרְתּוֹ אֵלָיו: וַיַּעֲזֹב אֶת־הַבָּקָר וַיָּרָץ אַחֲרֵי אֵלִיָּהוּ וַיֹּאמֶר
אֶשְּׁקָה־נָּא לְאָבִי וּלְאִמִּי וְאֵלְכָה אַחֲרֶיךָ וַיֹּאמֶר לוֹ לֵךְ שׁוּב כִּי מֶה־
כא עָשִׂיתִי לָךְ: וַיָּשָׁב מֵאַחֲרָיו וַיִּקַּח אֶת־צֶמֶד הַבָּקָר וַיִּזְבָּחֵהוּ וּבִכְלִי
הַבָּקָר בִּשְּׁלָם הַבָּשָׂר וַיִּתֵּן לָעָם וַיֹּאכֵלוּ וַיָּקָם וַיֵּלֶךְ אַחֲרֵי אֵלִיָּהוּ
כ א וַיְשָׁרְתֵהוּ: וּבֶן־הֲדַד מֶלֶךְ־אֲרָם קָבַץ אֶת־כָּל־חֵילוֹ
וּשְׁלֹשִׁים וּשְׁנַיִם מֶלֶךְ אִתּוֹ וְסוּס וָרָכֶב וַיַּעַל וַיָּצַר עַל־שֹׁמְרוֹן וַיִּלָּחֶם
ב ג בָּהּ: וַיִּשְׁלַח מַלְאָכִים אֶל־אַחְאָב מֶלֶךְ־יִשְׂרָאֵל הָעִירָה: וַיֹּאמֶר לוֹ
כֹּה אָמַר בֶּן־הֲדַד כַּסְפְּךָ וּזְהָבְךָ לִי־הוּא וְנָשֶׁיךָ וּבָנֶיךָ הַטּוֹבִים לִי־הֵם:
ד וַיַּעַן מֶלֶךְ־יִשְׂרָאֵל וַיֹּאמֶר כִּדְבָרְךָ אֲדֹנִי הַמֶּלֶךְ לְךָ אֲנִי וְכָל־אֲשֶׁר־לִי:
ה וַיָּשֻׁבוּ הַמַּלְאָכִים וַיֹּאמְרוּ כֹּה־אָמַר בֶּן־הֲדַד לֵאמֹר כִּי־שָׁלַחְתִּי אֵלֶיךָ
ו לֵאמֹר כַּסְפְּךָ וּזְהָבְךָ וְנָשֶׁיךָ וּבָנֶיךָ לִי תִתֵּן: כִּי ׀ אִם־כָּעֵת מָחָר אֶשְׁלַח
אֶת־עֲבָדַי אֵלֶיךָ וְחִפְּשׂוּ אֶת־בֵּיתְךָ וְאֵת בָּתֵּי עֲבָדֶיךָ וְהָיָה כָּל־מַחְמַד
ז עֵינֶיךָ יָשִׂימוּ בְיָדָם וְלָקָחוּ: וַיִּקְרָא מֶלֶךְ־יִשְׂרָאֵל לְכָל־זִקְנֵי הָאָרֶץ
וַיֹּאמֶר דְּעוּ־נָא וּרְאוּ כִּי רָעָה זֶה מְבַקֵּשׁ כִּי־שָׁלַח אֵלַי לְנָשַׁי וּלְבָנַי
ח וּלְכַסְפִּי וְלִזְהָבִי וְלֹא מָנַעְתִּי מִמֶּנּוּ: וַיֹּאמְרוּ אֵלָיו כָּל־הַזְּקֵנִים וְכָל־
הָעָם אַל־תִּשְׁמַע וְלוֹא תֹאבֶה: וַיֹּאמֶר לְמַלְאֲכֵי בֶן־הֲדַד אִמְרוּ לַאדֹנִי
הַמֶּלֶךְ כֹּל אֲשֶׁר־שָׁלַחְתָּ אֶל־עַבְדְּךָ בָרִאשֹׁנָה אֶעֱשֶׂה וְהַדָּבָר הַזֶּה
י לֹא אוּכַל לַעֲשׂוֹת וַיֵּלְכוּ הַמַּלְאָכִים וַיְשִׁבֻהוּ דָּבָר: וַיִּשְׁלַח אֵלָיו בֶּן־
הֲדַד וַיֹּאמֶר כֹּה־יַעֲשׂוּן לִי אֱלֹהִים וְכֹה יוֹסִפוּ אִם־יִשְׂפֹּק עֲפַר שֹׁמְרוֹן
יא לִשְׁעָלִים לְכָל־הָעָם אֲשֶׁר בְּרַגְלָי: וַיַּעַן מֶלֶךְ־יִשְׂרָאֵל וַיֹּאמֶר דַּבְּרוּ
יב אַל־יִתְהַלֵּל חֹגֵר כִּמְפַתֵּחַ: וַיְהִי כִּשְׁמֹעַ אֶת־הַדָּבָר הַזֶּה וְהוּא שֹׁתֶה
הוּא וְהַמְּלָכִים בַּסֻּכּוֹת וַיֹּאמֶר אֶל־עֲבָדָיו שִׂימוּ וַיָּשִׂימוּ עַל־הָעִיר:
יג וְהִנֵּה ׀ נָבִיא אֶחָד נִגַּשׁ אֶל־אַחְאָב מֶלֶךְ־יִשְׂרָאֵל וַיֹּאמֶר כֹּה אָמַר יז
יהוה הֲרָאִיתָ אֵת כָּל־הֶהָמוֹן הַגָּדוֹל הַזֶּה הִנְנִי נֹתְנוֹ בְיָדְךָ הַיּוֹם וְיָדַעְתָּ
יד כִּי־אֲנִי יהוה: וַיֹּאמֶר אַחְאָב בְּמִי וַיֹּאמֶר כֹּה־אָמַר יהוה בְּנַעֲרֵי שָׂרֵי
טו הַמְּדִינוֹת וַיֹּאמֶר מִי־יֶאְסֹר הַמִּלְחָמָה וַיֹּאמֶר אָתָּה: וַיִּפְקֹד אֶת־נַעֲרֵי
שָׂרֵי הַמְּדִינוֹת וַיִּהְיוּ מָאתַיִם שְׁנַיִם וּשְׁלֹשִׁים וְאַחֲרֵיהֶם פָּקַד אֶת־כָּל־
טז הָעָם כָּל־בְּנֵי יִשְׂרָאֵל שִׁבְעַת אֲלָפִים: וַיֵּצְאוּ בַּצָּהֳרָיִם וּבֶן־הֲדַד שֹׁתֶה
יז שִׁכּוֹר בַּסֻּכּוֹת הוּא וְהַמְּלָכִים שְׁלֹשִׁים־וּשְׁנַיִם מֶלֶךְ עֹזֵר אֹתוֹ: וַיֵּצְאוּ
נַעֲרֵי שָׂרֵי הַמְּדִינוֹת בָּרִאשֹׁנָה וַיִּשְׁלַח בֶּן־הֲדַד וַיַּגִּידוּ לוֹ לֵאמֹר אֲנָשִׁים

18 who told him, "Men have marched out of Shomron." "If they have come
out to surrender," he said, "capture them alive! And if they have come out
19 to fight – capture them alive!" Meanwhile, the junior district officers had
20 marched out of the city, followed by the troops, and each one struck down
his man. Aram fled, and Israel pursued them, but Ben Hadad, king of Aram,
21 escaped on horseback along with some riders. The king of Israel charged out
22 and attacked the horses and chariots and dealt Aram a crushing blow. Then
the prophet approached the king of Israel. "Go, and keep up your strength,"
he said, "and consider what course of action to take, for at the turn of the year,
the king of Aram will advance upon you."
23 Meanwhile, the servants of the king of Aram said to him, "Their God is a God
of mountains; that is why they overpowered us. But if we fight them in the
24 plain, we will surely overpower them. This is what you should do: Depose
25 every king from his position and appoint governors in their place. Then you
must amass a force, the same as your fallen force – horse for horse, chariot
for chariot – and we will fight them in the plain. We will surely overpower
26 them." And he listened to their advice and did just that. It was the
turn of the year, and Ben Hadad mustered Aram and marched up to Afek to
27 do battle with Israel. And the Israelites were rallied and provisioned, and they
set out toward them. When the Israelites set up camp opposite them, they
28 seemed like two vulnerable flocks of goats, while Aram filled the land. But
the man of God approached and said to the king of Israel, "Thus says the
LORD: Because Aram said that the LORD is a God of mountains and not a
God of valleys, I will hand all these vast hordes over to you. And you will
29 know that I am the LORD." They encamped opposite each other for seven
days. On the seventh day, battle broke out, and the Israelites struck down one
30 hundred thousand Aramean foot soldiers in a single day. The survivors fled
to Afek, to the city, but the wall came crashing down on the twenty-seven
thousand men who had survived. Ben Hadad managed to flee, and he entered
31 an inner chamber within the city. His officials said to him, "Look, we have
heard that the kings of the House of Israel are benevolent kings. Let us place
sackcloth around our waists and ropes around our heads, and let us go out
32 before the king of Israel; perhaps he will spare our lives." So they girded their
waists with sackcloth and placed ropes around their heads, and they came to
the king of Israel. "Your servant, Ben Hadad, asks, 'Please, spare my life,'" they
33 said. "Is he still alive?" he said. "He is my brother." The men took it as a good
omen and quickly seized their chance. "Ben Hadad is indeed your brother,"
they said. "Come, fetch him," he said. Ben Hadad went out to him, and he
34 had him mount the chariot. "I will give back the cities that my father seized
from your father," he said to him, "and you may set up markets in Damascus,
as my father did in Shomron." "Under this pact, I will set you free." And he
35 formed a pact with him and set him free. Now a certain man from
the brotherhood of the prophets said to another, by the word of the LORD,

יח יֵצְאוּ מִשֹּׁמְרוֹן׃ וַיֹּאמֶר אִם־לְשָׁלוֹם יָצְאוּ תִּפְשׂוּם חַיִּים וְאִם לְמִלְחָמָה
יט יָצְאוּ חַיִּים תִּפְשׂוּם׃ וְאֵלֶּה יָצְאוּ מִן־הָעִיר נַעֲרֵי שָׂרֵי הַמְּדִינוֹת וְהַחַיִל
כ אֲשֶׁר אַחֲרֵיהֶם׃ וַיַּכּוּ אִישׁ אִישׁוֹ וַיָּנֻסוּ אֲרָם וַיִּרְדְּפֵם יִשְׂרָאֵל וַיִּמָּלֵט
כא בֶּן־הֲדַד מֶלֶךְ אֲרָם עַל־סוּס וּפָרָשִׁים׃ וַיֵּצֵא מֶלֶךְ יִשְׂרָאֵל וַיַּךְ אֶת־
כב הַסּוּס וְאֶת־הָרֶכֶב וְהִכָּה בַאֲרָם מַכָּה גְדוֹלָה׃ וַיִּגַּשׁ הַנָּבִיא אֶל־
מֶלֶךְ יִשְׂרָאֵל וַיֹּאמֶר לוֹ לֵךְ הִתְחַזַּק וְדַע וּרְאֵה אֵת אֲשֶׁר־תַּעֲשֶׂה כִּי
לִתְשׁוּבַת הַשָּׁנָה מֶלֶךְ אֲרָם עֹלֶה עָלֶיךָ׃
כג וְעַבְדֵי מֶלֶךְ־אֲרָם אָמְרוּ אֵלָיו אֱלֹהֵי הָרִים אֱלֹהֵיהֶם עַל־כֵּן חָזְקוּ
כד מִמֶּנּוּ וְאוּלָם נִלָּחֵם אִתָּם בַּמִּישׁוֹר אִם־לֹא נֶחֱזַק מֵהֶם׃ וְאֶת־הַדָּבָר
כה הַזֶּה עֲשֵׂה הָסֵר הַמְּלָכִים אִישׁ מִמְּקֹמוֹ וְשִׂים פַּחוֹת תַּחְתֵּיהֶם׃ וְאַתָּה
תִמְנֶה־לְךָ ׀ חַיִל כַּחַיִל הַנֹּפֵל מֵאוֹתָךְ וְסוּס כַּסּוּס ׀ וְרֶכֶב כָּרֶכֶב
וְנִלָּחֲמָה אוֹתָם בַּמִּישׁוֹר אִם־לֹא נֶחֱזַק מֵהֶם וַיִּשְׁמַע לְקֹלָם וַיַּעַשׂ
כו כֵּן׃ וַיְהִי לִתְשׁוּבַת הַשָּׁנָה וַיִּפְקֹד בֶּן־הֲדַד אֶת־אֲרָם
כז וַיַּעַל אֲפֵקָה לַמִּלְחָמָה עִם־יִשְׂרָאֵל׃ וּבְנֵי יִשְׂרָאֵל הָתְפָּקְדוּ וְכָלְכְּלוּ
וַיֵּלְכוּ לִקְרָאתָם וַיַּחֲנוּ בְנֵי־יִשְׂרָאֵל נֶגְדָּם כִּשְׁנֵי חֲשִׂפֵי עִזִּים וַאֲרָם
כח מִלְאוּ אֶת־הָאָרֶץ׃ וַיִּגַּשׁ אִישׁ הָאֱלֹהִים וַיֹּאמֶר אֶל־מֶלֶךְ יִשְׂרָאֵל
וַיֹּאמֶר כֹּה־אָמַר יהוה יַעַן אֲשֶׁר אָמְרוּ אֲרָם אֱלֹהֵי הָרִים יהוה וְלֹא־
אֱלֹהֵי עֲמָקִים הוּא וְנָתַתִּי אֶת־כָּל־הֶהָמוֹן הַגָּדוֹל הַזֶּה בְּיָדֶךָ וִידַעְתֶּם
כט כִּי־אֲנִי יהוה׃ וַיַּחֲנוּ אֵלֶּה נֹכַח־אֵלֶּה שִׁבְעַת יָמִים וַיְהִי ׀ בַּיּוֹם הַשְּׁבִיעִי
וַתִּקְרַב הַמִּלְחָמָה וַיַּכּוּ בְנֵי־יִשְׂרָאֵל אֶת־אֲרָם מֵאָה־אֶלֶף רַגְלִי בְּיוֹם
ל אֶחָד׃ וַיָּנֻסוּ הַנּוֹתָרִים ׀ אֲפֵקָה אֶל־הָעִיר וַתִּפֹּל הַחוֹמָה עַל־עֶשְׂרִים
וְשִׁבְעָה אֶלֶף אִישׁ הַנּוֹתָרִים וּבֶן־הֲדַד נָס וַיָּבֹא אֶל־הָעִיר חֶדֶר בְּחָדֶר׃
לא וַיֹּאמְרוּ אֵלָיו עֲבָדָיו הִנֵּה־נָא שָׁמַעְנוּ כִּי מַלְכֵי בֵּית יִשְׂרָאֵל כִּי־מַלְכֵי
חֶסֶד הֵם נָשִׂימָה נָּא שַׂקִּים בְּמָתְנֵינוּ וַחֲבָלִים בְּרֹאשֵׁנוּ וְנֵצֵא אֶל־מֶלֶךְ
לב יִשְׂרָאֵל אוּלַי יְחַיֶּה אֶת־נַפְשֶׁךָ׃ וַיַּחְגְּרוּ שַׂקִּים בְּמָתְנֵיהֶם וַחֲבָלִים
בְּרָאשֵׁיהֶם וַיָּבֹאוּ אֶל־מֶלֶךְ יִשְׂרָאֵל וַיֹּאמְרוּ עַבְדְּךָ בֶן־הֲדַד אָמַר
לג תְּחִי־נָא נַפְשִׁי וַיֹּאמֶר הַעוֹדֶנּוּ חַי אָחִי הוּא׃ וְהָאֲנָשִׁים יְנַחֲשׁוּ וַיְמַהֲרוּ
וַיַּחְלְטוּ הֲמִמֶּנּוּ וַיֹּאמְרוּ אָחִיךָ בֶן־הֲדַד וַיֹּאמֶר בֹּאוּ קָחֻהוּ וַיֵּצֵא אֵלָיו
לד בֶּן־הֲדַד וַיַּעֲלֵהוּ עַל־הַמֶּרְכָּבָה׃ וַיֹּאמֶר אֵלָיו הֶעָרִים אֲשֶׁר־לָקַח־אָבִי
מֵאֵת אָבִיךָ אָשִׁיב וְחוּצוֹת תָּשִׂים לְךָ בְדַמֶּשֶׂק כַּאֲשֶׁר־שָׂם אָבִי בְּשֹׁמְרוֹן
לה וַאֲנִי בַּבְּרִית אֲשַׁלְּחֶךָּ וַיִּכְרָת־לוֹ בְרִית וַיְשַׁלְּחֵהוּ׃ וְאִישׁ
אֶחָד מִבְּנֵי הַנְּבִיאִים אָמַר אֶל־רֵעֵהוּ בִּדְבַר יהוה הַכֵּינִי נָא וַיְמָאֵן

36 "Now strike me," but the man refused to strike him. "Because you did not obey
the voice of the LORD," he said, "as soon as you leave me, you will be attacked
37 by a lion." And as soon as he left him, a lion found him and attacked him. He
found another man and said to him, "Now strike me," and the man struck
38 him a blow and wounded him. The prophet went and stood by the road
waiting for the king, and he disguised himself with a wrapping over his eyes.
39 When the king passed by, he shouted out to the king, "Your servant went out
into the thick of battle. Suddenly, a man turned around and brought someone
to me and said to me, 'Guard this man – if he goes missing, it will be your life
40 for his life, or you will have to weigh out a talent of silver.' But your servant
was busy with this and that, and he got away." "Well, that is your sentence,"
41 the king of Israel said to him. "You yourself pronounced it." He quickly
removed the wrapping from his eyes, and the king of Israel recognized him
42 as one of the prophets. "Thus says the LORD," he said to him. "Because you
freed the man I had marked for destruction, your life will be in place of his
43 life, and your people instead of his people." And the king of Israel went home,
21 1 dour and sullen, and he came to Shomron. Some time passed after
these events. Now Navot the Jezreelite owned a vineyard in Yizre'el next
2 to the palace of Aḥav, king of Shomron. Aḥav told Navot, "Give me your
vineyard so that I can use it as a vegetable garden, for it is right next to my
home. I will give you a better vineyard in its place, or, if you prefer, I will give
3 you its worth in silver." But Navot said to Aḥav, "The LORD forbid that I
4 should give up my ancestral share to you." Aḥav came home, dour and sullen
over what Navot the Jezreelite had told him: "I will not give up my ancestral
share to you." He lay down on his bed and turned his face away and would
5 not eat. Izevel, his wife, came to him. "What is this dour mood of yours?" she
6 asked him. "You won't even eat." "I spoke to Navot the Jezreelite," he told her,
"and I said to him, 'Give me your vineyard for silver, or, if you prefer, I will give
you a vineyard in its place,' but he said, 'I will not give you my vineyard.'"
7 "Why, you must now exercise your royal rights over Israel," his wife Izevel
said to him. "Get up and eat, and take heart. I will give you the vineyard of
8 Navot the Jezreelite." She wrote letters in Aḥav's name and sealed them with
his own seal. Then she sent the letters out to the elders and the nobles who
9 lived in the same town as Navot. "Proclaim a fast, and seat Navot in front of
10 the people," she had written in the letters. "Seat two depraved men opposite
him, and have them testify against Navot, declaring, 'You have "blessed"[71]
11 God and the king!' Then take him out, and stone him to death." And the men
of his town – the elders and nobles who lived in his town – did as Izevel
12 directed them, just as she had written in the letters she sent to them. They
13 proclaimed a fast and seated Navot in front of the people. Then came two

71 | "Bless" is a euphemism for "curse"; cf. Job 2:5, 9.

לו האיש להכתו: ויאמר לו יען אשר לא־שמעת בקול יהוה הנך הולך
לז מאתי והכך האריה וילך מאצלו וימצאהו האריה ויכהו: וימצא
לח איש אחר ויאמר הכיני נא ויכהו האיש הכה ופצע: וילך הנביא
לט ויעמד למלך על־הדרך ויתחפש באפר על־עיניו: ויהי המלך עבר
והוא צעק אל־המלך ויאמר עבדך ׀ יצא בקרב־המלחמה והנה־
איש סר ויבא אלי איש ויאמר שמר את־האיש הזה אם־הפקד
מ יפקד והיתה נפשך תחת נפשו או ככר־כסף תשקול: ויהי עבדך
עשה הנה והנה והוא איננו ויאמר אליו מלך־ישראל כן משפטך
מא אתה חרצת: וימהר ויסר את־האפר מעל עיניו ויכר אתו מלך
מב ישראל כי מהנביאים הוא: ויאמר אליו כה אמר יהוה יען שלחת
את־איש־חרמי מיד והיתה נפשך תחת נפשו ועמך תחת עמו:
כא מג א וילך מלך־ישראל על־ביתו סר וזעף ויבא שמרונה: ויהי
אחר הדברים האלה כרם היה לנבות היזרעאלי אשר ביזרעאל
ב אצל היכל אחאב מלך שמרון: וידבר אחאב אל־נבות ׀ לאמר ׀
תנה־לי את־כרמך ויהי־לי לגן־ירק כי הוא קרוב אצל ביתי ואתנה
לך תחתיו כרם טוב ממנו אם טוב בעיניך אתנה־לך כסף מחיר זה:
ג ויאמר נבות אל־אחאב חלילה לי מיהוה מתתי את־נחלת אבתי
ד לך: ויבא אחאב אל־ביתו סר וזעף על־הדבר אשר־דבר אליו נבות
היזרעאלי ויאמר לא־אתן לך את־נחלת אבותי וישכב על־מטתו
ה ויסב את־פניו ולא־אכל לחם: ותבא אליו איזבל אשתו ותדבר
ו אליו מה־זה רוחך סרה ואינך אכל לחם: וידבר אליה כי־אדבר
אל־נבות היזרעאלי ואמר לו תנה־לי את־כרמך בכסף או אם־חפץ
ז אתה אתנה־לך כרם תחתיו ויאמר לא־אתן לך את־כרמי: ותאמר
אליו איזבל אשתו אתה עתה תעשה מלוכה על־ישראל קום אכל־
ח לחם ויטב לבך אני אתן לך את־כרם נבות היזרעאלי: ותכתב
ספרים בשם אחאב ותחתם בחתמו ותשלח הספרים אל־הזקנים ספרים
ט ואל־החרים אשר בעירו הישבים את־נבות: ותכתב בספרים לאמר
י קראו־צום והשיבו את־נבות בראש העם: והושיבו שנים אנשים
בני־בליעל נגדו ויעדהו לאמר ברכת אלהים ומלך והוציאהו
יא וסקלהו וימת: ויעשו אנשי עירו הזקנים והחרים אשר הישבים
בעירו כאשר שלחה אליהם איזבל כאשר כתוב בספרים אשר
יב יג שלחה אליהם: קראו צום והשיבו את־נבות בראש העם: ויבאו

men – depraved men – who sat opposite him, and the depraved men testified
against Navot in front of the people, saying, "Navot has 'blessed' God and the
14 king!" Then they took him outside the city and stoned him to death and sent
15 to Izevel, "Navot has been stoned to death." When Izevel heard that Navot
had been stoned to death, Izevel said to Aḥav, "At once – take possession of
Navot the Jezreelite's vineyard, which he refused to sell to you for silver,
16 for Navot is no longer alive; he is dead." When Aḥav heard that Navot was
dead, he went straight down to the vineyard of Navot the Jezreelite to take
17 possession of it. And the word of the Lord came to Eliyahu the
18 Tishbite. "Go straight down to meet Aḥav, king of Israel, who is in Shomron.
He is now in the vineyard of Navot; he went down there to take possession
19 of it. Tell him, 'Thus says the Lord: Have you murdered, and also seized
possession? Thus says the Lord: In the very place that the dogs lapped up
20 the blood of Navot, the dogs will lap up your own blood, too.'" "So, you have
found me, my enemy?" Aḥav said to Eliyahu. "Yes, I have found you," he said.
21 "Because you have sold yourself to what is evil in the eyes of the Lord, I am
about to bring evil upon you, and I will burn up every last trace of you. I will
22 cut off every last male of Aḥav in Israel, bond and free, and I will make your
house like the house of Yorovam son of Nevat and like the house of Basha
son of Aḥiya because of the anger you have provoked by leading Israel to sin."
23 And the Lord has also spoken against Izevel: "The dogs will devour Izevel
24 within the bounds of Yizre'el. Those of Aḥav's who die in the city will be
devoured by dogs, and those of his who die in the field will be devoured by
25 the birds of the sky." Never again was there anyone like Aḥav, who sold himself
26 to what was evil in the eyes of the Lord, goaded on by Izevel his wife. Deeply
corrupt, he followed after idols just as the Amorites did, whom the Lord had
27 dispossessed before the Israelites. But when Aḥav heard these words, he rent
his clothes and put sackcloth on his body; he fasted and lay in sackcloth and
28 stumbled about in despair. Then the word of the Lord came to
29 Eliyahu the Tishbite: "Have you seen how Aḥav has humbled himself before
Me? Because he has humbled himself before Me, I will not bring the evil
about in his own time; I will bring the evil upon his house during his son's
22 1 time." For three years there was a respite, with no war between Aram and
Israel.
2 But in the third year, Yehoshafat, king of Yehuda, went down to the king of
3 Israel. "Are you aware that Ramot Gilad is ours," the king of Israel said to
his servants, "yet we have done nothing to take it back from the king of
4 Aram's hands? Will you go out to battle with me at Ramot Gilad?" he asked
Yehoshafat. "I am ready, as you are," Yehoshafat said to the king of Israel. "My
5 troops are your own troops; my horses are your own horses." Then Yehoshafat
6 said to the king of Israel, "Please, inquire of the Lord today." So the king of

שני האנשים בני־בליעל וישבו נגדו ויעדהו אנשי הבליעל את־נבות
נגד העם לאמר ברך נבות אלהים ומלך ויצאהו מחוץ לעיר
יד ויסקלהו באבנים וימת: וישלחו אל־איזבל לאמר סקל נבות וימת:
טו ויהי כשמע איזבל כי־סקל נבות וימת ותאמר איזבל אל־אחאב
קום רש את־כרם | נבות היזרעאלי אשר מאן לתת־לך בכסף כי
טז אין נבות חי כי־מת: ויהי כשמע אחאב כי מת נבות ויקם אחאב
יז לרדת אל־כרם נבות היזרעאלי לרשתו: ויהי דבר־
יח יהוה אל־אליהו התשבי לאמר: קום רד לקראת אחאב מלך־ יח
ישראל אשר בשמרון הנה בכרם נבות אשר־ירד שם לרשתו:
יט ודברת אליו לאמר כה אמר יהוה הרצחת וגם־ירשת ודברת
אליו לאמר כה אמר יהוה במקום אשר לקקו הכלבים את־דם
כ נבות ילקו הכלבים את־דמך גם־אתה: ויאמר אחאב אל־אליהו
המצאתני איבי ויאמר מצאתי יען התמכרך לעשות הרע בעיני
כא יהוה: הנני מבי אליך רעה ובערתי אחריך והכרתי לאחאב משתין
כב בקיר ועצור ועזוב בישראל: ונתתי את־ביתך כבית ירבעם בן־נבט
וכבית בעשא בן־אחיה אל־הכעס אשר הכעסת ותחטא את־
כג ישראל: וגם־לאיזבל דבר יהוה לאמר הכלבים יאכלו את־איזבל
כד בחל יזרעאל: המת לאחאב בעיר יאכלו הכלבים והמת בשדה
כה יאכלו עוף השמים: רק לא־היה כאחאב אשר התמכר לעשות
כו הרע בעיני יהוה אשר־הסתה אתו איזבל אשתו: ויתעב מאד ללכת
אחרי הגללים ככל אשר עשו האמרי אשר הוריש יהוה מפני בני
כז ישראל: ויהי כשמע אחאב את־הדברים האלה ויקרע בגדיו וישם־
כח שק על־בשרו ויצום וישכב בשק ויהלך אט: ויהי דבר־
כט יהוה אל־אליהו התשבי לאמר: הראית כי־נכנע אחאב מלפני יען
כב א כי־נכנע מפני לא־אבי הרעה בימיו בימי בנו אביא הרעה על־ביתו: אביא
וישבו שלש שנים אין מלחמה בין ארם ובין ישראל:
ב ויהי בשנה השלישית וירד יהושפט מלך־יהודה אל־מלך ישראל:
ג ויאמר מלך־ישראל אל־עבדיו הידעתם כי־לנו רמת גלעד ואנחנו
ד מחשים מקחת אתה מיד מלך ארם: ויאמר אל־יהושפט התלך
אתי למלחמה רמת גלעד ויאמר יהושפט אל־מלך ישראל כמוני
ה כמוך כעמי כעמך כסוסי כסוסיך: ויאמר יהושפט אל־מלך ישראל
ו דרש־נא כיום את־דבר יהוה: ויקבץ מלך־ישראל את־הנביאים

Israel gathered the prophets, about four hundred men, and said to them,
"Shall I go to battle over Ramot Gilad, or should I refrain?" "Advance!" they
7 said, "and the LORD will deliver them to the king's hand." "Is there no other
prophet of the LORD here?" said Yehoshafat. "Let us inquire through him."
8 "There is another man through whom we could inquire of the LORD," the
king of Israel said to Yehoshafat, "but I despise him; he has never prophesied
good for me, only evil – Mikhayehu son of Yimla." "Do not say such a thing,
9 O king," said Yehoshafat. So the king of Israel summoned one of the eunuchs
10 and said, "Bring Mikhayehu son of Yimla at once." The king of Israel and
Yehoshafat, king of Yehuda, each sat upon their thrones, attired in robes, at
the threshing floor at the entrance of the Shomron Gate, and all the prophets
11 were prophesying before them. Tzidkiya son of Kenaana had made himself
horns of iron. "Thus says the LORD," he said. "With these you shall gore Aram
12 until their demise." And all the prophets echoed his prophecy: "Advance to
Ramot Gilad, and be victorious," they were saying. "The LORD will deliver it
13 to the king's hand." Then the messenger who had gone to summon Mikhayehu
told him, "Look here – the words of the prophets are unanimous; they favor
14 the king. May your words be like theirs – speak favorably." "As the LORD lives,"
15 said Mikhayehu, "I will speak only what the LORD says to me." He came up
to the king, and the king said to him, "Mikhayehu – shall we go to battle over
Ramot Gilad, or should we refrain?" "Advance and be victorious," he said,
16 "and the LORD will deliver it to the king's hand." "How many times must I have
you swear?" the king said to him. "You must speak only the truth to me, by
17 the name of the LORD." "I saw all of Israel scattered over the hills," he said,
"like sheep without a shepherd. And the LORD said: These have no masters.
18 Let each man return home in peace." "Did I not tell you?" the king of Israel
19 said to Yehoshafat. "He never prophesies good for me – only evil! Therefore,
listen to the word of the LORD," he continued. "I saw the LORD sitting on His
throne, with all the heavenly hosts standing in attendance, to His right and
20 to His left. And the LORD said, 'Who will lure Aḥav so that he will advance
21 and fall at Ramot Gilad?' This one said this and that one said that. Then a
spirit came forward and stood before the LORD and said, 'I will lure him.'
22 'How?' said the LORD. 'I will go out and become a false spirit in the mouths
of all his prophets,' it said. 'Lure him – you will succeed.' He said: 'Go out and
23 do so.' And now, look – the LORD has placed a false spirit in the mouths of
all these prophets of yours, and the LORD has pronounced evil for you."
24 Tzidkiyahu son of Kenaana came forward and slapped Mikhayehu across the
cheek. "How did the spirit of the LORD pass from me to speak to you?" he
25 said. "Oh, you will see on that day," Mikhayehu said, "when you enter the
26 innermost room to hide." "Seize Mikhayehu!" said the king of Israel. "Hand
27 him over to Amon, the city governor, and to Yoash, the king's son, and say,
'Thus says the king: Put this one in prison, and feed him only scant bread and

כְּאַרְבַּע מֵאוֹת אִישׁ וַיֹּאמֶר אֲלֵהֶם הַאֵלֵךְ עַל־רָמֹת גִּלְעָד לַמִּלְחָמָה
ז אִם־אֶחְדָּל וַיֹּאמְרוּ עֲלֵה וְיִתֵּן אֲדֹנָי בְּיַד הַמֶּלֶךְ: וַיֹּאמֶר יְהוֹשָׁפָט הַאֵין
ח פֹּה נָבִיא לַיהוָה עוֹד וְנִדְרְשָׁה מֵאוֹתוֹ: וַיֹּאמֶר מֶלֶךְ־יִשְׂרָאֵל ׀ אֶל־
יְהוֹשָׁפָט עוֹד אִישׁ־אֶחָד לִדְרֹשׁ אֶת־יְהוָה מֵאֹתוֹ וַאֲנִי שְׂנֵאתִיו כִּי
לֹא־יִתְנַבֵּא עָלַי טוֹב כִּי אִם־רָע מִיכָיְהוּ בֶּן־יִמְלָה וַיֹּאמֶר יְהוֹשָׁפָט
ט אַל־יֹאמַר הַמֶּלֶךְ כֵּן: וַיִּקְרָא מֶלֶךְ יִשְׂרָאֵל אֶל־סָרִיס אֶחָד וַיֹּאמֶר
י מַהֲרָה מִיכָיְהוּ בֶן־יִמְלָה: וּמֶלֶךְ יִשְׂרָאֵל וִיהוֹשָׁפָט מֶלֶךְ־יְהוּדָה יֹשְׁבִים
אִישׁ עַל־כִּסְאוֹ מְלֻבָּשִׁים בְּגָדִים בְּגֹרֶן פֶּתַח שַׁעַר שֹׁמְרוֹן וְכָל־הַנְּבִיאִים
יא מִתְנַבְּאִים לִפְנֵיהֶם: וַיַּעַשׂ לוֹ צִדְקִיָּה בֶן־כְּנַעֲנָה קַרְנֵי בַרְזֶל וַיֹּאמֶר
יב כֹּה־אָמַר יְהוָה בְּאֵלֶּה תְּנַגַּח אֶת־אֲרָם עַד־כַּלֹּתָם: וְכָל־הַנְּבִאִים
נִבְּאִים כֵּן לֵאמֹר עֲלֵה רָמֹת גִּלְעָד וְהַצְלַח וְנָתַן יְהוָה בְּיַד הַמֶּלֶךְ:
יג וְהַמַּלְאָךְ אֲשֶׁר־הָלַךְ ׀ לִקְרֹא מִיכָיְהוּ דִּבֶּר אֵלָיו לֵאמֹר הִנֵּה־נָא דִּבְרֵי
הַנְּבִיאִים פֶּה־אֶחָד טוֹב אֶל־הַמֶּלֶךְ יְהִי־נָא דבריך כִּדְבַר אַחַד מֵהֶם דְבָרְךָ
יד וְדִבַּרְתָּ טּוֹב: וַיֹּאמֶר מִיכָיְהוּ חַי־יְהוָה כִּי אֶת־אֲשֶׁר יֹאמַר יְהוָה אֵלַי
טו אֹתוֹ אֲדַבֵּר: וַיָּבוֹא אֶל־הַמֶּלֶךְ וַיֹּאמֶר הַמֶּלֶךְ אֵלָיו מִיכָיְהוּ הֲנֵלֵךְ אֶל־
רָמֹת גִּלְעָד לַמִּלְחָמָה אִם־נֶחְדָּל וַיֹּאמֶר אֵלָיו עֲלֵה וְהַצְלַח וְנָתַן יְהוָה
טז בְּיַד הַמֶּלֶךְ: וַיֹּאמֶר אֵלָיו הַמֶּלֶךְ עַד־כַּמֶּה פְעָמִים אֲנִי מַשְׁבִּעֶךָ אֲשֶׁר
יז לֹא־תְדַבֵּר אֵלַי רַק־אֱמֶת בְּשֵׁם יְהוָה: וַיֹּאמֶר רָאִיתִי אֶת־כָּל־יִשְׂרָאֵל
נְפֹצִים אֶל־הֶהָרִים כַּצֹּאן אֲשֶׁר אֵין־לָהֶם רֹעֶה וַיֹּאמֶר יְהוָה לֹא־אֲדֹנִים
יח לָאֵלֶּה יָשׁוּבוּ אִישׁ־לְבֵיתוֹ בְּשָׁלוֹם: וַיֹּאמֶר מֶלֶךְ־יִשְׂרָאֵל אֶל־יְהוֹשָׁפָט
יט הֲלוֹא אָמַרְתִּי אֵלֶיךָ לוֹא־יִתְנַבֵּא עָלַי טוֹב כִּי אִם־רָע: וַיֹּאמֶר לָכֵן
שְׁמַע דְּבַר־יְהוָה רָאִיתִי אֶת־יְהוָה יֹשֵׁב עַל־כִּסְאוֹ וְכָל־צְבָא הַשָּׁמַיִם
כ עֹמֵד עָלָיו מִימִינוֹ וּמִשְּׂמֹאלוֹ: וַיֹּאמֶר יְהוָה מִי יְפַתֶּה אֶת־אַחְאָב וְיַעַל
כא וְיִפֹּל בְּרָמֹת גִּלְעָד וַיֹּאמֶר זֶה בְּכֹה וְזֶה אֹמֵר בְּכֹה: וַיֵּצֵא הָרוּחַ וַיַּעֲמֹד
כב לִפְנֵי יְהוָה וַיֹּאמֶר אֲנִי אֲפַתֶּנּוּ וַיֹּאמֶר יְהוָה אֵלָיו בַּמָּה: וַיֹּאמֶר אֵצֵא
וְהָיִיתִי רוּחַ שֶׁקֶר בְּפִי כָּל־נְבִיאָיו וַיֹּאמֶר תְּפַתֶּה וְגַם־תּוּכָל צֵא וַעֲשֵׂה־
כג כֵן: וְעַתָּה הִנֵּה נָתַן יְהוָה רוּחַ שֶׁקֶר בְּפִי כָּל־נְבִיאֶיךָ אֵלֶּה וַיהוָה
כד דִּבֶּר עָלֶיךָ רָעָה: וַיִּגַּשׁ צִדְקִיָּהוּ בֶן־כְּנַעֲנָה וַיַּכֶּה אֶת־מִיכָיְהוּ עַל־
כה הַלֶּחִי וַיֹּאמֶר אֵי־זֶה עָבַר רוּחַ־יְהוָה מֵאִתִּי לְדַבֵּר אוֹתָךְ: וַיֹּאמֶר
כו מִיכָיְהוּ הִנְּךָ רֹאֶה בַּיּוֹם הַהוּא אֲשֶׁר תָּבֹא חֶדֶר בְּחֶדֶר לְהֵחָבֵה: וַיֹּאמֶר
מֶלֶךְ יִשְׂרָאֵל קַח אֶת־מִיכָיְהוּ וַהֲשִׁיבֵהוּ אֶל־אָמֹן שַׂר־הָעִיר וְאֶל־
כז יוֹאָשׁ בֶּן־הַמֶּלֶךְ: וְאָמַרְתָּ כֹּה אָמַר הַמֶּלֶךְ שִׂימוּ אֶת־זֶה בֵּית הַכֶּלֶא

28 scant water until my safe arrival.'" "If you indeed return safely, then the
LORD did not speak through me," said Mikhayehu. And he added, "Listen, all
29 peoples!"[72] So the king of Israel and Yehoshafat, king of Yehuda, advanced to
30 Ramot Gilad. "I will disguise myself and go into battle," the king of Israel said
to Yehoshafat, "while you should wear your robes." And the king of Israel
31 disguised himself and went into battle. Now the king of Aram had instructed
his chariot commanders – they numbered thirty-two – as follows: "Do not
32 attack anyone, great or small, except for the king of Israel." When the chariot
commanders saw Yehoshafat, they thought, "Look: he must be the king of
33 Israel." They charged toward him to attack, but Yehoshafat cried out, and
when the chariot commanders realized that he was not the king of Israel, they
34 turned back away from him. But one man drew his bow at random, and he
struck the king of Israel between the joints of his armor. He called out to his
chariot driver, "Steer back around and get me out of the camp, for I am
35 wounded." As the battle raged that day, the king was propped up in his chariot
facing Aram. The blood from his wound trickled down into the hollow of the
36 chariot, and he died that evening. At sundown, the cry echoed through the
camp: "Every man back to his hometown; every man back to his own land."
37 But the king was dead and was brought to Shomron. They buried the king in
38 Shomron, and they rinsed out the chariot at the pool of Shomron; the dogs
lapped up his blood, and the whores bathed, fulfilling the word that the LORD
39 had spoken.[73] As for the rest of Aḥav's history and all his deeds and the ivory
palace that he built and all the cities that he built – they are recorded in the
40 book of the History of the Kings of Israel. And Aḥav slept with his ancestors,
41 and his son Aḥazya reigned in his place. Yehoshafat son of Asa
42 became king over Yehuda in the fourth year of Aḥav, king of Israel. Yehoshafat
was thirty-five years old when he became king, and for twenty-five years he
43 reigned in Jerusalem. His mother's name was Azuva daughter of Shilḥi. He
followed in all the ways of his father Asa and did not turn away from them,
44 doing what was right in the eyes of the LORD. Only the high shrines were not
removed; the people continued to offer sacrifices and incense at the high
45 46 shrines. Yehoshafat made peace with the king of Israel. As for the rest of
Yehoshafat's history, his exploits, and his battles – they are recorded in the
47 book of the History of the Kings of Yehuda. He purged every last trace of the
48 male ritual prostitutes who remained from the time of his father Asa. There
49 was no king in Edom; a governor served as king. Yehoshafat built a Tarshish[74]
fleet to set sail to Ofir for gold, but the ships were wrecked at Etzyon Gever,
50 and he never set sail. Then Aḥazyahu son of Aḥav proposed to Yehoshafat,
"Let my servants set out with your servants in the ships," but Yehoshafat would
51 not give his consent. And Yehoshafat slept with his ancestors and was buried
with his ancestors in the City of David, his ancestor. And his son Yehoram

72 | In his opening prophecy, the later prophet Mikha the Morashtite echoes these closing words of Mikhayehu son of Yimla; cf. Micah 1:2.

73 | See 21:19.

74 | See note on 10:22.

כח וְהַאֲכִלֻהוּ לֶחֶם לַחַץ וּמַיִם לַחַץ עַד בֹּאִי בְשָׁלוֹם: וַיֹּאמֶר מִיכָיְהוּ
אִם־שׁוֹב תָּשׁוּב בְּשָׁלוֹם לֹא־דִבֶּר יהוה בִּי וַיֹּאמֶר שִׁמְעוּ עַמִּים כֻּלָּם:
כט ל וַיַּעַל מֶלֶךְ־יִשְׂרָאֵל וִיהוֹשָׁפָט מֶלֶךְ־יְהוּדָה רָמֹת גִּלְעָד: וַיֹּאמֶר מֶלֶךְ
יִשְׂרָאֵל אֶל־יְהוֹשָׁפָט הִתְחַפֵּשׂ וָבֹא בַמִּלְחָמָה וְאַתָּה לְבַשׁ בְּגָדֶיךָ
לא וַיִּתְחַפֵּשׂ מֶלֶךְ יִשְׂרָאֵל וַיָּבוֹא בַּמִּלְחָמָה: וּמֶלֶךְ אֲרָם צִוָּה אֶת־שָׂרֵי
הָרֶכֶב אֲשֶׁר־לוֹ שְׁלֹשִׁים וּשְׁנַיִם לֵאמֹר לֹא תִּלָּחֲמוּ אֶת־קָטֹן וְאֶת־
לב גָּדוֹל כִּי אִם־אֶת־מֶלֶךְ יִשְׂרָאֵל לְבַדּוֹ: וַיְהִי כִּרְאוֹת שָׂרֵי הָרֶכֶב אֶת־
יְהוֹשָׁפָט וְהֵמָּה אָמְרוּ אַךְ מֶלֶךְ־יִשְׂרָאֵל הוּא וַיָּסֻרוּ עָלָיו לְהִלָּחֵם
לג וַיִּזְעַק יְהוֹשָׁפָט: וַיְהִי כִּרְאוֹת שָׂרֵי הָרֶכֶב כִּי־לֹא־מֶלֶךְ יִשְׂרָאֵל הוּא
לד וַיָּשׁוּבוּ מֵאַחֲרָיו: וְאִישׁ מָשַׁךְ בַּקֶּשֶׁת לְתֻמּוֹ וַיַּכֶּה אֶת־מֶלֶךְ יִשְׂרָאֵל
בֵּין הַדְּבָקִים וּבֵין הַשִּׁרְיָן וַיֹּאמֶר לְרַכָּבוֹ הֲפֹךְ יָדְךָ וְהוֹצִיאֵנִי מִן־הַמַּחֲנֶה
לה כִּי הָחֳלֵיתִי: וַתַּעַל הַמִּלְחָמָה בַּיּוֹם הַהוּא וְהַמֶּלֶךְ הָיָה מָעֳמָד
בַּמֶּרְכָּבָה נֹכַח אֲרָם וַיָּמָת בָּעֶרֶב וַיִּצֶק דַּם־הַמַּכָּה אֶל־חֵיק הָרָכֶב:
לו וַיַּעֲבֹר הָרִנָּה בַּמַּחֲנֶה כְּבֹא הַשֶּׁמֶשׁ לֵאמֹר אִישׁ אֶל־עִירוֹ וְאִישׁ אֶל־
לז לח אַרְצוֹ: וַיָּמָת הַמֶּלֶךְ וַיָּבוֹא שֹׁמְרוֹן וַיִּקְבְּרוּ אֶת־הַמֶּלֶךְ בְּשֹׁמְרוֹן: וַיִּשְׁטֹף
אֶת־הָרֶכֶב עַל ׀ בְּרֵכַת שֹׁמְרוֹן וַיָּלֹקּוּ הַכְּלָבִים אֶת־דָּמוֹ וְהַזֹּנוֹת רָחָצוּ
לט כִּדְבַר יהוה אֲשֶׁר דִּבֵּר: וְיֶתֶר דִּבְרֵי אַחְאָב וְכָל־אֲשֶׁר עָשָׂה וּבֵית הַשֵּׁן
אֲשֶׁר בָּנָה וְכָל־הֶעָרִים אֲשֶׁר בָּנָה הֲלוֹא־הֵם כְּתוּבִים עַל־סֵפֶר דִּבְרֵי
מ הַיָּמִים לְמַלְכֵי יִשְׂרָאֵל: וַיִּשְׁכַּב אַחְאָב עִם־אֲבֹתָיו וַיִּמְלֹךְ אֲחַזְיָהוּ בְנוֹ
מא תַּחְתָּיו: וִיהוֹשָׁפָט בֶּן־אָסָא מָלַךְ עַל־יְהוּדָה בִּשְׁנַת אַרְבַּע
מב לְאַחְאָב מֶלֶךְ יִשְׂרָאֵל: יְהוֹשָׁפָט בֶּן־שְׁלֹשִׁים וְחָמֵשׁ שָׁנָה בְּמָלְכוֹ
וְעֶשְׂרִים וְחָמֵשׁ שָׁנָה מָלַךְ בִּירוּשָׁלִָם וְשֵׁם אִמּוֹ עֲזוּבָה בַּת־שִׁלְחִי:
מג וַיֵּלֶךְ בְּכָל־דֶּרֶךְ אָסָא אָבִיו לֹא־סָר מִמֶּנּוּ לַעֲשׂוֹת הַיָּשָׁר בְּעֵינֵי יהוה: יט
מד מה אַךְ הַבָּמוֹת לֹא־סָרוּ עוֹד הָעָם מְזַבְּחִים וּמְקַטְּרִים בַּבָּמוֹת: וַיַּשְׁלֵם
מו יְהוֹשָׁפָט עִם־מֶלֶךְ יִשְׂרָאֵל: וְיֶתֶר דִּבְרֵי יְהוֹשָׁפָט וּגְבוּרָתוֹ אֲשֶׁר־עָשָׂה
וַאֲשֶׁר נִלְחָם הֲלֹא־הֵם כְּתוּבִים עַל־סֵפֶר דִּבְרֵי הַיָּמִים לְמַלְכֵי יְהוּדָה:
מז מח וְיֶתֶר הַקָּדֵשׁ אֲשֶׁר נִשְׁאַר בִּימֵי אָסָא אָבִיו בִּעֵר מִן־הָאָרֶץ: וּמֶלֶךְ
מט אֵין בֶּאֱדוֹם נִצָּב מֶלֶךְ: יְהוֹשָׁפָט עשר אֳנִיּוֹת תַּרְשִׁישׁ לָלֶכֶת אוֹפִירָה עָשָׂה
נ לַזָּהָב וְלֹא הָלָךְ כִּי־נשברה אֳנִיּוֹת בְּעֶצְיוֹן גָּבֶר: אָז אָמַר אֲחַזְיָהוּ נִשְׁבְּרוּ
בֶן־אַחְאָב אֶל־יְהוֹשָׁפָט יֵלְכוּ עֲבָדַי עִם־עֲבָדֶיךָ בָּאֳנִיּוֹת וְלֹא אָבָה
נא יְהוֹשָׁפָט: וַיִּשְׁכַּב יְהוֹשָׁפָט עִם־אֲבֹתָיו וַיִּקָּבֵר עִם־אֲבֹתָיו בְּעִיר דָּוִד

52 reigned in his place. Aḥazyahu son of Aḥav became king over Israel
in Shomron in the seventeenth year of Yehoshafat, king of Yehuda, and he
53 reigned over Israel for two years. He did what was evil in the eyes of the LORD
and followed in the ways of his father, the ways of his mother, and the ways
54 of Yorovam son of Nevat, who led Israel to sin. He served the Baal and
worshipped him and angered the LORD, God of Israel, just as his father did.
1 1 2 After Aḥav's death, Moav rebelled against Israel. Aḥazya fell through the II KINGS
lattice in his upper chamber at Shomron and was injured. He sent messengers,
instructing them, "Go, inquire of Baal Zevuv, the god of Ekron, whether I will
3 recover from this injury." But an angel of the LORD spoke to Eliyahu
the Tishbite, "Arise and go up to meet the messengers of the king of Shomron
and tell them, Is it for lack of a God in Israel that you go to inquire of Baal
4 Zevuv, the god of Ekron? Therefore, thus says the LORD: You will never rise
5 from your sickbed again – you will surely die!" And Eliyahu set out. When
6 the messengers returned to him, he said, "Why have you returned?" "A man
came up to meet us," they said to him, "and he said to us, 'Go back to the king
who sent you, and tell him, Thus says the LORD: Is it for lack of a God in Israel
that you sent to inquire of Baal Zevuv, god of Ekron? Therefore, you will never
7 rise from your sickbed again – you will surely die!'" "What kind of man came
8 up to meet you and told you these words?" he asked them. "A hairy man," they
said to him, "with a leather belt tied around his waist." "Why," he said, "it must
9 be Eliyahu the Tishbite!" And he sent his officer of fifty to him, together with
his company of fifty. He climbed up to him – for there he was, sitting on the
hilltop. "O man of God," he said to him, "the king has spoken: 'Come down!'"
10 "If I am a man of God," Eliyahu answered the officer of fifty, "let fire flare
down from heaven and consume you and your company of fifty." And fire
11 flared down from heaven and consumed him and his company of fifty. So
again, he sent another officer of fifty, together with his company of fifty, and
he addressed him. "O man of God," he said, "thus says the king: 'Come down
12 at once.'" "If I am a man of God," Eliyahu answered them, "let fire flare down
from heaven and consume you and your company of fifty." And a divine fire
13 flared down from heaven and consumed him and his company of fifty. So
again, he sent a third officer of fifty, together with his company of fifty. But
when the third officer of fifty arrived, he dropped down on his knees before
Eliyahu and pleaded with him. "O man of God," he said, "please – may my
life and the lives of these fifty servants of yours have some worth in your eyes.
14 Look – fire has just flared down from heaven and consumed the first two
officers of fifty, together with their companies of fifty. But now, may my life

נב אָבִיו וַיִּמְלֹךְ יְהוֹרָם בְּנוֹ תַּחְתָּיו׃ אֲחַזְיָהוּ בֶן־אַחְאָב מָלַךְ
עַל־יִשְׂרָאֵל בְּשֹׁמְרוֹן בִּשְׁנַת שְׁבַע עֶשְׂרֵה לִיהוֹשָׁפָט מֶלֶךְ יְהוּדָה
נג וַיִּמְלֹךְ עַל־יִשְׂרָאֵל שְׁנָתָיִם׃ וַיַּעַשׂ הָרַע בְּעֵינֵי יְהוָה וַיֵּלֶךְ בְּדֶרֶךְ
אָבִיו וּבְדֶרֶךְ אִמּוֹ וּבְדֶרֶךְ יָרָבְעָם בֶּן־נְבָט אֲשֶׁר הֶחֱטִיא אֶת־יִשְׂרָאֵל׃
נד וַיַּעֲבֹד אֶת־הַבַּעַל וַיִּשְׁתַּחֲוֶה לוֹ וַיַּכְעֵס אֶת־יְהוָה אֱלֹהֵי יִשְׂרָאֵל כְּכֹל

מלכים ב

א א ב אֲשֶׁר־עָשָׂה אָבִיו׃ וַיִּפְשַׁע מוֹאָב בְּיִשְׂרָאֵל אַחֲרֵי מוֹת אַחְאָב׃ וַיִּפֹּל
אֲחַזְיָה בְּעַד הַשְּׂבָכָה בַּעֲלִיָּתוֹ אֲשֶׁר בְּשֹׁמְרוֹן וַיָּחַל וַיִּשְׁלַח מַלְאָכִים
וַיֹּאמֶר אֲלֵהֶם לְכוּ דִרְשׁוּ בְּבַעַל זְבוּב אֱלֹהֵי עֶקְרוֹן אִם־אֶחְיֶה מֵחֳלִי
ג זֶה׃ וּמַלְאַךְ יְהוָה דִּבֶּר אֶל־אֵלִיָּה הַתִּשְׁבִּי קוּם עֲלֵה
לִקְרַאת מַלְאֲכֵי מֶלֶךְ־שֹׁמְרוֹן וְדַבֵּר אֲלֵהֶם הֲמִבְּלִי אֵין־אֱלֹהִים
ד בְּיִשְׂרָאֵל אַתֶּם הֹלְכִים לִדְרֹשׁ בְּבַעַל זְבוּב אֱלֹהֵי עֶקְרוֹן׃ וְלָכֵן כֹּה־
אָמַר יְהוָה הַמִּטָּה אֲשֶׁר־עָלִיתָ שָּׁם לֹא־תֵרֵד מִמֶּנָּה כִּי מוֹת תָּמוּת
ה וַיֵּלֶךְ אֵלִיָּה׃ וַיָּשׁוּבוּ הַמַּלְאָכִים אֵלָיו וַיֹּאמֶר אֲלֵיהֶם מַה־זֶּה שַׁבְתֶּם׃
ו וַיֹּאמְרוּ אֵלָיו אִישׁ ׀ עָלָה לִקְרָאתֵנוּ וַיֹּאמֶר אֵלֵינוּ לְכוּ שׁוּבוּ אֶל־הַמֶּלֶךְ
אֲשֶׁר־שָׁלַח אֶתְכֶם וְדִבַּרְתֶּם אֵלָיו כֹּה אָמַר יְהוָה הֲמִבְּלִי אֵין־אֱלֹהִים
בְּיִשְׂרָאֵל אַתָּה שֹׁלֵחַ לִדְרֹשׁ בְּבַעַל זְבוּב אֱלֹהֵי עֶקְרוֹן לָכֵן הַמִּטָּה
ז אֲשֶׁר־עָלִיתָ שָּׁם לֹא־תֵרֵד מִמֶּנָּה כִּי־מוֹת תָּמוּת׃ וַיְדַבֵּר אֲלֵהֶם מֶה
מִשְׁפַּט הָאִישׁ אֲשֶׁר עָלָה לִקְרַאתְכֶם וַיְדַבֵּר אֲלֵיכֶם אֶת־הַדְּבָרִים
ח הָאֵלֶּה׃ וַיֹּאמְרוּ אֵלָיו אִישׁ בַּעַל שֵׂעָר וְאֵזוֹר עוֹר אָזוּר בְּמָתְנָיו וַיֹּאמַר
ט אֵלִיָּה הַתִּשְׁבִּי הוּא׃ וַיִּשְׁלַח אֵלָיו שַׂר־חֲמִשִּׁים וַחֲמִשָּׁיו וַיַּעַל אֵלָיו
וְהִנֵּה יֹשֵׁב עַל־רֹאשׁ הָהָר וַיְדַבֵּר אֵלָיו אִישׁ הָאֱלֹהִים הַמֶּלֶךְ דִּבֶּר
י רֵדָה׃ וַיַּעֲנֶה אֵלִיָּהוּ וַיְדַבֵּר אֶל־שַׂר הַחֲמִשִּׁים וְאִם־אִישׁ אֱלֹהִים אָנִי
תֵּרֶד אֵשׁ מִן־הַשָּׁמַיִם וְתֹאכַל אֹתְךָ וְאֶת־חֲמִשֶּׁיךָ וַתֵּרֶד אֵשׁ מִן־
יא הַשָּׁמַיִם וַתֹּאכַל אֹתוֹ וְאֶת־חֲמִשָּׁיו׃ וַיָּשָׁב וַיִּשְׁלַח אֵלָיו שַׂר־חֲמִשִּׁים
אַחֵר וַחֲמִשָּׁיו וַיַּעַן וַיְדַבֵּר אֵלָיו אִישׁ הָאֱלֹהִים כֹּה־אָמַר הַמֶּלֶךְ
יב מְהֵרָה רֵדָה׃ וַיַּעַן אֵלִיָּה וַיְדַבֵּר אֲלֵיהֶם אִם־אִישׁ הָאֱלֹהִים אָנִי תֵּרֶד
אֵשׁ מִן־הַשָּׁמַיִם וְתֹאכַל אֹתְךָ וְאֶת־חֲמִשֶּׁיךָ וַתֵּרֶד אֵשׁ־אֱלֹהִים מִן־
יג הַשָּׁמַיִם וַתֹּאכַל אֹתוֹ וְאֶת־חֲמִשָּׁיו׃ וַיָּשָׁב וַיִּשְׁלַח שַׂר־חֲמִשִּׁים שְׁלִשִׁים
וַחֲמִשָּׁיו וַיַּעַל וַיָּבֹא שַׂר־הַחֲמִשִּׁים הַשְּׁלִישִׁי וַיִּכְרַע עַל־בִּרְכָּיו ׀ לְנֶגֶד
אֵלִיָּהוּ וַיִּתְחַנֵּן אֵלָיו וַיְדַבֵּר אֵלָיו אִישׁ הָאֱלֹהִים תִּיקַר־נָא נַפְשִׁי וְנֶפֶשׁ
יד עֲבָדֶיךָ אֵלֶּה חֲמִשִּׁים בְּעֵינֶיךָ׃ הִנֵּה יָרְדָה אֵשׁ מִן־הַשָּׁמַיִם וַתֹּאכַל
אֶת־שְׁנֵי שָׂרֵי הַחֲמִשִּׁים הָרִאשֹׁנִים וְאֶת־חֲמִשֵּׁיהֶם וְעַתָּה תִּיקַר נַפְשִׁי

15 have some worth in your eyes." Then an angel of the LORD spoke
to Eliyahu, "Go down with him; do not fear his presence." So he arose and
16 accompanied him down to the king. And he declared to him, "Thus says the
LORD: Because you sent messengers to inquire of Baal Zevuv, the god of
Ekron – was it for lack of a God in Israel whose word you could seek? – you
17 will never rise from your sickbed again; you will surely die!" And he died,
fulfilling the word of the LORD that Eliyahu had pronounced. Yehoram[75]
reigned in his place in the second year of King Yehoram son of
18 Yehoshafat of Yehuda, for he did not have a son. As for the rest of Aḥazyahu's
history and deeds – they are recorded in the book of the History of the Kings
2 1 of Israel. When the LORD was about to take Eliyahu up to heaven
2 in a whirlwind, Eliyahu and Elisha had just set out from Gilgal. "Stay here for
now," Eliyahu said to Elisha, "for the LORD has sent me to Beit El." "As the
LORD lives, and by your own life," said Elisha, "I will not leave you." So they
3 went down to Beit El. The brotherhood of the prophets in Beit El came out
to Elisha and said to him, "Do you know that the LORD will take your master
4 away from you today?" "Of course I know," he said. "Be silent!" Then Eliyahu
said to him, "Elisha, stay here for now, for the LORD has sent me to Yeriḥo."
"As the LORD lives, and by your own life," he said, "I will not leave you." So
5 they came to Yeriḥo. The brotherhood of the prophets in Yeriḥo approached
Elisha and said to him, "Do you know that the LORD will take your master
6 away from you today?" "Of course I know," he said. "Be silent!" Then Eliyahu
said to him, "Stay here for now, for the LORD has sent me to the Jordan."
"As the LORD lives, and by your own life," he said, "I will not leave you." So
7 the two of them went on. Fifty men from the brotherhood of the prophets
followed and stood by at a distance while the two of them stood by the Jordan.
8 Eliyahu took his cloak, rolled it up, and struck the waters; they split down the
9 middle, and the two of them crossed over on dry land. As they were crossing,
Eliyahu said to Elisha, "Ask what I may do for you before I am taken from you."
10 "Oh, if only twice of your spirit would rest upon me," said Elisha. "You have
made a difficult request," he said. "If you see me as I am taken from you, then
11 it will be granted for you, but if not, then it will not." And as they were walking
along, speaking to each other, a fiery chariot with fiery horses suddenly
appeared and parted the two of them, and Eliyahu rose up to heaven in a
12 whirlwind. As Elisha watched, he screamed, "Father! Father! The chariots of
Israel and its riders!" and then he saw him no more. Then he grasped hold of
13 his clothes and rent them in two. He picked up Eliyahu's cloak, which had
fallen from him, and he turned back and stood by the bank of the Jordan.
14 Grasping Eliyahu's cloak, which had fallen from him, he struck the waters.
"Oh, where is the LORD, God of Eliyahu?" he said. When he, too, struck the
15 waters, they split down the middle, and Elisha crossed over. When the
brotherhood of the prophets in Yeriḥo saw him from the other side, they said,
"The spirit of Eliyahu has settled on Elisha!" They came out toward him and

75 | Aḥazya's brother.

טו בְּעֵינֶיךָ: וַיְדַבֵּר מַלְאַךְ יהוה אֶל־אֵלִיָּהוּ רֵד אוֹתוֹ אַל־
טז תִּירָא מִפָּנָיו וַיָּקָם וַיֵּרֶד אוֹתוֹ אֶל־הַמֶּלֶךְ: וַיְדַבֵּר אֵלָיו כֹּה־אָמַר יהוה
יַעַן אֲשֶׁר־שָׁלַחְתָּ מַלְאָכִים לִדְרֹשׁ בְּבַעַל זְבוּב אֱלֹהֵי עֶקְרוֹן הֲמִבְּלִי
אֵין־אֱלֹהִים בְּיִשְׂרָאֵל לִדְרֹשׁ בִּדְבָרוֹ לָכֵן הַמִּטָּה אֲשֶׁר־עָלִיתָ שָּׁם
יז לֹא־תֵרֵד מִמֶּנָּה כִּי־מוֹת תָּמוּת: וַיָּמָת כִּדְבַר־יהוה | אֲשֶׁר־דִּבֶּר אֵלִיָּהוּ
וַיִּמְלֹךְ יְהוֹרָם תַּחְתָּיו בִּשְׁנַת שְׁתַּיִם לִיהוֹרָם בֶּן־יְהוֹשָׁפָט
יח מֶלֶךְ יְהוּדָה כִּי לֹא־הָיָה לוֹ בֵּן: וְיֶתֶר דִּבְרֵי אֲחַזְיָהוּ אֲשֶׁר עָשָׂה הֲלוֹא־
ב א הֵמָּה כְתוּבִים עַל־סֵפֶר דִּבְרֵי הַיָּמִים לְמַלְכֵי יִשְׂרָאֵל: וַיְהִי
בְּהַעֲלוֹת יהוה אֶת־אֵלִיָּהוּ בַּסְעָרָה הַשָּׁמָיִם וַיֵּלֶךְ אֵלִיָּהוּ וֶאֱלִישָׁע
ב מִן־הַגִּלְגָּל: וַיֹּאמֶר אֵלִיָּהוּ אֶל־אֱלִישָׁע שֵׁב־נָא פֹה כִּי יהוה שְׁלָחַנִי
עַד־בֵּית־אֵל וַיֹּאמֶר אֱלִישָׁע חַי־יהוה וְחֵי־נַפְשְׁךָ אִם־אֶעֶזְבֶךָּ וַיֵּרְדוּ
ג בֵּית־אֵל: וַיֵּצְאוּ בְנֵי־הַנְּבִיאִים אֲשֶׁר־בֵּית־אֵל אֶל־אֱלִישָׁע וַיֹּאמְרוּ
אֵלָיו הֲיָדַעְתָּ כִּי הַיּוֹם יהוה לֹקֵחַ אֶת־אֲדֹנֶיךָ מֵעַל רֹאשֶׁךָ וַיֹּאמֶר גַּם־
ד אֲנִי יָדַעְתִּי הֶחֱשׁוּ: וַיֹּאמֶר לוֹ אֵלִיָּהוּ אֱלִישָׁע | שֵׁב־נָא פֹה כִּי יהוה
שְׁלָחַנִי יְרִיחוֹ וַיֹּאמֶר חַי־יהוה וְחֵי־נַפְשְׁךָ אִם־אֶעֶזְבֶךָּ וַיָּבֹאוּ יְרִיחוֹ:
ה וַיִּגְּשׁוּ בְנֵי־הַנְּבִיאִים | אֲשֶׁר־בִּירִיחוֹ אֶל־אֱלִישָׁע וַיֹּאמְרוּ אֵלָיו הֲיָדַעְתָּ
כִּי הַיּוֹם יהוה לֹקֵחַ אֶת־אֲדֹנֶיךָ מֵעַל רֹאשֶׁךָ וַיֹּאמֶר גַּם־אֲנִי יָדַעְתִּי
ו הֶחֱשׁוּ: וַיֹּאמֶר לוֹ אֵלִיָּהוּ שֵׁב־נָא פֹה כִּי יהוה שְׁלָחַנִי הַיַּרְדֵּנָה וַיֹּאמֶר
ז חַי־יהוה וְחֵי־נַפְשְׁךָ אִם־אֶעֶזְבֶךָּ וַיֵּלְכוּ שְׁנֵיהֶם: וַחֲמִשִּׁים אִישׁ מִבְּנֵי
ח הַנְּבִיאִים הָלְכוּ וַיַּעַמְדוּ מִנֶּגֶד מֵרָחוֹק וּשְׁנֵיהֶם עָמְדוּ עַל־הַיַּרְדֵּן: וַיִּקַּח
אֵלִיָּהוּ אֶת־אַדַּרְתּוֹ וַיִּגְלֹם וַיַּכֶּה אֶת־הַמַּיִם וַיֵּחָצוּ הֵנָּה וָהֵנָּה וַיַּעַבְרוּ
ט שְׁנֵיהֶם בֶּחָרָבָה: וַיְהִי כְעָבְרָם וְאֵלִיָּהוּ אָמַר אֶל־אֱלִישָׁע שְׁאַל מָה
אֶעֱשֶׂה־לָּךְ בְּטֶרֶם אֶלָּקַח מֵעִמָּךְ וַיֹּאמֶר אֱלִישָׁע וִיהִי־נָא פִּי־שְׁנַיִם
י בְּרוּחֲךָ אֵלָי: וַיֹּאמֶר הִקְשִׁיתָ לִשְׁאוֹל אִם־תִּרְאֶה אֹתִי לֻקָּח מֵאִתָּךְ
יא יְהִי־לְךָ כֵן וְאִם־אַיִן לֹא יִהְיֶה: וַיְהִי הֵמָּה הֹלְכִים הָלוֹךְ וְדַבֵּר וְהִנֵּה
רֶכֶב־אֵשׁ וְסוּסֵי אֵשׁ וַיַּפְרִדוּ בֵּין שְׁנֵיהֶם וַיַּעַל אֵלִיָּהוּ בַּסְעָרָה הַשָּׁמָיִם:
יב וֶאֱלִישָׁע רֹאֶה וְהוּא מְצַעֵק אָבִי | אָבִי רֶכֶב יִשְׂרָאֵל וּפָרָשָׁיו וְלֹא רָאָהוּ
יג עוֹד וַיַּחֲזֵק בִּבְגָדָיו וַיִּקְרָעֵם לִשְׁנַיִם קְרָעִים: וַיָּרֶם אֶת־אַדֶּרֶת אֵלִיָּהוּ
יד אֲשֶׁר נָפְלָה מֵעָלָיו וַיָּשָׁב וַיַּעֲמֹד עַל־שְׂפַת הַיַּרְדֵּן: וַיִּקַּח אֶת־אַדֶּרֶת
אֵלִיָּהוּ אֲשֶׁר־נָפְלָה מֵעָלָיו וַיַּכֶּה אֶת־הַמַּיִם וַיֹּאמַר אַיֵּה יהוה אֱלֹהֵי
אֵלִיָּהוּ אַף־הוּא | וַיַּכֶּה אֶת־הַמַּיִם וַיֵּחָצוּ הֵנָּה וָהֵנָּה וַיַּעֲבֹר אֱלִישָׁע:
טו וַיִּרְאֻהוּ בְנֵי־הַנְּבִיאִים אֲשֶׁר־בִּירִיחוֹ מִנֶּגֶד וַיֹּאמְרוּ נָחָה רוּחַ אֵלִיָּהוּ כ

16 bowed low before him. "Please – your servants have fifty able men here with
them," they said to him. "Let them go and look for your master. Perhaps the
spirit of the LORD has carried him off and cast him upon some mountain or
17 into some valley." "Do not send them," he said. But they pressed him until it
grew late, and he said, "Send them!" They sent fifty men, and they searched
18 for him for three days, but they did not find him. He was staying in Yeriḥo
19 when they came back to him. "Well, I told you not to go," he said. Now the
townspeople said to Elisha, "Look, the town is a good place to live in, as my
20 lord can see, but the water is bad, and the land brings grief." "Fetch me a new
21 dish and put salt in it," he said, and they brought it to him. He went out to
the water source and flung the salt there. "Thus says the LORD," he said, "I
22 have healed these waters; no longer will death or grief issue from there." And
the waters have remained fresh ever since, fulfilling the word that Elisha
23 pronounced. From there, he went up to Beit El. As he was
making his way up, some young boys came out of the town and began to
24 taunt him. "Go away, baldy!" they said to him. "Go away, baldy!" He turned
around, and when he saw them, he cursed them in the name of the LORD –
and two bears came out of the forest and mauled forty-two of the children.
25 From there, he went on to Mount Carmel, and from there, he went back to
3 1 Shomron. Yehoram son of Aḥav became king over Israel in Shomron
in the eighteenth year of Yehoshafat, king of Yehuda, and he reigned for twelve
2 years. He did what was evil in the eyes of the LORD – though not to the same
extent as his father and mother, and he removed the pillar of Baal that his
3 father had made. But he clung to the sins of Yorovam son of Nevat, who led
4 Israel to sin, and did not turn away from them. Mesha, king of Moav,
was a sheep breeder, and he would pay tribute to the king of Israel with one
5 hundred thousand lambs and the wool of one hundred thousand rams. But
6 when Aḥav died, the king of Moav rebelled against the king of Israel. So at
7 that time King Yehoram set out from Shomron and rallied all of Israel. Then
he went and sent word to Yehoshafat, king of Yehuda: "The king of Moav has
rebelled against me. Will you go to war with me against Moav?" "I will," he
said. "I am ready, as you are; my troops are your own troops; my horses are
8 your own horses." "By which route shall we go up?" he asked. "By the road
9 through the wilderness of Edom," he said. So the king of Israel, the king of
Yehuda, and the king of Edom set out, but by the time they had made a circuit
of seven days' journey, there was no water for the camp or for the animals at
10 their heels. "Alas!" said the king of Israel. "The LORD has summoned these
11 three kings to hand them over to Moav." "Is there no prophet of the LORD
here?" said Yehoshafat. "Let us inquire of the LORD through him." One of the
king of Israel's officials spoke up. "Elisha son of Shafat is here," he said, "the
12 one who poured water on the hands of Eliyahu."[76] "He must have the word
of the LORD," said Yehoshafat, and the king of Israel, Yehoshafat, and the king

76 | That is, who served as an attendant to Eliyahu.

טז עַל־אֱלִישָׁע וַיָּבֹאוּ לִקְרָאתוֹ וַיִּשְׁתַּחֲווּ־לוֹ אָרְצָה׃ וַיֹּאמְרוּ אֵלָיו הִנֵּה־
נָא יֵשׁ־אֶת־עֲבָדֶיךָ חֲמִשִּׁים אֲנָשִׁים בְּנֵי־חַיִל יֵלְכוּ־נָא וִיבַקְשׁוּ אֶת־
אֲדֹנֶיךָ פֶּן־נְשָׂאוֹ רוּחַ יְהוָה וַיַּשְׁלִכֵהוּ בְּאַחַד הֶהָרִים אוֹ בְּאַחַת הגיאות הַגֵּאָיוֹת
יז וַיֹּאמֶר לֹא תִשְׁלָחוּ׃ וַיִּפְצְרוּ־בוֹ עַד־בֹּשׁ וַיֹּאמֶר שְׁלָחוּ וַיִּשְׁלְחוּ חֲמִשִּׁים
יח אִישׁ וַיְבַקְשׁוּ שְׁלֹשָׁה־יָמִים וְלֹא מְצָאֻהוּ׃ וַיָּשֻׁבוּ אֵלָיו וְהוּא יֹשֵׁב
יט בִּירִיחוֹ וַיֹּאמֶר אֲלֵהֶם הֲלוֹא־אָמַרְתִּי אֲלֵיכֶם אַל־תֵּלֵכוּ׃ וַיֹּאמְרוּ
אַנְשֵׁי הָעִיר אֶל־אֱלִישָׁע הִנֵּה־נָא מוֹשַׁב הָעִיר טוֹב כַּאֲשֶׁר אֲדֹנִי
כ רֹאֶה וְהַמַּיִם רָעִים וְהָאָרֶץ מְשַׁכָּלֶת׃ וַיֹּאמֶר קְחוּ־לִי צְלֹחִית חֲדָשָׁה
כא וְשִׂימוּ שָׁם מֶלַח וַיִּקְחוּ אֵלָיו׃ וַיֵּצֵא אֶל־מוֹצָא הַמַּיִם וַיַּשְׁלֶךְ־שָׁם מֶלַח
וַיֹּאמֶר כֹּה־אָמַר יְהוָה רִפִּאתִי לַמַּיִם הָאֵלֶּה לֹא־יִהְיֶה מִשָּׁם עוֹד
כב מָוֶת וּמְשַׁכָּלֶת׃ וַיֵּרָפוּ הַמַּיִם עַד הַיּוֹם הַזֶּה כִּדְבַר אֱלִישָׁע אֲשֶׁר
כג דִּבֵּר׃ וַיַּעַל מִשָּׁם בֵּית־אֵל וְהוּא ׀ עֹלֶה בַדֶּרֶךְ וּנְעָרִים
קְטַנִּים יָצְאוּ מִן־הָעִיר וַיִּתְקַלְּסוּ־בוֹ וַיֹּאמְרוּ לוֹ עֲלֵה קֵרֵחַ עֲלֵה קֵרֵחַ׃
כד וַיִּפֶן אַחֲרָיו וַיִּרְאֵם וַיְקַלְלֵם בְּשֵׁם יְהוָה וַתֵּצֶאנָה שְׁתַּיִם דֻּבִּים מִן־הַיַּעַר
כה וַתְּבַקַּעְנָה מֵהֶם אַרְבָּעִים וּשְׁנֵי יְלָדִים׃ וַיֵּלֶךְ מִשָּׁם אֶל־הַר הַכַּרְמֶל
ג א וּמִשָּׁם שָׁב שֹׁמְרוֹן׃ וִיהוֹרָם בֶּן־אַחְאָב מָלַךְ עַל־יִשְׂרָאֵל
בְּשֹׁמְרוֹן בִּשְׁנַת שְׁמֹנֶה עֶשְׂרֵה לִיהוֹשָׁפָט מֶלֶךְ יְהוּדָה וַיִּמְלֹךְ שְׁתֵּים־
ב עֶשְׂרֵה שָׁנָה׃ וַיַּעֲשֶׂה הָרַע בְּעֵינֵי יְהוָה רַק לֹא כְאָבִיו וּכְאִמּוֹ וַיָּסַר
ג אֶת־מַצְּבַת הַבַּעַל אֲשֶׁר עָשָׂה אָבִיו׃ רַק בְּחַטֹּאות יָרָבְעָם בֶּן־נְבָט
ד אֲשֶׁר־הֶחֱטִיא אֶת־יִשְׂרָאֵל דָּבֵק לֹא־סָר מִמֶּנָּה׃ וּמֵישַׁע
מֶלֶךְ־מוֹאָב הָיָה נֹקֵד וְהֵשִׁיב לְמֶלֶךְ־יִשְׂרָאֵל מֵאָה־אֶלֶף כָּרִים וּמֵאָה
ה אֶלֶף אֵילִים צָמֶר׃ וַיְהִי כְּמוֹת אַחְאָב וַיִּפְשַׁע מֶלֶךְ־מוֹאָב בְּמֶלֶךְ
ו יִשְׂרָאֵל׃ וַיֵּצֵא הַמֶּלֶךְ יְהוֹרָם בַּיּוֹם הַהוּא מִשֹּׁמְרוֹן וַיִּפְקֹד אֶת־כָּל־
ז יִשְׂרָאֵל׃ וַיֵּלֶךְ וַיִּשְׁלַח אֶל־יְהוֹשָׁפָט מֶלֶךְ־יְהוּדָה לֵאמֹר מֶלֶךְ מוֹאָב
פָּשַׁע בִּי הֲתֵלֵךְ אִתִּי אֶל־מוֹאָב לַמִּלְחָמָה וַיֹּאמֶר אֶעֱלֶה כָּמוֹנִי כָמוֹךָ
ח כְּעַמִּי כְעַמֶּךָ כְּסוּסַי כְּסוּסֶיךָ׃ וַיֹּאמֶר אֵי־זֶה הַדֶּרֶךְ נַעֲלֶה וַיֹּאמֶר דֶּרֶךְ
ט מִדְבַּר אֱדוֹם׃ וַיֵּלֶךְ מֶלֶךְ יִשְׂרָאֵל וּמֶלֶךְ יְהוּדָה וּמֶלֶךְ אֱדוֹם וַיָּסֹבּוּ דֶּרֶךְ
י שִׁבְעַת יָמִים וְלֹא־הָיָה מַיִם לַמַּחֲנֶה וְלַבְּהֵמָה אֲשֶׁר בְּרַגְלֵיהֶם׃ וַיֹּאמֶר
מֶלֶךְ יִשְׂרָאֵל אֲהָהּ כִּי־קָרָא יְהוָה לִשְׁלֹשֶׁת הַמְּלָכִים הָאֵלֶּה לָתֵת
יא אוֹתָם בְּיַד־מוֹאָב׃ וַיֹּאמֶר יְהוֹשָׁפָט הַאֵין פֹּה נָבִיא לַיהוָה וְנִדְרְשָׁה
אֶת־יְהוָה מֵאוֹתוֹ וַיַּעַן אֶחָד מֵעַבְדֵי מֶלֶךְ־יִשְׂרָאֵל וַיֹּאמֶר פֹּה אֱלִישָׁע
יב בֶּן־שָׁפָט אֲשֶׁר־יָצַק מַיִם עַל־יְדֵי אֵלִיָּהוּ׃ וַיֹּאמֶר יְהוֹשָׁפָט יֵשׁ אוֹתוֹ

13 of Edom went down to him. But Elisha said to the king of Israel, "What have
I to do with you? Go to the prophets of your father and to the prophets
of your mother." "No," the king of Israel said to him, "for the LORD has
14 summoned these three kings to hand them over to Moav." "As the LORD
of Hosts lives, whom I serve," said Elisha, "were it not for my regard for
Yehoshafat, king of Yehuda, I would not look at you or even glance at you.
15 Now fetch me a musician." And as the musician played, the hand of the LORD
16 settled upon him. "Thus says the LORD," he said. "This wadi shall fill up with
17 pool after pool. For thus says the LORD: You will see no wind and you will
see no rain, yet the wadi shall be filled with water, and you and your livestock
18 and your animals shall drink. But this is nothing in the eyes of the LORD, for
19 He will also hand Moav over to you. You will defeat every fortified city and
every illustrious city; you will fell every good tree and stop up every spring,
20 and you will wreck every good field with stones." And in the morning, at the
time of the grain offering, water suddenly came from the direction of Edom,
21 and the land was filled with water. When all of Moav heard that the kings had
marched up to fight them, everyone old enough to bear arms rallied and
22 stationed themselves at the border. When they rose early in the morning, the
sun rose over the water, and to the Moabites, the water in the distance seemed
23 as red as blood. "That's blood!" they said. "The kings must have fought among
24 themselves and slaughtered each other – now to the spoil, Moav!" But when
they reached the camp of Israel, Israel charged and attacked Moav, and they
25 fled from them. They advanced, constantly on the attack against Moav, and
destroyed their cities; each man flung stones at every good field until it was
filled up, and they stopped up every spring of water and felled every good tree,
leaving only the stone wall of Kir Ḥareset, which the slingers then surrounded
26 and attacked. When the king of Moav saw that the battle was too fierce for
him, he took seven hundred swordsmen with him to break through to the
27 king of Edom, but they could not. So he took his firstborn son, who was to
reign in his place, and he offered him up as a burnt offering on the wall.
Then there was great wrath against Israel, and they withdrew from him and
4 1 returned to the land. A woman – the wife of one of the brotherhood
of the prophets – cried out to Elisha, "Your servant, my husband, is dead! You
know that your servant always feared the LORD. Now a creditor has come to
2 take my two children away to be his slaves." "What can I do for you?" said
Elisha. "Tell me, what do you have in the house?" "Your servant has nothing
3 at all at home," she said, "except for a jar of oil." "Go out and borrow vessels
from all your neighbors," he said to her, "empty vessels – as many as you can.
4 When you come back in, close the door behind you and your sons. Then pour
5 away into all those vessels, setting them aside when they are full." And so
she left him. When she closed the door behind her and her sons, they kept

יג דְּבַר־יְהוָה וַיֵּרְדוּ אֵלָיו מֶלֶךְ יִשְׂרָאֵל וִיהוֹשָׁפָט וּמֶלֶךְ אֱדוֹם: וַיֹּאמֶר
אֱלִישָׁע אֶל־מֶלֶךְ יִשְׂרָאֵל מַה־לִּי וָלָךְ לֵךְ אֶל־נְבִיאֵי אָבִיךָ וְאֶל־נְבִיאֵי
אִמֶּךָ וַיֹּאמֶר לוֹ מֶלֶךְ יִשְׂרָאֵל אַל כִּי־קָרָא יְהוָה לִשְׁלֹשֶׁת הַמְּלָכִים
יד הָאֵלֶּה לָתֵת אוֹתָם בְּיַד מוֹאָב: וַיֹּאמֶר אֱלִישָׁע חַי־יְהוָה צְבָאוֹת אֲשֶׁר
עָמַדְתִּי לְפָנָיו כִּי לוּלֵי פְּנֵי־יְהוֹשָׁפָט מֶלֶךְ־יְהוּדָה אֲנִי נֹשֵׂא אִם־אַבִּיט
טו אֵלֶיךָ וְאִם־אֶרְאֶךָּ: וְעַתָּה קְחוּ־לִי מְנַגֵּן וְהָיָה כְּנַגֵּן הַמְנַגֵּן וַתְּהִי עָלָיו
טז יז יַד יְהוָה: וַיֹּאמֶר כֹּה אָמַר יְהוָה עָשֹׂה הַנַּחַל הַזֶּה גֵּבִים | גֵּבִים: כִּי־
כֹה | אָמַר יְהוָה לֹא־תִרְאוּ רוּחַ וְלֹא־תִרְאוּ גֶשֶׁם וְהַנַּחַל הַהוּא יִמָּלֵא
יח מַיִם וּשְׁתִיתֶם אַתֶּם וּמִקְנֵיכֶם וּבְהֶמְתְּכֶם: וְנָקַל זֹאת בְּעֵינֵי יְהוָה וְנָתַן
יט אֶת־מוֹאָב בְּיֶדְכֶם: וְהִכִּיתֶם כָּל־עִיר מִבְצָר וְכָל־עִיר מִבְחוֹר וְכָל־עֵץ
טוֹב תַּפִּילוּ וְכָל־מַעְיְנֵי־מַיִם תִּסְתֹּמוּ וְכֹל הַחֶלְקָה הַטּוֹבָה תַּכְאִבוּ
כ בָּאֲבָנִים: וַיְהִי בַבֹּקֶר כַּעֲלוֹת הַמִּנְחָה וְהִנֵּה־מַיִם בָּאִים מִדֶּרֶךְ אֱדוֹם
כא וַתִּמָּלֵא הָאָרֶץ אֶת־הַמָּיִם: וְכָל־מוֹאָב שָׁמְעוּ כִּי־עָלוּ הַמְּלָכִים לְהִלָּחֶם
כב בָּם וַיִּצָּעֲקוּ מִכֹּל חֹגֵר חֲגֹרָה וָמָעְלָה וַיַּעַמְדוּ עַל־הַגְּבוּל: וַיַּשְׁכִּימוּ
בַבֹּקֶר וְהַשֶּׁמֶשׁ זָרְחָה עַל־הַמָּיִם וַיִּרְאוּ מוֹאָב מִנֶּגֶד אֶת־הַמַּיִם אֲדֻמִּים
כג כַּדָּם: וַיֹּאמְרוּ דָּם זֶה הָחֳרֵב נֶחֶרְבוּ הַמְּלָכִים וַיַּכּוּ אִישׁ אֶת־רֵעֵהוּ
כד וְעַתָּה לַשָּׁלָל מוֹאָב: וַיָּבֹאוּ אֶל־מַחֲנֵה יִשְׂרָאֵל וַיָּקֻמוּ יִשְׂרָאֵל וַיַּכּוּ
כה אֶת־מוֹאָב וַיָּנֻסוּ מִפְּנֵיהֶם ויבו־בָהּ וְהַכּוֹת אֶת־מוֹאָב: וְהֶעָרִים יַהֲרֹסוּ וַיַּכּוּ־
וְכָל־חֶלְקָה טוֹבָה יַשְׁלִיכוּ אִישׁ־אַבְנוֹ וּמִלְאוּהָ וְכָל־מַעְיַן־מַיִם יִסְתְּמוּ
וְכָל־עֵץ־טוֹב יַפִּילוּ עַד־הִשְׁאִיר אֲבָנֶיהָ בַּקִּיר חֲרָשֶׂת וַיָּסֹבּוּ הַקַּלָּעִים
כו וַיַּכּוּהָ: וַיַּרְא מֶלֶךְ מוֹאָב כִּי־חָזַק מִמֶּנּוּ הַמִּלְחָמָה וַיִּקַּח אוֹתוֹ שְׁבַע־
כז מֵאוֹת אִישׁ שֹׁלֵף חֶרֶב לְהַבְקִיעַ אֶל־מֶלֶךְ אֱדוֹם וְלֹא יָכֹלוּ: וַיִּקַּח
אֶת־בְּנוֹ הַבְּכוֹר אֲשֶׁר־יִמְלֹךְ תַּחְתָּיו וַיַּעֲלֵהוּ עֹלָה עַל־הַחֹמָה וַיְהִי
ד א קֶצֶף־גָּדוֹל עַל־יִשְׂרָאֵל וַיִּסְעוּ מֵעָלָיו וַיָּשֻׁבוּ לָאָרֶץ: וְאִשָּׁה
אַחַת מִנְּשֵׁי בְנֵי־הַנְּבִיאִים צָעֲקָה אֶל־אֱלִישָׁע לֵאמֹר עַבְדְּךָ אִישִׁי
מֵת וְאַתָּה יָדַעְתָּ כִּי עַבְדְּךָ הָיָה יָרֵא אֶת־יְהוָה וְהַנֹּשֶׁה בָּא לָקַחַת
ב אֶת־שְׁנֵי יְלָדַי לוֹ לַעֲבָדִים: וַיֹּאמֶר אֵלֶיהָ אֱלִישָׁע מָה אֶעֱשֶׂה־לָּךְ
הַגִּידִי לִי מַה־יֶּשׁ־לכי בַּבָּיִת וַתֹּאמֶר אֵין לְשִׁפְחָתְךָ כֹל בַּבַּיִת כִּי לָךְ
ג אִם־אָסוּךְ שָׁמֶן: וַיֹּאמֶר לְכִי שַׁאֲלִי־לָךְ כֵּלִים מִן־הַחוּץ מֵאֵת כָּל־
ד שכניכי כֵּלִים רֵקִים אַל־תַּמְעִיטִי: וּבָאת וְסָגַרְתְּ הַדֶּלֶת בַּעֲדֵךְ וּבְעַד־ שְׁכֵנָיִךְ
ה בָּנַיִךְ וְיָצַקְתְּ עַל כָּל־הַכֵּלִים הָאֵלֶּה וְהַמָּלֵא תַּסִּיעִי: וַתֵּלֶךְ מֵאִתּוֹ
וַתִּסְגֹּר הַדֶּלֶת בַּעֲדָהּ וּבְעַד בָּנֶיהָ הֵם מַגִּשִׁים אֵלֶיהָ וְהִיא מיצקת: מוֹצָקֶת

6 bringing vessels to her while she kept pouring. When the vessels were full,
she said to her son, "Bring me another vessel," and he said to her, "There are
7 no more vessels" – and the oil stopped flowing. She came and told the man
of God, and he said, "Go, sell the oil and pay off your debt, and you and your
8 sons can live on the rest." One day, Elisha was passing through
Shunem, and a wealthy woman there urged him to have something to eat. So
9 whenever he passed through, he would stop there for some food. She said to
her husband, "Look, I am sure that the man who passes through here regularly
10 is a holy man of God. Let us make him a small enclosed upper chamber and
provide him with a bed, table, chair, and lamp there, so that whenever he
11 comes to us, he can turn in there." One day, he came by; he turned in to the
12 upper chamber and lay down there. He said to Geḥazi, his servant, "Call the
13 Shunamite woman." He called her, and she stood before him. He said to him,
"Please say to her, 'You have shown us so much concern. What can we do for
you? Shall I speak to the king on your behalf, or to the army commander?'"
14 "I live among my own people," she said. "Then what can be done for her?" he
15 said. "Well, she is childless," said Geḥazi, "and her husband is old." "Call her,"
16 he said, and he called her, and she stood in the entrance. "At this time next
year," he said, "you will be embracing a son." "No, my lord, man of God," she
17 said. "Do not delude your servant." But the woman did conceive, and she
bore a son at that time during the following year, just as Elisha had promised
18 her. The child grew up. One day, he went out to his father, who was with the
19 reapers. "My head! My head!" he said to his father, who said to the servant,
20 "Carry him to his mother." He carried him over and brought him to his
21 mother; he sat on her lap until noon, and then he died. She went up and laid
him on the man of God's bed, closed the door behind him, and went out.
22 Then she called to her husband. "Send me one of the servants and one of the
donkeys at once," she said. "I must rush over to the man of God and come
23 right back." "Why are you going to him today?" he said. "It is not the New
24 Moon, nor the Sabbath." "All is well," she said. She saddled the donkey and
said to her servant, "Drive! Be off! Do not stop riding on my account unless
25 I tell you." She set out and reached the man of God at Mount Carmel. When
the man of God saw her in the distance, he said to Geḥazi, his servant, "Look,
26 there is that Shunamite woman. Run to meet her straightaway and say to her,
'Are you well? Is your husband well? Is your child well?'" "All is well," she said.
27 But she came up to the man of God at the mountain and grasped his feet.
Geḥazi came forward to push her away, but the man of God said, "Leave her
be, for she is bitter of spirit, and the Lord has hidden this from me and did
28 not tell me." "Did I ask my lord for a son?" she said. "Did I not say, 'Do not
29 lead me on?'" "Hitch up your tunic," Elisha said to Geḥazi. "Take my staff in
your hand, and set out. If you meet anyone, do not greet them, and if anyone

ו ויהי | כמלאת הכלים ותאמר אל־בנה הגישה אלי עוד כלי ויאמר
ז אליה אין עוד כלי ויעמד השמן: ותבא ותגד לאיש האלהים
ויאמר לכי מכרי את־השמן ושלמי את־נשיכי ואת בניכי תחיי נשיך | ובניך
ח בנותר: ויהי היום ויעבר אלישע אל־שונם ושם אשה
גדולה ותחזק־בו לאכל־לחם ויהי מדי עברו יסר שמה לאכל־לחם:
ט ותאמר אל־אישה הנה־נא ידעתי כי איש אלהים קדוש הוא עבר
י עלינו תמיד: נעשה־נא עלית־קיר קטנה ונשים לו שם מטה ושלחן
יא וכסא ומנורה והיה בבאו אלינו יסור שמה: ויהי היום ויבא שמה
יב ויסר אל־העליה וישכב־שמה: ויאמר אל־גיחזי נערו קרא לשונמית
יג הזאת ויקרא־לה ותעמד לפניו: ויאמר לו אמר־נא אליה הנה
חרדת | אלינו את־כל־החרדה הזאת מה לעשות לך היש לדבר־
לך אל־המלך או אל־שר הצבא ותאמר בתוך עמי אנכי ישבת:
יד ויאמר ומה לעשות לה ויאמר גיחזי אבל בן אין־לה ואישה זקן:
טו טז ויאמר קרא־לה ויקרא־לה ותעמד בפתח: ויאמר למועד הזה כעת
חיה אתי חבקת בן ותאמר אל־אדני איש האלהים אל־תכזב את
יז בשפחתך: ותהר האשה ותלד בן למועד הזה כעת חיה אשר־דבר
יח אליה אלישע: ויגדל הילד ויהי היום ויצא אל־אביו אל־הקצרים:
יט ויאמר אל־אביו ראשי | ראשי ויאמר אל־הנער שאהו אל־אמו:
כ כא וישאהו ויביאהו אל־אמו וישב על־ברכיה עד־הצהרים וימת: ותעל
כב ותשכבהו על־מטת איש האלהים ותסגר בעדו ותצא: ותקרא
אל־אישה ותאמר שלחה נא לי אחד מן־הנערים ואחת האתנות
כג וארוצה עד־איש האלהים ואשובה: ויאמר מדוע אתי הלכתי אליו את הלכת
כד היום לא־חדש ולא שבת ותאמר שלום: ותחבש האתון ותאמר
כה אל־נערה נהג ולך אל־תעצר־לי לרכב כי אם־אמרתי לך: ותלך
ותבא אל־איש האלהים אל־הר הכרמל ויהי כראות איש־האלהים
כו אתה מנגד ויאמר אל־גיחזי נערו הנה השונמית הלז: עתה רוץ־ כא
נא לקראתה ואמר־לה השלום לך השלום לאישך השלום לילד
כז ותאמר שלום: ותבא אל־איש האלהים אל־ההר ותחזק ברגליו
ויגש גיחזי להדפה ויאמר איש האלהים הרפה־לה כי־נפשה מרה־
כח לה ויהוה העלים ממני ולא הגיד לי: ותאמר השאלתי בן מאת
כט אדני הלא אמרתי לא תשלה אתי: ויאמר לגיחזי חגר מתניך וקח
משענתי בידך ולך כי־תמצא איש לא תברכנו וכי־יברכך איש לא

30 greets you, do not answer them. Place my staff on the boy's face." "As the
Lord lives, and by your own life," said the boy's mother, "I will not leave you."
31 So he followed straight behind her. Geḥazi went on ahead of them and placed
the staff on the boy's face, but there was no sound and no response. He went
32 back to meet him and told him, "The boy did not wake." Elisha entered the
33 house, and there was the boy laid out on his bed – dead. He entered and
34 closed the door behind the two of them, and he prayed to the Lord. Then
he mounted the bed and lay on top of the boy; he placed his mouth on his
mouth and his eyes on his eyes and his palms on his palms, and he bent down
35 over him, and the child's body became warm. He went back down and paced
about the house, back and forth, then he climbed up and crouched down over
36 him. And the boy sneezed – seven times – and the boy opened his eyes. He
called to Geḥazi and said to him, "Call the Shunamite woman." He called her,
37 and she came to him. "Pick up your son," he said. And she came and fell at
his feet and bowed to the ground. Then she picked up her son and went
38 out. When Elisha returned to Gilgal, there was famine in the land.
As the brotherhood of the prophets sat before him, he said to his servant, "Set
39 up the large pot and cook a stew for the brotherhood of the prophets." One
of them went out to the field to gather herbs, and he found a wild vine. He
plucked its wild gourds and filled up his garment, then he came and diced
40 them into the pot of stew, for they did not realize what they were. They
poured it out for the people to eat, but as they were eating from the stew, they
began to shout, "There is death in the pot, O man of God!" and they could
41 not eat. "Fetch some flour," he said, and flung it into the pot. "Pour it out for
the people and let them eat," he said, and there was no longer anything
42 harmful in the pot. A man came from Baal Shalisha and brought the
man of God bread made of the first grain: twenty loaves of barley bread and
some fresh grain in his sack. "Give it to the people and let them eat," he said.
43 "How can I set this before a hundred people?" asked his attendant. "Give it
to the people and let them eat," he said, "for thus says the Lord: They will
44 eat and leave some over." So he set it before them and they ate, and there
5 1 was some left over, fulfilling the word of the Lord. Naaman, the
commander of the king of Aram's army, was highly esteemed by his master
and held in favor, for the Lord had granted victory to Aram through him.
2 But this powerful man suffered from an impure blight. Once, when the
Arameans were out raiding, they captured a young girl from the land of Israel,
3 and she became a servant of Naaman's wife. She said to her mistress, "If only
my master would present himself to the prophet in Shomron, he would cure
4 him of his blight." Naaman then went and told his own master about what
5 the girl from the land of Israel had said. "Prepare to set out," said the king of
Aram, "and I will send along a letter to the king of Israel." He set out, taking
ten talents of silver, six thousand pieces of gold, and ten sets of clothing with
6 him. And he brought the letter to the king of Israel, which read: "Now, as this
letter reaches you, I have sent my servant Naaman to you, that you may cure
7 him of his blight." When the king of Israel read the letter, he rent his clothes.

ל תעננו ושמת משענתי על־פני הנער: ותאמר אם הנער חי־יהוה
לא וחי־נפשך אם־אעזבך ויקם וילך אחריה: וגחזי עבר לפניהם וישם
את־המשענת על־פני הנער ואין קול ואין קשב וישב לקראתו
לב ויגד־לו לאמר לא הקיץ הנער: ויבא אלישע הביתה והנה הנער
לג מת משכב על־מטתו: ויבא ויסגר הדלת בעד שניהם ויתפלל
לד אל־יהוה: ויעל וישכב על־הילד וישם פיו על־פיו ועיניו על־עיניו
לה וכפיו על־כפו ויגהר עליו ויחם בשר הילד: וישב וילך בבית אחת
הנה ואחת הנה ויעל ויגהר עליו ויזורר הנער עד־שבע פעמים
לו ויפקח הנער את־עיניו: ויקרא אל־גיחזי ויאמר קרא אל־השנמית
לז הזאת ויקראה ותבוא אליו ויאמר שאי בנך: ותבא ותפל על־רגליו
לח ותשתחו ארצה ותשא את־בנה ותצא: ואלישע שב
הגלגלה והרעב בארץ ובני הנביאים ישבים לפניו ויאמר לנערו
לט שפת הסיר הגדולה ובשל נזיד לבני הנביאים: ויצא אחד אל־
השדה ללקט ארת וימצא גפן שדה וילקט ממנו פקעת שדה מלא
מ בגדו ויבא ויפלח אל־סיר הנזיד כי־לא ידעו: ויצקו לאנשים לאכול
ויהי כאכלם מהנזיד והמה צעקו ויאמרו מות בסיר איש האלהים
מא ולא יכלו לאכל: ויאמר וקחו־קמח וישלך אל־הסיר ויאמר צק
מב לעם ויאכלו ולא היה דבר רע בסיר: ואיש בא מבעל
שלשה ויבא לאיש האלהים לחם בכורים עשרים־לחם שערים
מג וכרמל בצקלנו ויאמר תן לעם ויאכלו: ויאמר משרתו מה אתן זה
לפני מאה איש ויאמר תן לעם ויאכלו כי כה אמר יהוה אכול והותר:
מד ויתן לפניהם ויאכלו ויותרו כדבר יהוה: ונעמן שר־צבא ה א
מלך־ארם היה איש גדול לפני אדניו ונשא פנים כי־בו נתן־יהוה
ב תשועה לארם והאיש היה גבור חיל מצרע: וארם יצאו גדודים
ג וישבו מארץ ישראל נערה קטנה ותהי לפני אשת נעמן: ותאמר
אל־גברתה אחלי אדני לפני הנביא אשר בשמרון אז יאסף אתו
ד מצרעתו: ויבא ויגד לאדניו לאמר כזאת וכזאת דברה הנערה אשר
ה מארץ ישראל: ויאמר מלך־ארם לך־בא ואשלחה ספר אל־
מלך ישראל וילך ויקח בידו עשר ככרי־כסף וששת אלפים זהב
ו ועשר חליפות בגדים: ויבא הספר אל־מלך ישראל לאמר ועתה
כבוא הספר הזה אליך הנה שלחתי אליך את־נעמן עבדי ואספתו
ז מצרעתו: ויהי כקרא מלך־ישראל את־הספר ויקרע בגדיו ויאמר

"Am I God, dealing death and granting life, that this one sends me a man to
cure his blight?" he said, "Be aware now, look – he must be provoking a
8 quarrel with me." When Elisha, the man of God, heard that the king of Israel
had rent his clothes, he sent to the king, saying, "Why have you rent your
clothes? Let him come to me now, and he will know that there is a prophet
9 in Israel." So Naaman came with his horses and chariots and halted at the
10 entrance of Elisha's house. And Elisha sent a messenger to him, saying, "Go
and bathe in the Jordan seven times; your skin will be restored to you, and
11 you will be cleansed." Naaman was furious and walked away. "I was certain
he would come out to me," he said, "and stand and invoke the name of the
Lord, his God, and wave his hand toward the affected area and cure my blight.
12 Why, Amana and Parpar, the rivers of Damascus, are better than all the waters
of Israel – if I bathe in them, will I not be cleansed?" And he turned and
13 stormed off in a rage. But his servants approached him and spoke to him.
"Father,"[77] they said, "had the prophet given you more difficult instructions,
would you not carry them out? All the more so when he has only said to you,
14 'Bathe and be cleansed.'" So he went down and immersed in the Jordan seven
times, fulfilling the instruction of the man of God, and his skin became like
15 the skin of a young boy, and he was cleansed. He went back to the man of
God along with all his company, and he came and stood before him. "Now I
know that there is no God in all the world except in Israel," he said. "Now,
16 please accept your servant's gift." "As the Lord lives, whom I serve," he said,
17 "I will not accept it." He urged him to accept, but he refused. "If not," said
Naaman, "may your servant be given two mule loads' worth of soil, for your
servant will no longer offer burnt offering or sacrifice to other gods, but
18 only to the Lord. But may the Lord forgive your servant this: when my
master comes to the temple of Rimon[78] to bow down there, he leans on my
hand so that I must bow down in the temple of Rimon. So when I bow down
19 in the temple of Rimon, may the Lord forgive your servant for this." "Go
in peace," he said to him. When he had traveled some distance away from
20 him, Geḥazi, the servant of the man of God, Elisha, thought, "Look,
my master has let that Aramean Naaman off without taking what he brought
with him. As the Lord lives, I will run after him and take something from
21 him." And Geḥazi chased after Naaman. When Naaman saw him running
behind him, he alighted from his chariot toward him. "Is all well?" he said.
22 "All is well," he said. "My master has sent me, saying, 'Two lads from the
brotherhood of the prophets in the Efrayim Hills have just come to me;
23 please let them have a talent of silver and two sets of clothing.'" "Please," said
Naaman, "be so kind as to accept two talents." He urged him and tied two
talents of silver in two bags with two sets of clothing and gave them to two
24 of his servants to bear before him. When he reached the Ofel, he took it off
their hands and deposited it inside. Then he dismissed the men and they left.
25 When he came to attend to his master, Elisha said to him, "Where have you

77 | A term of respect.

78 | Another name for Hadad, the Aramean god of storm and thunder.

הָאֱלֹהִים אָנִי לְהָמִית וּלְהַחֲיוֹת כִּי־זֶה שֹׁלֵחַ אֵלַי לֶאֱסֹף אִישׁ מִצָּרַעְתּוֹ
ח כִּי אַךְ־דְּעוּ־נָא וּרְאוּ כִּי־מִתְאַנֶּה הוּא לִי: וַיְהִי כִּשְׁמֹעַ ׀ אֱלִישָׁע אִישׁ־
הָאֱלֹהִים כִּי־קָרַע מֶלֶךְ־יִשְׂרָאֵל אֶת־בְּגָדָיו וַיִּשְׁלַח אֶל־הַמֶּלֶךְ לֵאמֹר
ט לָמָּה קָרַעְתָּ בְּגָדֶיךָ יָבֹא־נָא אֵלַי וְיֵדַע כִּי יֵשׁ נָבִיא בְּיִשְׂרָאֵל: וַיָּבֹא
י נַעֲמָן בְּסוּסָו וּבְרִכְבּוֹ וַיַּעֲמֹד פֶּתַח־הַבַּיִת לֶאֱלִישָׁע: וַיִּשְׁלַח אֵלָיו
אֱלִישָׁע מַלְאָךְ לֵאמֹר הָלוֹךְ וְרָחַצְתָּ שֶׁבַע־פְּעָמִים בַּיַּרְדֵּן וְיָשֹׁב בְּשָׂרְךָ
יא לְךָ וּטְהָר: וַיִּקְצֹף נַעֲמָן וַיֵּלַךְ וַיֹּאמֶר הִנֵּה אָמַרְתִּי אֵלַי ׀ יֵצֵא יָצוֹא
וְעָמַד וְקָרָא בְּשֵׁם־יְהוָה אֱלֹהָיו וְהֵנִיף יָדוֹ אֶל־הַמָּקוֹם וְאָסַף הַמְּצֹרָע:
יב הֲלֹא טוֹב אבנה וּפַרְפַּר נַהֲרוֹת דַּמֶּשֶׂק מִכֹּל מֵימֵי יִשְׂרָאֵל הֲלֹא־ אֲמָנָה
יג אֶרְחַץ בָּהֶם וְטָהָרְתִּי וַיִּפֶן וַיֵּלֶךְ בְּחֵמָה: וַיִּגְּשׁוּ עֲבָדָיו וַיְדַבְּרוּ אֵלָיו
וַיֹּאמְרוּ אָבִי דָּבָר גָּדוֹל הַנָּבִיא דִּבֶּר אֵלֶיךָ הֲלוֹא תַעֲשֶׂה וְאַף כִּי־
יד אָמַר אֵלֶיךָ רְחַץ וּטְהָר: וַיֵּרֶד וַיִּטְבֹּל בַּיַּרְדֵּן שֶׁבַע פְּעָמִים כִּדְבַר
טו אִישׁ הָאֱלֹהִים וַיָּשָׁב בְּשָׂרוֹ כִּבְשַׂר נַעַר קָטֹן וַיִּטְהָר: וַיָּשָׁב אֶל־אִישׁ
הָאֱלֹהִים הוּא וְכָל־מַחֲנֵהוּ וַיָּבֹא וַיַּעֲמֹד לְפָנָיו וַיֹּאמֶר הִנֵּה־נָא יָדַעְתִּי
כִּי אֵין אֱלֹהִים בְּכָל־הָאָרֶץ כִּי אִם־בְּיִשְׂרָאֵל וְעַתָּה קַח־נָא בְרָכָה
טז מֵאֵת עַבְדֶּךָ: וַיֹּאמֶר חַי־יְהוָה אֲשֶׁר־עָמַדְתִּי לְפָנָיו אִם־אֶקָּח וַיִּפְצַר־
יז בּוֹ לָקַחַת וַיְמָאֵן: וַיֹּאמֶר נַעֲמָן וָלֹא יֻתַּן־נָא לְעַבְדְּךָ מַשָּׂא צֶמֶד־
פְּרָדִים אֲדָמָה כִּי לוֹא־יַעֲשֶׂה עוֹד עַבְדְּךָ עֹלָה וָזֶבַח לֵאלֹהִים אֲחֵרִים
יח כִּי אִם־לַיהוָה: לַדָּבָר הַזֶּה יִסְלַח יְהוָה לְעַבְדֶּךָ בְּבוֹא אֲדֹנִי בֵית־
רִמּוֹן לְהִשְׁתַּחֲוֺת שָׁמָּה וְהוּא ׀ נִשְׁעָן עַל־יָדִי וְהִשְׁתַּחֲוֵיתִי בֵּית רִמֹּן
יט בְּהִשְׁתַּחֲוָיָתִי בֵּית רִמֹּן יִסְלַח־נָא יְהוָה לְעַבְדְּךָ בַּדָּבָר הַזֶּה: וַיֹּאמֶר
כ לוֹ לֵךְ לְשָׁלוֹם וַיֵּלֶךְ מֵאִתּוֹ כִּבְרַת אָרֶץ: וַיֹּאמֶר גֵּיחֲזִי נַעַר
אֱלִישָׁע אִישׁ־הָאֱלֹהִים הִנֵּה ׀ חָשַׂךְ אֲדֹנִי אֶת־נַעֲמָן הָאֲרַמִּי הַזֶּה
מִקַּחַת מִיָּדוֹ אֵת אֲשֶׁר־הֵבִיא חַי־יְהוָה כִּי־אִם־רַצְתִּי אַחֲרָיו וְלָקַחְתִּי
כא מֵאִתּוֹ מְאוּמָה: וַיִּרְדֹּף גֵּיחֲזִי אַחֲרֵי נַעֲמָן וַיִּרְאֶה נַעֲמָן רָץ אַחֲרָיו וַיִּפֹּל
כב מֵעַל הַמֶּרְכָּבָה לִקְרָאתוֹ וַיֹּאמֶר הֲשָׁלוֹם: וַיֹּאמֶר ׀ שָׁלוֹם אֲדֹנִי שְׁלָחַנִי
לֵאמֹר הִנֵּה עַתָּה זֶה בָּאוּ אֵלַי שְׁנֵי־נְעָרִים מֵהַר אֶפְרַיִם מִבְּנֵי הַנְּבִיאִים
כג תְּנָה־נָּא לָהֶם כִּכַּר־כֶּסֶף וּשְׁתֵּי חֲלִפוֹת בְּגָדִים: וַיֹּאמֶר נַעֲמָן הוֹאֵל
קַח כִּכָּרָיִם וַיִּפְרָץ־בּוֹ וַיָּצַר כִּכְּרַיִם כֶּסֶף בִּשְׁנֵי חֲרִטִים וּשְׁתֵּי חֲלִפוֹת
כד בְּגָדִים וַיִּתֵּן אֶל־שְׁנֵי נְעָרָיו וַיִּשְׂאוּ לְפָנָיו: וַיָּבֹא אֶל־הָעֹפֶל וַיִּקַּח מִיָּדָם
כה וַיִּפְקֹד בַּבָּיִת וַיְשַׁלַּח אֶת־הָאֲנָשִׁים וַיֵּלֵכוּ: וְהוּא־בָא וַיַּעֲמֹד אֶל־אֲדֹנָיו
וַיֹּאמֶר אֵלָיו אֱלִישָׁע מאן גֵּחֲזִי וַיֹּאמֶר לֹא־הָלַךְ עַבְדְּךָ אָנָה וָאָנָה: מֵאַיִן

26 been, Geḥazi?" "Your servant has not gone anywhere," he said. "Was I not
with you there in spirit when a man came down from his chariot to meet you?"
he said to him. "Is now the time to take silver and to take clothes, and olive
groves and vineyards, and sheep and cattle, and servants and maidservants?
27 Now, the blight of Naaman will cling to you and your descendants forever."
6 1 And he left his presence as a leper, as white as snow. The
brotherhood of the prophets said to Elisha, "Look – the place where we live
2 under your charge is too cramped for us. Let us go to the Jordan, and each
one of us will take a beam from there, and there we will build a meeting
3 place for us." "Yes, go," he said. "Please, be so kind as to accompany your
4 servants," one said. "I will come," he said, and he accompanied them. When
5 they reached the Jordan, they began to cut the wood. But as one of them was
felling a beam, the ax-head fell into the water. "Oh, no, Master!" he cried, "it
6 was borrowed." "Where did it fall?" asked the man of God. When he showed
him the place, he chopped off a stick and flung it in, and it made the ax-head
7 8 float. "Pick it up," he said, and he reached out and took it. Now the
king of Aram was at war with Israel, and he took counsel with his officials. "I
9 will set up camp in a certain hidden place," he said. The man of God sent word
to the king of Israel: "Beware of passing through that place, for the Arameans
10 have set up camp there." So the king of Israel sent warning to the place that
the man of God specified to him, and time and again he took precautions
11 there. This made the king of Aram seethe, and he summoned his officials.
"Tell me," he said to them, "who among us has defected to the king of Israel?"
12 "No, my lord the king," said one of his officials, "for it is Elisha, the prophet
in Israel, who has been informing the king of Israel of the words you speak in
13 your private chamber." "Go and find out where he is," he said, "and I will send
14 and seize him." When he was informed, "He is in Dotan," he sent out horses
and chariots and vast forces there. They arrived at night and surrounded the
15 city. The man of God's attendant rose early and went outside, to find that a
force with horses and chariots was surrounding the city. "Oh, no, Master," his
16 servant said to him, "what shall we do?" "Do not be afraid," he said, "for there
17 are many more with us than with them." And Elisha prayed. "O LORD," he
said, "open his eyes now, so he may see." The LORD opened the boy's eyes,
and suddenly, the hill was full of horses and fiery chariots all around Elisha.
18 As they came down to him, Elisha prayed to the LORD, "Strike this nation
with a blindness." And He struck them with a blindness, just as Elisha said.
19 "This is not the way, and this is not the city," Elisha said to them. "Follow
me, and I will lead you to the man you seek." And he led them to Shomron.
20 When they reached Shomron, Elisha said, "O LORD, open the eyes of these
men and let them see." And the LORD opened their eyes, and they found
21 themselves inside Shomron. When the king of Israel saw them, he said to

כו וַיֹּאמֶר אֵלָיו לֹא־לִבִּי הָלַךְ כַּאֲשֶׁר הָפַךְ־אִישׁ מֵעַל מֶרְכַּבְתּוֹ לִקְרָאתֶךָ
הַעֵת לָקַחַת אֶת־הַכֶּסֶף וְלָקַחַת בְּגָדִים וְזֵיתִים וּכְרָמִים וְצֹאן וּבָקָר
כז וַעֲבָדִים וּשְׁפָחוֹת: וְצָרַעַת נַעֲמָן תִּדְבַּק־בְּךָ וּבְזַרְעֲךָ לְעוֹלָם וַיֵּצֵא
ו א מִלְּפָנָיו מְצֹרָע כַּשָּׁלֶג: וַיֹּאמְרוּ בְנֵי־הַנְּבִיאִים אֶל־אֱלִישָׁע
ב הִנֵּה־נָא הַמָּקוֹם אֲשֶׁר אֲנַחְנוּ יֹשְׁבִים שָׁם לְפָנֶיךָ צַר מִמֶּנּוּ: נֵלְכָה־נָּא
עַד־הַיַּרְדֵּן וְנִקְחָה מִשָּׁם אִישׁ קוֹרָה אֶחָת וְנַעֲשֶׂה־לָּנוּ שָׁם מָקוֹם
ג לָשֶׁבֶת שָׁם וַיֹּאמֶר לֵכוּ: וַיֹּאמֶר הָאֶחָד הוֹאֶל נָא וְלֵךְ אֶת־עֲבָדֶיךָ
ד ה וַיֹּאמֶר אֲנִי אֵלֵךְ: וַיֵּלֶךְ אִתָּם וַיָּבֹאוּ הַיַּרְדֵּנָה וַיִּגְזְרוּ הָעֵצִים: וַיְהִי הָאֶחָד
מַפִּיל הַקּוֹרָה וְאֶת־הַבַּרְזֶל נָפַל אֶל־הַמָּיִם וַיִּצְעַק וַיֹּאמֶר אֲהָהּ אֲדֹנִי
ו וְהוּא שָׁאוּל: וַיֹּאמֶר אִישׁ־הָאֱלֹהִים אָנָה נָפָל וַיַּרְאֵהוּ אֶת־הַמָּקוֹם
ז וַיִּקְצָב־עֵץ וַיַּשְׁלֶךְ־שָׁמָּה וַיָּצֶף הַבַּרְזֶל: וַיֹּאמֶר הָרֶם לָךְ וַיִּשְׁלַח יָדוֹ
ח וַיִּקָּחֵהוּ: וּמֶלֶךְ אֲרָם הָיָה נִלְחָם בְּיִשְׂרָאֵל וַיִּוָּעַץ אֶל־
ט עֲבָדָיו לֵאמֹר אֶל־מְקוֹם פְּלֹנִי אַלְמֹנִי תַּחֲנֹתִי: וַיִּשְׁלַח אִישׁ הָאֱלֹהִים
אֶל־מֶלֶךְ יִשְׂרָאֵל לֵאמֹר הִשָּׁמֶר מֵעֲבֹר הַמָּקוֹם הַזֶּה כִּי־שָׁם אֲרָם
י נְחִתִּים: וַיִּשְׁלַח מֶלֶךְ יִשְׂרָאֵל אֶל־הַמָּקוֹם אֲשֶׁר אָמַר־לוֹ אִישׁ־
יא הָאֱלֹהִים וְהִזְהִירֹה וְנִשְׁמַר־שָׁם לֹא־אַחַת וְלֹא שְׁתָּיִם: וַיִּסָּעֵר לֵב
מֶלֶךְ־אֲרָם עַל־הַדָּבָר הַזֶּה וַיִּקְרָא אֶל־עֲבָדָיו וַיֹּאמֶר אֲלֵיהֶם הֲלוֹא
יב תַּגִּידוּ לִי מִי מִשֶּׁלָּנוּ אֶל־מֶלֶךְ יִשְׂרָאֵל: וַיֹּאמֶר אַחַד מֵעֲבָדָיו לוֹא
אֲדֹנִי הַמֶּלֶךְ כִּי־אֱלִישָׁע הַנָּבִיא אֲשֶׁר בְּיִשְׂרָאֵל יַגִּיד לְמֶלֶךְ יִשְׂרָאֵל
יג אֶת־הַדְּבָרִים אֲשֶׁר תְּדַבֵּר בַּחֲדַר מִשְׁכָּבֶךָ: וַיֹּאמֶר לְכוּ וּרְאוּ אֵיכֹה
יד הוּא וְאֶשְׁלַח וְאֶקָּחֵהוּ וַיֻּגַּד־לוֹ לֵאמֹר הִנֵּה בְדֹתָן: וַיִּשְׁלַח שָׁמָּה סוּסִים
טו וְרֶכֶב וְחַיִל כָּבֵד וַיָּבֹאוּ לַיְלָה וַיַּקִּפוּ עַל־הָעִיר: וַיַּשְׁכֵּם מְשָׁרֵת אִישׁ
הָאֱלֹהִים לָקוּם וַיֵּצֵא וְהִנֵּה־חַיִל סוֹבֵב אֶת־הָעִיר וְסוּס וָרָכֶב וַיֹּאמֶר
טז נַעֲרוֹ אֵלָיו אֲהָהּ אֲדֹנִי אֵיכָה נַעֲשֶׂה: וַיֹּאמֶר אַל־תִּירָא כִּי רַבִּים אֲשֶׁר
יז אִתָּנוּ מֵאֲשֶׁר אוֹתָם: וַיִּתְפַּלֵּל אֱלִישָׁע וַיֹּאמַר יְהוָה פְּקַח־נָא אֶת־עֵינָיו
וְיִרְאֶה וַיִּפְקַח יְהוָה אֶת־עֵינֵי הַנַּעַר וַיַּרְא וְהִנֵּה הָהָר מָלֵא סוּסִים
יח וְרֶכֶב אֵשׁ סְבִיבֹת אֱלִישָׁע: וַיֵּרְדוּ אֵלָיו וַיִּתְפַּלֵּל אֱלִישָׁע אֶל־יְהוָה
וַיֹּאמַר הַךְ־נָא אֶת־הַגּוֹי־הַזֶּה בַּסַּנְוֵרִים וַיַּכֵּם בַּסַּנְוֵרִים כִּדְבַר אֱלִישָׁע:
יט וַיֹּאמֶר אֲלֵהֶם אֱלִישָׁע לֹא־זֶה הַדֶּרֶךְ וְלֹא־זֹה הָעִיר לְכוּ אַחֲרַי וְאוֹלִיכָה
כ אֶתְכֶם אֶל־הָאִישׁ אֲשֶׁר תְּבַקֵּשׁוּן וַיֹּלֶךְ אוֹתָם שֹׁמְרוֹנָה: וַיְהִי כְּבֹאָם
שֹׁמְרוֹן וַיֹּאמֶר אֱלִישָׁע יְהוָה פְּקַח אֶת־עֵינֵי־אֵלֶּה וְיִרְאוּ וַיִּפְקַח יְהוָה
כא אֶת־עֵינֵיהֶם וַיִּרְאוּ וְהִנֵּה בְּתוֹךְ שֹׁמְרוֹן: וַיֹּאמֶר מֶלֶךְ־יִשְׂרָאֵל אֶל־

22 Elisha, "Shall I attack, Father?[79] Shall I attack?" "Do not attack," he said. "Did
you capture those you wish to attack with your own sword and bow? Place
bread and water before them, and let them eat and drink and go to their
23 master." So he prepared a great feast for them, and they ate and drank; then
he sent them off, and they went back to their master. And Aramean bands
24 stopped raiding the land of Israel. But some time later, Ben Hadad,
king of Aram, gathered all his forces and marched up to lay siege to Shomron.
25 Famine grew fierce in Shomron as the siege went on, until a donkey's head
fetched eighty pieces of silver, and a quarter kab of doves' droppings[80] fetched
26 five pieces of silver. Once, as the king of Israel was passing along the wall, a
27 woman screamed out to him, "Save me, O lord the king!" "If the LORD has
not saved you, how can I save you?" he said. "From the threshing floor, or
28 from the winepress?" Then the king said to her, "What is the matter?" "That
woman said to me, 'Give me your son, and we will eat him today; we will eat
29 my son tomorrow,'" she said, "so we cooked my son and ate him. But when I
said to her the next day, 'Give me your son and let us eat him,' she had hidden
30 her son." When the king heard the woman's words, he rent his clothes; and
as he passed along the wall, the people saw that he was wearing sackcloth
31 underneath. "So may the LORD do to me – and more," he said, "if the head
32 of Elisha son of Shafat remains on his shoulders today." And he sent a man
ahead of him. Elisha was sitting in his house, and the elders were sitting with
him. Before the messenger arrived, he said to the elders, "Do you see? That
son of a murderer has ordered my decapitation! Look, when the messenger
arrives, shut the door and hold the door fast against him – for no doubt, the
33 sound of his master's footsteps is close behind." And as he was still speaking
with them, the messenger descended upon him. "This evil is from the LORD,"[81]
7 1 he said. "How can I still have hope in the LORD?" And Elisha said,
"Hear the word of the LORD. Thus says the LORD: By this time tomorrow, a
se'a[82] of fine flour will sell for a shekel, and two *se'a* of barley will sell for
2 a shekel at the gate of Shomron." The adjutant upon whose arm the king
leaned spoke up and said to the man of God, "Even if the LORD were to make
floodgates in the heavens, how could this possibly come to pass?" "You will
3 see it with your own eyes," he said, "but you will not eat of it." There
were four men, who were lepers, at the entrance to the gate, and they said to
4 one another, "Why should we sit here until we die? If we decide to enter the
city when there is famine in the city, we will die there; and if we stay here, we
will die. So let us now defect to the Aramean camp; if they let us live, we will
5 live, and if they kill us, we will die." They set out at dusk to reach the Aramean
camp, but when they reached the edge of the Aramean camp, there was no
6 one there. For the LORD had caused the Aramean camp to hear the sound of
chariots, the sound of horses, the sound of a vast army – and the men had

79 | See note on 5:13.
80 | A popular term for carob husks.
81 | According to Rashi, Radak, and others, it is the king now speaking.
82 | See note on 1 Kings 18:32.

כב אֱלִישָׁע כְּרָאֹתוֹ אוֹתָם הַאַכֶּה אַכֶּה אָבִי: וַיֹּאמֶר לֹא תַכֶּה הַאֲשֶׁר
שָׁבִיתָ בְּחַרְבְּךָ וּבְקַשְׁתְּךָ אַתָּה מַכֶּה שִׂים לֶחֶם וָמַיִם לִפְנֵיהֶם וְיֹאכְלוּ
כג כב וְיִשְׁתּוּ וְיֵלְכוּ אֶל־אֲדֹנֵיהֶם: וַיִּכְרֶה לָהֶם כֵּרָה גְדוֹלָה וַיֹּאכְלוּ וַיִּשְׁתּוּ
וַיְשַׁלְּחֵם וַיֵּלְכוּ אֶל־אֲדֹנֵיהֶם וְלֹא־יָסְפוּ עוֹד גְּדוּדֵי אֲרָם לָבוֹא בְּאֶרֶץ
כד יִשְׂרָאֵל: וַיְהִי אַחֲרֵי־כֵן וַיִּקְבֹּץ בֶּן־הֲדַד מֶלֶךְ־אֲרָם אֶת־
כה כָּל־מַחֲנֵהוּ וַיַּעַל וַיָּצַר עַל־שֹׁמְרוֹן: וַיְהִי רָעָב גָּדוֹל בְּשֹׁמְרוֹן וְהִנֵּה
צָרִים עָלֶיהָ עַד הֱיוֹת רֹאשׁ־חֲמוֹר בִּשְׁמֹנִים כֶּסֶף וְרֹבַע הַקַּב חרייונים דִּבְיוֹנִים
כו בַּחֲמִשָּׁה כָסֶף: וַיְהִי מֶלֶךְ יִשְׂרָאֵל עֹבֵר עַל־הַחֹמָה וְאִשָּׁה צָעֲקָה
כז אֵלָיו לֵאמֹר הוֹשִׁיעָה אֲדֹנִי הַמֶּלֶךְ: וַיֹּאמֶר אַל־יוֹשִׁעֵךְ יְהוָה מֵאַיִן
כח אוֹשִׁיעֵךְ הֲמִן־הַגֹּרֶן אוֹ מִן־הַיָּקֶב: וַיֹּאמֶר־לָהּ הַמֶּלֶךְ מַה־לָּךְ וַתֹּאמֶר
הָאִשָּׁה הַזֹּאת אָמְרָה אֵלַי תְּנִי אֶת־בְּנֵךְ וְנֹאכְלֶנּוּ הַיּוֹם וְאֶת־בְּנִי נֹאכַל
כט מָחָר: וַנְּבַשֵּׁל אֶת־בְּנִי וַנֹּאכְלֵהוּ וָאֹמַר אֵלֶיהָ בַּיּוֹם הָאַחֵר תְּנִי אֶת־
ל בְּנֵךְ וְנֹאכְלֶנּוּ וַתַּחְבִּא אֶת־בְּנָהּ: וַיְהִי כִשְׁמֹעַ הַמֶּלֶךְ אֶת־דִּבְרֵי הָאִשָּׁה
וַיִּקְרַע אֶת־בְּגָדָיו וְהוּא עֹבֵר עַל־הַחֹמָה וַיַּרְא הָעָם וְהִנֵּה הַשַּׂק עַל־
לא בְּשָׂרוֹ מִבָּיִת: וַיֹּאמֶר כֹּה־יַעֲשֶׂה־לִּי אֱלֹהִים וְכֹה יוֹסִף אִם־יַעֲמֹד רֹאשׁ
לב אֱלִישָׁע בֶּן־שָׁפָט עָלָיו הַיּוֹם: וֶאֱלִישָׁע יֹשֵׁב בְּבֵיתוֹ וְהַזְּקֵנִים יֹשְׁבִים
אִתּוֹ וַיִּשְׁלַח אִישׁ מִלְּפָנָיו בְּטֶרֶם יָבֹא הַמַּלְאָךְ אֵלָיו וְהוּא ׀ אָמַר אֶל־
הַזְּקֵנִים הַרְּאִיתֶם כִּי־שָׁלַח בֶּן־הַמְרַצֵּחַ הַזֶּה לְהָסִיר אֶת־רֹאשִׁי רְאוּ ׀
כְּבֹא הַמַּלְאָךְ סִגְרוּ הַדֶּלֶת וּלְחַצְתֶּם אֹתוֹ בַּדֶּלֶת הֲלוֹא קוֹל רַגְלֵי
לג אֲדֹנָיו אַחֲרָיו: עוֹדֶנּוּ מְדַבֵּר עִמָּם וְהִנֵּה הַמַּלְאָךְ יֹרֵד אֵלָיו וַיֹּאמֶר
ז א הִנֵּה־זֹאת הָרָעָה מֵאֵת יְהוָה מָה־אוֹחִיל לַיהוָה עוֹד: וַיֹּאמֶר
אֱלִישָׁע שִׁמְעוּ דְּבַר־יְהוָה כֹּה ׀ אָמַר יְהוָה כָּעֵת ׀ מָחָר סְאָה־סֹלֶת
ב בְּשֶׁקֶל וְסָאתַיִם שְׂעֹרִים בְּשֶׁקֶל בְּשַׁעַר שֹׁמְרוֹן: וַיַּעַן הַשָּׁלִישׁ אֲשֶׁר
לַמֶּלֶךְ נִשְׁעָן עַל־יָדוֹ אֶת־אִישׁ הָאֱלֹהִים וַיֹּאמַר הִנֵּה יְהוָה עֹשֶׂה
אֲרֻבּוֹת בַּשָּׁמַיִם הֲיִהְיֶה הַדָּבָר הַזֶּה וַיֹּאמֶר הִנְּכָה רֹאֶה בְּעֵינֶיךָ וּמִשָּׁם
ג לֹא תֹאכֵל: וְאַרְבָּעָה אֲנָשִׁים הָיוּ מְצֹרָעִים פֶּתַח הַשָּׁעַר
ד וַיֹּאמְרוּ אִישׁ אֶל־רֵעֵהוּ מָה אֲנַחְנוּ יֹשְׁבִים פֹּה עַד־מָתְנוּ: אִם־אָמַרְנוּ
נָבוֹא הָעִיר וְהָרָעָב בָּעִיר וָמַתְנוּ שָׁם וְאִם־יָשַׁבְנוּ פֹה וָמָתְנוּ וְעַתָּה
לְכוּ וְנִפְּלָה אֶל־מַחֲנֵה אֲרָם אִם־יְחַיֻּנוּ נִחְיֶה וְאִם־יְמִיתֻנוּ וָמָתְנוּ:
ה וַיָּקֻמוּ בַנֶּשֶׁף לָבוֹא אֶל־מַחֲנֵה אֲרָם וַיָּבֹאוּ עַד־קְצֵה מַחֲנֵה אֲרָם וְהִנֵּה
ו אֵין־שָׁם אִישׁ: וַאדֹנָי הִשְׁמִיעַ ׀ אֶת־מַחֲנֵה אֲרָם קוֹל רֶכֶב קוֹל סוּס
קוֹל חַיִל גָּדוֹל וַיֹּאמְרוּ אִישׁ אֶל־אָחִיו הִנֵּה שָׂכַר־עָלֵינוּ מֶלֶךְ יִשְׂרָאֵל

said to one another, "Look, the king of Israel must have hired the Hittite kings
7 and the kings of Egypt against us, to attack us!" They rose and fled at dusk,
leaving their tents, their horses and their donkeys, and the camp as it was, and
8 they ran for their lives. When those lepers reached the edge of the camp, they
entered one tent and ate and drank. Then they carried off silver and gold and
garments from there and went and hid them. When they came back, they
9 went into another tent, carried off what was in it, and went and hid it. But
then one man said to another, "We are not doing what is right. This is a day
of good news, yet we are silent. If we wait until the light of morning, we will
10 be found guilty. We must go and report to the royal palace right now." When
they arrived, they called out to the city gatekeepers and reported to them,
"We came to the Aramean camp, but there was not a man or a human voice
there, with the horses still tied up and the donkeys still tied up and the tents
11 just as they were." The gatekeepers called out, and it was reported inside the
12 royal palace. The king rose in the night and said to his servants, "Let me tell
you what the Arameans are doing to us. They know we are starving, so they
have left the camp to hide in the field, planning, 'When they leave the city,
13 we will catch them alive and enter the city.'" One of his servants spoke up.
"Let them take five of the remaining horses that are still here," he said. "Look,
either they will be like all the masses of Israelites who remain or like all the
14 masses of Israelites who have perished. Let us send and find out." So they
took two chariots with horses, and the king sent them after the Aramean camp,
15 ordering them, "Go and find out." They followed them as far as the Jordan to
find that the whole road was full of garments and vessels that Aram had cast
aside in their haste, and the messengers went back and reported to the king.
16 Then the people went out and ransacked the Aramean camp, so that a *se'a* of
fine flour fetched a shekel, and two *se'a* of barley fetched a shekel, fulfilling
17 the word of the Lord. Meanwhile, the king had stationed the adjutant on
whose arm he leaned by the gate, and the people trampled him to death by
the gate – just as the man of God had pronounced when the king came down
18 to him. For when the man of God had told the king, "Two *se'a* of barley will
fetch a shekel, and a *se'a* of fine flour will fetch a shekel by this time tomorrow
19 at the gate of Shomron," the adjutant had retorted to the man of God, "Even
if the Lord were to make floodgates in the heavens, how could this possibly
come to pass?" "You will see it with your own eyes," he had said, "but you
20 will not eat of it." And that is exactly what happened to him – the people
8 1 trampled him to death by the gate. Now Elisha had told the woman
whose son he had revived, "Leave with your household right away and settle
wherever you can, for the Lord has decreed a seven-year famine on the
2 land, and it has already begun." The woman carried out the man of God's
instructions at once; she set out with her household and settled in the land
3 of the Philistines for seven years. At the end of seven years, the woman

ז אֶת־מַלְכֵי הַחִתִּים וְאֶת־מַלְכֵי מִצְרַיִם לָבוֹא עָלֵינוּ: וַיָּקוּמוּ וַיָּנוּסוּ
בַנֶּשֶׁף וַיַּעַזְבוּ אֶת־אָהֳלֵיהֶם וְאֶת־סוּסֵיהֶם וְאֶת־חֲמֹרֵיהֶם הַמַּחֲנֶה
ח כַּאֲשֶׁר הִיא וַיָּנֻסוּ אֶל־נַפְשָׁם: וַיָּבֹאוּ הַמְצֹרָעִים הָאֵלֶּה עַד־קְצֵה
הַמַּחֲנֶה וַיָּבֹאוּ אֶל־אֹהֶל אֶחָד וַיֹּאכְלוּ וַיִּשְׁתּוּ וַיִּשְׂאוּ מִשָּׁם כֶּסֶף וְזָהָב
וּבְגָדִים וַיֵּלְכוּ וַיַּטְמִנוּ וַיָּשֻׁבוּ וַיָּבֹאוּ אֶל־אֹהֶל אַחֵר וַיִּשְׂאוּ מִשָּׁם וַיֵּלְכוּ
ט וַיַּטְמִנוּ: וַיֹּאמְרוּ אִישׁ אֶל־רֵעֵהוּ לֹא־כֵן ׀ אֲנַחְנוּ עֹשִׂים הַיּוֹם הַזֶּה
יוֹם־בְּשֹׂרָה הוּא וַאֲנַחְנוּ מַחְשִׁים וְחִכִּינוּ עַד־אוֹר הַבֹּקֶר וּמְצָאָנוּ עָווֹן
י וְעַתָּה לְכוּ וְנָבֹאָה וְנַגִּידָה בֵּית הַמֶּלֶךְ: וַיָּבֹאוּ וַיִּקְרְאוּ אֶל־שֹׁעֵר הָעִיר
וַיַּגִּידוּ לָהֶם לֵאמֹר בָּאנוּ אֶל־מַחֲנֵה אֲרָם וְהִנֵּה אֵין־שָׁם אִישׁ וְקוֹל
יא אָדָם כִּי אִם־הַסּוּס אָסוּר וְהַחֲמוֹר אָסוּר וְאֹהָלִים כַּאֲשֶׁר הֵמָּה: וַיִּקְרָא
יב הַשֹּׁעֲרִים וַיַּגִּידוּ בֵּית הַמֶּלֶךְ פְּנִימָה: וַיָּקָם הַמֶּלֶךְ לַיְלָה וַיֹּאמֶר אֶל־
עֲבָדָיו אַגִּידָה־נָּא לָכֶם אֵת אֲשֶׁר־עָשׂוּ לָנוּ אֲרָם יָדְעוּ כִּי־רְעֵבִים
אֲנַחְנוּ וַיֵּצְאוּ מִן־הַמַּחֲנֶה לְהֵחָבֵה בהשדה לֵאמֹר כִּי־יֵצְאוּ מִן־הָעִיר בַשָּׂדֶה
יג וְנִתְפְּשֵׂם חַיִּים וְאֶל־הָעִיר נָבֹא: וַיַּעַן אֶחָד מֵעֲבָדָיו וַיֹּאמֶר וְיִקְחוּ־נָא
חֲמִשָּׁה מִן־הַסּוּסִים הַנִּשְׁאָרִים אֲשֶׁר נִשְׁאֲרוּ־בָהּ הִנָּם כְּכָל־ההמון הֶהָמוֹן
יִשְׂרָאֵל אֲשֶׁר נִשְׁאֲרוּ־בָהּ הִנָּם כְּכָל־הֲמוֹן יִשְׂרָאֵל אֲשֶׁר־תָּמּוּ וְנִשְׁלְחָה
יד וְנִרְאֶה: וַיִּקְחוּ שְׁנֵי רֶכֶב סוּסִים וַיִּשְׁלַח הַמֶּלֶךְ אַחֲרֵי מַחֲנֵה־אֲרָם
טו לֵאמֹר לְכוּ וּרְאוּ: וַיֵּלְכוּ אַחֲרֵיהֶם עַד־הַיַּרְדֵּן וְהִנֵּה כָל־הַדֶּרֶךְ מְלֵאָה
בְּגָדִים וְכֵלִים אֲשֶׁר־הִשְׁלִיכוּ אֲרָם בהחפזם וַיָּשֻׁבוּ הַמַּלְאָכִים וַיַּגִּדוּ בְּחָפְזָם
טז לַמֶּלֶךְ: וַיֵּצֵא הָעָם וַיָּבֹזּוּ אֵת מַחֲנֵה אֲרָם וַיְהִי סְאָה־סֹלֶת בְּשֶׁקֶל כג
יז וְסָאתַיִם שְׂעֹרִים בְּשֶׁקֶל כִּדְבַר יְהוָה: וְהַמֶּלֶךְ הִפְקִיד אֶת־הַשָּׁלִישׁ
אֲשֶׁר־נִשְׁעָן עַל־יָדוֹ עַל־הַשַּׁעַר וַיִּרְמְסֻהוּ הָעָם בַּשַּׁעַר וַיָּמֹת כַּאֲשֶׁר
יח דִּבֶּר אִישׁ הָאֱלֹהִים אֲשֶׁר דִּבֶּר בְּרֶדֶת הַמֶּלֶךְ אֵלָיו: וַיְהִי כְּדַבֵּר אִישׁ
הָאֱלֹהִים אֶל־הַמֶּלֶךְ לֵאמֹר סָאתַיִם שְׂעֹרִים בְּשֶׁקֶל וּסְאָה־סֹלֶת
יט בְּשֶׁקֶל יִהְיֶה כָּעֵת מָחָר בְּשַׁעַר שֹׁמְרוֹן: וַיַּעַן הַשָּׁלִישׁ אֶת־אִישׁ
הָאֱלֹהִים וַיֹּאמַר וְהִנֵּה יְהוָה עֹשֶׂה אֲרֻבּוֹת בַּשָּׁמַיִם הֲיִהְיֶה כַּדָּבָר הַזֶּה
כ וַיֹּאמֶר הִנְּךָ רֹאֶה בְּעֵינֶיךָ וּמִשָּׁם לֹא תֹאכֵל: וַיְהִי־לוֹ כֵן וַיִּרְמְסוּ אֹתוֹ
ח א הָעָם בַּשַּׁעַר וַיָּמֹת: וֶאֱלִישָׁע דִּבֶּר אֶל־הָאִשָּׁה אֲשֶׁר־הֶחֱיָה
אֶת־בְּנָהּ לֵאמֹר קוּמִי ולכי אתי וּבֵיתֵךְ וְגוּרִי בַּאֲשֶׁר תָּגוּרִי כִּי־קָרָא אַתְּ
ב יְהוָה לָרָעָב וְגַם־בָּא אֶל־הָאָרֶץ שֶׁבַע שָׁנִים: וַתָּקָם הָאִשָּׁה וַתַּעַשׂ
כִּדְבַר אִישׁ הָאֱלֹהִים וַתֵּלֶךְ הִיא וּבֵיתָהּ וַתָּגָר בְּאֶרֶץ־פְּלִשְׁתִּים שֶׁבַע
ג שָׁנִים: וַיְהִי מִקְצֵה שֶׁבַע שָׁנִים וַתָּשָׁב הָאִשָּׁה מֵאֶרֶץ פְּלִשְׁתִּים וַתֵּצֵא

returned from the land of the Philistines, and she went to appeal to the king
4 about her house and her field. Just then, the king was speaking with Geḥazi,
the man of God's servant, saying, "Please, tell me all about the great deeds
5 that Elisha has done." And as he was telling the king about how he had revived
the dead, the woman whose son he had revived came to appeal to the king
6 about her house and field. "My lord the king," said Geḥazi, "this is the very
woman, and this is her son whom Elisha revived." The king questioned the
woman, and she told him her story; then the king assigned a eunuch to her,
ordering: "Restore all that belongs to her and all the revenue from her field
from the day she left the land until now."
7 Elisha arrived in Damascus while Ben Hadad, king of Aram, was ill. When
8 he was informed, "The man of God has arrived here," the king said to Ḥazael,
"Take a gift with you, and go out to meet the man of God, and inquire of the
9 Lord through him, asking, 'Will I recover from this illness?'" Ḥazael went to
meet him, taking a gift with him: forty camel loads of all of Damascus's finest,
and he came and stood before him. "Your son Ben Hadad, king of Aram, has
10 sent me to you to ask, 'Will I recover from this illness?'" "Say to him, 'You
will certainly recover,'" said Elisha, "though the Lord has shown me that he
11 will certainly die." He managed to keep a stoic face for a long time, but then
12 the man of God began to weep. "Why does my lord weep?" asked Ḥazael.
"Because I know the evil you will inflict on Israel," said Elisha. "You will
set their fortresses on fire and put their young men to the sword and dash
13 their little ones to pieces and slash open their pregnant women." "But how
could your mere dog of a servant do such mighty deeds?" said Ḥazael. "The
14 Lord has shown me," said Elisha, "that you will be king over Aram." He left
Elisha and came to his lord. "What did Elisha say to you?" he asked him. "He
15 said to me, 'You will certainly recover,'" he said. But the next day, he took a
cloth, dipped it in water, and spread it over his face, and he died. And Ḥazael
16 reigned in his place. In the fifth year of Yoram son of Aḥav, king of
Israel – Yehoshafat had been king of Yehuda – Yehoram son of Yehoshafat
17 became king over Yehuda. He was thirty-two years old when he became king,
18 and for eight years he reigned in Jerusalem. He followed in the ways of the
kings of Israel, as the house of Aḥav had done, for Aḥav's daughter was his
19 wife; he did what was evil in the eyes of the Lord. But the Lord was not
willing to destroy Yehuda for the sake of His servant David, for He had
20 promised to grant him a lamp for his descendants for all time.[83] In his time
21 Edom rebelled against Yehuda and appointed their own king. Yoram crossed
over to Tza'ir with all his chariots; he advanced at night to attack Edom,
who had surrounded him and his chariot officers, but the troops fled back to
22 their homes. And Edom has rebelled against Yehuda ever since; Livna, too,

83 | See 1 Kings 15:4.

ד לִצְעֹק אֶל־הַמֶּלֶךְ אֶל־בֵּיתָהּ וְאֶל־שָׂדָהּ: וְהַמֶּלֶךְ מְדַבֵּר אֶל־גֵּחֲזִי נַעַר
אִישׁ־הָאֱלֹהִים לֵאמֹר סַפְּרָה־נָּא לִי אֵת כָּל־הַגְּדֹלוֹת אֲשֶׁר־עָשָׂה
ה אֱלִישָׁע: וַיְהִי הוּא מְסַפֵּר לַמֶּלֶךְ אֵת אֲשֶׁר־הֶחֱיָה אֶת־הַמֵּת וְהִנֵּה
הָאִשָּׁה אֲשֶׁר־הֶחֱיָה אֶת־בְּנָהּ צֹעֶקֶת אֶל־הַמֶּלֶךְ עַל־בֵּיתָהּ וְעַל־שָׂדָהּ
וַיֹּאמֶר גֵּחֲזִי אֲדֹנִי הַמֶּלֶךְ זֹאת הָאִשָּׁה וְזֶה־בְּנָהּ אֲשֶׁר־הֶחֱיָה אֱלִישָׁע:
ו וַיִּשְׁאַל הַמֶּלֶךְ לָאִשָּׁה וַתְּסַפֶּר־לוֹ וַיִּתֶּן־לָהּ הַמֶּלֶךְ סָרִיס אֶחָד לֵאמֹר
הָשֵׁיב אֶת־כָּל־אֲשֶׁר־לָהּ וְאֵת כָּל־תְּבוּאֹת הַשָּׂדֶה מִיּוֹם עָזְבָה אֶת־
הָאָרֶץ וְעַד־עָתָּה:
ז וַיָּבֹא אֱלִישָׁע דַּמֶּשֶׂק וּבֶן־הֲדַד מֶלֶךְ־אֲרָם חֹלֶה וַיֻּגַּד־לוֹ לֵאמֹר בָּא
ח אִישׁ הָאֱלֹהִים עַד־הֵנָּה: וַיֹּאמֶר הַמֶּלֶךְ אֶל־חֲזָהאֵל קַח בְּיָדְךָ מִנְחָה
וְלֵךְ לִקְרַאת אִישׁ הָאֱלֹהִים וְדָרַשְׁתָּ אֶת־יְהוָה מֵאוֹתוֹ לֵאמֹר הַאֶחְיֶה
ט מֵחֳלִי זֶה: וַיֵּלֶךְ חֲזָאֵל לִקְרָאתוֹ וַיִּקַּח מִנְחָה בְיָדוֹ וְכָל־טוּב דַּמֶּשֶׂק
מַשָּׂא אַרְבָּעִים גָּמָל וַיָּבֹא וַיַּעֲמֹד לְפָנָיו וַיֹּאמֶר בִּנְךָ בֶן־הֲדַד מֶלֶךְ־
י אֲרָם שְׁלָחַנִי אֵלֶיךָ לֵאמֹר הַאֶחְיֶה מֵחֳלִי זֶה: וַיֹּאמֶר אֵלָיו אֱלִישָׁע לֵךְ
יא אֱמָר־לא חָיֹה תִחְיֶה וְהִרְאַנִי יְהוָה כִּי־מוֹת יָמוּת: וַיַּעֲמֵד אֶת־פָּנָיו לְוֹ
יב וַיָּשֶׂם עַד־בֹּשׁ וַיֵּבְךְּ אִישׁ הָאֱלֹהִים: וַיֹּאמֶר חֲזָאֵל מַדּוּעַ אֲדֹנִי בֹכֶה
וַיֹּאמֶר כִּי־יָדַעְתִּי אֵת אֲשֶׁר־תַּעֲשֶׂה לִבְנֵי יִשְׂרָאֵל רָעָה מִבְצְרֵיהֶם
תְּשַׁלַּח בָּאֵשׁ וּבַחֻרֵיהֶם בַּחֶרֶב תַּהֲרֹג וְעֹלְלֵיהֶם תְּרַטֵּשׁ וְהָרֹתֵיהֶם
יג תְּבַקֵּעַ: וַיֹּאמֶר חֲזָהאֵל כִּי מָה עַבְדְּךָ הַכֶּלֶב כִּי יַעֲשֶׂה הַדָּבָר הַגָּדוֹל
יד הַזֶּה וַיֹּאמֶר אֱלִישָׁע הִרְאַנִי יְהוָה אֹתְךָ מֶלֶךְ עַל־אֲרָם: וַיֵּלֶךְ ׀ מֵאֵת
אֱלִישָׁע וַיָּבֹא אֶל־אֲדֹנָיו וַיֹּאמֶר לוֹ מָה־אָמַר לְךָ אֱלִישָׁע וַיֹּאמֶר אָמַר
טו לִי חָיֹה תִחְיֶה: וַיְהִי מִמָּחֳרָת וַיִּקַּח הַמַּכְבֵּר וַיִּטְבֹּל בַּמַּיִם וַיִּפְרֹשׂ
טז עַל־פָּנָיו וַיָּמֹת וַיִּמְלֹךְ חֲזָהאֵל תַּחְתָּיו: וּבִשְׁנַת חָמֵשׁ
לְיוֹרָם בֶּן־אַחְאָב מֶלֶךְ יִשְׂרָאֵל וִיהוֹשָׁפָט מֶלֶךְ יְהוּדָה מָלַךְ יְהוֹרָם
יז בֶּן־יְהוֹשָׁפָט מֶלֶךְ יְהוּדָה: בֶּן־שְׁלֹשִׁים וּשְׁתַּיִם שָׁנָה הָיָה בְמָלְכוֹ
יח וּשְׁמֹנֶה שָׁנָה מָלַךְ בִּירוּשָׁלָםִ: וַיֵּלֶךְ בְּדֶרֶךְ ׀ מַלְכֵי יִשְׂרָאֵל כַּאֲשֶׁר עָשׂוּ שָׁנִים
בֵּית אַחְאָב כִּי בַּת־אַחְאָב הָיְתָה־לּוֹ לְאִשָּׁה וַיַּעַשׂ הָרַע בְּעֵינֵי יְהוָה:
יט וְלֹא־אָבָה יְהוָה לְהַשְׁחִית אֶת־יְהוּדָה לְמַעַן דָּוִד עַבְדּוֹ כַּאֲשֶׁר אָמַר־
כ לוֹ לָתֵת לוֹ נִיר וּלְבָנָיו כָּל־הַיָּמִים: בְּיָמָיו פָּשַׁע אֱדוֹם מִתַּחַת יַד־יְהוּדָה
כא וַיַּמְלִכוּ עֲלֵיהֶם מֶלֶךְ: וַיַּעֲבֹר יוֹרָם צָעִירָה וְכָל־הָרֶכֶב עִמּוֹ וַיְהִי־הוּא
קָם לַיְלָה וַיַּכֶּה אֶת־אֱדוֹם הַסֹּבֵב אֵלָיו וְאֵת שָׂרֵי הָרֶכֶב וַיָּנָס הָעָם
כב לְאֹהָלָיו: וַיִּפְשַׁע אֱדוֹם מִתַּחַת יַד־יְהוּדָה עַד הַיּוֹם הַזֶּה אָז תִּפְשַׁע

23 rebelled at that time. As for the rest of Yoram's history and all his deeds – they
24 are recorded in the book of the History of the Kings of Yehuda. And Yoram
slept with his ancestors and was buried with his ancestors in the City of David.
25 And his son Aḥazyahu reigned in his place. In the twelfth year of
Yoram son of Aḥav, king of Israel, Aḥazyahu son of Yehoram became king
26 over Yehuda. Aḥazyahu was twenty-two years old when he became king, and
he reigned in Jerusalem for a single year; his mother's name was Atalyahu
27 daughter of Omri, the king of Israel.[84] He followed in the ways of the house
of Aḥav, doing what was evil in the eyes of the LORD just like the house of
28 Aḥav, for he was a son-in-law of the house of Aḥav. Together with Yoram son
of Aḥav, he went to war against Ḥazael, king of Aram, at Ramot Gilad, but
29 the Arameans defeated Yoram. King Yoram went back to Yizre'el to recover
from the wounds that the Arameans had inflicted upon him in Ramah when
he was fighting against Ḥazael, king of Aram. And Aḥazyahu son of Yehoram,
king of Yehuda, went down to visit Yoram son of Aḥav in Yizre'el while he
9 1 was injured. The prophet Elisha summoned one of the brotherhood
of the prophets. "Hitch up your tunic," he said to him, "take this flask of oil
2 in your hand, and go to Ramot Gilad. When you arrive there, you will see
Yehu son of Yehoshafat son of Nimshi there; go in and get him to leave his
3 comrades, and bring him into an inner room. Then take the flask of oil and
pour it on his head and say, 'Thus says the LORD: I have anointed you as king
4 of Israel.' Then open the door and flee; do not linger." So the lad, the prophet's
5 servant boy, set out for Ramot Gilad. When he arrived, there were the army
officers sitting together. "I have a message for you, officer," he said. "For which
6 one of us?" asked Yehu. "For you, officer," he said. He got up and came inside,
and he poured the oil on his head. "Thus says the LORD, God of Israel," he
7 said. "'I have anointed you as king of the LORD's people – of Israel! You will
strike down the house of Aḥav, your master; thus I will take vengeance on
Izevel for the blood of My servants the prophets and the blood of all the
8 LORD's servants. All the house of Aḥav will be lost; I will cut off every last
9 male of Aḥav in Israel, bond and free, and I will make the house of Aḥav like
the house of Yorovam son of Nevat and like the house of Basha son of Aḥiya.
10 As for Izevel – the dogs will devour her in the plot of Yizre'el, with no one to
11 bury her.'" And he opened the door and fled. When Yehu went out to his
lord's officials, they said to him, "Is all well? Why did that madman come
12 to you?" "Oh, you know the man and his talk," he said to them. "Lies!" they
said. "Tell us!" "This is what he said to me," he said. "Thus says the LORD: I
13 have anointed you as king of Israel." Each man quickly took his garment and
placed it beneath him[85] on the top step. They blasted the ram's horn and
14 proclaimed, "Yehu is king!" Thus Yehu son of Yehoshafat son of Nimshi
formed a conspiracy against Yoram. Yoram had been on the defense against

84 | Cf. verse 18; the term "daughter" in this verse is likely intended to mean "granddaughter."
85 | Beneath Yehu.

כג לִבְנָה בָּעֵת הַהִיא׃ וְיֶתֶר דִּבְרֵי יוֹרָם וְכָל־אֲשֶׁר עָשָׂה הֲלֹא־הֵם כְּתוּבִים
כד עַל־סֵפֶר דִּבְרֵי הַיָּמִים לְמַלְכֵי יְהוּדָה׃ וַיִּשְׁכַּב יוֹרָם עִם־אֲבֹתָיו וַיִּקָּבֵר
כה עִם־אֲבֹתָיו בְּעִיר דָּוִד וַיִּמְלֹךְ אֲחַזְיָהוּ בְנוֹ תַּחְתָּיו׃ בִּשְׁנַת
שְׁתֵּים־עֶשְׂרֵה שָׁנָה לְיוֹרָם בֶּן־אַחְאָב מֶלֶךְ יִשְׂרָאֵל מָלַךְ אֲחַזְיָהוּ בֶן־
כו יְהוֹרָם מֶלֶךְ יְהוּדָה׃ בֶּן־עֶשְׂרִים וּשְׁתַּיִם שָׁנָה אֲחַזְיָהוּ בְמָלְכוֹ וְשָׁנָה
אַחַת מָלַךְ בִּירוּשָׁלִָם וְשֵׁם אִמּוֹ עֲתַלְיָהוּ בַּת־עָמְרִי מֶלֶךְ יִשְׂרָאֵל׃
כז וַיֵּלֶךְ בְּדֶרֶךְ בֵּית אַחְאָב וַיַּעַשׂ הָרַע בְּעֵינֵי יְהוָה כְּבֵית אַחְאָב כִּי חֲתַן
כח בֵּית־אַחְאָב הוּא׃ וַיֵּלֶךְ אֶת־יוֹרָם בֶּן־אַחְאָב לַמִּלְחָמָה עִם־חֲזָאֵל
כט מֶלֶךְ־אֲרָם בְּרָמֹת גִּלְעָד וַיַּכּוּ אֲרַמִּים אֶת־יוֹרָם׃ וַיָּשָׁב יוֹרָם הַמֶּלֶךְ
לְהִתְרַפֵּא בְיִזְרְעֶאל מִן־הַמַּכִּים אֲשֶׁר יַכֻּהוּ אֲרַמִּים בָּרָמָה בְּהִלָּחֲמוֹ
אֶת־חֲזָהאֵל מֶלֶךְ אֲרָם וַאֲחַזְיָהוּ בֶן־יְהוֹרָם מֶלֶךְ יְהוּדָה יָרַד לִרְאוֹת
ט א אֶת־יוֹרָם בֶּן־אַחְאָב בְּיִזְרְעֶאל כִּי־חֹלֶה הוּא׃ וֶאֱלִישָׁע
הַנָּבִיא קָרָא לְאַחַד מִבְּנֵי הַנְּבִיאִים וַיֹּאמֶר לוֹ חֲגֹר מָתְנֶיךָ וְקַח פַּךְ
ב הַשֶּׁמֶן הַזֶּה בְּיָדֶךָ וְלֵךְ רָמֹת גִּלְעָד׃ וּבָאתָ שָׁמָּה וּרְאֵה־שָׁם יֵהוּא בֶן־
יְהוֹשָׁפָט בֶּן־נִמְשִׁי וּבָאתָ וַהֲקֵמֹתוֹ מִתּוֹךְ אֶחָיו וְהֵבֵיאתָ אֹתוֹ חֶדֶר
ג בְּחָדֶר׃ וְלָקַחְתָּ פַךְ־הַשֶּׁמֶן וְיָצַקְתָּ עַל־רֹאשׁוֹ וְאָמַרְתָּ כֹּה־אָמַר יְהוָה
מְשַׁחְתִּיךָ לְמֶלֶךְ אֶל־יִשְׂרָאֵל וּפָתַחְתָּ הַדֶּלֶת וְנַסְתָּה וְלֹא תְחַכֶּה׃
ד ה וַיֵּלֶךְ הַנַּעַר הַנָּבִיא רָמֹת גִּלְעָד׃ וַיָּבֹא וְהִנֵּה שָׂרֵי הַחַיִל יֹשְׁבִים
וַיֹּאמֶר דָּבָר לִי אֵלֶיךָ הַשָּׂר וַיֹּאמֶר יֵהוּא אֶל־מִי מִכֻּלָּנוּ וַיֹּאמֶר אֵלֶיךָ
ו הַשָּׂר׃ וַיָּקָם וַיָּבֹא הַבַּיְתָה וַיִּצֹק הַשֶּׁמֶן אֶל־רֹאשׁוֹ וַיֹּאמֶר לוֹ כֹּה־אָמַר
יְהוָה אֱלֹהֵי יִשְׂרָאֵל מְשַׁחְתִּיךָ לְמֶלֶךְ אֶל־עַם יְהוָה אֶל־יִשְׂרָאֵל׃
ז וְהִכִּיתָה אֶת־בֵּית אַחְאָב אֲדֹנֶיךָ וְנִקַּמְתִּי דְּמֵי ׀ עֲבָדַי הַנְּבִיאִים וּדְמֵי
ח כָּל־עַבְדֵי יְהוָה מִיַּד אִיזָבֶל׃ וְאָבַד כָּל־בֵּית אַחְאָב וְהִכְרַתִּי לְאַחְאָב
ט מַשְׁתִּין בְּקִיר וְעָצוּר וְעָזוּב בְּיִשְׂרָאֵל׃ וְנָתַתִּי אֶת־בֵּית אַחְאָב כְּבֵית
י יָרָבְעָם בֶּן־נְבָט וּכְבֵית בַּעְשָׁא בֶן־אֲחִיָּה׃ וְאֶת־אִיזֶבֶל יֹאכְלוּ הַכְּלָבִים
יא בְּחֵלֶק יִזְרְעֶאל וְאֵין קֹבֵר וַיִּפְתַּח הַדֶּלֶת וַיָּנֹס׃ וְיֵהוּא יָצָא אֶל־עַבְדֵי
אֲדֹנָיו וַיֹּאמֶר לוֹ הֲשָׁלוֹם מַדּוּעַ בָּא־הַמְשֻׁגָּע הַזֶּה אֵלֶיךָ וַיֹּאמֶר אֲלֵיהֶם
יב אַתֶּם יְדַעְתֶּם אֶת־הָאִישׁ וְאֶת־שִׂיחוֹ׃ וַיֹּאמְרוּ שֶׁקֶר הַגֶּד־נָא לָנוּ
וַיֹּאמֶר כָּזֹאת וְכָזֹאת אָמַר אֵלַי לֵאמֹר כֹּה אָמַר יְהוָה מְשַׁחְתִּיךָ לְמֶלֶךְ
יג אֶל־יִשְׂרָאֵל׃ וַיְמַהֲרוּ וַיִּקְחוּ אִישׁ בִּגְדוֹ וַיָּשִׂימוּ תַחְתָּיו אֶל־גֶּרֶם כד
יד הַמַּעֲלוֹת וַיִּתְקְעוּ בַּשּׁוֹפָר וַיֹּאמְרוּ מָלַךְ יֵהוּא׃ וַיִּתְקַשֵּׁר יֵהוּא בֶּן־
יְהוֹשָׁפָט בֶּן־נִמְשִׁי אֶל־יוֹרָם וְיוֹרָם הָיָה שֹׁמֵר בְּרָמֹת גִּלְעָד הוּא

15 Ḥazael, king of Aram, in Ramot Gilad, together with all of Israel. But Yoram
had come back to Yizre'el to recover from the wounds the Arameans had
inflicted upon him while he was fighting against Ḥazael, king of Aram. "If this
is indeed your will," said Yehu, "let no one escape from town to go and inform
16 in Yizre'el." And Yehu mounted a chariot and set out for Yizre'el, for there
17 Yoram lay, and Aḥazya, king of Yehuda, had gone down to visit Yoram. The
watchman stationed in the lookout tower in Yizre'el saw Yehu's company as
they approached and called out, "I see a company." "Fetch a rider and send
18 him out toward them," said Yoram, "and have him ask, 'Is all well?'" The rider
set out toward him on horseback and asked, "Thus says the king: 'Is all well?'"
"Does it matter to you if all is well?" said Yehu. "Fall in behind me." And the
watchman reported, "The messenger has reached them, but he has not come
19 back." He sent out a second rider on horseback. When he reached them, he
said, "'Thus says the king: 'Is all well?'" "Does it matter to you if all is well?"
20 said Yehu. "Fall in behind me." And the watchman reported, "He has reached
them, but he has not come back. It looks like the driving of Yehu son of
21 Nimshi – he drives like a madman." "Harness up," said Yehoram, and he
harnessed his chariot. Yehoram, king of Israel, and Aḥazyahu, king of Yehuda,
went out toward Yehu, each in his own chariot, and they met him at the plot
22 that belonged to Navot the Jezreelite. When Yehoram saw Yehu, he asked, "Is
all well, Yehu?" "How can all be well," he said, "while the whoring and endless
23 devilry of your mother Izevel continues?" Yehoram steered back around and
24 fled. "Treason, Aḥazya!" he called out to Aḥazyahu. But Yehu had drawn a
bow, and he struck Yoram between his arms – the arrow pierced his heart,
25 and he crumpled in his chariot. "Pick him up," he said to his adjutant Bidkar,
"and throw him in the field plot of Navot the Jezreelite. Remember how you
and I rode side by side behind his father Aḥav when the LORD made this
26 pronouncement against him: 'I swear, having seen the blood of Navot and
the blood of his children last night,' declares the LORD, 'I will pay you back
in this very plot,' declares the LORD, so now pick him up and throw him in
27 the plot, fulfilling the word of the LORD." When Aḥazya, king of Yehuda, saw,
he fled by the Beit HaGan Road, and Yehu chased after him. "Strike him as
well!" said Yehu, and they struck him[86] in his chariot by the Ascent of Gur
28 near Yivle'am. He fled to Megiddo, and there he died. His servants had him
driven to Jerusalem and buried him in his ancestral grave in the City of
29 David. In the eleventh year of Yoram son of Aḥav, Aḥazya had
30 become king over Yehuda. Meanwhile, Yehu arrived in Yizre'el. When Izevel
heard, she lined her eyes with kohl and dressed her hair and looked out
31 through the window. When Yehu entered the gate, she said, "Is all well, Zimri,
32 killer of his own master?"[87] He looked up to the window and said, "Who is
33 with me? Who?" Two or three eunuchs looked out at him. "Throw her down,"
he said, and they threw her down, and her blood spattered the walls and the
34 horses, and he trampled her. He came in and ate and drank and then said,

86 | The words "and they struck him" are not explicit in the Hebrew; see, e.g., Radak.
87 | See 1 Kings 16:8–10.

טו וְכָל־יִשְׂרָאֵל מִפְּנֵי חֲזָאֵל מֶלֶךְ אֲרָם: וַיָּשָׁב יְהוֹרָם הַמֶּלֶךְ לְהִתְרַפֵּא
בְיִזְרְעֶאל מִן־הַמַּכִּים אֲשֶׁר יַכֻּהוּ אֲרַמִּים בְּהִלָּחֲמוֹ אֶת־חֲזָהאֵל מֶלֶךְ
אֲרָם וַיֹּאמֶר יֵהוּא אִם־יֵשׁ נַפְשְׁכֶם אַל־יֵצֵא פָלִיט מִן־הָעִיר לָלֶכֶת
טז לגיד בְּיִזְרְעֶאל: וַיִּרְכַּב יֵהוּא וַיֵּלֶךְ יִזְרְעֶאלָה כִּי יוֹרָם שֹׁכֵב שָׁמָּה לְהַגִּיד
יז וַאֲחַזְיָה מֶלֶךְ יְהוּדָה יָרַד לִרְאוֹת אֶת־יוֹרָם: וְהַצֹּפֶה עֹמֵד עַל־הַמִּגְדָּל
בְּיִזְרְעֶאל וַיַּרְא אֶת־שִׁפְעַת יֵהוּא בְּבֹאוֹ וַיֹּאמֶר שִׁפְעַת אֲנִי רֹאֶה
יח וַיֹּאמֶר יְהוֹרָם קַח רַכָּב וּשְׁלַח לִקְרָאתָם וְיֹאמַר הֲשָׁלוֹם: וַיֵּלֶךְ רֹכֵב
הַסּוּס לִקְרָאתוֹ וַיֹּאמֶר כֹּה־אָמַר הַמֶּלֶךְ הֲשָׁלוֹם וַיֹּאמֶר יֵהוּא מַה־לְּךָ
וּלְשָׁלוֹם סֹב אֶל־אַחֲרָי וַיַּגֵּד הַצֹּפֶה לֵאמֹר בָּא־הַמַּלְאָךְ עַד־הֵם וְלֹא־
יט שָׁב: וַיִּשְׁלַח רֹכֵב סוּס שֵׁנִי וַיָּבֹא אֲלֵהֶם וַיֹּאמֶר כֹּה־אָמַר הַמֶּלֶךְ שָׁלוֹם
כ וַיֹּאמֶר יֵהוּא מַה־לְּךָ וּלְשָׁלוֹם סֹב אֶל־אַחֲרָי: וַיַּגֵּד הַצֹּפֶה לֵאמֹר בָּא
עַד־אֲלֵיהֶם וְלֹא־שָׁב וְהַמִּנְהָג כְּמִנְהַג יֵהוּא בֶן־נִמְשִׁי כִּי בְשִׁגָּעוֹן
כא יִנְהָג: וַיֹּאמֶר יְהוֹרָם אֱסֹר וַיֶּאְסֹר רִכְבּוֹ וַיֵּצֵא יְהוֹרָם מֶלֶךְ־יִשְׂרָאֵל
וַאֲחַזְיָהוּ מֶלֶךְ־יְהוּדָה אִישׁ בְּרִכְבּוֹ וַיֵּצְאוּ לִקְרַאת יֵהוּא וַיִּמְצָאֻהוּ
כב בְּחֶלְקַת נָבוֹת הַיִּזְרְעֵאלִי: וַיְהִי כִּרְאוֹת יְהוֹרָם אֶת־יֵהוּא וַיֹּאמֶר
הֲשָׁלוֹם יֵהוּא וַיֹּאמֶר מָה הַשָּׁלוֹם עַד־זְנוּנֵי אִיזֶבֶל אִמְּךָ וּכְשָׁפֶיהָ
כג הָרַבִּים: וַיַּהֲפֹךְ יְהוֹרָם יָדָיו וַיָּנֹס וַיֹּאמֶר אֶל־אֲחַזְיָהוּ מִרְמָה אֲחַזְיָה:
כד וְיֵהוּא מִלֵּא יָדוֹ בַקֶּשֶׁת וַיַּךְ אֶת־יְהוֹרָם בֵּין זְרֹעָיו וַיֵּצֵא הַחֵצִי מִלִּבּוֹ
כה וַיִּכְרַע בְּרִכְבּוֹ: וַיֹּאמֶר אֶל־בִּדְקַר שָׁלִשֹׁה שָׂא הַשְׁלִכֵהוּ בְּחֶלְקַת שְׂדֵה
נָבוֹת הַיִּזְרְעֵאלִי כִּי־זְכֹר אֲנִי וָאַתָּה אֵת רֹכְבִים צְמָדִים אַחֲרֵי אַחְאָב
כו אָבִיו וַיהוָה נָשָׂא עָלָיו אֶת־הַמַּשָּׂא הַזֶּה: אִם־לֹא אֶת־דְּמֵי נָבוֹת
וְאֶת־דְּמֵי בָנָיו רָאִיתִי אֶמֶשׁ נְאֻם־יְהוָה וְשִׁלַּמְתִּי לְךָ בַּחֶלְקָה הַזֹּאת
כז נְאֻם־יְהוָה וְעַתָּה שָׂא הַשְׁלִכֵהוּ בַּחֶלְקָה כִּדְבַר יְהוָה: וַאֲחַזְיָה מֶלֶךְ־
יְהוּדָה רָאָה וַיָּנָס דֶּרֶךְ בֵּית הַגָּן וַיִּרְדֹּף אַחֲרָיו יֵהוּא וַיֹּאמֶר גַּם־אֹתוֹ
הַכֻּהוּ אֶל־הַמֶּרְכָּבָה בְּמַעֲלֵה־גוּר אֲשֶׁר אֶת־יִבְלְעָם וַיָּנָס מְגִדּוֹ וַיָּמָת
כח שָׁם: וַיַּרְכִּבוּ אֹתוֹ עֲבָדָיו יְרוּשָׁלָמָה וַיִּקְבְּרוּ אֹתוֹ בִקְבֻרָתוֹ עִם־אֲבֹתָיו
כט בְּעִיר דָּוִד: וּבִשְׁנַת אַחַת עֶשְׂרֵה שָׁנָה לְיוֹרָם בֶּן־אַחְאָב
ל מָלַךְ אֲחַזְיָה עַל־יְהוּדָה: וַיָּבוֹא יֵהוּא יִזְרְעֶאלָה וְאִיזֶבֶל שָׁמְעָה וַתָּשֶׂם
לא בַּפּוּךְ עֵינֶיהָ וַתֵּיטֶב אֶת־רֹאשָׁהּ וַתַּשְׁקֵף בְּעַד הַחַלּוֹן: וְיֵהוּא בָּא
לב בַשָּׁעַר וַתֹּאמֶר הֲשָׁלוֹם זִמְרִי הֹרֵג אֲדֹנָיו: וַיִּשָּׂא פָנָיו אֶל־הַחַלּוֹן וַיֹּאמֶר
לג מִי אִתִּי מִי וַיַּשְׁקִיפוּ אֵלָיו שְׁנַיִם שְׁלֹשָׁה סָרִיסִים: וַיֹּאמֶר שמטוהו שִׁמְטֻהָ
לד וַיִּשְׁמְטוּהָ וַיִּז מִדָּמָהּ אֶל־הַקִּיר וְאֶל־הַסּוּסִים וַיִּרְמְסֶנָּה: וַיָּבֹא וַיֹּאכַל

"Take note of that cursed one, and bury her. After all, she was the daughter of
35 a king." But when they went to bury her, all they found of her was her skull,
36 her legs, and the palms of her hands. When they went back to tell him, he
said, "It is the word of the LORD, which He pronounced through His servant
Eliyahu the Tishbite: 'In the plot of Yizre'el, the dogs will devour Izevel's flesh.'
37 Now Izevel's corpse shall be like dung on the ground in the plot of Yizre'el,
10 1 so that none will ever say, 'This was Izevel.'" Now Aḥav had seventy
sons in Shomron. Yehu wrote letters and sent them to Shomron to the officers
2 of Yizre'el, the elders, and the guardians of Aḥav's sons, stating: "Now, when
this letter reaches you, as the sons of your lord are with you, and the chariots,
3 horses, fortified cities, and weapons are also with you, consider which is the
best and worthiest of your lord's sons, and set him on his father's throne. Then
4 fight for the house of your lord." They were absolutely terrified and said,
"Look, if two kings could not stand up to him, how can we take a stand?"
5 Those in charge of the palace, those in charge of the city, the elders, and the
guardians replied to Yehu, saying, "We are your servants, and whatever you
6 say to us we will do. We will not make anyone king; do as you please." So
he wrote them a second letter, stating: "If you are on my side, ready to obey
my command, then take the heads of the men, your master's sons, and come
to me this time tomorrow in Yizre'el." The king's sons numbered seventy
7 men, and the nobles of the city were raising them. When the letter reached
them, they seized the king's sons, massacred the seventy men, and placed
8 their heads in baskets, which they sent to him in Yizre'el. When the messenger
informed him, "They have brought the heads of the king's sons," he said,
9 "Place them in two heaps by the entrance to the gate until morning." In
the morning, he went out and stood by. "You are all innocent," he said to
all the people, "while it is I who formed a conspiracy against my lord and
10 killed him. Yet who killed all of these? Know, then, that not a word of what
the LORD pronounced for the house of Aḥav will fall through; the LORD
11 has fulfilled what He pronounced through His servant Eliyahu." And Yehu
struck down all who remained of the house of Aḥav in Yizre'el – all its nobles,
12 associates, and priests – until there were no survivors left. He then set out
13 toward Shomron, and on the way, at Beit Eked of the shepherds, Yehu
encountered the kinsmen of Aḥazyahu, the king of Yehuda. "Who are you?"
he asked, and they said, "We are Aḥazyahu's kinsmen, and we are going down
14 to visit the king's sons and the queen mother's sons." "Take them alive!" he
said, and they took them alive, and he massacred them by the Beit Eked
15 pit – forty-two men; he did not leave a single one of them. They
continued on from there. He met Yehonadav son of Rekhav coming toward
him and greeted him. "Is your heart truly with me, as my heart is with you?"
he said. "It is indeed," said Yehonadav. "If so, give me your hand." He held out

וַיֵּשְׁתְּ וַיֹּאמֶר פִּקְדוּ־נָא אֶת־הָאֲרוּרָה הַזֹּאת וְקִבְרוּהָ כִּי בַת־מֶלֶךְ
לה הִיא׃ וַיֵּלְכוּ לְקׇבְרָהּ וְלֹא־מָצְאוּ בָהּ כִּי אִם־הַגֻּלְגֹּלֶת וְהָרַגְלַיִם וְכַפּוֹת
לו הַיָּדָיִם׃ וַיָּשֻׁבוּ וַיַּגִּידוּ לוֹ וַיֹּאמֶר דְּבַר־יהוה הוּא אֲשֶׁר דִּבֶּר בְּיַד־עַבְדּוֹ
אֵלִיָּהוּ הַתִּשְׁבִּי לֵאמֹר בְּחֵלֶק יִזְרְעֶאל יֹאכְלוּ הַכְּלָבִים אֶת־בְּשַׂר
לז אִיזָבֶל׃ וְהָיְתָ נִבְלַת אִיזֶבֶל כְּדֹמֶן עַל־פְּנֵי הַשָּׂדֶה בְּחֵלֶק יִזְרְעֶאל אֲשֶׁר
י א לֹא־יֹאמְרוּ זֹאת אִיזָבֶל׃ וּלְאַחְאָב שִׁבְעִים בָּנִים
בְּשֹׁמְרוֹן וַיִּכְתֹּב יֵהוּא סְפָרִים וַיִּשְׁלַח שֹׁמְרוֹן אֶל־שָׂרֵי יִזְרְעֶאל הַזְּקֵנִים
ב וְאֶל־הָאֹמְנִים אַחְאָב לֵאמֹר׃ וְעַתָּה כְּבֹא הַסֵּפֶר הַזֶּה אֲלֵיכֶם וְאִתְּכֶם
ג בְּנֵי אֲדֹנֵיכֶם וְאִתְּכֶם הָרֶכֶב וְהַסּוּסִים וְעִיר מִבְצָר וְהַנָּשֶׁק׃ וּרְאִיתֶם
הַטּוֹב וְהַיָּשָׁר מִבְּנֵי אֲדֹנֵיכֶם וְשַׂמְתֶּם עַל־כִּסֵּא אָבִיו וְהִלָּחֲמוּ עַל־בֵּית
ד אֲדֹנֵיכֶם׃ וַיִּרְאוּ מְאֹד מְאֹד וַיֹּאמְרוּ הִנֵּה שְׁנֵי הַמְּלָכִים לֹא עָמְדוּ לְפָנָיו
ה וְאֵיךְ נַעֲמֹד אֲנָחְנוּ׃ וַיִּשְׁלַח אֲשֶׁר־עַל־הַבַּיִת וַאֲשֶׁר עַל־הָעִיר וְהַזְּקֵנִים
וְהָאֹמְנִים אֶל־יֵהוּא ׀ לֵאמֹר עֲבָדֶיךָ אֲנַחְנוּ וְכֹל אֲשֶׁר־תֹּאמַר אֵלֵינוּ
ו נַעֲשֶׂה לֹא־נַמְלִיךְ אִישׁ הַטּוֹב בְּעֵינֶיךָ עֲשֵׂה׃ וַיִּכְתֹּב אֲלֵיהֶם סֵפֶר ׀
שֵׁנִית לֵאמֹר אִם־לִי אַתֶּם וּלְקֹלִי ׀ אַתֶּם שֹׁמְעִים קְחוּ אֶת־רָאשֵׁי
אַנְשֵׁי בְנֵי־אֲדֹנֵיכֶם וּבֹאוּ אֵלַי כָּעֵת מָחָר יִזְרְעֶאלָה וּבְנֵי הַמֶּלֶךְ שִׁבְעִים
ז אִישׁ אֶת־גְּדֹלֵי הָעִיר מְגַדְּלִים אוֹתָם׃ וַיְהִי כְּבֹא הַסֵּפֶר אֲלֵיהֶם וַיִּקְחוּ
אֶת־בְּנֵי הַמֶּלֶךְ וַיִּשְׁחֲטוּ שִׁבְעִים אִישׁ וַיָּשִׂימוּ אֶת־רָאשֵׁיהֶם בַּדּוּדִים
ח וַיִּשְׁלְחוּ אֵלָיו יִזְרְעֶאלָה׃ וַיָּבֹא הַמַּלְאָךְ וַיַּגֶּד־לוֹ לֵאמֹר הֵבִיאוּ רָאשֵׁי
בְנֵי־הַמֶּלֶךְ וַיֹּאמֶר שִׂימוּ אֹתָם שְׁנֵי צִבֻּרִים פֶּתַח הַשַּׁעַר עַד־הַבֹּקֶר׃
ט וַיְהִי בַבֹּקֶר וַיֵּצֵא וַיַּעֲמֹד וַיֹּאמֶר אֶל־כׇּל־הָעָם צַדִּקִים אַתֶּם הִנֵּה אֲנִי
י קָשַׁרְתִּי עַל־אֲדֹנִי וָאֶהְרְגֵהוּ וּמִי הִכָּה אֶת־כׇּל־אֵלֶּה׃ דְּעוּ אֵפוֹא כִּי
לֹא יִפֹּל מִדְּבַר יהוה אַרְצָה אֲשֶׁר־דִּבֶּר יהוה עַל־בֵּית אַחְאָב וַיהוה
יא עָשָׂה אֵת אֲשֶׁר דִּבֶּר בְּיַד עַבְדּוֹ אֵלִיָּהוּ׃ וַיַּךְ יֵהוּא אֵת כׇּל־הַנִּשְׁאָרִים
לְבֵית־אַחְאָב בְּיִזְרְעֶאל וְכׇל־גְּדֹלָיו וּמְיֻדָּעָיו וְכֹהֲנָיו עַד־בִּלְתִּי הִשְׁאִיר־
יב לוֹ שָׂרִיד׃ וַיָּקָם וַיָּבֹא וַיֵּלֶךְ שֹׁמְרוֹן הוּא בֵּית־עֵקֶד הָרֹעִים בַּדָּרֶךְ׃
יג וְיֵהוּא מָצָא אֶת־אֲחֵי אֲחַזְיָהוּ מֶלֶךְ־יְהוּדָה וַיֹּאמֶר מִי אַתֶּם וַיֹּאמְרוּ
יד אֲחֵי אֲחַזְיָהוּ אֲנַחְנוּ וַנֵּרֶד לִשְׁלוֹם בְּנֵי־הַמֶּלֶךְ וּבְנֵי הַגְּבִירָה׃ וַיֹּאמֶר
תִּפְשׂוּם חַיִּים וַיִּתְפְּשׂוּם חַיִּים וַיִּשְׁחָטוּם אֶל־בּוֹר בֵּית־עֵקֶד אַרְבָּעִים
טו וּשְׁנַיִם אִישׁ וְלֹא־הִשְׁאִיר אִישׁ מֵהֶם׃ וַיֵּלֶךְ מִשָּׁם כה
וַיִּמְצָא אֶת־יְהוֹנָדָב בֶּן־רֵכָב לִקְרָאתוֹ וַיְבָרְכֵהוּ וַיֹּאמֶר אֵלָיו הֲיֵשׁ
אֶת־לְבָבְךָ יָשָׁר כַּאֲשֶׁר לְבָבִי עִם־לְבָבֶךָ וַיֹּאמֶר יְהוֹנָדָב יֵשׁ וָיֵשׁ תְּנָה

16 his hand, and Yehu hoisted him up into the chariot with him. "Come with
me and see my fervor for the LORD," he said, and drove him in his chariot.
17 When he arrived in Shomron, he struck down all those who were left to Aḥav
in Shomron until he had wiped him out, fulfilling the word that the LORD
18 had pronounced to Eliyahu. Yehu then gathered all the people and
19 said to them, "Aḥav hardly served the Baal; Yehu will serve him fully! Now,
summon all of Baal's prophets, worshippers, and priests to me; let no one be
absent, for I am making a great sacrifice for Baal, and whoever is absent will
not live." Yehu was staging deceit in order to destroy the worshippers of Baal.
20 "Declare a holy assembly for Baal," said Yehu, and so it was proclaimed. Yehu
21 sent throughout Israel, and all the worshippers of Baal came; not a single one
failed to come. They came to the temple of Baal, and the temple of Baal was
22 packed from end to end. "Bring out the vestments for all the worshippers of
Baal," he said to the man in charge of the raiment, and he brought vestments
23 out for them. Then Yehu and Yehonadav son of Rekhav entered the temple
of Baal. "Search carefully and make sure there are no worshippers of the LORD
here among you," he said to the worshippers of Baal. "There must only be
24 worshippers of Baal." And they went to offer sacrifices and burnt offerings.
Now Yehu had stationed eighty men outside, and he had said to them, "If a
single person escapes among those I hand over to you, it will be your life
25 for his life." And as he finished presenting the burnt offering, Yehu said to
the sentry and the adjutants, "Come in and strike them down! Let no man
escape!" They put them to the sword, then the sentry and the adjutants
26 threw them out and proceeded to the Baal temple compound. They brought
27 out the pillars of the temple of Baal and burned them, and they tore down
the sacred pillar of Baal, and they tore down the temple of Baal, and they
28 have used it as latrines ever since. Thus Yehu wiped out the Baal from
29 Israel. But as for the sins of Yorovam son of Nevat, who led Israel to sin
through the golden calves in Beit El and Dan – Yehu did not turn away from
30 them. The LORD said to Yehu, "Because you have accomplished
what was right in My eyes, executing all My intentions against the house of
31 Aḥav, four generations of your line will sit on the throne of Israel." But Yehu
did not follow the teaching of the LORD, God of Israel, with care, with all his
heart; he did not turn away from the sins of Yorovam, who led Israel to sin.
32 In those days, the LORD began to weaken Israel at the edges. Ḥazael attacked
33 Israel on every front: from east of the Jordan, all the land of the Gilad – the
Gadites, the Reubenites, and the Manassites – from Aroer by the Arnon
34 Stream to the Gilad and the Bashan. As for the rest of Yehu's history and all
his deeds and all his heroic feats – they are recorded in the book of the History
35 of the Kings of Israel. And Yehu slept with his ancestors, and they buried him
36 in Shomron. And his son Yehoaḥaz reigned in his place. Yehu had reigned

טז אֶת־יָדֶךָ וַיִּתֵּן יָדוֹ וַיַּעֲלֵהוּ אֵלָיו אֶל־הַמֶּרְכָּבָה: וַיֹּאמֶר לְכָה אִתִּי וּרְאֵה
יז בְּקִנְאָתִי לַיהוָה וַיַּרְכִּבוּ אֹתוֹ בְּרִכְבּוֹ: וַיָּבֹא שֹׁמְרוֹן וַיַּךְ אֶת־כָּל־
הַנִּשְׁאָרִים לְאַחְאָב בְּשֹׁמְרוֹן עַד־הִשְׁמִידוֹ כִּדְבַר יְהוָה אֲשֶׁר דִּבֶּר
יח אֶל־אֵלִיָּהוּ: וַיִּקְבֹּץ יֵהוּא אֶת־כָּל־הָעָם וַיֹּאמֶר אֲלֵהֶם
יט אַחְאָב עָבַד אֶת־הַבַּעַל מְעָט יֵהוּא יַעַבְדֶנּוּ הַרְבֵּה: וְעַתָּה כָל־נְבִיאֵי
הַבַּעַל כָּל־עֹבְדָיו וְכָל־כֹּהֲנָיו קִרְאוּ אֵלַי אִישׁ אַל־יִפָּקֵד כִּי זֶבַח גָּדוֹל
לִי לַבַּעַל כֹּל אֲשֶׁר־יִפָּקֵד לֹא יִחְיֶה וְיֵהוּא עָשָׂה בְעָקְבָּה לְמַעַן הַאֲבִיד
כ כא אֶת־עֹבְדֵי הַבָּעַל: וַיֹּאמֶר יֵהוּא קַדְּשׁוּ עֲצָרָה לַבַּעַל וַיִּקְרָאוּ: וַיִּשְׁלַח
יֵהוּא בְּכָל־יִשְׂרָאֵל וַיָּבֹאוּ כָּל־עֹבְדֵי הַבַּעַל וְלֹא־נִשְׁאַר אִישׁ אֲשֶׁר
כב לֹא־בָא וַיָּבֹאוּ בֵּית הַבַּעַל וַיִּמָּלֵא בֵית־הַבַּעַל פֶּה לָפֶה: וַיֹּאמֶר לַאֲשֶׁר
עַל־הַמֶּלְתָּחָה הוֹצֵא לְבוּשׁ לְכֹל עֹבְדֵי הַבָּעַל וַיֹּצֵא לָהֶם הַמַּלְבּוּשׁ:
כג וַיָּבֹא יֵהוּא וִיהוֹנָדָב בֶּן־רֵכָב בֵּית הַבָּעַל וַיֹּאמֶר לְעֹבְדֵי הַבַּעַל
חַפְּשׂוּ וּרְאוּ פֶּן־יֶשׁ־פֹּה עִמָּכֶם מֵעַבְדֵי יְהוָה כִּי אִם־עֹבְדֵי הַבַּעַל
כד לְבַדָּם: וַיָּבֹאוּ לַעֲשׂוֹת זְבָחִים וְעֹלוֹת וְיֵהוּא שָׂם־לוֹ בַחוּץ שְׁמֹנִים אִישׁ
וַיֹּאמֶר הָאִישׁ אֲשֶׁר־יִמָּלֵט מִן־הָאֲנָשִׁים אֲשֶׁר אֲנִי מֵבִיא עַל־יְדֵיכֶם
כה נַפְשׁוֹ תַּחַת נַפְשׁוֹ: וַיְהִי כְּכַלֹּתוֹ | לַעֲשׂוֹת הָעֹלָה וַיֹּאמֶר יֵהוּא לָרָצִים
וְלַשָּׁלִשִׁים בֹּאוּ הַכּוּם אִישׁ אַל־יֵצֵא וַיַּכּוּם לְפִי־חָרֶב וַיַּשְׁלִכוּ הָרָצִים
כו וְהַשָּׁלִשִׁים וַיֵּלְכוּ עַד־עִיר בֵּית־הַבָּעַל: וַיֹּצִאוּ אֶת־מַצְּבוֹת בֵּית־הַבַּעַל
כז וַיִּשְׂרְפוּהָ: וַיִּתְּצוּ אֵת מַצְּבַת הַבָּעַל וַיִּתְּצוּ אֶת־בֵּית הַבַּעַל וַיְשִׂמֻהוּ
כח כט למחראות עַד־הַיּוֹם: וַיַּשְׁמֵד יֵהוּא אֶת־הַבַּעַל מִיִּשְׂרָאֵל: רַק חֲטָאֵי לְמוֹצָאוֹת
יָרָבְעָם בֶּן־נְבָט אֲשֶׁר הֶחֱטִיא אֶת־יִשְׂרָאֵל לֹא־סָר יֵהוּא מֵאַחֲרֵיהֶם
ל עֶגְלֵי הַזָּהָב אֲשֶׁר בֵּית־אֵל וַאֲשֶׁר בְּדָן: וַיֹּאמֶר יְהוָה אֶל־
יֵהוּא יַעַן אֲשֶׁר־הֱטִיבֹתָ לַעֲשׂוֹת הַיָּשָׁר בְּעֵינַי כְּכֹל אֲשֶׁר בִּלְבָבִי
לא עָשִׂיתָ לְבֵית אַחְאָב בְּנֵי רְבִעִים יֵשְׁבוּ לְךָ עַל־כִּסֵּא יִשְׂרָאֵל: וְיֵהוּא
לֹא שָׁמַר לָלֶכֶת בְּתוֹרַת־יְהוָה אֱלֹהֵי־יִשְׂרָאֵל בְּכָל־לְבָבוֹ לֹא סָר מֵעַל
לב חַטֹּאות יָרָבְעָם אֲשֶׁר הֶחֱטִיא אֶת־יִשְׂרָאֵל: בַּיָּמִים הָהֵם הֵחֵל יְהוָה
לג לְקַצּוֹת בְּיִשְׂרָאֵל וַיַּכֵּם חֲזָאֵל בְּכָל־גְּבוּל יִשְׂרָאֵל: מִן־הַיַּרְדֵּן מִזְרַח
הַשֶּׁמֶשׁ אֵת כָּל־אֶרֶץ הַגִּלְעָד הַגָּדִי וְהָראוּבֵנִי וְהַמְנַשִּׁי מֵעֲרֹעֵר
לד אֲשֶׁר עַל־נַחַל אַרְנֹן וְהַגִּלְעָד וְהַבָּשָׁן: וְיֶתֶר דִּבְרֵי יֵהוּא וְכָל־אֲשֶׁר
עָשָׂה וְכָל־גְּבוּרָתוֹ הֲלוֹא־הֵם כְּתוּבִים עַל־סֵפֶר דִּבְרֵי הַיָּמִים לְמַלְכֵי
לה יִשְׂרָאֵל: וַיִּשְׁכַּב יֵהוּא עִם־אֲבֹתָיו וַיִּקְבְּרוּ אֹתוֹ בְּשֹׁמְרוֹן וַיִּמְלֹךְ יְהוֹאָחָז
לו בְּנוֹ תַּחְתָּיו: וְהַיָּמִים אֲשֶׁר מָלַךְ יֵהוּא עַל־יִשְׂרָאֵל עֶשְׂרִים־וּשְׁמֹנֶה

11 1 over Israel for twenty-eight years in Shomron. When Atalya, the
mother of Aḥazyahu, saw that her son was dead, she swiftly destroyed all
2 those of royal descent. But Yehosheva, the daughter of King Yoram and the
sister of Aḥazyahu, took Yoash, Aḥazya's son, and stole him away from where
the princes were being put to death to a bedchamber, together with his nurse.
3 They hid him from Atalya, so he was not put to death. He stayed with her in
the House of the LORD, hiding for six years, while Atalya reigned over the
4 land. In the seventh year, Yehoyada[88] sent for the Keretite[89] officers
of hundreds and the sentry and had them come to him in the House of the
LORD. He made a pact with them and had them swear an oath in the House
5 of the LORD; then he showed them the king's son. "This is what you must do,"
he instructed them. "A third of you on weekly duty will keep guard over the
6 royal palace, a third of you at the Sur Gate, and a third of you at the gate
7 behind the sentry post – maintain unrelenting watch over the House. As for
the two of your units who are off weekly duty – keep guard over the House
8 of the LORD for the sake of the king. Surround the king on all sides, and make
sure every man's weapon is poised, and whoever breaks through the ranks
9 must be killed. And stay with the king when he comes or goes." The officers
of hundreds did all that the priest Yehoyada instructed them, and each took
their men – those on weekly duty and those off weekly duty – and came
10 to the priest Yehoyada. The priest gave the officers of hundreds David's
11 own spears and quivers, which were in the House of the LORD. And the
sentry – each man with his weapon poised – were stationed from the south
end of the House to the north end of the House, by the altar and the House,
12 all around the king. He brought out the king's son and set the crown and the
royal insignia upon him. They declared him as king and anointed him and
13 clapped their hands and shouted, "Long live the king!" Atalya heard
the sound of the sentry, of the people, and she came to the people at the
14 House of the LORD. When Atalya looked up to find the king standing on the
platform, as was the custom, with officers with trumpets beside the king and
all the people of the land rejoicing and blowing the trumpets, Atalya rent her
15 clothes and called out, "Treason! Treason!" But Yehoyada gave orders to the
officers of hundreds, the force commanders. "Take her out between the ranks,"
he said to them, "and put anyone who follows to the sword," for the priest
16 thought, "She should not be put to death in the House of the LORD." They
cleared the way for her, and she entered the royal palace through the horses'
17 entrance, and there she was put to death. Then Yehoyada reinstated
the covenant between the LORD, the king, and the people, to be the LORD's
18 people; and between the king and the people. All the people of the land came
to the temple of Baal and tore it down and shattered its altars and images
through and through, and killed Matan, the priest of Baal, in front of the altars.
19 The priest set watchmen over the House of the LORD, and he had the officers

88 | The High Priest and Yehosheva's husband; see verse 9 and II Chronicles 22:11, 24:6.
89 | See note on I Kings 1:38.

יא א שָׁנָה בְּשֹׁמְרוֹן׃ וַעֲתַלְיָה אֵם אֲחַזְיָהוּ וראתה כִּי מֵת בְּנָהּ רָאֲתָה
ב וַתָּקָם וַתְּאַבֵּד אֵת כָּל־זֶרַע הַמַּמְלָכָה׃ וַתִּקַּח יְהוֹשֶׁבַע בַּת־הַמֶּלֶךְ־
יוֹרָם אֲחוֹת אֲחַזְיָהוּ אֶת־יוֹאָשׁ בֶּן־אֲחַזְיָה וַתִּגְנֹב אֹתוֹ מִתּוֹךְ בְּנֵי־
הַמֶּלֶךְ הממותתים אֹתוֹ וְאֶת־מֵינִקְתּוֹ בַּחֲדַר הַמִּטּוֹת וַיַּסְתִּרוּ אֹתוֹ הַמּוּמָתִים
ג מִפְּנֵי עֲתַלְיָהוּ וְלֹא הוּמָת׃ וַיְהִי אִתָּהּ בֵּית יְהוָה מִתְחַבֵּא שֵׁשׁ שָׁנִים
ד וַעֲתַלְיָה מֹלֶכֶת עַל־הָאָרֶץ׃ וּבַשָּׁנָה הַשְּׁבִיעִית שָׁלַח
יְהוֹיָדָע וַיִּקַּח ׀ אֶת־שָׂרֵי המאיות לַכָּרִי וְלָרָצִים וַיָּבֵא אֹתָם אֵלָיו בֵּית הַמֵּאוֹת
יְהוָה וַיִּכְרֹת לָהֶם בְּרִית וַיַּשְׁבַּע אֹתָם בְּבֵית יְהוָה וַיַּרְא אֹתָם אֶת־
ה בֶּן־הַמֶּלֶךְ׃ וַיְצַוֵּם לֵאמֹר זֶה הַדָּבָר אֲשֶׁר תַּעֲשׂוּן הַשְּׁלִשִׁית מִכֶּם
ו בָּאֵי הַשַּׁבָּת וְשֹׁמְרֵי מִשְׁמֶרֶת בֵּית הַמֶּלֶךְ׃ וְהַשְּׁלִשִׁית בְּשַׁעַר סוּר
וְהַשְּׁלִשִׁית בַּשַּׁעַר אַחַר הָרָצִים וּשְׁמַרְתֶּם אֶת־מִשְׁמֶרֶת הַבַּיִת מַסָּח׃
ז וּשְׁתֵּי הַיָּדוֹת בָּכֶם כֹּל יֹצְאֵי הַשַּׁבָּת וְשָׁמְרוּ אֶת־מִשְׁמֶרֶת בֵּית־יְהוָה
ח אֶל־הַמֶּלֶךְ׃ וְהִקַּפְתֶּם עַל־הַמֶּלֶךְ סָבִיב אִישׁ וְכֵלָיו בְּיָדוֹ וְהַבָּא אֶל־
ט הַשְּׂדֵרוֹת יוּמָת וִהְיוּ אֶת־הַמֶּלֶךְ בְּצֵאתוֹ וּבְבֹאוֹ׃ וַיַּעֲשׂוּ שָׂרֵי המאיות הַמֵּאוֹת
כְּכֹל אֲשֶׁר־צִוָּה יְהוֹיָדָע הַכֹּהֵן וַיִּקְחוּ אִישׁ אֶת־אֲנָשָׁיו בָּאֵי הַשַּׁבָּת
י עִם יֹצְאֵי הַשַּׁבָּת וַיָּבֹאוּ אֶל־יְהוֹיָדָע הַכֹּהֵן׃ וַיִּתֵּן הַכֹּהֵן לְשָׂרֵי המאיות הַמֵּאוֹת
אֶת־הַחֲנִית וְאֶת־הַשְּׁלָטִים אֲשֶׁר לַמֶּלֶךְ דָּוִד אֲשֶׁר בְּבֵית יְהוָה׃
יא וַיַּעַמְדוּ הָרָצִים אִישׁ ׀ וְכֵלָיו בְּיָדוֹ מִכֶּתֶף הַבַּיִת הַיְמָנִית עַד־כֶּתֶף
יב הַבַּיִת הַשְּׂמָאלִית לַמִּזְבֵּחַ וְלַבָּיִת עַל־הַמֶּלֶךְ סָבִיב׃ וַיּוֹצִא אֶת־בֶּן־
הַמֶּלֶךְ וַיִּתֵּן עָלָיו אֶת־הַנֵּזֶר וְאֶת־הָעֵדוּת וַיַּמְלִכוּ אֹתוֹ וַיִּמְשָׁחֻהוּ
יג וַיַּכּוּ־כָף וַיֹּאמְרוּ יְחִי הַמֶּלֶךְ׃ וַתִּשְׁמַע עֲתַלְיָה אֶת־קוֹל
יד הָרָצִין הָעָם וַתָּבֹא אֶל־הָעָם בֵּית יְהוָה׃ וַתֵּרֶא וְהִנֵּה הַמֶּלֶךְ עֹמֵד
עַל־הָעַמּוּד כַּמִּשְׁפָּט וְהַשָּׂרִים וְהַחֲצֹצְרוֹת אֶל־הַמֶּלֶךְ וְכָל־עַם הָאָרֶץ
שָׂמֵחַ וְתֹקֵעַ בַּחֲצֹצְרוֹת וַתִּקְרַע עֲתַלְיָה אֶת־בְּגָדֶיהָ וַתִּקְרָא קֶשֶׁר
טו קָשֶׁר׃ וַיְצַו יְהוֹיָדָע הַכֹּהֵן אֶת־שָׂרֵי המאיות ׀ פְּקֻדֵי הַחַיִל וַיֹּאמֶר הַמֵּאוֹת ׀
אֲלֵיהֶם הוֹצִיאוּ אֹתָהּ אֶל־מִבֵּית לַשְּׂדֵרֹת וְהַבָּא אַחֲרֶיהָ הָמֵת בֶּחָרֶב
טז כִּי אָמַר הַכֹּהֵן אַל־תּוּמַת בֵּית יְהוָה׃ וַיָּשִׂמוּ לָהּ יָדַיִם וַתָּבוֹא דֶּרֶךְ־
יז מְבוֹא הַסּוּסִים בֵּית הַמֶּלֶךְ וַתּוּמַת שָׁם׃ וַיִּכְרֹת יְהוֹיָדָע
אֶת־הַבְּרִית בֵּין יְהוָה וּבֵין הַמֶּלֶךְ וּבֵין הָעָם לִהְיוֹת לְעָם לַיהוָה וּבֵין
יח הַמֶּלֶךְ וּבֵין הָעָם׃ וַיָּבֹאוּ כָל־עַם הָאָרֶץ בֵּית־הַבַּעַל וַיִּתְּצֻהוּ אֶת־
מִזְבְּחֹתָו וְאֶת־צְלָמָיו שִׁבְּרוּ הֵיטֵב וְאֵת מַתָּן כֹּהֵן הַבַּעַל הָרְגוּ לִפְנֵי
יט הַמִּזְבְּחוֹת וַיָּשֶׂם הַכֹּהֵן פְּקֻדֹּת עַל־בֵּית יְהוָה׃ וַיִּקַּח אֶת־שָׂרֵי הַמֵּאוֹת

of the hundreds, the Keretites, the sentry, and all the people of the land escort
the king down from the House of the LORD. They came in through the sentry
20 gate of the royal palace, and he took his seat upon the royal throne. All the
people of the land rejoiced, and calm settled over the city. As for Atalya, they
12 1 had put her to death by sword in the royal palace. Yehoash was seven
2 years old when he became king; Yehoash became king in the seventh year of
Yehu, and for forty years, he reigned in Jerusalem. His mother's name was
3 Tzivya, of Be'er Sheva. Yehoash did what was right in the eyes of the LORD all
4 his days, as the priest Yehoyada had taught him. Yet the high shrines were not
removed; the people still offered sacrifices and incense at the high shrines.
5 Yehoash said to the priests, "All the dedicated money brought to the House
of the LORD – the money from the census, the money equivalent to a person's
worth,[90] or any money that a person is moved to bring to the House of the
6 LORD – let the priests accept it, each from his donor, and they will see to the
7 repair of the House wherever damage may be found." But by the
twenty-third year of King Yehoash, the priests had not seen to the repair of
8 the House, and King Yehoash summoned the priest Yehoyada and the priests.
"Why have you not kept the House in repair?" he said to them. "From now
on, do not take any money from your donors; rather, you must donate it
9 toward the repair of the House." The priests agreed that they would neither
10 take money from the people nor see to the House's repair. So the priest
Yehoyada took a chest, made a hole in its lid, and placed it to the right of
the altar, where people entered the House of the LORD. There, the priestly
guardians of the threshold placed all the money that was brought to the
11 House of the LORD. Whenever they saw that there was a considerable amount
of money in the chest, the royal scribe and the High Priest would come up,
tie it into a bundle, and count the money found in the House of the LORD.
12 They then gave the weighed-out money to the foremen in charge of the
House of the LORD, who would use it to pay the carpenters and the builders
13 who worked in the House of the LORD, and the masons and stonecutters, and
to purchase timber and quarry stones to keep the House of the LORD in repair,
14 and for any other expenses for maintenance of the House. However, no silver
bowls, shears, basins, or trumpets – or any golden or silver vessels – were
15 made from the money that was brought to the House of the LORD, as it was
given to the overseers, who used it to keep the House of the LORD in repair.
16 They did not need to keep track of the men who received the money to pay
17 out to the workers, for they dealt honestly. Money from guilt offerings and
money from purification offerings was not brought to the House of the
18 LORD; it belonged to the priests. At that time, Ḥazael, king of Aram,
marched up and attacked Gat, and he captured it; Ḥazael then set out to
19 march up against Jerusalem. So Yehoash, king of Yehuda, took all the sacred
objects that had been dedicated by his ancestors Yehoshafat, Yehoram, and
Aḥazya, the kings of Yehuda, along with his own sacred objects and all the
gold found in the treasuries of the House of the LORD and the royal palace.

90 | See Leviticus 27:1–8.

ואת־הכרי ואת־הרצים ואת ׀ כל־עם הארץ וירידו את־המלך מבית
יהוה ויבואו דרך־שער הרצים בית המלך וישב על־כסא המלכים:
כ וישמח כל־עם־הארץ והעיר שקטה ואת־עתליהו המיתו בחרב
יב א ב בית מלך: בן־שבע שנים יהואש במלכו: בשנת־שבע המלך
ליהוא מלך יהואש וארבעים שנה מלך בירושלם ושם אמו צביה
ג מבאר שבע: ויעש יהואש הישר בעיני יהוה כל־ימיו אשר הורהו כו
ד יהוידע הכהן: רק הבמות לא־סרו עוד העם מזבחים ומקטרים
ה בבמות: ויאמר יהואש אל־הכהנים כל כסף הקדשים אשר יובא
בית־יהוה כסף עובר איש כסף נפשות ערכו כל־כסף אשר יעלה
ו על לב־איש להביא בית יהוה: יקחו להם הכהנים איש מאת מכרו
ז והם יחזקו את־בדק הבית לכל אשר־ימצא שם בדק: ויהי
בשנת עשרים ושלש שנה למלך יהואש לא־חזקו הכהנים את־בדק
ח הבית: ויקרא המלך יהואש ליהוידע הכהן ולכהנים ויאמר אלהם
מדוע אינכם מחזקים את־בדק הבית ועתה אל־תקחו־כסף מאת
ט מכריכם כי־לבדק הבית תתנהו: ויאתו הכהנים לבלתי קחת־כסף
י מאת העם ולבלתי חזק את־בדק הבית: ויקח יהוידע הכהן ארון
אחד ויקב חר בדלתו ויתן אתו אצל המזבח בימין בבוא־איש בית מימין
יהוה ונתנו־שמה הכהנים שמרי הסף את־כל־הכסף המובא בית־
יא יהוה: ויהי כראותם כי־רב הכסף בארון ויעל ספר המלך והכהן
יב הגדול ויצרו וימנו את־הכסף הנמצא בית־יהוה: ונתנו את־הכסף
המתכן על־יד עשי המלאכה הפקדים בית יהוה ויוציאהו לחרשי המפקדים
יג העץ ולבנים העשים בית יהוה: ולגדרים ולחצבי האבן ולקנות
עצים ואבני מחצב לחזק את־בדק בית־יהוה ולכל אשר־יצא על־
יד הבית לחזקה: אך לא יעשה בית יהוה ספות כסף מזמרות מזרקות
טו חצצרות כל־כלי זהב וכלי־כסף מן־הכסף המובא בית־יהוה: כי־
טז לעשי המלאכה יתנהו וחזקו־בו את־בית יהוה: ולא יחשבו את־
האנשים אשר יתנו את־הכסף על־ידם לתת לעשי המלאכה כי
יז באמנה הם עשים: כסף אשם וכסף חטאות לא יובא בית יהוה
יח לכהנים יהיו: אז יעלה חזאל מלך ארם וילחם על־גת
יט וילכדה וישם חזאל פניו לעלות על־ירושלם: ויקח יהואש מלך־
יהודה את כל־הקדשים אשר־הקדישו יהושפט ויהורם ואחזיהו
אבתיו מלכי יהודה ואת־קדשיו ואת כל־הזהב הנמצא באצרות

20 He sent them to Ḥazael, king of Aram, and he withdrew from Jerusalem. As
for the rest of Yoash's history and all his deeds – they are recorded in the book
21 of the History of the Kings of Yehuda. His officials rose up and formed a
conspiracy, and they struck Yoash down in Beit Milo where it leads down to
22 Sila; Yozakhar son of Shimat and Yehozavad son of Shomer were the officials
who struck him down and killed him. They buried him with his ancestors in
13 1 the City of David, and his son Amatzya reigned in his place. In the
twenty-third year of Yehoash son of Aḥazyahu, king of Yehuda, Yehoaḥaz son
2 of Yehu became king over Israel in Shomron for seventeen years. He did what
was evil in the eyes of the LORD, following after the sins of Yorovam son of
3 Nevat, who led Israel to sin; he did not turn away from them. Then the LORD's
rage flared against Israel, and He handed them over to Ḥazael, king of Aram,
4 and to Ben Hadad, Ḥazael's son, for a long time. But Yehoaḥaz entreated the
LORD, and the LORD heeded him, for He saw Israel's oppression and how the
5 king of Aram oppressed them. So the LORD granted Israel a savior, and they
were freed from the hand of Aram, and the Israelites dwelled in their homes
6 as before. But they did not turn away from the sins of the house of Yorovam,
who had led Israel to sin – they followed them, and the sacred tree[91] still stood
7 in Shomron. Yehoaḥaz was left without an army save fifty riders, ten chariots,
and ten thousand foot soldiers, for the king of Aram had reduced them into
8 dust to be trampled. As for the rest of Yehoaḥaz's history and all his deeds
and heroic feats – they are recorded in the book of the History of the Kings
9 of Israel. And Yehoaḥaz slept with his ancestors, and they buried him in
Shomron. And his son Yoash reigned in his place.
10 In the thirty-seventh year of Yoash, king of Yehuda, Yehoash son of Yehoaḥaz
11 became king over Israel in Shomron for sixteen years. He did what was
evil in the eyes of the LORD; he did not turn away from all the sins of
12 Yorovam son of Nevat, who had led Israel to sin; he perpetuated them. As
for the rest of Yoash's history and all his deeds and heroic feats, and how he
fought with Amatzya, king of Yehuda – they are recorded in the book of
13 the History of the Kings of Israel. And Yoash slept with his ancestors, and
Yorovam ascended his throne. Yoash was buried in Shomron with the kings
14 of Israel. Elisha had fallen ill with the illness of which he was to die,
and Yoash, king of Israel, went down to him. He wept in his presence and
15 said, "Father! Father! The chariots of Israel and its riders!"[92] "Take a bow
and some arrows," Elisha said to him, and he fetched him a bow and some
16 arrows. "Position your hand on the bow," he said to the king of Israel, and he
17 positioned his hand, and Elisha put his hands over the king's hands. "Open
the window that faces east," he said, and he opened it. Then Elisha said,

91 | See I Kings 16:33.
92 | Cf. 2:12.

בֵּית־יהוה וּבֵית הַמֶּלֶךְ וַיִּשְׁלַח לַחֲזָאֵל מֶלֶךְ אֲרָם וַיַּעַל מֵעַל יְרוּשָׁלִָם׃
כ וְיֶתֶר דִּבְרֵי יוֹאָשׁ וְכָל־אֲשֶׁר עָשָׂה הֲלוֹא־הֵם כְּתוּבִים עַל־סֵפֶר דִּבְרֵי
כא הַיָּמִים לְמַלְכֵי יְהוּדָה׃ וַיָּקֻמוּ עֲבָדָיו וַיִּקְשְׁרוּ־קָשֶׁר וַיַּכּוּ אֶת־יוֹאָשׁ
כב בֵּית מִלֹּא הַיֹּרֵד סִלָּא׃ וְיוֹזָכָר בֶּן־שִׁמְעָת וִיהוֹזָבָד בֶּן־שֹׁמֵר ׀ עֲבָדָיו
הִכֻּהוּ וַיָּמֹת וַיִּקְבְּרוּ אֹתוֹ עִם־אֲבֹתָיו בְּעִיר דָּוִד וַיִּמְלֹךְ אֲמַצְיָה בְנוֹ
יג א תַּחְתָּיו׃ בִּשְׁנַת עֶשְׂרִים וְשָׁלֹשׁ שָׁנָה לְיוֹאָשׁ בֶּן־
אֲחַזְיָהוּ מֶלֶךְ יְהוּדָה מָלַךְ יְהוֹאָחָז בֶּן־יֵהוּא עַל־יִשְׂרָאֵל בְּשֹׁמְרוֹן
ב שְׁבַע עֶשְׂרֵה שָׁנָה׃ וַיַּעַשׂ הָרַע בְּעֵינֵי יהוה וַיֵּלֶךְ אַחַר חַטֹּאת יָרָבְעָם
ג בֶּן־נְבָט אֲשֶׁר־הֶחֱטִיא אֶת־יִשְׂרָאֵל לֹא־סָר מִמֶּנָּה׃ וַיִּחַר־אַף יהוה
בְּיִשְׂרָאֵל וַיִּתְּנֵם בְּיַד ׀ חֲזָאֵל מֶלֶךְ־אֲרָם וּבְיַד בֶּן־הֲדַד בֶּן־חֲזָאֵל
ד כָּל־הַיָּמִים׃ וַיְחַל יְהוֹאָחָז אֶת־פְּנֵי יהוה וַיִּשְׁמַע אֵלָיו יהוה כִּי רָאָה
ה אֶת־לַחַץ יִשְׂרָאֵל כִּי־לָחַץ אֹתָם מֶלֶךְ אֲרָם׃ וַיִּתֵּן יהוה לְיִשְׂרָאֵל
מוֹשִׁיעַ וַיֵּצְאוּ מִתַּחַת יַד־אֲרָם וַיֵּשְׁבוּ בְנֵי־יִשְׂרָאֵל בְּאָהֳלֵיהֶם כִּתְמוֹל
ו שִׁלְשׁוֹם׃ אַךְ לֹא־סָרוּ מֵחַטֹּאת בֵּית־יָרָבְעָם אֲשֶׁר־הֶחֱטִי אֶת־יִשְׂרָאֵל
ז בָּהּ הָלָךְ וְגַם הָאֲשֵׁרָה עָמְדָה בְּשֹׁמְרוֹן׃ כִּי לֹא הִשְׁאִיר לִיהוֹאָחָז
עָם כִּי אִם־חֲמִשִּׁים פָּרָשִׁים וַעֲשָׂרָה רֶכֶב וַעֲשֶׂרֶת אֲלָפִים רַגְלִי כִּי
ח אִבְּדָם מֶלֶךְ אֲרָם וַיְשִׂמֵם כֶּעָפָר לָדֻשׁ׃ וְיֶתֶר דִּבְרֵי יְהוֹאָחָז וְכָל־אֲשֶׁר
עָשָׂה וּגְבוּרָתוֹ הֲלוֹא־הֵם כְּתוּבִים עַל־סֵפֶר דִּבְרֵי הַיָּמִים לְמַלְכֵי
ט יִשְׂרָאֵל׃ וַיִּשְׁכַּב יְהוֹאָחָז עִם־אֲבֹתָיו וַיִּקְבְּרֻהוּ בְּשֹׁמְרוֹן וַיִּמְלֹךְ יוֹאָשׁ
בְּנוֹ תַּחְתָּיו׃
י בִּשְׁנַת שְׁלֹשִׁים וָשֶׁבַע שָׁנָה לְיוֹאָשׁ מֶלֶךְ יְהוּדָה מָלַךְ יְהוֹאָשׁ בֶּן־
יא יְהוֹאָחָז עַל־יִשְׂרָאֵל בְּשֹׁמְרוֹן שֵׁשׁ עֶשְׂרֵה שָׁנָה׃ וַיַּעֲשֶׂה הָרַע בְּעֵינֵי
יהוה לֹא סָר מִכָּל־חַטֹּאות יָרָבְעָם בֶּן־נְבָט אֲשֶׁר־הֶחֱטִיא אֶת־
יב יִשְׂרָאֵל בָּהּ הָלָךְ׃ וְיֶתֶר דִּבְרֵי יוֹאָשׁ וְכָל־אֲשֶׁר עָשָׂה וּגְבוּרָתוֹ אֲשֶׁר
נִלְחַם עִם אֲמַצְיָה מֶלֶךְ־יְהוּדָה הֲלוֹא־הֵם כְּתוּבִים עַל־סֵפֶר דִּבְרֵי
יג הַיָּמִים לְמַלְכֵי יִשְׂרָאֵל׃ וַיִּשְׁכַּב יוֹאָשׁ עִם־אֲבֹתָיו וְיָרָבְעָם יָשַׁב עַל־
יד כִּסְאוֹ וַיִּקָּבֵר יוֹאָשׁ בְּשֹׁמְרוֹן עִם מַלְכֵי יִשְׂרָאֵל׃ וֶאֱלִישָׁע
חָלָה אֶת־חָלְיוֹ אֲשֶׁר יָמוּת בּוֹ וַיֵּרֶד אֵלָיו יוֹאָשׁ מֶלֶךְ־יִשְׂרָאֵל וַיֵּבְךְּ
טו עַל־פָּנָיו וַיֹּאמַר אָבִי ׀ אָבִי רֶכֶב יִשְׂרָאֵל וּפָרָשָׁיו׃ וַיֹּאמֶר לוֹ אֱלִישָׁע
טז קַח קֶשֶׁת וְחִצִּים וַיִּקַּח אֵלָיו קֶשֶׁת וְחִצִּים׃ וַיֹּאמֶר ׀ לְמֶלֶךְ יִשְׂרָאֵל
הַרְכֵּב יָדְךָ עַל־הַקֶּשֶׁת וַיַּרְכֵּב יָדוֹ וַיָּשֶׂם אֱלִישָׁע יָדָיו עַל־יְדֵי הַמֶּלֶךְ׃
יז וַיֹּאמֶר פְּתַח הַחַלּוֹן קֵדְמָה וַיִּפְתָּח וַיֹּאמֶר אֱלִישָׁע יְרֵה וַיּוֹר וַיֹּאמֶר

"Shoot," and he shot. "An arrow of victory for the Lord; an arrow of victory
18 over Aram," he said. "You will defeat Aram at Afek – completely." He then
added, "Take the arrows," and he took them. "Now, strike the ground!" he
19 said to the king of Israel. He struck three times and stopped – and the
man of God grew furious with him. "Had you struck five or six times, you
would have defeated Aram completely," he said, "but now, you will defeat
20 Aram only three times." And Elisha died, and they buried him.
21 Now Moabite bands would raid the land at the start of every year. Once, as
they were burying someone, they suddenly saw the band, and they flung
the man into Elisha's grave. The moment the man's body touched Elisha's
22 bones, he sprang to life and stood on his feet. Ḥazael, king of Aram, oppressed
23 Israel throughout the days of Yehoaḥaz. But the Lord was gracious and
compassionate toward them; He turned to them for the sake of His covenant
with Avraham, Yitzḥak, and Yaakov, and He was unwilling to destroy them
24 or cast them away from His presence – for now. When Ḥazael, king of Aram,
25 died, and his son Ben Hadad reigned in his place, Yehoash son of Yehoaḥaz
managed to take back the cities from Ben Hadad son of Ḥazael – those that
had been taken from his father Yehoaḥaz in war. Yoash defeated him three
14 1 times and recaptured the cities of Israel. In the second year of
King Yoash son of Yoaḥaz of Israel, Amatzyahu son of Yoash, king of Yehuda,
2 became king. He was twenty-five years old when he became king, and for
twenty-nine years he reigned in Jerusalem. His mother's name was Yehoadan,
3 of Jerusalem. He did what was right in the eyes of the Lord, though not to
4 the extent of his ancestor David; he did all that his father Yoash had done. Yet
the high shrines were not removed; the people still offered sacrifices and
5 incense at the high shrines. Once the kingdom was firmly in his grasp, he
6 executed the officials who had struck down the king his father. But he did not
execute the sons of the assassins, fulfilling what is written in the book of the
teaching of Moshe, as the Lord commanded: "Parents shall not be put
to death for their children, nor shall children be put to death for their
7 parents. A person shall be put to death only for his own sin."[93] He defeated
ten thousand of Edom in the Valley of Salt, and he captured Sela in battle and
8 renamed it Yokte'el, as it has been called ever since. Then Amatzya
sent messengers to Yehoash son of Yehoaḥaz son of Yehu, king of Israel, saying,
9 "Come, let us meet face-to-face." Yehoash, king of Israel, sent a response to
Amatzyahu, king of Yehuda: "The thistle in Lebanon sent to the cedar in
Lebanon, saying, 'Give me your daughter as a wife for my son.' But a wild
10 beast in Lebanon passed by and trampled the thistle. Yes, you defeated
Edom, but you have grown arrogant – revel in your honor and stay at
home. Why should you provoke disaster and fall down together with
11 Yehuda?" But Amatzyahu paid no heed, and Yehoash, king of Israel, marched
up and met Amatzyahu, king of Yehuda, face-to-face in Beit Shemesh of
12 Yehuda. Yehuda was routed before Israel, and every man fled back to his

93 | Deuteronomy 24:16.

חֵץ־תְּשׁוּעָה לַיהוָה וְחֵץ־תְּשׁוּעָה בַּאֲרָם וְהִכִּיתָ אֶת־אֲרָם בַּאֲפֵק
יח עַד־כַּלֵּה: וַיֹּאמֶר קַח הַחִצִּים וַיִּקָּח וַיֹּאמֶר לְמֶלֶךְ־יִשְׂרָאֵל הַךְ־אַרְצָה
יט וַיַּךְ שָׁלֹשׁ־פְּעָמִים וַיַּעֲמֹד: וַיִּקְצֹף עָלָיו אִישׁ הָאֱלֹהִים וַיֹּאמֶר לְהַכּוֹת
חָמֵשׁ אוֹ־שֵׁשׁ פְּעָמִים אָז הִכִּיתָ אֶת־אֲרָם עַד־כַּלֵּה וְעַתָּה שָׁלֹשׁ
כ פְּעָמִים תַּכֶּה אֶת־אֲרָם: וַיָּמָת אֱלִישָׁע וַיִּקְבְּרֻהוּ וּגְדוּדֵי
כא מוֹאָב יָבֹאוּ בָאָרֶץ בָּא שָׁנָה: וַיְהִי הֵם | קֹבְרִים אִישׁ וְהִנֵּה רָאוּ אֶת־
הַגְּדוּד וַיַּשְׁלִיכוּ אֶת־הָאִישׁ בְּקֶבֶר אֱלִישָׁע וַיֵּלֶךְ וַיִּגַּע הָאִישׁ בְּעַצְמוֹת
כב אֱלִישָׁע וַיְחִי וַיָּקָם עַל־רַגְלָיו: וַחֲזָאֵל מֶלֶךְ אֲרָם לָחַץ אֶת־יִשְׂרָאֵל כֹּל
כג יְמֵי יְהוֹאָחָז: וַיָּחָן יְהוָה אֹתָם וַיְרַחֲמֵם וַיִּפֶן אֲלֵיהֶם לְמַעַן בְּרִיתוֹ כז
אֶת־אַבְרָהָם יִצְחָק וְיַעֲקֹב וְלֹא אָבָה הַשְׁחִיתָם וְלֹא־הִשְׁלִיכָם מֵעַל־
כד פָּנָיו עַד־עָתָּה: וַיָּמָת חֲזָאֵל מֶלֶךְ־אֲרָם וַיִּמְלֹךְ בֶּן־הֲדַד בְּנוֹ תַּחְתָּיו:
כה וַיָּשָׁב יְהוֹאָשׁ בֶּן־יְהוֹאָחָז וַיִּקַּח אֶת־הֶעָרִים מִיַּד בֶּן־הֲדַד בֶּן־חֲזָאֵל
אֲשֶׁר לָקַח מִיַּד יְהוֹאָחָז אָבִיו בַּמִּלְחָמָה שָׁלֹשׁ פְּעָמִים הִכָּהוּ יוֹאָשׁ
יד א וַיָּשֶׁב אֶת־עָרֵי יִשְׂרָאֵל: בִּשְׁנַת שְׁתַּיִם לְיוֹאָשׁ בֶּן־יוֹאָחָז
ב מֶלֶךְ יִשְׂרָאֵל מָלַךְ אֲמַצְיָהוּ בֶן־יוֹאָשׁ מֶלֶךְ יְהוּדָה: בֶּן־עֶשְׂרִים וְחָמֵשׁ
שָׁנָה הָיָה בְמָלְכוֹ וְעֶשְׂרִים וָתֵשַׁע שָׁנָה מָלַךְ בִּירוּשָׁלָ‍ִם וְשֵׁם אִמּוֹ
ג יהועדין מִן־יְרוּשָׁלָ‍ִם: וַיַּעַשׂ הַיָּשָׁר בְּעֵינֵי יְהוָה רַק לֹא כְּדָוִד אָבִיו יְהוֹעַדָּן
ד כְּכֹל אֲשֶׁר־עָשָׂה יוֹאָשׁ אָבִיו עָשָׂה: רַק הַבָּמוֹת לֹא־סָרוּ עוֹד הָעָם
ה מְזַבְּחִים וּמְקַטְּרִים בַּבָּמוֹת: וַיְהִי כַּאֲשֶׁר חָזְקָה הַמַּמְלָכָה בְּיָדוֹ וַיַּךְ
ו אֶת־עֲבָדָיו הַמַּכִּים אֶת־הַמֶּלֶךְ אָבִיו: וְאֶת־בְּנֵי הַמַּכִּים לֹא הֵמִית
כַּכָּתוּב בְּסֵפֶר תּוֹרַת־מֹשֶׁה אֲשֶׁר־צִוָּה יְהוָה לֵאמֹר לֹא־יוּמְתוּ אָבוֹת
עַל־בָּנִים וּבָנִים לֹא־יוּמְתוּ עַל־אָבוֹת כִּי אִם־אִישׁ בְּחֶטְאוֹ ימות: יוּמָת
ז הוּא־הִכָּה אֶת־אֱדוֹם בְּגֵיא־המלח עֲשֶׂרֶת אֲלָפִים וְתָפַשׂ אֶת־הַסֶּלַע מֶלַח
ח בַמִּלְחָמָה וַיִּקְרָא אֶת־שְׁמָהּ יָקְתְאֵל עַד הַיּוֹם הַזֶּה: אָז
שָׁלַח אֲמַצְיָה מַלְאָכִים אֶל־יְהוֹאָשׁ בֶּן־יְהוֹאָחָז בֶּן־יֵהוּא מֶלֶךְ יִשְׂרָאֵל
ט לֵאמֹר לְכָה נִתְרָאֶה פָנִים: וַיִּשְׁלַח יְהוֹאָשׁ מֶלֶךְ־יִשְׂרָאֵל אֶל־אֲמַצְיָהוּ
מֶלֶךְ־יְהוּדָה לֵאמֹר הַחוֹחַ אֲשֶׁר בַּלְּבָנוֹן שָׁלַח אֶל־הָאֶרֶז אֲשֶׁר בַּלְּבָנוֹן
לֵאמֹר תְּנָה־אֶת־בִּתְּךָ לִבְנִי לְאִשָּׁה וַתַּעֲבֹר חַיַּת הַשָּׂדֶה אֲשֶׁר בַּלְּבָנוֹן
י וַתִּרְמֹס אֶת־הַחוֹחַ: הַכֵּה הִכִּיתָ אֶת־אֱדוֹם וּנְשָׂאֲךָ לִבֶּךָ הִכָּבֵד וְשֵׁב
יא בְּבֵיתֶךָ וְלָמָּה תִתְגָּרֶה בְּרָעָה וְנָפַלְתָּה אַתָּה וִיהוּדָה עִמָּךְ: וְלֹא־
שָׁמַע אֲמַצְיָהוּ וַיַּעַל יְהוֹאָשׁ מֶלֶךְ־יִשְׂרָאֵל וַיִּתְרָאוּ פָנִים הוּא וַאֲמַצְיָהוּ
יב מֶלֶךְ־יְהוּדָה בְּבֵית שֶׁמֶשׁ אֲשֶׁר לִיהוּדָה: וַיִּנָּגֶף יְהוּדָה לִפְנֵי יִשְׂרָאֵל

13 tent. As for Amatzyahu, king of Yehuda, the son of Yehoash, the son of
Aḥazyahu – Yehoash, king of Israel, captured him in Beit Shemesh and then
marched on Jerusalem. He broke down the wall of Jerusalem from the
14 Efrayim Gate up to the Corner Gate, a distance of four hundred cubits. He
seized all the gold and silver and all the vessels that were in the House of the
Lord and the royal treasuries of the palace, along with hostages, and he
15 returned to Shomron. As for the rest of Yehoash's history, his deeds and his
heroic feats and how he fought with Amatzyahu, king of Yehuda – they are
16 recorded in the book of the History of the Kings of Israel. And Yehoash slept
with his ancestors and was buried in Shomron with the kings of Israel. And
17 his son Yorovam reigned in his place. Amatzyahu son of Yoash, king
of Yehuda, lived for fifteen years after the death of Yehoash son of Yehoaḥaz,
18 king of Israel. As for the rest of Amatzyahu's history – it is recorded in the
19 book of the History of the Kings of Yehuda. They formed a conspiracy against
him in Jerusalem, and he fled to Lakhish, but they sent after him to Lakhish
20 and assassinated him there. They conveyed his body back by horse, and he
21 was buried with his ancestors in Jerusalem, in the City of David. Then all the
people of Yehuda took Azarya, who was sixteen years old, and made him king
22 in place of his father Amatzyahu. He was the one who rebuilt Eilat and
23 restored it to Yehuda once the king slept with his ancestors. In
the fifteenth year of Amatzyahu son of Yoash, king of Yehuda, Yorovam son
24 of Yoash, king of Israel, became king in Shomron for forty-one years. He did
what was evil in the eyes of the Lord; he did not turn away from all the sins
25 of Yorovam son of Nevat, who led Israel to sin. He was the one who restored
Israel's border from Levo Ḥamat to the Arava Sea, fulfilling the word of the
Lord, God of Israel, as He had promised through His servant Yona son of
26 Amitai, the prophet from Gat Ḥefer. For the Lord had seen the depth of
Israel's bitter suffering, with neither bond nor free left and no helper for Israel.
27 But the Lord had not decreed to blot out Israel's name from under the
28 heavens, so He delivered them through Yorovam son of Yoash. As for the rest
of Yorovam's history and all his deeds and heroic feats in battle, and how he
restored Damascus and Ḥamat to Yehuda in Israel – they are recorded in the
29 book of the History of the Kings of Israel. And Yorovam slept with his
ancestors, with the kings of Israel, and his son Zekharya reigned in his
15 1 place. In the twenty-seventh year of Yorovam, king of Israel,
2 Azarya[94] son of Amatzya, king of Yehuda, became king. He was sixteen years
old when he became king, and for fifty-two years he reigned in Jerusalem.
3 His mother's name was Yekholyahu, of Jerusalem. He did what was right in
4 the eyes of the Lord, just as his father Amatzyahu had done. Yet the high
shrines were not removed; the people still offered sacrifices and incense at

94 | Also referred to as Uziya; see, e.g., verses 13, 30, 32, 34.

יג וַיָּנֻסוּ אִישׁ לְאֹהָלָו: וְאֵת אֲמַצְיָהוּ מֶלֶךְ־יְהוּדָה בֶּן־יְהוֹאָשׁ בֶּן־אֲחַזְיָהוּ
תָּפַשׂ יְהוֹאָשׁ מֶלֶךְ־יִשְׂרָאֵל בְּבֵית שָׁמֶשׁ וַיָּבֹאוּ יְרוּשָׁלַם וַיִּפְרֹץ ויבא
בְּחוֹמַת יְרוּשָׁלַם בְּשַׁעַר אֶפְרַיִם עַד־שַׁעַר הַפִּנָּה אַרְבַּע מֵאוֹת אַמָּה:
יד וְלָקַח אֶת־כָּל־הַזָּהָב וְהַכֶּסֶף וְאֵת כָּל־הַכֵּלִים הַנִּמְצְאִים בֵּית־יְהוָה
טו וּבְאֹצְרוֹת בֵּית הַמֶּלֶךְ וְאֵת בְּנֵי הַתַּעֲרֻבוֹת וַיָּשָׁב שֹׁמְרוֹנָה: וְיֶתֶר
דִּבְרֵי יְהוֹאָשׁ אֲשֶׁר עָשָׂה וּגְבוּרָתוֹ וַאֲשֶׁר נִלְחַם עִם אֲמַצְיָהוּ מֶלֶךְ־
יְהוּדָה הֲלֹא־הֵם כְּתוּבִים עַל־סֵפֶר דִּבְרֵי הַיָּמִים לְמַלְכֵי יִשְׂרָאֵל:
טז וַיִּשְׁכַּב יְהוֹאָשׁ עִם־אֲבֹתָיו וַיִּקָּבֵר בְּשֹׁמְרוֹן עִם מַלְכֵי יִשְׂרָאֵל וַיִּמְלֹךְ
יז יָרָבְעָם בְּנוֹ תַּחְתָּיו: וַיְחִי אֲמַצְיָהוּ בֶן־יוֹאָשׁ מֶלֶךְ יְהוּדָה
יח אַחֲרֵי מוֹת יְהוֹאָשׁ בֶּן־יְהוֹאָחָז מֶלֶךְ יִשְׂרָאֵל חֲמֵשׁ עֶשְׂרֵה שָׁנָה: וְיֶתֶר
דִּבְרֵי אֲמַצְיָהוּ הֲלֹא־הֵם כְּתֻבִים עַל־סֵפֶר דִּבְרֵי הַיָּמִים לְמַלְכֵי יְהוּדָה:
יט וַיִּקְשְׁרוּ עָלָיו קֶשֶׁר בִּירוּשָׁלַם וַיָּנָס לָכִישָׁה וַיִּשְׁלְחוּ אַחֲרָיו לָכִישָׁה
כ וַיְמִתֻהוּ שָׁם: וַיִּשְׂאוּ אֹתוֹ עַל־הַסּוּסִים וַיִּקָּבֵר בִּירוּשָׁלַם עִם־אֲבֹתָיו
כא בְּעִיר דָּוִד: וַיִּקְחוּ כָּל־עַם יְהוּדָה אֶת־עֲזַרְיָה וְהוּא בֶּן־שֵׁשׁ עֶשְׂרֵה
כב שָׁנָה וַיַּמְלִכוּ אֹתוֹ תַּחַת אָבִיו אֲמַצְיָהוּ: הוּא בָּנָה אֶת־אֵילַת וַיְשִׁבֶהָ
כג לִיהוּדָה אַחֲרֵי שְׁכַב־הַמֶּלֶךְ עִם־אֲבֹתָיו: בִּשְׁנַת חֲמֵשׁ־
עֶשְׂרֵה שָׁנָה לַאֲמַצְיָהוּ בֶן־יוֹאָשׁ מֶלֶךְ יְהוּדָה מָלַךְ יָרָבְעָם בֶּן־יוֹאָשׁ
כד מֶלֶךְ־יִשְׂרָאֵל בְּשֹׁמְרוֹן אַרְבָּעִים וְאַחַת שָׁנָה: וַיַּעַשׂ הָרַע בְּעֵינֵי יְהוָה
לֹא סָר מִכָּל־חַטֹּאות יָרָבְעָם בֶּן־נְבָט אֲשֶׁר הֶחֱטִיא אֶת־יִשְׂרָאֵל:
כה הוּא הֵשִׁיב אֶת־גְּבוּל יִשְׂרָאֵל מִלְּבוֹא חֲמָת עַד־יָם הָעֲרָבָה כִּדְבַר
יְהוָה אֱלֹהֵי יִשְׂרָאֵל אֲשֶׁר דִּבֶּר בְּיַד־עַבְדּוֹ יוֹנָה בֶן־אֲמִתַּי הַנָּבִיא אֲשֶׁר
כו מִגַּת הַחֵפֶר: כִּי־רָאָה יְהוָה אֶת־עֳנִי יִשְׂרָאֵל מֹרֶה מְאֹד וְאֶפֶס עָצוּר
כז וְאֶפֶס עָזוּב וְאֵין עֹזֵר לְיִשְׂרָאֵל: וְלֹא־דִבֶּר יְהוָה לִמְחוֹת אֶת־שֵׁם
כח יִשְׂרָאֵל מִתַּחַת הַשָּׁמָיִם וַיּוֹשִׁיעֵם בְּיַד יָרָבְעָם בֶּן־יוֹאָשׁ: וְיֶתֶר דִּבְרֵי
יָרָבְעָם וְכָל־אֲשֶׁר עָשָׂה וּגְבוּרָתוֹ אֲשֶׁר־נִלְחַם וַאֲשֶׁר הֵשִׁיב אֶת־
דַּמֶּשֶׂק וְאֶת־חֲמָת לִיהוּדָה בְּיִשְׂרָאֵל הֲלֹא־הֵם כְּתוּבִים עַל־סֵפֶר
כט דִּבְרֵי הַיָּמִים לְמַלְכֵי יִשְׂרָאֵל: וַיִּשְׁכַּב יָרָבְעָם עִם־אֲבֹתָיו עִם מַלְכֵי
טו א יִשְׂרָאֵל וַיִּמְלֹךְ זְכַרְיָה בְנוֹ תַּחְתָּיו: בִּשְׁנַת עֶשְׂרִים
וָשֶׁבַע שָׁנָה לְיָרָבְעָם מֶלֶךְ יִשְׂרָאֵל מָלַךְ עֲזַרְיָה בֶן־אֲמַצְיָה מֶלֶךְ
ב יְהוּדָה: בֶּן־שֵׁשׁ עֶשְׂרֵה שָׁנָה הָיָה בְמָלְכוֹ וַחֲמִשִּׁים וּשְׁתַּיִם שָׁנָה מָלַךְ
ג בִּירוּשָׁלָם וְשֵׁם אִמּוֹ יְכָלְיָהוּ מִירוּשָׁלָם: וַיַּעַשׂ הַיָּשָׁר בְּעֵינֵי יְהוָה כְּכֹל
ד אֲשֶׁר־עָשָׂה אֲמַצְיָהוּ אָבִיו: רַק הַבָּמוֹת לֹא־סָרוּ עוֹד הָעָם מְזַבְּחִים

5 the high shrines. The LORD struck the king with disease, and he became a
leper until his dying day. He remained in secluded quarters while Yotam,
the king's son, took charge of the palace and governed the people of the land.
6 As for the rest of Azaryahu's history and all his deeds – they are recorded in
7 the book of the History of the Kings of Yehuda. And Azarya slept with his
ancestors, and they buried him with his ancestors in the City of David.
8 And his son Yotam reigned in his place. In the thirty-eighth year of
Azaryahu, king of Yehuda, Zekharyahu son of Yorovam became king over
9 Israel in Shomron for six months. He did what was evil in the eyes of the LORD,
as his ancestors did; he did not turn away from the sins of Yorovam son of
10 Nevat, who led Israel to sin. Then Shalum son of Yavesh formed a conspiracy
against him; he struck him down before the people and assassinated him and
11 reigned in his place. As for the rest of Zekharya's history – it is recorded in
12 the book of the History of the Kings of Israel. This was the word of the LORD
as promised to Yehu: "Four generations of your line will sit on the throne of
13 Israel,"[95] and it had come to pass. Shalum son of Yavesh became king
in the thirty-ninth year of Uziya,[96] king of Yehuda, and for one month, he
14 reigned in Shomron. Then Menaḥem son of Gadi marched up from Tirtza
and entered Shomron. He struck down Shalum son of Yavesh in Shomron
15 and assassinated him, and he reigned in his place. As for the rest of Shalum's
history and the conspiracy that he formed – they are recorded in the book of
16 the History of the Kings of Israel. It was then that Menaḥem attacked Tifsaḥ
and everything in it and its territories from Tirtza; they would not yield, so
17 he attacked – he even slashed open its pregnant women. In the
thirty-ninth year of Azarya, king of Yehuda, Menaḥem son of Gadi became
18 king over Israel, for ten years in Shomron. He did what was evil in the eyes
of the LORD; all his days, he did not turn away from the sins of Yorovam son
19 of Nevat. When Pul,[97] king of Assyria, invaded the land, Menaḥem gave Pul
one thousand talents of silver to gain his support in maintaining control of
20 the kingdom. Menaḥem exacted the silver from Israel; every able man had
to pay fifty shekel of silver to the king of Assyria. Then the king of Assyria
21 withdrew and did not remain there in the land. As for the rest of Menaḥem's
history and all his deeds – they are recorded in the book of the History of the
22 Kings of Israel. And Menaḥem slept with his ancestors, and his son Pekaḥya
23 reigned in his place. In the fiftieth year of Azarya, king of Yehuda,
Pekaḥya son of Menaḥem became king over Israel in Shomron for two years.
24 He did what was evil in the eyes of the LORD; he did not turn away from the
25 sins of Yorovam son of Nevat, who led Israel to sin. Then Pekaḥ son of
Remalyahu, his adjutant, formed a conspiracy against him; he struck him
down in the citadel of the royal palace in Shomron. With him were Argov and
Aryeh[98] and fifty men of the Gileadites; they assassinated him, and he reigned

95 | See 10:30.
96 | See note on verse 1.
97 | A nickname of the Assyrian king Tiglat Pileser III.
98 | Perhaps names of warriors or military units.

ה וּמְקַטְּרִים בַּבָּמוֹת: וַיְנַגַּע יְהוָה אֶת־הַמֶּלֶךְ וַיְהִי מְצֹרָע עַד־יוֹם מֹתוֹ
וַיֵּשֶׁב בְּבֵית הַחָפְשִׁית וְיוֹתָם בֶּן־הַמֶּלֶךְ עַל־הַבַּיִת שֹׁפֵט אֶת־עַם
ו הָאָרֶץ: וְיֶתֶר דִּבְרֵי עֲזַרְיָהוּ וְכָל־אֲשֶׁר עָשָׂה הֲלֹא־הֵם כְּתוּבִים עַל־
ז סֵפֶר דִּבְרֵי הַיָּמִים לְמַלְכֵי יְהוּדָה: וַיִּשְׁכַּב עֲזַרְיָה עִם־אֲבֹתָיו וַיִּקְבְּרוּ כח
ח אֹתוֹ עִם־אֲבֹתָיו בְּעִיר דָּוִד וַיִּמְלֹךְ יוֹתָם בְּנוֹ תַּחְתָּיו: בִּשְׁנַת
שְׁלֹשִׁים וּשְׁמֹנֶה שָׁנָה לַעֲזַרְיָהוּ מֶלֶךְ יְהוּדָה מָלַךְ זְכַרְיָהוּ בֶן־יָרָבְעָם
ט עַל־יִשְׂרָאֵל בְּשֹׁמְרוֹן שִׁשָּׁה חֳדָשִׁים: וַיַּעַשׂ הָרַע בְּעֵינֵי יְהוָה כַּאֲשֶׁר
עָשׂוּ אֲבֹתָיו לֹא סָר מֵחַטֹּאות יָרָבְעָם בֶּן־נְבָט אֲשֶׁר הֶחֱטִיא אֶת־
י יִשְׂרָאֵל: וַיִּקְשֹׁר עָלָיו שַׁלֻּם בֶּן־יָבֵשׁ וַיַּכֵּהוּ קָבָל־עָם וַיְמִיתֵהוּ וַיִּמְלֹךְ
יא תַּחְתָּיו: וְיֶתֶר דִּבְרֵי זְכַרְיָה הִנָּם כְּתוּבִים עַל־סֵפֶר דִּבְרֵי הַיָּמִים לְמַלְכֵי
יב יִשְׂרָאֵל: הוּא דְבַר־יְהוָה אֲשֶׁר דִּבֶּר אֶל־יֵהוּא לֵאמֹר בְּנֵי רְבִיעִים
יג יֵשְׁבוּ לְךָ עַל־כִּסֵּא יִשְׂרָאֵל וַיְהִי־כֵן: שַׁלּוּם בֶּן־יָבֵישׁ מָלַךְ
בִּשְׁנַת שְׁלֹשִׁים וָתֵשַׁע שָׁנָה לְעֻזִּיָּה מֶלֶךְ יְהוּדָה וַיִּמְלֹךְ יֶרַח־יָמִים
יד בְּשֹׁמְרוֹן: וַיַּעַל מְנַחֵם בֶּן־גָּדִי מִתִּרְצָה וַיָּבֹא שֹׁמְרוֹן וַיַּךְ אֶת־שַׁלּוּם
טו בֶּן־יָבֵישׁ בְּשֹׁמְרוֹן וַיְמִיתֵהוּ וַיִּמְלֹךְ תַּחְתָּיו: וְיֶתֶר דִּבְרֵי שַׁלּוּם וְקִשְׁרוֹ
טז אֲשֶׁר קָשָׁר הִנָּם כְּתֻבִים עַל־סֵפֶר דִּבְרֵי הַיָּמִים לְמַלְכֵי יִשְׂרָאֵל: אָז
יַכֶּה־מְנַחֵם אֶת־תִּפְסַח וְאֶת־כָּל־אֲשֶׁר־בָּהּ וְאֶת־גְּבוּלֶיהָ מִתִּרְצָה כִּי
יז לֹא פָתַח וַיַּךְ אֵת כָּל־הֶהָרוֹתֶיהָ בִּקֵּעַ: בִּשְׁנַת שְׁלֹשִׁים
וָתֵשַׁע שָׁנָה לַעֲזַרְיָה מֶלֶךְ יְהוּדָה מָלַךְ מְנַחֵם בֶּן־גָּדִי עַל־יִשְׂרָאֵל
יח עֶשֶׂר שָׁנִים בְּשֹׁמְרוֹן: וַיַּעַשׂ הָרַע בְּעֵינֵי יְהוָה לֹא־סָר מֵעַל חַטֹּאות
יט יָרָבְעָם בֶּן־נְבָט אֲשֶׁר־הֶחֱטִיא אֶת־יִשְׂרָאֵל כָּל־יָמָיו: בָּא פוּל מֶלֶךְ־
אַשּׁוּר עַל־הָאָרֶץ וַיִּתֵּן מְנַחֵם לְפוּל אֶלֶף כִּכַּר־כָּסֶף לִהְיוֹת יָדָיו אִתּוֹ
כ לְהַחֲזִיק הַמַּמְלָכָה בְּיָדוֹ: וַיֹּצֵא מְנַחֵם אֶת־הַכֶּסֶף עַל־יִשְׂרָאֵל עַל
כָּל־גִּבּוֹרֵי הַחַיִל לָתֵת לְמֶלֶךְ אַשּׁוּר חֲמִשִּׁים שְׁקָלִים כֶּסֶף לְאִישׁ אֶחָד
כא וַיָּשָׁב מֶלֶךְ אַשּׁוּר וְלֹא־עָמַד שָׁם בָּאָרֶץ: וְיֶתֶר דִּבְרֵי מְנַחֵם וְכָל־אֲשֶׁר
עָשָׂה הֲלוֹא־הֵם כְּתוּבִים עַל־סֵפֶר דִּבְרֵי הַיָּמִים לְמַלְכֵי יִשְׂרָאֵל:
כב כג וַיִּשְׁכַּב מְנַחֵם עִם־אֲבֹתָיו וַיִּמְלֹךְ פְּקַחְיָה בְנוֹ תַּחְתָּיו: בִּשְׁנַת
חֲמִשִּׁים שָׁנָה לַעֲזַרְיָה מֶלֶךְ יְהוּדָה מָלַךְ פְּקַחְיָה בֶן־מְנַחֵם עַל־יִשְׂרָאֵל
כד בְּשֹׁמְרוֹן שְׁנָתָיִם: וַיַּעַשׂ הָרַע בְּעֵינֵי יְהוָה לֹא סָר מֵחַטֹּאות יָרָבְעָם
כה בֶּן־נְבָט אֲשֶׁר הֶחֱטִיא אֶת־יִשְׂרָאֵל: וַיִּקְשֹׁר עָלָיו פֶּקַח בֶּן־רְמַלְיָהוּ
שָׁלִישׁוֹ וַיַּכֵּהוּ בְשֹׁמְרוֹן בְּאַרְמוֹן בֵּית־מֶלֶךְ אֶת־אַרְגֹּב וְאֶת־הָאַרְיֵה הַמֶּלֶךְ

26 in his place. As for the rest of Pekaḥyahu's history and all his deeds – they are
27 recorded in the book of the History of the Kings of Israel. In the
fifty-second year of Azarya, king of Yehuda, Pekaḥ son of Remalyahu became
28 king over Israel in Shomron for twenty years. He did what was evil in the eyes
of the LORD; he did not turn away from the sins of Yorovam son of Nevat,
29 who led Israel to sin. In the days of Pekaḥ, king of Israel, Tiglat Pileser, king
of Assyria, came and seized Iyon, Avel Beit Maakha, Yanoaḥ, Kedesh, Ḥazor,
the Gilad, the Galil, and all the region of Naftali, and had them exiled to
30 Assyria. Then Hoshe'a son of Ela formed a conspiracy against Pekaḥ son of
Remalyahu; they struck him down and assassinated him, and he reigned in
31 his place in the twentieth year of Yotam son of Uziya. As for the rest of Pekaḥ's
history and all his deeds – they are recorded in the book of the History of the
32 Kings of Israel. In the second year of Pekaḥ son of Remalyahu, king
33 of Israel, Yotam son of Uziyahu, king of Yehuda, became king. He was twenty-
five years old when he became king, and for sixteen years he reigned in
34 Jerusalem. His mother's name was Yerusha daughter of Tzadok. He did what
35 was right in the eyes of the LORD, just as his father Uziyahu had done. Yet the
high shrines were not removed; the people still offered sacrifices and incense
36 at the high shrines. He built the upper gate of the House of the LORD. As for
the rest of Yotam's history and all his deeds – they are recorded in the book
37 of the History of the Kings of Yehuda. At that time the LORD began to rouse
38 Retzin, king of Aram, and Pekaḥ son of Remalyahu against Yehuda. And
Yotam slept with his ancestors and was buried with his ancestors in the City
16 1 of David, his ancestor. And his son Aḥaz reigned in his place. In the
seventeenth year of Pekaḥ son of Remalyahu, Aḥaz son of Yotam, king of
2 Yehuda, became king. Aḥaz was twenty years old when he became king, and
for sixteen years he reigned in Jerusalem. But he did not do what was right in
3 the eyes of the LORD his God, like his ancestor David; he followed in the
ways of the kings of Israel and even passed his son through the fire, imitating
the horrors of the nations whom the LORD had dispossessed before the
4 Israelites. He offered sacrifices and incense at the high shrines and on hilltops
5 and under every shady tree. It was then that Retzin, king of Aram, and Pekaḥ
son of Remalyahu, king of Israel, launched an attack on Jerusalem. They
6 besieged Aḥaz, but they could not conquer him. At that time, Retzin, king of
Aram, restored Eilat to Aram, and he drove out the Judahites from Eilat;
7 Edomites came to Eilat and have dwelled there ever since. Then Aḥaz sent
messengers to Tiglat Pileser, king of Assyria, saying, "I am your servant and
your son; come up and rescue me from the hand of the king of Aram and the
8 hand of the king of Israel, who threaten me." And Aḥaz took the silver and
gold that was in the House of the LORD and the royal treasuries of the palace,

כו וְעִמּוֹ חֲמִשִּׁים אִישׁ מִבְּנֵי גִלְעָדִים וַיְמִתֵהוּ וַיִּמְלֹךְ תַּחְתָּיו: וְיֶתֶר דִּבְרֵי
פְקַחְיָה וְכָל־אֲשֶׁר עָשָׂה הִנָּם כְּתוּבִים עַל־סֵפֶר דִּבְרֵי הַיָּמִים לְמַלְכֵי
כז יִשְׂרָאֵל: בִּשְׁנַת חֲמִשִּׁים וּשְׁתַּיִם שָׁנָה לַעֲזַרְיָה מֶלֶךְ
יְהוּדָה מָלַךְ פֶּקַח בֶּן־רְמַלְיָהוּ עַל־יִשְׂרָאֵל בְּשֹׁמְרוֹן עֶשְׂרִים שָׁנָה:
כח וַיַּעַשׂ הָרַע בְּעֵינֵי יְהוָה לֹא סָר מִן־חַטֹּאות יָרָבְעָם בֶּן־נְבָט אֲשֶׁר
כט הֶחֱטִיא אֶת־יִשְׂרָאֵל: בִּימֵי פֶּקַח מֶלֶךְ־יִשְׂרָאֵל בָּא תִּגְלַת פִּלְאֶסֶר
מֶלֶךְ אַשּׁוּר וַיִּקַּח אֶת־עִיּוֹן וְאֶת־אָבֵל בֵּית־מַעֲכָה וְאֶת־יָנוֹחַ וְאֶת־
קֶדֶשׁ וְאֶת־חָצוֹר וְאֶת־הַגִּלְעָד וְאֶת־הַגָּלִילָה כֹּל אֶרֶץ נַפְתָּלִי וַיַּגְלֵם
ל אַשּׁוּרָה: וַיִּקְשָׁר־קֶשֶׁר הוֹשֵׁעַ בֶּן־אֵלָה עַל־פֶּקַח בֶּן־רְמַלְיָהוּ וַיַּכֵּהוּ
לא וַיְמִיתֵהוּ וַיִּמְלֹךְ תַּחְתָּיו בִּשְׁנַת עֶשְׂרִים לְיוֹתָם בֶּן־עֻזִּיָּה: וְיֶתֶר דִּבְרֵי־
פֶקַח וְכָל־אֲשֶׁר עָשָׂה הִנָּם כְּתוּבִים עַל־סֵפֶר דִּבְרֵי הַיָּמִים לְמַלְכֵי
לב יִשְׂרָאֵל: בִּשְׁנַת שְׁתַּיִם לְפֶקַח בֶּן־רְמַלְיָהוּ מֶלֶךְ יִשְׂרָאֵל
לג מָלַךְ יוֹתָם בֶּן־עֻזִּיָּהוּ מֶלֶךְ יְהוּדָה: בֶּן־עֶשְׂרִים וְחָמֵשׁ שָׁנָה הָיָה בְמָלְכוֹ
וְשֵׁשׁ־עֶשְׂרֵה שָׁנָה מָלַךְ בִּירוּשָׁלִָם וְשֵׁם אִמּוֹ יְרוּשָׁא בַּת־צָדוֹק:
לד לה וַיַּעַשׂ הַיָּשָׁר בְּעֵינֵי יְהוָה כְּכֹל אֲשֶׁר־עָשָׂה עֻזִּיָּהוּ אָבִיו עָשָׂה: רַק
הַבָּמוֹת לֹא סָרוּ עוֹד הָעָם מְזַבְּחִים וּמְקַטְּרִים בַּבָּמוֹת הוּא בָּנָה אֶת־
לו שַׁעַר בֵּית־יְהוָה הָעֶלְיוֹן: וְיֶתֶר דִּבְרֵי יוֹתָם וְכָל־אֲשֶׁר עָשָׂה הֲלֹא־הֵם
לז כְּתוּבִים עַל־סֵפֶר דִּבְרֵי הַיָּמִים לְמַלְכֵי יְהוּדָה: בַּיָּמִים הָהֵם הֵחֵל
לח יְהוָה לְהַשְׁלִיחַ בִּיהוּדָה רְצִין מֶלֶךְ אֲרָם וְאֵת פֶּקַח בֶּן־רְמַלְיָהוּ: וַיִּשְׁכַּב
יוֹתָם עִם־אֲבֹתָיו וַיִּקָּבֵר עִם־אֲבֹתָיו בְּעִיר דָּוִד אָבִיו וַיִּמְלֹךְ אָחָז בְּנוֹ
טז א תַּחְתָּיו: בִּשְׁנַת שְׁבַע־עֶשְׂרֵה שָׁנָה לְפֶקַח בֶּן־רְמַלְיָהוּ מָלַךְ
ב אָחָז בֶּן־יוֹתָם מֶלֶךְ יְהוּדָה: בֶּן־עֶשְׂרִים שָׁנָה אָחָז בְּמָלְכוֹ וְשֵׁשׁ־עֶשְׂרֵה
שָׁנָה מָלַךְ בִּירוּשָׁלִָם וְלֹא־עָשָׂה הַיָּשָׁר בְּעֵינֵי יְהוָה אֱלֹהָיו כְּדָוִד אָבִיו:
ג וַיֵּלֶךְ בְּדֶרֶךְ מַלְכֵי יִשְׂרָאֵל וְגַם אֶת־בְּנוֹ הֶעֱבִיר בָּאֵשׁ כְּתֹעֲבוֹת הַגּוֹיִם
ד אֲשֶׁר הוֹרִישׁ יְהוָה אֹתָם מִפְּנֵי בְּנֵי יִשְׂרָאֵל: וַיְזַבֵּחַ וַיְקַטֵּר בַּבָּמוֹת
ה וְעַל־הַגְּבָעוֹת וְתַחַת כָּל־עֵץ רַעֲנָן: אָז יַעֲלֶה רְצִין מֶלֶךְ־אֲרָם וּפֶקַח
בֶּן־רְמַלְיָהוּ מֶלֶךְ־יִשְׂרָאֵל יְרוּשָׁלִַם לַמִּלְחָמָה וַיָּצֻרוּ עַל־אָחָז וְלֹא יָכְלוּ
ו לְהִלָּחֵם: בָּעֵת הַהִיא הֵשִׁיב רְצִין מֶלֶךְ־אֲרָם אֶת־אֵילַת לַאֲרָם וַיְנַשֵּׁל
אֶת־הַיְהוּדִים מֵאֵילוֹת וארומים בָּאוּ אֵילַת וַיֵּשְׁבוּ שָׁם עַד הַיּוֹם הַזֶּה: וַאֲדוֹמִים
ז וַיִּשְׁלַח אָחָז מַלְאָכִים אֶל־תִּגְלַת פְּלֶסֶר מֶלֶךְ־אַשּׁוּר לֵאמֹר עַבְדְּךָ
וּבִנְךָ אָנִי עֲלֵה וְהוֹשִׁעֵנִי מִכַּף מֶלֶךְ־אֲרָם וּמִכַּף מֶלֶךְ יִשְׂרָאֵל הַקּוֹמִים
ח עָלָי: וַיִּקַּח אָחָז אֶת־הַכֶּסֶף וְאֶת־הַזָּהָב הַנִּמְצָא בֵּית יְהוָה וּבְאֹצְרוֹת

9 and he sent them to the king of Assyria as a bribe. The king of Assyria acceded
to him; the king of Assyria launched an attack on Damascus, captured it, and
10 exiled its people to Kir. As for Retzin – he put him to death. King Aḥaz went
to meet Tiglat Pileser, king of Assyria, in Damascus. When he saw the altar
in Damascus, King Aḥaz sent an image of the altar to Uriya the priest with its
11 design, down to every last detail of its construction. The priest Uriya then
built the altar exactly as King Aḥaz had instructed from Damascus, and the
priest Uriya completed it by the time that King Aḥaz returned from Damascus.
12 When the king arrived from Damascus and saw the altar, he approached the
13 altar and ascended it and offered up his burnt offering and his grain offering,
poured out his libation, and dashed the blood of his peace offering against
14 the altar. As for the bronze altar before the Lord, he moved it from the front
of the House, between the new altar and the House of the Lord, and placed
15 it to the northern side of the new altar. King Aḥaz then instructed the priest
Uriya, "On the great altar, offer the morning burnt offering, the evening grain
offering, the royal burnt offering and grain offering, as well as the burnt
offering of all the people of the land and their grain offerings and libations;
and all blood from the burnt offerings and the blood from any sacrifices
16 should be dashed against it. As for the bronze altar, I have yet to decide." And
17 the priest Uriya did just as King Aḥaz instructed. King Aḥaz then stripped
off the frames of the washstands and removed their lavers, and he took the
Sea down from the bronze oxen that supported it and placed it on a stone
18 pavement. He also altered the Sabbath canopy that they had built in the
House, as well as the king's outer entrance to the House of the Lord – all
19 on account of the king of Assyria. As for the rest of Aḥaz's history and his
deeds – they are recorded in the book of the History of the Kings of Yehuda.
20 And Aḥaz slept with his ancestors and was buried with his ancestors in the
17 1 City of David. And his son Ḥizkiyahu reigned in his place. In the
twelfth year of Aḥaz, king of Yehuda, Hoshe'a son of Ela became king over
2 Israel in Shomron for nine years. He did what was evil in the eyes of the Lord,
3 though not to the extent of the kings of Israel who preceded him. Shalmaneser,
king of Assyria, marched up against him, and Hoshe'a became his vassal and
4 paid him tribute. But when the king of Assyria discovered that Hoshe'a had
betrayed him by sending envoys to So, king of Egypt, and by failing to pay
his annual tribute to the king of Assyria, he had him seized and thrown
5 into prison. Then the king of Assyria marched against the whole land and
6 marched up to Shomron and besieged it for three years. In the ninth year of
Hoshe'a, the king of Assyria captured Shomron. He exiled Israel to Assyria
and settled them in Ḥalaḥ, the Ḥavor, the Gozan River, and the cities of
7 Media. This came to pass because the Israelites had sinned against
the Lord their God – who had brought them out from the land of Egypt and

ט בֵּית הַמֶּלֶךְ וַיִּשְׁלַח לְמֶלֶךְ אַשּׁוּר שֹׁחַד: וַיִּשְׁמַע אֵלָיו מֶלֶךְ אַשּׁוּר וַיַּעַל
י מֶלֶךְ אַשּׁוּר אֶל־דַּמֶּשֶׂק וַיִּתְפְּשֶׂהָ וַיַּגְלֶהָ קִירָה וְאֶת־רְצִין הֵמִית: וַיֵּלֶךְ
הַמֶּלֶךְ אָחָז לִקְרַאת תִּגְלַת פִּלְאֶסֶר מֶלֶךְ־אַשּׁוּר דּוּמֶּשֶׂק וַיַּרְא אֶת־
הַמִּזְבֵּחַ אֲשֶׁר בְּדַמָּשֶׂק וַיִּשְׁלַח הַמֶּלֶךְ אָחָז אֶל־אוּרִיָּה הַכֹּהֵן אֶת־דְּמוּת
יא הַמִּזְבֵּחַ וְאֶת־תַּבְנִיתוֹ לְכָל־מַעֲשֵׂהוּ: וַיִּבֶן אוּרִיָּה הַכֹּהֵן אֶת־הַמִּזְבֵּחַ
כְּכֹל אֲשֶׁר־שָׁלַח הַמֶּלֶךְ אָחָז מִדַּמֶּשֶׂק כֵּן עָשָׂה אוּרִיָּה הַכֹּהֵן עַד־בּוֹא
יב הַמֶּלֶךְ־אָחָז מִדַּמָּשֶׂק: וַיָּבֹא הַמֶּלֶךְ מִדַּמֶּשֶׂק וַיַּרְא הַמֶּלֶךְ אֶת־הַמִּזְבֵּחַ
יג וַיִּקְרַב הַמֶּלֶךְ עַל־הַמִּזְבֵּחַ וַיַּעַל עָלָיו: וַיַּקְטֵר אֶת־עֹלָתוֹ וְאֶת־מִנְחָתוֹ
יד וַיַּסֵּךְ אֶת־נִסְכּוֹ וַיִּזְרֹק אֶת־דַּם־הַשְּׁלָמִים אֲשֶׁר־לוֹ עַל־הַמִּזְבֵּחַ: וְאֵת
הַמִּזְבַּח הַנְּחֹשֶׁת אֲשֶׁר לִפְנֵי יְהוָה וַיַּקְרֵב מֵאֵת פְּנֵי הַבַּיִת מִבֵּין הַמִּזְבֵּחַ
טו וּמִבֵּין בֵּית יְהוָה וַיִּתֵּן אֹתוֹ עַל־יֶרֶךְ הַמִּזְבֵּחַ צָפוֹנָה: ויצוהו הַמֶּלֶךְ וַיְצַוֶּה
אָחָז אֶת־אוּרִיָּה הַכֹּהֵן לֵאמֹר עַל הַמִּזְבֵּחַ הַגָּדוֹל הַקְטֵר אֶת־עֹלַת־
הַבֹּקֶר וְאֶת־מִנְחַת הָעֶרֶב וְאֶת־עֹלַת הַמֶּלֶךְ וְאֶת־מִנְחָתוֹ וְאֵת עֹלַת
כָּל־עַם הָאָרֶץ וּמִנְחָתָם וְנִסְכֵּיהֶם וְכָל־דַּם עֹלָה וְכָל־דַּם־זֶבַח עָלָיו
טז תִּזְרֹק וּמִזְבַּח הַנְּחֹשֶׁת יִהְיֶה־לִּי לְבַקֵּר: וַיַּעַשׂ אוּרִיָּה הַכֹּהֵן כְּכֹל אֲשֶׁר־
יז צִוָּה הַמֶּלֶךְ אָחָז: וַיְקַצֵּץ הַמֶּלֶךְ אָחָז אֶת־הַמִּסְגְּרוֹת הַמְּכֹנוֹת וַיָּסַר
מֵעֲלֵיהֶם ואת־הַכִּיֹּר וְאֶת־הַיָּם הוֹרִד מֵעַל הַבָּקָר הַנְּחֹשֶׁת אֲשֶׁר אֶת־
יח תַּחְתֶּיהָ וַיִּתֵּן אֹתוֹ עַל מַרְצֶפֶת אֲבָנִים: ואת־מיסך הַשַּׁבָּת אֲשֶׁר־בָּנוּ מוּסַךְ
בַבַּיִת וְאֶת־מְבוֹא הַמֶּלֶךְ הַחִיצוֹנָה הֵסֵב בֵּית יְהוָה מִפְּנֵי מֶלֶךְ אַשּׁוּר:
יט וְיֶתֶר דִּבְרֵי אָחָז אֲשֶׁר עָשָׂה הֲלֹא־הֵם כְּתוּבִים עַל־סֵפֶר דִּבְרֵי הַיָּמִים
כ לְמַלְכֵי יְהוּדָה: וַיִּשְׁכַּב אָחָז עִם־אֲבֹתָיו וַיִּקָּבֵר עִם־אֲבֹתָיו בְּעִיר דָּוִד כט
יז א וַיִּמְלֹךְ חִזְקִיָּהוּ בְנוֹ תַּחְתָּיו: בִּשְׁנַת שְׁתֵּים עֶשְׂרֵה לְאָחָז
מֶלֶךְ יְהוּדָה מָלַךְ הוֹשֵׁעַ בֶּן־אֵלָה בְשֹׁמְרוֹן עַל־יִשְׂרָאֵל תֵּשַׁע שָׁנִים:
ב ג וַיַּעַשׂ הָרַע בְּעֵינֵי יְהוָה רַק לֹא כְּמַלְכֵי יִשְׂרָאֵל אֲשֶׁר הָיוּ לְפָנָיו: עָלָיו
עָלָה שַׁלְמַנְאֶסֶר מֶלֶךְ אַשּׁוּר וַיְהִי־לוֹ הוֹשֵׁעַ עֶבֶד וַיָּשֶׁב לוֹ מִנְחָה:
ד וַיִּמְצָא מֶלֶךְ־אַשּׁוּר בְּהוֹשֵׁעַ קֶשֶׁר אֲשֶׁר שָׁלַח מַלְאָכִים אֶל־סוֹא
מֶלֶךְ־מִצְרַיִם וְלֹא־הֶעֱלָה מִנְחָה לְמֶלֶךְ אַשּׁוּר כְּשָׁנָה בְשָׁנָה וַיַּעַצְרֵהוּ
ה מֶלֶךְ אַשּׁוּר וַיַּאַסְרֵהוּ בֵּית כֶּלֶא: וַיַּעַל מֶלֶךְ־אַשּׁוּר בְּכָל־הָאָרֶץ וַיַּעַל
ו שֹׁמְרוֹן וַיָּצַר עָלֶיהָ שָׁלֹשׁ שָׁנִים: בִּשְׁנַת הַתְּשִׁיעִית לְהוֹשֵׁעַ לָכַד מֶלֶךְ־
אַשּׁוּר אֶת־שֹׁמְרוֹן וַיֶּגֶל אֶת־יִשְׂרָאֵל אַשּׁוּרָה וַיֹּשֶׁב אֹתָם בַּחְלַח
ז וּבְחָבוֹר נְהַר גּוֹזָן וְעָרֵי מָדָי: וַיְהִי כִּי־חָטְאוּ בְנֵי־
יִשְׂרָאֵל לַיהוָה אֱלֹהֵיהֶם הַמַּעֲלֶה אֹתָם מֵאֶרֶץ מִצְרַיִם מִתַּחַת יַד

8 the oppression of Pharaoh, king of Egypt – by revering other gods. They
followed the customs of the nations whom the LORD had dispossessed before
9 the Israelites and those that the kings of Israel had practiced. The Israelites
ascribed falsehoods to the LORD their God, and they built themselves high
10 shrines wherever they lived, from watchtower to fortified city. They set up
worship pillars and sacred trees for themselves on every high hill and under
11 every shady tree and made offerings there, at all the shrines, like the nations
whom the LORD had exiled before them. And they did evil things to anger
12 the LORD; they served idols though the LORD had told them, "You must not
13 do this thing." The LORD warned Israel and Yehuda through every prophet
and every seer, declaring: "Turn back from your evil ways and keep My
commandments and laws according to all the teachings that I commanded
your ancestors and that I conveyed to you through My servants the prophets."
14 But they would not listen; they were as stubborn as their ancestors, who did
15 not believe in the LORD their God. They spurned His laws and the covenant
He had made with their ancestors and the warnings He had given them;
they went after futilities until they themselves grew futile, imitating the
nations around them that the LORD had commanded them not to imitate.
16 They abandoned all the commandments of the LORD their God and made
themselves molten images of two calves; they made a sacred tree; they bowed
17 down to all the heavenly hosts; they worshipped the Baal. They passed their
sons and daughters through the fire and cast spells and practiced divination;
they sold themselves to do what was evil in the eyes of the LORD to anger
18 Him. And the LORD raged fiercely against Israel, and He banished them from
19 His presence; the tribe of Yehuda alone remained. Even Yehuda, though,
failed to keep the commandments of the LORD their God, and they followed
20 the customs that Israel had practiced. And the LORD rejected all of Israel's
seed, and He tormented them by handing them over to plunderers until He
21 had cast them away from His presence. For Israel had torn away from the
House of David, and they made Yorovam son of Nevat king. But Yorovam
22 drove Israel away from the LORD and led them to grave sin, and Israel
followed all the sins that Yorovam had committed and would not turn away
23 from them. Finally, the LORD banished Israel from His presence, as He had
promised through all His servants the prophets, and Israel was exiled from
24 its own soil to Assyria to this day. The king of Assyria brought in
people from Babylon, Kuta, Ava, Ḥamat, and Sefarvites, and he settled them
in the towns of Shomron instead of the Israelites. They took possession of
25 Shomron and settled its cities. When they first settled there, they had no
reverence for the LORD, so the LORD sent forth against them lions who killed
26 some of them. They reported to the king of Assyria, "The nations whom you
exiled and settled in the towns of Shomron do not know the customs of the
local God, and He has sent forth lions against them; they are now killing them

ח פַּרְעֹה מֶלֶךְ־מִצְרָיִם וַיִּירְאוּ אֱלֹהִים אֲחֵרִים: וַיֵּלְכוּ בְּחֻקּוֹת הַגּוֹיִם
אֲשֶׁר הוֹרִישׁ יְהוָה מִפְּנֵי בְּנֵי יִשְׂרָאֵל וּמַלְכֵי יִשְׂרָאֵל אֲשֶׁר עָשׂוּ:
ט וַיְחַפְּאוּ בְנֵי־יִשְׂרָאֵל דְּבָרִים אֲשֶׁר לֹא־כֵן עַל־יְהוָה אֱלֹהֵיהֶם וַיִּבְנוּ
י לָהֶם בָּמוֹת בְּכָל־עָרֵיהֶם מִמִּגְדַּל נוֹצְרִים עַד־עִיר מִבְצָר: וַיַּצִּבוּ לָהֶם
יא מַצֵּבוֹת וַאֲשֵׁרִים עַל כָּל־גִּבְעָה גְבֹהָה וְתַחַת כָּל־עֵץ רַעֲנָן: וַיְקַטְּרוּ־
שָׁם בְּכָל־בָּמוֹת כַּגּוֹיִם אֲשֶׁר־הֶגְלָה יְהוָה מִפְּנֵיהֶם וַיַּעֲשׂוּ דְּבָרִים רָעִים
יב לְהַכְעִיס אֶת־יְהוָה: וַיַּעַבְדוּ הַגִּלֻּלִים אֲשֶׁר אָמַר יְהוָה לָהֶם לֹא תַעֲשׂוּ
יג אֶת־הַדָּבָר הַזֶּה: וַיָּעַד יְהוָה בְּיִשְׂרָאֵל וּבִיהוּדָה בְּיַד כָּל־נביאו כָל־ נְבִיאֵי
חֹזֶה לֵאמֹר שֻׁבוּ מִדַּרְכֵיכֶם הָרָעִים וְשִׁמְרוּ מִצְוֺתַי חֻקּוֹתַי כְּכָל־הַתּוֹרָה
אֲשֶׁר צִוִּיתִי אֶת־אֲבֹתֵיכֶם וַאֲשֶׁר שָׁלַחְתִּי אֲלֵיכֶם בְּיַד עֲבָדַי הַנְּבִיאִים:
יד וְלֹא שָׁמֵעוּ וַיַּקְשׁוּ אֶת־עָרְפָּם כְּעֹרֶף אֲבוֹתָם אֲשֶׁר לֹא הֶאֱמִינוּ בַּיהוָה
טו אֱלֹהֵיהֶם: וַיִּמְאֲסוּ אֶת־חֻקָּיו וְאֶת־בְּרִיתוֹ אֲשֶׁר כָּרַת אֶת־אֲבוֹתָם
וְאֵת עֵדְוֺתָיו אֲשֶׁר הֵעִיד בָּם וַיֵּלְכוּ אַחֲרֵי הַהֶבֶל וַיֶּהְבָּלוּ וְאַחֲרֵי הַגּוֹיִם
טז אֲשֶׁר סְבִיבֹתָם אֲשֶׁר צִוָּה יְהוָה אֹתָם לְבִלְתִּי עֲשׂוֹת כָּהֶם: וַיַּעַזְבוּ
אֶת־כָּל־מִצְוֺת יְהוָה אֱלֹהֵיהֶם וַיַּעֲשׂוּ לָהֶם מַסֵּכָה שנים עֲגָלִים וַיַּעֲשׂוּ שְׁנֵי
יז אֲשֵׁירָה וַיִּשְׁתַּחֲווּ לְכָל־צְבָא הַשָּׁמַיִם וַיַּעַבְדוּ אֶת־הַבָּעַל: וַיַּעֲבִירוּ
אֶת־בְּנֵיהֶם וְאֶת־בְּנוֹתֵיהֶם בָּאֵשׁ וַיִּקְסְמוּ קְסָמִים וַיְנַחֵשׁוּ וַיִּתְמַכְּרוּ
יח לַעֲשׂוֹת הָרַע בְּעֵינֵי יְהוָה לְהַכְעִיסוֹ: וַיִּתְאַנַּף יְהוָה מְאֹד בְּיִשְׂרָאֵל
יט וַיְסִרֵם מֵעַל פָּנָיו לֹא נִשְׁאַר רַק שֵׁבֶט יְהוּדָה לְבַדּוֹ: גַּם־יְהוּדָה לֹא
שָׁמַר אֶת־מִצְוֺת יְהוָה אֱלֹהֵיהֶם וַיֵּלְכוּ בְּחֻקּוֹת יִשְׂרָאֵל אֲשֶׁר עָשׂוּ:
כ וַיִּמְאַס יְהוָה בְּכָל־זֶרַע יִשְׂרָאֵל וַיְעַנֵּם וַיִּתְּנֵם בְּיַד־שֹׁסִים עַד אֲשֶׁר
כא הִשְׁלִיכָם מִפָּנָיו: כִּי־קָרַע יִשְׂרָאֵל מֵעַל בֵּית דָּוִד וַיַּמְלִיכוּ אֶת־יָרָבְעָם
בֶּן־נְבָט וידא יָרָבְעָם אֶת־יִשְׂרָאֵל מֵאַחֲרֵי יְהוָה וְהֶחֱטִיאָם חֲטָאָה וַיַּדַּח
כב גְדוֹלָה: וַיֵּלְכוּ בְּנֵי יִשְׂרָאֵל בְּכָל־חַטֹּאות יָרָבְעָם אֲשֶׁר עָשָׂה לֹא־סָרוּ
כג מִמֶּנָּה: עַד אֲשֶׁר־הֵסִיר יְהוָה אֶת־יִשְׂרָאֵל מֵעַל פָּנָיו כַּאֲשֶׁר דִּבֶּר בְּיַד
כָּל־עֲבָדָיו הַנְּבִיאִים וַיִּגֶל יִשְׂרָאֵל מֵעַל אַדְמָתוֹ אַשּׁוּרָה עַד הַיּוֹם
כד הַזֶּה: וַיָּבֵא מֶלֶךְ־אַשּׁוּר מִבָּבֶל וּמִכּוּתָה וּמֵעַוָּא
וּמֵחֲמָת וספרוים וַיֹּשֶׁב בְּעָרֵי שֹׁמְרוֹן תַּחַת בְּנֵי יִשְׂרָאֵל וַיִּרְשׁוּ אֶת־ וּמִסְפַרְוַיִם
כה שֹׁמְרוֹן וַיֵּשְׁבוּ בְּעָרֶיהָ: וַיְהִי בִּתְחִלַּת שִׁבְתָּם שָׁם לֹא יָרְאוּ אֶת־יְהוָה
כו וַיְשַׁלַּח יְהוָה בָּהֶם אֶת־הָאֲרָיוֹת וַיִּהְיוּ הֹרְגִים בָּהֶם: וַיֹּאמְרוּ לְמֶלֶךְ
אַשּׁוּר לֵאמֹר הַגּוֹיִם אֲשֶׁר הִגְלִיתָ וַתּוֹשֶׁב בְּעָרֵי שֹׁמְרוֹן לֹא יָדְעוּ
אֶת־מִשְׁפַּט אֱלֹהֵי הָאָרֶץ וַיְשַׁלַּח־בָּם אֶת־הָאֲרָיוֹת וְהִנָּם מְמִיתִים

27 because they do not know the customs of the local God." So the king of
Assyria commanded, "Bring back one of the priests whom you exiled from
there; let them go and settle there to teach them the customs of the local God."
28 One of the priests who had been exiled from Shomron came and settled
29 in Beit El, and he taught them how to revere the LORD. Yet each nation
continued to make its own gods, and they placed them in the shrine temples
30 that the Samarians had made, each nation in the city where they settled. The
people of Babylon made Sukkot Benot; the people of Kut made Nergal; the
31 people of Ḥamat made Ashima; the Avites made Nivḥaz and Tartak; the
Sefarvites would burn their children with fire for Adramelekh and Anamelekh,
32 the gods of Sefarvites. Though they revered the LORD, they appointed some
of their own number as shrine priests, and they would officiate for them in
33 the shrine temples. Though they revered the LORD, they served their own
gods and followed the customs of the nations from which they had been
34 exiled. To this day, they follow their former customs; they do not truly
revere the LORD, and they do not follow the laws, customs, teachings, and
commandments that the LORD commanded the children of Yaakov, whose
35 name He changed to Yisrael. With them the LORD had made a covenant, and
He had commanded them, "Do not revere other gods; do not bow down to
36 them or serve them or make sacrifices to them. You shall revere only the
LORD who brought you out from the land of Egypt with great might and an
outstretched arm; to Him you shall bow down, and to Him you shall make
37 sacrifices. As for the laws, customs, teachings, and commandments He wrote
38 for you – keep them carefully forever, and do not revere other gods. Never
forget the covenant that I made with you, and do not revere other gods.
39 Revere only the LORD your God, and He will save you from the hands of all
40 your enemies." But they did not listen; they continued to follow their former
41 customs. Now, although these nations revered the LORD, they continued to
serve their idols – and their children and their children's children do just as
18 1 their ancestors did to this day. In the third year of Hoshe'a son of Ela,
2 king of Israel, Ḥizkiya son of Aḥaz, king of Yehuda, became king. He was
twenty-five years old when he became king, and for twenty-nine years he
3 reigned in Jerusalem. His mother's name was Avi daughter of Zekharya. He
4 did what was right in the eyes of the LORD just as his ancestor David did. He
removed the high shrines and tore down the worship pillars and cut down
the sacred tree. And he crushed the bronze serpent that Moshe had made,
for until that time the Israelites were making sacrifices to it and calling it
5 Neḥushtan.[99] In the LORD, God of Israel, he placed his trust; there were none
like him among all the kings of Yehuda who succeeded him or those who
6 came before him. He clung to the LORD and never turned away from him

99 | See Numbers 21:8–9.

כז אוֹתָם כַּאֲשֶׁר אֵינָם יֹדְעִים אֶת־מִשְׁפַּט אֱלֹהֵי הָאָרֶץ׃ וַיְצַו מֶלֶךְ־אַשּׁוּר
לֵאמֹר הֹלִיכוּ שָׁמָּה אֶחָד מֵהַכֹּהֲנִים אֲשֶׁר הִגְלִיתֶם מִשָּׁם וְיֵלְכוּ וְיֵשְׁבוּ
כח שָׁם וְיֹרֵם אֶת־מִשְׁפַּט אֱלֹהֵי הָאָרֶץ׃ וַיָּבֹא אֶחָד מֵהַכֹּהֲנִים אֲשֶׁר
הִגְלוּ מִשֹּׁמְרוֹן וַיֵּשֶׁב בְּבֵית־אֵל וַיְהִי מוֹרֶה אֹתָם אֵיךְ יִירְאוּ אֶת־יְהוָה׃
כט וַיִּהְיוּ עֹשִׂים גּוֹי גּוֹי אֱלֹהָיו וַיַּנִּיחוּ ׀ בְּבֵית הַבָּמוֹת אֲשֶׁר עָשׂוּ הַשֹּׁמְרֹנִים
ל גּוֹי גּוֹי בְּעָרֵיהֶם אֲשֶׁר הֵם יֹשְׁבִים שָׁם׃ וְאַנְשֵׁי בָבֶל עָשׂוּ אֶת־סֻכּוֹת
בְּנוֹת וְאַנְשֵׁי־כוּת עָשׂוּ אֶת־נֵרְגַל וְאַנְשֵׁי חֲמָת עָשׂוּ אֶת־אֲשִׁימָא׃
לא וְהָעַוִּים עָשׂוּ נִבְחַז וְאֶת־תַּרְתָּק וְהַסְפַרְוִים שֹׂרְפִים אֶת־בְּנֵיהֶם בָּאֵשׁ
לב לְאַדְרַמֶּלֶךְ וַעֲנַמֶּלֶךְ אלה ספרים׃ וַיִּהְיוּ יְרֵאִים אֶת־יְהוָה וַיַּעֲשׂוּ לָהֶם סְפַרְוָיִם
לג מִקְצוֹתָם כֹּהֲנֵי בָמוֹת וַיִּהְיוּ עֹשִׂים לָהֶם בְּבֵית הַבָּמוֹת׃ אֶת־יְהוָה הָיוּ
יְרֵאִים וְאֶת־אֱלֹהֵיהֶם הָיוּ עֹבְדִים כְּמִשְׁפַּט הַגּוֹיִם אֲשֶׁר־הִגְלוּ אֹתָם
לד מִשָּׁם׃ עַד הַיּוֹם הַזֶּה הֵם עֹשִׂים כַּמִּשְׁפָּטִים הָרִאשֹׁנִים אֵינָם יְרֵאִים
אֶת־יְהוָה וְאֵינָם עֹשִׂים כְּחֻקֹּתָם וּכְמִשְׁפָּטָם וְכַתּוֹרָה וְכַמִּצְוָה אֲשֶׁר
לה צִוָּה יְהוָה אֶת־בְּנֵי יַעֲקֹב אֲשֶׁר־שָׂם שְׁמוֹ יִשְׂרָאֵל׃ וַיִּכְרֹת יְהוָה אִתָּם
בְּרִית וַיְצַוֵּם לֵאמֹר לֹא תִירְאוּ אֱלֹהִים אֲחֵרִים וְלֹא־תִשְׁתַּחֲווּ לָהֶם
לו וְלֹא תַעַבְדוּם וְלֹא תִזְבְּחוּ לָהֶם׃ כִּי ׀ אִם־אֶת־יְהוָה אֲשֶׁר הֶעֱלָה אֶתְכֶם
מֵאֶרֶץ מִצְרַיִם בְּכֹחַ גָּדוֹל וּבִזְרוֹעַ נְטוּיָה אֹתוֹ תִירָאוּ וְלוֹ תִשְׁתַּחֲווּ
לז וְלוֹ תִזְבָּחוּ׃ וְאֶת־הַחֻקִּים וְאֶת־הַמִּשְׁפָּטִים וְהַתּוֹרָה וְהַמִּצְוָה אֲשֶׁר
כָּתַב לָכֶם תִּשְׁמְרוּן לַעֲשׂוֹת כָּל־הַיָּמִים וְלֹא תִירְאוּ אֱלֹהִים אֲחֵרִים׃
לח וְהַבְּרִית אֲשֶׁר־כָּרַתִּי אִתְּכֶם לֹא תִשְׁכָּחוּ וְלֹא תִירְאוּ אֱלֹהִים אֲחֵרִים׃
לט כִּי אִם־אֶת־יְהוָה אֱלֹהֵיכֶם תִּירָאוּ וְהוּא יַצִּיל אֶתְכֶם מִיַּד כָּל־אֹיְבֵיכֶם׃
מ מא וְלֹא שָׁמֵעוּ כִּי אִם־כְּמִשְׁפָּטָם הָרִאשׁוֹן הֵם עֹשִׂים׃ וַיִּהְיוּ ׀ הַגּוֹיִם הָאֵלֶּה
יְרֵאִים אֶת־יְהוָה וְאֶת־פְּסִילֵיהֶם הָיוּ עֹבְדִים גַּם־בְּנֵיהֶם ׀ וּבְנֵי בְנֵיהֶם
יח א כַּאֲשֶׁר עָשׂוּ אֲבֹתָם הֵם עֹשִׂים עַד הַיּוֹם הַזֶּה׃ וַיְהִי בִּשְׁנַת
שָׁלֹשׁ לְהוֹשֵׁעַ בֶּן־אֵלָה מֶלֶךְ יִשְׂרָאֵל מָלַךְ חִזְקִיָּה בֶן־אָחָז מֶלֶךְ
ב יְהוּדָה׃ בֶּן־עֶשְׂרִים וְחָמֵשׁ שָׁנָה הָיָה בְמָלְכוֹ וְעֶשְׂרִים וָתֵשַׁע שָׁנָה
ג מָלַךְ בִּירוּשָׁלִָם וְשֵׁם אִמּוֹ אֲבִי בַּת־זְכַרְיָה׃ וַיַּעַשׂ הַיָּשָׁר בְּעֵינֵי יְהוָה
ד כְּכֹל אֲשֶׁר־עָשָׂה דָּוִד אָבִיו׃ הוּא ׀ הֵסִיר אֶת־הַבָּמוֹת וְשִׁבַּר אֶת־
הַמַּצֵּבֹת וְכָרַת אֶת־הָאֲשֵׁרָה וְכִתַּת נְחַשׁ הַנְּחֹשֶׁת אֲשֶׁר־עָשָׂה מֹשֶׁה
כִּי עַד־הַיָּמִים הָהֵמָּה הָיוּ בְנֵי־יִשְׂרָאֵל מְקַטְּרִים לוֹ וַיִּקְרָא־לוֹ נְחֻשְׁתָּן׃
ה בַּיהוָה אֱלֹהֵי־יִשְׂרָאֵל בָּטָח וְאַחֲרָיו לֹא־הָיָה כָמֹהוּ בְּכֹל מַלְכֵי יְהוּדָה
ו וַאֲשֶׁר הָיוּ לְפָנָיו׃ וַיִּדְבַּק בַּיהוָה לֹא־סָר מֵאַחֲרָיו וַיִּשְׁמֹר מִצְוֹתָיו ל

7 and kept the commandments that the LORD had commanded Moshe. And
the LORD was with him; wherever he turned, he was successful. He rebelled
8 against the king of Assyria and did not serve him. He defeated the Philistines
9 up to Aza and its territories, from watchtower to fortified city. In the
fourth year of King Ḥizkiyahu – which was the seventh year of Hoshe'a son
of Ela, king of Israel – Shalmaneser, king of Assyria, marched up against
10 Shomron and besieged it. He captured it three years later during the sixth
year of Ḥizkiya; it was during the ninth year of Hoshe'a, king of Israel, that
11 Shomron was captured. And the king of Assyria exiled Israel to Assyria and
transferred them to Ḥalaḥ, the Ḥavor, the Gozan River, and the cities of
12 Media. This was because they would not heed the voice of the LORD their
God, and they violated His covenant – all that Moshe, the LORD's servant,
had commanded. They would not obey, and they would not comply.
13 In the fourteenth year of King Ḥizkiya, Sanḥeriv, king of Assyria, marched up
14 against all the fortified cities of Yehuda and seized them.[100] So Ḥizkiya, king
of Yehuda, sent to the king of Assyria at Lakhish, saying, "I have offended.
Withdraw from me, and I will bear whatever you impose on me." So the king
of Assyria charged Ḥizkiya, king of Yehuda, with three hundred talents of
15 silver and thirty talents of gold, and Ḥizkiya surrendered all the silver that was
to be found in the House of the LORD and in the royal treasuries of the palace.
16 It was then that Ḥizkiya stripped down the doors of the LORD's Sanctuary
and the doorposts that Ḥizkiya, king of Yehuda, had overlaid himself, and
17 he surrendered them to the king of Assyria. The king of Assyria
then sent the Tartan, the Rav-Saris, and the Rav-Shakeh[101] from Lakhish to
King Ḥizkiyahu in Jerusalem, along with vast forces; they marched up and
came to Jerusalem, and when they arrived, they stationed themselves by the
18 conduit of the Upper Pool, by the Fuller's Field Road. They summoned the
king, and Elyakim son of Ḥilkiyahu, who was in charge of the palace, Shevna
19 the scribe, and Yoaḥ son of Asaf, royal herald, went out to them. And the
Rav-Shakeh said to them, "Now, tell Ḥizkiyahu, 'Thus says the great king,
20 the king of Assyria: What is this display of trust? You talk as if mere chatter
were counsel and might in war! Now, in whom have you placed your trust,
21 that you rebel against me? Have you placed your trust in that crushed reed
of a staff, in Egypt, who pierces and punctures the palm of anyone who leans
upon it? For that is Pharaoh, king of Egypt, to all who place their trust in him.
22 And if you say to me, "We have placed our trust in the LORD, our God" – is
that not the one whose high shrines and altars Ḥizkiyahu removed, telling
23 Yehuda and Jerusalem, "Bow only before *this* altar, in Jerusalem"? Come, now,
make a wager with my lord, the king of Assyria: I will provide you with two
24 thousand horses if you are able to provide them with riders! How dare you

100 | Cf. this story in Isaiah, chapters 36–39.
101 | Titles of Assyrian officials.

ז אֲשֶׁר־צִוָּה יהוה אֶת־מֹשֶׁה: וְהָיָה יהוה עִמּוֹ בְּכֹל אֲשֶׁר־יֵצֵא יַשְׂכִּיל
ח וַיִּמְרֹד בְּמֶלֶךְ־אַשּׁוּר וְלֹא עֲבָדוֹ: הוּא־הִכָּה אֶת־פְּלִשְׁתִּים עַד־עַזָּה
ט וְאֶת־גְּבוּלֶיהָ מִמִּגְדַּל נוֹצְרִים עַד־עִיר מִבְצָר: וַיְהִי בַּשָּׁנָה
הָרְבִיעִית לַמֶּלֶךְ חִזְקִיָּהוּ הִיא הַשָּׁנָה הַשְּׁבִיעִית לְהוֹשֵׁעַ בֶּן־אֵלָה מֶלֶךְ
י יִשְׂרָאֵל עָלָה שַׁלְמַנְאֶסֶר מֶלֶךְ־אַשּׁוּר עַל־שֹׁמְרוֹן וַיָּצַר עָלֶיהָ: וַיִּלְכְּדֻהָ
מִקְצֵה שָׁלֹשׁ שָׁנִים בִּשְׁנַת־שֵׁשׁ לְחִזְקִיָּה הִיא שְׁנַת־תֵּשַׁע לְהוֹשֵׁעַ
יא מֶלֶךְ יִשְׂרָאֵל נִלְכְּדָה שֹׁמְרוֹן: וַיֶּגֶל מֶלֶךְ־אַשּׁוּר אֶת־יִשְׂרָאֵל אַשּׁוּרָה
יב וַיַּנְחֵם בַּחְלַח וּבְחָבוֹר נְהַר גּוֹזָן וְעָרֵי מָדָי: עַל ׀ אֲשֶׁר לֹא־שָׁמְעוּ בְּקוֹל
יהוה אֱלֹהֵיהֶם וַיַּעַבְרוּ אֶת־בְּרִיתוֹ אֵת כָּל־אֲשֶׁר צִוָּה מֹשֶׁה עֶבֶד יהוה
וְלֹא שָׁמְעוּ וְלֹא עָשׂוּ:
יג וּבְאַרְבַּע עֶשְׂרֵה שָׁנָה לַמֶּלֶךְ חִזְקִיָּה עָלָה סַנְחֵרִיב מֶלֶךְ־אַשּׁוּר עַל
יד כָּל־עָרֵי יְהוּדָה הַבְּצֻרוֹת וַיִּתְפְּשֵׂם: וַיִּשְׁלַח חִזְקִיָּה מֶלֶךְ־יְהוּדָה אֶל־
מֶלֶךְ־אַשּׁוּר ׀ לָכִישָׁה ׀ לֵאמֹר ׀ חָטָאתִי שׁוּב מֵעָלַי אֵת אֲשֶׁר־תִּתֵּן
עָלַי אֶשָּׂא וַיָּשֶׂם מֶלֶךְ־אַשּׁוּר עַל־חִזְקִיָּה מֶלֶךְ־יְהוּדָה שְׁלֹשׁ מֵאוֹת
טו כִּכַּר־כֶּסֶף וּשְׁלֹשִׁים כִּכַּר זָהָב: וַיִּתֵּן חִזְקִיָּה אֶת־כָּל־הַכֶּסֶף הַנִּמְצָא
טז בֵית־יהוה וּבְאֹצְרוֹת בֵּית הַמֶּלֶךְ: בָּעֵת הַהִיא קִצַּץ חִזְקִיָּה אֶת־
דַּלְתוֹת הֵיכַל יהוה וְאֶת־הָאֹמְנוֹת אֲשֶׁר צִפָּה חִזְקִיָּה מֶלֶךְ יְהוּדָה
יז וַיִּתְּנֵם לְמֶלֶךְ אַשּׁוּר: וַיִּשְׁלַח מֶלֶךְ־אַשּׁוּר אֶת־תַּרְתָּן
וְאֶת־רַב־סָרִיס ׀ וְאֶת־רַבְשָׁקֵה מִן־לָכִישׁ אֶל־הַמֶּלֶךְ חִזְקִיָּהוּ בְּחֵיל
כָּבֵד יְרוּשָׁלָם וַיַּעֲלוּ וַיָּבֹאוּ יְרוּשָׁלַם וַיַּעֲלוּ וַיָּבֹאוּ וַיַּעַמְדוּ בִּתְעָלַת
יח הַבְּרֵכָה הָעֶלְיוֹנָה אֲשֶׁר בִּמְסִלַּת שְׂדֵה כוֹבֵס: וַיִּקְרְאוּ אֶל־הַמֶּלֶךְ וַיֵּצֵא
אֲלֵהֶם אֶלְיָקִים בֶּן־חִלְקִיָּהוּ אֲשֶׁר עַל־הַבָּיִת וְשֶׁבְנָה הַסֹּפֵר וְיוֹאָח
יט בֶּן־אָסָף הַמַּזְכִּיר: וַיֹּאמֶר אֲלֵיהֶם רַבְשָׁקֵה אִמְרוּ־נָא אֶל־חִזְקִיָּהוּ
כֹּה־אָמַר הַמֶּלֶךְ הַגָּדוֹל מֶלֶךְ אַשּׁוּר מָה הַבִּטָּחוֹן הַזֶּה אֲשֶׁר בָּטָחְתָּ:
כ אָמַרְתָּ אַךְ־דְּבַר־שְׂפָתַיִם עֵצָה וּגְבוּרָה לַמִּלְחָמָה עַתָּה עַל־מִי בָטַחְתָּ
כא כִּי מָרַדְתָּ בִּי: עַתָּה הִנֵּה בָטַחְתָּ לְּךָ עַל־מִשְׁעֶנֶת הַקָּנֶה הָרָצוּץ הַזֶּה
עַל־מִצְרַיִם אֲשֶׁר יִסָּמֵךְ אִישׁ עָלָיו וּבָא בְכַפּוֹ וּנְקָבָהּ כֵּן פַּרְעֹה מֶלֶךְ־
כב מִצְרַיִם לְכָל־הַבֹּטְחִים עָלָיו: וְכִי־תֹאמְרוּן אֵלַי אֶל־יהוה אֱלֹהֵינוּ
בָּטָחְנוּ הֲלוֹא־הוּא אֲשֶׁר הֵסִיר חִזְקִיָּהוּ אֶת־בָּמֹתָיו וְאֶת־מִזְבְּחֹתָיו
וַיֹּאמֶר לִיהוּדָה וְלִירוּשָׁלַם לִפְנֵי הַמִּזְבֵּחַ הַזֶּה תִּשְׁתַּחֲווּ בִּירוּשָׁלָם:
כג וְעַתָּה הִתְעָרֶב נָא אֶת־אֲדֹנִי אֶת־מֶלֶךְ אַשּׁוּר וְאֶתְּנָה לְךָ אַלְפַּיִם
כד סוּסִים אִם־תּוּכַל לָתֶת לְךָ רֹכְבִים עֲלֵיהֶם: וְאֵיךְ תָּשִׁיב אֵת פְּנֵי פַחַת

slight even one of the deputies of my lord's lesser servants and place your trust
25 in Egypt for chariots and riders! What is more – was it without the LORD that
I marched up to destroy this place? It was the LORD Himself who said to me:
26 March up against this land and destroy it.'" Elyakim son of Ḥilkiyahu, Shevna,
and Yoaḥ said to the Rav-Shakeh, "Please, speak to your servants in Aramaic,
for we understand it. Do not speak with us in Hebrew[102] within earshot of
27 the people who are on the wall." "Was it to you and your master that my lord
sent me to speak these words?" the Rav-Shakeh told them, "Oh, but it was to
the very men who are stationed on the wall, who will have to eat their own
28 excrement and drink their own urine along with you." And the Rav-Shakeh
stood and shouted out in Hebrew: "Hear the word of the great king, the king
29 of Assyria," he proclaimed. "Thus says the king: Do not let Ḥizkiyahu deceive
30 you, for he cannot save you from my hand. Do not let Ḥizkiyahu convince
you to place your trust in the LORD, saying, 'The LORD will surely save us,
31 and this city will not be handed over to the king of Assyria.' Do not listen
to Ḥizkiyahu, for thus says the king of Assyria: Make peace with me; come
out to me, and each will eat from his own vine and his own fig tree, and each
32 will drink from his own cistern until I come and take you to a land like your
own – a land of grain and wine, a land of bread and vineyards, a land of olive
oil and honey, and you shall live and not die. Do not listen to Ḥizkiyahu, for
33 he misleads you by saying, 'The LORD will save us.' Have the gods of other
nations managed to save their own lands from the hand of the king of Assyria?
34 Where are the gods of Ḥamat and Arpad? Where are the gods of Sefarvites,
35 Hena, and Iva – did they save Shomron from my hand? Who among all the
gods of the lands saved their own land from my hands, that the LORD will save
36 Jerusalem from my hand?" And the people were silent and did not say a word,
37 for the king's order was, "Do not answer him." Then Elyakim son of Ḥilkiya,
who was in charge of the palace, Shevna the scribe, and Yoaḥ son of Asaf, the
royal herald, came to Ḥizkiyahu with their clothes rent and reported what
19 1 the Rav-Shakeh had said. When King Ḥizkiyahu heard, he rent his clothes
2 and covered himself in sackcloth and came to the House of the LORD. He
then sent Elyakim, who was in charge of the palace, and Shevna the scribe,
and the senior priests, covered in sackcloth, to the prophet Yeshayahu son of
3 Amotz. "Thus says Ḥizkiyahu," they said to him. "'Today is a day of distress
and reproach and disgrace, for children are about to be born, but there is no
4 strength left for the birth.[103] Perhaps the LORD your God will hear all the
words of the Rav-Shakeh, whom the king of Assyria, his lord, sent to taunt the
living God, and will condemn the words that the LORD your God heard – oh,
5 offer a prayer for the sake of the surviving remnant!'" Now, when the servants
6 of King Ḥizkiyahu came to Yeshayahu, Yeshayahu said to them, "This is what
you should tell your lord. Thus says the LORD: 'Do not be afraid of the words

102 | *Yehudit*, literally the language of Judah.
103 | A proverbial expression of distress and helplessness.

אַחַד עַבְדֵי אֲדֹנִי הַקְּטַנִּים וַתִּבְטַח לְךָ עַל־מִצְרַיִם לְרֶכֶב וּלְפָרָשִׁים:
כה עַתָּה הֲמִבַּלְעֲדֵי יְהוָה עָלִיתִי עַל־הַמָּקוֹם הַזֶּה לְהַשְׁחִתוֹ יְהוָה אָמַר
כו אֵלַי עֲלֵה עַל־הָאָרֶץ הַזֹּאת וְהַשְׁחִיתָהּ: וַיֹּאמֶר אֶלְיָקִים בֶּן־חִלְקִיָּהוּ
וְשֶׁבְנָה וְיוֹאָח אֶל־רַבְשָׁקֵה דַּבֶּר־נָא אֶל־עֲבָדֶיךָ אֲרָמִית כִּי שֹׁמְעִים
כז אֲנָחְנוּ וְאַל־תְּדַבֵּר עִמָּנוּ יְהוּדִית בְּאָזְנֵי הָעָם אֲשֶׁר עַל־הַחֹמָה: וַיֹּאמֶר
אֲלֵיהֶם רַבְשָׁקֵה הַעַל אֲדֹנֶיךָ וְאֵלֶיךָ שְׁלָחַנִי אֲדֹנִי לְדַבֵּר אֶת־הַדְּבָרִים
הָאֵלֶּה הֲלֹא עַל־הָאֲנָשִׁים הַיֹּשְׁבִים עַל־הַחֹמָה לֶאֱכֹל אֶת־חריהם צוֹאָתָם
כח וְלִשְׁתּוֹת אֶת־שיניהם עִמָּכֶם: וַיַּעֲמֹד רַבְשָׁקֵה וַיִּקְרָא בְקוֹל־גָּדוֹל מֵימֵי רַגְלֵיהֶם
כט יְהוּדִית וַיְדַבֵּר וַיֹּאמֶר שִׁמְעוּ דְּבַר־הַמֶּלֶךְ הַגָּדוֹל מֶלֶךְ אַשּׁוּר: כֹּה
אָמַר הַמֶּלֶךְ אַל־יַשִּׁא לָכֶם חִזְקִיָּהוּ כִּי־לֹא יוּכַל לְהַצִּיל אֶתְכֶם מִיָּדוֹ:
ל וְאַל־יַבְטַח אֶתְכֶם חִזְקִיָּהוּ אֶל־יְהוָה לֵאמֹר הַצֵּל יַצִּילֵנוּ יְהוָה וְלֹא
לא תִנָּתֵן אֶת־הָעִיר הַזֹּאת בְּיַד מֶלֶךְ אַשּׁוּר: אַל־תִּשְׁמְעוּ אֶל־חִזְקִיָּהוּ
כִּי כֹה אָמַר מֶלֶךְ אַשּׁוּר עֲשׂוּ אִתִּי בְרָכָה וּצְאוּ אֵלַי וְאִכְלוּ אִישׁ־גַּפְנוֹ
לב וְאִישׁ תְּאֵנָתוֹ וּשְׁתוּ אִישׁ מֵי־בֹרוֹ: עַד־בֹּאִי וְלָקַחְתִּי אֶתְכֶם אֶל־
אֶרֶץ כְּאַרְצְכֶם אֶרֶץ דָּגָן וְתִירוֹשׁ אֶרֶץ לֶחֶם וּכְרָמִים אֶרֶץ זֵית יִצְהָר
וּדְבַשׁ וִחְיוּ וְלֹא תָמֻתוּ וְאַל־תִּשְׁמְעוּ אֶל־חִזְקִיָּהוּ כִּי־יַסִּית אֶתְכֶם
לג לֵאמֹר יְהוָה יַצִּילֵנוּ: הַהַצֵּל הִצִּילוּ אֱלֹהֵי הַגּוֹיִם אִישׁ אֶת־אַרְצוֹ מִיַּד
לד מֶלֶךְ אַשּׁוּר: אַיֵּה אֱלֹהֵי חֲמָת וְאַרְפָּד אַיֵּה אֱלֹהֵי סְפַרְוַיִם הֵנַע וְעִוָּה
לה כִּי־הִצִּילוּ אֶת־שֹׁמְרוֹן מִיָּדִי: מִי בְּכָל־אֱלֹהֵי הָאֲרָצוֹת אֲשֶׁר־הִצִּילוּ
לו אֶת־אַרְצָם מִיָּדִי כִּי־יַצִּיל יְהוָה אֶת־יְרוּשָׁלִַם מִיָּדִי: וְהֶחֱרִישׁוּ הָעָם
לז וְלֹא־עָנוּ אֹתוֹ דָּבָר כִּי־מִצְוַת הַמֶּלֶךְ הִיא לֵאמֹר לֹא תַעֲנֻהוּ: וַיָּבֹא
אֶלְיָקִים בֶּן־חִלְקִיָּה אֲשֶׁר־עַל־הַבַּיִת וְשֶׁבְנָא הַסֹּפֵר וְיוֹאָח בֶּן־אָסָף
יט א הַמַּזְכִּיר אֶל־חִזְקִיָּהוּ קְרוּעֵי בְגָדִים וַיַּגִּדוּ לוֹ דִּבְרֵי רַבְשָׁקֵה: וַיְהִי
כִּשְׁמֹעַ הַמֶּלֶךְ חִזְקִיָּהוּ וַיִּקְרַע אֶת־בְּגָדָיו וַיִּתְכַּס בַּשָּׂק וַיָּבֹא בֵּית
ב יְהוָה: וַיִּשְׁלַח אֶת־אֶלְיָקִים אֲשֶׁר־עַל־הַבַּיִת וְשֶׁבְנָא הַסֹּפֵר וְאֵת זִקְנֵי
ג הַכֹּהֲנִים מִתְכַּסִּים בַּשַּׂקִּים אֶל־יְשַׁעְיָהוּ הַנָּבִיא בֶּן־אָמוֹץ: וַיֹּאמְרוּ
אֵלָיו כֹּה אָמַר חִזְקִיָּהוּ יוֹם־צָרָה וְתוֹכֵחָה וּנְאָצָה הַיּוֹם הַזֶּה כִּי בָאוּ
ד בָנִים עַד־מַשְׁבֵּר וְכֹחַ אַיִן לְלֵדָה: אוּלַי יִשְׁמַע יְהוָה אֱלֹהֶיךָ אֵת ׀
כָּל־דִּבְרֵי רַבְשָׁקֵה אֲשֶׁר שְׁלָחוֹ מֶלֶךְ־אַשּׁוּר ׀ אֲדֹנָיו לְחָרֵף אֱלֹהִים
חַי וְהוֹכִיחַ בַּדְּבָרִים אֲשֶׁר שָׁמַע יְהוָה אֱלֹהֶיךָ וְנָשָׂאתָ תְפִלָּה בְּעַד
ה ו הַשְּׁאֵרִית הַנִּמְצָאָה: וַיָּבֹאוּ עַבְדֵי הַמֶּלֶךְ חִזְקִיָּהוּ אֶל־יְשַׁעְיָהוּ: וַיֹּאמֶר
לָהֶם יְשַׁעְיָהוּ כֹּה תֹאמְרוּן אֶל־אֲדֹנֵיכֶם כֹּה ׀ אָמַר יְהוָה אַל־תִּירָא

7 you heard, which the king of Assyria's servant boys used to revile Me. I will
strike him with delusion so that he will hear a rumor and return to his own
8 land; then I will have him fall by the sword in his own land.'" The Rav-Shakeh
withdrew, for he heard that the king of Assyria had moved on from Lakhish,
9 and he found the king of Assyria attacking Livna. When the latter heard
rumor that Tirhaka, king of Kush, had set out to fight against him, he sent
10 messengers to Ḥizkiyahu once more, saying: "This is what you should tell
Ḥizkiyahu, king of Yehuda: Do not let your God in whom you trust deceive
11 you, saying, 'Jerusalem will not be handed over to the king of Assyria.' Look,
you have heard what the kings of Assyria have done to all the lands – they
12 have utterly destroyed them. Will you be saved? Did the gods of the nations
that my ancestors destroyed save them – Gozan and Ḥaran and Retzef and
13 the Edenites of Telasar? Where is the king of Ḥamat and the king of Arpad
14 and the king of La'ir, Sefarvites, Hena, and Iva?" When Ḥizkiyahu received
the letter from the messengers and read it, he went up to the House of the
Lord, and Ḥizkiyahu spread it open before the Lord.
15 Then Ḥizkiyahu prayed before the Lord: "O Lord, God of Israel, Enthroned
upon the Cherubim," he said, "You alone are God of all the kingdoms of the
16 earth; You made both heaven and earth. Incline Your ear, O Lord, and listen;
open Your eyes, O Lord, and see – listen to the words of Sanḥeriv, those he
17 sent to revile the living God. It is true, Lord, that the kings of Assyria have
18 laid the nations to waste, together with their lands. They have cast their gods
to the fire – for they are not gods but the work of human hands, wood and
19 stone – and destroyed them. But now, Lord our God, save us from his
hand, and all the kingdoms of the earth will see that You alone, O Lord, are
20 God." And Yeshayahu son of Amotz sent word to Ḥizkiyahu: "Thus
says the Lord, God of Israel: What you prayed to Me about Sanḥeriv, king
21 of Assyria, I have heard. This is the word the Lord has spoken of him: Virgin
daughter Zion scorns you, mocks you; she shakes her head behind your back,
22 daughter Jerusalem. Whom have you taunted, whom reviled; against whom
did you raise your voice, lifting your eyes haughtily against the Holy One of
23 Israel? By your messengers' hand you taunted the Lord; you said, 'With the
wealth of my chariots I climbed to the heights of the hills, the ends of Lebanon,
and I cut down its tallest cedars, its choicest junipers; I have reached its
24 farthest lodgings, its richest forests. I have dug down and drunk strange
25 waters; the passing soles of my feet have parched all the rivers of Egypt.' Did
you not hear of this long ago? I did this in ancient times; I formed the plan;
now I have brought it to be: towns crash to heaps of rubble, and the fortified
26 cities are ruined. The inhabitants are powerless, frozen in fear and ashamed,
like the field grasses, like green stalks, the grass of rooftops, blasted before
27 ripening. Your stops, your goings, your comings, I know them all, and your
28 raging against Me. Because you have raged against Me, your arrogance has
reached My ears; I shall put My ring in your nose, My bit between your lips,

ז מִפְּנֵי הַדְּבָרִים אֲשֶׁר שָׁמַעְתָּ אֲשֶׁר גִּדְּפוּ נַעֲרֵי מֶלֶךְ־אַשּׁוּר אֹתִי: הִנְנִי
ח נֹתֵן בּוֹ רוּחַ וְשָׁמַע שְׁמוּעָה וְשָׁב לְאַרְצוֹ וְהִפַּלְתִּיו בַּחֶרֶב בְּאַרְצוֹ: וַיָּשָׁב
רַבְשָׁקֵה וַיִּמְצָא אֶת־מֶלֶךְ אַשּׁוּר נִלְחָם עַל־לִבְנָה כִּי שָׁמַע כִּי נָסַע
ט מִלָּכִישׁ: וַיִּשְׁמַע אֶל־תִּרְהָקָה מֶלֶךְ־כּוּשׁ לֵאמֹר הִנֵּה יָצָא לְהִלָּחֵם
י אִתָּךְ וַיָּשָׁב וַיִּשְׁלַח מַלְאָכִים אֶל־חִזְקִיָּהוּ לֵאמֹר: כֹּה תֹאמְרוּן אֶל־
חִזְקִיָּהוּ מֶלֶךְ־יְהוּדָה לֵאמֹר אַל־יַשִּׁאֲךָ אֱלֹהֶיךָ אֲשֶׁר אַתָּה בֹּטֵחַ
יא בּוֹ לֵאמֹר לֹא תִנָּתֵן יְרוּשָׁלִַם בְּיַד מֶלֶךְ אַשּׁוּר: הִנֵּה | אַתָּה שָׁמַעְתָּ
אֵת אֲשֶׁר עָשׂוּ מַלְכֵי אַשּׁוּר לְכָל־הָאֲרָצוֹת לְהַחֲרִימָם וְאַתָּה תִּנָּצֵל:
יב הַהִצִּילוּ אֹתָם אֱלֹהֵי הַגּוֹיִם אֲשֶׁר שִׁחֲתוּ אֲבוֹתַי אֶת־גּוֹזָן וְאֶת־חָרָן
יג וְרֶצֶף וּבְנֵי־עֶדֶן אֲשֶׁר בִּתְלַאשָּׂר: אַיּוֹ מֶלֶךְ־חֲמָת וּמֶלֶךְ אַרְפָּד וּמֶלֶךְ
יד לָעִיר סְפַרְוָיִם הֵנַע וְעִוָּה: וַיִּקַּח חִזְקִיָּהוּ אֶת־הַסְּפָרִים מִיַּד הַמַּלְאָכִים
וַיִּקְרָאֵם וַיַּעַל בֵּית יְהוָה וַיִּפְרְשֵׂהוּ חִזְקִיָּהוּ לִפְנֵי יְהוָה:
טו וַיִּתְפַּלֵּל חִזְקִיָּהוּ לִפְנֵי יְהוָה וַיֹּאמַר יְהוָה אֱלֹהֵי יִשְׂרָאֵל יֹשֵׁב הַכְּרֻבִים
אַתָּה־הוּא הָאֱלֹהִים לְבַדְּךָ לְכֹל מַמְלְכוֹת הָאָרֶץ אַתָּה עָשִׂיתָ אֶת־
טז הַשָּׁמַיִם וְאֶת־הָאָרֶץ: הַטֵּה יְהוָה | אָזְנְךָ וּשְׁמָע פְּקַח יְהוָה עֵינֶיךָ וּרְאֵה
יז וּשְׁמַע אֵת דִּבְרֵי סַנְחֵרִיב אֲשֶׁר שְׁלָחוֹ לְחָרֵף אֱלֹהִים חָי: אָמְנָם יְהוָה
יח הֶחֱרִיבוּ מַלְכֵי אַשּׁוּר אֶת־הַגּוֹיִם וְאֶת־אַרְצָם: וְנָתְנוּ אֶת־אֱלֹהֵיהֶם
בָּאֵשׁ כִּי לֹא אֱלֹהִים הֵמָּה כִּי אִם־מַעֲשֵׂה יְדֵי־אָדָם עֵץ וָאֶבֶן וַיְאַבְּדוּם:
יט וְעַתָּה יְהוָה אֱלֹהֵינוּ הוֹשִׁיעֵנוּ נָא מִיָּדוֹ וְיֵדְעוּ כָּל־מַמְלְכוֹת הָאָרֶץ כִּי ל
כ אַתָּה יְהוָה אֱלֹהִים לְבַדֶּךָ: וַיִּשְׁלַח יְשַׁעְיָהוּ בֶן־אָמוֹץ
אֶל־חִזְקִיָּהוּ לֵאמֹר כֹּה־אָמַר יְהוָה אֱלֹהֵי יִשְׂרָאֵל אֲשֶׁר הִתְפַּלַּלְתָּ
כא אֵלַי אֶל־סַנְחֵרִב מֶלֶךְ־אַשּׁוּר שָׁמָעְתִּי: זֶה הַדָּבָר אֲשֶׁר־דִּבֶּר יְהוָה
עָלָיו בָּזָה לְךָ לָעֲגָה לְךָ בְּתוּלַת בַּת־צִיּוֹן אַחֲרֶיךָ רֹאשׁ הֵנִיעָה בַּת
כב יְרוּשָׁלִָם: אֶת־מִי חֵרַפְתָּ וְגִדַּפְתָּ וְעַל־מִי הֲרִימוֹתָ קּוֹל וַתִּשָּׂא מָרוֹם
כג עֵינֶיךָ עַל־קְדוֹשׁ יִשְׂרָאֵל: בְּיַד מַלְאָכֶיךָ חֵרַפְתָּ | אֲדֹנָי וַתֹּאמֶר ברכב בְּרֹב
רִכְבִּי אֲנִי עָלִיתִי מְרוֹם הָרִים יַרְכְּתֵי לְבָנוֹן וְאֶכְרֹת קוֹמַת אֲרָזָיו מִבְחוֹר
כד בְּרֹשָׁיו וְאָבוֹאָה מְלוֹן קִצֹּה יַעַר כַּרְמִלּוֹ: אֲנִי קַרְתִּי וְשָׁתִיתִי מַיִם
כה זָרִים וְאַחְרִב בְּכַף־פְּעָמַי כֹּל יְאֹרֵי מָצוֹר: הֲלֹא־שָׁמַעְתָּ לְמֵרָחוֹק
אֹתָהּ עָשִׂיתִי לְמִימֵי קֶדֶם וִיצַרְתִּיהָ עַתָּה הֲבֵיאתִיהָ וּתְהִי לְהַשְׁוֹת
כו גַּלִּים נִצִּים עָרִים בְּצֻרוֹת: וְיֹשְׁבֵיהֶן קִצְרֵי־יָד חַתּוּ וַיֵּבֹשׁוּ הָיוּ עֵשֶׂב
כז שָׂדֶה וִירַק דֶּשֶׁא חֲצִיר גַּגּוֹת וּשְׁדֵפָה לִפְנֵי קָמָה: וְשִׁבְתְּךָ וְצֵאתְךָ
כח וּבֹאֲךָ יָדָעְתִּי וְאֵת הִתְרַגֶּזְךָ אֵלָי: יַעַן הִתְרַגֶּזְךָ אֵלַי וְשַׁאֲנַנְךָ עָלָה

29 and drag you back along the road you came by. And this will be your sign:
This year you will eat what grows of itself, next year what grows from that, and
in the third year you will sow and harvest, plant vineyards and eat of their
30 fruit. Once more, the remaining survivors of the House of Yehuda will set
31 down roots below, bear fruits above. For a remnant will emerge from
Jerusalem, survivors from Mount Zion; the passion of the LORD of Hosts
32 will bring all this to be. And so, thus says the LORD of the king of
Assyria: He will not enter this city; he will not shoot one arrow there. He will
not advance upon her with the shield, nor pile up a siege mound against her.
33 The way he came he will return, but this city he will not enter. The LORD has
34 spoken. And I will protect this city, and deliver her, for My own sake and for
35 the sake of My servant David." And that night, an angel of the LORD
went out and struck down 185,000 in the Assyrian camp; by daybreak the next
36 morning, they were all dead bodies. And Sanḥeriv, king of Assyria, departed
37 at once and retreated and settled again in Nineveh. He was worshipping in
the temple of his god, Nisrokh, when his sons Adramelekh and Saretzer put
him to the sword. They fled to the land of Ararat, and his son Esar Ḥadon
20 1 reigned in his place. At that time, Ḥizkiyahu fell deathly ill, and
the prophet Yeshayahu son of Amotz came to him. "Thus says the LORD,"
he said. "Issue orders for your household, for you are dying; you will not
2 3 recover." And he turned his face to the wall and prayed to the LORD. "Please,
O LORD," he said, "please remember how I walked before You truly, with all
my heart, and how I did what is right in Your eyes." And Ḥizkiya wept bitter
4 tears. Yeshayahu had not yet left the middle courtyard when the
5 word of the LORD came to him: "Go back and say to Ḥizkiyahu, leader of My
people: Thus says the LORD, the God of your ancestor David: I have heard
your prayer; I have seen your tears. Now I will heal you – on the third day, you
6 will go up to the House of the LORD. And I will add fifteen years to your life;
and I will save you and this city from the hand of the king of Assyria – I will
7 protect this city for My sake and for the sake of My servant David." Then
Yeshayahu said, "Fetch a cake of dried figs," and they fetched one and placed
8 it on the boils, and he recovered. Ḥizkiyahu then said to Yeshayahu, "What
is the sign that the LORD will heal me so that I will go up to the House of the
9 LORD on the third day?" "Let this be a sign for you from the LORD that the
LORD will fulfill the promise He made," said Yeshayahu. "Shall the shadow
10 advance ten steps or recede ten steps?" "The shadow can easily lengthen by
11 ten steps," said Yeḥizkiyahu, "but it cannot recede by ten steps." And the
prophet Yeshayahu called out to the LORD, and He made the shadow that
12 had descended on the sundial of Aḥaz recede by ten steps. At that
time, Berodakh Baladan son of Baladan, king of Babylon, sent letters and a

בְאׇזְנָי וְשַׂמְתִּי חַחִי בְּאַפֶּךָ וּמִתְגִּי בִּשְׂפָתֶיךָ וַהֲשִׁבֹתִיךָ בַּדֶּרֶךְ אֲשֶׁר־
כט בָּאתָ בָּהּ׃ וְזֶה־לְּךָ הָאוֹת אָכוֹל הַשָּׁנָה סָפִיחַ וּבַשָּׁנָה הַשֵּׁנִית סָחִישׁ
ל וּבַשָּׁנָה הַשְּׁלִישִׁית זִרְעוּ וְקִצְרוּ וְנִטְעוּ כְרָמִים וְאִכְלוּ פִרְיָם׃ וְיָסְפָה
לא פְּלֵיטַת בֵּית־יְהוּדָה הַנִּשְׁאָרָה שֹׁרֶשׁ לְמָטָּה וְעָשָׂה פְרִי לְמָעְלָה׃
כִּי מִירוּשָׁלַ͏ִם תֵּצֵא שְׁאֵרִית וּפְלֵיטָה מֵהַר צִיּוֹן קִנְאַת יהוה צְבָאוֹת
לב תַּעֲשֶׂה־זֹּאת׃ לָכֵן כֹּה־אָמַר יהוה אֶל־מֶלֶךְ אַשּׁוּר לֹא
יָבֹא אֶל־הָעִיר הַזֹּאת וְלֹא־יוֹרֶה שָׁם חֵץ וְלֹא־יְקַדְּמֶנָּה מָגֵן וְלֹא־
לג יִשְׁפֹּךְ עָלֶיהָ סֹלְלָה׃ בַּדֶּרֶךְ אֲשֶׁר־יָבֹא בָּהּ יָשׁוּב וְאֶל־הָעִיר הַזֹּאת
לד לֹא יָבֹא נְאֻם־יהוה׃ וְגַנּוֹתִי אֶל־הָעִיר הַזֹּאת לְהוֹשִׁיעָהּ לְמַעֲנִי
לה וּלְמַעַן דָּוִד עַבְדִּי׃ וַיְהִי בַּלַּיְלָה הַהוּא וַיֵּצֵא ׀ מַלְאַךְ
יהוה וַיַּךְ בְּמַחֲנֵה אַשּׁוּר מֵאָה שְׁמוֹנִים וַחֲמִשָּׁה אָלֶף וַיַּשְׁכִּימוּ בַבֹּקֶר
לו וְהִנֵּה כֻלָּם פְּגָרִים מֵתִים׃ וַיִּסַּע וַיֵּלֶךְ וַיָּשָׁב סַנְחֵרִיב מֶלֶךְ־אַשּׁוּר
לז וַיֵּשֶׁב בְּנִינְוֵה׃ וַיְהִי הוּא מִשְׁתַּחֲוֶה בֵּית ׀ נִסְרֹךְ אֱלֹהָיו וְאַדְרַמֶּלֶךְ
וְשַׂרְאֶצֶר הִכֻּהוּ בַחֶרֶב וְהֵמָּה נִמְלְטוּ אֶרֶץ אֲרָרָט וַיִּמְלֹךְ אֵסַר־חַדֹּן בָּנָיו
כ א בְּנוֹ תַּחְתָּיו׃ בַּיָּמִים הָהֵם חָלָה חִזְקִיָּהוּ לָמוּת וַיָּבֹא אֵלָיו
יְשַׁעְיָהוּ בֶן־אָמוֹץ הַנָּבִיא וַיֹּאמֶר אֵלָיו כֹּה־אָמַר יהוה צַו לְבֵיתֶךָ כִּי
ב מֵת אַתָּה וְלֹא תִחְיֶה׃ וַיַּסֵּב אֶת־פָּנָיו אֶל־הַקִּיר וַיִּתְפַּלֵּל אֶל־יהוה
ג לֵאמֹר׃ אָנָּה יהוה זְכָר־נָא אֵת אֲשֶׁר הִתְהַלַּכְתִּי לְפָנֶיךָ בֶּאֱמֶת וּבְלֵבָב
ד שָׁלֵם וְהַטּוֹב בְּעֵינֶיךָ עָשִׂיתִי וַיֵּבְךְּ חִזְקִיָּהוּ בְּכִי גָדוֹל׃ וַיְהִי
ה יְשַׁעְיָהוּ לֹא יָצָא הָעִיר הַתִּיכֹנָה וּדְבַר־יהוה הָיָה אֵלָיו לֵאמֹר׃ שׁוּב חָצֵר
וְאָמַרְתָּ אֶל־חִזְקִיָּהוּ נְגִיד־עַמִּי כֹּה־אָמַר יהוה אֱלֹהֵי דָּוִד אָבִיךָ
שָׁמַעְתִּי אֶת־תְּפִלָּתֶךָ רָאִיתִי אֶת־דִּמְעָתֶךָ הִנְנִי רֹפֶא לָךְ בַּיּוֹם הַשְּׁלִישִׁי
ו תַּעֲלֶה בֵּית יהוה׃ וְהֹסַפְתִּי עַל־יָמֶיךָ חֲמֵשׁ עֶשְׂרֵה שָׁנָה וּמִכַּף מֶלֶךְ־
אַשּׁוּר אַצִּילְךָ וְאֵת הָעִיר הַזֹּאת וְגַנּוֹתִי עַל־הָעִיר הַזֹּאת לְמַעֲנִי וּלְמַעַן
ז דָּוִד עַבְדִּי׃ וַיֹּאמֶר יְשַׁעְיָהוּ קְחוּ דְּבֶלֶת תְּאֵנִים וַיִּקְחוּ וַיָּשִׂימוּ עַל־
ח הַשְּׁחִין וַיֶּחִי׃ וַיֹּאמֶר חִזְקִיָּהוּ אֶל־יְשַׁעְיָהוּ מָה אוֹת כִּי־יִרְפָּא יהוה לב
ט לִי וְעָלִיתִי בַּיּוֹם הַשְּׁלִישִׁי בֵּית יהוה׃ וַיֹּאמֶר יְשַׁעְיָהוּ זֶה־לְּךָ הָאוֹת
מֵאֵת יהוה כִּי יַעֲשֶׂה יהוה אֶת־הַדָּבָר אֲשֶׁר דִּבֵּר הָלַךְ הַצֵּל עֶשֶׂר
י מַעֲלוֹת אִם־יָשׁוּב עֶשֶׂר מַעֲלוֹת׃ וַיֹּאמֶר יְחִזְקִיָּהוּ נָקֵל לַצֵּל לִנְטוֹת
יא עֶשֶׂר מַעֲלוֹת לֹא כִּי יָשׁוּב הַצֵּל אֲחֹרַנִּית עֶשֶׂר מַעֲלוֹת׃ וַיִּקְרָא יְשַׁעְיָהוּ
הַנָּבִיא אֶל־יהוה וַיָּשֶׁב אֶת־הַצֵּל בַּמַּעֲלוֹת אֲשֶׁר יָרְדָה בְּמַעֲלוֹת אָחָז
יב אֲחֹרַנִּית עֶשֶׂר מַעֲלוֹת׃ בָּעֵת הַהִיא שָׁלַח בְּרֹאדַךְ בַּלְאֲדָן

13 gift to Ḥizkiyahu, for he had heard that Ḥizkiyahu had fallen ill. Ḥizkiyahu
received them and showed them all around his treasure house: the silver and
gold, the spices and fine oil, his armory, and everything that was kept in his
treasuries, in his palace, and all his realm; there was nothing that Ḥizkiyahu
14 did not show them. But the prophet Yeshayahu came to King Ḥizkiyahu and
said to him, "What did these people say, and from where did they come to
15 you?" "They came from a distant land," said Ḥizkiya, "from Babylon." "What
have they seen in your palace?" he asked. "Why, they have seen everything
in my palace," said Ḥizkiyahu. "There was nothing in my treasuries that I did
16 not show them." "Hear the word of the Lord," Yeshayahu said to Ḥizkiyahu.
17 "Behold – the days are coming when all that fills your palace and all that your
fathers amassed until this day will be borne away to Babylon, and nothing
18 will be left," the Lord has said, "while sons of yours who came forth from
you, who were born to you, will be borne far away, castrated slaves in the
19 palace of the king of Babylon." And Ḥizkiyahu said to Yeshayahu, "The word
of the Lord you have spoken is fair." For he thought, "At least peace and truth
20 will reign in my own time." As for the rest of Ḥizkiyahu's history and all his
heroic feats and how he constructed the pool and the conduit to bring water
into the city – they are recorded in the book of the History of the Kings
21 of Yehuda. And Ḥizkiyahu slept with his ancestors, and his son Menashe
21 1 reigned in his place. Menashe was twelve years old when he became
king, and for fifty-five years he reigned in Jerusalem. His mother's name was
2 Ḥeftziva. He did what was evil in the eyes of the Lord, imitating the horrors
3 of the nations whom the Lord had dispossessed before the Israelites. He
rebuilt the high shrines that his father Ḥizkiyahu had destroyed, and he
erected altars for Baal and made a sacred tree as Aḥav, king of Israel, had done;
4 he bowed down to all the heavenly hosts and served them. He even built
altars in the House of the Lord, of which the Lord had said, "In Jerusalem,
5 I will establish My name" – he built altars for all the heavenly hosts in both
6 courtyards of the House of the Lord. He passed his son through the fire and
practiced augury and divination and consulted ghosts and spirits; he did so
7 much that was evil in the eyes of the Lord, angering Him. He placed the
statue of Ashera that he had made in the very House of which the Lord said
to David and his son Shlomo: "In this House, and in Jerusalem, which I have
8 chosen out of all the tribes of Israel, I will establish My name forever. And
never again will I make the feet of Israel wander from the soil that I gave to
their ancestors – so long as they carefully observe all that I commanded them,
9 and all the teachings that My servant Moshe commanded them." But they
did not listen, and Menashe led them astray – to commit even worse evil than
10 the nations whom the Lord had destroyed before the Israelites. So the Lord
11 spoke through His servants the prophets: "Because Menashe, king of Yehuda,

בֶּן־בַּלְאֲדָן מֶלֶךְ־בָּבֶל סְפָרִים וּמִנְחָה אֶל־חִזְקִיָּהוּ כִּי שָׁמַע כִּי חָלָה
יג חִזְקִיָּהוּ: וַיִּשְׁמַע עֲלֵיהֶם חִזְקִיָּהוּ וַיַּרְאֵם אֶת־כָּל־בֵּית נְכֹתֹה אֶת־הַכֶּסֶף
וְאֶת־הַזָּהָב וְאֶת־הַבְּשָׂמִים וְאֵת ׀ שֶׁמֶן הַטּוֹב וְאֵת בֵּית כֵּלָיו וְאֵת
כָּל־אֲשֶׁר נִמְצָא בְּאוֹצְרֹתָיו לֹא־הָיָה דָבָר אֲשֶׁר לֹא־הֶרְאָם חִזְקִיָּהוּ
יד בְּבֵיתוֹ וּבְכָל־מֶמְשַׁלְתּוֹ: וַיָּבֹא יְשַׁעְיָהוּ הַנָּבִיא אֶל־הַמֶּלֶךְ חִזְקִיָּהוּ
וַיֹּאמֶר אֵלָיו מָה־אָמְרוּ ׀ הָאֲנָשִׁים הָאֵלֶּה וּמֵאַיִן יָבֹאוּ אֵלֶיךָ וַיֹּאמֶר
טו חִזְקִיָּהוּ מֵאֶרֶץ רְחוֹקָה בָּאוּ מִבָּבֶל: וַיֹּאמֶר מָה רָאוּ בְּבֵיתֶךָ וַיֹּאמֶר
חִזְקִיָּהוּ אֵת כָּל־אֲשֶׁר בְּבֵיתִי רָאוּ לֹא־הָיָה דָבָר אֲשֶׁר לֹא־הִרְאִיתִם
טז יז בְּאֹצְרֹתָי: וַיֹּאמֶר יְשַׁעְיָהוּ אֶל־חִזְקִיָּהוּ שְׁמַע דְּבַר־יהוה: הִנֵּה יָמִים
בָּאִים וְנִשָּׂא ׀ כָּל־אֲשֶׁר בְּבֵיתֶךָ וַאֲשֶׁר אָצְרוּ אֲבֹתֶיךָ עַד־הַיּוֹם הַזֶּה
יח בָּבֶלָה לֹא־יִוָּתֵר דָּבָר אָמַר יהוה: וּמִבָּנֶיךָ אֲשֶׁר יֵצְאוּ מִמְּךָ אֲשֶׁר
יט תּוֹלִיד יִקָּח וְהָיוּ סָרִיסִים בְּהֵיכַל מֶלֶךְ בָּבֶל: וַיֹּאמֶר חִזְקִיָּהוּ אֶל־
יְשַׁעְיָהוּ טוֹב דְּבַר־יהוה אֲשֶׁר דִּבַּרְתָּ וַיֹּאמֶר הֲלוֹא אִם־שָׁלוֹם וֶאֱמֶת
כ יִהְיֶה בְיָמָי: וְיֶתֶר דִּבְרֵי חִזְקִיָּהוּ וְכָל־גְּבוּרָתוֹ וַאֲשֶׁר עָשָׂה אֶת־הַבְּרֵכָה
וְאֶת־הַתְּעָלָה וַיָּבֵא אֶת־הַמַּיִם הָעִירָה הֲלֹא־הֵם כְּתוּבִים עַל־סֵפֶר
כא דִּבְרֵי הַיָּמִים לְמַלְכֵי יְהוּדָה: וַיִּשְׁכַּב חִזְקִיָּהוּ עִם־אֲבֹתָיו וַיִּמְלֹךְ מְנַשֶּׁה
כא א בְּנוֹ תַּחְתָּיו: בֶּן־שְׁתֵּים עֶשְׂרֵה שָׁנָה מְנַשֶּׁה בְמָלְכוֹ
ב וַחֲמִשִּׁים וְחָמֵשׁ שָׁנָה מָלַךְ בִּירוּשָׁלִָם וְשֵׁם אִמּוֹ חֶפְצִי־בָהּ: וַיַּעַשׂ הָרַע
בְּעֵינֵי יהוה כְּתוֹעֲבֹת הַגּוֹיִם אֲשֶׁר הוֹרִישׁ יהוה מִפְּנֵי בְּנֵי יִשְׂרָאֵל:
ג וַיָּשָׁב וַיִּבֶן אֶת־הַבָּמוֹת אֲשֶׁר אִבַּד חִזְקִיָּהוּ אָבִיו וַיָּקֶם מִזְבְּחֹת לַבַּעַל
וַיַּעַשׂ אֲשֵׁרָה כַּאֲשֶׁר עָשָׂה אַחְאָב מֶלֶךְ יִשְׂרָאֵל וַיִּשְׁתַּחוּ לְכָל־צְבָא
ד הַשָּׁמַיִם וַיַּעֲבֹד אֹתָם: וּבָנָה מִזְבְּחֹת בְּבֵית יהוה אֲשֶׁר אָמַר יהוה
ה בִּירוּשָׁלִַם אָשִׂים אֶת־שְׁמִי: וַיִּבֶן מִזְבְּחוֹת לְכָל־צְבָא הַשָּׁמָיִם בִּשְׁתֵּי
ו חַצְרוֹת בֵּית־יהוה: וְהֶעֱבִיר אֶת־בְּנוֹ בָּאֵשׁ וְעוֹנֵן וְנִחֵשׁ וְעָשָׂה אוֹב
ז וְיִדְּעֹנִים הִרְבָּה לַעֲשׂוֹת הָרַע בְּעֵינֵי יהוה לְהַכְעִיס: וַיָּשֶׂם אֶת־פֶּסֶל
הָאֲשֵׁרָה אֲשֶׁר עָשָׂה בַּבַּיִת אֲשֶׁר אָמַר יהוה אֶל־דָּוִד וְאֶל־שְׁלֹמֹה
בְנוֹ בַּבַּיִת הַזֶּה וּבִירוּשָׁלִַם אֲשֶׁר בָּחַרְתִּי מִכֹּל שִׁבְטֵי יִשְׂרָאֵל אָשִׂים
ח אֶת־שְׁמִי לְעוֹלָם: וְלֹא אֹסִיף לְהָנִיד רֶגֶל יִשְׂרָאֵל מִן־הָאֲדָמָה אֲשֶׁר
נָתַתִּי לַאֲבוֹתָם רַק ׀ אִם־יִשְׁמְרוּ לַעֲשׂוֹת כְּכֹל אֲשֶׁר צִוִּיתִים וּלְכָל־
ט הַתּוֹרָה אֲשֶׁר־צִוָּה אֹתָם עַבְדִּי מֹשֶׁה: וְלֹא שָׁמֵעוּ וַיַּתְעֵם מְנַשֶּׁה
לַעֲשׂוֹת אֶת־הָרָע מִן־הַגּוֹיִם אֲשֶׁר הִשְׁמִיד יהוה מִפְּנֵי בְּנֵי יִשְׂרָאֵל:
י יא וַיְדַבֵּר יהוה בְּיַד־עֲבָדָיו הַנְּבִיאִים לֵאמֹר: יַעַן אֲשֶׁר עָשָׂה מְנַשֶּׁה

has committed these abominations – worse than all the Amorites did before
12 him – and because he has led Yehuda to sin with his idols, thus says
the Lord, God of Israel: I am about to bring such evil on Jerusalem and
13 Yehuda that whoever hears of it – why, both his ears will ring. I will stretch
out the measuring line of Shomron and the plummet of the house of Aḥav
over Jerusalem, and I will wipe out Jerusalem as a dish is wiped clean and
14 turned upside down. I will abandon the remnant of My share and hand them
over to their enemies, and they will become plunder and prey to all their
15 enemies – because they have been doing what is evil in My eyes, angering
16 me from the day their ancestors left Egypt to this day." And what is more,
Menashe shed so much innocent blood until Jerusalem was brimming from
end to end; this was besides the sin of leading Yehuda to sin, doing what was
17 evil in the eyes of the Lord. As for the rest of Menashe's history and all he
did and the sins that he sinned – they are recorded in the book of the History
18 of the Kings of Yehuda. And Menashe slept with his ancestors and was buried
in his palace garden, in the garden of Uza. And his son Amon reigned in his
19 place. Amon was twenty-two years old when he became king, and
for two years he reigned in Jerusalem. His mother's name was Meshulemet,
20 daughter of Ḥarutz of Yotva. He did what was evil in the eyes of the Lord, as
21 his father Menashe had done; he followed in all the ways that his father had
followed, and he served the idols that his father had served and bowed down
22 to them. He left the Lord, the God of his ancestors, and he did not follow
23 in the ways of the Lord. Then the servants of Amon formed a conspiracy
24 against him, and they assassinated the king in his palace. But the people of
the land struck down all those who had conspired against King Amon, and
25 the people of the land appointed his son Yoshiyahu king in his place. As for
the rest of Amon's history and his deeds – they are recorded in the book of
26 the History of the Kings of Yehuda. They buried him in his burial plot in the
22 1 garden of Uza, and his son Yoshiyahu reigned in his place. Yoshiyahu
was eight years old when he became king, and for thirty-one years he
reigned in Jerusalem. His mother's name was Yedidya daughter of Adaya,
2 from Botzkat. He did what was right in the eyes of the Lord and followed
3 in all the ways of his ancestor David, straying neither right nor left. In the
eighteenth year of King Yoshiyahu, the king sent the scribe Shafan son of
4 Atzalyahu son of Meshulam to the House of the Lord with this message: "Go
up to Ḥilkiyahu the High Priest and have him calculate the silver that has
been brought to the House of the Lord, which the guardians of the threshold
5 have collected from the people. Have them give it to the foremen in charge
of the House of the Lord, and they will pay it out to the workers in the House
6 of the Lord to keep the House in repair – to the carpenters, builders, and
7 masons – and to purchase wood and quarry stones to repair the House. But
there is no need to keep track of the silver entrusted to them, for they deal

מֶלֶךְ־יְהוּדָה הַתֹּעֵבוֹת הָאֵלֶּה הֵרַע מִכֹּל אֲשֶׁר־עָשׂוּ הָאֱמֹרִי אֲשֶׁר
יב לְפָנָיו וַיַּחֲטִא גַם־אֶת־יְהוּדָה בְּגִלּוּלָיו׃ לָכֵן כֹּה־אָמַר יהוה
אֱלֹהֵי יִשְׂרָאֵל הִנְנִי מֵבִיא רָעָה עַל־יְרוּשָׁלִַם וִיהוּדָה אֲשֶׁר כָּל־שֹׁמְעָיו שֹׁמְעָהּ
יג תִּצַּלְנָה שְׁתֵּי אָזְנָיו׃ וְנָטִיתִי עַל־יְרוּשָׁלִַם אֵת קָו שֹׁמְרוֹן וְאֶת־מִשְׁקֹלֶת
בֵּית אַחְאָב וּמָחִיתִי אֶת־יְרוּשָׁלִַם כַּאֲשֶׁר־יִמְחֶה אֶת־הַצַּלַּחַת מָחָה
יד וְהָפַךְ עַל־פָּנֶיהָ׃ וְנָטַשְׁתִּי אֵת שְׁאֵרִית נַחֲלָתִי וּנְתַתִּים בְּיַד אֹיְבֵיהֶם
טו וְהָיוּ לְבַז וְלִמְשִׁסָּה לְכָל־אֹיְבֵיהֶם׃ יַעַן אֲשֶׁר עָשׂוּ אֶת־הָרַע בְּעֵינַי
וַיִּהְיוּ מַכְעִסִים אֹתִי מִן־הַיּוֹם אֲשֶׁר יָצְאוּ אֲבוֹתָם מִמִּצְרַיִם וְעַד הַיּוֹם
טז הַזֶּה׃ וְגַם דָּם נָקִי שָׁפַךְ מְנַשֶּׁה הַרְבֵּה מְאֹד עַד אֲשֶׁר־מִלֵּא אֶת־
יְרוּשָׁלִַם פֶּה לָפֶה לְבַד מֵחַטָּאתוֹ אֲשֶׁר הֶחֱטִיא אֶת־יְהוּדָה לַעֲשׂוֹת
יז הָרַע בְּעֵינֵי יהוה׃ וְיֶתֶר דִּבְרֵי מְנַשֶּׁה וְכָל־אֲשֶׁר עָשָׂה וְחַטָּאתוֹ
אֲשֶׁר חָטָא הֲלֹא־הֵם כְּתוּבִים עַל־סֵפֶר דִּבְרֵי הַיָּמִים לְמַלְכֵי יְהוּדָה׃
יח וַיִּשְׁכַּב מְנַשֶּׁה עִם־אֲבֹתָיו וַיִּקָּבֵר בְּגַן־בֵּיתוֹ בְּגַן־עֻזָּא וַיִּמְלֹךְ אָמוֹן בְּנוֹ
יט תַּחְתָּיו׃ בֶּן־עֶשְׂרִים וּשְׁתַּיִם שָׁנָה אָמוֹן בְּמָלְכוֹ וּשְׁתַּיִם
כ שָׁנִים מָלַךְ בִּירוּשָׁלִָם וְשֵׁם אִמּוֹ מְשֻׁלֶּמֶת בַּת־חָרוּץ מִן־יָטְבָה׃ וַיַּעַשׂ
כא הָרַע בְּעֵינֵי יהוה כַּאֲשֶׁר עָשָׂה מְנַשֶּׁה אָבִיו׃ וַיֵּלֶךְ בְּכָל־הַדֶּרֶךְ אֲשֶׁר־
כב הָלַךְ אָבִיו וַיַּעֲבֹד אֶת־הַגִּלֻּלִים אֲשֶׁר עָבַד אָבִיו וַיִּשְׁתַּחוּ לָהֶם׃ וַיַּעֲזֹב
כג אֶת־יהוה אֱלֹהֵי אֲבֹתָיו וְלֹא הָלַךְ בְּדֶרֶךְ יהוה׃ וַיִּקְשְׁרוּ עַבְדֵי־אָמוֹן
כד עָלָיו וַיָּמִיתוּ אֶת־הַמֶּלֶךְ בְּבֵיתוֹ׃ וַיַּךְ עַם־הָאָרֶץ אֵת כָּל־הַקֹּשְׁרִים
כה עַל־הַמֶּלֶךְ אָמוֹן וַיַּמְלִיכוּ עַם־הָאָרֶץ אֶת־יֹאשִׁיָּהוּ בְנוֹ תַּחְתָּיו׃ וְיֶתֶר
דִּבְרֵי אָמוֹן אֲשֶׁר עָשָׂה הֲלֹא־הֵם כְּתוּבִים עַל־סֵפֶר דִּבְרֵי הַיָּמִים
כו לְמַלְכֵי יְהוּדָה׃ וַיִּקְבֹּר אֹתוֹ בִּקְבֻרָתוֹ בְּגַן־עֻזָּא וַיִּמְלֹךְ יֹאשִׁיָּהוּ בְנוֹ
כב א תַּחְתָּיו׃ בֶּן־שְׁמֹנֶה שָׁנָה יֹאשִׁיָּהוּ בְמָלְכוֹ וּשְׁלֹשִׁים וְאַחַת
ב שָׁנָה מָלַךְ בִּירוּשָׁלִָם וְשֵׁם אִמּוֹ יְדִידָה בַת־עֲדָיָה מִבָּצְקַת׃ וַיַּעַשׂ לג
הַיָּשָׁר בְּעֵינֵי יהוה וַיֵּלֶךְ בְּכָל־דֶּרֶךְ דָּוִד אָבִיו וְלֹא־סָר יָמִין וּשְׂמֹאול׃
ג וַיְהִי בִּשְׁמֹנֶה עֶשְׂרֵה שָׁנָה לַמֶּלֶךְ יֹאשִׁיָּהוּ שָׁלַח הַמֶּלֶךְ אֶת־שָׁפָן בֶּן־
ד אֲצַלְיָהוּ בֶן־מְשֻׁלָּם הַסֹּפֵר בֵּית יהוה לֵאמֹר׃ עֲלֵה אֶל־חִלְקִיָּהוּ הַכֹּהֵן
הַגָּדוֹל וְיַתֵּם אֶת־הַכֶּסֶף הַמּוּבָא בֵּית יהוה אֲשֶׁר אָסְפוּ שֹׁמְרֵי הַסַּף
ה מֵאֵת הָעָם׃ וְיִתְּנֻה עַל־יַד עֹשֵׂי הַמְּלָאכָה הַמֻּפְקָדִים בבית יהוה בֵּית
וְיִתְּנוּ אֹתוֹ לְעֹשֵׂי הַמְּלָאכָה אֲשֶׁר בְּבֵית יהוה לְחַזֵּק בֶּדֶק הַבָּיִת׃
ו לֶחָרָשִׁים וְלַבֹּנִים וְלַגֹּדְרִים וְלִקְנוֹת עֵצִים וְאַבְנֵי מַחְצֵב לְחַזֵּק אֶת־
ז הַבָּיִת׃ אַךְ לֹא־יֵחָשֵׁב אִתָּם הַכֶּסֶף הַנִּתָּן עַל־יָדָם כִּי בֶאֱמוּנָה הֵם

8 honestly." Then the High Priest Ḥilkiyahu said to Shafan the scribe, "I found
a scroll of the Torah in the House of the LORD." Ḥilkiya gave the scroll to
9 Shafan, and he read it. Shafan the scribe came to the king, and reported back
to the king, "Your servants have melted down the silver found in the House,
and they have paid it out to the foremen in charge of the House of the LORD."
10 Then Shafan the scribe told the king, "The priest Ḥilkiya gave me a scroll,"
11 and Shafan read it out before the king. When the king heard the words of the
12 Torah scroll, he rent his clothes. And the king gave orders to Ḥilkiya the priest,
Aḥikam son of Shafan, Akhbor son of Mikhaya, Shafan the scribe, and Asaya,
13 the king's servant: "Go, inquire of the LORD on my behalf, and on behalf of
the people, and on behalf of all of Yehuda, about the words of this scroll that
has just been found. For great divine fury must have been kindled against us,
because our ancestors did not obey the words of this scroll and do all that
14 was prescribed for us." The priest Ḥilkiyahu, Aḥikam, Akhbor, Shafan, and
Asaya went to Ḥulda the prophet, the wife of Shalum son of Tikva son of
Ḥarḥas, keeper of the wardrobe – she lived in Jerusalem in the Mishneh[104] –
15 and they spoke to her. She said to them, "Thus says the LORD, God of Israel:
16 Say to the man who sent you to me: Thus says the LORD: I am about to bring
disaster upon this place and its inhabitants – fulfilling all the words of the
17 scroll that the king of Yehuda read. Because they left Me and made sacrifices
to other gods to anger Me with all their practices, My fury has been kindled
18 against this place, and it will not be extinguished. And to the king of Yehuda,
who sent you to inquire of the LORD, say this: Thus says the LORD, God of
19 Israel: Concerning the words that you heard, because you softened your heart
and humbled yourself before the LORD when you heard My promise that this
place and its people will become a desolation and a curse, and you rent
20 your clothes and wept before Me, I too have heard. The LORD has spoken. I
will gather you to your ancestors, and you will be gathered to your grave
peacefully; your own eyes will not see all the disaster I will bring upon this
23 1 place." And they reported back to the king. The king summoned all the elders
2 of Yehuda and Jerusalem, who gathered to him. And the king went up to the
House of the LORD, along with all the men of Yehuda and all the inhabitants
of Jerusalem, the priests and the prophets and all the people, from the smallest
to the greatest. And he read out to them all the words of the scroll of the
3 covenant that had been found in the House of the LORD. The king stood on
the platform and reinstated the covenant before the LORD: to follow the
LORD and to keep His commandments, decrees, and laws with all their
heart and all their soul; to fulfill the words of this covenant as written in this
4 book. And all the people pledged themselves to the covenant. The king then

104 | A quarter in the city.

ח עָשִׂים: וַיֹּאמֶר חִלְקִיָּהוּ הַכֹּהֵן הַגָּדוֹל עַל־שָׁפָן הַסֹּפֵר סֵפֶר הַתּוֹרָה
ט מָצָאתִי בְּבֵית יהוה וַיִּתֵּן חִלְקִיָּה אֶת־הַסֵּפֶר אֶל־שָׁפָן וַיִּקְרָאֵהוּ: וַיָּבֹא
שָׁפָן הַסֹּפֵר אֶל־הַמֶּלֶךְ וַיָּשֶׁב אֶת־הַמֶּלֶךְ דָּבָר וַיֹּאמֶר הִתִּיכוּ עֲבָדֶיךָ
אֶת־הַכֶּסֶף הַנִּמְצָא בַבַּיִת וַיִּתְּנֻהוּ עַל־יַד עֹשֵׂי הַמְּלָאכָה הַמֻּפְקָדִים
י בֵּית יהוה: וַיַּגֵּד שָׁפָן הַסֹּפֵר לַמֶּלֶךְ לֵאמֹר סֵפֶר נָתַן לִי חִלְקִיָּה הַכֹּהֵן
יא וַיִּקְרָאֵהוּ שָׁפָן לִפְנֵי הַמֶּלֶךְ: וַיְהִי כִּשְׁמֹעַ הַמֶּלֶךְ אֶת־דִּבְרֵי סֵפֶר הַתּוֹרָה
יב וַיִּקְרַע אֶת־בְּגָדָיו: וַיְצַו הַמֶּלֶךְ אֶת־חִלְקִיָּה הַכֹּהֵן וְאֶת־אֲחִיקָם בֶּן־
שָׁפָן וְאֶת־עַכְבּוֹר בֶּן־מִיכָיָה וְאֵת ׀ שָׁפָן הַסֹּפֵר וְאֵת עֲשָׂיָה עֶבֶד־הַמֶּלֶךְ
יג לֵאמֹר: לְכוּ דִרְשׁוּ אֶת־יהוה בַּעֲדִי וּבְעַד־הָעָם וּבְעַד כָּל־יְהוּדָה
עַל־דִּבְרֵי הַסֵּפֶר הַנִּמְצָא הַזֶּה כִּי־גְדוֹלָה חֲמַת יהוה אֲשֶׁר־הִיא נִצְּתָה
בָנוּ עַל אֲשֶׁר לֹא־שָׁמְעוּ אֲבֹתֵינוּ עַל־דִּבְרֵי הַסֵּפֶר הַזֶּה לַעֲשׂוֹת כְּכָל־
יד הַכָּתוּב עָלֵינוּ: וַיֵּלֶךְ חִלְקִיָּהוּ הַכֹּהֵן וַאֲחִיקָם וְעַכְבּוֹר וְשָׁפָן וַעֲשָׂיָה
אֶל־חֻלְדָּה הַנְּבִיאָה אֵשֶׁת ׀ שַׁלֻּם בֶּן־תִּקְוָה בֶּן־חַרְחַס שֹׁמֵר הַבְּגָדִים
טו וְהִיא יֹשֶׁבֶת בִּירוּשָׁלַםִ בַּמִּשְׁנֶה וַיְדַבְּרוּ אֵלֶיהָ: וַתֹּאמֶר אֲלֵיהֶם כֹּה־
טז אָמַר יהוה אֱלֹהֵי יִשְׂרָאֵל אִמְרוּ לָאִישׁ אֲשֶׁר־שָׁלַח אֶתְכֶם אֵלָי: כֹּה
אָמַר יהוה הִנְנִי מֵבִיא רָעָה אֶל־הַמָּקוֹם הַזֶּה וְעַל־יֹשְׁבָיו אֵת כָּל־
יז דִּבְרֵי הַסֵּפֶר אֲשֶׁר קָרָא מֶלֶךְ יְהוּדָה: תַּחַת ׀ אֲשֶׁר עֲזָבוּנִי וַיְקַטְּרוּ
לֵאלֹהִים אֲחֵרִים לְמַעַן הַכְעִיסֵנִי בְּכֹל מַעֲשֵׂה יְדֵיהֶם וְנִצְּתָה חֲמָתִי
יח בַּמָּקוֹם הַזֶּה וְלֹא תִכְבֶּה: וְאֶל־מֶלֶךְ יְהוּדָה הַשֹּׁלֵחַ אֶתְכֶם לִדְרֹשׁ
אֶת־יהוה כֹּה תֹאמְרוּ אֵלָיו כֹּה־אָמַר יהוה אֱלֹהֵי יִשְׂרָאֵל הַדְּבָרִים
יט אֲשֶׁר שָׁמָעְתָּ: יַעַן רַךְ־לְבָבְךָ וַתִּכָּנַע ׀ מִפְּנֵי יהוה בְּשָׁמְעֲךָ אֲשֶׁר
דִּבַּרְתִּי עַל־הַמָּקוֹם הַזֶּה וְעַל־יֹשְׁבָיו לִהְיוֹת לְשַׁמָּה וְלִקְלָלָה וַתִּקְרַע
כ אֶת־בְּגָדֶיךָ וַתִּבְכֶּה לְפָנָי וְגַם אָנֹכִי שָׁמַעְתִּי נְאֻם־יהוה: לָכֵן הִנְנִי
אֹסִפְךָ עַל־אֲבֹתֶיךָ וְנֶאֱסַפְתָּ אֶל־קִבְרֹתֶיךָ בְּשָׁלוֹם וְלֹא־תִרְאֶינָה עֵינֶיךָ
בְּכֹל הָרָעָה אֲשֶׁר־אֲנִי מֵבִיא עַל־הַמָּקוֹם הַזֶּה וַיָּשִׁבוּ אֶת־הַמֶּלֶךְ
כג א ב דָּבָר: וַיִּשְׁלַח הַמֶּלֶךְ וַיַּאַסְפוּ אֵלָיו כָּל־זִקְנֵי יְהוּדָה וִירוּשָׁלָםִ: וַיַּעַל
הַמֶּלֶךְ בֵּית־יהוה וְכָל־אִישׁ יְהוּדָה וְכָל־יֹשְׁבֵי יְרוּשָׁלַםִ אִתּוֹ וְהַכֹּהֲנִים
וְהַנְּבִיאִים וְכָל־הָעָם לְמִקָּטֹן וְעַד־גָּדוֹל וַיִּקְרָא בְאָזְנֵיהֶם אֶת־כָּל־דִּבְרֵי
ג סֵפֶר הַבְּרִית הַנִּמְצָא בְּבֵית יהוה: וַיַּעֲמֹד הַמֶּלֶךְ עַל־הָעַמּוּד וַיִּכְרֹת
אֶת־הַבְּרִית ׀ לִפְנֵי יהוה לָלֶכֶת אַחַר יהוה וְלִשְׁמֹר מִצְוֹתָיו וְאֶת־
עֵדְוֹתָיו וְאֶת־חֻקֹּתָיו בְּכָל־לֵב וּבְכָל־נֶפֶשׁ לְהָקִים אֶת־דִּבְרֵי הַבְּרִית
ד הַזֹּאת הַכְּתֻבִים עַל־הַסֵּפֶר הַזֶּה וַיַּעֲמֹד כָּל־הָעָם בַּבְּרִית: וַיְצַו הַמֶּלֶךְ

commanded Ḥilkiyahu, the High Priest, the deputy priests, and the guardians
of the threshold to remove from the LORD's Sanctuary all the vessels that had
been made for Baal, Ashera, and all the heavenly hosts. He burned them
outside of Jerusalem in the fields of Kidron and removed their ashes to
5 Beit El. He shut down the idolatrous priests whom the kings of Yehuda had
appointed to offer sacrifices at the high shrines in the towns of Yehuda and
the area around Jerusalem as well as those who offered sacrifices to Baal, to
6 the sun and moon and stars, and to all the heavenly hosts. He brought out
the Ashera from the House of the LORD to the Kidron Valley outside of
Jerusalem, and he burned it in the Kidron Valley and ground it to dust, then
7 he scattered the dust over the common burial ground. He tore down the
booths of the male ritual prostitutes in the House of the LORD, where the
8 women would weave coverings for Ashera. He brought in all the priests from
the towns of Yehuda and defiled the high shrines where the priests had offered
sacrifices from Geva to Be'er Sheva. And he tore down the high shrines by
the gates, those by the entrance to the gate of Joshua, the city governor; they
9 were on a person's left at the city gate. Though the shrine priests could not go
up to the Altar of the LORD in Jerusalem, they did eat of the unleavened bread
10 along with their kin. He defiled the Tofet in the Valley of Ben Hinom so that
11 no one could pass their son or daughter through the fire for Molekh. He put
down the horses that the kings of Yehuda had devoted to the sun from the
entrance of the House of the LORD to the chamber of the eunuch Natan
Melekh in the precincts; and as for the sun chariots, he burned them with fire.
12 As for the altars on the roof of Aḥaz's upper chamber that the kings of Yehuda
had made and the altars that Menashe had made in both courtyards of the
House of the LORD, the king tore them down, and from there he promptly
13 had the rubble scattered in the Kidron Valley. As for the high shrines facing
Jerusalem to the south of the Har HaMashḥit[105] – which Shlomo, king of Israel,
had built for Ashtoret, the abhorrence of the Sidonians, and for Kemosh, the
abhorrence of Moav, and for Milkom, the abomination of the Amonites[106] –
14 the king defiled them. He shattered the worship pillars and cut down the
15 sacred trees and covered their sites with human bones. As for the altar in Beit
El, the high shrine that Yorovam son of Nevat, who led Israel to sin, had
built – he tore down that altar and that high shrine as well. He burned down
the high shrine and ground it to dust and burned down the sacred tree.
16 Yoshiyahu then turned to see the graves that were there on the hillside. He
had the bones dug out of the graves, and he burned them on the altar to defile
it, fulfilling the word of the LORD that was pronounced by the man of God
17 who foretold these events.[107] When he asked, "What is the marker that I see
over there?" the townspeople told him, "It is the grave of the man of God who
came from Yehuda and foretold the very things you just did upon the altar of

105 | Literally "mountain of the destroyer"; this is a disparaging wordplay on Har HaMishḥa (Mount of Ointment), i.e., the Mount of Olives.

106 | Cf. 1 Kings 11:5–7.

107 | See 1 Kings 13:2.

אֶת־חִלְקִיָּהוּ הַכֹּהֵן הַגָּדוֹל וְאֶת־כֹּהֲנֵי הַמִּשְׁנֶה וְאֶת־שֹׁמְרֵי הַסַּף
לְהוֹצִיא מֵהֵיכַל יְהוָה אֵת כָּל־הַכֵּלִים הָעֲשׂוּיִם לַבַּעַל וְלָאֲשֵׁרָה וּלְכֹל
צְבָא הַשָּׁמָיִם וַיִּשְׂרְפֵם מִחוּץ לִירוּשָׁלַםִ בְּשַׁדְמוֹת קִדְרוֹן וְנָשָׂא אֶת
ה עֲפָרָם בֵּית־אֵל׃ וְהִשְׁבִּית אֶת־הַכְּמָרִים אֲשֶׁר נָתְנוּ מַלְכֵי יְהוּדָה
וַיְקַטֵּר בַּבָּמוֹת בְּעָרֵי יְהוּדָה וּמְסִבֵּי יְרוּשָׁלָםִ וְאֶת־הַמְקַטְּרִים לַבַּעַל
ו לַשֶּׁמֶשׁ וְלַיָּרֵחַ וְלַמַּזָּלוֹת וּלְכֹל צְבָא הַשָּׁמָיִם׃ וַיֹּצֵא אֶת־הָאֲשֵׁרָה מִבֵּית
יְהוָה מִחוּץ לִירוּשָׁלַםִ אֶל־נַחַל קִדְרוֹן וַיִּשְׂרֹף אֹתָהּ בְּנַחַל קִדְרוֹן וַיָּדֶק
ז לְעָפָר וַיַּשְׁלֵךְ אֶת־עֲפָרָהּ עַל־קֶבֶר בְּנֵי הָעָם׃ וַיִּתֹּץ אֶת־בָּתֵּי הַקְּדֵשִׁים
ח אֲשֶׁר בְּבֵית יְהוָה אֲשֶׁר הַנָּשִׁים אֹרְגוֹת שָׁם בָּתִּים לָאֲשֵׁרָה׃ וַיָּבֵא
אֶת־כָּל־הַכֹּהֲנִים מֵעָרֵי יְהוּדָה וַיְטַמֵּא אֶת־הַבָּמוֹת אֲשֶׁר קִטְּרוּ־שָׁמָּה
הַכֹּהֲנִים מִגֶּבַע עַד־בְּאֵר שָׁבַע וְנָתַץ אֶת־בָּמוֹת הַשְּׁעָרִים אֲשֶׁר־פֶּתַח
ט שַׁעַר יְהוֹשֻׁעַ שַׂר־הָעִיר אֲשֶׁר־עַל־שְׂמֹאול אִישׁ בְּשַׁעַר הָעִיר׃ אַךְ
לֹא יַעֲלוּ כֹּהֲנֵי הַבָּמוֹת אֶל־מִזְבַּח יְהוָה בִּירוּשָׁלָםִ כִּי אִם־אָכְלוּ מַצּוֹת
י בְּתוֹךְ אֲחֵיהֶם׃ וְטִמֵּא אֶת־הַתֹּפֶת אֲשֶׁר בְּגֵי בני־הִנֹּם לְבִלְתִּי לְהַעֲבִיר בֶּן־
יא אִישׁ אֶת־בְּנוֹ וְאֶת־בִּתּוֹ בָּאֵשׁ לַמֹּלֶךְ׃ וַיַּשְׁבֵּת אֶת־הַסּוּסִים אֲשֶׁר נָתְנוּ
מַלְכֵי יְהוּדָה לַשֶּׁמֶשׁ מִבֹּא בֵית־יְהוָה אֶל־לִשְׁכַּת נְתַן־מֶלֶךְ הַסָּרִיס
יב אֲשֶׁר בַּפַּרְוָרִים וְאֶת־מַרְכְּבוֹת הַשֶּׁמֶשׁ שָׂרַף בָּאֵשׁ׃ וְאֶת־הַמִּזְבְּחוֹת
אֲשֶׁר עַל־הַגָּג עֲלִיַּת אָחָז אֲשֶׁר־עָשׂוּ ׀ מַלְכֵי יְהוּדָה וְאֶת־הַמִּזְבְּחוֹת
אֲשֶׁר עָשָׂה מְנַשֶּׁה בִּשְׁתֵּי חַצְרוֹת בֵּית־יְהוָה נָתַץ הַמֶּלֶךְ וַיָּרָץ מִשָּׁם
יג וְהִשְׁלִיךְ אֶת־עֲפָרָם אֶל־נַחַל קִדְרוֹן׃ וְאֶת־הַבָּמוֹת אֲשֶׁר ׀ עַל־פְּנֵי
יְרוּשָׁלַםִ אֲשֶׁר מִימִין לְהַר־הַמַּשְׁחִית אֲשֶׁר בָּנָה שְׁלֹמֹה מֶלֶךְ־יִשְׂרָאֵל
לְעַשְׁתֹּרֶת ׀ שִׁקֻּץ צִידֹנִים וְלִכְמוֹשׁ שִׁקֻּץ מוֹאָב וּלְמִלְכֹּם תּוֹעֲבַת
יד בְּנֵי־עַמּוֹן טִמֵּא הַמֶּלֶךְ׃ וְשִׁבַּר אֶת־הַמַּצֵּבוֹת וַיִּכְרֹת אֶת־הָאֲשֵׁרִים
טו וַיְמַלֵּא אֶת־מְקוֹמָם עַצְמוֹת אָדָם׃ וְגַם אֶת־הַמִּזְבֵּחַ אֲשֶׁר בְּבֵית־
אֵל הַבָּמָה אֲשֶׁר עָשָׂה יָרָבְעָם בֶּן־נְבָט אֲשֶׁר הֶחֱטִיא אֶת־יִשְׂרָאֵל
גַּם אֶת־הַמִּזְבֵּחַ הַהוּא וְאֶת־הַבָּמָה נָתָץ וַיִּשְׂרֹף אֶת־הַבָּמָה הֵדַק
טז לְעָפָר וְשָׂרַף אֲשֵׁרָה׃ וַיִּפֶן יֹאשִׁיָּהוּ וַיַּרְא אֶת־הַקְּבָרִים אֲשֶׁר־שָׁם
בָּהָר וַיִּשְׁלַח וַיִּקַּח אֶת־הָעֲצָמוֹת מִן־הַקְּבָרִים וַיִּשְׂרֹף עַל־הַמִּזְבֵּחַ
וַיְטַמְּאֵהוּ כִּדְבַר יְהוָה אֲשֶׁר קָרָא אִישׁ הָאֱלֹהִים אֲשֶׁר קָרָא אֶת־
יז הַדְּבָרִים הָאֵלֶּה׃ וַיֹּאמֶר מָה הַצִּיּוּן הַלָּז אֲשֶׁר אֲנִי רֹאֶה וַיֹּאמְרוּ אֵלָיו
אַנְשֵׁי הָעִיר הַקֶּבֶר אִישׁ־הָאֱלֹהִים אֲשֶׁר־בָּא מִיהוּדָה וַיִּקְרָא אֶת־

18 Beit El." "Leave him be," he said. "Let no one disturb his bones." Thus they
spared his bones together with the bones of the prophet who came from
19 Shomron.[108] As for all the shrine temples in the towns of Shomron, which the
kings of Israel had made for provocation, Josiah removed them as well and
20 repeated all the procedures he had carried out at Beit El. He slaughtered all
the priests of the high shrines there on the altars, and he burned human bones
21 on them; then he went back to Jerusalem. The king then commanded all the
people: "Make the Passover sacrifice to the LORD your God, as it is written
22 in this book of the covenant." Now no such Passover sacrifice had been made
since the days of the judges who ruled Israel, nor throughout all the time of
23 the kings of Israel or the kings of Yehuda. But in the eighteenth year of King
24 Yoshiyahu, such a Passover sacrifice was made to the LORD in Jerusalem. As
for the necromancers, mediums, household gods, idols, and all the detestable
things that had appeared in the land of Yehuda and Jerusalem, Yoshiyahu
stamped them out in order to uphold the words of the teaching written in the
25 book that Ḥilkiyahu the priest had found in the House of the LORD. There
was none like him before him – a king who returned to the LORD with all his
heart, all his soul, and all his might, following all the teaching of Moshe, and
26 none like him ever arose after him. Yet the LORD did not turn back from His
great fury, the fury that raged against Yehuda because of all of Menashe's
27 provocations that angered Him. And the LORD said, "I will also remove
Yehuda from My presence, just as I removed Israel. I have rejected this city I
28 once chose, Jerusalem, and the House where I said My name would be." As
for the rest of Yoshiyahu's history and all his deeds – they are recorded in the
29 book of the History of the Kings of Yehuda. In his time, Pharaoh Nekho, the
king of Egypt, marched up against the king of Assyria at the Euphrates, and
King Yoshiyahu confronted him, but he killed him at Megiddo as soon as he
30 saw him. His servants had his body driven from Megiddo and brought him
to Jerusalem, and they buried him in his burial plot. Then the people of the
land took Yehoaḥaz son of Yoshiyahu, anointed him, and made him king in
31 his father's place. Yehoaḥaz was twenty-three years old when he
became king, and for three months he reigned in Jerusalem. His mother's
32 name was Ḥamutal daughter of Yirmeyahu, of Livna. He did what was evil
33 in the eyes of the LORD, just as his ancestors had done. Pharaoh Nekho
imprisoned him at Rivla in the land of Ḥamat to prevent him from reigning
in Jerusalem and placed a penalty on the land of one hundred talents of
34 silver and a talent of gold. Then Pharaoh Nekho made Elyakim son of
Yoshiyahu king in his father Yoshiyahu's place and changed his name to
Yehoyakim. As for Yehoaḥaz, he seized him; and he came to Egypt, where
35 he died. Yehoyakim paid the silver and gold to Pharaoh by assessing the
land to meet Pharaoh's demand for money; he exacted the silver and gold

108 | See 1 Kings 13:31–32.

יח הַדְּבָרִים הָאֵלֶּה אֲשֶׁר עָשִׂיתָ עַל הַמִּזְבַּח בֵּית־אֵל׃ וַיֹּאמֶר הַנִּיחוּ לוֹ
אִישׁ אַל־יָנַע עַצְמֹתָיו וַיְמַלְּטוּ עַצְמֹתָיו אֵת עַצְמוֹת הַנָּבִיא אֲשֶׁר־בָּא
יט מִשֹּׁמְרוֹן׃ וְגַם אֶת־כָּל־בָּתֵּי הַבָּמוֹת אֲשֶׁר ׀ בְּעָרֵי שֹׁמְרוֹן אֲשֶׁר עָשׂוּ
מַלְכֵי יִשְׂרָאֵל לְהַכְעִיס הֵסִיר יֹאשִׁיָּהוּ וַיַּעַשׂ לָהֶם כְּכָל־הַמַּעֲשִׂים
כ אֲשֶׁר עָשָׂה בְּבֵית־אֵל׃ וַיִּזְבַּח אֶת־כָּל־כֹּהֲנֵי הַבָּמוֹת אֲשֶׁר־שָׁם עַל־
כא הַמִּזְבְּחוֹת וַיִּשְׂרֹף אֶת־עַצְמוֹת אָדָם עֲלֵיהֶם וַיָּשָׁב יְרוּשָׁלִָם׃ וַיְצַו הַמֶּלֶךְ
אֶת־כָּל־הָעָם לֵאמֹר עֲשׂוּ פֶסַח לַיהוָה אֱלֹהֵיכֶם כַּכָּתוּב עַל סֵפֶר
כב הַבְּרִית הַזֶּה׃ כִּי לֹא נַעֲשָׂה כַּפֶּסַח הַזֶּה מִימֵי הַשֹּׁפְטִים אֲשֶׁר שָׁפְטוּ
כג אֶת־יִשְׂרָאֵל וְכֹל יְמֵי מַלְכֵי יִשְׂרָאֵל וּמַלְכֵי יְהוּדָה׃ כִּי אִם־בִּשְׁמֹנֶה
כד עֶשְׂרֵה שָׁנָה לַמֶּלֶךְ יֹאשִׁיָּהוּ נַעֲשָׂה הַפֶּסַח הַזֶּה לַיהוָה בִּירוּשָׁלִָם׃ וְגַם
אֶת־הָאֹבוֹת וְאֶת־הַיִּדְּעֹנִים וְאֶת־הַתְּרָפִים וְאֶת־הַגִּלֻּלִים וְאֵת כָּל־
הַשִּׁקֻּצִים אֲשֶׁר נִרְאוּ בְּאֶרֶץ יְהוּדָה וּבִירוּשָׁלִַם בִּעֵר יֹאשִׁיָּהוּ לְמַעַן
הָקִים אֶת־דִּבְרֵי הַתּוֹרָה הַכְּתֻבִים עַל־הַסֵּפֶר אֲשֶׁר מָצָא חִלְקִיָּהוּ
כה הַכֹּהֵן בֵּית יְהוָה׃ וְכָמֹהוּ לֹא־הָיָה לְפָנָיו מֶלֶךְ אֲשֶׁר־שָׁב אֶל־יְהוָה לד
בְּכָל־לְבָבוֹ וּבְכָל־נַפְשׁוֹ וּבְכָל־מְאֹדוֹ כְּכֹל תּוֹרַת מֹשֶׁה וְאַחֲרָיו לֹא־קָם
כו כָּמֹהוּ׃ אַךְ ׀ לֹא־שָׁב יְהוָה מֵחֲרוֹן אַפּוֹ הַגָּדוֹל אֲשֶׁר־חָרָה אַפּוֹ בִּיהוּדָה
כז עַל כָּל־הַכְּעָסִים אֲשֶׁר הִכְעִיסוֹ מְנַשֶּׁה׃ וַיֹּאמֶר יְהוָה גַּם אֶת־יְהוּדָה
אָסִיר מֵעַל פָּנַי כַּאֲשֶׁר הֲסִרֹתִי אֶת־יִשְׂרָאֵל וּמָאַסְתִּי אֶת־הָעִיר הַזֹּאת
אֲשֶׁר־בָּחַרְתִּי אֶת־יְרוּשָׁלִַם וְאֶת־הַבַּיִת אֲשֶׁר אָמַרְתִּי יִהְיֶה שְׁמִי שָׁם׃
כח וְיֶתֶר דִּבְרֵי יֹאשִׁיָּהוּ וְכָל־אֲשֶׁר עָשָׂה הֲלֹא־הֵם כְּתוּבִים עַל־סֵפֶר דִּבְרֵי
כט הַיָּמִים לְמַלְכֵי יְהוּדָה׃ בְּיָמָיו עָלָה פַרְעֹה נְכֹה מֶלֶךְ־מִצְרַיִם עַל־מֶלֶךְ
אַשּׁוּר עַל־נְהַר פְּרָת וַיֵּלֶךְ הַמֶּלֶךְ יֹאשִׁיָּהוּ לִקְרָאתוֹ וַיְמִיתֵהוּ בִּמְגִדּוֹ
ל כִּרְאֹתוֹ אֹתוֹ׃ וַיַּרְכִּבֻהוּ עֲבָדָיו מֵת מִמְּגִדּוֹ וַיְבִאֻהוּ יְרוּשָׁלִַם וַיִּקְבְּרֻהוּ
בִּקְבֻרָתוֹ וַיִּקַּח עַם־הָאָרֶץ אֶת־יְהוֹאָחָז בֶּן־יֹאשִׁיָּהוּ וַיִּמְשְׁחוּ אֹתוֹ
לא וַיַּמְלִיכוּ אֹתוֹ תַּחַת אָבִיו׃ בֶּן־עֶשְׂרִים וְשָׁלֹשׁ שָׁנָה
יְהוֹאָחָז בְּמָלְכוֹ וּשְׁלֹשָׁה חֳדָשִׁים מָלַךְ בִּירוּשָׁלִָם וְשֵׁם אִמּוֹ חֲמוּטַל
לב בַּת־יִרְמְיָהוּ מִלִּבְנָה׃ וַיַּעַשׂ הָרַע בְּעֵינֵי יְהוָה כְּכֹל אֲשֶׁר־עָשׂוּ אֲבֹתָיו׃
לג וַיַּאַסְרֵהוּ פַרְעֹה נְכֹה בְרִבְלָה בְּאֶרֶץ חֲמָת במלך בִּירוּשָׁלִָם וַיִּתֶּן־ מִמְּלֹךְ
לד עֹנֶשׁ עַל־הָאָרֶץ מֵאָה כִכַּר־כֶּסֶף וְכִכַּר זָהָב׃ וַיַּמְלֵךְ פַּרְעֹה נְכֹה אֶת־
אֶלְיָקִים בֶּן־יֹאשִׁיָּהוּ תַּחַת יֹאשִׁיָּהוּ אָבִיו וַיַּסֵּב אֶת־שְׁמוֹ יְהוֹיָקִים
לה וְאֶת־יְהוֹאָחָז לָקַח וַיָּבֹא מִצְרַיִם וַיָּמָת שָׁם׃ וְהַכֶּסֶף וְהַזָּהָב נָתַן יְהוֹיָקִים
לְפַרְעֹה אַךְ הֶעֱרִיךְ אֶת־הָאָרֶץ לָתֵת אֶת־הַכֶּסֶף עַל־פִּי פַרְעֹה אִישׁ

from the people of the land according to each man's worth to pay Pharaoh
36 Nekho. Yehoyakim was twenty-five years old when he became king,
and for eleven years he reigned in Jerusalem. His mother's name was Zevuda
37 daughter of Pedaya, of Ruma. He did what was evil in the eyes of the Lord,
24 1 all that his ancestors had done. In his time, Nevukhadnetzar, king of Babylon,
marched up, and Yehoyakim became his vassal for three years before he
2 turned and rebelled against him. But the Lord sent forth bands of Chaldeans,
bands of Arameans, bands of Moabites, and bands of Amonites against him;
He sent them forth against Yehuda to destroy it, to fulfill the word of the Lord
3 that He had pronounced through His servants the prophets. This was the
Lord's will – to remove Yehuda from His presence because of all the sins
4 Menashe committed, and because of all the innocent blood he spilled; he
filled Jerusalem with innocent blood, and the Lord was not willing to forgive.
5 As for the rest of Yehoyakim's history and all his deeds – they are recorded
6 in the book of the History of the Kings of Yehuda. And Yehoyakim slept
7 with his ancestors, and his son Yehoyakhin reigned in his place. The king of
Egypt no longer ventured out of his own land, for the king of Babylon had
seized all that belonged to the king of Egypt, from the Ravine of Egypt to
8 the Euphrates River. Yehoyakhin was eighteen years old when he
became king, and for three months he reigned in Jerusalem. His mother's
9 name was Neḥushta daughter of Elnatan, of Jerusalem. He did what was evil
10 in the eyes of the Lord, just as his father had done. At that time, the subjects
of Nevukhadnetzar, king of Babylon, marched up against Jerusalem, and the
11 city came under siege, and Nevukhadnetzar, king of Babylon, came to the
12 city while his army laid siege to it. Yehoyakhin, king of Yehuda, surrendered
to the king of Babylon, together with his mother, his officials, his ministers,
and his eunuchs, and the king of Babylon took him captive in the eighth year
13 of his reign. From there he carried off all the treasures of the House of the
Lord and the treasures of the palace, and he stripped off all the golden vessels
that Shlomo, king of Israel, had made in the Sanctuary of the Lord, as the
14 Lord had foretold. He exiled all of Jerusalem, all its ministers and all its
warriors – ten thousand exiles – including all the artisans and smiths; only
15 the very poorest people of the land remained. He exiled Yehoyakhin to
Babylon while the queen mother, the king's wives and eunuchs, and the
16 notables of the land were led in exile from Jerusalem to Babylon. The king
of Babylon led all the powerful men, numbering seven thousand, and one
thousand artisans and smiths – all strong and fit for battle – as exiles to
17 Babylon. And the king of Babylon made Matanyahu, Yehoyakhin's uncle, king
18 in his place, and he changed his name to Tzidkiyahu. Tzidkiyahu
was twenty-one years old when he became king, and for eleven years he
reigned in Jerusalem.[109] His mother's name was Ḥamutal, daughter of
19 Yirmeyahu of Livna. He did what was evil in the eyes of the Lord, just as
20 Yehoyakim had done. And because of the Lord's fury against Jerusalem and

109 | Cf. this story in Jeremiah, chapters 39 and 52.

כְּעֶרְכּוֹ נָגַשׂ אֶת־הַכֶּסֶף וְאֶת־הַזָּהָב אֶת־עַם הָאָרֶץ לָתֵת לְפַרְעֹה
לו נְכֹה׃ בֶּן־עֶשְׂרִים וְחָמֵשׁ שָׁנָה יְהוֹיָקִים בְּמָלְכוֹ וְאַחַת
עֶשְׂרֵה שָׁנָה מָלַךְ בִּירוּשָׁלִָם וְשֵׁם אִמּוֹ זבידה בַת־פְּדָיָה מִן־רוּמָה׃ זְבוּדָּה
לז כד א וַיַּעַשׂ הָרַע בְּעֵינֵי יְהוָה כְּכֹל אֲשֶׁר־עָשׂוּ אֲבֹתָיו׃ בְּיָמָיו עָלָה נְבֻכַדְנֶאצַּר
ב מֶלֶךְ בָּבֶל וַיְהִי־לוֹ יְהוֹיָקִים עֶבֶד שָׁלֹשׁ שָׁנִים וַיָּשָׁב וַיִּמְרָד־בּוֹ׃ וַיְשַׁלַּח
יְהוָה ׀ בּוֹ אֶת־גְּדוּדֵי כַשְׂדִּים וְאֶת־גְּדוּדֵי אֲרָם וְאֵת ׀ גְּדוּדֵי מוֹאָב וְאֵת
גְּדוּדֵי בְנֵי־עַמּוֹן וַיְשַׁלְּחֵם בִּיהוּדָה לְהַאֲבִידוֹ כִּדְבַר יְהוָה אֲשֶׁר דִּבֶּר
ג בְּיַד עֲבָדָיו הַנְּבִיאִים׃ אַךְ ׀ עַל־פִּי יְהוָה הָיְתָה בִּיהוּדָה לְהָסִיר מֵעַל
ד פָּנָיו בְּחַטֹּאת מְנַשֶּׁה כְּכֹל אֲשֶׁר עָשָׂה׃ וְגַם דַּם־הַנָּקִי אֲשֶׁר שָׁפָךְ וַיְמַלֵּא
ה אֶת־יְרוּשָׁלִַם דָּם נָקִי וְלֹא־אָבָה יְהוָה לִסְלֹחַ׃ וְיֶתֶר דִּבְרֵי יְהוֹיָקִים
וְכָל־אֲשֶׁר עָשָׂה הֲלֹא־הֵם כְּתוּבִים עַל־סֵפֶר דִּבְרֵי הַיָּמִים לְמַלְכֵי
ו ז יְהוּדָה׃ וַיִּשְׁכַּב יְהוֹיָקִים עִם־אֲבֹתָיו וַיִּמְלֹךְ יְהוֹיָכִין בְּנוֹ תַּחְתָּיו׃ וְלֹא־
הֹסִיף עוֹד מֶלֶךְ מִצְרַיִם לָצֵאת מֵאַרְצוֹ כִּי־לָקַח מֶלֶךְ בָּבֶל מִנַּחַל
ח מִצְרַיִם עַד־נְהַר פְּרָת כֹּל אֲשֶׁר הָיְתָה לְמֶלֶךְ מִצְרָיִם׃ בֶּן־
שְׁמֹנֶה עֶשְׂרֵה שָׁנָה יְהוֹיָכִין בְּמָלְכוֹ וּשְׁלֹשָׁה חֳדָשִׁים מָלַךְ בִּירוּשָׁלִָם
ט וְשֵׁם אִמּוֹ נְחֻשְׁתָּא בַת־אֶלְנָתָן מִירוּשָׁלִָם׃ וַיַּעַשׂ הָרַע בְּעֵינֵי יְהוָה
י כְּכֹל אֲשֶׁר־עָשָׂה אָבִיו׃ בָּעֵת הַהִיא עלה עַבְדֵי נְבֻכַדְנֶאצַּר מֶלֶךְ־בָּבֶל עָלוּ
יא יְרוּשָׁלִָם וַתָּבֹא הָעִיר בַּמָּצוֹר׃ וַיָּבֹא נְבוּכַדְנֶאצַּר מֶלֶךְ־בָּבֶל עַל־הָעִיר
יב וַעֲבָדָיו צָרִים עָלֶיהָ׃ וַיֵּצֵא יְהוֹיָכִין מֶלֶךְ־יְהוּדָה עַל־מֶלֶךְ בָּבֶל הוּא
וְאִמּוֹ וַעֲבָדָיו וְשָׂרָיו וְסָרִיסָיו וַיִּקַּח אֹתוֹ מֶלֶךְ בָּבֶל בִּשְׁנַת שְׁמֹנֶה
יג לְמָלְכוֹ׃ וַיּוֹצֵא מִשָּׁם אֶת־כָּל־אוֹצְרוֹת בֵּית יְהוָה וְאוֹצְרוֹת בֵּית הַמֶּלֶךְ
וַיְקַצֵּץ אֶת־כָּל־כְּלֵי הַזָּהָב אֲשֶׁר עָשָׂה שְׁלֹמֹה מֶלֶךְ־יִשְׂרָאֵל בְּהֵיכַל
יד יְהוָה כַּאֲשֶׁר דִּבֶּר יְהוָה׃ וְהִגְלָה אֶת־כָּל־יְרוּשָׁלִַם וְאֶת־כָּל־הַשָּׂרִים
וְאֵת ׀ כָּל־גִּבּוֹרֵי הַחַיִל עשרה אֲלָפִים גּוֹלֶה וְכָל־הֶחָרָשׁ וְהַמַּסְגֵּר עֲשֶׂרֶת
טו לֹא נִשְׁאַר זוּלַת דַּלַּת עַם־הָאָרֶץ׃ וַיֶּגֶל אֶת־יְהוֹיָכִין בָּבֶלָה וְאֶת־אֵם
הַמֶּלֶךְ וְאֶת־נְשֵׁי הַמֶּלֶךְ וְאֶת־סָרִיסָיו וְאֵת אולי הָאָרֶץ הוֹלִיךְ גּוֹלָה אֵילֵי
טז מִירוּשָׁלִַם בָּבֶלָה׃ וְאֵת כָּל־אַנְשֵׁי הַחַיִל שִׁבְעַת אֲלָפִים וְהֶחָרָשׁ
וְהַמַּסְגֵּר אֶלֶף הַכֹּל גִּבּוֹרִים עֹשֵׂי מִלְחָמָה וַיְבִיאֵם מֶלֶךְ־בָּבֶל גּוֹלָה
יז בָּבֶלָה׃ וַיַּמְלֵךְ מֶלֶךְ־בָּבֶל אֶת־מַתַּנְיָה דֹדוֹ תַּחְתָּיו וַיַּסֵּב אֶת־שְׁמוֹ
יח צִדְקִיָּהוּ׃ בֶּן־עֶשְׂרִים וְאַחַת שָׁנָה צִדְקִיָּהוּ בְמָלְכוֹ וְאַחַת לה
עֶשְׂרֵה שָׁנָה מָלַךְ בִּירוּשָׁלִָם וְשֵׁם אִמּוֹ חמיטל בַּת־יִרְמְיָהוּ מִלִּבְנָה׃ חֲמוּטַל
יט כ וַיַּעַשׂ הָרַע בְּעֵינֵי יְהוָה כְּכֹל אֲשֶׁר־עָשָׂה יְהוֹיָקִים׃ כִּי ׀ עַל־אַף יְהוָה

Yehuda, He cast them away from His presence. Now Tzidkiyahu rebelled
25 1 against the king of Babylon. In the ninth year of his reign, on the
tenth day of the tenth month, Nevukhadnetzar, king of Babylon, and all his
forces attacked Jerusalem. He encamped against it and built a siege wall all
2 around, and the city remained under siege until the eleventh year of King
3 Tzidkiyahu. By the ninth of the month,[110] famine raged so fiercely in the city
4 that there was no food for the people of the land. The city was breached, and
all the military men fled by the dark of night through the gate between the
double walls by the royal garden, as the Chaldeans surrounded the city, and
5 made toward the Arava. But the Chaldean force pursued the king and caught
up with him on the plains of Yeriḥo, and all his forces scattered and deserted
6 him. They seized the king and hauled him up before the king of Babylon at
7 Rivla, and they spoke harshly to him. They slaughtered Tzidkiyahu's sons
before his eyes and blinded Tzidkiyahu; then they chained him in bronze
8 fetters and brought him to Babylon. And on the seventh day of the
fifth month, in the nineteenth year of the reign of Nevukhadnetzar, king
of Babylon, Nevuzaradan, chief of the guard, the king of Babylon's official,
9 entered Jerusalem. He burned down the House of the Lord and the royal
palace and all the houses in Jerusalem; he set fire to every important building
10 in Jerusalem. As for the walls surrounding Jerusalem, all the Chaldean forces
11 with the chief of the guard tore them down. And as for the rest of the people
who remained in the city and those who defected to the king of Babylon and
12 the rest of the population, Nevuzaradan, chief of the guard, exiled them. But
the chief of the guard retained some of the poorest of the land as vinedressers
13 and field workers. The Chaldeans broke down the bronze pillars from the
House of the Lord, the stands, and the Bronze Sea that was in the House of
14 the Lord and carried the bronze off to Babylon. They took the pots, shovels,
shears, and spoons and all the bronze vessels that had been used in service,
15 while the chief of the guard took the firepans and the basins – whatever was
16 of gold, and whatever was of silver. The two pillars, the Molten Sea, and the
stands that Shlomo had made for the House of the Lord – the weight in
17 bronze of all these vessels was incalculable. Each pillar was eighteen cubits
high, and its capital was of bronze – the capital was three cubits high – and
meshwork and pomegranates surrounded the capital, all of bronze; and the
18 same on top of the second pillar atop the meshwork. The chief of the guard
seized Seraya, the head priest, and Tzefanyahu, the deputy priest, and the
19 three guardians of the threshold. And from the city, he took one official who
was in charge of the military men and five men among the king's personal
attendants who were left in the city, and the scribe of the army commander
whose duty was to rally the people of the land, and sixty of the people of the

110 | Referring to the fourth month; see Jeremiah 52:6.

הָיְתָה בִירוּשָׁלַםִ וּבִיהוּדָה עַד־הִשְׁלִכוֹ אֹתָם מֵעַל פָּנָיו וַיִּמְרֹד צִדְקִיָּהוּ
כה א בְּמֶלֶךְ בָּבֶל׃ וַיְהִי בִשְׁנַת הַתְּשִׁיעִית לְמָלְכוֹ בַּחֹדֶשׁ
הָעֲשִׂירִי בֶּעָשׂוֹר לַחֹדֶשׁ בָּא נְבֻכַדְנֶאצַּר מֶלֶךְ־בָּבֶל הוּא וְכָל־חֵילוֹ
ב עַל־יְרוּשָׁלַםִ וַיִּחַן עָלֶיהָ וַיִּבְנוּ עָלֶיהָ דָּיֵק סָבִיב׃ וַתָּבֹא הָעִיר בַּמָּצוֹר
ג עַד עַשְׁתֵּי עֶשְׂרֵה שָׁנָה לַמֶּלֶךְ צִדְקִיָּהוּ׃ בְּתִשְׁעָה לַחֹדֶשׁ וַיֶּחֱזַק הָרָעָב
ד בָּעִיר וְלֹא־הָיָה לֶחֶם לְעַם הָאָרֶץ׃ וַתִּבָּקַע הָעִיר וְכָל־אַנְשֵׁי הַמִּלְחָמָה ׀
הַלַּיְלָה דֶּרֶךְ שַׁעַר ׀ בֵּין הַחֹמֹתַיִם אֲשֶׁר עַל־גַּן הַמֶּלֶךְ וְכַשְׂדִּים עַל־
ה הָעִיר סָבִיב וַיֵּלֶךְ דֶּרֶךְ הָעֲרָבָה׃ וַיִּרְדְּפוּ חֵיל־כַּשְׂדִּים אַחַר הַמֶּלֶךְ
ו וַיַּשִּׂגוּ אֹתוֹ בְּעַרְבוֹת יְרֵחוֹ וְכָל־חֵילוֹ נָפֹצוּ מֵעָלָיו׃ וַיִּתְפְּשׂוּ אֶת־הַמֶּלֶךְ
ז וַיַּעֲלוּ אֹתוֹ אֶל־מֶלֶךְ בָּבֶל רִבְלָתָה וַיְדַבְּרוּ אִתּוֹ מִשְׁפָּט׃ וְאֶת־בְּנֵי
צִדְקִיָּהוּ שָׁחֲטוּ לְעֵינָיו וְאֶת־עֵינֵי צִדְקִיָּהוּ עִוֵּר וַיַּאַסְרֵהוּ בַנְחֻשְׁתַּיִם
ח וַיְבִאֵהוּ בָּבֶל׃ וּבַחֹדֶשׁ הַחֲמִישִׁי בְּשִׁבְעָה לַחֹדֶשׁ הִיא
שְׁנַת תְּשַׁע־עֶשְׂרֵה שָׁנָה לַמֶּלֶךְ נְבֻכַדְנֶאצַּר מֶלֶךְ־בָּבֶל בָּא נְבוּזַרְאֲדָן
ט רַב־טַבָּחִים עֶבֶד מֶלֶךְ־בָּבֶל יְרוּשָׁלָםִ׃ וַיִּשְׂרֹף אֶת־בֵּית יְהוָה וְאֶת־
בֵּית הַמֶּלֶךְ וְאֵת כָּל־בָּתֵּי יְרוּשָׁלַםִ וְאֶת־כָּל־בֵּית גָּדוֹל שָׂרַף בָּאֵשׁ׃
י וְאֶת־חוֹמֹת יְרוּשָׁלַםִ סָבִיב נָתְצוּ כָּל־חֵיל כַּשְׂדִּים אֲשֶׁר רַב־טַבָּחִים׃
יא וְאֵת יֶתֶר הָעָם הַנִּשְׁאָרִים בָּעִיר וְאֶת־הַנֹּפְלִים אֲשֶׁר נָפְלוּ עַל־הַמֶּלֶךְ
יב בָּבֶל וְאֵת יֶתֶר הֶהָמוֹן הֶגְלָה נְבוּזַרְאֲדָן רַב־טַבָּחִים׃ וּמִדַּלַּת הָאָרֶץ
יג הִשְׁאִיר רַב־טַבָּחִים לְכֹרְמִים ולגבים׃ וְאֶת־עַמּוּדֵי הַנְּחֹשֶׁת אֲשֶׁר וּלְיֹגְבִים
בֵּית־יְהוָה וְאֶת־הַמְּכֹנוֹת וְאֶת־יָם הַנְּחֹשֶׁת אֲשֶׁר בְּבֵית־יְהוָה שִׁבְּרוּ
יד כַשְׂדִּים וַיִּשְׂאוּ אֶת־נְחֻשְׁתָּם בָּבֶלָה׃ וְאֶת־הַסִּירֹת וְאֶת־הַיָּעִים וְאֶת־
הַמְזַמְּרוֹת וְאֶת־הַכַּפּוֹת וְאֵת כָּל־כְּלֵי הַנְּחֹשֶׁת אֲשֶׁר יְשָׁרְתוּ־בָם
טו לָקָחוּ׃ וְאֶת־הַמַּחְתּוֹת וְאֶת־הַמִּזְרָקוֹת אֲשֶׁר זָהָב זָהָב וַאֲשֶׁר־כֶּסֶף
טז כָּסֶף לָקַח רַב־טַבָּחִים׃ הָעַמּוּדִים ׀ שְׁנַיִם הַיָּם הָאֶחָד וְהַמְּכֹנוֹת אֲשֶׁר־
עָשָׂה שְׁלֹמֹה לְבֵית יְהוָה לֹא־הָיָה מִשְׁקָל לִנְחֹשֶׁת כָּל־הַכֵּלִים הָאֵלֶּה׃
יז שְׁמֹנֶה עֶשְׂרֵה אַמָּה קוֹמַת ׀ הָעַמּוּד הָאֶחָד וְכֹתֶרֶת עָלָיו ׀ נְחֹשֶׁת
וְקוֹמַת הַכֹּתֶרֶת שָׁלֹשׁ אמה וּשְׂבָכָה וְרִמֹּנִים עַל־הַכֹּתֶרֶת סָבִיב הַכֹּל אַמּוֹת
יח נְחֹשֶׁת וְכָאֵלֶּה לַעַמּוּד הַשֵּׁנִי עַל־הַשְּׂבָכָה׃ וַיִּקַּח רַב־טַבָּחִים אֶת־
שְׂרָיָה כֹּהֵן הָרֹאשׁ וְאֶת־צְפַנְיָהוּ כֹּהֵן מִשְׁנֶה וְאֶת־שְׁלֹשֶׁת שֹׁמְרֵי הַסַּף׃
יט וּמִן־הָעִיר לָקַח סָרִיס אֶחָד אֲשֶׁר־הוּא פָקִיד ׀ עַל־אַנְשֵׁי הַמִּלְחָמָה
וַחֲמִשָּׁה אֲנָשִׁים מֵרֹאֵי פְנֵי־הַמֶּלֶךְ אֲשֶׁר נִמְצְאוּ בָעִיר וְאֵת הַסֹּפֵר שַׂר
הַצָּבָא הַמַּצְבִּא אֶת־עַם הָאָרֶץ וְשִׁשִּׁים אִישׁ מֵעַם הָאָרֶץ הַנִּמְצְאִים

20 land who were left in the city. Nevuzaradan, the chief of the guard, took them
21 and led them to the king of Babylon in Rivla, and the king of Babylon struck
them down and put them to death in Rivla, in the land of Ḥamat. Thus
22 Yehuda was exiled from its own soil. As for the people who remained in
the land of Yehuda, whom Nevukhadnetzar, king of Babylon, had left, he
23 appointed Gedalyahu son of Aḥikam son of Shafan over them.[111] But when
all the army officers, they and their men, heard that the king of Babylon had
appointed Gedalyahu, they came to Gedalyahu at Mitzpa – Yishmael son of
Netanya, Yoḥanan son of Kare'aḥ, Seraya son of Tanḥumet the Netofatite,
24 and Yaazanyahu son of the Maakhatite, they and their men. "Do not fear the
Chaldean officials," Gedalyahu promised them and their men. "Stay in the
25 land and serve the king of Babylon, and all will be well for you." But
in the seventh month, Yishmael son of Netanya son of Elishama, of royal
descent, came with ten men and assassinated Gedalyahu, along with the
26 Judahites and Chaldeans who were with him in Mitzpa. Then all the
people – from the smallest to the greatest and the army officers – set out and
27 came to Egypt, for they were afraid of the Chaldeans. In
the thirty-seventh year following the exile of Yehoyakhin, king of Yehuda, on
the twenty-seventh of the twelfth month, Evvil Merodakh, king of Babylon,
in the year he became king, granted Yehoyakhin, king of Yehuda, pardon from
28 prison. He spoke kindly to him and set his throne above the thrones of
29 the kings who were with him in Babylon. He removed his prison garb, and
30 he dined in his presence for the rest of his life, and he was granted a permanent allowance from the king – a daily allowance – for the rest of his life.

111 | Cf. Jeremiah 40:7–41:18.

כ בָּעִיר: וַיִּקַּח אֹתָם נְבוּזַרְאֲדָן רַב־טַבָּחִים וַיֹּלֶךְ אֹתָם עַל־מֶלֶךְ בָּבֶל
כא רִבְלָתָה: וַיַּךְ אֹתָם מֶלֶךְ בָּבֶל וַיְמִיתֵם בְּרִבְלָה בְּאֶרֶץ חֲמָת וַיִּגֶל יְהוּדָה
כב מֵעַל אַדְמָתוֹ: וְהָעָם הַנִּשְׁאָר בְּאֶרֶץ יְהוּדָה אֲשֶׁר הִשְׁאִיר נְבוּכַדְנֶאצַּר
כג מֶלֶךְ בָּבֶל וַיַּפְקֵד עֲלֵיהֶם אֶת־גְּדַלְיָהוּ בֶּן־אֲחִיקָם בֶּן־שָׁפָן: וַיִּשְׁמְעוּ
כָל־שָׂרֵי הַחֲיָלִים הֵמָּה וְהָאֲנָשִׁים כִּי־הִפְקִיד מֶלֶךְ־בָּבֶל אֶת־גְּדַלְיָהוּ
וַיָּבֹאוּ אֶל־גְּדַלְיָהוּ הַמִּצְפָּה וְיִשְׁמָעֵאל בֶּן־נְתַנְיָה וְיוֹחָנָן בֶּן־קָרֵחַ
וּשְׂרָיָה בֶן־תַּנְחֻמֶת הַנְּטֹפָתִי וְיַאֲזַנְיָהוּ בֶּן־הַמַּעֲכָתִי הֵמָּה וְאַנְשֵׁיהֶם:
כד וַיִּשָּׁבַע לָהֶם גְּדַלְיָהוּ וּלְאַנְשֵׁיהֶם וַיֹּאמֶר לָהֶם אַל־תִּירְאוּ מֵעַבְדֵי
כה הַכַּשְׂדִּים שְׁבוּ בָאָרֶץ וְעִבְדוּ אֶת־מֶלֶךְ בָּבֶל וְיִטַב לָכֶם: וַיְהִי ׀
בַּחֹדֶשׁ הַשְּׁבִיעִי בָּא יִשְׁמָעֵאל בֶּן־נְתַנְיָה בֶן־אֱלִישָׁמָע מִזֶּרַע הַמְּלוּכָה
וַעֲשָׂרָה אֲנָשִׁים אִתּוֹ וַיַּכּוּ אֶת־גְּדַלְיָהוּ וַיָּמֹת וְאֶת־הַיְּהוּדִים וְאֶת־
כו הַכַּשְׂדִּים אֲשֶׁר־הָיוּ אִתּוֹ בַּמִּצְפָּה: וַיָּקֻמוּ כָל־הָעָם מִקָּטֹן וְעַד־גָּדוֹל
כז וְשָׂרֵי הַחֲיָלִים וַיָּבֹאוּ מִצְרָיִם כִּי יָרְאוּ מִפְּנֵי כַשְׂדִּים: וַיְהִי
בִשְׁלֹשִׁים וָשֶׁבַע שָׁנָה לְגָלוּת יְהוֹיָכִין מֶלֶךְ־יְהוּדָה בִּשְׁנֵים עָשָׂר
חֹדֶשׁ בְּעֶשְׂרִים וְשִׁבְעָה לַחֹדֶשׁ נָשָׂא אֱוִיל מְרֹדַךְ מֶלֶךְ בָּבֶל בִּשְׁנַת
כח מָלְכוֹ אֶת־רֹאשׁ יְהוֹיָכִין מֶלֶךְ־יְהוּדָה מִבֵּית כֶּלֶא: וַיְדַבֵּר אִתּוֹ
כט טֹבוֹת וַיִּתֵּן אֶת־כִּסְאוֹ מֵעַל כִּסֵּא הַמְּלָכִים אֲשֶׁר אִתּוֹ בְּבָבֶל:
ל וְשִׁנָּא אֵת בִּגְדֵי כִלְאוֹ וְאָכַל לֶחֶם תָּמִיד לְפָנָיו כָּל־יְמֵי חַיָּיו: וַאֲרֻחָתוֹ
אֲרֻחַת תָּמִיד נִתְּנָה־לּוֹ מֵאֵת הַמֶּלֶךְ דְּבַר־יוֹם בְּיוֹמוֹ כֹּל יְמֵי חַיָּו:

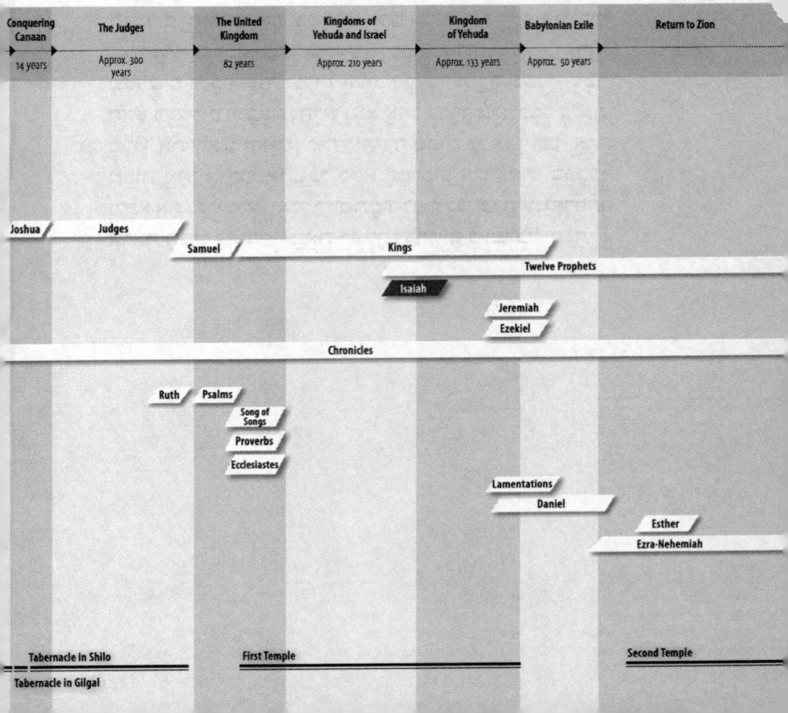

Conquering Canaan
14 years
The Judges
Approx. 300 years
The United Kingdom
82 years
Kingdoms of Yehuda and Israel
Approx. 210 years
Kingdom of Yehuda
Approx. 133 years
Babylonian Exile
Approx. 50 years
Return to Zion
Joshua
Judges
Samuel
Kings
Twelve Prophets
Isaiah
Jeremiah
Ezekiel
Chronicles
Ruth
Psalms
Song of Songs
Proverbs
Ecclesiastes
Lamentations
Daniel
Esther
Ezra-Nehemiah
Tabernacle in Shilo
Tabernacle in Gilgal
First Temple
Second Temple

ישעיה

YESHAYA/ISAIAH

ISAIAH	Rebuke to a corrupt affluent society	Military and spiritual evaluation of the ascent of Assyria	Prophecies regarding the nations	Prophecies of cataclysm and redemption	Yeshaya and Hizkiya	Prophecies of consolation and redemption
	Chs. 1–6	7–12	13–23	24–35	36–39	40–66

1 1 The vision of Yeshayahu son of Amotz, which he saw regarding Yehuda and
Jerusalem in the days of Uziyahu, Yotam, Aḥaz, and Ḥizkiyahu, kings of
2 Yehuda:[1] Listen, heavens, hear, O earth:[2] the LORD has spoken: I brought up
3 children, raised them; they rebelled against Me. Even an ox knows its owner,
an ass its master's trough. Israel does not know; My people does not try to
4 understand. Woe to the sinning nation, a people weighed down with iniquity,
seed of the wicked, vicious children, they forsook the LORD, defamed the
5 Holy One of Israel, fell away. Why should you suffer more beatings? Yet you
6 spawn more defiance, your head sickened, all, your whole heart ailing. From
sole to crown – nothing is sound; laceration, bruise, and open wound never
7 squeezed or bandaged; never eased with oil: your land is laid waste, your
towns burned up in fire; your own land – before your eyes strangers consume
8 it – laid waste: a vision of strangers' overturning.[3] Only daughter Zion stands
like the watchman's shack in a vineyard, like the hut in a cucumber field – a
9 town besieged. *Were it not for the LORD of Hosts, who left of us a bare remnant,*
10 *we would have been like Sedom, like Amora – gone.*[4] Listen to the
LORD's word, you officers of Sedom; hear the teaching of our God, you
11 townsmen of Amora. Why, says the LORD, would I want all these offerings?
I am sated with burnt offerings, with rams and fleshy creatures' fat, the blood
12 of bulls and sheep and goats – I do not want them. You come, appear before
Me. Who asked all this of you, who asked you for all this: trampling My
13 courtyards? Bring no more your empty gifts – they are foul incense to Me;
New Moon and Sabbath, the feast days you proclaim – I cannot endure these
14 sins and assemblies. Your New Moons and festivals, how I hate them; they
15 have become a burden to Me; I am weary, I cannot bear them. When you
spread your hands out skyward, I must turn My eyes away; when you pray
with such verbosity, I am not listening. Your hands, they are covered in blood.
16 Wash them, be clean now, remove your terrible deeds from My sight; stop
17 bringing about such evils. Learn to do good. Seek justice. Correct what is
18 cruel. Rule justice for orphans. Fight the widows' cause. Come, let
us argue this out; so says the LORD. Though your sins may be like scarlet, they
will grow whiter than snow. Though they redden you more than dye worms,
19 they will be clean wool again. If you will it and listen, the best of this earth is
20 yours to eat, but if you refuse and rebel against Me, the sword will devour
21 you; the LORD has spoken. How like a whore is she now, the faithful
metropolis. How full she was of justice once; righteousness lodged with her,
22 now murderers. Your silver has turned into dross, your wine is watered down,
23 your ministers are wayward, friends to thieves, loving corruption, all of them,
chasing bribes. They do not judge an orphan's case; a widow's claim does not
24 even come before them. And so, says the Master, the LORD of Hosts,

---

1 | This period saw the expansion of Assyria and its conquest of the Kingdom of Israel. The prophecies in most of the book are not arranged in chronological order, and it contains narrative accounts as well.

2 | Cf. Deuteronomy 32:1. This prophecy is best understood as a reference to the events of 701 BCE, in which Sanḥeriv, king of Assyria, destroyed many cities of Yehuda.

3 | Cf. the story of Sedom and Amora in Genesis, chapters 18–19.

4 | In Isaiah the translator has used italic font to indicate a change in voice or internal dialogue.

א א חֲזוֹן יְשַׁעְיָהוּ בֶן־אָמוֹץ אֲשֶׁר חָזָה עַל־יְהוּדָה וִירוּשָׁלִָם בִּימֵי עֻזִּיָּהוּ א
ב יוֹתָם אָחָז יְחִזְקִיָּהוּ מַלְכֵי יְהוּדָה׃ שִׁמְעוּ שָׁמַיִם וְהַאֲזִינִי אֶרֶץ כִּי יְהוָה
ג דִּבֵּר בָּנִים גִּדַּלְתִּי וְרוֹמַמְתִּי וְהֵם פָּשְׁעוּ בִי׃ יָדַע שׁוֹר קֹנֵהוּ וַחֲמוֹר
ד אֵבוּס בְּעָלָיו יִשְׂרָאֵל לֹא יָדַע עַמִּי לֹא הִתְבּוֹנָן׃ הוֹי ׀ גּוֹי חֹטֵא עַם
כֶּבֶד עָוֹן זֶרַע מְרֵעִים בָּנִים מַשְׁחִיתִים עָזְבוּ אֶת־יְהוָה נִאֲצוּ אֶת־קְדוֹשׁ
ה יִשְׂרָאֵל נָזֹרוּ אָחוֹר׃ עַל מֶה תֻכּוּ עוֹד תּוֹסִיפוּ סָרָה כָּל־רֹאשׁ לָחֳלִי
ו וְכָל־לֵבָב דַּוָּי׃ מִכַּף־רֶגֶל וְעַד־רֹאשׁ אֵין־בּוֹ מְתֹם פֶּצַע וְחַבּוּרָה וּמַכָּה
ז טְרִיָּה לֹא־זֹרוּ וְלֹא חֻבָּשׁוּ וְלֹא רֻכְּכָה בַּשָּׁמֶן׃ אַרְצְכֶם שְׁמָמָה עָרֵיכֶם
שְׂרֻפוֹת אֵשׁ אַדְמַתְכֶם לְנֶגְדְּכֶם זָרִים אֹכְלִים אֹתָהּ וּשְׁמָמָה כְּמַהְפֵּכַת
ח זָרִים׃ וְנוֹתְרָה בַת־צִיּוֹן כְּסֻכָּה בְכָרֶם כִּמְלוּנָה בְמִקְשָׁה כְּעִיר נְצוּרָה׃
ט לוּלֵי יְהוָה צְבָאוֹת הוֹתִיר לָנוּ שָׂרִיד כִּמְעָט כִּסְדֹם הָיִינוּ לַעֲמֹרָה
י דָּמִינוּ׃ שִׁמְעוּ דְבַר־יְהוָה קְצִינֵי סְדֹם הַאֲזִינוּ תּוֹרַת
יא אֱלֹהֵינוּ עַם עֲמֹרָה׃ לָמָּה לִּי רֹב־זִבְחֵיכֶם יֹאמַר יְהוָה שָׂבַעְתִּי עֹלוֹת
יב אֵילִים וְחֵלֶב מְרִיאִים וְדַם פָּרִים וּכְבָשִׂים וְעַתּוּדִים לֹא חָפָצְתִּי׃ כִּי
יג תָבֹאוּ לֵרָאוֹת פָּנָי מִי־בִקֵּשׁ זֹאת מִיֶּדְכֶם רְמֹס חֲצֵרָי׃ לֹא תוֹסִיפוּ
הָבִיא מִנְחַת־שָׁוְא קְטֹרֶת תּוֹעֵבָה הִיא לִי חֹדֶשׁ וְשַׁבָּת קְרֹא מִקְרָא
יד לֹא־אוּכַל אָוֶן וַעֲצָרָה׃ חָדְשֵׁיכֶם וּמוֹעֲדֵיכֶם שָׂנְאָה נַפְשִׁי הָיוּ עָלַי
טו לָטֹרַח נִלְאֵיתִי נְשֹׂא׃ וּבְפָרִשְׂכֶם כַּפֵּיכֶם אַעְלִים עֵינַי מִכֶּם גַּם כִּי־תַרְבּוּ
טז תְפִלָּה אֵינֶנִּי שֹׁמֵעַ יְדֵיכֶם דָּמִים מָלֵאוּ׃ רַחֲצוּ הִזַּכּוּ הָסִירוּ רֹעַ
יז מַעַלְלֵיכֶם מִנֶּגֶד עֵינָי חִדְלוּ הָרֵעַ׃ לִמְדוּ הֵיטֵב דִּרְשׁוּ מִשְׁפָּט אַשְּׁרוּ
יח חָמוֹץ שִׁפְטוּ יָתוֹם רִיבוּ אַלְמָנָה׃ לְכוּ־נָא וְנִוָּכְחָה יֹאמַר
יְהוָה אִם־יִהְיוּ חֲטָאֵיכֶם כַּשָּׁנִים כַּשֶּׁלֶג יַלְבִּינוּ אִם־יַאְדִּימוּ כַתּוֹלָע
יט כ כַּצֶּמֶר יִהְיוּ׃ אִם־תֹּאבוּ וּשְׁמַעְתֶּם טוּב הָאָרֶץ תֹּאכֵלוּ׃ וְאִם־תְּמָאֲנוּ
כא וּמְרִיתֶם חֶרֶב תְּאֻכְּלוּ כִּי פִּי יְהוָה דִּבֵּר׃ אֵיכָה הָיְתָה לְזוֹנָה
כב קִרְיָה נֶאֱמָנָה מְלֵאֲתִי מִשְׁפָּט צֶדֶק יָלִין בָּהּ וְעַתָּה מְרַצְּחִים׃ כַּסְפֵּךְ
כג הָיָה לְסִיגִים סָבְאֵךְ מָהוּל בַּמָּיִם׃ שָׂרַיִךְ סוֹרְרִים וְחַבְרֵי גַּנָּבִים כֻּלּוֹ
אֹהֵב שֹׁחַד וְרֹדֵף שַׁלְמֹנִים יָתוֹם לֹא יִשְׁפֹּטוּ וְרִיב אַלְמָנָה לֹא־יָבוֹא
כד אֲלֵיהֶם׃ לָכֵן נְאֻם הָאָדוֹן יְהוָה צְבָאוֹת אֲבִיר יִשְׂרָאֵל

the Mighty One of Israel: This woe! – I shall seek consolation, crush My foes,
25 wreak vengeance on My enemies. I shall set My hand against you again, as if
26 smelting, refining away your dross; all your lead will I remove. I shall set up
your judges again as first they were, your counselors as long ago. And then
27 you shall be called Righteous City, Faithful Metropolis. Zion will be redeemed
28 by justice, by righteousness – those who return to her; rebels and sinners will
29 all be broken, those who forsook the Lord all gone. How ashamed you will
be of the oaks that you longed for, how mortified over the gardens you chose.[5]
30 For you will be like an oak with withered leaves, like a garden that sees no
31 water. That mighty oak will become flax fibers and the one who once carved
them the spark; the two will burn together, and no one will be there to
2 1 quench the fire. The vision of Yeshayahu son of Amotz for Yehuda
2 and Jerusalem: This will be in days to come: The mountain of the Lord's
House will be rooted firm, the highest of mountains, raised high above all
3 hills, and all the nations will stream to it. Many peoples will come, saying:
"Come, let us go up to the mount of the Lord, to the House of Yaakov's God;
He will teach us of His ways; we will walk in His pathways," for teaching will
4 come forth from Zion, from Jerusalem, the Lord's word. He will judge
among nations and arbitrate for many peoples; they shall beat their swords
into plowshares, their spears into pruning hooks. Nation shall not raise sword
5 against nation; no more will they learn to make war.[6] House of
6 Yaakov, come, let us walk by the Lord's light. For you have forsaken your
people, House of Yaakov, full of what comes from the east, full of auguries
7 like the Philistines, glutted with customs of strangers. Their land is filled with
8 silver and gold, there is no end to their treasures; their land is filled with
horses, there is no end to their chariots. Their land is filled with false gods;
9 they bow to the works of their hands; their own fingers formed them. Man
falls on his face; a man degrades himself; You would not lift Your judgment.
10 Climb into the rock face; bury yourself in the dust for dread of the Lord
11 before the loftiness of His majesty. The proud eyes of man are fallen, man's
12 erect bearing bent low; the Lord alone will be exalted on that day. It
is the day of the Lord of Hosts for each exalted, each proud man, for each
13 man who is raised – to be brought down. For all the cedars of Lebanon, high
14 and exalted; for all the oaks of Bashan; for all the lofty mountains, all the high
15 16 hills; for each tall tower, each impenetrable wall; for all the boats of Tarshish,[7]
17 all the ships of longing. Man's arrogance will be thrown down, the pride of
18 men brought low; the Lord alone will be exalted on that day; all false gods
19 will cease to be. And people will run to the caves among the rocks, into the
caverns of dust, for fear of the Lord and His dazzling majesty as He comes
20 to strike dread across the earth. On that day, man will throw down his gods
21 of silver, gods of gold, that he made to worship, to the moles and the bats; he
will go into the rocks' clefts, the cliff's hidden places for fear of the Lord and

5 | See 65:3.
6 | Cf. Micah 4:1–3.
7 | A seagoing people who were skilled shipbuilders.

כה הוֹי אֶנָּחֵם מִצָּרַי וְאִנָּקְמָה מֵאוֹיְבָי: וְאָשִׁיבָה יָדִי עָלַיִךְ וְאֶצְרֹף כַּבֹּר
כו סִיגָיִךְ וְאָסִירָה כָּל־בְּדִילָיִךְ: וְאָשִׁיבָה שֹׁפְטַיִךְ כְּבָרִאשֹׁנָה וְיֹעֲצַיִךְ
כז כְּבַתְּחִלָּה אַחֲרֵי־כֵן יִקָּרֵא לָךְ עִיר הַצֶּדֶק קִרְיָה נֶאֱמָנָה: צִיּוֹן בְּמִשְׁפָּט
כח תִּפָּדֶה וְשָׁבֶיהָ בִּצְדָקָה: וְשֶׁבֶר פֹּשְׁעִים וְחַטָּאִים יַחְדָּו וְעֹזְבֵי יהוה
כט יִכְלוּ: כִּי יֵבֹשׁוּ מֵאֵילִים אֲשֶׁר חֲמַדְתֶּם וְתַחְפְּרוּ מֵהַגַּנּוֹת אֲשֶׁר
ל בְּחַרְתֶּם: כִּי תִהְיוּ כְּאֵלָה נֹבֶלֶת עָלֶהָ וּכְגַנָּה אֲשֶׁר־מַיִם אֵין לָהּ:
לא וְהָיָה הֶחָסֹן לִנְעֹרֶת וּפֹעֲלוֹ לְנִיצוֹץ וּבָעֲרוּ שְׁנֵיהֶם יַחְדָּו וְאֵין
ב א מְכַבֶּה: הַדָּבָר אֲשֶׁר חָזָה יְשַׁעְיָהוּ בֶּן־אָמוֹץ עַל־יְהוּדָה
ב וִירוּשָׁלִָם: וְהָיָה ׀ בְּאַחֲרִית הַיָּמִים נָכוֹן יִהְיֶה הַר בֵּית־יהוה בְּרֹאשׁ
ג הֶהָרִים וְנִשָּׂא מִגְּבָעוֹת וְנָהֲרוּ אֵלָיו כָּל־הַגּוֹיִם: וְהָלְכוּ עַמִּים רַבִּים
וְאָמְרוּ לְכוּ ׀ וְנַעֲלֶה אֶל־הַר־יהוה אֶל־בֵּית אֱלֹהֵי יַעֲקֹב וְיֹרֵנוּ מִדְּרָכָיו
וְנֵלְכָה בְּאֹרְחֹתָיו כִּי מִצִּיּוֹן תֵּצֵא תוֹרָה וּדְבַר־יהוה מִירוּשָׁלִָם:
ד וְשָׁפַט בֵּין הַגּוֹיִם וְהוֹכִיחַ לְעַמִּים רַבִּים וְכִתְּתוּ חַרְבוֹתָם לְאִתִּים
וַחֲנִיתוֹתֵיהֶם לְמַזְמֵרוֹת לֹא־יִשָּׂא גוֹי אֶל־גּוֹי חֶרֶב וְלֹא־יִלְמְדוּ עוֹד
ה ו מִלְחָמָה: בֵּית יַעֲקֹב לְכוּ וְנֵלְכָה בְּאוֹר יהוה: כִּי נָטַשְׁתָּה
עַמְּךָ בֵּית יַעֲקֹב כִּי מָלְאוּ מִקֶּדֶם וְעֹנְנִים כַּפְּלִשְׁתִּים וּבְיַלְדֵי נָכְרִים
ז יַשְׂפִּיקוּ: וַתִּמָּלֵא אַרְצוֹ כֶּסֶף וְזָהָב וְאֵין קֵצֶה לְאֹצְרֹתָיו וַתִּמָּלֵא אַרְצוֹ
ח סוּסִים וְאֵין קֵצֶה לְמַרְכְּבֹתָיו: וַתִּמָּלֵא אַרְצוֹ אֱלִילִים לְמַעֲשֵׂה יָדָיו
ט יִשְׁתַּחֲווּ לַאֲשֶׁר עָשׂוּ אֶצְבְּעֹתָיו: וַיִּשַּׁח אָדָם וַיִּשְׁפַּל־אִישׁ וְאַל־תִּשָּׂא
י יא לָהֶם: בּוֹא בַצּוּר וְהִטָּמֵן בֶּעָפָר מִפְּנֵי פַּחַד יהוה וּמֵהֲדַר גְּאֹנוֹ: עֵינֵי
גַּבְהוּת אָדָם שָׁפֵל וְשַׁח רוּם אֲנָשִׁים וְנִשְׂגַּב יהוה לְבַדּוֹ בַּיּוֹם
יב הַהוּא: כִּי יוֹם לַיהוה צְבָאוֹת עַל כָּל־גֵּאֶה וָרָם וְעַל
יג כָּל־נִשָּׂא וְשָׁפֵל: וְעַל כָּל־אַרְזֵי הַלְּבָנוֹן הָרָמִים וְהַנִּשָּׂאִים וְעַל כָּל־
יד אַלּוֹנֵי הַבָּשָׁן: וְעַל כָּל־הֶהָרִים הָרָמִים וְעַל כָּל־הַגְּבָעוֹת הַנִּשָּׂאוֹת:
טו טז וְעַל כָּל־מִגְדָּל גָּבֹהַּ וְעַל כָּל־חוֹמָה בְצוּרָה: וְעַל כָּל־אֳנִיּוֹת תַּרְשִׁישׁ
יז וְעַל כָּל־שְׂכִיּוֹת הַחֶמְדָּה: וְשַׁח גַּבְהוּת הָאָדָם וְשָׁפֵל רוּם אֲנָשִׁים
יח יט וְנִשְׂגַּב יהוה לְבַדּוֹ בַּיּוֹם הַהוּא: וְהָאֱלִילִים כָּלִיל יַחֲלֹף: וּבָאוּ בִּמְעָרוֹת
צֻרִים וּבִמְחִלּוֹת עָפָר מִפְּנֵי פַּחַד יהוה וּמֵהֲדַר גְּאוֹנוֹ בְּקוּמוֹ לַעֲרֹץ
כ הָאָרֶץ: בַּיּוֹם הַהוּא יַשְׁלִיךְ הָאָדָם אֵת אֱלִילֵי כַסְפּוֹ וְאֵת אֱלִילֵי זְהָבוֹ
כא אֲשֶׁר עָשׂוּ־לוֹ לְהִשְׁתַּחֲוֹת לַחְפֹּר פֵּרוֹת וְלָעֲטַלֵּפִים: לָבוֹא בְּנִקְרוֹת
הַצֻּרִים וּבִסְעִפֵי הַסְּלָעִים מִפְּנֵי פַּחַד יהוה וּמֵהֲדַר גְּאוֹנוֹ בְּקוּמוֹ לַעֲרֹץ

22 His dazzling majesty as He comes to strike dread across the earth. Stop; leave
3 1 man be who breathes – for what is his importance? For behold: the
Master, the LORD of Hosts, is taking from Jerusalem, from Yehuda all support,
2 all sustenance; all the bread they lean on, all the water; all the heroes, men of
3 war, judges, prophets, seers, elders, captains of fifties, and all who are respected,
4 advisors, artisans, whisperers of spells. I shall make children their princes;
5 infants will rule them. The people will be oppressed, one by another, each by
his friend; children will lord it over old men, and those who are contemptible
6 over those who merit honor. A man will grasp hold of his brother there in his
father's house. "You – you have a cloak: be our leader; let this ruin be in your
7 charge." And he, on that day, will raise his voice, "How can I be the one to
bandage you? In my house no bread, no cloak; do not make me a leader of
8 men." For Jerusalem and Yehuda have stumbled, fallen, their words, their
9 actions flouting the LORD, defying His glorious eyes. Their faces bear witness
against them; their sin is like that of Sedom. They say it outright, deny
10 nothing; woe to their souls, for they have done them wrong. Tell the righteous
11 that all is well, for they shall eat the fruits of their deeds. And woe to the
12 wicked man, evil; for what his hands have done will be done to him. My
people – their tyrants are infants; women rule over them. My people, those
13 who lead you, lead awry, confounding your pathways. The LORD is
14 ready for His case to be heard: He stands up now to judge nations. The LORD
is coming to trial with His people's elders, its princes: "It is you who ravaged
15 the vineyard; the plunder of the poor is in your homes. By what right do you
crush My people, grinding the faces of the poor?" So speaks the Lord GOD
16 of Hosts. The LORD says: Because the daughters of Zion are proud,
walking with their heads poised, casting their eyes around them, walking their
17 dainty walk, their feet ringing with anklets, the Lord will scab over the skulls
18 of the daughters of Zion; the LORD will lay their heads bare. On that
day, the Lord will pull off the glory of those anklets, those headbands and
19 20 moon pendants, earrings and bangles and scarves, those headdresses, silver
21 bands, and sashes, the perfume boxes and amulets, all those finger rings and
22 23 nose rings, the fine robes, the mantles, the stoles and the purses, the mirrors
24 and shawls, the turbans and veils. And where there was perfume, there shall
be stench, and where there were fine girdles, rope. Fine braided hair will fall
away to baldness; fine robes will fall to leave women wrapped in sacking;
25 this – where once there was beauty. Your men will fall to the sword, your valor
26 killed in action. Her gates will be weeping, lamenting, and empty will she sit
4 1 upon the ground. Seven women will take hold of any one man on that day;
they will say, "We will eat our own bread; we will wear our own clothes – only
2 let us be called by your name; only take away our disgrace." On that
day, the LORD's shoot will flower into beauty, into glory, and the fruit of the
3 land will be majesty, magnificence, for those of Israel who remain. And those
who are left in Zion, surviving in Jerusalem, "holy" will be said of them, of all
4 in Jerusalem who are inscribed to live after the Lord has cleaned the filth from

כב הָאָרֶץ: חִדְלוּ לָכֶם מִן־הָאָדָם אֲשֶׁר נְשָׁמָה בְּאַפּוֹ כִּי בַמֶּה נֶחְשָׁב
ג א הוּא: כִּי הִנֵּה הָאָדוֹן יהוה צְבָאוֹת מֵסִיר מִירוּשָׁלַם
ב וּמִיהוּדָה מַשְׁעֵן וּמַשְׁעֵנָה כֹּל מִשְׁעַן־לֶחֶם וְכֹל מִשְׁעַן־מָיִם: גִּבּוֹר
ג וְאִישׁ מִלְחָמָה שׁוֹפֵט וְנָבִיא וְקֹסֵם וְזָקֵן: שַׂר־חֲמִשִּׁים וּנְשׂוּא פָנִים
ד וְיוֹעֵץ וַחֲכַם חֲרָשִׁים וּנְבוֹן לָחַשׁ: וְנָתַתִּי נְעָרִים שָׂרֵיהֶם וְתַעֲלוּלִים
ה יִמְשְׁלוּ־בָם: וְנִגַּשׂ הָעָם אִישׁ בְּאִישׁ וְאִישׁ בְּרֵעֵהוּ יִרְהֲבוּ הַנַּעַר בַּזָּקֵן
ו וְהַנִּקְלֶה בַּנִּכְבָּד: כִּי־יִתְפֹּשׂ אִישׁ בְּאָחִיו בֵּית אָבִיו שִׂמְלָה לְכָה קָצִין
ז תִּהְיֶה־לָּנוּ וְהַמַּכְשֵׁלָה הַזֹּאת תַּחַת יָדֶךָ: יִשָּׂא בַיּוֹם הַהוּא ׀ לֵאמֹר
לֹא־אֶהְיֶה חֹבֵשׁ וּבְבֵיתִי אֵין לֶחֶם וְאֵין שִׂמְלָה לֹא תְשִׂימֻנִי קְצִין עָם:
ח כִּי כָשְׁלָה יְרוּשָׁלַם וִיהוּדָה נָפָל כִּי־לְשׁוֹנָם וּמַעַלְלֵיהֶם אֶל־יהוה
ט לַמְרוֹת עֵנֵי כְבוֹדוֹ: הַכָּרַת פְּנֵיהֶם עָנְתָה בָּם וְחַטָּאתָם כִּסְדֹם הִגִּידוּ
י לֹא כִחֵדוּ אוֹי לְנַפְשָׁם כִּי־גָמְלוּ לָהֶם רָעָה: אִמְרוּ צַדִּיק כִּי־טוֹב כִּי־
יא יב פְרִי מַעַלְלֵיהֶם יֹאכֵלוּ: אוֹי לְרָשָׁע רָע כִּי־גְמוּל יָדָיו יֵעָשֶׂה לּוֹ: עַמִּי
נֹגְשָׂיו מְעוֹלֵל וְנָשִׁים מָשְׁלוּ בוֹ עַמִּי מְאַשְּׁרֶיךָ מַתְעִים וְדֶרֶךְ אֹרְחֹתֶיךָ
יג יד בִּלֵּעוּ: נִצָּב לָרִיב יהוה וְעֹמֵד לָדִין עַמִּים: יהוה
בְּמִשְׁפָּט יָבוֹא עִם־זִקְנֵי עַמּוֹ וְשָׂרָיו וְאַתֶּם בִּעַרְתֶּם הַכֶּרֶם גְּזֵלַת הֶעָנִי
טו בְּבָתֵּיכֶם: מַלָּכֶם תְּדַכְּאוּ עַמִּי וּפְנֵי עֲנִיִּים תִּטְחָנוּ נְאֻם־אֲדֹנָי יֱהוִה מַה־לָּכֶם
טז צְבָאוֹת: וַיֹּאמֶר יהוה יַעַן כִּי גָבְהוּ בְּנוֹת צִיּוֹן וַתֵּלַכְנָה
נְטוּוֹת גָּרוֹן וּמְשַׂקְּרוֹת עֵינָיִם הָלוֹךְ וְטָפֹף תֵּלַכְנָה וּבְרַגְלֵיהֶם תְּעַכַּסְנָה: נְטוּיוֹת
יז יח וְשִׂפַּח אֲדֹנָי קָדְקֹד בְּנוֹת צִיּוֹן וַיהוה פָּתְהֵן יְעָרֶה: בַּיּוֹם
הַהוּא יָסִיר אֲדֹנָי אֵת תִּפְאֶרֶת הָעֲכָסִים וְהַשְּׁבִיסִים וְהַשַּׂהֲרֹנִים:
יט כ הַנְּטִפוֹת וְהַשֵּׁרוֹת וְהָרְעָלוֹת: הַפְּאֵרִים וְהַצְּעָדוֹת וְהַקִּשֻּׁרִים וּבָתֵּי
כא כב הַנֶּפֶשׁ וְהַלְּחָשִׁים: הַטַּבָּעוֹת וְנִזְמֵי הָאָף: הַמַּחֲלָצוֹת וְהַמַּעֲטָפוֹת
כג וְהַמִּטְפָּחוֹת וְהָחֲרִיטִים: הַגִּלְיֹנִים וְהַסְּדִינִים וְהַצְּנִיפוֹת וְהָרְדִידִים:
כד וְהָיָה תַחַת בֹּשֶׂם מַק יִהְיֶה וְתַחַת חֲגוֹרָה נִקְפָּה וְתַחַת מַעֲשֶׂה מִקְשֶׁה
כה קָרְחָה וְתַחַת פְּתִיגִיל מַחֲגֹרֶת שָׂק כִּי־תַחַת יֹפִי: מְתַיִךְ בַּחֶרֶב יִפֹּלוּ
כו וּגְבוּרָתֵךְ בַּמִּלְחָמָה: וְאָנוּ וְאָבְלוּ פְּתָחֶיהָ וְנִקָּתָה לָאָרֶץ תֵּשֵׁב:
ד א וְהֶחֱזִיקוּ שֶׁבַע נָשִׁים בְּאִישׁ אֶחָד בַּיּוֹם הַהוּא לֵאמֹר לַחְמֵנוּ נֹאכֵל
ב וְשִׂמְלָתֵנוּ נִלְבָּשׁ רַק יִקָּרֵא שִׁמְךָ עָלֵינוּ אֱסֹף חֶרְפָּתֵנוּ: בַּיּוֹם
הַהוּא יִהְיֶה צֶמַח יהוה לִצְבִי וּלְכָבוֹד וּפְרִי הָאָרֶץ לְגָאוֹן וּלְתִפְאֶרֶת
ג לִפְלֵיטַת יִשְׂרָאֵל: וְהָיָה ׀ הַנִּשְׁאָר בְּצִיּוֹן וְהַנּוֹתָר בִּירוּשָׁלַם קָדוֹשׁ ב
ד יֵאָמֶר לוֹ כָּל־הַכָּתוּב לַחַיִּים בִּירוּשָׁלָם: אִם ׀ רָחַץ אֲדֹנָי אֵת צֹאַת

the women of Zion, washed away Jerusalem's staining blood with a spirit of
5 judgment, a spirit that burns. And the LORD has formed over Mount Zion's
foundation and all her assemblies a cloud by day and smoke, brilliant light
6 and burning fire by night, for over all the glory, a canopy shields. And that
shelter will be shade all day from searing heat and a covering, a hiding place
5 1 from the deluge, from the rain. Let me sing a song for my friend, my
beloved's vineyard song: My beloved had a vineyard on the side of a rich hill.
2 He fenced it round, He cleared it, He planted it with vines. He built a
watchtower in it and hewed a winepress there. He hoped it would yield
3 grapes – it grew them rotten. "Now, man of Jerusalem, of Yehuda, judge
4 between Me and My vineyard. What more could I do for My vineyard, what,
that I have not done? Why did I hope to husband grapes where they grew
5 rotten? I tell you here and now what I must do to My vineyard. Tear up the
border hedge and leave it to be ravaged. Burst through the fence, to let them
6 trample it. I must turn this into wasteland, never pruned or hoed; brambles
and briars will take it over; I forbid the clouds ever to rain their rain upon it."
7 The LORD of Hosts' vineyard is the House of Israel, the people of Yehuda His
planting of joy; He hoped for justice: instead, disease; for kindness: instead,
8 the scream.[8] Woe to those who add house to house, join field to field
9 until no space is left; you are settled there alone on the face of the land. As
My ears hear it, I swear – I, the LORD of Hosts – a wealth of homes will
10 become desolation, great ones, fine ones, left without people. Ten *tzemed* of
11 vineyard will yield but one *bat*; ten omer of seed but one ephah.[9] Woe
to those who rise early to chase ale, whom wine lights up through the night,
12 who feast on lute and harp music, on timbrel, flutes, and wine, never once
turning to look at the LORD's workings, never once noticing the work of His
13 hands. And so – My people are exiled for want of knowledge, her glory shrunk
14 to men of hunger, her masses arid with thirst. And so – Sheol[10] spreads herself
wide; her mouth gapes wide without limit. And My people's glory, her crowds
15 and her noise, will all fall with those who rejoice in her. Humanity is humbled;
16 man is thrown down; proud eyes fall. For the LORD of Hosts rises up in
17 judgment: God most holy, made holy by justice. Sheep will graze then, as if
18 in their pasture, while wayfarers eat from the fat clans' ruins.[11] Woe
to those who draw iniquity with ropes of nothingness, pulling sin like a
19 harnessed carriage. "Let Him come quickly," they say. "Let Him bring His
works with haste, that we may see; let the plan of the Holy One of Israel draw
20 close and come to pass; then we will know." Woe to those who say
of evil, "good"; of good, "evil"; those who call darkness light and light dark-
21 ness; who consider sweetness bitter and bitter things sweet. Woe to
22 those who are wise in their own eyes, full of their own insight. Woe

8 | The Hebrew for "disease" (*mispaḥ*) echoes "justice" (*mishpat*). Likewise with "scream" (*tze'aka*) and "kindness" (*tzedaka*).

9 | These amounts express an acute crop failure.

10 | The netherworld.

11 | That is, tranquility will return to the land after the exile and destruction described in verses 13–14.

בְּנוֹת־צִיּוֹן וְאֶת־דְּמֵי יְרוּשָׁלִַם יָדִיחַ מִקִּרְבָּהּ בְּרוּחַ מִשְׁפָּט וּבְרוּחַ בָּעֵר׃
ה וּבָרָא יְהוָה עַל כָּל־מְכוֹן הַר־צִיּוֹן וְעַל־מִקְרָאֶהָ עָנָן ׀ יוֹמָם וְעָשָׁן וְנֹגַהּ
ו אֵשׁ לֶהָבָה לָיְלָה כִּי עַל־כָּל־כָּבוֹד חֻפָּה׃ וְסֻכָּה תִּהְיֶה לְצֵל־יוֹמָם
ה א מֵחֹרֶב וּלְמַחְסֶה וּלְמִסְתּוֹר מִזֶּרֶם וּמִמָּטָר׃ אָשִׁירָה נָּא
ב לִידִידִי שִׁירַת דּוֹדִי לְכַרְמוֹ כֶּרֶם הָיָה לִידִידִי בְּקֶרֶן בֶּן־שָׁמֶן׃ וַיְעַזְּקֵהוּ
וַיְסַקְּלֵהוּ וַיִּטָּעֵהוּ שֹׂרֵק וַיִּבֶן מִגְדָּל בְּתוֹכוֹ וְגַם־יֶקֶב חָצֵב בּוֹ וַיְקַו
ג לַעֲשׂוֹת עֲנָבִים וַיַּעַשׂ בְּאֻשִׁים׃ וְעַתָּה יוֹשֵׁב יְרוּשָׁלִַם וְאִישׁ יְהוּדָה
ד שִׁפְטוּ־נָא בֵּינִי וּבֵין כַּרְמִי׃ מַה־לַּעֲשׂוֹת עוֹד לְכַרְמִי וְלֹא עָשִׂיתִי בּוֹ
ה מַדּוּעַ קִוֵּיתִי לַעֲשׂוֹת עֲנָבִים וַיַּעַשׂ בְּאֻשִׁים׃ וְעַתָּה אוֹדִיעָה־נָּא אֶתְכֶם
אֵת אֲשֶׁר־אֲנִי עֹשֶׂה לְכַרְמִי הָסֵר מְשׂוּכָּתוֹ וְהָיָה לְבָעֵר פָּרֹץ גְּדֵרוֹ
ו וְהָיָה לְמִרְמָס׃ וַאֲשִׁיתֵהוּ בָתָה לֹא יִזָּמֵר וְלֹא יֵעָדֵר וְעָלָה שָׁמִיר וָשָׁיִת
ז וְעַל הֶעָבִים אֲצַוֶּה מֵהַמְטִיר עָלָיו מָטָר׃ כִּי כֶרֶם יְהוָה צְבָאוֹת בֵּית
יִשְׂרָאֵל וְאִישׁ יְהוּדָה נְטַע שַׁעֲשׁוּעָיו וַיְקַו לְמִשְׁפָּט וְהִנֵּה מִשְׂפָּח
ח לִצְדָקָה וְהִנֵּה צְעָקָה׃ הוֹי מַגִּיעֵי בַיִת בְּבַיִת שָׂדֶה בְשָׂדֶה
ט יַקְרִיבוּ עַד אֶפֶס מָקוֹם וְהוּשַׁבְתֶּם לְבַדְּכֶם בְּקֶרֶב הָאָרֶץ׃ בְּאָזְנָי
יְהוָה צְבָאוֹת אִם־לֹא בָּתִּים רַבִּים לְשַׁמָּה יִהְיוּ גְּדֹלִים וְטוֹבִים מֵאֵין
י יוֹשֵׁב׃ כִּי עֲשֶׂרֶת צִמְדֵּי־כֶרֶם יַעֲשׂוּ בַּת אֶחָת וְזֶרַע חֹמֶר יַעֲשֶׂה
יא אֵיפָה׃ הוֹי מַשְׁכִּימֵי בַבֹּקֶר שֵׁכָר יִרְדֹּפוּ מְאַחֲרֵי בַנֶּשֶׁף
יב יַיִן יַדְלִיקֵם׃ וְהָיָה כִנּוֹר וָנֶבֶל תֹּף וְחָלִיל וָיַיִן מִשְׁתֵּיהֶם וְאֵת פֹּעַל יְהוָה
יג לֹא יַבִּיטוּ וּמַעֲשֵׂה יָדָיו לֹא רָאוּ׃ לָכֵן גָּלָה עַמִּי מִבְּלִי־דָעַת וּכְבוֹדוֹ
יד מְתֵי רָעָב וַהֲמוֹנוֹ צִחֵה צָמָא׃ לָכֵן הִרְחִיבָה שְּׁאוֹל נַפְשָׁהּ וּפָעֲרָה פִיהָ
טו לִבְלִי־חֹק וְיָרַד הֲדָרָהּ וַהֲמוֹנָהּ וּשְׁאוֹנָהּ וְעָלֵז בָּהּ׃ וַיִּשַּׁח אָדָם וַיִּשְׁפַּל־
טז אִישׁ וְעֵינֵי גְבֹהִים תִּשְׁפַּלְנָה׃ וַיִּגְבַּהּ יְהוָה צְבָאוֹת בַּמִּשְׁפָּט וְהָאֵל
יז הַקָּדוֹשׁ נִקְדָּשׁ בִּצְדָקָה׃ וְרָעוּ כְבָשִׂים כְּדָבְרָם וְחָרְבוֹת מֵחִים גָּרִים
יח יֹאכֵלוּ׃ הוֹי מֹשְׁכֵי הֶעָוֺן בְּחַבְלֵי הַשָּׁוְא וְכַעֲבוֹת הָעֲגָלָה
יט חַטָּאָה׃ הָאֹמְרִים יְמַהֵר ׀ יָחִישָׁה מַעֲשֵׂהוּ לְמַעַן נִרְאֶה וְתִקְרַב
כ וְתָבוֹאָה עֲצַת קְדוֹשׁ יִשְׂרָאֵל וְנֵדָעָה׃ הוֹי הָאֹמְרִים לָרַע
טוֹב וְלַטּוֹב רָע שָׂמִים חֹשֶׁךְ לְאוֹר וְאוֹר לְחֹשֶׁךְ שָׂמִים מַר לְמָתוֹק
כא וּמָתוֹק לְמָר׃ הוֹי חֲכָמִים בְּעֵינֵיהֶם וְנֶגֶד פְּנֵיהֶם
כב נְבֹנִים׃ הוֹי גִּבּוֹרִים לִשְׁתּוֹת יָיִן וְאַנְשֵׁי־חַיִל לִמְסֹךְ שֵׁכָר׃

23 to the mighty drinkers of wine, heroes in the field of pouring liquor, who
vindicate the wicked for all they will pay and strip the righteous of their
24 rights. Just as a tongue of flame consumes the straw and chaff
collapses beneath the blaze, so will their root grow fetid, their flowers rising
as dust, for they reject the Lord of Hosts' teaching, debasing the word of
25 Israel's Holy One. So the Lord's fury rages against His people, and He
stretches His hand out over them and beats them, and the mountains quake,
and their corpses will be tossed aside like trash in the streets. *And still He has*
26 *not turned away His rage, and still He stretches forth His hand.* He will raise a
signal to the nations from afar and whistle them forth from the ends of the
27 earth; how swiftly they come. None weary, none stumbling among them –
28 they do not slumber, do not sleep; no belt slips, no sandal thong snaps, their
arrows sharp, and every last bow drawn; his[12] horses' hooves like flint and the
29 wheels like a storm wind. His growl like a lion's; like a young lion he growls,
30 roars, seizes his prey, hauls it away, and no one will be there to rescue it. On
that day he roars like the roaring of the sea, and he looks down to earth and
6 1 sees – darkness, pain, and light, darkening, across her clouded skies. In
the year in which King Uziyahu died I saw the Lord sitting on a high, raised
2 throne, the hem of His clothing filling the Sanctuary. There were seraphim
standing above Him, each with six wings – with two they covered their faces,
3 with two they covered their feet, and with two they were flying. And they
called out one to another, "Holy, holy, holy – the Lord of Hosts – all the
4 world's fullness His glory." The door pillars shook with the voice of him who
5 called – and smoke filled the House. And I said, "This ache – I am condemned,
for my mouth has been defiled,[13] one man among a people with their mouths
6 defiled, and my eyes see the King, the Lord of Hosts." One of the seraphim
flew to me, and in his hand was a coal, taken with tongs from the altar top.
7 With this he touched my lips and said, "When this has touched your lips, your
8 iniquity is gone, and all your sin forgiven." I heard the voice of the Lord saying,
"Whom shall I send, and who will go for us?" And I said, "I am here. Send me."
9 He said, "Go – tell this people: Hear, you shall hear but understand it not, see
10 it all but know it not. Fatten the heart of this people; make their ears heavy;
coat their eyes with plaster, lest they see with their eyes and hear with their
11 ears, and their hearts understand and they return – and are healed." I said,
"My Lord, how long?" And He said, "Until the towns are stripped of all who
12 live in them, houses left without people, the land stripped bare, and the Lord
13 dispatches man far hence, and swaths of land will be forsaken; if a tenth there
will survive, it will return and will be burnt like the terebinth and oak tree
that drop their leaves, and yet the trunk remains – and the trunk is holy
7 1 seed." In the days of Aḥaz[14] son of Yotam son of Uziyahu, king of
Yehuda, Retzin, king of Aram, and Pekaḥ son of Remalyahu, king of Israel,
2 launched an attack on Jerusalem, but they could not conquer it. The House

---

12 | The shift to the singular refers to the Assyrian king or to Assyria as an individual.
13 | That is, I have spoken impure words.
14 | See II Kings 16:5.

כג כד מַצְדִּיקֵי רָשָׁע עֵקֶב שֹׁחַד וְצִדְקַת צַדִּיקִים יָסִירוּ מִמֶּנּוּ׃ לָכֵן
כֶּאֱכֹל קַשׁ לְשׁוֹן אֵשׁ וַחֲשַׁשׁ לֶהָבָה יִרְפֶּה שָׁרְשָׁם כַּמָּק יִהְיֶה וּפִרְחָם
כָּאָבָק יַעֲלֶה כִּי מָאֲסוּ אֵת תּוֹרַת יְהוָה צְבָאוֹת וְאֵת אִמְרַת קְדוֹשׁ־
כה יִשְׂרָאֵל נִאֵצוּ׃ עַל־כֵּן חָרָה אַף־יְהוָה בְּעַמּוֹ וַיֵּט יָדוֹ עָלָיו וַיַּכֵּהוּ וַיִּרְגְּזוּ
הֶהָרִים וַתְּהִי נִבְלָתָם כַּסּוּחָה בְּקֶרֶב חוּצוֹת בְּכָל־זֹאת לֹא־שָׁב אַפּוֹ
כו וְעוֹד יָדוֹ נְטוּיָה׃ וְנָשָׂא־נֵס לַגּוֹיִם מֵרָחוֹק וְשָׁרַק לוֹ מִקְצֵה הָאָרֶץ וְהִנֵּה
כז מְהֵרָה קַל יָבוֹא׃ אֵין־עָיֵף וְאֵין־כּוֹשֵׁל בּוֹ לֹא יָנוּם וְלֹא יִישָׁן וְלֹא נִפְתַּח
כח אֵזוֹר חֲלָצָיו וְלֹא נִתַּק שְׂרוֹךְ נְעָלָיו׃ אֲשֶׁר חִצָּיו שְׁנוּנִים וְכָל־קַשְּׁתֹתָיו
כט דְּרֻכוֹת פַּרְסוֹת סוּסָיו כַּצַּר נֶחְשָׁבוּ וְגַלְגִּלָּיו כַּסּוּפָה׃ שְׁאָגָה לוֹ כַּלָּבִיא
ל ושאג כַּכְּפִירִים וְיִנְהֹם וְיֹאחֵז טֶרֶף וְיַפְלִיט וְאֵין מַצִּיל׃ וְיִנְהֹם עָלָיו יִשְׁאַג
בַּיּוֹם הַהוּא כְּנַהֲמַת־יָם וְנִבַּט לָאָרֶץ וְהִנֵּה־חֹשֶׁךְ צַר וָאוֹר חָשַׁךְ
ו א בַּעֲרִיפֶיהָ׃ בִּשְׁנַת־מוֹת הַמֶּלֶךְ עֻזִּיָּהוּ וָאֶרְאֶה אֶת־אֲדֹנָי
ב יֹשֵׁב עַל־כִּסֵּא רָם וְנִשָּׂא וְשׁוּלָיו מְלֵאִים אֶת־הַהֵיכָל׃ שְׂרָפִים עֹמְדִים ׀
מִמַּעַל לוֹ שֵׁשׁ כְּנָפַיִם שֵׁשׁ כְּנָפַיִם לְאֶחָד בִּשְׁתַּיִם ׀ יְכַסֶּה פָנָיו וּבִשְׁתַּיִם
ג יְכַסֶּה רַגְלָיו וּבִשְׁתַּיִם יְעוֹפֵף׃ וְקָרָא זֶה אֶל־זֶה וְאָמַר קָדוֹשׁ ׀ קָדוֹשׁ ג
ד קָדוֹשׁ יְהוָה צְבָאוֹת מְלֹא כָל־הָאָרֶץ כְּבוֹדוֹ׃ וַיָּנֻעוּ אַמּוֹת הַסִּפִּים
ה מִקּוֹל הַקּוֹרֵא וְהַבַּיִת יִמָּלֵא עָשָׁן׃ וָאֹמַר אוֹי־לִי כִי־נִדְמֵיתִי כִּי אִישׁ
טְמֵא־שְׂפָתַיִם אָנֹכִי וּבְתוֹךְ עַם־טְמֵא שְׂפָתַיִם אָנֹכִי יֹשֵׁב כִּי אֶת־הַמֶּלֶךְ
ו יְהוָה צְבָאוֹת רָאוּ עֵינָי׃ וַיָּעָף אֵלַי אֶחָד מִן־הַשְּׂרָפִים וּבְיָדוֹ רִצְפָּה
ז בְּמֶלְקַחַיִם לָקַח מֵעַל הַמִּזְבֵּחַ׃ וַיַּגַּע עַל־פִּי וַיֹּאמֶר הִנֵּה נָגַע זֶה עַל־
ח שְׂפָתֶיךָ וְסָר עֲוֺנֶךָ וְחַטָּאתְךָ תְּכֻפָּר׃ וָאֶשְׁמַע אֶת־קוֹל אֲדֹנָי אֹמֵר
ט אֶת־מִי אֶשְׁלַח וּמִי יֵלֶךְ־לָנוּ וָאֹמַר הִנְנִי שְׁלָחֵנִי׃ וַיֹּאמֶר לֵךְ וְאָמַרְתָּ
י לָעָם הַזֶּה שִׁמְעוּ שָׁמוֹעַ וְאַל־תָּבִינוּ וּרְאוּ רָאוֹ וְאַל־תֵּדָעוּ׃ הַשְׁמֵן
לֵב־הָעָם הַזֶּה וְאָזְנָיו הַכְבֵּד וְעֵינָיו הָשַׁע פֶּן־יִרְאֶה בְעֵינָיו וּבְאָזְנָיו
יא יִשְׁמָע וּלְבָבוֹ יָבִין וָשָׁב וְרָפָא לוֹ׃ וָאֹמַר עַד־מָתַי אֲדֹנָי וַיֹּאמֶר עַד
אֲשֶׁר אִם־שָׁאוּ עָרִים מֵאֵין יוֹשֵׁב וּבָתִּים מֵאֵין אָדָם וְהָאֲדָמָה תִּשָּׁאֶה
יב יג שְׁמָמָה׃ וְרִחַק יְהוָה אֶת־הָאָדָם וְרַבָּה הָעֲזוּבָה בְּקֶרֶב הָאָרֶץ׃ וְעוֹד
בָּהּ עֲשִׂרִיָּה וְשָׁבָה וְהָיְתָה לְבָעֵר כָּאֵלָה וְכָאַלּוֹן אֲשֶׁר בְּשַׁלֶּכֶת מַצֶּבֶת
ז א בָּם זֶרַע קֹדֶשׁ מַצַּבְתָּהּ׃ וַיְהִי בִּימֵי אָחָז בֶּן־יוֹתָם בֶּן־עֻזִּיָּהוּ
מֶלֶךְ יְהוּדָה עָלָה רְצִין מֶלֶךְ־אֲרָם וּפֶקַח בֶּן־רְמַלְיָהוּ מֶלֶךְ־יִשְׂרָאֵל
ב יְרוּשָׁלַםִ לַמִּלְחָמָה עָלֶיהָ וְלֹא יָכֹל לְהִלָּחֵם עָלֶיהָ׃ וַיֻּגַּד לְבֵית דָּוִד
לֵאמֹר נָחָה אֲרָם עַל־אֶפְרָיִם וַיָּנַע לְבָבוֹ וּלְבַב עַמּוֹ כְּנוֹעַ עֲצֵי־יַעַר

of David[15] was told, "Aram is allied with Efrayim." And his heart swayed,
and the hearts of his people, as trees of the forest will sway with the
3 wind. And the LORD said to Yeshayahu: Go out now to meet Aḥaz,
you and She'ar Yashuv[16] your son, to the end of the Upper Pool's conduit, by
4 the road to the Fuller's Field. And say to him: Be guarded, stay still, do not
fear, and let your heart not soften before these smoking tails of firebrands,
5 before the rage of Retzin and Aram and the son of Remalyahu. For Aram has
6 conspired to harm you, along with Efrayim and Remalyahu's son: "We shall
go up to Jerusalem, bring about her end; we shall break her walls open for
7 ourselves and set a new king over her: the son of Taval."[17] Thus says
8 the Lord GOD: It will not come to pass; it will not be. For the head of Aram
is Damascus, and the head of Damascus, Retzin, and in another five and sixty
9 years Efrayim will be shattered as a nation. The head of Efrayim is Shomron,
the head of Shomron is Remalyahu's son, and if you have no faith, you have
10 no future.
11 The LORD spoke again to Aḥaz and said, "Ask any sign of
12 the LORD your God; make it deep as Sheol or high as the heights." But Aḥaz
13 replied, "I shall not ask; I shall not test the LORD."[18] "Listen, House of David,"
Yeshayahu said. "Is it not enough to weary men? Must you weary my God
14 also? The Lord, then, will give you His sign. This maiden will conceive,[19] and
15 she will bear a son. She will call that child Imanu El.[20] Curds and honey will
16 he eat[21] when he knows to refuse what is evil and choose the good. For by
the time he knows to refuse what is evil, to choose the good, the lands of the
17 two kings you dread will all be forsaken, and the LORD will bring upon you,
your people, and your fathers' house, the king of Assyria, days such as never
18 have been since Efrayim left Yehuda." On that day, the LORD will
19 whistle to a fly at the Egyptian Nile's edge, to a bee in the land of Assyria, and
they will swarm and come to rest everywhere – in the crag ravines, in the
20 clefts of rock, on every thorn, in every pasture. On that day the Lord will take
a hired razor beyond the River – the king of Assyria – and shave: head,
21 nakedness, beard – utterly. On that day, each man will nurture one
22 calf, two goats; yet they will yield so much milk that he will live upon curds;
23 all those remaining on the land will live on curds and on honey. On that day,
in each place where once there grew a thousand vines worth a thousand silver
24 coins, briars and thorns will take over. One will need a bow and arrow to pass
25 through there, for the land will be wild with briars and thorns. But the hills
that the hoe turns over, no fear of briar or thorn will come there, for oven will
8 1 wander there and sheep will tread. The LORD said to me: Take a

15 | Aḥaz.
16 | The name means "a remnant will return." Symbolic names of sons appear also in verse 14 and 8:3.
17 | The "son of Taval" cannot be identified with certainty. The name might mean "someone good for us."
18 | Aḥaz offers a pious explanation for his refusal to ask for a sign; cf. the prohibition in Exodus 17:2.
19 | The "maiden" could refer to the wife of Yeshayahu or of the king, or possibly to a different young woman present. The sign is not the birth of the child itself, but the unusual food he will consume.
20 | Meaning "God is with us."
21 | The sign initially sounds positive. However, as verses 21–25 explain, the background is troubling: cultivation of the land will cease, and only these good but simple foods will remain.

ג מִפְּנֵי־רוּחַ׃ וַיֹּאמֶר יְהוָה אֶל־יְשַׁעְיָהוּ צֵא־נָא לִקְרַאת
אָחָז אַתָּה וּשְׁאָר יָשׁוּב בְּנֶךָ אֶל־קְצֵה תְּעָלַת הַבְּרֵכָה הָעֶלְיוֹנָה אֶל־
ד מְסִלַּת שְׂדֵה כוֹבֵס׃ וְאָמַרְתָּ אֵלָיו הִשָּׁמֵר וְהַשְׁקֵט אַל־תִּירָא וּלְבָבְךָ
אַל־יֵרַךְ מִשְּׁנֵי זַנְבוֹת הָאוּדִים הָעֲשֵׁנִים הָאֵלֶּה בָּחֳרִי־אַף רְצִין וַאֲרָם
ה וּבֶן־רְמַלְיָהוּ׃ יַעַן כִּי־יָעַץ עָלֶיךָ אֲרָם רָעָה אֶפְרַיִם וּבֶן־רְמַלְיָהוּ לֵאמֹר׃
ו נַעֲלֶה בִיהוּדָה וּנְקִיצֶנָּה וְנַבְקִעֶנָּה אֵלֵינוּ וְנַמְלִיךְ מֶלֶךְ בְּתוֹכָהּ אֵת
ז בֶּן־טָבְאַל׃ כֹּה אָמַר אֲדֹנָי יֱהוִה לֹא תָקוּם וְלֹא תִהְיֶה׃
ח כִּי רֹאשׁ אֲרָם דַּמֶּשֶׂק וְרֹאשׁ דַּמֶּשֶׂק רְצִין וּבְעוֹד שִׁשִּׁים וְחָמֵשׁ שָׁנָה
ט יֵחַת אֶפְרַיִם מֵעָם׃ וְרֹאשׁ אֶפְרַיִם שֹׁמְרוֹן וְרֹאשׁ שֹׁמְרוֹן בֶּן־רְמַלְיָהוּ
י אִם לֹא תַאֲמִינוּ כִּי לֹא תֵאָמֵנוּ׃ וַיּוֹסֶף יְהוָה דַּבֵּר אֶל־
יא אָחָז לֵאמֹר׃ שְׁאַל־לְךָ אוֹת מֵעִם יְהוָה אֱלֹהֶיךָ הַעְמֵק שְׁאָלָה אוֹ
יב יג הַגְבֵּהַּ לְמָעְלָה׃ וַיֹּאמֶר אָחָז לֹא־אֶשְׁאַל וְלֹא־אֲנַסֶּה אֶת־יְהוָה׃ וַיֹּאמֶר
שִׁמְעוּ־נָא בֵּית דָּוִד הַמְעַט מִכֶּם הַלְאוֹת אֲנָשִׁים כִּי תַלְאוּ גַּם אֶת־
יד אֱלֹהָי׃ לָכֵן יִתֵּן אֲדֹנָי הוּא לָכֶם אוֹת הִנֵּה הָעַלְמָה הָרָה וְיֹלֶדֶת בֵּן
טו וְקָרָאת שְׁמוֹ עִמָּנוּ אֵל׃ חֶמְאָה וּדְבַשׁ יֹאכֵל לְדַעְתּוֹ מָאוֹס בָּרָע וּבָחוֹר
טז בַּטּוֹב׃ כִּי בְּטֶרֶם יֵדַע הַנַּעַר מָאֹס בָּרָע וּבָחֹר בַּטּוֹב תֵּעָזֵב הָאֲדָמָה
יז אֲשֶׁר אַתָּה קָץ מִפְּנֵי שְׁנֵי מְלָכֶיהָ׃ יָבִיא יְהוָה עָלֶיךָ וְעַל־עַמְּךָ וְעַל־
בֵּית אָבִיךָ יָמִים אֲשֶׁר לֹא־בָאוּ לְמִיּוֹם סוּר־אֶפְרַיִם מֵעַל יְהוּדָה אֵת
יח מֶלֶךְ אַשּׁוּר׃ וְהָיָה ׀ בַּיּוֹם הַהוּא יִשְׁרֹק יְהוָה לַזְּבוּב אֲשֶׁר
יט בִּקְצֵה יְאֹרֵי מִצְרָיִם וְלַדְּבוֹרָה אֲשֶׁר בְּאֶרֶץ אַשּׁוּר׃ וּבָאוּ וְנָחוּ כֻלָּם
בְּנַחֲלֵי הַבַּתּוֹת וּבִנְקִיקֵי הַסְּלָעִים וּבְכֹל הַנַּעֲצוּצִים וּבְכֹל הַנַּהֲלֹלִים׃
כ בַּיּוֹם הַהוּא יְגַלַּח אֲדֹנָי בְּתַעַר הַשְּׂכִירָה בְּעֶבְרֵי נָהָר בְּמֶלֶךְ אַשּׁוּר
כא אֶת־הָרֹאשׁ וְשַׂעַר הָרַגְלָיִם וְגַם אֶת־הַזָּקָן תִּסְפֶּה׃ וְהָיָה
כב בַּיּוֹם הַהוּא יְחַיֶּה־אִישׁ עֶגְלַת בָּקָר וּשְׁתֵּי־צֹאן׃ וְהָיָה מֵרֹב עֲשׂוֹת
חָלָב יֹאכַל חֶמְאָה כִּי־חֶמְאָה וּדְבַשׁ יֹאכֵל כׇּל־הַנּוֹתָר בְּקֶרֶב הָאָרֶץ׃
כג וְהָיָה בַּיּוֹם הַהוּא יִהְיֶה כׇל־מָקוֹם אֲשֶׁר יִהְיֶה־שָּׁם אֶלֶף גֶּפֶן
כד בְּאֶלֶף כָּסֶף לַשָּׁמִיר וְלַשַּׁיִת יִהְיֶה׃ בַּחִצִּים וּבַקֶּשֶׁת יָבוֹא שָׁמָּה כִּי־
כה שָׁמִיר וָשַׁיִת תִּהְיֶה כׇל־הָאָרֶץ׃ וְכֹל הֶהָרִים אֲשֶׁר בַּמַּעְדֵּר יֵעָדֵרוּן
לֹא־תָבוֹא שָׁמָּה יִרְאַת שָׁמִיר וָשָׁיִת וְהָיָה לְמִשְׁלַח שׁוֹר וּלְמִרְמַס
ח א שֶׂה׃ וַיֹּאמֶר יְהוָה אֵלַי קַח־לְךָ גִּלָּיוֹן גָּדוֹל וּכְתֹב עָלָיו

large scroll and write upon it in common script: *Of Maher Shalal Ḥash*
2 *Baz.*[22] I called faithful witnesses to witness it for me: Uriya the priest and
3 Zekharya son of Berakhya. And so I came to my prophetess;[23] she conceived
and bore a son. And the LORD said to me, call him, name him, Maher Shalal
4 Ḥash Baz. For before the child knows how to call out "Mother," "Father," the
might of Damascus, the plunder of Shomron, will all be borne away before
5 6 the Assyrian king. The LORD spoke to me again: Because these
people shun the waters of Shiloaḥ,[24] flowing slow, in their frenzy over Retzin
7 and Remalyahu's son, the Lord will bring upon them the potent waters of the
great river – the king of Assyria in all his glory – to flood all the wadis, engulf
8 all the banks, to course over Yehuda, flood it in passing, steep it to the neck.
9 His wings spread over all your land's breadth, *Imanu El.*[25] Blast,
peoples, then fall apart; listen, far-off places of this world; gird yourselves,
10 then fall apart, gird, then fall apart. Plot and plan – you will fail; confer,
11 conspire; it will not come to be: *Imanu El.*[26] For the LORD said to
me, as if taking my hand, instructing me not to walk the path of this people:
12 "Do not say 'Conspiracy,' to all this people call conspiracy. Do not fear all
13 those they fear, nor pay them homage." The LORD of Hosts – it is Him you
14 must sanctify, Him that you fear; to Him you owe homage. And He is
Sanctuary and striking stone, stumbling block to both houses of Israel, trap
15 and snare to the people of Jerusalem. And many will stumble on these, and
16 many will fall and be broken, will be ensnared, be caught. *Bind up*
17 *the testimony; seal Teaching in My students*[27]; I wait for the LORD, who hides
18 His face from Yaakov; I long for Him. You see: I and all the children the LORD
gave me are messages, are signs, to Israel from the LORD of Hosts, who rests
19 upon Mount Zion. When they say to you, "Ask of the necromancers,
of the mediums, the chirpers and mutterers," say, "Does not a people ask its
20 God; why go to the dead for the living?" For teaching, for testimony; this is
21 what they will say, words the sun never rose upon. And one will pass through,
hardened, hungry, and when he has grown hungry, he will overflow with fury
22 and will curse his king, his God, and turn to look upward; he will look down
at the land and see: pain and darkness, dread dark of anguish, and be thrust
23 into the gloom. And the one does not weary who presses her to anguish. The
first lay light on the land of Zevulun, the land of Naftali, and the last weighs
9 1 heavy by the road to the sea, across the Jordan, to the Galilee of nations.[28] The
people who walked in darkness have seen abounding light; those who live in

22 | Meaning "hasten plunder, speed booty."

23 | Called so either because she was the wife of a prophet (Yeshayahu), or a prophetess in her own right.

24 | Jerusalem's only source of water, the modest Shiloaḥ pool, symbolized the city's self-sufficiency under God. The people, however, look to the brawn of Assyria, symbolized by the great Euphrates River.

25 | Meaning "God is with us"; this is the symbolic name given to the child in 7:14. Here it may refer to God's protection.

26 | See note to verse 8; here the term is not a name but a refrain.

27 | Yeshayahu's warnings are not heeded, nor are they vindicated in the short term. God has warned him of this frustration in 6:9.

28 | This is the route the conquerors would take in a campaign that would focus on the Galilee, which

ב בְּחֶרֶט אֱנוֹשׁ לְמַהֵר שָׁלָל חָשׁ בַּז׃ וְאָעִידָה לִּי עֵדִים נֶאֱמָנִים אֵת
ג אוּרִיָּה הַכֹּהֵן וְאֶת־זְכַרְיָהוּ בֶּן יְבֶרֶכְיָהוּ׃ וָאֶקְרַב אֶל־הַנְּבִיאָה וַתַּהַר
ד וַתֵּלֶד בֵּן וַיֹּאמֶר יהוה אֵלַי קְרָא שְׁמוֹ מַהֵר שָׁלָל חָשׁ בַּז׃ כִּי בְּטֶרֶם
יֵדַע הַנַּעַר קְרֹא אָבִי וְאִמִּי יִשָּׂא ׀ אֶת־חֵיל דַּמֶּשֶׂק וְאֵת שְׁלַל שֹׁמְרוֹן
ה ו לִפְנֵי מֶלֶךְ אַשּׁוּר׃ וַיֹּסֶף יהוה דַּבֵּר אֵלַי עוֹד לֵאמֹר׃ יַעַן
כִּי מָאַס הָעָם הַזֶּה אֵת מֵי הַשִּׁלֹחַ הַהֹלְכִים לְאַט וּמְשׂוֹשׂ אֶת־רְצִין
ז וּבֶן־רְמַלְיָהוּ׃ וְלָכֵן הִנֵּה אֲדֹנָי מַעֲלֶה עֲלֵיהֶם אֶת־מֵי הַנָּהָר הָעֲצוּמִים
וְהָרַבִּים אֶת־מֶלֶךְ אַשּׁוּר וְאֶת־כָּל־כְּבוֹדוֹ וְעָלָה עַל־כָּל־אֲפִיקָיו וְהָלַךְ
ח עַל־כָּל־גְּדוֹתָיו׃ וְחָלַף בִּיהוּדָה שָׁטַף וְעָבַר עַד־צַוָּאר יַגִּיעַ וְהָיָה מֻטּוֹת
ט כְּנָפָיו מְלֹא רֹחַב־אַרְצְךָ עִמָּנוּ אֵל׃ רֹעוּ עַמִּים וָחֹתּוּ וְהַאֲזִינוּ
י כֹּל מֶרְחַקֵּי־אָרֶץ הִתְאַזְּרוּ וָחֹתּוּ הִתְאַזְּרוּ וָחֹתּוּ׃ עֻצוּ עֵצָה וְתֻפָר דַּבְּרוּ
יא דָבָר וְלֹא יָקוּם כִּי עִמָּנוּ אֵל׃ כִּי כֹה אָמַר יהוה אֵלַי כְּחֶזְקַת
יב הַיָּד וְיִסְּרֵנִי מִלֶּכֶת בְּדֶרֶךְ הָעָם־הַזֶּה לֵאמֹר׃ לֹא־תֹאמְרוּן קֶשֶׁר לְכֹל
אֲשֶׁר־יֹאמַר הָעָם הַזֶּה קָשֶׁר וְאֶת־מוֹרָאוֹ לֹא־תִירְאוּ וְלֹא תַעֲרִיצוּ׃
יג אֶת־יהוה צְבָאוֹת אֹתוֹ תַקְדִּישׁוּ וְהוּא מוֹרַאֲכֶם וְהוּא מַעֲרִצְכֶם׃
יד וְהָיָה לְמִקְדָּשׁ וּלְאֶבֶן נֶגֶף וּלְצוּר מִכְשׁוֹל לִשְׁנֵי בָתֵּי יִשְׂרָאֵל לְפַח
טו וּלְמוֹקֵשׁ לְיוֹשֵׁב יְרוּשָׁלָ͏ִם׃ וְכָשְׁלוּ בָם רַבִּים וְנָפְלוּ וְנִשְׁבָּרוּ וְנוֹקְשׁוּ
טז יז וְנִלְכָּדוּ׃ צוֹר תְּעוּדָה חֲתוֹם תּוֹרָה בְּלִמֻּדָי׃ וְחִכִּיתִי לַיהוה
יח הַמַּסְתִּיר פָּנָיו מִבֵּית יַעֲקֹב וְקִוֵּיתִי־לוֹ׃ הִנֵּה אָנֹכִי וְהַיְלָדִים אֲשֶׁר נָתַן־
לִי יהוה לְאֹתוֹת וּלְמוֹפְתִים בְּיִשְׂרָאֵל מֵעִם יהוה צְבָאוֹת הַשֹּׁכֵן בְּהַר
יט צִיּוֹן׃ וְכִי־יֹאמְרוּ אֲלֵיכֶם דִּרְשׁוּ אֶל־הָאֹבוֹת וְאֶל־הַיִּדְּעֹנִים
הַמְצַפְצְפִים וְהַמַּהְגִּים הֲלוֹא־עַם אֶל־אֱלֹהָיו יִדְרֹשׁ בְּעַד הַחַיִּים אֶל־
כ הַמֵּתִים׃ לְתוֹרָה וְלִתְעוּדָה אִם־לֹא יֹאמְרוּ כַּדָּבָר הַזֶּה אֲשֶׁר אֵין־לוֹ
כא שָׁחַר׃ וְעָבַר בָּהּ נִקְשֶׁה וְרָעֵב וְהָיָה כִי־יִרְעַב וְהִתְקַצַּף וְקִלֵּל בְּמַלְכּוֹ
כב וּבֵאלֹהָיו וּפָנָה לְמָעְלָה׃ וְאֶל־אֶרֶץ יַבִּיט וְהִנֵּה צָרָה וַחֲשֵׁכָה מְעוּף
כג צוּקָה וַאֲפֵלָה מְנֻדָּח׃ כִּי לֹא מוּעָף לַאֲשֶׁר מוּצָק לָהּ כָּעֵת הָרִאשׁוֹן
הֵקַל אַרְצָה זְבֻלוּן וְאַרְצָה נַפְתָּלִי וְהָאַחֲרוֹן הִכְבִּיד דֶּרֶךְ הַיָּם עֵבֶר
ט א הַיַּרְדֵּן גְּלִיל הַגּוֹיִם׃ הָעָם הַהֹלְכִים בַּחֹשֶׁךְ רָאוּ אוֹר גָּדוֹל יֹשְׁבֵי בְּאֶרֶץ

2 a land of death's shadow – light now bathes them. For You have made great
Your nation, have raised up its joy; they rejoice before You, like harvest joy,
3 as a people celebrates dividing the spoils. For You have broken the yoke of
their suffering, the rod over their shoulders, the oppressor's staff, as on
4 Midyan's day.[29] For every boot that tramps like thunder, each mantle filthy
5 with blood, will be burned, will become the bonfire's fodder. For a child is
born to us, a son is given us; leadership rests on his shoulders, and he shall
be called Mighty God Is Planning Wonders, Eternal Father, Prince of Peace.[30]
6 To instill great leadership, peace without end, on the throne of David, and
over his kingdom, founding and supporting it with justice and with
righteousness now and forever; the passion of the LORD of Hosts will bring
7 all this to be. The Lord has sent word to Yaakov; it falls upon Israel,
8 and all the people know it, Efrayim and the people of Shomron in their pride,
9 in their swollen-headedness, even as they say: "Bricks have fallen; we will
rebuild in hewn stone; they chop down sycamores; we plant cedars in their
10 place." The LORD has raised Retzin's enemies high over him, stirs up his foes
11 to battle one another; Aram from the East, the Philistines west – they eat up
Israel, mouths agape, *and still He has not turned away His rage, and still He*
12 *stretches forth His hand.* And still the people do not turn to Him who beats
13 them, and do not seek to find the LORD of Hosts. The LORD has cut
14 off head and tail of Israel, palm and bulrush, all in a day. The elders and those
who are honored – they are the head, and the tail are the prophets, the
15 teachers of lies. Those who led this people, led awry, and those who were led
16 were confounded. And so the Lord takes no joy in its young people, nor
shows any compassion for its orphans, its widows. For all of them are godless,
evildoers, the words of each one poisoned. *And still He has not turned away*
17 *His rage, and still He stretches forth His hand.* For evil burns like fire here,
consuming briars and brambles, setting the forest undergrowth aflame,
18 sending them curling up in plumes of smoke. By the rage of the LORD of
Hosts, the land is blackened; the people are nothing but fuel for the fire;
19 brother cares nothing for brother. He on the right carves meat but stays
hungry; he on the left will eat but not feel full; a man will eat the flesh of his
20 own arm – Menashe on Efrayim, Efrayim on Menashe, and the two together
on Yehuda.[31] *And still He has not turned away His rage, and still He stretches*
10 1 *forth His hand.* Woe to the lawmakers who set abuse in stone, for
2 authors of unholy writ who turn justice away from the needy, stealing the
judgments of My people's poor, making widows their plunder and orphans
3 their spoils. What will you do on the day of judgment when, from far away,
calamity comes? To whom will you then flee for help; where will you leave

---

had a mixed population ("of nations"). This passage apparently refers to two separate invasions; see I Kings 15:20 and II Kings 15:29.

29 | See the victory described in Judges, chapters 6–8.

30 | The son mentioned in these verses may be Aḥaz's son Ḥizkiyahu or a future messianic leader; the verses may refer to his birth or to his coronation.

31 | This refers to internecine struggles that weakened both Israel and Yehuda and made it harder for them to withstand Assyrian attacks; see, e.g., II Kings 15:25, 16:5.

ב צַלְמָוֶת אוֹר נָגַהּ עֲלֵיהֶם׃ הִרְבִּיתָ הַגּוֹי לֹא הִגְדַּלְתָּ הַשִּׂמְחָה שָׂמְחוּ לו
ג לְפָנֶיךָ כְּשִׂמְחַת בַּקָּצִיר כַּאֲשֶׁר יָגִילוּ בְּחַלְּקָם שָׁלָל׃ כִּי ׀ אֶת־עֹל סֻבֳּלוֹ
ד וְאֵת מַטֵּה שִׁכְמוֹ שֵׁבֶט הַנֹּגֵשׂ בּוֹ הַחִתֹּתָ כְּיוֹם מִדְיָן׃ כִּי כָל־סְאוֹן סֹאֵן
ה בְּרַעַשׁ וְשִׂמְלָה מְגוֹלָלָה בְדָמִים וְהָיְתָה לִשְׂרֵפָה מַאֲכֹלֶת אֵשׁ׃ כִּי־יֶלֶד
יֻלַּד־לָנוּ בֵּן נִתַּן־לָנוּ וַתְּהִי הַמִּשְׂרָה עַל־שִׁכְמוֹ וַיִּקְרָא שְׁמוֹ פֶּלֶא יוֹעֵץ
ו אֵל גִּבּוֹר אֲבִי־עַד שַׂר־שָׁלוֹם׃ לםרבה הַמִּשְׂרָה וּלְשָׁלוֹם אֵין־קֵץ ד לְמַרְבֵּה
עַל־כִּסֵּא דָוִד וְעַל־מַמְלַכְתּוֹ לְהָכִין אֹתָהּ וּלְסַעֲדָהּ בְּמִשְׁפָּט וּבִצְדָקָה
ז מֵעַתָּה וְעַד־עוֹלָם קִנְאַת יְהוָה צְבָאוֹת תַּעֲשֶׂה־זֹּאת׃ דָּבָר
ח שָׁלַח אֲדֹנָי בְּיַעֲקֹב וְנָפַל בְּיִשְׂרָאֵל׃ וְיָדְעוּ הָעָם כֻּלּוֹ אֶפְרַיִם וְיוֹשֵׁב
ט שֹׁמְרוֹן בְּגַאֲוָה וּבְגֹדֶל לֵבָב לֵאמֹר׃ לְבֵנִים נָפָלוּ וְגָזִית נִבְנֶה שִׁקְמִים
י גֻּדָּעוּ וַאֲרָזִים נַחֲלִיף׃ וַיְשַׂגֵּב יְהוָה אֶת־צָרֵי רְצִין עָלָיו וְאֶת־אֹיְבָיו
יא יְסַכְסֵךְ׃ אֲרָם מִקֶּדֶם וּפְלִשְׁתִּים מֵאָחוֹר וַיֹּאכְלוּ אֶת־יִשְׂרָאֵל בְּכָל־פֶּה
יב בְּכָל־זֹאת לֹא־שָׁב אַפּוֹ וְעוֹד יָדוֹ נְטוּיָה׃ וְהָעָם לֹא־שָׁב עַד־הַמַּכֵּהוּ
יג וְאֶת־יְהוָה צְבָאוֹת לֹא דָרָשׁוּ׃ וַיַּכְרֵת יְהוָה מִיִּשְׂרָאֵל רֹאשׁ
יד וְזָנָב כִּפָּה וְאַגְמוֹן יוֹם אֶחָד׃ זָקֵן וּנְשׂוּא־פָנִים הוּא הָרֹאשׁ וְנָבִיא
טו מוֹרֶה־שֶּׁקֶר הוּא הַזָּנָב׃ וַיִּהְיוּ מְאַשְּׁרֵי הָעָם־הַזֶּה מַתְעִים וּמְאֻשָּׁרָיו
טז מְבֻלָּעִים׃ עַל־כֵּן עַל־בַּחוּרָיו לֹא־יִשְׂמַח ׀ אֲדֹנָי וְאֶת־יְתֹמָיו וְאֶת־
אַלְמְנֹתָיו לֹא יְרַחֵם כִּי כֻלּוֹ חָנֵף וּמֵרַע וְכָל־פֶּה דֹּבֵר נְבָלָה בְּכָל־זֹאת
יז לֹא־שָׁב אַפּוֹ וְעוֹד יָדוֹ נְטוּיָה׃ כִּי־בָעֲרָה כָאֵשׁ רִשְׁעָה שָׁמִיר וָשַׁיִת
יח תֹּאכֵל וַתִּצַּת בְּסִבְכֵי הַיַּעַר וַיִּתְאַבְּכוּ גֵּאוּת עָשָׁן׃ בְּעֶבְרַת יְהוָה
צְבָאוֹת נֶעְתַּם אָרֶץ וַיְהִי הָעָם כְּמַאֲכֹלֶת אֵשׁ אִישׁ אֶל־אָחִיו לֹא
יט יַחְמֹלוּ׃ וַיִּגְזֹר עַל־יָמִין וְרָעֵב וַיֹּאכַל עַל־שְׂמֹאול וְלֹא שָׂבֵעוּ אִישׁ
כ בְּשַׂר־זְרֹעוֹ יֹאכֵלוּ׃ מְנַשֶּׁה אֶת־אֶפְרַיִם וְאֶפְרַיִם אֶת־מְנַשֶּׁה יַחְדָּו הֵמָּה
י א עַל־יְהוּדָה בְּכָל־זֹאת לֹא־שָׁב אַפּוֹ וְעוֹד יָדוֹ נְטוּיָה׃ הוֹי
ב הַחֹקְקִים חִקְקֵי־אָוֶן וּמְכַתְּבִים עָמָל כִּתֵּבוּ׃ לְהַטּוֹת מִדִּין דַּלִּים וְלִגְזֹל
ג מִשְׁפַּט עֲנִיֵּי עַמִּי לִהְיוֹת אַלְמָנוֹת שְׁלָלָם וְאֶת־יְתוֹמִים יָבֹזּוּ׃ וּמַה־
תַּעֲשׂוּ לְיוֹם פְּקֻדָּה וּלְשׁוֹאָה מִמֶּרְחָק תָּבוֹא עַל־מִי תָּנוּסוּ לְעֶזְרָה

4 all your wealth behind? What then but to buckle as captives, among the fallen
to fall? *And still He has not turned away His rage, and still He stretches forth His*
5 *hand.* Woe to Assyria, staff of My fury; My rage is the rod in their
6 hand. I will set them loose upon a vile nation and command them against the
people of My wrath to plunder for plunder, to ravage for spoils,[32] to leave
7 them to be trampled like street mud. But this is not how he thinks of it; his
heart does not see it so; his heart is set on destruction, on cutting down not
8 9 a few nations, for he says, "Are not my ministers, all of them, kings?[33] Is Kalneh
not the same as Karkemish, Ḥamat like Arpad, Shomron just like Damascus?[34]
10 As my hand grasped the kingdoms of false gods, their idols more numerous
11 than Jerusalem's, Shomron's, will I not do as I did to Shomron and her gods,
12 Jerusalem and her images also?" It will be, when the Lord finishes
His work on Mount Zion and in Jerusalem, I shall come to judge what grows
from the swollen head of the king of Assyria, from the supremacy of his
13 haughty eyes, for he says, "By the power of my hands I act, and in my wisdom,
for I have insight; sweep away the borders of peoples and take their leaders
14 for plunder; like a wild bull I pull down all who preside. As if in a nest my
hand grasps the wealth of peoples, and as one might gather abandoned eggs,
I gather up all the world, yet none moves her wing to stop me; none opens a
15 beak or chirrups." Does the axe gloat over the one who wields it? Would a
saw place itself above the one who swings it? Does a staff swing the one who
16 lifts it? Does a rod lift Him who is not wood?[35] So the LORD God
of Hosts will send paucity to his fatness, and under his frame a burning will
17 burn as fire burns. The Light of Israel will be fire, their Holy One the flame,
18 and it will burn and consume the briars and thorns of him all in a day. All the
glory of his forest and pasture, man and beast, will be consumed, the standard
19 bearer melting away. As for the remnant of his forest, so few will be the trees,
20 a child could mark their tally. On that day this will be: No more will
the remnant of Israel, the fugitives of the House of Yaakov, return to lean upon
the one who beats them; they will lean upon the LORD in truth, the Holy
21 One of Israel. A remnant will return,[36] the remnant of Yaakov, to mighty God.
22 For though your people Israel may be like sands of the sea for number, but a
remnant will return of them, for annihilation is ordained, sweeping through
23 in justice, for annihilation ordained, the LORD of Hosts enforces all across
24 the earth. And so, thus says the Lord GOD of Hosts: Do not be
afraid, My people in Zion; fear not Assyria; they will beat you with the rod
25 and raise their staff against you on their way to Egypt. Let but a wisp of time
26 pass by, and the rage will be spent, My fury – over their destruction. And the
LORD of Hosts will awaken against him a whip – as when Midyan were lashed

---

32 | This echoes the symbolic name of Yeshayahu's son in 8:1, 3.

33 | Referring to the Assyrian practice of replacing local kings with Assyrian governors.

34 | These cities were conquered by Assyria around the time of the conquest of Shomron.

35 | That is, the king of Assyria is merely a tool God wields.

36 | This is the symbolic name of Yeshayahu's son in 7:3. "Mighty God" similarly refers back to the symbolic name in 9:5.

ד ואנה תעזבו כבודכם: בלתי כרע תחת אסיר ותחת הרוגים יפלו
ה בכל־זאת לא־שב אפו ועוד ידו נטויה: הוי אשור
ו שבט אפי ומטה־הוא בידם זעמי: בגוי חנף אשלחנו ועל־עם עברתי
ז אצונו לשלל שלל ולבז בז ולשימו מרמס כחמר חוצות: והוא לא־ [ולשומו]
כן ידמה ולבבו לא־כן יחשב כי להשמיד בלבבו ולהכרית גוים לא
ח ט מעט: כי יאמר הלא שרי יחדו מלכים: הלא ככרכמיש כלנו אם־לא
י כארפד חמת אם־לא כדמשק שמרון: כאשר מצאה ידי לממלכת
יא האליל ופסיליהם מירושלם ומשמרון: הלא כאשר עשיתי לשמרון
יב ולאליליה כן אעשה לירושלם ולעצביה: והיה כי־יבצע
אדני את־כל־מעשהו בהר ציון ובירושלם אפקד על־פרי־גדל לבב
יג מלך־אשור ועל־תפארת רום עיניו: כי אמר בכח ידי עשיתי
ובחכמתי כי נבנותי ואסיר | גבולת עמים ועתידתיהם שושתי [ועתודתיהם]
יד ואוריד כאביר יושבים: ותמצא כקן | ידי לחיל העמים וכאסף ביצים
עזבות כל־הארץ אני אספתי ולא היה נדד כנף ופצה פה ומצפצף:
טו היתפאר הגרזן על החצב בו אם־יתגדל המשור על־מניפו כהניף
טז שבט ואת־מרימיו כהרים מטה לא־עץ: לכן ישלח
האדון יהוה צבאות במשמניו רזון ותחת כבדו יקד יקד כיקוד אש:
יז והיה אור־ישראל לאש וקדושו ללהבה ובערה ואכלה שיתו ושמירו
יח ביום אחד: וכבוד יערו וכרמלו מנפש ועד־בשר יכלה והיה כמסס
יט כ נסס: ושאר עץ יערו מספר יהיו ונער יכתבם: והיה |
ביום ההוא לא־יוסיף עוד שאר ישראל ופליטת בית־יעקב להשען
כא על־מכהו ונשען על־יהוה קדוש ישראל באמת: שאר ישוב שאר
כב יעקב אל־אל גבור: כי אם־יהיה עמך ישראל כחול הים שאר ישוב
כג בו כליון חרוץ שוטף צדקה: כי כלה ונחרצה אדני יהוה צבאות
כד עשה בקרב כל־הארץ: לכן כה־אמר אדני יהוה צבאות
אל־תירא עמי ישב ציון מאשור בשבט יככה ומטהו ישא־עליך
כה בדרך מצרים: כי־עוד מעט מזער וכלה זעם ואפי על־תבליתם:
כו ועורר עליו יהוה צבאות שוט כמכת מדין בצור עורב ומטהו על־

at the Rock of Orev[37] – and raise His staff over the sea, bearing him away, as
27 He did to Egypt. On that day, this will be: his burden will drop from your
28 shoulders, his yoke from your neck; your heft will shatter the yoke. He comes
29 to Ayat,[38] marches through Migron, and stows His arms at Mikhmas. They
pass over the ford and lodge at Geva; Rama trembles; Givat Sha'ul has fled.
30 31 Cry out, daughter Galim; hear the cry, Laysha; scream, Anatot. Madmena
32 wanders; the people of Gevim seek refuge; this very day, he stands at
Nov, waving his hand toward the mount of daughter Zion, Jerusalem's
33 hill. Behold the Master, the LORD of Hosts, stirring dread, shearing
off branches. Those who held their heads high are brought down; the exalted
34 will be laid low. He fells the forest groves with iron, Lebanon falls to the blows
11 1 of majesty. A new shoot will grow from the stem of Yishai; from his
2 roots a branch will bud. And the spirit of the LORD will rest upon him – a
spirit of wisdom, of knowing, a spirit of guidance and might, a spirit of insight
3 and awe of the LORD. With awe of the LORD infusing his senses, he will not
4 judge by his eyes' perception, nor rule by what his ears can grasp; he will
judge poor people justly, render judgment rightly for oppressed ones in the
land; he will strike the land with the staff of his speech, and the spirit that
5 crosses his lips will execute those who do evil. He will gird his loins with
6 righteousness: his battle dress is truth. Wolf will lie down beside lamb, the
leopard will lie beside the young goat; calf, lion cub, fatted lamb together – a
7 little child will tend them. The cow and the bear will graze with their young
8 lying down together, and lion, like ox, will feed upon straw. A baby will play
9 at the cobra's hole, and an infant's hand will explore the viper's nest. There
will be no wrong or violence on all My holy mountain, for knowledge of the
10 LORD will fill the earth as waters cover the ocean. On that day, that
offshoot of Yishai that stands as a banner to all the peoples, nations will come
11 to seek him, and his resting place will be glorious. On that day this
will be: The Lord will stretch forth His hand again to take back the remnant
of His people, those who remain, from Assyria and Egypt, from Patros and
from Kush, from Eilam and from Shinar, Ḥamat and the islands of the sea.[39]
12 He will lift up a banner to nations and gather in the banished ones of Israel;
He will gather in the scattered ones of Israel from all four edges of the world.
13 Efrayim's jealousy will fall away, the enemies in Yehuda will be cut down,
Efrayim will no more be jealous of Yehuda; Yehuda will bear toward Efrayim
14 no more enmity. They will fly west to the Philistines, shoulder to shoulder;
together they will sack the people of the East; they will thrust their hand
15 against Edom and Moav, and the people of Amon will obey them. The LORD
will destroy the Egyptian Sea gulf and wave His hand over the River through
His fearsome wind; He will beat it into seven separate streams that people

37 | See Judges 7:25, and 9:3 above.

38 | This list maps an army's advance from the Assyrian province of Shomron southward toward Jerusalem.

39 | Patros and Kush are in the south of modern-day Egypt, Eilam is in Iran, and Shinar is southern Mesopotamia. Ḥamat is in northern Syria. Jews had spread out to all these areas around the time of the destruction of the First Temple.

הַיָּם וּנְשָׂאוֹ בְּדֶרֶךְ מִצְרָיִם: כז וְהָיָה ׀ בַּיּוֹם הַהוּא יָסוּר סֻבֳּלוֹ מֵעַל שִׁכְמֶךָ
כח וְעֻלּוֹ מֵעַל צַוָּארֶךָ וְחֻבַּל עֹל מִפְּנֵי־שָׁמֶן: בָּא עַל־עַיַּת עָבַר בְּמִגְרוֹן
כט לְמִכְמָשׂ יַפְקִיד כֵּלָיו: עָבְרוּ מַעְבָּרָה גֶּבַע מָלוֹן לָנוּ חָרְדָה הָרָמָה
ל גִּבְעַת שָׁאוּל נָסָה: צַהֲלִי קוֹלֵךְ בַּת־גַּלִּים הַקְשִׁיבִי לַיְשָׁה עֲנִיָּה עֲנָתוֹת:
לא לב נָדְדָה מַדְמֵנָה יֹשְׁבֵי הַגֵּבִים הֵעִיזוּ: עוֹד הַיּוֹם בְּנֹב לַעֲמֹד יְנֹפֵף יָדוֹ
לג הַר בֵּית־צִיּוֹן גִּבְעַת יְרוּשָׁלִָם: הִנֵּה הָאָדוֹן יְהוָה צְבָאוֹת בַּת־
לד מְסָעֵף פֻּארָה בְּמַעֲרָצָה וְרָמֵי הַקּוֹמָה גְּדֻעִים וְהַגְּבֹהִים יִשְׁפָּלוּ: וְנִקַּף
יא א סִבְכֵי הַיַּעַר בַּבַּרְזֶל וְהַלְּבָנוֹן בְּאַדִּיר יִפּוֹל: וְיָצָא חֹטֶר
ב מִגֵּזַע יִשָׁי וְנֵצֶר מִשָּׁרָשָׁיו יִפְרֶה: וְנָחָה עָלָיו רוּחַ יְהוָה רוּחַ חָכְמָה ה
ג וּבִינָה רוּחַ עֵצָה וּגְבוּרָה רוּחַ דַּעַת וְיִרְאַת יְהוָה: וַהֲרִיחוֹ בְּיִרְאַת יְהוָה
ד וְלֹא־לְמַרְאֵה עֵינָיו יִשְׁפּוֹט וְלֹא־לְמִשְׁמַע אָזְנָיו יוֹכִיחַ: וְשָׁפַט בְּצֶדֶק
דַּלִּים וְהוֹכִיחַ בְּמִישׁוֹר לְעַנְוֵי־אָרֶץ וְהִכָּה־אֶרֶץ בְּשֵׁבֶט פִּיו וּבְרוּחַ
ה שְׂפָתָיו יָמִית רָשָׁע: וְהָיָה צֶדֶק אֵזוֹר מָתְנָיו וְהָאֱמוּנָה אֵזוֹר חֲלָצָיו:
ו וְגָר זְאֵב עִם־כֶּבֶשׂ וְנָמֵר עִם־גְּדִי יִרְבָּץ וְעֵגֶל וּכְפִיר וּמְרִיא יַחְדָּו וְנַעַר
ז קָטֹן נֹהֵג בָּם: וּפָרָה וָדֹב תִּרְעֶינָה יַחְדָּו יִרְבְּצוּ יַלְדֵיהֶן וְאַרְיֵה כַּבָּקָר
ח יֹאכַל־תֶּבֶן: וְשִׁעֲשַׁע יוֹנֵק עַל־חֻר פָּתֶן וְעַל מְאוּרַת צִפְעוֹנִי גָּמוּל יָדוֹ
ט הָדָה: לֹא־יָרֵעוּ וְלֹא־יַשְׁחִיתוּ בְּכָל־הַר קָדְשִׁי כִּי־מָלְאָה הָאָרֶץ דֵּעָה
י אֶת־יְהוָה כַּמַּיִם לַיָּם מְכַסִּים: וְהָיָה בַּיּוֹם הַהוּא שֹׁרֶשׁ
יִשַׁי אֲשֶׁר עֹמֵד לְנֵס עַמִּים אֵלָיו גּוֹיִם יִדְרֹשׁוּ וְהָיְתָה מְנֻחָתוֹ
יא כָּבוֹד: וְהָיָה ׀ בַּיּוֹם הַהוּא יוֹסִיף אֲדֹנָי ׀ שֵׁנִית יָדוֹ לִקְנוֹת
אֶת־שְׁאָר עַמּוֹ אֲשֶׁר יִשָּׁאֵר מֵאַשּׁוּר וּמִמִּצְרַיִם וּמִפַּתְרוֹס וּמִכּוּשׁ
יב וּמֵעֵילָם וּמִשִּׁנְעָר וּמֵחֲמָת וּמֵאִיֵּי הַיָּם: וְנָשָׂא נֵס לַגּוֹיִם וְאָסַף נִדְחֵי
יג יִשְׂרָאֵל וּנְפֻצוֹת יְהוּדָה יְקַבֵּץ מֵאַרְבַּע כַּנְפוֹת הָאָרֶץ: וְסָרָה קִנְאַת
אֶפְרַיִם וְצֹרְרֵי יְהוּדָה יִכָּרֵתוּ אֶפְרַיִם לֹא־יְקַנֵּא אֶת־יְהוּדָה וִיהוּדָה
יד לֹא־יָצֹר אֶת־אֶפְרָיִם: וְעָפוּ בְכָתֵף פְּלִשְׁתִּים יָמָּה יַחְדָּו יָבֹזּוּ אֶת־בְּנֵי־
טו קֶדֶם אֱדוֹם וּמוֹאָב מִשְׁלוֹחַ יָדָם וּבְנֵי עַמּוֹן מִשְׁמַעְתָּם: וְהֶחֱרִים יְהוָה
אֵת לְשׁוֹן יַם־מִצְרַיִם וְהֵנִיף יָדוֹ עַל־הַנָּהָר בַּעְיָם רוּחוֹ וְהִכָּהוּ לְשִׁבְעָה

16 may cross in their shoes. A path will be there for the remnant of His people,
those who remain, from Assyria, as there was for the people of Israel on the
12 1 day they came up from the land of Egypt. And you will say on that day: *I
thank You, Lord for You raged against me, but You turned back Your rage, and*
2 *now You console me. Behold the God of my salvation; I trust and will not fear, for*
3 *God, the Lord, is my strength and song, and now my salvation.* With joy you
4 will draw water from the flowing springs of rescue. And you will say upon
that day: *Give thanks to the Lord; call on His name; proclaim His acts among*
5 *the peoples; recount: His name is transcendent. Sing out to the Lord: He has*
6 *performed grandeur; all across the world this thing is known. Cry out, sing out
joy, all you who dwell in Zion; for great in your midst is the Holy One of*
13 1 *Israel.* The burden of Babylon seen by Yeshayahu son of Amotz:
2 Raise a banner upon the high mountain, and lift your voice toward them;
3 gesture with your hand and let them come to the nobles' gates. I command
those I have consecrated and call up the mighty men of My rage, exuberant
4 with My own pride. The clamor of the horde fills the mountains, the image
of a mass of men, the roar of whole kingdoms, of nations called together: the
5 Lord of Hosts is gathering a host for war. They come from a distant land,
from the skies' edge, the Lord and His armaments of fury, to wreak violence
6 across the world. Wail, for the day of the Lord is nigh; like assault from
7 8 Shaddai it strikes, so all hands give way, so each mortal heart dissolves. The
throes take hold of them; agony grips them; they writhe like a woman in labor.
9 They stare in horror at each other as at faces dragged through the flames. Here
it is coming: the day of the Lord, cruel with fury, with flaming rage, turning
10 the land to desolation, routing out all her sinners, for the stars of the sky in
their patterns will shine no more their light; the sun will rise in darkness, and
11 the moon not beam its light. I shall repay this earth its evil, and the wicked
ones their wrongs. I shall halt the vicious ones' majesty and fell the tyrants'
12 pride. Human life will be prized higher than gold; I shall make it so: people
13 scarcer than fine gold. For this I shall jolt the heavens, shake the land out of
its resting place through the fury of the Lord of Hosts on the day His rage
14 flames high. And they will be like a hounded gazelle, a flock with none to
15 herd it; each man will turn to his people and flee back to his land. Whoever
is found will be run through with the sword, they will fall, all who are caught
16 in flight. Their little ones will be battered to death before their eyes, their
17 houses sacked, their women raped. I shall rouse Media against them, who
18 care not for silver, who have no desire for gold.[40] And their bows will crush
children; they will show infants no mercy, their eyes spare no one's child.
19 Babylon: splendor among kingdoms, crowning glory of Chaldean pride, her
20 end like God's overturning of Sedom and Amora, it will never again be
inhabited, and never be settled, in any generation, nor any Arab nomad pitch
21 his tent there, nor shepherds lay their flocks down in that place. Desert beasts
will lie down there and owls fill the houses. Ostriches will make their homes,

40 | Koresh (Cyrus) of Persia, which had been a vassal state of the Median empire, conquered Babylon in 539 BCE.

טז נְחָלִים וְהִדְרִיךְ בַּנְּעָלִים: וְהָיְתָה מְסִלָּה לִשְׁאָר עַמּוֹ אֲשֶׁר יִשָּׁאֵר
יב א מֵאַשּׁוּר כַּאֲשֶׁר הָיְתָה לְיִשְׂרָאֵל בְּיוֹם עֲלֹתוֹ מֵאֶרֶץ מִצְרָיִם: וְאָמַרְתָּ
ב בַּיּוֹם הַהוּא אוֹדְךָ יהוה כִּי אָנַפְתָּ בִּי יָשֹׁב אַפְּךָ וּתְנַחֲמֵנִי: הִנֵּה אֵל
יְשׁוּעָתִי אֶבְטַח וְלֹא אֶפְחָד כִּי־עָזִּי וְזִמְרָת יָהּ יהוה וַיְהִי־לִי לִישׁוּעָה:
ג ד וּשְׁאַבְתֶּם־מַיִם בְּשָׂשׂוֹן מִמַּעַיְנֵי הַיְשׁוּעָה: וַאֲמַרְתֶּם בַּיּוֹם הַהוּא הוֹדוּ
לַיהוה קִרְאוּ בִשְׁמוֹ הוֹדִיעוּ בָעַמִּים עֲלִילֹתָיו הַזְכִּירוּ כִּי נִשְׂגָּב שְׁמוֹ:
ה ו זַמְּרוּ יהוה כִּי גֵאוּת עָשָׂה מידעת זֹאת בְּכָל־הָאָרֶץ: צַהֲלִי וָרֹנִּי יוֹשֶׁבֶת מוּדַעַת
יג א צִיּוֹן כִּי־גָדוֹל בְּקִרְבֵּךְ קְדוֹשׁ יִשְׂרָאֵל: מַשָּׂא בָּבֶל אֲשֶׁר
ב חָזָה יְשַׁעְיָהוּ בֶּן־אָמוֹץ: עַל הַר־נִשְׁפֶּה שְׂאוּ־נֵס הָרִימוּ קוֹל לָהֶם
ג הָנִיפוּ יָד וְיָבֹאוּ פִּתְחֵי נְדִיבִים: אֲנִי צִוֵּיתִי לִמְקֻדָּשָׁי גַּם קָרָאתִי גִבּוֹרַי
ד לְאַפִּי עַלִּיזֵי גַּאֲוָתִי: קוֹל הָמוֹן בֶּהָרִים דְּמוּת עַם־רָב קוֹל שְׁאוֹן
ה מַמְלְכוֹת גּוֹיִם נֶאֱסָפִים יהוה צְבָאוֹת מְפַקֵּד צְבָא מִלְחָמָה: בָּאִים
מֵאֶרֶץ מֶרְחָק מִקְצֵה הַשָּׁמָיִם יהוה וּכְלֵי זַעְמוֹ לְחַבֵּל כָּל־הָאָרֶץ:
ו ז הֵילִילוּ כִּי קָרוֹב יוֹם יהוה כְּשֹׁד מִשַּׁדַּי יָבוֹא: עַל־כֵּן כָּל־יָדַיִם תִּרְפֶּינָה
ח וְכָל־לְבַב אֱנוֹשׁ יִמָּס: וְנִבְהָלוּ | צִירִים וַחֲבָלִים יֹאחֵזוּן כַּיּוֹלֵדָה יְחִילוּן
ט אִישׁ אֶל־רֵעֵהוּ יִתְמָהוּ פְּנֵי לְהָבִים פְּנֵיהֶם: הִנֵּה יוֹם־יהוה בָּא אַכְזָרִי
י וְעֶבְרָה וַחֲרוֹן אָף לָשׂוּם הָאָרֶץ לְשַׁמָּה וְחַטָּאֶיהָ יַשְׁמִיד מִמֶּנָּה: כִּי־
כוֹכְבֵי הַשָּׁמַיִם וּכְסִילֵיהֶם לֹא יָהֵלּוּ אוֹרָם חָשַׁךְ הַשֶּׁמֶשׁ בְּצֵאתוֹ וְיָרֵחַ
יא לֹא־יַגִּיהַּ אוֹרוֹ: וּפָקַדְתִּי עַל־תֵּבֵל רָעָה וְעַל־רְשָׁעִים עֲוֺנָם וְהִשְׁבַּתִּי
יב גְּאוֹן זֵדִים וְגַאֲוַת עָרִיצִים אַשְׁפִּיל: אוֹקִיר אֱנוֹשׁ מִפָּז וְאָדָם מִכֶּתֶם
יג אוֹפִיר: עַל־כֵּן שָׁמַיִם אַרְגִּיז וְתִרְעַשׁ הָאָרֶץ מִמְּקוֹמָהּ בְּעֶבְרַת יהוה
יד צְבָאוֹת וּבְיוֹם חֲרוֹן אַפּוֹ: וְהָיָה כִּצְבִי מֻדָּח וּכְצֹאן וְאֵין מְקַבֵּץ אִישׁ
טו אֶל־עַמּוֹ יִפְנוּ וְאִישׁ אֶל־אַרְצוֹ יָנוּסוּ: כָּל־הַנִּמְצָא יִדָּקֵר וְכָל־הַנִּסְפֶּה
טז יִפּוֹל בֶּחָרֶב: וְעֹלְלֵיהֶם יְרֻטְּשׁוּ לְעֵינֵיהֶם יִשַּׁסּוּ בָּתֵּיהֶם וּנְשֵׁיהֶם
יז תשגלנה: הִנְנִי מֵעִיר עֲלֵיהֶם אֶת־מָדָי אֲשֶׁר־כֶּסֶף לֹא יַחְשֹׁבוּ וְזָהָב תִּשָּׁכַבְנָה
יח לֹא יַחְפְּצוּ־בוֹ: וּקְשָׁתוֹת נְעָרִים תְּרַטַּשְׁנָה וּפְרִי־בֶטֶן לֹא יְרַחֵמוּ עַל־
יט בָּנִים לֹא־תָחוּס עֵינָם: וְהָיְתָה בָבֶל צְבִי מַמְלָכוֹת תִּפְאֶרֶת גְּאוֹן
כ כַּשְׂדִּים כְּמַהְפֵּכַת אֱלֹהִים אֶת־סְדֹם וְאֶת־עֲמֹרָה: לֹא־תֵשֵׁב לָנֶצַח
וְלֹא תִשְׁכֹּן עַד־דּוֹר וָדוֹר וְלֹא־יַהֵל שָׁם עֲרָבִי וְרֹעִים לֹא־יַרְבִּצוּ שָׁם:
כא וְרָבְצוּ־שָׁם צִיִּים וּמָלְאוּ בָתֵּיהֶם אֹחִים וְשָׁכְנוּ שָׁם בְּנוֹת יַעֲנָה וּשְׂעִירִים

22 and wild goats will dance. Wild cats will scream in her palaces and jackals in
her pleasure halls. Her time is coming close now; her days draw to a close.
14 1 For the LORD will show compassion to Yaakov, choose Israel again. He will
set them down upon their land, and strangers will join them – add themselves
2 to the House of Yaakov – while they will take of those peoples and bring them
to their place, and the House of Israel will possess them on the LORD's own
land, slaves and bondswomen; be captors to their captors and rule those who
3 oppressed them. On the day when the LORD lets you rest from your
4 pain and your turmoil, and all the hard labor to which you are subjected, then
you shall bear this speech to the king of Babylon; say: How could the
5 oppressor be halted so, the city of gold be halted? The LORD has broken the
6 staff of the wicked, the tyrants' scepter, the rod that beat peoples in fury,
beating and never letting up; the one who ruled nations by wrath is now
7 pursued unrelentingly. Now all the land rests, stilled, then breaks out in song.
8 Even the juniper trees rejoice over you; even cedars of Lebanon: "Since you
9 have fallen, no one will rise again to cut us down." Sheol shakes below you,
waiting for your coming. It rouses the shades to meet you, all leaders of this
10 earth, commanding the kings of all nations to rise up from their thrones. Each
one will speak up to you: "Are you fallen like us now? Are you like one of us?"
11 All your majesty has gone down to Sheol along with the crooning of your
12 harps; grubs are laid as sheets beneath you; worms are your covers. How you
have fallen from heaven now, shining one, son of the dawn light; how you are
13 cut down to earth, you who decided nations' fates. You once said in your heart,
"I shall ascend to the sky, raise my throne to the godly stars; I shall sit on the
14 mount where the gods meet, at the farthest reach of the north. I shall mount
15 the clouds' summits and be like the Most High."[41] Instead you fell down into
16 Sheol, to the lowest depths of the pit. Those who see it will gaze down; they
will scrutinize you well: "Is this really the man who shook the world, who
17 overturned all kingdoms, making the earth like a wasteland, razing its towns,
18 his captives never to come home?" All the kings of nations, each lies down
19 in glory in his home. But you – you are cast out of your grave like a rejected
branch, dressed in the dead whom the sword cut through, thrown down on
20 the rocks of the pit, a trampled carcass.[42] No, you will not be one with kings
in burial, for you have destroyed your own land, killed your own people; let
21 no child ever bear your evil-wreaking name. Prepare the slaughter for his sons
for their forefathers' iniquities; let them not rise to inherit the earth; let the
22 world be filled again with towns. I rise up against them, so says the LORD of
Hosts, and I shall cut off from Babylon name and remnant, child and child's
23 child, so says the LORD. I shall make her the inheritance of wild owls and
water bogs, sweep her with the broom of extinction: the LORD of Hosts has
24 spoken. The LORD of Hosts swears an oath: As I envisioned it,

41 | Hebrew "Elyon." This term is often used as an epithet for Israel's God, but here refers ambiguously to a Canaanite god of that name.

42 | Sargon II, king of Assyria, who deported Israelites from Shomron and then crowned himself king of Babylon, was killed on the battlefield in 705 BCE and not buried.

כב יַרְקְדוּ־שָׁם׃ וְעָנָה אִיִּים בְּאַלְמְנוֹתָיו וְתַנִּים בְּהֵיכְלֵי עֹנֶג וְקָרוֹב לָבוֹא
יד א עִתָּהּ וְיָמֶיהָ לֹא יִמָּשֵׁכוּ׃ כִּי יְרַחֵם יְהוָה אֶת־יַעֲקֹב וּבָחַר עוֹד בְּיִשְׂרָאֵל
וְהִנִּיחָם עַל־אַדְמָתָם וְנִלְוָה הַגֵּר עֲלֵיהֶם וְנִסְפְּחוּ עַל־בֵּית יַעֲקֹב׃
ב וּלְקָחוּם עַמִּים וֶהֱבִיאוּם אֶל־מְקוֹמָם וְהִתְנַחֲלוּם בֵּית־יִשְׂרָאֵל ו
עַל אַדְמַת יְהוָה לַעֲבָדִים וְלִשְׁפָחוֹת וְהָיוּ שֹׁבִים לְשֹׁבֵיהֶם וְרָדוּ
ג בְּנֹגְשֵׂיהֶם׃ וְהָיָה בְּיוֹם הָנִיחַ יְהוָה לְךָ מֵעָצְבְּךָ וּמֵרָגְזֶךָ
ד וּמִן־הָעֲבֹדָה הַקָּשָׁה אֲשֶׁר עֻבַּד־בָּךְ׃ וְנָשָׂאתָ הַמָּשָׁל הַזֶּה עַל־מֶלֶךְ
ה בָּבֶל וְאָמָרְתָּ אֵיךְ שָׁבַת נֹגֵשׂ שָׁבְתָה מַדְהֵבָה׃ שָׁבַר יְהוָה מַטֵּה רְשָׁעִים
ו שֵׁבֶט מֹשְׁלִים׃ מַכֶּה עַמִּים בְּעֶבְרָה מַכַּת בִּלְתִּי סָרָה רֹדֶה בָאַף גּוֹיִם
ז ח מֻרְדָּף בְּלִי חָשָׂךְ׃ נָחָה שָׁקְטָה כָּל־הָאָרֶץ פָּצְחוּ רִנָּה׃ גַּם־בְּרוֹשִׁים
ט שָׂמְחוּ לְךָ אַרְזֵי לְבָנוֹן מֵאָז שָׁכַבְתָּ לֹא־יַעֲלֶה הַכֹּרֵת עָלֵינוּ׃ שְׁאוֹל
מִתַּחַת רָגְזָה לְךָ לִקְרַאת בּוֹאֶךָ עוֹרֵר לְךָ רְפָאִים כָּל־עַתּוּדֵי אָרֶץ
י הֵקִים מִכִּסְאוֹתָם כֹּל מַלְכֵי גוֹיִם׃ כֻּלָּם יַעֲנוּ וְיֹאמְרוּ אֵלֶיךָ גַּם־אַתָּה
יא חֻלֵּיתָ כָמוֹנוּ אֵלֵינוּ נִמְשָׁלְתָּ׃ הוּרַד שְׁאוֹל גְּאוֹנֶךָ הֶמְיַת נְבָלֶיךָ תַּחְתֶּיךָ
יב יֻצַּע רִמָּה וּמְכַסֶּיךָ תּוֹלֵעָה׃ אֵיךְ נָפַלְתָּ מִשָּׁמַיִם הֵילֵל בֶּן־שָׁחַר נִגְדַּעְתָּ
יג לָאָרֶץ חוֹלֵשׁ עַל־גּוֹיִם׃ וְאַתָּה אָמַרְתָּ בִלְבָבְךָ הַשָּׁמַיִם אֶעֱלֶה מִמַּעַל
יד לְכוֹכְבֵי־אֵל אָרִים כִּסְאִי וְאֵשֵׁב בְּהַר־מוֹעֵד בְּיַרְכְּתֵי צָפוֹן׃ אֶעֱלֶה
טו עַל־בָּמֳתֵי עָב אֶדַּמֶּה לְעֶלְיוֹן׃ אַךְ אֶל־שְׁאוֹל תּוּרָד אֶל־יַרְכְּתֵי־בוֹר׃
טז רֹאֶיךָ אֵלֶיךָ יַשְׁגִּיחוּ אֵלֶיךָ יִתְבּוֹנָנוּ הֲזֶה הָאִישׁ מַרְגִּיז הָאָרֶץ מַרְעִישׁ
יז מַמְלָכוֹת׃ שָׂם תֵּבֵל כַּמִּדְבָּר וְעָרָיו הָרָס אֲסִירָיו לֹא־פָתַח בָּיְתָה׃
יח יט כָּל־מַלְכֵי גוֹיִם כֻּלָּם שָׁכְבוּ בְכָבוֹד אִישׁ בְּבֵיתוֹ׃ וְאַתָּה הָשְׁלַכְתָּ
מִקִּבְרְךָ כְּנֵצֶר נִתְעָב לְבֻשׁ הֲרֻגִים מְטֹעֲנֵי חָרֶב יוֹרְדֵי אֶל־אַבְנֵי־בוֹר
כ כְּפֶגֶר מוּבָס׃ לֹא־תֵחַד אִתָּם בִּקְבוּרָה כִּי־אַרְצְךָ שִׁחַתָּ עַמְּךָ הָרָגְתָּ
כא לֹא־יִקָּרֵא לְעוֹלָם זֶרַע מְרֵעִים׃ הָכִינוּ לְבָנָיו מַטְבֵּחַ בַּעֲוֹן אֲבוֹתָם
כב בַּל־יָקֻמוּ וְיָרְשׁוּ אָרֶץ וּמָלְאוּ פְנֵי־תֵבֵל עָרִים׃ וְקַמְתִּי עֲלֵיהֶם נְאֻם
כג יְהוָה צְבָאוֹת וְהִכְרַתִּי לְבָבֶל שֵׁם וּשְׁאָר וְנִין וָנֶכֶד נְאֻם־יְהוָה׃ וְשַׂמְתִּיהָ
לְמוֹרַשׁ קִפֹּד וְאַגְמֵי־מָיִם וְטֵאטֵאתִיהָ בְּמַטְאֲטֵא הַשְׁמֵד נְאֻם יְהוָה
כד צְבָאוֹת׃ נִשְׁבַּע יְהוָה צְבָאוֹת לֵאמֹר אִם־לֹא כַּאֲשֶׁר דִּמִּיתִי

25 always, has it not come to be? Just as I decide it, will it not always be? *To break*
Assyria in My land, I shall bring them down from My hills; I shall pull their yoke
26 *from this people, their burden down from their shoulders:* this is the plan that is
already plotted out for all the world, and this is the hand stretched forth over
27 all nations, for what the LORD of Hosts has planned, who can ever thwart it?
28 This His hand stretched forth, who can ever turn it back?" In the
29 year when King Aḥaz died, this burden was spoken: Do not rejoice, all of you
in Philistia, that the staff that beat you is broken. From the snake's severed
30 root a cobra will rise, its fruit a flying serpent. The firstborn of the poor will
graze as the powerless lie down in safety, but I will kill your root by hunger,
31 and those who survive will be slain. Wail at the gates; cry out, O town; melt,
all of you in Philistia, for smoke is billowing from the north, and not one man
32 breaks rank. What message back to the nation's messengers? That the LORD
has laid Zion's foundation, and there, the poor among His people will
15 1 shelter. The burden of Moav:[43] Massacre came to Ar in the night;
2 Moav is silenced. For massacre came in the night; Kir Moav was silenced. The
people of the House and of Divon climb to their high shrines in tears for Nevo
and for Meideva. Moav is wailing; every head is shaven, each beard shorn.[44]
3 They walk the streets in sackcloth; on the rooftops, in the squares, all is one
4 great wailing, poured out in tears. Ḥeshbon cries out, and Elaleh, and their
voices reach Yahatz. This is why Moav's warriors roar; their souls are screaming
5 for them. My heart cries out for Moav; the refugees reach Tzoar, Eglat
Shlishiya, climbing the slope of Luḥit weeping; all along the Ḥoronayim Road
6 rise the wails of brokenness, for the waters of Nimrim will become a
7 desolation; for grass will wither and plants will die: all green gone. And so,
the wealth they have accumulated, all that they have saved, they carry away
8 across the Stream of Willows. Her cries rise all around the border of Moav,
9 her wails as far as Agalim, her wails as far as Be'er Eilim. The waters of Dimon
are filled with blood; I will spill out yet more upon Dimon, set a lion upon
16 1 Moav's fugitives; those left will be swallowed by the ground. Send a sheep,
ruler of the land, from Sela into the desert, to the mount of daughter Zion:
2 Like a bird wandering, banished from the nest, the women of Moav on the
3 fords to Arnon. Bring counsel; act with judgment; cast your shade like night
4 over the noon heat. Hide these outcasts; do not expose the wanderers. Let
the outcasts of Moav bide among you; be their hiding place from the invading
mass until the oppressor is gone, the massacre over, brutality is ended all
5 across the land. There is a throne founded on kindness, presided
from in truth in David's tent, by a judge, a seeker of justice, one who hastens
6 righteousness. We have all heard Moav's arrogance, excessive arrogance: his
7 loftiness, his hubris, his wrath; his illusions came to naught. So Moav wails
for Moav, all of her wailing, for the grapes of Kir Ḥareshet low moans sound,[45]
8 for the vineyards of Ḥeshbon are pitiful, the vines of Sivma, its grapes were

43 | The locations mentioned in this passage were principle cities of Moav.
44 | Gestures of mourning or marks of enslavement.
45 | Cf. Jeremiah 48:29–33.

כה כֵּן הָיָתָה וְכַאֲשֶׁר יָעַצְתִּי הִיא תָקוּם׃ לִשְׁבֹּר אַשּׁוּר בְּאַרְצִי וְעַל־הָרַי
כו אֲבוּסֶנּוּ וְסָר מֵעֲלֵיהֶם עֻלּוֹ וְסֻבֳּלוֹ מֵעַל שִׁכְמוֹ יָסוּר׃ זֹאת הָעֵצָה
כז הַיְּעוּצָה עַל־כָּל־הָאָרֶץ וְזֹאת הַיָּד הַנְּטוּיָה עַל־כָּל־הַגּוֹיִם׃ כִּי־יְהוָה
כח צְבָאוֹת יָעָץ וּמִי יָפֵר וְיָדוֹ הַנְּטוּיָה וּמִי יְשִׁיבֶנָּה׃ בִּשְׁנַת־
כט מוֹת הַמֶּלֶךְ אָחָז הָיָה הַמַּשָּׂא הַזֶּה׃ אַל־תִּשְׂמְחִי פְלֶשֶׁת כֻּלֵּךְ כִּי נִשְׁבַּר
ל שֵׁבֶט מַכֵּךְ כִּי־מִשֹּׁרֶשׁ נָחָשׁ יֵצֵא צֶפַע וּפִרְיוֹ שָׂרָף מְעוֹפֵף׃ וְרָעוּ בְּכוֹרֵי
דַלִּים וְאֶבְיוֹנִים לָבֶטַח יִרְבָּצוּ וְהֵמַתִּי בָרָעָב שָׁרְשֵׁךְ וּשְׁאֵרִיתֵךְ יַהֲרֹג׃
לא הֵילִילִי שַׁעַר זַעֲקִי־עִיר נָמוֹג פְּלֶשֶׁת כֻּלֵּךְ כִּי מִצָּפוֹן עָשָׁן בָּא וְאֵין
לב בּוֹדֵד בְּמוֹעָדָיו׃ וּמַה־יַּעֲנֶה מַלְאֲכֵי־גוֹי כִּי יְהוָה יִסַּד צִיּוֹן וּבָהּ יֶחֱסוּ
טו א עֲנִיֵּי עַמּוֹ׃ מַשָּׂא מוֹאָב כִּי בְּלֵיל שֻׁדַּד עָר מוֹאָב נִדְמָה כִּי
ב בְּלֵיל שֻׁדַּד קִיר־מוֹאָב נִדְמָה׃ עָלָה הַבַּיִת וְדִיבֹן הַבָּמוֹת לְבֶכִי עַל־
נְבוֹ וְעַל מֵידְבָא מוֹאָב יְיֵלִיל בְּכָל־רֹאשָׁיו קָרְחָה כָּל־זָקָן גְּרוּעָה׃
ג בְּחוּצֹתָיו חָגְרוּ שָׂק עַל גַּגּוֹתֶיהָ וּבִרְחֹבֹתֶיהָ כֻּלֹּה יְיֵלִיל יֹרֵד בַּבֶּכִי׃
ד וַתִּזְעַק חֶשְׁבּוֹן וְאֶלְעָלֵה עַד־יַהַץ נִשְׁמַע קוֹלָם עַל־כֵּן חֲלֻצֵי מוֹאָב
ה יָרִיעוּ נַפְשׁוֹ יָרְעָה לּוֹ׃ לִבִּי לְמוֹאָב יִזְעָק בְּרִיחֶהָ עַד־צֹעַר עֶגְלַת
שְׁלִשִׁיָּה כִּי ׀ מַעֲלֵה הַלּוּחִית בִּבְכִי יַעֲלֶה־בּוֹ כִּי דֶּרֶךְ חוֹרֹנַיִם זַעֲקַת־
ו שֶׁבֶר יְעֹעֵרוּ׃ כִּי־מֵי נִמְרִים מְשַׁמּוֹת יִהְיוּ כִּי־יָבֵשׁ חָצִיר כָּלָה דֶשֶׁא
ז יֶרֶק לֹא הָיָה׃ עַל־כֵּן יִתְרָה עָשָׂה וּפְקֻדָּתָם עַל נַחַל הָעֲרָבִים יִשָּׂאוּם׃
ח כִּי־הִקִּיפָה הַזְּעָקָה אֶת־גְּבוּל מוֹאָב עַד־אֶגְלַיִם יִלְלָתָהּ וּבְאֵר אֵילִים
ט יִלְלָתָהּ׃ כִּי מֵי דִימוֹן מָלְאוּ דָם כִּי־אָשִׁית עַל־דִּימוֹן נוֹסָפוֹת לִפְלֵיטַת
טז א מוֹאָב אַרְיֵה וְלִשְׁאֵרִית אֲדָמָה׃ שִׁלְחוּ־כַר מֹשֵׁל־אֶרֶץ מִסֶּלַע מִדְבָּרָה
ב אֶל־הַר בַּת־צִיּוֹן׃ וְהָיָה כְעוֹף־נוֹדֵד קֵן מְשֻׁלָּח תִּהְיֶינָה בְּנוֹת מוֹאָב
ג מַעְבָּרֹת לְאַרְנוֹן׃ הביאו עֵצָה עשי פְלִילָה שִׁיתִי כַלַּיִל צִלֵּךְ בְּתוֹךְ הָבִיאִי | עֲשׂוּ
ד צָהֳרָיִם סַתְּרִי נִדָּחִים נֹדֵד אַל־תְּגַלִּי׃ יָגוּרוּ בָךְ נִדָּחַי מוֹאָב הֱוִי־
סֵתֶר לָמוֹ מִפְּנֵי שׁוֹדֵד כִּי־אָפֵס הַמֵּץ כָּלָה שֹׁד תַּמּוּ רֹמֵס מִן־
ה הָאָרֶץ׃ וְהוּכַן בַּחֶסֶד כִּסֵּא וְיָשַׁב עָלָיו בֶּאֱמֶת בְּאֹהֶל ז
ו דָּוִד שֹׁפֵט וְדֹרֵשׁ מִשְׁפָּט וּמְהִר צֶדֶק׃ שָׁמַעְנוּ גְאוֹן־מוֹאָב גֵּא מְאֹד
ז גַּאֲוָתוֹ וּגְאוֹנוֹ וְעֶבְרָתוֹ לֹא־כֵן בַּדָּיו׃ לָכֵן יְיֵלִיל מוֹאָב לְמוֹאָב כֻּלֹּה
ח יְיֵלִיל לַאֲשִׁישֵׁי קִיר־חֲרֶשֶׂת תֶּהְגּוּ אַךְ־נְכָאִים׃ כִּי שַׁדְמוֹת חֶשְׁבּוֹן
אֻמְלַל גֶּפֶן שִׂבְמָה בַּעֲלֵי גוֹיִם הָלְמוּ שְׂרוּקֶּיהָ עַד־יַעְזֵר נָגָעוּ תָּעוּ

fit for the masters of nations; they reached Yazer, wandered in the desert; their
9 tendrils spread and crossed the sea. So I weep the cries of Yazer for the vine
of Sivma; I would quench you with tears, Ḥeshbon and Elaleh, for over your
10 summer fruits and reaping the battle call has fallen. Joy and celebration are
dispelled from the fruitful field; no cheerful singing in vineyards; no more
trumpet song. The treaders do not tread the wine in the winepresses; I have
11 silenced those calls also. And so, for Moav, my being moans like a lute, and
12 all that is in me is with Kir Ḥareshet. And it will be: when Moav appears on
the high shrine, when he is wearied, he will climb to his sanctuary to pray – and
13 14 will not be able. This is what the LORD spoke of Moav long ago, and
now the LORD speaks – He says: Three more years, three hired workers' years,
and Moav's glory will fall to shame among all the vast multitude, the remnant
17 1 a thin trace, all eminence gone. The burden of Damascus: Behold:
2 Damascus is dismissed from the company of cities: piled up rubble; the Aroer
towns abandoned, left to the flocks lying down with none to trouble them.
3 No more fortresses in Efrayim; no more kingship in Damascus, and Aram
will be a remnant, like the children of Israel's glory; the LORD of Hosts has
4 spoken. On that day, slender will grow Yaakov's glory, the fat of his
5 body grown lean; it is as a man gathers up the standing corn at harvest, and
his arm slashes down the heads of grain, as the heads are collected in the
6 Refaim Valley, yet some will remain; as the olives are beaten down, but two
or three buds will be left at the very top of the tree; perhaps four or five on
7 the fruitful vine's limbs – so says the LORD, God of Israel. On that
day, man will turn to his Maker, and his eyes will see the Holy One of Israel.
8 No more will he turn to the altars his hands build to see what his own fingers
9 formed, the sacred trees and sun statues. On that day, his bastion
cities will be like fields forsaken, lapsed to groves and woods, like those they
10 forsook when Israel came; it will be wasteland, for you have forgotten God,
your rescue – you do not remember your bastion Rock. So you sow these
11 gorgeous shoots, plant cuttings from a stranger's branch; that day you bring
your shoots to flourish, by morning you see your seeds give flower; the fruits
12 will be waste on the day of your sickness: incurable pain. Woe to
the throngs of great peoples that roar the roar of oceans, that thunder the
13 thunder of nations, like the thunder of mighty waters. Nations thunder, the
thunder of great oceans; a voice dispels the flood; it flees far away, chased
14 away like hill chaff by the wind, like tumbleweed in a tempest. At evening,
horror; by morning it will be gone. This is the fate of those who plunder us,
18 1 the portion due to any who take us for their spoils. Woe to the land
2 of buzzing insect wings, far away beyond the Kushite rivers, that sends its
messengers out by sea, reed vessels crossing the waters: "Go now, swift
messengers, to a people pulled apart and mauled, to a people always fearsome
until now, a nation trampled piece by piece, despoiled by kings of the river
3 land."[46] All you who live upon this earth, all dwellers on the land, when the

---

46 | Verses 1–3 seem to refer to political leaders in upper Egypt who seek an alliance with Yehuda against Assyria.

ט מִדְבָּר שְׁלֻחוֹתֶיהָ נִטְּשׁוּ עָבְרוּ יָם׃ עַל־כֵּן אֶבְכֶּה בִּבְכִי יַעְזֵר גֶּפֶן שִׂבְמָה
אֲרַיָּוֶךְ דִּמְעָתִי חֶשְׁבּוֹן וְאֶלְעָלֵה כִּי עַל־קֵיצֵךְ וְעַל־קְצִירֵךְ הֵידָד נָפָל׃
י וְנֶאֱסַף שִׂמְחָה וָגִיל מִן־הַכַּרְמֶל וּבַכְּרָמִים לֹא־יְרֻנָּן לֹא יְרֹעָע יַיִן
יא בַּיְקָבִים לֹא־יִדְרֹךְ הַדֹּרֵךְ הֵידָד הִשְׁבַּתִּי׃ עַל־כֵּן מֵעַי לְמוֹאָב כַּכִּנּוֹר
יב יֶהֱמוּ וְקִרְבִּי לְקִיר חָרֶשׂ׃ וְהָיָה כִי־נִרְאָה כִּי־נִלְאָה מוֹאָב עַל־הַבָּמָה
יג וּבָא אֶל־מִקְדָּשׁוֹ לְהִתְפַּלֵּל וְלֹא יוּכָל׃ זֶה הַדָּבָר אֲשֶׁר דִּבֶּר
יד יְהוָה אֶל־מוֹאָב מֵאָז׃ וְעַתָּה דִּבֶּר יְהוָה לֵאמֹר בְּשָׁלֹשׁ שָׁנִים כִּשְׁנֵי
שָׂכִיר וְנִקְלָה כְּבוֹד מוֹאָב בְּכֹל הֶהָמוֹן הָרָב וּשְׁאָר מְעַט מִזְעָר לוֹא
יז א כַבִּיר׃ מַשָּׂא דַּמָּשֶׂק הִנֵּה דַמֶּשֶׂק מוּסָר מֵעִיר וְהָיְתָה
ב מְעִי מַפָּלָה׃ עֲזֻבוֹת עָרֵי עֲרֹעֵר לַעֲדָרִים תִּהְיֶינָה וְרָבְצוּ וְאֵין מַחֲרִיד׃
ג וְנִשְׁבַּת מִבְצָר מֵאֶפְרַיִם וּמַמְלָכָה מִדַּמֶּשֶׂק וּשְׁאָר אֲרָם כִּכְבוֹד בְּנֵי־
ד יִשְׂרָאֵל יִהְיוּ נְאֻם יְהוָה צְבָאוֹת׃ וְהָיָה בַּיּוֹם הַהוּא יִדַּל
ה כְּבוֹד יַעֲקֹב וּמִשְׁמַן בְּשָׂרוֹ יֵרָזֶה׃ וְהָיָה כֶּאֱסֹף קָצִיר קָמָה וּזְרֹעוֹ שִׁבֳּלִים
ו יִקְצוֹר וְהָיָה כִּמְלַקֵּט שִׁבֳּלִים בְּעֵמֶק רְפָאִים׃ וְנִשְׁאַר־בּוֹ עוֹלֵלֹת כְּנֹקֶף
זַיִת שְׁנַיִם שְׁלֹשָׁה גַּרְגְּרִים בְּרֹאשׁ אָמִיר אַרְבָּעָה חֲמִשָּׁה בִּסְעִפֶיהָ
ז פֹּרִיָּה נְאֻם־יְהוָה אֱלֹהֵי יִשְׂרָאֵל׃ בַּיּוֹם הַהוּא יִשְׁעֶה הָאָדָם
ח עַל־עֹשֵׂהוּ וְעֵינָיו אֶל־קְדוֹשׁ יִשְׂרָאֵל תִּרְאֶינָה׃ וְלֹא יִשְׁעֶה אֶל־
הַמִּזְבְּחוֹת מַעֲשֵׂה יָדָיו וַאֲשֶׁר עָשׂוּ אֶצְבְּעֹתָיו לֹא יִרְאֶה וְהָאֲשֵׁרִים
ט וְהַחַמָּנִים׃ בַּיּוֹם הַהוּא יִהְיוּ ׀ עָרֵי מָעֻזּוֹ כַּעֲזוּבַת הַחֹרֶשׁ
י וְהָאָמִיר אֲשֶׁר עָזְבוּ מִפְּנֵי בְּנֵי יִשְׂרָאֵל וְהָיְתָה שְׁמָמָה׃ כִּי שָׁכַחַתְּ אֱלֹהֵי
יִשְׁעֵךְ וְצוּר מָעֻזֵּךְ לֹא זָכָרְתְּ עַל־כֵּן תִּטְּעִי נִטְעֵי נַעֲמָנִים וּזְמֹרַת זָר
יא תִּזְרָעֶנּוּ׃ בְּיוֹם נִטְעֵךְ תְּשַׂגְשֵׂגִי וּבַבֹּקֶר זַרְעֵךְ תַּפְרִיחִי נֵד קָצִיר בְּיוֹם
יב נַחֲלָה וּכְאֵב אָנוּשׁ׃ הוֹי הֲמוֹן עַמִּים רַבִּים כַּהֲמוֹת יַמִּים
יג יֶהֱמָיוּן וּשְׁאוֹן לְאֻמִּים כִּשְׁאוֹן מַיִם כַּבִּירִים יִשָּׁאוּן׃ לְאֻמִּים כִּשְׁאוֹן
מַיִם רַבִּים יִשָּׁאוּן וְגָעַר בּוֹ וְנָס מִמֶּרְחָק וְרֻדַּף כְּמֹץ הָרִים לִפְנֵי־רוּחַ
יד וּכְגַלְגַּל לִפְנֵי סוּפָה׃ לְעֵת עֶרֶב וְהִנֵּה בַלָּהָה בְּטֶרֶם בֹּקֶר אֵינֶנּוּ זֶה
יח א חֵלֶק שׁוֹסֵינוּ וְגוֹרָל לְבֹזְזֵינוּ׃ הוֹי אֶרֶץ צִלְצַל כְּנָפָיִם אֲשֶׁר
ב מֵעֵבֶר לְנַהֲרֵי־כוּשׁ׃ הַשֹּׁלֵחַ בַּיָּם צִירִים וּבִכְלֵי־גֹמֶא עַל־פְּנֵי־מַיִם לְכוּ ׀
מַלְאָכִים קַלִּים אֶל־גּוֹי מְמֻשָּׁךְ וּמוֹרָט אֶל־עַם נוֹרָא מִן־הוּא וָהָלְאָה
ג גּוֹי קַו־קָו וּמְבוּסָה אֲשֶׁר־בָּזְאוּ נְהָרִים אַרְצוֹ׃ כָּל־יֹשְׁבֵי תֵבֵל וְשֹׁכְנֵי

banner is raised up on the mountains you shall see; when the horn sounds
4 its blast, then you shall hear. For this is what the Lord has told me:
Still I rest in My residence, gaze down as when pure heat rests on sunlight, or
5 on the harvest heat a cloud of dew, for before harvest comes, when the
blossom is gone, as the grape buds swell into young fruits, the trembling
stems shall fall to the pruning knife. The branches will be cleared, cut down,[47]
6 abandoned to mountain eagles, to beasts of the land. And birds of prey will
feed on this all summer, and all beasts of the land will see winter through on
7 this. At that time, tribute shall be brought to the Lord of Hosts from
this people pulled apart and mauled, from a people always fearsome until
now, a nation trampled piece by piece, despoiled by the kings of the river land,
19 1 to the place of the Lord of Hosts, His name: Mount Zion. The
burden of Egypt: Behold the Lord, riding upon swift cloud and coming to
Egypt. The gods of Egypt all sway before Him; the heart of Egypt will dissolve.
2 I shall make Egypt wrestle with Egypt; brother will fight against brother,
3 friend against friend, city against city, realm against realm. Egypt will empty
its spirit from within, and I shall confound all its plans. The people will seek
4 after their false gods and mutterers, necromancers, mediums. I shall dam
Egypt through a hard-handed master; a mighty king will tyrannize them, so
5 says the Master, Lord of Hosts. The sea will be emptied of water; the river
6 will be scorched dry. Rivers will be forsaken; Egypt's canals will dwindle and
7 dry, and rush and reed wither. Naked land on the Nile bed, naked the bank
of the Nile, and all that seeds and grows in the Nile will dry up, disperse, be
8 gone. The fishermen will lament; all who throw hooks to the river will mourn,
9 all who spread nets over water left waste. The many who work combed flax
10 will be shamed with all those who weave fine cotton; Egypt's founda-
11 tions – crushed, its dam builders mired spirits. The princes of Tzoan are fools;
the wisest of Pharaoh's advisors give idiots' counsel. How can you say to
12 Pharaoh, "I am a son of wise men, heir to the ancient kings"? Where,
then – where are these wise men of yours? Surely they would tell you, surely
13 they must know what the Lord of Hosts has planned for Egypt. The princes
of Tzoan are fools; the princes of Nof, deceived. They have led Egypt astray,
14 the very mainstay of its tribes. The Lord has poured into her a spirit of
madness, and they have led Egypt awry in all it does, like a drunk man lurching
15 through his vomit. Nothing in Egypt will be done that is done by head or by
16 tail, by palm or by bulrush of them.[48] On that day, Egypt will be like
women who quake and fear the Lord of Hosts' raised hand brandished over
17 them; the land of Yehuda will be the terror of Egypt. Whoever may mention
its name will strike them with fear of the Lord of Hosts' plan, of what He
18 has destined for them. On that day, five cities of Egypt shall speak
the language of Canaan and swear their oaths by the Lord of Hosts. City of
19 Calamity, one shall be named. On that day, in Egypt's heartlands,

---

47 | Possibly referring to the downfall of Assyria.

48 | Both the leadership and the masses will be rendered powerless, and Egyptian society will cease to function.

ד אֶרֶץ כִּנְשֹׂא־נֵס הָרִים תִּרְאוּ וְכִתְקֹעַ שׁוֹפָר תִּשְׁמָעוּ: כִּי כֹה
אָמַר יְהוָה אֵלַי אשקוטה וְאַבִּיטָה בִמְכוֹנִי כְּחֹם צַח עֲלֵי־אוֹר כְּעָב אֶשְׁקֳטָה
ה טַל בְּחֹם קָצִיר: כִּי־לִפְנֵי קָצִיר כְּתָם־פֶּרַח וּבֹסֶר גֹּמֵל יִהְיֶה נִצָּה וְכָרַת
ו הַזַּלְזַלִּים בַּמַּזְמֵרוֹת וְאֶת־הַנְּטִישׁוֹת הֵסִיר הֵתַז: יֵעָזְבוּ יַחְדָּו לְעֵיט
הָרִים וּלְבֶהֱמַת הָאָרֶץ וְקָץ עָלָיו הָעַיִט וְכָל־בֶּהֱמַת הָאָרֶץ עָלָיו
ז תֶּחֱרָף: בָּעֵת הַהִיא יוּבַל־שַׁי לַיהוָה צְבָאוֹת עַם מְמֻשָּׁךְ
וּמוֹרָט וּמֵעַם נוֹרָא מִן־הוּא וָהָלְאָה גּוֹי | קַו־קָו וּמְבוּסָה אֲשֶׁר בָּזְאוּ
יט א נְהָרִים אַרְצוֹ אֶל־מְקוֹם שֵׁם־יְהוָה צְבָאוֹת הַר־צִיּוֹן: מַשָּׂא
מִצְרָיִם הִנֵּה יְהוָה רֹכֵב עַל־עָב קַל וּבָא מִצְרַיִם וְנָעוּ אֱלִילֵי מִצְרַיִם
ב מִפָּנָיו וּלְבַב מִצְרַיִם יִמַּס בְּקִרְבּוֹ: וְסִכְסַכְתִּי מִצְרַיִם בְּמִצְרַיִם וְנִלְחֲמוּ
ג אִישׁ בְּאָחִיו וְאִישׁ בְּרֵעֵהוּ עִיר בְּעִיר מַמְלָכָה בְּמַמְלָכָה: וְנָבְקָה רוּחַ־
מִצְרַיִם בְּקִרְבּוֹ וַעֲצָתוֹ אֲבַלֵּעַ וְדָרְשׁוּ אֶל־הָאֱלִילִים וְאֶל־הָאִטִּים
ד וְאֶל־הָאֹבוֹת וְאֶל־הַיִּדְּעֹנִים: וְסִכַּרְתִּי אֶת־מִצְרַיִם בְּיַד אֲדֹנִים קָשֶׁה
ה וּמֶלֶךְ עַז יִמְשָׁל־בָּם נְאֻם הָאָדוֹן יְהוָה צְבָאוֹת: וְנִשְּׁתוּ־מַיִם מֵהַיָּם
ו וְנָהָר יֶחֱרַב וְיָבֵשׁ: וְהֶאֶזְנִיחוּ נְהָרוֹת דָּלְלוּ וְחָרְבוּ יְאֹרֵי מָצוֹר קָנֶה וָסוּף
ז קָמֵלוּ: עָרוֹת עַל־יְאוֹר עַל־פִּי יְאוֹר וְכֹל מִזְרַע יְאוֹר יִיבַשׁ נִדַּף וְאֵינֶנּוּ:
ח וְאָנוּ הַדַּיָּגִים וְאָבְלוּ כָּל־מַשְׁלִיכֵי בַיְאוֹר חַכָּה וּפֹרְשֵׂי מִכְמֹרֶת עַל־
ט י פְּנֵי־מַיִם אֻמְלָלוּ: וּבֹשׁוּ עֹבְדֵי פִשְׁתִּים שְׂרִיקוֹת וְאֹרְגִים חוֹרָי: וְהָיוּ
יא שָׁתֹתֶיהָ מְדֻכָּאִים כָּל־עֹשֵׂי שֶׂכֶר אַגְמֵי־נָפֶשׁ: אַךְ־אֱוִלִים שָׂרֵי צֹעַן
חַכְמֵי יֹעֲצֵי פַרְעֹה עֵצָה נִבְעָרָה אֵיךְ תֹּאמְרוּ אֶל־פַּרְעֹה בֶּן־חֲכָמִים
יב אֲנִי בֶּן־מַלְכֵי־קֶדֶם: אַיָּם אֵפוֹא חֲכָמֶיךָ וְיַגִּידוּ נָא לָךְ וְיֵדְעוּ מַה־יָּעַץ
יג יְהוָה צְבָאוֹת עַל־מִצְרָיִם: נוֹאֲלוּ שָׂרֵי צֹעַן נִשְּׁאוּ שָׂרֵי נֹף הִתְעוּ אֶת־
יד מִצְרַיִם פִּנַּת שְׁבָטֶיהָ: יְהוָה מָסַךְ בְּקִרְבָּהּ רוּחַ עִוְעִים וְהִתְעוּ אֶת־
טו מִצְרַיִם בְּכָל־מַעֲשֵׂהוּ כְּהִתָּעוֹת שִׁכּוֹר בְּקִיאוֹ: וְלֹא־יִהְיֶה לְמִצְרַיִם
טז מַעֲשֶׂה אֲשֶׁר יַעֲשֶׂה רֹאשׁ וְזָנָב כִּפָּה וְאַגְמוֹן: בַּיּוֹם הַהוּא
יִהְיֶה מִצְרַיִם כַּנָּשִׁים וְחָרַד | וּפָחַד מִפְּנֵי תְּנוּפַת יַד־יְהוָה צְבָאוֹת
יז אֲשֶׁר־הוּא מֵנִיף עָלָיו: וְהָיְתָה אַדְמַת יְהוּדָה לְמִצְרַיִם לְחָגָּא כֹּל אֲשֶׁר
יַזְכִּיר אֹתָהּ אֵלָיו יִפְחָד מִפְּנֵי עֲצַת יְהוָה צְבָאוֹת אֲשֶׁר־הוּא יוֹעֵץ
יח עָלָיו: בַּיּוֹם הַהוּא יִהְיוּ חָמֵשׁ עָרִים בְּאֶרֶץ מִצְרַיִם
מְדַבְּרוֹת שְׂפַת כְּנַעַן וְנִשְׁבָּעוֹת לַיהוָה צְבָאוֹת עִיר הַהֶרֶס יֵאָמֵר
יט לְאֶחָת: בַּיּוֹם הַהוּא יִהְיֶה מִזְבֵּחַ לַיהוָה בְּתוֹךְ אֶרֶץ מִצְרָיִם

20 an altar to the LORD will stand; at her borders a pillar to the LORD. They will
be sign and testament in the land of Egypt to the LORD of Hosts, for the
people shall cry out to the LORD because of their oppressors; He will send
21 them a rescuer, a fighter; he will save them. The LORD will be made known
to Egypt, and Egypt will know the LORD on that day. And they will serve by
22 sacrifice and offering; they will make the LORD vows and honor them. The
LORD will plague Egypt, plague it and heal. They will come back to the LORD,
23 and He will receive their appeal and heal. On that day a road will
run from Egypt to Assyria. Assyria will come to Egypt. Egypt will come to
24 Assyria, and Egypt with Assyria will worship. On that day, Israel will
25 be one with Egypt and Assyria, a blessing on this earth. For the LORD of
Hosts has blessed him, saying: Blessed are My people, Egypt; Assyria, work
20 1 of My hands; and Israel, My own possession. It was the year the
Tartan[49] came to Ashdod – dispatched by Sargon, king of Assyria – when he
2 fought against Ashdod and captured the city. At that time, the LORD spoke
through Yeshayahu son of Amotz: "Go, undo the sackcloth that covers your
loins, and take off the sandals on your feet." And that is what he did – naked
3 and barefoot would he walk. And the LORD said: My servant
Yeshayahu, walking naked and barefoot for these three years, is a message, a
4 sign, concerning Egypt and Kush. Just so will it be when the king of Assyria
leads away the captives of Egypt, the exiles of Kush, young and old, naked,
5 barefoot, backsides bare, that nakedness of Egypt, full of dread and shame
6 for Kush, their hope; for Egypt, their glory. The ruler of this shore will be
saying on that day, "Look where our hope is now: the place we would flee to
for aid, to be saved from the king of Assyria; now we – how will we
21 1 escape?" The burden of the Ocean Desert:[50] As storm winds sweep
on through the Negev, so from the wilderness it comes, from the terrible land.
2 A fierce vision is spoken to me: the traitors betraying, the plunderers
3 plunder – *Go up, Eilam; Media, lay siege; I have silenced all groaning.*[51] This is
why my hips are seized with sickness, why agonies take hold of me, like
agonies of birth. I writhe away from hearing, shrink, horrified, from seeing;
4 my heartbeat strays; I lurch with terror. He has turned the twilight of my
5 pleasure into dread. So lay a table now and raise the lamp, feast, drink. Now
6 get up, all you princes; grease your shields. For the Lord is saying
7 to me: Go now: set a watchman; let him tell you what he sees. He sees a
chariot, a pair of horses, a donkey rider, a camel rider; he listens, closely listens.
8 A lion roars. "At my post, Lord, always I stand, daylong at my watch, stationed
9 through the nights." And here they come: a chariot of men, a pair of horses.
Then He spoke and said: Fallen, fallen is Babylon; all the statues of her gods
10 are smashed into the ground. My downtrodden one, grain of my threshing
floor, what I hear from the LORD of Hosts, the God of Israel, I have spoken

49 | A title referring to the Assyrian king's second-in-command.

50 | Perhaps Babylon, where the banks of the Euphrates overflow into desert.

51 | The groans of Babylon, whom they are attacking. The italic font indicates God's voice, distinct from that of the prophet.

כ וּמַצֵּבָה אֵצֶל־גְּבוּלָהּ לַיהוה: וְהָיָה לְאוֹת וּלְעֵד לַיהוה צְבָאוֹת בְּאֶרֶץ
מִצְרָיִם כִּי־יִצְעֲקוּ אֶל־יהוה מִפְּנֵי לֹחֲצִים וְיִשְׁלַח לָהֶם מוֹשִׁיעַ וָרָב
כא וְהִצִּילָם: וְנוֹדַע יהוה לְמִצְרַיִם וְיָדְעוּ מִצְרַיִם אֶת־יהוה בַּיּוֹם הַהוּא
כב וְעָבְדוּ זֶבַח וּמִנְחָה וְנָדְרוּ־נֵדֶר לַיהוה וְשִׁלֵּמוּ: וְנָגַף יהוה אֶת־מִצְרַיִם
כג נָגֹף וְרָפוֹא וְשָׁבוּ עַד־יהוה וְנֶעְתַּר לָהֶם וּרְפָאָם: בַּיּוֹם הַהוּא
תִּהְיֶה מְסִלָּה מִמִּצְרַיִם אַשּׁוּרָה וּבָא־אַשּׁוּר בְּמִצְרַיִם וּמִצְרַיִם בְּאַשּׁוּר
כד וְעָבְדוּ מִצְרַיִם אֶת־אַשּׁוּר: בַּיּוֹם הַהוּא יִהְיֶה יִשְׂרָאֵל
כה שְׁלִישִׁיָּה לְמִצְרַיִם וּלְאַשּׁוּר בְּרָכָה בְּקֶרֶב הָאָרֶץ: אֲשֶׁר בֵּרְכוֹ יהוה ח
צְבָאוֹת לֵאמֹר בָּרוּךְ עַמִּי מִצְרַיִם וּמַעֲשֵׂה יָדַי אַשּׁוּר וְנַחֲלָתִי
כ א יִשְׂרָאֵל: בִּשְׁנַת בֹּא תַרְתָּן אַשְׁדּוֹדָה בִּשְׁלֹחַ אֹתוֹ סַרְגוֹן
ב מֶלֶךְ אַשּׁוּר וַיִּלָּחֶם בְּאַשְׁדּוֹד וַיִּלְכְּדָהּ: בָּעֵת הַהִיא דִּבֶּר יהוה בְּיַד
יְשַׁעְיָהוּ בֶן־אָמוֹץ לֵאמֹר לֵךְ וּפִתַּחְתָּ הַשַּׂק מֵעַל מָתְנֶיךָ וְנַעַלְךָ תַחֲלֹץ
ג מֵעַל רַגְלֶךָ וַיַּעַשׂ כֵּן הָלֹךְ עָרוֹם וְיָחֵף: וַיֹּאמֶר יהוה
כַּאֲשֶׁר הָלַךְ עַבְדִּי יְשַׁעְיָהוּ עָרוֹם וְיָחֵף שָׁלֹשׁ שָׁנִים אוֹת וּמוֹפֵת עַל־
ד מִצְרַיִם וְעַל־כּוּשׁ: כֵּן יִנְהַג מֶלֶךְ־אַשּׁוּר אֶת־שְׁבִי מִצְרַיִם וְאֶת־גָּלוּת
ה כּוּשׁ נְעָרִים וּזְקֵנִים עָרוֹם וְיָחֵף וַחֲשׂוּפַי שֵׁת עֶרְוַת מִצְרָיִם: וְחַתּוּ וָבֹשׁוּ
ו מִכּוּשׁ מַבָּטָם וּמִן־מִצְרַיִם תִּפְאַרְתָּם: וְאָמַר יֹשֵׁב הָאִי הַזֶּה בַּיּוֹם הַהוּא
הִנֵּה־כֹה מַבָּטֵנוּ אֲשֶׁר נַסְנוּ שָׁם לְעֶזְרָה לְהִנָּצֵל מִפְּנֵי מֶלֶךְ אַשּׁוּר
כא א וְאֵיךְ נִמָּלֵט אֲנָחְנוּ: מַשָּׂא מִדְבַּר־יָם כְּסוּפוֹת בַּנֶּגֶב
ב לַחֲלוֹף מִמִּדְבָּר בָּא מֵאֶרֶץ נוֹרָאָה: חָזוּת קָשָׁה הֻגַּד־לִי הַבּוֹגֵד ׀ בּוֹגֵד
ג וְהַשּׁוֹדֵד ׀ שׁוֹדֵד עֲלִי עֵילָם צוּרִי מָדַי כָּל־אַנְחָתָה הִשְׁבַּתִּי: עַל־כֵּן
מָלְאוּ מָתְנַי חַלְחָלָה צִירִים אֲחָזוּנִי כְּצִירֵי יוֹלֵדָה נַעֲוֵיתִי מִשְּׁמֹעַ
ד נִבְהַלְתִּי מֵרְאוֹת: תָּעָה לְבָבִי פַּלָּצוּת בִּעֲתָתְנִי אֵת נֶשֶׁף חִשְׁקִי שָׂם
ה לִי לַחֲרָדָה: עָרֹךְ הַשֻּׁלְחָן צָפֹה הַצָּפִית אָכוֹל שָׁתֹה קוּמוּ הַשָּׂרִים
ו מִשְׁחוּ מָגֵן: כִּי כֹה אָמַר אֵלַי אֲדֹנָי לֵךְ הַעֲמֵד הַמְצַפֶּה אֲשֶׁר
ז יִרְאֶה יַגִּיד: וְרָאָה רֶכֶב צֶמֶד פָּרָשִׁים רֶכֶב חֲמוֹר רֶכֶב גָּמָל וְהִקְשִׁיב
ח קֶשֶׁב רַב־קָשֶׁב: וַיִּקְרָא אַרְיֵה עַל־מִצְפֶּה ׀ אֲדֹנָי אָנֹכִי עֹמֵד תָּמִיד
ט יוֹמָם וְעַל־מִשְׁמַרְתִּי אָנֹכִי נִצָּב כָּל־הַלֵּילוֹת: וְהִנֵּה־זֶה בָא רֶכֶב אִישׁ
צֶמֶד פָּרָשִׁים וַיַּעַן וַיֹּאמֶר נָפְלָה נָפְלָה בָּבֶל וְכָל־פְּסִילֵי אֱלֹהֶיהָ שִׁבַּר
י לָאָרֶץ: מְדֻשָׁתִי וּבֶן־גָּרְנִי אֲשֶׁר שָׁמַעְתִּי מֵאֵת יהוה צְבָאוֹת אֱלֹהֵי

11 now to you. The burden of Duma:[52] A voice calling to me from Se'ir:
12 "What news does night bring, watchman? Watch, what news of night?" The
watch says, "Morning comes, and also night." If you would ask it, ask; turn
13 back, return. The burden of Arabia: In the forest of Arabia you spend
14 the night, nomads on the trail from Dedan.[53] People of Teima – meet the
15 thirsty with water, greet the travelers with bread; for they have fled the sword,
16 the drawn sword, the taut bow, the dead weight of war. For so the
Lord has said to me: One more year, a hired worker's year, and the glory of
17 Kedar[54] will be all gone, their bowmen a small remnant, Kedar's mighty men
22 1 left few; the LORD, God of Israel, has spoken. The burden of the
Valley of the Vision:[55] Why now, why have you all climbed up onto the
2 rooftops? You, full of bustle, buzzing metropolis, exuberant city? Not for your
3 fallen to fall to the sword, not yours to perish in warfare.[56] Now all Your
commanders have strayed, or been bound up by their bowstrings; all those
found in you were bound up together or fled from what comes from the
4 distance. So I say: Turn your gaze away; the tears I weep are bitter. Do not
5 rush in to comfort me for my maiden nation's ravaging. For a day of turmoil,
defeat, and shame is come from the Lord GOD of Hosts in the Valley of the
6 Vision. Kir cries carnage;[57] the call reaches the hills. Eilam bore ammunition
7 in horse-drawn chariots of men, and Kir drew out its shields. So it was: the
8 best of your valleys filled with chariots, and cavalry streamed to the gate. They
pulled away the city's cover: on that day you viewed all the weapons of the
9 Forest House,[58] the ruptures in the City of David – many – and you gathered
10 the waters to the Lower Pool and numbered Jerusalem's houses, then smashed
11 those houses down to reinforce the city wall. Yes, you dug a channel between
the walls for the waters of the ancient pool[59] and looked not once to the One
12 who made it; you saw not the One who, long since, formed it. On that day,
the Lord GOD of Hosts called for tears and eulogies, the baldness and
13 sackcloth of grief; but here: festivity and joy, the butchering of cattle, the
slaughter of flock. "Eat your meat, drink your wine; eat, drink; tomorrow we
14 die."[60] The LORD of Hosts' voice resounds in my ears: See if this sin can ever
15 be atoned for to the day you die, says the LORD of Hosts. So says the
Lord GOD of Hosts: Go; go to this minister, to Shevna in charge of the

---

52 | A kindom in what is now the northern part of Saudi Arabia. Se'ir is on the northern border of Duma.

53 | A kingdom in the northwestern Arabian Peninsula.

54 | The Kedarites were nomads whose areas of habitation included Dedan and Duma; Assyria fought these nomads several times.

55 | Apparently a reference to Jerusalem.

56 | But rather ingloriously from starvation and disease.

57 | Men from Kir (of Moav) and Eilam joined the Assyrian fighting forces.

58 | The royal palace; cf. 1 Kings 7:2–5.

59 | King Ḥizkiyahu fortified Jerusalem by building the broad wall, which necessitated the demolition of houses to clear space for it, and a channel to divert water into the city.

60 | The slaughter of the flock is a response to the siege, in which food and water for people and animals are lacking.

יא יִשְׂרָאֵל הִגַּדְתִּי לָכֶם׃ מַשָּׂא דּוּמָה אֵלַי קֹרֵא מִשֵּׂעִיר שֹׁמֵר
יב מַה־מִּלַּיְלָה שֹׁמֵר מַה־מִּלֵּיל׃ אָמַר שֹׁמֵר אָתָא בֹקֶר וְגַם־לָיְלָה אִם־
יג תִּבְעָיוּן בְּעָיוּ שֻׁבוּ אֵתָיוּ׃ מַשָּׂא בַּעְרָב בַּיַּעַר בַּעְרַב תָּלִינוּ
יד אֹרְחוֹת דְּדָנִים׃ לִקְרַאת צָמֵא הֵתָיוּ מָיִם יֹשְׁבֵי אֶרֶץ תֵּימָא בְּלַחְמוֹ
טו קִדְּמוּ נֹדֵד׃ כִּי־מִפְּנֵי חֲרָבוֹת נָדָדוּ מִפְּנֵי ׀ חֶרֶב נְטוּשָׁה וּמִפְּנֵי קֶשֶׁת
טז דְּרוּכָה וּמִפְּנֵי כֹּבֶד מִלְחָמָה׃ כִּי־כֹה אָמַר אֲדֹנָי אֵלָי בְּעוֹד
יז שָׁנָה כִּשְׁנֵי שָׂכִיר וְכָלָה כָּל־כְּבוֹד קֵדָר׃ וּשְׁאָר מִסְפַּר־קֶשֶׁת גִּבּוֹרֵי
כב א בְנֵי־קֵדָר יִמְעָטוּ כִּי יְהוָה אֱלֹהֵי־יִשְׂרָאֵל דִּבֵּר׃ מַשָּׂא גֵּיא
ב חִזָּיוֹן מַה־לָּךְ אֵפוֹא כִּי־עָלִית כֻּלָּךְ לַגַּגּוֹת׃ תְּשֻׁאוֹת ׀ מְלֵאָה עִיר
ג הוֹמִיָּה קִרְיָה עַלִּיזָה חֲלָלַיִךְ לֹא חַלְלֵי־חֶרֶב וְלֹא מֵתֵי מִלְחָמָה׃ כָּל־
קְצִינַיִךְ נָדְדוּ יַחַד מִקֶּשֶׁת אֻסָּרוּ כָּל־נִמְצָאַיִךְ אֻסְּרוּ יַחְדָּו מֵרָחוֹק
ד בָּרָחוּ׃ עַל־כֵּן אָמַרְתִּי שְׁעוּ מִנִּי אֲמָרֵר בַּבֶּכִי אַל־תָּאִיצוּ לְנַחֲמֵנִי עַל־
ה שֹׁד בַּת־עַמִּי׃ כִּי יוֹם מְהוּמָה וּמְבוּסָה וּמְבוּכָה לַאדֹנָי יֱהוִה צְבָאוֹת
ו בְּגֵי חִזָּיוֹן מְקַרְקַר קִר וְשׁוֹעַ אֶל־הָהָר׃ וְעֵילָם נָשָׂא אַשְׁפָּה בְּרֶכֶב
ז אָדָם פָּרָשִׁים וְקִיר עֵרָה מָגֵן׃ וַיְהִי מִבְחַר־עֲמָקַיִךְ מָלְאוּ רָכֶב
ח וְהַפָּרָשִׁים שֹׁת שָׁתוּ הַשָּׁעְרָה׃ וַיְגַל אֵת מָסַךְ יְהוּדָה וַתַּבֵּט בַּיּוֹם הַהוּא
ט אֶל־נֶשֶׁק בֵּית הַיָּעַר׃ וְאֵת בְּקִיעֵי עִיר־דָּוִד רְאִיתֶם כִּי־רָבּוּ וַתְּקַבְּצוּ
י אֶת־מֵי הַבְּרֵכָה הַתַּחְתּוֹנָה׃ וְאֶת־בָּתֵּי יְרוּשָׁלִַם סְפַרְתֶּם וַתִּתְצוּ הַבָּתִּים
יא לְבַצֵּר הַחוֹמָה׃ וּמִקְוָה עֲשִׂיתֶם בֵּין הַחֹמֹתַיִם לְמֵי הַבְּרֵכָה הַיְשָׁנָה
יב וְלֹא הִבַּטְתֶּם אֶל־עֹשֶׂיהָ וְיֹצְרָהּ מֵרָחוֹק לֹא רְאִיתֶם׃ וַיִּקְרָא אֲדֹנָי
יג יֱהוִה צְבָאוֹת בַּיּוֹם הַהוּא לִבְכִי וּלְמִסְפֵּד וּלְקָרְחָה וְלַחֲגֹר שָׂק׃ וְהִנֵּה ׀
שָׂשׂוֹן וְשִׂמְחָה הָרֹג ׀ בָּקָר וְשָׁחֹט צֹאן אָכֹל בָּשָׂר וְשָׁתוֹת יָיִן אָכוֹל
יד וְשָׁתוֹ כִּי מָחָר נָמוּת׃ וְנִגְלָה בְאָזְנָי יְהוָה צְבָאוֹת אִם־יְכֻפַּר הֶעָוֹן הַזֶּה
טו לָכֶם עַד־תְּמֻתוּן אָמַר אֲדֹנָי יֱהוִה צְבָאוֹת׃ כֹּה אָמַר אֲדֹנָי
יֱהוִה צְבָאוֹת לֶךְ־בֹּא אֶל־הַסֹּכֵן הַזֶּה עַל־שֶׁבְנָא אֲשֶׁר עַל־הַבָּיִת׃

16 palace: Why? What is yours here, and who here is yours that you hew yourself
a grave in this place? Hewing his grave on high, engraving his resting place
17 into the rock. See – the LORD will shake you, a masterful shake, will put you
18 on and wear you, will wind you, bind you, turn you around into an open-
handed land. It is there that you will die, there that your chariots of glory will
19 curse your master's house. I shall push you down from your high position,
20 destroy your standing. It will be on that day: I shall call upon my servant,
21 Elyakim son of Ḥilkiya.[61] I shall dress him in your tunic, with your breastplate
will protect him. I shall give over your rule into his hand, and he shall be father
22 to the people of Jerusalem, the House of Yehuda. I shall put the key to the
House of David upon his shoulder; what he opens, none will close; what he
23 closes, none will open. I shall set him as a peg in an enduring place and make
24 him a throne of glory to his father's house. All the glory of his father's house
will hang upon him,[62] children and progeny, small vessels, all, from barrels to
25 wine jars. On that day, says the LORD of Hosts, that peg, fixed in an enduring
place, will shift and be broken and fall, and the burden it carries will fall, for
23 1 the LORD has spoken. The burden of Tyre: Wail, ships of Tarshish,
for she is sacked: no home, no harbor; it was shown to them in the land of
2 Kitim. Stand silent, you, living on the island;[63] the merchant of Sidon, the sea
3 voyager once filled you up. Great waters bore the seed of the Shiḥor, the
4 River's crop her harvest, making her merchant to nations. Be humbled, Sidon,
for the sea speaks, the fortress sea – she says, "No! I never labored, never
5 birthed; I never brought up boys, nor raised young ladies."[64] When Egypt
6 hear, they will quake at the news of Tyre. Cross over then, back to Tarshish.
7 Wail, you who live on the island. Has it come to this, your exuberant city, old
8 as antiquity? Her feet will carry her far to seek haven. Who planned all this
for Tyre, who wore the crown? Tyre, whose merchants are princes, whose
9 tradesmen are nobles of this earth. It is the LORD of Hosts who planned it, to
10 desecrate all of splendor's eminence, to degrade all nobles of this earth. Pass
through your land like the Nile,[65] daughter Tarshish; there is no more landing.
11 He has stretched His hand out over the sea and whipped nations to a ferment.
12 The LORD has commanded Canaan to destroy her strongholds. He says: No
more will you exult, virgin daughter Sidon, downtrodden. Kitim – rise and
13 go there. You will find no rest there either. You see, land of Chaldeans, this is
the people that never was. Assyria built this land for desert beasts. They set
14 up their watchtowers, laid waste all her palaces, turned them to rubble. Now
15 wail, ships of Tarshish; your stronghold is sacked. It will be on
that day: Tyre will be forgotten for seventy years, the reign of a single king,
but at the end of seventy years, the strain of a harlot's song will come to Tyre.

61 | Also mentioned in 36:3 and II Kings 18:18.

62 | This will apparently be his downfall – despite a promising beginning he will start giving undue favor to his own family members.

63 | Tyre was an island until Alexander the Great made it a peninsula.

64 | The sea is either disowning, or perhaps mourning, her Tyrian "children."

65 | Referring, seemingly, to the seasonal flooding of the Nile bank, which displaces those on the shore.

טז מַה־לְּךָ פֹה וּמִי לְךָ פֹה כִּי־חָצַבְתָּ לְּךָ פֹּה קָבֶר חֹצְבִי מָרוֹם קִבְרוֹ
יז חֹקְקִי בַסֶּלַע מִשְׁכָּן לוֹ: הִנֵּה יהוה מְטַלְטֶלְךָ טַלְטֵלָה גָּבֶר וְעֹטְךָ
יח עָטֹה: צָנוֹף יִצְנָפְךָ צְנֵפָה כַּדּוּר אֶל־אֶרֶץ רַחֲבַת יָדָיִם שָׁמָּה תָמוּת
יט וְשָׁמָּה מַרְכְּבוֹת כְּבוֹדֶךָ קְלוֹן בֵּית אֲדֹנֶיךָ: וַהֲדַפְתִּיךָ מִמַּצָּבֶךָ
כ וּמִמַּעֲמָדְךָ יֶהֶרְסֶךָ: וְהָיָה בַּיּוֹם הַהוּא וְקָרָאתִי לְעַבְדִּי לְאֶלְיָקִים בֶּן־
כא חִלְקִיָּהוּ: וְהִלְבַּשְׁתִּיו כֻּתָּנְתֶּךָ וְאַבְנֵטְךָ אֲחַזְּקֶנּוּ וּמֶמְשַׁלְתְּךָ אֶתֵּן בְּיָדוֹ
כב וְהָיָה לְאָב לְיוֹשֵׁב יְרוּשָׁלַםִ וּלְבֵית יְהוּדָה: וְנָתַתִּי מַפְתֵּחַ בֵּית־דָּוִד
כג עַל־שִׁכְמוֹ וּפָתַח וְאֵין סֹגֵר וְסָגַר וְאֵין פֹּתֵחַ: וּתְקַעְתִּיו יָתֵד בְּמָקוֹם ט
כד נֶאֱמָן וְהָיָה לְכִסֵּא כָבוֹד לְבֵית אָבִיו: וְתָלוּ עָלָיו כֹּל ׀ כְּבוֹד בֵּית־אָבִיו
הַצֶּאֱצָאִים וְהַצְּפִעוֹת כֹּל כְּלֵי הַקָּטָן מִכְּלֵי הָאַגָּנוֹת וְעַד כָּל־כְּלֵי
כה הַנְּבָלִים: בַּיּוֹם הַהוּא נְאֻם יהוה צְבָאוֹת תָּמוּשׁ הַיָּתֵד הַתְּקוּעָה
בְּמָקוֹם נֶאֱמָן וְנִגְדְּעָה וְנָפְלָה וְנִכְרַת הַמַּשָּׂא אֲשֶׁר־עָלֶיהָ כִּי יהוה
כג א דִּבֵּר: מַשָּׂא צֹר הֵילִילוּ ׀ אֳנִיּוֹת תַּרְשִׁישׁ כִּי־שֻׁדַּד מִבַּיִת
ב מִבּוֹא מֵאֶרֶץ כִּתִּים נִגְלָה־לָמוֹ: דֹּמּוּ יֹשְׁבֵי אִי סֹחַר צִידוֹן עֹבֵר יָם
ג מִלְאוּךְ: וּבְמַיִם רַבִּים זֶרַע שִׁחֹר קְצִיר יְאוֹר תְּבוּאָתָהּ וַתְּהִי סְחַר
ד גּוֹיִם: בּוֹשִׁי צִידוֹן כִּי־אָמַר יָם מָעוֹז הַיָּם לֵאמֹר לֹא־חַלְתִּי וְלֹא־יָלַדְתִּי
ה וְלֹא גִדַּלְתִּי בַחוּרִים רוֹמַמְתִּי בְתוּלוֹת: כַּאֲשֶׁר שֵׁמַע לְמִצְרָיִם יָחִילוּ
ו ז כְּשֵׁמַע צֹר: עִבְרוּ תַּרְשִׁישָׁה הֵילִילוּ יֹשְׁבֵי אִי: הֲזֹאת לָכֶם עַלִּיזָה
ח מִימֵי־קֶדֶם קַדְמָתָהּ יֹבִלוּהָ רַגְלֶיהָ מֵרָחוֹק לָגוּר: מִי יָעַץ זֹאת עַל־צֹר
ט הַמַּעֲטִירָה אֲשֶׁר סֹחֲרֶיהָ שָׂרִים כִּנְעָנֶיהָ נִכְבַּדֵּי־אָרֶץ: יהוה צְבָאוֹת
י יְעָצָהּ לְחַלֵּל גְּאוֹן כָּל־צְבִי לְהָקֵל כָּל־נִכְבַּדֵּי־אָרֶץ: עִבְרִי אַרְצֵךְ כַּיְאֹר
יא בַּת־תַּרְשִׁישׁ אֵין מֵזַח עוֹד: יָדוֹ נָטָה עַל־הַיָּם הִרְגִּיז מַמְלָכוֹת יהוה
יב צִוָּה אֶל־כְּנַעַן לַשְׁמִד מָעֻזְנֶיהָ: וַיֹּאמֶר לֹא־תוֹסִיפִי עוֹד לַעְלוֹז
הַמְעֻשָּׁקָה בְּתוּלַת בַּת־צִידוֹן כתיים קוּמִי עֲבֹרִי גַּם־שָׁם לֹא־יָנוּחַ כִּתִּים
יג לָךְ: הֵן ׀ אֶרֶץ כַּשְׂדִּים זֶה הָעָם לֹא הָיָה אַשּׁוּר יְסָדָהּ לְצִיִּים הֵקִימוּ
יד בחיניו עֹרְרוּ אַרְמְנוֹתֶיהָ שָׂמָהּ לְמַפֵּלָה: הֵילִילוּ אֳנִיּוֹת תַּרְשִׁישׁ כִּי בַּחוּנָיו
טו שֻׁדַּד מָעֻזְּכֶן: וְהָיָה בַּיּוֹם הַהוּא וְנִשְׁכַּחַת צֹר שִׁבְעִים
שָׁנָה כִּימֵי מֶלֶךְ אֶחָד מִקֵּץ שִׁבְעִים שָׁנָה יִהְיֶה לְצֹר כְּשִׁירַת הַזּוֹנָה:

16 Take up your harp now; circle the town, forgotten harlot. Play your music
17 beautifully and fill the place with song, that you may be remembered. So it
will be, at the end of seventy years, the LORD will return to Tyre; she will go
to hire again. Now she can play harlot to all kingdoms of the land across the
18 world. But her merchandise, her hire, will be sacred to the LORD; it will
not be put by, will not be hoarded. For to all those who live in the LORD's
presence, her merchandise will be enough to eat their fill and dress in
24 1 finery. Behold the LORD pouring out the world, laying it waste,
2 warping its face, scattering all its dwellers. People and priest alike, servant and
master alike, maid and mistress, buyer, seller, lender and debtor, debtor and
3 usurer poured out – the world will be drained, sacked, and ransacked, for the
4 LORD has spoken this. The land has grieved and withered; pitiful, withered,
5 is the earth; the exalted of this land – pitiful. The land has turned vile beneath
its burden of humanity: they flout the teachings, overturn the laws; they
6 violate the ancient covenant,[66] so the country, a curse consumes it. The guilt
lies with her people, and the people dry up upon the land, humanity left a
7 bare remnant. New wine is mourning, the vine is pitiful, the merry-hearted
8 men are gone to groans. The joy of drums is frozen, the noise of exuberance
9 silenced, the joy of the harp is frozen. No more will they drink their wine in
10 song; strong drink has turned bitter to the drinker. The city of emptiness is
11 broken,[67] its homes shut off to all comers. In the streets, they cry out for
12 wine;[68] all joy has darkened to grief, the joy of the land in exile. Desolation
13 remains in the city, its gate beaten down to ruin, for so will it be: in the midst
of the earth, the peoples like the beatings of an olive tree, like gleanings left
14 at harvest's end. They will raise their voices in joyful song, singing out from
15 the ocean in the LORD's swelling majesty. So: Out of the fires, glorify the
LORD; in the coastlands of the ocean, the name of the LORD, of Israel's
16 God. From the edge of the world we hear songs come: "Glory to
the good man." But I say, "I am starving, starving, aching." Traitors betray;
17 betrayal – traitors betray; terror, trench, entrapment[69] for you who live on
18 earth. And he who flees the terror will fall into the trench, and he who rises
from the trench is caught up in the trap. Windows are opening to the heights,[70]
19 and earth's foundations shake. Shivering, shattering, the earth; the land
20 crumbles, crumbles, collapses – the land – collapsed. The land sways, sways
like a drunkard, shaking like a makeshift hut; its sin rests heavy on it, it is
21 falling, falling, nevermore to rise. On that day, the LORD will take
22 notice in heaven of the heavenly host, and on earth of the kings of earth; they
will be rounded up all together as captives are gathered to the pit; they will
23 be shut in under lock, but after many days they will be noticed. The moon
will be abashed, the sun ashamed, for the LORD of Hosts will rule, on Mount

---

66 | That is, that the land will provide sustenance while people will not pollute it with evil behavior.

67 | Perhaps morally bankrupt, or empty of life after the calamity.

68 | The party has ceased and the celebrants are suffering hangovers.

69 | The alliteration mirrors the Hebrew: *paḥad vafaḥat vafakh.*

70 | Cf. Genesis 7:12.

טז קְחִי כִנּוֹר סֹבִּי עִיר זוֹנָה נִשְׁכָּחָה הֵיטִיבִי נַגֵּן הַרְבִּי־שִׁיר לְמַעַן תִּזָּכֵרִי׃
יז וְהָיָה מִקֵּץ ׀ שִׁבְעִים שָׁנָה יִפְקֹד יְהוָה אֶת־צֹר וְשָׁבָה לְאֶתְנַנָּה וְזָנְתָה
יח אֶת־כָּל־מַמְלְכוֹת הָאָרֶץ עַל־פְּנֵי הָאֲדָמָה׃ וְהָיָה סַחְרָהּ וְאֶתְנַנָּהּ קֹדֶשׁ
לַיהוָה לֹא יֵאָצֵר וְלֹא יֵחָסֵן כִּי לַיֹּשְׁבִים לִפְנֵי יְהוָה יִהְיֶה סַחְרָהּ לֶאֱכֹל
כד א לְשָׂבְעָה וְלִמְכַסֶּה עָתִיק׃ הִנֵּה יְהוָה בּוֹקֵק הָאָרֶץ וּבוֹלְקָהּ
ב וְעִוָּה פָנֶיהָ וְהֵפִיץ יֹשְׁבֶיהָ׃ וְהָיָה כָעָם כַּכֹּהֵן כַּעֶבֶד כַּאדֹנָיו כַּשִּׁפְחָה
ג כַּגְּבִרְתָּהּ כַּקּוֹנֶה כַּמּוֹכֵר כַּמַּלְוֶה כַּלֹּוֶה כַּנֹּשֶׁה כַּאֲשֶׁר נֹשֶׁא בוֹ׃ הִבּוֹק ׀
ד תִּבּוֹק הָאָרֶץ וְהִבּוֹז ׀ תִּבּוֹז כִּי יְהוָה דִּבֶּר אֶת־הַדָּבָר הַזֶּה׃ אָבְלָה
ה נָבְלָה הָאָרֶץ אֻמְלְלָה נָבְלָה תֵבֵל אֻמְלָלוּ מְרוֹם עַם־הָאָרֶץ׃ וְהָאָרֶץ
חָנְפָה תַּחַת יֹשְׁבֶיהָ כִּי־עָבְרוּ תוֹרֹת חָלְפוּ חֹק הֵפֵרוּ בְּרִית עוֹלָם׃
ו עַל־כֵּן אָלָה אָכְלָה אֶרֶץ וַיֶּאְשְׁמוּ יֹשְׁבֵי בָהּ עַל־כֵּן חָרוּ יֹשְׁבֵי אֶרֶץ
ז וְנִשְׁאַר אֱנוֹשׁ מִזְעָר׃ אָבַל תִּירוֹשׁ אֻמְלְלָה־גָפֶן נֶאֶנְחוּ כָּל־שִׂמְחֵי־לֵב׃
ח ט שָׁבַת מְשׂוֹשׂ תֻּפִּים חָדַל שְׁאוֹן עַלִּיזִים שָׁבַת מְשׂוֹשׂ כִּנּוֹר׃ בַּשִּׁיר לֹא
י יִשְׁתּוּ־יָיִן יֵמַר שֵׁכָר לְשֹׁתָיו׃ נִשְׁבְּרָה קִרְיַת־תֹּהוּ סֻגַּר כָּל־בַּיִת מִבּוֹא׃
יא יב צְוָחָה עַל־הַיַּיִן בַּחוּצוֹת עָרְבָה כָּל־שִׂמְחָה גָּלָה מְשׂוֹשׂ הָאָרֶץ׃ נִשְׁאַר
יג בָּעִיר שַׁמָּה וּשְׁאִיָּה יֻכַּת־שָׁעַר׃ כִּי כֹה יִהְיֶה בְּקֶרֶב הָאָרֶץ בְּתוֹךְ
יד הָעַמִּים כְּנֹקֶף זַיִת כְּעוֹלֵלֹת אִם־כָּלָה בָצִיר׃ הֵמָּה יִשְׂאוּ קוֹלָם יָרֹנּוּ
טו בִּגְאוֹן יְהוָה צָהֲלוּ מִיָּם׃ עַל־כֵּן בָּאֻרִים כַּבְּדוּ יְהוָה בְּאִיֵּי הַיָּם שֵׁם
טז יְהוָה אֱלֹהֵי יִשְׂרָאֵל׃ מִכְּנַף הָאָרֶץ זְמִרֹת שָׁמַעְנוּ צְבִי
לַצַּדִּיק וָאֹמַר רָזִי־לִי רָזִי־לִי אוֹי לִי בֹּגְדִים בָּגָדוּ וּבֶגֶד בּוֹגְדִים בָּגָדוּ׃
יז יח פַּחַד וָפַחַת וָפָח עָלֶיךָ יוֹשֵׁב הָאָרֶץ׃ וְהָיָה הַנָּס מִקּוֹל הַפַּחַד יִפֹּל
אֶל־הַפַּחַת וְהָעוֹלֶה מִתּוֹךְ הַפַּחַת יִלָּכֵד בַּפָּח כִּי־אֲרֻבּוֹת מִמָּרוֹם
יט נִפְתָּחוּ וַיִּרְעֲשׁוּ מוֹסְדֵי אָרֶץ׃ רֹעָה הִתְרֹעֲעָה הָאָרֶץ פּוֹר הִתְפּוֹרְרָה
כ אֶרֶץ מוֹט הִתְמוֹטְטָה אָרֶץ׃ נוֹעַ תָּנוּעַ אֶרֶץ כַּשִּׁכּוֹר וְהִתְנוֹדְדָה
כא כַּמְּלוּנָה וְכָבַד עָלֶיהָ פִּשְׁעָהּ וְנָפְלָה וְלֹא־תֹסִיף קוּם׃ וְהָיָה
בַּיּוֹם הַהוּא יִפְקֹד יְהוָה עַל־צְבָא הַמָּרוֹם בַּמָּרוֹם וְעַל־מַלְכֵי הָאֲדָמָה
כב עַל־הָאֲדָמָה׃ וְאֻסְּפוּ אֲסֵפָה אַסִּיר עַל־בּוֹר וְסֻגְּרוּ עַל־מַסְגֵּר וּמֵרֹב
כג יָמִים יִפָּקֵדוּ׃ וְחָפְרָה הַלְּבָנָה וּבוֹשָׁה הַחַמָּה כִּי־מָלַךְ יְהוָה צְבָאוֹת ׀

25 1 Zion, Jerusalem, before His elders – in glory. LORD, You are my God,
and I exalt You, declare Your name, for You have worked wonders; commands
2 issued long since faithfully come true. You have turned town to rubble heap,
walled city to ruin, the palace of strangers to no more town, never to be rebuilt.
3 So You are glorified by a fearsome people; the cities of powerful nations fear
4 You. For You have been a stronghold to the vulnerable, the stronghold of the
poor man in his anguish, shelter from the storm, and shade from searing sun,
5 for the spirit of oppression is a storm against the wall, like searing heat in
desert land: You quell the roar of strangers. Like searing heat behind clouds'
6 shadows; the tyrants' song will be subdued. The LORD of Hosts – He
will lay out for all the nations on this hill[71] a feast of fats, a feast of wines; of
7 fats with the marrow, of wine refined. On this hill He will consume the
covering wrapped about the faces of all peoples, the weave that is woven to
8 shroud all nations. He will swallow up death forever; the Lord GOD, He will
wipe every tear from every face. He will sweep His people's shame away from
9 all the earth. The LORD has spoken. It will be said on that day:
This – this is our God; it is Him we waited for, and He has saved us. This, the
10 LORD we waited for, we exult, we rejoice in His salvation, for the hand of the
LORD will rest upon this hill. Moav is trampled beneath Him as straw is
11 trampled in the dung heap; He will spread His hands within her as one
spreads one's arms to swim; her pride will be brought low by the power of
12 His hands. The high defenses of your walls, He has brought them down, has
26 1 brought them low; and they have fallen down to earth, to dust. On
that day, this song will be sung in the land of Yehuda: How mighty – this our
2 city: He has turned wall and bulwark to salvation. Open wide the gates; let a
3 righteous nation in that kept its faith; for a faithful nature You keep peace,
4 peace, for it trusts in You. Trust in the LORD forever, for in God, the LORD,
5 you will find a Rock everlasting, for He has brought down those who dwelled
on high. Elevated city, He brought it low, brought it down to earth, to dust.
6 7 Feet trample it, poor men's feet, the footsteps of the beaten. The path is
smooth for a righteous man, and You level the straight road of the righteous.
8 But through all Your judgments, LORD, we wait for You, for Your name and
9 Your memory, for which the soul yearns. My soul yearns for You by night, and
with the spirit that is in me I rise to meet You early, for when Your judgment
10 comes to this world, all earth's dwellers will learn righteousness. Will He have
mercy on the wicked man who will not learn righteousness? Such a one
contorts what is upright in this world and never once sees the LORD's
11 grandeur. LORD, Your hand held high; they do not see it, but let
them see Your passion for a people – and be shamed; let the fire of your foes
12 consume them. LORD, set peace to warm[72] for us, for all the evil we wrought,
13 You brought back to us. LORD our God, other lords than You have mastered
14 us, but still it is Your name alone we speak. Deceased, they will not live again,
shades that will not rise. You have come, You will destroy them, and will wipe

---

71 | That is, Jerusalem.

72 | The same Hebrew word appears in Ezekiel 24:3 and describes the act of placing food on a fire to cook.

כה א בְּהַר צִיּוֹן וּבִירוּשָׁלִַם וְנֶגֶד זְקֵנָיו כָּבוֹד׃ יְהוָה אֱלֹהַי אַתָּה
ב אֲרוֹמִמְךָ אוֹדֶה שִׁמְךָ כִּי עָשִׂיתָ פֶּלֶא עֵצוֹת מֵרָחוֹק אֱמוּנָה אֹמֶן׃ כִּי
שַׂמְתָּ מֵעִיר לַגַּל קִרְיָה בְצוּרָה לְמַפֵּלָה אַרְמוֹן זָרִים מֵעִיר לְעוֹלָם לֹא
ג ד יִבָּנֶה׃ עַל־כֵּן יְכַבְּדוּךָ עַם־עָז קִרְיַת גּוֹיִם עָרִיצִים יִירָאוּךָ׃ כִּי־הָיִיתָ
מָעוֹז לַדָּל מָעוֹז לָאֶבְיוֹן בַּצַּר־לוֹ מַחְסֶה מִזֶּרֶם צֵל מֵחֹרֶב כִּי רוּחַ
ה עָרִיצִים כְּזֶרֶם קִיר׃ כְּחֹרֶב בְּצָיוֹן שְׁאוֹן זָרִים תַּכְנִיעַ חֹרֶב בְּצֵל עָב
ו זְמִיר עָרִיצִים יַעֲנֶה׃ וְעָשָׂה יְהוָה צְבָאוֹת לְכָל־הָעַמִּים
בָּהָר הַזֶּה מִשְׁתֵּה שְׁמָנִים מִשְׁתֵּה שְׁמָרִים שְׁמָנִים מְמֻחָיִם שְׁמָרִים
ז מְזֻקָּקִים׃ וּבִלַּע בָּהָר הַזֶּה פְּנֵי־הַלּוֹט ׀ הַלּוֹט עַל־כָּל־הָעַמִּים וְהַמַּסֵּכָה
ח הַנְּסוּכָה עַל־כָּל־הַגּוֹיִם׃ בִּלַּע הַמָּוֶת לָנֶצַח וּמָחָה אֲדֹנָי יֱהוִה
דִּמְעָה מֵעַל כָּל־פָּנִים וְחֶרְפַּת עַמּוֹ יָסִיר מֵעַל כָּל־הָאָרֶץ כִּי יְהוָה
ט דִּבֵּר׃ וְאָמַר בַּיּוֹם הַהוּא הִנֵּה אֱלֹהֵינוּ זֶה קִוִּינוּ לוֹ
י וְיוֹשִׁיעֵנוּ זֶה יְהוָה קִוִּינוּ לוֹ נָגִילָה וְנִשְׂמְחָה בִּישׁוּעָתוֹ׃ כִּי־תָנוּחַ יַד־
יְהוָה בָּהָר הַזֶּה וְנָדוֹשׁ מוֹאָב תַּחְתָּיו כְּהִדּוֹשׁ מַתְבֵּן במי מַדְמֵנָה׃ בְּמוֹ
יא וּפֵרַשׂ יָדָיו בְּקִרְבּוֹ כַּאֲשֶׁר יְפָרֵשׂ הַשֹּׂחֶה לִשְׂחוֹת וְהִשְׁפִּיל גַּאֲוָתוֹ עִם
יב אָרְבּוֹת יָדָיו׃ וּמִבְצַר מִשְׂגַּב חוֹמֹתֶיךָ הֵשַׁח הִשְׁפִּיל הִגִּיעַ לָאָרֶץ עַד־
כו א עָפָר׃ בַּיּוֹם הַהוּא יוּשַׁר הַשִּׁיר־הַזֶּה בְּאֶרֶץ יְהוּדָה עִיר
ב עָז־לָנוּ יְשׁוּעָה יָשִׁית חוֹמוֹת וָחֵל׃ פִּתְחוּ שְׁעָרִים וְיָבֹא גוֹי־צַדִּיק שֹׁמֵר
ג ד אֱמֻנִים׃ יֵצֶר סָמוּךְ תִּצֹּר שָׁלוֹם ׀ שָׁלוֹם כִּי בְךָ בָּטוּחַ׃ בִּטְחוּ בַיהוָה
ה עֲדֵי־עַד כִּי בְּיָהּ יְהוָה צוּר עוֹלָמִים׃ כִּי הֵשַׁח יֹשְׁבֵי מָרוֹם קִרְיָה נִשְׂגָּבָה
ו יַשְׁפִּילֶנָּה יַשְׁפִּילָהּ עַד־אֶרֶץ יַגִּיעֶנָּה עַד־עָפָר׃ תִּרְמְסֶנָּה רָגֶל רַגְלֵי עָנִי
ז ח פַּעֲמֵי דַלִּים׃ אֹרַח לַצַּדִּיק מֵישָׁרִים יָשָׁר מַעְגַּל צַדִּיק תְּפַלֵּס׃ אַף אֹרַח
ט מִשְׁפָּטֶיךָ יְהוָה קִוִּינוּךָ לְשִׁמְךָ וּלְזִכְרְךָ תַּאֲוַת־נָפֶשׁ׃ נַפְשִׁי אִוִּיתִךָ
בַּלַּיְלָה אַף־רוּחִי בְקִרְבִּי אֲשַׁחֲרֶךָּ כִּי כַּאֲשֶׁר מִשְׁפָּטֶיךָ לָאָרֶץ צֶדֶק
י לָמְדוּ יֹשְׁבֵי תֵבֵל׃ יֻחַן רָשָׁע בַּל־לָמַד צֶדֶק בְּאֶרֶץ נְכֹחוֹת יְעַוֵּל וּבַל־
יא יִרְאֶה גֵּאוּת יְהוָה׃ יְהוָה רָמָה יָדְךָ בַּל־יֶחֱזָיוּן יֶחֱזוּ וְיֵבֹשׁוּ
יב קִנְאַת־עָם אַף־אֵשׁ צָרֶיךָ תֹאכְלֵם׃ יְהוָה תִּשְׁפֹּת שָׁלוֹם לָנוּ כִּי גַּם
יג כָּל־מַעֲשֵׂינוּ פָּעַלְתָּ לָּנוּ׃ יְהוָה אֱלֹהֵינוּ בְּעָלוּנוּ אֲדֹנִים זוּלָתֶךָ לְבַד־בְּךָ
יד נַזְכִּיר שְׁמֶךָ׃ מֵתִים בַּל־יִחְיוּ רְפָאִים בַּל־יָקֻמוּ לָכֵן פָּקַדְתָּ וַתַּשְׁמִידֵם

15 away all memory. You have added to this people, LORD; You have added to
the people; You are glorified; You have pushed back all the borders of the
16 land. LORD – in anguish they came to You, pouring out whispers to
17 You even as You beat them. Like a woman with child, about to give birth,
18 writhing, crying out in her agonies, so have we been before You, LORD. We
carried, writhed, gave birth – as to the wind. We made no salvation in the
19 world, and those residing in the earth were not delivered. Let Your dead ones
live; let my own bodies rise. Wake up and rejoice, inhabitants of dust, for
droplets of light are Your dewfall, and You will fell the shades, down to the
20 earth. Go now, My people, into your inner chambers; close the doors
21 behind you and wait there – but a moment – until the rage has passed. For
here – the LORD – He comes out of His place to repay the land's dwellers for
their sin. The land is uncovering her blood now: no longer will she hide her
27 1 slain. On that day, the LORD will come with His sword, broad and
long and strong upon the Leviathan, the Fleeing Serpent, upon the Leviathan,
2 the Winding Serpent, and slay the great beast of the sea. On that day,
3 sing to her, "Vineyard of red wine…." I, the LORD, watch over her, moment
by moment will I water her, that no one may come to do harm; by night, by
4 day I watch her. There is no fury in Me now. Would that I could be those
briars and brambles in battle: in would I march and set them on fire as one.
5 But let them grasp My stronghold; then they will make peace with Me, peace,
6 will they make Me. In days to come, Yaakov will take root, Israel will put out
buds and flower, and all the land on all the earth will be covered with the
7 fruits. Was he beaten as are beaten those who beat him? Was his
8 slaying like the slaying of their slain? With a faithful measure, driving them
out You fight them; He blew them away with His blasting spirit on the day of
9 the gale. This, then, is how the iniquity of Israel may be atoned – and that, all
the fruit of removing his sin – by rendering all his altar stones smashed
10 limestone, no sacred trees or incense shrines rising again. The fortress city
will sit alone, a shelter left behind, lonely as desert. Calves will graze there,
11 there will they lie, and eat up all their branches. When their yield dries up
they will be broken down. Women will come and use them as firewood, for
this is not a wise people; and so its Maker will have no compassion, its Creator
12 will grant it no grace. On that day, the LORD will beat the branches
from the Euphrates's surge to the River of Egypt and gather you up one by
13 one, you children of Israel. It will be, on that day: a great ram's horn
will sound, and they will come, all those lost in the land of Assyria, and those
who are exiled to the land of Egypt, and bow low to the LORD on the holy
28 1 mount in Jerusalem. Woe to the proud garland of Efrayim's
drunkards, for the withered lotus flower that was the glorious supremacy
2 crowning the oiled valley of the wine benumbed. See what comes – something
strong and determined of the Lord, like pelting hail, like a cataclysmic storm,
like a river of great waters, flooding waters, heavy-handed, casting people
3 down to earth, trampling underfoot the garland pride of Efrayim's drunkards.
4 Like a withered lotus flower it shall be, its glorious supremacy that crowned
the fat valley like the first fig before harvest; the one that all who saw would

טו וְתְאַבֵּד כָּל־זֵכֶר לָמוֹ: יָסַפְתָּ לַגּוֹי יהוה יָסַפְתָּ לַגּוֹי נִכְבָּדְתָּ רִחַקְתָּ
טז כָּל־קַצְוֵי־אָרֶץ: יהוה בַּצַּר פְּקָדוּךָ צָקוּן לַחַשׁ מוּסָרְךָ לָמוֹ:
יז כְּמוֹ הָרָה תַּקְרִיב לָלֶדֶת תָּחִיל תִּזְעַק בַּחֲבָלֶיהָ כֵּן הָיִינוּ מִפָּנֶיךָ יהוה:
יח הָרִינוּ חַלְנוּ כְּמוֹ יָלַדְנוּ רוּחַ יְשׁוּעֹת בַּל־נַעֲשֶׂה אֶרֶץ וּבַל־יִפְּלוּ יֹשְׁבֵי
יט תֵבֵל: יִחְיוּ מֵתֶיךָ נְבֵלָתִי יְקוּמוּן הָקִיצוּ וְרַנְּנוּ שֹׁכְנֵי עָפָר כִּי טַל אוֹרֹת
כ טַלֶּךָ וָאָרֶץ רְפָאִים תַּפִּיל: לֵךְ עַמִּי בֹּא בַחֲדָרֶיךָ וּסְגֹר
כא דלתיך בַּעֲדֶךָ חֲבִי כִמְעַט־רֶגַע עַד־יעבור־זָעַם: כִּי־הִנֵּה יהוה יֹצֵא דְּלָתְךָ | יַעֲבָר־
מִמְּקוֹמוֹ לִפְקֹד עֲוֹן יֹשֵׁב־הָאָרֶץ עָלָיו וְגִלְּתָה הָאָרֶץ אֶת־דָּמֶיהָ וְלֹא־
כז א תְכַסֶּה עוֹד עַל־הֲרוּגֶיהָ: בַּיּוֹם הַהוּא יִפְקֹד יהוה בְּחַרְבּוֹ
הַקָּשָׁה וְהַגְּדוֹלָה וְהַחֲזָקָה עַל לִוְיָתָן נָחָשׁ בָּרִחַ וְעַל לִוְיָתָן נָחָשׁ
ב עֲקַלָּתוֹן וְהָרַג אֶת־הַתַּנִּין אֲשֶׁר בַּיָּם: בַּיּוֹם הַהוּא כֶּרֶם חֶמֶר
ג עַנּוּ־לָהּ: אֲנִי יהוה נֹצְרָהּ לִרְגָעִים אַשְׁקֶנָּה פֶּן יִפְקֹד עָלֶיהָ לַיְלָה וָיוֹם
ד אֶצֳּרֶנָּה: חֵמָה אֵין לִי מִי־יִתְּנֵנִי שָׁמִיר שַׁיִת בַּמִּלְחָמָה אֶפְשְׂעָה בָהּ
ה אֲצִיתֶנָּה יָּחַד: אוֹ יַחֲזֵק בְּמָעוּזִּי יַעֲשֶׂה שָׁלוֹם לִי שָׁלוֹם יַעֲשֶׂה־
ו לִּי: הַבָּאִים יַשְׁרֵשׁ יַעֲקֹב יָצִיץ וּפָרַח יִשְׂרָאֵל וּמָלְאוּ פְנֵי־תֵבֵל
ז תְּנוּבָה: הַכְּמַכַּת מַכֵּהוּ הִכָּהוּ אִם־כְּהֶרֶג הֲרֻגָיו
ח הֹרָג: בְּסַאסְּאָה בְּשַׁלְחָהּ תְּרִיבֶנָּה הָגָה בְּרוּחוֹ הַקָּשָׁה בְּיוֹם קָדִים:
ט לָכֵן בְּזֹאת יְכֻפַּר עֲוֹן־יַעֲקֹב וְזֶה כָּל־פְּרִי הָסִר חַטָּאתוֹ בְּשׂוּמוֹ ׀ כָּל־
י אַבְנֵי מִזְבֵּחַ כְּאַבְנֵי־גִר מְנֻפָּצוֹת לֹא־יָקֻמוּ אֲשֵׁרִים וְחַמָּנִים: כִּי עִיר
בְּצוּרָה בָּדָד נָוֶה מְשֻׁלָּח וְנֶעֱזָב כַּמִּדְבָּר שָׁם יִרְעֶה עֵגֶל וְשָׁם
יא יִרְבָּץ וְכִלָּה סְעִפֶיהָ: בִּיבֹשׁ קְצִירָהּ תִּשָּׁבַרְנָה נָשִׁים בָּאוֹת מְאִירוֹת
אוֹתָהּ כִּי לֹא עַם־בִּינוֹת הוּא עַל־כֵּן לֹא־יְרַחֲמֶנּוּ עֹשֵׂהוּ וְיֹצְרוֹ לֹא
יב יְחֻנֶּנּוּ: וְהָיָה בַּיּוֹם הַהוּא יַחְבֹּט יהוה מִשִּׁבֹּלֶת הַנָּהָר עַד־ יא
יג נַחַל מִצְרָיִם וְאַתֶּם תְּלֻקְּטוּ לְאַחַד אֶחָד בְּנֵי יִשְׂרָאֵל: וְהָיָה ׀
בַּיּוֹם הַהוּא יִתָּקַע בְּשׁוֹפָר גָּדוֹל וּבָאוּ הָאֹבְדִים בְּאֶרֶץ אַשּׁוּר וְהַנִּדָּחִים
כח א בְּאֶרֶץ מִצְרָיִם וְהִשְׁתַּחֲווּ לַיהוה בְּהַר הַקֹּדֶשׁ בִּירוּשָׁלִָם: הוֹי
עֲטֶרֶת גֵּאוּת שִׁכֹּרֵי אֶפְרַיִם וְצִיץ נֹבֵל צְבִי תִפְאַרְתּוֹ אֲשֶׁר עַל־רֹאשׁ
ב גֵיא־שְׁמָנִים הֲלוּמֵי יָיִן: הִנֵּה חָזָק וְאַמִּץ לַאדֹנָי כְּזֶרֶם בָּרָד שַׂעַר קָטֶב
ג כְּזֶרֶם מַיִם כַּבִּירִים שֹׁטְפִים הִנִּיחַ לָאָרֶץ בְּיָד: בְּרַגְלַיִם תֵּרָמַסְנָה עֲטֶרֶת
ד גֵּאוּת שִׁכּוֹרֵי אֶפְרָיִם: וְהָיְתָה צִיצַת נֹבֵל צְבִי תִפְאַרְתּוֹ אֲשֶׁר עַל־
רֹאשׁ גֵּיא שְׁמָנִים כְּבִכּוּרָהּ בְּטֶרֶם קַיִץ אֲשֶׁר יִרְאֶה הָרֹאֶה אוֹתָהּ

5 swallow up sooner than hold it. On that day the LORD of Hosts will
be a garland of splendor, the crown of supremacy, to the remnant of His
6 people, He will be the spirit of justice in those who preside over justice, and
7 of might in those who drive war back from the gate. For these men too[73] have
gone astray with wine, they have lost themselves in ale – priest and
prophet – gone astray with their ale, been swallowed up in wine, got lost by
8 their ale, gone astray in their vision, fallen over in judgment; the tables are
9 soaked, all, in vomit and filth, until there is no space left. Whom
would he teach knowledge, whom bring to comprehend his words? Those
10 barely weaned of milk, those just taken from the breast? *Law after law, law*
11 *after law, line after line, line after line, a little bit here, a little bit there* – in a babble
12 of words, in a different tongue he speaks to this people. He told them, "This
13 is rest: leave the weary be; this is calm." They would not hear.[74] So the word
of the LORD is to them law after law, law after law, line after line, line after line,
a little bit here, a little bit there, for them to walk and stumble on backward,
14 be broken, be beaten, be caught. And so, hear the word of the LORD,
15 you cynics, you leaders of this people in Jerusalem. "We have forged a
covenant with death," you say, "we have reached a seers' agreement with
Sheol.[75] When the whip cracks over us it will not touch us, for we have
16 delusion as a refuge; we will hide away inside the lie." And so, thus
says the Lord GOD: Behold: it is I who laid down a stone in Jerusalem, a tested
stele, precious cornerstone, foundation stone, and founded well; one who
17 believes will not act in haste. And I laid down law as the measuring line, and
justice as the plumb weight. And the hail will sweep off that delusion of cover,
18 and water will wash away the hiding place. Your covenant with death will be
swept away; your agreement with Sheol will not be honored. The whip will
19 crack and as it passes you will be trampled down. Ever as it passes it will take
you, and morning, early morning, it will pass, all day, all night. And only terror
20 comprehends what it hears. For the sheet is too short to be stretched out
21 upon, and the shroud too narrow to gather up under. For the LORD will rise
up as on Mount Peratzim, and will rage as in the Valley of Givon,[76] to do what
He shall do – and strange is what He does; to work His work – and foreign is
22 His work to you. Now – no more cynical speeches, lest your chains grip
firmer; for ordained annihilation, this is what I have heard from the Lord GOD
23 of Hosts for all the land. Listen now, and hear My voice; heed and
24 hear these words of Mine: Does the plowman plow all day to plant, opening
25 and breaking up the clods? Does he not then make the ground even and
scatter the black caraway, throw down the cumin, sow the wheat in line, the
26 barley in its place, the rye in bounds? This is the way his God trains him in
27 what is right, and teaches him; you cannot thresh caraway with a board, or

---

73 | The leaders of the Kingdom of Israel.

74 | To heed the prophet's message would bring peace and security, but his audience are as children, unable or unwilling to understand his words. Cf. 6:9ff.

75 | Apparently referring to a futile alliance with some foreign power.

76 | Victories narrated in II Samuel 5:20 and Joshua 10:10.

ה בְּעוֹדָהּ בְּכַפּוֹ יִבְלָעֶנָּה׃ בַּיּוֹם הַהוּא יִהְיֶה֙ יְהוָה צְבָאוֹת
ו לַעֲטֶרֶת צְבִי וְלִצְפִירַת תִּפְאָרָה לִשְׁאָר עַמּוֹ׃ וּלְרוּחַ מִשְׁפָּט לַיּוֹשֵׁב
ז עַל־הַמִּשְׁפָּט וְלִגְבוּרָה מְשִׁיבֵי מִלְחָמָה שָׁעְרָה׃ וְגַם־אֵלֶּה בַּיַּיִן שָׁגוּ
וּבַשֵּׁכָר תָּעוּ כֹּהֵן וְנָבִיא שָׁגוּ בַשֵּׁכָר נִבְלְעוּ מִן־הַיַּיִן תָּעוּ מִן־הַשֵּׁכָר
ח שָׁגוּ בָּרֹאֶה פָּקוּ פְּלִילִיָּה׃ כִּי כָּל־שֻׁלְחָנוֹת מָלְאוּ קִיא צֹאָה בְּלִי
ט מָקוֹם׃ אֶת־מִי יוֹרֶה דֵעָה וְאֶת־מִי יָבִין שְׁמוּעָה
י גְּמוּלֵי מֵחָלָב עַתִּיקֵי מִשָּׁדָיִם׃ כִּי צַו לָצָו צַו לָצָו קַו לָקָו קַו לָקָו זְעֵיר
יא שָׁם זְעֵיר שָׁם׃ כִּי בְּלַעֲגֵי שָׂפָה וּבְלָשׁוֹן אַחֶרֶת יְדַבֵּר אֶל־הָעָם הַזֶּה׃
יב אֲשֶׁר ׀ אָמַר אֲלֵיהֶם זֹאת הַמְּנוּחָה הָנִיחוּ לֶעָיֵף וְזֹאת הַמַּרְגֵּעָה וְלֹא
יג אָבוּא שְׁמוֹעַ׃ וְהָיָה לָהֶם דְּבַר־יְהוָה צַו לָצָו צַו לָצָו קַו לָקָו קַו
לָקָו זְעֵיר שָׁם זְעֵיר שָׁם לְמַעַן יֵלְכוּ וְכָשְׁלוּ אָחוֹר וְנִשְׁבָּרוּ וְנוֹקְשׁוּ
יד וְנִלְכָּדוּ׃ לָכֵן שִׁמְעוּ דְבַר־יְהוָה אַנְשֵׁי לָצוֹן מֹשְׁלֵי
טו הָעָם הַזֶּה אֲשֶׁר בִּירוּשָׁלִָם׃ כִּי אֲמַרְתֶּם כָּרַתְנוּ בְרִית אֶת־מָוֶת וְעִם־
שְׁאוֹל עָשִׂינוּ חֹזֶה שִׁיט שׁוֹטֵף כִּי־עבר לֹא יְבוֹאֵנוּ כִּי שַׂמְנוּ כָזָב מַחְסֵנוּ שׁוֹט | יַעֲבֹר
טז וּבַשֶּׁקֶר נִסְתָּרְנוּ׃ לָכֵן כֹּה אָמַר אֲדֹנָי יֱהוִה הִנְנִי יִסַּד
בְּצִיּוֹן אָבֶן אֶבֶן בֹּחַן פִּנַּת יִקְרַת מוּסָד מוּסָּד הַמַּאֲמִין לֹא יָחִישׁ׃
יז וְשַׂמְתִּי מִשְׁפָּט לְקָו וּצְדָקָה לְמִשְׁקָלֶת וְיָעָה בָרָד מַחְסֵה כָזָב וְסֵתֶר
יח מַיִם יִשְׁטֹפוּ׃ וְכֻפַּר בְּרִיתְכֶם אֶת־מָוֶת וְחָזוּתְכֶם אֶת־שְׁאוֹל לֹא תָקוּם
יט שׁוֹט שׁוֹטֵף כִּי יַעֲבֹר וִהְיִיתֶם לוֹ לְמִרְמָס׃ מִדֵּי עָבְרוֹ יִקַּח אֶתְכֶם כִּי־
בַבֹּקֶר בַּבֹּקֶר יַעֲבֹר בַּיּוֹם וּבַלָּיְלָה וְהָיָה רַק־זְוָעָה הָבִין שְׁמוּעָה׃
כ כא כִּי־קָצַר הַמַּצָּע מֵהִשְׂתָּרֵעַ וְהַמַּסֵּכָה צָרָה כְּהִתְכַּנֵּס׃ כִּי כְהַר־פְּרָצִים
יָקוּם יְהוָה כְּעֵמֶק בְּגִבְעוֹן יִרְגָּז לַעֲשׂוֹת מַעֲשֵׂהוּ זָר מַעֲשֵׂהוּ וְלַעֲבֹד
כב עֲבֹדָתוֹ נָכְרִיָּה עֲבֹדָתוֹ׃ וְעַתָּה אַל־תִּתְלוֹצָצוּ פֶּן־יֶחְזְקוּ מוֹסְרֵיכֶם
כִּי־כָלָה וְנֶחֱרָצָה שָׁמַעְתִּי מֵאֵת אֲדֹנָי יֱהוִה צְבָאוֹת עַל־כָּל־
כג הָאָרֶץ׃ הַאֲזִינוּ וְשִׁמְעוּ קוֹלִי הַקְשִׁיבוּ וְשִׁמְעוּ אִמְרָתִי׃
כד כה הֲכֹל הַיּוֹם יַחֲרֹשׁ הַחֹרֵשׁ לִזְרֹעַ יְפַתַּח וִישַׂדֵּד אַדְמָתוֹ׃ הֲלוֹא אִם־שִׁוָּה
פָנֶיהָ וְהֵפִיץ קֶצַח וְכַמֹּן יִזְרֹק וְשָׂם חִטָּה שׂוֹרָה וּשְׂעֹרָה נִסְמָן וְכֻסֶּמֶת
כו כז גְּבֻלָתוֹ׃ וְיִסְּרוֹ לַמִּשְׁפָּט אֱלֹהָיו יוֹרֶנּוּ׃ כִּי לֹא בֶחָרוּץ יוּדַשׁ קֶצַח וְאוֹפַן

roll a wagon wheel over cumin; black caraway must be beaten with a rod, and
28 cumin with a staff, and grain for bread must be ground fine, and not forever
does one thresh, pounding with the wheel of his carriage, crushing the seeds
29 under his horsemen. This too, then, came forth from the LORD of Hosts
29 1 whose plans are wondrous, and whose wisdom great.[77] Oh Ariel,
Ariel,[78] the city where David camped, add year to year, the festivals circling
2 round again, and I shall torment Ariel, and weeping and wailing there will
3 be; it will be like Ariel to Me.[79] I shall camp like a ring around you, besiege
4 you with a palisade, build the siege walls around you. Brought low, you speak
up from the ground, words spoken up from the dust, your voice a ghost rising
5 up from the ground; from the dust your speech gibbers. But then your many
invaders will become like thinnest sand, your many oppressors like transient
6 dust; it will be so very sudden from the LORD of Hosts, who will visit you
with thunder and earthquake and deafening voice, storm and tempest, and
7 the flame of consuming fire. It will all be as a dream, as a vision of the night:
all these, every nation, that mobbed Ariel, all her invading hordes and
8 entrapments tormenting her. It will be: as a hungry man dreams, and there
is food before him, but he wakes to find himself empty; as the thirsty man
dreams, he is drinking, but he wakes and is faint and is yearning; so will it be
9 for all the nations mobbing around Mount Zion.[80] Stop for a
moment dumbfounded; blind yourselves, and be blind, you who are drunk,
10 but not with wine, who sway, but not from ale; the LORD has poured over
you a spirit of sleep and closed your eyes; your prophets, your leaders who
11 see visions – He covered their eyes. The vision of everything will be like the
words of a sealed book to you; you would give such a book to a man who can
read: "Read to us from this," but he would say, "No, I cannot, because it is
12 sealed." Or give such a book to a man who cannot read: "Read to us from this,"
13 and all he would say is "I know not how to read." The Lord says:
Because this people comes with its mouth, with its lips gives Me honor while
its heart is far from Me, and the awe in which they hold Me is a precept people
14 taught them, I shall go on dazzling this people by wonder upon wonder until
their wise ones lose their wisdom, and the knowledge of their knowing ones
15 hides itself away. Gone, those who think to go deeper than the LORD,
to hide their counsel in the darkness of their deeds. "Who sees us?" they say.
16 "Who will know?" Oh, your reversals: Is the potter to be viewed as clay? Does
a thing say to its maker, "You did not make me," or the work of its artisan, "He
17 does not understand"? Soon, do you see it? Just a little longer; the Lebanon
18 will turn to fertile land and fertile land to forest. On that day, the deaf will
hear book words, and out of the gloom and darkness, blind men's eyes will
19 see. The humble will rejoice in the LORD, more and more; the most pitiful of

77 | Just as after a time, the plowman's preparation ends, so too will the time for the prophets' warnings. Then Israel must cease sinning or face the consequences.

78 | This term refers to the altar in the Temple and is a metonym for Jerusalem; cf. Ezekiel 43:15–16.

79 | Jerusalem will be like an altar of sacrifices.

80 | The siege will be but a dream. See chapters 37–38 and II Kings 18:17–19:37.

כח עֲגָלָה עַל־כַּמֹּן יוּסָּב כִּי בַמַּטֶּה יֵחָבֶט קֶצַח וְכַמֹּן בַּשָּׁבֶט: לֶחֶם
יוּדָק כִּי לֹא לָנֶצַח אָדוֹשׁ יְדוּשֶׁנּוּ וְהָמַם גִּלְגַּל עֶגְלָתוֹ וּפָרָשָׁיו לֹא
כט יְדֻקֶּנּוּ: גַּם־זֹאת מֵעִם יהוה צְבָאוֹת יָצָאָה הִפְלִא עֵצָה הִגְדִּיל
כט א תּוּשִׁיָּה: הוֹי אֲרִיאֵל אֲרִיאֵל קִרְיַת חָנָה דָוִד סְפוּ שָׁנָה
ב עַל־שָׁנָה חַגִּים יִנְקֹפוּ: וַהֲצִיקוֹתִי לַאֲרִיאֵל וְהָיְתָה תַאֲנִיָּה וַאֲנִיָּה וְהָיְתָה
ג לִּי כַּאֲרִיאֵל: וְחָנִיתִי כַדּוּר עָלָיִךְ וְצַרְתִּי עָלַיִךְ מֻצָּב וַהֲקִמֹתִי עָלַיִךְ
ד מְצֻרֹת: וְשָׁפַלְתְּ מֵאֶרֶץ תְּדַבֵּרִי וּמֵעָפָר תִּשַּׁח אִמְרָתֵךְ וְהָיָה כְּאוֹב
ה מֵאֶרֶץ קוֹלֵךְ וּמֵעָפָר אִמְרָתֵךְ תְּצַפְצֵף: וְהָיָה כְּאָבָק דַּק הֲמוֹן זָרָיִךְ
ו וּכְמֹץ עֹבֵר הֲמוֹן עָרִיצִים וְהָיָה לְפֶתַע פִּתְאֹם: מֵעִם יהוה צְבָאוֹת
תִּפָּקֵד בְּרַעַם וּבְרַעַשׁ וְקוֹל גָּדוֹל סוּפָה וּסְעָרָה וְלַהַב אֵשׁ אוֹכֵלָה:
ז וְהָיָה כַּחֲלוֹם חֲזוֹן לַיְלָה הֲמוֹן כָּל־הַגּוֹיִם הַצֹּבְאִים עַל־אֲרִיאֵל וְכָל־
ח צֹבֶיהָ וּמְצֹדָתָהּ וְהַמְּצִיקִים לָהּ: וְהָיָה כַּאֲשֶׁר יַחֲלֹם הָרָעֵב וְהִנֵּה אוֹכֵל
וְהֵקִיץ וְרֵיקָה נַפְשׁוֹ וְכַאֲשֶׁר יַחֲלֹם הַצָּמֵא וְהִנֵּה שֹׁתֶה וְהֵקִיץ וְהִנֵּה
עָיֵף וְנַפְשׁוֹ שׁוֹקֵקָה כֵּן יִהְיֶה הֲמוֹן כָּל־הַגּוֹיִם הַצֹּבְאִים עַל־הַר
ט צִיּוֹן: הִתְמַהְמְהוּ וּתְמָהוּ הִשְׁתַּעַשְׁעוּ וָשֹׁעוּ שָׁכְרוּ וְלֹא־יַיִן
י נָעוּ וְלֹא שֵׁכָר: כִּי־נָסַךְ עֲלֵיכֶם יהוה רוּחַ תַּרְדֵּמָה וַיְעַצֵּם אֶת־עֵינֵיכֶם
יא אֶת־הַנְּבִיאִים וְאֶת־רָאשֵׁיכֶם הַחֹזִים כִּסָּה: וַתְּהִי לָכֶם חָזוּת הַכֹּל
כְּדִבְרֵי הַסֵּפֶר הֶחָתוּם אֲשֶׁר־יִתְּנוּ אֹתוֹ אֶל־יוֹדֵעַ הספר לֵאמֹר קְרָא סֵפֶר
יב נָא־זֶה וְאָמַר לֹא אוּכַל כִּי חָתוּם הוּא: וְנִתַּן הַסֵּפֶר עַל אֲשֶׁר לֹא־יָדַע
יג סֵפֶר לֵאמֹר קְרָא נָא־זֶה וְאָמַר לֹא יָדַעְתִּי סֵפֶר: וַיֹּאמֶר
אֲדֹנָי יַעַן כִּי נִגַּשׁ הָעָם הַזֶּה בְּפִיו וּבִשְׂפָתָיו כִּבְּדוּנִי וְלִבּוֹ רִחַק מִמֶּנִּי
יד וַתְּהִי יִרְאָתָם אֹתִי מִצְוַת אֲנָשִׁים מְלֻמָּדָה: לָכֵן הִנְנִי יוֹסִף לְהַפְלִיא
אֶת־הָעָם־הַזֶּה הַפְלֵא וָפֶלֶא וְאָבְדָה חָכְמַת חֲכָמָיו וּבִינַת נְבֹנָיו
טו תִּסְתַּתָּר: הוֹי הַמַּעֲמִיקִים מֵיהוה לַסְתִּר עֵצָה וְהָיָה
טז בְמַחְשָׁךְ מַעֲשֵׂיהֶם וַיֹּאמְרוּ מִי רֹאֵנוּ וּמִי יוֹדְעֵנוּ: הַפְכְּכֶם אִם־כְּחֹמֶר
הַיֹּצֵר יֵחָשֵׁב כִּי־יֹאמַר מַעֲשֶׂה לְעֹשֵׂהוּ לֹא עָשָׂנִי וְיֵצֶר אָמַר לְיֹצְרוֹ לֹא
יז הֵבִין: הֲלוֹא־עוֹד מְעַט מִזְעָר וְשָׁב לְבָנוֹן לַכַּרְמֶל וְהַכַּרְמֶל לַיַּעַר יֵחָשֵׁב:
יח וְשָׁמְעוּ בַיּוֹם־הַהוּא הַחֵרְשִׁים דִּבְרֵי־סֵפֶר וּמֵאֹפֶל וּמֵחֹשֶׁךְ עֵינֵי עִוְרִים
יט תִּרְאֶינָה: וְיָסְפוּ עֲנָוִים בַּיהוה שִׂמְחָה וְאֶבְיוֹנֵי אָדָם בִּקְדוֹשׁ יִשְׂרָאֵל

20 men will celebrate the Holy One, for the oppressors – they are gone, the
cynical rulers are done for, and those who lie in wait to sin will all be severed,
21 those whose words bring men to sin, who entrap the man rebuking at the
22 gate and lead the good astray to follow emptiness. And so, this is
what the LORD has said – Avraham's redeemer – to the House of Yaakov: No
23 more will Yaakov be ashamed, his face no more grow pale, for when he sees
his children, the work of My hands, in his midst, sanctifying My name, it is
24 Yaakov's Holy One they sanctify; it is Israel's God they worship. Hearts that
go astray will know understanding, and those who murmured bitterly will
30 1 lay themselves open to learn. Woe to the wayward sons, so says the
LORD, who live by a plan that is not Mine, who pour out thoughts not of My
2 spirit, add sin upon sin, who set out to go down to Egypt, without having
sought My word, to seek refuge in Pharaoh's stronghold and shelter in the
3 shadow of Egypt. That stronghold of Pharaoh will be your shame; that shelter
4 of Egypt's shade, your disgrace, for his princes were at Tzoan; his emissaries
5 reached as far as Ḥanes;[81] shameful, reeking affair, this leaning on a people
that brings no benefit, no aid and no benefit, but only debasement and
6 shame. The burden of the southern beasts,[82] bound for a land of
trouble and anguish, of lions, great growling lions, of viper and flying serpent:
They carry their wealth on the backs of donkeys, their treasures on camels'
7 humps, to a nation that brings them no benefit. Egypt will help like hot air
8 and emptiness, and so I called her Rahav,[83] that is they, sitting still. Now, come
and write this on a stone with them and etch it in a scroll for it to be there to
9 the very last day, forever, for as long as there is time: that this is a rebellious
people, children who deny, children who refuse to hear the teaching of the
10 LORD, who say to the seers, "Do not see," to the men of the visions, "No
visions for us of uprightness; speak smooth words to us; bring visions of
11 deceit. Turn, turn from the path, go aside from that way, and remove from
12 our sight the Holy One of Israel." And so the Holy One of Israel
says: Because you have despised this word to place your trust in oppression
13 and strayed and leaned upon that, because of this, this sin shall be like the
crack lengthening, ready to bring down your exalted wall, the breaking of
14 which will come so very suddenly. That break is like the shattering of a wine
jar: shattering; no mercy; in its shattering you will not find a shard big
enough to take fire from the hearth, nor to scoop a little water from the
15 pool. For this is what the Lord GOD has said, the Holy One of Israel:
In stillness and in peace shall you be saved; in quiet and in trust, your might
16 will be, but you did not wish it. You say, "No, we will speed away on horses,"
and so you will flee. "We will mount the swiftest steeds," and so, swift will
17 your pursuers be. A thousand will flee at one man's harsh word, at the harsh

---

81 | Tzoan and Ḥanes were important Egyptian cities.

82 | Yeshayahu here derides those who send the animals bringing Judahite tribute to Egypt in an attempt to obtain that country's support against Assyria.

83 | A play on words. "Hot air and emptiness" (*hevel varik*) echoes "Rahav," a mythical beast sometimes associated with Egypt; cf. Psalms 87:4.

כ כא יָגִילוּ: כִּי־אָפֵס עָרִיץ וְכָלָה לֵץ וְנִכְרְתוּ כָּל־שֹׁקְדֵי אָוֶן: מַחֲטִיאֵי אָדָם
כב בְּדָבָר וְלַמּוֹכִיחַ בַּשַּׁעַר יְקֹשׁוּן וַיַּטּוּ בַתֹּהוּ צַדִּיק: לָכֵן כֹּה־
אָמַר יהוה אֶל־בֵּית יַעֲקֹב אֲשֶׁר פָּדָה אֶת־אַבְרָהָם לֹא־עַתָּה יֵבוֹשׁ
כג יַעֲקֹב וְלֹא עַתָּה פָּנָיו יֶחֱוָרוּ: כִּי בִרְאֹתוֹ יְלָדָיו מַעֲשֵׂה יָדַי בְּקִרְבּוֹ יב
יַקְדִּישׁוּ שְׁמִי וְהִקְדִּישׁוּ אֶת־קְדוֹשׁ יַעֲקֹב וְאֶת־אֱלֹהֵי יִשְׂרָאֵל יַעֲרִיצוּ:
כד ל א וְיָדְעוּ תֹעֵי־רוּחַ בִּינָה וְרוֹגְנִים יִלְמְדוּ־לֶקַח: הוֹי בָּנִים
סוֹרְרִים נְאֻם־יהוה לַעֲשׂוֹת עֵצָה וְלֹא מִנִּי וְלִנְסֹךְ מַסֵּכָה וְלֹא רוּחִי
ב לְמַעַן סְפוֹת חַטָּאת עַל־חַטָּאת: הַהֹלְכִים לָרֶדֶת מִצְרַיִם וּפִי לֹא
ג שָׁאָלוּ לָעוֹז בְּמָעוֹז פַּרְעֹה וְלַחְסוֹת בְּצֵל מִצְרָיִם: וְהָיָה לָכֶם מָעוֹז
ד פַּרְעֹה לְבֹשֶׁת וְהֶחָסוּת בְּצֵל־מִצְרַיִם לִכְלִמָּה: כִּי־הָיוּ בְצֹעַן שָׂרָיו
ה וּמַלְאָכָיו חָנֵס יַגִּיעוּ: כֹּל הִבְאִישׁ עַל־עַם לֹא־יוֹעִילוּ לָמוֹ לֹא לְעֵזֶר
ו וְלֹא לְהוֹעִיל כִּי לְבֹשֶׁת וְגַם־לְחֶרְפָּה: מַשָּׂא בַּהֲמוֹת נֶגֶב
בְּאֶרֶץ צָרָה וְצוּקָה לָבִיא וָלַיִשׁ מֵהֶם אֶפְעֶה וְשָׂרָף מְעוֹפֵף יִשְׂאוּ עַל־
כֶּתֶף עורים חֵילֵיהֶם וְעַל־דַּבֶּשֶׁת גְּמַלִּים אוֹצְרֹתָם עַל־עָם לֹא יוֹעִילוּ: עֲיָרִים
ז ח וּמִצְרַיִם הֶבֶל וָרִיק יַעְזֹרוּ לָכֵן קָרָאתִי לָזֹאת רַהַב הֵם שָׁבֶת: עַתָּה
בּוֹא כָתְבָהּ עַל־לוּחַ אִתָּם וְעַל־סֵפֶר חֻקָּהּ וּתְהִי לְיוֹם אַחֲרוֹן לָעַד
ט עַד־עוֹלָם: כִּי עַם מְרִי הוּא בָּנִים כֶּחָשִׁים בָּנִים לֹא־אָבוּ שְׁמוֹעַ תּוֹרַת
י יהוה: אֲשֶׁר אָמְרוּ לָרֹאִים לֹא תִרְאוּ וְלַחֹזִים לֹא תֶחֱזוּ־לָנוּ נְכֹחוֹת
יא דַּבְּרוּ־לָנוּ חֲלָקוֹת חֲזוּ מַהֲתַלּוֹת: סוּרוּ מִנֵּי־דֶרֶךְ הַטּוּ מִנֵּי־אֹרַח
יב הַשְׁבִּיתוּ מִפָּנֵינוּ אֶת־קְדוֹשׁ יִשְׂרָאֵל: לָכֵן כֹּה אָמַר
קְדוֹשׁ יִשְׂרָאֵל יַעַן מָאָסְכֶם בַּדָּבָר הַזֶּה וַתִּבְטְחוּ בְּעֹשֶׁק וְנָלוֹז וַתִּשָּׁעֲנוּ
יג עָלָיו: לָכֵן יִהְיֶה לָכֶם הֶעָוֹן הַזֶּה כְּפֶרֶץ נֹפֵל נִבְעֶה בְּחוֹמָה נִשְׂגָּבָה
יד אֲשֶׁר־פִּתְאֹם לְפֶתַע יָבוֹא שִׁבְרָהּ: וּשְׁבָרָהּ כְּשֵׁבֶר נֵבֶל יוֹצְרִים כָּתוּת
לֹא יַחְמֹל וְלֹא־יִמָּצֵא בִמְכִתָּתוֹ חֶרֶשׂ לַחְתּוֹת אֵשׁ מִיָּקוּד וְלַחְשֹׂף
טו מַיִם מִגֶּבֶא: כִּי כֹה־אָמַר אֲדֹנָי יֱהוִה קְדוֹשׁ יִשְׂרָאֵל
בְּשׁוּבָה וָנַחַת תִּוָּשֵׁעוּן בְּהַשְׁקֵט וּבְבִטְחָה תִּהְיֶה גְּבוּרַתְכֶם וְלֹא
טז אֲבִיתֶם: וַתֹּאמְרוּ לֹא־כִי עַל־סוּס נָנוּס עַל־כֵּן תְּנוּסוּן וְעַל־קַל נִרְכָּב
יז עַל־כֵּן יִקַּלּוּ רֹדְפֵיכֶם: אֶלֶף אֶחָד מִפְּנֵי גַּעֲרַת אֶחָד מִפְּנֵי גַּעֲרַת חֲמִשָּׁה

word of five until you are left like a flagpole at the hilltop, like a banner on
18 the mountain's peak.[84] So the LORD waits, that He may show You grace; He
lifts Himself aloof, that He may find compassion. For the LORD is a God of
19 judgment, and happy is the man who waits for Him. For a people
will live in Zion, Jerusalem; you will weep no more tears; favor – favor will
He show you at the sound of your cries; when He hears, He will answer you.
20 And though He feeds you bread of pain and water of oppression, your teacher
21 will hide Himself no more; your eyes will see your teacher, your ears will hear
22 a word behind you: "This is the path: now walk it whether right or left." You
will defile your silver-plated statues, the breastplates of your golden images.
23 You will cast them out like a menstruating woman. Tell them, "Go!" He will
grant rain for your seedlings that you will plant upon the land, the bread of
the land's bounty; it will become succulent, fat. Your livestock will graze on
24 that day, wide-open pasture. The oxen and the donkeys, the earth's workers,
25 seasoned hay they will eat, winnowed with spade and with fork. It will be: on
each high mountain, every elevated hill, streams, rivers of water,[85] on the day
26 of the terrible killing when all towers fall. The light of the moon will be like
the light of the sun, and the sun's light seven times the light of seven days, on
the day when the LORD bandages the breaking of His people and heals up
27 the gash from their beating. See: The LORD's name coming from far
hence, His rage burning and the heavy cloud of smoke. His mouth is full of
28 fury, His tongue, consuming fire. His breath a torrent overflowing, crossing
the land neck deep, sifting all the nations with a sieve of nothingness,[86] with
29 a false-leading bridle, holding nations by the jaw. How you will sing as on the
night when the festival begins; joy that fills the heart as when you walk out
30 with your flute to come to the LORD's mountain, to the Rock of Israel, when
the LORD sounds the glory of His voice, shows His arm coming down with
31 blazing rage, a flame of fire consuming, cloudburst, torrent, rocks of hail, for
32 at the LORD's voice Assyria will tremble, who once struck with their rod. In
every passage where the LORD plants down the staff, firmly, drums will sound,
33 and lutes, and the brandished hands of warfare; so will He fight them. For
the flaming valley[87] is prepared from yesterday, ready to receive even a king;
its hearth is full of fire and wood aplenty, and the LORD's breath like a river
31 1 of sulfur burns inside. Woe to those who go down to Egypt for
aid, relying on horses, placing their trust in chariots – so many – and
horsemen – how powerful they are – and do not turn to Israel's Holy One,
2 do not seek after the LORD. But He too is wise – He brings evil and does not
call back His words. He rises up against a house of those who harm and those
3 who abet the workers of iniquity. Egypt is human, not God, and their horses
are flesh, not spirit. The LORD will stretch out His hand: helper will trip, and

---

84 | Erected to give the soldiers a landmark to return to, the flagpole is left alone when the army flees.

85 | Geographical features will be transformed for the better, perhaps as a result of the earthquake that will quell the wicked.

86 | A sieve that lets nothing through; the enemy armies are not sifted but are completely wiped out.

87 | The Tofet altars in the Valley of Ben Hinom near Jerusalem are known from Jeremiah 7:31 as the location of abominable idolatrous practices. This location has become a metaphor for hell (*Gehinom*).

תָּנֻסוּ עַד אִם־נוֹתַרְתֶּם כַּתֹּרֶן עַל־רֹאשׁ הָהָר וְכַנֵּס עַל־הַגִּבְעָה׃
יח וְלָכֵן יְחַכֶּה יהוה לַחֲנַנְכֶם וְלָכֵן יָרוּם לְרַחֶמְכֶם כִּי־אֱלֹהֵי מִשְׁפָּט יהוה
יט אַשְׁרֵי כָּל־חוֹכֵי לוֹ׃ כִּי־עַם בְּצִיּוֹן יֵשֵׁב בִּירוּשָׁלָם בָּכוֹ לֹא־
כ תִבְכֶּה חָנוֹן יָחְנְךָ לְקוֹל זַעֲקֶךָ כְּשָׁמְעָתוֹ עָנָךְ׃ וְנָתַן לָכֶם אֲדֹנָי לֶחֶם
צָר וּמַיִם לָחַץ וְלֹא־יִכָּנֵף עוֹד מוֹרֶיךָ וְהָיוּ עֵינֶיךָ רֹאוֹת אֶת־מוֹרֶיךָ׃
כא וְאָזְנֶיךָ תִּשְׁמַעְנָה דָבָר מֵאַחֲרֶיךָ לֵאמֹר זֶה הַדֶּרֶךְ לְכוּ בוֹ כִּי תַאֲמִינוּ
כב וְכִי תַשְׂמְאִילוּ׃ וְטִמֵּאתֶם אֶת־צִפּוּי פְּסִילֵי כַסְפֶּךָ וְאֶת־אֲפֻדַּת מַסֵּכַת
כג זְהָבֶךָ תִּזְרֵם כְּמוֹ דָוָה צֵא תֹּאמַר לוֹ׃ וְנָתַן מְטַר זַרְעֲךָ אֲשֶׁר־תִּזְרַע
אֶת־הָאֲדָמָה וְלֶחֶם תְּבוּאַת הָאֲדָמָה וְהָיָה דָשֵׁן וְשָׁמֵן יִרְעֶה מִקְנֶיךָ
כד בַּיּוֹם הַהוּא כַּר נִרְחָב׃ וְהָאֲלָפִים וְהָעֲיָרִים עֹבְדֵי הָאֲדָמָה בְּלִיל חָמִיץ
כה יֹאכֵלוּ אֲשֶׁר־זֹרֶה בָרַחַת וּבַמִּזְרֶה׃ וְהָיָה ׀ עַל־כָּל־הַר גָּבֹהַּ וְעַל כָּל־
כו גִּבְעָה נִשָּׂאָה פְּלָגִים יִבְלֵי־מָיִם בְּיוֹם הֶרֶג רָב בִּנְפֹל מִגְדָּלִים׃ וְהָיָה
אוֹר־הַלְּבָנָה כְּאוֹר הַחַמָּה וְאוֹר הַחַמָּה יִהְיֶה שִׁבְעָתַיִם כְּאוֹר
שִׁבְעַת הַיָּמִים בְּיוֹם חֲבֹשׁ יהוה אֶת־שֶׁבֶר עַמּוֹ וּמַחַץ מַכָּתוֹ
כז יִרְפָּא׃ הִנֵּה שֵׁם־יהוה בָּא מִמֶּרְחָק בֹּעֵר אַפּוֹ וְכֹבֶד מַשָּׂאָה
כח שְׂפָתָיו מָלְאוּ זַעַם וּלְשׁוֹנוֹ כְּאֵשׁ אֹכָלֶת׃ וְרוּחוֹ כְּנַחַל שׁוֹטֵף עַד־צַוָּאר
כט יֶחֱצֶה לַהֲנָפָה גוֹיִם בְּנָפַת שָׁוְא וְרֶסֶן מַתְעֶה עַל לְחָיֵי עַמִּים׃ הַשִּׁיר
יִהְיֶה לָכֶם כְּלֵיל הִתְקַדֶּשׁ־חָג וְשִׂמְחַת לֵבָב כַּהוֹלֵךְ בֶּחָלִיל לָבוֹא
ל בְהַר־יהוה אֶל־צוּר יִשְׂרָאֵל׃ וְהִשְׁמִיעַ יהוה אֶת־הוֹד קוֹלוֹ וְנַחַת
לא זְרוֹעוֹ יַרְאֶה בְּזַעַף אַף וְלַהַב אֵשׁ אוֹכֵלָה נֶפֶץ וָזֶרֶם וְאֶבֶן בָּרָד׃ כִּי־
לב מִקּוֹל יהוה יֵחַת אַשּׁוּר בַּשֵּׁבֶט יַכֶּה׃ וְהָיָה כֹּל מַעֲבַר מַטֵּה מוּסָדָה
אֲשֶׁר יָנִיחַ יהוה עָלָיו בְּתֻפִּים וּבְכִנֹּרוֹת וּבְמִלְחֲמוֹת תְּנוּפָה נִלְחַם־בָּה׃ בָּם
לג כִּי־עָרוּךְ מֵאֶתְמוּל תָּפְתֶּה גַּם־הוּא לַמֶּלֶךְ הוּכָן הֶעְמִיק הִרְחִב הִיא
מְדֻרָתָהּ אֵשׁ וְעֵצִים הַרְבֵּה נִשְׁמַת יהוה כְּנַחַל גָּפְרִית בֹּעֲרָה
לא א בָּהּ׃ הוֹי הַיֹּרְדִים מִצְרַיִם לְעֶזְרָה עַל־סוּסִים יִשָּׁעֵנוּ
וַיִּבְטְחוּ עַל־רֶכֶב כִּי רָב וְעַל פָּרָשִׁים כִּי־עָצְמוּ מְאֹד וְלֹא שָׁעוּ עַל־
ב קְדוֹשׁ יִשְׂרָאֵל וְאֶת־יהוה לֹא דָרָשׁוּ׃ וְגַם־הוּא חָכָם וַיָּבֵא רָע וְאֶת־
ג דְּבָרָיו לֹא הֵסִיר וְקָם עַל־בֵּית מְרֵעִים וְעַל־עֶזְרַת פֹּעֲלֵי אָוֶן׃ וּמִצְרַיִם
אָדָם וְלֹא־אֵל וְסוּסֵיהֶם בָּשָׂר וְלֹא־רוּחַ וַיהוה יַטֶּה יָדוֹ וְכָשַׁל עוֹזֵר

4 helped will fall; both together will be destroyed. For so the LORD
has said to me: As a lion, a young lion, roars over his prey even as a band of
shepherds calls out over him, never pausing at their voice, a multitude
unanswered, so will the LORD of Hosts come down to camp over Mount Zion,
5 her hill. As a mother bird hovers above, so will the LORD of Hosts defend
6 Jerusalem, defending and saving, passing over and delivering. Come back to
7 the One whom they have gone so deep to turn from, Israel's children, for on
that day each man will recoil from his silver gods, his golden gods which your
8 hands made for you, sinning. Assyria will fall to a sword not of man; a sword
not of mortals will consume him. He will flee the sword, and still his youths
9 will be bonded laborers. His rock will fade away in terror, his princes will
freeze at the sight of the banner.[88] So says the LORD, who has a fire burning
32 1 in Zion, a furnace in Jerusalem. Then kings will govern to bring
2 goodness and ministers rule to bring justice. A man[89] will be a hiding place
from the gale, from the winter storm shelter, like streams of water in an arid
3 place, like the shade of a heavy rock on weary land. The eyes of those who see
4 will not be blinded, and the ears of those who hear, they will be listening. The
hearts of the hasty will understand and know; each stammering tongue will
5 swiftly speak clear truth. No more will fools be counted noble, nor villains
6 be named the elite, for the fool speaks felony; his heart works sin, working
vile deeds and speaking falsehoods of the LORD, emptying the hungry of their
7 life's bread and stealing all the thirsty have to drink. The devices of the devious
are wicked; they plot out their plans to do violence by lies to the oppressed
8 ones, talking the vulnerable out of their justice. But one who is noble forms
9 noble plans, and on his nobility he stands. Come, you sanguine
ladies, and listen to my words; you women of security, pay heed to what I say.
10 Mere days beyond a year and the safe ones will be shaken, for harvest is over,
11 and the crop will not come. Tremble, sanguine ladies; shake, women in safety;
12 strip yourselves bare and tie sack about your waists. Breasts are beaten in
13 mourning for the lovely meadows, the fruitful vine. All over My people's land
the sounds of thorn and briar rise to reach all joyous homes across the
14 exuberant city, for the palace is forsaken, the crowded city, bleak; citadel and
15 tower turned back to caves forever, wild donkeys' joy, pasture of flocks, until,
from above, the wind is bared to us, turning the wilderness to fertile land and
16 fertile land to woods. Justice will preside in the wilderness, and righteousness
17 rest across the fertile land. The act of goodness will be repaid with peace and
18 the work of righteousness with calm and safety, always. My people will
reside in a shelter of peace, in dwellings of safety, in sanguine harbor.
19 Hail will fall as the forest comes down, and low, low will the town then fall.
20 Happy you are who sow seeds by the water and send forth hoof falls of ox

---

88 | The rock stele on which the king engraves a record of his accomplishments is a symbol of Assyrian power; the banner is a symbol of the Assyrian army's presence.

89 | Referring to the just leaders referenced in the previous verse, who do not rely on foreign aid but rather on God.

ד וְנָפַל עָזֻר וְיַחְדָּו כֻּלָּם יִכְלָיוּן׃ כִּי כֹה אָמַר־יְהוָה ׀ אֵלַי כַּאֲשֶׁר
יֶהְגֶּה הָאַרְיֵה וְהַכְּפִיר עַל־טַרְפּוֹ אֲשֶׁר יִקָּרֵא עָלָיו מְלֹא רֹעִים מִקּוֹלָם
לֹא יֵחָת וּמֵהֲמוֹנָם לֹא יַעֲנֶה כֵּן יֵרֵד יְהוָה צְבָאוֹת לִצְבֹּא עַל־הַר־צִיּוֹן
ה וְעַל־גִּבְעָתָהּ׃ כְּצִפֳּרִים עָפוֹת כֵּן יָגֵן יְהוָה צְבָאוֹת עַל־יְרוּשָׁלִָם גָּנוֹן
ו ז וְהִצִּיל פָּסֹחַ וְהִמְלִיט׃ שׁוּבוּ לַאֲשֶׁר הֶעְמִיקוּ סָרָה בְּנֵי יִשְׂרָאֵל׃ כִּי
בַּיּוֹם הַהוּא יִמְאָסוּן אִישׁ אֱלִילֵי כַסְפּוֹ וֶאֱלִילֵי זְהָבוֹ אֲשֶׁר עָשׂוּ
ח לָכֶם יְדֵיכֶם חֵטְא׃ וְנָפַל אַשּׁוּר בְּחֶרֶב לֹא־אִישׁ וְחֶרֶב לֹא־
ט אָדָם תֹּאכְלֶנּוּ וְנָס לוֹ מִפְּנֵי־חֶרֶב וּבַחוּרָיו לָמַס יִהְיוּ׃ וְסַלְעוֹ מִמָּגוֹר
יַעֲבוֹר וְחַתּוּ מִנֵּס שָׂרָיו נְאֻם־יְהוָה אֲשֶׁר־אוּר לוֹ בְּצִיּוֹן וְתַנּוּר לוֹ
לב א בִּירוּשָׁלִָם׃ הֵן לְצֶדֶק יִמְלָךְ־מֶלֶךְ וּלְשָׂרִים לְמִשְׁפָּט יָשֹׂרוּ׃
ב וְהָיָה־אִישׁ כְּמַחֲבֵא־רוּחַ וְסֵתֶר זָרֶם כְּפַלְגֵי־מַיִם בְּצָיוֹן כְּצֵל סֶלַע־כָּבֵד
ג ד בְּאֶרֶץ עֲיֵפָה׃ וְלֹא תִשְׁעֶינָה עֵינֵי רֹאִים וְאָזְנֵי שֹׁמְעִים תִּקְשַׁבְנָה׃ וּלְבַב
ה נִמְהָרִים יָבִין לָדָעַת וּלְשׁוֹן עִלְּגִים תְּמַהֵר לְדַבֵּר צָחוֹת׃ לֹא־יִקָּרֵא
ו עוֹד לְנָבָל נָדִיב וּלְכִילַי לֹא יֵאָמֵר שׁוֹעַ׃ כִּי נָבָל נְבָלָה יְדַבֵּר וְלִבּוֹ
יַעֲשֶׂה־אָוֶן לַעֲשׂוֹת חֹנֶף וּלְדַבֵּר אֶל־יְהוָה תּוֹעָה לְהָרִיק נֶפֶשׁ רָעֵב
ז וּמַשְׁקֶה צָמֵא יַחְסִיר׃ וְכֵלַי כֵּלָיו רָעִים הוּא זִמּוֹת יָעָץ לְחַבֵּל ענוים עֲנִיִּים
ח בְּאִמְרֵי־שֶׁקֶר וּבְדַבֵּר אֶבְיוֹן מִשְׁפָּט׃ וְנָדִיב נְדִיבוֹת יָעָץ וְהוּא עַל־
ט נְדִיבוֹת יָקוּם׃ נָשִׁים שַׁאֲנַנּוֹת קֹמְנָה שְׁמַעְנָה קוֹלִי
י בָּנוֹת בֹּטְחוֹת הַאְזֵנָּה אִמְרָתִי׃ יָמִים עַל־שָׁנָה תִּרְגַּזְנָה בֹּטְחוֹת כִּי
יא כָּלָה בָצִיר אֹסֶף בְּלִי יָבוֹא׃ חִרְדוּ שַׁאֲנַנּוֹת רְגָזָה בֹּטְחוֹת פְּשֹׁטָה וְעֹרָה
יב וַחֲגוֹרָה עַל־חֲלָצָיִם׃ עַל־שָׁדַיִם סֹפְדִים עַל־שְׂדֵי־חֶמֶד עַל־גֶּפֶן פֹּרִיָּה׃
יג עַל אַדְמַת עַמִּי קוֹץ שָׁמִיר תַּעֲלֶה כִּי עַל־כָּל־בָּתֵּי מָשׂוֹשׂ קִרְיָה
יד עַלִּיזָה׃ כִּי־אַרְמוֹן נֻטָּשׁ הֲמוֹן עִיר עֻזָּב עֹפֶל וָבַחַן הָיָה בְעַד מְעָרוֹת
טו עַד־עוֹלָם מְשׂוֹשׂ פְּרָאִים מִרְעֵה עֲדָרִים׃ עַד־יֵעָרֶה עָלֵינוּ רוּחַ מִמָּרוֹם
טז וְהָיָה מִדְבָּר לַכַּרְמֶל וכרמל לַיַּעַר יֵחָשֵׁב׃ וְשָׁכַן בַּמִּדְבָּר מִשְׁפָּט וְהַכַּרְמֶל
יז וּצְדָקָה בַּכַּרְמֶל תֵּשֵׁב׃ וְהָיָה מַעֲשֵׂה הַצְּדָקָה שָׁלוֹם וַעֲבֹדַת הַצְּדָקָה
יח הַשְׁקֵט וָבֶטַח עַד־עוֹלָם׃ וְיָשַׁב עַמִּי בִּנְוֵה שָׁלוֹם וּבְמִשְׁכְּנוֹת יג
יט מִבְטַחִים וּבִמְנוּחֹת שַׁאֲנַנּוֹת׃ וּבָרַד בְּרֶדֶת הַיָּעַר וּבַשִּׁפְלָה
כ תִּשְׁפַּל הָעִיר׃ אַשְׁרֵיכֶם זֹרְעֵי עַל־כָּל־מָיִם מְשַׁלְּחֵי רֶגֶל־הַשּׁוֹר

33 1 and of ass. Woe to one who plundered though he had not been
plundered, who betrayed though none betrayed him. When you are done
plundering, you too shall be plundered; your betrayal at an end, you are
2 betrayed. Lord, be gracious to us; it is You we waited for; be the
3 people's arm, morning by morning, their rescue in times of distress. The
sound of the throng sent peoples adrift, nations scattered in the wake of
4 Your greatness. The plunder is ingathered as one would pluck up locusts,
5 spreading as locusts teem. The Lord is exalted, dwelling on high, filling Zion
6 with justice, with righteousness. He is constancy through time for you,
rescuing might, wisdom, knowledge; His treasure house is fear of the
7 Lord. The mighty cry out in the streets, and messengers of peace
8 weep in bitterness. The roads are desolate: no passersby. He has broken the
9 covenant, turned cities to scrap, counted people as nothing. The land is
mourning – misery, Lebanon disgraced and withered away, the Sharon dried
10 to desert, Bashan and Carmel shaken clear of all life. "Now I shall rise," says
11 the Lord. "Now shall I rise up, now be exalted." Conceive chaff; give birth
12 to straw; your breath of fire will consume you. The peoples around – they
13 will be a lime furnace, like broken thorns gone up in flames. You
who are far away, hear what I have done; you who are close, know My might.
14 Sinners in Zion have feared this; trembling catches hold of the vile. "Who of
us can abide through consuming fire; who of us can abide through everlasting
15 burning?" One who walks in righteousness, speaks the truth, rejects
oppression's profits, and shakes his hands clear of bolstering corruption,
blocks his ears from hearing violence, and closes his eyes to the allure of
16 wrong; he will reside on high, sheltered in strongholds of the rocks. His bread
17 is given to him; his water flows faithfully. Your eyes will see a king in his
18 splendor, will see his land from far away. Your heart will speak of awe: "Who
19 can count, who can measure; who can count the towers?" You will not see a
brazen people, a people whose speech is beyond hearing, a barbarian tongue
20 without sense. Look upon Zion, the city of our meeting: your eyes shall see
Jerusalem, sanguine shelter, the tent that need not be shifted, with stakes
21 that will never be lifted, none of its cords ever cut. For there the Lord is our
majesty in a place of broad-handed rivers where no sailing boat can pass,
22 and ships of majesty cannot cross, for the Lord is our judge, the Lord
23 our lawgiver, the Lord our King, and He will rescue us. Your ropes are
abandoned; they will not hold; their masts will not spread the banner. Then
will great plunder be shared about in plenty; those once limping will loot the
24 hoard. Her dwellers will not say, "I am ill"; all those who live there, their sins
34 1 will be forgiven. Come near, nations far away, and listen; peoples,
2 hear. The earth and her fill will listen, the world and all her children: The
Lord is filled with fury for all nations, rage for all their armies; He has
3 damned them and given them up to the slaughter. Their fallen will be cast
aside; the stench will rise up from their corpses as hills dissolve in their blood.
4 All the hosts of heaven will rot. The scroll of the heavens will be rolled shut.
All its hosts will wither away as leaves wither and fall from the vine, like a fig

לג א וְהַחֲמוֹר׃ הוֹי שׁוֹדֵד וְאַתָּה לֹא שָׁדוּד וּבוֹגֵד וְלֹא־בָגְדוּ בָךְ
ב כַּהֲתִמְךָ שׁוֹדֵד תּוּשַּׁד כַּנְּלֹתְךָ לִבְגֹּד יִבְגְּדוּ־בָךְ׃ יְהוָה חָנֵּנוּ
ג לְךָ קִוִּינוּ הֱיֵה זְרֹעָם לַבְּקָרִים אַף־יְשׁוּעָתֵנוּ בְּעֵת צָרָה׃ מִקּוֹל הָמוֹן
ד נָדְדוּ עַמִּים מֵרֹמְמֻתֶךָ נָפְצוּ גּוֹיִם׃ וְאֻסַּף שְׁלַלְכֶם אֹסֶף הֶחָסִיל כְּמַשַּׁק
ה גֵּבִים שֹׁקֵק בּוֹ׃ נִשְׂגָּב יְהוָה כִּי שֹׁכֵן מָרוֹם מִלֵּא צִיּוֹן מִשְׁפָּט וּצְדָקָה׃
ו וְהָיָה אֱמוּנַת עִתֶּיךָ חֹסֶן יְשׁוּעֹת חָכְמַת וָדָעַת יִרְאַת יְהוָה הִיא
ז אוֹצָרוֹ׃ הֵן אֶרְאֶלָּם צָעֲקוּ חֻצָה מַלְאֲכֵי שָׁלוֹם מַר יִבְכָּיוּן׃
ח נָשַׁמּוּ מְסִלּוֹת שָׁבַת עֹבֵר אֹרַח הֵפֵר בְּרִית מָאַס עָרִים לֹא חָשַׁב אֱנוֹשׁ׃
ט אָבַל אֻמְלְלָה אָרֶץ הֶחְפִּיר לְבָנוֹן קָמַל הָיָה הַשָּׁרוֹן כָּעֲרָבָה וְנֹעֵר בָּשָׁן
י יא וְכַרְמֶל׃ עַתָּה אָקוּם יֹאמַר יְהוָה עַתָּה אֵרוֹמָם עַתָּה אֶנָּשֵׂא׃ תַּהֲרוּ
יב חֲשַׁשׁ תֵּלְדוּ קַשׁ רוּחֲכֶם אֵשׁ תֹּאכַלְכֶם׃ וְהָיוּ עַמִּים מִשְׂרְפוֹת שִׂיד
יג קוֹצִים כְּסוּחִים בָּאֵשׁ יִצַּתּוּ׃ שִׁמְעוּ רְחוֹקִים אֲשֶׁר עָשִׂיתִי
יד וּדְעוּ קְרוֹבִים גְּבֻרָתִי׃ פָּחֲדוּ בְצִיּוֹן חַטָּאִים אָחֲזָה רְעָדָה חֲנֵפִים מִי
טו יָגוּר לָנוּ אֵשׁ אוֹכֵלָה מִי־יָגוּר לָנוּ מוֹקְדֵי עוֹלָם׃ הֹלֵךְ צְדָקוֹת וְדֹבֵר
מֵישָׁרִים מֹאֵס בְּבֶצַע מַעֲשַׁקּוֹת נֹעֵר כַּפָּיו מִתְּמֹךְ בַּשֹּׁחַד אֹטֵם אָזְנוֹ
טז מִשְּׁמֹעַ דָּמִים וְעֹצֵם עֵינָיו מֵרְאוֹת בְּרָע׃ הוּא מְרוֹמִים יִשְׁכֹּן מְצָדוֹת
יז סְלָעִים מִשְׂגַּבּוֹ לַחְמוֹ נִתָּן מֵימָיו נֶאֱמָנִים׃ מֶלֶךְ בְּיָפְיוֹ תֶּחֱזֶינָה עֵינֶיךָ
יח תִּרְאֶינָה אֶרֶץ מַרְחַקִּים׃ לִבְּךָ יֶהְגֶּה אֵימָה אַיֵּה סֹפֵר אַיֵּה שֹׁקֵל אַיֵּה
יט סֹפֵר אֶת־הַמִּגְדָּלִים׃ אֶת־עַם נוֹעָז לֹא תִרְאֶה עַם עִמְקֵי שָׂפָה מִשְּׁמוֹעַ
כ נִלְעַג לָשׁוֹן אֵין בִּינָה׃ חֲזֵה צִיּוֹן קִרְיַת מוֹעֲדֵנוּ עֵינֶיךָ תִרְאֶינָה יְרוּשָׁלִַם
נָוֶה שַׁאֲנָן אֹהֶל בַּל־יִצְעָן בַּל־יִסַּע יְתֵדֹתָיו לָנֶצַח וְכָל־חֲבָלָיו בַּל־
כא יִנָּתֵקוּ׃ כִּי אִם־שָׁם אַדִּיר יְהוָה לָנוּ מְקוֹם־נְהָרִים יְאֹרִים רַחֲבֵי יָדָיִם
כב בַּל־תֵּלֶךְ בּוֹ אֳנִי־שַׁיִט וְצִי אַדִּיר לֹא יַעַבְרֶנּוּ׃ כִּי יְהוָה שֹׁפְטֵנוּ יְהוָה
כג מְחֹקְקֵנוּ יְהוָה מַלְכֵּנוּ הוּא יוֹשִׁיעֵנוּ׃ נִטְּשׁוּ חֲבָלָיִךְ בַּל־יְחַזְּקוּ כֵן־תָּרְנָם
כד בַּל־פָּרְשׂוּ נֵס אָז חֻלַּק עַד־שָׁלָל מַרְבֶּה פִּסְחִים בָּזְזוּ בַז׃ וּבַל־יֹאמַר
לד א שָׁכֵן חָלִיתִי הָעָם הַיֹּשֵׁב בָּהּ נְשֻׂא עָוֺן׃ קִרְבוּ גוֹיִם לִשְׁמֹעַ
ב וּלְאֻמִּים הַקְשִׁיבוּ תִּשְׁמַע הָאָרֶץ וּמְלֹאָהּ תֵּבֵל וְכָל־צֶאֱצָאֶיהָ׃ כִּי קֶצֶף
לַיהוָה עַל־כָּל־הַגּוֹיִם וְחֵמָה עַל־כָּל־צְבָאָם הֶחֱרִימָם נְתָנָם לַטָּבַח׃
ג ד וְחַלְלֵיהֶם יֻשְׁלָכוּ וּפִגְרֵיהֶם יַעֲלֶה בָאְשָׁם וְנָמַסּוּ הָרִים מִדָּמָם׃ וְנָמַקּוּ
כָּל־צְבָא הַשָּׁמַיִם וְנָגֹלּוּ כַסֵּפֶר הַשָּׁמָיִם וְכָל־צְבָאָם יִבּוֹל כִּנְבֹל עָלֶה

5 that falls too soon, for My sword has slaked its thirst from the skies; see: it
6 comes down upon Edom, upon the people I have damned in judgment. The
LORD – His sword is sated with blood, fleshed out with fat, with the blood
of rams and goats, the fat parts of rams' livers, for the LORD receives His
7 offering in Botzra, a great slaughter in the land of Edom. The wild oxen go
down with them, bullocks along with wild bulls, and all their land is slaked
8 with blood, their dust fleshed out with fat, for the LORD has had His day of
9 vengeance, a year of repayment for Zion's cause. Her[90] streams will turn to
10 pitch, her dust to sulfur, and all her land will be burning tar. Night and day
the burning will not stop; her smoke will rise forever; from one generation
to the next, she will be devastation; from one age to the next, no passersby.
11 The pelican and fish owl will take up possession; the long-eared owl and raven
will take up residence; He will stretch out across her a measuring line of chaos,
12 hung down with weights of emptiness. Her nobles – they will not be there,
13 they will not be called royalty; her ministers will turn to nothing. Thorns will
come up in her palaces, milk thistle, oyster thistle filling her fortresses. It will
14 be a jackals' shelter, the ostriches' pasture. Desert beasts will meet there with
the wildcats, night birds will call out for each other, and brown owls too will
15 take their ease, finally finding a resting place. There will the great owl build
her nest, lay her eggs and hatch them to warm in her shadow; there will the
16 kites gather too, one to another. Seek out the Book of the LORD and read: not
one will be missing.[91] None will seek her neighbor in vain, for it is My mouth
17 that charged them, My spirit that gathered them in. He has cast the lots for
them; His hand has divided them up; He has settled their legacy forever; age
35 1 after age they will live on there. The desert, the parched land, will
2 celebrate, and the arid plain rejoice and blossom like a dune flower, flowering,
blossoming, rejoicing – rejoicing and singing – she is given the glory of
Lebanon, the splendor of Carmel and Sharon, that the LORD's glory may be
seen, the splendor of our God. Sustain your weakened hands; hold
4 firm your failing knees. Say to those whose pulse beats fast, "Do not fear; here
is your God, coming for vengeance; God's repayment comes; this will save you."
5 The eyes of the blind will be opened, and the ears of the deaf will be unlocked.
6 Then will lame men skip like deer, while the tongues of those who could not
speak will sing. For the desert will be split across with water, streams across the
7 arid plain. Parched ground will turn to lakes and thirst to springs of water. In
8 the shelter of jackals, where they lay: grasses, reeds, and rushes. There will a
path, a road run by, and Holy Road will they call it. No impure person will pass
along it; it will be theirs, theirs who walk the road; even fools will not mistake
9 it. No lion will be there; no ravaging creature will dare ascend; they will not be
10 there, and the redeemed ones will walk on. Those the LORD has claimed will
return, arriving in Zion in song, crowned with everlasting joy; they will have
found joy and happiness, and sorrow and moaning will flee.

90 | Edom's.

91 | That is, all the animals predicted in the prophecy ("the Book") will indeed come to roost in Edom's ruins.

ה מְגֻפֶּן וּכְנֹבֶלֶת מִתְּאֵנָה׃ כִּי־רִוְּתָה בַשָּׁמַיִם חַרְבִּי הִנֵּה עַל־אֱדוֹם תֵּרֵד
ו וְעַל־עַם חֶרְמִי לְמִשְׁפָּט׃ חֶרֶב לַיהוָה מָלְאָה דָם הֻדַּשְּׁנָה מֵחֵלֶב מִדַּם
כָּרִים וְעַתּוּדִים מֵחֵלֶב כִּלְיוֹת אֵילִים כִּי זֶבַח לַיהוָה בְּבָצְרָה וְטֶבַח
ז גָּדוֹל בְּאֶרֶץ אֱדוֹם׃ וְיָרְדוּ רְאֵמִים עִמָּם וּפָרִים עִם־אַבִּירִים וְרִוְּתָה
ח אַרְצָם מִדָּם וַעֲפָרָם מֵחֵלֶב יְדֻשָּׁן׃ כִּי יוֹם נָקָם לַיהוָה שְׁנַת שִׁלּוּמִים
ט לְרִיב צִיּוֹן׃ וְנֶהֶפְכוּ נְחָלֶיהָ לְזֶפֶת וַעֲפָרָהּ לְגָפְרִית וְהָיְתָה אַרְצָהּ לְזֶפֶת
י בֹּעֵרָה׃ לַיְלָה וְיוֹמָם לֹא תִכְבֶּה לְעוֹלָם יַעֲלֶה עֲשָׁנָהּ מִדּוֹר לָדוֹר תֶּחֱרָב
יא לְנֵצַח נְצָחִים אֵין עֹבֵר בָּהּ׃ וִירֵשׁוּהָ קָאַת וְקִפּוֹד וְיַנְשׁוֹף וְעֹרֵב יִשְׁכְּנוּ־
יב בָהּ וְנָטָה עָלֶיהָ קַו־תֹהוּ וְאַבְנֵי־בֹהוּ׃ חֹרֶיהָ וְאֵין־שָׁם מְלוּכָה יִקְרָאוּ
יג וְכָל־שָׂרֶיהָ יִהְיוּ אָפֶס׃ וְעָלְתָה אַרְמְנֹתֶיהָ סִירִים קִמּוֹשׂ וָחוֹחַ בְּמִבְצָרֶיהָ
יד וְהָיְתָה נְוֵה תַנִּים חָצִיר לִבְנוֹת יַעֲנָה׃ וּפָגְשׁוּ צִיִּים אֶת־אִיִּים וְשָׂעִיר
טו עַל־רֵעֵהוּ יִקְרָא אַךְ־שָׁם הִרְגִּיעָה לִּילִית וּמָצְאָה לָהּ מָנוֹחַ׃ שָׁמָּה
קִנְּנָה קִפּוֹז וַתְּמַלֵּט וּבָקְעָה וְדָגְרָה בְצִלָּהּ אַךְ־שָׁם נִקְבְּצוּ דַיּוֹת אִשָּׁה
טז רְעוּתָהּ׃ דִּרְשׁוּ מֵעַל־סֵפֶר יְהוָה וּקְרָאוּ אַחַת מֵהֵנָּה לֹא נֶעְדָּרָה אִשָּׁה
יז רְעוּתָהּ לֹא פָקָדוּ כִּי־פִי הוּא צִוָּה וְרוּחוֹ הוּא קִבְּצָן׃ וְהוּא־הִפִּיל לָהֶן
גּוֹרָל וְיָדוֹ חִלְּקַתָּה לָהֶם בַּקָּו עַד־עוֹלָם יִירָשׁוּהָ לְדוֹר וָדוֹר יִשְׁכְּנוּ־
א בָהּ׃ יְשֻׂשׂוּם מִדְבָּר וְצִיָּה וְתָגֵל עֲרָבָה וְתִפְרַח כַּחֲבַצָּלֶת׃ לה
ב פָּרֹחַ תִּפְרַח וְתָגֵל אַף גִּילַת וְרַנֵּן כְּבוֹד הַלְּבָנוֹן נִתַּן־לָהּ הֲדַר הַכַּרְמֶל
ג וְהַשָּׁרוֹן הֵמָּה יִרְאוּ כְבוֹד־יְהוָה הֲדַר אֱלֹהֵינוּ׃ חַזְּקוּ
ד יָדַיִם רָפוֹת וּבִרְכַּיִם כֹּשְׁלוֹת אַמֵּצוּ׃ אִמְרוּ לְנִמְהֲרֵי־לֵב חִזְקוּ אַל־
ה תִּירָאוּ הִנֵּה אֱלֹהֵיכֶם נָקָם יָבוֹא גְּמוּל אֱלֹהִים הוּא יָבוֹא וְיֹשַׁעֲכֶם׃ אָז
ו תִּפָּקַחְנָה עֵינֵי עִוְרִים וְאָזְנֵי חֵרְשִׁים תִּפָּתַחְנָה׃ אָז יְדַלֵּג כָּאַיָּל פִּסֵּחַ
ז וְתָרֹן לְשׁוֹן אִלֵּם כִּי־נִבְקְעוּ בַמִּדְבָּר מַיִם וּנְחָלִים בָּעֲרָבָה׃ וְהָיָה הַשָּׁרָב
לַאֲגַם וְצִמָּאוֹן לְמַבּוּעֵי מָיִם בִּנְוֵה תַנִּים רִבְצָהּ חָצִיר לְקָנֶה וָגֹמֶא׃
ח וְהָיָה־שָׁם מַסְלוּל וָדֶרֶךְ וְדֶרֶךְ הַקֹּדֶשׁ יִקָּרֵא לָהּ לֹא־יַעַבְרֶנּוּ טָמֵא
ט וְהוּא־לָמוֹ הֹלֵךְ דֶּרֶךְ וֶאֱוִילִים לֹא יִתְעוּ׃ לֹא־יִהְיֶה שָׁם אַרְיֵה וּפְרִיץ
י חַיּוֹת בַּל־יַעֲלֶנָּה לֹא תִמָּצֵא שָׁם וְהָלְכוּ גְּאוּלִים׃ וּפְדוּיֵי יְהוָה יְשֻׁבוּן יד
וּבָאוּ צִיּוֹן בְּרִנָּה וְשִׂמְחַת עוֹלָם עַל־רֹאשָׁם שָׂשׂוֹן וְשִׂמְחָה יַשִּׂיגוּ וְנָסוּ
יָגוֹן וַאֲנָחָה׃

36 1 In the fourteenth year of King Ḥizkiyahu, Sanḥeriv, king of Assyria, marched
2 up against all the fortified cities of Yehuda and seized them.[92] And the king
of Assyria sent the Rav-Shakeh[93] from Lakhish to King Ḥizkiyahu in Jerusalem,
along with vast forces; they marched up and came to Jerusalem, and stationed
themselves by the conduit of the Upper Pool, by the Fuller's Field Road.
3 Elyakim son of Ḥilkiyahu, who was in charge of the palace, Shevna the scribe,
4 and Yoaḥ son of Asaf, royal herald, went out to them. And the Rav-Shakeh
said to them, "Now, tell Ḥizkiyahu: 'Thus says the Great King, the king of
5 Assyria: What is this display of trust? You talk as if mere chatter were counsel
and might in war! Now, in whom have you placed your trust, that you rebel
6 against me? Have you placed your trust in that crushed reed of a staff, in Egypt,
who pierces and punctures the palm of anyone who leans upon it? For that
7 is Pharaoh, king of Egypt, to all who place their trust in him. And if you say
to me, "We have placed our trust in the LORD, our God," is that not the one
whose high shrines and altars Ḥizkiyahu removed, telling Yehuda and
8 Jerusalem, "Bow only before *this* altar"? Come, now, make a wager with my
lord, the king of Assyria: I will provide you with two thousand horses if you
9 are able to provide them with riders! How dare you slight even one of the
deputies of my lord's lesser servants and place your trust in Egypt for chariots
10 and riders! What is more – was it without the LORD that I marched up to
destroy this land? It was the LORD Himself who said to me: March up against
11 this land and destroy it.'" Elyakim, Shevna, and Yoaḥ said to the Rav-Shakeh,
"Please, speak to your servants in Aramaic, for we understand it. Do not speak
12 to us in Hebrew within earshot of the people who are on the wall." "Was it to
you and your master that my lord sent me to speak these words?" the Rav-
Shakeh said. "Oh, but it was to the very men who are stationed on the wall,
who will have to eat their own excrement and drink their own urine along
13 with you."[94] And the Rav-Shakeh stood and shouted out in Hebrew: "Hear
14 the words of the Great King, the king of Assyria," he proclaimed. "Thus says
15 the king: Do not let Ḥizkiyahu deceive you, for he cannot save you. Do not
let Ḥizkiyahu convince you to place your trust in the LORD, saying, 'The LORD
will surely save us, and this city will not be handed over to the king of Assyria.'
16 Do not listen to Ḥizkiyahu, for thus says the king of Assyria: Make peace with
me; come out to me, and each will eat from his own vine and his own fig tree,
17 and each will drink from his own cistern until I come and take you to a land
like your own – a land of grain and wine, a land of bread and vineyards, a land
18 of olive oil and honey. Do not listen to Ḥizkiyahu, for he misleads you by
saying, 'The LORD will save us.' Have the gods of other nations managed to
19 save their own lands from the hand of the king of Assyria? Where are the
gods of Ḥamat and Arpad? Where are the gods of Sefarvites? Did they save
20 Shomron from my hand? Who among all the gods of the lands saved their

---

92 | Regarding chapters 36–39, cf. II Kings 18:13–20:19.

93 | The title of an Assyrian official.

94 | The translation follows the vocalized version, the *keri*. The terminology of the *ketiv* (written version) is more vulgar.

לו א וַיְהִי בְּאַרְבַּע עֶשְׂרֵה שָׁנָה לַמֶּלֶךְ חִזְקִיָּהוּ עָלָה סַנְחֵרִיב מֶלֶךְ־אַשּׁוּר
ב עַל כָּל־עָרֵי יְהוּדָה הַבְּצֻרוֹת וַיִּתְפְּשֵׂם: וַיִּשְׁלַח מֶלֶךְ־אַשּׁוּר | אֶת־
רַבְשָׁקֵה מִלָּכִישׁ יְרוּשָׁלַמָה אֶל־הַמֶּלֶךְ חִזְקִיָּהוּ בְּחֵיל כָּבֵד וַיַּעֲמֹד
ג בִּתְעָלַת הַבְּרֵכָה הָעֶלְיוֹנָה בִּמְסִלַּת שְׂדֵה כוֹבֵס: וַיֵּצֵא אֵלָיו אֶלְיָקִים
בֶּן־חִלְקִיָּהוּ אֲשֶׁר עַל־הַבָּיִת וְשֶׁבְנָא הַסֹּפֵר וְיוֹאָח בֶּן־אָסָף הַמַּזְכִּיר:
ד וַיֹּאמֶר אֲלֵיהֶם רַבְשָׁקֵה אִמְרוּ־נָא אֶל־חִזְקִיָּהוּ כֹּה־אָמַר הַמֶּלֶךְ הַגָּדוֹל
ה מֶלֶךְ אַשּׁוּר מָה הַבִּטָּחוֹן הַזֶּה אֲשֶׁר בָּטָחְתָּ: אָמַרְתִּי אַךְ־דְּבַר־שְׂפָתַיִם
ו עֵצָה וּגְבוּרָה לַמִּלְחָמָה עַתָּה עַל־מִי בָטַחְתָּ כִּי מָרַדְתָּ בִּי: הִנֵּה בָטַחְתָּ
עַל־מִשְׁעֶנֶת הַקָּנֶה הָרָצוּץ הַזֶּה עַל־מִצְרַיִם אֲשֶׁר יִסָּמֵךְ אִישׁ עָלָיו
ז וּבָא בְכַפּוֹ וּנְקָבָהּ כֵּן פַּרְעֹה מֶלֶךְ־מִצְרַיִם לְכָל־הַבֹּטְחִים עָלָיו: וְכִי־
תֹאמַר אֵלַי אֶל־יְהוָה אֱלֹהֵינוּ בָּטָחְנוּ הֲלוֹא הוּא אֲשֶׁר הֵסִיר חִזְקִיָּהוּ
אֶת־בָּמֹתָיו וְאֶת־מִזְבְּחֹתָיו וַיֹּאמֶר לִיהוּדָה וְלִירוּשָׁלִַם לִפְנֵי הַמִּזְבֵּחַ
ח הַזֶּה תִּשְׁתַּחֲווּ: וְעַתָּה הִתְעָרֶב נָא אֶת־אֲדֹנִי הַמֶּלֶךְ אַשּׁוּר וְאֶתְּנָה לְךָ
ט אַלְפַּיִם סוּסִים אִם־תּוּכַל לָתֶת לְךָ רֹכְבִים עֲלֵיהֶם: וְאֵיךְ תָּשִׁיב אֵת
פְּנֵי פַחַת אַחַד עַבְדֵי אֲדֹנִי הַקְּטַנִּים וַתִּבְטַח לְךָ עַל־מִצְרַיִם לְרֶכֶב
י וּלְפָרָשִׁים: וְעַתָּה הֲמִבַּלְעֲדֵי יְהוָה עָלִיתִי עַל־הָאָרֶץ הַזֹּאת לְהַשְׁחִיתָהּ
יא יְהוָה אָמַר אֵלַי עֲלֵה אֶל־הָאָרֶץ הַזֹּאת וְהַשְׁחִיתָהּ: וַיֹּאמֶר אֶלְיָקִים
וְשֶׁבְנָא וְיוֹאָח אֶל־רַבְשָׁקֵה דַּבֶּר־נָא אֶל־עֲבָדֶיךָ אֲרָמִית כִּי שֹׁמְעִים
אֲנָחְנוּ וְאַל־תְּדַבֵּר אֵלֵינוּ יְהוּדִית בְּאָזְנֵי הָעָם אֲשֶׁר עַל־הַחוֹמָה:
יב וַיֹּאמֶר רַבְשָׁקֵה הַאֶל אֲדֹנֶיךָ וְאֵלֶיךָ שְׁלָחַנִי אֲדֹנִי לְדַבֵּר אֶת־הַדְּבָרִים
הָאֵלֶּה הֲלֹא עַל־הָאֲנָשִׁים הַיֹּשְׁבִים עַל־הַחוֹמָה לֶאֱכֹל אֶת־חראיהם צוֹאָתָם
יג וְלִשְׁתּוֹת אֶת־שיניהם עִמָּכֶם: וַיַּעֲמֹד רַבְשָׁקֵה וַיִּקְרָא בְקוֹל־גָּדוֹל מֵימֵי רַגְלֵיהֶם
יד יְהוּדִית וַיֹּאמֶר שִׁמְעוּ אֶת־דִּבְרֵי הַמֶּלֶךְ הַגָּדוֹל מֶלֶךְ אַשּׁוּר: כֹּה אָמַר
טו הַמֶּלֶךְ אַל־יַשִּׁא לָכֶם חִזְקִיָּהוּ כִּי לֹא־יוּכַל לְהַצִּיל אֶתְכֶם: וְאַל־יַבְטַח
אֶתְכֶם חִזְקִיָּהוּ אֶל־יְהוָה לֵאמֹר הַצֵּל יַצִּילֵנוּ יְהוָה לֹא תִנָּתֵן הָעִיר
טז הַזֹּאת בְּיַד מֶלֶךְ אַשּׁוּר: אַל־תִּשְׁמְעוּ אֶל־חִזְקִיָּהוּ כִּי כֹה אָמַר הַמֶּלֶךְ
אַשּׁוּר עֲשׂוּ אִתִּי בְרָכָה וּצְאוּ אֵלַי וְאִכְלוּ אִישׁ־גַּפְנוֹ וְאִישׁ תְּאֵנָתוֹ
יז וּשְׁתוּ אִישׁ מֵי־בוֹרוֹ: עַד־בֹּאִי וְלָקַחְתִּי אֶתְכֶם אֶל־אֶרֶץ כְּאַרְצְכֶם
יח אֶרֶץ דָּגָן וְתִירוֹשׁ אֶרֶץ לֶחֶם וּכְרָמִים: פֶּן־יַסִּית אֶתְכֶם חִזְקִיָּהוּ לֵאמֹר
יְהוָה יַצִּילֵנוּ הַהִצִּילוּ אֱלֹהֵי הַגּוֹיִם אִישׁ אֶת־אַרְצוֹ מִיַּד מֶלֶךְ אַשּׁוּר:
יט אַיֵּה אֱלֹהֵי חֲמָת וְאַרְפָּד אַיֵּה אֱלֹהֵי סְפַרְוָיִם וְכִי־הִצִּילוּ אֶת־שֹׁמְרוֹן
כ מִיָּדִי: מִי בְּכָל־אֱלֹהֵי הָאֲרָצוֹת הָאֵלֶּה אֲשֶׁר־הִצִּילוּ אֶת־אַרְצָם מִיָּדִי

own land from my hands, that the LORD will save Jerusalem from my hand?"
21 And the people were silent and did not say a word, for the king's order was,
22 "Do not answer him." Then Elyakim son of Ḥilkiyahu, who was in charge of
the palace, Shevna the scribe, and Yoaḥ son of Asaf, the royal herald, came to
Ḥizkiyahu with their clothes rent and reported what the Rav-Shakeh had
37 1 said. When King Ḥizkiyahu heard, he rent his clothes and
2 covered himself in sackcloth and came to the House of the LORD. He then
sent Elyakim, who was in charge of the palace, and Shevna the scribe, and the
senior priests, covered in sackcloth, to the prophet Yeshayahu son of Amotz.
3 "Thus says Ḥizkiyahu," they said to him. "'Today is a day of distress and
reproach and disgrace, for children are about to be born, but there is no
4 strength left for the birth.[95] Perhaps the LORD your God will hear the words
of the Rav-Shakeh, whom the king of Assyria, his lord, sent to taunt the Living
God, and will condemn the words that the LORD your God heard – Oh, offer
5 a prayer for the sake of the surviving remnant!'" Now, when the servants of
6 King Ḥizkiyahu came to Yeshayahu, Yeshayahu said to them, "This is what
you should tell your lord. Thus says the LORD: Do not be afraid of the words
7 you heard, which the king of Assyria's servant boys used to revile Me. I will
strike him with delusion so that he will hear a rumor and return to his own
8 land; then I will have him fall by the sword in his own land." The Rav-Shakeh
withdrew, for he heard that the king of Assyria had moved on from Lakhish,
9 and he found the king of Assyria attacking Livna. When the latter heard
rumor that King Tirhaka, king of Kush, had set out to fight against him –
10 when he heard, he sent messengers to Ḥizkiyahu, saying: "This is what you
should tell Ḥizkiyahu, king of Yehuda: Do not let your God in whom you
trust deceive you, saying, 'Jerusalem will not be handed over to the king of
11 Assyria.' Look, you have heard what the kings of Assyria have done to all the
12 lands – they have utterly destroyed them. Will you be saved? Did the gods of
the nations that my ancestors destroyed save them – Gozan and Ḥaran and
13 Retzef and the Edenites of Telasar? Where is the king of Ḥamat and the king
14 of Arpad and the king of La'ir, Sefarvites, Hena, and Iva?" When Ḥizkiyahu
received the letter from the messengers and read it, he went up to the House
15 of the LORD, and Ḥizkiyahu spread it open before the LORD. Then Ḥizkiyahu
16 prayed to the LORD. "LORD of Hosts, God of Israel, Enthroned upon the
Cherubim," he said, "You alone are God of all the kingdoms of the earth; You
17 made both heaven and earth. Incline Your ear, O LORD, and listen; open Your
eyes, O LORD, and see; listen to the words of Sanḥeriv, those he sent to revile
18 the Living God. It is true, LORD, that the kings of Assyria have laid countries
19 to waste, with their lands. They have cast their gods to the fire – for they are
not gods but the work of human hands, wood and stone – and destroyed
20 them. But now, LORD our God, save us from his hand, and all the kingdoms

95 | A proverbial expression of distress and helplessness.

כא כִּי־יַצִּיל יְהוָה אֶת־יְרוּשָׁלַ͏ִם מִיָּדִי: וַיַּחֲרִישׁוּ וְלֹא־עָנוּ אֹתוֹ דָּבָר כִּי־
כב מִצְוַת הַמֶּלֶךְ הִיא לֵאמֹר לֹא תַעֲנֻהוּ: וַיָּבֹא אֶלְיָקִים בֶּן־חִלְקִיָּהוּ
אֲשֶׁר־עַל־הַבַּיִת וְשֶׁבְנָא הַסּוֹפֵר וְיוֹאָח בֶּן־אָסָף הַמַּזְכִּיר אֶל־חִזְקִיָּהוּ
לז א קְרוּעֵי בְגָדִים וַיַּגִּידוּ לוֹ אֵת דִּבְרֵי רַבְשָׁקֵה: וַיְהִי כִּשְׁמֹעַ
ב הַמֶּלֶךְ חִזְקִיָּהוּ וַיִּקְרַע אֶת־בְּגָדָיו וַיִּתְכַּס בַּשָּׂק וַיָּבֹא בֵּית יְהוָה: וַיִּשְׁלַח
אֶת־אֶלְיָקִים אֲשֶׁר־עַל־הַבַּיִת וְאֵת ׀ שֶׁבְנָא הַסּוֹפֵר וְאֵת זִקְנֵי הַכֹּהֲנִים
ג מִתְכַּסִּים בַּשַּׂקִּים אֶל־יְשַׁעְיָהוּ בֶן־אָמוֹץ הַנָּבִיא: וַיֹּאמְרוּ אֵלָיו כֹּה
אָמַר חִזְקִיָּהוּ יוֹם־צָרָה וְתוֹכֵחָה וּנְאָצָה הַיּוֹם הַזֶּה כִּי בָאוּ בָנִים עַד־
ד מַשְׁבֵּר וְכֹחַ אַיִן לְלֵדָה: אוּלַי יִשְׁמַע יְהוָה אֱלֹהֶיךָ אֵת ׀ דִּבְרֵי רַבְשָׁקֵה
אֲשֶׁר שְׁלָחוֹ מֶלֶךְ־אַשּׁוּר ׀ אֲדֹנָיו לְחָרֵף אֱלֹהִים חַי וְהוֹכִיחַ בַּדְּבָרִים
אֲשֶׁר שָׁמַע יְהוָה אֱלֹהֶיךָ וְנָשָׂאתָ תְפִלָּה בְּעַד הַשְּׁאֵרִית הַנִּמְצָאָה:
ה ו וַיָּבֹאוּ עַבְדֵי הַמֶּלֶךְ חִזְקִיָּהוּ אֶל־יְשַׁעְיָהוּ: וַיֹּאמֶר אֲלֵיהֶם יְשַׁעְיָהוּ כֹּה
תֹאמְרוּן אֶל־אֲדֹנֵיכֶם כֹּה ׀ אָמַר יְהוָה אַל־תִּירָא מִפְּנֵי הַדְּבָרִים אֲשֶׁר
ז שָׁמַעְתָּ אֲשֶׁר גִּדְּפוּ נַעֲרֵי מֶלֶךְ־אַשּׁוּר אוֹתִי: הִנְנִי נוֹתֵן בּוֹ רוּחַ וְשָׁמַע
ח שְׁמוּעָה וְשָׁב אֶל־אַרְצוֹ וְהִפַּלְתִּיו בַּחֶרֶב בְּאַרְצוֹ: וַיָּשָׁב רַבְשָׁקֵה וַיִּמְצָא
ט אֶת־מֶלֶךְ אַשּׁוּר נִלְחָם עַל־לִבְנָה כִּי שָׁמַע כִּי נָסַע מִלָּכִישׁ: וַיִּשְׁמַע
עַל־תִּרְהָקָה מֶלֶךְ־כּוּשׁ לֵאמֹר יָצָא לְהִלָּחֵם אִתָּךְ וַיִּשְׁמַע וַיִּשְׁלַח
י מַלְאָכִים אֶל־חִזְקִיָּהוּ לֵאמֹר: כֹּה תֹאמְרוּן אֶל־חִזְקִיָּהוּ מֶלֶךְ־יְהוּדָה
לֵאמֹר אַל־יַשִּׁאֲךָ אֱלֹהֶיךָ אֲשֶׁר אַתָּה בּוֹטֵחַ בּוֹ לֵאמֹר לֹא תִנָּתֵן
יא יְרוּשָׁלַ͏ִם בְּיַד מֶלֶךְ אַשּׁוּר: הִנֵּה ׀ אַתָּה שָׁמַעְתָּ אֲשֶׁר עָשׂוּ מַלְכֵי אַשּׁוּר
יב לְכָל־הָאֲרָצוֹת לְהַחֲרִימָם וְאַתָּה תִּנָּצֵל: הַהִצִּילוּ אוֹתָם אֱלֹהֵי הַגּוֹיִם
אֲשֶׁר הִשְׁחִיתוּ אֲבוֹתַי אֶת־גּוֹזָן וְאֶת־חָרָן וְרֶצֶף וּבְנֵי־עֶדֶן אֲשֶׁר
יג בִּתְלַשָּׂר: אַיֵּה מֶלֶךְ־חֲמָת וּמֶלֶךְ אַרְפָּד וּמֶלֶךְ לָעִיר סְפַרְוָיִם הֵנַע
יד וְעִוָּה: וַיִּקַּח חִזְקִיָּהוּ אֶת־הַסְּפָרִים מִיַּד הַמַּלְאָכִים וַיִּקְרָאֵהוּ וַיַּעַל בֵּית
טו יְהוָה וַיִּפְרְשֵׂהוּ חִזְקִיָּהוּ לִפְנֵי יְהוָה: וַיִּתְפַּלֵּל חִזְקִיָּהוּ אֶל־יְהוָה לֵאמֹר:
טז יְהוָה צְבָאוֹת אֱלֹהֵי יִשְׂרָאֵל יֹשֵׁב הַכְּרֻבִים אַתָּה־הוּא הָאֱלֹהִים לְבַדְּךָ
יז לְכֹל מַמְלְכוֹת הָאָרֶץ אַתָּה עָשִׂיתָ אֶת־הַשָּׁמַיִם וְאֶת־הָאָרֶץ: הַטֵּה
יְהוָה ׀ אָזְנְךָ וּשְׁמָע פְּקַח יְהוָה עֵינְךָ וּרְאֵה וּשְׁמַע אֵת כָּל־דִּבְרֵי
יח סַנְחֵרִיב אֲשֶׁר שָׁלַח לְחָרֵף אֱלֹהִים חָי: אָמְנָם יְהוָה הֶחֱרִיבוּ מַלְכֵי
יט אַשּׁוּר אֶת־כָּל־הָאֲרָצוֹת וְאֶת־אַרְצָם: וְנָתֹן אֶת־אֱלֹהֵיהֶם בָּאֵשׁ כִּי
כ לֹא אֱלֹהִים הֵמָּה כִּי אִם־מַעֲשֵׂה יְדֵי־אָדָם עֵץ וָאֶבֶן וַיְאַבְּדוּם: וְעַתָּה טו
יְהוָה אֱלֹהֵינוּ הוֹשִׁיעֵנוּ מִיָּדוֹ וְיֵדְעוּ כָּל־מַמְלְכוֹת הָאָרֶץ כִּי־אַתָּה יְהוָה

21 of the earth will see that You alone are LORD." And Yeshayahu son of Amotz
sent word to Ḥizkiyahu: "Thus says the LORD, God of Israel: Because you
22 prayed to Me about Sanḥeriv, king of Assyria, this is the word the LORD has
spoken of him: Virgin daughter Zion scorns you, mocks you; she shakes her
23 head behind your back, daughter Jerusalem. Whom have you taunted, whom
reviled; against whom did you raise your voice, lifting your eyes haughtily
24 against the Holy One of Israel? By your servants' hand you taunted the Lord;
you said, 'With the wealth of my chariots I climbed to the heights of the hills,
the ends of Lebanon, and I cut down its tallest cedars, its choicest junipers;
25 I attained its farthest reaches, its richest forests. I have dug down and drunk
the waters; the passing soles of my feet have parched all the rivers of Egypt.'
26 Did you not hear of this long ago? I did this in ancient times; I formed the
plan; now I have brought it to be: towns crash to heaps of rubble, and fortified
27 cities are ruined. The inhabitants are powerless, frozen in fear and ashamed,
like field grasses, like green stalks, the grass of rooftops, and fields before
28 harvest. Your stops, your goings, your comings, I know them all, and your
29 raging against Me. Because you have raged against Me, your arrogance has
reached My ears; I shall put My ring in your nose, My bit between your lips,
30 and drag you back along the road you came by. And this will be your sign:[96]
This year you will eat what grows of itself, next year what grows from that, and
in the third year you will sow and harvest, plant vineyards and eat of their
31 fruit. Once more, the remaining survivors of the House of Yehuda will set
32 down roots below, bear fruits above. For a remnant will emerge from
Jerusalem, survivors from Mount Zion; the passion of the LORD of Hosts will
33 bring all this to be. And so, thus says the LORD of the king of Assyria:
He will not enter this city; he will not shoot one arrow there. He will not
34 advance upon her with the shield nor pile up a siege mound against her. The
way he came he will return, but this city he will not enter. The LORD has
35 spoken. And I will protect this city, and deliver her, for My own sake and for
36 My servant, David." An angel of the LORD went out then and struck
down 185,000 in the Assyrian camp; by daybreak the next morning they were
37 all dead bodies. And Sanḥeriv, king of Assyria, departed at once and retreated
38 and settled again in Nineveh. He was worshipping in the temple of his god,
Nisrokh, when his sons Adramelekh and Saretzer put him to the sword.
They fled to the land of Ararat, and his son Esar Ḥadon reigned in his
38 1 place. At that time, Ḥizkiyahu fell deathly ill, and the prophet
Yeshayahu son of Amotz came to him. "Thus says the LORD," he said. "Issue
2 orders for your household, for you are dying; you will not recover." And
3 Ḥizkiyahu turned his face to the wall and prayed to the LORD. "Please, O
LORD," he said, "please remember how I walked before You truly, with all my
heart, and how I did what is right in Your eyes." And Ḥizkiyahu wept bitter
4 tears. And the word of the LORD came to Yeshayahu: "Go and say
5 to Ḥizkiyahu, leader of My people: Thus says the LORD, the God of your

96 | Ḥizkiyahu is now addressed.

כא לְבַדֶּךָ: וַיִּשְׁלַח יְשַׁעְיָהוּ בֶן־אָמוֹץ אֶל־חִזְקִיָּהוּ לֵאמֹר כֹּה־אָמַר יהוה
כב אֱלֹהֵי יִשְׂרָאֵל אֲשֶׁר הִתְפַּלַּלְתָּ אֵלַי אֶל־סַנְחֵרִיב מֶלֶךְ אַשּׁוּר: זֶה
הַדָּבָר אֲשֶׁר־דִּבֶּר יהוה עָלָיו בָּזָה לְךָ לָעֲגָה לְךָ בְּתוּלַת בַּת־צִיּוֹן
כג אַחֲרֶיךָ רֹאשׁ הֵנִיעָה בַּת יְרוּשָׁלָםִ: אֶת־מִי חֵרַפְתָּ וְגִדַּפְתָּ וְעַל־מִי
כד הֲרִימוֹתָה קּוֹל וַתִּשָּׂא מָרוֹם עֵינֶיךָ אֶל־קְדוֹשׁ יִשְׂרָאֵל: בְּיַד עֲבָדֶיךָ
חֵרַפְתָּ ׀ אֲדֹנָי וַתֹּאמֶר בְּרֹב רִכְבִּי אֲנִי עָלִיתִי מְרוֹם הָרִים יַרְכְּתֵי לְבָנוֹן
וְאֶכְרֹת קוֹמַת אֲרָזָיו מִבְחַר בְּרֹשָׁיו וְאָבוֹא מְרוֹם קִצּוֹ יַעַר כַּרְמִלּוֹ:
כה כו אֲנִי קַרְתִּי וְשָׁתִיתִי מָיִם וְאַחְרִב בְּכַף־פְּעָמַי כֹּל יְאֹרֵי מָצוֹר: הֲלוֹא־
שָׁמַעְתָּ לְמֵרָחוֹק אוֹתָהּ עָשִׂיתִי מִימֵי קֶדֶם וִיצַרְתִּיהָ עַתָּה הֲבֵאתִיהָ
כז וּתְהִי לְהַשְׁאוֹת גַּלִּים נִצִּים עָרִים בְּצֻרוֹת: וְיֹשְׁבֵיהֶן קִצְרֵי־יָד חַתּוּ
וָבֹשׁוּ הָיוּ עֵשֶׂב שָׂדֶה וִירַק דֶּשֶׁא חֲצִיר גַּגּוֹת וּשְׁדֵמָה לִפְנֵי קָמָה:
כח כט וְשִׁבְתְּךָ וְצֵאתְךָ וּבוֹאֲךָ יָדָעְתִּי וְאֵת הִתְרַגֶּזְךָ אֵלָי: יַעַן הִתְרַגֶּזְךָ אֵלַי
וְשַׁאֲנַנְךָ עָלָה בְאָזְנָי וְשַׂמְתִּי חַחִי בְּאַפֶּךָ וּמִתְגִּי בִּשְׂפָתֶיךָ וַהֲשִׁיבֹתִיךָ
ל בַּדֶּרֶךְ אֲשֶׁר־בָּאתָ בָּהּ: וְזֶה־לְּךָ הָאוֹת אָכוֹל הַשָּׁנָה סָפִיחַ וּבַשָּׁנָה
הַשֵּׁנִית שָׁחִיס וּבַשָּׁנָה הַשְּׁלִישִׁית זִרְעוּ וְקִצְרוּ וְנִטְעוּ כְרָמִים ואכול וְאִכְלוּ
לא פִּרְיָם: וְיָסְפָה פְּלֵיטַת בֵּית־יְהוּדָה הַנִּשְׁאָרָה שֹׁרֶשׁ לְמָטָּה וְעָשָׂה פְרִי
לב לְמָעְלָה: כִּי מִירוּשָׁלַםִ תֵּצֵא שְׁאֵרִית וּפְלֵיטָה מֵהַר צִיּוֹן קִנְאַת יהוה
לג צְבָאוֹת תַּעֲשֶׂה־זֹּאת: לָכֵן כֹּה־אָמַר יהוה אֶל־מֶלֶךְ אַשּׁוּר
לֹא יָבוֹא אֶל־הָעִיר הַזֹּאת וְלֹא־יוֹרֶה שָׁם חֵץ וְלֹא־יְקַדְּמֶנָּה מָגֵן וְלֹא־
לד יִשְׁפֹּךְ עָלֶיהָ סֹלְלָה: בַּדֶּרֶךְ אֲשֶׁר־בָּא בָּהּ יָשׁוּב וְאֶל־הָעִיר הַזֹּאת לֹא
לה יָבוֹא נְאֻם־יהוה: וְגַנּוֹתִי עַל־הָעִיר הַזֹּאת לְהוֹשִׁיעָהּ לְמַעֲנִי וּלְמַעַן
לו דָּוִד עַבְדִּי: וַיֵּצֵא ׀ מַלְאַךְ יהוה וַיַּכֶּה בְּמַחֲנֵה אַשּׁוּר מֵאָה
לז וּשְׁמֹנִים וַחֲמִשָּׁה אָלֶף וַיַּשְׁכִּימוּ בַבֹּקֶר וְהִנֵּה כֻלָּם פְּגָרִים מֵתִים: וַיִּסַּע
לח וַיֵּלֶךְ וַיָּשָׁב סַנְחֵרִיב מֶלֶךְ־אַשּׁוּר וַיֵּשֶׁב בְּנִינְוֵה: וַיְהִי הוּא מִשְׁתַּחֲוֶה
בֵּית ׀ נִסְרֹךְ אֱלֹהָיו וְאַדְרַמֶּלֶךְ וְשַׂרְאֶצֶר בָּנָיו הִכֻּהוּ בַחֶרֶב וְהֵמָּה
לח א נִמְלְטוּ אֶרֶץ אֲרָרָט וַיִּמְלֹךְ אֵסַר־חַדֹּן בְּנוֹ תַּחְתָּיו: בַּיָּמִים
הָהֵם חָלָה חִזְקִיָּהוּ לָמוּת וַיָּבוֹא אֵלָיו יְשַׁעְיָהוּ בֶן־אָמוֹץ הַנָּבִיא וַיֹּאמֶר
ב אֵלָיו כֹּה־אָמַר יהוה צַו לְבֵיתֶךָ כִּי מֵת אַתָּה וְלֹא תִחְיֶה: וַיַּסֵּב חִזְקִיָּהוּ
ג פָּנָיו אֶל־הַקִּיר וַיִּתְפַּלֵּל אֶל־יהוה: וַיֹּאמַר אָנָּה יהוה זְכָר־נָא אֵת
אֲשֶׁר הִתְהַלַּכְתִּי לְפָנֶיךָ בֶּאֱמֶת וּבְלֵב שָׁלֵם וְהַטּוֹב בְּעֵינֶיךָ עָשִׂיתִי
ד וַיֵּבְךְּ חִזְקִיָּהוּ בְּכִי גָדוֹל: וַיְהִי דְּבַר־יהוה אֶל־יְשַׁעְיָהוּ
ה לֵאמֹר: הָלוֹךְ וְאָמַרְתָּ אֶל־חִזְקִיָּהוּ כֹּה־אָמַר יהוה אֱלֹהֵי דָּוִד אָבִיךָ

ancestor David: I have heard your prayer; I have seen your tears. I will add
6 fifteen years to your life; and I will save you and this city from the hand of the
7 king of Assyria – I will protect this city. This will be a sign for you from the
8 LORD that the LORD will fulfill the promise He made: I shall turn back the
shadow that has fallen on the sundial of Aḥaz by ten steps" – and the sun
9 receded by ten steps on which it had cast its shadow. The inscription
10 of Ḥizkiyahu, king of Yehuda, when he was ill and survived his illness: In the
full blood of my days, I said, I must leave this place, committed to the gates
11 of Sheol for all of my years that remained. I said, I shall not see the LORD, the
LORD in the land of the living; never again will I see a human face, any one
12 of those who live upon this mortal earth. My generation wanders on; they
have moved away from me like a shepherd's tent; I cut off my life like a
13 weaver – cut it off the threads – from day to night You finish me. Until the
dawn it was as though a lion were breaking all my bones; from day to night
14 You will finish me. Like a swift, like a swallow I chirp; like a dove I call. My
15 eyes hang on the heights: Lord, in my oppression, be security to me. What
can I say? He told me it is He who did this. I trudged through all my years
16 with the bitterness of my soul. Lord, this is what a person lives upon, and my
17 life's spirit depends on this; heal me and let me live. Longing for peace, my
life is bitter, bitter; You willed My soul away from destruction and oblivion,
18 throwing all my sins behind Your back, for Sheol does not acknowledge You;
death does not praise You; those who have descended to the pit will not look
19 toward Your faithfulness. The living, the living acknowledge You as I do today;
20 a father of children, he will speak Your truth. The LORD is here to save me;
let us sing these songs of mine all the days of our lives in the House of the
21 LORD. Yeshayahu said, "Let them bring a cake of dried figs and rub it over the
22 boils, and he will recover." But Ḥizkiyahu said, "What is the sign to assure
39 1 me that I shall go up to the House of the LORD?" At that time,
Merodakh Baladan son of Baladan, king of Babylon, sent letters and a gift to
2 Ḥizkiyahu, for he had heard that he had fallen ill and recovered. Ḥizkiyahu
received them joyfully and showed them around his treasure house: the silver
and gold, the spices and fine oil, his armory, and everything that was kept in
his treasuries, in his palace, and all his realm; there was nothing that
3 Ḥizkiyahu did not show them. But the prophet Yeshayahu came to King
Ḥizkiyahu and said to him, "What did these people say, and from where did
they come to you?" "They came to me from a distant land," said Ḥizkiyahu,
4 "from Babylon." "What have they seen in your palace?" he asked. "Why, they
have seen everything in my palace," said Ḥizkiyahu. "There was nothing in
5 my treasuries that I did not show them." "Hear the word of the LORD of Hosts,"
6 Yeshayahu said to Ḥizkiyahu. "Behold – the days are coming when all that
fills your palace and all that your fathers amassed until this day will be borne
7 away to Babylon, and nothing will be left, the LORD has said it, while sons of
yours who came forth from you, who were born to you, will be borne far away,

שָׁמַעְתִּי אֶת־תְּפִלָּתֶךָ רָאִיתִי אֶת־דִּמְעָתֶךָ הִנְנִי יוֹסִף עַל־יָמֶיךָ חֲמֵשׁ
ו עֶשְׂרֵה שָׁנָה: וּמִכַּף מֶלֶךְ־אַשּׁוּר אַצִּילְךָ וְאֵת הָעִיר הַזֹּאת וְגַנּוֹתִי
ז עַל־הָעִיר הַזֹּאת: וְזֶה־לְּךָ הָאוֹת מֵאֵת יהוה אֲשֶׁר יַעֲשֶׂה יהוה אֶת־
ח הַדָּבָר הַזֶּה אֲשֶׁר דִּבֵּר: הִנְנִי מֵשִׁיב אֶת־צֵל הַמַּעֲלוֹת אֲשֶׁר יָרְדָה
בְמַעֲלוֹת אָחָז בַּשֶּׁמֶשׁ אֲחֹרַנִּית עֶשֶׂר מַעֲלוֹת וַתָּשָׁב הַשֶּׁמֶשׁ עֶשֶׂר
ט מַעֲלוֹת בַּמַּעֲלוֹת אֲשֶׁר יָרָדָה: מִכְתָּב לְחִזְקִיָּהוּ מֶלֶךְ־
י יְהוּדָה בַּחֲלֹתוֹ וַיְחִי מֵחָלְיוֹ: אֲנִי אָמַרְתִּי בִּדְמִי יָמַי אֵלֵכָה בְּשַׁעֲרֵי
יא שְׁאוֹל פֻּקַּדְתִּי יֶתֶר שְׁנוֹתָי: אָמַרְתִּי לֹא־אֶרְאֶה יָהּ יָהּ בְּאֶרֶץ הַחַיִּים
יב לֹא־אַבִּיט אָדָם עוֹד עִם־יוֹשְׁבֵי חָדֶל: דּוֹרִי נִסַּע וְנִגְלָה מִנִּי כְּאֹהֶל
יג רֹעִי קִפַּדְתִּי כָאֹרֵג חַיַּי מִדַּלָּה יְבַצְּעֵנִי מִיּוֹם עַד־לַיְלָה תַּשְׁלִימֵנִי: שִׁוִּיתִי
יד עַד־בֹּקֶר כָּאֲרִי כֵּן יְשַׁבֵּר כָּל־עַצְמוֹתָי מִיּוֹם עַד־לַיְלָה תַּשְׁלִימֵנִי: כְּסוּס
עָגוּר כֵּן אֲצַפְצֵף אֶהְגֶּה כַּיּוֹנָה דַּלּוּ עֵינַי לַמָּרוֹם אֲדֹנָי עָשְׁקָה־לִּי עָרְבֵנִי:
טו מָה־אֲדַבֵּר וְאָמַר־לִי וְהוּא עָשָׂה אֶדַּדֶּה כָל־שְׁנוֹתַי עַל־מַר נַפְשִׁי:
טז יז אֲדֹנָי עֲלֵיהֶם יִחְיוּ וּלְכָל־בָּהֶן חַיֵּי רוּחִי וְתַחֲלִימֵנִי וְהַחֲיֵנִי: הִנֵּה לְשָׁלוֹם
מַר־לִי מָר וְאַתָּה חָשַׁקְתָּ נַפְשִׁי מִשַּׁחַת בְּלִי כִּי הִשְׁלַכְתָּ אַחֲרֵי גֵוְךָ
יח כָּל־חֲטָאָי: כִּי לֹא שְׁאוֹל תּוֹדֶךָּ מָוֶת יְהַלְלֶךָּ לֹא־יְשַׂבְּרוּ יוֹרְדֵי־בוֹר
יט אֶל־אֲמִתֶּךָ: חַי חַי הוּא יוֹדֶךָ כָּמוֹנִי הַיּוֹם אָב לְבָנִים יוֹדִיעַ אֶל־אֲמִתֶּךָ:
כ כא יהוה לְהוֹשִׁיעֵנִי וּנְגִנוֹתַי נְנַגֵּן כָּל־יְמֵי חַיֵּינוּ עַל־בֵּית יהוה: וַיֹּאמֶר
כב יְשַׁעְיָהוּ יִשְׂאוּ דְּבֶלֶת תְּאֵנִים וְיִמְרְחוּ עַל־הַשְּׁחִין וְיֶחִי: וַיֹּאמֶר חִזְקִיָּהוּ
לט א מָה אוֹת כִּי אֶעֱלֶה בֵּית יהוה: בָּעֵת הַהִוא שָׁלַח מְרֹדַךְ
בַּלְאֲדָן בֶּן־בַּלְאֲדָן מֶלֶךְ־בָּבֶל סְפָרִים וּמִנְחָה אֶל־חִזְקִיָּהוּ וַיִּשְׁמַע כִּי
ב חָלָה וַיֶּחֱזָק: וַיִּשְׂמַח עֲלֵיהֶם חִזְקִיָּהוּ וַיַּרְאֵם אֶת־בֵּית נְכֹתֹה אֶת־הַכֶּסֶף
וְאֶת־הַזָּהָב וְאֶת־הַבְּשָׂמִים וְאֵת ׀ הַשֶּׁמֶן הַטּוֹב וְאֵת כָּל־בֵּית כֵּלָיו
וְאֵת כָּל־אֲשֶׁר נִמְצָא בְּאוֹצְרֹתָיו לֹא־הָיָה דָבָר אֲשֶׁר לֹא־הֶרְאָם
ג חִזְקִיָּהוּ בְּבֵיתוֹ וּבְכָל־מֶמְשַׁלְתּוֹ: וַיָּבֹא יְשַׁעְיָהוּ הַנָּבִיא אֶל־הַמֶּלֶךְ
חִזְקִיָּהוּ וַיֹּאמֶר אֵלָיו מָה אָמְרוּ ׀ הָאֲנָשִׁים הָאֵלֶּה וּמֵאַיִן יָבֹאוּ אֵלֶיךָ
ד וַיֹּאמֶר חִזְקִיָּהוּ מֵאֶרֶץ רְחוֹקָה בָּאוּ אֵלַי מִבָּבֶל: וַיֹּאמֶר מָה רָאוּ
בְּבֵיתֶךָ וַיֹּאמֶר חִזְקִיָּהוּ אֵת כָּל־אֲשֶׁר בְּבֵיתִי רָאוּ לֹא־הָיָה דָבָר אֲשֶׁר
ה לֹא־הִרְאִיתִים בְּאוֹצְרֹתָי: וַיֹּאמֶר יְשַׁעְיָהוּ אֶל־חִזְקִיָּהוּ שְׁמַע דְּבַר־
ו יהוה צְבָאוֹת: הִנֵּה יָמִים בָּאִים וְנִשָּׂא ׀ כָּל־אֲשֶׁר בְּבֵיתֶךָ וַאֲשֶׁר אָצְרוּ
ז אֲבֹתֶיךָ עַד־הַיּוֹם הַזֶּה בָּבֶל לֹא־יִוָּתֵר דָּבָר אָמַר יהוה: וּמִבָּנֶיךָ
אֲשֶׁר יֵצְאוּ מִמְּךָ אֲשֶׁר תּוֹלִיד יִקָּחוּ וְהָיוּ סָרִיסִים בְּהֵיכַל מֶלֶךְ בָּבֶל:

8 castrated slaves in the palace of the king of Babylon." And Ḥizkiyahu said
to Yeshayahu, "The word of the LORD you have spoken is good." For he
40 1 thought, "Truth and peace will reign in my days." Comfort, comfort,
2 My people – these are your God's words[97] – speak to Jerusalem's heart and
call out to her that her term is served, her guilt appeased, that she has received
3 at the LORD's hand twice over for all her sins. A voice calls out:
"Clear the LORD's way in the desert: smooth across the arid plain a road for
4 our God." Every valley will be raised, each hill and mountain leveled; the
5 twisted road will be made straight; the mountain ranges, open land, to let the
LORD's glory be revealed, and all flesh see as one – the voice of the LORD has
6 spoken. A voice speaks: "Call out!" I say, "What shall I call?" All life
7 is nothing more than grass, and all its love, green shoots upon the land. And
grass dries up; shoots wither, when the LORD's breath blows over them and
8 yes – this people is but grass. Grass dries up, and shoots will wither, but the
9 word of our God stands firm; always. O lady, ascend the high
mountain, you who bear tidings to Zion; raise your voice in strength, with
tidings to Jerusalem. Raise it – do not fear – call out loud to the cities of
10 Yehuda: "Behold: your God." Behold: the LORD your God coming in all His
strength, His mighty arm ruling. Behold: with Him, His prize; His reward
11 walks before Him; like a shepherd He pastures His flock, gathering the lambs
12 into His arms, bearing them in His embrace, guiding His young. Who
was it who measured out the waters in His palm and gauged the skies by His
handspan? Who measured in His fingers all the dust of earth; who weighed
13 out the hills on His balance and the mountains upon a hand scale? Who could
14 survey the wind? The LORD. Who is the confidant He would tell? To gain
His insight, with whom did He hold counsel; who taught Him the path of
justice? Who ever taught Him awareness; who showed Him the way of
15 insight? Whole nations are like the drop left in His bucket, as inconsequential
16 as dust on the balance. He sweeps up the distant isles like powder. All
17 Lebanon has not wood enough, or animals, for the burnt offering. All
the nations are as nothing before Him, less than absence, than emptiness, to
18 19 Him. And what will you liken to God; what image will you draw of Him? A
smith molds a statue; the jeweler plates it with gold and fashions chains of
20 silver for it. Mulberry wood his offering, he chooses a tree that will not rot;
21 he chooses a skilled craftsman to build a statue that cannot fall. Do you not
know it, have you not heard, was it not told to you long before? Have you
22 paid no attention to the world's foundations? He sits over the dome of the
sky, its dwellers like grasshoppers below; He spreads out the skies like a
23 canvas and pulls them taut like a tent to dwell in. He turns great rulers to
24 nothing, the judges of this earth to emptiness, as if they were not planted,
were not sown, as if their stem had no root within the earth. He breathes on
them and they dry up to nothing; the storm will sweep them all away like
25 straw. Whom can you compare Me to – so speaks the Holy

97 | The rest of the book of Isaiah relates to the period of the return to Zion, detailed in Ezra and Nehemiah.

ח וַיֹּאמֶר חִזְקִיָּהוּ אֶל־יְשַׁעְיָהוּ טוֹב דְּבַר־יְהוָה אֲשֶׁר דִּבַּרְתָּ וַיֹּאמֶר כִּי
מ א יִהְיֶה שָׁלוֹם וֶאֱמֶת בְּיָמָי׃ נַחֲמוּ נַחֲמוּ עַמִּי יֹאמַר אֱלֹהֵיכֶם׃ טז
ב דַּבְּרוּ עַל־לֵב יְרוּשָׁלִַם וְקִרְאוּ אֵלֶיהָ כִּי מָלְאָה צְבָאָהּ כִּי נִרְצָה עֲוֺנָהּ
ג כִּי לָקְחָה מִיַּד יְהוָה כִּפְלַיִם בְּכָל־חַטֹּאתֶיהָ׃ קוֹל קוֹרֵא
ד בַּמִּדְבָּר פַּנּוּ דֶּרֶךְ יְהוָה יַשְּׁרוּ בָּעֲרָבָה מְסִלָּה לֵאלֹהֵינוּ׃ כָּל־גֶּיא יִנָּשֵׂא
ה וְכָל־הַר וְגִבְעָה יִשְׁפָּלוּ וְהָיָה הֶעָקֹב לְמִישׁוֹר וְהָרְכָסִים לְבִקְעָה׃ וְנִגְלָה
ו כְּבוֹד יְהוָה וְרָאוּ כָל־בָּשָׂר יַחְדָּו כִּי פִּי יְהוָה דִּבֵּר׃ קוֹל
אֹמֵר קְרָא וְאָמַר מָה אֶקְרָא כָּל־הַבָּשָׂר חָצִיר וְכָל־חַסְדּוֹ כְּצִיץ הַשָּׂדֶה׃
ז ח יָבֵשׁ חָצִיר נָבֵל צִיץ כִּי רוּחַ יְהוָה נָשְׁבָה בּוֹ אָכֵן חָצִיר הָעָם׃ יָבֵשׁ
ט חָצִיר נָבֵל צִיץ וּדְבַר אֱלֹהֵינוּ יָקוּם לְעוֹלָם׃ עַל הַר־גָּבֹהַּ
עֲלִי־לָךְ מְבַשֶּׂרֶת צִיּוֹן הָרִימִי בַכֹּחַ קוֹלֵךְ מְבַשֶּׂרֶת יְרוּשָׁלִָם הָרִימִי
י אַל־תִּירָאִי אִמְרִי לְעָרֵי יְהוּדָה הִנֵּה אֱלֹהֵיכֶם׃ הִנֵּה אֲדֹנָי יְהוִה בְּחָזָק
יא יָבוֹא וּזְרֹעוֹ מֹשְׁלָה לוֹ הִנֵּה שְׂכָרוֹ אִתּוֹ וּפְעֻלָּתוֹ לְפָנָיו׃ כְּרֹעֶה עֶדְרוֹ
יב יִרְעֶה בִּזְרֹעוֹ יְקַבֵּץ טְלָאִים וּבְחֵיקוֹ יִשָּׂא עָלוֹת יְנַהֵל׃ מִי־
מָדַד בְּשָׁעֳלוֹ מַיִם וְשָׁמַיִם בַּזֶּרֶת תִּכֵּן וְכָל בַּשָּׁלִשׁ עֲפַר הָאָרֶץ וְשָׁקַל
יג בַּפֶּלֶס הָרִים וּגְבָעוֹת בְּמֹאזְנָיִם׃ מִי־תִכֵּן אֶת־רוּחַ יְהוָה וְאִישׁ עֲצָתוֹ
יד יוֹדִיעֶנּוּ׃ אֶת־מִי נוֹעָץ וַיְבִינֵהוּ וַיְלַמְּדֵהוּ בְּאֹרַח מִשְׁפָּט וַיְלַמְּדֵהוּ
טו דַעַת וְדֶרֶךְ תְּבוּנוֹת יוֹדִיעֶנּוּ׃ הֵן גּוֹיִם כְּמַר מִדְּלִי וּכְשַׁחַק מֹאזְנַיִם
טז נֶחְשָׁבוּ הֵן אִיִּים כַּדַּק יִטּוֹל׃ וּלְבָנוֹן אֵין דֵּי בָּעֵר וְחַיָּתוֹ אֵין דֵּי
יז יח עוֹלָה׃ כָּל־הַגּוֹיִם כְּאַיִן נֶגְדּוֹ מֵאֶפֶס וָתֹהוּ נֶחְשְׁבוּ־לוֹ׃ וְאֶל־
יט מִי תְּדַמְּיוּן אֵל וּמַה־דְּמוּת תַּעַרְכוּ־לוֹ׃ הַפֶּסֶל נָסַךְ חָרָשׁ וְצֹרֵף בַּזָּהָב
כ יְרַקְּעֶנּוּ וּרְתֻקוֹת כֶּסֶף צוֹרֵף׃ הַמְסֻכָּן תְּרוּמָה עֵץ לֹא־יִרְקַב יִבְחָר חָרָשׁ
כא חָכָם יְבַקֶּשׁ־לוֹ לְהָכִין פֶּסֶל לֹא יִמּוֹט׃ הֲלוֹא תֵדְעוּ הֲלוֹא תִשְׁמָעוּ
כב הֲלוֹא הֻגַּד מֵרֹאשׁ לָכֶם הֲלוֹא הֲבִינֹתֶם מוֹסְדוֹת הָאָרֶץ׃ הַיֹּשֵׁב עַל־
חוּג הָאָרֶץ וְיֹשְׁבֶיהָ כַּחֲגָבִים הַנּוֹטֶה כַדֹּק שָׁמַיִם וַיִּמְתָּחֵם כָּאֹהֶל
כג כד לָשָׁבֶת׃ הַנּוֹתֵן רוֹזְנִים לְאָיִן שֹׁפְטֵי אֶרֶץ כַּתֹּהוּ עָשָׂה׃ אַף בַּל־נִטָּעוּ
אַף בַּל־זֹרָעוּ אַף בַּל־שֹׁרֵשׁ בָּאָרֶץ גִּזְעָם וְגַם־נָשַׁף בָּהֶם וַיִּבָשׁוּ וּסְעָרָה
כה כַּקַּשׁ תִּשָּׂאֵם׃ וְאֶל־מִי תְדַמְּיוּנִי וְאֶשְׁוֶה יֹאמַר קָדוֹשׁ׃

26 One – and find them equal? Raise your eyes skyward and see: Who created
all these? Who summons their legions by number and calls each man by
name? In His great might, His adamantine strength, not one of them is
27 lost. Why do you say, Yaakov; Israel, why declare, "My way is hidden
28 from the LORD; my God overlooks my claim"? Do you not know this; have
you not heard? The LORD is God eternal, Creator of all horizons; He does
29 not weary, does not tire; no one can plumb His understanding. He gives the
30 weary strength, the helpless, power: more and more. Youths will tire, grow
31 weary; young men will falter and fall, but those who wait for the LORD, their
strength will be renewed; they will rise on their wings like eagles, will run
41 1 and never grow weary, will walk on and never grow tired. Hush
before Me, coastlands and nations; renew your strength, and then come
2 forward, speak, draw close; let us come into judgment. Who roused the one
from the east[98] and called victory to his feet? Who herded nations before him,
laid their kings low, and made his swords numerous as dust, his bowshots like
3 chaff in the wind? He pursued them and came through in peace on paths that
4 his feet never walked. Who was it who acted and did this, who called forth
generations long before? I, the LORD, am the first, and I shall be, I, with the
5 last who will be. Coastlands witness this and fear, earth's horizons witness,
6 tremble, draw near, come. *Each man helps his fellow and tells his brother, "Be*
7 *strong." "Strong," says the wright to the goldsmith, the hammerman to him who*
beats. He says of the glue, "This is good," and firms it up with nails, never to
8 *fall.*[99] And you, Israel, My servant, Yaakov whom I chose, children
9 of Avraham who loved Me, whom I lifted and brought from the ends of the
earth, calling you forth from its furthest corners, telling you: You are My
10 servant; You have I chosen, and I will not reject you; do not fear, for I am
with you; do not be afraid: I am your God; I strengthen you and help you,
11 uphold you with My right hand of righteousness. All who rage against you
will be shamed, debased; become like nothing, lost, all those who fight you.
12 Look for them then – you will not find them – the men with whom you are
13 wrestling, adversaries in war, like nothing, like no more. For I am the LORD
your God, holding your right hand, telling you: Do not fear, for I am here: I
14 help you. Yaakov: worm,[100] men of Israel, do not fear; I will help
15 you, so speaks the LORD, the Holy One of Israel, your redeemer. You shall
see: I have made you a slotted threshing board, new and razor edged; you will
16 thresh mountains, turn them to powder, and hills into chaff. As you winnow,
the wind will lift them, and the storm will spread them far; you will rejoice
17 in the LORD and will, through the Holy One of Israel, be praised. The
oppressed, impoverished, beg for water – there is none; their tongues are
seared with thirst. I am the LORD; I will answer them; Israel's God, I will not
18 leave them. Unlocking rivers upon the high mountains and springs in the

98 | Koresh of Persia, who conquered Babylon and allowed the exiles to return to Yehuda.

99 | These verses appear to ridicule those who fashion idols. The message of the passage as a whole is that God alone gives power to kings.

100 | A reflection of Israel's perception of its own weakness.

כו שְׂאוּ־מָרוֹם עֵינֵיכֶם וּרְאוּ מִי־בָרָא אֵלֶּה הַמּוֹצִיא בְמִסְפָּר צְבָאָם לְכֻלָּם
כז בְּשֵׁם יִקְרָא מֵרֹב אוֹנִים וְאַמִּיץ כֹּחַ אִישׁ לֹא נֶעְדָּר׃ לָמָּה
תֹאמַר יַעֲקֹב וּתְדַבֵּר יִשְׂרָאֵל נִסְתְּרָה דַרְכִּי מֵיהוה וּמֵאֱלֹהַי מִשְׁפָּטִי
כח יַעֲבוֹר׃ הֲלוֹא יָדַעְתָּ אִם־לֹא שָׁמַעְתָּ אֱלֹהֵי עוֹלָם ׀ יהוה בּוֹרֵא קְצוֹת
כט הָאָרֶץ לֹא יִיעַף וְלֹא יִיגָע אֵין חֵקֶר לִתְבוּנָתוֹ׃ נֹתֵן לַיָּעֵף כֹּחַ וּלְאֵין
ל לא אוֹנִים עָצְמָה יַרְבֶּה׃ וְיִעֲפוּ נְעָרִים וְיִגָעוּ וּבַחוּרִים כָּשׁוֹל יִכָּשֵׁלוּ׃ וְקוֹיֵ
יהוה יַחֲלִיפוּ כֹחַ יַעֲלוּ אֵבֶר כַּנְּשָׁרִים יָרוּצוּ וְלֹא יִיגָעוּ יֵלְכוּ וְלֹא
מא א יִיעָפוּ׃ הַחֲרִישׁוּ אֵלַי אִיִּים וּלְאֻמִּים יַחֲלִיפוּ כֹחַ יִגְּשׁוּ אָז
ב יְדַבֵּרוּ יַחְדָּו לַמִּשְׁפָּט נִקְרָבָה׃ מִי הֵעִיר מִמִּזְרָח צֶדֶק יִקְרָאֵהוּ לְרַגְלוֹ
ג יִתֵּן לְפָנָיו גּוֹיִם וּמְלָכִים יַרְדְּ יִתֵּן כֶּעָפָר חַרְבּוֹ כְּקַשׁ נִדָּף קַשְׁתּוֹ׃ יִרְדְּפֵם
ד יַעֲבוֹר שָׁלוֹם אֹרַח בְּרַגְלָיו לֹא יָבוֹא׃ מִי־פָעַל וְעָשָׂה קֹרֵא הַדֹּרוֹת
ה מֵרֹאשׁ אֲנִי יהוה רִאשׁוֹן וְאֶת־אַחֲרֹנִים אֲנִי־הוּא׃ רָאוּ אִיִּים וְיִירָאוּ
ו קְצוֹת הָאָרֶץ יֶחֱרָדוּ קָרְבוּ וַיֶּאֱתָיוּן׃ אִישׁ אֶת־רֵעֵהוּ יַעְזֹרוּ וּלְאָחִיו
ז יֹאמַר חֲזָק׃ וַיְחַזֵּק חָרָשׁ אֶת־צֹרֵף מַחֲלִיק פַּטִּישׁ אֶת־הוֹלֶם פָּעַם אֹמֵר
ח לַדֶּבֶק טוֹב הוּא וַיְחַזְּקֵהוּ בְמַסְמְרִים לֹא יִמּוֹט׃ וְאַתָּה
ט יִשְׂרָאֵל עַבְדִּי יַעֲקֹב אֲשֶׁר בְּחַרְתִּיךָ זֶרַע אַבְרָהָם אֹהֲבִי׃ אֲשֶׁר
הֶחֱזַקְתִּיךָ מִקְצוֹת הָאָרֶץ וּמֵאֲצִילֶיהָ קְרָאתִיךָ וָאֹמַר לְךָ עַבְדִּי־אַתָּה
י בְּחַרְתִּיךָ וְלֹא מְאַסְתִּיךָ׃ אַל־תִּירָא כִּי עִמְּךָ־אָנִי אַל־תִּשְׁתָּע כִּי־אֲנִי
יא אֱלֹהֶיךָ אִמַּצְתִּיךָ אַף־עֲזַרְתִּיךָ אַף־תְּמַכְתִּיךָ בִּימִין צִדְקִי׃ הֵן יֵבֹשׁוּ
יב וְיִכָּלְמוּ כֹּל הַנֶּחֱרִים בָּךְ יִהְיוּ כְאַיִן וְיֹאבְדוּ אַנְשֵׁי רִיבֶךָ׃ תְּבַקְשֵׁם וְלֹא
יג תִמְצָאֵם אַנְשֵׁי מַצֻּתֶךָ יִהְיוּ כְאַיִן וּכְאֶפֶס אַנְשֵׁי מִלְחַמְתֶּךָ׃ כִּי אֲנִי יהוה
יד אֱלֹהֶיךָ מַחֲזִיק יְמִינֶךָ הָאֹמֵר לְךָ אַל־תִּירָא אֲנִי עֲזַרְתִּיךָ׃ אַל־
תִּירְאִי תּוֹלַעַת יַעֲקֹב מְתֵי יִשְׂרָאֵל אֲנִי עֲזַרְתִּיךְ נְאֻם־יהוה וְגֹאֲלֵךְ
טו קְדוֹשׁ יִשְׂרָאֵל׃ הִנֵּה שַׂמְתִּיךְ לְמוֹרַג חָרוּץ חָדָשׁ בַּעַל פִּיפִיּוֹת תָּדוּשׁ
טז הָרִים וְתָדֹק וּגְבָעוֹת כַּמֹּץ תָּשִׂים׃ תִּזְרֵם וְרוּחַ תִּשָּׂאֵם וּסְעָרָה תָּפִיץ
יז אוֹתָם וְאַתָּה תָּגִיל בַּיהוה בִּקְדוֹשׁ יִשְׂרָאֵל תִּתְהַלָּל׃ הָעֲנִיִּים
וְהָאֶבְיוֹנִים מְבַקְשִׁים מַיִם וָאַיִן לְשׁוֹנָם בַּצָּמָא נָשָׁתָּה אֲנִי יהוה אֶעֱנֵם
יח אֱלֹהֵי יִשְׂרָאֵל לֹא אֶעֶזְבֵם׃ אֶפְתַּח עַל־שְׁפָיִים נְהָרוֹת וּבְתוֹךְ בְּקָעוֹת

open land, I shall turn the very desert into a lake of water; parched land will
19 bring forth water; I will fill the desert with cedars, acacia trees, with myrtle,
pine, and will plant the arid plain with junipers, with cypress trees and pencil
20 pines together – all this for people to see, to know, to take to heart, growing
aware that the LORD's hand has done all this: this, created by Israel's Holy
21 One. Bring forth your claim, so says the LORD; present your case,
22 says Yaakov's King.[101] Let them lay it out and tell us what is yet to be. The
long-gone past – what happened then? Tell. Let us listen closely and know
23 their future also; let us hear what is to come. Tell over the signs so that we
know that you are gods, know that you bring good and harm; let us tell and
24 confront one another. You come from nowhere; your works are nothing;
25 to choose you would be contemptible. I roused him from the
north – he came; [102] from the place of sunrise he called My name, and he
walks over captains as if they were clay, like the potter tramping, mixing muck.
26 Who said this would happen before; who let us know; who, long ago? We
would declare him victor. But none were there to say, and none to voice, and
27 none to hear your words.[103] I was first to speak to Zion: Here, these things
28 are come; I have sent one to break news to Jerusalem. No man could I see to
29 speak, no counselor among all these to question, that he might answer. I see:
all of them worthless, nothing all their deeds, cold wind and emptiness their
42 1 molten images. My servant, I uphold him, the one I chose, I wanted.
2 I have placed My spirit over him to draw justice out to nations; he will not
3 shout nor raise his voice; in the street he will not be heard;[104] not one crushed
reed will break beneath him, no dimming wick be quelled; he will open
4 out judgment to truth, never himself dimmed or crushed until he has
brought the world justice, and all the distant coastlands quake before his
5 teaching. So says God, the LORD, who created the skies, who
stretched them across and set down the land and all her children, and gave
6 humanity upon her breath, and spirit to those who walk her. I, the LORD, call
you forth in victory, and I will hold your hand; I shall form you and make you
7 a covenant people, make you a light unto nations, to open blinded eyes, to
bring prisoners out of captivity, and those who dwell in darkness from their
8 jail.[105] I am the LORD; this is My name, and I share not My glory with others,
9 My praise with idols. What I said at the beginning: see, it has come, and I tell
you now what will be afresh before it pushes through the earth;[106] you will
10 hear it first from Me. Sing out to the LORD a new song, His praise
from the ends of the earth, You who go to sea, and all that fill it, distant

---

101 | Here God presses His case against other gods, arguing they are powerless and cannot predict the future.

102 | A reference to Koresh.

103 | The opponents did not contest the case; they did not argue against God.

104 | God's servant does not resort to shouted demagoguery. The appellation of God's "servant" can refer to many different characters, such as Koresh here and Israel in 42:18–25.

105 | Koresh claimed to have released the subjects of Babylon from their enslavement.

106 | God predicts the return to Zion before it happens, just as if He had predicted a plant's sprouting while it was still in the ground.

יט מַעְיָנוֹת אָשִׂים מִדְבָּר לַאֲגַם־מַיִם וְאֶרֶץ צִיָּה לְמוֹצָאֵי מָיִם: אֶתֵּן
בַּמִּדְבָּר אֶרֶז שִׁטָּה וַהֲדַס וְעֵץ שָׁמֶן אָשִׂים בָּעֲרָבָה בְּרוֹשׁ תִּדְהָר
כ וּתְאַשּׁוּר יַחְדָּו: לְמַעַן יִרְאוּ וְיֵדְעוּ וְיָשִׂימוּ וְיַשְׂכִּילוּ יַחְדָּו כִּי יַד־יְהוָה
כא עָשְׂתָה זֹּאת וּקְדוֹשׁ יִשְׂרָאֵל בְּרָאָהּ: קָרְבוּ רִיבְכֶם יֹאמַר
כב יְהוָה הַגִּישׁוּ עֲצֻמוֹתֵיכֶם יֹאמַר מֶלֶךְ יַעֲקֹב: יַגִּישׁוּ וְיַגִּידוּ לָנוּ אֵת אֲשֶׁר
תִּקְרֶינָה הָרִאשֹׁנוֹת ׀ מָה הֵנָּה הַגִּידוּ וְנָשִׂימָה לִבֵּנוּ וְנֵדְעָה אַחֲרִיתָן
כג אוֹ הַבָּאוֹת הַשְׁמִיעֻנוּ: הַגִּידוּ הָאֹתִיּוֹת לְאָחוֹר וְנֵדְעָה כִּי אֱלֹהִים אַתֶּם
כד אַף־תֵּיטִיבוּ וְתָרֵעוּ וְנִשְׁתָּעָה וְנִרְא יַחְדָּו: הֵן־אַתֶּם מֵאַיִן וּפָעָלְכֶם
כה מֵאָפַע תּוֹעֵבָה יִבְחַר בָּכֶם: הַעִירוֹתִי מִצָּפוֹן וַיַּאת מִמִּזְרַח־
שֶׁמֶשׁ יִקְרָא בִשְׁמִי וְיָבֹא סְגָנִים כְּמוֹ־חֹמֶר וּכְמוֹ יוֹצֵר יִרְמָס־טִיט:
כו מִי־הִגִּיד מֵרֹאשׁ וְנֵדָעָה וּמִלְּפָנִים וְנֹאמַר צַדִּיק אַף אֵין־מַגִּיד אַף אֵין
כז מַשְׁמִיעַ אַף אֵין־שֹׁמֵעַ אִמְרֵיכֶם: רִאשׁוֹן לְצִיּוֹן הִנֵּה הִנָּם וְלִירוּשָׁלִַם יז
כח מְבַשֵּׂר אֶתֵּן: וְאֵרֶא וְאֵין אִישׁ וּמֵאֵלֶּה וְאֵין יוֹעֵץ וְאֶשְׁאָלֵם וְיָשִׁיבוּ
כט דָבָר: הֵן כֻּלָּם אָוֶן אֶפֶס מַעֲשֵׂיהֶם רוּחַ וָתֹהוּ נִסְכֵּיהֶם: הֵן מב א
עַבְדִּי אֶתְמָךְ־בּוֹ בְּחִירִי רָצְתָה נַפְשִׁי נָתַתִּי רוּחִי עָלָיו מִשְׁפָּט לַגּוֹיִם
ב ג יוֹצִיא: לֹא יִצְעַק וְלֹא יִשָּׂא וְלֹא־יַשְׁמִיעַ בַּחוּץ קוֹלוֹ: קָנֶה רָצוּץ לֹא
ד יִשְׁבּוֹר וּפִשְׁתָּה כֵהָה לֹא יְכַבֶּנָּה לֶאֱמֶת יוֹצִיא מִשְׁפָּט: לֹא יִכְהֶה וְלֹא
ה יָרוּץ עַד־יָשִׂים בָּאָרֶץ מִשְׁפָּט וּלְתוֹרָתוֹ אִיִּים יְיַחֵלוּ: כֹּה־
אָמַר הָאֵל ׀ יְהוָה בּוֹרֵא הַשָּׁמַיִם וְנוֹטֵיהֶם רֹקַע הָאָרֶץ וְצֶאֱצָאֶיהָ נֹתֵן
ו נְשָׁמָה לָעָם עָלֶיהָ וְרוּחַ לַהֹלְכִים בָּהּ: אֲנִי יְהוָה קְרָאתִיךָ בְצֶדֶק וְאַחְזֵק
ז בְּיָדֶךָ וְאֶצָּרְךָ וְאֶתֶּנְךָ לִבְרִית עָם לְאוֹר גּוֹיִם: לִפְקֹחַ עֵינַיִם עִוְרוֹת
ח לְהוֹצִיא מִמַּסְגֵּר אַסִּיר מִבֵּית כֶּלֶא יֹשְׁבֵי חֹשֶׁךְ: אֲנִי יְהוָה הוּא שְׁמִי
ט וּכְבוֹדִי לְאַחֵר לֹא־אֶתֵּן וּתְהִלָּתִי לַפְּסִילִים: הָרִאשֹׁנוֹת הִנֵּה־בָאוּ
י וַחֲדָשׁוֹת אֲנִי מַגִּיד בְּטֶרֶם תִּצְמַחְנָה אַשְׁמִיעַ אֶתְכֶם: שִׁירוּ
לַיהוָה שִׁיר חָדָשׁ תְּהִלָּתוֹ מִקְצֵה הָאָרֶץ יוֹרְדֵי הַיָּם וּמְלֹאוֹ אִיִּים

11 coastlands and you who live there. Desert and its towns, raise your voices,
Kedarites in their scattered camps; those who dwell in the rocks must sing
12 out joy from the mountaintops, shout and give the LORD His glory; His
13 praise will be spoken in the distant coastlands. The LORD sets out like a hero,
rousing His passion like a man of war; He gives the war cry, bellows the war
14 cry, overthrows His enemies. Always I held still and was silent, held
back; I will bellow out like one giving birth, breathing out, breathing in all
15 together, will vanquish hills and mountains and will dry up all the green; I
16 shall turn the rivers into coastlands and desiccate the lakes, and lead the blind
along a way they know not, on paths unknown shall guide them; I shall
turn darkness to light before them, the treacherous road to open highway;
17 these things I will perform, and will not fail. Those who trust in idols will
step back ashamed, those who say to molded statuary, "You – you are our
18 gods." All you deaf ones – listen, and you who are blind – now see.
19 Who is blind if not My servant, who deaf like the messenger I send?[107] Who
could be blind like him – who is devoted, blind like this, the LORD's servant?
20 Many things seen, but you remember not, with open ears, hear nothing. Yet
21 the LORD has desired them, that His righteousness be known, to raise aloft
22 His teachings, to confer majesty. He is with this plundered, this torn-apart
people, who are trapped away in pits, hidden in prison, plunder with none to
23 save them, given over to looters with none to cry, "Give back!" Who among
24 you will listen to this, will hear it and heed for the future? Who was it who
gave Yaakov up for looting, Israel for plunder – was it not the LORD? Him
against whom we sinned; whose ways they cared not to follow, whose Law
25 they did not heed. He poured out the fire of His rage against them, His
terrible warfare, and flames raged all around them, yet they did not know;
43 1 they burned but still they took it not to heart. And now, Yaakov,
so says the LORD, your Creator, the One who formed you, Israel: Do not
2 fear: I redeem you; I name you: you are Mine. Though you pass through
waters – I am with you; through rivers – they will not wash you away. Though
you walk right through the fire, you will not be burned, and no flame will take
3 hold of you, for I am the LORD your God, the Holy One of Israel, your rescuer.
4 I have paid Egypt as your ransom, Kush and Seva in your place.[108] Because
you are valued in My eyes, you are honored. I love you enough to give up
5 other men for you, whole nations in your place. Do not fear, for I am with
you. I will bring your children from the east, will gather you back from the
6 west. To the north I will say, "Give over"; to the south, "Imprison no more."
Bring My sons from far away, My daughters back from the ends of the earth,
7 all the people I called by My name, created for My glory; I formed them, I
8 made them. He brought out a people – blind though they have eyes, deaf

107 | In verse 18, God addresses the people and accuses them of being deaf and blind, unable to realize that God is sending Koresh to return them to Zion. In verse 19, the people respond: they think it is not they but the prophet who is blind.

108 | Three kingdoms along the Nile are here said to be given by God to the king of Persia in return for releasing Israel.

יא וְיֹשְׁבֵיהֶם׃ יִשְׂאוּ מִדְבָּר וְעָרָיו חֲצֵרִים תֵּשֵׁב קֵדָר יָרֹנּוּ יֹשְׁבֵי סֶלַע
יב יג מֵרֹאשׁ הָרִים יִצְוָחוּ׃ יָשִׂימוּ לַיהוָה כָּבוֹד וּתְהִלָּתוֹ בָּאִיִּים יַגִּידוּ׃ יְהוָה
כַּגִּבּוֹר יֵצֵא כְּאִישׁ מִלְחָמוֹת יָעִיר קִנְאָה יָרִיעַ אַף־יַצְרִיחַ עַל־אֹיְבָיו
יד יִתְגַּבָּר׃ הֶחֱשֵׁיתִי מֵעוֹלָם אַחֲרִישׁ אֶתְאַפָּק כַּיּוֹלֵדָה אֶפְעֶה
טו אֶשֹּׁם וְאֶשְׁאַף יָחַד׃ אַחֲרִיב הָרִים וּגְבָעוֹת וְכָל־עֶשְׂבָּם אוֹבִישׁ וְשַׂמְתִּי
טז נְהָרוֹת לָאִיִּים וַאֲגַמִּים אוֹבִישׁ׃ וְהוֹלַכְתִּי עִוְרִים בְּדֶרֶךְ לֹא יָדָעוּ
בִּנְתִיבוֹת לֹא־יָדְעוּ אַדְרִיכֵם אָשִׂים מַחְשָׁךְ לִפְנֵיהֶם לָאוֹר וּמַעֲקַשִּׁים
יז לְמִישׁוֹר אֵלֶּה הַדְּבָרִים עֲשִׂיתִם וְלֹא עֲזַבְתִּים׃ נָסֹגוּ אָחוֹר יֵבֹשׁוּ בֹשֶׁת
יח הַבֹּטְחִים בַּפָּסֶל הָאֹמְרִים לְמַסֵּכָה אַתֶּם אֱלֹהֵינוּ׃ הַחֵרְשִׁים
יט שְׁמָעוּ וְהַעִוְרִים הַבִּיטוּ לִרְאוֹת׃ מִי עִוֵּר כִּי אִם־עַבְדִּי וְחֵרֵשׁ כְּמַלְאָכִי
כ אֶשְׁלָח מִי עִוֵּר כִּמְשֻׁלָּם וְעִוֵּר כְּעֶבֶד יְהוָה׃ ראית רַבּוֹת וְלֹא תִשְׁמֹר רָאוֹת
כא פָּקוֹחַ אָזְנַיִם וְלֹא יִשְׁמָע׃ יְהוָה חָפֵץ לְמַעַן צִדְקוֹ יַגְדִּיל תּוֹרָה וְיַאְדִּיר׃
כב וְהוּא עַם־בָּזוּז וְשָׁסוּי הָפֵחַ בַּחוּרִים כֻּלָּם וּבְבָתֵּי כְלָאִים הָחְבָּאוּ הָיוּ
כג לָבַז וְאֵין מַצִּיל מְשִׁסָּה וְאֵין־אֹמֵר הָשַׁב׃ מִי בָכֶם יַאֲזִין זֹאת יַקְשִׁב
כד וְיִשְׁמַע לְאָחוֹר׃ מִי־נָתַן למשוסה יַעֲקֹב וְיִשְׂרָאֵל לְבֹזְזִים הֲלוֹא יְהוָה לִמְשִׁסָּה
כה זוּ חָטָאנוּ לוֹ וְלֹא־אָבוּ בִדְרָכָיו הָלוֹךְ וְלֹא שָׁמְעוּ בְּתוֹרָתוֹ׃ וַיִּשְׁפֹּךְ
עָלָיו חֵמָה אַפּוֹ וֶעֱזוּז מִלְחָמָה וַתְּלַהֲטֵהוּ מִסָּבִיב וְלֹא יָדָע וַתִּבְעַר־בּוֹ
מג א וְלֹא־יָשִׂים עַל־לֵב׃ וְעַתָּה כֹּה־אָמַר יְהוָה בֹּרַאֲךָ
יַעֲקֹב וְיֹצֶרְךָ יִשְׂרָאֵל אַל־תִּירָא כִּי גְאַלְתִּיךָ קָרָאתִי בְשִׁמְךָ לִי־אָתָּה׃
ב כִּי־תַעֲבֹר בַּמַּיִם אִתְּךָ אָנִי וּבַנְּהָרוֹת לֹא יִשְׁטְפוּךָ כִּי־תֵלֵךְ בְּמוֹ־
ג אֵשׁ לֹא תִכָּוֶה וְלֶהָבָה לֹא תִבְעַר־בָּךְ׃ כִּי אֲנִי יְהוָה אֱלֹהֶיךָ קְדוֹשׁ
ד יִשְׂרָאֵל מוֹשִׁיעֶךָ נָתַתִּי כָפְרְךָ מִצְרַיִם כּוּשׁ וּסְבָא תַּחְתֶּיךָ׃ מֵאֲשֶׁר
יָקַרְתָּ בְעֵינַי נִכְבַּדְתָּ וַאֲנִי אֲהַבְתִּיךָ וְאֶתֵּן אָדָם תַּחְתֶּיךָ וּלְאֻמִּים
ה תַּחַת נַפְשֶׁךָ׃ אַל־תִּירָא כִּי אִתְּךָ־אָנִי מִמִּזְרָח אָבִיא זַרְעֶךָ
ו וּמִמַּעֲרָב אֲקַבְּצֶךָּ׃ אֹמַר לַצָּפוֹן תֵּנִי וּלְתֵימָן אַל־תִּכְלָאִי הָבִיאִי בָנַי
ז מֵרָחוֹק וּבְנוֹתַי מִקְצֵה הָאָרֶץ׃ כֹּל הַנִּקְרָא בִשְׁמִי וְלִכְבוֹדִי בְּרָאתִיו
ח יְצַרְתִּיו אַף־עֲשִׂיתִיו׃ הוֹצִיא עַם־עִוֵּר וְעֵינַיִם יֵשׁ וְחֵרְשִׁים וְאָזְנַיִם לָמוֹ׃

9 though they have ears.[109] Were all the nations to gather, the peoples to come
into session, who of them could tell of this? Who could speak of this before?
Let them bring their witnesses to vindicate them, so that hearers may say,
10 "This is truth." No – you are My witnesses, so says the LORD, My servants
whom I chose, so that you should know, and trust in Me and understand that
11 I am He; before Me, no god was made, and after Me – no other. I, I
12 am the LORD; aside from Me there is no rescue; I spoke, and I rescued; I gave
voice; no stranger stood among you; you are My witnesses, so says the LORD,
13 and I am God. And still from this day onward, I am He, and from My hands
14 there is no rescue; I act, and what I do, who, who can undo? So says
the LORD, your redeemer, the Holy One of Israel: for Your sake I sent one[110]
to Babylon; I will bring down all their bars and the Chaldeans in the ships of
15 16 their joy. I am the LORD, your Holy One, Creator of Israel, King. So
says the LORD, who forges a way through the ocean, who sets a path through
17 raging waters, who destroys mighty horse and chariot of war, to make them
18 lie down never to rise; they died down like a flaxen wick, snuffed out. Do not
19 remember the earliest things nor look upon the beginnings, for I am making
something new; even now it grows, and will you not know it? I shall make a
20 way through desert land and rivers across the wilderness; wild beasts will
glorify Me, jackals and ostriches, for I have given the desert water and rivers
21 in the wilderness to give My people, My chosen one, to drink, the people I
22 have formed for Me, who are to tell My praises. It is not Me you call for,
23 Yaakov; Israel, you wearied of Me. You did not bring Me the lamb of your
offering; it was not Me your sacrifice honored; I did not enslave you to My
24 gifts or weary you with frankincense. You did not pay silver for calamus[111] for
Me or slake My thirst with fat of the sacrifice, yet you enslaved Me to your
25 iniquity and wearied Me with your sins. I am I, who expunge your offenses
26 for My own sake and will not keep your sins in mind. Recall Me now; let us
27 argue this out; tell Me so that you may be vindicated. Your first father sinned,
28 and those who spoke for you rebelled against Me, so I desecrated your
Sanctuary's ministers and marked you for destruction, Yaakov; Israel, to be
44 1 denounced. And now listen, Yaakov My servant, Israel whom I
2 chose; so says the LORD who made you, the One who made you in the womb,
who helps you: Do not fear, My servant Yaakov, Yeshurun[112] whom I chose.
3 As I pour water on thirsty earth, water upon parched land, I shall pour forth
4 My spirit upon your children, upon your offspring My blessing. They will
5 sprout among the grasses, like willows on streams of water, and a man will
say, "I am the LORD's," while another invokes the name of Yaakov, and a third
6 one will inscribe on his hand, "The LORD's," to name himself Israel. So
says the LORD, King of Israel, its rescue, the LORD of Hosts: I am the first and
7 I the last; beside Me is no God. Who like Me calls the future forth and tells
it? Let them lay their claim before Me. I have formed an eternal people, so let

---

109 | See 42:18.

110 | That is, Koresh.

111 | An element in the incense offering.

112 | An appellation for Israel; see, e.g., Numbers 23:10.

ט כָּל־הַגּוֹיִם נִקְבְּצוּ יַחְדָּו וְיֵאָסְפוּ לְאֻמִּים מִי בָהֶם יַגִּיד זֹאת וְרִאשֹׁנוֹת
י יַשְׁמִיעֻנוּ יִתְּנוּ עֵדֵיהֶם וְיִצְדָּקוּ וְיִשְׁמְעוּ וְיֹאמְרוּ אֱמֶת׃ אַתֶּם עֵדַי
נְאֻם־יְהוָה וְעַבְדִּי אֲשֶׁר בָּחָרְתִּי לְמַעַן תֵּדְעוּ וְתַאֲמִינוּ לִי וְתָבִינוּ כִּי־
יא אֲנִי הוּא לְפָנַי לֹא־נוֹצַר אֵל וְאַחֲרַי לֹא יִהְיֶה׃ אָנֹכִי אָנֹכִי
יב יְהוָה וְאֵין מִבַּלְעָדַי מוֹשִׁיעַ׃ אָנֹכִי הִגַּדְתִּי וְהוֹשַׁעְתִּי וְהִשְׁמַעְתִּי וְאֵין
יג בָּכֶם זָר וְאַתֶּם עֵדַי נְאֻם־יְהוָה וַאֲנִי־אֵל׃ גַּם־מִיּוֹם אֲנִי הוּא וְאֵין מִיָּדִי
יד מַצִּיל אֶפְעַל וּמִי יְשִׁיבֶנָּה׃ כֹּה־אָמַר יְהוָה גֹּאַלְכֶם קְדוֹשׁ
יִשְׂרָאֵל לְמַעַנְכֶם שִׁלַּחְתִּי בָבֶלָה וְהוֹרַדְתִּי בָרִיחִים כֻּלָּם וְכַשְׂדִּים
טו טז בָּאֳנִיּוֹת רִנָּתָם׃ אֲנִי יְהוָה קְדוֹשְׁכֶם בּוֹרֵא יִשְׂרָאֵל מַלְכְּכֶם׃ כֹּה
יז אָמַר יְהוָה הַנּוֹתֵן בַּיָּם דָּרֶךְ וּבְמַיִם עַזִּים נְתִיבָה׃ הַמּוֹצִיא רֶכֶב־וָסוּס
יח חַיִל וְעִזּוּז יַחְדָּו יִשְׁכְּבוּ בַּל־יָקוּמוּ דָּעֲכוּ כַּפִּשְׁתָּה כָבוּ׃ אַל־תִּזְכְּרוּ
יט רִאשֹׁנוֹת וְקַדְמֹנִיּוֹת אַל־תִּתְבֹּנָנוּ׃ הִנְנִי עֹשֶׂה חֲדָשָׁה עַתָּה תִצְמָח
כ הֲלוֹא תֵדָעוּהָ אַף אָשִׂים בַּמִּדְבָּר דֶּרֶךְ בִּישִׁמֹן נְהָרוֹת׃ תְּכַבְּדֵנִי חַיַּת
הַשָּׂדֶה תַּנִּים וּבְנוֹת יַעֲנָה כִּי־נָתַתִּי בַמִּדְבָּר מַיִם נְהָרוֹת בִּישִׁימֹן
כא כב לְהַשְׁקוֹת עַמִּי בְחִירִי׃ עַם־זוּ יָצַרְתִּי לִי תְּהִלָּתִי יְסַפֵּרוּ׃ וְלֹא־אֹתִי
כג קָרָאתָ יַעֲקֹב כִּי־יָגַעְתָּ בִּי יִשְׂרָאֵל׃ לֹא־הֵבֵיאתָ לִּי שֵׂה עֹלֹתֶיךָ וּזְבָחֶיךָ
כד לֹא כִבַּדְתָּנִי לֹא הֶעֱבַדְתִּיךָ בְּמִנְחָה וְלֹא הוֹגַעְתִּיךָ בִּלְבוֹנָה׃ לֹא־קָנִיתָ
לִּי בַכֶּסֶף קָנֶה וְחֵלֶב זְבָחֶיךָ לֹא הִרְוִיתָנִי אַךְ הֶעֱבַדְתַּנִי בְּחַטֹּאותֶיךָ
כה הוֹגַעְתַּנִי בַּעֲוֺנֹתֶיךָ׃ אָנֹכִי אָנֹכִי הוּא מֹחֶה פְשָׁעֶיךָ לְמַעֲנִי וְחַטֹּאתֶיךָ
כו כז לֹא אֶזְכֹּר׃ הַזְכִּירֵנִי נִשָּׁפְטָה יָחַד סַפֵּר אַתָּה לְמַעַן תִּצְדָּק׃ אָבִיךָ
כח הָרִאשׁוֹן חָטָא וּמְלִיצֶיךָ פָּשְׁעוּ בִי׃ וַאֲחַלֵּל שָׂרֵי קֹדֶשׁ וְאֶתְּנָה לַחֵרֶם
מד א יַעֲקֹב וְיִשְׂרָאֵל לְגִדּוּפִים׃ וְעַתָּה שְׁמַע יַעֲקֹב עַבְדִּי
ב וְיִשְׂרָאֵל בָּחַרְתִּי בוֹ׃ כֹּה־אָמַר יְהוָה עֹשֶׂךָ וְיֹצֶרְךָ מִבֶּטֶן יַעְזְרֶךָּ אַל־
ג תִּירָא עַבְדִּי יַעֲקֹב וִישֻׁרוּן בָּחַרְתִּי בוֹ׃ כִּי אֶצָּק־מַיִם עַל־צָמֵא וְנֹזְלִים
ד עַל־יַבָּשָׁה אֶצֹּק רוּחִי עַל־זַרְעֶךָ וּבִרְכָתִי עַל־צֶאֱצָאֶיךָ׃ וְצָמְחוּ בְּבֵין
ה חָצִיר כַּעֲרָבִים עַל־יִבְלֵי־מָיִם׃ זֶה יֹאמַר לַיהוָה אָנִי וְזֶה יִקְרָא בְשֵׁם־
ו יַעֲקֹב וְזֶה יִכְתֹּב יָדוֹ לַיהוָה וּבְשֵׁם יִשְׂרָאֵל יְכַנֶּה׃ כֹּה־אָמַר יח
יְהוָה מֶלֶךְ־יִשְׂרָאֵל וְגֹאֲלוֹ יְהוָה צְבָאוֹת אֲנִי רִאשׁוֹן וַאֲנִי אַחֲרוֹן
ז וּמִבַּלְעָדַי אֵין אֱלֹהִים׃ וּמִי־כָמוֹנִי יִקְרָא וְיַגִּידֶהָ וְיַעְרְכֶהָ לִי מִשּׂוּמִי

8 them bring out signs and tell what is to come. Do not fear, do not lose faith;
have I not let you hear this from the start? I told it, and you are My witnesses:
9 Is there any God but Me? There is no rock I do not know. All those makers
of images – all emptiness, their gorgeous objects useless, and all their
10 witnesses see nothing and know not and are shamed. Who has made a god
11 and molded an idol to bring him no good? All his company will be shamed;
craftsmen – they are human; let them come together, all, and stand and fear
12 and feel their shame together, for the craftsman in iron makes a chisel, works
it over the coals and forms it with hammers, works it with his arms' strength,
grows hungry and has no strength, fails to drink water until he grows faint.
13 The carpenter stretches out his line and marks it with a thread; he forms it
with his planes and marks it with a compass. He is making it into the form of
14 a man, a supreme human frame, to sit in a house. He cuts down cedars for his
work or chooses a cypress or oak and sees it grow strong in the forest, plants
15 a bay laurel and lets rain nourish it to grow. These become firewood for a man;
he takes them and warms himself, kindles them and bakes bread, and works
16 the rest into a god, and worships a statue and prostrates himself before it. Half
of it he burns in the fire; thanks to that half he eats meat, roasts the roast, feels
17 fullness, warms himself, says, "Ah – I am warmed; I have seen the flames." And
with what is left over, he makes a god, a statue to prostrate himself in front of
18 and to worship, pray to, say, "Save me, please: you are my god." They know
not; they do not comprehend, for their eyes are smeared over, not to see, not
19 to let understanding into their hearts, so they do not take it to heart, nor find
mind or wisdom to say, "I burned half in the fire; I baked bread on the coals;
I roasted meat and ate it; with the rest should I make this disgusting thing,
20 this slab of wood, and bow down?" He courts ashes; his deceived heart has
misled him; he cannot save himself; he cannot say, "This in my right hand – it
21 is a lie." Hold these things in mind, Yaakov, Israel, for you are My
22 servant. I made you – you are My servant; do not forget Me, Israel. I dispelled
your offenses like mist, like a cloud all your sins – come back to Me, for I have
23 redeemed you. Sing out, heavens, for the LORD has acted. Sound the trumpets,
lowest depths of earth; hills, break out in song, and forests, all their trees, for
24 the LORD has redeemed Yaakov; in Israel is He glorified. For so says
the LORD, your redeemer, the One who formed you in the womb: "I the LORD
am Maker of all, stretching out the heavens alone, firming the earth with My
25 own power. It is I who unravels the necromancers' signs, who turns the
sorcerers mad, who turns the wise men back, confounding their knowledge.
26 It is I who bring My servants' words to be, My messengers' plans to be fulfilled,
who tells Jerusalem: Let her be settled, and the cities of Yehuda: Let them be
27 built up; I shall raise up all her ruins; I who say to the deeps: be arid; I shall
28 dry up your rivers; who says of Koresh: he is My shepherd, fulfilling all My
will, that he should tell Jerusalem, 'She shall be built,' and the Sanctuary, 'Let
45 1 her be founded.'" Thus says the LORD to His anointed one, to
Koresh, into whose right hand I invested strength to subjugate nations before

ח עַם־עוֹלָם וְאֹתִיּוֹת וַאֲשֶׁר תָּבֹאנָה יַגִּידוּ לָמוֹ׃ אַל־תִּפְחֲדוּ וְאַל־תִּרְהוּ
הֲלֹא מֵאָז הִשְׁמַעְתִּיךָ וְהִגַּדְתִּי וְאַתֶּם עֵדָי הֲיֵשׁ אֱלוֹהַּ מִבַּלְעָדַי וְאֵין
ט צוּר בַּל־יָדָעְתִּי׃ יֹצְרֵי־פֶסֶל כֻּלָּם תֹּהוּ וַחֲמוּדֵיהֶם בַּל־יוֹעִילוּ וְעֵדֵיהֶם
י הֵמָּה בַּל־יִרְאוּ וּבַל־יֵדְעוּ לְמַעַן יֵבֹשׁוּ׃ מִי־יָצַר אֵל וּפֶסֶל נָסָךְ לְבִלְתִּי
יא הוֹעִיל׃ הֵן כָּל־חֲבֵרָיו יֵבֹשׁוּ וְחָרָשִׁים הֵמָּה מֵאָדָם יִתְקַבְּצוּ כֻלָּם יַעֲמֹדוּ
יב יִפְחֲדוּ יֵבֹשׁוּ יָחַד׃ חָרַשׁ בַּרְזֶל מַעֲצָד וּפָעַל בַּפֶּחָם וּבַמַּקָּבוֹת יִצְּרֵהוּ
יג וַיִּפְעָלֵהוּ בִּזְרוֹעַ כֹּחוֹ גַּם־רָעֵב וְאֵין כֹּחַ לֹא־שָׁתָה מַיִם וַיִּיעָף׃ חָרַשׁ
עֵצִים נָטָה קָו יְתָאֲרֵהוּ בַשֶּׂרֶד יַעֲשֵׂהוּ בַּמַּקְצֻעוֹת וּבַמְּחוּגָה יְתָאֳרֵהוּ
יד וַיַּעֲשֵׂהוּ כְּתַבְנִית אִישׁ כְּתִפְאֶרֶת אָדָם לָשֶׁבֶת בָּיִת׃ לִכְרָת־לוֹ אֲרָזִים
טו וַיִּקַּח תִּרְזָה וְאַלּוֹן וַיְאַמֶּץ־לוֹ בַּעֲצֵי־יָעַר נָטַע אֹרֶן וְגֶשֶׁם יְגַדֵּל׃ וְהָיָה
לְאָדָם לְבָעֵר וַיִּקַּח מֵהֶם וַיָּחָם אַף־יַשִּׂיק וְאָפָה לָחֶם אַף־יִפְעַל־אֵל
טז וַיִּשְׁתָּחוּ עָשָׂהוּ פֶסֶל וַיִּסְגָּד־לָמוֹ׃ חֶצְיוֹ שָׂרַף בְּמוֹ־אֵשׁ עַל־חֶצְיוֹ בָּשָׂר
יֹאכֵל יִצְלֶה צָלִי וְיִשְׂבָּע אַף־יָחֹם וְיֹאמַר הֶאָח חַמּוֹתִי רָאִיתִי אוּר׃
יז וּשְׁאֵרִיתוֹ לְאֵל עָשָׂה לְפִסְלוֹ יסגוד־לוֹ וְיִשְׁתַּחוּ וְיִתְפַּלֵּל אֵלָיו וְיֹאמַר יִסְגָּד־
יח הַצִּילֵנִי כִּי אֵלִי אָתָּה׃ לֹא יָדְעוּ וְלֹא יָבִינוּ כִּי טַח מֵרְאוֹת עֵינֵיהֶם
יט מֵהַשְׂכִּיל לִבֹּתָם׃ וְלֹא־יָשִׁיב אֶל־לִבּוֹ וְלֹא דַעַת וְלֹא־תְבוּנָה לֵאמֹר
חֶצְיוֹ שָׂרַפְתִּי בְמוֹ־אֵשׁ וְאַף אָפִיתִי עַל־גֶּחָלָיו לֶחֶם אֶצְלֶה בָשָׂר וְאֹכֵל
כ וְיִתְרוֹ לְתוֹעֵבָה אֶעֱשֶׂה לְבוּל עֵץ אֶסְגּוֹד׃ רֹעֶה אֵפֶר לֵב הוּתַל הִטָּהוּ
כא וְלֹא־יַצִּיל אֶת־נַפְשׁוֹ וְלֹא יֹאמַר הֲלוֹא שֶׁקֶר בִּימִינִי׃ זְכָר־
אֵלֶּה יַעֲקֹב וְיִשְׂרָאֵל כִּי עַבְדִּי־אָתָּה יְצַרְתִּיךָ עֶבֶד־לִי אַתָּה יִשְׂרָאֵל
כב לֹא תִנָּשֵׁנִי׃ מָחִיתִי כָעָב פְּשָׁעֶיךָ וְכֶעָנָן חַטֹּאותֶיךָ שׁוּבָה אֵלַי כִּי
כג גְאַלְתִּיךָ׃ רָנּוּ שָׁמַיִם כִּי־עָשָׂה יהוה הָרִיעוּ תַּחְתִּיּוֹת אָרֶץ פִּצְחוּ
הָרִים רִנָּה יַעַר וְכָל־עֵץ בּוֹ כִּי־גָאַל יהוה יַעֲקֹב וּבְיִשְׂרָאֵל
כד יִתְפָּאָר׃ כֹּה־אָמַר יהוה גֹּאֲלֶךָ וְיֹצֶרְךָ מִבָּטֶן אָנֹכִי יהוה
כה עֹשֶׂה כֹּל נֹטֶה שָׁמַיִם לְבַדִּי רֹקַע הָאָרֶץ מי אתי׃ מֵפֵר אֹתוֹת בַּדִּים מֵאִתִּי
כו וְקֹסְמִים יְהוֹלֵל מֵשִׁיב חֲכָמִים אָחוֹר וְדַעְתָּם יְסַכֵּל׃ מֵקִים דְּבַר עַבְדּוֹ
וַעֲצַת מַלְאָכָיו יַשְׁלִים הָאֹמֵר לִירוּשָׁלִַם תּוּשָׁב וּלְעָרֵי יְהוּדָה תִּבָּנֶינָה
כז כח וְחָרְבוֹתֶיהָ אֲקוֹמֵם׃ הָאֹמֵר לַצּוּלָה חֳרָבִי וְנַהֲרֹתַיִךְ אוֹבִישׁ׃ הָאֹמֵר
לְכוֹרֶשׁ רֹעִי וְכָל־חֶפְצִי יַשְׁלִם וְלֵאמֹר לִירוּשָׁלִַם תִּבָּנֶה וְהֵיכָל
מה א תִּוָּסֵד׃ כֹּה־אָמַר יהוה לִמְשִׁיחוֹ לְכוֹרֶשׁ אֲשֶׁר־הֶחֱזַקְתִּי
בִימִינוֹ לְרַד־לְפָנָיו גּוֹיִם וּמָתְנֵי מְלָכִים אֲפַתֵּחַ לִפְתֹּחַ לְפָנָיו דְּלָתַיִם

him, and I shall loosen the girdles of kings[113] to unlock doors before him, open
2 city gates, never to be closed: I walk before you; I will level out mountain
3 lands; I will break through doors of bronze and cut down iron bars. I give to
you treasures of darkness, buried hoards in hidden places, for you to know
4 that it is I the LORD who calls your name – I, the God of Israel – all for My
servant Yaakov, for Israel, My chosen. For them I call you by your name and
5 give you your title though you know Me not. I am the LORD – there is no
other, no gods aside from Me – and I gird you though you do not know Me
6 so that they all should know, from the east of the sun's rising to the west of its
7 dusk, that there is none but I: I am the LORD; there is no other, forming light,
creating darkness, making peace, creating evil; I, the LORD, make all of
8 these. Skies above, form drops, and let the heavens rain down victory.
Land, open; let triumph bear her fruit; let vindication flourish, for I, the LORD,
9 created this. Woe to one who fights his Maker – for this potsherd
among shards upon the earth. Does clay ask its maker, "What would you now
10 do? This work of yours lacks handles"? Woe to one who asks a father,
"Why did you conceive?" Who asks a woman, "What then did you labor so
11 to birth?" Thus says the LORD, the Holy One of Israel, its Maker:
Would you ask Me for the signs; would you command Me about My children,
12 about My own hands' work? I made the earth, and I created mankind on it. I,
13 My hands, stretched out the skies, commanded all their armies forth. I roused
him[114] for victory and will smooth out all his paths. He will build My city; he
will send My exile forth, not for silver, not for pay: so speaks the LORD of
14 Hosts. Thus says the LORD: The fruits of Egypt's labor, the wares of
Kush, and Sabeans,[115] lofty men, will come to join you, will be yours and
follow you, pass across in chains and pray through you: "It is you that God
15 resides in; there are no more gods, none. You are, indeed, a hidden God, God
16 of Israel, rescuer." They are all shamed, debased, walking together debased,
17 all who crafted images. Israel's rescue is in the LORD, rescue everlasting. They
18 will not be shamed, will never be debased to the end of time. For
thus says the LORD, God, who created the skies, who formed the earth, forged
it, sets its foundation; He did not create it for emptiness; He formed it for life:
19 I am the LORD – there is no other. I did not speak in hiding somewhere away
in a land of darkness; I did not say to the seed of Yaakov, "Seek Me amid
20 emptiness." I am the LORD – I tell of justice, speak clear truth. Gather together,
come, draw near together, survivors of nations. They have no knowledge, they
21 who bear the wood of images and pray to a god who affords no rescue. Speak,
bring your case and make your plans together. Who spoke of this long ago;
who told it from the beginning? Was it not I, the LORD? There is no other
22 god but Me – righteous God, rescue, and there is none beside Me. Turn to
23 Me; be saved from all ends of the earth, for I am God; there is no other. By
My own self I swore; justice issued from My lips, and not one word will be

113 | Weaken and hinder them before Koresh.
114 | Koresh.
115 | Cf. 43:3.

ב וּשְׁעָרִים לֹא יִסָּגֵרוּ: אֲנִי לְפָנֶיךָ אֵלֵךְ וַהֲדוּרִים אושר דַּלְתוֹת נְחוּשָׁה אֲיַשֵּׁר
ג אֲשַׁבֵּר וּבְרִיחֵי בַרְזֶל אֲגַדֵּעַ: וְנָתַתִּי לְךָ אוֹצְרוֹת חֹשֶׁךְ וּמַטְמֻנֵי
מִסְתָּרִים לְמַעַן תֵּדַע כִּי אֲנִי יהוה הַקּוֹרֵא בְשִׁמְךָ אֱלֹהֵי יִשְׂרָאֵל:
ד לְמַעַן עַבְדִּי יַעֲקֹב וְיִשְׂרָאֵל בְּחִירִי וָאֶקְרָא לְךָ בִּשְׁמֶךָ אֲכַנְּךָ וְלֹא
ה יְדַעְתָּנִי: אֲנִי יהוה וְאֵין עוֹד זוּלָתִי אֵין אֱלֹהִים אֲאַזֶּרְךָ וְלֹא יְדַעְתָּנִי:
ו לְמַעַן יֵדְעוּ מִמִּזְרַח־שֶׁמֶשׁ וּמִמַּעֲרָבָה כִּי־אֶפֶס בִּלְעָדָי אֲנִי יהוה וְאֵין
ז עוֹד: יוֹצֵר אוֹר וּבוֹרֵא חֹשֶׁךְ עֹשֶׂה שָׁלוֹם וּבוֹרֵא רָע אֲנִי יהוה עֹשֶׂה
ח כָל־אֵלֶּה: הַרְעִיפוּ שָׁמַיִם מִמַּעַל וּשְׁחָקִים יִזְּלוּ־
צֶדֶק תִּפְתַּח־אֶרֶץ וְיִפְרוּ־יֶשַׁע וּצְדָקָה תַצְמִיחַ יַחַד אֲנִי יהוה
ט בְּרָאתִיו: הוֹי רָב אֶת־יֹצְרוֹ חֶרֶשׂ אֶת־חַרְשֵׂי אֲדָמָה
י הֲיֹאמַר חֹמֶר לְיֹצְרוֹ מַה־תַּעֲשֶׂה וּפָעָלְךָ אֵין־יָדַיִם לוֹ: הוֹי
יא אֹמֵר לְאָב מַה־תּוֹלִיד וּלְאִשָּׁה מַה־תְּחִילִין: כֹּה־
אָמַר יהוה קְדוֹשׁ יִשְׂרָאֵל וְיֹצְרוֹ הָאֹתִיּוֹת שְׁאָלוּנִי עַל־בָּנַי וְעַל־
יב פֹּעַל יָדַי תְּצַוֻּנִי: אָנֹכִי עָשִׂיתִי אֶרֶץ וְאָדָם עָלֶיהָ בָרָאתִי אֲנִי יָדַי נָטוּ
יג שָׁמַיִם וְכָל־צְבָאָם צִוֵּיתִי: אָנֹכִי הַעִירֹתִהוּ בְצֶדֶק וְכָל־דְּרָכָיו אֲיַשֵּׁר
הוּא־יִבְנֶה עִירִי וְגָלוּתִי יְשַׁלֵּחַ לֹא בִמְחִיר וְלֹא בְשֹׁחַד אָמַר יהוה
יד צְבָאוֹת: כֹּה ׀ אָמַר יהוה יְגִיעַ מִצְרַיִם וּסְחַר־כּוּשׁ וּסְבָאִים
אַנְשֵׁי מִדָּה עָלַיִךְ יַעֲבֹרוּ וְלָךְ יִהְיוּ אַחֲרַיִךְ יֵלֵכוּ בַּזִּקִּים יַעֲבֹרוּ וְאֵלַיִךְ
טו יִשְׁתַּחֲווּ אֵלַיִךְ יִתְפַּלָּלוּ אַךְ בָּךְ אֵל וְאֵין עוֹד אֶפֶס אֱלֹהִים: אָכֵן אַתָּה
טז אֵל מִסְתַּתֵּר אֱלֹהֵי יִשְׂרָאֵל מוֹשִׁיעַ: בּוֹשׁוּ וְגַם־נִכְלְמוּ כֻּלָּם יַחְדָּו הָלְכוּ
יז בַכְּלִמָּה חָרָשֵׁי צִירִים: יִשְׂרָאֵל נוֹשַׁע בַּיהוה תְּשׁוּעַת עוֹלָמִים לֹא־ יט
יח תֵבֹשׁוּ וְלֹא־תִכָּלְמוּ עַד־עוֹלְמֵי עַד: כִּי כֹה אָמַר־יהוה
בּוֹרֵא הַשָּׁמַיִם הוּא הָאֱלֹהִים יֹצֵר הָאָרֶץ וְעֹשָׂהּ הוּא כוֹנְנָהּ לֹא־תֹהוּ
יט בְרָאָהּ לָשֶׁבֶת יְצָרָהּ אֲנִי יהוה וְאֵין עוֹד: לֹא בַסֵּתֶר דִּבַּרְתִּי בִּמְקוֹם
אֶרֶץ חֹשֶׁךְ לֹא אָמַרְתִּי לְזֶרַע יַעֲקֹב תֹּהוּ בַקְּשׁוּנִי אֲנִי יהוה דֹּבֵר צֶדֶק
כ מַגִּיד מֵישָׁרִים: הִקָּבְצוּ וָבֹאוּ הִתְנַגְּשׁוּ יַחְדָּו פְּלִיטֵי הַגּוֹיִם לֹא יָדְעוּ
כא הַנֹּשְׂאִים אֶת־עֵץ פִּסְלָם וּמִתְפַּלְלִים אֶל־אֵל לֹא יוֹשִׁיעַ: הַגִּידוּ וְהַגִּישׁוּ
אַף יִוָּעֲצוּ יַחְדָּו מִי הִשְׁמִיעַ זֹאת מִקֶּדֶם מֵאָז הִגִּידָהּ הֲלוֹא אֲנִי יהוה
כב וְאֵין־עוֹד אֱלֹהִים מִבַּלְעָדַי אֵל־צַדִּיק וּמוֹשִׁיעַ אַיִן זוּלָתִי: פְּנוּ־אֵלַי
כג וְהִוָּשְׁעוּ כָּל־אַפְסֵי־אָרֶץ כִּי אֲנִי־אֵל וְאֵין עוֹד: בִּי נִשְׁבַּעְתִּי יָצָא מִפִּי

returned, for every knee should bend before Me; every tongue should swear
24 its oath and say, "In the LORD alone can I find righteousness and power." To
25 Him they will come, and all who rage against Him now be shamed. In the
LORD will be proved victorious, all the seed of Israel, they will glorify
46 1 themselves. Bel is prostrate; Nevo falls; their statues are loaded on beasts, on
2 cattle;[116] your bearers are weighed down beneath their weary burden. The
gods fell, were laid prostrate together; they cannot deliver this burden; they
3 themselves are prisoners. Listen to Me, House of Yaakov, all of you
remaining of the House of Israel, you whom I bore from the womb, whom I
4 have carried since before your birth and into your old age: I am He, and in
your white-haired years I shall still bear you. I made you; I shall carry and
5 bear you, shall deliver. To whom will you compare and liken Me,
6 with whom match Me and find us equal? Men pour out gold from their
pouches, weigh silver in reed baskets, hire a smith – he makes a god, and they
7 worship it, worship. They carry it on their shoulders, bear it away, then set it
down, and there it stands; it will not move an inch from its place; when he
cries out to it, it will not answer and will not deliver him from all his
8 troubles. Remember this: be strong, transgressors; call this to
9 your hearts. Remember the first, the earliest things, for I am God, there is no
10 other; God, there is none like Me, telling of the end from the beginning,
telling long since of what was not yet made, saying, "My plan, it will arise; I
11 shall bring about all that I desire," calling the kite from the east, from a far-off
land – the man who carries My design. I have spoken, and I shall bring to be,
12 have formed and shall perform it. Listen to Me, mighty hearts, far
13 away from righteousness; I will bring close My victory; it never will be far
from you; My rescue will not come too late. I shall grant in Zion My rescue,
47 1 grant Israel My glory. Go down, sit in the dust, virgin daughter
Babylon; sit upon the ground, no throne, Chaldean daughter,[117] for no more
2 will you be called delicate lady, refined. Take a millstone; grind some flour;
3 expose your tresses, lift your hem, and show your legs to cross the rivers. Your
nakedness will be exposed and your abjection seen; I shall take vengeance; I
4 shall not accept the prayers of man. Our redeemer, His name is the
5 LORD of Hosts, Israel's Holy One. Sit silent; come into the dark, Chaldean
6 daughter, for no more are you to be called a lady among kingdoms. I raged
against My people, defiled My estate; I gave them over to your hands. You
bore them no compassion; you laid your heavy yoke upon the backs of aged
7 men. You thought, "I am, always, the lady," so you did not lay this on your
8 heart, did not consider that lady's future. Listen now to this,
delicate lady, living without cares, saying in your heart, "I: there is none but
9 me; I will not live a widow's life, will not know the loss of children." These
two came to you all in a moment, in one day: child grief, widowhood, whole

116 | A description of the collapse of the Babylonian gods, who are here said to have fled Babylon when Koresh conquered the city.

117 | The chapter is a mocking lament of Babylon on the occasion of its fall to Koresh. The Chaldeans were an ethnic group prominent around Babylon.

כד צְדָקָה דָּבָר וְלֹא יָשׁוּב כִּי־לִי תִּכְרַע כָּל־בֶּרֶךְ תִּשָּׁבַע כָּל־לָשׁוֹן׃ אַךְ
כה בַּיהוָה לִי אָמַר צְדָקוֹת וָעֹז עָדָיו יָבוֹא וְיֵבֹשׁוּ כֹּל הַנֶּחֱרִים בּוֹ׃ בַּיהוָה
מו א יִצְדְּקוּ וְיִתְהַלְלוּ כָּל־זֶרַע יִשְׂרָאֵל׃ כָּרַע בֵּל קֹרֵס נְבוֹ הָיוּ עֲצַבֵּיהֶם
ב לַחַיָּה וְלַבְּהֵמָה נְשֻׂאֹתֵיכֶם עֲמוּסוֹת מַשָּׂא לַעֲיֵפָה׃ קָרְסוּ כָרְעוּ יַחְדָּו
ג לֹא יָכְלוּ מַלֵּט מַשָּׂא וְנַפְשָׁם בַּשְּׁבִי הָלָכָה׃ שִׁמְעוּ אֵלַי בֵּית
יַעֲקֹב וְכָל־שְׁאֵרִית בֵּית יִשְׂרָאֵל הָעֲמֻסִים מִנִּי־בֶטֶן הַנְּשֻׂאִים מִנִּי־
ד רָחַם׃ וְעַד־זִקְנָה אֲנִי הוּא וְעַד־שֵׂיבָה אֲנִי אֶסְבֹּל אֲנִי עָשִׂיתִי וַאֲנִי
ה אֶשָּׂא וַאֲנִי אֶסְבֹּל וַאֲמַלֵּט׃ לְמִי תְדַמְּיוּנִי וְתַשְׁווּ וְתַמְשִׁלוּנִי
ו וְנִדְמֶה׃ הַזָּלִים זָהָב מִכִּיס וְכֶסֶף בַּקָּנֶה יִשְׁקֹלוּ יִשְׂכְּרוּ צוֹרֵף וְיַעֲשֵׂהוּ
ז אֵל יִסְגְּדוּ אַף־יִשְׁתַּחֲווּ׃ יִשָּׂאֻהוּ עַל־כָּתֵף יִסְבְּלֻהוּ וְיַנִּיחֻהוּ תַחְתָּיו
וְיַעֲמֹד מִמְּקוֹמוֹ לֹא יָמִישׁ אַף־יִצְעַק אֵלָיו וְלֹא יַעֲנֶה מִצָּרָתוֹ לֹא
ח יוֹשִׁיעֶנּוּ׃ זִכְרוּ־זֹאת וְהִתְאֹשָׁשׁוּ הָשִׁיבוּ פוֹשְׁעִים עַל־לֵב׃
ט זִכְרוּ רִאשֹׁנוֹת מֵעוֹלָם כִּי אָנֹכִי אֵל וְאֵין עוֹד אֱלֹהִים וְאֶפֶס כָּמוֹנִי׃
י מַגִּיד מֵרֵאשִׁית אַחֲרִית וּמִקֶּדֶם אֲשֶׁר לֹא־נַעֲשׂוּ אֹמֵר עֲצָתִי תָקוּם
יא וְכָל־חֶפְצִי אֶעֱשֶׂה׃ קֹרֵא מִמִּזְרָח עַיִט מֵאֶרֶץ מֶרְחָק אִישׁ עצתו אַף־ עֲצָתִי
יב דִּבַּרְתִּי אַף־אֲבִיאֶנָּה יָצַרְתִּי אַף־אֶעֱשֶׂנָּה׃ שִׁמְעוּ אֵלַי אַבִּירֵי
יג לֵב הָרְחוֹקִים מִצְּדָקָה׃ קֵרַבְתִּי צִדְקָתִי לֹא תִרְחָק וּתְשׁוּעָתִי לֹא
מז א תְאַחֵר וְנָתַתִּי בְצִיּוֹן תְּשׁוּעָה לְיִשְׂרָאֵל תִּפְאַרְתִּי׃ רְדִי ׀
וּשְׁבִי עַל־עָפָר בְּתוּלַת בַּת־בָּבֶל שְׁבִי־לָאָרֶץ אֵין־כִּסֵּא בַּת־כַּשְׂדִּים
ב כִּי לֹא תוֹסִיפִי יִקְרְאוּ־לָךְ רַכָּה וַעֲנֻגָּה׃ קְחִי רֵחַיִם וְטַחֲנִי קָמַח גַּלִּי
ג צַמָּתֵךְ חֶשְׂפִּי־שֹׁבֶל גַּלִּי־שׁוֹק עִבְרִי נְהָרוֹת׃ תִּגָּל עֶרְוָתֵךְ גַּם תֵּרָאֶה
ד חֶרְפָּתֵךְ נָקָם אֶקָּח וְלֹא אֶפְגַּע אָדָם׃ גֹּאֲלֵנוּ יְהוָה צְבָאוֹת
ה שְׁמוֹ קְדוֹשׁ יִשְׂרָאֵל׃ שְׁבִי דוּמָם וּבֹאִי בַחֹשֶׁךְ בַּת־כַּשְׂדִּים כִּי לֹא
ו תוֹסִיפִי יִקְרְאוּ־לָךְ גְּבֶרֶת מַמְלָכוֹת׃ קָצַפְתִּי עַל־עַמִּי חִלַּלְתִּי נַחֲלָתִי
וָאֶתְּנֵם בְּיָדֵךְ לֹא־שַׂמְתְּ לָהֶם רַחֲמִים עַל־זָקֵן הִכְבַּדְתְּ עֻלֵּךְ מְאֹד׃
ז וַתֹּאמְרִי לְעוֹלָם אֶהְיֶה גְבָרֶת עַד לֹא־שַׂמְתְּ אֵלֶּה עַל־לִבֵּךְ לֹא זָכַרְתְּ
ח אַחֲרִיתָהּ׃ וְעַתָּה שִׁמְעִי־זֹאת עֲדִינָה הַיּוֹשֶׁבֶת לָבֶטַח
הָאֹמְרָה בִּלְבָבָהּ אֲנִי וְאַפְסִי עוֹד לֹא אֵשֵׁב אַלְמָנָה וְלֹא אֵדַע שְׁכוֹל׃
ט וְתָבֹאנָה לָּךְ שְׁתֵּי־אֵלֶּה רֶגַע בְּיוֹם אֶחָד שְׁכוֹל וְאַלְמֹן כְּתֻמָּם בָּאוּ

10 and pure, for all your witchcraft, for the mighty force of your wizardry. You
felt secure in your evil: "No one sees me," so you said. It is your very wisdom,
your knowledge, that led you astray, "I" – you said in your heart – "there is
11 no other." Evil came to you; you knew not how to meet it; calamity fell on
you that you cannot cover over; suddenly it came to you, catastrophe you
12 have not known. Cling now to your magic, to all the forms of witchcraft that
you have worked so hard at perfecting since your youth; perhaps you will do
13 some good; perhaps you can strike dread again. How you have wearied of all
your counsels; let them stand up now and rescue you – diviners by the skies,
stargazers, tellers of tidings by the shape of the moon – let them save you
14 from what will come. No; they are become like straw burned up in fire; they
cannot even save themselves from the flames' hold. No ember remains to
15 warm yourself by, no fire to sit before. So did they become to you, those for
whom you labored, those who peddled spells from your first youth; each has
48 1 gone astray in his own way; not one will be your rescue. Listen,
people of Yaakov, to this, you who are called by the name Israel, you who
emerged from Judahite waters, who swear by the name of the LORD, calling
on the name of Israel's God but neither in truth nor in righteousness – know:
2 you are called from the holy city forth, depend upon Israel's God, the LORD
3 of Hosts is His name. From the first I told you all of this; it issued
from My mouth, resounded; suddenly I brought these things about; they
4 came to be from My own mind, for you are tough, your neck an iron sinew,
5 your forehead bronze. I told you from the start, before they came to be,
resounded them to you, lest you say, "It was my idol that did these things, my
6 statue, my cast image, that issued the command." You have heard; now see it
all, and now, will you not speak it? I told you of this newness that now comes
7 and guarded secrets you knew not. Now they have been made, and not before,
8 but yesterday you could not hear it – lest you tell me, "This I knew." You did
not hear; you did not know; even then your ears were opened not; I knew
9 you would betray Me – you were named a rebel from the womb. For My
name's sake I shall hold back My rage; for My praise I will hold back and will
10 not sever you from life. I have refined you, not like silver; in the furnace of
11 oppression you are chosen. For My sake shall I act, for Mine, for how can I be
12 profaned, and how could I give over of My glory to another? Listen
to Me, Yaakov, and Israel, named for Me. It is I – I am the first, and I shall be
13 the last; My hand laid down the land and My right hand spread the heavens;
14 when I call to them, they stand, all, to attention. Gather, listen all – who
among you spoke of this? It is the LORD who loved him: He shall do his
15 will in Babylon, raise his arm over Kasdim. I, it is I who spoke this, I who
16 called him forth, who brought him and made his way prosper. Come close
to Me and hear this: Long ago, and not in secret, did I speak; ever since it
began, I was there. And now the LORD my God has sent me, and His
17 spirit. Thus says the LORD, your redeemer, Israel's Holy One: I am
the LORD your God, who taught you in order to better you, who showed you
18 the path to walk. Would you but heed My charge, your peace would flow like

י עָלַיִךְ בְּרֹב כְּשָׁפַיִךְ בְּעָצְמַת חֲבָרַיִךְ מְאֹד׃ וַתִּבְטְחִי בְרָעָתֵךְ אָמַרְתְּ
אֵין רֹאָנִי חָכְמָתֵךְ וְדַעְתֵּךְ הִיא שׁוֹבְבָתֶךְ וַתֹּאמְרִי בְלִבֵּךְ אֲנִי וְאַפְסִי
יא עוֹד׃ וּבָא עָלַיִךְ רָעָה לֹא תֵדְעִי שַׁחְרָהּ וְתִפֹּל עָלַיִךְ הֹוָה לֹא תוּכְלִי
יב כַּפְּרָהּ וְתָבֹא עָלַיִךְ פִּתְאֹם שׁוֹאָה לֹא תֵדָעִי׃ עִמְדִי־נָא בַחֲבָרַיִךְ וּבְרֹב
כְּשָׁפַיִךְ בַּאֲשֶׁר יָגַעַתְּ מִנְּעוּרָיִךְ אוּלַי תּוּכְלִי הוֹעִיל אוּלַי תַּעֲרוֹצִי׃
יג נִלְאֵית בְּרֹב עֲצָתָיִךְ יַעַמְדוּ־נָא וְיוֹשִׁיעֻךְ הברו שָׁמַיִם הַחֹזִים בַּכּוֹכָבִים הֹבְרֵי
יד מוֹדִיעִם לֶחֳדָשִׁים מֵאֲשֶׁר יָבֹאוּ עָלָיִךְ׃ הִנֵּה הָיוּ כְקַשׁ אֵשׁ שְׂרָפָתַם
לֹא־יַצִּילוּ אֶת־נַפְשָׁם מִיַּד לֶהָבָה אֵין־גַּחֶלֶת לַחְמָם אוּר לָשֶׁבֶת נֶגְדּוֹ׃
טו כֵּן הָיוּ־לָךְ אֲשֶׁר יָגָעַתְּ סֹחֲרַיִךְ מִנְּעוּרַיִךְ אִישׁ לְעֶבְרוֹ תָּעוּ אֵין
מח א מוֹשִׁיעֵךְ׃ שִׁמְעוּ־זֹאת בֵּית־יַעֲקֹב הַנִּקְרָאִים בְּשֵׁם
יִשְׂרָאֵל וּמִמֵּי יְהוּדָה יָצָאוּ הַנִּשְׁבָּעִים ׀ בְּשֵׁם יְהוָה וּבֵאלֹהֵי יִשְׂרָאֵל
ב יַזְכִּירוּ לֹא בֶאֱמֶת וְלֹא בִצְדָקָה׃ כִּי־מֵעִיר הַקֹּדֶשׁ נִקְרָאוּ וְעַל־אֱלֹהֵי כ
ג יִשְׂרָאֵל נִסְמָכוּ יְהוָה צְבָאוֹת שְׁמוֹ׃ הָרִאשֹׁנוֹת מֵאָז הִגַּדְתִּי
ד וּמִפִּי יָצְאוּ וְאַשְׁמִיעֵם פִּתְאֹם עָשִׂיתִי וַתָּבֹאנָה׃ מִדַּעְתִּי כִּי קָשֶׁה אָתָּה
ה וְגִיד בַּרְזֶל עָרְפֶּךָ וּמִצְחֲךָ נְחוּשָׁה׃ וָאַגִּיד לְךָ מֵאָז בְּטֶרֶם תָּבוֹא
ו הִשְׁמַעְתִּיךָ פֶּן־תֹּאמַר עָצְבִּי עָשָׂם וּפִסְלִי וְנִסְכִּי צִוָּם׃ שָׁמַעְתָּ חֲזֵה
כֻּלָּהּ וְאַתֶּם הֲלוֹא תַגִּידוּ הִשְׁמַעְתִּיךָ חֲדָשׁוֹת מֵעַתָּה וּנְצֻרוֹת וְלֹא
ז יְדַעְתָּם׃ עַתָּה נִבְרְאוּ וְלֹא מֵאָז וְלִפְנֵי־יוֹם וְלֹא שְׁמַעְתָּם פֶּן־תֹּאמַר
ח הִנֵּה יְדַעְתִּין׃ גַּם לֹא־שָׁמַעְתָּ גַּם לֹא יָדַעְתָּ גַּם מֵאָז לֹא־פִתְּחָה אָזְנֶךָ
ט כִּי יָדַעְתִּי בָּגוֹד תִּבְגּוֹד וּפֹשֵׁעַ מִבֶּטֶן קֹרָא לָךְ׃ לְמַעַן שְׁמִי אַאֲרִיךְ
י אַפִּי וּתְהִלָּתִי אֶחֱטָם־לָךְ לְבִלְתִּי הַכְרִיתֶךָ׃ הִנֵּה צְרַפְתִּיךָ וְלֹא בְכָסֶף
יא בְּחַרְתִּיךָ בְּכוּר עֹנִי׃ לְמַעֲנִי לְמַעֲנִי אֶעֱשֶׂה כִּי אֵיךְ יֵחָל וּכְבוֹדִי לְאַחֵר
יב לֹא־אֶתֵּן׃ שְׁמַע אֵלַי יַעֲקֹב וְיִשְׂרָאֵל מְקֹרָאִי אֲנִי־הוּא אֲנִי
יג רִאשׁוֹן אַף אֲנִי אַחֲרוֹן׃ אַף־יָדִי יָסְדָה אֶרֶץ וִימִינִי טִפְּחָה שָׁמָיִם קֹרֵא
יד אֲנִי אֲלֵיהֶם יַעַמְדוּ יַחְדָּו׃ הִקָּבְצוּ כֻלְּכֶם וּשְׁמָעוּ מִי בָהֶם הִגִּיד אֶת־
טו אֵלֶּה יְהוָה אֲהֵבוֹ יַעֲשֶׂה חֶפְצוֹ בְּבָבֶל וּזְרֹעוֹ כַּשְׂדִּים׃ אֲנִי אֲנִי דִּבַּרְתִּי
טז אַף־קְרָאתִיו הֲבִיאֹתִיו וְהִצְלִיחַ דַּרְכּוֹ׃ קִרְבוּ אֵלַי שִׁמְעוּ־זֹאת לֹא
מֵרֹאשׁ בַּסֵּתֶר דִּבַּרְתִּי מֵעֵת הֱיוֹתָהּ שָׁם אָנִי וְעַתָּה אֲדֹנָי יְהוִה שְׁלָחַנִי
יז וְרוּחוֹ׃ כֹּה־אָמַר יְהוָה גֹּאַלְךָ קְדוֹשׁ יִשְׂרָאֵל אֲנִי יְהוָה
יח אֱלֹהֶיךָ מְלַמֶּדְךָ לְהוֹעִיל מַדְרִיכְךָ בְּדֶרֶךְ תֵּלֵךְ׃ לוּא הִקְשַׁבְתָּ לְמִצְוֺתָי

19 a river, your righteousness waves on the ocean. Like sand would your children
be, the fruit of your womb abundant as its grains, their name never severed,
20 never rendered extinct before Me. Go forth from Babylon; flee
Kasdim; call out joyful song; resound, spread the word to the ends of the
21 earth; say it: "the LORD has redeemed His servant Yaakov."[118] They did not
thirst; He led them through dry ruins but poured water from the rock. The
22 rock burst open, and out coursed water. There is no peace, the LORD says, for
49 1 the wicked. Listen to me, distant coastlands; hear me, nations far
away: From the womb the LORD called me; when I was in my mother still,
2 He spoke my name and made my mouth a dagger, sharp, concealed in the
shadow of His hand. He made me a sheer arrowhead and hid me in His quiver.
3 He said to me: You are My servant, Israel; through you I am glorious. And I
4 say: I toiled for nothing; in breath and emptiness I spent my strength, but the
5 LORD retains my rightful share; my reward is with my God. Now
the LORD has spoken, the One who made me in the womb to serve Him, to
bring Yaakov back to Him, to gather Israel in to Him, and in the LORD's eyes
6 I found honor; my God became my strength. It is not enough, He said, that
you serve Me, raising up Yaakov's tribes, restoring those of Israel I protected;
I made you to be a light unto nations; My rescue must reach the ends of this
7 earth. Thus says the LORD, redeemer of Israel, his Holy One, to a
soul reviled, a nation's abhorrence, slave of rulers; kings will see and rise to
their feet, ministers bow low for the sake of the LORD who is faithful, of
8 Israel's Holy One who chooses you. Thus says the LORD: At a time
of favor I answered you; on a day ripe for rescue I was there for your aid. I
guarded you and made you a covenant people, ready to build up a land, to
9 take possession of a lost estate, to say to prisoners, "Leave," and to people in
darkness, "Come to light." They will graze along the way, with all the hills their
10 pasture. They will know no hunger, know no thirst; searing heat and sun will
never harm them, for the One who cares for them will be their guide, leading
11 them by springs of water. I shall make all mountains a path to walk and build
12 up My roads. Here – from far away they come, all of these, from the north,
13 from the west, all of these, from the land of Sinim. Sing out, skies, and land,
rejoice; hills, break out in song, for the LORD has brought His people comfort;
14 He will care for the oppressed ones who are His. Zion speaks: "The
15 LORD has forsaken me; my Lord, He has forgotten me." Can a mother forget
her own baby; can she fail to care for the child of her womb? These too may
16 yet forget, but I will not forget you. I have etched you on My palms; your
17 walls are before My eyes always. Your children will run to you; your destroyers,
18 your demolishers, will all be gone from you. Raise your eyes; look around
and see: the children all gathered and coming back to you. As I live, so says
the LORD, you will wear them all as jewels, which you will bind on like a bride.
19 For your ruins, for your wastelands, for the land of your destruction, for you
will be too narrow for your dwellers, while those who would destroy you will

118 | A reference to the moment the exiles departed from Babylon, headed for Yehuda.

יט וַיְהִי כַנָּהָר שְׁלוֹמֶךָ וְצִדְקָתְךָ כְּגַלֵּי הַיָּם: וַיְהִי כַחוֹל זַרְעֶךָ וְצֶאֱצָאֵי
כ מֵעֶיךָ כִּמְעֹתָיו לֹא־יִכָּרֵת וְלֹא־יִשָּׁמֵד שְׁמוֹ מִלְּפָנָי: צְאוּ
מִבָּבֶל בִּרְחוּ מִכַּשְׂדִּים בְּקוֹל רִנָּה הַגִּידוּ הַשְׁמִיעוּ זֹאת הוֹצִיאוּהָ עַד־
כא קְצֵה הָאָרֶץ אִמְרוּ גָּאַל יהוה עַבְדּוֹ יַעֲקֹב: וְלֹא צָמְאוּ בָּחֳרָבוֹת
כב הוֹלִיכָם מַיִם מִצּוּר הִזִּיל לָמוֹ וַיִּבְקַע־צוּר וַיָּזֻבוּ מָיִם: אֵין שָׁלוֹם אָמַר
מט א יהוה לָרְשָׁעִים: שִׁמְעוּ אִיִּים אֵלַי וְהַקְשִׁיבוּ לְאֻמִּים
ב מֵרָחוֹק יהוה מִבֶּטֶן קְרָאָנִי מִמְּעֵי אִמִּי הִזְכִּיר שְׁמִי: וַיָּשֶׂם פִּי כְּחֶרֶב
חַדָּה בְּצֵל יָדוֹ הֶחְבִּיאָנִי וַיְשִׂימֵנִי לְחֵץ בָּרוּר בְּאַשְׁפָּתוֹ הִסְתִּירָנִי:
ג ד וַיֹּאמֶר לִי עַבְדִּי־אָתָּה יִשְׂרָאֵל אֲשֶׁר־בְּךָ אֶתְפָּאָר: וַאֲנִי אָמַרְתִּי לְרִיק
יָגַעְתִּי לְתֹהוּ וְהֶבֶל כֹּחִי כִלֵּיתִי אָכֵן מִשְׁפָּטִי אֶת־יהוה וּפְעֻלָּתִי אֶת־
ה אֱלֹהָי: וְעַתָּה | אָמַר יהוה יֹצְרִי מִבֶּטֶן לְעֶבֶד לוֹ
לְשׁוֹבֵב יַעֲקֹב אֵלָיו וְיִשְׂרָאֵל לא יֵאָסֵף וְאֶכָּבֵד בְּעֵינֵי יהוה וֵאלֹהַי לוֹ
ו הָיָה עֻזִּי: וַיֹּאמֶר נָקֵל מִהְיוֹתְךָ לִי עֶבֶד לְהָקִים אֶת־שִׁבְטֵי יַעֲקֹב
ונצירי יִשְׂרָאֵל לְהָשִׁיב וּנְתַתִּיךָ לְאוֹר גּוֹיִם לִהְיוֹת יְשׁוּעָתִי עַד־קְצֵה וּנְצוּרֵי
ז הָאָרֶץ: כֹּה אָמַר־יהוה גֹּאֵל יִשְׂרָאֵל קְדוֹשׁוֹ לִבְזֹה־נֶפֶשׁ
לִמְתָעֵב גּוֹי לְעֶבֶד מֹשְׁלִים מְלָכִים יִרְאוּ וָקָמוּ שָׂרִים וְיִשְׁתַּחֲווּ לְמַעַן
ח יהוה אֲשֶׁר נֶאֱמָן קְדֹשׁ יִשְׂרָאֵל וַיִּבְחָרֶךָּ: כֹּה | אָמַר יהוה
בְּעֵת רָצוֹן עֲנִיתִיךָ וּבְיוֹם יְשׁוּעָה עֲזַרְתִּיךָ וְאֶצָּרְךָ וְאֶתֶּנְךָ לִבְרִית עָם
ט לְהָקִים אֶרֶץ לְהַנְחִיל נְחָלוֹת שֹׁמֵמוֹת: לֵאמֹר לַאֲסוּרִים צֵאוּ לַאֲשֶׁר
י בַּחֹשֶׁךְ הִגָּלוּ עַל־דְּרָכִים יִרְעוּ וּבְכָל־שְׁפָיִים מַרְעִיתָם: לֹא יִרְעָבוּ
וְלֹא יִצְמָאוּ וְלֹא־יַכֵּם שָׁרָב וָשָׁמֶשׁ כִּי־מְרַחֲמָם יְנַהֲגֵם וְעַל־מַבּוּעֵי
יא יב מַיִם יְנַהֲלֵם: וְשַׂמְתִּי כָל־הָרַי לַדָּרֶךְ וּמְסִלֹּתַי יְרֻמוּן: הִנֵּה־אֵלֶּה
יג מֵרָחוֹק יָבֹאוּ וְהִנֵּה־אֵלֶּה מִצָּפוֹן וּמִיָּם וְאֵלֶּה מֵאֶרֶץ סִינִים: רָנּוּ
שָׁמַיִם וְגִילִי אֶרֶץ יפצחו הָרִים רִנָּה כִּי־נִחַם יהוה עַמּוֹ וַעֲנִיָּו וּפִצְחוּ
יד טו יְרַחֵם: וַתֹּאמֶר צִיּוֹן עֲזָבַנִי יהוה וַאדֹנָי שְׁכֵחָנִי: הֲתִשְׁכַּח
אִשָּׁה עוּלָהּ מֵרַחֵם בֶּן־בִּטְנָהּ גַּם־אֵלֶּה תִשְׁכַּחְנָה וְאָנֹכִי לֹא אֶשְׁכָּחֵךְ:
טז יז הֵן עַל־כַּפַּיִם חַקֹּתִיךְ חוֹמֹתַיִךְ נֶגְדִּי תָּמִיד: מִהֲרוּ בָּנָיִךְ מְהָרְסַיִךְ
יח וּמַחֲרִבַיִךְ מִמֵּךְ יֵצֵאוּ: שְׂאִי־סָבִיב עֵינַיִךְ וּרְאִי כֻּלָּם נִקְבְּצוּ בָאוּ־לָךְ
יט חַי־אָנִי נְאֻם־יהוה כִּי כֻלָּם כַּעֲדִי תִלְבָּשִׁי וּתְקַשְּׁרִים כַּכַּלָּה: כִּי חָרְבֹתַיִךְ

20 be far away from you. You will yet hear the children say, of whom you were
21 bereaved, "The place is too tight for me; make space for me to sit," while you
say in your heart, "Who bore these children, mine, to me, bereft and left alone,
exiled and expelled; these children – who has raised them? I was left all alone,
22 and these – who can they be?" So says the Lord God: Behold: I shall
raise My hands to nations, lift My banner toward peoples; they will bring your
sons back in the folds of their robes, bearing your daughters upon their
23 shoulders; kings will be your caregivers, their princesses your nursemaids.
They will bow to the ground before you and kiss the dust you tread upon, and
you will know: I am the Lord, and those who wait for Me will not be
24 shamed. Can a mighty warrior be plundered; can a victor's captives
25 flee? For so says the Lord: The mighty man's captives may yet be taken, the
tyrant's plunder flee, but I shall fight against those who fight you, I will save
26 your children. To those who wrong you, I will feed their own flesh; their
blood will intoxicate them like wine, and all flesh will know then that I am
50 1 the Lord, your rescue, your redeemer, Mighty One of Yaakov. So
says the Lord: Where is your mother's bill of divorce with which I banished
her? Which one of My creditors have I, then, sold you to? No, it was for your
sins that you were sold; for your faithlessness your mother was sent hence.
2 Why is it that I came, and no man was here; I cried out, and no one answered?
Does My arm fall short to redeem you; have I not strength to rescue? No – at
My rebuke I dry the sea; I turn whole rivers to desert land. Their fish will stink
3 for lack of water, dead of thirst. I will dress the skies in darkness and make
4 mourning sack their covering. The Lord my God made me a
learning tongue to sustain the weary with words; morning, early morning,
5 He wakens my ears, He wakes them, like students, to hear. The Lord my God
6 opened my ears, and I did not reject Him; I never shrank back; I gave up my
back to beating, my cheeks to those who scratched them. I never hid my face
7 from humiliations, spittle, but the Lord my God will help me, and so no
8 humiliation; I set my face as flint and know I will not be ashamed. He is near
who shows me righteous. Who, then, will contend with me? Let us stand up
9 opposing one another. Who has a claim against me? Let him come to me, for
the Lord God, He will help me; who then can condemn me? They will wear
10 out like an old cloak; moths will eat them. Who of you reveres the
Lord, and listens to His servant's voice? Let one who walked in darkness,
nothing shining for him, trust in the Lord's name, and lean on his God.
11 You – you light your fire and gird yourselves with torchlight. Walk by the light
of your own fire, by torches that you burn. From My hand, all this came to
51 1 you; you will lie down in pain. You who chase righteousness,
2 listen to Me, you who seek the Lord: Look to the rock you are hewed from,
the quarry from which you were carved; look to your father, Avraham, to Sara
who gave you birth, for I called him, one alone, and blessed him, made
3 him many. And the Lord has comforted Zion, brought comfort to all her
ruins; He has made her desert like Eden, her arid land like the Lord's

כ וְשֹׁמְמֹתַיִךְ וְאֶרֶץ הֲרִסֻתֵךְ כִּי עַתָּה תֵּצְרִי מִיּוֹשֵׁב וְרָחֲקוּ מְבַלְּעָיִךְ: עוֹד
כא יֹאמְרוּ בְאָזְנַיִךְ בְּנֵי שִׁכֻּלָיִךְ צַר־לִי הַמָּקוֹם גְּשָׁה־לִּי וְאֵשֵׁבָה: וְאָמַרְתְּ
בִּלְבָבֵךְ מִי יָלַד־לִי אֶת־אֵלֶּה וַאֲנִי שְׁכוּלָה וְגַלְמוּדָה גֹּלָה ׀ וְסוּרָה
כב וְאֵלֶּה מִי גִדֵּל הֵן אֲנִי נִשְׁאַרְתִּי לְבַדִּי אֵלֶּה אֵיפֹה הֵם: כֹּה־
אָמַר אֲדֹנָי יֱהוִה הִנֵּה אֶשָּׂא אֶל־גּוֹיִם יָדִי וְאֶל־עַמִּים אָרִים נִסִּי וְהֵבִיאוּ
כג בָנַיִךְ בְּחֹצֶן וּבְנֹתַיִךְ עַל־כָּתֵף תִּנָּשֶׂאנָה: וְהָיוּ מְלָכִים אֹמְנַיִךְ וְשָׂרוֹתֵיהֶם
מֵינִיקֹתַיִךְ אַפַּיִם אֶרֶץ יִשְׁתַּחֲווּ לָךְ וַעֲפַר רַגְלַיִךְ יְלַחֵכוּ וְיָדַעַתְּ כִּי־אֲנִי
כד יְהוָה אֲשֶׁר לֹא־יֵבֹשׁוּ קֹוָי: הֲיֻקַּח מִגִּבּוֹר מַלְקוֹחַ וְאִם־
כה שְׁבִי צַדִּיק יִמָּלֵט: כִּי־כֹה ׀ אָמַר יְהוָה גַּם־שְׁבִי גִבּוֹר יֻקָּח וּמַלְקוֹחַ
כו עָרִיץ יִמָּלֵט וְאֶת־יְרִיבֵךְ אָנֹכִי אָרִיב וְאֶת־בָּנַיִךְ אָנֹכִי אוֹשִׁיעַ: וְהַאֲכַלְתִּי **כא**
אֶת־מוֹנַיִךְ אֶת־בְּשָׂרָם וְכֶעָסִיס דָּמָם יִשְׁכָּרוּן וְיָדְעוּ כָל־בָּשָׂר כִּי אֲנִי
נ א יְהוָה מוֹשִׁיעֵךְ וְגֹאֲלֵךְ אֲבִיר יַעֲקֹב: כֹּה ׀ אָמַר יְהוָה אֵי
זֶה סֵפֶר כְּרִיתוּת אִמְּכֶם אֲשֶׁר שִׁלַּחְתִּיהָ אוֹ מִי מִנּוֹשַׁי אֲשֶׁר־מָכַרְתִּי
ב אֶתְכֶם לוֹ הֵן בַּעֲוֺנֹתֵיכֶם נִמְכַּרְתֶּם וּבְפִשְׁעֵיכֶם שֻׁלְּחָה אִמְּכֶם: מַדּוּעַ
בָּאתִי וְאֵין אִישׁ קָרָאתִי וְאֵין עוֹנֶה הֲקָצוֹר קָצְרָה יָדִי מִפְּדוּת וְאִם־
אֵין־בִּי כֹחַ לְהַצִּיל הֵן בְּגַעֲרָתִי אַחֲרִיב יָם אָשִׂים נְהָרוֹת מִדְבָּר תִּבְאַשׁ
ג דְּגָתָם מֵאֵין מַיִם וְתָמֹת בַּצָּמָא: אַלְבִּישׁ שָׁמַיִם קַדְרוּת וְשַׂק אָשִׂים
ד כְּסוּתָם: אֲדֹנָי יֱהוִה נָתַן לִי לְשׁוֹן לִמּוּדִים לָדַעַת לָעוּת
ה אֶת־יָעֵף דָּבָר יָעִיר ׀ בַּבֹּקֶר בַּבֹּקֶר יָעִיר לִי אֹזֶן לִשְׁמֹעַ כַּלִּמּוּדִים: אֲדֹנָי
ו יֱהוִה פָּתַח־לִי אֹזֶן וְאָנֹכִי לֹא מָרִיתִי אָחוֹר לֹא נְסוּגֹתִי: גֵּוִי נָתַתִּי
ז לְמַכִּים וּלְחָיַי לְמֹרְטִים פָּנַי לֹא הִסְתַּרְתִּי מִכְּלִמּוֹת וָרֹק: וַאדֹנָי יֱהוִה
יַעֲזָר־לִי עַל־כֵּן לֹא נִכְלָמְתִּי עַל־כֵּן שַׂמְתִּי פָנַי כַּחַלָּמִישׁ וָאֵדַע כִּי־לֹא
ח אֵבוֹשׁ: קָרוֹב מַצְדִּיקִי מִי־יָרִיב אִתִּי נַעַמְדָה יָּחַד מִי־בַעַל מִשְׁפָּטִי
ט יִגַּשׁ אֵלָי: הֵן אֲדֹנָי יֱהוִה יַעֲזָר־לִי מִי־הוּא יַרְשִׁיעֵנִי הֵן כֻּלָּם כַּבֶּגֶד יִבְלוּ
י עָשׁ יֹאכְלֵם: מִי בָכֶם יְרֵא יְהוָה שֹׁמֵעַ בְּקוֹל עַבְדּוֹ אֲשֶׁר ׀
יא הָלַךְ חֲשֵׁכִים וְאֵין נֹגַהּ לוֹ יִבְטַח בְּשֵׁם יְהוָה וְיִשָּׁעֵן בֵּאלֹהָיו: הֵן כֻּלְּכֶם
קֹדְחֵי אֵשׁ מְאַזְּרֵי זִיקוֹת לְכוּ ׀ בְּאוּר אֶשְׁכֶם וּבְזִיקוֹת בִּעַרְתֶּם מִיָּדִי
נא א הָיְתָה־זֹּאת לָכֶם לְמַעֲצֵבָה תִּשְׁכָּבוּן: שִׁמְעוּ אֵלַי רֹדְפֵי
צֶדֶק מְבַקְשֵׁי יְהוָה הַבִּיטוּ אֶל־צוּר חֻצַּבְתֶּם וְאֶל־מַקֶּבֶת בּוֹר נֻקַּרְתֶּם:
ב הַבִּיטוּ אֶל־אַבְרָהָם אֲבִיכֶם וְאֶל־שָׂרָה תְּחוֹלֶלְכֶם כִּי־אֶחָד קְרָאתִיו
ג וַאֲבָרְכֵהוּ וְאַרְבֵּהוּ: כִּי־נִחַם יְהוָה צִיּוֹן נִחַם כָּל־חָרְבֹתֶיהָ וַיָּשֶׂם מִדְבָּרָהּ
כְּעֵדֶן וְעַרְבָתָהּ כְּגַן־יְהוָה שָׂשׂוֹן וְשִׂמְחָה יִמָּצֵא בָהּ תּוֹדָה וְקוֹל

garden;[119] celebration, joy are found in her, and thanks, and sounds of
4 song. My people, listen to Me; heed Me, nation Mine, for teaching
will come forth from Me; in a moment I bring My judgment, light for all
5 peoples; My victory is close; My rescue has come forth; My arms' strength
brings judgment to peoples. The coastlands wait for Me; for My strong arm
6 they long. Lift your eyes to the heavens and gaze at the earth below: the
heavens fade away like smoke; like an old cloak, the land wears out, and those
who dwell upon her likewise die, but My rescue is forever; My justice will not
7 be broken. Listen to Me, you who know what is right, people with
My teaching at your heart: do not fear disgrace from men, nor break when
8 they abuse you, for moths will eat them up like cloth, like wool, the grubs
will eat them while My justice, that will always be, My rescue through all
9 ages. Rise, rise, and don your dress of might, the LORD's strong arm.
Rise as long ago in the earliest time – was it not You who cleaved Rahav, beat
10 the Serpent down?[120] Was it not You who dried the ocean, the waters of
endless deeps, making the depths of the ocean a path for redeemed ones to
11 travel? They will return, those the LORD has claimed, arriving in Zion in song,
crowned with everlasting joy; they will have found joy and happiness, and
12 sorrow and moaning will flee. It is I, I who comfort you. Who are
13 you to fear mortal man, humanity, that ends like grass, forgetting the LORD
who made you, who stretches out the skies, lays down the earth? All day you
fear the oppressor's rage as he makes his schemes of violence, yet where is
14 the oppressor's rage? The man bent under his burden – how fast will he be
15 freed; he[121] will not die into the pit, nor will his bread be lacking. I am the
LORD your God. I trouble the ocean; its waves roar; the LORD of Hosts is My
16 name. I have placed My words in your mouth and covered you in My hand's
shade, planting the skies, laying down the earth, and saying to Zion: "You are
17 My people." Rouse, rouse yourself and rise, Jerusalem, you who have
drunk from the LORD's hand His full cup of rage, the poisoned goblet, drunk
18 and drained it. No one will guide her back, of all the children she has borne;
19 of all the sons she raised there is none to hold her hand.[122] Two things came
to you, but who is moved for you? Massacre and breaking, hunger and the
20 sword; through whom may I comfort you? Your children fainted, fallen at
every street corner, like netted wild oxen, full of the LORD's rage, your God's
21 22 rebuke. So listen, woman oppressed and drunk but not with wine. So
says the LORD, your Lord; so your God fights His people's cause: Behold: I
have taken the poisoned cup from your hand, the goblet of My rage; you will
23 drink from it no more. I shall place it in the hands of those who torment you,
who have said to your face, "Bow down to let us pass." You made your back
52 1 like earth, like the road to be walked over. Rise, rise, Zion, and don
your dress of might; wear your garb of glory, Jerusalem, holy town, for no

119 | Cf. Genesis 13:10.

120 | Rahav was a mythical monster of the sea (see 30:7 above and cf. Ps. 89:11; Job 9:13, 26:12).

121 | The bent-over prisoner is a metaphor for Israel in exile.

122 | This may refer to the trope of a drunken parent whose children will not steady her but leave her helpless in her debasement; cf. Genesis 9:20–27.

ד זִמְרָה׃ הַקְשִׁיבוּ אֵלַי עַמִּי וּלְאוּמִּי אֵלַי הַאֲזִינוּ כִּי תוֹרָה
ה מֵאִתִּי תֵצֵא וּמִשְׁפָּטִי לְאוֹר עַמִּים אַרְגִּיעַ׃ קָרוֹב צִדְקִי יָצָא יִשְׁעִי
ו וּזְרֹעַי עַמִּים יִשְׁפֹּטוּ אֵלַי אִיִּים יְקַוּוּ וְאֶל־זְרֹעִי יְיַחֵלוּן׃ שְׂאוּ לַשָּׁמַיִם
עֵינֵיכֶם וְהַבִּיטוּ אֶל־הָאָרֶץ מִתַּחַת כִּי־שָׁמַיִם כֶּעָשָׁן נִמְלָחוּ וְהָאָרֶץ
כַּבֶּגֶד תִּבְלֶה וְיֹשְׁבֶיהָ כְּמוֹ־כֵן יְמוּתוּן וִישׁוּעָתִי לְעוֹלָם תִּהְיֶה וְצִדְקָתִי
ז לֹא תֵחָת׃ שִׁמְעוּ אֵלַי יֹדְעֵי צֶדֶק עַם תּוֹרָתִי בְלִבָּם
ח אַל־תִּירְאוּ חֶרְפַּת אֱנוֹשׁ וּמִגִּדֻּפֹתָם אַל־תֵּחָתּוּ׃ כִּי כַבֶּגֶד יֹאכְלֵם
עָשׁ וְכַצֶּמֶר יֹאכְלֵם סָס וְצִדְקָתִי לְעוֹלָם תִּהְיֶה וִישׁוּעָתִי לְדוֹר
ט דּוֹרִים׃ עוּרִי עוּרִי לִבְשִׁי־עֹז זְרוֹעַ יהוה עוּרִי כִּימֵי קֶדֶם
י דֹּרוֹת עוֹלָמִים הֲלוֹא אַתְּ־הִיא הַמַּחְצֶבֶת רַהַב מְחוֹלֶלֶת תַּנִּין׃ הֲלוֹא
אַתְּ־הִיא הַמַּחֲרֶבֶת יָם מֵי תְּהוֹם רַבָּה הַשָּׂמָה מַעֲמַקֵּי־יָם דֶּרֶךְ לַעֲבֹר
יא גְּאוּלִים׃ וּפְדוּיֵי יהוה יְשׁוּבוּן וּבָאוּ צִיּוֹן בְּרִנָּה וְשִׂמְחַת עוֹלָם עַל־
יב רֹאשָׁם שָׂשׂוֹן וְשִׂמְחָה יַשִּׂיגוּן נָסוּ יָגוֹן וַאֲנָחָה׃ אָנֹכִי
אָנֹכִי הוּא מְנַחֶמְכֶם מִי־אַתְּ וַתִּירְאִי מֵאֱנוֹשׁ יָמוּת וּמִבֶּן־אָדָם חָצִיר
יג יִנָּתֵן׃ וַתִּשְׁכַּח יהוה עֹשֶׂךָ נוֹטֶה שָׁמַיִם וְיֹסֵד אָרֶץ וַתְּפַחֵד תָּמִיד כָּל־
הַיּוֹם מִפְּנֵי חֲמַת הַמֵּצִיק כַּאֲשֶׁר כּוֹנֵן לְהַשְׁחִית וְאַיֵּה חֲמַת הַמֵּצִיק׃
יד טו מִהַר צֹעֶה לְהִפָּתֵחַ וְלֹא־יָמוּת לַשַּׁחַת וְלֹא יֶחְסַר לַחְמוֹ׃ וְאָנֹכִי יהוה
טז אֱלֹהֶיךָ רֹגַע הַיָּם וַיֶּהֱמוּ גַּלָּיו יהוה צְבָאוֹת שְׁמוֹ׃ וָאָשִׂם דְּבָרַי בְּפִיךָ
וּבְצֵל יָדִי כִּסִּיתִיךָ לִנְטֹעַ שָׁמַיִם וְלִיסֹד אָרֶץ וְלֵאמֹר לְצִיּוֹן עַמִּי־
יז אָתָּה׃ הִתְעוֹרְרִי הִתְעוֹרְרִי קוּמִי יְרוּשָׁלַםִ אֲשֶׁר שָׁתִית
מִיַּד יהוה אֶת־כּוֹס חֲמָתוֹ אֶת־קֻבַּעַת כּוֹס הַתַּרְעֵלָה שָׁתִית מָצִית׃
יח אֵין־מְנַהֵל לָהּ מִכָּל־בָּנִים יָלָדָה וְאֵין מַחֲזִיק בְּיָדָהּ מִכָּל־בָּנִים גִּדֵּלָה׃
יט שְׁתַּיִם הֵנָּה קֹרְאֹתַיִךְ מִי יָנוּד לָךְ הַשֹּׁד וְהַשֶּׁבֶר וְהָרָעָב וְהַחֶרֶב מִי
כ אֲנַחֲמֵךְ׃ בָּנַיִךְ עֻלְּפוּ שָׁכְבוּ בְּרֹאשׁ כָּל־חוּצוֹת כְּתוֹא מִכְמָר הַמְלֵאִים
כא חֲמַת־יהוה גַּעֲרַת אֱלֹהָיִךְ׃ לָכֵן שִׁמְעִי־נָא זֹאת עֲנִיָּה וּשְׁכֻרַת וְלֹא
כב מִיָּיִן׃ כֹּה־אָמַר אֲדֹנַיִךְ יהוה וֵאלֹהַיִךְ יָרִיב עַמּוֹ הִנֵּה לָקַחְתִּי
מִיָּדֵךְ אֶת־כּוֹס הַתַּרְעֵלָה אֶת־קֻבַּעַת כּוֹס חֲמָתִי לֹא־תוֹסִיפִי לִשְׁתּוֹתָהּ
כג עוֹד׃ וְשַׂמְתִּיהָ בְּיַד־מוֹגַיִךְ אֲשֶׁר־אָמְרוּ לְנַפְשֵׁךְ שְׁחִי וְנַעֲבֹרָה וַתָּשִׂימִי
נב א כָאָרֶץ גֵּוֵךְ וְכַחוּץ לַעֹבְרִים׃ עוּרִי עוּרִי לִבְשִׁי עֻזֵּךְ צִיּוֹן
לִבְשִׁי ׀ בִּגְדֵי תִפְאַרְתֵּךְ יְרוּשָׁלַםִ עִיר הַקֹּדֶשׁ כִּי לֹא יוֹסִיף יָבֹא־בָךְ

2 more will uncircumcised, impure ones enter you. Shake yourself free of the
dust; rise up to take your place, Jerusalem. Break free of the chains around
3 your neck, captive daughter Jerusalem. For so says the LORD:
You were sold away for nothing, and it is not for silver[123] that you will be
4 redeemed. For so says the Lord GOD: My people went down long
ago to Egypt, to live there for a time; for nothing, Assyria oppressed them,
5 and now, what is there here for Me? So says the LORD: For nothing My people
is taken captive, its rulers baying. So says the LORD: Unceasingly, all day, My
6 name is defamed, and so – My people will know My name, and so – on that
7 day – they will know that it is I who spoke, that I am here. How
lovely upon the mountains: the steps of the bringer of tidings, resounding
with peace, tidings of good, resounding of rescue, saying to Zion: "Your God
8 has ascended the throne." The voice of your watchmen, their voices rise as
one, singing, for they will see with their own eyes the LORD's return to Zion.
9 Break out in song; sing out together, ruins of Jerusalem, for the LORD has
10 comforted His people, redeemed His Jerusalem. The LORD has uncovered
His holy arm before the eyes of all nations, and all ends of this earth will see
11 rescue from our God. Turn, turn aside – leave that place without
touching the defiled. Go out from there; cleanse yourselves, you who bear
12 the LORD's vessels;[124] this time you will not leave in haste,[125] you will not leave
in flight. The LORD will go before you, the God of Israel your rear guard
13 behind. My servant will prevail,[126] be elevated, raised, attain great
14 height. As everyone was aghast at you, racked beyond recognition as a man,
15 face no longer human, just so: many nations leap in fear, their kings silenced
before him, for they have seen what they were never told of and witnessed
53 1 what they never heard. Who would believe what we have to tell? To whom
2 is the LORD's strong arm revealed? He came up like a tender shoot before
Him, like a slip from a desert land; he has no appearance or manifest glory,
3 no beauty for us to desire, scorned and forsaken by men, a being of pain,
schooled in sickness, one whom we would hide our faces from, scorned – we
4 never considered him. But yes: he has borne our own sickness, has suffered
5 our own pain, and we thought him polluted, God-beaten, abused, but it was
our betrayals that desecrated him, our iniquities that crushed him down; the
anguish of our peace is on his shoulders, and in his bruises – we are healed.
6 All of us have strayed like sheep, each man turning his own way, and the LORD
7 has thrust upon him the iniquity of us all. He was battered and oppressed and
opened not his mouth; led like a lamb to the slaughter, mute as a ewe before
8 the shearer, he opened not his mouth. Taken from imprisonment and
judgment, who of his time will talk to him? For he is expelled from the land

123 | They will be redeemed for free, which will restore God's dignity among nations.

124 | Probably a reference to the carrying of the Temple vessels from Babylon to Jerusalem as ordered in Ezra 6:5.

125 | As you did from Egypt; cf. Deuteronomy 16:3.

126 | The servant described in this passage is the Jewish people, who made the difficult journey from Babylon to Yehuda, only to find suffering and poverty in their homeland.

ב עוֹד עָרֵל וְטָמֵא: הִתְנַעֲרִי מֵעָפָר קוּמִי שְּׁבִי יְרוּשָׁלָ͏ִם הִתְפַּתְּחוּ מוֹסְרֵי הִתְפַּתְּחִי
ג צַוָּארֵךְ שְׁבִיָּה בַּת־צִיּוֹן: כִּי־כֹה אָמַר יְהוָה חִנָּם נִמְכַּרְתֶּם
ד וְלֹא בְכֶסֶף תִּגָּאֵלוּ: כִּי כֹה אָמַר אֲדֹנָי יֱהוִה מִצְרַיִם יָרַד־
ה עַמִּי בָרִאשֹׁנָה לָגוּר שָׁם וְאַשּׁוּר בְּאֶפֶס עֲשָׁקוֹ: וְעַתָּה מַה־לִּי־פֹה
נְאֻם־יְהוָה כִּי־לֻקַּח עַמִּי חִנָּם מֹשְׁלָו יְהֵילִילוּ נְאֻם־יְהוָה וְתָמִיד כָּל־
ו הַיּוֹם שְׁמִי מִנֹּאָץ: לָכֵן יֵדַע עַמִּי שְׁמִי לָכֵן בַּיּוֹם הַהוּא כִּי־אֲנִי־הוּא
ז הַמְדַבֵּר הִנֵּנִי: מַה־נָּאווּ עַל־הֶהָרִים רַגְלֵי מְבַשֵּׂר מַשְׁמִיעַ כב
ח שָׁלוֹם מְבַשֵּׂר טוֹב מַשְׁמִיעַ יְשׁוּעָה אֹמֵר לְצִיּוֹן מָלַךְ אֱלֹהָיִךְ: קוֹל
ט צֹפַיִךְ נָשְׂאוּ קוֹל יַחְדָּו יְרַנֵּנוּ כִּי עַיִן בְּעַיִן יִרְאוּ בְּשׁוּב יְהוָה צִיּוֹן: פִּצְחוּ
י רַנְּנוּ יַחְדָּו חָרְבוֹת יְרוּשָׁלָ͏ִם כִּי־נִחַם יְהוָה עַמּוֹ גָּאַל יְרוּשָׁלָ͏ִם: חָשַׂף
יְהוָה אֶת־זְרוֹעַ קָדְשׁוֹ לְעֵינֵי כָּל־הַגּוֹיִם וְרָאוּ כָּל־אַפְסֵי־אָרֶץ אֵת
יא יְשׁוּעַת אֱלֹהֵינוּ: סוּרוּ סוּרוּ צְאוּ מִשָּׁם טָמֵא אַל־תִּגָּעוּ צְאוּ
יב מִתּוֹכָהּ הִבָּרוּ נֹשְׂאֵי כְּלֵי יְהוָה: כִּי לֹא בְחִפָּזוֹן תֵּצֵאוּ וּבִמְנוּסָה לֹא
יג תֵלֵכוּן כִּי־הֹלֵךְ לִפְנֵיכֶם יְהוָה וּמְאַסִּפְכֶם אֱלֹהֵי יִשְׂרָאֵל: הִנֵּה
יד יַשְׂכִּיל עַבְדִּי יָרוּם וְנִשָּׂא וְגָבַהּ מְאֹד: כַּאֲשֶׁר שָׁמְמוּ עָלֶיךָ רַבִּים כֵּן־
טו מִשְׁחַת מֵאִישׁ מַרְאֵהוּ וְתֹאֳרוֹ מִבְּנֵי אָדָם: כֵּן יַזֶּה גּוֹיִם רַבִּים עָלָיו
יִקְפְּצוּ מְלָכִים פִּיהֶם כִּי אֲשֶׁר לֹא־סֻפַּר לָהֶם רָאוּ וַאֲשֶׁר לֹא־שָׁמְעוּ
נג א ב הִתְבּוֹנָנוּ: מִי הֶאֱמִין לִשְׁמֻעָתֵנוּ וּזְרוֹעַ יְהוָה עַל־מִי נִגְלָתָה: וַיַּעַל
כַּיּוֹנֵק לְפָנָיו וְכַשֹּׁרֶשׁ מֵאֶרֶץ צִיָּה לֹא־תֹאַר לוֹ וְלֹא הָדָר וְנִרְאֵהוּ וְלֹא־
ג מַרְאֶה וְנֶחְמְדֵהוּ: נִבְזֶה וַחֲדַל אִישִׁים אִישׁ מַכְאֹבוֹת וִידוּעַ חֹלִי
ד וּכְמַסְתֵּר פָּנִים מִמֶּנּוּ נִבְזֶה וְלֹא חֲשַׁבְנֻהוּ: אָכֵן חֳלָיֵנוּ הוּא נָשָׂא
ה וּמַכְאֹבֵינוּ סְבָלָם וַאֲנַחְנוּ חֲשַׁבְנֻהוּ נָגוּעַ מֻכֵּה אֱלֹהִים וּמְעֻנֶּה: וְהוּא
מְחֹלָל מִפְּשָׁעֵנוּ מְדֻכָּא מֵעֲוֺנֹתֵינוּ מוּסַר שְׁלוֹמֵנוּ עָלָיו וּבַחֲבֻרָתוֹ
ו נִרְפָּא־לָנוּ: כֻּלָּנוּ כַּצֹּאן תָּעִינוּ אִישׁ לְדַרְכּוֹ פָּנִינוּ וַיהוָה הִפְגִּיעַ בּוֹ אֵת
ז עֲוֺן כֻּלָּנוּ: נִגַּשׂ וְהוּא נַעֲנֶה וְלֹא יִפְתַּח־פִּיו כַּשֶּׂה לַטֶּבַח יוּבָל וּכְרָחֵל
ח לִפְנֵי גֹזְזֶיהָ נֶאֱלָמָה וְלֹא יִפְתַּח פִּיו: מֵעֹצֶר וּמִמִּשְׁפָּט לֻקָּח וְאֶת־דּוֹרוֹ

9 of life, wounded for My people's sin. His grave is with the sinners'; he will be
with the wealthy in death[127] for no violence at his hands, for no deceit at his
10 lips.[128] The LORD has desired to crush him with sickness; if you offer him up
for guilt,[129] then he shall see children, live long, and the LORD's desire will
11 flourish at his hand. From his soul's very burden he will see and feel fullness;
of his mind, My servant will vindicate the righteous before many and bear
12 their iniquities himself. And so I shall give him his share among the great;
with the mighty he will share the spoils, for he has offered up his soul to death,
been numbered among sinners, and borne the guilt of many while pleading
54 1 for the sinners' good. Barren woman, never a mother, rejoice; break
out in joyful song though you have not given birth, for the children of the
2 forsaken woman will outnumber those of the wife, so says the LORD. Broaden
the site of your tent; stretch out your canvas home; do not hold back; lengthen
3 your tent cords, and strengthen its pegs: you shall overflow rightward and
4 left, your children possessing nations, and filling forsaken towns with life. Do
not fear – you will not be shamed; fear not, for none can disgrace you. You
will forget your youthful abjection; the debasement of your widowhood you
5 will call no more to mind, for your husband, He who made you – the LORD
of Hosts is His name, and your redeemer, Israel's Holy One – will be named
6 God of all the world, for as a woman abandoned, of sorrowful spirit, the LORD
7 has called to you: Can the young bride ever be rejected? says your God; for
8 one small moment I left you; with infinite care shall I gather you back; in the
flash of My fury I hid My face from you for just a moment, and in everlasting
9 love will I care for you now. So speaks the LORD, your redeemer. For
these are the waters of Noaḥ to Me, and I swore that the waters of Noaḥ would
never sweep again over the earth. And so did I swear no more to be furious
10 with you, no more to rebuke you. For mountains may move, hills may
crumble away; but My love for you will not be moved, nor My pact of peace
11 crumble. So speaks the LORD, who cares for you. Oppressed and
storm swept, never comforted; behold: I am paving your ground with garnet,
12 lapis lazuli your foundations. I am fitting your windows with rubies, your
13 gates with glowing granite, marking your borders with stones men covet. All
your children will be students of the LORD, and great will be your children's
14 peace. On righteousness will you be founded; stay far from oppression; you
15 will not fear, and terror will never come near you. No strife can arise without
16 My assent; who among you fears one who could come upon you? For I create
the craftsman who blows the charcoal fire and brings forth the tools of his
17 trade; I create also the destroyer to do harm. No weapon made to harm you
can prevail; any tongue that calls you into judgment, you will prove its fault.
This is the birthright of the LORD's servants, for their innocence is Mine; so

127 | This is a punishment because wealthy people's graves were more likely to be plundered by grave robbers.

128 | That is, he did not deserve this punishment.

129 | If you confess (following Rabbi Isaiah miTrani); cf. Numbers 5:6–7.

ט מִי יְשׂוֹחֵחַ כִּי נִגְזַר מֵאֶרֶץ חַיִּים מִפֶּשַׁע עַמִּי נֶגַע לָמוֹ: וַיִּתֵּן אֶת־רְשָׁעִים
י קִבְרוֹ וְאֶת־עָשִׁיר בְּמֹתָיו עַל לֹא־חָמָס עָשָׂה וְלֹא מִרְמָה בְּפִיו: וַיהוָה
חָפֵץ דַּכְּאוֹ הֶחֱלִי אִם־תָּשִׂים אָשָׁם נַפְשׁוֹ יִרְאֶה זֶרַע יַאֲרִיךְ יָמִים וְחֵפֶץ
יא יְהוָה בְּיָדוֹ יִצְלָח: מֵעֲמַל נַפְשׁוֹ יִרְאֶה יִשְׂבָּע בְּדַעְתּוֹ יַצְדִּיק צַדִּיק
יב עַבְדִּי לָרַבִּים וַעֲוֺנֹתָם הוּא יִסְבֹּל: לָכֵן אֲחַלֶּק־לוֹ בָרַבִּים וְאֶת־עֲצוּמִים
יְחַלֵּק שָׁלָל תַּחַת אֲשֶׁר הֶעֱרָה לַמָּוֶת נַפְשׁוֹ וְאֶת־פֹּשְׁעִים נִמְנָה וְהוּא
נד א חֵטְא־רַבִּים נָשָׂא וְלַפֹּשְׁעִים יַפְגִּיעַ: רָנִּי עֲקָרָה לֹא יָלָדָה
פִּצְחִי רִנָּה וְצַהֲלִי לֹא־חָלָה כִּי־רַבִּים בְּנֵי־שׁוֹמֵמָה מִבְּנֵי בְעוּלָה אָמַר
ב יְהוָה: הַרְחִיבִי ׀ מְקוֹם אָהֳלֵךְ וִירִיעוֹת מִשְׁכְּנוֹתַיִךְ יַטּוּ אַל־תַּחְשֹׂכִי
ג הַאֲרִיכִי מֵיתָרַיִךְ וִיתֵדֹתַיִךְ חַזֵּקִי: כִּי־יָמִין וּשְׂמֹאול תִּפְרֹצִי וְזַרְעֵךְ
ד גּוֹיִם יִירָשׁ וְעָרִים נְשַׁמּוֹת יוֹשִׁיבוּ: אַל־תִּירְאִי כִּי־לֹא תֵבוֹשִׁי וְאַל־
תִּכָּלְמִי כִּי לֹא תַחְפִּירִי כִּי בֹשֶׁת עֲלוּמַיִךְ תִּשְׁכָּחִי וְחֶרְפַּת אַלְמְנוּתַיִךְ
ה לֹא תִזְכְּרִי־עוֹד: כִּי בֹעֲלַיִךְ עֹשַׂיִךְ יְהוָה צְבָאוֹת שְׁמוֹ וְגֹאֲלֵךְ קְדוֹשׁ
ו יִשְׂרָאֵל אֱלֹהֵי כָל־הָאָרֶץ יִקָּרֵא: כִּי־כְאִשָּׁה עֲזוּבָה וַעֲצוּבַת רוּחַ קְרָאָךְ
ז יְהוָה וְאֵשֶׁת נְעוּרִים כִּי תִמָּאֵס אָמַר אֱלֹהָיִךְ: בְּרֶגַע קָטֹן עֲזַבְתִּיךְ
ח וּבְרַחֲמִים גְּדֹלִים אֲקַבְּצֵךְ: בְּשֶׁצֶף קֶצֶף הִסְתַּרְתִּי פָנַי רֶגַע מִמֵּךְ
ט וּבְחֶסֶד עוֹלָם רִחַמְתִּיךְ אָמַר גֹּאֲלֵךְ יְהוָה: כִּי־מֵי
נֹחַ זֹאת לִי אֲשֶׁר נִשְׁבַּעְתִּי מֵעֲבֹר מֵי־נֹחַ עוֹד עַל־הָאָרֶץ כֵּן
י נִשְׁבַּעְתִּי מִקְּצֹף עָלַיִךְ וּמִגְּעָר־בָּךְ: כִּי הֶהָרִים יָמוּשׁוּ וְהַגְּבָעוֹת
תְּמוּטֶינָה וְחַסְדִּי מֵאִתֵּךְ לֹא־יָמוּשׁ וּבְרִית שְׁלוֹמִי לֹא תָמוּט אָמַר
יא מְרַחֲמֵךְ יְהוָה: עֲנִיָּה סֹעֲרָה לֹא נֻחָמָה הִנֵּה אָנֹכִי מַרְבִּיץ
יב בַּפּוּךְ אֲבָנַיִךְ וִיסַדְתִּיךְ בַּסַּפִּירִים: וְשַׂמְתִּי כַּדְכֹד שִׁמְשֹׁתַיִךְ וּשְׁעָרַיִךְ
יג לְאַבְנֵי אֶקְדָּח וְכָל־גְּבוּלֵךְ לְאַבְנֵי־חֵפֶץ: וְכָל־בָּנַיִךְ לִמּוּדֵי יְהוָה וְרַב
יד שְׁלוֹם בָּנָיִךְ: בִּצְדָקָה תִּכּוֹנָנִי רַחֲקִי מֵעֹשֶׁק כִּי־לֹא תִירָאִי וּמִמְּחִתָּה
טו כִּי לֹא־תִקְרַב אֵלָיִךְ: הֵן גּוֹר יָגוּר אֶפֶס מֵאוֹתִי מִי־גָר אִתָּךְ עָלַיִךְ יִפּוֹל:
טז הֵן אָנֹכִי בָּרָאתִי חָרָשׁ נֹפֵחַ בְּאֵשׁ פֶּחָם וּמוֹצִיא כְלִי לְמַעֲשֵׂהוּ וְאָנֹכִי הִנֵּה
יז בָּרָאתִי מַשְׁחִית לְחַבֵּל: כָּל־כְּלִי יוּצַר עָלַיִךְ לֹא יִצְלָח וְכָל־לָשׁוֹן
תָּקוּם־אִתָּךְ לַמִּשְׁפָּט תַּרְשִׁיעִי זֹאת נַחֲלַת עַבְדֵי יְהוָה וְצִדְקָתָם מֵאִתִּי

55 1 says the LORD. You who are thirsty, all, come to water; you who have
no silver, come, take food and eat; come and take food without silver, wine
2 and milk without cost, for why should you weigh out your silver for no bread,
your labor bringing you no fullness? Listen – listen to Me: let goodness
3 nourish you, and let your souls delight in plenty. Turn your ear to Me and
come; listen, that your souls may live; let Me forge an everlasting covenant
4 with you, like David's faithful promises, for I make him a witness to nations,
5 a leader, a ruler of nations; for you shall call out, call, to a people you know
not, and a people who know you not will come running out to you for the
6 sake of the LORD your God, the Holy One of Israel, your glory. Seek
out the LORD while He is to be found; call to Him – now, when He is close.
7 Let the wrongdoer turn from his path, the corrupt man abandon his thoughts
and return to the LORD, who shows compassion, to our God, who forgives
8 much, for My thoughts, they are not your thoughts and nor are your ways
9 Mine; so says the LORD. As high as the sky is raised above the land, so are My
10 ways above yours, My thoughts above your thoughts; just as rain and snow
fall from the skies and will not there return before quenching the earth's thirst,
before seeing her birth and flourish, yielding seed to the sower and bread to
11 the one who eats, just so My word, when it leaves My mouth, will not come
back to Me unanswered without working My desire, without bearing the fruit
12 of My message, for you will go forth in joy, be led on in peace; the mountains
and the hills will break out in song before you as all the wild trees clap their
13 hands. In place of the thorn tree, juniper will grow, and where there were
nettles, myrtle. This will be, for the LORD, a monument, an everlasting sign,
56 1 that will not be severed. So says the LORD: Guard close the Law; do
what is right. My salvation is close at hand, My righteousness will be revealed.
2 Happy the man who does this, the person who clings to this: guarding My
3 Sabbath from being profaned, guarding his hand from performing evil. Let
not the son of strangers say, who has come to walk with the LORD, "The LORD
has separated me from His people." Let the castrated slave not say, "I am a
4 tree dried up." For thus says the LORD of those castrated slaves who
have guarded My Sabbath, who chose what I desire and hold fast to My
5 covenant: To these I am giving, in My house between My walls, a monument
and name better than sons and than daughters; I give them a name everlasting
6 that will not be severed. And the children of strangers who have
come to join the LORD, to serve Him, to love the LORD's name and be His
servants, all who guard the Sabbath from being profaned and hold fast to My
7 covenant, I shall bring them to My holy mount, show them joy in My house
of prayer. Their offerings and sacrifices are desired on My altar, for My House
8 will be called a house of prayer for all peoples. So says the Lord GOD, who
gathers back the banished ones of Israel: I shall gather yet more with those
9 who have been gathered. All the wild animals, come and eat, you creatures
10 of the forest. All his watchmen[130] are blind, do not know, mute dogs

130 | The people's leaders or false prophets.

נה א נאם־יהוה: הוי כל־צמא לכו למים ואשר אין־לו כסף
ב לכו שברו ואכלו ולכו שברו בלוא־כסף ובלוא מחיר יין וחלב: למה
תשקלו־כסף בלוא־לחם ויגיעכם בלוא לשבעה שמעו שמוע אלי
ג ואכלו־טוב ותתענג בדשן נפשכם: הטו אזנכם ולכו אלי שמעו
ד ותחי נפשכם ואכרתה לכם ברית עולם חסדי דוד הנאמנים: הן
ה עד לאומים נתתיו נגיד ומצוה לאמים: הן גוי לא־תדע תקרא
וגוי לא־ידעוך אליך ירוצו למען יהוה אלהיך ולקדוש ישראל כי
ו ז פארך: דרשו יהוה בהמצאו קראהו בהיותו קרוב: יעזב
רשע דרכו ואיש און מחשבתיו וישב אל־יהוה וירחמהו ואל־אלהינו
ח כי־ירבה לסלוח: כי לא מחשבותי מחשבותיכם ולא דרכיכם דרכי
ט נאם יהוה: כי־גבהו שמים מארץ כן גבהו דרכי מדרכיכם ומחשבתי
י ממחשבתיכם: כי כאשר ירד הגשם והשלג מן־השמים ושמה לא
ישוב כי אם־הרוה את־הארץ והולידה והצמיחה ונתן זרע לזרע
יא ולחם לאכל: כן יהיה דברי אשר יצא מפי לא־ישוב אלי ריקם כי
יב אם־עשה את־אשר חפצתי והצליח אשר שלחתיו: כי־בשמחה
תצאו ובשלום תובלון ההרים והגבעות יפצחו לפניכם רנה וכל־עצי
יג השדה ימחאו־כף: תחת הנעצוץ יעלה ברוש תחת הסרפד יעלה כג ותחת
נו א הדס והיה ליהוה לשם לאות עולם לא יכרת: כה
אמר יהוה שמרו משפט ועשו צדקה כי־קרובה ישועתי לבוא
ב וצדקתי להגלות: אשרי אנוש יעשה־זאת ובן־אדם יחזיק בה שמר
ג שבת מחללו ושמר ידו מעשות כל־רע: ואל־יאמר בן־הנכר הנלוה
אל־יהוה לאמר הבדל יבדילני יהוה מעל עמו ואל־יאמר הסריס
ד הן אני עץ יבש: כי־כה | אמר יהוה לסריסים אשר
ה ישמרו את־שבתותי ובחרו באשר חפצתי ומחזיקים בבריתי: ונתתי
להם בביתי ובחומתי יד ושם טוב מבנים ומבנות שם עולם אתן־לו
ו אשר לא יכרת: ובני הנכר הנלוים על־יהוה לשרתו
ולאהבה את־שם יהוה להיות לו לעבדים כל־שמר שבת מחללו
ז ומחזיקים בבריתי: והביאותים אל־הר קדשי ושמחתים בבית
תפלתי עולתיהם וזבחיהם לרצון על־מזבחי כי ביתי בית־תפלה
ח יקרא לכל־העמים: נאם אדני יהוה מקבץ נדחי ישראל עוד
ט אקבץ עליו לנקבציו: כל חיתו שדי אתיו לאכל כל־חיתו
י ביער: צפו עורים כלם לא ידעו כלם כלבים אלמים

11 all, no bark, full of dreams, lying down, lovers of slumber, like brazen dogs
who know no fullness. These shepherds, who know not how to understand,
12 each turns to his own way, every man to his own profit: *"Here: I bring the wine;*
57 1 *let us get us drunk on ale; let the morrow be like today, and greater still."* The
righteous man is gone; none take it to heart; all good people are gathered
up,[131] with none to understand: it is this evil that causes the righteous to be
2 gathered up. Yet peace will come: they lie still in their resting place, those
3 who walked upright. Now draw close, you children of sorcery, sons
4 of a philanderer and an adulterous wife. To whom do you go for your delight;
to whom do you open wide your mouth and make your mocking tongue
5 long? Are you not children of sin, the offspring of lies, in heat with the false
gods under every leafy tree, slaughtering children in rivers and under the
6 crags of the rocks. You took your share amid the riverbeds' smooth stones;
they are your destiny; to them as well you poured out offerings, brought
7 sacrifices. Am I to be comforted for that? Upon the high and lofty mountains
you laid down your bed; there too you went up to make your offerings.
8 Behind the door, the doorpost, you mounted your keepsakes, for you are
uncovered and gone from Me;[132] you made your bed broad, forged your
covenant with them; you have loved to lie with them, loved every hand you
9 saw.[133] Daubed in oils, you paid your court to kings; how great your perfumery
is; you sent your messengers out afar and lowered yourself as deep as Sheol;
10 you put great efforts into your path, [134] never admitting despair. Your hands
11 made their livelihood and did not give way to sickness; whom did you regard
or fear throughout your deception? Me you did not remember or take to your
12 heart. I have held still, always, and so you did not fear Me. Let Me recount
13 your righteousness.... [135] Your actions do you no good. When you call out, let
them rescue you, the gods that you collected. The wind will carry them all
away; empty breath will take them. But those who shelter in Me will possess
14 the earth and inherit My holy mountain; they will say, "Mark, mark a road
here;[136] clear a way. Lift out of My people's way all that could make them
15 fall." Thus says the high, the exalted One, abiding forever, whose
name is holy: High and holy I abide, yet I am with the crushed and humbled,
16 giving life to the humbled, giving life to crushed men's hearts. I will not
forever contend with you, will not rage to the bitter end. When the spirit
17 faints before Me, I created these souls. I have raged at the sin behind their
profits, have struck them, have hidden My face and raged as they went
18 wayward on the path their hearts beat out. I have seen their ways and will
heal them. I will lead them, will reward them in comfort, them and their
19 mourners; I form the words: Peace, peace to those far away and near – so the

131 | That is, they perish.
132 | The "wife" has gone from the marital bed to embrace her lovers.
133 | You looked favorably upon anyone who reached out to embrace you.
134 | The "path" and "livelihood" allude to prostitutes to the wealthy, whose custom was to advertise through messengers.
135 | This is said in irony.
136 | Stones would be cleared to the two sides of the dirt path, forming the road.

יא לֹא יוּכְלוּ לִנְבֹּחַ הֹזִים שֹׁכְבִים אֹהֲבֵי לָנוּם: וְהַכְּלָבִים עַזֵּי־נֶפֶשׁ לֹא
יָדְעוּ שָׂבְעָה וְהֵמָּה רֹעִים לֹא יָדְעוּ הָבִין כֻּלָּם לְדַרְכָּם פָּנוּ אִישׁ לְבִצְעוֹ
יב מִקָּצֵהוּ: אֵתָיוּ אֶקְחָה־יַיִן וְנִסְבְּאָה שֵׁכָר וְהָיָה כָזֶה יוֹם מָחָר גָּדוֹל יֶתֶר
נז א מְאֹד: הַצַּדִּיק אָבָד וְאֵין אִישׁ שָׂם עַל־לֵב וְאַנְשֵׁי־חֶסֶד נֶאֱסָפִים בְּאֵין
ב מֵבִין כִּי־מִפְּנֵי הָרָעָה נֶאֱסַף הַצַּדִּיק: יָבוֹא שָׁלוֹם יָנוּחוּ עַל־מִשְׁכְּבוֹתָם
ג הֹלֵךְ נְכֹחוֹ: וְאַתֶּם קִרְבוּ־הֵנָּה בְּנֵי עֹנְנָה זֶרַע מְנָאֵף וַתִּזְנֶה:
ד עַל־מִי תִּתְעַנָּגוּ עַל־מִי תַּרְחִיבוּ פֶה תַּאֲרִיכוּ לָשׁוֹן הֲלוֹא־אַתֶּם יִלְדֵי־
ה פֶשַׁע זֶרַע שָׁקֶר: הַנֵּחָמִים בָּאֵלִים תַּחַת כָּל־עֵץ רַעֲנָן שֹׁחֲטֵי הַיְלָדִים
ו בַּנְּחָלִים תַּחַת סְעִפֵי הַסְּלָעִים: בְּחַלְּקֵי־נַחַל חֶלְקֵךְ הֵם הֵם גּוֹרָלֵךְ
ז גַּם־לָהֶם שָׁפַכְתְּ נֶסֶךְ הֶעֱלִית מִנְחָה הַעַל אֵלֶּה אֶנָּחֵם: עַל הַר־גָּבֹהַּ
ח וְנִשָּׂא שַׂמְתְּ מִשְׁכָּבֵךְ גַּם־שָׁם עָלִית לִזְבֹּחַ זָבַח: וְאַחַר הַדֶּלֶת וְהַמְּזוּזָה
שַׂמְתְּ זִכְרוֹנֵךְ כִּי מֵאִתִּי גִּלִּית וַתַּעֲלִי הִרְחַבְתְּ מִשְׁכָּבֵךְ וַתִּכְרָת־לָךְ
ט מֵהֶם אָהַבְתְּ מִשְׁכָּבָם יָד חָזִית: וַתָּשֻׁרִי לַמֶּלֶךְ בַּשֶּׁמֶן וַתַּרְבִּי רִקֻּחָיִךְ
י וַתְּשַׁלְּחִי צִרַיִךְ עַד־מֵרָחֹק וַתַּשְׁפִּילִי עַד־שְׁאוֹל: בְּרֹב דַּרְכֵּךְ יָגַעַתְּ
יא לֹא אָמַרְתְּ נוֹאָשׁ חַיַּת יָדֵךְ מָצָאת עַל־כֵּן לֹא חָלִית: וְאֶת־מִי דָּאַגְתְּ
וַתִּירְאִי כִּי תְכַזֵּבִי וְאוֹתִי לֹא זָכַרְתְּ לֹא־שַׂמְתְּ עַל־לִבֵּךְ הֲלֹא אֲנִי
יב מַחְשֶׁה וּמֵעֹלָם וְאוֹתִי לֹא תִירָאִי: אֲנִי אַגִּיד צִדְקָתֵךְ וְאֶת־מַעֲשַׂיִךְ
יג וְלֹא יוֹעִילוּךְ: בְּזַעֲקֵךְ יַצִּילֻךְ קִבּוּצַיִךְ וְאֶת־כֻּלָּם יִשָּׂא־רוּחַ יִקַּח־הָבֶל
יד וְהַחוֹסֶה בִי יִנְחַל־אֶרֶץ וְיִירַשׁ הַר־קָדְשִׁי: וְאָמַר סֹלּוּ־סֹלּוּ פַּנּוּ־דָרֶךְ
טו הָרִימוּ מִכְשׁוֹל מִדֶּרֶךְ עַמִּי: כִּי כֹה אָמַר רָם וְנִשָּׂא שֹׁכֵן
עַד וְקָדוֹשׁ שְׁמוֹ מָרוֹם וְקָדוֹשׁ אֶשְׁכּוֹן וְאֶת־דַּכָּא וּשְׁפַל־רוּחַ לְהַחֲיוֹת
טז רוּחַ שְׁפָלִים וּלְהַחֲיוֹת לֵב נִדְכָּאִים: כִּי לֹא לְעוֹלָם אָרִיב וְלֹא לָנֶצַח
יז אֶקְּצוֹף כִּי־רוּחַ מִלְּפָנַי יַעֲטוֹף וּנְשָׁמוֹת אֲנִי עָשִׂיתִי: בַּעֲוֹן בִּצְעוֹ קָצַפְתִּי
יח וְאַכֵּהוּ הַסְתֵּר וְאֶקְצֹף וַיֵּלֶךְ שׁוֹבָב בְּדֶרֶךְ לִבּוֹ: דְּרָכָיו רָאִיתִי וְאֶרְפָּאֵהוּ
יט וְאַנְחֵהוּ וַאֲשַׁלֵּם נִחֻמִים לוֹ וְלַאֲבֵלָיו: בּוֹרֵא נוב שְׂפָתָיִם שָׁלוֹם ׀ נִיב

20 LORD speaks – I will heal them. The wicked are like the ocean surging, unable
21 to be still; its waters fling up mud and filth. There is no peace, says my God,
58 1 for the wicked. Shout out loud; do not hold back; raise up your
voice like a ram's horn. Tell My people of their rebellion; tell the House of
2 Yaakov their sins. Day after day they search for Me; they desire to know My
ways,[137] like a nation that always did right and never forsook its God's justice.
They ask for rulings in law. They say that being close to God is all that interests
3 them. "Why do we fast and You not see it, oppress ourselves and You
acknowledge it not?" But even on your fast days you press your interests,
4 extort a profit on all that you own. Contending and fighting each other, you
fast while you beat with the fist of evil. The fast you perform today will not
5 carry your voice on high. Is this the fast I have chosen, a day for man to
oppress himself? To bow his head like a rush in the wind, to lay his bed with
sackcloth and ashes? Is this what you call a fast, "a day for the LORD's favor"?
6 No! This is the fast I choose: Loosen the bindings of evil, and break the
slavery chain. Those who were crushed, release to freedom, and shatter every
7 yoke of slavery. Break your bread for the starving; bring dispossessed
wanderers home. When you see a man naked, clothe him; do not avert your
8 eyes from your own flesh.[138] Then will your light break forth like sunrise, and
healing will grow fast over your wound. Your righteousness will go before
9 you, with the LORD's presence your rear guard behind. Then you will call, and
10 the LORD will answer; when you cry out, He will say, "I am here"; if you give
of your soul to the starving and answer the hunger of souls oppressed, then
your light will shine out in darkness; your very night will shine like noontide.
11 The LORD will fortify your bones. You will be like a watered garden, like a
12 spring of waters that will not fail. Places ruined long ago will be rebuilt in you;
you will raise up houses from age-old foundations, be known as mender of
13 the ruptured wall, as the one who restored the paths for living. If you keep
your feet from roving on the Sabbath,[139] from pursuing your interests on My
holy day, if you call the Sabbath a delight, the LORD's holy day to be honored,
if you honor it by not going your own way, attending to your own affairs, or
14 speaking idle words, then you will find joy in the LORD; I will set you astride
the heights of the earth to feast on the inheritance of your father Yaakov, for
59 1 the mouth of the LORD has spoken. The LORD's hand does not
2 fall short of rescue; His ear is not so dull as not to hear. It is your sins that
separated you from your God, your iniquities that hid His face from you, Him
3 from your hearing, the palms of your hands disgusting with blood, your
fingers with iniquity; your lips have spoken lies, and your tongue frames
4 violence. No one calls out in integrity; none come honestly to be judged; they
trust in emptiness, speak hollow words, pregnant with treachery, breeding
5 sin.[140] They hatch out adders' eggs and weave spiders' webs. Anyone eating

137 | That is, they falsely claim to seek God's ways.
138 | A play on words; as in English, "flesh" can refer to the naked body or to one's relatives.
139 | Following the instruction in Exodus 16:29.
140 | Cf. Psalms 7:15; Job 15:35.

כ שָׁלוֹם לָרָחוֹק וְלַקָּרוֹב אָמַר יְהוָה וּרְפָאתִיו׃ וְהָרְשָׁעִים כַּיָּם נִגְרָשׁ כִּי
כא הַשְׁקֵט לֹא יוּכָל וַיִּגְרְשׁוּ מֵימָיו רֶפֶשׁ וָטִיט׃ אֵין שָׁלוֹם אָמַר אֱלֹהַי
נח א לָרְשָׁעִים׃ קְרָא בְגָרוֹן אַל־תַּחְשֹׂךְ כַּשּׁוֹפָר הָרֵם קוֹלֶךָ
ב וְהַגֵּד לְעַמִּי פִּשְׁעָם וּלְבֵית יַעֲקֹב חַטֹּאתָם׃ וְאוֹתִי יוֹם יוֹם יִדְרֹשׁוּן
וְדַעַת דְּרָכַי יֶחְפָּצוּן כְּגוֹי אֲשֶׁר־צְדָקָה עָשָׂה וּמִשְׁפַּט אֱלֹהָיו לֹא עָזָב
ג יִשְׁאָלוּנִי מִשְׁפְּטֵי־צֶדֶק קִרְבַת אֱלֹהִים יֶחְפָּצוּן׃ לָמָּה צַּמְנוּ וְלֹא רָאִיתָ
עִנִּינוּ נַפְשֵׁנוּ וְלֹא תֵדָע הֵן בְּיוֹם צֹמְכֶם תִּמְצְאוּ־חֵפֶץ וְכָל־עַצְּבֵיכֶם
ד תִּנְגֹּשׂוּ׃ הֵן לְרִיב וּמַצָּה תָּצוּמוּ וּלְהַכּוֹת בְּאֶגְרֹף רֶשַׁע לֹא־תָצוּמוּ כַיּוֹם
ה לְהַשְׁמִיעַ בַּמָּרוֹם קוֹלְכֶם׃ הֲכָזֶה יִהְיֶה צוֹם אֶבְחָרֵהוּ יוֹם עַנּוֹת אָדָם
נַפְשׁוֹ הֲלָכֹף כְּאַגְמֹן רֹאשׁוֹ וְשַׂק וָאֵפֶר יַצִּיעַ הֲלָזֶה תִּקְרָא־צוֹם וְיוֹם
ו רָצוֹן לַיהוָה׃ הֲלוֹא זֶה צוֹם אֶבְחָרֵהוּ פַּתֵּחַ חַרְצֻבּוֹת רֶשַׁע הַתֵּר אֲגֻדּוֹת
ז מוֹטָה וְשַׁלַּח רְצוּצִים חָפְשִׁים וְכָל־מוֹטָה תְּנַתֵּקוּ׃ הֲלוֹא פָרֹס לָרָעֵב
לַחְמֶךָ וַעֲנִיִּים מְרוּדִים תָּבִיא בָיִת כִּי־תִרְאֶה עָרֹם וְכִסִּיתוֹ וּמִבְּשָׂרְךָ
ח לֹא תִתְעַלָּם׃ אָז יִבָּקַע כַּשַּׁחַר אוֹרֶךָ וַאֲרֻכָתְךָ מְהֵרָה תִצְמָח וְהָלַךְ
ט לְפָנֶיךָ צִדְקֶךָ כְּבוֹד יְהוָה יַאַסְפֶךָ׃ אָז תִּקְרָא וַיהוָה יַעֲנֶה תְּשַׁוַּע וְיֹאמַר
י הִנֵּנִי אִם־תָּסִיר מִתּוֹכְךָ מוֹטָה שְׁלַח אֶצְבַּע וְדַבֶּר־אָוֶן׃ וְתָפֵק לָרָעֵב
נַפְשֶׁךָ וְנֶפֶשׁ נַעֲנָה תַּשְׂבִּיעַ וְזָרַח בַּחֹשֶׁךְ אוֹרֶךָ וַאֲפֵלָתְךָ כַּצָּהֳרָיִם׃
יא וְנָחֲךָ יְהוָה תָּמִיד וְהִשְׂבִּיעַ בְּצַחְצָחוֹת נַפְשֶׁךָ וְעַצְמֹתֶיךָ יַחֲלִיץ וְהָיִיתָ
יב כְּגַן רָוֶה וּכְמוֹצָא מַיִם אֲשֶׁר לֹא־יְכַזְּבוּ מֵימָיו׃ וּבָנוּ מִמְּךָ חָרְבוֹת עוֹלָם
מוֹסְדֵי דוֹר־וָדוֹר תְּקוֹמֵם וְקֹרָא לְךָ גֹּדֵר פֶּרֶץ מְשֹׁבֵב נְתִיבוֹת לָשָׁבֶת׃
יג אִם־תָּשִׁיב מִשַּׁבָּת רַגְלֶךָ עֲשׂוֹת חֲפָצֶךָ בְּיוֹם קָדְשִׁי וְקָרָאתָ לַשַּׁבָּת
עֹנֶג לִקְדוֹשׁ יְהוָה מְכֻבָּד וְכִבַּדְתּוֹ מֵעֲשׂוֹת דְּרָכֶיךָ מִמְּצוֹא חֶפְצְךָ וְדַבֵּר
יד דָּבָר׃ אָז תִּתְעַנַּג עַל־יְהוָה וְהִרְכַּבְתִּיךָ עַל־בָּמוֹתֵי אָרֶץ וְהַאֲכַלְתִּיךָ כד בָּמֳתֵי
נט א נַחֲלַת יַעֲקֹב אָבִיךָ כִּי פִּי יְהוָה דִּבֵּר׃ הֵן לֹא־קָצְרָה יַד־
ב יְהוָה מֵהוֹשִׁיעַ וְלֹא־כָבְדָה אָזְנוֹ מִשְּׁמוֹעַ׃ כִּי אִם־עֲוֺנֹתֵיכֶם הָיוּ
מַבְדִּלִים בֵּינֵכֶם לְבֵין אֱלֹהֵיכֶם וְחַטֹּאותֵיכֶם הִסְתִּירוּ פָנִים מִכֶּם
ג מִשְּׁמוֹעַ׃ כִּי כַפֵּיכֶם נְגֹאֲלוּ בַדָּם וְאֶצְבְּעוֹתֵיכֶם בֶּעָוֺן שִׂפְתוֹתֵיכֶם דִּבְּרוּ־
ד שֶׁקֶר לְשׁוֹנְכֶם עַוְלָה תֶהְגֶּה׃ אֵין־קֹרֵא בְצֶדֶק וְאֵין נִשְׁפָּט בֶּאֱמוּנָה
ה בָּטוֹחַ עַל־תֹּהוּ וְדַבֶּר־שָׁוְא הָרוֹ עָמָל וְהוֹלֵיד אָוֶן׃ בֵּיצֵי צִפְעוֹנִי בִּקֵּעוּ
וְקוּרֵי עַכָּבִישׁ יֶאֱרֹגוּ הָאֹכֵל מִבֵּיצֵיהֶם יָמוּת וְהַזּוּרֶה תִּבָּקַע אֶפְעֶה׃

6 those eggs will die; kicked apart, they will hatch out vipers. Those webs will
not make them a garment, nor will their actions hide them. Their actions are
7 acts of wickedness, and violence is in their hands. Their feet race toward
evil; they rush to spill innocent blood;[141] their thoughts are thoughts of
8 wickedness, with violent destruction strewn along their road. They do not
know the way of peace; their byways know no justice; their paths turn crooked
9 before them: no one who treads these will ever know peace. This is why
justice is far from them, and they will not reach goodness. "We hope for light,
10 and here is darkness; for brightness, yet we walk in gloom. We feel our way
like blind men against the wall; we stumble on as if eyeless. We have fallen at
11 noontime as if it were night; we walk among the healthy as if dead. All of us
growl like bears, moan like doves, hope for judgment, but none comes; for
12 rescue, but it is far from us, for our crimes in Your presence are many; our
sins have spoken against us. Our crimes are with us always; we know our
13 iniquities well: rebelling against the Lord, denying Him, fleeing away from
our God, speaking oppression and waywardness, conceiving and speaking a
14 mind's lies. Justice has fled back, and righteousness stands distant, for truth
15 has fallen down in the town square, and uprightness gains no entry; truth is
absent; those who turn from evil are gone away from us." The Lord sees it
16 all; it is evil in His eyes, for there is no justice. He sees there is no man
here – aghast, for there is none to intercede – so His own arm brings rescue;
17 His righteousness brings strength. He dons righteousness as armor, with a
helmet of rescue on His head; He dons the clothes of vengeance and His
18 passion as a mantle. A rightful punishment, rightly paid, rage against His foes,
19 punishment of enemies, punishment to far-off coastlands He shall pay. From
the western horizon they will fear the Lord's name; from the rising of the
sun, revere His glory, for the foe will come flooding like a river, but from the
20 spirit of the Lord he will flee. A redeemer is coming to Zion, to those among
21 Yaakov who turn back from sin; the Lord has spoken. And I, this is My
covenant with them – so says the Lord – My spirit, which is upon you, My
words, which I planted in your mouths, will not fade from your mouths or
the mouths of your children or of your children's children – so speaks the
60 1 Lord – from now until the end of time. Rise, give light, for your
2 light has come: the glory of the Lord shines over you, for darkness may cover
the earth, and clouds shroud nations, but over you, the Lord will be shining,
3 His glory manifest over you; nations will walk toward your light, and kings
4 into the brilliance you shine forth. Raise your eyes; look around and see: all
of them gathered in, and come to you; your sons have come from far away,
5 your daughters as if clinging to nursemaids' hips.[142] Then you will see and
shine; your heart will fill with awe and open wide, for the ocean's abundance
6 will turn to you; the wealth of nations will come to you; herds of camels will
cover your land, young camels from Midyan and Eifa, all having come to you
from Sheba, carrying gold and frankincense and tidings of the Lord's praise.

141 | Cf. Proverbs 1:16.
142 | As if carried by their nursemaids; cf. 49:23.

ו קוּרֵיהֶם לֹא־יִהְיוּ לְבֶגֶד וְלֹא יִתְכַּסּוּ בְּמַעֲשֵׂיהֶם מַעֲשֵׂיהֶם מַעֲשֵׂי־אָוֶן
ז וּפֹעַל חָמָס בְּכַפֵּיהֶם: רַגְלֵיהֶם לָרַע יָרֻצוּ וִימַהֲרוּ לִשְׁפֹּךְ דָּם נָקִי
ח מַחְשְׁבוֹתֵיהֶם מַחְשְׁבוֹת אָוֶן שֹׁד וָשֶׁבֶר בִּמְסִלּוֹתָם: דֶּרֶךְ שָׁלוֹם לֹא
יָדָעוּ וְאֵין מִשְׁפָּט בְּמַעְגְּלוֹתָם נְתִיבוֹתֵיהֶם עִקְּשׁוּ לָהֶם כֹּל דֹּרֵךְ בָּהּ
ט לֹא יָדַע שָׁלוֹם: עַל־כֵּן רָחַק מִשְׁפָּט מִמֶּנּוּ וְלֹא תַשִּׂיגֵנוּ צְדָקָה נְקַוֶּה
י לָאוֹר וְהִנֵּה־חֹשֶׁךְ לִנְגֹהוֹת בָּאֲפֵלוֹת נְהַלֵּךְ: נְגַשְׁשָׁה כַעִוְרִים קִיר
יא וּכְאֵין עֵינַיִם נְגַשֵּׁשָׁה כָּשַׁלְנוּ בַצָּהֳרַיִם כַּנֶּשֶׁף בָּאַשְׁמַנִּים כַּמֵּתִים: נֶהֱמֶה
כַדֻּבִּים כֻּלָּנוּ וְכַיּוֹנִים הָגֹה נֶהְגֶּה נְקַוֶּה לַמִּשְׁפָּט וָאַיִן לִישׁוּעָה רָחֲקָה
יב מִמֶּנּוּ: כִּי־רַבּוּ פְשָׁעֵינוּ נֶגְדֶּךָ וְחַטֹּאותֵינוּ עָנְתָה בָּנוּ כִּי־פְשָׁעֵינוּ אִתָּנוּ
יג וַעֲוֺנֹתֵינוּ יְדַעֲנוּם: פָּשֹׁעַ וְכַחֵשׁ בַּיהוה וְנָסוֹג מֵאַחַר אֱלֹהֵינוּ דַּבֶּר־עֹשֶׁק
יד וְסָרָה הֹרוֹ וְהֹגוֹ מִלֵּב דִּבְרֵי־שָׁקֶר: וְהֻסַּג אָחוֹר מִשְׁפָּט וּצְדָקָה מֵרָחוֹק
טו תַּעֲמֹד כִּי־כָשְׁלָה בָרְחוֹב אֱמֶת וּנְכֹחָה לֹא־תוּכַל לָבוֹא: וַתְּהִי הָאֱמֶת
נֶעְדֶּרֶת וְסָר מֵרָע מִשְׁתּוֹלֵל וַיַּרְא יהוה וַיֵּרַע בְּעֵינָיו כִּי־אֵין מִשְׁפָּט:
טז וַיַּרְא כִּי־אֵין אִישׁ וַיִּשְׁתּוֹמֵם כִּי אֵין מַפְגִּיעַ וַתּוֹשַׁע לוֹ זְרֹעוֹ וְצִדְקָתוֹ
יז הִיא סְמָכָתְהוּ: וַיִּלְבַּשׁ צְדָקָה כַּשִּׁרְיָן וְכוֹבַע יְשׁוּעָה בְּרֹאשׁוֹ וַיִּלְבַּשׁ
יח בִּגְדֵי נָקָם תִּלְבֹּשֶׁת וַיַּעַט כַּמְעִיל קִנְאָה: כְּעַל גְּמֻלוֹת כְּעַל יְשַׁלֵּם
יט חֵמָה לְצָרָיו גְּמוּל לְאֹיְבָיו לָאִיִּים גְּמוּל יְשַׁלֵּם: וְיִירְאוּ מִמַּעֲרָב אֶת־
שֵׁם יהוה וּמִמִּזְרַח־שֶׁמֶשׁ אֶת־כְּבוֹדוֹ כִּי־יָבוֹא כַנָּהָר צָר רוּחַ יהוה
כ כא נֹסְסָה בוֹ: וּבָא לְצִיּוֹן גּוֹאֵל וּלְשָׁבֵי פֶשַׁע בְּיַעֲקֹב נְאֻם יהוה: וַאֲנִי זֹאת
בְּרִיתִי אוֹתָם אָמַר יהוה רוּחִי אֲשֶׁר עָלֶיךָ וּדְבָרַי אֲשֶׁר־שַׂמְתִּי בְּפִיךָ
לֹא־יָמוּשׁוּ מִפִּיךָ וּמִפִּי זַרְעֲךָ וּמִפִּי זֶרַע זַרְעֲךָ אָמַר יהוה מֵעַתָּה וְעַד־
ס א עוֹלָם: קוּמִי אוֹרִי כִּי בָא אוֹרֵךְ וּכְבוֹד יהוה עָלַיִךְ
ב זָרָח: כִּי־הִנֵּה הַחֹשֶׁךְ יְכַסֶּה־אֶרֶץ וַעֲרָפֶל לְאֻמִּים וְעָלַיִךְ יִזְרַח יהוה
ג ד וּכְבוֹדוֹ עָלַיִךְ יֵרָאֶה: וְהָלְכוּ גוֹיִם לְאוֹרֵךְ וּמְלָכִים לְנֹגַהּ זַרְחֵךְ: שְׂאִי־
סָבִיב עֵינַיִךְ וּרְאִי כֻּלָּם נִקְבְּצוּ בָאוּ־לָךְ בָּנַיִךְ מֵרָחוֹק יָבֹאוּ וּבְנֹתַיִךְ
ה עַל־צַד תֵּאָמַנָה: אָז תִּרְאִי וְנָהַרְתְּ וּפָחַד וְרָחַב לְבָבֵךְ כִּי־יֵהָפֵךְ
ו עָלַיִךְ הֲמוֹן יָם חֵיל גּוֹיִם יָבֹאוּ לָךְ: שִׁפְעַת גְּמַלִּים תְּכַסֵּךְ בִּכְרֵי מִדְיָן
וְעֵיפָה כֻּלָּם מִשְּׁבָא יָבֹאוּ זָהָב וּלְבוֹנָה יִשָּׂאוּ וּתְהִלֹּת יהוה יְבַשֵּׂרוּ:

7 All the flocks of Kedar will be gathered in to you; the rams of Nevayot will
be in your service. Offered on My altar, they will be desired; I shall glorify
8 the House of My glory. Who are these sailing like clouds, like doves come
9 back to their roosting cote? It is Me the distant islands wait for; ships of
Tarshish come the first,[143] to bring your children from far away, their silver
and gold with them, for the name of the LORD your God, the Holy One of
10 Israel: He has glorified you. The children of strangers will build your walls;[144]
their kings will be in your service, for in My fury I beat you, but, desiring you
11 now, I show you mercy, and your gates will be always open, day and night,
never closed,[145] as the wealth of nations is brought in to you, their kings led
12 to you,[146] for the nations and kingdoms that do not serve you will be lost,
13 nations desolate, destroyed. Lebanon's glory will come to you: junipers,
cypress trees, and pencil pines together, to lend the place of My Sanctuary
14 splendor; I shall glorify the place of My footstool.[147] The children of those
who once oppressed you will come before you prostrate, bowing themselves
to the soles of your feet; all who once denounced you, they will call you The
15 LORD's City, Zion of Israel's Holy One. Where once you were forsaken, hated,
never even passed through, I have made you everlasting majesty, the joy of
16 generations. You shall suckle the milk of nations, suckle at kings' breasts,[148]
and know that I am the LORD, your rescue, your redeemer, the Mighty One
17 of Yaakov. Where once there was bronze, I shall bring gold, and where there
was iron, silver. Where once there was wood, I shall bring bronze, and where
there was stone, now iron. I shall make peace your commander, your ruling
18 class: righteousness. No more will violence be heard of in your land, nor
plunder or destruction in your borders. You shall name your walls Rescue,
19 and your gates, Praise. No more, by day, will the sun be your light, nor the
moon's radiance shine for you, for the LORD will be your light forever; your
20 God will be your glory. Your sun will set no longer, nor your moon be
gathered in, for the LORD is your light forever; the days of your mourning are
21 done. Your people, all of them righteous, will inherit the land forever, the
shoots of My planting, works of My hands, spreading branches in glory.[149]
22 The little son will become a thousand strong, the youngest child a mighty
nation; I am the LORD: when the time is right, in a flash I will bring it all to
61 1 be. The spirit of the Lord GOD is with me: the LORD has anointed
me to bring to oppressed ones tidings; has sent me to bandage broken hearts,
2 to cry freedom to captives, and to break the prisoners' bonds; to call forth a
year of the LORD's favor, a day for the vengeance of our God, to comfort all

143 | A symbol of wealth and power; see note on 2:16 and 1 Kings 10:23.

144 | Rather than toiling over them yourselves while foreigners attempt to hinder you; contrast with Nehemiah 2:19–20, 4:1–17.

145 | A sign of prosperity and security.

146 | To bring tribute.

147 | That is, the Temple, where God's presence resides on earth.

148 | The Hebrew contains a wordplay between the similar words for "breast" (*shad*) and "loot" (*shod*).

149 | The verb *lehitpaer* means both "to spread branches" and "to be glorified."

ז כָּל־צֹאן קֵדָר יִקָּבְצוּ לָךְ אֵילֵי נְבָיוֹת יְשָׁרְתוּנֶךְ יַעֲלוּ עַל־רָצוֹן מִזְבְּחִי
ח וּבֵית תִּפְאַרְתִּי אֲפָאֵר׃ מִי־אֵלֶּה כָּעָב תְּעוּפֶינָה וְכַיּוֹנִים אֶל־אֲרֻבֹּתֵיהֶם׃
ט כִּי־לִי ׀ אִיִּים יְקַוּוּ וָאֳנִיּוֹת תַּרְשִׁישׁ בָּרִאשֹׁנָה לְהָבִיא בָנַיִךְ מֵרָחוֹק
כַּסְפָּם וּזְהָבָם אִתָּם לְשֵׁם יהוה אֱלֹהַיִךְ וְלִקְדוֹשׁ יִשְׂרָאֵל כִּי פֵאֲרָךְ׃
י וּבָנוּ בְנֵי־נֵכָר חֹמֹתַיִךְ וּמַלְכֵיהֶם יְשָׁרְתוּנֶךְ כִּי בְקִצְפִּי הִכִּיתִיךְ וּבִרְצוֹנִי
יא רִחַמְתִּיךְ׃ וּפִתְּחוּ שְׁעָרַיִךְ תָּמִיד יוֹמָם וָלַיְלָה לֹא יִסָּגֵרוּ לְהָבִיא אֵלַיִךְ
יב חֵיל גּוֹיִם וּמַלְכֵיהֶם נְהוּגִים׃ כִּי־הַגּוֹי וְהַמַּמְלָכָה אֲשֶׁר לֹא־יַעַבְדוּךְ
יג יֹאבֵדוּ וְהַגּוֹיִם חָרֹב יֶחֱרָבוּ׃ כְּבוֹד הַלְּבָנוֹן אֵלַיִךְ יָבוֹא בְּרוֹשׁ תִּדְהָר
יד וּתְאַשּׁוּר יַחְדָּו לְפָאֵר מְקוֹם מִקְדָּשִׁי וּמְקוֹם רַגְלַי אֲכַבֵּד׃ וְהָלְכוּ אֵלַיִךְ
שְׁחוֹחַ בְּנֵי מְעַנַּיִךְ וְהִשְׁתַּחֲווּ עַל־כַּפּוֹת רַגְלַיִךְ כָּל־מְנַאֲצָיִךְ וְקָרְאוּ לָךְ
טו עִיר יהוה צִיּוֹן קְדוֹשׁ יִשְׂרָאֵל׃ תַּחַת הֱיוֹתֵךְ עֲזוּבָה וּשְׂנוּאָה וְאֵין עוֹבֵר
טז וְשַׂמְתִּיךְ לִגְאוֹן עוֹלָם מְשׂוֹשׂ דּוֹר וָדוֹר׃ וְיָנַקְתְּ חֲלֵב גּוֹיִם וְשֹׁד מְלָכִים
יז תִּינָקִי וְיָדַעַתְּ כִּי אֲנִי יהוה מוֹשִׁיעֵךְ וְגֹאֲלֵךְ אֲבִיר יַעֲקֹב׃ תַּחַת הַנְּחֹשֶׁת
אָבִיא זָהָב וְתַחַת הַבַּרְזֶל אָבִיא כֶסֶף וְתַחַת הָעֵצִים נְחֹשֶׁת וְתַחַת
יח הָאֲבָנִים בַּרְזֶל וְשַׂמְתִּי פְקֻדָּתֵךְ שָׁלוֹם וְנֹגְשַׂיִךְ צְדָקָה׃ לֹא־יִשָּׁמַע עוֹד
חָמָס בְּאַרְצֵךְ שֹׁד וָשֶׁבֶר בִּגְבוּלָיִךְ וְקָרָאת יְשׁוּעָה חוֹמֹתַיִךְ וּשְׁעָרַיִךְ
יט תְּהִלָּה׃ לֹא־יִהְיֶה־לָּךְ עוֹד הַשֶּׁמֶשׁ לְאוֹר יוֹמָם וּלְנֹגַהּ הַיָּרֵחַ לֹא־יָאִיר
כ לָךְ וְהָיָה־לָךְ יהוה לְאוֹר עוֹלָם וֵאלֹהַיִךְ לְתִפְאַרְתֵּךְ׃ לֹא־יָבוֹא עוֹד
שִׁמְשֵׁךְ וִירֵחֵךְ לֹא יֵאָסֵף כִּי יהוה יִהְיֶה־לָּךְ לְאוֹר עוֹלָם וְשָׁלְמוּ יְמֵי
כא אֶבְלֵךְ׃ וְעַמֵּךְ כֻּלָּם צַדִּיקִים לְעוֹלָם יִירְשׁוּ אָרֶץ נֵצֶר מטעו מַעֲשֵׂה מַטָּעַי
כב יָדַי לְהִתְפָּאֵר׃ הַקָּטֹן יִהְיֶה לָאֶלֶף וְהַצָּעִיר לְגוֹי עָצוּם אֲנִי יהוה בְּעִתָּהּ
סא א אֲחִישֶׁנָּה׃ רוּחַ אֲדֹנָי יֱהוִה עָלָי יַעַן מָשַׁח יהוה אֹתִי לְבַשֵּׂר
עֲנָוִים שְׁלָחַנִי לַחֲבֹשׁ לְנִשְׁבְּרֵי־לֵב לִקְרֹא לִשְׁבוּיִם דְּרוֹר וְלַאֲסוּרִים
ב פְּקַח־קוֹחַ׃ לִקְרֹא שְׁנַת־רָצוֹן לַיהוה וְיוֹם נָקָם לֵאלֹהֵינוּ לְנַחֵם כָּל־

3 mourners; to give to the mourners of Zion, to crown them in splendor where
once there was ash,[150] where once there was mourning, oil of joy, a mantle of
praise where there were dark spirits, calling them oaks of righteousness, the
4 LORD's planting, grown for His splendor. Ancient ruins will be rebuilt, from
the first desolations will rise again; deserted cities will be renewed, those
5 desolate age after age. Foreigners will stand up to pasture your flocks, children
6 of strangers your farm and vineyard laborers. You will be called the LORD's
priests; "These are our God's servants," will be said of you. You will eat of the
7 wealth of nations and boast of their glory. Where once you had shame, you
will twice have goodness; instead of disgrace, you will sing of your share. And
8 so, in their land, they will inherit twofold: everlasting joy will be theirs, for I
the LORD love justice, rejecting stolen offerings. I shall give those who are
true, return for their work; I shall forge an everlasting covenant with them;
9 their children will be well known among the nations, their offspring among
peoples, for all those who see them will know who they are: children of the
10 LORD's own blessing. I shall rejoice, rejoice in the LORD; my soul
exults in my God; He has wrapped me in garb of rescue, on my shoulders the
mantle of righteousness, as a bridegroom attends in splendor, and a bride
11 puts on her jewels; just as the land brings forth green life, having all that is
planted in her flower like a garden, so will the Lord GOD bring forth
62 1 righteousness and glory before all the nations. For Zion's sake I cannot be
silent, for Jerusalem's I cannot be still until righteousness bursts forth shining,
2 and rescue burns like a brand, and all nations see your righteousness, all the
kings your glory. They will call you by a new name spoken from the LORD's
3 own mouth.[151] You will be a crown of glory in the LORD's hand, a kingly
4 diadem in your God's palms. No more will they say of you, "Abandoned,"
"Desolate" of your land, for you shall be called "My Desire," your land renamed
"Embraced," for it is you the LORD desires, and your land shall be embraced;
5 as a young man embraces a maid, so will your children embrace you, while
the joy of a bridegroom over his bride is the joy your God will take in you.
6 Over your walls, Jerusalem, I have appointed watchmen, all day, all night long,
always, and they will not keep silence; you who call the LORD by name, none
7 of you be quiet, and do not give Him quiet until He has established, until He
8 has raised Jerusalem to be the glory of this earth. The LORD has sworn by His
right hand and by His mighty arm: never again to give away your grain as your
foes' food, never to let strangers drink the wine that you have labored for.
9 No – the ones who harvest it will eat and sing out the LORD's praise, and those
10 He has gathered in will drink[152] within My sacred courtyards. Pass,
pass through the gates, and make way for the people. Mark, mark a road here;
11 clear the stones; raise a banner above all peoples. Behold: the LORD
resounding to the earth's ends; tell daughter Zion, your rescue is come, and

150 | The word "splendor" (*pe'er*) is an anagram of "ash" (*efer*) in Hebrew.

151 | In place of the derogatory names that have been used by the nations until now.

152 | Referring to the consumption of tithes in Jerusalem; see Deuteronomy 14:22–27.

ג אֲבֵלִים: לָשׂוּם ׀ לַאֲבֵלֵי צִיּוֹן לָתֵת לָהֶם פְּאֵר תַּחַת אֵפֶר שֶׁמֶן שָׂשׂוֹן
תַּחַת אֵבֶל מַעֲטֵה תְהִלָּה תַּחַת רוּחַ כֵּהָה וְקֹרָא לָהֶם אֵילֵי הַצֶּדֶק
ד מַטַּע יְהוָה לְהִתְפָּאֵר: וּבָנוּ חָרְבוֹת עוֹלָם שֹׁמְמוֹת רִאשֹׁנִים יְקוֹמֵמוּ
ה וְחִדְּשׁוּ עָרֵי חֹרֶב שֹׁמְמוֹת דּוֹר וָדוֹר: וְעָמְדוּ זָרִים וְרָעוּ צֹאנְכֶם וּבְנֵי
ו נֵכָר אִכָּרֵיכֶם וְכֹרְמֵיכֶם: וְאַתֶּם כֹּהֲנֵי יְהוָה תִּקָּרֵאוּ מְשָׁרְתֵי אֱלֹהֵינוּ
ז יֵאָמֵר לָכֶם חֵיל גּוֹיִם תֹּאכֵלוּ וּבִכְבוֹדָם תִּתְיַמָּרוּ: תַּחַת בָּשְׁתְּכֶם מִשְׁנֶה
וּכְלִמָּה יָרֹנּוּ חֶלְקָם לָכֵן בְּאַרְצָם מִשְׁנֶה יִירָשׁוּ שִׂמְחַת עוֹלָם תִּהְיֶה
ח לָהֶם: כִּי אֲנִי יְהוָה אֹהֵב מִשְׁפָּט שֹׂנֵא גָזֵל בְּעוֹלָה וְנָתַתִּי פְעֻלָּתָם
ט בֶּאֱמֶת וּבְרִית עוֹלָם אֶכְרוֹת לָהֶם: וְנוֹדַע בַּגּוֹיִם זַרְעָם וְצֶאֱצָאֵיהֶם כה
י בְּתוֹךְ הָעַמִּים כָּל־רֹאֵיהֶם יַכִּירוּם כִּי הֵם זֶרַע בֵּרַךְ יְהוָה: שׂוֹשׂ
אָשִׂישׂ בַּיהוָה תָּגֵל נַפְשִׁי בֵּאלֹהַי כִּי הִלְבִּישַׁנִי בִּגְדֵי־יֶשַׁע מְעִיל צְדָקָה
יא יְעָטָנִי כֶּחָתָן יְכַהֵן פְּאֵר וְכַכַּלָּה תַּעְדֶּה כֵלֶיהָ: כִּי כָאָרֶץ תּוֹצִיא צִמְחָהּ
וּכְגַנָּה זֵרוּעֶיהָ תַצְמִיחַ כֵּן ׀ אֲדֹנָי יְהוִה יַצְמִיחַ צְדָקָה וּתְהִלָּה נֶגֶד כָּל־
א הַגּוֹיִם: לְמַעַן צִיּוֹן לֹא אֶחֱשֶׁה וּלְמַעַן יְרוּשָׁלִַם לֹא אֶשְׁקוֹט עַד־יֵצֵא סב
ב כַנֹּגַהּ צִדְקָהּ וִישׁוּעָתָהּ כְּלַפִּיד יִבְעָר: וְרָאוּ גוֹיִם צִדְקֵךְ וְכָל־מְלָכִים
ג כְּבוֹדֵךְ וְקֹרָא לָךְ שֵׁם חָדָשׁ אֲשֶׁר פִּי יְהוָה יִקֳּבֶנּוּ: וְהָיִית עֲטֶרֶת
ד תִּפְאֶרֶת בְּיַד־יְהוָה וּצְנוּף מְלוּכָה בְּכַף־אֱלֹהָיִךְ: לֹא־יֵאָמֵר לָךְ עוֹד וּצְנִיף
עֲזוּבָה וּלְאַרְצֵךְ לֹא־יֵאָמֵר עוֹד שְׁמָמָה כִּי לָךְ יִקָּרֵא חֶפְצִי־בָהּ וּלְאַרְצֵךְ
ה בְּעוּלָה כִּי־חָפֵץ יְהוָה בָּךְ וְאַרְצֵךְ תִּבָּעֵל: כִּי־יִבְעַל בָּחוּר בְּתוּלָה
ו יִבְעָלוּךְ בָּנָיִךְ וּמְשׂוֹשׂ חָתָן עַל־כַּלָּה יָשִׂישׂ עָלַיִךְ אֱלֹהָיִךְ: עַל־חוֹמֹתַיִךְ
יְרוּשָׁלִַם הִפְקַדְתִּי שֹׁמְרִים כָּל־הַיּוֹם וְכָל־הַלַּיְלָה תָּמִיד לֹא יֶחֱשׁוּ
ז הַמַּזְכִּרִים אֶת־יְהוָה אַל־דֳּמִי לָכֶם: וְאַל־תִּתְּנוּ דֳמִי לוֹ עַד־יְכוֹנֵן
ח וְעַד־יָשִׂים אֶת־יְרוּשָׁלִַם תְּהִלָּה בָּאָרֶץ: נִשְׁבַּע יְהוָה בִּימִינוֹ וּבִזְרוֹעַ
עֻזּוֹ אִם־אֶתֵּן אֶת־דְּגָנֵךְ עוֹד מַאֲכָל לְאֹיְבַיִךְ וְאִם־יִשְׁתּוּ בְנֵי־נֵכָר
ט תִּירוֹשֵׁךְ אֲשֶׁר יָגַעַתְּ בּוֹ: כִּי מְאַסְפָיו יֹאכְלֻהוּ וְהִלְלוּ אֶת־יְהוָה וּמְקַבְּצָיו
י יִשְׁתֻּהוּ בְּחַצְרוֹת קָדְשִׁי: עִבְרוּ עִבְרוּ בַּשְּׁעָרִים פַּנּוּ דֶּרֶךְ
יא הָעָם סֹלּוּ סֹלּוּ הַמְסִלָּה סַקְּלוּ מֵאֶבֶן הָרִימוּ נֵס עַל־הָעַמִּים: הִנֵּה יְהוָה
הִשְׁמִיעַ אֶל־קְצֵה הָאָרֶץ אִמְרוּ לְבַת־צִיּוֹן הִנֵּה יִשְׁעֵךְ בָּא הִנֵּה שְׂכָרוֹ

12 with Him, His prize: His work walking before Him.[153] They will call them a
holy people, redeemed ones of the LORD. And you – you shall be called the
63 1 One Sought After, the City That Will Never Be Abandoned. "Who
is this, coming from Edom, from Botzra, in reddened clothes?[154] Who, His
clothing glorious, striding forth in might?" It is I who speak with rectitude,
2 powerful to rescue. "And why is Your clothing red, your garments, as if You
3 trod the winepress?" I have trodden the vat alone; no man of any nation was
there with Me; I trod them in My fury, trampling them in rage, until their
4 lifeblood steeped My clothes, befouling all My garments, for today in My
5 heart is a day of vengeance; My year of redemption is come. I look, and no
one is there to help; with dismay I see – no aid;[155] so My arm will bear My
6 rescue; My rage is My support. My fury will tread peoples low; in My rage I
7 shall make them drunk and pour down their lifeblood to earth. Let
me speak the LORD's acts of kindness, praises of the LORD for all the LORD
has done for us, for His great goodness to Israel, performed in all compassion,
8 in all His loving-kindness. He said: They, they are My people, My children
9 who would not lie to Me – and He was their rescue. Wherever they suffered,
He too suffered,[156] and His presence, its emissary rescued them; in His love,
in His mercy He redeemed them and took them up and bore them through
10 all those long-past days. And they rebelled and saddened His holy spirit, and
11 He became their enemy; He fought against them. Then they remembered
those long-past days, and Moshe, and His people; where is He, who brought
them up from the sea[157] with the shepherds of His flock? Where is He who
12 placed among them His holy spirit, leading, at Moshe's right hand, and with
His arm of glory? He split the waters before them to make Him a name
13 everlasting, leading them through the deep like a horse riding the desert,
14 never to fall; as cattle descend the valley, the LORD's spirit would guide them.
15 Thus You led Your people to make You a name for glory. Look down from the
heavens and see, from Your Sanctuary in its holiness and glory, where, now,
is all Your passion and might? All Your great fervor and care are held back
16 now from me. You are our Father though Avraham would not know us,[158]
Yisrael would not recognize us. You, LORD, are our Father, named our
17 redeemer since time began. Why, LORD, have you led us astray from Your
path and hardened our hearts from fearing You? Come back for Your servants'
18 sake, to the tribes of Your possession. For such a short time Your holy people
19 held it, then enemies trampled down Your Sanctuary. We have become as
ones You never ruled, as ones never given Your name. Would You but tear

153 | Cf. 40:10.

154 | *Edom* means red (see Gen. 25:30); Botzra, a city in ancient Edom, derives from the root meaning "grape harvest."

155 | Cf. 59:16.

156 | Translation follows the *keri*. The *ketiv*: "Whenever they suffered, He did not cause them to suffer greatly."

157 | The name *Moshe* literally means "one who draws out"; see Exodus 2:10.

158 | Neither Avraham nor Yaakov rescued us, but God.

יב אֹתוֹ וּפְעֻלָּתוֹ לְפָנָיו: וְקָרְאוּ לָהֶם עַם־הַקֹּדֶשׁ גְּאוּלֵי יהוה וְלָךְ יִקָּרֵא
סג א דְרוּשָׁה עִיר לֹא נֶעֱזָבָה: מִי־זֶה ׀ בָּא מֵאֱדוֹם חֲמוּץ בְּגָדִים
מִבָּצְרָה זֶה הָדוּר בִּלְבוּשׁוֹ צֹעֶה בְּרֹב כֹּחוֹ אֲנִי מְדַבֵּר בִּצְדָקָה רַב
ב ג לְהוֹשִׁיעַ: מַדּוּעַ אָדֹם לִלְבוּשֶׁךָ וּבְגָדֶיךָ כְּדֹרֵךְ בְּגַת: פּוּרָה ׀ דָּרַכְתִּי
לְבַדִּי וּמֵעַמִּים אֵין־אִישׁ אִתִּי וְאֶדְרְכֵם בְּאַפִּי וְאֶרְמְסֵם בַּחֲמָתִי וְיֵז
ד נִצְחָם עַל־בְּגָדַי וְכָל־מַלְבּוּשַׁי אֶגְאָלְתִּי: כִּי יוֹם נָקָם בְּלִבִּי וּשְׁנַת גְּאוּלַי
ה בָּאָה: וְאַבִּיט וְאֵין עֹזֵר וְאֶשְׁתּוֹמֵם וְאֵין סוֹמֵךְ וַתּוֹשַׁע לִי זְרֹעִי וַחֲמָתִי
ו הִיא סְמָכָתְנִי: וְאָבוּס עַמִּים בְּאַפִּי וַאֲשַׁכְּרֵם בַּחֲמָתִי וְאוֹרִיד לָאָרֶץ
ז נִצְחָם: חַסְדֵי יהוה ׀ אַזְכִּיר תְּהִלֹּת יהוה כְּעַל כֹּל אֲשֶׁר־
גְּמָלָנוּ יהוה וְרַב־טוּב לְבֵית יִשְׂרָאֵל אֲשֶׁר־גְּמָלָם כְּרַחֲמָיו וּכְרֹב חֲסָדָיו:
ח ט וַיֹּאמֶר אַךְ־עַמִּי הֵמָּה בָּנִים לֹא יְשַׁקֵּרוּ וַיְהִי לָהֶם לְמוֹשִׁיעַ: בְּכָל־
צָרָתָם ׀ לא צָר וּמַלְאַךְ פָּנָיו הוֹשִׁיעָם בְּאַהֲבָתוֹ וּבְחֶמְלָתוֹ הוּא גְאָלָם לוֹ
י וַיְנַטְּלֵם וַיְנַשְּׂאֵם כָּל־יְמֵי עוֹלָם: וְהֵמָּה מָרוּ וְעִצְּבוּ אֶת־רוּחַ קָדְשׁוֹ
יא וַיֵּהָפֵךְ לָהֶם לְאוֹיֵב הוּא נִלְחַם־בָּם: וַיִּזְכֹּר יְמֵי־עוֹלָם מֹשֶׁה עַמּוֹ אַיֵּה ׀
יב הַמַּעֲלֵם מִיָּם אֵת רֹעֵה צֹאנוֹ אַיֵּה הַשָּׂם בְּקִרְבּוֹ אֶת־רוּחַ קָדְשׁוֹ: מוֹלִיךְ
לִימִין מֹשֶׁה זְרוֹעַ תִּפְאַרְתּוֹ בּוֹקֵעַ מַיִם מִפְּנֵיהֶם לַעֲשׂוֹת לוֹ שֵׁם עוֹלָם:
יג יד מוֹלִיכָם בַּתְּהֹמוֹת כַּסּוּס בַּמִּדְבָּר לֹא יִכָּשֵׁלוּ: כַּבְּהֵמָה בַּבִּקְעָה תֵרֵד
טו רוּחַ יהוה תְּנִיחֶנּוּ כֵּן נִהַגְתָּ עַמְּךָ לַעֲשׂוֹת לְךָ שֵׁם תִּפְאָרֶת: הַבֵּט
מִשָּׁמַיִם וּרְאֵה מִזְּבֻל קָדְשְׁךָ וְתִפְאַרְתֶּךָ אַיֵּה קִנְאָתְךָ וּגְבוּרֹתֶךָ הֲמוֹן
טז מֵעֶיךָ וְרַחֲמֶיךָ אֵלַי הִתְאַפָּקוּ: כִּי־אַתָּה אָבִינוּ כִּי אַבְרָהָם לֹא יְדָעָנוּ
יז וְיִשְׂרָאֵל לֹא יַכִּירָנוּ אַתָּה יהוה אָבִינוּ גֹּאֲלֵנוּ מֵעוֹלָם שְׁמֶךָ: לָמָּה
תַתְעֵנוּ יהוה מִדְּרָכֶיךָ תַּקְשִׁיחַ לִבֵּנוּ מִיִּרְאָתֶךָ שׁוּב לְמַעַן עֲבָדֶיךָ
יח שִׁבְטֵי נַחֲלָתֶךָ: לַמִּצְעָר יָרְשׁוּ עַם־קָדְשֶׁךָ צָרֵינוּ בּוֹסְסוּ מִקְדָּשֶׁךָ:
יט הָיִינוּ מֵעוֹלָם לֹא־מָשַׁלְתָּ בָּם לֹא־נִקְרָא שִׁמְךָ עֲלֵיהֶם לוּא־קָרַעְתָּ

64 1 through the skies and come down, the hills would melt before You[159] as fire
burns to liquefy, as water boils amid fire, to make Your name known to Your
2 foes, and nations would quake before You. Then, when You performed
wonders we never could have hoped for, when You came down, the hills
3 melted before You, and never has anyone heard, anyone heeded, has any eye
borne witness to any god but You with all that You perform for those who
4 wait for You. You struck down even those who rejoice in doing justice, who
recall You, following Your ways, for You raged; we sinned; it was through
5 them, always, that we were spared. All of us are defiled now, the best of our
actions a bleeding cloth and all of us withered like leaves until, like the wind,
6 our sin bore us away, and none call on Your name or rouse themselves to grasp
You, for You have hidden Your face from us and let our iniquities melt us away.
7 Now, LORD, You are our Father; we are the clay, You our potter, and all of us
8 are Your hands' work. Do not rage against us, LORD, with such a fury, or
remember forever our sin. Please – look on and see – all of us, Your people.
9 Your holy cities have turned to wilderness; Zion has turned to wilderness,
10 Jerusalem to wasteland; our holy House, our glory, where our ancestors
sang Your praise become a great conflagration; and all we hold dear – ruin.
11 LORD, from all this, will You yet hold back, keep silence, torment us
65 1 so? Though no one looked for Me, still I was found. For those who
did not seek Me, I was there. I am here – I said – am here, to a nation that
2 never called My name; I spread My hands out all the day to a people that
3 turned away, walking the path to no good after their wandering thoughts. The
people anger Me, always there before Me sacrificing in gardens, burning
4 incense on the slabs, sitting among the graves and passing the nights in
caverns, eating the meat of pigs and filling their bowls with a broth of foulness,
5 saying, "Stand with your own kind; do not come near me; I am holier than
you"; these people are smoke in My nostrils from fire burning all the day.
6 Behold: it is written before Me: I shall not be silent until I have repaid, thrust
7 everything back into their arms, your iniquities with those of your parents,
so says the LORD. Your parents who burned incense on the hills and
blasphemed Me from the mountaintops, I have measured their payment out
8 from the first into their arms. So says the LORD: Just as there is yet
wine in the bunch, so that one will say, "Do not destroy this one, for there is
blessing in it yet," so will I intervene for My servants not to destroy them all;
9 I will deprive Yaakov of progeny, Yehuda of an heir to My mountains, and My
10 chosen ones will take possession; My servants will live there; the Sharon will
be pasture to flocks, the Valley of the Scourge[160] a resting place for cattle for
11 those of My people who sought Me out. While you who forsake the LORD,
forgetting My holy mountain while laying a table for Gad, pouring lavish
12 libations to Meni,[161] I have marked you out for the sword; you will all bow to

159 | Cf. Judges 5:5.

160 | See Joshua 7:24–26.

161 | Gad was a god of fortune worshipped throughout the Near East, and Meni was a god worshipped by the Nabateans.

סד א שָׁמַיִם יָרַדְתָּ מִפָּנֶיךָ הָרִים נָזֹלּוּ׃ כִּקְדֹחַ אֵשׁ הֲמָסִים מַיִם תִּבְעֶה־אֵשׁ
ב לְהוֹדִיעַ שִׁמְךָ לְצָרֶיךָ מִפָּנֶיךָ גּוֹיִם יִרְגָּזוּ׃ בַּעֲשׂוֹתְךָ נוֹרָאוֹת לֹא נְקַוֶּה
ג יָרַדְתָּ מִפָּנֶיךָ הָרִים נָזֹלּוּ׃ וּמֵעוֹלָם לֹא־שָׁמְעוּ לֹא הֶאֱזִינוּ עַיִן לֹא־
ד רָאָתָה אֱלֹהִים זוּלָתְךָ יַעֲשֶׂה לִמְחַכֵּה־לוֹ׃ פָּגַעְתָּ אֶת־שָׂשׂ וְעֹשֵׂה צֶדֶק
ה בִּדְרָכֶיךָ יִזְכְּרוּךָ הֵן־אַתָּה קָצַפְתָּ וַנֶּחֱטָא בָּהֶם עוֹלָם וְנִוָּשֵׁעַ׃ וַנְּהִי
כַטָּמֵא כֻּלָּנוּ וּכְבֶגֶד עִדִּים כָּל־צִדְקֹתֵינוּ וַנָּבֶל כֶּעָלֶה כֻּלָּנוּ וַעֲוֺנֵנוּ כָּרוּחַ
ו יִשָּׂאֻנוּ׃ וְאֵין־קוֹרֵא בְשִׁמְךָ מִתְעוֹרֵר לְהַחֲזִיק בָּךְ כִּי־הִסְתַּרְתָּ פָנֶיךָ
ז מִמֶּנּוּ וַתְּמוּגֵנוּ בְּיַד־עֲוֺנֵנוּ׃ וְעַתָּה יְהוָה אָבִינוּ אָתָּה אֲנַחְנוּ הַחֹמֶר
ח וְאַתָּה יֹצְרֵנוּ וּמַעֲשֵׂה יָדְךָ כֻּלָּנוּ׃ אַל־תִּקְצֹף יְהוָה עַד־מְאֹד וְאַל־לָעַד
ט תִּזְכֹּר עָוֺן הֵן הַבֶּט־נָא עַמְּךָ כֻלָּנוּ׃ עָרֵי קָדְשְׁךָ הָיוּ מִדְבָּר צִיּוֹן מִדְבָּר
י הָיָתָה יְרוּשָׁלִַם שְׁמָמָה׃ בֵּית קָדְשֵׁנוּ וְתִפְאַרְתֵּנוּ אֲשֶׁר הִלְלוּךָ אֲבֹתֵינוּ
יא הָיָה לִשְׂרֵפַת אֵשׁ וְכָל־מַחֲמַדֵּינוּ הָיָה לְחָרְבָּה׃ הַעַל־אֵלֶּה תִתְאַפַּק
סה א יְהוָה תֶּחֱשֶׁה וּתְעַנֵּנוּ עַד־מְאֹד׃ נִדְרַשְׁתִּי לְלוֹא שָׁאָלוּ
נִמְצֵאתִי לְלֹא בִקְשֻׁנִי אָמַרְתִּי הִנֵּנִי הִנֵּנִי אֶל־גּוֹי לֹא־קֹרָא בִשְׁמִי׃
ב פֵּרַשְׂתִּי יָדַי כָּל־הַיּוֹם אֶל־עַם סוֹרֵר הַהֹלְכִים הַדֶּרֶךְ לֹא־טוֹב אַחַר
ג מַחְשְׁבֹתֵיהֶם׃ הָעָם הַמַּכְעִיסִים אוֹתִי עַל־פָּנַי תָּמִיד זֹבְחִים בַּגַּנּוֹת
ד וּמְקַטְּרִים עַל־הַלְּבֵנִים׃ הַיֹּשְׁבִים בַּקְּבָרִים וּבַנְּצוּרִים יָלִינוּ הָאֹכְלִים
ה בְּשַׂר הַחֲזִיר וּפרק פִּגֻּלִים כְּלֵיהֶם׃ הָאֹמְרִים קְרַב אֵלֶיךָ אַל־תִּגַּשׁ־בִּי וּמְרַק
ו כִּי קְדַשְׁתִּיךָ אֵלֶּה עָשָׁן בְּאַפִּי אֵשׁ יֹקֶדֶת כָּל־הַיּוֹם׃ הִנֵּה כְתוּבָה לְפָנָי
ז לֹא אֶחֱשֶׁה כִּי אִם־שִׁלַּמְתִּי וְשִׁלַּמְתִּי עַל־חֵיקָם׃ עֲוֺנֹתֵיכֶם וַעֲוֺנֹת
אֲבוֹתֵיכֶם יַחְדָּו אָמַר יְהוָה אֲשֶׁר קִטְּרוּ עַל־הֶהָרִים וְעַל־הַגְּבָעוֹת
ח חֵרְפוּנִי וּמַדֹּתִי פְּעֻלָּתָם רִאשֹׁנָה עַל־חֵיקָם׃ כֹּה ׀ אָמַר אֶל־
יְהוָה כַּאֲשֶׁר יִמָּצֵא הַתִּירוֹשׁ בָּאֶשְׁכּוֹל וְאָמַר אַל־תַּשְׁחִיתֵהוּ כִּי בְרָכָה
ט בּוֹ כֵּן אֶעֱשֶׂה לְמַעַן עֲבָדַי לְבִלְתִּי הַשְׁחִית הַכֹּל׃ וְהוֹצֵאתִי מִיַּעֲקֹב כו
י זֶרַע וּמִיהוּדָה יוֹרֵשׁ הָרָי וִירֵשׁוּהָ בְחִירַי וַעֲבָדַי יִשְׁכְּנוּ־שָׁמָּה׃ וְהָיָה
יא הַשָּׁרוֹן לִנְוֵה־צֹאן וְעֵמֶק עָכוֹר לְרֵבֶץ בָּקָר לְעַמִּי אֲשֶׁר דְּרָשׁוּנִי׃ וְאַתֶּם
עֹזְבֵי יְהוָה הַשְּׁכֵחִים אֶת־הַר קָדְשִׁי הַעֹרְכִים לַגַּד שֻׁלְחָן וְהַמְמַלְאִים
יב לַמְנִי מִמְסָךְ׃ וּמָנִיתִי אֶתְכֶם לַחֶרֶב וְכֻלְּכֶם לַטֶּבַח תִּכְרָעוּ יַעַן קָרָאתִי

the slaughter, for I have called out to you, and you did not answer; I spoke,
but you were not listening; you did what was evil in My sight and chose what
13 I never desired. And so, thus says the Lord God: My servants will
eat, but you will hunger; My servants will drink, but you will thirst. My
14 servants will rejoice, but you will be shamed; My servants will sing out
contentment, but you will cry out in heartache, will wail with a broken spirit.
15 You will leave behind your name for My chosen few to swear by, for the Lord
16 God will annihilate you and call His servants by a different name, for those
who bless themselves in the land will bless themselves invoking the ever-
faithful God, and those who swear their oaths in the land will swear by ever-
faithful God, for the early trials will be forgotten, hidden away from My sight;
17 for I am creating new heavens, a new earth, and the first ones will not be
18 remembered, will not be taken to heart. Rejoice, exult forever in that which
19 I create, for I am creating Jerusalem as happiness, her people as joy, and I shall
exult in Jerusalem, rejoice in My people, and no more will you hear in her the
20 sounds of weeping, of crying out. There will not be any youth or old person
who does not live out his days; a man will die young one hundred years old,
21 and a sinner a hundred years old die accursed.[162] They will build their houses
22 and live, plant vineyards, eat the fruit; they will not build houses for others
to dwell in or plant and have others consume. My people's lifetime is like that
of a tree, and those I have chosen will wear out the works of their hands.[163]
23 They will not toil for nothing, will not bear children to know horror,[164] for
24 they are the children the Lord has blessed, their descendants with them, and
before they call out to Me, I shall answer – while they are yet speaking, I shall
25 respond. Wolf and lamb will pasture as one, and lion, like ox, will feed upon
straw, and dust will be the serpent's bread.[165] There will be no wrong or
66 1 violence on all My holy mountain, says the Lord. Thus speaks the
Lord: The heavens are My throne; the world, My footstool. What house,
2 then, would You build for Me, where could I rest? All this – My own hands
made, all these are Mine, so says the Lord. And these are the ones I look
3 toward: the poor, of humbled spirit, who tremble at My words. While he,
killing his ox is like a murderer of men, the one who offers up a lamb might
so well behead a dog; the offering brought may just as well be pigs' blood;
and his remembrance incense is a blessing of iniquity. These men, they choose
4 their paths, their souls desire their disgusting things, and so I too will
choose – will choose their torments, and bring to them what they most fear.
I called out – no one answered; I spoke, but none was listening. They did what
5 was evil in My sight, and chose what I never desired.[166] You who
tremble to hear His word, listen to the Lord's word: Your brothers said, the
ones who hated you, who cast you out, "Because of my name, the Lord is

162 | Death at the age of one hundred will be assumed to be the fulfillment of a curse on a sinner, as most people will live much longer.

163 | The tools and vessels they fashion will wear out long before the person who made them dies.

164 | Children will not die in their parents' lifetime.

165 | Cf. 11:6–9.

166 | Cf. 65:12.

וְלֹא עֲנִיתֶם דִּבַּרְתִּי וְלֹא שְׁמַעְתֶּם וַתַּעֲשׂוּ הָרַע בְּעֵינַי וּבַאֲשֶׁר לֹא־
יג חָפַצְתִּי בְּחַרְתֶּם׃ לָכֵן כֹּה־אָמַר ׀ אֲדֹנָי יֱהֹוִה הִנֵּה עֲבָדַי ׀
יֹאכֵלוּ וְאַתֶּם תִּרְעָבוּ הִנֵּה עֲבָדַי יִשְׁתּוּ וְאַתֶּם תִּצְמָאוּ הִנֵּה עֲבָדַי
יד יִשְׂמָחוּ וְאַתֶּם תֵּבֹשׁוּ׃ הִנֵּה עֲבָדַי יָרֹנּוּ מִטּוּב לֵב וְאַתֶּם תִּצְעֲקוּ מִכְּאֵב
טו לֵב וּמִשֵּׁבֶר רוּחַ תְּיֵלִילוּ׃ וְהִנַּחְתֶּם שִׁמְכֶם לִשְׁבוּעָה לִבְחִירַי וֶהֱמִיתְךָ
טז אֲדֹנָי יֱהֹוִה וְלַעֲבָדָיו יִקְרָא שֵׁם אַחֵר׃ אֲשֶׁר הַמִּתְבָּרֵךְ בָּאָרֶץ יִתְבָּרֵךְ
בֵּאלֹהֵי אָמֵן וְהַנִּשְׁבָּע בָּאָרֶץ יִשָּׁבַע בֵּאלֹהֵי אָמֵן כִּי נִשְׁכְּחוּ הַצָּרוֹת
יז הָרִאשֹׁנוֹת וְכִי נִסְתְּרוּ מֵעֵינָי׃ כִּי־הִנְנִי בוֹרֵא שָׁמַיִם חֲדָשִׁים וָאָרֶץ
יח חֲדָשָׁה וְלֹא תִזָּכַרְנָה הָרִאשֹׁנוֹת וְלֹא תַעֲלֶינָה עַל־לֵב׃ כִּי־אִם־שִׂישׂוּ
וְגִילוּ עֲדֵי־עַד אֲשֶׁר אֲנִי בוֹרֵא כִּי הִנְנִי בוֹרֵא אֶת־יְרוּשָׁלִַם גִּילָה וְעַמָּהּ
יט מָשׂוֹשׂ׃ וְגַלְתִּי בִירוּשָׁלִַם וְשַׂשְׂתִּי בְעַמִּי וְלֹא־יִשָּׁמַע בָּהּ עוֹד קוֹל בְּכִי
כ וְקוֹל זְעָקָה׃ לֹא־יִהְיֶה מִשָּׁם עוֹד עוּל יָמִים וְזָקֵן אֲשֶׁר לֹא־יְמַלֵּא
אֶת־יָמָיו כִּי הַנַּעַר בֶּן־מֵאָה שָׁנָה יָמוּת וְהַחוֹטֶא בֶּן־מֵאָה שָׁנָה יְקֻלָּל׃
כא כב וּבָנוּ בָתִּים וְיָשָׁבוּ וְנָטְעוּ כְרָמִים וְאָכְלוּ פִּרְיָם׃ לֹא יִבְנוּ וְאַחֵר יֵשֵׁב
לֹא יִטְּעוּ וְאַחֵר יֹאכֵל כִּי־כִימֵי הָעֵץ יְמֵי עַמִּי וּמַעֲשֵׂה יְדֵיהֶם יְבַלּוּ
כג בְחִירָי׃ לֹא יִיגְעוּ לָרִיק וְלֹא יֵלְדוּ לַבֶּהָלָה כִּי זֶרַע בְּרוּכֵי יְהוָה הֵמָּה
כד וְצֶאֱצָאֵיהֶם אִתָּם׃ וְהָיָה טֶרֶם יִקְרָאוּ וַאֲנִי אֶעֱנֶה עוֹד הֵם מְדַבְּרִים
כה וַאֲנִי אֶשְׁמָע׃ זְאֵב וְטָלֶה יִרְעוּ כְאֶחָד וְאַרְיֵה כַּבָּקָר יֹאכַל־תֶּבֶן
וְנָחָשׁ עָפָר לַחְמוֹ לֹא־יָרֵעוּ וְלֹא־יַשְׁחִיתוּ בְּכָל־הַר קָדְשִׁי אָמַר
סו א יְהוָה׃ כֹּה אָמַר יְהוָה הַשָּׁמַיִם כִּסְאִי וְהָאָרֶץ הֲדֹם רַגְלָי
ב אֵי־זֶה בַיִת אֲשֶׁר תִּבְנוּ־לִי וְאֵי־זֶה מָקוֹם מְנוּחָתִי׃ וְאֶת־כָּל־אֵלֶּה יָדִי
עָשָׂתָה וַיִּהְיוּ כָל־אֵלֶּה נְאֻם־יְהוָה וְאֶל־זֶה אַבִּיט אֶל־עָנִי וּנְכֵה־רוּחַ
ג וְחָרֵד עַל־דְּבָרִי׃ שׁוֹחֵט הַשּׁוֹר מַכֵּה־אִישׁ זוֹבֵחַ הַשֶּׂה עֹרֵף כֶּלֶב מַעֲלֵה
מִנְחָה דַּם־חֲזִיר מַזְכִּיר לְבֹנָה מְבָרֵךְ אָוֶן גַּם־הֵמָּה בָּחֲרוּ בְּדַרְכֵיהֶם
ד וּבְשִׁקּוּצֵיהֶם נַפְשָׁם חָפֵצָה׃ גַּם־אֲנִי אֶבְחַר בְּתַעֲלֻלֵיהֶם וּמְגוּרֹתָם
אָבִיא לָהֶם יַעַן קָרָאתִי וְאֵין עוֹנֶה דִּבַּרְתִּי וְלֹא שָׁמֵעוּ וַיַּעֲשׂוּ הָרַע
ה בְּעֵינַי וּבַאֲשֶׁר לֹא־חָפַצְתִּי בָּחָרוּ׃ שִׁמְעוּ דְּבַר־יְהוָה
הַחֲרֵדִים אֶל־דְּבָרוֹ אָמְרוּ אֲחֵיכֶם שֹׂנְאֵיכֶם מְנַדֵּיכֶם לְמַעַן שְׁמִי יִכְבַּד

6 honored." We will see your joy, and they will be shamefaced.[167] A voice
roaring out from the city, a voice, out of the Sanctuary, a voice – it is the
7 LORD's, as He repays His enemies. Before she had writhed in labor she gave
8 birth; before the agonies took her she was delivered of a boy. Who ever heard
of anything like this? Who ever saw such happenings as these? Can the land
give birth in a day? Can a nation be born at a single step? Yet Zion has labored,
9 and has birthed her children. Would I bring on the labor and not deliver? So
the LORD speaks: Would I who fathered close the womb? So your God
10 speaks. Bring Jerusalem joy, exult in her, all of you who love her;
11 celebrate her joy with her, all of you who mourned her. That you may suck
your fill from the bosom of her comforting; may suckle, take delight in the
12 brilliance of her glory. For thus says the LORD: See Me make peace
flow to her like a river, and the substance of nations – like a rushing brook – and
13 you shall suckle. You will be borne upon hips, playing upon loving laps; as a
man is consoled by his mother, just so shall I comfort you, and in Jerusalem,
14 you shall be consoled. You shall look on, your heart rejoicing, while your
bones grow vigorous, like grass, and the hand of the LORD becomes known
15 to His servants, and His rage known to all His foes. For see: the LORD is
coming in fire, His chariots a storm wind, to slake His fury in rage, His rebuke
16 in flames of fire. For in fire, the LORD comes to judgment, and by the sword,
17 to all flesh, and many are those the LORD will execute. Those in the gardens,
sanctifying and cleansing themselves, one after the other in the midst of it,[168]
while eating the flesh of pigs and pests and mice, they will all be gathered in
18 together: so the LORD has spoken. For I – I know their works, their thoughts;
and time will come, to gather all nations and tongues, and they will come,
19 and look upon My glory. I shall place a sign among them, send out survivors
from them to all nations, to Tarshish, Pul, and Lud, to the great archers, Tuval,
Yavan,[169] to the distant coastlands where none ever heard tell of Me or saw
20 My glory, and they will tell of My glory to the nations. And they will bring
back all your brothers from among all other nations, an offering to the LORD,
on horseback and on chariot, on camels, mules, dromedaries, to My holy
mount, Jerusalem – so says the LORD – just as the children of Israel would
21 bring up their offerings in pure vessels, to the LORD's House, and from among
22 them also I shall take priests and Levites, so says the LORD. For just as the
new heavens, the new earth that I am now forming, will stand forever before
23 Me, so says the LORD, so will stand your children, your name. And it will
be – every New Moon, every Sabbath – all flesh will come to worship Me, so
24 says the LORD. Going out, they will see bodies of those people who sinned
against Me, for the worms will not die nor the fire be quenched, and they will
be repugnant to all flesh.

And it will be – every New Moon, every Sabbath –
all flesh will come to worship Me: so says the LORD.

---

167 | These are the prophet's words of reassurance to those mocked by the hateful brothers, apparently a reference to Jews who rejected other Jews.

168 | Cf. 65:3.

169 | Lands on the coasts of Asia Minor.

ו יְהוָה וְנִרְאֶה בְשִׂמְחַתְכֶם וְהֵם יֵבֹשׁוּ׃ קוֹל שָׁאוֹן מֵעִיר קוֹל מֵהֵיכָל
ז קוֹל יְהוָה מְשַׁלֵּם גְּמוּל לְאֹיְבָיו׃ בְּטֶרֶם תָּחִיל יָלָדָה בְּטֶרֶם יָבוֹא חֵבֶל
ח לָהּ וְהִמְלִיטָה זָכָר׃ מִי־שָׁמַע כָּזֹאת מִי רָאָה כָּאֵלֶּה הֲיוּחַל אֶרֶץ בְּיוֹם
ט אֶחָד אִם־יִוָּלֵד גּוֹי פַּעַם אֶחָת כִּי־חָלָה גַּם־יָלְדָה צִיּוֹן אֶת־בָּנֶיהָ׃ הַאֲנִי
אַשְׁבִּיר וְלֹא אוֹלִיד יֹאמַר יְהוָה אִם־אֲנִי הַמּוֹלִיד וְעָצַרְתִּי אָמַר
י אֱלֹהָיִךְ׃ שִׂמְחוּ אֶת־יְרוּשָׁלִַם וְגִילוּ בָהּ כָּל־אֹהֲבֶיהָ שִׂישׂוּ
יא אִתָּהּ מָשׂוֹשׂ כָּל־הַמִּתְאַבְּלִים עָלֶיהָ׃ לְמַעַן תִּינְקוּ וּשְׂבַעְתֶּם מִשֹּׁד
יב תַּנְחֻמֶיהָ לְמַעַן תָּמֹצּוּ וְהִתְעַנַּגְתֶּם מִזִּיז כְּבוֹדָהּ׃ כִּי־כֹה ׀
אָמַר יְהוָה הִנְנִי נֹטֶה־אֵלֶיהָ כְּנָהָר שָׁלוֹם וּכְנַחַל שׁוֹטֵף כְּבוֹד גּוֹיִם
יג וִינַקְתֶּם עַל־צַד תִּנָּשֵׂאוּ וְעַל־בִּרְכַּיִם תְּשָׁעֳשָׁעוּ׃ כְּאִישׁ אֲשֶׁר אִמּוֹ
יד תְּנַחֲמֶנּוּ כֵּן אָנֹכִי אֲנַחֶמְכֶם וּבִירוּשָׁלִַם תְּנֻחָמוּ׃ וּרְאִיתֶם וְשָׂשׂ לִבְּכֶם
וְעַצְמוֹתֵיכֶם כַּדֶּשֶׁא תִפְרַחְנָה וְנוֹדְעָה יַד־יְהוָה אֶת־עֲבָדָיו וְזָעַם אֶת־
טו אֹיְבָיו׃ כִּי־הִנֵּה יְהוָה בָּאֵשׁ יָבוֹא וְכַסּוּפָה מַרְכְּבֹתָיו לְהָשִׁיב בְּחֵמָה
טז אַפּוֹ וְגַעֲרָתוֹ בְּלַהֲבֵי־אֵשׁ׃ כִּי בָאֵשׁ יְהוָה נִשְׁפָּט וּבְחַרְבּוֹ אֶת־כָּל־בָּשָׂר
יז וְרַבּוּ חַלְלֵי יְהוָה׃ הַמִּתְקַדְּשִׁים וְהַמִּטַּהֲרִים אֶל־הַגַּנּוֹת אַחַר אחד אַחַת
בַּתָּוֶךְ אֹכְלֵי בְּשַׂר הַחֲזִיר וְהַשֶּׁקֶץ וְהָעַכְבָּר יַחְדָּו יָסֻפוּ נְאֻם־יְהוָה׃
יח וְאָנֹכִי מַעֲשֵׂיהֶם וּמַחְשְׁבֹתֵיהֶם בָּאָה לְקַבֵּץ אֶת־כָּל־הַגּוֹיִם וְהַלְּשֹׁנוֹת
יט וּבָאוּ וְרָאוּ אֶת־כְּבוֹדִי׃ וְשַׂמְתִּי בָהֶם אוֹת וְשִׁלַּחְתִּי מֵהֶם ׀ פְּלֵיטִים
אֶל־הַגּוֹיִם תַּרְשִׁישׁ פּוּל וְלוּד מֹשְׁכֵי קֶשֶׁת תֻּבַל וְיָוָן הָאִיִּים הָרְחֹקִים
אֲשֶׁר לֹא־שָׁמְעוּ אֶת־שִׁמְעִי וְלֹא־רָאוּ אֶת־כְּבוֹדִי וְהִגִּידוּ אֶת־כְּבוֹדִי
כ בַּגּוֹיִם׃ וְהֵבִיאוּ אֶת־כָּל־אֲחֵיכֶם ׀ מִכָּל־הַגּוֹיִם ׀ מִנְחָה ׀ לַיהוָה בַּסּוּסִים
וּבָרֶכֶב וּבַצַּבִּים וּבַפְּרָדִים וּבַכִּרְכָּרוֹת עַל הַר קָדְשִׁי יְרוּשָׁלִַם אָמַר
יְהוָה כַּאֲשֶׁר יָבִיאוּ בְנֵי יִשְׂרָאֵל אֶת־הַמִּנְחָה בִּכְלִי טָהוֹר בֵּית יְהוָה׃
כא כב וְגַם־מֵהֶם אֶקַּח לַכֹּהֲנִים לַלְוִיִּם אָמַר יְהוָה׃ כִּי כַאֲשֶׁר הַשָּׁמַיִם
הַחֲדָשִׁים וְהָאָרֶץ הַחֲדָשָׁה אֲשֶׁר אֲנִי עֹשֶׂה עֹמְדִים לְפָנַי נְאֻם־יְהוָה
כג כֵּן יַעֲמֹד זַרְעֲכֶם וְשִׁמְכֶם׃ וְהָיָה מִדֵּי־חֹדֶשׁ בְּחָדְשׁוֹ וּמִדֵּי שַׁבָּת בְּשַׁבַּתּוֹ
כד יָבוֹא כָל־בָּשָׂר לְהִשְׁתַּחֲוֺת לְפָנַי אָמַר יְהוָה׃ וְיָצְאוּ וְרָאוּ בְּפִגְרֵי
הָאֲנָשִׁים הַפֹּשְׁעִים בִּי כִּי תוֹלַעְתָּם לֹא תָמוּת וְאִשָּׁם לֹא תִכְבֶּה
וְהָיוּ דֵרָאוֹן לְכָל־בָּשָׂר׃

והיה מדי חדש בחדשו ומדי שבת בשבתו
יבוא כל בשר להשתחות לפני
אמר יהוה

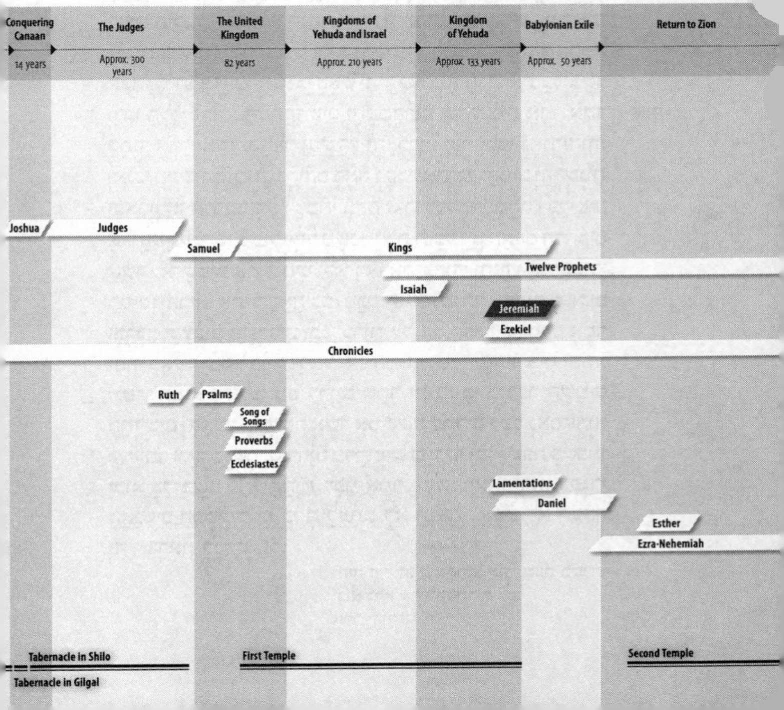
Conquering Canaan
14 years
The Judges
Approx. 300 years
The United Kingdom
82 years
Kingdoms of Yehuda and Israel
Approx. 210 years
Kingdom of Yehuda
Approx. 133 years
Babylonian Exile
Approx. 50 years
Return to Zion
Joshua
Judges
Samuel
Kings
Twelve Prophets
Isaiah
Jeremiah
Ezekiel
Chronicles
Ruth
Psalms
Song of Songs
Proverbs
Ecclesiastes
Lamentations
Daniel
Esther
Ezra-Nehemiah
Tabernacle in Shilo
Tabernacle in Gilgal
First Temple
Second Temple

ירמיה

YIRMEYA/JEREMIAH

JEREMIAH							
	The prophetic mission to establish an improved reality	Causes of the destruction and Yirmeya's attempts to prevent it	Yirmeya in conflict with the kings and false prophets	Prophecies of consolation and redemption	The period immediately before the destruction and its aftermath	Prophecies about the nations	Depiction of the destruction of Jerusalem and the Temple, and hints of hope
	Chs. 1–6	7–24	25–29	30–33	34–45	46–51	52
	Approx. 42 years						

1 1 The words of Yirmeyahu, son of Ḥilkiyahu, one of the priests who were in
2 Anatot in the land of Binyamin, to whom the word of the LORD came in the
days of Yoshiyahu son of Amon, king of Yehuda, in the thirteenth year of his
3 reign, and continued during the days of Yehoyakim son of Yoshiyahu, king
of Yehuda, until the end of the eleventh year of Tzidkiyahu son of Yoshiyahu,
4 king of Yehuda – until the exile of Jerusalem in the fifth month: The
5 word of the LORD came to me: "Before I formed you in the womb I knew
you. Before you were born I consecrated you. I placed you as a prophet to the
6 nations." I said, "Please, Lord GOD, I am not capable of speaking, for I am
7 still only a boy." The LORD replied to me, "Do not say, 'I am a boy,' for you
8 shall go to all to whom I send you, and you shall speak as I instruct you. Do
9 not fear them, for I am with you to rescue you, declares the LORD." The LORD
10 extended His hand and touched my mouth and the LORD said to me, "Look,
I have placed My words in your mouth. I have appointed you this day against
the kingdoms and against the nations to uproot and tear down, to destroy
11 and demolish, to build and to plant." The word of the LORD came
to me: "What do you see, Yirmeyahu?" I replied, "I see the branch of an
12 almond tree." And the LORD said to me: "You have seen well, for I am watchful
13 about keeping My word."[1] The word of the LORD came to me a
second time: "What do you see?" I answered, "I see a boiling cauldron facing
14 the north." And the LORD said to me: "From the north disaster shall burst
15 forth upon all the inhabitants of the land, for I am about to summon all the
tribes of the kingdoms of the north," declares the LORD. "They shall come;
each shall set up a throne at the entrance of the gates of Jerusalem against
16 her ramparts roundabout and against all the cities of Yehuda. Thus will I
pronounce My judgment upon them on account of their wickedness: they
abandoned Me, sacrificed to other gods, and worshipped the works of their
17 own hands. As for you, be courageous; stand up and speak to them as I will
instruct you. Do not break down because of them lest I break you down
18 before them. I have made you today a fortress city, an iron column, and walls
of bronze against the entire land – against the kings of Yehuda, its princes,
19 its priests, and the people of the land. They will wage battle against you, but
they will not prevail, for I am with you," declares the LORD, "to rescue
2 1 2 you." The word of the LORD came to me: "Go and proclaim to the
people of Jerusalem: 'This is what the LORD has said: I recall on your behalf
the devotion of your youth, your bridal love, when you followed Me into the
3 wilderness, a land unseeded. Israel is a treasure to the LORD, His choice
harvest. All who eat of it will be held to account. Evil will befall them, declares
4 the LORD.'" Listen to the word of the LORD, House of Yaakov and
5 all the tribes of the House of Israel. This is what the LORD said: What fault
did your forefathers find with Me that they distanced themselves from Me?
6 They followed nothingness and became nothing. They did not say, "Where
is the LORD who lifted us up from the land of Egypt, who guided us in the

1 | The Hebrew *shoked* (watchful) resonates with *shaked* (almond tree).

א א דִּבְרֵי יִרְמְיָהוּ בֶּן־חִלְקִיָּהוּ מִן־הַכֹּהֲנִים אֲשֶׁר בַּעֲנָתוֹת בְּאֶרֶץ בִּנְיָמִן: א
ב אֲשֶׁר הָיָה דְבַר־יְהוָה אֵלָיו בִּימֵי יֹאשִׁיָּהוּ בֶן־אָמוֹן מֶלֶךְ יְהוּדָה
ג בִּשְׁלֹשׁ־עֶשְׂרֵה שָׁנָה לְמָלְכוֹ: וַיְהִי בִּימֵי יְהוֹיָקִים בֶּן־יֹאשִׁיָּהוּ מֶלֶךְ
יְהוּדָה עַד־תֹּם עַשְׁתֵּי־עֶשְׂרֵה שָׁנָה לְצִדְקִיָּהוּ בֶן־יֹאשִׁיָּהוּ מֶלֶךְ יְהוּדָה
ד עַד־גְּלוֹת יְרוּשָׁלִַם בַּחֹדֶשׁ הַחֲמִישִׁי: וַיְהִי דְבַר־
ה יְהוָה אֵלַי לֵאמֹר: בְּטֶרֶם אצורך בַבֶּטֶן יְדַעְתִּיךָ וּבְטֶרֶם תֵּצֵא מֵרֶחֶם אֶצָּרְךָ
ו הִקְדַּשְׁתִּיךָ נָבִיא לַגּוֹיִם נְתַתִּיךָ: וָאֹמַר אֲהָהּ אֲדֹנָי יְהוִה הִנֵּה לֹא־
ז יָדַעְתִּי דַּבֵּר כִּי־נַעַר אָנֹכִי: וַיֹּאמֶר יְהוָה אֵלַי אַל־תֹּאמַר נַעַר אָנֹכִי כִּי
ח עַל־כָּל־אֲשֶׁר אֶשְׁלָחֲךָ תֵּלֵךְ וְאֵת כָּל־אֲשֶׁר אֲצַוְּךָ תְּדַבֵּר: אַל־תִּירָא
ט מִפְּנֵיהֶם כִּי־אִתְּךָ אֲנִי לְהַצִּלֶךָ נְאֻם־יְהוָה: וַיִּשְׁלַח יְהוָה אֶת־יָדוֹ וַיַּגַּע
י עַל־פִּי וַיֹּאמֶר יְהוָה אֵלַי הִנֵּה נָתַתִּי דְבָרַי בְּפִיךָ: רְאֵה הִפְקַדְתִּיךָ ׀
הַיּוֹם הַזֶּה עַל־הַגּוֹיִם וְעַל־הַמַּמְלָכוֹת לִנְתוֹשׁ וְלִנְתוֹץ וּלְהַאֲבִיד
יא וְלַהֲרוֹס לִבְנוֹת וְלִנְטוֹעַ: וַיְהִי דְבַר־יְהוָה אֵלַי לֵאמֹר
יב מָה־אַתָּה רֹאֶה יִרְמְיָהוּ וָאֹמַר מַקֵּל שָׁקֵד אֲנִי רֹאֶה: וַיֹּאמֶר יְהוָה אֵלַי
יג הֵיטַבְתָּ לִרְאוֹת כִּי־שֹׁקֵד אֲנִי עַל־דְּבָרִי לַעֲשֹׂתוֹ: וַיְהִי
דְבַר־יְהוָה ׀ אֵלַי שֵׁנִית לֵאמֹר מָה אַתָּה רֹאֶה וָאֹמַר סִיר נָפוּחַ אֲנִי
יד רֹאֶה וּפָנָיו מִפְּנֵי צָפוֹנָה: וַיֹּאמֶר יְהוָה אֵלָי מִצָּפוֹן תִּפָּתַח הָרָעָה עַל
טו כָּל־יֹשְׁבֵי הָאָרֶץ: כִּי ׀ הִנְנִי קֹרֵא לְכָל־מִשְׁפְּחוֹת מַמְלְכוֹת צָפוֹנָה
נְאֻם־יְהוָה וּבָאוּ וְנָתְנוּ אִישׁ כִּסְאוֹ פֶּתַח ׀ שַׁעֲרֵי יְרוּשָׁלִַם וְעַל כָּל־
טז חוֹמֹתֶיהָ סָבִיב וְעַל כָּל־עָרֵי יְהוּדָה: וְדִבַּרְתִּי מִשְׁפָּטַי אוֹתָם עַל כָּל־
רָעָתָם אֲשֶׁר עֲזָבוּנִי וַיְקַטְּרוּ לֵאלֹהִים אֲחֵרִים וַיִּשְׁתַּחֲווּ לְמַעֲשֵׂי יְדֵיהֶם:
יז וְאַתָּה תֶּאְזֹר מָתְנֶיךָ וְקַמְתָּ וְדִבַּרְתָּ אֲלֵיהֶם אֵת כָּל־אֲשֶׁר אָנֹכִי אֲצַוֶּךָּ
יח אַל־תֵּחַת מִפְּנֵיהֶם פֶּן־אֲחִתְּךָ לִפְנֵיהֶם: וַאֲנִי הִנֵּה נְתַתִּיךָ הַיּוֹם לְעִיר
מִבְצָר וּלְעַמּוּד בַּרְזֶל וּלְחֹמוֹת נְחֹשֶׁת עַל־כָּל־הָאָרֶץ לְמַלְכֵי יְהוּדָה
יט לְשָׂרֶיהָ לְכֹהֲנֶיהָ וּלְעַם הָאָרֶץ: וְנִלְחֲמוּ אֵלֶיךָ וְלֹא־יוּכְלוּ לָךְ כִּי־אִתְּךָ
ב א אֲנִי נְאֻם־יְהוָה לְהַצִּילֶךָ: וַיְהִי דְבַר־יְהוָה אֵלַי לֵאמֹר:
ב הָלֹךְ וְקָרָאתָ בְאָזְנֵי יְרוּשָׁלִַם לֵאמֹר כֹּה אָמַר יְהוָה זָכַרְתִּי לָךְ חֶסֶד
נְעוּרַיִךְ אַהֲבַת כְּלוּלֹתָיִךְ לֶכְתֵּךְ אַחֲרַי בַּמִּדְבָּר בְּאֶרֶץ לֹא זְרוּעָה:
ג קֹדֶשׁ יִשְׂרָאֵל לַיהוָה רֵאשִׁית תְּבוּאָתֹה כָּל־אֹכְלָיו יֶאְשָׁמוּ רָעָה
ד תָּבֹא אֲלֵיהֶם נְאֻם־יְהוָה: שִׁמְעוּ דְבַר־יְהוָה בֵּית יַעֲקֹב
ה וְכָל־מִשְׁפְּחוֹת בֵּית יִשְׂרָאֵל: כֹּה ׀ אָמַר יְהוָה מַה־מָּצְאוּ אֲבוֹתֵיכֶם
ו בִי עָוֶל כִּי רָחֲקוּ מֵעָלָי וַיֵּלְכוּ אַחֲרֵי הַהֶבֶל וַיֶּהְבָּלוּ: וְלֹא אָמְרוּ אַיֵּה

wilderness, a land of deserts and pits, an arid land, deathly dark, a land never
7 traversed by man, where no one ever dwelt?" I brought you to a fertile land,
to eat its fruits and bounty, but you came and defiled My land, and made My
8 heritage an abomination. The priests did not say, "Where is the LORD?" The
teachers of the Torah did not know Me. The shepherds[2] betrayed Me. The
prophets prophesied in the name of Baal. They pursued that which was
9 useless. Therefore, I will continue to contend with them, declares the LORD.
10 I will contend with their children's children. Cross over to the islands of the
Kittites[3] and observe. Send emissaries to Kedar[4] and ponder well. See if
11 anything like this ever happened before. Has a people ever exchanged its gods,
and they are non-gods? Yet my nation exchanged its glory for something
12 useless. Heavens, be astounded by this. Storm and become utterly desolate,
13 declares the LORD. For My nation has performed two wrongs: they have
forsaken Me, the source of living waters, to dig wells, broken wells that cannot
14 hold water. Is Israel a slave? Is he born to a maidservant? Why has he become
15 an object of plunder? Young lions roar at him. They voiced their cries. They
16 laid waste to his land. His cities have been set afire, with no inhabitants. Even
17 the men of Nof and Taḥpanḥes[5] crush your skull. This has been done to you
because you deserted the LORD your God during the time He guided you
18 upon the journey. Now of what use is it to you to approach Egypt to drink
the waters of Shiḥor? Of what use is it to you to approach Assyria to drink
19 the waters of the river?[6] Your own evil will discipline you; your own
waywardness will rebuke you. Know and see that your abandonment of
the LORD your God has been bad and bitter. There is no fear of Me in you,
20 says the Almighty, LORD of Hosts. I broke your yoke long ago. I tore your
restraints asunder. You said, "I will never again transgress!" Yet on every high
21 hilltop and under every leafy tree you recline like a harlot. I planted you as a
choice grape: perfect and genuine seed. How did you change on Me into a
22 weed? Rotten grapes of a strange vine! Although you scrub yourself with
natron[7] and heap soap on yourselves, your guilt is stained before Me, declares
23 the Lord GOD. How can you say that you were never defiled? That you never
followed the Be'alim? Look back upon your path in the valley. Recognize what
24 you did, like a young she-camel clinging to her wild ways. Like a wild ass
accustomed to the wilderness; inhaling wind as she pleases, her wailing
cannot be silenced. Yet those who seek her need not be weary. In her month
25 they will find her. Spare your foot from becoming bare and your throat from
suffering thirst! But you said, "Never mind. No. I have loved strangers; it is
26 them whom I will follow." Like the shame of a thief when he is found out, so
will the House of Israel be shamed: They, their kings, their noblemen, their

---

2 | A metaphor for the rulers.

3 | Islands to the west.

4 | A desert tribe to the east.

5 | Cities in Lower Egypt to whom the Israelites looked as allies against Nevukhadnetzar.

6 | *Shiḥor* is usually understood as the Nile, and "the River" is the Euphrates.

7 | A mineral used in ancient times as a cleanser. Cf. Proverbs 25:20.

יְהוָה הַמַּעֲלֶה אֹתָנוּ מֵאֶרֶץ מִצְרָיִם הַמּוֹלִיךְ אֹתָנוּ בַּמִּדְבָּר בְּאֶרֶץ
עֲרָבָה וְשׁוּחָה בְּאֶרֶץ צִיָּה וְצַלְמָוֶת בְּאֶרֶץ לֹא־עָבַר בָּהּ אִישׁ וְלֹא־
ז יָשַׁב אָדָם שָׁם: וָאָבִיא אֶתְכֶם אֶל־אֶרֶץ הַכַּרְמֶל לֶאֱכֹל פִּרְיָהּ וְטוּבָהּ
ח וַתָּבֹאוּ וַתְּטַמְּאוּ אֶת־אַרְצִי וְנַחֲלָתִי שַׂמְתֶּם לְתוֹעֵבָה: הַכֹּהֲנִים לֹא
אָמְרוּ אַיֵּה יְהוָה וְתֹפְשֵׂי הַתּוֹרָה לֹא יְדָעוּנִי וְהָרֹעִים פָּשְׁעוּ בִי וְהַנְּבִיאִים
ט נִבְּאוּ בַבַּעַל וְאַחֲרֵי לֹא־יוֹעִלוּ הָלָכוּ: לָכֵן עֹד אָרִיב אִתְּכֶם נְאֻם־יְהוָה
י וְאֶת־בְּנֵי בְנֵיכֶם אָרִיב: כִּי עִבְרוּ אִיֵּי כִתִּיִּים וּרְאוּ וְקֵדָר שִׁלְחוּ וְהִתְבּוֹנְנוּ
יא מְאֹד וּרְאוּ הֵן הָיְתָה כָּזֹאת: הַהֵימִיר גּוֹי אֱלֹהִים וְהֵמָּה לֹא אֱלֹהִים
יב וְעַמִּי הֵמִיר כְּבוֹדוֹ בְּלוֹא יוֹעִיל: שֹׁמּוּ שָׁמַיִם עַל־זֹאת וְשַׂעֲרוּ חָרְבוּ
יג מְאֹד נְאֻם־יְהוָה: כִּי־שְׁתַּיִם רָעוֹת עָשָׂה עַמִּי אֹתִי עָזְבוּ מְקוֹר | מַיִם
חַיִּים לַחְצֹב לָהֶם בֹּארוֹת בֹּארֹת נִשְׁבָּרִים אֲשֶׁר לֹא־יָכִלוּ הַמָּיִם:
יד טו הַעֶבֶד יִשְׂרָאֵל אִם־יְלִיד בַּיִת הוּא מַדּוּעַ הָיָה לָבַז: עָלָיו יִשְׁאֲגוּ כְפִרִים
טז נָתְנוּ קוֹלָם וַיָּשִׁיתוּ אַרְצוֹ לְשַׁמָּה עָרָיו נצתה מִבְּלִי יֹשֵׁב: גַּם־בְּנֵי־נֹף נִצְּתוּ
יז ותחפנס יִרְעוּךְ קָדְקֹד: הֲלוֹא־זֹאת תַּעֲשֶׂה־לָּךְ עָזְבֵךְ אֶת־יְהוָה אֱלֹהַיִךְ וְתַחְפַּנְחֵס
יח בְּעֵת מוֹלִכֵךְ בַּדָּרֶךְ: וְעַתָּה מַה־לָּךְ לְדֶרֶךְ מִצְרַיִם לִשְׁתּוֹת מֵי שִׁחוֹר
יט וּמַה־לָּךְ לְדֶרֶךְ אַשּׁוּר לִשְׁתּוֹת מֵי נָהָר: תְּיַסְּרֵךְ רָעָתֵךְ וּמְשֻׁבוֹתַיִךְ
תּוֹכִחֻךְ וּדְעִי וּרְאִי כִּי־רַע וָמָר עָזְבֵךְ אֶת־יְהוָה אֱלֹהָיִךְ וְלֹא פַחְדָּתִי
כ אֵלַיִךְ נְאֻם־אֲדֹנָי יְהוִה צְבָאוֹת: כִּי מֵעוֹלָם שָׁבַרְתִּי עֻלֵּךְ נִתַּקְתִּי
מוֹסְרוֹתַיִךְ וַתֹּאמְרִי לֹא אעבוד כִּי עַל־כָּל־גִּבְעָה גְּבֹהָה וְתַחַת כָּל־ אֶעֱבוֹר
כא עֵץ רַעֲנָן אַתְּ צֹעָה זֹנָה: וְאָנֹכִי נְטַעְתִּיךְ שׂוֹרֵק כֻּלֹּה זֶרַע אֱמֶת וְאֵיךְ
כב נֶהְפַּכְתְּ לִי סוּרֵי הַגֶּפֶן נָכְרִיָּה: כִּי אִם־תְּכַבְּסִי בַּנֶּתֶר וְתַרְבִּי־לָךְ בֹּרִית
כג נִכְתָּם עֲוֺנֵךְ לְפָנַי נְאֻם אֲדֹנָי יְהוִה: אֵיךְ תֹּאמְרִי לֹא נִטְמֵאתִי אַחֲרֵי
הַבְּעָלִים לֹא הָלַכְתִּי רְאִי דַרְכֵּךְ בַּגַּיְא דְּעִי מֶה עָשִׂית בִּכְרָה קַלָּה
כד מְשָׂרֶכֶת דְּרָכֶיהָ: פֶּרֶה | לִמֻּד מִדְבָּר בְּאַוַּת נפשו שָׁאֲפָה רוּחַ תַּאֲנָתָהּ נַפְשָׁהּ
כה מִי יְשִׁיבֶנָּה כָּל־מְבַקְשֶׁיהָ לֹא יִיעָפוּ בְּחָדְשָׁהּ יִמְצָאוּנְהָ: מִנְעִי רַגְלֵךְ
מִיָּחֵף וגורנך מִצִּמְאָה וַתֹּאמְרִי נוֹאָשׁ לוֹא כִּי־אָהַבְתִּי זָרִים וְאַחֲרֵיהֶם וּגְרוֹנֵךְ
כו אֵלֵךְ: כְּבֹשֶׁת גַּנָּב כִּי יִמָּצֵא כֵּן הֹבִישׁוּ בֵּית יִשְׂרָאֵל הֵמָּה מַלְכֵיהֶם

27 priests, and their prophets. They say to the tree, "You are my father!" And to
the stone, "You gave birth to me!" They have turned their backs to me, not
28 their faces but in their time of trouble they say, "Arise and save us!" Where
are the gods that you have crafted for yourself? Let them rise if they can save
you in your time of trouble. For your gods, Yehuda, are as numerous as your
29 cities. Why do you contend with Me? You have all rebelled against
30 Me, declares the Lord. I have punished your sons for naught, for they did
not learn their lesson. Your sword has devoured your prophets like a vicious
31 lion. I call upon this generation to acknowledge the word of the Lord! Have
I been a wilderness for Israel, or a land of great darkness? Why has My nation
32 said, "We have strayed; we will never again approach You"? Does a maiden
forget her ornaments? A bride her braided ribbons? Yet My nation has
33 forgotten Me for days without number. You have perfected the ways in which
you search for love so well that you have even taught those ways to sinful
34 women. The blood of the innocent poor can be found on your skirts, yet you
35 did not find them tunneling into your home. Despite all of this you dare
declare: "I am innocent; surely He has turned His anger away from me!" Be
36 aware: I will judge you for saying, "I did not sin." How you have degraded
yourself by perverting your ways. You will yet be shamed by Egypt too, just
37 as you were shamed by Assyria. From this[8] too you will depart with your
hands on your head. The Lord despises those in whom you trust; You will
3 1 not succeed with them. That is to say: [9] If a man sent away his wife, and she
walked away from him and married another man, would he return to her
again? Such a land would be utterly defiled. You have strayed after many lovers,
2 and yet you dare return to Me? demands the Lord. Raise your eyes to the
heights and observe: Where have you not been debauched? By the roadsides
you sat in wait for them like a nomad in the desert. You defiled the land with
3 your promiscuity and your wickedness. The rains were withheld, and the
spring rain did not come, yet yours was the forehead[10] of a promiscuous
4 woman; you refused to be shamed. By now, you should have called Me:
5 "Father! You were my childhood companion!" Did you think He would bear
a grudge forever or preserve it for eternity? Instead you spoke, did evil, and
6 you had your way. The Lord spoke to me in the days of King
Yoshiyahu:[11] "Have you seen what wayward Israel has done? She walks along
7 every high mountain and under every leafy tree; she plays the harlot there. I
hoped that, having done all this, she would return to Me; but she did not return,
8 and her sister, treacherous Yehuda, took note. I saw. For all the adulteries
committed by wayward Israel I sent her away and delivered a bill of divorce to
her. But treacherous Yehuda, her sister, still showed no fear. Instead, she too
9 went off and played the harlot. With her casual promiscuity she defiled the
10 land; she debauched both stone and tree. In spite of all this, her treacherous

---

8 | That is, from your alliance with Egypt.

9 | The voice in verses 1–5 is now the prophet's.

10 | Meaning willfulness.

11 | By which time the Ten Tribes of Israel had already been exiled (see II Kings, ch. 17, 18:1–9).

כז שָׂרֵיהֶם וְכֹהֲנֵיהֶם וּנְבִיאֵיהֶם׃ אֹמְרִים לָעֵץ אָבִי אַתָּה וְלָאֶבֶן אַתְּ
ילדתני כִּי־פָנוּ אֵלַי עֹרֶף וְלֹא פָנִים וּבְעֵת רָעָתָם יֹאמְרוּ קוּמָה יְלִדְתָּנוּ
כח וְהוֹשִׁיעֵנוּ׃ וְאַיֵּה אֱלֹהֶיךָ אֲשֶׁר עָשִׂיתָ לָּךְ יָקוּמוּ אִם־יוֹשִׁיעוּךָ בְּעֵת
כט רָעָתֶךָ כִּי מִסְפַּר עָרֶיךָ הָיוּ אֱלֹהֶיךָ יְהוּדָה׃ לָמָּה תָרִיבוּ
ל אֵלָי כֻּלְּכֶם פְּשַׁעְתֶּם בִּי נְאֻם־יְהוָה׃ לַשָּׁוְא הִכֵּיתִי אֶת־בְּנֵיכֶם מוּסָר
לא לֹא לָקָחוּ אָכְלָה חַרְבְּכֶם נְבִיאֵיכֶם כְּאַרְיֵה מַשְׁחִית׃ הַדּוֹר אַתֶּם רְאוּ
דְבַר־יְהוָה הֲמִדְבָּר הָיִיתִי לְיִשְׂרָאֵל אִם אֶרֶץ מַאְפֵּלְיָה מַדּוּעַ אָמְרוּ
לב עַמִּי רַדְנוּ לוֹא־נָבוֹא עוֹד אֵלֶיךָ׃ הֲתִשְׁכַּח בְּתוּלָה עֶדְיָהּ כַּלָּה קִשֻּׁרֶיהָ
לג וְעַמִּי שְׁכֵחוּנִי יָמִים אֵין מִסְפָּר׃ מַה־תֵּיטִבִי דַּרְכֵּךְ לְבַקֵּשׁ אַהֲבָה לָכֵן
לד גַּם אֶת־הָרָעוֹת למדתי אֶת־דְּרָכָיִךְ׃ גַּם בִּכְנָפַיִךְ נִמְצְאוּ דַּם נַפְשׁוֹת לִמַּדְתְּ
לה אֶבְיוֹנִים נְקִיִּים לֹא־בַמַּחְתֶּרֶת מְצָאתִים כִּי עַל־כָּל־אֵלֶּה׃ וַתֹּאמְרִי
כִּי נִקֵּיתִי אַךְ שָׁב אַפּוֹ מִמֶּנִּי הִנְנִי נִשְׁפָּט אוֹתָךְ עַל־אָמְרֵךְ לֹא חָטָאתִי׃
לו מַה־תֵּזְלִי מְאֹד לְשַׁנּוֹת אֶת־דַּרְכֵּךְ גַּם מִמִּצְרַיִם תֵּבֹשִׁי כַּאֲשֶׁר־בֹּשְׁתְּ
לז מֵאַשּׁוּר׃ גַּם מֵאֵת זֶה תֵּצְאִי וְיָדַיִךְ עַל־רֹאשֵׁךְ כִּי־מָאַס יְהוָה בְּמִבְטַחַיִךְ
ג א וְלֹא תַצְלִיחִי לָהֶם׃ לֵאמֹר הֵן יְשַׁלַּח אִישׁ אֶת־אִשְׁתּוֹ וְהָלְכָה מֵאִתּוֹ
וְהָיְתָה לְאִישׁ־אַחֵר הֲיָשׁוּב אֵלֶיהָ עוֹד הֲלוֹא חָנוֹף תֶּחֱנַף הָאָרֶץ
ב הַהִיא וְאַתְּ זָנִית רֵעִים רַבִּים וְשׁוֹב אֵלַי נְאֻם־יְהוָה׃ שְׂאִי־עֵינַיִךְ עַל־
שְׁפָיִם וּרְאִי אֵיפֹה לֹא שגלת עַל־דְּרָכִים יָשַׁבְתְּ לָהֶם כַּעֲרָבִי בַּמִּדְבָּר שֻׁכַּבְתְּ
ג וַתַּחֲנִיפִי אֶרֶץ בִּזְנוּתַיִךְ וּבְרָעָתֵךְ׃ וַיִּמָּנְעוּ רְבִבִים וּמַלְקוֹשׁ לוֹא הָיָה
ד וּמֵצַח אִשָּׁה זוֹנָה הָיָה לָךְ מֵאַנְתְּ הִכָּלֵם׃ הֲלוֹא מֵעַתָּה קראתי לִי ב קָרָאת
ה אָבִי אַלּוּף נְעֻרַי אָתָּה׃ הֲיִנְטֹר לְעוֹלָם אִם־יִשְׁמֹר לָנֶצַח הִנֵּה דִבַּרְתְּ
ו וַתַּעֲשִׂי הָרָעוֹת וַתּוּכָל׃ וַיֹּאמֶר יְהוָה אֵלַי בִּימֵי
יֹאשִׁיָּהוּ הַמֶּלֶךְ הֲרָאִיתָ אֲשֶׁר עָשְׂתָה מְשֻׁבָה יִשְׂרָאֵל הֹלְכָה הִיא
ז עַל־כָּל־הַר גָּבֹהַּ וְאֶל־תַּחַת כָּל־עֵץ רַעֲנָן וַתִּזְנִי־שָׁם׃ וָאֹמַר אַחֲרֵי
עֲשׂוֹתָהּ אֶת־כָּל־אֵלֶּה אֵלַי תָּשׁוּב וְלֹא־שָׁבָה ותראה בָּגוֹדָה אֲחוֹתָהּ וַתֵּרֶא
ח יְהוּדָה׃ וָאֵרֶא כִּי עַל־כָּל־אֹדוֹת אֲשֶׁר נִאֲפָה מְשֻׁבָה יִשְׂרָאֵל שִׁלַּחְתִּיהָ
וָאֶתֵּן אֶת־סֵפֶר כְּרִיתֻתֶיהָ אֵלֶיהָ וְלֹא יָרְאָה בֹּגֵדָה יְהוּדָה אֲחוֹתָהּ
ט וַתֵּלֶךְ וַתִּזֶן גַּם־הִיא׃ וְהָיָה מִקֹּל זְנוּתָהּ וַתֶּחֱנַף אֶת־הָאָרֶץ וַתִּנְאַף
י אֶת־הָאֶבֶן וְאֶת־הָעֵץ׃ וְגַם־בְּכָל־זֹאת לֹא־שָׁבָה אֵלַי בָּגוֹדָה אֲחוֹתָהּ

sister Yehuda did not return to Me with all her heart, but with deception,
11 declares the LORD." The LORD said to me: "Wayward Israel was
12 more justified than treacherous Yehuda. Go, proclaim these words to the
north, and say: Return, wayward Israel – declares the LORD. I will not frown
upon you, for I am compassionate, declares the LORD; I will not bear a grudge
13 forever. Acknowledge your sin, for you have betrayed the LORD your God.
You scattered your paths, following strangers under every leafy tree. You did
14 not heed My voice, declares the LORD. Return, wayward children, declares
the LORD, for I am your Master. I will take you, one from a city, two from a
15 family, and I will bring you back to Zion. I will provide you with shepherds
16 true to My heart who will shepherd you with wisdom and skill. It will come
to pass that you will multiply and be fruitful in the land. Then, declares the
LORD, there will no longer be a call for the Ark of the LORD's Covenant. It will
neither enter anyone's mind nor be remembered nor be missed; nor will it be
17 replaced by another. At that time, they will call Jerusalem 'the LORD's throne';
all nations will assemble in the LORD's name in Jerusalem and will no longer
18 follow the stubbornness of their evil hearts. In those days the House
of Yehuda will join the House of Israel. They will come together from the
19 north to the land that I bequeathed to your ancestors. I had resolved that I
would award you a special place among My children and that I would grant
you a precious land, a glorious heritage for all nations. I said: 'Call Me "my
20 Father" and never turn away from Me.' But – as a woman betrays her lover –
21 so have you, the House of Israel, betrayed Me, declares the LORD. A clamor
is heard from the hilltops, the tearful supplications of the children of Israel,
for they have perverted their ways, and they have forgotten the LORD their
22 God. Return, wayward children! I will heal your waywardness." Here we are.
23 We come to You, for You are the LORD our God. In truth, false were the hopes
offered by the hills and the tumult upon the mountains.[12] In truth, only in the
24 LORD our God is Israel's salvation. The Shame[13] devoured the efforts of our
ancestors from the time of our youth: their sheep, their cattle, their sons, and
25 their daughters. We wallow in our shame; our disgrace envelops us; we sinned
against the LORD our God, we and our ancestors. From the time of our youth
4 1 until this very day we did not heed the voice of the LORD our God. If you,
Israel, return to Me, declares the LORD, I will welcome your return. If you
2 remove your abominations from My presence, you shall not suffer exile.
You will utter oaths – exclaiming "as the LORD lives" truthfully, justly, and
righteously – so that other nations will bless themselves by Him and come
3 to take pride in Him. For this is what the LORD said to the people
of Yehuda and to Jerusalem: Plow your untilled field well, and do not sow
4 among thorns. Men of Yehuda and inhabitants of Jerusalem: Circumcise
yourselves before the LORD, and remove the hardness of your hearts[14] lest
your evil deeds cause My wrath to spread like a fire burning out of control.

12 | Places where idols were worshipped.

13 | The word "Shame" (*boshet*) is a derogatory substitute for "Baal."

14 | Cf. Deuteronomy 10:16.

יא יהודה בכל־לבה כי אם־בשקר נאם־יהוה: ויאמר
יב יהוה אלי צדקה נפשה משבה ישראל מבגדה יהודה: הלך וקראת
את־הדברים האלה צפונה ואמרת שובה משבה ישראל נאם־יהוה
יג לוא־אפיל פני בכם כי־חסיד אני נאם־יהוה לא אטור לעולם: אך
דעי עונך כי ביהוה אלהיך פשעת ותפזרי את־דרכיך לזרים תחת
יד כל־עץ רענן ובקולי לא־שמעתם נאם־יהוה: שובו בנים שובבים
נאם־יהוה כי אנכי בעלתי בכם ולקחתי אתכם אחד מעיר ושנים
טו ממשפחה והבאתי אתכם ציון: ונתתי לכם רעים כלבי ורעו אתכם
טז דעה והשכיל: והיה כי תרבו ופריתם בארץ בימים ההמה נאם־
יהוה לא־יאמרו עוד ארון ברית־יהוה ולא יעלה על־לב ולא יזכרו־
יז בו ולא יפקדו ולא יעשה עוד: בעת ההיא יקראו לירושלם כסא
יהוה ונקוו אליה כל־הגוים לשם יהוה לירושלם ולא־ילכו עוד
יח אחרי שררות לבם הרע: בימים ההמה ילכו בית־יהודה
על־בית ישראל ויבאו יחדו מארץ צפון על־הארץ אשר הנחלתי
יט את־אבותיכם: ואנכי אמרתי איך אשיתך בבנים ואתן־לך ארץ
חמדה נחלת צבי צבאות גוים ואמר אבי תקראו־לי ומאחרי לא תקראי־
כ תשובו: אכן בגדה אשה מרעה כן בגדתם בי בית ישראל נאם־ תשובי
כא יהוה: קול על־שפיים נשמע בכי תחנוני בני ישראל כי העוו
כב את־דרכם שכחו את־יהוה אלהיהם: שובו בנים שובבים ארפה
כג משובתיכם הננו אתנו לך כי אתה יהוה אלהינו: אכן לשקר
כד מגבעות המון הרים אכן ביהוה אלהינו תשועת ישראל: והבשת
אכלה את־יגיע אבותינו מנעורינו את־צאנם ואת־בקרם את־בניהם
כה ואת־בנותיהם: נשכבה בבשתנו ותכסנו כלמתנו כי ליהוה אלהינו
חטאנו אנחנו ואבותינו מנעורינו ועד־היום הזה ולא שמענו בקול
ד א יהוה אלהינו: אם־תשוב ישראל ׀ נאם־יהוה אלי תשוב ואם־
ב תסיר שקוציך מפני ולא תנוד: ונשבעת חי־יהוה באמת במשפט
ג ובצדקה והתברכו בו גוים ובו יתהללו: כי־כה ׀
אמר יהוה לאיש יהודה ולירושלם נירו לכם ניר ואל־תזרעו אל־
ד קצים: המלו ליהוה והסרו ערלות לבבכם איש יהודה וישבי
ירושלם פן־תצא כאש חמתי ובערה ואין מכבה מפני רע מעלליכם:

5 Tell it in Yehuda; let it be heard in Jerusalem. Say: "Sound the ram's horn in
the land." Call out loudly and tell one another, "Let us gather and enter to the
6 fortified cities." Raise a flag over Zion. Take flight; do not stand still. I am about
7 to deliver evil from the north – a terrible destruction. The Lion has come up
from his lair. The Destroyer of Nations has set forth. He has departed from his
place in order to lay waste to your land. Your cities will become desolate, with
8 no inhabitant. For this reason, don sackcloth, lament, and wail, for the LORD's
9 wrath has not left us. On that day – declares the LORD –
the king will lose heart; so will the princes; the priests will be stunned, the
10 prophets stupefied. I said: "Oh, Lord GOD, in fact You deceived this people
and Jerusalem by telling them that there would be peace for them, but the
11 sword has reached the throat." At that time it will be told to this people and
to Jerusalem that a desiccating wind will come from hill and desert on the
12 way to my people. It will come neither to winnow nor to cleanse. A wind so
13 forceful will come upon us that now,[15] I too will rebuke them harshly: Behold,
He rises like the clouds, His chariots like the whirlwind; His steeds are swifter
14 than eagles. Woe to us, for we have been despoiled. Jerusalem: Cleanse your
heart from evil so that you will be saved. How long will your schemes of
15 corruption abide in you? For a voice proclaims from Dan; it announces
16 misfortune from the Efrayim hills: Let the nations be informed; let it be
announced about Jerusalem: Besiegers are approaching from a distant
17 land. They have sounded their voices throughout the cities of Yehuda. Like
watchmen around the fields, so have they encircled her because she has
18 rebelled against Me, declares the LORD. Your path and your deeds have done
this to you. This is your punishment so bitter. It has touched your very
19 heart. My innards, my innards quake, as do the chambers of my
heart. My heart pounds; I cannot silence it, for my soul has heard the call of
20 the ram's horn, the signal of war. Destruction upon destruction has transpired.
The entire land has been despoiled. Suddenly, my tents have been despoiled;
21 and so, in an instant, have my tent curtains. How much longer will I see the
22 flag[16] and hear the call of the ram's horn? For My nation is a fool;
they do not know Me. They are stupid children; they are not intelligent. They
23 are clever at doing evil, but to do good? That they do not know. I gazed at the
land – it was void and desolate;[17] and at the heavens, but gone was their light.
24 25 I gazed at the mountains – they were shaking; all the hills were aquiver. I
gazed, and behold: mankind was gone. All the birds of the skies had flown
26 away. I gazed, and behold: the Carmel was the wilderness; all its cities were
27 torn down before the LORD, before His fiery wrath. This is what the
LORD has said: The entire land will be desolate, but I will not completely
28 eradicate it. For this shall the land be ruined and the heavens above darkened,
for I have declared My intentions; I have not come to regret them, nor will I
29 retract them. The entire city flees from the sound of the horseman and the

15 | That is, even before the wind has come.
16 | The flag of war.
17 | Cf. Genesis 1:2.

ה הַגִּידוּ בִיהוּדָה וּבִירוּשָׁלִַם הַשְׁמִיעוּ וְאִמְרוּ ותקעו שׁוֹפָר בָּאָרֶץ קִרְאוּ תִּקְעוּ
ו מַלְאוּ וְאִמְרוּ הֵאָסְפוּ וְנָבוֹאָה אֶל־עָרֵי הַמִּבְצָר׃ שְׂאוּ־נֵס צִיּוֹנָה הָעִיזוּ
ז אַל־תַּעֲמֹדוּ כִּי רָעָה אָנֹכִי מֵבִיא מִצָּפוֹן וְשֶׁבֶר גָּדוֹל׃ עָלָה אַרְיֵה
מִסֻּבְּכוֹ וּמַשְׁחִית גּוֹיִם נָסַע יָצָא מִמְּקֹמוֹ לָשׂוּם אַרְצֵךְ לְשַׁמָּה עָרַיִךְ
ח תִּצֶּינָה מֵאֵין יוֹשֵׁב׃ עַל־זֹאת חִגְרוּ שַׂקִּים סִפְדוּ וְהֵילִילוּ כִּי לֹא־שָׁב
ט חֲרוֹן אַף־יְהוָה מִמֶּנּוּ׃ וְהָיָה בַיּוֹם־הַהוּא נְאֻם־יְהוָה יֹאבַד
י לֵב־הַמֶּלֶךְ וְלֵב הַשָּׂרִים וְנָשַׁמּוּ הַכֹּהֲנִים וְהַנְּבִאִים יִתְמָהוּ׃ וָאֹמַר
אֲהָהּ ׀ אֲדֹנָי יְהוִה אָכֵן הַשֵּׁא הִשֵּׁאתָ לָעָם הַזֶּה וְלִירוּשָׁלִַם לֵאמֹר
יא שָׁלוֹם יִהְיֶה לָכֶם וְנָגְעָה חֶרֶב עַד־הַנָּפֶשׁ׃ בָּעֵת הַהִיא יֵאָמֵר לָעָם־הַזֶּה
וְלִירוּשָׁלִַם רוּחַ צַח שְׁפָיִם בַּמִּדְבָּר דֶּרֶךְ בַּת־עַמִּי לוֹא לִזְרוֹת וְלוֹא
יב לְהָבַר׃ רוּחַ מָלֵא מֵאֵלֶּה יָבוֹא לִי עַתָּה גַּם־אֲנִי אֲדַבֵּר מִשְׁפָּטִים
יג אוֹתָם׃ הִנֵּה ׀ כַּעֲנָנִים יַעֲלֶה וְכַסּוּפָה מַרְכְּבוֹתָיו קַלּוּ מִנְּשָׁרִים סוּסָיו
יד אוֹי לָנוּ כִּי שֻׁדָּדְנוּ׃ כַּבְּסִי מֵרָעָה לִבֵּךְ יְרוּשָׁלִַם לְמַעַן תִּוָּשֵׁעִי עַד־מָתַי
טו תָּלִין בְּקִרְבֵּךְ מַחְשְׁבוֹת אוֹנֵךְ׃ כִּי קוֹל מַגִּיד מִדָּן וּמַשְׁמִיעַ אָוֶן מֵהַר
טז אֶפְרָיִם׃ הַזְכִּירוּ לַגּוֹיִם הִנֵּה הַשְׁמִיעוּ עַל־יְרוּשָׁלִַם נֹצְרִים בָּאִים מֵאֶרֶץ
יז הַמֶּרְחָק וַיִּתְּנוּ עַל־עָרֵי יְהוּדָה קוֹלָם׃ כְּשֹׁמְרֵי שָׂדַי הָיוּ עָלֶיהָ מִסָּבִיב
יח כִּי־אֹתִי מָרָתָה נְאֻם־יְהוָה׃ דַּרְכֵּךְ וּמַעֲלָלַיִךְ עָשׂוֹ אֵלֶּה לָךְ זֹאת רָעָתֵךְ
יט כִּי מָר כִּי נָגַע עַד־לִבֵּךְ׃ מֵעַי ׀ מֵעַי ׀ אחולה קִירוֹת לִבִּי אוֹחִילָה
הֹמֶה־לִּי לִבִּי לֹא אַחֲרִישׁ כִּי קוֹל שׁוֹפָר שמעתי נַפְשִׁי תְּרוּעַת מִלְחָמָה׃ שָׁמַעַתְּ
כ שֶׁבֶר עַל־שֶׁבֶר נִקְרָא כִּי שֻׁדְּדָה כָּל־הָאָרֶץ פִּתְאֹם שֻׁדְּדוּ אֹהָלַי רֶגַע
כא כב יְרִיעֹתָי׃ עַד־מָתַי אֶרְאֶה־נֵּס אֶשְׁמְעָה קוֹל שׁוֹפָר׃ כִּי ׀
אֱוִיל עַמִּי אוֹתִי לֹא יָדָעוּ בָּנִים סְכָלִים הֵמָּה וְלֹא נְבוֹנִים הֵמָּה
כג חֲכָמִים הֵמָּה לְהָרַע וּלְהֵיטִיב לֹא יָדָעוּ׃ רָאִיתִי אֶת־הָאָרֶץ וְהִנֵּה־תֹהוּ
כד וָבֹהוּ וְאֶל־הַשָּׁמַיִם וְאֵין אוֹרָם׃ רָאִיתִי הֶהָרִים וְהִנֵּה רֹעֲשִׁים וְכָל־
כה הַגְּבָעוֹת הִתְקַלְקָלוּ׃ רָאִיתִי וְהִנֵּה אֵין הָאָדָם וְכָל־עוֹף הַשָּׁמַיִם נָדָדוּ׃
כו רָאִיתִי וְהִנֵּה הַכַּרְמֶל הַמִּדְבָּר וְכָל־עָרָיו נִתְּצוּ מִפְּנֵי יְהוָה מִפְּנֵי חֲרוֹן
כז אַפּוֹ׃ כִּי־כֹה אָמַר יְהוָה שְׁמָמָה תִהְיֶה כָּל־הָאָרֶץ וְכָלָה
כח לֹא אֶעֱשֶׂה׃ עַל־זֹאת תֶּאֱבַל הָאָרֶץ וְקָדְרוּ הַשָּׁמַיִם מִמָּעַל עַל כִּי־
כט דִּבַּרְתִּי זַמֹּתִי וְלֹא נִחַמְתִּי וְלֹא־אָשׁוּב מִמֶּנָּה׃ מִקּוֹל פָּרָשׁ וְרֹמֵה קֶשֶׁת

archer. They have gone to the thick forests; they climbed the cliffs. The entire
30 city is abandoned; no man dwells there. And you, despoiled one, what will
you do? Will you wear scarlet and bedeck yourself with golden ornaments?
Will you line your eyes with kohl? You will beautify yourself in vain. Your
31 lovers have rejected you. They seek your death. For I hear a voice like that of
a sick person, anguish like a woman delivering her firstborn. It is the sound
of Zion's daughter, gasping and spreading her palms: "Woe is me; my soul is
5 1 exhausted by these murderers." Roam the streets of
Jerusalem; look about and determine; search in her squares. If you find a man,
if there is anyone who upholds justice, who seeks faithfulness, then I will
2 forgive her. Even those who exclaim, "As the LORD lives," do so in order to
3 swear falsely. LORD, Your eyes seek faithfulness.[18] You struck them, but they
were not pained. You consumed them, yet they failed to take instruction. They
4 stiffened their faces harder than rock. They refused to return. I said to myself,
"These are but lowly folk. They are foolish. They know not the way of the LORD,
5 the Law of their God. Instead, let me go to great men and speak to them.
They surely know the way of the LORD, the Law of their God." But they too
6 broke the yoke and ripped apart what bound them. Therefore the lion from
the forest has mauled them; the wolf of the plains will despoil them; the
leopard lies in wait over their cities. Whoever escapes will be torn apart.
For their sins have been numerous, and mighty have been their wayward
7 acts. How then can I forgive you? Your children have abandoned Me. They
swear by non-gods. I fed them well, but they turned adulterous. They trooped
8 together to the harlot's house. Like well-fed horses they awaken; each has
9 reveled with his neighbor's wife. Should I not hold such people to account?
declares the LORD. From a nation such as this should I not exact retribu-
10 tion? Climb the rows of her vineyards and do damage, but do not
totally destroy them. Remove their spreading vines, for they are no longer
11 the LORD's. For the House of Israel and the House of Yehuda have utterly
12 betrayed Me, declares the LORD. They have denied the LORD and said, "He
13 is nothing. No harm will befall us; we shall see neither sword nor famine. The
prophets shall be but wind; the Word is not in them. May what they prophesy
14 be done to them." Therefore, so says the LORD, God of
Hosts: Because you have said such words, I will convert My words into fire
in your mouth. This people will be as kindling wood, and it will consume
15 them. I will bring upon them, the House of Israel, a nation from afar, declares
the LORD, a powerful nation, an ancient nation, a nation whose language you
16 will not know[19] and whose speech you will not understand. His quiver is like
17 an open grave. They are all warriors. He will devour your harvest and your
bread; they will devour your sons and daughters. He will devour your flocks
and your herds, your vine and your fig tree. He will devastate your fortress
18 cities – those in which you place such confidence – by the sword. Yet even in
19 those days, declares the LORD, I will not make a full end of you. And if you

18 | Meaning honest people who will accept rebuke.

19 | Cf. Deuteronomy 28:49.

בְּרַחַת כָּל־הָעִיר בָּאוּ בֶּעָבִים וּבַכֵּפִים עָלוּ כָּל־הָעִיר עֲזוּבָה וְאֵין־יוֹשֵׁב
ל בָּהֵן אִישׁ: ואתי שָׁדוּד מַה־תַּעֲשִׂי כִּי־תִלְבְּשִׁי שָׁנִי כִּי־תַעְדִּי עֲדִי־זָהָב וְאַתְּ
כִּי־תִקְרְעִי בַפּוּךְ עֵינַיִךְ לַשָּׁוְא תִּתְיַפִּי מָאֲסוּ־בָךְ עֹגְבִים נַפְשֵׁךְ יְבַקֵּשׁוּ:
לא כִּי קוֹל כְּחוֹלָה שָׁמַעְתִּי צָרָה כְּמַבְכִּירָה קוֹל בַּת־צִיּוֹן תִּתְיַפֵּחַ תְּפָרֵשׂ
ה א כַּפֶּיהָ אוֹי־נָא לִי כִּי־עָיְפָה נַפְשִׁי לְהֹרְגִים: שׁוֹטְטוּ בְּחוּצוֹת ג
יְרוּשָׁלַ͏ִם וּרְאוּ־נָא וּדְעוּ וּבַקְשׁוּ בִרְחוֹבוֹתֶיהָ אִם־תִּמְצְאוּ אִישׁ אִם־יֵשׁ
ב עֹשֶׂה מִשְׁפָּט מְבַקֵּשׁ אֱמוּנָה וְאֶסְלַח לָהּ: וְאִם חַי־יְהוָה יֹאמֵרוּ לָכֵן
ג לַשֶּׁקֶר יִשָּׁבֵעוּ: יְהוָה עֵינֶיךָ הֲלוֹא לֶאֱמוּנָה הִכִּיתָה אֹתָם וְלֹא־חָלוּ
ד כִּלִּיתָם מֵאֲנוּ קַחַת מוּסָר חִזְּקוּ פְנֵיהֶם מִסֶּלַע מֵאֲנוּ לָשׁוּב: וַאֲנִי
אָמַרְתִּי אַךְ־דַּלִּים הֵם נוֹאֲלוּ כִּי לֹא יָדְעוּ דֶּרֶךְ יְהוָה מִשְׁפַּט אֱלֹהֵיהֶם:
ה אֵלֲכָה־לִּי אֶל־הַגְּדֹלִים וַאֲדַבְּרָה אוֹתָם כִּי הֵמָּה יָדְעוּ דֶּרֶךְ יְהוָה
ו מִשְׁפַּט אֱלֹהֵיהֶם אַךְ הֵמָּה יַחְדָּו שָׁבְרוּ עֹל נִתְּקוּ מוֹסֵרוֹת: עַל־כֵּן
הִכָּם אַרְיֵה מִיַּעַר זְאֵב עֲרָבוֹת יְשָׁדְדֵם נָמֵר שֹׁקֵד עַל־עָרֵיהֶם כָּל־
ז הַיּוֹצֵא מֵהֵנָּה יִטָּרֵף כִּי רַבּוּ פִּשְׁעֵיהֶם עָצְמוּ מְשֻׁבוֹתֵיהֶם: אֵי לָזֹאת
אסלוח־לָךְ בָּנַיִךְ עֲזָבוּנִי וַיִּשָּׁבְעוּ בְּלֹא אֱלֹהִים וָאַשְׂבִּעַ אוֹתָם וַיִּנְאָפוּ אֶסְלַח־
ח וּבֵית זוֹנָה יִתְגּוֹדָדוּ: סוּסִים מוזנים מַשְׁכִּים הָיוּ אִישׁ אֶל־אֵשֶׁת רֵעֵהוּ מְיֻזָּנִים
ט יִצְהָלוּ: הַעַל־אֵלֶּה לוֹא־אֶפְקֹד נְאֻם־יְהוָה וְאִם בְּגוֹי אֲשֶׁר־כָּזֶה לֹא
י תִתְנַקֵּם נַפְשִׁי: עֲלוּ בְשָׁרוֹתֶיהָ וְשַׁחֵתוּ וְכָלָה אַל־תַּעֲשׂוּ
יא הָסִירוּ נְטִישׁוֹתֶיהָ כִּי לוֹא לַיהוָה הֵמָּה: כִּי בָּגוֹד בָּגְדוּ בִּי בֵּית יִשְׂרָאֵל
יב וּבֵית יְהוּדָה נְאֻם־יְהוָה: כִּחֲשׁוּ בַּיהוָה וַיֹּאמְרוּ לוֹא־הוּא וְלֹא־תָבוֹא
יג עָלֵינוּ רָעָה וְחֶרֶב וְרָעָב לוֹא נִרְאֶה: וְהַנְּבִיאִים יִהְיוּ לְרוּחַ וְהַדִּבֵּר אֵין
יד בָּהֶם כֹּה יֵעָשֶׂה לָהֶם: לָכֵן כֹּה־אָמַר יְהוָה אֱלֹהֵי צְבָאוֹת
יַעַן דַּבֶּרְכֶם אֶת־הַדָּבָר הַזֶּה הִנְנִי נֹתֵן דְּבָרַי בְּפִיךָ לְאֵשׁ וְהָעָם הַזֶּה
טו עֵצִים וַאֲכָלָתַם: הִנְנִי מֵבִיא עֲלֵיכֶם גּוֹי מִמֶּרְחָק בֵּית יִשְׂרָאֵל נְאֻם־
יְהוָה גּוֹי ׀ אֵיתָן הוּא גּוֹי מֵעוֹלָם הוּא גּוֹי לֹא־תֵדַע לְשֹׁנוֹ וְלֹא תִשְׁמַע
טז יז מַה־יְדַבֵּר: אַשְׁפָּתוֹ כְּקֶבֶר פָּתוּחַ כֻּלָּם גִּבּוֹרִים: וְאָכַל קְצִירְךָ וְלַחְמֶךָ
יֹאכְלוּ בָּנֶיךָ וּבְנוֹתֶיךָ יֹאכַל צֹאנְךָ וּבְקָרֶךָ יֹאכַל גַּפְנְךָ וּתְאֵנָתֶךָ יְרֹשֵׁשׁ
יח עָרֵי מִבְצָרֶיךָ אֲשֶׁר אַתָּה בּוֹטֵחַ בָּהֵנָּה בֶּחָרֶב: וְגַם בַּיָּמִים הָהֵמָּה
יט נְאֻם־יְהוָה לֹא־אֶעֱשֶׂה אִתְּכֶם כָּלָה: וְהָיָה כִּי תֹאמְרוּ תַּחַת מֶה עָשָׂה

will ask, "For what reason did the LORD our God do all this to us?" Then you
shall say to them that just as you have abandoned Me and worshipped alien
gods in your land, so shall you worship strangers in a land which is not
20 yours. Proclaim this in the House of Yaakov, and let it be heard in
21 Yehuda: Listen well to this, stupid people without heart, who have eyes but
22 do not see and ears but do not hear. Me you will not fear? declares the LORD.
Will you not tremble before Me, who set the sand as a boundary to the sea,
an eternal boundary that it cannot pass? The waters may rage, but they are
23 impotent; the waves may roar, but they cannot pass over it. This people had
24 a wayward and rebellious heart; they turned aside and went their way, and
they did not say in their hearts, "Let us revere the LORD our God who has
given us rain, early and late, in the proper time, who protects for us the weeks
25 reserved for harvest." Your sins have ended these things; your transgressions
26 have withheld the good from you. For among My people wicked men are to
be found. They watch for the trap to come down; they set up an ambush in
27 order to catch men. Like a cage full of fowl, so are their homes full of deceit.
28 That is how they have grown great and become wealthy. They have become
fat and sleek. They have surpassed the deeds of the wicked. They have not
judged justly, even on behalf of the orphan, and yet they prosper. They did
29 not judge the case of the poor. Should I not hold such people to account?
declares the LORD. Against a nation such as this should I not avenge
30 Myself? An astonishing and ugly thing has happened in the land.
31 The prophets prophesy falsehood; the priests govern at their direction. My
6 1 people love it that way. What will you do when it all ends? Take refuge,
Benjaminites, out of the midst of Jerusalem; in Tekoa, blow the ram's horn;[20]
Above Beit HaKerem, raise a signal, for evil looms from the north, a great
2 disaster. I once likened you to a beautiful and delicate woman, daughter Zion.
3 But now shepherds and their flocks approach her. Against her they pitch their
4 tents roundabout. They graze, each in his place. "Prepare for war against her.
Rise and let us go up at noon." But woe to us – the day is departing. The
5 shadows of evening are growing long. "Rise and let us go up at night. Let us
6 destroy her palaces." For this is what the LORD of Hosts said: Cut
down trees, cast up a siege ramp against Jerusalem, for she is a city called to
7 account, ridden with oppression. As a well flows with its water, so does her
wickedness flow. Violence and plunder are heard within her. Before Me
8 constantly are sickness and suffering. Correct yourself, Jerusalem, lest My
favor be withdrawn from you, lest I render you desolate, a land never
9 inhabited. This is what the LORD of Hosts said: "Let the remnant of
Israel be gleaned like grapes off the vine. Bring back your hand again like a
10 grape picker over his baskets."[21] Whom can I address? Whom can I forewarn
and expect that they will take heed? Their ears are closed; they cannot listen.
The word of the LORD has become a mockery to them. They want none of it.
11 I am filled with the LORD's wrath and am too weak to contain it. Pour it upon

20 | The city name Tekoa resonates with the Hebrew *tiku* (blow).

21 | The grape harvesters return to the vine to pluck every last grape.

יְהוָה אֱלֹהֵינוּ לָנוּ אֶת־כָּל־אֵלֶּה וְאָמַרְתָּ אֲלֵיהֶם כַּאֲשֶׁר עֲזַבְתֶּם
אוֹתִי וַתַּעַבְדוּ אֱלֹהֵי נֵכָר בְּאַרְצְכֶם כֵּן תַּעַבְדוּ זָרִים בְּאֶרֶץ לֹא
כ לָכֶם׃ הַגִּידוּ זֹאת בְּבֵית יַעֲקֹב וְהַשְׁמִיעוּהָ בִיהוּדָה
כא לֵאמֹר׃ שִׁמְעוּ־נָא זֹאת עַם סָכָל וְאֵין לֵב עֵינַיִם לָהֶם וְלֹא יִרְאוּ אָזְנַיִם
כב לָהֶם וְלֹא יִשְׁמָעוּ׃ הַאוֹתִי לֹא־תִירָאוּ נְאֻם־יְהוָה אִם מִפָּנַי לֹא תָחִילוּ
אֲשֶׁר־שַׂמְתִּי חוֹל גְּבוּל לַיָּם חָק־עוֹלָם וְלֹא יַעַבְרֶנְהוּ וַיִּתְגָּעֲשׁוּ וְלֹא
כג יוּכָלוּ וְהָמוּ גַלָּיו וְלֹא יַעַבְרֻנְהוּ׃ וְלָעָם הַזֶּה הָיָה לֵב סוֹרֵר וּמוֹרֶה סָרוּ
כד וַיֵּלֵכוּ׃ וְלוֹא־אָמְרוּ בִלְבָבָם נִירָא נָא אֶת־יְהוָה אֱלֹהֵינוּ הַנֹּתֵן גֶּשֶׁם
כה וירה וּמַלְקוֹשׁ בְּעִתּוֹ שְׁבֻעֹת חֻקּוֹת קָצִיר יִשְׁמָר־לָנוּ׃ עֲוֺנוֹתֵיכֶם הִטּוּ־ יוֹרֶה
כו אֵלֶּה וְחַטֹּאותֵיכֶם מָנְעוּ הַטּוֹב מִכֶּם׃ כִּי־נִמְצְאוּ בְעַמִּי רְשָׁעִים יָשׁוּר
כז כְּשַׁךְ יְקוּשִׁים הִצִּיבוּ מַשְׁחִית אֲנָשִׁים יִלְכֹּדוּ׃ כִּכְלוּב מָלֵא עוֹף כֵּן
כח בָּתֵּיהֶם מְלֵאִים מִרְמָה עַל־כֵּן גָּדְלוּ וַיַּעֲשִׁירוּ׃ שָׁמְנוּ עָשְׁתוּ גַּם עָבְרוּ
דִבְרֵי־רָע דִּין לֹא־דָנוּ דִּין יָתוֹם וְיַצְלִיחוּ וּמִשְׁפַּט אֶבְיוֹנִים לֹא שָׁפָטוּ׃
כט הַעַל־אֵלֶּה לֹא־אֶפְקֹד נְאֻם־יְהוָה אִם בְּגוֹי אֲשֶׁר־כָּזֶה לֹא תִתְנַקֵּם
ל לא נַפְשִׁי׃ שַׁמָּה וְשַׁעֲרוּרָה נִהְיְתָה בָּאָרֶץ׃ הַנְּבִאִים
נִבְּאוּ בַשֶּׁקֶר וְהַכֹּהֲנִים יִרְדּוּ עַל־יְדֵיהֶם וְעַמִּי אָהֲבוּ כֵן וּמַה־תַּעֲשׂוּ
ו א לְאַחֲרִיתָהּ׃ הָעִזוּ ׀ בְּנֵי בִנְיָמִן מִקֶּרֶב יְרוּשָׁלִַם וּבִתְקוֹעַ תִּקְעוּ שׁוֹפָר
וְעַל־בֵּית הַכֶּרֶם שְׂאוּ מַשְׂאֵת כִּי רָעָה נִשְׁקְפָה מִצָּפוֹן וְשֶׁבֶר גָּדוֹל׃
ב ג הַנָּוָה וְהַמְּעֻנָּגָה דָּמִיתִי בַּת־צִיּוֹן׃ אֵלֶיהָ יָבֹאוּ רֹעִים וְעֶדְרֵיהֶם תָּקְעוּ ג
ד עָלֶיהָ אֹהָלִים סָבִיב רָעוּ אִישׁ אֶת־יָדוֹ׃ קַדְּשׁוּ עָלֶיהָ מִלְחָמָה קוּמוּ
ה וְנַעֲלֶה בַצָּהֳרָיִם אוֹי לָנוּ כִּי־פָנָה הַיּוֹם כִּי־יִנָּטוּ צִלְלֵי־עָרֶב׃ קוּמוּ
ו וְנַעֲלֶה בַלָּיְלָה וְנַשְׁחִיתָה אַרְמְנוֹתֶיהָ׃ כִּי כֹה אָמַר יְהוָה
צְבָאוֹת כִּרְתוּ עֵצָה וְשִׁפְכוּ עַל־יְרוּשָׁלִַם סֹלְלָה הִיא הָעִיר הָפְקַד כֻּלָּהּ
ז עֹשֶׁק בְּקִרְבָּהּ׃ כְּהָקִיר בור מֵימֶיהָ כֵּן הֵקֵרָה רָעָתָהּ חָמָס וָשֹׁד יִשָּׁמַע בַּיִר
ח בָּהּ עַל־פָּנַי תָּמִיד חֳלִי וּמַכָּה׃ הִוָּסְרִי יְרוּשָׁלִַם פֶּן־תֵּקַע נַפְשִׁי מִמֵּךְ
ט פֶּן־אֲשִׂימֵךְ שְׁמָמָה אֶרֶץ לוֹא נוֹשָׁבָה׃ כֹּה אָמַר יְהוָה
צְבָאוֹת עוֹלֵל יְעוֹלְלוּ כַגֶּפֶן שְׁאֵרִית יִשְׂרָאֵל הָשֵׁב יָדְךָ כְּבוֹצֵר עַל־
י סַלְסִלּוֹת׃ עַל־מִי אֲדַבְּרָה וְאָעִידָה וְיִשְׁמָעוּ הִנֵּה עֲרֵלָה אָזְנָם וְלֹא
יוּכְלוּ לְהַקְשִׁיב הִנֵּה דְבַר־יְהוָה הָיָה לָהֶם לְחֶרְפָּה לֹא יַחְפְּצוּ־בוֹ׃
יא וְאֵת חֲמַת יְהוָה ׀ מָלֵאתִי נִלְאֵיתִי הָכִיל שְׁפֹךְ עַל־עוֹלָל בַּחוּץ וְעַל

a young child in the outdoors, upon a group of young men joined together.
Husband and wife will be captured, as will be the old man and the one full of
12 days. Their houses will be passed on to others, fields and wives together, for
I will stretch out My hand against the inhabitants of the land, declares the
13 LORD. From their smallest to their greatest, all are greedy for gain. From
14 prophet to priest, all commit fraud. They heal My people's brokenness
15 dismissively, saying, "Peace, peace," when there is no peace. Were they
ashamed when they performed abominations? They showed no shame and
knew no embarrassment; therefore they will fall along with all who will fall.
16 When I hold them to account they will falter, said the LORD. This is
what the LORD said: Stand upon the roads and reflect. Inquire about the
ancient paths. What is the good way? Walk in it. You will find tranquility for
17 your souls. But you said, "We will not walk." I set up watchmen over you:
"Listen to the call of the ram's horn." But you said, "We will not listen."
18 19 Therefore, hear, O nations, and know, O community, what awaits them. Hear,
earth. I am about to bring evil upon this people, the fruit of their schemes.
20 For they did not listen to My words, and as for My Law, they rejected it. For
what purpose do I need frankincense brought from Sheba or choice cane
from some distant land? Your burnt offerings are not desirable, nor do I find
21 pleasure in your sacrifices. Therefore, this is what the LORD said: I
am about to place obstacles before this people so that fathers and sons will
22 stumble together. The neighbor and his friend will perish. This is
what the LORD said: A nation is about to come from the land of the north, a
23 powerful nation, awakened from the ends of the earth. They will grip both
bow and spear. They are cruel and will have no pity. Their sound will rage like
the sea. They will ride upon horses, each equipped to wage war against you,
24 daughter Zion. We heard word of him, and our hands weakened. Distress
25 gripped us: a writhing, as of a woman giving birth. Do not go out to the field.
Do not wander on the road, for the enemy has a sword, and terror is all around.
26 My dear nation, gird yourself in sackcloth and roll in the ash. Mourn as if for
an only child, a bitter lament, for the despoiler will come upon us suddenly.
27 I have made you a tower of strength for My people, a fortress.[22] You will know
28 how to assess their ways. They are all masters of rebellion, talebearers.
29 They are bronze and iron. They are all corrupt.[23] The bellows is charred; the
lead has dissolved in fire. The refiner has refined in vain. The dross has not
30 been removed. They are called rejected silver, for the LORD has rejected
7 1 2 them. The word that came to Yirmeyahu from the LORD: "Stand at
the gate of the House of the LORD and announce this message there. Say:
Hear the word of the LORD, all you people of Yehuda who enter these gates
3 in order to worship the LORD." This is what the LORD of Hosts, the
God of Israel, has said: Rectify your ways and your deeds, and I shall allow
4 you to dwell in this place. Do not rely upon words of false assurance that say:

22 | Cf. 1:18.

23 | As metal contains impurities.

סוֹד בַּחוּרִים יַחְדָּו כִּי־גַם־אִישׁ עִם־אִשָּׁה יִלָּכֵדוּ זָקֵן עִם־מְלֵא יָמִים׃
יב וְנָסַבּוּ בָתֵּיהֶם לַאֲחֵרִים שָׂדוֹת וְנָשִׁים יַחְדָּו כִּי־אַטֶּה אֶת־יָדִי עַל־יֹשְׁבֵי
יג הָאָרֶץ נְאֻם־יהוה׃ כִּי מִקְּטַנָּם וְעַד־גְּדוֹלָם כֻּלּוֹ בּוֹצֵעַ בָּצַע וּמִנָּבִיא
יד וְעַד־כֹּהֵן כֻּלּוֹ עֹשֶׂה שָּׁקֶר׃ וַיְרַפְּאוּ אֶת־שֶׁבֶר עַמִּי עַל־נְקַלָּה לֵאמֹר
טו שָׁלוֹם ׀ שָׁלוֹם וְאֵין שָׁלוֹם׃ הוֹבִשׁוּ כִּי־תוֹעֵבָה עָשׂוּ גַּם־בּוֹשׁ לֹא־
יֵבוֹשׁוּ גַּם־הַכְלִים לֹא יָדָעוּ לָכֵן יִפְּלוּ בַנֹּפְלִים בְּעֵת־פְּקַדְתִּים יִכָּשְׁלוּ
טז אָמַר יהוה׃ כֹּה אָמַר יהוה עִמְדוּ עַל־דְּרָכִים וּרְאוּ
וְשַׁאֲלוּ ׀ לִנְתִבוֹת עוֹלָם אֵי־זֶה דֶרֶךְ הַטּוֹב וּלְכוּ־בָהּ וּמִצְאוּ מַרְגּוֹעַ
יז לְנַפְשְׁכֶם וַיֹּאמְרוּ לֹא נֵלֵךְ׃ וַהֲקִמֹתִי עֲלֵיכֶם צֹפִים הַקְשִׁיבוּ לְקוֹל
יח שׁוֹפָר וַיֹּאמְרוּ לֹא נַקְשִׁיב׃ לָכֵן שִׁמְעוּ הַגּוֹיִם וּדְעִי עֵדָה אֶת־אֲשֶׁר־
יט בָּם׃ שִׁמְעִי הָאָרֶץ הִנֵּה אָנֹכִי מֵבִיא רָעָה אֶל־הָעָם הַזֶּה פְּרִי מַחְשְׁבוֹתָם
כ כִּי עַל־דְּבָרַי לֹא הִקְשִׁיבוּ וְתוֹרָתִי וַיִּמְאֲסוּ־בָהּ׃ לָמָּה־זֶּה לִי לְבוֹנָה
מִשְּׁבָא תָבוֹא וְקָנֶה הַטּוֹב מֵאֶרֶץ מֶרְחָק עֹלוֹתֵיכֶם לֹא לְרָצוֹן וְזִבְחֵיכֶם
כא לֹא־עָרְבוּ לִי׃ לָכֵן כֹּה אָמַר יהוה הִנְנִי נֹתֵן
אֶל־הָעָם הַזֶּה מִכְשֹׁלִים וְכָשְׁלוּ בָם אָבוֹת וּבָנִים יַחְדָּו שָׁכֵן וְרֵעוֹ
כב יאבדו׃ כֹּה אָמַר יהוה הִנֵּה עַם בָּא מֵאֶרֶץ צָפוֹן וְגוֹי גָּדוֹל וְאָבָדוּ
כג יֵעוֹר מִיַּרְכְּתֵי־אָרֶץ׃ קֶשֶׁת וְכִידוֹן יַחֲזִיקוּ אַכְזָרִי הוּא וְלֹא יְרַחֵמוּ קוֹלָם
כַּיָּם יֶהֱמֶה וְעַל־סוּסִים יִרְכָּבוּ עָרוּךְ כְּאִישׁ לַמִּלְחָמָה עָלַיִךְ בַּת־
כד כה צִיּוֹן׃ שָׁמַעְנוּ אֶת־שָׁמְעוֹ רָפוּ יָדֵינוּ צָרָה הֶחֱזִקַתְנוּ חִיל כַּיּוֹלֵדָה׃ אַל־
כו תצאי השדה ובדרך אל־תלכי כִּי חֶרֶב לְאֹיֵב מָגוֹר מִסָּבִיב׃ בַּת־עַמִּי תֵּצְאוּ | תֵּלֵכוּ
חִגְרִי־שָׂק וְהִתְפַּלְּשִׁי בָאֵפֶר אֵבֶל יָחִיד עֲשִׂי־לָךְ מִסְפַּד תַּמְרוּרִים כִּי
כז פִּתְאֹם יָבֹא הַשֹּׁדֵד עָלֵינוּ׃ בָּחוֹן נְתַתִּיךָ בְעַמִּי מִבְצָר וְתֵדַע וּבָחַנְתָּ
כח אֶת־דַּרְכָּם׃ כֻּלָּם סָרֵי סוֹרְרִים הֹלְכֵי רָכִיל נְחֹשֶׁת וּבַרְזֶל כֻּלָּם מַשְׁחִיתִים
כט הֵמָּה׃ נָחַר מַפֻּחַ מאשתם עֹפָרֶת לַשָּׁוְא צָרַף צָרוֹף וְרָעִים לֹא נִתָּקוּ׃ מֵאֵשׁ תַּם
ל
ז א כֶּסֶף נִמְאָס קָרְאוּ לָהֶם כִּי־מָאַס יהוה בָּהֶם׃ הַדָּבָר
ב אֲשֶׁר הָיָה אֶל־יִרְמְיָהוּ מֵאֵת יהוה לֵאמֹר׃ עֲמֹד בְּשַׁעַר בֵּית יהוה
וְקָרָאתָ שָּׁם אֶת־הַדָּבָר הַזֶּה וְאָמַרְתָּ שִׁמְעוּ דְבַר־יהוה כָּל־יְהוּדָה
ג הַבָּאִים בַּשְּׁעָרִים הָאֵלֶּה לְהִשְׁתַּחֲוֺת לַיהוה׃ כֹּה־אָמַר
יהוה צְבָאוֹת אֱלֹהֵי יִשְׂרָאֵל הֵיטִיבוּ דַרְכֵיכֶם וּמַעַלְלֵיכֶם וַאֲשַׁכְּנָה
ד אֶתְכֶם בַּמָּקוֹם הַזֶּה׃ אַל־תִּבְטְחוּ לָכֶם אֶל־דִּבְרֵי הַשֶּׁקֶר לֵאמֹר הֵיכַל

This is the Temple of the Lord, the Temple of the Lord, the Temple of the
5 Lord.[24] For, if you indeed rectify your ways and your deeds, if you indeed
6 perform justice between a man and his fellow, if you do not oppress the
stranger, the orphan, and the widow, if you do not spill innocent blood in this
7 place, and if you do not pursue alien gods to your detriment, then I shall allow
you to dwell in this place, in the land that I gave to your forefathers for ever
8 and ever. But here you are, relying upon words of false assurance that are
9 useless. Will you steal, murder, fornicate, swear falsely, offer sacrifices to Baal,
10 and pursue other gods that you have not known, then come and stand before
Me in this House, which is called by My name, and say, "We are saved," so
11 that you might continue to commit all of these abominations? Has this House
that is called by My name become a den of robbers in your eyes? I myself have
12 observed this, declares the Lord. But go now to My place which was in Shilo,
where I first made a dwelling for My name. Observe what I did to it on
13 account of the wickedness of My people Israel.[25] Now, because you have done
all these deeds, declares the Lord, after I spoke to you repeatedly and you
14 did not listen, after I called to you and you did not respond, I will do to this
House that is called by My name, and in which you place your trust, and to
15 the place that I gave to you and to your forefathers, just as I did to Shilo. I will
cast you from My presence just as I cast away all of your brothers, all the seed
16 of Efrayim.[26] As for you, do not pray for this people, do not raise a
cry or a plea on their behalf, and do not beseech Me, for I will not listen to
17 you. Do you not see what they are doing in the cities of Yehuda and in the
18 streets of Jerusalem? The children gather kindling wood, the fathers ignite
the fire, and the women knead the dough to bake cakes to the queen of the
19 heavens.[27] They pour libations to alien gods in order to anger Me. Is it Me
that they anger? demands the Lord. Is it not themselves whom they harm,
20 bringing shame upon themselves? Therefore, so said the Lord
God: My wrath and My fury are about to be poured out upon this place, upon
man and beast, upon the trees of the field and the fruit of the earth. It shall
21 burn and not be extinguished. This is what the Lord of Hosts, the
God of Israel, said: Heap your burnt offerings upon your other sacrifices and
22 eat the meat. For when I brought your forefathers out of Egypt, I did not
speak to them, Nor did I command them about matters of burnt offerings
23 and sacrifices. Rather, this is what I commanded them: Heed my voice so
that I will be your God and you will be My people. Walk in all the ways as I
24 will command you so that it will be good for you. But they did not listen, nor
even bend an ear. They followed their own counsel, their stubborn, wicked
25 hearts. They went backward, not forward. From the day your forefathers left

24 | Meaning that God would never allow His Temple to be destroyed.

25 | See 1 Samuel, chapter 4.

26 | That is, the exiled Ten Tribes.

27 | A foreign deity (see also ch. 44).

ה יְהוָה הֵיכַל יְהוָה הֵיכַל יְהוָה הֵמָּה: כִּי אִם־הֵיטֵיב תֵּיטִיבוּ אֶת־דַּרְכֵיכֶם
ו וְאֶת־מַעַלְלֵיכֶם אִם־עָשׂוֹ תַעֲשׂוּ מִשְׁפָּט בֵּין אִישׁ וּבֵין רֵעֵהוּ: גֵּר יָתוֹם
וְאַלְמָנָה לֹא תַעֲשֹׁקוּ וְדָם נָקִי אַל־תִּשְׁפְּכוּ בַּמָּקוֹם הַזֶּה וְאַחֲרֵי אֱלֹהִים
ז אֲחֵרִים לֹא תֵלְכוּ לְרַע לָכֶם: וְשִׁכַּנְתִּי אֶתְכֶם בַּמָּקוֹם הַזֶּה בָּאָרֶץ אֲשֶׁר
ח נָתַתִּי לַאֲבוֹתֵיכֶם לְמִן־עוֹלָם וְעַד־עוֹלָם: הִנֵּה אַתֶּם בֹּטְחִים לָכֶם
ט עַל־דִּבְרֵי הַשָּׁקֶר לְבִלְתִּי הוֹעִיל: הֲגָנֹב ׀ רָצֹחַ וְנָאֹף וְהִשָּׁבֵעַ לַשֶּׁקֶר
י וְקַטֵּר לַבָּעַל וְהָלֹךְ אַחֲרֵי אֱלֹהִים אֲחֵרִים אֲשֶׁר לֹא־יְדַעְתֶּם: וּבָאתֶם
וַעֲמַדְתֶּם לְפָנַי בַּבַּיִת הַזֶּה אֲשֶׁר נִקְרָא־שְׁמִי עָלָיו וַאֲמַרְתֶּם נִצַּלְנוּ לְמַעַן
יא עֲשׂוֹת אֵת כָּל־הַתּוֹעֵבֹת הָאֵלֶּה: הַמְעָרַת פָּרִצִים הָיָה הַבַּיִת הַזֶּה
אֲשֶׁר־נִקְרָא־שְׁמִי עָלָיו בְּעֵינֵיכֶם גַּם אָנֹכִי הִנֵּה רָאִיתִי נְאֻם־יְהוָה:
יב כִּי לְכוּ־נָא אֶל־מְקוֹמִי אֲשֶׁר בְּשִׁילוֹ אֲשֶׁר שִׁכַּנְתִּי שְׁמִי שָׁם בָּרִאשׁוֹנָה
יג וּרְאוּ אֵת אֲשֶׁר־עָשִׂיתִי לוֹ מִפְּנֵי רָעַת עַמִּי יִשְׂרָאֵל: וְעַתָּה יַעַן עֲשׂוֹתְכֶם
אֶת־כָּל־הַמַּעֲשִׂים הָאֵלֶּה נְאֻם־יְהוָה וָאֲדַבֵּר אֲלֵיכֶם הַשְׁכֵּם וְדַבֵּר
יד וְלֹא שְׁמַעְתֶּם וָאֶקְרָא אֶתְכֶם וְלֹא עֲנִיתֶם: וְעָשִׂיתִי לַבַּיִת ׀ אֲשֶׁר
נִקְרָא־שְׁמִי עָלָיו אֲשֶׁר אַתֶּם בֹּטְחִים בּוֹ וְלַמָּקוֹם אֲשֶׁר־נָתַתִּי לָכֶם
טו וְלַאֲבוֹתֵיכֶם כַּאֲשֶׁר עָשִׂיתִי לְשִׁלוֹ: וְהִשְׁלַכְתִּי אֶתְכֶם מֵעַל פָּנָי כַּאֲשֶׁר
טז הִשְׁלַכְתִּי אֶת־כָּל־אֲחֵיכֶם אֵת כָּל־זֶרַע אֶפְרָיִם: וְאַתָּה
אַל־תִּתְפַּלֵּל ׀ בְּעַד־הָעָם הַזֶּה וְאַל־תִּשָּׂא בַעֲדָם רִנָּה וּתְפִלָּה וְאַל־
יז תִּפְגַּע־בִּי כִּי־אֵינֶנִּי שֹׁמֵעַ אֹתָךְ: הַאֵינְךָ רֹאֶה מָה הֵמָּה עֹשִׂים בְּעָרֵי
יח יְהוּדָה וּבְחֻצוֹת יְרוּשָׁלִָם: הַבָּנִים מְלַקְּטִים עֵצִים וְהָאָבוֹת מְבַעֲרִים
אֶת־הָאֵשׁ וְהַנָּשִׁים לָשׁוֹת בָּצֵק לַעֲשׂוֹת כַּוָּנִים לִמְלֶכֶת הַשָּׁמַיִם
יט וְהַסֵּךְ נְסָכִים לֵאלֹהִים אֲחֵרִים לְמַעַן הַכְעִסֵנִי: הַאֹתִי הֵם מַכְעִסִים
כ נְאֻם־יְהוָה הֲלוֹא אֹתָם לְמַעַן בֹּשֶׁת פְּנֵיהֶם: לָכֵן כֹּה־
אָמַר ׀ אֲדֹנָי יֱהוִה הִנֵּה אַפִּי וַחֲמָתִי נִתֶּכֶת אֶל־הַמָּקוֹם הַזֶּה עַל־
הָאָדָם וְעַל־הַבְּהֵמָה וְעַל־עֵץ הַשָּׂדֶה וְעַל־פְּרִי הָאֲדָמָה וּבָעֲרָה וְלֹא
כא תִכְבֶּה: כֹּה אָמַר יְהוָה צְבָאוֹת אֱלֹהֵי יִשְׂרָאֵל עֹלוֹתֵיכֶם
כב סְפוּ עַל־זִבְחֵיכֶם וְאִכְלוּ בָשָׂר: כִּי לֹא־דִבַּרְתִּי אֶת־אֲבוֹתֵיכֶם וְלֹא
כג צִוִּיתִים בְּיוֹם הוֹצִיאִ אוֹתָם מֵאֶרֶץ מִצְרָיִם עַל־דִּבְרֵי עוֹלָה וָזָבַח: כִּי ה
אִם־אֶת־הַדָּבָר הַזֶּה צִוִּיתִי אוֹתָם לֵאמֹר שִׁמְעוּ בְקוֹלִי וְהָיִיתִי לָכֶם
לֵאלֹהִים וְאַתֶּם תִּהְיוּ־לִי לְעָם וַהֲלַכְתֶּם בְּכָל־הַדֶּרֶךְ אֲשֶׁר אֲצַוֶּה
כד אֶתְכֶם לְמַעַן יִיטַב לָכֶם: וְלֹא שָׁמְעוּ וְלֹא־הִטּוּ אֶת־אָזְנָם וַיֵּלְכוּ
כה בְּמֹעֵצוֹת בִּשְׁרִרוּת לִבָּם הָרָע וַיִּהְיוּ לְאָחוֹר וְלֹא לְפָנִים: לְמִן־הַיּוֹם

the land of Egypt until this very day, I sent to them all of My servants, the
26 prophets – early every day, and persistently. But they did not listen to Me, nor
even bend an ear. They stiffened their necks. They did worse than their fathers.
27 You will speak all these words to them, but they will not hear you. You will
28 call to them, but they will not answer you. You shall say to them: "This is the
nation that did not obey the voice of the LORD its God and that did not accept
29 correction. Gone is faithfulness, severed from their mouths." Shear
your hair and throw it away. Raise a lament upon the high places, for the LORD
30 has despised and has abandoned the generation that enraged Him. For the
children of Yehuda have done evil in My eyes, declares the LORD. They have
placed their vile objects in the House which is called by My name, thereby
31 defiling it. They have built the altars of Tofet, which are in the Valley of Ben
Hinom,[28] to burn their sons and daughters in fire, something that I did not
32 command and that never entered My mind. Therefore, days are fast
approaching, declares the LORD, when men will no longer speak of "Tofet"
and "Valley of Ben Hinom" but rather of "Valley of Slaughter." They will bury
33 in Tofet for lack of space elsewhere. The carcasses of this people will become
food for the birds of the heavens and the beasts of the earth, and none will
34 frighten them away. I will silence from the cities of Yehuda and the streets of
Jerusalem the sound of joy and the sound of happiness, the voice of the groom
8 1 and the voice of the bride, for the land shall come to ruin. At that time,
declares the LORD, they will remove the bones of the kings of Yehuda and
the bones of its princes, the bones of the priests, and the bones of the prophets,
2 and the bones of the inhabitants of Jerusalem from their graves. They will
spread them beneath the sun, the moon, and all the host of heaven that they
loved, and that they served, after which they followed, and which they sought,
and to which they bowed. They will neither be collected nor reburied but
3 shall remain as dung upon the face of the earth. Death will be preferable to
life for all the surviving remnant of this evil clan in all the other places to
4 which I have expelled them, declares the LORD of Hosts. Say to
them: This is what the LORD said: Did they ever fall and not rise again?
5 Whenever they returned, did He not return? Why, then, do these people,
Jerusalem, rebel in an everlasting rebellion? They hold fast to deceit. They
6 refuse to return. I listened carefully, and I understood. They do not speak
properly. No one regrets his misdeed and says, "What have I done?" They all
7 persist in their course like a horse plunging headlong into battle. Even the
stork in the sky knows its seasons; the turtledove, the swallow, and the crane
know their time of arrival. Yet my people do not know the judgment of the
8 LORD. How dare you assert, "We are wise; with us is the LORD's teaching. For
9 naught was the pen fashioned, and for naught is the scribes' rebuke"! The
wise men are put to shame, broken and ensnared. They have rejected the word
10 of the LORD. Theirs is an empty wisdom. Therefore, I will give their wives
over to others, their fields to dispossessors. From small to great, all are greedy

28 | The valley bounding Jerusalem to the west.

אֲשֶׁר יָצְאוּ אֲבוֹתֵיכֶם֙ מֵאֶרֶץ מִצְרַיִם עַד הַיּוֹם הַזֶּה וָאֶשְׁלַח אֲלֵיכֶם֙
אֶת־כָּל־עֲבָדַי הַנְּבִיאִים יוֹם הַשְׁכֵּם וְשָׁלֹחַ׃ וְלוֹא שָׁמְעוּ֙ אֵלַי וְלֹא הִטּוּ כו
אֶת־אָזְנָם וַיַּקְשׁוּ֙ אֶת־עָרְפָּם הֵרֵעוּ מֵאֲבוֹתָם׃ וְדִבַּרְתָּ אֲלֵיהֶם֙ אֶת־ כז
כָּל־הַדְּבָרִים הָאֵלֶּה וְלֹא יִשְׁמְעוּ אֵלֶיךָ וְקָרָאתָ אֲלֵיהֶם וְלֹא יַעֲנוּכָה׃
וְאָמַרְתָּ אֲלֵיהֶם זֶה הַגּוֹי֙ אֲשֶׁר לוֹא־שָׁמְעוּ בְּקוֹל֙ יְהוָה אֱלֹהָיו וְלֹא כח
לָקְחוּ מוּסָר אָבְדָה֙ הָאֱמוּנָה וְנִכְרְתָה מִפִּיהֶם׃ גָּזִּי כט
נִזְרֵךְ֙ וְהַשְׁלִיכִי וּשְׂאִי עַל־שְׁפָיִם קִינָה כִּי מָאַס יְהוָה וַיִּטֹּשׁ אֶת־דּוֹר
עֶבְרָתוֹ׃ כִּי־עָשׂוּ בְנֵי־יְהוּדָה הָרַע בְּעֵינַי נְאֻם־יְהוָה שָׂמוּ שִׁקּוּצֵיהֶם ל
בַּבַּיִת אֲשֶׁר־נִקְרָא־שְׁמִי עָלָיו לְטַמְּאוֹ׃ וּבָנוּ בָּמוֹת הַתֹּפֶת אֲשֶׁר֙ בְּגֵיא לא
בֶן־הִנֹּם לִשְׂרֹף אֶת־בְּנֵיהֶם וְאֶת־בְּנֹתֵיהֶם בָּאֵשׁ אֲשֶׁר֙ לֹא צִוִּיתִי וְלֹא
עָלְתָה עַל־לִבִּי׃ לָכֵן הִנֵּה יָמִים בָּאִים֙ נְאֻם־יְהוָה וְלֹא־ לב
יֵאָמֵר עוֹד הַתֹּפֶת֙ וְגֵיא בֶן־הִנֹּם כִּי אִם־גֵּיא הַהֲרֵגָה וְקָבְרוּ בְתֹפֶת
מֵאֵין מָקוֹם׃ וְהָיְתָה נִבְלַת הָעָם הַזֶּה֙ לְמַאֲכָל לְעוֹף הַשָּׁמַיִם וּלְבֶהֱמַת לג
הָאָרֶץ וְאֵין מַחֲרִיד׃ וְהִשְׁבַּתִּי ׀ מֵעָרֵי יְהוּדָה וּמֵחֻצוֹת֙ יְרוּשָׁלִַם קוֹל לד
שָׂשׂוֹן֙ וְקוֹל שִׂמְחָה קוֹל חָתָן וְקוֹל כַּלָּה כִּי לְחָרְבָּה תִּהְיֶה הָאָרֶץ׃
ח א בָּעֵת הַהִיא נְאֻם־יְהוָה ויוציאו אֶת־עַצְמוֹת מַלְכֵי־יְהוּדָה וְאֶת־ יוֹצִיאוּ
עַצְמוֹת שָׂרָיו וְאֶת־עַצְמוֹת הַכֹּהֲנִים וְאֵת ׀ עַצְמוֹת הַנְּבִיאִים וְאֵת
עַצְמוֹת יוֹשְׁבֵי־יְרוּשָׁלִָם מִקִּבְרֵיהֶם׃ וּשְׁטָחוּם לַשֶּׁמֶשׁ וְלַיָּרֵחַ וּלְכֹל ׀ ב
צְבָא הַשָּׁמַיִם אֲשֶׁר אֲהֵבוּם וַאֲשֶׁר עֲבָדוּם וַאֲשֶׁר הָלְכוּ אַחֲרֵיהֶם֙
וַאֲשֶׁר דְּרָשׁוּם וַאֲשֶׁר הִשְׁתַּחֲווּ לָהֶם לֹא יֵאָסְפוּ֙ וְלֹא יִקָּבֵרוּ לְדֹמֶן
עַל־פְּנֵי הָאֲדָמָה יִהְיוּ׃ וְנִבְחַר מָוֶת֙ מֵחַיִּים לְכֹל הַשְּׁאֵרִית֙ הַנִּשְׁאָרִים ג
מִן־הַמִּשְׁפָּחָה הָרָעָה הַזֹּאת בְּכָל־הַמְּקֹמוֹת הַנִּשְׁאָרִים֙ אֲשֶׁר הִדַּחְתִּים
שָׁם נְאֻם יְהוָה צְבָאוֹת׃ וְאָמַרְתָּ אֲלֵיהֶם כֹּה אָמַר יְהוָה ד
הֲיִפְּלוּ וְלֹא יָקוּמוּ אִם־יָשׁוּב וְלֹא יָשׁוּב׃ מַדּוּעַ שׁוֹבְבָה הָעָם הַזֶּה ה
יְרוּשָׁלִַם מְשֻׁבָה נִצַּחַת הֶחֱזִיקוּ֙ בַּתַּרְמִת מֵאֲנוּ לָשׁוּב׃ הִקְשַׁבְתִּי ו
וָאֶשְׁמָע לוֹא־כֵן יְדַבֵּרוּ֙ אֵין אִישׁ נִחָם֙ עַל־רָעָתוֹ לֵאמֹר מֶה עָשִׂיתִי
כֻּלֹּה שָׁב במרצותם כְּסוּס שׁוֹטֵף בַּמִּלְחָמָה׃ גַּם־חֲסִידָה בַשָּׁמַיִם ז בִּמְרוּצָתָם
יָדְעָה֙ מוֹעֲדֶיהָ וְתֹר וסוס וְעָגוּר שָׁמְרוּ אֶת־עֵת בֹּאָנָה וְעַמִּי לֹא יָדְעוּ וְסִיס
אֵת מִשְׁפַּט יְהוָה׃ אֵיכָה תֹאמְרוּ֙ חֲכָמִים אֲנַחְנוּ וְתוֹרַת יְהוָה אִתָּנוּ ח
אָכֵן֙ הִנֵּה לַשֶּׁקֶר עָשָׂה עֵט שֶׁקֶר סֹפְרִים׃ הֹבִישׁוּ חֲכָמִים חַתּוּ וַיִּלָּכֵדוּ ט
הִנֵּה בִדְבַר־יְהוָה֙ מָאָסוּ וְחָכְמַת־מֶה לָהֶם׃ לָכֵן֩ אֶתֵּן אֶת־נְשֵׁיהֶם י
לַאֲחֵרִים שְׂדוֹתֵיהֶם֙ לְיוֹרְשִׁים כִּי מִקָּטֹן֙ וְעַד־גָּדוֹל כֻּלֹּה בֹּצֵעַ בָּצַע

11 for gain. From prophet to priest, all commit fraud.[29] They wish to heal my
people's brokenness with ease, saying, "Peace, peace," when there is no peace.
12 Were they ashamed when they performed abominations? They showed no
shame and knew no embarrassment. Therefore, they will fall along with
all who will fall. When I hold them to account they will falter, said the
13 LORD. I will eradicate them thoroughly, declares the LORD. No
grapes on the vine. No figs on the fig tree. Even the leaf is withered. That
14 which I gave them will pass them by. For what purpose do we sit still?
Assemble, and let us approach the fortress cities and sit silently there. The
LORD our God has silenced us and given us poisonous water to drink, for we
15 have sinned against the LORD. We hope for peace, but no good awaits us; for
16 a time of healing, but instead – horror. From Dan[30] the snorting of his horses
can be heard. The entire land shudders from the neighing of his steeds. They
have come and have devoured the land and its bounty, the city and its
17 inhabitants. I am about to let loose upon you snakes, vipers against which
18 there is no charm, and they will bite you, declares the LORD. Though
19 I struggle to contain my torment, my heart is overwhelmed by woe. Behold
the sound of my people's cry from a distant land. "Is the LORD no longer in
Zion? Is her King no longer there?" "Why have they angered Me with their
20 idols, with their alien vanities?" The harvest is over. The summer is gone, but
21 we have not been saved. Because of the collapse of my precious people, I have
22 collapsed. I am despondent. Desolation has possessed me. Is there no balm
in Gilad?[31] Is there no healer there? Why then has there not arisen a cure for
23 my precious people? If only my head were water and my eye a
fountain of tears, then I would weep day and night for the slain of my precious
9 1 people. If only I were granted a wayfarer's lodging in the wilderness, I would
abandon my people and walk away from them, for they are all adulterers, a
2 band of traitors. They have drawn their tongue, their bow is falsehood. Not
for faithfulness have they become powerful in the land. From evil to evil they
3 have advanced, but Me they did not know, declares the LORD. Let each man
be on guard against his fellow, and let no one trust his own brother, for every
4 brother acts deceitfully, and every friend spreads slander. Each man defrauds
his fellow and speaks untruth; they have trained their tongues to speak lies.
5 They weary themselves with perversions. You dwell in the midst of deceit. In
6 deceit they have refused to know Me – declares the LORD. Therefore,
thus said the LORD of Hosts: I am about to smelt them and test them,[32]
7 for what else can I do on behalf of My precious people? Their tongue is a
sharpened arrow, speaking deceit. One speaks peaceably to another but
8 secretly plots an ambush. Should I not hold them to account for these
things? demands the LORD. For a nation such as this, should I not exact
9 retribution? Over the mountains I will raise a cry and a wail, and

29 | Cf. 6:12–15.

30 | In the north of Israel. The enemy would come from the north.

31 | Gilad was known for this substance (see, e.g., 46:11; Genesis 37:25).

32 | As metal is tested for quality after smelting.

יא מִנָּבִיא֙ וְעַד־כֹּהֵ֔ן כֻּלֹּ֖ה עֹ֥שֶׂה שָּֽׁקֶר׃ וַיְרַפּ֞וּ אֶת־שֶׁ֤בֶר בַּת־עַמִּי֙ עַל־
יב נְקַלָּ֔ה לֵאמֹ֖ר שָׁל֣וֹם ׀ שָׁל֑וֹם וְאֵ֖ין שָׁלֽוֹם׃ הֹבִ֕שׁוּ כִּ֥י תוֹעֵבָ֖ה עָשׂ֑וּ גַּם־בּ֣וֹשׁ
לֹֽא־יֵבֹ֗שׁוּ וְהִכָּלֵם֙ לֹ֣א יָדָ֔עוּ לָכֵ֞ן יִפְּל֣וּ בַנֹּפְלִ֗ים בְּעֵ֧ת פְּקֻדָּתָ֛ם יִכָּשְׁל֖וּ
יג אָמַ֥ר יהוה׃ אָסֹ֥ף אֲסִיפֵ֖ם נְאֻם־יהוה אֵין֩ עֲנָבִ֨ים בַּגֶּ֜פֶן וְאֵ֧ין
יד תְּאֵנִ֣ים בַּתְּאֵנָ֗ה וְהֶֽעָלֶה֙ נָבֵ֔ל וָאֶתֵּ֥ן לָהֶ֖ם יַעַבְרֽוּם׃ עַל־מָה֙ אֲנַ֣חְנוּ
יֹֽשְׁבִ֔ים הֵאָֽסְפ֗וּ וְנָב֛וֹא אֶל־עָרֵ֥י הַמִּבְצָ֖ר וְנִדְּמָה־שָּׁ֑ם כִּי֩ יהוה אֱלֹהֵ֤ינוּ
טו הֲדִמָּ֙נוּ֙ וַיַּשְׁקֵ֣נוּ מֵי־רֹ֔אשׁ כִּ֥י חָטָ֖אנוּ לַיהוָֽה׃ קַוֵּ֥ה לְשָׁל֖וֹם וְאֵ֣ין ט֑וֹב
טז לְעֵ֥ת מַרְפֵּ֖ה וְהִנֵּ֥ה בְעָתָֽה׃ מִדָּ֣ן נִשְׁמַע֮ נַחְרַ֣ת סוּסָיו֒ מִקּוֹל֙ מִצְהֲל֣וֹת
אַבִּירָ֔יו רָעֲשָׁ֖ה כָּל־הָאָ֑רֶץ וַיָּב֗וֹאוּ וַיֹּֽאכְלוּ֙ אֶ֣רֶץ וּמְלוֹאָ֔הּ עִ֖יר וְיֹ֥שְׁבֵי
יז בָֽהּ׃ כִּי֩ הִנְנִ֨י מְשַׁלֵּ֜חַ בָּכֶ֗ם נְחָשִׁים֙ צִפְעֹנִ֔ים אֲשֶׁ֥ר אֵין־לָהֶ֖ם לָ֑חַשׁ וְנִשְּׁכ֥וּ
יח אֶתְכֶ֖ם נְאֻם־יהוה׃ מַבְלִ֥יגִיתִ֖י עֲלֵ֣י יָג֑וֹן עָלַ֖י לִבִּ֥י דַוָּֽי׃
יט הִנֵּה־ק֞וֹל שַֽׁוְעַ֣ת בַּת־עַמִּ֗י מֵאֶ֙רֶץ֙ מַרְחַקִּ֔ים הַיהוָה֙ אֵ֣ין בְּצִיּ֔וֹן אִם־
כ מַלְכָּ֖הּ אֵ֣ין בָּ֑הּ מַדּ֗וּעַ הִכְעִס֛וּנִי בִּפְסִלֵיהֶ֖ם בְּהַבְלֵ֥י נֵכָֽר׃ עָבַ֥ר קָצִ֖יר
כא כָּ֣לָה קָ֑יִץ וַאֲנַ֖חְנוּ ל֥וֹא נוֹשָֽׁעְנוּ׃ עַל־שֶׁ֥בֶר בַּת־עַמִּ֖י הָשְׁבָּ֑רְתִּי קָדַ֕רְתִּי
כב שַׁמָּ֖ה הֶחֱזִקָֽתְנִי׃ הַצֳרִי֙ אֵ֣ין בְּגִלְעָ֔ד אִם־רֹפֵ֖א אֵ֣ין שָׁ֑ם כִּ֗י מַדּ֙וּעַ֙ לֹ֣א
כג עָֽלְתָ֔ה אֲרֻכַ֖ת בַּת־עַמִּֽי׃ מִֽי־יִתֵּ֤ן רֹאשִׁי֙ מַ֔יִם וְעֵינִ֖י מְק֣וֹר
ט א דִּמְעָ֑ה וְאֶבְכֶּה֙ יוֹמָ֣ם וָלַ֔יְלָה אֵ֖ת חַֽלְלֵ֥י בַת־עַמִּֽי׃ מִֽי־יִתְּנֵ֣נִי בַמִּדְבָּ֗ר
מְלוֹן֮ אֹֽרְחִים֒ וְאֶֽעֶזְבָה֙ אֶת־עַמִּ֔י וְאֵלְכָ֖ה מֵאִתָּ֑ם כִּ֤י כֻלָּם֙ מְנָ֣אֲפִ֔ים עֲצֶ֖רֶת
ב בֹּגְדִֽים׃ וַיַּדְרְכ֤וּ אֶת־לְשׁוֹנָם֙ קַשְׁתָּ֣ם שֶׁ֔קֶר וְלֹ֥א לֶאֱמוּנָ֖ה גָּבְר֣וּ בָאָ֑רֶץ
ג כִּי֩ מֵרָעָ֨ה אֶל־רָעָ֧ה ׀ יָצָ֛אוּ וְאֹתִ֥י לֹא־יָדָ֖עוּ נְאֻם־יהוה׃ אִ֤ישׁ מֵרֵעֵ֙הוּ֙
הִשָּׁמֵ֔רוּ וְעַל־כָּל־אָ֖ח אַל־תִּבְטָ֑חוּ כִּ֤י כָל־אָח֙ עָק֣וֹב יַעְקֹ֔ב וְכָל־רֵ֖עַ
ד רָכִ֥יל יַהֲלֹֽךְ׃ וְאִ֤ישׁ בְּרֵעֵ֙הוּ֙ יְהָתֵ֔לּוּ וֶאֱמֶ֖ת לֹ֣א יְדַבֵּ֑רוּ לִמְּד֧וּ לְשׁוֹנָ֛ם
ה דַּבֶּר־שֶׁ֖קֶר הַעֲוֵ֥ה נִלְאֽוּ׃ שִׁבְתְּךָ֖ בְּת֣וֹךְ מִרְמָ֑ה בְּמִרְמָ֛ה מֵאֲנ֥וּ דַֽעַת־
ו אוֹתִ֖י נְאֻם־יהוה׃ לָכֵ֗ן כֹּ֤ה אָמַר֙ יהוה צְבָא֔וֹת הִנְנִ֥י
ז צוֹרְפָ֖ם וּבְחַנְתִּ֑ים כִּֽי־אֵ֣יךְ אֶעֱשֶׂ֔ה מִפְּנֵ֖י בַּת־עַמִּֽי׃ חֵ֥ץ שׁוחט לְשׁוֹנָ֖ם שָׁח֑וּט
ח מִרְמָ֣ה דִבֵּ֑ר בְּפִ֗יו שָׁל֤וֹם אֶת־רֵעֵ֙הוּ֙ יְדַבֵּ֔ר וּבְקִרְבּ֖וֹ יָשִׂ֥ים אָרְבּֽוֹ׃ הַעַל־
אֵ֥לֶּה לֹֽא־אֶפְקָד־בָּ֖ם נְאֻם־יהוה אִ֚ם בְּג֣וֹי אֲשֶׁר־כָּזֶ֔ה לֹ֥א תִתְנַקֵּ֖ם
ט נַפְשִֽׁי׃ עַל־הֶהָרִ֞ים אֶשָּׂ֤א בְכִי֙ וָנֶ֔הִי וְעַל־נְא֤וֹת מִדְבָּר֙

over pastures in the wilderness I will lament. For they have been laid waste
with not even a passerby. The sound of cattle is no longer to be heard. From
10 the bird in the sky to the beast, all have wandered, all are gone. I will reduce
Jerusalem to piles of rubble, a dwelling place for jackals. I will make the towns
11 of Yehuda desolate, with no inhabitant. Every wise man knows this.
Let all to whom the Lord has spoken confirm it: Why has the land been
12 destroyed, laid waste like a wilderness with no passerby? The Lord
said: For they abandoned the teaching that I gave them. They did not heed
13 Me, nor did they follow it. Instead they followed the waywardness of their
14 hearts and the Be'alim, as their fathers taught them. Therefore, thus
said the Lord of Hosts, the God of Israel: "I am about to feed this people
15 wormwood and give them poisoned water to drink. I will scatter them among
nations that neither they nor their ancestors ever knew. I will send the sword
16 after them until I finish them off." Thus said the Lord
of Hosts: Consider, then summon dirge singers and let them come, and
17 send for skilled women[33] and let them come. Let them hurry and sound a
18 wailing for us so that our eyes shed tears and our pupils drip water. For the
sound of wailing has been heard in Zion: how we have been despoiled! We
are put to shame, for we have left the land, and they have cast down our
19 dwellings. Women, hear the word of the Lord, and let your ears
absorb the word of His mouth. Teach your daughters wailing and one another
20 lamentation. For death has climbed into our windows, arrived in our palaces,
to cut down babes from the outdoors and youth from the town squares.
21 "Speak!" Thus declares the Lord: The carcasses of men will fall like dung
upon the open field, like sheaves behind the reaper, with no one to gather
22 them. Thus said the Lord: Let not the wise man boast of his wisdom.
Let not the mighty man boast of his might. Let not the wealthy boast of his
23 wealth. Someone may boast only of his conscious devotion to Me, for I the
Lord act with loving-kindness, justice, and righteousness in the world. For
24 it is these things that I desire, declares the Lord. Days are coming,
declares the Lord, when I will call to account all those who are circumcised
25 only in foreskin:[34] Egypt, Yehuda, Edom, the Amonites, Moav, and all whose
hair is shaven at the temples, who dwell in the wilderness. For all these
nations are uncircumcised, but all of the House of Israel is uncircumcised at
10 1 heart. Listen to the word that the Lord has spoken concerning you,
2 House of Israel. This is what the Lord said: Do not learn the ways of the
3 nations; do not fear heavenly portents, even if the nations fear them, for the
laws of the nations are delusions. It[35] is cut from a tree in the forest; it is the
4 handiwork of a craftsman with a chisel. He embellishes it with silver and gold.
5 He fastens it with nails and hammers so that it does not totter. They are like
a scarecrow in a cucumber patch; they do not speak. They must be carried,

---

33 | Skilled in singing or composing dirges.
34 | That is, whose hearts are not "circumcised" (cf. Deut. 10:16).
35 | Their god.

קִינָה כִּי נִצְּתוּ מִבְּלִי־אִישׁ עֹבֵר וְלֹא שָׁמְעוּ קוֹל מִקְנֶה מֵעוֹף הַשָּׁמַיִם
י וְעַד־בְּהֵמָה נָדְדוּ הָלָכוּ׃ וְנָתַתִּי אֶת־יְרוּשָׁלִַם לְגַלִּים מְעוֹן תַּנִּים וְאֶת־
יא עָרֵי יְהוּדָה אֶתֵּן שְׁמָמָה מִבְּלִי יוֹשֵׁב׃ מִי־הָאִישׁ הֶחָכָם
וְיָבֵן אֶת־זֹאת וַאֲשֶׁר דִּבֶּר פִּי־יהוה אֵלָיו וְיַגִּדָהּ עַל־מָה אָבְדָה הָאָרֶץ
יב נִצְּתָה כַמִּדְבָּר מִבְּלִי עֹבֵר׃ וַיֹּאמֶר יהוה עַל־
עָזְבָם אֶת־תּוֹרָתִי אֲשֶׁר נָתַתִּי לִפְנֵיהֶם וְלֹא־שָׁמְעוּ בְקוֹלִי וְלֹא־
יג הָלְכוּ בָהּ׃ וַיֵּלְכוּ אַחֲרֵי שְׁרִרוּת לִבָּם וְאַחֲרֵי הַבְּעָלִים אֲשֶׁר לִמְּדוּם
יד אֲבוֹתָם׃ לָכֵן כֹּה־אָמַר יהוה צְבָאוֹת אֱלֹהֵי יִשְׂרָאֵל
טו הִנְנִי מַאֲכִילָם אֶת־הָעָם הַזֶּה לַעֲנָה וְהִשְׁקִיתִים מֵי־רֹאשׁ׃ וַהֲפִצוֹתִים
בַּגּוֹיִם אֲשֶׁר לֹא יָדְעוּ הֵמָּה וַאֲבוֹתָם וְשִׁלַּחְתִּי אַחֲרֵיהֶם אֶת־הַחֶרֶב
טז עַד כַּלּוֹתִי אוֹתָם׃ כֹּה אָמַר יהוה צְבָאוֹת
הִתְבּוֹנְנוּ וְקִרְאוּ לַמְקוֹנְנוֹת וּתְבוֹאֶינָה וְאֶל־הַחֲכָמוֹת שִׁלְחוּ וְתָבוֹאנָה׃
יז וּתְמַהֵרְנָה וְתִשֶּׂנָה עָלֵינוּ נֶהִי וְתֵרַדְנָה עֵינֵינוּ דִּמְעָה וְעַפְעַפֵּינוּ יִזְּלוּ־
יח מָיִם׃ כִּי קוֹל נְהִי נִשְׁמַע מִצִּיּוֹן אֵיךְ שֻׁדָּדְנוּ בֹּשְׁנוּ מְאֹד כִּי־עָזַבְנוּ אָרֶץ
יט כִּי הִשְׁלִיכוּ מִשְׁכְּנוֹתֵינוּ׃ כִּי־שְׁמַעְנָה נָשִׁים דְּבַר־יהוה
כ וְתִקַּח אָזְנְכֶם דְּבַר־פִּיו וְלַמֵּדְנָה בְנוֹתֵיכֶם נֶהִי וְאִשָּׁה רְעוּתָהּ קִינָה׃
כִּי־עָלָה מָוֶת בְּחַלּוֹנֵינוּ בָּא בְּאַרְמְנוֹתֵינוּ לְהַכְרִית עוֹלָל מִחוּץ בַּחוּרִים
כא מֵרְחֹבוֹת׃ דַּבֵּר כֹּה נְאֻם־יהוה וְנָפְלָה נִבְלַת הָאָדָם כְּדֹמֶן עַל־פְּנֵי
כב הַשָּׂדֶה וּכְעָמִיר מֵאַחֲרֵי הַקֹּצֵר וְאֵין מְאַסֵּף׃ כֹּה ׀
אָמַר יהוה אַל־יִתְהַלֵּל חָכָם בְּחָכְמָתוֹ וְאַל־יִתְהַלֵּל הַגִּבּוֹר בִּגְבוּרָתוֹ
כג אַל־יִתְהַלֵּל עָשִׁיר בְּעָשְׁרוֹ׃ כִּי אִם־בְּזֹאת יִתְהַלֵּל הַמִּתְהַלֵּל הַשְׂכֵּל ו
וְיָדֹעַ אוֹתִי כִּי אֲנִי יהוה עֹשֶׂה חֶסֶד מִשְׁפָּט וּצְדָקָה בָּאָרֶץ כִּי־בְאֵלֶּה
כד חָפַצְתִּי נְאֻם־יהוה׃ הִנֵּה יָמִים בָּאִים נְאֻם־יהוה וּפָקַדְתִּי
כה עַל־כָּל־מוּל בְּעָרְלָה׃ עַל־מִצְרַיִם וְעַל־יְהוּדָה וְעַל־אֱדוֹם וְעַל־בְּנֵי
עַמּוֹן וְעַל־מוֹאָב וְעַל כָּל־קְצוּצֵי פֵאָה הַיֹּשְׁבִים בַּמִּדְבָּר כִּי כָל־הַגּוֹיִם
י א עֲרֵלִים וְכָל־בֵּית יִשְׂרָאֵל עַרְלֵי־לֵב׃ שִׁמְעוּ אֶת־הַדָּבָר
ב אֲשֶׁר דִּבֶּר יהוה עֲלֵיכֶם בֵּית יִשְׂרָאֵל׃ כֹּה ׀ אָמַר יהוה אֶל־דֶּרֶךְ הַגּוֹיִם
אַל־תִּלְמָדוּ וּמֵאֹתוֹת הַשָּׁמַיִם אַל־תֵּחָתּוּ כִּי־יֵחַתּוּ הַגּוֹיִם מֵהֵמָּה׃
ג כִּי־חֻקּוֹת הָעַמִּים הֶבֶל הוּא כִּי־עֵץ מִיַּעַר כְּרָתוֹ מַעֲשֵׂה יְדֵי־חָרָשׁ
ד בַּמַּעֲצָד׃ בְּכֶסֶף וּבְזָהָב יְיַפֵּהוּ בְּמַסְמְרוֹת וּבְמַקָּבוֹת יְחַזְּקוּם וְלוֹא
ה יָפִיק׃ כְּתֹמֶר מִקְשָׁה הֵמָּה וְלֹא יְדַבֵּרוּ נָשׂוֹא יִנָּשׂוּא כִּי לֹא יִצְעָדוּ

for they cannot walk. Do not fear them, for they can do no harm. Neither is
6 doing good in their capacity. LORD, there is none like You – You are
7 great, and Your name is great in strength. Who would not fear You, King of
the nations? For it befits You. For among all the wise of the nations, and
8 among all their kingdoms, there is none like You. All together they are
senseless and foolish. Their code of conduct is a delusion made of wood.
9 Beaten silver is brought from Tarshish, and gold from Ufaz, work of a
craftsman and of a goldsmith's hands, bedecked with blue and purple: all the
10 labor of skilled men. But the LORD God is true. He is the living God, the
eternal King. At His wrath the earth trembles. Nations cannot endure His
11 fury. "This is what you must say to them: A god who did not create
heaven and earth shall perish from the earth and from under these
12 heavens."[36] He makes the earth by His power, establishes the world
13 by His wisdom, and stretches out the heavens by His understanding. As He
makes His voice heard, there is rumbling water in the heavens, and He raises
clouds from the end of the earth. He makes lightning bolts with the rain and
14 brings out wind from His storehouses.[37] All humans are foolish, without
knowledge. Every goldsmith is disappointed in his idol; his molten image is
15 a sham. No breath animates them. They are delusions, works of mockery.
16 When they are called to account, they will perish. Not like these is the portion
of Yaakov, for He formed all things. Israel is the tribe He possesses. LORD of
17 Hosts is His name. Gather your wares in from the land, you who
18 dwell under siege. For thus said the LORD: This time I will fling away
those who dwell in the land and confine them to close quarters so that they
19 can easily be found. Woe unto me for my collapse. My wound is
20 severe. I once thought: This is my affliction; I can bear it. My tent is despoiled;
all its cords are severed. My children have left me; they are gone. There is no
21 longer anyone to stretch out my tent, no one to hang up my curtains. For the
shepherds became foolish. They did not seek out the LORD; therefore, they
22 did not succeed, and all their flocks have scattered. Hark! What we
heard is now approaching, a great commotion from a northern land to render
23 the cities of Yehuda desolate, a dwelling place for jackals. LORD, I know that
man does not determine his path. No man who walks controls his footsteps.
24 LORD, discipline me, but with justice, not with Your wrath, lest You reduce
25 me to nothing. Pour out Your fury on the nations that do not know You on
those clans that do not invoke Your name, for they have devoured Yaakov,
11 1 devoured him and finished him off and laid his homeland waste.[38] The
2 word which came to Yirmeyahu from the LORD: "Hear the terms of this
covenant and speak to the men of Yehuda and to those who dwell in Jerusalem.
3 Say to them: This is what the LORD, God of Israel, has said: Cursed is the man
4 who shall not heed the words of this covenant, which I commanded your

36 | This verse is in Aramaic. It is perhaps a message from Yirmeyahu to the exiles in Babylon, whose spoken language was Aramaic.

37 | Cf. Psalms 135:7.

38 | Cf. Psalms 79:6–7.

ו אַל־תִּירְאוּ מֵהֶם כִּי־לֹא יָרֵעוּ וְגַם־הֵיטֵיב אֵין אוֹתָם׃ מֵאֵין
ז כָּמוֹךָ יְהוָה גָּדוֹל אַתָּה וְגָדוֹל שִׁמְךָ בִּגְבוּרָה׃ מִי לֹא יִרָאֲךָ מֶלֶךְ הַגּוֹיִם
ח כִּי לְךָ יָאָתָה כִּי בְכָל־חַכְמֵי הַגּוֹיִם וּבְכָל־מַלְכוּתָם מֵאֵין כָּמוֹךָ׃ וּבְאַחַת
ט יִבְעֲרוּ וְיִכְסָלוּ מוּסַר הֲבָלִים עֵץ הוּא׃ כֶּסֶף מְרֻקָּע מִתַּרְשִׁישׁ יוּבָא
וְזָהָב מֵאוּפָז מַעֲשֵׂה חָרָשׁ וִידֵי צוֹרֵף תְּכֵלֶת וְאַרְגָּמָן לְבוּשָׁם מַעֲשֵׂה
י חֲכָמִים כֻּלָּם׃ וַיהוָה אֱלֹהִים אֱמֶת הוּא־אֱלֹהִים חַיִּים וּמֶלֶךְ עוֹלָם
יא מִקִּצְפּוֹ תִּרְעַשׁ הָאָרֶץ וְלֹא־יָכִלוּ גוֹיִם זַעְמוֹ׃ כִּדְנָה
תֵּאמְרוּן לְהוֹם אֱלָהַיָּא דִּי־שְׁמַיָּא וְאַרְקָא לָא עֲבַדוּ יֵאבַדוּ מֵאַרְעָא
יב וּמִן־תְּחוֹת שְׁמַיָּא אֵלֶּה׃ עֹשֵׂה אֶרֶץ בְּכֹחוֹ
יג מֵכִין תֵּבֵל בְּחָכְמָתוֹ וּבִתְבוּנָתוֹ נָטָה שָׁמָיִם׃ לְקוֹל תִּתּוֹ הֲמוֹן מַיִם
בַּשָּׁמַיִם וַיַּעֲלֶה נְשִׂאִים מִקְצֵה ארץ בְּרָקִים לַמָּטָר עָשָׂה וַיּוֹצֵא רוּחַ הָאָרֶץ
יד מֵאֹצְרֹתָיו׃ נִבְעַר כָּל־אָדָם מִדַּעַת הֹבִישׁ כָּל־צוֹרֵף מִפָּסֶל כִּי שֶׁקֶר
טו נִסְכּוֹ וְלֹא־רוּחַ בָּם׃ הֶבֶל הֵמָּה מַעֲשֵׂה תַּעְתֻּעִים בְּעֵת פְּקֻדָּתָם יֹאבֵדוּ׃
טז לֹא־כְאֵלֶּה חֵלֶק יַעֲקֹב כִּי־יוֹצֵר הַכֹּל הוּא וְיִשְׂרָאֵל שֵׁבֶט נַחֲלָתוֹ יְהוָה
יז צְבָאוֹת שְׁמוֹ׃ אִסְפִּי מֵאֶרֶץ כִּנְעָתֵךְ ישבתי יֹשֶׁבֶת
יח בַּמָּצוֹר׃ כִּי־כֹה אָמַר יְהוָה הִנְנִי קוֹלֵעַ אֶת־יוֹשְׁבֵי
יט הָאָרֶץ בַּפַּעַם הַזֹּאת וַהֲצֵרוֹתִי לָהֶם לְמַעַן יִמְצָאוּ׃ אוֹי
כ לִי עַל־שִׁבְרִי נַחְלָה מַכָּתִי וַאֲנִי אָמַרְתִּי אַךְ זֶה חֳלִי וְאֶשָּׂאֶנּוּ׃ אָהֳלִי
שֻׁדָּד וְכָל־מֵיתָרַי נִתָּקוּ בָּנַי יְצָאֻנִי וְאֵינָם אֵין־נֹטֶה עוֹד אָהֳלִי וּמֵקִים
כא יְרִיעוֹתָי׃ כִּי נִבְעֲרוּ הָרֹעִים וְאֶת־יְהוָה לֹא דָרָשׁוּ עַל־כֵּן לֹא הִשְׂכִּילוּ
כב וְכָל־מַרְעִיתָם נְפוֹצָה׃ קוֹל שְׁמוּעָה הִנֵּה בָאָה וְרַעַשׁ גָּדוֹל
כג מֵאֶרֶץ צָפוֹן לָשׂוּם אֶת־עָרֵי יְהוּדָה שְׁמָמָה מְעוֹן תַּנִּים׃ יָדַעְתִּי יְהוָה
כד כִּי לֹא לָאָדָם דַּרְכּוֹ לֹא־לְאִישׁ הֹלֵךְ וְהָכִין אֶת־צַעֲדוֹ׃ יַסְּרֵנִי יְהוָה אַךְ
כה בְּמִשְׁפָּט אַל־בְּאַפְּךָ פֶּן־תַּמְעִטֵנִי׃ שְׁפֹךְ חֲמָתְךָ עַל־הַגּוֹיִם אֲשֶׁר לֹא־
יְדָעוּךָ וְעַל מִשְׁפָּחוֹת אֲשֶׁר בְּשִׁמְךָ לֹא קָרָאוּ כִּי־אָכְלוּ אֶת־יַעֲקֹב
יא א וַאֲכָלֻהוּ וַיְכַלֻּהוּ וְאֶת־נָוֵהוּ הֵשַׁמּוּ׃ הַדָּבָר
ב אֲשֶׁר הָיָה אֶל־יִרְמְיָהוּ מֵאֵת יְהוָה לֵאמֹר׃ שִׁמְעוּ אֶת־דִּבְרֵי הַבְּרִית
ג הַזֹּאת וְדִבַּרְתָּם אֶל־אִישׁ יְהוּדָה וְעַל־יֹשְׁבֵי יְרוּשָׁלִָם׃ וְאָמַרְתָּ אֲלֵיהֶם
כֹּה־אָמַר יְהוָה אֱלֹהֵי יִשְׂרָאֵל אָרוּר הָאִישׁ אֲשֶׁר לֹא יִשְׁמַע אֶת־דִּבְרֵי
ד הַבְּרִית הַזֹּאת׃ אֲשֶׁר צִוִּיתִי אֶת־אֲבוֹתֵיכֶם בְּיוֹם הוֹצִיאִי־אוֹתָם

fathers to keep at the time I delivered them from the land of Egypt, the iron
furnace, when I told them, 'Heed My voice, and perform them exactly as I
5 commanded you. Then you will be My people, and I will be your God in
order to uphold the oath which I swore to your fathers, to give them a land
flowing with milk and honey as at this day.'" I responded and said: "Amen,
6 LORD." The LORD said to me, "Proclaim all these words in the cities
of Yehuda and in the streets of Jerusalem: Heed the terms of this covenant
7 and perform them. For I have forewarned your fathers from the day I raised
them up out of Egypt until this very day, consistently admonishing them:
8 'Heed My voice!' But they did not listen, they did not even bend an ear. They
followed the stubbornness of their evil hearts, so I brought over them the
terms of this covenant, which I commanded them to follow, but they did not
9 follow." The LORD said to me, "A conspiracy is to be found among
10 the men of Yehuda and the inhabitants of Jerusalem. They have returned to
the sins of their forefathers, who refused to heed My words. They followed
other gods and worshipped them. The House of Israel and the House of
11 Yehuda have broken My covenant that I made with their fathers." This
is what the LORD therefore said: "I am about to bring upon them a disaster from
which they will not be able to extricate themselves. They will cry out to Me, but
12 I will pay them no heed. The cities of Yehuda and the inhabitants of Jerusalem
will then go and cry out to the gods to whom they offer sacrifices. But they will
13 certainly not save them in the time of their disaster. For your gods have been
equal to the number of your cities, Yehuda, and the altars you erected to
Shame[39] are as many as the streets of Jerusalem – altars upon which to
14 offer sacrifices to the Baal. As for you, do not pray on behalf of this
people, and do not raise on their behalf a song or a prayer, for I will not pay
15 heed at the time they call out to Me on account of their disaster." For
what purpose does My dear one come to My House? Is it to perform her many
sinful schemes? Will sacral flesh absolve you? For when you do evil, that is
16 when you rejoice! A verdant olive tree – beautiful, with lovely fruit – the
LORD did call your name. To the sound of a great roar He has set fire to her
17 and crushed her branches. The LORD of Hosts, who planted you, has spoken
evil against you on account of the evil that the House of Israel and the House
of Yehuda have done to themselves, angering Me by burning offerings to the
18 Baal. The LORD informed me, and so I knew. Then You showed me
19 their actions. I was like a choice lamb led to slaughter. I did not know that
they plotted schemes against me: "Let us poison his bread with a poisonous
plant and cut him off from the land of the living. Let his name be mentioned
20 no longer." The LORD of Hosts is a righteous judge; He discerns
both mind and heart. I will yet witness Your vengeance upon them, for to You
21 I have disclosed my disputes. This is what the LORD therefore said
concerning the men of Anatot who seek your life, demanding, "You shall

39 | See note on 3:24.

מֵאֶרֶץ־מִצְרַיִם מִכּוּר הַבַּרְזֶל לֵאמֹר שִׁמְעוּ בְקוֹלִי וַעֲשִׂיתֶם אוֹתָם
כְּכֹל אֲשֶׁר־אֲצַוֶּה אֶתְכֶם וִהְיִיתֶם לִי לְעָם וְאָנֹכִי אֶהְיֶה לָכֶם
ה לֵאלֹהִים: לְמַעַן הָקִים אֶת־הַשְּׁבוּעָה אֲשֶׁר־נִשְׁבַּעְתִּי לַאֲבוֹתֵיכֶם
לָתֵת לָהֶם אֶרֶץ זָבַת חָלָב וּדְבַשׁ כַּיּוֹם הַזֶּה וָאַעַן וָאֹמַר אָמֵן ׀
ו יְהוָה: וַיֹּאמֶר יְהוָה אֵלַי קְרָא אֶת־כָּל־הַדְּבָרִים הָאֵלֶּה
בְּעָרֵי יְהוּדָה וּבְחֻצוֹת יְרוּשָׁלִַם לֵאמֹר שִׁמְעוּ אֶת־דִּבְרֵי הַבְּרִית
ז הַזֹּאת וַעֲשִׂיתֶם אוֹתָם: כִּי הָעֵד הַעִדֹתִי בַּאֲבוֹתֵיכֶם בְּיוֹם הַעֲלוֹתִי
אוֹתָם מֵאֶרֶץ מִצְרַיִם עַד־הַיּוֹם הַזֶּה הַשְׁכֵּם וְהָעֵד לֵאמֹר שִׁמְעוּ בְּקוֹלִי:
ח וְלֹא שָׁמְעוּ וְלֹא־הִטּוּ אֶת־אָזְנָם וַיֵּלְכוּ אִישׁ בִּשְׁרִירוּת לִבָּם הָרָע
וָאָבִיא עֲלֵיהֶם אֶת־כָּל־דִּבְרֵי הַבְּרִית־הַזֹּאת אֲשֶׁר־צִוִּיתִי לַעֲשׂוֹת וְלֹא
ט עָשׂוּ: וַיֹּאמֶר יְהוָה אֵלָי נִמְצָא־קֶשֶׁר בְּאִישׁ יְהוּדָה וּבְיֹשְׁבֵי
י יְרוּשָׁלִָם: שָׁבוּ עַל־עֲוֺנֹת אֲבוֹתָם הָרִאשֹׁנִים אֲשֶׁר מֵאֲנוּ לִשְׁמוֹעַ אֶת־
דְּבָרַי וְהֵמָּה הָלְכוּ אַחֲרֵי אֱלֹהִים אֲחֵרִים לְעָבְדָם הֵפֵרוּ בֵית־יִשְׂרָאֵל
יא וּבֵית יְהוּדָה אֶת־בְּרִיתִי אֲשֶׁר כָּרַתִּי אֶת־אֲבוֹתָם: לָכֵן
כֹּה אָמַר יְהוָה הִנְנִי מֵבִיא אֲלֵיהֶם רָעָה אֲשֶׁר לֹא־יוּכְלוּ לָצֵאת מִמֶּנָּה
יב וְזָעֲקוּ אֵלַי וְלֹא אֶשְׁמַע אֲלֵיהֶם: וְהָלְכוּ עָרֵי יְהוּדָה וְיֹשְׁבֵי יְרוּשָׁלִַם
וְזָעֲקוּ אֶל־הָאֱלֹהִים אֲשֶׁר הֵם מְקַטְּרִים לָהֶם וְהוֹשֵׁעַ לֹא־יוֹשִׁיעוּ לָהֶם
יג בְּעֵת רָעָתָם: כִּי מִסְפַּר עָרֶיךָ הָיוּ אֱלֹהֶיךָ יְהוּדָה וּמִסְפַּר חֻצוֹת יְרוּשָׁלִַם
יד שַׂמְתֶּם מִזְבְּחוֹת לַבֹּשֶׁת מִזְבְּחוֹת לְקַטֵּר לַבָּעַל: וְאַתָּה
אַל־תִּתְפַּלֵּל בְּעַד־הָעָם הַזֶּה וְאַל־תִּשָּׂא בַעֲדָם רִנָּה וּתְפִלָּה כִּי ׀ אֵינֶנִּי
טו שֹׁמֵעַ בְּעֵת קָרְאָם אֵלַי בְּעַד רָעָתָם: מֶה לִידִידִי בְּבֵיתִי
עֲשׂוֹתָהּ הַמְזִמָּתָה הָרַבִּים וּבְשַׂר־קֹדֶשׁ יַעַבְרוּ מֵעָלָיִךְ כִּי רָעָתֵכִי אָז
טז תַּעֲלֹזִי: זַיִת רַעֲנָן יְפֵה פְרִי־תֹאַר קָרָא יְהוָה שְׁמֵךְ לְקוֹל ׀ הֲמוּלָּה
יז גְדֹלָה הִצִּית אֵשׁ עָלֶיהָ וְרָעוּ דָּלִיּוֹתָיו: וַיהוָה צְבָאוֹת הַנּוֹטֵעַ אוֹתָךְ
דִּבֶּר עָלַיִךְ רָעָה בִּגְלַל רָעַת בֵּית־יִשְׂרָאֵל וּבֵית יְהוּדָה אֲשֶׁר עָשׂוּ
יח לָהֶם לְהַכְעִסֵנִי לְקַטֵּר לַבָּעַל: וַיהוָה הוֹדִיעַנִי וָאֵדָעָה
יט אָז הִרְאִיתַנִי מַעַלְלֵיהֶם: וַאֲנִי כְּכֶבֶשׂ אַלּוּף יוּבַל לִטְבוֹחַ וְלֹא־יָדַעְתִּי
כִּי־עָלַי ׀ חָשְׁבוּ מַחֲשָׁבוֹת נַשְׁחִיתָה עֵץ בְּלַחְמוֹ וְנִכְרְתֶנּוּ מֵאֶרֶץ
כ חַיִּים וּשְׁמוֹ לֹא־יִזָּכֵר עוֹד: וַיהוָה צְבָאוֹת שֹׁפֵט
צֶדֶק בֹּחֵן כְּלָיוֹת וָלֵב אֶרְאֶה נִקְמָתְךָ מֵהֶם כִּי אֵלֶיךָ גִּלִּיתִי אֶת־
כא רִיבִי: לָכֵן כֹּה־אָמַר יְהוָה עַל־אַנְשֵׁי עֲנָתוֹת

not prophesy in the name of the LORD so that you will not die by our
22 hand." This is what the LORD of Hosts therefore said: I am about to
hold them to account: the young men will die by the sword; their sons and
23 their daughters will die by famine. There will be no remnant of them, for
I will bring a disaster upon the men of Anatot during the year of their
12 1 retribution. You are in the right, LORD, when I dispute with You.
Nevertheless, I will express my arguments with You: Why does the way of
2 the wicked prosper? And why does every faithless traitor live securely? You
have planted them, and they have taken root. They have even gone on to bear
3 fruit. You are near in their mouths but distant from their inner thoughts. You,
LORD, know me. You see me; You have discerned that my heart is with You.
Drive them out like sheep to the slaughter and assign them to the day of
4 slaying. How long must the land mourn and the grass of every field
wither? Must beasts and birds perish because of the evil of those who dwell
5 there, who say, "He does not see our future"? You ran with foot runners, and
they exhausted you; how do you presume to compete with horses? In a
peaceful land you were confident, but how will you fare in the depths of the
6 Jordan? For even your brothers and your father's house, even they have
betrayed you. Even they have summoned a mob against you. Do not trust
7 them when they speak well of you. I have abandoned My House; I
have deserted My heritage. I have given over My dear beloved into the hands
8 of her enemies. My heritage has become for Me like a lion in the forest. She
9 raised her cry toward Me; therefore I despised her. Has My heritage become
like a bloodied bird of prey, like a bird of prey with all circling around her?
10 Go and gather all the beasts of the field; let them come and eat their fill. Many
shepherds have destroyed My vineyard, trampled My portion, turned My
11 precious portion into a desolate wasteland. It has been rendered a desolation;
the desolate one pins her grief on Me. The entire land has become desolate
12 yet no one takes it to heart. The despoilers have come upon every hilltop in
the wilderness, for the LORD's sword devours from one end of the earth to
13 the other. There is no peace for anyone. They have sown wheat, and they have
reaped thorns. They suffered pain to no avail. Be ashamed of your harvests
14 because of the burning wrath of the LORD. This is what the LORD
said: As for all My evil neighbors who have harmed the heritage that I
bequeathed to My people Israel, I am about to uproot them from their land,
15 and I will uproot the House of Yehuda from among them. Then, after I have
uprooted them, I will again show them compassion, and I will return them,
16 each to his heritage and each to his land. Then, if they study well the ways of
My people, to swear by My name, "As the LORD lives," just as they taught My
17 people to swear by Baal, then they will flourish together with My people. But
if they will not take heed, then I will uproot that nation, uproot it and destroy
13 1 it, declares the LORD. This is what the LORD said: "Go and purchase
2 a linen loincloth and place it on your loins. Do not bring it into water." I
purchased the loincloth as the LORD instructed, and I placed it on my
3 loins. The word of the LORD came to me a second time, saying,

הַֽמְבַקְשִׁים אֶת־נַפְשְׁךָ לֵאמֹר לֹא תִנָּבֵא בְּשֵׁם יהוה וְלֹא תָמוּת
כב בְּיָדֵנוּ׃ לָכֵן כֹּה אָמַר יהוה צְבָאוֹת הִנְנִי פֹקֵד
עֲלֵיהֶם הַבַּחוּרִים יָמֻתוּ בַחֶרֶב בְּנֵיהֶם וּבְנוֹתֵיהֶם יָמֻתוּ בָּרָעָב׃
כג וּשְׁאֵרִית לֹא תִהְיֶה לָהֶם כִּי־אָבִיא רָעָה אֶל־אַנְשֵׁי עֲנָתוֹת שְׁנַת
יב א פְּקֻדָּתָם׃ צַדִּיק אַתָּה יהוה כִּי אָרִיב אֵלֶיךָ אַךְ מִשְׁפָּטִים
ב אֲדַבֵּר אוֹתָךְ מַדּוּעַ דֶּרֶךְ רְשָׁעִים צָלֵחָה שָׁלוּ כָּל־בֹּגְדֵי בָגֶד׃ נְטַעְתָּם
גַּם־שֹׁרָשׁוּ יֵלְכוּ גַּם־עָשׂוּ פֶרִי קָרוֹב אַתָּה בְּפִיהֶם וְרָחוֹק מִכִּלְיוֹתֵיהֶם׃
ג וְאַתָּה יהוה יְדַעְתָּנִי תִּרְאֵנִי וּבָחַנְתָּ לִבִּי אִתָּךְ הַתִּקֵם כְּצֹאן לְטִבְחָה
ד וְהַקְדִּשֵׁם לְיוֹם הֲרֵגָה׃ עַד־מָתַי תֶּאֱבַל הָאָרֶץ וְעֵשֶׂב
כָּל־הַשָּׂדֶה יִיבָשׁ מֵרָעַת יֹשְׁבֵי־בָהּ סָפְתָה בְהֵמוֹת וָעוֹף כִּי אָמְרוּ לֹא
ה יִרְאֶה אֶת־אַחֲרִיתֵנוּ׃ כִּי אֶת־רַגְלִים ׀ רַצְתָּה וַיַּלְאוּךָ וְאֵיךְ תְּתַחֲרֶה
אֶת־הַסּוּסִים וּבְאֶרֶץ שָׁלוֹם אַתָּה בוֹטֵחַ וְאֵיךְ תַּעֲשֶׂה בִּגְאוֹן הַיַּרְדֵּן׃
ו כִּי גַם־אַחֶיךָ וּבֵית־אָבִיךָ גַּם־הֵמָּה בָּגְדוּ בָךְ גַּם־הֵמָּה קָרְאוּ אַחֲרֶיךָ
ז מָלֵא אַל־תַּאֲמֵן בָּם כִּי־יְדַבְּרוּ אֵלֶיךָ טוֹבוֹת׃ עָזַבְתִּי
אֶת־בֵּיתִי נָטַשְׁתִּי אֶת־נַחֲלָתִי נָתַתִּי אֶת־יְדִדוּת נַפְשִׁי בְּכַף אֹיְבֶיהָ׃
ח הָיְתָה־לִּי נַחֲלָתִי כְּאַרְיֵה בַיָּעַר נָתְנָה עָלַי בְּקוֹלָהּ עַל־כֵּן שְׂנֵאתִיהָ׃
ט הַעַיִט צָבוּעַ נַחֲלָתִי לִי הַעַיִט סָבִיב עָלֶיהָ לְכוּ אִסְפוּ כָּל־חַיַּת הַשָּׂדֶה
י הֵתָיוּ לְאָכְלָה׃ רֹעִים רַבִּים שִׁחֲתוּ כַרְמִי בֹּסְסוּ אֶת־חֶלְקָתִי נָתְנוּ אֶת־
יא חֶלְקַת חֶמְדָּתִי לְמִדְבַּר שְׁמָמָה׃ שָׂמָהּ לִשְׁמָמָה אָבְלָה עָלַי שְׁמֵמָה
יב נָשַׁמָּה כָּל־הָאָרֶץ כִּי אֵין אִישׁ שָׂם עַל־לֵב׃ עַל־כָּל־שְׁפָיִם בַּמִּדְבָּר בָּאוּ
שֹׁדְדִים כִּי חֶרֶב לַיהוה אֹכְלָה מִקְצֵה אֶרֶץ וְעַד־קְצֵה הָאָרֶץ אֵין
יג שָׁלוֹם לְכָל־בָּשָׂר׃ זָרְעוּ חִטִּים וְקֹצִים קָצָרוּ נֶחְלוּ לֹא יוֹעִלוּ וּבֹשׁוּ
יד מִתְּבוּאֹתֵיכֶם מֵחֲרוֹן אַף־יהוה׃ כֹּה ׀ אָמַר יהוה
עַל־כָּל־שְׁכֵנַי הָרָעִים הַנֹּגְעִים בַּנַּחֲלָה אֲשֶׁר־הִנְחַלְתִּי אֶת־עַמִּי
אֶת־יִשְׂרָאֵל הִנְנִי נֹתְשָׁם מֵעַל אַדְמָתָם וְאֶת־בֵּית יְהוּדָה אֶתּוֹשׁ
טו מִתּוֹכָם׃ וְהָיָה אַחֲרֵי נָתְשִׁי אוֹתָם אָשׁוּב וְרִחַמְתִּים וַהֲשִׁבֹתִים אִישׁ ז
טז לְנַחֲלָתוֹ וְאִישׁ לְאַרְצוֹ׃ וְהָיָה אִם־לָמֹד יִלְמְדוּ אֶת־דַּרְכֵי עַמִּי לְהִשָּׁבֵעַ
בִּשְׁמִי חַי־יהוה כַּאֲשֶׁר לִמְּדוּ אֶת־עַמִּי לְהִשָּׁבֵעַ בַּבָּעַל וְנִבְנוּ בְּתוֹךְ
יז עַמִּי׃ וְאִם לֹא יִשְׁמָעוּ וְנָתַשְׁתִּי אֶת־הַגּוֹי הַהוּא נָתוֹשׁ וְאַבֵּד נְאֻם־
יג א יהוה׃ כֹּה־אָמַר יהוה אֵלַי הָלוֹךְ וְקָנִיתָ לְּךָ אֵזוֹר פִּשְׁתִּים
ב וְשַׂמְתּוֹ עַל־מָתְנֶיךָ וּבַמַּיִם לֹא תְבִאֵהוּ׃ וָאֶקְנֶה אֶת־הָאֵזוֹר כִּדְבַר
ג יהוה וָאָשִׂם עַל־מָתְנָי׃ וַיְהִי דְבַר־יהוה אֵלַי שֵׁנִית

4 "Take the loincloth that you purchased, that is on your loins, and get up and
5 go to Perat,[40] and hide it there in the crevice of a rock." I went and hid it at
6 Perat, just as the LORD commanded me. After many days the LORD said to
me, "Get up and go to Perat and remove from there the loincloth that I
7 commanded you to hide there." I went to Perat and dug up the loincloth from
the place where I had hidden it, and behold, the loincloth was ruined, good
8 for nothing. The word of the LORD came to me. This is what the
9 LORD said: "Thus shall I bring ruin to the pride of Yehuda and the great pride
10 of Jerusalem. This evil people who refuse to heed My words, who follow their
own stubborn hearts, who have gone after other gods and serve them and
11 worship them, shall become like this loincloth – good for nothing. For just
as a loincloth clings to a man's loins, so have I made all the House of Israel
and all the House of Yehuda cling to Me," declares the LORD, "to become My
12 people for fame, praise, and glory. But they would not take heed. Say to them
this word: This is what the LORD, God of Israel, has said: Every jug shall be
filled with wine. When they respond, 'Do we not know that every
13 jug should be filled with wine?' say to them: This is what the LORD has said:
I am about to fill with drunkenness all who dwell in this land, and the kings
who sit upon David's throne, and the priests and the prophets, and all who
14 dwell in Jerusalem. I will smash them, each man against his brother, fathers
and sons together, declares the LORD; I will neither pity nor show mercy nor
15 spare them from ruin." Take heed, listen, and be not
16 haughty, for the LORD has spoken. Give honor to the LORD your God before
He brings darkness, before your feet stumble upon the mountains of the night.
You will hope for light, but He will make it deathly dark and turn it into thick
17 cloud. If you will not take heed, my soul will secretly weep because of your
pride; my eyes will well up and drop tears, for the LORD's flock is held
18 captive. Say to the king and to the queen mother: Be humbled, be
19 seated, for your headpiece has come down, the crown of your glory. The cities
of the south are enclosed; there is no one to open them. All of Yehuda has
20 been exiled, exiled completely. Lift your eyes and see those who
approach from the north. Where is the flock that you were given, the sheep
21 in which you took such pride? What will you say when he holds you to
account? You taught them to rule over you like princes. Will not pangs of pain
22 grip you like a woman in childbirth? And when you say to yourselves, "Why
has all this happened to me?" It is because of your many sins that your skirts
23 are exposed, your heels laid bare. Can the Kushite change his skin? Or the
leopard its spots? Neither will you be able to do good, so accustomed you are
24 to doing evil. I will scatter them like straw that tumbles before the desert wind.
25 This is your lot, your measure meted out by Me, declares the LORD, because
26 you forgot Me and trusted in falsehood. I too will lift your skirts upon your

40 | This likely refers to Wadi Kelt, located in the hills east of Jerusalem and Yirmeyahu's hometown of Anatot, rather than the Euphrates River.

ד לֵאמֹר: קַח אֶת־הָאֵזוֹר אֲשֶׁר קָנִיתָ אֲשֶׁר עַל־מָתְנֶיךָ וְקוּם לֵךְ פְּרָתָה
ה וְטָמְנֵהוּ שָׁם בִּנְקִיק הַסָּלַע: וָאֵלֵךְ וָאֶטְמְנֵהוּ בִּפְרָת כַּאֲשֶׁר צִוָּה יְהוָה
ו אוֹתִי: וַיְהִי מִקֵּץ יָמִים רַבִּים וַיֹּאמֶר יְהוָה אֵלַי קוּם לֵךְ פְּרָתָה וְקַח
ז מִשָּׁם אֶת־הָאֵזוֹר אֲשֶׁר צִוִּיתִיךָ לְטָמְנוֹ־שָׁם: וָאֵלֵךְ פְּרָתָה וָאֶחְפֹּר
וָאֶקַּח אֶת־הָאֵזוֹר מִן־הַמָּקוֹם אֲשֶׁר־טְמַנְתִּיו שָׁמָּה וְהִנֵּה נִשְׁחַת
ח ט הָאֵזוֹר לֹא יִצְלַח לַכֹּל: וַיְהִי דְבַר־יְהוָה אֵלַי לֵאמֹר: כֹּה
אָמַר יְהוָה כָּכָה אַשְׁחִית אֶת־גְּאוֹן יְהוּדָה וְאֶת־גְּאוֹן יְרוּשָׁלִַם הָרָב:
י הָעָם הַזֶּה הָרָע הַמֵּאֲנִים | לִשְׁמוֹעַ אֶת־דְּבָרַי הַהֹלְכִים בִּשְׁרִרוּת לִבָּם
וַיֵּלְכוּ אַחֲרֵי אֱלֹהִים אֲחֵרִים לְעָבְדָם וּלְהִשְׁתַּחֲוֹת לָהֶם וִיהִי כָּאֵזוֹר
יא הַזֶּה אֲשֶׁר לֹא־יִצְלַח לַכֹּל: כִּי כַּאֲשֶׁר יִדְבַּק הָאֵזוֹר אֶל־מָתְנֵי אִישׁ
כֵּן הִדְבַּקְתִּי אֵלַי אֶת־כָּל־בֵּית יִשְׂרָאֵל וְאֶת־כָּל־בֵּית יְהוּדָה נְאֻם־
יב יְהוָה לִהְיוֹת לִי לְעָם וּלְשֵׁם וְלִתְהִלָּה וּלְתִפְאָרֶת וְלֹא שָׁמֵעוּ: וְאָמַרְתָּ
אֲלֵיהֶם אֶת־הַדָּבָר הַזֶּה כֹּה־אָמַר יְהוָה אֱלֹהֵי יִשְׂרָאֵל כָּל־נֵבֶל יִמָּלֵא
יָיִן וְאָמְרוּ אֵלֶיךָ הֲיָדֹעַ לֹא נֵדַע כִּי כָל־נֵבֶל יִמָּלֵא יָיִן:
יג וְאָמַרְתָּ אֲלֵיהֶם כֹּה־אָמַר יְהוָה הִנְנִי מְמַלֵּא אֶת־כָּל־יֹשְׁבֵי הָאָרֶץ
הַזֹּאת וְאֶת־הַמְּלָכִים הַיֹּשְׁבִים לְדָוִד עַל־כִּסְאוֹ וְאֶת־הַכֹּהֲנִים וְאֶת־
יד הַנְּבִיאִים וְאֵת כָּל־יֹשְׁבֵי יְרוּשָׁלִָם שִׁכָּרוֹן: וְנִפַּצְתִּים אִישׁ אֶל־אָחִיו
וְהָאָבוֹת וְהַבָּנִים יַחְדָּו נְאֻם־יְהוָה לֹא־אֶחְמוֹל וְלֹא־אָחוּס וְלֹא אֲרַחֵם
טו מֵהַשְׁחִיתָם: שִׁמְעוּ וְהַאֲזִינוּ אַל־תִּגְבָּהוּ כִּי יְהוָה
טז דִּבֵּר: תְּנוּ לַיהוָה אֱלֹהֵיכֶם כָּבוֹד בְּטֶרֶם יַחְשִׁךְ וּבְטֶרֶם יִתְנַגְּפוּ רַגְלֵיכֶם
יז עַל־הָרֵי נָשֶׁף וְקִוִּיתֶם לְאוֹר וְשָׂמָהּ לְצַלְמָוֶת ישית לַעֲרָפֶל: וְאִם לֹא   וְשִׁית
תִשְׁמָעוּהָ בְּמִסְתָּרִים תִּבְכֶּה־נַפְשִׁי מִפְּנֵי גֵוָה וְדָמֹעַ תִּדְמַע וְתֵרַד עֵינִי
יח דִּמְעָה כִּי נִשְׁבָּה עֵדֶר יְהוָה: אֱמֹר לַמֶּלֶךְ וְלַגְּבִירָה
יט הַשְׁפִּילוּ שֵׁבוּ כִּי יָרַד מַרְאֲשׁוֹתֵיכֶם עֲטֶרֶת תִּפְאַרְתְּכֶם: עָרֵי הַנֶּגֶב
כ סֻגְּרוּ וְאֵין פֹּתֵחַ הָגְלָת יְהוּדָה כֻּלָּהּ הָגְלָת שְׁלוֹמִים: שאי   שְׂאוּ
כא עֵינֵיכֶם וראי הַבָּאִים מִצָּפוֹן אַיֵּה הָעֵדֶר נִתַּן־לָךְ צֹאן תִּפְאַרְתֵּךְ: מַה־   וּרְאוּ
תֹּאמְרִי כִּי־יִפְקֹד עָלַיִךְ וְאַתְּ לִמַּדְתְּ אֹתָם עָלַיִךְ אַלֻּפִים לְרֹאשׁ הֲלוֹא
כב חֲבָלִים יֹאחֱזוּךְ כְּמוֹ אֵשֶׁת לֵדָה: וְכִי תֹאמְרִי בִּלְבָבֵךְ מַדּוּעַ קְרָאֻנִי
כג אֵלֶּה בְּרֹב עֲוֺנֵךְ נִגְלוּ שׁוּלַיִךְ נֶחְמְסוּ עֲקֵבָיִךְ: הֲיַהֲפֹךְ כּוּשִׁי עוֹרוֹ וְנָמֵר
כד חֲבַרְבֻּרֹתָיו גַּם־אַתֶּם תּוּכְלוּ לְהֵיטִיב לִמֻּדֵי הָרֵעַ: וַאֲפִיצֵם כְּקַשׁ עוֹבֵר
כה לְרוּחַ מִדְבָּר: זֶה גוֹרָלֵךְ מְנָת־מִדַּיִךְ מֵאִתִּי נְאֻם־יְהוָה אֲשֶׁר שָׁכַחַתְּ
כו אוֹתִי וַתִּבְטְחִי בַּשָּׁקֶר: וְגַם־אֲנִי חָשַׂפְתִּי שׁוּלַיִךְ עַל־פָּנָיִךְ וְנִרְאָה

27 face, and your shame will be seen, your adulteries and your loud orgies, the
lewdness of your harlotry; on the hills in the fields I saw your abominations.
Woe to you, Jerusalem. If you will not become pure after all this, when,
14 1 then? The word of the LORD came to Yirmeyahu concerning
2 the matter of the droughts: Yehuda is aggrieved, her gates weakened, her
3 inhabitants bent to the earth; Jerusalem's screams rose. The master shepherds
sent their apprentices for water. They came to the water holes but did not find
water. They returned with their vessels empty. They were humiliated and
4 ashamed, and they covered their heads.[41] Because the earth was parched, for
there had been no rain in the land, the farmers were humiliated. They covered
5 their heads. Indeed, even the hind in the field gives birth but abandons its
6 young because there is no grass. The wild asses stand upon the heights panting
7 as jackals do. Their eyes fail because there is no vegetation. If our sins testify
against us – then, LORD, act on behalf of Your name. Our rebellious deeds
8 are many. We have sinned against You. Hope of Israel, its redeemer in times
of trouble, why be like a stranger in the land, like a guest who stops by for a
9 night? Why be like a man taken by surprise, like a warrior who cannot help?
You are in our midst, O LORD, and we are called by Your name. Do not desert
10 us. This is what the LORD said concerning this people: "Just as they
love to wander and never restrained their feet, so too does the LORD not
accept them. Now He will remember their transgressions and hold them to
11 account for their sins." The LORD said to me: "Do not pray for the
12 benefit of this people. When they fast, I will not hear their cry; if they offer a
burnt offering or a grain offering I will not accept them, for I will finish them
13 off by the sword and by famine and by plague." I protested, "Wait, Lord GOD!
The prophets say to them: 'You shall not see the sword, and no famine shall
14 befall you, but I will grant you true peace in this place.'" The LORD
said to me: "These prophets prophesy falsehood in My name. I did not send
them, I did not command them, and I did not speak to them. A false vision,
sorcery, idolatry, and the fraudulence of their hearts – that is what they
15 prophesy to you." This is what the LORD therefore said: "About the
prophets who prophesy in My name although I have not sent them, those
who say, 'There will be neither sword nor famine in this land,' those very
16 prophets shall perish by sword and famine. And the people to whom they
prophesy will be thrown about the streets of Jerusalem as a consequence of
famine and the sword, with no one to bury them: not them, nor their wives,
17 nor their sons or daughters. I will pour out their evil upon them. This is what
you should say to them: Let my eyes flow with tears night and day and not
cease, for the maiden daughter, my people has suffered a great collapse, a most
18 painful wound. If I went out to the field, those slain by the sword were there.
If I entered the city, those struck ill by famine were there. For even the priest
19 and the prophet circle about a land that they do not know." Have
You totally rejected Yehuda? Have You become disgusted with Zion? Why
did You strike us so that we have no cure? We hope for peace, but no good

41 | As was the custom of mourners.

כז קְלוֹנֵךְ: נִאֻפַיִךְ וּמִצְהֲלוֹתַיִךְ זִמַּת זְנוּתֵךְ עַל־גְּבָעוֹת בַּשָּׂדֶה רָאִיתִי
יד א שִׁקּוּצָיִךְ אוֹי לָךְ יְרוּשָׁלַםִ לֹא תִטְהֲרִי אַחֲרֵי מָתַי עֹד: אֲשֶׁר
ב הָיָה דְבַר־יְהוָה אֶל־יִרְמְיָהוּ עַל־דִּבְרֵי הַבַּצָּרוֹת: אָבְלָה יְהוּדָה
ג וּשְׁעָרֶיהָ אֻמְלְלוּ קָדְרוּ לָאָרֶץ וְצִוְחַת יְרוּשָׁלַםִ עָלָתָה: וְאַדִּרֵיהֶם שָׁלְחוּ
צעוריהם לַמָּיִם בָּאוּ עַל־גֵּבִים לֹא־מָצְאוּ מַיִם שָׁבוּ כְלֵיהֶם רֵיקָם בֹּשׁוּ צְעִירֵיהֶם
ד וְהָכְלְמוּ וְחָפוּ רֹאשָׁם: בַּעֲבוּר הָאֲדָמָה חַתָּה כִּי לֹא־הָיָה גֶשֶׁם בָּאָרֶץ
ה בֹּשׁוּ אִכָּרִים חָפוּ רֹאשָׁם: כִּי גַם־אַיֶּלֶת בַּשָּׂדֶה יָלְדָה וְעָזוֹב כִּי לֹא־הָיָה
ו דֶּשֶׁא: וּפְרָאִים עָמְדוּ עַל־שְׁפָיִם שָׁאֲפוּ רוּחַ כַּתַּנִּים כָּלוּ עֵינֵיהֶם כִּי־אֵין
ז עֵשֶׂב: אִם־עֲוֺנֵינוּ עָנוּ בָנוּ יְהוָה עֲשֵׂה לְמַעַן שְׁמֶךָ כִּי־רַבּוּ מְשׁוּבֹתֵינוּ
ח לְךָ חָטָאנוּ: מִקְוֵה יִשְׂרָאֵל מוֹשִׁיעוֹ בְּעֵת צָרָה לָמָּה תִהְיֶה כְּגֵר בָּאָרֶץ
ט וּכְאֹרֵחַ נָטָה לָלוּן: לָמָּה תִהְיֶה כְּאִישׁ נִדְהָם כְּגִבּוֹר לֹא־יוּכַל לְהוֹשִׁיעַ
י וְאַתָּה בְקִרְבֵּנוּ יְהוָה וְשִׁמְךָ עָלֵינוּ נִקְרָא אַל־תַּנִּחֵנוּ: כֹּה־
אָמַר יְהוָה לָעָם הַזֶּה כֵּן אָהֲבוּ לָנוּעַ רַגְלֵיהֶם לֹא חָשָׂכוּ וַיהוָה לֹא
יא רָצָם עַתָּה יִזְכֹּר עֲוֺנָם וְיִפְקֹד חַטֹּאתָם: וַיֹּאמֶר יְהוָה אֵלָי
יב אַל־תִּתְפַּלֵּל בְּעַד־הָעָם הַזֶּה לְטוֹבָה: כִּי יָצֻמוּ אֵינֶנִּי שֹׁמֵעַ אֶל־רִנָּתָם
וְכִי יַעֲלוּ עֹלָה וּמִנְחָה אֵינֶנִּי רֹצָם כִּי בַּחֶרֶב וּבָרָעָב וּבַדֶּבֶר אָנֹכִי מְכַלֶּה
יג אוֹתָם: וָאֹמַר אֲהָהּ ׀ אֲדֹנָי יְהוִה הִנֵּה הַנְּבִאִים אֹמְרִים לָהֶם לֹא־
תִרְאוּ חֶרֶב וְרָעָב לֹא־יִהְיֶה לָכֶם כִּי־שְׁלוֹם אֱמֶת אֶתֵּן לָכֶם בַּמָּקוֹם
יד הַזֶּה: וַיֹּאמֶר יְהוָה אֵלַי שֶׁקֶר הַנְּבִאִים נִבְּאִים בִּשְׁמִי לֹא
שְׁלַחְתִּים וְלֹא צִוִּיתִים וְלֹא דִבַּרְתִּי אֲלֵיהֶם חֲזוֹן שֶׁקֶר וְקֶסֶם ואלול וֶאֱלִיל
טו ותרמות לִבָּם הֵמָּה מִתְנַבְּאִים לָכֶם: לָכֵן כֹּה־אָמַר יְהוָה וְתַרְמִית
עַל־הַנְּבִאִים הַנִּבְּאִים בִּשְׁמִי וַאֲנִי לֹא־שְׁלַחְתִּים וְהֵמָּה אֹמְרִים חֶרֶב
וְרָעָב לֹא יִהְיֶה בָּאָרֶץ הַזֹּאת בַּחֶרֶב וּבָרָעָב יִתַּמּוּ הַנְּבִאִים הָהֵמָּה:
טז וְהָעָם אֲשֶׁר־הֵמָּה נִבְּאִים לָהֶם יִהְיוּ מֻשְׁלָכִים בְּחֻצוֹת יְרוּשָׁלַםִ מִפְּנֵי ׀
הָרָעָב וְהַחֶרֶב וְאֵין מְקַבֵּר לָהֵמָּה הֵמָּה נְשֵׁיהֶם וּבְנֵיהֶם וּבְנֹתֵיהֶם
יז וְשָׁפַכְתִּי עֲלֵיהֶם אֶת־רָעָתָם: וְאָמַרְתָּ אֲלֵיהֶם אֶת־הַדָּבָר הַזֶּה תֵּרַדְנָה
עֵינַי דִּמְעָה לַיְלָה וְיוֹמָם וְאַל־תִּדְמֶינָה כִּי שֶׁבֶר גָּדוֹל נִשְׁבְּרָה בְּתוּלַת
יח בַּת־עַמִּי מַכָּה נַחְלָה מְאֹד: אִם־יָצָאתִי הַשָּׂדֶה וְהִנֵּה חַלְלֵי־חֶרֶב
וְאִם בָּאתִי הָעִיר וְהִנֵּה תַּחֲלוּאֵי רָעָב כִּי גַם־נָבִיא גַם־כֹּהֵן סָחֲרוּ אֶל־
יט אֶרֶץ וְלֹא יָדָעוּ: הֲמָאֹס מָאַסְתָּ אֶת־יְהוּדָה אִם־בְּצִיּוֹן
גָּעֲלָה נַפְשֶׁךָ מַדּוּעַ הִכִּיתָנוּ וְאֵין לָנוּ מַרְפֵּא קַוֵּה לְשָׁלוֹם וְאֵין טוֹב

20 awaits us; for a time of healing, but instead – horror. LORD, we acknowledge
our wickedness and the iniquity of our fathers, for we have sinned against
21 You. Do not spurn us for Your name's sake. Do not dishonor the throne of
22 Your glory. Remember, do not annul Your covenant with us. Are there among
the false gods of the nations any that give rain? Do the heavens give showers
by themselves? It is You, the LORD our God, so we place our hope in You, for
15 1 it is You who made all these things. The LORD then said to me, "Even
if Moshe and Shmuel were to stand before Me, I would not show favor to this
2 people. Send them away from My presence, and let them depart. Should they
then say to you, 'Where shall we go?' tell them that this is what the LORD said:
Those destined for death, to death; for the sword, to the sword; for hunger,
3 to hunger; and for captivity, to captivity. I will appoint four families over them,
declares the LORD: the sword to slay, the dogs to drag away, the birds of the
4 sky and the beasts of the earth to devour and to destroy. I shall make them
an object of horror for all the kingdoms of the earth on account of Menashe
the son of Ḥizkiyahu, king of Yehuda, because of what he did in Jerusalem.[42]
5 For who will have pity upon you, Jerusalem? Who will console you? Who
6 will turn aside to inquire about your well-being? You abandoned Me," declares
the LORD. "You went backward. I stretched out My hand against you and
7 destroyed you. I had become tired of relenting. I will scatter them with a
winnowing fork to all the cities of the world. I, bereaved, I destroyed My
8 people. They did not repent of their ways. Their widows are more numerous
to Me than the sand of the seas. I brought down upon mother and young lad
a marauder at noon. I cast down upon them, suddenly, anguish and horrors.
9 Diminished is she who gave birth to seven. Her spirit is weakened. Her sun
set while it was yet day. She is shamed and humiliated. I will deliver their
10 remnant to the sword, to their enemies," declares the LORD. Woe is
me, my mother, that you gave birth to me – a contentious man, a quarrelsome
man, throughout the whole land. I have no claims on anyone, nor do they
11 have claims on me. Yet they all curse me. The LORD responded: "I swear that
I will yet spare you for good, and I swear that I will cause the enemy to appeal
12 to you in the time of evil and the time of distress. Can iron shatter northern
13 iron reinforced with bronze? I will turn your wealth and your treasure into
booty with no compensation because of all your sins in all your territories.
14 I will bring you with your enemies into a land you never knew, for a fire
15 is kindled in My nostrils, blazing against you." LORD, You know.
Remember me, take me into account. Take revenge for me upon my pursuers.
Do not be overly patient in taking up my cause. Know that I have borne
16 humiliation for Your sake. Your words were found, and I devoured them. Your
word was for me a joy and a source of happiness for my heart, for I have been
17 called by Your name, O LORD, God of Hosts. I never sat among a band of
revelers and made merry. Because of Your hand,[43] I sat alone, for You have
18 filled me with a prophecy of wrath. Why has my pain become endless and

42 | See II Kings 21:1–16.

43 | Meaning God's prophecy, or perhaps God's wrath.

כ וּלְעֵת מַרְפֵּא וְהִנֵּה בְעָתָה: יָדַעְנוּ יְהוָה רִשְׁעֵנוּ עֲוֺן אֲבוֹתֵינוּ כִּי חָטָאנוּ
כא לָךְ: אַל־תִּנְאַץ לְמַעַן שִׁמְךָ אַל־תְּנַבֵּל כִּסֵּא כְבוֹדֶךָ זְכֹר אַל־תָּפֵר
כב בְּרִיתְךָ אִתָּנוּ: הֲיֵשׁ בְּהַבְלֵי הַגּוֹיִם מַגְשִׁמִים וְאִם־הַשָּׁמַיִם יִתְּנוּ רְבִבִים ח
הֲלֹא אַתָּה־הוּא יְהוָה אֱלֹהֵינוּ וּנְקַוֶּה־לָּךְ כִּי־אַתָּה עָשִׂיתָ אֶת־כָּל־
טו א אֵלֶּה: וַיֹּאמֶר יְהוָה אֵלַי אִם־יַעֲמֹד מֹשֶׁה וּשְׁמוּאֵל
ב לְפָנַי אֵין נַפְשִׁי אֶל־הָעָם הַזֶּה שַׁלַּח מֵעַל־פָּנַי וְיֵצֵאוּ: וְהָיָה כִּי־יֹאמְרוּ
אֵלֶיךָ אָנָה נֵצֵא וְאָמַרְתָּ אֲלֵיהֶם כֹּה־אָמַר יְהוָה אֲשֶׁר לַמָּוֶת לַמָּוֶת
ג וַאֲשֶׁר לַחֶרֶב לַחֶרֶב וַאֲשֶׁר לָרָעָב לָרָעָב וַאֲשֶׁר לַשְּׁבִי לַשֶּׁבִי: וּפָקַדְתִּי
עֲלֵיהֶם אַרְבַּע מִשְׁפָּחוֹת נְאֻם־יְהוָה אֶת־הַחֶרֶב לַהֲרֹג וְאֶת־הַכְּלָבִים
לִסְחֹב וְאֶת־עוֹף הַשָּׁמַיִם וְאֶת־בֶּהֱמַת הָאָרֶץ לֶאֱכֹל וּלְהַשְׁחִית:
ד וּנְתַתִּים לזועה לְכֹל מַמְלְכוֹת הָאָרֶץ בִּגְלַל מְנַשֶּׁה בֶן־יְחִזְקִיָּהוּ מֶלֶךְ לְזַעֲוָה
ה יְהוּדָה עַל אֲשֶׁר־עָשָׂה בִּירוּשָׁלָםִ: כִּי מִי־יַחְמֹל עָלַיִךְ יְרוּשָׁלַםִ וּמִי
ו יָנוּד לָךְ וּמִי יָסוּר לִשְׁאֹל לְשָׁלֹם לָךְ: אַתְּ נָטַשְׁתְּ אֹתִי נְאֻם־יְהוָה
ז אָחוֹר תֵּלֵכִי וָאַט אֶת־יָדִי עָלַיִךְ וָאַשְׁחִיתֵךְ נִלְאֵיתִי הִנָּחֵם: וָאֶזְרֵם
בְּמִזְרֶה בְּשַׁעֲרֵי הָאָרֶץ שִׁכַּלְתִּי אִבַּדְתִּי אֶת־עַמִּי מִדַּרְכֵיהֶם לוֹא שָׁבוּ:
ח עָצְמוּ־לִי אַלְמְנוֹתָו מֵחוֹל יַמִּים הֵבֵאתִי לָהֶם עַל־אֵם בָּחוּר שֹׁדֵד
ט בַּצָּהֳרָיִם הִפַּלְתִּי עָלֶיהָ פִּתְאֹם עִיר וּבֶהָלוֹת: אֻמְלְלָה יֹלֶדֶת הַשִּׁבְעָה
נָפְחָה נַפְשָׁהּ באה שִׁמְשָׁהּ בְּעֹד יוֹמָם בּוֹשָׁה וְחָפֵרָה וּשְׁאֵרִיתָם לַחֶרֶב בָּא
י אֶתֵּן לִפְנֵי אֹיְבֵיהֶם נְאֻם־יְהוָה: אוֹי־לִי אִמִּי כִּי יְלִדְתִּנִי
אִישׁ רִיב וְאִישׁ מָדוֹן לְכָל־הָאָרֶץ לֹא־נָשִׁיתִי וְלֹא־נָשׁוּ־בִי כֻּלֹּה
יא מְקַלְלַונִי: אָמַר יְהוָה אִם־לֹא שרותך לְטוֹב אִם־לוֹא | הִפְגַּעְתִּי בְךָ שֵׁרִיתִיךָ
יב בְּעֵת־רָעָה וּבְעֵת צָרָה אֶת־הָאֹיֵב: הֲיָרֹעַ בַּרְזֶל | בַּרְזֶל מִצָּפוֹן וּנְחֹשֶׁת:
יג חֵילְךָ וְאוֹצְרוֹתֶיךָ לָבַז אֶתֵּן לֹא בִמְחִיר וּבְכָל־חַטֹּאותֶיךָ וּבְכָל־גְּבוּלֶיךָ:
יד וְהַעֲבַרְתִּי אֶת־אֹיְבֶיךָ בְּאֶרֶץ לֹא יָדָעְתָּ כִּי־אֵשׁ קָדְחָה בְאַפִּי עֲלֵיכֶם
טו תּוּקָד: אַתָּה יָדַעְתָּ יְהוָה זָכְרֵנִי וּפָקְדֵנִי וְהִנָּקֶם לִי מֵרֹדְפַי
טז אַל־לְאֶרֶךְ אַפְּךָ תִּקָּחֵנִי דַּע שְׂאֵתִי עָלֶיךָ חֶרְפָּה: נִמְצְאוּ דְבָרֶיךָ וָאֹכְלֵם
וַיְהִי דבריך לִי לְשָׂשׂוֹן וּלְשִׂמְחַת לְבָבִי כִּי־נִקְרָא שִׁמְךָ עָלַי יְהוָה דְּבָרְךָ
יז אֱלֹהֵי צְבָאוֹת: לֹא־יָשַׁבְתִּי בְסוֹד־מְשַׂחֲקִים וָאֶעְלֹז מִפְּנֵי יָדְךָ בָּדָד
יח יָשַׁבְתִּי כִּי־זַעַם מִלֵּאתָנִי: לָמָּה הָיָה כְאֵבִי נֶצַח וּמַכָּתִי אֲנוּשָׁה מֵאֲנָה

my wound incurable, refusing to heal? You have become for me a deceptive
19 stream, waters that cannot be trusted. Therefore, this is what the
Lord said: "If you return I will take you back, and you will stand before Me.
If you will extract preciousness from rubbish, you will have done as I decreed.
But let them return to you, and do not allow yourselves to return to them.
20 Against these people I will make you like a fortified bronze wall. They will
wage battle against you, but they shall not prevail, for I am with you to deliver
21 you and rescue you," declares the Lord.[44] "I will rescue you from the hands
16 1 of the evil ones and redeem you from the grasp of the violent." The
2 Lord's word came to me: "Do not take a wife, so that you will have no sons
3 or daughters in this place." For this is what the Lord said of sons
and daughters born in this place and of their mothers who bear them and of
4 their fathers who beget them in this land: "They will die of deadly diseases.
They will not be eulogized and they will not be buried. They will be like dung
on the face of the earth. They will be annihilated by the sword and by famine.
Their corpses will be food for the birds of the sky and for the beasts of the
5 earth." For this is what the Lord said: "Do not enter the house of
funeral feasting, do not go to eulogize, and do not lament for them, for I have
withdrawn My peace from this people," declares the Lord, "My kindness and
6 compassion. Great and small alike will perish in this land and not be buried.
7 There will be no eulogies for them, no slashing, no hair torn out for them. No
one will break bread for a mourner to comfort them over the dead. No one
8 will offer to drink with them a cup of consolation for father or for mother. Do
9 not enter the festival hall to sit with them to eat and to drink." For
this is what the Lord of Hosts, the God of Israel, said: "I am about to banish
from this place, before your eyes and in your days, the sound of joy and the
10 sound of happiness, the voice of the groom and the voice of the bride. When
you tell all these things to this people and they say to you, 'For what reason
did the Lord pronounce all this great evil over us? What is our transgression,
11 and what sin have we sinned against the Lord our God?' say to them: It is
because your fathers abandoned Me, declares the Lord. They followed other
gods, served them, and worshipped them. They abandoned Me and did not
12 keep My teaching. And you did worse than your fathers. Each of you pursues
13 the stubbornness of his evil heart so as not to obey Me. I will hurl you
out of this land onto a land that neither you nor your fathers ever knew.
There you will serve other gods day and night, for I will grant you no
14 mercy." Therefore, days are approaching, declares the Lord, when
it will no longer be said, "As the Lord lives who has brought the Israelites up
15 from the land of Egypt," but rather, "As the Lord lives who has brought the
Israelites up from the land of the north and from all the lands to which He
had expelled them"; I will return them to their own soil, which I gave to their

---

44 | Cf. 1:18–19.

יט הַרְפָּא הָיוֹ תִהְיֶה לִי כְּמוֹ אַכְזָב מַיִם לֹא נֶאֱמָנוּ׃ לָכֵן כֹּה־
אָמַר יְהוָה אִם־תָּשׁוּב וַאֲשִׁיבְךָ לְפָנַי תַּעֲמֹד וְאִם־תּוֹצִיא יָקָר מִזּוֹלֵל
כ כְּפִי תִהְיֶה יָשֻׁבוּ הֵמָּה אֵלֶיךָ וְאַתָּה לֹא־תָשׁוּב אֲלֵיהֶם׃ וּנְתַתִּיךָ לָעָם
הַזֶּה לְחוֹמַת נְחֹשֶׁת בְּצוּרָה וְנִלְחֲמוּ אֵלֶיךָ וְלֹא־יוּכְלוּ לָךְ כִּי־אִתְּךָ אֲנִי
כא לְהוֹשִׁיעֲךָ וּלְהַצִּילֶךָ נְאֻם־יְהוָה׃ וְהִצַּלְתִּיךָ מִיַּד רָעִים וּפְדִתִיךָ מִכַּף
טז א ב עָרִצִים׃ וַיְהִי דְבַר־יְהוָה אֵלַי לֵאמֹר׃ לֹא־תִקַּח לְךָ אִשָּׁה
ג וְלֹא־יִהְיוּ לְךָ בָּנִים וּבָנוֹת בַּמָּקוֹם הַזֶּה׃ כִּי־כֹה ׀ אָמַר
יְהוָה עַל־הַבָּנִים וְעַל־הַבָּנוֹת הַיִּלּוֹדִים בַּמָּקוֹם הַזֶּה וְעַל־אִמֹּתָם
ד הַיֹּלְדוֹת אוֹתָם וְעַל־אֲבוֹתָם הַמּוֹלִדִים אוֹתָם בָּאָרֶץ הַזֹּאת׃ מְמוֹתֵי
תַחֲלֻאִים יָמֻתוּ לֹא יִסָּפְדוּ וְלֹא יִקָּבֵרוּ לְדֹמֶן עַל־פְּנֵי הָאֲדָמָה יִהְיוּ
וּבַחֶרֶב וּבָרָעָב יִכְלוּ וְהָיְתָה נִבְלָתָם לְמַאֲכָל לְעוֹף הַשָּׁמַיִם וּלְבֶהֱמַת
ה הָאָרֶץ׃ כִּי־כֹה ׀ אָמַר יְהוָה אַל־תָּבוֹא בֵּית מַרְזֵחַ
וְאַל־תֵּלֵךְ לִסְפּוֹד וְאַל־תָּנֹד לָהֶם כִּי־אָסַפְתִּי אֶת־שְׁלוֹמִי מֵאֵת הָעָם
ו הַזֶּה נְאֻם־יְהוָה אֶת־הַחֶסֶד וְאֶת־הָרַחֲמִים׃ וּמֵתוּ גְדֹלִים וּקְטַנִּים
בָּאָרֶץ הַזֹּאת לֹא יִקָּבֵרוּ וְלֹא־יִסְפְּדוּ לָהֶם וְלֹא יִתְגֹּדַד וְלֹא יִקָּרֵחַ
ז לָהֶם׃ וְלֹא־יִפְרְסוּ לָהֶם עַל־אֵבֶל לְנַחֲמוֹ עַל־מֵת וְלֹא־יַשְׁקוּ אוֹתָם
ח כּוֹס תַּנְחוּמִים עַל־אָבִיו וְעַל־אִמּוֹ׃ וּבֵית־מִשְׁתֶּה לֹא־תָבוֹא לָשֶׁבֶת
ט אוֹתָם לֶאֱכֹל וְלִשְׁתּוֹת׃ כִּי כֹה אָמַר יְהוָה צְבָאוֹת
אֱלֹהֵי יִשְׂרָאֵל הִנְנִי מַשְׁבִּית מִן־הַמָּקוֹם הַזֶּה לְעֵינֵיכֶם וּבִימֵיכֶם קוֹל
י שָׂשׂוֹן וְקוֹל שִׂמְחָה קוֹל חָתָן וְקוֹל כַּלָּה׃ וְהָיָה כִּי תַגִּיד לָעָם הַזֶּה אֵת
כָּל־הַדְּבָרִים הָאֵלֶּה וְאָמְרוּ אֵלֶיךָ עַל־מֶה דִבֶּר יְהוָה עָלֵינוּ אֵת כָּל־
הָרָעָה הַגְּדוֹלָה הַזֹּאת וּמֶה עֲוֹנֵנוּ וּמֶה חַטָּאתֵנוּ אֲשֶׁר חָטָאנוּ לַיהוָה
יא אֱלֹהֵינוּ׃ וְאָמַרְתָּ אֲלֵיהֶם עַל אֲשֶׁר־עָזְבוּ אֲבוֹתֵיכֶם אוֹתִי נְאֻם־יְהוָה
וַיֵּלְכוּ אַחֲרֵי אֱלֹהִים אֲחֵרִים וַיַּעַבְדוּם וַיִּשְׁתַּחֲווּ לָהֶם וְאֹתִי עָזָבוּ וְאֶת־
יב תּוֹרָתִי לֹא שָׁמָרוּ׃ וְאַתֶּם הֲרֵעֹתֶם לַעֲשׂוֹת מֵאֲבוֹתֵיכֶם וְהִנְּכֶם הֹלְכִים
יג אִישׁ אַחֲרֵי שְׁרִרוּת לִבּוֹ־הָרָע לְבִלְתִּי שְׁמֹעַ אֵלָי׃ וְהֵטַלְתִּי אֶתְכֶם
מֵעַל הָאָרֶץ הַזֹּאת עַל־הָאָרֶץ אֲשֶׁר לֹא יְדַעְתֶּם אַתֶּם וַאֲבוֹתֵיכֶם
וַעֲבַדְתֶּם־שָׁם אֶת־אֱלֹהִים אֲחֵרִים יוֹמָם וָלַיְלָה אֲשֶׁר לֹא־אֶתֵּן לָכֶם
יד חֲנִינָה׃ לָכֵן הִנֵּה־יָמִים בָּאִים נְאֻם־יְהוָה וְלֹא־
יֵאָמֵר עוֹד חַי־יְהוָה אֲשֶׁר הֶעֱלָה אֶת־בְּנֵי יִשְׂרָאֵל מֵאֶרֶץ מִצְרָיִם׃
טו כִּי אִם־חַי־יְהוָה אֲשֶׁר הֶעֱלָה אֶת־בְּנֵי יִשְׂרָאֵל מֵאֶרֶץ צָפוֹן וּמִכֹּל
הָאֲרָצוֹת אֲשֶׁר הִדִּיחָם שָׁמָּה וַהֲשִׁבֹתִים עַל־אַדְמָתָם אֲשֶׁר נָתַתִּי

16 fathers. I am about to send for many fishermen, declares the LORD,
and they will fish for them. Afterward I will send for many hunters, and they
will hunt them down from atop every mountain and from atop every hill and
17 from the crevices in the rocks. For My eyes are upon all their ways; they are
not hidden from My presence, and their sins are not concealed from before
18 My eyes. I will first exact retribution for double their transgressions and sins –
for defiling My land with the carcasses of their repulsive things and their
19 abominations with which they filled My inheritance. The
LORD is my strength and my might, my refuge in a day of trouble. To You
the nations will come from the ends of the earth, and they will say: "Our
20 ancestors inherited nothing but falsehood, futility, and things of no use. Can
21 a human make gods for himself when they are not gods?" Therefore, I
am about to make them know; this time I will make them know of My
power and My strength, and they shall come to know that My name is the
17 1 LORD. Yehuda's sin is written with an iron pen with a diamond point,
engraved upon the tablets of their hearts and upon the corners of your altars.
2 As they yearn for their children, so do they for their altars and their sacred trees[45]
3 beside verdant trees upon the high hills. Mountain dweller[46] – because of the
sin of your high places in all your territories, I will turn your wealth and all your
4 treasures into booty upon the field. You will forfeit, by your own fault, the
heritage which I have given you. I will make you a slave to your enemies in a
land that you never knew, for you kindled a fire in My nostrils which shall blaze
5 forever. This is what the LORD said: Cursed is he who trusts in man,
who makes flesh his strength and who turns his heart away from the LORD.
6 He will be like a shrub in the desert, never witnessing prosperity. He will
7 dwell scorched in the wilderness, a salty, uninhabited land. Blessed
8 is the person who trusts in the LORD. The LORD will be his protector. He will
be like a tree planted beside the water, its roots spreading along the stream. It
need not be concerned when heat comes, for its leaves will remain verdant.
It need not worry in a year of drought, for it will never cease to produce fruit.
9 More devious is the heart than all else, and it is hopelessly sick. Who can
10 know it? I, the LORD, search out the heart and examine inner thoughts so as
to treat each person according to his ways, according to the fruits of his
11 actions. Like the bird that hatches what she did not lay, so is he who
accumulated his wealth unjustly. After half of his days, his fortune will leave
12 him, and in the end he will be proven a fool. Like the throne of glory, elevated
13 from the beginning, so is the place of our Temple. The hope of Israel is the
LORD. All who forsake You will be humiliated. Those who stray from Me will
be written in the earth, for they have forsaken the source of living waters,
14 declares the LORD. Heal me, LORD, so that I may be healed. Save
15 me so that I may be saved, for it is You whom I praise. "See," they say to me,
16 "where is the LORD's word? Let it come now!" I did not rush to serve as Your

45 | Used in the worship of the goddess Ashera.
46 | Jerusalem is situated in the mountains of Yehuda.

טו לַאֲבוֹתָם׃ הִנְנִי שֹׁלֵחַ לדוגים רַבִּים נְאֻם־יְהוָה לְדַיָּגִים
וְדִיגוּם וְאַחֲרֵי־כֵן אֶשְׁלַח לְרַבִּים צַיָּדִים וְצָדוּם מֵעַל כָּל־הַר וּמֵעַל
יז כָּל־גִּבְעָה וּמִנְּקִיקֵי הַסְּלָעִים׃ כִּי עֵינַי עַל־כָּל־דַּרְכֵיהֶם לֹא נִסְתְּרוּ
יח מִלְּפָנָי וְלֹא־נִצְפַּן עֲוֺנָם מִנֶּגֶד עֵינָי׃ וְשִׁלַּמְתִּי רִאשׁוֹנָה מִשְׁנֵה עֲוֺנָם
וְחַטָּאתָם עַל חַלְּלָם אֶת־אַרְצִי בְּנִבְלַת שִׁקּוּצֵיהֶם וְתוֹעֲבוֹתֵיהֶם
יט מָלְאוּ אֶת־נַחֲלָתִי׃ יְהוָה עֻזִּי וּמָעֻזִּי וּמְנוּסִי בְּיוֹם צָרָה
אֵלֶיךָ גּוֹיִם יָבֹאוּ מֵאַפְסֵי־אָרֶץ וְיֹאמְרוּ אַךְ־שֶׁקֶר נָחֲלוּ אֲבוֹתֵינוּ הֶבֶל
כ כא וְאֵין־בָּם מוֹעִיל׃ הֲיַעֲשֶׂה־לּוֹ אָדָם אֱלֹהִים וְהֵמָּה לֹא אֱלֹהִים׃ לָכֵן
הִנְנִי מוֹדִיעָם בַּפַּעַם הַזֹּאת אוֹדִיעֵם אֶת־יָדִי וְאֶת־גְּבוּרָתִי וְיָדְעוּ כִּי־
יז א שְׁמִי יְהוָה׃ חַטַּאת יְהוּדָה כְּתוּבָה בְּעֵט בַּרְזֶל בְּצִפֹּרֶן
ב שָׁמִיר חֲרוּשָׁה עַל־לוּחַ לִבָּם וּלְקַרְנוֹת מִזְבְּחוֹתֵיכֶם׃ כִּזְכֹּר בְּנֵיהֶם
ג מִזְבְּחוֹתָם וַאֲשֵׁרֵיהֶם עַל־עֵץ רַעֲנָן עַל גְּבָעוֹת הַגְּבֹהוֹת׃ הֲרָרִי
בַּשָּׂדֶה חֵילְךָ כָל־אוֹצְרוֹתֶיךָ לָבַז אֶתֵּן בָּמֹתֶיךָ בְּחַטָּאת בְּכָל־גְּבוּלֶיךָ׃
ד וְשָׁמַטְתָּה וּבְךָ מִנַּחֲלָתְךָ אֲשֶׁר נָתַתִּי לָךְ וְהַעֲבַדְתִּיךָ אֶת־אֹיְבֶיךָ בָּאָרֶץ
ה אֲשֶׁר לֹא־יָדָעְתָּ כִּי־אֵשׁ קְדַחְתֶּם בְּאַפִּי עַד־עוֹלָם תּוּקָד׃ כֹּה ׀
אָמַר יְהוָה אָרוּר הַגֶּבֶר אֲשֶׁר יִבְטַח בָּאָדָם וְשָׂם בָּשָׂר זְרֹעוֹ וּמִן־יְהוָה
ו יָסוּר לִבּוֹ׃ וְהָיָה כְּעַרְעָר בָּעֲרָבָה וְלֹא יִרְאֶה כִּי־יָבוֹא טוֹב וְשָׁכַן חֲרֵרִים
ז בַּמִּדְבָּר אֶרֶץ מְלֵחָה וְלֹא תֵשֵׁב׃ בָּרוּךְ הַגֶּבֶר אֲשֶׁר ט
ח יִבְטַח בַּיהוָה וְהָיָה יְהוָה מִבְטַחוֹ׃ וְהָיָה כְּעֵץ ׀ שָׁתוּל עַל־מַיִם וְעַל־
יוּבַל יְשַׁלַּח שָׁרָשָׁיו וְלֹא יִרְא כִּי־יָבֹא חֹם וְהָיָה עָלֵהוּ רַעֲנָן וּבִשְׁנַת
ט בַּצֹּרֶת לֹא יִדְאָג וְלֹא יָמִישׁ מֵעֲשׂוֹת פֶּרִי׃ עָקֹב הַלֵּב מִכֹּל וְאָנֻשׁ הוּא
י מִי יֵדָעֶנּוּ׃ אֲנִי יְהוָה חֹקֵר לֵב בֹּחֵן כְּלָיוֹת וְלָתֵת לְאִישׁ כִּדְרָכָו כִּפְרִי
יא מַעֲלָלָיו׃ קֹרֵא דָגַר וְלֹא יָלָד עֹשֶׂה עֹשֶׁר וְלֹא בְמִשְׁפָּט
יב בַּחֲצִי יָמָו יַעַזְבֶנּוּ וּבְאַחֲרִיתוֹ יִהְיֶה נָבָל׃ כִּסֵּא כָבוֹד מָרוֹם מֵרִאשׁוֹן
יג מְקוֹם מִקְדָּשֵׁנוּ׃ מִקְוֵה יִשְׂרָאֵל יְהוָה כָּל־עֹזְבֶיךָ יֵבֹשׁוּ יסורי בָּאָרֶץ וְסוּרַי
יד יִכָּתֵבוּ כִּי עָזְבוּ מְקוֹר מַיִם־חַיִּים אֶת־יְהוָה׃ רְפָאֵנִי יְהוָה
טו וְאֵרָפֵא הוֹשִׁיעֵנִי וְאִוָּשֵׁעָה כִּי תְהִלָּתִי אָתָּה׃ הִנֵּה־הֵמָּה אֹמְרִים אֵלָי
טז אַיֵּה דְבַר־יְהוָה יָבוֹא נָא׃ וַאֲנִי לֹא־אַצְתִּי ׀ מֵרֹעֶה אַחֲרֶיךָ וְיוֹם אָנוּשׁ

shepherd, and I did not desire that fateful day.[47] You know that! The utterance
17 of my lips was apparent to You. Do not be a source of terror for me; You are
18 my protection in a day of evil. Let my pursuers be humiliated, but let me not
be humiliated. Let them be terrified, but let me not be terrified. Bring upon
19 them the day of evil and shatter them repeatedly. This is what the
LORD said to me: "Go and stand in the people's gate where the kings of
Yehuda enter and through which they leave, and in all the gates of Jerusalem.
20 Say to them: Listen to the LORD, you kings of Yehuda, and all of Yehuda, and
21 all the inhabitants of Jerusalem who enter through these gates. This is what
the LORD said: Be careful for your lives, and do not carry any burden on the
22 Sabbath day, nor bring them into the gates of Jerusalem. Do not bring out a
burden from your houses on the Sabbath day, perform no work, and hallow
23 the Sabbath day, as I commanded your fathers." But they did not listen nor
even bend an ear. They stiffened their necks so as not to listen and so as not
24 to take instruction. If you obey Me, declares the LORD, so as not to bring any
burden through the gates of this city on the Sabbath day, and you hallow the
25 Sabbath day, so as not to perform any work on it, then through the gates of
this city shall come kings and princes, those sitting upon the throne of David,
riding chariots and horses, they and their princes, men of Yehuda and
26 dwellers in Jerusalem, and this city shall dwell forever. They shall come from
the towns of Yehuda and the environs of Jerusalem, from the land of Binyamin,
from the lowland and from the mountain and from the south, bringing
burnt offerings and sacrifices, grain offerings and frankincense, and bearing
27 thanksgiving offerings to the House of the LORD. But if you do not obey
Me to hallow the Sabbath day, so as not to carry in any burden through
the gates of Jerusalem on the Sabbath day, then I will send a fire against
her gates, and it will consume the fortresses of Jerusalem and not be extin-
18 1 guished. The word that came to Yirmeyahu from the LORD:
2 "Rise and go down to the house of the potter; there I will tell you My words."
3 So I went down to the potter's house and found him doing work upon his
4 wheel. Whenever the vessel that he was fashioning of clay would break in the
hands of the potter, he would remake it into a different vessel such as it
5 6 pleased the potter to fashion. The LORD's word came to me:
"Can I not do to you, House of Israel," declares the LORD, "what this potter
does? Like clay in the hand of the potter, so are you in My hand, House of
7 Israel. At one moment I may decree that a nation or a kingdom be
8 uprooted, shattered, and destroyed. But should that nation turn back because
of the evil that I pronounced upon it, I change My mind concerning the evil
9 that I had planned to do to it. And at one moment I may decree that
10 a nation or a kingdom be built and planted. But if it does what is evil in My
eyes, not heeding My voice, I change My mind about the good that I had
11 thought to bestow upon it. Now, tell the men of Yehuda and those who dwell

47 | When I was called to prophecy.

יז לֹא הִתְאַוֵּיתִי אַתָּה יָדָעְתָּ מוֹצָא שְׂפָתַי נֹכַח פָּנֶיךָ הָיָה׃ אַל־תִּהְיֵה־
יח לִי לִמְחִתָּה מַחְסִי־אַתָּה בְּיוֹם רָעָה׃ יֵבֹשׁוּ רֹדְפַי וְאַל־אֵבֹשָׁה אָנִי
יֵחַתּוּ הֵמָּה וְאַל־אֵחַתָּה אָנִי הָבִיא עֲלֵיהֶם יוֹם רָעָה וּמִשְׁנֶה שִׁבָּרוֹן
יט שָׁבְרֵם׃ כֹּה־אָמַר יהוה אֵלַי הָלֹךְ וְעָמַדְתָּ
בְּשַׁעַר בְּנֵי־עָם אֲשֶׁר יָבֹאוּ בוֹ מַלְכֵי יְהוּדָה וַאֲשֶׁר יֵצְאוּ בוֹ וּבְכֹל הָעָם
כ שַׁעֲרֵי יְרוּשָׁלָםִ׃ וְאָמַרְתָּ אֲלֵיהֶם שִׁמְעוּ דְבַר־יהוה מַלְכֵי יְהוּדָה וְכָל־
כא יְהוּדָה וְכֹל יֹשְׁבֵי יְרוּשָׁלָםִ הַבָּאִים בַּשְּׁעָרִים הָאֵלֶּה׃ כֹּה אָמַר יהוה
הִשָּׁמְרוּ בְּנַפְשׁוֹתֵיכֶם וְאַל־תִּשְׂאוּ מַשָּׂא בְּיוֹם הַשַּׁבָּת וַהֲבֵאתֶם בְּשַׁעֲרֵי
כב יְרוּשָׁלָםִ׃ וְלֹא־תוֹצִיאוּ מַשָּׂא מִבָּתֵּיכֶם בְּיוֹם הַשַּׁבָּת וְכָל־מְלָאכָה לֹא
כג תַעֲשׂוּ וְקִדַּשְׁתֶּם אֶת־יוֹם הַשַּׁבָּת כַּאֲשֶׁר צִוִּיתִי אֶת־אֲבוֹתֵיכֶם׃ וְלֹא
שָׁמְעוּ וְלֹא הִטּוּ אֶת־אָזְנָם וַיַּקְשׁוּ אֶת־עָרְפָּם לְבִלְתִּי שומע וּלְבִלְתִּי שְׁמוֹעַ
כד קַחַת מוּסָר׃ וְהָיָה אִם־שָׁמֹעַ תִּשְׁמְעוּן אֵלַי נְאֻם־יהוה לְבִלְתִּי ׀ הָבִיא
מַשָּׂא בְּשַׁעֲרֵי הָעִיר הַזֹּאת בְּיוֹם הַשַּׁבָּת וּלְקַדֵּשׁ אֶת־יוֹם הַשַּׁבָּת
כה לְבִלְתִּי עֲשׂוֹת־בּוֹ כָּל־מְלָאכָה׃ וּבָאוּ בְשַׁעֲרֵי הָעִיר הַזֹּאת מְלָכִים ׀
וְשָׂרִים יֹשְׁבִים עַל־כִּסֵּא דָוִד רֹכְבִים ׀ בָּרֶכֶב וּבַסּוּסִים הֵמָּה וְשָׂרֵיהֶם
כו אִישׁ יְהוּדָה וְיֹשְׁבֵי יְרוּשָׁלָםִ וְיָשְׁבָה הָעִיר הַזֹּאת לְעוֹלָם׃ וּבָאוּ מֵעָרֵי־
יְהוּדָה וּמִסְּבִיבוֹת יְרוּשָׁלַםִ וּמֵאֶרֶץ בִּנְיָמִן וּמִן־הַשְּׁפֵלָה וּמִן־הָהָר
וּמִן־הַנֶּגֶב מְבִאִים עֹלָה וְזֶבַח וּמִנְחָה וּלְבוֹנָה וּמְבִאֵי תוֹדָה בֵּית
כז יהוה׃ וְאִם־לֹא תִשְׁמְעוּ אֵלַי לְקַדֵּשׁ אֶת־יוֹם הַשַּׁבָּת וּלְבִלְתִּי ׀ שְׂאֵת
מַשָּׂא וּבֹא בְּשַׁעֲרֵי יְרוּשָׁלַםִ בְּיוֹם הַשַּׁבָּת וְהִצַּתִּי אֵשׁ בִּשְׁעָרֶיהָ וְאָכְלָה
יח א אַרְמְנוֹת יְרוּשָׁלַםִ וְלֹא תִכְבֶּה׃ הַדָּבָר אֲשֶׁר הָיָה אֶל־
ב יִרְמְיָהוּ מֵאֵת יהוה לֵאמֹר׃ קוּם וְיָרַדְתָּ בֵּית הַיּוֹצֵר וְשָׁמָּה אַשְׁמִיעֲךָ
ג אֶת־דְּבָרָי׃ וָאֵרֵד בֵּית הַיּוֹצֵר והנהו עֹשֶׂה מְלָאכָה עַל־הָאָבְנָיִם׃ וְהִנֵּה־הוּא
ד וְנִשְׁחַת הַכְּלִי אֲשֶׁר הוּא עֹשֶׂה בַּחֹמֶר בְּיַד הַיּוֹצֵר וְשָׁב וַיַּעֲשֵׂהוּ כְּלִי
ה אַחֵר כַּאֲשֶׁר יָשַׁר בְּעֵינֵי הַיּוֹצֵר לַעֲשׂוֹת׃ וַיְהִי
ו דְבַר־יהוה אֵלַי לֵאמוֹר׃ הֲכַיּוֹצֵר הַזֶּה לֹא־אוּכַל לַעֲשׂוֹת לָכֶם בֵּית
יִשְׂרָאֵל נְאֻם־יהוה הִנֵּה כַחֹמֶר בְּיַד הַיּוֹצֵר כֵּן־אַתֶּם בְּיָדִי בֵּית
ז יִשְׂרָאֵל׃ רֶגַע אֲדַבֵּר עַל־גּוֹי וְעַל־מַמְלָכָה לִנְתוֹשׁ
ח וְלִנְתוֹץ וּלְהַאֲבִיד׃ וְשָׁב הַגּוֹי הַהוּא מֵרָעָתוֹ אֲשֶׁר דִּבַּרְתִּי עָלָיו וְנִחַמְתִּי
ט עַל־הָרָעָה אֲשֶׁר חָשַׁבְתִּי לַעֲשׂוֹת לוֹ׃ וְרֶגַע אֲדַבֵּר עַל־
י גּוֹי וְעַל־מַמְלָכָה לִבְנֹת וְלִנְטֹעַ׃ וְעָשָׂה הרעה בְּעֵינַי לְבִלְתִּי שְׁמֹעַ הָרַע
יא בְּקוֹלִי וְנִחַמְתִּי עַל־הַטּוֹבָה אֲשֶׁר אָמַרְתִּי לְהֵיטִיב אוֹתוֹ׃ וְעַתָּה

in Jerusalem that this is what the LORD said: I am about to fashion[48] a disaster
for you, and I am devising a plan against you. Return now, each of you from
12 his evil way, and mend your ways and your actions. But they will say, 'It is
futile. We will follow our own plans, and each of us will do as his evil heart
13 sees fit.'" This is what the LORD therefore said: "Inquire now among
the nations: Who has heard of such things? She has committed a terrible
14 scandal, maiden Israel. Would one forsake the snow from Lebanon now
flowing among the rocks in My field? Would waters from afar, cold and
15 flowing, be abandoned? For My people have forgotten Me. They offer incense
to vanity. They were made to stumble in their ways and forsake the ancient
16 paths, to walk on byways, on a way not cleared of stones, to make their land
a desolation, a place of perpetual hissing. Every passerby will gasp and shake
17 his head. Like the east wind I will scatter them before the enemy. I will look
18 upon their neck and not upon their face on their fateful day." They
said, "Let us devise plans against Yirmeyahu, for surely the Law will not cease
from the priest, nor counsel from the wise man, nor the word from the
prophet. Let us go and strike him with the tongue so that we need no longer
19 listen to all his words." LORD, listen to me and hear the voice of my adversaries.
20 Will good be repaid with evil? They dug a pit to kill me. Remember how I
stood before You to speak well of them, to remove Your anger from them?
21 Therefore, give their children over to hunger. Let their blood flow by the hand
of the sword. May their women become childless, bereaved, and widowed,
their men slain by pestilence, and their young men struck down in battle
22 by the sword. May a scream be heard from their houses when You bring
troops upon them suddenly, for they have dug a pit to trap me and hidden
23 snares for my feet. You, LORD, know all their schemes to kill me. Do not
forgive their iniquity. Do not erase their sin from Your presence, and may
they be made to stumble before You. Act against them in Your moment of
19 1 wrath. This is what the LORD said: "Go along with some of the elders
2 of the people and some of the elders of the priests, and get a potter's jug. Then
go out to the Valley of Ben Hinom – it is by the entry to the Potsherd Gate –
3 and there proclaim the words which I will speak to you. Say: Hear the word
of the LORD, kings of Yehuda and residents of Jerusalem. This is what the
LORD of Hosts, the God of Israel, has said: I am about to bring such evil upon
4 this place that the ears of all who hear of it shall ring, because they have
abandoned Me and made this into an alien place. They sacrificed there to
other gods whom neither they nor their ancestors nor the kings of Yehuda
5 ever knew. They filled this place with the blood of innocents. They built altars
for the Baal, to burn their children in fire as burnt offerings to the Baal –
something I never commanded or spoke about and that never entered My
6 mind. Therefore, days are soon coming, declares the LORD, when
this place will no longer be called the Tofet or the Valley of Ben Hinom, but
7 rather the Valley of Slaughter. I will spoil the scheme of Yehuda and Jerusalem
in this place. I will cause them to fall by the sword before their enemies, into

48 | Hebrew *yotzer*, which also means "potter" in the preceding verses.

אֱמָר־נָא אֶל־אִישׁ יְהוּדָה וְעַל־יוֹשְׁבֵי יְרוּשָׁלִַם לֵאמֹר כֹּה אָמַר יְהוָה
הִנֵּה אָנֹכִי יוֹצֵר עֲלֵיכֶם רָעָה וְחֹשֵׁב עֲלֵיכֶם מַחֲשָׁבָה שׁוּבוּ נָא אִישׁ
יב מִדַּרְכּוֹ הָרָעָה וְהֵיטִיבוּ דַרְכֵיכֶם וּמַעַלְלֵיכֶם: וְאָמְרוּ נוֹאָשׁ כִּי־אַחֲרֵי
יג מַחְשְׁבוֹתֵינוּ נֵלֵךְ וְאִישׁ שְׁרִרוּת לִבּוֹ־הָרָע נַעֲשֶׂה: לָכֵן כֹּה
אָמַר יְהוָה שַׁאֲלוּ־נָא בַּגּוֹיִם מִי שָׁמַע כָּאֵלֶּה שַׁעֲרֻרִת עָשְׂתָה מְאֹד
יד בְּתוּלַת יִשְׂרָאֵל: הֲיַעֲזֹב מִצּוּר שָׂדַי שֶׁלֶג לְבָנוֹן אִם־יִנָּתְשׁוּ מַיִם זָרִים
טו קָרִים נוֹזְלִים: כִּי־שְׁכֵחֻנִי עַמִּי לַשָּׁוְא יְקַטֵּרוּ וַיַּכְשִׁלוּם בְּדַרְכֵיהֶם שבולי שְׁבִילֵי
טז עוֹלָם לָלֶכֶת נְתִיבוֹת דֶּרֶךְ לֹא סְלוּלָה: לָשׂוּם אַרְצָם לְשַׁמָּה שרוקת שְׁרִיקוֹת
יז עוֹלָם כֹּל עוֹבֵר עָלֶיהָ יִשֹּׁם וְיָנִיד בְּרֹאשׁוֹ: כְּרוּחַ־קָדִים אֲפִיצֵם לִפְנֵי
יח אוֹיֵב עֹרֶף וְלֹא־פָנִים אַרְאֵם בְּיוֹם אֵידָם: וַיֹּאמְרוּ לְכוּ
וְנַחְשְׁבָה עַל־יִרְמְיָהוּ מַחֲשָׁבוֹת כִּי לֹא־תֹאבַד תּוֹרָה מִכֹּהֵן וְעֵצָה
מֵחָכָם וְדָבָר מִנָּבִיא לְכוּ וְנַכֵּהוּ בַלָּשׁוֹן וְאַל־נַקְשִׁיבָה אֶל־כָּל־דְּבָרָיו:
יט כ הַקְשִׁיבָה יְהוָה אֵלָי וּשְׁמַע לְקוֹל יְרִיבָי: הַיְשֻׁלַּם תַּחַת־טוֹבָה רָעָה
כִּי־כָרוּ שׁוּחָה לְנַפְשִׁי זְכֹר | עָמְדִי לְפָנֶיךָ לְדַבֵּר עֲלֵיהֶם טוֹבָה לְהָשִׁיב
כא אֶת־חֲמָתְךָ מֵהֶם: לָכֵן תֵּן אֶת־בְּנֵיהֶם לָרָעָב וְהַגִּרֵם עַל־יְדֵי־חֶרֶב
וְתִהְיֶנָה נְשֵׁיהֶם שַׁכֻּלוֹת וְאַלְמָנוֹת וְאַנְשֵׁיהֶם יִהְיוּ הֲרֻגֵי מָוֶת בַּחוּרֵיהֶם
כב מֻכֵּי־חֶרֶב בַּמִּלְחָמָה: תִּשָּׁמַע זְעָקָה מִבָּתֵּיהֶם כִּי־תָבִיא עֲלֵיהֶם גְּדוּד
כג פִּתְאֹם כִּי־כָרוּ שיחה לְלָכְדֵנִי וּפַחִים טָמְנוּ לְרַגְלָי: וְאַתָּה יְהוָה יָדַעְתָּ שׁוּחָה
אֶת־כָּל־עֲצָתָם עָלַי לַמָּוֶת אַל־תְּכַפֵּר עַל־עֲוֺנָם וְחַטָּאתָם מִלְּפָנֶיךָ
יט א אַל־תֶּמְחִי והיו מֻכְשָׁלִים לְפָנֶיךָ בְּעֵת אַפְּךָ עֲשֵׂה בָהֶם: כֹּה וְיִהְיוּ
אָמַר יְהוָה הָלֹךְ וְקָנִיתָ בַקְבֻּק יוֹצֵר חָרֶשׂ וּמִזִּקְנֵי הָעָם וּמִזִּקְנֵי הַכֹּהֲנִים:
ב וְיָצָאתָ אֶל־גֵּיא בֶן־הִנֹּם אֲשֶׁר פֶּתַח שַׁעַר החרסות וְקָרָאתָ שָּׁם אֶת־ הַחַרְסִית
ג הַדְּבָרִים אֲשֶׁר־אֲדַבֵּר אֵלֶיךָ: וְאָמַרְתָּ שִׁמְעוּ דְבַר־יְהוָה מַלְכֵי יְהוּדָה
וְיֹשְׁבֵי יְרוּשָׁלִָם כֹּה־אָמַר יְהוָה צְבָאוֹת אֱלֹהֵי יִשְׂרָאֵל הִנְנִי מֵבִיא
ד רָעָה עַל־הַמָּקוֹם הַזֶּה אֲשֶׁר כָּל־שֹׁמְעָהּ תִּצַּלְנָה אָזְנָיו: יַעַן | אֲשֶׁר
עֲזָבֻנִי וַיְנַכְּרוּ אֶת־הַמָּקוֹם הַזֶּה וַיְקַטְּרוּ־בוֹ לֵאלֹהִים אֲחֵרִים אֲשֶׁר
לֹא־יְדָעוּם הֵמָּה וַאֲבוֹתֵיהֶם וּמַלְכֵי יְהוּדָה וּמָלְאוּ אֶת־הַמָּקוֹם הַזֶּה
ה דַּם נְקִיִּם: וּבָנוּ אֶת־בָּמוֹת הַבַּעַל לִשְׂרֹף אֶת־בְּנֵיהֶם בָּאֵשׁ עֹלוֹת לַבָּעַל
ו אֲשֶׁר לֹא־צִוִּיתִי וְלֹא דִבַּרְתִּי וְלֹא עָלְתָה עַל־לִבִּי: לָכֵן
הִנֵּה־יָמִים בָּאִים נְאֻם־יְהוָה וְלֹא־יִקָּרֵא לַמָּקוֹם הַזֶּה עוֹד הַתֹּפֶת
ז וְגֵיא בֶן־הִנֹּם כִּי אִם־גֵּיא הַהֲרֵגָה: וּבַקֹּתִי אֶת־עֲצַת יְהוּדָה וִירוּשָׁלִַם
בַּמָּקוֹם הַזֶּה וְהִפַּלְתִּים בַּחֶרֶב לִפְנֵי אֹיְבֵיהֶם וּבְיַד מְבַקְשֵׁי נַפְשָׁם וְנָתַתִּי

the hands of those who seek their lives. I will give their carcasses as food to
8 the birds of the heavens and the beasts of the earth. I will make of this city a
place of desolation and shrieking, for everyone who passes it by will be
9 horrified and will shriek over all its wounds. I will make them eat the flesh of
their sons and the flesh of their daughters. Everyone will devour the flesh of
his fellow during the siege and in the plight inflicted upon them by their
10 enemies, by those that seek their lives. Then smash the jug in front of those
11 who accompanied you. Say to them: This is what the Lord of Hosts said:
This is how I will smash this people and this city, as one smashes a potter's
vessel, so that it can never again be repaired. They will be buried in the Tofet,
12 there being no place to bury them elsewhere. This is what I will do to this
place," declares the Lord, "and to its residents. This city will become a Tofet.[49]
13 The houses of Jerusalem and the houses of the kings of Yehuda will become
impure like the place of the Tofet – all those houses where they offered
sacrifices on their rooftops to all the hosts of heaven and poured libations to
14 other gods." Yirmeyahu returned from the Tofet, where the Lord
had sent him to prophesy, and he stood in the court of the House of the Lord
15 and said to all the people: "This is what the Lord of Hosts, the
God of Israel, said: I am about to bring upon this city and upon all of her
surrounding cities all the evil which I have decreed against her. For they have
20 1 stiffened their necks so as not to heed My words." Pashḥur son of Imer the
priest, a high official in the House of the Lord, heard Yirmeyahu prophesying
2 these words. Pashḥur struck Yirmeyahu the prophet and placed him in the
stocks that were in the upper Binyamin Gate, that was in the House of the
3 Lord. The next day Pashḥur released Yirmeyahu from the stocks, whereupon
Yirmeyahu said to him, "The Lord did not call your name Pashḥur, but rather
4 Terror All Around.[50] For this is what the Lord said: I am about to
make of you a source of terror for yourself and for all your friends. They will
fall before the sword of their enemies as your eyes look on. I will deliver all
of Yehuda into the hand of the king of Babylon. Some he will exile to Babylon;
5 others he will slay by the sword. I will deliver all the wealth of this city – all
the fruit of its toil and all it holds dear and all the treasures of the kings
of Yehuda – into the hands of their enemies. They will plunder them and
6 confiscate them and bring them to Babylon. You, Pashḥur, and your entire
household will go into captivity. You will come to Babylon. There you will
die, and there you will be buried, you and all your friends for whom you
7 prophesied falsely." You persuaded me, Lord, and I let myself
be persuaded. You overpowered me, and You prevailed. I have become a
8 laughingstock all day long: they all mock me. For whenever I speak prophecy,
I shout; I call out, Injustice! Violence! The Lord's word has brought upon
9 me derision and scorn all day long. I said to myself: I will not make mention

49 | See 7:31.

50 | The name Pashḥur can have any of several positive meanings, e.g., *pash* meaning "great" and *ḥur* meaning "nobleman." Or it can be interpreted negatively: *pash* meaning "many (enemies)" and *seḥor* meaning "all around."

ח אֶת־נִבְלָתָם לְמַאֲכָל לְעוֹף הַשָּׁמַיִם וּלְבֶהֱמַת הָאָרֶץ: וְשַׂמְתִּי אֶת־
הָעִיר הַזֹּאת לְשַׁמָּה וְלִשְׁרֵקָה כֹּל עֹבֵר עָלֶיהָ יִשֹּׁם וְיִשְׁרֹק עַל־כָּל־
ט מַכֹּתֶהָ: וְהַאֲכַלְתִּים אֶת־בְּשַׂר בְּנֵיהֶם וְאֵת בְּשַׂר בְּנֹתֵיהֶם וְאִישׁ
בְּשַׂר־רֵעֵהוּ יֹאכֵלוּ בְּמָצוֹר וּבְמָצוֹק אֲשֶׁר יָצִיקוּ לָהֶם אֹיְבֵיהֶם וּמְבַקְשֵׁי
י יא נַפְשָׁם: וְשָׁבַרְתָּ הַבַּקְבֻּק לְעֵינֵי הָאֲנָשִׁים הַהֹלְכִים אוֹתָךְ: וְאָמַרְתָּ
אֲלֵיהֶם כֹּה־אָמַר ׀ יְהוָה צְבָאוֹת כָּכָה אֶשְׁבֹּר אֶת־הָעָם הַזֶּה
וְאֶת־הָעִיר הַזֹּאת כַּאֲשֶׁר יִשְׁבֹּר אֶת־כְּלִי הַיּוֹצֵר אֲשֶׁר לֹא־יוּכַל
יב לְהֵרָפֵה עוֹד וּבְתֹפֶת יִקְבְּרוּ מֵאֵין מָקוֹם לִקְבּוֹר: כֵּן־אֶעֱשֶׂה לַמָּקוֹם
יג הַזֶּה נְאֻם־יְהוָה וּלְיוֹשְׁבָיו וְלָתֵת אֶת־הָעִיר הַזֹּאת כְּתֹפֶת: וְהָיוּ
בָּתֵּי יְרוּשָׁלַםִ וּבָתֵּי מַלְכֵי יְהוּדָה כִּמְקוֹם הַתֹּפֶת הַטְּמֵאִים לְכֹל
הַבָּתִּים אֲשֶׁר קִטְּרוּ עַל־גַּגֹּתֵיהֶם לְכֹל צְבָא הַשָּׁמַיִם וְהַסֵּךְ נְסָכִים
יד לֵאלֹהִים אֲחֵרִים: וַיָּבֹא יִרְמְיָהוּ מֵהַתֹּפֶת אֲשֶׁר
שְׁלָחוֹ יְהוָה שָׁם לְהִנָּבֵא וַיַּעֲמֹד בַּחֲצַר בֵּית־יְהוָה וַיֹּאמֶר אֶל־כָּל־
טו הָעָם: כֹּה־אָמַר יְהוָה צְבָאוֹת אֱלֹהֵי יִשְׂרָאֵל הִנְנִי מֵבִי
אֶל־הָעִיר הַזֹּאת וְעַל־כָּל־עָרֶיהָ אֵת כָּל־הָרָעָה אֲשֶׁר דִּבַּרְתִּי עָלֶיהָ
כ א כִּי הִקְשׁוּ אֶת־עָרְפָּם לְבִלְתִּי שְׁמוֹעַ אֶת־דְּבָרָי: וַיִּשְׁמַע פַּשְׁחוּר בֶּן־אִמֵּר
הַכֹּהֵן וְהוּא־פָקִיד נָגִיד בְּבֵית יְהוָה אֶת־יִרְמְיָהוּ נִבָּא אֶת־הַדְּבָרִים
ב הָאֵלֶּה: וַיַּכֶּה פַשְׁחוּר אֵת יִרְמְיָהוּ הַנָּבִיא וַיִּתֵּן אֹתוֹ עַל־הַמַּהְפֶּכֶת
ג אֲשֶׁר בְּשַׁעַר בִּנְיָמִן הָעֶלְיוֹן אֲשֶׁר בְּבֵית יְהוָה: וַיְהִי מִמָּחֳרָת וַיֹּצֵא
פַשְׁחוּר אֶת־יִרְמְיָהוּ מִן־הַמַּהְפָּכֶת וַיֹּאמֶר אֵלָיו יִרְמְיָהוּ לֹא פַשְׁחוּר
ד קָרָא יְהוָה שְׁמֶךָ כִּי אִם־מָגוֹר מִסָּבִיב: כִּי כֹה אָמַר
יְהוָה הִנְנִי נֹתֶנְךָ לְמָגוֹר לְךָ וּלְכָל־אֹהֲבֶיךָ וְנָפְלוּ בְּחֶרֶב אֹיְבֵיהֶם וְעֵינֶיךָ
רֹאוֹת וְאֶת־כָּל־יְהוּדָה אֶתֵּן בְּיַד מֶלֶךְ־בָּבֶל וְהִגְלָם בָּבֶלָה וְהִכָּם בֶּחָרֶב:
ה וְנָתַתִּי אֶת־כָּל־חֹסֶן הָעִיר הַזֹּאת וְאֶת־כָּל־יְגִיעָהּ וְאֶת־כָּל־יְקָרָהּ
וְאֵת כָּל־אוֹצְרוֹת מַלְכֵי יְהוּדָה אֶתֵּן בְּיַד אֹיְבֵיהֶם וּבְזָזוּם וּלְקָחוּם
ו וֶהֱבִיאוּם בָּבֶלָה: וְאַתָּה פַשְׁחוּר וְכֹל יֹשְׁבֵי בֵיתֶךָ תֵּלְכוּ בַּשֶּׁבִי וּבָבֶל
תָּבוֹא וְשָׁם תָּמוּת וְשָׁם תִּקָּבֵר אַתָּה וְכָל־אֹהֲבֶיךָ אֲשֶׁר־נִבֵּאתָ לָהֶם
ז בַּשָּׁקֶר: פִּתִּיתַנִי יְהוָה וָאֶפָּת חֲזַקְתַּנִי וַתּוּכָל הָיִיתִי לִשְׂחוֹק
ח כָּל־הַיּוֹם כֻּלֹּה לֹעֵג לִי: כִּי־מִדֵּי אֲדַבֵּר אֶזְעָק חָמָס וָשֹׁד אֶקְרָא כִּי־הָיָה
ט דְבַר־יְהוָה לִי לְחֶרְפָּה וּלְקֶלֶס כָּל־הַיּוֹם: וְאָמַרְתִּי לֹא־אֶזְכְּרֶנּוּ וְלֹא־

of it. I will no longer speak in His name. But it resides within me like a flaming
10 fire, locked into my bones. I wearied of holding it back. I could not. I have
overheard the slanderous whispers, a terror all around: "Testify and let us
testify." All of my trusted friends await my collapse. They say, "Perhaps we can
11 entrap him, overcome him, and thereby take our revenge upon him." But the
LORD is with me like a mighty warrior. Therefore my pursuers will stumble
and not prevail. They will suffer great shame and not succeed, an eternal
12 disgrace, never to be forgotten. The LORD of Hosts discerns who is righteous.
He sees into both heart and mind. I will yet witness Your revenge upon them,
13 for to You I have disclosed my disputes. Sing to the LORD,
praise the LORD, for He has rescued the helpless from the hands of
14 evildoers. Cursed be the day that I was born. May the day that my
15 mother gave birth to me not be blessed. Cursed be the man who informed
16 my father, saying, "A son was born to you." He caused him so much joy. May
that man be like the cities that the LORD overturned without regret.[51] May he
17 hear shrieking each morning and sobbing in the afternoon. He should have
killed me as I left the womb. Then my mother would have been my grave and
18 her womb forever pregnant. Why did I leave the womb to see only misery
21 1 and agony? My days have ended in shame. This is the word
that came to Yirmeyahu from the LORD when King Tzidkiyahu sent him
Pashḥur son of Malkiya and Tzefanya son of Maaseya the priest. They said,
2 "Please inquire of the LORD on our behalf because Nevukhadretzar, king of
Babylon, is waging war against us. Perhaps the LORD will act with us in
accordance with all His wonders, so that our enemy will withdraw from
3 us." Yirmeyahu said to them, "This is what you shall say to
4 Tzidkiyahu: This is what the LORD, God of Israel, said: I am about to turn
back the weapons that are in your hands with which you battle the king of
Babylon and the Chaldeans[52] who are besieging you from outside the wall,
5 and I will gather them in the midst of this city. I Myself will fight you with a
hand stretched forth and a with mighty arm, with anger and wrath and rage.
6 I will smite those who dwell in this city, man and beast – they shall die by a
7 great pestilence. After that, declares the LORD, I will deliver Tzidkiyahu, king
of Yehuda, his servants, the people, and all those in this city who survive the
pestilence, the sword, and the hunger into the hands of Nevukhadretzar, king
of Babylon, into the hands of their enemies, and into the hands of those who
seek their lives. He will smite them by the sword and not have pity upon them,
8 nor show mercy, nor show compassion. To this people you shall say: This is
what the LORD said: Look, I am placing before you the way of life and the
9 way of death. Whoever remains in this city will die by sword or famine or
pestilence, but whoever leaves and surrenders to the Chaldeans, who are now
10 besieging you, will live, and his life will be their prize of war. I will set My face
against this city for evil, not for good, declares the LORD. It shall be given into
11 the hand of the king of Babylon, and he will burn it with fire. And

51 | Referring to Sedom and Amora.
52 | An Aramean tribe prominent in Babylonia.

אֲדַבֵּר עוֹד בִּשְׁמוֹ וְהָיָה בְלִבִּי כְּאֵשׁ בֹּעֶרֶת עָצֻר בְּעַצְמֹתָי וְנִלְאֵיתִי
י כַּלְכֵל וְלֹא אוּכָל: כִּי שָׁמַעְתִּי דִּבַּת רַבִּים מָגוֹר מִסָּבִיב הַגִּידוּ וְנַגִּידֶנּוּ
כֹּל אֱנוֹשׁ שְׁלֹמִי שֹׁמְרֵי צַלְעִי אוּלַי יְפֻתֶּה וְנוּכְלָה לוֹ וְנִקְחָה נִקְמָתֵנוּ
יא מִמֶּנּוּ: ויהוה אוֹתִי כְּגִבּוֹר עָרִיץ עַל־כֵּן רֹדְפַי יִכָּשְׁלוּ וְלֹא יֻכָלוּ בֹּשׁוּ
יב מְאֹד כִּי־לֹא הִשְׂכִּילוּ כְּלִמַּת עוֹלָם לֹא תִשָּׁכֵחַ: וַיהוה צְבָאוֹת בֹּחֵן
צַדִּיק רֹאֶה כְלָיוֹת וָלֵב אֶרְאֶה נִקְמָתְךָ מֵהֶם כִּי אֵלֶיךָ גִּלִּיתִי אֶת־
יג רִיבִי: שִׁירוּ לַיהוה הַלְלוּ אֶת־יהוה כִּי הִצִּיל אֶת־נֶפֶשׁ
יד אֶבְיוֹן מִיַּד מְרֵעִים: אָרוּר הַיּוֹם אֲשֶׁר יֻלַּדְתִּי בּוֹ
טו יוֹם אֲשֶׁר־יְלָדַתְנִי אִמִּי אַל־יְהִי בָרוּךְ: אָרוּר הָאִישׁ אֲשֶׁר בִּשַּׂר
טז אֶת־אָבִי לֵאמֹר יֻלַּד־לְךָ בֵּן זָכָר שַׂמֵּחַ שִׂמְּחָהוּ: וְהָיָה הָאִישׁ הַהוּא
כֶּעָרִים אֲשֶׁר־הָפַךְ יהוה וְלֹא נִחָם וְשָׁמַע זְעָקָה בַּבֹּקֶר וּתְרוּעָה בְּעֵת
יז צָהֳרָיִם: אֲשֶׁר לֹא־מוֹתְתַנִי מֵרָחֶם וַתְּהִי־לִי אִמִּי קִבְרִי וְרַחְמָה הֲרַת
יח עוֹלָם: לָמָּה זֶּה מֵרֶחֶם יָצָאתִי לִרְאוֹת עָמָל וְיָגוֹן וַיִּכְלוּ בְּבֹשֶׁת
כא א יָמָי: הַדָּבָר אֲשֶׁר־הָיָה אֶל־יִרְמְיָהוּ מֵאֵת יהוה בִּשְׁלֹחַ
אֵלָיו הַמֶּלֶךְ צִדְקִיָּהוּ אֶת־פַּשְׁחוּר בֶּן־מַלְכִּיָּה וְאֶת־צְפַנְיָה בֶן־מַעֲשֵׂיָה
ב הַכֹּהֵן לֵאמֹר: דְּרָשׁ־נָא בַעֲדֵנוּ אֶת־יהוה כִּי נְבוּכַדְרֶאצַּר מֶלֶךְ־
בָּבֶל נִלְחָם עָלֵינוּ אוּלַי יַעֲשֶׂה יהוה אוֹתָנוּ כְּכָל־נִפְלְאֹתָיו וְיַעֲלֶה
ג מֵעָלֵינוּ: וַיֹּאמֶר יִרְמְיָהוּ אֲלֵיהֶם כֹּה תֹאמְרֻן אֶל־
ד צִדְקִיָּהוּ: כֹּה־אָמַר יהוה אֱלֹהֵי יִשְׂרָאֵל הִנְנִי מֵסֵב אֶת־כְּלֵי הַמִּלְחָמָה
אֲשֶׁר בְּיֶדְכֶם אֲשֶׁר אַתֶּם נִלְחָמִים בָּם אֶת־מֶלֶךְ בָּבֶל וְאֶת־הַכַּשְׂדִּים
הַצָּרִים עֲלֵיכֶם מִחוּץ לַחוֹמָה וְאָסַפְתִּי אוֹתָם אֶל־תּוֹךְ הָעִיר הַזֹּאת:
ה וְנִלְחַמְתִּי אֲנִי אִתְּכֶם בְּיָד נְטוּיָה וּבִזְרוֹעַ חֲזָקָה וּבְאַף וּבְחֵמָה וּבְקֶצֶף
ו גָּדוֹל: וְהִכֵּיתִי אֶת־יוֹשְׁבֵי הָעִיר הַזֹּאת וְאֶת־הָאָדָם וְאֶת־הַבְּהֵמָה
ז בְּדֶבֶר גָּדוֹל יָמֻתוּ: וְאַחֲרֵי־כֵן נְאֻם־יהוה אֶתֵּן אֶת־צִדְקִיָּהוּ מֶלֶךְ־
יְהוּדָה | וְאֶת־עֲבָדָיו | וְאֶת־הָעָם וְאֶת־הַנִּשְׁאָרִים בָּעִיר הַזֹּאת מִן־
הַדֶּבֶר | מִן־הַחֶרֶב וּמִן־הָרָעָב בְּיַד נְבוּכַדְרֶאצַּר מֶלֶךְ־בָּבֶל וּבְיַד
אֹיְבֵיהֶם וּבְיַד מְבַקְשֵׁי נַפְשָׁם וְהִכָּם לְפִי־חֶרֶב לֹא־יָחוּס עֲלֵיהֶם וְלֹא
ח יַחְמֹל וְלֹא יְרַחֵם: וְאֶל־הָעָם הַזֶּה תֹּאמַר כֹּה אָמַר יהוה הִנְנִי נֹתֵן
ט לִפְנֵיכֶם אֶת־דֶּרֶךְ הַחַיִּים וְאֶת־דֶּרֶךְ הַמָּוֶת: הַיֹּשֵׁב בָּעִיר הַזֹּאת יָמוּת
בַּחֶרֶב וּבָרָעָב וּבַדָּבֶר וְהַיּוֹצֵא וְנָפַל עַל־הַכַּשְׂדִּים הַצָּרִים עֲלֵיכֶם יחיה וְחָיָה
י וְהָיְתָה־לּוֹ נַפְשׁוֹ לְשָׁלָל: כִּי שַׂמְתִּי פָנַי בָּעִיר הַזֹּאת לְרָעָה וְלֹא לְטוֹבָה
יא נְאֻם־יהוה בְּיַד מֶלֶךְ־בָּבֶל תִּנָּתֵן וּשְׂרָפָהּ בָּאֵשׁ: וּלְבֵית

12 to the house of the king of Yehuda: Listen to the word of the Lord. House
of David, this is what the Lord said: Sit in judgment each morning and save
the victim of theft from the hand of his oppressor, lest My wrath burst forth
13 like a fire and burn with none to quench it because of your evil actions. Look,
I am against you, valley dwellers, rock upon the plain, declares the Lord, who
14 say, 'Who can descend upon us? Who can enter our homes?' I will punish
you as your deeds deserve, declares the Lord. I will kindle a fire in her forest
22 1 that will consume all her surroundings." This is what the Lord said:
2 "Go down to the palace of the king of Yehuda and speak this word there. Say:
King of Yehuda, who sits upon the throne of David, heed the word of the
3 Lord – you, your servants, and your people who enter these gates. This is
what the Lord said: Do justice and righteousness; protect the victim of theft
from the perpetrator; do not deceive and do not cheat the stranger, the
4 orphan, and the widow; and spill no innocent blood in this place. If you will
act in accordance with this word, then kings who sit on David's throne will
enter the gates of this palace riding upon chariots and horses – he, his servants,
5 and his people. But if you do not heed these words, then by My own self I
6 swear, declares the Lord, that this palace will become a ruin. For
this is what the Lord said concerning the palace of the king of Yehuda:
Although you are like Gilad to Me, like the peak of Mount Lebanon,
7 nevertheless I will make of you a wilderness, cities uninhabited. I will
designate destroyers against you, each man and his tools – they will cut down
8 your choicest cedars and cast them onto the fire. Many nations will pass by
this city, and one person will say to the other: 'For what reason did the Lord
9 do this to this great city?' And they will say, 'Because they abandoned the
covenant of the Lord their God; they bowed to other gods and worshipped
10 them.'" Weep not for the dead; do not bemoan him. Weep
instead for him who departs, never to return again to see the land of his
11 birth. For this is what the Lord said concerning Shalum son of
Yoshiyahu, king of Yehuda, who reigned after his father Yoshiyahu: He who
12 left this place will never return again. For in that place where they will exile
13 him, there he shall die, and he will never see this land again: Woe
to him who builds his house without righteousness and his lofts without
14 justice; who works his fellow for no pay and never gives him his wages. Who
says, "I will build myself a house of grand dimensions, with spacious lofts."
15 He makes himself windows covered with cedarwood, coated with precious
paint. Do you presume to reign because you compete in cedarwood? Indeed,
your father ate and drank, but he dispensed justice and righteousness;
16 therefore, things went well for him. He took up the cause of the poor and the
17 destitute with good results. That is the way to know Me, declares the Lord.
But your eyes and your heart are concerned with nothing but your own
gain, with spilling the blood of the innocent, with cheating and oppres-
18 sion. Therefore, this is what the Lord said concerning
Yehoyakim the son of Yoshiyahu, king of Yehuda: They will not eulogize him
saying, "Woe, my brother, my sister." They will not eulogize him saying, "Woe

יב מֶלֶךְ יְהוּדָה שִׁמְעוּ דְּבַר־יְהוָה׃ בֵּית דָּוִד כֹּה אָמַר יְהוָה דִּינוּ לַבֹּקֶר
מִשְׁפָּט וְהַצִּילוּ גָזוּל מִיַּד עוֹשֵׁק פֶּן־תֵּצֵא כָאֵשׁ חֲמָתִי וּבָעֲרָה וְאֵין
יג מְכַבֶּה מִפְּנֵי רֹעַ מעלליהם׃ הִנְנִי אֵלַיִךְ יֹשֶׁבֶת הָעֵמֶק צוּר הַמִּישֹׁר מַעַלְלֵיכֶם
יד נְאֻם־יְהוָה הָאֹמְרִים מִי־יֵחַת עָלֵינוּ וּמִי יָבוֹא בִּמְעוֹנוֹתֵינוּ׃ וּפָקַדְתִּי
עֲלֵיכֶם כִּפְרִי מַעַלְלֵיכֶם נְאֻם־יְהוָה וְהִצַּתִּי אֵשׁ בְּיַעְרָהּ וְאָכְלָה כָּל־
כב א סְבִיבֶיהָ׃ כֹּה אָמַר יְהוָה רֵד בֵּית־מֶלֶךְ יְהוּדָה וְדִבַּרְתָּ
ב שָׁם אֶת־הַדָּבָר הַזֶּה׃ וְאָמַרְתָּ שְׁמַע דְּבַר־יְהוָה מֶלֶךְ יְהוּדָה הַיֹּשֵׁב
ג עַל־כִּסֵּא דָוִד אַתָּה וַעֲבָדֶיךָ וְעַמְּךָ הַבָּאִים בַּשְּׁעָרִים הָאֵלֶּה׃ כֹּה ׀
אָמַר יְהוָה עֲשׂוּ מִשְׁפָּט וּצְדָקָה וְהַצִּילוּ גָזוּל מִיַּד עָשׁוֹק וְגֵר יָתוֹם
ד וְאַלְמָנָה אַל־תֹּנוּ אַל־תַּחְמֹסוּ וְדָם נָקִי אַל־תִּשְׁפְּכוּ בַּמָּקוֹם הַזֶּה׃ כִּי
אִם־עָשׂוֹ תַּעֲשׂוּ אֶת־הַדָּבָר הַזֶּה וּבָאוּ בְשַׁעֲרֵי הַבַּיִת הַזֶּה מְלָכִים
יֹשְׁבִים לְדָוִד עַל־כִּסְאוֹ רֹכְבִים בָּרֶכֶב וּבַסּוּסִים הוּא וַעֲבָדָו וְעַמּוֹ׃
ה וְאִם לֹא תִשְׁמְעוּ אֶת־הַדְּבָרִים הָאֵלֶּה בִּי נִשְׁבַּעְתִּי נְאֻם־יְהוָה כִּי־
ו לְחָרְבָּה יִהְיֶה הַבַּיִת הַזֶּה׃ כִּי־כֹה ׀ אָמַר יְהוָה עַל־בֵּית
מֶלֶךְ יְהוּדָה גִּלְעָד אַתָּה לִי רֹאשׁ הַלְּבָנוֹן אִם־לֹא אֲשִׁיתְךָ מִדְבָּר
ז עָרִים לֹא נושבה׃ וְקִדַּשְׁתִּי עָלֶיךָ מַשְׁחִתִים אִישׁ וְכֵלָיו וְכָרְתוּ מִבְחַר נוֹשָׁבוּ
ח אֲרָזֶיךָ וְהִפִּילוּ עַל־הָאֵשׁ׃ וְעָבְרוּ גּוֹיִם רַבִּים עַל הָעִיר הַזֹּאת וְאָמְרוּ
ט אִישׁ אֶל־רֵעֵהוּ עַל־מֶה עָשָׂה יְהוָה כָּכָה לָעִיר הַגְּדוֹלָה הַזֹּאת׃ וְאָמְרוּ
עַל אֲשֶׁר עָזְבוּ אֶת־בְּרִית יְהוָה אֱלֹהֵיהֶם וַיִּשְׁתַּחֲווּ לֵאלֹהִים אֲחֵרִים
י וַיַּעַבְדוּם׃ אַל־תִּבְכּוּ לְמֵת וְאַל־תָּנֻדוּ לוֹ בְּכוּ בָכוֹ לַהֹלֵךְ
יא כִּי לֹא יָשׁוּב עוֹד וְרָאָה אֶת־אֶרֶץ מוֹלַדְתּוֹ׃ כִּי־כֹה אָמַר־
יְהוָה אֶל־שַׁלֻּם בֶּן־יֹאשִׁיָּהוּ מֶלֶךְ יְהוּדָה הַמֹּלֵךְ תַּחַת יֹאשִׁיָּהוּ אָבִיו
יב אֲשֶׁר יָצָא מִן־הַמָּקוֹם הַזֶּה לֹא־יָשׁוּב שָׁם עוֹד׃ כִּי בִּמְקוֹם אֲשֶׁר־הִגְלוּ
יג אֹתוֹ שָׁם יָמוּת וְאֶת־הָאָרֶץ הַזֹּאת לֹא־יִרְאֶה עוֹד׃ הוֹי
בֹּנֶה בֵיתוֹ בְּלֹא־צֶדֶק וַעֲלִיּוֹתָיו בְּלֹא מִשְׁפָּט בְּרֵעֵהוּ יַעֲבֹד חִנָּם וּפֹעֲלוֹ
יד לֹא יִתֶּן־לוֹ׃ הָאֹמֵר אֶבְנֶה־לִּי בֵּית מִדּוֹת וַעֲלִיּוֹת מְרֻוָּחִים וְקָרַע לוֹ
טו חַלּוֹנָי וְסָפוּן בָּאָרֶז וּמָשׁוֹחַ בַּשָּׁשַׁר׃ הֲתִמְלֹךְ כִּי אַתָּה מְתַחֲרֶה בָאָרֶז
טז אָבִיךָ הֲלוֹא אָכַל וְשָׁתָה וְעָשָׂה מִשְׁפָּט וּצְדָקָה אָז טוֹב לוֹ׃ דָּן דִּין־עָנִי
יז וְאֶבְיוֹן אָז טוֹב הֲלוֹא־הִיא הַדַּעַת אֹתִי נְאֻם־יְהוָה׃ כִּי אֵין עֵינֶיךָ וְלִבְּךָ
כִּי אִם־עַל־בִּצְעֶךָ וְעַל דַּם־הַנָּקִי לִשְׁפּוֹךְ וְעַל־הָעֹשֶׁק וְעַל־הַמְּרוּצָה
יח לַעֲשׂוֹת׃ לָכֵן כֹּה־אָמַר יְהוָה אֶל־יְהוֹיָקִים בֶּן־יֹאשִׁיָּהוּ
מֶלֶךְ יְהוּדָה לֹא־יִסְפְּדוּ לוֹ הוֹי אָחִי וְהוֹי אָחוֹת לֹא־יִסְפְּדוּ לוֹ הוֹי אָדוֹן

19 master, woe majesty." Like the burial of a donkey will he be buried, then
20 dragged and flung outside the gates of Jerusalem. Climb upon
Lebanon and shout; raise your voice upon Bashan; shout in all directions – all
21 your lovers have collapsed. I spoke to you in your tranquil moments, but you
said, "I will not listen." This has been your way since your youth: you will not
22 heed My voice. Your shepherds will all be crushed by the wind; your lovers
will go into captivity. Then you will be ashamed and humiliated by all your
23 evil. Dweller in Lebanon, nestled among cedars, how much grace will you
24 retain when pains come upon you – pangs as if to a woman in childbirth? By
My life, declares the LORD, even if Konyahu[53] son of Yehoyakim, king of
Yehuda, were a signet ring on My right hand, even from there I would dislodge
25 you. I will deliver you into the hands of those who seek your life, into the
hands of those of whom you are terrified, into the hand of Nevukhadretzar,
26 king of Babylon, and into the hands of the Chaldeans. I will cast you and your
mother who bore you into another land where you were not born, and there
27 you will both die. But to the land where they greatly desire to return, there
28 they will not return. Is he a disgraced and broken idol,
this man Konyahu? Is he an unwanted vessel? Why have he and his seed been
29 cast out and flung into a land that they did not know? Land, land, land – heed
30 the word of the LORD. This is what the LORD said: Write this man down
as sterile, a person who will not succeed in his lifetime, for none of his
descendants will rise to sit upon the throne of David, to reign ever again in
23 1 Yehuda. Woe to the shepherds who misguide and disperse the flock
2 of My pasture, declares the LORD.[54] Consequently, this is what the LORD, God
of Israel, said concerning the shepherds who now tend to my people: You
have dispersed My sheep; you drove them away. You did not guide them. I
3 am about to punish you for your evil deeds, declares the LORD. I will gather
the remnant of My flock from all the lands into which I have driven them, and
4 I will bring them to their home, where they will be fruitful and multiply. And
I will raise up shepherds who will tend to them so that they will no longer
5 fear, nor feel panic, and none shall be missing, declares the LORD. Days
are soon approaching, declares the LORD, when I will raise up a righteous
scion for David. He will reign as king and prosper and dispense justice and
6 righteousness in the land. In his days Yehuda will be saved, and Israel will
dwell in safety. And this is the name by which the LORD will call him: Our
7 Righteous One. Therefore, days are approaching, declares the LORD,
when they will no longer say, "As the LORD lives, who has brought the
8 Israelites up from the land of Egypt," but rather, "As the LORD lives, who
brought up and delivered the descendants of the House of Israel from the
northern land, and from the lands to which I had expelled them," and they
9 shall dwell upon their own soil. As for these prophets:
my heart breaks within me; my bones all shudder; I have become like a
drunkard, a man overcome by wine, on behalf of the LORD and His holy words.

---

53 | Perhaps Yekhonya.
54 | Cf. Ezekiel 34:1–15.

יט וַחֲמוֹר הֹדֹה: קְבוּרַת חֲמוֹר יִקָּבֵר סָחוֹב וְהַשְׁלֵךְ מֵהָלְאָה לְשַׁעֲרֵי
כ יְרוּשָׁלִָם: עֲלִי הַלְּבָנוֹן וּצְעָקִי וּבַבָּשָׁן תְּנִי קוֹלֵךְ וְצַעֲקִי
כא מֵעֲבָרִים כִּי נִשְׁבְּרוּ כָּל־מְאַהֲבָיִךְ: דִּבַּרְתִּי אֵלַיִךְ בְּשַׁלְוֺתַיִךְ אָמַרְתְּ לֹא
כב אֶשְׁמָע זֶה דַרְכֵּךְ מִנְּעוּרַיִךְ כִּי לֹא־שָׁמַעַתְּ בְּקוֹלִי: כָּל־רֹעַיִךְ תִּרְעֶה־
כג רוּחַ וּמְאַהֲבַיִךְ בַּשְּׁבִי יֵלֵכוּ כִּי אָז תֵּבֹשִׁי וְנִכְלַמְתְּ מִכֹּל רָעָתֵךְ: ישבתי יֹשַׁבְתְּ
בַּלְּבָנוֹן מקננתי בָּאֲרָזִים מַה־נֵּחַנְתְּ בְּבֹא־לָךְ חֲבָלִים חִיל כַּיֹּלֵדָה: מְקֻנַּנְתְּ
כד חַי־אָנִי נְאֻם־יְהוָה כִּי אִם־יִהְיֶה כָּנְיָהוּ בֶן־יְהוֹיָקִים מֶלֶךְ יְהוּדָה חוֹתָם
כה עַל־יַד יְמִינִי כִּי מִשָּׁם אֶתְּקֶנְךָּ: וּנְתַתִּיךָ בְּיַד מְבַקְשֵׁי נַפְשֶׁךָ וּבְיַד
אֲשֶׁר־אַתָּה יָגוֹר מִפְּנֵיהֶם וּבְיַד נְבוּכַדְרֶאצַּר מֶלֶךְ־בָּבֶל וּבְיַד הַכַּשְׂדִּים:
כו וְהֵטַלְתִּי אֹתְךָ וְאֶת־אִמְּךָ אֲשֶׁר יְלָדַתְךָ עַל הָאָרֶץ אַחֶרֶת אֲשֶׁר לֹא־
כז יֻלַּדְתֶּם שָׁם וְשָׁם תָּמוּתוּ: וְעַל־הָאָרֶץ אֲשֶׁר הֵם מְנַשְּׂאִים אֶת־נַפְשָׁם
כח לָשׁוּב שָׁם שָׁמָּה לֹא יָשׁוּבוּ: הַעֶצֶב נִבְזֶה נָפוּץ הָאִישׁ
הַזֶּה כָּנְיָהוּ אִם־כְּלִי אֵין חֵפֶץ בּוֹ מַדּוּעַ הוּטְלוּ הוּא וְזַרְעוֹ וְהֻשְׁלְכוּ עַל־
כט ל הָאָרֶץ אֲשֶׁר לֹא־יָדָעוּ: אֶרֶץ אֶרֶץ אָרֶץ שִׁמְעִי דְּבַר־יְהוָה: כֹּה ׀ אָמַר
יְהוָה כִּתְבוּ אֶת־הָאִישׁ הַזֶּה עֲרִירִי גֶּבֶר לֹא־יִצְלַח בְּיָמָיו כִּי לֹא יִצְלַח
מִזַּרְעוֹ אִישׁ יֹשֵׁב עַל־כִּסֵּא דָוִד וּמֹשֵׁל עוֹד בִּיהוּדָה: הוֹי
כג א
ב רֹעִים מְאַבְּדִים וּמְפִצִים אֶת־צֹאן מַרְעִיתִי נְאֻם־יְהוָה: לָכֵן כֹּה־אָמַר
יְהוָה אֱלֹהֵי יִשְׂרָאֵל עַל־הָרֹעִים הָרֹעִים אֶת־עַמִּי אַתֶּם הֲפִצֹתֶם אֶת־
צֹאנִי וַתַּדִּחוּם וְלֹא פְקַדְתֶּם אֹתָם הִנְנִי פֹקֵד עֲלֵיכֶם אֶת־רֹעַ מַעַלְלֵיכֶם
ג נְאֻם־יְהוָה: וַאֲנִי אֲקַבֵּץ אֶת־שְׁאֵרִית צֹאנִי מִכֹּל הָאֲרָצוֹת אֲשֶׁר־
ד הִדַּחְתִּי אֹתָם שָׁם וַהֲשִׁבֹתִי אֶתְהֶן עַל־נְוֵהֶן וּפָרוּ וְרָבוּ: וַהֲקִמֹתִי
עֲלֵיהֶם רֹעִים וְרָעוּם וְלֹא־יִירְאוּ עוֹד וְלֹא־יֵחַתּוּ וְלֹא יִפָּקֵדוּ נְאֻם־
ה יְהוָה: הִנֵּה יָמִים בָּאִים נְאֻם־יְהוָה וַהֲקִמֹתִי לְדָוִד
צֶמַח צַדִּיק וּמָלַךְ מֶלֶךְ וְהִשְׂכִּיל וְעָשָׂה מִשְׁפָּט וּצְדָקָה בָּאָרֶץ:
ו בְּיָמָיו תִּוָּשַׁע יְהוּדָה וְיִשְׂרָאֵל יִשְׁכֹּן לָבֶטַח וְזֶה־שְּׁמוֹ אֲשֶׁר־יִקְרְאוֹ יב
ז יְהוָה ׀ צִדְקֵנוּ: לָכֵן הִנֵּה־יָמִים בָּאִים נְאֻם־יְהוָה
וְלֹא־יֹאמְרוּ עוֹד חַי־יְהוָה אֲשֶׁר הֶעֱלָה אֶת־בְּנֵי יִשְׂרָאֵל מֵאֶרֶץ
ח מִצְרָיִם: כִּי אִם־חַי־יְהוָה אֲשֶׁר הֶעֱלָה וַאֲשֶׁר הֵבִיא אֶת־זֶרַע בֵּית
יִשְׂרָאֵל מֵאֶרֶץ צָפוֹנָה וּמִכֹּל הָאֲרָצוֹת אֲשֶׁר הִדַּחְתִּים שָׁם וְיָשְׁבוּ
ט עַל־אַדְמָתָם: לַנְּבִאִים נִשְׁבַּר לִבִּי בְקִרְבִּי רָחֲפוּ כָּל־
עַצְמוֹתַי הָיִיתִי כְּאִישׁ שִׁכּוֹר וּכְגֶבֶר עֲבָרוֹ יָיִן מִפְּנֵי יְהוָה וּמִפְּנֵי דִּבְרֵי

10 For adulterers fill the land; the land is in ruins because of false oaths; pastures
in the wilderness have withered. Their pursuits are evil, their heroism
11 improper. Even the prophet and even the priest act deceitfully. Even in My
12 House I discovered their evil, declares the LORD. Therefore their path shall
become for them like slippery ground in the darkness; they shall be driven
there, and there they shall fall, for I will bring evil upon them in their year of
13 retribution, declares the LORD. Among the prophets of Shomron I
have witnessed inanity. They have prophesied for the Baal and have misled
14 My people, Israel. Among the prophets of Jerusalem I have witnessed scandal,
adultery, walking in falsehood. They support the hands of the wicked so that
no man repents his wickedness. They have all become to Me like Sedom, their
15 inhabitants like Amora. Consequently, this is what the LORD of
Hosts said concerning the prophets:[55] I am about to feed them wormwood
and give them poison water to drink, for from the prophets of Jerusalem
16 hypocrisy has gone forth to the entire land. This is what the LORD
of Hosts has said: Do not heed the words of the prophets who prophesy to
you; they are telling you nonsense. They speak of the visions of their own
17 hearts, not from the mouth of the LORD. Indeed, they say to those who
despise Me, "The LORD has spoken; there will peace for you." And to all who
18 follow the desires of their own hearts they say, "No evil shall befall you." For
who has stood in the counsel of the LORD, and seen and heard His word?
19 Who has listened to His word and heeded it? Behold, the tempest
of the LORD shall go forth with fury. An earthshaking storm will come down
20 upon the heads of the wicked. The LORD's wrath will not turn away until it
carries out and fulfills His heart's intentions. In the days to come you will
21 understand this fully. I did not send these prophets, and yet they responded
22 hastily; I did not speak to them, and yet they prophesied. Had they stood in
My counsel, they would have let My people hear My words and brought them
23 back from their wicked ways and from their evil actions. Am I a God
only for those who are close, declares the LORD, but not a God for those who
24 are distant? If a person conceals himself in a hiding place, will I not see him?
demands the LORD. Do I not fill the heavens and the earth? demands the
25 LORD. I have heard what the prophets who prophesy falsely in My name
26 declare: "I dreamed, I dreamed." How long will these prophets persist with
these false prophesies in their hearts, these prophets with fraudulent hearts?
27 They plan to make My people forget My name with the dreams that they tell
28 one another, just as their fathers forgot My name because of the Baal. The
prophet who has a dream, let him relate the dream; but he who has received
My word, let him speak My true word. How can straw compare to grain?
29 demands the LORD. Behold, My word is like fire, declares the LORD, and like
30 a hammer that will shatter a rock. Therefore, I am against these prophets,
31 declares the LORD, who steal My words, one from the other. I am against
these prophets, declares the LORD, who use their own language to speak as
32 if I had spoken. I am against those who prophesy false dreams, declares the

55 | That is, the false prophets.

י קָדְשׁוֹ: כִּי מְנָאֲפִים מָלְאָה הָאָרֶץ כִּי־מִפְּנֵי אָלָה אָבְלָה הָאָרֶץ יָבְשׁוּ
יא נְאוֹת מִדְבָּר וַתְּהִי מְרוּצָתָם רָעָה וּגְבוּרָתָם לֹא־כֵן: כִּי־גַם־נָבִיא
יב גַם־כֹּהֵן חָנֵפוּ גַּם־בְּבֵיתִי מָצָאתִי רָעָתָם נְאֻם־יהוה: לָכֵן יִהְיֶה דַרְכָּם
לָהֶם כַּחֲלַקְלַקּוֹת בָּאֲפֵלָה יִדַּחוּ וְנָפְלוּ בָהּ כִּי־אָבִיא עֲלֵיהֶם רָעָה
יג שְׁנַת פְּקֻדָּתָם נְאֻם־יהוה: וּבִנְבִיאֵי שֹׁמְרוֹן רָאִיתִי
יד תִפְלָה הִנַּבְּאוּ בַבַּעַל וַיַּתְעוּ אֶת־עַמִּי אֶת־יִשְׂרָאֵל: וּבִנְבִאֵי יְרוּשָׁלַםִ
רָאִיתִי שַׁעֲרוּרָה נָאוֹף וְהָלֹךְ בַּשֶּׁקֶר וְחִזְּקוּ יְדֵי מְרֵעִים לְבִלְתִּי־שָׁבוּ
טו אִישׁ מֵרָעָתוֹ הָיוּ־לִי כֻלָּם כִּסְדֹם וְיֹשְׁבֶיהָ כַּעֲמֹרָה: לָכֵן
כֹּה־אָמַר יהוה צְבָאוֹת עַל־הַנְּבִאִים הִנְנִי מַאֲכִיל אוֹתָם לַעֲנָה
וְהִשְׁקִתִים מֵי־רֹאשׁ כִּי מֵאֵת נְבִיאֵי יְרוּשָׁלַםִ יָצְאָה חֲנֻפָּה לְכָל־
טז הָאָרֶץ: כֹּה־אָמַר יהוה צְבָאוֹת אַל־תִּשְׁמְעוּ
עַל־דִּבְרֵי הַנְּבִאִים הַנִּבְּאִים לָכֶם מַהְבִּלִים הֵמָּה אֶתְכֶם חֲזוֹן לִבָּם
יז יְדַבֵּרוּ לֹא מִפִּי יהוה: אֹמְרִים אָמוֹר לִמְנַאֲצַי דִּבֶּר יהוה שָׁלוֹם
יִהְיֶה לָכֶם וְכֹל הֹלֵךְ בִּשְׁרִרוּת לִבּוֹ אָמְרוּ לֹא־תָבוֹא עֲלֵיכֶם רָעָה:
יח כִּי מִי עָמַד בְּסוֹד יהוה וְיֵרֶא וְיִשְׁמַע אֶת־דְּבָרוֹ מִי־הִקְשִׁיב דברי דְּבָרוֹ
יט וַיִּשְׁמָע: הִנֵּה ׀ סַעֲרַת יהוה חֵמָה יָצְאָה וְסַעַר
כ מִתְחוֹלֵל עַל רֹאשׁ רְשָׁעִים יָחוּל: לֹא יָשׁוּב אַף־יהוה עַד־עֲשֹׂתוֹ
כא וְעַד־הֲקִימוֹ מְזִמּוֹת לִבּוֹ בְּאַחֲרִית הַיָּמִים תִּתְבּוֹנְנוּ בָהּ בִּינָה: לֹא־
כב שָׁלַחְתִּי אֶת־הַנְּבִאִים וְהֵם רָצוּ לֹא־דִבַּרְתִּי אֲלֵיהֶם וְהֵם נִבָּאוּ: וְאִם־
עָמְדוּ בְּסוֹדִי וְיַשְׁמִעוּ דְבָרַי אֶת־עַמִּי וִישִׁבוּם מִדַּרְכָּם הָרָע וּמֵרֹעַ
כג מַעַלְלֵיהֶם: הַאֱלֹהֵי מִקָּרֹב אָנִי נְאֻם־יהוה וְלֹא אֱלֹהֵי
כד מֵרָחֹק: אִם־יִסָּתֵר אִישׁ בַּמִּסְתָּרִים וַאֲנִי לֹא־אֶרְאֶנּוּ נְאֻם־יהוה הֲלוֹא
כה אֶת־הַשָּׁמַיִם וְאֶת־הָאָרֶץ אֲנִי מָלֵא נְאֻם־יהוה: שָׁמַעְתִּי אֵת אֲשֶׁר־
כו אָמְרוּ הַנְּבִאִים הַנִּבְּאִים בִּשְׁמִי שֶׁקֶר לֵאמֹר חָלַמְתִּי חָלָמְתִּי: עַד־מָתַי
כז הֲיֵשׁ בְּלֵב הַנְּבִאִים נִבְּאֵי הַשָּׁקֶר וּנְבִיאֵי תַּרְמִת לִבָּם: הַחֹשְׁבִים
לְהַשְׁכִּיחַ אֶת־עַמִּי שְׁמִי בַּחֲלוֹמֹתָם אֲשֶׁר יְסַפְּרוּ אִישׁ לְרֵעֵהוּ כַּאֲשֶׁר
כח שָׁכְחוּ אֲבוֹתָם אֶת־שְׁמִי בַּבָּעַל: הַנָּבִיא אֲשֶׁר־אִתּוֹ חֲלוֹם יְסַפֵּר חֲלוֹם
וַאֲשֶׁר דְּבָרִי אִתּוֹ יְדַבֵּר דְּבָרִי אֱמֶת מַה־לַתֶּבֶן אֶת־הַבָּר נְאֻם־יהוה:
כט ל הֲלוֹא כֹה דְבָרִי כָּאֵשׁ נְאֻם־יהוה וּכְפַטִּישׁ יְפֹצֵץ סָלַע: לָכֵן הִנְנִי עַל־
לא הַנְּבִאִים נְאֻם־יהוה מְגַנְּבֵי דְבָרַי אִישׁ מֵאֵת רֵעֵהוּ: הִנְנִי עַל־הַנְּבִיאִם
לב נְאֻם־יהוה הַלֹּקְחִים לְשׁוֹנָם וַיִּנְאֲמוּ נְאֻם: הִנְנִי עַל־נִבְּאֵי חֲלֹמוֹת

LORD, those who relate them and mislead My people with their falsehood
and carelessness. I have neither sent them nor commanded them, nor will
33 they at all benefit My people, declares the LORD. If this people, or a prophet
or a priest, should ask of you, "What is the burden of the LORD?"[56] you shall
34 say to them, "What burden? I will abandon you!" declares the LORD. The
prophet or priest or the people who shall say to you "burden of the LORD," I
35 will punish that person and his household. This is what each person shall say
to his neighbor and each person to his kinsman: "What did the LORD answer?
36 What did the LORD say?" But as for "burden of the LORD," never mention
that again, for "burden" is but a word that people use. You have perverted the
37 words of the living God, the LORD of Hosts, our God. This is how you should
speak to the prophet: "What did the LORD answer you? What did the LORD
38 say?" If you continue to say "burden of the LORD," then this is what the LORD
said: Because you say this phrase, "burden of the LORD," after I have sent
39 word to you never to say "burden of the LORD," I am therefore about to eject
you totally and remove from My presence you and the city that I gave to you
40 and your fathers. I will place upon you eternal shame, eternal humiliation,
24 1 that will not be forgotten. The LORD showed me two baskets of figs
placed before the Temple of the LORD. This was after Nevukhadretzar, king
of Babylon, had exiled Yekhonyahu son of Yehoyakim, king of Yehuda, and
the officers of Yehuda, and the artisans and smiths,[57] from Jerusalem, and had
2 brought them to Babylon. In one basket were very fine figs, like well-ripened
figs; in the other basket were very bad figs, so bad that they could not be
3 eaten. The LORD said to me, "What do you see, Yirmeyahu?" And
I replied, "Figs! The fine ones are very fine, and the bad ones very bad, so bad
4 that they cannot be eaten." The word of the LORD came to me: This
5 is what the LORD, God of Israel, said: "Like these fine figs, so will I show favor
to the exiles of Yehuda whom I have sent forth from this place to the land of
6 the Chaldeans for their benefit. I will watch over them benevolently and bring
them back to this land; I will build them up and not tear them down; I will
7 plant them and not uproot them. I will grant them the heart to know Me, for
I am the LORD. They will be My people, and I will be their God, for they will
8 return to Me with all their heart." But of the bad figs, so bad that they
cannot be eaten, the LORD said, "Like those I will make Tzidkiyahu, king of
Yehuda, his officers, and the remnant of Jerusalem that has remained in this
9 land, and those who dwell in the land of Egypt.[58] I will make them a horror,
an evil, for all the kingdoms of the earth; a disgrace and an epithet, a sharp
10 word and a curse, in all the places to which I shall banish them. And I will
send against them the sword and famine and pestilence until they are finished

---

56 | The word "burden" (*masa*) also means "oracle," e.g., Isaiah 13:1.

57 | See II Kings 24:14.

58 | Egypt was viewed as a place of refuge (see 41:16–17).

שֶׁקֶר נְאֻם־יְהוָה וַיְסַפְּרוּם וַיַּתְעוּ אֶת־עַמִּי בְּשִׁקְרֵיהֶם וּבְפַחֲזוּתָם
וְאָנֹכִי לֹא־שְׁלַחְתִּים וְלֹא צִוִּיתִים וְהוֹעֵיל לֹא־יוֹעִילוּ לָעָם־הַזֶּה נְאֻם־
לג יְהוָה: וְכִי־יִשְׁאָלְךָ הָעָם הַזֶּה אוֹ־הַנָּבִיא אוֹ־כֹהֵן לֵאמֹר מַה־מַּשָּׂא
יְהוָה וְאָמַרְתָּ אֲלֵיהֶם אֶת־מַה־מַּשָּׂא וְנָטַשְׁתִּי אֶתְכֶם נְאֻם־יְהוָה:
לד וְהַנָּבִיא וְהַכֹּהֵן וְהָעָם אֲשֶׁר יֹאמַר מַשָּׂא יְהוָה וּפָקַדְתִּי עַל־הָאִישׁ
לה הַהוּא וְעַל־בֵּיתוֹ: כֹּה תֹאמְרוּ אִישׁ עַל־רֵעֵהוּ וְאִישׁ אֶל־אָחִיו מֶה־
לו עָנָה יְהוָה וּמַה־דִּבֶּר יְהוָה: וּמַשָּׂא יְהוָה לֹא תִזְכְּרוּ־עוֹד כִּי הַמַּשָּׂא
יִהְיֶה לְאִישׁ דְּבָרוֹ וַהֲפַכְתֶּם אֶת־דִּבְרֵי אֱלֹהִים חַיִּים יְהוָה צְבָאוֹת
לז לח אֱלֹהֵינוּ: כֹּה תֹאמַר אֶל־הַנָּבִיא מֶה־עָנָךְ יְהוָה וּמַה־דִּבֶּר יְהוָה: וְאִם־
מַשָּׂא יְהוָה תֹּאמֵרוּ לָכֵן כֹּה אָמַר יְהוָה יַעַן אֲמָרְכֶם אֶת־הַדָּבָר הַזֶּה
לט מַשָּׂא יְהוָה וָאֶשְׁלַח אֲלֵיכֶם לֵאמֹר לֹא תֹאמְרוּ מַשָּׂא יְהוָה: לָכֵן הִנְנִי
וְנָשִׁיתִי אֶתְכֶם נָשֹׁא וְנָטַשְׁתִּי אֶתְכֶם וְאֶת־הָעִיר אֲשֶׁר נָתַתִּי לָכֶם
מ וְלַאֲבוֹתֵיכֶם מֵעַל פָּנָי: וְנָתַתִּי עֲלֵיכֶם חֶרְפַּת עוֹלָם וּכְלִמּוּת עוֹלָם
כד א אֲשֶׁר לֹא תִשָּׁכֵחַ: הִרְאַנִי יְהוָה וְהִנֵּה שְׁנֵי דּוּדָאֵי
תְאֵנִים מוּעָדִים לִפְנֵי הֵיכַל יְהוָה אַחֲרֵי הַגְלוֹת נְבוּכַדְרֶאצַּר מֶלֶךְ־
בָּבֶל אֶת־יְכָנְיָהוּ בֶן־יְהוֹיָקִים מֶלֶךְ־יְהוּדָה וְאֶת־שָׂרֵי יְהוּדָה וְאֶת־
ב הֶחָרָשׁ וְאֶת־הַמַּסְגֵּר מִירוּשָׁלִַם וַיְבִאֵם בָּבֶל: הַדּוּד אֶחָד תְּאֵנִים טֹבוֹת
מְאֹד כִּתְאֵנֵי הַבַּכֻּרוֹת וְהַדּוּד אֶחָד תְּאֵנִים רָעוֹת מְאֹד אֲשֶׁר לֹא־
ג תֵאָכַלְנָה מֵרֹעַ: וַיֹּאמֶר יְהוָה אֵלַי מָה־אַתָּה רֹאֶה יִרְמְיָהוּ
וָאֹמַר תְּאֵנִים הַתְּאֵנִים הַטֹּבוֹת טֹבוֹת מְאֹד וְהָרָעוֹת רָעוֹת מְאֹד
ד אֲשֶׁר לֹא־תֵאָכַלְנָה מֵרֹעַ: וַיְהִי דְבַר־יְהוָה אֵלַי לֵאמֹר:
ה כֹּה־אָמַר יְהוָה אֱלֹהֵי יִשְׂרָאֵל כַּתְּאֵנִים הַטֹּבוֹת הָאֵלֶּה כֵּן אַכִּיר אֶת־
גָּלוּת יְהוּדָה אֲשֶׁר שִׁלַּחְתִּי מִן־הַמָּקוֹם הַזֶּה אֶרֶץ כַּשְׂדִּים לְטוֹבָה:
ו וְשַׂמְתִּי עֵינִי עֲלֵיהֶם לְטוֹבָה וַהֲשִׁבֹתִים עַל־הָאָרֶץ הַזֹּאת וּבְנִיתִים
יג ז וְלֹא אֶהֱרֹס וּנְטַעְתִּים וְלֹא אֶתּוֹשׁ: וְנָתַתִּי לָהֶם לֵב לָדַעַת אֹתִי כִּי אֲנִי
יְהוָה וְהָיוּ־לִי לְעָם וְאָנֹכִי אֶהְיֶה לָהֶם לֵאלֹהִים כִּי־יָשֻׁבוּ אֵלַי בְּכָל־
ח לִבָּם: וְכַתְּאֵנִים הָרָעוֹת אֲשֶׁר לֹא־תֵאָכַלְנָה מֵרֹעַ
כִּי־כֹה ׀ אָמַר יְהוָה כֵּן אֶתֵּן אֶת־צִדְקִיָּהוּ מֶלֶךְ־יְהוּדָה וְאֶת־שָׂרָיו וְאֵת ׀
שְׁאֵרִית יְרוּשָׁלִַם הַנִּשְׁאָרִים בָּאָרֶץ הַזֹּאת וְהַיֹּשְׁבִים בְּאֶרֶץ מִצְרָיִם:
ט וּנְתַתִּים לזועה לְרָעָה לְכֹל מַמְלְכוֹת הָאָרֶץ לְחֶרְפָּה וּלְמָשָׁל לִשְׁנִינָה לְזַעֲוָה
י וְלִקְלָלָה בְּכָל־הַמְּקֹמוֹת אֲשֶׁר־אַדִּיחֵם שָׁם: וְשִׁלַּחְתִּי בָם אֶת־הַחֶרֶב
אֶת־הָרָעָב וְאֶת־הַדָּבֶר עַד־תֻּמָּם מֵעַל הָאֲדָמָה אֲשֶׁר־נָתַתִּי לָהֶם

25 1 off within the land which I gave them and their fathers." The word
that came to Yirmeyahu concerning the entire people of Yehuda in the fourth
year of Yehoyakim son of Yoshiyahu, king of Yehuda, that being the first year
2 of Nevukhadretzar, king of Babylon. This is what Yirmeyahu the prophet
spoke to the entire people of Yehuda and to all those dwelling in Jerusalem:
3 From the thirteenth year of Yoshiyahu son of Amon, king of Yehuda, until
this very day, it has been twenty-three years that the word of the LORD has
4 come to me. I have spoken to you diligently, but you have not listened. The
LORD sent you all of His servants, the prophets – early and persistently – yet
5 you did not listen, nor even bend your ear to hear. They said, "Please turn
back, each of you, from his wicked ways and evil deeds, so that you may for
ever and ever dwell upon the soil which the LORD gave to you and to your
6 fathers." Do not follow other gods, serving them and worshipping them, so
7 as not to anger Me with your actions and so that I do not harm you. But you
did not listen to Me, declares the LORD, and thereby angered Me by your
8 actions, to your detriment. Consequently, this is what the LORD of
9 Hosts said: Because you have not listened to My words, I am about to send
for My servant Nevukhadnetzar, king of Babylon, and I shall take all the tribes
of the north, declares the LORD, and bring them upon this land, upon its
inhabitants, and upon all these nations surrounding them. I will destroy them
10 and make of them a wasteland and a place of shrieking, an eternal ruin. I shall
abolish from them the sound of joy and the sound of happiness, the voice of
the groom and the voice of the bride, the sound of the mill and the light of
11 the lamp. The entire land shall become a ruin and a wasteland, and these
12 nations shall serve the king of Babylon for seventy years. When these seventy
years are completed, I will visit retribution upon the king of Babylon and that
nation, declares the LORD, for their sin, and as for the land of the Chaldeans,
13 I shall make it an eternal wasteland. I will bring upon that land all that I have
spoken against her, all that is written in this book, which was prophesied
14 by Yirmeyahu concerning all the nations. For they too shall serve many
nations and great kings, and I will repay them according to their actions and
15 handiwork. For this is what the LORD, God of Israel, said to me:
"Take this cup of the wine of wrath from My hand, and give it to drink to all
16 the nations to whom I am sending you. They will drink and shiver and act
17 foolishly because of the sword that I am sending among them." I took the cup
from the hand of the LORD and I gave it to drink to all the nations to whom
18 the LORD had sent me. To Jerusalem and to the cities of Yehuda, to her kings
and to her officers, to lead them into destruction, waste, and shrieking, and
19 to a curse, just as on this very day. To Pharaoh, king of Egypt, to his servants
20 and officers, and to his entire nation. To the conglomeration of peoples
and to all the kings of the land of Utz; to all the kings of the land of the

כה א וְלַאֲבוֹתֵיהֶם׃ הַדָּבָר אֲשֶׁר־הָיָה עַל־יִרְמְיָהוּ עַל־כָּל־
עַם יְהוּדָה בַּשָּׁנָה הָרְבִעִית לִיהוֹיָקִים בֶּן־יֹאשִׁיָּהוּ מֶלֶךְ יְהוּדָה הִיא
ב הַשָּׁנָה הָרִאשֹׁנִית לִנְבוּכַדְרֶאצַּר מֶלֶךְ בָּבֶל׃ אֲשֶׁר דִּבֶּר יִרְמְיָהוּ הַנָּבִיא
ג עַל־כָּל־עַם יְהוּדָה וְאֶל כָּל־יֹשְׁבֵי יְרוּשָׁלִַם לֵאמֹר׃ מִן־שְׁלֹשׁ עֶשְׂרֵה
שָׁנָה לְיֹאשִׁיָּהוּ בֶן־אָמוֹן מֶלֶךְ יְהוּדָה וְעַד ׀ הַיּוֹם הַזֶּה זֶה שָׁלֹשׁ וְעֶשְׂרִים
שָׁנָה הָיָה דְבַר־יְהוָה אֵלָי וָאֲדַבֵּר אֲלֵיכֶם אַשְׁכֵּים וְדַבֵּר וְלֹא שְׁמַעְתֶּם׃
ד וְשָׁלַח יְהוָה אֲלֵיכֶם אֶת־כָּל־עֲבָדָיו הַנְּבִאִים הַשְׁכֵּם וְשָׁלֹחַ וְלֹא
ה שְׁמַעְתֶּם וְלֹא־הִטִּיתֶם אֶת־אָזְנְכֶם לִשְׁמֹעַ׃ לֵאמֹר שׁוּבוּ־נָא אִישׁ
מִדַּרְכּוֹ הָרָעָה וּמֵרֹעַ מַעַלְלֵיכֶם וּשְׁבוּ עַל־הָאֲדָמָה אֲשֶׁר נָתַן יְהוָה
ו לָכֶם וְלַאֲבוֹתֵיכֶם לְמִן־עוֹלָם וְעַד־עוֹלָם׃ וְאַל־תֵּלְכוּ אַחֲרֵי אֱלֹהִים
אֲחֵרִים לְעָבְדָם וּלְהִשְׁתַּחֲוֺת לָהֶם וְלֹא־תַכְעִיסוּ אוֹתִי בְּמַעֲשֵׂה יְדֵיכֶם
ז וְלֹא אָרַע לָכֶם׃ וְלֹא־שְׁמַעְתֶּם אֵלַי נְאֻם־יְהוָה לְמַעַן הכעסוני בְּמַעֲשֵׂה הַכְעִיסֵנִי
ח יְדֵיכֶם לְרַע לָכֶם׃ לָכֵן כֹּה אָמַר יְהוָה צְבָאוֹת יַעַן אֲשֶׁר
ט לֹא־שְׁמַעְתֶּם אֶת־דְּבָרָי׃ הִנְנִי שֹׁלֵחַ וְלָקַחְתִּי אֶת־כָּל־מִשְׁפְּחוֹת צָפוֹן
נְאֻם־יְהוָה וְאֶל־נְבוּכַדְרֶאצַּר מֶלֶךְ־בָּבֶל עַבְדִּי וַהֲבִאֹתִים עַל־הָאָרֶץ
הַזֹּאת וְעַל־יֹשְׁבֶיהָ וְעַל כָּל־הַגּוֹיִם הָאֵלֶּה סָבִיב וְהַחֲרַמְתִּים וְשַׂמְתִּים
י לְשַׁמָּה וְלִשְׁרֵקָה וּלְחָרְבוֹת עוֹלָם׃ וְהַאֲבַדְתִּי מֵהֶם קוֹל שָׂשׂוֹן וְקוֹל
יא שִׂמְחָה קוֹל חָתָן וְקוֹל כַּלָּה קוֹל רֵחַיִם וְאוֹר נֵר׃ וְהָיְתָה כָּל־הָאָרֶץ
הַזֹּאת לְחָרְבָּה לְשַׁמָּה וְעָבְדוּ הַגּוֹיִם הָאֵלֶּה אֶת־מֶלֶךְ בָּבֶל שִׁבְעִים
יב שָׁנָה׃ וְהָיָה כִמְלֹאות שִׁבְעִים שָׁנָה אֶפְקֹד עַל־מֶלֶךְ־בָּבֶל וְעַל־הַגּוֹי
הַהוּא נְאֻם־יְהוָה אֶת־עֲוֺנָם וְעַל־אֶרֶץ כַּשְׂדִּים וְשַׂמְתִּי אֹתוֹ לְשִׁמְמוֹת
יג עוֹלָם׃ והבאותי עַל־הָאָרֶץ הַהִיא אֶת־כָּל־דְּבָרַי אֲשֶׁר־דִּבַּרְתִּי עָלֶיהָ וְהֵבֵאתִי
יד אֵת כָּל־הַכָּתוּב בַּסֵּפֶר הַזֶּה אֲשֶׁר־נִבָּא יִרְמְיָהוּ עַל־כָּל־הַגּוֹיִם׃ כִּי
עָבְדוּ־בָם גַּם־הֵמָּה גּוֹיִם רַבִּים וּמְלָכִים גְּדוֹלִים וְשִׁלַּמְתִּי לָהֶם כְּפָעֳלָם
טו וּכְמַעֲשֵׂה יְדֵיהֶם׃ כִּי כֹה אָמַר יְהוָה אֱלֹהֵי יִשְׂרָאֵל
אֵלַי קַח אֶת־כּוֹס הַיַּיִן הַחֵמָה הַזֹּאת מִיָּדִי וְהִשְׁקִיתָה אֹתוֹ אֶת־כָּל־
טז הַגּוֹיִם אֲשֶׁר אָנֹכִי שֹׁלֵחַ אוֹתְךָ אֲלֵיהֶם׃ וְשָׁתוּ וְהִתְגֹּעֲשׁוּ וְהִתְהֹלָלוּ
יז מִפְּנֵי הַחֶרֶב אֲשֶׁר אָנֹכִי שֹׁלֵחַ בֵּינֹתָם׃ וָאֶקַּח אֶת־הַכּוֹס מִיַּד יְהוָה
יח וָאַשְׁקֶה אֶת־כָּל־הַגּוֹיִם אֲשֶׁר־שְׁלָחַנִי יְהוָה אֲלֵיהֶם׃ אֶת־יְרוּשָׁלִַם
וְאֶת־עָרֵי יְהוּדָה וְאֶת־מְלָכֶיהָ אֶת־שָׂרֶיהָ לָתֵת אֹתָם לְחָרְבָּה לְשַׁמָּה
יט לִשְׁרֵקָה וְלִקְלָלָה כַּיּוֹם הַזֶּה׃ אֶת־פַּרְעֹה מֶלֶךְ־מִצְרַיִם וְאֶת־עֲבָדָיו
כ וְאֶת־שָׂרָיו וְאֶת־כָּל־עַמּוֹ׃ וְאֵת כָּל־הָעֶרֶב וְאֵת כָּל־מַלְכֵי אֶרֶץ הָעוּץ

21 Philistines – Ashkelon, Aza, Ekron, and the remnant of Ashdod. To Edom
22 and Moav and the Amonites. To all the kings of Tyre, and to all the kings of
23 Sidon; to the kings of the islands across the sea. To Dedan and to Tema and
24 to Buz, and to all in the distant reaches. To all the kings of Arabia, and to all
25 the kings of the conglomeration of peoples that dwell in the desert. To all the
26 kings of Zimri, and all the kings of Elam, and all the kings of Media. To all
the kings of the north, those who are near and those who are far from each
other, and to the kingdoms of all the lands on the face of the earth, and the
27 king of Sheshakh[59] will drink after them. "You shall say to them: This is what
the LORD of Hosts, God of Israel, has said: Drink, become drunk and vomit,
fall and do not rise because of the sword that I am sending into your midst.
28 Should they refuse to take the cup from your hand to drink, say to them: This
29 is what the LORD of Hosts said: You must drink! For I am about to bring evil
upon the city that is called by My name, and you expect to be absolved? You
will not be absolved, for I summon a sword to fall upon all the inhabitants of
30 the land, declares the LORD of Hosts. Now, you are to prophesy all these
words to them and say to them: The LORD roars from on high; from His holy
dwelling place He raises His voice; He roars and roars above His abode; He
31 shouts '*heidad*'[60] like the grape treaders to all who dwell on earth. A clamor
has reached the end of the earth, for the LORD has a dispute with the nations.
He enters into judgment with all flesh. He has delivered them, the wicked, to
32 the sword," declares the LORD. This is what the LORD of Hosts said:
Evil is about to go forth from nation to nation, and a great storm from the
33 ends of the earth will awaken them. On that day, those slain by the LORD will
spread from one end of the earth to the other end of the earth – they will not
be eulogized; they will not be gathered; they will not be buried. They will be
34 like dung upon the face of the earth. Wail, shepherds, and scream. Roll in the
dust, you masters of the flock, for the days before your slaughter have expired.
35 I will smash you, and you will fall like a precious vessel. Flight shall be denied
36 to the shepherds; escape shall be denied to the masters of the flock. Listen!
Oh, the shouts of the shepherds and the wails of the masters of the flock, for
37 the LORD has ruined their pasture. The peaceful meadows will be demolished
38 by the burning anger of the LORD. The young lion has left his lair, for their
land will soon be laid waste by the wrath of the oppressor and by His burning
26 1 anger. At the beginning of the reign of Yehoyakim son of Yoshiyahu,
2 king of Yehuda, this word came from the LORD. This is what the LORD said:
"Stand in the courtyard of the House of the LORD and speak to all who dwell
in the cities of Yehuda, who come to worship in the House of the LORD, all
the words which I commanded you to speak to them. Do not omit a word.
3 Perhaps they will listen and repent, each person from his evil way, so that I
will reconsider the evil that I plan to do to them because of the evil of their
4 deeds. Say to them: This is what the LORD said: If you do not listen to Me to

59 | Babylon (*Bavel*), written in the *atbash* cipher.

60 | An exclamation of effort or celebration, typically over the grape harvest, or a battle cry.

וְאֵת֙ כׇּל־מַלְכֵי֙ אֶ֣רֶץ פְּלִשְׁתִּ֔ים וְאֶת־אַשְׁקְל֤וֹן וְאֶת־עַזָּה֙ וְאֶת־עֶקְר֔וֹן
כא כב וְאֵ֖ת שְׁאֵרִ֥ית אַשְׁדּֽוֹד׃ אֶת־אֱד֥וֹם וְאֶת־מוֹאָ֖ב וְאֶת־בְּנֵ֥י עַמּֽוֹן׃ וְאֵת֙
כׇּל־מַלְכֵי־צֹ֔ר וְאֵ֖ת כׇּל־מַלְכֵ֣י צִיד֑וֹן וְאֵת֙ מַלְכֵ֣י הָאִ֔י אֲשֶׁ֖ר בְּעֵ֥בֶר הַיָּֽם׃
כג כד וְאֶת־דְּדָ֤ן וְאֶת־תֵּימָא֙ וְאֶת־בּ֔וּז וְאֵ֖ת כׇּל־קְצוּצֵ֥י פֵאָֽה׃ וְאֵ֖ת כׇּל־מַלְכֵ֣י
כה עֲרָ֑ב וְאֵת֙ כׇּל־מַלְכֵ֣י הָעֶ֔רֶב הַשֹּׁכְנִ֖ים בַּמִּדְבָּֽר׃ וְאֵ֣ת ׀ כׇּל־מַלְכֵ֣י זִמְרִ֗י
כו וְאֵת֙ כׇּל־מַלְכֵ֣י עֵילָ֔ם וְאֵ֖ת כׇּל־מַלְכֵ֥י מָדָֽי׃ וְאֵ֣ת ׀ כׇּל־מַלְכֵ֣י הַצָּפ֗וֹן
הַקְּרֹבִ֤ים וְהָֽרְחֹקִים֙ אִ֣ישׁ אֶל־אָחִ֔יו וְאֵת֙ כׇּל־הַמַּמְלְכ֣וֹת הָאָ֔רֶץ אֲשֶׁ֖ר
כז עַל־פְּנֵ֣י הָאֲדָמָ֑ה וּמֶ֥לֶךְ שֵׁשַׁ֖ךְ יִשְׁתֶּ֥ה אַחֲרֵיהֶֽם׃ וְאָמַרְתָּ֣ אֲלֵיהֶ֡ם כֹּֽה־
אָמַר֩ יהוה צְבָא֨וֹת אֱלֹהֵ֜י יִשְׂרָאֵ֗ל שְׁת֤וּ וְשִׁכְרוּ֙ וּקְי֔וּ וְנִפְל֖וּ וְלֹ֣א תָק֑וּמוּ
כח מִפְּנֵ֣י הַחֶ֔רֶב אֲשֶׁ֛ר אָנֹכִ֥י שֹׁלֵ֖חַ בֵּינֵיכֶֽם׃ וְהָיָ֛ה כִּ֧י יְמָאֲנ֛וּ לָקַֽחַת־הַכּ֥וֹס
מִיָּדְךָ֖ לִשְׁתּ֑וֹת וְאָמַרְתָּ֣ אֲלֵיהֶ֗ם כֹּ֥ה אָמַ֛ר יהוה צְבָא֖וֹת שָׁת֥וֹ תִשְׁתּֽוּ׃
כט כִּ֣י הִנֵּה֩ בָעִ֨יר אֲשֶׁ֤ר נִֽקְרָא־שְׁמִי֙ עָלֶ֔יהָ אָנֹכִי֙ מֵחֵ֣ל לְהָרַ֔ע וְאַתֶּ֖ם הִנָּקֵ֣ה
תִנָּק֑וּ לֹ֣א תִנָּק֔וּ כִּ֣י חֶ֗רֶב אֲנִ֥י קֹרֵא֙ עַל־כׇּל־יֹשְׁבֵ֣י הָאָ֔רֶץ נְאֻ֖ם יהוה
ל צְבָאֽוֹת׃ וְאַתָּה֙ תִּנָּבֵ֣א אֲלֵיהֶ֔ם אֵ֥ת כׇּל־הַדְּבָרִ֖ים הָאֵ֑לֶּה וְאָמַרְתָּ֣ אֲלֵיהֶ֗ם
יהוה מִמָּר֤וֹם יִשְׁאָג֙ וּמִמְּע֤וֹן קׇדְשׁוֹ֙ יִתֵּ֣ן קוֹל֔וֹ שָׁאֹ֤ג יִשְׁאַג֙ עַל־נָוֵ֔הוּ
לא הֵידָד֙ כְּדֹרְכִ֣ים יַעֲנֶ֔ה אֶ֖ל כׇּל־יֹשְׁבֵ֥י הָאָֽרֶץ׃ בָּ֤א שָׁאוֹן֙ עַד־קְצֵ֣ה הָאָ֔רֶץ
כִּ֣י רִ֤יב לַֽיהוה֙ בַּגּוֹיִ֔ם נִשְׁפָּ֥ט ה֖וּא לְכׇל־בָּשָׂ֑ר הָרְשָׁעִ֛ים נְתָנָ֥ם לַחֶ֖רֶב
לב נְאֻם־יהוה׃ כֹּ֤ה אָמַר֙ יהוה צְבָא֔וֹת הִנֵּ֥ה רָעָ֛ה יֹצֵ֖את
לג מִגּ֣וֹי אֶל־גּ֑וֹי וְסַ֣עַר גָּד֔וֹל יֵע֖וֹר מִיַּרְכְּתֵי־אָֽרֶץ׃ וְהָי֨וּ חַלְלֵ֤י יהוה֙ בַּיּ֣וֹם
הַה֔וּא מִקְצֵ֥ה הָאָ֖רֶץ וְעַד־קְצֵ֣ה הָאָ֑רֶץ לֹ֣א יִסָּפְד֗וּ וְלֹ֤א יֵאָֽסְפוּ֙ וְלֹ֣א
לד יִקָּבֵ֔רוּ לְדֹ֛מֶן עַל־פְּנֵ֥י הָאֲדָמָ֖ה יִהְיֽוּ׃ הֵילִ֨ילוּ הָרֹעִ֜ים וְזַעֲק֗וּ וְהִֽתְפַּלְּשׁוּ֙
אַדִּירֵ֣י הַצֹּ֔אן כִּֽי־מָלְא֥וּ יְמֵיכֶ֖ם לִטְב֑וֹחַ וּתְפוֹצ֣וֹתִיכֶ֔ם וּנְפַלְתֶּ֖ם כִּכְלִ֥י
לה לו חֶמְדָּֽה׃ וְאָבַ֥ד מָנ֖וֹס מִן־הָרֹעִ֑ים וּפְלֵיטָ֖ה מֵאַדִּירֵ֥י הַצֹּֽאן׃ ק֚וֹל צַעֲקַ֣ת
לז הָרֹעִ֔ים וִֽילְלַ֖ת אַדִּירֵ֣י הַצֹּ֑אן כִּֽי־שֹׁדֵ֥ד יהוה אֶת־מַרְעִיתָֽם׃ וְנָדַ֖מּוּ נְא֣וֹת
לח הַשָּׁל֑וֹם מִפְּנֵ֖י חֲר֥וֹן אַף־יהוה׃ עָזַ֤ב כַּכְּפִיר֙ סֻכּ֔וֹ כִּֽי־הָיְתָ֤ה אַרְצָם֙
כו א לְשַׁמָּ֔ה מִפְּנֵי֙ חֲר֣וֹן הַיּוֹנָ֔ה וּמִפְּנֵ֖י חֲר֥וֹן אַפּֽוֹ׃ בְּרֵאשִׁ֗ית יד
מַמְלְכ֛וּת יְהוֹיָקִ֥ים בֶּן־יֹאשִׁיָּ֖הוּ מֶ֣לֶךְ יְהוּדָ֑ה הָיָ֛ה הַדָּבָ֥ר הַזֶּ֖ה מֵאֵ֥ת יהוה
ב לֵאמֹֽר׃ כֹּ֣ה ׀ אָמַ֣ר יהוה עֲמֹד֮ בַּחֲצַ֣ר בֵּית־יהוה֒ וְדִבַּרְתָּ֞ עַל־כׇּל־עָרֵ֣י
יְהוּדָ֗ה הַבָּאִים֙ לְהִשְׁתַּחֲוֺ֣ת בֵּית־יהוה אֵ֚ת כׇּל־הַדְּבָרִ֔ים אֲשֶׁ֥ר צִוִּיתִ֖יךָ
ג לְדַבֵּ֣ר אֲלֵיהֶ֑ם אַל־תִּגְרַ֖ע דָּבָֽר׃ אוּלַ֣י יִשְׁמְע֔וּ וְיָשֻׁ֕בוּ אִ֖ישׁ מִדַּרְכּ֣וֹ
הָרָעָ֑ה וְנִחַמְתִּ֣י אֶל־הָרָעָ֗ה אֲשֶׁ֨ר אָנֹכִ֤י חֹשֵׁב֙ לַעֲשׂ֣וֹת לָהֶ֔ם מִפְּנֵ֖י רֹ֥עַ
ד מַעַלְלֵיהֶֽם׃ וְאָמַרְתָּ֖ אֲלֵיהֶ֑ם כֹּ֚ה אָמַ֣ר יהוה אִם־לֹ֤א תִשְׁמְעוּ֙ אֵלַ֔י

5 follow the teaching that I have placed before you, to obey the words of My
servants the prophets, whom I have sent to you early and repeatedly – though
6 you did not obey – I will make this House like Shilo, and this city I will turn
7 into a curse for all the nations of the earth." The priests and
the prophets and all the people heard Yirmeyahu speak these words in the
8 House of the Lord. When Yirmeyahu finished speaking all that the Lord
commanded him to speak to all the people, the priests and the prophets and
9 all the people seized him, saying, "You shall die! Why did you prophesy in
the name of the Lord, saying that this House will be like Shilo and that this
city will be destroyed, leaving no inhabitant?" All the people crowded about
10 Yirmeyahu in the House of the Lord. The officers of Yehuda heard these
words, and they went up from the king's house to the House of the Lord and
11 sat at the entrance of the new gate of the Lord. The priests and the prophets
said to the officers and to all the people, "This man deserves the death penalty,
for he prophesied against this city, as you have heard with your own ears."
12 Yirmeyahu said to all the officers and to all the people, "The Lord sent me
to prophesy against this House and against this city all the words that you
13 heard. Now, rectify your ways and your deeds, and heed the voice of the Lord
your God. Then the Lord will reconsider the evil which He has spoken
14 against you. As for me, I am in your hands. Do to me whatever is good and
15 proper in your eyes. But know well that if you kill me, you will have brought
the blood of an innocent man upon yourselves and upon this city and its
inhabitants. For, truthfully, the Lord did send me to you to speak all these
16 words to you." The officers and all the people said to the priests and
the prophets, "This man does not deserve the death penalty, for he spoke to
17 us in the name of the Lord our God." Some men from among the elders of
18 the land stood up and said to all the assembled people, "Mikha the Morashtite
would prophesy in the days of Ḥizkiyahu, king of Yehuda. He addressed all
the people of Yehuda, saying, 'This is what the Lord of Hosts said: Zion will
be plowed over like a field, Jerusalem will come to be a mound of ruins, and
19 the Temple Mount an overgrown hilltop shrine.'[61] Did Ḥizkiyahu, king of
Yehuda, and all of Yehuda put him to death? Did he not fear the Lord and
beseech the Lord, so that the Lord reconsidered the evil that He had spoken
20 concerning them? We would be bringing great evil upon ourselves. Another
man would prophesy in the name of the Lord – Uriyahu son of Shemayahu
of Kiryat Ye'arim. He too prophesied against this city and against this land as
21 all of Yirmeyahu's words did. King Yehoyakim and all his soldiers and all his
officers heard his words, and the king sought to put him to death, but Uriyahu
22 heard and was afraid. He took flight and went to Egypt. King Yehoyakim sent
men to Egypt; he sent Elnatan son of Akhbor and his companions to Egypt.

61 | Cf. Micah 3:12.

ה לָלֶכֶת בְּתוֹרָתִי אֲשֶׁר נָתַתִּי לִפְנֵיכֶם: לִשְׁמֹעַ עַל־דִּבְרֵי עֲבָדַי הַנְּבִאִים
ו אֲשֶׁר אָנֹכִי שֹׁלֵחַ אֲלֵיכֶם וְהַשְׁכֵּם וְשָׁלֹחַ וְלֹא שְׁמַעְתֶּם: וְנָתַתִּי
אֶת־הַבַּיִת הַזֶּה כְּשִׁלֹה וְאֶת־הָעִיר הזאתה אֶתֵּן לִקְלָלָה לְכֹל גּוֹיֵי הַזֹּאת
ז הָאָרֶץ: וַיִּשְׁמְעוּ הַכֹּהֲנִים וְהַנְּבִאִים וְכָל־הָעָם אֶת־יִרְמְיָהוּ
ח מְדַבֵּר אֶת־הַדְּבָרִים הָאֵלֶּה בְּבֵית יהוה: וַיְהִי ׀ כְּכַלּוֹת יִרְמְיָהוּ לְדַבֵּר
אֵת כָּל־אֲשֶׁר־צִוָּה יהוה לְדַבֵּר אֶל־כָּל־הָעָם וַיִּתְפְּשׂוּ אֹתוֹ הַכֹּהֲנִים
ט וְהַנְּבִאִים וְכָל־הָעָם לֵאמֹר מוֹת תָּמוּת: מַדּוּעַ נִבֵּיתָ בְשֵׁם־יהוה
לֵאמֹר כְּשִׁלוֹ יִהְיֶה הַבַּיִת הַזֶּה וְהָעִיר הַזֹּאת תֶּחֱרַב מֵאֵין יוֹשֵׁב וַיִּקָּהֵל
י כָּל־הָעָם אֶל־יִרְמְיָהוּ בְּבֵית יהוה: וַיִּשְׁמְעוּ ׀ שָׂרֵי יְהוּדָה אֵת הַדְּבָרִים
הָאֵלֶּה וַיַּעֲלוּ מִבֵּית־הַמֶּלֶךְ בֵּית יהוה וַיֵּשְׁבוּ בְּפֶתַח שַׁעַר־יהוה
יא הֶחָדָשׁ: וַיֹּאמְרוּ הַכֹּהֲנִים וְהַנְּבִאִים אֶל־הַשָּׂרִים וְאֶל־כָּל־הָעָם לֵאמֹר
מִשְׁפַּט־מָוֶת לָאִישׁ הַזֶּה כִּי נִבָּא אֶל־הָעִיר הַזֹּאת כַּאֲשֶׁר שְׁמַעְתֶּם
יב בְּאָזְנֵיכֶם: וַיֹּאמֶר יִרְמְיָהוּ אֶל־כָּל־הַשָּׂרִים וְאֶל־כָּל־הָעָם לֵאמֹר יהוה
שְׁלָחַנִי לְהִנָּבֵא אֶל־הַבַּיִת הַזֶּה וְאֶל־הָעִיר הַזֹּאת אֵת כָּל־הַדְּבָרִים
יג אֲשֶׁר שְׁמַעְתֶּם: וְעַתָּה הֵיטִיבוּ דַרְכֵיכֶם וּמַעַלְלֵיכֶם וְשִׁמְעוּ בְּקוֹל
יד יהוה אֱלֹהֵיכֶם וְיִנָּחֵם יהוה אֶל־הָרָעָה אֲשֶׁר דִּבֶּר עֲלֵיכֶם: וַאֲנִי הִנְנִי
טו בְיֶדְכֶם עֲשׂוּ־לִי כַּטּוֹב וְכַיָּשָׁר בְּעֵינֵיכֶם: אַךְ ׀ יָדֹעַ תֵּדְעוּ כִּי אִם־מְמִתִים
אַתֶּם אֹתִי כִּי־דָם נָקִי אַתֶּם נֹתְנִים עֲלֵיכֶם וְאֶל־הָעִיר הַזֹּאת וְאֶל־
יֹשְׁבֶיהָ כִּי בֶאֱמֶת שְׁלָחַנִי יהוה עֲלֵיכֶם לְדַבֵּר בְּאָזְנֵיכֶם אֵת כָּל־
טז הַדְּבָרִים הָאֵלֶּה: וַיֹּאמְרוּ הַשָּׂרִים וְכָל־הָעָם אֶל־הַכֹּהֲנִים
וְאֶל־הַנְּבִיאִים אֵין־לָאִישׁ הַזֶּה מִשְׁפַּט־מָוֶת כִּי בְּשֵׁם יהוה אֱלֹהֵינוּ
יז דִּבֶּר אֵלֵינוּ: וַיָּקֻמוּ אֲנָשִׁים מִזִּקְנֵי הָאָרֶץ וַיֹּאמְרוּ אֶל־כָּל־קְהַל הָעָם
יח לֵאמֹר: מיכיה הַמּוֹרַשְׁתִּי הָיָה נִבָּא בִּימֵי חִזְקִיָּהוּ מֶלֶךְ־יְהוּדָה וַיֹּאמֶר מִיכָה
אֶל־כָּל־עַם יְהוּדָה לֵאמֹר כֹּה־אָמַר ׀ יהוה צְבָאוֹת צִיּוֹן שָׂדֶה תֵחָרֵשׁ
יט וִירוּשָׁלַיִם עִיִּים תִּהְיֶה וְהַר הַבַּיִת לְבָמוֹת יָעַר: הֶהָמֵת הֱמִתֻהוּ חִזְקִיָּהוּ
מֶלֶךְ־יְהוּדָה וְכָל־יְהוּדָה הֲלֹא יָרֵא אֶת־יהוה וַיְחַל אֶת־פְּנֵי יהוה
וַיִּנָּחֶם יהוה אֶל־הָרָעָה אֲשֶׁר־דִּבֶּר עֲלֵיהֶם וַאֲנַחְנוּ עֹשִׂים רָעָה גְדוֹלָה
כ עַל־נַפְשׁוֹתֵינוּ: וְגַם־אִישׁ הָיָה מִתְנַבֵּא בְּשֵׁם יהוה אוּרִיָּהוּ בֶּן־שְׁמַעְיָהוּ
מִקִּרְיַת הַיְּעָרִים וַיִּנָּבֵא עַל־הָעִיר הַזֹּאת וְעַל־הָאָרֶץ הַזֹּאת כְּכֹל דִּבְרֵי
כא יִרְמְיָהוּ: וַיִּשְׁמַע הַמֶּלֶךְ יְהוֹיָקִים וְכָל־גִּבּוֹרָיו וְכָל־הַשָּׂרִים אֶת־דְּבָרָיו
וַיְבַקֵּשׁ הַמֶּלֶךְ הֲמִיתוֹ וַיִּשְׁמַע אוּרִיָּהוּ וַיִּרָא וַיִּבְרַח וַיָּבֹא מִצְרָיִם:
כב וַיִּשְׁלַח הַמֶּלֶךְ יְהוֹיָקִים אֲנָשִׁים מִצְרָיִם אֶת־אֶלְנָתָן בֶּן־עַכְבּוֹר וַאֲנָשִׁים

23 They brought Uriyahu out of Egypt and delivered him to Yehoyakim, who
smote him by sword. He threw his carcass into the graves of the common
24 people." But the power of Aḥikam son of Shafan stood by Yirmeyahu, refusing
27 1 to surrender him to the hands of the people who would kill him. At
the beginning of the reign of Yehoyakim son of Yoshiyahu, king of Yehuda,
2 this word came to Yirmeya from the LORD. This is what the LORD said to me:
"Make yourself the reins and bars of a yoke,[62] and place them upon your neck,
3 and send them to the king of Edom, the king of Moav, the king of the Amonites,
the king of Tyre, and the king of Sidon, and by way of the emissaries who
4 come to Jerusalem, to Tzidkiyahu, king of Yehuda. And instruct them to tell
their masters: This is what the LORD of Hosts, God of Israel, has said, and
5 this is what you should say to your masters: It is I who made the earth – the
humans and the animals upon the face of the earth – with My great might
6 and My arm stretched forth, and I gave it to whom I saw fit. And now, I have
delivered all these lands into the hands of Nevukhadnetzar, king of Babylon,
7 My servant. I have even given him the beasts of the field to serve him. All the
nations will serve him, his son, and his son's son, until his land's time will also
8 come, and many nations and great kings will subjugate him. The nation and
kingdom that will not serve him – Nevukhadnetzar, king of Babylon – and
will not submit its neck to the yoke of the king of Babylon, I will visit sword,
famine, and pestilence upon that nation, declares the LORD, until I finish
9 them off by his hands. As for you, do not listen to your prophets and diviners,
your dreamers and soothsayers and sorcerers, who tell you not to serve the
10 king of Babylon. For what they prophesy to you is false, with the result that
it will remove you from your land. I will drive you away, and you will be lost.
11 But the nation that will submit its neck to the yoke of the king of Babylon
and serve him, that nation I will leave upon its soil," declares the LORD. "They
12 shall till it and dwell on it." I spoke similarly to King Tzidkiya of Yehuda,
saying, "Submit your necks to the yoke of the king of Babylon, serve him and
13 his people, and survive. Why should you and your people perish by the sword,
by famine, and by pestilence, as the LORD has spoken regarding that nation
14 that will not serve the king of Babylon? Do not listen to the words of those
prophets who tell you not to serve the king of Babylon, for falsehood is what
15 they are prophesying to you. For I did not send them, declares the LORD.
They prophesy falsehood in My name, with the result that I will drive you
16 away and you will be lost – you and the prophets who prophesy to you." And
to the priests, and to all these people, I said, "This is what the LORD said: Do
not listen to the words of your prophets, who prophesy to you saying that the
vessels of the LORD's House are about to be returned from Babylon – now,

62 | See also 28:10.

כג אֹתוֹ אֶל־מִצְרָיִם׃ וַיּוֹצִיאוּ אֶת־אוּרִיָּהוּ מִמִּצְרַיִם וַיְבִאֻהוּ אֶל־הַמֶּלֶךְ
כד יְהוֹיָקִים וַיַּכֵּהוּ בֶּחָרֶב וַיַּשְׁלֵךְ אֶת־נִבְלָתוֹ אֶל־קִבְרֵי בְּנֵי הָעָם׃ אַךְ יַד
אֲחִיקָם בֶּן־שָׁפָן הָיְתָה אֶת־יִרְמְיָהוּ לְבִלְתִּי תֶּת־אֹתוֹ בְיַד־הָעָם
כז א לַהֲמִיתוֹ׃ בְּרֵאשִׁית מַמְלְכוּת יְהוֹיָקִם בֶּן־יֹאושִׁיָּהוּ מֶלֶךְ
ב יְהוּדָה הָיָה הַדָּבָר הַזֶּה אֶל־יִרְמְיָה מֵאֵת יהוה לֵאמֹר׃ כֹּה־אָמַר יהוה
ג אֵלַי עֲשֵׂה לְךָ מוֹסֵרוֹת וּמֹטוֹת וּנְתַתָּם עַל־צַוָּארֶךָ׃ וְשִׁלַּחְתָּם אֶל־
מֶלֶךְ אֱדוֹם וְאֶל־מֶלֶךְ מוֹאָב וְאֶל־מֶלֶךְ בְּנֵי עַמּוֹן וְאֶל־מֶלֶךְ צֹר וְאֶל־
מֶלֶךְ צִידוֹן בְּיַד מַלְאָכִים הַבָּאִים יְרוּשָׁלַםִ אֶל־צִדְקִיָּהוּ מֶלֶךְ יְהוּדָה׃
ד וְצִוִּיתָ אֹתָם אֶל־אֲדֹנֵיהֶם לֵאמֹר כֹּה־אָמַר יהוה צְבָאוֹת אֱלֹהֵי יִשְׂרָאֵל
ה כֹּה תֹאמְרוּ אֶל־אֲדֹנֵיכֶם׃ אָנֹכִי עָשִׂיתִי אֶת־הָאָרֶץ אֶת־הָאָדָם וְאֶת־ טו
הַבְּהֵמָה אֲשֶׁר עַל־פְּנֵי הָאָרֶץ בְּכֹחִי הַגָּדוֹל וּבִזְרוֹעִי הַנְּטוּיָה וּנְתַתִּיהָ
ו לַאֲשֶׁר יָשַׁר בְּעֵינָי׃ וְעַתָּה אָנֹכִי נָתַתִּי אֶת־כָּל־הָאֲרָצוֹת הָאֵלֶּה בְּיַד
נְבוּכַדְנֶאצַּר מֶלֶךְ־בָּבֶל עַבְדִּי וְגַם אֶת־חַיַּת הַשָּׂדֶה נָתַתִּי לוֹ לְעָבְדוֹ׃
ז וְעָבְדוּ אֹתוֹ כָּל־הַגּוֹיִם וְאֶת־בְּנוֹ וְאֶת־בֶּן־בְּנוֹ עַד בֹּא־עֵת אַרְצוֹ גַּם־
ח הוּא וְעָבְדוּ בוֹ גּוֹיִם רַבִּים וּמְלָכִים גְּדֹלִים׃ וְהָיָה הַגּוֹי וְהַמַּמְלָכָה אֲשֶׁר
לֹא־יַעַבְדוּ אֹתוֹ אֶת־נְבוּכַדְנֶאצַּר מֶלֶךְ־בָּבֶל וְאֵת אֲשֶׁר לֹא־יִתֵּן אֶת־
צַוָּארוֹ בְּעֹל מֶלֶךְ בָּבֶל בַּחֶרֶב וּבָרָעָב וּבַדֶּבֶר אֶפְקֹד עַל־הַגּוֹי הַהוּא
ט נְאֻם־יהוה עַד־תֻּמִּי אֹתָם בְּיָדוֹ׃ וְאַתֶּם אַל־תִּשְׁמְעוּ אֶל־נְבִיאֵיכֶם
וְאֶל־קֹסְמֵיכֶם וְאֶל חֲלֹמֹתֵיכֶם וְאֶל־עֹנְנֵיכֶם וְאֶל־כַּשָּׁפֵיכֶם אֲשֶׁר־הֵם
י אֹמְרִים אֲלֵיכֶם לֵאמֹר לֹא תַעַבְדוּ אֶת־מֶלֶךְ בָּבֶל׃ כִּי שֶׁקֶר הֵם נִבְּאִים
לָכֶם לְמַעַן הַרְחִיק אֶתְכֶם מֵעַל אַדְמַתְכֶם וְהִדַּחְתִּי אֶתְכֶם וַאֲבַדְתֶּם׃
יא וְהַגּוֹי אֲשֶׁר יָבִיא אֶת־צַוָּארוֹ בְּעֹל מֶלֶךְ־בָּבֶל וַעֲבָדוֹ וְהִנַּחְתִּיו עַל־
יב אַדְמָתוֹ נְאֻם־יהוה וַעֲבָדָהּ וְיָשַׁב בָּהּ׃ וְאֶל־צִדְקִיָּה מֶלֶךְ־יְהוּדָה
דִּבַּרְתִּי כְּכָל־הַדְּבָרִים הָאֵלֶּה לֵאמֹר הָבִיאוּ אֶת־צַוְּארֵיכֶם בְּעֹל
יג מֶלֶךְ בָּבֶל וְעִבְדוּ אֹתוֹ וְעַמּוֹ וִחְיוּ׃ לָמָּה תָמוּתוּ אַתָּה וְעַמֶּךָ בַּחֶרֶב
בָּרָעָב וּבַדָּבֶר כַּאֲשֶׁר דִּבֶּר יהוה אֶל־הַגּוֹי אֲשֶׁר לֹא־יַעֲבֹד אֶת־מֶלֶךְ
יד בָּבֶל׃ וְאַל־תִּשְׁמְעוּ אֶל־דִּבְרֵי הַנְּבִאִים הָאֹמְרִים אֲלֵיכֶם לֵאמֹר לֹא
טו תַעַבְדוּ אֶת־מֶלֶךְ בָּבֶל כִּי שֶׁקֶר הֵם נִבְּאִים לָכֶם׃ כִּי לֹא שְׁלַחְתִּים
נְאֻם־יהוה וְהֵם נִבְּאִים בִּשְׁמִי לַשָּׁקֶר לְמַעַן הַדִּיחִי אֶתְכֶם וַאֲבַדְתֶּם
טז אַתֶּם וְהַנְּבִאִים הַנִּבְּאִים לָכֶם׃ וְאֶל־הַכֹּהֲנִים וְאֶל־כָּל־הָעָם הַזֶּה
דִּבַּרְתִּי לֵאמֹר כֹּה אָמַר יהוה אַל־תִּשְׁמְעוּ אֶל־דִּבְרֵי נְבִיאֵיכֶם
הַנִּבְּאִים לָכֶם לֵאמֹר הִנֵּה כְלֵי בֵית־יהוה מוּשָׁבִים מִבָּבֶלָה עַתָּה

17 quickly. For they prophesy falsehood to you. Do not listen to them. Serve the
18 king of Babylon and survive. Why should the city become a ruin? If they are
indeed prophets, and if the word of the LORD is indeed with them, let them
beg of the LORD of Hosts not to allow the vessels that remain in the House
of the LORD, and in the palace of the king of Yehuda, and in Jerusalem, to go
19 to Babylon. For this is what the LORD of Hosts has said about the
pillars, and the Sea, and the stands, and the other vessels that remain in this
20 city,[63] those that Nevukhadnetzar, king of Babylon, did not take when he
exiled Yekhonya son of Yehoyakim, king of Yehuda, from Jerusalem to
21 Babylon, along with all the nobles of Yehuda and Jerusalem. For this
is what the LORD of Hosts, God of Israel, had said regarding the vessels that
remain in the LORD's House, and in the palace of the king of Yehuda, and
22 Jerusalem: To Babylon they shall be brought, and there they shall remain
until the day that I appoint for them, declares the LORD. Then I will bring
28 1 them up and return them to this place." It was that year, at the
beginning of the reign of Tzidkiya, king of Yehuda, in the fifth month of the
fourth year, that Ḥananya son of Azur the prophet, who was from Givon,
spoke to me in the House of the LORD, in full view of the priests and all the
2 people. He said, "This is what the LORD of Hosts, God of Israel, said: I have
3 broken the yoke of the king of Babylon. In two years I will restore all the
vessels of the LORD's House to this place, those that Nevukhadnetzar king of
4 Babylon took from here and brought to Babylon. I will return Yekhonya son
of Yehoyakim, king of Yehuda, and all of Yehuda's exiles who have gone to
Babylon, to this place – declares the LORD – for I shall break the yoke of the
5 king of Babylon." Then Yirmeya the prophet spoke to Ḥananya the prophet
in full view of the priests and in full view of all the people who were standing
6 in the LORD's House. Yirmeya the prophet said, "Amen. May the LORD do
that. May He uphold the words that you prophesied regarding the return of
the vessels of the LORD's House and of all the exiles from Babylon to this
7 place. But please listen to the word that I am speaking in your ears, and in the
8 ears of all the people. The prophets who were before me and before you long
ago – they prophesied war, catastrophe, and pestilence to many lands and to
9 great kingdoms. The prophet who shall prophesy peace, when his words
come true, that prophet shall be acknowledged as one whom the LORD has
10 truly sent." Then Ḥananya the prophet took the bar[64] from the neck of
11 Yirmeya the prophet and broke it. And Ḥananya spoke in full view of all the
people and said, "This is what the LORD said: Thus shall I break the yoke of
Nevukhadnetzar, king of Babylon, in two years, from the necks of all nations."
12 Yirmeya the prophet went on his way. The word of the LORD came
to Yirmeya after Ḥananya the prophet broke the bar from the neck of Yirmeya

---

63 | See 1 Kings 7:13–50.

64 | The yoke mentioned in 27:2.

יז מְהֵרָ֑ה כִּ֥י שֶׁ֖קֶר הֵ֥מָּה נִבְּאִ֥ים לָכֶֽם׃ אַל־תִּשְׁמְע֣וּ אֲלֵיהֶ֗ם עִבְד֛וּ אֶת־
יח מֶֽלֶךְ־בָּבֶ֖ל וִֽחְי֑וּ לָ֧מָּה תִֽהְיֶ֛ה הָעִ֥יר הַזֹּ֖את חׇרְבָּֽה׃ וְאִם־נְבִאִ֣ים הֵ֔ם
וְאִם־יֵ֥שׁ דְּבַר־יְהֹוָ֖ה אִתָּ֑ם יִפְגְּעוּ־נָ֞א בַּֽיהֹוָ֣ה צְבָא֗וֹת לְבִלְתִּי־בֹ֜אוּ
הַכֵּלִ֣ים ׀ הַנּוֹתָרִ֣ים בְּבֵית־יְהֹוָ֗ה וּבֵ֛ית מֶ֥לֶךְ יְהוּדָ֖ה וּבִירוּשָׁלַ֖͏ִם
יט בָּבֶֽלָה׃ כִּ֣י כֹ֥ה אָמַ֛ר יְהֹוָ֥ה צְבָא֖וֹת אֶל־הָֽעַמֻּדִ֑ים וְעַל־הַיָּ֗ם
כ וְעַל־הַמְּכֹנ֔וֹת וְעַל֙ יֶ֣תֶר הַכֵּלִ֔ים הַנּוֹתָרִ֖ים בָּעִ֥יר הַזֹּֽאת׃ אֲשֶׁר֙ לֹֽא־
לְקָחָ֗ם נְבוּכַדְנֶאצַּר֙ מֶ֣לֶךְ בָּבֶ֔ל בַּגְלוֹת֩ אֶת־יכוניה בֶן־יְהוֹיָקִ֨ים מֶֽלֶךְ־ יְכׇנְיָ֣ה
כא יְהוּדָ֜ה מִירוּשָׁלַ֛͏ִם בָּבֶ֖לָה וְאֵ֥ת כׇּל־חֹרֵ֥י יְהוּדָ֖ה וִירוּשָׁלָֽ͏ִם׃ כִּ֣י
כֹ֥ה אָמַ֛ר יְהֹוָ֥ה צְבָא֖וֹת אֱלֹהֵ֣י יִשְׂרָאֵ֑ל עַל־הַכֵּלִים֙ הַנּֽוֹתָרִ֔ים בֵּ֥ית
כב יְהֹוָ֛ה וּבֵ֥ית מֶֽלֶךְ־יְהוּדָ֖ה וִירוּשָׁלָֽ͏ִם׃ בָּבֶ֥לָה יוּבָ֖אוּ וְשָׁ֣מָּה יִֽהְי֑וּ עַ֠ד
י֣וֹם פָּקְדִ֤י אֹתָם֙ נְאֻם־יְהֹוָ֔ה וְהַעֲלִיתִים֙ וַהֲשִׁ֣יבֹתִ֔ים אֶל־הַמָּק֖וֹם
כח א הַזֶּֽה׃ וַיְהִ֣י ׀ בַּשָּׁנָ֣ה הַהִ֗יא בְּרֵאשִׁית֙ מַמְלֶ֙כֶת֙ צִדְקִיָּ֣ה
מֶֽלֶךְ־יְהוּדָ֔ה בשנת הָרְבִעִ֖ית בַּחֹ֣דֶשׁ הַחֲמִישִׁ֑י אָמַ֣ר אֵלַ֡י חֲנַנְיָה֩ בֶן־ בַּשָּׁנָ֣ה
עַזּ֨וּר הַנָּבִ֜יא אֲשֶׁ֣ר מִגִּבְע֗וֹן בְּבֵ֣ית יְהֹוָ֔ה לְעֵינֵ֧י הַכֹּהֲנִ֛ים וְכׇל־הָעָ֖ם
ב לֵאמֹֽר׃ כֹּֽה־אָמַ֛ר יְהֹוָ֥ה צְבָא֖וֹת אֱלֹהֵ֣י יִשְׂרָאֵ֣ל לֵאמֹ֑ר שָׁבַ֕רְתִּי אֶת־עֹ֖ל
ג מֶ֥לֶךְ בָּבֶֽל׃ בְּע֣וֹד ׀ שְׁנָתַ֣יִם יָמִ֗ים אֲנִ֤י מֵשִׁיב֙ אֶל־הַמָּק֣וֹם הַזֶּ֔ה אֶֽת־כׇּל־
כְּלֵ֖י בֵּ֣ית יְהֹוָ֑ה אֲשֶׁר֩ לָקַ֨ח נְבוּכַדְנֶאצַּ֤ר מֶֽלֶךְ־בָּבֶל֙ מִן־הַמָּק֣וֹם הַזֶּ֔ה
ד וַיְבִיאֵ֖ם בָּבֶֽל׃ וְאֶת־יְכׇנְיָ֨ה בֶן־יְהוֹיָקִ֤ים מֶֽלֶךְ־יְהוּדָה֙ וְאֶת־כׇּל־גָּל֤וּת
יְהוּדָ֙ה הַבָּאִ֣ים בָּבֶ֔לָה אֲנִ֥י מֵשִׁ֛יב אֶל־הַמָּק֥וֹם הַזֶּ֖ה נְאֻם־יְהֹוָ֑ה כִּ֣י
ה אֶשְׁבֹּ֔ר אֶת־עֹ֖ל מֶ֥לֶךְ בָּבֶֽל׃ וַיֹּ֙אמֶר֙ יִרְמְיָ֣ה הַנָּבִ֔יא אֶל־חֲנַנְיָ֖ה הַנָּבִ֑יא
ו לְעֵינֵ֤י הַכֹּֽהֲנִים֙ וּלְעֵינֵ֣י כׇל־הָעָ֔ם הָעֹמְדִ֖ים בְּבֵ֥ית יְהֹוָֽה׃ וַיֹּ֙אמֶר֙ יִרְמְיָ֣ה
הַנָּבִ֔יא אָמֵ֕ן כֵּ֖ן יַעֲשֶׂ֣ה יְהֹוָ֑ה יָקֵ֤ם יְהֹוָה֙ אֶת־דְּבָרֶ֔יךָ אֲשֶׁ֣ר נִבֵּ֔אתָ לְהָשִׁ֞יב
ז כְּלֵ֤י בֵית־יְהֹוָה֙ וְכׇל־הַגּוֹלָ֔ה מִבָּבֶ֖ל אֶל־הַמָּק֥וֹם הַזֶּֽה׃ אַךְ־שְׁמַֽע־נָ֗א
ח הַדָּבָ֤ר הַזֶּה֙ אֲשֶׁ֣ר אָנֹכִ֔י דֹּבֵ֖ר בְּאׇזְנֶ֑יךָ וּבְאׇזְנֵ֖י כׇּל־הָעָֽם׃ הַנְּבִיאִ֗ים אֲשֶׁ֨ר
הָי֤וּ לְפָנַי֙ וּלְפָנֶ֔יךָ מִן־הָעוֹלָ֑ם וַיִּנָּ֨בְא֜וּ אֶל־אֲרָצ֤וֹת רַבּוֹת֙ וְעַל־מַמְלָכ֣וֹת
ט גְּדֹל֔וֹת לְמִלְחָמָ֖ה וּלְרָעָ֥ה וּלְדָֽבֶר׃ הַנָּבִ֕יא אֲשֶׁ֥ר יִנָּבֵ֖א לְשָׁל֑וֹם בְּבֹא֙
י דְּבַ֣ר הַנָּבִ֔יא יִוָּדַע֙ הַנָּבִ֔יא אֲשֶׁר־שְׁלָח֥וֹ יְהֹוָ֖ה בֶּאֱמֶֽת׃ וַיִּקַּ֞ח חֲנַנְיָ֤ה
יא הַנָּבִיא֙ אֶת־הַמּוֹטָ֔ה מֵעַ֕ל צַוַּ֖אר יִרְמְיָ֣ה הַנָּבִ֑יא וַֽיִּשְׁבְּרֵֽהוּ׃ וַיֹּ֣אמֶר
חֲנַנְיָה֮ לְעֵינֵ֣י כׇל־הָעָם֮ לֵאמֹר֒ כֹּ֣ה אָמַ֣ר יְהֹוָ֗ה כָּ֠כָה אֶשְׁבֹּ֞ר אֶת־עֹ֣ל ׀
נְבֻכַדְנֶאצַּ֣ר מֶלֶךְ־בָּבֶ֗ל בְּעוֹד֙ שְׁנָתַ֣יִם יָמִ֔ים מֵעַ֖ל צַוַּ֣אר כׇּל־הַגּוֹיִ֑ם וַיֵּ֛לֶךְ
יב יִרְמְיָ֥ה הַנָּבִ֖יא לְדַרְכּֽוֹ׃ וַיְהִ֥י דְבַר־יְהֹוָ֖ה אֶל־יִרְמְיָ֑ה
אַחֲרֵ֡י שְׁבוֹר֩ חֲנַנְיָ֨ה הַנָּבִ֜יא אֶת־הַמּוֹטָ֗ה מֵעַל֙ צַוַּ֣אר יִרְמְיָ֣ה הַנָּבִ֔יא

13 the prophet, and He said, "Go and say to Ḥananya: This is what the LORD
said: You have broken bars of wood, but in their stead you shall fashion bars
14 of iron. For this is what the LORD of Hosts, the God of Israel, had said: I
have placed a yoke of iron upon the necks of all these nations to serve
Nevukhadnetzar, king of Babylon, and they shall indeed serve him. I have
15 even given him the beasts of the field." Then Yirmeya the prophet said to
Ḥananya the prophet, "Listen well, Ḥananya. The LORD did not send you,
16 and you have assured this people of a lie. Therefore, this is what the LORD
has said: I am about to send you away from the earth. This year you shall die,
17 for you preached insubordination against the LORD." And Ḥananya the
29 1 prophet died that year in the seventh month. These are the words
of the letter that Yirmeya the prophet sent from Jerusalem to the remaining
elders of the exiles, and to the priests and the prophets, and to all the people
2 that Nevukhadnetzar had exiled from Jerusalem to Babylon. This was after
King Yekhonya and the queen mother and the courtiers, the officers of
Yehuda and Jerusalem, and the craftsmen and artisans had departed from
3 Jerusalem. This letter was sent by the hand of Elasa son of Shafan and Gemarya
son of Ḥilkiya, who were sent to Babylon by King Tzidkiya of Yehuda to King
4 Nevukhadnetzar of Babylon. It said: "This is what the LORD of Hosts, God
of Israel, said to all the exiles that I have exiled from Jerusalem to Babylon:
5 6 Build houses and dwell in them; plant gardens and eat their fruit. Take wives,
and beget sons and daughters. Take wives for your sons and give your
daughters to husbands so that they may give birth to sons and daughters.
7 Multiply there; do not be diminished. Seek the welfare of the city to which I
have exiled you, and pray on its behalf to the LORD, for in its peace there shall
8 be peace for you. For this is what the LORD of Hosts, God of Israel,
has said: Do not allow the prophets among you and your diviners to mislead
9 you. Do not heed your dreams, those that you yourselves inspired. For they
prophesy to you falsely in My name. I did not send them, declares the
10 LORD. But this is what the LORD has said: Only when Babylon's
seventy years are completed will I take note of you and will I fulfill for you
11 My good word, to bring you back to this place. For surely I know the plans
that I have in store for you – declares the LORD – plans for welfare and not
12 for harm, to grant you a hopeful future. Then, when you call upon Me and
13 follow and pray to Me, I will hear you. And when you search you will find Me,
14 if you seek Me with all your heart. I shall be accessible to you – declares the
LORD – and I shall bring back your captives and gather you from all the
nations and from all the places to which I have driven you, declares the LORD.
15 I will bring you back to the place from which I have exiled you. And yet you
16 say, 'The LORD has raised up prophets for us in Babylon.' But this is

יג לֵאמֹר: הָלוֹךְ וְאָמַרְתָּ אֶל־חֲנַנְיָה לֵאמֹר כֹּה אָמַר יְהוָה מוֹטֹת עֵץ
יד שָׁבָרְתָּ וְעָשִׂיתָ תַחְתֵּיהֶן מֹטוֹת בַּרְזֶל: כִּי כֹה־אָמַר יְהוָה צְבָאוֹת
אֱלֹהֵי יִשְׂרָאֵל עֹל בַּרְזֶל נָתַתִּי עַל־צַוַּאר ׀ כָּל־הַגּוֹיִם הָאֵלֶּה לַעֲבֹד
אֶת־נְבֻכַדְנֶאצַּר מֶלֶךְ־בָּבֶל וַעֲבָדֻהוּ וְגַם אֶת־חַיַּת הַשָּׂדֶה נָתַתִּי
טו לוֹ: וַיֹּאמֶר יִרְמְיָה הַנָּבִיא אֶל־חֲנַנְיָה הַנָּבִיא שְׁמַע־נָא חֲנַנְיָה לֹא־
טז שְׁלָחֲךָ יְהוָה וְאַתָּה הִבְטַחְתָּ אֶת־הָעָם הַזֶּה עַל־שָׁקֶר: לָכֵן כֹּה
אָמַר יְהוָה הִנְנִי מְשַׁלֵּחֲךָ מֵעַל פְּנֵי הָאֲדָמָה הַשָּׁנָה אַתָּה מֵת כִּי־
יז סָרָה דִבַּרְתָּ אֶל־יְהוָה: וַיָּמָת חֲנַנְיָה הַנָּבִיא בַּשָּׁנָה הַהִיא בַּחֹדֶשׁ
כט א הַשְּׁבִיעִי: וְאֵלֶּה דִּבְרֵי הַסֵּפֶר אֲשֶׁר שָׁלַח יִרְמְיָה הַנָּבִיא
מִירוּשָׁלָםִ אֶל־יֶתֶר זִקְנֵי הַגּוֹלָה וְאֶל־הַכֹּהֲנִים וְאֶל־הַנְּבִיאִים וְאֶל־
ב כָּל־הָעָם אֲשֶׁר הֶגְלָה נְבוּכַדְנֶאצַּר מִירוּשָׁלַםִ בָּבֶלָה: אַחֲרֵי צֵאת
יְכָנְיָה הַמֶּלֶךְ וְהַגְּבִירָה וְהַסָּרִיסִים שָׂרֵי יְהוּדָה וִירוּשָׁלַםִ וְהֶחָרָשׁ
ג וְהַמַּסְגֵּר מִירוּשָׁלָםִ: בְּיַד אֶלְעָשָׂה בֶן־שָׁפָן וּגְמַרְיָה בֶּן־חִלְקִיָּה אֲשֶׁר
שָׁלַח צִדְקִיָּה מֶלֶךְ־יְהוּדָה אֶל־נְבוּכַדְנֶאצַּר מֶלֶךְ בָּבֶל בָּבֶלָה לֵאמֹר:
ד כֹּה אָמַר יְהוָה צְבָאוֹת אֱלֹהֵי יִשְׂרָאֵל לְכָל־הַגּוֹלָה אֲשֶׁר־הִגְלֵיתִי
ה ו מִירוּשָׁלַםִ בָּבֶלָה: בְּנוּ בָתִּים וְשֵׁבוּ וְנִטְעוּ גַנּוֹת וְאִכְלוּ אֶת־פִּרְיָן: קְחוּ
נָשִׁים וְהוֹלִידוּ בָּנִים וּבָנוֹת וּקְחוּ לִבְנֵיכֶם נָשִׁים וְאֶת־בְּנוֹתֵיכֶם תְּנוּ
ז לַאֲנָשִׁים וְתֵלַדְנָה בָּנִים וּבָנוֹת וּרְבוּ־שָׁם וְאַל־תִּמְעָטוּ: וְדִרְשׁוּ אֶת־ טז
שְׁלוֹם הָעִיר אֲשֶׁר הִגְלֵיתִי אֶתְכֶם שָׁמָּה וְהִתְפַּלְלוּ בַעֲדָהּ אֶל־יְהוָה
ח כִּי בִשְׁלוֹמָהּ יִהְיֶה לָכֶם שָׁלוֹם: כִּי כֹה אָמַר יְהוָה צְבָאוֹת
אֱלֹהֵי יִשְׂרָאֵל אַל־יַשִּׁיאוּ לָכֶם נְבִיאֵיכֶם אֲשֶׁר־בְּקִרְבְּכֶם וְקֹסְמֵיכֶם
ט וְאַל־תִּשְׁמְעוּ אֶל־חֲלֹמֹתֵיכֶם אֲשֶׁר אַתֶּם מַחְלְמִים: כִּי בְשֶׁקֶר הֵם
י נִבְּאִים לָכֶם בִּשְׁמִי לֹא שְׁלַחְתִּים נְאֻם־יְהוָה: כִּי־כֹה
אָמַר יְהוָה כִּי לְפִי מְלֹאת לְבָבֶל שִׁבְעִים שָׁנָה אֶפְקֹד אֶתְכֶם וַהֲקִמֹתִי
יא עֲלֵיכֶם אֶת־דְּבָרִי הַטּוֹב לְהָשִׁיב אֶתְכֶם אֶל־הַמָּקוֹם הַזֶּה: כִּי אָנֹכִי
יָדַעְתִּי אֶת־הַמַּחֲשָׁבֹת אֲשֶׁר אָנֹכִי חֹשֵׁב עֲלֵיכֶם נְאֻם־יְהוָה מַחְשְׁבוֹת
יב שָׁלוֹם וְלֹא לְרָעָה לָתֵת לָכֶם אַחֲרִית וְתִקְוָה: וּקְרָאתֶם אֹתִי וַהֲלַכְתֶּם
יג וְהִתְפַּלַּלְתֶּם אֵלָי וְשָׁמַעְתִּי אֲלֵיכֶם: וּבִקַּשְׁתֶּם אֹתִי וּמְצָאתֶם כִּי תִדְרְשֻׁנִי
יד בְּכָל־לְבַבְכֶם: וְנִמְצֵאתִי לָכֶם נְאֻם־יְהוָה וְשַׁבְתִּי אֶת־שביתכם וְקִבַּצְתִּי שְׁבוּתְכֶם
אֶתְכֶם מִכָּל־הַגּוֹיִם וּמִכָּל־הַמְּקוֹמוֹת אֲשֶׁר הִדַּחְתִּי אֶתְכֶם שָׁם נְאֻם־
טו יְהוָה וַהֲשִׁבֹתִי אֶתְכֶם אֶל־הַמָּקוֹם אֲשֶׁר־הִגְלֵיתִי אֶתְכֶם מִשָּׁם: כִּי
טז אֲמַרְתֶּם הֵקִים לָנוּ יְהוָה נְבִאִים בָּבֶלָה: כִּי־

what the LORD said with regard to the king who sits upon David's throne and
with regard to all the people who dwell in this city, your brothers, who did
17 not go out into exile with you: This is what the LORD of Hosts said:
I am about to send down upon you sword, famine, and pestilence and treat
18 you like putrid figs, so bad that they cannot be eaten. I will chase after you
with sword, famine, and pestilence. I will make them into a source of trembling
for all the kingdoms of the earth, as a curse and an object of horror and
shrieking and derision among all the nations to which I will have driven you.
19 Because they did not hear My words – declares the LORD – when I sent them
My servants, the prophets, early and repeatedly, and yet you did not listen,
20 declares the LORD. But you, the entire exiled community, whom I sent off
21 from Jerusalem to Babylon, heed the LORD's word. This is what the
LORD of Hosts, God of Israel, said concerning Aḥav son of Kolaya and
Tzidkiyahu son of Maaseya – who prophesy to you falsely in My name. I am
about to surrender them to the hand of King Nevukhadnetzar of Babylon,
22 and he will slay them before your eyes. From them a curse will be taken up
by all of Yehuda's exiles who are in Babylon. They will say, 'May the LORD
make you as Tzidkiyahu and Aḥav, whom the king of Babylon roasted in fire.'
23 Because they performed a vile deed in Israel, committing adultery with the
wives of others and speaking false words in My name, which I did not com-
24 mand them. I know, and I am a witness, declares the LORD." "And
25 you[65] should say to Shemayahu the Nehelamite: This is what the LORD of
Hosts, God of Israel, said: Because you sent letters in your name to the people
in Jerusalem and to Tzefanya son of Maaseya the priest and to all the priests,
26 saying, 'The LORD has appointed you as priest in place of Yehoyada the priest,
to be overseers of the LORD's House over every madman who pretends he is
27 a prophet, whom you should consign to the stocks and to the iron collar. Now,
why have you not excoriated Yirmeyahu the Anatotite, who pretends to be a
28 prophet for you? For he did indeed send a message to us in Babylon declaring:
"The exile will be a long one, so build houses and dwell in them, and plant
29 gardens and eat their fruit."'" And Tzefanya the priest read this letter to the
30 ears of Yirmeyahu the prophet. Then the LORD's word came
31 to Yirmeyahu, saying, "Send a message to all the exiles, saying: This is what
the LORD said regarding Shemaya the Nehelamite: Because Shemaya has
prophesied to you although I did not send him, and has made you trust in a
32 lie, therefore, this is what the LORD said: I am about to punish Shemaya
the Nehelamite and his descendants so that he will have no one dwelling
among this people; no one to see the good that I am going to do for My
people – declares the LORD – for he has preached insubordination against
30 1 the LORD." The word that came to Yirmeyahu from the LORD: This
2 is what the LORD, God of Israel, said: "Write all the words that I speak to you
3 in a scroll. For look, days are coming," declares the LORD, "when I will bring

65 | Yirmeyahu.

כֹּה ׀ אָמַר יְהוָה אֶל־הַמֶּלֶךְ הַיּוֹשֵׁב אֶל־כִּסֵּא דָוִד וְאֶל־כָּל־הָעָם הַיּוֹשֵׁב
יז בָּעִיר הַזֹּאת אֲחֵיכֶם אֲשֶׁר לֹא־יָצְאוּ אִתְּכֶם בַּגּוֹלָה׃ כֹּה
אָמַר יְהוָה צְבָאוֹת הִנְנִי מְשַׁלֵּחַ בָּם אֶת־הַחֶרֶב אֶת־הָרָעָב וְאֶת־
הַדָּבֶר וְנָתַתִּי אוֹתָם כַּתְּאֵנִים הַשֹּׁעָרִים אֲשֶׁר לֹא־תֵאָכַלְנָה מֵרֹעַ׃
יח וְרָדַפְתִּי אַחֲרֵיהֶם בַּחֶרֶב בָּרָעָב וּבַדָּבֶר וּנְתַתִּים לזועה לְכֹל ׀ מַמְלְכוֹת לְזַעֲוָה
הָאָרֶץ לְאָלָה וּלְשַׁמָּה וְלִשְׁרֵקָה וּלְחֶרְפָּה בְּכָל־הַגּוֹיִם אֲשֶׁר־הִדַּחְתִּים
יט שָׁם׃ תַּחַת אֲשֶׁר־לֹא־שָׁמְעוּ אֶל־דְּבָרַי נְאֻם־יְהוָה אֲשֶׁר שָׁלַחְתִּי
אֲלֵיהֶם אֶת־עֲבָדַי הַנְּבִאִים הַשְׁכֵּם וְשָׁלֹחַ וְלֹא שְׁמַעְתֶּם נְאֻם־
כ יְהוָה׃ וְאַתֶּם שִׁמְעוּ דְבַר־יְהוָה כָּל־הַגּוֹלָה אֲשֶׁר־שִׁלַּחְתִּי מִירוּשָׁלַ͏ִם
כא בָּבֶלָה׃ כֹּה־אָמַר יְהוָה צְבָאוֹת אֱלֹהֵי יִשְׂרָאֵל אֶל־אַחְאָב
בֶּן־קוֹלָיָה וְאֶל־צִדְקִיָּהוּ בֶן־מַעֲשֵׂיָה הַנִּבְּאִים לָכֶם בִּשְׁמִי שָׁקֶר הִנְנִי ׀
כב נֹתֵן אֹתָם בְּיַד נְבוּכַדְרֶאצַּר מֶלֶךְ־בָּבֶל וְהִכָּם לְעֵינֵיכֶם׃ וְלֻקַּח מֵהֶם
קְלָלָה לְכֹל גָּלוּת יְהוּדָה אֲשֶׁר בְּבָבֶל לֵאמֹר יְשִׂמְךָ יְהוָה כְּצִדְקִיָּהוּ
כג וּכְאֶחָב אֲשֶׁר־קָלָם מֶלֶךְ־בָּבֶל בָּאֵשׁ׃ יַעַן אֲשֶׁר עָשׂוּ נְבָלָה בְּיִשְׂרָאֵל
וַיְנַאֲפוּ אֶת־נְשֵׁי רֵעֵיהֶם וַיְדַבְּרוּ דָבָר בִּשְׁמִי שֶׁקֶר אֲשֶׁר לוֹא צִוִּיתִם
כד וְאָנֹכִי הוידע וָעֵד נְאֻם־יְהוָה׃ וְאֶל־שְׁמַעְיָהוּ הַנֶּחֱלָמִי הַיּוֹדֵעַ
כה תֹּאמַר לֵאמֹר׃ כֹּה־אָמַר יְהוָה צְבָאוֹת אֱלֹהֵי יִשְׂרָאֵל לֵאמֹר יַעַן אֲשֶׁר
אַתָּה שָׁלַחְתָּ בְשִׁמְכָה סְפָרִים אֶל־כָּל־הָעָם אֲשֶׁר בִּירוּשָׁלַ͏ִם וְאֶל־
כו צְפַנְיָה בֶן־מַעֲשֵׂיָה הַכֹּהֵן וְאֶל־כָּל־הַכֹּהֲנִים לֵאמֹר׃ יְהוָה נְתָנְךָ כֹהֵן
תַּחַת יְהוֹיָדָע הַכֹּהֵן לִהְיוֹת פְּקִדִים בֵּית יְהוָה לְכָל־אִישׁ מְשֻׁגָּע וּמִתְנַבֵּא
כז וְנָתַתָּה אֹתוֹ אֶל־הַמַּהְפֶּכֶת וְאֶל־הַצִּינֹק׃ וְעַתָּה לָמָּה לֹא גָעַרְתָּ
כח בְּיִרְמְיָהוּ הָעַנְּתֹתִי הַמִּתְנַבֵּא לָכֶם׃ כִּי עַל־כֵּן שָׁלַח אֵלֵינוּ בָּבֶל לֵאמֹר
כט אֲרֻכָּה הִיא בְּנוּ בָתִּים וְשֵׁבוּ וְנִטְעוּ גַנּוֹת וְאִכְלוּ אֶת־פְּרִיהֶן׃ וַיִּקְרָא
ל צְפַנְיָה הַכֹּהֵן אֶת־הַסֵּפֶר הַזֶּה בְּאָזְנֵי יִרְמְיָהוּ הַנָּבִיא׃ וַיְהִי
לא דְּבַר־יְהוָה אֶל־יִרְמְיָהוּ לֵאמֹר׃ שְׁלַח עַל־כָּל־הַגּוֹלָה לֵאמֹר כֹּה אָמַר
יְהוָה אֶל־שְׁמַעְיָה הַנֶּחֱלָמִי יַעַן אֲשֶׁר נִבָּא לָכֶם שְׁמַעְיָה וַאֲנִי לֹא
לב שְׁלַחְתִּיו וַיַּבְטַח אֶתְכֶם עַל־שָׁקֶר׃ לָכֵן כֹּה־אָמַר יְהוָה הִנְנִי פֹקֵד
עַל־שְׁמַעְיָה הַנֶּחֱלָמִי וְעַל־זַרְעוֹ לֹא־יִהְיֶה לוֹ אִישׁ ׀ יוֹשֵׁב ׀ בְּתוֹךְ־הָעָם
הַזֶּה וְלֹא־יִרְאֶה בַטּוֹב אֲשֶׁר־אֲנִי עֹשֶׂה־לְעַמִּי נְאֻם־יְהוָה כִּי־סָרָה
ל א דִבֶּר עַל־יְהוָה׃ הַדָּבָר אֲשֶׁר הָיָה אֶל־יִרְמְיָהוּ מֵאֵת
ב יְהוָה לֵאמֹר׃ כֹּה־אָמַר יְהוָה אֱלֹהֵי יִשְׂרָאֵל לֵאמֹר כְּתָב־לְךָ אֵת
ג כָּל־הַדְּבָרִים אֲשֶׁר־דִּבַּרְתִּי אֵלֶיךָ אֶל־סֵפֶר׃ כִּי הִנֵּה יָמִים בָּאִים נְאֻם־

back from captivity My people Israel and Yehuda," said the LORD, "and I will
restore them to the land that I gave to their fathers, and they shall possess
4 it." And these are the words that the LORD spoke concerning Israel
5 and Yehuda: Thus said the LORD: We heard the sound of trembling, terror,
6 and no peace. Ask now and observe. Do males give birth? Why then do I see
every man with his hands upon his loins like a woman in labor and every face
7 turned green? O! That day is great; there is none like it! It is a time of distress
8 for Yaakov, but he shall be delivered from it. It will happen on that day,
declares the LORD of Hosts, that I will break his[66] yoke from upon your neck,
and I will tear apart your bonds, and strangers will no longer make you
9 servants. Rather, they will serve the LORD their God, and David their king,
10 whom I shall raise up for them. As for you, My servant Yaakov, do
not fear, declares the LORD, and Israel, do not be terrified, for I will deliver
you from a distant land and your descendants from their land of captivity. For
11 Yaakov it will again be quiet and tranquil with none to frighten him. For I am
with you, declares the LORD, to deliver you. For I will make an end of all the
nations among whom I have scattered you, but of you I will not make an end.
12 I will discipline you justly, but I will surely not annihilate you. For
13 thus said the LORD: Your bruise is incurable, your wound severe. There is
14 none to plead your cause for healing. You have no curative medicine. All your
supposed lovers have forgotten you; they do not seek you out. For I have
struck you with an enemy's blow, a cruel rebuke for your many iniquities, for
15 your numerous sins. Why do you cry out over your affliction? Why is your
pain incurable? It is because of your many iniquities, your numerous sins, that
16 I have done these things to you. Therefore, all who devoured you will be
devoured, and all of your oppressors, every one, will fall into captivity. Those
who laid waste to you will be laid waste, and all who despoiled you, I will
17 make spoils of them. I will surely raise up a cure for you, and I will heal you
of your wounds, declares the LORD, for they have called you an outcast, saying,
18 "This Zion, there is none to seek her out." Thus said the LORD: I am
about to bring back the captives of Yaakov's tents and will show compassion
for his dwelling places. The city will be rebuilt upon its mound, and its citadel
19 will be set upon its rightful place. Out of them shall come thanksgiving and
the sound of merrymakers. I will multiply them, and they will not be
20 diminished; I will make them honored, and they shall not be degraded. Its
children will be as before, and its community will be established before Me.
21 I will punish all of its oppressors. His leader shall be one of his own, and
his ruler shall come forth from his midst. I will draw him near, and he
shall approach Me, for who is it who will otherwise dare to approach Me?
22 declares the LORD. And you shall become My people, and I will be your
23 God. Behold, the tempest of the LORD shall go forth with fury. An
24 earthshaking storm will whirl down upon the heads of the wicked. The
LORD's burning wrath will not turn away until it carries out and fulfills His

66 | Nevukhadnetzar's.

יְהוָה וְשַׁבְתִּי אֶת־שְׁבוּת עַמִּי יִשְׂרָאֵל וִיהוּדָה אָמַר יְהוָה וַהֲשִׁבֹתִים
ד אֶל־הָאָרֶץ אֲשֶׁר־נָתַתִּי לַאֲבוֹתָם וִירֵשׁוּהָ: וְאֵלֶּה הַדְּבָרִים
ה אֲשֶׁר דִּבֶּר יְהוָה אֶל־יִשְׂרָאֵל וְאֶל־יְהוּדָה: כִּי־כֹה אָמַר יְהוָה קוֹל
ו חֲרָדָה שָׁמָעְנוּ פַּחַד וְאֵין שָׁלוֹם: שַׁאֲלוּ־נָא וּרְאוּ אִם־יֹלֵד זָכָר מַדּוּעַ
ז רָאִיתִי כָל־גֶּבֶר יָדָיו עַל־חֲלָצָיו כַּיּוֹלֵדָה וְנֶהֶפְכוּ כָל־פָּנִים לְיֵרָקוֹן: הוֹי
כִּי גָדוֹל הַיּוֹם הַהוּא מֵאַיִן כָּמֹהוּ וְעֵת־צָרָה הִיא לְיַעֲקֹב וּמִמֶּנָּה יִוָּשֵׁעַ:
ח וְהָיָה בַיּוֹם הַהוּא נְאֻם ׀ יְהוָה צְבָאוֹת אֶשְׁבֹּר עֻלּוֹ מֵעַל צַוָּארֶךָ
ט וּמוֹסְרוֹתֶיךָ אֲנַתֵּק וְלֹא־יַעַבְדוּ־בוֹ עוֹד זָרִים: וְעָבְדוּ אֵת יְהוָה אֱלֹהֵיהֶם יז
י וְאֵת דָּוִד מַלְכָּם אֲשֶׁר אָקִים לָהֶם: וְאַתָּה אַל־תִּירָא עַבְדִּי
יַעֲקֹב נְאֻם־יְהוָה וְאַל־תֵּחַת יִשְׂרָאֵל כִּי הִנְנִי מוֹשִׁיעֲךָ מֵרָחוֹק וְאֶת־
יא זַרְעֲךָ מֵאֶרֶץ שִׁבְיָם וְשָׁב יַעֲקֹב וְשָׁקַט וְשַׁאֲנַן וְאֵין מַחֲרִיד: כִּי־אִתְּךָ
אֲנִי נְאֻם־יְהוָה לְהוֹשִׁיעֶךָ כִּי אֶעֱשֶׂה כָלָה בְּכָל־הַגּוֹיִם ׀ אֲשֶׁר הֲפִצוֹתִיךָ
שָׁם אַךְ אֹתְךָ לֹא־אֶעֱשֶׂה כָלָה וְיִסַּרְתִּיךָ לַמִּשְׁפָּט וְנַקֵּה לֹא
יב אֲנַקֶּךָּ: כִּי כֹה אָמַר יְהוָה אָנוּשׁ לְשִׁבְרֵךְ נַחְלָה
יג יד מַכָּתֵךְ: אֵין־דָּן דִּינֵךְ לְמָזוֹר רְפֻאוֹת תְּעָלָה אֵין לָךְ: כָּל־מְאַהֲבַיִךְ
שְׁכֵחוּךְ אוֹתָךְ לֹא יִדְרֹשׁוּ כִּי מַכַּת אוֹיֵב הִכִּיתִיךְ מוּסַר אַכְזָרִי עַל רֹב
טו עֲוֺנֵךְ עָצְמוּ חַטֹּאתָיִךְ: מַה־תִּזְעַק עַל־שִׁבְרֵךְ אָנוּשׁ מַכְאֹבֵךְ עַל ׀ רֹב
טז עֲוֺנֵךְ עָצְמוּ חַטֹּאתַיִךְ עָשִׂיתִי אֵלֶּה לָךְ: לָכֵן כָּל־אֹכְלַיִךְ יֵאָכֵלוּ וְכָל־
יז צָרַיִךְ כֻּלָּם בַּשְּׁבִי יֵלֵכוּ וְהָיוּ שֹׁאסַיִךְ לִמְשִׁסָּה וְכָל־בֹּזְזַיִךְ אֶתֵּן לָבַז: כִּי
אַעֲלֶה אֲרֻכָה לָךְ וּמִמַּכּוֹתַיִךְ אֶרְפָּאֵךְ נְאֻם־יְהוָה כִּי נִדָּחָה קָרְאוּ לָךְ
יח צִיּוֹן הִיא דֹּרֵשׁ אֵין לָהּ: כֹּה ׀ אָמַר יְהוָה הִנְנִי־שָׁב שְׁבוּת
אָהֳלֵי יַעֲקוֹב וּמִשְׁכְּנֹתָיו אֲרַחֵם וְנִבְנְתָה עִיר עַל־תִּלָּהּ וְאַרְמוֹן עַל־
יט מִשְׁפָּטוֹ יֵשֵׁב: וְיָצָא מֵהֶם תּוֹדָה וְקוֹל מְשַׂחֲקִים וְהִרְבִּתִים וְלֹא יִמְעָטוּ
כ וְהִכְבַּדְתִּים וְלֹא יִצְעָרוּ: וְהָיוּ בָנָיו כְּקֶדֶם וַעֲדָתוֹ לְפָנַי תִּכּוֹן וּפָקַדְתִּי
כא עַל כָּל־לֹחֲצָיו: וְהָיָה אַדִּירוֹ מִמֶּנּוּ וּמֹשְׁלוֹ מִקִּרְבּוֹ יֵצֵא וְהִקְרַבְתִּיו
כב וְנִגַּשׁ אֵלָי כִּי מִי הוּא־זֶה עָרַב אֶת־לִבּוֹ לָגֶשֶׁת אֵלַי נְאֻם־יְהוָה: וִהְיִיתֶם
כג לִי לְעָם וְאָנֹכִי אֶהְיֶה לָכֶם לֵאלֹהִים: הִנֵּה ׀ סַעֲרַת יְהוָה
כד חֵמָה יָצְאָה סַעַר מִתְגּוֹרֵר עַל רֹאשׁ רְשָׁעִים יָחוּל: לֹא יָשׁוּב חֲרוֹן
אַף־יְהוָה עַד־עֲשֹׂתוֹ וְעַד־הֲקִימוֹ מְזִמּוֹת לִבּוֹ בְּאַחֲרִית הַיָּמִים

25 heart's intentions. In the days to come you will understand this.[67] At that time,
declares the LORD, I will be God to all the families of Israel, and they will be
31 1 My people. This is what the LORD said: The people who escaped
the sword found favor in the wilderness – Israel, on the way to its place of rest.
2 From afar the LORD appeared to me: I have loved you with an everlasting
3 love and thereby drew you close with loving-kindness. I will again rebuild
you, and you shall remain rebuilt, maiden Israel. You will again adorn yourself
4 with timbrels and go out to dance a dance of merrymakers. You will again
plant vineyards on the hills of Shomron. Planters will plant and enjoy the
5 fruit. Indeed, there is a day when sentinels shall call out over the Efrayim hills:
6 "Come, and let us go up to Zion, to the LORD our God." For this is
what the LORD said: Sing joyously for Yaakov and shout publicly to the
nations. Give voice, give praise, and say, "LORD, deliver Your people, the
7 remnant of Israel." I am about to bring them from the northern land and
gather them from the ends of the earth. The blind and the lame among them,
the pregnant woman together with one who has just given birth. A great
8 assembly will return here. They will come weeping, and with compassion I
shall lead them. I will guide them along streams of water on a level path upon
which they will not stumble, for I have become a Father to Israel, and Efrayim
9 is My firstborn. Nations, hear the word of the LORD, and
tell it to the distant isles. Say, "He who has scattered Israel will gather him and
10 will watch over him as a shepherd does his flock." For the LORD has released
11 Yaakov and has rescued him from the hands of one mightier than him. They
will come and sing on the heights of Zion and will stream toward the LORD's
goodness, because of the grain and the new wine and olive oil, and because
of the young sheep and cattle. Their lives will be like a well-watered garden;
12 they will no longer languish ever again. Then maidens shall rejoice in dance,
young men and old together. I shall turn their grief into joy; I shall console
13 them and gladden them in their grief. I shall give the priests their fill of
fatness, and My people shall be satiated with My goodness, declares the
14 LORD. This is what the LORD said: A sound is heard in Rama:[69]
wailing, bitter weeping. It is Raḥel, weeping for her children. She refuses to
15 be consoled for her children, for they are gone. This is what the
LORD said: Restrain your voice from crying and your eyes from tears, for
there is a reward for your labor, declares the LORD, and they will return from
16 the land of the enemy. There is hope for your future, declares the LORD, and
17 your children will return to their own country. I have indeed heard Efrayim
moaning for himself: "You have disciplined me and I accepted the discipline,
like an untamed calf. Bring me back and I shall return, for You are the LORD,
18 my God. After I turned back, I was remorseful, and after I became aware, I
struck myself upon my thigh. I was ashamed and even humiliated, for I carry

---

67 | Cf. 23:19–20.

68 | Note that many English Bibles number the last verse of chapter 30 as the first verse of chapter 31, so that our verse 1 is their verse 2, and so on throughout the chapter.

69 | A town north of Jerusalem (see 40:1).

כה תִּתְבּוֹנְנוּ בָהּ׃ בָּעֵת הַהִיא נְאֻם־יְהוָה אֶהְיֶה לֵאלֹהִים לְכֹל מִשְׁפְּחוֹת
לא א יִשְׂרָאֵל וְהֵמָּה יִהְיוּ־לִי לְעָם׃ כֹּה אָמַר יְהוָה
ב מָצָא חֵן בַּמִּדְבָּר עַם שְׂרִידֵי חָרֶב הָלוֹךְ לְהַרְגִּיעוֹ יִשְׂרָאֵל׃ מֵרָחוֹק
ג יְהוָה נִרְאָה לִי וְאַהֲבַת עוֹלָם אֲהַבְתִּיךְ עַל־כֵּן מְשַׁכְתִּיךְ חָסֶד׃ עוֹד
אֶבְנֵךְ וְנִבְנֵית בְּתוּלַת יִשְׂרָאֵל עוֹד תַּעְדִּי תֻפַּיִךְ וְיָצָאת בִּמְחוֹל
ד מְשַׂחֲקִים׃ עוֹד תִּטְּעִי כְרָמִים בְּהָרֵי שֹׁמְרוֹן נָטְעוּ נֹטְעִים וְחִלֵּלוּ׃
ה כִּי יֶשׁ־יוֹם קָרְאוּ נֹצְרִים בְּהַר אֶפְרָיִם קוּמוּ וְנַעֲלֶה צִיּוֹן אֶל־יְהוָה
ו אֱלֹהֵינוּ׃ כִּי־כֹה ׀ אָמַר יְהוָה רָנּוּ לְיַעֲקֹב שִׂמְחָה
וְצַהֲלוּ בְּרֹאשׁ הַגּוֹיִם הַשְׁמִיעוּ הַלְלוּ וְאִמְרוּ הוֹשַׁע יְהוָה אֶת־עַמְּךָ
ז אֵת שְׁאֵרִית יִשְׂרָאֵל׃ הִנְנִי מֵבִיא אוֹתָם מֵאֶרֶץ צָפוֹן וְקִבַּצְתִּים
מִיַּרְכְּתֵי־אָרֶץ בָּם עִוֵּר וּפִסֵּחַ הָרָה וְיֹלֶדֶת יַחְדָּו קָהָל גָּדוֹל יָשׁוּבוּ
ח הֵנָּה׃ בִּבְכִי יָבֹאוּ וּבְתַחֲנוּנִים אוֹבִילֵם אוֹלִיכֵם אֶל־נַחֲלֵי מַיִם
בְּדֶרֶךְ יָשָׁר לֹא יִכָּשְׁלוּ בָּהּ כִּי־הָיִיתִי לְיִשְׂרָאֵל לְאָב וְאֶפְרַיִם בְּכֹרִי
ט הוּא׃ שִׁמְעוּ דְבַר־יְהוָה גּוֹיִם וְהַגִּידוּ בָאִיִּים מִמֶּרְחָק וְאִמְרוּ
י מְזָרֵה יִשְׂרָאֵל יְקַבְּצֶנּוּ וּשְׁמָרוֹ כְּרֹעֶה עֶדְרוֹ׃ כִּי־פָדָה יְהוָה אֶת־יַעֲקֹב
יא וּגְאָלוֹ מִיַּד חָזָק מִמֶּנּוּ׃ וּבָאוּ וְרִנְּנוּ בִמְרוֹם־צִיּוֹן וְנָהֲרוּ אֶל־טוּב יְהוָה
עַל־דָּגָן וְעַל־תִּירֹשׁ וְעַל־יִצְהָר וְעַל־בְּנֵי־צֹאן וּבָקָר וְהָיְתָה נַפְשָׁם
יב כְּגַן רָוֶה וְלֹא־יוֹסִיפוּ לְדַאֲבָה עוֹד׃ אָז תִּשְׂמַח בְּתוּלָה בְּמָחוֹל
וּבַחֻרִים וּזְקֵנִים יַחְדָּו וְהָפַכְתִּי אֶבְלָם לְשָׂשׂוֹן וְנִחַמְתִּים וְשִׂמַּחְתִּים
יג מִיגוֹנָם׃ וְרִוֵּיתִי נֶפֶשׁ הַכֹּהֲנִים דָּשֶׁן וְעַמִּי אֶת־טוּבִי יִשְׂבָּעוּ נְאֻם־
יד יְהוָה׃ כֹּה ׀ אָמַר יְהוָה קוֹל בְּרָמָה נִשְׁמָע נְהִי
בְּכִי תַמְרוּרִים רָחֵל מְבַכָּה עַל־בָּנֶיהָ מֵאֲנָה לְהִנָּחֵם עַל־בָּנֶיהָ כִּי
טו אֵינֶנּוּ׃ כֹּה ׀ אָמַר יְהוָה מִנְעִי קוֹלֵךְ מִבֶּכִי וְעֵינַיִךְ מִדִּמְעָה
טז כִּי יֵשׁ שָׂכָר לִפְעֻלָּתֵךְ נְאֻם־יְהוָה וְשָׁבוּ מֵאֶרֶץ אוֹיֵב׃ וְיֵשׁ־תִּקְוָה
יז לְאַחֲרִיתֵךְ נְאֻם־יְהוָה וְשָׁבוּ בָנִים לִגְבוּלָם׃ שָׁמוֹעַ שָׁמַעְתִּי אֶפְרַיִם
מִתְנוֹדֵד יִסַּרְתַּנִי וָאִוָּסֵר כְּעֵגֶל לֹא לֻמָּד הֲשִׁבֵנִי וְאָשׁוּבָה כִּי אַתָּה
יח יְהוָה אֱלֹהָי׃ כִּי־אַחֲרֵי שׁוּבִי נִחַמְתִּי וְאַחֲרֵי הִוָּדְעִי סָפַקְתִּי עַל־יָרֵךְ

19 the disgrace of my youth." Is Efrayim not a precious son to me, a delightful
child? Whenever I speak of him I remember him all the more. Therefore I
long for him inwardly. I will show him great compassion, declares the
20 LORD. Set up road markers for yourself, place high guideposts for
yourself, take note of the path by which you traveled. Return, maiden Israel.
21 Return to these, your cities. How long will you turn away, wayward daughter?
For the LORD will create something new in the world: A woman will go about
22 in search of a man! This is what the LORD of Hosts, God of Israel,
said: They will again say these words in the land of Yehuda and in its cities,
when I bring them back from their captivity: "May the LORD bless you, abode
23 of righteousness, holy mountain." And they shall dwell there, in Yehuda and
24 in all its cities, farmers and those who move about with their flocks. I will
25 refresh the weary and replenish every languishing person. At this I awoke and
26 understood; I had slept pleasantly. Days are soon coming,
declares the LORD, when I will sow the House of Israel and the House of
27 Yehuda with the seed of people and the seed of cattle. It will come to pass that
just as I was watchful over them to uproot, to tear down, to demolish, to
destroy, and to harm, so will I be watchful over them to build and to plant,
28 declares the LORD. In those days they will no longer say, "Fathers eat sour
29 grapes, but the teeth of the children are set on edge." Instead, everyone will
perish for his own sins; anyone who eats sour grapes, only his own teeth shall
30 be set on edge. Days are soon coming, declares the LORD, when I
31 will make a new covenant with the House of Israel and the House of Yehuda,
not like the covenant that I made with their fathers at the time that I held fast
to their hands in order to take them out of Egypt; they broke that covenant
32 with Me although I was master over them, declares the LORD. For this
covenant, which I will make with the House of Israel after these days, declares
the LORD, I will deliver My teaching into their midst and inscribe it upon
33 their hearts, and I will be their God, and they will be My people. No longer
will each person teach a neighbor and each person a brother, saying, "Know
the LORD!" For they will all know Me, from the least of them to their greatest,
declares the LORD. For I will forgive their iniquities and no longer remember
34 their transgressions. This is what the LORD said: He who assigns the
sun to shine by day and regulates the moon and stars to shine at night, who
35 first calms the sea and then makes its waves roar, LORD of Hosts is His name.
If these statutes vanish from before Me, declares the LORD, then will the seed
36 of Israel cease to be a nation before Me for all time. This is what the
LORD said: If the heavens above be measured, and the foundation of the earth
below be explored, only then will I reject all the seed of Israel for all that they
37 have done, declares the LORD. For days are soon coming, declares
the LORD, when the city will be rebuilt for the LORD from the Tower of
38 Ḥananel to the Corner Gate. And a measuring line shall go out again in front
39 of it to the Hill of Garev and continue toward Goa. And the entire valley of
the corpses and ashes, and all the meadows up to the Kidron Valley, up to the

יט בָּשְׁתִּי וְגַם־נִכְלַמְתִּי כִּי נָשָׂאתִי חֶרְפַּת נְעוּרָי׃ הֲבֵן יַקִּיר לִי אֶפְרַיִם אִם
יֶלֶד שַׁעֲשֻׁעִים כִּי־מִדֵּי דַבְּרִי בּוֹ זָכֹר אֶזְכְּרֶנּוּ עוֹד עַל־כֵּן הָמוּ מֵעַי לוֹ
כ רַחֵם אֲרַחֲמֶנּוּ נְאֻם־יְהוָה׃ הַצִּיבִי לָךְ צִיֻּנִים שִׂמִי לָךְ
תַּמְרוּרִים שִׁתִי לִבֵּךְ לַמְסִלָּה דֶּרֶךְ הלכתי שׁוּבִי בְּתוּלַת יִשְׂרָאֵל שֻׁבִי הָלָכְתְּ
כא אֶל־עָרַיִךְ אֵלֶּה׃ עַד־מָתַי תִּתְחַמָּקִין הַבַּת הַשּׁוֹבֵבָה כִּי־בָרָא יְהוָה
כב חֲדָשָׁה בָּאָרֶץ נְקֵבָה תְּסוֹבֵב גָּבֶר׃ כֹּה־אָמַר יְהוָה צְבָאוֹת
אֱלֹהֵי יִשְׂרָאֵל עוֹד יֹאמְרוּ אֶת־הַדָּבָר הַזֶּה בְּאֶרֶץ יְהוּדָה וּבְעָרָיו
כג בְּשׁוּבִי אֶת־שְׁבוּתָם יְבָרֶכְךָ יְהוָה נְוֵה־צֶדֶק הַר הַקֹּדֶשׁ׃ וְיָשְׁבוּ בָהּ
כד יְהוּדָה וְכָל־עָרָיו יַחְדָּו אִכָּרִים וְנָסְעוּ בַּעֵדֶר׃ כִּי הִרְוֵיתִי נֶפֶשׁ עֲיֵפָה
כה וְכָל־נֶפֶשׁ דָּאֲבָה מִלֵּאתִי׃ עַל־זֹאת הֱקִיצֹתִי וָאֶרְאֶה וּשְׁנָתִי עָרְבָה
כו לִי׃ הִנֵּה יָמִים בָּאִים נְאֻם־יְהוָה וְזָרַעְתִּי אֶת־בֵּית יִשְׂרָאֵל
כז וְאֶת־בֵּית יְהוּדָה זֶרַע אָדָם וְזֶרַע בְּהֵמָה׃ וְהָיָה כַּאֲשֶׁר שָׁקַדְתִּי עֲלֵיהֶם
לִנְתוֹשׁ וְלִנְתוֹץ וְלַהֲרֹס וּלְהַאֲבִיד וּלְהָרֵעַ כֵּן אֶשְׁקֹד עֲלֵיהֶם לִבְנוֹת
כח וְלִנְטוֹעַ נְאֻם־יְהוָה׃ בַּיָּמִים הָהֵם לֹא־יֹאמְרוּ עוֹד אָבוֹת אָכְלוּ בֹסֶר
כט וְשִׁנֵּי בָנִים תִּקְהֶינָה׃ כִּי אִם־אִישׁ בַּעֲוֺנוֹ יָמוּת כָּל־הָאָדָם הָאֹכֵל הַבֹּסֶר
ל תִּקְהֶינָה שִׁנָּיו׃ הִנֵּה יָמִים בָּאִים נְאֻם־יְהוָה וְכָרַתִּי אֶת־
לא בֵּית יִשְׂרָאֵל וְאֶת־בֵּית יְהוּדָה בְּרִית חֲדָשָׁה׃ לֹא כַבְּרִית אֲשֶׁר כָּרַתִּי
אֶת־אֲבוֹתָם בְּיוֹם הֶחֱזִיקִי בְיָדָם לְהוֹצִיאָם מֵאֶרֶץ מִצְרָיִם אֲשֶׁר־הֵמָּה
לב הֵפֵרוּ אֶת־בְּרִיתִי וְאָנֹכִי בָּעַלְתִּי בָם נְאֻם־יְהוָה׃ כִּי זֹאת הַבְּרִית אֲשֶׁר יח
אֶכְרֹת אֶת־בֵּית יִשְׂרָאֵל אַחֲרֵי הַיָּמִים הָהֵם נְאֻם־יְהוָה נָתַתִּי אֶת־
תּוֹרָתִי בְּקִרְבָּם וְעַל־לִבָּם אֶכְתֲּבֶנָּה וְהָיִיתִי לָהֶם לֵאלֹהִים וְהֵמָּה
לג יִהְיוּ־לִי לְעָם׃ וְלֹא יְלַמְּדוּ עוֹד אִישׁ אֶת־רֵעֵהוּ וְאִישׁ אֶת־אָחִיו לֵאמֹר
דְּעוּ אֶת־יְהוָה כִּי כוּלָּם יֵדְעוּ אוֹתִי לְמִקְּטַנָּם וְעַד־גְּדוֹלָם נְאֻם־יְהוָה
לד כִּי אֶסְלַח לַעֲוֺנָם וּלְחַטָּאתָם לֹא אֶזְכָּר־עוֹד׃ כֹּה ׀ אָמַר
יְהוָה נֹתֵן שֶׁמֶשׁ לְאוֹר יוֹמָם חֻקֹּת יָרֵחַ וְכוֹכָבִים לְאוֹר לָיְלָה רֹגַע
לה הַיָּם וַיֶּהֱמוּ גַלָּיו יְהוָה צְבָאוֹת שְׁמוֹ׃ אִם־יָמֻשׁוּ הַחֻקִּים הָאֵלֶּה
מִלְּפָנַי נְאֻם־יְהוָה גַּם זֶרַע יִשְׂרָאֵל יִשְׁבְּתוּ מִהְיוֹת גּוֹי לְפָנַי כָּל־
לו הַיָּמִים׃ כֹּה ׀ אָמַר יְהוָה אִם־יִמַּדּוּ שָׁמַיִם מִלְמַעְלָה וְיֵחָקְרוּ
מוֹסְדֵי־אֶרֶץ לְמָטָּה גַּם־אֲנִי אֶמְאַס בְּכָל־זֶרַע יִשְׂרָאֵל עַל־כָּל־אֲשֶׁר
לז עָשׂוּ נְאֻם־יְהוָה׃ הִנֵּה יָמִים נְאֻם־יְהוָה וְנִבְנְתָה הָעִיר בָּאִים
לח לַיהוָה מִמִּגְדַּל חֲנַנְאֵל עַד־שַׁעַר הַפִּנָּה׃ וְיָצָא עוֹד קוה הַמִּדָּה נֶגְדּוֹ קָו
לט עַל גִּבְעַת גָּרֵב וְנָסַב גֹּעָתָה׃ וְכָל־הָעֵמֶק הַפְּגָרִים ׀ וְהַדֶּשֶׁן וְכָל־

corner of the Horse Gate to the east, will be holy to the Lord, never again to
32 1 be uprooted or demolished. The word that came to Yirmeyahu from
the Lord during the tenth year of Tzidkiyahu, king of Yehuda, that being the
2 eighteenth year of Nevukhadnetzar. The army of the king of Babylon was
then besieging Jerusalem, and Yirmeyahu the prophet was confined to the
3 prison courtyard near the palace of the king of Yehuda.[70] He had been
confined by Tzidkiyahu, king of Yehuda, who had said, "How dare you
prophesy?" This is what the Lord said: "I am about to give the city into the
4 hand of the king of Babylon, and he shall capture it. And Tzidkiyahu, king of
Yehuda, shall not escape the hand of the Chaldeans but shall certainly be
delivered into the hand of the king of Babylon, and will speak to him mouth
5 to mouth and see him eye to eye. He will lead Tzidkiyahu to Babylon, and
there he will remain until I call him to account," declares the Lord. "If you
6 wage war against the Chaldeans, you shall not be successful." And
7 Yirmeyahu said: The word of the Lord came to me: Ḥanamel, son of your
uncle Shalum, shall come to you and say, "Purchase for yourself my field that
8 is in Anatot, for yours is the right of redemption by purchase."[71] Ḥanamel, my
uncle's son, came to me – just as the Lord had said – to the prison courtyard,
and said to me, "Please purchase my field in Anatot, in the territory of
Binyamin, for yours is the right of inheritance, and it is your right to redeem
it. Purchase it for yourself." Then I knew that this was the word of the Lord.
9 And so I purchased the field that was in Anatot from my uncle's son Ḥanamel.
10 I weighed out the silver to him: seven shekel and ten silver coins. I wrote it
upon a scroll and sealed it, and I had it witnessed; and I weighed out the silver
11 on a scale. I took the deed of purchase, sealed as prescribed by law and custom,
12 along with the unsealed document.[72] And I gave the deed of purchase to
Barukh son of Neriya son of Maḥseya in the presence of Ḥanamel my uncle,
in the presence of the witnesses who were listed in the deed of purchase, and
in the presence of all the men of Yehuda who were sitting in the prison
13 14 courtyard. In their presence I instructed Barukh, saying, "This is what the
Lord of Hosts, God of Israel, said: Take these scrolls, this deed of purchase,
the sealed section and the unsealed section, and place it in a clay vessel, so that
15 it might be preserved for many days." For this is what the Lord of
Hosts, God of Israel, has said: Houses, fields, and vineyards shall once again
16 be purchased in this land. After I gave this deed of purchase to Barukh
17 son of Neriya, I prayed to the Lord, saying, "O Lord God! You made the
heavens and the earth with Your great strength and with Your arm stretched
18 forth. Nothing is too wonderful for You. You perform loving-kindness to
thousands but repay the sins of fathers unto the bosoms of their children after
19 them. The great and mighty God, Lord of Hosts is His name. Great in counsel,
mighty in deed, Your eyes are open to all of the ways of humans, to give each

70 | See 37:21.
71 | See Leviticus 25:25.
72 | Common practice was to have both a sealed and an open copy of a deed.

הַשְּׁרֵמוֹת עַד־נַחַל קִדְרוֹן עַד־פִּנַּת שַׁעַר הַסּוּסִים מִזְרָחָה קֹדֶשׁ הַשְּׁדֵמוֹת
לב א לַיהוה לֹא־יִנָּתֵשׁ וְלֹא־יֵהָרֵס עוֹד לְעוֹלָם: הַדָּבָר אֲשֶׁר
הָיָה אֶל־יִרְמְיָהוּ מֵאֵת יהוה בשנת הָעֲשִׂרִית לְצִדְקִיָּהוּ מֶלֶךְ יְהוּדָה בַּשָּׁנָה
ב הִיא הַשָּׁנָה שְׁמֹנֶה־עֶשְׂרֵה שָׁנָה לִנְבוּכַדְרֶאצַּר: וְאָז חֵיל מֶלֶךְ בָּבֶל
צָרִים עַל־יְרוּשָׁלִָם וְיִרְמְיָהוּ הַנָּבִיא הָיָה כָלוּא בַּחֲצַר הַמַּטָּרָה אֲשֶׁר
ג בֵּית־מֶלֶךְ יְהוּדָה: אֲשֶׁר כְּלָאוֹ צִדְקִיָּהוּ מֶלֶךְ־יְהוּדָה לֵאמֹר מַדּוּעַ
אַתָּה נִבָּא לֵאמֹר כֹּה אָמַר יהוה הִנְנִי נֹתֵן אֶת־הָעִיר הַזֹּאת בְּיַד
ד מֶלֶךְ־בָּבֶל וּלְכָדָהּ: וְצִדְקִיָּהוּ מֶלֶךְ יְהוּדָה לֹא יִמָּלֵט מִיַּד הַכַּשְׂדִּים
כִּי־הִנָּתֹן יִנָּתֵן בְּיַד מֶלֶךְ־בָּבֶל וְדִבֶּר־פִּיו עִם־פִּיו וְעֵינָיו אֶת־עֵינָו
ה תִּרְאֶינָה: וּבָבֶל יוֹלִךְ אֶת־צִדְקִיָּהוּ וְשָׁם יִהְיֶה עַד־פָּקְדִי אֹתוֹ נְאֻם־
ו יהוה כִּי תִלָּחֲמוּ אֶת־הַכַּשְׂדִּים לֹא תַצְלִיחוּ: וַיֹּאמֶר
ז יִרְמְיָהוּ הָיָה דְּבַר־יהוה אֵלַי לֵאמֹר: הִנֵּה חֲנַמְאֵל בֶּן־שַׁלֻּם דֹּדְךָ בָּא
אֵלֶיךָ לֵאמֹר קְנֵה לְךָ אֶת־שָׂדִי אֲשֶׁר בַּעֲנָתוֹת כִּי לְךָ מִשְׁפַּט הַגְּאֻלָּה
ח לִקְנוֹת: וַיָּבֹא אֵלַי חֲנַמְאֵל בֶּן־דֹּדִי כִּדְבַר יהוה אֶל־חֲצַר הַמַּטָּרָה
וַיֹּאמֶר אֵלַי קְנֵה נָא אֶת־שָׂדִי אֲשֶׁר־בַּעֲנָתוֹת אֲשֶׁר ׀ בְּאֶרֶץ בִּנְיָמִין
כִּי־לְךָ מִשְׁפַּט הַיְרֻשָּׁה וּלְךָ הַגְּאֻלָּה קְנֵה־לָךְ וָאֵדַע כִּי דְבַר־יהוה הוּא:
ט וָאֶקְנֶה אֶת־הַשָּׂדֶה מֵאֵת חֲנַמְאֵל בֶּן־דֹּדִי אֲשֶׁר בַּעֲנָתוֹת וָאֶשְׁקֲלָה־
י לּוֹ אֶת־הַכֶּסֶף שִׁבְעָה שְׁקָלִים וַעֲשָׂרָה הַכָּסֶף: וָאֶכְתֹּב בַּסֵּפֶר וָאֶחְתֹּם
יא וָאָעֵד עֵדִים וָאֶשְׁקֹל הַכֶּסֶף בְּמֹאזְנָיִם: וָאֶקַּח אֶת־סֵפֶר הַמִּקְנָה אֶת־
יב הֶחָתוּם הַמִּצְוָה וְהַחֻקִּים וְאֶת־הַגָּלוּי: וָאֶתֵּן אֶת־הַסֵּפֶר הַמִּקְנָה אֶל־
בָּרוּךְ בֶּן־נֵרִיָּה בֶּן־מַחְסֵיָה לְעֵינֵי חֲנַמְאֵל דֹּדִי וּלְעֵינֵי הָעֵדִים הַכֹּתְבִים
יג בְּסֵפֶר הַמִּקְנָה לְעֵינֵי כָּל־הַיְּהוּדִים הַיֹּשְׁבִים בַּחֲצַר הַמַּטָּרָה: וָאֲצַוֶּה
יד אֶת־בָּרוּךְ לְעֵינֵיהֶם לֵאמֹר: כֹּה־אָמַר יהוה צְבָאוֹת אֱלֹהֵי יִשְׂרָאֵל
לָקוֹחַ אֶת־הַסְּפָרִים הָאֵלֶּה אֵת סֵפֶר הַמִּקְנָה הַזֶּה וְאֵת הֶחָתוּם
וְאֵת סֵפֶר הַגָּלוּי הַזֶּה וּנְתַתָּם בִּכְלִי־חָרֶשׂ לְמַעַן יַעַמְדוּ יָמִים
טו רַבִּים: כִּי כֹה אָמַר יהוה צְבָאוֹת אֱלֹהֵי יִשְׂרָאֵל עוֹד
טז יִקָּנוּ בָתִּים וְשָׂדוֹת וּכְרָמִים בָּאָרֶץ הַזֹּאת: וָאֶתְפַּלֵּל
אֶל־יהוה אַחֲרֵי תִתִּי אֶת־סֵפֶר הַמִּקְנָה אֶל־בָּרוּךְ בֶּן־נֵרִיָּה לֵאמֹר:
יז אֲהָהּ אֲדֹנָי יֱהֹוִה הִנֵּה ׀ אַתָּה עָשִׂיתָ אֶת־הַשָּׁמַיִם וְאֶת־הָאָרֶץ בְּכֹחֲךָ
יח הַגָּדוֹל וּבִזְרֹעֲךָ הַנְּטוּיָה לֹא־יִפָּלֵא מִמְּךָ כָּל־דָּבָר: עֹשֶׂה חֶסֶד לַאֲלָפִים
וּמְשַׁלֵּם עֲוֹן אָבוֹת אֶל־חֵיק בְּנֵיהֶם אַחֲרֵיהֶם הָאֵל הַגָּדוֹל הַגִּבּוֹר
יט יהוה צְבָאוֹת שְׁמוֹ: גְּדֹל הָעֵצָה וְרַב הָעֲלִילִיָּה אֲשֶׁר־עֵינֶיךָ פְקֻחוֹת

one according to his ways, to each according to the fruits of his actions.
20 You set signs and wonders in the land of Egypt to this day[73] for Israel and for
21 humankind, and You made a name for Yourself as on this day. You brought
out Your people Israel from the land of Egypt with signs and wonders, a
22 mighty hand and an arm stretched forth, and with terrifying power. You gave
them this land that You swore to their fathers that You would give them, a
23 land flowing with milk and honey. They came and possessed it, but they
neither heeded Your voice nor followed Your teaching. All that You had
commanded them to do they did not do, and so You caused all this disaster
24 to come upon them. The siege ramps have come near the city in order to
capture it, and the city is about to be delivered, because of the sword and the
famine and the pestilence, into the hands of the Chaldeans who are attacking
25 it. That which you spoke about has happened, and You see it for Yourself. And
yet You say to me, Lord God, 'Purchase this field for yourself for silver and
have it witnessed, when the city is about to be delivered into the hands of the
26 27 Chaldeans'?" And the word of the Lord came to Yirmeyahu: "Look,
28 I am the Lord, God of all flesh. Is anything beyond My power?" Therefore,
this is what the Lord said: "I am about to deliver this city into the hands of
the Chaldeans and into the hands of Nevukhadretzar, king of Babylon, and
29 he will capture it. The Chaldeans, who are attacking this city, will come and
set fire to city and burn it down along with the houses that offered incense
to the Baal on their rooftops and poured libations to other gods, thereby
30 arousing My anger. For the Israelites and the people of Yehuda have been
doing nothing but that which is evil in My eyes from the time of their youth;
for the Israelites are only arousing My anger with their actions," declares the
31 Lord. "This city, from the time they built it until this very day, has aroused
32 My anger and My wrath so that it must be removed from My presence
on account of all the evil that the Israelites and the people of Yehuda did to
anger Me: them, their kings, their officials, their priests, and their prophets,
33 the prominent men of Yehuda, and the inhabitants of Jerusalem. They
turned their backs to Me, not their faces. I taught them early and repeatedly;
34 nevertheless, they neither listened nor took instruction. They placed their
35 vile objects in the very house which is called by My name, to defile it. They
built the altars for the Baal that are in the Valley of Ben Hinom, to give over
their sons and daughters to Molekh – something that I did not command
them and that never entered My mind – to perform such a detestable thing,
36 and so they corrupted Yehuda. But now," so said the Lord, God of
Israel, "about this city that you say is delivered into the hands of the king of
37 Babylon by the sword, by famine, and by pestilence, I will gather them from
all the lands to which I have driven them in My anger and in My wrath and
with great rage, and I will return them to this place and settle them here in
38 39 safety. They will be My people, and I will be their God. I will give them one

73 | That are still spoken about today.

כ עַל־כָּל־דַּרְכֵי בְּנֵי אָדָם לָתֵת לְאִישׁ כִּדְרָכָיו וְכִפְרִי מַעֲלָלָיו׃ אֲשֶׁר
שַׂמְתָּ אֹתוֹת וּמֹפְתִים בְּאֶרֶץ מִצְרַיִם עַד־הַיּוֹם הַזֶּה וּבְיִשְׂרָאֵל וּבָאָדָם
כא וַתַּעֲשֶׂה־לְּךָ שֵׁם כַּיּוֹם הַזֶּה׃ וַתֹּצֵא אֶת־עַמְּךָ אֶת־יִשְׂרָאֵל מֵאֶרֶץ
מִצְרָיִם בְּאֹתוֹת וּבְמוֹפְתִים וּבְיָד חֲזָקָה וּבְאֶזְרוֹעַ נְטוּיָה וּבְמוֹרָא גָּדוֹל׃ יט
כב וַתִּתֵּן לָהֶם אֶת־הָאָרֶץ הַזֹּאת אֲשֶׁר־נִשְׁבַּעְתָּ לַאֲבוֹתָם לָתֵת לָהֶם
כג אֶרֶץ זָבַת חָלָב וּדְבָשׁ׃ וַיָּבֹאוּ וַיִּרְשׁוּ אֹתָהּ וְלֹא־שָׁמְעוּ בְקוֹלֶךָ ובתרותך וּבְתוֹרָתְךָ
לֹא־הָלָכוּ אֵת כָּל־אֲשֶׁר צִוִּיתָה לָהֶם לַעֲשׂוֹת לֹא עָשׂוּ וַתַּקְרֵא אֹתָם
כד אֵת כָּל־הָרָעָה הַזֹּאת׃ הִנֵּה הַסֹּלְלוֹת בָּאוּ הָעִיר לְלָכְדָהּ וְהָעִיר נִתְּנָה
בְּיַד הַכַּשְׂדִּים הַנִּלְחָמִים עָלֶיהָ מִפְּנֵי הַחֶרֶב וְהָרָעָב וְהַדָּבֶר וַאֲשֶׁר
כה דִּבַּרְתָּ הָיָה וְהִנְּךָ רֹאֶה׃ וְאַתָּה אָמַרְתָּ אֵלַי אֲדֹנָי יְהוִה קְנֵה־לְךָ הַשָּׂדֶה
כו בַּכֶּסֶף וְהָעֵד עֵדִים וְהָעִיר נִתְּנָה בְּיַד הַכַּשְׂדִּים׃ וַיְהִי
כז דְּבַר־יְהוָה אֶל־יִרְמְיָהוּ לֵאמֹר׃ הִנֵּה אֲנִי יְהוָה אֱלֹהֵי כָּל־בָּשָׂר הֲמִמֶּנִּי
כח יִפָּלֵא כָּל־דָּבָר׃ לָכֵן כֹּה אָמַר יְהוָה הִנְנִי נֹתֵן אֶת־הָעִיר הַזֹּאת
כט בְּיַד הַכַּשְׂדִּים וּבְיַד נְבוּכַדְרֶאצַּר מֶלֶךְ־בָּבֶל וּלְכָדָהּ׃ וּבָאוּ הַכַּשְׂדִּים
הַנִּלְחָמִים עַל־הָעִיר הַזֹּאת וְהִצִּיתוּ אֶת־הָעִיר הַזֹּאת בָּאֵשׁ וּשְׂרָפוּהָ
וְאֵת הַבָּתִּים אֲשֶׁר קִטְּרוּ עַל־גַּגּוֹתֵיהֶם לַבַּעַל וְהִסִּכוּ נְסָכִים לֵאלֹהִים
ל אֲחֵרִים לְמַעַן הַכְעִסֵנִי׃ כִּי־הָיוּ בְנֵי־יִשְׂרָאֵל וּבְנֵי יְהוּדָה אַךְ עֹשִׂים
הָרַע בְּעֵינַי מִנְּעֻרֹתֵיהֶם כִּי בְנֵי־יִשְׂרָאֵל אַךְ מַכְעִסִים אֹתִי בְּמַעֲשֵׂה
לא יְדֵיהֶם נְאֻם־יְהוָה׃ כִּי עַל־אַפִּי וְעַל־חֲמָתִי הָיְתָה לִּי הָעִיר הַזֹּאת
לב לְמִן־הַיּוֹם אֲשֶׁר בָּנוּ אוֹתָהּ וְעַד הַיּוֹם הַזֶּה לַהֲסִירָהּ מֵעַל פָּנָי׃ עַל
כָּל־רָעַת בְּנֵי־יִשְׂרָאֵל וּבְנֵי יְהוּדָה אֲשֶׁר עָשׂוּ לְהַכְעִסֵנִי הֵמָּה מַלְכֵיהֶם
לג שָׂרֵיהֶם כֹּהֲנֵיהֶם וּנְבִיאֵיהֶם וְאִישׁ יְהוּדָה וְיֹשְׁבֵי יְרוּשָׁלִָם׃ וַיִּפְנוּ אֵלַי
עֹרֶף וְלֹא פָנִים וְלַמֵּד אֹתָם הַשְׁכֵּם וְלַמֵּד וְאֵינָם שֹׁמְעִים לָקַחַת מוּסָר׃
לד לה וַיָּשִׂימוּ שִׁקּוּצֵיהֶם בַּבַּיִת אֲשֶׁר־נִקְרָא־שְׁמִי עָלָיו לְטַמְּאוֹ׃ וַיִּבְנוּ אֶת־
בָּמוֹת הַבַּעַל אֲשֶׁר ׀ בְּגֵיא בֶן־הִנֹּם לְהַעֲבִיר אֶת־בְּנֵיהֶם וְאֶת־בְּנוֹתֵיהֶם
לַמֹּלֶךְ אֲשֶׁר לֹא־צִוִּיתִים וְלֹא עָלְתָה עַל־לִבִּי לַעֲשׂוֹת הַתּוֹעֵבָה הַזֹּאת
לו לְמַעַן הַחֲטִי אֶת־יְהוּדָה׃ וְעַתָּה לָכֵן כֹּה־אָמַר יְהוָה אֱלֹהֵי
יִשְׂרָאֵל אֶל־הָעִיר הַזֹּאת אֲשֶׁר ׀ אַתֶּם אֹמְרִים נִתְּנָה בְּיַד מֶלֶךְ־בָּבֶל
לז בַּחֶרֶב וּבָרָעָב וּבַדָּבֶר׃ הִנְנִי מְקַבְּצָם מִכָּל־הָאֲרָצוֹת אֲשֶׁר הִדַּחְתִּים
שָׁם בְּאַפִּי וּבַחֲמָתִי וּבְקֶצֶף גָּדוֹל וַהֲשִׁבֹתִים אֶל־הַמָּקוֹם הַזֶּה וְהֹשַׁבְתִּים
לח לט לָבֶטַח׃ וְהָיוּ לִי לְעָם וַאֲנִי אֶהְיֶה לָהֶם לֵאלֹהִים׃ וְנָתַתִּי לָהֶם לֵב אֶחָד

heart and one way to revere Me always in order to benefit them and their
40 children after them. I will make an eternal covenant with them and never
draw back from them, from benefiting them. I will instill reverence for Me in
41 their hearts so that they will never turn aside from Me. I will rejoice over them
to their benefit, and I will plant them in this land faithfully, with all My heart
42 and with all My soul." For this is what the LORD said: "Just as I
brought upon this people this great disaster, so will I bring them all the good
43 fortune that I have assured them. Fields will be purchased in this land of which
you say, 'It is desolate, devoid of man and beast, delivered to the Chaldeans.'
44 Fields will be purchased for silver, written in a scroll, and sealed and witnessed
in the land of Binyamin and in the surroundings of Jerusalem, and in the cities
of Yehuda and the cities in the mountains, in the cities of the lowland and the
cities of the south, for I will bring them back from their captivity," declares the
33 1 LORD. The word of the LORD came to Yirmeyahu a second time
2 while he was still shut in the prison courtyard: This is what the LORD, who
is performing it, said – the LORD is crafting it to make it last; the LORD is His
3 name – Call to Me and I will answer you. I will tell you great and unattainable
4 things, things that you never knew. For this is what the LORD,
God of Israel, said regarding the houses of this city and the palaces that are
5 being demolished on account of the siege ramps and the sword: The kings
of Yehuda are coming to do battle with the Chaldeans, but they themselves
fill the city with the corpses of the people whom I struck in My anger and
6 in My wrath, having hidden My face from this city on account of all their
wickedness.I shall offer her cure and healing, and I shall heal them. I shall
7 impart to them abundant and abiding peace. I will bring them back from the
8 captivity of Yehuda and the captivity of Israel and will build them up as before.
I will purify them from all their sins that they sinned against Me. I shall forgive
9 them for all the sins that they sinned against Me and for their rebellion against
Me. She shall become for Me a symbol of joy, praise, and glory for all nations
of the earth, who shall learn of the great good that I have done for them and
will fear and tremble over all the great good and peace that I shall accomplish
10 for her. This is what the LORD said: Again will be heard in this place,
that you say is ruined and devoid of man and beast, the cities of Yehuda and
the streets of Jerusalem that are deserted, devoid of man and inhabitant and
11 beast, the sound of joy and the sound of happiness, the voice of the groom
and the voice of the bride, the voice of those who proclaim, "Give thanks to
the LORD of Hosts, for the LORD is good and His loving-kindness is forever,"
and the voice of those who bring offerings of thanksgiving to the House
of the LORD, for I will return the captives to the land as before, says the
12 LORD. This is what the LORD of Hosts said: There will again be in
this place – now a ruin with neither man nor beast in all of its cities – an abode
13 for shepherds resting their sheep. In the towns of the hills, in the cities of the
lowlands, and in the cities of the south, and in the territory of Binyamin, and

וְדֶרֶךְ אֶחָד לְיִרְאָה אוֹתִי כָּל־הַיָּמִים לְטוֹב לָהֶם וְלִבְנֵיהֶם אַחֲרֵיהֶם׃
מ וְכָרַתִּי לָהֶם בְּרִית עוֹלָם אֲשֶׁר לֹא־אָשׁוּב מֵאַחֲרֵיהֶם לְהֵיטִיבִי
מא אוֹתָם וְאֶת־יִרְאָתִי אֶתֵּן בִּלְבָבָם לְבִלְתִּי סוּר מֵעָלָי׃ וְשַׂשְׂתִּי עֲלֵיהֶם
לְהֵטִיב אוֹתָם וּנְטַעְתִּים בָּאָרֶץ הַזֹּאת בֶּאֱמֶת בְּכָל־לִבִּי וּבְכָל־
מב נַפְשִׁי׃ כִּי־כֹה אָמַר יהוה כַּאֲשֶׁר הֵבֵאתִי אֶל־הָעָם הַזֶּה
אֵת כָּל־הָרָעָה הַגְּדוֹלָה הַזֹּאת כֵּן אָנֹכִי מֵבִיא עֲלֵיהֶם אֶת־כָּל־הַטּוֹבָה
מג אֲשֶׁר אָנֹכִי דֹּבֵר עֲלֵיהֶם׃ וְנִקְנָה הַשָּׂדֶה בָּאָרֶץ הַזֹּאת אֲשֶׁר ׀ אַתֶּם
מד אֹמְרִים שְׁמָמָה הִיא מֵאֵין אָדָם וּבְהֵמָה נִתְּנָה בְּיַד הַכַּשְׂדִּים׃ שָׂדוֹת
בַּכֶּסֶף יִקְנוּ וְכָתוֹב בַּסֵּפֶר ׀ וְחָתוֹם וְהָעֵד עֵדִים בְּאֶרֶץ בִּנְיָמִן וּבִסְבִיבֵי
יְרוּשָׁלַ͏ִם וּבְעָרֵי יְהוּדָה וּבְעָרֵי הָהָר וּבְעָרֵי הַשְּׁפֵלָה וּבְעָרֵי הַנֶּגֶב כִּי־
לג א אָשִׁיב אֶת־שְׁבוּתָם נְאֻם־יהוה׃ וַיְהִי דְבַר־יהוה אֶל־
ב יִרְמְיָהוּ שֵׁנִית וְהוּא עוֹדֶנּוּ עָצוּר בַּחֲצַר הַמַּטָּרָה לֵאמֹר׃ כֹּה־אָמַר
ג יהוה עֹשָׂהּ יהוה יוֹצֵר אוֹתָהּ לַהֲכִינָהּ יהוה שְׁמוֹ׃ קְרָא אֵלַי וְאֶעֱנֶךָּ
ד וְאַגִּידָה לְךָ גְּדֹלוֹת וּבְצֻרוֹת לֹא יְדַעְתָּם׃ כִּי כֹה אָמַר יהוה
אֱלֹהֵי יִשְׂרָאֵל עַל־בָּתֵּי הָעִיר הַזֹּאת וְעַל־בָּתֵּי מַלְכֵי יְהוּדָה הַנְּתֻצִים
ה אֶל־הַסֹּלְלוֹת וְאֶל־הֶחָרֶב׃ בָּאִים לְהִלָּחֵם אֶת־הַכַּשְׂדִּים וּלְמַלְאָם
אֶת־פִּגְרֵי הָאָדָם אֲשֶׁר־הִכֵּיתִי בְאַפִּי וּבַחֲמָתִי וַאֲשֶׁר הִסְתַּרְתִּי פָנַי
ו מֵהָעִיר הַזֹּאת עַל כָּל־רָעָתָם׃ הִנְנִי מַעֲלֶה־לָּהּ אֲרֻכָה וּמַרְפֵּא וּרְפָאתִים
ז וְגִלֵּיתִי לָהֶם עֲתֶרֶת שָׁלוֹם וֶאֱמֶת׃ וַהֲשִׁבֹתִי אֶת־שְׁבוּת יְהוּדָה וְאֵת
ח שְׁבוּת יִשְׂרָאֵל וּבְנִתִים כְּבָרִאשֹׁנָה׃ וְטִהַרְתִּים מִכָּל־עֲוֺנָם אֲשֶׁר
חָטְאוּ־לִי וְסָלַחְתִּי לכול־עֲוֺנוֹתֵיהֶם אֲשֶׁר חָטְאוּ־לִי וַאֲשֶׁר פָּשְׁעוּ לְכָל־
ט בִי׃ וְהָיְתָה לִּי לְשֵׁם שָׂשׂוֹן לִתְהִלָּה וּלְתִפְאֶרֶת לְכֹל גּוֹיֵי הָאָרֶץ אֲשֶׁר
יִשְׁמְעוּ אֶת־כָּל־הַטּוֹבָה אֲשֶׁר אָנֹכִי עֹשֶׂה אֹתָם וּפָחֲדוּ וְרָגְזוּ עַל כָּל־
י הַטּוֹבָה וְעַל כָּל־הַשָּׁלוֹם אֲשֶׁר אָנֹכִי עֹשֶׂה לָּהּ׃ כֹּה ׀
אָמַר יהוה עוֹד יִשָּׁמַע בַּמָּקוֹם־הַזֶּה אֲשֶׁר אַתֶּם אֹמְרִים חָרֵב הוּא
מֵאֵין אָדָם וּמֵאֵין בְּהֵמָה בְּעָרֵי יְהוּדָה וּבְחֻצוֹת יְרוּשָׁלַ͏ִם הַנְשַׁמּוֹת
יא מֵאֵין אָדָם וּמֵאֵין יוֹשֵׁב וּמֵאֵין בְּהֵמָה׃ קוֹל שָׂשׂוֹן וְקוֹל שִׂמְחָה קוֹל
חָתָן וְקוֹל כַּלָּה קוֹל אֹמְרִים הוֹדוּ אֶת־יהוה צְבָאוֹת כִּי־טוֹב יהוה
כִּי־לְעוֹלָם חַסְדּוֹ מְבִאִים תּוֹדָה בֵּית יהוה כִּי־אָשִׁיב אֶת־שְׁבוּת־הָאָרֶץ
יב כְּבָרִאשֹׁנָה אָמַר יהוה׃ כֹּה אָמַר יהוה צְבָאוֹת עוֹד יִהְיֶה ׀
בַּמָּקוֹם הַזֶּה הֶחָרֵב מֵאֵין־אָדָם וְעַד־בְּהֵמָה וּבְכָל־עָרָיו נְוֵה רֹעִים
יג מַרְבִּצִים צֹאן׃ בְּעָרֵי הָהָר בְּעָרֵי הַשְּׁפֵלָה וּבְעָרֵי הַנֶּגֶב וּבְאֶרֶץ בִּנְיָמִן

in the environs of Jerusalem, and in the cities of Yehuda, sheep will again pass
14 under the hands of the one numbering them, says the LORD. Days
are approaching, declares the LORD, when I will fulfill the good promise that
15 I made to the House of Israel and the House of Yehuda. In those days and in
that time, I will make a righteous scion blossom forth from David, and he will
16 dispense justice and righteousness in the land. In those days Yehuda will be
saved, and Jerusalem will dwell in safety, and this is what He will call her:
17 "The LORD is our righteous one." For this is what the LORD said:
There will never cease to be someone of David's line to sit upon the throne
18 of the House of Israel. And for the Levitical priests there will never cease
to be someone to offer burnt offerings, burn grain offerings, and perform
19 sacrifices before Me for all time. The word of the LORD came to
20 Yirmeyahu: This is what the LORD said: If you are able to break My covenant
with the day and My covenant with the night, causing day and night not to
21 occur in their designated times, only then can My covenant with My servant
David, that his son will reign upon his throne, be broken, and similarly for
22 the Levitical priests, My ministrants. Just as the heavenly bodies cannot be
counted, and the sand of the sea cannot be measured, so will I increase the
23 seed of my servant David and of the Levites who minister to Me. The
24 word of the LORD came to Yirmeyahu: Have you not observed what this
people have said? "The LORD has rejected these two families which He had
once chosen."[74] They have scorned My people, so that they will never again
25 be a nation in their eyes. This is what the LORD said: Only if I had
no covenant with day and night, and if I had not established the laws of
26 heaven and earth, would I reject the offspring of Yaakov and of David My
servant, and not select any of his offspring as rulers over the offspring of
Avraham, Yisḥak,[75] and Yaakov – for I will bring them back from their captivity
34 1 and have compassion for them. The word that came to Yirmeyahu
from the LORD while Nevukhadretzar, king of Babylon, his army, all the
kingdoms under his dominion, and all the peoples were attacking Jerusalem
2 and its towns – this is what the LORD, God of Israel, said: "Go and speak to
Tzidkiyahu, king of Yehuda, and say to him: This is what the LORD said: I am
about to deliver this city into the hands of the king of Babylon, and he will
3 burn it down by fire. You will not escape him. You will be seized and delivered
into his hands. Your eyes will see the eyes of the king of Babylon, and you
4 will speak directly to each other. You will be brought to Babylon. But hear
the word of the LORD, Tzidkiyahu, king of Yehuda. This is what the LORD
5 said regarding you: You will not perish by the sword. Rather, you will die
peacefully. Just as incense was burned for your ancestors, the kings of old who
came before you, so will they burn spices for you. They will eulogize you,
saying, 'Alas, master!' For this is the word that I asserted," declares the
6 LORD. Yirmeyahu the prophet related all these words to Tzidkiyahu,

74 | The dynasties of the priesthood and the kingship referred to in verse 21 above.

75 | A variant spelling of Yitzḥak. The verb "to laugh," on which the name is based, can itself appear in Biblical Hebrew both as *tzaḥak* and *saḥak*.

ובסביבי ירושלם ובערי יהודה עד תעברנה הצאן על־ידי מונה
יד אמר יהוה: הנה ימים באים נאם־יהוה והקמתי את־
טו הדבר הטוב אשר דברתי אל־בית ישראל ועל־בית יהודה: בימים
ההם ובעת ההיא אצמיח לדוד צמח צדקה ועשה משפט וצדקה
טז בארץ: בימים ההם תושע יהודה וירושלם תשכון לבטח וזה ב
יז אשר־יקרא־לה יהוה ׀ צדקנו: כי־כה אמר יהוה לא־
יח יכרת לדוד איש ישב על־כסא בית־ישראל: ולכהנים הלוים לא־
יכרת איש מלפני מעלה עולה ומקטיר מנחה ועשה זבח כל־
יט הימים: ויהי דבר־יהוה אל־ירמיהו לאמור: כ כה אמר
יהוה אם־תפרו את־בריתי היום ואת־בריתי הלילה ולבלתי היות
כא יומם־ולילה בעתם: גם־בריתי תפר את־דוד עבדי מהיות־לו בן
כב מלך על־כסאו ואת־הלוים הכהנים משרתי: אשר לא־יספר צבא
השמים ולא ימד חול הים כן ארבה את־זרע דוד עבדי ואת־
כג הלוים משרתי אתי: ויהי דבר־יהוה אל־ירמיהו
כד לאמר: הלוא ראית מה־העם הזה דברו לאמר שתי המשפחות
אשר בחר יהוה בהם וימאסם ואת־עמי ינאצון מהיות עוד גוי
כה לפניהם: כה אמר יהוה אם־לא בריתי יומם ולילה חקות
כו שמים וארץ לא־שמתי: גם־זרע יעקוב ודוד עבדי אמאס מקחת
מזרעו משלים אל־זרע אברהם ישחק ויעקב כי־אשוב את־שבותם (אשיב)
לד א ורחמתים: הדבר אשר־היה אל־ירמיהו מאת יהוה
ונבוכדראצר מלך־בבל ׀ וכל־חילו וכל־ממלכות ארץ ממשלת
ב ידו וכל־העמים נלחמים על־ירושלם ועל־כל־עריה לאמר: כה־
אמר יהוה אלהי ישראל הלך ואמרת אל־צדקיהו מלך יהודה
ואמרת אליו כה אמר יהוה הנני נתן את־העיר הזאת ביד מלך־בבל
ג ושרפה באש: ואתה לא תמלט מידו כי תפש תתפש ובידו תנתן
ועיניך את־עיני מלך־בבל תראינה ופיהו את־פיך ידבר ובבל תבוא:
ד אך שמע דבר־יהוה צדקיהו מלך יהודה כה־אמר יהוה עליך לא
ה תמות בחרב: בשלום תמות ובמשרפות אבותיך המלכים הראשנים
אשר־היו לפניך כן ישרפו־לך והוי אדון יספדו־לך כי־דבר אני־
ו דברתי נאם־יהוה: וידבר ירמיהו הנביא אל־צדקיהו

7 king of Yehuda, in Jerusalem while the army of the king of Babylon continued
to attack Jerusalem and all the remaining cities of Yehuda, Lakhish and Azeka,
8 for they alone were the fortified cities left of the cities of Yehuda. The
word that came to Yirmeyahu from the Lord after King Tzidkiyahu had
9 made a covenant with all the people of Jerusalem, proclaiming their freedom:
Everyone was to set free his Hebrew manservant and his Hebrew maidservant.
10 No one was to enslave his fellow man of Yehuda. All the officials and all the
people who had entered into the covenant obeyed in that each person set free
his manservant and his maidservant, Hebrew males and females, never to
11 enslave them again. They obeyed and set them free. After a time, they regressed.
They recovered the manservants and maidservants that they had set free and
12 forced them to be manservants and maidservants. Then the word of
13 the Lord came to Yirmeyahu from the Lord. This is what the Lord, God of
Israel, said: "I made a covenant with your ancestors at the time I took them
14 out of the land of Egypt, the house of bondage, saying, 'At the beginning of
the seventh year[76] each of you should set free your brother Hebrew who had
been sold to you and who served you for six years – send him forth from you
free.' But your ancestors did not heed Me and did not even bend their ears.
15 You repented today and did what was proper in My eyes, proclaiming freedom,
every person for his fellow, and you made a covenant in My presence in the
16 house which is called by My name. But you regressed and profaned My name.
Each of you recovered his manservant and his maidservant, whom you had
set free to do as they desire, and you forced them to remain manservants and
17 maidservants for yourselves." Therefore, this is what the Lord said:
"Because you did not heed Me to proclaim freedom, everyone for his brother
and everyone for his fellow, so will I set free against you," declares the Lord,
"the sword, the pestilence, and the famine, and render you an object of
18 shuddering for all the kingdoms of the earth. And I will deliver to all the
people who violated My covenant and did not uphold the words of the
covenant that they made in My presence, the calf that they cut in two,[77] the
19 sections of which they passed between – the officials of Yehuda and the
officials of Jerusalem, the courtiers and the priests, and all the folk of the land
20 who passed between the sections of the calf – I will deliver them into the
hands of their enemies, the hands of those that seek their lives, and their
corpses shall become fodder for the birds of the skies and the beasts of the
21 earth. I will deliver Tzidkiyahu, king of Yehuda, and his officials into the hands
of their enemies and into the hands of those who seek their lives and into the
22 army of the king of Babylon, which is withdrawing from you.[78] I shall now
utter a command," declares the Lord, "and I shall bring them back to this city.
They will attack it, capture it, and burn it down by fire. The cities of Yehuda I
35 1 shall render desolate, without an inhabitant." The word that came
to Yirmeyahu from the Lord in the days of Yehoyakim, son of Yoshiyahu,

76 | See Exodus 21:2–3.

77 | An important covenantal ritual (see, e.g., Gen., ch. 15).

78 | Referring to when the Chaldeans were temporarily diverted from the siege (see ch. 37).

ז מֶלֶךְ יְהוּדָה אֵת כׇּל־הַדְּבָרִים הָאֵלֶּה בִּירוּשָׁלִָם׃ וְחֵיל מֶלֶךְ־בָּבֶל
נִלְחָמִים עַל־יְרוּשָׁלִַם וְעַל כׇּל־עָרֵי יְהוּדָה הַנּוֹתָרוֹת אֶל־לָכִישׁ וְאֶל־
ח עֲזֵקָה כִּי הֵנָּה נִשְׁאֲרוּ בְּעָרֵי יְהוּדָה עָרֵי מִבְצָר׃ הַדָּבָר
אֲשֶׁר־הָיָה אֶל־יִרְמְיָהוּ מֵאֵת יהוה אַחֲרֵי כְּרֹת הַמֶּלֶךְ צִדְקִיָּהוּ בְּרִית
ט אֶת־כׇּל־הָעָם אֲשֶׁר בִּירוּשָׁלִַם לִקְרֹא לָהֶם דְּרוֹר׃ לְשַׁלַּח אִישׁ אֶת־
עַבְדּוֹ וְאִישׁ אֶת־שִׁפְחָתוֹ הָעִבְרִי וְהָעִבְרִיָּה חׇפְשִׁים לְבִלְתִּי עֲבׇד־
י בָּם בִּיהוּדִי אָחִיהוּ אִישׁ׃ וַיִּשְׁמְעוּ כׇּל־הַשָּׂרִים וְכׇל־הָעָם אֲשֶׁר־
בָּאוּ בַבְּרִית לְשַׁלַּח אִישׁ אֶת־עַבְדּוֹ וְאִישׁ אֶת־שִׁפְחָתוֹ חׇפְשִׁים
יא לְבִלְתִּי עֲבׇד־בָּם עוֹד וַיִּשְׁמְעוּ וַיְשַׁלֵּחוּ׃ וַיָּשׁוּבוּ אַחֲרֵי־כֵן וַיָּשִׁבוּ אֶת־
הָעֲבָדִים וְאֶת־הַשְּׁפָחוֹת אֲשֶׁר שִׁלְּחוּ חׇפְשִׁים ויכבישום לַעֲבָדִים וַיִּכְבְּשׁוּם
יב וְלִשְׁפָחוֹת׃ וַיְהִי דְבַר־יהוה אֶל־יִרְמְיָהוּ מֵאֵת יהוה
יג לֵאמֹר׃ כֹּה־אָמַר יהוה אֱלֹהֵי יִשְׂרָאֵל אָנֹכִי כָּרַתִּי בְרִית אֶת־אֲבוֹתֵיכֶם
יד בְּיוֹם הוֹצִאִי אוֹתָם מֵאֶרֶץ מִצְרַיִם מִבֵּית עֲבָדִים לֵאמֹר׃ מִקֵּץ שֶׁבַע
שָׁנִים תְּשַׁלְּחוּ אִישׁ אֶת־אָחִיו הָעִבְרִי אֲשֶׁר־יִמָּכֵר לְךָ וַעֲבָדְךָ שֵׁשׁ
שָׁנִים וְשִׁלַּחְתּוֹ חׇפְשִׁי מֵעִמָּךְ וְלֹא־שָׁמְעוּ אֲבוֹתֵיכֶם אֵלַי וְלֹא הִטּוּ
טו אֶת־אׇזְנָם׃ וַתָּשֻׁבוּ אַתֶּם הַיּוֹם וַתַּעֲשׂוּ אֶת־הַיָּשָׁר בְּעֵינַי לִקְרֹא דְרוֹר
אִישׁ לְרֵעֵהוּ וַתִּכְרְתוּ בְרִית לְפָנַי בַּבַּיִת אֲשֶׁר־נִקְרָא שְׁמִי עָלָיו׃
טז וַתָּשֻׁבוּ וַתְּחַלְּלוּ אֶת־שְׁמִי וַתָּשִׁבוּ אִישׁ אֶת־עַבְדּוֹ וְאִישׁ אֶת־שִׁפְחָתוֹ
אֲשֶׁר־שִׁלַּחְתֶּם חׇפְשִׁים לְנַפְשָׁם וַתִּכְבְּשׁוּ אֹתָם לִהְיוֹת לָכֶם לַעֲבָדִים
יז וְלִשְׁפָחוֹת׃ לָכֵן כֹּה־אָמַר יהוה אַתֶּם לֹא־שְׁמַעְתֶּם אֵלַי
לִקְרֹא דְּרוֹר אִישׁ לְאָחִיו וְאִישׁ לְרֵעֵהוּ הִנְנִי קֹרֵא לָכֶם דְּרוֹר נְאֻם־
יהוה אֶל־הַחֶרֶב אֶל־הַדֶּבֶר וְאֶל־הָרָעָב וְנָתַתִּי אֶתְכֶם לזועה לְכֹל לְזַעֲוָה
יח מַמְלְכוֹת הָאָרֶץ׃ וְנָתַתִּי אֶת־הָאֲנָשִׁים הָעֹבְרִים אֶת־בְּרִתִי אֲשֶׁר
לֹא־הֵקִימוּ אֶת־דִּבְרֵי הַבְּרִית אֲשֶׁר כָּרְתוּ לְפָנָי הָעֵגֶל אֲשֶׁר כָּרְתוּ
יט לִשְׁנַיִם וַיַּעַבְרוּ בֵּין בְּתָרָיו׃ שָׂרֵי יְהוּדָה וְשָׂרֵי יְרוּשָׁלִַם הַסָּרִסִים
כ וְהַכֹּהֲנִים וְכֹל עַם הָאָרֶץ הָעֹבְרִים בֵּין בִּתְרֵי הָעֵגֶל׃ וְנָתַתִּי אוֹתָם
בְּיַד אֹיְבֵיהֶם וּבְיַד מְבַקְשֵׁי נַפְשָׁם וְהָיְתָה נִבְלָתָם לְמַאֲכָל לְעוֹף
כא הַשָּׁמַיִם וּלְבֶהֱמַת הָאָרֶץ׃ וְאֶת־צִדְקִיָּהוּ מֶלֶךְ־יְהוּדָה וְאֶת־שָׂרָיו אֶתֵּן
בְּיַד אֹיְבֵיהֶם וּבְיַד מְבַקְשֵׁי נַפְשָׁם וּבְיַד חֵיל מֶלֶךְ בָּבֶל הָעֹלִים
כב מֵעֲלֵיכֶם׃ הִנְנִי מְצַוֶּה נְאֻם־יהוה וַהֲשִׁבֹתִים אֶל־הָעִיר הַזֹּאת וְנִלְחֲמוּ
עָלֶיהָ וּלְכָדוּהָ וּשְׂרָפֻהָ בָאֵשׁ וְאֶת־עָרֵי יְהוּדָה אֶתֵּן שְׁמָמָה מֵאֵין
לה א יֹשֵׁב׃ הַדָּבָר אֲשֶׁר־הָיָה אֶל־יִרְמְיָהוּ מֵאֵת יהוה בִּימֵי

2 king of Yehuda: "Go to the house of the descendants of Rekhav[79] and speak
to them. Bring them to the House of the LORD, to one of the chambers, and
3 give them wine to drink." I took Yaazanya son of Yirmeyahu son of Ḥavatzinya,
his brothers and all his children and the entire house of the descendants of
4 Rekhav, and I brought them to the House of the LORD, to the chamber of the
sons of Ḥanan son of Yigdalyahu, the man of God, that was adjacent to the
chamber of the officials and above the chamber of Maaseyahu son of Shalum,
5 the gatekeeper. I placed goblets full of wine and cups before the sons of the
6 house of Rekhav and said to them, "Drink wine." They said, "We will not drink
wine because Yonadav son of Rekhav, our ancestor, commanded us: 'Do not
7 drink wine, neither you nor your children, forever! You are not to build houses,
nor sow seed, nor plant vineyards, nor even possess them for yourselves.
Instead, you are to live in tents all your lives so that you will thrive for many
8 days upon the land where you will reside.' We heeded the voice of Yehonadav
son of Rekhav our forefather in all that he commanded us, never to drink
9 wine, neither ourselves nor our wives, nor our sons and daughters, and not
to build houses in which to live, and not to have vineyard, field, or seed.
10 Rather, we live in tents. We heeded Yonadav our ancestor, and we have done
11 all that he commanded us. However, when Nevukhadretzar, king of Babylon,
rose up against the land, we said, 'Come and let us go up to Jerusalem because
of the army of the Chaldeans and because of the army of Aram.' And so we
12 live in Jerusalem." Then the word of the LORD came to Yirmeyahu.
13 This is what the LORD of Hosts, God of Israel, said: "Go and say to the men
of Yehuda and to those that dwell in Jerusalem: It would befit you to take
14 instruction to heed my words, declares the LORD. Fulfilled are the words
of Yehonadav son of Rekhav, who commanded his descendants not to
drink wine. They have not drunk wine to this very day, for they heeded the
command of their ancestor. But I spoke to you persistently, and yet you did
15 not heed Me. I sent to you My servants, the prophets, again and again, to tell
every one of you to turn away from his evil path, to correct his actions, and
not to follow other gods to worship them. Then you would live upon the land
which I gave you and your ancestors. But you did not bend your ears. You did
16 not listen to Me. For the children of Yehonadav son of Rekhav obeyed their
ancestor's command just as he had commanded them, but this people have
17 not obeyed Me. Therefore, this is what the LORD, God of Hosts,
God of Israel, said: Now I will bring upon Yehuda, and upon all who dwell
in Jerusalem, every disaster which I have decreed upon them, for I spoke to
them and they did not listen; I called to them and they did not respond."
18 Yirmeyahu said to the house of the Rekhabites, "This is what the LORD of
Hosts, God of Israel, said: Because you listened to the command of Yehonadav
your ancestor, and kept all his precepts, and did exactly as he commanded
19 you, this is what the LORD of Hosts, God of Israel, therefore said: There will

79 | See II Kings 10:15; I Chronicles 2:55.

ב יְהוֹיָקִים בֶּן־יֹאשִׁיָּהוּ מֶלֶךְ יְהוּדָה לֵאמֹר׃ הָלוֹךְ אֶל־בֵּית הָרֵכָבִים
וְדִבַּרְתָּ אוֹתָם וַהֲבֵאוֹתָם בֵּית יהוה אֶל־אַחַת הַלְּשָׁכוֹת וְהִשְׁקִיתָ
ג אוֹתָם יָיִן׃ וָאֶקַּח אֶת־יַאֲזַנְיָה בֶן־יִרְמְיָהוּ בֶּן־חֲבַצִּנְיָה וְאֶת־אֶחָיו וְאֶת־
ד כָּל־בָּנָיו וְאֵת כָּל־בֵּית הָרֵכָבִים׃ וָאָבִא אֹתָם בֵּית יהוה אֶל־לִשְׁכַּת
בְּנֵי חָנָן בֶּן־יִגְדַּלְיָהוּ אִישׁ הָאֱלֹהִים אֲשֶׁר־אֵצֶל לִשְׁכַּת הַשָּׂרִים אֲשֶׁר
ה מִמַּעַל לְלִשְׁכַּת מַעֲשֵׂיָהוּ בֶן־שַׁלֻּם שֹׁמֵר הַסַּף׃ וָאֶתֵּן לִפְנֵי ׀ בְּנֵי בֵית־
ו הָרֵכָבִים גְּבִעִים מְלֵאִים יַיִן וְכֹסוֹת וָאֹמַר אֲלֵיהֶם שְׁתוּ־יָיִן׃ וַיֹּאמְרוּ
לֹא נִשְׁתֶּה־יָּיִן כִּי יוֹנָדָב בֶּן־רֵכָב אָבִינוּ צִוָּה עָלֵינוּ לֵאמֹר לֹא תִשְׁתּוּ־
ז יַיִן אַתֶּם וּבְנֵיכֶם עַד־עוֹלָם׃ וּבַיִת לֹא־תִבְנוּ וְזֶרַע לֹא־תִזְרָעוּ וְכֶרֶם
לֹא־תִטָּעוּ וְלֹא יִהְיֶה לָכֶם כִּי בָּאֳהָלִים תֵּשְׁבוּ כָּל־יְמֵיכֶם לְמַעַן תִּחְיוּ
ח יָמִים רַבִּים עַל־פְּנֵי הָאֲדָמָה אֲשֶׁר אַתֶּם גָּרִים שָׁם׃ וַנִּשְׁמַע בְּקוֹל
יְהוֹנָדָב בֶּן־רֵכָב אָבִינוּ לְכֹל אֲשֶׁר צִוָּנוּ לְבִלְתִּי שְׁתוֹת־יַיִן כָּל־יָמֵינוּ
ט אֲנַחְנוּ נָשֵׁינוּ בָּנֵינוּ וּבְנֹתֵינוּ׃ וּלְבִלְתִּי בְּנוֹת בָּתִּים לְשִׁבְתֵּנוּ וְכֶרֶם וְשָׂדֶה
י וָזֶרַע לֹא יִהְיֶה־לָּנוּ׃ וַנֵּשֶׁב בָּאֳהָלִים וַנִּשְׁמַע וַנַּעַשׂ כְּכֹל אֲשֶׁר־צִוָּנוּ כא
יא יוֹנָדָב אָבִינוּ׃ וַיְהִי בַּעֲלוֹת נְבוּכַדְרֶאצַּר מֶלֶךְ־בָּבֶל אֶל־הָאָרֶץ וַנֹּאמֶר
בֹּאוּ וְנָבוֹא יְרוּשָׁלִַם מִפְּנֵי חֵיל הַכַּשְׂדִּים וּמִפְּנֵי חֵיל אֲרָם וַנֵּשֶׁב
יב יג בִּירוּשָׁלִָם׃ וַיְהִי דְבַר־יהוה אֶל־יִרְמְיָהוּ לֵאמֹר׃ כֹּה־
אָמַר יהוה צְבָאוֹת אֱלֹהֵי יִשְׂרָאֵל הָלֹךְ וְאָמַרְתָּ לְאִישׁ יְהוּדָה וּלְיוֹשְׁבֵי
יד יְרוּשָׁלִָם הֲלוֹא תִקְחוּ מוּסָר לִשְׁמֹעַ אֶל־דְּבָרַי נְאֻם־יהוה׃ הוּקַם
אֶת־דִּבְרֵי יְהוֹנָדָב בֶּן־רֵכָב אֲשֶׁר־צִוָּה אֶת־בָּנָיו לְבִלְתִּי שְׁתוֹת־יַיִן וְלֹא
שָׁתוּ עַד־הַיּוֹם הַזֶּה כִּי שָׁמְעוּ אֵת מִצְוַת אֲבִיהֶם וְאָנֹכִי דִּבַּרְתִּי אֲלֵיכֶם
טו הַשְׁכֵּם וְדַבֵּר וְלֹא שְׁמַעְתֶּם אֵלָי׃ וָאֶשְׁלַח אֲלֵיכֶם אֶת־כָּל־עֲבָדַי
הַנְּבִאִים ׀ הַשְׁכֵּים וְשָׁלֹחַ ׀ לֵאמֹר שֻׁבוּ־נָא אִישׁ מִדַּרְכּוֹ הָרָעָה וְהֵיטִיבוּ
מַעַלְלֵיכֶם וְאַל־תֵּלְכוּ אַחֲרֵי אֱלֹהִים אֲחֵרִים לְעָבְדָם וּשְׁבוּ אֶל־
הָאֲדָמָה אֲשֶׁר־נָתַתִּי לָכֶם וְלַאֲבֹתֵיכֶם וְלֹא הִטִּיתֶם אֶת־אָזְנְכֶם וְלֹא
טז שְׁמַעְתֶּם אֵלָי׃ כִּי הֵקִימוּ בְּנֵי יְהוֹנָדָב בֶּן־רֵכָב אֶת־מִצְוַת אֲבִיהֶם אֲשֶׁר
יז צִוָּם וְהָעָם הַזֶּה לֹא שָׁמְעוּ אֵלָי׃ לָכֵן כֹּה־אָמַר יהוה אֱלֹהֵי
צְבָאוֹת אֱלֹהֵי יִשְׂרָאֵל הִנְנִי מֵבִיא אֶל־יְהוּדָה וְאֶל כָּל־יוֹשְׁבֵי יְרוּשָׁלִָם
אֵת כָּל־הָרָעָה אֲשֶׁר דִּבַּרְתִּי עֲלֵיהֶם יַעַן דִּבַּרְתִּי אֲלֵיהֶם וְלֹא שָׁמֵעוּ
יח וָאֶקְרָא לָהֶם וְלֹא עָנוּ׃ וּלְבֵית הָרֵכָבִים אָמַר יִרְמְיָהוּ כֹּה־אָמַר יהוה
צְבָאוֹת אֱלֹהֵי יִשְׂרָאֵל יַעַן אֲשֶׁר שְׁמַעְתֶּם עַל־מִצְוַת יְהוֹנָדָב אֲבִיכֶם
יט וַתִּשְׁמְרוּ אֶת־כָּל־מִצְוֹתָיו וַתַּעֲשׂוּ כְּכֹל אֲשֶׁר־צִוָּה אֶתְכֶם׃ לָכֵן כֹּה

never cease to be a descendant of Yonadav son of Rekhav who will stand
36 1 before Me, for all time." In the fourth year of Yehoyakim son of
Yoshiyahu, king of Yehuda, this word came to Yirmeyahu from the LORD:
2 "Take for yourself a scroll and write upon it all the words that I have spoken
to you concerning Israel, Yehuda, and all the nations from the time I spoke
3 to you in the days of Yoshiyahu until today. Perhaps the House of Yehuda
will hear of all the disasters that I plan to bring upon them, and each of
them will turn back from his evil way. I would then forgive their sins and
4 transgressions." So Yirmeyahu summoned Barukh son of Neriya.
From the mouth of Yirmeyahu, Barukh wrote upon a scroll all of the LORD's
5 words that He had spoken to him. Yirmeyahu instructed Barukh, "I am
6 constrained; I cannot go to the House of the LORD. You go and read the scroll
upon which you wrote from my mouth the words of the LORD – in the
hearing of the people in the House of the LORD on a fast day. In doing so, you
will be reading it in the hearing of the people of Yehuda who come there from
7 their towns. Perhaps their pleas will be accepted by the LORD and each of
them will turn back from his evil ways, for great is the anger and wrath with
8 which the LORD has spoken against this people." Barukh son of Neriya did
just as Yirmeyahu the prophet instructed him, reading from the scroll the
9 words of the LORD in the House of the LORD. In the fifth year of
Yehoyakim son of Yoshiyahu, king of Yehuda, in the ninth month, all the
people of Jerusalem and all the people who came from the towns of Yehuda
10 to Jerusalem proclaimed a fast before the LORD. Barukh read the words of
Yirmeyahu from the scroll in the House of the LORD in the chamber of
Gemaryahu son of Shafan the scribe, in the upper courtyard by the entrance
of the New Gate of the House of the LORD, in the hearing of all the people.
11 Mikhayehu son of Gemaryahu son of Shafan heard all the words of the LORD
12 from the scroll. He went down to the king's palace to the scribe's chamber
where all the officials had gathered: Elishama the scribe, Delayahu son of
Shemayahu, Elnatan son of Akhbor, Gemaryahu son of Shafan, Tzidkiyahu
13 son of Ḥananyahu, and all the officials. Mikhayehu told them all that he had
14 heard when Barukh read the scroll in the hearing of the people. All the
officials sent Yehudi son of Netanyahu son of Shelemyahu son of Kushi to
Barukh to say, "Come, and bring the scroll that you read in the hearing of the
people with you." Barukh son of Neriyahu took the scroll with him and came
15 to them. They said to him, "Be seated, please, and read it in our presence." So
16 Barukh read it in their presence. As they heard everything, they looked at
each other fearfully and said to Barukh, "We must certainly tell the king about
17 all this." They asked Barukh, "Please, tell us how you were able to write all
18 this from his mouth." Barukh replied, "He dictated all these words to me from

אָמַר יהוה צְבָאוֹת אֱלֹהֵי יִשְׂרָאֵל לֹא־יִכָּרֵת אִישׁ לְיוֹנָדָב בֶּן־רֵכָב
לו א עֹמֵד לְפָנַי כָּל־הַיָּמִים׃ וַיְהִי בַּשָּׁנָה הָרְבִעִית לִיהוֹיָקִים
בֶּן־יֹאשִׁיָּהוּ מֶלֶךְ יְהוּדָה הָיָה הַדָּבָר הַזֶּה אֶל־יִרְמְיָהוּ מֵאֵת יהוה
ב לֵאמֹר׃ קַח־לְךָ מְגִלַּת־סֵפֶר וְכָתַבְתָּ אֵלֶיהָ אֵת כָּל־הַדְּבָרִים אֲשֶׁר
דִּבַּרְתִּי אֵלֶיךָ עַל־יִשְׂרָאֵל וְעַל־יְהוּדָה וְעַל־כָּל־הַגּוֹיִם מִיּוֹם דִּבַּרְתִּי
ג אֵלֶיךָ מִימֵי יֹאשִׁיָּהוּ וְעַד הַיּוֹם הַזֶּה׃ אוּלַי יִשְׁמְעוּ בֵּית יְהוּדָה אֵת
כָּל־הָרָעָה אֲשֶׁר אָנֹכִי חֹשֵׁב לַעֲשׂוֹת לָהֶם לְמַעַן יָשׁוּבוּ אִישׁ מִדַּרְכּוֹ
ד הָרָעָה וְסָלַחְתִּי לַעֲוֺנָם וּלְחַטָּאתָם׃ וַיִּקְרָא יִרְמְיָהוּ אֶת־
בָּרוּךְ בֶּן־נֵרִיָּה וַיִּכְתֹּב בָּרוּךְ מִפִּי יִרְמְיָהוּ אֵת כָּל־דִּבְרֵי יהוה אֲשֶׁר־
ה דִּבֶּר אֵלָיו עַל־מְגִלַּת־סֵפֶר׃ וַיְצַוֶּה יִרְמְיָהוּ אֶת־בָּרוּךְ לֵאמֹר אֲנִי עָצוּר
ו לֹא אוּכַל לָבוֹא בֵּית יהוה׃ וּבָאתָ אַתָּה וְקָרָאתָ בַמְּגִלָּה אֲשֶׁר־כָּתַבְתָּ
מִפִּי אֶת־דִּבְרֵי יהוה בְּאָזְנֵי הָעָם בֵּית יהוה בְּיוֹם צוֹם וְגַם בְּאָזְנֵי כָל־
ז יְהוּדָה הַבָּאִים מֵעָרֵיהֶם תִּקְרָאֵם׃ אוּלַי תִּפֹּל תְּחִנָּתָם לִפְנֵי יהוה
וְיָשֻׁבוּ אִישׁ מִדַּרְכּוֹ הָרָעָה כִּי־גָדוֹל הָאַף וְהַחֵמָה אֲשֶׁר־דִּבֶּר יהוה
ח אֶל־הָעָם הַזֶּה׃ וַיַּעַשׂ בָּרוּךְ בֶּן־נֵרִיָּה כְּכֹל אֲשֶׁר־צִוָּהוּ יִרְמְיָהוּ הַנָּבִיא
ט לִקְרֹא בַסֵּפֶר דִּבְרֵי יהוה בֵּית יהוה׃ וַיְהִי בַשָּׁנָה
הַחֲמִשִׁית לִיהוֹיָקִים בֶּן־יֹאשִׁיָּהוּ מֶלֶךְ־יְהוּדָה בַּחֹדֶשׁ הַתְּשִׁעִי קָרְאוּ
צוֹם לִפְנֵי יהוה כָּל־הָעָם בִּירוּשָׁלָ͏ִם וְכָל־הָעָם הַבָּאִים מֵעָרֵי יְהוּדָה
י בִּירוּשָׁלָ͏ִם׃ וַיִּקְרָא בָרוּךְ בַּסֵּפֶר אֶת־דִּבְרֵי יִרְמְיָהוּ בֵּית יהוה בְּלִשְׁכַּת
גְּמַרְיָהוּ בֶן־שָׁפָן הַסֹּפֵר בֶּחָצֵר הָעֶלְיוֹן פֶּתַח שַׁעַר בֵּית־יהוה הֶחָדָשׁ
יא בְּאָזְנֵי כָּל־הָעָם׃ וַיִּשְׁמַע מִכָיְהוּ בֶן־גְּמַרְיָהוּ בֶן־שָׁפָן אֶת־כָּל־דִּבְרֵי
יב יהוה מֵעַל הַסֵּפֶר׃ וַיֵּרֶד בֵּית־הַמֶּלֶךְ עַל־לִשְׁכַּת הַסֹּפֵר וְהִנֵּה־שָׁם
כָּל־הַשָּׂרִים יוֹשְׁבִים אֱלִישָׁמָע הַסֹּפֵר וּדְלָיָהוּ בֶן־שְׁמַעְיָהוּ וְאֶלְנָתָן
יג בֶּן־עַכְבּוֹר וּגְמַרְיָהוּ בֶן־שָׁפָן וְצִדְקִיָּהוּ בֶן־חֲנַנְיָהוּ וְכָל־הַשָּׂרִים׃ וַיַּגֵּד
לָהֶם מִיכָיְהוּ אֵת כָּל־הַדְּבָרִים אֲשֶׁר שָׁמֵעַ בִּקְרֹא בָרוּךְ בַּסֵּפֶר בְּאָזְנֵי
יד הָעָם׃ וַיִּשְׁלְחוּ כָל־הַשָּׂרִים אֶל־בָּרוּךְ אֶת־יְהוּדִי בֶּן־נְתַנְיָהוּ בֶּן־
שֶׁלֶמְיָהוּ בֶן־כּוּשִׁי לֵאמֹר הַמְּגִלָּה אֲשֶׁר קָרָאתָ בָּהּ בְּאָזְנֵי הָעָם קָחֶנָּה
טו בְיָדְךָ וָלֵךְ וַיִּקַּח בָּרוּךְ בֶּן־נֵרִיָּהוּ אֶת־הַמְּגִלָּה בְּיָדוֹ וַיָּבֹא אֲלֵיהֶם׃
טז וַיֹּאמְרוּ אֵלָיו שֵׁב נָא וּקְרָאֶנָּה בְּאָזְנֵינוּ וַיִּקְרָא בָרוּךְ בְּאָזְנֵיהֶם׃ וַיְהִי
כְּשָׁמְעָם אֶת־כָּל־הַדְּבָרִים פָּחֲדוּ אִישׁ אֶל־רֵעֵהוּ וַיֹּאמְרוּ אֶל־בָּרוּךְ
יז הַגֵּיד נַגִּיד לַמֶּלֶךְ אֵת כָּל־הַדְּבָרִים הָאֵלֶּה׃ וְאֶת־בָּרוּךְ שָׁאֲלוּ לֵאמֹר
יח הַגֶּד־נָא לָנוּ אֵיךְ כָּתַבְתָּ אֶת־כָּל־הַדְּבָרִים הָאֵלֶּה מִפִּיו׃ וַיֹּאמֶר לָהֶם

19 his mouth, and I wrote onto the scroll in ink." The officials said to
20 Barukh, "Go hide, you and Yirmeyahu. Let no one know where you are." They
approached the king in the courtyard, having deposited the scroll in the
21 chamber of Elishama the scribe. They told the king everything. The king sent
Yehudi to retrieve the scroll, and he retrieved it from the chamber of Elishama
the scribe. Yehudi read it in the presence of the king and in the presence of
22 all the officials who were in attendance on the king. The king was sitting in
the winter quarters, it being the ninth month.[80] The hearth was ablaze before
23 him. As soon as Yehudi had read three or four columns, he would cut them
off with a scribe's knife and cast them into the fire in the hearth until the entire
24 scroll was consumed in the fire of the hearth. The king and all his servants,
having heard all of it, showed no fear and did not rend their garments.
25 Although Elnatan, Delayahu, and Gemaryahu had begged the king not
26 to burn the scroll, he did not listen to them. The king ordered Yeraḥme'el
the king's son, Serayahu son of Azriel, and Shelemyahu son of Avde'el to
seize Barukh the scribe and Yirmeyahu the prophet. But the Lord hid
27 them. After the king had burned the scroll and the words that
Barukh had written from the mouth of Yirmeyahu, the word of the Lord
28 came to Yirmeyahu, saying: "Do it again; take another scroll for yourself and
write upon it all the earlier words that were upon the first scroll that Yehoyakim,
29 king of Yehuda, burned. Concerning Yehoyakim, king of Yehuda, you shall
say: Thus said the Lord: You burned this scroll, asking how did you dare
write upon it that the king of Babylon would come and lay waste to this land
30 and eradicate from it humans and animals? Therefore, this is what
the Lord said concerning Yehoyakim, king of Yehuda: He will have no heir
to sit upon the throne of David, and his corpse will be exposed to the heat of
31 day and the frost of night. I will hold him and his offspring and his servants
accountable for their sins. I shall bring upon them and upon those who dwell
in Jerusalem and upon every man of Yehuda every disaster of which I have
32 spoken to them, but they did not listen." Yirmeyahu took another
scroll and gave it to Barukh son of Neriyahu the scribe, who wrote upon it
from the mouth of Yirmeyahu all the words of the message that Yehoyakim,
king of Yehuda, burned in the fire, with many more words similar to them
37 1 added. Tzidkiyahu son of Yoshiyahu reigned as king instead of
Konyahu[81] son of Yehoyakim, for Nevukhadretzar, king of Babylon, made him
2 king of the land of Yehuda. Neither he nor his servants nor the people of
the land heeded the words of the Lord as spoken through Yirmeyahu the
3 prophet. Nevertheless, King Tzidkiyahu sent Yehukhal son of Shelemyahu

80 | The month of Kislev, which generally coincides with December.
81 | Yekhonya, who reigned for only three months (see 24:1; II Kings 24:8–17).

בָּרוּךְ מִפִּיו יִקְרָא אֵלַי אֵת כׇּל־הַדְּבָרִים הָאֵלֶּה וַאֲנִי כֹּתֵב עַל־הַסֵּפֶר
יט בַּדְּיוֹ׃ וַיֹּאמְרוּ הַשָּׂרִים אֶל־בָּרוּךְ לֵךְ הִסָּתֵר אַתָּה וְיִרְמְיָהוּ
כ וְאִישׁ אַל־יֵדַע אֵיפֹה אַתֶּם׃ וַיָּבֹאוּ אֶל־הַמֶּלֶךְ חָצֵרָה וְאֶת־הַמְּגִלָּה
הִפְקִדוּ בְּלִשְׁכַּת אֱלִישָׁמָע הַסֹּפֵר וַיַּגִּידוּ בְּאׇזְנֵי הַמֶּלֶךְ אֵת כׇּל־הַדְּבָרִים׃
כא וַיִּשְׁלַח הַמֶּלֶךְ אֶת־יְהוּדִי לָקַחַת אֶת־הַמְּגִלָּה וַיִּקָּחֶהָ מִלִּשְׁכַּת
אֱלִישָׁמָע הַסֹּפֵר וַיִּקְרָאֶהָ יְהוּדִי בְּאׇזְנֵי הַמֶּלֶךְ וּבְאׇזְנֵי כׇּל־הַשָּׂרִים
כב הָעֹמְדִים מֵעַל הַמֶּלֶךְ׃ וְהַמֶּלֶךְ יוֹשֵׁב בֵּית הַחֹרֶף בַּחֹדֶשׁ הַתְּשִׁיעִי
כג וְאֶת־הָאָח לְפָנָיו מְבֹעָרֶת׃ וַיְהִי ׀ כִּקְרוֹא יְהוּדִי שָׁלֹשׁ דְּלָתוֹת וְאַרְבָּעָה
יִקְרָעֶהָ בְּתַעַר הַסֹּפֵר וְהַשְׁלֵךְ אֶל־הָאֵשׁ אֲשֶׁר אֶל־הָאָח עַד־תֹּם כׇּל־
כד הַמְּגִלָּה עַל־הָאֵשׁ אֲשֶׁר עַל־הָאָח׃ וְלֹא פָחֲדוּ וְלֹא קָרְעוּ אֶת־בִּגְדֵיהֶם
כה הַמֶּלֶךְ וְכׇל־עֲבָדָיו הַשֹּׁמְעִים אֵת כׇּל־הַדְּבָרִים הָאֵלֶּה׃ וְגַם אֶלְנָתָן
וּדְלָיָהוּ וּגְמַרְיָהוּ הִפְגִּעוּ בַמֶּלֶךְ לְבִלְתִּי שְׂרֹף אֶת־הַמְּגִלָּה וְלֹא שָׁמַע
כו אֲלֵיהֶם׃ וַיְצַוֶּה הַמֶּלֶךְ אֶת־יְרַחְמְאֵל בֶּן־הַמֶּלֶךְ וְאֶת־שְׂרָיָהוּ בֶן־ כב
עַזְרִיאֵל וְאֶת־שֶׁלֶמְיָהוּ בֶּן־עַבְדְּאֵל לָקַחַת אֶת־בָּרוּךְ הַסֹּפֵר וְאֵת
כז יִרְמְיָהוּ הַנָּבִיא וַיַּסְתִּרֵם יְהוָה׃ וַיְהִי דְבַר־יְהוָה אֶל־יִרְמְיָהוּ
אַחֲרֵי ׀ שְׂרֹף הַמֶּלֶךְ אֶת־הַמְּגִלָּה וְאֶת־הַדְּבָרִים אֲשֶׁר כָּתַב בָּרוּךְ מִפִּי
כח יִרְמְיָהוּ לֵאמֹר׃ שׁוּב קַח־לְךָ מְגִלָּה אַחֶרֶת וּכְתֹב עָלֶיהָ אֵת כׇּל־
הַדְּבָרִים הָרִאשֹׁנִים אֲשֶׁר הָיוּ עַל־הַמְּגִלָּה הָרִאשֹׁנָה אֲשֶׁר שָׂרַף
כט יְהוֹיָקִים מֶלֶךְ־יְהוּדָה׃ וְעַל־יְהוֹיָקִים מֶלֶךְ־יְהוּדָה תֹּאמַר כֹּה אָמַר
יְהוָה אַתָּה שָׂרַפְתָּ אֶת־הַמְּגִלָּה הַזֹּאת לֵאמֹר מַדּוּעַ כָּתַבְתָּ עָלֶיהָ
לֵאמֹר בֹּא־יָבוֹא מֶלֶךְ־בָּבֶל וְהִשְׁחִית אֶת־הָאָרֶץ הַזֹּאת וְהִשְׁבִּית
ל מִמֶּנָּה אָדָם וּבְהֵמָה׃ לָכֵן כֹּה־אָמַר יְהוָה עַל־יְהוֹיָקִים מֶלֶךְ
יְהוּדָה לֹא־יִהְיֶה־לּוֹ יוֹשֵׁב עַל־כִּסֵּא דָוִד וְנִבְלָתוֹ תִּהְיֶה מֻשְׁלֶכֶת לַחֹרֶב
לא בַּיּוֹם וְלַקֶּרַח בַּלָּיְלָה׃ וּפָקַדְתִּי עָלָיו וְעַל־זַרְעוֹ וְעַל־עֲבָדָיו אֶת־עֲוֺנָם
וְהֵבֵאתִי עֲלֵיהֶם וְעַל־יֹשְׁבֵי יְרוּשָׁלַםִ וְאֶל־אִישׁ יְהוּדָה אֵת כׇּל־הָרָעָה
לב אֲשֶׁר־דִּבַּרְתִּי אֲלֵיהֶם וְלֹא שָׁמֵעוּ׃ וְיִרְמְיָהוּ לָקַח ׀ מְגִלָּה
אַחֶרֶת וַיִּתְּנָהּ אֶל־בָּרוּךְ בֶּן־נֵרִיָּהוּ הַסֹּפֵר וַיִּכְתֹּב עָלֶיהָ מִפִּי יִרְמְיָהוּ
אֵת כׇּל־דִּבְרֵי הַסֵּפֶר אֲשֶׁר שָׂרַף יְהוֹיָקִים מֶלֶךְ־יְהוּדָה בָּאֵשׁ וְעוֹד
לז א נוֹסַף עֲלֵיהֶם דְּבָרִים רַבִּים כָּהֵמָּה׃ וַיִּמְלׇךְ־מֶלֶךְ צִדְקִיָּהוּ
בֶּן־יֹאשִׁיָּהוּ תַּחַת כׇּנְיָהוּ בֶּן־יְהוֹיָקִים אֲשֶׁר הִמְלִיךְ נְבוּכַדְרֶאצַּר מֶלֶךְ־
ב בָּבֶל בְּאֶרֶץ יְהוּדָה׃ וְלֹא שָׁמַע הוּא וַעֲבָדָיו וְעַם הָאָרֶץ אֶל־דִּבְרֵי
ג יְהוָה אֲשֶׁר דִּבֶּר בְּיַד יִרְמְיָהוּ הַנָּבִיא׃ וַיִּשְׁלַח הַמֶּלֶךְ צִדְקִיָּהוּ אֶת־

and Tzefanyahu son of Maaseya the priest to Yirmeyahu the prophet,
4 saying, "Please pray on our behalf to the LORD our God." At that time
Yirmeyahu walked about freely among the people, for they had not placed
5 him in prison. Now Pharaoh's army set out from Egypt, and when the
Chaldeans who were besieging Jerusalem heard of this, they withdrew from
6 Jerusalem.
7 The word of the LORD came to Yirmeyahu. This
is what the LORD, God of Israel, said: "This is what you are to say to the king
of Yehuda, who sent you to Me to inquire of Me: Pharaoh's army, which set
8 out to help you, is about to return to his land, to Egypt. The Chaldeans will
return and attack this city. They will capture it and burn it down with
9 fire. This is what the LORD said: Do not deceive yourselves by
10 assuming that the Chaldeans will depart from us, for they will not depart. For
even if you were to smite the entire Chaldean army that is attacking you,
leaving behind only the gravely wounded, each of them would rise up from
11 his tent and burn down this city with fire." When the Chaldean army had
12 withdrawn from Jerusalem because of Pharaoh's army, Yirmeyahu
went out from the city to go toward the land of Binyamin, to flee from there
13 into the midst of the people. He was at the Binyamin Gate. An appointed
guard was there whose name was Yiriya son of Shelemya son of Ḥananya. He
seized Yirmeyahu the prophet, saying, "You are surrendering to the Chaldeans."
14 Yirmeyahu said, "That is a lie! I am not surrendering to the Chaldeans." But
Yiriya paid him no heed and held onto Yirmeyahu and brought him to the
15 officials. The officials were furious at Yirmeyahu and beat him. They put him
in a prison house, the house of Yehonatan the scribe, for they had made it
16 into a jail. Thus did Yirmeyahu come to the cistern house, to the prison cells.
17 He remained there for many days. King Tzidkiyahu sent for him and brought
him and questioned him secretly in his palace: "Is there any word from the
LORD?" Yirmeyahu replied, "There is," and continued, "you shall be delivered
18 into the hands of the king of Babylon." Yirmeyahu further said to King
Tzidkiyahu, "What crime did I commit against you, your servants, or this
19 people that you have put me into prison? Where are your prophets who
prophesied to you saying that the king of Babylon will not come upon you
20 and upon this land? And now, my master the king, please listen. May my plea
be acceptable to you. Do not send me back to the house of Yehonatan the
21 scribe, lest I die there." King Tzidkiyahu gave commands, and Yirmeyahu was
confined in the prisoners' courtyard. He was given a loaf of bread each day
from the bakers' street; until all the bread in the city was gone, Yirmeyahu
38 1 remained in the prisoners' courtyard. Shefatya son of Matan, Gedalyahu son
of Pashḥur, Yukhal son of Shelemyahu, and Pashḥur son of Malkiya heard
2 the words that Yirmeyahu was speaking to all the people: "This is what the
LORD said: Whoever remains in this city will die by sword or famine or

יְהוּכַל בֶּן־שֶׁלֶמְיָה וְאֶת־צְפַנְיָהוּ בֶן־מַעֲשֵׂיָה הַכֹּהֵן אֶל־יִרְמְיָהוּ הַנָּבִיא
ד לֵאמֹר הִתְפַּלֶּל־נָא בַעֲדֵנוּ אֶל־יְהוָה אֱלֹהֵינוּ: וְיִרְמְיָהוּ בָּא וְיֹצֵא
ה בְּתוֹךְ הָעָם וְלֹא־נָתְנוּ אֹתוֹ בֵּית הכליא: וְחֵיל פַּרְעֹה יָצָא מִמִּצְרָיִם הַכְּלוּא
וַיִּשְׁמְעוּ הַכַּשְׂדִּים הַצָּרִים עַל־יְרוּשָׁלִַם אֶת־שִׁמְעָם וַיֵּעָלוּ מֵעַל
ו ז יְרוּשָׁלִָם: וַיְהִי דְּבַר־יְהוָה אֶל־יִרְמְיָהוּ הַנָּבִיא לֵאמֹר: כֹּה־
אָמַר יְהוָה אֱלֹהֵי יִשְׂרָאֵל כֹּה תֹאמְרוּ אֶל־מֶלֶךְ יְהוּדָה הַשֹּׁלֵחַ אֶתְכֶם
אֵלַי לְדָרְשֵׁנִי הִנֵּה ׀ חֵיל פַּרְעֹה הַיֹּצֵא לָכֶם לְעֶזְרָה שָׁב לְאַרְצוֹ
ח מִצְרָיִם: וְשָׁבוּ הַכַּשְׂדִּים וְנִלְחֲמוּ עַל־הָעִיר הַזֹּאת וּלְכָדֻהָ וּשְׂרָפֻהָ
ט בָאֵשׁ: כֹּה ׀ אָמַר יְהוָה אַל־תַּשִּׁאוּ נַפְשֹׁתֵיכֶם לֵאמֹר הָלֹךְ
י יֵלְכוּ מֵעָלֵינוּ הַכַּשְׂדִּים כִּי־לֹא יֵלֵכוּ: כִּי אִם־הִכִּיתֶם כָּל־חֵיל כַּשְׂדִּים
הַנִּלְחָמִים אִתְּכֶם וְנִשְׁאֲרוּ־בָם אֲנָשִׁים מְדֻקָּרִים אִישׁ בְּאָהֳלוֹ יָקוּמוּ
יא וְשָׂרְפוּ אֶת־הָעִיר הַזֹּאת בָּאֵשׁ: וְהָיָה בְּהֵעָלוֹת חֵיל הַכַּשְׂדִּים מֵעַל
יב יְרוּשָׁלִָם מִפְּנֵי חֵיל פַּרְעֹה: וַיֵּצֵא יִרְמְיָהוּ מִירוּשָׁלִַם לָלֶכֶת
יג אֶרֶץ בִּנְיָמִן לַחֲלִק מִשָּׁם בְּתוֹךְ הָעָם: וַיְהִי־הוּא בְּשַׁעַר בִּנְיָמִן וְשָׁם
בַּעַל פְּקִדֻת וּשְׁמוֹ יִרְאִיָּיה בֶּן־שֶׁלֶמְיָה בֶּן־חֲנַנְיָה וַיִּתְפֹּשׂ אֶת־יִרְמְיָהוּ
יד הַנָּבִיא לֵאמֹר אֶל־הַכַּשְׂדִּים אַתָּה נֹפֵל: וַיֹּאמֶר יִרְמְיָהוּ שֶׁקֶר אֵינֶנִּי
נֹפֵל עַל־הַכַּשְׂדִּים וְלֹא שָׁמַע אֵלָיו וַיִּתְפֹּשׂ יִרְאִיָּיה בְּיִרְמְיָהוּ וַיְבִאֵהוּ
טו אֶל־הַשָּׂרִים: וַיִּקְצְפוּ הַשָּׂרִים עַל־יִרְמְיָהוּ וְהִכּוּ אֹתוֹ וְנָתְנוּ אוֹתוֹ בֵּית
טז הָאֵסוּר בֵּית יְהוֹנָתָן הַסֹּפֵר כִּי־אֹתוֹ עָשׂוּ לְבֵית הַכֶּלֶא: כִּי בָא יִרְמְיָהוּ
יז אֶל־בֵּית הַבּוֹר וְאֶל־הַחֲנֻיוֹת וַיֵּשֶׁב־שָׁם יִרְמְיָהוּ יָמִים רַבִּים: וַיִּשְׁלַח
הַמֶּלֶךְ צִדְקִיָּהוּ וַיִּקָּחֵהוּ וַיִּשְׁאָלֵהוּ הַמֶּלֶךְ בְּבֵיתוֹ בַּסֵּתֶר וַיֹּאמֶר הֲיֵשׁ
דָּבָר מֵאֵת יְהוָה וַיֹּאמֶר יִרְמְיָהוּ יֵשׁ וַיֹּאמֶר בְּיַד מֶלֶךְ־בָּבֶל תִּנָּתֵן:
יח וַיֹּאמֶר יִרְמְיָהוּ אֶל־הַמֶּלֶךְ צִדְקִיָּהוּ מֶה חָטָאתִי לְךָ וְלַעֲבָדֶיךָ וְלָעָם
יט הַזֶּה כִּי־נְתַתֶּם אוֹתִי אֶל־בֵּית הַכֶּלֶא: ואיו נְבִיאֵיכֶם אֲשֶׁר־נִבְּאוּ לָכֶם וְאַיֵּה
כ לֵאמֹר לֹא־יָבֹא מֶלֶךְ־בָּבֶל עֲלֵיכֶם וְעַל הָאָרֶץ הַזֹּאת: וְעַתָּה שְׁמַע־
נָא אֲדֹנִי הַמֶּלֶךְ תִּפָּל־נָא תְחִנָּתִי לְפָנֶיךָ וְאַל־תְּשִׁבֵנִי בֵּית יְהוֹנָתָן
כא הַסֹּפֵר וְלֹא אָמוּת שָׁם: וַיְצַוֶּה הַמֶּלֶךְ צִדְקִיָּהוּ וַיַּפְקִדוּ אֶת־יִרְמְיָהוּ
בַּחֲצַר הַמַּטָּרָה וְנָתֹן לוֹ כִכַּר־לֶחֶם לַיּוֹם מִחוּץ הָאֹפִים עַד־תֹּם כָּל־
לח א הַלֶּחֶם מִן־הָעִיר וַיֵּשֶׁב יִרְמְיָהוּ בַּחֲצַר הַמַּטָּרָה: וַיִּשְׁמַע שְׁפַטְיָה בֶן־
מַתָּן וּגְדַלְיָהוּ בֶּן־פַּשְׁחוּר וְיוּכַל בֶּן־שֶׁלֶמְיָהוּ וּפַשְׁחוּר בֶּן־מַלְכִּיָּה
ב אֶת־הַדְּבָרִים אֲשֶׁר יִרְמְיָהוּ מְדַבֵּר אֶל־כָּל־הָעָם לֵאמֹר: כֹּה אָמַר
יְהוָה הַיֹּשֵׁב בָּעִיר הַזֹּאת יָמוּת בַּחֶרֶב בָּרָעָב וּבַדָּבֶר וְהַיֹּצֵא אֶל־

pestilence, but whoever goes out to the Chaldeans will live. His life will be
3 his prize in war, and he will live. This is what the LORD said: This
city shall surely be delivered into the hands of the army of the king of Babylon,
4 and he shall capture it." The officials said to the king, "Let this man be put to
death, for he demoralizes the men of war who remain in this city as well as
all the people, speaking such words to them. This man does not seek the
5 welfare of this people, but only disaster." King Tzidkiyahu said, "He is in your
6 hands, for the king can do nothing against your will." So they took Yirmeyahu
and cast him into the pit of Malkiyahu the king's son, which was in the prison
courtyard. They lowered Yirmeyahu with ropes. There was no water in the
7 pit, only mud. Yirmeyahu sank into the mud. Eved Melekh the Kushite, a
eunuch, who was in the king's palace, heard that Yirmeyahu was put into the
8 pit. The king was then at the Binyamin Gate. Eved Melekh left the king's
9 palace and spoke to the king, saying, "My lord the king, these men have done
wrong by treating Yirmeyahu the prophet this way, by casting him into
the pit. He will surely die of hunger right where he is, for there is no
10 longer any bread in the city." The king ordered Eved Melekh the Kushite as
follows: "Take thirty men from here under your authority and have them
11 raise Yirmeyahu the prophet from the pit before he dies." Eved Melekh took
the men under his authority and went to the king's palace to a room beneath
the treasury. From there they took ragged and worn-out clothes and lowered
12 them with ropes to Yirmeyahu in the pit. Eved Melekh the Kushite said to
Yirmeyahu, "Now place the ragged and worn-out clothes under your armpits,
13 under the ropes," and Yirmeyahu did just that. They pulled Yirmeyahu out
with the ropes and lifted him up from the pit. Yirmeyahu stayed in the prison
14 courtyard. King Tzidkiyahu sent for Yirmeyahu, and they took the
prophet to him near the third entrance of the House of the LORD. The king
said to Yirmeyahu, "I ask you about the word of the Lord. Hold nothing
15 back." Yirmeyahu replied to Tzidkiyahu, "If I tell you, you will surely kill me;
16 if I advise you, you will not listen to me." King Tzidkiyahu swore to Yirmeyahu
in secret, saying, "As the LORD lives, who made this life for us, I will not kill
you, and I will not deliver you into the hands of these men who seek your
17 life." Yirmeyahu said to Tzidkiyahu, "This is what the LORD, God of
Hosts, God of Israel, said: If you will go out to the officers of the king of
Babylon, your life will be spared, and this city will not be burned with fire.
18 You and your household will live. But if you do not go out to the officers of
the king of Babylon, then this city shall be delivered into the hands of the
Chaldeans; they shall burn it with fire, and you shall not escape from their
19 hands." King Tzidkiyahu said to Yirmeyahu, "I worry about the

ג הַכַּשְׂדִּים יחיה וְהָיְתָה־לּוֹ נַפְשׁוֹ לְשָׁלָל וָחָי׃ כֹּה אָמַר יְהוָה וְחָיָה
ד הִנָּתֹן תִּנָּתֵן הָעִיר הַזֹּאת בְּיַד חֵיל מֶלֶךְ־בָּבֶל וּלְכָדָהּ׃ וַיֹּאמְרוּ הַשָּׂרִים
אֶל־הַמֶּלֶךְ יוּמַת נָא אֶת־הָאִישׁ הַזֶּה כִּי עַל־כֵּן הוּא־מְרַפֵּא אֶת־יְדֵי
אַנְשֵׁי הַמִּלְחָמָה הַנִּשְׁאָרִים ׀ בָּעִיר הַזֹּאת וְאֵת יְדֵי כָל־הָעָם לְדַבֵּר
אֲלֵיהֶם כַּדְּבָרִים הָאֵלֶּה כִּי ׀ הָאִישׁ הַזֶּה אֵינֶנּוּ דֹרֵשׁ לְשָׁלוֹם לָעָם הַזֶּה
ה כִּי אִם־לְרָעָה׃ וַיֹּאמֶר הַמֶּלֶךְ צִדְקִיָּהוּ הִנֵּה־הוּא בְּיֶדְכֶם כִּי־אֵין הַמֶּלֶךְ
ו יוּכַל אֶתְכֶם דָּבָר׃ וַיִּקְחוּ אֶת־יִרְמְיָהוּ וַיַּשְׁלִכוּ אֹתוֹ אֶל־הַבּוֹר ׀ מַלְכִּיָּהוּ
בֶן־הַמֶּלֶךְ אֲשֶׁר בַּחֲצַר הַמַּטָּרָה וַיְשַׁלְּחוּ אֶת־יִרְמְיָהוּ בַּחֲבָלִים וּבַבּוֹר
ז אֵין־מַיִם כִּי אִם־טִיט וַיִּטְבַּע יִרְמְיָהוּ בַּטִּיט׃ וַיִּשְׁמַע עֶבֶד־מֶלֶךְ הַכּוּשִׁי
אִישׁ סָרִיס וְהוּא בְּבֵית הַמֶּלֶךְ כִּי־נָתְנוּ אֶת־יִרְמְיָהוּ אֶל־הַבּוֹר וְהַמֶּלֶךְ
ח יוֹשֵׁב בְּשַׁעַר בִּנְיָמִן׃ וַיֵּצֵא עֶבֶד־מֶלֶךְ מִבֵּית הַמֶּלֶךְ וַיְדַבֵּר אֶל־הַמֶּלֶךְ כג
ט לֵאמֹר׃ אֲדֹנִי הַמֶּלֶךְ הֵרֵעוּ הָאֲנָשִׁים הָאֵלֶּה אֵת כָּל־אֲשֶׁר עָשׂוּ לְיִרְמְיָהוּ
הַנָּבִיא אֵת אֲשֶׁר־הִשְׁלִיכוּ אֶל־הַבּוֹר וַיָּמָת תַּחְתָּיו מִפְּנֵי הָרָעָב כִּי
י אֵין הַלֶּחֶם עוֹד בָּעִיר׃ וַיְצַוֶּה הַמֶּלֶךְ אֵת עֶבֶד־מֶלֶךְ הַכּוּשִׁי לֵאמֹר
קַח בְּיָדְךָ מִזֶּה שְׁלֹשִׁים אֲנָשִׁים וְהַעֲלִיתָ אֶת־יִרְמְיָהוּ הַנָּבִיא מִן־הַבּוֹר
יא בְּטֶרֶם יָמוּת׃ וַיִּקַּח ׀ עֶבֶד־מֶלֶךְ אֶת־הָאֲנָשִׁים בְּיָדוֹ וַיָּבֹא בֵית־הַמֶּלֶךְ
אֶל־תַּחַת הָאוֹצָר וַיִּקַּח מִשָּׁם בְּלוֹיֵ הסחבות וּבְלוֹיֵ מְלָחִים וַיְשַׁלְּחֵם סְחָבוֹת
יב אֶל־יִרְמְיָהוּ אֶל־הַבּוֹר בַּחֲבָלִים׃ וַיֹּאמֶר עֶבֶד־מֶלֶךְ הַכּוּשִׁי אֶל־יִרְמְיָהוּ
שִׂים נָא בְּלוֹאֵי הַסְּחָבוֹת וְהַמְּלָחִים תַּחַת אַצִּלוֹת יָדֶיךָ מִתַּחַת
יג לַחֲבָלִים וַיַּעַשׂ יִרְמְיָהוּ כֵּן׃ וַיִּמְשְׁכוּ אֶת־יִרְמְיָהוּ בַּחֲבָלִים וַיַּעֲלוּ אֹתוֹ
יד מִן־הַבּוֹר וַיֵּשֶׁב יִרְמְיָהוּ בַּחֲצַר הַמַּטָּרָה׃ וַיִּשְׁלַח הַמֶּלֶךְ
צִדְקִיָּהוּ וַיִּקַּח אֶת־יִרְמְיָהוּ הַנָּבִיא אֵלָיו אֶל־מָבוֹא הַשְּׁלִישִׁי אֲשֶׁר
בְּבֵית יְהוָה וַיֹּאמֶר הַמֶּלֶךְ אֶל־יִרְמְיָהוּ שֹׁאֵל אֲנִי אֹתְךָ דָּבָר אַל־תְּכַחֵד
טו מִמֶּנִּי דָּבָר׃ וַיֹּאמֶר יִרְמְיָהוּ אֶל־צִדְקִיָּהוּ כִּי אַגִּיד לְךָ הֲלוֹא הָמֵת
טז תְּמִיתֵנִי וְכִי אִיעָצְךָ לֹא תִשְׁמַע אֵלָי׃ וַיִּשָּׁבַע הַמֶּלֶךְ צִדְקִיָּהוּ אֶל־
יִרְמְיָהוּ בַּסֵּתֶר לֵאמֹר חַי־יְהוָה אֵת אֲשֶׁר עָשָׂה־לָנוּ אֶת־הַנֶּפֶשׁ הַזֹּאת
אִם־אֲמִיתֶךָ וְאִם־אֶתֶּנְךָ בְּיַד הָאֲנָשִׁים הָאֵלֶּה אֲשֶׁר מְבַקְשִׁים אֶת־
יז נַפְשֶׁךָ׃ וַיֹּאמֶר יִרְמְיָהוּ אֶל־צִדְקִיָּהוּ כֹּה־אָמַר יְהוָה אֱלֹהֵי
צְבָאוֹת אֱלֹהֵי יִשְׂרָאֵל אִם־יָצֹא תֵצֵא אֶל־שָׂרֵי מֶלֶךְ־בָּבֶל וְחָיְתָה
יח נַפְשֶׁךָ וְהָעִיר הַזֹּאת לֹא תִשָּׂרֵף בָּאֵשׁ וְחָיִתָה אַתָּה וּבֵיתֶךָ׃ וְאִם לֹא־
תֵצֵא אֶל־שָׂרֵי מֶלֶךְ בָּבֶל וְנִתְּנָה הָעִיר הַזֹּאת בְּיַד הַכַּשְׂדִּים וּשְׂרָפוּהָ
יט בָּאֵשׁ וְאַתָּה לֹא־תִמָּלֵט מִיָּדָם׃ וַיֹּאמֶר הַמֶּלֶךְ צִדְקִיָּהוּ

people of Yehuda who have deserted to the Chaldeans lest they hand me over
20 to them and they torture me." Yirmeyahu said, "They will not hand
you over. Heed now the voice of the LORD in what I say to you. It will benefit
21 you, and your life will be spared. But if you refuse to go out, this is what the
22 LORD has shown me – look, all the women remaining in the palace of the
king of Yehuda are being led out to the officers of the king of Babylon. And
look, this is what they say: 'Your allies have seduced you, and they have
prevailed. Now that your feet have sunk into the mire, they have retreated
23 backward.' All your wives and sons are being taken to the Chaldeans, and
even you shall not escape their hands, for you shall be caught by the hand of
the king of Babylon, and you shall cause this city to be burned down by
24 fire." Tzidkiyahu said to Yirmeyahu, "Let no one else know of this
25 conversation, and you shall not die. Should the officials hear that I spoke to
you, and should they come to you and say, 'Tell us now what you said to the
king – hold nothing back and we will not kill you – and what the king said to
26 you,' tell them, 'I was presenting my plea before the king that he not send me
27 back to the house of Yonatan to die there.'" All the officials did come
to Yirmeyahu, and they interrogated him. He told them precisely everything
that the king had instructed him to tell. They ceased speaking with him, for
28 none of the conversation had been overheard. Yirmeyahu stayed in
the prison courtyard until the day that Jerusalem was captured. It
39 1 transpired when Jerusalem was captured... In the ninth year of Tzidkiyahu,
king of Yehuda, in the tenth month, Nevukhadretzar, king of Babylon, and
2 all his forces came to Jerusalem and laid siege to it. In the eleventh year of
3 Tzidkiyahu, on the ninth day of the fourth month, the city was breached. All
the officers of the king of Babylon came and sat at the middle gate – Nergal
Saretzer, Samgar Nevo, Sarsekhim the Rav-Saris, Nergal Saretzer the Rav-
4 Mag, and all the other officers of the king of Babylon. When Tzidkiyahu, king
of Yehuda, and all the men of war saw them, they fled. They left the city by
dark of night by way of the royal garden through the gate between the double
5 walls. They went in the direction of the Arava.[82] But the Chaldean force
pursued them and caught up with Tzidkiyahu on the plains of Yeriḥo. They
took him and hauled him up before Nevukhadretzar, king of Babylon, at Rivla
6 in the land of Ḥamat, and he spoke harshly to him. The king of Babylon
slaughtered the sons of Tzidkiyahu before his eyes in Rivla. The king of
7 Babylon also slaughtered all the nobles of Yehuda. He blinded Tzidkiyahu
8 and chained him in bronze fetters to bring him to Babylon. The Chaldeans
burned down the royal palace and the people's houses with fire, and they tore
9 down the walls of Jerusalem. As for the rest of the people who remained in
the city and those that had defected to him and the rest of the people who
10 survived – Nevuzaradan, chief of the guard, exiled them to Babylon. But
Nevuzaradan, chief of the guard, retained some of the poor people, who had

82 | Eastward, toward the Jordan River.

אֶל־יִרְמְיָהוּ אֲנִי דֹאֵג אֶת־הַיְּהוּדִים אֲשֶׁר נָפְלוּ אֶל־הַכַּשְׂדִּים פֶּן־יִתְּנוּ
כ אֹתִי בְּיָדָם וְהִתְעַלְּלוּ־בִי׃ וַיֹּאמֶר יִרְמְיָהוּ לֹא יִתֵּנוּ
שְׁמַע־נָא ׀ בְּקוֹל יהוה לַאֲשֶׁר אֲנִי דֹּבֵר אֵלֶיךָ וְיִיטַב לְךָ וּתְחִי נַפְשֶׁךָ׃
כא כב וְאִם־מָאֵן אַתָּה לָצֵאת זֶה הַדָּבָר אֲשֶׁר הִרְאַנִי יהוה׃ וְהִנֵּה כָל־הַנָּשִׁים
אֲשֶׁר נִשְׁאֲרוּ בְּבֵית מֶלֶךְ־יְהוּדָה מוּצָאוֹת אֶל־שָׂרֵי מֶלֶךְ בָּבֶל וְהֵנָּה
אֹמְרוֹת הִסִּיתוּךָ וְיָכְלוּ לְךָ אַנְשֵׁי שְׁלֹמֶךָ הָטְבְּעוּ בַבֹּץ רַגְלֶךָ נָסֹגוּ
כג אָחוֹר׃ וְאֶת־כָּל־נָשֶׁיךָ וְאֶת־בָּנֶיךָ מוֹצִאִים אֶל־הַכַּשְׂדִּים וְאַתָּה לֹא־
תִמָּלֵט מִיָּדָם כִּי בְיַד מֶלֶךְ־בָּבֶל תִּתָּפֵשׂ וְאֶת־הָעִיר הַזֹּאת תִּשְׂרֹף
כד בָּאֵשׁ׃ וַיֹּאמֶר צִדְקִיָּהוּ אֶל־יִרְמְיָהוּ אִישׁ אַל־יֵדַע בַּדְּבָרִים־
כה הָאֵלֶּה וְלֹא תָמוּת׃ וְכִי־יִשְׁמְעוּ הַשָּׂרִים כִּי־דִבַּרְתִּי אִתָּךְ וּבָאוּ אֵלֶיךָ
וְאָמְרוּ אֵלֶיךָ הַגִּידָה־נָּא לָנוּ מַה־דִּבַּרְתָּ אֶל־הַמֶּלֶךְ אַל־תְּכַחֵד מִמֶּנּוּ
כו וְלֹא נְמִיתֶךָ וּמַה־דִּבֶּר אֵלֶיךָ הַמֶּלֶךְ׃ וְאָמַרְתָּ אֲלֵיהֶם מַפִּיל־אֲנִי תְחִנָּתִי
כז לִפְנֵי הַמֶּלֶךְ לְבִלְתִּי הֲשִׁיבֵנִי בֵּית יְהוֹנָתָן לָמוּת שָׁם׃ וַיָּבֹאוּ
כָל־הַשָּׂרִים אֶל־יִרְמְיָהוּ וַיִּשְׁאֲלוּ אֹתוֹ וַיַּגֵּד לָהֶם כְּכָל־הַדְּבָרִים הָאֵלֶּה
כח אֲשֶׁר צִוָּה הַמֶּלֶךְ וַיַּחֲרִשׁוּ מִמֶּנּוּ כִּי לֹא־נִשְׁמַע הַדָּבָר׃ וַיֵּשֶׁב
יִרְמְיָהוּ בַּחֲצַר הַמַּטָּרָה עַד־יוֹם אֲשֶׁר־נִלְכְּדָה יְרוּשָׁלִָם וְהָיָה
לט א כַּאֲשֶׁר נִלְכְּדָה יְרוּשָׁלִָם׃ בַּשָּׁנָה הַתְּשִׁעִית לְצִדְקִיָּהוּ מֶלֶךְ־יְהוּדָה
בַּחֹדֶשׁ הָעֲשִׂרִי בָּא נְבוּכַדְרֶאצַּר מֶלֶךְ־בָּבֶל וְכָל־חֵילוֹ אֶל־יְרוּשָׁלִַם
ב וַיָּצֻרוּ עָלֶיהָ׃ בְּעַשְׁתֵּי־עֶשְׂרֵה שָׁנָה לְצִדְקִיָּהוּ בַּחֹדֶשׁ הָרְבִיעִי בְּתִשְׁעָה
ג לַחֹדֶשׁ הָבְקְעָה הָעִיר׃ וַיָּבֹאוּ כֹּל שָׂרֵי מֶלֶךְ־בָּבֶל וַיֵּשְׁבוּ בְּשַׁעַר הַתָּוֶךְ
נֵרְגַל שַׂרְאֶצֶר סַמְגַּר־נְבוּ שַׂרְסְכִים רַב־סָרִיס נֵרְגַל שַׂרְאֶצֶר רַב־מָג
ד וְכָל־שְׁאֵרִית שָׂרֵי מֶלֶךְ־בָּבֶל׃ וַיְהִי כַּאֲשֶׁר רָאָם צִדְקִיָּהוּ מֶלֶךְ־יְהוּדָה
וְכֹל ׀ אַנְשֵׁי הַמִּלְחָמָה וַיִּבְרְחוּ וַיֵּצְאוּ לַיְלָה מִן־הָעִיר דֶּרֶךְ גַּן הַמֶּלֶךְ
ה בְּשַׁעַר בֵּין הַחֹמֹתָיִם וַיֵּצֵא דֶּרֶךְ הָעֲרָבָה׃ וַיִּרְדְּפוּ חֵיל־כַּשְׂדִּים אַחֲרֵיהֶם
וַיַּשִּׂגוּ אֶת־צִדְקִיָּהוּ בְּעַרְבוֹת יְרֵחוֹ וַיִּקְחוּ אֹתוֹ וַיַּעֲלֻהוּ אֶל־נְבוּכַדְרֶאצַּר
ו מֶלֶךְ־בָּבֶל רִבְלָתָה בְּאֶרֶץ חֲמָת וַיְדַבֵּר אִתּוֹ מִשְׁפָּטִים׃ וַיִּשְׁחַט מֶלֶךְ
בָּבֶל אֶת־בְּנֵי צִדְקִיָּהוּ בְּרִבְלָה לְעֵינָיו וְאֵת כָּל־חֹרֵי יְהוּדָה שָׁחַט מֶלֶךְ
ז בָּבֶל׃ וְאֶת־עֵינֵי צִדְקִיָּהוּ עִוֵּר וַיַּאַסְרֵהוּ בַּנְחֻשְׁתַּיִם לָבִיא אֹתוֹ בָּבֶלָה׃
ח וְאֶת־בֵּית הַמֶּלֶךְ וְאֶת־בֵּית הָעָם שָׂרְפוּ הַכַּשְׂדִּים בָּאֵשׁ וְאֶת־חֹמוֹת
ט יְרוּשָׁלִַם נָתָצוּ׃ וְאֵת יֶתֶר הָעָם הַנִּשְׁאָרִים בָּעִיר וְאֶת־הַנֹּפְלִים אֲשֶׁר
נָפְלוּ עָלָיו וְאֵת יֶתֶר הָעָם הַנִּשְׁאָרִים הֶגְלָה נְבוּזַרְאֲדָן רַב־טַבָּחִים
י בָּבֶל׃ וּמִן־הָעָם הַדַּלִּים אֲשֶׁר אֵין־לָהֶם מְאוּמָה הִשְׁאִיר נְבוּזַרְאֲדָן

nothing, in the land of Yehuda and gave them vineyards and fields at that
11 time. As for Yirmeyahu, Nevukhadretzar, king of Babylon, ordered Nevuza-
12 radan, chief of the guard, as follows: "Release him[83] and treat him with care.
Do nothing harmful to him; rather, do for him whatever he asks of
13 you." Nevuzaradan, chief of the guard, sent word along with Nevushazban
the Rav-Saris, Nergal Saretzer the Rav-Mag, and all the commanders of
14 the king of Babylon. They sent word and had Yirmeyahu released from the
prison courtyard. They entrusted him to Gedalyahu son of Aḥikam[84] son
of Shafan so that he would be taken to his house. He stayed among the
15 people. The word of the LORD had come to Yirmeyahu while he was
16 still confined to the prison courtyard: "Go and tell Eved Melekh the Kushite
that this is what the LORD of Hosts, God of Israel, said: I will bring My words
to pass upon this city, for disaster and not for good, and you will witness it at
17 that time. I will save you at that time, declares the LORD. You will not be
18 turned over to the hands of the men whom you dread. I will surely rescue
you so that you will not fall by the sword. Your own life will be your prize in
40 1 war because you trusted in Me, declares the LORD." The word came
to Yirmeyahu from the LORD after Nevuzaradan, chief of the guard, set him
free from Rama, when he had taken him bound in chains in the midst of all
2 those of Jerusalem and Yehuda who were being exiled to Babylon. The chief
of the guard took Yirmeyahu and said to him, "The LORD, your God, ordered
3 disaster for this place. The LORD brought it about as He had promised, for
you all sinned against the LORD and did not heed His voice, and this is what
4 has happened to you. But now I have freed you from the chains that were
upon your hands. If it pleases you to come with me to Babylon, I will take
good care of you. If it displeases you to come with me to Babylon, then do
not. See this: the entire land is before you. Go wherever pleases you and
5 wherever seems proper to you to go." And before Yirmeyahu turned to go,
Nevuzaradan continued, "Go back to Gedalya son of Aḥikam son of Shafan,
whom the king of Babylon has appointed over the towns of Yehuda, and stay
together with him among the people, or go wherever it seems proper for you
to go." The chief of the guard gave him food, provisions, and a gift and sent
6 him off. Yirmeyahu came to Gedalya son of Aḥikam at Mitzpa and stayed
7 with him among the people who were left in the land. When all the
army officers who were scattered in the countryside, they and their men,
heard that the king of Babylon had appointed Gedalyahu son of Aḥikam over
the land and that he had entrusted him with the men, women, and children
8 who were among the poor of the land who were not exiled to Babylon, they
came to Gedalya at Mitzpa – Yishmael son of Netanyahu, Yoḥanan and
Yonatan sons of Kare'aḥ, Seraya son of Tanḥumet, the sons of Ofai the
9 Netofatite, and Yezanyahu son of the Maakhatite, they and their men. "Do
not be afraid to serve the Chaldeans," Gedalyahu son of Aḥikam son of Shafan

83 | From the prison courtyard.

84 | See 26:24.

רַב־טַבָּחִים בְּאֶרֶץ יְהוּדָה וַיִּתֵּן לָהֶם כְּרָמִים וִיגֵבִים בַּיּוֹם הַהוּא׃
יא וַיְצַו נְבוּכַדְרֶאצַּר מֶלֶךְ־בָּבֶל עַל־יִרְמְיָהוּ בְּיַד נְבוּזַרְאֲדָן רַב־טַבָּחִים
יב לֵאמֹר׃ קָחֶנּוּ וְעֵינֶיךָ שִׂים עָלָיו וְאַל־תַּעַשׂ לוֹ מְאוּמָה רָּע כִּי אִם כַּאֲשֶׁר
יג יְדַבֵּר אֵלֶיךָ כֵּן עֲשֵׂה עִמּוֹ׃ וַיִּשְׁלַח נְבוּזַרְאֲדָן רַב־טַבָּחִים וּנְבוּשַׁזְבָּן
יד רַב־סָרִיס וְנֵרְגַל שַׂרְאֶצֶר רַב־מָג וְכֹל רַבֵּי מֶלֶךְ־בָּבֶל׃ וַיִּשְׁלְחוּ וַיִּקְחוּ
אֶת־יִרְמְיָהוּ מֵחֲצַר הַמַּטָּרָה וַיִּתְּנוּ אֹתוֹ אֶל־גְּדַלְיָהוּ בֶּן־אֲחִיקָם בֶּן־
טו שָׁפָן לְהוֹצִאֵהוּ אֶל־הַבָּיִת וַיֵּשֶׁב בְּתוֹךְ הָעָם׃ וְאֶל־
טז יִרְמְיָהוּ הָיָה דְבַר־יְהוָה בִּהְיֹתוֹ עָצוּר בַּחֲצַר הַמַּטָּרָה לֵאמֹר׃ הָלוֹךְ
וְאָמַרְתָּ לְעֶבֶד־מֶלֶךְ הַכּוּשִׁי לֵאמֹר כֹּה־אָמַר יְהוָה צְבָאוֹת אֱלֹהֵי
יִשְׂרָאֵל הִנְנִי מֵבִי אֶת־דְּבָרַי אֶל־הָעִיר הַזֹּאת לְרָעָה וְלֹא לְטוֹבָה וְהָיוּ
יז לְפָנֶיךָ בַּיּוֹם הַהוּא׃ וְהִצַּלְתִּיךָ בַיּוֹם־הַהוּא נְאֻם־יְהוָה וְלֹא תִנָּתֵן בְּיַד
יח הָאֲנָשִׁים אֲשֶׁר־אַתָּה יָגוֹר מִפְּנֵיהֶם׃ כִּי מַלֵּט אֲמַלֶּטְךָ וּבַחֶרֶב לֹא תִפֹּל כד
מ א וְהָיְתָה לְךָ נַפְשְׁךָ לְשָׁלָל כִּי־בָטַחְתָּ בִּי נְאֻם־יְהוָה׃ הַדָּבָר
אֲשֶׁר־הָיָה אֶל־יִרְמְיָהוּ מֵאֵת יְהוָה אַחַר ׀ שַׁלַּח אֹתוֹ נְבוּזַרְאֲדָן רַב־
טַבָּחִים מִן־הָרָמָה בְּקַחְתּוֹ אֹתוֹ וְהוּא־אָסוּר בָּאזִקִּים בְּתוֹךְ כָּל־גָּלוּת
ב יְרוּשָׁלִַם וִיהוּדָה הַמֻּגְלִים בָּבֶלָה׃ וַיִּקַּח רַב־טַבָּחִים לְיִרְמְיָהוּ וַיֹּאמֶר
ג אֵלָיו יְהוָה אֱלֹהֶיךָ דִּבֶּר אֶת־הָרָעָה הַזֹּאת אֶל־הַמָּקוֹם הַזֶּה׃ וַיָּבֵא
וַיַּעַשׂ יְהוָה כַּאֲשֶׁר דִּבֵּר כִּי־חֲטָאתֶם לַיהוָה וְלֹא־שְׁמַעְתֶּם בְּקוֹלוֹ
ד וְהָיָה לָכֶם דבר הַזֶּה׃ וְעַתָּה הִנֵּה פִתַּחְתִּיךָ הַיּוֹם מִן־הָאזִקִּים אֲשֶׁר הַדָּבָר
עַל־יָדֶךָ אִם־טוֹב בְּעֵינֶיךָ לָבוֹא אִתִּי בָבֶל בֹּא וְאָשִׂים אֶת־עֵינִי
עָלֶיךָ וְאִם־רַע בְּעֵינֶיךָ לָבוֹא־אִתִּי בָבֶל חֲדָל רְאֵה כָּל־הָאָרֶץ לְפָנֶיךָ
ה אֶל־טוֹב וְאֶל־הַיָּשָׁר בְּעֵינֶיךָ לָלֶכֶת שָׁמָּה לֵךְ׃ וְעוֹדֶנּוּ לֹא־יָשׁוּב
וְשֻׁבָה אֶל־גְּדַלְיָה בֶן־אֲחִיקָם בֶּן־שָׁפָן אֲשֶׁר הִפְקִיד מֶלֶךְ־בָּבֶל בְּעָרֵי
יְהוּדָה וְשֵׁב אִתּוֹ בְּתוֹךְ הָעָם אוֹ אֶל־כָּל־הַיָּשָׁר בְּעֵינֶיךָ לָלֶכֶת לֵךְ
ו וַיִּתֶּן־לוֹ רַב־טַבָּחִים אֲרֻחָה וּמַשְׂאֵת וַיְשַׁלְּחֵהוּ׃ וַיָּבֹא יִרְמְיָהוּ אֶל־
גְּדַלְיָה בֶן־אֲחִיקָם הַמִּצְפָּתָה וַיֵּשֶׁב אִתּוֹ בְּתוֹךְ הָעָם הַנִּשְׁאָרִים
ז בָּאָרֶץ׃ וַיִּשְׁמְעוּ כָל־שָׂרֵי הַחֲיָלִים אֲשֶׁר בַּשָּׂדֶה הֵמָּה
וְאַנְשֵׁיהֶם כִּי־הִפְקִיד מֶלֶךְ־בָּבֶל אֶת־גְּדַלְיָהוּ בֶן־אֲחִיקָם בָּאָרֶץ וְכִי ׀
הִפְקִיד אִתּוֹ אֲנָשִׁים וְנָשִׁים וָטָף וּמִדַּלַּת הָאָרֶץ מֵאֲשֶׁר לֹא־הָגְלוּ
ח בָּבֶלָה׃ וַיָּבֹאוּ אֶל־גְּדַלְיָה הַמִּצְפָּתָה וְיִשְׁמָעֵאל בֶּן־נְתַנְיָהוּ וְיוֹחָנָן
וְיוֹנָתָן בְּנֵי־קָרֵחַ וּשְׂרָיָה בֶן־תַּנְחֻמֶת וּבְנֵי ׀ עופי הַנְּטֹפָתִי וִיזַנְיָהוּ בֶּן־ עֵיפַי
ט הַמַּעֲכָתִי הֵמָּה וְאַנְשֵׁיהֶם׃ וַיִּשָּׁבַע לָהֶם גְּדַלְיָהוּ בֶן־אֲחִיקָם בֶּן־

promised them and their men. "Stay in the land and serve the king of Babylon,
10 and all will be well for you. I intend to remain in Mitzpa to represent you
before the Chaldeans when they come to us. As for you, gather wine and
summer fruit and oil and store them in your vessels, and settle in the towns
11 that you have occupied." Likewise, when all the people of Yehuda who were
in Moav and among the Amonites and in Edom and in all other lands heard
that the king of Babylon had granted a remnant in Yehuda and had appointed
12 Gedalyahu son of Aḥikam son of Shafan over them, all the people of Yehuda
returned from all the places where they had been dispersed and came to the
land of Yehuda, to Gedalyahu in Mitzpa. They gathered a great deal of wine
13 and summer fruit. Yoḥanan son of Kare'aḥ and all the army officers
14 who were in the countryside came to Gedalyahu at Mitzpa. They said to him,
"Are you aware that Baalis, king of the Amonites, has sent Yishmael son of
Netanya to take your life?" But Gedalyahu son of Aḥikam did not believe
15 them. Yoḥanan son of Kare'aḥ secretly said to Gedalyahu in Mitzpa, "Let me
go now and slay Yishmael son of Netanya, and no one will know. Why should
he take your life? Then all of Yehuda who have gathered to you will scatter,
16 and the remnant of Yehuda will be lost!" Gedalyahu son of Aḥikam said to
Yoḥanan son of Kare'aḥ, "Do not do such a thing. You are telling a lie about
41 1 Yishmael." In the seventh month, Yishmael son of Netanya son of
Elishama, of royal descent and among the king's chief officers, came with ten
men to Mitzpa to Gedalyahu son of Aḥikam. They ate a meal together there
2 in Mitzpa. Yishmael son of Netanya stood up, along with the ten men with
him, and they struck Gedalyahu son of Aḥikam son of Shafan with swords
and killed him because the king of Babylon had put him in charge of the land,
3 and all the men of Yehuda who were with Gedalyahu in Mitzpa and the
4 Chaldeans who were stationed there, the men of war, Yishmael killed. It was
5 the second day after Gedalyahu was killed, yet no one knew. Eighty men came
from Shekhem, Shilo, and Shomron with shaven beards and torn clothing,
having gashed themselves. They had grain offerings and incense with them
6 to bring to the House of the Lord. Yishmael son of Netanya went out to
greet them from Mitzpa, weeping as he went. When he met them, he said to
7 them, "Come to Gedalyahu son of Aḥikam." When they came into the town,
Yishmael son of Netanya – he and his ten men – killed them and threw their
8 bodies into the pit. There were ten men among them who said to Yishmael,
"Do not kill us, for we have hidden treasures in the field – wheat, barley, oil,
9 and honey." He desisted and did not kill them along with their comrades. The
pit into which Yishmael cast the corpses of all the men whom he murdered

שפן ולאנשיהם לאמר אל־תיראו מעבוד הכשדים שבו בארץ
י ועבדו את־מלך בבל וייטב לכם: ואני הנני ישב במצפה לעמד
לפני הכשדים אשר יבאו אלינו ואתם אספו יין וקיץ ושמן ושמו
יא בכליכם ושבו בעריכם אשר־תפשתם: וגם כל־היהודים אשר־
במואב ׀ ובבני־עמון ובאדום ואשר בכל־הארצות שמעו כי־נתן
מלך־בבל שארית ליהודה וכי הפקיד עליהם את־גדליהו בן־
יב אחיקם בן־שפן: וישבו כל־היהודים מכל־המקמות אשר נדחו־שם
ויבאו ארץ־יהודה אל־גדליהו המצפתה ויאספו יין וקיץ הרבה
יג מאד: ויוחנן בן־קרח וכל־שרי החילים אשר
יד בשדה באו אל־גדליהו המצפתה: ויאמרו אליו הידע תדע כי
בעליס ׀ מלך בני־עמון שלח את־ישמעאל בן־נתניה להכתך נפש
טו ולא־האמין להם גדליהו בן־אחיקם: ויוחנן בן־קרח אמר אל־
גדליהו בסתר במצפה לאמר אלכה נא ואכה את־ישמעאל בן־
נתניה ואיש לא ידע למה יככה נפש ונפצו כל־יהודה הנקבצים
טז אליך ואבדה שארית יהודה: ויאמר גדליהו בן־אחיקם אל־
יוחנן בן־קרח אל־תעש את־הדבר הזה כי־שקר אתה דבר אל־
מא א ישמעאל: ויהי ׀ בחדש השביעי בא ישמעאל בן־נתניה
בן־אלישמע מזרע המלוכה ורבי המלך ועשרה אנשים אתו אל־
ב גדליהו בן־אחיקם המצפתה ויאכלו שם לחם יחדו במצפה: ויקם
ישמעאל בן־נתניה ועשרת האנשים ׀ אשר־היו אתו ויכו את־
גדליהו בן־אחיקם בן־שפן בחרב וימת אתו אשר־הפקיד מלך־בבל
ג בארץ: ואת כל־היהודים אשר־היו אתו את־גדליהו במצפה ואת־
ד הכשדים אשר נמצאו־שם את אנשי המלחמה הכה ישמעאל: ויהי
ה ביום השני להמית את־גדליהו ואיש לא ידע: ויבאו אנשים משכם
משלו ומשמרון שמנים איש מגלחי זקן וקרעי בגדים ומתגדדים
ו ומנחה ולבונה בידם להביא בית יהוה: ויצא ישמעאל בן־נתניה
לקראתם מן־המצפה הלך הלך ובכה ויהי כפגש אתם ויאמר
ז אליהם באו אל־גדליהו בן־אחיקם: ויהי כבואם אל־תוך העיר
וישחטם ישמעאל בן־נתניה אל־תוך הבור הוא והאנשים אשר־
ח אתו: ועשרה אנשים נמצאו־בם ויאמרו אל־ישמעאל אל־תמתנו
כי־יש־לנו מטמנים בשדה חטים ושערים ושמן ודבש ויחדל ולא
ט המיתם בתוך אחיהם: והבור אשר השליך שם ישמעאל את ׀ כל־

because of Gedalyahu was the very pit that King Asa had made to defend
himself against Baasha, king of Israel.[85] Yishmael son of Netanyahu filled it
10 with dead bodies. Yishmael made captives of the rest of the people who were
in Mitzpa – the daughters of the king and all the people remaining in Mitzpa
whom Nevuzaradan, chief of the guard, had entrusted to Gedalyahu son of
Aḥikam. Yishmael son of Netanya took them captive and set out to cross over
11 to the Amonites. Yoḥanan son of Kare'aḥ, along with all his
12 army officers, heard of all the evil that Yishmael son of Netanya had done.
They took all their men and set out to do battle with Yishmael son of Netanya,
13 and found him by the great pool near Givon. When the people who were
14 held by Yishmael saw Yoḥanan son of Kare'aḥ and all his army officers, they
rejoiced. All the people whom Yishmael had taken captive from Mitzpa
15 turned and went over to Yoḥanan son of Kare'aḥ. Yishmael son of Netanya
along with eight of his men escaped from Yoḥanan and set out toward the
16 Amonites. Yoḥanan son of Kare'aḥ, along with all his army officers,
took from Mitzpa all the rest of the people whom he had recovered from
Yishmael son of Netanya after he had murdered Gedalya son of Aḥikam: men,
soldiers, women, children, and courtiers whom he, Yoḥanan, had recovered
17 from Givon. They left and stayed in the dwelling place of Kimham, near Beit
18 Leḥem, on their way to go to Egypt because of the Chaldeans, for they feared
them, for Yishmael son of Netanya had murdered Gedalyahu son of Aḥikam,
42 1 whom the king had put in charge of the land. All the army officers,
Yoḥanan son of Kare'aḥ, Yezanya son of Hoshaya, and all the people from the
2 least to the greatest, stepped forward. They said to Yirmeyahu the prophet,
"Please accept our plea and pray to the Lord your God on our behalf – on
behalf of this entire remnant, for we remain but a few of many, as your eyes
3 can see. May the Lord your God tell us what path we are to follow and what
4 we are to do." Yirmeyahu the prophet said to them, "I hear you. I will pray to
the Lord your God as you have requested. I will tell you every word that the
5 Lord will declare to you. I will hold nothing back." They said to Yirmeyahu,
"May the Lord be a true and trusted witness against us if we do not do
6 everything that the Lord your God will send you to tell us. Whether good
or bad in our eyes, we shall heed the voice of the Lord our God to whom we
have sent you so that it will go well with us, for we shall obey the voice of the
7 Lord our God." At the end of ten days the word of the Lord came
8 to Yirmeyahu. He summoned Yoḥanan son of Kare'aḥ, all the army officers

85 | See 1 Kings 15:16–22.

פִּגְרֵי הָאֲנָשִׁים אֲשֶׁר הִכָּה בְּיַד־גְּדַלְיָהוּ הוּא אֲשֶׁר עָשָׂה הַמֶּלֶךְ אָסָא
מִפְּנֵי בַּעְשָׁא מֶלֶךְ־יִשְׂרָאֵל אֹתוֹ מִלֵּא יִשְׁמָעֵאל בֶּן־נְתַנְיָהוּ חֲלָלִים:
י וַיִּשְׁבְּ ׀ יִשְׁמָעֵאל אֶת־כָּל־שְׁאֵרִית הָעָם אֲשֶׁר בַּמִּצְפָּה אֶת־בְּנוֹת
הַמֶּלֶךְ וְאֶת־כָּל־הָעָם הַנִּשְׁאָרִים בַּמִּצְפָּה אֲשֶׁר הִפְקִיד נְבוּזַרְאֲדָן
רַב־טַבָּחִים אֶת־גְּדַלְיָהוּ בֶּן־אֲחִיקָם וַיִּשְׁבֵּם יִשְׁמָעֵאל בֶּן־נְתַנְיָה וַיֵּלֶךְ
יא לַעֲבֹר אֶל־בְּנֵי עַמּוֹן: וַיִּשְׁמַע יוֹחָנָן בֶּן־קָרֵחַ וְכָל־שָׂרֵי
יב הַחֲיָלִים אֲשֶׁר אִתּוֹ אֵת כָּל־הָרָעָה אֲשֶׁר עָשָׂה יִשְׁמָעֵאל בֶּן־נְתַנְיָה:
וַיִּקְחוּ אֶת־כָּל־הָאֲנָשִׁים וַיֵּלְכוּ לְהִלָּחֵם עִם־יִשְׁמָעֵאל בֶּן־נְתַנְיָה
יג וַיִּמְצְאוּ אֹתוֹ אֶל־מַיִם רַבִּים אֲשֶׁר בְּגִבְעוֹן: וַיְהִי כִּרְאוֹת כָּל־הָעָם
אֲשֶׁר אֶת־יִשְׁמָעֵאל אֶת־יוֹחָנָן בֶּן־קָרֵחַ וְאֵת כָּל־שָׂרֵי הַחֲיָלִים אֲשֶׁר
יד אִתּוֹ וַיִּשְׂמָחוּ: וַיָּסֹבּוּ כָּל־הָעָם אֲשֶׁר־שָׁבָה יִשְׁמָעֵאל מִן־הַמִּצְפָּה
טו וַיָּשֻׁבוּ וַיֵּלְכוּ אֶל־יוֹחָנָן בֶּן־קָרֵחַ: וְיִשְׁמָעֵאל בֶּן־נְתַנְיָה נִמְלַט בִּשְׁמֹנָה
טז אֲנָשִׁים מִפְּנֵי יוֹחָנָן וַיֵּלֶךְ אֶל־בְּנֵי עַמּוֹן: וַיִּקַּח
יוֹחָנָן בֶּן־קָרֵחַ וְכָל־שָׂרֵי הַחֲיָלִים אֲשֶׁר־אִתּוֹ אֵת כָּל־שְׁאֵרִית הָעָם
אֲשֶׁר הֵשִׁיב מֵאֵת יִשְׁמָעֵאל בֶּן־נְתַנְיָה מִן־הַמִּצְפָּה אַחַר הִכָּה אֶת־
גְּדַלְיָה בֶּן־אֲחִיקָם גְּבָרִים אַנְשֵׁי הַמִּלְחָמָה וְנָשִׁים וְטַף וְסָרִסִים אֲשֶׁר
יז הֵשִׁיב מִגִּבְעוֹן: וַיֵּלְכוּ וַיֵּשְׁבוּ בְּגֵרוּת כמוהם אֲשֶׁר־אֵצֶל בֵּית לָחֶם כִּמְהָם
יח לָלֶכֶת לָבוֹא מִצְרָיִם: מִפְּנֵי הַכַּשְׂדִּים כִּי יָרְאוּ מִפְּנֵיהֶם כִּי־הִכָּה
יִשְׁמָעֵאל בֶּן־נְתַנְיָה אֶת־גְּדַלְיָהוּ בֶּן־אֲחִיקָם אֲשֶׁר־הִפְקִיד מֶלֶךְ־
מב א בָּבֶל בָּאָרֶץ: וַיִּגְּשׁוּ כָּל־שָׂרֵי הַחֲיָלִים וְיוֹחָנָן בֶּן־קָרֵחַ
ב וִיזַנְיָה בֶּן־הוֹשַׁעְיָה וְכָל־הָעָם מִקָּטֹן וְעַד־גָּדוֹל: וַיֹּאמְרוּ אֶל־יִרְמְיָהוּ
הַנָּבִיא תִּפָּל־נָא תְחִנָּתֵנוּ לְפָנֶיךָ וְהִתְפַּלֵּל בַּעֲדֵנוּ אֶל־יְהוָה אֱלֹהֶיךָ
בְּעַד כָּל־הַשְּׁאֵרִית הַזֹּאת כִּי־נִשְׁאַרְנוּ מְעַט מֵהַרְבֵּה כַּאֲשֶׁר עֵינֶיךָ
ג רֹאוֹת אֹתָנוּ: וְיַגֶּד־לָנוּ יְהוָה אֱלֹהֶיךָ אֶת־הַדֶּרֶךְ אֲשֶׁר נֵלֶךְ־בָּהּ וְאֶת־
ד הַדָּבָר אֲשֶׁר נַעֲשֶׂה: וַיֹּאמֶר אֲלֵיהֶם יִרְמְיָהוּ הַנָּבִיא שָׁמַעְתִּי הִנְנִי
מִתְפַּלֵּל אֶל־יְהוָה אֱלֹהֵיכֶם כְּדִבְרֵיכֶם וְהָיָה כָּל־הַדָּבָר אֲשֶׁר־יַעֲנֶה
ה יְהוָה אֶתְכֶם אַגִּיד לָכֶם לֹא־אֶמְנַע מִכֶּם דָּבָר: וְהֵמָּה אָמְרוּ אֶל־יִרְמְיָהוּ
יְהִי יְהוָה בָּנוּ לְעֵד אֱמֶת וְנֶאֱמָן אִם־לֹא כְּכָל־הַדָּבָר אֲשֶׁר יִשְׁלָחֲךָ
ו יְהוָה אֱלֹהֶיךָ אֵלֵינוּ כֵּן נַעֲשֶׂה: אִם־טוֹב וְאִם־רָע בְּקוֹל ׀ יְהוָה אֱלֹהֵינוּ
אֲשֶׁר אנו שֹׁלְחִים אֹתְךָ אֵלָיו נִשְׁמָע לְמַעַן אֲשֶׁר יִיטַב־לָנוּ כִּי נִשְׁמַע אֲנַחְנוּ
ז בְּקוֹל יְהוָה אֱלֹהֵינוּ: וַיְהִי מִקֵּץ עֲשֶׂרֶת יָמִים וַיְהִי דְבַר־יְהוָה
ח אֶל־יִרְמְיָהוּ: וַיִּקְרָא אֶל־יוֹחָנָן בֶּן־קָרֵחַ וְאֶל כָּל־שָׂרֵי הַחֲיָלִים אֲשֶׁר

9 who were with him, and all the people from the least to the greatest. He told
them, "This is what the LORD, God of Israel, to whom you sent me to present
10 your plea, said: If you will indeed dwell in this land, I will rebuild you and not
tear you down. I will plant you and not uproot you, for I have come to regret
11 the disaster that I inflicted upon you. No longer fear the king of Babylon as
you fear him now. Do not fear him, declares the LORD, for I am with you to
12 save you and to rescue you from his hands. I will grant you mercy, and he will
13 show mercy toward you and return you to your land. But if you say that you
shall not dwell in this land, and that you shall not heed the voice of the LORD
14 your God – if you will say, 'No! We will go to Egypt, where we will not see
war, nor hear the sound of trumpets, and not hunger for bread. There we shall
15 dwell!' – in that case, listen to the word of the LORD, remnant of Yehuda. This
is what the LORD of Hosts, God of Israel, said: If you indeed direct your
16 course toward Egypt and come to settle there, the sword that you fear will
overtake you in the land of Egypt, and the famine that you worry over shall
17 pursue you there in Egypt, and there you shall die. All those who directed
their course toward Egypt to settle there shall die by sword, famine, and
pestilence. There shall be neither remnant nor survivor from the disaster that
18 I shall bring upon them. For this is what the LORD of Hosts, God of Israel,
said: Just as My anger and My wrath poured out upon the inhabitants of
Jerusalem, so will My wrath pour out upon you when you arrive in Egypt.
You will become an object of swearing and horror, of curses and vilification.
19 You shall never see this place again. The LORD has told you, remnant of
20 Yehuda: Do not go to Egypt. Know this well, for I warn you today. For you
have misled me deliberately. You sent me to the LORD your God, saying, 'Pray
to the LORD our God on our behalf. Tell us all that the LORD our God says,
21 and we will do it.' Today I told you. But you did not heed the voice of the
22 LORD your God, hearing all that I was sent to say to you. Now know this well:
You will die by sword, famine, and pestilence in the very place where you so
43 1 desired to go and settle." It was after Yirmeyahu had finished telling
all the people all the words of the LORD their God that the LORD their God
2 had sent him to tell them, all those words, that Azarya son
of Hoshaya and Yoḥanan son of Kare'aḥ and all the insolent men said to
Yirmeyahu, "You tell a lie! The LORD our God did not send you to say, 'Do
3 not come to settle in Egypt.' Rather, Barukh son of Neriya incited you against
us in order to give us over to the hands of the Chaldeans to kill us or to exile
4 us to Babylon." Yoḥanan son of Kare'aḥ and all the army officers and all the

ט אֹת֔וֹ וּלְכָל־הָעָ֖ם לְמִקָּטֹ֥ן וְעַד־גָּדֽוֹל׃ וַיֹּ֣אמֶר אֲלֵיהֶ֔ם כֹּֽה־אָמַ֥ר יְהוָ֖ה
אֱלֹהֵ֣י יִשְׂרָאֵ֑ל אֲשֶׁ֨ר שְׁלַחְתֶּ֤ם אֹתִי֙ אֵלָ֔יו לְהַפִּ֥יל תְּחִנַּתְכֶ֖ם לְפָנָֽיו׃
י אִם־שׁ֤וֹב תֵּשְׁבוּ֙ בָּאָ֣רֶץ הַזֹּ֔את וּבָנִ֤יתִי אֶתְכֶם֙ וְלֹ֣א אֶהֱרֹ֔ס וְנָטַעְתִּ֥י
יא אֶתְכֶ֖ם וְלֹ֣א אֶתּ֑וֹשׁ כִּ֤י נִחַ֙מְתִּי֙ אֶל־הָ֣רָעָ֔ה אֲשֶׁ֥ר עָשִׂ֖יתִי לָכֶֽם׃ אַל־
תִּֽירְא֗וּ מִפְּנֵי֙ מֶ֣לֶךְ בָּבֶ֔ל אֲשֶׁר־אַתֶּ֖ם יְרֵאִ֣ים מִפָּנָ֑יו אַל־תִּֽירְא֤וּ מִמֶּ֙נּוּ֙
כה יב נְאֻם־יְהוָ֔ה כִּֽי־אִתְּכֶ֣ם אָ֔נִי לְהוֹשִׁ֧יעַ אֶתְכֶ֛ם וּלְהַצִּ֥יל אֶתְכֶ֖ם מִיָּדֽוֹ׃ וְאֶתֵּ֥ן
יג לָכֶ֛ם רַחֲמִ֖ים וְרִחַ֣ם אֶתְכֶ֑ם וְהֵשִׁ֥יב אֶתְכֶ֖ם אֶל־אַדְמַתְכֶֽם׃ וְאִם־אֹמְרִ֣ים
אַתֶּ֔ם לֹ֥א נֵשֵׁ֖ב בָּאָ֣רֶץ הַזֹּ֑את לְבִלְתִּ֣י שְׁמֹ֔עַ בְּק֖וֹל יְהוָ֥ה אֱלֹהֵיכֶֽם׃
יד לֵאמֹ֗ר לֹ֚א כִּ֣י אֶ֤רֶץ מִצְרַ֙יִם֙ נָב֔וֹא אֲשֶׁ֨ר לֹא־נִרְאֶ֤ה מִלְחָמָה֙ וְק֥וֹל שׁוֹפָ֖ר
טו לֹ֣א נִשְׁמָ֑ע וְלַלֶּ֥חֶם לֹא־נִרְעַ֖ב וְשָׁ֥ם נֵשֵֽׁב׃ וְעַתָּ֕ה לָכֵ֛ן שִׁמְע֥וּ דְבַר־יְהוָ֖ה
שְׁאֵרִ֣ית יְהוּדָ֑ה כֹּֽה־אָמַ֞ר יְהוָ֤ה צְבָאוֹת֙ אֱלֹהֵ֣י יִשְׂרָאֵ֔ל אִם־אַתֶּ֞ם שׂ֣וֹם
טז תְּשִׂמ֤וּן פְּנֵיכֶם֙ לָבֹ֣א מִצְרַ֔יִם וּבָאתֶ֖ם לָג֥וּר שָֽׁם׃ וְהָיְתָ֣ה הַחֶ֗רֶב אֲשֶׁ֤ר
אַתֶּם֙ יְרֵאִ֣ים מִמֶּ֔נָּה שָׁ֛ם תַּשִּׂ֥יג אֶתְכֶ֖ם בְּאֶ֣רֶץ מִצְרָ֑יִם וְהָרָעָ֞ב אֲשֶׁר־
יז אַתֶּ֣ם ׀ דֹּאֲגִ֣ים מִמֶּ֗נּוּ שָׁ֣ם יִדְבַּ֥ק אַחֲרֵיכֶ֛ם מִצְרַ֖יִם וְשָׁ֥ם תָּמֻֽתוּ׃ וְיִהְי֣וּ
כָל־הָאֲנָשִׁ֞ים אֲשֶׁר־שָׂ֤מוּ אֶת־פְּנֵיהֶם֙ לָב֣וֹא מִצְרַ֔יִם לָג֣וּר שָׁ֔ם יָמ֕וּתוּ
בַּחֶ֖רֶב בָּרָעָ֣ב וּבַדָּ֑בֶר וְלֹא־יִהְיֶ֤ה לָהֶם֙ שָׂרִ֣יד וּפָלִ֔יט מִפְּנֵי֙ הָֽרָעָ֔ה אֲשֶׁ֥ר
יח אֲנִ֖י מֵבִ֥יא עֲלֵיהֶֽם׃ כִּ֣י כֹה֩ אָמַ֨ר יְהוָ֤ה צְבָאוֹת֙ אֱלֹהֵ֣י יִשְׂרָאֵ֔ל כַּאֲשֶׁ֙ר
נִתַּ֨ךְ אַפִּ֜י וַחֲמָתִ֗י עַל־יֹֽשְׁבֵי֙ יְר֣וּשָׁלִַ֔ם כֵּ֣ן תִּתַּ֤ךְ חֲמָתִי֙ עֲלֵיכֶ֔ם בְּבֹאֲכֶ֖ם
מִצְרָ֑יִם וִהְיִיתֶ֡ם לְאָלָ֣ה וּלְשַׁמָּ֗ה וְלִקְלָלָה֙ וּלְחֶרְפָּ֔ה וְלֹא־תִרְא֣וּ ע֔וֹד
יט אֶת־הַמָּק֖וֹם הַזֶּֽה׃ דִּבֶּ֨ר יְהוָ֤ה עֲלֵיכֶם֙ שְׁאֵרִ֣ית יְהוּדָ֔ה אַל־תָּבֹ֖אוּ מִצְרָ֑יִם
כ יָדֹ֙עַ֙ תֵּֽדְע֔וּ כִּֽי־הַעִידֹ֥תִי בָכֶ֖ם הַיּֽוֹם׃ כִּ֣י התעתים בְּנַפְשֽׁוֹתֵיכֶם֒ כִּֽי־אַתֶּ֞ם הִתְעֵיתֶ֖ם
שְׁלַחְתֶּ֣ם אֹתִ֗י אֶל־יְהוָ֤ה אֱלֹֽהֵיכֶם֙ לֵאמֹ֔ר הִתְפַּלֵּ֣ל בַּעֲדֵ֔נוּ אֶל־יְהוָ֖ה
כא אֱלֹהֵ֑ינוּ וּכְכֹל֩ אֲשֶׁ֨ר יֹאמַ֜ר יְהוָ֧ה אֱלֹהֵ֛ינוּ כֵּ֥ן הַגֶּד־לָ֖נוּ וְעָשִֽׂינוּ׃ וָאַגִּ֥ד
לָכֶ֖ם הַיּ֑וֹם וְלֹ֣א שְׁמַעְתֶּ֗ם בְּקוֹל֙ יְהוָ֣ה אֱלֹֽהֵיכֶ֔ם וּלְכֹ֖ל אֲשֶׁר־שְׁלָחַ֥נִי
כב אֲלֵיכֶֽם׃ וְעַתָּה֙ יָדֹ֣עַ תֵּֽדְע֔וּ כִּ֗י בַּחֶ֛רֶב בָּרָעָ֥ב וּבַדֶּ֖בֶר תָּמ֑וּתוּ בַּמָּקוֹם֙
מג א אֲשֶׁ֣ר חֲפַצְתֶּ֔ם לָב֖וֹא לָג֥וּר שָֽׁם׃ וַיְהִ֞י כְּכַלּ֣וֹת יִרְמְיָ֗הוּ לְדַבֵּ֤ר
אֶל־כָּל־הָעָם֙ אֶת־כָּל־דִּבְרֵי֙ יְהוָ֣ה אֱלֹהֵיהֶ֔ם אֲשֶׁ֧ר שְׁלָח֛וֹ יְהוָ֥ה אֱלֹהֵיהֶ֖ם
ב אֲלֵיהֶ֑ם אֵ֥ת כָּל־הַדְּבָרִ֖ים הָאֵֽלֶּה׃ וַיֹּ֨אמֶר עֲזַרְיָ֤ה בֶן־
הוֹשַׁעְיָה֙ וְיוֹחָנָ֣ן בֶּן־קָרֵ֔חַ וְכָל־הָאֲנָשִׁ֖ים הַזֵּדִ֑ים אֹמְרִ֣ים אֶֽל־יִרְמְיָ֗הוּ
שֶׁ֚קֶר אַתָּ֣ה מְדַבֵּ֔ר לֹ֣א שְׁלָחֲךָ֞ יְהוָ֤ה אֱלֹהֵ֙ינוּ֙ לֵאמֹ֔ר לֹא־תָבֹ֥אוּ מִצְרַ֖יִם
ג לָג֥וּר שָֽׁם׃ כִּ֗י בָּר֤וּךְ בֶּן־נֵֽרִיָּה֙ מַסִּ֣ית אֹתְךָ֔ בָּ֑נוּ לְמַ֜עַן תֵּ֧ת אֹתָ֣נוּ בְיַד־
ד הַכַּשְׂדִּים֙ לְהָמִ֣ית אֹתָ֔נוּ וּלְהַגְל֥וֹת אֹתָ֖נוּ בָּבֶֽל׃ וְלֹֽא־שָׁמַ֨ע יוֹחָנָ֤ן בֶּן־

people did not heed the voice of the LORD telling them to dwell in the land
5 of Yehuda. Yoḥanan son of Kare'aḥ and all the army officers led the entire
remnant of Yehuda who had returned from all the nations where they had
6 been driven to settle in the land of Yehuda – along with the men, women, and
children; the daughters of the king; every person whom Nevuzaradan, chief
of the guard, had left with Gedalyahu son of Aḥikam son of Shafan; Yirmeyahu
7 the prophet; and Barukh son of Neriyahu – and they went to the land of
Egypt, for they did not heed the voice of the LORD, and they arrived at
8 Taḥpanḥes. The word of the LORD came to Yirmeyahu in Taḥpanḥes:
9 "In the presence of the men of Yehuda, take some large stones in your hands
and conceal them in the mortar in the square that is at the entrance to
10 Pharaoh's palace in Taḥpanḥes. Say to them: This is what the LORD of Hosts,
God of Israel, said: I will soon send forth and lead Nevukhadnetzar, king of
Babylon, My servant, here. I will set his throne above these stones that I have
11 concealed, and he will raise his scepter over them. He will come and smite
the land of Egypt. Those destined for death will die, those destined for
captivity will be taken captive, and those destined for the sword will fall
12 victim to the sword. I will set fire to the temples of the gods of Egypt, and
Nevukhadnetzar will burn them and take the gods captive. He will wrap
himself up in the land of Egypt as a shepherd wraps himself up in his garment,
13 and he will depart from there in peace. He will smash the monuments at the
house of the sun,[86] which is in the land of Egypt, and he will burn the buildings
44 1 of the gods of Egypt by fire." This was the word that came to
Yirmeyahu for all the people of Yehuda living in the land of Egypt, who lived
2 in Migdol, Taḥpanḥes, and Nof, and in the land of Patros; this is what the
LORD of Hosts, God of Israel, said: You yourselves have witnessed the entire
disaster that I brought upon Jerusalem and upon all the cities of Yehuda.
3 Today they are a ruin with no one living in them because of their evil that
they perpetrated in order to anger Me, burning incense to serve other gods
4 whom they never knew – neither they nor you nor your ancestors. I sent to
them all My servants, the prophets, persistently, imploring them not to
5 commit this abomination that I despise. But they took no heed, never even
inclining their ears to turn away from their evil and not burn incense to other
6 gods. My anger and My wrath poured out and blazed in the towns of Yehuda
and in the streets of Jerusalem. They became a ruin and desolation, as they
7 are today. Now this is what the LORD, God of Hosts, God of Israel,
said: Why do you do this terrible harm to yourselves, cutting off man and
woman, child and suckling babe, from the midst of Yehuda, not leaving
8 yourselves any remnant? For you anger Me with your actions by burning
incense to other gods in the land of Egypt where you have come to settle,
causing yourselves to be cut off and to become a curse and a disgrace among
9 all the nations of the earth. Have you forgotten the evils of your ancestors,

86 | Temples to the sun god.

קֹרֵחַ וְכָל־שָׂרֵי הַחֲיָלִים וְכָל־הָעָם בְּקוֹל יְהוָה לָשֶׁבֶת בְּאֶרֶץ יְהוּדָה׃
ה וַיִּקַּח יוֹחָנָן בֶּן־קָרֵחַ וְכָל־שָׂרֵי הַחֲיָלִים אֵת כָּל־שְׁאֵרִית יְהוּדָה אֲשֶׁר־
ו שָׁבוּ מִכָּל־הַגּוֹיִם אֲשֶׁר נִדְּחוּ־שָׁם לָגוּר בְּאֶרֶץ יְהוּדָה׃ אֶת־הַגְּבָרִים
וְאֶת־הַנָּשִׁים וְאֶת־הַטַּף וְאֶת־בְּנוֹת הַמֶּלֶךְ וְאֵת כָּל־הַנֶּפֶשׁ אֲשֶׁר הִנִּיחַ
נְבוּזַרְאֲדָן רַב־טַבָּחִים אֶת־גְּדַלְיָהוּ בֶּן־אֲחִיקָם בֶּן־שָׁפָן וְאֵת יִרְמְיָהוּ
ז הַנָּבִיא וְאֶת־בָּרוּךְ בֶּן־נֵרִיָּהוּ׃ וַיָּבֹאוּ אֶרֶץ מִצְרַיִם כִּי לֹא שָׁמְעוּ בְּקוֹל
ח יְהוָה וַיָּבֹאוּ עַד־תַּחְפַּנְחֵס׃ וַיְהִי דְבַר־יְהוָה אֶל־יִרְמְיָהוּ
ט בְּתַחְפַּנְחֵס לֵאמֹר׃ קַח בְּיָדְךָ אֲבָנִים גְּדֹלוֹת וּטְמַנְתָּם בַּמֶּלֶט בַּמַּלְבֵּן
י אֲשֶׁר בְּפֶתַח בֵּית־פַּרְעֹה בְּתַחְפַּנְחֵס לְעֵינֵי אֲנָשִׁים יְהוּדִים׃ וְאָמַרְתָּ
אֲלֵיהֶם כֹּה־אָמַר יְהוָה צְבָאוֹת אֱלֹהֵי יִשְׂרָאֵל הִנְנִי שֹׁלֵחַ וְלָקַחְתִּי
אֶת־נְבוּכַדְרֶאצַּר מֶלֶךְ־בָּבֶל עַבְדִּי וְשַׂמְתִּי כִסְאוֹ מִמַּעַל לָאֲבָנִים
יא הָאֵלֶּה אֲשֶׁר טָמָנְתִּי וְנָטָה אֶת־שפרורו עֲלֵיהֶם׃ ובאה וְהִכָּה אֶת־אֶרֶץ — שַׁפְרִירוֹ וּבָא
מִצְרָיִם אֲשֶׁר לַמָּוֶת לַמָּוֶת וַאֲשֶׁר לַשְּׁבִי לַשֶּׁבִי וַאֲשֶׁר לַחֶרֶב לֶחָרֶב׃
יב וְהִצַּתִּי אֵשׁ בְּבָתֵּי אֱלֹהֵי מִצְרַיִם וּשְׂרָפָם וְשָׁבָם וְעָטָה אֶת־אֶרֶץ מִצְרַיִם
יג כַּאֲשֶׁר־יַעְטֶה הָרֹעֶה אֶת־בִּגְדוֹ וְיָצָא מִשָּׁם בְּשָׁלוֹם׃ וְשִׁבַּר אֶת־
מַצְּבוֹת בֵּית שֶׁמֶשׁ אֲשֶׁר בְּאֶרֶץ מִצְרָיִם וְאֶת־בָּתֵּי אֱלֹהֵי־מִצְרַיִם יִשְׂרֹף
מד א בָּאֵשׁ׃ הַדָּבָר אֲשֶׁר הָיָה אֶל־יִרְמְיָהוּ אֶל כָּל־הַיְּהוּדִים
הַיֹּשְׁבִים בְּאֶרֶץ מִצְרָיִם הַיֹּשְׁבִים בְּמִגְדֹּל וּבְתַחְפַּנְחֵס וּבְנֹף וּבְאֶרֶץ
ב פַּתְרוֹס לֵאמֹר׃ כֹּה־אָמַר יְהוָה צְבָאוֹת אֱלֹהֵי יִשְׂרָאֵל אַתֶּם רְאִיתֶם
אֵת כָּל־הָרָעָה אֲשֶׁר הֵבֵאתִי עַל־יְרוּשָׁלִַם וְעַל כָּל־עָרֵי יְהוּדָה וְהִנָּם
ג חָרְבָּה הַיּוֹם הַזֶּה וְאֵין בָּהֶם יוֹשֵׁב׃ מִפְּנֵי רָעָתָם אֲשֶׁר עָשׂוּ לְהַכְעִסֵנִי
לָלֶכֶת לְקַטֵּר לַעֲבֹד לֵאלֹהִים אֲחֵרִים אֲשֶׁר לֹא יְדָעוּם הֵמָּה אַתֶּם
ד וַאֲבֹתֵיכֶם׃ וָאֶשְׁלַח אֲלֵיכֶם אֶת־כָּל־עֲבָדַי הַנְּבִיאִים הַשְׁכֵּים וְשָׁלֹחַ
ה לֵאמֹר אַל־נָא תַעֲשׂוּ אֵת דְּבַר־הַתֹּעֵבָה הַזֹּאת אֲשֶׁר שָׂנֵאתִי׃ וְלֹא
שָׁמְעוּ וְלֹא־הִטּוּ אֶת־אָזְנָם לָשׁוּב מֵרָעָתָם לְבִלְתִּי קַטֵּר לֵאלֹהִים
ו אֲחֵרִים׃ וַתִּתַּךְ חֲמָתִי וְאַפִּי וַתִּבְעַר בְּעָרֵי יְהוּדָה וּבְחֻצוֹת יְרוּשָׁלִָם
ז וַתִּהְיֶינָה לְחָרְבָּה לִשְׁמָמָה כַּיּוֹם הַזֶּה׃ וְעַתָּה כֹּה־אָמַר
יְהוָה אֱלֹהֵי צְבָאוֹת אֱלֹהֵי יִשְׂרָאֵל לָמָה אַתֶּם עֹשִׂים רָעָה גְדוֹלָה
אֶל־נַפְשֹׁתֵכֶם לְהַכְרִית לָכֶם אִישׁ־וְאִשָּׁה עוֹלֵל וְיוֹנֵק מִתּוֹךְ יְהוּדָה
ח לְבִלְתִּי הוֹתִיר לָכֶם שְׁאֵרִית׃ לְהַכְעִסֵנִי בְּמַעֲשֵׂי יְדֵיכֶם לְקַטֵּר לֵאלֹהִים
אֲחֵרִים בְּאֶרֶץ מִצְרַיִם אֲשֶׁר־אַתֶּם בָּאִים לָגוּר שָׁם לְמַעַן הַכְרִית לָכֶם
ט וּלְמַעַן הֱיוֹתְכֶם לִקְלָלָה וּלְחֶרְפָּה בְּכֹל גּוֹיֵי הָאָרֶץ׃ הֲשְׁכַחְתֶּם אֶת־

the evils of the kings of Yehuda and the evils of their wives, your own evils
and the evils of your wives that you committed in the land of Yehuda and in
10 the streets of Jerusalem? To this very day you have not been humbled; you
do not fear; you do not follow My teaching and My statutes that I placed
11 before you and before your ancestors. This is what the LORD of
Hosts, God of Israel, therefore said: I am about to direct My face toward you
12 for harm and to cut off all of Yehuda. I will seize the remnant of Yehuda that
directed their course to go to the land of Egypt to settle there. They shall all
be finished off in the land of Egypt; they shall fall by sword and famine; they
shall be finished off from the least to the greatest. By sword and by famine
they shall die; they shall become objects of swearing and horror, of curses
13 and vilification. I will punish those who dwell in the land of Egypt just as I
14 punished Jerusalem – with the sword, with famine, and with pestilence. There
will be neither refugee nor survivor from the remnant of Yehuda who have
come to settle in the land of Egypt. As for returning to the land of Yehuda,
where they so strongly desire to return to dwell, none but refugees shall
15 return. All the men who knew that their wives had burned incense
to other gods along with the great throng of women who were standing there
and all the people living in the land of Egypt, in Patros, responded to
16 Yirmeyahu, "We will not listen to you regarding the matter that you have told
17 us in the name of the LORD. We will continue to do all that we said we would,
to burn incense to the queen of the heavens and to pour libations to her
exactly as we, our ancestors, our kings, and our officials did in the towns of
Yehuda and in the streets of Jerusalem. There we had plenty of food, and we
18 were successful and suffered no harm. But when we ceased to burn incense
to the queen of the heavens and to pour libations to her, only then did we lack
19 everything and were finished off by the sword and by famine. When we burn
incense to the queen of the heavens and pour libations to her, is it without
our husbands' consent that we make wafers in order to sadden[87] her and pour
20 libations to her?" Yirmeyahu spoke to all the people including the
men and women and to all the people who had responded to him with those
21 words: "With regard to your actions burning incense in the towns of Yehuda
and in the streets of Jerusalem – you, your ancestors, your kings, your officials,
and the people of the land – the LORD remembered those actions, and they
22 remain upon His heart. When the LORD could no longer forbear because of
the wickedness of your actions and because of the abominations that you
performed, then your land became a ruin, a desolation, and a curse with
23 no one living there, as it is today. Because you burned incense and sinned
against the LORD, did not heed the LORD's voice, and did not follow His
teaching, statutes, and testimonies, disaster therefore afflicted you, as it does
24 today." Yirmeyahu said to all the people and to all the women: "Heed
25 the word of the LORD, all of Yehuda that is in the land of Egypt. This is what

87 | Expecting that the saddening of the deity would cause her to rescue them.

רָעוֹת אֲבוֹתֵיכֶם וְאֶת־רָעוֹת ׀ מַלְכֵי יְהוּדָה וְאֵת רָעוֹת נָשָׁיו וְאֵת
רָעֹתֵכֶם וְאֵת רָעֹת נְשֵׁיכֶם אֲשֶׁר עָשׂוּ בְּאֶרֶץ יְהוּדָה וּבְחֻצוֹת יְרוּשָׁלָםִ׃
י לֹא דֻכְּאוּ עַד הַיּוֹם הַזֶּה וְלֹא יָרְאוּ וְלֹא־הָלְכוּ בְתוֹרָתִי וּבְחֻקֹּתַי אֲשֶׁר־
יא נָתַתִּי לִפְנֵיכֶם וְלִפְנֵי אֲבוֹתֵיכֶם׃ לָכֵן כֹּה־אָמַר יְהוָה
צְבָאוֹת אֱלֹהֵי יִשְׂרָאֵל הִנְנִי שָׂם פָּנַי בָּכֶם לְרָעָה וּלְהַכְרִית אֶת־כָּל־
יב יְהוּדָה׃ וְלָקַחְתִּי אֶת־שְׁאֵרִית יְהוּדָה אֲשֶׁר־שָׂמוּ פְנֵיהֶם לָבוֹא אֶרֶץ־
מִצְרַיִם לָגוּר שָׁם וְתַמּוּ כֹל בְּאֶרֶץ מִצְרַיִם יִפֹּלוּ בַּחֶרֶב בָּרָעָב יִתַּמּוּ
מִקָּטֹן וְעַד־גָּדוֹל בַּחֶרֶב וּבָרָעָב יָמֻתוּ וְהָיוּ לְאָלָה לְשַׁמָּה וְלִקְלָלָה
יג וּלְחֶרְפָּה׃ וּפָקַדְתִּי עַל הַיּוֹשְׁבִים בְּאֶרֶץ מִצְרַיִם כַּאֲשֶׁר פָּקַדְתִּי עַל־
יד יְרוּשָׁלָםִ בַּחֶרֶב בָּרָעָב וּבַדָּבֶר׃ וְלֹא יִהְיֶה פָּלִיט וְשָׂרִיד לִשְׁאֵרִית
יְהוּדָה הַבָּאִים לָגוּר־שָׁם בְּאֶרֶץ מִצְרָיִם וְלָשׁוּב ׀ אֶרֶץ יְהוּדָה אֲשֶׁר־
הֵמָּה מְנַשְּׂאִים אֶת־נַפְשָׁם לָשׁוּב לָשֶׁבֶת שָׁם כִּי לֹא־יָשׁוּבוּ כִּי אִם־
טו פְּלֵטִים׃ וַיַּעֲנוּ אֶת־יִרְמְיָהוּ כָּל־הָאֲנָשִׁים הַיֹּדְעִים
כִּי־מְקַטְּרוֹת נְשֵׁיהֶם לֵאלֹהִים אֲחֵרִים וְכָל־הַנָּשִׁים הָעֹמְדוֹת קָהָל
טז גָּדוֹל וְכָל־הָעָם הַיֹּשְׁבִים בְּאֶרֶץ־מִצְרַיִם בְּפַתְרוֹס לֵאמֹר׃ הַדָּבָר
יז אֲשֶׁר־דִּבַּרְתָּ אֵלֵינוּ בְּשֵׁם יְהוָה אֵינֶנּוּ שֹׁמְעִים אֵלֶיךָ׃ כִּי עָשֹׂה נַעֲשֶׂה
אֶת־כָּל־הַדָּבָר ׀ אֲשֶׁר־יָצָא מִפִּינוּ לְקַטֵּר לִמְלֶכֶת הַשָּׁמַיִם וְהַסֵּיךְ־לָהּ
נְסָכִים כַּאֲשֶׁר עָשִׂינוּ אֲנַחְנוּ וַאֲבֹתֵינוּ מְלָכֵינוּ וְשָׂרֵינוּ בְּעָרֵי יְהוּדָה
יח וּבְחֻצוֹת יְרוּשָׁלָםִ וַנִּשְׂבַּע־לֶחֶם וַנִּהְיֶה טוֹבִים וְרָעָה לֹא רָאִינוּ׃ וּמִן־
אָז חָדַלְנוּ לְקַטֵּר לִמְלֶכֶת הַשָּׁמַיִם וְהַסֵּךְ־לָהּ נְסָכִים חָסַרְנוּ כֹל וּבַחֶרֶב
יט וּבָרָעָב תָּמְנוּ׃ וְכִי־אֲנַחְנוּ מְקַטְּרִים לִמְלֶכֶת הַשָּׁמַיִם וּלְהַסֵּךְ לָהּ
נְסָכִים הֲמִבַּלְעֲדֵי אֲנָשֵׁינוּ עָשִׂינוּ לָהּ כַּוָּנִים לְהַעֲצִבָה וְהַסֵּךְ לָהּ
כ נְסָכִים׃ וַיֹּאמֶר יִרְמְיָהוּ אֶל־כָּל־הָעָם עַל־הַגְּבָרִים כו
כא וְעַל־הַנָּשִׁים וְעַל־כָּל־הָעָם הָעֹנִים אֹתוֹ דָּבָר לֵאמֹר׃ הֲלוֹא אֶת־הַקִּטֵּר
אֲשֶׁר קִטַּרְתֶּם בְּעָרֵי יְהוּדָה וּבְחֻצוֹת יְרוּשָׁלַםִ אַתֶּם וַאֲבוֹתֵיכֶם מַלְכֵיכֶם
כב וְשָׂרֵיכֶם וְעַם הָאָרֶץ אֹתָם זָכַר יְהוָה וַתַּעֲלֶה עַל־לִבּוֹ׃ וְלֹא־יוּכַל יְהוָה
עוֹד לָשֵׂאת מִפְּנֵי רֹעַ מַעַלְלֵיכֶם מִפְּנֵי הַתּוֹעֵבֹת אֲשֶׁר עֲשִׂיתֶם וַתְּהִי
כג אַרְצְכֶם לְחָרְבָּה וּלְשַׁמָּה וְלִקְלָלָה מֵאֵין יוֹשֵׁב כְּהַיּוֹם הַזֶּה׃ מִפְּנֵי אֲשֶׁר
קִטַּרְתֶּם וַאֲשֶׁר חֲטָאתֶם לַיהוָה וְלֹא שְׁמַעְתֶּם בְּקוֹל יְהוָה וּבְתֹרָתוֹ
וּבְחֻקֹּתָיו וּבְעֵדְוֹתָיו לֹא הֲלַכְתֶּם עַל־כֵּן קָרָאת אֶתְכֶם הָרָעָה הַזֹּאת
כד כַּיּוֹם הַזֶּה׃ וַיֹּאמֶר יִרְמְיָהוּ אֶל־כָּל־הָעָם וְאֶל כָּל־הַנָּשִׁים
כה שִׁמְעוּ דְּבַר־יְהוָה כָּל־יְהוּדָה אֲשֶׁר בְּאֶרֶץ מִצְרָיִם׃ כֹּה־אָמַר יְהוָה־

the Lord of Hosts, God of Israel, said: You and your wives have spoken with
your mouth and have acted with your hands, saying, 'We shall comply with
our vows, having vowed to burn incense to the queen of the heavens and to
26 pour libations to her.' So fulfill your vows; comply with your vows. Therefore,
listen to the word of the Lord, all people of Yehuda living in the land of
Egypt: I have sworn by My great name, said the Lord, that My name will no
longer be invoked by any man of Yehuda anywhere in Egypt saying, 'As the
27 Lord God lives.' I will be watchful over them for harm and not for good.
Every man of Yehuda that is in the land of Egypt will be finished off by the
28 sword and by famine until they are gone. Those who escape the sword shall
return from the land of Egypt to the land of Yehuda few in number, and the
entire remnant of Yehuda that came to settle in the land of Egypt shall know
29 whose word shall stand, Mine or theirs. This will be the sign for you – declares
the Lord – that I will punish you in this place so that you shall know that My
30 promise to inflict harm upon you shall stand. This is what the Lord
said: I shall deliver Pharaoh Ḥofra, king of Egypt, into the hands of his
enemies and those who seek his life, just as I delivered Tzidkiyahu, king of
Yehuda, into the hands of Nevukhadretzar, king of Babylon, his enemy, who
45 1 sought his life." The word that Yirmeyahu the prophet spoke to
Barukh son of Neriya when he was writing these words from Yirmeyahu's
mouth on a scroll in the fourth year of the reign of Yehoyakim, son of
2 Yoshiyahu, king of Yehuda: "This is what the Lord, God of Israel, said about
3 you, Barukh: You said, 'Woe to me now, for the Lord has added agony to my
4 pain. I am exhausted by my sighing and have found no rest.' This is also what
you shall say to Him. But this is what the Lord said: That which I have built
I will tear down, and that which I have planted I will uproot. This applies to
5 the entire land. Yet you seek greatness for yourself? Do not seek it, for I am
about to inflict disaster upon all flesh – declares the Lord – but I will grant
46 1 you your life as a prize of war everywhere that you may go." This
came to Yirmeyahu the prophet as the word of the Lord concerning the
2 nations: Of Egypt, concerning the army of Pharaoh Nekho, king of Egypt,
located at the Euphrates River near Karkemish and which Nevukhadretzar,
king of Babylon, attacked during the fourth year of Yehoyakim son of
3 Yoshiyahu, king of Yehuda: Prepare shield and buckler, and approach the
4 battle. Harness the horses; let the riders mount them. Polish the spears; put
5 on armor; stand erect with helmets on. Why have I seen them thus: frightened,
retreating, moving backward, their mighty ones crushed, desperately fleeing
6 and not looking back, terror all around? so says the Lord. Let the swift not
flee, and let the mighty not escape. Up north, beside the Euphrates River, they
7 stumble; they fall. Who is this that rises like the Nile, whose waters pour forth
8 like rivers? It is Egypt that rises like the Nile, whose water pours forth like
rivers, and who says, "I will rise and cover the earth; I will destroy cities and

צְבָאוֹת אֱלֹהֵי יִשְׂרָאֵל לֵאמֹר אַתֶּם וּנְשֵׁיכֶם וַתְּדַבֵּרְנָה בְּפִיכֶם וּבִידֵיכֶם
מִלֵּאתֶם ׀ לֵאמֹר עָשֹׂה נַעֲשֶׂה אֶת־נְדָרֵינוּ אֲשֶׁר נָדַרְנוּ לְקַטֵּר לִמְלֶכֶת
הַשָּׁמַיִם וּלְהַסֵּךְ לָהּ נְסָכִים הָקֵים תָּקִימְנָה אֶת־נִדְרֵיכֶם וְעָשֹׂה תַעֲשֶׂינָה
כו אֶת־נִדְרֵיכֶם׃ לָכֵן שִׁמְעוּ דְבַר־יְהוָה כָּל־יְהוּדָה הַיֹּשְׁבִים בְּאֶרֶץ מִצְרָיִם
הִנְנִי נִשְׁבַּעְתִּי בִּשְׁמִי הַגָּדוֹל אָמַר יְהוָה אִם־יִהְיֶה עוֹד שְׁמִי נִקְרָא ׀
כז בְּפִי ׀ כָּל־אִישׁ יְהוּדָה אֹמֵר חַי־אֲדֹנָי יְהוִה בְּכָל־אֶרֶץ מִצְרָיִם׃ הִנְנִי
שֹׁקֵד עֲלֵיהֶם לְרָעָה וְלֹא לְטוֹבָה וְתַמּוּ כָל־אִישׁ יְהוּדָה אֲשֶׁר בְּאֶרֶץ־
כח מִצְרַיִם בַּחֶרֶב וּבָרָעָב עַד־כְּלוֹתָם׃ וּפְלִיטֵי חֶרֶב יְשֻׁבוּן מִן־אֶרֶץ מִצְרַיִם
אֶרֶץ יְהוּדָה מְתֵי מִסְפָּר וְיָדְעוּ כָּל־שְׁאֵרִית יְהוּדָה הַבָּאִים לְאֶרֶץ־
כט מִצְרַיִם לָגוּר שָׁם דְּבַר־מִי יָקוּם מִמֶּנִּי וּמֵהֶם׃ וְזֹאת לָכֶם הָאוֹת נְאֻם־
יְהוָה כִּי־פֹקֵד אֲנִי עֲלֵיכֶם בַּמָּקוֹם הַזֶּה לְמַעַן תֵּדְעוּ כִּי קוֹם יָקוּמוּ
ל דְבָרַי עֲלֵיכֶם לְרָעָה׃ כֹּה ׀ אָמַר יְהוָה הִנְנִי נֹתֵן אֶת־פַּרְעֹה
חָפְרַע מֶלֶךְ־מִצְרַיִם בְּיַד אֹיְבָיו וּבְיַד מְבַקְשֵׁי נַפְשׁוֹ כַּאֲשֶׁר נָתַתִּי אֶת־
צִדְקִיָּהוּ מֶלֶךְ־יְהוּדָה בְּיַד נְבוּכַדְרֶאצַּר מֶלֶךְ־בָּבֶל אֹיְבוֹ וּמְבַקֵּשׁ
מה א נַפְשׁוֹ׃ הַדָּבָר אֲשֶׁר דִּבֶּר יִרְמְיָהוּ הַנָּבִיא אֶל־בָּרוּךְ בֶּן־
נֵרִיָּה בְּכָתְבוֹ אֶת־הַדְּבָרִים הָאֵלֶּה עַל־סֵפֶר מִפִּי יִרְמְיָהוּ בַּשָּׁנָה
ב הָרְבִעִית לִיהוֹיָקִים בֶּן־יֹאשִׁיָּהוּ מֶלֶךְ יְהוּדָה לֵאמֹר׃ כֹּה־אָמַר יְהוָה
ג אֱלֹהֵי יִשְׂרָאֵל עָלֶיךָ בָּרוּךְ׃ אָמַרְתָּ אוֹי־נָא לִי כִּי־יָסַף יְהוָה יָגוֹן עַל־
ד מַכְאֹבִי יָגַעְתִּי בְּאַנְחָתִי וּמְנוּחָה לֹא מָצָאתִי׃ כֹּה ׀ תֹּאמַר אֵלָיו כֹּה
אָמַר יְהוָה הִנֵּה אֲשֶׁר־בָּנִיתִי אֲנִי הֹרֵס וְאֵת אֲשֶׁר־נָטַעְתִּי אֲנִי נֹתֵשׁ
ה וְאֶת־כָּל־הָאָרֶץ הִיא׃ וְאַתָּה תְּבַקֶּשׁ־לְךָ גְדֹלוֹת אַל־תְּבַקֵּשׁ כִּי הִנְנִי
מֵבִיא רָעָה עַל־כָּל־בָּשָׂר נְאֻם־יְהוָה וְנָתַתִּי לְךָ אֶת־נַפְשְׁךָ לְשָׁלָל
מו א עַל כָּל־הַמְּקֹמוֹת אֲשֶׁר תֵּלֶךְ־שָׁם׃ אֲשֶׁר הָיָה דְבַר־יְהוָה
ב אֶל־יִרְמְיָהוּ הַנָּבִיא עַל־הַגּוֹיִם׃ לְמִצְרַיִם עַל־חֵיל פַּרְעֹה נְכוֹ מֶלֶךְ
מִצְרַיִם אֲשֶׁר־הָיָה עַל־נְהַר־פְּרָת בְּכַרְכְּמִשׁ אֲשֶׁר הִכָּה נְבוּכַדְרֶאצַּר
ג מֶלֶךְ בָּבֶל בִּשְׁנַת הָרְבִיעִית לִיהוֹיָקִים בֶּן־יֹאשִׁיָּהוּ מֶלֶךְ יְהוּדָה׃ עִרְכוּ
ד מָגֵן וְצִנָּה וּגְשׁוּ לַמִּלְחָמָה׃ אִסְרוּ הַסּוּסִים וַעֲלוּ הַפָּרָשִׁים וְהִתְיַצְּבוּ
ה בְּכוֹבָעִים מִרְקוּ הָרְמָחִים לִבְשׁוּ הַסִּרְיֹנֹת׃ מַדּוּעַ רָאִיתִי הֵמָּה חַתִּים
נְסֹגִים אָחוֹר וְגִבּוֹרֵיהֶם יֻכַּתּוּ וּמָנוֹס נָסוּ וְלֹא הִפְנוּ מָגוֹר מִסָּבִיב נְאֻם־
ו יְהוָה׃ אַל־יָנוּס הַקַּל וְאַל־יִמָּלֵט הַגִּבּוֹר צָפוֹנָה עַל־יַד נְהַר־פְּרָת
ז ח כָּשְׁלוּ וְנָפָלוּ׃ מִי־זֶה כַּיְאֹר יַעֲלֶה כַּנְּהָרוֹת יִתְגָּעֲשׁוּ מֵימָיו׃ מִצְרַיִם
כַּיְאֹר יַעֲלֶה וְכַנְּהָרוֹת יִתְגֹּעֲשׁוּ מָיִם וַיֹּאמֶר אַעֲלֶה אֲכַסֶּה־אֶרֶץ אֹבִידָה

9 their inhabitants." Let the horses advance and the chariots charge madly, and
let the mighty go forth; Kush and Put, who grasp the shield, and the Lydians,
10 who grasp and draw the bow. That day will be a day of vengeance for the Lord
God of Hosts, to take revenge upon His enemies. The sword will devour, be
sated, and overflow with their blood; a sacrifice for the Lord God of Hosts,
11 in the northern land, by the Euphrates River. Go up to Gilad and take balm,
virgin daughter Egypt. For naught will you apply many remedies; there is no
12 cure for you. The nations have heard of your disgrace, and your screams have
filled the earth. One mighty man has stumbled over the other mighty man;
13 together both have fallen. The word that the Lord spoke to
Yirmeyahu the prophet – how Nevukhadretzar, king of Babylon, would come
14 to attack the land of Egypt: Tell it in Egypt, let it be heard in Migdol, and let
it be heard in Nof and in Taḥpanḥes! Say, "Stand firm and prepare yourself,
15 for the sword has devoured your surroundings." Why have your warriors been
16 swept away? They did not stand because the Lord pushed them down. He
made many falter. Each man fell upon his comrade and said, "Get up and let
us return to our people and to the land of our birth, away from the sword of
17 the oppressor." There they will taunt: "Pharaoh, king of Egypt, king over a
18 multitude, allowed the appointed time to go by." As I live – declares the King,
Lord of Hosts is His name – just as Tabor is among the mountains, and
19 Carmel is by the sea, so will he come. Make for yourselves baggage for exile,
you who dwell securely, daughter Egypt, for Nof will become a desolation,
20 laid waste, with no inhabitant. A very beautiful calf was Egypt, but
21 a murderous enemy attacks her from the north. Even her hired soldiers within
her army are like fattened calves. They too shall turn away, flee together, and
not stand firm. Their day of doom has arrived, when they will meet their fate.
22 Her voice will go forth like a snake's, for they will attack her with force and
23 come upon her with axes like woodcutters. They shall cut down her forest,
declares the Lord, although it cannot be fathomed. There are more of them
24 than locusts; they are innumerable. Shamed is daughter Egypt, given over
25 into the hands of the northern people. Said the Lord of Hosts, the God of
Israel, I will inflict punishment upon Amon of No,[88] and upon Pharaoh, and
upon Egypt, upon her gods and upon her kings, upon Pharaoh and all who
26 trust in him. I will give them over into the hands of those who seek their lives
and into the hands of Nevukhadretzar, king of Babylon, and into the hands
of his servants. Afterward, she shall be inhabited as in days of old, declares
27 the Lord. As for you, My servant Yaakov, do not fear, and Israel, do
not be terrified, for I will deliver you from a distant land and your descendants
from their land of captivity. For Yaakov it will again be quiet and tranquil, with
28 none to frighten him. And you, My servant Yaakov, do not fear, declares the
Lord, for I am with you. For I will make an end of all the nations among
whom I have scattered you, but of you I will not make an end. I will discipline
47 1 you justly, but I will surely not annihilate you.[89] The word of the

88 | A prominent Egyptian god.
89 | Cf. 30:10–11.

ט עִיר וְיֹשְׁבֵי בָהּ: עֲלוּ הַסּוּסִים וְהִתְהֹלְלוּ הָרֶכֶב וְיֵצְאוּ הַגִּבּוֹרִים כּוּשׁ
י וּפוּט תֹּפְשֵׂי מָגֵן וְלוּדִים תֹּפְשֵׂי דֹּרְכֵי קָשֶׁת: וְהַיּוֹם הַהוּא לַאדֹנָי יֱהֹוִה
צְבָאוֹת יוֹם נְקָמָה לְהִנָּקֵם מִצָּרָיו וְאָכְלָה חֶרֶב וְשָׂבְעָה וְרָוְתָה מִדָּמָם
יא כִּי זֶבַח לַאדֹנָי יֱהֹוִה צְבָאוֹת בְּאֶרֶץ צָפוֹן אֶל־נְהַר־פְּרָת: עֲלִי גִלְעָד
וּקְחִי צֳרִי בְּתוּלַת בַּת־מִצְרָיִם לַשָּׁוְא הרביתי רְפֻאוֹת תְּעָלָה אֵין לָךְ: הִרְבֵּית
יב שָׁמְעוּ גוֹיִם קְלוֹנֵךְ וְצִוְחָתֵךְ מָלְאָה הָאָרֶץ כִּי־גִבּוֹר בְּגִבּוֹר כָּשָׁלוּ יַחְדָּיו
יג נָפְלוּ שְׁנֵיהֶם: הַדָּבָר אֲשֶׁר דִּבֶּר יְהֹוָה אֶל־יִרְמְיָהוּ
יד הַנָּבִיא לָבוֹא נְבוּכַדְרֶאצַּר מֶלֶךְ בָּבֶל לְהַכּוֹת אֶת־אֶרֶץ מִצְרָיִם: הַגִּידוּ
בְמִצְרַיִם וְהַשְׁמִיעוּ בְמִגְדּוֹל וְהַשְׁמִיעוּ בְנֹף וּבְתַחְפַּנְחֵס אִמְרוּ הִתְיַצֵּב
טו וְהָכֵן לָךְ כִּי־אָכְלָה חֶרֶב סְבִיבֶיךָ: מַדּוּעַ נִסְחַף אַבִּירֶיךָ לֹא עָמַד
טז כִּי יְהֹוָה הֲדָפוֹ: הִרְבָּה כּוֹשֵׁל גַּם־נָפַל אִישׁ אֶל־רֵעֵהוּ וַיֹּאמְרוּ קוּמָה ׀
יז וְנָשֻׁבָה אֶל־עַמֵּנוּ וְאֶל־אֶרֶץ מוֹלַדְתֵּנוּ מִפְּנֵי חֶרֶב הַיּוֹנָה: קָרְאוּ
יח שָׁם פַּרְעֹה מֶלֶךְ־מִצְרַיִם שָׁאוֹן הֶעֱבִיר הַמּוֹעֵד: חַי־אָנִי נְאֻם־
יט הַמֶּלֶךְ יְהֹוָה צְבָאוֹת שְׁמוֹ כִּי כְּתָבוֹר בֶּהָרִים וּכְכַרְמֶל בַּיָּם יָבוֹא: כְּלֵי
גוֹלָה עֲשִׂי לָךְ יוֹשֶׁבֶת בַּת־מִצְרָיִם כִּי־נֹף לְשַׁמָּה תִהְיֶה וְנִצְּתָה מֵאֵין
כ יוֹשֵׁב: עֶגְלָה יְפֵה־פִיָּה מִצְרָיִם קֶרֶץ מִצָּפוֹן בָּא בָא:
כא גַּם־שְׂכִרֶיהָ בְקִרְבָּהּ כְּעֶגְלֵי מַרְבֵּק כִּי־גַם־הֵמָּה הִפְנוּ נָסוּ יַחְדָּיו לֹא
כב עָמָדוּ כִּי יוֹם אֵידָם בָּא עֲלֵיהֶם עֵת פְּקֻדָּתָם: קוֹלָהּ כַּנָּחָשׁ יֵלֵךְ כִּי־
כג בְחַיִל יֵלֵכוּ וּבְקַרְדֻּמּוֹת בָּאוּ לָהּ כְּחֹטְבֵי עֵצִים: כָּרְתוּ יַעְרָהּ נְאֻם־יְהֹוָה
כד כִּי לֹא יֵחָקֵר כִּי רַבּוּ מֵאַרְבֶּה וְאֵין לָהֶם מִסְפָּר: הֹבִישָׁה בַּת־מִצְרָיִם
כה נִתְּנָה בְּיַד עַם־צָפוֹן: אָמַר יְהֹוָה צְבָאוֹת אֱלֹהֵי יִשְׂרָאֵל הִנְנִי פוֹקֵד
אֶל־אָמוֹן מִנֹּא וְעַל־פַּרְעֹה וְעַל־מִצְרַיִם וְעַל־אֱלֹהֶיהָ וְעַל־מְלָכֶיהָ
כו וְעַל־פַּרְעֹה וְעַל הַבֹּטְחִים בּוֹ: וּנְתַתִּים בְּיַד מְבַקְשֵׁי נַפְשָׁם וּבְיַד
נְבוּכַדְרֶאצַּר מֶלֶךְ־בָּבֶל וּבְיַד־עֲבָדָיו וְאַחֲרֵי־כֵן תִּשְׁכֹּן כִּימֵי־קֶדֶם
כז נְאֻם־יְהֹוָה: וְאַתָּה אַל־תִּירָא עַבְדִּי יַעֲקֹב וְאַל־תֵּחַת כז
יִשְׂרָאֵל כִּי הִנְנִי מוֹשִׁעֲךָ מֵרָחוֹק וְאֶת־זַרְעֲךָ מֵאֶרֶץ שִׁבְיָם וְשָׁב יַעֲקוֹב
כח וְשָׁקַט וְשַׁאֲנַן וְאֵין מַחֲרִיד: אַתָּה אַל־תִּירָא עַבְדִּי יַעֲקֹב נְאֻם־יְהֹוָה
כִּי אִתְּךָ אָנִי כִּי אֶעֱשֶׂה כָלָה בְּכָל־הַגּוֹיִם ׀ אֲשֶׁר הִדַּחְתִּיךָ שָׁמָּה וְאֹתְךָ
מז א לֹא־אֶעֱשֶׂה כָלָה וְיִסַּרְתִּיךָ לַמִּשְׁפָּט וְנַקֵּה לֹא אֲנַקֶּךָּ: אֲשֶׁר

Lord that came to Yirmeyahu the prophet concerning the Philistines before
2 Pharaoh attacked Aza:[90] Thus said the Lord: Waters are about to rise from
the north[91] that will become like an overflowing river. They shall flood the
land and those who fill it, the town and its inhabitants. People will cry out;
3 all the land's inhabitants shall wail. At the sound of the pounding hooves of
his stallions, the roar of his chariots, and the rumbling of his wheels, fathers
will not turn around to save their children because of their enfeebled hands,
4 because of the day that is coming to devastate all the Philistines, to cut off
from Tyre and Sidon every last ally. For the Lord is devastating the Philistines,
5 the remnant of the island of Kaftor. Aza has been shorn; Ashkelon has been
6 severed. O remnant of her valley, how long will you gash yourselves?[92] O
sword of the Lord, how long will you be unquiet? Withdraw into your
7 scabbard; rest and be silent. How can she be quiet when the Lord has
ordered her against Ashkelon and has selected the seacoast as her tar-
48 1 get? Concerning Moav, this is what the Lord of Hosts, God of
Israel, said: Woe to Nevo, for she has been devastated; shamed, captured is
2 Kiryatayim; the fortress is shamed and shattered. There shall no longer be
glory for Moav. In Ḥeshbon they have plotted disaster against her: "Come
and let us cut her off from being a nation." You too, Madmen,[93] shall be
3 silenced; the sword shall pursue you. The sound of a scream from Ḥoronayim,
4 devastation, and a great collapse – Moav is broken; her young people have
5 let loose a great scream. On the ascent to Luḥit weeping shall follow weeping;
6 on the descent from Ḥoronayim enemies heard sounds of collapse. Flee, save
7 your lives, and let them be like shrubs in the wilderness. Because you have
trusted in your achievements and in your storehouses, you shall also be taken
captive, and Kemosh[94] shall go into exile together with his priests and his
8 officials. The marauder shall come to every town – no town will be spared;
9 the valley ruined, the plain destroyed, as the Lord has said. Give wings to
Moav so that she can take flight, and her towns become a desolation with no
10 inhabitant in them. Cursed is the one who performs the Lord's work
deceitfully, and cursed is the one who restrains his sword from shedding
11 blood. Moav has been tranquil from his youth and has rested quietly upon
his lees. He has not been emptied from vessel to vessel and has never gone
into exile so that his flavor has remained fresh, and his fragrance has never
12 altered. Therefore, days are approaching, declares the Lord, when
I will send forth spoilers who will despoil him. They will empty his vessels,
13 and they will smash his jugs. And Moav will be shamed because of Kemosh,
just as the House of Israel was shamed because of Beit El,[95] in whom they
14 trusted. How dare you say: "We are mighty men, soldiers adept at war"?

---

90 | A chief Philistine city.

91 | Whence the invaders would come.

92 | In mourning.

93 | A city in the region of Moav.

94 | The god of Moav.

95 | A reference to the idolatrous calf situated there.

הָיָה דְבַר־יְהוָה אֶל־יִרְמְיָהוּ הַנָּבִיא אֶל־פְּלִשְׁתִּים בְּטֶרֶם יַכֶּה פַּרְעֹה
ב אֶת־עַזָּה: כֹּה ׀ אָמַר יְהוָה הִנֵּה־מַיִם עֹלִים מִצָּפוֹן וְהָיוּ לְנַחַל שׁוֹטֵף
וְיִשְׁטְפוּ אֶרֶץ וּמְלוֹאָהּ עִיר וְיֹשְׁבֵי בָהּ וְזָעֲקוּ הָאָדָם וְהֵילִל כֹּל יוֹשֵׁב
ג הָאָרֶץ: מִקּוֹל שַׁעֲטַת פַּרְסוֹת אַבִּירָיו מֵרַעַשׁ לְרִכְבּוֹ הֲמוֹן גַּלְגִּלָּיו
ד לֹא־הִפְנוּ אָבוֹת אֶל־בָּנִים מֵרִפְיוֹן יָדָיִם: עַל־הַיּוֹם הַבָּא לִשְׁדוֹד אֶת־
כָּל־פְּלִשְׁתִּים לְהַכְרִית לְצֹר וּלְצִידוֹן כֹּל שָׂרִיד עֹזֵר כִּי־שֹׁדֵד יְהוָה
ה אֶת־פְּלִשְׁתִּים שְׁאֵרִית אִי כַפְתּוֹר: בָּאָה קָרְחָה אֶל־עַזָּה נִדְמְתָה
ו אַשְׁקְלוֹן שְׁאֵרִית עִמְקָם עַד־מָתַי תִּתְגּוֹדָדִי: הוֹי חֶרֶב לַיהוָה עַד־
ז אָנָה לֹא תִשְׁקֹטִי הֵאָסְפִי אֶל־תַּעְרֵךְ הֵרָגְעִי וָדֹמִּי: אֵיךְ תִּשְׁקֹטִי וַיהוָה
מח א צִוָּה־לָהּ אֶל־אַשְׁקְלוֹן וְאֶל־חוֹף הַיָּם שָׁם יְעָדָהּ: לְמוֹאָב
כֹּה־אָמַר יְהוָה צְבָאוֹת אֱלֹהֵי יִשְׂרָאֵל הוֹי אֶל־נְבוֹ כִּי שֻׁדָּדָה הֹבִישָׁה
ב נִלְכְּדָה קִרְיָתָיִם הֹבִישָׁה הַמִּשְׂגָּב וָחָתָּה: אֵין עוֹד תְּהִלַּת מוֹאָב
בְּחֶשְׁבּוֹן חָשְׁבוּ עָלֶיהָ רָעָה לְכוּ וְנַכְרִיתֶנָּה מִגּוֹי גַּם־מַדְמֵן תִּדֹּמִּי
ג ד אַחֲרַיִךְ תֵּלֶךְ חָרֶב: קוֹל צְעָקָה מֵחוֹרֹנָיִם שֹׁד וָשֶׁבֶר גָּדוֹל: נִשְׁבְּרָה
ה מוֹאָב הִשְׁמִיעוּ זְּעָקָה צעוריה: כִּי מַעֲלֵה הלחות בִּבְכִי יַעֲלֶה־בֶּכִי צְעִירֶיהָ
ו כִּי בְּמוֹרַד חוֹרֹנַיִם צָרֵי צַעֲקַת־שֶׁבֶר שָׁמֵעוּ: נֻסוּ מַלְּטוּ נַפְשְׁכֶם וְתִהְיֶינָה הַלּוּחִית
ז כַּעֲרוֹעֵר בַּמִּדְבָּר: כִּי יַעַן בִּטְחֵךְ בְּמַעֲשַׂיִךְ וּבְאוֹצְרוֹתַיִךְ גַּם־אַתְּ תִּלָּכֵדִי
ח וְיָצָא כמיש בַּגּוֹלָה כֹּהֲנָיו וְשָׂרָיו יחד: וְיָבֹא שֹׁדֵד אֶל־כָּל־עִיר וְעִיר כְּמוֹשׁ
ט לֹא תִמָּלֵט וְאָבַד הָעֵמֶק וְנִשְׁמַד הַמִּישֹׁר אֲשֶׁר אָמַר יְהוָה: תְּנוּ־צִיץ יַחְדָּו
י לְמוֹאָב כִּי נָצֹא תֵּצֵא וְעָרֶיהָ לְשַׁמָּה תִהְיֶינָה מֵאֵין יוֹשֵׁב בָּהֵן: אָרוּר
יא עֹשֶׂה מְלֶאכֶת יְהוָה רְמִיָּה וְאָרוּר מֹנֵעַ חַרְבּוֹ מִדָּם: שַׁאֲנַן מוֹאָב
מִנְּעוּרָיו וְשֹׁקֵט הוּא אֶל־שְׁמָרָיו וְלֹא־הוּרַק מִכְּלִי אֶל־כֶּלִי וּבַגּוֹלָה
יב לֹא הָלָךְ עַל־כֵּן עָמַד טַעְמוֹ בּוֹ וְרֵיחוֹ לֹא נָמָר: לָכֵן
הִנֵּה־יָמִים בָּאִים נְאֻם־יְהוָה וְשִׁלַּחְתִּי־לוֹ צֹעִים וְצֵעֻהוּ וְכֵלָיו יָרִיקוּ
יג וְנִבְלֵיהֶם יְנַפֵּצוּ: וּבֹשׁ מוֹאָב מִכְּמוֹשׁ כַּאֲשֶׁר־בֹּשׁוּ בֵּית יִשְׂרָאֵל מִבֵּית
יד אֵל מִבְטֶחָם: אֵיךְ תֹּאמְרוּ גִּבּוֹרִים אֲנָחְנוּ וְאַנְשֵׁי־חַיִל לַמִּלְחָמָה:

15 Moav is devastated; his towns are gone. His finest youths have gone down to
16 the slaughter, declares the King – LORD of Hosts is his name. Moav's doom
17 comes near; his disaster hastens swiftly. Grieve, all who dwell around him
and all who know his fame. Say: "How has this mighty scepter, this splendid
18 staff, been broken?!" Descend from glory and sit in thirst, she who dwells in
daughter Dibon. He who has devastated Moav has come upon you. He has
19 destroyed your fortresses. Stand by the road and stare, dweller in Aroer. Ask
20 of him who flees and of her who escapes: say, "What has happened?" Shamed
is Moav, for she is broken; wail and shriek. Tell it at the Arnon: Moav is
21 devastated. Judgment has reached the tableland upon Ḥolon, Yahatz, and
22 23 Meifaat; and upon Divon, Nevo, and Beit Divlatayim; and upon Kiryatayim,
24 Beit Gamul, and Beit Meon; and upon Keriyot and Botzra – and upon all the
25 towns of the land of Moav, far and near. The horn of Moav has been cut off,
26 its arm broken, declares the LORD. Make him drunk, for he has puffed himself
up against the LORD. Let him roll about in his vomit so that he too becomes
27 a laughingstock. Was not Israel a laughingstock to you? Was he found among
28 thieves? For whenever you spoke about him, you shook with scorn. Abandon
towns and dwell among rocks, inhabitants of Moav. Become like a dove
29 that nests in the sides of the entrance of a crevice. We have heard of Moav's
arrogance – excessive arrogance – his loftiness, his hubris, his pride, and his
30 haughty heart.[96] I know, declares the LORD, that his wrath has no basis, and
31 that his illusions have come to naught. Therefore I will wail for Moav; I will
shriek on behalf of all of Moav; for the people of Kir Ḥeres I will whimper.
32 Even more than weeping for Yazer I weep for you, vineyards of Sivma, whose
branches once extended over the waters and reached the Yazer Sea. The
33 devastator has fallen upon your summer fruits and vintage. Joy and gaiety are
dispelled from the fruitful field and from the land of Moav. I have made an
end to the wine in the winepresses. No one treads them with shouts of
34 "*heidad*" – the "*heidad*" is no longer the same "*heidad*." The screams reached
from Ḥeshbon to Elaleh. They raised their voices as far as Yahatz, from Tzoar
up to Ḥoronayim and up to Eglat Shlishiya. Even the waters of Nimrim shall
35 become a desolation. I will make an end in Moav, declares the LORD, of the
one who gives an offering upon a high place or burns incense to his god.
36 Therefore my heart moans for Moav like flutes; my heart moans for Kir Ḥeres
37 like flutes; all the wealth it accumulated is lost. For every head is shaved,
38 every beard shorn. On all hands there are gashes, and on the loins sackcloth.
On all the rooftops of Moav and in her squares there is only lament, for
39 I have broken Moav like an unwanted vessel, declares the LORD. "How
shattered!" they wailed. How Moav has turned his back in shame and become
40 a laughingstock and a source of horror for all around him. For this
is what the LORD said: He will soar like an eagle and spread his wings toward
41 Moav. The towns are captured and the fortresses seized. On that day the heart
42 of the mighty of Moav will become like the heart of a woman in labor. Moav

96 | Cf. Isaiah, chapters 15–16.

טו שֻׁדַּד מוֹאָב וְעָרֶיהָ עָלָה וּמִבְחַר בַּחוּרָיו יָרְדוּ לַטָּבַח נְאֻם־הַמֶּלֶךְ
טז יז יְהוָה צְבָאוֹת שְׁמוֹ׃ קָרוֹב אֵיד־מוֹאָב לָבוֹא וְרָעָתוֹ מִהֲרָה מְאֹד׃ נֻדוּ
לוֹ כָּל־סְבִיבָיו וְכֹל יֹדְעֵי שְׁמוֹ אִמְרוּ אֵיכָה נִשְׁבַּר מַטֵּה־עֹז מַקֵּל
יח תִּפְאָרָה׃ רְדִי מִכָּבוֹד ישבי בַצָּמָא יֹשֶׁבֶת בַּת־דִּיבוֹן כִּי־שֹׁדֵד מוֹאָב וּשְׁבִי
יט עָלָה בָךְ שִׁחֵת מִבְצָרָיִךְ׃ אֶל־דֶּרֶךְ עִמְדִי וְצַפִּי יוֹשֶׁבֶת עֲרוֹעֵר שַׁאֲלִי־
כ נָס וְנִמְלָטָה אִמְרִי מַה־נִּהְיָתָה׃ הֹבִישׁ מוֹאָב כִּי־חַתָּה הילילי ׀ וזעקי הֵילִילוּ ׀ וּזְעָקוּ
כא הַגִּידוּ בְאַרְנוֹן כִּי שֻׁדַּד מוֹאָב׃ וּמִשְׁפָּט בָּא אֶל־אֶרֶץ הַמִּישֹׁר אֶל־חֹלוֹן
כב כג וְאֶל־יַהְצָה וְעַל־מופעת׃ וְעַל־דִּיבוֹן וְעַל־נְבוֹ וְעַל־בֵּית דִּבְלָתָיִם׃ וְעַל מֵיפָעַת
כד קִרְיָתַיִם וְעַל־בֵּית גָּמוּל וְעַל־בֵּית מְעוֹן׃ וְעַל־קְרִיּוֹת וְעַל־בָּצְרָה וְעַל
כה כָּל־עָרֵי אֶרֶץ מוֹאָב הָרְחֹקוֹת וְהַקְּרֹבוֹת׃ נִגְדְּעָה קֶרֶן מוֹאָב וּזְרֹעוֹ
כו נִשְׁבָּרָה נְאֻם יְהוָה׃ הַשְׁכִּירֻהוּ כִּי עַל־יְהוָה הִגְדִּיל וְסָפַק מוֹאָב בְּקִיאוֹ
כז וְהָיָה לִשְׂחֹק גַּם־הוּא׃ וְאִם ׀ לוֹא הַשְּׂחֹק הָיָה לְךָ יִשְׂרָאֵל אִם־בְּגַנָּבִים
כח נמצאה כִּי־מִדֵּי דְבָרֶיךָ בּוֹ תִּתְנוֹדָד׃ עִזְבוּ עָרִים וְשִׁכְנוּ בַּסֶּלַע יֹשְׁבֵי נִמְצָא
כט מוֹאָב וִהְיוּ כְיוֹנָה תְּקַנֵּן בְּעֶבְרֵי פִי־פָחַת׃ שָׁמַעְנוּ גְאוֹן־מוֹאָב גֵּאֶה
ל מְאֹד גָּבְהוֹ וּגְאוֹנוֹ וְגַאֲוָתוֹ וְרֻם לִבּוֹ׃ אֲנִי יָדַעְתִּי נְאֻם־יְהוָה עֶבְרָתוֹ
לא וְלֹא־כֵן בַּדָּיו לֹא־כֵן עָשׂוּ׃ עַל־כֵּן עַל־מוֹאָב אֲיֵלִיל וּלְמוֹאָב כֻּלֹּה
לב אֶזְעָק אֶל־אַנְשֵׁי קִיר־חֶרֶשׂ יֶהְגֶּה׃ מִבְּכִי יַעְזֵר אֶבְכֶּה־לָּךְ הַגֶּפֶן שִׂבְמָה
נְטִישֹׁתַיִךְ עָבְרוּ יָם עַד יָם יַעְזֵר נָגָעוּ עַל־קֵיצֵךְ וְעַל־בְּצִירֵךְ שֹׁדֵד נָפָל׃
לג וְנֶאֶסְפָה שִׂמְחָה וָגִיל מִכַּרְמֶל וּמֵאֶרֶץ מוֹאָב וְיַיִן מִיקָבִים הִשְׁבַּתִּי
לד לֹא־יִדְרֹךְ הֵידָד הֵידָד לֹא הֵידָד׃ מִזַּעֲקַת חֶשְׁבּוֹן עַד־אֶלְעָלֵה עַד־
יַהַץ נָתְנוּ קוֹלָם מִצֹּעַר עַד־חֹרֹנַיִם עֶגְלַת שְׁלִשִׁיָּה כִּי גַּם־מֵי נִמְרִים
לה לִמְשַׁמּוֹת יִהְיוּ׃ וְהִשְׁבַּתִּי לְמוֹאָב נְאֻם־יְהוָה מַעֲלֶה בָמָה וּמַקְטִיר
לו לֵאלֹהָיו׃ עַל־כֵּן לִבִּי לְמוֹאָב כַּחֲלִלִים יֶהֱמֶה וְלִבִּי אֶל־אַנְשֵׁי קִיר־חֶרֶשׂ
לז כַּחֲלִילִים יֶהֱמֶה עַל־כֵּן יִתְרַת עָשָׂה אָבָדוּ׃ כִּי כָל־רֹאשׁ קָרְחָה וְכָל־
לח זָקָן גְּרֻעָה עַל כָּל־יָדַיִם גְּדֻדֹת וְעַל־מָתְנַיִם שָׂק׃ עַל כָּל־גַּגּוֹת מוֹאָב
וּבִרְחֹבֹתֶיהָ כֻּלֹּה מִסְפֵּד כִּי־שָׁבַרְתִּי אֶת־מוֹאָב כִּכְלִי אֵין־חֵפֶץ בּוֹ
לט נְאֻם־יְהוָה׃ אֵיךְ חַתָּה הֵילִילוּ אֵיךְ הִפְנָה־עֹרֶף מוֹאָב בּוֹשׁ וְהָיָה
מ מוֹאָב לִשְׂחֹק וְלִמְחִתָּה לְכָל־סְבִיבָיו׃ כִּי־כֹה אָמַר יְהוָה
מא הִנֵּה כַנֶּשֶׁר יִדְאֶה וּפָרַשׂ כְּנָפָיו אֶל־מוֹאָב׃ נִלְכְּדָה הַקְּרִיּוֹת וְהַמְּצָדוֹת
מב נִתְפָּשָׂה וְהָיָה לֵב גִּבּוֹרֵי מוֹאָב בַּיּוֹם הַהוּא כְּלֵב אִשָּׁה מְצֵרָה׃ וְנִשְׁמַד

43 is denied peoplehood, for he has puffed himself up against the LORD. Panic,
44 pit, and a snare upon you, inhabitant of Moav, declares the LORD. Whoever
flees from the panic shall fall into the pit, and whoever climbs out of the pit
shall be caught in the snare, for I shall bring upon her, upon Moav, the year
45 of its retribution, declares the LORD. Those who fled from the power stood
in the shadow of Ḥeshbon, but a fire came forth from Ḥeshbon, a flame from
the midst of Siḥon. It consumed the brow of Moav and the foreheads of
46 Shaon.[97] Woe for you, Moav; Kemosh's people are destroyed, for they have
47 taken your sons captive and your daughters into captivity. I will return the
captives of Moav in the days to come, declares the LORD. Thus far this is the
49 1 judgment on Moav. Concerning the Amonites, this is what the LORD
said: Does Israel have no children? Does he have no heir? Why then did their
2 king possess Gad and their people settle in its towns? Therefore, days are
approaching, declares the LORD, when I shall let the trumpet blasts of war be
heard over Raba of the Amonites, and she shall become a desolate mound,
her villages set on fire, and Israel shall dispossess those who possessed him,
3 says the LORD. Wail, Ḥeshbon, for Ai has been devastated. Shout, daughters
of Raba; gird sackcloth, lament, rush about inside the fences, for their king
4 shall go into exile together with his priests and princes. Why do you boast
about the valleys? Your valley flows away, wayward daughter, she who trusts
5 in her treasures, saying, "Who dares come upon me?" I am about to bring
terror upon you, declares the Lord GOD of Hosts, from every direction.
Everyone will be driven forward with none to gather the one who wanders
6 off. Afterward, I will return the captives of the Amonites, declares the
7 LORD. Concerning Edom, this is what the LORD of Hosts said:
Is there no longer wisdom in Teiman? Has good counsel been lost to those
8 with understanding? Has their wisdom decayed? Inhabitants of Dedan, flee,
clear out, dwell in the depths, for I have brought Esav's fate upon you at the
9 time I punished him. If grape gatherers come upon you, do they not leave
10 gleanings? Do not thieves of the night consume only their fill?[98] For I have
exposed Esav; I have revealed his secret places so that he cannot hide. His
11 seed has been ravaged, his brothers, his neighbors – he is gone. Leave your
orphans to Me, and I shall keep them alive, and your widows shall come to
12 rely on Me. For this is what the LORD said: Even those who are not
sentenced to drink the cup of wrath must drink it, and yet you expect to be
13 absolved? You will certainly not be absolved. You shall certainly drink it. For
by My own self have I sworn, declares the LORD, Botzra[99] will become a
desolation, a disgrace, a wasteland, and a curse, and all her towns shall be
14 ruins forever. I heard tidings from the LORD, and an envoy is sent out among
15 the nations: "Assemble and come upon her; rise up for battle."[100] Look, I have
16 made you small among nations, scorned by humanity. Your dreadfulness and

97 | Cf. Numbers 21:27–30.
98 | Cf. Obadiah 1:5–6.
99 | An important city in Edom.
100 | Cf. Obadiah 1:1–2.

מג מואב מעם כי על־יהוה הגדיל: פחד ופחת ופח עליך יושב מואב
מד נאם־יהוה: הניס מפני הפחד יפל אל־הפחת והעלה מן־הפחת הנס
מה ילכד בפח כי־אביא אליה אל־מואב שנת פקדתם נאם־יהוה: בצל
חשבון עמדו מכח נסים כי־אש יצא מחשבון ולהבה מבין סיחון
מו ותאכל פאת מואב וקדקד בני שאון: אוי־לך מואב אבד עם־כמוש
מז כי־לקחו בניך בשבי ובנתיך בשביה: ושבתי שבות־מואב באחרית
מט א הימים נאם־יהוה עד־הנה משפט מואב: לבני עמון
כה אמר יהוה הבנים אין לישראל אם־יורש אין לו מדוע ירש מלכם
ב את־גד ועמו בעריו ישב: לכן הנה ימים באים נאם־יהוה והשמעתי כח
אל־רבת בני־עמון תרועת מלחמה והיתה לתל שממה ובנתיה
ג באש תצתנה וירש ישראל את־ירשיו אמר יהוה: הילילי חשבון
כי שדדה־עי צעקנה בנות רבה חגרנה שקים ספדנה והתשוטטנה
ד בגדרות כי מלכם בגולה ילך כהניו ושריו יחדיו: מה־תתהללי
בעמקים זב עמקך הבת השובבה הבטחה באצרתיה מי יבוא אלי:
ה הנני מביא עליך פחד נאם־אדני יהוה צבאות מכל־סביביך ונדחתם
ו איש לפניו ואין מקבץ לנדד: ואחרי־כן אשיב את־שבות בני־עמון
ז נאם־יהוה: לאדום כה אמר יהוה צבאות האין עוד
ח חכמה בתימן אבדה עצה מבנים נסרחה חכמתם: נסו הפנו העמקו
ט לשבת ישבי דדן כי איד עשו הבאתי עליו עת פקדתיו: אם־
בצרים באו לך לא ישארו עוללות אם־גנבים בלילה השחיתו דים:
י כי־אני חשפתי את־עשו גליתי את־מסתריו ונחבה לא יוכל שדד
יא זרעו ואחיו ושכניו ואיננו: עזבה יתמיך אני אחיה ואלמנותיך עלי
יב תבטחו: כי־כה | אמר יהוה הנה אשר־אין משפטם
לשתות הכוס שתו ישתו ואתה הוא נקה תנקה לא תנקה כי שתה
יג תשתה: כי בי נשבעתי נאם־יהוה כי־לשמה לחרפה לחרב ולקללה
יד תהיה בצרה וכל־עריה תהיינה לחרבות עולם: שמועה שמעתי
מאת יהוה וציר בגוים שלוח התקבצו ובאו עליה וקומו למלחמה:
טו טז כי־הנה קטן נתתיך בגוים בזוי באדם: תפלצתך השיא אתך זדון

your haughty heart deceived you, you who dwell in the cliff's niches, who
hold on to the height of the hill. Should you raise your nest as high as the
17 eagle's, I shall bring you down from there, declares the LORD. Edom shall
become a source of astonishment. Whoever passes her by shall be astonished
18 and shall shriek over all her wounds. As in the overturning of Sedom and
Amora and their neighbors, says the LORD, no one shall live there, and no
19 human shall stay there. Look, like a lion coming up from a thicket of the
Jordan against the secure pasture, in a moment I will drive him[101] away from
it. I will appoint over her whomever I choose, for who is like Me, and who
can summon Me? Who is the shepherd who can stand up against Me?[102]
20 Therefore, hear the counsel that the LORD has taken against Edom and
His plans regarding the inhabitants of Teiman: Surely the weakest of sheep
21 shall drag him away; surely he will render their pastures desolate. The earth
trembles at the sound of their collapse, a shout, the sound of which will
22 be heard at the Sea of Reeds. Look, he will fly up and soar like an eagle
and spread his wings over Botzra. On that day the heart of the mighty of
23 Edom will become like the heart of a woman in labor. Concerning
Damascus: Ḥamat and Arpad are put to shame, for they heard bad tidings
24 and quivered, fearful as if at sea, unable to be calm. Damascus has become
feeble. She has turned around to flee. A shudder has possessed her; anguish
25 and pangs have seized her like a woman giving birth. "Why was the city of
26 glory not fortified, the town of my delight?" Therefore, her young men will
fall in her squares, and all men of war will be cut down on that day, declares
27 the LORD of Hosts. I will set fire to the wall of Damascus, and it shall devour
28 the citadels of Ben Hadad. Concerning Kedar[103] and the kingdoms
of Ḥatzor that Nevukhadretzar king of Babylon attacked, this is what the
LORD said: Rise! Go up against Kedar and plunder the peoples of the East.
29 They will take away their tents and their sheep; their curtains, all their utensils,
and their camels they shall carry off for themselves, and they will cry out at
30 them, "Terror all around." Flee, wander far, dwell in the depths, inhabitants
of Ḥatzor, declares the LORD, for Nevukhadretzar, king of Babylon, has taken
31 counsel against you. He has devised a scheme against you. Rise and go up
against the tranquil nation that dwells securely, declares the LORD, that has
32 neither gates nor bars, that dwells alone. Their camels shall be booty, and
their many cattle shall be spoils. I shall scatter them in every direction, to the
end of every corner. From every side I shall deliver their doom, declares the
33 LORD. Ḥatzor shall become a jackals' haunt, an eternal desolation. No one
34 shall live there, and no human shall reside there. The word of the
LORD that came to Yirmeyahu the prophet concerning Eilam at the beginning
35 of the reign of Tzidkiya, king of Yehuda – this is what the LORD of Hosts said:
36 I am about to break the bow of Eilam, the mainstay of their might. I shall
bring upon Eilam four winds from the four corners of the heavens, and I shall

101 | Referring to Edom.
102 | Cf. 50:44–46.
103 | Kedar was a kingdom in the eastern desert; Ḥatzor was probably in the same area.

לִבֶּךָ שֹׁכְנִי בְּחַגְוֵי הַסֶּלַע תֹּפְשִׂי מְרוֹם גִּבְעָה כִּי־תַגְבִּיהַּ כַּנֶּשֶׁר קִנֶּךָ
יז מִשָּׁם אוֹרִידְךָ נְאֻם־יְהוָה: וְהָיְתָה אֱדוֹם לְשַׁמָּה כֹּל עֹבֵר עָלֶיהָ יִשֹּׁם
יח וְיִשְׁרֹק עַל־כׇּל־מַכּוֹתֶהָ: כְּמַהְפֵּכַת סְדֹם וַעֲמֹרָה וּשְׁכֵנֶיהָ אָמַר יְהוָה
יט לֹא־יֵשֵׁב שָׁם אִישׁ וְלֹא־יָגוּר בָּהּ בֶּן־אָדָם: הִנֵּה כְּאַרְיֵה יַעֲלֶה מִגְּאוֹן
הַיַּרְדֵּן אֶל־נְוֵה אֵיתָן כִּי־אַרְגִּיעָה אֲרִיצֶנּוּ מֵעָלֶיהָ וּמִי בָחוּר אֵלֶיהָ
כ אֶפְקֹד כִּי מִי כָמוֹנִי וּמִי יֹעִידֶנִּי וּמִי־זֶה רֹעֶה אֲשֶׁר יַעֲמֹד לְפָנָי: לָכֵן
שִׁמְעוּ עֲצַת־יְהוָה אֲשֶׁר יָעַץ אֶל־אֱדוֹם וּמַחְשְׁבוֹתָיו אֲשֶׁר חָשַׁב אֶל־
יֹשְׁבֵי תֵימָן אִם־לוֹא יִסְחָבוּם צְעִירֵי הַצֹּאן אִם־לֹא יַשִּׁים עֲלֵיהֶם נְוֵהֶם:
כא כב מִקּוֹל נִפְלָם רָעֲשָׁה הָאָרֶץ צְעָקָה בְּיַם־סוּף נִשְׁמַע קוֹלָהּ: הִנֵּה כַנֶּשֶׁר
יַעֲלֶה וְיִדְאֶה וְיִפְרֹשׂ כְּנָפָיו עַל־בׇּצְרָה וְהָיָה לֵב גִּבּוֹרֵי אֱדוֹם בַּיּוֹם
כג הַהוּא כְּלֵב אִשָּׁה מְצֵרָה: לְדַמֶּשֶׂק בּוֹשָׁה חֲמָת וְאַרְפָּד
כד כִּי־שְׁמֻעָה רָעָה שָׁמְעוּ נָמֹגוּ בַּיָּם דְּאָגָה הַשְׁקֵט לֹא יוּכָל: רָפְתָה
דַמֶּשֶׂק הִפְנְתָה לָנוּס וְרֶטֶט ׀ הֶחֱזִיקָה צָרָה וַחֲבָלִים אֲחָזַתָּה כַּיּוֹלֵדָה:
כה כו אֵיךְ לֹא־עֻזְּבָה עִיר תהלה קִרְיַת מְשׂוֹשִׂי: לָכֵן יִפְּלוּ בַחוּרֶיהָ בִּרְחֹבֹתֶיהָ תְּהִלָּת
כז וְכׇל־אַנְשֵׁי הַמִּלְחָמָה יִדַּמּוּ בַּיּוֹם הַהוּא נְאֻם יְהוָה צְבָאוֹת: וְהִצַּתִּי
כח אֵשׁ בְּחוֹמַת דַּמָּשֶׂק וְאָכְלָה אַרְמְנוֹת בֶּן־הֲדָד: לְקֵדָר ׀
וּלְמַמְלְכוֹת חָצוֹר אֲשֶׁר הִכָּה נבוכדראצור מֶלֶךְ־בָּבֶל כֹּה אָמַר יְהוָה נְבוּכַדְרֶאצַּר
כט קוּמוּ עֲלוּ אֶל־קֵדָר וְשָׁדְדוּ אֶת־בְּנֵי־קֶדֶם: אׇהֳלֵיהֶם וְצֹאנָם יִקָּחוּ
יְרִיעוֹתֵיהֶם וְכׇל־כְּלֵיהֶם וּגְמַלֵּיהֶם יִשְׂאוּ לָהֶם וְקָרְאוּ עֲלֵיהֶם מָגוֹר
ל מִסָּבִיב: נֻסוּ נֻּדוּ מְאֹד הֶעְמִיקוּ לָשֶׁבֶת יֹשְׁבֵי חָצוֹר נְאֻם־יְהוָה כִּי־יָעַץ
לא עֲלֵיכֶם נְבוּכַדְרֶאצַּר מֶלֶךְ־בָּבֶל עֵצָה וְחָשַׁב עליהם מַחֲשָׁבָה: קוּמוּ עֲלֵיכֶם
עֲלוּ אֶל־גּוֹי שְׁלֵיו יוֹשֵׁב לָבֶטַח נְאֻם־יְהוָה לֹא־דְלָתַיִם וְלֹא־בְרִיחַ לוֹ
לב בָּדָד יִשְׁכֹּנוּ: וְהָיוּ גְמַלֵּיהֶם לָבַז וַהֲמוֹן מִקְנֵיהֶם לְשָׁלָל וְזֵרִתִים לְכׇל־
לג רוּחַ קְצוּצֵי פֵאָה וּמִכׇּל־עֲבָרָיו אָבִיא אֶת־אֵידָם נְאֻם־יְהוָה: וְהָיְתָה
חָצוֹר לִמְעוֹן תַּנִּים שְׁמָמָה עַד־עוֹלָם לֹא־יֵשֵׁב שָׁם אִישׁ וְלֹא־יָגוּר בָּהּ
לד בֶּן־אָדָם: אֲשֶׁר הָיָה דְבַר־יְהוָה אֶל־יִרְמְיָהוּ הַנָּבִיא אֶל־
לה עֵילָם בְּרֵאשִׁית מַלְכוּת צִדְקִיָּה מֶלֶךְ־יְהוּדָה לֵאמֹר: כֹּה אָמַר יְהוָה
לו צְבָאוֹת הִנְנִי שֹׁבֵר אֶת־קֶשֶׁת עֵילָם רֵאשִׁית גְּבוּרָתָם: וְהֵבֵאתִי אֶל־
עֵילָם אַרְבַּע רוּחוֹת מֵאַרְבַּע קְצוֹת הַשָּׁמַיִם וְזֵרִתִים לְכֹל הָרֻחוֹת הָאֵלֶּה

scatter them to all those winds so that there shall be no nation to which those
37 driven from Eilam shall not come. I shall shatter Eilam before their foes and
before those who seek their lives, and I shall bring upon them disaster, My
wrath, declares the LORD. I shall send the sword after them until I finish them
38 off. I shall place My throne in Eilam, and I shall remove from there kings and
39 princes, declares the LORD. In the days to come I shall return the captives of
50 1 Eilam, declares the LORD. The word that the LORD spoke concerning
2 Babylon, the land of the Chaldeans, through Yirmeyahu the prophet: Tell it
among the nations, and let it be heard. Raise a banner. Let it be heard, and
hold nothing back. Say, "Babylon is captured, Bel is shamed, Merodakh[104]
3 broken; her statues shamed, her idols broken." For a nation from the north
has come upon her. He shall render her land desolate, and there shall be no
inhabitant within her. Humans and animals alike shall wander off and be gone.
4 In those days, and at that time, declares the LORD, the people of Israel shall
come, they and the people of Yehuda together. They shall go, weeping all the
5 while, and shall seek the LORD their God. They shall ask for the way to Zion
with their faces turned toward it. Come and let us join ourselves to the LORD
6 in an eternal covenant, never to be forgotten. My people were lost
sheep. Their shepherds misled them and set them loose in the mountains.
They wandered from mountain to hilltop and forgot their own resting place.
7 All who encountered them devoured them. Her tormentors said, "We are not
to blame because they sinned against the LORD, Righteous Pasture; the LORD,
8 the hope of their ancestors." Wander away from the midst of Babylon,
depart from the land of the Chaldeans, and be like male goats at the head of
9 the flock. For I am about to arouse and bring up against Babylon an assembly
of great nations from the land of the north. They will array themselves in
battle formation about her and capture her there. Their arrows are those of a
10 murderous warrior who does not miss his mark. The Chaldeans shall become
11 spoils, and all those that spoil her will be sated, declares the LORD. For you
have rejoiced, you have celebrated, you who pillage My possession. You
12 stomped like a threshing calf and neighed like stallions. Your mother is greatly
shamed; the one who gave birth to you is disgraced. Look, the end of the
13 nations will be wilderness, parched land, and desert. Because of the LORD's
anger, she will not be inhabited and shall become entirely desolate. All who
14 pass by Babylon shall be stunned and shall shriek over her wounds. Array
yourselves in battle formation surrounding Babylon, all you that bend the
bow. Shoot at her and spare no arrow, for she has sinned against the LORD.
15 Shout against her from all sides; she has raised her hand in surrender. Her
foundations have fallen; her walls are destroyed. It is the LORD's revenge, so
16 take revenge on her. What she did, do to her. Cut off the sower from Babylon
and he who wields the scythe at the time of the harvest. Because of the sword
of the oppressor, everyone will turn back to his people and everyone will flee
17 to his land. A scattered sheep is Israel; lions have driven it away. The
king of Assyria was the first to devour it, and now this last one, Nevukhadretzar,

104 | Two names for the chief Babylonian god.

לז וְלֹא־יִהְיֶה הַגּוֹי אֲשֶׁר לֹא־יָבוֹא שָׁם נִדְּחֵי עוֹלָם: וְהַחְתַּתִּי אֶת־עֵילָם עֵילָם
לִפְנֵי אֹיְבֵיהֶם וְלִפְנֵי ׀ מְבַקְשֵׁי נַפְשָׁם וְהֵבֵאתִי עֲלֵיהֶם ׀ רָעָה אֶת־חֲרוֹן
לח אַפִּי נְאֻם־יְהוָה וְשִׁלַּחְתִּי אַחֲרֵיהֶם אֶת־הַחֶרֶב עַד כַּלּוֹתִי אוֹתָם: וְשַׂמְתִּי
לט כִסְאִי בְּעֵילָם וְהַאֲבַדְתִּי מִשָּׁם מֶלֶךְ וְשָׂרִים נְאֻם־יְהוָה: וְהָיָה ׀ בְּאַחֲרִית
נ א הַיָּמִים אשוב אֶת־שבית עֵילָם נְאֻם־יְהוָה: הַדָּבָר אֲשֶׁר אָשִׁיב | שְׁבוּת
ב דִּבֶּר יְהוָה אֶל־בָּבֶל אֶל־אֶרֶץ כַּשְׂדִּים בְּיַד יִרְמְיָהוּ הַנָּבִיא: הַגִּידוּ
בַגּוֹיִם וְהַשְׁמִיעוּ וּשְׂאוּ־נֵס הַשְׁמִיעוּ אַל־תְּכַחֵדוּ אִמְרוּ נִלְכְּדָה בָבֶל
ג הֹבִישׁ בֵּל חַת מְרֹדָךְ הֹבִישׁוּ עֲצַבֶּיהָ חַתּוּ גִּלּוּלֶיהָ: כִּי עָלָה עָלֶיהָ גּוֹי
מִצָּפוֹן הוּא־יָשִׁית אֶת־אַרְצָהּ לְשַׁמָּה וְלֹא־יִהְיֶה יוֹשֵׁב בָּהּ מֵאָדָם
ד וְעַד־בְּהֵמָה נָדוּ הָלָכוּ: בַּיָּמִים הָהֵמָּה וּבָעֵת הַהִיא נְאֻם־יְהוָה יָבֹאוּ
בְנֵי־יִשְׂרָאֵל הֵמָּה וּבְנֵי־יְהוּדָה יַחְדָּו הָלוֹךְ וּבָכוֹ יֵלֵכוּ וְאֶת־יְהוָה
ה אֱלֹהֵיהֶם יְבַקֵּשׁוּ: צִיּוֹן יִשְׁאָלוּ דֶּרֶךְ הֵנָּה פְנֵיהֶם בֹּאוּ וְנִלְווּ אֶל־יְהוָה כט
ו בְּרִית עוֹלָם לֹא תִשָּׁכֵחַ: צֹאן אֹבְדוֹת היה עַמִּי רֹעֵיהֶם הָיוּ
ז התעום הָרִים שׁובבים מֵהַר אֶל־גִּבְעָה הָלָכוּ שָׁכְחוּ רִבְצָם: כָּל־ שׁוֹבְבוּם
מוֹצְאֵיהֶם אֲכָלוּם וְצָרֵיהֶם אָמְרוּ לֹא נֶאְשָׁם תַּחַת אֲשֶׁר חָטְאוּ לַיהוָה
ח נְוֵה־צֶדֶק וּמִקְוֵה אֲבוֹתֵיהֶם יְהוָה: נֻדוּ מִתּוֹךְ בָּבֶל
ט וּמֵאֶרֶץ כַּשְׂדִּים יצאו וִהְיוּ כְּעַתּוּדִים לִפְנֵי־צֹאן: כִּי הִנֵּה אָנֹכִי מֵעִיר צֵאוּ
וּמַעֲלֶה עַל־בָּבֶל קְהַל־גּוֹיִם גְּדֹלִים מֵאֶרֶץ צָפוֹן וְעָרְכוּ לָהּ מִשָּׁם תִּלָּכֵד
י חִצָּיו כְּגִבּוֹר מַשְׁכִּיל לֹא יָשׁוּב רֵיקָם: וְהָיְתָה כַשְׂדִּים לְשָׁלָל כָּל־שֹׁלְלֶיהָ תִשְׂמְחוּ
יא יִשְׂבָּעוּ נְאֻם־יְהוָה: כִּי תשמחי כִּי תעלזי שֹׁסֵי נַחֲלָתִי כִּי תפושי כְּעֶגְלָה תַעַלְזוּ | תָפוּשׁוּ
יב דָשָׁה ותצהלי כָּאֲבִּרִים: בּוֹשָׁה אִמְּכֶם מְאֹד חָפְרָה יוֹלַדְתְּכֶם הִנֵּה וְתִצְהֲלוּ
יג אַחֲרִית גּוֹיִם מִדְבָּר צִיָּה וַעֲרָבָה: מִקֶּצֶף יְהוָה לֹא תֵשֵׁב וְהָיְתָה שְׁמָמָה
יד כֻּלָּהּ כֹּל עֹבֵר עַל־בָּבֶל יִשֹּׁם וְיִשְׁרֹק עַל־כָּל־מַכּוֹתֶיהָ: עִרְכוּ עַל־בָּבֶל ׀
סָבִיב כָּל־דֹּרְכֵי קֶשֶׁת יְדוּ אֵלֶיהָ אַל־תַּחְמְלוּ אֶל־חֵץ כִּי לַיהוָה חָטָאָה:
טו הָרִיעוּ עָלֶיהָ סָבִיב נָתְנָה יָדָהּ נָפְלוּ אשויתיה נֶהֶרְסוּ חוֹמוֹתֶיהָ כִּי אָשְׁיוֹתֶיהָ
טז נִקְמַת יְהוָה הִיא הִנָּקְמוּ בָהּ כַּאֲשֶׁר עָשְׂתָה עֲשׂוּ־לָהּ: כִּרְתוּ זוֹרֵעַ
מִבָּבֶל וְתֹפֵשׂ מַגָּל בְּעֵת קָצִיר מִפְּנֵי חֶרֶב הַיּוֹנָה אִישׁ אֶל־עַמּוֹ יִפְנוּ
יז וְאִישׁ לְאַרְצוֹ יָנֻסוּ: שֶׂה פְזוּרָה יִשְׂרָאֵל אֲרָיוֹת הִדִּיחוּ
הָרִאשׁוֹן אֲכָלוֹ מֶלֶךְ אַשּׁוּר וְזֶה הָאַחֲרוֹן עִצְּמוֹ נְבוּכַדְרֶאצַּר מֶלֶךְ

18 king of Babylon, has gnawed its bones. Therefore, this is what the LORD of
Hosts, God of Israel, said: I shall now bring retribution upon the king of
19 Babylon and upon his land just as I did to the king of Assyria. I shall return
Israel to his pasture; he shall graze on the Carmel and the Bashan and will
20 satisfy himself upon the Efrayim hills and Gilad. In those days and at that
time, declares the LORD, the sin of Israel will be sought but will be gone; and
the sins of Yehuda too, but they will not be found, for I will forgive those
21 whom I will spare. Go up against her, the land of Meratayim, and
against the inhabitants of Pekod;[105] attack them by the sword and destroy
them wherever they flee, declares the LORD. Do exactly as I command you.
22 There is the sound of war in the land and of a great collapse. How the hammer
23 of the entire earth has been cut down and broken! How Babylon has become
24 an astonishment among nations! I set a trap for you, and you were ensnared,
Babylon! You were caught by surprise. You were discovered, and you were
25 seized, for you strove against the LORD. The LORD has opened His armory
and extracted the weapons of His wrath, for this is a mission that the Lord
26 GOD of Hosts is pursuing in the land of the Chaldeans. Come upon her from
the farthest border; open her granaries, tread upon her as upon bundles of
27 grain, and destroy her completely. Let there be no remnant of her. Slay all her
young bulls. Let them go down to the slaughter. Woe to them, for their day
28 has come, the moment of their retribution. The sound of those who flee,
refugees from the land of Babylon, to tell in Zion of the vengeance of the
29 LORD our God, vengeance for His Temple. Summon archers against Babylon;
let everyone who bends the bow encamp around her; let none escape. Repay
her according to her actions; do to her all that she did, for she has acted
30 arrogantly toward the LORD, toward the Holy One of Israel. Therefore her
young lads shall lie fallen in her squares, and all who fought in her war shall
31 be still on that day, declares the LORD. I am against you, arrogant
one, declares the Lord GOD of Hosts, for your day has come, the moment
32 when I will hold you to account. The arrogant one will stumble and fall and
will have no one to lift him. I shall set fire to his cities, and it will consume all
33 its surroundings. This is what the LORD of Hosts said: The people
of Israel are oppressed, and the people of Yehuda along with them. Their
34 captors have all held them fast and have refused to set them free. Their
redeemer is strong; the LORD of Hosts is His name. He will take up their
35 cause: He will calm the land and disquiet the inhabitants of Babylon. A sword
upon the Chaldeans, declares the LORD, and upon the inhabitants of Babylon,
36 its officials, and its wise men. A sword upon the diviners; they shall be made
37 fools. A sword upon her mighty men; they shall be broken. A sword upon his
horses and chariots and upon the foreign troops in her midst; they shall
become as weak as women. A sword upon her treasuries; they shall be looted.
38 A drought upon her waters; they shall dry up. For it is a land of graven images
39 and acts as if mad before its dreadful deities. Therefore, weasels shall dwell
there with wildcats, and owls shall dwell there, but it will never again be

105 | The location of Meratayim is unknown. Pekod is a region of southern Babylonia.

יח בָּבֶל: לָכֵן כֹּה־אָמַר יהוה צְבָאוֹת אֱלֹהֵי יִשְׂרָאֵל הִנְנִי פֹקֵד אֶל־
יט מֶלֶךְ בָּבֶל וְאֶל־אַרְצוֹ כַּאֲשֶׁר פָּקַדְתִּי אֶל־מֶלֶךְ אַשּׁוּר: וְשֹׁבַבְתִּי
אֶת־יִשְׂרָאֵל אֶל־נָוֵהוּ וְרָעָה הַכַּרְמֶל וְהַבָּשָׁן וּבְהַר אֶפְרַיִם וְהַגִּלְעָד
כ תִּשְׂבַּע נַפְשׁוֹ: בַּיָּמִים הָהֵם וּבָעֵת הַהִיא נְאֻם־יהוה יְבֻקַּשׁ אֶת־עֲוֺן
יִשְׂרָאֵל וְאֵינֶנּוּ וְאֶת־חַטֹּאת יְהוּדָה וְלֹא תִמָּצֶאינָה כִּי אֶסְלַח לַאֲשֶׁר
כא אַשְׁאִיר: עַל־הָאָרֶץ מְרָתַיִם עֲלֵה עָלֶיהָ וְאֶל־יוֹשְׁבֵי
פְּקוֹד חֲרֹב וְהַחֲרֵם אַחֲרֵיהֶם נְאֻם־יהוה וַעֲשֵׂה כְּכֹל אֲשֶׁר צִוִּיתִיךָ:
כב כג קוֹל מִלְחָמָה בָּאָרֶץ וְשֶׁבֶר גָּדוֹל: אֵיךְ נִגְדַּע וַיִּשָּׁבֵר פַּטִּישׁ כָּל־הָאָרֶץ
כד אֵיךְ הָיְתָה לְשַׁמָּה בָּבֶל בַּגּוֹיִם: יָקֹשְׁתִּי לָךְ וְגַם־נִלְכַּדְתְּ בָּבֶל וְאַתְּ לֹא
כה יָדָעַתְּ נִמְצֵאת וְגַם־נִתְפַּשְׂתְּ כִּי בַיהוה הִתְגָּרִית: פָּתַח יהוה אֶת־
אוֹצָרוֹ וַיּוֹצֵא אֶת־כְּלֵי זַעְמוֹ כִּי־מְלָאכָה הִיא לַאדֹנָי יֱהוִה צְבָאוֹת
כו בְּאֶרֶץ כַּשְׂדִּים: בֹּאוּ־לָהּ מִקֵּץ פִּתְחוּ מַאֲבֻסֶיהָ סָלּוּהָ כְמוֹ־עֲרֵמִים
כז וְהַחֲרִימוּהָ אַל־תְּהִי־לָהּ שְׁאֵרִית: חִרְבוּ כָּל־פָּרֶיהָ יֵרְדוּ לַטָּבַח הוֹי
כח עֲלֵיהֶם כִּי־בָא יוֹמָם עֵת פְּקֻדָּתָם: קוֹל נָסִים וּפְלֵטִים מֵאֶרֶץ בָּבֶל
כט לְהַגִּיד בְּצִיּוֹן אֶת־נִקְמַת יהוה אֱלֹהֵינוּ נִקְמַת הֵיכָלוֹ: הַשְׁמִיעוּ אֶל־
בָּבֶל | רַבִּים כָּל־דֹּרְכֵי קֶשֶׁת חֲנוּ עָלֶיהָ סָבִיב אַל־יְהִי־ פְּלֵיטָה לָהּ
שַׁלְּמוּ־לָהּ כְּפָעֳלָהּ כְּכֹל אֲשֶׁר עָשְׂתָה עֲשׂוּ־לָהּ כִּי אֶל־יהוה זָדָה
ל אֶל־קְדוֹשׁ יִשְׂרָאֵל: לָכֵן יִפְּלוּ בַחוּרֶיהָ בִּרְחֹבֹתֶיהָ וְכָל־אַנְשֵׁי מִלְחַמְתָּהּ
לא יִדַּמּוּ בַּיּוֹם הַהוּא נְאֻם־יהוה: הִנְנִי אֵלֶיךָ זָדוֹן נְאֻם־אֲדֹנָי
לב יֱהוִה צְבָאוֹת כִּי בָּא יוֹמְךָ עֵת פְּקַדְתִּיךָ: וְכָשַׁל זָדוֹן וְנָפַל וְאֵין לוֹ
לג מֵקִים וְהִצַּתִּי אֵשׁ בְּעָרָיו וְאָכְלָה כָּל־סְבִיבֹתָיו: כֹּה אָמַר
יהוה צְבָאוֹת עֲשׁוּקִים בְּנֵי־יִשְׂרָאֵל וּבְנֵי־יְהוּדָה יַחְדָּו וְכָל־שֹׁבֵיהֶם
לד הֶחֱזִיקוּ בָם מֵאֲנוּ שַׁלְּחָם: גֹּאֲלָם | חָזָק יהוה צְבָאוֹת שְׁמוֹ רִיב יָרִיב
לה אֶת־רִיבָם לְמַעַן הִרְגִּיעַ אֶת־הָאָרֶץ וְהִרְגִּיז לְיֹשְׁבֵי בָבֶל: חֶרֶב עַל־
לו כַּשְׂדִּים נְאֻם־יהוה וְאֶל־יֹשְׁבֵי בָבֶל וְאֶל־שָׂרֶיהָ וְאֶל־חֲכָמֶיהָ: חֶרֶב
לז אֶל־הַבַּדִּים וְנֹאָלוּ חֶרֶב אֶל־גִּבּוֹרֶיהָ וָחָתּוּ: חֶרֶב אֶל־סוּסָיו וְאֶל־רִכְבּוֹ
וְאֶל־כָּל־הָעֶרֶב אֲשֶׁר בְּתוֹכָהּ וְהָיוּ לְנָשִׁים חֶרֶב אֶל־אוֹצְרֹתֶיהָ וּבֻזָּזוּ:
לח לט חֹרֶב אֶל־מֵימֶיהָ וְיָבֵשׁוּ כִּי אֶרֶץ פְּסִלִים הִיא וּבָאֵימִים יִתְהֹלָלוּ: לָכֵן
יֵשְׁבוּ צִיִּים אֶת־אִיִּים וְיָשְׁבוּ בָהּ בְּנוֹת יַעֲנָה וְלֹא־תֵשֵׁב עוֹד לָנֶצַח וְלֹא

40 inhabited by humans and never be settled, in any generation. As God
overthrew Sedom and Amora and their neighbors, declares the LORD, so shall
41 no one dwell there, and no human stay within her. A people is coming down
from the north; a great nation with many kings awakens from the remote
42 parts of the earth. They shall grasp bow and spear; they are cruel and have no
mercy. The sound of them roars like the sea, and they ride upon horses
43 arrayed like men of war against you, daughter Babylon. The king of Babylon
heard a report of them, and his hands became feeble. Anguish gripped him;
44 he shook like a woman in childbirth. Look, like a lion rising up from the
thicket of the Jordan against the secure pasture, in a moment I will drive him
away from it. I will visit upon him whomever I choose, for who is like Me, and
who can summon Me? Who is the shepherd who can stand up against Me?
45 Therefore, hear the counsel that the LORD has taken against Babylon and His
thoughts regarding the land of the Chaldeans: Surely the weakest of the sheep
46 shall drive him away; surely he will render their pasture desolate. The land
trembles at the sound of Babylon's capture, and a cry is heard among the
51 1 nations. This is what the LORD said: I am about to stir up against
Babylon, and against the hearts of those who dwell there and oppose Me,[106] a
2 destructive spirit. I shall incite foreigners against Babylon who shall scatter
3 her and empty out her land as they encircle her on the day of disaster. To him
who bends his bow and to him who takes pride in his armor: do not pity her
4 young men; completely destroy her army. Let them fall as corpses in the land
5 of the Chaldeans and as wounded in her streets. For Israel has not been
forsaken, nor Yehuda by his God, by the LORD of Hosts, although their land
6 is full of sin against the Holy One of Israel. Flee from the midst of Babylon;
let each one save his own life lest he be cut down along with her[107] sin, for this
is a moment of vengeance for the LORD; He is paying her that which she
7 deserves. Babylon is like a golden cup in the hand of the LORD, intoxicating
the entire land. The nations drank of her wine; therefore the nations have
8 gone mad. Suddenly Babylon fell and has been broken. Wail for her; apply
9 balm to her pain – perhaps she will be healed. We have tended to Babylon,
but she has not been healed. Abandon her, and let each one of us return to
his land, for her judgment has reached heavenward and has been lifted into
10 the skies. The LORD has brought forth our vindication. Come! Let us relate
11 in Zion the deeds of the LORD our God. Polish the arrows; gather the shields.
The LORD has stirred up the spirit of the kings of Media,[108] for He has designs
upon Babylon to destroy her. This is the LORD's vengeance, vengeance for
12 His Temple. Raise a banner upon the walls of Babylon. Strengthen the watch,
set up watchmen, and prepare ambushes, for the LORD planned and has
13 carried out what He had spoken against the inhabitants of Babylon. You who
dwelled upon mighty waters, rich in treasures – your end has come, retribution
14 for your crime. The LORD of Hosts has sworn by Himself that He will fill

---

106 | Hebrew *lev kamai*, i.e., the Chaldeans (*Kasdim*), written in the *atbash* cipher.

107 | Babylon's.

108 | Media was located east of Babylon. Babylon would later be conquered by Cyrus, the king of Media.

מ תִשְׁכּוֹן עַד־דּוֹר וָדֹר׃ כְּמַהְפֵּכַת אֱלֹהִים אֶת־סְדֹם וְאֶת־עֲמֹרָה וְאֶת־
מא שְׁכֵנֶיהָ נְאֻם־יהוה לֹא־יֵשֵׁב שָׁם אִישׁ וְלֹא־יָגוּר בָּהּ בֶּן־אָדָם׃ הִנֵּה
מב עַם בָּא מִצָּפוֹן וְגוֹי גָּדוֹל וּמְלָכִים רַבִּים יֵעֹרוּ מִיַּרְכְּתֵי־אָרֶץ׃ קֶשֶׁת
וְכִידֹן יַחֲזִיקוּ אַכְזָרִי הֵמָּה וְלֹא יְרַחֵמוּ קוֹלָם כַּיָּם יֶהֱמֶה וְעַל־סוּסִים
מג יִרְכָּבוּ עָרוּךְ כְּאִישׁ לַמִּלְחָמָה עָלַיִךְ בַּת־בָּבֶל׃ שָׁמַע מֶלֶךְ־בָּבֶל אֶת־
מד שִׁמְעָם וְרָפוּ יָדָיו צָרָה הֶחֱזִיקַתְהוּ חִיל כַּיּוֹלֵדָה׃ הִנֵּה כְּאַרְיֵה יַעֲלֶה
מִגְּאוֹן הַיַּרְדֵּן אֶל־נְוֵה אֵיתָן כִּי־אַרְגִּעָה ארוצם מֵעָלֶיהָ וּמִי בָחוּר אֲרִיצֵם
אֵלֶיהָ אֶפְקֹד כִּי מִי כָמוֹנִי וּמִי יוֹעִדֶנִּי וּמִי־זֶה רֹעֶה אֲשֶׁר יַעֲמֹד
מה לְפָנָי׃ לָכֵן שִׁמְעוּ עֲצַת־יהוה אֲשֶׁר יָעַץ אֶל־בָּבֶל וּמַחְשְׁבוֹתָיו אֲשֶׁר
חָשַׁב אֶל־אֶרֶץ כַּשְׂדִּים אִם־לֹא יִסְחָבוּם צְעִירֵי הַצֹּאן אִם־לֹא יַשִּׁים
מו עֲלֵיהֶם נָוֶה׃ מִקּוֹל נִתְפְּשָׂה בָבֶל נִרְעֲשָׁה הָאָרֶץ וּזְעָקָה בַּגּוֹיִם
נא א נִשְׁמָע׃ כֹּה אָמַר יהוה הִנְנִי מֵעִיר עַל־בָּבֶל וְאֶל־
ב יֹשְׁבֵי לֵב קָמָי רוּחַ מַשְׁחִית׃ וְשִׁלַּחְתִּי לְבָבֶל ׀ זָרִים וְזֵרוּהָ וִיבֹקְקוּ
ג אֶת־אַרְצָהּ כִּי־הָיוּ עָלֶיהָ מִסָּבִיב בְּיוֹם רָעָה׃ אֶל־ידרך יִדְרֹךְ הַדֹּרֵךְ
קַשְׁתּוֹ וְאֶל־יִתְעַל בְּסִרְיֹנוֹ וְאַל־תַּחְמְלוּ אֶל־בַּחֻרֶיהָ הַחֲרִימוּ כָּל־
ד ה צְבָאָהּ׃ וְנָפְלוּ חֲלָלִים בְּאֶרֶץ כַּשְׂדִּים וּמְדֻקָּרִים בְּחוּצוֹתֶיהָ׃ כִּי לֹא־
אַלְמָן יִשְׂרָאֵל וִיהוּדָה מֵאֱלֹהָיו מֵיהוה צְבָאוֹת כִּי אַרְצָם מָלְאָה אָשָׁם
ו מִקְּדוֹשׁ יִשְׂרָאֵל׃ נֻסוּ ׀ מִתּוֹךְ בָּבֶל וּמַלְּטוּ אִישׁ נַפְשׁוֹ אַל־תִּדַּמּוּ בַּעֲוֺנָהּ
ז כִּי עֵת נְקָמָה הִיא לַיהוה גְּמוּל הוּא מְשַׁלֵּם לָהּ׃ כּוֹס־זָהָב בָּבֶל בְּיַד־
יהוה מְשַׁכֶּרֶת כָּל־הָאָרֶץ מִיֵּינָהּ שָׁתוּ גוֹיִם עַל־כֵּן יִתְהֹלְלוּ גוֹיִם׃
ח פִּתְאֹם נָפְלָה בָבֶל וַתִּשָּׁבֵר הֵילִילוּ עָלֶיהָ קְחוּ צֳרִי לְמַכְאוֹבָהּ אוּלַי
ט תֵּרָפֵא׃ רִפִּאנוּ אֶת־בָּבֶל וְלֹא נִרְפָּתָה עִזְבוּהָ וְנֵלֵךְ אִישׁ לְאַרְצוֹ כִּי־
י נָגַע אֶל־הַשָּׁמַיִם מִשְׁפָּטָהּ וְנִשָּׂא עַד־שְׁחָקִים׃ הוֹצִיא יהוה אֶת־ ל
יא צִדְקֹתֵינוּ בֹּאוּ וּנְסַפְּרָה בְצִיּוֹן אֶת־מַעֲשֵׂה יהוה אֱלֹהֵינוּ׃ הָבֵרוּ הַחִצִּים
מִלְאוּ הַשְּׁלָטִים הֵעִיר יהוה אֶת־רוּחַ מַלְכֵי מָדַי כִּי־עַל־בָּבֶל מְזִמָּתוֹ
יב לְהַשְׁחִיתָהּ כִּי־נִקְמַת יהוה הִיא נִקְמַת הֵיכָלוֹ׃ אֶל־חוֹמֹת בָּבֶל שְׂאוּ־
נֵס הַחֲזִיקוּ הַמִּשְׁמָר הָקִימוּ שֹׁמְרִים הָכִינוּ הָאֹרְבִים כִּי גַּם־זָמַם יהוה
יג גַּם־עָשָׂה אֵת אֲשֶׁר־דִּבֶּר אֶל־יֹשְׁבֵי בָבֶל׃ שכנתי עַל־מַיִם רַבִּים רַבַּת שֹׁכַנְתְּ
יד אוֹצָרֹת בָּא קִצֵּךְ אַמַּת בִּצְעֵךְ׃ נִשְׁבַּע יהוה צְבָאוֹת בְּנַפְשׁוֹ כִּי אִם־

you with men as numerous as locusts, and they will shout over you, "*Hei-*
15 *dad*!"[109] He makes the earth by His power, establishes the world by
16 His wisdom, and stretches out the heavens by His understanding.[110] As He
makes His voice heard, there is rumbling water in the heavens, and clouds
rise from the ends of the earth. He makes lightning bolts with the rain and
17 brings out winds from His storehouses. All humans are foolish, without
knowledge. Every goldsmith is disappointed in his idol: his molten image is
18 a sham; no breath animates them. They are delusions, works of mockery.
19 When they are called to account, they will perish. Not like these is the portion
of Yaakov, for He formed all things, and Israel is the tribe He possesses; LORD
20 of Hosts is His name. You are a sledgehammer for Me, a weapon of
21 war. With you I will shatter nations; with you I will destroy kingdoms. With
you I will shatter horse and rider; with you I will shatter chariot and driver.
22 With you I will shatter man and woman; with you I will shatter old and young;
23 with you I will shatter lad and lass. With you I will shatter the shepherd and
his flock; with you I will shatter the farmer and his team; with you I will
24 shatter governors and deputies. I will repay Babylon and all the inhabitants
of Chaldea for all the evil they did to Zion before your eyes, declares the
25 LORD. Look, I am against you, destructive mountain, declares the
LORD, that destroys all the earth. I shall stretch out My hand against you and
roll you down from the cliffs. I shall make of you a burned-out mountain.
26 They shall not take from you even a cornerstone or a foundation stone, for
27 you shall remain a wasteland forever, declares the LORD. Raise a banner in
the land, sound a ram's horn among the nations, prepare nations against her,
assemble upon her the kingdoms of Ararat, Mini, and Ashkenaz,[111] appoint a
chieftain over her, and bring up horses like a swarm of bristling locusts.
28 Prepare nations for war against her: the kings of Media, her governors and
29 all her deputies, and all the lands under their rule. The land will shake and
tremble, for the LORD's designs against Babylon shall stand: to make of the
30 land of Babylon a desolation with no inhabitant. The mighty of Babylon have
ceased waging war. They remain in fortresses. Their strength is gone. They
have become like women: her dwellings were set on fire; her bolts are broken.
31 Runner runs to meet runner and herald to meet herald, to tell the king of
32 Babylon that his city has been taken from end to end. The river crossings are
33 seized, the marshes burned in fire; the men of war feel panic. For
this is what the LORD of Hosts, God of Israel, said: Daughter Babylon is like
a threshing floor at the time we tread upon it. In but an instant her reaping
34 season will arrive. "Nevukhadretzar, the king of Babylon, has devoured me,
crushed me, set me up as an empty vessel, swallowed me as a crocodile does,
35 filled his belly with my delicacies, cast me away. My stolen possessions and
my flesh are upon Babylon," says she who dwells in Zion. "My blood is upon
36 the inhabitants of Chaldea," says Jerusalem. Therefore, this is what

109 | See note on 25:30.
110 | Cf. 10:12–16.
111 | Three kingdoms located north of Mesopotamia, allies or subjects of the Medes.

טו מִלֵּאתִיךְ אָדָם כַּיֶּלֶק וְעָנוּ עָלַיִךְ הֵידָד׃ עֹשֵׂה אֶרֶץ בְּכֹחוֹ
טז מֵכִין תֵּבֵל בְּחָכְמָתוֹ וּבִתְבוּנָתוֹ נָטָה שָׁמָיִם׃ לְקוֹל תִּתּוֹ הֲמוֹן מַיִם
בַּשָּׁמַיִם וַיַּעַל נְשִׂאִים מִקְצֵה־אָרֶץ בְּרָקִים לַמָּטָר עָשָׂה וַיּוֹצֵא רוּחַ
יז מֵאֹצְרֹתָיו׃ נִבְעַר כָּל־אָדָם מִדַּעַת הֹבִישׁ כָּל־צֹרֵף מִפָּסֶל כִּי שֶׁקֶר
יח נִסְכּוֹ וְלֹא־רוּחַ בָּם׃ הֶבֶל הֵמָּה מַעֲשֵׂה תַּעְתֻּעִים בְּעֵת פְּקֻדָּתָם יֹאבֵדוּ׃
יט לֹא־כְאֵלֶּה חֵלֶק יַעֲקוֹב כִּי־יוֹצֵר הַכֹּל הוּא וְשֵׁבֶט נַחֲלָתוֹ יְהוָה צְבָאוֹת
כ שְׁמוֹ׃ מַפֵּץ־אַתָּה לִי כְּלֵי מִלְחָמָה וְנִפַּצְתִּי בְךָ גּוֹיִם וְהִשְׁחַתִּי
כא כב בְךָ מַמְלָכוֹת׃ וְנִפַּצְתִּי בְךָ סוּס וְרֹכְבוֹ וְנִפַּצְתִּי בְךָ רֶכֶב וְרֹכְבוֹ׃ וְנִפַּצְתִּי
בְךָ אִישׁ וְאִשָּׁה וְנִפַּצְתִּי בְךָ זָקֵן וָנָעַר וְנִפַּצְתִּי בְךָ בָּחוּר וּבְתוּלָה׃
כג וְנִפַּצְתִּי בְךָ רֹעֶה וְעֶדְרוֹ וְנִפַּצְתִּי בְךָ אִכָּר וְצִמְדּוֹ וְנִפַּצְתִּי בְךָ פַּחוֹת
כד וּסְגָנִים׃ וְשִׁלַּמְתִּי לְבָבֶל וּלְכֹל ׀ יוֹשְׁבֵי כַשְׂדִּים אֵת כָּל־רָעָתָם אֲשֶׁר־
כה עָשׂוּ בְצִיּוֹן לְעֵינֵיכֶם נְאֻם יְהוָה׃ הִנְנִי אֵלֶיךָ הַר הַמַּשְׁחִית
נְאֻם־יְהוָה הַמַּשְׁחִית אֶת־כָּל־הָאָרֶץ וְנָטִיתִי אֶת־יָדִי עָלֶיךָ וְגִלְגַּלְתִּיךָ
כו מִן־הַסְּלָעִים וּנְתַתִּיךָ לְהַר שְׂרֵפָה׃ וְלֹא־יִקְחוּ מִמְּךָ אֶבֶן לְפִנָּה וְאֶבֶן
כז לְמוֹסָדוֹת כִּי־שִׁמְמוֹת עוֹלָם תִּהְיֶה נְאֻם־יְהוָה׃ שְׂאוּ־נֵס בָּאָרֶץ תִּקְעוּ
שׁוֹפָר בַּגּוֹיִם קַדְּשׁוּ עָלֶיהָ גּוֹיִם הַשְׁמִיעוּ עָלֶיהָ מַמְלְכוֹת אֲרָרַט מִנִּי
כח וְאַשְׁכְּנָז פִּקְדוּ עָלֶיהָ טִפְסָר הַעֲלוּ־סוּס כְּיֶלֶק סָמָר׃ קַדְּשׁוּ עָלֶיהָ גוֹיִם
אֶת־מַלְכֵי מָדַי אֶת־פַּחוֹתֶיהָ וְאֶת־כָּל־סְגָנֶיהָ וְאֵת כָּל־אֶרֶץ מֶמְשַׁלְתּוֹ׃
כט וַתִּרְעַשׁ הָאָרֶץ וַתָּחֹל כִּי קָמָה עַל־בָּבֶל מַחְשְׁבוֹת יְהוָה לָשׂוּם
ל אֶת־אֶרֶץ בָּבֶל לְשַׁמָּה מֵאֵין יוֹשֵׁב׃ חָדְלוּ גִבּוֹרֵי בָבֶל לְהִלָּחֵם יָשְׁבוּ
בַּמְּצָדוֹת נָשְׁתָה גְבוּרָתָם הָיוּ לְנָשִׁים הִצִּיתוּ מִשְׁכְּנֹתֶיהָ נִשְׁבְּרוּ
לא בְרִיחֶיהָ׃ רָץ לִקְרַאת־רָץ יָרוּץ וּמַגִּיד לִקְרַאת מַגִּיד לְהַגִּיד לְמֶלֶךְ
לב בָּבֶל כִּי־נִלְכְּדָה עִירוֹ מִקָּצֶה׃ וְהַמַּעְבָּרוֹת נִתְפָּשׂוּ וְאֶת־הָאֲגַמִּים
לג שָׂרְפוּ בָאֵשׁ וְאַנְשֵׁי הַמִּלְחָמָה נִבְהָלוּ׃ כִּי כֹה
אָמַר יְהוָה צְבָאוֹת אֱלֹהֵי יִשְׂרָאֵל בַּת־בָּבֶל כְּגֹרֶן עֵת הִדְרִיכָהּ עוֹד
לד מְעַט וּבָאָה עֵת־הַקָּצִיר לָהּ׃ אכלנו הממנו נְבוּכַדְרֶאצַּר מֶלֶךְ בָּבֶל
לה הציגנו כְּלִי רִיק בלענו כַּתַּנִּין מִלָּא כְרֵשׂוֹ מֵעֲדָנָי הדיחנו׃ חֲמָסִי
וּשְׁאֵרִי עַל־בָּבֶל תֹּאמַר יֹשֶׁבֶת צִיּוֹן וְדָמִי אֶל־יֹשְׁבֵי כַשְׂדִּים תֹּאמַר
לו יְרוּשָׁלָםִ׃ לָכֵן כֹּה אָמַר יְהוָה הִנְנִי־רָב אֶת־רִיבֵךְ

אֲכָלַנִי הֲמָמַנִי
הִצִּיגַנִי
בְּלָעַנִי | הֱדִיחָנִי

the LORD said: I will take up your cause and take vengeance on your behalf.
37 I will dry up her sea and cause her fountain to evaporate. Babylon will become
heaps of stones, a haunt of jackals, a desolation and a place of shrieking, with
38 no inhabitant. They will roar in unison like young lions and bray like lion
39 cubs. When they are warm, I shall set out their drink. I shall intoxicate them
so that they will revel. They shall sleep an everlasting sleep and never awaken,
40 declares the LORD. I shall lead them down like sheep to be slaughtered, like
41 rams together with male goats. How Sheshakh[112] has been taken captive; the
praise of all the earth been seized! How Babylon has become a desolation
42 among nations! The sea has overcome Babylon; she is enveloped by its raging
43 waves. Her towns have become desolate, parched land and desert. No one
44 dwells in them, and no person passes through them. I shall bring retribution
upon Bel in Babylon; I shall make what he swallowed come up from his
mouth. No longer shall nations stream toward him. Even the wall of Babylon
45 has fallen. Depart from its midst, My people; let each one save himself from
46 the LORD's wrath. Do not be faint of heart and fearful at the rumor that is
heard in the land, and later that year the rumor, and in the next year the rumor
47 and violence in the land, ruler against ruler. Therefore, days are coming when
I shall take retribution upon the graven images of Babylon; its entire land
48 shall be shamed, and all her slain shall fall within her. Heaven and earth and
all that is in them shall rejoice over Babylon, for marauders shall come against
49 her from the north, declares the LORD. Because of Babylon the slain of Israel
50 lie fallen. Because of Babylon the slain of the entire land lie fallen. Survivors
of the sword, go! Do not stand there. Remember the LORD from afar, and
51 call Jerusalem to mind. We are ashamed because we have heard of our disgrace.
Embarrassment has covered our faces, for strangers attacked the holy places
52 of the LORD's House. Therefore, days are coming, declares the LORD,
when I shall take retribution upon her graven images, and all over her land,
53 the slain shall gasp their last gasp. Even should Babylon ascend to the heavens
and fortify the heights of her strength, marauders shall descend upon her
54 from Me, declares the LORD. The sound of a cry from Babylon and of a great
55 collapse from the land of the Chaldeans, for the LORD is marauding Babylon.
Gone from her is her great sound, their waves that would rage like great waters,
56 giving forth their loud sound, for a marauder is coming upon Babylon. Her
mighty men will be taken captive, their bows broken, for a God of recompense
57 is the LORD; He will indeed repay them. I will intoxicate her officials and her
wise men, her governors and her deputies, and her mighty men. They shall
sleep an everlasting sleep and never awaken, declares the King; LORD of
58 Hosts is His name. This is what the LORD of Hosts said: The broad
wall of Babylon shall be demolished, and her high gates shall be set afire.
Peoples shall toil for naught, nations shall earn fiery destruction, and they
59 shall become exhausted. The word that Yirmeyahu the prophet
commanded to Seraya son of Neriya son of Maḥseya when he went with
Tzidkiyahu to Babylon in the fourth year of his reign, and Seraya was his

112 | Babylon; cf. 25:26.

וְנִקַּמְתִּי אֶת־נִקְמָתֵךְ וְהַחֲרַבְתִּי אֶת־יַמָּהּ וְהֹבַשְׁתִּי אֶת־מְקוֹרָהּ׃
לז לח וְהָיְתָה בָבֶל ׀ לְגַלִּים ׀ מְעוֹן־תַּנִּים שַׁמָּה וּשְׁרֵקָה מֵאֵין יוֹשֵׁב׃ יַחְדָּו
לט כַּכְּפִרִים יִשְׁאָגוּ נָעֲרוּ כְּגוֹרֵי אֲרָיוֹת׃ בְּחֻמָּם אָשִׁית אֶת־מִשְׁתֵּיהֶם
וְהִשְׁכַּרְתִּים לְמַעַן יַעֲלֹזוּ וְיָשְׁנוּ שְׁנַת־עוֹלָם וְלֹא יָקִיצוּ נְאֻם יְהוָה׃
מ מא אוֹרִידֵם כְּכָרִים לִטְבוֹחַ כְּאֵילִים עִם־עַתּוּדִים׃ אֵיךְ נִלְכְּדָה שֵׁשַׁךְ
מב וַתִּתָּפֵשׂ תְּהִלַּת כָּל־הָאָרֶץ אֵיךְ הָיְתָה לְשַׁמָּה בָּבֶל בַּגּוֹיִם׃ עָלָה עַל־
מג בָּבֶל הַיָּם בַּהֲמוֹן גַּלָּיו נִכְסָתָה׃ הָיוּ עָרֶיהָ לְשַׁמָּה אֶרֶץ צִיָּה וַעֲרָבָה
מד אֶרֶץ לֹא־יֵשֵׁב בָּהֵן כָּל־אִישׁ וְלֹא־יַעֲבֹר בָּהֵן בֶּן־אָדָם׃ וּפָקַדְתִּי עַל־בֵּל
בְּבָבֶל וְהֹצֵאתִי אֶת־בִּלְעוֹ מִפִּיו וְלֹא־יִנְהֲרוּ אֵלָיו עוֹד גּוֹיִם גַּם־חוֹמַת
מה בָּבֶל נָפָלָה׃ צְאוּ מִתּוֹכָהּ עַמִּי וּמַלְּטוּ אִישׁ אֶת־נַפְשׁוֹ מֵחֲרוֹן אַף־
מו יְהוָה׃ וּפֶן־יֵרַךְ לְבַבְכֶם וְתִירְאוּ בַּשְּׁמוּעָה הַנִּשְׁמַעַת בָּאָרֶץ וּבָא בַשָּׁנָה
הַשְּׁמוּעָה וְאַחֲרָיו בַּשָּׁנָה הַשְּׁמוּעָה וְחָמָס בָּאָרֶץ מֹשֵׁל עַל־מֹשֵׁל׃
מז לָכֵן הִנֵּה יָמִים בָּאִים וּפָקַדְתִּי עַל־פְּסִילֵי בָבֶל וְכָל־אַרְצָהּ תֵּבוֹשׁ
מח וְכָל־חֲלָלֶיהָ יִפְּלוּ בְתוֹכָהּ׃ וְרִנְּנוּ עַל־בָּבֶל שָׁמַיִם וָאָרֶץ וְכֹל אֲשֶׁר בָּהֶם
מט כִּי מִצָּפוֹן יָבוֹא־לָהּ הַשּׁוֹדְדִים נְאֻם־יְהוָה׃ גַּם־בָּבֶל לִנְפֹּל חַלְלֵי
נ יִשְׂרָאֵל גַּם־לְבָבֶל נָפְלוּ חַלְלֵי כָל־הָאָרֶץ׃ פְּלֵטִים מֵחֶרֶב הִלְכוּ אַל־
נא תַּעֲמֹדוּ זִכְרוּ מֵרָחוֹק אֶת־יְהוָה וִירוּשָׁלִַם תַּעֲלֶה עַל־לְבַבְכֶם׃ בֹּשְׁנוּ
כִּי־שָׁמַעְנוּ חֶרְפָּה כִּסְּתָה כְלִמָּה פָּנֵינוּ כִּי בָּאוּ זָרִים עַל־מִקְדְּשֵׁי בֵּית
נב יְהוָה׃ לָכֵן הִנֵּה־יָמִים בָּאִים נְאֻם־יְהוָה וּפָקַדְתִּי עַל־
נג פְּסִילֶיהָ וּבְכָל־אַרְצָהּ יֶאֱנֹק חָלָל׃ כִּי־תַעֲלֶה בָבֶל הַשָּׁמַיִם וְכִי תְבַצֵּר
נד מְרוֹם עֻזָּהּ מֵאִתִּי יָבֹאוּ שֹׁדְדִים לָהּ נְאֻם־יְהוָה׃ קוֹל זְעָקָה מִבָּבֶל
נה וְשֶׁבֶר גָּדוֹל מֵאֶרֶץ כַּשְׂדִּים׃ כִּי־שֹׁדֵד יְהוָה אֶת־בָּבֶל וְאִבַּד מִמֶּנָּה קוֹל
נו גָּדוֹל וְהָמוּ גַלֵּיהֶם כְּמַיִם רַבִּים נִתַּן שְׁאוֹן קוֹלָם׃ כִּי בָא עָלֶיהָ עַל־בָּבֶל
שׁוֹדֵד וְנִלְכְּדוּ גִּבּוֹרֶיהָ חִתְּתָה קַשְּׁתוֹתָם כִּי אֵל גְּמֻלוֹת יְהוָה שַׁלֵּם
נז יְשַׁלֵּם׃ וְהִשְׁכַּרְתִּי שָׂרֶיהָ וַחֲכָמֶיהָ פַּחוֹתֶיהָ וּסְגָנֶיהָ וְגִבּוֹרֶיהָ וְיָשְׁנוּ שְׁנַת־
נח עוֹלָם וְלֹא יָקִיצוּ נְאֻם־הַמֶּלֶךְ יְהוָה צְבָאוֹת שְׁמוֹ׃ כֹּה־
אָמַר יְהוָה צְבָאוֹת חֹמוֹת בָּבֶל הָרְחָבָה עַרְעֵר תִּתְעַרְעָר וּשְׁעָרֶיהָ
הַגְּבֹהִים בָּאֵשׁ יִצַּתּוּ וְיִגְעוּ עַמִּים בְּדֵי־רִיק וּלְאֻמִּים בְּדֵי־אֵשׁ
נט וְיָעֵפוּ׃ הַדָּבָר אֲשֶׁר־צִוָּה ׀ יִרְמְיָהוּ הַנָּבִיא אֶת־שְׂרָיָה לא
בֶּן־נֵרִיָּה בֶּן־מַחְסֵיָה בְּלֶכְתּוֹ אֶת־צִדְקִיָּהוּ מֶלֶךְ־יְהוּדָה בָּבֶל בִּשְׁנַת

60 confidant: Yirmeyahu wrote down all the disasters that would befall Babylon
61 in one scroll; all these words were written concerning Babylon. Yirmeyahu
said to Seraya, "When you arrive in Babylon, see that you read out all these
62 words. Say, 'LORD, You declared that this place shall be cut off, so that there
shall be no inhabitant, neither human nor beast, for it shall be an eternal
63 wasteland.' When you finish reading this scroll, tie a stone to it, cast it into
64 the Euphrates, and say, 'So shall Babylon sink and never rise from the disaster
that I shall bring upon her, and they shall become exhausted.'" The words of
52 1 Yirmeyahu extend to here. Tzidkiyahu was twenty-one years old
when he became king, and for eleven years he reigned in Jerusalem.[113] His
2 mother's name was Ḥamutal, daughter of Yirmeyahu of Livna. He did what
3 was evil in the eyes of the LORD, just as Yehoyakim had done. And because of
the LORD's fury against Jerusalem and Yehuda, He cast them away from His
4 presence. Now Tzidkiyahu rebelled against the king of Babylon. In the
ninth year of his reign, on the tenth day of the tenth month, Nevukhadretzar,
king of Babylon, and all his forces attacked Jerusalem. They encamped against
5 it and built a siege wall all around, and the city remained under siege until
6 the eleventh year of King Tzidkiyahu. By the ninth day of the fourth month,
famine raged so fiercely in the city that there was no food for the people of
7 the land. The city was breached, and all the military men fled and left the city
by the dark of night through the gate between the double walls by the royal
garden, as the Chaldeans surrounded the city, and made toward the Arava.
8 But the Chaldean force pursued the king and caught up with Tzidkiyahu on
9 the plains of Yeriḥo, and all his forces scattered and deserted him. They seized
the king and hauled him up before the king of Babylon at Rivla in the land of
10 Ḥamat, where he spoke harshly to him. The king of Babylon slaughtered
Tzidkiyahu's sons before his eyes. He also slaughtered all the officials of
11 Yehuda in Rivla. He blinded Tzidkiyahu and chained him in bronze fetters,
and the king of Babylon brought him to Babylon and put him in prison until
12 the day of his death. On the tenth day of the fifth month, in the
nineteenth year of the reign of Nevukhadretzar, king of Babylon, Nevuzaradan,
13 chief of the guard, who served the king of Babylon, entered Jerusalem. He
burned down the House of the LORD and the royal palace and all the houses
14 in Jerusalem; he set fire to every important building in Jerusalem. As for all
the walls surrounding Jerusalem, all the Chaldean forces with the chief of the
15 guard tore them down. As for some of the poor people, the rest of the people
who remained in the city, those who defected to the king of Babylon, and
16 the rest of the artisans, Nevuzaradan, chief of the guard, exiled them. But

113 | Cf. 39:1–7; II Kings 24:18–25:7.

ס הָרְבִיעִית לְמָלְכוֹ וּשְׂרָיָה שַׂר מְנוּחָה: וַיִּכְתֹּב יִרְמְיָהוּ אֵת כָּל־הָרָעָה
אֲשֶׁר־תָּבוֹא אֶל־בָּבֶל אֶל־סֵפֶר אֶחָד אֵת כָּל־הַדְּבָרִים הָאֵלֶּה הַכְּתֻבִים
סא אֶל־בָּבֶל: וַיֹּאמֶר יִרְמְיָהוּ אֶל־שְׂרָיָה כְּבֹאֲךָ בָבֶל וְרָאִיתָ וְקָרָאתָ אֵת
סב כָּל־הַדְּבָרִים הָאֵלֶּה: וְאָמַרְתָּ יְהוָה אַתָּה דִבַּרְתָּ אֶל־הַמָּקוֹם הַזֶּה
לְהַכְרִיתוֹ לְבִלְתִּי הֱיוֹת־בּוֹ יוֹשֵׁב לְמֵאָדָם וְעַד־בְּהֵמָה כִּי־שִׁמְמוֹת
סג עוֹלָם תִּהְיֶה: וְהָיָה כְּכַלֹּתְךָ לִקְרֹא אֶת־הַסֵּפֶר הַזֶּה תִּקְשֹׁר עָלָיו
סד אֶבֶן וְהִשְׁלַכְתּוֹ אֶל־תּוֹךְ פְּרָת: וְאָמַרְתָּ כָּכָה תִּשְׁקַע בָּבֶל וְלֹא־
תָקוּם מִפְּנֵי הָרָעָה אֲשֶׁר אָנֹכִי מֵבִיא עָלֶיהָ וְיָעֵפוּ עַד־הֵנָּה דִּבְרֵי
נב א יִרְמְיָהוּ: בֶּן־עֶשְׂרִים וְאַחַת שָׁנָה צִדְקִיָּהוּ בְמָלְכוֹ וְאַחַת
עֶשְׂרֵה שָׁנָה מָלַךְ בִּירוּשָׁלִָם וְשֵׁם אִמּוֹ חמיטל בַּת־יִרְמְיָהוּ מִלִּבְנָה: [חֲמוּטַל]
ב ג וַיַּעַשׂ הָרַע בְּעֵינֵי יְהוָה כְּכֹל אֲשֶׁר־עָשָׂה יְהוֹיָקִים: כִּי ׀ עַל־אַף יְהוָה
הָיְתָה בִירוּשָׁלִַם וִיהוּדָה עַד־הִשְׁלִיכוֹ אוֹתָם מֵעַל פָּנָיו וַיִּמְרֹד צִדְקִיָּהוּ
ד בְּמֶלֶךְ בָּבֶל: וַיְהִי בַשָּׁנָה הַתְּשִׁעִית לְמָלְכוֹ בַּחֹדֶשׁ הָעֲשִׂירִי
בֶּעָשׂוֹר לַחֹדֶשׁ בָּא נְבוּכַדְרֶאצַּר מֶלֶךְ־בָּבֶל הוּא וְכָל־חֵילוֹ עַל־
ה יְרוּשָׁלִַם וַיַּחֲנוּ עָלֶיהָ וַיִּבְנוּ עָלֶיהָ דָּיֵק סָבִיב: וַתָּבֹא הָעִיר בַּמָּצוֹר עַד
ו עַשְׁתֵּי עֶשְׂרֵה שָׁנָה לַמֶּלֶךְ צִדְקִיָּהוּ: בַּחֹדֶשׁ הָרְבִיעִי בְּתִשְׁעָה לַחֹדֶשׁ
ז וַיֶּחֱזַק הָרָעָב בָּעִיר וְלֹא־הָיָה לֶחֶם לְעַם הָאָרֶץ: וַתִּבָּקַע הָעִיר וְכָל־
אַנְשֵׁי הַמִּלְחָמָה יִבְרְחוּ וַיֵּצְאוּ מֵהָעִיר לַיְלָה דֶּרֶךְ שַׁעַר בֵּין־הַחֹמֹתַיִם
אֲשֶׁר עַל־גַּן הַמֶּלֶךְ וְכַשְׂדִּים עַל־הָעִיר סָבִיב וַיֵּלְכוּ דֶּרֶךְ הָעֲרָבָה:
ח וַיִּרְדְּפוּ חֵיל־כַּשְׂדִּים אַחֲרֵי הַמֶּלֶךְ וַיַּשִּׂיגוּ אֶת־צִדְקִיָּהוּ בְּעַרְבֹת יְרֵחוֹ
ט וְכָל־חֵילוֹ נָפֹצוּ מֵעָלָיו: וַיִּתְפְּשׂוּ אֶת־הַמֶּלֶךְ וַיַּעֲלוּ אֹתוֹ אֶל־מֶלֶךְ בָּבֶל
י רִבְלָתָה בְּאֶרֶץ חֲמָת וַיְדַבֵּר אִתּוֹ מִשְׁפָּטִים: וַיִּשְׁחַט מֶלֶךְ־בָּבֶל אֶת־
יא בְּנֵי צִדְקִיָּהוּ לְעֵינָיו וְגַם אֶת־כָּל־שָׂרֵי יְהוּדָה שָׁחַט בְּרִבְלָתָה: וְאֶת־עֵינֵי
צִדְקִיָּהוּ עִוֵּר וַיַּאַסְרֵהוּ בַנְחֻשְׁתַּיִם וַיְבִאֵהוּ מֶלֶךְ־בָּבֶל בָּבֶלָה וַיִּתְּנֵהוּ
יב בבית־הַפְּקֻדֹּת עַד־יוֹם מוֹתוֹ: וּבַחֹדֶשׁ הַחֲמִישִׁי [בֵית־]
בֶּעָשׂוֹר לַחֹדֶשׁ הִיא שְׁנַת תְּשַׁע־עֶשְׂרֵה שָׁנָה לַמֶּלֶךְ נְבוּכַדְרֶאצַּר
מֶלֶךְ־בָּבֶל בָּא נְבוּזַרְאֲדָן רַב־טַבָּחִים עָמַד לִפְנֵי מֶלֶךְ־בָּבֶל בִּירוּשָׁלִָם:
יג וַיִּשְׂרֹף אֶת־בֵּית־יְהוָה וְאֶת־בֵּית הַמֶּלֶךְ וְאֵת כָּל־בָּתֵּי יְרוּשָׁלִַם וְאֶת־
יד כָּל־בֵּית הַגָּדוֹל שָׂרַף בָּאֵשׁ: וְאֶת־כָּל־חֹמוֹת יְרוּשָׁלִַם סָבִיב נָתְצוּ
טו כָּל־חֵיל כַּשְׂדִּים אֲשֶׁר אֶת־רַב־טַבָּחִים: וּמִדַּלּוֹת הָעָם וְאֶת־יֶתֶר
הָעָם ׀ הַנִּשְׁאָרִים בָּעִיר וְאֶת־הַנֹּפְלִים אֲשֶׁר נָפְלוּ אֶל־מֶלֶךְ בָּבֶל וְאֵת
טז יֶתֶר הָאָמוֹן הֶגְלָה נְבוּזַרְאֲדָן רַב־טַבָּחִים: וּמִדַּלּוֹת הָאָרֶץ הִשְׁאִיר

Nevuzaradan, chief of the guard, retained some of the poorest of the land as
17 vine dressers and field workers. The Chaldeans broke down the bronze pillars
of the House of the LORD, the stands, and the Bronze Sea that was in the
18 House of the LORD, and carried all the bronze off to Babylon. They took the
pots, shovels, shears, basins, and spoons and all the bronze vessels that had
19 been used in service, while the chief of the guard took the bowls, firepan,
basins, pots, candelabra, spoons, and jars – whatever was of gold and whatever
20 was of silver. The two pillars, the Molten Sea, the twelve bronze oxen that
were underneath, and the stands that King Shlomo had made for the House
21 of the LORD – the weight in bronze of all these vessels was incalculable. As
for the pillars, each pillar was eighteen cubits high and twelve cubits in
22 circumference. It was four fingers thick and hollow. Its capital was of bronze.
The height of each capital was five cubits. Meshwork and pomegranates
surrounded the capital, all of bronze; and the same for the second pillar and
23 the pomegranates. There were ninety-six pomegranates facing all directions,
24 with room for one hundred pomegranates around the meshwork. The chief
of the guard seized Seraya, the head priest, and Tzefanya, the deputy priest,
25 and the three guardians of the threshold. And from the city, he took one
official who was in charge of the military men, and seven men among the
king's personal attendants who were left in the city, the scribe of the army
commander whose duty was to rally the people of the land, and sixty of the
26 people of the land who were left inside the city. Nevuzaradan, the chief of the
27 guard, took them and led them to the king of Babylon in Rivla, and the king
of Babylon struck them down and put them to death in Rivla, in the land of
28 Ḥamat. Thus Yehuda was exiled from its own soil. These are the people whom
29 Nevukhadretzar exiled in the seventh year: 3,023 people of Yehuda. In the
30 eighteenth year of Nevukhadretzar: 832 persons from Jerusalem. In the
twenty-third year of Nevukhadretzar, Nevuzaradan, chief of the guard, exiled
31 745 people of Yehuda. All the people totaled 4,600. In the thirty-
seventh year following the exile of Yehoyakhin, king of Yehuda, on the twenty-
fifth of the twelfth month, Evvil Merodakh, king of Babylon, in the year he
32 became king, granted Yehoyakhin, king of Yehuda, pardon from prison. He
spoke kindly to him and set his throne above the thrones of the kings who
33 were with him in Babylon. He removed his prison garb, and he dined in his
34 presence for the rest of his life, and he was granted a permanent allowance
from the king of Babylon – a daily allowance for the rest of his life until the
day of his death.

יז נְבוּזַרְאֲדָן רַב־טַבָּחִים לְכֹרְמִים וּלְיֹגְבִים: וְאֶת־עַמּוּדֵי הַנְּחֹשֶׁת אֲשֶׁר
לְבֵית־יְהוָה וְאֶת־הַמְּכֹנוֹת וְאֶת־יָם הַנְּחֹשֶׁת אֲשֶׁר בְּבֵית־יְהוָה שִׁבְּרוּ
יח כַשְׂדִּים וַיִּשְׂאוּ אֶת־כָּל־נְחֻשְׁתָּם בָּבֶלָה: וְאֶת־הַסִּרוֹת וְאֶת־הַיָּעִים
וְאֶת־הַמְזַמְּרוֹת וְאֶת־הַמִּזְרָקֹת וְאֶת־הַכַּפּוֹת וְאֵת כָּל־כְּלֵי הַנְּחֹשֶׁת
יט אֲשֶׁר־יְשָׁרְתוּ בָהֶם לָקָחוּ: וְאֶת־הַסִּפִּים וְאֶת־הַמַּחְתּוֹת וְאֶת־הַמִּזְרָקוֹת
וְאֶת־הַסִּירוֹת וְאֶת־הַמְּנֹרוֹת וְאֶת־הַכַּפּוֹת וְאֶת־הַמְּנַקִּיּוֹת אֲשֶׁר זָהָב
כ זָהָב וַאֲשֶׁר־כֶּסֶף כָּסֶף לָקַח רַב־טַבָּחִים: הָעַמּוּדִים ׀ שְׁנַיִם הַיָּם אֶחָד
וְהַבָּקָר שְׁנֵים־עָשָׂר נְחֹשֶׁת אֲשֶׁר־תַּחַת הַמְּכֹנוֹת אֲשֶׁר עָשָׂה הַמֶּלֶךְ
שְׁלֹמֹה לְבֵית יְהוָה לֹא־הָיָה מִשְׁקָל לִנְחֻשְׁתָּם כָּל־הַכֵּלִים הָאֵלֶּה:
כא וְהָעַמּוּדִים שְׁמֹנֶה עֶשְׂרֵה אַמָּה קומה הָעַמֻּד הָאֶחָד וְחוּט שְׁתֵּים־ (קוֹמַת)
כב עֶשְׂרֵה אַמָּה יְסֻבֶּנּוּ וְעָבְיוֹ אַרְבַּע אֶצְבָּעוֹת נָבוּב: וְכֹתֶרֶת עָלָיו נְחֹשֶׁת
וְקוֹמַת הַכֹּתֶרֶת הָאַחַת חָמֵשׁ אַמּוֹת וּשְׂבָכָה וְרִמּוֹנִים עַל־הַכּוֹתֶרֶת
כג סָבִיב הַכֹּל נְחֹשֶׁת וְכָאֵלֶּה לַעַמּוּד הַשֵּׁנִי וְרִמּוֹנִים: וַיִּהְיוּ הָרִמֹּנִים תִּשְׁעִים
כד וְשִׁשָּׁה רוּחָה כָּל־הָרִמּוֹנִים מֵאָה עַל־הַשְּׂבָכָה סָבִיב: וַיִּקַּח רַב־
טַבָּחִים אֶת־שְׂרָיָה כֹּהֵן הָרֹאשׁ וְאֶת־צְפַנְיָה כֹּהֵן הַמִּשְׁנֶה וְאֶת־שְׁלֹשֶׁת
כה שֹׁמְרֵי הַסַּף: וּמִן־הָעִיר לָקַח סָרִיס אֶחָד אֲשֶׁר־הָיָה פָקִיד ׀ עַל־אַנְשֵׁי
הַמִּלְחָמָה וְשִׁבְעָה אֲנָשִׁים מֵרֹאֵי פְנֵי־הַמֶּלֶךְ אֲשֶׁר נִמְצְאוּ בָעִיר וְאֵת
סֹפֵר שַׂר הַצָּבָא הַמַּצְבִּא אֶת־עַם הָאָרֶץ וְשִׁשִּׁים אִישׁ מֵעַם הָאָרֶץ
כו הַנִּמְצְאִים בְּתוֹךְ הָעִיר: וַיִּקַּח אוֹתָם נְבוּזַרְאֲדָן רַב־טַבָּחִים וַיֵּלֶךְ אוֹתָם
כז אֶל־מֶלֶךְ בָּבֶל רִבְלָתָה: וַיַּכֶּה אוֹתָם מֶלֶךְ בָּבֶל וַיְמִתֵם בְּרִבְלָה בְּאֶרֶץ
כח חֲמָת וַיִּגֶל יְהוּדָה מֵעַל אַדְמָתוֹ: זֶה הָעָם אֲשֶׁר הֶגְלָה נְבוּכַדְרֶאצַּר
כט בִּשְׁנַת־שֶׁבַע יְהוּדִים שְׁלֹשֶׁת אֲלָפִים וְעֶשְׂרִים וּשְׁלֹשָׁה: בִּשְׁנַת שְׁמוֹנֶה
עֶשְׂרֵה לִנְבוּכַדְרֶאצַּר מִירוּשָׁלַם נֶפֶשׁ שְׁמֹנֶה מֵאוֹת שְׁלֹשִׁים וּשְׁנָיִם:
ל בִּשְׁנַת שָׁלֹשׁ וְעֶשְׂרִים לִנְבוּכַדְרֶאצַּר הֶגְלָה נְבוּזַרְאֲדָן רַב־טַבָּחִים
יְהוּדִים נֶפֶשׁ שְׁבַע מֵאוֹת אַרְבָּעִים וַחֲמִשָּׁה כָּל־נֶפֶשׁ אַרְבַּעַת אֲלָפִים
לא וְשֵׁשׁ מֵאוֹת: וַיְהִי בִשְׁלֹשִׁים וָשֶׁבַע שָׁנָה לְגָלוּת יְהוֹיָכִן
מֶלֶךְ־יְהוּדָה בִּשְׁנֵים עָשָׂר חֹדֶשׁ בְּעֶשְׂרִים וַחֲמִשָּׁה לַחֹדֶשׁ נָשָׂא אֱוִיל
מְרֹדַךְ מֶלֶךְ בָּבֶל בִּשְׁנַת מַלְכֻתוֹ אֶת־רֹאשׁ יְהוֹיָכִין מֶלֶךְ־יְהוּדָה וַיֹּצֵא
לב אֹתוֹ מִבֵּית הכליא: וַיְדַבֵּר אִתּוֹ טֹבוֹת וַיִּתֵּן אֶת־כִּסְאוֹ מִמַּעַל לְכִסֵּא (הַכְּלוּא)
לג מלכים אֲשֶׁר אִתּוֹ בְּבָבֶל: וְשִׁנָּה אֵת בִּגְדֵי כִלְאוֹ וְאָכַל לֶחֶם לְפָנָיו (הַמְּלָכִים)
לד תָּמִיד כָּל־יְמֵי חַיָּו: וַאֲרֻחָתוֹ אֲרֻחַת תָּמִיד נִתְּנָה־לּוֹ מֵאֵת מֶלֶךְ־בָּבֶל
דְּבַר־יוֹם בְּיוֹמוֹ עַד־יוֹם מוֹתוֹ כֹּל יְמֵי חַיָּיו:

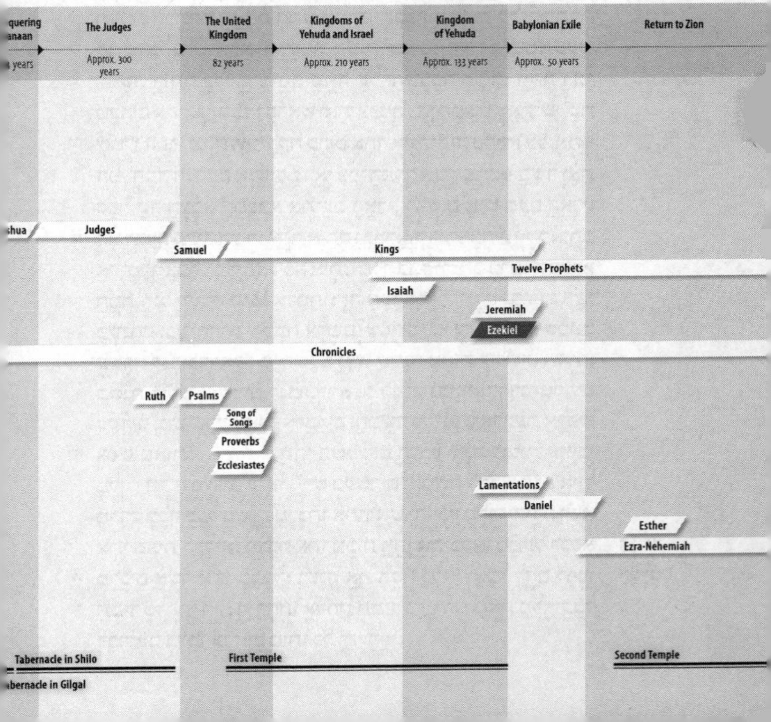

quering
anaan
years
The Judges
Approx. 300 years
The United Kingdom
82 years
Kingdoms of Yehuda and Israel
Approx. 210 years
Kingdom of Yehuda
Approx. 133 years
Babylonian Exile
Approx. 50 years
Return to Zion
shua
Judges
Samuel
Kings
Twelve Prophets
Isaiah
Jeremiah
Ezekiel
Chronicles
Ruth
Psalms
Song of Songs
Proverbs
Ecclesiastes
Lamentations
Daniel
Esther
Ezra-Nehemiah
Tabernacle in Shilo
abernacle in Gilgal
First Temple
Second Temple

יחזקאל

YEHEZKEL/EZEKIEL

EZEKIEL

Initiation into prophecy, and the first message	Prophecies predicting the imminent destruction	Prophetic journey to Jerusalem – the destruction and its environment	Conflict with the people and the false prophets who denied the imminent destruction	Dramatizing the destruction and its environment through parables and descriptions	Prophecies concerning the nations	From destruction to consolation and redemption
Chs. 1–3	4–7	8–11	12–15	16–24	25–32	36–48

Approx. 22 years

1 1 It was in the thirtieth year in the fourth month on the fifth day of the month.
I was in the exile, by the Kevar River; the heavens opened up, and I saw Godly
2 visions. On the fifth day of the month, the fifth year of the exile of King
3 Yoyakhin,[1] so it was: the word of the LORD came to Yeḥezkel son of Buzi the
priest, in the land of the Chaldeans by the Kevar River; there the hand of the
4 LORD was upon him. And I looked: Behold, a storm wind came from the
north, a great cloud and a flaring fire with a radiance around it, and inside it,
5 within the fire, the look of something luminous, and within that was the form
of four living beings. This was their appearance: they had the form of a man;
6 each one had four faces, and each one of them had four wings; their legs were
7 straight-standing, and their feet were like a calf's hoof, gleaming with a look
8 of burnished bronze; they had man's hands beneath their wings on their four
9 sides, and the four of them had faces and wings. Their wings were joined to
each other; they did not turn when they moved but moved in the direction
10 of one of the faces. Their faces were in the form of the face of a man with the
face of a lion on the right of the four, the face of an ox on the left of the four,
11 and the face of an eagle[2] on all four of them. Their faces and their wings were
separated above: each one had two joining it to the others and two covering
12 its body; each moved in the direction of one of the faces – wherever the spirit
13 would move, they moved – they did not turn when they moved. The form of
the living beings, their appearance, was like coals burning, like the appearance
of torch flames; it passed among the living beings; the fire had a radiance,
14 lightning flashed out from the fire, and the living beings ran forward and back
15 with the appearance of darting flames. I looked at the living beings, and
there, a wheel was on the ground beside each of the living beings with the
16 four faces. The appearance of the wheels and their design had the look of an
aquamarine gem, all four of them with the same form; their appearance and
17 their design were as though one wheel were inside the other. When they
moved, they moved on any of their four sides; they did not turn as they
18 moved. Their rims, towering, inspired fear; and the rims of all four of them
19 were covered, all around, with eyes. When the living beings moved, the
wheels moved beside them, and when the living beings rose above the ground,
20 the wheels also rose; wherever the spirit would move, they moved; there
where the spirit moved, the wheels rose with them, for the spirit of the living
21 being was also in the wheels: when they moved, they too moved, and when
they stood still, they too stood still, and when they rose from the ground, the
wheels too rose with them because the spirit of the living being was in the
22 wheels. Above the head of the living being was the form of an expanse with
23 a look of ice, its overawing glare, suspended over their heads from above, and
beneath the expanse, their wings reached out toward each other. Each had a
24 pair covering them; each had a pair covering their bodies. I heard the sound
of their wings when they moved; it was like the sound of great rushing waters,
like the voice of Shaddai, a clamor like the noise of a gathered army. Standing

1 | The year 592 BCE; see II Kings 24:11–17. "The thirtieth year" (v. 1) may be in reference to the Jubilee.
2 | Literally "vulture."

א א וַיְהִי ׀ בִּשְׁלֹשִׁים שָׁנָה בָּרְבִיעִי בַּחֲמִשָּׁה לַחֹדֶשׁ וַאֲנִי בְתוֹךְ־הַגּוֹלָה א
ב עַל־נְהַר־כְּבָר נִפְתְּחוּ הַשָּׁמַיִם וָאֶרְאֶה מַרְאוֹת אֱלֹהִים׃ בַּחֲמִשָּׁה
ג לַחֹדֶשׁ הִיא הַשָּׁנָה הַחֲמִישִׁית לְגָלוּת הַמֶּלֶךְ יוֹיָכִין׃ הָיֹה הָיָה דְבַר־
יְהוָה אֶל־יְחֶזְקֵאל בֶּן־בּוּזִי הַכֹּהֵן בְּאֶרֶץ כַּשְׂדִּים עַל־נְהַר־כְּבָר וַתְּהִי
ד עָלָיו שָׁם יַד־יְהוָה׃ וָאֵרֶא וְהִנֵּה רוּחַ סְעָרָה בָּאָה מִן־הַצָּפוֹן עָנָן גָּדוֹל
וְאֵשׁ מִתְלַקַּחַת וְנֹגַהּ לוֹ סָבִיב וּמִתּוֹכָהּ כְּעֵין הַחַשְׁמַל מִתּוֹךְ הָאֵשׁ׃
ה ו וּמִתּוֹכָהּ דְּמוּת אַרְבַּע חַיּוֹת וְזֶה מַרְאֵיהֶן דְּמוּת אָדָם לָהֵנָּה׃ וְאַרְבָּעָה
ז פָנִים לְאֶחָת וְאַרְבַּע כְּנָפַיִם לְאַחַת לָהֶם׃ וְרַגְלֵיהֶם רֶגֶל יְשָׁרָה וְכַף
ח רַגְלֵיהֶם כְּכַף רֶגֶל עֵגֶל וְנֹצְצִים כְּעֵין נְחֹשֶׁת קָלָל׃ וידו אָדָם מִתַּחַת וִידֵי
ט כַּנְפֵיהֶם עַל אַרְבַּעַת רִבְעֵיהֶם וּפְנֵיהֶם וְכַנְפֵיהֶם לְאַרְבַּעְתָּם׃ חֹבְרֹת
אִשָּׁה אֶל־אֲחוֹתָהּ כַּנְפֵיהֶם לֹא־יִסַּבּוּ בְלֶכְתָּן אִישׁ אֶל־עֵבֶר פָּנָיו יֵלֵכוּ׃
י וּדְמוּת פְּנֵיהֶם פְּנֵי אָדָם וּפְנֵי אַרְיֵה אֶל־הַיָּמִין לְאַרְבַּעְתָּם וּפְנֵי־שׁוֹר
יא מֵהַשְּׂמֹאול לְאַרְבַּעְתָּן וּפְנֵי־נֶשֶׁר לְאַרְבַּעְתָּן׃ וּפְנֵיהֶם וְכַנְפֵיהֶם פְּרֻדוֹת
מִלְמָעְלָה לְאִישׁ שְׁתַּיִם חֹבְרוֹת אִישׁ וּשְׁתַּיִם מְכַסּוֹת אֵת גְּוִיֹתֵיהֶנָה׃
יב וְאִישׁ אֶל־עֵבֶר פָּנָיו יֵלֵכוּ אֶל אֲשֶׁר יִהְיֶה־שָּׁמָּה הָרוּחַ לָלֶכֶת יֵלֵכוּ לֹא
יג יִסַּבּוּ בְּלֶכְתָּן׃ וּדְמוּת הַחַיּוֹת מַרְאֵיהֶם כְּגַחֲלֵי־אֵשׁ בֹּעֲרוֹת כְּמַרְאֵה
הַלַּפִּדִים הִיא מִתְהַלֶּכֶת בֵּין הַחַיּוֹת וְנֹגַהּ לָאֵשׁ וּמִן־הָאֵשׁ יוֹצֵא בָרָק׃
יד טו וְהַחַיּוֹת רָצוֹא וָשׁוֹב כְּמַרְאֵה הַבָּזָק׃ וָאֵרֶא הַחַיּוֹת וְהִנֵּה אוֹפַן אֶחָד
טז בָּאָרֶץ אֵצֶל הַחַיּוֹת לְאַרְבַּעַת פָּנָיו׃ מַרְאֵה הָאוֹפַנִּים וּמַעֲשֵׂיהֶם כְּעֵין
תַּרְשִׁישׁ וּדְמוּת אֶחָד לְאַרְבַּעְתָּן וּמַרְאֵיהֶם וּמַעֲשֵׂיהֶם כַּאֲשֶׁר יִהְיֶה
יז הָאוֹפַן בְּתוֹךְ הָאוֹפָן׃ עַל־אַרְבַּעַת רִבְעֵיהֶן בְּלֶכְתָּם יֵלֵכוּ לֹא יִסַּבּוּ
יח בְּלֶכְתָּן׃ וְגַבֵּיהֶן וְגֹבַהּ לָהֶם וְיִרְאָה לָהֶם וְגַבֹּתָם מְלֵאֹת עֵינַיִם סָבִיב
יט לְאַרְבַּעְתָּן׃ וּבְלֶכֶת הַחַיּוֹת יֵלְכוּ הָאוֹפַנִּים אֶצְלָם וּבְהִנָּשֵׂא הַחַיּוֹת
כ מֵעַל הָאָרֶץ יִנָּשְׂאוּ הָאוֹפַנִּים׃ עַל אֲשֶׁר יִהְיֶה־שָּׁם הָרוּחַ לָלֶכֶת יֵלֵכוּ
שָׁמָּה הָרוּחַ לָלֶכֶת וְהָאוֹפַנִּים יִנָּשְׂאוּ לְעֻמָּתָם כִּי רוּחַ הַחַיָּה בָּאוֹפַנִּים׃
כא בְּלֶכְתָּם יֵלֵכוּ וּבְעָמְדָם יַעֲמֹדוּ וּבְהִנָּשְׂאָם מֵעַל הָאָרֶץ יִנָּשְׂאוּ הָאוֹפַנִּים
כב לְעֻמָּתָם כִּי רוּחַ הַחַיָּה בָּאוֹפַנִּים׃ וּדְמוּת עַל־רָאשֵׁי הַחַיָּה רָקִיעַ
כג כְּעֵין הַקֶּרַח הַנּוֹרָא נָטוּי עַל־רָאשֵׁיהֶם מִלְמָעְלָה׃ וְתַחַת הָרָקִיעַ
כַּנְפֵיהֶם יְשָׁרוֹת אִשָּׁה אֶל־אֲחוֹתָהּ לְאִישׁ שְׁתַּיִם מְכַסּוֹת לָהֵנָּה וּלְאִישׁ
כד שְׁתַּיִם מְכַסּוֹת לָהֵנָּה אֵת גְּוִיֹּתֵיהֶם׃ וָאֶשְׁמַע אֶת־קוֹל כַּנְפֵיהֶם כְּקוֹל
מַיִם רַבִּים כְּקוֹל־שַׁדַּי בְּלֶכְתָּם קוֹל הֲמֻלָּה כְּקוֹל מַחֲנֶה בְּעָמְדָם

25 still, they lowered their wings; a voice came from upon the expanse which
26 was over their heads – standing still, they lowered their wings. Above the film
which was over their heads, with the appearance of a sapphire, was the form
of a throne; and upon the form of the throne – upon it, above – was a form
27 with the appearance of a man. And I saw: something that looked luminous,
the appearance of fire encasing it from what appeared to be his waist and
above; and from what appeared to be his waist and below, I saw an appearance
28 like fire with a radiance around it; it was like the appearance of a rainbow in
the clouds on a rainy day; the radiance around it had that appearance. This
was the appearance of the form of the glory of the LORD. I saw it and I fell
2 1 upon my face, and I heard a voice speak. He said to me: "Man, stand
2 on your feet, and I will speak to you." As He spoke to me, a spirit came into
3 me and set me on my feet, and I heard him speaking to me. He said
to me: "Man, I am sending you to the sons of Israel, a nation of rebels who
have rebelled against me; they – and their fathers – have transgressed against
4 me until this very day. The sons are hard faced, tough hearted – I am sending
5 you to them, and you will say to them: 'So says the Lord GOD.' Whether they
listen or refuse, they are a defiant house, and they will know that a prophet
6 was among them. You, Man, do not fear them and their words – do
not fear; thorns and thistles surround you and you sit among scorpions;
their words do not fear, before them do not quail, for they are a defiant
7 house; speak My words to them whether they listen or refuse, for they are
8 defiant. You, Man, listen to what I say to you – do not be defiant like
9 this defiant house; open your mouth and eat what I give you." I looked – there
10 was a hand reaching toward me, and there, within it, was a written scroll. He
spread it out in front of me and it had writing on the front and on the back,
3 1 and on it were written laments, keening, and woe. And He
said to me: "Man, what you find here, eat – eat this scroll and then go, speak
2 to the House of Israel." I opened my mouth, and He fed it to me, this scroll,
3 and said to me: "Man, feed your stomach; fill your insides with this scroll
that I am giving you." I ate it, and in my mouth it had the sweetness of
4 honey.[3] And He said to me: "Man, go now! Come to the House of
5 Israel and speak My words to them. You are not being sent to a people of
6 unfathomable speech, of heavy tongue, but to the House of Israel; not to the
many peoples of unfathomable speech and heavy tongue whose words you
cannot understand – if I were to send you to them, they would listen to you.
7 The House of Israel will not agree to listen to you, for they are not prepared
to listen to Me – the whole of the House of Israel are tough browed and hard-
8 hearted. Behold – I have made your face tough before their faces and your

---

3 | Perhaps indicating an eventual positive outcome to the destruction.

כה תְּרַפֶּינָה כַנְפֵיהֶן: וַיְהִי־קוֹל מֵעַל לָרָקִיעַ אֲשֶׁר עַל־רֹאשָׁם בְּעָמְדָם
כו תְּרַפֶּינָה כַנְפֵיהֶן: וּמִמַּעַל לָרָקִיעַ אֲשֶׁר עַל־רֹאשָׁם כְּמַרְאֵה אֶבֶן־סַפִּיר
דְּמוּת כִּסֵּא וְעַל דְּמוּת הַכִּסֵּא דְּמוּת כְּמַרְאֵה אָדָם עָלָיו מִלְמָעְלָה:
כז וָאֵרֶא ׀ כְּעֵין חַשְׁמַל כְּמַרְאֵה־אֵשׁ בֵּית־לָהּ סָבִיב מִמַּרְאֵה מָתְנָיו
וּלְמָעְלָה וּמִמַּרְאֵה מָתְנָיו וּלְמַטָּה רָאִיתִי כְּמַרְאֵה־אֵשׁ וְנֹגַהּ לוֹ סָבִיב:
כח כְּמַרְאֵה הַקֶּשֶׁת אֲשֶׁר יִהְיֶה בֶעָנָן בְּיוֹם הַגֶּשֶׁם כֵּן מַרְאֵה הַנֹּגַהּ סָבִיב
הוּא מַרְאֵה דְּמוּת כְּבוֹד־יְהוָה וָאֶרְאֶה וָאֶפֹּל עַל־פָּנַי וָאֶשְׁמַע קוֹל
ב א מְדַבֵּר: וַיֹּאמֶר אֵלָי בֶּן־אָדָם עֲמֹד עַל־רַגְלֶיךָ וַאֲדַבֵּר
ב אֹתָךְ: וַתָּבֹא בִי רוּחַ כַּאֲשֶׁר דִּבֶּר אֵלַי וַתַּעֲמִדֵנִי עַל־רַגְלָי וָאֶשְׁמַע
ג אֵת מִדַּבֵּר אֵלָי: וַיֹּאמֶר אֵלַי בֶּן־אָדָם שׁוֹלֵחַ
אֲנִי אוֹתְךָ אֶל־בְּנֵי יִשְׂרָאֵל אֶל־גּוֹיִם הַמּוֹרְדִים אֲשֶׁר מָרְדוּ־בִי הֵמָּה
ד וַאֲבוֹתָם פָּשְׁעוּ בִי עַד־עֶצֶם הַיּוֹם הַזֶּה: וְהַבָּנִים קְשֵׁי פָנִים וְחִזְקֵי־
לֵב אֲנִי שׁוֹלֵחַ אוֹתְךָ אֲלֵיהֶם וְאָמַרְתָּ אֲלֵיהֶם כֹּה אָמַר אֲדֹנָי יְהוִה:
ה וְהֵמָּה אִם־יִשְׁמְעוּ וְאִם־יֶחְדָּלוּ כִּי בֵּית מְרִי הֵמָּה וְיָדְעוּ כִּי נָבִיא הָיָה
ו בְתוֹכָם: וְאַתָּה בֶן־אָדָם אַל־תִּירָא מֵהֶם וּמִדִּבְרֵיהֶם אַל־
תִּירָא כִּי סָרָבִים וְסַלּוֹנִים אוֹתָךְ וְאֶל־עַקְרַבִּים אַתָּה יוֹשֵׁב מִדִּבְרֵיהֶם
ז אַל־תִּירָא וּמִפְּנֵיהֶם אַל־תֵּחָת כִּי בֵּית מְרִי הֵמָּה: וְדִבַּרְתָּ אֶת־דְּבָרַי
ח אֲלֵיהֶם אִם־יִשְׁמְעוּ וְאִם־יֶחְדָּלוּ כִּי מְרִי הֵמָּה: וְאַתָּה
בֶן־אָדָם שְׁמַע אֵת אֲשֶׁר־אֲנִי מְדַבֵּר אֵלֶיךָ אַל־תְּהִי־מֶרִי כְּבֵית הַמֶּרִי
ט פְּצֵה פִיךָ וֶאֱכֹל אֵת אֲשֶׁר־אֲנִי נֹתֵן אֵלֶיךָ: וָאֶרְאֶה וְהִנֵּה־יָד שְׁלוּחָה
י אֵלָי וְהִנֵּה־בוֹ מְגִלַּת־סֵפֶר: וַיִּפְרֹשׂ אוֹתָהּ לְפָנַי וְהִיא כְתוּבָה פָּנִים
ג א וְאָחוֹר וְכָתוּב אֵלֶיהָ קִנִים וָהֶגֶה וָהִי: וַיֹּאמֶר אֵלַי בֶּן־
אָדָם אֵת אֲשֶׁר־תִּמְצָא אֱכוֹל אֱכוֹל אֶת־הַמְּגִלָּה הַזֹּאת וְלֵךְ דַּבֵּר
ב ג אֶל־בֵּית יִשְׂרָאֵל: וָאֶפְתַּח אֶת־פִּי וַיַּאֲכִלֵנִי אֵת הַמְּגִלָּה הַזֹּאת: וַיֹּאמֶר
אֵלַי בֶּן־אָדָם בִּטְנְךָ תַאֲכֵל וּמֵעֶיךָ תְמַלֵּא אֵת הַמְּגִלָּה הַזֹּאת אֲשֶׁר
ד אֲנִי נֹתֵן אֵלֶיךָ וָאֹכְלָה וַתְּהִי בְּפִי כִּדְבַשׁ לְמָתוֹק: וַיֹּאמֶר
ה אֵלַי בֶּן־אָדָם לֶךְ־בֹּא אֶל־בֵּית יִשְׂרָאֵל וְדִבַּרְתָּ בִדְבָרַי אֲלֵיהֶם: כִּי
לֹא אֶל־עַם עִמְקֵי שָׂפָה וְכִבְדֵי לָשׁוֹן אַתָּה שָׁלוּחַ אֶל־בֵּית יִשְׂרָאֵל:
ו לֹא ׀ אֶל־עַמִּים רַבִּים עִמְקֵי שָׂפָה וְכִבְדֵי לָשׁוֹן אֲשֶׁר לֹא־תִשְׁמַע
ז דִּבְרֵיהֶם אִם־לֹא אֲלֵיהֶם שְׁלַחְתִּיךָ הֵמָּה יִשְׁמְעוּ אֵלֶיךָ: וּבֵית יִשְׂרָאֵל
לֹא יֹאבוּ לִשְׁמֹעַ אֵלֶיךָ כִּי־אֵינָם אֹבִים לִשְׁמֹעַ אֵלָי כִּי כָּל־בֵּית יִשְׂרָאֵל
ח חִזְקֵי־מֵצַח וּקְשֵׁי־לֵב הֵמָּה: הִנֵּה נָתַתִּי אֶת־פָּנֶיךָ חֲזָקִים לְעֻמַּת פְּנֵיהֶם

9 brow tough before their brows; like adamant, harder than flint I have made
your brow. Do not fear them; do not quail before them – they are a defiant
10 house." And He said to me: "Man, everything that I say to you, take
11 it into your heart; let your ears hear it. Go now – come to the exiles, to the
sons of your people, and speak to them; say to them, 'So says the Lord
12 GOD' – whether they listen or refuse." A spirit then lifted me up, and I heard
a great, thunderous noise behind me: "Blessed is the LORD's glory from its
13 place!" – the sound of the wings of the living beings brushing against each
14 other and the sound of the wheels beside them, a great, thunderous noise. A
spirit lifted me up and took me away, and I went away bitter, my spirit raging,
15 with the hand of the LORD firm upon me, and I came to the exiles in Tel Aviv[4]
who were living on the Kevar River, and there, where they sit, I sat there
16 among them for seven days, desolate. At the end of seven
17 days... the word of the LORD came to me, saying: "Man, I have
made you watchman for the House of Israel; when you hear a word from My
18 mouth, give them warning from Me. "If I say to the wicked one, 'You will
surely die,' and you do not warn him, if you do not speak out to warn the
wicked one off his wicked course so that he should live, and he remains
wicked, he will die for his iniquity – but I will seek redress for his blood from
19 your hands. But if you warn the wicked one and he still does not turn from
his wickedness, from his wicked course, he will die for his iniquity – but you
20 will have saved your own life. If the righteous one turns from his
righteousness and does wrong, I will put obstacles before him, and he will
die; if you do not warn him, he will die for his sin, and the righteousness that
he has done will not be remembered – and you, his blood will be on your
21 hands. But if you warn the righteous one so that he does not sin, if he remains
righteous and does not sin because he has been warned, then he will surely
22 live – and you will save your own soul."[5] And the hand of the LORD
came upon me there, and He said to me: "Get up, go out to the valley, and I
23 will speak to you there." I got up and went out to the valley, and there was the
glory of the LORD standing there – like the glory that I saw on the Kevar
24 River[6] – and I fell upon my face. A spirit came into me and set me on my feet,
25 and He spoke to me and said: "Come, shut yourself in your house. You,
Man, they have put ropes on you, they have bound you with them, and you
26 will not get out of them. I will stick your tongue to the roof of your mouth,
you will be struck silent, and you will not be a man of rebuke to them – they
27 are a defiant house. But when I speak to you, I will open your mouth, and
you will say to them, 'So says the Lord GOD.' The one who listens will listen,
4 1 and the one who refuses will refuse, for they are a defiant house. Now
you, Man, take a clay block, place it before you, and carve on it a city: Jerusa-
2 lem. Lay siege to her: build a siege wall against her, throw up earthworks
against her, set up encampments against her, and position battering rams

4 | Literally "hill of new grain," this was an ancient Mesopotamian city whose precise location is unknown.
5 | The prophecy of the "watchman" here in verses 16–21 is expanded in 33:1–20.
6 | See chapter 1.

ט וְאֶת־מִצְחֲךָ חָזָק לְעֻמַּת מִצְחָם׃ כְּשָׁמִיר חָזָק מִצֹּר נָתַתִּי מִצְחֶךָ לֹא־
י תִירָא אוֹתָם וְלֹא־תֵחַת מִפְּנֵיהֶם כִּי בֵּית מְרִי הֵמָּה׃ וַיֹּאמֶר
אֵלָי בֶּן־אָדָם אֶת־כָּל־דְּבָרַי אֲשֶׁר אֲדַבֵּר אֵלֶיךָ קַח בִּלְבָבְךָ וּבְאָזְנֶיךָ
יא שְׁמָע׃ וְלֵךְ בֹּא אֶל־הַגּוֹלָה אֶל־בְּנֵי עַמֶּךָ וְדִבַּרְתָּ אֲלֵיהֶם וְאָמַרְתָּ
ב יב אֲלֵיהֶם כֹּה אָמַר אֲדֹנָי יֱהֹוִה אִם־יִשְׁמְעוּ וְאִם־יֶחְדָּלוּ׃ וַתִּשָּׂאֵנִי רוּחַ
יג וָאֶשְׁמַע אַחֲרַי קוֹל רַעַשׁ גָּדוֹל בָּרוּךְ כְּבוֹד־יְהֹוָה מִמְּקוֹמוֹ׃ וְקוֹל ׀
כַּנְפֵי הַחַיּוֹת מַשִּׁיקוֹת אִשָּׁה אֶל־אֲחוֹתָהּ וְקוֹל הָאוֹפַנִּים לְעֻמָּתָם
יד וְקוֹל רַעַשׁ גָּדוֹל׃ וְרוּחַ נְשָׂאַתְנִי וַתִּקָּחֵנִי וָאֵלֵךְ מַר בַּחֲמַת רוּחִי
טו וְיַד־יְהֹוָה עָלַי חָזָקָה׃ וָאָבוֹא אֶל־הַגּוֹלָה תֵּל אָבִיב הַיֹּשְׁבִים אֶל־נְהַר־
כְּבָר ואשר הֵמָּה יוֹשְׁבִים שָׁם וָאֵשֵׁב שָׁם שִׁבְעַת יָמִים מַשְׁמִים וָאֵשֵׁב
טז בְּתוֹכָם׃ וַיְהִי מִקְצֵה שִׁבְעַת יָמִים וַיְהִי
יז דְבַר־יְהֹוָה אֵלַי לֵאמֹר׃ בֶּן־אָדָם צֹפֶה נְתַתִּיךָ לְבֵית יִשְׂרָאֵל וְשָׁמַעְתָּ
יח מִפִּי דָּבָר וְהִזְהַרְתָּ אוֹתָם מִמֶּנִּי׃ בְּאָמְרִי לָרָשָׁע מוֹת תָּמוּת וְלֹא
הִזְהַרְתּוֹ וְלֹא דִבַּרְתָּ לְהַזְהִיר רָשָׁע מִדַּרְכּוֹ הָרְשָׁעָה לְחַיֹּתוֹ הוּא
יט רָשָׁע בַּעֲוֺנוֹ יָמוּת וְדָמוֹ מִיָּדְךָ אֲבַקֵּשׁ׃ וְאַתָּה כִּי־הִזְהַרְתָּ רָשָׁע וְלֹא־
שָׁב מֵרִשְׁעוֹ וּמִדַּרְכּוֹ הָרְשָׁעָה הוּא בַּעֲוֺנוֹ יָמוּת וְאַתָּה אֶת־נַפְשְׁךָ
כ הִצַּלְתָּ׃ וּבְשׁוּב צַדִּיק מִצִּדְקוֹ וְעָשָׂה עָוֶל וְנָתַתִּי מִכְשׁוֹל
לְפָנָיו הוּא יָמוּת כִּי לֹא הִזְהַרְתּוֹ בְּחַטָּאתוֹ יָמוּת וְלֹא תִזָּכַרְןָ צִדְקֹתָו
כא אֲשֶׁר עָשָׂה וְדָמוֹ מִיָּדְךָ אֲבַקֵּשׁ׃ וְאַתָּה כִּי הִזְהַרְתּוֹ צַדִּיק לְבִלְתִּי
חֲטֹא צַדִּיק וְהוּא לֹא־חָטָא חָיוֹ יִחְיֶה כִּי נִזְהָר וְאַתָּה אֶת־נַפְשְׁךָ
כב הִצַּלְתָּ׃ וַתְּהִי עָלַי שָׁם יַד־יְהֹוָה וַיֹּאמֶר אֵלַי קוּם צֵא אֶל־
כג הַבִּקְעָה וְשָׁם אֲדַבֵּר אוֹתָךְ׃ וָאָקוּם וָאֵצֵא אֶל־הַבִּקְעָה וְהִנֵּה־שָׁם
כְּבוֹד־יְהֹוָה עֹמֵד כַּכָּבוֹד אֲשֶׁר רָאִיתִי עַל־נְהַר־כְּבָר וָאֶפֹּל עַל־פָּנָי׃
כד וַתָּבֹא־בִי רוּחַ וַתַּעֲמִדֵנִי עַל־רַגְלָי וַיְדַבֵּר אֹתִי וַיֹּאמֶר אֵלַי בֹּא הִסָּגֵר
כה בְּתוֹךְ בֵּיתֶךָ׃ וְאַתָּה בֶן־אָדָם הִנֵּה נָתְנוּ עָלֶיךָ עֲבוֹתִים
כו וַאֲסָרוּךָ בָּהֶם וְלֹא תֵצֵא בְּתוֹכָם׃ וּלְשׁוֹנְךָ אַדְבִּיק אֶל־חִכֶּךָ וְנֶאֱלַמְתָּ
כז וְלֹא־תִהְיֶה לָהֶם לְאִישׁ מוֹכִיחַ כִּי בֵּית מְרִי הֵמָּה׃ וּבְדַבְּרִי אוֹתְךָ
אֶפְתַּח אֶת־פִּיךָ וְאָמַרְתָּ אֲלֵיהֶם כֹּה אָמַר אֲדֹנָי יֱהֹוִה הַשֹּׁמֵעַ ׀ יִשְׁמָע
ד א וְהֶחָדֵל ׀ יֶחְדָּל כִּי בֵּית מְרִי הֵמָּה׃ וְאַתָּה בֶן־אָדָם קַח־לְךָ
ב לְבֵנָה וְנָתַתָּה אוֹתָהּ לְפָנֶיךָ וְחַקּוֹתָ עָלֶיהָ עִיר אֶת־יְרוּשָׁלִָם׃ וְנָתַתָּה
עָלֶיהָ מָצוֹר וּבָנִיתָ עָלֶיהָ דָּיֵק וְשָׁפַכְתָּ עָלֶיהָ סֹלְלָה וְנָתַתָּה עָלֶיהָ

3 around her. Take an iron griddle and place it as an iron wall between you and
the city, and turn your face upon her – she will be under siege, and you will
4 besiege her. This is a sign for the House of Israel. And you, lie on
your left side and let it bear the weight of the sins of the House of Israel: you
5 will bear their sin for the number of days that you lie upon it. I set you as many
days as the years of their sin: for 390 days you will bear the sin of the House
6 of Israel, and when you have completed these, lie for a second time – on your
right side – and bear the sin of the House of Yehuda for forty days: a day for
7 a year, I have set this for you, a day for each year. Turn your face upon the
8 siege of Jerusalem; bare your arm and prophesy about her. Behold, I have
bound you with ropes – you shall not turn over from one side to the other
9 until your days of siege are complete. And you – take wheat, barley, beans,
lentils, millet, and emmer wheat, put them all into one utensil, and make
bread for yourself from them. All the days that you will be lying on your
10 side – 390 days – you shall eat this. You will eat this, your food, at a weight of
11 twenty shekel a day; you will eat this from one day to the next, and you will
drink a small measure of water: you will drink a sixth of a hin from one day
12 to the next. You will eat it as though it were a barley cake, and you will bake
13 it over dung – human excrement – before their eyes." And the LORD
said: "This is how the children of Israel will eat their bread, impure, among
14 the nations that I will banish them to." And I said, "Ah, my Lord GOD! Never
before has my throat been defiled; I have never eaten flesh from a carcass or
mauled animal even as a youth, never until now, and fouled meat has never
15 entered my mouth." And He said to me: "I will allow you
cattle dung in place of human excrement; you shall make your bread over
16 that." And He said to me: "See, I am going to break the staff of bread
they lean on in Jerusalem; they will eat bread weighed out, anxious; water
17 measured out, desolate, they will drink; and so, they will lack bread and
water; each man and his brother desolate, they will waste away in their
5 1 sin. And you, Man, take a sharp blade – a barber's razor – pass it over
2 your head and beard; take scales for weighing and divide up the hair. One-
third set aflame inside your city once the days of siege are over, one-third take
and strike with a sword on all sides, and one-third scatter to the winds and I
3 shall draw the sword after them. From this take a small measure, bind it up
4 in the hem of your garment, and again take from this and fling it into the fire,
5 burn it in the fire; fire will spread to all the House of Israel from this. So
says the Lord GOD: This is Jerusalem. Amidst the nations I have placed her,
6 all around her the lands. She has rebelled against My laws with a wickedness
greater than the other nations' and against My statutes even more than the

ג מַחֲנוֹת וְשִׂים־עָלֶיהָ כָרִים סָבִיב: וְאַתָּה קַח־לְךָ מַחֲבַת בַּרְזֶל וְנָתַתָּה
אוֹתָהּ קִיר בַּרְזֶל בֵּינְךָ וּבֵין הָעִיר וַהֲכִינֹתָה אֶת־פָּנֶיךָ אֵלֶיהָ וְהָיְתָה
ד בַמָּצוֹר וְצַרְתָּ עָלֶיהָ אוֹת הִיא לְבֵית יִשְׂרָאֵל: וְאַתָּה שְׁכַב
עַל־צִדְּךָ הַשְּׂמָאלִי וְשַׂמְתָּ אֶת־עֲוֺן בֵּית־יִשְׂרָאֵל עָלָיו מִסְפַּר הַיָּמִים
ה אֲשֶׁר תִּשְׁכַּב עָלָיו תִּשָּׂא אֶת־עֲוֺנָם: וַאֲנִי נָתַתִּי לְךָ אֶת־שְׁנֵי עֲוֺנָם
לְמִסְפַּר יָמִים שְׁלֹשׁ־מֵאוֹת וְתִשְׁעִים יוֹם וְנָשָׂאתָ עֲוֺן בֵּית־יִשְׂרָאֵל:
ו וְכִלִּיתָ אֶת־אֵלֶּה וְשָׁכַבְתָּ עַל־צִדְּךָ הימיני שֵׁנִית וְנָשָׂאתָ אֶת־עֲוֺן הַיְמָנִי
ז בֵּית־יְהוּדָה אַרְבָּעִים יוֹם יוֹם לַשָּׁנָה יוֹם לַשָּׁנָה נְתַתִּיו לָךְ: וְאֶל־מְצוֹר
ח יְרוּשָׁלִַם תָּכִין פָּנֶיךָ וּזְרֹעֲךָ חֲשׂוּפָה וְנִבֵּאתָ עָלֶיהָ: וְהִנֵּה נָתַתִּי עָלֶיךָ
ט עֲבוֹתִים וְלֹא־תֵהָפֵךְ מִצִּדְּךָ אֶל־צִדֶּךָ עַד־כַּלּוֹתְךָ יְמֵי מְצוּרֶךָ: וְאַתָּה
קַח־לְךָ חִטִּין וּשְׂעֹרִים וּפוֹל וַעֲדָשִׁים וְדֹחַן וְכֻסְּמִים וְנָתַתָּה אוֹתָם
בִּכְלִי אֶחָד וְעָשִׂיתָ אוֹתָם לְךָ לְלָחֶם מִסְפַּר הַיָּמִים אֲשֶׁר־אַתָּה ׀ שׁוֹכֵב
י עַל־צִדְּךָ שְׁלֹשׁ־מֵאוֹת וְתִשְׁעִים יוֹם תֹּאכְלֶנּוּ: וּמַאֲכָלְךָ אֲשֶׁר תֹּאכְלֶנּוּ
יא בְּמִשְׁקוֹל עֶשְׂרִים שֶׁקֶל לַיּוֹם מֵעֵת עַד־עֵת תֹּאכְלֶנּוּ: וּמַיִם בִּמְשׂוּרָה
יב תִשְׁתֶּה שִׁשִּׁית הַהִין מֵעֵת עַד־עֵת תִּשְׁתֶּה: וְעֻגַת שְׂעֹרִים תֹּאכְלֶנָּה
יג וְהִיא בְּגֶלְלֵי צֵאַת הָאָדָם תְּעֻגֶנָה לְעֵינֵיהֶם: וַיֹּאמֶר יְהוָה
כָּכָה יֹאכְלוּ בְנֵי־יִשְׂרָאֵל אֶת־לַחְמָם טָמֵא בַּגּוֹיִם אֲשֶׁר אַדִּיחֵם שָׁם:
יד וָאֹמַר אֲהָהּ אֲדֹנָי יֱהוִה הִנֵּה נַפְשִׁי לֹא מְטֻמָּאָה וּנְבֵלָה וּטְרֵפָה לֹא־
טו אָכַלְתִּי מִנְּעוּרַי וְעַד־עַתָּה וְלֹא־בָא בְּפִי בְּשַׂר פִּגּוּל: וַיֹּאמֶר
אֵלַי רְאֵה נָתַתִּי לְךָ אֶת־צפועי הַבָּקָר תַּחַת גֶּלְלֵי הָאָדָם וְעָשִׂיתָ צְפִיעֵי
טז אֶת־לַחְמְךָ עֲלֵיהֶם: וַיֹּאמֶר אֵלַי בֶּן־אָדָם הִנְנִי שֹׁבֵר
מַטֵּה־לֶחֶם בִּירוּשָׁלִַם וְאָכְלוּ־לֶחֶם בְּמִשְׁקָל וּבִדְאָגָה וּמַיִם בִּמְשׂוּרָה
יז וּבְשִׁמָּמוֹן יִשְׁתּוּ: לְמַעַן יַחְסְרוּ לֶחֶם וָמָיִם וְנָשַׁמּוּ אִישׁ וְאָחִיו וְנָמַקּוּ
ה א בַּעֲוֺנָם: וְאַתָּה בֶן־אָדָם קַח־לְךָ ׀ חֶרֶב חַדָּה תַּעַר הַגַּלָּבִים
תִּקָּחֶנָּה לָּךְ וְהַעֲבַרְתָּ עַל־רֹאשְׁךָ וְעַל־זְקָנֶךָ וְלָקַחְתָּ לְךָ מֹאזְנֵי מִשְׁקָל
ב וְחִלַּקְתָּם: שְׁלִשִׁית בָּאוּר תַּבְעִיר בְּתוֹךְ הָעִיר כִּמְלֹאת יְמֵי הַמָּצוֹר
וְלָקַחְתָּ אֶת־הַשְּׁלִשִׁית תַּכֶּה בַחֶרֶב סְבִיבוֹתֶיהָ וְהַשְּׁלִשִׁית תִּזְרֶה
ג לָרוּחַ וְחֶרֶב אָרִיק אַחֲרֵיהֶם: וְלָקַחְתָּ מִשָּׁם מְעַט בְּמִסְפָּר וְצַרְתָּ אוֹתָם
ד בִּכְנָפֶיךָ: וּמֵהֶם עוֹד תִּקָּח וְהִשְׁלַכְתָּ אוֹתָם אֶל־תּוֹךְ הָאֵשׁ וְשָׂרַפְתָּ
ה אֹתָם בָּאֵשׁ מִמֶּנּוּ תֵצֵא־אֵשׁ אֶל־כָּל־בֵּית יִשְׂרָאֵל: כֹּה
אָמַר אֲדֹנָי יֱהוִה זֹאת יְרוּשָׁלִַם בְּתוֹךְ הַגּוֹיִם שַׂמְתִּיהָ וּסְבִיבוֹתֶיהָ
ו אֲרָצוֹת: וַתֶּמֶר אֶת־מִשְׁפָּטַי לְרִשְׁעָה מִן־הַגּוֹיִם וְאֶת־חֻקּוֹתַי מִן־

lands all around her, for they rejected My laws and did not follow My
7 statutes. So the Lord GOD says this: Because you have surpassed
even those nations around you – you did not follow My statutes, you did not
perform My laws – and you did not even perform the laws of the nations
8 around you. So the Lord GOD says this: See, I am upon you – I, too,
9 I will execute My judgments among you before the eyes of the nations; I will
do to you what I have not ever done, the like of which I will never do again,
10 because of your abominations. Parents will eat children among you,
children will eat their parents; I will execute judgments upon you, and I will
11 scatter all that remains of you to the winds. And so, declares the Lord GOD,
surely as I live, because you defiled My Sanctuary with all your detestable
things, all your abominations, I, I too, will draw Myself back, and My eye will
12 not pity; I will not show mercy: One-third of you will die of the plague and
destroyed by the famine among you, one-third will fall to the sword on all
sides, and one-third I will scatter to the winds and draw the sword behind
13 them. My anger will be exhausted, I will let My fury at them die down, and I
will find relief; they will know that I am the LORD; I have spoken – in the
14 passion of My anger, in exhausting My anger upon them. And I will give you
over to ruin and reproach among the nations around you in the sight of every
15 passerby; it will be a reproach and a disgrace, a warning and a horror to the
nations who are around you when I execute judgments upon you in anger, in
16 fury, in furious rebuke. I am the LORD; I have spoken. When I set loose the
terrible arrows of famine among them to destroy them, I will set them loose
to destroy you, and I will pile more famine upon you and break the staff of
17 bread you lean on. I will set loose upon you famine and savage animals, and
they will bereave you; plague and blood will pass through you; I will bring
the sword down upon you. I am the LORD; I have spoken." 6 1 And the
2 word of the LORD came to me, saying: "Man, set your face to the mountains
3 of Israel and prophesy to them; say: Mountains of Israel, listen to the word
of the Lord GOD. So says the Lord GOD to the mountains and hills, to the
ravines and valleys: Behold, it is I – I will bring the sword down on you, I will
4 completely destroy your high places. Your altars will be devastated, your sun
shrines will be smashed. I will cut them down, your slain, in front of your
5 idols, I will leave the corpses of the children of Israel before their idols,
6 and I will scatter your bones around your altars. Everywhere you live your
cities will be laid waste, and the high places will be devastated so that your
altars will be laid waste, desolate, your idols smashed to pieces, your sun
7 shrines crushed, and what you have crafted wiped out entirely; the slain will
8 fall there among you, and you will know that I am the LORD. I will leave a
remnant, some survivors of the sword among the nations, when you are
9 scattered across the lands; your survivors will remember Me among the
nations they are taken to as captives – that I was grieved by their whoring
heart that turned away from Me, their eyes whoring after their idols, and they

הָאֲרָצוֹת אֲשֶׁר סְבִיבוֹתֶיהָ כִּי בְמִשְׁפָּטַי מָאָסוּ וְחֻקּוֹתַי לֹא־הָלְכוּ
ז בָהֶם: לָכֵן כֹּה־אָמַר | אֲדֹנָי יֱהֹוִה יַעַן הֲמָנְכֶם מִן־הַגּוֹיִם
אֲשֶׁר סְבִיבוֹתֵיכֶם בְּחֻקּוֹתַי לֹא הֲלַכְתֶּם וְאֶת־מִשְׁפָּטַי לֹא עֲשִׂיתֶם
ח וּכְמִשְׁפְּטֵי הַגּוֹיִם אֲשֶׁר סְבִיבוֹתֵיכֶם לֹא עֲשִׂיתֶם: לָכֵן כֹּה
אָמַר אֲדֹנָי יֱהֹוִה הִנְנִי עָלַיִךְ גַּם־אָנִי וְעָשִׂיתִי בְתוֹכֵךְ מִשְׁפָּטִים לְעֵינֵי
ט הַגּוֹיִם: וְעָשִׂיתִי בָךְ אֵת אֲשֶׁר לֹא־עָשִׂיתִי וְאֵת אֲשֶׁר־לֹא־אֶעֱשֶׂה
י כָמֹהוּ עוֹד יַעַן כָּל־תּוֹעֲבֹתָיִךְ: לָכֵן אָבוֹת יֹאכְלוּ בָנִים
בְּתוֹכֵךְ וּבָנִים יֹאכְלוּ אֲבוֹתָם וְעָשִׂיתִי בָךְ שְׁפָטִים וְזֵרִיתִי אֶת־כָּל־
יא שְׁאֵרִיתֵךְ לְכָל־רוּחַ: לָכֵן חַי־אָנִי נְאֻם אֲדֹנָי יֱהֹוִה אִם־לֹא יַעַן אֶת־
מִקְדָּשִׁי טִמֵּאת בְּכָל־שִׁקּוּצַיִךְ וּבְכָל־תּוֹעֲבֹתָיִךְ וְגַם־אֲנִי אֶגְרַע וְלֹא־
יב תָחוֹס עֵינִי וְגַם־אֲנִי לֹא אֶחְמוֹל: שְׁלִשִׁתַיִךְ בַּדֶּבֶר יָמוּתוּ וּבָרָעָב יִכְלוּ
בְתוֹכֵךְ וְהַשְּׁלִשִׁית בַּחֶרֶב יִפְּלוּ סְבִיבוֹתָיִךְ וְהַשְּׁלִישִׁית לְכָל־רוּחַ אֱזָרֶה
יג וְחֶרֶב אָרִיק אַחֲרֵיהֶם: וְכָלָה אַפִּי וַהֲנִחוֹתִי חֲמָתִי בָּם וְהִנֶּחָמְתִּי וְיָדְעוּ
יד כִּי־אֲנִי יְהוָה דִּבַּרְתִּי בְּקִנְאָתִי בְּכַלּוֹתִי חֲמָתִי בָּם: וְאֶתְּנֵךְ לְחָרְבָּה
טו וּלְחֶרְפָּה בַּגּוֹיִם אֲשֶׁר סְבִיבוֹתָיִךְ לְעֵינֵי כָּל־עוֹבֵר: וְהָיְתָה חֶרְפָּה וּגְדוּפָה
מוּסָר וּמְשַׁמָּה לַגּוֹיִם אֲשֶׁר סְבִיבוֹתָיִךְ בַּעֲשׂוֹתִי בָךְ שְׁפָטִים בְּאַף
טז וּבְחֵמָה וּבְתֹכְחוֹת חֵמָה אֲנִי יְהוָה דִּבַּרְתִּי: בְּשַׁלְּחִי אֶת־חִצֵּי הָרָעָב
הָרָעִים בָּהֶם אֲשֶׁר הָיוּ לְמַשְׁחִית אֲשֶׁר־אֲשַׁלַּח אוֹתָם לְשַׁחֶתְכֶם
יז וְרָעָב אֹסֵף עֲלֵיכֶם וְשָׁבַרְתִּי לָכֶם מַטֵּה־לָחֶם: וְשִׁלַּחְתִּי עֲלֵיכֶם רָעָב
וְחַיָּה רָעָה וְשִׁכְּלֻךְ וְדֶבֶר וָדָם יַעֲבָר־בָּךְ וְחֶרֶב אָבִיא עָלַיִךְ אֲנִי יְהוָה
ו א ב דִּבַּרְתִּי: וַיְהִי דְבַר־יְהוָה אֵלַי לֵאמֹר: בֶּן־אָדָם שִׂים ג
ג פָּנֶיךָ אֶל־הָרֵי יִשְׂרָאֵל וְהִנָּבֵא אֲלֵיהֶם: וְאָמַרְתָּ הָרֵי יִשְׂרָאֵל שִׁמְעוּ
דְּבַר־אֲדֹנָי יֱהֹוִה כֹּה־אָמַר אֲדֹנָי יֱהֹוִה לֶהָרִים וְלַגְּבָעוֹת לָאֲפִיקִים
ד ולגאות הִנְנִי אֲנִי מֵבִיא עֲלֵיכֶם חֶרֶב וְאִבַּדְתִּי בָּמוֹתֵיכֶם: וְנָשַׁמּוּ וְלַגֵּאָיוֹת
ה מִזְבְּחוֹתֵיכֶם וְנִשְׁבְּרוּ חַמָּנֵיכֶם וְהִפַּלְתִּי חַלְלֵיכֶם לִפְנֵי גִּלּוּלֵיכֶם: וְנָתַתִּי
אֶת־פִּגְרֵי בְּנֵי יִשְׂרָאֵל לִפְנֵי גִּלּוּלֵיהֶם וְזֵרִיתִי אֶת־עַצְמוֹתֵיכֶם סְבִיבוֹת
ו מִזְבְּחוֹתֵיכֶם: בְּכֹל מוֹשְׁבוֹתֵיכֶם הֶעָרִים תֶּחֱרַבְנָה וְהַבָּמוֹת תִּישָׁמְנָה
לְמַעַן יֶחֶרְבוּ וְיֶאְשְׁמוּ מִזְבְּחוֹתֵיכֶם וְנִשְׁבְּרוּ וְנִשְׁבְּתוּ גִּלּוּלֵיכֶם וְנִגְדְּעוּ
ז חַמָּנֵיכֶם וְנִמְחוּ מַעֲשֵׂיכֶם: וְנָפַל חָלָל בְּתוֹכְכֶם וִידַעְתֶּם כִּי־אֲנִי יְהוָה:
ח ט וְהוֹתַרְתִּי בִּהְיוֹת לָכֶם פְּלִיטֵי חֶרֶב בַּגּוֹיִם בְּהִזָּרוֹתֵיכֶם בָּאֲרָצוֹת: וְזָכְרוּ
פְלִיטֵיכֶם אוֹתִי בַּגּוֹיִם אֲשֶׁר נִשְׁבּוּ־שָׁם אֲשֶׁר נִשְׁבַּרְתִּי אֶת־לִבָּם הַזּוֹנֶה
אֲשֶׁר־סָר מֵעָלַי וְאֵת עֵינֵיהֶם הַזֹּנוֹת אַחֲרֵי גִּלּוּלֵיהֶם וְנָקֹטּוּ בִּפְנֵיהֶם

10 will hate themselves for the evils they did, for all their abominations. They
will know that I am the LORD; not for nothing have I said that I would inflict
11 this great evil upon them. So says the Lord GOD: Beat with
your hands, stamp with your feet, and cry out at all the evil abominations of
the House of Israel for which they will fall to sword, famine, and plague.
12 Those far away will die from plague, those close by will fall by the sword, and
those who remain, under siege, will die of famine; I will exhaust My fury upon
13 them, and you will know that I am the LORD – when their slain are among
their idols, surrounding their altars, on every high hill, every mountain peak,
beneath every green tree, beneath every lush oak, that place where they burnt
14 a sweet fragrance to all their idols. I will stretch out My hand over them; I
will turn the land over to waste and desolation from the desert up to Divla,[7]
7 1 everywhere they live. And they will know that I am the LORD." And
2 the word of the LORD came to me, saying: "And you, Man – so says the Lord
GOD to the land of Israel: End, the end is come to the four edges of the land;
3 now the end is upon you. I will set loose My anger against you and judge you
4 according to your ways, bring down on you all your abominations. My eye
will not pity you; I will not show mercy, but I will bring your ways down upon
you; your abominations will be there in your midst, and you will know that
5 I am the LORD. So says the Lord GOD: Evil, a unique evil, see, it is
6 come; an end is come; it comes, the end, awakened against you; see, it is come.
7 The sun has set for you who live in the land; the time is come, it is near, the
8 day of panicked and not joyous cries on the hills. It is close now. I will pour
My fury over you; I will exhaust My anger upon you; I will judge you according
9 to your ways and bring down upon you all your abominations. My eye will
not pity; I will not show mercy; in accordance with your ways will I bring it
down upon you; your abominations will be there in your midst, and you will
10 know that I, the LORD, strike. See – the day, here, it has come: the dawn breaks,
11 the rod blossoms, and insolence has budded, violence grown into a rod of
evil. Nothing of them, none of their masses, nothing of theirs, and none
12 wailing for them. The time is come, the day is here: the buyer is not to rejoice,
13 nor need the seller mourn,[8] for wrath is upon her masses. For the seller will
not return to his sale again while they both live, for the prophecy to her
masses will not be withdrawn, and each man caught in his sin will not hold
14 fast to his life. They blast the horns and make everything ready, but none go
15 to war, for My wrath is upon her masses. The sword out there, plague and
famine within; whoever is in the field, by the sword he will die; whoever is
16 in the city, famine and plague will destroy; their fugitives will escape to the
mountains like doves of the valley, crying, all of them, each man caught in his
17 18 sin. All hands will go limp, all thighs wet with fear; they will put on sackcloth,
19 they will be stifled with horror, on every face shame, all heads shaved. Their
silver they will fling into the streets; their gold will be a thing defiled. Their

---

7 | Referring to Rivla, a city in Syria that served as a Babylonian army center.

8 | The seller should not mourn the sale of his property, nor should the buyer rejoice about acquiring it, because neither will derive benefit from it in the impending exile.

י אֶל־הָרָעוֹת אֲשֶׁר עָשׂוּ לְכֹל תּוֹעֲבֹתֵיהֶם: וְיָדְעוּ כִּי־אֲנִי יהוה לֹא אֶל־
יא חִנָּם דִּבַּרְתִּי לַעֲשׂוֹת לָהֶם הָרָעָה הַזֹּאת: כֹּה־אָמַר אֲדֹנָי
יֱהוִה הַכֵּה בְכַפְּךָ וּרְקַע בְּרַגְלְךָ וֶאֱמָר־אָח אֶל כָּל־תּוֹעֲבוֹת רָעוֹת
יב בֵּית יִשְׂרָאֵל אֲשֶׁר בַּחֶרֶב בָּרָעָב וּבַדֶּבֶר יִפֹּלוּ: הָרָחוֹק בַּדֶּבֶר יָמוּת
וְהַקָּרוֹב בַּחֶרֶב יִפּוֹל וְהַנִּשְׁאָר וְהַנָּצוּר בָּרָעָב יָמוּת וְכִלֵּיתִי חֲמָתִי
יג בָּם: וִידַעְתֶּם כִּי־אֲנִי יהוה בִּהְיוֹת חַלְלֵיהֶם בְּתוֹךְ גִּלּוּלֵיהֶם סְבִיבוֹת
מִזְבְּחוֹתֵיהֶם אֶל כָּל־גִּבְעָה רָמָה בְּכֹל ׀ רָאשֵׁי הֶהָרִים וְתַחַת כָּל־עֵץ
רַעֲנָן וְתַחַת כָּל־אֵלָה עֲבֻתָּה מְקוֹם אֲשֶׁר נָתְנוּ־שָׁם רֵיחַ נִיחֹחַ לְכֹל
יד גִּלּוּלֵיהֶם: וְנָטִיתִי אֶת־יָדִי עֲלֵיהֶם וְנָתַתִּי אֶת־הָאָרֶץ שְׁמָמָה וּמְשַׁמָּה
ז א מִמִּדְבַּר דִּבְלָתָה בְּכֹל מוֹשְׁבוֹתֵיהֶם וְיָדְעוּ כִּי־אֲנִי יהוה: וַיְהִי
ב דְבַר־יהוה אֵלַי לֵאמֹר: וְאַתָּה בֶן־אָדָם כֹּה־אָמַר אֲדֹנָי יֱהוִה לְאַדְמַת
ג יִשְׂרָאֵל קֵץ בָּא הַקֵּץ עַל־ארבעת כַּנְפוֹת הָאָרֶץ: עַתָּה הַקֵּץ עָלַיִךְ אַרְבַּע
וְשִׁלַּחְתִּי אַפִּי בָּךְ וּשְׁפַטְתִּיךְ כִּדְרָכָיִךְ וְנָתַתִּי עָלַיִךְ אֵת כָּל־תּוֹעֲבֹתָיִךְ:
ד וְלֹא־תָחוֹס עֵינִי עָלַיִךְ וְלֹא אֶחְמוֹל כִּי דְרָכַיִךְ עָלַיִךְ אֶתֵּן וְתוֹעֲבוֹתַיִךְ
ה בְּתוֹכֵךְ תִּהְיֶיןָ וִידַעְתֶּם כִּי־אֲנִי יהוה: כֹּה אָמַר אֲדֹנָי יֱהוִה
ו רָעָה אַחַת רָעָה הִנֵּה בָאָה: קֵץ בָּא בָּא הַקֵּץ הֵקִיץ אֵלָיִךְ הִנֵּה בָּאָה:
ז בָּאָה הַצְּפִירָה אֵלֶיךָ יוֹשֵׁב הָאָרֶץ בָּא הָעֵת קָרוֹב הַיּוֹם מְהוּמָה וְלֹא־
ח הֵד הָרִים: עַתָּה מִקָּרוֹב אֶשְׁפּוֹךְ חֲמָתִי עָלַיִךְ וְכִלֵּיתִי אַפִּי בָּךְ וּשְׁפַטְתִּיךְ
ט כִּדְרָכָיִךְ וְנָתַתִּי עָלַיִךְ אֵת כָּל־תּוֹעֲבוֹתָיִךְ: וְלֹא־תָחוֹס עֵינִי וְלֹא אֶחְמוֹל
כִּדְרָכַיִךְ עָלַיִךְ אֶתֵּן וְתוֹעֲבוֹתַיִךְ בְּתוֹכֵךְ תִּהְיֶיןָ וִידַעְתֶּם כִּי אֲנִי יהוה
י מַכֶּה: הִנֵּה הַיּוֹם הִנֵּה בָאָה יָצְאָה הַצְּפִרָה צָץ הַמַּטֶּה פָּרַח הַזָּדוֹן:
יא הֶחָמָס ׀ קָם לְמַטֵּה־רֶשַׁע לֹא־מֵהֶם וְלֹא מֵהֲמוֹנָם וְלֹא מֶהֱמֵהֶם וְלֹא־נֹהַּ
יב בָּהֶם: בָּא הָעֵת הִגִּיעַ הַיּוֹם הַקּוֹנֶה אַל־יִשְׂמָח וְהַמּוֹכֵר אַל־יִתְאַבָּל
יג כִּי חָרוֹן אֶל־כָּל־הֲמוֹנָהּ: כִּי הַמּוֹכֵר אֶל־הַמִּמְכָּר לֹא יָשׁוּב וְעוֹד בַּחַיִּים
חַיָּתָם כִּי־חָזוֹן אֶל־כָּל־הֲמוֹנָהּ לֹא יָשׁוּב וְאִישׁ בַּעֲוֺנוֹ חַיָּתוֹ לֹא־
יד יִתְחַזָּקוּ: תָּקְעוּ בַתָּקוֹעַ וְהָכִין הַכֹּל וְאֵין הֹלֵךְ לַמִּלְחָמָה כִּי חֲרוֹנִי
טו אֶל־כָּל־הֲמוֹנָהּ: הַחֶרֶב בַּחוּץ וְהַדֶּבֶר וְהָרָעָב מִבָּיִת אֲשֶׁר בַּשָּׂדֶה
טז בַּחֶרֶב יָמוּת וַאֲשֶׁר בָּעִיר רָעָב וָדֶבֶר יֹאכְלֶנּוּ: וּפָלְטוּ פְּלִיטֵיהֶם וְהָיוּ
יז אֶל־הֶהָרִים כְּיוֹנֵי הַגֵּאָיוֹת כֻּלָּם הֹמוֹת אִישׁ בַּעֲוֺנוֹ: כָּל־הַיָּדַיִם תִּרְפֶּינָה
יח וְכָל־בִּרְכַּיִם תֵּלַכְנָה מָּיִם: וְחָגְרוּ שַׂקִּים וְכִסְּתָה אוֹתָם פַּלָּצוּת וְאֶל
יט כָּל־פָּנִים בּוּשָׁה וּבְכָל־רָאשֵׁיהֶם קָרְחָה: כַּסְפָּם בַּחוּצוֹת יַשְׁלִיכוּ וּזְהָבָם

silver and gold will not save them on the day of the LORD's rage; their
souls will not be satisfied, their bellies not filled, for this was the stumbling
20 block of their sin. He bestowed upon them majesty, the splendor from His
adornment, but they used it for their abominable, detestable things, and so I
21 will make it a thing defiled for them; I will give it over into the hands of
strangers to pillage, to the wicked ones of the earth as spoil, and they will
22 desecrate it. I will turn My face away from them, and they will desecrate My
23 treasured place; hooligans will come into her and desecrate her. Forge
24 the chains, for the land is filled with blood crimes, the city with violence; I
will bring the evil of the nations and they will take possession of their houses;
I will put an end to the majesty of the powerful; their sanctified places will
25 be desecrated. Terror is coming; they will search for peace, but – nothing.
26 Disaster upon disaster will come, there will be report after report; they will
search for a vision from the prophet; teaching will be lost from the priests
27 and counsel from the elders. The king will mourn, the prince wear ruin, and
the hands of landed folk will quake; according to their own ways will I deal
with them, with their own judgments will I judge them, and they will know
8 1 that I am the LORD." It was in the sixth year in the sixth month on
the fifth day of the month: I was sitting in my house with the elders of Yehuda
2 sitting before me when the hand of the Lord GOD fell upon me there. And I
looked: There was a form with the appearance of fire: from what appeared to
be his waist and below, fire, and from his waist and above the appearance of
3 brilliance, the look of something luminous.[9] He stretched out the figure of a
hand, which took hold of me by the locks of my head, and a spirit lifted me
up between the land and the heavens and brought me to Jerusalem in a Godly
vision, to the entrance of the inner gate facing north where the statue of
4 jealousy – that incites jealous anger – stands. And there was the glory of the
5 God of Israel as in the vision that I saw in the valley,[10] and He said to me, "Man,
lift your eyes up toward the north." I lifted my eyes up toward the north, and
there, to the north of the gate of the altar, was this statue of jealousy at the
6 entry. He said to me, "Man, do you see what they are doing – that the House
of Israel is committing great abominations here to drive Me away from My
7 Sanctuary? You will see yet greater abominations." He brought me to the
8 entrance to the court, and I saw there a single hole in the wall, and He said
to me, "Man, dig through the wall." I dug through the wall, and there was
9 a single entrance. He said to me, "Come through; look at the evil abomina-
10 tions that they are carrying out here." I came through, and there I saw every
form of creeping thing and detestable animal and all the idols of the House
11 of Israel, all carved out on the surrounding walls. Seventy men from the elders
of the House of Israel were standing before them, with Yaazanyahu son of
Shafan[11] standing among them; each man had his censer in his hand, and a
12 dense cloud of incense was ascending. And He said to me, "Do you see what

9 | Cf. the vision in 1:26–27; see also 43:3–4.

10 | Referring to 3:22–23, which refers in turn to chapter 1.

11 | Possibly a descendant of Shafan the scribe, mentioned in II Kings, chapter 22.

לְנִדָּה יִהְיֶה כַּסְפָּם וּזְהָבָם לֹא־יוּכַל לְהַצִּילָם בְּיוֹם עֶבְרַת יְהוָה נַפְשָׁם
כ לֹא יְשַׂבֵּעוּ וּמְעֵיהֶם לֹא יְמַלֵּאוּ כִּי־מִכְשׁוֹל עֲוֺנָם הָיָה: וּצְבִי עֶדְיוֹ לְגָאוֹן
שָׂמָהוּ וְצַלְמֵי תוֹעֲבֹתָם שִׁקּוּצֵיהֶם עָשׂוּ בוֹ עַל־כֵּן נְתַתִּיו לָהֶם לְנִדָּה:
כא כב וּנְתַתִּיו בְּיַד־הַזָּרִים לָבַז וּלְרִשְׁעֵי הָאָרֶץ לְשָׁלָל וְחִלְּלוּהָ: וַהֲסִבּוֹתִי פָנַי
כג מֵהֶם וְחִלְּלוּ אֶת־צְפוּנִי וּבָאוּ־בָהּ פָּרִיצִים וְחִלְּלוּהָ: עֲשֵׂה
כד הָרַתּוֹק כִּי הָאָרֶץ מָלְאָה מִשְׁפַּט דָּמִים וְהָעִיר מָלְאָה חָמָס: וְהֵבֵאתִי
רָעֵי גוֹיִם וְיָרְשׁוּ אֶת־בָּתֵּיהֶם וְהִשְׁבַּתִּי גְּאוֹן עַזִּים וְנִחֲלוּ מְקַדְשֵׁיהֶם:
כה כו קְפָדָה־בָא וּבִקְשׁוּ שָׁלוֹם וָאָיִן: הֹוָה עַל־הֹוָה תָּבוֹא וּשְׁמֻעָה אֶל־
שְׁמוּעָה תִּהְיֶה וּבִקְשׁוּ חָזוֹן מִנָּבִיא וְתוֹרָה תֹּאבַד מִכֹּהֵן וְעֵצָה מִזְּקֵנִים:
כז הַמֶּלֶךְ יִתְאַבָּל וְנָשִׂיא יִלְבַּשׁ שְׁמָמָה וִידֵי עַם־הָאָרֶץ תִּבָּהַלְנָה מִדַּרְכָּם
ח א אֶעֱשֶׂה אוֹתָם וּבְמִשְׁפְּטֵיהֶם אֶשְׁפְּטֵם וְיָדְעוּ כִּי־אֲנִי יְהוָה: וַיְהִי | ד
בַּשָּׁנָה הַשִּׁשִּׁית בַּשִּׁשִּׁי בַּחֲמִשָּׁה לַחֹדֶשׁ אֲנִי יוֹשֵׁב בְּבֵיתִי וְזִקְנֵי יְהוּדָה
ב יוֹשְׁבִים לְפָנָי וַתִּפֹּל עָלַי שָׁם יַד אֲדֹנָי יְהוִה: וָאֶרְאֶה וְהִנֵּה דְמוּת
כְּמַרְאֵה־אֵשׁ מִמַּרְאֵה מָתְנָיו וּלְמַטָּה אֵשׁ וּמִמָּתְנָיו וּלְמַעְלָה כְּמַרְאֵה־
ג זֹהַר כְּעֵין הַחַשְׁמַלָה: וַיִּשְׁלַח תַּבְנִית יָד וַיִּקָּחֵנִי בְּצִיצִת רֹאשִׁי וַתִּשָּׂא
אֹתִי רוּחַ | בֵּין־הָאָרֶץ וּבֵין הַשָּׁמַיִם וַתָּבֵא אֹתִי יְרוּשָׁלְַמָה בְּמַרְאוֹת
אֱלֹהִים אֶל־פֶּתַח שַׁעַר הַפְּנִימִית הַפּוֹנֶה צָפוֹנָה אֲשֶׁר־שָׁם מוֹשַׁב
ד סֵמֶל הַקִּנְאָה הַמַּקְנֶה: וְהִנֵּה־שָׁם כְּבוֹד אֱלֹהֵי יִשְׂרָאֵל כַּמַּרְאֶה אֲשֶׁר
ה רָאִיתִי בַּבִּקְעָה: וַיֹּאמֶר אֵלַי בֶּן־אָדָם שָׂא־נָא עֵינֶיךָ דֶּרֶךְ צָפוֹנָה
וָאֶשָּׂא עֵינַי דֶּרֶךְ צָפוֹנָה וְהִנֵּה מִצָּפוֹן לְשַׁעַר הַמִּזְבֵּחַ סֵמֶל הַקִּנְאָה
ו הַזֶּה בַּבִּאָה: וַיֹּאמֶר אֵלַי בֶּן־אָדָם הֲרֹאֶה אַתָּה מהם עֹשִׂים תּוֹעֵבוֹת מָה הֵם
גְּדֹלוֹת אֲשֶׁר בֵּית־יִשְׂרָאֵל | עֹשִׂים פֹּה לְרָחֳקָה מֵעַל מִקְדָּשִׁי וְעוֹד
ז תָּשׁוּב תִּרְאֶה תּוֹעֵבוֹת גְּדֹלוֹת: וַיָּבֵא אֹתִי אֶל־פֶּתַח הֶחָצֵר וָאֶרְאֶה
ח וְהִנֵּה חֹר־אֶחָד בַּקִּיר: וַיֹּאמֶר אֵלַי בֶּן־אָדָם חֲתָר־נָא בַקִּיר וָאֶחְתֹּר
ט בַּקִּיר וְהִנֵּה פֶּתַח אֶחָד: וַיֹּאמֶר אֵלָי בֹּא וּרְאֵה אֶת־הַתּוֹעֵבוֹת הָרָעוֹת
י אֲשֶׁר הֵם עֹשִׂים פֹּה: וָאָבוֹא וָאֶרְאֶה וְהִנֵּה כָל־תַּבְנִית רֶמֶשׂ וּבְהֵמָה
יא שֶׁקֶץ וְכָל־גִּלּוּלֵי בֵּית יִשְׂרָאֵל מְחֻקֶּה עַל־הַקִּיר סָבִיב | סָבִיב: וְשִׁבְעִים
אִישׁ מִזִּקְנֵי בֵית־יִשְׂרָאֵל וְיַאֲזַנְיָהוּ בֶן־שָׁפָן עֹמֵד בְּתוֹכָם עֹמְדִים
יב לִפְנֵיהֶם וְאִישׁ מִקְטַרְתּוֹ בְּיָדוֹ וַעֲתַר עֲנַן־הַקְּטֹרֶת עֹלֶה: וַיֹּאמֶר אֵלַי
הֲרָאִיתָ בֶן־אָדָם אֲשֶׁר זִקְנֵי בֵית־יִשְׂרָאֵל עֹשִׂים בַּחֹשֶׁךְ אִישׁ בְּחַדְרֵי

the elders of the House of Israel are doing in the dark, each in his room of
graven images? For they say: 'The LORD does not see us; the LORD has gone
13 from the land.'" And He said to me, "You will soon see greater abominations
14 that they are committing." He brought me to the entrance of the northern
gate of the House of the LORD, and there women were sitting, wailing over
15 Tamuz.[12] And He said to me: "Do you see, Man? You will yet see
16 even greater abominations than these." And He brought me to the inner court
of the House of the LORD, and there, at the entrance to the Sanctuary of the
LORD, between its hallway and the altar, were about twenty-five men with
their backs to the Sanctuary of the LORD and their faces to the east, and they
17 were bowing down eastward – bowing to the sun. And He said to me, "Man,
do you see? Is it so light a thing to the House of Yehuda – the practice of these
abominations here – that they have filled the land with violence and anger
18 Me further and even raised the branch to their noses?![13] I, too, will act – with
fury. My eye will not pity, I will not show mercy; though loudly they call out
9 1 to Me, I will not hear them." And He called out loudly in my hearing, "Come
out, officers of forces in the city, each with his weapon of destruction in his
2 hand!" And six men came forward through the upper gate that faces north,
each with his bludgeon in his hand; among them was a man dressed in linen
with a scribe's instruments at his waist. They came forward and stood beside
3 the bronze altar. Now the glory of the God of Israel had moved off the cherub
it had rested upon to the threshold of the House.[14] He called to the man
4 dressed in linen with the scribe's instruments at his waist. The LORD
said to him, "Pass through the city, through Jerusalem, and put a mark on the
foreheads of the people sighing and crying over all the abominations that are
5 being done in her very midst." And to the others He said in my hearing, "Pass
through the city after him and strike – do not let your eye pity, do not show
6 mercy. The elderly, young men, young girls, small children, women – kill,
destroy, but do not go near any person who has the mark upon them; begin
with My Temple." And they began with the elders who were before the House.
7 He said to them, "Defile the House; fill the courts with slain; go out!" And
8 they went out; they struck the city. And as they were striking it down, I alone
was left; I fell on my face, and I cried, "But my Lord GOD! Will you destroy
9 all that remains of Israel, pouring Your fury out over Jerusalem?" And He said
to me: "The iniquity of the House of Israel and Yehuda is extremely great; the
land is filled with blood, and the city is full of corruption, for they have said,
10 'The LORD has gone from the land; the LORD does not see.' And so I will
not let My eye pity, I will not show mercy; their ways I will bring down on
11 their heads." Then the man dressed in linen with the scribe's instruments at
his waist returned and reported, "I have done that which you commanded
10 1 me." I looked – there, upon the expanse that was above the heads of

12 | In Mesopotamian mythology, a god who dies every year when vegetation wilts; mourning aims to restore the vegetation.

13 | Possibly an idolatrous ritual or an offensive gesture.

14 | Beginning its gradual movement out of the city. See also 10:4, 18–19, and 11:22–23.

מַשְׂכִּיתוֹ כִּי אֹמְרִים אֵין יהוה רֹאֶה אֹתָנוּ עָזַב יהוה אֶת־הָאָרֶץ׃
יג וַיֹּאמֶר אֵלָי עוֹד תָּשׁוּב תִּרְאֶה תּוֹעֵבוֹת גְּדֹלוֹת אֲשֶׁר־הֵמָּה עֹשִׂים׃
יד וַיָּבֵא אֹתִי אֶל־פֶּתַח שַׁעַר בֵּית־יהוה אֲשֶׁר אֶל־הַצָּפוֹנָה וְהִנֵּה־שָׁם
טו הַנָּשִׁים יֹשְׁבוֹת מְבַכּוֹת אֶת־הַתַּמּוּז׃ וַיֹּאמֶר אֵלַי
טז הֲרָאִיתָ בֶן־אָדָם עוֹד תָּשׁוּב תִּרְאֶה תּוֹעֵבוֹת גְּדֹלוֹת מֵאֵלֶּה׃ וַיָּבֵא
אֹתִי אֶל־חֲצַר בֵּית־יהוה הַפְּנִימִית וְהִנֵּה־פֶתַח הֵיכַל יהוה בֵּין הָאוּלָם
וּבֵין הַמִּזְבֵּחַ כְּעֶשְׂרִים וַחֲמִשָּׁה אִישׁ אֲחֹרֵיהֶם אֶל־הֵיכַל יהוה וּפְנֵיהֶם
יז קֵדְמָה וְהֵמָּה מִשְׁתַּחֲוִיתֶם קֵדְמָה לַשָּׁמֶשׁ׃ וַיֹּאמֶר אֵלַי הֲרָאִיתָ בֶן־
אָדָם הֲנָקֵל לְבֵית יְהוּדָה מֵעֲשׂוֹת אֶת־הַתּוֹעֵבוֹת אֲשֶׁר עָשׂוּ־פֹה
כִּי־מָלְאוּ אֶת־הָאָרֶץ חָמָס וַיָּשֻׁבוּ לְהַכְעִיסֵנִי וְהִנָּם שֹׁלְחִים אֶת־
יח הַזְּמוֹרָה אֶל־אַפָּם׃ וְגַם־אֲנִי אֶעֱשֶׂה בְחֵמָה לֹא־תָחוֹס עֵינִי וְלֹא אֶחְמֹל
ט א וְקָרְאוּ בְאָזְנַי קוֹל גָּדוֹל וְלֹא אֶשְׁמַע אוֹתָם׃ וַיִּקְרָא בְאָזְנַי קוֹל גָּדוֹל
ב לֵאמֹר קָרְבוּ פְּקֻדּוֹת הָעִיר וְאִישׁ כְּלִי מַשְׁחֵתוֹ בְּיָדוֹ׃ וְהִנֵּה שִׁשָּׁה
אֲנָשִׁים בָּאִים ׀ מִדֶּרֶךְ־שַׁעַר הָעֶלְיוֹן אֲשֶׁר ׀ מָפְנֶה צָפוֹנָה וְאִישׁ כְּלִי
מַפָּצוֹ בְּיָדוֹ וְאִישׁ־אֶחָד בְּתוֹכָם לָבֻשׁ בַּדִּים וְקֶסֶת הַסֹּפֵר בְּמָתְנָיו
ג וַיָּבֹאוּ וַיַּעַמְדוּ אֵצֶל מִזְבַּח הַנְּחֹשֶׁת׃ וּכְבוֹד ׀ אֱלֹהֵי יִשְׂרָאֵל נַעֲלָה
מֵעַל הַכְּרוּב אֲשֶׁר הָיָה עָלָיו אֶל מִפְתַּן הַבָּיִת וַיִּקְרָא אֶל־הָאִישׁ
ד הַלָּבֻשׁ הַבַּדִּים אֲשֶׁר קֶסֶת הַסֹּפֵר בְּמָתְנָיו׃ וַיֹּאמֶר
יהוה אֵלָו עֲבֹר בְּתוֹךְ הָעִיר בְּתוֹךְ יְרוּשָׁלָם וְהִתְוִיתָ תָּו עַל־מִצְחוֹת
הָאֲנָשִׁים הַנֶּאֱנָחִים וְהַנֶּאֱנָקִים עַל כָּל־הַתּוֹעֵבוֹת הַנַּעֲשׂוֹת בְּתוֹכָהּ׃
ה וּלְאֵלֶּה אָמַר בְּאָזְנַי עִבְרוּ בָעִיר אַחֲרָיו וְהַכּוּ עַל־תָּחֹס עֵינֵיכֶם וְאַל־ אַל־ | עֵינְכֶם
ו תַּחְמֹלוּ׃ זָקֵן בָּחוּר וּבְתוּלָה וְטַף וְנָשִׁים תַּהַרְגוּ לְמַשְׁחִית וְעַל־כָּל־אִישׁ
אֲשֶׁר־עָלָיו הַתָּו אַל־תִּגַּשׁוּ וּמִמִּקְדָּשִׁי תָּחֵלּוּ וַיָּחֵלּוּ בָּאֲנָשִׁים הַזְּקֵנִים
ז אֲשֶׁר לִפְנֵי הַבָּיִת׃ וַיֹּאמֶר אֲלֵיהֶם טַמְּאוּ אֶת־הַבַּיִת וּמַלְאוּ אֶת־
ח הַחֲצֵרוֹת חֲלָלִים צֵאוּ וְיָצְאוּ וְהִכּוּ בָעִיר׃ וַיְהִי כְּהַכּוֹתָם וְנֵאשֲׁאַר אָנִי
וָאֶפְּלָה עַל־פָּנַי וָאֶזְעַק וָאֹמַר אֲהָהּ אֲדֹנָי יֱהוִה הֲמַשְׁחִית אַתָּה אֵת
ט כָּל־שְׁאֵרִית יִשְׂרָאֵל בְּשָׁפְכְּךָ אֶת־חֲמָתְךָ עַל־יְרוּשָׁלָם׃ וַיֹּאמֶר אֵלַי
עֲוֺן בֵּית־יִשְׂרָאֵל וִיהוּדָה גָּדוֹל בִּמְאֹד מְאֹד וַתִּמָּלֵא הָאָרֶץ דָּמִים
וְהָעִיר מָלְאָה מֻטֶּה כִּי אָמְרוּ עָזַב יהוה אֶת־הָאָרֶץ וְאֵין יהוה רֹאֶה׃
י וְגַם־אֲנִי לֹא־תָחוֹס עֵינִי וְלֹא אֶחְמֹל דַּרְכָּם בְּרֹאשָׁם נָתָתִּי׃ וְהִנֵּה
הָאִישׁ ׀ לְבֻשׁ הַבַּדִּים אֲשֶׁר הַקֶּסֶת בְּמָתְנָיו מֵשִׁיב דָּבָר לֵאמֹר עָשִׂיתִי
י א כַּאֲשֶׁר צִוִּיתָנִי׃ וָאֶרְאֶה וְהִנֵּה אֶל־הָרָקִיעַ אֲשֶׁר עַל־רֹאשׁ ה כְּכֹל אֲשֶׁר

the cherubim, something like a sapphire, like the appearance of the form of
2 a throne, could be seen above them.[15] He spoke to the man dressed in linen;
He said, "Go into the space between the wheelworks, beneath the cherub;
fill your hands with burning coals from between the cherubim and scatter
3 them over the city." And he went in before my eyes. The cherubim were
standing to the right of the House; the man went in, and the cloud filled the
4 inner court. The glory of the LORD rose from the cherub upon the threshold
of the House; the House was filled with the cloud, and the radiance of the
5 glory of the LORD filled the court; the sound from the wings of the cherubim
could be heard all the way to the outer court – like the voice of El Shaddai
6 when He speaks. When He commanded the man dressed in linen, saying,
"Take fire from between the wheelworks, from between the cherubim," the
7 man came and stood by the wheel. One of the cherubim reached his hand
between the cherubim and into the fire between the cherubim; he picked it
up and put it into the hands of the man dressed in linen, who took it and then
8 came out. The cherubim appeared to have the figure of a man's hand under
9 their wings. And I looked: There were four wheels alongside the cherubim,
one wheel by this cherub and one wheel by that cherub,[16] and the appearance
10 of the wheels was bright like a topaz gem. In their appearance, all four had
11 the same form of a wheel within a wheel; when they moved, they moved in
the direction of any of their four sides; they did not turn when they moved,
for they moved toward whichever place their head turned toward; they did
12 not turn when they moved. All of their bodies, their backs, their hands, their
wings, and the wheels were filled, all over, with eyes – the wheels of the four
13 14 of them. It is these wheels that were called wheelworks in my hearing. Each
one had four faces: the first face was the face of a cherub, the second was the
face of a man, the third was the face of a lion, and the fourth was the face of
15 an eagle. And the cherubim rose up – these were the living beings that I saw
16 by the Kevar River[17] – and when the cherubim moved, the wheels moved
with them; and when the cherubim lifted up their wings so that they could
17 rise up above the land, the wheels that were with them did not turn: when
they stood, they too stood, and when they rose up, they too rose up, for the
18 spirit of the living beings was in them. And the glory of the LORD left the
19 threshold of the House to stand upon the cherubim; the cherubim lifted their
wings, and they rose up from the ground to leave – before my very eyes – with
the wheels beside them; they stood at the entrance of the eastern gate of the
House of the LORD, and the glory of the God of Israel was resting upon them
20 from above. These are the living beings that I saw beneath the God of Israel
21 by the Kevar River, and I knew that they were cherubim – four, each one had
four faces, and each one had four wings, and the form of a man's hand was
22 beneath their wings; the forms of their faces were those of the faces that I saw
by the Kevar River both in their appearance and in themselves; each moved

15 | Cf. 1:26.
16 | Cf. 1:15–21.
17 | See chapter 1.

ב הַכְּרֻבִים כְּאֶבֶן סַפִּיר כְּמַרְאֵה דְּמוּת כִּסֵּא נִרְאָה עֲלֵיהֶם׃ וַיֹּאמֶר אֶל־
הָאִישׁ ׀ לְבֻשׁ הַבַּדִּים וַיֹּאמֶר בֹּא אֶל־בֵּינוֹת לַגַּלְגַּל אֶל־תַּחַת לַכְּרוּב
וּמַלֵּא חָפְנֶיךָ גַחֲלֵי־אֵשׁ מִבֵּינוֹת לַכְּרֻבִים וּזְרֹק עַל־הָעִיר וַיָּבֹא לְעֵינָי׃
ג וְהַכְּרֻבִים עֹמְדִים מִימִין לַבַּיִת בְּבֹאוֹ הָאִישׁ וְהֶעָנָן מָלֵא אֶת־הֶחָצֵר
ד הַפְּנִימִית׃ וַיָּרָם כְּבוֹד־יְהוָה מֵעַל הַכְּרוּב עַל מִפְתַּן הַבָּיִת וַיִּמָּלֵא
ה הַבַּיִת אֶת־הֶעָנָן וְהֶחָצֵר מָלְאָה אֶת־נֹגַהּ כְּבוֹד יְהוָה׃ וְקוֹל כַּנְפֵי
ו הַכְּרוּבִים נִשְׁמַע עַד־הֶחָצֵר הַחִיצֹנָה כְּקוֹל אֵל־שַׁדַּי בְּדַבְּרוֹ׃ וַיְהִי
בְּצַוֹּתוֹ אֶת־הָאִישׁ לְבֻשׁ־הַבַּדִּים לֵאמֹר קַח אֵשׁ מִבֵּינוֹת לַגַּלְגַּל
ז מִבֵּינוֹת לַכְּרוּבִים וַיָּבֹא וַיַּעֲמֹד אֵצֶל הָאוֹפָן׃ וַיִּשְׁלַח הַכְּרוּב אֶת־יָדוֹ
מִבֵּינוֹת לַכְּרוּבִים אֶל־הָאֵשׁ אֲשֶׁר בֵּינוֹת הַכְּרֻבִים וַיִּשָּׂא וַיִּתֵּן אֶל־
ח חָפְנֵי לְבֻשׁ הַבַּדִּים וַיִּקַּח וַיֵּצֵא׃ וַיֵּרָא לַכְּרֻבִים תַּבְנִית יַד־אָדָם תַּחַת
ט כַּנְפֵיהֶם׃ וָאֶרְאֶה וְהִנֵּה אַרְבָּעָה אוֹפַנִּים אֵצֶל הַכְּרוּבִים אוֹפַן אֶחָד
אֵצֶל הַכְּרוּב אֶחָד וְאוֹפַן אֶחָד אֵצֶל הַכְּרוּב אֶחָד וּמַרְאֵה הָאוֹפַנִּים
י כְּעֵין אֶבֶן תַּרְשִׁישׁ׃ וּמַרְאֵיהֶם דְּמוּת אֶחָד לְאַרְבַּעְתָּם כַּאֲשֶׁר יִהְיֶה
יא הָאוֹפַן בְּתוֹךְ הָאוֹפָן׃ בְּלֶכְתָּם אֶל־אַרְבַּעַת רִבְעֵיהֶם יֵלֵכוּ לֹא יִסַּבּוּ
בְּלֶכְתָּם כִּי הַמָּקוֹם אֲשֶׁר־יִפְנֶה הָרֹאשׁ אַחֲרָיו יֵלֵכוּ לֹא יִסַּבּוּ בְּלֶכְתָּם׃
יב וְכָל־בְּשָׂרָם וְגַבֵּהֶם וִידֵיהֶם וְכַנְפֵיהֶם וְהָאוֹפַנִּים מְלֵאִים עֵינַיִם סָבִיב
יג יד לְאַרְבַּעְתָּם אוֹפַנֵּיהֶם׃ לָאוֹפַנִּים לָהֶם קוֹרָא הַגַּלְגַּל בְּאָזְנָי׃ וְאַרְבָּעָה
פָנִים לְאֶחָד פְּנֵי הָאֶחָד פְּנֵי הַכְּרוּב וּפְנֵי הַשֵּׁנִי פְּנֵי אָדָם וְהַשְּׁלִישִׁי
טו פְּנֵי אַרְיֵה וְהָרְבִיעִי פְּנֵי־נָשֶׁר׃ וַיֵּרֹמּוּ הַכְּרוּבִים הִיא הַחַיָּה אֲשֶׁר
טז רָאִיתִי בִּנְהַר־כְּבָר׃ וּבְלֶכֶת הַכְּרוּבִים יֵלְכוּ הָאוֹפַנִּים אֶצְלָם וּבִשְׂאֵת
הַכְּרוּבִים אֶת־כַּנְפֵיהֶם לָרוּם מֵעַל הָאָרֶץ לֹא־יִסַּבּוּ הָאוֹפַנִּים גַּם־
יז הֵם מֵאֶצְלָם׃ בְּעָמְדָם יַעֲמֹדוּ וּבְרוֹמָם יֵרוֹמּוּ אוֹתָם כִּי רוּחַ הַחַיָּה
יח יט בָּהֶם׃ וַיֵּצֵא כְּבוֹד יְהוָה מֵעַל מִפְתַּן הַבָּיִת וַיַּעֲמֹד עַל־הַכְּרוּבִים׃ וַיִּשְׂאוּ
הַכְּרוּבִים אֶת־כַּנְפֵיהֶם וַיֵּרוֹמּוּ מִן־הָאָרֶץ לְעֵינַי בְּצֵאתָם וְהָאוֹפַנִּים
לְעֻמָּתָם וַיַּעֲמֹד פֶּתַח שַׁעַר בֵּית־יְהוָה הַקַּדְמוֹנִי וּכְבוֹד אֱלֹהֵי־
כ יִשְׂרָאֵל עֲלֵיהֶם מִלְמָעְלָה׃ הִיא הַחַיָּה אֲשֶׁר רָאִיתִי תַּחַת אֱלֹהֵי־יִשְׂרָאֵל
כא בִּנְהַר־כְּבָר וָאֵדַע כִּי כְרוּבִים הֵמָּה׃ אַרְבָּעָה אַרְבָּעָה פָנִים לְאֶחָד
כב וְאַרְבַּע כְּנָפַיִם לְאֶחָד וּדְמוּת יְדֵי אָדָם תַּחַת כַּנְפֵיהֶם׃ וּדְמוּת פְּנֵיהֶם
הֵמָּה הַפָּנִים אֲשֶׁר רָאִיתִי עַל־נְהַר־כְּבָר מַרְאֵיהֶם וְאוֹתָם אִישׁ אֶל־

11 1 in the direction of one of the faces. And a spirit lifted me up and brought me
to the eastern gate of the House of the LORD, which faces east, and there
at the entrance to the gate were twenty-five men. And I saw among them
Yaazanya the son of Azur and Pelatyahu son of Benayahu, officials of the
2 people. And He said to me: "Man, these are the men plotting sin
3 and giving evil advice in this city. They say, 'There is no need now for building
4 houses; the city, she is the pot – we are the meat!'[18] And so, prophesy
5 against them; prophesy, Man." And so the spirit of the LORD fell upon me,
and He said to me, "Say this: So says the LORD: This is what you said, House
6 of Israel; I know what comes up in your minds. You have made your slain ever
7 more numerous in this city; you have filled her streets with slain. So
the Lord GOD says this: The slain you have put in her midst, they are the meat,
8 and she is the pot, and you, I will remove from her midst.[19] You feared the
9 sword; I will bring the sword down upon you, declares the Lord GOD. I will
take you out from her midst; I will give you over into the hands of strangers,
10 and I will execute judgments upon you. You will fall by the sword, upon the
11 border of Israel I will judge you, and you will know that I am the LORD. She
will not be a pot for you, but you will be the meat in her; I will judge you
12 in the borders of Israel and you will know that I am the LORD. You did not
follow My statutes, you did not practice My laws, but you acted according to
13 the laws of the nations around you." As I was prophesying, Pelatyahu son of
Benaya fell dead, and I fell on my face and cried a great cry: "Ah, my Lord
14 GOD, You are destroying all that remains of Israel!" And the word
15 of the LORD came to me, saying: "Man, your brothers, your brothers, your
very kinsmen, all of the House of Israel, entirely, the inhabitants of Jerusalem
say to them: 'They are far from the LORD; this land has been given to us as a
16 possession!'[20] And so, say: So says the Lord GOD: Though I have
placed them far away among the nations, though I have scattered them over
the lands and am but a small sanctuary for them in whichever lands they come
17 to... So say: So says the Lord GOD: I will gather you in from these
other nations; I will bring you in from the countries where you have been
18 scattered, and I will give you the land of Israel. And they will come there, and
19 they will remove all the detestable things, all the abominations, from her. I
will give them one heart, I will put a new spirit into you. I will remove the
20 heart of stone from their flesh and give them a heart of flesh, so that they will
follow My decrees and keep My laws and fulfill them; they will be My people,
21 and I will be their God. And those whose hearts are drawn to the heart of
their detestable things and abominations, I will bring their ways down on
22 their heads, declares the Lord GOD." The cherubim lifted up their wings with
the wheels beside them, and above, upon them, the glory of the God of Israel.

---

18 | That is, the city walls will protect us from destruction like the pot protects the meat.
19 | That is, I will remove you from the city like cooked meat is removed from a pot.
20 | The current inhabitants of Jerusalem claim exclusive ownership of the city, since those exiled are far away.

יא א עֵבֶר פָּנָיו יֵלֵכוּ: וַתִּשָּׂא אֹתִי רוּחַ וַתָּבֵא אֹתִי אֶל־שַׁעַר בֵּית־יְהוָה
הַקַּדְמוֹנִי הַפּוֹנֶה קָדִימָה וְהִנֵּה בְּפֶתַח הַשַּׁעַר עֶשְׂרִים וַחֲמִשָּׁה אִישׁ
וָאֶרְאֶה בְתוֹכָם אֶת־יַאֲזַנְיָה בֶן־עַזֻּר וְאֶת־פְּלַטְיָהוּ בֶן־בְּנָיָהוּ שָׂרֵי
ב הָעָם: וַיֹּאמֶר אֵלָי בֶּן־אָדָם אֵלֶּה הָאֲנָשִׁים הַחֹשְׁבִים אָוֶן
ג וְהַיֹּעֲצִים עֲצַת־רָע בָּעִיר הַזֹּאת: הָאֹמְרִים לֹא בְקָרוֹב בְּנוֹת בָּתִּים
ד הִיא הַסִּיר וַאֲנַחְנוּ הַבָּשָׂר: לָכֵן הִנָּבֵא עֲלֵיהֶם הִנָּבֵא
ה בֶּן־אָדָם: וַתִּפֹּל עָלַי רוּחַ יְהוָה וַיֹּאמֶר אֵלַי אֱמֹר כֹּה־אָמַר יְהוָה כֵּן
ו אֲמַרְתֶּם בֵּית יִשְׂרָאֵל וּמַעֲלוֹת רוּחֲכֶם אֲנִי יְדַעְתִּיהָ: הִרְבֵּיתֶם חַלְלֵיכֶם
ז בָּעִיר הַזֹּאת וּמִלֵּאתֶם חוּצֹתֶיהָ חָלָל: לָכֵן כֹּה־
אָמַר אֲדֹנָי יֱהוִה חַלְלֵיכֶם אֲשֶׁר שַׂמְתֶּם בְּתוֹכָהּ הֵמָּה הַבָּשָׂר וְהִיא
ח הַסִּיר וְאֶתְכֶם הוֹצִיא מִתּוֹכָהּ: חֶרֶב יְרֵאתֶם וְחֶרֶב אָבִיא עֲלֵיכֶם
ט נְאֻם אֲדֹנָי יֱהוִה: וְהוֹצֵאתִי אֶתְכֶם מִתּוֹכָהּ וְנָתַתִּי אֶתְכֶם בְּיַד־זָרִים
י וְעָשִׂיתִי בָכֶם שְׁפָטִים: בַּחֶרֶב תִּפֹּלוּ עַל־גְּבוּל יִשְׂרָאֵל אֶשְׁפּוֹט אֶתְכֶם
יא וִידַעְתֶּם כִּי־אֲנִי יְהוָה: הִיא לֹא־תִהְיֶה לָכֶם לְסִיר וְאַתֶּם תִּהְיוּ בְתוֹכָהּ
יב לְבָשָׂר אֶל־גְּבוּל יִשְׂרָאֵל אֶשְׁפֹּט אֶתְכֶם: וִידַעְתֶּם כִּי־אֲנִי יְהוָה אֲשֶׁר
בְּחֻקַּי לֹא הֲלַכְתֶּם וּמִשְׁפָּטַי לֹא עֲשִׂיתֶם וּכְמִשְׁפְּטֵי הַגּוֹיִם אֲשֶׁר
יג סְבִיבוֹתֵיכֶם עֲשִׂיתֶם: וַיְהִי כְּהִנָּבְאִי וּפְלַטְיָהוּ בֶן־בְּנָיָה מֵת וָאֶפֹּל
עַל־פָּנַי וָאֶזְעַק ׀ קוֹל גָּדוֹל וָאֹמַר אֲהָהּ אֲדֹנָי יֱהוִה כָּלָה אַתָּה עֹשֶׂה
יד אֵת שְׁאֵרִית יִשְׂרָאֵל: וַיְהִי דְבַר־יְהוָה אֵלַי לֵאמֹר:
טו בֶּן־אָדָם אַחֶיךָ אַחֶיךָ אַנְשֵׁי גְאֻלָּתֶךָ וְכָל־בֵּית יִשְׂרָאֵל כֻּלֹּה אֲשֶׁר
אָמְרוּ לָהֶם יֹשְׁבֵי יְרוּשָׁלִַם רַחֲקוּ מֵעַל יְהוָה לָנוּ הִיא נִתְּנָה הָאָרֶץ
טז לְמוֹרָשָׁה: לָכֵן אֱמֹר כֹּה אָמַר אֲדֹנָי יֱהוִה כִּי הִרְחַקְתִּים
בַּגּוֹיִם וְכִי הֲפִיצוֹתִים בָּאֲרָצוֹת וָאֱהִי לָהֶם לְמִקְדָּשׁ מְעַט בָּאֲרָצוֹת
יז אֲשֶׁר־בָּאוּ שָׁם: לָכֵן אֱמֹר כֹּה־אָמַר אֲדֹנָי יֱהוִה
וְקִבַּצְתִּי אֶתְכֶם מִן־הָעַמִּים וְאָסַפְתִּי אֶתְכֶם מִן־הָאֲרָצוֹת אֲשֶׁר נְפֹצוֹתֶם
יח בָּהֶם וְנָתַתִּי לָכֶם אֶת־אַדְמַת יִשְׂרָאֵל: וּבָאוּ־שָׁמָּה וְהֵסִירוּ אֶת־כָּל־
יט שִׁקּוּצֶיהָ וְאֶת־כָּל־תּוֹעֲבוֹתֶיהָ מִמֶּנָּה: וְנָתַתִּי לָהֶם לֵב אֶחָד וְרוּחַ
חֲדָשָׁה אֶתֵּן בְּקִרְבְּכֶם וַהֲסִרֹתִי לֵב הָאֶבֶן מִבְּשָׂרָם וְנָתַתִּי לָהֶם לֵב בָּשָׂר:
כ לְמַעַן בְּחֻקֹּתַי יֵלֵכוּ וְאֶת־מִשְׁפָּטַי יִשְׁמְרוּ וְעָשׂוּ אֹתָם וְהָיוּ־לִי לְעָם ו
כא וַאֲנִי אֶהְיֶה לָהֶם לֵאלֹהִים: וְאֶל־לֵב שִׁקּוּצֵיהֶם וְתוֹעֲבוֹתֵיהֶם לִבָּם
כב הֹלֵךְ דַּרְכָּם בְּרֹאשָׁם נָתַתִּי נְאֻם אֲדֹנָי יֱהוִה: וַיִּשְׂאוּ הַכְּרוּבִים אֶת־
כַּנְפֵיהֶם וְהָאוֹפַנִּים לְעֻמָּתָם וּכְבוֹד אֱלֹהֵי־יִשְׂרָאֵל עֲלֵיהֶם מִלְמָעְלָה:

23 The glory of the LORD rose from within the city and stood upon the mountain
24 east of the city. And a spirit lifted me up and brought back me to the Chaldeans,
to the exile, in a vision by the spirit of God, and the vision I had seen rose off
25 me. And to the exiles I related all the things that the LORD had shown
12 1 me. 2 And the word of the LORD came to me, saying: "Man, you are
living in the midst of this defiant house; they have eyes to see with, but they
do not see; they have ears to hear with, but they do not hear,[21] for they are
3 a defiant house. You, Man, make an exile's bundle for yourself, and
go into exile by day before their eyes; you will go into exile from your home
to another place before their eyes; perhaps they will see it, for they are a
4 defiant house. Bring out your belongings as an exile's bundle by day before
their eyes; by night you will go out before their eyes like one going into exile.
5 Before their eyes burrow through the wall and take your bundle out through
6 it, before their eyes carry it on your shoulder; bring it out in the dark. Cover
your face so that you cannot see the land, for I am making you a sign for the
7 House of Israel." I did as I had been commanded: I brought my belongings
out as an exile's bundle by day, and by night I burrowed through the wall with
my hand; in the dark I took it out and carried it on my shoulder before their
8 eyes. And the word of the LORD came to me in the morning, saying:
9 "Man, has not the House of Israel, that defiant house, asked you, 'What are
10 you doing?' Say to them: So says the Lord GOD: The prince is this burden in
11 Jerusalem,[22] and the whole of the House of Israel who are in its midst. Say: I
am your sign; just as I have done, this is what will be done to them: they will
12 go into exile in captivity. The prince who is in their midst will carry the bundle
on his shoulder in darkness and go out; they will burrow through the wall to
take him out through it; his face will be covered so that he will not see the
13 land with his eyes. I will spread My net over him; he will be caught in My trap.
I will take him to Babylon, the land of the Chaldeans, but he will not see it,
14 and there he will die. All who are around him, his attendants, all his forces, I
15 will scatter to the winds; I will draw the sword after them. They will know
that I am the LORD when I strew them among the nations and scatter them
16 over the lands. I will leave a small number of them after sword, famine, and
plague to tell of all their abominations among the nations that they go to, and
17 they will know that I am the LORD." And the word of the LORD came
18 to me, saying: "Man, eat your bread trembling; drink your water quaking and
19 anxious. Say to the people of the land: So says the Lord GOD to the inhabitants
of Jerusalem in the land of Israel: They will eat their bread anxious; they will
drink their water aghast. And so, the land will be devastated of all that fills her
20 because of the lawlessness of all who inhabit her; the populated cities will be
laid waste, and the land will be desolate; and you will know that I am the
21 LORD." 22 And the word of the LORD came to me, saying: "Man, to
you on the soil of Israel, what does this saying mean: 'Time passes; every

---

21 | Cf. Psalms 115:5–6; Isaiah 6:9–10.

22 | The prince is Tzidkiya, who would be exiled (II Kings 24:18–25:21). *Masa* (burden) resonates with *nasi* (prince) and derives from the same Hebrew root.

כג וַיַּעַל כְּבוֹד יהוה מֵעַל תּוֹךְ הָעִיר וַיַּעֲמֹד עַל־הָהָר אֲשֶׁר מִקֶּדֶם לָעִיר:
כד וְרוּחַ נְשָׂאַתְנִי וַתְּבִיאֵנִי כַשְׂדִּימָה אֶל־הַגּוֹלָה בַּמַּרְאֶה בְּרוּחַ אֱלֹהִים
כה וַיַּעַל מֵעָלַי הַמַּרְאֶה אֲשֶׁר רָאִיתִי: וָאֲדַבֵּר אֶל־הַגּוֹלָה אֵת כָּל־דִּבְרֵי
יב א ב יהוה אֲשֶׁר הֶרְאָנִי: וַיְהִי דְבַר־יהוה אֵלַי לֵאמֹר: בֶּן־אָדָם
בְּתוֹךְ בֵּית־הַמֶּרִי אַתָּה יֹשֵׁב אֲשֶׁר עֵינַיִם לָהֶם לִרְאוֹת וְלֹא רָאוּ אָזְנַיִם
ג לָהֶם לִשְׁמֹעַ וְלֹא שָׁמֵעוּ כִּי בֵּית מְרִי הֵם: וְאַתָּה בֶן־
אָדָם עֲשֵׂה לְךָ כְּלֵי גוֹלָה וּגְלֵה יוֹמָם לְעֵינֵיהֶם וְגָלִיתָ מִמְּקוֹמְךָ אֶל־
ד מָקוֹם אַחֵר לְעֵינֵיהֶם אוּלַי יִרְאוּ כִּי בֵּית מְרִי הֵמָּה: וְהוֹצֵאתָ כֵלֶיךָ
כִּכְלֵי גוֹלָה יוֹמָם לְעֵינֵיהֶם וְאַתָּה תֵּצֵא בָעֶרֶב לְעֵינֵיהֶם כְּמוֹצָאֵי גּוֹלָה:
ה ו לְעֵינֵיהֶם חֲתָר־לְךָ בַקִּיר וְהוֹצֵאתָ בּוֹ: לְעֵינֵיהֶם עַל־כָּתֵף תִּשָּׂא
בָּעֲלָטָה תוֹצִיא פָּנֶיךָ תְכַסֶּה וְלֹא תִרְאֶה אֶת־הָאָרֶץ כִּי־מוֹפֵת נְתַתִּיךָ
ז לְבֵית יִשְׂרָאֵל: וָאַעַשׂ כֵּן כַּאֲשֶׁר צֻוֵּיתִי כֵּלַי הוֹצֵאתִי כִּכְלֵי גוֹלָה יוֹמָם
וּבָעֶרֶב חָתַרְתִּי־לִי בַקִּיר בְּיָד בָּעֲלָטָה הוֹצֵאתִי עַל־כָּתֵף נָשָׂאתִי
ח לְעֵינֵיהֶם: וַיְהִי דְבַר־יהוה אֵלַי בַּבֹּקֶר לֵאמֹר:
ט בֶּן־אָדָם הֲלֹא אָמְרוּ אֵלֶיךָ בֵּית יִשְׂרָאֵל בֵּית הַמֶּרִי מָה אַתָּה עֹשֶׂה:
י אֱמֹר אֲלֵיהֶם כֹּה אָמַר אֲדֹנָי יֱהוִה הַנָּשִׂיא הַמַּשָּׂא הַזֶּה בִּירוּשָׁלִַם
יא וְכָל־בֵּית יִשְׂרָאֵל אֲשֶׁר־הֵמָּה בְתוֹכָם: אֱמֹר אֲנִי מוֹפֶתְכֶם כַּאֲשֶׁר
יב עָשִׂיתִי כֵּן יֵעָשֶׂה לָהֶם בַּגּוֹלָה בַשְּׁבִי יֵלֵכוּ: וְהַנָּשִׂיא אֲשֶׁר־בְּתוֹכָם
אֶל־כָּתֵף יִשָּׂא בָּעֲלָטָה וְיֵצֵא בַּקִּיר יַחְתְּרוּ לְהוֹצִיא בוֹ פָּנָיו יְכַסֶּה יַעַן
יג אֲשֶׁר לֹא־יִרְאֶה לַעַיִן הוּא אֶת־הָאָרֶץ: וּפָרַשְׂתִּי אֶת־רִשְׁתִּי עָלָיו
וְנִתְפַּשׂ בִּמְצוּדָתִי וְהֵבֵאתִי אֹתוֹ בָבֶלָה אֶרֶץ כַּשְׂדִּים וְאוֹתָהּ לֹא־יִרְאֶה
יד וְשָׁם יָמוּת: וְכֹל אֲשֶׁר סְבִיבֹתָיו עֶזְרֹה וְכָל־אֲגַפָּיו אֱזָרֶה לְכָל־רוּחַ
טו וְחֶרֶב אָרִיק אַחֲרֵיהֶם: וְיָדְעוּ כִּי־אֲנִי יהוה בַּהֲפִיצִי אוֹתָם בַּגּוֹיִם וְזֵרִיתִי
טז אוֹתָם בָּאֲרָצוֹת: וְהוֹתַרְתִּי מֵהֶם אַנְשֵׁי מִסְפָּר מֵחֶרֶב מֵרָעָב וּמִדָּבֶר
לְמַעַן יְסַפְּרוּ אֶת־כָּל־תּוֹעֲבוֹתֵיהֶם בַּגּוֹיִם אֲשֶׁר־בָּאוּ שָׁם וְיָדְעוּ כִּי־
יז יח אֲנִי יהוה: וַיְהִי דְבַר־יהוה אֵלַי לֵאמֹר: בֶּן־אָדָם לַחְמְךָ
יט בְּרַעַשׁ תֹּאכֵל וּמֵימֶיךָ בְּרָגְזָה וּבִדְאָגָה תִּשְׁתֶּה: וְאָמַרְתָּ אֶל־עַם הָאָרֶץ
כֹּה־אָמַר אֲדֹנָי יֱהוִה לְיוֹשְׁבֵי יְרוּשָׁלִַם אֶל־אַדְמַת יִשְׂרָאֵל לַחְמָם
בִּדְאָגָה יֹאכֵלוּ וּמֵימֵיהֶם בְּשִׁמָּמוֹן יִשְׁתּוּ לְמַעַן תֵּשַׁם אַרְצָהּ מִמְּלֹאָהּ
כ מֵחֲמַס כָּל־הַיֹּשְׁבִים בָּהּ: וְהֶעָרִים הַנּוֹשָׁבוֹת תֶּחֱרַבְנָה וְהָאָרֶץ שְׁמָמָה
כא תִהְיֶה וִידַעְתֶּם כִּי־אֲנִי יהוה: וַיְהִי דְבַר־יהוה אֵלַי
כב לֵאמֹר: בֶּן־אָדָם מָה־הַמָּשָׁל הַזֶּה לָכֶם עַל־אַדְמַת יִשְׂרָאֵל לֵאמֹר

23 vision comes to nothing'? And so, say to them: So says the Lord God: I will
bring an end to this saying; they will no longer use it in Israel; instead, say to
24 them: 'The days are near, each word of every vision.' Never again will there
25 be any false visions or fawning divinations among the House of Israel. For I,
the Lord, will speak; every word that I speak will be fulfilled; it will no longer
be held off; in your days, defiant house, I will speak a word and fulfill it,
26 declares the Lord God." And the word of the Lord came to me,
27 saying: "Man, the House of Israel says, 'The vision he sees is for many days
28 in the future; he prophesies for a far-off time.' So say to them: So
says the Lord God: All My words will no longer be held off; every word I
13 1 speak will be fulfilled, declares the Lord God." And the word
2 of the Lord came to me, saying: "Man, prophesy against those prophets of
Israel who prophesy; say to those who prophesy their own hearts: Hear the
3 word of the Lord. So says the Lord God: Woe to those depraved prophets
4 who go after their own spirit, who have seen nothing. Like foxes among ruins
5 your prophets have become, Israel. You have not gone up into the breaches
or built a fence for the House of Israel so that they can stand strong in
6 battle on the day of the Lord. They profess false visions, lying divinations,
saying, 'So declares the Lord,' when the Lord had not sent them, and
7 expecting their words to be fulfilled. Have you not professed false visions,
uttered lying divinations, and said, 'So declares the Lord,' when I have not
8 spoken? So the Lord God says this: Because you speak falsehood
9 and profess lies, behold, I am upon you, declares the Lord God. My hand
will be against the prophets who assert false visions, those who divine lies;
they will not be part of the company of My people; they will not be written
in the annals of the House of Israel; they will not come back to the soil of
10 Israel; you will know that I am the Lord God. For the very reason that they
have misled my people, saying, 'All is well,' when all is not well, the people
11 build a thin wall, and they daub it with whitewash. Say to those daubing on
the whitewash: It will fall; there will be torrential rain; you, hailstones, will
12 fall; storm winds will burst forth; and when the wall falls, will they not ask
13 of you, 'Where is the whitewash that you daubed?' So the Lord
God says this: I will make storm winds burst forth in My fury; there will be
14 torrential rain in My anger; and hailstones in fury, for destruction. I will tear
down the wall you daubed with whitewash; I will raze it to the ground, bare
its foundation; it will fall, and you will be destroyed in her midst, and you
15 will know that I am the Lord. I will exhaust My fury upon the wall, upon
those who daubed her with whitewash; I will say to you: Gone is the wall,
16 gone are those who daubed it, prophets of Israel who prophesy to Jerusalem,
asserting visions to her that all is well when all is not well, declares the Lord
17 God. And you, Man, turn your face to the daughters of your people

כג יַאַרְכוּ הַיָּמִים וְאָבַד כָּל־חָזוֹן: לָכֵן אֱמֹר אֲלֵיהֶם כֹּה־אָמַר אֲדֹנָי יֱהֹוִה
הִשְׁבַּתִּי אֶת־הַמָּשָׁל הַזֶּה וְלֹא־יִמְשְׁלוּ אֹתוֹ עוֹד בְּיִשְׂרָאֵל כִּי אִם־דַּבֵּר
כד אֲלֵיהֶם קָרְבוּ הַיָּמִים וּדְבַר כָּל־חָזוֹן: כִּי לֹא יִהְיֶה עוֹד כָּל־חֲזוֹן שָׁוְא
כה וּמִקְסַם חָלָק בְּתוֹךְ בֵּית יִשְׂרָאֵל: כִּי | אֲנִי יְהוָה אֲדַבֵּר אֵת אֲשֶׁר
אֲדַבֵּר דָּבָר וְיֵעָשֶׂה לֹא תִמָּשֵׁךְ עוֹד כִּי בִימֵיכֶם בֵּית הַמֶּרִי אֲדַבֵּר דָּבָר
כו וַעֲשִׂיתִיו נְאֻם אֲדֹנָי יֱהֹוִה: וַיְהִי דְבַר־יְהוָה אֵלַי לֵאמֹר:
כז בֶּן־אָדָם הִנֵּה בֵית־יִשְׂרָאֵל אֹמְרִים הֶחָזוֹן אֲשֶׁר־הוּא חֹזֶה לְיָמִים
כח רַבִּים וּלְעִתִּים רְחוֹקוֹת הוּא נִבָּא: לָכֵן אֱמֹר אֲלֵיהֶם כֹּה
אָמַר אֲדֹנָי יֱהֹוִה לֹא־תִמָּשֵׁךְ עוֹד כָּל־דְּבָרָי אֲשֶׁר אֲדַבֵּר דָּבָר וְיֵעָשֶׂה
יג א ב נְאֻם אֲדֹנָי יֱהֹוִה: וַיְהִי דְבַר־יְהוָה אֵלַי לֵאמֹר: בֶּן־אָדָם
הִנָּבֵא אֶל־נְבִיאֵי יִשְׂרָאֵל הַנִּבָּאִים וְאָמַרְתָּ לִנְבִיאֵי מִלִּבָּם שִׁמְעוּ
ג דְּבַר־יְהוָה: כֹּה אָמַר אֲדֹנָי יֱהֹוִה הוֹי עַל־הַנְּבִיאִים הַנְּבָלִים אֲשֶׁר
ד הֹלְכִים אַחַר רוּחָם וּלְבִלְתִּי רָאוּ: כְּשֻׁעָלִים בָּחֳרָבוֹת נְבִיאֶיךָ יִשְׂרָאֵל
ה הָיוּ: לֹא עֲלִיתֶם בַּפְּרָצוֹת וַתִּגְדְּרוּ גָדֵר עַל־בֵּית יִשְׂרָאֵל לַעֲמֹד
ו בַּמִּלְחָמָה בְּיוֹם יְהוָה: חָזוּ שָׁוְא וְקֶסֶם כָּזָב הָאֹמְרִים נְאֻם־יְהוָה וַיהוָה
ז לֹא שְׁלָחָם וְיִחֲלוּ לְקַיֵּם דָּבָר: הֲלוֹא מַחֲזֵה־שָׁוְא חֲזִיתֶם וּמִקְסַם כָּזָב
ח אֲמַרְתֶּם וְאֹמְרִים נְאֻם־יְהוָה וַאֲנִי לֹא דִבַּרְתִּי: לָכֵן כֹּה
אָמַר אֲדֹנָי יֱהֹוִה יַעַן דַּבֶּרְכֶם שָׁוְא וַחֲזִיתֶם כָּזָב לָכֵן הִנְנִי אֲלֵיכֶם נְאֻם
ט אֲדֹנָי יֱהֹוִה: וְהָיְתָה יָדִי אֶל־הַנְּבִיאִים הַחֹזִים שָׁוְא וְהַקֹּסְמִים כָּזָב
בְּסוֹד עַמִּי לֹא־יִהְיוּ וּבִכְתָב בֵּית־יִשְׂרָאֵל לֹא יִכָּתֵבוּ וְאֶל־אַדְמַת
י יִשְׂרָאֵל לֹא יָבֹאוּ וִידַעְתֶּם כִּי אֲנִי אֲדֹנָי יֱהֹוִה: יַעַן וּבְיַעַן הִטְעוּ אֶת־
עַמִּי לֵאמֹר שָׁלוֹם וְאֵין שָׁלוֹם וְהוּא בֹּנֶה חַיִץ וְהִנָּם טָחִים אֹתוֹ תָּפֵל:
יא אֱמֹר אֶל־טָחֵי תָפֵל וְיִפֹּל הָיָה | גֶּשֶׁם שׁוֹטֵף וְאַתֵּנָה אַבְנֵי אֶלְגָּבִישׁ
יב תִּפֹּלְנָה וְרוּחַ סְעָרוֹת תְּבַקֵּעַ: וְהִנֵּה נָפַל הַקִּיר הֲלוֹא יֵאָמֵר אֲלֵיכֶם
יג אַיֵּה הַטִּיחַ אֲשֶׁר טַחְתֶּם: לָכֵן כֹּה אָמַר אֲדֹנָי יֱהֹוִה
וּבִקַּעְתִּי רוּחַ־סְעָרוֹת בַּחֲמָתִי וְגֶשֶׁם שֹׁטֵף בְּאַפִּי יִהְיֶה וְאַבְנֵי אֶלְגָּבִישׁ
יד בְּחֵמָה לְכָלָה: וְהָרַסְתִּי אֶת־הַקִּיר אֲשֶׁר־טַחְתֶּם תָּפֵל וְהִגַּעְתִּיהוּ
אֶל־הָאָרֶץ וְנִגְלָה יְסֹדוֹ וְנָפְלָה וְכִלִּיתֶם בְּתוֹכָהּ וִידַעְתֶּם כִּי־אֲנִי יְהוָה:
טו וְכִלֵּיתִי אֶת־חֲמָתִי בַּקִּיר וּבַטָּחִים אֹתוֹ תָּפֵל וְאֹמַר לָכֶם אֵין הַקִּיר
טז וְאֵין הַטָּחִים אֹתוֹ: נְבִיאֵי יִשְׂרָאֵל הַנִּבְּאִים אֶל־יְרוּשָׁלִַם וְהַחֹזִים לָהּ
יז חֲזוֹן שָׁלֹם וְאֵין שָׁלֹם נְאֻם אֲדֹנָי יֱהֹוִה: וְאַתָּה בֶן־
אָדָם שִׂים פָּנֶיךָ אֶל־בְּנוֹת עַמְּךָ הַמִּתְנַבְּאוֹת מִלִּבְּהֶן וְהִנָּבֵא עֲלֵיהֶן:

18 who prophesy their own hearts; prophesy to them and say: So says the
Lord God: Woe to those women who sew ribbon-amulets onto the joints of
every arm, who make veils for the heads of people of every stature, in order
to hunt others' lives; you hunt the lives of My people, but your own lives
19 you preserve? You have profaned Me to my people for handfuls of barley
and crumbs of bread, proclaiming death to those who should not die and
life to those who should not live, in your lies to My people, who listen to
20 lies. So the Lord God says this: Behold, I am against your ribbon-
amulets that you use to hunt people like birds; I will rip them off your arms;
21 I will set free the people whose lives you hunt like birds; I will tear off your
veils and save My people from your grasp; they will never again be prey in
22 your grasp, and you will know that I am the Lord, for with lies you depress
the hearts of the righteous whom I would not cause pain and strengthen
the actions of the wicked so that he does not turn from his evil course
23 and live. And so, you will never profess false visions or divine divinations
again; I will save My people from your grasp, and you will know that I am
14 1 the Lord." Men from the elders of Israel came to me, and they sat before
2 3 me. And the word of the Lord came to me, saying: "Man, these
men have brought their idols close to their hearts; they have placed the
obstacle that is their sin right before their faces; should they now be allowed
4 to consult Me? So, speak to them, say to them: So says the Lord God: Any
man from the House of Israel who brings his idols close to his heart and who
places the obstacle that is his sin before his own face and who then comes to
the prophet – I am the Lord – I will answer him when he comes with his
5 many idols in order to regain the hearts of the House of Israel, who have all
6 become estranged from Me with all their idols. So say to the
House of Israel: So says the Lord God: Return, turn from your idols; from
7 all of your abominations turn your faces! For any man from the House of
Israel or the stranger who dwells in Israel who becomes estranged from Me,
brings his idols close to his heart, places the obstacle that is his sin before his
own face, and comes to the prophet to consult Me through him, I am the
8 Lord; it is I who will answer him. I will set My face against that man; I will
make him a sign, a cautionary tale; I will cut him off from amongst My people,
9 and you will know that I am the Lord. And if a prophet is tempted
and speaks a word, I am the Lord; I have tempted that prophet, and I will
10 stretch My hand out over him and destroy him from among My people Israel.
They will bear their sin; the punishment of the inquirer will also be that of
11 the prophet, and so the House of Israel will no longer stray from Me and no
longer defile themselves with all their transgressions. They will be My people,
12 and I will be their God, declares the Lord God." And the word
13 of the Lord came to me, saying: "Man, if a land sins against Me by her
faithlessness, and I stretch My hand out over her and break the staff of bread

יח וְאָמַרְתָּ כֹּה־אָמַר ׀ אֲדֹנָי יֱהֹוִה הוֹי לִמְתַפְּרוֹת כְּסָתוֹת עַל ׀ כָּל־
אַצִּילֵי יָדַי וְעֹשׂוֹת הַמִּסְפָּחוֹת עַל־רֹאשׁ כָּל־קוֹמָה לְצוֹדֵד נְפָשׁוֹת
יט הַנְּפָשׁוֹת תְּצוֹדֵדְנָה לְעַמִּי וּנְפָשׁוֹת לָכֶנָה תְחַיֶּינָה: וַתְּחַלֶּלְנָה אֹתִי
אֶל־עַמִּי בְּשַׁעֲלֵי שְׂעֹרִים וּבִפְתוֹתֵי לֶחֶם לְהָמִית נְפָשׁוֹת אֲשֶׁר לֹא־
תְמוּתֶנָה וּלְחַיּוֹת נְפָשׁוֹת אֲשֶׁר לֹא־תִחְיֶינָה בְּכַזֶּבְכֶם לְעַמִּי שֹׁמְעֵי
כ כָזָב: לָכֵן כֹּה־אָמַר ׀ אֲדֹנָי יֱהֹוִה הִנְנִי אֶל־כִּסְּתוֹתֵיכֶנָה
אֲשֶׁר אַתֵּנָה מְצֹדְדוֹת שָׁם אֶת־הַנְּפָשׁוֹת לְפֹרְחוֹת וְקָרַעְתִּי אֹתָם מֵעַל
זְרוֹעֹתֵיכֶם וְשִׁלַּחְתִּי אֶת־הַנְּפָשׁוֹת אֲשֶׁר אַתֶּם מְצֹדְדוֹת אֶת־נְפָשִׁים
כא לְפֹרְחֹת: וְקָרַעְתִּי אֶת־מִסְפְּחֹתֵיכֶם וְהִצַּלְתִּי אֶת־עַמִּי מִיֶּדְכֶן וְלֹא־
כב יִהְיוּ עוֹד בְּיֶדְכֶן לִמְצוּדָה וִידַעְתֶּן כִּי־אֲנִי יְהֹוָה: יַעַן הַכְאוֹת לֵב־צַדִּיק
שֶׁקֶר וַאֲנִי לֹא הִכְאַבְתִּיו וּלְחַזֵּק יְדֵי רָשָׁע לְבִלְתִּי־שׁוּב מִדַּרְכּוֹ הָרָע
כג לְהַחֲיֹתוֹ: לָכֵן שָׁוְא לֹא תֶחֱזֶינָה וְקֶסֶם לֹא־תִקְסַמְנָה עוֹד וְהִצַּלְתִּי
יד א אֶת־עַמִּי מִיֶּדְכֶן וִידַעְתֶּן כִּי־אֲנִי יְהֹוָה: וַיָּבוֹא אֵלַי אֲנָשִׁים מִזִּקְנֵי יִשְׂרָאֵל ז
ב ג וַיֵּשְׁבוּ לְפָנָי: וַיְהִי דְבַר־יְהֹוָה אֵלַי לֵאמֹר: בֶּן־אָדָם הָאֲנָשִׁים
הָאֵלֶּה הֶעֱלוּ גִלּוּלֵיהֶם עַל־לִבָּם וּמִכְשׁוֹל עֲוֺנָם נָתְנוּ נֹכַח פְּנֵיהֶם
ד הַאִדָּרֹשׁ אִדָּרֵשׁ לָהֶם: לָכֵן דַּבֵּר־אוֹתָם וְאָמַרְתָּ אֲלֵיהֶם כֹּה־אָמַר ׀
אֲדֹנָי יֱהֹוִה אִישׁ אִישׁ מִבֵּית יִשְׂרָאֵל אֲשֶׁר יַעֲלֶה אֶת־גִּלּוּלָיו אֶל־לִבּוֹ
וּמִכְשׁוֹל עֲוֺנוֹ יָשִׂים נֹכַח פָּנָיו וּבָא אֶל־הַנָּבִיא אֲנִי יְהֹוָה נַעֲנֵיתִי לוֹ בה בָּא
ה בְרֹב גִּלּוּלָיו: לְמַעַן תְּפֹשׂ אֶת־בֵּית־יִשְׂרָאֵל בְּלִבָּם אֲשֶׁר נָזֹרוּ מֵעָלַי
ו בְּגִלּוּלֵיהֶם כֻּלָּם: לָכֵן אֱמֹר ׀ אֶל־בֵּית יִשְׂרָאֵל כֹּה אָמַר
אֲדֹנָי יֱהֹוִה שׁוּבוּ וְהָשִׁיבוּ מֵעַל גִּלּוּלֵיכֶם וּמֵעַל כָּל־תּוֹעֲבֹתֵיכֶם הָשִׁיבוּ
ז פְנֵיכֶם: כִּי אִישׁ אִישׁ מִבֵּית יִשְׂרָאֵל וּמֵהַגֵּר אֲשֶׁר־יָגוּר בְּיִשְׂרָאֵל וְיִנָּזֵר
מֵאַחֲרַי וְיַעַל גִּלּוּלָיו אֶל־לִבּוֹ וּמִכְשׁוֹל עֲוֺנוֹ יָשִׂים נֹכַח פָּנָיו וּבָא אֶל־
ח הַנָּבִיא לִדְרָשׁ־לוֹ בִי אֲנִי יְהֹוָה נַעֲנֶה־לּוֹ בִּי: וְנָתַתִּי פָנַי בָּאִישׁ הַהוּא
וַהֲשִׁמֹתִיהוּ לְאוֹת וְלִמְשָׁלִים וְהִכְרַתִּיו מִתּוֹךְ עַמִּי וִידַעְתֶּם כִּי־אֲנִי
ט יְהֹוָה: וְהַנָּבִיא כִי־יְפֻתֶּה וְדִבֶּר דָּבָר אֲנִי יְהֹוָה פִּתֵּיתִי אֵת
הַנָּבִיא הַהוּא וְנָטִיתִי אֶת־יָדִי עָלָיו וְהִשְׁמַדְתִּיו מִתּוֹךְ עַמִּי יִשְׂרָאֵל:
י יא וְנָשְׂאוּ עֲוֺנָם כַּעֲוֺן הַדֹּרֵשׁ כַּעֲוֺן הַנָּבִיא יִהְיֶה: לְמַעַן לֹא־יִתְעוּ עוֹד
בֵּית־יִשְׂרָאֵל מֵאַחֲרַי וְלֹא־יִטַּמְּאוּ עוֹד בְּכָל־פִּשְׁעֵיהֶם וְהָיוּ־לִי לְעָם
יב וַאֲנִי אֶהְיֶה לָהֶם לֵאלֹהִים נְאֻם אֲדֹנָי יֱהֹוִה: וַיְהִי דְבַר־יְהֹוָה
יג אֵלַי לֵאמֹר: בֶּן־אָדָם אֶרֶץ כִּי תֶחֱטָא־לִי לִמְעָל־מַעַל וְנָטִיתִי יָדִי
עָלֶיהָ וְשָׁבַרְתִּי לָהּ מַטֵּה־לָחֶם וְהִשְׁלַחְתִּי־בָהּ רָעָב וְהִכְרַתִּי מִמֶּנָּה

14 she leans on, send her famine, and cut man and beast off from her, if these
three men were in her midst – Noaḥ, Daniel, and Iyov – their righteousness
15 would save them, declares the Lord God. And if I make wild animals pass
through the land and bereave her, a devastation none can pass through
16 because of these beasts, if these three men were there within her, surely as I
live, declares the Lord God, even if they would save sons and daughters – only
17 they themselves would be saved, and the land would be devastated. Or if I
bring the sword down on that land and say, 'The sword will pass through the
18 land and cut man and beast off from her,' and these three men were there
within her, surely as I live, declares the Lord God, they would not save sons
19 or daughters; they alone would be saved. Or if I send a plague to that land
and pour My fury out upon her in blood, to cut man and beast off from her,
20 and Noaḥ, Daniel, and Iyov were there within her, surely as I live, declares
the Lord God, they would save neither son nor daughter – their righteousness
21 would save their own souls. So says the Lord God: How much more
so when I unleash on Jerusalem My four terrible judgments: sword, famine,
22 wild animals, and plague, to cut off man and beast from her. And yet, a
remnant will be left in her, will be brought out, sons and daughters; they will
come out to you, and you will see their ways and their deeds, and you will be
comforted over the evil that I have brought upon Jerusalem, all that I have
23 brought down on her. They will comfort you – for when you see their ways
and their deeds, you will know that not for nothing have I done all that I have
15 1 done to her, declares the Lord God." And the word of the
2 Lord came to me, saying: "Man, of all trees what is the grapevine, the vine
3 branch, among the trees of the forest? Can wood be taken from it to be put
4 to use? Can you take a peg from it to hang utensils on? See: given as fuel to
fire, both ends the fire consumes; its insides are charred. Is it then fit for use?
5 See: when whole it cannot be put to use, even less so when consumed by fire
6 and charred; how could it be put to further use? So the Lord God
says this: Like the grapevine among the trees of the forest, which I have given
7 as fuel to fire, so have I given over the inhabitants of Jerusalem. I will fix My
face against them; they have escaped from fire, but fire will consume them;
8 you will know that I am the Lord when I set My face against them. I will turn
the land over to desolation because of their faithlessness, declares the Lord
16 1 2 God." The word of the Lord came to me, saying: "Man, make
3 known to Jerusalem her abominations and say: So says the Lord God to
Jerusalem: Your ancestry and your birth were in the land of the Canaanites.
4 Your father was Amorite, your mother Hittite; and as for your birth, on the
day you were born your cord was not cut, you were not washed clean with
5 water, you were not rubbed with salt, and you were not swaddled. No eye
took enough pity on you to do any of these things out of compassion for you.

יד אָדָם וּבְהֵמָה: וְהָיוּ שְׁלֹשֶׁת הָאֲנָשִׁים הָאֵלֶּה בְּתוֹכָהּ נֹחַ דנאל וְאִיּוֹב דָּנִיֵּאל
טו הֵמָּה בְצִדְקָתָם יְנַצְּלוּ נַפְשָׁם נְאֻם אֲדֹנָי יֱהֹוִה: לוּ־חַיָּה רָעָה אַעֲבִיר
טז בָּאָרֶץ וְשִׁכְּלָתָּה וְהָיְתָה שְׁמָמָה מִבְּלִי עוֹבֵר מִפְּנֵי הַחַיָּה: שְׁלֹשֶׁת
הָאֲנָשִׁים הָאֵלֶּה בְּתוֹכָהּ חַי־אָנִי נְאֻם אֲדֹנָי יֱהֹוִה אִם־בָּנִים וְאִם־בָּנוֹת
יז יַצִּילוּ הֵמָּה לְבַדָּם יִנָּצֵלוּ וְהָאָרֶץ תִּהְיֶה שְׁמָמָה: אוֹ חֶרֶב אָבִיא עַל־
הָאָרֶץ הַהִיא וְאָמַרְתִּי חֶרֶב תַּעֲבֹר בָּאָרֶץ וְהִכְרַתִּי מִמֶּנָּה אָדָם וּבְהֵמָה:
יח וּשְׁלֹשֶׁת הָאֲנָשִׁים הָאֵלֶּה בְּתוֹכָהּ חַי־אָנִי נְאֻם אֲדֹנָי יֱהֹוִה לֹא יַצִּילוּ
יט בָּנִים וּבָנוֹת כִּי הֵם לְבַדָּם יִנָּצֵלוּ: אוֹ דֶּבֶר אֲשַׁלַּח אֶל־הָאָרֶץ הַהִיא
כ וְשָׁפַכְתִּי חֲמָתִי עָלֶיהָ בְּדָם לְהַכְרִית מִמֶּנָּה אָדָם וּבְהֵמָה: וְנֹחַ דנאל דָּנִיֵּאל
וְאִיּוֹב בְּתוֹכָהּ חַי־אָנִי נְאֻם אֲדֹנָי יֱהֹוִה אִם־בֵּן אִם־בַּת יַצִּילוּ הֵמָּה
כא בְצִדְקָתָם יַצִּילוּ נַפְשָׁם: כִּי כֹה אָמַר אֲדֹנָי יֱהֹוִה אַף כִּי־
אַרְבַּעַת שְׁפָטַי ׀ הָרָעִים חֶרֶב וְרָעָב וְחַיָּה רָעָה וָדֶבֶר שִׁלַּחְתִּי אֶל־
כב יְרוּשָׁלָ‍ִם לְהַכְרִית מִמֶּנָּה אָדָם וּבְהֵמָה: וְהִנֵּה נוֹתְרָה־בָּהּ פְּלֵטָה
הַמּוּצָאִים בָּנִים וּבָנוֹת הִנָּם יוֹצְאִים אֲלֵיכֶם וּרְאִיתֶם אֶת־דַּרְכָּם וְאֶת־
עֲלִילוֹתָם וְנִחַמְתֶּם עַל־הָרָעָה אֲשֶׁר הֵבֵאתִי עַל־יְרוּשָׁלַ‍ִם אֵת כָּל־
כג אֲשֶׁר הֵבֵאתִי עָלֶיהָ: וְנִחֲמוּ אֶתְכֶם כִּי־תִרְאוּ אֶת־דַּרְכָּם וְאֶת־עֲלִילוֹתָם
וִידַעְתֶּם כִּי לֹא חִנָּם עָשִׂיתִי אֵת כָּל־אֲשֶׁר־עָשִׂיתִי בָהּ נְאֻם אֲדֹנָי
טו א ב יֱהֹוִה: וַיְהִי דְבַר־יְהוָה אֵלַי לֵאמֹר: בֶּן־אָדָם מַה־
ג יִּהְיֶה עֵץ־הַגֶּפֶן מִכָּל־עֵץ הַזְּמוֹרָה אֲשֶׁר הָיָה בַּעֲצֵי הַיָּעַר: הֲיֻקַּח מִמֶּנּוּ
עֵץ לַעֲשׂוֹת לִמְלָאכָה אִם־יִקְחוּ מִמֶּנּוּ יָתֵד לִתְלוֹת עָלָיו כָּל־כֶּלִי:
ד הִנֵּה לָאֵשׁ נִתַּן לְאָכְלָה אֵת שְׁנֵי קְצוֹתָיו אָכְלָה הָאֵשׁ וְתוֹכוֹ נָחָר
ה הֲיִצְלַח לִמְלָאכָה: הִנֵּה בִּהְיוֹתוֹ תָמִים לֹא יֵעָשֶׂה לִמְלָאכָה אַף כִּי־
ו אֵשׁ אֲכָלַתְהוּ וַיֵּחָר וְנַעֲשָׂה עוֹד לִמְלָאכָה: לָכֵן כֹּה אָמַר
אֲדֹנָי יֱהֹוִה כַּאֲשֶׁר עֵץ־הַגֶּפֶן בְּעֵץ הַיַּעַר אֲשֶׁר־נְתַתִּיו לָאֵשׁ לְאָכְלָה
ז כֵּן נָתַתִּי אֶת־יֹשְׁבֵי יְרוּשָׁלָ‍ִם: וְנָתַתִּי אֶת־פָּנַי בָּהֶם מֵהָאֵשׁ יָצָאוּ וְהָאֵשׁ
ח תֹּאכְלֵם וִידַעְתֶּם כִּי־אֲנִי יְהוָה בְּשׂוּמִי אֶת־פָּנַי בָּהֶם: וְנָתַתִּי אֶת־
טז א הָאָרֶץ שְׁמָמָה יַעַן מָעֲלוּ מַעַל נְאֻם אֲדֹנָי יֱהֹוִה: וַיְהִי
ב דְבַר־יְהוָה אֵלַי לֵאמֹר: בֶּן־אָדָם הוֹדַע אֶת־יְרוּשָׁלַ‍ִם אֶת־תּוֹעֲבֹתֶיהָ:
ג וְאָמַרְתָּ כֹּה־אָמַר אֲדֹנָי יֱהֹוִה לִירוּשָׁלַ‍ִם מְכֹרֹתַיִךְ וּמֹלְדֹתַיִךְ מֵאֶרֶץ
ד הַכְּנַעֲנִי אָבִיךְ הָאֱמֹרִי וְאִמֵּךְ חִתִּית: וּמוֹלְדוֹתַיִךְ בְּיוֹם הוּלֶּדֶת אוֹתָךְ
לֹא־כָרַּת שָׁרֵּךְ וּבְמַיִם לֹא־רֻחַצְתְּ לְמִשְׁעִי וְהָמְלֵחַ לֹא הֻמְלַחַתְּ
ה וְהָחְתֵּל לֹא חֻתָּלְתְּ: לֹא־חָסָה עָלַיִךְ עַיִן לַעֲשׂוֹת לָךְ אַחַת מֵאֵלֶּה

You were thrown out into the open field, loathed, on the day you were born.
6 And when I passed by you, I saw you floundering in your own blood, and I
7 said to you, 'In your blood, live'; I said to you, 'In your blood, live!' I made
you flourish like the shoots of the field. You grew up, matured, were beautifully
adorned – your breasts were firm, your hair grew long – but you were naked
8 and bare. Then I passed by you and saw that you had reached the age of love,
so I spread my mantle out over you[23] and covered your nakedness. I made My
vow to you, entered into a covenant with you, declares the Lord GOD, and
9 you became Mine. I washed you with water, I rinsed your blood off you, and
10 I anointed you with oil. I clothed you in embroidered cloth, I placed on you
leather shoes, I wound about your head fine linen, and I covered you with
11 silk. I adorned you with jewelry; I put bracelets upon your arms and a
12 necklace around your neck. I put a nose ring in your nose, earrings in your
13 ears, and a glorious crown upon your head. You were adorned with gold and
silver; your clothing was fine linen, silk, and embroidered cloth; you ate fine
flour, honey, and oil; and you were exceptionally beautiful, fit to be a queen.
14 You became known among the nations for your beauty, for with the splendor
15 I placed upon you it was perfect, declares the Lord GOD. But you trusted in
your beauty, and you used your fame to play the whore; you showered your
16 whoring upon every passerby – his for the taking! You used your clothes to
make yourself multicolored platforms that you whored upon – such things
17 will not come about, will not happen again. You took your glorious jewelry,
made from the gold and silver I had given you. You made yourself male images,
18 and you whored with them. You took your embroidered clothing to cover
19 them. My oil and My incense you set before them. The food I had given
you – the fine flour, oil, and honey I fed you – you set before them as a sweet
20 fragrance; it was so, declares the Lord GOD. You took the sons and the
daughters you bore Me and sacrificed them to them to devour – were your
21 whorings not enough? You slaughtered My children; you offered them up by
22 passing them over to them. With all your abominations, all your whoring,
you did not remember the days of your youth when you were naked and
23 bare, when you were floundering in your own blood. After all this, your
24 wickedness – oh, what woe will come to you! declares the Lord GOD – you
then built yourself a platform, made yourself a raised place in every square.
25 At every crossroad you built raised places and made your beauty disgusting,
26 opening your legs to every passerby; you escalated your whoring. You whored
with the sons of Egypt, your large-membered neighbors; you escalated your
27 whoring to anger Me. So I stretched out My hand against you, reduced your
portion and gave you over to the will of your enemies, the daughters of the
28 Philistines who are themselves embarrassed at your depraved ways. Unsated,
you whored with the Assyrians; you whored with them, but you were
29 still not satisfied. You broadened your whoring to the land of merchants,
30 Chaldea, but even with this you were not satisfied. How languid is your
heart, declares the Lord GOD, to have done all these things, the acts of a

23 | A metaphor for marriage (cf. Ruth 3:9).

לְחֻמְלָה עָלָיִךְ וַתֻּשְׁלְכִי אֶל־פְּנֵי הַשָּׂדֶה בְּגֹעַל נַפְשֵׁךְ בְּיוֹם הֻלֶּדֶת
ו אֹתָךְ: וָאֶעֱבֹר עָלַיִךְ וָאֶרְאֵךְ מִתְבּוֹסֶסֶת בְּדָמָיִךְ וָאֹמַר לָךְ בְּדָמַיִךְ חֲיִי
ז וָאֹמַר לָךְ בְּדָמַיִךְ חֲיִי: רְבָבָה כְּצֶמַח הַשָּׂדֶה נְתַתִּיךְ וַתִּרְבִּי וַתִּגְדְּלִי
וַתָּבֹאִי בַּעֲדִי עֲדָיִים שָׁדַיִם נָכֹנוּ וּשְׂעָרֵךְ צִמֵּחַ וְאַתְּ עֵרֹם וְעֶרְיָה:
ח וָאֶעֱבֹר עָלַיִךְ וָאֶרְאֵךְ וְהִנֵּה עִתֵּךְ עֵת דֹּדִים וָאֶפְרֹשׂ כְּנָפִי עָלַיִךְ וָאֲכַסֶּה
עֶרְוָתֵךְ וָאֶשָּׁבַע לָךְ וָאָבוֹא בִבְרִית אֹתָךְ נְאֻם אֲדֹנָי יֱהֹוִה וַתִּהְיִי־לִי:
ט י וָאֶרְחָצֵךְ בַּמַּיִם וָאֶשְׁטֹף דָּמַיִךְ מֵעָלָיִךְ וָאֲסֻכֵךְ בַּשָּׁמֶן: וָאַלְבִּישֵׁךְ רִקְמָה
יא וָאֶנְעֲלֵךְ תָּחַשׁ וָאֶחְבְּשֵׁךְ בַּשֵּׁשׁ וַאֲכַסֵּךְ מֶשִׁי: וָאֶעְדֵּךְ עֶדִי וָאֶתְּנָה
יב צְמִידִים עַל־יָדַיִךְ וְרָבִיד עַל־גְּרוֹנֵךְ: וָאֶתֵּן נֶזֶם עַל־אַפֵּךְ וַעֲגִילִים
יג עַל־אָזְנָיִךְ וַעֲטֶרֶת תִּפְאֶרֶת בְּרֹאשֵׁךְ: וַתַּעְדִּי זָהָב וָכֶסֶף וּמַלְבּוּשֵׁךְ
ששי וָמֶשִׁי וְרִקְמָה סֹלֶת וּדְבַשׁ וָשֶׁמֶן אכלתי וַתִּיפִי בִּמְאֹד מְאֹד שֵׁשׁ | אָכָלְתְּ
יד וַתִּצְלְחִי לִמְלוּכָה: וַיֵּצֵא לָךְ שֵׁם בַּגּוֹיִם בְּיָפְיֵךְ כִּי ׀ כָּלִיל הוּא בַּהֲדָרִי ח
טו אֲשֶׁר־שַׂמְתִּי עָלַיִךְ נְאֻם אֲדֹנָי יֱהֹוִה: וַתִּבְטְחִי בְיָפְיֵךְ וַתִּזְנִי עַל־שְׁמֵךְ
טז וַתִּשְׁפְּכִי אֶת־תַּזְנוּתַיִךְ עַל־כָּל־עוֹבֵר לוֹ־יֶהִי: וַתִּקְחִי מִבְּגָדַיִךְ וַתַּעֲשִׂי־
יז לָךְ בָּמוֹת טְלֻאוֹת וַתִּזְנִי עֲלֵיהֶם לֹא בָאוֹת וְלֹא יִהְיֶה: וַתִּקְחִי כְּלֵי
תִפְאַרְתֵּךְ מִזְּהָבִי וּמִכַּסְפִּי אֲשֶׁר נָתַתִּי לָךְ וַתַּעֲשִׂי־לָךְ צַלְמֵי זָכָר
יח וַתִּזְנִי־בָם: וַתִּקְחִי אֶת־בִּגְדֵי רִקְמָתֵךְ וַתְּכַסִּים וְשַׁמְנִי וּקְטָרְתִּי נתתי נָתַתְּ
יט לִפְנֵיהֶם: וְלַחְמִי אֲשֶׁר־נָתַתִּי לָךְ סֹלֶת וָשֶׁמֶן וּדְבַשׁ הֶאֱכַלְתִּיךְ וּנְתַתִּיהוּ
כ לִפְנֵיהֶם לְרֵיחַ נִיחֹחַ וַיֶּהִי נְאֻם אֲדֹנָי יֱהֹוִה: וַתִּקְחִי אֶת־בָּנַיִךְ וְאֶת־
בְּנוֹתַיִךְ אֲשֶׁר יָלַדְתְּ לִי וַתִּזְבָּחִים לָהֶם לֶאֱכוֹל הַמְעַט מתזנותך: מִתַּזְנוּתָיִךְ
כא כב וַתִּשְׁחֲטִי אֶת־בָּנָי וַתִּתְּנִים בְּהַעֲבִיר אוֹתָם לָהֶם: וְאֵת כָּל־תּוֹעֲבֹתַיִךְ
וְתַזְנֻתַיִךְ לֹא זכרתי אֶת־יְמֵי נְעוּרָיִךְ בִּהְיוֹתֵךְ עֵרֹם וְעֶרְיָה מִתְבּוֹסֶסֶת זָכַרְתְּ
כג בְּדָמֵךְ הָיִית: וַיְהִי אַחֲרֵי כָּל־רָעָתֵךְ אוֹי אוֹי לָךְ נְאֻם אֲדֹנָי יֱהֹוִה:
כד כה וַתִּבְנִי־לָךְ גָּב וַתַּעֲשִׂי־לָךְ רָמָה בְּכָל־רְחוֹב: אֶל־כָּל־רֹאשׁ דֶּרֶךְ בָּנִית
רָמָתֵךְ וַתְּתַעֲבִי אֶת־יָפְיֵךְ וַתְּפַשְּׂקִי אֶת־רַגְלַיִךְ לְכָל־עוֹבֵר וַתַּרְבִּי
כו אֶת־תזנותך: וַתִּזְנִי אֶל־בְּנֵי־מִצְרַיִם שְׁכֵנַיִךְ גִּדְלֵי בָשָׂר וַתַּרְבִּי אֶת־ תַּזְנוּתָיִךְ
כז תַּזְנֻתֵךְ לְהַכְעִיסֵנִי: וְהִנֵּה נָטִיתִי יָדִי עָלַיִךְ וָאֶגְרַע חֻקֵּךְ וָאֶתְּנֵךְ בְּנֶפֶשׁ
כח שֹׂנְאוֹתַיִךְ בְּנוֹת פְּלִשְׁתִּים הַנִּכְלָמוֹת מִדַּרְכֵּךְ זִמָּה: וַתִּזְנִי אֶל־בְּנֵי
כט אַשּׁוּר מִבִּלְתִּי שָׂבְעָתֵךְ וַתִּזְנִים וְגַם לֹא שָׂבָעַתְּ: וַתַּרְבִּי אֶת־תַּזְנוּתֵךְ
ל אֶל־אֶרֶץ כְּנַעַן כַּשְׂדִּימָה וְגַם־בְּזֹאת לֹא שָׂבָעַתְּ: מָה אֲמֻלָה לִבָּתֵךְ
נְאֻם אֲדֹנָי יֱהֹוִה בַּעֲשׂוֹתֵךְ אֶת־כָּל־אֵלֶּה מַעֲשֵׂה אִשָּׁה־זוֹנָה שַׁלָּטֶת:

31 brazen prostitute! Building platforms at every crossroad, constructing raised
places in every square. But you were not like a regular whore; you scorned
32 33 payment, the adulterous wife who takes strangers instead of her husband. All
prostitutes are given gifts, but you in your whoring gave gifts to all your lovers,
34 bribing them on every side to come to you. You have been the opposite
of other women – by whoring unsolicited, by paying and not being paid
35 a prostitute's fee, you were the opposite. So, whore, hear the word of the
36 LORD. So says the Lord GOD: Because your lust was poured out and
your nakedness bared in your whoring with your lovers, and for all the idols
37 of your abominations, and as you gave them your children's blood, behold: I
will gather together all the lovers you pleased, all those you loved along with
all those you hated; I will gather them against you from all around, and I will
38 bare your nakedness to them – they will see you in all your nakedness. I will
condemn you to the punishment of the adulterous woman and the murderess,
39 give you over to bloody fury and passionate anger. I will give you over into
their hands, and they will tear down your platforms, pull down your raised
places; they will strip you of your clothes; they will take your glorious jewelry
40 and leave you naked and bare. They will bring against you a horde; they will
41 stone you and cut you down with their swords. They will burn down your
houses; they will execute judgments on you before the eyes of many women.
Thus will I put an end to your whoring; you will no longer pay a prostitute's
42 fee. I will let My fury at you die down; My passionate anger will turn away
43 from you; I will be silent, no longer will I be angry. Because you did not recall
the days of your youth but enraged Me with all of this – here, I will bring your
ways down upon your head, declares the Lord GOD, for have you not acted
44 with depravity on top of all your other abominations? Behold, all who use
45 sayings will say of you, 'Like mother, like daughter.' You are the daughter of
the mother who despised her husband and children; you are the sister of
sisters who despised their husbands and children. Your mother was a Hittite,
46 your father an Amorite. Your older sister Shomron and her daughters live to
the north; your younger sister lives to the south, Sedom and her daughters.
47 Did you not follow their ways and act out their abominations? Within a short
48 time, you became more corrupt than they were in all your ways. As I live,
declares the Lord GOD, your sister Sedom and her daughters did not act as
49 you and your daughters have acted. The sin of your sister Sedom was this:
pride. She and her daughters had enough bread and an easy tranquility and
50 yet did not aid the hands of the poor and needy. They were haughty and
committed abominations before Me, and so, when I beheld them, I did away
51 with them. As for Shomron, she has not committed half of the sins
you have. You committed more abominations than they did; with all the
52 abominations you committed you made your sisters appear righteous! And
so, bear your disgrace: you have advocated for your sisters – because your
sins were more abominable than theirs, they appeared more righteous than
you! So, you, be ashamed; bear the disgrace of making your sisters appear

לא בִּבְנוֹתַיִךְ גַּבֵּךְ בְּרֹאשׁ כָּל־דֶּרֶךְ וְרָמָתֵךְ עָשִׂיתי בְּכָל־רְחוֹב וְלֹא־הָיִיתי עָשִׂית | הָיִית
לב כַּזּוֹנָה לְקַלֵּס אֶתְנָן׃ הָאִשָּׁה הַמְנָאָפֶת תַּחַת אִישָׁהּ תִּקַּח אֶת־זָרִים׃
לג לְכָל־זֹנוֹת יִתְּנוּ־נֵדֶה וְאַתְּ נָתַתְּ אֶת־נְדָנַיִךְ לְכָל־מְאַהֲבַיִךְ וַתִּשְׁחֳדִי
לד אוֹתָם לָבוֹא אֵלַיִךְ מִסָּבִיב בְּתַזְנוּתָיִךְ׃ וַיְהִי־בָךְ הֶפֶךְ מִן־הַנָּשִׁים
בְּתַזְנוּתַיִךְ וְאַחֲרַיִךְ לֹא זוּנָּה וּבְתִתֵּךְ אֶתְנָן וְאֶתְנַן לֹא נִתַּן־לָךְ וַתְּהִי
לה לו לְהֶפֶךְ׃ לָכֵן זוֹנָה שִׁמְעִי דְּבַר־יְהוָה׃ כֹּה־אָמַר אֲדֹנָי
יֱהֹוִה יַעַן הִשָּׁפֵךְ נְחֻשְׁתֵּךְ וַתִּגָּלֶה עֶרְוָתֵךְ בְּתַזְנוּתַיִךְ עַל־מְאַהֲבָיִךְ
לז וְעַל כָּל־גִּלּוּלֵי תוֹעֲבוֹתַיִךְ וְכִדְמֵי בָנַיִךְ אֲשֶׁר נָתַתְּ לָהֶם׃ לָכֵן הִנְנִי
מְקַבֵּץ אֶת־כָּל־מְאַהֲבַיִךְ אֲשֶׁר עָרַבְתְּ עֲלֵיהֶם וְאֵת כָּל־אֲשֶׁר אָהַבְתְּ
עַל כָּל־אֲשֶׁר שָׂנֵאת וְקִבַּצְתִּי אֹתָם עָלַיִךְ מִסָּבִיב וְגִלֵּיתִי עֶרְוָתֵךְ
לח אֲלֵהֶם וְרָאוּ אֶת־כָּל־עֶרְוָתֵךְ׃ וּשְׁפַטְתִּיךְ מִשְׁפְּטֵי נֹאֲפוֹת וְשֹׁפְכֹת דָּם
לט וּנְתַתִּיךְ דַּם חֵמָה וְקִנְאָה׃ וְנָתַתִּי אוֹתָךְ בְּיָדָם וְהָרְסוּ גַבֵּךְ וְנִתְּצוּ
רָמֹתַיִךְ וְהִפְשִׁיטוּ אוֹתָךְ בְּגָדַיִךְ וְלָקְחוּ כְּלֵי תִפְאַרְתֵּךְ וְהִנִּיחוּךְ עֵירֹם
מ וְעֶרְיָה׃ וְהֶעֱלוּ עָלַיִךְ קָהָל וְרָגְמוּ אוֹתָךְ בָּאָבֶן וּבִתְּקוּךְ בְּחַרְבוֹתָם׃
מא וְשָׂרְפוּ בָתַּיִךְ בָּאֵשׁ וְעָשׂוּ־בָךְ שְׁפָטִים לְעֵינֵי נָשִׁים רַבּוֹת וְהִשְׁבַּתִּיךְ
מב מִזּוֹנָה וְגַם־אֶתְנַן לֹא תִתְּנִי־עוֹד׃ וַהֲנִחֹתִי חֲמָתִי בָּךְ וְסָרָה קִנְאָתִי
מג מִמֵּךְ וְשָׁקַטְתִּי וְלֹא אֶכְעַס עוֹד׃ יַעַן אֲשֶׁר לֹא־זָכַרְתי אֶת־יְמֵי זָכַרְתְּ
נְעוּרַיִךְ וַתִּרְגְּזִי־לִי בְּכָל־אֵלֶּה וְגַם־אֲנִי הֵא דַּרְכֵּךְ ׀ בְּרֹאשׁ נָתַתִּי נְאֻם
מד אֲדֹנָי יֱהֹוִה וְלֹא עָשִׂיתי אֶת־הַזִּמָּה עַל כָּל־תּוֹעֲבֹתָיִךְ׃ הִנֵּה כָּל־ עָשִׂית
מה הַמֹּשֵׁל עָלַיִךְ יִמְשֹׁל לֵאמֹר כְּאִמָּה בִּתָּהּ׃ בַּת־אִמֵּךְ אַתְּ גֹּעֶלֶת אִישָׁהּ
וּבָנֶיהָ וַאֲחוֹת אֲחוֹתֵךְ אַתְּ אֲשֶׁר גָּעֲלוּ אַנְשֵׁיהֶן וּבְנֵיהֶן אִמְּכֶן חִתִּית
מו וַאֲבִיכֶן אֱמֹרִי׃ וַאֲחוֹתֵךְ הַגְּדוֹלָה שֹׁמְרוֹן הִיא וּבְנוֹתֶיהָ הַיּוֹשֶׁבֶת עַל־
שְׂמֹאולֵךְ וַאֲחוֹתֵךְ הַקְּטַנָּה מִמֵּךְ הַיּוֹשֶׁבֶת מִימִינֵךְ סְדֹם וּבְנוֹתֶיהָ׃
מז וְלֹא בְדַרְכֵיהֶן הָלַכְתְּ וּבְתוֹעֲבוֹתֵיהֶן עָשִׂיתי כִּמְעַט קָט וַתַּשְׁחִתִי מֵהֵן עָשִׂית
מח בְּכָל־דְּרָכָיִךְ׃ חַי־אָנִי נְאֻם אֲדֹנָי יֱהֹוִה אִם־עָשְׂתָה סְדֹם אֲחוֹתֵךְ הִיא
מט וּבְנוֹתֶיהָ כַּאֲשֶׁר עָשִׂית אַתְּ וּבְנוֹתָיִךְ׃ הִנֵּה־זֶה הָיָה עֲוֹן סְדֹם אֲחוֹתֵךְ
גָּאוֹן שִׂבְעַת־לֶחֶם וְשַׁלְוַת הַשְׁקֵט הָיָה לָהּ וְלִבְנוֹתֶיהָ וְיַד־עָנִי וְאֶבְיוֹן
נ לֹא הֶחֱזִיקָה׃ וַתִּגְבְּהֶינָה וַתַּעֲשֶׂינָה תוֹעֵבָה לְפָנָי וָאָסִיר אֶתְהֶן כַּאֲשֶׁר
נא רָאִיתִי׃ וְשֹׁמְרוֹן כַּחֲצִי חַטֹּאתַיִךְ לֹא חָטָאָה וַתַּרְבִּי
אֶת־תּוֹעֲבוֹתַיִךְ מֵהֵנָּה וַתְּצַדְּקִי אֶת־אֲחוֹתַךְ בְּכָל־תּוֹעֲבֹתַיִךְ אֲשֶׁר אֲחוֹתַיִךְ
נב עָשִׂיתי׃ גַּם־אַתְּ ׀ שְׂאִי כְלִמָּתֵךְ אֲשֶׁר פִּלַּלְתְּ לַאֲחוֹתֵךְ בְּחַטֹּאתַיִךְ עָשִׂית
אֲשֶׁר־הִתְעַבְתְּ מֵהֵן תִּצְדַּקְנָה מִמֵּךְ וְגַם־אַתְּ בּוֹשִׁי וּשְׂאִי כְלִמָּתֵךְ

53 righteous. I will restore their fortunes, the fortune of Sedom and her daughters
and the fortune of Shomron and her daughters – and your fortune among
54 them – so that you will bear your disgrace and be disgraced by what you have
55 done in providing this comfort to them. Your sister Sedom and her daughters
will return to their former state; Shomron and her daughters will return to
their former state; and you and your daughters will return to your former
56 state. Was not Sedom, your sister, a byword in your mouth during your proud
57 days, before your own wickedness was revealed? Now you are reproached
by the daughters of Aram and all those around her, the daughters of the
58 Philistines, who treat you with contempt from all sides. Your depravity, your
59 abominations – you will bear them, declares the LORD. So says the
Lord GOD: I will do to you as you, who flouted the oath and violated the
60 covenant, have done, but I will remember My covenant with you from the
61 days of your youth, and I shall establish an everlasting covenant with you. You
will remember your ways; you will feel disgraced when you receive your older
sisters with your younger ones – I will give them to you as daughters though
62 they are not included in your covenant. I will establish My covenant with
63 you; you will know that I am the LORD. And so you will remember and be
ashamed; your voice will be silenced in the face of your disgrace when I
17 1 forgive you for all that you have done, declares the Lord GOD." And
2 the word of the LORD came to me: "Man, pose a riddle; tell a parable to the
3 House of Israel; say: So says the Lord GOD: A great eagle with great wings,
long pinions, his dense plumage a rich tapestry, came to Lebanon and took
4 the crown of the cedar. He plucked the topmost stalk and carried it to the
5 land of merchants, placed it in a city of traders. He took a seed from that land
and placed it in a field ready for seeding, planted it on great flowing waters,
6 positioned it like a willow. And it grew; it became a vine, sprawling, low-
growing, bending its arms toward him, its roots spreading below; it became
7 a vine, it grew shoots, and stretched out boughs. And another great eagle with
great wings and full plumage – behold, this vine reached its roots out toward
8 him to be watered, stretched its arms out to him from its planting bed – planted
in a rich field by great flowing waters to grow branches, bear fruit, become a
9 majestic vine. Say: So says the Lord GOD: Will it thrive? Surely he will tear
up its roots, he will rip off its fruit, and it will wither. All fresh leaves will
wither; it will take neither a strong arm nor a great army to tear it from its
10 roots. Even planted as it is, will it thrive? Surely when the east wind strikes it
11 will wither away; upon the bed where it has grown it will wither." And
12 the word of the LORD came to me: "Say this now to the defiant house: Do
you not know what these things mean? Say: Behold, the king of Babylon came
to Jerusalem and took her king and officials, and he brought them to Babylon.
13 He took one of the royal seed and made a covenant with him; he brought

נג בְּצַדֶּקְתֵּךְ אַחְיוֹתֵךְ: וְשַׁבְתִּי אֶת־שְׁבִיתְהֶן אֶת־שבית סְדֹם וּבְנוֹתֶיהָ שְׁבוּת
נד וְאֶת־שבית שֹׁמְרוֹן וּבְנוֹתֶיהָ ושבית שְׁבִיתַיִךְ בְּתוֹכָהְנָה: לְמַעַן תִּשְׂאִי שְׁבוּת | וּשְׁבוּת
נה כְלִמָּתֵךְ וְנִכְלַמְתְּ מִכֹּל אֲשֶׁר עָשִׂית בְּנַחֲמֵךְ אֹתָן: וַאֲחוֹתַיִךְ סְדֹם
וּבְנוֹתֶיהָ תָּשֹׁבְןָ לְקַדְמָתָן וְשֹׁמְרוֹן וּבְנוֹתֶיהָ תָּשֹׁבְןָ לְקַדְמָתָן וְאַתְּ
נו וּבְנוֹתַיִךְ תְּשֻׁבֶינָה לְקַדְמַתְכֶן: וְלוֹא הָיְתָה סְדֹם אֲחוֹתֵךְ לִשְׁמוּעָה
נז בְּפִיךְ בְּיוֹם גְּאוֹנָיִךְ: בְּטֶרֶם תִּגָּלֶה רָעָתֵךְ כְּמוֹ עֵת חֶרְפַּת בְּנוֹת־אֲרָם
נח וְכָל־סְבִיבוֹתֶיהָ בְּנוֹת פְּלִשְׁתִּים הַשָּׁאטוֹת אוֹתָךְ מִסָּבִיב: אֶת־זִמָּתֵךְ
נט וְאֶת־תּוֹעֲבוֹתַיִךְ אַתְּ נְשָׂאתִים נְאֻם יְהוָה: כִּי כֹה אָמַר
אֲדֹנָי יֱהוִה וְעָשִׂית אוֹתָךְ כַּאֲשֶׁר עָשִׂית אֲשֶׁר־בָּזִית אָלָה לְהָפֵר בְּרִית:
ס וְזָכַרְתִּי אֲנִי אֶת־בְּרִיתִי אוֹתָךְ בִּימֵי נְעוּרָיִךְ וַהֲקִימוֹתִי לָךְ בְּרִית עוֹלָם: ט
סא וְזָכַרְתְּ אֶת־דְּרָכַיִךְ וְנִכְלַמְתְּ בְּקַחְתֵּךְ אֶת־אֲחוֹתַיִךְ הַגְּדֹלוֹת מִמֵּךְ
סב אֶל־הַקְּטַנּוֹת מִמֵּךְ וְנָתַתִּי אֶתְהֶן לָךְ לְבָנוֹת וְלֹא מִבְּרִיתֵךְ: וַהֲקִימוֹתִי
סג אֲנִי אֶת־בְּרִיתִי אִתָּךְ וְיָדַעַתְּ כִּי־אֲנִי יְהוָה: לְמַעַן תִּזְכְּרִי וָבֹשְׁתְּ וְלֹא
יִהְיֶה־לָּךְ עוֹד פִּתְחוֹן פֶּה מִפְּנֵי כְּלִמָּתֵךְ בְּכַפְּרִי־לָךְ לְכָל־אֲשֶׁר עָשִׂית
יז א ב נְאֻם אֲדֹנָי יֱהוִה: וַיְהִי דְבַר־יְהוָה אֵלַי לֵאמֹר: בֶּן־אָדָם
ג חוּד חִידָה וּמְשֹׁל מָשָׁל אֶל־בֵּית יִשְׂרָאֵל: וְאָמַרְתָּ כֹּה־אָמַר ׀ אֲדֹנָי
יֱהוִה הַנֶּשֶׁר הַגָּדוֹל גְּדוֹל הַכְּנָפַיִם אֶרֶךְ הָאֵבֶר מָלֵא הַנּוֹצָה אֲשֶׁר־לוֹ
ד הָרִקְמָה בָּא אֶל־הַלְּבָנוֹן וַיִּקַּח אֶת־צַמֶּרֶת הָאָרֶז: אֵת רֹאשׁ יְנִיקוֹתָיו
ה קָטָף וַיְבִיאֵהוּ אֶל־אֶרֶץ כְּנַעַן בְּעִיר רֹכְלִים שָׂמוֹ: וַיִּקַּח מִזֶּרַע הָאָרֶץ
ו וַיִּתְּנֵהוּ בִּשְׂדֵה־זָרַע קָח עַל־מַיִם רַבִּים צַפְצָפָה שָׂמוֹ: וַיִּצְמַח וַיְהִי
לְגֶפֶן סֹרַחַת שִׁפְלַת קוֹמָה לִפְנוֹת דָּלִיּוֹתָיו אֵלָיו וְשָׁרָשָׁיו תַּחְתָּיו יִהְיוּ
ז וַתְּהִי לְגֶפֶן וַתַּעַשׂ בַּדִּים וַתְּשַׁלַּח פֹּארוֹת: וַיְהִי נֶשֶׁר־אֶחָד גָּדוֹל גְּדוֹל
כְּנָפַיִם וְרַב נוֹצָה וְהִנֵּה הַגֶּפֶן הַזֹּאת כָּפְנָה שָׁרָשֶׁיהָ עָלָיו וְדָלִיּוֹתָיו
ח שִׁלְּחָה־לּוֹ לְהַשְׁקוֹת אוֹתָהּ מֵעֲרֻגוֹת מַטָּעָהּ: אֶל־שָׂדֶה טּוֹב אֶל־מַיִם
רַבִּים הִיא שְׁתוּלָה לַעֲשׂוֹת עָנָף וְלָשֵׂאת פֶּרִי לִהְיוֹת לְגֶפֶן אַדָּרֶת:
ט אֱמֹר כֹּה אָמַר אֲדֹנָי יֱהוִה תִּצְלָח הֲלוֹא אֶת־שָׁרָשֶׁיהָ יְנַתֵּק וְאֶת־
פִּרְיָהּ ׀ יְקוֹסֵס וְיָבֵשׁ כָּל־טַרְפֵּי צִמְחָהּ תִּיבָשׁ וְלֹא־בִזְרֹעַ גְּדוֹלָה וּבְעַם
י רָב לְמַשְׂאוֹת אוֹתָהּ מִשָּׁרָשֶׁיהָ: וְהִנֵּה שְׁתוּלָה הֲתִצְלָח הֲלֹא כְגַעַת
יא בָּהּ רוּחַ הַקָּדִים תִּיבַשׁ יָבֹשׁ עַל־עֲרֻגֹת צִמְחָהּ תִּיבָשׁ: וַיְהִי
יב דְבַר־יְהוָה אֵלַי לֵאמֹר: אֱמָר־נָא לְבֵית הַמֶּרִי הֲלֹא יְדַעְתֶּם מָה־אֵלֶּה
אֱמֹר הִנֵּה־בָא מֶלֶךְ־בָּבֶל יְרוּשָׁלִַם וַיִּקַּח אֶת־מַלְכָּהּ וְאֶת־שָׂרֶיהָ וַיָּבֵא
יג אוֹתָם אֵלָיו בָּבֶלָה: וַיִּקַּח מִזֶּרַע הַמְּלוּכָה וַיִּכְרֹת אִתּוֹ בְּרִית וַיָּבֵא

14 him under oath and took away the leaders of the land so that it would be a
lowly kingdom that could not rise up, that would keep his covenant to
15 preserve itself. But he rebelled against him, sending his messengers to Egypt
for horses and a great army.[24] Will he thrive? Will he who does these things
16 escape? Will he violate a covenant and escape? As I live, declares the Lord
God, in the domain of that king who made him king, whose oath he flouted,
17 whose covenant he broke with him – in Babylon he will die. And in war
Pharaoh will assist him with neither numerous troops nor great hordes, nor
when earthworks are thrown up or a siege wall built against them for the
18 destruction of numerous people. He flouted the oath by breaking the
covenant; he gave his word and yet still did all these things; he will not
19 escape. So the Lord God says this: As I live, My oath that he has
flouted, My covenant that he has broken I will bring back down upon his head.
20 I will spread My net over him; he will be caught in My trap; I will take him
to Babylon and enter into judgment with him there for his betrayal, through
21 which he betrayed Me. All his fugitives from all his forces will fall by the sword,
and those who remain will be scattered to the winds, and you will know that
22 I, the Lord, have spoken. So says the Lord God: I will take from
the soaring crown of the cedar and place it, I will pluck from the topmost,
23 tender stalks, and I will plant it upon a high and lofty mountain; in the
mountainous height of Israel I will plant it. It will bear branches, grow fruit;
it will become a majestic cedar, and every bird of every type will settle beneath
24 it; in the shade of its arms they will dwell. And all the trees of the field will
know that I, the Lord, have brought down the high tree and raised the lowly
tree; I have withered the green tree and made the withered tree bloom; I, the
18 1 Lord, have spoken and will do it." And the word of the Lord came
2 to me, saying: "What are you doing, using this proverb on the soil of Israel:
3 'Fathers eat sour grapes, but the teeth of the children are set on edge'? As I
live, declares the Lord God, you will no longer use this proverb in Israel.
4 Behold: all lives are Mine; the life of father and son alike are Mine; that person
5 who sins will die. The person who is righteous, who acts in a way
6 that is just and right – he does not eat on the mountains or look up to the
idols of the House of Israel, he does not defile another's wife or approach a
7 menstruating woman,[25] he mistreats no one, he returns his debtor's pledge to
him, he commits no robbery, he gives his bread to the hungry, he covers the
8 naked with clothes, he does not lend with advanced interest or take accrued
interest,[26] he resists doing wrong, he judges between man and man with true
9 justice, he follows My statutes, keeps My laws, acts with truth – he is righteous;
10 he will live, declares the Lord God. If he bears a violent son, a bloodshedder,
11 who commits any one of these – although he himself committed none of
12 these – who eats on the mountains, who defiles another's wife, who mistreats
the poor and needy, commits robbery, does not return his debtor's pledge,

24 | See II Kings 24:20.
25 | Leviticus 18:19.
26 | Leviticus 25:36.

יד אֹתוֹ בְּאָלָה וְאֶת־אֵילֵי הָאָרֶץ לָקָח׃ לִהְיוֹת מַמְלָכָה שְׁפָלָה לְבִלְתִּי
טו הִתְנַשֵּׂא לִשְׁמֹר אֶת־בְּרִיתוֹ לְעָמְדָהּ׃ וַיִּמְרָד־בּוֹ לִשְׁלֹחַ מַלְאָכָיו
מִצְרַיִם לָתֶת־לוֹ סוּסִים וְעַם־רָב הֲיִצְלָח הֲיִמָּלֵט הָעֹשֵׂה אֵלֶּה וְהֵפֵר
טז בְּרִית וְנִמְלָט׃ חַי־אָנִי נְאֻם אֲדֹנָי יֱהֹוִה אִם־לֹא בִּמְקוֹם הַמֶּלֶךְ הַמַּמְלִיךְ
אֹתוֹ אֲשֶׁר בָּזָה אֶת־אָלָתוֹ וַאֲשֶׁר הֵפֵר אֶת־בְּרִיתוֹ אִתּוֹ בְתוֹךְ־בָּבֶל
יז יָמוּת׃ וְלֹא בְחַיִל גָּדוֹל וּבְקָהָל רָב יַעֲשֶׂה אוֹתוֹ פַרְעֹה בַּמִּלְחָמָה
יח בִּשְׁפֹּךְ סֹלְלָה וּבִבְנוֹת דָּיֵק לְהַכְרִית נְפָשׁוֹת רַבּוֹת׃ וּבָזָה אָלָה לְהָפֵר
יט בְּרִית וְהִנֵּה נָתַן יָדוֹ וְכָל־אֵלֶּה עָשָׂה לֹא יִמָּלֵט׃ לָכֵן כֹּה־
אָמַר אֲדֹנָי יֱהֹוִה חַי־אָנִי אִם־לֹא אָלָתִי אֲשֶׁר בָּזָה וּבְרִיתִי אֲשֶׁר הֵפִיר
כ וּנְתַתִּיו בְּרֹאשׁוֹ׃ וּפָרַשְׂתִּי עָלָיו רִשְׁתִּי וְנִתְפַּשׂ בִּמְצוּדָתִי וַהֲבִיאוֹתִיהוּ
כא בָבֶלָה וְנִשְׁפַּטְתִּי אִתּוֹ שָׁם מַעֲלוֹ אֲשֶׁר מָעַל־בִּי׃ וְאֵת כָּל־מִבְרָחוֹ
בְּכָל־אֲגַפָּיו בַּחֶרֶב יִפֹּלוּ וְהַנִּשְׁאָרִים לְכָל־רוּחַ יִפָּרֵשׂוּ וִידַעְתֶּם כִּי אֲנִי
כב יְהֹוָה דִּבַּרְתִּי׃ כֹּה אָמַר אֲדֹנָי יֱהֹוִה וְלָקַחְתִּי אָנִי
מִצַּמֶּרֶת הָאֶרֶז הָרָמָה וְנָתָתִּי מֵרֹאשׁ יֹנְקוֹתָיו רַךְ אֶקְטֹף וְשָׁתַלְתִּי אָנִי
כג עַל הַר־גָּבֹהַּ וְתָלוּל׃ בְּהַר מְרוֹם יִשְׂרָאֵל אֶשְׁתֳּלֶנּוּ וְנָשָׂא עָנָף וְעָשָׂה
פֶרִי וְהָיָה לְאֶרֶז אַדִּיר וְשָׁכְנוּ תַחְתָּיו כֹּל צִפּוֹר כָּל־כָּנָף בְּצֵל דָּלִיּוֹתָיו
כד תִּשְׁכֹּנָּה׃ וְיָדְעוּ כָּל־עֲצֵי הַשָּׂדֶה כִּי אֲנִי יְהֹוָה הִשְׁפַּלְתִּי ׀ עֵץ גָּבֹהַּ
הִגְבַּהְתִּי עֵץ שָׁפָל הוֹבַשְׁתִּי עֵץ לָח וְהִפְרַחְתִּי עֵץ יָבֵשׁ אֲנִי יְהֹוָה
יח א ב דִּבַּרְתִּי וְעָשִׂיתִי׃ וַיְהִי דְבַר־יְהֹוָה אֵלַי לֵאמֹר׃ מַה־לָּכֶם
אַתֶּם מֹשְׁלִים אֶת־הַמָּשָׁל הַזֶּה עַל־אַדְמַת יִשְׂרָאֵל לֵאמֹר אָבוֹת
ג יֹאכְלוּ בֹסֶר וְשִׁנֵּי הַבָּנִים תִּקְהֶינָה׃ חַי־אָנִי נְאֻם אֲדֹנָי יֱהֹוִה אִם־יִהְיֶה
ד לָכֶם עוֹד מְשֹׁל הַמָּשָׁל הַזֶּה בְּיִשְׂרָאֵל׃ הֵן כָּל־הַנְּפָשׁוֹת לִי הֵנָּה כְּנֶפֶשׁ
ה הָאָב וּכְנֶפֶשׁ הַבֵּן לִי־הֵנָּה הַנֶּפֶשׁ הַחֹטֵאת הִיא תָמוּת׃ וְאִישׁ
ו כִּי־יִהְיֶה צַדִּיק וְעָשָׂה מִשְׁפָּט וּצְדָקָה׃ אֶל־הֶהָרִים לֹא אָכָל וְעֵינָיו
לֹא נָשָׂא אֶל־גִּלּוּלֵי בֵּית יִשְׂרָאֵל וְאֶת־אֵשֶׁת רֵעֵהוּ לֹא טִמֵּא וְאֶל־
ז אִשָּׁה נִדָּה לֹא יִקְרָב׃ וְאִישׁ לֹא יוֹנֶה חֲבֹלָתוֹ חוֹב יָשִׁיב גְּזֵלָה לֹא יִגְזֹל
ח לַחְמוֹ לְרָעֵב יִתֵּן וְעֵירֹם יְכַסֶּה־בָּגֶד׃ בַּנֶּשֶׁךְ לֹא־יִתֵּן וְתַרְבִּית לֹא יִקָּח
ט מֵעָוֶל יָשִׁיב יָדוֹ מִשְׁפַּט אֱמֶת יַעֲשֶׂה בֵּין אִישׁ לְאִישׁ׃ בְּחֻקּוֹתַי יְהַלֵּךְ
וּמִשְׁפָּטַי שָׁמַר לַעֲשׂוֹת אֱמֶת צַדִּיק הוּא חָיֹה יִחְיֶה נְאֻם אֲדֹנָי יֱהֹוִה׃
י יא וְהוֹלִיד בֵּן־פָּרִיץ שֹׁפֵךְ דָּם וְעָשָׂה אָח מֵאַחַד מֵאֵלֶּה׃ וְהוּא אֶת־כָּל־
יב אֵלֶּה לֹא עָשָׂה כִּי גַם אֶל־הֶהָרִים אָכַל וְאֶת־אֵשֶׁת רֵעֵהוּ טִמֵּא׃ עָנִי
וְאֶבְיוֹן הוֹנָה גְּזֵלוֹת גָּזָל חֲבֹל לֹא יָשִׁיב וְאֶל־הַגִּלּוּלִים נָשָׂא עֵינָיו

13 who looks up to the idols, who commits abominable things, who lends with
advanced interest and takes accrued interest, will he live? He will not live; he
has committed all these abominable acts; he will die – his blood is on his own
14 head. And if he bears a son, who sees all the sins that his father has committed,
15 who considers them but does not act similarly – he does not eat on the
mountains, he does not look up to the idols of the House of Israel, he does
16 not defile another's wife, he mistreats no one, he does not retain his debtor's
pledge, he does not commit robbery, he gives his bread to the hungry,
17 he covers the naked with clothes, he refrains from harming the poor, he
takes neither advanced nor accrued interest, he keeps My laws, follows My
18 statutes – he will not die for the iniquity of his father; he will live. Because
his father practiced extortion, robbed his own brother, acted in a way that
19 was no good among his people, behold: he will die in his iniquity. And you
say: Why does the son not bear the iniquity of the father? The son has acted
in a way that is just and right, has kept all My statutes, has performed them – he
20 will live. That person who sins will die; the son will not bear the iniquity of
the father, and the father will not bear the iniquity of the son; the righteous
one's righteousness will be on him, and the wicked one's wickedness will be
21 on him. The wicked one who turns back from all the sins he
committed and keeps all My statutes and acts in a way that is just and right –
22 he will live; he will not die. All the transgressions he committed will not be
remembered against him; through the righteousness he has performed he
23 will live. Do I desire the death of the wicked, declares the Lord God, not that
24 he should turn from his ways and live? And the righteous
one who turns from his righteousness and does wrong similar to all the
abominable acts the wicked one committed, shall he live? None of the
righteous deeds he has done will be remembered; his betrayal and the sins
25 that he has sinned – because of these he will die. You say, 'The way of the Lord
is not fair.' Listen, House of Israel: Is My way not fair? Surely, your ways are
26 not fair. When the righteous one turns from his righteousness and does
27 wrong and dies for it, he dies for that which he has done wrong. And
when the wicked one turns from the wickedness that he has done and acts
28 in a way that is just and right, he preserves his life. When he considers them
and turns from all the transgressions he has committed, he will live; he will
29 not die. And the House of Israel says, 'The way of the Lord is not fair.' Are My
30 ways not fair, House of Israel? It is your ways that are not fair. So I will judge
you, House of Israel, each man according to his ways, declares the Lord
God; return – turn back from all your transgressions so that they will not be
31 the obstacle that is sin for you. Throw off all the transgressions you have
committed; make yourselves a new heart, a new spirit. Why should you die,
32 House of Israel? For I do not desire the death of those who die, declares the
19 1 Lord God; turn back and live! And you, raise a lament about the
2 leaders of Israel; say: What a lioness was your mother; among lions she lay;
3 among young lions she reared her cubs. She raised one of her cubs as a young
4 lion, and he learned to tear apart prey and devour men. But the nations heard

יג תּוֹעֵבָה עָשָׂה׃ בַּנֶּשֶׁךְ נָתַן וְתַרְבִּית לָקַח וָחָי לֹא יִחְיֶה אֵת כָּל־
יד הַתּוֹעֵבוֹת הָאֵלֶּה עָשָׂה מוֹת יוּמָת דָּמָיו בּוֹ יִהְיֶה׃ וְהִנֵּה הוֹלִיד בֵּן
טו וַיַּרְא אֶת־כָּל־חַטֹּאת אָבִיו אֲשֶׁר עָשָׂה וַיִּרְאֶה וְלֹא יַעֲשֶׂה כָּהֵן׃ עַל־
הֶהָרִים לֹא אָכָל וְעֵינָיו לֹא נָשָׂא אֶל־גִּלּוּלֵי בֵּית יִשְׂרָאֵל אֶת־אֵשֶׁת
טז רֵעֵהוּ לֹא טִמֵּא׃ וְאִישׁ לֹא הוֹנָה חֲבֹל לֹא חָבָל וּגְזֵלָה לֹא גָזָל לַחְמוֹ
יז לְרָעֵב נָתָן וְעֵרוֹם כִּסָּה־בָגֶד׃ מֵעָנִי הֵשִׁיב יָדוֹ נֶשֶׁךְ וְתַרְבִּית לֹא
לָקָח מִשְׁפָּטַי עָשָׂה בְּחֻקּוֹתַי הָלָךְ הוּא לֹא יָמוּת בַּעֲוֺן אָבִיו חָיֹה
יח יִחְיֶה׃ אָבִיו כִּי־עָשַׁק עֹשֶׁק גָּזַל גֵּזֶל אָח וַאֲשֶׁר לֹא־טוֹב עָשָׂה בְּתוֹךְ
יט עַמָּיו וְהִנֵּה־מֵת בַּעֲוֺנוֹ׃ וַאֲמַרְתֶּם מַדֻּעַ לֹא־נָשָׂא הַבֵּן בַּעֲוֺן הָאָב
וְהַבֵּן מִשְׁפָּט וּצְדָקָה עָשָׂה אֵת כָּל־חֻקּוֹתַי שָׁמַר וַיַּעֲשֶׂה אֹתָם חָיֹה
כ יִחְיֶה׃ הַנֶּפֶשׁ הַחֹטֵאת הִיא תָמוּת בֵּן לֹא־יִשָּׂא ׀ בַּעֲוֺן הָאָב וְאָב
לֹא יִשָּׂא בַּעֲוֺן הַבֵּן צִדְקַת הַצַּדִּיק עָלָיו תִּהְיֶה וְרִשְׁעַת רשע עָלָיו הָרָשָׁע
כא תִּהְיֶה׃ וְהָרָשָׁע כִּי יָשׁוּב מִכָּל־חַטֹּאתָו אֲשֶׁר
עָשָׂה וְשָׁמַר אֶת־כָּל־חֻקּוֹתַי וְעָשָׂה מִשְׁפָּט וּצְדָקָה חָיֹה יִחְיֶה לֹא
כב יָמוּת׃ כָּל־פְּשָׁעָיו אֲשֶׁר עָשָׂה לֹא יִזָּכְרוּ לוֹ בְּצִדְקָתוֹ אֲשֶׁר־עָשָׂה יִחְיֶה׃
כג הֶחָפֹץ אֶחְפֹּץ מוֹת רָשָׁע נְאֻם אֲדֹנָי יֱהֹוִה הֲלוֹא בְּשׁוּבוֹ מִדְּרָכָיו
כד וְחָיָה׃ וּבְשׁוּב צַדִּיק מִצִּדְקָתוֹ וְעָשָׂה עָוֶל כְּכֹל הַתּוֹעֵבוֹת
אֲשֶׁר־עָשָׂה הָרָשָׁע יַעֲשֶׂה וָחָי כָּל־צִדְקֹתָו אֲשֶׁר־עָשָׂה לֹא תִזָּכַרְנָה
כה בְּמַעֲלוֹ אֲשֶׁר־מָעַל וּבְחַטָּאתוֹ אֲשֶׁר־חָטָא בָּם יָמוּת׃ וַאֲמַרְתֶּם לֹא
יִתָּכֵן דֶּרֶךְ אֲדֹנָי שִׁמְעוּ־נָא בֵּית יִשְׂרָאֵל הֲדַרְכִּי לֹא יִתָּכֵן הֲלֹא דַרְכֵיכֶם
כו לֹא יִתָּכֵנוּ׃ בְּשׁוּב־צַדִּיק מִצִּדְקָתוֹ וְעָשָׂה עָוֶל וּמֵת עֲלֵיהֶם בְּעַוְלוֹ
כז אֲשֶׁר־עָשָׂה יָמוּת׃ וּבְשׁוּב רָשָׁע מֵרִשְׁעָתוֹ אֲשֶׁר עָשָׂה
כח וַיַּעַשׂ מִשְׁפָּט וּצְדָקָה הוּא אֶת־נַפְשׁוֹ יְחַיֶּה׃ וַיִּרְאֶה וישוב מִכָּל־פְּשָׁעָיו וַיָּשָׁב
כט אֲשֶׁר עָשָׂה חָיוֹ יִחְיֶה לֹא יָמוּת׃ וְאָמְרוּ בֵּית יִשְׂרָאֵל לֹא יִתָּכֵן דֶּרֶךְ
ל אֲדֹנָי הַדְּרָכַי לֹא יִתָּכְנוּ בֵּית יִשְׂרָאֵל הֲלֹא דַרְכֵיכֶם לֹא יִתָּכֵן׃ לָכֵן
אִישׁ כִּדְרָכָיו אֶשְׁפֹּט אֶתְכֶם בֵּית יִשְׂרָאֵל נְאֻם אֲדֹנָי יֱהֹוִה שׁוּבוּ וְהָשִׁיבוּ
לא מִכָּל־פִּשְׁעֵיכֶם וְלֹא־יִהְיֶה לָכֶם לְמִכְשׁוֹל עָוֺן׃ הַשְׁלִיכוּ מֵעֲלֵיכֶם אֶת־
כָּל־פִּשְׁעֵיכֶם אֲשֶׁר פְּשַׁעְתֶּם בָּם וַעֲשׂוּ לָכֶם לֵב חָדָשׁ וְרוּחַ חֲדָשָׁה
לב וְלָמָּה תָמֻתוּ בֵּית יִשְׂרָאֵל׃ כִּי לֹא אֶחְפֹּץ בְּמוֹת הַמֵּת נְאֻם אֲדֹנָי יֱהֹוִה
יט א ב וְהָשִׁיבוּ וִחְיוּ׃ וְאַתָּה שָׂא קִינָה אֶל־נְשִׂיאֵי יִשְׂרָאֵל׃ וְאָמַרְתָּ
ג מָה אִמְּךָ לְבִיָּא בֵּין אֲרָיוֹת רָבָצָה בְּתוֹךְ כְּפִרִים רִבְּתָה גוּרֶיהָ׃ וַתַּעַל
ד אֶחָד מִגֻּרֶיהָ כְּפִיר הָיָה וַיִּלְמַד לִטְרָף־טֶרֶף אָדָם אָכָל׃ וַיִּשְׁמְעוּ אֵלָיו

about him, and he was captured in their pit; with hooks they brought him in
5 to the land of Egypt.[27] She saw that in vain she waited, that hope was lost, so
6 she took another of her cubs; she made him the young lion. And he prowled
among the lions as a young lion; he learned to tear apart prey; he devoured
7 men. He seduced their widows, destroyed their cities; the land and all within
8 it were devastated at the sound of his roar. But the nations set upon him from
surrounding provinces; they spread their net over him; he was captured in
9 their pit. With hooks they locked him in a cage and brought him to the king
of Babylon; they brought him trapped in nets so that his voice would no
10 longer be heard on the mountains of Israel.[28] Your mother was like
a vine, like you, planted by the water, full of fruit and with full branches from
11 the great flowing waters. She had strong branches for the scepters of rulers;
her heights towered among the clouds; in her height and abundant arms, she
12 was striking. But she was uprooted in fury and hurled down to the ground;
the east wind withered her fruit; they broke off, they withered, the branches
13 of her strength; fire devoured her. Now, planted in the desert in a land of
14 drought and thirst, fire burst out from the branch holding her shoots and
consumed her fruit; no strong branch remained on her, no scepter to rule
with. This is a lament and has become a lament."

20 1 And it was in the seventh year in the fifth month on the tenth day of the
month that men from the elders of Israel came and sat before me to consult
2 the LORD. 3 And the word of the LORD came to me: "Man, speak to
the elders of Israel; say to them: So says the Lord GOD: Have you come to
4 seek Me? As I live, I will not be sought by you, declares the Lord GOD. Will
you accuse them, Man, will you accuse them? Make known to them their
5 fathers' abominations. Say to them: So says the Lord GOD: On the day that
I chose Israel, raising My hand in promise to the descendants of the House
of Yaakov and making Myself known to them in the land of Egypt, I raised
6 My hand in promise to them, saying: 'I the LORD am your God.' On that day,
I raised My hand in promise to them to take them from the land of Egypt to
the land that flows with milk and honey, the most beautiful of all lands, that
7 I had sought out for them. I said to them: 'Throw off, each of you, the
detestable things before your eyes; do not defile yourselves with Egyptian
8 idols: I the LORD am your God.' But they defied Me; they were not prepared
to listen to Me; none threw off the detestable things before their eyes; they
did not relinquish their Egyptian idols. And I thought of pouring out My fury,
9 exhausting My anger upon them in the midst of the land of Egypt. But I acted
for the sake of My name so that it would not be desecrated in the eyes of the
nations among whom they were – and before whose eyes I had made Myself
10 known in taking them out from the land of Egypt. I took them out from the
11 land of Egypt and brought them into the wilderness. I gave them My statutes,
12 made My laws known to them, by which a person shall live. I even gave them
My Sabbaths as a sign between Myself and them so that they should know

27 | Referring to Yehoaḥaz (see II Kings 23:33).
28 | Referring to Yehoyakhin (see II Kings 24:8–16).

ה גוים בשחתם נתפש ויבאהו בחחים אל־ארץ מצרים: ותרא כי
ו נוחלה אבדה תקותה ותקח אחד מגריה כפיר שמתהו: ויתהלך
ז בתוך־אריות כפיר היה וילמד לטרף־טרף אדם אכל: וידע אלמנותיו
ח ועריהם החריב ותשם ארץ ומלאה מקול שאגתו: ויתנו עליו גוים
ט סביב ממדינות ויפרשו עליו רשתם בשחתם נתפש: ויתנהו בסוגר
בחחים ויבאהו אל־מלך בבל יבאהו במצדות למען לא־ישמע
י קולו עוד אל־הרי ישראל: אמך כגפן בדמך על־מים
יא שתולה פריה וענפה היתה ממים רבים: ויהיו־לה מטות עז אל־
שבטי משלים ותגבה קומתו על־בין עבתים וירא בגבהו ברב
יב דליתיו: ותתש בחמה לארץ השלכה ורוח הקדים הוביש פריה
יג התפרקו ויבשו מטה עזה אש אכלתהו: ועתה שתולה במדבר
יד בארץ ציה וצמא: ותצא אש ממטה בדיה פריה אכלה ולא־היה
בה מטה עז שבט למשול קינה היא ותהי לקינה:
כ א ויהי | בשנה השביעית בחמשי בעשור לחדש באו אנשים מזקני יא
ב ישראל לדרש את־יהוה וישבו לפני: ויהי דבר־יהוה
ג אלי לאמר: בן־אדם דבר את־זקני ישראל ואמרת אלהם כה אמר
אדני יהוה הלדרש אתי אתם באים חי־אני אם־אדרש לכם נאם
ד אדני יהוה: התשפט אתם התשפוט בן־אדם את־תועבת אבותם
ה הודיעם: ואמרת אליהם כה־אמר אדני יהוה ביום בחרי בישראל
ואשא ידי לזרע בית יעקב ואודע להם בארץ מצרים ואשא ידי
ו להם לאמר אני יהוה אלהיכם: ביום ההוא נשאתי ידי להם להוציאם
מארץ מצרים אל־ארץ אשר־תרתי להם זבת חלב ודבש צבי היא
ז לכל־הארצות: ואמר אלהם איש שקוצי עיניו השליכו ובגלולי
ח מצרים אל־תטמאו אני יהוה אלהיכם: וימרו־בי ולא אבו לשמע
אלי איש את־שקוצי עיניהם לא השליכו ואת־גלולי מצרים לא
עזבו ואמר לשפך חמתי עליהם לכלות אפי בהם בתוך ארץ מצרים:
ט ואעש למען שמי לבלתי החל לעיני הגוים אשר־המה בתוכם אשר
י נודעתי אליהם לעיניהם להוציאם מארץ מצרים: ואוציאם מארץ
יא מצרים ואבאם אל־המדבר: ואתן להם את־חקותי ואת־משפטי
יב הודעתי אותם אשר יעשה אותם האדם וחי בהם: וגם את־שבתותי
נתתי להם להיות לאות ביני וביניהם לדעת כי אני יהוה מקדשם:

13 that I, the LORD, make them holy. But the House of Israel defied me in the
wilderness. They did not follow My statutes; they rejected My laws, by which
each person was to live; they wholly desecrated My Sabbaths. I thought of
14 pouring out My fury upon them in the wilderness and destroying them, but
I acted for the sake of My name so that it would not be desecrated in the
15 eyes of the nations before whose eyes I had taken them out. I even raised My
hand in promise to them in the desert not to bring them to the land that
flows with milk and honey, the most beautiful of all lands, which I had given
16 them, because they rejected My laws, did not follow My statutes, desecrated
17 My Sabbaths – for their hearts followed after their idols. But My eye pitied
them, and I could not destroy them; I did not bring them to their end in the
18 wilderness. I said to their children in the wilderness: 'Do not follow the
statutes of your fathers, do not keep their laws; do not be defiled by their idols.
19 I the LORD am your God: follow My statutes, keep My laws, perform them,
20 make My Sabbaths holy – it will be a sign between Me and you to know that
21 I the LORD am your God.' But the children defied me: they did not follow
My statutes, they did not take care to keep My laws, by which a person shall
live, they desecrated My Sabbaths, and I thought to pour out My fury upon
22 them, exhausting My anger upon them there in the wilderness. But I drew
back My hand; I acted for the sake of My name so that it would not be
desecrated in the eyes of the nations before whose eyes I had taken them out.
23 Nevertheless, I raised My hand in promise to them in the wilderness – to
24 scatter them among the nations and strew them through the lands because
they did not perform My laws, they rejected My statutes, and they desecrated
25 My Sabbaths, their eyes bent toward the idols of their fathers. So I further
gave them statutes that were no good and laws they could not live through;
26 I defiled them through their gifts of giving over all the first to emerge from
the womb so that I might devastate them, so that they might know that I am
27 the LORD. And so, speak to the House of Israel, Man, and say to
them: So says the Lord GOD: In this, too, your fathers acted toward Me with
28 contempt in their betrayal of Me. I brought them to the land which I raised
My hand in promise to give to them; they saw each high hill, every lush tree,
and there offered up their offerings, there gave their enraging sacrifices with
29 the sweet fragrances they made, and there poured their libations. I said
to them: What is the high place that you hurry to? To this day it is called
30 Bama.[29] So say to the House of Israel: So says the Lord GOD: Do
you defile yourselves in the way that your fathers did; do you whore after their
31 detestable things? You defile yourselves when you offer your children through
fire as presents to all your idols – to this very day; shall I allow you to seek Me,
House of Israel? As I live, declares the Lord GOD, I will not allow you to seek
32 Me. And that which is in your thoughts will never be. You say: We will be like

29 | The name Bama (high place) can be read as a compound of *ba* (hurry) and *ma* (what).

יג וַיַּמְרוּ־בִי בֵית־יִשְׂרָאֵל בַּמִּדְבָּר בְּחֻקּוֹתַי לֹא־הָלָכוּ וְאֶת־מִשְׁפָּטַי מָאָסוּ
אֲשֶׁר יַעֲשֶׂה אֹתָם הָאָדָם וָחַי בָּהֶם וְאֶת־שַׁבְּתֹתַי חִלְּלוּ מְאֹד וָאֹמַר
יד לִשְׁפֹּךְ חֲמָתִי עֲלֵיהֶם בַּמִּדְבָּר לְכַלּוֹתָם: וָאֶעֱשֶׂה לְמַעַן שְׁמִי לְבִלְתִּי
טו הֵחֵל לְעֵינֵי הַגּוֹיִם אֲשֶׁר הוֹצֵאתִים לְעֵינֵיהֶם: וְגַם־אֲנִי נָשָׂאתִי יָדִי
לָהֶם בַּמִּדְבָּר לְבִלְתִּי הָבִיא אוֹתָם אֶל־הָאָרֶץ אֲשֶׁר־נָתַתִּי זָבַת חָלָב
טז וּדְבַשׁ צְבִי הִיא לְכָל־הָאֲרָצוֹת: יַעַן בְּמִשְׁפָּטַי מָאָסוּ וְאֶת־חֻקּוֹתַי
לֹא־הָלְכוּ בָהֶם וְאֶת־שַׁבְּתוֹתַי חִלֵּלוּ כִּי אַחֲרֵי גִלּוּלֵיהֶם לִבָּם הֹלֵךְ:
יז יח וַתָּחָס עֵינִי עֲלֵיהֶם מִשַּׁחֲתָם וְלֹא־עָשִׂיתִי אוֹתָם כָּלָה בַּמִּדְבָּר: וָאֹמַר
אֶל־בְּנֵיהֶם בַּמִּדְבָּר בְּחוּקֵּי אֲבוֹתֵיכֶם אַל־תֵּלֵכוּ וְאֶת־מִשְׁפְּטֵיהֶם
יט אַל־תִּשְׁמֹרוּ וּבְגִלּוּלֵיהֶם אַל־תִּטַּמָּאוּ: אֲנִי יְהוָה אֱלֹהֵיכֶם בְּחֻקּוֹתַי
כ לֵכוּ וְאֶת־מִשְׁפָּטַי שִׁמְרוּ וַעֲשׂוּ אוֹתָם: וְאֶת־שַׁבְּתוֹתַי קַדֵּשׁוּ וְהָיוּ
כא לְאוֹת בֵּינִי וּבֵינֵיכֶם לָדַעַת כִּי אֲנִי יְהוָה אֱלֹהֵיכֶם: וַיַּמְרוּ־בִי הַבָּנִים
בְּחֻקּוֹתַי לֹא־הָלָכוּ וְאֶת־מִשְׁפָּטַי לֹא־שָׁמְרוּ לַעֲשׂוֹת אוֹתָם אֲשֶׁר
יַעֲשֶׂה אוֹתָם הָאָדָם וָחַי בָּהֶם אֶת־שַׁבְּתוֹתַי חִלֵּלוּ וָאֹמַר לִשְׁפֹּךְ חֲמָתִי
כב עֲלֵיהֶם לְכַלּוֹת אַפִּי בָּם בַּמִּדְבָּר: וַהֲשִׁבֹתִי אֶת־יָדִי וָאַעַשׂ לְמַעַן
שְׁמִי לְבִלְתִּי הֵחֵל לְעֵינֵי הַגּוֹיִם אֲשֶׁר־הוֹצֵאתִי אוֹתָם לְעֵינֵיהֶם:
כג גַּם־אֲנִי נָשָׂאתִי אֶת־יָדִי לָהֶם בַּמִּדְבָּר לְהָפִיץ אֹתָם בַּגּוֹיִם וּלְזָרוֹת
כד אוֹתָם בָּאֲרָצוֹת: יַעַן מִשְׁפָּטַי לֹא־עָשׂוּ וְחֻקּוֹתַי מָאָסוּ וְאֶת־שַׁבְּתוֹתַי
כה חִלֵּלוּ וְאַחֲרֵי גִּלּוּלֵי אֲבוֹתָם הָיוּ עֵינֵיהֶם: וְגַם־אֲנִי נָתַתִּי לָהֶם חֻקִּים
כו לֹא טוֹבִים וּמִשְׁפָּטִים לֹא יִחְיוּ בָּהֶם: וָאֲטַמֵּא אוֹתָם בְּמַתְּנוֹתָם
בְּהַעֲבִיר כָּל־פֶּטֶר רָחַם לְמַעַן אֲשִׁמֵּם לְמַעַן אֲשֶׁר יֵדְעוּ אֲשֶׁר אֲנִי
כז יְהוָה: לָכֵן דַּבֵּר אֶל־בֵּית יִשְׂרָאֵל בֶּן־אָדָם וְאָמַרְתָּ אֲלֵיהֶם
כֹּה אָמַר אֲדֹנָי יֱהֹוִה עוֹד זֹאת גִּדְּפוּ אוֹתִי אֲבוֹתֵיכֶם בְּמַעֲלָם בִּי מָעַל:
כח וָאֲבִיאֵם אֶל־הָאָרֶץ אֲשֶׁר נָשָׂאתִי אֶת־יָדִי לָתֵת אוֹתָהּ לָהֶם וַיִּרְאוּ
כָל־גִּבְעָה רָמָה וְכָל־עֵץ עָבֹת וַיִּזְבְּחוּ־שָׁם אֶת־זִבְחֵיהֶם וַיִּתְּנוּ־שָׁם
כַּעַס קָרְבָּנָם וַיָּשִׂימוּ שָׁם רֵיחַ נִיחוֹחֵיהֶם וַיַּסִּיכוּ שָׁם אֶת־נִסְכֵּיהֶם:
כט וָאֹמַר אֲלֵהֶם מָה הַבָּמָה אֲשֶׁר־אַתֶּם הַבָּאִים שָׁם וַיִּקָּרֵא שְׁמָהּ בָּמָה
ל עַד הַיּוֹם הַזֶּה: לָכֵן אֱמֹר ׀ אֶל־בֵּית יִשְׂרָאֵל כֹּה אָמַר
אֲדֹנָי יֱהֹוִה הַבְדֶרֶךְ אֲבוֹתֵיכֶם אַתֶּם נִטְמְאִים וְאַחֲרֵי שִׁקּוּצֵיהֶם אַתֶּם
לא זֹנִים: וּבִשְׂאֵת מַתְּנֹתֵיכֶם בְּהַעֲבִיר בְּנֵיכֶם בָּאֵשׁ אַתֶּם נִטְמְאִים לְכָל־
גִּלּוּלֵיכֶם עַד־הַיּוֹם וַאֲנִי אִדָּרֵשׁ לָכֶם בֵּית יִשְׂרָאֵל חַי־אָנִי נְאֻם אֲדֹנָי
לב יֱהֹוִה אִם־אִדָּרֵשׁ לָכֶם: וְהָעֹלָה עַל־רוּחֲכֶם הָיוֹ לֹא תִהְיֶה אֲשֶׁר ׀ אַתֶּם

33 the nations, like the families of the lands, serving wood and stone. As I live,
declares the Lord God, with a strong hand, with an outstretched arm, and
34 with an outpouring of fury, I will rule over you. I will take you out from the
nations; I will gather you in from the countries where you have been scattered;
with a strong hand, with an outstretched arm, and with an outpouring of
35 fury I will bring you into the wilderness of the nations, and I will enter
36 into judgment with you there, face-to-face. Just as I entered into judgment
with your fathers in the wilderness of the land of Egypt, so will I enter into
37 judgment with you, declares the Lord God. I will make you pass beneath the
38 rod;[30] I will bring you into the bond of the covenant. I will purge you of the
rebellious and of those who transgress against Me; I will take them out of the
land in which they are living, but they will not come onto the soil of Israel.
39 So you will know that I am the Lord. And you, House of Israel – so says
the Lord God: Go each of you to worship his idols, now and beyond, if you
will not listen to Me; you will no longer desecrate My holy name with your
40 gifts and your idols, because on My holy mountain – on Israel's high mountain,
declares the Lord God – there, all of the House of Israel in its entirety
will serve Me in the land; there I will receive them; there I will seek your
41 contributions and your most choice offerings, with all your holy things. As
with a sweet fragrance I will accept you when I take you out from among the
nations and gather you in from the lands that you were scattered among; I
42 will be sanctified through you in the eyes of the nations. And you will know
that I am the Lord when I bring you to the soil of Israel, to the land that I
43 raised My hand in promise to give to your fathers. There you will remember
your ways, all your deeds through which you were defiled, and you will loathe
44 yourselves for all the evil things that you have done. And you will know that
I am the Lord when I act toward you for the sake of My name, not for
your evil ways and your corrupt deeds, House of Israel, declares the Lord
21 1 God." 2 And the word of the Lord came to me: "Man, set your face
toward Teiman, proclaim to Darom, prophesy to the forestland of the Negev.[31]
3 Say to the forest of the Negev: Listen to the word of the Lord. So says the
Lord God: See, I will kindle in you a fire; it will devour in you every new tree
and every withered tree; it will not go out, this raging blaze. They, every face,
4 will be scorched by it, from the Negev up to the north. All flesh will see that
5 I, the Lord, set it alight; it will not be extinguished." And I said: "Ah, but my
6 Lord God! They say of me, 'He is just a teller of parables.'" And
7 the word of the Lord came to me: "Man, set your face toward Jerusalem and
8 proclaim to the sanctuaries; prophesy against the soil of Israel. Say to the soil
of Israel: So says the Lord: Behold, I am coming down upon you; I will draw
My sword from its sheath; I will cut off from you both righteous and wicked.
9 Since I will cut off from you righteous and wicked, My sword will come

30 | As a shepherd counts his flock (cf. Lev. 27:32).

31 | Teiman, Darom, and Negev are terms for south, denoting the land of Israel from Yeḥezkel's vantage point.

לג אֹמְרִים נִהְיֶה כַגּוֹיִם כְּמִשְׁפְּחוֹת הָאֲרָצוֹת לְשָׁרֵת עֵץ וָאָבֶן: חַי־אָנִי
נְאֻם אֲדֹנָי יֱהֹוִה אִם־לֹא בְּיָד חֲזָקָה וּבִזְרוֹעַ נְטוּיָה וּבְחֵמָה שְׁפוּכָה
לד אֶמְלוֹךְ עֲלֵיכֶם: וְהוֹצֵאתִי אֶתְכֶם מִן־הָעַמִּים וְקִבַּצְתִּי אֶתְכֶם מִן־
הָאֲרָצוֹת אֲשֶׁר נְפוֹצוֹתֶם בָּם בְּיָד חֲזָקָה וּבִזְרוֹעַ נְטוּיָה וּבְחֵמָה שְׁפוּכָה:
לה וְהֵבֵאתִי אֶתְכֶם אֶל־מִדְבַּר הָעַמִּים וְנִשְׁפַּטְתִּי אִתְּכֶם שָׁם פָּנִים אֶל־
לו פָּנִים: כַּאֲשֶׁר נִשְׁפַּטְתִּי אֶת־אֲבוֹתֵיכֶם בְּמִדְבַּר אֶרֶץ מִצְרָיִם כֵּן אִשָּׁפֵט
לז אִתְּכֶם נְאֻם אֲדֹנָי יֱהֹוִה: וְהַעֲבַרְתִּי אֶתְכֶם תַּחַת הַשָּׁבֶט וְהֵבֵאתִי
לח אֶתְכֶם בְּמָסֹרֶת הַבְּרִית: וּבָרוֹתִי מִכֶּם הַמֹּרְדִים וְהַפּוֹשְׁעִים בִּי מֵאֶרֶץ
מְגוּרֵיהֶם אוֹצִיא אוֹתָם וְאֶל־אַדְמַת יִשְׂרָאֵל לֹא יָבוֹא וִידַעְתֶּם כִּי־אֲנִי
לט יְהֹוָה: וְאַתֶּם בֵּית־יִשְׂרָאֵל כֹּה־אָמַר ׀ אֲדֹנָי יֱהֹוִה אִישׁ גִּלּוּלָיו לְכוּ
עֲבֹדוּ וְאַחַר אִם־אֵינְכֶם שֹׁמְעִים אֵלָי וְאֶת־שֵׁם קָדְשִׁי לֹא תְחַלְּלוּ־עוֹד
מ בְּמַתְּנוֹתֵיכֶם וּבְגִלּוּלֵיכֶם: כִּי בְהַר־קָדְשִׁי בְּהַר ׀ מְרוֹם יִשְׂרָאֵל נְאֻם
אֲדֹנָי יֱהֹוִה שָׁם יַעַבְדֻנִי כָּל־בֵּית יִשְׂרָאֵל כֻּלֹּה בָּאָרֶץ שָׁם אֶרְצֵם וְשָׁם
אֶדְרוֹשׁ אֶת־תְּרוּמֹתֵיכֶם וְאֶת־רֵאשִׁית מַשְׂאוֹתֵיכֶם בְּכָל־קָדְשֵׁיכֶם:
מא בְּרֵיחַ נִיחֹחַ אֶרְצֶה אֶתְכֶם בְּהוֹצִיאִי אֶתְכֶם מִן־הָעַמִּים וְקִבַּצְתִּי אֶתְכֶם יב
מב מִן־הָאֲרָצוֹת אֲשֶׁר נְפֹצֹתֶם בָּם וְנִקְדַּשְׁתִּי בָכֶם לְעֵינֵי הַגּוֹיִם: וִידַעְתֶּם
כִּי־אֲנִי יְהֹוָה בַּהֲבִיאִי אֶתְכֶם אֶל־אַדְמַת יִשְׂרָאֵל אֶל־הָאָרֶץ אֲשֶׁר
מג נָשָׂאתִי אֶת־יָדִי לָתֵת אוֹתָהּ לַאֲבוֹתֵיכֶם: וּזְכַרְתֶּם־שָׁם אֶת־דַּרְכֵיכֶם
וְאֵת כָּל־עֲלִילוֹתֵיכֶם אֲשֶׁר נִטְמֵאתֶם בָּם וּנְקֹטֹתֶם בִּפְנֵיכֶם בְּכָל־
מד רָעוֹתֵיכֶם אֲשֶׁר עֲשִׂיתֶם: וִידַעְתֶּם כִּי־אֲנִי יְהֹוָה בַּעֲשׂוֹתִי אִתְּכֶם לְמַעַן
שְׁמִי לֹא כְדַרְכֵיכֶם הָרָעִים וְכַעֲלִילוֹתֵיכֶם הַנִּשְׁחָתוֹת בֵּית יִשְׂרָאֵל
כא א ב נְאֻם אֲדֹנָי יֱהֹוִה: וַיְהִי דְבַר־יְהֹוָה אֵלַי לֵאמֹר: בֶּן־אָדָם
שִׂים פָּנֶיךָ דֶּרֶךְ תֵּימָנָה וְהַטֵּף אֶל־דָּרוֹם וְהִנָּבֵא אֶל־יַעַר הַשָּׂדֶה נֶגֶב:
ג וְאָמַרְתָּ לְיַעַר הַנֶּגֶב שְׁמַע דְּבַר־יְהֹוָה כֹּה־אָמַר אֲדֹנָי יֱהֹוִה הִנְנִי
מַצִּית־בְּךָ ׀ אֵשׁ וְאָכְלָה בְךָ כָל־עֵץ־לַח וְכָל־עֵץ יָבֵשׁ לֹא־תִכְבֶּה
ד לַהֶבֶת שַׁלְהֶבֶת וְנִצְרְבוּ־בָהּ כָּל־פָּנִים מִנֶּגֶב צָפוֹנָה: וְרָאוּ כָּל־בָּשָׂר
ה כִּי אֲנִי יְהֹוָה בִּעַרְתִּיהָ לֹא תִּכְבֶּה: וָאֹמַר אֲהָהּ אֲדֹנָי יֱהֹוִה הֵמָּה אֹמְרִים
ו לִי הֲלֹא מְמַשֵּׁל מְשָׁלִים הוּא: וַיְהִי דְבַר־יְהֹוָה אֵלַי
ז לֵאמֹר: בֶּן־אָדָם שִׂים פָּנֶיךָ אֶל־יְרוּשָׁלִַם וְהַטֵּף אֶל־מִקְדָּשִׁים וְהִנָּבֵא
ח אֶל־אַדְמַת יִשְׂרָאֵל: וְאָמַרְתָּ לְאַדְמַת יִשְׂרָאֵל כֹּה אָמַר יְהֹוָה הִנְנִי
ט אֵלַיִךְ וְהוֹצֵאתִי חַרְבִּי מִתַּעְרָהּ וְהִכְרַתִּי מִמֵּךְ צַדִּיק וְרָשָׁע: יַעַן אֲשֶׁר־
הִכְרַתִּי מִמֵּךְ צַדִּיק וְרָשָׁע לָכֵן תֵּצֵא חַרְבִּי מִתַּעְרָהּ אֶל־כָּל־בָּשָׂר

10 out of its sheath against all flesh, from south to north. All flesh will know
that I am the LORD; I have drawn My sword from its sheath; it will not be
11 returned. And you, Man: Groan with a body shattered; in bitterness
12 groan before their eyes. And when they say, 'Why are you groaning?' say:
Because of a report that is coming: Every heart will melt; all hands will go
limp; every spirit will faint, all thighs run wet with fear; behold: it is coming;
13 it will be, declares the Lord GOD." And the word of the LORD came
14 to me: "Man, prophesy and say: So says the Lord: Say: A sword, a sword has
15 been sharpened, polished, to commit slaughter; sharpened, and so that it will
16 flash, polished. Will we rejoice, rod of My son that despises every tree? It was
given to be polished, to be wielded, the sword was sharpened, polished, to
17 be given into the hand of a killer. Cry out, wail, Man, for it is against My
people, it is against all the leaders of Israel – they are thrown to the sword
18 with My people, so slap your thigh in grief; it is assured. What is? That even
19 the rod that despises will not be spared, declares the Lord GOD. And
you, Man, prophesy; clap your hands: The sword will come again and a third
20 time, the sword of slaying, the sword of a great massacre enclosing them; so
that hearts will crumble, and many will fall at each of their gates. I have
allowed sword slaughter; O, shined so that it will flash, honed for slaughter.
21 22 Sharp, to the right! To the left! Where is your blade aimed? I, too, will clap
23 My hands, then let My fury die down. I, the LORD, have spoken." And
24 the word of the LORD came to me: "And you, Man, mark out two roads for
the sword of the king of Babylon to advance upon, both exiting from the
same land, and clear space for a sign at the beginning of the road leading to
25 each city; clear space. Mark out a road for the sword to advance upon –
26 to Raba of the Amonites[32] and to Yehuda in fortified Jerusalem. For the
king of Babylon stands at the fork in the road, at the beginning of the two
roads, to perform a divination: shaking arrows, inquiring of household gods,
27 scrutinizing the liver. In his right hand is the omen that signals Jerusalem:
to post battering rams, to demand slaughter, to shout out war cries; to
post battering rams at the gates, to throw up earthworks, to build a siege
28 wall. It will be seen as a false divination in their eyes – for they have had
reassuring oaths sworn to them which recall the sin for which they will be
29 seized. So the Lord GOD says this: since you have recalled
your sin by uncovering your transgressions to reveal the iniquities in
all your deeds – because your sin has been recalled, by hand you will be
30 seized. To you, disgraced, wicked leader of Israel whose day, the
31 'time of final punishment, has come, so says the Lord GOD: Remove
the royal turban; lift off the crown! This will no longer be thus; exalt the lowly,
32 and lower the exalted. Ruin, ruined, wrecked I will make it. This, too, will not
33 be until he with just claim comes, and I hand it to him. And you,

32 | Raba, modern Aman, was the Amonite capital.

י מִנֶּגֶב צָפוֹן׃ וְיָדְעוּ כָּל־בָּשָׂר כִּי אֲנִי יְהוָה הוֹצֵאתִי חַרְבִּי מִתַּעְרָהּ לֹא
יא תָשׁוּב עוֹד׃ וְאַתָּה בֶן־אָדָם הֵאָנַח בְּשִׁבְרוֹן מָתְנַיִם
יב וּבִמְרִירוּת תֵּאָנַח לְעֵינֵיהֶם׃ וְהָיָה כִּי־יֹאמְרוּ אֵלֶיךָ עַל־מָה אַתָּה
נֶאֱנָח וְאָמַרְתָּ אֶל־שְׁמוּעָה כִי־בָאָה וְנָמֵס כָּל־לֵב וְרָפוּ כָל־יָדַיִם
וְכִהֲתָה כָל־רוּחַ וְכָל־בִּרְכַּיִם תֵּלַכְנָה מַּיִם הִנֵּה בָאָה וְנִהְיָתָה נְאֻם
יג יד אֲדֹנָי יְהוִה׃ וַיְהִי דְבַר־יְהוָה אֵלַי לֵאמֹר׃ בֶּן־אָדָם הִנָּבֵא
טו וְאָמַרְתָּ כֹּה אָמַר אֲדֹנָי אֱמֹר חֶרֶב חֶרֶב הוּחַדָּה וְגַם־מְרוּטָה׃ לְמַעַן
טְבֹחַ טֶבַח הוּחַדָּה לְמַעַן־הֱיֵה־לָהּ בָּרָק מֹרָטָּה אוֹ נָשִׂישׂ שֵׁבֶט בְּנִי
טז מֹאֶסֶת כָּל־עֵץ׃ וַיִּתֵּן אֹתָהּ לְמָרְטָה לִתְפֹּשׂ בַּכָּף הִיא־הוּחַדָּה חֶרֶב
יז וְהִיא מֹרָטָּה לָתֵת אוֹתָהּ בְּיַד־הוֹרֵג׃ זְעַק וְהֵילֵל בֶּן־אָדָם כִּי־הִיא
הָיְתָה בְעַמִּי הִיא בְּכָל־נְשִׂיאֵי יִשְׂרָאֵל מְגוּרֵי אֶל־חֶרֶב הָיוּ אֶת־עַמִּי
יח לָכֵן סְפֹק אֶל־יָרֵךְ׃ כִּי בֹחַן וּמָה אִם־גַּם־שֵׁבֶט מֹאֶסֶת לֹא יִהְיֶה נְאֻם
יט אֲדֹנָי יְהוִה׃ וְאַתָּה בֶן־אָדָם הִנָּבֵא וְהַךְ כַּף אֶל־כָּף וְתִכָּפֵל
חֶרֶב שְׁלִישִׁתָה חֶרֶב חֲלָלִים הִיא חֶרֶב חָלָל הַגָּדוֹל הַחֹדֶרֶת לָהֶם׃
כ לְמַעַן ׀ לָמוּג לֵב וְהַרְבֵּה הַמִּכְשֹׁלִים עַל כָּל־שַׁעֲרֵיהֶם נָתַתִּי אִבְחַת־
כא חָרֶב אָח עֲשׂוּיָה לְבָרָק מְעֻטָּה לְטָבַח׃ הִתְאַחֲדִי הֵימִינִי הָשִׂימִי
כב הַשְׂמִילִי אָנָה פָּנַיִךְ מֻעָדוֹת׃ וְגַם־אֲנִי אַכֶּה כַפִּי אֶל־כַּפִּי וַהֲנִחֹתִי חֲמָתִי
כג כד אֲנִי יְהוָה דִּבַּרְתִּי׃ וַיְהִי דְבַר־יְהוָה אֵלַי לֵאמֹר׃ וְאַתָּה בֶן־
אָדָם שִׂים־לְךָ ׀ שְׁנַיִם דְּרָכִים לָבוֹא חֶרֶב מֶלֶךְ־בָּבֶל מֵאֶרֶץ אֶחָד יֵצְאוּ
כה שְׁנֵיהֶם וְיָד בָּרֵא בְּרֹאשׁ דֶּרֶךְ־עִיר בָּרֵא׃ דֶּרֶךְ תָּשִׂים לָבוֹא חֶרֶב אֵת
כו רַבַּת בְּנֵי־עַמּוֹן וְאֶת־יְהוּדָה בִירוּשָׁלִַם בְּצוּרָה׃ כִּי־עָמַד מֶלֶךְ־בָּבֶל
אֶל־אֵם הַדֶּרֶךְ בְּרֹאשׁ שְׁנֵי הַדְּרָכִים לִקְסָם־קָסֶם קִלְקַל בַּחִצִּים שָׁאַל
כז בַּתְּרָפִים רָאָה בַּכָּבֵד׃ בִּימִינוֹ הָיָה ׀ הַקֶּסֶם יְרוּשָׁלִַם לָשׂוּם כָּרִים
לִפְתֹּחַ פֶּה בְּרֶצַח לְהָרִים קוֹל בִּתְרוּעָה לָשׂוּם כָּרִים עַל־שְׁעָרִים
כח לִשְׁפֹּךְ סֹלְלָה לִבְנוֹת דָּיֵק׃ וְהָיָה לָהֶם כִּקְסוֹם־שָׁוְא בְּעֵינֵיהֶם שְׁבֻעֵי כְּקָסָם־
כט שְׁבֻעוֹת לָהֶם וְהוּא־מַזְכִּיר עָוֺן לְהִתָּפֵשׂ׃ לָכֵן כֹּה־אָמַר
אֲדֹנָי יְהוִה יַעַן הַזְכַּרְכֶם עֲוֺנְכֶם בְּהִגָּלוֹת פִּשְׁעֵיכֶם לְהֵרָאוֹת חַטֹּאותֵיכֶם
ל בְּכֹל עֲלִילוֹתֵיכֶם יַעַן הִזָּכֶרְכֶם בַּכַּף תִּתָּפֵשׂוּ׃ וְאַתָּה חָלָל
לא רָשָׁע נְשִׂיא יִשְׂרָאֵל אֲשֶׁר־בָּא יוֹמוֹ בְּעֵת עֲוֺן קֵץ׃ כֹּה אָמַר
אֲדֹנָי יְהוִה הָסִיר הַמִּצְנֶפֶת וְהָרִים הָעֲטָרָה זֹאת לֹא־זֹאת הַשָּׁפָלָה
לב הַגְבֵּהַ וְהַגָּבֹהַּ הַשְׁפִּיל׃ עַוָּה עַוָּה עַוָּה אֲשִׂימֶנָּה גַּם־זֹאת לֹא הָיָה
לג עַד־בֹּא אֲשֶׁר־לוֹ הַמִּשְׁפָּט וּנְתַתִּיו׃ וְאַתָּה בֶן־אָדָם הִנָּבֵא

Man, prophesy – say: So says the Lord GOD concerning the Amonites and
their taunts: Sword, sword, unsheathed, for slaughter polished to its utmost
34 so that it flashes, professing false visions and lying predictions about you,
sword, have brought you down instead onto the necks of the disgraced
35 wicked, whose day has come, the time of final punishment. Return it to its
sheath! In the place you were created, in the land of your origin, I will judge
36 you. I will pour out My rage upon you, I will blast through you the fire of My
wrath, I will give you over into the hands of brutish men, skilled at destruction.
37 You will be fuel for the fire, your blood will be shed there in the land; you will
22 1 not be remembered – for I, the LORD, have spoken." The word of
2 the LORD came to me, saying, "And you, Man, will you accuse – will you
3 accuse the bloody city? Make all her abominations known to her. Say: So says
the Lord GOD: City that spills blood in her own midst, hastening her time
4 and making idols in her to defile her, in spilling your own blood, you have
become guilty; in making your own idols, you have been defiled. You have
brought your days near; you have come to the end of your years, so I give you
5 over as a reproach to the nations, a mockery to all the lands. Those near and
6 far will mock you, you of impure name, filled with panic. Here are the leaders
7 of Israel: each used his power to spill blood among you; they have dishonored
mother and father within you; they have oppressed the foreigner in your
8 midst; they have mistreated orphan and widow within you. You despised My
9 holy things; you desecrated My Sabbaths. Slanderers have been among you
so as to spill blood; on the mountains they have eaten among you; depravities
10 they have performed in your midst. Their father's nakedness they have
uncovered within you; the impure, menstrual woman they have forced within
11 you. One man committed abominations with another's wife; another has
defiled his daughter-in-law with depravity; another in you has forced his sister,
12 the daughter of his father – within you! They have taken bribes within you
so as to spill blood; you have taken both advanced and accrued interest; you
have taken advantage of your friend with extortion; and Me you have
13 forgotten, declares the Lord GOD. See: I clap My hands over the dishonest
14 gain you have taken and over the bloodshed that were in your midst. Will
your heart stand firm, will your hands stay strong for the days when I deal
15 with you? I am the LORD; I have spoken and will do it. I will strew you among
the nations, scatter you over the lands: I will purge your impurity from you.
16 You will be debased in yourself before the eyes of nations, and you will know
17 that I am the LORD." And the word of the LORD came to me, saying,
18 "Man, to Me the House of Israel are dross; they are bronze, tin, iron, and lead
19 in a crucible; they are the dross of silver. So the Lord GOD says this:
20 Because you have all become dross, I am gathering you in to Jerusalem. Like
silver and bronze, iron, lead, and tin gathered into a crucible to blast with fire
to melt it – so will I gather you in My anger and My fury and put you in and
21 melt you. I will collect you together and blast the fire of My wrath upon you;
22 you will be melted down within her. Like the smelting of silver in a crucible,
this is how you will be smelted within her; you will know that I am the LORD

וְאָמַרְתָּ כֹּה אָמַר אֲדֹנָי יֱהוִה אֶל־בְּנֵי עַמּוֹן וְאֶל־חֶרְפָּתָם וְאָמַרְתָּ חֶרֶב
לד חֶרֶב פְּתוּחָה לְטֶבַח מְרוּטָה לְהָכִיל לְמַעַן בָּרָק׃ בַּחֲזוֹת לָךְ שָׁוְא
בִּקְסָם־לָךְ כָּזָב לָתֵת אוֹתָךְ אֶל־צַוְּארֵי חַלְלֵי רְשָׁעִים אֲשֶׁר־בָּא יוֹמָם
לה בְּעֵת עֲוֺן קֵץ׃ הָשַׁב אֶל־תַּעְרָהּ בִּמְקוֹם אֲשֶׁר־נִבְרֵאת בְּאֶרֶץ מְכֻרוֹתַיִךְ
לו אֶשְׁפֹּט אֹתָךְ׃ וְשָׁפַכְתִּי עָלַיִךְ זַעְמִי בְּאֵשׁ עֶבְרָתִי אָפִיחַ עָלָיִךְ וּנְתַתִּיךְ
לז בְּיַד אֲנָשִׁים בֹּעֲרִים חָרָשֵׁי מַשְׁחִית׃ לָאֵשׁ תִּהְיֶה לְאָכְלָה דָּמֵךְ יִהְיֶה
כב א בְּתוֹךְ הָאָרֶץ לֹא תִזָּכֵרִי כִּי אֲנִי יְהוָה דִּבַּרְתִּי׃ וַיְהִי דְבַר־
ב יְהוָה אֵלַי לֵאמֹר׃ וְאַתָּה בֶן־אָדָם הֲתִשְׁפֹּט הֲתִשְׁפֹּט אֶת־עִיר הַדָּמִים
ג וְהוֹדַעְתָּהּ אֵת כָּל־תּוֹעֲבוֹתֶיהָ׃ וְאָמַרְתָּ כֹּה אָמַר אֲדֹנָי יֱהוִה עִיר
ד שֹׁפֶכֶת דָּם בְּתוֹכָהּ לָבוֹא עִתָּהּ וְעָשְׂתָה גִלּוּלִים עָלֶיהָ לְטָמְאָה׃ בְּדָמֵךְ
אֲשֶׁר־שָׁפַכְתְּ אָשַׁמְתְּ וּבְגִלּוּלַיִךְ אֲשֶׁר־עָשִׂית טָמֵאת וַתַּקְרִיבִי יָמַיִךְ
וַתָּבוֹא עַד־שְׁנוֹתָיִךְ עַל־כֵּן נְתַתִּיךְ חֶרְפָּה לַגּוֹיִם וְקַלָּסָה לְכָל־
ה הָאֲרָצוֹת׃ הַקְּרֹבוֹת וְהָרְחֹקוֹת מִמֵּךְ יִתְקַלְּסוּ־בָךְ טְמֵאַת הַשֵּׁם רַבַּת
ו הַמְּהוּמָה׃ הִנֵּה נְשִׂיאֵי יִשְׂרָאֵל אִישׁ לִזְרֹעוֹ הָיוּ בָךְ לְמַעַן שְׁפָךְ־דָּם׃
ז אָב וָאֵם הֵקַלּוּ בָךְ לַגֵּר עָשׂוּ בַעֹשֶׁק בְּתוֹכֵךְ יָתוֹם וְאַלְמָנָה הוֹנוּ בָךְ׃
ח ט קָדָשַׁי בָּזִית וְאֶת־שַׁבְּתֹתַי חִלָּלְתְּ׃ אַנְשֵׁי רָכִיל הָיוּ בָךְ לְמַעַן שְׁפָךְ־דָּם
י וְאֶל־הֶהָרִים אָכְלוּ בָךְ זִמָּה עָשׂוּ בְתוֹכֵךְ׃ עֶרְוַת־אָב גִּלָּה־בָךְ טְמֵאַת
יא הַנִּדָּה עִנּוּ־בָךְ׃ וְאִישׁ ׀ אֶת־אֵשֶׁת רֵעֵהוּ עָשָׂה תּוֹעֵבָה וְאִישׁ אֶת־כַּלָּתוֹ
יב טִמֵּא בְזִמָּה וְאִישׁ אֶת־אֲחֹתוֹ בַת־אָבִיו עִנָּה־בָךְ׃ שֹׁחַד לָקְחוּ־בָךְ
לְמַעַן שְׁפָךְ־דָּם נֶשֶׁךְ וְתַרְבִּית לָקַחַתְּ וַתְּבַצְּעִי רֵעַיִךְ בַּעֹשֶׁק וְאֹתִי
יג שָׁכַחַתְּ נְאֻם אֲדֹנָי יְהוִה׃ וְהִנֵּה הִכֵּיתִי כַפִּי אֶל־בִּצְעֵךְ אֲשֶׁר עָשִׂית
יד וְעַל־דָּמֵךְ אֲשֶׁר הָיוּ בְּתוֹכֵךְ׃ הֲיַעֲמֹד לִבֵּךְ אִם־תֶּחֱזַקְנָה יָדַיִךְ לַיָּמִים
טו אֲשֶׁר אֲנִי עֹשֶׂה אוֹתָךְ אֲנִי יְהוָה דִּבַּרְתִּי וְעָשִׂיתִי׃ וַהֲפִיצוֹתִי אוֹתָךְ
טז בַגּוֹיִם וְזֵרִיתִיךְ בָּאֲרָצוֹת וַהֲתִמֹּתִי טֻמְאָתֵךְ מִמֵּךְ׃ וְנִחַלְתְּ בָּךְ לְעֵינֵי יג
יז גוֹיִם וְיָדַעַתְּ כִּי־אֲנִי יְהוָה׃ וַיְהִי דְבַר־יְהוָה אֵלַי לֵאמֹר׃
יח בֶּן־אָדָם הָיוּ־לִי בֵית־יִשְׂרָאֵל לְסוּג כֻּלָּם נְחֹשֶׁת וּבְדִיל וּבַרְזֶל וְעוֹפֶרֶת לְסִיג
יט בְּתוֹךְ כּוּר סִגִים כֶּסֶף הָיוּ׃ לָכֵן כֹּה אָמַר אֲדֹנָי יְהוִה
כ יַעַן הֱיוֹת כֻּלְּכֶם לְסִגִים לָכֵן הִנְנִי קֹבֵץ אֶתְכֶם אֶל־תּוֹךְ יְרוּשָׁלִָם׃ קְבֻצַת
כֶּסֶף וּנְחֹשֶׁת וּבַרְזֶל וְעוֹפֶרֶת וּבְדִיל אֶל־תּוֹךְ כּוּר לָפַחַת־עָלָיו אֵשׁ
כא לְהַנְתִּיךְ כֵּן אֶקְבֹּץ בְּאַפִּי וּבַחֲמָתִי וְהִנַּחְתִּי וְהִתַּכְתִּי אֶתְכֶם׃ וְכִנַּסְתִּי
כב אֶתְכֶם וְנָפַחְתִּי עֲלֵיכֶם בְּאֵשׁ עֶבְרָתִי וְנִתַּכְתֶּם בְּתוֹכָהּ׃ כְּהִתּוּךְ כֶּסֶף
בְּתוֹךְ כּוּר כֵּן תֻּתְּכוּ בְתוֹכָהּ וִידַעְתֶּם כִּי־אֲנִי יְהוָה שָׁפַכְתִּי חֲמָתִי

23 and that I have poured My fury out upon you." And the word
24 of the LORD came to me, saying: "Man, say to her: You are a land not cleansed,
25 not swept with rain on the day of rage. Her prophets are a conspiracy in her
midst: like a roaring lion that tears apart its prey, they have devoured people;
they have taken treasures and precious things; they have made numerous
26 widows in her midst. Her priests have abused My teaching, desecrated My
holy things; they have not distinguished between sacred and profane; they
have not taught the difference between impure and pure; they have hidden
27 their eyes from My Sabbaths, and I have been profaned in their midst. The
leaders in her midst have been like wolves tearing their prey, spilling blood,
28 destroying people for malicious gain. For them, her prophets have daubed
with whitewash, asserted false visions, and predicted lies, saying, 'So says the
29 Lord GOD,' when the LORD has not spoken. The people of the land practiced
extortion and committed robbery, mistreated the poor and needy, and
30 oppressed the foreigner without redress. I searched for a man among them
to build a fence, to stand in the breach before Me on behalf of the land so that
31 I would not have to ruin her, but I found no one. I have poured My rage out
upon them, destroyed them in the fire of My wrath; I have brought their ways
23 1 down on their heads, declares the Lord GOD." And the word of the
2 LORD came to me, saying: "Man, there were two women, daughters of one
3 mother, and they whored in Egypt. In their youth they whored; there were
4 their breasts caressed; there they fondled their virgin's nipples. Their names:
the older one was Ohola, and Oholiva was her sister. And they became Mine
and bore sons and daughters. Their names: Shomron is Ohola, and Jerusalem
5 is Oholiva.[33] Even while still Mine, Ohola whored and lusted after her lovers,
6 the Assyrians. They were warriors attired in blue, governors and officials,
7 young desirable men all of them, cavalrymen on horseback. She lavished her
whoring upon them, the finest of all the Assyrians, and defiled herself with
8 all the idols of each of those she lusted after. Still she did not abandon her
whoring with Egypt – for they had lain with her in her youth; they had
9 fondled her virgin's nipples and poured all their lusting onto her. So I gave
her over into the hands of her lovers, into the hands of the Assyrians after
10 whom she lusted. They exposed her nakedness; they took her sons and
daughters, and by sword they killed her. The punishments they inflicted on
11 her made her infamous among women. Her sister Oholiva
saw this – yet she still made her lusting and her whoring even more perverted
12 than her sister's. She lusted after the Assyrians, governors and officials,
warriors impeccably attired, cavalrymen on horseback – all of them dashing
13 men. I saw that she defiled herself – both of them took the same course. Then
14 she added to her whoring: she saw carved figures of men on the walls, images
15 of Chaldeans imprinted in bright red, girded at their waists with cloth belts,
trailing turbans on their heads, all with the appearance of officers, forms of
16 Babylonians born in Chaldea. As soon as she saw them she lusted after them
17 and sent messengers to them in Chaldea. And the Babylonians came to her

33 | Ohola literally means "tent"; Oholiva, "my tent is therein."

כג כד עֲלֵיכֶם׃ וַיְהִי דְבַר־יְהוָה אֵלַי לֵאמֹר׃ בֶּן־אָדָם אֱמָר־לָהּ
כה אַתְּ אֶרֶץ לֹא מְטֹהָרָה הִיא לֹא גֻשְׁמָהּ בְּיוֹם זָעַם׃ קֶשֶׁר נְבִיאֶיהָ בְּתוֹכָהּ
כַּאֲרִי שׁוֹאֵג טֹרֵף טָרֶף נֶפֶשׁ אָכָלוּ חֹסֶן וִיקָר יִקָּחוּ אַלְמְנוֹתֶיהָ הִרְבּוּ
כו בְתוֹכָהּ׃ כֹּהֲנֶיהָ חָמְסוּ תוֹרָתִי וַיְחַלְּלוּ קָדָשַׁי בֵּין־קֹדֶשׁ לְחֹל לֹא הִבְדִּילוּ
וּבֵין־הַטָּמֵא לְטָהוֹר לֹא הוֹדִיעוּ וּמִשַּׁבְּתוֹתַי הֶעְלִימוּ עֵינֵיהֶם וָאֵחַל
כז בְּתוֹכָם׃ שָׂרֶיהָ בְקִרְבָּהּ כִּזְאֵבִים טֹרְפֵי טָרֶף לִשְׁפָּךְ־דָּם לְאַבֵּד נְפָשׁוֹת
כח לְמַעַן בְּצֹעַ בָּצַע׃ וּנְבִיאֶיהָ טָחוּ לָהֶם תָּפֵל חֹזִים שָׁוְא וְקֹסְמִים לָהֶם
כט כָּזָב אֹמְרִים כֹּה אָמַר אֲדֹנָי יְהוִה וַיהוָה לֹא דִבֵּר׃ עַם הָאָרֶץ עָשְׁקוּ
עֹשֶׁק וְגָזְלוּ גָּזֵל וְעָנִי וְאֶבְיוֹן הוֹנוּ וְאֶת־הַגֵּר עָשְׁקוּ בְּלֹא מִשְׁפָּט׃
ל וָאֲבַקֵּשׁ מֵהֶם אִישׁ גֹּדֵר־גָּדֵר וְעֹמֵד בַּפֶּרֶץ לְפָנַי בְּעַד הָאָרֶץ לְבִלְתִּי
לא שַׁחֲתָהּ וְלֹא מָצָאתִי׃ וָאֶשְׁפֹּךְ עֲלֵיהֶם זַעְמִי בְּאֵשׁ עֶבְרָתִי כִּלִּיתִים
כג א דַּרְכָּם בְּרֹאשָׁם נָתַתִּי נְאֻם אֲדֹנָי יְהוִה׃ וַיְהִי
ב דְבַר־יְהוָה אֵלַי לֵאמֹר׃ בֶּן־אָדָם שְׁתַּיִם נָשִׁים בְּנוֹת אֵם־אַחַת הָיוּ׃
ג וַתִּזְנֶינָה בְמִצְרַיִם בִּנְעוּרֵיהֶן זָנוּ שָׁמָּה מֹעֲכוּ שְׁדֵיהֶן וְשָׁם עִשּׂוּ דַּדֵּי
ד בְּתוּלֵיהֶן׃ וּשְׁמוֹתָן אָהֳלָה הַגְּדוֹלָה וְאָהֳלִיבָה אֲחוֹתָהּ וַתִּהְיֶינָה לִי
ה וַתֵּלַדְנָה בָּנִים וּבָנוֹת וּשְׁמוֹתָן שֹׁמְרוֹן אָהֳלָה וִירוּשָׁלִַם אָהֳלִיבָה׃ וַתִּזֶן
ו אָהֳלָה תַּחְתָּי וַתַּעְגַּב עַל־מְאַהֲבֶיהָ אֶל־אַשּׁוּר קְרוֹבִים׃ לְבֻשֵׁי תְכֵלֶת
ז פַּחוֹת וּסְגָנִים בַּחוּרֵי חֶמֶד כֻּלָּם פָּרָשִׁים רֹכְבֵי סוּסִים׃ וַתִּתֵּן תַּזְנוּתֶיהָ
עֲלֵיהֶם מִבְחַר בְּנֵי־אַשּׁוּר כֻּלָּם וּבְכֹל אֲשֶׁר־עָגְבָה בְּכָל־גִּלּוּלֵיהֶם
ח נִטְמָאָה׃ וְאֶת־תַּזְנוּתֶיהָ מִמִּצְרַיִם לֹא עָזָבָה כִּי אוֹתָהּ שָׁכְבוּ בִנְעוּרֶיהָ
ט וְהֵמָּה עִשּׂוּ דַּדֵּי בְתוּלֶיהָ וַיִּשְׁפְּכוּ תַזְנוּתָם עָלֶיהָ׃ לָכֵן נְתַתִּיהָ בְּיַד־
י מְאַהֲבֶיהָ בְּיַד בְּנֵי אַשּׁוּר אֲשֶׁר עָגְבָה עֲלֵיהֶם׃ הֵמָּה גִּלּוּ עֶרְוָתָהּ בָּנֶיהָ
וּבְנוֹתֶיהָ לָקָחוּ וְאוֹתָהּ בַּחֶרֶב הָרָגוּ וַתְּהִי־שֵׁם לַנָּשִׁים וּשְׁפוּטִים עָשׂוּ
יא בָהּ׃ וַתֵּרֶא אֲחוֹתָהּ אָהֳלִיבָה וַתַּשְׁחֵת עַגְבָתָהּ מִמֶּנָּה וְאֶת־
יב תַּזְנוּתֶיהָ מִזְּנוּנֵי אֲחוֹתָהּ׃ אֶל־בְּנֵי אַשּׁוּר עָגָבָה פַּחוֹת וּסְגָנִים קְרֹבִים
יג לְבֻשֵׁי מִכְלוֹל פָּרָשִׁים רֹכְבֵי סוּסִים בַּחוּרֵי חֶמֶד כֻּלָּם׃ וָאֵרֶא כִּי נִטְמָאָה
יד דֶּרֶךְ אֶחָד לִשְׁתֵּיהֶן׃ וַתּוֹסֶף אֶל־תַּזְנוּתֶיהָ וַתֵּרֶא אַנְשֵׁי מְחֻקֶּה עַל־
טו הַקִּיר צַלְמֵי כשדיים חֲקֻקִים בַּשָּׁשַׁר׃ חֲגוֹרֵי אֵזוֹר בְּמָתְנֵיהֶם סְרוּחֵי כַּשְׂדִּים
טְבוּלִים בְּרָאשֵׁיהֶם מַרְאֵה שָׁלִשִׁים כֻּלָּם דְּמוּת בְּנֵי־בָבֶל כַּשְׂדִּים
טז אֶרֶץ מוֹלַדְתָּם׃ וַתַּעְגַּב עֲלֵיהֶם לְמַרְאֵה עֵינֶיהָ וַתִּשְׁלַח מַלְאָכִים
יז אֲלֵיהֶם כַּשְׂדִּימָה׃ וַיָּבֹאוּ אֵלֶיהָ בְנֵי־בָבֶל לְמִשְׁכַּב דֹּדִים וַיְטַמְּאוּ אוֹתָהּ

for lovemaking, and they defiled her with their lusting – she defiled herself
18 with them, then she recoiled from them. She flaunted her whoring, flaunted
19 her nakedness, and I recoiled from her – as I had recoiled from her sister. She
escalated her whoring – remembering the days of her youth, whoring in the
20 land of Egypt. And she lusted after their lovers whose members were like a
21 donkey's, whose emissions were like a horse's. You sought out the depravity
of your youth when the men of Egypt fondled your nipples because of your
22 young breasts. So, Oholiva, so says the Lord God: See
that I will stir your lovers up against you, those from whom you recoiled. I
23 will bring them against you from all around: Babylonians and all of the
Chaldeans, Pekod, Shoa, and Koa,[34] and all of the Assyrians along with them –
dashing men, all of them governors and officials, officers and dignitaries, all
24 of them on horseback. They will come down upon you – weapon, chariot,
and wheel – with a horde of armies; they will accost you all around with shield,
buckler, and helmet. I will give punishment over to them, and they will judge
25 you with their laws. I will bring down My passionate anger upon you: They
will deal with you with fury; your nose and your ears they will cut away, and
what remains of you will fall by the sword; they will take your sons and your
26 daughters, and what remains of you will be consumed by fire. They will strip
27 you of your clothes; they will take your glorious jewelry. I will put an end to
your depravity and your whoring with the land of Egypt; you will not set your
28 eyes upon them, and you will remember Egypt no more. For so
says the Lord God: See that I am handing you over into the hands of those
29 you hate, into the hands of those from whom you recoil. They will deal with
you with hatred; they will take all you have worked for; they will leave you
naked and bare with the nakedness of your whoring, your depravity and your
30 licentiousness exposed. For whoring after nations this will be done to you
31 because you defiled yourself with their idols. You followed in the ways of your
32 sister, so I will put her cup into your hand. So says the Lord God:
You will drink from the deep, wide cup of your sister, the cup of derision
33 and contempt spilling over. With drunkenness and grief you will be filled, the
34 cup of ruin and desolation, the cup of your sister Shomron; you will drink it,
you will drain it, you will gnaw at its shards, and you will tear at your breasts;
35 for I have spoken, declares the Lord God. So the Lord God says
this: Because you forgot Me and cast Me behind your back, you must now
36 bear the consequences of your depravity and whoring." And the
Lord said to me: "Man, will you accuse Ohola and Oholiva? Tell them of
37 their abominations, for they have committed adultery, and blood is on their
hands; they committed adultery with their idols, and the children that they
38 bore Me they also passed over to their idols to devour. What is more, this
they have done to Me: on that same day they defiled My Sanctuary, and they
39 desecrated My Sabbaths; when they slaughtered their children for their idols,
on that same day they would then come to My Sanctuary and desecrate it!
40 See, this is what they did in My House. And even more: they sent for men

34 | Groups of Babylonian allies.

יח בְּתַזְנוּתָם וַתִּטְמָא־בָם וַתֵּקַע נַפְשָׁהּ מֵהֶם: וַתְּגַל תַּזְנוּתֶיהָ וַתְּגַל אֶת־
יט עֶרְוָתָהּ וַתֵּקַע נַפְשִׁי מֵעָלֶיהָ כַּאֲשֶׁר נָקְעָה נַפְשִׁי מֵעַל אֲחוֹתָהּ: וַתַּרְבֶּה
אֶת־תַּזְנוּתֶיהָ לִזְכֹּר אֶת־יְמֵי נְעוּרֶיהָ אֲשֶׁר זָנְתָה בְּאֶרֶץ מִצְרָיִם:
כ וַתַּעְגְּבָה עַל פִּלַגְשֵׁיהֶם אֲשֶׁר בְּשַׂר־חֲמוֹרִים בְּשָׂרָם וְזִרְמַת סוּסִים
כא זִרְמָתָם: וַתִּפְקְדִי אֵת זִמַּת נְעוּרָיִךְ בַּעְשׂוֹת מִמִּצְרַיִם דַּדַּיִךְ לְמַעַן שְׁדֵי
כב נְעוּרָיִךְ: לָכֵן אָהֳלִיבָה כֹּה־אָמַר אֲדֹנָי יֱהֹוִה הִנְנִי
מֵעִיר אֶת־מְאַהֲבַיִךְ עָלַיִךְ אֵת אֲשֶׁר־נָקְעָה נַפְשֵׁךְ מֵהֶם וַהֲבֵאתִים
כג עָלַיִךְ מִסָּבִיב: בְּנֵי בָבֶל וְכָל־כַּשְׂדִּים פְּקוֹד וְשׁוֹעַ וְקוֹעַ כָּל־בְּנֵי אַשּׁוּר
אוֹתָם בַּחוּרֵי חֶמֶד פַּחוֹת וּסְגָנִים כֻּלָּם שָׁלִשִׁים וּקְרוּאִים רֹכְבֵי סוּסִים
כד כֻּלָּם: וּבָאוּ עָלַיִךְ הֹצֶן רֶכֶב וְגַלְגַּל וּבִקְהַל עַמִּים צִנָּה וּמָגֵן וְקוֹבַע
יָשִׂימוּ עָלַיִךְ סָבִיב וְנָתַתִּי לִפְנֵיהֶם מִשְׁפָּט וּשְׁפָטוּךְ בְּמִשְׁפְּטֵיהֶם:
כה וְנָתַתִּי קִנְאָתִי בָּךְ וְעָשׂוּ אוֹתָךְ בְּחֵמָה אַפֵּךְ וְאָזְנַיִךְ יָסִירוּ וְאַחֲרִיתֵךְ
בַּחֶרֶב תִּפּוֹל הֵמָּה בָּנַיִךְ וּבְנוֹתַיִךְ יִקָּחוּ וְאַחֲרִיתֵךְ תֵּאָכֵל בָּאֵשׁ:
כו כז וְהִפְשִׁיטוּךְ אֶת־בְּגָדָיִךְ וְלָקְחוּ כְּלֵי תִפְאַרְתֵּךְ: וְהִשְׁבַּתִּי זִמָּתֵךְ מִמֵּךְ יד
וְאֶת־זְנוּתֵךְ מֵאֶרֶץ מִצְרָיִם וְלֹא־תִשְׂאִי עֵינַיִךְ אֲלֵיהֶם וּמִצְרַיִם לֹא
כח תִזְכְּרִי־עוֹד: כִּי כֹה אָמַר אֲדֹנָי יֱהֹוִה הִנְנִי נֹתְנָךְ בְּיַד אֲשֶׁר
כט שָׂנֵאת בְּיַד אֲשֶׁר־נָקְעָה נַפְשֵׁךְ מֵהֶם: וְעָשׂוּ אוֹתָךְ בְּשִׂנְאָה וְלָקְחוּ
כָּל־יְגִיעֵךְ וַעֲזָבוּךְ עֵירֹם וְעֶרְיָה וְנִגְלָה עֶרְוַת זְנוּנַיִךְ וְזִמָּתֵךְ וְתַזְנוּתָיִךְ:
ל עָשֹׂה אֵלֶּה לָךְ בִּזְנוֹתֵךְ אַחֲרֵי גוֹיִם עַל אֲשֶׁר־נִטְמֵאת בְּגִלּוּלֵיהֶם:
לא לב בְּדֶרֶךְ אֲחוֹתֵךְ הָלָכְתְּ וְנָתַתִּי כוֹסָהּ בְּיָדֵךְ: כֹּה אָמַר
אֲדֹנָי יֱהֹוִה כּוֹס אֲחוֹתֵךְ תִּשְׁתִּי הָעֲמֻקָּה וְהָרְחָבָה תִּהְיֶה לִצְחֹק וּלְלַעַג
לג מִרְבָּה לְהָכִיל: שִׁכָּרוֹן וְיָגוֹן תִּמָּלֵאִי כּוֹס שַׁמָּה וּשְׁמָמָה כּוֹס אֲחוֹתֵךְ
לד שֹׁמְרוֹן: וְשָׁתִית אוֹתָהּ וּמָצִית וְאֶת־חֲרָשֶׂיהָ תְּגָרֵמִי וְשָׁדַיִךְ תְּנַתֵּקִי
לה כִּי אֲנִי דִבַּרְתִּי נְאֻם אֲדֹנָי יֱהֹוִה: לָכֵן כֹּה אָמַר אֲדֹנָי
יֱהֹוִה יַעַן שָׁכַחַתְּ אוֹתִי וַתַּשְׁלִיכִי אוֹתִי אַחֲרֵי גַוֵּךְ וְגַם־אַתְּ שְׂאִי זִמָּתֵךְ
לו וְאֶת־תַּזְנוּתָיִךְ: וַיֹּאמֶר יְהוָה אֵלַי בֶּן־אָדָם הֲתִשְׁפּוֹט
לז אֶת־אָהֳלָה וְאֶת־אָהֳלִיבָה וְהַגֵּד לָהֶן אֵת תּוֹעֲבוֹתֵיהֶן: כִּי נִאֵפוּ וְדָם
בִּידֵיהֶן וְאֶת־גִּלּוּלֵיהֶן נִאֵפוּ וְגַם אֶת־בְּנֵיהֶן אֲשֶׁר יָלְדוּ־לִי הֶעֱבִירוּ
לח לָהֶם לְאָכְלָה: עוֹד זֹאת עָשׂוּ לִי טִמְּאוּ אֶת־מִקְדָּשִׁי בַּיּוֹם הַהוּא
לט וְאֶת־שַׁבְּתוֹתַי חִלֵּלוּ: וּבְשַׁחֲטָם אֶת־בְּנֵיהֶם לְגִלּוּלֵיהֶם וַיָּבֹאוּ אֶל־
מ מִקְדָּשִׁי בַּיּוֹם הַהוּא לְחַלְּלוֹ וְהִנֵּה־כֹה עָשׂוּ בְּתוֹךְ בֵּיתִי: וְאַף כִּי

from afar to come; a messenger was sent to them – and they came! For them
41 you bathed, painted your eyes, adorned yourself with jewelry. You sat on a
lavish bed with a table set before it, and you put My incense and My oil upon
42 it. And the murmur of a careless crowd was there; to the men among the mass
of people they brought wines from the desert; they placed bracelets on their
43 arms and glorious crowns on their heads. I thought the desire for whoring
44 would leave her, haggard from adultery, but she is unchanged. They came to
her as though coming to a prostitute; this is how they came to Ohola and
45 Oholiva, depraved women. Righteous people will sentence them to the
punishment of the adulteress and the punishment of the murderess – for they
46 are adulteresses, and they have blood on their hands. So says the
47 Lord God: Bring a horde against them! Give them over to terror, pillage! The
horde will stone them with rocks, cut them down with their swords, kill their
48 sons and daughters; they will burn their houses down with fire. I will put an
end to depravity in the land; all women will be warned not to imitate your
49 depravity. They will inflict upon you the outcome of your depravity, you will
bear the consequences of your idolatrous sin, and you will know that I am
24 1 the Lord God." And the word of the Lord came to me in the ninth
2 year in the tenth month on the tenth of the month:[35] "Man, write down the
name of the day, of this very day; the king of Babylon laid siege to Jerusalem
3 on this very day. Recount a parable to the defiant house; say to them: So says
the Lord God: Put the pot onto the fire; put it on, then pour water into it;
4 gather its carcass pieces into it, every choice piece, thigh and shoulder; fill it
5 with the best bones. Take the best of the flock, then pile the bones up under
6 it and bring it to boil, then cook the bones in it. So the Lord God
says this: Woe, bloody city, pot with its insides rusted, whose rust will not
7 come off it; empty it piece by piece; the lot has not fallen to her, for her blood
is within her; she placed it upon the bare rock and did not spill it onto the
8 ground to cover it with earth. To stir up fury, to take vengeance, I put her
9 blood upon the bare rock, not to be covered up. So the
10 Lord God says this: Woe, bloody city; I, in turn, will build up the pile. Heap
on more wood, light the fire, cook the flesh well, mix the compound; the
11 bones will be charred. Stand it upon the coals, empty, so that the bronze heats
up, scorches, and her impurity melts down within her so that her filth is gone
12 completely. Worn with useless toil, its pervasive filth will not come off it even
13 through fire, such filth. In your depraved impurity – because I cleansed
you, but you did not become pure – you will never be purified of your
14 impurity until My fury against you dies down. I am the Lord; I have spoken;
it is coming; I will do it; I will not refrain, I will not pity, I will not relent;
according to your ways, your deeds, will you be judged, declares the Lord

35 | The tenth of Tevet.

תִּשְׁלַחְנָה לַאֲנָשִׁים בָּאִים מִמֶּרְחָק אֲשֶׁר מַלְאָךְ שָׁלוּחַ אֲלֵיהֶם וְהִנֵּה־
מא בָאוּ לַאֲשֶׁר רָחַצְתְּ כָּחַלְתְּ עֵינַיִךְ וְעָדִית עֶדִי׃ וְיָשַׁבְתְּ עַל־מִטָּה כְבוּדָּה
מב וְשֻׁלְחָן עָרוּךְ לְפָנֶיהָ וּקְטָרְתִּי וְשַׁמְנִי שַׂמְתְּ עָלֶיהָ׃ וְקוֹל הָמוֹן שָׁלֵו
בָהּ וְאֶל־אֲנָשִׁים מֵרֹב אָדָם מוּבָאִים סובאים מִמִּדְבָּר וַיִּתְּנוּ צְמִידִים סָבָאִים
מג אֶל־יְדֵיהֶן וַעֲטֶרֶת תִּפְאֶרֶת עַל־רָאשֵׁיהֶן׃ וָאֹמַר לַבָּלָה נִאוּפִים עַתָּ
מד יזנה תַזְנוּתֶיהָ וָהִיא׃ וַיָּבוֹא אֵלֶיהָ כְּבוֹא אֶל־אִשָּׁה זוֹנָה כֵּן בָּאוּ אֶל־ יִזְנוּ
מה אָהֳלָה וְאֶל־אָהֳלִיבָה אִשֹּׁת הַזִּמָּה׃ וַאֲנָשִׁים צַדִּיקִם הֵמָּה יִשְׁפְּטוּ
אוֹתְהֶם מִשְׁפַּט נֹאֲפוֹת וּמִשְׁפַּט שֹׁפְכוֹת דָּם כִּי נֹאֲפֹת הֵנָּה וְדָם
מו בִּידֵיהֶן׃ כִּי כֹה אָמַר אֲדֹנָי יֱהֹוִה הַעֲלֵה עֲלֵיהֶם קָהָל
מז וְנָתֹן אֶתְהֶן לְזַעֲוָה וָלָבַז׃ וְרָגְמוּ עֲלֵיהֶן אֶבֶן קָהָל וּבָרֵא אוֹתְהֶן
מח בְּחַרְבוֹתָם בְּנֵיהֶם וּבְנוֹתֵיהֶם יַהֲרֹגוּ וּבָתֵּיהֶן בָּאֵשׁ יִשְׂרֹפוּ׃ וְהִשְׁבַּתִּי
מט זִמָּה מִן־הָאָרֶץ וְנִוַּסְּרוּ כָּל־הַנָּשִׁים וְלֹא תַעֲשֶׂינָה כְּזִמַּתְכֶנָה׃ וְנָתְנוּ
זִמַּתְכֶנָה עֲלֵיכֶן וַחֲטָאֵי גִלּוּלֵיכֶן תִּשֶּׂאינָה וִידַעְתֶּם כִּי אֲנִי אֲדֹנָי
כד א יֱהֹוִה׃ וַיְהִי דְבַר־יְהֹוָה אֵלַי בַּשָּׁנָה הַתְּשִׁיעִית בַּחֹדֶשׁ הָעֲשִׂירִי
ב בֶּעָשׂוֹר לַחֹדֶשׁ לֵאמֹר׃ בֶּן־אָדָם כתוב־לְךָ אֶת־שֵׁם הַיּוֹם אֶת־עֶצֶם כְּתָב־
ג הַיּוֹם הַזֶּה סָמַךְ מֶלֶךְ־בָּבֶל אֶל־יְרוּשָׁלִַם בְּעֶצֶם הַיּוֹם הַזֶּה׃ וּמְשֹׁל
אֶל־בֵּית־הַמֶּרִי מָשָׁל וְאָמַרְתָּ אֲלֵיהֶם כֹּה אָמַר אֲדֹנָי יֱהֹוִה שְׁפֹת הַסִּיר
ד שְׁפֹת וְגַם־יְצֹק בּוֹ מָיִם׃ אֱסֹף נְתָחֶיהָ אֵלֶיהָ כָּל־נֵתַח טוֹב יָרֵךְ וְכָתֵף
ה מִבְחַר עֲצָמִים מַלֵּא׃ מִבְחַר הַצֹּאן לָקוֹחַ וְגַם דּוּר הָעֲצָמִים תַּחְתֶּיהָ
ו רַתַּח רְתָחֶיהָ גַּם־בָּשְׁלוּ עֲצָמֶיהָ בְּתוֹכָהּ׃ לָכֵן כֹּה־אָמַר ׀
אֲדֹנָי יֱהֹוִה אוֹי עִיר הַדָּמִים סִיר אֲשֶׁר חֶלְאָתָה בָהּ וְחֶלְאָתָהּ לֹא
ז יָצְאָה מִמֶּנָּה לִנְתָחֶיהָ לִנְתָחֶיהָ הוֹצִיאָהּ לֹא־נָפַל עָלֶיהָ גּוֹרָל׃ כִּי דָמָהּ
בְּתוֹכָהּ הָיָה עַל־צְחִיחַ סֶלַע שָׂמָתְהוּ לֹא שְׁפָכַתְהוּ עַל־הָאָרֶץ לְכַסּוֹת
ח עָלָיו עָפָר׃ לְהַעֲלוֹת חֵמָה לִנְקֹם נָקָם נָתַתִּי אֶת־דָּמָהּ עַל־צְחִיחַ
ט סָלַע לְבִלְתִּי הִכָּסוֹת׃ לָכֵן כֹּה אָמַר אֲדֹנָי יֱהֹוִה אוֹי עִיר
י הַדָּמִים גַּם־אֲנִי אַגְדִּיל הַמְּדוּרָה׃ הַרְבֵּה הָעֵצִים הַדְלֵק הָאֵשׁ הָתֵם
יא הַבָּשָׂר וְהַרְקַח הַמֶּרְקָחָה וְהָעֲצָמוֹת יֵחָרוּ׃ וְהַעֲמִידֶהָ עַל־גֶּחָלֶיהָ רֵקָה
לְמַעַן תֵּחַם וְחָרָה נְחֻשְׁתָּהּ וְנִתְּכָה בְתוֹכָהּ טֻמְאָתָהּ תִּתֹּם חֶלְאָתָהּ׃
יב תְּאֻנִים הֶלְאָת וְלֹא־תֵצֵא מִמֶּנָּה רַבַּת חֶלְאָתָהּ בְּאֵשׁ חֶלְאָתָהּ׃
יג בְּטֻמְאָתֵךְ זִמָּה יַעַן טִהַרְתִּיךְ וְלֹא טָהַרְתְּ מִטֻּמְאָתֵךְ לֹא תִטְהֲרִי־עוֹד
יד עַד־הֲנִיחִי אֶת־חֲמָתִי בָּךְ׃ אֲנִי יְהֹוָה דִּבַּרְתִּי בָּאָה וְעָשִׂיתִי לֹא־
אֶפְרַע וְלֹא־אָחוּס וְלֹא אֶנָּחֵם כִּדְרָכַיִךְ וְכַעֲלִילוֹתַיִךְ שְׁפָטוּךְ נְאֻם אֲדֹנָי

15 16 GOD." And the word of the LORD came to me: "Man, behold: I
am taking from you your eyes' delight with a sudden blow; you will not
17 lament, you will not cry, your tears will not fall. Moan silently for the dead
but do not mourn: bind on your turban, put your shoes on your feet; do
18 not cover your mouth, do not eat others' bread." And I spoke to the people
in the morning; my wife died in the evening; in the morning I did as I was
19 commanded. And the people said to me, "Tell us, what do these things
20 mean for us that you are doing?" And I said to them: "The word of the LORD
21 came to me: 'Say to the House of Israel: So says the Lord GOD: I am going
to desecrate My Sanctuary – your power's majesty, your eyes' delight, your
soul's tenderness – and your sons and your daughters whom you have left
22 behind will fall to the sword. You will do as I have done: Your mouth you
23 will not cover; the bread of others you will not eat; your turbans will remain
on your heads, your shoes on your feet. You will not lament, you will not cry;
24 you will waste away in your sins and groan to each other. And Yeḥezkel will
be a sign to you: everything that he has done, so will you do when it comes,
25 and you will know that I am the Lord GOD. And you, Man, on
the day that I take away from them their stronghold, their glory's joy, their
26 eyes' delight, their soul's yearning, their sons and daughters, on that day, a
27 fugitive will come to you, for you to hear it with your own ears. On that day
your mouth will be opened with the fugitive, and you will speak; you will no
longer be struck silent; you will be a sign to them, and they will know that
25 1 2 I am the LORD.'"[36] And the word of the LORD came to me: "Man,
3 set your face to the Amonites; prophesy against them; say to the Amonites:
Listen to the word of the Lord GOD: So says the Lord GOD: Because you
said, 'Ha!' about My Sanctuary when it was desecrated, about the soil of
Israel when it was devastated, about the House of Yehuda when they went
4 into exile, so I will give you over to the people of the East[37] as a possession; in
you they will set up their camps, in you put up their dwellings; they will eat
5 your fruits; they will drink your milk. I will turn Raba into a grazing place for
camels, Amon into a resting place for sheep, and you will know that I am the
6 LORD. For so says the Lord GOD: Because you clapped your hands,
stamped your feet, grew joyous with such absolute contempt about the soil
7 of Israel,[38] for this I am stretching My arm out over you – giving you over as
spoil to the nations; I will cut you off from among the peoples, I will make
you perish from among the lands, I will decimate you, and you will know that
8 I am the LORD. So says the Lord GOD: Because Moav and Se'ir have
9 said, 'See, the House of Yehuda is just like all the other nations,' for this I am
exposing Moav's flank, its cities, the cities at its edges, the glory of the land,
10 Beit HaYeshimot, Baal Meon, Kiryatayim. To the people of the East, together
with the Amonites, I will give it as a possession so that the Amonites will not
11 be remembered among the nations, and over Moav I will execute judgments;

---

36 | This ends the period of Yeḥezkel's muteness described in 3:24–27.

37 | Nomads from the Arabian Desert.

38 | Moav and Amon were enemies of Israel at this time (see II Kings 24:2).

טו טז יְהוִה: וַיְהִי דְבַר־יְהוָה אֵלַי לֵאמֹר: בֶּן־אָדָם הִנְנִי
לֹקֵחַ מִמְּךָ אֶת־מַחְמַד עֵינֶיךָ בְּמַגֵּפָה וְלֹא תִסְפֹּד וְלֹא תִבְכֶּה וְלוֹא
יז תָבוֹא דִּמְעָתֶךָ: הֵאָנֵק ׀ דֹּם מֵתִים אֵבֶל לֹא־תַעֲשֶׂה פְּאֵרְךָ חֲבוֹשׁ
עָלֶיךָ וּנְעָלֶיךָ תָּשִׂים בְּרַגְלֶיךָ וְלֹא תַעְטֶה עַל־שָׂפָם וְלֶחֶם אֲנָשִׁים לֹא
יח תֹאכֵל: וָאֲדַבֵּר אֶל־הָעָם בַּבֹּקֶר וַתָּמָת אִשְׁתִּי בָּעָרֶב וָאַעַשׂ בַּבֹּקֶר
יט כַּאֲשֶׁר צֻוֵּיתִי: וַיֹּאמְרוּ אֵלַי הָעָם הֲלֹא־תַגִּיד לָנוּ מָה־אֵלֶּה לָּנוּ כִּי
כ כא אַתָּה עֹשֶׂה: וָאֹמַר אֲלֵיהֶם דְּבַר־יְהוָה הָיָה אֵלַי לֵאמֹר: אֱמֹר ׀ לְבֵית
יִשְׂרָאֵל כֹּה־אָמַר אֲדֹנָי יְהוִה הִנְנִי מְחַלֵּל אֶת־מִקְדָּשִׁי גְּאוֹן עֻזְּכֶם
מַחְמַד עֵינֵיכֶם וּמַחְמַל נַפְשְׁכֶם וּבְנֵיכֶם וּבְנוֹתֵיכֶם אֲשֶׁר עֲזַבְתֶּם בַּחֶרֶב
כב יִפֹּלוּ: וַעֲשִׂיתֶם כַּאֲשֶׁר עָשִׂיתִי עַל־שָׂפָם לֹא תַעְטוּ וְלֶחֶם אֲנָשִׁים לֹא
כג תֹאכֵלוּ: וּפְאֵרֵכֶם עַל־רָאשֵׁיכֶם וְנַעֲלֵיכֶם בְּרַגְלֵיכֶם לֹא תִסְפְּדוּ וְלֹא
כד תִבְכּוּ וּנְמַקֹּתֶם בַּעֲוֺנֹתֵיכֶם וּנְהַמְתֶּם אִישׁ אֶל־אָחִיו: וְהָיָה יְחֶזְקֵאל טו
לָכֶם לְמוֹפֵת כְּכֹל אֲשֶׁר־עָשָׂה תַּעֲשׂוּ בְּבֹאָהּ וִידַעְתֶּם כִּי אֲנִי אֲדֹנָי
כה יְהוִה: וְאַתָּה בֶן־אָדָם הֲלוֹא בְּיוֹם קַחְתִּי מֵהֶם אֶת־
מָעֻזָּם מְשׂוֹשׂ תִּפְאַרְתָּם אֶת־מַחְמַד עֵינֵיהֶם וְאֶת־מַשָּׂא נַפְשָׁם בְּנֵיהֶם
כו כז וּבְנוֹתֵיהֶם: בַּיּוֹם הַהוּא יָבוֹא הַפָּלִיט אֵלֶיךָ לְהַשְׁמָעוּת אָזְנָיִם: בַּיּוֹם
הַהוּא יִפָּתַח פִּיךָ אֶת־הַפָּלִיט וּתְדַבֵּר וְלֹא תֵאָלֵם עוֹד וְהָיִיתָ לָהֶם
כה א לְמוֹפֵת וְיָדְעוּ כִּי־אֲנִי יְהוָה: וַיְהִי דְבַר־יְהוָה אֵלַי לֵאמֹר:
ב ג בֶּן־אָדָם שִׂים פָּנֶיךָ אֶל־בְּנֵי עַמּוֹן וְהִנָּבֵא עֲלֵיהֶם: וְאָמַרְתָּ לִבְנֵי עַמּוֹן
שִׁמְעוּ דְּבַר־אֲדֹנָי יְהוִה כֹּה־אָמַר אֲדֹנָי יְהוִה יַעַן אָמְרֵךְ הֶאָח אֶל־
מִקְדָּשִׁי כִי־נִחָל וְאֶל־אַדְמַת יִשְׂרָאֵל כִּי נָשַׁמָּה וְאֶל־בֵּית יְהוּדָה כִּי
ד הָלְכוּ בַּגּוֹלָה: לָכֵן הִנְנִי נֹתְנָךְ לִבְנֵי־קֶדֶם לְמוֹרָשָׁה וְיִשְּׁבוּ טִירוֹתֵיהֶם
ה בָּךְ וְנָתְנוּ בָךְ מִשְׁכְּנֵיהֶם הֵמָּה יֹאכְלוּ פִרְיֵךְ וְהֵמָּה יִשְׁתּוּ חֲלָבֵךְ: וְנָתַתִּי
אֶת־רַבָּה לִנְוֵה גְמַלִּים וְאֶת־בְּנֵי עַמּוֹן לְמִרְבַּץ־צֹאן וִידַעְתֶּם כִּי־אֲנִי
ו יְהוָה: כִּי כֹה אָמַר אֲדֹנָי יְהוִה יַעַן מַחְאֵךְ יָד וְרַקְעֵךְ בְּרָגֶל
ז וַתִּשְׂמַח בְּכָל־שָׁאטְךָ בְּנֶפֶשׁ אֶל־אַדְמַת יִשְׂרָאֵל: לָכֵן הִנְנִי נָטִיתִי
אֶת־יָדִי עָלֶיךָ וּנְתַתִּיךָ לבג לַגּוֹיִם וְהִכְרַתִּיךָ מִן־הָעַמִּים וְהַאֲבַדְתִּיךָ לְבַז
ח מִן־הָאֲרָצוֹת אַשְׁמִידְךָ וְיָדַעְתָּ כִּי־אֲנִי יְהוָה: כֹּה אָמַר
ט אֲדֹנָי יְהוִה יַעַן אָמַר מוֹאָב וְשֵׂעִיר הִנֵּה כְּכָל־הַגּוֹיִם בֵּית יְהוּדָה: לָכֵן
הִנְנִי פֹתֵחַ אֶת־כֶּתֶף מוֹאָב מֵהֶעָרִים מֵעָרָיו מִקָּצֵהוּ צְבִי אֶרֶץ בֵּית
י הַיְשִׁימֹת בַּעַל מְעוֹן וקריתמה: לִבְנֵי־קֶדֶם עַל־בְּנֵי עַמּוֹן וּנְתַתִּיהָ וְקִרְיָתָיְמָה
יא לְמוֹרָשָׁה לְמַעַן לֹא־תִזָּכֵר בְּנֵי־עַמּוֹן בַּגּוֹיִם: וּבְמוֹאָב אֶעֱשֶׂה שְׁפָטִים

12 they will know that I am the LORD. So says the Lord GOD: Because
of how Edom acted, taking their vengeance against the House of Yehuda and
13 incurring great guilt for their vengeance upon them, for this, so says the Lord
GOD: I will stretch My arm out against Edom and cut every man and beast
off from her. I will give her over to destruction; from Teiman to Dedan they
14 will fall by the sword.[39] My vengeance against Edom will be carried out by
My people Israel; they will act with My anger, My fury, against Edom; they
15 will know My vengeance, declares the Lord GOD. So says the Lord
GOD: Because the Philistines acted in vengeance, took their vengeance with
16 absolute contempt, and wrought destruction with an abiding hatred, for this,
so says the Lord GOD: I am stretching My hand out against the Philistines;
I will cut off the Keretites;[40] I will cause the remaining coastland to perish.
17 I will carry out great acts of vengeance against them with furious rebukes,
and they will know that I am the LORD when I take My vengeance against
them."

26 1 And it was in the eleventh year on the first of the month, the word of the LORD
2 came to me: "Man, because Tyre said of Jerusalem: 'Aha! She has been broken,
the doorway of the peoples; it has passed round to me; I will be filled now
3 that she is laid waste,' for this, so says the Lord GOD: Behold: I am upon you,
4 Tyre; I will heave many nations upon you as the sea heaves up its waves. They
will destroy the walls; they will demolish her towers; I will strip her rubble
5 off her, turn her into a bare rock; a place for spreading nets to dry, she will be
in the midst of the sea, for I have spoken, declares the Lord GOD. She will
6 become spoil for the nations, her daughters in the fields will be killed by the
7 sword, and they will know that I am the LORD. For so says the Lord
GOD: Against Tyre I will bring Nevukhadretzar, king of Babylon, from the
north, a kings of kings, with horse, chariot, cavalrymen, with a horde and a
8 great army. By sword he will kill your daughters in the field; he will construct
a siege wall against you; he will throw up earthworks against you, set shields
9 up against you. He will pound his battering ram against your walls; he will
10 tear down your towers with his weapons. From his legion of horses the dust
will cover you; from the sound of cavalrymen, wheel, and chariot your walls
will tremble when he enters through your gates like men charging a breached
11 city. With the hooves of his horses he will trample all of your streets; he will
12 kill your people by sword; your strong pillars will fall to the ground. They
will plunder your riches, pillage your merchandise, tear down your walls, pull
down your delightful houses, and your stones, your wood, your rubble they
13 will throw into the water. I will put an end to the noise of your songs; the
14 sound of your lyres will be heard no more. I will make you a bald, glaring
rock; you will be a place for spreading nets to dry; you will never be rebuilt,
15 for I the LORD have spoken, declares the Lord GOD. So says the Lord
GOD to Tyre: Surely, from the sound of your downfall, at the groaning of
the slain, when killing is raging in your midst, the coastlands will tremble.

---

39 | Teiman and Dedan were settlements in the desert of Edom.

40 | The Philistines are also called the Keretites and the dwellers of the coastland (e.g., Zeph. 2:5).

יב וְיָדְעוּ כִּי־אֲנִי יְהוָה: כֹּה אָמַר אֲדֹנָי יֱהֹוִה יַעַן עֲשׂוֹת
יג אֱדוֹם בִּנְקֹם נָקָם לְבֵית יְהוּדָה וַיֶּאְשְׁמוּ אָשׁוֹם וְנִקְּמוּ בָהֶם: לָכֵן כֹּה
אָמַר אֲדֹנָי יֱהֹוִה וְנָטִתִי יָדִי עַל־אֱדוֹם וְהִכְרַתִּי מִמֶּנָּה אָדָם וּבְהֵמָה
יד וּנְתַתִּיהָ חָרְבָּה מִתֵּימָן וּדְדָנֶה בַּחֶרֶב יִפֹּלוּ: וְנָתַתִּי אֶת־נִקְמָתִי בֶּאֱדוֹם
בְּיַד עַמִּי יִשְׂרָאֵל וְעָשׂוּ בֶאֱדוֹם כְּאַפִּי וְכַחֲמָתִי וְיָדְעוּ אֶת־נִקְמָתִי נְאֻם
טו אֲדֹנָי יֱהֹוִה: כֹּה אָמַר אֲדֹנָי יֱהֹוִה יַעַן עֲשׂוֹת פְּלִשְׁתִּים
טז בִּנְקָמָה וַיִּנָּקְמוּ נָקָם בִּשְׁאָט בְּנֶפֶשׁ לְמַשְׁחִית אֵיבַת עוֹלָם: לָכֵן כֹּה
אָמַר אֲדֹנָי יֱהֹוִה הִנְנִי נוֹטֶה יָדִי עַל־פְּלִשְׁתִּים וְהִכְרַתִּי אֶת־כְּרֵתִים
יז וְהַאֲבַדְתִּי אֶת־שְׁאֵרִית חוֹף הַיָּם: וְעָשִׂיתִי בָם נְקָמוֹת גְּדֹלוֹת בְּתוֹכְחוֹת
חֵמָה וְיָדְעוּ כִּי־אֲנִי יְהוָה בְּתִתִּי אֶת־נִקְמָתִי בָּם:
כו א וַיְהִי בְּעַשְׁתֵּי־עֶשְׂרֵה שָׁנָה בְּאֶחָד לַחֹדֶשׁ הָיָה דְבַר־יְהוָה אֵלַי לֵאמֹר:
ב בֶּן־אָדָם יַעַן אֲשֶׁר־אָמְרָה צֹּר עַל־יְרוּשָׁלִַם הֶאָח נִשְׁבְּרָה דַּלְתוֹת
ג הָעַמִּים נָסֵבָּה אֵלָי אִמָּלְאָה הָחֳרָבָה: לָכֵן כֹּה אָמַר אֲדֹנָי יֱהֹוִה הִנְנִי
ד עָלַיִךְ צֹר וְהַעֲלֵיתִי עָלַיִךְ גּוֹיִם רַבִּים כְּהַעֲלוֹת הַיָּם לְגַלָּיו: וְשִׁחֲתוּ
חֹמוֹת צֹר וְהָרְסוּ מִגְדָּלֶיהָ וְסִחֵיתִי עֲפָרָהּ מִמֶּנָּה וְנָתַתִּי אוֹתָהּ לִצְחִיחַ
ה סָלַע: מִשְׁטַח חֲרָמִים תִּהְיֶה בְּתוֹךְ הַיָּם כִּי אֲנִי דִבַּרְתִּי נְאֻם אֲדֹנָי
ו יֱהֹוִה וְהָיְתָה לְבַז לַגּוֹיִם: וּבְנוֹתֶיהָ אֲשֶׁר בַּשָּׂדֶה בַּחֶרֶב תֵּהָרַגְנָה וְיָדְעוּ
ז כִּי־אֲנִי יְהוָה: כִּי כֹה אָמַר אֲדֹנָי יֱהֹוִה הִנְנִי מֵבִיא אֶל־
צֹר נְבוּכַדְרֶאצַּר מֶלֶךְ־בָּבֶל מִצָּפוֹן מֶלֶךְ מְלָכִים בְּסוּס וּבְרֶכֶב וּבְפָרָשִׁים
ח וְקָהָל וְעַם־רָב: בְּנוֹתַיִךְ בַּשָּׂדֶה בַּחֶרֶב יַהֲרֹג וְנָתַן עָלַיִךְ דָּיֵק וְשָׁפַךְ
ט עָלַיִךְ סֹלְלָה וְהֵקִים עָלַיִךְ צִנָּה: וּמְחִי קָבָלּוֹ יִתֵּן בְּחֹמוֹתָיִךְ וּמִגְדְּלֹתַיִךְ
י יִתֹּץ בְּחַרְבוֹתָיו: מִשִּׁפְעַת סוּסָיו יְכַסֵּךְ אֲבָקָם מִקּוֹל פָּרָשׁ וְגַלְגַּל וָרֶכֶב
יא תִּרְעַשְׁנָה חוֹמוֹתַיִךְ בְּבֹאוֹ בִּשְׁעָרַיִךְ כִּמְבוֹאֵי עִיר מְבֻקָּעָה: בְּפַרְסוֹת
סוּסָיו יִרְמֹס אֶת־כָּל־חוּצוֹתָיִךְ עַמֵּךְ בַּחֶרֶב יַהֲרֹג וּמַצְּבוֹת עֻזֵּךְ לָאָרֶץ
יב תֵּרֵד: וְשָׁלְלוּ חֵילֵךְ וּבָזְזוּ רְכֻלָּתֵךְ וְהָרְסוּ חוֹמוֹתַיִךְ וּבָתֵּי חֶמְדָּתֵךְ יִתֹּצוּ
יג וַאֲבָנַיִךְ וְעֵצַיִךְ וַעֲפָרֵךְ בְּתוֹךְ מַיִם יָשִׂימוּ: וְהִשְׁבַּתִּי הֲמוֹן שִׁירָיִךְ וְקוֹל
יד כִּנּוֹרַיִךְ לֹא יִשָּׁמַע עוֹד: וּנְתַתִּיךְ לִצְחִיחַ סֶלַע מִשְׁטַח חֲרָמִים תִּהְיֶה
טו לֹא תִבָּנֶה עוֹד כִּי אֲנִי יְהוָה דִּבַּרְתִּי נְאֻם אֲדֹנָי יֱהֹוִה: כֹּה
אָמַר אֲדֹנָי יֱהֹוִה לְצוֹר הֲלֹא | מִקּוֹל מַפַּלְתֵּךְ בֶּאֱנֹק חָלָל בֵּהָרֵג הֶרֶג

16 They will descend from their thrones, all the princes of the sea; they will
take off their robes, pull off their embroidered clothes, dress themselves in
quaking; they will sit on the ground, they will quake unceasingly, they will
17 be aghast at you. They will raise a lament over you; they will say to you: 'How
you have perished, you praised city, who were settled from the seas, who was
so mighty on the seas – she was, along with her habitants – who inspired
18 terror over all its habitants.' Now the coastlands quake on the day of your
19 downfall; the coastlands by the sea are terrified at your demise. For
so says the Lord God: When I turn you into a destroyed city like cities that
lie unsettled, when I heave the deep upon you and the great rushing waters
20 cover you over, I will take you down with those descending to the Pit, to the
ancient dead; I will settle you there in the netherworld of the dead, like
ancient ruins, with those who descend to the Pit, so that you will no longer
21 be settled, and I will make the land of the living glorious. I will make you a
horror; you will cease to be; you will be searched for but will be not be found
27 1 ever again, declares the Lord God." And the word of the Lord came
2 3 to me: "Man, raise a lament about Tyre. Say to Tyre, who inhabits the gateway
to the sea, who is trader of the peoples to many coastlands: So says the Lord
4 God: Tyre, you have said, 'I am perfect in beauty'; in the heart of the sea were
5 your borders; builders perfected your beauty; cypresses from Senir they used
6 to build your planks; cedars from Lebanon they used for your mast; out of
oaks from Bashan they made your oars, your deck of ivory-inlaid boxwood
7 from the islands of the Kittites; embroidered linen from Egypt was your sail,
8 set as your flag, blue and purple from the islands of Elisha[41] your awnings. The
inhabitants of Sidon and Arvad were your oarsmen; the wise men in you, Tyre,
9 were your sailors, the elders of Geval,[42] her wise men among you, repaired
your breaches; all the seafaring ships and her sailors were among you to bring
10 you imports. Persia, Lydia, and Put[43] peopled your army, served as your men
11 of combat; they hung shield and helmet upon you, making you splendid; the
sons of Arvad and Ḥeilekh were on the perimeter of your walls; there were
Gamadim in your towers; they hung their quivers upon the perimeter of your
12 walls, and it made your beauty perfect. Tarshish was your trader – due to your
13 great wealth, silver, iron, tin, and lead they gave for your wares. Ionia, Tuval,
and Meshekh[44] were your merchants – living men and bronze vessels they
14 gave you as imports. From Beit Togarma,[45] horses, steeds, and mules they
15 gave for your wares. The sons of Dedan were your merchants; numerous
islands traded under your aegis; ivory tusks and ebony they brought as
16 tributes. Aram was your trader due to your abundant goods; emerald, purple
and embroidered cloths, fine linen, corals, and rubies they gave for your wares.

---

41 | Cyprus.
42 | Byblos, on the Lebanese coast.
43 | Put refers to Libya.
44 | Tuval and Meshekh are in Anatolia.
45 | Modern-day Gürün in central Turkey.

טז בְּתוֹכֵךְ יִרְעֲשׁוּ הָאִיִּים: וְיָרְדוּ מֵעַל כִּסְאוֹתָם כֹּל נְשִׂיאֵי הַיָּם וְהֵסִירוּ
אֶת־מְעִילֵיהֶם וְאֶת־בִּגְדֵי רִקְמָתָם יִפְשֹׁטוּ חֲרָדוֹת ׀ יִלְבָּשׁוּ עַל־הָאָרֶץ
יז יֵשֵׁבוּ וְחָרְדוּ לִרְגָעִים וְשָׁמְמוּ עָלָיִךְ: וְנָשְׂאוּ עָלַיִךְ קִינָה וְאָמְרוּ לָךְ אֵיךְ
אָבַדְתְּ נוֹשֶׁבֶת מִיַּמִּים הָעִיר הַהֻלָּלָה אֲשֶׁר הָיְתָה חֲזָקָה בַיָּם הִיא
יח וְיֹשְׁבֶיהָ אֲשֶׁר־נָתְנוּ חִתִּיתָם לְכָל־יוֹשְׁבֶיהָ: עַתָּה יֶחֶרְדוּ הָאִיִּן יוֹם
יט מַפַּלְתֵּךְ וְנִבְהֲלוּ הָאִיִּים אֲשֶׁר־בַּיָּם מִצֵּאתֵךְ: כִּי כֹה אָמַר
אֲדֹנָי יֱהֹוִה בְּתִתִּי אֹתָךְ עִיר נֶחֱרֶבֶת כֶּעָרִים אֲשֶׁר לֹא־נוֹשָׁבוּ בְּהַעֲלוֹת
כ עָלַיִךְ אֶת־תְּהוֹם וְכִסּוּךְ הַמַּיִם הָרַבִּים: וְהוֹרַדְתִּיךְ אֶת־יוֹרְדֵי בוֹר טז
אֶל־עַם עוֹלָם וְהוֹשַׁבְתִּיךְ בְּאֶרֶץ תַּחְתִּיּוֹת כָּחֳרָבוֹת מֵעוֹלָם אֶת־יוֹרְדֵי
כא בוֹר לְמַעַן לֹא תֵשֵׁבִי וְנָתַתִּי צְבִי בְּאֶרֶץ חַיִּים: בַּלָּהוֹת אֶתְּנֵךְ וְאֵינֵךְ
כז א וּתְבֻקְשִׁי וְלֹא־תִמָּצְאִי עוֹד לְעוֹלָם נְאֻם אֲדֹנָי יֱהֹוִה: וַיְהִי
ב ג דְבַר־יְהוָה אֵלַי לֵאמֹר: וְאַתָּה בֶן־אָדָם שָׂא עַל־צֹר קִינָה: וְאָמַרְתָּ
לְצוֹר הישבתי עַל־מְבוֹאֹת יָם רֹכֶלֶת הָעַמִּים אֶל־אִיִּים רַבִּים כֹּה הַיֹּשֶׁבֶת
ד אָמַר אֲדֹנָי יֱהֹוִה צוֹר אַתְּ אָמַרְתְּ אֲנִי כְּלִילַת יֹפִי: בְּלֵב יַמִּים גְּבוּלָיִךְ
ה בֹּנַיִךְ כָּלְלוּ יָפְיֵךְ: בְּרוֹשִׁים מִשְּׂנִיר בָּנוּ לָךְ אֵת כָּל־לֻחֹתָיִם אֶרֶז מִלְּבָנוֹן
ו לָקָחוּ לַעֲשׂוֹת תֹּרֶן עָלָיִךְ: אַלּוֹנִים מִבָּשָׁן עָשׂוּ מִשּׁוֹטָיִךְ קַרְשֵׁךְ עָשׂוּ־
ז שֵׁן בַּת־אֲשֻׁרִים מֵאִיֵּי כִּתִּים: שֵׁשׁ בְּרִקְמָה מִמִּצְרַיִם הָיָה מִפְרָשֵׂךְ
ח לִהְיוֹת לָךְ לְנֵס תְּכֵלֶת וְאַרְגָּמָן מֵאִיֵּי אֱלִישָׁה הָיָה מְכַסֵּךְ: יֹשְׁבֵי צִידוֹן
ט וְאַרְוַד הָיוּ שָׁטִים לָךְ חֲכָמַיִךְ צוֹר הָיוּ בָךְ הֵמָּה חֹבְלָיִךְ: זִקְנֵי גְבַל
וַחֲכָמֶיהָ הָיוּ בָךְ מַחֲזִיקֵי בִּדְקֵךְ כָּל־אֳנִיּוֹת הַיָּם וּמַלָּחֵיהֶם הָיוּ בָךְ
י לַעֲרֹב מַעֲרָבֵךְ: פָּרַס וְלוּד וּפוּט הָיוּ בְחֵילֵךְ אַנְשֵׁי מִלְחַמְתֵּךְ מָגֵן
יא וְכוֹבַע תִּלּוּ־בָךְ הֵמָּה נָתְנוּ הֲדָרֵךְ: בְּנֵי אַרְוַד וְחֵילֵךְ עַל־חוֹמוֹתַיִךְ
סָבִיב וְגַמָּדִים בְּמִגְדְּלוֹתַיִךְ הָיוּ שִׁלְטֵיהֶם תִּלּוּ עַל־חוֹמוֹתַיִךְ סָבִיב
יב הֵמָּה כָּלְלוּ יָפְיֵךְ: תַּרְשִׁישׁ סֹחַרְתֵּךְ מֵרֹב כָּל־הוֹן בְּכֶסֶף בַּרְזֶל בְּדִיל
יג וְעוֹפֶרֶת נָתְנוּ עִזְבוֹנָיִךְ: יָוָן תֻּבַל וָמֶשֶׁךְ הֵמָּה רֹכְלָיִךְ בְּנֶפֶשׁ אָדָם וּכְלֵי
יד נְחֹשֶׁת נָתְנוּ מַעֲרָבֵךְ: מִבֵּית תּוֹגַרְמָה סוּסִים וּפָרָשִׁים וּפְרָדִים נָתְנוּ
טו עִזְבוֹנָיִךְ: בְּנֵי דְדָן רֹכְלַיִךְ אִיִּים רַבִּים סְחֹרַת יָדֵךְ קַרְנוֹת שֵׁן והובנים וְהָבְנִים
טז הֵשִׁיבוּ אֶשְׁכָּרֵךְ: אֲרָם סֹחַרְתֵּךְ מֵרֹב מַעֲשָׂיִךְ בְּנֹפֶךְ אַרְגָּמָן וְרִקְמָה

17 Yehuda and the land of Israel were your merchants; wheat of Minit,[46] millet,
18 honey, oil, and balm they gave you as imports. Damascus was your trader,
because of your abundant goods and great wealth, in wine of Ḥelbon and
19 wool of Sahar. Vedan and Ionia, from Uzal, for your wares gave polished iron,
20 cassia, and calamus as imports. Dedan was your merchant of saddlecloths for
21 riding. Arabia and all the chiefs of Kedar[47] were traders under your aegis; in
22 lambs, rams, and goats they traded with you. The merchants of Sheba[48] and
Rama were your merchants in all perfumes, all precious stones, and gold that
23 they gave for your wares. Ḥaran, Kaneh, and Eden, merchants of Sheba,
24 Assyria, and Kilmad were your merchants; they were your merchants for
exquisite clothing, blue and embroidered cloaks, many-colored carpets
25 bound with cords, preserved with cedar – in your marketplace. The ships of
Tarshish transported your imports; you were filled, heavily laden, in the heart
26 of the sea. They rowed you,[49] brought you to great rushing waters; the east
27 wind smashed you apart in the heart of the sea. Your wealth, your wares, and
your imports, your sailors and your pilots, those who repair your breaches
and who bring your imports, and all your men of combat among you, all the
crew who are within you will plummet into the heart of the sea on the day of
28 29 your downfall. At the sound of your pilot's shouts the billows will churn, and
all your oarsmen and sailors, all your pilots will debark from their ships, will
30 stand on dry land. They will make their voices heard over you, and they will
cry out bitterly; they will put dirt on their heads, dust themselves with ashes.
31 They will make themselves bald over you, gird themselves with sackcloth;
32 they will cry over you, their spirits bitter, a bitter lament. And in their wailing,
they will raise a lament over you; they will lament over you: 'Who was like
33 Tyre, silenced in the midst of the sea?' When your wares were sent out on the
seas, you brought abundance to numerous peoples; with your great wealth
34 and imports you made the kings of the earth rich. Now, broken by the seas,
there in the depths of the water, your imports and all of the crew within you
35 have plummeted down. All the inhabitants of the coastlands are aghast
36 at your fate, their kings appalled, their faces thunderous. Merchants among
the other peoples hiss at you; a horror you have become; you are gone,
28 1 2 forever." And the word of the LORD came to me: "Man,
say to the ruler of Tyre: So says the Lord GOD: Because your heart grew
arrogant, you said, 'I am a god; I sit upon the seat of a god in the heart of the
sea' – but you are a man and not a god; you consider your heart to be the
3 heart of a god, but are you wiser than Daniel? Is no obscure matter hidden
4 from you? With your wisdom and understanding you made yourself powerful;
5 you amassed silver and gold in your treasuries; with your great wisdom in
commerce you increased your riches, and you heart grew arrogant with your
6 riches. So the Lord GOD says this: Because you consider your heart

---

46 | In Amon (see Judges 11:33).

47 | A nomadic kingdom in the Arabian Desert.

48 | A kingdom in the southern Arabian Peninsula (see 1 Kings 10:1).

49 | Tyre is represented here as a ship.

יז וּבוּץ וְרָאמֹת וְכַדְכֹּד נָתְנוּ בְּעִזְבוֹנָיִךְ: יְהוּדָה וְאֶרֶץ יִשְׂרָאֵל הֵמָּה
יח רֹכְלָיִךְ בְּחִטֵּי מִנִּית וּפַנַּג וּדְבַשׁ וָשֶׁמֶן וָצֹרִי נָתְנוּ מַעֲרָבֵךְ: דַּמֶּשֶׂק
יט סֹחַרְתֵּךְ בְּרֹב מַעֲשַׂיִךְ מֵרֹב כָּל־הוֹן בְּיֵין חֶלְבּוֹן וְצֶמֶר צָחַר: וְדָן וְיָוָן
כ מְאוּזָּל בְּעִזְבוֹנַיִךְ נָתָנּוּ בַּרְזֶל עָשׁוֹת קִדָּה וְקָנֶה בְּמַעֲרָבֵךְ הָיָה: דְּדָן
כא רֹכַלְתֵּךְ בְּבִגְדֵי־חֹפֶשׁ לְרִכְבָּה: עֲרַב וְכָל־נְשִׂיאֵי קֵדָר הֵמָּה סֹחֲרֵי יָדֵךְ
כב בְּכָרִים וְאֵילִם וְעַתּוּדִים בָּם סֹחֲרָיִךְ: רֹכְלֵי שְׁבָא וְרַעְמָה הֵמָּה רֹכְלָיִךְ
כג בְּרֹאשׁ כָּל־בֹּשֶׂם וּבְכָל־אֶבֶן יְקָרָה וְזָהָב נָתְנוּ עִזְבוֹנָיִךְ: חָרָן וְכַנֵּה
כד וָעֶדֶן רֹכְלֵי שְׁבָא אַשּׁוּר כִּלְמַד רֹכַלְתֵּךְ: הֵמָּה רֹכְלַיִךְ בְמַכְלֻלִים בִּגְלוֹמֵי
תְּכֵלֶת וְרִקְמָה וּבְגִנְזֵי בְּרֹמִים בַּחֲבָלִים חֲבֻשִׁים וַאֲרֻזִים בְּמַרְכֻלְתֵּךְ:
כה אֳנִיּוֹת תַּרְשִׁישׁ שָׁרוֹתַיִךְ מַעֲרָבֵךְ וַתִּמָּלְאִי וַתִּכְבְּדִי מְאֹד בְּלֵב יַמִּים:
כו בְּמַיִם רַבִּים הֱבִאוּךְ הַשָּׁטִים אוֹתָךְ רוּחַ הַקָּדִים שְׁבָרֵךְ בְּלֵב יַמִּים:
כז הוֹנֵךְ וְעִזְבוֹנַיִךְ מַעֲרָבֵךְ מַלָּחַיִךְ וְחֹבְלָיִךְ מַחֲזִיקֵי בִדְקֵךְ וְעֹרְבֵי מַעֲרָבֵךְ
וְכָל־אַנְשֵׁי מִלְחַמְתֵּךְ אֲשֶׁר־בָּךְ וּבְכָל־קְהָלֵךְ אֲשֶׁר בְּתוֹכֵךְ יִפְּלוּ בְּלֵב
כח כט יַמִּים בְּיוֹם מַפַּלְתֵּךְ: לְקוֹל זַעֲקַת חֹבְלָיִךְ יִרְעֲשׁוּ מִגְרֹשׁוֹת: וְיָרְדוּ
מֵאֳנִיּוֹתֵיהֶם כֹּל תֹּפְשֵׂי מָשׁוֹט מַלָּחִים כֹּל חֹבְלֵי הַיָּם אֶל־הָאָרֶץ יַעֲמֹדוּ:
ל וְהִשְׁמִיעוּ עָלַיִךְ בְּקוֹלָם וְיִזְעֲקוּ מָרָה וְיַעֲלוּ עָפָר עַל־רָאשֵׁיהֶם בָּאֵפֶר
לא יִתְפַּלָּשׁוּ: וְהִקְרִיחוּ אֵלַיִךְ קָרְחָה וְחָגְרוּ שַׂקִּים וּבָכוּ אֵלַיִךְ בְּמַר־נֶפֶשׁ
לב מִסְפֵּד מָר: וְנָשְׂאוּ אֵלַיִךְ בְּנִיהֶם קִינָה וְקוֹנְנוּ עָלָיִךְ מִי כְצוֹר כְּדֻמָה
לג בְּתוֹךְ הַיָּם: בְּצֵאת עִזְבוֹנַיִךְ מִיַּמִּים הִשְׂבַּעַתְּ עַמִּים רַבִּים בְּרֹב הוֹנַיִךְ
לד וּמַעֲרָבַיִךְ הֶעֱשַׁרְתְּ מַלְכֵי־אָרֶץ: עֵת נִשְׁבֶּרֶת מִיַּמִּים בְּמַעֲמַקֵּי־מָיִם
לה מַעֲרָבֵךְ וְכָל־קְהָלֵךְ בְּתוֹכֵךְ נָפָלוּ: כֹּל יֹשְׁבֵי הָאִיִּים שָׁמְמוּ עָלָיִךְ
לו וּמַלְכֵיהֶם שָׂעֲרוּ שַׂעַר רָעֲמוּ פָּנִים: סֹחֲרִים בָּעַמִּים שָׁרְקוּ עָלָיִךְ בַּלָּהוֹת
כח א ב הָיִית וְאֵינֵךְ עַד־עוֹלָם: וַיְהִי דְבַר־יְהוָה אֵלַי לֵאמֹר: בֶּן־
אָדָם אֱמֹר לִנְגִיד צֹר כֹּה־אָמַר ׀ אֲדֹנָי יֱהוִה יַעַן גָּבַהּ לִבְּךָ וַתֹּאמֶר אֵל
אָנִי מוֹשַׁב אֱלֹהִים יָשַׁבְתִּי בְּלֵב יַמִּים וְאַתָּה אָדָם וְלֹא־אֵל וַתִּתֵּן לִבְּךָ
ג ד כְּלֵב אֱלֹהִים: הִנֵּה חָכָם אַתָּה מִדָּנִאֵל כָּל־סָתוּם לֹא עֲמָמוּךָ: בְּחָכְמָתְךָ מִדָּנִיֵּאל
ה וּבִתְבוּנָתְךָ עָשִׂיתָ לְּךָ חָיִל וַתַּעַשׂ זָהָב וָכֶסֶף בְּאוֹצְרוֹתֶיךָ: בְּרֹב חָכְמָתְךָ
ו בִּרְכֻלָּתְךָ הִרְבִּיתָ חֵילֶךָ וַיִּגְבַּהּ לְבָבְךָ בְּחֵילֶךָ: לָכֵן כֹּה אָמַר

7 to be the heart of a god, so will I bring strangers upon you, the most terrifying
of nations; they will draw their swords upon the beauty of your wisdom; they
8 will defile your radiance. They will take you down to the Pit; you will die the
9 death of the slain in the heart of the sea. Will you still say 'I am a god' before
10 your slayer? You are a man, not a god, in the hands of your killers. You will
die the death of the uncircumcised at the hands of strangers; thus have I
11 spoken, declares the Lord God." And the word of the Lord came
12 to me: "Man, raise a lament over the king of Tyre; say to him: So says the
Lord God: You were the model of flawlessness, full of wisdom, perfect in
13 beauty. You were there in Eden, the garden of God, every precious stone as
your wrapping, carnelian, olivine, and green quartz, aquamarine, rock crystal,
and jasper, sapphire, emerald, and garnet,[50] gold the handiwork of your
14 settings and grooves that were set on the day you were created. You were a
sublime, shielding cherub; I placed you there; you were on the holy mountain
15 of God; you walked among the stones of fire. You were faultless in your ways
16 from the day you were created until wrongdoing was found in you; because
of your vast commerce your midst was filled with corruption, and you sinned.
I struck you from the mountain of God; I have banished you, shielding cherub,
17 from among the stones of fire. Your heart grew arrogant because of your
beauty; you perverted your wisdom along with your radiance; I flung you
18 to the ground, brought you before kings to look on you. Because of your
many sins, your dishonesty in commerce, you desecrated your sanctuaries. I
brought fire from within your midst – it consumed you; I turned you into
19 ashes on the ground before the eyes of all who looked on you. All your
acquaintances among the peoples are aghast at your fate; a horror you have
20 become; you are gone, forever." And the word of the Lord came
21 to me: "Man, set your face toward Sidon, prophesy against her and say: So
22 says the Lord God: I am upon you, Sidon; I will gain glory in your midst.
They will know that I am the Lord when I execute judgments upon her, when
23 I am sanctified through her. I will set plague and blood loose against her in
her streets, the slain will fall within her when the sword is bearing down on
24 her from all around, and they will know that I am the Lord. The House of
Israel will no longer suffer stabbing briers, scratching thorns, from those in
their surroundings who scorn them, and they will know that I am the Lord
25 God. So says the Lord God: When I gather the House of Israel in
from the peoples where they have been scattered and I am sanctified through
them in the eyes of the nations, when they live on their land that I gave to My
26 servant Yaakov – they will live on it in safety; they will build houses, plant
vineyards, live safely; when I execute judgments over all those from their
surroundings who scorn them, they will know that I am the Lord, their
29 1 God." In the tenth year in the tenth month on the
2 twelfth of the month, the word of the Lord came to me: "Man, set your face
against Pharaoh, king of Egypt; prophesy against him and against all of Egypt.
3 Speak and say: So says the Lord God: Behold, I am upon you, Pharaoh, king

50 | Cf. Exodus 28:17–20.

ז אֲדֹנָי יֱהוִה יַעַן תִּתְּךָ אֶת־לְבָבְךָ כְּלֵב אֱלֹהִים׃ לָכֵן הִנְנִי מֵבִיא עָלֶיךָ
זָרִים עָרִיצֵי גּוֹיִם וְהֵרִיקוּ חַרְבוֹתָם עַל־יְפִי חָכְמָתֶךָ וְחִלְּלוּ יִפְעָתֶךָ׃
ח ט לַשַּׁחַת יוֹרִדוּךָ וָמַתָּה מְמוֹתֵי חָלָל בְּלֵב יַמִּים׃ הֶאָמֹר תֹּאמַר אֱלֹהִים
י אָנִי לִפְנֵי הֹרְגֶךָ וְאַתָּה אָדָם וְלֹא־אֵל בְּיַד מְחַלְלֶיךָ׃ מוֹתֵי עֲרֵלִים
יא תָּמוּת בְּיַד זָרִים כִּי אֲנִי דִבַּרְתִּי נְאֻם אֲדֹנָי יֱהוִה׃ וַיְהִי
יב דְבַר־יְהוָה אֵלַי לֵאמֹר׃ בֶּן־אָדָם שָׂא קִינָה עַל־מֶלֶךְ צוֹר וְאָמַרְתָּ לּוֹ
יג כֹּה אָמַר אֲדֹנָי יֱהוִה אַתָּה חוֹתֵם תָּכְנִית מָלֵא חָכְמָה וּכְלִיל יֹפִי׃ בְּעֵדֶן יז
גַּן־אֱלֹהִים הָיִיתָ כָּל־אֶבֶן יְקָרָה מְסֻכָתֶךָ אֹדֶם פִּטְדָה וְיָהֲלֹם תַּרְשִׁישׁ
שֹׁהַם וְיָשְׁפֵה סַפִּיר נֹפֶךְ וּבָרְקַת וְזָהָב מְלֶאכֶת תֻּפֶּיךָ וּנְקָבֶיךָ בָּךְ
יד בְּיוֹם הִבָּרַאֲךָ כּוֹנָנוּ׃ אַתְּ־כְּרוּב מִמְשַׁח הַסּוֹכֵךְ וּנְתַתִּיךָ בְּהַר קֹדֶשׁ
טו אֱלֹהִים הָיִיתָ בְּתוֹךְ אַבְנֵי־אֵשׁ הִתְהַלָּכְתָּ׃ תָּמִים אַתָּה בִּדְרָכֶיךָ מִיּוֹם
טז הִבָּרְאָךְ עַד־נִמְצָא עַוְלָתָה בָּךְ׃ בְּרֹב רְכֻלָּתְךָ מָלוּ תוֹכְךָ חָמָס וַתֶּחֱטָא
יז וָאֲחַלֶּלְךָ מֵהַר אֱלֹהִים וָאַבֶּדְךָ כְּרוּב הַסֹּכֵךְ מִתּוֹךְ אַבְנֵי־אֵשׁ׃ גָּבַהּ
לִבְּךָ בְּיָפְיֶךָ שִׁחַתָּ חָכְמָתְךָ עַל־יִפְעָתֶךָ עַל־אֶרֶץ הִשְׁלַכְתִּיךָ לִפְנֵי
יח מְלָכִים נְתַתִּיךָ לְרַאֲוָה בָךְ׃ מֵרֹב עֲוֺנֶיךָ בְּעֶוֶל רְכֻלָּתְךָ חִלַּלְתָּ מִקְדָּשֶׁיךָ
וָאוֹצִא־אֵשׁ מִתּוֹכְךָ הִיא אֲכָלַתְךָ וָאֶתֶּנְךָ לְאֵפֶר עַל־הָאָרֶץ לְעֵינֵי
יט כָּל־רֹאֶיךָ׃ כָּל־יוֹדְעֶיךָ בָּעַמִּים שָׁמְמוּ עָלֶיךָ בַּלָּהוֹת הָיִיתָ וְאֵינְךָ עַד־
כ כא עוֹלָם׃ וַיְהִי דְבַר־יְהוָה אֵלַי לֵאמֹר׃ בֶּן־אָדָם שִׂים פָּנֶיךָ
כב אֶל־צִידוֹן וְהִנָּבֵא עָלֶיהָ׃ וְאָמַרְתָּ כֹּה אָמַר אֲדֹנָי יֱהוִה הִנְנִי עָלַיִךְ
צִידוֹן וְנִכְבַּדְתִּי בְּתוֹכֵךְ וְיָדְעוּ כִּי־אֲנִי יְהוָה בַּעֲשׂוֹתִי בָהּ שְׁפָטִים
כג וְנִקְדַּשְׁתִּי בָהּ׃ וְשִׁלַּחְתִּי־בָהּ דֶּבֶר וָדָם בְּחוּצוֹתֶיהָ וְנִפְלַל חָלָל בְּתוֹכָהּ
כד בְּחֶרֶב עָלֶיהָ מִסָּבִיב וְיָדְעוּ כִּי־אֲנִי יְהוָה׃ וְלֹא־יִהְיֶה עוֹד לְבֵית יִשְׂרָאֵל
סִלּוֹן מַמְאִיר וְקוֹץ מַכְאִב מִכֹּל סְבִיבֹתָם הַשָּׁאטִים אוֹתָם וְיָדְעוּ כִּי
כה אֲנִי אֲדֹנָי יֱהוִה׃ כֹּה־אָמַר אֲדֹנָי יֱהוִה בְּקַבְּצִי ׀ אֶת־בֵּית
יִשְׂרָאֵל מִן־הָעַמִּים אֲשֶׁר נָפֹצוּ בָם וְנִקְדַּשְׁתִּי בָם לְעֵינֵי הַגּוֹיִם וְיָשְׁבוּ
כו עַל־אַדְמָתָם אֲשֶׁר נָתַתִּי לְעַבְדִּי לְיַעֲקֹב׃ וְיָשְׁבוּ עָלֶיהָ לָבֶטַח וּבָנוּ
בָתִּים וְנָטְעוּ כְרָמִים וְיָשְׁבוּ לָבֶטַח בַּעֲשׂוֹתִי שְׁפָטִים בְּכֹל הַשָּׁאטִים
כט א אֹתָם מִסְּבִיבוֹתָם וְיָדְעוּ כִּי אֲנִי יְהוָה אֱלֹהֵיהֶם׃ בַּשָּׁנָה
הָעֲשִׂרִית בָּעֲשִׂרִי בִּשְׁנֵים עָשָׂר לַחֹדֶשׁ הָיָה דְבַר־יְהוָה אֵלַי לֵאמֹר׃
ב בֶּן־אָדָם שִׂים פָּנֶיךָ עַל־פַּרְעֹה מֶלֶךְ מִצְרָיִם וְהִנָּבֵא עָלָיו וְעַל־מִצְרַיִם
ג כֻּלָּהּ׃ דַּבֵּר וְאָמַרְתָּ כֹּה־אָמַר ׀ אֲדֹנָי יֱהוִה הִנְנִי עָלֶיךָ פַּרְעֹה מֶלֶךְ־

of Egypt, great crocodile crouching in his Nile streams who says, 'It is mine,
4 this Nile; I made it for myself.' I will fix hooks into your jaw; I will make the
fish from your streams stick to your scales; I will drag you up out of your
5 streams, and all the fish from your streams will stick to your scales; I will
abandon you in the desert, you and all the fish of your streams. You will fall
in the open field and be neither collected nor gathered up; to the animals
6 of the land and the birds of the skies I will give you over as food. All the
inhabitants of Egypt will know that I am the LORD – for they were a reed
7 staff to the House of Israel: when they grasped hold of you, you crumbled,
tearing their shoulders; when they leaned upon you, you broke, buckling their
8 loins. So the Lord GOD says this: I will bring the sword down upon
9 you, cut off man and beast from you. The land of Egypt will be desolate,
ruined, and they will know that I am the LORD. Because he said, 'The Nile is
10 mine; I made it,' for this, I am coming down upon you and your Nile streams.
I will turn the land of Egypt into a waste of desolate ruins from Migdol to
11 Sevene and to the border with Kush.[51] The foot of no man will pass through
her; the foot of no animal will pass through her; she will not be inhabited for
12 forty years. For forty years I will make the land of Egypt desolate among
desolate lands, and her cities will lie desolate among ruined cities. I will strew
13 Egypt among the nations, scatter them over the lands. Yet, so says
the Lord GOD, at the end of forty years I will gather Egypt in from the people
14 among whom they were scattered. I will restore the fortunes of Egypt; I will
restore them to the land of Patros, the land of their origin, and there they will
15 be a lowly kingdom. She will be the lowest of the kingdoms and will never
again elevate herself above the nations; I will reduce them to a state where
16 they cannot dominate among the nations. They will no longer be a source of
trust for the House of Israel but merely a reminder of Israel's sin in turning
17 to them, and they will know that I am the Lord GOD." It was in the
twenty-seventh year in the first month on the first day of the month that the
18 word of the LORD came to me: "Man: Nevukhadretzar, king of Babylon,
exerted his army to labor hard against Tyre. Every head was rubbed raw, every
shoulder worn down bare, but from Tyre neither he nor his army received
19 pay for the hard work with which they toiled against her. So the Lord
GOD says this: See that to Nevukhadretzar, king of Babylon, I will give the
land of Egypt. He will carry off her wealth, ransack her spoils, and seize her
20 loot; she will be the pay for his army. I shall give him the land of Egypt as his
payment, for which he has labored, which he has done for Me, declares the
21 Lord GOD. On that day I will make a horn of strength grow for the House of
Israel, and you – I will let your voice be heard among them, and they will
30 1 know that I am the LORD." And the word of the LORD came
2 to me: "Man, prophesy; say: So says the Lord GOD. Howl it: 'Alas, the day!'
3 For a day is near; the day of the LORD is near; a day of cloud, a time of nations

51 | Migdol is in northern Egypt (see Ex. 14:2). Sevene is Aswan, in southern Egypt, near the border with Kush.

מִצְרַיִם הַתַּנִּים הַגָּדוֹל הָרֹבֵץ בְּתוֹךְ יְאֹרָיו אֲשֶׁר אָמַר לִי יְאֹרִי וַאֲנִי
ד עֲשִׂיתִנִי: וְנָתַתִּי חחיים בִּלְחָיֶיךָ וְהִדְבַּקְתִּי דְגַת־יְאֹרֶיךָ בְּקַשְׂקְשֹׂתֶיךָ חַחִים
וְהַעֲלִיתִיךָ מִתּוֹךְ יְאֹרֶיךָ וְאֵת כָּל־דְּגַת יְאֹרֶיךָ בְּקַשְׂקְשֹׂתֶיךָ תִּדְבָּק:
ה וּנְטַשְׁתִּיךָ הַמִּדְבָּרָה אוֹתְךָ וְאֵת כָּל־דְּגַת יְאֹרֶיךָ עַל־פְּנֵי הַשָּׂדֶה תִּפּוֹל
לֹא תֵאָסֵף וְלֹא תִקָּבֵץ לְחַיַּת הָאָרֶץ וּלְעוֹף הַשָּׁמַיִם נְתַתִּיךָ לְאָכְלָה:
ו וְיָדְעוּ כָּל־יֹשְׁבֵי מִצְרַיִם כִּי אֲנִי יְהוָה יַעַן הֱיוֹתָם מִשְׁעֶנֶת קָנֶה לְבֵית
ז יִשְׂרָאֵל: בְּתָפְשָׂם בְּךָ בכפך תֵּרוֹץ וּבָקַעְתָּ לָהֶם כָּל־כָּתֵף וּבְהִשָּׁעֲנָם בַכַּף
ח עָלֶיךָ תִּשָּׁבֵר וְהַעֲמַדְתָּ לָהֶם כָּל־מָתְנָיִם: לָכֵן כֹּה אָמַר
ט אֲדֹנָי יְהוִה הִנְנִי מֵבִיא עָלַיִךְ חָרֶב וְהִכְרַתִּי מִמֵּךְ אָדָם וּבְהֵמָה: וְהָיְתָה
אֶרֶץ־מִצְרַיִם לִשְׁמָמָה וְחָרְבָּה וְיָדְעוּ כִּי־אֲנִי יְהוָה יַעַן אָמַר יְאֹר לִי
י וַאֲנִי עָשִׂיתִי: לָכֵן הִנְנִי אֵלֶיךָ וְאֶל־יְאֹרֶיךָ וְנָתַתִּי אֶת־אֶרֶץ מִצְרַיִם
יא לְחָרְבוֹת חֹרֶב שְׁמָמָה מִמִּגְדֹּל סְוֵנֵה וְעַד־גְּבוּל כּוּשׁ: לֹא תַעֲבָר־בָּהּ
יב רֶגֶל אָדָם וְרֶגֶל בְּהֵמָה לֹא תַעֲבָר־בָּהּ וְלֹא תֵשֵׁב אַרְבָּעִים שָׁנָה: וְנָתַתִּי
אֶת־אֶרֶץ מִצְרַיִם שְׁמָמָה בְּתוֹךְ ׀ אֲרָצוֹת נְשַׁמּוֹת וְעָרֶיהָ בְּתוֹךְ עָרִים
מָחֳרָבוֹת תִּהְיֶיןָ שְׁמָמָה אַרְבָּעִים שָׁנָה וַהֲפִצֹתִי אֶת־מִצְרַיִם בַּגּוֹיִם
יג וְזֵרִיתִים בָּאֲרָצוֹת: כִּי כֹּה אָמַר אֲדֹנָי יְהוִה מִקֵּץ אַרְבָּעִים
יד שָׁנָה אֲקַבֵּץ אֶת־מִצְרַיִם מִן־הָעַמִּים אֲשֶׁר־נָפֹצוּ שָׁמָּה: וְשַׁבְתִּי אֶת־
שְׁבוּת מִצְרַיִם וַהֲשִׁבֹתִי אֹתָם אֶרֶץ פַּתְרוֹס עַל־אֶרֶץ מְכוּרָתָם וְהָיוּ
טו שָׁם מַמְלָכָה שְׁפָלָה: מִן־הַמַּמְלָכוֹת תִּהְיֶה שְׁפָלָה וְלֹא־תִתְנַשֵּׂא עוֹד
טז עַל־הַגּוֹיִם וְהִמְעַטְתִּים לְבִלְתִּי רְדוֹת בַּגּוֹיִם: וְלֹא יִהְיֶה־עוֹד לְבֵית
יִשְׂרָאֵל לְמִבְטָח מַזְכִּיר עָוֺן בִּפְנוֹתָם אַחֲרֵיהֶם וְיָדְעוּ כִּי אֲנִי אֲדֹנָי
יז יְהוִה: וַיְהִי בְּעֶשְׂרִים וָשֶׁבַע שָׁנָה בָּרִאשׁוֹן בְּאֶחָד
יח לַחֹדֶשׁ הָיָה דְבַר־יְהוָה אֵלַי לֵאמֹר: בֶּן־אָדָם נְבוּכַדְרֶאצַּר מֶלֶךְ־בָּבֶל
הֶעֱבִיד אֶת־חֵילוֹ עֲבֹדָה גְדוֹלָה אֶל־צֹר כָּל־רֹאשׁ מֻקְרָח וְכָל־כָּתֵף
מְרוּטָה וְשָׂכָר לֹא־הָיָה לוֹ וּלְחֵילוֹ מִצֹּר עַל־הָעֲבֹדָה אֲשֶׁר־עָבַד
יט עָלֶיהָ: לָכֵן כֹּה אָמַר אֲדֹנָי יְהוִה הִנְנִי נֹתֵן לִנְבוּכַדְרֶאצַּר
מֶלֶךְ־בָּבֶל אֶת־אֶרֶץ מִצְרָיִם וְנָשָׂא הֲמֹנָהּ וְשָׁלַל שְׁלָלָהּ וּבָזַז בִּזָּהּ
כ וְהָיְתָה שָׂכָר לְחֵילוֹ: פְּעֻלָּתוֹ אֲשֶׁר־עָבַד בָּהּ נָתַתִּי לוֹ אֶת־אֶרֶץ מִצְרָיִם
כא אֲשֶׁר עָשׂוּ לִי נְאֻם אֲדֹנָי יְהוִה: בַּיּוֹם הַהוּא אַצְמִיחַ קֶרֶן לְבֵית יִשְׂרָאֵל יח
ל א וּלְךָ אֶתֵּן פִּתְחוֹן־פֶּה בְּתוֹכָם וְיָדְעוּ כִּי־אֲנִי יְהוָה: וַיְהִי
ב דְבַר־יְהוָה אֵלַי לֵאמֹר: בֶּן־אָדָם הִנָּבֵא וְאָמַרְתָּ כֹּה אָמַר אֲדֹנָי יְהוִה
ג הֵילִילוּ הָהּ לַיּוֹם: כִּי־קָרוֹב יוֹם וְקָרוֹב יוֹם לַיהוָה יוֹם עָנָן עֵת גּוֹיִם

4 it will be. The sword will come to Egypt; there will be anguish in Kush; when
the slain in Egypt fall, they will take her wealth, and her foundations will be
5 torn up. Kush and Put and Lydia, all the mixed peoples and Kub,[52] and people
6 of allied lands with them will fall by the sword. So says the LORD:
Those defending Egypt will fall; the majesty of her power will collapse from
Migdol to Sevene; there they will fall by the sword, declares the Lord GOD.
7 They will be desolate among desolate lands, her cities among the cities laid
8 waste; they will know that I am the LORD when I set Egypt afire and all those
9 who assist her are broken. On that day messengers from Me will go forth in
ships to make secure Kush quake; anguish will be among them on Egypt's
10 day, for see, it is coming. So says the Lord GOD: I will put an end to
11 the crowds of Egypt by the hand of Nevukhadretzar, king of Babylon. He
along with his troops, the most terrifying of nations, will be brought to
destroy the land; they will draw their swords upon Egypt and fill the land
12 with the slain. I will turn the streams to dry ground; I will sell the land into
the hands of evil people; at the hands of strangers I will devastate the land
13 and everything in it; I, the LORD, have spoken. So says the Lord
GOD: I will destroy idols and end the false gods of Nof;[53] there will no longer
14 be a prince in the land of Egypt; I will put fear into the land of Egypt. I will
15 devastate Patros; I will set Tzoan afire and execute judgments in No. I will
pour out My fury upon Sin, stronghold of Egypt; I will cut off the masses of
16 No. I will set Egypt afire, Sin will quiver in terror, No will be broken open,
17 and Nof will face enemies daily. The young men of Aven and Pi Beset will fall
18 by the sword; they will go into captivity. In Taḥpanḥes day will darken when
I break Egypt's bars there and the majesty of her power is put to an end; cloud
19 will cover her up, and her daughters will go into captivity. I will execute
20 judgments in Egypt, and they will know: I am the LORD." And it was
in the eleventh year in the first month on the seventh of the month that the
21 word of the LORD came to me: "Man, I have broken the arm of Pharaoh, king
of Egypt; see, it has not been bound up to heal nor bound with a bandage to
22 strengthen it enough to wield a sword. So the Lord GOD says this:
Behold, I am against Pharaoh, king of Egypt; I will break his arms, the strong
23 one along with the broken one; I will make the sword fall from his hand. I
24 will strew Egypt among the nations, scatter them over the lands. I will make
the arms of the king of Babylon strong; I will place My sword into his hands,
and I will break Pharaoh's arms; he will groan with the moans of the mortally
25 wounded before him. I will support the arms of the king of Babylon, and the
arms of Pharaoh will fall slack, and they will know that I am the LORD when
I put My sword into the hand of the king of Babylon and stretch it forth
26 against the land of Egypt. I will strew Egypt across the nations, scatter them

52 | Kush is in the south of Egypt, Put (Libya) is in its west, "the mixed peoples" (*kol ha'erev*) refers to Arabia to the east, and Lydia is in the north. Kub is otherwise unknown.

53 | This and the following are all major cities and regions in Egypt.

ד יהיה: ובאה חרב במצרים והיתה חלחלה בכוש בנפל חלל במצרים
ה ולקחו המונה ונהרסו יסודתיה: כוש ופוט ולוד וכל־הערב וכוב
ו ובני ארץ הברית אתם בחרב יפלו: כה אמר יהוה ונפלו
סמכי מצרים וירד גאון עזה ממגדל סונה בחרב יפלו־בה נאם אדני
ז יהוה: ונשמו בתוך ארצות נשמות ועריו בתוך־ערים נחרבות
ח תהיינה: וידעו כי־אני יהוה בתתי־אש במצרים ונשברו כל־עזריה:
ט ביום ההוא יצאו מלאכים מלפני בצים להחריד את־כוש בטח
י והיתה חלחלה בהם כיום מצרים כי הנה באה: כה אמר
אדני יהוה והשבתי את־המון מצרים ביד נבוכדראצר מלך־בבל:
יא הוא ועמו אתו עריצי גוים מובאים לשחת הארץ והריקו חרבותם
יב על־מצרים ומלאו את־הארץ חלל: ונתתי יארים חרבה ומכרתי
את־הארץ ביד־רעים והשמתי ארץ ומלאה ביד־זרים אני יהוה
יג דברתי: כה־אמר אדני יהוה והאבדתי גלולים והשבתי
אלילים מנף ונשיא מארץ־מצרים לא יהיה־עוד ונתתי יראה בארץ
יד מצרים: והשמתי את־פתרוס ונתתי אש בצען ועשיתי שפטים
טו בנא: ושפכתי חמתי על־סין מעוז מצרים והכרתי את־המון נא:
טז ונתתי אש במצרים חול תחיל סין ונא תהיה להבקע ונף צרי יומם: תחול
יז יח בחורי און ופי־בסת בחרב יפלו והנה בשבי תלכנה: ובתחפנחס
חשך היום בשברי־שם את־מטות מצרים ונשבת־בה גאון עזה
יט היא ענן יכסנה ובנותיה בשבי תלכנה: ועשיתי שפטים במצרים
כ וידעו כי־אני יהוה: ויהי באחת עשרה שנה בראשון
כא בשבעה לחדש היה דבר־יהוה אלי לאמר: בן־אדם את־זרוע
פרעה מלך־מצרים שברתי והנה לא־חבשה לתת רפאות לשום
כב חתול לחבשה לחזקה לתפש בחרב: לכן כה־אמר ׀
אדני יהוה הנני אל־פרעה מלך־מצרים ושברתי את־זרעתיו את־
כג החזקה ואת־הנשברת והפלתי את־החרב מידו: והפצותי את־
כד מצרים בגוים וזריתם בארצות: וחזקתי את־זרעות מלך בבל ונתתי
את־חרבי בידו ושברתי את־זרעות פרעה ונאק נאקות חלל לפניו:
כה והחזקתי את־זרעות מלך בבל וזרעות פרעה תפלנה וידעו כי־אני
יהוה בתתי חרבי ביד מלך־בבל ונטה אותה אל־ארץ מצרים:
כו והפצותי את־מצרים בגוים וזריתי אותם בארצות וידעו כי־אני

31 1 among the lands, and they will know: I am the LORD." It was in the
eleventh year in the third month on the first of the month that the word of
2 the LORD came to me: "Man, say to Pharaoh, king of Egypt, and to his crowds:
3 Who are you comparable to in your greatness? Here is Assyria, a cedar in
Lebanon with beautiful branches, a wood giving shade with towering heights,
4 his crown among the clouds; water made him grow; the deep waters made
him soar; her rivers ran around his plantings; she sent her waterways out to
5 all trees of the field. And so, his height towered above all other trees of the
field; his branches became many, his boughs grew long from the abundant
6 water in his channel. Upon his limbs nested every bird of the sky, beneath his
boughs birthed every animal of the field, and in his shade lived each of the
7 many nations. He was beautiful in his greatness, in the length of his branches,
8 for his roots reached down to abundant waters. In the garden of God, the
cedars could not overshadow him, the cypress trees could not compare to his
limbs, and the plane trees could not equal his boughs; none of the trees in
9 the garden of God could compare to him in beauty. I made him beautiful with
his abundant branches, and all the trees of Eden that were in the garden of
10 God envied him. So the Lord GOD says this: Because he became
towering in height and placed his crown up among the clouds, he grew
11 arrogant because of his height. I gave him over into the hands of the leader
of the nations, who dealt with him; I drove him out due to his wickedness.
12 Strangers, the most terrifying of nations, have cut him down and abandoned
him; his branches fell on the mountains, in all the valleys; his boughs broke
in all the land's ravines; all the peoples of the land stepped out from under
13 his shade; they abandoned him. Every bird of the sky will settle on his fallen
14 trunk, every animal of the field will nestle upon his boughs; so that no watered
trees will become towering in their height or place their own crowns up
among the clouds, and of all drinkers of water, none of their mighty trees will
stand at their full height, for all of them will give in to death, to the nether-
15 world, among men who descend to the Pit. So says the Lord GOD:
On the day of his descent into Sheol, I closed the deep waters upon him,
covered him; I held back her rivers, and abundant waters were restrained. For
him I cast Lebanon into darkness; for him all the trees of the field languished.
16 With the sound of his fall I made the nations tremble when I took him down
to Sheol with those gone down into the Pit; in the netherworld all the
trees of Eden – the best, most choice of Lebanon, all richly watered – were
17 comforted. They too descended to Sheol with him, to those slain by the
18 sword and his allies who sat in his shade among the nations. To whom were
you comparable like this in glory and in greatness among the trees of Eden?
You will be brought down, too, with the trees of Eden, to the netherworld;
you will lie among the uncircumcised with those slain by the sword, Pharaoh
32 1 and all his crowds, declares the Lord GOD." It was in the
twelfth year in the twelfth month on the first of the month that the word of
2 the LORD came to me: "Man, say a lament over Pharaoh, king of Egypt; say
to him: You think yourself a young lion among the nations, but you are like

לא א יְהוָה: וַיְהִי בְּאַחַת עֶשְׂרֵה שָׁנָה בַּשְּׁלִישִׁי בְּאֶחָד לַחֹדֶשׁ
ב הָיָה דְבַר־יְהוָה אֵלַי לֵאמֹר: בֶּן־אָדָם אֱמֹר אֶל־פַּרְעֹה מֶלֶךְ־מִצְרַיִם
ג וְאֶל־הֲמוֹנוֹ אֶל־מִי דָּמִיתָ בְגָדְלֶךָ: הִנֵּה אַשּׁוּר אֶרֶז בַּלְּבָנוֹן יְפֵה עָנָף
ד וְחֹרֶשׁ מֵצַל וּגְבַהּ קוֹמָה וּבֵין עֲבֹתִים הָיְתָה צַמַּרְתּוֹ: מַיִם גִּדְּלוּהוּ
תְּהוֹם רֹמְמָתְהוּ אֶת־נַהֲרֹתֶיהָ הֹלֵךְ סְבִיבוֹת מַטָּעָהּ וְאֶת־תְּעָלֹתֶיהָ
ה שִׁלְחָה אֶל כָּל־עֲצֵי הַשָּׂדֶה: עַל־כֵּן גָּבְהָא קֹמָתוֹ מִכֹּל עֲצֵי הַשָּׂדֶה
ו וַתִּרְבֶּינָה סַרְעַפֹּתָיו וַתֶּאֱרַכְנָה פֹארֹתָיו מִמַּיִם רַבִּים בְּשַׁלְּחוֹ: בִּסְעַפֹּתָיו
קִנְנוּ כָּל־עוֹף הַשָּׁמַיִם וְתַחַת פֹּארֹתָיו יָלְדוּ כֹּל חַיַּת הַשָּׂדֶה וּבְצִלּוֹ
ז יֵשְׁבוּ כֹּל גּוֹיִם רַבִּים: וַיְּיף בְּגָדְלוֹ בְּאֹרֶךְ דָּלִיּוֹתָיו כִּי־הָיָה שָׁרְשׁוֹ אֶל־
ח מַיִם רַבִּים: אֲרָזִים לֹא־עֲמָמֻהוּ בְּגַן־אֱלֹהִים בְּרוֹשִׁים לֹא דָמוּ אֶל־
סְעַפֹּתָיו וְעַרְמֹנִים לֹא־הָיוּ כְּפֹארֹתָיו כָּל־עֵץ בְּגַן־אֱלֹהִים לֹא־דָמָה
ט אֵלָיו בְּיָפְיוֹ: יָפֶה עֲשִׂיתִיו בְּרֹב דָּלִיּוֹתָיו וַיְקַנְאֻהוּ כָּל־עֲצֵי־עֵדֶן אֲשֶׁר
י בְּגַן הָאֱלֹהִים: לָכֵן כֹּה אָמַר אֲדֹנָי יְהוִה יַעַן אֲשֶׁר
גָּבַהְתָּ בְּקוֹמָה וַיִּתֵּן צַמַּרְתּוֹ אֶל־בֵּין עֲבוֹתִים וְרָם לְבָבוֹ בְּגָבְהוֹ:
יא יב וְאֶתְּנֵהוּ בְּיַד אֵיל גּוֹיִם עָשׂוֹ יַעֲשֶׂה לוֹ כְּרִשְׁעוֹ גֵּרַשְׁתִּהוּ: וַיִּכְרְתֻהוּ
זָרִים עָרִיצֵי גוֹיִם וַיִּטְּשֻׁהוּ אֶל־הֶהָרִים וּבְכָל־גֵּאָיוֹת נָפְלוּ דָלִיּוֹתָיו
וַתִּשָּׁבַרְנָה פֹארֹתָיו בְּכֹל אֲפִיקֵי הָאָרֶץ וַיֵּרְדוּ מִצִּלּוֹ כָּל־עַמֵּי הָאָרֶץ
יג וַיִּטְּשֻׁהוּ: עַל־מַפַּלְתּוֹ יִשְׁכְּנוּ כָּל־עוֹף הַשָּׁמָיִם וְאֶל־פֹּארֹתָיו הָיוּ כֹּל
יד חַיַּת הַשָּׂדֶה: לְמַעַן אֲשֶׁר לֹא־יִגְבְּהוּ בְקוֹמָתָם כָּל־עֲצֵי־מַיִם וְלֹא־יִתְּנוּ
אֶת־צַמַּרְתָּם אֶל־בֵּין עֲבֹתִים וְלֹא־יַעַמְדוּ אֵלֵיהֶם בְּגָבְהָם כָּל־שֹׁתֵי
מָיִם כִּי כֻלָּם נִתְּנוּ לַמָּוֶת אֶל־אֶרֶץ תַּחְתִּית בְּתוֹךְ בְּנֵי אָדָם אֶל־יוֹרְדֵי
טו בוֹר: כֹּה־אָמַר אֲדֹנָי יְהוִה בְּיוֹם רִדְתּוֹ שְׁאוֹלָה הֶאֱבַלְתִּי
כִּסֵּתִי עָלָיו אֶת־תְּהוֹם וָאֶמְנַע נַהֲרוֹתֶיהָ וַיִּכָּלְאוּ מַיִם רַבִּים וָאַקְדִּר
טז עָלָיו לְבָנוֹן וְכָל־עֲצֵי הַשָּׂדֶה עָלָיו עֻלְפֶּה: מִקּוֹל מַפַּלְתּוֹ הִרְעַשְׁתִּי
גוֹיִם בְּהוֹרִדִי אֹתוֹ שְׁאוֹלָה אֶת־יוֹרְדֵי בוֹר וַיִּנָּחֲמוּ בְּאֶרֶץ תַּחְתִּית
יז כָּל־עֲצֵי־עֵדֶן מִבְחַר וְטוֹב־לְבָנוֹן כָּל־שֹׁתֵי מָיִם: גַּם־הֵם אִתּוֹ יָרְדוּ
יח שְׁאוֹלָה אֶל־חַלְלֵי־חָרֶב וּזְרֹעוֹ יָשְׁבוּ בְצִלּוֹ בְּתוֹךְ גּוֹיִם: אֶל־מִי דָמִיתָ
כָּכָה בְּכָבוֹד וּבְגֹדֶל בַּעֲצֵי־עֵדֶן וְהוּרַדְתָּ אֶת־עֲצֵי־עֵדֶן אֶל־אֶרֶץ
תַּחְתִּית בְּתוֹךְ עֲרֵלִים תִּשְׁכַּב אֶת־חַלְלֵי־חֶרֶב הוּא פַרְעֹה וְכָל־הֲמוֹנֹה
לב א נְאֻם אֲדֹנָי יְהוִה: וַיְהִי בִּשְׁתֵּי עֶשְׂרֵה שָׁנָה בִּשְׁנֵי־ יט
ב עָשָׂר חֹדֶשׁ בְּאֶחָד לַחֹדֶשׁ הָיָה דְבַר־יְהוָה אֵלַי לֵאמֹר: בֶּן־אָדָם
שָׂא קִינָה עַל־פַּרְעֹה מֶלֶךְ־מִצְרַיִם וְאָמַרְתָּ אֵלָיו כְּפִיר גּוֹיִם נִדְמֵיתָ

a crocodile in the seas, pouncing in your rivers, churning the waters with your
3 feet, turning up the mud of their rivers. So says the Lord GOD: I will
spread My net over you with a horde of many people; they will bring you up
4 in My fishing net. I will dash you to the ground, I will hurl you onto the open
field, I will make every bird of the sky settle on you, I will make all the animals
5 of the land gorge upon you, I will disperse your limbs over the mountains, I
6 will fill the valleys with your carcasses, I will drench your floodlands with
7 your blood up to the mountains, and the ravines will be filled with you. When
you are extinguished, I will cover over the heavens, I will darken their stars, I
8 will cover the sun over with clouds, and the moon will not shine its light. I
will darken all the lights that shine in the sky, for you, I will place your land
9 in darkness, declares the Lord GOD. I will cause alarm in the hearts of many
peoples when I bring news of your collapse among the nations, among lands
10 you have never known. I will make many peoples appalled at you; their kings
will bristle in horror when I brandish My sword before them; every man will
11 quake in constant fear of his life on the day of your downfall. So the
Lord GOD says this: The sword of the king of Babylon will come upon you;
12 I will bring down your hordes with the swords of warriors, all the most
terrifying of the nations; they will devastate the majesty of Egypt; all her
13 hordes will be decimated. I will cause all her livestock to perish from beside
abundant waters; the feet of men will no longer churn them, nor will the
14 hooves of livestock churn them. Then will I settle their waters and make their
15 rivers flow like oil, declares the Lord GOD. When I render the land of Egypt
desolate, the land will be devastated of everything in it; when I strike all her
16 inhabitants, then they will know that I am the LORD. This is a lament – they
will keen it; the women of the nations will keen it; over Egypt and all her
hordes they will keen it, declares the Lord GOD."
17 It was in the twelfth year on the fifteenth of the month that the word of the
18 LORD came to me: "Man, lament over the hordes of Egypt; take them – take
her, Egypt, and the daughters of majestic nations, down to the netherworld
19 with those gone down into the Pit. Are you more pleasant than anyone else?
20 Go down; be laid to rest with the uncircumcised! They will fall among those
slain by the sword; she has been given over to the sword; pull her and her
21 hordes down. From within Sheol, leaders of warriors will say of him and those
who help him, 'They have gone down and lie with the uncircumcised, slain
22 by the sword.' There is Assyria and all her crowds; all around him are his
23 graves; all of them the slain, fallen by the sword, whose graves lie at the far
edge of the Pit; her crowds are around her grave, all of them the slain, fallen
24 by the sword, those who struck terror in the land of the living. There is Eilam,
all her hordes around her grave, all of them the slain, fallen by the sword, who
went down uncircumcised to the netherworld, who spread their terror in the
land of the living and now bear their disgrace with those gone down into the
25 Pit. Among the slain they have made a bed for her with all her hordes; her
graves are all around him, all of them uncircumcised, slain by the sword, for

וְאַתָּה כַּתַּנִּים בַּיַּמִּים וַתָּגַח בְּנַהֲרוֹתֶיךָ וַתִּדְלַח־מַיִם בְּרַגְלֶיךָ וַתִּרְפֹּס
ג נַהֲרוֹתָם: כֹּה אָמַר אֲדֹנָי יֱהֹוִה וּפָרַשְׂתִּי עָלֶיךָ אֶת־רִשְׁתִּי
ד בִּקְהַל עַמִּים רַבִּים וְהֶעֱלוּךָ בְּחֶרְמִי: וּנְטַשְׁתִּיךָ בָאָרֶץ עַל־פְּנֵי הַשָּׂדֶה
אֲטִילֶךָ וְהִשְׁכַּנְתִּי עָלֶיךָ כָּל־עוֹף הַשָּׁמַיִם וְהִשְׂבַּעְתִּי מִמְּךָ חַיַּת כָּל־
ה הָאָרֶץ: וְנָתַתִּי אֶת־בְּשָׂרְךָ עַל־הֶהָרִים וּמִלֵּאתִי הַגֵּאָיוֹת רָמוּתֶךָ:
ו וְהִשְׁקֵיתִי אֶרֶץ צָפָתְךָ מִדָּמְךָ אֶל־הֶהָרִים וַאֲפִקִים יִמָּלְאוּן מִמֶּךָּ:
ז וְכִסֵּיתִי בְכַבּוֹתְךָ שָׁמַיִם וְהִקְדַּרְתִּי אֶת־כֹּכְבֵיהֶם שֶׁמֶשׁ בֶּעָנָן אֲכַסֶּנּוּ
ח וְיָרֵחַ לֹא־יָאִיר אוֹרוֹ: כָּל־מְאוֹרֵי אוֹר בַּשָּׁמַיִם אַקְדִּירֵם עָלֶיךָ וְנָתַתִּי
ט חֹשֶׁךְ עַל־אַרְצְךָ נְאֻם אֲדֹנָי יֱהֹוִה: וְהִכְעַסְתִּי לֵב עַמִּים רַבִּים בַּהֲבִיאִי
י שִׁבְרְךָ בַּגּוֹיִם עַל־אֲרָצוֹת אֲשֶׁר לֹא־יְדַעְתָּם: וַהֲשִׁמּוֹתִי עָלֶיךָ עַמִּים
רַבִּים וּמַלְכֵיהֶם יִשְׂעֲרוּ עָלֶיךָ שַׂעַר בְּעוֹפְפִי חַרְבִּי עַל־פְּנֵיהֶם וְחָרְדוּ
יא לִרְגָעִים אִישׁ לְנַפְשׁוֹ בְּיוֹם מַפַּלְתֶּךָ: כִּי כֹה אָמַר אֲדֹנָי יֱהֹוִה
יב חֶרֶב מֶלֶךְ־בָּבֶל תְּבוֹאֶךָ: בְּחַרְבוֹת גִּבּוֹרִים אַפִּיל הֲמוֹנֶךָ עָרִיצֵי גוֹיִם
יג כֻּלָּם וְשָׁדְדוּ אֶת־גְּאוֹן מִצְרַיִם וְנִשְׁמַד כָּל־הֲמוֹנָהּ: וְהַאֲבַדְתִּי אֶת־
כָּל־בְּהֶמְתָּהּ מֵעַל מַיִם רַבִּים וְלֹא תִדְלָחֵם רֶגֶל־אָדָם עוֹד וּפַרְסוֹת
יד בְּהֵמָה לֹא תִדְלָחֵם: אָז אַשְׁקִיעַ מֵימֵיהֶם וְנַהֲרוֹתָם כַּשֶּׁמֶן אוֹלִיךְ נְאֻם
טו אֲדֹנָי יֱהֹוִה: בְּתִתִּי אֶת־אֶרֶץ מִצְרַיִם שְׁמָמָה וּנְשַׁמָּה אֶרֶץ מִמְּלֹאָהּ
טז בְּהַכּוֹתִי אֶת־כָּל־יוֹשְׁבֵי בָהּ וְיָדְעוּ כִּי־אֲנִי יְהוָה: קִינָה הִיא וְקוֹנְנוּהָ
בְּנוֹת הַגּוֹיִם תְּקוֹנֵנָּה אוֹתָהּ עַל־מִצְרַיִם וְעַל־כָּל־הֲמוֹנָהּ תְּקוֹנֵנָּה
אוֹתָהּ נְאֻם אֲדֹנָי יֱהֹוִה:

יז וַיְהִי בִּשְׁתֵּי עֶשְׂרֵה שָׁנָה בַּחֲמִשָּׁה עָשָׂר לַחֹדֶשׁ הָיָה דְבַר־יְהוָה אֵלַי
יח לֵאמֹר: בֶּן־אָדָם נְהֵה עַל־הֲמוֹן מִצְרַיִם וְהוֹרִדֵהוּ אוֹתָהּ וּבְנוֹת גּוֹיִם
יט אַדִּרִם אֶל־אֶרֶץ תַּחְתִּיּוֹת אֶת־יוֹרְדֵי בוֹר: מִמִּי נָעָמְתְּ רְדָה וְהָשְׁכְּבָה
כ אֶת־עֲרֵלִים: בְּתוֹךְ חַלְלֵי־חֶרֶב יִפֹּלוּ חֶרֶב נִתָּנָה מָשְׁכוּ אוֹתָהּ וְכָל־
כא הֲמוֹנֶיהָ: יְדַבְּרוּ־לוֹ אֵלֵי גִבּוֹרִים מִתּוֹךְ שְׁאוֹל אֶת־עֹזְרָיו יָרְדוּ שָׁכְבוּ
כב הָעֲרֵלִים חַלְלֵי־חָרֶב: שָׁם אַשּׁוּר וְכָל־קְהָלָהּ סְבִיבוֹתָיו קִבְרֹתָיו כֻּלָּם
כג חֲלָלִים הַנֹּפְלִים בֶּחָרֶב: אֲשֶׁר נִתְּנוּ קִבְרֹתֶיהָ בְּיַרְכְּתֵי־בוֹר וַיְהִי קְהָלָהּ
סְבִיבוֹת קְבֻרָתָהּ כֻּלָּם חֲלָלִים נֹפְלִים בַּחֶרֶב אֲשֶׁר־נָתְנוּ חִתִּית בְּאֶרֶץ
כד חַיִּים: שָׁם עֵילָם וְכָל־הֲמוֹנָהּ סְבִיבוֹת קְבֻרָתָהּ כֻּלָּם חֲלָלִים הַנֹּפְלִים
בַּחֶרֶב אֲשֶׁר־יָרְדוּ עֲרֵלִים ׀ אֶל־אֶרֶץ תַּחְתִּיּוֹת אֲשֶׁר נָתְנוּ חִתִּיתָם
כה בְּאֶרֶץ חַיִּים וַיִּשְׂאוּ כְלִמָּתָם אֶת־יוֹרְדֵי בוֹר: בְּתוֹךְ חֲלָלִים נָתְנוּ מִשְׁכָּב
לָהּ בְּכָל־הֲמוֹנָהּ סְבִיבוֹתָיו קִבְרֹתֶהָ כֻּלָּם עֲרֵלִים חַלְלֵי־חֶרֶב כִּי־נִתַּן

though their terror spread through the land of the living, they now bear their
26 disgrace, placed among the slain with those gone down into the Pit. There is
Meshekh and Tuval and all her horde; her graves are all around him, all of
them uncircumcised, pierced by the sword, though they spread their terror
27 in the land of the living. They do not lie with warriors felled by the uncircumcised, who went down to Sheol with their weapons of war, their swords placed
beneath their heads; their sins are upon their bones, for terror of the mighty
28 was in the land of the living. But you: among the uncircumcised you will be
29 broken, and you will lie with those slain by the sword. There is Edom, her
kings and all her princes, who, for all their might, are placed with those slain
by the sword; they will lie with the uncircumcised and those gone down into
30 the Pit. There are all the princes of the north and all the Sidonians, who went
down with the slain, shamed despite the terror caused by their might, lying
uncircumcised with those slain by the sword, bearing their disgrace with
31 those gone down into the Pit. Pharaoh will see them and be comforted for
all his hordes, Pharaoh and all his army, slain by the sword, declares the Lord
32 God. For I have spread terror of Me through the land of the living: he will be
laid among the uncircumcised with those slain by the sword – Pharaoh and
33 1 all his hordes, declares the Lord God." The word of the Lord
2 came to me:[36] "Man, speak to your people; say to them: When I bring the
sword upon a land, and the people of that land choose a man from among
3 them and appoint him as watchman for them, and he sees the sword bearing
4 down on the land, and he sounds the horn and warns the people, if someone
hears the sound of this horn and does not heed the warning, and the sword
5 comes and claims him – his blood is on his own head. He heard the sound
of the horn and did not heed the warning; he is to blame for his blood: had
6 he taken heed of the warning, his life would have been saved. The watchman
who sees the sword coming but does not sound the horn, so that the people
are not warned – if the sword comes and claims one of them, that person's
life has been claimed for his own iniquity, but I will seek redress for his blood
7 from the hand of the watchman. Man, I have made you the
watchman of the House of Israel; when you hear word from My mouth, give
8 them warning from Me. If I say to the wicked, 'Wicked man, you will surely
die,' but you do not speak out to warn the wicked one from his course – that
wicked man will die for his iniquity, but I will seek redress for his blood from
9 your hands. But if you warn the wicked man to turn from his course and he
still does not turn from it – he will die for his iniquity, but you will have saved
10 your own life. You, Man, say to the House of Israel: You have all
been saying, 'Our sins and iniquities are upon us; we are wasting away in
11 them; how can we live?' Say to them: Surely as I live, declares the Lord God,
I do not desire the death of the wicked one but that he should turn from his
course and live – turn, return from your evil ways! Why should you die,
12 House of Israel? You, Man, say to your people: The righteous
person's righteousness will not save him on the day he transgresses; the

36 | Verses 1–20 here are a longer version of the prophecy of the watchman, which appears in 3:17–21.

חִתִּיתָם בְּאֶרֶץ חַיִּים וַיִּשְׂאוּ כְלִמָּתָם אֶת־יוֹרְדֵי בוֹר בְּתוֹךְ חֲלָלִים
כו נִתָּן׃ שָׁם מֶשֶׁךְ תֻּבַל וְכָל־הֲמוֹנָהּ סְבִיבוֹתָיו קִבְרוֹתֶיהָ כֻּלָּם עֲרֵלִים
כז מְחֻלְלֵי חֶרֶב כִּי־נָתְנוּ חִתִּיתָם בְּאֶרֶץ חַיִּים׃ וְלֹא יִשְׁכְּבוּ אֶת־גִּבּוֹרִים
נֹפְלִים מֵעֲרֵלִים אֲשֶׁר יָרְדוּ־שְׁאוֹל בִּכְלֵי־מִלְחַמְתָּם וַיִּתְּנוּ אֶת־
חַרְבוֹתָם תַּחַת רָאשֵׁיהֶם וַתְּהִי עֲוֺנֹתָם עַל־עַצְמוֹתָם כִּי־חִתִּית גִּבּוֹרִים
כח בְּאֶרֶץ חַיִּים׃ וְאַתָּה בְּתוֹךְ עֲרֵלִים תִּשָּׁבַר וְתִשְׁכַּב אֶת־חַלְלֵי־חָרֶב׃
כט שָׁמָּה אֱדוֹם מְלָכֶיהָ וְכָל־נְשִׂיאֶיהָ אֲשֶׁר־נִתְּנוּ בִגְבוּרָתָם אֶת־חַלְלֵי־
ל חָרֶב הֵמָּה אֶת־עֲרֵלִים יִשְׁכָּבוּ וְאֶת־יֹרְדֵי בוֹר׃ שָׁמָּה נְסִיכֵי צָפוֹן כֻּלָּם
וְכָל־צִדֹנִי אֲשֶׁר־יָרְדוּ אֶת־חֲלָלִים בְּחִתִּיתָם מִגְּבוּרָתָם בּוֹשִׁים וַיִּשְׁכְּבוּ
לא עֲרֵלִים אֶת־חַלְלֵי־חֶרֶב וַיִּשְׂאוּ כְלִמָּתָם אֶת־יוֹרְדֵי בוֹר׃ אוֹתָם יִרְאֶה
פַרְעֹה וְנִחַם עַל־כָּל־הֲמוֹנֹה חַלְלֵי־חֶרֶב פַּרְעֹה וְכָל־חֵילוֹ נְאֻם אֲדֹנָי
לב יֱהוִה׃ כִּי־נָתַתִּי אֶת־חתיתו בְּאֶרֶץ חַיִּים וְהֻשְׁכַּב בְּתוֹךְ עֲרֵלִים אֶת־ חִתִּיתִי
לג א חַלְלֵי־חֶרֶב פַּרְעֹה וְכָל־הֲמוֹנֹה נְאֻם אֲדֹנָי יֱהוִה׃ וַיְהִי
ב דְבַר־יְהוָה אֵלַי לֵאמֹר׃ בֶּן־אָדָם דַּבֵּר אֶל־בְּנֵי־עַמְּךָ וְאָמַרְתָּ אֲלֵיהֶם
אֶרֶץ כִּי־אָבִיא עָלֶיהָ חָרֶב וְלָקְחוּ עַם־הָאָרֶץ אִישׁ אֶחָד מִקְצֵיהֶם וְנָתְנוּ
ג אֹתוֹ לָהֶם לְצֹפֶה׃ וְרָאָה אֶת־הַחֶרֶב בָּאָה עַל־הָאָרֶץ וְתָקַע בַּשּׁוֹפָר
ד וְהִזְהִיר אֶת־הָעָם׃ וְשָׁמַע הַשֹּׁמֵעַ אֶת־קוֹל הַשּׁוֹפָר וְלֹא נִזְהָר וַתָּבוֹא
ה חֶרֶב וַתִּקָּחֵהוּ דָּמוֹ בְרֹאשׁוֹ יִהְיֶה׃ אֵת קוֹל הַשּׁוֹפָר שָׁמַע וְלֹא נִזְהָר
ו דָּמוֹ בּוֹ יִהְיֶה וְהוּא נִזְהָר נַפְשׁוֹ מִלֵּט׃ וְהַצֹּפֶה כִּי־יִרְאֶה אֶת־הַחֶרֶב
בָּאָה וְלֹא־תָקַע בַּשּׁוֹפָר וְהָעָם לֹא־נִזְהָר וַתָּבוֹא חֶרֶב וַתִּקַּח מֵהֶם נָפֶשׁ
ז הוּא בַּעֲוֺנוֹ נִלְקָח וְדָמוֹ מִיַּד־הַצֹּפֶה אֶדְרֹשׁ׃ וְאַתָּה בֶן־אָדָם
צֹפֶה נְתַתִּיךָ לְבֵית יִשְׂרָאֵל וְשָׁמַעְתָּ מִפִּי דָּבָר וְהִזְהַרְתָּ אֹתָם מִמֶּנִּי׃
ח בְּאָמְרִי לָרָשָׁע רָשָׁע מוֹת תָּמוּת וְלֹא דִבַּרְתָּ לְהַזְהִיר רָשָׁע מִדַּרְכּוֹ
ט הוּא רָשָׁע בַּעֲוֺנוֹ יָמוּת וְדָמוֹ מִיָּדְךָ אֲבַקֵּשׁ׃ וְאַתָּה כִּי־הִזְהַרְתָּ רָשָׁע
מִדַּרְכּוֹ לָשׁוּב מִמֶּנָּה וְלֹא־שָׁב מִדַּרְכּוֹ הוּא בַּעֲוֺנוֹ יָמוּת וְאַתָּה נַפְשְׁךָ
י הִצַּלְתָּ׃ וְאַתָּה בֶן־אָדָם אֱמֹר אֶל־בֵּית יִשְׂרָאֵל כֵּן
אֲמַרְתֶּם לֵאמֹר כִּי־פְשָׁעֵינוּ וְחַטֹּאתֵינוּ עָלֵינוּ וּבָם אֲנַחְנוּ נְמַקִּים וְאֵיךְ
יא נִחְיֶה׃ אֱמֹר אֲלֵיהֶם חַי־אָנִי ׀ נְאֻם ׀ אֲדֹנָי יֱהוִה אִם־אֶחְפֹּץ בְּמוֹת
הָרָשָׁע כִּי אִם־בְּשׁוּב רָשָׁע מִדַּרְכּוֹ וְחָיָה שׁוּבוּ שׁוּבוּ מִדַּרְכֵיכֶם הָרָעִים
יב וְלָמָּה תָמוּתוּ בֵּית יִשְׂרָאֵל׃ וְאַתָּה בֶן־אָדָם אֱמֹר אֶל־בְּנֵי־
עַמְּךָ צִדְקַת הַצַּדִּיק לֹא תַצִּילֶנּוּ בְּיוֹם פִּשְׁעוֹ וְרִשְׁעַת הָרָשָׁע לֹא־יִכָּשֶׁל

wicked person's wickedness – he will not stumble over it on the day he turns
away from his wickedness; the righteous person will not be able to live by his
13 righteousness on the day he sins. If I say to the righteous person, 'You will
surely live,' but he relies on his righteousness and does wrong, then of all his
righteousness, none of it will be remembered, and through the iniquity he
14 has done he will die. If I say to the wicked person, 'You will surely die,' and
15 he turns from his sin and does what is right and just – the wicked person
restores a pledge, pays back what he has stolen, and follows the laws of life,
16 doing no wrong – he will surely live; he will not die. All his sins that he
committed will not be remembered of him if he does what is just and right:
17 he will surely live. Your people say, 'The way of the Lord is not fair,' but
18 it is their ways that are not fair! When the righteous man turns from his
19 righteousness and does wrong, he will die for it; when the wicked man turns
from his wickedness and does that which is just and right, by virtue of these
20 deeds will he live. You have all said, 'The way of the Lord is not fair,' but I will
21 judge you, each man according to his ways, House of Israel." It was
in the twelfth year of our exile in the tenth month on the fifth of the month
that a fugitive came to me from Jerusalem and said, "The city has been taken."
22 The hand of the LORD had been upon me the evening before the fugitive
arrived and had opened my mouth by the time he came to me in the morning;
23 my mouth was opened; I was no longer struck silent.[37] The word of
24 the LORD came to me: "Man, the inhabitants of these ruins on the soil of
Israel say, 'Avraham was one person, and he inherited the land; we are many,
25 and to us the land has been given as a possession.'[38] So say to them:
So says the Lord GOD: You eat with the blood, you lift your eyes up to your
26 idols, you shed blood – and you would inherit the land? You stood by your
sword, you practiced abominations, each of you defiled others' wives – and
27 you would inherit the land? So you will say to them: So says the Lord GOD:
As I live, those who are in the ruins will fall by the sword; those who are in
the open field I will give over to animals as food; those who are in strongholds
28 and caves will die by plague. I will hand the land over to waste and desolation,
the majesty of her power will cease to be, the mountains of Israel will be
29 desolate, none will pass through, and they will know that I am the LORD when
I hand the land over to waste and desolation because of all the abominations
30 they practiced. As for you, Man, your people who speak of you by
the walls and in the entrances of houses, who speak with one another, with
31 each other, saying, 'Come and hear what word has come from the LORD,'
they come to you as a gathering of people, and they sit before you – My
people – and hear your words, but they do not perform them; they turn them
into lustful talk in their mouths while their hearts pursue their own gains.
32 To them you are like a singer of lustful songs with a lovely voice, playing
33 music with skill; they hear your words but perform none of them. When
it comes – see, it is coming – they will know that a prophet was in their

37 | See 3:22–27 and 24:27.

38 | This statement is attributed to those who remained in the land after the exile.

בָּהּ בְּיוֹם שׁוּבוֹ מֵרִשְׁעוֹ וְצַדִּיק לֹא יוּכַל לִחְיוֹת בָּהּ בְּיוֹם חֲטֹאתוֹ׃
יג בְּאָמְרִי לַצַּדִּיק חָיֹה יִחְיֶה וְהוּא־בָטַח עַל־צִדְקָתוֹ וְעָשָׂה עָוֶל כָּל־
יד צִדְקֹתָו לֹא תִזָּכַרְנָה וּבְעַוְלוֹ אֲשֶׁר־עָשָׂה בּוֹ יָמוּת׃ וּבְאָמְרִי לָרָשָׁע
טו מוֹת תָּמוּת וְשָׁב מֵחַטָּאתוֹ וְעָשָׂה מִשְׁפָּט וּצְדָקָה׃ חֲבֹל יָשִׁיב רָשָׁע
גְּזֵלָה יְשַׁלֵּם בְּחֻקּוֹת הַחַיִּים הָלַךְ לְבִלְתִּי עֲשׂוֹת עָוֶל חָיוֹ יִחְיֶה לֹא
טז יָמוּת׃ כָּל־חַטֹּאתָו אֲשֶׁר חָטָא לֹא תִזָּכַרְנָה לוֹ מִשְׁפָּט וּצְדָקָה עָשָׂה כ
יז חָיוֹ יִחְיֶה׃ וְאָמְרוּ בְּנֵי עַמְּךָ לֹא יִתָּכֵן דֶּרֶךְ אֲדֹנָי וְהֵמָּה דַּרְכָּם לֹא־יִתָּכֵן׃
יח יט בְּשׁוּב־צַדִּיק מִצִּדְקָתוֹ וְעָשָׂה עָוֶל וּמֵת בָּהֶם׃ וּבְשׁוּב רָשָׁע מֵרִשְׁעָתוֹ
כ וְעָשָׂה מִשְׁפָּט וּצְדָקָה עֲלֵיהֶם הוּא יִחְיֶה׃ וַאֲמַרְתֶּם לֹא יִתָּכֵן דֶּרֶךְ
כא אֲדֹנָי אִישׁ כִּדְרָכָיו אֶשְׁפּוֹט אֶתְכֶם בֵּית יִשְׂרָאֵל׃ וַיְהִי
בִּשְׁתֵּי עֶשְׂרֵה שָׁנָה בָּעֲשִׂרִי בַּחֲמִשָּׁה לַחֹדֶשׁ לְגָלוּתֵנוּ בָּא־אֵלַי הַפָּלִיט
כב מִירוּשָׁלַםִ לֵאמֹר הֻכְּתָה הָעִיר׃ וְיַד־יהוה הָיְתָה אֵלַי בָּעֶרֶב לִפְנֵי בּוֹא
הַפָּלִיט וַיִּפְתַּח אֶת־פִּי עַד־בּוֹא אֵלַי בַּבֹּקֶר וַיִּפָּתַח פִּי וְלֹא נֶאֱלַמְתִּי
כג כד עוֹד׃ וַיְהִי דְבַר־יהוה אֵלַי לֵאמֹר׃ בֶּן־אָדָם יֹשְׁבֵי הֶחֳרָבוֹת
הָאֵלֶּה עַל־אַדְמַת יִשְׂרָאֵל אֹמְרִים לֵאמֹר אֶחָד הָיָה אַבְרָהָם וַיִּירַשׁ
כה אֶת־הָאָרֶץ וַאֲנַחְנוּ רַבִּים לָנוּ נִתְּנָה הָאָרֶץ לְמוֹרָשָׁה׃ לָכֵן
אֱמֹר אֲלֵיהֶם כֹּה־אָמַר ׀ אֲדֹנָי יֱהוִה עַל־הַדָּם ׀ תֹּאכֵלוּ וְעֵינֵכֶם תִּשְׂאוּ
כו אֶל־גִּלּוּלֵיכֶם וְדָם תִּשְׁפֹּכוּ וְהָאָרֶץ תִּירָשׁוּ׃ עֲמַדְתֶּם עַל־חַרְבְּכֶם עֲשִׂיתֶן
כז תּוֹעֵבָה וְאִישׁ אֶת־אֵשֶׁת רֵעֵהוּ טִמֵּאתֶם וְהָאָרֶץ תִּירָשׁוּ׃ כֹּה־תֹאמַר
אֲלֵהֶם כֹּה־אָמַר אֲדֹנָי יהוה חַי־אָנִי אִם־לֹא אֲשֶׁר בֶּחֳרָבוֹת בַּחֶרֶב יִפֹּלוּ
וַאֲשֶׁר עַל־פְּנֵי הַשָּׂדֶה לַחַיָּה נְתַתִּיו לְאָכְלוֹ וַאֲשֶׁר בַּמְּצָדוֹת וּבַמְּעָרוֹת
כח בַּדֶּבֶר יָמוּתוּ׃ וְנָתַתִּי אֶת־הָאָרֶץ שְׁמָמָה וּמְשַׁמָּה וְנִשְׁבַּת גְּאוֹן עֻזָּהּ
כט וְשָׁמְמוּ הָרֵי יִשְׂרָאֵל מֵאֵין עוֹבֵר׃ וְיָדְעוּ כִּי־אֲנִי יהוה בְּתִתִּי אֶת־הָאָרֶץ
ל שְׁמָמָה וּמְשַׁמָּה עַל כָּל־תּוֹעֲבֹתָם אֲשֶׁר עָשׂוּ׃ וְאַתָּה
בֶן־אָדָם בְּנֵי עַמְּךָ הַנִּדְבָּרִים בְּךָ אֵצֶל הַקִּירוֹת וּבְפִתְחֵי הַבָּתִּים וְדִבֶּר־
חַד אֶת־אַחַד אִישׁ אֶת־אָחִיו לֵאמֹר בֹּאוּ־נָא וְשִׁמְעוּ מָה הַדָּבָר הַיּוֹצֵא
לא מֵאֵת יהוה׃ וְיָבוֹאוּ אֵלֶיךָ כִּמְבוֹא־עָם וְיֵשְׁבוּ לְפָנֶיךָ עַמִּי וְשָׁמְעוּ אֶת־
דְּבָרֶיךָ וְאוֹתָם לֹא יַעֲשׂוּ כִּי־עֲגָבִים בְּפִיהֶם הֵמָּה עֹשִׂים אַחֲרֵי בִצְעָם
לב לִבָּם הֹלֵךְ׃ וְהִנְּךָ לָהֶם כְּשִׁיר עֲגָבִים יְפֵה קוֹל וּמֵטִב נַגֵּן וְשָׁמְעוּ אֶת־
לג דְּבָרֶיךָ וְעֹשִׂים אֵינָם אוֹתָם׃ וּבְבֹאָהּ הִנֵּה בָאָה וְיָדְעוּ כִּי נָבִיא הָיָה

34 1 midst." The word of the LORD came to me: "Man, prophesy
2 against the shepherds of Israel;[39] prophesy and say to them, to the shepherds:
So says the Lord GOD: Woe, shepherds of Israel who have been tending
3 themselves when surely it is the sheep the shepherds should tend. You ate
the fat, you wore the wool, and you slaughtered the fattest, but you did not
4 tend the sheep: you did not strengthen the weak, you did not nurse the sick,
you did not bind the broken, you did not recover the stray, and you did not
5 search for the lost; you ruled over them with force and with harshness. They
scattered, for they had no shepherd; they became food for every animal of
6 the field and scattered. My sheep are wandering upon all the mountains, all
the high hills; My sheep have scattered over the face of the earth; no one
7 searches for them; no one seeks them out. So, shepherds, listen to the word
8 of the LORD: Surely as I live, declares the Lord GOD, because My sheep were
spoils, My sheep became the food of every animal of the field for want of a
shepherd, and because My shepherds did not search for My sheep but tended
9 themselves and did not tend My sheep, so, shepherds, listen to the word of
10 the LORD: So says the Lord GOD: Behold, I am coming down upon
the shepherds; I will seek redress for My sheep from their hands and put an
end to their shepherding; no more will the shepherds tend themselves; I will
11 save My sheep from their mouths; it will not be their food. For so
says the Lord GOD: Behold, it is I; I will search for My sheep and care for
12 them; just as a shepherd cares for his flock when he is among his sheep who
have dispersed, so will I care for My sheep. I will save them from all the
13 places they have been scattered on a day of heavy cloud, thick fog. I will take
them out from the nations; I will gather them in from the lands and bring
them to their soil. I will tend them on the mountains of Israel, in the ravines,
14 in all the settled parts of the land. I will tend them on good grazing-land; the
high hills of Israel will be their pasture; there will they lie down on lush
15 pasture; they will graze on rich grazing-land in the hills of Israel. I Myself will
16 tend My sheep: I will lay them down, declares the Lord GOD; I will seek the
lost, I will recover the stray, I will bind the broken, I will strengthen the sick,
17 but the robust, the strong, I will destroy; I will tend them with justice. As for
you, My sheep, so says the Lord GOD: Behold that I will judge between one
18 sheep and another, rams and he-goats. Is it not enough for you to graze on
good grazing-land; must your feet trample the rest of your grazing-land? And
19 when you drink clear waters, must you muddy the rest with your feet? My
sheep graze on what has been trampled by your feet and drink from what has
20 been muddied by your feet. So the Lord GOD says this to them:
21 Behold, it is I – I will judge between the fat sheep and the thin sheep. Because
you pushed with flank and shoulder and rammed all the weak with your horns
22 until you scattered them, I will save My sheep; they will no longer be spoils;

39 | Verses 1–16 are directed against the pre-exilic kings of Israel, referred to metaphorically as shepherds.

לד א ב בְּתוֹכָם׃ וַיְהִי דְבַר־יְהוָה אֵלַי לֵאמֹר׃ בֶּן־אָדָם הִנָּבֵא
עַל־רוֹעֵי יִשְׂרָאֵל הִנָּבֵא וְאָמַרְתָּ אֲלֵיהֶם לָרֹעִים כֹּה אָמַר ׀ אֲדֹנָי יֱהוִה
הוֹי רֹעֵי יִשְׂרָאֵל אֲשֶׁר הָיוּ רֹעִים אוֹתָם הֲלוֹא הַצֹּאן יִרְעוּ הָרֹעִים׃
ג אֶת־הַחֵלֶב תֹּאכֵלוּ וְאֶת־הַצֶּמֶר תִּלְבָּשׁוּ הַבְּרִיאָה תִּזְבָּחוּ הַצֹּאן לֹא
ד תִרְעוּ׃ אֶת־הַנַּחְלוֹת לֹא חִזַּקְתֶּם וְאֶת־הַחוֹלָה לֹא־רִפֵּאתֶם וְלַנִּשְׁבֶּרֶת
לֹא חֲבַשְׁתֶּם וְאֶת־הַנִּדַּחַת לֹא הֲשֵׁבֹתֶם וְאֶת־הָאֹבֶדֶת לֹא בִקַּשְׁתֶּם
ה וּבְחָזְקָה רְדִיתֶם אֹתָם וּבְפָרֶךְ׃ וַתְּפוּצֶינָה מִבְּלִי רֹעֶה וַתִּהְיֶינָה לְאָכְלָה
ו לְכָל־חַיַּת הַשָּׂדֶה וַתְּפוּצֶינָה׃ יִשְׁגּוּ צֹאנִי בְּכָל־הֶהָרִים וְעַל כָּל־גִּבְעָה
ז רָמָה וְעַל כָּל־פְּנֵי הָאָרֶץ נָפֹצוּ צֹאנִי וְאֵין דּוֹרֵשׁ וְאֵין מְבַקֵּשׁ׃ לָכֵן
ח רֹעִים שִׁמְעוּ אֶת־דְּבַר יְהוָה׃ חַי־אָנִי נְאֻם ׀ אֲדֹנָי יֱהוִה אִם־לֹא יַעַן
הֱיוֹת־צֹאנִי ׀ לָבַז וַתִּהְיֶינָה צֹאנִי לְאָכְלָה לְכָל־חַיַּת הַשָּׂדֶה מֵאֵין רֹעֶה
וְלֹא־דָרְשׁוּ רֹעַי אֶת־צֹאנִי וַיִּרְעוּ הָרֹעִים אוֹתָם וְאֶת־צֹאנִי לֹא רָעוּ׃
ט י לָכֵן הָרֹעִים שִׁמְעוּ דְּבַר־יְהוָה׃ כֹּה־אָמַר אֲדֹנָי יֱהוִה
הִנְנִי אֶל־הָרֹעִים וְדָרַשְׁתִּי אֶת־צֹאנִי מִיָּדָם וְהִשְׁבַּתִּים מֵרְעוֹת צֹאן
וְלֹא־יִרְעוּ עוֹד הָרֹעִים אוֹתָם וְהִצַּלְתִּי צֹאנִי מִפִּיהֶם וְלֹא־תִהְיֶיןָ
יא לָהֶם לְאָכְלָה׃ כִּי כֹּה אָמַר אֲדֹנָי יֱהוִה הִנְנִי־אָנִי
יב וְדָרַשְׁתִּי אֶת־צֹאנִי וּבִקַּרְתִּים׃ כְּבַקָּרַת רֹעֶה עֶדְרוֹ בְּיוֹם־הֱיוֹתוֹ בְתוֹךְ־
צֹאנוֹ נִפְרָשׁוֹת כֵּן אֲבַקֵּר אֶת־צֹאנִי וְהִצַּלְתִּי אֶתְהֶם מִכָּל־הַמְּקוֹמֹת
יג אֲשֶׁר נָפֹצוּ שָׁם בְּיוֹם עָנָן וַעֲרָפֶל׃ וְהוֹצֵאתִים מִן־הָעַמִּים וְקִבַּצְתִּים
מִן־הָאֲרָצוֹת וַהֲבִיאֹתִים אֶל־אַדְמָתָם וּרְעִיתִים אֶל־הָרֵי יִשְׂרָאֵל
יד בָּאֲפִיקִים וּבְכֹל מוֹשְׁבֵי הָאָרֶץ׃ בְּמִרְעֶה־טּוֹב אֶרְעֶה אֹתָם וּבְהָרֵי
מְרוֹם־יִשְׂרָאֵל יִהְיֶה נְוֵהֶם שָׁם תִּרְבַּצְנָה בְּנָוֶה טּוֹב וּמִרְעֶה שָׁמֵן תִּרְעֶינָה
טו אֶל־הָרֵי יִשְׂרָאֵל׃ אֲנִי אֶרְעֶה צֹאנִי וַאֲנִי אַרְבִּיצֵם נְאֻם אֲדֹנָי יֱהוִה׃
טז אֶת־הָאֹבֶדֶת אֲבַקֵּשׁ וְאֶת־הַנִּדַּחַת אָשִׁיב וְלַנִּשְׁבֶּרֶת אֶחֱבֹשׁ וְאֶת־
הַחוֹלָה אֲחַזֵּק וְאֶת־הַשְּׁמֵנָה וְאֶת־הַחֲזָקָה אַשְׁמִיד אֶרְעֶנָּה בְמִשְׁפָּט׃
יז וְאַתֵּנָה צֹאנִי כֹּה אָמַר אֲדֹנָי יֱהוִה הִנְנִי שֹׁפֵט בֵּין־שֶׂה לָשֶׂה לָאֵילִים
יח וְלָעַתּוּדִים׃ הַמְעַט מִכֶּם הַמִּרְעֶה הַטּוֹב תִּרְעוּ וְיֶתֶר מִרְעֵיכֶם תִּרְמְסוּ
יט בְּרַגְלֵיכֶם וּמִשְׁקַע־מַיִם תִּשְׁתּוּ וְאֵת הַנּוֹתָרִים בְּרַגְלֵיכֶם תִּרְפֹּשׂוּן׃ וְצֹאנִי
כ מִרְמַס רַגְלֵיכֶם תִּרְעֶינָה וּמִרְפַּשׂ רַגְלֵיכֶם תִּשְׁתֶּינָה׃ לָכֵן
כֹּה אָמַר אֲדֹנָי יֱהוִה אֲלֵיהֶם הִנְנִי־אָנִי וְשָׁפַטְתִּי בֵּין־שֶׂה בִרְיָה וּבֵין
כא שֶׂה רָזָה׃ יַעַן בְּצַד וּבְכָתֵף תֶּהְדֹּפוּ וּבְקַרְנֵיכֶם תְּנַגְּחוּ כָּל־הַנַּחְלוֹת עַד
כב אֲשֶׁר הֲפִיצוֹתֶם אוֹתָנָה אֶל־הַחוּצָה׃ וְהוֹשַׁעְתִּי לְצֹאנִי וְלֹא־תִהְיֶינָה

23 I will judge between one sheep and another. I will establish over them one
single shepherd who will tend them; My servant, David, he will tend them;
24 he will be a shepherd to them; I, the LORD, will be their God, and My servant
25 David will be prince among them; I, the LORD, have spoken. I will make a
covenant of peace with them, I will rid the land of wild animals, and even in
26 the wilderness they will live securely and sleep in the forests. I will make them
and all around My hill a blessing; I will make rain fall at its right time – they
27 will be blessed rains; the trees of the field will bear their fruit, and the land
will yield its produce. They will be secure upon their soil, and they will know
that I am the LORD when I break the bars of their yoke and save them from
28 those who enslave them. They will no longer be spoils for the nations; the
animals of the land will not eat them; they will live securely and without fear.
29 I will establish for them a planting of renown; they will no longer be claimed
30 by famine in the land; they will no longer bear the insults of the nations, and
they will know that I, the LORD their God, I am with them, and that they,
31 the House of Israel, are My people, declares the Lord GOD. You, My sheep,
sheep of My tending, are people, and I am your God, declares the Lord
35 1 2 GOD." The word of the LORD came to me: "Man, set your face
3 against Mount Se'ir and prophesy against it; say to it: So says the Lord GOD:
Behold, I am coming down upon you, Mount Se'ir; I will stretch My hand
4 out over you and turn you into waste, desolation. I will make your cities ruins,
5 you will be desolate; you will know that I am the LORD. Because you have
displayed an endless enmity and delivered the Israelites up to the sword at
6 the time of their ruin,[40] at the time of final punishment, so, as I live, declares
the Lord GOD: I will turn you to blood and blood will pursue you; as you did
7 not hate bloodshed, blood will pursue you. I will turn Mount Se'ir over to
8 complete desolation and cut off from it those who come and go. I will fill its
mountains with its slain; your hills, your valleys, all your ravines – those slain
9 by the sword will fall into them. I will turn you over to perpetual desolation;
10 your cities will not be reinhabited, and you will know: I am the LORD. Because
you said, 'The two nations and the two lands will be mine; we will possess
11 it,' and the LORD was there, so, as I live, declares the Lord GOD, I will act
according to the anger and the jealousy with which you acted because of your
hatred of them; I will make Myself known among them when I judge you.
12 You will know that I am the LORD. I have heard all your abuse that you uttered
against the mountains of Israel, saying, 'They are desolate; they have been
13 given to us to consume.' You opened your mouths wide against Me; you
14 multiplied your words against Me – I have heard it. So says the
15 Lord GOD: As the entire earth rejoices, I will make you desolate. Just as you
rejoiced when the heritage of the House of Israel was made desolate, so will
I do to you: you will be desolate, Mount Se'ir and the whole of Edom. They
36 1 will know: I am the LORD. And you, Man, prophesy to the mountains
2 of Israel and say: Mountains of Israel, hear the word of the LORD: So says the

40 | See Obadiah and Psalms 137:7.

כג עוֹד לָבַז וְשָׁפַטְתִּי בֵּין שֶׂה לָשֶׂה: וַהֲקִמֹתִי עֲלֵיהֶם רֹעֶה אֶחָד וְרָעָה
כד אֶתְהֶן אֵת עַבְדִּי דָוִיד הוּא יִרְעֶה אֹתָם וְהוּא יִהְיֶה לָהֶן לְרֹעֶה: וַאֲנִי
יְהוָה אֶהְיֶה לָהֶם לֵאלֹהִים וְעַבְדִּי דָוִד נָשִׂיא בְתוֹכָם אֲנִי יְהוָה דִּבַּרְתִּי:
כה וְכָרַתִּי לָהֶם בְּרִית שָׁלוֹם וְהִשְׁבַּתִּי חַיָּה־רָעָה מִן־הָאָרֶץ וְיָשְׁבוּ בַמִּדְבָּר
כו לָבֶטַח וְיָשְׁנוּ ביעורים: וְנָתַתִּי אוֹתָם וּסְבִיבוֹת גִּבְעָתִי בְּרָכָה וְהוֹרַדְתִּי כא בַּיְּעָרִים
כז הַגֶּשֶׁם בְּעִתּוֹ גִּשְׁמֵי בְרָכָה יִהְיוּ: וְנָתַן עֵץ הַשָּׂדֶה אֶת־פִּרְיוֹ וְהָאָרֶץ
תִּתֵּן יְבוּלָהּ וְהָיוּ עַל־אַדְמָתָם לָבֶטַח וְיָדְעוּ כִּי־אֲנִי יְהוָה בְּשִׁבְרִי אֶת־
כח מֹטוֹת עֻלָּם וְהִצַּלְתִּים מִיַּד הָעֹבְדִים בָּהֶם: וְלֹא־יִהְיוּ עוֹד בַּז לַגּוֹיִם
כט וְחַיַּת הָאָרֶץ לֹא תֹאכְלֵם וְיָשְׁבוּ לָבֶטַח וְאֵין מַחֲרִיד: וַהֲקִמֹתִי לָהֶם
מַטָּע לְשֵׁם וְלֹא־יִהְיוּ עוֹד אֲסֻפֵי רָעָב בָּאָרֶץ וְלֹא־יִשְׂאוּ עוֹד כְּלִמַּת
ל הַגּוֹיִם: וְיָדְעוּ כִּי אֲנִי יְהוָה אֱלֹהֵיהֶם אִתָּם וְהֵמָּה עַמִּי בֵּית יִשְׂרָאֵל
לא נְאֻם אֲדֹנָי יֱהוִה: וְאַתֵּן צֹאנִי צֹאן מַרְעִיתִי אָדָם אַתֶּם אֲנִי אֱלֹהֵיכֶם
לה א נְאֻם אֲדֹנָי יֱהוִה: וַיְהִי דְבַר־יְהוָה אֵלַי לֵאמֹר:
ב ג בֶּן־אָדָם שִׂים פָּנֶיךָ עַל־הַר שֵׂעִיר וְהִנָּבֵא עָלָיו: וְאָמַרְתָּ לּוֹ כֹּה אָמַר
אֲדֹנָי יֱהוִה הִנְנִי אֵלֶיךָ הַר־שֵׂעִיר וְנָטִיתִי יָדִי עָלֶיךָ וּנְתַתִּיךָ שְׁמָמָה
ד וּמְשַׁמָּה: עָרֶיךָ חָרְבָּה אָשִׂים וְאַתָּה שְׁמָמָה תִהְיֶה וְיָדַעְתָּ כִּי־אֲנִי
ה יְהוָה: יַעַן הֱיוֹת לְךָ אֵיבַת עוֹלָם וַתַּגֵּר אֶת־בְּנֵי־יִשְׂרָאֵל עַל־יְדֵי־חָרֶב
ו בְּעֵת אֵידָם בְּעֵת עֲוֺן קֵץ: לָכֵן חַי־אָנִי נְאֻם אֲדֹנָי יֱהוִה כִּי־לְדָם אֶעֶשְׂךָ
ז וְדָם יִרְדֲּפֶךָ אִם־לֹא דָם שָׂנֵאתָ וְדָם יִרְדֲּפֶךָ: וְנָתַתִּי אֶת־הַר שֵׂעִיר
ח לְשִׁמְמָה וּשְׁמָמָה וְהִכְרַתִּי מִמֶּנּוּ עֹבֵר וָשָׁב: וּמִלֵּאתִי אֶת־הָרָיו חֲלָלָיו
ט גִּבְעוֹתֶיךָ וְגֵאוֹתֶיךָ וְכָל־אֲפִיקֶיךָ חַלְלֵי־חֶרֶב יִפְּלוּ בָהֶם: שִׁמְמוֹת
י עוֹלָם אֶתֶּנְךָ וְעָרֶיךָ לֹא תישבנה וִידַעְתֶּם כִּי־אֲנִי יְהוָה: יַעַן אֲמָרְךָ תָּשֹׁבְנָה
אֶת־שְׁנֵי הַגּוֹיִם וְאֶת־שְׁתֵּי הָאֲרָצוֹת לִי תִהְיֶינָה וִירַשְׁנוּהָ וַיהוָה שָׁם
יא הָיָה: לָכֵן חַי־אָנִי נְאֻם אֲדֹנָי יֱהוִה וְעָשִׂיתִי כְּאַפְּךָ וּכְקִנְאָתְךָ אֲשֶׁר
יב עָשִׂיתָה מִשִּׂנְאָתֶיךָ בָּם וְנוֹדַעְתִּי בָם כַּאֲשֶׁר אֶשְׁפְּטֶךָ: וְיָדַעְתָּ כִּי
אֲנִי יְהוָה שָׁמַעְתִּי | אֶת־כָּל־נֶאָצוֹתֶיךָ אֲשֶׁר אָמַרְתָּ עַל־הָרֵי יִשְׂרָאֵל
יג לֵאמֹר | שממה לָנוּ נִתְּנוּ לְאָכְלָה: וַתַּגְדִּילוּ עָלַי בְּפִיכֶם וְהַעְתַּרְתֶּם שָׁמֵמוּ
יד עָלַי דִּבְרֵיכֶם אֲנִי שָׁמָעְתִּי: כֹּה אָמַר אֲדֹנָי יֱהוִה
טו כִּשְׂמֹחַ כָּל־הָאָרֶץ שְׁמָמָה אֶעֱשֶׂה־לָּךְ: כְּשִׂמְחָתְךָ לְנַחֲלַת בֵּית־
יִשְׂרָאֵל עַל אֲשֶׁר־שָׁמֵמָה כֵּן אֶעֱשֶׂה־לָּךְ שְׁמָמָה תִהְיֶה הַר־שֵׂעִיר
לו א וְכָל־אֱדוֹם כֻּלָּהּ וְיָדְעוּ כִּי־אֲנִי יְהוָה: וְאַתָּה בֶן־אָדָם
ב הִנָּבֵא אֶל־הָרֵי יִשְׂרָאֵל וְאָמַרְתָּ הָרֵי יִשְׂרָאֵל שִׁמְעוּ דְּבַר־יְהוָה: כֹּה

Lord God: Because the enemy said about you, 'Ha! The ancient high places
3 have become our possession,' so, prophesy; say: So says the Lord God: For
this very reason, they desolated and hounded you from all around so that you
would become a possession to the other nations and a topic of slander and
4 common gossip. So, mountains of Israel, listen to the word of the Lord God:
So says the Lord God to the mountains and hills, to the ravines and valleys,
to the desolate ruins and abandoned cities that were objects of pillaging and
5 derision to the other nations all around. So the Lord God says this:
Surely in the fiery passion of My anger have I spoken against the other nations
and against all of Edom – who, with wholehearted joy and absolute contempt,
gave My land to them as a possession so that her pastureland would be spoils.
6 So, prophesy about the soil of Israel; say to the mountains and hills, to the
ravines and valleys: So says the Lord God: See that I have spoken, in the
passion of My anger and My fury, because you have borne disgrace from the
7 nations. So the Lord God says this: I raise My hand in promise that the
8 nations who are all around you will surely bear their own disgrace. And
you, mountains of Israel, you will extend your branches; you will bear your
9 fruit for My people Israel, for they are almost come. For I am with you; I will
10 turn toward you, and you will be tilled and sown. I will make you densely
populated, the whole of the House of Israel; the cities will be reinhabited, the
11 ruins will be rebuilt. I will make you densely populated with people and
animals; they will multiply and be fertile, and I will make you inhabited just
as you were formerly and make you thrive more than before, and you will
12 know: I am the Lord. I will make people, My people Israel, walk on you; they
will possess you, and you will be their heritage, and you will no longer bereave
13 them. So says the Lord God: Because they said of you, 'You
14 consume people; you bereave your nations,' so: you will no longer consume
15 people; you will not bereave your nations again, declares the Lord God. I will
no longer allow the insults of the nations to be heard against you, you will no
longer bear the reproaches of peoples, and you will not cause your own
16 nations to stumble again, declares the Lord God." The word of the
17 Lord came to me: "Man, the House of Israel dwelled upon their soil and
defiled it with their ways and their deeds – their ways were like the impurity
18 of the menstrual woman before Me. I poured out My fury upon them for
the blood they spilled upon the land and the idols they defiled her with.
19 I scattered them among the nations – they were strewn across the countries –
20 and I punished them according to their ways and their deeds. There, in
whichever nations they came to, they desecrated My holy name because it
was said of them, 'These are the Lord's people, and they have left His land.'[41]
21 And I am concerned for My holy name, which the House of Israel has
22 desecrated among the nations to which they have come. So, say to
the House of Israel: So says the Lord God: It is not for your sake that I do
this, House of Israel, but for My holy name that you desecrated among the

41 | The implication being that God could not defend His people in their land, and that God was somehow "defeated" by the Babylonians.

אָמַר אֲדֹנָי יֱהֹוִה יַעַן אָמַר הָאוֹיֵב עֲלֵיכֶם הֶאָח וּבָמוֹת עוֹלָם לְמוֹרָשָׁה
ג הָיְתָה לָּנוּ׃ לָכֵן הִנָּבֵא וְאָמַרְתָּ כֹּה אָמַר אֲדֹנָי יֱהֹוִה יַעַן בְּיַעַן שַׁמּוֹת
וְשָׁאֹף אֶתְכֶם מִסָּבִיב לִהְיוֹתְכֶם מוֹרָשָׁה לִשְׁאֵרִית הַגּוֹיִם וַתֵּעֲלוּ עַל־
ד שְׂפַת לָשׁוֹן וְדִבַּת־עָם׃ לָכֵן הָרֵי יִשְׂרָאֵל שִׁמְעוּ דְּבַר־אֲדֹנָי יֱהֹוִה
כֹּה־אָמַר אֲדֹנָי יֱהֹוִה לֶהָרִים וְלַגְּבָעוֹת לָאֲפִיקִים וְלַגֵּאָיוֹת וְלֶחֳרָבוֹת
הַשֹּׁמְמוֹת וְלֶעָרִים הַנֶּעֱזָבוֹת אֲשֶׁר הָיוּ לְבַז וּלְלַעַג לִשְׁאֵרִית הַגּוֹיִם
ה אֲשֶׁר מִסָּבִיב׃ לָכֵן כֹּה־אָמַר אֲדֹנָי יֱהֹוִה אִם־
לֹא בְּאֵשׁ קִנְאָתִי דִבַּרְתִּי עַל־שְׁאֵרִית הַגּוֹיִם וְעַל־אֱדוֹם כֻּלָּא אֲשֶׁר
נָתְנוּ־אֶת־אַרְצִי ׀ לָהֶם לְמוֹרָשָׁה בְּשִׂמְחַת כָּל־לֵבָב בִּשְׁאָט נֶפֶשׁ
ו לְמַעַן מִגְרָשָׁהּ לָבַז׃ לָכֵן הִנָּבֵא עַל־אַדְמַת יִשְׂרָאֵל וְאָמַרְתָּ לֶהָרִים
וְלַגְּבָעוֹת לָאֲפִיקִים וְלַגֵּאָיוֹת כֹּה־אָמַר ׀ אֲדֹנָי יֱהֹוִה הִנְנִי בְקִנְאָתִי
ז וּבַחֲמָתִי דִּבַּרְתִּי יַעַן כְּלִמַּת גּוֹיִם נְשָׂאתֶם׃ לָכֵן כֹּה אָמַר אֲדֹנָי יֱהֹוִה
אֲנִי נָשָׂאתִי אֶת־יָדִי אִם־לֹא הַגּוֹיִם אֲשֶׁר לָכֶם מִסָּבִיב הֵמָּה כְּלִמָּתָם
ח יִשָּׂאוּ׃ וְאַתֶּם הָרֵי יִשְׂרָאֵל עַנְפְּכֶם תִּתֵּנוּ וּפֶרְיְכֶם תִּשְׂאוּ לְעַמִּי יִשְׂרָאֵל
ט כִּי קֵרְבוּ לָבוֹא׃ כִּי הִנְנִי אֲלֵיכֶם וּפָנִיתִי אֲלֵיכֶם וְנֶעֱבַדְתֶּם וְנִזְרַעְתֶּם׃
י וְהִרְבֵּיתִי עֲלֵיכֶם אָדָם כָּל־בֵּית יִשְׂרָאֵל כֻּלֹּה וְנֹשְׁבוּ הֶעָרִים וְהֶחֳרָבוֹת
יא תִּבָּנֶינָה׃ וְהִרְבֵּיתִי עֲלֵיכֶם אָדָם וּבְהֵמָה וְרָבוּ וּפָרוּ וְהוֹשַׁבְתִּי אֶתְכֶם
יב כְּקַדְמוֹתֵיכֶם וְהֵטִבֹתִי מֵרִאשֹׁתֵיכֶם וִידַעְתֶּם כִּי־אֲנִי יְהוָה׃ וְהוֹלַכְתִּי
עֲלֵיכֶם אָדָם אֶת־עַמִּי יִשְׂרָאֵל וִירֵשׁוּךָ וְהָיִיתָ לָהֶם לְנַחֲלָה וְלֹא־תוֹסִף
יג עוֹד לְשַׁכְּלָם׃ כֹּה אָמַר אֲדֹנָי יֱהֹוִה יַעַן אֹמְרִים לָכֶם
יד אֹכֶלֶת אָדָם אתי וּמְשַׁכֶּלֶת גויך הָיִית׃ לָכֵן אָדָם לֹא־תֹאכְלִי עוֹד — אַתְּ | גּוֹיַיִךְ
טו וגויך לֹא תכשלי־עוֹד נְאֻם אֲדֹנָי יֱהֹוִה׃ וְלֹא־אַשְׁמִיעַ אֵלַיִךְ עוֹד כְּלִמַּת — וְגוֹיַיִךְ | תְשַׁכְּלִי־
הַגּוֹיִם וְחֶרְפַּת עַמִּים לֹא תִשְׂאִי־עוֹד וגויך לֹא־תַכְשְׁלִי עוֹד נְאֻם אֲדֹנָי — וְגוֹיַיִךְ
טז יז יֱהֹוִה׃ וַיְהִי דְבַר־יְהוָה אֵלַי לֵאמֹר׃ בֶּן־אָדָם בֵּית
יִשְׂרָאֵל יֹשְׁבִים עַל־אַדְמָתָם וַיְטַמְּאוּ אוֹתָהּ בְּדַרְכָּם וּבַעֲלִילוֹתָם
יח כְּטֻמְאַת הַנִּדָּה הָיְתָה דַרְכָּם לְפָנָי׃ וָאֶשְׁפֹּךְ חֲמָתִי עֲלֵיהֶם עַל־הַדָּם
יט אֲשֶׁר־שָׁפְכוּ עַל־הָאָרֶץ וּבְגִלּוּלֵיהֶם טִמְּאוּהָ׃ וָאָפִיץ אֹתָם בַּגּוֹיִם
כ וַיִּזָּרוּ בָּאֲרָצוֹת כְּדַרְכָּם וְכַעֲלִילוֹתָם שְׁפַטְתִּים׃ וַיָּבוֹא אֶל־הַגּוֹיִם אֲשֶׁר־
בָּאוּ שָׁם וַיְחַלְּלוּ אֶת־שֵׁם קָדְשִׁי בֶּאֱמֹר לָהֶם עַם־יְהוָה אֵלֶּה וּמֵאַרְצוֹ
כא יָצָאוּ׃ וָאֶחְמֹל עַל־שֵׁם קָדְשִׁי אֲשֶׁר חִלְּלֻהוּ בֵּית יִשְׂרָאֵל בַּגּוֹיִם אֲשֶׁר־
כב בָּאוּ שָׁמָּה׃ לָכֵן אֱמֹר לְבֵית־יִשְׂרָאֵל כֹּה אָמַר אֲדֹנָי יֱהֹוִה
לֹא לְמַעַנְכֶם אֲנִי עֹשֶׂה בֵּית יִשְׂרָאֵל כִּי אִם־לְשֵׁם־קָדְשִׁי אֲשֶׁר חִלַּלְתֶּם

23 nations to which you came. I will sanctify My great name that has been
desecrated among the nations – that you desecrated among them. The nations
will know that I am the LORD, declares the Lord GOD, when I am sanctified
24 through you before their eyes. I will take you from the nations; I will gather
25 you from all the countries and bring you to your land. I will sprinkle over
you purifying waters, and you will be cleansed; I will cleanse you of all your
26 impurities and all your idols. I will give you a new heart and put a new spirit
into you; I will remove the heart of stone from your flesh and give you a heart
27 of flesh; I will put My spirit into you; make sure that you follow My decrees
28 and that you keep My laws and fulfill them. You will live in the land that I gave
29 to your fathers; you will be My people, and I will be your God. I will deliver
you from all your impurities; I will summon the grain, make it plentiful; I will
30 not bring famine upon you. I will make the fruit of the trees and the produce
of the fields plentiful so that you will no longer have to endure the reproach
31 of famine among the nations. You will remember your evil ways and your
actions that were no good; you will loathe yourselves for your iniquities and
32 your abominations. Not for your sake do I act, declares the Lord GOD; let
that be known to you; be ashamed, disgraced by your own ways, House of
Israel.
33 So says the Lord GOD: On the day when I cleanse you of all your iniquities,
34 I will reinhabit the cities; the ruins will be rebuilt. The desolate land will
35 be tilled there, where she was desolate in the sight of every passerby. They
will say, 'This land that was desolate has become like the garden of Eden; its
towns that were ruined, devastated, and destroyed have been fortified and
36 inhabited.' And the nations that remain around you will know that I, the
LORD, have rebuilt what was destroyed, have sown what was desolated; I the
37 LORD have spoken and will do it. So says the Lord GOD: This, too – I
will respond to the House of Israel's request to do this for them: I will multiply
38 their people like a flock of sheep, like the flocks for sacred offerings, like the
flocks of Jerusalem during her holy times; this is how the ruined cities will be,
filled with flocks of people, and they will know that I am the LORD."
37 1 And the hand of the LORD came upon me. He brought me out by the spirit
2 of the LORD and set me down in the valley. It was full of bones. He led
me around through them all; there were so very many of them out upon the
3 valley, and they were utterly dry. And He said to me, "Man, can they come to
4 life, these bones?" And I said, "My Lord GOD, You know." He said to me:
"Prophesy to these bones; say to them: Dry bones – hear the word of the
5 LORD! So says the Lord GOD to these bones: See – I will bring breath into
6 you, and you will come to life. I will give you sinews, I will make flesh grow
on you, I will spread skin over you, I will put breath into you, you will come
7 to life, and you will know that I am the LORD." I prophesied as I had been

כג בַּגּוֹיִם אֲשֶׁר־בָּאתֶם שָׁם׃ וְקִדַּשְׁתִּי אֶת־שְׁמִי הַגָּדוֹל הַמְחֻלָּל בַּגּוֹיִם
אֲשֶׁר חִלַּלְתֶּם בְּתוֹכָם וְיָדְעוּ הַגּוֹיִם כִּי־אֲנִי יְהוָה נְאֻם אֲדֹנָי יֱהוִה
כד בְּהִקָּדְשִׁי בָכֶם לְעֵינֵיהֶם׃ וְלָקַחְתִּי אֶתְכֶם מִן־הַגּוֹיִם וְקִבַּצְתִּי אֶתְכֶם
כה מִכָּל־הָאֲרָצוֹת וְהֵבֵאתִי אֶתְכֶם אֶל־אַדְמַתְכֶם׃ וְזָרַקְתִּי עֲלֵיכֶם מַיִם כב
טְהוֹרִים וּטְהַרְתֶּם מִכֹּל טֻמְאוֹתֵיכֶם וּמִכָּל־גִּלּוּלֵיכֶם אֲטַהֵר אֶתְכֶם׃
כו וְנָתַתִּי לָכֶם לֵב חָדָשׁ וְרוּחַ חֲדָשָׁה אֶתֵּן בְּקִרְבְּכֶם וַהֲסִרֹתִי אֶת־לֵב
כז הָאֶבֶן מִבְּשַׂרְכֶם וְנָתַתִּי לָכֶם לֵב בָּשָׂר׃ וְאֶת־רוּחִי אֶתֵּן בְּקִרְבְּכֶם
כח וְעָשִׂיתִי אֵת אֲשֶׁר־בְּחֻקַּי תֵּלֵכוּ וּמִשְׁפָּטַי תִּשְׁמְרוּ וַעֲשִׂיתֶם׃ וִישַׁבְתֶּם
בָּאָרֶץ אֲשֶׁר נָתַתִּי לַאֲבֹתֵיכֶם וִהְיִיתֶם לִי לְעָם וְאָנֹכִי אֶהְיֶה לָכֶם
כט לֵאלֹהִים׃ וְהוֹשַׁעְתִּי אֶתְכֶם מִכֹּל טֻמְאוֹתֵיכֶם וְקָרָאתִי אֶל־הַדָּגָן
ל וְהִרְבֵּיתִי אֹתוֹ וְלֹא־אֶתֵּן עֲלֵיכֶם רָעָב׃ וְהִרְבֵּיתִי אֶת־פְּרִי הָעֵץ וּתְנוּבַת
לא הַשָּׂדֶה לְמַעַן אֲשֶׁר לֹא תִקְחוּ עוֹד חֶרְפַּת רָעָב בַּגּוֹיִם׃ וּזְכַרְתֶּם אֶת־
דַּרְכֵיכֶם הָרָעִים וּמַעַלְלֵיכֶם אֲשֶׁר לֹא־טוֹבִים וּנְקֹטֹתֶם בִּפְנֵיכֶם עַל
לב עֲוֺנֹתֵיכֶם וְעַל תּוֹעֲבוֹתֵיכֶם׃ לֹא לְמַעַנְכֶם אֲנִי־עֹשֶׂה נְאֻם אֲדֹנָי יֱהוִה
יִוָּדַע לָכֶם בּוֹשׁוּ וְהִכָּלְמוּ מִדַּרְכֵיכֶם בֵּית יִשְׂרָאֵל׃
לג כֹּה אָמַר אֲדֹנָי יֱהוִה בְּיוֹם טַהֲרִי אֶתְכֶם מִכֹּל עֲוֺנוֹתֵיכֶם וְהוֹשַׁבְתִּי
לד אֶת־הֶעָרִים וְנִבְנוּ הֶחֳרָבוֹת׃ וְהָאָרֶץ הַנְּשַׁמָּה תֵּעָבֵד תַּחַת אֲשֶׁר
לה הָיְתָה שְׁמָמָה לְעֵינֵי כָּל־עוֹבֵר׃ וְאָמְרוּ הָאָרֶץ הַלֵּזוּ הַנְּשַׁמָּה הָיְתָה
כְּגַן־עֵדֶן וְהֶעָרִים הֶחֳרֵבוֹת וְהַנְשַׁמּוֹת וְהַנֶּהֱרָסוֹת בְּצוּרוֹת יָשָׁבוּ׃
לו וְיָדְעוּ הַגּוֹיִם אֲשֶׁר יִשָּׁאֲרוּ סְבִיבוֹתֵיכֶם כִּי ׀ אֲנִי יְהוָה בָּנִיתִי הַנֶּהֱרָסוֹת
לז נָטַעְתִּי הַנְּשַׁמָּה אֲנִי יְהוָה דִּבַּרְתִּי וְעָשִׂיתִי׃ כֹּה אָמַר
אֲדֹנָי יֱהוִה עוֹד זֹאת אִדָּרֵשׁ לְבֵית־יִשְׂרָאֵל לַעֲשׂוֹת לָהֶם אַרְבֶּה אֹתָם
לח כַּצֹּאן אָדָם׃ כְּצֹאן קָדָשִׁים כְּצֹאן יְרוּשָׁלַםִ בְּמוֹעֲדֶיהָ כֵּן תִּהְיֶינָה הֶעָרִים
הֶחֳרֵבוֹת מְלֵאוֹת צֹאן אָדָם וְיָדְעוּ כִּי־אֲנִי יְהוָה׃

לז א הָיְתָה עָלַי יַד־יְהוָה וַיּוֹצִאֵנִי בְרוּחַ יְהוָה וַיְנִיחֵנִי בְּתוֹךְ הַבִּקְעָה וְהִיא
ב מְלֵאָה עֲצָמוֹת׃ וְהֶעֱבִירַנִי עֲלֵיהֶם סָבִיב ׀ סָבִיב וְהִנֵּה רַבּוֹת מְאֹד
ג עַל־פְּנֵי הַבִּקְעָה וְהִנֵּה יְבֵשׁוֹת מְאֹד׃ וַיֹּאמֶר אֵלַי בֶּן־אָדָם הֲתִחְיֶינָה
ד הָעֲצָמוֹת הָאֵלֶּה וָאֹמַר אֲדֹנָי יֱהוִה אַתָּה יָדָעְתָּ׃ וַיֹּאמֶר אֵלַי הִנָּבֵא
עַל־הָעֲצָמוֹת הָאֵלֶּה וְאָמַרְתָּ אֲלֵיהֶם הָעֲצָמוֹת הַיְבֵשׁוֹת שִׁמְעוּ דְּבַר־
ה יְהוָה׃ כֹּה אָמַר אֲדֹנָי יֱהוִה לָעֲצָמוֹת הָאֵלֶּה הִנֵּה אֲנִי מֵבִיא בָכֶם רוּחַ
ו וִחְיִיתֶם׃ וְנָתַתִּי עֲלֵיכֶם גִּידִים וְהַעֲלֵתִי עֲלֵיכֶם בָּשָׂר וְקָרַמְתִּי עֲלֵיכֶם
ז עוֹר וְנָתַתִּי בָכֶם רוּחַ וִחְיִיתֶם וִידַעְתֶּם כִּי־אֲנִי יְהוָה׃ וְנִבֵּאתִי כַּאֲשֶׁר

commanded. There was a noise as I was prophesying, and then a rattling, and
8 the bones moved together, each bone to its bone. And I saw there on them
sinews, flesh forming, and skin spreading a cover over them – but there
9 was no breath in them. And He said to me: "Prophesy to the breath; Man,
prophesy and say to the breath: So says the Lord God: From the four winds,
10 come; breath, breathe into these slain so that they come to life." I prophesied
as He had commanded me, and the breath entered them, and they came to
11 life; they stood upon their feet, a vast army. And He said to me: "Man, these
bones are the whole House of Israel. See, they say, 'Our bones are dried out,
12 our hope is lost, and we are completely cut off.' So, prophesy; say to them: So
says the Lord God: See, I am opening up your graves; I will lift you out of
13 your graves, My people, and I will bring you to the soil of Israel. You will know
that I am the Lord when I open up your graves, when I lift you out of your
14 graves, My people. I will put My breath into you, and you will come to life; I
will set you upon your soil, and you will know that I am the Lord; I have
15 spoken, and I will do it, declares the Lord." The word of the Lord
16 came to me, saying: "And you, Man, take a branch and write on it, 'For Yehuda
and the children of Israel associated with him.' Then take one branch and
write on it, 'For Yosef – the branch of Efrayim – and all of the House of Israel
17 associated with him.' Bring them together to make one branch, so that they
18 are one in your hand. When your people say to you, 'Tell us, what do these
19 mean to you?' say to them: So says the Lord God: See, I am going to take the
branch of Yosef, which is in the hand of Efrayim, and the tribes of Israel who
are associated with him, and join them with him, with the branch of Yehuda;
20 I will make them into one branch, and they will be one in My hand. Let these
21 branches that you write upon be in your hand before their eyes. Speak to
them: So says the Lord God: See that I am taking the children of Israel from
among the nations that they went to; I will gather them from all around, and
22 I will bring them to their land. I will make them into one nation in the land,
in the mountains of Israel; one king will be king for all of them, and they will
no longer be two nations; they will no longer be split into two kingdoms.
23 They will no longer be defiled by their idols or by their detestable things and
all their transgressions; I will deliver them from all the dwelling places where
they have sinned; I will purify them, and they will be My people, and I will
24 be their God. My servant David will be king over them; there shall be one
shepherd for all, and they will follow My laws, and they will keep My statutes
25 and perform them. They will live on the land that I gave to My servant Yaakov,
where your ancestors lived. They will live upon it, they and their children and
their children's children, for eternity, and David My servant will be their
26 prince for eternity. I will make a covenant of peace with them; it will be an
everlasting covenant with them. I will place them securely there, I will make
them ever more numerous; I will place My Sanctuary among them for eternity.

צִוֵּיתִי וַיְהִי־קוֹל כְּהִנָּבְאִי וְהִנֵּה־רַעַשׁ וַתִּקְרְבוּ עֲצָמוֹת עֶצֶם אֶל־עַצְמוֹ׃
ח וְרָאִיתִי וְהִנֵּה־עֲלֵיהֶם גִּדִים וּבָשָׂר עָלָה וַיִּקְרַם עֲלֵיהֶם עוֹר מִלְמָעְלָה
ט וְרוּחַ אֵין בָּהֶם׃ וַיֹּאמֶר אֵלַי הִנָּבֵא אֶל־הָרוּחַ הִנָּבֵא בֶן־אָדָם וְאָמַרְתָּ
אֶל־הָרוּחַ כֹּה־אָמַר ׀ אֲדֹנָי יֱהוִה מֵאַרְבַּע רוּחוֹת בֹּאִי הָרוּחַ וּפְחִי
י בַּהֲרוּגִים הָאֵלֶּה וְיִחְיוּ׃ וְהִנַּבֵּאתִי כַּאֲשֶׁר צִוָּנִי וַתָּבוֹא בָהֶם הָרוּחַ וַיִּחְיוּ
יא וַיַּעַמְדוּ עַל־רַגְלֵיהֶם חַיִל גָּדוֹל מְאֹד מְאֹד׃ וַיֹּאמֶר אֵלַי בֶּן־אָדָם
הָעֲצָמוֹת הָאֵלֶּה כָּל־בֵּית יִשְׂרָאֵל הֵמָּה הִנֵּה אֹמְרִים יָבְשׁוּ עַצְמוֹתֵינוּ
יב וְאָבְדָה תִקְוָתֵנוּ נִגְזַרְנוּ לָנוּ׃ לָכֵן הִנָּבֵא וְאָמַרְתָּ אֲלֵיהֶם כֹּה־אָמַר
אֲדֹנָי יֱהוִה הִנֵּה אֲנִי פֹתֵחַ אֶת־קִבְרוֹתֵיכֶם וְהַעֲלֵיתִי אֶתְכֶם מִקִּבְרוֹתֵיכֶם
יג עַמִּי וְהֵבֵאתִי אֶתְכֶם אֶל־אַדְמַת יִשְׂרָאֵל׃ וִידַעְתֶּם כִּי־אֲנִי יְהוָה
יד בְּפִתְחִי אֶת־קִבְרוֹתֵיכֶם וּבְהַעֲלוֹתִי אֶתְכֶם מִקִּבְרוֹתֵיכֶם עַמִּי׃ וְנָתַתִּי
רוּחִי בָכֶם וִחְיִיתֶם וְהִנַּחְתִּי אֶתְכֶם עַל־אַדְמַתְכֶם וִידַעְתֶּם כִּי אֲנִי
טו יְהוָה דִּבַּרְתִּי וְעָשִׂיתִי נְאֻם־יְהוָה׃ וַיְהִי דְבַר־יְהוָה אֵלַי
טז לֵאמֹר׃ וְאַתָּה בֶן־אָדָם קַח־לְךָ עֵץ אֶחָד וּכְתֹב עָלָיו לִיהוּדָה וְלִבְנֵי
יִשְׂרָאֵל חֲבֵרָו וּלְקַח עֵץ אֶחָד וּכְתוֹב עָלָיו לְיוֹסֵף עֵץ אֶפְרַיִם וְכָל־בֵּית
יז יִשְׂרָאֵל חֲבֵרָו׃ וְקָרַב אֹתָם אֶחָד אֶל־אֶחָד לְךָ לְעֵץ אֶחָד וְהָיוּ לַאֲחָדִים
יח בְּיָדֶךָ׃ וְכַאֲשֶׁר יֹאמְרוּ אֵלֶיךָ בְּנֵי עַמְּךָ לֵאמֹר הֲלוֹא־תַגִּיד לָנוּ מָה־
יט אֵלֶּה לָּךְ׃ דַּבֵּר אֲלֵהֶם כֹּה־אָמַר אֲדֹנָי יֱהוִה הִנֵּה אֲנִי לֹקֵחַ אֶת־עֵץ
יוֹסֵף אֲשֶׁר בְּיַד־אֶפְרַיִם וְשִׁבְטֵי יִשְׂרָאֵל חֲבֵרָו וְנָתַתִּי אוֹתָם עָלָיו
כ אֶת־עֵץ יְהוּדָה וַעֲשִׂיתִם לְעֵץ אֶחָד וְהָיוּ אֶחָד בְּיָדִי׃ וְהָיוּ הָעֵצִים
כא אֲשֶׁר־תִּכְתֹּב עֲלֵיהֶם בְּיָדְךָ לְעֵינֵיהֶם׃ וְדַבֵּר אֲלֵיהֶם כֹּה־אָמַר אֲדֹנָי
יֱהוִה הִנֵּה אֲנִי לֹקֵחַ אֶת־בְּנֵי יִשְׂרָאֵל מִבֵּין הַגּוֹיִם אֲשֶׁר הָלְכוּ־שָׁם
כב וְקִבַּצְתִּי אֹתָם מִסָּבִיב וְהֵבֵאתִי אוֹתָם אֶל־אַדְמָתָם׃ וְעָשִׂיתִי אֹתָם
לְגוֹי אֶחָד בָּאָרֶץ בְּהָרֵי יִשְׂרָאֵל וּמֶלֶךְ אֶחָד יִהְיֶה לְכֻלָּם לְמֶלֶךְ וְלֹא
כג יהיה־עוֹד לִשְׁנֵי גוֹיִם וְלֹא יֵחָצוּ עוֹד לִשְׁתֵּי מַמְלָכוֹת עוֹד׃ וְלֹא יִטַּמְּאוּ יִהְיוּ
עוֹד בְּגִלּוּלֵיהֶם וּבְשִׁקּוּצֵיהֶם וּבְכֹל פִּשְׁעֵיהֶם וְהוֹשַׁעְתִּי אֹתָם מִכֹּל
מוֹשְׁבֹתֵיהֶם אֲשֶׁר חָטְאוּ בָהֶם וְטִהַרְתִּי אוֹתָם וְהָיוּ־לִי לְעָם וַאֲנִי
כד אֶהְיֶה לָהֶם לֵאלֹהִים׃ וְעַבְדִּי דָוִד מֶלֶךְ עֲלֵיהֶם וְרוֹעֶה אֶחָד יִהְיֶה
כה לְכֻלָּם וּבְמִשְׁפָּטַי יֵלֵכוּ וְחֻקֹּתַי יִשְׁמְרוּ וְעָשׂוּ אוֹתָם׃ וְיָשְׁבוּ עַל־הָאָרֶץ
אֲשֶׁר נָתַתִּי לְעַבְדִּי לְיַעֲקֹב אֲשֶׁר יָשְׁבוּ־בָהּ אֲבוֹתֵיכֶם וְיָשְׁבוּ עָלֶיהָ
הֵמָּה וּבְנֵיהֶם וּבְנֵי בְנֵיהֶם עַד־עוֹלָם וְדָוִד עַבְדִּי נָשִׂיא לָהֶם לְעוֹלָם׃
כו וְכָרַתִּי לָהֶם בְּרִית שָׁלוֹם בְּרִית עוֹלָם יִהְיֶה אוֹתָם וּנְתַתִּים וְהִרְבֵּיתִי

27 My presence will be upon them; I will be their God, and they will be My
28 people. And the nations will know that I the LORD make Israel holy when
38 1 My Sanctuary is among them for all eternity." The word of the LORD
2 came to me: "Man, set your face toward Gog of the land of Magog, the chief
3 prince of Meshekh and Tuval.[60] Prophesy against him; say: So says the Lord
4 GOD: Behold – I am against you, Gog, chief prince of Meshekh and Tuval. I
will turn you around, fix hooks into your jaw, and bring you out with all your
troops, horses, and cavalry in complete regalia, a great horde with shields and
5 bucklers, all wielding swords. And with them Persia, Kush, and Put, all with
6 shields and helmets; Gomer and all her forces; Beit Togarma from the far
7 edges of the north and all her forces – many peoples with you. Prepare, ready
yourself, you and all of the hordes assembled around you; you are their
8 guarding commander. After many days you will be summoned; at the end of
years, you will come against the land which has been restored after the sword,
which has been gathered back from many nations upon the mountains of
Israel that long lay in ruins – she who will have been brought out from the
9 nations, a people who all now live securely. You will advance, you will come
like a devastating storm, and you will be like a cloud covering the land – you,
10 all your forces, and the many peoples with you. So says the
Lord GOD: On that day, certain thoughts will occur to you; you will devise
11 an evil scheme. You will say, 'I will advance against the land of open villages;
I will come upon those who are tranquil, living securely, all of whom live
12 in unwalled towns and without bars or gates,' to ransack spoils and seize
loot, to turn your hand against reinhabited ruins and a people gathered in
from the nations who have built up livestock and possessions, who live at the
13 center of the land. Sheba, Dedan, and the merchants of Tarshish and all her
young warriors will say to you, 'Have you come to ransack spoils? Have you
assembled your hordes to seize loot – to carry off silver and gold, to take
14 livestock and possessions, to ransack great spoils?' So, prophesy,
Man; say to Gog: So says the Lord GOD: Surely, on the day that My people
15 Israel lives securely, you will know it, and you will come from your place, from
the far edges of the north, you and many peoples with you, all of them on
16 horseback, with a great horde and a mighty army. You will advance against
My people Israel like a cloud covering the land. This is what will be in the end
of days, and I will bring you to My land so that the nations will know Me
17 when I am sanctified through you before their eyes, Gog. So says
the Lord GOD: It is you whom I spoke of in former days through My servants
the prophets of Israel, who in those days, for years, prophesied that I would
18 bring you against them. And it shall be, on that day, on the day that
19 Gog comes onto the soil of Israel, says the Lord GOD: My fury will blaze; in
My passionate anger, in the fire of My rage I have spoken: Surely on that day

60 | Gog and Magog cannot be identified as real people or places. Meshekh, Tuval, and the other kingdoms mentioned here are located throughout the lands surrounding the Mediterranean (many are mentioned in chapter 27 above).

כז אוֹתָם וְנָתַתִּי אֶת־מִקְדָּשִׁי בְּתוֹכָם לְעוֹלָם׃ וְהָיָה מִשְׁכָּנִי עֲלֵיהֶם וְהָיִיתִי
כג כח לָהֶם לֵאלֹהִים וְהֵמָּה יִהְיוּ־לִי לְעָם׃ וְיָדְעוּ הַגּוֹיִם כִּי אֲנִי יְהֹוָה מְקַדֵּשׁ
לח א אֶת־יִשְׂרָאֵל בִּהְיוֹת מִקְדָּשִׁי בְּתוֹכָם לְעוֹלָם׃ וַיְהִי דְבַר־
ב יְהֹוָה אֵלַי לֵאמֹר׃ בֶּן־אָדָם שִׂים פָּנֶיךָ אֶל־גּוֹג אֶרֶץ הַמָּגוֹג נְשִׂיא רֹאשׁ
ג מֶשֶׁךְ וְתֻבָל וְהִנָּבֵא עָלָיו׃ וְאָמַרְתָּ כֹּה אָמַר אֲדֹנָי יֱהֹוִה הִנְנִי אֵלֶיךָ
ד גּוֹג נְשִׂיא רֹאשׁ מֶשֶׁךְ וְתֻבָל׃ וְשׁוֹבַבְתִּיךָ וְנָתַתִּי חַחִים בִּלְחָיֶיךָ וְהוֹצֵאתִי
אוֹתְךָ וְאֶת־כׇּל־חֵילֶךָ סוּסִים וּפָרָשִׁים לְבֻשֵׁי מִכְלוֹל כֻּלָּם קָהָל רָב
ה צִנָּה וּמָגֵן תֹּפְשֵׂי חֲרָבוֹת כֻּלָּם׃ פָּרַס כּוּשׁ וּפוּט אִתָּם כֻּלָּם מָגֵן וְכוֹבָע׃
ו גֹּמֶר וְכׇל־אֲגַפֶּיהָ בֵּית תּוֹגַרְמָה יַרְכְּתֵי צָפוֹן וְאֶת־כׇּל־אֲגַפָּיו עַמִּים
ז רַבִּים אִתָּךְ׃ הִכֹּן וְהָכֵן לְךָ אַתָּה וְכׇל־קְהָלֶךָ הַנִּקְהָלִים עָלֶיךָ וְהָיִיתָ
ח לָהֶם לְמִשְׁמָר׃ מִיָּמִים רַבִּים תִּפָּקֵד בְּאַחֲרִית הַשָּׁנִים תָּבוֹא ׀ אֶל־
אֶרֶץ ׀ מְשׁוֹבֶבֶת מֵחֶרֶב מְקֻבֶּצֶת מֵעַמִּים רַבִּים עַל הָרֵי יִשְׂרָאֵל
אֲשֶׁר־הָיוּ לְחׇרְבָּה תָּמִיד וְהִיא מֵעַמִּים הוּצָאָה וְיָשְׁבוּ לָבֶטַח כֻּלָּם׃
ט וְעָלִיתָ כַּשֹּׁאָה תָבוֹא כֶּעָנָן לְכַסּוֹת הָאָרֶץ תִּהְיֶה אַתָּה וְכׇל־אֲגַפֶּיךָ
י וְעַמִּים רַבִּים אוֹתָךְ׃ כֹּה אָמַר אֲדֹנָי יֱהֹוִה וְהָיָה ׀ בַּיּוֹם
יא הַהוּא יַעֲלוּ דְבָרִים עַל־לְבָבֶךָ וְחָשַׁבְתָּ מַחֲשֶׁבֶת רָעָה׃ וְאָמַרְתָּ אֶעֱלֶה
עַל־אֶרֶץ פְּרָזוֹת אָבוֹא הַשֹּׁקְטִים יֹשְׁבֵי לָבֶטַח כֻּלָּם יֹשְׁבִים בְּאֵין
יב חוֹמָה וּבְרִיחַ וּדְלָתַיִם אֵין לָהֶם׃ לִשְׁלֹל שָׁלָל וְלָבֹז בַּז לְהָשִׁיב יָדְךָ
עַל־חֳרָבוֹת נוֹשָׁבֹת וְאֶל־עַם מְאֻסָּף מִגּוֹיִם עֹשֶׂה מִקְנֶה וְקִנְיָן יֹשְׁבֵי
יג עַל־טַבּוּר הָאָרֶץ׃ שְׁבָא וּדְדָן וְסֹחֲרֵי תַרְשִׁישׁ וְכׇל־כְּפִרֶיהָ יֹאמְרוּ
לְךָ הֲלִשְׁלֹל שָׁלָל אַתָּה בָא הֲלָבֹז בַּז הִקְהַלְתָּ קְהָלֶךָ לָשֵׂאת ׀ כֶּסֶף
יד וְזָהָב לָקַחַת מִקְנֶה וְקִנְיָן לִשְׁלֹל שָׁלָל גָּדוֹל׃ לָכֵן
הִנָּבֵא בֶן־אָדָם וְאָמַרְתָּ לְגוֹג כֹּה אָמַר אֲדֹנָי יֱהֹוִה הֲלוֹא ׀ בַּיּוֹם הַהוּא
טו בְּשֶׁבֶת עַמִּי יִשְׂרָאֵל לָבֶטַח תֵּדָע׃ וּבָאתָ מִמְּקוֹמְךָ מִיַּרְכְּתֵי צָפוֹן
אַתָּה וְעַמִּים רַבִּים אִתָּךְ רֹכְבֵי סוּסִים כֻּלָּם קָהָל גָּדוֹל וְחַיִל רָב׃
טז וְעָלִיתָ עַל־עַמִּי יִשְׂרָאֵל כֶּעָנָן לְכַסּוֹת הָאָרֶץ בְּאַחֲרִית הַיָּמִים תִּהְיֶה
וַהֲבִאוֹתִיךָ עַל־אַרְצִי לְמַעַן דַּעַת הַגּוֹיִם אֹתִי בְּהִקָּדְשִׁי בְךָ לְעֵינֵיהֶם
יז גּוֹג׃ כֹּה־אָמַר אֲדֹנָי יֱהֹוִה הַאַתָּה־הוּא אֲשֶׁר־דִּבַּרְתִּי בְּיָמִים
קַדְמוֹנִים בְּיַד עֲבָדַי נְבִיאֵי יִשְׂרָאֵל הַנִּבְּאִים בַּיָּמִים הָהֵם שָׁנִים לְהָבִיא
יח אֹתְךָ עֲלֵיהֶם׃ וְהָיָה ׀ בַּיּוֹם הַהוּא בְּיוֹם בּוֹא גוֹג עַל־
יט אַדְמַת יִשְׂרָאֵל נְאֻם אֲדֹנָי יֱהֹוִה תַּעֲלֶה חֲמָתִי בְּאַפִּי׃ וּבְקִנְאָתִי בְאֵשׁ־
עֶבְרָתִי דִּבַּרְתִּי אִם־לֹא ׀ בַּיּוֹם הַהוּא יִהְיֶה רַעַשׁ גָּדוֹל עַל אַדְמַת

20 there will be a great quaking upon the soil of Israel; they will quake before
Me: the fish of the seas and the birds of the sky, the animals of the field, every
creeping thing that crawls upon the earth, and every man on the face of the
earth; the mountains will be demolished, the terraces will collapse, and every
21 wall shall fall to the ground. I will call the sword down against him across My
mountains, says the Lord God; each man's sword will be turned against
22 his brother. I will execute judgment on him with pestilence and blood; I
will pour down torrential rain and crystal hailstone, fire and sulfur over
23 him and his troops, and over the many peoples who are with him. I will be
magnified, I will be sanctified, and I will make Myself known in the eyes of
39 1 many nations – and they will know that I am the Lord. And
you, Man, prophesy against Gog and say: So says the Lord God: Behold – I
2 am against you, Gog, chief prince of Meshekh and Tuval. I will turn you
around; I will drive you forward; I will make you advance from the far edges
3 of the north and bring you to the mountains of Israel. I will strike your bow
4 from your left hand; I will make the arrows fall from your right; upon the
mountains of Israel you will fall – you, all your troops, and the peoples who
are with you. I will give you up to birds of prey of every kind and to the
5 animals of the field as food; upon the open field you will fall, for I have spoken,
6 says the Lord God. I will set loose fire on Magog and on those living securely
7 in the coastlands, and they will know that I am the Lord. I will make My holy
name known among My people Israel; I will no longer allow My holy name
to be desecrated, and the nations will know that I am the Lord, holy in Israel.
8 Behold: it is coming, it will be, says the Lord God: This is the day I have
9 spoken of. The inhabitants of the cities of Israel will come out, and they
will kindle and burn the weapons, the shields and bucklers, the bows and
arrows, and the clubs and spears; they will burn them as fuel for fire for seven
10 years. They will not take wood from the fields or chop down trees from
the forests, for they will fuel their fires with weapons. They will ransack
those who despoiled them and loot those who looted them, says the Lord
11 God. And it will happen on that day: I will grant Gog a burial place
there in Israel, the Valley of the Travelers, east of the sea, and it will block the
travelers. Here they will bury Gog and his horde; they will call it the Valley
12 of the Horde of Gog. For seven months the House of Israel will bury them
13 to purify the land. All the people in the land shall bury them, and it will make
14 them renowned on the day of My glory, says the Lord God. They shall select
men to cross the land constantly, burying the invaders' remains that lie upon
the ground – to purify it. They will search for a period of seven months.
15 Whenever these men assigned to cross the land see a human bone, they shall
place a sign next to it until the buriers have buried it in the Valley of the Horde
16 of Gog. There will also be a city named Horde. Thus they shall purify the
17 land. And you, Man, so says the Lord God, say to every type of bird
and every animal of the field: Assemble, come, gather from all around, for the
sacrificial feast that I am preparing for you, a great sacrificial feast upon the
18 mountains of Israel; you will eat flesh; you will drink blood. You will eat the

כ יִשְׂרָאֵל: וְרָעֲשׁוּ מִפָּנַי דְּגֵי הַיָּם וְעוֹף הַשָּׁמַיִם וְחַיַּת הַשָּׂדֶה וְכָל־הָרֶמֶשׂ
הָרֹמֵשׂ עַל־הָאֲדָמָה וְכֹל הָאָדָם אֲשֶׁר עַל־פְּנֵי הָאֲדָמָה וְנֶהֶרְסוּ הֶהָרִים
כא וְנָפְלוּ הַמַּדְרֵגוֹת וְכָל־חוֹמָה לָאָרֶץ תִּפּוֹל: וְקָרָאתִי עָלָיו לְכָל־הָרַי
כב חֶרֶב נְאֻם אֲדֹנָי יֱהֹוִה חֶרֶב אִישׁ בְּאָחִיו תִּהְיֶה: וְנִשְׁפַּטְתִּי אִתּוֹ
בְּדֶבֶר וּבְדָם וְגֶשֶׁם שׁוֹטֵף וְאַבְנֵי אֶלְגָּבִישׁ אֵשׁ וְגָפְרִית אַמְטִיר עָלָיו
כג וְעַל־אֲגַפָּיו וְעַל־עַמִּים רַבִּים אֲשֶׁר אִתּוֹ: וְהִתְגַּדִּלְתִּי וְהִתְקַדִּשְׁתִּי
לט א וְנוֹדַעְתִּי לְעֵינֵי גּוֹיִם רַבִּים וְיָדְעוּ כִּי־אֲנִי יְהֹוָה: וְאַתָּה
בֶן־אָדָם הִנָּבֵא עַל־גּוֹג וְאָמַרְתָּ כֹּה אָמַר אֲדֹנָי יֱהֹוִה הִנְנִי אֵלֶיךָ גּוֹג
ב נְשִׂיא רֹאשׁ מֶשֶׁךְ וְתֻבָל: וְשֹׁבַבְתִּיךָ וְשִׁשֵּׁאתִיךָ וְהַעֲלִיתִיךָ מִיַּרְכְּתֵי
ג צָפוֹן וַהֲבִאוֹתִךָ עַל־הָרֵי יִשְׂרָאֵל: וְהִכֵּיתִי קַשְׁתְּךָ מִיַּד שְׂמֹאולֶךָ
ד וְחִצֶּיךָ מִיַּד יְמִינְךָ אַפִּיל: עַל־הָרֵי יִשְׂרָאֵל תִּפּוֹל אַתָּה וְכָל־אֲגַפֶּיךָ
וְעַמִּים אֲשֶׁר אִתָּךְ לְעֵיט צִפּוֹר כָּל־כָּנָף וְחַיַּת הַשָּׂדֶה נְתַתִּיךָ לְאָכְלָה:
ה ו עַל־פְּנֵי הַשָּׂדֶה תִּפּוֹל כִּי אֲנִי דִבַּרְתִּי נְאֻם אֲדֹנָי יֱהֹוִה: וְשִׁלַּחְתִּי־אֵשׁ
ז בְּמָגוֹג וּבְיֹשְׁבֵי הָאִיִּים לָבֶטַח וְיָדְעוּ כִּי־אֲנִי יְהֹוָה: וְאֶת־שֵׁם קָדְשִׁי
אוֹדִיעַ בְּתוֹךְ עַמִּי יִשְׂרָאֵל וְלֹא־אַחֵל אֶת־שֵׁם־קָדְשִׁי עוֹד וְיָדְעוּ הַגּוֹיִם
ח כִּי־אֲנִי יְהֹוָה קָדוֹשׁ בְּיִשְׂרָאֵל: הִנֵּה בָאָה וְנִהְיָתָה נְאֻם אֲדֹנָי יֱהֹוִה
ט הוּא הַיּוֹם אֲשֶׁר דִּבַּרְתִּי: וְיָצְאוּ יֹשְׁבֵי ׀ עָרֵי יִשְׂרָאֵל וּבִעֲרוּ וְהִשִּׂיקוּ
בְּנֶשֶׁק וּמָגֵן וְצִנָּה בְּקֶשֶׁת וּבְחִצִּים וּבְמַקֵּל יָד וּבְרֹמַח וּבִעֲרוּ בָהֶם אֵשׁ
י שֶׁבַע שָׁנִים: וְלֹא־יִשְׂאוּ עֵצִים מִן־הַשָּׂדֶה וְלֹא יַחְטְבוּ מִן־הַיְּעָרִים כִּי
בַנֶּשֶׁק יְבַעֲרוּ־אֵשׁ וְשָׁלְלוּ אֶת־שֹׁלְלֵיהֶם וּבָזְזוּ אֶת־בֹּזְזֵיהֶם נְאֻם אֲדֹנָי
יא יֱהֹוִה: וְהָיָה בַיּוֹם הַהוּא אֶתֵּן לְגוֹג ׀ מְקוֹם־שָׁם קֶבֶר
בְּיִשְׂרָאֵל גֵּי הָעֹבְרִים קִדְמַת הַיָּם וְחֹסֶמֶת הִיא אֶת־הָעֹבְרִים וְקָבְרוּ
יב שָׁם אֶת־גּוֹג וְאֶת־כָּל־הֲמוֹנֹה וְקָרְאוּ גֵּיא הֲמוֹן גּוֹג: וּקְבָרוּם בֵּית
יג יִשְׂרָאֵל לְמַעַן טַהֵר אֶת־הָאָרֶץ שִׁבְעָה חֳדָשִׁים: וְקָבְרוּ כָּל־עַם הָאָרֶץ
יד וְהָיָה לָהֶם לְשֵׁם יוֹם הִכָּבְדִי נְאֻם אֲדֹנָי יֱהֹוִה: וְאַנְשֵׁי תָמִיד יַבְדִּילוּ
עֹבְרִים בָּאָרֶץ מְקַבְּרִים אֶת־הָעֹבְרִים אֶת־הַנּוֹתָרִים עַל־פְּנֵי הָאָרֶץ
טו לְטַהֲרָהּ מִקְצֵה שִׁבְעָה־חֳדָשִׁים יַחְקֹרוּ: וְעָבְרוּ הָעֹבְרִים בָּאָרֶץ וְרָאָה
עֶצֶם אָדָם וּבָנָה אֶצְלוֹ צִיּוּן עַד קָבְרוּ אֹתוֹ הַמְקַבְּרִים אֶל־גֵּיא הֲמוֹן
טז יז גּוֹג: וְגַם שֶׁם־עִיר הֲמוֹנָה וְטִהֲרוּ הָאָרֶץ: וְאַתָּה בֶן־אָדָם
כֹּה־אָמַר ׀ אֲדֹנָי יֱהֹוִה אֱמֹר לְצִפּוֹר כָּל־כָּנָף וּלְכֹל ׀ חַיַּת הַשָּׂדֶה הִקָּבְצוּ
וָבֹאוּ הֵאָסְפוּ מִסָּבִיב עַל־זִבְחִי אֲשֶׁר אֲנִי זֹבֵחַ לָכֶם זֶבַח גָּדוֹל עַל הָרֵי
יח יִשְׂרָאֵל וַאֲכַלְתֶּם בָּשָׂר וּשְׁתִיתֶם דָּם: בְּשַׂר גִּבּוֹרִים תֹּאכֵלוּ וְדַם־נְשִׂיאֵי

flesh of warriors; you will drink the blood of the princes of the earth, rams,
19 lambs, he-goats, and bulls – all fatlings of Bashan. You will eat fat until you
are full, you will drink blood until you are drunk from the sacrificial feast I
20 will prepare for you. At My table you will fill yourselves on horses and chariots,
21 warriors and all men of war, declares the Lord God. I will manifest My glory
among the nations; all the nations will see the judgment that I have executed
22 and the hand that I have placed upon them. The House of Israel will know
23 that I the Lord am their God – from that day on. And the nations will know
that it was for their iniquity that the House of Israel was exiled. Because they
betrayed me, I hid My face from them and gave them over into the hand of
24 their enemies, and they fell by the sword, all of them. I have dealt with them
according to their impurity and transgressions; I have hidden My face from
25 them. So the Lord God says this: Now I will restore the fortunes of
Yaakov; I will have compassion for the whole of the House of Israel and
26 passionate anger for the sake of My holy name. They will forget their disgrace
and all the betrayals by which they betrayed me – when they live in the land
27 securely and without fear, when I bring them back from among the nations,
when I gather them in from the lands of their enemies, and when I am
28 sanctified through them in the eyes of the many nations. They will know that
I the Lord am their God because I exiled them among the nations and then
29 collected them back to their land, leaving none of them behind. I will not
hide My face from them again, for I have poured out My spirit upon the
40 1 House of Israel, declares the Lord God." It was in the twenty-fifth
year of our exile, at the beginning of the year, on the tenth of the month, in
the fourteenth year after the city was destroyed; on that very day the hand of
2 the Lord was upon me, and He brought me there. In visions of God He
brought me to the land of Israel and set me down near a very high mountain
3 upon which, to the south, was something like the structure of a city. He
brought me over there and – behold! – there was a man who looked as if made
of bronze, and in his hand was a string of flax and a measuring reed, and he
4 was standing at the gate. The man spoke to me: "Man, see with your eyes and
listen with your ears, and pay close attention to everything that I am showing
you, for you have been brought here in order that they be shown to you; tell
5 the House of Israel about everything you see." And behold – there was a wall
outside the house roundabout, and the man had in his hand a measuring reed,
six cubits long plus one more handbreadth, and he measured the width of
6 the structure, one reed wide; and the height, one reed.[61] He came to the gate
that faced eastward, climbing its steps. He measured the doorpost of the gate,
7 one reed deep, and the other doorpost, one reed deep. And each of its side
chambers was one reed long and one reed wide, and between the side
chambers were five cubits. And the doorpost of the gate, between the entrance

---

61 | Many points in Yeḥezkel's vision are unclear, leading to a variety of interpretations of the Temple layout, but the scale of the Temple is clearly much larger than Shlomo Temple; cf. 1 Kings, chapter 6. Note that the terms "width" and "length" refer to the shorter and longer measure of an object or area regardless of its orientation. For a diagram of the Temple in Yeḥezkel's vision, see the appendices.

יט הָאָרֶץ תִּשְׁתּוּ אֵילִים כָּרִים וְעַתּוּדִים פָּרִים מְרִיאֵי בָשָׁן כֻּלָּם׃ וַאֲכַלְתֶּם־
חֵלֶב לְשָׂבְעָה וּשְׁתִיתֶם דָּם לְשִׁכָּרוֹן מִזִּבְחִי אֲשֶׁר־זָבַחְתִּי לָכֶם׃
כ וּשְׂבַעְתֶּם עַל־שֻׁלְחָנִי סוּס וָרֶכֶב גִּבּוֹר וְכָל־אִישׁ מִלְחָמָה נְאֻם אֲדֹנָי
כא יֱהוִה׃ וְנָתַתִּי אֶת־כְּבוֹדִי בַּגּוֹיִם וְרָאוּ כָל־הַגּוֹיִם אֶת־מִשְׁפָּטִי אֲשֶׁר
כב עָשִׂיתִי וְאֶת־יָדִי אֲשֶׁר־שַׂמְתִּי בָהֶם׃ וְיָדְעוּ בֵּית יִשְׂרָאֵל כִּי אֲנִי יְהוָה כד
כג אֱלֹהֵיהֶם מִן־הַיּוֹם הַהוּא וָהָלְאָה׃ וְיָדְעוּ הַגּוֹיִם כִּי בַעֲוֺנָם גָּלוּ בֵית־
יִשְׂרָאֵל עַל אֲשֶׁר מָעֲלוּ־בִי וָאַסְתִּר פָּנַי מֵהֶם וָאֶתְּנֵם בְּיַד צָרֵיהֶם
כד וַיִּפְּלוּ בַחֶרֶב כֻּלָּם׃ כְּטֻמְאָתָם וּכְפִשְׁעֵיהֶם עָשִׂיתִי אֹתָם וָאַסְתִּר פָּנַי
כה מֵהֶם׃ לָכֵן כֹּה אָמַר אֲדֹנָי יֱהוִה עַתָּה אָשִׁיב אֶת־שבית שְׁבוּת
כו יַעֲקֹב וְרִחַמְתִּי כָּל־בֵּית יִשְׂרָאֵל וְקִנֵּאתִי לְשֵׁם קָדְשִׁי׃ וְנָשׂוּ אֶת־
כְּלִמָּתָם וְאֶת־כָּל־מַעֲלָם אֲשֶׁר מָעֲלוּ־בִי בְּשִׁבְתָּם עַל־אַדְמָתָם לָבֶטַח
כז וְאֵין מַחֲרִיד׃ בְּשׁוֹבְבִי אוֹתָם מִן־הָעַמִּים וְקִבַּצְתִּי אֹתָם מֵאַרְצוֹת
כח אֹיְבֵיהֶם וְנִקְדַּשְׁתִּי בָם לְעֵינֵי הַגּוֹיִם רַבִּים׃ וְיָדְעוּ כִּי אֲנִי יְהוָה אֱלֹהֵיהֶם
בְּהַגְלוֹתִי אֹתָם אֶל־הַגּוֹיִם וְכִנַּסְתִּים עַל־אַדְמָתָם וְלֹא־אוֹתִיר עוֹד
כט מֵהֶם שָׁם׃ וְלֹא־אַסְתִּיר עוֹד פָּנַי מֵהֶם אֲשֶׁר שָׁפַכְתִּי אֶת־רוּחִי עַל־בֵּית
מ א יִשְׂרָאֵל נְאֻם אֲדֹנָי יֱהוִה׃ בְּעֶשְׂרִים וְחָמֵשׁ שָׁנָה לְגָלוּתֵנוּ
בְּרֹאשׁ הַשָּׁנָה בֶּעָשׂוֹר לַחֹדֶשׁ בְּאַרְבַּע עֶשְׂרֵה שָׁנָה אַחַר אֲשֶׁר הֻכְּתָה
ב הָעִיר בְּעֶצֶם ׀ הַיּוֹם הַזֶּה הָיְתָה עָלַי יַד־יְהוָה וַיָּבֵא אֹתִי שָׁמָּה׃ בְּמַרְאוֹת
אֱלֹהִים הֱבִיאַנִי אֶל־אֶרֶץ יִשְׂרָאֵל וַיְנִיחֵנִי אֶל־הַר גָּבֹהַּ מְאֹד וְעָלָיו
ג כְּמִבְנֵה־עִיר מִנֶּגֶב׃ וַיָּבִיא אוֹתִי שָׁמָּה וְהִנֵּה־אִישׁ מַרְאֵהוּ כְּמַרְאֵה
ד נְחֹשֶׁת וּפְתִיל־פִּשְׁתִּים בְּיָדוֹ וּקְנֵה הַמִּדָּה וְהוּא עֹמֵד בַּשָּׁעַר׃ וַיְדַבֵּר
אֵלַי הָאִישׁ בֶּן־אָדָם רְאֵה בְעֵינֶיךָ וּבְאָזְנֶיךָ שְּׁמָע וְשִׂים לִבְּךָ לְכֹל
אֲשֶׁר־אֲנִי מַרְאֶה אוֹתָךְ כִּי לְמַעַן הַרְאוֹתְכָה הֻבָאתָה הֵנָּה הַגֵּד אֶת־
ה כָּל־אֲשֶׁר־אַתָּה רֹאֶה לְבֵית יִשְׂרָאֵל׃ וְהִנֵּה חוֹמָה מִחוּץ לַבַּיִת סָבִיב ׀
סָבִיב וּבְיַד הָאִישׁ קְנֵה הַמִּדָּה שֵׁשׁ־אַמּוֹת בָּאַמָּה וָטֹפַח וַיָּמָד אֶת־
ו רֹחַב הַבִּנְיָן קָנֶה אֶחָד וְקוֹמָה קָנֶה אֶחָד׃ וַיָּבוֹא אֶל־שַׁעַר אֲשֶׁר פָּנָיו
דֶּרֶךְ הַקָּדִימָה וַיַּעַל בְּמַעֲלוֹתָו וַיָּמָד ׀ אֶת־סַף הַשַּׁעַר קָנֶה אֶחָד רֹחַב
ז וְאֵת סַף אֶחָד קָנֶה אֶחָד רֹחַב׃ וְהַתָּא קָנֶה אֶחָד אֹרֶךְ וְקָנֶה אֶחָד
רֹחַב וּבֵין הַתָּאִים חָמֵשׁ אַמּוֹת וְסַף הַשַּׁעַר מֵאֵצֶל אֻלָם הַשַּׁעַר מֵהַבָּיִת

8 hall and the inside one, was one reed. He measured the entrance hall of the
9 inner gate, one reed. He measured the entrance hall of the gate, eight cubits;
and its doorway columns, two cubits, this being the entrance hall of the gate
10 of the inner gate. And the side chambers of the eastern gate were three on
this side and three on the other. Each cluster of three measured the same, and
there was one measure for each of their doorway columns, one on each side.
11 He measured the width of the opening in the gate, ten cubits; the length of
12 the gate was thirteen cubits. And there was a border of one cubit in front of
the side chambers and a border of one cubit on the other side, and each side
13 chamber was six cubits by six cubits. He measured the gate from the roof of
one side chamber to the roof of the opposite side chamber, a width of twenty-
14 five cubits; each doorway was directly across from another doorway. Then
he did the doorway columns, sixty cubits high, as well as the columns of the
15 courtyard all around the gate. The distance from the front of the entry gate
16 to the front of the entrance hall of the inner gate was fifty cubits. And there
were windows narrowing into the side chambers and into their doorway
columns within the gate roundabout, and into the halls as well; and there
were windows roundabout within, and on each doorway column were
17 decorations in the form of palm trees. Then he brought me to the outer
courtyard and behold – there were chambers and a tiled pavement for the
courtyard roundabout: there were thirty chambers upon the tiled pavement.
18 And the tiled pavement continued to the sides of the gates along the length
19 of the gates: this was the lower tiled pavement. He measured the width from
in front of the lower gate to the outside of the inner courtyard, one hundred
20 cubits both eastward and northward. He measured the length and width of
21 the gate facing northward toward the outer courtyard. Its side chambers were
three on one side and three on the other, and its doorway columns and
its entrance hall had the same measurements as the first gate: fifty cubits
22 in length, and twenty-five cubits wide. And its windows and its entrance hall
and its decorations of palm trees were the same as those of the gate facing
eastward; people would rise to it on seven steps, and its entrance hall would
23 be before them. And a gate to the inner courtyard was across from the gate
facing north as from the one facing east; he measured one hundred cubits
24 from gate to gate. He led me southward, and behold, there was a gate leading
south, and he measured its doorway columns and its entrance hall to be the
25 same as the measurements of the others. And it had windows roundabout,
as did its entrance hall, like those other windows. Its length was fifty cubits
26 and its width twenty-five cubits. People would ascend to it on seven steps,
and its entrance hall would be before them; and it had palm tree decorations
27 upon its doorpost columns, one on this side and one on the other. There was
a gate leading to the inner courtyard by way of the south and he measured
28 from gate to gate toward the south: one hundred cubits. He brought me to
the inner courtyard through the southern gate. He measured the southern
29 gate to be of the same measurements as the others. And its side chambers
and its doorway columns and its entrance hall shared the measurements of

ח ט קָנֶה אֶחָד: וַיָּמָד אֶת־אֻלָם הַשַּׁעַר מֵהַבַּיִת קָנֶה אֶחָד: וַיָּמָד אֶת־אֻלָם
י הַשַּׁעַר שְׁמֹנֶה אַמּוֹת וְאֵילָו שְׁתַּיִם אַמּוֹת וְאֻלָם הַשַּׁעַר מֵהַבָּיִת: וְתָאֵי
הַשַּׁעַר דֶּרֶךְ הַקָּדִים שְׁלֹשָׁה מִפֹּה וּשְׁלֹשָׁה מִפֹּה מִדָּה אַחַת לִשְׁלָשְׁתָּם
יא וּמִדָּה אַחַת לָאֵילִם מִפֹּה וּמִפּוֹ: וַיָּמָד אֶת־רֹחַב פֶּתַח־הַשַּׁעַר עֶשֶׂר
יב אַמּוֹת אֹרֶךְ הַשַּׁעַר שְׁלוֹשׁ עֶשְׂרֵה אַמּוֹת: וּגְבוּל לִפְנֵי הַתָּאוֹת אַמָּה
אֶחָת וְאַמָּה־אַחַת גְּבוּל מִפֹּה וְהַתָּא שֵׁשׁ־אַמּוֹת מִפּוֹ וְשֵׁשׁ אַמּוֹת
יג מִפּוֹ: וַיָּמָד אֶת־הַשַּׁעַר מִגַּג הַתָּא לְגַגּוֹ רֹחַב עֶשְׂרִים וְחָמֵשׁ אַמּוֹת
יד פֶּתַח נֶגֶד פָּתַח: וַיַּעַשׂ אֶת־אֵילִים שִׁשִּׁים אַמָּה וְאֶל־אֵיל הֶחָצֵר הַשַּׁעַר
טו סָבִיב ׀ סָבִיב: וְעַל־פְּנֵי הַשַּׁעַר היאתון עַל־לִפְנֵי אֻלָם הַשַּׁעַר הַפְּנִימִי הָאִיתוֹן
טז חֲמִשִּׁים אַמָּה: וְחַלֹּנוֹת אֲטֻמוֹת אֶל־הַתָּאִים וְאֶל אֵלֵיהֵמָה לִפְנִימָה
לַשַּׁעַר סָבִיב ׀ סָבִיב וְכֵן לָאֵלַמּוֹת וְחַלּוֹנוֹת סָבִיב ׀ סָבִיב לִפְנִימָה
יז וְאֶל־אַיִל תִּמֹרִים: וַיְבִיאֵנִי אֶל־הֶחָצֵר הַחִיצוֹנָה וְהִנֵּה לְשָׁכוֹת וְרִצְפָה
יח עָשׂוּי לֶחָצֵר סָבִיב ׀ סָבִיב שְׁלֹשִׁים לְשָׁכוֹת אֶל־הָרִצְפָה: וְהָרִצְפָה
יט אֶל־כֶּתֶף הַשְּׁעָרִים לְעֻמַּת אֹרֶךְ הַשְּׁעָרִים הָרִצְפָה הַתַּחְתּוֹנָה: וַיָּמָד
רֹחַב מִלִּפְנֵי הַשַּׁעַר הַתַּחְתּוֹנָה לִפְנֵי הֶחָצֵר הַפְּנִימִי מִחוּץ מֵאָה אַמָּה
כ הַקָּדִים וְהַצָּפוֹן: וְהַשַּׁעַר אֲשֶׁר פָּנָיו דֶּרֶךְ הַצָּפוֹן לֶחָצֵר הַחִיצוֹנָה מָדַד
כא אָרְכּוֹ וְרָחְבּוֹ: וְתָאוֹ שְׁלוֹשָׁה מִפּוֹ וּשְׁלֹשָׁה מִפּוֹ וְאֵילָו וְאֵלַמָּו הָיָה
כְּמִדַּת הַשַּׁעַר הָרִאשׁוֹן חֲמִשִּׁים אַמָּה אָרְכּוֹ וְרֹחַב חָמֵשׁ וְעֶשְׂרִים
כב בָּאַמָּה: וְחַלּוֹנוֹ וְאֵילַמּוֹ וְתִמֹרוֹ כְּמִדַּת הַשַּׁעַר אֲשֶׁר פָּנָיו דֶּרֶךְ הַקָּדִים
כג וּבְמַעֲלוֹת שֶׁבַע יַעֲלוּ־בוֹ וְאֵילַמּוֹ לִפְנֵיהֶם: וְשַׁעַר לֶחָצֵר הַפְּנִימִי נֶגֶד
כד הַשַּׁעַר לַצָּפוֹן וְלַקָּדִים וַיָּמָד מִשַּׁעַר אֶל־שַׁעַר מֵאָה אַמָּה: וַיּוֹלִכֵנִי
דֶּרֶךְ הַדָּרוֹם וְהִנֵּה־שַׁעַר דֶּרֶךְ הַדָּרוֹם וּמָדַד אֵילָו וְאֵילַמָּו כַּמִּדּוֹת
כה הָאֵלֶּה: וְחַלּוֹנִים לוֹ וּלְאֵילַמּוֹ סָבִיב ׀ סָבִיב כְּהַחַלֹּנוֹת הָאֵלֶּה חֲמִשִּׁים
כו אַמָּה אֹרֶךְ וְרֹחַב חָמֵשׁ וְעֶשְׂרִים אַמָּה: וּמַעֲלוֹת שִׁבְעָה עֹלוֹתָו וְאֵלַמָּו
כז לִפְנֵיהֶם וְתִמֹרִים לוֹ אֶחָד מִפּוֹ וְאֶחָד מִפּוֹ אֶל־אֵילָו: וְשַׁעַר לֶחָצֵר
הַפְּנִימִי דֶּרֶךְ הַדָּרוֹם וַיָּמָד מִשַּׁעַר אֶל־הַשַּׁעַר דֶּרֶךְ הַדָּרוֹם מֵאָה
כח אַמּוֹת: וַיְבִיאֵנִי אֶל־חָצֵר הַפְּנִימִי בְּשַׁעַר הַדָּרוֹם וַיָּמָד אֶת־הַשַּׁעַר
כט הַדָּרוֹם כַּמִּדּוֹת הָאֵלֶּה: וְתָאָו וְאֵלָו וְאֵלַמָּו כַּמִּדּוֹת הָאֵלֶּה וְחַלּוֹנוֹת

the others; and it and its entrance hall had windows roundabout. It was fifty
30 cubits in length, and its width was twenty-five cubits. And there were halls
31 all around, with a length of twenty-five cubits and a width of five cubits. Its
entrance hall faced the outer courtyard and had palm tree decorations on its
doorway columns on both sides, and people would ascend to it on eight
32 steps. Then he brought me to the inner courtyard by way of the east, and he
33 measured the gate to be the same as the others. And its side chambers and
its doorway columns and its entrance hall shared the measurements of the
others, and it had windows roundabout, a height of fifty cubits and a width
34 of twenty-five cubits. And its entrance hall faced the outer courtyard and had
palm tree decorations on its doorway columns on both sides, and people
35 would ascend to it on eight steps. He brought me to the northern gate and
36 measured it to be the same as the others – its chambers, its doorway columns,
and its entrance hall – and it had windows roundabout, a length of fifty
37 cubits and a width of twenty-five cubits. And its doorway columns led to
the outer courtyard, and there were palm tree decorations on its doorway
38 columns on both sides, and people would ascend to it on eight steps. There
was a chamber that had its entrance at the doorway columns of the gate where
39 the animals for burnt offerings were washed. And the entrance hall of the
gate had two tables on each side on which to slaughter the animals brought
40 to be burnt offerings, purification offerings, or guilt offerings. And there were
two tables outside on the slope rising toward the northward gate, and there
41 were two tables on the other side, at the entrance hall of the gate. Four tables
on this side and four tables on the other side, alongside the gate; in all, eight
42 tables upon which they would slaughter. And there were four tables made of
cut stone for the burnt offering: they were one and a half cubits in length, one
and a half cubits wide, and one cubit high. On these they would also lay
out the instruments with which they slaughtered the burnt offering or the
43 sacrifice. The rack of double hooks of one handbreadth, to aid in the flaying
of the animal, were installed on the inside wall all around; the flesh of the
44 animal would then be brought to the tables. And outside the inner gate were
the chambers for the singers in the inner courtyard to the side of the northern
gate, and they faced toward the south; one chamber was to the side of the
45 eastern gate, facing north. And he spoke to me: "This chamber which faces
46 southward is for the priests who are guardians in charge of the house. And
the chamber which faces northward is for the priests who are guardians in
charge of the altar. These are the sons of Tzadok, of the sons of Levi, who
47 approach the LORD to serve Him."[62] He measured the court to be a square
one hundred cubits in length and one hundred cubits in width; the altar
48 was in front of the house. He took me to the entrance hall of the house, he
measured each doorway column of the hall to be five cubits on this side and
five cubits on that, and the width of the gate was three cubits on this side and
49 three cubits on that. The length of the entrance hall was twenty cubits and
its width was eleven cubits, and there were steps by which people would

62 | Tzadok was one of the priests in the period of David, and was loyal to Shlomo (1 Kings 1:44).

לוֹ וּלְאֵלַמָּו סָבִיב ׀ סָבִיב חֲמִשִּׁים אַמָּה אֹרֶךְ וְרֹחַב עֶשְׂרִים וְחָמֵשׁ
ל אַמּוֹת׃ וְאֵלַמּוֹת סָבִיב ׀ סָבִיב אֹרֶךְ חָמֵשׁ וְעֶשְׂרִים אַמָּה וְרֹחַב חָמֵשׁ
לא אַמּוֹת׃ וְאֵלַמָּו אֶל־חָצֵר הַחִיצוֹנָה וְתִמֹרִים אֶל־אֵילָו וּמַעֲלוֹת שְׁמוֹנֶה
לב מַעֲלוֹ׃ וַיְבִיאֵנִי אֶל־הֶחָצֵר הַפְּנִימִי דֶּרֶךְ הַקָּדִים וַיָּמָד אֶת־הַשַּׁעַר
לג כַּמִּדּוֹת הָאֵלֶּה׃ וְתָאָו וְאֵלָו וְאֵלַמָּו כַּמִּדּוֹת הָאֵלֶּה וְחַלּוֹנוֹת לוֹ וּלְאֵלַמָּו
לד סָבִיב ׀ סָבִיב אֹרֶךְ חֲמִשִּׁים אַמָּה וְרֹחַב חָמֵשׁ וְעֶשְׂרִים אַמָּה׃ וְאֵלַמָּו
לֶחָצֵר הַחִיצוֹנָה וְתִמֹרִים אֶל־אֵילָו מִפּוֹ וּמִפּוֹ וּשְׁמֹנֶה מַעֲלוֹת מַעֲלוֹ׃
לה לו וַיְבִיאֵנִי אֶל־שַׁעַר הַצָּפוֹן וּמָדַד כַּמִּדּוֹת הָאֵלֶּה׃ תָּאָו אֵלָו וְאֵלַמָּו
וְחַלּוֹנוֹת לוֹ סָבִיב ׀ סָבִיב אֹרֶךְ חֲמִשִּׁים אַמָּה וְרֹחַב חָמֵשׁ וְעֶשְׂרִים
לז אַמָּה׃ וְאֵילָו לֶחָצֵר הַחִיצוֹנָה וְתִמֹרִים אֶל־אֵילָו מִפּוֹ וּמִפּוֹ וּשְׁמֹנֶה
לח מַעֲלוֹת מַעֲלוֹ׃ וְלִשְׁכָּה וּפִתְחָהּ בְּאֵילִים הַשְּׁעָרִים שָׁם יָדִיחוּ אֶת־
לט הָעֹלָה׃ וּבְאֻלָם הַשַּׁעַר שְׁנַיִם שֻׁלְחָנוֹת מִפּוֹ וּשְׁנַיִם שֻׁלְחָנוֹת מִפֹּה
מ לִשְׁחוֹט אֲלֵיהֶם הָעוֹלָה וְהַחַטָּאת וְהָאָשָׁם׃ וְאֶל־הַכָּתֵף מִחוּצָה
לָעוֹלֶה לְפֶתַח הַשַּׁעַר הַצָּפוֹנָה שְׁנַיִם שֻׁלְחָנוֹת וְאֶל־הַכָּתֵף הָאַחֶרֶת
מא אֲשֶׁר לְאֻלָם הַשַּׁעַר שְׁנַיִם שֻׁלְחָנוֹת׃ אַרְבָּעָה שֻׁלְחָנוֹת מִפֹּה וְאַרְבָּעָה
שֻׁלְחָנוֹת מִפֹּה לְכֶתֶף הַשָּׁעַר שְׁמוֹנָה שֻׁלְחָנוֹת אֲלֵיהֶם יִשְׁחָטוּ׃
מב וְאַרְבָּעָה שֻׁלְחָנוֹת לָעוֹלָה אַבְנֵי גָזִית אֹרֶךְ אַמָּה אַחַת וָחֵצִי וְרֹחַב
אַמָּה אַחַת וָחֵצִי וְגֹבַהּ אַמָּה אֶחָת אֲלֵיהֶם וְיַנִּיחוּ אֶת־הַכֵּלִים אֲשֶׁר
מג יִשְׁחֲטוּ אֶת־הָעוֹלָה בָּם וְהַזָּבַח׃ וְהַשְׁפַתַּיִם טֹפַח אֶחָד מוּכָנִים בַּבַּיִת
מד סָבִיב ׀ סָבִיב וְאֶל־הַשֻּׁלְחָנוֹת בְּשַׂר הַקָּרְבָּן׃ וּמִחוּצָה לְשַׁעַר הַפְּנִימִי
לִשְׁכוֹת שָׁרִים בֶּחָצֵר הַפְּנִימִי אֲשֶׁר אֶל־כֶּתֶף שַׁעַר הַצָּפוֹן וּפְנֵיהֶם
מה דֶּרֶךְ הַדָּרוֹם אֶחָד אֶל־כֶּתֶף שַׁעַר הַקָּדִים פְּנֵי דֶּרֶךְ הַצָּפֹן׃ וַיְדַבֵּר אֵלַי כה
זֹה הַלִּשְׁכָּה אֲשֶׁר פָּנֶיהָ דֶּרֶךְ הַדָּרוֹם לַכֹּהֲנִים שֹׁמְרֵי מִשְׁמֶרֶת הַבָּיִת׃
מו וְהַלִּשְׁכָּה אֲשֶׁר פָּנֶיהָ דֶּרֶךְ הַצָּפוֹן לַכֹּהֲנִים שֹׁמְרֵי מִשְׁמֶרֶת הַמִּזְבֵּחַ
מז הֵמָּה בְנֵי־צָדוֹק הַקְּרֵבִים מִבְּנֵי־לֵוִי אֶל־יהוה לְשָׁרְתוֹ׃ וַיָּמָד אֶת־
הֶחָצֵר אֹרֶךְ ׀ מֵאָה אַמָּה וְרֹחַב מֵאָה אַמָּה מְרֻבָּעַת וְהַמִּזְבֵּחַ לִפְנֵי
מח הַבָּיִת׃ וַיְבִאֵנִי אֶל־אֻלָם הַבַּיִת וַיָּמָד אֵל אֻלָם חָמֵשׁ אַמּוֹת מִפֹּה וְחָמֵשׁ
מט אַמּוֹת מִפֹּה וְרֹחַב הַשַּׁעַר שָׁלֹשׁ אַמּוֹת מִפּוֹ וְשָׁלֹשׁ אַמּוֹת מִפּוֹ׃ אֹרֶךְ
הָאֻלָם עֶשְׂרִים אַמָּה וְרֹחַב עַשְׁתֵּי עֶשְׂרֵה אַמָּה וּבַמַּעֲלוֹת אֲשֶׁר יַעֲלוּ

ascend to it, and there were pillars at each of the doorways, one on this side
41 1 and one on that. He then brought me to the Sanctuary. He measured the
doorway columns to be six cubits wide on this side and six cubits wide on
2 the other; these narrowed the width of the opening. And the width of the
entranceway was ten cubits, and the sides of the entranceway were five cubits
long on this side and five cubits on the other. He measured the Sanctuary's
3 length to be forty cubits and its width to be twenty cubits. And he came to
the inner sanctum and measured the doorway column of the door, two cubits,
and the entranceway, six cubits high; and the width of the entranceway was
4 seven cubits. He measured the inner sanctum's length, twenty cubits, and
width, twenty cubits, along the width of the Sanctuary. He said to me: "This
5 is the Holy of Holies." He measured the wall of the House, six cubits, and the
width of each side chamber, four cubits: so it was roundabout the House on
6 every side. And the side chambers adjoined each other, thirty-three, and there
were recesses in the wall of the House roundabout for the side chamber
ceilings to attach to, so they would not be attached to the wall of the House.
7 The side chambers became progressively wider as they went up because the
House was surrounded by an inner system of stairs, which added width to the
House as it rose. A person would thus ascend from the lowermost level to the
8 topmost level by way of the middle level. And so, I saw, the House had a raised
platform roundabout: the foundations of the side chambers were a full reed
9 of six extended cubits. The width of the side chamber wall on the outside was
five cubits, as was the measure of the open space between the outside wall of
10 the side chamber structure and the House. And separating all this from the
11 chamber building were twenty cubits, surrounding the House on all sides. The
side chambers' doors, which opened onto the open space, were one door
to the north and another door to the south, and the width of the open
12 space was five cubits all around. Now the structure, facing the main enclosure
along its western edge, was seventy cubits wide, and the wall of the structure
13 was five cubits wide roundabout, and its length was ninety cubits. And he
measured the length of the House to be one hundred cubits; including the
main enclosure and the structure with its walls, it was one hundred cubits in
14 length. The width of the front of the House and the main enclosure facing east
15 was also one hundred cubits. He then measured the length of the structure
in front of the main enclosure, as he came back, along with its supporting
walls on both sides, to be one hundred cubits. Now the Sanctuary, the
16 inner sanctum, and the entrance hall of the courtyard – all three of them
had thresholds, and narrowing windows, and supporting walls all around.
Across the thresholds there was wooden paneling all around and this overlay
extended from the ground up to the windows, as well as between the
17 windows; similarly, the space over the door all the way to the inner House
and outside, and all the wall roundabout, on the inside and on the outside,
18 were paneled to measure. And they were decorated with cherubim and palm
trees, with a palm tree in between one cherub and the next. And each cherub
19 had two faces, such that a human face faced the palm tree on this side and a

מא א אֵלָיו וְעַמֻּדִים אֶל־הָאֵילִים אֶחָד מִפֹּה וְאֶחָד מִפֹּה׃ וַיְבִיאֵנִי אֶל־הַהֵיכָל
וַיָּמָד אֶת־הָאֵילִים שֵׁשׁ־אַמּוֹת רֹחַב מִפּוֹ וְשֵׁשׁ־אַמּוֹת רֹחַב־מִפּוֹ רֹחַב
ב הָאֹהֶל׃ וְרֹחַב הַפֶּתַח עֶשֶׂר אַמּוֹת וְכִתְפוֹת הַפֶּתַח חָמֵשׁ אַמּוֹת מִפּוֹ
וְחָמֵשׁ אַמּוֹת מִפּוֹ וַיָּמָד אָרְכּוֹ אַרְבָּעִים אַמָּה וְרֹחַב עֶשְׂרִים אַמָּה׃
ג וּבָא לִפְנִימָה וַיָּמָד אֵיל־הַפֶּתַח שְׁתַּיִם אַמּוֹת וְהַפֶּתַח שֵׁשׁ אַמּוֹת
ד וְרֹחַב הַפֶּתַח שֶׁבַע אַמּוֹת׃ וַיָּמָד אֶת־אָרְכּוֹ עֶשְׂרִים אַמָּה וְרֹחַב עֶשְׂרִים
ה אַמָּה אֶל־פְּנֵי הַהֵיכָל וַיֹּאמֶר אֵלַי זֶה קֹדֶשׁ הַקֳּדָשִׁים׃ וַיָּמָד קִיר־הַבַּיִת
שֵׁשׁ אַמּוֹת וְרֹחַב הַצֵּלָע אַרְבַּע אַמּוֹת סָבִיב ׀ סָבִיב לַבַּיִת סָבִיב׃
ו וְהַצְּלָעוֹת צֵלָע אֶל־צֵלָע שָׁלוֹשׁ וּשְׁלֹשִׁים פְּעָמִים וּבָאוֹת בַּקִּיר אֲשֶׁר־
לַבַּיִת לַצְּלָעוֹת סָבִיב ׀ סָבִיב לִהְיוֹת אֲחוּזִים וְלֹא־יִהְיוּ אֲחוּזִים בְּקִיר
ז הַבָּיִת׃ וְרָחֲבָה וְנָסְבָה לְמַעְלָה לְמַעְלָה לַצְּלָעוֹת כִּי מוּסַב־הַבַּיִת
לְמַעְלָה לְמַעְלָה סָבִיב ׀ סָבִיב לַבַּיִת עַל־כֵּן רֹחַב־לַבַּיִת לְמָעְלָה וְכֵן
ח הַתַּחְתּוֹנָה יַעֲלֶה עַל־הָעֶלְיוֹנָה לַתִּיכוֹנָה׃ וְרָאִיתִי לַבַּיִת גֹּבַהּ סָבִיב ׀
ט סָבִיב מיסדות הַצְּלָעוֹת מְלוֹ הַקָּנֶה שֵׁשׁ אַמּוֹת אַצִּילָה׃ רֹחַב הַקִּיר מוּסְדוֹת
אֲשֶׁר־לַצֵּלָע אֶל־הַחוּץ חָמֵשׁ אַמּוֹת וַאֲשֶׁר מֻנָּח בֵּית צְלָעוֹת אֲשֶׁר
י לַבָּיִת׃ וּבֵין הַלְּשָׁכוֹת רֹחַב עֶשְׂרִים אַמָּה סָבִיב לַבַּיִת סָבִיב ׀ סָבִיב׃
יא וּפֶתַח הַצֵּלָע לַמֻּנָּח פֶּתַח אֶחָד דֶּרֶךְ הַצָּפוֹן וּפֶתַח אֶחָד לַדָּרוֹם וְרֹחַב
יב מְקוֹם הַמֻּנָּח חָמֵשׁ אַמּוֹת סָבִיב ׀ סָבִיב׃ וְהַבִּנְיָן אֲשֶׁר אֶל־פְּנֵי הַגִּזְרָה
פְּאַת דֶּרֶךְ־הַיָּם רֹחַב שִׁבְעִים אַמָּה וְקִיר הַבִּנְיָן חָמֵשׁ־אַמּוֹת רֹחַב
יג סָבִיב ׀ סָבִיב וְאָרְכּוֹ תִּשְׁעִים אַמָּה׃ וּמָדַד אֶת־הַבַּיִת אֹרֶךְ מֵאָה אַמָּה
יד וְהַגִּזְרָה וְהַבִּנְיָה וְקִירוֹתֶיהָ אֹרֶךְ מֵאָה אַמָּה׃ וְרֹחַב פְּנֵי הַבַּיִת וְהַגִּזְרָה
טו לַקָּדִים מֵאָה אַמָּה׃ וּמָדַד אֹרֶךְ־הַבִּנְיָן אֶל־פְּנֵי הַגִּזְרָה אֲשֶׁר עַל־
אַחֲרֶיהָ ואתוקיהא מִפּוֹ וּמִפּוֹ מֵאָה אַמָּה וְהַהֵיכָל הַפְּנִימִי וְאֻלַמֵּי וְאַתִּיקֶיהָ
טז הֶחָצֵר׃ הַסִּפִּים וְהַחַלּוֹנִים הָאֲטֻמוֹת וְהָאַתִּיקִים ׀ סָבִיב לִשְׁלָשְׁתָּם
נֶגֶד הַסַּף שְׂחִיף עֵץ סָבִיב ׀ סָבִיב וְהָאָרֶץ עַד־הַחַלֹּנוֹת וְהַחַלֹּנוֹת
יז מְכֻסּוֹת׃ עַל־מֵעַל הַפֶּתַח וְעַד־הַבַּיִת הַפְּנִימִי וְלַחוּץ וְאֶל־כָּל־הַקִּיר
יח סָבִיב ׀ סָבִיב בַּפְּנִימִי וּבַחִיצוֹן מִדּוֹת׃ וְעָשׂוּי כְּרוּבִים וְתִמֹרִים וְתִמֹרָה
יט בֵּין־כְּרוּב לִכְרוּב וּשְׁנַיִם פָּנִים לַכְּרוּב׃ וּפְנֵי אָדָם אֶל־הַתִּמֹרָה מִפּוֹ

lion's face faced the palm tree on the other side. Thus was the whole House
20 decorated roundabout. Cherubim and palm trees were carved from the
21 ground and up over the door as well as along the wall of the Sanctuary. The
Sanctuary had square doorposts, as did the front of the inner sanctum: the
22 appearance of one pair was like that of the other. The altar was of wood three
cubits high, and its length was two cubits, and its legs were of a piece with it.
And its length and its sides were wood. The man spoke to me: "This is the
23 table placed before the Lord." The Sanctuary and the inner sanctum each
24 had double doors and each door had two panels, two folding panels: two
25 panels for one door and two panels for the other. The doors of the Sanctuary
were carved with cherubim and palm tree carvings just like the decoration
on the walls, and there was thick wood paneling on the front of the entrance
26 hall from the outside. And there were narrowing windows with palm tree
decorations on this side and on that on the sides of the entrance hall, on the
42 1 side chambers of the House, and on the thick wood paneling. He took me
out to the outer courtyard; the path led to the north. He brought me to the
chamber building that ran alongside the main enclosure and parallel to the
2 structure, to the north. We faced a length of one hundred cubits and entered
3 by a door leading north; the width of the building was fifty cubits. It ran
alongside the space, twenty cubits across, belonging to the inner courtyard,
and paralleled the tiled pavement of the outer courtyard. Its supporting
4 walls faced one another in thirds. In front of the chamber building was a
walkway ten cubits wide leading to the inner courtyard, a path of one cubit.
5 The chamber doors faced north. And the walls of the upper chambers were
narrower than those of the lower and central floors of the building because
6 the inner supporting walls consumed space. For these were three stories high
and did not have pillars like the courtyard pillars. Therefore, the lower and
7 middle floors lost floor space. There was a fence parallel to the chamber
building, extending by way of the outer courtyard to the front of the chamber
8 building. Its length was fifty cubits. For the length of the chamber building
belonging to the outer courtyard was fifty cubits, and behold, the one across
9 from the Sanctuary was one hundred cubits. Below these chambers there
was an entrance on the east side for a person approaching from the outer
10 courtyard. And there were chambers set into the thickness of the eastward
11 courtyard wall, facing the sacred enclosure and facing the building. There was
a passageway in front of them, and they looked just like the chambers on the
northern passageway; their lengths were the same, as well as their widths, as
12 were their exits with their rules, and their entranceways. And as with the
entranceways to the chamber building on the southward passageway, there
was an entranceway at the main approach. This faced the platform for singers,
13 closest to those entering from the east. Then he said to me: "The northern
chambers and the southern chambers which face the main enclosure are holy
chambers where the priests who approach the Lord may eat the holiest
of sacrifices. There shall they place the holiest of sacrifices, the grain offering
and the purification offering and the guilt offering, for the place is holy.

וּפְנֵי־כְפִיר אֶל־הַתִּמֹרָה מִפּוֹ עָשׂוּי אֶל־כָּל־הַבַּיִת סָבִיב ׀ סָבִיב׃
כ מֵהָאָרֶץ עַד־מֵעַל הַפֶּתַח הַכְּרוּבִים וְהַתִּמֹרִים עֲשׂוּיִם וְקִיר הַהֵיכָל׃
כא כב הַהֵיכָל מְזוּזַת רְבֻעָה וּפְנֵי הַקֹּדֶשׁ הַמַּרְאֶה כַּמַּרְאֶה׃ הַמִּזְבֵּחַ עֵץ שָׁלוֹשׁ
אַמּוֹת גָּבֹהַּ וְאָרְכּוֹ שְׁתַּיִם־אַמּוֹת וּמִקְצֹעוֹתָיו לוֹ וְאָרְכּוֹ וְקִירֹתָיו עֵץ
כג וַיְדַבֵּר אֵלַי זֶה הַשֻּׁלְחָן אֲשֶׁר לִפְנֵי יְהוָה׃ וּשְׁתַּיִם דְּלָתוֹת לַהֵיכָל
כד וְלַקֹּדֶשׁ׃ וּשְׁתַּיִם דְּלָתוֹת לַדְּלָתוֹת שְׁתַּיִם מוּסַבּוֹת דְּלָתוֹת שְׁתַּיִם
כה לְדֶלֶת אֶחָת וּשְׁתֵּי דְלָתוֹת לָאַחֶרֶת׃ וַעֲשׂוּיָה אֲלֵיהֶן אֶל־דַּלְתוֹת
הַהֵיכָל כְּרוּבִים וְתִמֹרִים כַּאֲשֶׁר עֲשׂוּיִם לַקִּירוֹת וְעָב עֵץ אֶל־פְּנֵי
כו הָאוּלָם מֵהַחוּץ׃ וְחַלּוֹנִים אֲטֻמוֹת וְתִמֹרִים מִפּוֹ וּמִפּוֹ אֶל־כִּתְפוֹת
א הָאוּלָם וְצַלְעוֹת הַבַּיִת וְהָעֻבִּים׃ וַיּוֹצִאֵנִי אֶל־הֶחָצֵר הַחִיצוֹנָה הַדֶּרֶךְ מב
דֶּרֶךְ הַצָּפוֹן וַיְבִאֵנִי אֶל־הַלִּשְׁכָּה אֲשֶׁר נֶגֶד הַגִּזְרָה וַאֲשֶׁר־נֶגֶד הַבִּנְיָן
ב אֶל־הַצָּפוֹן׃ אֶל־פְּנֵי אֹרֶךְ אַמּוֹת הַמֵּאָה פֶּתַח הַצָּפוֹן וְהָרֹחַב חֲמִשִּׁים
ג אַמּוֹת׃ נֶגֶד הָעֶשְׂרִים אֲשֶׁר לֶחָצֵר הַפְּנִימִי וְנֶגֶד רִצְפָה אֲשֶׁר לֶחָצֵר
ד הַחִיצוֹנָה אַתִּיק אֶל־פְּנֵי־אַתִּיק בַּשְּׁלִשִׁים׃ וְלִפְנֵי הַלְּשָׁכוֹת מַהֲלַךְ
עֶשֶׂר אַמּוֹת רֹחַב אֶל־הַפְּנִימִית דֶּרֶךְ אַמָּה אֶחָת וּפִתְחֵיהֶם לַצָּפוֹן׃
ה וְהַלְּשָׁכוֹת הָעֶלְיוֹנֹת קְצֻרוֹת כִּי־יוֹכְלוּ אַתִּיקִים מֵהֵנָּה מֵהַתַּחְתֹּנוֹת
ו וּמֵהַתִּכֹנוֹת בִּנְיָן׃ כִּי מְשֻׁלָּשׁוֹת הֵנָּה וְאֵין לָהֶן עַמּוּדִים כְּעַמּוּדֵי
ז הַחֲצֵרוֹת עַל־כֵּן נֶאֱצַל מֵהַתַּחְתּוֹנוֹת וּמֵהַתִּיכֹנוֹת מֵהָאָרֶץ׃ וְגָדֵר
אֲשֶׁר־לַחוּץ לְעֻמַּת הַלְּשָׁכוֹת דֶּרֶךְ הֶחָצֵר הַחִצוֹנָה אֶל־פְּנֵי הַלְּשָׁכוֹת
ח אָרְכּוֹ חֲמִשִּׁים אַמָּה׃ כִּי־אֹרֶךְ הַלְּשָׁכוֹת אֲשֶׁר לֶחָצֵר הַחִצוֹנָה חֲמִשִּׁים
ט אַמָּה וְהִנֵּה עַל־פְּנֵי הַהֵיכָל מֵאָה אַמָּה׃ וּמִתַּחְתָּה לְשָׁכוֹת הָאֵלֶּה וּמִתַּחַת הַלְּשָׁכוֹת
י הַמָּבוֹא מֵהַקָּדִים בְּבֹאוֹ לָהֵנָּה מֵהֶחָצֵר הַחִצֹנָה׃ בְּרֹחַב ׀ גֶּדֶר הֶחָצֵר הַמֵּבִיא
יא דֶּרֶךְ הַקָּדִים אֶל־פְּנֵי הַגִּזְרָה וְאֶל־פְּנֵי הַבִּנְיָן לְשָׁכוֹת׃ וְדֶרֶךְ לִפְנֵיהֶם
כְּמַרְאֵה הַלְּשָׁכוֹת אֲשֶׁר דֶּרֶךְ הַצָּפוֹן כְּאָרְכָּן כֵּן רָחְבָּן וְכֹל מוֹצָאֵיהֶן
יב וּכְמִשְׁפְּטֵיהֶן וּכְפִתְחֵיהֶן׃ וּכְפִתְחֵי הַלְּשָׁכוֹת אֲשֶׁר דֶּרֶךְ הַדָּרוֹם פֶּתַח
יג בְּרֹאשׁ דָּרֶךְ דֶּרֶךְ בִּפְנֵי הַגְּדֶרֶת הֲגִינָה דֶּרֶךְ הַקָּדִים בְּבוֹאָן׃ וַיֹּאמֶר כו
אֵלַי לִשְׁכוֹת הַצָּפוֹן לִשְׁכוֹת הַדָּרוֹם אֲשֶׁר אֶל־פְּנֵי הַגִּזְרָה הֵנָּה ׀
לִשְׁכוֹת הַקֹּדֶשׁ אֲשֶׁר יֹאכְלוּ־שָׁם הַכֹּהֲנִים אֲשֶׁר־קְרוֹבִים לַיהוָה קָדְשֵׁי
הַקֳּדָשִׁים שָׁם יַנִּיחוּ ׀ קָדְשֵׁי הַקֳּדָשִׁים וְהַמִּנְחָה וְהַחַטָּאת וְהָאָשָׁם כִּי

14 Once the priests enter, they may not leave the holy area to go to the outer
courtyard; first they shall leave the garments in which they minister there, for
they are holy. They are to put on other clothes and after that may approach
15 the area designated for the nation." He finished the measurements of the inner
House and took me out through the gate looking out eastward and measured
16 the whole perimeter. He measured the eastern side with his measuring
17 reed – five hundred cubits with the measuring reed all around. He measured
the northern side – five hundred cubits with the measuring reed all around.
18 He measured the southern side – five hundred reeds with the measuring reed.
19 He turned to the western side and measured five hundred reeds with the
20 measuring reed. He measured it in four directions; it had a wall roundabout
running a length of five hundred and a width of five hundred, to separate the
43 1 holy from the ordinary. He led me to the gate, the gate facing out eastward.
2 And behold! The glory of the God of Israel was approaching by the eastern
path with a sound like the roar of vast waters, and the earth was lit up with
3 His glory! It looked like the vision that I had seen, like the vision I saw when
I came to prophesy the city's destruction,[63] visions like the vision I had seen
4 at the Kevar River,[64] and I fell upon my face. Then the glory of the LORD
5 entered the House by way of the gate facing eastward. And a wind lifted me
up and brought me to the inner courtyard, and behold – the glory of the LORD
6 filled the House. I heard Him speaking to me from the House, then there was
7 a man standing next to me. He said to me: "Man, this is the site of My throne
and the place of My footstool, where I will dwell among the children of Israel
forever. And the House of Israel will no longer defile My holy name, they and
their kings with their whoring, and with the graves of their kings' corpses
8 decorated with altars. When they placed their thresholds near My threshold
and their doorposts near My doorposts, with only a wall between Me and
them, they polluted My holy name by the disgusting things they did, so I
9 destroyed them in My anger. This time they must keep their whoring and the
corpses of their kings far away from Me, so that I may dwell among them
10 forever.[65] You, Man, describe this House to the House of Israel so that
they feel ashamed of their sins, and let them take measure of the plan. And if
11 they do feel shame about all they have done, then make known to them the
design of the House and its architectural plan: its exits and entrances, all of its
structures and all of its rules, all its decorative shapes and all the instructions
about it. And write it down in front of them so that they can preserve everything about its design and its rules so that they can carry them out. This is the
12 teaching of the House: the top of the mountain, all its boundary roundabout,
13 is holy of holies. Behold – this is the teaching of the House: These are
the dimensions of the altar[66] in cubits, each cubit being a five-handbreadth

63 | Literally "to destroy the city"; see the visions in chapters 8–11, which depict God's glory leaving Jerusalem as it is destroyed.

64 | See chapter 1.

65 | Cf. Exodus 25:8.

66 | See diagram of the Temple in Yeḥezkel's vision in the appendices.

יד הַמָּקוֹם קֹדֶשׁ: בְּבֹאָם הַכֹּהֲנִים וְלֹא־יֵצְאוּ מֵהַקֹּדֶשׁ אֶל־הֶחָצֵר הַחִיצוֹנָה
וְשָׁם יַנִּיחוּ בִגְדֵיהֶם אֲשֶׁר־יְשָׁרְתוּ בָהֶן כִּי־קֹדֶשׁ הֵנָּה ילבשו בְּגָדִים וְלָבְשׁוּ
טו אֲחֵרִים וְקָרְבוּ אֶל־אֲשֶׁר לָעָם: וְכִלָּה אֶת־מִדּוֹת הַבַּיִת הַפְּנִימִי
טז וְהוֹצִיאַנִי דֶּרֶךְ הַשַּׁעַר אֲשֶׁר פָּנָיו דֶּרֶךְ הַקָּדִים וּמְדָדוֹ סָבִיב | סָבִיב: מָדַד
רוּחַ הַקָּדִים בִּקְנֵה הַמִּדָּה חֲמֵשׁ־אמות קָנִים בִּקְנֵה הַמִּדָּה סָבִיב: מֵאוֹת
יז יח מָדַד רוּחַ הַצָּפוֹן חֲמֵשׁ־מֵאוֹת קָנִים בִּקְנֵה הַמִּדָּה סָבִיב: אֵת רוּחַ
יט הַדָּרוֹם מָדָד חֲמֵשׁ־מֵאוֹת קָנִים בִּקְנֵה הַמִּדָּה: סָבַב אֶל־רוּחַ הַיָּם
כ מָדַד חֲמֵשׁ־מֵאוֹת קָנִים בִּקְנֵה הַמִּדָּה: לְאַרְבַּע רוּחוֹת מְדָדוֹ חוֹמָה
לוֹ סָבִיב | סָבִיב אֹרֶךְ חֲמֵשׁ מֵאוֹת וְרֹחַב חֲמֵשׁ מֵאוֹת לְהַבְדִּיל בֵּין
מג א ב הַקֹּדֶשׁ לְחֹל: וַיּוֹלִכֵנִי אֶל־הַשָּׁעַר שַׁעַר אֲשֶׁר פֹּנֶה דֶּרֶךְ הַקָּדִים: וְהִנֵּה
כְּבוֹד אֱלֹהֵי יִשְׂרָאֵל בָּא מִדֶּרֶךְ הַקָּדִים וְקוֹלוֹ כְּקוֹל מַיִם רַבִּים וְהָאָרֶץ
ג הֵאִירָה מִכְּבֹדוֹ: וּכְמַרְאֵה הַמַּרְאֶה אֲשֶׁר רָאִיתִי כַּמַּרְאֶה אֲשֶׁר־רָאִיתִי
בְּבֹאִי לְשַׁחֵת אֶת־הָעִיר וּמַרְאוֹת כַּמַּרְאֶה אֲשֶׁר רָאִיתִי אֶל־נְהַר כְּבָר
ד וָאֶפֹּל אֶל־פָּנָי: וּכְבוֹד יְהוָה בָּא אֶל־הַבָּיִת דֶּרֶךְ שַׁעַר אֲשֶׁר פָּנָיו
ה דֶּרֶךְ הַקָּדִים: וַתִּשָּׂאֵנִי רוּחַ וַתְּבִאֵנִי אֶל־הֶחָצֵר הַפְּנִימִי וְהִנֵּה מָלֵא
ו כְבוֹד־יְהוָה הַבָּיִת: וָאֶשְׁמַע מִדַּבֵּר אֵלַי מֵהַבָּיִת וְאִישׁ הָיָה עֹמֵד
ז אֶצְלִי: וַיֹּאמֶר אֵלַי בֶּן־אָדָם אֶת־מְקוֹם כִּסְאִי וְאֶת־מְקוֹם כַּפּוֹת
רַגְלַי אֲשֶׁר אֶשְׁכָּן־שָׁם בְּתוֹךְ בְּנֵי־יִשְׂרָאֵל לְעוֹלָם וְלֹא יְטַמְּאוּ עוֹד
בֵית־יִשְׂרָאֵל שֵׁם קָדְשִׁי הֵמָּה וּמַלְכֵיהֶם בִּזְנוּתָם וּבְפִגְרֵי מַלְכֵיהֶם
ח בָּמוֹתָם: בְּתִתָּם סִפָּם אֶת־סִפִּי וּמְזוּזָתָם אֵצֶל מְזוּזָתִי וְהַקִּיר בֵּינִי
וּבֵינֵיהֶם וְטִמְּאוּ | אֶת־שֵׁם קָדְשִׁי בְּתוֹעֲבוֹתָם אֲשֶׁר עָשׂוּ וָאֲכַל אֹתָם
ט בְּאַפִּי: עַתָּה יְרַחֲקוּ אֶת־זְנוּתָם וּפִגְרֵי מַלְכֵיהֶם מִמֶּנִּי וְשָׁכַנְתִּי בְתוֹכָם
י לְעוֹלָם: אַתָּה בֶן־אָדָם הַגֵּד אֶת־בֵּית־יִשְׂרָאֵל אֶת־
יא הַבַּיִת וְיִכָּלְמוּ מֵעֲוֺנוֹתֵיהֶם וּמָדְדוּ אֶת־תָּכְנִית: וְאִם־נִכְלְמוּ מִכֹּל
אֲשֶׁר־עָשׂוּ צוּרַת הַבַּיִת וּתְכוּנָתוֹ וּמוֹצָאָיו וּמוֹבָאָיו וְכָל־צורתו וְאֵת
כָּל־חֻקֹּתָיו וְכָל־צורתו וְכָל־תורתו הוֹדַע אוֹתָם וּכְתֹב לְעֵינֵיהֶם
יב וְיִשְׁמְרוּ אֶת־כָּל־צוּרָתוֹ וְאֶת־כָּל־חֻקֹּתָיו וְעָשׂוּ אוֹתָם: זֹאת תּוֹרַת
הַבָּיִת עַל־רֹאשׁ הָהָר כָּל־גְּבֻלוֹ סָבִיב | סָבִיב קֹדֶשׁ קָדָשִׁים הִנֵּה־זֹאת
יג תּוֹרַת הַבָּיִת: וְאֵלֶּה מִדּוֹת הַמִּזְבֵּחַ בָּאַמּוֹת אַמָּה אַמָּה וָטֹפַח וְחֵיק

cubit plus a handbreadth. But the base is a smaller cubit, as is the cubit of its
width, and the border at its edge all around is one half-cubit, the same as for
14 the top level of the altar. Now from the base on the ground up to the lower
ledge there are two cubits, and its excess width is one cubit, and from the
smaller ledge up to the top of the large ledge there are four cubits, with an
15 excess width of one cubit. Now the Harel hearth is four cubits, and from this
16 Ariel upward, there rise four horns. And the Ariel is twelve cubits long by
17 twelve cubits wide, square on its four sides. And the ledge is fourteen in
length by fourteen in width on its four sides, and the border surrounding it
is half a small cubit. A cubit of its base extends all around, and its ramp
18 is off-center, shifted eastward." Then He said to me: "Man, thus says the
Lord GOD: These are the statutes pertaining to the altar on the day that it is
fashioned, to enable you to bring burnt offerings upon it and to sprinkle blood
19 upon it. You will pass on to the priests, the Levites who are of the seed of
Tzadok who approach Me to serve Me, the word of the Lord GOD: a young
20 bull from the cattle herd shall be a purification offering. Take from its blood
and put some on the four altar horns and four corners of the ledge and upon
the border all around: you shall purify it so that it can provide atonement.
21 Then take the bull of the purification offering and burn it in its designated
22 place in the bounds of the House, outside the Sanctuary. And from the
second day onward, you shall sacrifice a flawless male goat for a purification
offering. They shall purify the altar as they purified it before, by sacrificing
23 the bull. When you have finished the purification process, sacrifice a flawless
24 young bull from among the cattle and a flawless ram from among the sheep.
You shall bring them near the LORD, and the priests shall throw salt upon
25 them and offer them up as a burnt offering to the LORD. For seven days you
shall bring the goat of a purification offering daily, as well as a young bull from
26 the cattle and a ram from the sheep; they are all to be flawless. For seven days
27 they shall cleanse the altar and purify it and consecrate it. When these days
are over, from the eighth day onward, the priests may prepare your burnt
offerings and your peace offerings on the altar, and I shall respond favorably
44 1 to you. So spoke the Lord GOD.[67] He brought me back by way of the
2 outer gate of the Sanctuary that faces eastward, and it was closed. The LORD
said to me: This gate will stay shut; it shall not be opened, and no man may
enter through it; because the LORD, God of Israel, entered through it, it shall
3 remain closed. Regarding the prince: as prince, he will sit within it to eat
bread before the LORD, arriving by way of the entrance hall of that gate and
4 leaving the same way." He brought me toward the northern gate to the front
of the House. I looked, and behold – the LORD's glory filled the House of the
5 LORD, and I fell on my face. The LORD said to me: "Man, pay attention, and
see with your eyes and hear with your ears all that I am saying to you about
the laws of the House of the LORD and all its teachings; and pay attention to
6 the rules about entering the House, about exiting the Sanctuary. And you

67 | Compare to the dedication of the altar in the Tabernacle in Leviticus 8:11–21; there, too, the ceremony lasts seven days (Lev. 9:34).

האמה ואמה-רחב וגבולה אל-שפתה סביב זרת האחד וזה גב
יד המזבח: ומחיק הארץ עד-העזרה התחתונה שתים אמות ורחב
אמה אחת ומהעזרה הקטנה עד-העזרה הגדולה ארבע אמות
טו ורחב האמה: וההראל ארבע אמות ומהאראיל ולמעלה הקרנות
טז ארבע: והאראיל שתים עשרה ארך בשתים עשרה רחב רבוע אל
יז ארבעת רבעיו: והעזרה ארבע עשרה ארך בארבע עשרה רחב
אל ארבעת רבעיה והגבול סביב אותה חצי האמה והחיק-לה אמה
יח סביב ומעלתהו פנות קדים: ויאמר אלי בן-אדם כה אמר אדני
יהוה אלה חקות המזבח ביום העשותו להעלות עליו עולה ולזרק
יט עליו דם: ונתתה אל-הכהנים הלוים אשר הם מזרע צדוק הקרבים
כ אלי נאם אדני יהוה לשרתני פר בן-בקר לחטאת: ולקחת מדמו
ונתתה על-ארבע קרנתיו ואל-ארבע פנות העזרה ואל-הגבול
כא סביב וחטאת אותו וכפרתהו: ולקחת את הפר החטאת ושרפו
כב במפקד הבית מחוץ למקדש: וביום השני תקריב שעיר-עזים תמים
כג לחטאת וחטאו את-המזבח כאשר חטאו בפר: בכלותך מחטא
כד תקריב פר בן-בקר תמים ואיל מן-הצאן תמים: והקרבתם לפני
יהוה והשליכו הכהנים עליהם מלח והעלו אותם עלה ליהוה:
כה שבעת ימים תעשה שעיר-חטאת ליום ופר בן-בקר ואיל מן-הצאן
כו תמימים יעשו: שבעת ימים יכפרו את-המזבח וטהרו אתו ומלאו
כז ידו: ויכלו את-הימים והיה ביום השמיני והלאה יעשו הכהנים כז
על-המזבח את-עולותיכם ואת-שלמיכם ורצאתי אתכם נאם אדני
מד א יהוה: וישב אתי דרך שער המקדש החיצון הפנה
ב קדים והוא סגור: ויאמר אלי יהוה השער הזה סגור יהיה לא יפתח
ג ואיש לא-יבא בו כי יהוה אלהי-ישראל בא בו והיה סגור: את-
הנשיא נשיא הוא ישב-בו לאכול-לחם לפני יהוה מדרך אולם לאכל-
ד השער יבוא ומדרכו יצא: ויביאני דרך-שער הצפון אל-פני הבית
ה וארא והנה מלא כבוד-יהוה את-בית יהוה ואפל אל-פני: ויאמר
אלי יהוה בן-אדם שים לבך וראה בעיניך ובאזניך שמע את כל-
אשר אני מדבר אתך לכל-חקות בית-יהוה ולכל-תורתו ושמת
ו לבך למבוא הבית בכל מוצאי המקדש: ואמרת אל-מרי אל-בית

shall say to the rebels, to the House of Israel: Thus says the Lord God: Enough
7 with your disgusting activities, House of Israel, with your bringing of strangers,
uncircumcised of heart and uncircumcised of flesh, into My Sanctuary to
desecrate My House, offering up My bread, fat, and blood; with your breaking
8 of My covenant with all your disgusting deeds! You did not dutifully protect
My holy things. As guardians of My precious things in My Sanctuary, you
9 turned them into your own property! Thus says the Lord God: No
stranger uncircumcised of heart or uncircumcised of flesh shall enter My
Sanctuary; this applies to any estranged person among the children of Israel.
10 But the Levites who became distanced from Me when Israel went astray, who
11 strayed from Me to follow their idols, they shall bear their sin. They may be
ministers in My Sanctuary, in charge of the gates of the House and attending
to the House; they shall slaughter burnt offerings and sacrifices for the people,
12 and they shall stand before them to minister to them. But because they
ministered to them in front of their idols and became a stumbling block of
sin to the House of Israel, I have raised My hand against them; this is the word
13 of the Lord God, and they shall bear their sin.[68] Thus they shall not come
near Me to serve Me as a priest, nor approach any of My holy offerings or the
holy of holy offerings; let them bear their shame for the disgusting things they
14 did. I appoint them custodians of the duties of the House, in charge of all its
15 services and everything that is done within it. But the priests who
are Levites descended from Tzadok, who protected the preciousness of My
Sanctuary when the children of Israel strayed from Me, they are the ones who
may draw near Me in order to serve Me, and they shall stand before Me to
16 offer Me fat and blood: this is the word of the Lord God. They are the ones
who will enter My Sanctuary, and they shall approach My table to serve Me;
17 they shall dutifully protect My precious things. This is how it shall be when
they approach the gates of the inner courtyard: they will wear linen garments,
and no wool shall be upon them when they serve at the gates of the inner
18 courtyard and within. There will be linen turbans on their heads and linen
trousers on their loins; they shall not gird themselves in a way that causes
19 perspiration. And when they leave to go to the outer courtyard – to the outer
courtyard to the people – they shall remove the garments in which they serve,
leaving them in the holy chambers, and put on other clothing, in order not
to give the impression, by mingling with them wearing their holy garments,
20 that the people are equal to them in sanctity. They shall not shave their heads
nor grow their hair long in disarray; they shall keep their heads carefully
21 trimmed. Nor shall any priest drink wine when they enter the inner courtyard.
22 And they shall not take as a wife a widow or a divorcée.[69] Rather, they shall
take as wives only virgins of the seed of the House of Israel, or a widow
23 who is the widow of a priest. And they shall teach My people the difference
between the sacred and the profane and make known to them the difference
24 between impure and pure. When there is controversy, they shall stand in

68 | This idea does not appear in the Torah (Five Books of Moses), but see, e.g., Judges, chapter 17.

69 | Cf. Leviticus 21:7, which does not include the restriction on widows.

יִשְׂרָאֵל כֹּה אָמַר אֲדֹנָי יֱהֹוִה רַב־לָכֶם מִכָּל־תּוֹעֲבוֹתֵיכֶם בֵּית יִשְׂרָאֵל׃ ז
בַּהֲבִיאֲכֶם בְּנֵי־נֵכָר עַרְלֵי־לֵב וְעַרְלֵי בָשָׂר לִהְיוֹת בְּמִקְדָּשִׁי לְחַלְּלוֹ
אֶת־בֵּיתִי בְּהַקְרִיבְכֶם אֶת־לַחְמִי חֵלֶב וָדָם וַיָּפֵרוּ אֶת־בְּרִיתִי אֶל כָּל־
תּוֹעֲבוֹתֵיכֶם׃ וְלֹא שְׁמַרְתֶּם מִשְׁמֶרֶת קָדָשָׁי וַתְּשִׂימוּן לְשֹׁמְרֵי מִשְׁמַרְתִּי ח
בְּמִקְדָּשִׁי לָכֶם׃ כֹּה־אָמַר אֲדֹנָי יֱהֹוִה כָּל־בֶּן־נֵכָר עֶרֶל ט
לֵב וְעֶרֶל בָּשָׂר לֹא יָבוֹא אֶל־מִקְדָּשִׁי לְכָל־בֶּן־נֵכָר אֲשֶׁר בְּתוֹךְ בְּנֵי
יִשְׂרָאֵל׃ כִּי אִם־הַלְוִיִּם אֲשֶׁר רָחֲקוּ מֵעָלַי בִּתְעוֹת יִשְׂרָאֵל אֲשֶׁר תָּעוּ י
מֵעָלַי אַחֲרֵי גִּלּוּלֵיהֶם וְנָשְׂאוּ עֲוֺנָם׃ וְהָיוּ בְמִקְדָּשִׁי מְשָׁרְתִים פְּקֻדּוֹת יא
אֶל־שַׁעֲרֵי הַבַּיִת וּמְשָׁרְתִים אֶת־הַבָּיִת הֵמָּה יִשְׁחֲטוּ אֶת־הָעֹלָה
וְאֶת־הַזֶּבַח לָעָם וְהֵמָּה יַעַמְדוּ לִפְנֵיהֶם לְשָׁרְתָם׃ יַעַן אֲשֶׁר יְשָׁרְתוּ יב
אוֹתָם לִפְנֵי גִלּוּלֵיהֶם וְהָיוּ לְבֵית־יִשְׂרָאֵל לְמִכְשׁוֹל עָוֺן עַל־כֵּן נָשָׂאתִי
יָדִי עֲלֵיהֶם נְאֻם אֲדֹנָי יֱהֹוִה וְנָשְׂאוּ עֲוֺנָם׃ וְלֹא־יִגְּשׁוּ אֵלַי לְכַהֵן לִי יג
וְלָגֶשֶׁת עַל־כָּל־קָדָשַׁי אֶל־קָדְשֵׁי הַקְּדָשִׁים וְנָשְׂאוּ כְּלִמָּתָם וְתוֹעֲבוֹתָם
אֲשֶׁר עָשׂוּ׃ וְנָתַתִּי אוֹתָם שֹׁמְרֵי מִשְׁמֶרֶת הַבָּיִת לְכֹל עֲבֹדָתוֹ וּלְכֹל יד
אֲשֶׁר יֵעָשֶׂה בּוֹ׃ וְהַכֹּהֲנִים הַלְוִיִּם בְּנֵי צָדוֹק אֲשֶׁר שָׁמְרוּ טו
אֶת־מִשְׁמֶרֶת מִקְדָּשִׁי בִּתְעוֹת בְּנֵי־יִשְׂרָאֵל מֵעָלַי הֵמָּה יִקְרְבוּ אֵלַי
לְשָׁרְתֵנִי וְעָמְדוּ לְפָנַי לְהַקְרִיב לִי חֵלֶב וָדָם נְאֻם אֲדֹנָי יֱהֹוִה׃ הֵמָּה טז
יָבֹאוּ אֶל־מִקְדָּשִׁי וְהֵמָּה יִקְרְבוּ אֶל־שֻׁלְחָנִי לְשָׁרְתֵנִי וְשָׁמְרוּ אֶת־
מִשְׁמַרְתִּי׃ וְהָיָה בְּבוֹאָם אֶל־שַׁעֲרֵי הֶחָצֵר הַפְּנִימִית בִּגְדֵי פִשְׁתִּים יז
יִלְבָּשׁוּ וְלֹא־יַעֲלֶה עֲלֵיהֶם צֶמֶר בְּשָׁרְתָם בְּשַׁעֲרֵי הֶחָצֵר הַפְּנִימִית
וָבָיְתָה׃ פַּאֲרֵי פִשְׁתִּים יִהְיוּ עַל־רֹאשָׁם וּמִכְנְסֵי פִשְׁתִּים יִהְיוּ עַל־ יח
מָתְנֵיהֶם לֹא יַחְגְּרוּ בַּיָּזַע׃ וּבְצֵאתָם אֶל־הֶחָצֵר הַחִיצוֹנָה אֶל־הֶחָצֵר יט
הַחִיצוֹנָה אֶל־הָעָם יִפְשְׁטוּ אֶת־בִּגְדֵיהֶם אֲשֶׁר־הֵמָּה מְשָׁרְתִם בָּם
וְהִנִּיחוּ אוֹתָם בְּלִשְׁכֹת הַקֹּדֶשׁ וְלָבְשׁוּ בְּגָדִים אֲחֵרִים וְלֹא־יְקַדְּשׁוּ
אֶת־הָעָם בְּבִגְדֵיהֶם׃ וְרֹאשָׁם לֹא יְגַלֵּחוּ וּפֶרַע לֹא יְשַׁלֵּחוּ כָּסוֹם יִכְסְמוּ כ
אֶת־רָאשֵׁיהֶם׃ וְיַיִן לֹא־יִשְׁתּוּ כָּל־כֹּהֵן בְּבוֹאָם אֶל־הֶחָצֵר הַפְּנִימִית׃ כא
וְאַלְמָנָה וּגְרוּשָׁה לֹא־יִקְחוּ לָהֶם לְנָשִׁים כִּי אִם־בְּתוּלֹת מִזֶּרַע בֵּית כב
יִשְׂרָאֵל וְהָאַלְמָנָה אֲשֶׁר תִּהְיֶה אַלְמָנָה מִכֹּהֵן יִקָּחוּ׃ וְאֶת־עַמִּי יוֹרוּ כג
בֵּין קֹדֶשׁ לְחֹל וּבֵין־טָמֵא לְטָהוֹר יוֹדִעֻם׃ וְעַל־רִיב הֵמָּה יַעַמְדוּ כד

judgment, adjudicating it according to My laws. And they shall keep My
teachings and My statutes at all the times I have appointed, and sanctify My
25 Sabbaths. The priest shall not approach a human corpse and become impure
because of it, though for a father or a mother, for a son or a daughter, for a
26 brother or for a sister who is unmarried, they may become impure.[70] After a
27 priest's purification process begins, seven days are counted for him. And on
the day he comes to the Sanctuary, into the inner courtyard to minister in the
Sanctuary, he is to bring his purification offering – this is the word of the Lord
28 God. And this shall be the priests' inheritance: I am their inheritance. Give
29 them no territory to possess in the land of Israel; I am their possession.[71] They
shall eat the grain offering and the purification offering and the guilt offering,
30 and everything consecrated by vow in Israel shall be theirs.[72] The choicest of
all first fruits of every kind and every gift offering out of all your various
donations belongs to the priests. And your first kneading you shall give to the
31 priest so that a blessing settles upon your home.[73] Whether it be bird or beast,
the priests may not eat any creature that died on its own or was torn to pieces
45 1 as prey. When you allot the land as inheritance, you shall raise up a
portion of it as a gift to the Lord, a holy portion of the land measuring
twenty-five thousand reeds in length and ten thousand reeds in width. This
2 is consecrated ground within all of its boundary roundabout. Out of this,
there shall be dedicated a square plot for the Sanctuary, five hundred by five
3 hundred roundabout, with an open space of fifty cubits surrounding it. And
by this same measure you shall measure out a length of twenty-five thousand
and a width of ten thousand, and in it will be the Sanctuary, the Holy of
4 Holies.[74] This consecrated portion of the land belongs to the priests who
minister in the Sanctuary, those who approach to serve the Lord. It shall give
5 them a place for their houses as well as holy ground for the Sanctuary. Another
area twenty-five thousand long by ten thousand wide shall be the heritable
possession of the Levites who minister in the House, to be divided into
6 twenty sections. For the property of the city, set an area of five thousand wide
by twenty-five thousand long alongside the consecrated portion: this shall
7 belong to the entire House of Israel. And the prince's portion shall be on both
sides of the consecrated area and the city's landholding, facing the consecrated
area and facing the city's landholding; on the west side extending westward,
and on the east side, eastward. And its length will parallel one of the tribes'
8 portions, from the western boundary to the eastern boundary. This is the
prince's territorial possession in Israel so that My princes will no longer
maltreat My nation; instead, the rest of the land will be given to the House
9 of Israel, according to their tribes. Thus says the Lord God: You
have gone far enough, O princes of Israel! Stop your violence and robbery,

70 | Cf. Leviticus 21:1–4.

71 | Cf. Deuteronomy 10:9.

72 | For this and the next verse, cf. Numbers 18:8–14.

73 | Cf. Numbers 15:20–21.

74 | That is, the Temple, which includes the Holy of Holies.

לשפט בְּמִשְׁפָּטַי ושפטהו וְאֶת־תּוֹרֹתַי וְאֶת־חֻקֹּתַי בְּכָל־מוֹעֲדַי יִשְׁמֹרוּ לְמִשְׁפָּט יִשְׁפְּטֻהוּ
כה וְאֶת־שַׁבְּתוֹתַי יְקַדֵּשׁוּ: וְאֶל־מֵת אָדָם לֹא יָבוֹא לְטָמְאָה כִּי אִם־לְאָב
וּלְאֵם וּלְבֵן וּלְבַת לְאָח וּלְאָחוֹת אֲשֶׁר־לֹא־הָיְתָה לְאִישׁ יִטַּמָּאוּ:
כו כז וְאַחֲרֵי טָהֳרָתוֹ שִׁבְעַת יָמִים יִסְפְּרוּ־לוֹ: וּבְיוֹם בֹּאוֹ אֶל־הַקֹּדֶשׁ אֶל־
הֶחָצֵר הַפְּנִימִית לְשָׁרֵת בַּקֹּדֶשׁ יַקְרִיב חַטָּאתוֹ נְאֻם אֲדֹנָי יֱהוִה:
כח וְהָיְתָה לָהֶם לְנַחֲלָה אֲנִי נַחֲלָתָם וַאֲחֻזָּה לֹא־תִתְּנוּ לָהֶם בְּיִשְׂרָאֵל
כט אֲנִי אֲחֻזָּתָם: הַמִּנְחָה וְהַחַטָּאת וְהָאָשָׁם הֵמָּה יֹאכְלוּם וְכָל־חֵרֶם
ל בְּיִשְׂרָאֵל לָהֶם יִהְיֶה: וְרֵאשִׁית כָּל־בִּכּוּרֵי כֹל וְכָל־תְּרוּמַת כֹּל מִכֹּל
תְּרוּמוֹתֵיכֶם לַכֹּהֲנִים יִהְיֶה וְרֵאשִׁית עֲרִסוֹתֵיכֶם תִּתְּנוּ לַכֹּהֵן לְהָנִיחַ
לא בְּרָכָה אֶל־בֵּיתֶךָ: כָּל־נְבֵלָה וּטְרֵפָה מִן־הָעוֹף וּמִן־הַבְּהֵמָה לֹא יֹאכְלוּ
מה א הַכֹּהֲנִים: וּבְהַפִּילְכֶם אֶת־הָאָרֶץ בְּנַחֲלָה תָּרִימוּ תְרוּמָה
לַיהוָה ׀ קֹדֶשׁ מִן־הָאָרֶץ אֹרֶךְ חֲמִשָּׁה וְעֶשְׂרִים אֶלֶף אֹרֶךְ וְרֹחַב עֲשָׂרָה
ב אָלֶף קֹדֶשׁ־הוּא בְכָל־גְּבוּלָהּ סָבִיב: יִהְיֶה מִזֶּה אֶל־הַקֹּדֶשׁ חֲמֵשׁ
מֵאוֹת בַּחֲמֵשׁ מֵאוֹת מְרֻבָּע סָבִיב וַחֲמִשִּׁים אַמָּה מִגְרָשׁ לוֹ סָבִיב:
ג וּמִן־הַמִּדָּה הַזֹּאת תָּמוֹד אֹרֶךְ חֲמֵשׁ וְעֶשְׂרִים אֶלֶף וְרֹחַב עֲשֶׂרֶת
ד אֲלָפִים וּבוֹ־יִהְיֶה הַמִּקְדָּשׁ קֹדֶשׁ קֳדָשִׁים: קֹדֶשׁ מִן־הָאָרֶץ הוּא
לַכֹּהֲנִים מְשָׁרְתֵי הַמִּקְדָּשׁ יִהְיֶה הַקְּרֵבִים לְשָׁרֵת אֶת־יְהוָה וְהָיָה לָהֶם
ה מָקוֹם לְבָתִּים וּמִקְדָּשׁ לַמִּקְדָּשׁ: וַחֲמִשָּׁה וְעֶשְׂרִים אֶלֶף אֹרֶךְ וַעֲשֶׂרֶת
אֲלָפִים רֹחַב יהיה לַלְוִיִּם מְשָׁרְתֵי הַבַּיִת לָהֶם לַאֲחֻזָּה עֶשְׂרִים לְשָׁכֹת: וְהָיָה
ו וַאֲחֻזַּת הָעִיר תִּתְּנוּ חֲמֵשֶׁת אֲלָפִים רֹחַב וְאֹרֶךְ חֲמִשָּׁה וְעֶשְׂרִים אֶלֶף
ז לְעֻמַּת תְּרוּמַת הַקֹּדֶשׁ לְכָל־בֵּית יִשְׂרָאֵל יִהְיֶה: וְלַנָּשִׂיא מִזֶּה וּמִזֶּה
לִתְרוּמַת הַקֹּדֶשׁ וְלַאֲחֻזַּת הָעִיר אֶל־פְּנֵי תְרוּמַת־הַקֹּדֶשׁ וְאֶל־פְּנֵי
אֲחֻזַּת הָעִיר מִפְּאַת יָם יָמָּה וּמִפְּאַת קֵדְמָה קָדִימָה וְאֹרֶךְ לְעֻמּוֹת
ח אַחַד הַחֲלָקִים מִגְּבוּל יָם אֶל־גְּבוּל קָדִימָה: לָאָרֶץ יִהְיֶה־לּוֹ לַאֲחֻזָּה
בְּיִשְׂרָאֵל וְלֹא־יוֹנוּ עוֹד נְשִׂיאַי אֶת־עַמִּי וְהָאָרֶץ יִתְּנוּ לְבֵית־יִשְׂרָאֵל
ט לְשִׁבְטֵיהֶם: כֹּה־אָמַר אֲדֹנָי יֱהוִה רַב־לָכֶם נְשִׂיאֵי
יִשְׂרָאֵל חָמָס וָשֹׁד הָסִירוּ וּמִשְׁפָּט וּצְדָקָה עֲשׂוּ הָרִימוּ גְרֻשֹׁתֵיכֶם

do what is just and right! Remove from My people your exacting taxes that
10 evict them from their land, says the Lord God. You shall have honest scales
11 and honest measures of the ephah and the *bat*.[75] The ephah and the *bat*
contain the same amount, so the *bat* contains one-tenth of a homer, and one-
12 tenth of a homer is also an ephah: their measure is relative to the homer. Now
the shekel is twenty gerah. Twenty shekel, twenty-five shekel, fifteen shekel
13 together shall be your maneh.[76] This is the contribution that you shall offer
up: one-sixth of an ephah per homer of wheat and one-sixth of an ephah per
14 homer of barley. The rule regarding oil: the *bat* is the measure of oil; you shall
offer one-tenth of a *bat* out of the *kor*, which is a homer of ten *bat*, for ten *bat*
15 make up a homer. And you shall offer one lamb out of two hundred from
your flock in the well-watered pastureland of Israel. These shall serve as the
grain offering and as the burnt offering and as the peace offering to atone for
16 them, says the Lord God. All the people of the land
17 shall give this contribution to the prince of Israel. And it shall be the prince's
duty to provide burnt offerings and grain offerings and libations on festivals,
New Moons, and Sabbaths; at all the times appointed for the House of
Israel, he shall prepare the purification offering and the grain offering and the
burnt offering and the peace offering to provide atonement for the House of
18 Israel. Thus says the Lord God: In the first month, on the first
day of the month, you shall take a young bull with no blemish to purify
19 the Sanctuary. And the priest shall take from the blood of this purification
offering and put it on the doorposts of the House, on the four corners of the
20 ledge of the altar, and on the doorpost of the gate of the inner courtyard.[77] And
so shall you do on the seventh day of the month for anyone who has sinned
by mistake or due to ignorance: thus you shall provide atonement for the
21 House. In the first month, on the fourteenth day of the month, you shall bring
the Passover sacrifice, for a festival of seven days, unleavened bread shall be
22 eaten. On that day the prince shall prepare a bull as a purification offering for
23 himself and for all the people of the land. And on every one of the seven days
of the festival he shall prepare a burnt offering to the Lord: seven bulls and
seven rams with no blemish every day for seven days, and a daily purification
24 offering consisting of one male goat. And he shall prepare a grain offering
consisting of one ephah for each bull and one ephah for each ram and a hin
25 of oil for each ephah.[78] In the seventh month, on the fifteenth day of the
month, during the festival, he shall prepare offerings just like those on the
seven days: a similar purification offering, a similar burnt offering, and a
46 1 similar grain offering, and a like amount of oil. Thus says the Lord
God: The gate of the inner courtyard that faces eastward shall be closed

75 | The ephah is a dry measure and the *bat* a liquid measure; each contained approximately 22 liters (cf. Lev. 19:35).

76 | The maneh and the shekel were measurements of weight. The shekel of pre-exilic Yehuda weighed 11.3 grams.

77 | Cf. Exodus 12:7, 22.

78 | A hin is one-sixth of a *bat*.

י מֵעַל עַמִּי נְאֻם אֲדֹנָי יֱהוִה: מֹאזְנֵי־צֶדֶק וְאֵיפַת־צֶדֶק וּבַת־צֶדֶק יְהִי
יא לָכֶם: הָאֵיפָה וְהַבַּת תֹּכֶן אֶחָד יִהְיֶה לָשֵׂאת מַעְשַׂר הַחֹמֶר הַבָּת
יב וַעֲשִׂירִת הַחֹמֶר הָאֵיפָה אֶל־הַחֹמֶר יִהְיֶה מַתְכֻּנְתּוֹ: וְהַשֶּׁקֶל עֶשְׂרִים
גֵּרָה עֶשְׂרִים שְׁקָלִים חֲמִשָּׁה וְעֶשְׂרִים שְׁקָלִים עֲשָׂרָה וַחֲמִשָּׁה שֶׁקֶל
יג הַמָּנֶה יִהְיֶה לָכֶם: זֹאת הַתְּרוּמָה אֲשֶׁר תָּרִימוּ שִׁשִּׁית הָאֵיפָה מֵחֹמֶר
יד הַחִטִּים וְשִׁשִּׁיתֶם הָאֵיפָה מֵחֹמֶר הַשְּׂעֹרִים: וְחֹק הַשֶּׁמֶן הַבַּת הַשֶּׁמֶן
מַעְשַׂר הַבַּת מִן־הַכֹּר עֲשֶׂרֶת הַבַּתִּים חֹמֶר כִּי־עֲשֶׂרֶת הַבַּתִּים חֹמֶר:
טו כח וְשֶׂה־אַחַת מִן־הַצֹּאן מִן־הַמָּאתַיִם מִמַּשְׁקֵה יִשְׂרָאֵל לְמִנְחָה וּלְעוֹלָה
טז וְלִשְׁלָמִים לְכַפֵּר עֲלֵיהֶם נְאֻם אֲדֹנָי יֱהוִה: כֹּל הָעָם
יז הָאָרֶץ יִהְיוּ אֶל־הַתְּרוּמָה הַזֹּאת לַנָּשִׂיא בְּיִשְׂרָאֵל: וְעַל־הַנָּשִׂיא יִהְיֶה
הָעוֹלוֹת וְהַמִּנְחָה וְהַנֵּסֶךְ בַּחַגִּים וּבֶחֳדָשִׁים וּבַשַּׁבָּתוֹת בְּכָל־מוֹעֲדֵי
בֵּית יִשְׂרָאֵל הוּא־יַעֲשֶׂה אֶת־הַחַטָּאת וְאֶת־הַמִּנְחָה וְאֶת־הָעוֹלָה
יח וְאֶת־הַשְּׁלָמִים לְכַפֵּר בְּעַד בֵּית־יִשְׂרָאֵל: כֹּה־אָמַר אֲדֹנָי
יֱהוִה בָּרִאשׁוֹן בְּאֶחָד לַחֹדֶשׁ תִּקַּח פַּר־בֶּן־בָּקָר תָּמִים וְחִטֵּאתָ אֶת־
יט הַמִּקְדָּשׁ: וְלָקַח הַכֹּהֵן מִדַּם הַחַטָּאת וְנָתַן אֶל־מְזוּזַת הַבַּיִת וְאֶל־
כ אַרְבַּע פִּנּוֹת הָעֲזָרָה לַמִּזְבֵּחַ וְעַל־מְזוּזַת שַׁעַר הֶחָצֵר הַפְּנִימִית: וְכֵן
תַּעֲשֶׂה בְּשִׁבְעָה בַחֹדֶשׁ מֵאִישׁ שֹׁגֶה וּמִפֶּתִי וְכִפַּרְתֶּם אֶת־הַבָּיִת:
כא בָּרִאשׁוֹן בְּאַרְבָּעָה עָשָׂר יוֹם לַחֹדֶשׁ יִהְיֶה לָכֶם הַפָּסַח חָג שְׁבֻעוֹת
כב יָמִים מַצּוֹת יֵאָכֵל: וְעָשָׂה הַנָּשִׂיא בַּיּוֹם הַהוּא בַּעֲדוֹ וּבְעַד כָּל־עַם
כג הָאָרֶץ פַּר חַטָּאת: וְשִׁבְעַת יְמֵי־הֶחָג יַעֲשֶׂה עוֹלָה לַיהוָה שִׁבְעַת
פָּרִים וְשִׁבְעַת אֵילִים תְּמִימִם לַיּוֹם שִׁבְעַת הַיָּמִים וְחַטָּאת שְׂעִיר
כד עִזִּים לַיּוֹם: וּמִנְחָה אֵיפָה לַפָּר וְאֵיפָה לָאַיִל יַעֲשֶׂה וְשֶׁמֶן הִין לָאֵיפָה:
כה בַּשְּׁבִיעִי בַּחֲמִשָּׁה עָשָׂר יוֹם לַחֹדֶשׁ בֶּחָג יַעֲשֶׂה כָאֵלֶּה שִׁבְעַת הַיָּמִים
מו א כַּחַטָּאת כָּעֹלָה וְכַמִּנְחָה וְכַשָּׁמֶן: כֹּה־אָמַר אֲדֹנָי
יֱהוִה שַׁעַר הֶחָצֵר הַפְּנִימִית הַפֹּנֶה קָדִים יִהְיֶה סָגוּר שֵׁשֶׁת יְמֵי

during the six days of labor, but on the Sabbath it shall be opened, and on the
2 day of the New Moon it shall be opened. The prince shall enter from outside
by way of the entrance hall of the gate and shall stand by the doorpost of the
gate. The priests shall prepare his burnt offering and his peace offering, and
he shall bow down at the threshold of the gate and then leave, but the gate
3 shall not be closed until the evening so that the ordinary people can also bow
down before the LORD at the threshold of that gate on Sabbaths and New
4 Moons. The burnt offering that the prince shall offer to the LORD on every
Sabbath day consists of six lambs with no blemish and a ram with no blemish.
5 And his accompanying grain offering shall be one ephah for the ram; as for
the lambs, his grain offering shall be whatever he chooses to give as well as a
6 hin of oil for each ephah of grain. And on the day of the New Moon his
offering shall consist of a young bull with no blemish as well as six lambs and
7 a ram, all without blemish. He shall prepare a grain offering of one ephah for
the bull and one ephah for the ram; as for the lambs, his grain offering shall
be whatever he chooses to give as well as a hin of oil for each ephah of grain.
8 And when the prince comes, he shall enter by way of the entrance hall of the
9 gate – and by way of it shall he exit. But when the people come before the
LORD on festivals, a person who enters by way of the northern gate in order
to bow down shall exit by the southern gate, and a person who enters by way
of the southern gate shall exit by way of the northern gate. He shall not return
by way of the gate through which he entered but shall exit through the one
10 across from it. And the prince shall be among the people on those days: when
11 they enter, he enters, and when they leave, they leave together. And on the
festivals and at the appointed times the grain offering shall be an ephah for
the bull, an ephah for the ram, and as for the lambs, whatever he chooses to
12 give as well as a hin of oil for each ephah of grain. Now, should
the prince make a voluntary offering, a burnt offering or peace offering,
voluntarily offered to the LORD on a weekday, the gate facing eastward shall
be open for him, and he shall prepare his burnt offering or peace offering
just as he would do on the Sabbath, but when he leaves, the gate will be
13 closed after his exit. And you shall prepare a daily burnt offering to the LORD
consisting of a lamb in its first year without blemish; you shall prepare it every
14 morning. And you shall prepare a grain offering for it every morning: one-
sixth of an ephah and one-third of a hin of oil to moisten the finely ground
15 flour as a grain offering to the LORD: a perpetual, everlasting decree.[79] Thus
shall they prepare the lamb and the grain offering with the oil every morning
16 as a regular burnt offering. Thus says the Lord GOD: Should the
prince give a gift to one of his sons, it is his estate that will belong to his sons;
17 it is their possession by inheritance. But should he give a gift from his estate
to one of his servants, the servant owns it until the year of freedom,[80] when
18 it returns to the prince, for his heritors are his sons: it belongs to them. This
is so that the prince does not take anything from the people's inheritance,

79 | Cf. Numbers 28:1–8.
80 | See Leviticus 25:9–24.

ב הַמַּעֲשֶׂה וּבְיוֹם הַשַּׁבָּת יִפָּתֵחַ וּבְיוֹם הַחֹדֶשׁ יִפָּתֵחַ: וּבָא הַנָּשִׂיא דֶּרֶךְ
אוּלָם הַשַּׁעַר מִחוּץ וְעָמַד עַל־מְזוּזַת הַשַּׁעַר וְעָשׂוּ הַכֹּהֲנִים אֶת־
עוֹלָתוֹ וְאֶת־שְׁלָמָיו וְהִשְׁתַּחֲוָה עַל־מִפְתַּן הַשַּׁעַר וְיָצָא וְהַשַּׁעַר לֹא־
ג יִסָּגֵר עַד־הָעָרֶב: וְהִשְׁתַּחֲווּ עַם־הָאָרֶץ פֶּתַח הַשַּׁעַר הַהוּא בַּשַּׁבָּתוֹת
ד וּבֶחֳדָשִׁים לִפְנֵי יהוה: וְהָעֹלָה אֲשֶׁר־יַקְרִב הַנָּשִׂיא לַיהוה בְּיוֹם הַשַּׁבָּת
ה שִׁשָּׁה כְבָשִׂים תְּמִימִם וְאַיִל תָּמִים: וּמִנְחָה אֵיפָה לָאַיִל וְלַכְּבָשִׂים
ו מִנְחָה מַתַּת יָדוֹ וְשֶׁמֶן הִין לָאֵיפָה: וּבְיוֹם הַחֹדֶשׁ פַּר בֶּן־בָּקָר תְּמִימִם
ז וְשֵׁשֶׁת כְּבָשִׂם וָאַיִל תְּמִימִם יִהְיוּ: וְאֵיפָה לַפָּר וְאֵיפָה לָאַיִל יַעֲשֶׂה
ח מִנְחָה וְלַכְּבָשִׂים כַּאֲשֶׁר תַּשִּׂיג יָדוֹ וְשֶׁמֶן הִין לָאֵיפָה: וּבְבוֹא הַנָּשִׂיא
ט דֶּרֶךְ אוּלָם הַשַּׁעַר יָבוֹא וּבְדַרְכּוֹ יֵצֵא: וּבְבוֹא עַם־הָאָרֶץ לִפְנֵי יהוה
בַּמּוֹעֲדִים הַבָּא דֶּרֶךְ שַׁעַר צָפוֹן לְהִשְׁתַּחֲוֹת יֵצֵא דֶּרֶךְ־שַׁעַר נֶגֶב
וְהַבָּא דֶּרֶךְ־שַׁעַר נֶגֶב יֵצֵא דֶּרֶךְ־שַׁעַר צָפוֹנָה לֹא יָשׁוּב דֶּרֶךְ הַשַּׁעַר
י אֲשֶׁר־בָּא בוֹ כִּי נִכְחוֹ יצאו: וְהַנָּשִׂיא בְּתוֹכָם בְּבוֹאָם יָבוֹא וּבְצֵאתָם יֵצֵא
יא יֵצֵאוּ: וּבַחַגִּים וּבַמּוֹעֲדִים תִּהְיֶה הַמִּנְחָה אֵיפָה לַפָּר וְאֵיפָה לָאַיִל
יב וְלַכְּבָשִׂים מַתַּת יָדוֹ וְשֶׁמֶן הִין לָאֵיפָה: וְכִי־יַעֲשֶׂה
הַנָּשִׂיא נְדָבָה עוֹלָה אוֹ־שְׁלָמִים נְדָבָה לַיהוה וּפָתַח לוֹ אֶת־הַשַּׁעַר
הַפֹּנֶה קָדִים וְעָשָׂה אֶת־עֹלָתוֹ וְאֶת־שְׁלָמָיו כַּאֲשֶׁר יַעֲשֶׂה בְּיוֹם הַשַּׁבָּת
יג וְיָצָא וְסָגַר אֶת־הַשַּׁעַר אַחֲרֵי צֵאתוֹ: וְכֶבֶשׂ בֶּן־שְׁנָתוֹ תָּמִים תַּעֲשֶׂה
יד עוֹלָה לַיּוֹם לַיהוה בַּבֹּקֶר בַּבֹּקֶר תַּעֲשֶׂה אֹתוֹ: וּמִנְחָה תַעֲשֶׂה עָלָיו
בַּבֹּקֶר בַּבֹּקֶר שִׁשִּׁית הָאֵיפָה וְשֶׁמֶן שְׁלִישִׁית הַהִין לָרֹס אֶת־הַסֹּלֶת
טו מִנְחָה לַיהוה חֻקּוֹת עוֹלָם תָּמִיד: ועשו אֶת־הַכֶּבֶשׂ וְאֶת־הַמִּנְחָה יַעֲשׂוּ
טז וְאֶת־הַשֶּׁמֶן בַּבֹּקֶר בַּבֹּקֶר עוֹלַת תָּמִיד: כֹּה־
אָמַר אֲדֹנָי יהוה כִּי־יִתֵּן הַנָּשִׂיא מַתָּנָה לְאִישׁ מִבָּנָיו נַחֲלָתוֹ הִיא לְבָנָיו
יז תִּהְיֶה אֲחֻזָּתָם הִיא בְּנַחֲלָה: וְכִי־יִתֵּן מַתָּנָה מִנַּחֲלָתוֹ לְאַחַד מֵעֲבָדָיו
וְהָיְתָה לּוֹ עַד־שְׁנַת הַדְּרוֹר וְשָׁבַת לַנָּשִׂיא אַךְ נַחֲלָתוֹ בָּנָיו לָהֶם
יח תִּהְיֶה: וְלֹא־יִקַּח הַנָּשִׂיא מִנַּחֲלַת הָעָם לְהוֹנֹתָם מֵאֲחֻזָּתָם מֵאֲחֻזָּתוֹ

throwing them wrongfully out of their landholding. He shall pass his own
landholding onto his sons so that My people will not be scattered, each ousted
19 from his landholding." Then he led me through the entry passage at the side
of the gate to the holy chambers of the priests, which faced northward, and
20 behold – there was a space over there at the western end. He said to me: "This
is the place where the priests will cook the guilt offerings and the purification
offerings, where they will bake the grain offerings, so that they do not need
to carry them out to the outer courtyard to mingle with the people as if they
21 were holy, too." He took me outside to the outer courtyard and had me pass
by the four corners of the courtyard, and behold, at every corner of the
22 courtyard there was another courtyard. In the four corners of the courtyard
there were roofless courtyards that were forty cubits long and thirty wide.
23 All four corner courtyards had the same measurements. And there was a
stonework platform roundabout inside them, roundabout each of the four,
and underneath the stonework platform there were cooking hearths all
24 around. He said to me: "This is the cooks' house, where those who serve in
47 1 the House cook the sacrifices of the people." Then he brought me back to the
entrance of the House, and behold, there was water coming out from under
the threshold of the House eastward, for the House faced east, and the water
flowed downward beneath the right-hand wall of the House, south of the altar.
2 He took me out through the northern gate and led me around the outside
path to the outer gate in an eastward direction, and behold – water was
3 trickling from the right-hand wall. As the man went out eastward with the
measuring line in his hand, he measured off one thousand cubits. Then he
4 led me through the water there, ankle-deep water. He measured off one
thousand cubits and led me through the water there, knee-deep water. He
5 measured off a thousand and led me through water up to my loins. Then he
measured off a thousand, and there was a stream I could not cross – for the
waters had risen to become swimming waters, a stream that could not be
6 walked through. He said to me: "Have you seen this, Man?" He led me and
7 brought me back to the edge of the stream. When I got back there – behold!
8 there was a vast profusion of trees on both banks of the stream. He said to
me: "These waters flow out toward the eastern region, descending to the
Arava. Then they enter the sea;[81] it is to this sea that these waters are sent forth,
9 and the sea's waters will be healed thereby from their saltiness. It shall come
to pass that every living creature that swarms shall survive wherever these
streams flow, and there will be a great abundance of fish because these waters
will have arrived, and they will be healed. Everything will live wherever this
10 stream reaches. It shall come to pass that fishermen will stand over the stream
from Ein Gedi all the way to Ein Eglayim. There will be an area to spread
nets. The fish they catch will be as varied as the fish of the Great Sea, and so
11 abundant! But its swamps and its marshes will not be healed; they are set
12 aside for salt. Beside the stream, rising on both banks, every kind of food tree
shall grow, whose leaves will never wither and whose fruit will never fail; it

81 | Referring to the Dead Sea.

יט יַנְחִל אֶת־בָּנָיו לְמַעַן אֲשֶׁר לֹא־יָפֻצוּ עַמִּי אִישׁ מֵאֲחֻזָּתוֹ: וַיְבִיאֵנִי
בַמָּבוֹא אֲשֶׁר עַל־כֶּתֶף הַשַּׁעַר אֶל־הַלְּשָׁכוֹת הַקֹּדֶשׁ אֶל־הַכֹּהֲנִים
כ הַפֹּנוֹת צָפוֹנָה וְהִנֵּה־שָׁם מָקוֹם בירכתם יָמָּה: וַיֹּאמֶר אֵלַי זֶה הַמָּקוֹם בְּיַרְכָתָיִם
אֲשֶׁר יְבַשְּׁלוּ־שָׁם הַכֹּהֲנִים אֶת־הָאָשָׁם וְאֶת־הַחַטָּאת אֲשֶׁר יֹאפוּ
אֶת־הַמִּנְחָה לְבִלְתִּי הוֹצִיא אֶל־הֶחָצֵר הַחִיצוֹנָה לְקַדֵּשׁ אֶת־הָעָם:
כא וַיּוֹצִיאֵנִי אֶל־הֶחָצֵר הַחִיצֹנָה וַיַּעֲבִירֵנִי אֶל־אַרְבַּעַת מִקְצוֹעֵי הֶחָצֵר
כב וְהִנֵּה חָצֵר בְּמִקְצֹעַ הֶחָצֵר חָצֵר בְּמִקְצֹעַ הֶחָצֵר: בְּאַרְבַּעַת מִקְצֹעוֹת
הֶחָצֵר חֲצֵרוֹת קְטֻרוֹת אַרְבָּעִים אֹרֶךְ וּשְׁלֹשִׁים רֹחַב מִדָּה אַחַת
כג לְאַרְבַּעְתָּם מְהֻקְצָעוֹת: וְטוּר סָבִיב בָּהֶם סָבִיב לְאַרְבַּעְתָּם וּמְבַשְּׁלוֹת
כד עָשׂוּי מִתַּחַת הַטִּירוֹת סָבִיב: וַיֹּאמֶר אֵלָי אֵלֶּה בֵּית הַמְבַשְּׁלִים אֲשֶׁר
מז א יְבַשְּׁלוּ־שָׁם מְשָׁרְתֵי הַבַּיִת אֶת־זֶבַח הָעָם: וַיְשִׁבֵנִי אֶל־פֶּתַח הַבַּיִת
וְהִנֵּה־מַיִם יֹצְאִים מִתַּחַת מִפְתַּן הַבַּיִת קָדִימָה כִּי־פְנֵי הַבַּיִת קָדִים
ב וְהַמַּיִם יֹרְדִים מִתַּחַת מִכֶּתֶף הַבַּיִת הַיְמָנִית מִנֶּגֶב לַמִּזְבֵּחַ: וַיּוֹצִאֵנִי
דֶּרֶךְ־שַׁעַר צָפוֹנָה וַיְסִבֵּנִי דֶּרֶךְ חוּץ אֶל־שַׁעַר הַחוּץ דֶּרֶךְ הַפּוֹנֶה קָדִים
ג וְהִנֵּה־מַיִם מְפַכִּים מִן־הַכָּתֵף הַיְמָנִית: בְּצֵאת־הָאִישׁ קָדִים וְקָו בְּיָדוֹ
ד וַיָּמָד אֶלֶף בָּאַמָּה וַיַּעֲבִרֵנִי בַמַּיִם מֵי אָפְסָיִם: וַיָּמָד אֶלֶף וַיַּעֲבִרֵנִי בַמַּיִם
ה מַיִם בִּרְכָּיִם וַיָּמָד אֶלֶף וַיַּעֲבִרֵנִי מֵי מָתְנָיִם: וַיָּמָד אֶלֶף נַחַל אֲשֶׁר
ו לֹא־אוּכַל לַעֲבֹר כִּי־גָאוּ הַמַּיִם מֵי שָׂחוּ נַחַל אֲשֶׁר לֹא־יֵעָבֵר: וַיֹּאמֶר
ז אֵלַי הֲרָאִיתָ בֶן־אָדָם וַיּוֹלִכֵנִי וַיְשִׁבֵנִי שְׂפַת הַנָּחַל: בְּשׁוּבֵנִי וְהִנֵּה אֶל־
ח שְׂפַת הַנַּחַל עֵץ רַב מְאֹד מִזֶּה וּמִזֶּה: וַיֹּאמֶר אֵלַי הַמַּיִם הָאֵלֶּה יוֹצְאִים
אֶל־הַגְּלִילָה הַקַּדְמוֹנָה וְיָרְדוּ עַל־הָעֲרָבָה וּבָאוּ הַיָּמָּה אֶל־הַיָּמָּה
ט הַמּוּצָאִים וְנִרְפְּאוּ הַמָּיִם: וְהָיָה כָל־נֶפֶשׁ חַיָּה ׀ אֲשֶׁר־יִשְׁרֹץ אֶל כָּל־
אֲשֶׁר יָבוֹא שָׁם נַחֲלַיִם יִחְיֶה וְהָיָה הַדָּגָה רַבָּה מְאֹד כִּי בָאוּ שָׁמָּה הַמַּיִם
י הָאֵלֶּה וְיֵרָפְאוּ וָחָי כֹּל אֲשֶׁר־יָבוֹא שָׁמָּה הַנָּחַל: וְהָיָה יעמדו עָלָיו דַּוָּגִים עָמְדוּ
מֵעֵין גֶּדִי וְעַד־עֵין עֶגְלַיִם מִשְׁטוֹחַ לַחֲרָמִים יִהְיוּ לְמִינָה תִּהְיֶה דְגָתָם
יא כִּדְגַת הַיָּם הַגָּדוֹל רַבָּה מְאֹד: בִּצֹּאתָו וּגְבָאָיו וְלֹא יֵרָפְאוּ לְמֶלַח נִתָּנוּ:
יב וְעַל־הַנַּחַל יַעֲלֶה עַל־שְׂפָתוֹ מִזֶּה ׀ וּמִזֶּה ׀ כָּל־עֵץ־מַאֲכָל לֹא־יִבּוֹל כט

will bring forth new fruit every month because its waters emanate from the
13 Sanctuary. Its fruit shall yield food, and its leaves, medicine. Thus
says the Lord God: This shall be the border according to which you shall give
the land as inheritance to the twelve tribes of Israel. Yosef shall receive two
14 portions. You shall inherit it equally, one person like another; as I swore
to give it to your forefathers, so shall this land become your possession.
15 Now, this is the boundary of the land: On the northern side: from the Great
16 Sea by way of Ḥetlon, Levo, Tzedad. Ḥamat, Berota; Sivrayim, located
between the border of Damascus and the border of Ḥamat; Ḥatzer HaTikhon,
17 which lies near the border of Ḥavran. The border shall continue from the Sea
up to Ḥatzar Einon at the border of Damascus and everything northward,
18 including the border of Ḥamat. That is the northern side. As for the eastern
side: between Ḥavran and Damascus, between the Gilad and the land of Israel,
the Jordan. You shall measure from the border at the eastern sea. That is the
19 eastern side. And the southern side: southward from Tamar up to the waters
of Merivot Kadesh, a wadi leading to the Great Sea. That is the south side,
20 toward the Negev. The west side shall be the Great Sea, from the border until
21 opposite Levo Ḥamat. That is the western side. You shall divide this land for
22 yourselves according to the tribes of Israel. You shall allot it as an inheritance
for yourselves and for the strangers who live amongst you, who bear children
in your midst. These shall be considered by you as citizens among the children
23 of Israel. They shall be allotted an inheritance among the tribes of Israel. It
shall be that in whatever tribe's territory the stranger lives, there shall you give
48 1 him his inheritance," says the Lord God. "Now, these are the names
of the tribes: From the northern edge, near the Ḥetlon Road toward Levo
Ḥamat, Ḥatzar Einan, the border of Damascus northward near Ḥamat, this
2 shall be his from the eastern edge to the sea: one portion for Dan. And
bordering Dan, from the eastern edge to the western edge, one portion for
3 Asher. And bordering Asher, from the eastern edge to the western edge, one
4 portion for Naftali. And bordering Naftali, from the eastern edge to the
5 western edge, one portion for Menashe. And bordering Menashe, from the
6 eastern edge to the western edge, one portion for Efrayim. And bordering
Efrayim, from the eastern edge to the western edge, one portion for Reuven.
7 And bordering Reuven, from the eastern edge to the western edge, one
8 portion for Yehuda. And bordering Yehuda, from the eastern edge to the
western edge, shall be the gift portion that you shall designate, twenty-five
thousand wide and as long as any of the other portions – from the eastern
9 edge to the western edge – and the Sanctuary shall be within it. The gift
portion that you shall designate for the Lord shall be twenty-five thousand
10 in length and ten thousand wide. And to these shall the holy gift portion
belong. To the priests – to the north a length of twenty-five thousand, to the
west a width of ten thousand, and to the east a width of ten thousand, and to
the south a length of twenty-five thousand; and the Sanctuary of the Lord
11 shall be within it. This sacred place shall belong to the priests descended from

עלהו ולא־יתם פריו לחדשיו יבכר כי מימיו מן־המקדש המה
יג יוצאים והיו פריו למאכל ועלהו לתרופה: כה אמר והיה
אדני יהוה גה גבול אשר תתנחלו את־הארץ לשני עשר שבטי
יד ישראל יוסף חבלים: ונחלתם אותה איש כאחיו אשר נשאתי את־
טו ידי לתתה לאבתיכם ונפלה הארץ הזאת לכם בנחלה: וזה גבול
הארץ לפאת צפונה מן־הים הגדול הדרך חתלן לבוא צדדה:
טז חמת ׀ ברותה סברים אשר בין־גבול דמשק ובין גבול חמת חצר
יז התיכון אשר אל־גבול חורן: והיה גבול מן־הים חצר עינון גבול
יח דמשק וצפון ׀ צפונה וגבול חמת ואת פאת צפון: ופאת קדים מבין
חורן ומבין דמשק ומבין הגלעד ומבין ארץ ישראל הירדן מגבול
יט על־הים הקדמוני תמדו ואת פאת קדימה: ופאת נגב תימנה מתמר
עד־מי מריבות קדש נחלה אל־הים הגדול ואת פאת־תימנה נגבה:
כ ופאת־ים הים הגדול מגבול עד־נכח לבוא חמת זאת פאת־ים:
כא כב וחלקתם את־הארץ הזאת לכם לשבטי ישראל: והיה תפלו אותה
בנחלה לכם ולהגרים הגרים בתוככם אשר־הולדו בנים בתוככם
והיו לכם כאזרח בבני ישראל אתכם יפלו בנחלה בתוך שבטי
כג ישראל: והיה בשבט אשר־גר הגר אתו שם תתנו נחלתו נאם אדני
מח א יהוה: ואלה שמות השבטים מקצה צפונה אל־יד דרך־
חתלן ׀ לבוא־חמת חצר עינן גבול דמשק צפונה אל־יד חמת
ב והיו־לו פאת־קדים הים דן אחד: ועל ׀ גבול דן מפאת קדים עד־
ג פאת־ימה אשר אחד: ועל ׀ גבול אשר מפאת קדימה ועד־פאת־
ד ימה נפתלי אחד: ועל ׀ גבול נפתלי מפאת קדמה עד־פאת־ימה
ה מנשה אחד: ועל ׀ גבול מנשה מפאת קדמה עד־פאת ימה אפרים
ו ז אחד: ועל ׀ גבול אפרים מפאת קדים ועד־פאת־ימה ראובן אחד:
ח ועל ׀ גבול ראובן מפאת קדים עד־פאת ימה יהודה אחד: ועל
גבול יהודה מפאת קדים עד־פאת ימה תהיה התרומה אשר־תרימו
חמשה ועשרים אלף רחב וארך כאחד החלקים מפאת קדימה
ט עד־פאת־ימה והיה המקדש בתוכו: התרומה אשר תרימו ליהוה
י ארך חמשה ועשרים אלף ורחב עשרת אלפים: ולאלה תהיה
תרומת־הקדש לכהנים צפונה חמשה ועשרים אלף וימה רחב
עשרת אלפים וקדימה רחב עשרת אלפים ונגבה ארך חמשה
יא ועשרים אלף והיה מקדש־יהוה בתוכו: לכהנים המקדש מבני

Tzadok, who were guardians of My precious things and who did not stray
12 when the children of Israel went astray as the other Levites did. And it shall
be for them God's gift from the gift portion of the land, holy of holies and
13 bordering the Levites. The Levites, alongside the border with the priests shall
have an area twenty-five thousand in length with a width of ten thousand;
14 the entire length of twenty-five thousand and width of ten thousand. And
they shall not sell any part of it or exchange or transfer this choicest piece of
15 the land, for it is consecrated to the LORD. The five thousand that remain
of the width, along the twenty-five thousand, are for ordinary use for the
16 city – for dwelling and for open space – and the city shall be within this. And
these are the city's dimensions: the northern side, four thousand five hundred; the southern side, four thousand five hundred; the eastern side, four
17 thousand five hundred; the western side, four thousand five hundred. The
city shall have an open space – to the north, two hundred and fifty; to the
south, two hundred and fifty; eastward, two hundred and fifty; northward,
18 two hundred and fifty. And the remainder in length parallel to the holy gift
portion shall measure ten thousand to the east and ten thousand to the west.
This shall extend alongside the holy gift portion, and its produce shall be food
19 for people who work in the city. The people who work in the city shall come
20 from all the tribes of Israel to cultivate it. The entire gift portion is twenty-five
thousand by twenty-five thousand, a square; and this shall you designate as
21 the holy gift portion, with the city property in it. What remains on both sides
of the holy gift portion and the property of the city belongs to the prince.
Along the twenty-five thousand of the gift portion up to the eastern border,
and to the west along the twenty-five thousand up to the western border,
parallel to the tribes' portions, shall be the prince's; the holy gift portion with
22 the Sanctuary of the House are within it. Thus the property of the Levites
and the property of the city are in the middle of that which belongs to the
prince. The portion of the prince shall be between the border of Yehuda and
23 the border of Binyamin. And for the rest of the tribes, from the eastern side
24 to the western side, one portion for Binyamin. And bordering Binyamin, from
25 the eastern side to the western side, one portion for Shimon. And bordering
Shimon, from the eastern side to the western side, one portion for Yissakhar.
26 And bordering Yissakhar, from the eastern side to the western side, one
27 portion for Zevulun. And bordering Zevulun, from the eastern side to the
28 western side, one portion for Gad. And bordering Gad, at the Negev side
southward, the border shall run from Tamar by the waters of Merivat Kadesh
29 to the wadi leading to the Great Sea. This is the land which you shall allot as
inheritance to the tribes of Israel, and these are their portions, says the Lord
30 GOD. And these are the exits from the city: From the northern side,
31 which measures four thousand five hundred – the gates of the city shall be
named after the tribes of Israel – three gates northward: one the Reuven Gate,
32 one the Yehuda Gate, one the Levi Gate. And toward the eastern side, which
measures four thousand five hundred, three gates: one the Yosef Gate, one

צָדוֹק אֲשֶׁר שָׁמְרוּ מִשְׁמַרְתִּי אֲשֶׁר לֹא־תָעוּ בִּתְעוֹת בְּנֵי יִשְׂרָאֵל כַּאֲשֶׁר
יב תָּעוּ הַלְוִיִּם׃ וְהָיְתָה לָהֶם תְּרוּמִיָּה מִתְּרוּמַת הָאָרֶץ קֹדֶשׁ קָדָשִׁים
יג אֶל־גְּבוּל הַלְוִיִּם׃ וְהַלְוִיִּם לְעֻמַּת גְּבוּל הַכֹּהֲנִים חֲמִשָּׁה וְעֶשְׂרִים אֶלֶף
אֹרֶךְ וְרֹחַב עֲשֶׂרֶת אֲלָפִים כָּל־אֹרֶךְ חֲמִשָּׁה וְעֶשְׂרִים אֶלֶף וְרֹחַב עֲשֶׂרֶת
יד אֲלָפִים׃ וְלֹא־יִמְכְּרוּ מִמֶּנּוּ וְלֹא יָמֵר וְלֹא יעבור רֵאשִׁית הָאָרֶץ כִּי־ יַעֲבִיר
טו קֹדֶשׁ לַיהוָה׃ וַחֲמֵשֶׁת אֲלָפִים הַנּוֹתָר בָּרֹחַב עַל־פְּנֵי חֲמִשָּׁה וְעֶשְׂרִים
טז אֶלֶף חֹל־הוּא לָעִיר לְמוֹשָׁב וּלְמִגְרָשׁ וְהָיְתָה הָעִיר בְּתוֹכֹה׃ וְאֵלֶּה
מִדּוֹתֶיהָ פְּאַת צָפוֹן חֲמֵשׁ מֵאוֹת וְאַרְבַּעַת אֲלָפִים וּפְאַת־נֶגֶב חֲמֵשׁ
חמש מֵאוֹת וְאַרְבַּעַת אֲלָפִים וּמִפְּאַת קָדִים חֲמֵשׁ מֵאוֹת וְאַרְבַּעַת
יז אֲלָפִים וּפְאַת־יָמָּה חֲמֵשׁ מֵאוֹת וְאַרְבַּעַת אֲלָפִים׃ וְהָיָה מִגְרָשׁ לָעִיר
צָפוֹנָה חֲמִשִּׁים וּמָאתַיִם וְנֶגְבָּה חֲמִשִּׁים וּמָאתָיִם וְקָדִימָה חֲמִשִּׁים
יח וּמָאתַיִם וְיָמָּה חֲמִשִּׁים וּמָאתָיִם׃ וְהַנּוֹתָר בָּאֹרֶךְ לְעֻמַּת ׀ תְּרוּמַת
הַקֹּדֶשׁ עֲשֶׂרֶת אֲלָפִים קָדִימָה וַעֲשֶׂרֶת אֲלָפִים יָמָּה וְהָיָה לְעֻמַּת
יט תְּרוּמַת הַקֹּדֶשׁ וְהָיְתָה תְבוּאָתֹה לְלֶחֶם לְעֹבְדֵי הָעִיר׃ וְהָעֹבֵד הָעִיר
כ יַעַבְדוּהוּ מִכֹּל שִׁבְטֵי יִשְׂרָאֵל׃ כָּל־הַתְּרוּמָה חֲמִשָּׁה וְעֶשְׂרִים אֶלֶף
בַּחֲמִשָּׁה וְעֶשְׂרִים אָלֶף רְבִיעִית תָּרִימוּ אֶת־תְּרוּמַת הַקֹּדֶשׁ אֶל־אֲחֻזַּת
כא הָעִיר׃ וְהַנּוֹתָר לַנָּשִׂיא מִזֶּה ׀ וּמִזֶּה ׀ לִתְרוּמַת־הַקֹּדֶשׁ וְלַאֲחֻזַּת הָעִיר
אֶל־פְּנֵי חֲמִשָּׁה וְעֶשְׂרִים אֶלֶף ׀ תְּרוּמָה עַד־גְּבוּל קָדִימָה וְיָמָּה עַל־
פְּנֵי חֲמִשָּׁה וְעֶשְׂרִים אֶלֶף עַל־גְּבוּל יָמָּה לְעֻמַּת חֲלָקִים לַנָּשִׂיא וְהָיְתָה
כב תְּרוּמַת הַקֹּדֶשׁ וּמִקְדַּשׁ הַבַּיִת בְּתוֹכֹה׃ וּמֵאֲחֻזַּת הַלְוִיִּם וּמֵאֲחֻזַּת
הָעִיר בְּתוֹךְ אֲשֶׁר לַנָּשִׂיא יִהְיֶה בֵּין ׀ גְּבוּל יְהוּדָה וּבֵין גְּבוּל בִּנְיָמִן
כג לַנָּשִׂיא יִהְיֶה׃ וְיֶתֶר הַשְּׁבָטִים מִפְּאַת קָדִימָה עַד־פְּאַת־יָמָּה בִּנְיָמִן
כד אֶחָד׃ וְעַל ׀ גְּבוּל בִּנְיָמִן מִפְּאַת קָדִימָה עַד־פְּאַת־יָמָּה שִׁמְעוֹן אֶחָד׃
כה כו וְעַל ׀ גְּבוּל שִׁמְעוֹן מִפְּאַת קָדִימָה עַד־פְּאַת־יָמָּה יִשָּׂשכָר אֶחָד׃ וְעַל ׀
כז גְּבוּל יִשָּׂשכָר מִפְּאַת קָדִימָה עַד־פְּאַת־יָמָּה זְבוּלֻן אֶחָד׃ וְעַל ׀ גְּבוּל
כח זְבוּלֻן מִפְּאַת קָדִמָה עַד־פְּאַת־יָמָּה גָּד אֶחָד׃ וְעַל גְּבוּל גָּד אֶל־פְּאַת
נֶגֶב תֵּימָנָה וְהָיָה גְבוּל מִתָּמָר מֵי מְרִיבַת קָדֵשׁ נַחֲלָה עַל־הַיָּם הַגָּדוֹל׃
כט זֹאת הָאָרֶץ אֲשֶׁר־תַּפִּילוּ מִנַּחֲלָה לְשִׁבְטֵי יִשְׂרָאֵל וְאֵלֶּה מַחְלְקוֹתָם
ל נְאֻם אֲדֹנָי יְהוִה׃ וְאֵלֶּה תּוֹצְאֹת הָעִיר מִפְּאַת צָפוֹן חֲמֵשׁ
לא מֵאוֹת וְאַרְבַּעַת אֲלָפִים מִדָּה׃ וְשַׁעֲרֵי הָעִיר עַל־שְׁמוֹת שִׁבְטֵי יִשְׂרָאֵל
שְׁעָרִים שְׁלוֹשָׁה צָפוֹנָה שַׁעַר רְאוּבֵן אֶחָד שַׁעַר יְהוּדָה אֶחָד שַׁעַר
לֵוִי אֶחָד׃ וְאֶל־פְּאַת קָדִימָה חֲמֵשׁ מֵאוֹת וְאַרְבַּעַת אֲלָפִים וּשְׁעָרִים

33 the Binyamin Gate, one the Dan Gate. And the southern side, which measures
four thousand five hundred, three gates: one the Shimon Gate, one the
34 Yissakhar Gate, one the Zevulun Gate. Finally, the western side, four thousand
five hundred, will have three gates: one the Gad Gate, one the Asher Gate,
35 one the Naftali Gate. All around the city shall measure eighteen thousand,
and its name from that day on shall be: The LORD Is There."

לב שְׁלֹשָׁה וְשַׁעַר יוֹסֵף אֶחָד שַׁעַר בִּנְיָמִן אֶחָד שַׁעַר דָּן אֶחָד: וּפְאַת־
לג נֶגְבָּה חֲמֵשׁ מֵאוֹת וְאַרְבַּעַת אֲלָפִים מִדָּה וּשְׁעָרִים שְׁלֹשָׁה שַׁעַר
שִׁמְעוֹן אֶחָד שַׁעַר יִשָּׂשכָר אֶחָד שַׁעַר זְבוּלֻן אֶחָד: פְּאַת־יָמָּה חֲמֵשׁ
לד מֵאוֹת וְאַרְבַּעַת אֲלָפִים שַׁעֲרֵיהֶם שְׁלֹשָׁה שַׁעַר גָּד אֶחָד שַׁעַר אָשֵׁר
אֶחָד שַׁעַר נַפְתָּלִי אֶחָד: סָבִיב שְׁמֹנָה עָשָׂר אָלֶף וְשֵׁם־הָעִיר מִיּוֹם
לה יְהוָה ׀ שָׁמָּה:

HAGGAI	Encouraging those who returned to Zion to rebuild the Temple Chs. 1–2		
ZECHARIAH	Zekharya's visions Chs. 1–6	Fasting over the destruction in an era of redemption 7–8	Regarding the kingdoms of Israel and the nations of the world 9–14
MALACHI	The poor spiritual state of those who returned to Zion Chs. 1–3		

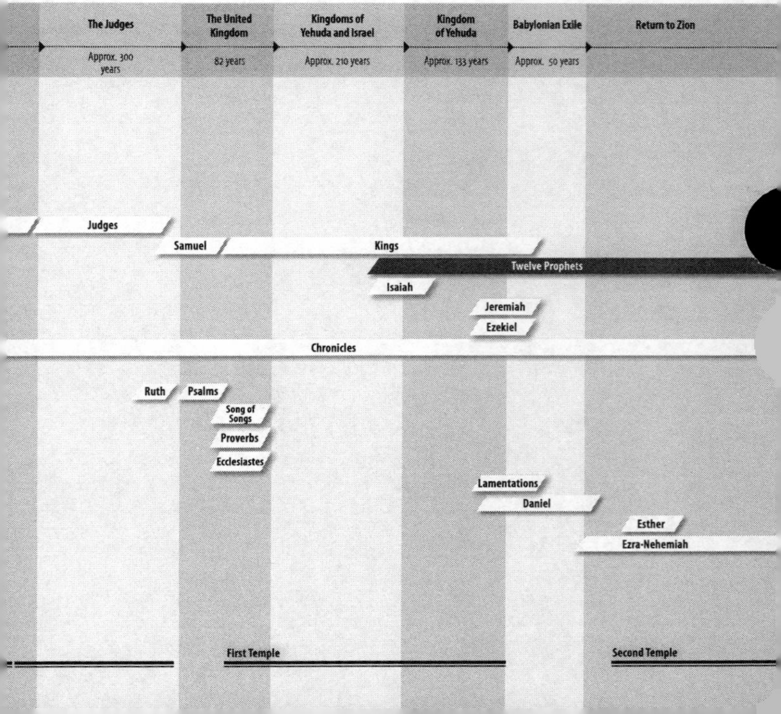

שנים עשר
SHENEIM ASAR/ TWELVE PROPHETS

HOSEA	Relations between husband and wife as an allegory for relations between God and Israel Chs. 1–3	Rebuke and calls to repentance 4–14	
JOEL	The plague of locusts and its results Chs. 1–2	Promise of salvation for Israel and justice for the nations 3–4	
AMOS	Prophecies concerning the nations Chs. 1–2	Rebuke to a corrupt affluent society 3–6	From calamities to consolation 7–9
OBADIAH	Esav's relationship with Yaakov, and his judgment		
JONAH	Yona in the presence of God – flight and return Chs. 1–2	Yona in Nineveh – the argument over the fate of the city 3–4	
MICAH	Rebuke of a corrupt affluent society Chs. 1–3	Prophecies of redemption and ethics 4–7	
NAHUM	Punishment and destruction of Assyria – redemption for those enslaved by it Chs. 1–3		
HABAKKUK	The prophet's protest against the success of the wicked Ch. 1	God's response 2	The prophet's prayer 3
ZEPHANIAH	God judges the world – rebuke, punishment, and redemption Chs. 1–3		

HOSHE'A/ HOSEA

1 1 This is the word of the LORD which came to Hoshe'a son of Be'eri in the days
of Uziya, Yotam, Aḥaz, and Yeḥizkiya, kings of Yehuda, and in the days of
2 Yorovam son of Yoash, king of Israel. When the LORD first spoke to Hoshe'a,
the LORD said to Hoshe'a, "Go, take for yourself a whoring woman and have
3 children of a whore, for the land is whoring itself away from the LORD." So he
went and married Gomer, daughter of Divlayim, and she conceived and bore
4 him a son. And the LORD said to him, "Call him by the name of Yizre'el, for
soon I will punish the house of Yehu for the blood of Yizre'el,[1] and I will put
5 an end to the kingdom of the House of Israel. And it will be on that day that
6 I will break the bow of Israel in the Yizre'el Valley." Again she conceived and
gave birth to a daughter, and He said, "Call her by the name of Unloved, for
no longer will I have compassion on the House of Israel, no more will I bear
7 the burden of their sins; but I will have compassion on the House of Yehuda,
and they will be saved by the LORD their God. I will not save them by bow,
8 nor by sword or battle, not by horses nor by horsemen." She weaned Unloved;
9 then she conceived and gave birth to a son. And He said, "Call him Not My
2 1 People, for you are not My people, and I will not be for you." Yet the
children of Israel will number like the sands of the sea, not measurable or
countable, and rather than being told, "You are Not My People," they will be
2 told, "You are the sons of the living God." Then the children of Yehuda and
the children of Israel will gather together; they will designate one leader and
3 escape from the land, for the day of Yizre'el will be a great one. Say then to
4 your brothers "People," and to your sisters "Loved." Berate your mother, for
she is not my wife, nor I her husband. Let her remove her prostitute's rouge
5 from her face, her adulterous acts from between her breasts, lest I strip her
naked as the day she was born and make her as a desert wilderness. I will make
6 her into parched wasteland and let her die from thirst. As for her sons, I will
7 have no mercy, for they are the sons of a harlot, for their mother has whored;
she has conceived them in shame. She said, "I will follow after my lovers; it is
they who give me bread and water, keep me in wools and linens, lotions and
8 wines," so I will obstruct her path with prickly shrubs; I will fence her in with
9 walls; her way will be lost to her. She will pursue her lovers but not catch
them; she will search them out but never find them. Then she will say, "I will
10 go and return to my first husband, for I fared better then than now." But she
did not care to know that it was I who furnished her with grain, wine, and oil,
11 I who lavished silver upon her and gold which they used for Baal. Hence I
will take back My grain as it ripens in its season, My wine as it ages; I will seize
12 My wools and My linens meant to cover her nakedness. And now I will expose
her indecency for her lovers to see, and there will be no one to rescue her
13 from My hand. I will put an end to all her joyous occasions – her holidays,
14 her New Moons, her Sabbaths, and all her festive seasons. I will ravage her
vines and fig trees, of which she once said, "These are my harlot's favors, given
to me by my lovers." I will make them into abandoned woodlands, and wild

1 | The site of Yehu's bloody revolt; see II Kings 9–10.

א הושע

א א דְּבַר־יְהוָה ׀ אֲשֶׁר הָיָה אֶל־הוֹשֵׁעַ בֶּן־בְּאֵרִי בִּימֵי עֻזִּיָּה יוֹתָם אָחָז
ב יְחִזְקִיָּה מַלְכֵי יְהוּדָה וּבִימֵי יָרָבְעָם בֶּן־יוֹאָשׁ מֶלֶךְ יִשְׂרָאֵל: תְּחִלַּת
דִּבֶּר־יְהוָה בְּהוֹשֵׁעַ וַיֹּאמֶר יְהוָה אֶל־הוֹשֵׁעַ לֵךְ קַח־לְךָ אֵשֶׁת זְנוּנִים
ג וְיַלְדֵי זְנוּנִים כִּי־זָנֹה תִזְנֶה הָאָרֶץ מֵאַחֲרֵי יְהוָה: וַיֵּלֶךְ וַיִּקַּח אֶת־גֹּמֶר
ד בַּת־דִּבְלָיִם וַתַּהַר וַתֵּלֶד־לוֹ בֵּן: וַיֹּאמֶר יְהוָה אֵלָיו קְרָא שְׁמוֹ יִזְרְעֶאל
כִּי־עוֹד מְעַט וּפָקַדְתִּי אֶת־דְּמֵי יִזְרְעֶאל עַל־בֵּית יֵהוּא וְהִשְׁבַּתִּי
ה מַמְלְכוּת בֵּית יִשְׂרָאֵל: וְהָיָה בַּיּוֹם הַהוּא וְשָׁבַרְתִּי אֶת־קֶשֶׁת יִשְׂרָאֵל
ו בְּעֵמֶק יִזְרְעֶאל: וַתַּהַר עוֹד וַתֵּלֶד בַּת וַיֹּאמֶר לוֹ קְרָא שְׁמָהּ לֹא רֻחָמָה
כִּי לֹא אוֹסִיף עוֹד אֲרַחֵם אֶת־בֵּית יִשְׂרָאֵל כִּי־נָשֹׂא אֶשָּׂא לָהֶם:
ז וְאֶת־בֵּית יְהוּדָה אֲרַחֵם וְהוֹשַׁעְתִּים בַּיהוָה אֱלֹהֵיהֶם וְלֹא אוֹשִׁיעֵם
ח בְּקֶשֶׁת וּבְחֶרֶב וּבְמִלְחָמָה בְּסוּסִים וּבְפָרָשִׁים: וַתִּגְמֹל אֶת־לֹא רֻחָמָה
ט וַתַּהַר וַתֵּלֶד בֵּן: וַיֹּאמֶר קְרָא שְׁמוֹ לֹא עַמִּי כִּי אַתֶּם לֹא עַמִּי וְאָנֹכִי
ב א לֹא־אֶהְיֶה לָכֶם: וְהָיָה מִסְפַּר בְּנֵי־יִשְׂרָאֵל כְּחוֹל
הַיָּם אֲשֶׁר לֹא־יִמַּד וְלֹא יִסָּפֵר וְהָיָה בִּמְקוֹם אֲשֶׁר־יֵאָמֵר לָהֶם לֹא־
ב עַמִּי אַתֶּם יֵאָמֵר לָהֶם בְּנֵי אֵל־חָי: וְנִקְבְּצוּ בְּנֵי־יְהוּדָה וּבְנֵי־יִשְׂרָאֵל
יַחְדָּו וְשָׂמוּ לָהֶם רֹאשׁ אֶחָד וְעָלוּ מִן־הָאָרֶץ כִּי גָדוֹל יוֹם יִזְרְעֶאל:
ג ד אִמְרוּ לַאֲחֵיכֶם עַמִּי וְלַאֲחוֹתֵיכֶם רֻחָמָה: רִיבוּ בְאִמְּכֶם רִיבוּ כִּי־
הִיא לֹא אִשְׁתִּי וְאָנֹכִי לֹא אִישָׁהּ וְתָסֵר זְנוּנֶיהָ מִפָּנֶיהָ וְנַאֲפוּפֶיהָ
ה מִבֵּין שָׁדֶיהָ: פֶּן־אַפְשִׁיטֶנָּה עֲרֻמָּה וְהִצַּגְתִּיהָ כְּיוֹם הִוָּלְדָהּ וְשַׂמְתִּיהָ
ו כַמִּדְבָּר וְשַׁתִּהָ כְּאֶרֶץ צִיָּה וַהֲמִתִּיהָ בַּצָּמָא: וְאֶת־בָּנֶיהָ לֹא אֲרַחֵם
ז כִּי־בְנֵי זְנוּנִים הֵמָּה: כִּי זָנְתָה אִמָּם הֹבִישָׁה הוֹרָתָם כִּי אָמְרָה אֵלְכָה
ח אַחֲרֵי מְאַהֲבַי נֹתְנֵי לַחְמִי וּמֵימַי צַמְרִי וּפִשְׁתִּי שַׁמְנִי וְשִׁקּוּיָי: לָכֵן
הִנְנִי־שָׂךְ אֶת־דַּרְכֵּךְ בַּסִּירִים וְגָדַרְתִּי אֶת־גְּדֵרָהּ וּנְתִיבוֹתֶיהָ לֹא
ט תִמְצָא: וְרִדְּפָה אֶת־מְאַהֲבֶיהָ וְלֹא־תַשִּׂיג אֹתָם וּבִקְשָׁתַם וְלֹא תִמְצָא
וְאָמְרָה אֵלְכָה וְאָשׁוּבָה אֶל־אִישִׁי הָרִאשׁוֹן כִּי טוֹב לִי אָז מֵעָתָּה:
י וְהִיא לֹא יָדְעָה כִּי אָנֹכִי נָתַתִּי לָהּ הַדָּגָן וְהַתִּירוֹשׁ וְהַיִּצְהָר וְכֶסֶף
יא הִרְבֵּיתִי לָהּ וְזָהָב עָשׂוּ לַבָּעַל: לָכֵן אָשׁוּב וְלָקַחְתִּי דְגָנִי בְּעִתּוֹ וְתִירוֹשִׁי
יב בְּמוֹעֲדוֹ וְהִצַּלְתִּי צַמְרִי וּפִשְׁתִּי לְכַסּוֹת אֶת־עֶרְוָתָהּ: וְעַתָּה אֲגַלֶּה
יג אֶת־נַבְלֻתָהּ לְעֵינֵי מְאַהֲבֶיהָ וְאִישׁ לֹא־יַצִּילֶנָּה מִיָּדִי: וְהִשְׁבַּתִּי כָּל־
יד מְשׂוֹשָׂהּ חַגָּהּ חָדְשָׁהּ וְשַׁבַּתָּהּ וְכֹל מוֹעֲדָהּ: וַהֲשִׁמֹּתִי גַּפְנָהּ וּתְאֵנָתָהּ
אֲשֶׁר אָמְרָה אֶתְנָה הֵמָּה לִי אֲשֶׁר נָתְנוּ־לִי מְאַהֲבָי וְשַׂמְתִּים לְיַעַר

15 animals will feed on them. I will revisit upon her the days of the Baalim,[2]
for whom she burned incense and adorned herself with earrings and
jewels, how she followed after her lovers and forgot Me. So declares the
16 LORD. Behold, now I will coax her, I will lead her back to the open
17 desert, and I will speak to her heart. Then and there I will give her vineyards
to her, and the Valley of the Scourge[3] will be a doorway to hope; she will
return to Me in song as in the first days of her youth, as on the day when she
18 came up out of the land of Egypt. It will be on that day, says the
LORD: you will call Me "my Husband";[4] no longer will you call Me "my
19 Master."[5] I will eradicate the names of the Baalim from her mouth; no more
20 will they be mentioned by name. On that day I will make a covenant with
them: with the beasts of the fields, and the birds of heaven, and the crawling
creatures of the ground. I will break the bow and the sword; I will crush
21 conflict out from the land, and you will rest in safety. I will betroth you to Me
forever; I will betroth you to Me in righteousness and justice, in kindness and
22 compassion. I will betroth you to Me in faithfulness, and you will know the
23 LORD. And it will be on that day: I will answer, declares the LORD;
24 I will answer the heavens, the heavens will answer the earth, and the earth
will answer the grain and the wine and the oil, and they will answer to Yizre'el.
25 And I will sow her as My own in the land, and I will have compassion on
Unloved, and I will say to Lo Ami,[6] "You are My people," and he will then say,
3 1 "You are my God." The LORD said to me, "Furthermore, go and love
a woman loved by another, and she an adulteress," as the LORD loves Israel
2 even as they turn to other gods and adore their own drunken indulgence. So
then I paid her dowry of fifteen silver pieces and a homer[7] and a half of barley,
3 and I said to her, "Sit alone and wait for me for many days; do not make a
4 whore of yourself or be with any man; neither will I come to you." So too the
children of Israel will wait alone for many days with neither king nor leader,
5 without sacrifice or altars, with no priestly garments or household shrines. In
time, the children of Israel will return; they will seek the LORD their God. and
David their king; they will come trembling in awe back to the LORD and His
4 1 goodness in the end of days. Hear the word of the LORD, children
of Israel, for the LORD has a dispute with the people of this land – for there
2 is no truthfulness or kindness and no awareness of God in the land. False
swearing and lying, murder, thievery, and prostitution are rampant, raging,
3 and bloodshed spills over into bloodshed. For this the land will be laid waste,
all who dwell there wiped out: beasts of the field and birds of heaven, even
4 the fish in the seas will be swept away. Still no man disputes another nor
admonishes his fellow man; indeed, yours is like a nation at strife with their

2 | Canaanite gods mentioned frequently as objects of idolatrous worship by Israel.
3 | See Joshua 7:24–26.
4 | Hebrew *ishi*.
5 | Hebrew *baali*. Both *baali* and *ishi* mean "my husband," but *baali* carries a connotation of dominance and evokes the Canaanite deity.
6 | "Not My people"; cf. 1:9.
7 | A dry measure equaling approximately 220 liters.

טו וְאָכָלָתַם חַיַּת הַשָּׂדֶה: וּפָקַדְתִּי עָלֶיהָ אֶת־יְמֵי הַבְּעָלִים אֲשֶׁר תַּקְטִיר
לָהֶם וַתַּעַד נִזְמָהּ וְחֶלְיָתָהּ וַתֵּלֶךְ אַחֲרֵי מְאַהֲבֶיהָ וְאֹתִי שָׁכְחָה נְאֻם־
טז יְהוָה: לָכֵן הִנֵּה אָנֹכִי מְפַתֶּיהָ וְהֹלַכְתִּיהָ הַמִּדְבָּר
יז וְדִבַּרְתִּי עַל־לִבָּהּ: וְנָתַתִּי לָהּ אֶת־כְּרָמֶיהָ מִשָּׁם וְאֶת־עֵמֶק עָכוֹר
לְפֶתַח תִּקְוָה וְעָנְתָה שָּׁמָּה כִּימֵי נְעוּרֶיהָ וּכְיוֹם עֲלוֹתָהּ מֵאֶרֶץ־
יח מִצְרָיִם: וְהָיָה בַיּוֹם־הַהוּא נְאֻם־יְהוָה תִּקְרְאִי אִישִׁי
יט וְלֹא־תִקְרְאִי־לִי עוֹד בַּעְלִי: וַהֲסִרֹתִי אֶת־שְׁמוֹת הַבְּעָלִים מִפִּיהָ
כ וְלֹא־יִזָּכְרוּ עוֹד בִּשְׁמָם: וְכָרַתִּי לָהֶם בְּרִית בַּיּוֹם הַהוּא עִם־חַיַּת
הַשָּׂדֶה וְעִם־עוֹף הַשָּׁמַיִם וְרֶמֶשׂ הָאֲדָמָה וְקֶשֶׁת וְחֶרֶב וּמִלְחָמָה
כא אֶשְׁבּוֹר מִן־הָאָרֶץ וְהִשְׁכַּבְתִּים לָבֶטַח: וְאֵרַשְׂתִּיךְ לִי לְעוֹלָם וְאֵרַשְׂתִּיךְ
כב לִי בְּצֶדֶק וּבְמִשְׁפָּט וּבְחֶסֶד וּבְרַחֲמִים: וְאֵרַשְׂתִּיךְ לִי בֶּאֱמוּנָה וְיָדַעַתְּ
כג אֶת־יְהוָה: וְהָיָה ׀ בַּיּוֹם הַהוּא אֶעֱנֶה נְאֻם־יְהוָה אֶעֱנֶה
כד אֶת־הַשָּׁמָיִם וְהֵם יַעֲנוּ אֶת־הָאָרֶץ: וְהָאָרֶץ תַּעֲנֶה אֶת־הַדָּגָן וְאֶת־
כה הַתִּירוֹשׁ וְאֶת־הַיִּצְהָר וְהֵם יַעֲנוּ אֶת־יִזְרְעֶאל: וּזְרַעְתִּיהָ לִּי בָּאָרֶץ
וְרִחַמְתִּי אֶת־לֹא רֻחָמָה וְאָמַרְתִּי לְלֹא־עַמִּי עַמִּי־אַתָּה וְהוּא יֹאמַר
ג א אֱלֹהָי: וַיֹּאמֶר יְהוָה אֵלַי עוֹד לֵךְ אֱהַב־אִשָּׁה אֲהֻבַת רֵעַ
וּמְנָאָפֶת כְּאַהֲבַת יְהוָה אֶת־בְּנֵי יִשְׂרָאֵל וְהֵם פֹּנִים אֶל־אֱלֹהִים אֲחֵרִים
ב וְאֹהֲבֵי אֲשִׁישֵׁי עֲנָבִים: וָאֶכְּרֶהָ לִּי בַּחֲמִשָּׁה עָשָׂר כָּסֶף וְחֹמֶר שְׂעֹרִים
ג וְלֶתֶךְ שְׂעֹרִים: וָאֹמַר אֵלֶיהָ יָמִים רַבִּים תֵּשְׁבִי לִי לֹא תִזְנִי וְלֹא תִהְיִי
ד לְאִישׁ וְגַם־אֲנִי אֵלָיִךְ: כִּי ׀ יָמִים רַבִּים יֵשְׁבוּ בְּנֵי יִשְׂרָאֵל אֵין מֶלֶךְ וְאֵין
ה שָׂר וְאֵין זֶבַח וְאֵין מַצֵּבָה וְאֵין אֵפוֹד וּתְרָפִים: אַחַר יָשֻׁבוּ בְּנֵי יִשְׂרָאֵל
וּבִקְשׁוּ אֶת־יְהוָה אֱלֹהֵיהֶם וְאֵת דָּוִד מַלְכָּם וּפָחֲדוּ אֶל־יְהוָה וְאֶל־
ד א טוּבוֹ בְּאַחֲרִית הַיָּמִים: שִׁמְעוּ דְבַר־יְהוָה בְּנֵי יִשְׂרָאֵל
כִּי רִיב לַיהוָה עִם־יוֹשְׁבֵי הָאָרֶץ כִּי אֵין־אֱמֶת וְאֵין־חֶסֶד וְאֵין־דַּעַת
ב אֱלֹהִים בָּאָרֶץ: אָלֹה וְכַחֵשׁ וְרָצֹחַ וְגָנֹב וְנָאֹף פָּרָצוּ וְדָמִים בְּדָמִים
ג נָגָעוּ: עַל־כֵּן ׀ תֶּאֱבַל הָאָרֶץ וְאֻמְלַל כָּל־יוֹשֵׁב בָּהּ בְּחַיַּת הַשָּׂדֶה
ד וּבְעוֹף הַשָּׁמָיִם וְגַם־דְּגֵי הַיָּם יֵאָסֵפוּ: אַךְ אִישׁ אַל־יָרֵב וְאַל־יוֹכַח

5 priests. For this you will fall over in daylight, and the false prophet with you
6 at nightfall, and I will cut off your nation. My people are cut off for being
unaware, for as you spurned this awareness, I too will spurn you as My priest;
as you have forgotten the Law of your God, I too will forget your children.
7 The greater they became, the greater their sins against Me; I will turn their
8 dignity into disgrace. The priests feed on the purification offerings of My
9 people and yearn for their iniquity. As the people so too the priests; I will
10 punish each according to their ways, and each will get what they deserve. They
will eat but not be satisfied; they will whore but no offspring will come forth,
11 for they left the LORD and did not heed His laws. Their heart leads them to
12 harlotry and drunkenness. My people look to their wooden figures for
counsel, to their sticks of magic to guide them, for the prostituting spirit has
13 steered them wrong, and they whore themselves away from their God. They
sacrifice on the mountaintops, offer incense on the hills beneath the oak, the
poplar, and the terebinth, for their shade is bountiful. And so your daughters
14 will whore, and your daughters-in-law will be adulterous. But no, I will not
punish your daughters for their whoring, nor your daughters-in-law for their
adultery, for their men go with the whores and sacrifice with the harlots;
15 surely a nation with no awareness will fall to its ruin. Though you, Israel,
whore yourself, do not let Yehuda become guilty. Do not come to Gilgal, or
16 make a pilgrimage to Beit Aven,[8] or swear:[9] "As the LORD lives." For Israel is
as rebellious as an obstinate cow; the LORD will graze them as a lone sheep
17 18 in a wide pasture. Efrayim[10] is entwined with idols; leave him be. When their
drunkenness is done, they whore with the harlots; her leaders love nothing
19 more than disgrace. The wind will bind her in its billowing wings, and they
5 1 will come to be ashamed of their sacrifices. Hear this, priests; heed,
House of Israel; listen now, house of the king, for judgment was entrusted to
2 you, but you set traps at Mitzpa and spread nets out on Tavor.[11] Those who
strayed from Me are deep in the slaughter; I will bring suffering on them all.
3 For I know all about Efrayim, and Israel is not concealed from Me; now you,
4 Efrayim, have pursued prostitution, and Israel has become defiled. Their evil
actions do not allow them to return to their God, for a whoring spirit has
5 taken them over, and they do not know the LORD. The pride of Israel will bear
witness against them. The sins of Israel and Efrayim will make them falter,
6 and Yehuda too will falter with them. They will go with their flocks and herds
to seek[12] the LORD but will not find Him, for He has turned away from them.
7 They betrayed the LORD, for they begot foreign children, so soon there will
8 come a month,[13] and your fields will be consumed. Blast the ram's

---

8 | A derogatory name for Beit El. Beit El and Gilgal were places of worship, sometimes idolatrous; see Amos 5:5.

9 | That is, swear falsely.

10 | A recurring metonym for the Kingdom of Israel.

11 | Mitzpa and Har Tavor were respectively the southern and northern reaches of the Kingdom of Israel at the time.

12 | That is, by offering sacrifices.

13 | Meaning a month of destruction.

ה אִישׁ וְעַמְּךָ כִּמְרִיבֵי כֹהֵן: וְכָשַׁלְתָּ הַיּוֹם וְכָשַׁל גַּם־נָבִיא עִמְּךָ לָיְלָה
ו וְדָמִיתִי אִמֶּךָ: נִדְמוּ עַמִּי מִבְּלִי הַדָּעַת כִּי אַתָּה הַדַּעַת מָאַסְתָּ
ואמאסאך מִכַּהֵן לִי וַתִּשְׁכַּח תּוֹרַת אֱלֹהֶיךָ אֶשְׁכַּח בָּנֶיךָ גַּם־אָנִי: וְאֶמְאָסְךָ
ז ח כְּרֻבָּם כֵּן חָטְאוּ־לִי כְּבוֹדָם בְּקָלוֹן אָמִיר: חַטַּאת עַמִּי יֹאכֵלוּ וְאֶל־
ט עֲוֺנָם יִשְׂאוּ נַפְשׁוֹ: וְהָיָה כָעָם כַּכֹּהֵן וּפָקַדְתִּי עָלָיו דְּרָכָיו וּמַעֲלָלָיו
י אָשִׁיב לוֹ: וְאָכְלוּ וְלֹא יִשְׂבָּעוּ הִזְנוּ וְלֹא יִפְרֹצוּ כִּי־אֶת־יהוה עָזְבוּ
יא יב לִשְׁמֹר: זְנוּת וְיַיִן וְתִירוֹשׁ יִקַּח־לֵב: עַמִּי בְּעֵצוֹ יִשְׁאָל וּמַקְלוֹ יַגִּיד לוֹ
יג כִּי רוּחַ זְנוּנִים הִתְעָה וַיִּזְנוּ מִתַּחַת אֱלֹהֵיהֶם: עַל־רָאשֵׁי הֶהָרִים יְזַבֵּחוּ
וְעַל־הַגְּבָעוֹת יְקַטֵּרוּ תַּחַת אַלּוֹן וְלִבְנֶה וְאֵלָה כִּי טוֹב צִלָּהּ עַל־כֵּן
יד תִּזְנֶינָה בְּנוֹתֵיכֶם וְכַלּוֹתֵיכֶם תְּנָאַפְנָה: לֹא־אֶפְקוֹד עַל־בְּנוֹתֵיכֶם כִּי
תִזְנֶינָה וְעַל־כַּלּוֹתֵיכֶם כִּי תְנָאַפְנָה כִּי־הֵם עִם־הַזֹּנוֹת יְפָרֵדוּ וְעִם־
טו הַקְּדֵשׁוֹת יְזַבֵּחוּ וְעָם לֹא־יָבִין יִלָּבֵט: אִם־זֹנֶה אַתָּה יִשְׂרָאֵל אַל־יֶאְשַׁם
יְהוּדָה וְאַל־תָּבֹאוּ הַגִּלְגָּל וְאַל־תַּעֲלוּ בֵּית אָוֶן וְאַל־תִּשָּׁבְעוּ חַי־יהוה:
טז יז כִּי כְּפָרָה סֹרֵרָה סָרַר יִשְׂרָאֵל עַתָּה יִרְעֵם יהוה כְּכֶבֶשׂ בַּמֶּרְחָב: חֲבוּר
יח עֲצַבִּים אֶפְרָיִם הַנַּח־לוֹ: סָר סָבְאָם הַזְנֵה הִזְנוּ אָהֲבוּ הֵבוּ קָלוֹן מָגִנֶּיהָ:
יט ה א צָרַר רוּחַ אוֹתָהּ בִּכְנָפֶיהָ וְיֵבֹשׁוּ מִזִּבְחוֹתָם: שִׁמְעוּ־
זֹאת הַכֹּהֲנִים וְהַקְשִׁיבוּ ׀ בֵּית יִשְׂרָאֵל וּבֵית הַמֶּלֶךְ הַאֲזִינוּ כִּי לָכֶם
ב הַמִּשְׁפָּט כִּי־פַח הֱיִיתֶם לְמִצְפָּה וְרֶשֶׁת פְּרוּשָׂה עַל־תָּבוֹר: וְשַׁחֲטָה
ג שֵׂטִים הֶעְמִיקוּ וַאֲנִי מוּסָר לְכֻלָּם: אֲנִי יָדַעְתִּי אֶפְרַיִם וְיִשְׂרָאֵל
ד לֹא־נִכְחַד מִמֶּנִּי כִּי עַתָּה הִזְנֵיתָ אֶפְרַיִם נִטְמָא יִשְׂרָאֵל: לֹא יִתְּנוּ
מַעַלְלֵיהֶם לָשׁוּב אֶל־אֱלֹהֵיהֶם כִּי רוּחַ זְנוּנִים בְּקִרְבָּם וְאֶת־יהוה לֹא
ה יָדָעוּ: וְעָנָה גְאוֹן־יִשְׂרָאֵל בְּפָנָיו וְיִשְׂרָאֵל וְאֶפְרַיִם יִכָּשְׁלוּ בַּעֲוֺנָם כָּשַׁל
ו גַּם־יְהוּדָה עִמָּם: בְּצֹאנָם וּבִבְקָרָם יֵלְכוּ לְבַקֵּשׁ אֶת־יהוה וְלֹא יִמְצָאוּ
ז חָלַץ מֵהֶם: בַּיהוה בָּגָדוּ כִּי־בָנִים זָרִים יָלָדוּ עַתָּה יֹאכְלֵם חֹדֶשׁ אֶת־
ח חֶלְקֵיהֶם: תִּקְעוּ שׁוֹפָר בַּגִּבְעָה חֲצֹצְרָה בָּרָמָה הָרִיעוּ

horn in Giva,[14] the trumpet in Rama; sound the battle cry in Beit Aven; they
9 are closing in on you, Binyamin. Efrayim will become desolate on the day of
punishment; to the tribes of Israel I have declared the truth of what will be.
10 The princes of Yehuda have become like those who move back the boundary
11 stones; upon them I will pour out My wrath like water. Efrayim is oppressed,
crushed by decrees, for he readily chose to follow the commands of others.
12 And so I will be like a moth and eat away at Efrayim and cause the House of
13 Yehuda to rot from within. Then Efrayim saw his sickness, and Yehuda his
oozing wound; Efrayim hailed Assyria and dispatched messengers to the great
14 king,[15] but he cannot heal you, nor can he cure your wound. For I will be like
a lion to Efrayim and like a young lion to the House of Yehuda. For I – yes, I –
will tear them to pieces and leave; I will carry them off, and none will rescue
15 them. I will go and return to My place until they realize their guilt and seek
6 1 Me out, for only in their distress will they long for Me. Come, let us return to
the LORD, for though He has ripped us apart, He will heal us, for though He
2 battered us, He will bandage us up. After two days He will revive us; on the
3 third He will raise us up, and we will live before Him. Let us know, let us strive
and eagerly seek knowledge of the LORD, for as dawn breaks, He is surely
there. He will come to us as the rain, as the final winter rains that replenish
4 the earth. What can I do for you, Efrayim; what can I do for you, Yehuda?
Your goodness dissolves like morning mist; like dew at daybreak it swiftly
5 fades. For this I have hewed at them by way of the prophets; I have killed them
with the strength of My words, and your judgment will emerge like the
6 morning light. For it is goodness I yearn for, not sacrifice; awareness of God
7 rather than burnt offerings. But they breached the covenant, as men do;
8 there they betrayed Me. Gilad, a city full of sinners, is stained with tracks of
9 blood. As gangs of thieves stalk men, bands of priests murder on the path
10 to Shekhem,[16] so purposeful is their evil. In the House of Israel I have
11 seen an appalling sight, in Efrayim – prostitution, Israel – defiled. You too,
Yehuda, reaped your harvest[17] when I was ready to restore My people from
7 1 captivity.[18] When I would have wanted to heal Israel, the iniquity
of Efrayim and the sinfulness of Shomron was exposed, for they acted
2 deceitfully; so the thief barges in, and gangs raid the open streets. They do
not think to themselves that I remember all their wicked actions; now they
3 are besieged by their very misdeeds, and they stand clearly before Me. The
4 king rejoices in their evil deeds, the officials in their lies. Adulterers, all of
them: their passions burn like an oven stoked by the baker, barely pausing
5 from the time the dough is kneaded until rising. On the day of our king,
officials make themselves ill from drinking skins of wine; he too joins his hand

---

14 | These were three cities in the tribal territory of Binyamin.

15 | This was the title of the Assyrian king.

16 | Shekhem and Gilad were prominent Israelite cities.

17 | Received the punishment you deserved.

18 | This verse is unclear and subject to a wide variety of interpretations. The translation follows Radak and Metzudat David.

ט בֵּית אָוֶן אַחֲרֶיךָ בִּנְיָמִין: אֶפְרַיִם לְשַׁמָּה תִהְיֶה בְּיוֹם תּוֹכֵחָה בְּשִׁבְטֵי
י יִשְׂרָאֵל הוֹדַעְתִּי נֶאֱמָנָה: הָיוּ שָׂרֵי יְהוּדָה כְּמַסִּיגֵי גְּבוּל עֲלֵיהֶם אֶשְׁפּוֹךְ
יא כַּמַּיִם עֶבְרָתִי: עָשׁוּק אֶפְרַיִם רְצוּץ מִשְׁפָּט כִּי הוֹאִיל הָלַךְ אַחֲרֵי־צָו:
יב יג וַאֲנִי כָעָשׁ לְאֶפְרָיִם וְכָרָקָב לְבֵית יְהוּדָה: וַיַּרְא אֶפְרַיִם אֶת־חָלְיוֹ
וִיהוּדָה אֶת־מְזֹרוֹ וַיֵּלֶךְ אֶפְרַיִם אֶל־אַשּׁוּר וַיִּשְׁלַח אֶל־מֶלֶךְ יָרֵב וְהוּא
יד לֹא יוּכַל לִרְפֹּא לָכֶם וְלֹא־יִגְהֶה מִכֶּם מָזוֹר: כִּי אָנֹכִי כַשַּׁחַל לְאֶפְרַיִם
טו וְכַכְּפִיר לְבֵית יְהוּדָה אֲנִי אֲנִי אֶטְרֹף וְאֵלֵךְ אֶשָּׂא וְאֵין מַצִּיל: אֵלֵךְ
אָשׁוּבָה אֶל־מְקוֹמִי עַד אֲשֶׁר־יֶאְשְׁמוּ וּבִקְשׁוּ פָנָי בַּצַּר לָהֶם יְשַׁחֲרֻנְנִי:
ו א ב לְכוּ וְנָשׁוּבָה אֶל־יְהוָה כִּי הוּא טָרָף וְיִרְפָּאֵנוּ יַךְ וְיַחְבְּשֵׁנוּ: יְחַיֵּנוּ מִיֹּמָיִם ב
ג בַּיּוֹם הַשְּׁלִישִׁי יְקִמֵנוּ וְנִחְיֶה לְפָנָיו: וְנֵדְעָה נִרְדְּפָה לָדַעַת אֶת־יְהוָה
ד כְּשַׁחַר נָכוֹן מֹצָאוֹ וְיָבוֹא כַגֶּשֶׁם לָנוּ כְּמַלְקוֹשׁ יוֹרֶה אָרֶץ: מָה אֶעֱשֶׂה־
לְּךָ אֶפְרַיִם מָה אֶעֱשֶׂה־לְּךָ יְהוּדָה וְחַסְדְּכֶם כַּעֲנַן־בֹּקֶר וְכַטַּל מַשְׁכִּים
ה הֹלֵךְ: עַל־כֵּן חָצַבְתִּי בַּנְּבִיאִים הֲרַגְתִּים בְּאִמְרֵי־פִי וּמִשְׁפָּטֶיךָ אוֹר
ו ז יֵצֵא: כִּי חֶסֶד חָפַצְתִּי וְלֹא־זָבַח וְדַעַת אֱלֹהִים מֵעֹלוֹת: וְהֵמָּה כְּאָדָם
ח ט עָבְרוּ בְרִית שָׁם בָּגְדוּ בִי: גִּלְעָד קִרְיַת פֹּעֲלֵי אָוֶן עֲקֻבָּה מִדָּם: וּכְחַכֵּי
י אִישׁ גְּדוּדִים חֶבֶר כֹּהֲנִים דֶּרֶךְ יְרַצְּחוּ־שֶׁכְמָה כִּי זִמָּה עָשׂוּ: בְּבֵית
יא יִשְׂרָאֵל רָאִיתִי שערוריה שָׁם זְנוּת לְאֶפְרַיִם נִטְמָא יִשְׂרָאֵל: גַּם־יְהוּדָה שַׁעֲרוּרִיָּה
ז א שָׁת קָצִיר לָךְ בְּשׁוּבִי שְׁבוּת עַמִּי: כְּרָפְאִי
לְיִשְׂרָאֵל וְנִגְלָה עֲוֺן אֶפְרַיִם וְרָעוֹת שֹׁמְרוֹן כִּי פָעֲלוּ שָׁקֶר וְגַנָּב יָבוֹא
ב פָּשַׁט גְּדוּד בַּחוּץ: וּבַל־יֹאמְרוּ לִלְבָבָם כָּל־רָעָתָם זָכָרְתִּי עַתָּה סְבָבוּם
ג מַעַלְלֵיהֶם נֶגֶד פָּנַי הָיוּ: בְּרָעָתָם יְשַׂמְּחוּ־מֶלֶךְ וּבְכַחֲשֵׁיהֶם שָׂרִים:
ד כֻּלָּם מְנָאֲפִים כְּמוֹ תַנּוּר בֹּעֵרָה מֵאֹפֶה יִשְׁבּוֹת מֵעִיר מִלּוּשׁ בָּצֵק
ה עַד־חֻמְצָתוֹ: יוֹם מַלְכֵּנוּ הֶחֱלוּ שָׂרִים חֲמַת מִיָּיִן מָשַׁךְ יָדוֹ אֶת־לֹצְצִים:

6 with scoffers. Their heart, like an oven, burns as they lie in wait; all night their
7 baker sleeps; come morning, it burns like a raging blaze. All of them heat up
like an oven and feed upon their judges; their kings all fall; not one cries out
8 to Me. Efrayim mixes with the nations; unturned on a griddle, Efrayim has
9 become like a burnt cake. Foreign nations ate away his strength, and he was
10 unaware. Old and frail, strewn with gray – and he was unaware. The pride of
Israel will bear witness against them, yet they do not return to the LORD their
11 God nor even seek Him out. And so Efrayim has become like an easily wooed,
12 witless dove. They appeal to Egypt, and to Assyria they run. Wherever they
go, I will snag them with My net; I will bring them down like birds in the
13 skies; I will afflict them as was heard by the whole assembly. Woe to
them who have strayed from Me; ruin unto them, for they have sinned against
14 Me. And I, how can I save them when they speak lies against Me? They do
not cry out to Me in sincerity but wail from their beds; they gather over grain
15 and wine and rebel against Me. I honed and strengthened their arms, but they
16 devise evil against Me. They return, though not toward heaven, and are
misdirected like a faulty bow; their leaders will fall by the sword for the fire
8 1 of their tongues; for this they will be mocked in the land of Egypt.[19] Set the
ram's horn to your lips:[20] he will swoop like a vulture onto the House of the
2 LORD, for they have violated My covenant, revolted against My Law. To Me
3 they will cry, "O, our God, it is You; Israel knows You." But Israel rejected the
4 good; so will be hounded by the enemy. They have crowned kings without
My sanction, appointed princes without My say; with their wealth and gold
5 they made themselves idols, bringing about their own demise. Your calf has
forsaken you, Shomron! My anger burns against them; how long until they
6 become clean from this sin? For this has been done by Israel – the work of a
craftsman; it is not God; so too, the calf of Shomron will be reduced to shards.
7 For wind they will sow, gales they will reap; wheat stalks will not stand, grains
8 will not yield flour, and were they to yield, strangers would consume it. Israel
has been consumed and now has become to the nations like an object of no
9 value. As they went up to Assyria like an unruly donkey roaming aloof, so
10 Efrayim sold himself for lovers' favors. Even as they sell themselves to the
nations, I will gather the nations against them, and they will shudder under
11 the burden of the king and ministers. For Efrayim has increased altars for
12 sinning; indeed, these altars have spawned his sins. And though for him
I wrote down My laws in their greatness, they are considered as foreign
13 by him. As for the burnt sacrifices they offer Me, that burning flesh – let
them eat it; the LORD does not accept them. Now He will remember their
transgressions and hold them to account for their sins; to Egypt they will
14 return.[21] For Israel has forgotten his Maker; he has built palaces, and Yehuda
has increased fortified cities. I will send a fire to his cities to consume his
9 1 castles. Israel, do not celebrate; you will know no joy like other

19 | To whom they appeal for aid.
20 | In other words, warn of an impending attack.
21 | See Deuteronomy 28:68.

ו כִּי־קֵרְבוּ כַתַּנּוּר לִבָּם בְּאָרְבָּם כָּל־הַלַּיְלָה יָשֵׁן אֹפֵהֶם בֹּקֶר הוּא בֹעֵר
ז כְּאֵשׁ לֶהָבָה׃ כֻּלָּם יֵחַמּוּ כַּתַּנּוּר וְאָכְלוּ אֶת־שֹׁפְטֵיהֶם כָּל־מַלְכֵיהֶם
ח נָפָלוּ אֵין־קֹרֵא בָהֶם אֵלָי׃ אֶפְרַיִם בָּעַמִּים הוּא יִתְבּוֹלָל אֶפְרַיִם הָיָה
ט עֻגָה בְּלִי הֲפוּכָה׃ אָכְלוּ זָרִים כֹּחוֹ וְהוּא לֹא יָדָע גַּם־שֵׂיבָה זָרְקָה בּוֹ
י וְהוּא לֹא יָדָע׃ וְעָנָה גְאוֹן־יִשְׂרָאֵל בְּפָנָיו וְלֹא־שָׁבוּ אֶל־יְהוָה אֱלֹהֵיהֶם
יא וְלֹא בִקְשֻׁהוּ בְּכָל־זֹאת׃ וַיְהִי אֶפְרַיִם כְּיוֹנָה פוֹתָה אֵין לֵב מִצְרַיִם
יב קָרָאוּ אַשּׁוּר הָלָכוּ׃ כַּאֲשֶׁר יֵלֵכוּ אֶפְרוֹשׂ עֲלֵיהֶם רִשְׁתִּי כְּעוֹף הַשָּׁמַיִם
יג אוֹרִידֵם אַיְסִרֵם כְּשֵׁמַע לַעֲדָתָם׃ אוֹי לָהֶם כִּי־נָדְדוּ
מִמֶּנִּי שֹׁד לָהֶם כִּי־פָשְׁעוּ בִי וְאָנֹכִי אֶפְדֵּם וְהֵמָּה דִּבְּרוּ עָלַי כְּזָבִים׃
יד וְלֹא־זָעֲקוּ אֵלַי בְּלִבָּם כִּי יְיֵלִילוּ עַל־מִשְׁכְּבוֹתָם עַל־דָּגָן וְתִירוֹשׁ
טו יִתְגּוֹרָרוּ יָסוּרוּ בִי׃ וַאֲנִי יִסַּרְתִּי חִזַּקְתִּי זְרוֹעֹתָם וְאֵלַי יְחַשְּׁבוּ־רָע׃
טז יָשׁוּבוּ ׀ לֹא עָל הָיוּ כְּקֶשֶׁת רְמִיָּה יִפְּלוּ בַחֶרֶב שָׂרֵיהֶם מִזַּעַם לְשׁוֹנָם
ח א זוֹ לַעְגָּם בְּאֶרֶץ מִצְרָיִם׃ אֶל־חִכְּךָ שֹׁפָר כַּנֶּשֶׁר עַל־בֵּית יְהוָה יַעַן
ב עָבְרוּ בְרִיתִי וְעַל־תּוֹרָתִי פָּשָׁעוּ׃ לִי יִזְעָקוּ אֱלֹהַי יְדַעֲנוּךָ יִשְׂרָאֵל׃
ג ד זָנַח יִשְׂרָאֵל טוֹב אוֹיֵב יִרְדְּפוֹ׃ הֵם הִמְלִיכוּ וְלֹא מִמֶּנִּי הֵשִׂירוּ וְלֹא
ה יָדָעְתִּי כַּסְפָּם וּזְהָבָם עָשׂוּ לָהֶם עֲצַבִּים לְמַעַן יִכָּרֵת׃ זָנַח עֶגְלֵךְ שֹׁמְרוֹן
ו חָרָה אַפִּי בָּם עַד־מָתַי לֹא יוּכְלוּ נִקָּיֹן׃ כִּי מִיִּשְׂרָאֵל וְהוּא חָרָשׁ עָשָׂהוּ
ז וְלֹא אֱלֹהִים הוּא כִּי־שְׁבָבִים יִהְיֶה עֵגֶל שֹׁמְרוֹן׃ כִּי רוּחַ יִזְרָעוּ וְסוּפָתָה
יִקְצֹרוּ קָמָה אֵין־לוֹ צֶמַח בְּלִי יַעֲשֶׂה־קֶּמַח אוּלַי יַעֲשֶׂה זָרִים יִבְלָעֻהוּ׃
ח ט נִבְלַע יִשְׂרָאֵל עַתָּה הָיוּ בַגּוֹיִם כִּכְלִי אֵין־חֵפֶץ בּוֹ׃ כִּי־הֵמָּה עָלוּ אַשּׁוּר
י פֶּרֶא בּוֹדֵד לוֹ אֶפְרַיִם הִתְנוּ אֲהָבִים׃ גַּם כִּי־יִתְנוּ בַגּוֹיִם עַתָּה אֲקַבְּצֵם
יא וַיָּחֵלּוּ מְּעָט מִמַּשָּׂא מֶלֶךְ שָׂרִים׃ כִּי־הִרְבָּה אֶפְרַיִם מִזְבְּחֹת לַחֲטֹא
יב הָיוּ־לוֹ מִזְבְּחוֹת לַחֲטֹא׃ אֶכְתּוֹב־לוֹ רֻבּוֹ תּוֹרָתִי כְּמוֹ־זָר נֶחְשָׁבוּ׃ אֶכְתָּב־ רִבֵּי
יג זִבְחֵי הַבְהָבַי יִזְבְּחוּ בָשָׂר וַיֹּאכֵלוּ יְהוָה לֹא רָצָם עַתָּה יִזְכֹּר עֲוֹנָם
יד וְיִפְקֹד חַטֹּאותָם הֵמָּה מִצְרַיִם יָשׁוּבוּ׃ וַיִּשְׁכַּח יִשְׂרָאֵל אֶת־עֹשֵׂהוּ וַיִּבֶן
הֵיכָלוֹת וִיהוּדָה הִרְבָּה עָרִים בְּצֻרוֹת וְשִׁלַּחְתִּי־אֵשׁ בְּעָרָיו וְאָכְלָה
ט א אַרְמְנֹתֶיהָ׃ אַל־תִּשְׂמַח יִשְׂרָאֵל ׀ אֶל־גִּיל כָּעַמִּים כִּי זָנִיתָ

peoples, for you have whored; away from your God, you have loved the
2 harlot's payments found on every thresher's floor. The threshing floor and
3 winepress will yield them no fodder, and the new wine will fall short. No
more will they dwell in the LORD's land; Efrayim will go again to Egypt and
4 into Assyria, where they will eat impure food. They will not pour wine in
offering to the LORD, nor will their sacrifices find favor with Him; like the
bread of grievers it will be; all who eat of it will be defiled, for their bread is
merely to feed their hunger and will not be brought to the House of the LORD.
5 What then will you offer on festival days, on days of sacrifice to the LORD?
6 Though they have run from ruin, Egypt will collect them, Mof bury them;
their treasure-filled houses will be overrun by thistles, and thorns will be in
7 their tents. Know, Israel: the days of reckoning have come; the days of requital
are here. You said, "This prophet is a fool; the man with God's spirit is a
madman"; as the enormity of your sins, so the magnitude of the hatred.[22]
8 Efrayim's watchman[23] stands with his god; he, a prophet, sets snares for all
9 who follow his paths, bringing hatred into the house of his god. They have
delved deeply into corruption as in the days of the Giva.[24] He will remember
10 their iniquity; He will punish their sins. When I found Israel, they
were as grapes in the desert; your fathers were to Me like the first, ripe figs of
the new season, but when they arrived at Baal Peor, they devoted themselves
11 to shame[25] and became detested – just as they had been loved. As for Efrayim,
their glory will take flight like a bird, leaving nothing: no birth, none with
12 child, not even conception. Even were they to raise their children, they would
13 mourn every last one, for woe to them when I turn from them. Efrayim
seemed to Me like Tyre nested in a lush haven,[26] but no, Efrayim will send his
14 sons to the slaughter. Give them, O LORD – what can I ask you to give them?
15 Give them a grieving womb and shriveled breasts gone dry. Their wickedness,
all of it was rooted in Gilgal;[27] it is there that I hated them on account of the
evil of their ways. I will banish them from My House; no longer can I love
16 them; their leaders are all rebellious. Efrayim has been struck down; their
roots have withered; no longer can they bear fruit – and even were they to
17 give birth, I would slay the treasured fruit of their womb. He, my God, will
reject them, for they did not heed Him, and they will be wanderers among
10 1 the nations. Israel is a withered, barren vine; will he ever bear fruit
again? As he yielded fruit in plenty, so he built altars profuse; as his land filled
2 with favor, so pagan shrines flourished. Their heart severed from Me, now
they will be held guilty. He[28] will break down their altars, bring ruin upon their
3 pagan shrines. For now they will say, "We have no king, for we feared not the
4 LORD. And the king? What could he do for us?" They spoke deceptive words,

22 | Referring to divine hatred and rejection.
23 | Perhaps a reference to false prophets.
24 | See Judges 19:14–30.
25 | Hebrew *boshet*, a common epithet for the foreign god Baal.
26 | Tyre was seen as a paragon of peace and security; cf. Ezekiel 28:2.
27 | Where Israelite sovereignty and monarchy originated; see Joshua, chapter 5; 1 Samuel 11:14–12:25.
28 | That is, the enemy.

ב מעל אלהיך אהבת אתנן על כל־גרנות דגן: גרן ויקב לא ירעם
ג ותירוש יכחש בה: לא ישבו בארץ יהוה ושב אפרים מצרים ובאשור
ד טמא יאכלו: לא־יסכו ליהוה ׀ יין ולא יערבו־לו זבחיהם כלחם
אונים להם כל־אכליו יטמאו כי־לחמם לנפשם לא יבוא בית יהוה:
ה ו מה־תעשו ליום מועד וליום חג־יהוה: כי־הנה הלכו משד מצרים
תקבצם מף תקברם מחמד לכספם קמוש יירשם חוח באהליהם:
ז באו ׀ ימי הפקדה באו ימי השלם ידעו ישראל אויל הנביא משגע
ח איש הרוח על רב עונך ורבה משטמה: צפה אפרים עם־אלהי נביא
ט פח יקוש על־כל־דרכיו משטמה בבית אלהיו: העמיקו שחתו כימי
י הגבעה יזכור עונם יפקוד חטאתם: כענבים במדבר
מצאתי ישראל כבכורה בתאנה בראשיתה ראיתי אבותיכם המה
יא באו בעל־פעור וינזרו לבשת ויהיו שקוצים כאהבם: אפרים כעוף
יב יתעופף כבודם מלדה ומבטן ומהריון: כי אם־יגדלו את־בניהם
יג ושכלתים מאדם כי־גם־אוי להם בשורי מהם: אפרים כאשר־ראיתי
יד לצור שתולה בנוה ואפרים להוציא אל־הרג בניו: תן־להם יהוה
טו מה־תתן תן־להם רחם משכיל ושדים צמקים: כל־רעתם בגלגל
כי־שם שנאתים על רע מעלליהם מביתי אגרשם לא אוסף אהבתם
טז כל־שריהם סוררים: הכה אפרים שרשם יבש פרי בלי־יעשון גם בל־
יז כי ילדון והמתי מחמדי בטנם: ימאסם אלהי כי לא שמעו לו ויהיו
י א נדדים בגוים: גפן בוקק ישראל פרי ישוה־לו כרב
ב לפריו הרבה למזבחות כטוב לארצו היטיבו מצבות: חלק לבם עתה
ג יאשמו הוא יערף מזבחותם ישדד מצבותם: כי עתה יאמרו אין
ד מלך לנו כי לא יראנו את־יהוה והמלך מה־יעשה־לנו: דברו

made covenants with hollow oaths; their false justice crops up like poison
5 weeds in the ruts of the field. The residents of Shomron are afraid for the
golden calf of Beit Aven;[29] the people will mourn for it, as will the priests who
6 once rejoiced in its honor, for it will be banished from them. It too will be
brought to Assyria as tribute to the great king. Efrayim will be seized with
7 shame, and Israel will be shamed by the counsel they gave. Shomron's king
8 will cease to be, like froth on the water's surface. The hilltop shrines of Aven
will be ravaged, that place of Israel's sin. Thorns and thistles will sprout up
over their altars; to the mountains they will say, "Conceal us," to the hills,
9 "Descend upon us." You have sinned, Israel, ever since the days of
Giva;[30] unchanged they remain, still believing that they will not be overtaken
10 at Giva in war against the wicked ones. At My will I will lash out at them, and
the nations will rally against them when they are bound like two plowing
11 cows. Efrayim is a well-trained young cow who loves to thresh; I will stroke
his fattened, strong neck; I will harness Efrayim and make Yehuda plow;
12 Yaakov will break up the dirt clods in the field. Sow within yourselves honesty;
reap by the rule of goodness; till the unbroken ground; for now it is time to
13 seek the LORD until He comes to shower you with justice. But instead, you
have cultivated wickedness, reaped wrongdoing, eaten the fruit of your lies,
14 for your faith was in your own path, in the might of your warriors. And so the
roar of battle will rise against your people, and all your fortresses will be
ravaged as in the ravaging of Shalman[31] at Beit Arbel on that day of war when
15 mothers were crushed to pieces with their children. So this, then, is what Beit
El has made of you as a result of your great evildoing; at dawn the king of
11 1 Israel will be no more. When Israel was a child, I already loved him; from Egypt
2 I called him to Me to be My son. They[32] called to them, but they only turned
3 further away to sacrifice to the Baalim, to burn incense to the idols. It was I
who guided Efrayim's first steps, carrying them in My arms, but they never
4 grasped that I was the one who tended them. I led them with reins of human
compassion, with ties of love; I was to them like him who lifts the harness
5 from their mouths, and I gently bent down to feed them. I vowed that they
would never return to Egypt, but now Assyria is their king, and to Me they
6 refuse to return. The sword will linger in their cities; it will consume all their
7 villages and devour them because of their evil designs. My people waver –
whether to turn back to Me, although Israel is summoned upward, they will
8 not praise Him together. How can I relinquish you, Efrayim; hand you over,
Israel? How can I make you like Adma[33] and treat you like Tzevoyim? My heart
9 has turned upon Me; My compassion has been kindled. No, I will not unleash
My burning wrath, I will not turn again to destroy Efrayim – for I am God, I
am not a man; within you, My holiness dwells; I will not enter the city with

29 | See note on 4:15.
30 | See above, 9:9.
31 | Perhaps Shalmaneser III of Assyria.
32 | That is, My prophets.
33 | Adma and Tzevoyim were destroyed along with Sedom and Amora; see Deuteronomy 29:22.

דְבָרִים אָלוֹת שָׁוְא כָּרֹת בְּרִית וּפָרַח כָּרֹאשׁ מִשְׁפָּט עַל תַּלְמֵי שָׂדָי׃
ה לְעֶגְלוֹת בֵּית אָוֶן יָגוּרוּ שְׁכַן שֹׁמְרוֹן כִּי־אָבַל עָלָיו עַמּוֹ וּכְמָרָיו
ו עָלָיו יָגִילוּ עַל־כְּבוֹדוֹ כִּי־גָלָה מִמֶּנּוּ׃ גַּם־אוֹתוֹ לְאַשּׁוּר יוּבָל מִנְחָה
ז לְמֶלֶךְ יָרֵב בָּשְׁנָה אֶפְרַיִם יִקָּח וְיֵבוֹשׁ יִשְׂרָאֵל מֵעֲצָתוֹ׃ נִדְמֶה שֹׁמְרוֹן
ח מַלְכָּהּ כְּקֶצֶף עַל־פְּנֵי־מָיִם׃ וְנִשְׁמְדוּ בָּמוֹת אָוֶן חַטַּאת יִשְׂרָאֵל קוֹץ
וְדַרְדַּר יַעֲלֶה עַל־מִזְבְּחוֹתָם וְאָמְרוּ לֶהָרִים כַּסּוּנוּ וְלַגְּבָעוֹת נִפְלוּ
ט עָלֵינוּ׃ מִימֵי הַגִּבְעָה חָטָאתָ יִשְׂרָאֵל שָׁם עָמָדוּ לֹא־תַשִּׂיגֵם
י בַגִּבְעָה מִלְחָמָה עַל־בְּנֵי עֹלָה׃ בְּאַוָּתִי וְאֶסֳּרֵם וְאֻסְּפוּ עֲלֵיהֶם עַמִּים
יא בְּאָסְרָם לִשְׁתֵּי עינתם׃ וְאֶפְרַיִם עֶגְלָה מְלֻמָּדָה אֹהַבְתִּי לָדוּשׁ וַאֲנִי עֲוֹנֹתָם
עָבַרְתִּי עַל־טוּב צַוָּארָהּ אַרְכִּיב אֶפְרַיִם יַחֲרוֹשׁ יְהוּדָה יְשַׂדֶּד־לוֹ
יב יַעֲקֹב׃ זִרְעוּ לָכֶם לִצְדָקָה קִצְרוּ לְפִי־חֶסֶד נִירוּ לָכֶם נִיר וְעֵת לִדְרוֹשׁ ג
יג אֶת־יְהוָה עַד־יָבוֹא וְיֹרֶה צֶדֶק לָכֶם׃ חֲרַשְׁתֶּם־רֶשַׁע עַוְלָתָה קְצַרְתֶּם
יד אֲכַלְתֶּם פְּרִי־כָחַשׁ כִּי־בָטַחְתָּ בְדַרְכְּךָ בְּרֹב גִּבּוֹרֶיךָ׃ וְקָאם שָׁאוֹן
בְּעַמֶּךָ וְכָל־מִבְצָרֶיךָ יוּשַּׁד כְּשֹׁד שַׁלְמַן בֵּית אַרְבֵאל בְּיוֹם מִלְחָמָה
טו אֵם עַל־בָּנִים רֻטָּשָׁה׃ כָּכָה עָשָׂה לָכֶם בֵּית־אֵל מִפְּנֵי רָעַת רָעַתְכֶם
יא א בַּשַּׁחַר נִדְמֹה נִדְמָה מֶלֶךְ יִשְׂרָאֵל׃ כִּי נַעַר יִשְׂרָאֵל וָאֹהֲבֵהוּ וּמִמִּצְרַיִם
ב קָרָאתִי לִבְנִי׃ קָרְאוּ לָהֶם כֵּן הָלְכוּ מִפְּנֵיהֶם לַבְּעָלִים יְזַבֵּחוּ וְלַפְּסִלִים
ג יְקַטֵּרוּן׃ וְאָנֹכִי תִרְגַּלְתִּי לְאֶפְרַיִם קָחָם עַל־זְרוֹעֹתָיו וְלֹא יָדְעוּ כִּי
ד רְפָאתִים׃ בְּחַבְלֵי אָדָם אֶמְשְׁכֵם בַּעֲבֹתוֹת אַהֲבָה וָאֶהְיֶה לָהֶם כִּמְרִימֵי
ה עֹל עַל לְחֵיהֶם וְאַט אֵלָיו אוֹכִיל׃ לֹא יָשׁוּב אֶל־אֶרֶץ מִצְרַיִם וְאַשּׁוּר
ו הוּא מַלְכּוֹ כִּי מֵאֲנוּ לָשׁוּב׃ וְחָלָה חֶרֶב בְּעָרָיו וְכִלְּתָה בַדָּיו וְאָכָלָה
ז מִמֹּעֲצוֹתֵיהֶם׃ וְעַמִּי תְלוּאִים לִמְשׁוּבָתִי וְאֶל־עַל יִקְרָאֻהוּ יַחַד לֹא
ח יְרוֹמֵם׃ אֵיךְ אֶתֶּנְךָ אֶפְרַיִם אֲמַגֶּנְךָ יִשְׂרָאֵל אֵיךְ אֶתֶּנְךָ כְאַדְמָה אֲשִׂימְךָ
ט כִּצְבֹאיִם נֶהְפַּךְ עָלַי לִבִּי יַחַד נִכְמְרוּ נִחוּמָי׃ לֹא אֶעֱשֶׂה חֲרוֹן אַפִּי לֹא
אָשׁוּב לְשַׁחֵת אֶפְרָיִם כִּי אֵל אָנֹכִי וְלֹא־אִישׁ בְּקִרְבְּךָ קָדוֹשׁ וְלֹא

10 hatred. They will follow after the LORD; He will roar like a lion. When He
11 roars, His children will rush forth from the west. They will be like a frightened
bird coming out of Egypt, like a dove leaving the land of Assyria. I will bring
12 1 them to settle safely in their homes. So declares the LORD. Efrayim
besieges Me with lies, the House of Israel with deception, but Yehuda still
2 walks with God and remains faithful to the Holy One. Efrayim shepherds the
wind;[34] he chases the east winds. Day and night he increases lies and ruin; he
3 makes pacts with Assyria and to Egypt bears oil.[35] But also with Yehuda the
LORD has a dispute: He will visit upon Yaakov as he deserves, as befits his
4 deeds – He will repay him. In the womb he grasped his brother by the heel,[36]
5 and with all his strength he struggled with God.[37] He struggled with an angel
and prevailed; he cried and pleaded with him; in Beit El He found him,[38] and
6 there He spoke to us. But the LORD, God of Hosts, the LORD is His name.
7 Now you, too, return to your God, uphold compassion and justice, and long
8 for your God forever more. Still the merchant possesses false scales; he loves
9 to exploit. Efrayim exclaims, "I have become wealthy; I have found fortune
from my own labors; in all the fruits of my toil they will find neither sin nor
10 iniquity." I am the LORD your God from the time you were in the land of
11 Egypt; once more I will settle you safely in tents as in days of old. I have
spoken by way of the prophets; I endowed them with many visions, and
12 through images I communicated with the prophets. As Gilad is rampant with
iniquity, so too they are empty and vain; in Gilgal they sacrifice oxen, and
their altars too will become like rocks piled high in furrows of the fields.
13 Yaakov fled to the lands of Aram, and Yisrael labored to acquire a bride; for
14 a bride he kept sheep.[39] With a prophet the LORD brought Israel up out of
15 Egypt, and with a prophet He kept watch over us. Efrayim has provoked bitter
anger; the guilt from the blood he shed will remain, and the Lord will turn
13 1 his scorn back upon him. So it was: when Efrayim spoke, they trembled in
fear; he was esteemed in Israel, but when found guilty of worshipping Baal,
2 he was as dead. Now their sinning goes on and on; they cast graven images
from their silver, mold idols as they understood, each entirely the craft of men;
3 of them they say, "Men who offer sacrifices must kiss calves."[40] So they will
dissolve like morning mist, like dew at daybreak that swiftly fades. They will
4 scatter like chaff from the threshing floor, like smoke from the window. I am
the LORD your God from the land of Egypt; you know no God other than
5 Me; no one can save you except for Me. I knew you, cared for you in the
6 desert, in the parched, bereft land. But when they grazed, they became sated
7 and satisfied; their hearts became haughty – then they forgot Me. Therefore
8 I will be as a lion to them; as a leopard I will watch, lurking on the path. I will

34 | A reference to useless activity; cf., e.g., Ecclesiastes 1:14.

35 | As a tribute.

36 | See Genesis 25:26.

37 | See Genesis 32:25–31.

38 | See Genesis 28:10–22; 35:1–8.

39 | See Genesist, chapter 29.

40 | The idolatrous priests compel the worshippers to kiss golden calves as a sign of devotion.

י אָבוֹא בְּעִיר׃ אַחֲרֵי יהוה יֵלְכוּ כְּאַרְיֵה יִשְׁאָג כִּי־הוּא יִשְׁאַג וְיֶחֶרְדוּ
יא בָנִים מִיָּם׃ יֶחֶרְדוּ כְצִפּוֹר מִמִּצְרַיִם וּכְיוֹנָה מֵאֶרֶץ אַשּׁוּר וְהוֹשַׁבְתִּים
יב א עַל־בָּתֵּיהֶם נְאֻם־יהוה׃ סְבָבֻנִי בְכַחַשׁ אֶפְרַיִם וּבְמִרְמָה
ב בֵּית יִשְׂרָאֵל וִיהוּדָה עֹד רָד עִם־אֵל וְעִם־קְדוֹשִׁים נֶאֱמָן׃ אֶפְרַיִם
רֹעֶה רוּחַ וְרֹדֵף קָדִים כָּל־הַיּוֹם כָּזָב וָשֹׁד יַרְבֶּה וּבְרִית עִם־אַשּׁוּר
ג יִכְרֹתוּ וְשֶׁמֶן לְמִצְרַיִם יוּבָל׃ וְרִיב לַיהוה עִם־יְהוּדָה וְלִפְקֹד עַל־יַעֲקֹב
ד כִּדְרָכָיו כְּמַעֲלָלָיו יָשִׁיב לוֹ׃ בַּבֶּטֶן עָקַב אֶת־אָחִיו וּבְאוֹנוֹ שָׂרָה אֶת־
ה אֱלֹהִים׃ וַיָּשַׂר אֶל־מַלְאָךְ וַיֻּכָל בָּכָה וַיִּתְחַנֶּן־לוֹ בֵּית־אֵל יִמְצָאֶנּוּ
ו ז וְשָׁם יְדַבֵּר עִמָּנוּ׃ וַיהוה אֱלֹהֵי הַצְּבָאוֹת יהוה זִכְרוֹ׃ וְאַתָּה בֵּאלֹהֶיךָ
ח תָשׁוּב חֶסֶד וּמִשְׁפָּט שְׁמֹר וְקַוֵּה אֶל־אֱלֹהֶיךָ תָּמִיד׃ כְּנַעַן בְּיָדוֹ מֹאזְנֵי
ט מִרְמָה לַעֲשֹׁק אָהֵב׃ וַיֹּאמֶר אֶפְרַיִם אַךְ עָשַׁרְתִּי מָצָאתִי אוֹן לִי כָּל־
י יְגִיעַי לֹא יִמְצְאוּ־לִי עָוֹן אֲשֶׁר־חֵטְא׃ וְאָנֹכִי יהוה אֱלֹהֶיךָ מֵאֶרֶץ
יא מִצְרָיִם עֹד אוֹשִׁיבְךָ בָאֳהָלִים כִּימֵי מוֹעֵד׃ וְדִבַּרְתִּי עַל־הַנְּבִיאִים
יב וְאָנֹכִי חָזוֹן הִרְבֵּיתִי וּבְיַד הַנְּבִיאִים אֲדַמֶּה׃ אִם־גִּלְעָד אָוֶן אַךְ־שָׁוְא
יג הָיוּ בַּגִּלְגָּל שְׁוָרִים זִבֵּחוּ גַּם מִזְבְּחוֹתָם כְּגַלִּים עַל תַּלְמֵי שָׂדָי׃ וַיִּבְרַח
יד יַעֲקֹב שְׂדֵה אֲרָם וַיַּעֲבֹד יִשְׂרָאֵל בְּאִשָּׁה וּבְאִשָּׁה שָׁמָר׃ וּבְנָבִיא הֶעֱלָה
טו יהוה אֶת־יִשְׂרָאֵל מִמִּצְרָיִם וּבְנָבִיא נִשְׁמָר׃ הִכְעִיס אֶפְרַיִם תַּמְרוּרִים
יג א וְדָמָיו עָלָיו יִטּוֹשׁ וְחֶרְפָּתוֹ יָשִׁיב לוֹ אֲדֹנָיו׃ כְּדַבֵּר אֶפְרַיִם רְתֵת נָשָׂא
ב הוּא בְּיִשְׂרָאֵל וַיֶּאְשַׁם בַּבַּעַל וַיָּמֹת׃ וְעַתָּה ׀ יוֹסִפוּ לַחֲטֹא וַיַּעֲשׂוּ לָהֶם
מַסֵּכָה מִכַּסְפָּם כִּתְבוּנָם עֲצַבִּים מַעֲשֵׂה חָרָשִׁים כֻּלֹּה לָהֶם הֵם אֹמְרִים
ג זֹבְחֵי אָדָם עֲגָלִים יִשָּׁקוּן׃ לָכֵן יִהְיוּ כַּעֲנַן־בֹּקֶר וְכַטַּל מַשְׁכִּים הֹלֵךְ
ד כְּמֹץ יְסֹעֵר מִגֹּרֶן וּכְעָשָׁן מֵאֲרֻבָּה׃ וְאָנֹכִי יהוה אֱלֹהֶיךָ מֵאֶרֶץ מִצְרָיִם
ה וֵאלֹהִים זוּלָתִי לֹא תֵדָע וּמוֹשִׁיעַ אַיִן בִּלְתִּי׃ אֲנִי יְדַעְתִּיךָ בַּמִּדְבָּר
ו בְּאֶרֶץ תַּלְאֻבוֹת׃ כְּמַרְעִיתָם וַיִּשְׂבָּעוּ שָׂבְעוּ וַיָּרָם לִבָּם עַל־כֵּן שְׁכֵחוּנִי׃
ז ח וָאֱהִי לָהֶם כְּמוֹ־שָׁחַל כְּנָמֵר עַל־דֶּרֶךְ אָשׁוּר׃ אֶפְגְּשֵׁם כְּדֹב שַׁכּוּל

fall upon them like a bear who mourns her whelps and tear apart their sealed
hearts; there I will consume them like a lion; wild beasts will shred them to
9 pieces. You have brought ruin upon yourself, Israel, for your help is to be
10 found in Me. I am your King, then who will save you in all your cities, and
11 what of your judges of whom you said, "Appoint me a king and officers"? In
12 My rage I gave you a king, and in My wrath I will take him away. The
13 sinfulness of Efrayim is tied together; his sins are stored away. Pangs of birth
will overcome him, but he is not a wise son, for when the moment of birth
14 comes, he will break and not survive. I will rescue them from Sheol;[41] I will
redeem them from the clutches of death. I shall be your plague, O Death; I
will be your destruction, O Sheol; any qualms will be concealed from My
15 eyes. For though he will flourish wildly among the reeds, an east wind will
come; a gust from the LORD will rise from the wilderness. His fountain will
dry up; his spring will parch; his enemy will plunder all of his treasures.
14 1 Shomron will be held guilty, for she has rebelled against her God; she will fall
by the sword, her young smashed to pieces, her women with child ripped
2 apart. O Israel, return, go back to the LORD your God, for
3 you have stumbled in your own sinfulness. Take words of remorse with you
and return to the LORD; say to Him, "Forgive all of our sins; accept our
4 goodness – instead of calves we offer You our words of prayer. Assyria will
not save us; no more will we ride upon horses;[42] never again will we say, 'You
are our god' to the work of our hands, for only in You will the orphan find
5 mercy." I will mend their rebellion with gracious love, for I have turned My
6 anger away from them. I will be as dew to Israel; he will bloom like a lily
7 and set down roots as deep as the trees of Lebanon. His branches will spread
wide; his splendor will be as the olive tree, and his fragrance as the trees of
8 Lebanon. They who return will dwell beneath his shade; they will revive once
again as grain and flower like vines; their acclaim will linger as the scent of
9 the wine of Lebanon. Efrayim will say, "What need do I have of these idols?"
And I will answer him; I will look after him. I will be as a cypress tree, lush
10 and leafy; you will find in Me your source of fruit. He who is wise will fathom
these words; the insightful will grasp them, for the ways of the LORD are just,
and the righteous will walk in them, but sinners will stumble over them.

YOEL/JOEL

1 1 This is the word of the LORD that came to Yoel the son of Petuel: Listen, O
2 elders; take heed, all those who live on the land. Has there been anything like
3 this in your lifetimes or in the lifetimes of your parents? You will tell your
children of this, and your children will tell their children of this, and their
4 children will tell a different generation of this: "What remains after the chewer-
locusts will be eaten by the locusts; what remains after the locusts will be
eaten by the springing-locusts; what remains after the springing-locusts

41 | Meaning the grave or the underworld.
42 | Symbolizing Egypt; cf., e.g., II Kings 18:24.

ט וְאֶקְרַע סְגוֹר לִבָּם וְאֹכְלֵם שָׁם כְּלָבִיא חַיַּת הַשָּׂדֶה תְּבַקְּעֵם׃ שִׁחֶתְךָ
י יִשְׂרָאֵל כִּי־בִי בְעֶזְרֶךָ׃ אֱהִי מַלְכְּךָ אֵפוֹא וְיוֹשִׁיעֲךָ בְּכָל־עָרֶיךָ וְשֹׁפְטֶיךָ
יא אֲשֶׁר אָמַרְתָּ תְּנָה־לִּי מֶלֶךְ וְשָׂרִים׃ אֶתֶּן־לְךָ מֶלֶךְ בְּאַפִּי וְאֶקַּח
יב יג בְּעֶבְרָתִי׃ צָרוּר עֲוֺן אֶפְרָיִם צְפוּנָה חַטָּאתוֹ׃ חֶבְלֵי יוֹלֵדָה
יד יָבֹאוּ לוֹ הוּא־בֵן לֹא חָכָם כִּי־עֵת לֹא־יַעֲמֹד בְּמִשְׁבַּר בָּנִים׃ מִיַּד
שְׁאוֹל אֶפְדֵּם מִמָּוֶת אֶגְאָלֵם אֱהִי דְבָרֶיךָ מָוֶת אֱהִי קָטָבְךָ שְׁאוֹל נֹחַם
טו יִסָּתֵר מֵעֵינָי׃ כִּי הוּא בֵּין אַחִים יַפְרִיא יָבוֹא קָדִים רוּחַ יְהוָה מִמִּדְבָּר
עֹלֶה וְיֵבוֹשׁ מְקוֹרוֹ וְיֶחֱרַב מַעְיָנוֹ הוּא יִשְׁסֶה אוֹצַר כָּל־כְּלִי חֶמְדָּה׃
יד א תֶּאְשַׁם שֹׁמְרוֹן כִּי מָרְתָה בֵּאלֹהֶיהָ בַּחֶרֶב יִפְּלוּ עֹלְלֵיהֶם יְרֻטָּשׁוּ
ב וְהָרִיּוֹתָיו יְבֻקָּעוּ׃ שׁוּבָה יִשְׂרָאֵל עַד יְהוָה
ג אֱלֹהֶיךָ כִּי כָשַׁלְתָּ בַּעֲוֺנֶךָ׃ קְחוּ עִמָּכֶם דְּבָרִים וְשׁוּבוּ אֶל־יְהוָה אִמְרוּ
ד אֵלָיו כָּל־תִּשָּׂא עָוֺן וְקַח־טוֹב וּנְשַׁלְּמָה פָרִים שְׂפָתֵינוּ׃ אַשּׁוּר ׀ לֹא
יוֹשִׁיעֵנוּ עַל־סוּס לֹא נִרְכָּב וְלֹא־נֹאמַר עוֹד אֱלֹהֵינוּ לְמַעֲשֵׂה יָדֵינוּ
ה אֲשֶׁר־בְּךָ יְרֻחַם יָתוֹם׃ אֶרְפָּא מְשׁוּבָתָם אֹהֲבֵם נְדָבָה כִּי שָׁב אַפִּי
ו ז מִמֶּנּוּ׃ אֶהְיֶה כַטַּל לְיִשְׂרָאֵל יִפְרַח כַּשּׁוֹשַׁנָּה וְיַךְ שָׁרָשָׁיו כַּלְּבָנוֹן׃ יֵלְכוּ ד
ח יֹנְקוֹתָיו וִיהִי כַזַּיִת הוֹדוֹ וְרֵיחַ לוֹ כַּלְּבָנוֹן׃ יָשֻׁבוּ יֹשְׁבֵי בְצִלּוֹ יְחַיּוּ דָגָן
ט וְיִפְרְחוּ כַגָּפֶן זִכְרוֹ כְּיֵין לְבָנוֹן׃ אֶפְרַיִם מַה־לִּי עוֹד לָעֲצַבִּים אֲנִי עָנִיתִי
י וַאֲשׁוּרֶנּוּ אֲנִי כִּבְרוֹשׁ רַעֲנָן מִמֶּנִּי פֶּרְיְךָ נִמְצָא׃ מִי חָכָם וְיָבֵן אֵלֶּה נָבוֹן
וְיֵדָעֵם כִּי־יְשָׁרִים דַּרְכֵי יְהוָה וְצַדִּקִים יֵלְכוּ בָם וּפֹשְׁעִים יִכָּשְׁלוּ בָם׃

יואל

א ב דְּבַר־יְהוָה אֲשֶׁר הָיָה אֶל־יוֹאֵל בֶּן־פְּתוּאֵל׃ שִׁמְעוּ־זֹאת הַזְּקֵנִים
וְהַאֲזִינוּ כֹּל יוֹשְׁבֵי הָאָרֶץ הֶהָיְתָה זֹּאת בִּימֵיכֶם וְאִם בִּימֵי אֲבֹתֵיכֶם׃
ג ד עָלֶיהָ לִבְנֵיכֶם סַפֵּרוּ וּבְנֵיכֶם לִבְנֵיהֶם וּבְנֵיהֶם לְדוֹר אַחֵר׃ יֶתֶר הַגָּזָם
אָכַל הָאַרְבֶּה וְיֶתֶר הָאַרְבֶּה אָכַל הַיָּלֶק וְיֶתֶר הַיֶּלֶק אָכַל הֶחָסִיל׃

5 will be eaten by the finisher-locusts." Wake, drunkards, and weep; wail,
6 drinkers of wine, over the sweet wine you are denied drinking. For a nation
has risen up against My land – innumerable, mighty, with lion's teeth – its
7 fangs the fangs of a lioness. It has laid My vines to waste and splintered
My fig trees. It has stripped them bare and cast them down, their cuttings
8 bleached. Wail like a young woman donning sackcloth for her husband in
9 her youth. Grain offerings and libations have been cut off from the House
10 of the LORD. The priests, attendants of the LORD, are in mourning. The
field has been devastated; the earth is in mourning. The grain is devastated,
11 the young wine has dried up, and the oil languishes. Farmers, be ashamed;
vintners, bewail the wheat, the barley, the harvest of the field – destroyed.
12 The vine has withered, and the fig tree languishes; the pomegranate; also
the date. The apple and all the orchard trees wither. Truly man is parched of
13 joy. Don sackcloth – mourn, O priests. Wail, attendants of the
altar. Come sleep in sackcloth, attendants of my God, for grain offerings and
14 libations have been cut off from the House of your God. Sanctify a fast day,
convene an assembly, gather the elders and all those who live on the land to
15 the House of the LORD, your God, and cry out to the LORD. O, for the day,
16 the day of the LORD is nigh; like havoc from Shaddai it will come. Is not food
cut off in front of our very eyes; happiness and joy from the House of our
17 God? The seeds have shriveled under the clods. The storehouses are desolate.
18 The granaries have been destroyed; the grain has dried up. O, the animals,
how they moan. Herds of cattle are in confusion, for they are without
19 pasturage; even the flocks of sheep suffer. To You, my LORD, I cry out. Fire
has consumed the desert pasture, and flame has been ignited in all the orchard
20 trees. Even the animals of the fields long for You – for the riverbeds are dry,
2 1 and fire has consumed the desert pasture. Blow a ram's horn in Zion;
sound a horn on My holy mountain. Let all those who live on the land tremble,
2 for the day of the LORD is coming; it is nigh. It is a day of darkness and
blinding black, a day of clouds and mist like dawn spread over the mountains.
There will be a great and mighty nation, the likes of which has never been
3 before nor will ever be again until the end of time. Before it, the consuming
fire; after it, a burning flame. The land, like Eden, before it; after it, a barren
4 desert. It leaves not one survivor. Its resemblance is to horses – like war-
5 horses, so they run. Theirs is the pounding of chariots dancing over the
mountain peaks; theirs is the crackle of a flame as it consumes straw; theirs
6 is the shout of a vast nation ready for battle. Nations tremble before them;
7 they are all ashen faced. They race like warriors; like soldiers they ascend the
wall: Every soldier moving forward in position, not one strays from the route.
8 They advance untouching, every warrior moving forward in position along
9 the track. They fall on the sword but are not wounded. They rush into the
city, race over the wall, ascend into the houses like thieves through the
10 windows. The earth trembles before Him, the skies thunder, the sun and the
11 moon go dark, and the stars draw in their light. Then the LORD raises His
voice before His troops – for His camp is vast, and mighty are the ones who

ה הקיצו שכורים ובכו והילילו כל־שתי יין על־עסיס כי נכרת מפיכם:
ו כי־גוי עלה על־ארצי עצום ואין מספר שניו שני אריה ומתלעות
ז לביא לו: שם גפני לשמה ותאנתי לקצפה חשף חשפה והשליך
ח ט הלבינו שריגיה: אלי כבתולה חגרת־שק על־בעל נעוריה: הכרת
י מנחה ונסך מבית יהוה אבלו הכהנים משרתי יהוה: שדד שדה
יא אבלה אדמה כי שדד דגן הוביש תירוש אמלל יצהר: הבישו אכרים
יב הילילו כרמים על־חטה ועל־שערה כי אבד קציר שדה: הגפן
הובישה והתאנה אמללה רמון גם־תמר ותפוח כל־עצי השדה
יג יבשו כי־הביש ששון מן־בני אדם: חגרו וספדו
הכהנים הילילו משרתי מזבח באו לינו בשקים משרתי אלהי כי
יד נמנע מבית אלהיכם מנחה ונסך: קדשו־צום קראו עצרה אספו
טו זקנים כל ישבי הארץ בית יהוה אלהיכם וזעקו אל־יהוה: אהה
טז ליום כי קרוב יום יהוה וכשד משדי יבוא: הלוא נגד עינינו אכל
יז נכרת מבית אלהינו שמחה וגיל: עבשו פרדות תחת מגרפתיהם
יח נשמו אצרות נהרסו ממגרות כי הביש דגן: מה־נאנחה בהמה נבכו
יט עדרי בקר כי אין מרעה להם גם־עדרי הצאן נאשמו: אליך יהוה
אקרא כי־אש אכלה נאות מדבר ולהבה להטה כל־עצי השדה:
כ גם־בהמות שדה תערוג אליך כי יבשו אפיקי מים ואש אכלה נאות
ב א המדבר: תקעו שופר בציון והריעו בהר קדשי ירגזו
ב כל ישבי הארץ כי־בא יום־יהוה כי קרוב: יום חשך ואפלה יום ענן
וערפל כשחר פרש על־ההרים עם רב ועצום כמהו לא נהיה מן־
ג העולם ואחריו לא יוסף עד־שני דור ודור: לפניו אכלה אש ואחריו
תלהט להבה כגן־עדן הארץ לפניו ואחריו מדבר שממה וגם־
ד פליטה לא־היתה לו: כמראה סוסים מראהו וכפרשים כן ירוצון:
ה כקול מרכבות על־ראשי ההרים ירקדון כקול להב אש אכלה קש
ו כעם עצום ערוך מלחמה: מפניו יחילו עמים כל־פנים קבצו פארור:
ז כגבורים ירצון כאנשי מלחמה יעלו חומה ואיש בדרכיו ילכון ולא
ח יעבטון ארחותם: ואיש אחיו לא ידחקון גבר במסלתו ילכון ובעד
ט השלח יפלו לא יבצעו: בעיר ישקו בחומה ירצון בבתים יעלו בעד
י החלונים יבאו כגנב: לפניו רגזה ארץ רעשו שמים שמש וירח קדרו
יא וכוכבים אספו נגהם: ויהוה נתן קולו לפני חילו כי רב מאד מחנהו

carry out His words. For great and terrifying is the day of the LORD – who
12 could withstand it? Even now, so says the LORD, return to Me wholeheartedly,
13 with fasting, weeping, and grief. Rend your hearts, not your clothing, and
come back to the LORD your God. For He is gracious and compassionate,
slow to anger and abounding in kindness; He may well relent and forswear
14 the evil. Who knows? Maybe He will reconsider and relent[1] and leave
behind blessings; offer grain offerings and libations to the LORD, your
15 God. Blow a ram's horn in Zion, sanctify a fast day, convene an
16 assembly, gather the people, sanctify the masses, convene the old, and gather
the children and infants. Let the groom come from his room and the bride
17 from her wedding chamber. Let the priests, attendants of the LORD, weep
between the hallway and the altar. Let them say: "Have compassion, O LORD,
upon Your people, and do not allow Your possession to become a reproach –
ruled by nations." Why should it be said among the peoples, "Where is their
18 God?" Then the LORD will be fiercely zealous toward His land, and He will
19 have mercy upon His nation. He will reply and say to His nation: So I will
send to you grain, and sweet wine, and young oil. You will be sated with it. I
20 will no longer allow you to become a reproach among the nations. I will drive
the northerner[2] away from you – I will banish them to a dry and desolate
land; their vanguard to the east sea, their rearguard to the west sea.[3] Their
foul smell will ascend, their stench will rise, for they have done terrible things.
21 22 Fear not, earth. Rejoice! Be glad! For the LORD has done great things. Fear
not, animals of My fields, for the desert pasture is green with grass; the tree
23 has borne fruit: the fig and vine have blossomed. Rejoice and be glad in the
LORD, your God, children of Zion. For He has given you the first rain out of
generosity. He will rain down for you the first and last rain as it was in the
24 beginning. The granaries will fill with grain, and the press will overflow with
25 sweet wine and young oil. I will repay you for all the seasons consumed by the
locusts, the springing-locusts, the finisher-locusts, and the chewer-locusts –
26 My great army, which I sent among you. You will eat, eat and be sated, and
you will praise the name of the LORD, your God, who has done wonders for
27 you, for My nation will never be ashamed. You will know that I am among
Israel, and I am the LORD, your God; there is no other. My nation will never
3 1 be ashamed. Afterward, this is what will be: I will pour My spirit out
over humankind: your sons and your daughters will speak prophecy, your
2 elders will dream dreams, your young men will see visions. In those days,
3 even over the slaves and bondswomen I will pour My spirit out. I will turn
4 the skies and land into omens: blood and fire and plumes of smoke. The sun
will go dark, the moon bloody, before the coming great and terrifying day of
5 the LORD. And all those who call on the name of the LORD will escape, for
there will be a remnant on Mount Zion and in Jerusalem as the LORD has

1 | Cf. Jonah 3:9.
2 | Meaning the invading horde.
3 | The Dead Sea is located in the east of the land of Israel, and the Mediterranean to the west.

יב כִּי עָצוּם עֹשֵׂה דְבָרוֹ כִּי־גָדוֹל יוֹם־יְהוָה וְנוֹרָא מְאֹד וּמִי יְכִילֶנּוּ: וְגַם־
עַתָּה נְאֻם־יְהוָה שֻׁבוּ עָדַי בְּכָל־לְבַבְכֶם וּבְצוֹם וּבִבְכִי וּבְמִסְפֵּד:
יג וְקִרְעוּ לְבַבְכֶם וְאַל־בִּגְדֵיכֶם וְשׁוּבוּ אֶל־יְהוָה אֱלֹהֵיכֶם כִּי־חַנּוּן וְרַחוּם
יד הוּא אֶרֶךְ אַפַּיִם וְרַב־חֶסֶד וְנִחָם עַל־הָרָעָה: מִי יוֹדֵעַ יָשׁוּב וְנִחָם
טו וְהִשְׁאִיר אַחֲרָיו בְּרָכָה מִנְחָה וָנֶסֶךְ לַיהוָה אֱלֹהֵיכֶם: תִּקְעוּ
טז שׁוֹפָר בְּצִיּוֹן קַדְּשׁוּ־צוֹם קִרְאוּ עֲצָרָה: אִסְפוּ־עָם קַדְּשׁוּ קָהָל קִבְצוּ
זְקֵנִים אִסְפוּ עוֹלָלִים וְיֹנְקֵי שָׁדָיִם יֵצֵא חָתָן מֵחֶדְרוֹ וְכַלָּה מֵחֻפָּתָהּ:
יז בֵּין הָאוּלָם וְלַמִּזְבֵּחַ יִבְכּוּ הַכֹּהֲנִים מְשָׁרְתֵי יְהוָה וְיֹאמְרוּ חוּסָה יְהוָה
עַל־עַמֶּךָ וְאַל־תִּתֵּן נַחֲלָתְךָ לְחֶרְפָּה לִמְשָׁל־בָּם גּוֹיִם לָמָּה יֹאמְרוּ
יח יט בָעַמִּים אַיֵּה אֱלֹהֵיהֶם: וַיְקַנֵּא יְהוָה לְאַרְצוֹ וַיַּחְמֹל עַל־עַמּוֹ: וַיַּעַן
יְהוָה וַיֹּאמֶר לְעַמּוֹ הִנְנִי שֹׁלֵחַ לָכֶם אֶת־הַדָּגָן וְהַתִּירוֹשׁ וְהַיִּצְהָר
כ וּשְׂבַעְתֶּם אֹתוֹ וְלֹא־אֶתֵּן אֶתְכֶם עוֹד חֶרְפָּה בַּגּוֹיִם: וְאֶת־הַצְּפוֹנִי
אַרְחִיק מֵעֲלֵיכֶם וְהִדַּחְתִּיו אֶל־אֶרֶץ צִיָּה וּשְׁמָמָה אֶת־פָּנָיו אֶל־הַיָּם
הַקַּדְמֹנִי וְסֹפוֹ אֶל־הַיָּם הָאַחֲרוֹן וְעָלָה בָאְשׁוֹ וְתַעַל צַחֲנָתוֹ כִּי הִגְדִּיל
כא לַעֲשׂוֹת: אַל־תִּירְאִי אֲדָמָה גִּילִי וּשְׂמָחִי כִּי־הִגְדִּיל יְהוָה לַעֲשׂוֹת:
כב אַל־תִּירְאוּ בַּהֲמוֹת שָׂדַי כִּי דָשְׁאוּ נְאוֹת מִדְבָּר כִּי־עֵץ נָשָׂא פִרְיוֹ
כג תְּאֵנָה וָגֶפֶן נָתְנוּ חֵילָם: וּבְנֵי צִיּוֹן גִּילוּ וְשִׂמְחוּ בַּיהוָה אֱלֹהֵיכֶם כִּי־נָתַן
לָכֶם אֶת־הַמּוֹרֶה לִצְדָקָה וַיּוֹרֶד לָכֶם גֶּשֶׁם מוֹרֶה וּמַלְקוֹשׁ בָּרִאשׁוֹן:
כד כה וּמָלְאוּ הַגֳּרָנוֹת בָּר וְהֵשִׁיקוּ הַיְקָבִים תִּירוֹשׁ וְיִצְהָר: וְשִׁלַּמְתִּי לָכֶם
אֶת־הַשָּׁנִים אֲשֶׁר אָכַל הָאַרְבֶּה הַיֶּלֶק וְהֶחָסִיל וְהַגָּזָם חֵילִי הַגָּדוֹל
כו אֲשֶׁר שִׁלַּחְתִּי בָּכֶם: וַאֲכַלְתֶּם אָכוֹל וְשָׂבוֹעַ וְהִלַּלְתֶּם אֶת־שֵׁם יְהוָה
אֱלֹהֵיכֶם אֲשֶׁר־עָשָׂה עִמָּכֶם לְהַפְלִיא וְלֹא־יֵבֹשׁוּ עַמִּי לְעוֹלָם:
כז וִידַעְתֶּם כִּי בְקֶרֶב יִשְׂרָאֵל אָנִי וַאֲנִי יְהוָה אֱלֹהֵיכֶם וְאֵין עוֹד וְלֹא־יֵבֹשׁוּ ה
ג א עַמִּי לְעוֹלָם: וְהָיָה אַחֲרֵי־כֵן אֶשְׁפּוֹךְ אֶת־רוּחִי
עַל־כָּל־בָּשָׂר וְנִבְּאוּ בְּנֵיכֶם וּבְנוֹתֵיכֶם זִקְנֵיכֶם חֲלֹמוֹת יַחֲלֹמוּן בַּחוּרֵיכֶם
ב חֶזְיֹנוֹת יִרְאוּ: וְגַם עַל־הָעֲבָדִים וְעַל־הַשְּׁפָחוֹת בַּיָּמִים הָהֵמָּה אֶשְׁפּוֹךְ
ג אֶת־רוּחִי: וְנָתַתִּי מוֹפְתִים בַּשָּׁמַיִם וּבָאָרֶץ דָּם וָאֵשׁ וְתִימְרוֹת עָשָׁן:
ד הַשֶּׁמֶשׁ יֵהָפֵךְ לְחֹשֶׁךְ וְהַיָּרֵחַ לְדָם לִפְנֵי בּוֹא יוֹם יְהוָה הַגָּדוֹל וְהַנּוֹרָא:
ה וְהָיָה כֹּל אֲשֶׁר־יִקְרָא בְּשֵׁם יְהוָה יִמָּלֵט כִּי בְּהַר־צִיּוֹן וּבִירוּשָׁלַםִ

said; even among the survivors called by the LORD there will be a remnant.[4]
4 1 For it will be in those days and at that time that I will restore those held captive
2 from Yehuda and Jerusalem. I will gather all the nations and bring them down
to the Valley of Yehoshafat. There I will carry out judgment against them for
the sake of My people – My possession Israel, whom they scattered among
the nations – and for the sake of My land, which they divided among
3 themselves. They cast lots for My nation,[5] and handed over young boys for
4 the hire of a harlot, and sold young girls for wine, and they drank. But what
are you to Me, Tyre and Sidon, all the Philistine regions? Do you deign to
retaliate against Me? And if you retaliate, how quickly and easily I will repay
5 your deeds upon your head. You took My silver and gold and carried My
6 precious things away to your temples. You sold the Judahites and Jerusalemites
7 to the Ionians to cast them far from their borders. But I will rouse them from
the place to which you sold them, and I will repay your deeds upon your
8 head. I will sell your sons and daughters into the hands of the Judahites, who
will sell them to the people of Sheba – a far-off nation. For the LORD has
9 spoken. Call this out to the nations: Declare a war[6] and let the
10 warriors stir. Let all the men of war approach, ascend. Beat your plowshares
into swords and your pruning hooks into spears.[7] Let the weak say, "I am
11 mighty." Come swiftly, all you surrounding nations, and gather together there.
12 O LORD, let Your warriors descend. Let the nations stir and go up to the
Valley of Yehoshafat, for it is there that I will sit and judge all the surrounding
13 nations.[8] Hoist the sickle; the harvest is ripe. Come, trample; the winepress
14 is full. The vats of wine overflow, so great is the evil they have done. Masses
upon masses in the Valley of Decision, for the day of the LORD is nigh in the
15 Valley of Decision. The sun and moon go dark, and the stars draw in their
16 light. The LORD roars from Zion;[9] from Jerusalem He raises His voice. The
heavens and the earth tremble. But the LORD will be a shelter for His people,
17 a stronghold for the children of Israel. So you will know that I am the LORD,
your God – the One who resides in Zion, My holy mountain. Jerusalem will
18 be sacred; strangers will pass through her no longer. On that day,
the mountains will drip with sweet wine,[10] the hills will flow with milk, and
all of Yehuda's rivers will flow, full of water. A spring will surge forth from the
19 House of the LORD and irrigate the Valley of Acacias. Egypt will be desolate,
Edom a barren desert, because of the violence they have perpetrated against
20 Yehuda – because of the innocent blood they spilled in their land. But Yehuda
21 will be forever settled, Jerusalem to the end of time. Even though I pardon, I
will not pardon the spilling of their blood, for the LORD resides in Zion.

4 | Cf. Obadiah 1:17; Isaiah 37:32; II Kings 19:31.
5 | In order to divide up Israel's land.
6 | That is, commence a war; cf. Micah 3:5; Jeremiah 6:4.
7 | Cf. Isaiah 2:4; Micah 4:3.
8 | *Yehoshafat* literally means "the Lord judges."
9 | Cf. Amos 1:2; Jeremiah 25:30.
10 | Cf. Amos 9:13.

ד א תִּהְיֶה פְלֵיטָה כַּאֲשֶׁר אָמַר יְהוָה וּבַשְּׂרִידִים אֲשֶׁר יְהוָה קֹרֵא׃ כִּי הִנֵּה
בַּיָּמִים הָהֵמָּה וּבָעֵת הַהִיא אֲשֶׁר אָשׁוּב אֶת־שְׁבוּת יְהוּדָה וִירוּשָׁלִָם׃ אָשִׁיב
ב וְקִבַּצְתִּי אֶת־כָּל־הַגּוֹיִם וְהוֹרַדְתִּים אֶל־עֵמֶק יְהוֹשָׁפָט וְנִשְׁפַּטְתִּי עִמָּם
שָׁם עַל־עַמִּי וְנַחֲלָתִי יִשְׂרָאֵל אֲשֶׁר פִּזְּרוּ בַגּוֹיִם וְאֶת־אַרְצִי חִלֵּקוּ׃
ג ד וְאֶל־עַמִּי יַדּוּ גוֹרָל וַיִּתְּנוּ הַיֶּלֶד בַּזּוֹנָה וְהַיַּלְדָּה מָכְרוּ בַיַּיִן וַיִּשְׁתּוּ׃ וְגַם
מָה־אַתֶּם לִי צֹר וְצִידוֹן וְכֹל גְּלִילוֹת פְּלָשֶׁת הַגְּמוּל אַתֶּם מְשַׁלְּמִים
עָלָי וְאִם־גֹּמְלִים אַתֶּם עָלַי קַל מְהֵרָה אָשִׁיב גְּמֻלְכֶם בְּרֹאשְׁכֶם׃
ה אֲשֶׁר־כַּסְפִּי וּזְהָבִי לְקַחְתֶּם וּמַחֲמַדַּי הַטֹּבִים הֲבֵאתֶם לְהֵיכְלֵיכֶם׃
ו וּבְנֵי יְהוּדָה וּבְנֵי יְרוּשָׁלִַם מְכַרְתֶּם לִבְנֵי הַיְּוָנִים לְמַעַן הַרְחִיקָם מֵעַל
ז גְּבוּלָם׃ הִנְנִי מְעִירָם מִן־הַמָּקוֹם אֲשֶׁר־מְכַרְתֶּם אֹתָם שָׁמָּה וַהֲשִׁבֹתִי
ח גְמֻלְכֶם בְּרֹאשְׁכֶם׃ וּמָכַרְתִּי אֶת־בְּנֵיכֶם וְאֶת־בְּנוֹתֵיכֶם בְּיַד בְּנֵי יְהוּדָה
ט וּמְכָרוּם לִשְׁבָאיִם אֶל־גּוֹי רָחוֹק כִּי יְהוָה דִּבֵּר׃ קִרְאוּ־זֹאת
בַגּוֹיִם קַדְּשׁוּ מִלְחָמָה הָעִירוּ הַגִּבּוֹרִים יִגְּשׁוּ יַעֲלוּ כֹּל אַנְשֵׁי הַמִּלְחָמָה׃
י כֹּתּוּ אִתֵּיכֶם לַחֲרָבוֹת וּמַזְמְרֹתֵיכֶם לִרְמָחִים הַחַלָּשׁ יֹאמַר גִּבּוֹר אָנִי׃
יא עוּשׁוּ וָבֹאוּ כָל־הַגּוֹיִם מִסָּבִיב וְנִקְבָּצוּ שָׁמָּה הַנְחַת יְהוָה גִּבּוֹרֶיךָ׃
יב יֵעוֹרוּ וְיַעֲלוּ הַגּוֹיִם אֶל־עֵמֶק יְהוֹשָׁפָט כִּי שָׁם אֵשֵׁב לִשְׁפֹּט אֶת־כָּל־
יג הַגּוֹיִם מִסָּבִיב׃ שִׁלְחוּ מַגָּל כִּי בָשַׁל קָצִיר בֹּאוּ רְדוּ כִּי־מָלְאָה גַּת
יד הֵשִׁיקוּ הַיְקָבִים כִּי רַבָּה רָעָתָם׃ הֲמוֹנִים הֲמוֹנִים בְּעֵמֶק הֶחָרוּץ כִּי
טו קָרוֹב יוֹם יְהוָה בְּעֵמֶק הֶחָרוּץ׃ שֶׁמֶשׁ וְיָרֵחַ קָדָרוּ וְכוֹכָבִים אָסְפוּ
טז נָגְהָם׃ וַיהוָה מִצִּיּוֹן יִשְׁאָג וּמִירוּשָׁלִַם יִתֵּן קוֹלוֹ וְרָעֲשׁוּ שָׁמַיִם וָאָרֶץ
יז וַיהוָה מַחֲסֶה לְעַמּוֹ וּמָעוֹז לִבְנֵי יִשְׂרָאֵל׃ וִידַעְתֶּם כִּי אֲנִי יְהוָה אֱלֹהֵיכֶם
שֹׁכֵן בְּצִיּוֹן הַר־קָדְשִׁי וְהָיְתָה יְרוּשָׁלִַם קֹדֶשׁ וְזָרִים לֹא־יַעַבְרוּ־בָהּ
יח עוֹד׃ וְהָיָה בַיּוֹם הַהוּא יִטְּפוּ הֶהָרִים עָסִיס וְהַגְּבָעוֹת תֵּלַכְנָה
חָלָב וְכָל־אֲפִיקֵי יְהוּדָה יֵלְכוּ מָיִם וּמַעְיָן מִבֵּית יְהוָה יֵצֵא וְהִשְׁקָה אֶת־
יט נַחַל הַשִּׁטִּים׃ מִצְרַיִם לִשְׁמָמָה תִהְיֶה וֶאֱדוֹם לְמִדְבַּר שְׁמָמָה תִּהְיֶה
כ מֵחֲמַס בְּנֵי יְהוּדָה אֲשֶׁר־שָׁפְכוּ דָם־נָקִיא בְּאַרְצָם׃ וִיהוּדָה לְעוֹלָם תֵּשֵׁב
כא וִירוּשָׁלִַם לְדוֹר וָדוֹר׃ וְנִקֵּיתִי דָּמָם לֹא־נִקֵּיתִי וַיהוָה שֹׁכֵן בְּצִיּוֹן׃

1 1 These are the words of Amos of the herdsmen of Tekoa, who prophesied AMOS
regarding Israel during the days of Uziya, king of Yehuda, and Yorovam the
2 son of Yoash, king of Israel, two years before the earthquake.[1] He said: The
LORD roars from Zion; from Jerusalem He raises His voice: The shepherds'
3 pastures are in mourning, and the peak of the Carmel withers. So
says the LORD: On account of Damascus's three crimes and on account of
the fourth, I will not forgive them:[2] they threshed through Gilad with
4 threshing sledges of iron,[3] so I will send a fire against the house of Ḥazael. It
5 will consume the fortresses of Ben Ḥadad.[4] I will shatter the barred gates
of Damascus.[5] I will cut off any ruler from the Aven Valley and any staff-
bearer from Beit Eden. The nation of Aram will be exiled to Kir,[6] says the
6 LORD. So says the LORD: On account of Aza's three crimes and on
account of the fourth, I will not forgive them: they exiled an entire group of
7 exiles, handing them over to Edom, so I will send a fire against Aza's wall. It
8 will consume her fortresses. I will cut off any ruler from Ashdod and any
staff-bearer from Ashkelon. I will set My hand against Ekron, and the remnant
9 of Philistines will be lost, says the Lord GOD. So says the LORD:
On account of Tyre's three crimes and on account of the fourth, I will not
forgive them: they handed over an entire group of exiles to Edom and did not
10 remember the brotherly covenant.[7] So I will send a fire against Tyre's wall.
11 It will consume her fortresses. So says the LORD: On account
of Edom's three crimes and on account of the fourth, I will not forgive
them: They have pursued their brother[8] in war and suppressed their own
mercy. They have allowed their anger to rage forever and nursed their wrath
12 unending, so I will send a fire against Yemen. It will consume the fortresses
13 of Botzra. So says the LORD: On account of the children of Amon's
three crimes and on account of the fourth, I will not forgive them: to expand
14 their borders, they sliced open the pregnant women of the Gilad, so I will
send a fire against the walls of Raba. It will consume her fortresses with a
15 shout on a day of war, a gale on a day of a storm. Their king shall be taken into
2 1 exile, he and his princes together, says the LORD. So says the LORD:
On account of Moav's three crimes and on account of the fourth, I will not
forgive them: they immolated the corpse of the king of Edom down to lime,
2 so I will send a fire against Moav. It will consume the fortresses of the cities.

---

1 | See Zechariah 14:5.

2 | This is a common rhetorical device in Tanakh; cf., e.g., Proverbs 30:15. The last (or in these cases, only) item of the list mentioned is generally different or more extreme, roughly equivalent to "the final straw" in English.

3 | They used these machines to torture Gilad's inhabitants.

4 | Ḥazael and Ben Ḥadad were powerful kings of Damascus. See, e.g., I Kings 20; II Kings 8:7–15.

5 | This and the following were major Aramean cities. The following prophecies as well foretell doom for the major cities of the peoples in question.

6 | The place of their origins; see 9:7.

7 | Perhaps a reference to the covenant between David and Shlomo and the rulers of Tyre; see I Kings 5:21–25.

8 | Referring to Yisrael (Yaakov), who was the brother of Edom (Esav); see Genesis, chapter 23.

עמוס

א א דִּבְרֵי עָמוֹס אֲשֶׁר־הָיָה בַנֹּקְדִים מִתְּקוֹעַ אֲשֶׁר חָזָה עַל־יִשְׂרָאֵל בִּימֵי ׀
עֻזִּיָּה מֶלֶךְ־יְהוּדָה וּבִימֵי יָרָבְעָם בֶּן־יוֹאָשׁ מֶלֶךְ יִשְׂרָאֵל שְׁנָתַיִם לִפְנֵי
ב הָרָעַשׁ׃ וַיֹּאמַר ׀ יהוה מִצִּיּוֹן יִשְׁאָג וּמִירוּשָׁלִַם יִתֵּן קוֹלוֹ וְאָבְלוּ נְאוֹת
ג הָרֹעִים וְיָבֵשׁ רֹאשׁ הַכַּרְמֶל׃ כֹּה אָמַר יהוה עַל־שְׁלֹשָׁה
פִּשְׁעֵי דַמֶּשֶׂק וְעַל־אַרְבָּעָה לֹא אֲשִׁיבֶנּוּ עַל־דּוּשָׁם בַּחֲרֻצוֹת הַבַּרְזֶל
ד אֶת־הַגִּלְעָד׃ וְשִׁלַּחְתִּי אֵשׁ בְּבֵית חֲזָאֵל וְאָכְלָה אַרְמְנוֹת בֶּן־הֲדָד׃
ה וְשָׁבַרְתִּי בְּרִיחַ דַּמֶּשֶׂק וְהִכְרַתִּי יוֹשֵׁב מִבִּקְעַת־אָוֶן וְתוֹמֵךְ שֵׁבֶט מִבֵּית
ו עֶדֶן וְגָלוּ עַם־אֲרָם קִירָה אָמַר יהוה׃ כֹּה אָמַר יהוה
עַל־שְׁלֹשָׁה פִּשְׁעֵי עַזָּה וְעַל־אַרְבָּעָה לֹא אֲשִׁיבֶנּוּ עַל־הַגְלוֹתָם גָּלוּת
ז שְׁלֵמָה לְהַסְגִּיר לֶאֱדוֹם׃ וְשִׁלַּחְתִּי אֵשׁ בְּחוֹמַת עַזָּה וְאָכְלָה אַרְמְנֹתֶיהָ׃
ח וְהִכְרַתִּי יוֹשֵׁב מֵאַשְׁדּוֹד וְתוֹמֵךְ שֵׁבֶט מֵאַשְׁקְלוֹן וַהֲשִׁיבוֹתִי יָדִי עַל־
ט עֶקְרוֹן וְאָבְדוּ שְׁאֵרִית פְּלִשְׁתִּים אָמַר אֲדֹנָי יֱהוִה׃ כֹּה
אָמַר יהוה עַל־שְׁלֹשָׁה פִּשְׁעֵי־צֹר וְעַל־אַרְבָּעָה לֹא אֲשִׁיבֶנּוּ עַל־
י הַסְגִּירָם גָּלוּת שְׁלֵמָה לֶאֱדוֹם וְלֹא זָכְרוּ בְּרִית אַחִים׃ וְשִׁלַּחְתִּי אֵשׁ
יא בְּחוֹמַת צֹר וְאָכְלָה אַרְמְנוֹתֶיהָ׃ כֹּה אָמַר יהוה עַל־שְׁלֹשָׁה
פִּשְׁעֵי אֱדוֹם וְעַל־אַרְבָּעָה לֹא אֲשִׁיבֶנּוּ עַל־רָדְפוֹ בַחֶרֶב אָחִיו וְשִׁחֵת
יב רַחֲמָיו וַיִּטְרֹף לָעַד אַפּוֹ וְעֶבְרָתוֹ שְׁמָרָה נֶצַח׃ וְשִׁלַּחְתִּי אֵשׁ בְּתֵימָן
יג וְאָכְלָה אַרְמְנוֹת בָּצְרָה׃ כֹּה אָמַר יהוה עַל־שְׁלֹשָׁה פִּשְׁעֵי
בְנֵי־עַמּוֹן וְעַל־אַרְבָּעָה לֹא אֲשִׁיבֶנּוּ עַל־בִּקְעָם הָרוֹת הַגִּלְעָד לְמַעַן
יד הַרְחִיב אֶת־גְּבוּלָם׃ וְהִצַּתִּי אֵשׁ בְּחוֹמַת רַבָּה וְאָכְלָה אַרְמְנוֹתֶיהָ
טו בִּתְרוּעָה בְּיוֹם מִלְחָמָה בְּסַעַר בְּיוֹם סוּפָה׃ וְהָלַךְ מַלְכָּם בַּגּוֹלָה הוּא
ב א וְשָׂרָיו יַחְדָּו אָמַר יהוה׃ כֹּה אָמַר יהוה עַל־שְׁלֹשָׁה פִּשְׁעֵי
מוֹאָב וְעַל־אַרְבָּעָה לֹא אֲשִׁיבֶנּוּ עַל־שָׂרְפוֹ עַצְמוֹת מֶלֶךְ־אֱדוֹם לַשִּׂיד׃
ב וְשִׁלַּחְתִּי־אֵשׁ בְּמוֹאָב וְאָכְלָה אַרְמְנוֹת הַקְּרִיּוֹת וּמֵת בְּשָׁאוֹן מוֹאָב

3 Moav will die in an uproar with shouting, the sound of a ram's horn. I will cut
off any chieftain from within her, and I will kill all her princes along with him,
4 says the LORD. So says the LORD: On account of Yehuda's three
crimes and on account of the fourth, I will not forgive them: they despised
the LORD's Torah and did not keep His statutes. Their own lies – the ones
5 their fathers followed – led them astray, so I will send a fire against Yehuda.
6 It will consume the fortresses of Jerusalem. So says the LORD:
On account of Israel's three crimes and on account of the fourth, I will not
forgive them. They sold the righteous for silver and the poor for the price of
7 shoes. They are those who trample the dust of the earth atop the heads of the
poor; they turn the humble away from the path. A man and his father visit
8 the same girl to desecrate My holy name. They spread confiscated clothing
beside every altar and drink wine bought with fines in the house of their gods.
9 But I had destroyed before them the Amorite, whose height was as tall as
cedars and whose strength was like that of oaks. Yet I obliterated their fruit
10 above and their roots below. I brought you up from the land of Egypt and led
11 you in the desert for forty years to inherit Amorite lands. I raised up into
prophets some of your sons and into nazirites some of your young men.
12 Is this not so, children of Israel? said the LORD. But you made the nazirites
13 drink wine and ordered the prophets not to prophesy.[9] Behold, I will hold
14 you back in your place, as a wagon loaded with sheaves is held back. The swift
will lose the ability to flee; the strong will not gather their strength; the
15 warrior will not escape with his life. The bowman will not stand; the fleet of
16 foot will not escape; the horse rider will not escape with his life. He who
considers himself strongest among warriors will flee naked on that day, says
3 1 the LORD. Hear this word, which the LORD has spoken about you,
children of Israel: About the whole family I brought up from the land of
2 Egypt, it is only you that I have known from among all the families on earth,
3 so I will visit all your sins upon you. Would two walk together if they had not
4 met? Would a lion roar in the forest if it had not caught prey? Would a young
5 lion raise its voice from its den if it had not seized prey? Would a bird plunge
into a trap on the ground if it were not baited? Would the trap spring up from
6 the earth if it had not trapped quarry? Would a warning horn blow in the city
and the people not be afraid? Would disaster come upon the city were it not
7 an act of the LORD? The Lord GOD does not do anything without revealing
8 His secret to His servants, the prophets. A lion roars; who would not fear?
9 The Lord GOD speaks; who would not prophesy? Cause this to be heard in
the fortresses of Ashdod and the fortresses of Egypt. Gather against the hills
of Shomron and witness much tumult within her and the oppressed in her
10 midst. They do not know how to act honestly, says the LORD, those who hoard
11 violence and theft in their palaces. Therefore, says the Lord GOD,
an enemy will surround the land and remove from you your defenses, and

9 | The nazirite is forbidden to drink wine (Num. 6:1–21).

ג בַתְּרוּעָה בְּקוֹל שׁוֹפָר׃ וְהִכְרַתִּי שׁוֹפֵט מִקִּרְבָּהּ וְכָל־שָׂרֶיהָ אֶהֱרוֹג
ד עִמּוֹ אָמַר יְהוָה׃ כֹּה אָמַר יְהוָה עַל־שְׁלֹשָׁה פִּשְׁעֵי יְהוּדָה
וְעַל־אַרְבָּעָה לֹא אֲשִׁיבֶנּוּ עַל־מָאֳסָם אֶת־תּוֹרַת יְהוָה וְחֻקָּיו לֹא שָׁמָרוּ
ה וַיַּתְעוּם כִּזְבֵיהֶם אֲשֶׁר־הָלְכוּ אֲבוֹתָם אַחֲרֵיהֶם׃ וְשִׁלַּחְתִּי אֵשׁ בִּיהוּדָה
ו וְאָכְלָה אַרְמְנוֹת יְרוּשָׁלִָם׃ כֹּה אָמַר יְהוָה עַל־שְׁלֹשָׁה
פִּשְׁעֵי יִשְׂרָאֵל וְעַל־אַרְבָּעָה לֹא אֲשִׁיבֶנּוּ עַל־מִכְרָם בַּכֶּסֶף צַדִּיק
ז וְאֶבְיוֹן בַּעֲבוּר נַעֲלָיִם׃ הַשֹּׁאֲפִים עַל־עֲפַר־אֶרֶץ בְּרֹאשׁ דַּלִּים וְדֶרֶךְ
עֲנָוִים יַטּוּ וְאִישׁ וְאָבִיו יֵלְכוּ אֶל־הַנַּעֲרָה לְמַעַן חַלֵּל אֶת־שֵׁם קָדְשִׁי׃
ח וְעַל־בְּגָדִים חֲבֻלִים יַטּוּ אֵצֶל כָּל־מִזְבֵּחַ וְיֵין עֲנוּשִׁים יִשְׁתּוּ בֵּית
ט אֱלֹהֵיהֶם׃ וְאָנֹכִי הִשְׁמַדְתִּי אֶת־הָאֱמֹרִי מִפְּנֵיהֶם אֲשֶׁר כְּגֹבַהּ אֲרָזִים
גָּבְהוֹ וְחָסֹן הוּא כָּאַלּוֹנִים וָאַשְׁמִיד פִּרְיוֹ מִמַּעַל וְשָׁרָשָׁיו מִתָּחַת׃
י וְאָנֹכִי הֶעֱלֵיתִי אֶתְכֶם מֵאֶרֶץ מִצְרָיִם וָאוֹלֵךְ אֶתְכֶם בַּמִּדְבָּר אַרְבָּעִים ו
יא שָׁנָה לָרֶשֶׁת אֶת־אֶרֶץ הָאֱמֹרִי׃ וָאָקִים מִבְּנֵיכֶם לִנְבִיאִים וּמִבַּחוּרֵיכֶם
יב לִנְזִרִים הַאַף אֵין־זֹאת בְּנֵי יִשְׂרָאֵל נְאֻם־יְהוָה׃ וַתַּשְׁקוּ אֶת־הַנְּזִרִים
יג יָיִן וְעַל־הַנְּבִיאִים צִוִּיתֶם לֵאמֹר לֹא תִּנָּבְאוּ׃ הִנֵּה אָנֹכִי מֵעִיק תַּחְתֵּיכֶם
יד כַּאֲשֶׁר תָּעִיק הָעֲגָלָה הַמְלֵאָה לָהּ עָמִיר׃ וְאָבַד מָנוֹס מִקָּל וְחָזָק
טו לֹא־יְאַמֵּץ כֹּחוֹ וְגִבּוֹר לֹא־יְמַלֵּט נַפְשׁוֹ׃ וְתֹפֵשׂ הַקֶּשֶׁת לֹא יַעֲמֹד וְקַל
טז בְּרַגְלָיו לֹא יְמַלֵּט וְרֹכֵב הַסּוּס לֹא יְמַלֵּט נַפְשׁוֹ׃ וְאַמִּיץ לִבּוֹ בַּגִּבּוֹרִים
ג א עָרוֹם יָנוּס בַּיּוֹם־הַהוּא נְאֻם־יְהוָה׃ שִׁמְעוּ אֶת־הַדָּבָר הַזֶּה
אֲשֶׁר דִּבֶּר יְהוָה עֲלֵיכֶם בְּנֵי יִשְׂרָאֵל עַל כָּל־הַמִּשְׁפָּחָה אֲשֶׁר הֶעֱלֵיתִי
ב מֵאֶרֶץ מִצְרַיִם לֵאמֹר׃ רַק אֶתְכֶם יָדַעְתִּי מִכֹּל מִשְׁפְּחוֹת הָאֲדָמָה
ג עַל־כֵּן אֶפְקֹד עֲלֵיכֶם אֵת כָּל־עֲוֺנֹתֵיכֶם׃ הֲיֵלְכוּ שְׁנַיִם יַחְדָּו בִּלְתִּי
ד אִם־נוֹעָדוּ׃ הֲיִשְׁאַג אַרְיֵה בַּיַּעַר וְטֶרֶף אֵין לוֹ הֲיִתֵּן כְּפִיר קוֹלוֹ מִמְּעֹנָתוֹ
ה בִּלְתִּי אִם־לָכָד׃ הֲתִפֹּל צִפּוֹר עַל־פַּח הָאָרֶץ וּמוֹקֵשׁ אֵין לָהּ הֲיַעֲלֶה־
ו פַּח מִן־הָאֲדָמָה וְלָכוֹד לֹא יִלְכּוֹד׃ אִם־יִתָּקַע שׁוֹפָר בְּעִיר וְעָם לֹא
ז יֶחֱרָדוּ אִם־תִּהְיֶה רָעָה בְּעִיר וַיהוָה לֹא עָשָׂה׃ כִּי לֹא יַעֲשֶׂה אֲדֹנָי
ח יְהוִה דָּבָר כִּי אִם־גָּלָה סוֹדוֹ אֶל־עֲבָדָיו הַנְּבִיאִים׃ אַרְיֵה שָׁאָג מִי לֹא
ט יִירָא אֲדֹנָי יְהוִה דִּבֶּר מִי לֹא יִנָּבֵא׃ הַשְׁמִיעוּ עַל־אַרְמְנוֹת בְּאַשְׁדּוֹד
וְעַל־אַרְמְנוֹת בְּאֶרֶץ מִצְרָיִם וְאִמְרוּ הֵאָסְפוּ עַל־הָרֵי שֹׁמְרוֹן וּרְאוּ
י מְהוּמֹת רַבּוֹת בְּתוֹכָהּ וַעֲשׁוּקִים בְּקִרְבָּהּ׃ וְלֹא־יָדְעוּ עֲשׂוֹת־נְכֹחָה
יא נְאֻם־יְהוָה הָאוֹצְרִים חָמָס וָשֹׁד בְּאַרְמְנוֹתֵיהֶם׃ לָכֵן כֹּה
אָמַר אֲדֹנָי יְהוִה צַר וּסְבִיב הָאָרֶץ וְהוֹרִד מִמֵּךְ עֻזֵּךְ וְנָבֹזּוּ אַרְמְנוֹתָיִךְ׃

12 your fortresses will be plundered. So says the LORD: Just as a shepherd
salvages two thighs or a scrap of an ear from a lion, so will the children of
Israel, those who reside in Shomron, be saved with the edge of the bed, with
13 the cradle of Damascus.[10] Proclaim; bear witness against the House of Yaakov,
14 says the Lord GOD, God of Hosts: For on the day on which I visit Israel's
crimes upon them, I will visit them upon the altars of Beit El. The altar horns
15 will be hewn; they will fall to the ground. I will strike the winter palace along
with the summer palace: the palaces of ivory will be lost. Many are the palaces
4 1 that will be swept away. Hear this, O cows of the Bashan who are
on Mount Shomron, who oppress the poor, who break the poverty stricken,
2 who say to their masters, "Bring wine[11] and let us drink." The Lord GOD
swears by His holiness: Days are coming upon you; you will be carried away
impaled on hooks, and in fishing pots your children will be dragged away.
3 Women will flee through the breaches and be cast into the palaces,[12] says
4 the LORD. Come to Beit El and sin, to the Gilgal and sin greatly. Bring
5 your sacrifices in the morning and your tithes on the third day. Burn your
thanksgiving offering of leaven; call for donations; let it be heard, for this is
6 what you love doing, children of Israel, says the Lord GOD. Yet I gave you
clean teeth in all your cities, a lack of bread in your places, but you did not
7 return to Me, says the LORD. And I held back the rain from you three months
before the harvest, caused rain to fall on one city and not another; one plot
will be rained upon, and one in which there will be no rain will wither away.
8 The residents of two or three cities will wander to one city for water to drink,
9 but their thirst is not slaked, yet you did not return to Me, says the LORD. I
struck you with blight and mildew, your many gardens and vineyards, your
fig and olive trees devoured by the chewer-locusts, but you did not return to
10 Me, says the LORD. I sent a plague upon you like that which I sent against
Egypt; I slew your young men by the sword during the capture of your horses.
The stench of your slain camp rises in your noses, but you did not return to
11 Me, says the LORD. I overturned you as God overturned Sedom and Amora.
You became like a firebrand saved from the fire, but you did not return to Me,
12 says the LORD. Therefore, this is what I will do to you, Israel –
because of the above, this is what I will do: prepare yourselves to meet your
13 God, O Israel, for it is He, Mountain-shaper, Wind-creator, the One who tells
man his thoughts. He turns the dawn to dark and treads over mountain
5 1 heights; the LORD, God of Hosts, is His name. Hear these words
2 that I raise as a lament over you, House of Israel: She has fallen, maiden of
Israel; she will not rise again. She has been abandoned in her land; there is
3 no one to raise her up, for so says the Lord GOD. A city one thousand

10 | The end of this verse is difficult. The word *eres* literally means bed. It may be a reference to Nergal Eresh, the Assyrian magnate in Damascus in the early eighth century who was a leader of the campaign (narrated in II Kings 13:5, without reference to Assyria) that ended the oppression of Israel by the Aramean Ḥazael and his successor Ben Hadad.

11 | "Wine" missing from the Hebrew, but implied.

12 | Of the enemy.

יב כֹּה אָמַר יְהוָה כַּאֲשֶׁר יַצִּיל הָרֹעֶה מִפִּי הָאֲרִי שְׁתֵּי כְרָעַיִם אוֹ בְדַל־
אֹזֶן כֵּן יִנָּצְלוּ בְּנֵי יִשְׂרָאֵל הַיֹּשְׁבִים בְּשֹׁמְרוֹן בִּפְאַת מִטָּה וּבִדְמֶשֶׁק
יג עָרֶשׂ׃ שִׁמְעוּ וְהָעִידוּ בְּבֵית יַעֲקֹב נְאֻם־אֲדֹנָי יְהוִה אֱלֹהֵי הַצְּבָאוֹת׃
יד כִּי בְּיוֹם פָּקְדִי פִשְׁעֵי־יִשְׂרָאֵל עָלָיו וּפָקַדְתִּי עַל־מִזְבְּחוֹת בֵּית־אֵל
טו וְנִגְדְּעוּ קַרְנוֹת הַמִּזְבֵּחַ וְנָפְלוּ לָאָרֶץ׃ וְהִכֵּיתִי בֵית־הַחֹרֶף עַל־בֵּית
ד א הַקָּיִץ וְאָבְדוּ בָּתֵּי הַשֵּׁן וְסָפוּ בָּתִּים רַבִּים נְאֻם־יְהוָה׃ שִׁמְעוּ
הַדָּבָר הַזֶּה פָּרוֹת הַבָּשָׁן אֲשֶׁר בְּהַר שֹׁמְרוֹן הָעֹשְׁקוֹת דַּלִּים הָרֹצְצוֹת
ב אֶבְיוֹנִים הָאֹמְרֹת לַאֲדֹנֵיהֶם הָבִיאָה וְנִשְׁתֶּה׃ נִשְׁבַּע אֲדֹנָי יְהוִה
בְּקָדְשׁוֹ כִּי הִנֵּה יָמִים בָּאִים עֲלֵיכֶם וְנִשָּׂא אֶתְכֶם בְּצִנּוֹת וְאַחֲרִיתְכֶן
ג בְּסִירוֹת דּוּגָה׃ וּפְרָצִים תֵּצֶאנָה אִשָּׁה נֶגְדָּהּ וְהִשְׁלַכְתֶּנָה הַהַרְמוֹנָה
ד נְאֻם־יְהוָה׃ בֹּאוּ בֵית־אֵל וּפִשְׁעוּ הַגִּלְגָּל הַרְבּוּ לִפְשֹׁעַ וְהָבִיאוּ לַבֹּקֶר
ה זִבְחֵיכֶם לִשְׁלֹשֶׁת יָמִים מַעְשְׂרֹתֵיכֶם׃ וְקַטֵּר מֵחָמֵץ תּוֹדָה וְקִרְאוּ
ו נְדָבוֹת הַשְׁמִיעוּ כִּי כֵן אֲהַבְתֶּם בְּנֵי יִשְׂרָאֵל נְאֻם אֲדֹנָי יְהוִה׃ וְגַם־אֲנִי
נָתַתִּי לָכֶם נִקְיוֹן שִׁנַּיִם בְּכָל־עָרֵיכֶם וְחֹסֶר לֶחֶם בְּכֹל מְקוֹמֹתֵיכֶם
ז וְלֹא־שַׁבְתֶּם עָדַי נְאֻם־יְהוָה׃ וְגַם אָנֹכִי מָנַעְתִּי מִכֶּם אֶת־הַגֶּשֶׁם בְּעוֹד
שְׁלֹשָׁה חֳדָשִׁים לַקָּצִיר וְהִמְטַרְתִּי עַל־עִיר אֶחָת וְעַל־עִיר אַחַת
לֹא אַמְטִיר חֶלְקָה אַחַת תִּמָּטֵר וְחֶלְקָה אֲשֶׁר־לֹא־תַמְטִיר עָלֶיהָ
ח תִּיבָשׁ׃ וְנָעוּ שְׁתַּיִם שָׁלֹשׁ עָרִים אֶל־עִיר אַחַת לִשְׁתּוֹת מַיִם וְלֹא
ט יִשְׂבָּעוּ וְלֹא־שַׁבְתֶּם עָדַי נְאֻם־יְהוָה׃ הִכֵּיתִי אֶתְכֶם בַּשִּׁדָּפוֹן וּבַיֵּרָקוֹן
הַרְבּוֹת גַּנּוֹתֵיכֶם וְכַרְמֵיכֶם וּתְאֵנֵיכֶם וְזֵיתֵיכֶם יֹאכַל הַגָּזָם וְלֹא־שַׁבְתֶּם
י עָדַי נְאֻם־יְהוָה׃ שִׁלַּחְתִּי בָכֶם דֶּבֶר בְּדֶרֶךְ מִצְרַיִם הָרַגְתִּי בַחֶרֶב
בַּחוּרֵיכֶם עִם שְׁבִי סוּסֵיכֶם וָאַעֲלֶה בְּאֹשׁ מַחֲנֵיכֶם וּבְאַפְּכֶם וְלֹא־
יא שַׁבְתֶּם עָדַי נְאֻם־יְהוָה׃ הָפַכְתִּי בָכֶם כְּמַהְפֵּכַת אֱלֹהִים אֶת־סְדֹם
וְאֶת־עֲמֹרָה וַתִּהְיוּ כְּאוּד מֻצָּל מִשְּׂרֵפָה וְלֹא־שַׁבְתֶּם עָדַי נְאֻם־
יב יְהוָה׃ לָכֵן כֹּה אֶעֱשֶׂה־לְּךָ יִשְׂרָאֵל עֵקֶב כִּי־זֹאת אֶעֱשֶׂה־
יג לָּךְ הִכּוֹן לִקְרַאת־אֱלֹהֶיךָ יִשְׂרָאֵל׃ כִּי הִנֵּה יוֹצֵר הָרִים וּבֹרֵא רוּחַ
וּמַגִּיד לְאָדָם מַה־שֵּׂחוֹ עֹשֵׂה שַׁחַר עֵיפָה וְדֹרֵךְ עַל־בָּמֳתֵי אָרֶץ יְהוָה
ה א אֱלֹהֵי־צְבָאוֹת שְׁמוֹ׃ שִׁמְעוּ אֶת־הַדָּבָר הַזֶּה אֲשֶׁר אָנֹכִי
ב נֹשֵׂא עֲלֵיכֶם קִינָה בֵּית יִשְׂרָאֵל׃ נָפְלָה לֹא־תוֹסִיף קוּם בְּתוּלַת יִשְׂרָאֵל
ג נִטְּשָׁה עַל־אַדְמָתָהּ אֵין מְקִימָהּ׃ כִּי כֹה אָמַר אֲדֹנָי יְהוִה

strong will remain only one hundred strong, and a city one hundred strong
4 will remain only ten strong for the House of Israel, for so says the
5 LORD to the House of Israel. Seek Me and live. Do not go to Beit El seeking,
do not come to the Gilgal, and pass not through Be'er Sheva.[13] For the Gilgal
6 will surely be exiled, and Beit El will be as nothing. Seek the LORD and live
lest the House of Yosef be split like fire and Beit El be devoured with no one
7 to extinguish it. O, those who turn justice bitter and cast righteousness to
8 the ground. O, He who formed Pleiades and Orion, who turns morning to
dread dark; day to night He darkens; He who calls to the ocean waters and
9 pours them out over the face of the earth, the LORD is His name: He who
10 rains ruin upon the stronghold so that ruin upon the fortress will come, for
they have hated the reprimander at their gates and loathed the honest speaker.
11 Therefore, because you trample the poor and confiscate their allotment of
grain, you have built houses of hewn stone but will not live in them; you have
12 planted choice vineyards but will not drink the wine, for I know that your
crimes are many and your sins vast – you, enemies of the innocent, bribe
13 takers; they turn aside the poor at the gates. Therefore, the wise are silent at
14 this time, for it is an evil time. Seek good and not evil so that you may live.
15 And if you do so, the LORD, God of Hosts, will be with you as you said. Hate
evil, love good; present justice at your gates. Maybe the LORD, God of Hosts,
16 will have pity upon the remnant of Yosef. Therefore – so says the
LORD, God of Hosts, the Lord – mourning in all the squares, groaning in
all the streets: oh, oh. They will call the farmer to lament, and the skilled
17 mourners to mourn. Mourning in all the vineyards, for I will pass among you,
18 says the LORD. Hie, all those who long for the day of the LORD.
What is the day of the LORD to you, and why do you want it? The day of
19 the LORD is darkness and not light. Like a man who runs from a lion, then
encounters a bear, then comes home, lays a hand on the wall, and a snake bites
20 him, is not the day of the LORD darkness and not light? It has dimness and
21 no shine. I have hated, I have loathed your holiday sacrifices, and I will not
22 take in the scent of your festival offerings. For even if you proffer Me burnt
offerings and your grain offerings, I will not desire them, and I will not look
23 at your peace offerings of fat cows. Take away your clamoring songs; I will
24 not hear your harp tunes. But let justice roll on like water and righteousness
25 like a roaring river. Did you offer Me sacrifices and grain offerings all those
26 forty years in the desert, House of Israel? Yet you bore Sikut, your king, and
27 Kiyun, your idol, the star of your god which you made for yourselves.[14] So I
will send you into exile beyond Damascus, says the LORD. God of Hosts is
6 1 His name. Woe, you who are settled secure in Zion, who rest assured
on Mount Shomron, who are called "chief among nations"; the House of Israel
2 flocks to them. Yet go to Kalneh and look, and from there to Ḥamat Raba; go

13 | All these cities contained shrines and sites of illicit worship.

14 | The identity of these foreign deities is unclear. Some have suggested that these are two Akkadian names for Saturn, vocalized as the Hebrew *shikkutz*, "abomination."

הָעִיר הַיֹּצֵאת אֶלֶף תַּשְׁאִיר מֵאָה וְהַיּוֹצֵאת מֵאָה תַּשְׁאִיר עֲשָׂרָה
ד לְבֵית יִשְׂרָאֵל: כִּי כֹה אָמַר יהוה לְבֵית יִשְׂרָאֵל
ה דִּרְשׁוּנִי וִחְיוּ: וְאַל־תִּדְרְשׁוּ בֵּית־אֵל וְהַגִּלְגָּל לֹא תָבֹאוּ וּבְאֵר שֶׁבַע
ו לֹא תַעֲבֹרוּ כִּי הַגִּלְגָּל גָּלֹה יִגְלֶה וּבֵית אֵל יִהְיֶה לְאָוֶן: דִּרְשׁוּ אֶת־יהוה
ז וִחְיוּ פֶּן־יִצְלַח כָּאֵשׁ בֵּית יוֹסֵף וְאָכְלָה וְאֵין־מְכַבֶּה לְבֵית־אֵל: הַהֹפְכִים
ח לְלַעֲנָה מִשְׁפָּט וּצְדָקָה לָאָרֶץ הִנִּיחוּ: עֹשֵׂה כִימָה וּכְסִיל וְהֹפֵךְ לַבֹּקֶר
צַלְמָוֶת וְיוֹם לַיְלָה הֶחְשִׁיךְ הַקּוֹרֵא לְמֵי־הַיָּם וַיִּשְׁפְּכֵם עַל־פְּנֵי הָאָרֶץ
ט י יהוה שְׁמוֹ: הַמַּבְלִיג שֹׁד עַל־עָז וְשֹׁד עַל־מִבְצָר יָבוֹא: שָׂנְאוּ בַשַּׁעַר
יא מוֹכִיחַ וְדֹבֵר תָּמִים יְתָעֵבוּ: לָכֵן יַעַן בּוֹשַׁסְכֶם עַל־דָּל וּמַשְׂאַת־בַּר
תִּקְחוּ מִמֶּנּוּ בָּתֵּי גָזִית בְּנִיתֶם וְלֹא־תֵשְׁבוּ בָם כַּרְמֵי־חֶמֶד נְטַעְתֶּם
יב וְלֹא תִשְׁתּוּ אֶת־יֵינָם: כִּי יָדַעְתִּי רַבִּים פִּשְׁעֵיכֶם וַעֲצֻמִים חַטֹּאתֵיכֶם
יג צֹרְרֵי צַדִּיק לֹקְחֵי כֹפֶר וְאֶבְיוֹנִים בַּשַּׁעַר הִטּוּ: לָכֵן הַמַּשְׂכִּיל בָּעֵת
יד הַהִיא יִדֹּם כִּי עֵת רָעָה הִיא: דִּרְשׁוּ־טוֹב וְאַל־רָע לְמַעַן תִּחְיוּ וִיהִי־ ז
טו כֵן יהוה אֱלֹהֵי־צְבָאוֹת אִתְּכֶם כַּאֲשֶׁר אֲמַרְתֶּם: שִׂנְאוּ־רָע וְאֶהֱבוּ
טוֹב וְהַצִּיגוּ בַשַּׁעַר מִשְׁפָּט אוּלַי יֶחֱנַן יהוה אֱלֹהֵי־צְבָאוֹת שְׁאֵרִית
טז יוֹסֵף: לָכֵן כֹּה־אָמַר יהוה אֱלֹהֵי צְבָאוֹת אֲדֹנָי בְּכָל־
רְחֹבוֹת מִסְפֵּד וּבְכָל־חוּצוֹת יֹאמְרוּ הוֹ־הוֹ וְקָרְאוּ אִכָּר אֶל־אֵבֶל
יז וּמִסְפֵּד אֶל־יוֹדְעֵי נֶהִי: וּבְכָל־כְּרָמִים מִסְפֵּד כִּי־אֶעֱבֹר בְּקִרְבְּךָ אָמַר
יח יהוה: הוֹי הַמִּתְאַוִּים אֶת־יוֹם יהוה לָמָּה־זֶּה לָכֶם יוֹם יהוה
יט הוּא־חֹשֶׁךְ וְלֹא־אוֹר: כַּאֲשֶׁר יָנוּס אִישׁ מִפְּנֵי הָאֲרִי וּפְגָעוֹ הַדֹּב וּבָא
כ הַבַּיִת וְסָמַךְ יָדוֹ עַל־הַקִּיר וּנְשָׁכוֹ הַנָּחָשׁ: הֲלֹא־חֹשֶׁךְ יוֹם יהוה וְלֹא־
כא אוֹר וְאָפֵל וְלֹא־נֹגַהּ לוֹ: שָׂנֵאתִי מָאַסְתִּי חַגֵּיכֶם וְלֹא אָרִיחַ בְּעַצְּרֹתֵיכֶם:
כב כִּי אִם־תַּעֲלוּ־לִי עֹלוֹת וּמִנְחֹתֵיכֶם לֹא אֶרְצֶה וְשֶׁלֶם מְרִיאֵיכֶם לֹא
כג כד אַבִּיט: הָסֵר מֵעָלַי הֲמוֹן שִׁרֶיךָ וְזִמְרַת נְבָלֶיךָ לֹא אֶשְׁמָע: וְיִגַּל כַּמַּיִם
כה מִשְׁפָּט וּצְדָקָה כְּנַחַל אֵיתָן: הַזְּבָחִים וּמִנְחָה הִגַּשְׁתֶּם־לִי בַמִּדְבָּר
כו אַרְבָּעִים שָׁנָה בֵּית יִשְׂרָאֵל: וּנְשָׂאתֶם אֵת סִכּוּת מַלְכְּכֶם וְאֵת כִּיּוּן
כז צַלְמֵיכֶם כּוֹכַב אֱלֹהֵיכֶם אֲשֶׁר עֲשִׂיתֶם לָכֶם: וְהִגְלֵיתִי אֶתְכֶם מֵהָלְאָה
ו א לְדַמָּשֶׂק אָמַר יהוה אֱלֹהֵי־צְבָאוֹת שְׁמוֹ: הוֹי הַשַּׁאֲנַנִּים
בְּצִיּוֹן וְהַבֹּטְחִים בְּהַר שֹׁמְרוֹן נְקֻבֵי רֵאשִׁית הַגּוֹיִם וּבָאוּ לָהֶם בֵּית
ב יִשְׂרָאֵל: עִבְרוּ כַלְנֵה וּרְאוּ וּלְכוּ מִשָּׁם חֲמַת רַבָּה וּרְדוּ גַת־פְּלִשְׁתִּים

down to the Philistine Gat.[15] Are you better than these kingdoms? Is their
3 territory greater than yours? You who dismiss the day of evil but embrace
4 violent rule, who lie on beds of ivory, lounge upon your couches, feasting on
5 the choicest of sheep and calves taken from their feeding stalls, who play the
6 harp – with instruments they think themselves like David – who guzzle wine
from bowls, anoint yourselves with the finest of oils, but are not heartsick
7 over Yosef's ruin; therefore, you will now be the first of exiles, a coterie of
8 loungers removed, the Lord GOD swears by Himself; the LORD, God of
Hosts, has spoken. I despise the pride of Yaakov, hate his palaces, so I will
9 hand over a city in its fullness. This is what will be: If ten people initially
10 survive by hiding in a house, even so, they will die. Then the dead man's
relative and loved one, stirring themselves, will go and remove the corpses
from the house. One of them will call to the other, searching at the back of
the house, "Is anyone alive there?" "Not one,"[16] he will say. "Hush! Do not
11 utter the name of the LORD," he will say. For indeed, the LORD
commands and will shatter the great house to pieces and the small house to
12 slabs. Can horses gallop over rock? Can anyone plow there with oxen? Yet
13 you have turned justice to poison and the fruits of righteousness bitter. Those
who rejoice over Lo Davar, who say that by our own strength we took
14 Karnayim.[17] Indeed I will raise a nation against you, House of Israel. The
LORD, God of Hosts, has spoken. They will drive you from Levo Ḥamat down
7 1 to Arava Ravine. The Lord GOD showed me this: He was forming
a horde of locusts just as the late wheat started to grow, the late wheat that
2 sprouts after the king's mowers have mowed. And as they consumed the land's
greenery completely, I said, "My Lord GOD, please forgive. How could
3 Yaakov survive this – he, who is so small?" And the LORD relented: "This shall
4 not be," said the LORD. The Lord GOD showed me this: He was
calling to fight with fire. It consumed the mighty deep; it consumed the
5 allotted land. I said, "My Lord GOD, please stop. How could Yaakov survive
6 this – he, who is so small?" And the LORD relented: "This, too, shall not be,"
7 said the Lord GOD. He showed me this: The LORD was standing
8 high upon a plumb line[18] in Hand. The LORD said to me, "What do you see,
Amos?" and I said, "A plumb line." Then the Lord said, "I will place a plumb
9 line among My people, Israel. I will spare them no longer. Yisḥak's[19] altars will
be desolate, and Israel's temples will be destroyed. I will rise up against the
10 house of Yorovam with a sword." Then Amatzya, priest of Beit El,
sent the following message to Yorovam, king of Israel: "Amos has conspired

15 | Ḥamat and Gat had been centers of powerful city-states before being vanquished and destroyed.

16 | This cryptic phrase is explained by Radak and others as follows: The speaker is implying that this catastrophe has befallen us because we failed to mention the name of the Lord in our prayers and instead referred to idols. Therefore, let us now simply hush and suffer in silence.

17 | Cities in Transjordan.

18 | The "plumb line" is a tool by which one makes an exact and precise determination of the angle of a wall. Thus, "plumb line" here is a metaphor for justice that is exact and precise, i.e., strict.

19 | A variant spelling of Yitzḥak. The verb "to laugh," on which the name is based, can itself appear in Biblical Hebrew both as *tzaḥak* and *saḥak*.

ג הֲטוֹבִים מִן־הַמַּמְלָכוֹת הָאֵלֶּה אִם־רַב גְּבוּלָם מִגְּבֻלְכֶם׃ הַמְנַדִּים
ד לְיוֹם רָע וַתַּגִּשׁוּן שֶׁבֶת חָמָס׃ הַשֹּׁכְבִים עַל־מִטּוֹת שֵׁן וּסְרֻחִים עַל־
ה עַרְשׂוֹתָם וְאֹכְלִים כָּרִים מִצֹּאן וַעֲגָלִים מִתּוֹךְ מַרְבֵּק׃ הַפֹּרְטִים עַל־פִּי
ו הַנָּבֶל כְּדָוִיד חָשְׁבוּ לָהֶם כְּלֵי־שִׁיר׃ הַשֹּׁתִים בְּמִזְרְקֵי יַיִן וְרֵאשִׁית
ז שְׁמָנִים יִמְשָׁחוּ וְלֹא נֶחְלוּ עַל־שֵׁבֶר יוֹסֵף׃ לָכֵן עַתָּה יִגְלוּ בְּרֹאשׁ גֹּלִים
ח וְסָר מִרְזַח סְרוּחִים׃ נִשְׁבַּע אֲדֹנָי יֱהוִה בְּנַפְשׁוֹ נְאֻם־יְהוָה אֱלֹהֵי צְבָאוֹת
מְתָאֵב אָנֹכִי אֶת־גְּאוֹן יַעֲקֹב וְאַרְמְנֹתָיו שָׂנֵאתִי וְהִסְגַּרְתִּי עִיר וּמְלֹאָהּ׃
ט י וְהָיָה אִם־יִוָּתְרוּ עֲשָׂרָה אֲנָשִׁים בְּבַיִת אֶחָד וָמֵתוּ׃ וּנְשָׂאוֹ דּוֹדוֹ וּמְסָרְפוֹ
לְהוֹצִיא עֲצָמִים מִן־הַבַּיִת וְאָמַר לַאֲשֶׁר בְּיַרְכְּתֵי הַבַּיִת הַעוֹד עִמָּךְ
יא וְאָמַר אָפֶס וְאָמַר הָס כִּי לֹא לְהַזְכִּיר בְּשֵׁם יְהוָה׃ כִּי־
הִנֵּה יְהוָה מְצַוֶּה וְהִכָּה הַבַּיִת הַגָּדוֹל רְסִיסִים וְהַבַּיִת הַקָּטֹן בְּקִעִים׃
יב הַיְרֻצוּן בַּסֶּלַע סוּסִים אִם־יַחֲרוֹשׁ בַּבְּקָרִים כִּי־הֲפַכְתֶּם לְרֹאשׁ
יג מִשְׁפָּט וּפְרִי צְדָקָה לְלַעֲנָה׃ הַשְּׂמֵחִים לְלֹא דָבָר הָאֹמְרִים הֲלוֹא
יד בְחָזְקֵנוּ לָקַחְנוּ לָנוּ קַרְנָיִם׃ כִּי הִנְנִי מֵקִים עֲלֵיכֶם בֵּית יִשְׂרָאֵל נְאֻם־
יְהוָה אֱלֹהֵי הַצְּבָאוֹת גּוֹי וְלָחֲצוּ אֶתְכֶם מִלְּבוֹא חֲמָת עַד־נַחַל
ז א הָעֲרָבָה׃ כֹּה הִרְאַנִי אֲדֹנָי יֱהוִה וְהִנֵּה יוֹצֵר גֹּבַי בִּתְחִלַּת
ב עֲלוֹת הַלָּקֶשׁ וְהִנֵּה־לֶקֶשׁ אַחַר גִּזֵּי הַמֶּלֶךְ׃ וְהָיָה אִם־כִּלָּה לֶאֱכוֹל
אֶת־עֵשֶׂב הָאָרֶץ וָאֹמַר אֲדֹנָי יֱהוִה סְלַח־נָא מִי יָקוּם יַעֲקֹב כִּי קָטֹן
ג ד הוּא׃ נִחַם יְהוָה עַל־זֹאת לֹא תִהְיֶה אָמַר יְהוָה׃ כֹּה
הִרְאַנִי אֲדֹנָי יֱהוִה וְהִנֵּה קֹרֵא לָרִב בָּאֵשׁ אֲדֹנָי יֱהוִה וַתֹּאכַל אֶת־תְּהוֹם
ה רַבָּה וְאָכְלָה אֶת־הַחֵלֶק׃ וָאֹמַר אֲדֹנָי יֱהוִה חֲדַל־נָא מִי יָקוּם יַעֲקֹב
ו כִּי קָטֹן הוּא׃ נִחַם יְהוָה עַל־זֹאת גַּם־הִיא לֹא תִהְיֶה אָמַר אֲדֹנָי
ז יֱהוִה׃ כֹּה הִרְאַנִי וְהִנֵּה אֲדֹנָי נִצָּב עַל־חוֹמַת אֲנָךְ וּבְיָדוֹ
ח אֲנָךְ׃ וַיֹּאמֶר יְהוָה אֵלַי מָה־אַתָּה רֹאֶה עָמוֹס וָאֹמַר אֲנָךְ וַיֹּאמֶר אֲדֹנָי
ט הִנְנִי שָׂם אֲנָךְ בְּקֶרֶב עַמִּי יִשְׂרָאֵל לֹא־אוֹסִיף עוֹד עֲבוֹר לוֹ׃ וְנָשַׁמּוּ
בָּמוֹת יִשְׂחָק וּמִקְדְּשֵׁי יִשְׂרָאֵל יֶחֱרָבוּ וְקַמְתִּי עַל־בֵּית יָרָבְעָם
י בֶּחָרֶב׃ וַיִּשְׁלַח אֲמַצְיָה כֹּהֵן בֵּית־אֵל אֶל־יָרָבְעָם
מֶלֶךְ־יִשְׂרָאֵל לֵאמֹר קָשַׁר עָלֶיךָ עָמוֹס בְּקֶרֶב בֵּית יִשְׂרָאֵל לֹא־תוּכַל

11 against you within the House of Israel. The land cannot bear all he says. For
this is what Amos says: 'Yorovam will surely die by the sword, and Israel will
12 be exiled from their land.'" And to Amos, Amatzya said: "Seer, flee
to the land of Yehuda. It is there that you should eat your bread, and it is there
13 that you should prophesy. Prophesy no longer in Beit El, for it is a royal temple
14 and a king's shrine." Amos replied and said to Amatzya, "I am not a prophet
15 nor of prophets but a herdsman and a splicer of sycamore figs. It was the LORD
who took me from behind the flock of sheep and told me, 'Go, prophesy to
16 My people Israel.' And now, heed the word of the LORD: You say, 'Do not
17 prophesy to Israel; do not speak regarding the House of Yisḥak.' Therefore,
says the LORD, your wife will sell herself in the city, your sons and daughters
will be slaughtered by the sword, and your land will be divided. And as for
you, you will die in an impure land, and Israel will surely be exiled from their
8 1 land." This is what the Lord GOD showed me: a basket of summer
2 fruit. He said, "What do you see, Amos?" and I said, "A basket of summer
fruit." Then the LORD said to me, "The end[20] is coming for My people, Israel.
3 I will spare them no longer. On that day" – the Lord GOD has spoken –
"Temple songs will become wails. Many corpses everywhere, and those who
4 dispose of them calling out, 'Silence.'" Hear this, those who trample
5 the poor, who would decimate the destitute of the land, those who say,
"When will the New Moon pass so we can sell grain, and the Sabbath so we
can open the storehouses,[21] so we can diminish the weight of an ephah but
6 enlarge the shekel,[22] skew false scales, sell the needy for silver and the poor
7 for the price of shoes? Let us sell chaff as grain." The LORD swears by the pride
8 of Yaakov: I will forever remember what they have done. Would the earth not
shudder for this and all its inhabitants mourn? The earth will rise like the Nile,
9 churn and sink like the Nile of Egypt. This is what will be on
that day – the Lord GOD has spoken – I will cause the sun to set at noon and
10 the earth to go dark on a sunny day. I will turn your holidays into mourning
days and all your songs to dirges. I will cause sackcloth to be girded around
every waist and every forehead to be shorn bare. I will make the grief of this
day like the grief of the loss of an only child, with a day of bitterness at its
11 end. Yes, days are coming – the Lord GOD has spoken – I will cast
hunger over the land: not hunger for bread nor thirst for water, but hunger to
12 hear the words of the LORD. They will wander from sea to sea and from the
13 north to the east to seek the word of the LORD, but they will not find it. On
14 that day, beautiful young women and young men will faint of thirst. O, those
who swear by Shomron's sin and say, "By the life of your god, Dan; by the life
9 1 of the way to Be'er Sheva,"[23] They will fall and never stand again. I
saw my Lord standing beside the altar. He said: "Strike the lintel, and let the
doorposts quake. Their riches first, then, by the sword, their children. None

---

20 | Hebrew *ketz*, echoing "summer fruit" (*kayitz*).
21 | The verse reflects a practice to avoid work on the Sabbath and New Moon.
22 | Dishonestly skewing weights and measures; cf., e.g., Deuteronomy 25:13–16.
23 | See note on 5:5.

יא הָאָרֶץ לְהָכִיל אֶת־כָּל־דְּבָרָיו׃ כִּי־כֹה אָמַר עָמוֹס בַּחֶרֶב יָמוּת יָרָבְעָם
יב וְיִשְׂרָאֵל גָּלֹה יִגְלֶה מֵעַל אַדְמָתוֹ׃ וַיֹּאמֶר אֲמַצְיָה אֶל־
עָמוֹס חֹזֶה לֵךְ בְּרַח־לְךָ אֶל־אֶרֶץ יְהוּדָה וֶאֱכָל־שָׁם לֶחֶם וְשָׁם תִּנָּבֵא׃
יג וּבֵית־אֵל לֹא־תוֹסִיף עוֹד לְהִנָּבֵא כִּי מִקְדַּשׁ־מֶלֶךְ הוּא וּבֵית מַמְלָכָה
יד הוּא׃ וַיַּעַן עָמוֹס וַיֹּאמֶר אֶל־אֲמַצְיָה לֹא־נָבִיא אָנֹכִי וְלֹא בֶן־נָבִיא
טו אָנֹכִי כִּי־בוֹקֵר אָנֹכִי וּבוֹלֵס שִׁקְמִים׃ וַיִּקָּחֵנִי יְהוָה מֵאַחֲרֵי הַצֹּאן ח
טז וַיֹּאמֶר אֵלַי יְהוָה לֵךְ הִנָּבֵא אֶל־עַמִּי יִשְׂרָאֵל׃ וְעַתָּה שְׁמַע דְּבַר־יְהוָה
יז אַתָּה אֹמֵר לֹא תִנָּבֵא עַל־יִשְׂרָאֵל וְלֹא תַטִּיף עַל־בֵּית יִשְׂחָק׃ לָכֵן
כֹּה־אָמַר יְהוָה אִשְׁתְּךָ בָּעִיר תִּזְנֶה וּבָנֶיךָ וּבְנֹתֶיךָ בַּחֶרֶב יִפֹּלוּ וְאַדְמָתְךָ
בַּחֶבֶל תְּחֻלָּק וְאַתָּה עַל־אֲדָמָה טְמֵאָה תָּמוּת וְיִשְׂרָאֵל גָּלֹה יִגְלֶה
ח א מֵעַל אַדְמָתוֹ׃ כֹּה הִרְאַנִי אֲדֹנָי יְהוִה וְהִנֵּה כְּלוּב
ב קָיִץ׃ וַיֹּאמֶר מָה־אַתָּה רֹאֶה עָמוֹס וָאֹמַר כְּלוּב קָיִץ וַיֹּאמֶר יְהוָה אֵלַי
ג בָּא הַקֵּץ אֶל־עַמִּי יִשְׂרָאֵל לֹא־אוֹסִיף עוֹד עֲבוֹר לוֹ׃ וְהֵילִילוּ שִׁירוֹת
הֵיכָל בַּיּוֹם הַהוּא נְאֻם אֲדֹנָי יְהוִה רַב הַפֶּגֶר בְּכָל־מָקוֹם הִשְׁלִיךְ
ד הָס׃ שִׁמְעוּ־זֹאת הַשֹּׁאֲפִים אֶבְיוֹן וְלַשְׁבִּית ענוי־ עֲנִיֵּי־
ה אָרֶץ׃ לֵאמֹר מָתַי יַעֲבֹר הַחֹדֶשׁ וְנַשְׁבִּירָה שֶּׁבֶר וְהַשַּׁבָּת וְנִפְתְּחָה־
ו בָּר לְהַקְטִין אֵיפָה וּלְהַגְדִּיל שֶׁקֶל וּלְעַוֵּת מֹאזְנֵי מִרְמָה׃ לִקְנוֹת
ז בַּכֶּסֶף דַּלִּים וְאֶבְיוֹן בַּעֲבוּר נַעֲלָיִם וּמַפַּל בַּר נַשְׁבִּיר׃ נִשְׁבַּע יְהוָה
ח בִּגְאוֹן יַעֲקֹב אִם־אֶשְׁכַּח לָנֶצַח כָּל־מַעֲשֵׂיהֶם׃ הַעַל זֹאת לֹא־תִרְגַּז
הָאָרֶץ וְאָבַל כָּל־יוֹשֵׁב בָּהּ וְעָלְתָה כָאֹר כֻּלָּהּ וְנִגְרְשָׁה ונשקה כִּיאוֹר וְנִשְׁקְעָה
ט מִצְרָיִם׃ וְהָיָה ׀ בַּיּוֹם הַהוּא נְאֻם אֲדֹנָי יְהוִה וְהֵבֵאתִי
י הַשֶּׁמֶשׁ בַּצָּהֳרָיִם וְהַחֲשַׁכְתִּי לָאָרֶץ בְּיוֹם אוֹר׃ וְהָפַכְתִּי חַגֵּיכֶם לְאֵבֶל
וְכָל־שִׁירֵיכֶם לְקִינָה וְהַעֲלֵיתִי עַל־כָּל־מָתְנַיִם שָׂק וְעַל־כָּל־רֹאשׁ
יא קָרְחָה וְשַׂמְתִּיהָ כְּאֵבֶל יָחִיד וְאַחֲרִיתָהּ כְּיוֹם מָר׃ הִנֵּה ׀
יָמִים בָּאִים נְאֻם אֲדֹנָי יְהוִה וְהִשְׁלַחְתִּי רָעָב בָּאָרֶץ לֹא־רָעָב לַלֶּחֶם
יב וְלֹא־צָמָא לַמַּיִם כִּי אִם־לִשְׁמֹעַ אֵת דִּבְרֵי יְהוָה׃ וְנָעוּ מִיָּם עַד־יָם
יג וּמִצָּפוֹן וְעַד־מִזְרָח יְשׁוֹטְטוּ לְבַקֵּשׁ אֶת־דְּבַר־יְהוָה וְלֹא יִמְצָאוּ׃ בַּיּוֹם
יד הַהוּא תִּתְעַלַּפְנָה הַבְּתוּלֹת הַיָּפוֹת וְהַבַּחוּרִים בַּצָּמָא׃ הַנִּשְׁבָּעִים
בְּאַשְׁמַת שֹׁמְרוֹן וְאָמְרוּ חֵי אֱלֹהֶיךָ דָּן וְחֵי דֶּרֶךְ בְּאֵר־שָׁבַע וְנָפְלוּ
ט א וְלֹא־יָקוּמוּ עוֹד׃ רָאִיתִי אֶת־אֲדֹנָי נִצָּב עַל־הַמִּזְבֵּחַ וַיֹּאמֶר
הַךְ הַכַּפְתּוֹר וְיִרְעֲשׁוּ הַסִּפִּים וּבְצַעַם בְּרֹאשׁ כֻּלָּם וְאַחֲרִיתָם בַּחֶרֶב

2 who flee will escape; no refugee will find safety. Even if they burrow down to
Sheol,[24] there My hand will seize them; even if they ascend to heaven, from
3 there I will pull them down; even if they hide on the Carmel's peak, there I
will seek and seize them; even if they secret themselves away from My eyes on
4 the sea-floor, there I will command the snake to bite them; even if they are
taken captive, marched before their enemies, there I will command the sword
5 to kill them; I will set My eyes upon them for evil, not good." And my Lord,
God of Hosts – it is He – who but touches the earth, and it dissolves; all
inhabitants in mourning; He makes all the earth rise like the Nile and sink like
6 the river of Egypt. He who built His heavenly dome and established His
myriad forces upon the earth, He calls to the sea and spills it out over the
7 land – the Lord is His name. Are you not to Me like the
children of Kush, O children of Israel? Did I not bring up Israel from the land
of Egypt as I brought the Philistines up from Kaftor and Aram from Kir?[25]
8 Yes, the eyes of the Lord God are upon the sinning kingdom; I will wipe it
off the face of the earth, but the House of Yaakov I will never destroy,[26] says
9 the Lord. For I will but command, and I will shake the House of Israel among
10 all the nations as one shakes a sieve;[27] not one pebble will fall to the earth. All
the sinners of My nation will be killed by the sword – those who say, "Disaster
11 will not reach, will not advance upon us." On that day, I will lift up David's
fallen tabernacle, repair its breaches, and lift up its ruins, rebuild it as it
12 was in days of yore. And so they will possess the remnants of Edom and
all the nations who are called in My name, says the Lord who does
13 this. Behold, days are coming. The Lord has spoken. The
plow man will meet the reaper, and the grape crusher the seed sower;[28] the
14 mountains will drip with sweet wine, and all the hills will dissolve. I will bring
back the exiled of My nation, Israel. They will build ruined cities and settle.
They will plant vineyards and drink their wine. They will grow gardens and
15 eat their fruit. I will plant them on their land, and never again will they be
uprooted from the land which I gave to them, says the Lord, your God.

OVADYA/ OBADIAH

1 1 This is Ovadya's vision: So says the Lord God to Edom – we have heard
tidings from the Lord: and an envoy has been sent among the nations,
2 "Come, let us rise up in battle against her." Look, I have made you small
3 among nations; you are utterly scorned. The arrogance of your heart deceived
you, you who dwell in the cliff's niches, your lofty abode, saying in your
4 heart, "Who could bring me down to earth?" But even if you rise as high as

24 | The netherworld.
25 | All these migrations occurred around the same time.
26 | The sinners will be destroyed, and the remnant of Israel will be restored.
27 | Separating the worthy from the unworthy.
28 | Due to the great bounty, the summer reaping will last until the time of plowing in the late fall. Likewise for late-summer grape crushing and winter sowing.

ב אֶהֱרֹג לֹא־יָנוּס לָהֶם נָס וְלֹא־יִמָּלֵט לָהֶם פָּלִיט: אִם־יַחְתְּרוּ בִשְׁאוֹל
ג מִשָּׁם יָדִי תִקָּחֵם וְאִם־יַעֲלוּ הַשָּׁמַיִם מִשָּׁם אוֹרִידֵם: וְאִם־יֵחָבְאוּ
בְּרֹאשׁ הַכַּרְמֶל מִשָּׁם אֲחַפֵּשׂ וּלְקַחְתִּים וְאִם־יִסָּתְרוּ מִנֶּגֶד עֵינַי בְּקַרְקַע
ד הַיָּם מִשָּׁם אֲצַוֶּה אֶת־הַנָּחָשׁ וּנְשָׁכָם: וְאִם־יֵלְכוּ בַשְּׁבִי לִפְנֵי אֹיְבֵיהֶם
מִשָּׁם אֲצַוֶּה אֶת־הַחֶרֶב וַהֲרָגָתַם וְשַׂמְתִּי עֵינִי עֲלֵיהֶם לְרָעָה וְלֹא
ה לְטוֹבָה: וַאדֹנָי יֱהֹוִה הַצְּבָאוֹת הַנּוֹגֵעַ בָּאָרֶץ וַתָּמוֹג וְאָבְלוּ כָּל־יוֹשְׁבֵי
ו בָהּ וְעָלְתָה כַיְאֹר כֻּלָּהּ וְשָׁקְעָה כִּיאֹר מִצְרָיִם: הַבּוֹנֶה בַשָּׁמַיִם מַעֲלוֹתָו
וַאֲגֻדָּתוֹ עַל־אֶרֶץ יְסָדָהּ הַקֹּרֵא לְמֵי־הַיָּם וַיִּשְׁפְּכֵם עַל־פְּנֵי הָאָרֶץ
ז יְהֹוָה שְׁמוֹ: הֲלוֹא כִבְנֵי כֻשִׁיִּים אַתֶּם לִי בְּנֵי יִשְׂרָאֵל נְאֻם־
יְהֹוָה הֲלוֹא אֶת־יִשְׂרָאֵל הֶעֱלֵיתִי מֵאֶרֶץ מִצְרַיִם וּפְלִשְׁתִּיִּים מִכַּפְתּוֹר
ח וַאֲרָם מִקִּיר: הִנֵּה עֵינֵי ׀ אֲדֹנָי יֱהֹוִה בַּמַּמְלָכָה הַחַטָּאָה וְהִשְׁמַדְתִּי
אֹתָהּ מֵעַל פְּנֵי הָאֲדָמָה אֶפֶס כִּי לֹא הַשְׁמֵיד אַשְׁמִיד אֶת־בֵּית יַעֲקֹב
ט נְאֻם־יְהֹוָה: כִּי־הִנֵּה אָנֹכִי מְצַוֶּה וַהֲנִעוֹתִי בְכָל־הַגּוֹיִם אֶת־בֵּית
י יִשְׂרָאֵל כַּאֲשֶׁר יִנּוֹעַ בַּכְּבָרָה וְלֹא־יִפּוֹל צְרוֹר אָרֶץ: בַּחֶרֶב יָמוּתוּ כֹּל
יא חַטָּאֵי עַמִּי הָאֹמְרִים לֹא־תַגִּישׁ וְתַקְדִּים בַּעֲדֵינוּ הָרָעָה: בַּיּוֹם הַהוּא
אָקִים אֶת־סֻכַּת דָּוִיד הַנֹּפֶלֶת וְגָדַרְתִּי אֶת־פִּרְצֵיהֶן וַהֲרִסֹתָיו אָקִים
יב וּבְנִיתִיהָ כִּימֵי עוֹלָם: לְמַעַן יִירְשׁוּ אֶת־שְׁאֵרִית אֱדוֹם וְכָל־הַגּוֹיִם
יג אֲשֶׁר־נִקְרָא שְׁמִי עֲלֵיהֶם נְאֻם־יְהֹוָה עֹשֶׂה זֹּאת: הִנֵּה
יָמִים בָּאִים נְאֻם־יְהֹוָה וְנִגַּשׁ חוֹרֵשׁ בַּקֹּצֵר וְדֹרֵךְ עֲנָבִים בְּמֹשֵׁךְ
יד הַזָּרַע וְהִטִּיפוּ הֶהָרִים עָסִיס וְכָל־הַגְּבָעוֹת תִּתְמוֹגַגְנָה: וְשַׁבְתִּי אֶת־
שְׁבוּת עַמִּי יִשְׂרָאֵל וּבָנוּ עָרִים נְשַׁמּוֹת וְיָשָׁבוּ וְנָטְעוּ כְרָמִים וְשָׁתוּ
טו אֶת־יֵינָם וְעָשׂוּ גַנּוֹת וְאָכְלוּ אֶת־פְּרִיהֶם: וּנְטַעְתִּים עַל־אַדְמָתָם
וְלֹא יִנָּתְשׁוּ עוֹד מֵעַל אַדְמָתָם אֲשֶׁר נָתַתִּי לָהֶם אָמַר יְהֹוָה אֱלֹהֶיךָ:

עובדיה

א א חֲזוֹן עֹבַדְיָה כֹּה־אָמַר אֲדֹנָי יֱהֹוִה לֶאֱדוֹם שְׁמוּעָה שָׁמַעְנוּ מֵאֵת
ב יְהֹוָה וְצִיר בַּגּוֹיִם שֻׁלָּח קוּמוּ וְנָקוּמָה עָלֶיהָ לַמִּלְחָמָה: הִנֵּה קָטֹן
ג נְתַתִּיךָ בַּגּוֹיִם בָּזוּי אַתָּה מְאֹד: זְדוֹן לִבְּךָ הִשִּׁיאֶךָ שֹׁכְנִי בְחַגְוֵי־סֶלַע
ד מְרוֹם שִׁבְתּוֹ אֹמֵר בְּלִבּוֹ מִי יוֹרִדֵנִי אָרֶץ: אִם־תַּגְבִּיהַ כַּנֶּשֶׁר וְאִם־

an eagle, if you make your nest among the stars, I shall bring you down from
5 there, declares the LORD. If thieves come upon you, bandits in the night,
do they not take only their fill? If grape gatherers[1] come upon you, do they
6 not leave gleanings? Yet how has Esav been ransacked, his hidden treasures
7 laid bare. Your allies all have forced you to the borders; those with whom
you had made peace all deceived you, defeated you. Those with whom you
8 broke your bread laid a snare for you, bereft of awareness. Behold, on that
day, says the LORD, I will purge Edom of wise men, The mountains of Esav
9 of awareness. Your warriors will be frightened, Teiman, for the mountains of
10 Esav will be unmanned by slaughter. For the violence you wrought against
11 your brother Yaakov shame will cover you, and you will be cut off forever. The
day you stood aside, the day strangers took captive his forces, and foreigners
entered his gates, casting lots for Jerusalem – you too were like one of them.
12 Do not gloat over the day of your brother's destruction, the day he becomes
a stranger. Do not rejoice over the children of Yehuda on the day of their
13 destruction. Do not open your mouth on the day of trouble. Do not enter
My people's gate on the day of their ruin. Do not gloat over its misfortune
on the day of its ruin. Do not extend your hands to take its wealth on the
14 day of his ruin. Do not stand at the crossroads to cut down his refugees. Do
15 not surrender his survivors on the day of trouble. For the day of the LORD
draws near for all the nations. What you have done shall be done to you;
16 what you have wrought will return upon your head. What you drank on My
holy mountain, all the nations will always drink. They will drink and they will
17 swallow, and they will be as if they never were. There will be a remnant on
Mount Zion, and it will be holy, and the House of Yaakov will possess their
18 inheritance. The House of Yaakov will be fire, the House of Yosef, flame; the
House of Esav, straw. They will blaze among them and consume them, and
there will be no survivors of the House of Esav, for the LORD has spoken.
19 They will take possession of the Negev, along with the mountains of Esav, and
the Shefela, from the Philistines. And they will take possession of the land
of Efrayim and the land of Shomron; and Binyamin, along with the Gilad –
20 they, the exiled force of the children of Israel who are among the Canaanites
as far as Tzarfat[2] and the exiled of Jerusalem who are in Sepharad[3] will
21 take possession of the cities of the Negev. And saviors shall go up to Mount
Zion to judge the mountains of Esav, and dominion shall be the LORD's.

YONA/JONAH

1 1 The word of the LORD came to Yona son of Amitai: "Rise up – go to the great
2 city of Nineveh and cry out against it, for its cruel evil has come into My sight."
3 But Yona rose instead to flee to Tarshish, away from the LORD's presence.
He went down to Yafo, found a ship bound for Tarshish, paid the fare, and

1 | Hebrew *botzerim,* evoking the Edomite city of Botzra (see, e.g., Gen. 36:33; Is. 34:6, 63:1).
2 | A town on the Phoenician coast (see 1 Kings 17:9).
3 | Possibly a reference to Sardis, in Asia Minor.

ה בֵּין כּוֹכָבִים שִׂים קִנֶּךָ מִשָּׁם אוֹרִידְךָ נְאֻם־יְהוָה: אִם־גַּנָּבִים בָּאוּ־לְךָ
אִם־שׁוֹדְדֵי לַיְלָה אֵיךְ נִדְמֵיתָה הֲלוֹא יִגְנְבוּ דַּיָּם אִם־בֹּצְרִים בָּאוּ לָךְ
ו ז הֲלוֹא יַשְׁאִירוּ עֹלֵלוֹת: אֵיךְ נֶחְפְּשׂוּ עֵשָׂו נִבְעוּ מַצְפֻּנָיו: עַד־הַגְּבוּל
שִׁלְּחוּךָ כֹּל אַנְשֵׁי בְרִיתֶךָ הִשִּׁיאוּךָ יָכְלוּ לְךָ אַנְשֵׁי שְׁלֹמֶךָ לַחְמְךָ
ח יָשִׂימוּ מָזוֹר תַּחְתֶּיךָ אֵין תְּבוּנָה בּוֹ: הֲלוֹא בַּיּוֹם הַהוּא נְאֻם־יְהוָה
ט וְהַאֲבַדְתִּי חֲכָמִים מֵאֱדוֹם וּתְבוּנָה מֵהַר עֵשָׂו: וְחַתּוּ גִבּוֹרֶיךָ תֵּימָן
י לְמַעַן יִכָּרֶת־אִישׁ מֵהַר עֵשָׂו מִקָּטֶל: מֵחֲמַס אָחִיךָ יַעֲקֹב תְּכַסְּךָ
יא בוּשָׁה וְנִכְרַתָּ לְעוֹלָם: בְּיוֹם עֲמָדְךָ מִנֶּגֶד בְּיוֹם שְׁבוֹת זָרִים חֵילוֹ
וְנָכְרִים בָּאוּ שְׁעָרָו וְעַל־יְרוּשָׁלַםִ יַדּוּ גוֹרָל גַּם־אַתָּה כְּאַחַד מֵהֶם:
יב וְאַל־תֵּרֶא בְיוֹם־אָחִיךָ בְּיוֹם נָכְרוֹ וְאַל־תִּשְׂמַח לִבְנֵי־יְהוּדָה בְּיוֹם
יג אָבְדָם וְאַל־תַּגְדֵּל פִּיךָ בְּיוֹם צָרָה: אַל־תָּבוֹא בְשַׁעַר־עַמִּי בְּיוֹם
אֵידָם אַל־תֵּרֶא גַם־אַתָּה בְּרָעָתוֹ בְּיוֹם אֵידוֹ וְאַל־תִּשְׁלַחְנָה בְחֵילוֹ
יד בְּיוֹם אֵידוֹ: וְאַל־תַּעֲמֹד עַל־הַפֶּרֶק לְהַכְרִית אֶת־פְּלִיטָיו וְאַל־תַּסְגֵּר
טו שְׂרִידָיו בְּיוֹם צָרָה: כִּי־קָרוֹב יוֹם־יְהוָה עַל־כָּל־הַגּוֹיִם כַּאֲשֶׁר עָשִׂיתָ
טז יֵעָשֶׂה לָּךְ גְּמֻלְךָ יָשׁוּב בְּרֹאשֶׁךָ: כִּי כַּאֲשֶׁר שְׁתִיתֶם עַל־הַר קָדְשִׁי
יז יִשְׁתּוּ כָל־הַגּוֹיִם תָּמִיד וְשָׁתוּ וְלָעוּ וְהָיוּ כְּלוֹא הָיוּ: וּבְהַר צִיּוֹן תִּהְיֶה
יח פְלֵיטָה וְהָיָה קֹדֶשׁ וְיָרְשׁוּ בֵּית יַעֲקֹב אֵת מוֹרָשֵׁיהֶם: וְהָיָה בֵית־
יַעֲקֹב אֵשׁ וּבֵית יוֹסֵף לֶהָבָה וּבֵית עֵשָׂו לְקַשׁ וְדָלְקוּ בָהֶם וַאֲכָלוּם
יט וְלֹא־יִהְיֶה שָׂרִיד לְבֵית עֵשָׂו כִּי יְהוָה דִּבֵּר: וְיָרְשׁוּ הַנֶּגֶב אֶת־הַר עֵשָׂו
וְהַשְּׁפֵלָה אֶת־פְּלִשְׁתִּים וְיָרְשׁוּ אֶת־שְׂדֵה אֶפְרַיִם וְאֵת שְׂדֵה שֹׁמְרוֹן
כ וּבִנְיָמִן אֶת־הַגִּלְעָד: וְגָלֻת הַחֵל־הַזֶּה לִבְנֵי יִשְׂרָאֵל אֲשֶׁר־כְּנַעֲנִים
כא עַד־צָרְפַת וְגָלֻת יְרוּשָׁלַםִ אֲשֶׁר בִּסְפָרַד יִרְשׁוּ אֵת עָרֵי הַנֶּגֶב: וְעָלוּ ט
מוֹשִׁעִים בְּהַר צִיּוֹן לִשְׁפֹּט אֶת־הַר עֵשָׂו וְהָיְתָה לַיהוָה הַמְּלוּכָה:

יונה

א א ב וַיְהִי דְּבַר־יְהוָה אֶל־יוֹנָה בֶן־אֲמִתַּי לֵאמֹר: קוּם לֵךְ אֶל־נִינְוֵה הָעִיר
ג הַגְּדוֹלָה וּקְרָא עָלֶיהָ כִּי־עָלְתָה רָעָתָם לְפָנָי: וַיָּקָם יוֹנָה לִבְרֹחַ
תַּרְשִׁישָׁה מִלִּפְנֵי יְהוָה וַיֵּרֶד יָפוֹ וַיִּמְצָא אָנִיָּה ׀ בָּאָה תַרְשִׁישׁ וַיִּתֵּן

went down inside the ship to sail away with them to Tarshish, away from the
4 Lord's presence. But the Lord hurled a great wind across the sea; a great
5 storm overcame the sea, and the ship threatened to break apart. The sailors
were afraid and cried out, each to his god,[1] and they cast the ship's cargo out
into the sea to lighten the load, but Yona went down to the bottom of the boat,
6 lay down, and fell asleep. The captain came up to him: "How can you sleep?"
he said. "Rise up! Cry out to your god! Perhaps your god will think kindly of
7 us, and we will not be lost." The sailors said to one another, "Let us cast lots
so that we may know on whose account this cruel evil has come upon us."
8 And they cast their lot, and the lot fell upon Yona. "Tell us," they said to him,
"you from whom this cruel thing has come – what is your trade, and where
are you coming from? Which country is yours, and which is your people?"
9 And he said to them, "I am a Hebrew, and it is the Lord God of the heavens
10 that I fear – He who made both sea and dry land." The men were filled with
great fear and said, "What have you done?" for they knew that he was fleeing
11 the Lord's presence; he had told them. They said, "What must we do to you
12 to calm the sea for us?" – and the sea was storming ever more fiercely. "Lift
me up," he said, "cast me out into the sea, and the sea will be still for you, for I
13 know it is on my account that this great storm has come upon you." The men
oared toward dry land but could not reach it, for the sea was storming ever
14 more fiercely around them. And they cried out to the Lord and said, "Please,
Lord, please – do not let us be lost on account of this man's life, and do not
stain our hands with innocent blood, for You are the Lord, and whatever
15 You desire, You perform." Then they lifted Yona up and cast him out into the
16 sea, and the sea ceased raging and grew still. And the men were filled with a
great fear of the Lord, and they offered up a sacrifice to the Lord, and made
2 1 vows. The Lord sent a great fish to swallow up Yona; and Yona was inside
2 the belly of the fish for three days and three nights. And Yona prayed to the
3 Lord his God from the belly of the fish: "From a narrow place[2] I cry out to
the Lord,[3] and He will answer. From the belly of Sheol[4] I beg – You hear
4 my words. You have cast me down into deep waters, the heart of the sea – the
5 current engulfs me – all Your torrents and storm waves crash over me. I said
to myself, I am flung away out of Your presence – but I will yet see Your holy
6 Sanctuary again.[5] The waters rush around me to my very life's edge, deeps
7 surround me, weeds crown me. I have sunk down to the roots of the hills; the
earth is forever barred before me.[6] Yet You raise my life up from the abyss, O
8 Lord my God. As my life closes over me the Lord comes to my mind – then
9 my prayer comes to You, comes to Your holy Sanctuary. Those who cleave

1 | The crew was multi-ethnic. A person's origin was identified by the god he worshipped.

2 | Meaning from a position of distress.

3 | The prayer is here translated in the present tense, rather than the past tense of the Hebrew. This makes it a prayer for rescue, which is immediately forthcoming. Alternatively, rendering in the past tense suggests that the great fish had rescued Yona from drowning in the sea and this is a prayer of thanksgiving.

4 | Sheol is the realm of death, the netherworld, the lowest place on earth.

5 | The Temple is where one is in God's presence. It is the antipode of Sheol.

6 | That is, the gates of Sheol are locked behind me and I cannot return to the living.

ד שְׂכָרָהּ וַיֵּרֶד בָּהּ לָבוֹא עִמָּהֶם תַּרְשִׁישָׁה מִלִּפְנֵי יְהוָה: וַיהוָה הֵטִיל
רֽוּחַ־גְּדוֹלָה אֶל־הַיָּם וַיְהִי סַעַר־גָּדוֹל בַּיָּם וְהָאֳנִיָּה חִשְּׁבָה לְהִשָּׁבֵר:
ה וַיִּירְאוּ הַמַּלָּחִים וַיִּזְעֲקוּ אִישׁ אֶל־אֱלֹהָיו וַיָּטִלוּ אֶת־הַכֵּלִים אֲשֶׁר
בָּאֳנִיָּה אֶל־הַיָּם לְהָקֵל מֵעֲלֵיהֶם וְיוֹנָה יָרַד אֶל־יַרְכְּתֵי הַסְּפִינָה וַיִּשְׁכַּב
ו וַיֵּרָדַם: וַיִּקְרַב אֵלָיו רַב הַחֹבֵל וַיֹּאמֶר לוֹ מַה־לְּךָ נִרְדָּם קוּם קְרָא
ז אֶל־אֱלֹהֶיךָ אוּלַי יִתְעַשֵּׁת הָאֱלֹהִים לָנוּ וְלֹא נֹאבֵד: וַיֹּאמְרוּ אִישׁ
אֶל־רֵעֵהוּ לְכוּ וְנַפִּילָה גוֹרָלוֹת וְנֵדְעָה בְּשֶׁלְּמִי הָרָעָה הַזֹּאת לָנוּ וַיַּפִּלוּ
ח גּוֹרָלוֹת וַיִּפֹּל הַגּוֹרָל עַל־יוֹנָה: וַיֹּאמְרוּ אֵלָיו הַגִּידָה־נָּא לָנוּ בַּאֲשֶׁר
לְמִי־הָרָעָה הַזֹּאת לָנוּ מַה־מְּלַאכְתְּךָ וּמֵאַיִן תָּבוֹא מָה אַרְצֶךָ וְאֵי־
ט מִזֶּה עַם אָתָּה: וַיֹּאמֶר אֲלֵיהֶם עִבְרִי אָנֹכִי וְאֶת־יְהוָה אֱלֹהֵי הַשָּׁמַיִם
י אֲנִי יָרֵא אֲשֶׁר־עָשָׂה אֶת־הַיָּם וְאֶת־הַיַּבָּשָׁה: וַיִּירְאוּ הָאֲנָשִׁים יִרְאָה
גְדוֹלָה וַיֹּאמְרוּ אֵלָיו מַה־זֹּאת עָשִׂיתָ כִּי־יָדְעוּ הָאֲנָשִׁים כִּי־מִלִּפְנֵי
יא יְהוָה הוּא בֹרֵחַ כִּי הִגִּיד לָהֶם: וַיֹּאמְרוּ אֵלָיו מַה־נַּעֲשֶׂה לָּךְ וְיִשְׁתֹּק
יב הַיָּם מֵעָלֵינוּ כִּי הַיָּם הוֹלֵךְ וְסֹעֵר: וַיֹּאמֶר אֲלֵיהֶם שָׂאוּנִי וַהֲטִילֻנִי
אֶל־הַיָּם וְיִשְׁתֹּק הַיָּם מֵעֲלֵיכֶם כִּי יוֹדֵעַ אָנִי כִּי בְשֶׁלִּי הַסַּעַר הַגָּדוֹל
יג הַזֶּה עֲלֵיכֶם: וַיַּחְתְּרוּ הָאֲנָשִׁים לְהָשִׁיב אֶל־הַיַּבָּשָׁה וְלֹא יָכֹלוּ כִּי הַיָּם
יד הוֹלֵךְ וְסֹעֵר עֲלֵיהֶם: וַיִּקְרְאוּ אֶל־יְהוָה וַיֹּאמְרוּ אָנָּה יְהוָה אַל־נָא
נֹאבְדָה בְּנֶפֶשׁ הָאִישׁ הַזֶּה וְאַל־תִּתֵּן עָלֵינוּ דָּם נָקִיא כִּי־אַתָּה יְהוָה
טו כַּאֲשֶׁר חָפַצְתָּ עָשִׂיתָ: וַיִּשְׂאוּ אֶת־יוֹנָה וַיְטִלֻהוּ אֶל־הַיָּם וַיַּעֲמֹד הַיָּם
טז מִזַּעְפּוֹ: וַיִּירְאוּ הָאֲנָשִׁים יִרְאָה גְדוֹלָה אֶת־יְהוָה וַיִּזְבְּחוּ־זֶבַח לַיהוָה
ב א וַיִּדְּרוּ נְדָרִים: וַיְמַן יְהוָה דָּג גָּדוֹל לִבְלֹעַ אֶת־יוֹנָה וַיְהִי יוֹנָה בִּמְעֵי
ב הַדָּג שְׁלֹשָׁה יָמִים וּשְׁלֹשָׁה לֵילוֹת: וַיִּתְפַּלֵּל יוֹנָה אֶל־יְהוָה אֱלֹהָיו
ג מִמְּעֵי הַדָּגָה: וַיֹּאמֶר קָרָאתִי מִצָּרָה לִי אֶל־יְהוָה וַיַּעֲנֵנִי מִבֶּטֶן שְׁאוֹל
ד שִׁוַּעְתִּי שָׁמַעְתָּ קוֹלִי: וַתַּשְׁלִיכֵנִי מְצוּלָה בִּלְבַב יַמִּים וְנָהָר יְסֹבְבֵנִי
ה כָּל־מִשְׁבָּרֶיךָ וְגַלֶּיךָ עָלַי עָבָרוּ: וַאֲנִי אָמַרְתִּי נִגְרַשְׁתִּי מִנֶּגֶד עֵינֶיךָ
ו אַךְ אוֹסִיף לְהַבִּיט אֶל־הֵיכַל קָדְשֶׁךָ: אֲפָפוּנִי מַיִם עַד־נֶפֶשׁ תְּהוֹם
ז יְסֹבְבֵנִי סוּף חָבוּשׁ לְרֹאשִׁי: לְקִצְבֵי הָרִים יָרַדְתִּי הָאָרֶץ בְּרִחֶיהָ
ח בַעֲדִי לְעוֹלָם וַתַּעַל מִשַּׁחַת חַיַּי יְהוָה אֱלֹהָי: בְּהִתְעַטֵּף עָלַי נַפְשִׁי
ט אֶת־יְהוָה זָכָרְתִּי וַתָּבוֹא אֵלֶיךָ תְּפִלָּתִי אֶל־הֵיכַל קָדְשֶׁךָ: מְשַׁמְּרִים

10 to empty folly will yet forsake their faithfulness.[7] But I, voicing thanks, shall
bring You offerings. I shall fulfill what I have vowed. Rescue belongs to the
11 LORD." And the LORD spoke to the fish, and it vomited Yona out
3 1 onto dry land. So the word of the LORD came to Yona for a second
2 time: "Rise up – go to the great city of Nineveh and cry out to it the call that
3 I convey to you." And Yona rose and went to Nineveh as the LORD had said.
4 Nineveh was an immensely great city, three days' walk across. Yona began
his journey, a day's walk into Nineveh, and cried out, "Forty more days, and
5 Nineveh will be overturned!" And the people of Nineveh believed in God,
and declared a fast, and dressed themselves in sackcloth, from the greatest
6 of them to the least. When word reached the king of Nineveh, he rose from
his throne, took off his mantle, covered himself with sackcloth, and sat down
7 upon ashes. And he had this proclaimed in Nineveh in the name of the
king and his nobles: "No person or animal – cattle or flock – may taste any
8 morsel; they may not pasture; they may drink no water. All must be covered
in sackcloth, man and beast, and must cry out to God with all their strength.
Let every man turn back from his cruel practices, from the violence that stains
9 his hands. Who knows? Perhaps God, too, will turn back and relent, will turn
10 back from His burning rage before we are all lost." And God saw their actions –
that they had turned away from their cruel practices – and God relented
from the evil He had spoken of bringing upon them, and brought it not.
4 1 To Yona, this was a cruel evil, and he raged against it. And he prayed to the
2 LORD: "Please, LORD, is this not just what I said while I was still in my own
land? This is why I first fled toward Tarshish – because I knew that You are
a gracious and compassionate God, slow to anger, abounding in kindness,
3 and relenting from evil. Now, LORD, please take my soul away from me, for
4 death would be better than my life." "Are you so enraged?" said the LORD.
5 Yona left the city and sat down to its east. He made himself a shelter and
sat in the shade beneath it, waiting to see what would become of the city.
6 The LORD God sent a gourd plant, which grew up above Yona to shade his
head, to shield him from the cruel heat, and Yona rejoiced over this gourd
7 plant with great joy. But God sent a worm as dawn broke the next day, and
8 it attacked the gourd plant until it dried up entirely. As the sun rose, God
sent a scorching east wind, and the sun beat down on Yona's head. He grew
faint and longed in his soul to die. "Death," he said, "would be better than
9 my life." God said to Yona, "Are you so enraged about the gourd plant?" Said
10 Yona, "I am enraged enough to die." And the LORD said, "You cared about
that gourd plant, which you did not toil for and did not grow, which was
11 born overnight and was lost overnight. Am I not to care for the great city of
Nineveh, which has in it more than one hundred and twenty thousand people
who do not know their right hands from their left, and so many animals?"

7 | They will renounce their belief in other gods, or their expectation of receiving favor from those gods.

י הבלי־שוא חסדם יעזבו: ואני בקול תודה אזבחה־לך אשר נדרתי
יא אשלמה ישועתה ליהוה: ויאמר יהוה לדג ויקא את־
ג א יונה אל־היבשה: ויהי דבר־יהוה אל־יונה שנית לאמר:
ב קום לך אל־נינוה העיר הגדולה וקרא אליה את־הקריאה אשר
ג אנכי דבר אליך: ויקם יונה וילך אל־נינוה כדבר יהוה ונינוה היתה
ד עיר־גדולה לאלהים מהלך שלשת ימים: ויחל יונה לבוא בעיר
מהלך יום אחד ויקרא ויאמר עוד ארבעים יום ונינוה נהפכת:
ה ויאמינו אנשי נינוה באלהים ויקראו־צום וילבשו שקים מגדולם
ו ועד־קטנם: ויגע הדבר אל־מלך נינוה ויקם מכסאו ויעבר אדרתו
ז מעליו ויכס שק וישב על־האפר: ויזעק ויאמר בנינוה מטעם המלך
וגדליו לאמר האדם והבהמה הבקר והצאן אל־יטעמו מאומה
ח אל־ירעו ומים אל־ישתו: ויתכסו שקים האדם והבהמה ויקראו
אל־אלהים בחזקה וישבו איש מדרכו הרעה ומן־החמס אשר
ט בכפיהם: מי־יודע ישוב ונחם האלהים ושב מחרון אפו ולא נאבד:
י וירא האלהים את־מעשיהם כי־שבו מדרכם הרעה וינחם האלהים
ד א על־הרעה אשר־דבר לעשות־להם ולא עשה: וירע אל־יונה רעה
ב גדולה ויחר לו: ויתפלל אל־יהוה ויאמר אנה יהוה הלוא־זה דברי
עד־היותי על־אדמתי על־כן קדמתי לברח תרשישה כי ידעתי
כי אתה אל־חנון ורחום ארך אפים ורב־חסד ונחם על־הרעה:
ג ד ועתה יהוה קח־נא את־נפשי ממני כי טוב מותי מחיי: ויאמר
ה יהוה ההיטב חרה לך: ויצא יונה מן־העיר וישב מקדם לעיר ויעש
לו שם סכה וישב תחתיה בצל עד אשר יראה מה־יהיה בעיר:
ו וימן יהוה־אלהים קיקיון ויעל | מעל ליונה להיות צל על־ראשו
ז להציל לו מרעתו וישמח יונה על־הקיקיון שמחה גדולה: וימן
האלהים תולעת בעלות השחר למחרת ותך את־הקיקיון וייבש:
ח ויהי | כזרח השמש וימן אלהים רוח קדים חרישית ותך השמש
על־ראש יונה ויתעלף וישאל את־נפשו למות ויאמר טוב מותי
ט מחיי: ויאמר אלהים אל־יונה ההיטב חרה־לך על־הקיקיון ויאמר
י היטב חרה־לי עד־מות: ויאמר יהוה אתה חסת על־הקיקיון אשר
יא לא־עמלת בו ולא גדלתו שבן־לילה היה ובן־לילה אבד: ואני
לא אחוס על־נינוה העיר הגדולה אשר יש־בה הרבה משתים־
עשרה רבו אדם אשר לא־ידע בין־ימינו לשמאלו ובהמה רבה:

MIKHA/MICAH

1 1 This is the word of the LORD that came to Mikha the Morashtite in the days
of Yotam, Aḥaz, and Yeḥizkiya, kings of Yehuda, in a vision concerning
2 Shomron and Jerusalem. Listen, all peoples; give heed, O earth and all its
fullness. May the Lord GOD be a witness against you, the Lord from His
3 holy Temple. For behold the LORD – He is coming out of His place; He will
4 go down and tread upon the highest places of the earth. The mountains
dissolve beneath Him, and the valleys split open like wax melting before fire,
5 like waters surging down a steep slope. All this owing to Yaakov's sins, to the
wrongdoings of the House of Israel. What then is the sin of Yaakov if not
6 Shomron? Who is behind the hilltop shrines in Yehuda if not Jerusalem? I
will turn Shomron into a mass of stones in the fields, a place for planting
vineyards, and will hurl her ruins into the valley and bare her foundations.
7 All her statues will be shattered; all her tainted payment will go up in flames;
all her idols I will lay waste, for she amassed it all from harlot's payment,
8 and to harlot's payment it will return. Over this I will wail and lament; I will
walk barefoot, stripped bare, my grief the cry of jackals, my mourning like
9 ostriches.[1] For her blows are mortal; they come all the way to Yehuda,
10 reaching the gates of my people, even to Jerusalem. Do not tell of this in Gat,[2]
nor break out in tears. But within Beit Le'afra immerse yourself in mourner's
11 ashes. Go then, residents of Shafir, naked and shamed; the dwellers of Tzaanan
could not escape; so too the mourning in Beit HaEtzel will be great, and your
12 seat of safety will be snatched from you, for though the residents of Marot
hoped for good, disaster came down from the LORD just to the gates of
13 Jerusalem. Hitch the chariot to the horses, lady of Lakhish – inciter of sin for
daughter Zion – the rebellious acts of Israel were first embraced in your midst.
14 So, then, give your gifts[3] to Moreshet Gat; the houses of Akhziv deceive,
15 disappoint[4] the kings of Israel. I will yet bring a conqueror upon you, O
residents of Maresha; the esteemed men of Israel will flee even to Adulam.
16 Shave your head; pull out your hair in mourning over the children of your
delight. Make yourself bald like the vulture, for they are gone from you into
2 1 exile. Woe to those who plot wicked deeds, who plan evildoing from
their beds; come morning light they carry it out merely because they have
2 the power. They lust for others' fields and seize them, eye others' homes and
assume them as theirs; they exploit men and their households, both man and
3 his estate. So says the LORD: I too plot evil against this tribe of
people, for you will not be able to move your necks from there, nor will you
4 walk with your heads held high, for the time of disaster has come. On that
day you will be made an object of ridicule; a woeful wail will arise, and it will
be said, "We are raided and ruined, our people's portion seized. How then

---

1 | These animals lived in the wasteland and were considered despicable.

2 | The following are localities in the Kingdom of Yehuda.

3 | That is, parting tokens.

4 | Hebrew *le'akhzav*, resonating with *Akhziv*.

א א דבר־יהוה ׀ אשר היה אל־מיכה המרשתי בימי יותם אחז יחזקיה י מיכה
ב מלכי יהודה אשר־חזה על־שמרון וירושלם: שמעו עמים כלם
הקשיבי ארץ ומלאה ויהי אדני יהוה בכם לעד אדני מהיכל קדשו:
ג ד כי־הנה יהוה יצא ממקומו וירד ודרך על־במותי־ארץ: ונמסו במתי־
ההרים תחתיו והעמקים יתבקעו כדונג מפני האש כמים מגרים
ה במורד: בפשע יעקב כל־זאת ובחטאות בית ישראל מי־פשע יעקב
ו הלוא שמרון ומי במות יהודה הלוא ירושלם: ושמתי שמרון לעי
ז השדה למטעי כרם והגרתי לגי אבניה ויסדיה אגלה: וכל־פסיליה
יכתו וכל־אתנניה ישרפו באש וכל־עצביה אשים שממה כי מאתנן
ח זונה קבצה ועד־אתנן זונה ישובו: על־זאת אספדה ואילילה אילכה
ט שילל וערום אעשה מספד כתנים ואבל כבנות יענה: כי אנושה שולל
מכותיה כי־באה עד־יהודה נגע עד־שער עמי עד־ירושלם:
י בגת אל־תגידו בכו אל־תבכו בבית לעפרה עפר התפלשתי: התפלשי
יא עברי לכם יושבת שפיר עריה־בשת לא יצאה יושבת צאנן
יב מספד בית האצל יקח מכם עמדתו: כי־חלה לטוב יושבת מרות
יג כי־ירד רע מאת יהוה לשער ירושלם: רתם המרכבה לרכש
יושבת לכיש ראשית חטאת היא לבת־ציון כי־בך נמצאו פשעי
יד ישראל: לכן תתני שלוחים על מורשת גת בתי אכזיב לאכזב למלכי
טו ישראל: עד הירש אבי לך יושבת מרשה עד־עדלם יבוא כבוד אביא
טז ישראל: קרחי וגזי על־בני תענוגיך הרחבי קרחתך כנשר כי־גלו
ב א ממך: הוי חשבי־און ופעלי רע על־משכבותם באור
ב הבקר יעשוה כי יש־לאל ידם: וחמדו שדות וגזלו ובתים ונשאו
ג ועשקו גבר וביתו ואיש ונחלתו: לכן כה אמר יהוה הנני
חשב על־המשפחה הזאת רעה אשר לא־תמישו משם צואריתכם
ד ולא תלכו רומה כי עת רעה היא: ביום ההוא ישא עליכם משל ונהה
נהי נהיה אמר שדוד נשדנו חלק עמי ימיר איך ימיש לי לשובב

5 does he take what is mine and divide up our fields?"[5] So then you will have
no one to cast the lots for dividing the land among the community of the
6 LORD. "Do not preach," they preach, for they will not be reproved nor shrink
7 back in shame. Will it then be said in the House of Yaakov, "Is the LORD's
spirit wanting? Can these truly be His deeds?" Will My words not grant
8 goodness to those who walk righteously? But instead, My people arise as their
own enemy; they strip fine outer garments from passersby; those who felt
9 safe become like hopeless men returning from war. You drive out the wives
of My people from their secure and joyful homes, from their young children;
10 you forever remove the honor I gave them. So get up and go; this is not your
place to rest, for the defilement you brought will destroy; it will bring down
11 a harsh line of destruction. For if there were a man with a spirit of falsehood
and lies who would preach toward drink and drunkenness, he would be
12 welcomed as preacher of this people. Gather – I will gather all of you, Yaakov;
collect – indeed I will collect the remnant of Israel. I will place them together;
sheltered as sheep in a paddock and as a flock in their pasture, they will
13 clamor, a commotion of men. He, the breaker of the gate, will rise up before
them; they will burst through and cross over, and their king will lead them
3 1 with the LORD at their head. And I say: Hear me, heads of Yaakov,
2 rulers of the House of Israel: Is it not for you to know what is just? Haters of
3 good, lovers of evil, you rip off their skin, the flesh from their very bones, you
who feast on the flesh of my people, who strip off their skins and crack their
4 bones, carving them like pieces into a pot like meat in a caldron. Then they[6]
will call out to the LORD, but He will not answer. He will hide His face from
5 them at that time, for they have ingrained evil in their ways. So
says the LORD: As to those prophets who mislead My people, who call for
peace while sinking in their teeth[7] but declare war on those who do not feed
6 them their fill, thus night will come to end your vision; darkness will fall upon
your divination; the sun will set on the prophets, and their day will darken
7 upon them. The seers will be ashamed, the diviners disgraced; they will veil
8 their mouths,[8] every one – God does not answer. But I, I am filled with the
strength of the LORD's spirit of justice and courage to declare to Yaakov his
9 transgressions, to Israel his sins. And I say: Hear me now, heads of
Yaakov, leaders of the House of Israel who abhor justice and all that is straight
10 11 turn twisted, who build Zion with bloodshed, Jerusalem with iniquity. Her
leaders arbitrate for bribes, her priests will teach for a price, and her prophets
for dividends will divine, yet they rely upon the LORD, saying, "Surely the
12 LORD is in our midst; no calamity can befall us." And so because of you Zion
will be plowed over like a field; Jerusalem will come to be a mound of ruins
4 1 and the Temple Mount an overgrown hilltop shrine. This will be in
days to come: The mountain of the LORD's House will be rooted firm, the

5 | As booty.
6 | The rulers.
7 | When satiated.
8 | In mourning.

ה שְׂדֵינוּ יְחַלֵּק׃ לָכֵן לֹא־יִהְיֶה לְךָ מַשְׁלִיךְ חֶבֶל בְּגוֹרָל בִּקְהַל יְהוָה׃
ו ז אַל־תַּטִּפוּ יַטִּיפוּן לֹא־יַטִּפוּ לָאֵלֶּה לֹא יִסַּג כְּלִמּוֹת׃ הֶאָמוּר בֵּית־יַעֲקֹב
הֲקָצַר רוּחַ יְהוָה אִם־אֵלֶּה מַעֲלָלָיו הֲלוֹא דְבָרַי יֵיטִיבוּ עִם הַיָּשָׁר הוֹלֵךְ׃
ח וְאֶתְמוּל עַמִּי לְאוֹיֵב יְקוֹמֵם מִמּוּל שַׂלְמָה אֶדֶר תַּפְשִׁטוּן מֵעֹבְרִים
ט בֶּטַח שׁוּבֵי מִלְחָמָה׃ נְשֵׁי עַמִּי תְּגָרְשׁוּן מִבֵּית תַּעֲנֻגֶיהָ מֵעַל עֹלָלֶיהָ
י תִּקְחוּ הֲדָרִי לְעוֹלָם׃ קוּמוּ וּלְכוּ כִּי לֹא־זֹאת הַמְּנוּחָה בַּעֲבוּר טָמְאָה
יא תְּחַבֵּל וְחֶבֶל נִמְרָץ׃ לוּ־אִישׁ הֹלֵךְ רוּחַ וָשֶׁקֶר כִּזֵּב אַטִּף לְךָ לַיַּיִן
יב וְלַשֵּׁכָר וְהָיָה מַטִּיף הָעָם הַזֶּה׃ אָסֹף אֶאֱסֹף יַעֲקֹב כֻּלָּךְ קַבֵּץ אֲקַבֵּץ
שְׁאֵרִית יִשְׂרָאֵל יַחַד אֲשִׂימֶנּוּ כְּצֹאן בָּצְרָה כְּעֵדֶר בְּתוֹךְ הַדָּבְרוֹ
יג תְּהִימֶנָה מֵאָדָם׃ עָלָה הַפֹּרֵץ לִפְנֵיהֶם פָּרְצוּ וַיַּעֲבֹרוּ שַׁעַר וַיֵּצְאוּ בוֹ
ג א וַיַּעֲבֹר מַלְכָּם לִפְנֵיהֶם וַיהוָה בְּרֹאשָׁם׃ וָאֹמַר
שִׁמְעוּ־נָא רָאשֵׁי יַעֲקֹב וּקְצִינֵי בֵּית יִשְׂרָאֵל הֲלוֹא לָכֶם לָדַעַת אֶת־
ב הַמִּשְׁפָּט׃ שֹׂנְאֵי טוֹב וְאֹהֲבֵי רעה גֹּזְלֵי עוֹרָם מֵעֲלֵיהֶם וּשְׁאֵרָם מֵעַל רָע
ג עַצְמוֹתָם׃ וַאֲשֶׁר אָכְלוּ שְׁאֵר עַמִּי וְעוֹרָם מֵעֲלֵיהֶם הִפְשִׁיטוּ וְאֶת־
ד עַצְמֹתֵיהֶם פִּצֵּחוּ וּפָרְשׂוּ כַּאֲשֶׁר בַּסִּיר וּכְבָשָׂר בְּתוֹךְ קַלָּחַת׃ אָז יִזְעֲקוּ
אֶל־יְהוָה וְלֹא יַעֲנֶה אוֹתָם וְיַסְתֵּר פָּנָיו מֵהֶם בָּעֵת הַהִיא כַּאֲשֶׁר הֵרֵעוּ
ה מַעַלְלֵיהֶם׃ כֹּה אָמַר יְהוָה עַל־הַנְּבִיאִים הַמַּתְעִים
אֶת־עַמִּי הַנֹּשְׁכִים בְּשִׁנֵּיהֶם וְקָרְאוּ שָׁלוֹם וַאֲשֶׁר לֹא־יִתֵּן עַל־פִּיהֶם
ו וְקִדְּשׁוּ עָלָיו מִלְחָמָה׃ לָכֵן לַיְלָה לָכֶם מֵחָזוֹן וְחָשְׁכָה לָכֶם מִקְּסֹם
ז וּבָאָה הַשֶּׁמֶשׁ עַל־הַנְּבִיאִים וְקָדַר עֲלֵיהֶם הַיּוֹם׃ וּבֹשׁוּ הַחֹזִים וְחָפְרוּ
ח הַקֹּסְמִים וְעָטוּ עַל־שָׂפָם כֻּלָּם כִּי אֵין מַעֲנֵה אֱלֹהִים׃ וְאוּלָם אָנֹכִי
מָלֵאתִי כֹחַ אֶת־רוּחַ יְהוָה וּמִשְׁפָּט וּגְבוּרָה לְהַגִּיד לְיַעֲקֹב פִּשְׁעוֹ
ט וּלְיִשְׂרָאֵל חַטָּאתוֹ׃ שִׁמְעוּ־נָא זֹאת רָאשֵׁי בֵּית יַעֲקֹב
י וּקְצִינֵי בֵּית יִשְׂרָאֵל הַמְתַעֲבִים מִשְׁפָּט וְאֵת כָּל־הַיְשָׁרָה יְעַקֵּשׁוּ׃ בֹּנֶה
יא צִיּוֹן בְּדָמִים וִירוּשָׁלִַם בְּעַוְלָה׃ רָאשֶׁיהָ בְּשֹׁחַד יִשְׁפֹּטוּ וְכֹהֲנֶיהָ בִּמְחִיר
יוֹרוּ וּנְבִיאֶיהָ בְּכֶסֶף יִקְסֹמוּ וְעַל־יְהוָה יִשָּׁעֵנוּ לֵאמֹר הֲלוֹא יְהוָה
יב בְּקִרְבֵּנוּ לֹא־תָבוֹא עָלֵינוּ רָעָה׃ לָכֵן בִּגְלַלְכֶם צִיּוֹן שָׂדֶה תֵחָרֵשׁ
ד א וִירוּשָׁלִַם עִיִּין תִּהְיֶה וְהַר הַבַּיִת לְבָמוֹת יָעַר׃ וְהָיָה ׀
בְּאַחֲרִית הַיָּמִים יִהְיֶה הַר בֵּית־יְהוָה נָכוֹן בְּרֹאשׁ הֶהָרִים וְנִשָּׂא הוּא

highest of mountains, raised high above all hills, and all the peoples will
2 stream to it.[9] Many nations will come, saying: "Come, let us go up to the
mount of the LORD, to the House of Yaakov's God; He will teach us of His
ways; we will walk in His pathways" – for teaching will come forth from Zion,
3 from Jerusalem the LORD's word. He will judge among peoples and arbitrate
for mighty nations, far away; they shall beat their swords into plowshares,
their spears into pruning hooks. Nation shall not raise sword against nation;
4 no more will they learn to make war. Every man will sit beneath his grapevine,
under his fig tree with none to trouble him, for the LORD of Hosts has spoken.
5 For all peoples follow, each the call of his god; we will follow the LORD our
6 God, His call, for ever and ever. On that day, so says the LORD: I
7 will gather the lame, draw close those driven away and any I have afflicted. I
will set the lame as the remnant and her who was far removed as a great
nation, and the LORD will reign over them in Mount Zion from then and
8 forever. And now you, Migdal Eder,[10] the tower of daughter Zion
to you will come; the ruling power will return as first it was, and the crown
9 to daughter Jerusalem. Now then, why do you cry out loud? Have you no
king among you? Is your advisor lost to you that your agony overcomes you
10 like a woman in labor? Suffer and strain as a laboring woman, daughter Zion,
for now you will leave the city and dwell in the open field. You will go as far
as Babylon; there you will be rescued; it is there the LORD will redeem you
11 from the hand of your enemies. though now many nations rally against you,
12 saying: "Let her be violated; we will watch and gawk at Zion."[11] But they
know nothing of the LORD's thoughts; they do not realize His design, for He
13 has gathered them like sheaves on the threshing floor. Rise and trample them,
daughter Zion, for I will make your horns iron, your hoofs bronze. You will
crush multitudes of peoples. You will dedicate their spoils to the LORD, their
14 riches to the Master of all the earth. Now then, muster the warriors, O warrior
daughter – they have laid siege against us; with their staff they lash the face
5 1 of the Judge of Israel. You, Beit Leḥem Efrata, minor among the clans
of Yehuda – from you, one will emerge to rule Israel for Me, one whose
2 descent is from an earlier time, from ancient days. So, then, He will give them
over until that time when the laboring woman delivers. Only then will the
3 remaining brothers return to the children of Israel. And he will rise up and
lead his flock with the strength of the LORD, with the majesty of the name
of the LORD his God, and they will reside in safety, for His greatness will
4 be known to the ends of the earth. This, then, will be peace when Assyria
comes to invade our land, to trample our fortresses; we will set against him
5 seven shepherds and eight commanders of men. They will ravage the land of
Assyria by sword and the land of Nimrod[12] with the drawn blade, and he
will deliver us from Assyria when they invade our land and trample our

9 | Cf. Isaiah 2:2–4.

10 | A town in the region of Beit Leḥem; see Genesis 35:21.

11 | That is, at Zion's downfall.

12 | Assyria or Babylon (see Gen. 10:8–12).

ב מִגְּבָעוֹת וְנָהֲרוּ עָלָיו עַמִּים: וְהָלְכוּ גּוֹיִם רַבִּים וְאָמְרוּ לְכוּ ׀ וְנַעֲלֶה
אֶל־הַר־יְהוָה וְאֶל־בֵּית אֱלֹהֵי יַעֲקֹב וְיוֹרֵנוּ מִדְּרָכָיו וְנֵלְכָה בְּאֹרְחֹתָיו
ג כִּי מִצִּיּוֹן תֵּצֵא תוֹרָה וּדְבַר־יְהוָה מִירוּשָׁלִָם: וְשָׁפַט בֵּין עַמִּים רַבִּים
וְהוֹכִיחַ לְגוֹיִם עֲצֻמִים עַד־רָחוֹק וְכִתְּתוּ חַרְבֹתֵיהֶם לְאִתִּים וַחֲנִיתֹתֵיהֶם
ד לְמַזְמֵרוֹת לֹא־יִשְׂאוּ גּוֹי אֶל־גּוֹי חֶרֶב וְלֹא־יִלְמְדוּן עוֹד מִלְחָמָה: וְיָשְׁבוּ
אִישׁ תַּחַת גַּפְנוֹ וְתַחַת תְּאֵנָתוֹ וְאֵין מַחֲרִיד כִּי־פִי יְהוָה צְבָאוֹת דִּבֵּר:
ה כִּי כָּל־הָעַמִּים יֵלְכוּ אִישׁ בְּשֵׁם אֱלֹהָיו וַאֲנַחְנוּ נֵלֵךְ בְּשֵׁם־יְהוָה אֱלֹהֵינוּ יא
ו לְעוֹלָם וָעֶד: בַּיּוֹם הַהוּא נְאֻם־יְהוָה אֹסְפָה הַצֹּלֵעָה
ז וְהַנִּדָּחָה אֲקַבֵּצָה וַאֲשֶׁר הֲרֵעֹתִי: וְשַׂמְתִּי אֶת־הַצֹּלֵעָה לִשְׁאֵרִית
וְהַנַּהֲלָאָה לְגוֹי עָצוּם וּמָלַךְ יְהוָה עֲלֵיהֶם בְּהַר צִיּוֹן מֵעַתָּה וְעַד־
ח עוֹלָם: וְאַתָּה מִגְדַּל־עֵדֶר עֹפֶל בַּת־צִיּוֹן עָדֶיךָ תֵּאתֶה
ט וּבָאָה הַמֶּמְשָׁלָה הָרִאשֹׁנָה מַמְלֶכֶת לְבַת־יְרוּשָׁלִָם: עַתָּה לָמָּה תָרִיעִי
י רֵעַ הֲמֶלֶךְ אֵין־בָּךְ אִם־יוֹעֲצֵךְ אָבָד כִּי־הֶחֱזִיקֵךְ חִיל כַּיּוֹלֵדָה: חוּלִי
וָגֹחִי בַּת־צִיּוֹן כַּיּוֹלֵדָה כִּי עַתָּה תֵצְאִי מִקִּרְיָה וְשָׁכַנְתְּ בַּשָּׂדֶה וּבָאת
יא עַד־בָּבֶל שָׁם תִּנָּצֵלִי שָׁם יִגְאָלֵךְ יְהוָה מִכַּף אֹיְבָיִךְ: וְעַתָּה נֶאֶסְפוּ
יב עָלַיִךְ גּוֹיִם רַבִּים הָאֹמְרִים תֶּחֱנָף וְתַחַז בְּצִיּוֹן עֵינֵינוּ: וְהֵמָּה לֹא יָדְעוּ
יג מַחְשְׁבוֹת יְהוָה וְלֹא הֵבִינוּ עֲצָתוֹ כִּי קִבְּצָם כֶּעָמִיר גֹּרְנָה: קוּמִי וָדוֹשִׁי
בַת־צִיּוֹן כִּי קַרְנֵךְ אָשִׂים בַּרְזֶל וּפַרְסֹתַיִךְ אָשִׂים נְחוּשָׁה וַהֲדִקּוֹת
יד עַמִּים רַבִּים וְהַחֲרַמְתִּי לַיהוָה בִּצְעָם וְחֵילָם לַאֲדוֹן כָּל־הָאָרֶץ: עַתָּה
תִּתְגֹּדְדִי בַת־גְּדוּד מָצוֹר שָׂם עָלֵינוּ בַּשֵּׁבֶט יַכּוּ עַל־הַלְּחִי אֵת שֹׁפֵט
ה א יִשְׂרָאֵל: וְאַתָּה בֵּית־לֶחֶם אֶפְרָתָה צָעִיר לִהְיוֹת בְּאַלְפֵי
יְהוּדָה מִמְּךָ לִי יֵצֵא לִהְיוֹת מוֹשֵׁל בְּיִשְׂרָאֵל וּמוֹצָאֹתָיו מִקֶּדֶם מִימֵי
ב עוֹלָם: לָכֵן יִתְּנֵם עַד־עֵת יוֹלֵדָה יָלָדָה וְיֶתֶר אֶחָיו יְשׁוּבוּן עַל־בְּנֵי
ג יִשְׂרָאֵל: וְעָמַד וְרָעָה בְּעֹז יְהוָה בִּגְאוֹן שֵׁם יְהוָה אֱלֹהָיו וְיָשָׁבוּ כִּי־
ד עַתָּה יִגְדַּל עַד־אַפְסֵי־אָרֶץ: וְהָיָה זֶה שָׁלוֹם אַשּׁוּר ׀ כִּי־יָבוֹא בְאַרְצֵנוּ
וְכִי יִדְרֹךְ בְּאַרְמְנוֹתֵינוּ וַהֲקֵמֹנוּ עָלָיו שִׁבְעָה רֹעִים וּשְׁמֹנָה נְסִיכֵי
ה אָדָם: וְרָעוּ אֶת־אֶרֶץ אַשּׁוּר בַּחֶרֶב וְאֶת־אֶרֶץ נִמְרֹד בִּפְתָחֶיהָ וְהִצִּיל

6 borders. And the remnant of Yaakov will be found amid countless
peoples as dew brought down from the LORD, as ample rains shower upon
7 grass; they will not look to any man, nor place their hopes in humankind. The
remnant of Yaakov will be among nations, amid countless peoples, like a lion
among wild beasts of the forest, like a young lion among flocks of sheep
whom, as they pass, he tramples and rips to pieces; there is no one to save
8 them. Your hand shall be raised over your foes; your enemies will be cut
9 down. On that day, so says the LORD: I will cut out the horses from
10 among you, I will destroy your chariots, and I will cut down the fortified cities
11 of your land and demolish all your fortresses. I will cut out all practice of
12 witchcraft, and there will be no more fortune-tellers among you. I will cut
down your idols, the worship pillars from your midst; no longer will you bow
13 down to the craft of your hands. I will rip out the Ashera[13] from your midst,
14 and I will destroy your cities. I will lash out with My anger and wrath in
6 1 vengeance against nations who did not heed My words. Hear now
what the LORD says: Arise; argue your case before the mountains; let the hills
2 hear your plea. Hear, O mountains, the LORD's dispute – you, earth's everlasting
foundations. For the LORD has a dispute with His people; He will contend
3 with Israel: My people! How have I wronged you? How have I worn you
4 down? Bear witness against Me, for I brought you up from the land of Egypt;
I redeemed you from the house of slavery; I sent Moshe, Aharon, and Miriam
5 to lead you. My people, remember now how Balak, king of Moav, schemed,
and how Bilam son of Beor responded;[14] remember from Shitim to Gilgal[15]
6 so that you may come to realize the righteous ways of the LORD. What then
can I offer the LORD when I bow low to the God Most High? Should I come
7 before Him with burnt offerings, with year-old calves? Would the LORD want
a thousand rams, untold rivulets of oil? Should I offer my firstborn as payment
8 for my crimes, the fruit of my womb for the sins of my being? Man, God has
told you what is good and what the LORD seeks from you: only to do justice,
9 love goodness, and walk modestly with your God. The LORD's voice
cries out to the city; wise men will perceive Your name. Heed the staff[16] and
10 Him who sanctioned it. Are storerooms of evil still found in the homes of the
11 wicked? And the scant measure so detested by God? Shall I be found innocent
12 while using false scales and a bag full of deceptive weights? Her wealthy are
filled with corruption; her residents speak lies with tongues of deceit in their
13 14 mouths. And so I will strike you with sickness, ruin you for your sins. You
will eat and never be sated; sickness will settle in your innards. You will
conceive but bear no young, and what you do bring forth I will give over to
15 the sword. You will plant but not reap, you will tread olives but have no oil to
16 anoint, and you will crush grapes but drink no wine. For the laws of Omri are

---

13 | A prominent Canaanite goddess and the tree used in her worship.

14 | See Numbers, chapters 22–25.

15 | Meaning the crossing of the Jordan in Joshua, chapters 2–5.

16 | The rod of punishment.

ו מֵאַשּׁוּר כִּי־יָבוֹא בְאַרְצֵנוּ וְכִי יִדְרֹךְ בִּגְבוּלֵנוּ׃ וְהָיָה ׀
שְׁאֵרִית יַעֲקֹב בְּקֶרֶב עַמִּים רַבִּים כְּטַל מֵאֵת יְהוָה כִּרְבִיבִים עֲלֵי־
ז עֵשֶׂב אֲשֶׁר לֹא־יְקַוֶּה לְאִישׁ וְלֹא יְיַחֵל לִבְנֵי אָדָם׃ וְהָיָה שְׁאֵרִית יַעֲקֹב
בַּגּוֹיִם בְּקֶרֶב עַמִּים רַבִּים כְּאַרְיֵה בְּבַהֲמוֹת יַעַר כִּכְפִיר בְּעֶדְרֵי־צֹאן
ח אֲשֶׁר אִם עָבַר וְרָמַס וְטָרַף וְאֵין מַצִּיל׃ תָּרֹם יָדְךָ עַל־צָרֶיךָ וְכָל־אֹיְבֶיךָ
ט יִכָּרֵתוּ׃ וְהָיָה בַיּוֹם־הַהוּא נְאֻם־יְהוָה וְהִכְרַתִּי סוּסֶיךָ
י מִקִּרְבֶּךָ וְהַאֲבַדְתִּי מַרְכְּבֹתֶיךָ׃ וְהִכְרַתִּי עָרֵי אַרְצֶךָ וְהָרַסְתִּי כָּל־
יא יב מִבְצָרֶיךָ׃ וְהִכְרַתִּי כְשָׁפִים מִיָּדֶךָ וּמְעוֹנְנִים לֹא יִהְיוּ־לָךְ׃ וְהִכְרַתִּי
פְסִילֶיךָ וּמַצֵּבוֹתֶיךָ מִקִּרְבֶּךָ וְלֹא־תִשְׁתַּחֲוֶה עוֹד לְמַעֲשֵׂה יָדֶיךָ׃
יג יד וְנָתַשְׁתִּי אֲשֵׁירֶיךָ מִקִּרְבֶּךָ וְהִשְׁמַדְתִּי עָרֶיךָ׃ וְעָשִׂיתִי בְּאַף וּבְחֵמָה
ו א נָקָם אֶת־הַגּוֹיִם אֲשֶׁר לֹא שָׁמֵעוּ׃ שִׁמְעוּ־נָא אֵת אֲשֶׁר־
ב יְהוָה אֹמֵר קוּם רִיב אֶת־הֶהָרִים וְתִשְׁמַעְנָה הַגְּבָעוֹת קוֹלֶךָ׃ שִׁמְעוּ
הָרִים אֶת־רִיב יְהוָה וְהָאֵתָנִים מֹסְדֵי אָרֶץ כִּי רִיב לַיהוָה עִם־עַמּוֹ
ג ד וְעִם־יִשְׂרָאֵל יִתְוַכָּח׃ עַמִּי מֶה־עָשִׂיתִי לְךָ וּמָה הֶלְאֵתִיךָ עֲנֵה בִי׃ כִּי
הֶעֱלִתִיךָ מֵאֶרֶץ מִצְרַיִם וּמִבֵּית עֲבָדִים פְּדִיתִיךָ וָאֶשְׁלַח לְפָנֶיךָ אֶת־
ה מֹשֶׁה אַהֲרֹן וּמִרְיָם׃ עַמִּי זְכָר־נָא מַה־יָּעַץ בָּלָק מֶלֶךְ מוֹאָב וּמֶה־עָנָה
אֹתוֹ בִּלְעָם בֶּן־בְּעוֹר מִן־הַשִּׁטִּים עַד־הַגִּלְגָּל לְמַעַן דַּעַת צִדְקוֹת
ו יְהוָה׃ בַּמָּה אֲקַדֵּם יְהוָה אִכַּף לֵאלֹהֵי מָרוֹם הַאֲקַדְּמֶנּוּ בְעוֹלוֹת
ז בַּעֲגָלִים בְּנֵי שָׁנָה׃ הֲיִרְצֶה יְהוָה בְּאַלְפֵי אֵילִים בְּרִבְבוֹת נַחֲלֵי־שָׁמֶן
ח הַאֶתֵּן בְּכוֹרִי פִּשְׁעִי פְּרִי בִטְנִי חַטַּאת נַפְשִׁי׃ הִגִּיד לְךָ אָדָם מַה־טּוֹב
וּמָה־יְהוָה דּוֹרֵשׁ מִמְּךָ כִּי אִם־עֲשׂוֹת מִשְׁפָּט וְאַהֲבַת חֶסֶד וְהַצְנֵעַ
ט לֶכֶת עִם־אֱלֹהֶיךָ׃ קוֹל יְהוָה לָעִיר יִקְרָא וְתוּשִׁיָּה יִרְאֶה
י שְׁמֶךָ שִׁמְעוּ מַטֶּה וּמִי יְעָדָהּ׃ עוֹד הַאִשׁ בֵּית רָשָׁע אֹצְרוֹת רֶשַׁע
יא יב וְאֵיפַת רָזוֹן זְעוּמָה׃ הַאֶזְכֶּה בְּמֹאזְנֵי רֶשַׁע וּבְכִיס אַבְנֵי מִרְמָה׃ אֲשֶׁר
עֲשִׁירֶיהָ מָלְאוּ חָמָס וְיֹשְׁבֶיהָ דִּבְּרוּ־שָׁקֶר וּלְשׁוֹנָם רְמִיָּה בְּפִיהֶם׃
יג יד וְגַם־אֲנִי הֶחֱלֵיתִי הַכּוֹתֶךָ הַשְׁמֵם עַל־חַטֹּאתֶךָ׃ אַתָּה תֹאכַל וְלֹא
תִשְׂבָּע וְיֶשְׁחֲךָ בְּקִרְבֶּךָ וְתַסֵּג וְלֹא תַפְלִיט וַאֲשֶׁר תְּפַלֵּט לַחֶרֶב אֶתֵּן׃
טו אַתָּה תִזְרַע וְלֹא תִקְצוֹר אַתָּה תִדְרֹךְ־זַיִת וְלֹא־תָסוּךְ שֶׁמֶן וְתִירוֹשׁ
טז וְלֹא תִשְׁתֶּה־יָּיִן׃ וְיִשְׁתַּמֵּר חֻקּוֹת עָמְרִי וְכֹל מַעֲשֵׂה בֵית־אַחְאָב וַתֵּלְכוּ

upheld, the conventions of Aḥav's house kept;[17] you follow their counsel. So
then I will lay waste to you, turn the people of this land into objects of disdain;
7 1 you will bear the shame of My people. Woe is me! I am like the last
of summer fruit, the gleanings of harvest. No cluster of grapes is left to eat,
2 no first, ripe fig that I long for. The righteous man is gone from the land; no
upright men remain; all lie in wait for blood, each snaring his brother in a net.
3 They extend their hands to enhance evil; the official makes his request, the
judge names his price, and the powerful man states his heart's evil wish;
4 together they weave it. The best of them are only prickly shrubs, the most
righteous worse than a thorn hedge. The day you awaited will be the day of
5 your reckoning; now is your time of confusion. Do not put your faith in a
friend nor place trust in a confidant; guard your words from her who lies in
6 your arms. For a son denigrates his father; daughter rises up against mother;
women stand against their husbands' mothers; a man's own household are
7 his enemies. Yet I, I will look toward the Lord; I will await my God who will
8 save me, my God who will heed me. My enemies, do not revel over me;
9 though I fall I will rise; though I sit in darkness, the Lord is my light. I
will bear the rage of the Lord's anger, for I have sinned against Him, until He
upholds my case and favors my justice. He will bring me out into the light; I
10 will behold His righteousness. When my enemy sees this, she will be covered
with shame, she who once said to me, "Where is the Lord your God?" My
eyes will behold her defeat, how she is now trampled like mud in the streets.
11 12 The day for mending your walls, that day is far away. There will be a day when
they will come to you from Assyria and the cities of Egypt, and from Egypt
13 to the river, from sea to sea and from mountain to mountain. And their
lands will be devastated along with their people; this is the fruit of their
14 actions. Shepherd Your people with Your staff, the flock of Your
legacy; they will dwell safely in lush forest lands, pasture in Bashan and
15 Gilad[18] as in ancient days. As in the days when you came out of Egypt, I will
16 show My wonders. Nations will see and be shamed by the might they wielded;
17 they will place their hands over their mouths; their ears will be deafened. Like
snakes they will lick the dust, like slithering creatures of earth; they will come
quivering out from their holes in terror; they will come before the Lord our
18 God, and they will fear You. Is there any God like You who forgives iniquities,
who looks beyond the sins of the remnant of His own people, who does not
19 hold onto His wrath forever because He desires kindness? He will again have
compassion for us; He will subdue our iniquities and hurl all of our sins into
20 the deepest of seas. You will show truth to Yaakov, kindness to Avraham, as
You swore to our fathers in the earliest days.

---

17 | For these kings' abuses, see 1 Kings, chapters 16–22.

18 | Rich pastureland east of the Jordan River; see Numbers 32:1–4.

בְּמֹעֲצוֹתָם לְמַעַן תִּתִּי אֹתְךָ לְשַׁמָּה וְיֹשְׁבֶיהָ לִשְׁרֵקָה וְחֶרְפַּת עַמִּי
ז א תִּשָּׂאוּ׃ אַלְלַי לִי כִּי הָיִיתִי כְּאָסְפֵּי־קַיִץ כְּעֹלְלֹת
ב בָּצִיר אֵין־אֶשְׁכּוֹל לֶאֱכוֹל בִּכּוּרָה אִוְּתָה נַפְשִׁי׃ אָבַד חָסִיד מִן־הָאָרֶץ
וְיָשָׁר בָּאָדָם אָיִן כֻּלָּם לְדָמִים יֶאֱרֹבוּ אִישׁ אֶת־אָחִיהוּ יָצוּדוּ חֵרֶם׃
ג עַל־הָרַע כַּפַּיִם לְהֵיטִיב הַשַּׂר שֹׁאֵל וְהַשֹּׁפֵט בַּשִּׁלּוּם וְהַגָּדוֹל דֹּבֵר
ד הַוַּת נַפְשׁוֹ הוּא וַיְעַבְּתוּהָ׃ טוֹבָם כְּחֵדֶק יָשָׁר מִמְּסוּכָה יוֹם מְצַפֶּיךָ
ה פְּקֻדָּתְךָ בָאָה עַתָּה תִהְיֶה מְבוּכָתָם׃ אַל־תַּאֲמִינוּ בְרֵעַ אַל־תִּבְטְחוּ
ו בְּאַלּוּף מִשֹּׁכֶבֶת חֵיקֶךָ שְׁמֹר פִּתְחֵי־פִיךָ׃ כִּי־בֵן מְנַבֵּל אָב בַּת קָמָה
ז בְאִמָּהּ כַּלָּה בַּחֲמֹתָהּ אֹיְבֵי אִישׁ אַנְשֵׁי בֵיתוֹ׃ וַאֲנִי בַּיהוה אֲצַפֶּה
ח אוֹחִילָה לֵאלֹהֵי יִשְׁעִי יִשְׁמָעֵנִי אֱלֹהָי׃ אַל־תִּשְׂמְחִי אֹיַבְתִּי לִי כִּי
ט נָפַלְתִּי קָמְתִּי כִּי־אֵשֵׁב בַּחֹשֶׁךְ יהוה אוֹר לִי׃ זַעַף יהוה
אֶשָּׂא כִּי חָטָאתִי לוֹ עַד אֲשֶׁר יָרִיב רִיבִי וְעָשָׂה מִשְׁפָּטִי יוֹצִיאֵנִי לָאוֹר
י אֶרְאֶה בְּצִדְקָתוֹ׃ וְתֵרֶא אֹיַבְתִּי וּתְכַסֶּהָ בוּשָׁה הָאֹמְרָה אֵלַי אַיּוֹ יהוה
יא אֱלֹהָיִךְ עֵינַי תִּרְאֶינָּה בָּהּ עַתָּה תִּהְיֶה לְמִרְמָס כְּטִיט חוּצוֹת׃ יוֹם
יב לִבְנוֹת גְּדֵרָיִךְ יוֹם הַהוּא יִרְחַק־חֹק׃ יוֹם הוּא וְעָדֶיךָ יָבוֹא לְמִנִּי אַשּׁוּר
יג וְעָרֵי מָצוֹר וּלְמִנִּי מָצוֹר וְעַד־נָהָר וְיָם מִיָּם וְהַר הָהָר׃ וְהָיְתָה הָאָרֶץ
יד לִשְׁמָמָה עַל־יֹשְׁבֶיהָ מִפְּרִי מַעַלְלֵיהֶם׃ רְעֵה עַמְּךָ
בְשִׁבְטֶךָ צֹאן נַחֲלָתֶךָ שֹׁכְנִי לְבָדָד יַעַר בְּתוֹךְ כַּרְמֶל יִרְעוּ בָשָׁן וְגִלְעָד
טו טז כִּימֵי עוֹלָם׃ כִּימֵי צֵאתְךָ מֵאֶרֶץ מִצְרָיִם אַרְאֶנּוּ נִפְלָאוֹת׃ יִרְאוּ גוֹיִם
יז וְיֵבֹשׁוּ מִכֹּל גְּבוּרָתָם יָשִׂימוּ יָד עַל־פֶּה אָזְנֵיהֶם תֶּחֱרַשְׁנָה׃ יְלַחֲכוּ עָפָר
כַּנָּחָשׁ כְּזֹחֲלֵי אֶרֶץ יִרְגְּזוּ מִמִּסְגְּרֹתֵיהֶם אֶל־יהוה אֱלֹהֵינוּ יִפְחָדוּ וְיִרְאוּ
יח מִמֶּךָּ׃ מִי־אֵל כָּמוֹךָ נֹשֵׂא עָוֹן וְעֹבֵר עַל־פֶּשַׁע לִשְׁאֵרִית נַחֲלָתוֹ לֹא־
יט הֶחֱזִיק לָעַד אַפּוֹ כִּי־חָפֵץ חֶסֶד הוּא׃ יָשׁוּב יְרַחֲמֵנוּ יִכְבֹּשׁ עֲוֺנֹתֵינוּ
כ וְתַשְׁלִיךְ בִּמְצֻלוֹת יָם כָּל־חַטֹּאתָם׃ תִּתֵּן אֱמֶת לְיַעֲקֹב חֶסֶד לְאַבְרָהָם יב
אֲשֶׁר־נִשְׁבַּעְתָּ לַאֲבֹתֵינוּ מִימֵי קֶדֶם׃

NAḤUM/NAHUM

1 1 2 The oracle of Nineveh, a visionary book by Naḥum the Elkoshite. The LORD
is envious, an avenging God;revengeful is the LORD, filled with burning fury;
the LORD takes vengeance on His foes; He restrains His scorching wrath and
3 awaits His enemies. The LORD is slow to anger, immense in power. Never
will He let the guilty go unpunished. The way of the LORD will be a raging
4 whirlwind, clouds as dust beneath His feet. God berates the sea, parching it
dry. Each and every river He depletes. Bashan and Carmel lie despondent,
5 the flowers of Lebanon despondent, dying. Mountains convulse before Him
and hills crumble; the earth staggers from God's presence, the world with all
6 who live in it. Who could possibly stand up to His rage? Who could endure
the fierceness of His fury? His wrath rages like fire; rocks shatter before Him.
7 Goodness is the LORD; He, a refuge in days of distress, knows who seeks His
8 shelter. With a ravaging flood He will bring an utter end to this place. As for
9 His enemies, He will pursue them into darkness. What then do you contrive
against the LORD? He wreaks utter destruction so that trouble will not strike
10 a second time. For they are ensnared as if by thorns, soaked and soused with
11 drink, to be consumed entirely like the driest of straw. It is from you[1] that
the architect of evil came, he who plotted against the LORD, who counseled
12 to evil. So says the LORD: Though they are numerous and mighty,
still they shall be mowed down and disappear, and as surely as I afflicted
13 you,[2] I will afflict you no more. And now I will break off his yoke from you;
14 the straps of your shackles I will slash. The LORD has ruled against you,[3]
that no seed will come from your name. I will wipe out all idols and images
from the temple of your gods; there I will prepare your grave, for you are as
2 1 nothing. Behold: a messenger – his feet tread upon the mountain;
he bears tidings of peace. O Yehuda, go ahead, celebrate your feasts; once
again you may fulfill your vows. Never again will the wicked pass through
2 you; they will be utterly destroyed. The hammer of war is rising against you;
fortify your defenses, guard your roads, ready yourself for battle, summon all
3 your strength. For the LORD will restore the pride of Yaakov like the pride
of Israel. For the plunderers have drained them bare; they have trampled
4 their vineyards. The shields of his brave warriors are colored red; his heroic
troops are clad in crimson. On this day as he prepares for battle, the steel of
5 the chariots glitters; the cypress spears are poisoned and ready. The chariots
rush frenzied on the roadways, clanging and ramming in the streets; they
6 appear like torches flashing, strikes of lightning racing about. He summons his
warriors; they stumble in their advance; hastening to defend the walls, they
7 find the shielding barrier already in place. The dams of the channels have been
8 opened; the palace washed away. The queen, exposed in her disgrace, is taken
away, and like mournful doves, her handmaids wail and beat their breasts in
9 mourning. Though Nineveh was a brimming pool from ancient times,[4] now

1 | The prophet begins to address Nineveh, the capital of Assyria.
2 | The prophet now addresses Israel.
3 | The prophet returns to addressing Assyria.
4 | Meaning abundant in water and life.

א א ב מַשָּׂא נִינְוֵה סֵפֶר חֲזוֹן נַחוּם הָאֶלְקֹשִׁי: אֵל קַנּוֹא וְנֹקֵם יְהוָה נֹקֵם נחום
ג יְהוָה וּבַעַל חֵמָה נֹקֵם יְהוָה לְצָרָיו וְנוֹטֵר הוּא לְאֹיְבָיו: יְהוָה אֶרֶךְ
אַפַּיִם וגדול־כֹּחַ וְנַקֵּה לֹא יְנַקֶּה יְהוָה בְּסוּפָה וּבִשְׂעָרָה דַּרְכּוֹ וְעָנָן וּגְדָל־
ד אֲבַק רַגְלָיו: גּוֹעֵר בַּיָּם וַיַּבְּשֵׁהוּ וְכָל־הַנְּהָרוֹת הֶחֱרִיב אֻמְלַל בָּשָׁן
ה וְכַרְמֶל וּפֶרַח לְבָנוֹן אֻמְלָל: הָרִים רָעֲשׁוּ מִמֶּנּוּ וְהַגְּבָעוֹת הִתְמֹגָגוּ
ו וַתִּשָּׂא הָאָרֶץ מִפָּנָיו וְתֵבֵל וְכָל־יֹשְׁבֵי בָהּ: לִפְנֵי זַעְמוֹ מִי יַעֲמוֹד וּמִי
ז יָקוּם בַּחֲרוֹן אַפּוֹ חֲמָתוֹ נִתְּכָה כָאֵשׁ וְהַצֻּרִים נִתְּצוּ מִמֶּנּוּ: טוֹב יְהוָה
ח לְמָעוֹז בְּיוֹם צָרָה וְיֹדֵעַ חֹסֵי בוֹ: וּבְשֶׁטֶף עֹבֵר כָּלָה יַעֲשֶׂה מְקוֹמָהּ
ט וְאֹיְבָיו יְרַדֶּף־חֹשֶׁךְ: מַה־תְּחַשְּׁבוּן אֶל־יְהוָה כָּלָה הוּא עֹשֶׂה לֹא־תָקוּם
י פַּעֲמַיִם צָרָה: כִּי עַד־סִירִים סְבֻכִים וּכְסָבְאָם סְבוּאִים אֻכְּלוּ כְּקַשׁ יָבֵשׁ
יא יב מָלֵא: מִמֵּךְ יָצָא חֹשֵׁב עַל־יְהוָה רָעָה יֹעֵץ בְּלִיָּעַל: כֹּה ׀
אָמַר יְהוָה אִם־שְׁלֵמִים וְכֵן רַבִּים וְכֵן נָגֹזּוּ וְעָבָר וְעִנִּתִךְ לֹא אֲעַנֵּךְ
יג יד עוֹד: וְעַתָּה אֶשְׁבֹּר מֹטֵהוּ מֵעָלָיִךְ וּמוֹסְרֹתַיִךְ אֲנַתֵּק: וְצִוָּה עָלֶיךָ
יְהוָה לֹא־יִזָּרַע מִשִּׁמְךָ עוֹד מִבֵּית אֱלֹהֶיךָ אַכְרִית פֶּסֶל וּמַסֵּכָה אָשִׂים
ב א קִבְרֶךָ כִּי קַלּוֹתָ: הִנֵּה עַל־הֶהָרִים רַגְלֵי מְבַשֵּׂר מַשְׁמִיעַ
שָׁלוֹם חָגִּי יְהוּדָה חַגַּיִךְ שַׁלְּמִי נְדָרָיִךְ כִּי לֹא יוֹסִיף עוֹד לעבור־בָּךְ לַעֲבָר־
ב בְּלִיַּעַל כֻּלֹּה נִכְרָת: עָלָה מֵפִיץ עַל־פָּנַיִךְ נָצוֹר מְצֻרָה צַפֵּה־דֶרֶךְ חַזֵּק
ג מָתְנַיִם אַמֵּץ כֹּחַ מְאֹד: כִּי שָׁב יְהוָה אֶת־גְּאוֹן יַעֲקֹב כִּגְאוֹן יִשְׂרָאֵל
ד כִּי בְקָקוּם בֹּקְקִים וּזְמֹרֵיהֶם שִׁחֵתוּ: מָגֵן גִּבֹּרֵיהוּ מְאָדָּם אַנְשֵׁי־חַיִל
ה מְתֻלָּעִים בְּאֵשׁ־פְּלָדוֹת הָרֶכֶב בְּיוֹם הֲכִינוֹ וְהַבְּרֹשִׁים הָרְעָלוּ: בַּחוּצוֹת
יִתְהוֹלְלוּ הָרֶכֶב יִשְׁתַּקְשְׁקוּן בָּרְחֹבוֹת מַרְאֵיהֶן כַּלַּפִּידִם כַּבְּרָקִים
ו יְרוֹצֵצוּ: יִזְכֹּר אַדִּירָיו יִכָּשְׁלוּ בהלוכתם יְמַהֲרוּ חוֹמָתָהּ וְהֻכַן הַסֹּכֵךְ: בַּהֲלִיכָתָם
ז ח שַׁעֲרֵי הַנְּהָרוֹת נִפְתָּחוּ וְהַהֵיכָל נָמוֹג: וְהֻצַּב גֻּלְּתָה הֹעֲלָתָה וְאַמְהֹתֶיהָ
ט מְנַהֲגוֹת כְּקוֹל יוֹנִים מְתֹפְפֹת עַל־לִבְבֵהֶן: וְנִינְוֵה כִבְרֵכַת־מַיִם מִימֵי

10 all flee from her. "Stay, stay!" but no one even looks back. Plunder the silver,
plunder the gold. Indeed, there is no limit to the storehouse of riches, the
11 endless articles of wealth. She is devoid; she is devastated and drained; their[5]
hearts turn faint, knees buckle in fear; their loins are seized with trembling; all
12 gather, their faces blackened with ashes. What then has become of the lion's
den, the pasture for grazing cubs where the lion and lioness roamed freely
13 with their whelp and feared no one? What then has become of the lion who
ripped apart his prey, plentiful for his cubs, who strangled victims for his
14 lionesses, who filled his caves with game, his lair with spoils? Behold, I will
oppose you, says the Lord of Hosts. I will burn your chariots up into smoke;
your young lions will be devoured by My sword, I will sever your prey from
3 1 the land, the calls of your emissaries never again to be heard. Woe to
the bloodstained city, the utterly treacherous place, suffused with plundering,
2 never lacking prey. Hear the cracking whips, the rattling wheels; hear the
3 pounding of stampeding horses, the clatter of lurching chariots. Mounted
soldiers charge – flame of the swords, flash of the spears; masses lay slain,
corpses upon corpses; so endless are the carcasses that they are stumbled
4 over. All this because of the many whorings of the prostitute – this beautifully
charming mistress of witchcraft, who sells nations through her whoring, and
5 clans in her witchcraft. Behold, I will oppose you, says the Lord of Hosts;
I will lift your skirts over your faces in disgrace; I will reveal your nakedness
6 to the nations, to the kingdoms your shame I will hurl abhorrent filth upon
you and disgrace you; I will make you into a repulsive, detestable public
7 display. So it will be that all who look upon you will flee and say: Nineveh has
been sacked, but who will mourn for her? Where could I ever find someone
8 to comfort you? Are you any better than Thebes, situated amidst rivers,
surrounded by water, whose protective walls were the waters and whose
9 ramparts came from the depths of the sea? The kingdom of Kush served as her
strength; the power of Egypt knew no limits. She counted Put and Libyans
10 among her allies. Yet even she was taken into exile, carried into captivity;
her babies were smashed to pieces at every street corner; onlookers drew
lots for her prominent people; her powerful men were chained in shackles.
11 You too will be in a drunken stupor, shriveled in hiding; you too will beg
12 for refuge from the enemy. All your fortresses will be like the ripened first
fruits of the fig tree: lightly shaken, they drop easily into the enemy's mouth.
13 Behold: your troops sit submissively like women; in your midst the gates to
your land fall gaping, open to your enemies; fire consumes the bars of your
14 gates. Draw yourself water for the siege; secure your strongholds; prepare the
15 clay and trample the mortar; cast the bricks for the fortress. But no matter
what, there in your fortresses, fire will consume you; the enemy sword will
cut you down, consume you like swarms of young locusts. O, go ahead and
16 multiply like young locusts; make yourself many like banding locusts. As
you thrived, your traders were more than the stars in the sky; as locusts
17 they stormed and flew on. Your rulers are like locusts, your generals like

---

5 | The remaining people of Nineveh.

י הִיא וְהֵמָּה נָסִים עִמְדוּ עֲמֹדוּ וְאֵין מַפְנֶה: בֹּזּוּ כֶסֶף בֹּזּוּ זָהָב וְאֵין קֵצֶה
יא לַתְּכוּנָה כָּבֹד מִכֹּל כְּלִי חֶמְדָּה: בּוּקָה וּמְבוּקָה וּמְבֻלָּקָה וְלֵב נָמֵס
יב וּפַק בִּרְכַּיִם וְחַלְחָלָה בְּכָל־מָתְנַיִם וּפְנֵי כֻלָּם קִבְּצוּ פָארוּר: אַיֵּה מְעוֹן
אֲרָיוֹת וּמִרְעֶה הוּא לַכְּפִרִים אֲשֶׁר הָלַךְ אַרְיֵה לָבִיא שָׁם גּוּר אַרְיֵה
יג וְאֵין מַחֲרִיד: אַרְיֵה טֹרֵף בְּדֵי גֹרוֹתָיו וּמְחַנֵּק לְלִבְאֹתָיו וַיְמַלֵּא־טֶרֶף
יד חֹרָיו וּמְעֹנֹתָיו טְרֵפָה: הִנְנִי אֵלַיִךְ נְאֻם יְהוָה צְבָאוֹת וְהִבְעַרְתִּי בֶעָשָׁן
רִכְבָּהּ וּכְפִירַיִךְ תֹּאכַל חָרֶב וְהִכְרַתִּי מֵאֶרֶץ טַרְפֵּךְ וְלֹא־יִשָּׁמַע עוֹד
ג א קוֹל מַלְאָכֵכֵה: הוֹי עִיר דָּמִים כֻּלָּהּ כַּחַשׁ פֶּרֶק מְלֵאָה לֹא
ב יָמִישׁ טָרֶף: קוֹל שׁוֹט וְקוֹל רַעַשׁ אוֹפָן וְסוּס דֹּהֵר וּמֶרְכָּבָה מְרַקֵּדָה:
ג פָּרָשׁ מַעֲלֶה וְלַהַב חֶרֶב וּבְרַק חֲנִית וְרֹב חָלָל וְכֹבֶד פָּגֶר וְאֵין קֵצֶה
ד לַגְּוִיָּה יכשלו בִּגְוִיָּתָם: מֵרֹב זְנוּנֵי זוֹנָה טוֹבַת חֵן בַּעֲלַת כְּשָׁפִים הַמֹּכֶרֶת וְכָשְׁלוּ
ה גּוֹיִם בִּזְנוּנֶיהָ וּמִשְׁפָּחוֹת בִּכְשָׁפֶיהָ: הִנְנִי אֵלַיִךְ נְאֻם יְהוָה צְבָאוֹת
וְגִלֵּיתִי שׁוּלַיִךְ עַל־פָּנָיִךְ וְהַרְאֵיתִי גוֹיִם מַעְרֵךְ וּמַמְלָכוֹת קְלוֹנֵךְ:
ו ז וְהִשְׁלַכְתִּי עָלַיִךְ שִׁקֻּצִים וְנִבַּלְתִּיךְ וְשַׂמְתִּיךְ כְּרֹאִי: וְהָיָה כָל־רֹאַיִךְ
יִדּוֹד מִמֵּךְ וְאָמַר שָׁדְּדָה נִינְוֵה מִי יָנוּד לָהּ מֵאַיִן אֲבַקֵּשׁ מְנַחֲמִים לָךְ:
ח הֲתֵיטְבִי מִנֹּא אָמוֹן הַיֹּשְׁבָה בַּיְאֹרִים מַיִם סָבִיב לָהּ אֲשֶׁר־חֵיל יָם מִיָּם
ט חוֹמָתָהּ: כּוּשׁ עָצְמָה וּמִצְרַיִם וְאֵין קֵצֶה פּוּט וְלוּבִים הָיוּ בְּעֶזְרָתֵךְ:
י גַּם־הִיא לַגֹּלָה הָלְכָה בַשֶּׁבִי גַּם עֹלָלֶיהָ יְרֻטְּשׁוּ בְּרֹאשׁ כָּל־חוּצוֹת
יא וְעַל־נִכְבַּדֶּיהָ יַדּוּ גוֹרָל וְכָל־גְּדוֹלֶיהָ רֻתְּקוּ בַזִּקִּים: גַּם־אַתְּ תִּשְׁכְּרִי
יב תְּהִי נַעֲלָמָה גַּם־אַתְּ תְּבַקְשִׁי מָעוֹז מֵאוֹיֵב: כָּל־מִבְצָרַיִךְ תְּאֵנִים עִם־
יג בִּכּוּרִים אִם־יִנּוֹעוּ וְנָפְלוּ עַל־פִּי אוֹכֵל: הִנֵּה עַמֵּךְ נָשִׁים בְּקִרְבֵּךְ לְאֹיְבַיִךְ
יד פָּתוֹחַ נִפְתְּחוּ שַׁעֲרֵי אַרְצֵךְ אָכְלָה אֵשׁ בְּרִיחָיִךְ: מֵי מָצוֹר שַׁאֲבִי־לָךְ
טו חַזְּקִי מִבְצָרָיִךְ בֹּאִי בַטִּיט וְרִמְסִי בַחֹמֶר הַחֲזִיקִי מַלְבֵּן: שָׁם תֹּאכְלֵךְ
אֵשׁ תַּכְרִיתֵךְ חֶרֶב תֹּאכְלֵךְ כַּיָּלֶק הִתְכַּבֵּד כַּיֶּלֶק הִתְכַּבְּדִי כָּאַרְבֶּה:
טז יז הִרְבֵּית רֹכְלַיִךְ מִכּוֹכְבֵי הַשָּׁמָיִם יֶלֶק פָּשַׁט וַיָּעֹף: מִנְּזָרַיִךְ כָּאַרְבֶּה

plagues of grasshoppers who camp in hedges on cold days, but as soon as
18 the sun rises they swiftly flee, who knows to where? O king of Assyria, your
shepherds sleep on duty; your leaders are lounging; your nation is scattered
19 upon the mountains with no one to gather them. There is no healing your
pain; your blow is mortal. All who hear what has become of you will applaud
your fall – for are there any who have not suffered your unrelenting evil?

ḤAVAKUK/HABAKKUK

1 1 The burden Ḥavakuk the prophet saw in a vision: How much longer must
2 I implore You, O Lord, though You do not listen. I scream out to You
3 "violence!" yet You bring no salvation. Why then do You show me this evil?
You who see the oppression, why are ruin and corruption before me so
4 that strife endures and contention rises? This then is why law will cease to
exist and justice will never prevail, for the wicked besiege the righteous,
5 and justice becomes twisted. Look around at the nations and witness: feel
stunned, bewildered, for I will perform a deed in these very days that you
6 would not believe if you were told. For behold, I am raising up the Chaldeans,
that harsh and impetuous nation that sweeps the span of the earth seizing
7 homes not theirs – they the dreaded and terrifying who alone dictate law
8 and power. Their horses run faster even than leopards, fiercer than wolves of
the night; their horsemen advance all over. They come from far; horsemen
9 come flying like a vulture swooping swiftly to devour its prey. They come
intent on violence, their faces relentless as the east wind, and amass captives
10 countless as sand. They ridicule kings and scorn rulers; every fortress is a
11 mockery to them; they pile dirt for siege ramps, and the city falls. But then
they will pass through as the wind blows and be held guilty, they who made
12 their power their god. But surely You are eternal, O Lord my God, my Holy
One, You who will never die. You, Lord, have assigned them to judge; You,
13 my Rock, have appointed them to rebuke. You, with eyes too pure for seeing
evil, who cannot witness oppression, how then can You look upon the wicked
and remain silent? How can You allow the evil man to devour a person more
14 righteous than he? How could You make man like fish in the sea, like creeping
15 creatures with none watching over them? For they will all be caught by the
fishhook, entangled in their net and gathered up into their trawl; this will
16 bring them happiness, make them rejoice. And so they worship their net,
make offerings to their trawl; because of them their portions are plump, their
17 food plentiful. And so they empty their nets and with no mercy return to
2 1 slaughtering nations. I stand watch at my post; I will not move from
my lookout; I wait to see what God will say to me and how I will respond to
2 the rebuke. And the Lord answered me saying: Write the vison clearly onto
3 the tablets so that all may read it readily. For there will be yet another vision
in due time; it will be a witness to the end and not deceive. Though it lingers,

וְטַפְסְרַיִךְ כְּגוֹב גֹּבָי הַחוֹנִים בַּגְּדֵרוֹת בְּיוֹם קָרָה שֶׁמֶשׁ זָרְחָה וְנוֹדַד
יח וְלֹא־נוֹדַע מְקוֹמוֹ אַיָּם׃ נָמוּ רֹעֶיךָ מֶלֶךְ אַשּׁוּר יִשְׁכְּנוּ אַדִּירֶיךָ נָפֹשׁוּ
יט עַמְּךָ עַל־הֶהָרִים וְאֵין מְקַבֵּץ׃ אֵין־כֵּהָה לְשִׁבְרֶךָ נַחְלָה מַכָּתֶךָ כֹּל ׀
שֹׁמְעֵי שִׁמְעֲךָ תָּקְעוּ כַף עָלֶיךָ כִּי עַל־מִי לֹא־עָבְרָה רָעָתְךָ תָּמִיד׃

יג חבקוק

א א ב הַמַּשָּׂא אֲשֶׁר חָזָה חֲבַקּוּק הַנָּבִיא׃ עַד־אָנָה יְהוָה שִׁוַּעְתִּי וְלֹא תִשְׁמָע
ג אֶזְעַק אֵלֶיךָ חָמָס וְלֹא תוֹשִׁיעַ׃ לָמָּה תַרְאֵנִי אָוֶן וְעָמָל תַּבִּיט וְשֹׁד
ד וְחָמָס לְנֶגְדִּי וַיְהִי רִיב וּמָדוֹן יִשָּׂא׃ עַל־כֵּן תָּפוּג תּוֹרָה וְלֹא־יֵצֵא לָנֶצַח
ה מִשְׁפָּט כִּי רָשָׁע מַכְתִּיר אֶת־הַצַּדִּיק עַל־כֵּן יֵצֵא מִשְׁפָּט מְעֻקָּל׃ רְאוּ
בַגּוֹיִם וְהַבִּיטוּ וְהִתַּמְּהוּ תְּמָהוּ כִּי־פֹעַל פֹּעֵל בִּימֵיכֶם לֹא תַאֲמִינוּ
ו כִּי יְסֻפָּר׃ כִּי־הִנְנִי מֵקִים אֶת־הַכַּשְׂדִּים הַגּוֹי הַמַּר וְהַנִּמְהָר הַהוֹלֵךְ
ז לְמֶרְחֲבֵי־אֶרֶץ לָרֶשֶׁת מִשְׁכָּנוֹת לֹּא־לוֹ׃ אָיֹם וְנוֹרָא הוּא מִמֶּנּוּ מִשְׁפָּטוֹ
ח וּשְׂאֵתוֹ יֵצֵא׃ וְקַלּוּ מִנְּמֵרִים סוּסָיו וְחַדּוּ מִזְּאֵבֵי עֶרֶב וּפָשׁוּ פָּרָשָׁיו
ט וּפָרָשָׁיו מֵרָחוֹק יָבֹאוּ יָעֻפוּ כְּנֶשֶׁר חָשׁ לֶאֱכוֹל׃ כֻּלֹּה לְחָמָס יָבוֹא
י מְגַמַּת פְּנֵיהֶם קָדִימָה וַיֶּאֱסֹף כַּחוֹל שֶׁבִי׃ וְהוּא בַּמְּלָכִים יִתְקַלָּס וְרֹזְנִים
יא מִשְׂחָק לוֹ הוּא לְכָל־מִבְצָר יִשְׂחָק וַיִּצְבֹּר עָפָר וַיִּלְכְּדָהּ׃ אָז חָלַף רוּחַ
יב וַיַּעֲבֹר וְאָשֵׁם זוּ כֹחוֹ לֵאלֹהוֹ׃ הֲלוֹא אַתָּה מִקֶּדֶם יְהוָה אֱלֹהַי קְדֹשִׁי
יג לֹא נָמוּת יְהוָה לְמִשְׁפָּט שַׂמְתּוֹ וְצוּר לְהוֹכִיחַ יְסַדְתּוֹ׃ טְהוֹר עֵינַיִם
מֵרְאוֹת רָע וְהַבִּיט אֶל־עָמָל לֹא תוּכָל לָמָּה תַבִּיט בּוֹגְדִים תַּחֲרִישׁ
יד בְּבַלַּע רָשָׁע צַדִּיק מִמֶּנּוּ׃ וַתַּעֲשֶׂה אָדָם כִּדְגֵי הַיָּם כְּרֶמֶשׂ לֹא־מֹשֵׁל
טו בּוֹ׃ כֻּלֹּה בְּחַכָּה הֵעֲלָה יְגֹרֵהוּ בְחֶרְמוֹ וְיַאַסְפֵהוּ בְּמִכְמַרְתּוֹ עַל־כֵּן
טז יִשְׂמַח וְיָגִיל׃ עַל־כֵּן יְזַבֵּחַ לְחֶרְמוֹ וִיקַטֵּר לְמִכְמַרְתּוֹ כִּי בָהֵמָּה שָׁמֵן
יז חֶלְקוֹ וּמַאֲכָלוֹ בְּרִאָה׃ הַעַל כֵּן יָרִיק חֶרְמוֹ וְתָמִיד לַהֲרֹג גּוֹיִם לֹא
ב א יַחְמוֹל׃ עַל־מִשְׁמַרְתִּי אֶעֱמֹדָה וְאֶתְיַצְּבָה עַל־מָצוֹר
ב וַאֲצַפֶּה לִרְאוֹת מַה־יְדַבֶּר־בִּי וּמָה אָשִׁיב עַל־תּוֹכַחְתִּי׃ וַיַּעֲנֵנִי יְהוָה
ג וַיֹּאמֶר כְּתֹב חָזוֹן וּבָאֵר עַל־הַלֻּחוֹת לְמַעַן יָרוּץ קוֹרֵא בוֹ׃ כִּי עוֹד חָזוֹן
לַמּוֹעֵד וְיָפֵחַ לַקֵּץ וְלֹא יְכַזֵּב אִם־יִתְמַהְמַהּ חַכֵּה־לוֹ כִּי־בֹא יָבֹא לֹא

4 wait for it, for when the time is right it will come; it will not delay. For behold –
the arrogant man his life will not be upright but the righteous man lives on
5 by his faith. And just as wine betrays its drinker, so too the haughty man is
betrayed by his pride and knows no peace. His greedy mouth gapes wide
like Sheol;[1] like death he swallows and is never sated. Yet he conquers all
6 nations around him and amasses all peoples to himself. Surely all these people
tell tales of him, sneer and mock him, saying: Woe unto him who greedily
takes what is not his; for how long will he weigh himself down, heavily in
7 debt? Suddenly your moneylenders will rise against you; they will wake you
8 and shake you, and you will be their spoils. And as you plundered countless
nations, so too all remaining nations will plunder you for men's blood you
9 spilt, for your assault upon lands, the city, and all its inhabitants. Woe
to him who garners evil gains, who brings ruin upon his home, who places
10 his nest up high to keep himself out of harm's way. You brought shame upon
your household; you destroyed many nations; you are a sinner in your
11 essence. Even the stone set in the wall cries out, and the wooden rafters
12 answer. Woe to him who builds a city with bloodshed, who founds
13 a town upon iniquity. Is this not then from the LORD of Hosts when peoples
14 toil for the flames and nations weary themselves for naught? For then, the
earth will be filled with knowledge of the LORD's splendor as waters cover the
15 ocean floor.[2] Woe to him who offers his companions drink, spiking
it with wrath; he draws them into a drunken stupor to see their nakedness.
16 You, sated by scandal rather than filled with glory, now you too drink from the
poisoned cup and become exposed; the cup of the LORD's right hand will turn
17 upon you, and shame will replace your glory. Your destruction of Lebanon
will cover you with disgrace, and the beasts you reduced to ruin will make
you afraid for men's blood you spilt, for your assault upon lands, the city, and
18 all its inhabitants. Of what value is an idol created by a craftsman, an
image by a master of falsehood? For the craftsman puts faith in his handiwork
19 but instead crafts mute idols. Woe unto him that says to the wood,
"Awake!" To the lifeless stone, "Arise!" Can it teach us? Behold, it is wrapped
20 with gold and with silver, but no spirit breathes within it. But the LORD is in
3 1 His heavenly dwelling. All the earth, be silent before Him. A prayer
2 Ḥavakuk the prophet sung with *shiggayon*:[3] LORD, I have heard accounts of
You and am afraid. O LORD, in the coming years renew Your deeds; in the
3 coming years, make Yourself known; in wrath, remember mercy. God appears
from Teiman, the Holy One from Mount Paran.[4] Selah[5] His splendor
4 covers the heavens; the earth is filled with His glory. His radiance illuminates
like light; rays emanate from His every side; therein lies His hidden strength.
5 6 Before Him will come plague, fiery blight at His feet. He stands and the earth

1 | The netherworld.
2 | Cf. Isaiah 11:9.
3 | Perhaps a tune or musical instrument; cf. Psalms 7:1.
4 | Localities in the southern desert.
5 | A liturgical or musical term of unknown meaning.

ד ה יְאַחֵר׃ הִנֵּה עֻפְּלָה לֹא־יָשְׁרָה נַפְשׁוֹ בּוֹ וְצַדִּיק בֶּאֱמוּנָתוֹ יִחְיֶה׃ וְאַף
כִּי־הַיַּיִן בֹּגֵד גֶּבֶר יָהִיר וְלֹא יִנְוֶה אֲשֶׁר הִרְחִיב כִּשְׁאוֹל נַפְשׁוֹ וְהוּא
כַמָּוֶת וְלֹא יִשְׂבָּע וַיֶּאֱסֹף אֵלָיו כָּל־הַגּוֹיִם וַיִּקְבֹּץ אֵלָיו כָּל־הָעַמִּים׃
ו הֲלוֹא־אֵלֶּה כֻלָּם עָלָיו מָשָׁל יִשָּׂאוּ וּמְלִיצָה חִידוֹת לוֹ וְיֹאמַר הוֹי
ז הַמַּרְבֶּה לֹּא־לוֹ עַד־מָתַי וּמַכְבִּיד עָלָיו עַבְטִיט׃ הֲלוֹא פֶתַע יָקוּמוּ
ח נֹשְׁכֶיךָ וְיִקְצוּ מְזַעְזְעֶיךָ וְהָיִיתָ לִמְשִׁסּוֹת לָמוֹ׃ כִּי־אַתָּה שַׁלּוֹתָ גּוֹיִם
רַבִּים יְשָׁלּוּךָ כָּל־יֶתֶר עַמִּים מִדְּמֵי אָדָם וַחֲמַס־אֶרֶץ קִרְיָה וְכָל־יֹשְׁבֵי
ט בָהּ׃ הוֹי בֹּצֵעַ בֶּצַע רָע לְבֵיתוֹ לָשׂוּם בַּמָּרוֹם קִנּוֹ לְהִנָּצֵל
י יא מִכַּף־רָע׃ יָעַצְתָּ בֹּשֶׁת לְבֵיתֶךָ קְצוֹת־עַמִּים רַבִּים וְחוֹטֵא נַפְשֶׁךָ׃ כִּי־
יב אֶבֶן מִקִּיר תִּזְעָק וְכָפִיס מֵעֵץ יַעֲנֶנָּה׃ הוֹי בֹּנֶה עִיר בְּדָמִים
יג וְכוֹנֵן קִרְיָה בְּעַוְלָה׃ הֲלוֹא הִנֵּה מֵאֵת יְהוָה צְבָאוֹת וְיִיגְעוּ עַמִּים בְּדֵי־
יד אֵשׁ וּלְאֻמִּים בְּדֵי־רִיק יִעָפוּ׃ כִּי תִּמָּלֵא הָאָרֶץ לָדַעַת אֶת־כְּבוֹד יְהוָה
טו כַּמַּיִם יְכַסּוּ עַל־יָם׃ הוֹי מַשְׁקֵה רֵעֵהוּ מְסַפֵּחַ חֲמָתְךָ וְאַף
טז שַׁכֵּר לְמַעַן הַבִּיט עַל־מְעוֹרֵיהֶם׃ שָׂבַעְתָּ קָלוֹן מִכָּבוֹד שְׁתֵה גַם־אַתָּה
יז וְהֵעָרֵל תִּסּוֹב עָלֶיךָ כּוֹס יְמִין יְהוָה וְקִיקָלוֹן עַל־כְּבוֹדֶךָ׃ כִּי־חֲמַס לְבָנוֹן
יְכַסֶּךָּ וְשֹׁד בְּהֵמוֹת יְחִיתַן מִדְּמֵי אָדָם וַחֲמַס־אֶרֶץ קִרְיָה וְכָל־יֹשְׁבֵי
יח בָהּ׃ מָה־הוֹעִיל פֶּסֶל כִּי פְסָלוֹ יֹצְרוֹ מַסֵּכָה וּמוֹרֶה שָּׁקֶר
יט כִּי בָטַח יֹצֵר יִצְרוֹ עָלָיו לַעֲשׂוֹת אֱלִילִים אִלְּמִים׃ הוֹי
אֹמֵר לָעֵץ הָקִיצָה עוּרִי לְאֶבֶן דּוּמָם הוּא יוֹרֶה הִנֵּה־הוּא תָּפוּשׂ
כ זָהָב וָכֶסֶף וְכָל־רוּחַ אֵין בְּקִרְבּוֹ׃ וַיהוָה בְּהֵיכַל קָדְשׁוֹ הַס מִפָּנָיו כָּל־
ג א ב הָאָרֶץ׃ תְּפִלָּה לַחֲבַקּוּק הַנָּבִיא עַל שִׁגְיֹנוֹת׃ יְהוָה
שָׁמַעְתִּי שִׁמְעֲךָ יָרֵאתִי יְהוָה פָּעָלְךָ בְּקֶרֶב שָׁנִים חַיֵּיהוּ בְּקֶרֶב שָׁנִים
ג תּוֹדִיעַ בְּרֹגֶז רַחֵם תִּזְכּוֹר׃ אֱלוֹהַּ מִתֵּימָן יָבוֹא וְקָדוֹשׁ מֵהַר־פָּארָן סֶלָה
ד כִּסָּה שָׁמַיִם הוֹדוֹ וּתְהִלָּתוֹ מָלְאָה הָאָרֶץ׃ וְנֹגַהּ כָּאוֹר תִּהְיֶה קַרְנַיִם
ה ו מִיָּדוֹ לוֹ וְשָׁם חֶבְיוֹן עֻזֹּה׃ לְפָנָיו יֵלֶךְ דָּבֶר וְיֵצֵא רֶשֶׁף לְרַגְלָיו׃ עָמַד ׀

shakes; He looks and nations tremble; age-old mountains shatter; everlasting
7 hills bow low; all the world's ways are His. I saw Kushan's tents afflicted for
8 sinning, the curtains[6] in the land of Midyan quiver. Is the LORD
angry at the rivers; is it against the rivers that You rage? Is Your fury against the
ocean so that You ride upon Your horses of war, Your chariots of deliverance?
9 Your bow is unsheathed; You keep Your word, Your oath to the tribes, Selah,
10 and split the earth open with rivers. When the mountains see You they shiver;
streams of water flow through; the deep sounds with thunder, lifting its hands
11 up high. The sun, the moon stand still in their spheres;by the light of Your
12 bolts the world will march, by the glow of Your flashing spear. In rage, You
13 tread the earth; in wrath, You trample nations. You emerge to liberate Your
people, to liberate Your king. You crush the head of the house of evil, stripping
14 it from the core up to its neck, Selah. You pierce heads
of cities with their own spears, they who come in a storm to shatter me,
15 rejoicing as though secretly devouring the needy. You trample the ocean
16 floor with Your steeds, stirring mighty seas. I hear this, and my gut churns;
my lips tremble at the sound. Rot eats at my bones; I shudder in my place.
Could I rest on the day of terror, the day God rises up for His nation?
17 Though the fig tree will not flower, nor will fruit fill the vines, olives will
grow gaunt and grain fields yield no produce, sheep will be removed from
18 their pens, and cattle will not be found in the sheds, yet I will delight in
19 the LORD; I will rejoice in the God who will save me. GOD, my Lord,
my strength, He makes my legs like a deer's and guides me to stride to
the heights. This song is for the conductor; to Him I offer my melodies.

TZEFANYA/ZEPHANIAH

1 1 This is the word of the LORD that came to Tzefanya son of Kushi son of
Gedalya son of Amarya son of Ḥizkiya in the days of Yoshiyahu son of Amon,
2 king of Yehuda: I will erase everything utterly from the face of the earth,
3 declares the LORD. I will erase man and animal, birds of the sky and fish of
the sea; misfortune will find the evil men. I will sever man from the face of
4 the earth, so the LORD declares. My hand will strike Yehuda and all who dwell
in Jerusalem. I will sever every trace of Baal from this place, every mention of
5 pagan priests among priests; those who bow before the hosts of the heavens
on rooftops and those who serve and swear loyalty to the LORD and to
6 Malkam[1] side by side; those who have renounced the LORD and those who
7 never sought out the LORD nor entreated Him. Fall silent before the Lord
GOD, for the day of the LORD is near; the LORD has readied a sacrificial feast;
8 His guests have been selected. On the day of the LORD's
feast I will punish ministers, and kings' sons, and all who dress in foreign
9 clothes. On that day I will punish all who leap over the threshold in the

6 | That is, tent canvases.

1 | God of the Amonites; see II Kings 23:13.

וַיְמֹדֶד אֶרֶץ רָאָה וַיַּתֵּר גּוֹיִם וַיִּתְפֹּצְצוּ הַרְרֵי־עַד שַׁחוּ גִּבְעוֹת עוֹלָם
ז הֲלִיכוֹת עוֹלָם לוֹ׃ תַּחַת אָוֶן רָאִיתִי אׇהֳלֵי כוּשָׁן יִרְגְּזוּן יְרִיעוֹת אֶרֶץ
ח מִדְיָן׃ הֲבִנְהָרִים חָרָה יְהוָה אִם בַּנְּהָרִים אַפֶּךָ אִם־בַּיָּם
ט עֶבְרָתֶךָ כִּי תִרְכַּב עַל־סוּסֶיךָ מַרְכְּבֹתֶיךָ יְשׁוּעָה׃ עֶרְיָה תֵעוֹר קַשְׁתֶּךָ
י שְׁבֻעוֹת מַטּוֹת אֹמֶר סֶלָה נְהָרוֹת תְּבַקַּע־אָרֶץ׃ רָאוּךָ יָחִילוּ הָרִים
יא זֶרֶם מַיִם עָבָר נָתַן תְּהוֹם קוֹלוֹ רוֹם יָדֵיהוּ נָשָׂא׃ שֶׁמֶשׁ יָרֵחַ עָמַד זְבֻלָה
יב לְאוֹר חִצֶּיךָ יְהַלֵּכוּ לְנֹגַהּ בְּרַק חֲנִיתֶךָ׃ בְּזַעַם תִּצְעַד־אָרֶץ בְּאַף תָּדוּשׁ
יג גּוֹיִם׃ יָצָאתָ לְיֵשַׁע עַמֶּךָ לְיֵשַׁע אֶת־מְשִׁיחֶךָ מָחַצְתָּ רֹּאשׁ מִבֵּית רָשָׁע
יד עָרוֹת יְסוֹד עַד־צַוָּאר סֶלָה׃ נָקַבְתָּ בְמַטָּיו רֹאשׁ
טו פְּרָזָו יִסְעֲרוּ לַהֲפִיצֵנִי עֲלִיצֻתָם כְּמוֹ־לֶאֱכֹל עָנִי בַּמִּסְתָּר׃ דָּרַכְתָּ
טז בַיָּם סוּסֶיךָ חֹמֶר מַיִם רַבִּים׃ שָׁמַעְתִּי ׀ וַתִּרְגַּז בִּטְנִי לְקוֹל צָלְלוּ
שְׂפָתַי יָבוֹא רָקָב בַּעֲצָמַי וְתַחְתַּי אֶרְגָּז אֲשֶׁר אָנוּחַ לְיוֹם צָרָה
יז לַעֲלוֹת לְעַם יְגוּדֶנּוּ׃ כִּי־תְאֵנָה לֹא־תִפְרָח וְאֵין יְבוּל בַּגְּפָנִים כִּחֵשׁ
מַעֲשֵׂה־זַיִת וּשְׁדֵמוֹת לֹא־עָשָׂה אֹכֶל גָּזַר מִמִּכְלָה צֹאן וְאֵין בָּקָר
יח יט בָּרְפָתִים׃ וַאֲנִי בַּיהוָה אֶעְלוֹזָה אָגִילָה בֵּאלֹהֵי יִשְׁעִי׃ יְהוִה אֲדֹנָי
חֵילִי וַיָּשֶׂם רַגְלַי כָּאַיָּלוֹת וְעַל־בָּמוֹתַי יַדְרִכֵנִי לַמְנַצֵּחַ בִּנְגִינוֹתָי׃

יד צפניה

א א דְּבַר־יְהוָה ׀ אֲשֶׁר הָיָה אֶל־צְפַנְיָה בֶּן־כּוּשִׁי בֶן־גְּדַלְיָה בֶּן־אֲמַרְיָה
ב בֶּן־חִזְקִיָּה בִּימֵי יֹאשִׁיָּהוּ בֶן־אָמוֹן מֶלֶךְ יְהוּדָה׃ אָסֹף אָסֵף כֹּל מֵעַל
ג פְּנֵי הָאֲדָמָה נְאֻם־יְהוָה׃ אָסֵף אָדָם וּבְהֵמָה אָסֵף עוֹף־הַשָּׁמַיִם וּדְגֵי
הַיָּם וְהַמַּכְשֵׁלוֹת אֶת־הָרְשָׁעִים וְהִכְרַתִּי אֶת־הָאָדָם מֵעַל פְּנֵי הָאֲדָמָה
ד נְאֻם־יְהוָה׃ וְנָטִיתִי יָדִי עַל־יְהוּדָה וְעַל כׇּל־יוֹשְׁבֵי יְרוּשָׁלָ͏ִם וְהִכְרַתִּי
מִן־הַמָּקוֹם הַזֶּה אֶת־שְׁאָר הַבַּעַל אֶת־שֵׁם הַכְּמָרִים עִם־הַכֹּהֲנִים׃
ה וְאֶת־הַמִּשְׁתַּחֲוִים עַל־הַגַּגּוֹת לִצְבָא הַשָּׁמָיִם וְאֶת־הַמִּשְׁתַּחֲוִים
ו הַנִּשְׁבָּעִים לַיהוָה וְהַנִּשְׁבָּעִים בְּמַלְכָּם׃ וְאֶת־הַנְּסוֹגִים מֵאַחֲרֵי יְהוָה
ז וַאֲשֶׁר לֹא־בִקְשׁוּ אֶת־יְהוָה וְלֹא דְרָשֻׁהוּ׃ הַס מִפְּנֵי אֲדֹנָי יְהוִה כִּי קָרוֹב
ח יוֹם יְהוָה כִּי־הֵכִין יְהוָה זֶבַח הִקְדִּישׁ קְרֻאָיו׃ וְהָיָה בְּיוֹם
זֶבַח יְהוָה וּפָקַדְתִּי עַל־הַשָּׂרִים וְעַל־בְּנֵי הַמֶּלֶךְ וְעַל כׇּל־הַלֹּבְשִׁים
ט מַלְבּוּשׁ נׇכְרִי׃ וּפָקַדְתִּי עַל כׇּל־הַדּוֹלֵג עַל־הַמִּפְתָּן בַּיּוֹם הַהוּא

manner of idolaters,[2] and all who fill their master's palace with violence and
10 vice. On this day, the LORD declares, a cry will be heard from the
Fish Gate,[3] wailing from the second quarter, and a shattering heartbreak from
11 the hills. Wail, you residents of the Makhtesh: the merchants have been
12 destroyed; those weighed down by silver have been cut down. And
it shall come to pass: I shall search Jerusalem with lamps; I will punish men
who have settled like sediment, saying in their hearts that the LORD can do
13 neither good nor harm. Their wealth will be pillaged, their homes laid waste;
they will build houses but not dwell in them, plant vineyards but not drink
14 of their wine.[4] The terrible day of the LORD is near; swiftly it draws near. The
15 LORD's day will resound with bitter cries of brave men. That day will be a day
of wrath, a day of trouble and torment, a day of destruction and desolation,
16 a day of darkness and dread, a day of concealment and clouds, a day of
blasting horns and trumpets of battle against the fortified cities and fortressed
17 towers. I will besiege men with troubles; they shall walk as if blind, for
they have sinned against the LORD, and their blood shall spill like dust, their
18 flesh scattered like dung. Neither their silver nor their gold will save them.
On the day of the LORD's wrath, in the fire of His fury, all the land will be
consumed; for He will bring an end, a shocking end to all who dwell in the
2 1 land. Gather yourselves together, collect yourselves, O you unwanted
2 nation, before the ruling bears down upon you, and the moment blows away
like chaff, before the LORD's wrath befalls you, before the day of the LORD's
3 rage comes upon you. Seek out the LORD, all you humble folk who have
followed His Law. Pursue righteousness, pursue decency; possibly you might
4 find refuge on the day of the LORD's wrath. For Aza shall be deserted and
Ashkelon desolate; Ashdod will be purged of its people in broad daylight and
5 Ekron ripped from its roots.[5] Woe, coastland dwellers, people of
Keretim; the word of the LORD is averse to you; O Canaan, land of the
6 Philistines, I shall destroy you until no man remains. And the coastland will
7 serve as pastures for shepherds, pens and sheepfolds for flocks. Those left of
the House of Yehuda will be allotted this land; here their flocks will feed.
Come evening their animals will lie down to rest in the houses of Ashkelon,
when the LORD their God will remember them and will restore them to their
8 richness. I have heard the slanderous smears of Moav and the children of
Amon's taunting as they ridiculed My people and gloated over their borders.
9 So says the LORD of Hosts, the God of Israel: As surely as I live, Moav shall
become as Sedom and the children of Amon as Amora – a land of rustling
thorny thistles and stark salt pits, a desolation everlasting. My returning
nation shall savor their spoils; the survivors of My people shall stake their
10 claim. This, then, is what they will receive for their arrogance, their slandering,
11 their gloating over the nation of the LORD of Hosts. The LORD will inflict His

2 | See, e.g., I Samuel 5:5 for this practice.
3 | This and the following were localities in Jerusalem.
4 | Cf. Deuteronomy 20:5–7 and 28:30. Contrast with Deuteronomy 6:10–11.
5 | These curses are alliterative in Hebrew (e.g., *Azza azuva*).

י הַמְמַלְאִים בֵּית אֲדֹנֵיהֶם חָמָס וּמִרְמָה׃ וְהָיָה בַיּוֹם הַהוּא
נְאֻם־יְהֹוָה קוֹל צְעָקָה מִשַּׁעַר הַדָּגִים וִילָלָה מִן־הַמִּשְׁנֶה וְשֶׁבֶר גָּדוֹל
יא מֵהַגְּבָעוֹת׃ הֵילִילוּ יֹשְׁבֵי הַמַּכְתֵּשׁ כִּי נִדְמָה כָּל־עַם כְּנַעַן נִכְרְתוּ כָּל־
יב נְטִילֵי כָסֶף׃ וְהָיָה בָּעֵת הַהִיא אֲחַפֵּשׂ אֶת־יְרוּשָׁלִַם בַּנֵּרוֹת
וּפָקַדְתִּי עַל־הָאֲנָשִׁים הַקֹּפְאִים עַל־שִׁמְרֵיהֶם הָאֹמְרִים בִּלְבָבָם
יג לֹא־יֵיטִיב יְהֹוָה וְלֹא יָרֵעַ׃ וְהָיָה חֵילָם לִמְשִׁסָּה וּבָתֵּיהֶם לִשְׁמָמָה
יד וּבָנוּ בָתִּים וְלֹא יֵשֵׁבוּ וְנָטְעוּ כְרָמִים וְלֹא יִשְׁתּוּ אֶת־יֵינָם׃ קָרוֹב יוֹם־
טו יְהֹוָה הַגָּדוֹל קָרוֹב וּמַהֵר מְאֹד קוֹל יוֹם יְהֹוָה מַר צֹרֵחַ שָׁם גִּבּוֹר׃ יוֹם
עֶבְרָה הַיּוֹם הַהוּא יוֹם צָרָה וּמְצוּקָה יוֹם שֹׁאָה וּמְשׁוֹאָה יוֹם חֹשֶׁךְ
טז וַאֲפֵלָה יוֹם עָנָן וַעֲרָפֶל׃ יוֹם שׁוֹפָר וּתְרוּעָה עַל הֶעָרִים הַבְּצֻרוֹת וְעַל
יז הַפִּנּוֹת הַגְּבֹהוֹת׃ וַהֲצֵרֹתִי לָאָדָם וְהָלְכוּ כַּעִוְרִים כִּי לַיהֹוָה חָטָאוּ
יח וְשֻׁפַּךְ דָּמָם כֶּעָפָר וּלְחֻמָם כַּגְּלָלִים׃ גַּם־כַּסְפָּם גַּם־זְהָבָם לֹא־יוּכַל
לְהַצִּילָם בְּיוֹם עֶבְרַת יְהֹוָה וּבְאֵשׁ קִנְאָתוֹ תֵּאָכֵל כָּל־הָאָרֶץ כִּי־כָלָה
ב א אַךְ־נִבְהָלָה יַעֲשֶׂה אֵת כָּל־יֹשְׁבֵי הָאָרֶץ׃ הִתְקוֹשְׁשׁוּ וָקוֹשּׁוּ
ב הַגּוֹי לֹא נִכְסָף׃ בְּטֶרֶם לֶדֶת חֹק כְּמֹץ עָבַר יוֹם בְּטֶרֶם ׀ לֹא־יָבוֹא
ג עֲלֵיכֶם חֲרוֹן אַף־יְהֹוָה בְּטֶרֶם לֹא־יָבוֹא עֲלֵיכֶם יוֹם אַף־יְהֹוָה׃ בַּקְּשׁוּ
אֶת־יְהֹוָה כָּל־עַנְוֵי הָאָרֶץ אֲשֶׁר מִשְׁפָּטוֹ פָּעָלוּ בַּקְּשׁוּ־צֶדֶק בַּקְּשׁוּ
ד עֲנָוָה אוּלַי תִּסָּתְרוּ בְּיוֹם אַף־יְהֹוָה׃ כִּי עַזָּה עֲזוּבָה תִהְיֶה וְאַשְׁקְלוֹן
ה לִשְׁמָמָה אַשְׁדּוֹד בַּצָּהֳרַיִם יְגָרְשׁוּהָ וְעֶקְרוֹן תֵּעָקֵר׃ הוֹי
יֹשְׁבֵי חֶבֶל הַיָּם גּוֹי כְּרֵתִים דְּבַר־יְהֹוָה עֲלֵיכֶם כְּנַעַן אֶרֶץ פְּלִשְׁתִּים
ו וְהַאֲבַדְתִּיךְ מֵאֵין יוֹשֵׁב׃ וְהָיְתָה חֶבֶל הַיָּם נְוֹת כְּרֹת רֹעִים וְגִדְרוֹת צֹאן׃
ז וְהָיָה חֶבֶל לִשְׁאֵרִית בֵּית יְהוּדָה עֲלֵיהֶם יִרְעוּן בְּבָתֵּי אַשְׁקְלוֹן בָּעֶרֶב
ח יִרְבָּצוּן כִּי יִפְקְדֵם יְהֹוָה אֱלֹהֵיהֶם וְשָׁב שבותם׃ שָׁמַעְתִּי חֶרְפַּת מוֹאָב שְׁבִיתָם
ט וְגִדּוּפֵי בְּנֵי עַמּוֹן אֲשֶׁר חֵרְפוּ אֶת־עַמִּי וַיַּגְדִּילוּ עַל־גְּבוּלָם׃ לָכֵן חַי־אָנִי
נְאֻם יְהֹוָה צְבָאוֹת אֱלֹהֵי יִשְׂרָאֵל כִּי מוֹאָב כִּסְדֹם תִּהְיֶה וּבְנֵי עַמּוֹן
כַּעֲמֹרָה מִמְשַׁק חָרוּל וּמִכְרֵה־מֶלַח וּשְׁמָמָה עַד־עוֹלָם שְׁאֵרִית עַמִּי
י יְבָזּוּם וְיֶתֶר גּוֹי יִנְחָלוּם׃ זֹאת לָהֶם תַּחַת גְּאוֹנָם כִּי חֵרְפוּ וַיַּגְדִּלוּ עַל־
יא עַם יְהֹוָה צְבָאוֹת׃ נוֹרָא יְהֹוָה עֲלֵיהֶם כִּי רָזָה אֵת כָּל־אֱלֹהֵי הָאָרֶץ

terror upon them, causing every earthly god to wither and nations widespread
12 to kneel down to Him, each person from where he stands. Even you Kushites,
13 you too will become victims of My sword. He will reach His hand out to the
North and destroy Assyria; He will reduce Nineveh to a desolate wasteland,
14 to parched desert dryness. Herds from every land will lie down in her midst;
both the pelican and the short-eared owl will nest in the crevices of her
columns, their caws heard from the windows, destruction seen from her
15 doorways, for the cedar rooftops have crumbled to ruins. This, then, was the
joyous city, living without a care, saying in her heart, "I am superior; there is
none beside me." Alas, she has become a desolate lair for beasts, with every
passerby hissing and scornfully waving her off with his hand.
3 1 Woe
2 to her who is sullied and stained, this city of deceit. She who did not heed the
voice, she refused reproach. In the LORD she has not placed her trust; to her
3 God she has not drawn herself close. Sitting amidst her, her rulers roar like
lions over their prey; her judges, wolves of the night, do not leave even a bone
4 for morning. Her prophets are brazen men of treachery; her priests have
5 profaned the holy, pillaged the Law. The LORD, righteous within her midst,
does no wrong; morning after morning, unfailingly, His judgment comes
6 to light – but still the culprit knows no shame. I have severed nations; their
fortresses lie abandoned. I have turned their bustling boulevards into ruins
empty of passersby; their cities, destroyed, have become desolate – no
7 man remains. I said to Myself: Surely this will bring you to fear Me, to heed
My reproaches; then her home will not be wiped out, and all that I have
designed against her will not befall – but alas, eagerly they arose and remained
8 unrelenting in their corrupt ways. So says the LORD: Only wait for Me, wait
for the day when I stand up in judgment once and for all. For it is My decree
to gather the nations, to amass the kingdoms; I will pour out My wrath upon
them, all My burning anger, and all the earth shall be consumed by the fire of
9 My rage. Then I will transform the people's language and turn their words
into clear, clean speech so that they may call upon the name of the LORD and
10 serve Him shoulder to shoulder. From beyond the rivers of Kush, even the
11 peoples of Atarai and the daughter of Putzai[6] will pay Me tribute. On that day
you will no longer know shame for all the corrupt ways in which you have
sinned against Me, for I will remove from your midst those elated with pride,
12 and you shall no longer stand haughtily on My sacred mountain. I will leave
the humble and destitute among you, and they will find refuge in the LORD's
13 name. They who remain of Israel shall do no wrong; they will speak no lies,
and words of deceit will not be found upon their lips. Like sheep they will
graze and lie down, and none shall cause them alarm.
14 Sing out,
daughter Zion; shout for joy, Israel; be jubilant and rejoice wholeheartedly,
15 daughter Jerusalem. The LORD has withdrawn His judgment; He has banished
your foes. The LORD, King of Israel, is within you; you will no longer fear
evil.
16 Jerusalem on that day will be told: Zion, do not be afraid; do

6 | The identities of these peoples are unclear. Others understand *atarai* to mean "my supplicants" and *bat putzai* as "my scattered people."

יב וְיִשְׁתַּחֲווּ־לוֹ אִישׁ מִמְּקוֹמוֹ כֹּל אִיֵּי הַגּוֹיִם: גַּם־אַתֶּם כּוּשִׁים חַלְלֵי חַרְבִּי
יג הֵמָּה: וְיֵט יָדוֹ עַל־צָפוֹן וִיאַבֵּד אֶת־אַשּׁוּר וְיָשֵׂם אֶת־נִינְוֵה לִשְׁמָמָה
יד צִיָּה כַּמִּדְבָּר: וְרָבְצוּ בְתוֹכָהּ עֲדָרִים כָּל־חַיְתוֹ־גוֹי גַּם־קָאַת גַּם־
קִפֹּד בְּכַפְתֹּרֶיהָ יָלִינוּ קוֹל יְשׁוֹרֵר בַּחַלּוֹן חֹרֶב בַּסַּף כִּי אַרְזָה עֵרָה:
טו זֹאת הָעִיר הָעַלִּיזָה הַיּוֹשֶׁבֶת לָבֶטַח הָאֹמְרָה בִּלְבָבָהּ אֲנִי וְאַפְסִי
עוֹד אֵיךְ ׀ הָיְתָה לְשַׁמָּה מַרְבֵּץ לַחַיָּה כֹּל עוֹבֵר עָלֶיהָ יִשְׁרֹק יָנִיעַ
ג א ב יָדוֹ: הוֹי מֹרְאָה וְנִגְאָלָה הָעִיר הַיּוֹנָה: לֹא שָׁמְעָה בְּקוֹל לֹא
ג לָקְחָה מוּסָר בַּיהוה לֹא בָטָחָה אֶל־אֱלֹהֶיהָ לֹא קָרֵבָה: שָׂרֶיהָ בְקִרְבָּהּ
ד אֲרָיוֹת שֹׁאֲגִים שֹׁפְטֶיהָ זְאֵבֵי עֶרֶב לֹא גָרְמוּ לַבֹּקֶר: נְבִיאֶיהָ פֹּחֲזִים
ה אַנְשֵׁי בֹּגְדוֹת כֹּהֲנֶיהָ חִלְּלוּ־קֹדֶשׁ חָמְסוּ תּוֹרָה: יהוה צַדִּיק בְּקִרְבָּהּ
לֹא יַעֲשֶׂה עַוְלָה בַּבֹּקֶר בַּבֹּקֶר מִשְׁפָּטוֹ יִתֵּן לָאוֹר לֹא נֶעְדָּר וְלֹא־
ו יוֹדֵעַ עַוָּל בֹּשֶׁת: הִכְרַתִּי גוֹיִם נָשַׁמּוּ פִּנּוֹתָם הֶחֱרַבְתִּי חוּצוֹתָם מִבְּלִי
ז עוֹבֵר נִצְדּוּ עָרֵיהֶם מִבְּלִי־אִישׁ מֵאֵין יוֹשֵׁב: אָמַרְתִּי אַךְ־תִּירְאִי אוֹתִי
תִּקְחִי מוּסָר וְלֹא־יִכָּרֵת מְעוֹנָהּ כֹּל אֲשֶׁר־פָּקַדְתִּי עָלֶיהָ אָכֵן הִשְׁכִּימוּ
ח הִשְׁחִיתוּ כֹּל עֲלִילוֹתָם: לָכֵן חַכּוּ־לִי נְאֻם־יהוה לְיוֹם קוּמִי לְעַד כִּי
מִשְׁפָּטִי לֶאֱסֹף גּוֹיִם לְקָבְצִי מַמְלָכוֹת לִשְׁפֹּךְ עֲלֵיהֶם זַעְמִי כֹּל חֲרוֹן
ט אַפִּי כִּי בְּאֵשׁ קִנְאָתִי תֵּאָכֵל כָּל־הָאָרֶץ: כִּי־אָז אֶהְפֹּךְ אֶל־עַמִּים שָׂפָה
י בְרוּרָה לִקְרֹא כֻלָּם בְּשֵׁם יהוה לְעָבְדוֹ שְׁכֶם אֶחָד: מֵעֵבֶר לְנַהֲרֵי־כוּשׁ
יא עֲתָרַי בַּת־פּוּצַי יוֹבִלוּן מִנְחָתִי: בַּיּוֹם הַהוּא לֹא תֵבוֹשִׁי מִכֹּל עֲלִילֹתַיִךְ
אֲשֶׁר פָּשַׁעַתְּ בִּי כִּי־אָז ׀ אָסִיר מִקִּרְבֵּךְ עַלִּיזֵי גַּאֲוָתֵךְ וְלֹא־תוֹסִפִי
יב לְגָבְהָה עוֹד בְּהַר קָדְשִׁי: וְהִשְׁאַרְתִּי בְקִרְבֵּךְ עַם עָנִי וָדָל וְחָסוּ בְּשֵׁם
יג יהוה: שְׁאֵרִית יִשְׂרָאֵל לֹא־יַעֲשׂוּ עַוְלָה וְלֹא־יְדַבְּרוּ כָזָב וְלֹא־יִמָּצֵא
יד בְּפִיהֶם לְשׁוֹן תַּרְמִית כִּי־הֵמָּה יִרְעוּ וְרָבְצוּ וְאֵין מַחֲרִיד: רָנִּי
טו בַּת־צִיּוֹן הָרִיעוּ יִשְׂרָאֵל שִׂמְחִי וְעָלְזִי בְּכָל־לֵב בַּת יְרוּשָׁלָםִ: הֵסִיר
יהוה מִשְׁפָּטַיִךְ פִּנָּה אֹיְבֵךְ מֶלֶךְ יִשְׂרָאֵל ׀ יהוה בְּקִרְבֵּךְ לֹא־תִירְאִי רָע
טז עוֹד: בַּיּוֹם הַהוּא יֵאָמֵר לִירוּשָׁלַםִ אַל־תִּירָאִי צִיּוֹן אַל־יִרְפּוּ

17 not throw your hands up in despair. The LORD your God is among you; He
who is strong will bring salvation. He rejoices, takes pleasure in you. His love
18 leads Him to be silent, then He joyfully sings you songs of praise. I will gather
the mournful – those who grieved for your lost celebrations and all those
19 burdened with shame. Behold, I will confront all who then caused you to
suffer. I will rescue the lame and draw close those driven away. I will replace
20 their shame with glory and make them acclaimed throughout the lands. At
that time I will gather you together and bring you home; indeed, I will make
you legendary and praised among all the people of the earth. Thus I will restore
you and your people to your place before your very eyes. So says the LORD.

ḤAGAI/HAGGAI

1 1 In the second year of King Daryavesh's reign, in the sixth month, on the first
day of the month, the word of the LORD came through Ḥagai the prophet
to Zerubavel son of She'altiel, governor of Yehuda, and to Yehoshua son of
2 Yehotzadak, the High Priest. "So says the LORD of Hosts: This people says, 'The
3 time has not come – the time for the LORD's House to be built.'" Then
4 the word of the LORD came through the hand of Ḥagai the prophet: "Is it the
time for you yourselves to sit under roofs in your homes while this House
5 6 lies desolate? Now says the LORD of Hosts: Take your ways to heart. You
sow much but bring in little, eat but are not satisfied, drink but remain sober.
You clothe yourselves but are not warmed, and anyone who earns wages
7 receives them into a pouch full of holes. So says the LORD of Hosts:
8 Pay heed to your ways. Go up onto the mountain, bring wood, and build My
9 House. I will desire it and be glorified by it, says the LORD. You expect much
but receive little. You bring it home; I cause it to wither. Why? Because of
My House which remains desolate while each of you keeps running back to
10 his own house, says the LORD of Hosts. Therefore, the skies lock up the dew
11 above you;[1] the land locks up its produce. I will call forth a drought over
the land and the mountains; over the grains, the young wine, and the fresh
oil; over everything the land produces. I will declare a drought over man
12 and animal, even over the labor of their hands." Zerubavel son of
She'altiel, Yehoshua son of Yehotzadak, the High Priest, and all the remnant
of the people listened to the voice of the LORD their God and to the words
of Ḥagai the prophet, for he was sent by the LORD their God. The people
13 feared the LORD. Then Ḥagai, messenger of the LORD, sent by the
14 LORD to the people, spoke: "So says the LORD: I am with you." Then the
LORD roused the spirit of Zerubavel son of She'altiel, governor of Yehuda,
the spirit of Yehoshua son of Yehotzadak, the High Priest, and the spirits of
all the remnant of the people. They came and they carried out the work on
15 the House of the LORD of Hosts, their God. This happened on the
twenty-fourth day of the sixth month in the second year of King Daryavesh's

1 | Cf. Deuteronomy 11:17.

יז יָדָיִךְ׃ יְהוָה אֱלֹהַיִךְ בְּקִרְבֵּךְ גִּבּוֹר יוֹשִׁיעַ יָשִׂישׂ עָלַיִךְ בְּשִׂמְחָה יַחֲרִישׁ
יח בְּאַהֲבָתוֹ יָגִיל עָלַיִךְ בְּרִנָּה׃ נוּגֵי מִמּוֹעֵד אָסַפְתִּי מִמֵּךְ הָיוּ מַשְׂאֵת
יט עָלֶיהָ חֶרְפָּה׃ הִנְנִי עֹשֶׂה אֶת־כָּל־מְעַנַּיִךְ בָּעֵת הַהִיא וְהוֹשַׁעְתִּי אֶת־
הַצֹּלֵעָה וְהַנִּדָּחָה אֲקַבֵּץ וְשַׂמְתִּים לִתְהִלָּה וּלְשֵׁם בְּכָל־הָאָרֶץ בָּשְׁתָּם׃
כ בָּעֵת הַהִיא אָבִיא אֶתְכֶם וּבָעֵת קַבְּצִי אֶתְכֶם כִּי־אֶתֵּן אֶתְכֶם לְשֵׁם טו
וְלִתְהִלָּה בְּכֹל עַמֵּי הָאָרֶץ בְּשׁוּבִי אֶת־שְׁבוּתֵיכֶם לְעֵינֵיכֶם אָמַר יְהוָה׃

חגי

א א בִּשְׁנַת שְׁתַּיִם לְדָרְיָוֶשׁ הַמֶּלֶךְ בַּחֹדֶשׁ הַשִּׁשִּׁי בְּיוֹם אֶחָד לַחֹדֶשׁ
הָיָה דְבַר־יְהוָה בְּיַד־חַגַּי הַנָּבִיא אֶל־זְרֻבָּבֶל בֶּן־שְׁאַלְתִּיאֵל פַּחַת
ב יְהוּדָה וְאֶל־יְהוֹשֻׁעַ בֶּן־יְהוֹצָדָק הַכֹּהֵן הַגָּדוֹל לֵאמֹר׃ כֹּה אָמַר
יְהוָה צְבָאוֹת לֵאמֹר הָעָם הַזֶּה אָמְרוּ לֹא עֶת־בֹּא עֶת־בֵּית יְהוָה
ג ד לְהִבָּנוֹת׃ וַיְהִי דְּבַר־יְהוָה בְּיַד־חַגַּי הַנָּבִיא לֵאמֹר׃ הַעֵת
ה לָכֶם אַתֶּם לָשֶׁבֶת בְּבָתֵּיכֶם סְפוּנִים וְהַבַּיִת הַזֶּה חָרֵב׃ וְעַתָּה כֹּה אָמַר
ו יְהוָה צְבָאוֹת שִׂימוּ לְבַבְכֶם עַל־דַּרְכֵיכֶם׃ זְרַעְתֶּם הַרְבֵּה וְהָבֵא מְעָט
אָכוֹל וְאֵין־לְשָׂבְעָה שָׁתוֹ וְאֵין־לְשָׁכְרָה לָבוֹשׁ וְאֵין־לְחֹם לוֹ וְהַמִּשְׂתַּכֵּר
ז מִשְׂתַּכֵּר אֶל־צְרוֹר נָקוּב׃ כֹּה אָמַר יְהוָה צְבָאוֹת שִׂימוּ
ח לְבַבְכֶם עַל־דַּרְכֵיכֶם׃ עֲלוּ הָהָר וַהֲבֵאתֶם עֵץ וּבְנוּ הַבָּיִת וְאֶרְצֶה־בּוֹ
ט וְאֶכָּבְדָ אָמַר יְהוָה׃ פָּנֹה אֶל־הַרְבֵּה וְהִנֵּה לִמְעָט וַהֲבֵאתֶם הַבַּיִת
וְנָפַחְתִּי בוֹ יַעַן מֶה נְאֻם יְהוָה צְבָאוֹת יַעַן בֵּיתִי אֲשֶׁר־הוּא חָרֵב וְאַתֶּם
י רָצִים אִישׁ לְבֵיתוֹ׃ עַל־כֵּן עֲלֵיכֶם כָּלְאוּ שָׁמַיִם מִטָּל וְהָאָרֶץ כָּלְאָה
יא יְבוּלָהּ׃ וָאֶקְרָא חֹרֶב עַל־הָאָרֶץ וְעַל־הֶהָרִים וְעַל־הַדָּגָן וְעַל־הַתִּירוֹשׁ
וְעַל־הַיִּצְהָר וְעַל אֲשֶׁר תּוֹצִיא הָאֲדָמָה וְעַל־הָאָדָם וְעַל־הַבְּהֵמָה
יב וְעַל כָּל־יְגִיעַ כַּפָּיִם׃ וַיִּשְׁמַע זְרֻבָּבֶל ׀ בֶּן־שַׁלְתִּיאֵל
וִיהוֹשֻׁעַ בֶּן־יְהוֹצָדָק הַכֹּהֵן הַגָּדוֹל וְכֹל ׀ שְׁאֵרִית הָעָם בְּקוֹל יְהוָה
אֱלֹהֵיהֶם וְעַל־דִּבְרֵי חַגַּי הַנָּבִיא כַּאֲשֶׁר שְׁלָחוֹ יְהוָה אֱלֹהֵיהֶם וַיִּירְאוּ
יג הָעָם מִפְּנֵי יְהוָה׃ וַיֹּאמֶר חַגַּי מַלְאַךְ יְהוָה בְּמַלְאֲכוּת
יד יְהוָה לָעָם לֵאמֹר אֲנִי אִתְּכֶם נְאֻם־יְהוָה׃ וַיָּעַר יְהוָה אֶת־רוּחַ זְרֻבָּבֶל
בֶּן־שַׁלְתִּיאֵל פַּחַת יְהוּדָה וְאֶת־רוּחַ יְהוֹשֻׁעַ בֶּן־יְהוֹצָדָק הַכֹּהֵן הַגָּדוֹל
וְאֶת־רוּחַ כֹּל שְׁאֵרִית הָעָם וַיָּבֹאוּ וַיַּעֲשׂוּ מְלָאכָה בְּבֵית־יְהוָה צְבָאוֹת
טו אֱלֹהֵיהֶם׃ בְּיוֹם עֶשְׂרִים וְאַרְבָּעָה לַחֹדֶשׁ בַּשִּׁשִּׁי בִּשְׁנַת

2 1 reign. In the seventh month, on the twenty-first day of the month, the word
2 of the Lord came through Ḥagai the prophet: "Say now to Zerubavel son
of She'altiel, governor of Yehuda, and to Yehoshua son of Yehotzadak, the
3 High Priest, and to the remnant of the people: Who is there still among you
who saw this House in its first glory? As you see it now, it must seem like
4 nothing to you.[2] Now be strong, Zerubavel; the Lord has spoken. Be strong,
Yehoshua son of Yehotzadak, the High Priest; be strong, people of the land;
the Lord has spoken. Act, for I am with you; the Lord of Hosts has spoken.
5 That which I made into a covenant with you when you left Egypt, that and
6 My Spirit, stand here among you. Do not fear. For so says the Lord
of Hosts: One more thing, but a small thing,[3] and I will shake the heavens
7 and the earth, the sea and the dry land. I will shake all the nations, they will
come with the riches of all the nations, and I will fill this House with glory,
8 says the Lord of Hosts. For Mine is the silver and Mine the gold; the Lord
9 of Hosts has spoken. The glory of this latter House will be greater than the
glory of the first, says the Lord of Hosts, and I will bestow peace upon this
10 place. The Lord of Hosts has spoken." On the twenty-fourth
day of the ninth month,[4] in the second year of Daryavesh's reign, the word
11 of the Lord came to Ḥagai the prophet: "So says the Lord of Hosts: Now
12 ask the priests for a ruling of Law: 'If a man carries consecrated meat in
the fold of his garment and with that fold touches bread, or a cooked dish,
or wine, or oil, or any other food, does it become sanctified?'" The priests
13 answered and said, "No." Ḥagai said, "And if someone who has become
impure through contact with the dead touches any one of these things, does
14 it become impure?" The priests answered and said, "It becomes impure." Then
Ḥagai spoke and said, "The Lord has spoken: So too is this people, this nation
before Me, and so is all the labor of their hands. Everything they might offer
15 there is impure. And now, pay heed from this day forward: Before stone was
16 placed upon stone in the Temple of the Lord, when you would come for a
grain pile of twenty, it was ten; and when you came to the vineyard to draw
17 fifty measures from a winepress, it would be twenty. I struck you with blight
and mildew; I struck you with hail. I struck all the labor of your hands. And
18 still you are not with Me – the Lord has spoken. Pay heed: From this day
forward, from the twenty-fourth day of the ninth month, from the day of
19 the foundation of the Temple of the Lord, pay heed. Is the seed still in the
storehouse? Even the vine, fig, pomegranate, and olive tree have not borne
20 fruit. But from this day on, I will bless you." Then on the twenty-
fourth day of the month, the word of the Lord came to Ḥagai a second time:
21 "Tell Zerubavel, governor of Yehuda: I am going to shake the heavens and
22 earth, I will overturn the thrones of kingdoms, and I will destroy the mighty
dominion of nations; I will overturn the chariot and its riders. The horses
and their riders will fall, every man cut down by the sword of his brother.

2 | See Ezra 3:12.

3 | A small impediment; alternatively, "very soon."

4 | On the day the foundations for the Temple were laid; see verse 18.

ב א שְׁתַּיִם לְדָרְיָוֶשׁ הַמֶּלֶךְ׃ בַּשְּׁבִיעִי בְּעֶשְׂרִים וְאֶחָד לַחֹדֶשׁ הָיָה דְּבַר־
ב יְהוָה בְּיַד־חַגַּי הַנָּבִיא לֵאמֹר׃ אֱמָר־נָא אֶל־זְרֻבָּבֶל בֶּן־שַׁלְתִּיאֵל
פַּחַת יְהוּדָה וְאֶל־יְהוֹשֻׁעַ בֶּן־יְהוֹצָדָק הַכֹּהֵן הַגָּדוֹל וְאֶל־שְׁאֵרִית הָעָם
ג לֵאמֹר׃ מִי בָכֶם הַנִּשְׁאָר אֲשֶׁר רָאָה אֶת־הַבַּיִת הַזֶּה בִּכְבוֹדוֹ הָרִאשׁוֹן
ד וּמָה אַתֶּם רֹאִים אֹתוֹ עַתָּה הֲלוֹא כָמֹהוּ כְּאַיִן בְּעֵינֵיכֶם׃ וְעַתָּה חֲזַק
זְרֻבָּבֶל ׀ נְאֻם־יְהוָה וַחֲזַק יְהוֹשֻׁעַ בֶּן־יְהוֹצָדָק הַכֹּהֵן הַגָּדוֹל וַחֲזַק כָּל־
ה עַם הָאָרֶץ נְאֻם־יְהוָה וַעֲשׂוּ כִּי־אֲנִי אִתְּכֶם נְאֻם יְהוָה צְבָאוֹת׃ אֶת־
הַדָּבָר אֲשֶׁר כָּרַתִּי אִתְּכֶם בְּצֵאתְכֶם מִמִּצְרַיִם וְרוּחִי עֹמֶדֶת בְּתוֹכְכֶם
ו אַל־תִּירָאוּ׃ כִּי כֹה אָמַר יְהוָה צְבָאוֹת עוֹד אַחַת מְעַט
הִיא וַאֲנִי מַרְעִישׁ אֶת־הַשָּׁמַיִם וְאֶת־הָאָרֶץ וְאֶת־הַיָּם וְאֶת־הֶחָרָבָה׃
ז וְהִרְעַשְׁתִּי אֶת־כָּל־הַגּוֹיִם וּבָאוּ חֶמְדַּת כָּל־הַגּוֹיִם וּמִלֵּאתִי אֶת־הַבַּיִת
ח הַזֶּה כָּבוֹד אָמַר יְהוָה צְבָאוֹת׃ לִי הַכֶּסֶף וְלִי הַזָּהָב נְאֻם יְהוָה צְבָאוֹת׃
ט גָּדוֹל יִהְיֶה כְּבוֹד הַבַּיִת הַזֶּה הָאַחֲרוֹן מִן־הָרִאשׁוֹן אָמַר יְהוָה צְבָאוֹת
י וּבַמָּקוֹם הַזֶּה אֶתֵּן שָׁלוֹם נְאֻם יְהוָה צְבָאוֹת׃ בְּעֶשְׂרִים
וְאַרְבָּעָה לַתְּשִׁיעִי בִּשְׁנַת שְׁתַּיִם לְדָרְיָוֶשׁ הָיָה דְּבַר־יְהוָה בְּיַד־חַגַּי
יא הַנָּבִיא לֵאמֹר׃ כֹּה אָמַר יְהוָה צְבָאוֹת שְׁאַל־נָא אֶת־הַכֹּהֲנִים תּוֹרָה
יב לֵאמֹר׃ הֵן ׀ יִשָּׂא־אִישׁ בְּשַׂר־קֹדֶשׁ בִּכְנַף בִּגְדוֹ וְנָגַע בִּכְנָפוֹ אֶל־הַלֶּחֶם
וְאֶל־הַנָּזִיד וְאֶל־הַיַּיִן וְאֶל־שֶׁמֶן וְאֶל־כָּל־מַאֲכָל הֲיִקְדָּשׁ וַיַּעֲנוּ הַכֹּהֲנִים
יג וַיֹּאמְרוּ לֹא׃ וַיֹּאמֶר חַגַּי אִם־יִגַּע טְמֵא־נֶפֶשׁ בְּכָל־אֵלֶּה הֲיִטְמָא וַיַּעֲנוּ
יד הַכֹּהֲנִים וַיֹּאמְרוּ יִטְמָא׃ וַיַּעַן חַגַּי וַיֹּאמֶר כֵּן הָעָם־הַזֶּה וְכֵן־הַגּוֹי הַזֶּה
לְפָנַי נְאֻם־יְהוָה וְכֵן כָּל־מַעֲשֵׂה יְדֵיהֶם וַאֲשֶׁר יַקְרִיבוּ שָׁם טָמֵא הוּא׃
טו וְעַתָּה שִׂימוּ־נָא לְבַבְכֶם מִן־הַיּוֹם הַזֶּה וָמָעְלָה מִטֶּרֶם שׂוּם־אֶבֶן אֶל־
טז אֶבֶן בְּהֵיכַל יְהוָה׃ מִהְיוֹתָם בָּא אֶל־עֲרֵמַת עֶשְׂרִים וְהָיְתָה עֲשָׂרָה
יז בָּא אֶל־הַיֶּקֶב לַחְשֹׂף חֲמִשִּׁים פּוּרָה וְהָיְתָה עֶשְׂרִים׃ הִכֵּיתִי אֶתְכֶם
בַּשִּׁדָּפוֹן וּבַיֵּרָקוֹן וּבַבָּרָד אֵת כָּל־מַעֲשֵׂה יְדֵיכֶם וְאֵין־אֶתְכֶם אֵלַי נְאֻם־
יח יְהוָה׃ שִׂימוּ־נָא לְבַבְכֶם מִן־הַיּוֹם הַזֶּה וָמָעְלָה מִיּוֹם עֶשְׂרִים וְאַרְבָּעָה
יט לַתְּשִׁיעִי לְמִן־הַיּוֹם אֲשֶׁר־יֻסַּד הֵיכַל־יְהוָה שִׂימוּ לְבַבְכֶם׃ הַעוֹד הַזֶּרַע
בַּמְּגוּרָה וְעַד־הַגֶּפֶן וְהַתְּאֵנָה וְהָרִמּוֹן וְעֵץ הַזַּיִת לֹא נָשָׂא מִן־הַיּוֹם הַזֶּה
כ אֲבָרֵךְ׃ וַיְהִי דְבַר־יְהוָה ׀ שֵׁנִית אֶל־חַגַּי בְּעֶשְׂרִים וְאַרְבָּעָה
כא לַחֹדֶשׁ לֵאמֹר׃ אֱמֹר אֶל־זְרֻבָּבֶל פַּחַת־יְהוּדָה לֵאמֹר אֲנִי מַרְעִישׁ אֶת־
כב הַשָּׁמַיִם וְאֶת־הָאָרֶץ׃ וְהָפַכְתִּי כִּסֵּא מַמְלָכוֹת וְהִשְׁמַדְתִּי חֹזֶק מַמְלְכוֹת
הַגּוֹיִם וְהָפַכְתִּי מֶרְכָּבָה וְרֹכְבֶיהָ וְיָרְדוּ סוּסִים וְרֹכְבֵיהֶם אִישׁ בְּחֶרֶב

23 On that day – the Lord of Hosts has spoken – I will take you, Zerubavel son of She'altiel, My servant – the Lord has spoken – and wear you close like a signet ring, for it is you whom I have chosen. The Lord of Hosts has spoken."

ZEKHARYA/ ZECHARIAH

1 1 In the eighth month of the second year of Daryavesh's reign, the word of the
2 Lord came to Zekharya son of Berekhya son of Ido the prophet: "The Lord
3 overflowed with fury against your forefathers. Say to them: So says the Lord
of Hosts: Come back to Me – the Lord of Hosts has said – and I will come
4 back to you, so says the Lord of Hosts. O, do not be like your forefathers, to
whom the earlier prophets called, saying: So says the Lord of Hosts: Return,
please, from your evil ways and your evil deeds. They did not hear; they did
5 not listen to Me – the Lord has spoken. Where are your forefathers? Even
6 the prophets – do they live forever? Yet My words and the rulings with which
I charged My servants, the prophets, did they not overtake your forefathers?
They returned. They said: 'That which the Lord of Hosts devised to do to us,
7 befitting our ways and our deeds, indeed, He did with us.'" On the
twenty-fourth day of the eleventh month – which is the month of Shevat – in
the second year of Daryavesh's reign, the word of the Lord came to Zekharya
8 son of Berekhya son of Ido the prophet: I saw in the darkness: a man mounted
on a blood bay horse stood among the myrtles in the deep, with blood bay,
9 sorrel, and white horses behind him. I said, "What are these, my lord?" The
10 angel with whom I spoke said to me, "I will show you what these are." Then
the man standing among the myrtles spoke. He said, "These are the ones that
11 the Lord sent to rove the land." They spoke to the angel of the Lord, standing
among the myrtles. "We have roved the land. The whole land sits settled and
12 quiet," they said. The angel of the Lord spoke and said, "Lord of Hosts, how
long will You have no mercy on Jerusalem and the cities of Yehuda against
13 whom You have been filled with wrath these seventy years?" Then the Lord
answered the angel with whom I spoke with good words, words of comfort.
14 So the angel with whom I spoke said to me, "Call out: So says the Lord of
15 Hosts: I have been greatly zealous on behalf of Jerusalem and Zion, and I
have been greatly furious at those complacent nations. I was only somewhat
furious, but they aided evil.
16 Therefore, so says the Lord: I have returned to Jerusalem in mercy. My
House will be built in it – the Lord of Hosts has spoken – and a measuring
17 cord will be drawn over Jerusalem. Call out again: So says the Lord of Hosts:
Once again My city will brim over with good, and the Lord will again

כג אַחִיו: בַּיּוֹם הַהוּא נְאֻם־יְהוָה צְבָאוֹת אֶקָּחֲךָ זְרֻבָּבֶל בֶּן־שְׁאַלְתִּיאֵל טז
עַבְדִּי נְאֻם־יְהוָה וְשַׂמְתִּיךָ כַּחוֹתָם כִּי־בְךָ בָחַרְתִּי נְאֻם יְהוָה צְבָאוֹת:

א א בַּחֹדֶשׁ הַשְּׁמִינִי בִּשְׁנַת שְׁתַּיִם לְדָרְיָוֶשׁ הָיָה דְבַר־יְהוָה אֶל־זְכַרְיָה זכריה
ב בֶּן־בֶּרֶכְיָה בֶּן־עִדּוֹ הַנָּבִיא לֵאמֹר: קָצַף יְהוָה עַל־אֲבוֹתֵיכֶם קָצֶף:
ג וְאָמַרְתָּ אֲלֵהֶם כֹּה אָמַר יְהוָה צְבָאוֹת שׁוּבוּ אֵלַי נְאֻם יְהוָה צְבָאוֹת
ד וְאָשׁוּב אֲלֵיכֶם אָמַר יְהוָה צְבָאוֹת: אַל־תִּהְיוּ כַאֲבֹתֵיכֶם אֲשֶׁר קָרְאוּ־
אֲלֵיהֶם הַנְּבִיאִים הָרִאשֹׁנִים לֵאמֹר כֹּה אָמַר יְהוָה צְבָאוֹת שׁוּבוּ נָא
מִדַּרְכֵיכֶם הָרָעִים ומעליליכם הָרָעִים וְלֹא שָׁמְעוּ וְלֹא־הִקְשִׁיבוּ אֵלַי וּמַעַלְלֵיכֶם
ה ו נְאֻם־יְהוָה: אֲבוֹתֵיכֶם אַיֵּה־הֵם וְהַנְּבִאִים הַלְעוֹלָם יִחְיוּ: אַךְ | דְּבָרַי
וְחֻקַּי אֲשֶׁר צִוִּיתִי אֶת־עֲבָדַי הַנְּבִיאִים הֲלוֹא הִשִּׂיגוּ אֲבֹתֵיכֶם וַיָּשׁוּבוּ
וַיֹּאמְרוּ כַּאֲשֶׁר זָמַם יְהוָה צְבָאוֹת לַעֲשׂוֹת לָנוּ כִּדְרָכֵינוּ וּכְמַעֲלָלֵינוּ
ז כֵּן עָשָׂה אִתָּנוּ: בְּיוֹם עֶשְׂרִים וְאַרְבָּעָה לְעַשְׁתֵּי־
עָשָׂר חֹדֶשׁ הוּא־חֹדֶשׁ שְׁבָט בִּשְׁנַת שְׁתַּיִם לְדָרְיָוֶשׁ הָיָה דְבַר־יְהוָה
ח אֶל־זְכַרְיָה בֶּן־בֶּרֶכְיָהוּ בֶּן־עִדּוֹא הַנָּבִיא לֵאמֹר: רָאִיתִי | הַלַּיְלָה
וְהִנֵּה־אִישׁ רֹכֵב עַל־סוּס אָדֹם וְהוּא עֹמֵד בֵּין הַהֲדַסִּים אֲשֶׁר בַּמְּצֻלָה
ט וְאַחֲרָיו סוּסִים אֲדֻמִּים שְׂרֻקִּים וּלְבָנִים: וָאֹמַר מָה־אֵלֶּה אֲדֹנִי וַיֹּאמֶר
י אֵלַי הַמַּלְאָךְ הַדֹּבֵר בִּי אֲנִי אַרְאֶךָּ מָה־הֵמָּה אֵלֶּה: וַיַּעַן הָאִישׁ הָעֹמֵד
יא בֵּין־הַהֲדַסִּים וַיֹּאמַר אֵלֶּה אֲשֶׁר שָׁלַח יְהוָה לְהִתְהַלֵּךְ בָּאָרֶץ: וַיַּעֲנוּ
אֶת־מַלְאַךְ יְהוָה הָעֹמֵד בֵּין הַהֲדַסִּים וַיֹּאמְרוּ הִתְהַלַּכְנוּ בָאָרֶץ וְהִנֵּה
יב כָל־הָאָרֶץ יֹשֶׁבֶת וְשֹׁקָטֶת: וַיַּעַן מַלְאַךְ־יְהוָה וַיֹּאמַר יְהוָה צְבָאוֹת
עַד־מָתַי אַתָּה לֹא־תְרַחֵם אֶת־יְרוּשָׁלִַם וְאֵת עָרֵי יְהוּדָה אֲשֶׁר זָעַמְתָּה
יג זֶה שִׁבְעִים שָׁנָה: וַיַּעַן יְהוָה אֶת־הַמַּלְאָךְ הַדֹּבֵר בִּי דְּבָרִים טוֹבִים
יד דְּבָרִים נִחֻמִים: וַיֹּאמֶר אֵלַי הַמַּלְאָךְ הַדֹּבֵר בִּי קְרָא לֵאמֹר כֹּה אָמַר
טו יְהוָה צְבָאוֹת קִנֵּאתִי לִירוּשָׁלִַם וּלְצִיּוֹן קִנְאָה גְדוֹלָה: וְקֶצֶף גָּדוֹל
אֲנִי קֹצֵף עַל־הַגּוֹיִם הַשַּׁאֲנַנִּים אֲשֶׁר אֲנִי קָצַפְתִּי מְּעָט וְהֵמָּה עָזְרוּ
לְרָעָה:
טז לָכֵן כֹּה־אָמַר יְהוָה שַׁבְתִּי לִירוּשָׁלִַם בְּרַחֲמִים בֵּיתִי יִבָּנֶה בָּהּ נְאֻם
יז יְהוָה צְבָאוֹת וקוה יִנָּטֶה עַל־יְרוּשָׁלִָם: עוֹד | קְרָא לֵאמֹר כֹּה אָמַר וְקָו
יְהוָה צְבָאוֹת עוֹד תְּפוּצֶנָה עָרַי מִטּוֹב וְנִחַם יְהוָה עוֹד אֶת־צִיּוֹן וּבָחַר

2 1 comfort Zion; again He will choose Jerusalem." I lifted my eyes and
2 saw: There were four horns. I said to the angel with whom I spoke: "What
are these?" He said, "These are the horns that scattered Yehuda, Israel, and
3 4 Jerusalem."[1] The LORD showed me four craftsmen. I said, "What
are these coming to do?" He said, "These are the horns that scattered Yehuda
so that no man could lift his head. And those, they are coming to terrify them,
to cast down the horns of the nations who lifted their horns against the land
5 of Yehuda, scattering her."[2] I raised my eyes and saw: there was a
6 man with a measuring cord in his hand. "Where are you going?" I said. He
7 said, "To measure Jerusalem. To see how wide and how long she is." Suddenly
the angel with whom I spoke emerged, and another angel came out to meet
8 him. He told him, "Run, tell that attendant that Jerusalem shall be settled
9 beyond her walls from the abundance of people and animals within her." I
will be for her – the LORD has spoken – an encircling wall of fire. I will be the
10 Glory within her. Hie, hie, and flee from the northland – the LORD
has spoken – for like the four winds I have spread you far – the LORD has
11 12 spoken. Hie, Zion, escape, O dweller with daughter Babylon, for so
says the LORD of Hosts: In the wake of Glory He sent me to the nations that
have plundered you, for he who harms you harms that which is reflected in
13 His eyes. I will brandish My hand over them, and they will be plundered by
14 their slaves. You will know that the LORD of Hosts sent me. Shout
out and be joyful, daughter Zion, for I am coming, and I will dwell in your
15 midst – the LORD has spoken. Many nations will join themselves to the LORD
on that day, and they will be My people. I will dwell in your midst, and you
16 will know that the LORD of Hosts sent me to you. The LORD will take
possession of Yehuda as His portion of holy ground, and He will choose
17 Jerusalem once again. Hush, all flesh, before the LORD, for He has stirred from
3 1 His holy abode. Then He showed me Yehoshua the High Priest
standing before an angel of the LORD with the Adversary on his right to
2 oppose him.[3] The LORD said to the Adversary: The LORD drives you away,
Adversary. The LORD, who has chosen Jerusalem, drives you away. Yes, this
3 is a firebrand saved from the fire. And Yehoshua, wearing filthy clothing, was
4 standing before the angel, who spoke and said to those standing before him,
"Take those filthy clothes off him." Then the angel said to him, "See, I have
5 removed your guilt from you and dressed you in finery." I said, "Place a pure
turban on his head," and they placed a pure turban on his head. They dressed
6 him in clothing.[4] The angel of the LORD remained standing. Then that angel
7 of the LORD testified regarding Yehoshua: "So says the LORD of Hosts: If you
walk in My ways, if you keep My watch, if you judge My House, and guard

1 | The Hebrew word *keranot* (horns) can also mean "corners." This could refer to the kings of Mesopotamia, who claimed to rule the four corners of the earth.

2 | The craftsmen might symbolize the rebuilding of the Temple, which took place at this time.

3 | Cf. Psalms 109:6.

4 | The priestly garments, symbolizing investiture (see Lev., ch. 8).

ב א עוֹד בִּירוּשָׁלִָם׃ וָאֶשָּׂא אֶת־עֵינַי וָאֵרֶא וְהִנֵּה אַרְבַּע קְרָנוֹת׃
ב וָאֹמַר אֶל־הַמַּלְאָךְ הַדֹּבֵר בִּי מָה־אֵלֶּה וַיֹּאמֶר אֵלַי אֵלֶּה הַקְּרָנוֹת
ג אֲשֶׁר זֵרוּ אֶת־יְהוּדָה אֶת־יִשְׂרָאֵל וִירוּשָׁלִָם׃ וַיַּרְאֵנִי יְהוָה
ד אַרְבָּעָה חָרָשִׁים׃ וָאֹמַר מָה אֵלֶּה בָאִים לַעֲשׂוֹת וַיֹּאמֶר לֵאמֹר אֵלֶּה
הַקְּרָנוֹת אֲשֶׁר־זֵרוּ אֶת־יְהוּדָה כְּפִי־אִישׁ לֹא־נָשָׂא רֹאשׁוֹ וַיָּבֹאוּ אֵלֶּה
לְהַחֲרִיד אֹתָם לְיַדּוֹת אֶת־קַרְנוֹת הַגּוֹיִם הַנֹּשְׂאִים קֶרֶן אֶל־אֶרֶץ
ה יְהוּדָה לְזָרוֹתָהּ׃ וָאֶשָּׂא עֵינַי וָאֵרֶא וְהִנֵּה־אִישׁ וּבְיָדוֹ חֶבֶל
ו מִדָּה׃ וָאֹמַר אָנָה אַתָּה הֹלֵךְ וַיֹּאמֶר אֵלַי לָמֹד אֶת־יְרוּשָׁלִַם לִרְאוֹת
ז כַּמָּה־רָחְבָּהּ וְכַמָּה אָרְכָּהּ׃ וְהִנֵּה הַמַּלְאָךְ הַדֹּבֵר בִּי יֹצֵא וּמַלְאָךְ אַחֵר
ח יֹצֵא לִקְרָאתוֹ׃ וַיֹּאמֶר אֵלָו רֻץ דַּבֵּר אֶל־הַנַּעַר הַלָּז לֵאמֹר פְּרָזוֹת
ט תֵּשֵׁב יְרוּשָׁלִַם מֵרֹב אָדָם וּבְהֵמָה בְּתוֹכָהּ׃ וַאֲנִי אֶהְיֶה־לָּהּ נְאֻם־יְהוָה
י חוֹמַת אֵשׁ סָבִיב וּלְכָבוֹד אֶהְיֶה בְתוֹכָהּ׃ הוֹי הוֹי וְנֻסוּ
מֵאֶרֶץ צָפוֹן נְאֻם־יְהוָה כִּי כְּאַרְבַּע רוּחוֹת הַשָּׁמַיִם פֵּרַשְׂתִּי אֶתְכֶם
יא יב נְאֻם־יְהוָה׃ הוֹי צִיּוֹן הִמָּלְטִי יוֹשֶׁבֶת בַּת־בָּבֶל׃ כִּי כֹה
אָמַר יְהוָה צְבָאוֹת אַחַר כָּבוֹד שְׁלָחַנִי אֶל־הַגּוֹיִם הַשֹּׁלְלִים אֶתְכֶם כִּי
יג הַנֹּגֵעַ בָּכֶם נֹגֵעַ בְּבָבַת עֵינוֹ׃ כִּי הִנְנִי מֵנִיף אֶת־יָדִי עֲלֵיהֶם וְהָיוּ שָׁלָל
יד לְעַבְדֵיהֶם וִידַעְתֶּם כִּי־יְהוָה צְבָאוֹת שְׁלָחָנִי׃ רָנִּי
טו וְשִׂמְחִי בַּת־צִיּוֹן כִּי הִנְנִי־בָא וְשָׁכַנְתִּי בְתוֹכֵךְ נְאֻם־יְהוָה׃ וְנִלְווּ גוֹיִם
רַבִּים אֶל־יְהוָה בַּיּוֹם הַהוּא וְהָיוּ לִי לְעָם וְשָׁכַנְתִּי בְתוֹכֵךְ וְיָדַעַתְּ כִּי־
טז יְהוָה צְבָאוֹת שְׁלָחַנִי אֵלָיִךְ׃ וְנָחַל יְהוָה אֶת־יְהוּדָה חֶלְקוֹ עַל אַדְמַת
יז הַקֹּדֶשׁ וּבָחַר עוֹד בִּירוּשָׁלִָם׃ הַס כָּל־בָּשָׂר מִפְּנֵי יְהוָה כִּי נֵעוֹר מִמְּעוֹן
ג א קָדְשׁוֹ׃ וַיַּרְאֵנִי אֶת־יְהוֹשֻׁעַ הַכֹּהֵן הַגָּדוֹל עֹמֵד לִפְנֵי
ב מַלְאַךְ יְהוָה וְהַשָּׂטָן עֹמֵד עַל־יְמִינוֹ לְשִׂטְנוֹ׃ וַיֹּאמֶר יְהוָה אֶל־הַשָּׂטָן
יִגְעַר יְהוָה בְּךָ הַשָּׂטָן וְיִגְעַר יְהוָה בְּךָ הַבֹּחֵר בִּירוּשָׁלִָם הֲלוֹא זֶה אוּד
ג מֻצָּל מֵאֵשׁ׃ וִיהוֹשֻׁעַ הָיָה לָבֻשׁ בְּגָדִים צוֹאִים וְעֹמֵד לִפְנֵי הַמַּלְאָךְ׃
ד וַיַּעַן וַיֹּאמֶר אֶל־הָעֹמְדִים לְפָנָיו לֵאמֹר הָסִירוּ הַבְּגָדִים הַצֹּאִים מֵעָלָיו
וַיֹּאמֶר אֵלָיו רְאֵה הֶעֱבַרְתִּי מֵעָלֶיךָ עֲוֺנֶךָ וְהַלְבֵּשׁ אֹתְךָ מַחֲלָצוֹת׃
ה וָאֹמַר יָשִׂימוּ צָנִיף טָהוֹר עַל־רֹאשׁוֹ וַיָּשִׂימוּ הַצָּנִיף הַטָּהוֹר עַל־רֹאשׁוֹ
ו וַיַּלְבִּשֻׁהוּ בְּגָדִים וּמַלְאַךְ יְהוָה עֹמֵד׃ וַיָּעַד מַלְאַךְ יְהוָה בִּיהוֹשֻׁעַ
ז לֵאמֹר׃ כֹּה־אָמַר יְהוָה צְבָאוֹת אִם־בִּדְרָכַי תֵּלֵךְ וְאִם אֶת־מִשְׁמַרְתִּי
תִשְׁמֹר וְגַם־אַתָּה תָּדִין אֶת־בֵּיתִי וְגַם תִּשְׁמֹר אֶת־חֲצֵרָי וְנָתַתִּי לְךָ

My courtyards, then I will give you walkers among these who are standing.[5]
8 Listen, Yehoshua the High Priest, you and your friends who sit before you,
for they are men of wonders: Behold, I am bringing My servant Tzemaḥ.[6]
9 Upon the stone that I set before Yehoshua, one stone with seven eyes,[7] I will
engrave its inscription, and I will wipe away the guilt of this land in one
10 day. On that day – the LORD of Hosts has spoken – you will call one to
another: Come under the shade of the vine; come under the shade of the
4 1 fig." Then the angel with whom I had spoken returned and roused me
2 like a man stirring from his sleep. He said to me, "What do you see?" I said, "I
see a candelabrum of pure gold, its bowl at the top. It has seven lamps –
3 seven – and seven indentations for the lamps, which are at the top.[8] Next to
4 it are two olive trees, one to the right of the bowl and one to its left." I spoke
5 and said to the angel with whom I spoke, "What are these, my lord?" And the
angel with whom I spoke replied and said, "You know what these are." I said,
6 "No, my lord." Then he spoke and said to me, "This is the word of the LORD
to Zerubavel: Not with valor and not with strength, but with My spirit, says
7 the LORD of Hosts. Who are you, great mountain before Zerubavel? Surely
it will become a level plain. He will remove the re-foundation stone[9] with
8 clamor: Favor, favor to her!" Then the word of the LORD came to
9 me: "Zerubavel's hands founded this House, and his hands will complete it.
10 You will know that the LORD of Hosts sent me to you, for whosoever scorned
the day of small things[10] will rejoice seeing the measuring stone in Zerubavel's
hand. These seven, they are the eyes of the LORD, roaming throughout the
11 land." Then I spoke and said to him, "What are those two olive trees to the
12 right and to the left of the candelabrum?" And again I spoke. I said, "What
are these two olive branches next to the golden pipes that stream golden oil
13 from above?" He said to me, "You know what these are." I said, "No, my lord."
14 He said, "These are the two sons of the anointed ones[11] who stand beside
5 1 the Lord of all the land." Once again I raised my eyes and saw a flying
2 scroll. He said to me, "What do you see?" I said, "I see a flying scroll twenty
3 cubits long and ten cubits wide." And He said to me, "This is the curse
emerging all over the land; every thief has been spared what is written here.
4 Every person who swears has been spared what is written here. But I have
brought it out – the LORD of Hosts has spoken – and it will come into the
house of the thief and the house of the one who swears falsely in My name.
5 It will lodge in his house and destroy it, wood and stones and all." Then the
angel with whom I spoke approached and said to me, "Raise your eyes and
6 see. What is that approaching?" I said, "What is it?" He said, "This is the

5 | That is, Yehoshua will be able to stand among the angels.
6 | *Tzemaḥ* means "plant" or "shoot," referring to a royal heir (cf. Is. 11:1).
7 | The eyes may symbolize God's providence and protection.
8 | Cf. Exodus 25:31–37.
9 | Referring to a stone from the old, ruined palace or temple that served as a symbolic foundation for the new.
10 | Meaning the day on which construction for the Second Temple was undertaken (see Hag. 2:3).
11 | Zerubavel and Yehoshua, anointed king and priest, respectively.

ח מְהַלְּכִים בֵּין הָעֹמְדִים הָאֵלֶּה׃ שְׁמַע־נָא יְהוֹשֻׁעַ ׀ הַכֹּהֵן הַגָּדוֹל אַתָּה
וְרֵעֶיךָ הַיֹּשְׁבִים לְפָנֶיךָ כִּי־אַנְשֵׁי מוֹפֵת הֵמָּה כִּי־הִנְנִי מֵבִיא אֶת־עַבְדִּי
ט צֶמַח׃ כִּי ׀ הִנֵּה הָאֶבֶן אֲשֶׁר נָתַתִּי לִפְנֵי יְהוֹשֻׁעַ עַל־אֶבֶן אַחַת שִׁבְעָה
עֵינָיִם הִנְנִי מְפַתֵּחַ פִּתֻּחָהּ נְאֻם יְהוָה צְבָאוֹת וּמַשְׁתִּי אֶת־עֲוֺן הָאָרֶץ־
י הַהִיא בְּיוֹם אֶחָד׃ בַּיּוֹם הַהוּא נְאֻם יְהוָה צְבָאוֹת תִּקְרְאוּ אִישׁ לְרֵעֵהוּ
ד א אֶל־תַּחַת גֶּפֶן וְאֶל־תַּחַת תְּאֵנָה׃ וַיָּשָׁב הַמַּלְאָךְ
ב הַדֹּבֵר בִּי וַיְעִירֵנִי כְּאִישׁ אֲשֶׁר־יֵעוֹר מִשְּׁנָתוֹ׃ וַיֹּאמֶר אֵלַי מָה אַתָּה יז
רֹאֶה ויאמר רָאִיתִי ׀ וְהִנֵּה מְנוֹרַת זָהָב כֻּלָּהּ וְגֻלָּהּ עַל־רֹאשָׁהּ וְשִׁבְעָה וָאֹמַר
נֵרֹתֶיהָ עָלֶיהָ שִׁבְעָה וְשִׁבְעָה מוּצָקוֹת לַנֵּרוֹת אֲשֶׁר עַל־רֹאשָׁהּ׃
ג ד וּשְׁנַיִם זֵיתִים עָלֶיהָ אֶחָד מִימִין הַגֻּלָּה וְאֶחָד עַל־שְׂמֹאלָהּ׃ וָאַעַן
ה וָאֹמַר אֶל־הַמַּלְאָךְ הַדֹּבֵר בִּי לֵאמֹר מָה־אֵלֶּה אֲדֹנִי׃ וַיַּעַן הַמַּלְאָךְ
הַדֹּבֵר בִּי וַיֹּאמֶר אֵלַי הֲלוֹא יָדַעְתָּ מָה־הֵמָּה אֵלֶּה וָאֹמַר לֹא אֲדֹנִי׃
ו וַיַּעַן וַיֹּאמֶר אֵלַי לֵאמֹר זֶה דְּבַר־יְהוָה אֶל־זְרֻבָּבֶל לֵאמֹר לֹא בְחַיִל
ז וְלֹא בְכֹחַ כִּי אִם־בְּרוּחִי אָמַר יְהוָה צְבָאוֹת׃ מִי־אַתָּה הַר־הַגָּדוֹל
לִפְנֵי זְרֻבָּבֶל לְמִישֹׁר וְהוֹצִיא אֶת־הָאֶבֶן הָרֹאשָׁה תְּשֻׁאוֹת חֵן ׀ חֵן
ח ט לָהּ׃ וַיְהִי דְבַר־יְהוָה אֵלַי לֵאמֹר׃ יְדֵי זְרֻבָּבֶל יִסְּדוּ הַבַּיִת
י הַזֶּה וְיָדָיו תְּבַצַּעְנָה וְיָדַעְתָּ כִּי־יְהוָה צְבָאוֹת שְׁלָחַנִי אֲלֵיכֶם׃ כִּי מִי
בַז לְיוֹם קְטַנּוֹת וְשָׂמְחוּ וְרָאוּ אֶת־הָאֶבֶן הַבְּדִיל בְּיַד זְרֻבָּבֶל שִׁבְעָה־
יא אֵלֶּה עֵינֵי יְהוָה הֵמָּה מְשׁוֹטְטִים בְּכָל־הָאָרֶץ׃ וָאַעַן וָאֹמַר אֵלָיו
יב מַה־שְּׁנֵי הַזֵּיתִים הָאֵלֶּה עַל־יְמִין הַמְּנוֹרָה וְעַל־שְׂמֹאולָהּ׃ וָאַעַן שֵׁנִית
וָאֹמַר אֵלָיו מַה־שְׁתֵּי שִׁבֲּלֵי הַזֵּיתִים אֲשֶׁר בְּיַד שְׁנֵי צַנְתְּרוֹת הַזָּהָב
יג הַמְרִיקִים מֵעֲלֵיהֶם הַזָּהָב׃ וַיֹּאמֶר אֵלַי לֵאמֹר הֲלוֹא יָדַעְתָּ מָה־אֵלֶּה
יד וָאֹמַר לֹא אֲדֹנִי׃ וַיֹּאמֶר אֵלֶּה שְׁנֵי בְנֵי־הַיִּצְהָר הָעֹמְדִים עַל־אֲדוֹן
ה א כָּל־הָאָרֶץ׃ וָאָשׁוּב וָאֶשָּׂא עֵינַי וָאֶרְאֶה וְהִנֵּה מְגִלָּה עָפָה׃
ב וַיֹּאמֶר אֵלַי מָה אַתָּה רֹאֶה וָאֹמַר אֲנִי רֹאֶה מְגִלָּה עָפָה אָרְכָּהּ עֶשְׂרִים
ג בָּאַמָּה וְרָחְבָּהּ עֶשֶׂר בָּאַמָּה׃ וַיֹּאמֶר אֵלַי זֹאת הָאָלָה הַיּוֹצֵאת עַל־
פְּנֵי כָל־הָאָרֶץ כִּי כָל־הַגֹּנֵב מִזֶּה כָּמוֹהָ נִקָּה וְכָל־הַנִּשְׁבָּע מִזֶּה כָּמוֹהָ
ד נִקָּה׃ הוֹצֵאתִיהָ נְאֻם יְהוָה צְבָאוֹת וּבָאָה אֶל־בֵּית הַגַּנָּב וְאֶל־בֵּית
הַנִּשְׁבָּע בִּשְׁמִי לַשָּׁקֶר וְלָנָה בְּתוֹךְ בֵּיתוֹ וְכִלַּתּוּ וְאֶת־עֵצָיו וְאֶת־אֲבָנָיו׃
ה וַיֵּצֵא הַמַּלְאָךְ הַדֹּבֵר בִּי וַיֹּאמֶר אֵלַי שָׂא נָא עֵינֶיךָ וּרְאֵה מָה הַיּוֹצֵאת
ו הַזֹּאת׃ וָאֹמַר מַה־הִיא וַיֹּאמֶר זֹאת הָאֵיפָה הַיּוֹצֵאת וַיֹּאמֶר זֹאת

7 ephah[12] emerging." He said, "This is their seeing eye all over the land." A lead
8 weight is lifted. There is a lone woman sitting in the ephah. He said, "She
is the evil." He cast her into the ephah, then dropped the lead stone onto
9 its opening. I raised my eyes and saw: there were two women
approaching, wind in their wings, and their wings were like the wings of a
10 stork. They lifted the ephah up between the earth and the heavens. I said to
11 the angel with whom I spoke, "Where are they taking the ephah?" He said to
me, "To build it a house in the land of Shinar,[13] established and placed there
6 1 on its foundation." Once again I lifted my eyes and saw: four chariots
2 emerging from between two mountains. The mountains were of bronze. The
first chariot was hitched to blood bay horses; the second chariot was hitched
3 to black horses; the third chariot was hitched to white horses; and the fourth
4 one was hitched to brindle horses, mighty ones. Then I spoke and said to the
5 angel with whom I spoke, "What are these, my lord?" The angel spoke and
said, "They are the four winds of the skies, stationing themselves before the
6 Lord of all the earth. The chariot with the black horses is going out to the
northland, the white ones behind them. The brindle horses are going out to
7 the southland." Then these mighty ones went out and sought to go, to rove
the earth. So He said, "Go, rove the earth." And the chariots went and roved
8 the earth. He spurred me on and spoke to me, saying: "See, those going out
9 to the northland, they set My spirit upon the northland."[14] Then
10" the word of the LORD came to me: "Take from the exiles – from Ḥeldai, from
Tuvya, from Yedaya who came from Babylon – and come, you yourself, on
11 that day; come to the house of Yoshiya son of Tzefanya. Take silver and gold;
make crowns and set one on the head of Yehoshua son of Yehotzadak the
12 High Priest. Tell him, so says the LORD of Hosts: There is a man; Tzemaḥ is
his name. He will come to flower from where he is and build the Sanctuary
13 of the LORD. Lo, he will build the Sanctuary of the LORD. He will wear
majesty; he will sit and rule on his throne. The priest, also, will sit on his own
14 throne, and between them there will be peaceful counsel. Let these crowns
be a monument for Ḥelem, Tuvya, Yedaya, and Ḥen son of Tzefanya in
15 the Sanctuary of the LORD. Then those from afar will come and build the
Sanctuary of the LORD, and you will know that the LORD of Hosts sent me
to you. This is what will be if you indeed heed the voice of the LORD your
7 1 God." In the fourth year of King Daryavesh's reign, on the fourth
2 of the ninth month, Kislev, the word of the LORD came to Zekharya: Beit-El,
3 Saretzer, and Regem Melekh[15] and his men sent to entreat the LORD, to
ask the priests at the House of the LORD of Hosts and the prophets, too:
Should I weep in the fifth month,[16] deny myself as I have done these many

12 | A dry measure, equivalent to approximately 25 liters.
13 | Another name for Bavel (see, e.g., Gen. 10:10).
14 | Conquerors such as the Babylonians generally invaded from the north (cf. Jer. 1:13–14).
15 | Presumably Jewish leaders in the Babylonian exile.
16 | The fast of the Ninth of Av, commemorating the destruction of the Temple (II Kings 25:8).

ז עֵינָם בְּכָל־הָאָרֶץ: וְהִנֵּה כִּכַּר עֹפֶרֶת נִשֵּׂאת וְזֹאת אִשָּׁה אַחַת יוֹשֶׁבֶת
ח בְּתוֹךְ הָאֵיפָה: וַיֹּאמֶר זֹאת הָרִשְׁעָה וַיַּשְׁלֵךְ אֹתָהּ אֶל־תּוֹךְ הָאֵיפָה
ט וַיַּשְׁלֵךְ אֶת־אֶבֶן הָעֹפֶרֶת אֶל־פִּיהָ: וָאֶשָּׂא עֵינַי וָאֵרֶא וְהִנֵּה
שְׁתַּיִם נָשִׁים יוֹצְאוֹת וְרוּחַ בְּכַנְפֵיהֶם וְלָהֵנָּה כְנָפַיִם כְּכַנְפֵי הַחֲסִידָה
י וַתִּשֶּׂאנָה אֶת־הָאֵיפָה בֵּין הָאָרֶץ וּבֵין הַשָּׁמָיִם: וָאֹמַר אֶל־הַמַּלְאָךְ
יא הַדֹּבֵר בִּי אָנָה הֵמָּה מוֹלִכוֹת אֶת־הָאֵיפָה: וַיֹּאמֶר אֵלַי לִבְנוֹת־לָה
ו א בַיִת בְּאֶרֶץ שִׁנְעָר וְהוּכַן וְהֻנִּיחָה שָּׁם עַל־מְכֻנָתָהּ: וָאָשֻׁב
וָאֶשָּׂא עֵינַי וָאֶרְאֶה וְהִנֵּה אַרְבַּע מַרְכָּבוֹת יֹצְאוֹת מִבֵּין שְׁנֵי הֶהָרִים
ב וְהֶהָרִים הָרֵי נְחֹשֶׁת: בַּמֶּרְכָּבָה הָרִאשֹׁנָה סוּסִים אֲדֻמִּים וּבַמֶּרְכָּבָה
ג הַשֵּׁנִית סוּסִים שְׁחֹרִים: וּבַמֶּרְכָּבָה הַשְּׁלִשִׁית סוּסִים לְבָנִים וּבַמֶּרְכָּבָה
ד הָרְבִעִית סוּסִים בְּרֻדִּים אֲמֻצִּים: וָאַעַן וָאֹמַר אֶל־הַמַּלְאָךְ הַדֹּבֵר בִּי
ה מָה־אֵלֶּה אֲדֹנִי: וַיַּעַן הַמַּלְאָךְ וַיֹּאמֶר אֵלָי אֵלֶּה אַרְבַּע רֻחוֹת הַשָּׁמַיִם
ו יוֹצְאוֹת מֵהִתְיַצֵּב עַל־אֲדוֹן כָּל־הָאָרֶץ: אֲשֶׁר־בָּהּ הַסּוּסִים הַשְּׁחֹרִים
יֹצְאִים אֶל־אֶרֶץ צָפוֹן וְהַלְּבָנִים יָצְאוּ אֶל־אַחֲרֵיהֶם וְהַבְּרֻדִּים יָצְאוּ
ז אֶל־אֶרֶץ הַתֵּימָן: וְהָאֲמֻצִּים יָצְאוּ וַיְבַקְשׁוּ לָלֶכֶת לְהִתְהַלֵּךְ בָּאָרֶץ
ח וַיֹּאמֶר לְכוּ הִתְהַלְּכוּ בָאָרֶץ וַתִּתְהַלַּכְנָה בָּאָרֶץ: וַיַּזְעֵק אֹתִי וַיְדַבֵּר
אֵלַי לֵאמֹר רְאֵה הַיּוֹצְאִים אֶל־אֶרֶץ צָפוֹן הֵנִיחוּ אֶת־רוּחִי בְּאֶרֶץ
ט צָפוֹן: וַיְהִי דְבַר־יְהוָה אֵלַי לֵאמֹר: לָקוֹחַ מֵאֵת
הַגּוֹלָה מֵחֶלְדַּי וּמֵאֵת טוֹבִיָּה וּמֵאֵת יְדַעְיָה וּבָאתָ אַתָּה בַּיּוֹם הַהוּא
יא וּבָאתָ בֵּית יֹאשִׁיָּה בֶן־צְפַנְיָה אֲשֶׁר־בָּאוּ מִבָּבֶל: וְלָקַחְתָּ כֶסֶף־וְזָהָב
וְעָשִׂיתָ עֲטָרוֹת וְשַׂמְתָּ בְּרֹאשׁ יְהוֹשֻׁעַ בֶּן־יְהוֹצָדָק הַכֹּהֵן הַגָּדוֹל:
יב וְאָמַרְתָּ אֵלָיו לֵאמֹר כֹּה אָמַר יְהוָה צְבָאוֹת לֵאמֹר הִנֵּה־אִישׁ צֶמַח
יג שְׁמוֹ וּמִתַּחְתָּיו יִצְמָח וּבָנָה אֶת־הֵיכַל יְהוָה: וְהוּא יִבְנֶה אֶת־הֵיכַל
יְהוָה וְהוּא־יִשָּׂא הוֹד וְיָשַׁב וּמָשַׁל עַל־כִּסְאוֹ וְהָיָה כֹהֵן עַל־כִּסְאוֹ
יד וַעֲצַת שָׁלוֹם תִּהְיֶה בֵּין שְׁנֵיהֶם: וְהָעֲטָרֹת תִּהְיֶה לְחֵלֶם וּלְטוֹבִיָּה יח
טו וְלִידַעְיָה וּלְחֵן בֶּן־צְפַנְיָה לְזִכָּרוֹן בְּהֵיכַל יְהוָה: וּרְחוֹקִים ׀ יָבֹאוּ וּבָנוּ
בְּהֵיכַל יְהוָה וִידַעְתֶּם כִּי־יְהוָה צְבָאוֹת שְׁלָחַנִי אֲלֵיכֶם וְהָיָה אִם־
ז א שָׁמוֹעַ תִּשְׁמְעוּן בְּקוֹל יְהוָה אֱלֹהֵיכֶם: וַיְהִי בִּשְׁנַת
אַרְבַּע לְדָרְיָוֶשׁ הַמֶּלֶךְ הָיָה דְבַר־יְהוָה אֶל־זְכַרְיָה בְּאַרְבָּעָה לַחֹדֶשׁ
ב הַתְּשִׁעִי בְּכִסְלֵו: וַיִּשְׁלַח בֵּית־אֵל שַׂר־אֶצֶר וְרֶגֶם מֶלֶךְ וַאֲנָשָׁיו לְחַלּוֹת
ג אֶת־פְּנֵי יְהוָה: לֵאמֹר אֶל־הַכֹּהֲנִים אֲשֶׁר לְבֵית־יְהוָה צְבָאוֹת וְאֶל־
הַנְּבִיאִים לֵאמֹר הַאֶבְכֶּה בַּחֹדֶשׁ הַחֲמִשִׁי הִנָּזֵר כַּאֲשֶׁר עָשִׂיתִי זֶה

4 5 years? Then the word of the LORD came to me: "Tell all the people
of the land and the priests as well: When you fasted and mourned during the
fifth and seventh[17] months these seventy years, was it for Me? Was it for Me
6 that you fasted? When you eat and when you drink, are you not the ones
7 eating and drinking?" Were these not the words called by the LORD through
the earlier prophets when Jerusalem was settled and serene, her cities around
8 her, too; when the Negev and the lowlands were settled? Then the
9 word of the LORD came to Zekharya: "So says the LORD of Hosts: Judge
10 truthful justice; show kindness and compassion to one another. Do not
oppress the widow or orphan, stranger or poor person, and do not think evil
11 of your brother in your hearts. But they refused to listen. They turned a
12 stubborn shoulder and closed their ears so that they could not hear; they set
their hearts like adamant so as not to hear the Torah and the words sent
through the earlier prophets by the spirit of the LORD of Hosts. Then a terrible
13 fury arose from the LORD of Hosts: Because when He called they did not
14 hear Him, so they call and I do not hear, says the LORD of Hosts. So in a
storm I blew them away to all the nations who do not know them. They
left behind them a land barren of wayfarers. They laid this desired land
8 1 2 waste." Then the word of the LORD of Hosts came: So says the LORD
of Hosts: I was fiercely zealous on Zion's behalf; on behalf of her I was zealous
3 with a great wrath. So says the LORD: I have returned to Zion and dwelled
within Jerusalem. Jerusalem will be called City of Truth, the Mountain of the
4 LORD of Hosts, the Holy Mountain. So says the LORD of Hosts:
Once again old men and old women will sit in the squares of Jerusalem. In
5 old age a man will lean on the staff in his hand, and the city squares will be
6 full and alive with young boys and girls playing in her open squares. So
says the LORD of Hosts: Though it was wondrous in the eyes of this nation
in those days, would it be wondrous to My eyes? The LORD of Hosts has
7 spoken. So says the LORD of Hosts: Behold, I will deliver My nation
8 from the east land and the land of the setting sun. I will bring them back, and
they will dwell within Jerusalem. They will be My nation, and I will be their
9 God in truth and beneficence. So says the LORD of Hosts: Be strong!
Be like those who heard these words in those days from the prophets who
were present on the day the foundations were laid for the House of the LORD
10 of Hosts, for His Sanctuary to be built.[18] Previously, in those days, there were
neither wages for man nor recompense for animals; there was no peace from
the enemy for those who came and went. I set all of humanity against one
11 another. But now I will not be as in those first days for the remnant of this
12 people – the LORD of Hosts has spoken. These are the seeds of peace: the
vine will give its fruit, the land its produce, and the skies their dew. I will give

17 | The fast of Gedalya, commemorating his assassination (Jer., ch. 41).
18 | See Haggai 2:2–4 and Ezra, chapter 3.

ד ה כמה שנים: ויהי דבר־יהוה צבאות אלי לאמר: אמר
אל־כל־עם הארץ ואל־הכהנים לאמר כי־צמתם וספוד בחמישי
ו ובשביעי וזה שבעים שנה הצום צמתני אני: וכי תאכלו וכי תשתו
ז הלוא אתם האכלים ואתם השתים: הלוא את־הדברים אשר קרא
יהוה ביד הנביאים הראשנים בהיות ירושלם ישבת ושלוה ועריה
ח סביבתיה והנגב והשפלה ישב: ויהי דבר־יהוה אל־
ט זכריה לאמר: כה אמר יהוה צבאות לאמר משפט אמת שפטו
י וחסד ורחמים עשו איש את־אחיו: ואלמנה ויתום גר ועני אל־
יא תעשקו ורעת איש אחיו אל־תחשבו בלבבכם: וימאנו להקשיב
יב ויתנו כתף סררת ואזניהם הכבידו משמוע: ולבם שמו שמיר משמוע
את־התורה ואת־הדברים אשר שלח יהוה צבאות ברוחו ביד
יג הנביאים הראשנים ויהי קצף גדול מאת יהוה צבאות: ויהי כאשר־
יד קרא ולא שמעו כן יקראו ולא אשמע אמר יהוה צבאות: ואסערם
על כל־הגוים אשר לא־ידעום והארץ נשמה אחריהם מעבר ומשב
ח א וישימו ארץ־חמדה לשמה: ויהי דבר־יהוה
ב צבאות לאמר: כה אמר יהוה צבאות קנאתי לציון קנאה גדולה
ג וחמה גדולה קנאתי לה: כה אמר יהוה שבתי אל־ציון ושכנתי
בתוך ירושלם ונקראה ירושלם עיר האמת והר־יהוה צבאות הר
ד הקדש: כה אמר יהוה צבאות עד ישבו זקנים וזקנות
ה ברחבות ירושלם ואיש משענתו בידו מרב ימים: ורחבות העיר
ו ימלאו ילדים וילדות משחקים ברחבתיה: כה אמר
יהוה צבאות כי יפלא בעיני שארית העם הזה בימים ההם גם־בעיני
ז יפלא נאם יהוה צבאות: כה אמר יהוה צבאות הנני
ח מושיע את־עמי מארץ מזרח ומארץ מבוא השמש: והבאתי אתם
ושכנו בתוך ירושלם והיו־לי לעם ואני אהיה להם לאלהים באמת
ט ובצדקה: כה־אמר יהוה צבאות תחזקנה ידיכם
השמעים בימים האלה את הדברים האלה מפי הנביאים אשר
י ביום יסד בית־יהוה צבאות ההיכל להבנות: כי לפני הימים ההם
שכר האדם לא נהיה ושכר הבהמה איננה וליוצא ולבא אין־שלום
יא מן־הצר ואשלח את־כל־האדם איש ברעהו: ועתה לא כימים
יב הראשנים אני לשארית העם הזה נאם יהוה צבאות: כי־זרע השלום
הגפן תתן פריה והארץ תתן את־יבולה והשמים יתנו טלם והנחלתי

13 all of this to the remnant of this people to possess. Just as you were a curse
among the nations, House of Yehuda and House of Israel, to that degree I will
14 deliver you, and you will be a blessing. Do not fear. Be strong. For
so says the Lord of Hosts: Insofar as I planned to cause you trouble when
15 your forefathers angered Me, says the Lord of Hosts, and did not relent, to
that degree I have again planned in these days to do good with Jerusalem and
16 the House of Yehuda. Do not fear. This is what you should do: Speak truthfully,
17 one to another. In your gates render judgments of truth and peace. Think not
evil of one another in your hearts. Do not love the false oath. I hate all of
18 these – the Lord has spoken. The word of the Lord of Hosts came
19 to me: So says the Lord of Hosts: The fasts of the fourth month and of the
fifth and the seventh and the tenth – all of these will be for the House of
Yehuda joy and happiness, and times set aside for good. Therefore, love truth
20 and peace.[19] So says the Lord of Hosts: Once again nations,
21 dwellers of many cities, will come, and the dwellers of one city will go, saying
one to another, one by one, "Let us go entreat the face of the Lord, beseech
22 the Lord of Hosts. I too will go." Then many nations will come – great
peoples – to beseech the Lord of Hosts in Jerusalem, to entreat the face of
23 the Lord. So says the Lord of Hosts: It will be in those days
that ten men of many languages will cling, they will cling to the hem of a
Jewish man and say, "Let us go with you, for we have heard that God is with
9 1 you." An oracle: The word of the Lord is in Ḥadrakh;[20] Damascus
is its resting place. For the eyes of man turn to the Lord and to the tribes of
2 Israel. Even Ḥamat will be bordered by it, Tyre and Sidon, for in great wisdom
3 Tyre built herself a tower; she hoarded silver like dust and gold like street
4 mud, but the Lord will dispossess her, strike her forces at sea, while she
5 herself will be consumed by flame. Ashkelon will look on in fear; Aza will
shudder and shake; Ekron too, for the one she looks to will be debased: A
6 king will be lost in Aza, Ashkelon will be unpeopled, a bastard will sit in
7 Ashdod, and I will cut off the majesty of the Philistines. But I will wash away
the blood in his mouth, the detestable things between his teeth, and he, he
too will remain for our God and be like a chieftain in Yehuda, while Ekron
8 will be like a Jebusite. I will be an encampment around My House against
armies, against those who come and go. No more shall any oppressor overrun
9 them, for now I have seen with My eyes. Rejoice mightily, daughter
Zion; call out joyfully, daughter Jerusalem. Yes, your king is coming to you.
He is righteous and has prevailed – humble, riding a donkey, a yearling,
10 purebred. There will be no more chariots in Efrayim, nor horses in Jerusalem.
No longer will there be bows of war. For he will speak words of peace with
the nations, and his rule will span from sea to sea, from the river to the ends
11 of the earth. You too: for the sake of the blood of your covenant, I released

---

19 | See notes on 7:3–5. The fast of the fourth month is the Seventeenth of Tammuz, commemorating the breach of Jerusalem's walls (see Jer. 39:2). That of the tenth month is the Tenth of Tevet, commemorating the beginning of the siege (see ii Kings 25:1 and Ezek. 24:2).

20 | A town in the region of Damascus.

יג אֶת־שְׁאֵרִית הָעָם הַזֶּה אֶת־כָּל־אֵלֶּה׃ וְהָיָה כַּאֲשֶׁר הֱיִיתֶם קְלָלָה
בַּגּוֹיִם בֵּית יְהוּדָה וּבֵית יִשְׂרָאֵל כֵּן אוֹשִׁיעַ אֶתְכֶם וִהְיִיתֶם בְּרָכָה
יד אַל־תִּירָאוּ תֶּחֱזַקְנָה יְדֵיכֶם׃ כִּי כֹה אָמַר יְהוָה צְבָאוֹת
כַּאֲשֶׁר זָמַמְתִּי לְהָרַע לָכֶם בְּהַקְצִיף אֲבֹתֵיכֶם אֹתִי אָמַר יְהוָה צְבָאוֹת
טו וְלֹא נִחָמְתִּי׃ כֵּן שַׁבְתִּי זָמַמְתִּי בַּיָּמִים הָאֵלֶּה לְהֵיטִיב אֶת־יְרוּשָׁלַםִ
טז וְאֶת־בֵּית יְהוּדָה אַל־תִּירָאוּ׃ אֵלֶּה הַדְּבָרִים אֲשֶׁר תַּעֲשׂוּ דַּבְּרוּ אֱמֶת
יז אִישׁ אֶת־רֵעֵהוּ אֱמֶת וּמִשְׁפַּט שָׁלוֹם שִׁפְטוּ בְּשַׁעֲרֵיכֶם׃ וְאִישׁ ׀ אֶת־
רָעַת רֵעֵהוּ אַל־תַּחְשְׁבוּ בִּלְבַבְכֶם וּשְׁבֻעַת שֶׁקֶר אַל־תֶּאֱהָבוּ כִּי
יח אֶת־כָּל־אֵלֶּה אֲשֶׁר שָׂנֵאתִי נְאֻם־יְהוָה׃ וַיְהִי דְּבַר־
יט יְהוָה צְבָאוֹת אֵלַי לֵאמֹר׃ כֹּה־אָמַר יְהוָה צְבָאוֹת צוֹם הָרְבִיעִי וְצוֹם
הַחֲמִישִׁי וְצוֹם הַשְּׁבִיעִי וְצוֹם הָעֲשִׂירִי יִהְיֶה לְבֵית־יְהוּדָה לְשָׂשׂוֹן
כ וּלְשִׂמְחָה וּלְמֹעֲדִים טוֹבִים וְהָאֱמֶת וְהַשָּׁלוֹם אֱהָבוּ׃ כֹּה
כא אָמַר יְהוָה צְבָאוֹת עֹד אֲשֶׁר יָבֹאוּ עַמִּים וְיֹשְׁבֵי עָרִים רַבּוֹת׃ וְהָלְכוּ
יֹשְׁבֵי אַחַת אֶל־אַחַת לֵאמֹר נֵלְכָה הָלוֹךְ לְחַלּוֹת אֶת־פְּנֵי יְהוָה
כב וּלְבַקֵּשׁ אֶת־יְהוָה צְבָאוֹת אֵלְכָה גַּם־אָנִי׃ וּבָאוּ עַמִּים רַבִּים וְגוֹיִם
עֲצוּמִים לְבַקֵּשׁ אֶת־יְהוָה צְבָאוֹת בִּירוּשָׁלָםִ וּלְחַלּוֹת אֶת־פְּנֵי
כג יְהוָה׃ כֹּה־אָמַר יְהוָה צְבָאוֹת בַּיָּמִים הָהֵמָּה אֲשֶׁר יַחֲזִיקוּ יט
עֲשָׂרָה אֲנָשִׁים מִכֹּל לְשֹׁנוֹת הַגּוֹיִם וְהֶחֱזִיקוּ בִּכְנַף אִישׁ יְהוּדִי לֵאמֹר
ט א נֵלְכָה עִמָּכֶם כִּי שָׁמַעְנוּ אֱלֹהִים עִמָּכֶם׃ מַשָּׂא דְבַר־יְהוָה
בְּאֶרֶץ חַדְרָךְ וְדַמֶּשֶׂק מְנֻחָתוֹ כִּי לַיהוָה עֵין אָדָם וְכֹל שִׁבְטֵי יִשְׂרָאֵל׃
ב ג וְגַם־חֲמָת תִּגְבָּל־בָּהּ צֹר וְצִידוֹן כִּי חָכְמָה מְאֹד׃ וַתִּבֶן צֹר מָצוֹר לָהּ
ד וַתִּצְבָּר־כֶּסֶף כֶּעָפָר וְחָרוּץ כְּטִיט חוּצוֹת׃ הִנֵּה אֲדֹנָי יוֹרִשֶׁנָּה וְהִכָּה
ה בַיָּם חֵילָהּ וְהִיא בָּאֵשׁ תֵּאָכֵל׃ תֵּרֶא אַשְׁקְלוֹן וְתִירָא וְעַזָּה וְתָחִיל
מְאֹד וְעֶקְרוֹן כִּי־הֹבִישׁ מֶבָּטָהּ וְאָבַד מֶלֶךְ מֵעַזָּה וְאַשְׁקְלוֹן לֹא תֵשֵׁב׃
ו ז וְיָשַׁב מַמְזֵר בְּאַשְׁדּוֹד וְהִכְרַתִּי גְּאוֹן פְּלִשְׁתִּים׃ וַהֲסִרֹתִי דָמָיו מִפִּיו
וְשִׁקֻּצָיו מִבֵּין שִׁנָּיו וְנִשְׁאַר גַּם־הוּא לֵאלֹהֵינוּ וְהָיָה כְּאַלֻּף בִּיהוּדָה
ח וְעֶקְרוֹן כִּיבוּסִי׃ וְחָנִיתִי לְבֵיתִי מִצָּבָה מֵעֹבֵר וּמִשָּׁב וְלֹא־יַעֲבֹר עֲלֵיהֶם
ט עוֹד נֹגֵשׂ כִּי עַתָּה רָאִיתִי בְעֵינָי׃ גִּילִי מְאֹד בַּת־צִיּוֹן הָרִיעִי
בַּת יְרוּשָׁלַםִ הִנֵּה מַלְכֵּךְ יָבוֹא לָךְ צַדִּיק וְנוֹשָׁע הוּא עָנִי וְרֹכֵב עַל־
י חֲמוֹר וְעַל־עַיִר בֶּן־אֲתֹנוֹת׃ וְהִכְרַתִּי־רֶכֶב מֵאֶפְרַיִם וְסוּס מִירוּשָׁלַםִ
וְנִכְרְתָה קֶשֶׁת מִלְחָמָה וְדִבֶּר שָׁלוֹם לַגּוֹיִם וּמָשְׁלוֹ מִיָּם עַד־יָם וּמִנָּהָר
יא עַד־אַפְסֵי־אָרֶץ׃ גַּם־אַתְּ בְּדַם־בְּרִיתֵךְ שִׁלַּחְתִּי אֲסִירַיִךְ מִבּוֹר אֵין

12 your prisoners from a waterless pit. Return to the stronghold, O prisoners of
13 hope. Even today I will answer you, messenger after messenger. I aimed
Yehuda like a bow; Efrayim I filled like a quiver. I roused your children, Zion,
14 against your children, Ionia,[21] and wielded you like a warrior's sword. The
LORD GOD will appear above them; His arrow flies like a strike of lightning.
15 The Lord GOD will sound a ram's horn and rush in on southern storms. The
LORD of Hosts will protect them. They will consume; they will conquer
slingstones. They will drink, clamor as if with wine brimming over like a bowl,
16 like the corners of the altar. On that day the LORD their God will save them
like sheep, His people, for they are crown jewels displayed above His land.
17 For how good is His good, how lovely His beauty: Young men like wheat;
10 1 young women blossoming with wine. Ask the LORD for rain in the time of
spring showers, and the LORD will strike lightning; He will bring down
2 torrents of rain; He will give grass in the field to man. For the household idols
spoke deceit, and the seers falsely saw. They tell of empty dreams; their
comfort means nothing. Therefore they wandered like sheep; they were
3 defeated, for they were without a shepherd. My wrath is upon those
shepherds, and I will visit punishment upon those goat sires, for the LORD of
Hosts has redeemed His flock; He has redeemed the House of Yehuda and
4 made them like His magnificent horse charging in battle. From Him the
cornerstone; from Him the tent peg; from Him the bow of war; from Him
5 every ruler emerges together. They will be like heroes treading through field
mud in battle. They will fight, for the LORD is with them, and they will put
6 riders of horses to shame. I will strengthen the House of Yehuda and deliver
the House of Yosef. I will bring them back to roost with My mercy upon them,
and they will be as if I never abandoned them. For I am the LORD, their God,
7 who will answer them. Efrayim will be like a hero. Their hearts will be glad
like wine. Their children will see and be glad. Their hearts will rejoice in the
8 LORD. I will surely whistle for them, gather them in, for I will redeem them,
9 and they will multiply as once they multiplied. I will scatter them like seeds
among the nations; in far-off places they will remember Me. They will live
10 along with their children and return. I will bring them back from the land of
Egypt; from Ashur, I will gather them in and bring them to the land of Gilad
11 and Lebanon, and still, it will not be enough for them. He will trawl trouble
through the sea, strike the ocean waves, and dry will be the depths of the Nile.
12 Ashur's majesty will be cast down, and rule shall pass away from Egypt. I will
strengthen them in the LORD, and they will walk with His name – the LORD
11 1 has spoken. Lebanon, open your doors, and fire will consume
2 your cedar trees. Wail, O juniper tree, for the cedar, devastated by august ones,
has fallen. Wail, O oaks of the Bashan, for the fortified forest has been felled.
3 O, the sound, the wail of the shepherds for their devastated glory. O, the
sound, the roar of young lions for the devastated lush thicket along the
4 Jordan. So says the LORD, my God: "Herd the sheep marked

21 | Ionia was a region in Asia Minor inhabited by Hellenic (Greek-speaking) peoples; the name Yavan eventually came to refer in Hebrew to the Greek lands and peoples in general.

יב מַיִם בּוֹ: שׁוּבוּ לְבִצָּרוֹן אֲסִירֵי הַתִּקְוָה גַּם־הַיּוֹם מַגִּיד מִשְׁנֶה אָשִׁיב
יג לָךְ: כִּי־דָרַכְתִּי לִי יְהוּדָה קֶשֶׁת מִלֵּאתִי אֶפְרַיִם וְעוֹרַרְתִּי בָנַיִךְ צִיּוֹן
יד עַל־בָּנַיִךְ יָוָן וְשַׂמְתִּיךְ כְּחֶרֶב גִּבּוֹר: וַיהוָה עֲלֵיהֶם יֵרָאֶה וְיָצָא כַבָּרָק
טו חִצּוֹ וַאדֹנָי יֱהוִה בַּשּׁוֹפָר יִתְקָע וְהָלַךְ בְּסַעֲרוֹת תֵּימָן: יְהוָה צְבָאוֹת
יָגֵן עֲלֵיהֶם וְאָכְלוּ וְכָבְשׁוּ אַבְנֵי־קֶלַע וְשָׁתוּ הָמוּ כְּמוֹ־יָיִן וּמָלְאוּ כַּמִּזְרָק
טז כְּזָוִיּוֹת מִזְבֵּחַ: וְהוֹשִׁיעָם יְהוָה אֱלֹהֵיהֶם בַּיּוֹם הַהוּא כְּצֹאן עַמּוֹ כִּי
יז אַבְנֵי־נֵזֶר מִתְנוֹסְסוֹת עַל־אַדְמָתוֹ: כִּי מַה־טּוּבוֹ וּמַה־יָּפְיוֹ דָּגָן בַּחוּרִים
י א וְתִירוֹשׁ יְנוֹבֵב בְּתֻלוֹת: שַׁאֲלוּ מֵיְהוָה מָטָר בְּעֵת מַלְקוֹשׁ יְהוָה עֹשֶׂה
ב חֲזִיזִים וּמְטַר־גֶּשֶׁם יִתֵּן לָהֶם לְאִישׁ עֵשֶׂב בַּשָּׂדֶה: כִּי הַתְּרָפִים דִּבְּרוּ־
אָוֶן וְהַקּוֹסְמִים חָזוּ שֶׁקֶר וַחֲלֹמוֹת הַשָּׁוא יְדַבֵּרוּ הֶבֶל יְנַחֵמוּן עַל־כֵּן
ג נָסְעוּ כְמוֹ־צֹאן יַעֲנוּ כִּי־אֵין רֹעֶה: עַל־הָרֹעִים חָרָה
אַפִּי וְעַל־הָעַתּוּדִים אֶפְקוֹד כִּי־פָקַד יְהוָה צְבָאוֹת אֶת־עֶדְרוֹ אֶת־בֵּית
ד יְהוּדָה וְשָׂם אוֹתָם כְּסוּס הוֹדוֹ בַּמִּלְחָמָה: מִמֶּנּוּ פִנָּה מִמֶּנּוּ יָתֵד מִמֶּנּוּ
ה קֶשֶׁת מִלְחָמָה מִמֶּנּוּ יֵצֵא כָל־נוֹגֵשׂ יַחְדָּו: וְהָיוּ כְגִבֹּרִים בּוֹסִים בְּטִיט
חוּצוֹת בַּמִּלְחָמָה וְנִלְחֲמוּ כִּי יְהוָה עִמָּם וְהֹבִישׁוּ רֹכְבֵי סוּסִים:
ו וְגִבַּרְתִּי | אֶת־בֵּית יְהוּדָה וְאֶת־בֵּית יוֹסֵף אוֹשִׁיעַ וְהוֹשְׁבוֹתִים כִּי
ז רִחַמְתִּים וְהָיוּ כַּאֲשֶׁר לֹא־זְנַחְתִּים כִּי אֲנִי יְהוָה אֱלֹהֵיהֶם וְאֶעֱנֵם: וְהָיוּ
כְגִבּוֹר אֶפְרַיִם וְשָׂמַח לִבָּם כְּמוֹ־יָיִן וּבְנֵיהֶם יִרְאוּ וְשָׂמֵחוּ יָגֵל לִבָּם
ח ט בַּיהוָה: אֶשְׁרְקָה לָהֶם וַאֲקַבְּצֵם כִּי פְדִיתִים וְרָבוּ כְּמוֹ רָבוּ: וְאֶזְרָעֵם
י בָּעַמִּים וּבַמֶּרְחַקִּים יִזְכְּרוּנִי וְחָיוּ אֶת־בְּנֵיהֶם וָשָׁבוּ: וַהֲשִׁבוֹתִים מֵאֶרֶץ
מִצְרַיִם וּמֵאַשּׁוּר אֲקַבְּצֵם וְאֶל־אֶרֶץ גִּלְעָד וּלְבָנוֹן אֲבִיאֵם וְלֹא יִמָּצֵא
יא לָהֶם: וְעָבַר בַּיָּם צָרָה וְהִכָּה בַיָּם גַּלִּים וְהֹבִישׁוּ כֹּל מְצוּלוֹת יְאֹר וְהוּרַד
יב גְּאוֹן אַשּׁוּר וְשֵׁבֶט מִצְרַיִם יָסוּר: וְגִבַּרְתִּים בַּיהוָה וּבִשְׁמוֹ יִתְהַלָּכוּ
יא א נְאֻם יְהוָה: פְּתַח לְבָנוֹן דְּלָתֶיךָ וְתֹאכַל אֵשׁ בַּאֲרָזֶיךָ:
ב הֵילֵל בְּרוֹשׁ כִּי־נָפַל אֶרֶז אֲשֶׁר אַדִּרִים שֻׁדָּדוּ הֵילִילוּ אַלּוֹנֵי בָשָׁן כִּי
ג יָרַד יַעַר הַבָּצוּר: קוֹל יִלְלַת הָרֹעִים כִּי שֻׁדְּדָה אַדַּרְתָּם קוֹל שַׁאֲגַת הַבָּצִיר
ד כְּפִירִים כִּי שֻׁדַּד גְּאוֹן הַיַּרְדֵּן: כֹּה אָמַר יְהוָה

5 for slaughter, those whom buyers will kill and feel no guilt, whose sellers will
say, 'Blessed be the LORD, I will be rich'; whose shepherds have no mercy
6 upon them. For I will no longer spare the people of the land – the LORD has
spoken – but indeed, I will hand over every person into the hands of their
fellows, into the hand of their king. They will harrow the earth. I will deliver
7 no one from their hands." So I herded the sheep marked for slaughter, for they
were ailing sheep. I took two staffs – one I called Pleasant; the other I called
8 Harmful. I herded the sheep with them. I removed three shepherds in the
space of one month, for I had lost my patience with them, and they too were
9 disgusted with me. I said, "I will not herd for you; the dying will die, the lost
will remain lost, and as for those ewes that remain, they will eat one another's
10 flesh." I took my staff, I took Pleasant, and snapped it so as to annul my
11 covenant, the one I made with all the nations. Yes, on that day it will be
annulled, and those ailing sheep whom I guarded will indeed know that this
12 is the word of the LORD. I said to them, "If you wish, pay me, but if not, do
13 not." So they measured out my salary of thirty shekel. Then the LORD said to
me, "Throw it away to the treasury in that eminent place where I granted them
eminence." So I took the thirty shekel and threw them into Temple treasury.
14 Then I snapped my second staff, Harmful, so as to annul the brotherhood
15 between Yehuda and Israel. Then the LORD said to me, "Once again,
16 take up the instrument of a foolish shepherd, for I am going to establish a
shepherd in this land: He will not render an account of the lost, nor seek out
the young one. He will not heal the broken, nor provide for the lame. But he
17 will consume the healthy fleshed and break their hooves. Hie, worthless
shepherd, abandoner of sheep. A sword be upon his arm, and his right eye!
12 1 His arm will surely wither, his right eye surely darken." An oracle,
which is the word of the LORD regarding Israel: The LORD who spread out
heaven, laid the foundations of earth, and created the spirit of man within
2 him, has spoken: So it will be: that I will make Jerusalem as a cup of reeling
for all those nations surrounding her, even for Yehuda it will be so by a siege
3 upon Jerusalem. On that day when the nations of the land gather against her,
I will make Jerusalem a boulder to all the nations; all those who dare lift it
4 will surely be deeply wounded. On that day – the LORD has spoken – I will
strike every horse with terror and their riders with insanity. I will keep an
open eye on the House of Yehuda but strike all the nations' horses with
5 blindness. Then the chieftains of Yehuda will say in their hearts: "I take
strength from the strength that the residents of Jerusalem find in the LORD
6 of Hosts, their God." On that day, I will make the chieftains of Yehuda like a
fire basin alight among the trees, like a flaming torch among the sheaves, and
they will consume everything to the right and to the left of them: all the
surrounding nations. Then Jerusalem will still remain in its place, in Jerusalem,
7 and the LORD will save the tents of Yehuda first so that the glory of the House
of David and the glory of the residents of Jerusalem does not become greater

ה אֱלֹהָי רְעֵה אֶת־צֹאן הַהֲרֵגָה׃ אֲשֶׁר קֹנֵיהֶן יַהַרְגֻן וְלֹא יֶאְשָׁמוּ וּמֹכְרֵיהֶן
ו יֹאמַר בָּרוּךְ יהוה וַאעְשִׁר וְרֹעֵיהֶם לֹא יַחְמוֹל עֲלֵיהֶן׃ כִּי לֹא אֶחְמוֹל
עוֹד עַל־יֹשְׁבֵי הָאָרֶץ נְאֻם־יהוה וְהִנֵּה אָנֹכִי מַמְצִיא אֶת־הָאָדָם אִישׁ
ז בְּיַד־רֵעֵהוּ וּבְיַד מַלְכּוֹ וְכִתְּתוּ אֶת־הָאָרֶץ וְלֹא אַצִּיל מִיָּדָם׃ וָאֶרְעֶה
אֶת־צֹאן הַהֲרֵגָה לָכֵן עֲנִיֵּי הַצֹּאן וָאֶקַּח־לִי שְׁנֵי מַקְלוֹת לְאַחַד
ח קָרָאתִי נֹעַם וּלְאַחַד קָרָאתִי חֹבְלִים וָאֶרְעֶה אֶת־הַצֹּאן׃ וָאַכְחִד אֶת־
שְׁלֹשֶׁת הָרֹעִים בְּיֶרַח אֶחָד וַתִּקְצַר נַפְשִׁי בָּהֶם וְגַם־נַפְשָׁם בָּחֲלָה בִי׃
ט וָאֹמַר לֹא אֶרְעֶה אֶתְכֶם הַמֵּתָה תָמוּת וְהַנִּכְחֶדֶת תִּכָּחֵד וְהַנִּשְׁאָרוֹת
י תֹּאכַלְנָה אִשָּׁה אֶת־בְּשַׂר רְעוּתָהּ׃ וָאֶקַּח אֶת־מַקְלִי אֶת־נֹעַם וָאֶגְדַּע
יא אֹתוֹ לְהָפֵיר אֶת־בְּרִיתִי אֲשֶׁר כָּרַתִּי אֶת־כָּל־הָעַמִּים׃ וַתֻּפַר בַּיּוֹם
יב הַהוּא וַיֵּדְעוּ כֵן עֲנִיֵּי הַצֹּאן הַשֹּׁמְרִים אֹתִי כִּי דְבַר־יהוה הוּא׃ וָאֹמַר
אֲלֵיהֶם אִם־טוֹב בְּעֵינֵיכֶם הָבוּ שְׂכָרִי וְאִם־לֹא ׀ חֲדָלוּ וַיִּשְׁקְלוּ אֶת־
יג שְׂכָרִי שְׁלֹשִׁים כָּסֶף׃ וַיֹּאמֶר יהוה אֵלַי הַשְׁלִיכֵהוּ אֶל־הַיּוֹצֵר אֶדֶר
הַיְקָר אֲשֶׁר יָקַרְתִּי מֵעֲלֵיהֶם וָאֶקְחָה שְׁלֹשִׁים הַכֶּסֶף וָאַשְׁלִיךְ אֹתוֹ
יד בֵּית יהוה אֶל־הַיּוֹצֵר׃ וָאֶגְדַּע אֶת־מַקְלִי הַשֵּׁנִי אֵת הַחֹבְלִים לְהָפֵר
טו אֶת־הָאַחֲוָה בֵּין יְהוּדָה וּבֵין יִשְׂרָאֵל׃ וַיֹּאמֶר יהוה אֵלָי
טז עוֹד קַח־לְךָ כְּלִי רֹעֶה אֱוִלִי׃ כִּי הִנֵּה־אָנֹכִי מֵקִים רֹעֶה בָּאָרֶץ הַנִּכְחָדוֹת
לֹא־יִפְקֹד הַנַּעַר לֹא־יְבַקֵּשׁ וְהַנִּשְׁבֶּרֶת לֹא יְרַפֵּא הַנִּצָּבָה לֹא יְכַלְכֵּל
יז וּבְשַׂר הַבְּרִיאָה יֹאכַל וּפַרְסֵיהֶן יְפָרֵק׃ הוֹי רֹעִי הָאֱלִיל עֹזְבִי הַצֹּאן
חֶרֶב עַל־זְרוֹעוֹ וְעַל־עֵין יְמִינוֹ זְרֹעוֹ יָבוֹשׁ תִּיבָשׁ וְעֵין יְמִינוֹ כָּהֹה
יב א תִכְהֶה׃ מַשָּׂא דְבַר־יהוה עַל־יִשְׂרָאֵל נְאֻם־יהוה כ
ב נֹטֶה שָׁמַיִם וְיֹסֵד אָרֶץ וְיֹצֵר רוּחַ־אָדָם בְּקִרְבּוֹ׃ הִנֵּה אָנֹכִי שָׂם אֶת־
יְרוּשָׁלִַם סַף־רַעַל לְכָל־הָעַמִּים סָבִיב וְגַם עַל־יְהוּדָה יִהְיֶה בַמָּצוֹר
ג עַל־יְרוּשָׁלִָם׃ וְהָיָה בַיּוֹם־הַהוּא אָשִׂים אֶת־יְרוּשָׁלִַם אֶבֶן מַעֲמָסָה
לְכָל־הָעַמִּים כָּל־עֹמְסֶיהָ שָׂרוֹט יִשָּׂרֵטוּ וְנֶאֶסְפוּ עָלֶיהָ כֹּל גּוֹיֵי הָאָרֶץ׃
ד בַּיּוֹם הַהוּא נְאֻם־יהוה אַכֶּה כָל־סוּס בַּתִּמָּהוֹן וְרֹכְבוֹ בַּשִּׁגָּעוֹן וְעַל־
ה בֵּית יְהוּדָה אֶפְקַח אֶת־עֵינַי וְכֹל סוּס הָעַמִּים אַכֶּה בַּעִוָּרוֹן׃ וְאָמְרוּ
אַלֻּפֵי יְהוּדָה בְּלִבָּם אַמְצָה לִי יֹשְׁבֵי יְרוּשָׁלִַם בַּיהוה צְבָאוֹת אֱלֹהֵיהֶם׃
ו בַּיּוֹם הַהוּא אָשִׂים אֶת־אַלֻּפֵי יְהוּדָה כְּכִיּוֹר אֵשׁ בְּעֵצִים וּכְלַפִּיד אֵשׁ
בְּעָמִיר וְאָכְלוּ עַל־יָמִין וְעַל־שְׂמֹאול אֶת־כָּל־הָעַמִּים סָבִיב וְיָשְׁבָה
ז יְרוּשָׁלִַם עוֹד תַּחְתֶּיהָ בִּירוּשָׁלִָם׃ וְהוֹשִׁיעַ יהוה אֶת־אָהֳלֵי יְהוּדָה
בָּרִאשֹׁנָה לְמַעַן לֹא־תִגְדַּל תִּפְאֶרֶת בֵּית־דָּוִיד וְתִפְאֶרֶת יֹשֵׁב יְרוּשָׁלִַם

8 than that of Yehuda. On that day the LORD will protect the residents of
Jerusalem. On that day the most stumbling of them will be like David, and
9 the House of David will be like a god, an angel of the LORD, before them. On
10 that day I will seek to destroy all the nations coming against Jerusalem. Then
I will pour out a spirit of favor and supplication over the House of David and
the residents of Jerusalem, and they will look to Me regarding the one whom
they stabbed. They will mourn for him as a person mourns for an only child,
11 and their bitterness will be the bitterness of the loss of a firstborn. On that
day the mourning in Jerusalem will be greater than the mourning of Hadad-
12 Rimon[22] in the Valley of Megidon. The whole land will mourn, every family
on its own: the family of the House of David on its own, the women on their
own, the family of the house of Natan on its own, the women on their own,
13 the family of the House of Levi on its own, the women on their own, the
14 Shimi family on its own, the women on their own, all the remaining families,
13 1 every family, on its own, all the women on their own. On that day a spring
will flow for the House of David and the residents of Jerusalem, providing for
2 water of lustration[23] and purification offering. On that day – the LORD of
Hosts has spoken – I will eradicate the names of the idols from the land. They
will never be spoken of again. I will remove the prophets and the spirit of
3 impurity from the land. And should a person prophesy still, then his father
and mother, those who bore him, will say, "You shall not live, for you have
spoken falsely in the name of the LORD." Then his father and mother, those
4 who bore him, will stab him in the act of his prophecy. On that day the
prophets will be ashamed of their vision, each one of them, when they
5 prophesy. They will no longer wear a mantle of hair to deceive. He will say, "I
am not a prophet; I am a worker of the land, made a herdsman in my youth."
6 And if someone should ask him, "What are those bruises between your
shoulders?" he will reply, "Those are the bruises I received in the house of
7 those who love me." Awake, O sword, against My shepherd, against
the man beside Me – the LORD of Hosts has spoken. Strike the shepherd and
let the sheep be scattered, while I, I will set My Hand against the little ones.
8 This is what will be all over the land – the LORD has spoken – two-thirds of
9 the population will be cut down; they will die. One-third will remain. I will
pass that third through fire and refine them as one refines silver, and test them
as one tests gold. He will call in My name, and I will answer him. I will say,
14 1 "He is My nation," and he will say, "The LORD is my God."[24] Behold,
2 a day of the LORD is coming; your spoil will be divided up in your midst. I
will gather all the nations to Jerusalem in war: the city will be taken, the
houses will be plundered, and the women will be raped; half of the city will
go into exile, but the remainder of the people will not be cut off from the city.
3 The LORD will go out, and He will fight against these nations as He has fought
4 on days of battle. On that day His feet will stand upon the Mount of Olives

22 | Hadad and Rimon were names of Aramean gods; the verse may refer to an idolatrous rite.
23 | See Numbers 19:9.
24 | Cf. Hosea 2:25.

ח עַל־יְהוּדָה: בַּיּוֹם הַהוּא יָגֵן יְהוָה בְּעַד יוֹשֵׁב יְרוּשָׁלִַם וְהָיָה הַנִּכְשָׁל
בָּהֶם בַּיּוֹם הַהוּא כְּדָוִיד וּבֵית דָּוִיד כֵּאלֹהִים כְּמַלְאַךְ יְהוָה לִפְנֵיהֶם:
ט וְהָיָה בַּיּוֹם הַהוּא אֲבַקֵּשׁ לְהַשְׁמִיד אֶת־כָּל־הַגּוֹיִם הַבָּאִים עַל־
י יְרוּשָׁלִָם: וְשָׁפַכְתִּי עַל־בֵּית דָּוִיד וְעַל | יוֹשֵׁב יְרוּשָׁלִַם רוּחַ חֵן וְתַחֲנוּנִים
וְהִבִּיטוּ אֵלַי אֵת אֲשֶׁר־דָּקָרוּ וְסָפְדוּ עָלָיו כְּמִסְפֵּד עַל־הַיָּחִיד וְהָמֵר
יא עָלָיו כְּהָמֵר עַל־הַבְּכוֹר: בַּיּוֹם הַהוּא יִגְדַּל הַמִּסְפֵּד בִּירוּשָׁלִַם כְּמִסְפַּד
יב הֲדַדְרִמּוֹן בְּבִקְעַת מְגִדּוֹן: וְסָפְדָה הָאָרֶץ מִשְׁפָּחוֹת מִשְׁפָּחוֹת לְבָד
מִשְׁפַּחַת בֵּית־דָּוִיד לְבָד וּנְשֵׁיהֶם לְבָד מִשְׁפַּחַת בֵּית־נָתָן לְבָד וּנְשֵׁיהֶם
יג לְבָד: מִשְׁפַּחַת בֵּית־לֵוִי לְבָד וּנְשֵׁיהֶם לְבָד מִשְׁפַּחַת הַשִּׁמְעִי לְבָד
יד וּנְשֵׁיהֶם לְבָד: כֹּל הַמִּשְׁפָּחוֹת הַנִּשְׁאָרוֹת מִשְׁפָּחֹת מִשְׁפָּחֹת לְבָד
יג א וּנְשֵׁיהֶם לְבָד: בַּיּוֹם הַהוּא יִהְיֶה מָקוֹר נִפְתָּח לְבֵית דָּוִיד וּלְיֹשְׁבֵי
ב יְרוּשָׁלִָם לְחַטֵּאת וּלְנִדָּה: וְהָיָה בַיּוֹם הַהוּא נְאֻם | יְהוָה צְבָאוֹת
אַכְרִית אֶת־שְׁמוֹת הָעֲצַבִּים מִן־הָאָרֶץ וְלֹא יִזָּכְרוּ עוֹד וְגַם אֶת־
ג הַנְּבִיאִים וְאֶת־רוּחַ הַטֻּמְאָה אַעֲבִיר מִן־הָאָרֶץ: וְהָיָה כִּי־יִנָּבֵא אִישׁ
עוֹד וְאָמְרוּ אֵלָיו אָבִיו וְאִמּוֹ יֹלְדָיו לֹא תִחְיֶה כִּי שֶׁקֶר דִּבַּרְתָּ בְּשֵׁם
ד יְהוָה וּדְקָרֻהוּ אָבִיהוּ וְאִמּוֹ יֹלְדָיו בְּהִנָּבְאוֹ: וְהָיָה | בַּיּוֹם הַהוּא יֵבֹשׁוּ
הַנְּבִיאִים אִישׁ מֵחֶזְיֹנוֹ בְּהִנָּבְאֹתוֹ וְלֹא יִלְבְּשׁוּ אַדֶּרֶת שֵׂעָר לְמַעַן
ה כַּחֵשׁ: וְאָמַר לֹא נָבִיא אָנֹכִי אִישׁ־עֹבֵד אֲדָמָה אָנֹכִי כִּי־אָדָם הִקְנַנִי
ו מִנְּעוּרָי: וְאָמַר אֵלָיו מָה הַמַּכּוֹת הָאֵלֶּה בֵּין יָדֶיךָ וְאָמַר אֲשֶׁר הֻכֵּיתִי
ז בֵּית מְאַהֲבָי: חֶרֶב עוּרִי עַל־רֹעִי וְעַל־גֶּבֶר עֲמִיתִי נְאֻם
יְהוָה צְבָאוֹת הַךְ אֶת־הָרֹעֶה וּתְפוּצֶיןָ הַצֹּאן וַהֲשִׁבֹתִי יָדִי עַל־הַצֹּעֲרִים:
ח וְהָיָה בְכָל־הָאָרֶץ נְאֻם־יְהוָה פִּי־שְׁנַיִם בָּהּ יִכָּרְתוּ יִגְוָעוּ וְהַשְּׁלִשִׁית
ט יִוָּתֶר בָּהּ: וְהֵבֵאתִי אֶת־הַשְּׁלִשִׁית בָּאֵשׁ וּצְרַפְתִּים כִּצְרֹף אֶת־הַכֶּסֶף
וּבְחַנְתִּים כִּבְחֹן אֶת־הַזָּהָב הוּא | יִקְרָא בִשְׁמִי וַאֲנִי אֶעֱנֶה אֹתוֹ אָמַרְתִּי
יד א עַמִּי הוּא וְהוּא יֹאמַר יְהוָה אֱלֹהָי: הִנֵּה יוֹם־בָּא
ב לַיהוָה וְחֻלַּק שְׁלָלֵךְ בְּקִרְבֵּךְ: וְאָסַפְתִּי אֶת־כָּל־הַגּוֹיִם | אֶל־יְרוּשָׁלִַם
לַמִּלְחָמָה וְנִלְכְּדָה הָעִיר וְנָשַׁסּוּ הַבָּתִּים וְהַנָּשִׁים תשגלנה וְיָצָא חֲצִי תִּשָּׁכַבְנָה
ג הָעִיר בַּגּוֹלָה וְיֶתֶר הָעָם לֹא יִכָּרֵת מִן־הָעִיר: וְיָצָא יְהוָה וְנִלְחַם בַּגּוֹיִם
ד הָהֵם כְּיוֹם הִלָּחֲמוֹ בְּיוֹם קְרָב: וְעָמְדוּ רַגְלָיו בַּיּוֹם־הַהוּא עַל־הַר

which faces Jerusalem on the east, and the Mount of Olives will split through
its middle – into a great valley – from east to west. Half the mountain will
5 shift northward and half southward. And you will flee from this Valley of the
Mountains, for the Valley of the Mountains will reach as far as Atzal; you will
flee as you fled from the earthquake in the days of Uziya, the king of Yehuda,
6 and the LORD will come – my God, and all the holy ones with You. This is
what will be: on that day there will be neither bright light nor thick darkness.
7 This is what will be: there will be a day known to the LORD; it will be neither
8 day nor night, but at evening time there will be light. This is what will be: on
that day living waters will flow out from Jerusalem, half to the eastern sea and
9 half to the western sea; in summer and winter it will be so. Then the LORD
shall be King over all the earth; on that day the LORD shall be One and His
10 name One. Then the land will be smoothed out like a plain from Geva[25] to
Rimon, until the area south of Jerusalem, and Jerusalem will be lifted up in
her place. From the Gate of Binyamin to the site of the First Gate and to
the Corner Gate, from the Tower of Ḥananel to the king's winery, they will
11 inhabit her. There will be no more devastation, and Jerusalem will live in
12 safety. This will be the plague that the LORD will bring upon all the
peoples who fought against Jerusalem: their flesh will rot away as they stand
on their feet, their eyes will rot in their sockets, and their tongues will rot in
13 their mouths. This is what will be: on that day the turmoil the LORD brings
on them will be great, and each man will seize another by the arm and raise
14 his fist against his neighbor's fist. And Yehuda too will fight in Jerusalem, and
the wealth of all the surrounding nations, great quantities of gold, silver, and
15 clothing, will be gathered in. There will be a plague just like this plague on
the horses, the mules, the camels, and the donkeys, and on every animal in
16 those camps. This is what will be: all those remaining from all the nations
who came up against Jerusalem will go up year after year to bow down to
17 the King, LORD of Hosts, and to celebrate the Festival of Tabernacles. This
is what will be: the families of the land who do not go up to Jerusalem and
18 bow down to the King, LORD of Hosts, rain shall not fall for them. If the
family of Egypt does not go up, does not come, it shall not be upon them.
This will be the plague that the LORD will bring upon the nations who do
19 not go up to celebrate the Festival of Tabernacles. Such will be the punishment of Egypt and the punishment of all the nations who do not come up
20 to celebrate the Festival of Tabernacles. On that day even the bells of the
horses will be inscribed "sacred to the LORD," and the pots in the House of
21 the LORD will be like basins before the Altar. This is what will be: every
pot in Jerusalem and in Yehuda will be sacred to the LORD of Hosts, and all
those who come to sacrifice will take them and will cook in them. On that
day, there will be no more need for traders in the House of the LORD of Hosts.

25 | North of Jerusalem.

הַזֵּיתִים אֲשֶׁר עַל־פְּנֵי יְרוּשָׁלִַם מִקֶּדֶם וְנִבְקַע הַר הַזֵּיתִים מֵחֶצְיוֹ
מִזְרָחָה וָיָמָּה גֵּיא גְּדוֹלָה מְאֹד וּמָשׁ חֲצִי הָהָר צָפוֹנָה וְחֶצְיוֹ נֶגְבָּה׃
ה וְנַסְתֶּם גֵּיא־הָרַי כִּי־יַגִּיעַ גֵּי־הָרִים אֶל־אָצַל וְנַסְתֶּם כַּאֲשֶׁר נַסְתֶּם מִפְּנֵי
הָרַעַשׁ בִּימֵי עֻזִּיָּה מֶלֶךְ־יְהוּדָה וּבָא יהוה אֱלֹהַי כָּל־קְדֹשִׁים עִמָּךְ׃
ו ז וְהָיָה בַּיּוֹם הַהוּא לֹא־יִהְיֶה אוֹר יְקָרוֹת יקפאון׃ וְהָיָה יוֹם־אֶחָד הוּא וְקִפָּאוֹן
ח יִוָּדַע לַיהוה לֹא־יוֹם וְלֹא־לָיְלָה וְהָיָה לְעֵת־עֶרֶב יִהְיֶה־אוֹר׃ וְהָיָה ׀
בַּיּוֹם הַהוּא יֵצְאוּ מַיִם־חַיִּים מִירוּשָׁלִַם חֶצְיָם אֶל־הַיָּם הַקַּדְמוֹנִי וְחֶצְיָם
ט אֶל־הַיָּם הָאַחֲרוֹן בַּקַּיִץ וּבָחֹרֶף יִהְיֶה׃ וְהָיָה יהוה לְמֶלֶךְ עַל־כָּל־
י הָאָרֶץ בַּיּוֹם הַהוּא יִהְיֶה יהוה אֶחָד וּשְׁמוֹ אֶחָד׃ יִסּוֹב כָּל־הָאָרֶץ
כָּעֲרָבָה מִגֶּבַע לְרִמּוֹן נֶגֶב יְרוּשָׁלִָם וְרָאֲמָה וְיָשְׁבָה תַחְתֶּיהָ לְמִשַּׁעַר
בִּנְיָמִן עַד־מְקוֹם שַׁעַר הָרִאשׁוֹן עַד־שַׁעַר הַפִּנִּים וּמִגְדַּל חֲנַנְאֵל
יא עַד יִקְבֵי הַמֶּלֶךְ׃ וְיָשְׁבוּ בָהּ וְחֵרֶם לֹא יִהְיֶה־עוֹד וְיָשְׁבָה יְרוּשָׁלִַם
יב לָבֶטַח׃ וְזֹאת ׀ תִּהְיֶה הַמַּגֵּפָה אֲשֶׁר יִגֹּף יהוה אֶת־כָּל־
הָעַמִּים אֲשֶׁר צָבְאוּ עַל־יְרוּשָׁלִָם הָמֵק ׀ בְּשָׂרוֹ וְהוּא עֹמֵד עַל־רַגְלָיו
יג וְעֵינָיו תִּמַּקְנָה בְחֹרֵיהֶן וּלְשׁוֹנוֹ תִּמַּק בְּפִיהֶם׃ וְהָיָה בַּיּוֹם הַהוּא תִּהְיֶה
מְהוּמַת־יהוה רַבָּה בָּהֶם וְהֶחֱזִיקוּ אִישׁ יַד רֵעֵהוּ וְעָלְתָה יָדוֹ עַל־יַד
יד רֵעֵהוּ׃ וְגַם־יְהוּדָה תִּלָּחֵם בִּירוּשָׁלִָם וְאֻסַּף חֵיל כָּל־הַגּוֹיִם סָבִיב זָהָב
טו וָכֶסֶף וּבְגָדִים לָרֹב מְאֹד׃ וְכֵן תִּהְיֶה מַגֵּפַת הַסּוּס הַפֶּרֶד הַגָּמָל
וְהַחֲמוֹר וְכָל־הַבְּהֵמָה אֲשֶׁר יִהְיֶה בַּמַּחֲנוֹת הָהֵמָּה כַּמַּגֵּפָה הַזֹּאת׃
טז וְהָיָה כָּל־הַנּוֹתָר מִכָּל־הַגּוֹיִם הַבָּאִים עַל־יְרוּשָׁלִָם וְעָלוּ מִדֵּי שָׁנָה
יז בְשָׁנָה לְהִשְׁתַּחֲוֺת לְמֶלֶךְ יהוה צְבָאוֹת וְלָחֹג אֶת־חַג הַסֻּכּוֹת׃ וְהָיָה
אֲשֶׁר לֹא־יַעֲלֶה מֵאֵת מִשְׁפְּחוֹת הָאָרֶץ אֶל־יְרוּשָׁלִַם לְהִשְׁתַּחֲוֺת
יח לְמֶלֶךְ יהוה צְבָאוֹת וְלֹא עֲלֵיהֶם יִהְיֶה הַגָּשֶׁם׃ וְאִם־מִשְׁפַּחַת
מִצְרַיִם לֹא־תַעֲלֶה וְלֹא בָאָה וְלֹא עֲלֵיהֶם תִּהְיֶה הַמַּגֵּפָה אֲשֶׁר יִגֹּף
יט יהוה אֶת־הַגּוֹיִם אֲשֶׁר לֹא יַעֲלוּ לָחֹג אֶת־חַג הַסֻּכּוֹת׃ זֹאת תִּהְיֶה
חַטַּאת מִצְרָיִם וְחַטַּאת כָּל־הַגּוֹיִם אֲשֶׁר לֹא יַעֲלוּ לָחֹג אֶת־חַג
כ הַסֻּכּוֹת׃ בַּיּוֹם הַהוּא יִהְיֶה עַל־מְצִלּוֹת הַסּוּס קֹדֶשׁ לַיהוה וְהָיָה
כא הַסִּירוֹת בְּבֵית יהוה כַּמִּזְרָקִים לִפְנֵי הַמִּזְבֵּחַ׃ וְהָיָה כָּל־סִיר בִּירוּשָׁלִַם כא
וּבִיהוּדָה קֹדֶשׁ לַיהוה צְבָאוֹת וּבָאוּ כָּל־הַזֹּבְחִים וְלָקְחוּ מֵהֶם
וּבִשְּׁלוּ בָהֶם וְלֹא־יִהְיֶה כְנַעֲנִי עוֹד בְּבֵית־יהוה צְבָאוֹת בַּיּוֹם הַהוּא׃

MALAKHI/MALACHI

1 1 An oracle: the word of the LORD to Israel through Malakhi.[1] The LORD says,
2 "I have loved you." But you say, "How have You loved us?" Is Esav not a
3 brother to Yaakov? So says the LORD: Yet I loved Yaakov and hated Esav, so
I made his mountains desolate and gave his inheritance over to desert jackals.
4 Even should Edom say, "We have been destroyed, but we will return and
rebuild the ruins," says the LORD of Hosts, they will build; I will destroy, and
they will be called the territory of evil and the nation that suffers the LORD's
5 wrath forever. Your eyes will see this, and you will say, "The LORD is great
6 beyond the territory of Israel." A son honors his father, and a slave his master;
if I am a Father, where is My honor, and if I am the Master, where is My
reverence? So says the LORD of Hosts to you, the priests who scorn My name.
7 Yet you say, "How have we scorned Your name?" You offer defiled bread on
My altar. Yet you say, "How have we defiled You?" In saying the LORD's table
8 is repugnant. When you offer a blind animal to be sacrificed, is this no evil?[2]
And when you offer the lame and the sick, is this no evil? Offer it if you will
to your governor. Would he then accept you – let you lift your face to him?
9 So says the LORD of Hosts. Now, please, beseech God, and let Him be gracious
to us. This was in your hands – would He turn His face for any one of you?
10 So says the LORD of Hosts: O, who is there among you who would close the
doors so that you might not light My altar for naught? I have no desire for
11 you, says the LORD of Hosts. I will accept no offering from your hands. For
from one end of the earth to the other, My name is great among the nations.
Incense is offered in My name, a pure offering everywhere, for My name is
12 great among the nations, says the LORD of Hosts. Yet you desecrate it by
saying that the Lord's table is defiled and its fruit too repugnant to be
13 consumed. You say, "O, how wearisome," and you snort at it, says the LORD
of Hosts. You bring what is stolen, the LORD says, what is lame, what is ill;
14 you bring this offering. Am I to accept it from your hands? Cursed is the knave
who has a ram in his flock but pledges and sacrifices a damaged animal to the
Lord. For I am a great King, says the LORD of Hosts, and My name is revered
2 1 among the nations. Now, this is your command, priests: If you do not listen,
2 if you do not take it to heart to honor My name, says the LORD of Hosts, then
I will set a curse on you, and I will curse your blessings – indeed, I have cursed
3 your blessing, for you do not take it to heart. I will drive away the crops
because of you, and I will scatter filth in your face, the filth of your holiday
4 sacrifices, and you will be carried away after it. And you will know that I sent
you this command so that My covenant may endure with Levi, says the LORD
5 of Hosts. My covenant endures in him – life and peace. I gave them to him so
6 as to be revered. He revered Me and was in awe of My name. True teaching
was in his mouth, no sin from his lips; he walked with Me in peace and
7 uprightness and returned many from iniquity. For a priest's lips should
safeguard knowledge, and the people should seek teaching from his mouth,
8 for he is a messenger of the LORD of Hosts. But you have strayed from the

1 | Either the prophet's name or a title: "My servant."

2 | See the prohibition in Deuteronomy 17:1.

מלאכי

א א ב מַשָּׂא דְבַר־יְהוָה אֶל־יִשְׂרָאֵל בְּיַד מַלְאָכִי: אָהַבְתִּי אֶתְכֶם אָמַר יְהוָה
וַאֲמַרְתֶּם בַּמָּה אֲהַבְתָּנוּ הֲלוֹא־אָח עֵשָׂו לְיַעֲקֹב נְאֻם־יְהוָה וָאֹהַב
ג אֶת־יַעֲקֹב: וְאֶת־עֵשָׂו שָׂנֵאתִי וָאָשִׂים אֶת־הָרָיו שְׁמָמָה וְאֶת־נַחֲלָתוֹ
ד לְתַנּוֹת מִדְבָּר: כִּי־תֹאמַר אֱדוֹם רֻשַּׁשְׁנוּ וְנָשׁוּב וְנִבְנֶה חֳרָבוֹת כֹּה
אָמַר יְהוָה צְבָאוֹת הֵמָּה יִבְנוּ וַאֲנִי אֶהֱרוֹס וְקָרְאוּ לָהֶם גְּבוּל רִשְׁעָה
ה וְהָעָם אֲשֶׁר־זָעַם יְהוָה עַד־עוֹלָם: וְעֵינֵיכֶם תִּרְאֶינָה וְאַתֶּם תֹּאמְרוּ
ו יִגְדַּל יְהוָה מֵעַל לִגְבוּל יִשְׂרָאֵל: בֵּן יְכַבֵּד אָב וְעֶבֶד אֲדֹנָיו וְאִם־אָב
אָנִי אַיֵּה כְבוֹדִי וְאִם־אֲדוֹנִים אָנִי אַיֵּה מוֹרָאִי אָמַר ׀ יְהוָה צְבָאוֹת
ז לָכֶם הַכֹּהֲנִים בּוֹזֵי שְׁמִי וַאֲמַרְתֶּם בַּמֶּה בָזִינוּ אֶת־שְׁמֶךָ: מַגִּישִׁים
עַל־מִזְבְּחִי לֶחֶם מְגֹאָל וַאֲמַרְתֶּם בַּמֶּה גֵאַלְנוּךָ בֶּאֱמָרְכֶם שֻׁלְחַן יְהוָה
ח נִבְזֶה הוּא: וְכִי־תַגִּשׁוּן עִוֵּר לִזְבֹּחַ אֵין רָע וְכִי תַגִּישׁוּ פִּסֵּחַ וְחֹלֶה אֵין
רָע הַקְרִיבֵהוּ נָא לְפֶחָתֶךָ הֲיִרְצְךָ אוֹ הֲיִשָּׂא פָנֶיךָ אָמַר יְהוָה צְבָאוֹת:
ט וְעַתָּה חַלּוּ־נָא פְנֵי־אֵל וִיחָנֵנוּ מִיֶּדְכֶם הָיְתָה זֹּאת הֲיִשָּׂא מִכֶּם פָּנִים
י אָמַר יְהוָה צְבָאוֹת: מִי גַם־בָּכֶם וְיִסְגֹּר דְּלָתַיִם וְלֹא־תָאִירוּ מִזְבְּחִי
חִנָּם אֵין־לִי חֵפֶץ בָּכֶם אָמַר יְהוָה צְבָאוֹת וּמִנְחָה לֹא־אֶרְצֶה מִיֶּדְכֶם:
יא כִּי מִמִּזְרַח־שֶׁמֶשׁ וְעַד־מְבוֹאוֹ גָּדוֹל שְׁמִי בַּגּוֹיִם וּבְכָל־מָקוֹם מֻקְטָר
מֻגָּשׁ לִשְׁמִי וּמִנְחָה טְהוֹרָה כִּי־גָדוֹל שְׁמִי בַּגּוֹיִם אָמַר יְהוָה צְבָאוֹת:
יב וְאַתֶּם מְחַלְּלִים אוֹתוֹ בֶּאֱמָרְכֶם שֻׁלְחַן אֲדֹנָי מְגֹאָל הוּא וְנִיבוֹ נִבְזֶה
יג אָכְלוֹ: וַאֲמַרְתֶּם הִנֵּה מַתְּלָאָה וְהִפַּחְתֶּם אוֹתוֹ אָמַר יְהוָה צְבָאוֹת
וַהֲבֵאתֶם גָּזוּל וְאֶת־הַפִּסֵּחַ וְאֶת־הַחוֹלֶה וַהֲבֵאתֶם אֶת־הַמִּנְחָה
יד הַאֶרְצֶה אוֹתָהּ מִיֶּדְכֶם אָמַר יְהוָה: וְאָרוּר נוֹכֵל וְיֵשׁ בְּעֶדְרוֹ זָכָר וְנֹדֵר
וְזֹבֵחַ מָשְׁחָת לַאדֹנָי כִּי מֶלֶךְ גָּדוֹל אָנִי אָמַר יְהוָה צְבָאוֹת וּשְׁמִי נוֹרָא
ב א ב בַגּוֹיִם: וְעַתָּה אֲלֵיכֶם הַמִּצְוָה הַזֹּאת הַכֹּהֲנִים: אִם־לֹא תִשְׁמְעוּ וְאִם־
לֹא תָשִׂימוּ עַל־לֵב לָתֵת כָּבוֹד לִשְׁמִי אָמַר יְהוָה צְבָאוֹת וְשִׁלַּחְתִּי
בָכֶם אֶת־הַמְּאֵרָה וְאָרוֹתִי אֶת־בִּרְכוֹתֵיכֶם וְגַם אָרוֹתִיהָ כִּי אֵינְכֶם
ג שָׂמִים עַל־לֵב: הִנְנִי גֹעֵר לָכֶם אֶת־הַזֶּרַע וְזֵרִיתִי פֶרֶשׁ עַל־פְּנֵיכֶם פֶּרֶשׁ
ד חַגֵּיכֶם וְנָשָׂא אֶתְכֶם אֵלָיו: וִידַעְתֶּם כִּי שִׁלַּחְתִּי אֲלֵיכֶם אֵת הַמִּצְוָה
ה הַזֹּאת לִהְיוֹת בְּרִיתִי אֶת־לֵוִי אָמַר יְהוָה צְבָאוֹת: בְּרִיתִי ׀ הָיְתָה אִתּוֹ
הַחַיִּים וְהַשָּׁלוֹם וָאֶתְּנֵם־לוֹ מוֹרָא וַיִּירָאֵנִי וּמִפְּנֵי שְׁמִי נִחַת הוּא:
ו תּוֹרַת אֱמֶת הָיְתָה בְּפִיהוּ וְעַוְלָה לֹא־נִמְצָא בִשְׂפָתָיו בְּשָׁלוֹם וּבְמִישׁוֹר
ז הָלַךְ אִתִּי וְרַבִּים הֵשִׁיב מֵעָוֺן: כִּי־שִׂפְתֵי כֹהֵן יִשְׁמְרוּ־דַעַת וְתוֹרָה
ח יְבַקְשׁוּ מִפִּיהוּ כִּי מַלְאַךְ יְהוָה־צְבָאוֹת הוּא: וְאַתֶּם סַרְתֶּם מִן־הַדֶּרֶךְ

path and caused many to stumble by your teaching. You have destroyed the
9 covenant of Levi, says the LORD of Hosts. So indeed I will make you scorned
and degraded before the whole nation because you do not safeguard My ways,
10 and you distort the face of the Torah. Do we not all have one Father? Were
we not all created by one God? Why should a man be faithless to his brother,
11 desecrating the covenant of our fathers? For Yehuda has been faithless, and
an abomination has been perpetrated in Israel and Jerusalem. For Yehuda,
whom He loves, has desecrated that which is holy to the LORD and married
12 the daughter of a foreign god. Let the man who does this be cut off by the
LORD – kith and kin[3] – from the tents of Yaakov – even one who brings
13 offerings to the LORD of Hosts. And this you also do: flood the
LORD's altar with tears – weeping and sighing because He no longer turns
14 toward the offerings nor accepts favor from your hands. And you say, "Why?"
For the LORD is witness between you and the wife of your youth, to whom
you have been faithless, though she is your companion and your covenantal
15 wife. Did He not make them one being? All remaining spirit accords with
that. And what does the One seek? Children of God. So take care of your
16 spirits, and let none of you be faithless to the wife of your youth. If anyone
hates and sends her away, says the LORD, God of Israel, corruption covers his
wedding clothes, says the LORD of Hosts, and so, take care with your spirit
17 and be not faithless. You have wearied the LORD with your talk. But
you say, "How have we wearied Him?" By saying every evildoer is good in the
eyes of the LORD and it is them whom He desires; or, "Where is the God of
3 1 justice?" Behold: I am sending My messenger, and he will clear a path before
Me.[4] Suddenly, the Lord whom you seek will arrive at His Temple. The
angel of the covenant whom you desire – behold, he is coming, says the LORD
2 of Hosts. Who can survive the day of His coming, and who can remain
standing when He appears? For He is like the smelter's fire and the washers'
3 lye. And He will sit smelting and purifying silver, and He will purify the sons
of Levi and refine them like gold and silver, and they will be the LORD's –
4 bringing offerings in righteousness. Then the offering of Yehuda and Jerusalem
5 will be pleasing to the LORD as in days of old and years past. I will draw close
to you in judgment, and I will be a swift witness against the sorcerers and
adulterers and those who falsely swear; against those who withhold payment
from the worker or the widow or the orphan; against those who turn away
6 the stranger. They do not fear Me,[5] says the LORD of Hosts. For I am the
LORD. I have not changed. And you, children of Yaakov, you have not perished.
7 Ever since the days of your forefathers you have strayed from My statutes, and
you did not keep them. Come back to Me, and I will come back to you, says
8 the LORD of Hosts. But you say, "How shall we come back?" Can a person
steal[6] from God? Yet you steal from Me. But you say, "What have we stolen

---

3 | Hebrew *er ve'ona*, possibly echoing the children of Yehuda, Er and Onan (see Gen., ch. 38).

4 | Cf. Exodus 23:20.

5 | Cf. the prohibitions in Leviticus, chapter 19, especially verses 12–14.

6 | The Hebrew *yikba* echoes the name Yaakov (v. 6).

הִכְשַׁלְתֶּם רַבִּים בַּתּוֹרָה שִׁחַתֶּם בְּרִית הַלֵּוִי אָמַר יְהוָה צְבָאוֹת:
ט וְגַם־אֲנִי נָתַתִּי אֶתְכֶם נִבְזִים וּשְׁפָלִים לְכָל־הָעָם כְּפִי אֲשֶׁר אֵינְכֶם
י שֹׁמְרִים אֶת־דְּרָכַי וְנֹשְׂאִים פָּנִים בַּתּוֹרָה: הֲלוֹא אָב אֶחָד לְכֻלָּנוּ הֲלוֹא
יא אֵל אֶחָד בְּרָאָנוּ מַדּוּעַ נִבְגַּד אִישׁ בְּאָחִיו לְחַלֵּל בְּרִית אֲבֹתֵינוּ: בָּגְדָה
יְהוּדָה וְתוֹעֵבָה נֶעֶשְׂתָה בְיִשְׂרָאֵל וּבִירוּשָׁלִָם כִּי | חִלֵּל יְהוּדָה קֹדֶשׁ
יב יְהוָה אֲשֶׁר אָהֵב וּבָעַל בַּת־אֵל נֵכָר: יַכְרֵת יְהוָה לָאִישׁ אֲשֶׁר יַעֲשֶׂנָּה
יג עֵר וְעֹנֶה מֵאָהֳלֵי יַעֲקֹב וּמַגִּישׁ מִנְחָה לַיהוָה צְבָאוֹת: וְזֹאת
שֵׁנִית תַּעֲשׂוּ כַּסּוֹת דִּמְעָה אֶת־מִזְבַּח יְהוָה בְּכִי וַאֲנָקָה מֵאֵין עוֹד
יד פְּנוֹת אֶל־הַמִּנְחָה וְלָקַחַת רָצוֹן מִיֶּדְכֶם: וַאֲמַרְתֶּם עַל־מָה עַל כִּי־
יְהוָה הֵעִיד בֵּינְךָ וּבֵין | אֵשֶׁת נְעוּרֶיךָ אֲשֶׁר אַתָּה בָּגַדְתָּה בָּהּ וְהִיא
טו חֲבֶרְתְּךָ וְאֵשֶׁת בְּרִיתֶךָ: וְלֹא־אֶחָד עָשָׂה וּשְׁאָר רוּחַ לוֹ וּמָה הָאֶחָד
מְבַקֵּשׁ זֶרַע אֱלֹהִים וְנִשְׁמַרְתֶּם בְּרוּחֲכֶם וּבְאֵשֶׁת נְעוּרֶיךָ אַל־יִבְגֹּד:
טז כִּי־שָׂנֵא שַׁלַּח אָמַר יְהוָה אֱלֹהֵי יִשְׂרָאֵל וְכִסָּה חָמָס עַל־לְבוּשׁוֹ אָמַר
יז יְהוָה צְבָאוֹת וְנִשְׁמַרְתֶּם בְּרוּחֲכֶם וְלֹא תִבְגֹּדוּ: הוֹגַעְתֶּם
יְהוָה בְּדִבְרֵיכֶם וַאֲמַרְתֶּם בַּמָּה הוֹגָעְנוּ בֶּאֱמָרְכֶם כָּל־עֹשֵׂה רָע טוֹב |
ג א בְּעֵינֵי יְהוָה וּבָהֶם הוּא חָפֵץ אוֹ אַיֵּה אֱלֹהֵי הַמִּשְׁפָּט: הִנְנִי שֹׁלֵחַ
מַלְאָכִי וּפִנָּה־דֶרֶךְ לְפָנָי וּפִתְאֹם יָבוֹא אֶל־הֵיכָלוֹ הָאָדוֹן | אֲשֶׁר־אַתֶּם
מְבַקְשִׁים וּמַלְאַךְ הַבְּרִית אֲשֶׁר־אַתֶּם חֲפֵצִים הִנֵּה־בָא אָמַר יְהוָה
ב צְבָאוֹת: וּמִי מְכַלְכֵּל אֶת־יוֹם בּוֹאוֹ וּמִי הָעֹמֵד בְּהֵרָאוֹתוֹ כִּי־הוּא
ג כְּאֵשׁ מְצָרֵף וּכְבֹרִית מְכַבְּסִים: וְיָשַׁב מְצָרֵף וּמְטַהֵר כֶּסֶף וְטִהַר אֶת־
בְּנֵי־לֵוִי וְזִקַּק אֹתָם כַּזָּהָב וְכַכָּסֶף וְהָיוּ לַיהוָה מַגִּישֵׁי מִנְחָה בִּצְדָקָה:
ד וְעָרְבָה לַיהוָה מִנְחַת יְהוּדָה וִירוּשָׁלִָם כִּימֵי עוֹלָם וּכְשָׁנִים קַדְמֹנִיּוֹת:
ה וְקָרַבְתִּי אֲלֵיכֶם לַמִּשְׁפָּט וְהָיִיתִי | עֵד מְמַהֵר בַּמְכַשְּׁפִים וּבַמְנָאֲפִים
וּבַנִּשְׁבָּעִים לַשָּׁקֶר וּבְעֹשְׁקֵי שְׂכַר־שָׂכִיר אַלְמָנָה וְיָתוֹם וּמַטֵּי־גֵר וְלֹא
ו יְרֵאוּנִי אָמַר יְהוָה צְבָאוֹת: כִּי אֲנִי יְהוָה לֹא שָׁנִיתִי וְאַתֶּם בְּנֵי־יַעֲקֹב
ז לֹא כְלִיתֶם: לְמִימֵי אֲבֹתֵיכֶם סַרְתֶּם מֵחֻקַּי וְלֹא שְׁמַרְתֶּם שׁוּבוּ אֵלַי
ח וְאָשׁוּבָה אֲלֵיכֶם אָמַר יְהוָה צְבָאוֹת וַאֲמַרְתֶּם בַּמֶּה נָשׁוּב: הֲיִקְבַּע
אָדָם אֱלֹהִים כִּי אַתֶּם קֹבְעִים אֹתִי וַאֲמַרְתֶּם בַּמֶּה קְבַעֲנוּךָ הַמַּעֲשֵׂר

9 from You?" The tithes and donations. You are being cursed with the curse
10 because you steal from Me – the whole nation. Bring the entire tithe to the
treasury, and it will be food for My House, and put Me to the test, please,
in this, says the LORD of Hosts. See if I do not open up the floodgates of
11 heaven for you and pour out blessings upon you endlessly. I will drive away
for you that which devours. Your produce will not be destroyed, and your
12 vines in the field will not be barren, says the LORD of Hosts. All the nations
will call you happy, for you, yours will be a desired land, says the LORD of
13 Hosts. The LORD says, "You have spoken harshly against Me." Yet
14 you say, "What have we said of You?" You say, "It is useless to serve God, and
what do we gain in keeping His watch, or by walking in dark sorrow before
15 the LORD of Hosts? Now we call the arrogant happy; evildoers have built
16 themselves up; they have tested God and escaped." Then those who fear the
LORD spoke one to another, and the LORD listened and He heard, and it was
written – a book of remembrance before Him for those who fear the LORD
17 and keep His name in mind. And they shall be Mine, says the LORD of Hosts,
on the day on which I choose My cherished possession, and I will take pity
18 on them as a man takes pity on his son who serves him. And you will once
again distinguish between the righteous and the wicked, between one who
19 serves God and one who does not serve Him. For behold, the day
is coming, burning like an oven; the arrogant and the evildoers will be straw,
and the coming day will consume them, says the LORD of Hosts, so that
20 neither root nor branch will remain of them. But for you, fearers of My name,
a sun of righteousness will shine with healing under its wings, and you will
21 go out and frolic like stall-fatted calves. You will trample evildoers – for they
will be ashes under the soles of your feet on the day on which I act, says the
22 LORD of Hosts. Remember the Teaching of Moshe My servant,
23 which I commanded to him at Ḥorev, statutes and laws for all of Israel. Behold,
I will send you Eliya the prophet before the great and terrible day of the LORD.
24 And he will return the hearts of parents back to their children and the hearts
of children back to their parents, lest I come and lay the earth waste.

Behold, I will send you Eliya the prophet before the great
and terrible day of the LORD.

ט וְהַתְּרוּמָה: בַּמְּאֵרָה אַתֶּם נֵאָרִים וְאֹתִי אַתֶּם קֹבְעִים הַגּוֹי כֻּלּוֹ: הָבִיאוּ
אֶת־כָּל־הַמַּעֲשֵׂר אֶל־בֵּית הָאוֹצָר וִיהִי טֶרֶף בְּבֵיתִי וּבְחָנוּנִי נָא בָּזֹאת
אָמַר יְהוָה צְבָאוֹת אִם־לֹא אֶפְתַּח לָכֶם אֵת אֲרֻבּוֹת הַשָּׁמַיִם וַהֲרִיקֹתִי
יא לָכֶם בְּרָכָה עַד־בְּלִי־דָי: וְגָעַרְתִּי לָכֶם בָּאֹכֵל וְלֹא־יַשְׁחִת לָכֶם אֶת־
פְּרִי הָאֲדָמָה וְלֹא־תְשַׁכֵּל לָכֶם הַגֶּפֶן בַּשָּׂדֶה אָמַר יְהוָה צְבָאוֹת:
יב וְאִשְּׁרוּ אֶתְכֶם כָּל־הַגּוֹיִם כִּי־תִהְיוּ אַתֶּם אֶרֶץ חֵפֶץ אָמַר יְהוָה
יג צְבָאוֹת: חָזְקוּ עָלַי דִּבְרֵיכֶם אָמַר יְהוָה וַאֲמַרְתֶּם
יד מַה־נִּדְבַּרְנוּ עָלֶיךָ: אֲמַרְתֶּם שָׁוְא עֲבֹד אֱלֹהִים וּמַה־בֶּצַע כִּי שָׁמַרְנוּ
טו מִשְׁמַרְתּוֹ וְכִי הָלַכְנוּ קְדֹרַנִּית מִפְּנֵי יְהוָה צְבָאוֹת: וְעַתָּה אֲנַחְנוּ
טז מְאַשְּׁרִים זֵדִים גַּם־נִבְנוּ עֹשֵׂי רִשְׁעָה גַּם בָּחֲנוּ אֱלֹהִים וַיִּמָּלֵטוּ: אָז
נִדְבְּרוּ יִרְאֵי יְהוָה אִישׁ אֶל־רֵעֵהוּ וַיַּקְשֵׁב יְהוָה וַיִּשְׁמָע וַיִּכָּתֵב סֵפֶר
יז זִכָּרוֹן לְפָנָיו לְיִרְאֵי יְהוָה וּלְחֹשְׁבֵי שְׁמוֹ: וְהָיוּ לִי אָמַר יְהוָה צְבָאוֹת
לַיּוֹם אֲשֶׁר אֲנִי עֹשֶׂה סְגֻלָּה וְחָמַלְתִּי עֲלֵיהֶם כַּאֲשֶׁר יַחְמֹל אִישׁ עַל־
יח בְּנוֹ הָעֹבֵד אֹתוֹ: וְשַׁבְתֶּם וּרְאִיתֶם בֵּין צַדִּיק לְרָשָׁע בֵּין עֹבֵד אֱלֹהִים
יט לַאֲשֶׁר לֹא עֲבָדוֹ: כִּי־הִנֵּה הַיּוֹם בָּא בֹּעֵר כַּתַּנּוּר וְהָיוּ
כָל־זֵדִים וְכָל־עֹשֵׂה רִשְׁעָה קַשׁ וְלִהַט אֹתָם הַיּוֹם הַבָּא אָמַר יְהוָה
כ צְבָאוֹת אֲשֶׁר לֹא־יַעֲזֹב לָהֶם שֹׁרֶשׁ וְעָנָף: וְזָרְחָה לָכֶם יִרְאֵי שְׁמִי
כא שֶׁמֶשׁ צְדָקָה וּמַרְפֵּא בִּכְנָפֶיהָ וִיצָאתֶם וּפִשְׁתֶּם כְּעֶגְלֵי מַרְבֵּק: וְעַסּוֹתֶם
רְשָׁעִים כִּי־יִהְיוּ אֵפֶר תַּחַת כַּפּוֹת רַגְלֵיכֶם בַּיּוֹם אֲשֶׁר אֲנִי עֹשֶׂה אָמַר
כב יְהוָה צְבָאוֹת: זִכְרוּ תּוֹרַת מֹשֶׁה עַבְדִּי אֲשֶׁר
כג צִוִּיתִי אוֹתוֹ בְחֹרֵב עַל־כָּל־יִשְׂרָאֵל חֻקִּים וּמִשְׁפָּטִים: הִנֵּה אָנֹכִי שֹׁלֵחַ
כד לָכֶם אֵת אֵלִיָּה הַנָּבִיא לִפְנֵי בּוֹא יוֹם יְהוָה הַגָּדוֹל וְהַנּוֹרָא: וְהֵשִׁיב
לֵב־אָבוֹת עַל־בָּנִים וְלֵב בָּנִים עַל־אֲבוֹתָם פֶּן־אָבוֹא וְהִכֵּיתִי אֶת־
הָאָרֶץ חֵרֶם:

הנה אנכי שלח לכם את אליה הנביא לפני בוא
יום יהוה הגדול והנורא

כתובים
KETUVIM/WRITINGS

תהלים	TEHILLIM/PSALMS
משלי	MISHLE/PROVERBS
איוב	IYOV/JOB
שיר השירים	SHIR HASHIRIM/SONG OF SONGS
רות	RUT/RUTH
איכה	EIKHA/LAMENTATIONS
קהלת	KOHELET/ECCLESIASTES
אסתר	ESTER/ESTHER
דניאל	DANIEL
עזרא • נחמיה	EZRA • NEḤEMYA/NEHEMIAH
דברי הימים	DIVREI HAYAMIM/CHRONICLES

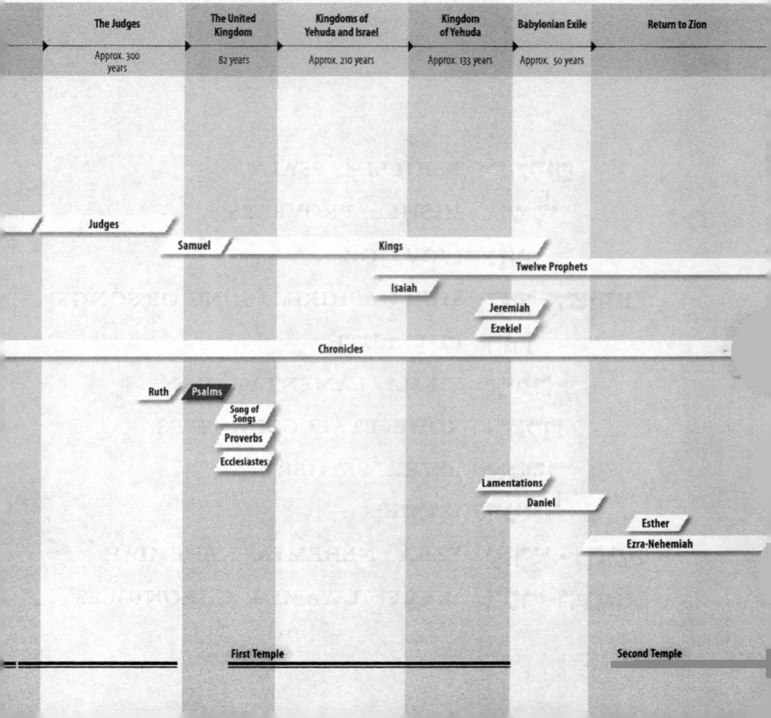

The Judges
Approx. 300 years
The United Kingdom
82 years
Kingdoms of Yehuda and Israel
Approx. 210 years
Kingdom of Yehuda
Approx. 133 years
Babylonian Exile
Approx. 50 years
Return to Zion
Judges
Samuel
Kings
Twelve Prophets
Isaiah
Jeremiah
Ezekiel
Chronicles
Ruth
Psalms
Song of Songs
Proverbs
Ecclesiastes
Lamentations
Daniel
Esther
Ezra-Nehemiah
First Temple
Second Temple

תהלים

TEHILLIM/PSALMS

PSALMS	Book One	Book Two	Book Three	Book Four	Book Five
	Chs. 1–41	42–72	73–89	90–106	107–150

BOOK ONE

1 1 Happy is the one who does not walk in the counsel of the wicked, who
does not stand on the path of sinners, who does not sit among the jeering
2 cynics – instead, the LORD's teaching is all his desire, and he contemplates
3 that teaching day and night. He is like a tree planted on streams of water
yielding fruit in its season, its leaves never withering – all it produces thrives.
4 5 Not so the wicked – they are like chaff blown away by the wind. Therefore,
the wicked will not endure judgment, nor the sinners among the righteous
6 crowd. For the LORD cares for the way of the righteous, while the way of the
wicked will be lost forever.
2 1 2 Why do the nations clamor; why do the peoples plot futilities? Kings of the
earth stand ready; leaders have bonded together against the LORD and His
3 4 anointed – "Let us sever their bonds and cast away their cords." The One who
5 dwells in heaven shall laugh; the Lord will mock them, then He will speak
6 to them in His fury; He will fill them with terror in His rage: "I have set My
7 king over Zion My holy mountain." I tell now of the LORD's decree: He told
8 me, "You are My child; this very day I fathered you. Just ask of Me – I shall
9 give you nations for your inheritance, estate to the ends of the earth. You will
10 crush them with an iron rod; You will shatter them like pottery." And now,
11 kings, be wise; be warned, judges of the earth: Serve the LORD with reverence
12 and tremble as you exalt. Pay homage sincerely lest He grow angry and you
lose your way, for His fury flares up in a moment. Happy are all who seek
refuge in Him.
3 1 2 *A psalm of David, when he fled from his son Avshalom.*[1] LORD, my foes are so
3 many – so many rise up against me; so many say of me, "He has no salvation
4 in God" – Selah[2] – but You, LORD, are the shield that protects me, my honor;
5 the One who raises my head. My voice cries out to the LORD; He answers
6 me from His holy mountain – Selah. I lie down to sleep; I wake again, for
7 the LORD sustains me. I do not fear the myriads of men, those encamped
8 all around me. Rise up, LORD; save me, my God! You have smashed all my
9 foes across the jaw; You have broken the teeth of the wicked. Salvation is the
LORD's – Your blessing rests on Your people – Selah.
4 1 2 *To the lead singer,*[3] *accompanied by music*[4] *– a psalm of David.* When I call out,
answer me, O God of my vindication; in my distress You set me free – show
3 me grace and hear my prayer. All you people – how long will my honor be
disgraced; how long will you love emptiness; how long will you seek illusions? –
4 Selah. Know that the LORD singles out those who are faithful to Him; when
5 I cry out to the LORD, He will hear. Tremble and do not sin; contemplate as
6 you lie awake; stay silent – Selah. Offer sincere offerings, and place Your trust
7 in the LORD. So many say, "Who will show us goodness?" Direct the light of
8 Your face upon us, LORD. You have filled my heart with more joy than others

---

1 | See II Samuel, chapters 15–19.

2 | A term of uncertain meaning. It is most likely an instruction related to musical performance.

3 | The precise meaning of the Hebrew term *menatze'aḥ* remains unknown. It is often understood to refer to the leader of a group of musical performers.

4 | Hebrew *binginot,* another term of uncertain meaning referring to musical performance.

ספר ראשון

א א אַשְׁרֵי־הָאִישׁ אֲשֶׁר ׀ לֹא הָלַךְ בַּעֲצַת רְשָׁעִים וּבְדֶרֶךְ חַטָּאִים לֹא
ב עָמָד וּבְמוֹשַׁב לֵצִים לֹא יָשָׁב׃ כִּי אִם בְּתוֹרַת יהוה חֶפְצוֹ וּבְתוֹרָתוֹ
ג יֶהְגֶּה יוֹמָם וָלָיְלָה׃ וְהָיָה כְּעֵץ שָׁתוּל עַל־פַּלְגֵי מָיִם אֲשֶׁר פִּרְיוֹ ׀ יִתֵּן
ד בְּעִתּוֹ וְעָלֵהוּ לֹא־יִבּוֹל וְכֹל אֲשֶׁר־יַעֲשֶׂה יַצְלִיחַ׃ לֹא־כֵן הָרְשָׁעִים
ה כִּי אִם־כַּמֹּץ אֲשֶׁר־תִּדְּפֶנּוּ רוּחַ׃ עַל־כֵּן ׀ לֹא־יָקֻמוּ רְשָׁעִים בַּמִּשְׁפָּט
ו וְחַטָּאִים בַּעֲדַת צַדִּיקִים׃ כִּי־יוֹדֵעַ יהוה דֶּרֶךְ צַדִּיקִים וְדֶרֶךְ רְשָׁעִים
תֹּאבֵד׃

ב א ב לָמָּה רָגְשׁוּ גוֹיִם וּלְאֻמִּים יֶהְגּוּ־רִיק׃ יִתְיַצְּבוּ ׀ מַלְכֵי־אֶרֶץ וְרוֹזְנִים
ג נוֹסְדוּ־יָחַד עַל־יהוה וְעַל־מְשִׁיחוֹ׃ נְנַתְּקָה אֶת־מוֹסְרוֹתֵימוֹ וְנַשְׁלִיכָה
ד ה מִמֶּנּוּ עֲבֹתֵימוֹ׃ יוֹשֵׁב בַּשָּׁמַיִם יִשְׂחָק אֲדֹנָי יִלְעַג־לָמוֹ׃ אָז יְדַבֵּר אֵלֵימוֹ
ו בְאַפּוֹ וּבַחֲרוֹנוֹ יְבַהֲלֵמוֹ׃ וַאֲנִי נָסַכְתִּי מַלְכִּי עַל־צִיּוֹן הַר־קָדְשִׁי׃
ז ח אֲסַפְּרָה אֶל חֹק יהוה אָמַר אֵלַי בְּנִי אַתָּה אֲנִי הַיּוֹם יְלִדְתִּיךָ׃ שְׁאַל
ט מִמֶּנִּי וְאֶתְּנָה גוֹיִם נַחֲלָתֶךָ וַאֲחֻזָּתְךָ אַפְסֵי־אָרֶץ׃ תְּרֹעֵם בְּשֵׁבֶט בַּרְזֶל
י יא כִּכְלִי יוֹצֵר תְּנַפְּצֵם׃ וְעַתָּה מְלָכִים הַשְׂכִּילוּ הִוָּסְרוּ שֹׁפְטֵי אָרֶץ׃ עִבְדוּ
יב אֶת־יהוה בְּיִרְאָה וְגִילוּ בִּרְעָדָה׃ נַשְּׁקוּ־בַר פֶּן־יֶאֱנַף ׀ וְתֹאבְדוּ דֶרֶךְ
כִּי־יִבְעַר כִּמְעַט אַפּוֹ אַשְׁרֵי כָּל־חוֹסֵי בוֹ׃

ג א ב מִזְמוֹר לְדָוִד בְּבָרְחוֹ מִפְּנֵי ׀ אַבְשָׁלוֹם בְּנוֹ׃ יהוה מָה־רַבּוּ צָרָי רַבִּים
ג קָמִים עָלָי׃ רַבִּים אֹמְרִים לְנַפְשִׁי אֵין יְשׁוּעָתָה לּוֹ בֵאלֹהִים סֶלָה׃
ד ה וְאַתָּה יהוה מָגֵן בַּעֲדִי כְּבוֹדִי וּמֵרִים רֹאשִׁי׃ קוֹלִי אֶל־יהוה אֶקְרָא
ו וַיַּעֲנֵנִי מֵהַר קָדְשׁוֹ סֶלָה׃ אֲנִי שָׁכַבְתִּי וָאִישָׁנָה הֱקִיצוֹתִי כִּי יהוה
ז ח יִסְמְכֵנִי׃ לֹא־אִירָא מֵרִבְבוֹת עָם אֲשֶׁר סָבִיב שָׁתוּ עָלָי׃ קוּמָה יהוה ׀
הוֹשִׁיעֵנִי אֱלֹהַי כִּי־הִכִּיתָ אֶת־כָּל־אֹיְבַי לֶחִי שִׁנֵּי רְשָׁעִים שִׁבַּרְתָּ׃
ט לַיהוה הַיְשׁוּעָה עַל־עַמְּךָ בִרְכָתֶךָ סֶּלָה׃

ד א ב לַמְנַצֵּחַ בִּנְגִינוֹת מִזְמוֹר לְדָוִד׃ בְּקָרְאִי עֲנֵנִי ׀ אֱלֹהֵי צִדְקִי בַּצָּר הִרְחַבְתָּ
ג לִּי חָנֵּנִי וּשְׁמַע תְּפִלָּתִי׃ בְּנֵי־אִישׁ עַד־מֶה כְבוֹדִי לִכְלִמָּה תֶּאֱהָבוּן
ד רִיק תְּבַקְשׁוּ כָזָב סֶלָה׃ וּדְעוּ כִּי־הִפְלָה יהוה חָסִיד לוֹ יהוה יִשְׁמַע
ה בְּקָרְאִי אֵלָיו׃ רִגְזוּ וְאַל־תֶּחֱטָאוּ אִמְרוּ בִלְבַבְכֶם עַל־מִשְׁכַּבְכֶם וְדֹמּוּ
ו ז סֶלָה׃ זִבְחוּ זִבְחֵי־צֶדֶק וּבִטְחוּ אֶל־יהוה׃ רַבִּים אֹמְרִים מִי־יַרְאֵנוּ
ח טוֹב נְסָה־עָלֵינוּ אוֹר פָּנֶיךָ יהוה׃ נָתַתָּה שִׂמְחָה בְלִבִּי מֵעֵת דְּגָנָם

9 feel in their abundance of grain and wine. In peace I shall lie down and sleep
soundly, for You alone, Lord, keep me safe.
5 1 2 *To the lead singer, on the* neḥilot[5] *– a psalm of David.* Give ear to my words,
3 Lord; understand my reflections; listen to the sound of my plea, my King
4 and God, for to You I pray. Lord, hear my voice in the morning; in the
5 morning I plead before You in expectation, for You are not a God who desires
6 wickedness; evil cannot abide with You. The brazen will not stand before
7 Your eyes; You hate all evildoers. You destroy those who speak lies; men of
8 blood and deceit the Lord despises. But I, with Your great loving-kindness,
will come to Your House; I will worship at Your holy Sanctuary in reverence
9 of You. Lord, lead me in Your righteousness because of my oppressors. Make
10 Your path straight before me, for there is not a true word on their lips; their
insides churn with malice; their slippery tongues lead to the open grave of
11 their throats. Condemn them, God; let them fall by their own counsel. Drive
12 them away for their many crimes, for they have rebelled against You. Let all
those who take refuge in You rejoice; let them ever sing for joy as You shelter
13 them; let those who love Your name exult in You, for You bless the righteous,
O Lord, sheathing them with favor like a shield.
6 1 *To the lead singer, accompanied by music on the* sheminit[6] *– a psalm of David.*
2 Lord, do not reproach me in Your anger; do not punish me in Your fury.
3 Be gracious to me, Lord, for I am wretched; heal me, Lord, for my bones
4 shake with agony. My soul is in grave agony – and You, O Lord – oh, how
5 long? Come back, Lord – rescue my soul; save me for the sake of Your love,
6 for there is no mention of You in death; who can praise You from the grave?
7 I am weary with sighing – each night I flood my bed with weeping; I drench
8 my couch in tears. My eye grows dim from grief, worn out from all my foes.
9 Leave me, all you evildoers, for the Lord has heard the sound of my weeping;
10 11 The Lord has heard my pleas; the Lord will accept my prayer. Shame and
agony will seize all my foes; they will turn back in sudden shame.
7 1 *A shiggayon[7] of David, which he sang to the Lord concerning Kush,[8] a Benjaminite.*
2 O Lord my God, in You I take refuge. Save me and deliver me from all my
3 foes lest they ravage me like a lion, tearing me apart, with no one to save me.
4 5 O Lord, my God, if I have done this, if there is guilt on my hands, if I have
6 repaid my allies with harm or plundered my rivals without cause, then let
my enemies pursue and overtake me; let them trample me into the ground
7 and lay my body in the dust – Selah. Arise, O Lord, in Your anger; rear up in
wrath against my enemies and rouse, for my sake, the judgment You decreed.
8 The assembly of peoples will surround You; take Your seat over them on
9 high. The Lord will judge nations; vindicate me, O Lord, according to my
10 righteousness and integrity. Let the evil of the wicked come to an end, and let

---

5 | A term of uncertain meaning, which many commentators relate to musical performance.

6 | A term of unknown meaning, perhaps a musical instrument with eight strings.

7 | A term of uncertain meaning that may pertain to musical performance. Cf. Habakkuk 3:1.

8 | Perhaps a reference to Sha'ul, son of Kish, who had persecuted David; see 1 Samuel, chapter 18 and onward.

ט וְתִירוֹשָׁם רָבּוּ: בְּשָׁלוֹם יַחְדָּו אֶשְׁכְּבָה וְאִישָׁן כִּי־אַתָּה יהוה לְבָדָד
לָבֶטַח תּוֹשִׁיבֵנִי:
ה א ב לַמְנַצֵּחַ אֶל־הַנְּחִילוֹת מִזְמוֹר לְדָוִד: אֲמָרַי הַאֲזִינָה ׀ יהוה בִּינָה
ג ד הֲגִיגִי: הַקְשִׁיבָה ׀ לְקוֹל שַׁוְעִי מַלְכִּי וֵאלֹהָי כִּי־אֵלֶיךָ אֶתְפַּלָּל: יהוה
ה בֹּקֶר תִּשְׁמַע קוֹלִי בֹּקֶר אֶעֱרָךְ־לְךָ וַאֲצַפֶּה: כִּי ׀ לֹא אֵל־חָפֵץ רֶשַׁע ׀
ו אָתָּה לֹא יְגֻרְךָ רָע: לֹא־יִתְיַצְּבוּ הוֹלְלִים לְנֶגֶד עֵינֶיךָ שָׂנֵאתָ כָּל־פֹּעֲלֵי
ז ח אָוֶן: תְּאַבֵּד דֹּבְרֵי כָזָב אִישׁ־דָּמִים וּמִרְמָה יְתָעֵב ׀ יהוה: וַאֲנִי בְּרֹב
ט חַסְדְּךָ אָבוֹא בֵיתֶךָ אֶשְׁתַּחֲוֶה אֶל־הֵיכַל־קָדְשְׁךָ בְּיִרְאָתֶךָ: יהוה ׀
י נְחֵנִי בְצִדְקָתֶךָ לְמַעַן שׁוֹרְרָי הושר לְפָנַי דַּרְכֶּךָ: כִּי אֵין בְּפִיהוּ נְכוֹנָה הַיְשַׁר
יא קִרְבָּם הַוּוֹת קֶבֶר־פָּתוּחַ גְּרוֹנָם לְשׁוֹנָם יַחֲלִיקוּן: הַאֲשִׁימֵם ׀ אֱלֹהִים
יב יִפְּלוּ מִמֹּעֲצוֹתֵיהֶם בְּרֹב פִּשְׁעֵיהֶם הַדִּיחֵמוֹ כִּי מָרוּ בָךְ: וְיִשְׂמְחוּ
יג כָל־חוֹסֵי בָךְ לְעוֹלָם יְרַנֵּנוּ וְתָסֵךְ עָלֵימוֹ וְיַעְלְצוּ בְךָ אֹהֲבֵי שְׁמֶךָ: כִּי־
אַתָּה תְּבָרֵךְ צַדִּיק יהוה כַּצִּנָּה רָצוֹן תַּעְטְרֶנּוּ:
ו א ב לַמְנַצֵּחַ בִּנְגִינוֹת עַל־הַשְּׁמִינִית מִזְמוֹר לְדָוִד: יהוה אַל־בְּאַפְּךָ תוֹכִיחֵנִי
ג וְאַל־בַּחֲמָתְךָ תְיַסְּרֵנִי: חָנֵּנִי יהוה כִּי אֻמְלַל אָנִי רְפָאֵנִי יהוה כִּי נִבְהֲלוּ
ד ה עֲצָמָי: וְנַפְשִׁי נִבְהֲלָה מְאֹד וְאַתְּ יהוה עַד־מָתָי: שׁוּבָה יהוה חַלְּצָה
ו נַפְשִׁי הוֹשִׁיעֵנִי לְמַעַן חַסְדֶּךָ: כִּי אֵין בַּמָּוֶת זִכְרֶךָ בִּשְׁאוֹל מִי יוֹדֶה־לָּךְ:
ז יָגַעְתִּי ׀ בְּאַנְחָתִי אַשְׂחֶה בְכָל־לַיְלָה מִטָּתִי בְּדִמְעָתִי עַרְשִׂי אַמְסֶה:
ח ט עָשְׁשָׁה מִכַּעַס עֵינִי עָתְקָה בְּכָל־צוֹרְרָי: סוּרוּ מִמֶּנִּי כָּל־פֹּעֲלֵי אָוֶן
י כִּי־שָׁמַע יהוה קוֹל בִּכְיִי: שָׁמַע יהוה תְּחִנָּתִי יהוה תְּפִלָּתִי יִקָּח:
יא יֵבֹשׁוּ ׀ וְיִבָּהֲלוּ מְאֹד כָּל־אֹיְבָי יָשֻׁבוּ יֵבֹשׁוּ רָגַע:
ז א ב שִׁגָּיוֹן לְדָוִד אֲשֶׁר־שָׁר לַיהוה עַל־דִּבְרֵי־כוּשׁ בֶּן־יְמִינִי: יהוה אֱלֹהַי
ג בְּךָ חָסִיתִי הוֹשִׁיעֵנִי מִכָּל־רֹדְפַי וְהַצִּילֵנִי: פֶּן־יִטְרֹף כְּאַרְיֵה נַפְשִׁי פֹּרֵק
ד ה וְאֵין מַצִּיל: יהוה אֱלֹהַי אִם־עָשִׂיתִי זֹאת אִם־יֶשׁ־עָוֶל בְּכַפָּי: אִם־
ו גָּמַלְתִּי שׁוֹלְמִי רָע וָאֲחַלְּצָה צוֹרְרִי רֵיקָם: יִרַדֹּף אוֹיֵב ׀ נַפְשִׁי וְיַשֵּׂג
ז וְיִרְמֹס לָאָרֶץ חַיָּי וּכְבוֹדִי ׀ לֶעָפָר יַשְׁכֵּן סֶלָה: קוּמָה יהוה ׀ בְּאַפֶּךָ
ח הִנָּשֵׂא בְּעַבְרוֹת צוֹרְרָי וְעוּרָה אֵלַי מִשְׁפָּט צִוִּיתָ: וַעֲדַת לְאֻמִּים
ט תְּסוֹבְבֶךָּ וְעָלֶיהָ לַמָּרוֹם שׁוּבָה: יהוה יָדִין עַמִּים שָׁפְטֵנִי יהוה כְּצִדְקִי
י וּכְתֻמִּי עָלָי: יִגְמָר־נָא רַע ׀ רְשָׁעִים וּתְכוֹנֵן צַדִּיק וּבֹחֵן לִבּוֹת וּכְלָיוֹת

the righteous stand firm – You who search hearts and minds,[9] O Righteous
11 12 God. My shield is God,[10] who saves the upright of heart. God vindicates the
13 righteous, growing livid every day. If someone fails to repent and sharpens
14 his sword and draws his bow and aims, then he has prepared the instruments
15 of his own death; he has poisoned his arrows for himself, for he has spawned
16 evil, he is pregnant with treachery, and he breeds falsehood.[11] He has dug a
17 pit and hollowed it out, and he himself will fall into that hole. His treachery
will come back on his own head; his violence will crash down on his own
18 skull. I will praise the Lord for His righteousness; I will sing to the name of
the Lord Most High.

8 1 2 *To the lead singer, on the* gittit[12] *– a psalm of David.* O Lord our Master, how
mighty is Your name throughout the earth; Your majesty extends across the
3 heavens! From the coos of little ones and babies You founded power against
4 Your foes, silencing enemies and avengers. When I behold Your heavens,
5 the work of Your fingertips, the moon and stars that You designed, what are
mortals, that You should be mindful of them; human beings, that You should
6 take note of them? Yet You have set them just below God[13] and crowned them
7 with glory and splendor. You made them rulers over Your handiwork; You set
8 9 it all beneath their feet – all flocks and herds, beasts of the field, birds of the
10 skies, and fish of the sea – whatever travels the paths of the seas. O Lord our
Master, how mighty is Your name throughout the earth!

9 1 2 *To the lead singer,* Al Mot Labben[14] *– a psalm of David.* I thank You, Lord,
3 with all my heart; let me tell of all Your wonders. I rejoice and exult in You; let
4 me sing praise to Your name, Most High. My enemies retreat; they stumble
5 and perish before You, for You have upheld my case and my cause; You have
6 sat enthroned as righteous judge; You have blasted nations and destroyed
7 the wicked, blotting out their names for ever and all time. The enemies are
finished, ruined forever; You have overthrown their cities – every trace of
8 them is lost. But the Lord abides forever; He has established His throne for
9 judgment. He will judge the world with justice and try the cause of peoples
10 fairly. The Lord is a stronghold for the downtrodden, a stronghold in times
11 of trouble. Those who know Your name trust in You, for You never forsake
12 those who seek You, Lord. Sing praise to the Lord who dwells in Zion;
13 tell of His deeds among the peoples. For the avenger of blood remembers;
14 He does not forget the cry of the suffering. Show me grace, Lord – see how
15 my enemies make me suffer, You who lift me up from the gates of death, so
that I may sing all Your praises at the gates of daughter Zion and rejoice in
16 Your deliverance. The nations have fallen into their own pit; their feet are
17 tangled in their own hidden net. The Lord is famed for His justice while the

---

9 | Literally "kidneys."
10 | Literally "my shield is upon God."
11 | Cf. Isaiah 59:4; Job 15:35.
12 | An unknown musical term.
13 | Or "the angels."
14 | The meaning of this phrase remains uncertain; perhaps it is related to the death (*mot*) of a son (*ben*) or someone called Labben.

יא יב אֱלֹהִים צַדִּיק: מָגִנִּי עַל־אֱלֹהִים מוֹשִׁיעַ יִשְׁרֵי־לֵב: אֱלֹהִים שׁוֹפֵט
יג צַדִּיק וְאֵל זֹעֵם בְּכָל־יוֹם: אִם־לֹא יָשׁוּב חַרְבּוֹ יִלְטוֹשׁ קַשְׁתּוֹ דָרַךְ
יד טו וַיְכוֹנְנֶהָ: וְלוֹ הֵכִין כְּלֵי־מָוֶת חִצָּיו לְדֹלְקִים יִפְעָל: הִנֵּה יְחַבֶּל־אָוֶן
טז יז וְהָרָה עָמָל וְיָלַד שָׁקֶר: בּוֹר כָּרָה וַיַּחְפְּרֵהוּ וַיִּפֹּל בְּשַׁחַת יִפְעָל: יָשׁוּב
יח עֲמָלוֹ בְרֹאשׁוֹ וְעַל קָדְקֳדוֹ חֲמָסוֹ יֵרֵד: אוֹדֶה יְהוָה כְּצִדְקוֹ וַאֲזַמְּרָה
שֵׁם־יְהוָה עֶלְיוֹן:

ח א ב לַמְנַצֵּחַ עַל־הַגִּתִּית מִזְמוֹר לְדָוִד: יְהוָה אֲדֹנֵינוּ מָה־אַדִּיר שִׁמְךָ בְּכָל־
ג הָאָרֶץ אֲשֶׁר תְּנָה הוֹדְךָ עַל־הַשָּׁמָיִם: מִפִּי עוֹלְלִים ׀ וְיֹנְקִים יִסַּדְתָּ
ד עֹז לְמַעַן צוֹרְרֶיךָ לְהַשְׁבִּית אוֹיֵב וּמִתְנַקֵּם: כִּי־אֶרְאֶה שָׁמֶיךָ מַעֲשֵׂה
ה אֶצְבְּעֹתֶיךָ יָרֵחַ וְכוֹכָבִים אֲשֶׁר כּוֹנָנְתָּה: מָה־אֱנוֹשׁ כִּי־תִזְכְּרֶנּוּ וּבֶן־
ו אָדָם כִּי תִפְקְדֶנּוּ: וַתְּחַסְּרֵהוּ מְּעַט מֵאֱלֹהִים וְכָבוֹד וְהָדָר תְּעַטְּרֵהוּ:
ז ח תַּמְשִׁילֵהוּ בְּמַעֲשֵׂי יָדֶיךָ כֹּל שַׁתָּה תַחַת־רַגְלָיו: צֹנֶה וַאֲלָפִים כֻּלָּם
ט י וְגַם בַּהֲמוֹת שָׂדָי: צִפּוֹר שָׁמַיִם וּדְגֵי הַיָּם עֹבֵר אָרְחוֹת יַמִּים: יְהוָה
אֲדֹנֵינוּ מָה־אַדִּיר שִׁמְךָ בְּכָל־הָאָרֶץ:

ט א ב לַמְנַצֵּחַ עַל־מוּת לַבֵּן מִזְמוֹר לְדָוִד: אוֹדֶה יְהוָה בְּכָל־לִבִּי אֲסַפְּרָה
ג ד כָּל־נִפְלְאוֹתֶיךָ: אֶשְׂמְחָה וְאֶעֶלְצָה בָךְ אֲזַמְּרָה שִׁמְךָ עֶלְיוֹן: בְּשׁוּב־
ה אוֹיְבַי אָחוֹר יִכָּשְׁלוּ וְיֹאבְדוּ מִפָּנֶיךָ: כִּי־עָשִׂיתָ מִשְׁפָּטִי וְדִינִי יָשַׁבְתָּ
ו לְכִסֵּא שׁוֹפֵט צֶדֶק: גָּעַרְתָּ גוֹיִם אִבַּדְתָּ רָשָׁע שְׁמָם מָחִיתָ לְעוֹלָם וָעֶד:
ז ח הָאוֹיֵב ׀ תַּמּוּ חֳרָבוֹת לָנֶצַח וְעָרִים נָתַשְׁתָּ אָבַד זִכְרָם הֵמָּה: וַיהוָה
ט לְעוֹלָם יֵשֵׁב כּוֹנֵן לַמִּשְׁפָּט כִּסְאוֹ: וְהוּא יִשְׁפֹּט־תֵּבֵל בְּצֶדֶק יָדִין לְאֻמִּים
י יא בְּמֵישָׁרִים: וִיהִי יְהוָה מִשְׂגָּב לַדָּךְ מִשְׂגָּב לְעִתּוֹת בַּצָּרָה: וְיִבְטְחוּ בְךָ
יב יוֹדְעֵי שְׁמֶךָ כִּי לֹא־עָזַבְתָּ דֹרְשֶׁיךָ יְהוָה: זַמְּרוּ לַיהוָה יֹשֵׁב צִיּוֹן הַגִּידוּ
יג בָעַמִּים עֲלִילוֹתָיו: כִּי־דֹרֵשׁ דָּמִים אוֹתָם זָכָר לֹא־שָׁכַח צַעֲקַת עניים: עֲנָוִים
יד טו חָנְנֵנִי יְהוָה רְאֵה עָנְיִי מִשֹּׂנְאָי מְרוֹמְמִי מִשַּׁעֲרֵי־מָוֶת: לְמַעַן אֲסַפְּרָה
טז כָּל־תְּהִלָּתֶיךָ בְּשַׁעֲרֵי בַת־צִיּוֹן אָגִילָה בִּישׁוּעָתֶךָ: טָבְעוּ גוֹיִם בְּשַׁחַת
יז עָשׂוּ בְּרֶשֶׁת־זוּ טָמָנוּ נִלְכְּדָה רַגְלָם: נוֹדַע ׀ יְהוָה מִשְׁפָּט עָשָׂה בְּפֹעַל

18 wicked are ensnared by the work of their own hands – *higgayon*[15] – Selah. The
19 wicked return to Sheol,[16] all nations that forget God, but the needy will not be
20 forgotten for long; the hope of the suffering will never be lost. Arise, LORD;
21 do not let mortals prevail – let the nations be judged before You. Strike them
with fear, LORD; let the nations know they are but mortal – Selah.
10 1 2 Why, LORD, do You stand far off, hiding Yourself in times of trouble? The
proud wicked persecute the poor – let them be trapped by their own devious
3 schemes! – for the wicked boast of their lust; the avaricious curse and revile
4 the LORD. In their sheer arrogance, the wicked say, "He will never call us
5 to account"; in all their scheming, they say, "There is no God." Their ways
always prosper – Your justice is far above them. As for their foes, they snort
6 at them. They say to themselves, "I will not be shaken; I will never encounter
7 trouble." Curses fill their mouths, deceit and malice; treachery and cruelty lie
8 beneath their tongues. They lurk in backwater places, murdering innocents
9 where no one sees; their eyes stalk the helpless. They lurk, hidden like a lion
in its lair, lurk to snatch away the poor; they snatch away the poor and drag
10 them off in their net. They stoop, they crouch, and the helpless fall prey to
11 their clutches. They say to themselves, "God has forgotten – He has hidden
12 His face and averted His gaze forever." Rise up, LORD; God, raise Your hand –
13 do not forget the poor! Why do the wicked revile God, thinking, "You will
14 never call us to account"? You do see! You do note treachery and torment
and take them into Your hands; the helpless commit themselves to You; You
15 have always helped the orphan. Break the arms of the wicked; call the evil to
16 account for their wickedness until it is gone. The LORD is King for ever and
17 ever; the nations shall perish from His land. You have heard what the lowly
18 desire, LORD; strengthen their hearts and lend Your ear to bring justice to
the orphan and the downtrodden so that mere earthly mortals will never
spread terror again.
11 1 *To the lead singer, of David.* In the LORD I take shelter – how can you say to me,
2 "Flee your mountain like a bird – for look, the wicked, they draw their bows
3 taut, set their arrows on the string to shoot from the shadows at the upright –
for the foundations will soon be destroyed." What are the righteous to do?
4 The LORD is in His holy Sanctuary; the LORD is on His heavenly throne;
5 His eyes gaze down; He examines humanity; the LORD examines righteous
6 and wicked. He despises the lover of violence; He will rain down soot and
7 fire and sulfur on the wicked; scorching winds are their portion. For the
LORD is righteous; He loves what is right. The upright will gaze upon His
face.
12 1 2 *To the lead singer, on the* sheminit[17] *– a psalm of David.* Help, LORD, for the
3 godly are no more, for the faithful have faded from humanity. People tell
4 each other lies; they are smooth talking and two faced. May the LORD cut
5 off all these smooth lips, these arrogant wagging tongues that declare, "Our

15 | A term of uncertain meaning, probably a musical notation.
16 | The underworld, the abode of the dead.
17 | See note on 6:1.

יח כַּפָּיו נוֹקֵשׁ רָשָׁע הִגָּיוֹן סֶלָה: יָשׁוּבוּ רְשָׁעִים לִשְׁאוֹלָה כָּל־גּוֹיִם שְׁכֵחֵי
יט כ אֱלֹהִים: כִּי לֹא לָנֶצַח יִשָּׁכַח אֶבְיוֹן תִּקְוַת ענוים תֹּאבַד לָעַד: קוּמָה עֲנִיִּים
כא יְהוָה אַל־יָעֹז אֱנוֹשׁ יִשָּׁפְטוּ גוֹיִם עַל־פָּנֶיךָ: שִׁיתָה יְהוָה | מוֹרָה לָהֶם
יֵדְעוּ גוֹיִם אֱנוֹשׁ הֵמָּה סֶּלָה:

י א ב לָמָה יְהוָה תַּעֲמֹד בְּרָחוֹק תַּעְלִים לְעִתּוֹת בַּצָּרָה: בְּגַאֲוַת רָשָׁע יִדְלַק
ג עָנִי יִתָּפְשׂוּ | בִּמְזִמּוֹת זוּ חָשָׁבוּ: כִּי־הִלֵּל רָשָׁע עַל־תַּאֲוַת נַפְשׁוֹ וּבֹצֵעַ
ד בֵּרֵךְ נִאֵץ | יְהוָה: רָשָׁע כְּגֹבַהּ אַפּוֹ בַּל־יִדְרֹשׁ אֵין אֱלֹהִים כָּל־מְזִמּוֹתָיו:
ה יָחִילוּ דְרָכָו | בְּכָל־עֵת מָרוֹם מִשְׁפָּטֶיךָ מִנֶּגְדּוֹ כָּל־צוֹרְרָיו יָפִיחַ בָּהֶם:
ו ז אָמַר בְּלִבּוֹ בַּל־אֶמּוֹט לְדֹר וָדֹר אֲשֶׁר לֹא־בְרָע: אָלָה | פִּיהוּ מָלֵא
ח וּמִרְמוֹת וָתֹךְ תַּחַת לְשׁוֹנוֹ עָמָל וָאָוֶן: יֵשֵׁב | בְּמַאְרַב חֲצֵרִים בַּמִּסְתָּרִים
ט יַהֲרֹג נָקִי עֵינָיו לְחֵלְכָה יִצְפֹּנוּ: יֶאֱרֹב בַּמִּסְתָּר | כְּאַרְיֵה בְסֻכֹּה יֶאֱרֹב
י לַחֲטוֹף עָנִי יַחְטֹף עָנִי בְּמָשְׁכוֹ בְרִשְׁתּוֹ: ודכה יָשֹׁחַ וְנָפַל בַּעֲצוּמָיו יִדְכֶּה
יא יב חלכאים: אָמַר בְּלִבּוֹ שָׁכַח אֵל הִסְתִּיר פָּנָיו בַּל־רָאָה לָנֶצַח: קוּמָה חֵל כָּאִים
יג יְהוָה אֵל נְשָׂא יָדֶךָ אַל־תִּשְׁכַּח עניים: עַל־מֶה | נִאֵץ רָשָׁע | אֱלֹהִים עֲנָוִים
יד אָמַר בְּלִבּוֹ לֹא תִּדְרֹשׁ: רָאִתָה כִּי־אַתָּה | עָמָל וָכַעַס | תַּבִּיט לָתֵת
טו בְּיָדֶךָ עָלֶיךָ יַעֲזֹב חֵלְכָה יָתוֹם אַתָּה | הָיִיתָ עוֹזֵר: שְׁבֹר זְרוֹעַ רָשָׁע
טז וָרָע תִּדְרוֹשׁ־רִשְׁעוֹ בַל־תִּמְצָא: יְהוָה מֶלֶךְ עוֹלָם וָעֶד אָבְדוּ גוֹיִם
יז יח מֵאַרְצוֹ: תַּאֲוַת עֲנָוִים שָׁמַעְתָּ יְהוָה תָּכִין לִבָּם תַּקְשִׁיב אָזְנֶךָ: לִשְׁפֹּט
יָתוֹם וָדָךְ בַּל־יוֹסִיף עוֹד לַעֲרֹץ אֱנוֹשׁ מִן־הָאָרֶץ:

יא א לַמְנַצֵּחַ לְדָוִד בַּיהוָה | חָסִיתִי אֵיךְ תֹּאמְרוּ לְנַפְשִׁי נודו הַרְכֶם צִפּוֹר: נוּדִי
ב כִּי הִנֵּה הָרְשָׁעִים יִדְרְכוּן קֶשֶׁת כּוֹנְנוּ חִצָּם עַל־יֶתֶר לִירוֹת בְּמוֹ־אֹפֶל
ג ד לְיִשְׁרֵי־לֵב: כִּי הַשָּׁתוֹת יֵהָרֵסוּן צַדִּיק מַה־פָּעָל: יְהוָה | בְּהֵיכַל קָדְשׁוֹ
ה יְהוָה בַּשָּׁמַיִם כִּסְאוֹ עֵינָיו יֶחֱזוּ עַפְעַפָּיו יִבְחֲנוּ בְּנֵי אָדָם: יְהוָה צַדִּיק
ו יִבְחָן וְרָשָׁע וְאֹהֵב חָמָס שָׂנְאָה נַפְשׁוֹ: יַמְטֵר עַל־רְשָׁעִים פַּחִים אֵשׁ
ב ז וְגָפְרִית וְרוּחַ זִלְעָפוֹת מְנָת כּוֹסָם: כִּי־צַדִּיק יְהוָה צְדָקוֹת אָהֵב יָשָׁר
יֶחֱזוּ פָנֵימוֹ:

יב א ב לַמְנַצֵּחַ עַל־הַשְּׁמִינִית מִזְמוֹר לְדָוִד: הוֹשִׁיעָה יְהוָה כִּי־גָמַר חָסִיד
ג כִּי־פַסּוּ אֱמוּנִים מִבְּנֵי אָדָם: שָׁוְא | יְדַבְּרוּ אִישׁ אֶת־רֵעֵהוּ שְׂפַת
ד חֲלָקוֹת בְּלֵב וָלֵב יְדַבֵּרוּ: יַכְרֵת יְהוָה כָּל־שִׂפְתֵי חֲלָקוֹת לָשׁוֹן מְדַבֶּרֶת
ה גְּדֹלוֹת: אֲשֶׁר אָמְרוּ | לִלְשֹׁנֵנוּ נַגְבִּיר שְׂפָתֵינוּ אִתָּנוּ מִי אָדוֹן לָנוּ:

6 tongues shall prevail; our lips are our own – who is our master?" "Because
of the oppression of the poor, the groans of the needy, I will now rise up,"
7 declares the LORD. "I will grant them the safety they sigh for." The LORD's
words are pure words, like silver refined in an earthen furnace, purified seven
8 times over. You, LORD, will watch over them and protect them from this
9 generation forever – as the wicked strut around, and obscenity is prized
among humanity.
13 1 2 *To the lead singer – a psalm of David.* For how long, LORD, will You forget me?
3 Forever? For how long will You hide Your face from me? For how long will
I have worries in my mind and sorrow in my heart each day? For how long
4 will my enemy triumph over me? Look at me; answer me, O LORD my God.
5 Light up my eyes lest I fall into a death sleep, lest my enemy declare, "I have
6 bested him!" – lest my foes delight at my collapse. But I have placed my trust
in Your loyalty; my heart will delight in Your salvation. I will sing to the LORD,
for He has been good to me.
14 1 *To the lead singer, of David.*[18] The brute says in his heart, "There is no God."
They are corrupt; they wreak vile schemes; there is no one who does good.
2 The LORD looks down from heaven at humanity to see if someone has the
3 sense to seek out God, but all have turned away, altogether tainted; there is
4 no one who does good, not even one. Have they no knowledge, all those
evildoers, who devour My people as if devouring bread, who do not call
5 out to the LORD? There they will be struck with terror, for God is among
6 the abodes of the righteous. You would rebuff the counsel of the poor, but
7 the LORD is their shelter. Oh, that Israel's salvation might come from Zion!
When the LORD restores His people's fortune, Yaakov will rejoice; Israel will
be glad.
15 1 *A psalm of David.* LORD, who may dwell in Your tent? Who may live on
2 Your holy mountain? The one whose ways are blameless, who does what is
3 right, who speaks truth from the heart; the one who has no malice on his
tongue, who does no wrong to his fellow, who does not cast a slur against his
4 neighbor; the one who scorns those who are vile, who honors those who fear
5 the LORD, who keeps an oath even when it hurts; the one who does not loan
money for interest, who does not take a bribe against the innocent – anyone
who acts thus will never be shaken.
16 1 2 A mikhtam[19] *of David.* Protect me, God, for in You I take refuge. I said to the
3 LORD, "You are my Lord; My favor comes from none but You." As for the holy
4 ones in the land, the mighty who were all my delight, may those who court
other gods suffer many sorrows – I will not pour out their libations of blood;
5 I will not bear their names on my lips. The LORD is my chosen portion and
6 my cup. You direct my fate. A sweet heritage has fallen to my lot; my share is
7 delightful to me. I will bless the LORD who has guided me; even at night, my
8 conscience stirs me. I have set the LORD before me always; He is at my right
9 hand; I shall not be shaken. Therefore my heart is glad, my spirit rejoices,

18 | Cf. Psalm 53, a slightly different version of this psalm.
19 | Meaning is uncertain.

ו מִשֹּׁד עֲנִיִּים מֵאַנְקַת אֶבְיוֹנִים עַתָּה אָקוּם יֹאמַר יהוה אָשִׁית בְּיֵשַׁע
ז יָפִיחַ לוֹ: אִמְרוֹת יהוה אֲמָרוֹת טְהֹרוֹת כֶּסֶף צָרוּף בַּעֲלִיל לָאָרֶץ
ח מְזֻקָּק שִׁבְעָתָיִם: אַתָּה־יהוה תִּשְׁמְרֵם תִּצְּרֶנּוּ ׀ מִן־הַדּוֹר זוּ לְעוֹלָם:
ט סָבִיב רְשָׁעִים יִתְהַלָּכוּן כְּרֻם זֻלּוּת לִבְנֵי אָדָם:
יג א ב לַמְנַצֵּחַ מִזְמוֹר לְדָוִד: עַד־אָנָה יהוה תִּשְׁכָּחֵנִי נֶצַח עַד־אָנָה ׀ תַּסְתִּיר
ג אֶת־פָּנֶיךָ מִמֶּנִּי: עַד־אָנָה אָשִׁית עֵצוֹת בְּנַפְשִׁי יָגוֹן בִּלְבָבִי יוֹמָם עַד־
ד אָנָה ׀ יָרוּם אֹיְבִי עָלָי: הַבִּיטָה עֲנֵנִי יהוה אֱלֹהָי הָאִירָה עֵינַי פֶּן־אִישַׁן
ה ו הַמָּוֶת: פֶּן־יֹאמַר אֹיְבִי יְכָלְתִּיו צָרַי יָגִילוּ כִּי אֶמּוֹט: וַאֲנִי ׀ בְּחַסְדְּךָ
בָטַחְתִּי יָגֵל לִבִּי בִּישׁוּעָתֶךָ אָשִׁירָה לַיהוה כִּי גָמַל עָלָי:
יד א לַמְנַצֵּחַ לְדָוִד אָמַר נָבָל בְּלִבּוֹ אֵין אֱלֹהִים הִשְׁחִיתוּ הִתְעִיבוּ עֲלִילָה
ב אֵין עֹשֵׂה־טוֹב: יהוה מִשָּׁמַיִם הִשְׁקִיף עַל־בְּנֵי־אָדָם לִרְאוֹת הֲיֵשׁ
ג מַשְׂכִּיל דֹּרֵשׁ אֶת־אֱלֹהִים: הַכֹּל סָר יַחְדָּו נֶאֱלָחוּ אֵין עֹשֵׂה־טוֹב אֵין
ד גַּם־אֶחָד: הֲלֹא יָדְעוּ כָּל־פֹּעֲלֵי אָוֶן אֹכְלֵי עַמִּי אָכְלוּ לֶחֶם יהוה לֹא
ה ו קָרָאוּ: שָׁם ׀ פָּחֲדוּ פָחַד כִּי־אֱלֹהִים בְּדוֹר צַדִּיק: עֲצַת־עָנִי תָבִישׁוּ
ז כִּי יהוה מַחְסֵהוּ: מִי יִתֵּן מִצִּיּוֹן יְשׁוּעַת יִשְׂרָאֵל בְּשׁוּב יהוה שְׁבוּת
עַמּוֹ יָגֵל יַעֲקֹב יִשְׂמַח יִשְׂרָאֵל:
טו א ב מִזְמוֹר לְדָוִד יהוה מִי־יָגוּר בְּאָהֳלֶךָ מִי־יִשְׁכֹּן בְּהַר קָדְשֶׁךָ: הוֹלֵךְ
ג תָּמִים וּפֹעֵל צֶדֶק וְדֹבֵר אֱמֶת בִּלְבָבוֹ: לֹא־רָגַל ׀ עַל־לְשֹׁנוֹ לֹא־עָשָׂה
ד לְרֵעֵהוּ רָעָה וְחֶרְפָּה לֹא־נָשָׂא עַל־קְרֹבוֹ: נִבְזֶה ׀ בְּעֵינָיו נִמְאָס וְאֶת־
ה יִרְאֵי יהוה יְכַבֵּד נִשְׁבַּע לְהָרַע וְלֹא יָמִר: כַּסְפּוֹ ׀ לֹא־נָתַן בְּנֶשֶׁךְ וְשֹׁחַד
עַל־נָקִי לֹא־לָקָח עֹשֵׂה אֵלֶּה לֹא יִמּוֹט לְעוֹלָם:
טז א ב מִכְתָּם לְדָוִד שָׁמְרֵנִי אֵל כִּי־חָסִיתִי בָךְ: אָמַרְתְּ לַיהוה אֲדֹנָי אָתָּה
ג טוֹבָתִי בַּל־עָלֶיךָ: לִקְדוֹשִׁים אֲשֶׁר־בָּאָרֶץ הֵמָּה וְאַדִּירֵי כָּל־חֶפְצִי־
ד בָם: יִרְבּוּ עַצְּבוֹתָם אַחֵר מָהָרוּ בַּל־אַסִּיךְ נִסְכֵּיהֶם מִדָּם וּבַל־אֶשָּׂא
ה אֶת־שְׁמוֹתָם עַל־שְׂפָתָי: יהוה מְנָת־חֶלְקִי וְכוֹסִי אַתָּה תּוֹמִיךְ גּוֹרָלִי:
ו ז חֲבָלִים נָפְלוּ־לִי בַּנְּעִמִים אַף־נַחֲלָת שָׁפְרָה עָלָי: אֲבָרֵךְ אֶת־יהוה
ח אֲשֶׁר יְעָצָנִי אַף־לֵילוֹת יִסְּרוּנִי כִלְיוֹתָי: שִׁוִּיתִי יהוה לְנֶגְדִּי תָמִיד כִּי
ט מִימִינִי בַּל־אֶמּוֹט: לָכֵן ׀ שָׂמַח לִבִּי וַיָּגֶל כְּבוֹדִי אַף־בְּשָׂרִי יִשְׁכֹּן לָבֶטַח:

10 and my body rests secure, for You will not abandon me to Sheol nor let Your
11 devoted one see the Pit. You will teach me the path of life. In Your presence
is fullness of joy; at Your right hand, bliss for evermore.
17 1 *A prayer of David.* Hear, LORD, what is just; listen to my plea; give ear to my
2 prayer, mouthed without deceit. May I be vindicated before You – Your eyes
3 will behold what is right. You have searched my heart, visited me by night,
tried me, and found nothing amiss. I shut my mouth tight against offense.
4 As for what others do, by the words of Your lips I myself keep away from the
5 paths of the violent. My steps have adhered to Your pathways; my feet have
6 never faltered. I call on You for You will answer me, God; lend Your ear to
7 me; listen to my words. Show Your wondrous loyalty, You who save with
8 Your right hand those who seek refuge from adversaries. Guard me like the
9 apple of Your eye; hide me in the shade of Your wings from the wicked who
10 assault me, my deadly enemies who encircle me. Their hearts are callous;
11 their mouths flaunt and gloat. Now they close in around our steps, combing
12 the ground with their gaze like a lion hungering for prey, like a young lion
13 crouching in ambush. Rise up, LORD; confront them; bring them down.
14 Rescue me from the wicked with Your sword, from people, O LORD, by Your
hand, from people whose share in life is fleeting. As for those You treasure, fill
their bellies; their children, too, will be sated and leave what remains for their
15 own little ones. As for me, in justice I will gaze upon Your face; wide awake,
I am sated with Your image.
18 1 *To the lead singer – of the LORD's servant, of David,*[20] *who uttered these words of*
song to the LORD; on the day that the LORD saved him from the hands of all his
2 *enemies and from the hands of Sha'ul, he said,* I love You, O LORD, my strength.
3 The LORD is my Rock, my fortress, my rescuer; my God is the Rock of my
4 refuge, my shield, the horn of my salvation, my haven. Praise! When I call
5 on the LORD, I am saved from my enemies. The cords of death assailed me;
6 deadly torrents engulfed me; the cords of Sheol entangled me; snares of death
7 confronted me. In my distress I called on the LORD; I cried out to my God; He
8 heard my voice from His Temple, and my cry rang in His ears. Then the earth
shook and shuddered; the very mountain beds trembled; they shuddered
9 from His wrath. Smoke issued from His nostrils; devouring flames flared from
10 His mouth; from Him gleaming coals blazed forth. He bent the heavens and
11 descended, dense cloud beneath His feet; He mounted a cherub and flew,
12 soaring on wings of wind. He enveloped Himself in darkness, a shelter all
13 around Him of heavy storm clouds dark with rain. The brilliant glow of His
14 presence pierced His clouds with hail and fiery coals. The LORD thundered
from the heavens; the Most High raised His voice with hail and fiery coals.
15 He shot His arrows and scattered them; He hurled lightning bolts and routed
16 them. The ocean bed was exposed, the foundations of the world laid bare
17 by Your onslaught, LORD, from the blast of Your breath. From on high He
18 reached down and took me; He drew me out of the mighty waters. He saved
19 me from my fierce enemy, from foes too strong for me. They confronted

20 | Cf. II Samuel, chapter 22.

י יא כִּי ׀ לֹא־תַעֲזֹב נַפְשִׁי לִשְׁאוֹל לֹא־תִתֵּן חסידיך לִרְאוֹת שָׁחַת: תּוֹדִיעֵנִי חֲסִידְךָ
אֹרַח חַיִּים שֹׂבַע שְׂמָחוֹת אֶת־פָּנֶיךָ נְעִמוֹת בִּימִינְךָ נֶצַח:
יז א תְּפִלָּה לְדָוִד שִׁמְעָה יהוה ׀ צֶדֶק הַקְשִׁיבָה רִנָּתִי הַאֲזִינָה תְפִלָּתִי
ב בְּלֹא שִׂפְתֵי מִרְמָה: מִלְּפָנֶיךָ מִשְׁפָּטִי יֵצֵא עֵינֶיךָ תֶּחֱזֶינָה מֵישָׁרִים:
ג בָּחַנְתָּ לִבִּי ׀ פָּקַדְתָּ לַּיְלָה צְרַפְתַּנִי בַל־תִּמְצָא זַמֹּתִי בַּל־יַעֲבָר־פִּי:
ד ה לִפְעֻלּוֹת אָדָם בִּדְבַר שְׂפָתֶיךָ אֲנִי שָׁמַרְתִּי אָרְחוֹת פָּרִיץ: תָּמֹךְ אֲשֻׁרַי
ו בְּמַעְגְּלוֹתֶיךָ בַּל־נָמוֹטּוּ פְעָמָי: אֲנִי־קְרָאתִיךָ כִי־תַעֲנֵנִי אֵל הַט־אָזְנְךָ
ז לִי שְׁמַע אִמְרָתִי: הַפְלֵה חֲסָדֶיךָ מוֹשִׁיעַ חוֹסִים מִמִּתְקוֹמְמִים בִּימִינֶךָ:
ח ט שָׁמְרֵנִי כְּאִישׁוֹן בַּת־עָיִן בְּצֵל כְּנָפֶיךָ תַּסְתִּירֵנִי: מִפְּנֵי רְשָׁעִים זוּ שַׁדּוּנִי
י יא אֹיְבַי בְּנֶפֶשׁ יַקִּיפוּ עָלָי: חֶלְבָּמוֹ סָּגְרוּ פִּימוֹ דִּבְּרוּ בְגֵאוּת: אַשֻּׁרֵינוּ עַתָּה
יב סבבוני עֵינֵיהֶם יָשִׁיתוּ לִנְטוֹת בָּאָרֶץ: דִּמְיֹנוֹ כְּאַרְיֵה יִכְסוֹף לִטְרֹף סְבָבוּנוּ
יג וְכִכְפִיר יֹשֵׁב בְּמִסְתָּרִים: קוּמָה יהוה קַדְּמָה פָנָיו הַכְרִיעֵהוּ פַּלְּטָה
יד נַפְשִׁי מֵרָשָׁע חַרְבֶּךָ: מִמְתִים יָדְךָ ׀ יהוה מִמְתִים מֵחֶלֶד חֶלְקָם בַּחַיִּים
טו וצפינך תְּמַלֵּא בִטְנָם יִשְׂבְּעוּ בָנִים וְהִנִּיחוּ יִתְרָם לְעוֹלְלֵיהֶם: אֲנִי וּצְפוּנְךָ
בְּצֶדֶק אֶחֱזֶה פָנֶיךָ אֶשְׂבְּעָה בְהָקִיץ תְּמוּנָתֶךָ:
יח א לַמְנַצֵּחַ לְעֶבֶד יהוה לְדָוִד אֲשֶׁר דִּבֶּר ׀ לַיהוה אֶת־דִּבְרֵי הַשִּׁירָה
ב הַזֹּאת בְּיוֹם ׀ הִצִּיל־יהוה אוֹתוֹ מִכַּף כָּל־אֹיְבָיו וּמִיַּד שָׁאוּל: וַיֹּאמַר
ג אֶרְחָמְךָ יהוה חִזְקִי: יהוה ׀ סַלְעִי וּמְצוּדָתִי וּמְפַלְטִי אֵלִי צוּרִי אֶחֱסֶה־
ד בּוֹ מָגִנִּי וְקֶרֶן־יִשְׁעִי מִשְׂגַּבִּי: מְהֻלָּל אֶקְרָא יהוה וּמִן־אֹיְבַי אִוָּשֵׁעַ:
ה ו אֲפָפוּנִי חֶבְלֵי־מָוֶת וְנַחֲלֵי בְלִיַּעַל יְבַעֲתוּנִי: חֶבְלֵי שְׁאוֹל סְבָבוּנִי
ז קִדְּמוּנִי מוֹקְשֵׁי מָוֶת: בַּצַּר־לִי ׀ אֶקְרָא יהוה וְאֶל־אֱלֹהַי אֲשַׁוֵּעַ יִשְׁמַע
ח מֵהֵיכָלוֹ קוֹלִי וְשַׁוְעָתִי לְפָנָיו ׀ תָּבוֹא בְאָזְנָיו: וַתִּגְעַשׁ וַתִּרְעַשׁ ׀ הָאָרֶץ
ט וּמוֹסְדֵי הָרִים יִרְגָּזוּ וַיִּתְגָּעֲשׁוּ כִּי־חָרָה לוֹ: עָלָה עָשָׁן ׀ בְּאַפּוֹ וְאֵשׁ־מִפִּיו
י יא תֹּאכֵל גֶּחָלִים בָּעֲרוּ מִמֶּנּוּ: וַיֵּט שָׁמַיִם וַיֵּרַד וַעֲרָפֶל תַּחַת רַגְלָיו: וַיִּרְכַּב
יב עַל־כְּרוּב וַיָּעֹף וַיֵּדֶא עַל־כַּנְפֵי־רוּחַ: יָשֶׁת חֹשֶׁךְ ׀ סִתְרוֹ סְבִיבוֹתָיו
יג סֻכָּתוֹ חֶשְׁכַת־מַיִם עָבֵי שְׁחָקִים: מִנֹּגַהּ נֶגְדּוֹ עָבָיו עָבְרוּ בָּרָד וְגַחֲלֵי־
יד טו אֵשׁ: וַיַּרְעֵם בַּשָּׁמַיִם ׀ יהוה וְעֶלְיוֹן יִתֵּן קֹלוֹ בָּרָד וְגַחֲלֵי־אֵשׁ: וַיִּשְׁלַח
טז חִצָּיו וַיְפִיצֵם וּבְרָקִים רָב וַיְהֻמֵּם: וַיֵּרָאוּ ׀ אֲפִיקֵי מַיִם וַיִּגָּלוּ מוֹסְדוֹת
יז תֵּבֵל מִגַּעֲרָתְךָ יהוה מִנִּשְׁמַת רוּחַ אַפֶּךָ: יִשְׁלַח מִמָּרוֹם יִקָּחֵנִי יַמְשֵׁנִי
יח יט מִמַּיִם רַבִּים: יַצִּילֵנִי מֵאֹיְבִי עָז וּמִשֹּׂנְאַי כִּי־אָמְצוּ מִמֶּנִּי: יְקַדְּמוּנִי

20 me on my direst day, but the LORD was my support. He brought me out to
21 freedom; He rescued me because He delighted in me. The LORD rewarded
22 me as I deserved; as my hands were clean, He repaid me, for I kept the ways
23 of the LORD and did not betray my God, for all His laws are before me; I will
24 not cast aside His statutes. I am blameless to Him and keep myself from sin,
25 so the LORD repaid me as I deserved, as my hands were clean in His sight.
26 You deal loyally with those who are loyal; to the blameless You show Yourself
27 blameless; You are pure with those who are pure, but with the crooked,
28 You twist and turn, for it is You who brings salvation to a humble people
29 but humiliate haughty eyes, for it is You who lights my lamp. The LORD my
30 God lights up my darkness; with You I can rush a ridge; with my God I can
31 leap over a wall. God's ways are blameless, the LORD's words are pure; He is
32 a shield to all who take refuge in Him. For who is a god besides the LORD;
33 who is a Rock besides our God? God is the one who girds me with power;
34 He makes my way sound. He makes my legs like a deer's and stands me on
35 the heights; He trains my hands for battle so that my arms can bend a bow of
36 bronze. You gave me the shield of Your victory; Your right hand sustained me;
37 Your gentleness made me great. You made my steps broad and firm; my feet
38 never faltered. I pursued my enemies and overtook them, never turning back
39 until they perished. I crushed them until they could rise no more; they fell
40 beneath my feet. You girded me with power for battle and sunk my adversaries
41 far beneath me; You made my enemies turn tail before me; my foes, too, I
42 destroyed. They cried out, but there was no savior – out to the LORD, but He
43 did not answer them – while I ground them up like dust in the wind; I poured
44 them out like street mud. You rescued me from civil strife; You have set me
45 as the head of nations; peoples I never knew of serve me. They merely hear
46 of me and obey; foreign peoples come cringing before me. Foreign peoples
47 lose heart and come trembling out of their forts. The LORD lives! Blessed is
48 my Rock; exalted is the God of my rescue! – the God who grants vengeance
49 to me, who subjugates people under me. My rescuer from my enemies, You
raise me above those who rise against me; You save me from violent men,
50 so I praise You among the nations, LORD, and sing to Your name. He grants
51 great victories to His king and shows loyalty to His anointed, to David and
his seed forever.

19 1 *To the lead singer – a psalm of David.* The heavens tell of God's glory; the
2 skies proclaim His handiwork. Day to day pours forth speech; night to night
3 expresses knowledge. There is no speech; there are no words; their voice is
4 not heard, yet their music carries across the land, their words to the end of
5 the earth. In them[21] He has set a tent for the sun, which emerges like a groom
6 from his marriage chamber, glowing like a champion about to run his course.
7 It rises at one end of the heaven and circuits to the other; nothing can hide
8 from its heat. The LORD's teaching is perfect, reviving the spirit; the LORD's
9 decree is steadfast, making the simple wise. The LORD's precepts are just,
cheering the heart; the LORD's commandment is radiant, lighting up the eyes.

21 | Meaning in the heavens.

כ בְיוֹם־אֵידִי וַיְהִי־יְהוָה לְמִשְׁעָן לִי׃ וַיּוֹצִיאֵנִי לַמֶּרְחָב יְחַלְּצֵנִי כִּי חָפֵץ
כא כב בִּי׃ יִגְמְלֵנִי יְהוָה כְּצִדְקִי כְּבֹר יָדַי יָשִׁיב לִי׃ כִּי־שָׁמַרְתִּי דַּרְכֵי יְהוָה
כג וְלֹא־רָשַׁעְתִּי מֵאֱלֹהָי׃ כִּי כָל־מִשְׁפָּטָיו לְנֶגְדִּי וְחֻקֹּתָיו לֹא־אָסִיר מֶנִּי׃
כד כה וָאֱהִי תָמִים עִמּוֹ וָאֶשְׁתַּמֵּר מֵעֲוֺנִי׃ וַיָּשֶׁב־יְהוָה לִי כְצִדְקִי כְּבֹר יָדַי
כו כז לְנֶגֶד עֵינָיו׃ עִם־חָסִיד תִּתְחַסָּד עִם־גְּבַר תָּמִים תִּתַּמָּם׃ עִם־נָבָר
כח תִּתְבָּרָר וְעִם־עִקֵּשׁ תִּתְפַּתָּל׃ כִּי־אַתָּה עַם־עָנִי תוֹשִׁיעַ וְעֵינַיִם רָמוֹת
כט ל תַּשְׁפִּיל׃ כִּי־אַתָּה תָּאִיר נֵרִי יְהוָה אֱלֹהַי יַגִּיהַּ חָשְׁכִּי׃ כִּי־בְךָ אָרֻץ
לא גְּדוּד וּבֵאלֹהַי אֲדַלֶּג־שׁוּר׃ הָאֵל תָּמִים דַּרְכּוֹ אִמְרַת־יְהוָה צְרוּפָה מָגֵן
לב הוּא לְכֹל ׀ הַחֹסִים בּוֹ׃ כִּי מִי אֱלוֹהַּ מִבַּלְעֲדֵי יְהוָה וּמִי צוּר זוּלָתִי
לג לד אֱלֹהֵינוּ׃ הָאֵל הַמְאַזְּרֵנִי חָיִל וַיִּתֵּן תָּמִים דַּרְכִּי׃ מְשַׁוֶּה רַגְלַי כָּאַיָּלוֹת
לה וְעַל בָּמֹתַי יַעֲמִידֵנִי׃ מְלַמֵּד יָדַי לַמִּלְחָמָה וְנִחֲתָה קֶשֶׁת־נְחוּשָׁה
לו לז זְרוֹעֹתָי׃ וַתִּתֶּן־לִי מָגֵן יִשְׁעֶךָ וִימִינְךָ תִסְעָדֵנִי וְעַנְוַתְךָ תַרְבֵּנִי׃ תַּרְחִיב
לח צַעֲדִי תַחְתָּי וְלֹא מָעֲדוּ קַרְסֻלָּי׃ אֶרְדּוֹף אוֹיְבַי וְאַשִּׂיגֵם וְלֹא־אָשׁוּב
לט מ עַד־כַּלּוֹתָם׃ אֶמְחָצֵם וְלֹא־יֻכְלוּ קוּם יִפְּלוּ תַּחַת רַגְלָי׃ וַתְּאַזְּרֵנִי חַיִל
מא לַמִּלְחָמָה תַּכְרִיעַ קָמַי תַּחְתָּי׃ וְאֹיְבַי נָתַתָּה לִּי עֹרֶף וּמְשַׂנְאַי אַצְמִיתֵם׃
מב מג יְשַׁוְּעוּ וְאֵין־מוֹשִׁיעַ עַל־יְהוָה וְלֹא עָנָם׃ וְאֶשְׁחָקֵם כְּעָפָר עַל־פְּנֵי־רוּחַ
מד כְּטִיט חוּצוֹת אֲרִיקֵם׃ תְּפַלְּטֵנִי מֵרִיבֵי עָם תְּשִׂימֵנִי לְרֹאשׁ גּוֹיִם עַם
מה מו לֹא־יָדַעְתִּי יַעַבְדוּנִי׃ לְשֵׁמַע אֹזֶן יִשָּׁמְעוּ לִי בְּנֵי־נֵכָר יְכַחֲשׁוּ־לִי׃ בְּנֵי־
מז נֵכָר יִבֹּלוּ וְיַחְרְגוּ מִמִּסְגְּרוֹתֵיהֶם׃ חַי־יְהוָה וּבָרוּךְ צוּרִי וְיָרוּם אֱלוֹהֵי
מח מט יִשְׁעִי׃ הָאֵל הַנּוֹתֵן נְקָמוֹת לִי וַיַּדְבֵּר עַמִּים תַּחְתָּי׃ מְפַלְּטִי מֵאֹיְבָי
נ אַף מִן־קָמַי תְּרוֹמְמֵנִי מֵאִישׁ חָמָס תַּצִּילֵנִי׃ עַל־כֵּן ׀ אוֹדְךָ בַגּוֹיִם ׀
נא יְהוָה וּלְשִׁמְךָ אֲזַמֵּרָה׃ מַגְדִּל יְשׁוּעוֹת מַלְכּוֹ וְעֹשֶׂה חֶסֶד ׀ לִמְשִׁיחוֹ
לְדָוִד וּלְזַרְעוֹ עַד־עוֹלָם׃

יט א ב לַמְנַצֵּחַ מִזְמוֹר לְדָוִד׃ הַשָּׁמַיִם מְסַפְּרִים כְּבוֹד־אֵל וּמַעֲשֵׂה יָדָיו מַגִּיד
ג ד הָרָקִיעַ׃ יוֹם לְיוֹם יַבִּיעַ אֹמֶר וְלַיְלָה לְּלַיְלָה יְחַוֶּה־דָּעַת׃ אֵין־אֹמֶר
ה וְאֵין דְּבָרִים בְּלִי נִשְׁמָע קוֹלָם׃ בְּכָל־הָאָרֶץ ׀ יָצָא קַוָּם וּבִקְצֵה תֵבֵל
ו מִלֵּיהֶם לַשֶּׁמֶשׁ שָׂם־אֹהֶל בָּהֶם׃ וְהוּא כְּחָתָן יֹצֵא מֵחֻפָּתוֹ יָשִׂישׂ
ז כְּגִבּוֹר לָרוּץ אֹרַח׃ מִקְצֵה הַשָּׁמַיִם ׀ מוֹצָאוֹ וּתְקוּפָתוֹ עַל־קְצוֹתָם
ח וְאֵין נִסְתָּר מֵחַמָּתוֹ׃ תּוֹרַת יְהוָה תְּמִימָה מְשִׁיבַת נָפֶשׁ עֵדוּת יְהוָה
ט נֶאֱמָנָה מַחְכִּימַת פֶּתִי׃ פִּקּוּדֵי יְהוָה יְשָׁרִים מְשַׂמְּחֵי־לֵב מִצְוַת יְהוָה

10 Fear of the Lord is pure, enduring forever; the Lord's judgments are true
11 and righteous without exception – more precious than gold, than boundless
12 fine gold, sweeter than honey, than nectar from the honeycomb. Your servant,
13 too, is careful of them; in keeping them there is great reward. Yet who can
14 discern his errors? Cleanse me of hidden faults. Spare Your servant from the
insolent; let them rule me not. Then shall I be blameless, cleansed of grave
15 sin. May the words of my mouth and my heart's reflections please You, Lord,
my Rock and redeemer.

20 1 2 *To the lead singer – a psalm of David.* May the Lord answer you in times of
3 trouble; may the name of Yaakov's God protect you. May He send you help
4 from the Sanctuary and support you from Zion. May He recall all your grain
5 offerings and accept your burnt offerings – Selah. May He give you your
6 heart's desire and ensure that all your plans succeed. We will shout for joy at
Your salvation and raise a banner in our God's name. May the Lord grant
7 all your requests. Now I know that the Lord saves His anointed, that He
answers him from His holy heaven with the saving power of His right hand.
8 Some trust in chariots, others in horses, but we call on the name of the Lord
9 10 our God. They crumple and fall, but we rise up and stand firm. Lord, grant
victory! May the King answer us when we call.

21 1 2 *To the lead singer – a psalm of David.* Lord, the king rejoices in Your might;
3 how he delights in Your victory! You have granted him his heart's desire and
4 not denied the requests of his lips – Selah. You have welcomed him with
5 rich blessing and set a golden crown upon his head. He asked You for life,
6 and You have granted it – long life for evermore. His glory is great through
7 Your victory; You lavish majesty and splendor upon him, bestowing upon
8 him eternal blessing, cheering him with the joy of Your presence, for the
king trusts in the Lord; with the loyalty of the Most High he will never be
9 shaken. Your hand reaches all Your enemies; Your right hand reaches those
10 who hate You. You set them ablaze like a furnace when You appear; in His
11 wrath, the Lord will engulf them, and fire will consume them. You wipe
12 their offspring from the earth, their seed from among men, for they plotted
13 evil toward You; they devised schemes but could not succeed. You will put
14 them to flight, aiming Your bow at their faces. Rise up, Lord, in Your might;
we will sing and praise Your power.

22 1 2 *To the lead singer, a dawn song*[22] *– a psalm of David.* O God, my God – why have
3 You forsaken me? So far from my salvation are the words that I roar. My God,
I cry out to You by day, but You do not answer, and by night – without relief.
4 5 But You are the Holy One, enthroned on Israel's praises. In You our ancestors
6 placed their trust; they trusted, and You delivered them. To You they cried out
7 and were saved; in You they trusted and were not let down. But I am a worm,
8 not human – scorned by men, disgraced among people. Whoever sees me
9 mocks me; they curl their lips and shake their heads. "Look to the Lord – let
10 Him deliver; let Him save him, if He delights in him," for it is You who drew
11 me out from the womb, You who kept me safe at my mother's breast. I have

22 | The meaning of the Hebrew *ayelet hashaḥar* is uncertain. It is possibly a musical term.

י בָּרָה מְאִירַת עֵינָיִם: יִרְאַת יְהוָה ׀ טְהוֹרָה עוֹמֶדֶת לָעַד מִשְׁפְּטֵי־יְהוָה
יא אֱמֶת צָדְקוּ יַחְדָּו: הַנֶּחֱמָדִים מִזָּהָב וּמִפַּז רָב וּמְתוּקִים מִדְּבַשׁ וְנֹפֶת
יב יג צוּפִים: גַּם־עַבְדְּךָ נִזְהָר בָּהֶם בְּשָׁמְרָם עֵקֶב רָב: שְׁגִיאוֹת מִי־יָבִין
יד מִנִּסְתָּרוֹת נַקֵּנִי: גַּם מִזֵּדִים ׀ חֲשֹׂךְ עַבְדֶּךָ אַל־יִמְשְׁלוּ־בִי אָז אֵיתָם
טו וְנִקֵּיתִי מִפֶּשַׁע רָב: יִהְיוּ לְרָצוֹן ׀ אִמְרֵי־פִי וְהֶגְיוֹן לִבִּי לְפָנֶיךָ יְהוָה
צוּרִי וְגֹאֲלִי:
כ א ב לַמְנַצֵּחַ מִזְמוֹר לְדָוִד: יַעַנְךָ יְהוָה בְּיוֹם צָרָה יְשַׂגֶּבְךָ שֵׁם ׀ אֱלֹהֵי
ג ד יַעֲקֹב: יִשְׁלַח־עֶזְרְךָ מִקֹּדֶשׁ וּמִצִּיּוֹן יִסְעָדֶךָּ: יִזְכֹּר כָּל־מִנְחֹתֶךָ וְעוֹלָתְךָ
ה ו יְדַשְּׁנֶה סֶלָה: יִתֶּן־לְךָ כִלְבָבֶךָ וְכָל־עֲצָתְךָ יְמַלֵּא: נְרַנְּנָה ׀ בִּישׁוּעָתֶךָ
ז וּבְשֵׁם־אֱלֹהֵינוּ נִדְגֹּל יְמַלֵּא יְהוָה כָּל־מִשְׁאֲלוֹתֶיךָ: עַתָּה יָדַעְתִּי כִּי
הוֹשִׁיעַ ׀ יְהוָה מְשִׁיחוֹ יַעֲנֵהוּ מִשְּׁמֵי קָדְשׁוֹ בִּגְבֻרוֹת יֵשַׁע יְמִינוֹ:
ח ט אֵלֶּה בָרֶכֶב וְאֵלֶּה בַסּוּסִים וַאֲנַחְנוּ ׀ בְּשֵׁם־יְהוָה אֱלֹהֵינוּ נַזְכִּיר: הֵמָּה
י כָּרְעוּ וְנָפָלוּ וַאֲנַחְנוּ קַּמְנוּ וַנִּתְעוֹדָד: יְהוָה הוֹשִׁיעָה הַמֶּלֶךְ יַעֲנֵנוּ
בְיוֹם־קָרְאֵנוּ:
כא א ב לַמְנַצֵּחַ מִזְמוֹר לְדָוִד: יְהוָה בְּעָזְּךָ יִשְׂמַח־מֶלֶךְ וּבִישׁוּעָתְךָ מַה־יָּגִיל יָגֶל
ג ד מְאֹד: תַּאֲוַת לִבּוֹ נָתַתָּה לּוֹ וַאֲרֶשֶׁת שְׂפָתָיו בַּל־מָנַעְתָּ סֶּלָה: כִּי־
ה תְקַדְּמֶנּוּ בִּרְכוֹת טוֹב תָּשִׁית לְרֹאשׁוֹ עֲטֶרֶת פָּז: חַיִּים ׀ שָׁאַל מִמְּךָ
ו נָתַתָּה לּוֹ אֹרֶךְ יָמִים עוֹלָם וָעֶד: גָּדוֹל כְּבוֹדוֹ בִּישׁוּעָתֶךָ הוֹד וְהָדָר
ז ח תְּשַׁוֶּה עָלָיו: כִּי־תְשִׁיתֵהוּ בְרָכוֹת לָעַד תְּחַדֵּהוּ בְשִׂמְחָה אֶת־פָּנֶיךָ: כִּי־
ט הַמֶּלֶךְ בֹּטֵחַ בַּיהוָה וּבְחֶסֶד עֶלְיוֹן בַּל־יִמּוֹט: תִּמְצָא יָדְךָ לְכָל־אֹיְבֶיךָ
י יְמִינְךָ תִּמְצָא שֹׂנְאֶיךָ: תְּשִׁיתֵמוֹ ׀ כְּתַנּוּר אֵשׁ לְעֵת פָּנֶיךָ יְהוָה בְּאַפּוֹ
יא יב יְבַלְּעֵם וְתֹאכְלֵם אֵשׁ: פִּרְיָמוֹ מֵאֶרֶץ תְּאַבֵּד וְזַרְעָם מִבְּנֵי אָדָם: כִּי־נָטוּ
יג עָלֶיךָ רָעָה חָשְׁבוּ מְזִמָּה בַּל־יוּכָלוּ: כִּי תְּשִׁיתֵמוֹ שֶׁכֶם בְּמֵיתָרֶיךָ תְּכוֹנֵן
יד עַל־פְּנֵיהֶם: רוּמָה יְהוָה בְעֻזֶּךָ נָשִׁירָה וּנְזַמְּרָה גְּבוּרָתֶךָ:
כב א ב לַמְנַצֵּחַ עַל־אַיֶּלֶת הַשַּׁחַר מִזְמוֹר לְדָוִד: אֵלִי אֵלִי לָמָה עֲזַבְתָּנִי רָחוֹק
ג מִישׁוּעָתִי דִּבְרֵי שַׁאֲגָתִי: אֱלֹהַי אֶקְרָא יוֹמָם וְלֹא תַעֲנֶה וְלַיְלָה וְלֹא־
ד ה דֻמִיָּה לִי: וְאַתָּה קָדוֹשׁ יוֹשֵׁב תְּהִלּוֹת יִשְׂרָאֵל: בְּךָ בָּטְחוּ אֲבֹתֵינוּ
ו ז בָּטְחוּ וַתְּפַלְּטֵמוֹ: אֵלֶיךָ זָעֲקוּ וְנִמְלָטוּ בְּךָ בָטְחוּ וְלֹא־בוֹשׁוּ: וְאָנֹכִי
ח תוֹלַעַת וְלֹא־אִישׁ חֶרְפַּת אָדָם וּבְזוּי עָם: כָּל־רֹאַי יַלְעִגוּ לִי יַפְטִירוּ
ט י בְשָׂפָה יָנִיעוּ רֹאשׁ: גֹּל אֶל־יְהוָה יְפַלְּטֵהוּ יַצִּילֵהוּ כִּי חָפֵץ בּוֹ: כִּי־אַתָּה
יא גֹחִי מִבָּטֶן מַבְטִיחִי עַל־שְׁדֵי אִמִּי: עָלֶיךָ הָשְׁלַכְתִּי מֵרָחֶם מִבֶּטֶן אִמִּי

been in Your care since birth; from my mother's womb, You have been my
12 13 God. Do not stray far from me, for trouble is near, with no one to help. Many
14 bulls surround me; fierce beasts of the Bashan[23] close in on me. Their jaws
15 open wide against me like ravenous roaring lions. I dissolve like water, all my
16 limbs falling to pieces, my heart melting like wax within me. My strength is
dried up like clay shards; my tongue sticks to my palate; You lay me down in
17 the dust of death, for hounds are all around me; a vicious pack encircles me, at
18 my hands and feet like a lion. I count all my bones as they look on and gloat.
19 They divide up my garments among themselves and cast lots for my clothing.
20 21 But You, LORD – do not be distant, O my help; rush to my aid; save my life
22 from the sword, my precious soul from those hounds; rescue me from the
23 lions' jaws; deliver me from the horns of wild bulls. I will tell of Your name to
24 my kin; I will praise You in the midst of the assembly. You who fear the LORD,
praise Him; honor Him, all you seed of Yaakov; revere Him, all you seed of
25 Israel, for He has not spurned or scorned the suffering of the lowly; He has
not hidden His face from them; when they cried out to Him, He listened.
26 You inspire my praise before the great assembly; I will pay my vows before
27 those who revere Him. The lowly will eat and be satisfied; those who seek the
28 LORD will praise Him – may your hearts rejoice forever! Let all the ends of
the earth remember and turn to the LORD; let all families of the nations bow
29 30 before You, for the kingship is the LORD's; He rules over the nations. All those
who thrive on the land will feast and worship; all those who descend to the
31 dust shall kneel before Him – those who cannot endure. Posterity will serve
32 Him; future generations will be told about the Lord, and they, in turn, will
tell of His righteousness, of His deeds, to the people yet unborn.
23 1 2 *A psalm of David*. The LORD is my Shepherd; I lack nothing. He lets me lie
3 down in green pastures; He leads me beside still waters. He refreshes my
4 soul, guiding me along the right paths for the sake of His name. Though I
walk through the valley of the shadow of death, I fear no evil, for You are with
5 me; Your rod and Your staff encourage me. You set a table before me in the
6 face of my foes; You anoint my head with oil; my cup brims over. May only
goodness and kindness follow me all the days of my life; let me live in the
LORD's House for evermore.
24 1 *Of David – a psalm*. The LORD owns the earth and all it contains, the world
2 3 and all who live in it, for He founded it on the seas, set it on the streams. Who
4 may ascend the LORD's mountain? Who may stand in His holy place? Those
who have clean hands and pure hearts, who do not take false oaths by My life,
5 who have not sworn deceitfully, they shall receive blessing from the LORD,
6 due reward from the God of their salvation. Such is the generation who seek
7 Him – Yaakov who seek Your presence, Selah. Lift up your heads, O gates;
8 rise up, eternal doors, so that the King of glory may enter. Who is the King
9 of glory? It is the LORD, strong and mighty, the LORD mighty in battle. Lift
up your heads, O gates; lift them up, eternal doors, so that the King of glory

23 | A territory notable for its pasture; see Numbers, chapter 32.

יב יג אֵלִי אָתָּה: אַל־תִּרְחַק מִמֶּנִּי כִּי־צָרָה קְרוֹבָה כִּי־אֵין עוֹזֵר: סְבָבוּנִי
יד פָּרִים רַבִּים אַבִּירֵי בָשָׁן כִּתְּרוּנִי: פָּצוּ עָלַי פִּיהֶם אַרְיֵה טֹרֵף וְשֹׁאֵג:
טו כַּמַּיִם נִשְׁפַּכְתִּי וְהִתְפָּרְדוּ כָּל־עַצְמוֹתָי הָיָה לִבִּי כַּדּוֹנָג נָמֵס בְּתוֹךְ
טז מֵעָי: יָבֵשׁ כַּחֶרֶשׂ ׀ כֹּחִי וּלְשׁוֹנִי מֻדְבָּק מַלְקוֹחָי וְלַעֲפַר־מָוֶת תִּשְׁפְּתֵנִי:
יז יח כִּי סְבָבוּנִי כְּלָבִים עֲדַת מְרֵעִים הִקִּיפוּנִי כָּאֲרִי יָדַי וְרַגְלָי: אֲסַפֵּר כָּל־
יט עַצְמוֹתָי הֵמָּה יַבִּיטוּ יִרְאוּ־בִי: יְחַלְּקוּ בְגָדַי לָהֶם וְעַל־לְבוּשִׁי יַפִּילוּ
כ כא גוֹרָל: וְאַתָּה יְהוָה אַל־תִּרְחָק אֱיָלוּתִי לְעֶזְרָתִי חוּשָׁה: הַצִּילָה מֵחֶרֶב
כב נַפְשִׁי מִיַּד־כֶּלֶב יְחִידָתִי: הוֹשִׁיעֵנִי מִפִּי אַרְיֵה וּמִקַּרְנֵי רֵמִים עֲנִיתָנִי:
כג כד אֲסַפְּרָה שִׁמְךָ לְאֶחָי בְּתוֹךְ קָהָל אֲהַלְלֶךָּ: יִרְאֵי יְהוָה ׀ הַלְלוּהוּ כָּל־
כה זֶרַע יַעֲקֹב כַּבְּדוּהוּ וְגוּרוּ מִמֶּנּוּ כָּל־זֶרַע יִשְׂרָאֵל: כִּי לֹא־בָזָה וְלֹא
כו שִׁקַּץ עֱנוּת עָנִי וְלֹא־הִסְתִּיר פָּנָיו מִמֶּנּוּ וּבְשַׁוְּעוֹ אֵלָיו שָׁמֵעַ: מֵאִתְּךָ
כז תְּהִלָּתִי בְּקָהָל רָב נְדָרַי אֲשַׁלֵּם נֶגֶד יְרֵאָיו: יֹאכְלוּ עֲנָוִים ׀ וְיִשְׂבָּעוּ
כח יְהַלְלוּ יְהוָה דֹּרְשָׁיו יְחִי לְבַבְכֶם לָעַד: יִזְכְּרוּ ׀ וְיָשֻׁבוּ אֶל־יְהוָה כָּל־
כט אַפְסֵי־אָרֶץ וְיִשְׁתַּחֲווּ לְפָנֶיךָ כָּל־מִשְׁפְּחוֹת גּוֹיִם: כִּי לַיהוָה הַמְּלוּכָה
ל וּמֹשֵׁל בַּגּוֹיִם: אָכְלוּ וַיִּשְׁתַּחֲווּ ׀ כָּל־דִּשְׁנֵי־אֶרֶץ לְפָנָיו יִכְרְעוּ כָּל־יוֹרְדֵי
לא לב עָפָר וְנַפְשׁוֹ לֹא חִיָּה: זֶרַע יַעַבְדֶנּוּ יְסֻפַּר לַאדֹנָי לַדּוֹר: יָבֹאוּ וְיַגִּידוּ
צִדְקָתוֹ לְעַם נוֹלָד כִּי עָשָׂה:

כג א ב מִזְמוֹר לְדָוִד יְהוָה רֹעִי לֹא אֶחְסָר: בִּנְאוֹת דֶּשֶׁא יַרְבִּיצֵנִי עַל־מֵי
ג ד מְנֻחוֹת יְנַהֲלֵנִי: נַפְשִׁי יְשׁוֹבֵב יַנְחֵנִי בְמַעְגְּלֵי־צֶדֶק לְמַעַן שְׁמוֹ: גַּם
כִּי־אֵלֵךְ בְּגֵיא צַלְמָוֶת לֹא־אִירָא רָע כִּי־אַתָּה עִמָּדִי שִׁבְטְךָ וּמִשְׁעַנְתֶּךָ
ה הֵמָּה יְנַחֲמֻנִי: תַּעֲרֹךְ לְפָנַי ׀ שֻׁלְחָן נֶגֶד צֹרְרָי דִּשַּׁנְתָּ בַשֶּׁמֶן רֹאשִׁי
ו כּוֹסִי רְוָיָה: אַךְ ׀ טוֹב וָחֶסֶד יִרְדְּפוּנִי כָּל־יְמֵי חַיָּי וְשַׁבְתִּי בְּבֵית־יְהוָה
לְאֹרֶךְ יָמִים:

כד א ב לְדָוִד מִזְמוֹר לַיהוָה הָאָרֶץ וּמְלוֹאָהּ תֵּבֵל וְיֹשְׁבֵי בָהּ: כִּי־הוּא עַל־יַמִּים
ג יְסָדָהּ וְעַל־נְהָרוֹת יְכוֹנְנֶהָ: מִי־יַעֲלֶה בְהַר־יְהוָה וּמִי־יָקוּם בִּמְקוֹם
ד קָדְשׁוֹ: נְקִי כַפַּיִם וּבַר־לֵבָב אֲשֶׁר לֹא־נָשָׂא לַשָּׁוְא נַפְשׁוֹ וְלֹא נִשְׁבַּע נַפְשִׁי
ה ו לְמִרְמָה: יִשָּׂא בְרָכָה מֵאֵת יְהוָה וּצְדָקָה מֵאֱלֹהֵי יִשְׁעוֹ: זֶה דּוֹר
ז דֹּרְשָׁו מְבַקְשֵׁי פָנֶיךָ יַעֲקֹב סֶלָה: שְׂאוּ שְׁעָרִים ׀ רָאשֵׁיכֶם וְהִנָּשְׂאוּ
ח פִּתְחֵי עוֹלָם וְיָבוֹא מֶלֶךְ הַכָּבוֹד: מִי זֶה מֶלֶךְ הַכָּבוֹד יְהוָה עִזּוּז וְגִבּוֹר
ט יְהוָה גִּבּוֹר מִלְחָמָה: שְׂאוּ שְׁעָרִים ׀ רָאשֵׁיכֶם וּשְׂאוּ פִּתְחֵי עוֹלָם

10 may enter. Who is this King of glory? The LORD of Hosts – He is the King
of glory – Selah.
25 1 2 *Of David.*[24] To You, O LORD, I lift up my soul; in You, my God, I place my
trust. Do not let me be put to shame; do not let my enemies gloat over me.
3 Let none who hope for You be put to shame, but let traitors, empty-handed,
4 5 be ashamed. Show me Your ways, LORD; teach me Your paths. Guide me in
Your truth; teach me, for You are the God of my salvation; I constantly look
6 to You in hope. Remember Your compassion, LORD, Your loyalty, for they
7 have always been. Do not remember the sins of my youth or my offenses, but
remember me in keeping with Your loyalty, in keeping with Your goodness,
8 LORD. Good and upright is the LORD; therefore He shows sinners the way;
9 10 He guides the lowly along the right path and teaches the lowly His way. All
the ways of the LORD are loyal and true to those who keep His covenant, His
11 12 rules. For the sake of Your name, LORD, forgive my sin though it is great. Who,
then, is one who fears the LORD? He will show them which path to choose.
13 14 They will live good lives, and their children will inherit the earth. The LORD
15 confides in those who fear Him; to them He reveals His covenant. My eyes
16 are ever on the LORD, for only He can free my feet from the net. Turn to me
17 and show me favor, for I am lonely and suffering; my heart swells with grief;
18 relieve me from my agony; see my suffering and my pain, and forgive all
19 my sins. See how many enemies I have and their violent hatred toward me.
20 Protect me and save me; let me not be put to shame, for in You I take refuge.
21 22 Let integrity and decency keep me, for I look to You in hope. May God free
Israel from all its grief.
26 1 *Of David.* Judge me, LORD, for I have walked blamelessly; I place my trust
2 in the LORD; I do not waver. Test me, LORD; try me; probe my heart and
3 4 mind,[25] for Your loyalty is before my eyes, and I walk in Your truth. I do not
5 sit with corrupt people or associate with hypocrites; I despise the company of
6 evildoers and will not tolerate the wicked. I wash my hands in innocence and
7 walk around Your altar, LORD, raising my voice in thanksgiving and telling of
8 all Your wonders. O LORD, I love the abode of Your House, the dwelling place
9 of Your glory! Do not sweep me away with sinners, my life with the men of
10 11 blood in whose hands are evil schemes, their right hands full of bribes, for I
12 will walk on blamelessly; redeem me and show me grace. My feet stand on
even ground; among the crowd, I bless the LORD.
27 1 *Of David.* The LORD is my light and my salvation – whom need I fear? The
2 LORD is the stronghold of my life – whom need I dread? When evildoers close
in on me to devour my flesh, it is they, my enemies and foes, who stumble and
3 fall. Should an army besiege me, my heart would not fear. Should war break
4 out against me, I would still be confident. One thing I ask of the LORD; this
alone I seek: to live in the LORD's House all the days of my life, to gaze on the
5 beauty of the LORD, and to worship in His Temple, for He will keep me safe

---

24 | This psalm takes the form of an alphabetical acrostic, with a few letters omitted.

25 | Literally "my kidneys and heart."

י וְיָבוֹא מֶלֶךְ הַכָּבוֹד: מִי הוּא זֶה מֶלֶךְ הַכָּבוֹד יְהוָה צְבָאוֹת הוּא מֶלֶךְ
הַכָּבוֹד סֶלָה:

כה א ב לְדָוִד אֵלֶיךָ יְהוָה נַפְשִׁי אֶשָּׂא: אֱלֹהַי בְּךָ בָטַחְתִּי אַל־אֵבוֹשָׁה אַל־
ג ד יַעַלְצוּ אוֹיְבַי לִי: גַּם כָּל־קֹוֶיךָ לֹא יֵבֹשׁוּ יֵבֹשׁוּ הַבּוֹגְדִים רֵיקָם: דְּרָכֶיךָ
ה יְהוָה הוֹדִיעֵנִי אֹרְחוֹתֶיךָ לַמְּדֵנִי: הַדְרִיכֵנִי בַאֲמִתֶּךָ וְלַמְּדֵנִי כִּי־אַתָּה
ו אֱלֹהֵי יִשְׁעִי אוֹתְךָ קִוִּיתִי כָּל־הַיּוֹם: זְכֹר־רַחֲמֶיךָ יְהוָה וַחֲסָדֶיךָ כִּי
ז מֵעוֹלָם הֵמָּה: חַטֹּאות נְעוּרַי וּפְשָׁעַי אַל־תִּזְכֹּר כְּחַסְדְּךָ זְכָר־לִי־אַתָּה
ח ט לְמַעַן טוּבְךָ יְהוָה: טוֹב־וְיָשָׁר יְהוָה עַל־כֵּן יוֹרֶה חַטָּאִים בַּדָּרֶךְ: יַדְרֵךְ
י עֲנָוִים בַּמִּשְׁפָּט וִילַמֵּד עֲנָוִים דַּרְכּוֹ: כָּל־אָרְחוֹת יְהוָה חֶסֶד וֶאֱמֶת
יא לְנֹצְרֵי בְרִיתוֹ וְעֵדֹתָיו: לְמַעַן־שִׁמְךָ יְהוָה וְסָלַחְתָּ לַעֲוֹנִי כִּי רַב־הוּא:
יב יג מִי־זֶה הָאִישׁ יְרֵא יְהוָה יוֹרֶנּוּ בְּדֶרֶךְ יִבְחָר: נַפְשׁוֹ בְּטוֹב תָּלִין וְזַרְעוֹ
יד טו יִירַשׁ אָרֶץ: סוֹד יְהוָה לִירֵאָיו וּבְרִיתוֹ לְהוֹדִיעָם: עֵינַי תָּמִיד אֶל־יְהוָה
טז יז כִּי הוּא־יוֹצִיא מֵרֶשֶׁת רַגְלָי: פְּנֵה־אֵלַי וְחָנֵּנִי כִּי־יָחִיד וְעָנִי אָנִי: צָרוֹת
יח לְבָבִי הִרְחִיבוּ מִמְּצוּקוֹתַי הוֹצִיאֵנִי: רְאֵה עָנְיִי וַעֲמָלִי וְשָׂא לְכָל־
יט כ חַטֹּאותָי: רְאֵה־אוֹיְבַי כִּי־רָבּוּ וְשִׂנְאַת חָמָס שְׂנֵאוּנִי: שָׁמְרָה נַפְשִׁי
כא כב וְהַצִּילֵנִי אַל־אֵבוֹשׁ כִּי־חָסִיתִי בָךְ: תֹּם־וָיֹשֶׁר יִצְּרוּנִי כִּי קִוִּיתִיךָ: פְּדֵה
אֱלֹהִים אֶת־יִשְׂרָאֵל מִכֹּל צָרוֹתָיו:

כו א לְדָוִד ׀ שָׁפְטֵנִי יְהוָה כִּי־אֲנִי בְּתֻמִּי הָלַכְתִּי וּבַיהוָה בָּטַחְתִּי לֹא אֶמְעָד:
ב ג בְּחָנֵנִי יְהוָה וְנַסֵּנִי צרופה כִלְיוֹתַי וְלִבִּי: כִּי־חַסְדְּךָ לְנֶגֶד עֵינָי וְהִתְהַלַּכְתִּי צָרְפָה
ד ה בַּאֲמִתֶּךָ: לֹא־יָשַׁבְתִּי עִם־מְתֵי־שָׁוְא וְעִם נַעֲלָמִים לֹא אָבוֹא: שָׂנֵאתִי
ו קְהַל מְרֵעִים וְעִם־רְשָׁעִים לֹא אֵשֵׁב: אֶרְחַץ בְּנִקָּיוֹן כַּפָּי וַאֲסֹבְבָה
ז ח אֶת־מִזְבַּחֲךָ יְהוָה: לַשְׁמִעַ בְּקוֹל תּוֹדָה וּלְסַפֵּר כָּל־נִפְלְאוֹתֶיךָ: יְהוָה
ט אָהַבְתִּי מְעוֹן בֵּיתֶךָ וּמְקוֹם מִשְׁכַּן כְּבוֹדֶךָ: אַל־תֶּאֱסֹף עִם־חַטָּאִים
י נַפְשִׁי וְעִם־אַנְשֵׁי דָמִים חַיָּי: אֲשֶׁר־בִּידֵיהֶם זִמָּה וִימִינָם מָלְאָה
יא יב שֹּׁחַד: וַאֲנִי בְּתֻמִּי אֵלֵךְ פְּדֵנִי וְחָנֵּנִי: רַגְלִי עָמְדָה בְמִישׁוֹר בְּמַקְהֵלִים
אֲבָרֵךְ יְהוָה:

כז א לְדָוִד ׀ יְהוָה ׀ אוֹרִי וְיִשְׁעִי מִמִּי אִירָא יְהוָה מָעוֹז־חַיַּי מִמִּי אֶפְחָד:
ב בִּקְרֹב עָלַי ׀ מְרֵעִים לֶאֱכֹל אֶת־בְּשָׂרִי צָרַי וְאֹיְבַי לִי הֵמָּה כָשְׁלוּ וְנָפָלוּ:
ג אִם־תַּחֲנֶה עָלַי ׀ מַחֲנֶה לֹא־יִירָא לִבִּי אִם־תָּקוּם עָלַי מִלְחָמָה בְּזֹאת
ד אֲנִי בוֹטֵחַ: אַחַת ׀ שָׁאַלְתִּי מֵאֵת־יְהוָה אוֹתָהּ אֲבַקֵּשׁ שִׁבְתִּי בְּבֵית־
ה יְהוָה כָּל־יְמֵי חַיַּי לַחֲזוֹת בְּנֹעַם־יְהוָה וּלְבַקֵּר בְּהֵיכָלוֹ: כִּי יִצְפְּנֵנִי ׀

in His shelter in times of terror; He will hide me under the cover of His tent;
6 He will set me high upon a rock. Now my head is high above the enemies
around me – I will sacrifice in His tent with shouts of joy; I will sing and chant
7 praises to the LORD. Hear my voice, LORD, when I call; show me grace and
8 answer me. Of You my heart whispers, "Seek My presence" – Your presence,
9 LORD, I will seek. Do not hide Your face from me; do not turn Your servant
away in anger. You have been my help – do not reject or forsake me, God,
10 my savior. Were my father and my mother to forsake me, the LORD would
11 take me in. Teach me Your way, LORD; lead me on a level path because of my
12 oppressors. Do not abandon me to the will of my foes, for false witnesses
13 have risen against me, breathing violence. Were it not for my faith that I will
14 see the LORD's goodness in the land of the living.... Hope in the LORD; be
strong and brave of heart, and hope in the LORD.
28 1 *Of David.* To You, O LORD, I call; O my Rock, be not deaf to my cry, for if You
2 remain silent, I shall be like those who plummet to the Pit. Hear the sound
of my plea when I cry out to You, when I lift my hands toward Your holiest
3 Sanctuary. Do not pull me away with the wicked, with evildoers who feign
4 peace with one another but harbor malice in their hearts. Pay them back
for their actions, for their malicious acts; pay them back for their deeds –
5 treat them as they deserve, for they do not recognize the LORD's acts or His
6 handiwork. May He break them down, not build them up. Blessed is the
7 LORD, who has heard the sound of my plea; the LORD is my might and my
protector; my heart trusted Him, and I received help. My heart exults, and I
8 praise Him with my song. The LORD is their strength, the saving stronghold
9 of His anointed. Save Your people; bless Your heritage; tend them and sustain
them forever.
29 1 *A psalm of David.* Render to the LORD, you angelic beings – render to the
2 LORD glory and might. Render to the LORD the glory due His name; bow
3 to the LORD in the splendor of holiness. The LORD's voice echoes over the
waters; the God of glory thunders; the LORD thunders over the mighty
4 waters. The LORD's voice rings with power; the LORD's voice rings with
5 splendor! The LORD's voice breaks cedars; the LORD shatters the cedars of
6 Lebanon – He makes them skip like a calf, Lebanon and Siryon[26] like a young
7 8 wild ox. The LORD's voice sparks fiery flames! The LORD's voice shakes the
9 desert; the LORD shakes the desert of Kadesh. The LORD's voice terrifies
10 the deer and strips the forests bare, and in His Temple all say, "Glory!" The
LORD sat enthroned at the flood; the LORD sits enthroned as King forever.
11 May the LORD give might to His people; may the LORD bless His people
with peace.
30 1 2 *A psalm of David – a song for the dedication of the House.*[27] I will exalt You,
3 LORD, for You have lifted me up; You have not let my enemies gloat over me.
4 LORD, my God, I cried out to You, and You healed me; LORD, You lifted me
5 from Sheol; You saved me from plummeting to the Pit. Sing to the LORD, you

---

26 | Mountainous areas.

27 | Likely the Temple of Jerusalem.

ו בְּסֻכֹּה בְּיוֹם רָעָה יַסְתִּרֵנִי בְּסֵתֶר אָהֳלוֹ בְּצוּר יְרוֹמְמֵנִי: וְעַתָּה יָרוּם
רֹאשִׁי עַל אֹיְבַי סְבִיבוֹתַי וְאֶזְבְּחָה בְאָהֳלוֹ זִבְחֵי תְרוּעָה אָשִׁירָה
ז ח וַאֲזַמְּרָה לַיהוה: שְׁמַע־יהוה קוֹלִי אֶקְרָא וְחָנֵּנִי וַעֲנֵנִי: לְךָ ׀ אָמַר
ט לִבִּי בַּקְּשׁוּ פָנָי אֶת־פָּנֶיךָ יהוה אֲבַקֵּשׁ: אַל־תַּסְתֵּר פָּנֶיךָ ׀ מִמֶּנִּי אַל
תַּט־בְּאַף עַבְדֶּךָ עֶזְרָתִי הָיִיתָ אַל־תִּטְּשֵׁנִי וְאַל־תַּעַזְבֵנִי אֱלֹהֵי יִשְׁעִי:
י יא כִּי־אָבִי וְאִמִּי עֲזָבוּנִי וַיהוה יַאַסְפֵנִי: הוֹרֵנִי יהוה דַּרְכֶּךָ וּנְחֵנִי בְּאֹרַח
יב מִישׁוֹר לְמַעַן שׁוֹרְרָי: אַל־תִּתְּנֵנִי בְּנֶפֶשׁ צָרָי כִּי קָמוּ־בִי עֵדֵי־שֶׁקֶר
יג יד וִיפֵחַ חָמָס: לוּלֵא הֶאֱמַנְתִּי לִרְאוֹת בְּטוּב־יהוה בְּאֶרֶץ חַיִּים: קַוֵּה
אֶל־יהוה חֲזַק וְיַאֲמֵץ לִבֶּךָ וְקַוֵּה אֶל־יהוה:
כח א לְדָוִד אֵלֶיךָ יהוה ׀ אֶקְרָא צוּרִי אַל־תֶּחֱרַשׁ מִמֶּנִּי פֶּן־תֶּחֱשֶׁה מִמֶּנִּי
ב וְנִמְשַׁלְתִּי עִם־יוֹרְדֵי בוֹר: שְׁמַע קוֹל תַּחֲנוּנַי בְּשַׁוְּעִי אֵלֶיךָ בְּנָשְׂאִי יָדַי
ג אֶל־דְּבִיר קָדְשֶׁךָ: אַל־תִּמְשְׁכֵנִי עִם־רְשָׁעִים וְעִם־פֹּעֲלֵי אָוֶן דֹּבְרֵי
ד שָׁלוֹם עִם־רֵעֵיהֶם וְרָעָה בִּלְבָבָם: תֶּן־לָהֶם כְּפָעֳלָם וּכְרֹעַ מַעַלְלֵיהֶם
ה כְּמַעֲשֵׂה יְדֵיהֶם תֵּן לָהֶם הָשֵׁב גְּמוּלָם לָהֶם: כִּי לֹא יָבִינוּ אֶל־פְּעֻלֹּת
ו יהוה וְאֶל־מַעֲשֵׂה יָדָיו יֶהֶרְסֵם וְלֹא יִבְנֵם: בָּרוּךְ יהוה כִּי־שָׁמַע קוֹל
ז תַּחֲנוּנָי: יהוה ׀ עֻזִּי וּמָגִנִּי בּוֹ בָטַח לִבִּי וְנֶעֱזָרְתִּי וַיַּעֲלֹז לִבִּי וּמִשִּׁירִי
ח ט אֲהוֹדֶנּוּ: יהוה עֹז־לָמוֹ וּמָעוֹז יְשׁוּעוֹת מְשִׁיחוֹ הוּא: הוֹשִׁיעָה ׀ אֶת־
עַמֶּךָ וּבָרֵךְ אֶת־נַחֲלָתֶךָ וּרְעֵם וְנַשְּׂאֵם עַד־הָעוֹלָם:
כט א ב מִזְמוֹר לְדָוִד הָבוּ לַיהוה בְּנֵי אֵלִים הָבוּ לַיהוה כָּבוֹד וָעֹז: הָבוּ
ג לַיהוה כְּבוֹד שְׁמוֹ הִשְׁתַּחֲווּ לַיהוה בְּהַדְרַת־קֹדֶשׁ: קוֹל יהוה עַל־
ד הַמָּיִם אֵל־הַכָּבוֹד הִרְעִים יהוה עַל־מַיִם רַבִּים: קוֹל־יהוה בַּכֹּחַ קוֹל
ה יהוה בֶּהָדָר: קוֹל יהוה שֹׁבֵר אֲרָזִים וַיְשַׁבֵּר יהוה אֶת־אַרְזֵי הַלְּבָנוֹן:
ו ז וַיַּרְקִידֵם כְּמוֹ־עֵגֶל לְבָנוֹן וְשִׂרְיֹן כְּמוֹ בֶן־רְאֵמִים: קוֹל־יהוה חֹצֵב
ח ט לַהֲבוֹת אֵשׁ: קוֹל יהוה יָחִיל מִדְבָּר יָחִיל יהוה מִדְבַּר קָדֵשׁ: קוֹל
י יהוה ׀ יְחוֹלֵל אַיָּלוֹת וַיֶּחֱשֹׂף יְעָרוֹת וּבְהֵיכָלוֹ כֻּלּוֹ אֹמֵר כָּבוֹד: יהוה
יא לַמַּבּוּל יָשָׁב וַיֵּשֶׁב יהוה מֶלֶךְ לְעוֹלָם: יהוה עֹז לְעַמּוֹ יִתֵּן יהוה ׀ יְבָרֵךְ ד
אֶת־עַמּוֹ בַשָּׁלוֹם:
ל א ב מִזְמוֹר שִׁיר־חֲנֻכַּת הַבַּיִת לְדָוִד: אֲרוֹמִמְךָ יהוה כִּי דִלִּיתָנִי וְלֹא־
ג ד שִׂמַּחְתָּ אֹיְבַי לִי: יהוה אֱלֹהָי שִׁוַּעְתִּי אֵלֶיךָ וַתִּרְפָּאֵנִי: יהוה הֶעֱלִיתָ
ה מִן־שְׁאוֹל נַפְשִׁי חִיִּיתַנִי מיורדי־בוֹר: זַמְּרוּ לַיהוה חֲסִידָיו וְהוֹדוּ לְזֵכֶר מִיָּרְדִי־

6 His devoted; give thanks to His holy name, for His wrath lasts but a moment,
but His favor a lifetime; at night there may be weeping, but the morning
7 8 brings joy. In my serenity I said, "I shall never be shaken." In Your favor, LORD,
You made me stand firm as a mountain, but when You hid Your face, I was
9 10 terrified. To You, LORD, I called; to my Lord I pleaded, "What gain would
there be in my death[28] if I went down to the grave? Can dust praise You? Can
11 it declare Your truth? Hear, LORD, and show me grace; LORD, be my help."
12 You have turned my mourning into dancing; You have untied my sackcloth
13 and clothed me with joy so that my soul[29] may sing to You and not be silent.
LORD my God, I will praise You forever.
31 1 2 *To the lead singer – a psalm of David.* In You, LORD, I take refuge; may I never
3 be put to shame; rescue me in Your righteousness. Lend Your ear to me;
4 swiftly save me; be my Rock of refuge, a stronghold of salvation, for You are
my Rock and my fortress. Lead me and guide me for the sake of Your name.
5 6 Free me from this net they laid for me, for You are my stronghold. I place my
7 spirit in Your hand – You set me free, LORD, God of truth. I despise those
8 who rely on futilities – as for me, I trust in the LORD. I will delight and rejoice
9 in Your loyalty: You saw my suffering; You knew of my grave danger; You
10 did not disclose me to enemy hands; You let me go free.[30] Show me grace,
LORD, for I am in danger; torment wastes my eyes, my being, my insides.
11 My life is spent with sorrow; my years seep away in sighs; my strength fades
12 because of my sin; my bones waste away. I am the scorn of all my foes, even
more so to my neighbors; I am a horror to my friends; whoever sees me on
13 the streets shrinks away from me. I have been forgotten like the dead, like a
14 long-discarded vessel, for I have heard the whispers of many – terror on every
15 side![31] – as they all conspire against me, scheming to take my life. But I place
16 my trust in You, O LORD; I say, "You are my God." My fate is in Your hands;
17 save me from the hands of my enemies and pursuers. Shine Your face on Your
18 servant; save me in Your loyalty. Let me not be put to shame, LORD, for I
19 call upon You; let the wicked be shamed and silenced to Sheol. Let deceitful
lips be stilled that speak brashly against the righteous with arrogance and
20 contempt. How great is the goodness You keep in store for those who fear
21 You; You act for those who take refuge in You in the full view of all. Shelter
them in Your safe presence from human guile; shield them within Your cover
22 from scathing tongues. Blessed is the LORD who has shown me His wondrous
23 loyalty in a city under siege. Even when I said rashly, "I am cut off from Your
24 sight," You still heard the sound of my plea when I cried out to You. Love the
LORD, all you His devoted ones; the LORD protects the faithful and amply
25 punishes those who act in arrogance. Be strong and of determined hearts, all
you who wait for the LORD.

---

28 | Literally "in my blood."

29 | Literally "glory."

30 | Literally "You set my feet in a broad place."

31 | Cf. Jeremiah 20:10.

ו קָדְשׁוֹ: כִּי רֶגַע ׀ בְּאַפּוֹ חַיִּים בִּרְצוֹנוֹ בָּעֶרֶב יָלִין בֶּכִי וְלַבֹּקֶר רִנָּה:
ז ח וַאֲנִי אָמַרְתִּי בְשַׁלְוִי בַּל־אֶמּוֹט לְעוֹלָם: יְהוָה בִּרְצוֹנְךָ הֶעֱמַדְתָּה
ט לְהַרְרִי עֹז הִסְתַּרְתָּ פָנֶיךָ הָיִיתִי נִבְהָל: אֵלֶיךָ יְהוָה אֶקְרָא וְאֶל־
י אֲדֹנָי אֶתְחַנָּן: מַה־בֶּצַע בְּדָמִי בְּרִדְתִּי אֶל שָׁחַת הֲיוֹדְךָ עָפָר הֲיַגִּיד
יא יב אֲמִתֶּךָ: שְׁמַע־יְהוָה וְחָנֵּנִי יְהוָה הֱיֵה־עֹזֵר לִי: הָפַכְתָּ מִסְפְּדִי לְמָחוֹל
יג לִי פִּתַּחְתָּ שַׂקִּי וַתְּאַזְּרֵנִי שִׂמְחָה: לְמַעַן ׀ יְזַמֶּרְךָ כָבוֹד וְלֹא יִדֹּם יְהוָה
אֱלֹהַי לְעוֹלָם אוֹדֶךָּ:

לא

א ב לַמְנַצֵּחַ מִזְמוֹר לְדָוִד: בְּךָ־יְהוָה חָסִיתִי אַל־אֵבוֹשָׁה לְעוֹלָם בְּצִדְקָתְךָ
ג פַלְּטֵנִי: הַטֵּה אֵלַי ׀ אָזְנְךָ מְהֵרָה הַצִּילֵנִי הֱיֵה לִי ׀ לְצוּר־מָעוֹז לְבֵית
ד מְצוּדוֹת לְהוֹשִׁיעֵנִי: כִּי־סַלְעִי וּמְצוּדָתִי אָתָּה וּלְמַעַן שִׁמְךָ תַּנְחֵנִי
ה ו וּתְנַהֲלֵנִי: תּוֹצִיאֵנִי מֵרֶשֶׁת זוּ טָמְנוּ לִי כִּי־אַתָּה מָעוּזִּי: בְּיָדְךָ אַפְקִיד
ז רוּחִי פָּדִיתָה אוֹתִי יְהוָה אֵל אֱמֶת: שָׂנֵאתִי הַשֹּׁמְרִים הַבְלֵי־שָׁוְא וַאֲנִי
ח אֶל־יְהוָה בָּטָחְתִּי: אָגִילָה וְאֶשְׂמְחָה בְּחַסְדֶּךָ אֲשֶׁר רָאִיתָ אֶת־עָנְיִי
ט יָדַעְתָּ בְּצָרוֹת נַפְשִׁי: וְלֹא הִסְגַּרְתַּנִי בְּיַד־אוֹיֵב הֶעֱמַדְתָּ בַמֶּרְחָב רַגְלָי:
י יא חָנֵּנִי יְהוָה כִּי צַר־לִי עָשְׁשָׁה בְכַעַס עֵינִי נַפְשִׁי וּבִטְנִי: כִּי כָלוּ בְיָגוֹן חַיַּי
יב וּשְׁנוֹתַי בַּאֲנָחָה כָּשַׁל בַּעֲוֺנִי כֹחִי וַעֲצָמַי עָשֵׁשׁוּ: מִכָּל־צֹרְרַי הָיִיתִי
יג חֶרְפָּה וְלִשְׁכֵנַי ׀ מְאֹד וּפַחַד לִמְיֻדָּעָי רֹאַי בַּחוּץ נָדְדוּ מִמֶּנִּי: נִשְׁכַּחְתִּי
יד כְּמֵת מִלֵּב הָיִיתִי כִּכְלִי אֹבֵד: כִּי שָׁמַעְתִּי ׀ דִּבַּת רַבִּים מָגוֹר מִסָּבִיב
טו בְּהִוָּסְדָם יַחַד עָלַי לָקַחַת נַפְשִׁי זָמָמוּ: וַאֲנִי ׀ עָלֶיךָ בָטַחְתִּי יְהוָה
טז יז אָמַרְתִּי אֱלֹהַי אָתָּה: בְּיָדְךָ עִתֹּתָי הַצִּילֵנִי מִיַּד־אוֹיְבַי וּמֵרֹדְפָי: הָאִירָה
יח פָנֶיךָ עַל־עַבְדֶּךָ הוֹשִׁיעֵנִי בְחַסְדֶּךָ: יְהוָה אַל־אֵבוֹשָׁה כִּי קְרָאתִיךָ
יט יֵבֹשׁוּ רְשָׁעִים יִדְּמוּ לִשְׁאוֹל: תֵּאָלַמְנָה שִׂפְתֵי שָׁקֶר הַדֹּבְרוֹת עַל־צַדִּיק
כ עָתָק בְּגַאֲוָה וָבוּז: מָה רַב טוּבְךָ אֲשֶׁר־צָפַנְתָּ לִּירֵאֶיךָ פָּעַלְתָּ לַחֹסִים
כא בָּךְ נֶגֶד בְּנֵי אָדָם: תַּסְתִּירֵם ׀ בְּסֵתֶר פָּנֶיךָ מֵרֻכְסֵי אִישׁ תִּצְפְּנֵם בְּסֻכָּה
כב כג מֵרִיב לְשֹׁנוֹת: בָּרוּךְ יְהוָה כִּי הִפְלִיא חַסְדּוֹ לִי בְּעִיר מָצוֹר: וַאֲנִי ׀
אָמַרְתִּי בְחָפְזִי נִגְרַזְתִּי מִנֶּגֶד עֵינֶיךָ אָכֵן שָׁמַעְתָּ קוֹל תַּחֲנוּנַי בְּשַׁוְּעִי
כד אֵלֶיךָ: אֶהֱבוּ אֶת־יְהוָה כָּל־חֲסִידָיו אֱמוּנִים נֹצֵר יְהוָה וּמְשַׁלֵּם עַל־יֶתֶר
כה עֹשֵׂה גַאֲוָה: חִזְקוּ וְיַאֲמֵץ לְבַבְכֶם כָּל־הַמְיַחֲלִים לַיהוָה:

32 1 *Of David – a* maskil.[32] Happy is the one whose offense has been forgiven,
2 whose sin has been covered over. Happy is the one whom the LORD does
3 not hold guilty, whose spirit is devoid of deceit. When I remained silent,
4 my body wasted away from my howling all day long, for day and night, Your
hand weighed down upon me; my vitality dried up as if scorched by summer
5 heat – Selah. I admitted my sin to You and did not cover up my guilt; I said,
"I confess my offenses to the LORD," and You forgave the guilt of my sin –
6 Selah. Thus let all those pray to You at the moment of discovery[33] so that
7 the rush of mighty waters will not reach them. You are my shelter; You keep
8 me from danger; You surround me with glad shouts of rescue – Selah. I will
instruct you and guide you along the path you should follow; I will counsel
9 you and keep My eye on you. Do not be senseless like a horse or mule that
10 must be curbed by bit and bridle – far be it from you! Many are the torments
of the wicked, while those who trust in the LORD are surrounded by loving-
11 kindness. Rejoice in the LORD; delight, righteous ones; sing out loud, all you
upright of heart!

33 1 Sing joyfully to the LORD, you righteous ones; praise from the upright is
2 beautiful. Give thanks to the LORD with the harp; sing praise to Him with the
3 4 ten-stringed lute. Sing Him a new song; play your best with joyous shout, for
5 the LORD's word is right, and all His deeds are faithful. He loves righteousness
6 and justice; the earth is full of the LORD's loving-kindness. By the LORD's
7 word the heavens were made, by His breath all their starry host. He gathers
8 the sea waters as if in a heap and stores the depths in treasuries. Let all the
9 earth fear the LORD; let all inhabitants of the world revere Him, for He spoke
10 and it came to be at His command; it stood firm. The LORD foils the plans
11 of nations; He thwarts the intentions of peoples. The LORD's plans endure
12 forever, His heart's intents for all generations. Happy is the nation whose God
13 is the LORD, the people He has chosen as His own. The LORD looks down
14 from heaven and sees all of humanity; from His dwelling place He watches
15 over all inhabitants of the earth. He forms the hearts of all and discerns all
16 their deeds. A king is not saved by a vast force; a warrior is not delivered by
17 great strength. A horse is a vain hope for victory; despite its great strength, it
18 cannot bring salvation. Yes, the eye of the LORD is on those who fear Him,
19 on those who place their hopes in His kindness, rescuing them from death,
20 keeping them alive in famine. We await the LORD; He is our help and shield.
21 22 In Him our hearts rejoice, for we trust in His holy name. May Your loving-
kindness be upon us, LORD, for we place our hope in You.

34 1 *Of David, when he feigned insanity before Avimelekh,*[34] *who drove him away,*
2 *and he left.*[35] I will bless the LORD at all times; His praise will be always on
3 my lips. My soul will glory in the LORD; let the lowly hear this and rejoice.

---

32 | A musical term of uncertain meaning, perhaps related to instruction. Compare the use of this verb in verse 8.

33 | Meaning discovery of their sins.

34 | See 1 Samuel 21:11–16, which refers to the person here called Avimelekh as Akhish, king of Gat.

35 | This psalm takes the form of an alphabetical acrostic.

לב א ב לְדָוִד מַשְׂכִּיל אַשְׁרֵי נְשׂוּי־פֶּשַׁע כְּסוּי חֲטָאָה: אַשְׁרֵי־אָדָם לֹא יַחְשֹׁב
ג יהוה לוֹ עָוֺן וְאֵין בְּרוּחוֹ רְמִיָּה: כִּי־הֶחֱרַשְׁתִּי בָּלוּ עֲצָמָי בְּשַׁאֲגָתִי
ד כָּל־הַיּוֹם: כִּי ׀ יוֹמָם וָלַיְלָה תִּכְבַּד עָלַי יָדֶךָ נֶהְפַּךְ לְשַׁדִּי בְּחַרְבֹנֵי קַיִץ
ה סֶלָה: חַטָּאתִי אוֹדִיעֲךָ וַעֲוֺנִי לֹא־כִסִּיתִי אָמַרְתִּי אוֹדֶה עֲלֵי פְשָׁעַי
ו לַיהוה וְאַתָּה נָשָׂאתָ עֲוֺן חַטָּאתִי סֶלָה: עַל־זֹאת יִתְפַּלֵּל כָּל־חָסִיד ׀
ז אֵלֶיךָ לְעֵת מְצֹא רַק לְשֵׁטֶף מַיִם רַבִּים אֵלָיו לֹא יַגִּיעוּ: אַתָּה ׀ סֵתֶר
ח לִי מִצַּר תִּצְּרֵנִי רָנֵּי פַלֵּט תְּסוֹבְבֵנִי סֶלָה: אַשְׂכִּילְךָ ׀ וְאוֹרְךָ בְּדֶרֶךְ־זוּ
ט תֵלֵךְ אִיעֲצָה עָלֶיךָ עֵינִי: אַל־תִּהְיוּ ׀ כְּסוּס כְּפֶרֶד אֵין הָבִין בְּמֶתֶג־
י וָרֶסֶן עֶדְיוֹ לִבְלוֹם בַּל קְרֹב אֵלֶיךָ: רַבִּים מַכְאוֹבִים לָרָשָׁע וְהַבּוֹטֵחַ
יא בַּיהוה חֶסֶד יְסוֹבְבֶנּוּ: שִׂמְחוּ בַיהוה וְגִילוּ צַדִּיקִים וְהַרְנִינוּ כָּל־
יִשְׁרֵי־לֵב:

לג א ב רַנְּנוּ צַדִּיקִים בַּיהוה לַיְשָׁרִים נָאוָה תְהִלָּה: הוֹדוּ לַיהוה בְּכִנּוֹר בְּנֵבֶל
ג ד עָשׂוֹר זַמְּרוּ־לוֹ: שִׁירוּ־לוֹ שִׁיר חָדָשׁ הֵיטִיבוּ נַגֵּן בִּתְרוּעָה: כִּי־יָשָׁר
ה דְּבַר־יהוה וְכָל־מַעֲשֵׂהוּ בֶּאֱמוּנָה: אֹהֵב צְדָקָה וּמִשְׁפָּט חֶסֶד יהוה
ו ז מָלְאָה הָאָרֶץ: בִּדְבַר יהוה שָׁמַיִם נַעֲשׂוּ וּבְרוּחַ פִּיו כָּל־צְבָאָם: כֹּנֵס
ח כַּנֵּד מֵי הַיָּם נֹתֵן בְּאֹצָרוֹת תְּהוֹמוֹת: יִירְאוּ מֵיהוה כָּל־הָאָרֶץ מִמֶּנּוּ
ט י יָגוּרוּ כָּל־יֹשְׁבֵי תֵבֵל: כִּי הוּא אָמַר וַיֶּהִי הוּא־צִוָּה וַיַּעֲמֹד: יהוה הֵפִיר
יא עֲצַת־גּוֹיִם הֵנִיא מַחְשְׁבוֹת עַמִּים: עֲצַת יהוה לְעוֹלָם תַּעֲמֹד מַחְשְׁבוֹת
יב לִבּוֹ לְדֹר וָדֹר: אַשְׁרֵי הַגּוֹי אֲשֶׁר־יהוה אֱלֹהָיו הָעָם ׀ בָּחַר לְנַחֲלָה לוֹ:
יג יד מִשָּׁמַיִם הִבִּיט יהוה רָאָה אֶת־כָּל־בְּנֵי הָאָדָם: מִמְּכוֹן־שִׁבְתּוֹ הִשְׁגִּיחַ
טו טז אֶל כָּל־יֹשְׁבֵי הָאָרֶץ: הַיֹּצֵר יַחַד לִבָּם הַמֵּבִין אֶל־כָּל־מַעֲשֵׂיהֶם: אֵין־
יז הַמֶּלֶךְ נוֹשָׁע בְּרָב־חָיִל גִּבּוֹר לֹא־יִנָּצֵל בְּרָב־כֹּחַ: שֶׁקֶר הַסּוּס לִתְשׁוּעָה
יח וּבְרֹב חֵילוֹ לֹא יְמַלֵּט: הִנֵּה עֵין יהוה אֶל־יְרֵאָיו לַמְיַחֲלִים לְחַסְדּוֹ:
יט כ לְהַצִּיל מִמָּוֶת נַפְשָׁם וּלְחַיּוֹתָם בָּרָעָב: נַפְשֵׁנוּ חִכְּתָה לַיהוה עֶזְרֵנוּ
כא כב וּמָגִנֵּנוּ הוּא: כִּי־בוֹ יִשְׂמַח לִבֵּנוּ כִּי בְשֵׁם קָדְשׁוֹ בָטָחְנוּ: יְהִי־חַסְדְּךָ
יהוה עָלֵינוּ כַּאֲשֶׁר יִחַלְנוּ לָךְ:

לד א ב לְדָוִד בְּשַׁנּוֹתוֹ אֶת־טַעְמוֹ לִפְנֵי אֲבִימֶלֶךְ וַיְגָרְשֵׁהוּ וַיֵּלַךְ: אֲבָרְכָה
ג אֶת־יהוה בְּכָל־עֵת תָּמִיד תְּהִלָּתוֹ בְּפִי: בַּיהוה תִּתְהַלֵּל נַפְשִׁי יִשְׁמְעוּ

4 5 Glorify the LORD with me; let us exalt His name together. I sought the LORD,
6 and He answered me; He saved me from all my fears. Those who look to Him
7 are radiant; let their faces not be downcast. This poor person called, and the
8 LORD heard; He saved him from all his troubles. The LORD's angel encamps
9 around those who fear Him and comes to their rescue. Taste for yourselves;
10 see that the LORD is good; happy are those who take refuge in Him. Fear the
11 LORD, you His holy ones, for those who fear Him lack nothing. Lions may
grow weak and hungry, but those who seek the LORD will never lack any
12 good. Come, my children, listen to me; I will teach you the fear of the LORD.
13 14 Who among you desires life; who longs to see many good years? Then keep
15 your tongue from evil, your lips from speaking deceit. Turn away from evil
16 and do good; strive for peace and pursue it. The eyes of the LORD are on the
17 righteous; His ears are attuned to their cry. The LORD's face is set against
18 those who do evil, to erase their memory from the earth. The LORD hears
19 when they[36] cry out; He delivers them from all their troubles. The LORD is
20 close to the brokenhearted; He saves those who are crushed in spirit. Many
troubles may befall the righteous, but the LORD delivers him from all of them;
21 22 He protects every one of his bones so that none of them will be broken. Evil
23 will slay the wicked; the enemies of the righteous will be condemned. The
LORD redeems the lives of His servants; none who take refuge in Him will
be condemned.

35 1 *Of David.* Contend with those who contend with me, LORD; fight those who
2 3 fight me; take up shield and armor and rise up to help me; unsheathe spear
4 and javelin against my pursuers. Tell me, "I am your salvation." Let those who
seek my life be shamed and humiliated; let those who plot my ruin retreat
5 in disgrace. Let them be like chaff in the wind, driven by the LORD's angel;
6 7 let their way be dark and slippery, with the LORD's angel in pursuit, for they
8 laid a trap for me without cause; without cause they dug a pit for me; let
ruin ravage them suddenly; let them be caught in their own trap and fall into
9 it to their utter ruin, but my soul will delight in the LORD, rejoicing in His
10 salvation. Every inch of my being declares, "O LORD, who is like You? You
save the poor from those too strong for them, the poor and needy from those
11 who exploit them." False witnesses suddenly come forward, interrogating
12 me about things I know not; they repay good with evil – I am left bereaved,
13 for when they were ill I donned sackcloth, made myself suffer with fasting,
14 prayer surging in my chest; I went about as if it were my own friend, my own
15 brother, bowed in gloom as if mourning for my mother, but when I stumbled,
they swarmed in glee; wretches suddenly swarmed about me, tearing at me
16 17 without cease. With a vile, mocking leer they gnash their teeth at me. How
long, Lord, will You look on? Save me from their onslaught, my precious life
18 from lions. I will thank You before a great assembly; I will praise You before
19 a mighty throng. Do not let my treacherous enemies gloat over me or those
20 who hate me without cause narrow their eyes, for they do not speak words
of peace; they devise treacherous schemes against the harmless of the land.

36 | This pronoun refers back to the righteous mentioned in verse 16.

ד ה עֲנָוִים וְיִשְׂמָחוּ׃ גַּדְּלוּ לַיהוָה אִתִּי וּנְרוֹמְמָה שְׁמוֹ יַחְדָּו׃ דָּרַשְׁתִּי אֶת־
ו יְהוָה וְעָנָנִי וּמִכׇּל־מְגוּרוֹתַי הִצִּילָנִי׃ הִבִּיטוּ אֵלָיו וְנָהָרוּ וּפְנֵיהֶם אַל־
ז ח יֶחְפָּרוּ׃ זֶה עָנִי קָרָא וַיהוָה שָׁמֵעַ וּמִכׇּל־צָרוֹתָיו הוֹשִׁיעוֹ׃ חֹנֶה מַלְאַךְ־
ט יְהוָה סָבִיב לִירֵאָיו וַיְחַלְּצֵם׃ טַעֲמוּ וּרְאוּ כִּי־טוֹב יְהוָה אַשְׁרֵי הַגֶּבֶר
י יא יֶחֱסֶה־בּוֹ׃ יְראוּ אֶת־יְהוָה קְדֹשָׁיו כִּי־אֵין מַחְסוֹר לִירֵאָיו׃ כְּפִירִים רָשׁוּ
יב וְרָעֵבוּ וְדֹרְשֵׁי יְהוָה לֹא־יַחְסְרוּ כׇל־טוֹב׃ לְכוּ־בָנִים שִׁמְעוּ־לִי יִרְאַת
יג יד יְהוָה אֲלַמֶּדְכֶם׃ מִי־הָאִישׁ הֶחָפֵץ חַיִּים אֹהֵב יָמִים לִרְאוֹת טוֹב׃ נְצֹר
טו לְשׁוֹנְךָ מֵרָע וּשְׂפָתֶיךָ מִדַּבֵּר מִרְמָה׃ סוּר מֵרָע וַעֲשֵׂה־טוֹב בַּקֵּשׁ שָׁלוֹם
טז יז וְרׇדְפֵהוּ׃ עֵינֵי יְהוָה אֶל־צַדִּיקִים וְאׇזְנָיו אֶל־שַׁוְעָתָם׃ פְּנֵי יְהוָה בְּעֹשֵׂי
יח רָע לְהַכְרִית מֵאֶרֶץ זִכְרָם׃ צָעֲקוּ וַיהוָה שָׁמֵעַ וּמִכׇּל־צָרוֹתָם הִצִּילָם׃
יט כ קָרוֹב יְהוָה לְנִשְׁבְּרֵי־לֵב וְאֶת־דַּכְּאֵי־רוּחַ יוֹשִׁיעַ׃ רַבּוֹת רָעוֹת צַדִּיק
כא וּמִכֻּלָּם יַצִּילֶנּוּ יְהוָה׃ שֹׁמֵר כׇּל־עַצְמוֹתָיו אַחַת מֵהֵנָּה לֹא נִשְׁבָּרָה׃
כב כג תְּמוֹתֵת רָשָׁע רָעָה וְשֹׂנְאֵי צַדִּיק יֶאְשָׁמוּ׃ פּוֹדֶה יְהוָה נֶפֶשׁ עֲבָדָיו
וְלֹא יֶאְשְׁמוּ כׇּל־הַחֹסִים בּוֹ׃

לה א ב לְדָוִד ׀ רִיבָה יְהוָה אֶת־יְרִיבַי לְחַם אֶת־לֹחֲמָי׃ הַחֲזֵק מָגֵן וְצִנָּה וְקוּמָה
ג בְּעֶזְרָתִי׃ וְהָרֵק חֲנִית וּסְגֹר לִקְרַאת רֹדְפָי אֱמֹר לְנַפְשִׁי יְשֻׁעָתֵךְ אָנִי׃
ד ה יֵבֹשׁוּ וְיִכָּלְמוּ מְבַקְשֵׁי נַפְשִׁי יִסֹּגוּ אָחוֹר וְיַחְפְּרוּ חֹשְׁבֵי רָעָתִי׃ יִהְיוּ
ו כְּמֹץ לִפְנֵי־רוּחַ וּמַלְאַךְ יְהוָה דּוֹחֶה׃ יְהִי־דַרְכָּם חֹשֶׁךְ וַחֲלַקְלַקֹּת
ז וּמַלְאַךְ יְהוָה רֹדְפָם׃ כִּי־חִנָּם טָמְנוּ־לִי שַׁחַת רִשְׁתָּם חִנָּם חָפְרוּ לְנַפְשִׁי׃
ח תְּבוֹאֵהוּ שׁוֹאָה לֹא־יֵדָע וְרִשְׁתּוֹ אֲשֶׁר־טָמַן תִּלְכְּדוֹ בְּשׁוֹאָה יִפׇּל־בָּהּ׃
ט י וְנַפְשִׁי תָּגִיל בַּיהוָה תָּשִׂישׂ בִּישׁוּעָתוֹ׃ כׇּל עַצְמוֹתַי ׀ תֹּאמַרְנָה יְהוָה
יא מִי כָמוֹךָ מַצִּיל עָנִי מֵחָזָק מִמֶּנּוּ וְעָנִי וְאֶבְיוֹן מִגֹּזְלוֹ׃ יְקוּמוּן עֵדֵי חָמָס
יב אֲשֶׁר לֹא־יָדַעְתִּי יִשְׁאָלוּנִי׃ יְשַׁלְּמוּנִי רָעָה תַּחַת טוֹבָה שְׁכוֹל לְנַפְשִׁי׃
יג וַאֲנִי ׀ בַּחֲלוֹתָם לְבוּשִׁי שָׂק עִנֵּיתִי בַצּוֹם נַפְשִׁי וּתְפִלָּתִי עַל־חֵיקִי
יד טו תָשׁוּב׃ כְּרֵעַ־כְּאָח לִי הִתְהַלָּכְתִּי כַּאֲבֶל־אֵם קֹדֵר שַׁחוֹתִי׃ וּבְצַלְעִי
טז שָׂמְחוּ וְנֶאֱסָפוּ נֶאֶסְפוּ עָלַי נֵכִים וְלֹא יָדַעְתִּי קָרְעוּ וְלֹא־דָמּוּ׃ בְּחַנְפֵי
יז לַעֲגֵי מָעוֹג חָרֹק עָלַי שִׁנֵּימוֹ׃ אֲדֹנָי כַּמָּה תִּרְאֶה הָשִׁיבָה נַפְשִׁי מִשֹּׁאֵיהֶם
יח יט מִכְּפִירִים יְחִידָתִי׃ אוֹדְךָ בְּקָהָל רָב בְּעַם עָצוּם אֲהַלְלֶךָּ׃ אַל־יִשְׂמְחוּ־
כ לִי אֹיְבַי שֶׁקֶר שֹׂנְאַי חִנָּם יִקְרְצוּ־עָיִן׃ כִּי לֹא שָׁלוֹם יְדַבֵּרוּ וְעַל רִגְעֵי־

21 Their mouths open wide against me, calling "Aha! Aha! Our eyes have seen
22 it!" You have seen it, LORD; do not remain silent; O Lord, do not be far
23 from me. Awake and rise to my defense; contend for me, my God, my Lord.
24 Vindicate me in Your justice, LORD my God; do not let them gloat over
25 me; do not let them tell themselves, "Aha! As we wished!" Do not let them
26 say, "We have swallowed him up!" Let those who gloat at my misfortune be
altogether shamed and disgraced; let those who boast over me don shame and
27 humiliation. May those who delight in my vindication sing and rejoice; may
they always say, "Great be the LORD who delights in His servants' success."
28 Then will my tongue express Your justice, Your praises all day long.

36 1 2 *To the lead singer – of the LORD's servant, of David.* Well do I know what
3 vice whispers to the wicked; there is no fear of God before their eyes. They
flatter themselves in their own eyes that their sin will not be discovered and
4 hated. The words they mouth are treacherous and deceitful; they cannot
5 contemplate doing good; in bed they plot treachery; they are set on a path
6 of no good, never spurning evil. O LORD, Your loyalty reaches the heavens,
7 Your faithfulness the skies; Your justice is like the mighty mountains, Your
judgment like the great deep; O LORD, You save both human and beast.
8 How precious is Your loyalty, God; people find refuge in the shade of Your
9 wings; they feast on the rich plenty of Your House; You quench their thirst
10 with Your river of delights, for the fountain of life is with You; by Your light
11 we see light. Extend Your loyalty to those who know You, Your justice to the
12 upright of heart. Let no arrogant foot trample me; let no wicked hand drive
13 me away – there evildoers lie fallen, forced down, unable to rise.

37 1 *Of David.*[37] Do not be incensed at the wicked or let your envy be kindled by
2 evildoers, for they will soon wither like grass and fade away like greenery.
3 Trust in the LORD and do good – you will be settled in the land, secure in
4 your pasture. Delight in the LORD, and He will grant you your heart's desire.
5 6 Commit your way to the LORD; trust in Him, and He will act: He will bring
out your vindication to light, the justice of your cause like the noonday
7 sun. Wait for the LORD silently, patiently; do not be incensed at those who
8 succeed through devious plots. Release your anger; abandon your wrath;
9 do not be incensed – it leads only to harm, for the wicked will be cut off,
10 while those who hope for the LORD shall inherit the earth. Very soon, the
11 wicked will be no more; you will look at their place to find them gone, but
12 the lowly shall inherit the earth; they will delight in the wealth of peace. The
13 wicked scheme against the righteous, gnashing their teeth at them, but the
14 Lord laughs at them; He knows their day will come. The wicked unsheathe
their swords and draw their bows to bring down the poor and the needy, to
15 slaughter those whose path is straight. Their swords will pierce their own
16 hearts; their bows will be shattered. The righteous person's precious little is
17 better than the vast wealth of the many wicked, for the arms of the wicked
18 will be broken, while the LORD supports the righteous. The LORD cares for

37 | The first letters of every second verse of this psalm form an alphabetical acrostic.

כא אֶרֶץ דִּבְרֵי מִרְמוֹת יַחֲשֹׁבוּן: וַיַּרְחִיבוּ עָלַי פִּיהֶם אָמְרוּ הֶאָח ׀ הֶאָח
כב כג רָאֲתָה עֵינֵנוּ: רָאִיתָה יהוה אַל־תֶּחֱרַשׁ אֲדֹנָי אַל־תִּרְחַק מִמֶּנִּי: הָעִירָה
כד וְהָקִיצָה לְמִשְׁפָּטִי אֱלֹהַי וַאדֹנָי לְרִיבִי: שָׁפְטֵנִי כְצִדְקְךָ יהוה אֱלֹהָי
כה וְאַל־יִשְׂמְחוּ־לִי: אַל־יֹאמְרוּ בְלִבָּם הֶאָח נַפְשֵׁנוּ אַל־יֹאמְרוּ בִּלַּעֲנוּהוּ:
כו יֵבֹשׁוּ וְיַחְפְּרוּ ׀ יַחְדָּו שְׂמֵחֵי רָעָתִי יִלְבְּשׁוּ־בֹשֶׁת וּכְלִמָּה הַמַּגְדִּילִים
כז עָלָי: יָרֹנּוּ וְיִשְׂמְחוּ חֲפֵצֵי צִדְקִי וְיֹאמְרוּ תָמִיד יִגְדַּל יהוה הֶחָפֵץ
כח שְׁלוֹם עַבְדּוֹ: וּלְשׁוֹנִי תֶּהְגֶּה צִדְקֶךָ כָּל־הַיּוֹם תְּהִלָּתֶךָ: ה
לו א ב לַמְנַצֵּחַ ׀ לְעֶבֶד־יהוה לְדָוִד: נְאֻם־פֶּשַׁע לָרָשָׁע בְּקֶרֶב לִבִּי אֵין־
ג פַּחַד אֱלֹהִים לְנֶגֶד עֵינָיו: כִּי־הֶחֱלִיק אֵלָיו בְּעֵינָיו לִמְצֹא עֲוֺנוֹ לִשְׂנֹא:
ד ה דִּבְרֵי־פִיו אָוֶן וּמִרְמָה חָדַל לְהַשְׂכִּיל לְהֵיטִיב: אָוֶן ׀ יַחְשֹׁב עַל־
ו מִשְׁכָּבוֹ יִתְיַצֵּב עַל־דֶּרֶךְ לֹא־טוֹב רָע לֹא יִמְאָס: יהוה בְּהַשָּׁמַיִם
ז חַסְדֶּךָ אֱמוּנָתְךָ עַד־שְׁחָקִים: צִדְקָתְךָ ׀ כְּהַרְרֵי־אֵל מִשְׁפָּטֶךָ תְּהוֹם
ח רַבָּה אָדָם וּבְהֵמָה תוֹשִׁיעַ ׀ יהוה: מַה־יָּקָר חַסְדְּךָ אֱלֹהִים וּבְנֵי אָדָם
ט י בְּצֵל כְּנָפֶיךָ יֶחֱסָיוּן: יִרְוְיֻן מִדֶּשֶׁן בֵּיתֶךָ וְנַחַל עֲדָנֶיךָ תַשְׁקֵם: כִּי־עִמְּךָ
יא מְקוֹר חַיִּים בְּאוֹרְךָ נִרְאֶה־אוֹר: מְשֹׁךְ חַסְדְּךָ לְיֹדְעֶיךָ וְצִדְקָתְךָ
יב יג לְיִשְׁרֵי־לֵב: אַל־תְּבוֹאֵנִי רֶגֶל גַּאֲוָה וְיַד־רְשָׁעִים אַל־תְּנִדֵנִי: שָׁם נָפְלוּ
פֹּעֲלֵי אָוֶן דֹּחוּ וְלֹא־יָכְלוּ קוּם:
לז א ב לְדָוִד ׀ אַל־תִּתְחַר בַּמְּרֵעִים אַל־תְּקַנֵּא בְּעֹשֵׂי עַוְלָה: כִּי כֶחָצִיר
ג מְהֵרָה יִמָּלוּ וּכְיֶרֶק דֶּשֶׁא יִבּוֹלוּן: בְּטַח בַּיהוה וַעֲשֵׂה־טוֹב שְׁכָן־אֶרֶץ
ד ה וּרְעֵה אֱמוּנָה: וְהִתְעַנַּג עַל־יהוה וְיִתֶּן־לְךָ מִשְׁאֲלֹת לִבֶּךָ: גּוֹל עַל־
ו יהוה דַּרְכֶּךָ וּבְטַח עָלָיו וְהוּא יַעֲשֶׂה: וְהוֹצִיא כָאוֹר צִדְקֶךָ וּמִשְׁפָּטֶךָ
ז כַּצָּהֳרָיִם: דּוֹם ׀ לַיהוה וְהִתְחוֹלֵל לוֹ אַל־תִּתְחַר בְּמַצְלִיחַ דַּרְכּוֹ
ח בְּאִישׁ עֹשֶׂה מְזִמּוֹת: הֶרֶף מֵאַף וַעֲזֹב חֵמָה אַל־תִּתְחַר אַךְ־לְהָרֵעַ:
ט י כִּי־מְרֵעִים יִכָּרֵתוּן וְקֹוֵי יהוה הֵמָּה יִירְשׁוּ־אָרֶץ: וְעוֹד מְעַט וְאֵין רָשָׁע
יא וְהִתְבּוֹנַנְתָּ עַל־מְקוֹמוֹ וְאֵינֶנּוּ: וַעֲנָוִים יִירְשׁוּ־אָרֶץ וְהִתְעַנְּגוּ עַל־רֹב
יב יג שָׁלוֹם: זֹמֵם רָשָׁע לַצַּדִּיק וְחֹרֵק עָלָיו שִׁנָּיו: אֲדֹנָי יִשְׂחַק־לוֹ כִּי־רָאָה
יד כִּי־יָבֹא יוֹמוֹ: חֶרֶב ׀ פָּתְחוּ רְשָׁעִים וְדָרְכוּ קַשְׁתָּם לְהַפִּיל עָנִי וְאֶבְיוֹן
טו טז לִטְבוֹחַ יִשְׁרֵי־דָרֶךְ: חַרְבָּם תָּבוֹא בְלִבָּם וְקַשְּׁתוֹתָם תִּשָּׁבַרְנָה: טוֹב־
יז מְעַט לַצַּדִּיק מֵהֲמוֹן רְשָׁעִים רַבִּים: כִּי זְרוֹעוֹת רְשָׁעִים תִּשָּׁבַרְנָה
יח וְסוֹמֵךְ צַדִּיקִים יהוה: יוֹדֵעַ יהוה יְמֵי תְמִימִם וְנַחֲלָתָם לְעוֹלָם תִּהְיֶה:

19 the days of the blameless; their heritage will last forever. They will not suffer
20 shame when times are hard; in famine they will still be sated, but the wicked
will perish; the LORD's enemies are like meadow grass: they vanish away like
21 vanishing smoke. The wicked borrows and does not repay; the righteous
22 are generous; they give and give, for His blessed ones shall inherit the earth,
23 while those cursed by Him will be cut off. It is the LORD who makes people's
24 footsteps firm when He delights in their way; when they stumble, they will
25 not fall, for the LORD holds their hand. I was once young; now I am old,
yet I have never seen the righteous forsaken, with their children begging for
26 bread. They are always generous, lending freely, and their children become a
27 blessing. Turn away from evil and do good, and you will always dwell secure,
28 for the LORD loves justice; He will never abandon His devoted ones. They
29 will always be kept safe, while the children of the wicked will be cut off. The
30 righteous will inherit the earth and be settled upon it forever. Righteous
31 mouths speak words of wisdom; their tongues express justice. Their God's
32 teaching is in their hearts; their steps will never falter. The wicked lie in wait
33 for the righteous, seeking their death; the LORD will not abandon them to
34 their hands or condemn them when they are judged. Place your hope in the
LORD and keep His way – He will raise you up to inherit the earth as you will
35 see when the wicked are cut off. I have seen a tyrant in his prime, well rooted
36 like a verdant native tree, yet suddenly he passes on and is no more; I looked
37 for him, but he was nowhere to be found. Watch and see, you blameless and
38 upright, that a future awaits the peaceful person while sinners will be utterly
39 destroyed; the future of the wicked will be cut off. The righteous's deliverance
40 is from the LORD; He is their refuge in times of trouble. The LORD will help
them and rescue them – rescue them from the wicked and deliver them, for
they seek refuge in Him.

38 1 2 *A psalm of David,* lehazkir.[38] LORD, do not reproach me in Your rage or punish
3 4 me in Your fury, for Your arrows strike me; Your hand strikes me! My body is
5 not sound because of Your wrath; my bones are not well because of my sin. My
offenses have piled up above my head like a heavy burden, too heavy to bear.
6 7 My wounds reek and fester because of my foolishness. I am utterly stooped
8 over, hunched up, my gait gloomy all day long, for my insides burn fiercely;
9 my body is not sound. I have grown so weak, so broken; I roar out from the
10 uproar in my mind, "Lord, all I ache for is known to You; My groans are not
11 hidden from You." My heart is throbbing; my strength has left me; the light is
12 long gone from my eyes. My loved ones, my friends – they shrink away at my
13 suffering; those I was close to keep their distance while those who seek my
life lay their snares; those who seek my harm scheme viciously, plotting their
14 treacherous plots all day, but I am like a deaf person who cannot hear, like a
15 dumb person who cannot speak; I am like one who cannot hear and cannot
16 answer back, yet for You, LORD, I wait in hope; You will answer me, Lord
17 my God, for I fear they will gloat over me and, when my foot slips, swagger
18 19 over me – for I am on the verge of collapse and constantly in pain. I admit

38 | A musical term of uncertain meaning, literally "to evoke."

יט כ לֹא־יֵבֹשׁוּ בְּעֵת רָעָה וּבִימֵי רְעָבוֹן יִשְׂבָּעוּ׃ כִּי רְשָׁעִים ׀ יֹאבֵדוּ וְאֹיְבֵי
כא יְהוָה כִּיקַר כָּרִים כָּלוּ בֶעָשָׁן כָּלוּ׃ לֹוֶה רָשָׁע וְלֹא יְשַׁלֵּם וְצַדִּיק חוֹנֵן
כב כג וְנוֹתֵן׃ כִּי מְבֹרָכָיו יִירְשׁוּ אָרֶץ וּמְקֻלָּלָיו יִכָּרֵתוּ׃ מֵיְהוָה מִצְעֲדֵי־גֶבֶר
כד כה כּוֹנָנוּ וְדַרְכּוֹ יֶחְפָּץ׃ כִּי־יִפֹּל לֹא־יוּטָל כִּי־יְהוָה סוֹמֵךְ יָדוֹ׃ נַעַר ׀ הָיִיתִי
כו גַּם־זָקַנְתִּי וְלֹא־רָאִיתִי צַדִּיק נֶעֱזָב וְזַרְעוֹ מְבַקֶּשׁ־לָחֶם׃ כָּל־הַיּוֹם
כז חוֹנֵן וּמַלְוֶה וְזַרְעוֹ לִבְרָכָה׃ סוּר מֵרָע וַעֲשֵׂה־טוֹב וּשְׁכֹן לְעוֹלָם׃
כח כִּי יְהוָה ׀ אֹהֵב מִשְׁפָּט וְלֹא־יַעֲזֹב אֶת־חֲסִידָיו לְעוֹלָם נִשְׁמָרוּ וְזֶרַע
כט ל רְשָׁעִים נִכְרָת׃ צַדִּיקִים יִירְשׁוּ־אָרֶץ וְיִשְׁכְּנוּ לָעַד עָלֶיהָ׃ פִּי־צַדִּיק
לא יֶהְגֶּה חָכְמָה וּלְשׁוֹנוֹ תְּדַבֵּר מִשְׁפָּט׃ תּוֹרַת אֱלֹהָיו בְּלִבּוֹ לֹא תִמְעַד
לב לג אֲשֻׁרָיו׃ צוֹפֶה רָשָׁע לַצַּדִּיק וּמְבַקֵּשׁ לַהֲמִיתוֹ׃ יְהוָה לֹא־יַעַזְבֶנּוּ בְיָדוֹ
לד וְלֹא יַרְשִׁיעֶנּוּ בְּהִשָּׁפְטוֹ׃ קַוֵּה אֶל־יְהוָה ׀ וּשְׁמֹר דַּרְכּוֹ וִירוֹמִמְךָ לָרֶשֶׁת
לה אָרֶץ בְּהִכָּרֵת רְשָׁעִים תִּרְאֶה׃ רָאִיתִי רָשָׁע עָרִיץ וּמִתְעָרֶה כְּאֶזְרָח
לו לז רַעֲנָן׃ וַיַּעֲבֹר וְהִנֵּה אֵינֶנּוּ וָאֲבַקְשֵׁהוּ וְלֹא נִמְצָא׃ שְׁמָר־תָּם וּרְאֵה
לח יָשָׁר כִּי־אַחֲרִית לְאִישׁ שָׁלוֹם׃ וּפֹשְׁעִים נִשְׁמְדוּ יַחְדָּו אַחֲרִית רְשָׁעִים
לט מ נִכְרָתָה׃ וּתְשׁוּעַת צַדִּיקִים מֵיְהוָה מָעוּזָּם בְּעֵת צָרָה׃ וַיַּעְזְרֵם יְהוָה
וַיְפַלְּטֵם יְפַלְּטֵם מֵרְשָׁעִים וְיוֹשִׁיעֵם כִּי־חָסוּ בוֹ׃

לח א ב מִזְמוֹר לְדָוִד לְהַזְכִּיר׃ יְהוָה אַל־בְּקֶצְפְּךָ תוֹכִיחֵנִי וּבַחֲמָתְךָ תְיַסְּרֵנִי׃
ג ד כִּי־חִצֶּיךָ נִחֲתוּ בִי וַתִּנְחַת עָלַי יָדֶךָ׃ אֵין־מְתֹם בִּבְשָׂרִי מִפְּנֵי זַעְמֶךָ
ה אֵין־שָׁלוֹם בַּעֲצָמַי מִפְּנֵי חַטָּאתִי׃ כִּי עֲוֺנֹתַי עָבְרוּ רֹאשִׁי כְּמַשָּׂא
ו ז כָבֵד יִכְבְּדוּ מִמֶּנִּי׃ הִבְאִישׁוּ נָמַקּוּ חַבּוּרֹתָי מִפְּנֵי אִוַּלְתִּי׃ נַעֲוֵיתִי
ח שַׁחֹתִי עַד־מְאֹד כָּל־הַיּוֹם קֹדֵר הִלָּכְתִּי׃ כִּי־כְסָלַי מָלְאוּ נִקְלֶה וְאֵין
ט י מְתֹם בִּבְשָׂרִי׃ נְפוּגוֹתִי וְנִדְכֵּיתִי עַד־מְאֹד שָׁאַגְתִּי מִנַּהֲמַת לִבִּי׃ אֲדֹנָי
יא נֶגְדְּךָ כָל־תַּאֲוָתִי וְאַנְחָתִי מִמְּךָ לֹא־נִסְתָּרָה׃ לִבִּי סְחַרְחַר עֲזָבַנִי
יב כֹחִי וְאוֹר־עֵינַי גַּם־הֵם אֵין אִתִּי׃ אֹהֲבַי ׀ וְרֵעַי מִנֶּגֶד נִגְעִי יַעֲמֹדוּ
יג וּקְרוֹבַי מֵרָחֹק עָמָדוּ׃ וַיְנַקְשׁוּ ׀ מְבַקְשֵׁי נַפְשִׁי וְדֹרְשֵׁי רָעָתִי דִּבְּרוּ הַוּוֹת
יד וּמִרְמוֹת כָּל־הַיּוֹם יֶהְגּוּ׃ וַאֲנִי כְחֵרֵשׁ לֹא אֶשְׁמָע וּכְאִלֵּם לֹא יִפְתַּח־
טו טז פִּיו׃ וָאֱהִי כְּאִישׁ אֲשֶׁר לֹא־שֹׁמֵעַ וְאֵין בְּפִיו תּוֹכָחוֹת׃ כִּי־לְךָ יְהוָה
יז הוֹחָלְתִּי אַתָּה תַעֲנֶה אֲדֹנָי אֱלֹהָי׃ כִּי־אָמַרְתִּי פֶּן־יִשְׂמְחוּ־לִי בְּמוֹט
יח יט רַגְלִי עָלַי הִגְדִּילוּ׃ כִּי־אֲנִי לְצֶלַע נָכוֹן וּמַכְאוֹבִי נֶגְדִּי תָמִיד׃ כִּי־עֲוֺנִי

20 my guilt; I regret my sin. My mortal enemies are fierce; so many hate me
21 without cause. Those who repay good with evil oppose me for pursuing good.
22 23 Do not abandon me, LORD; My God, do not stray far from me. Rush to my
help, O Lord, my salvation.

39 1 2 *For the lead singer, for Yedutun*[39] *– a psalm of David.* I was determined to watch
my ways and not to sin with my tongue; I would keep my mouth shut tight
3 so long as the wicked were in my presence. I remained silent; I kept perfectly
4 still, but my pain grew intense – my heart burned within me, my thoughts
5 blazed, and I spoke up: "Tell me when it will end, LORD, the number of my
6 days – that I may know how fleeting I am." You have measured out my days in
handbreadths, and my life span is as nothing before You. Alas, all humanity,
7 however firm it stands, is but a mere breath – Selah. Alas, people are but
walking shadows, their restless bustle but mere breath; they hoard without
8 knowing who will gather in. And now, what can I wait for, Lord? My only
9 hope is You. Save me from all my sins; do not let me be scorned by fools.
10 11 I will keep silent; I will not open my mouth, for it is Your doing. Remove
12 Your scourge from me; I waste away from the blows of Your hand. Punishing
offense, You bring suffering, crumbling people's treasures like a moth. Alas,
13 all humanity is but fleeting breath – Selah. Hear my prayer, LORD; give ear
to my cry; do not remain silent at my tears, for to You I am but a passerby, a
14 mere transient like all my ancestors. Let me be, so I may smile again before I
pass away and am no more.

40 1 2 *To the lead singer – of David, a psalm.* I put all my hope in the LORD; He bent
3 down to me; He heard my cry. He raised me out of the pit of despair from
the oozing mud; He set my feet on solid stone and steadied my footsteps.
4 He placed a new song on my lips, a song of praise for our God; the crowds
5 will see and be struck with awe and place their trust in the LORD. Happy are
those who make the LORD their trust instead of turning to the pompous, to
6 followers of falsehood, for You have done great things, O LORD my God; You
have devised such wonders for us; none can compare to You – were I to tell of
7 them, to speak of them, there would be far too many to count. For sacrifice or
gift You have no desire – that You have made clear.[40] You never asked for burnt
8 offering or purification offering, so I decided, "Here – I come with the scroll
9 that was written for me." To do Your will, God, is my desire; Your teachings
10 course through my insides. I proclaimed Your righteousness before the great
11 assembly; see – I have not sealed my lips, LORD, as You know. I have not kept
Your justice secret in my heart; I proclaim Your devotion and salvation; I
12 have not denied Your loyalty and truth before the great assembly. As for You,
LORD, do not withhold Your compassion from me; let Your loyalty and truth
13 keep me always, for endless evil has beset me; my offenses have caught up
with me, blurring my vision; they far outnumber the hairs on my head, and
14 my heart fails within me. Show me favor, LORD, and save me; rush to my help,
15 LORD! Let those who seek to snatch away my life be shamed and disgraced;

39 | A famed Temple musician; cf. Psalms 62, 77; I Chronicles 16:42, 25:6.
40 | Literally "You have hollowed out ears for me."

כ כא אַגִּיד אֶדְאַג מֵחַטָּאתִי׃ וְאֹיְבַי חַיִּים עָצֵמוּ וְרַבּוּ שֹׂנְאַי שָׁקֶר׃ וּמְשַׁלְּמֵי
כב רָעָה תַּחַת טוֹבָה יִשְׂטְנוּנִי תַּחַת רדופי־טוֹב׃ אַל־תַּעַזְבֵנִי יְהוָה אֱלֹהַי רָדְפִי־
כג אַל־תִּרְחַק מִמֶּנִּי׃ חוּשָׁה לְעֶזְרָתִי אֲדֹנָי תְּשׁוּעָתִי׃

לט א ב לַמְנַצֵּחַ לידיתון מִזְמוֹר לְדָוִד׃ אָמַרְתִּי אֶשְׁמְרָה דְרָכַי מֵחֲטוֹא בִלְשׁוֹנִי לִידוּתוּן
ג אֶשְׁמְרָה־לְפִי מַחְסוֹם בְּעֹד רָשָׁע לְנֶגְדִּי׃ נֶאֱלַמְתִּי דוּמִיָּה הֶחֱשֵׁיתִי
ד מִטּוֹב וּכְאֵבִי נֶעְכָּר׃ חַם־לִבִּי | בְּקִרְבִּי בַּהֲגִיגִי תִבְעַר־אֵשׁ דִּבַּרְתִּי
ה בִּלְשׁוֹנִי׃ הוֹדִיעֵנִי יְהוָה | קִצִּי וּמִדַּת יָמַי מַה־הִיא אֵדְעָה מֶה־חָדֵל
ו אָנִי׃ הִנֵּה טְפָחוֹת | נָתַתָּה יָמַי וְחֶלְדִּי כְאַיִן נֶגְדֶּךָ אַךְ־כׇּל־הֶבֶל כׇּל־
ז אָדָם נִצָּב סֶלָה׃ אַךְ־בְּצֶלֶם | יִתְהַלֶּךְ־אִישׁ אַךְ־הֶבֶל יֶהֱמָיוּן יִצְבֹּר
ח ט וְלֹא־יֵדַע מִי־אֹסְפָם׃ וְעַתָּה מַה־קִּוִּיתִי אֲדֹנָי תּוֹחַלְתִּי לְךָ הִיא׃ מִכׇּל־
י פְּשָׁעַי הַצִּילֵנִי חֶרְפַּת נָבָל אַל־תְּשִׂימֵנִי׃ נֶאֱלַמְתִּי לֹא אֶפְתַּח־פִּי כִּי
יא יב אַתָּה עָשִׂיתָ׃ הָסֵר מֵעָלַי נִגְעֶךָ מִתִּגְרַת יָדְךָ אֲנִי כָלִיתִי׃ בְּתוֹכָחוֹת
עַל־עָוֺן | יִסַּרְתָּ אִישׁ וַתֶּמֶס כָּעָשׁ חֲמוּדוֹ אַךְ הֶבֶל כׇּל־אָדָם סֶלָה׃
יג שִׁמְעָה תְפִלָּתִי | יְהוָה וְשַׁוְעָתִי | הַאֲזִינָה אֶל־דִּמְעָתִי אַל־תֶּחֱרַשׁ
יד כִּי גֵר אָנֹכִי עִמָּךְ תּוֹשָׁב כְּכׇל־אֲבוֹתָי׃ הָשַׁע מִמֶּנִּי וְאַבְלִיגָה בְּטֶרֶם
אֵלֵךְ וְאֵינֶנִּי׃

מ א ב לַמְנַצֵּחַ לְדָוִד מִזְמוֹר׃ קַוֺּה קִוִּיתִי יְהוָה וַיֵּט אֵלַי וַיִּשְׁמַע שַׁוְעָתִי׃
ג וַיַּעֲלֵנִי | מִבּוֹר שָׁאוֹן מִטִּיט הַיָּוֵן וַיָּקֶם עַל־סֶלַע רַגְלַי כּוֹנֵן אֲשֻׁרָי׃
ד וַיִּתֵּן בְּפִי | שִׁיר חָדָשׁ תְּהִלָּה לֵאלֹהֵינוּ יִרְאוּ רַבִּים וְיִירָאוּ וְיִבְטְחוּ
ה בַּיהוָה׃ אַשְׁרֵי־הַגֶּבֶר אֲשֶׁר־שָׂם יְהוָה מִבְטַחוֹ וְלֹא־פָנָה אֶל־רְהָבִים
ו וְשָׂטֵי כָזָב׃ רַבּוֹת עָשִׂיתָ | אַתָּה | יְהוָה אֱלֹהַי נִפְלְאֹתֶיךָ וּמַחְשְׁבֹתֶיךָ
ז אֵלֵינוּ אֵין | עֲרֹךְ אֵלֶיךָ אַגִּידָה וַאֲדַבֵּרָה עָצְמוּ מִסַּפֵּר׃ זֶבַח וּמִנְחָה |
ח לֹא־חָפַצְתָּ אׇזְנַיִם כָּרִיתָ לִּי עוֹלָה וַחֲטָאָה לֹא שָׁאָלְתָּ׃ אָז אָמַרְתִּי
ט הִנֵּה־בָאתִי בִּמְגִלַּת־סֵפֶר כָּתוּב עָלָי׃ לַעֲשׂוֹת־רְצוֹנְךָ אֱלֹהַי חָפָצְתִּי
י וְתוֹרָתְךָ בְּתוֹךְ מֵעָי׃ בִּשַּׂרְתִּי צֶדֶק | בְּקָהָל רָב הִנֵּה שְׂפָתַי לֹא אֶכְלָא
יא יְהוָה אַתָּה יָדָעְתָּ׃ צִדְקָתְךָ לֹא־כִסִּיתִי | בְּתוֹךְ לִבִּי אֱמוּנָתְךָ וּתְשׁוּעָתְךָ
יב אָמָרְתִּי לֹא־כִחַדְתִּי חַסְדְּךָ וַאֲמִתְּךָ לְקָהָל רָב׃ אַתָּה יְהוָה לֹא־תִכְלָא
יג רַחֲמֶיךָ מִמֶּנִּי חַסְדְּךָ וַאֲמִתְּךָ תָּמִיד יִצְּרוּנִי׃ כִּי אָפְפוּ־עָלַי | רָעוֹת עַד־
אֵין מִסְפָּר הִשִּׂיגוּנִי עֲוֺנֹתַי וְלֹא־יָכֹלְתִּי לִרְאוֹת עָצְמוּ מִשַּׂעֲרוֹת רֹאשִׁי
יד טו וְלִבִּי עֲזָבָנִי׃ רְצֵה יְהוָה לְהַצִּילֵנִי יְהוָה לְעֶזְרָתִי חוּשָׁה׃ יֵבֹשׁוּ וְיַחְפְּרוּ |

16 let those who wish me harm retreat in humiliation; let those who leer at me –
17 "Aha! Aha!" – wallow in their shame. May all those who seek You rejoice
and delight in You. May those who long for Your salvation always proclaim,
18 "The LORD is great!" As for me, I am poor and needy; may the Lord call me
to mind. You are my help and my rescuer – my God, do not delay.[41]

41 1 2 *To the lead singer – a psalm of David.* Happy are those who give thought to
3 the weak; may the LORD spare them in times of misery. May the LORD keep
them and give them life so that they will be happy in the land, rather than give
4 them up to the will of their enemies. May the LORD sustain them on their
5 sickbeds; You completely turned back their suffering. I prayed, "O LORD,
6 show me mercy; heal me, for I sinned against You." My enemies speak of me
7 with spite: "When will he die and his name perish?" If they visit, they babble
insincerely while malice swells in their heart – as soon as they leave, they
8 speak out. All those who hate me whisper about me, imagining the worst for
9 me: "Something deadly courses through him; he will never rise from his bed
10 again." Even my trusted friend – who ate of my bread! – has treated me with
11 cruel deceit.[42] But You, LORD, show me grace; raise me up so that I may pay
12 them back – by this I shall know that You delight in me; my enemies will not
13 crow over me. As for me, because I am blameless You support me; You let
14 me stand firm before You forever. Blessed is the LORD, God of Israel, for ever
and ever, Amen and Amen.

BOOK TWO

42 1 2 *To the lead singer – of the sons of Korah,*[43] *a* maskil.[44] As a deer pines for flowing
3 streams, my soul pines for You, God; my soul thirsts for God, the living God –
4 oh, when will I come and appear before God? My tears have been my fare
5 day and night as people ever taunt me, "Where is your God?" Oh, the things
I remember as I pour out my soul: how I would join the crowd and march
along to the House of God with elated song and the hum of praise from the
6 reveling throngs. Why are you miserable, my soul? Why do you grieve so
within me? Hope for God – that I will yet praise Him in the salvation of His
7 presence. My God – my soul is miserable within me; therefore I think of You
in the land of Jordan, in the Hermon range, from the Humble Mountain,
8 where deep calls to deep in the roar of Your waterfalls; all Your torrents and
9 storm waves crashed over me.[45] By day, the LORD commands His loyalty;
10 by night, His song is with me – a prayer to the God of my life. Let me say
to God, my Rock, "Why have You forgotten me? Why must I walk bent in
11 gloom, oppressed by my enemies?" My enemies' scorn pierces my bones as
12 they ever taunt me, "Where is your God?" Why are you miserable, my soul?
Why do you grieve so within me? Hope for God – that I will yet praise Him,
my salvation and my God.

---

41 | Cf. Psalm 70, which parallels (with variants) the text of verses 14–18.
42 | Literally "has made his heel great against me."
43 | A group of Levitical Temple singers; see II Chronicles 20:19.
44 | See note on 32:1.
45 | Cf. Jonah 2:4.

טז יַחַד מְבַקְשֵׁי נַפְשִׁי לִסְפּוֹתָהּ יִסֹּגוּ אָחוֹר וְיִכָּלְמוּ חֲפֵצֵי רָעָתִי: יָשֹׁמּוּ
יז עַל־עֵקֶב בָּשְׁתָּם הָאֹמְרִים לִי הֶאָח | הֶאָח: יָשִׂישׂוּ וְיִשְׂמְחוּ | בְּךָ כָּל־
יח מְבַקְשֶׁיךָ יֹאמְרוּ תָמִיד יִגְדַּל יהוה אֹהֲבֵי תְּשׁוּעָתֶךָ: וַאֲנִי | עָנִי וְאֶבְיוֹן
אֲדֹנָי יַחֲשָׁב לִי עֶזְרָתִי וּמְפַלְטִי אַתָּה אֱלֹהַי אַל־תְּאַחַר:

מא א ב לַמְנַצֵּחַ מִזְמוֹר לְדָוִד: אַשְׁרֵי מַשְׂכִּיל אֶל־דָּל בְּיוֹם רָעָה יְמַלְּטֵהוּ יהוה:
ג ד יהוה | יִשְׁמְרֵהוּ וִיחַיֵּהוּ יאשר בָּאָרֶץ וְאַל־תִּתְּנֵהוּ בְּנֶפֶשׁ אֹיְבָיו: יהוה וְאֻשַּׁר
ה יִסְעָדֶנּוּ עַל־עֶרֶשׂ דְּוָי כָּל־מִשְׁכָּבוֹ הָפַכְתָּ בְחָלְיוֹ: אֲנִי־אָמַרְתִּי יהוה
ו חָנֵּנִי רְפָאָה נַפְשִׁי כִּי־חָטָאתִי לָךְ: אוֹיְבַי יֹאמְרוּ רַע לִי מָתַי יָמוּת
ז וְאָבַד שְׁמוֹ: וְאִם־בָּא לִרְאוֹת | שָׁוְא יְדַבֵּר לִבּוֹ יִקְבָּץ־אָוֶן לוֹ יֵצֵא
ח ט לַחוּץ יְדַבֵּר: יַחַד עָלַי יִתְלַחֲשׁוּ כָּל־שֹׂנְאָי עָלַי | יַחְשְׁבוּ רָעָה לִי: דְּבַר־
י בְּלִיַּעַל יָצוּק בּוֹ וַאֲשֶׁר שָׁכַב לֹא־יוֹסִיף לָקוּם: גַּם־אִישׁ שְׁלוֹמִי | אֲשֶׁר־
יא בָּטַחְתִּי בוֹ אוֹכֵל לַחְמִי הִגְדִּיל עָלַי עָקֵב: וְאַתָּה יהוה חָנֵּנִי וַהֲקִימֵנִי
יב יג וַאֲשַׁלְּמָה לָהֶם: בְּזֹאת יָדַעְתִּי כִּי־חָפַצְתָּ בִּי כִּי לֹא־יָרִיעַ אֹיְבִי עָלָי: וַאֲנִי
יד בְּתֻמִּי תָּמַכְתָּ בִּי וַתַּצִּיבֵנִי לְפָנֶיךָ לְעוֹלָם: בָּרוּךְ יהוה | אֱלֹהֵי יִשְׂרָאֵל ו
מֵהָעוֹלָם וְעַד־הָעוֹלָם אָמֵן | וְאָמֵן:

מב א ב לַמְנַצֵּחַ מַשְׂכִּיל לִבְנֵי־קֹרַח: כְּאַיָּל תַּעֲרֹג עַל־אֲפִיקֵי־מָיִם כֵּן נַפְשִׁי ספר שני
ג תַעֲרֹג אֵלֶיךָ אֱלֹהִים: צָמְאָה נַפְשִׁי | לֵאלֹהִים לְאֵל חָי מָתַי אָבוֹא
ד וְאֵרָאֶה פְּנֵי אֱלֹהִים: הָיְתָה־לִּי דִמְעָתִי לֶחֶם יוֹמָם וָלָיְלָה בֶּאֱמֹר
ה אֵלַי כָּל־הַיּוֹם אַיֵּה אֱלֹהֶיךָ: אֵלֶּה אֶזְכְּרָה | וְאֶשְׁפְּכָה עָלַי | נַפְשִׁי כִּי
אֶעֱבֹר | בַּסָּךְ אֶדַּדֵּם עַד־בֵּית אֱלֹהִים בְּקוֹל־רִנָּה וְתוֹדָה הָמוֹן חוֹגֵג:
ו מַה־תִּשְׁתּוֹחֲחִי | נַפְשִׁי וַתֶּהֱמִי עָלָי הוֹחִילִי לֵאלֹהִים כִּי־עוֹד אוֹדֶנּוּ
ז יְשׁוּעוֹת פָּנָיו: אֱלֹהַי עָלַי נַפְשִׁי תִשְׁתּוֹחָח עַל־כֵּן אֶזְכָּרְךָ מֵאֶרֶץ יַרְדֵּן
ח וְחֶרְמוֹנִים מֵהַר מִצְעָר: תְּהוֹם־אֶל־תְּהוֹם קוֹרֵא לְקוֹל צִנּוֹרֶיךָ כָּל־
ט מִשְׁבָּרֶיךָ וְגַלֶּיךָ עָלַי עָבָרוּ: יוֹמָם | יְצַוֶּה יהוה | חַסְדּוֹ וּבַלַּיְלָה שִׁירֹה
י עִמִּי תְּפִלָּה לְאֵל חַיָּי: אוֹמְרָה | לְאֵל סַלְעִי לָמָה שְׁכַחְתָּנִי לָמָּה־קֹדֵר
יא אֵלֵךְ בְּלַחַץ אוֹיֵב: בְּרֶצַח | בְּעַצְמוֹתַי חֵרְפוּנִי צוֹרְרָי בְּאָמְרָם אֵלַי כָּל־
יב הַיּוֹם אַיֵּה אֱלֹהֶיךָ: מַה־תִּשְׁתּוֹחֲחִי | נַפְשִׁי וּמַה־תֶּהֱמִי עָלָי הוֹחִילִי
לֵאלֹהִים כִּי־עוֹד אוֹדֶנּוּ יְשׁוּעֹת פָּנַי וֵאלֹהָי:

43 1 Vindicate me, God;[46] contend on my behalf against an ungodly nation; from
2 treacherous, corrupt people rescue me, for You are the God of my refuge. Why
do You forsake me? Why must I walk about bent in gloom, oppressed by my
3 enemies? Send forth Your light and Your truth – they will guide me; they will
4 bring me to Your holy mountain, to Your dwelling place, and I will come to the
altar of God – to God, my joy, my delight. I will praise You with the lyre, God,
5 O my God! Why are you miserable, my soul? Why do you grieve so within me?
Hope for God – that I will yet praise Him, my salvation and my God.
44 1 2 *To the lead singer – of the sons of Koraḥ, a* maskil. God, we heard with our own
3 ears; our ancestors told us of the deeds You did in their days, in days of old. By
Your hand You planted them, dispossessing nations; You brought evil upon
4 peoples and drove them out. Not by their swords did they win the land, nor
did their arms bring them victory. It was Your right hand, Your arm, the light
5 of Your face, for You showed them favor. You are my King, God – command
6 victory for Yaakov. Through You we will gore our foes, in Your name trample
7 our adversaries, for I do not place my trust in my bow; it is not my sword that
8 will bring me victory. It is You who bring us victory over our foes, who bring
9 shame to those who hate us. In God we glory all day long, and we will ever
10 praise Your name – Selah. Yet You have forsaken us and disgraced us; You no
11 longer accompany our armies. You make us retreat before foes while those
12 who hate us plunder away. You have allowed us to be devoured like sheep
13 and scattered us among the nations, selling Your people for next to nothing,
14 making no profit from their sale. You have made us the scorn of our neighbors,
15 the laughingstock of those around us, a cautionary tale among the nations –
16 the peoples shake their heads. All day long my disgrace haunts me; my face
17 is draped in shame from the shouts of those who taunt and revile, from the
18 enemy and avenger. All this has befallen us, but we have not forgotten You;
19 we have not betrayed Your covenant. Our hearts have not turned back; our
20 steps have not strayed from Your path although You have broken us where
21 jackals prowl and draped us in death-shadow. Had we forgotten the name
22 of our God or spread out our hands toward an alien god, would God fail
23 to discover this? For He knows the secrets of the heart. For Your sake we
24 constantly face death; we are considered mere sheep for the slaughter. Stir –
25 why do You sleep, Lord? Rouse Yourself! Do not forsake us forever. Why
26 do You hide Your face; why do You forget our suffering and misery? We are
27 dragged down to the dust, our bodies pressed to the earth. Arise to help us;
redeem us for the sake of Your loyalty.
45 1 *To the lead singer – of the sons of Koraḥ, set to* shoshanim[47] – *a* maskil, *a love*
2 *song.* My heart is astir with glad words; I dedicate this work to the king; my
3 tongue runs like a skilled scribe's pen. You are the fairest of mortals; your lips
4 brim with grace; for this, God has blessed you forever. Fasten your sword
5 on your thigh, mighty one, in your majesty and splendor. In your splendor,
ride on triumphant for the sake of truth, humility, and justice, and may your

46 | This psalm represents the continuation of Psalm 42; note the shared refrain in 42:6, 42:12, and 43:5.
47 | A musical term of uncertain meaning, perhaps related to the meaning "lilies."

מג א שָׁפְטֵנִי אֱלֹהִים ׀ וְרִיבָה רִיבִי מִגּוֹי לֹא־חָסִיד מֵאִישׁ־מִרְמָה וְעַוְלָה
ב תְפַלְּטֵנִי׃ כִּי־אַתָּה ׀ אֱלֹהֵי מָעוּזִּי לָמָה זְנַחְתָּנִי לָמָּה־קֹדֵר אֶתְהַלֵּךְ
ג בְּלַחַץ אוֹיֵב׃ שְׁלַח־אוֹרְךָ וַאֲמִתְּךָ הֵמָּה יַנְחוּנִי יְבִיאוּנִי אֶל־הַר־קָדְשְׁךָ
ד וְאֶל־מִשְׁכְּנוֹתֶיךָ׃ וְאָבוֹאָה ׀ אֶל־מִזְבַּח אֱלֹהִים אֶל־אֵל שִׂמְחַת גִּילִי
ה וְאוֹדְךָ בְכִנּוֹר אֱלֹהִים אֱלֹהָי׃ מַה־תִּשְׁתּוֹחֲחִי ׀ נַפְשִׁי וּמַה־תֶּהֱמִי
עָלָי הוֹחִילִי לֵאלֹהִים כִּי־עוֹד אוֹדֶנּוּ יְשׁוּעֹת פָּנַי וֵאלֹהָי׃
מד א ב לַמְנַצֵּחַ לִבְנֵי־קֹרַח מַשְׂכִּיל׃ אֱלֹהִים ׀ בְּאָזְנֵינוּ שָׁמַעְנוּ אֲבוֹתֵינוּ סִפְּרוּ־
ג לָנוּ פֹּעַל־פָּעַלְתָּ בִימֵיהֶם בִּימֵי קֶדֶם׃ אַתָּה ׀ יָדְךָ גּוֹיִם הוֹרַשְׁתָּ וַתִּטָּעֵם
ד תָּרַע לְאֻמִּים וַתְּשַׁלְּחֵם׃ כִּי לֹא בְחַרְבָּם יָרְשׁוּ אָרֶץ וּזְרוֹעָם לֹא־
ה הוֹשִׁיעָה לָּמוֹ כִּי־יְמִינְךָ וּזְרוֹעֲךָ וְאוֹר פָּנֶיךָ כִּי רְצִיתָם׃ אַתָּה־הוּא
ו מַלְכִּי אֱלֹהִים צַוֵּה יְשׁוּעוֹת יַעֲקֹב׃ בְּךָ צָרֵינוּ נְנַגֵּחַ בְּשִׁמְךָ נָבוּס קָמֵינוּ׃
ז ח כִּי לֹא בְקַשְׁתִּי אֶבְטָח וְחַרְבִּי לֹא תוֹשִׁיעֵנִי׃ כִּי הוֹשַׁעְתָּנוּ מִצָּרֵינוּ
ט וּמְשַׂנְאֵינוּ הֱבִישׁוֹתָ׃ בֵּאלֹהִים הִלַּלְנוּ כָל־הַיּוֹם וְשִׁמְךָ ׀ לְעוֹלָם נוֹדֶה
י יא סֶלָה׃ אַף־זָנַחְתָּ וַתַּכְלִימֵנוּ וְלֹא־תֵצֵא בְּצִבְאוֹתֵינוּ׃ תְּשִׁיבֵנוּ אָחוֹר
יב מִנִּי־צָר וּמְשַׂנְאֵינוּ שָׁסוּ לָמוֹ׃ תִּתְּנֵנוּ כְּצֹאן מַאֲכָל וּבַגּוֹיִם זֵרִיתָנוּ׃
יג יד תִּמְכֹּר־עַמְּךָ בְלֹא־הוֹן וְלֹא־רִבִּיתָ בִּמְחִירֵיהֶם׃ תְּשִׂימֵנוּ חֶרְפָּה
טו לִשְׁכֵנֵינוּ לַעַג וָקֶלֶס לִסְבִיבוֹתֵינוּ׃ תְּשִׂימֵנוּ מָשָׁל בַּגּוֹיִם מְנוֹד־רֹאשׁ
טז יז בַּלְאֻמִּים׃ כָּל־הַיּוֹם כְּלִמָּתִי נֶגְדִּי וּבֹשֶׁת פָּנַי כִּסָּתְנִי׃ מִקּוֹל מְחָרֵף
יח וּמְגַדֵּף מִפְּנֵי אוֹיֵב וּמִתְנַקֵּם׃ כָּל־זֹאת בָּאַתְנוּ וְלֹא שְׁכַחֲנוּךָ וְלֹא־
יט כ שִׁקַּרְנוּ בִּבְרִיתֶךָ׃ לֹא־נָסוֹג אָחוֹר לִבֵּנוּ וַתֵּט אֲשֻׁרֵינוּ מִנִּי אָרְחֶךָ׃ כִּי
כא דִכִּיתָנוּ בִּמְקוֹם תַּנִּים וַתְּכַס עָלֵינוּ בְצַלְמָוֶת׃ אִם־שָׁכַחְנוּ שֵׁם אֱלֹהֵינוּ
כב וַנִּפְרֹשׂ כַּפֵּינוּ לְאֵל זָר׃ הֲלֹא אֱלֹהִים יַחֲקָר־זֹאת כִּי־הוּא יֹדֵעַ תַּעֲלֻמוֹת
כג כד לֵב׃ כִּי־עָלֶיךָ הֹרַגְנוּ כָל־הַיּוֹם נֶחְשַׁבְנוּ כְּצֹאן טִבְחָה׃ עוּרָה ׀ לָמָּה
כה תִישַׁן ׀ אֲדֹנָי הָקִיצָה אַל־תִּזְנַח לָנֶצַח׃ לָמָּה־פָנֶיךָ תַסְתִּיר תִּשְׁכַּח
כו כז עָנְיֵנוּ וְלַחֲצֵנוּ׃ כִּי שָׁחָה לֶעָפָר נַפְשֵׁנוּ דָּבְקָה לָאָרֶץ בִּטְנֵנוּ׃ קוּמָה
עֶזְרָתָה לָּנוּ וּפְדֵנוּ לְמַעַן חַסְדֶּךָ׃
מה א ב לַמְנַצֵּחַ עַל־שֹׁשַׁנִּים לִבְנֵי־קֹרַח מַשְׂכִּיל שִׁיר יְדִידֹת׃ רָחַשׁ לִבִּי ׀ דָּבָר
ג טוֹב אֹמֵר אָנִי מַעֲשַׂי לְמֶלֶךְ לְשׁוֹנִי עֵט ׀ סוֹפֵר מָהִיר׃ יָפְיָפִיתָ מִבְּנֵי
ד אָדָם הוּצַק חֵן בְּשְׂפְתוֹתֶיךָ עַל־כֵּן בֵּרַכְךָ אֱלֹהִים לְעוֹלָם׃ חֲגוֹר־חַרְבְּךָ
ה עַל־יָרֵךְ גִּבּוֹר הוֹדְךָ וַהֲדָרֶךָ׃ וַהֲדָרְךָ ׀ צְלַח רְכַב עַל־דְּבַר־אֱמֶת

6 right hand lead you to wondrous deeds. Your arrows are sharp in the hearts
7 of the king's enemies; peoples fall at your feet. Your divine throne is eternal;
8 your royal scepter is a scepter of equity. You love justice and despise evil – for
this, God – your God – has anointed you out of all your fellows with oil of
9 bliss. Your robes are all fragrant with myrrh and aloe and cinnamon. Lutes
10 echo from ivory chambers, delighting you. The daughters of kings are among
11 your noble ladies; on your right stands the queen in gold of Ofir. Hear me,
daughter; look around and listen; forget your own people and your father's
12 house, and let the king crave your beauty. He is your master now; bow to
13 him. Daughter of Tyre, the richest of peoples will seek your favor with gifts.
14 15 In all her glory, the princess is inside, adorned in golden filigree; she is led
to the king in embroidered finery, maidens, her friends, in her train; they
16 17 are brought to you, led in gladness and joy; they enter the king's palace.
Your sons will succeed your fathers; you will make them princes throughout
18 the land. I have perpetuated your name for all generations; therefore peoples
shall praise you for ever and for all time.

46 1 2 *To the lead singer – a song of the sons of Koraḥ, on* alamot.[48] God is our refuge
3 and might, ever present to help in times of trouble, so we need not fear
when the world shifts, when mountains crumble into the heart of the sea –
4 though its waters rage and foam, though the mountains shudder at its surge –
5 Selah. There is a river whose streams bring joy to the city of God, to the holy
6 dwelling place of the Most High. God is in its midst; it will never crumble;
7 God will come to its aid at the break of day. Nations rage; kingdoms crumble;
8 He sounds His voice, and the earth dissolves. The LORD of Hosts is with us;
9 the God of Yaakov is our refuge – Selah. Come, gaze at the works of the LORD,
10 at the desolation He has wrought upon the earth. He has ended war all over
11 the earth, breaking bow and snapping spear, burning chariots with fire. Desist
12 and know that I am God, exalted among nations, exalted over the earth. The
LORD of Hosts is with us; the God of Yaakov is our refuge – Selah.

47 1 2 *To the lead singer – a psalm of the sons of Koraḥ.* Clap your hands together, all
3 peoples; shout out joyfully to God, for the LORD, Most High, is fearsome, the
4 great King over all the earth. It is He who subjugates peoples under us, nations
5 beneath our feet. He chooses our legacy for us: the pride of Yaakov, whom
6 He loves – Selah. God ascends amid shouts of joy – the LORD – to the blast
7 8 of the ram's horn. Sing out to God, sing! Sing out to our King, sing! For God
9 is King over all the earth – sing a psalm of praise![49] God reigns over nations;
10 God is seated on His holy throne. The rulers of peoples have gathered, the
people of Avraham's God, for all the earth's protectors are God's; He is raised
high above.

48 1 2 *A song – a psalm of the sons of Koraḥ.* Great is the LORD, of highest praise in the
3 city of our God, His holy mountain, beautiful in its heights, the delight
of all the earth, Mount Zion, the slopes of Tzafon,[50] city of the great King.

---

48 | A musical term of uncertain meaning; cf. 1 Chronicles 15:20.

49 | Hebrew *maskil.* See note on 32:1.

50 | Literally "the North." The peak of Mount Zion (Moriah) was situated at the northern end of the city of Jerusalem, which was built on its southern slopes.

ו וְעַנְוָה־צֶדֶק וְתוֹרְךָ נוֹרָאוֹת יְמִינֶךָ: חִצֶּיךָ שְׁנוּנִים עַמִּים תַּחְתֶּיךָ
ז יִפְּלוּ בְּלֵב אוֹיְבֵי הַמֶּלֶךְ: כִּסְאֲךָ אֱלֹהִים עוֹלָם וָעֶד שֵׁבֶט מִישֹׁר שֵׁבֶט
ח מַלְכוּתֶךָ: אָהַבְתָּ צֶּדֶק וַתִּשְׂנָא רֶשַׁע עַל־כֵּן ׀ מְשָׁחֲךָ אֱלֹהִים אֱלֹהֶיךָ
ט שֶׁמֶן שָׂשׂוֹן מֵחֲבֵרֶךָ: מֹר־וַאֲהָלוֹת קְצִיעוֹת כָּל־בִּגְדֹתֶיךָ מִן־הֵיכְלֵי
י שֵׁן מִנִּי שִׂמְּחוּךָ: בְּנוֹת מְלָכִים בְּיִקְּרוֹתֶיךָ נִצְּבָה שֵׁגַל לִימִינְךָ בְּכֶתֶם
יא יב אוֹפִיר: שִׁמְעִי־בַת וּרְאִי וְהַטִּי אָזְנֵךְ וְשִׁכְחִי עַמֵּךְ וּבֵית אָבִיךְ: וְיִתְאָו
יג הַמֶּלֶךְ יָפְיֵךְ כִּי־הוּא אֲדֹנַיִךְ וְהִשְׁתַּחֲוִי־לוֹ: וּבַת־צֹר ׀ בְּמִנְחָה פָּנַיִךְ יְחַלּוּ
יד עֲשִׁירֵי עָם: כָּל־כְּבוּדָּה בַת־מֶלֶךְ פְּנִימָה מִמִּשְׁבְּצוֹת זָהָב לְבוּשָׁהּ:
טו טז לִרְקָמוֹת תּוּבַל לַמֶּלֶךְ בְּתוּלוֹת אַחֲרֶיהָ רֵעוֹתֶיהָ מוּבָאוֹת לָךְ: תּוּבַלְנָה
יז בִּשְׂמָחֹת וָגִיל תְּבֹאֶינָה בְּהֵיכַל מֶלֶךְ: תַּחַת אֲבֹתֶיךָ יִהְיוּ בָנֶיךָ תְּשִׁיתֵמוֹ
יח לְשָׂרִים בְּכָל־הָאָרֶץ: אַזְכִּירָה שִׁמְךָ בְּכָל־דֹּר וָדֹר עַל־כֵּן עַמִּים יְהוֹדֻךָ
לְעֹלָם וָעֶד:
מו א ב לַמְנַצֵּחַ לִבְנֵי־קֹרַח עַל־עֲלָמוֹת שִׁיר: אֱלֹהִים לָנוּ מַחֲסֶה וָעֹז עֶזְרָה
ג בְצָרוֹת נִמְצָא מְאֹד: עַל־כֵּן לֹא־נִירָא בְּהָמִיר אָרֶץ וּבְמוֹט הָרִים
ד ה בְּלֵב יַמִּים: יֶהֱמוּ יֶחְמְרוּ מֵימָיו יִרְעֲשׁוּ־הָרִים בְּגַאֲוָתוֹ סֶלָה: נָהָר
ו פְּלָגָיו יְשַׂמְּחוּ עִיר־אֱלֹהִים קְדֹשׁ מִשְׁכְּנֵי עֶלְיוֹן: אֱלֹהִים בְּקִרְבָּהּ
ז בַּל־תִּמּוֹט יַעְזְרֶהָ אֱלֹהִים לִפְנוֹת בֹּקֶר: הָמוּ גוֹיִם מָטוּ מַמְלָכוֹת
ח נָתַן בְּקוֹלוֹ תָּמוּג אָרֶץ: יְהוָה צְבָאוֹת עִמָּנוּ מִשְׂגָּב לָנוּ אֱלֹהֵי יַעֲקֹב
ט י סֶלָה: לְכוּ־חֲזוּ מִפְעֲלוֹת יְהוָה אֲשֶׁר־שָׂם שַׁמּוֹת בָּאָרֶץ: מַשְׁבִּית
מִלְחָמוֹת עַד־קְצֵה הָאָרֶץ קֶשֶׁת יְשַׁבֵּר וְקִצֵּץ חֲנִית עֲגָלוֹת יִשְׂרֹף
יא יב בָּאֵשׁ: הַרְפּוּ וּדְעוּ כִּי־אָנֹכִי אֱלֹהִים אָרוּם בַּגּוֹיִם אָרוּם בָּאָרֶץ: יְהוָה
צְבָאוֹת עִמָּנוּ מִשְׂגָּב לָנוּ אֱלֹהֵי יַעֲקֹב סֶלָה:
מז א ב לַמְנַצֵּחַ לִבְנֵי־קֹרַח מִזְמוֹר: כָּל־הָעַמִּים תִּקְעוּ־כָף הָרִיעוּ לֵאלֹהִים
ג ד בְּקוֹל רִנָּה: כִּי־יְהוָה עֶלְיוֹן נוֹרָא מֶלֶךְ גָּדוֹל עַל־כָּל־הָאָרֶץ: יַדְבֵּר
ה עַמִּים תַּחְתֵּינוּ וּלְאֻמִּים תַּחַת רַגְלֵינוּ: יִבְחַר־לָנוּ אֶת־נַחֲלָתֵנוּ אֶת
ו גְּאוֹן יַעֲקֹב אֲשֶׁר־אָהֵב סֶלָה: עָלָה אֱלֹהִים בִּתְרוּעָה יְהוָה בְּקוֹל
ז ח שׁוֹפָר: זַמְּרוּ אֱלֹהִים זַמֵּרוּ זַמְּרוּ לְמַלְכֵּנוּ זַמֵּרוּ: כִּי מֶלֶךְ כָּל־הָאָרֶץ
ט אֱלֹהִים זַמְּרוּ מַשְׂכִּיל: מָלַךְ אֱלֹהִים עַל־גּוֹיִם אֱלֹהִים יָשַׁב ׀ עַל־כִּסֵּא
י קָדְשׁוֹ: נְדִיבֵי עַמִּים ׀ נֶאֱסָפוּ עַם אֱלֹהֵי אַבְרָהָם כִּי לֵאלֹהִים מָגִנֵּי־
אֶרֶץ מְאֹד נַעֲלָה:
מח א ב שִׁיר מִזְמוֹר לִבְנֵי־קֹרַח: גָּדוֹל יְהוָה וּמְהֻלָּל מְאֹד בְּעִיר אֱלֹהֵינוּ הַר־
ג קָדְשׁוֹ: יְפֵה נוֹף מְשׂוֹשׂ כָּל־הָאָרֶץ הַר־צִיּוֹן יַרְכְּתֵי צָפוֹן קִרְיַת מֶלֶךְ

4 5 6 7 God is known as the protector of its palaces. See how the kings joined forces,
advancing together. Astounded at the sight, they panicked and fled – there fear
8 seized them, the agony of a woman in childbirth, like ships of Tarshish
9 wrecked by eastern winds.[51] The tales are all true – we have seen for ourselves –
in the city of the LORD of Hosts, in the city of our God. May God preserve it
10 11 forever – Selah. Within Your Temple, God, we meditate on Your love. Your
name, God, like Your praise, reaches the ends of the earth; Your right hand
12 is filled with righteousness. Let Mount Zion rejoice; let the towns of Yehuda
13 be glad because of Your judgments. Walk around Zion and encircle it; count
14 its towers; note its strong walls; make your way through its citadels so that
15 you may tell future generations that this is God, our God, for ever and ever;
He will guide us for evermore.

49 1 2 *To the lead singer – a psalm of the sons of Koraḥ.* Hear this, all you peoples;
3 4 listen, all dwellers of this world, low and high, rich and poor alike. My mouth
5 will speak words of wisdom; my heart's utterance, understanding. I listen with
6 care to a parable; I expound my theme to the music of the harp. Why should
7 I fear when evil days come, when wicked deceivers surround me – those
8 who trust in their wealth, who boast of their great riches? No person can ever
9 redeem another or pay God the price of his release; the ransom of a life is
10 costly; no payment will ever be enough to let him live forever, never seeing the
11 grave. For all can see that wise men die and that the foolish and senseless all
12 perish, leaving their wealth to others. They think their houses will last forever,
13 their dwellings for all generations – they give their names to their estates, but
a person, despite his wealth, cannot linger; he is like the beasts that perish.
14 Such is the fate of the foolish, the end of those pleased with their own words –
15 Selah. They go down to Sheol like sheep; death will be their shepherd. The
upright will rule over them in the morning. Their forms will decay in Sheol,
16 far from their noble mansions. But God will redeem my life from Sheol, for
17 He will take me – Selah. Fear not when people grow rich, when their houses
18 rise in esteem, for they will take nothing with them in death; their esteem
19 will not descend with them. Though they counted themselves blessed in
20 life, for people praise you when you prosper, they too will join the ranks of
21 their ancestors, who will never see the light again. A person with wealth but
without understanding is like the beasts that perish.

50 1 *A psalm of Asaf.*[52] God, the LORD God, speaks and summons the earth from
2 where the sun rises to where it sets. From Zion, pure beauty, God shines
3 forth. Let our God come; let Him not hold back – a devouring fire flares
4 before Him; a wild storm rages around Him. He calls on the earth and the
5 heavens above for the judgment of His people: "Gather My devoted ones to
6 Me, those who forged a covenant with Me by sacrifice." The heavens tell of
7 His justice, for God Himself is the judge – Selah. Listen, My people, and I will
8 speak; Israel, I will testify against you: I am God, your God. I do not rebuke
9 you for your sacrifices or for your burnt offerings ever before Me. I claim no

51 | Cf. 1 Kings 22:49.

52 | A prominent Levitical Temple singer; see 1 Chronicles 16:7, 25:1–9; Nehemiah 7:44.

ד ה רַב׃ אֱלֹהִים בְּאַרְמְנוֹתֶיהָ נוֹדַע לְמִשְׂגָּב׃ כִּי־הִנֵּה הַמְּלָכִים נוֹעֲדוּ
ו ז עָבְרוּ יַחְדָּו׃ הֵמָּה רָאוּ כֵּן תָּמָהוּ נִבְהֲלוּ נֶחְפָּזוּ׃ רְעָדָה אֲחָזָתַם שָׁם
ח ט חִיל כַּיּוֹלֵדָה׃ בְּרוּחַ קָדִים תְּשַׁבֵּר אֳנִיּוֹת תַּרְשִׁישׁ׃ כַּאֲשֶׁר שָׁמַעְנוּ ׀
כֵּן רָאִינוּ בְּעִיר־יְהוָה צְבָאוֹת בְּעִיר אֱלֹהֵינוּ אֱלֹהִים יְכוֹנְנֶהָ עַד־עוֹלָם
י יא סֶלָה׃ דִּמִּינוּ אֱלֹהִים חַסְדֶּךָ בְּקֶרֶב הֵיכָלֶךָ׃ כְּשִׁמְךָ ׀ אֱלֹהִים כֵּן
יב תְּהִלָּתְךָ עַל־קַצְוֵי־אֶרֶץ צֶדֶק מָלְאָה יְמִינֶךָ׃ יִשְׂמַח ׀ הַר־צִיּוֹן תָּגֵלְנָה
יג בְּנוֹת יְהוּדָה לְמַעַן מִשְׁפָּטֶיךָ׃ סֹבּוּ צִיּוֹן וְהַקִּיפוּהָ סִפְרוּ מִגְדָּלֶיהָ׃
יד שִׁיתוּ לִבְּכֶם ׀ לְחֵילָה פַּסְּגוּ אַרְמְנוֹתֶיהָ לְמַעַן תְּסַפְּרוּ לְדוֹר אַחֲרוֹן׃
טו כִּי זֶה ׀ אֱלֹהִים אֱלֹהֵינוּ עוֹלָם וָעֶד הוּא יְנַהֲגֵנוּ עַל־מוּת׃
מט א ב לַמְנַצֵּחַ לִבְנֵי־קֹרַח מִזְמוֹר׃ שִׁמְעוּ־זֹאת כָּל־הָעַמִּים הַאֲזִינוּ כָּל־יֹשְׁבֵי
ג ד חָלֶד׃ גַּם־בְּנֵי אָדָם גַּם־בְּנֵי־אִישׁ יַחַד עָשִׁיר וְאֶבְיוֹן׃ פִּי יְדַבֵּר חָכְמוֹת
ה ו וְהָגוּת לִבִּי תְבוּנוֹת׃ אַטֶּה לְמָשָׁל אָזְנִי אֶפְתַּח בְּכִנּוֹר חִידָתִי׃ לָמָּה
ז אִירָא בִּימֵי רָע עֲוֺן עֲקֵבַי יְסוּבֵּנִי׃ הַבֹּטְחִים עַל־חֵילָם וּבְרֹב עָשְׁרָם
ח ט יִתְהַלָּלוּ׃ אָח לֹא־פָדֹה יִפְדֶּה אִישׁ לֹא־יִתֵּן לֵאלֹהִים כָּפְרוֹ׃ וְיֵקַר פִּדְיוֹן
י יא נַפְשָׁם וְחָדַל לְעוֹלָם׃ וִיחִי־עוֹד לָנֶצַח לֹא יִרְאֶה הַשָּׁחַת׃ כִּי יִרְאֶה ׀
יב חֲכָמִים יָמוּתוּ יַחַד כְּסִיל וָבַעַר יֹאבֵדוּ וְעָזְבוּ לַאֲחֵרִים חֵילָם׃ קִרְבָּם
בָּתֵּימוֹ ׀ לְעוֹלָם מִשְׁכְּנֹתָם לְדֹר וָדֹר קָרְאוּ בִשְׁמוֹתָם עֲלֵי אֲדָמוֹת׃
יג יד וְאָדָם בִּיקָר בַּל־יָלִין נִמְשַׁל כַּבְּהֵמוֹת נִדְמוּ׃ זֶה דַרְכָּם כֵּסֶל לָמוֹ
טו וְאַחֲרֵיהֶם ׀ בְּפִיהֶם יִרְצוּ סֶלָה׃ כַּצֹּאן ׀ לִשְׁאוֹל שַׁתּוּ מָוֶת יִרְעֵם וַיִּרְדּוּ
טז בָם יְשָׁרִים ׀ לַבֹּקֶר וצירם לְבַלּוֹת שְׁאוֹל מִזְּבֻל לוֹ׃ אַךְ־אֱלֹהִים יִפְדֶּה וְצוּרָם
יז נַפְשִׁי מִיַּד שְׁאוֹל כִּי יִקָּחֵנִי סֶלָה׃ אַל־תִּירָא כִּי־יַעֲשִׁר אִישׁ כִּי־יִרְבֶּה
יח יט כְּבוֹד בֵּיתוֹ׃ כִּי לֹא בְמוֹתוֹ יִקַּח הַכֹּל לֹא־יֵרֵד אַחֲרָיו כְּבוֹדוֹ׃ כִּי־נַפְשׁוֹ ז
כ בְּחַיָּיו יְבָרֵךְ וְיוֹדֻךָ כִּי־תֵיטִיב לָךְ׃ תָּבוֹא עַד־דּוֹר אֲבוֹתָיו עַד־נֵצַח לֹא
כא יִרְאוּ־אוֹר׃ אָדָם בִּיקָר וְלֹא יָבִין נִמְשַׁל כַּבְּהֵמוֹת נִדְמוּ׃
נ א מִזְמוֹר לְאָסָף אֵל ׀ אֱלֹהִים יְהוָה דִּבֶּר וַיִּקְרָא־אָרֶץ מִמִּזְרַח־שֶׁמֶשׁ
ב ג עַד־מְבֹאוֹ׃ מִצִּיּוֹן מִכְלַל־יֹפִי אֱלֹהִים הוֹפִיעַ׃ יָבֹא אֱלֹהֵינוּ וְאַל־יֶחֱרַשׁ
ד אֵשׁ־לְפָנָיו תֹּאכֵל וּסְבִיבָיו נִשְׂעֲרָה מְאֹד׃ יִקְרָא אֶל־הַשָּׁמַיִם מֵעָל
ה ו וְאֶל־הָאָרֶץ לָדִין עַמּוֹ׃ אִסְפוּ־לִי חֲסִידָי כֹּרְתֵי בְרִיתִי עֲלֵי־זָבַח׃ וַיַּגִּידוּ
ז שָׁמַיִם צִדְקוֹ כִּי־אֱלֹהִים ׀ שֹׁפֵט הוּא סֶלָה׃ שִׁמְעָה עַמִּי ׀ וַאֲדַבֵּרָה
ח יִשְׂרָאֵל וְאָעִידָה בָּךְ אֱלֹהִים אֱלֹהֶיךָ אָנֹכִי׃ לֹא עַל־זְבָחֶיךָ אוֹכִיחֶךָ
ט וְעוֹלֹתֶיךָ לְנֶגְדִּי תָמִיד׃ לֹא־אֶקַּח מִבֵּיתְךָ פָר מִמִּכְלְאֹתֶיךָ עַתּוּדִים׃

10 bulls of your house, no he-goats from your folds, for all the forest beasts are
11 Mine, the cattle of a thousand hills; I know every bird of the mountains; the
12 creatures of the fields belong to Me. Were I to hunger, I would not tell you,
13 for Mine is the world and all that fills it. Do I eat the flesh of bulls? Do I drink
14 the blood of he-goats? Offer to God a thanksgiving sacrifice; pay your vows
15 to the Most High. When you call Me in times of trouble, I will rescue you,
16 and you will honor Me. But to the wicked, God says, "How dare you recite
17 My laws or bear My covenant on your lips – you who despise discipline and
18 toss My words behind you? When you see a thief, you are drawn to him; you
19 associate with adulterers; you speak evil freely; your tongue adheres to deceit;
20 you sit and slander your brother, maligning the child of your own mother.
21 If all this you do and I hold back, You might imagine I am like you, so I will
22 rebuke you and charge you outright. Consider this, you who forget God,
23 lest I tear you apart, with no one to save you: those who bring Me offerings
of thanksgiving honor Me, and as for those who are following My way, I will
show them God's salvation."

51 1 2 *To the lead singer – a psalm of David, when the prophet Natan came to him after*
3 *he came to Batsheva.*[53] Show me grace, God, in Your loyalty; in Your great
4 mercy, erase my offense; wash me well of my guilt; purify me of my sin,
5 6 for I am aware of my transgression, and my sin is ever before me. I sinned
against You alone; I committed what is evil in Your eyes, so Your sentence
7 is just, and Your judgment is fair. Yes, with guilt I came to be; in sin did my
8 mother conceive me. Yes, You desire truth to course deep within me – to
9 teach wisdom to my innermost self. Purge me with hyssop, and I will be
10 pure; wash me, and I will be whiter than snow. Let me hear gladness and joy;
11 let the bones You have crushed rejoice. Hide Your face from my sins; erase
12 all my guilt. Create a pure heart for me, God; renew a firm spirit within me.
13 Do not cast me away from Your presence or take Your holy spirit away from
14 15 me. Restore your glad salvation to me; let a willing spirit sustain me. I will
16 teach offenders Your ways, and sinners will come back to You. Save me from
bloodshed, God, God of my salvation; my tongue will sing of Your justice.
17 18 O Lord, open my lips, and my mouth will declare Your praise. You have no
19 desire for me to bring sacrifice; You do not want burnt offerings. To God, a
broken spirit is an offering; a crushed and broken heart, God, You will not
20 21 spurn. Favor Zion with Your goodness; rebuild the walls of Jerusalem. Then
You will delight in sincere sacrifices, burnt offerings and whole offerings; then
bulls will be offered up on Your altar.

52 1 2 *To the lead singer – of David, a* maskil, *when Doeg the Edomite came and informed*
3 *Sha'ul, telling him, "David went to the house of Avimelekh."*[54] Why do you
4 boast of evil, powerful one? God's loyalty is everlasting. Your tongue wreaks
5 malice, carving mischief like a sharpened razor; you love evil more than
6 good, lying more than speaking truth – Selah. You love all words of carnage,
7 all treacherous speech, but God will tear you down once and for all; He will

53 | See II Samuel, chapter 12.

54 | See I Samuel 22:9.

יא כי־לי כל־חיתו־יער בהמות בהררי־אלף: ידעתי כל־עוף הרים וזיז
יב יג שדי עמדי: אם־ארעב לא־אמר לך כי־לי תבל ומלאה: האוכל
יד בשר אבירים ודם עתודים אשתה: זבח לאלהים תודה ושלם
טו טז לעליון נדריך: וקראני ביום צרה אחלצך ותכבדני: ולרשע | אמר
יז אלהים מה־לך לספר חקי ותשא בריתי עלי־פיך: ואתה שנאת
יח מוסר ותשלך דברי אחריך: אם־ראית גנב ותרץ עמו ועם מנאפים
יט כ חלקך: פיך שלחת ברעה ולשונך תצמיד מרמה: תשב באחיך
כא תדבר בבן־אמך תתן־דפי: אלה עשית | והחרשתי דמית היות־
כב אהיה כמוך אוכיחך ואערכה לעיניך: בינו־נא זאת שכחי אלוה
כג פן־אטרף ואין מציל: זבח תודה יכבדנני ושם דרך אראנו בישע
אלהים:

נא א ב למנצח מזמור לדוד: בבוא־אליו נתן הנביא כאשר־בא אל־בת־
ג ד שבע: חנני אלהים כחסדך כרב רחמיך מחה פשעי: הרבה כבסני הרב
ה מעוני ומחטאתי טהרני: כי־פשעי אני אדע וחטאתי נגדי תמיד:
ו לך לבדך | חטאתי והרע בעיניך עשיתי למען תצדק בדברך תזכה
ז ח בשפטך: הן־בעוון חוללתי ובחטא יחמתני אמי: הן־אמת חפצת
ט בטחות ובסתם חכמה תודיעני: תחטאני באזוב ואטהר תכבסני
י יא ומשלג אלבין: תשמיעני ששון ושמחה תגלנה עצמות דכית: הסתר
יב פניך מחטאי וכל־עונתי מחה: לב טהור ברא־לי אלהים ורוח נכון
יג חדש בקרבי: אל־תשליכני מלפניך ורוח קדשך אל־תקח ממני:
יד טו השיבה לי ששון ישעך ורוח נדיבה תסמכני: אלמדה פשעים דרכיך
טז וחטאים אליך ישובו: הצילני מדמים | אלהים אלהי תשועתי תרנן
יז יח לשוני צדקתך: אדני שפתי תפתח ופי יגיד תהלתך: כי | לא־תחפץ
יט זבח ואתנה עולה לא תרצה: זבחי אלהים רוח נשברה לב־נשבר
כ ונדכה אלהים לא תבזה: היטיבה ברצונך את־ציון תבנה חומות
כא ירושלם: אז תחפץ זבחי־צדק עולה וכליל אז יעלו על־מזבחך
פרים:

נב א ב למנצח משכיל לדוד: בבוא | דואג האדמי ויגד לשאול ויאמר לו
ג בא דוד אל־בית אחימלך: מה־תתהלל ברעה הגבור חסד אל
ד ה כל־היום: הוות תחשב לשונך כתער מלטש עשה רמיה: אהבת
ו רע מטוב שקר | מדבר צדק סלה: אהבת כל־דברי־בלע לשון
ז מרמה: גם־אל יתצך לנצח יחתך ויסחך מאהל ושרשך מארץ

snatch you up and uproot you from your home, your roots from the land of
8 the living – Selah. Then the righteous will look on in awe, and they will mock
9 him: "Here is someone who would not make God his refuge but trusted in his
10 great wealth and grew powerful through malice." But I am like a flourishing
olive tree in the House of God; I will trust in God's loyalty for ever and for
11 all time. I will praise You forever for what You have done; I will proclaim that
Your name is good in the presence of Your devoted ones.

53 1 2 *To the lead singer, on* maḥalat[55] *– of David, a* maskil.[56] The brute says in his heart,
"There is no God." They are corrupt; they wreak vile schemes; there is no one
3 who does good. God looks down from heaven at humanity to see if someone
4 has the sense to seek out God, but all are treacherous, altogether tainted;
5 there is no one who does good, not even one. Have they no knowledge, those
evildoers who devour my people as if devouring bread, who do not call out to
6 God? There they were struck with terror, such terror as never before, for God
scattered the bones of your attackers; You have put them to shame, for God has
7 rejected them. Oh, that Israel's salvation might come from Zion; when God
restores His people's fortune, Yaakov will rejoice; Israel will be glad.

54 1 2 *To the lead singer, accompanied by music – of David, a* maskil, *when the Zifites*
3 *came and told Sha'ul, "David is hiding among us."*[57] God, save me by Your name;
4 with Your might, vindicate me. God, hear my prayer; give ear to the words I
5 mouth, for strangers have risen up against me; cruel men seek my life, men
6 who have no regard for God – Selah. Look – God is my helper; the Lord is
7 the one who sustains my life. He will repay my oppressors for their evil. By
8 Your truth, destroy them. To You I will offer a freewill sacrifice; I will praise
9 Your name, LORD, for it is good, for He has saved me from all danger; my eyes
have seen my enemies' downfall.

55 1 2 *To the lead singer, accompanied by music – of David, a* maskil. Give ear, God,
3 to my prayer; do not ignore my plea; hear me and answer me. Restless, I
4 wail and cry out – at the clamor of the enemy, at the cruelty of the wicked,
5 for they bring evil crashing down on me; they pounce on me with fury. My
6 heart trembles within me; I am gripped with death terror; fear and shaking
7 seize me; I am stifled with horror. And I cried, "If only I had wings like a
8 dove, I would fly away and find rest; O, I would roam far away and alight in
9 the wilderness – Selah. I would soon find shelter from the raging wind and
10 storm." Thwart them, Lord; confound their speech, for I see violence and
11 strife in the city. Day and night they patrol its walls; evil and suffering are in
12 its midst. In its midst is corruption; treachery and deceit never cease to haunt
13 its square, but it is not an enemy who taunts me – that I could bear – it is not
14 a foe who looms over me, for then I could hide. It is you, a person like me –
15 my companion, my friend. We shared sweet closeness as we walked among
16 the crowd at the House of God. May He set death upon them; may they go
down to Sheol alive, for evil has permeated their minds, their very being.

---

55 | An unknown musical term. See also 88:1.

56 | Cf. Psalm 14, a slightly different version of this psalm.

57 | See 1 Samuel 23:19.

ח ט חַיִּים סֶלָה׃ וְיִרְאוּ צַדִּיקִים וְיִירָאוּ וְעָלָיו יִשְׂחָקוּ׃ הִנֵּה הַגֶּבֶר לֹא
י יָשִׂים אֱלֹהִים מָעוּזּוֹ וַיִּבְטַח בְּרֹב עָשְׁרוֹ יָעֹז בְּהַוָּתוֹ׃ וַאֲנִי | כְּזַיִת רַעֲנָן
יא בְּבֵית אֱלֹהִים בָּטַחְתִּי בְחֶסֶד־אֱלֹהִים עוֹלָם וָעֶד׃ אוֹדְךָ לְעוֹלָם כִּי
עָשִׂיתָ וַאֲקַוֶּה שִׁמְךָ כִי־טוֹב נֶגֶד חֲסִידֶיךָ׃

נג א ב לַמְנַצֵּחַ עַל־מָחֲלַת מַשְׂכִּיל לְדָוִד׃ אָמַר נָבָל בְּלִבּוֹ אֵין אֱלֹהִים הִשְׁחִיתוּ
ג וְהִתְעִיבוּ עָוֶל אֵין עֹשֵׂה־טוֹב׃ אֱלֹהִים מִשָּׁמַיִם הִשְׁקִיף עַל־בְּנֵי־אָדָם
ד לִרְאוֹת הֲיֵשׁ מַשְׂכִּיל דֹּרֵשׁ אֶת־אֱלֹהִים׃ כֻּלּוֹ סָג יַחְדָּו נֶאֱלָחוּ אֵין
ה עֹשֵׂה־טוֹב אֵין גַּם־אֶחָד׃ הֲלֹא יָדְעוּ פֹּעֲלֵי אָוֶן אֹכְלֵי עַמִּי אָכְלוּ לֶחֶם
ו אֱלֹהִים לֹא קָרָאוּ׃ שָׁם | פָּחֲדוּ־פַחַד לֹא־הָיָה פָחַד כִּי־אֱלֹהִים פִּזַּר
ז עַצְמוֹת חֹנָךְ הֱבִשֹׁתָה כִּי־אֱלֹהִים מְאָסָם׃ מִי יִתֵּן מִצִּיּוֹן יְשֻׁעוֹת יִשְׂרָאֵל
בְּשׁוּב אֱלֹהִים שְׁבוּת עַמּוֹ יָגֵל יַעֲקֹב יִשְׂמַח יִשְׂרָאֵל׃

נד א ב לַמְנַצֵּחַ בִּנְגִינֹת מַשְׂכִּיל לְדָוִד׃ בְּבוֹא הַזִּיפִים וַיֹּאמְרוּ לְשָׁאוּל הֲלֹא
ג דָוִד מִסְתַּתֵּר עִמָּנוּ׃ אֱלֹהִים בְּשִׁמְךָ הוֹשִׁיעֵנִי וּבִגְבוּרָתְךָ תְדִינֵנִי׃
ד ה אֱלֹהִים שְׁמַע תְּפִלָּתִי הַאֲזִינָה לְאִמְרֵי־פִי׃ כִּי זָרִים | קָמוּ עָלַי וְעָרִיצִים
ו בִּקְשׁוּ נַפְשִׁי לֹא שָׂמוּ אֱלֹהִים לְנֶגְדָּם סֶלָה׃ הִנֵּה אֱלֹהִים עֹזֵר לִי
ז ח אֲדֹנָי בְּסֹמְכֵי נַפְשִׁי׃ ישוב הָרַע לְשֹׁרְרָי בַּאֲמִתְּךָ הַצְמִיתֵם׃ בִּנְדָבָה יָשִׁיב
ט אֶזְבְּחָה־לָּךְ אוֹדֶה שִּׁמְךָ יְהוָה כִּי־טוֹב׃ כִּי מִכָּל־צָרָה הִצִּילָנִי וּבְאֹיְבַי
רָאֲתָה עֵינִי׃

נה א ב לַמְנַצֵּחַ בִּנְגִינֹת מַשְׂכִּיל לְדָוִד׃ הַאֲזִינָה אֱלֹהִים תְּפִלָּתִי וְאַל־תִּתְעַלַּם
ג ד מִתְּחִנָּתִי׃ הַקְשִׁיבָה לִּי וַעֲנֵנִי אָרִיד בְּשִׂיחִי וְאָהִימָה׃ מִקּוֹל אוֹיֵב
ה מִפְּנֵי עָקַת רָשָׁע כִּי־יָמִיטוּ עָלַי אָוֶן וּבְאַף יִשְׂטְמוּנִי׃ לִבִּי יָחִיל בְּקִרְבִּי
ו ז וְאֵימוֹת מָוֶת נָפְלוּ עָלָי׃ יִרְאָה וָרַעַד יָבֹא בִי וַתְּכַסֵּנִי פַּלָּצוּת׃ וָאֹמַר
ח מִי־יִתֶּן־לִּי אֵבֶר כַּיּוֹנָה אָעוּפָה וְאֶשְׁכֹּנָה׃ הִנֵּה אַרְחִיק נְדֹד אָלִין
ט י בַּמִּדְבָּר סֶלָה׃ אָחִישָׁה מִפְלָט לִי מֵרוּחַ סֹעָה מִסָּעַר׃ בַּלַּע אֲדֹנָי פַּלַּג
יא לְשׁוֹנָם כִּי־רָאִיתִי חָמָס וְרִיב בָּעִיר׃ יוֹמָם וָלַיְלָה יְסוֹבְבֻהָ עַל־חוֹמֹתֶיהָ
יב וְאָוֶן וְעָמָל בְּקִרְבָּהּ׃ הַוּוֹת בְּקִרְבָּהּ וְלֹא־יָמִישׁ מֵרְחֹבָהּ תֹּךְ וּמִרְמָה׃
יג כִּי לֹא־אוֹיֵב יְחָרְפֵנִי וְאֶשָּׂא לֹא־מְשַׂנְאִי עָלַי הִגְדִּיל וְאֶסָּתֵר מִמֶּנּוּ׃
יד טו וְאַתָּה אֱנוֹשׁ כְּעֶרְכִּי אַלּוּפִי וּמְיֻדָּעִי׃ אֲשֶׁר יַחְדָּו נַמְתִּיק סוֹד בְּבֵית
טז אֱלֹהִים נְהַלֵּךְ בְּרָגֶשׁ׃ ישימות | עָלֵימוֹ יֵרְדוּ שְׁאוֹל חַיִּים כִּי־רָעוֹת יַשִּׁיא מָוֶת

17 18 I will call out to God; the LORD will save me. Evening, morning, noon I wail
19 and cry out, and He hears my voice. He redeems me unharmed from the
20 battle I wage as if many are on my side. God, enthroned as of old, will hear
and humble them – Selah – for they will never change; they will never fear
21 22 God. That man[58] lashed out at his own allies; he violated his pact. His speech
was smooth as butter, but war was in his heart; his words seemed soft as oil,
23 but they were drawn swords. Cast your burden upon the LORD, and He will
24 sustain you; He will never let the righteous be shaken, but You, God, will
plunge them down the deepest pit – men of blood, deceitful men will not
live out half their days, while I will trust in You.

56 1 *To the lead singer, on* yonat elem reḥokim[59] *– a* mikhtam[60] *of David, when the*
2 *Philistines seized him in Gat.*[61] Show me grace, God, for mortals hound me;
3 all day long my foes oppress me; all day long my oppressors trample me; so
4 5 many attack me, Exalted One! When I fear, I trust in You – in God, whose
word I praise, in God I trust; I do not fear – what can mere flesh do to me?
6 7 All day long they move me to grief; all their plans against me are evil; they
8 lie in wait, tracing my footsteps, eager to take my life. Uproot them for their
9 evil; cast down such people in Your wrath, God! You count my wanderings;
10 You store my tears in Your vial; are they not in Your records? Then, on the day
11 that I call, my enemies will retreat; this I know, for God is with me. In God,
12 whose word I praise, in the LORD, whose word I praise, in God I trust; I do
13 not fear – what can man do to me? I must fulfill my vows to You, God; I will
14 give thank offerings to You, for You have saved me from death, my feet from
stumbling, that I may walk before God in the light of life.

57 1 *To the lead singer,* al tashḥet[62] *– a* mikhtam *of David in the cave, when he was*
2 *fleeing from Sha'ul.*[63] Show me grace, God; show me grace, for in You I take
refuge. I will take refuge in the shade of Your wings until disaster has passed.
3 4 I will call on God, the Most High, to the God who grants me fulfillment. He
will send from heaven and save me; He will bring those who crush me to
5 shame – Selah. God will send His loyalty and truth. I am bounded by lions,
forced to dwell among ravenous beasts, men whose teeth are spears and
6 arrows, their tongues sharpened swords. Rise up, God, over the heavens;
7 unleash Your glory over all the earth. They rigged a net to trip me up, to entrap
8 me; they dug a pit in my path but fell into it themselves – Selah. My heart is
9 sound, God; my heart is sound – I will sing and chant praises. Stir, my soul!
10 Stir, harp and lyre! I will stir the dawn. I will praise You among the peoples,
11 Lord; I will chant Your praise among the nations, for Your loyalty is as high
12 as the heavens; Your truth reaches the skies. Rise up, God, over the heavens;
unleash Your glory over all the earth.[64]

---

58 | Referring to the duplicitous companion of verse 14.
59 | The meaning of this phrase is uncertain.
60 | See note on 16:1.
61 | Perhaps referring to 1 Samuel 21:11–16.
62 | Perhaps "do not destroy." The meaning of the phrase in this context is uncertain.
63 | See 1 Samuel, chapters 24, 26.
64 | Regarding verses 8–12, cf. 108:2–6.

יז יח בְּמִגּוֹרָם בְּקִרְבָּם׃ אֲנִי אֶל־אֱלֹהִים אֶקְרָא וַיהוָה יוֹשִׁיעֵנִי׃ עֶרֶב וָבֹקֶר
יט וְצָהֳרַיִם אָשִׂיחָה וְאֶהֱמֶה וַיִּשְׁמַע קוֹלִי׃ פָּדָה בְשָׁלוֹם נַפְשִׁי מִקְּרָב־
כ לִי כִּי־בְרַבִּים הָיוּ עִמָּדִי׃ יִשְׁמַע ׀ אֵל ׀ וְיַעֲנֵם וְיֹשֵׁב קֶדֶם סֶלָה אֲשֶׁר
כא אֵין חֲלִיפוֹת לָמוֹ וְלֹא יָרְאוּ אֱלֹהִים׃ שָׁלַח יָדָיו בִּשְׁלֹמָיו חִלֵּל בְּרִיתוֹ׃
כב חָלְקוּ ׀ מַחְמָאֹת פִּיו וּקְרָב־לִבּוֹ רַכּוּ דְבָרָיו מִשֶּׁמֶן וְהֵמָּה פְתִחוֹת׃
כג הַשְׁלֵךְ עַל־יְהוָה ׀ יְהָבְךָ וְהוּא יְכַלְכְּלֶךָ לֹא־יִתֵּן לְעוֹלָם מוֹט לַצַּדִּיק׃
כד וְאַתָּה אֱלֹהִים ׀ תּוֹרִדֵם לִבְאֵר שַׁחַת אַנְשֵׁי דָמִים וּמִרְמָה לֹא־יֶחֱצוּ
יְמֵיהֶם וַאֲנִי אֶבְטַח־בָּךְ׃

נו א לַמְנַצֵּחַ ׀ עַל־יוֹנַת אֵלֶם רְחֹקִים לְדָוִד מִכְתָּם בֶּאֱחֹז אֹתוֹ פְלִשְׁתִּים
ב ג בְּגַת׃ חָנֵּנִי אֱלֹהִים כִּי־שְׁאָפַנִי אֱנוֹשׁ כָּל־הַיּוֹם לֹחֵם יִלְחָצֵנִי׃ שָׁאֲפוּ
ד שׁוֹרְרַי כָּל־הַיּוֹם כִּי־רַבִּים לֹחֲמִים לִי מָרוֹם׃ יוֹם אִירָא אֲנִי אֵלֶיךָ
ה אֶבְטָח׃ בֵּאלֹהִים אֲהַלֵּל דְּבָרוֹ בֵּאלֹהִים בָּטַחְתִּי לֹא אִירָא מַה־
ו יַּעֲשֶׂה בָשָׂר לִי׃ כָּל־הַיּוֹם דְּבָרַי יְעַצֵּבוּ עָלַי כָּל־מַחְשְׁבֹתָם לָרָע׃
ז ח יָגוּרוּ ׀ יצפינו הֵמָּה עֲקֵבַי יִשְׁמֹרוּ כַּאֲשֶׁר קִוּוּ נַפְשִׁי׃ עַל־אָוֶן פַּלֶּט־לָמוֹ יִצְפֹּנוּ
ט בְּאַף עַמִּים ׀ הוֹרֵד אֱלֹהִים׃ נֹדִי סָפַרְתָּה אָתָּה שִׂימָה דִמְעָתִי בְנֹאדֶךָ
י הֲלֹא בְּסִפְרָתֶךָ׃ אָז ׀ יָשׁוּבוּ אוֹיְבַי אָחוֹר בְּיוֹם אֶקְרָא זֶה־יָדַעְתִּי
יא יב כִּי־אֱלֹהִים לִי׃ בֵּאלֹהִים אֲהַלֵּל דָּבָר בַּיהוָה אֲהַלֵּל דָּבָר׃ בֵּאלֹהִים
יג בָּטַחְתִּי לֹא אִירָא מַה־יַּעֲשֶׂה אָדָם לִי׃ עָלַי אֱלֹהִים נְדָרֶיךָ אֲשַׁלֵּם
יד תּוֹדֹת לָךְ׃ כִּי הִצַּלְתָּ נַפְשִׁי מִמָּוֶת הֲלֹא רַגְלַי מִדֶּחִי לְהִתְהַלֵּךְ לִפְנֵי
אֱלֹהִים בְּאוֹר הַחַיִּים׃

נז א ב לַמְנַצֵּחַ אַל־תַּשְׁחֵת לְדָוִד מִכְתָּם בְּבָרְחוֹ מִפְּנֵי־שָׁאוּל בַּמְּעָרָה׃ חָנֵּנִי
אֱלֹהִים ׀ חָנֵּנִי כִּי בְךָ חָסָיָה נַפְשִׁי וּבְצֵל־כְּנָפֶיךָ אֶחְסֶה עַד יַעֲבֹר הַוּוֹת׃
ג ד אֶקְרָא לֵאלֹהִים עֶלְיוֹן לָאֵל גֹּמֵר עָלָי׃ יִשְׁלַח מִשָּׁמַיִם ׀ וְיוֹשִׁיעֵנִי
ה חֵרֵף שֹׁאֲפִי סֶלָה יִשְׁלַח אֱלֹהִים חַסְדּוֹ וַאֲמִתּוֹ׃ נַפְשִׁי ׀ בְּתוֹךְ לְבָאִם
אֶשְׁכְּבָה לֹהֲטִים בְּנֵי־אָדָם שִׁנֵּיהֶם חֲנִית וְחִצִּים וּלְשׁוֹנָם חֶרֶב חַדָּה׃
ו ז רוּמָה עַל־הַשָּׁמַיִם אֱלֹהִים עַל כָּל־הָאָרֶץ כְּבוֹדֶךָ׃ רֶשֶׁת ׀ הֵכִינוּ
ח לִפְעָמַי כָּפַף נַפְשִׁי כָּרוּ לְפָנַי שִׁיחָה נָפְלוּ בְתוֹכָהּ סֶלָה׃ נָכוֹן לִבִּי
ט אֱלֹהִים נָכוֹן לִבִּי אָשִׁירָה וַאֲזַמֵּרָה׃ עוּרָה כְבוֹדִי עוּרָה הַנֵּבֶל וְכִנּוֹר
י יא אָעִירָה שָּׁחַר׃ אוֹדְךָ בָעַמִּים ׀ אֲדֹנָי אֲזַמֶּרְךָ בַּלְאֻמִּים׃ כִּי־גָדֹל עַד־
יב שָׁמַיִם חַסְדֶּךָ וְעַד־שְׁחָקִים אֲמִתֶּךָ׃ רוּמָה עַל־שָׁמַיִם אֱלֹהִים עַל ח
כָּל־הָאָרֶץ כְּבוֹדֶךָ׃

58 1 2 *To the lead singer,* al tashḥet – *a* mikhtam *of David.* Do you truly decree justice,
3 powerful ones? Do you judge people with equity? No, your hearts churn
4 out injustice; your hands mete out violence in the land. The wicked have
5 been wayward since birth – those liars, astray from the womb. Their venom
6 is like snake venom; they are as deaf as the cobra that stops its ears to tune
7 out the whispers of the charmer, the most skilled of enchanters. God, crush
8 the teeth in their mouths; smash the fangs of these young lions, LORD. May
they melt away like water and vanish; when they aim their arrows, let them
9 crumble like a snail dissolving as it moves, like a stillborn that never sees the
10 sun. Before your thorns harden to bramble, He will whirl them away in wild
11 fury. The righteous will rejoice at the sight of vengeance and rinse their feet
12 in the blood of the wicked. People will say, "The righteous do harvest fruit;
there is, after all, divine justice on earth."

59 1 *To the lead singer,* al tashḥet – *a* mikhtam *of David when Sha'ul sent guards to*
2 *David's house to kill him.*[65] Save me from my enemies, God; protect me from
3 those who rise against me. Save me from evildoers; deliver me from men of
4 blood, for look – they lurk in ambush – fierce men lie in wait for me for no
5 crime or offense of mine, LORD; for no fault of mine they rush at me, ready
6 to attack. Look – rouse Yourself for my sake. You, LORD God of Hosts, are
the God of Israel; stir and call all the nations to account; show no mercy to
7 evil traitors – Selah. They come out at nightfall, growling like dogs, prowling
8 about the city. See how they rant, their lips like swords, thinking, "Who can
9 hear us?" But You, LORD, mock them; You hold all the nations in contempt.
10 11 O Mighty One,[66] I watch for You, for God is my stronghold. My loyal God
12 will go out before me; God will show me my enemies' downfall. Do not kill
them lest my people forget, but send them staggering by Your force; bring
13 them down, Lord, our shield. For the sins of their mouths, for the words of
their lips, let them be trapped by their own arrogance, by the curses and lies
14 they utter. Destroy them in Your fury; destroy them until they are no more.
Then it will be known to the ends of the earth that God rules over Yaakov –
15 Selah. They come out at nightfall, growling like dogs, prowling about the
16 17 city. They stagger about, scavenging, whining when they are discontent, but
I will sing of Your might; each morning I will laud Your loving-kindness, for
18 You have been my stronghold, my haven in times of trouble. My Mighty One,
to You I will chant praise, for God is my stronghold, the God who shows
me loyalty.

60 1 2 *To the lead singer, on* shushan edut,[67] *a* mikhtam *of David, for instruction, when*
he fought against Aram Naharayim and Aram Tzova, while Yoav returned and
3 *defeated twelve thousand men of Edom in the Valley of Salt.*[68] God, You have
4 forsaken us, shattered us, shown Your anger. Now restore us! You have made

---

65 | See I Samuel 19:11.
66 | Literally "His strength"; cf. verse 18.
67 | A musical term of uncertain meaning.
68 | See II Samuel, chapter 8, and I Chronicles, chapter 18.

נח א ב לַמְנַצֵּחַ אַל־תַּשְׁחֵת לְדָוִד מִכְתָּם׃ הַאֻמְנָם אֵלֶם צֶדֶק תְּדַבֵּרוּן מֵישָׁרִים
ג תִּשְׁפְּטוּ בְּנֵי אָדָם׃ אַף־בְּלֵב עוֹלֹת תִּפְעָלוּן בָּאָרֶץ חֲמַס יְדֵיכֶם
ד ה תְּפַלֵּסוּן׃ זֹרוּ רְשָׁעִים מֵרָחֶם תָּעוּ מִבֶּטֶן דֹּבְרֵי כָזָב׃ חֲמַת־לָמוֹ
ו כִּדְמוּת חֲמַת־נָחָשׁ כְּמוֹ־פֶתֶן חֵרֵשׁ יַאְטֵם אָזְנוֹ׃ אֲשֶׁר לֹא־יִשְׁמַע
ז לְקוֹל מְלַחֲשִׁים חוֹבֵר חֲבָרִים מְחֻכָּם׃ אֱלֹהִים הֲרָס־שִׁנֵּימוֹ בְּפִימוֹ
ח מַלְתְּעוֹת כְּפִירִים נְתֹץ ׀ יְהוָה׃ יִמָּאֲסוּ כְמוֹ־מַיִם יִתְהַלְּכוּ־לָמוֹ יִדְרֹךְ
ט חִצָּו כְּמוֹ יִתְמֹלָלוּ׃ כְּמוֹ שַׁבְּלוּל תֶּמֶס יַהֲלֹךְ נֵפֶל אֵשֶׁת בַּל־חָזוּ שָׁמֶשׁ׃
י יא בְּטֶרֶם יָבִינוּ סִּירֹתֵיכֶם אָטָד כְּמוֹ־חַי כְּמוֹ־חָרוֹן יִשְׂעָרֶנּוּ׃ יִשְׂמַח צַדִּיק
יב כִּי־חָזָה נָקָם פְּעָמָיו יִרְחַץ בְּדַם הָרָשָׁע׃ וְיֹאמַר אָדָם אַךְ־פְּרִי לַצַּדִּיק
אַךְ יֵשׁ־אֱלֹהִים שֹׁפְטִים בָּאָרֶץ׃

נט א לַמְנַצֵּחַ אַל־תַּשְׁחֵת לְדָוִד מִכְתָּם בִּשְׁלֹחַ שָׁאוּל וַיִּשְׁמְרוּ אֶת־הַבַּיִת
ב ג לַהֲמִיתוֹ׃ הַצִּילֵנִי מֵאֹיְבַי ׀ אֱלֹהָי מִמִּתְקוֹמְמַי תְּשַׂגְּבֵנִי׃ הַצִּילֵנִי מִפֹּעֲלֵי
ד אָוֶן וּמֵאַנְשֵׁי דָמִים הוֹשִׁיעֵנִי׃ כִּי הִנֵּה אָרְבוּ לְנַפְשִׁי יָגוּרוּ עָלַי עַזִּים
ה לֹא־פִשְׁעִי וְלֹא־חַטָּאתִי יְהוָה׃ בְּלִי־עָוֺן יְרוּצוּן וְיִכּוֹנָנוּ עוּרָה לִקְרָאתִי
ו וּרְאֵה׃ וְאַתָּה יְהוָה־אֱלֹהִים ׀ צְבָאוֹת אֱלֹהֵי יִשְׂרָאֵל הָקִיצָה לִפְקֹד כָּל־
ז הַגּוֹיִם אַל־תָּחֹן כָּל־בֹּגְדֵי אָוֶן סֶלָה׃ יָשׁוּבוּ לָעֶרֶב יֶהֱמוּ כַכָּלֶב וִיסוֹבְבוּ
ח ט עִיר׃ הִנֵּה ׀ יַבִּיעוּן בְּפִיהֶם חֲרָבוֹת בְּשִׂפְתוֹתֵיהֶם כִּי־מִי שֹׁמֵעַ׃ וְאַתָּה
י יְהוָה תִּשְׂחַק־לָמוֹ תִּלְעַג לְכָל־גּוֹיִם׃ עֻזּוֹ אֵלֶיךָ אֶשְׁמֹרָה כִּי־אֱלֹהִים
יא יב מִשְׂגַּבִּי׃ אֱלֹהֵי חסדו יְקַדְּמֵנִי אֱלֹהִים יַרְאֵנִי בְשֹׁרְרָי׃ אַל־תַּהַרְגֵם ׀ חַסְדִּי
יג פֶּן־יִשְׁכְּחוּ עַמִּי הֲנִיעֵמוֹ בְחֵילְךָ וְהוֹרִידֵמוֹ מָגִנֵּנוּ אֲדֹנָי׃ חַטַּאת־פִּימוֹ
יד דְּבַר־שְׂפָתֵימוֹ וְיִלָּכְדוּ בִגְאוֹנָם וּמֵאָלָה וּמִכַּחַשׁ יְסַפֵּרוּ׃ כַּלֵּה בְחֵמָה
כַּלֵּה וְאֵינֵמוֹ וְיֵדְעוּ כִּי־אֱלֹהִים מֹשֵׁל בְּיַעֲקֹב לְאַפְסֵי הָאָרֶץ סֶלָה׃
טו טז וְיָשֻׁבוּ לָעֶרֶב יֶהֱמוּ כַכָּלֶב וִיסוֹבְבוּ עִיר׃ הֵמָּה ינועון לֶאֱכֹל אִם־ יְנִיעוּן
יז לֹא יִשְׂבְּעוּ וַיָּלִינוּ׃ וַאֲנִי ׀ אָשִׁיר עֻזֶּךָ וַאֲרַנֵּן לַבֹּקֶר חַסְדֶּךָ כִּי־הָיִיתָ
יח מִשְׂגָּב לִי וּמָנוֹס בְּיוֹם צַר־לִי׃ עֻזִּי אֵלֶיךָ אֲזַמֵּרָה כִּי־אֱלֹהִים מִשְׂגַּבִּי
אֱלֹהֵי חַסְדִּי׃

ס א ב לַמְנַצֵּחַ עַל־שׁוּשַׁן עֵדוּת מִכְתָּם לְדָוִד לְלַמֵּד׃ בְּהַצּוֹתוֹ ׀ אֶת אֲרַם
נַהֲרַיִם וְאֶת־אֲרַם צוֹבָה וַיָּשָׁב יוֹאָב וַיַּךְ אֶת־אֱדוֹם בְּגֵיא־מֶלַח שְׁנֵים
ג ד עָשָׂר אָלֶף׃ אֱלֹהִים זְנַחְתָּנוּ פְרַצְתָּנוּ אָנַפְתָּ תְּשׁוֹבֵב לָנוּ׃ הִרְעַשְׁתָּה

5 the land shudder and split it open; mend its cracks, for it is falling apart. You
6 have made Your people suffer; You have poured us poisoned wine, but You
have given those who revere You a waving banner beyond bowshot – Selah.
7 That Your dear ones may be rescued, let Your right hand bring victory –
8 answer me! God promised in His Sanctuary that I would triumph. I will
9 divide up Shekhem and measure out the Valley of Sukkot; Gilad and Menashe
10 will be mine; Efrayim will be my chief stronghold, Yehuda my scepter. Moav
11 will be my washbasin; at Edom I'll fling my shoe; Philistia, applaud me! But
12 who will bring me to the besieged cities? Who will lead me to Edom? Have
You not forsaken us, God? God, You no longer march out with our forces.
13 14 Come to our aid against the enemy, for human help is worthless. With God,
we will triumph valiantly, and He will trample our enemies.[69]
61 1 2 *To the lead singer, accompanied by music – of David.* Hear my plea, God; listen
3 to my prayer. From the end of the earth I call to You when my heart is faint;
4 lead me up to a rock far above me, for You have been my refuge, a tower of
5 strength against the enemy. Let me dwell in Your tent forever and take refuge
6 in the shelter of Your wings – Selah – for You, God, hear my vows. Grant
7 me the legacy of those who revere Your name. Add days to the days of the
8 king; may he live on for many generations! May he ever be seated in God's
9 presence; appoint loyalty and truth to keep him, so I will ever sing praises to
Your name, fulfilling my vows day after day.
62 1 2 *To the lead singer, for Yedutun[70] – a psalm of David.* For God alone my soul
3 waits silently; from Him is my salvation. He alone is my Rock and salvation,
4 my stronghold – I will never be shaken. How long will you come crashing
down on people, all you murderous men, like a crooked wall, a tottering fence?
5 Scheming to topple the people from their height, they relish lies; their mouths
6 bless while their insides curse – Selah. Wait for God in silence, my soul, for
7 my hope is from Him. He alone is my Rock and salvation, my stronghold – I
8 will not be shaken. My deliverance and honor rest on God, the Rock of my
9 strength; in God is my refuge. Trust in Him at all times, O people; pour out
10 your hearts before Him; God is our refuge – Selah. But people are mere
breath; humans are but an illusion; placed on a scale all together, they are
11 lighter than a breath. Place not trust in extortion or false hopes in robbery;
12 should force pay off, give it no heed. God made one pronouncement, I heard
13 these two: That power belongs to God; and that loyalty, Lord, is Yours, for
You will reward each person according to his deeds.
63 1 2 *A psalm of David, when he was in the Wilderness of Yehuda.[71]* O God, You are
my God; I seek You desperately. My soul thirsts for You; my flesh longs for
3 You in a parched and weary land that has no water, so I have visions of You in
4 the Sanctuary of Your might and glory. Your loving-kindness is better than
5 life, so my lips praise You, so I will bless You as long as I live, as I lift up my
6 hands in Your name. My soul will be nourished as with a rich feast; my mouth

---

69 | Cf. 108:7–14.

70 | See note on 39:1.

71 | See 1 Samuel 23:14.

ה אֶרֶץ פִּצַמְתָּהּ רְפָה שְׁבָרֶיהָ כִי־מָטָה׃ הִרְאִיתָ עַמְּךָ קָשָׁה הִשְׁקִיתָנוּ
ו ז יַיִן תַּרְעֵלָה׃ נָתַתָּה לִּירֵאֶיךָ נֵּס לְהִתְנוֹסֵס מִפְּנֵי קֹשֶׁט סֶלָה׃ לְמַעַן
ח יֵחָלְצוּן יְדִידֶיךָ הוֹשִׁיעָה יְמִינְךָ ועננו׃ אֱלֹהִים ׀ דִּבֶּר בְּקָדְשׁוֹ אֶעְלֹזָה וַעֲנֵנִי
ט אֲחַלְּקָה שְׁכֶם וְעֵמֶק סֻכּוֹת אֲמַדֵּד׃ לִי גִלְעָד ׀ וְלִי מְנַשֶּׁה וְאֶפְרַיִם
י מָעוֹז רֹאשִׁי יְהוּדָה מְחֹקְקִי׃ מוֹאָב ׀ סִיר רַחְצִי עַל־אֱדוֹם אַשְׁלִיךְ
יא נַעֲלִי עָלַי פְּלֶשֶׁת הִתְרוֹעָעִי׃ מִי יֹבִלֵנִי עִיר מָצוֹר מִי נָחַנִי עַד־
יב אֱדוֹם׃ הֲלֹא־אַתָּה אֱלֹהִים זְנַחְתָּנוּ וְלֹא־תֵצֵא אֱלֹהִים בְּצִבְאוֹתֵינוּ׃
יג יד הָבָה־לָּנוּ עֶזְרָת מִצָּר וְשָׁוְא תְּשׁוּעַת אָדָם׃ בֵּאלֹהִים נַעֲשֶׂה־חָיִל
וְהוּא יָבוּס צָרֵינוּ׃

סא א ב לַמְנַצֵּחַ ׀ עַל־נְגִינַת לְדָוִד׃ שִׁמְעָה אֱלֹהִים רִנָּתִי הַקְשִׁיבָה תְּפִלָּתִי׃
ג מִקְצֵה הָאָרֶץ ׀ אֵלֶיךָ אֶקְרָא בַּעֲטֹף לִבִּי בְּצוּר־יָרוּם מִמֶּנִּי תַנְחֵנִי׃
ד ה כִּי־הָיִיתָ מַחְסֶה לִי מִגְדַּל־עֹז מִפְּנֵי אוֹיֵב׃ אָגוּרָה בְאָהָלְךָ עוֹלָמִים
ו אֶחֱסֶה בְסֵתֶר כְּנָפֶיךָ סֶּלָה׃ כִּי־אַתָּה אֱלֹהִים שָׁמַעְתָּ לִנְדָרָי נָתַתָּ
ז יְרֻשַּׁת יִרְאֵי שְׁמֶךָ׃ יָמִים עַל־יְמֵי־מֶלֶךְ תּוֹסִיף שְׁנוֹתָיו כְּמוֹ־דֹר וָדֹר׃
ח ט יֵשֵׁב עוֹלָם לִפְנֵי אֱלֹהִים חֶסֶד וֶאֱמֶת מַן יִנְצְרֻהוּ׃ כֵּן אֲזַמְּרָה שִׁמְךָ
לָעַד לְשַׁלְּמִי נְדָרַי יוֹם ׀ יוֹם׃

סב א ב לַמְנַצֵּחַ עַל־יְדוּתוּן מִזְמוֹר לְדָוִד׃ אַךְ אֶל־אֱלֹהִים דּוּמִיָּה נַפְשִׁי
ג מִמֶּנּוּ יְשׁוּעָתִי׃ אַךְ־הוּא צוּרִי וִישׁוּעָתִי מִשְׂגַּבִּי לֹא־אֶמּוֹט רַבָּה׃
ד עַד־אָנָה ׀ תְּהוֹתְתוּ עַל־אִישׁ תְּרָצְּחוּ כֻלְּכֶם כְּקִיר נָטוּי גָּדֵר הַדְּחוּיָה׃
ה אַךְ מִשְּׂאֵתוֹ ׀ יָעֲצוּ לְהַדִּיחַ יִרְצוּ כָזָב בְּפִיו יְבָרֵכוּ וּבְקִרְבָּם יְקַלְלוּ־סֶלָה׃
ו ז אַךְ לֵאלֹהִים דּוֹמִּי נַפְשִׁי כִּי־מִמֶּנּוּ תִּקְוָתִי׃ אַךְ־הוּא צוּרִי וִישׁוּעָתִי
ח מִשְׂגַּבִּי לֹא אֶמּוֹט׃ עַל־אֱלֹהִים יִשְׁעִי וּכְבוֹדִי צוּר־עֻזִּי מַחְסִי בֵּאלֹהִים׃
ט בִּטְחוּ בוֹ בְכָל־עֵת ׀ עָם שִׁפְכוּ־לְפָנָיו לְבַבְכֶם אֱלֹהִים מַחֲסֶה־לָּנוּ סֶלָה׃
י אַךְ ׀ הֶבֶל בְּנֵי־אָדָם כָּזָב בְּנֵי אִישׁ בְּמֹאזְנַיִם לַעֲלוֹת הֵמָּה מֵהֶבֶל יָחַד׃
יא אַל־תִּבְטְחוּ בְעֹשֶׁק וּבְגָזֵל אַל־תֶּהְבָּלוּ חַיִל ׀ כִּי־יָנוּב אַל־תָּשִׁיתוּ
יב יג לֵב׃ אַחַת ׀ דִּבֶּר אֱלֹהִים שְׁתַּיִם־זוּ שָׁמָעְתִּי כִּי עֹז לֵאלֹהִים׃ וּלְךָ־אֲדֹנָי
חָסֶד כִּי־אַתָּה תְשַׁלֵּם לְאִישׁ כְּמַעֲשֵׂהוּ׃

סג א ב מִזְמוֹר לְדָוִד בִּהְיוֹתוֹ בְּמִדְבַּר יְהוּדָה׃ אֱלֹהִים ׀ אֵלִי אַתָּה אֲשַׁחֲרֶךָּ
ג צָמְאָה לְךָ ׀ נַפְשִׁי כָּמַהּ לְךָ בְשָׂרִי בְּאֶרֶץ־צִיָּה וְעָיֵף בְּלִי־מָיִם׃ כֵּן בַּקֹּדֶשׁ
ד חֲזִיתִךָ לִרְאוֹת עֻזְּךָ וּכְבוֹדֶךָ׃ כִּי־טוֹב חַסְדְּךָ מֵחַיִּים שְׂפָתַי יְשַׁבְּחוּנְךָ׃
ה ו כֵּן אֲבָרֶכְךָ בְחַיָּי בְּשִׁמְךָ אֶשָּׂא כַפָּי׃ כְּמוֹ חֵלֶב וָדֶשֶׁן תִּשְׂבַּע נַפְשִׁי

7 will sing praises with joyful lips. I think of You upon my bed; I contemplate
8 You in the vigil of night, for You have been my help, and I revel in the shade
9 10 of Your wings. My soul clings to You; Your right hand supports me. As for
those who seek to destroy my life, may they reach the lowest depths of the
11 12 earth. May the sword spill their blood; may they be the prey of foxes, but the
king will rejoice in God; all who swear by Him will glory, while the mouths
of liars will be stopped up.

64 1 2 *To the lead singer – a psalm of David.* Hear my voice, God, in my lament; keep
3 my life from the terror of the enemy. Hide me from the band of wicked men,
4 from the riotous mob of evildoers who sharpen their tongues like swords,
5 who aim bitter words like arrows and shoot from ambush at the blameless,
6 shooting suddenly, without fear. They arm themselves with evil schemes;
7 they plot to lay secret snares, thinking, "Who can see them?" They seek out
vile crimes, exhausting every possible plan in the depths of the human mind
8 and heart, but God will shoot them down; with a sudden arrow they will be
9 wounded; their own tongues will trip them up, and all who see them will
10 shudder. Then all people will be struck with fear; they will tell of God's works
11 and contemplate His deeds. The righteous will rejoice in the Lord and take
refuge in Him; all the upright of heart will exult.

65 1 2 *To the lead singer, a psalm – a song of David.* Praise awaits You in Zion, God;
3 4 to You vows are paid. Hearer of prayer, to You all flesh will come. When acts
5 of sin overwhelm me, You forgive our transgressions. Happy are those whom
You choose, those You bring close to dwell in Your courtyards. May we be
6 sated with the goodness of Your House, Your holy Sanctuary. Answer us with
wondrous deeds in Your righteousness, O God, our savior – hope of all the
7 ends of the earth and the distant seas, who set down the mountains in His
8 power, so girded in strength is He; who stills the roaring seas, the roaring of
9 the waves, the clamor of the nations. Those who live at the ends of the earth
are awed by Your signs. The lands of sunrise and sunset You move to joyful
10 song. You care for the land and water it and make it very rich, with God-given
streams brimming with water; You provide the people's grain – thus You have
11 arranged it all. Water its furrows; level its ridges; soften it with showers; bless
12 its growth. You have crowned the year with Your goodness; Your pathways
13 overflow with richness. The wild pasturelands overflow; the hills are girded
14 with joy. The meadows are clothed with sheep; the valleys are decked with
grain – they shout for joy; they burst into song.

66 1 2 *To the lead singer, a song – a psalm.* Shout for joy to God, all the earth; sing the
3 glory of His name; laud Him with glorious praise. Proclaim to God, "How
wondrous are Your deeds! In Your sheer strength, Your enemies come cringing
4 before You." All the earth bows down before You and sings to You, singing to
5 Your name – Selah. Come, see the works of God, the acts that move humanity
6 to awe. He turned sea to dry land; they crossed the river on foot – there we
7 rejoiced in Him. He rules over the world in His might, His eyes keeping watch
8 over the nations so that the rebellious will not rise up – Selah. Bless our God,
9 O you peoples; let His praise resound. He keeps us among the living, never

ז וְשִׂפְתֵי רְנָנוֹת יְהַלֶּל־פִּי: אִם־זְכַרְתִּיךָ עַל־יְצוּעָי בְּאַשְׁמֻרוֹת אֶהְגֶּה־
ח ט בָךְ: כִּי־הָיִיתָ עֶזְרָתָה לִּי וּבְצֵל כְּנָפֶיךָ אֲרַנֵּן: דָּבְקָה נַפְשִׁי אַחֲרֶיךָ בִּי
י תָּמְכָה יְמִינֶךָ: וְהֵמָּה לְשׁוֹאָה יְבַקְשׁוּ נַפְשִׁי יָבֹאוּ בְּתַחְתִּיּוֹת הָאָרֶץ:
יא יב יַגִּירֻהוּ עַל־יְדֵי־חָרֶב מְנָת שֻׁעָלִים יִהְיוּ: וְהַמֶּלֶךְ יִשְׂמַח בֵּאלֹהִים
יִתְהַלֵּל כָּל־הַנִּשְׁבָּע בּוֹ כִּי יִסָּכֵר פִּי דוֹבְרֵי־שָׁקֶר:

סד א ב לַמְנַצֵּחַ מִזְמוֹר לְדָוִד: שְׁמַע־אֱלֹהִים קוֹלִי בְשִׂיחִי מִפַּחַד אוֹיֵב תִּצֹּר
ג ד חַיָּי: תַּסְתִּירֵנִי מִסּוֹד מְרֵעִים מֵרִגְשַׁת פֹּעֲלֵי אָוֶן: אֲשֶׁר שָׁנְנוּ כַחֶרֶב
ה לְשׁוֹנָם דָּרְכוּ חִצָּם דָּבָר מָר: לִירוֹת בַּמִּסְתָּרִים תָּם פִּתְאֹם יֹרֻהוּ וְלֹא
ו יִירָאוּ: יְחַזְּקוּ־לָמוֹ ׀ דָּבָר רָע יְסַפְּרוּ לִטְמוֹן מוֹקְשִׁים אָמְרוּ מִי יִרְאֶה־
ז ח לָּמוֹ: יַחְפְּשׂוּ־עוֹלֹת תַּמְנוּ חֵפֶשׂ מְחֻפָּשׂ וְקֶרֶב אִישׁ וְלֵב עָמֹק: וַיֹּרֵם
ט אֱלֹהִים חֵץ פִּתְאוֹם הָיוּ מַכּוֹתָם: וַיַּכְשִׁילֻהוּ עָלֵימוֹ לְשׁוֹנָם יִתְנֹדְדוּ
י כָּל־רֹאֵה בָם: וַיִּירְאוּ כָּל־אָדָם וַיַּגִּידוּ פֹּעַל אֱלֹהִים וּמַעֲשֵׂהוּ הִשְׂכִּילוּ:
יא יִשְׂמַח צַדִּיק בַּיהוָה וְחָסָה בוֹ וְיִתְהַלְלוּ כָּל־יִשְׁרֵי־לֵב:

סה א ב לַמְנַצֵּחַ מִזְמוֹר לְדָוִד שִׁיר: לְךָ דֻמִיָּה תְהִלָּה אֱלֹהִים בְּצִיּוֹן וּלְךָ יְשֻׁלַּם־
ג ד נֶדֶר: שֹׁמֵעַ תְּפִלָּה עָדֶיךָ כָּל־בָּשָׂר יָבֹאוּ: דִּבְרֵי עֲוֹנֹת גָּבְרוּ מֶנִּי פְּשָׁעֵינוּ
ה אַתָּה תְכַפְּרֵם: אַשְׁרֵי ׀ תִּבְחַר וּתְקָרֵב יִשְׁכֹּן חֲצֵרֶיךָ נִשְׂבְּעָה בְּטוּב
ו בֵּיתֶךָ קְדֹשׁ הֵיכָלֶךָ: נוֹרָאוֹת ׀ בְּצֶדֶק תַּעֲנֵנוּ אֱלֹהֵי יִשְׁעֵנוּ מִבְטָח כָּל־
ז ח קַצְוֵי־אֶרֶץ וְיָם רְחֹקִים: מֵכִין הָרִים בְּכֹחוֹ נֶאְזָר בִּגְבוּרָה: מַשְׁבִּיחַ ׀
ט שְׁאוֹן יַמִּים שְׁאוֹן גַּלֵּיהֶם וַהֲמוֹן לְאֻמִּים: וַיִּירְאוּ ׀ יֹשְׁבֵי קְצָוֺת מֵאוֹתֹתֶיךָ
י מוֹצָאֵי־בֹקֶר וָעֶרֶב תַּרְנִין: פָּקַדְתָּ הָאָרֶץ ׀ וַתְּשֹׁקְקֶהָ רַבַּת תַּעְשְׁרֶנָּה
יא פֶּלֶג אֱלֹהִים מָלֵא מָיִם תָּכִין דְּגָנָם כִּי־כֵן תְּכִינֶהָ: תְּלָמֶיהָ רַוֵּה נַחֵת
יב גְּדוּדֶהָ בִּרְבִיבִים תְּמֹגְגֶנָּה צִמְחָהּ תְּבָרֵךְ: עִטַּרְתָּ שְׁנַת טוֹבָתֶךָ וּמַעְגָּלֶיךָ
יג יד יִרְעֲפוּן דָּשֶׁן: יִרְעֲפוּ נְאוֹת מִדְבָּר וְגִיל גְּבָעוֹת תַּחְגֹּרְנָה: לָבְשׁוּ כָרִים ׀
הַצֹּאן וַעֲמָקִים יַעַטְפוּ־בָר יִתְרוֹעֲעוּ אַף־יָשִׁירוּ:

סו א ב לַמְנַצֵּחַ שִׁיר מִזְמוֹר הָרִיעוּ לֵאלֹהִים כָּל־הָאָרֶץ: זַמְּרוּ כְבוֹד־שְׁמוֹ
ג שִׂימוּ כָבוֹד תְּהִלָּתוֹ: אִמְרוּ לֵאלֹהִים מַה־נּוֹרָא מַעֲשֶׂיךָ בְּרֹב עֻזְּךָ
ד יְכַחֲשׁוּ לְךָ אֹיְבֶיךָ: כָּל־הָאָרֶץ ׀ יִשְׁתַּחֲווּ לְךָ וִיזַמְּרוּ־לָךְ יְזַמְּרוּ שִׁמְךָ
ה ו סֶלָה: לְכוּ וּרְאוּ מִפְעֲלוֹת אֱלֹהִים נוֹרָא עֲלִילָה עַל־בְּנֵי אָדָם: הָפַךְ
ז יָם ׀ לְיַבָּשָׁה בַּנָּהָר יַעַבְרוּ בְרָגֶל שָׁם נִשְׂמְחָה־בּוֹ: מֹשֵׁל בִּגְבוּרָתוֹ ׀
ח עוֹלָם עֵינָיו בַּגּוֹיִם תִּצְפֶּינָה הַסּוֹרְרִים ׀ אַל־יָרִימוּ לָמוֹ סֶלָה: בָּרְכוּ יָרוּמוּ
ט עַמִּים ׀ אֱלֹהֵינוּ וְהַשְׁמִיעוּ קוֹל תְּהִלָּתוֹ: הַשָּׂם נַפְשֵׁנוּ בַּחַיִּים וְלֹא־נָתַן

10 letting our feet slip. For You, God, have tested us, refining us as silver is refined:
11 12 You led us into a trap, placing shackles around our waists; You let people ride
over us; we have been through fire and water, but You brought us out to
13 freedom. I will enter Your House with burnt offerings; to You I will honor my
14 15 vows – those that crossed my lips, that my mouth uttered in my distress. Fat
burnt offerings I will offer up to You, the rich aroma of roasting rams; I will
16 prepare bulls and he-goats – Selah. Come, listen, all you who fear God; I will
17 tell of what He did for me. My mouth called out to Him, high praise upon
18 19 my tongue; had evil been in my heart, the Lord would not have listened, but
20 God did listen – He paid heed to my prayer. Blessed is God, who has not
turned away my prayer, nor His loyalty from me.

67 1 2 *To the lead singer, accompanied by stringed instruments – a psalm, a song.* May
God be gracious to us and bless us. May He shine His face upon us[72] – Selah.
3 Then will Your way be known on earth, Your salvation among all the nations.
4 5 Let the peoples praise You, God; let all peoples praise You. Let nations rejoice
and sing for joy, for You judge the peoples justly and guide the nations of the
6 7 earth – Selah. Let the peoples praise You, God; let all peoples praise You. The
8 earth has yielded its harvest; may God, our God, bless us. God will bless us,
and all will revere Him to the ends of the earth.

68 1 2 *To the lead singer, of David – a psalm, a song.* Let God arise and His enemies
3 be scattered; let His foes flee before Him.[73] As smoke disperses, disperse
4 them; as wax melts before fire, may the wicked perish before God, while the
5 righteous rejoice and exult before God, delighted and joyful. Sing to God;
sing praises to His name. Laud Him who rides the clouds – the LORD is His
6 name – and exult before Him. Father of orphans, judge of widows, God is
7 in His holy abode. God brings the lonely back home and sets captives free,
8 to their delight, but the rebellious must dwell in a parched wasteland. O
God, when You went out before Your people, when You strode through the
9 wilderness – Selah – the earth shook; the heavens, too, poured down before
10 God, Sinai itself before God, God of Israel![74] You, God, unleashed a lavish
11 rain, reviving Your weary heritage. Your own flock settled there; in Your
12 goodness, God, You provided for the lowly. The Lord made His decree; a
13 great host of women spread the news: "Kings with their armies are fleeing,
14 fleeing, while housewives share out the spoil." Even for those of you who lie
among the sheepfolds, the wings of the dove are inlaid with silver, her pinions
15 with glittering gold. When Shaddai scattered the kings there, it was like
16 snow falling on Tzalmon.[75] O mighty mountain, Mount Bashan,[76] O Mount
17 Bashan of many peaks, why do you glare so, O many-peaked mountains, at
the mountain God desires for His abode? Yes, the LORD will dwell there

---

72 | Cf. the priestly blessing in Numbers 6:24–26.

73 | Cf. Numbers 10:35.

74 | Cf. Judges 5:4–5.

75 | Perhaps a mountain in the vicinity of Shekhem mentioned in Judges 9:48.

76 | Located in the northern Transjordan region.

י יא לַמּוֹט רַגְלֵנוּ: כִּי־בְחַנְתָּנוּ אֱלֹהִים צְרַפְתָּנוּ כִּצְרָף־כָּסֶף: הֲבֵאתָנוּ
יב בַמְּצוּדָה שַׂמְתָּ מוּעָקָה בְמָתְנֵינוּ: הִרְכַּבְתָּ אֱנוֹשׁ לְרֹאשֵׁנוּ בָּאנוּ־בָאֵשׁ
יג וּבַמַּיִם וַתּוֹצִיאֵנוּ לָרְוָיָה: אָבוֹא בֵיתְךָ בְעוֹלוֹת אֲשַׁלֵּם לְךָ נְדָרָי:
יד טו אֲשֶׁר־פָּצוּ שְׂפָתָי וְדִבֶּר־פִּי בַּצַּר־לִי: עֹלוֹת מֵחִים אַעֲלֶה־לָּךְ עִם־
טז קְטֹרֶת אֵילִים אֶעֱשֶׂה בָקָר עִם־עַתּוּדִים סֶלָה: לְכוּ־שִׁמְעוּ וַאֲסַפְּרָה
יז כָּל־יִרְאֵי אֱלֹהִים אֲשֶׁר עָשָׂה לְנַפְשִׁי: אֵלָיו פִּי־קָרָאתִי וְרוֹמַם תַּחַת
יח יט לְשׁוֹנִי: אָוֶן אִם־רָאִיתִי בְלִבִּי לֹא יִשְׁמַע | אֲדֹנָי: אָכֵן שָׁמַע אֱלֹהִים
כ הִקְשִׁיב בְּקוֹל תְּפִלָּתִי: בָּרוּךְ אֱלֹהִים אֲשֶׁר לֹא־הֵסִיר תְּפִלָּתִי וְחַסְדּוֹ
מֵאִתִּי:

סז א ב לַמְנַצֵּחַ בִּנְגִינֹת מִזְמוֹר שִׁיר: אֱלֹהִים יְחָנֵּנוּ וִיבָרְכֵנוּ יָאֵר פָּנָיו אִתָּנוּ
ג ד סֶלָה: לָדַעַת בָּאָרֶץ דַּרְכֶּךָ בְּכָל־גּוֹיִם יְשׁוּעָתֶךָ: יוֹדוּךָ עַמִּים | אֱלֹהִים
ה יוֹדוּךָ עַמִּים כֻּלָּם: יִשְׂמְחוּ וִירַנְּנוּ לְאֻמִּים כִּי־תִשְׁפֹּט עַמִּים מִישׁוֹר
ו וּלְאֻמִּים | בָּאָרֶץ תַּנְחֵם סֶלָה: יוֹדוּךָ עַמִּים | אֱלֹהִים יוֹדוּךָ עַמִּים כֻּלָּם:
ז ח אֶרֶץ נָתְנָה יְבוּלָהּ יְבָרְכֵנוּ אֱלֹהִים אֱלֹהֵינוּ: יְבָרְכֵנוּ אֱלֹהִים וְיִירְאוּ ט
אוֹתוֹ כָּל־אַפְסֵי־אָרֶץ:

סח א ב לַמְנַצֵּחַ לְדָוִד מִזְמוֹר שִׁיר: יָקוּם אֱלֹהִים יָפוּצוּ אוֹיְבָיו וְיָנוּסוּ מְשַׂנְאָיו
ג מִפָּנָיו: כְּהִנְדֹּף עָשָׁן תִּנְדֹּף כְּהִמֵּס דּוֹנַג מִפְּנֵי־אֵשׁ יֹאבְדוּ רְשָׁעִים מִפְּנֵי
ד ה אֱלֹהִים: וְצַדִּיקִים יִשְׂמְחוּ יַעַלְצוּ לִפְנֵי אֱלֹהִים וְיָשִׂישׂוּ בְשִׂמְחָה: שִׁירוּ |
ו לֵאלֹהִים זַמְּרוּ שְׁמוֹ סֹלּוּ לָרֹכֵב בָּעֲרָבוֹת בְּיָהּ שְׁמוֹ וְעִלְזוּ לְפָנָיו: אֲבִי
ז יְתוֹמִים וְדַיַּן אַלְמָנוֹת אֱלֹהִים בִּמְעוֹן קָדְשׁוֹ: אֱלֹהִים | מוֹשִׁיב יְחִידִים |
ח בַּיְתָה מוֹצִיא אֲסִירִים בַּכּוֹשָׁרוֹת אַךְ סוֹרְרִים שָׁכְנוּ צְחִיחָה: אֱלֹהִים
ט בְּצֵאתְךָ לִפְנֵי עַמֶּךָ בְּצַעְדְּךָ בִישִׁימוֹן סֶלָה: אֶרֶץ רָעָשָׁה | אַף־שָׁמַיִם
י נָטְפוּ מִפְּנֵי אֱלֹהִים זֶה סִינַי מִפְּנֵי אֱלֹהִים אֱלֹהֵי יִשְׂרָאֵל: גֶּשֶׁם נְדָבוֹת
יא תָּנִיף אֱלֹהִים נַחֲלָתְךָ וְנִלְאָה אַתָּה כוֹנַנְתָּהּ: חַיָּתְךָ יָשְׁבוּ־בָהּ תָּכִין
יב יג בְּטוֹבָתְךָ לֶעָנִי אֱלֹהִים: אֲדֹנָי יִתֶּן־אֹמֶר הַמְבַשְּׂרוֹת צָבָא רָב: מַלְכֵי
יד צְבָאוֹת יִדֹּדוּן יִדֹּדוּן וּנְוַת־בַּיִת תְּחַלֵּק שָׁלָל: אִם־תִּשְׁכְּבוּן בֵּין שְׁפַתָּיִם
טו כַּנְפֵי יוֹנָה נֶחְפָּה בַכֶּסֶף וְאֶבְרוֹתֶיהָ בִּירַקְרַק חָרוּץ: בְּפָרֵשׂ שַׁדַּי מְלָכִים
טז יז בָּהּ תַּשְׁלֵג בְּצַלְמוֹן: הַר־אֱלֹהִים הַר־בָּשָׁן הַר גַּבְנֻנִּים הַר־בָּשָׁן: לָמָּה |
תְּרַצְּדוּן הָרִים גַּבְנֻנִּים הָהָר חָמַד אֱלֹהִים לְשִׁבְתּוֹ אַף־יְהוָה יִשְׁכֹּן

18 forever. God's chariots are many myriads, thousands upon thousands; the
19 Lord is among them as at Sinai in holiness. You ascended the heights and
carried off captives; You received tributes from people, even from those
20 rebellious against the LORD God's dwelling there. Blessed be the Lord, who
21 bears our burdens every day; God is our salvation – Selah. Our God is for us
22 a saving God; God, the LORD, provides an escape from death, but God will
crush the heads of His enemies, the hairy scalps of those who walk about in
23 guilt. The Lord decreed, "I will bring them back from Bashan; I will bring
24 them back from the depths of the sea, so that your feet may wade through
blood, so that the tongues of your dogs may take their share of the enemy."
25 They saw Your processions, God, the processions of my God, of my King,
26 into the Sanctuary. First came the singers; next came the musicians amid
27 the girls playing tambourines. Bless God in chorus, the Lord, you of Israel's
28 fountain! There young Binyamin leads them, the princes of Yehuda in their
29 throngs, princes of Zevulun, princes of Naftali. Your God has commanded
30 your might, the might, God, that You have shown us! For Your Temple over
31 Jerusalem, kings will come to You bearing gifts. Tame the beast of the marsh,
the herd of fierce bulls, of feisty young calves, the peoples; until they come
32 cringing with pieces of silver, scatter the peoples who delight in battle. Let the
33 nobles of Egypt come; let Kush swiftly reach out its hands to God. Kingdoms
34 of earth, sing to God; sing praise to the Lord – Selah. To Him who rides the
35 highest heavens of old, listen! His voice rings out with might. Ascribe might
36 to God, whose majesty is over Israel, whose might fills the skies. Your awe,
God, emanates from Your Sanctuaries, It is Israel's God who gives might and
power to the people. Blessed is God!

69 1 2 *To the lead singer, set to* shoshanim[77] – *of David*. Save me, God, for the waters
3 have reached my neck; I am drowning in the mire of the deep with nowhere
to stand; I have reached the watery depths, and the current has swept me
4 away. I am weary from calling out; my throat is hoarse; my eyes are dim from
5 searching for my God. There are more who hate me without cause than there
are hairs on my head, so many treacherous foes who long to destroy me. Must
6 I return what I have not stolen? God, You know my folly; my guilt is not
7 hidden from You. Let not those who hope for You be shamed through me,
Lord GOD of Hosts; let not those who seek You be disgraced through me,
8 God of Israel. For Your sake I bear taunting; my face is draped in disgrace.
9 I have become a stranger to my brothers, an alien to my mother's children,
10 for fervor for Your House has destroyed me; the taunts of Your taunters have
11 12 fallen on me. When I wept and fasted, I was taunted for it; when I clothed
13 myself in sackcloth, I became a cautionary tale for them. Loiterers at the gate
14 gossip about me; drunkards sing about me, but as for me, may my prayer
come to You, LORD, in a moment of favor. God, in Your great loyalty, answer
15 me with Your true salvation. Save me from drowning in the mud; let me be
16 saved from my haters, from the watery depths. Do not let me be swept away
in the current or swallowed by the deep; do not let the Pit close its mouth

77 | See note on 45:1.

יח יט לָנֶצַח: רֶכֶב אֱלֹהִים רִבֹּתַיִם אַלְפֵי שִׁנְאָן אֲדֹנָי בָם סִינַי בַּקֹּדֶשׁ: עָלִיתָ
לַמָּרוֹם ׀ שָׁבִיתָ שֶּׁבִי לָקַחְתָּ מַתָּנוֹת בָּאָדָם וְאַף סוֹרְרִים לִשְׁכֹּן ׀ יָהּ
כ כא אֱלֹהִים: בָּרוּךְ אֲדֹנָי יוֹם ׀ יוֹם יַעֲמָס־לָנוּ הָאֵל יְשׁוּעָתֵנוּ סֶלָה: הָאֵל ׀
כב לָנוּ אֵל לְמוֹשָׁעוֹת וְלֵיהוִה אֲדֹנָי לַמָּוֶת תּוֹצָאוֹת: אַךְ־אֱלֹהִים יִמְחַץ
כג רֹאשׁ אֹיְבָיו קָדְקֹד שֵׂעָר מִתְהַלֵּךְ בַּאֲשָׁמָיו: אָמַר אֲדֹנָי מִבָּשָׁן אָשִׁיב
כד אָשִׁיב מִמְּצֻלוֹת יָם: לְמַעַן ׀ תִּמְחַץ רַגְלְךָ בְּדָם לְשׁוֹן כְּלָבֶיךָ מֵאֹיְבִים
כה כו מִנֵּהוּ: רָאוּ הֲלִיכוֹתֶיךָ אֱלֹהִים הֲלִיכוֹת אֵלִי מַלְכִּי בַקֹּדֶשׁ: קִדְּמוּ
כז שָׁרִים אַחַר נֹגְנִים בְּתוֹךְ עֲלָמוֹת תּוֹפֵפוֹת: בְּמַקְהֵלוֹת בָּרְכוּ אֱלֹהִים
כח אֲדֹנָי מִמְּקוֹר יִשְׂרָאֵל: שָׁם בִּנְיָמִן ׀ צָעִיר רֹדֵם שָׂרֵי יְהוּדָה רִגְמָתָם
כט שָׂרֵי זְבֻלוּן שָׂרֵי נַפְתָּלִי: צִוָּה אֱלֹהֶיךָ עֻזֶּךָ עוּזָּה אֱלֹהִים זוּ פָּעַלְתָּ לָּנוּ:
ל לא מֵהֵיכָלֶךָ עַל־יְרוּשָׁלִָם לְךָ יוֹבִילוּ מְלָכִים שָׁי: גְּעַר חַיַּת קָנֶה עֲדַת
אַבִּירִים ׀ בְּעֶגְלֵי עַמִּים מִתְרַפֵּס בְּרַצֵּי־כָסֶף בִּזַּר עַמִּים קְרָבוֹת יֶחְפָּצוּ:
לב לג יֶאֱתָיוּ חַשְׁמַנִּים מִנִּי מִצְרָיִם כּוּשׁ תָּרִיץ יָדָיו לֵאלֹהִים: מַמְלְכוֹת הָאָרֶץ
לד שִׁירוּ לֵאלֹהִים זַמְּרוּ אֲדֹנָי סֶלָה: לָרֹכֵב בִּשְׁמֵי שְׁמֵי־קֶדֶם הֵן יִתֵּן
לה בְּקוֹלוֹ קוֹל עֹז: תְּנוּ עֹז לֵאלֹהִים עַל־יִשְׂרָאֵל גַּאֲוָתוֹ וְעֻזּוֹ בַּשְּׁחָקִים:
לו נוֹרָא אֱלֹהִים ׀ מִמִּקְדָּשֶׁיךָ אֵל יִשְׂרָאֵל הוּא נֹתֵן ׀ עֹז וְתַעֲצֻמוֹת לָעָם
בָּרוּךְ אֱלֹהִים:

סט א ב לַמְנַצֵּחַ עַל־שׁוֹשַׁנִּים לְדָוִד: הוֹשִׁיעֵנִי אֱלֹהִים כִּי בָאוּ מַיִם עַד־נָפֶשׁ:
ג טָבַעְתִּי ׀ בִּיוֵן מְצוּלָה וְאֵין מָעֳמָד בָּאתִי בְמַעֲמַקֵּי־מַיִם וְשִׁבֹּלֶת
ד ה שְׁטָפָתְנִי: יָגַעְתִּי בְקָרְאִי נִחַר גְּרוֹנִי כָּלוּ עֵינַי מְיַחֵל לֵאלֹהָי: רַבּוּ ׀
מִשַּׂעֲרוֹת רֹאשִׁי שֹׂנְאַי חִנָּם עָצְמוּ מַצְמִיתַי אֹיְבַי שֶׁקֶר אֲשֶׁר לֹא־גָזַלְתִּי
ו אָז אָשִׁיב: אֱלֹהִים אַתָּה יָדַעְתָּ לְאִוַּלְתִּי וְאַשְׁמוֹתַי מִמְּךָ לֹא־נִכְחָדוּ:
ז אַל־יֵבֹשׁוּ בִי ׀ קֹוֶיךָ אֲדֹנָי יֱהֹוִה צְבָאוֹת אַל־יִכָּלְמוּ בִי מְבַקְשֶׁיךָ אֱלֹהֵי
ח ט יִשְׂרָאֵל: כִּי־עָלֶיךָ נָשָׂאתִי חֶרְפָּה כִּסְּתָה כְלִמָּה פָנָי: מוּזָר הָיִיתִי לְאֶחָי
י וְנָכְרִי לִבְנֵי אִמִּי: כִּי־קִנְאַת בֵּיתְךָ אֲכָלָתְנִי וְחֶרְפּוֹת חוֹרְפֶיךָ נָפְלוּ
יא יב עָלָי: וָאֶבְכֶּה בַצּוֹם נַפְשִׁי וַתְּהִי לַחֲרָפוֹת לִי: וָאֶתְּנָה לְבוּשִׁי שָׂק
יג יד וָאֱהִי לָהֶם לְמָשָׁל: יָשִׂיחוּ בִי יֹשְׁבֵי שָׁעַר וּנְגִינוֹת שׁוֹתֵי שֵׁכָר: וַאֲנִי
תְפִלָּתִי־לְךָ ׀ יְהוָה עֵת רָצוֹן אֱלֹהִים בְּרָב־חַסְדֶּךָ עֲנֵנִי בֶּאֱמֶת יִשְׁעֶךָ:
טו טז הַצִּילֵנִי מִטִּיט וְאַל־אֶטְבָּעָה אִנָּצְלָה מִשֹּׂנְאַי וּמִמַּעֲמַקֵּי־מָיִם: אַל־
תִּשְׁטְפֵנִי ׀ שִׁבֹּלֶת מַיִם וְאַל־תִּבְלָעֵנִי מְצוּלָה וְאַל־תֶּאְטַר־עָלַי בְּאֵר

17 over me. Answer me, LORD, in Your good loyalty; turn to me in Your great
18 compassion. Do not hide Your face from Your servant, for I am in danger –
19 hurry, answer me! Draw near to me; redeem me; free me from my enemies.
20 You know of how I am taunted, of my shame and disgrace – all my foes are
21 before You. Taunts have broken my heart, and I am deathly ill; I hope for
22 consolation, but there is none; for comforters, but find none – they gave me
23 poison for my fare and vinegar to quench my thirst. Let their own table be
24 a deathtrap to them, a snare for their friends. May their eyes grow too dark
25 to see; may their loins ever tremble. Pour Your wrath upon them; let Your
26 blazing fury overcome them. May their encampment be laid waste, their tents
27 stand empty, for they persecuted those You struck down and recounted the
28 pain of Your victims. Add that offense to their offenses; never let them share
29 in Your favor. Let them be blotted out from the book of life, not ever inscribed
30 among the righteous, but as for me, I am lowly and in pain; Your salvation,
31 God, will lift me up. I will praise God's name with song; I will glorify Him in
32 thanksgiving. This will please the LORD more than any ox or any horned and
33 cloven-hooved bull. The lowly will see and rejoice; take heart, you who seek
34 God – for the LORD listens to the needy and does not neglect His captives.
35 36 Let heaven and earth praise Him, the seas and all that stir within them, for
God will save Zion and rebuild the towns of Yehuda; they will settle there
37 and take possession. The seed of His servants will inherit it, and those who
love His name will dwell there.

70 1 2 *To the lead singer – of David,* lehazkir.[78] O God, save me; O LORD, rush to my
3 help – let those who seek my life be shamed and disgraced; let those who
4 wish me harm retreat in humiliation; let those who leer "Aha! Aha!" turn
5 away in shame. May all who seek You rejoice and delight in You; may those
6 who long for Your salvation always proclaim, "God is great." As for me, I am
poor and needy – God, rush to me; You are my help and my rescuer; LORD,
do not delay.

71 1 2 In You, LORD, I take refuge; may I never be put to shame. Deliver me; rescue
3 me in Your righteousness; lend Your ear to me and save me. Be a Rock of
refuge where I may always come; command my salvation, for You are my
4 Rock and my fortress. My God, rescue me from the hands of the wicked,
5 from the grip of the evil and the violent, for You are my hope, O Lord GOD,
6 my trust since my youth. I have relied upon You since conception; from my
7 mother's womb You brought me out; I will praise You always. I have set an
8 example for many while You have been my mighty refuge; may my mouth be
9 filled with Your praise, Your glory, all day long. Do not cast me away in old
10 age; when my strength fails, do not abandon me, for my enemies say of me,
11 those who stalk me and conspire together, "God has abandoned him. Chase
12 him and catch him, for no one will save him." God, do not stray far from
13 me; my God, rush to my help. Let my accusers be shamed and ruined; let
14 those who seek my harm be cloaked in disgrace and humiliation. As for me,
15 I shall always hope and praise You ever more and more. My mouth will tell

78 | See note on 38:1. This psalm is paralleled with slight variants in Psalms 40:14–18.

יז יח פִּיהָ: עֲנֵנִי יהוה כִּי־טוֹב חַסְדֶּךָ כְּרֹב רַחֲמֶיךָ פְּנֵה אֵלָי: וְאַל־תַּסְתֵּר
יט פָּנֶיךָ מֵעַבְדֶּךָ כִּי־צַר־לִי מַהֵר עֲנֵנִי: קָרְבָה אֶל־נַפְשִׁי גְאָלָהּ לְמַעַן
כ אֹיְבַי פְּדֵנִי: אַתָּה יָדַעְתָּ חֶרְפָּתִי וּבָשְׁתִּי וּכְלִמָּתִי נֶגְדְּךָ כָּל־צוֹרְרָי:
כא חֶרְפָּה ׀ שָׁבְרָה לִבִּי וָאָנוּשָׁה וָאֲקַוֶּה לָנוּד וָאַיִן וְלַמְנַחֲמִים וְלֹא
כב כג מָצָאתִי: וַיִּתְּנוּ בְּבָרוּתִי רֹאשׁ וְלִצְמָאִי יַשְׁקוּנִי חֹמֶץ: יְהִי־שֻׁלְחָנָם
כד לִפְנֵיהֶם לְפָח וְלִשְׁלוֹמִים לְמוֹקֵשׁ: תֶּחְשַׁכְנָה עֵינֵיהֶם מֵרְאוֹת וּמָתְנֵיהֶם
כה כו תָּמִיד הַמְעַד: שְׁפָךְ־עֲלֵיהֶם זַעְמֶךָ וַחֲרוֹן אַפְּךָ יַשִּׂיגֵם: תְּהִי־טִירָתָם
כז נְשַׁמָּה בְּאָהֳלֵיהֶם אַל־יְהִי יֹשֵׁב: כִּי־אַתָּה אֲשֶׁר־הִכִּיתָ רָדָפוּ וְאֶל־
כח מַכְאוֹב חֲלָלֶיךָ יְסַפֵּרוּ: תְּנָה־עָוֺן עַל־עֲוֺנָם וְאַל־יָבֹאוּ בְּצִדְקָתֶךָ:
כט ל יִמָּחוּ מִסֵּפֶר חַיִּים וְעִם צַדִּיקִים אַל־יִכָּתֵבוּ: וַאֲנִי עָנִי וְכוֹאֵב יְשׁוּעָתְךָ
לא אֱלֹהִים תְּשַׂגְּבֵנִי: אֲהַלְלָה שֵׁם־אֱלֹהִים בְּשִׁיר וַאֲגַדְּלֶנּוּ בְתוֹדָה:
לב לג וְתִיטַב לַיהוה מִשּׁוֹר פָּר מַקְרִן מַפְרִיס: רָאוּ עֲנָוִים יִשְׂמָחוּ דֹּרְשֵׁי
לד אֱלֹהִים וִיחִי לְבַבְכֶם: כִּי־שֹׁמֵעַ אֶל־אֶבְיוֹנִים יהוה וְאֶת־אֲסִירָיו לֹא
לה לו בָזָה: יְהַלְלוּהוּ שָׁמַיִם וָאָרֶץ יַמִּים וְכָל־רֹמֵשׂ בָּם: כִּי אֱלֹהִים ׀ יוֹשִׁיעַ
לז צִיּוֹן וְיִבְנֶה עָרֵי יְהוּדָה וְיָשְׁבוּ שָׁם וִירֵשׁוּהָ: וְזֶרַע עֲבָדָיו יִנְחָלוּהָ וְאֹהֲבֵי
שְׁמוֹ יִשְׁכְּנוּ־בָהּ:

ע א ב ג לַמְנַצֵּחַ לְדָוִד לְהַזְכִּיר: אֱלֹהִים לְהַצִּילֵנִי יהוה לְעֶזְרָתִי חוּשָׁה: יֵבֹשׁוּ
ד וְיַחְפְּרוּ מְבַקְשֵׁי נַפְשִׁי יִסֹּגוּ אָחוֹר וְיִכָּלְמוּ חֲפֵצֵי רָעָתִי: יָשׁוּבוּ עַל־עֵקֶב
ה בָּשְׁתָּם הָאֹמְרִים הֶאָח ׀ הֶאָח: יָשִׂישׂוּ וְיִשְׂמְחוּ ׀ בְּךָ כָּל־מְבַקְשֶׁיךָ
ו וְיֹאמְרוּ תָמִיד יִגְדַּל אֱלֹהִים אֹהֲבֵי יְשׁוּעָתֶךָ: וַאֲנִי ׀ עָנִי וְאֶבְיוֹן אֱלֹהִים
חוּשָׁה לִּי עֶזְרִי וּמְפַלְטִי אַתָּה יהוה אַל־תְּאַחַר:

עא א ב בְּךָ־יהוה חָסִיתִי אַל־אֵבוֹשָׁה לְעוֹלָם: בְּצִדְקָתְךָ תַּצִּילֵנִי וּתְפַלְּטֵנִי
ג הַטֵּה־אֵלַי אָזְנְךָ וְהוֹשִׁיעֵנִי: הֱיֵה לִי ׀ לְצוּר מָעוֹן לָבוֹא תָּמִיד צִוִּיתָ
ד לְהוֹשִׁיעֵנִי כִּי־סַלְעִי וּמְצוּדָתִי אָתָּה: אֱלֹהַי פַּלְּטֵנִי מִיַּד רָשָׁע מִכַּף
ה ו מְעַוֵּל וְחוֹמֵץ: כִּי־אַתָּה תִקְוָתִי אֲדֹנָי יֱהוִה מִבְטַחִי מִנְּעוּרָי: עָלֶיךָ ׀
ז נִסְמַכְתִּי מִבֶּטֶן מִמְּעֵי אִמִּי אַתָּה גוֹזִי בְּךָ תְהִלָּתִי תָמִיד: כְּמוֹפֵת הָיִיתִי
ח ט לְרַבִּים וְאַתָּה מַחֲסִי־עֹז: יִמָּלֵא פִי תְּהִלָּתֶךָ כָּל־הַיּוֹם תִּפְאַרְתֶּךָ: אַל־
י תַּשְׁלִיכֵנִי לְעֵת זִקְנָה כִּכְלוֹת כֹּחִי אַל־תַּעַזְבֵנִי: כִּי־אָמְרוּ אוֹיְבַי לִי
יא וְשֹׁמְרֵי נַפְשִׁי נוֹעֲצוּ יַחְדָּו: לֵאמֹר אֱלֹהִים עֲזָבוֹ רִדְפוּ וְתִפְשׂוּהוּ כִּי־אֵין
יב יג מַצִּיל: אֱלֹהִים אַל־תִּרְחַק מִמֶּנִּי אֱלֹהַי לְעֶזְרָתִי חִישָׁה: יֵבֹשׁוּ יִכְלוּ חוּשָׁה
יד שֹׂטְנֵי נַפְשִׁי יַעֲטוּ חֶרְפָּה וּכְלִמָּה מְבַקְשֵׁי רָעָתִי: וַאֲנִי תָּמִיד אֲיַחֵל
טו וְהוֹסַפְתִּי עַל־כָּל־תְּהִלָּתֶךָ: פִּי ׀ יְסַפֵּר צִדְקָתֶךָ כָּל־הַיּוֹם תְּשׁוּעָתֶךָ

of Your righteousness, Your salvation all day long, though it is immeasurable.
16 I will come tell of Your powerful deeds, O Lord God; I will proclaim Your
17 righteousness – Yours alone. God, You have taught me since my youth; to this
18 day I tell of Your wonders. Now that I am old and gray, God, do not abandon
me until I tell the next generation of Your power, all those to come of Your
19 power. Your righteousness, God, reaches the highest heights, for You have
20 done great things. O God, who is like You? You who have shown me great and
terrible troubles will revive me once more; from the depths of the earth You
21 will once more raise me up. You will increase my greatness and comfort me
22 again; then I will praise You with the lyre for Your faithfulness, my God; I will
23 sing praises to You with the harp, O Holy One of Israel. My lips will delight
24 in singing praise to You, my very being, whom You redeemed. My tongue,
too, will express Your righteousness all day long, how those who sought my
harm were shamed and reviled.

72 1 *Of Shlomo.*[79] God, grant Your judgment to the king, Your justice to the king's
2 son, so that he may judge Your people fairly, Your lowly ones with justice.
3 4 May the mountains yield peace for the people, the hills righteousness; may
he bring justice to the lowly people, save the children of the needy, and crush
5 the oppressor. May they revere You as long as the sun shines, as long as the
6 moon glows, for generations untold. May he be like rain falling on mown
7 grass, like showers watering the earth. In his time, may the righteous bloom;
8 may peace abound until the moon ceases to be. May he rule from sea to sea,
9 from the river to the ends of the earth.[80] Let the desert nomads kneel before
10 him; let his enemies lick the dust; let kings of Tarshish and the isles pay him
11 tribute, kings of Sheba and Seba offer gifts; let all kings bow down to him,
12 and let all nations serve him, for he brings salvation to the needy who cry
13 out, to the lowly with none to help them. He pities the poor and the needy
14 and saves the lives of the needy, redeeming them from deceit and violence,
15 for their blood is precious in his sight. Long may he live! May he be granted
the gold of Sheba; may they always pray on his behalf, blessing him all day
16 long. May there be a wealth of grain in the land, even on the mountaintops;
let its fruit rustle like Lebanon and the people[81] thrive in the towns like field
17 grass. May his name be forever; may his name endure as long as the sun; let all
18 nations be blessed through him and praise his fortune. Blessed be the Lord
19 God, God of Israel, who alone does wonders; blessed be His glorious name
20 forever. May the whole world be filled with His glory! Amen and Amen! *Here
end the prayers of David, son of Yishai.*

BOOK THREE

73 1 2 *A psalm of Asaf.*[82] God is truly good to Israel, to those pure of heart; but as for
3 me, my feet nearly strayed, my steps had all but slipped, for I was envious of

79 | See also Psalm 127.
80 | Cf. Exodus 23:31.
81 | The word "people" does not appear in Hebrew and is taken as implied.
82 | See note on 50:1. Psalms 73–83 all mention Asaf in their titles.

טז כִּי לֹא יָדַעְתִּי סְפֹרוֹת׃ אָבוֹא בִּגְבֻרוֹת אֲדֹנָי יֱהֹוִה אַזְכִּיר צִדְקָתְךָ
יז יח לְבַדֶּךָ׃ אֱלֹהִים לִמַּדְתַּנִי מִנְּעוּרָי וְעַד־הֵנָּה אַגִּיד נִפְלְאוֹתֶיךָ׃ וְגַם
עַד־זִקְנָה ׀ וְשֵׂיבָה אֱלֹהִים אַל־תַּעַזְבֵנִי עַד־אַגִּיד זְרוֹעֲךָ לְדוֹר לְכָל־
יט יָבוֹא גְּבוּרָתֶךָ׃ וְצִדְקָתְךָ אֱלֹהִים עַד־מָרוֹם אֲשֶׁר־עָשִׂיתָ גְדֹלוֹת
כ אֱלֹהִים מִי כָמוֹךָ׃ אֲשֶׁר הראיתנו ׀ צָרוֹת רַבּוֹת וְרָעוֹת תָּשׁוּב תחיינו הִרְאִיתַנִי תְּחַיֵּנִי
כא כב וּמִתְּהֹמוֹת הָאָרֶץ תָּשׁוּב תעלנו׃ תֶּרֶב ׀ גְּדֻלָּתִי וְתִסֹּב תְּנַחֲמֵנִי׃ גַּם־ תַּעֲלֵנִי
אֲנִי ׀ אוֹדְךָ בִכְלִי־נֶבֶל אֲמִתְּךָ אֱלֹהָי אֲזַמְּרָה לְךָ בְכִנּוֹר קְדוֹשׁ יִשְׂרָאֵל׃
כג כד תְּרַנֵּנָּה שְׂפָתַי כִּי אֲזַמְּרָה־לָּךְ וְנַפְשִׁי אֲשֶׁר פָּדִיתָ׃ גַּם־לְשׁוֹנִי כָּל־הַיּוֹם
תֶּהְגֶּה צִדְקָתֶךָ כִּי־בֹשׁוּ כִי־חָפְרוּ מְבַקְשֵׁי רָעָתִי׃

עב א ב לִשְׁלֹמֹה ׀ אֱלֹהִים מִשְׁפָּטֶיךָ לְמֶלֶךְ תֵּן וְצִדְקָתְךָ לְבֶן־מֶלֶךְ׃ יָדִין עַמְּךָ
ג בְצֶדֶק וַעֲנִיֶּיךָ בְמִשְׁפָּט׃ יִשְׂאוּ הָרִים שָׁלוֹם לָעָם וּגְבָעוֹת בִּצְדָקָה׃
ד ה יִשְׁפֹּט ׀ עֲנִיֵּי־עָם יוֹשִׁיעַ לִבְנֵי אֶבְיוֹן וִידַכֵּא עוֹשֵׁק׃ יִירָאוּךָ עִם־שָׁמֶשׁ
ו ז וְלִפְנֵי יָרֵחַ דּוֹר דּוֹרִים׃ יֵרֵד כְּמָטָר עַל־גֵּז כִּרְבִיבִים זַרְזִיף אָרֶץ׃ יִפְרַח־
ח בְּיָמָיו צַדִּיק וְרֹב שָׁלוֹם עַד־בְּלִי יָרֵחַ׃ וְיֵרְדְּ מִיָּם עַד־יָם וּמִנָּהָר עַד־
ט י אַפְסֵי־אָרֶץ׃ לְפָנָיו יִכְרְעוּ צִיִּים וְאֹיְבָיו עָפָר יְלַחֵכוּ׃ מַלְכֵי תַרְשִׁישׁ
יא וְאִיִּים מִנְחָה יָשִׁיבוּ מַלְכֵי שְׁבָא וּסְבָא אֶשְׁכָּר יַקְרִיבוּ׃ וְיִשְׁתַּחֲווּ־לוֹ
יב כָל־מְלָכִים כָּל־גּוֹיִם יַעַבְדוּהוּ׃ כִּי־יַצִּיל אֶבְיוֹן מְשַׁוֵּעַ וְעָנִי וְאֵין־עֹזֵר
יג יד לוֹ׃ יָחֹס עַל־דַּל וְאֶבְיוֹן וְנַפְשׁוֹת אֶבְיוֹנִים יוֹשִׁיעַ׃ מִתּוֹךְ וּמֵחָמָס יִגְאַל
טו נַפְשָׁם וְיֵיקַר דָּמָם בְּעֵינָיו׃ וִיחִי וְיִתֶּן־לוֹ מִזְּהַב שְׁבָא וְיִתְפַּלֵּל בַּעֲדוֹ
טז תָמִיד כָּל־הַיּוֹם יְבָרֲכֶנְהוּ׃ יְהִי פִסַּת־בַּר ׀ בָּאָרֶץ בְּרֹאשׁ הָרִים יִרְעַשׁ
יז כַּלְּבָנוֹן פִּרְיוֹ וְיָצִיצוּ מֵעִיר כְּעֵשֶׂב הָאָרֶץ׃ יְהִי שְׁמוֹ ׀ לְעוֹלָם לִפְנֵי־שֶׁמֶשׁ
יח ינין שְׁמוֹ וְיִתְבָּרְכוּ בוֹ כָּל־גּוֹיִם יְאַשְּׁרוּהוּ׃ בָּרוּךְ ׀ יְהֹוָה אֱלֹהִים אֱלֹהֵי יִנּוֹן
יט יִשְׂרָאֵל עֹשֵׂה נִפְלָאוֹת לְבַדּוֹ׃ וּבָרוּךְ ׀ שֵׁם כְּבוֹדוֹ לְעוֹלָם וְיִמָּלֵא כְבוֹדוֹ
כ אֶת־כֹּל הָאָרֶץ אָמֵן ׀ וְאָמֵן׃ כָּלּוּ תְפִלּוֹת דָּוִד בֶּן־יִשָׁי׃

עג א ב מִזְמוֹר לְאָסָף אַךְ טוֹב לְיִשְׂרָאֵל אֱלֹהִים לְבָרֵי לֵבָב׃ וַאֲנִי כִּמְעַט ספר שלישי
ג נטוי רַגְלָי כְּאַיִן שפכה אֲשֻׁרָי׃ כִּי־קִנֵּאתִי בַּהוֹלְלִים שְׁלוֹם רְשָׁעִים נָטָיוּ | שֻׁפְּכוּ

4 the revelers; I saw the well-being of the wicked, how they were free of death's
5 torments with their sound, healthy forms, with no part in human misery, not
6 suffering like other people. Therefore they wear arrogance like a necklace and
7 drape themselves in violence; their eyes bulge out; their hearts overflow with
8 fancies. They mock and speak with malice; from on high they plan oppression.
9 Their lips are aimed against the heavens; their tongues prowl over the earth.
10 11 Thus His people are drawn back to them, and they lap up their words. They
12 say, "How could God know? What knowledge has the Most High?" Look
13 at these wicked people – always at ease, amassing wealth. All in vain have I
14 kept my heart pure and washed my hands in innocence – when all day long
15 I suffer from pain, tormented each morning anew. Were I to speak out in this
16 way, I would betray the circle of Your children. When I tried to understand
17 this, it made me miserable until I came to God's Sanctuary and realized what
18 their end would be. You set them on a slippery path and plunge them into
19 20 devastation; how they suddenly come to ruin, swept away by utter terror, like
21 a dream upon waking, O Lord. Upon rising You despise their image. When
22 my heart was sour and my conscience pricked,[83] I was stupid and ignorant –
23 like a brute beast before You. Yet I am always with You; You hold my right
24 25 hand. You guide me with Your counsel; You take me toward glory. Whom
26 else do I have in heaven? With You, I desire nothing else on earth. Though
my flesh and heart waste away, God is the Rock of my heart and my portion
27 forever, for look – those far from You are lost; You destroy all those who stray
28 from You, but as for me, God's closeness is good for me. I have made the Lord
God my refuge, to tell of all Your works.

74 1 *A maskil of Asaf.* Why, God, have You forsaken us forever? Your wrath
2 smolders against the flock You tend. Remember the congregation You made
Yours long ago, the tribe You redeemed as Your share, Mount Zion where
3 You dwell. Rush over[84] to the endless devastation, all the evil the enemy
4 has wrought in the Sanctuary. Your foes roared out in Your meeting place,
5 displaying their own signs as signs. They are renowned as wielders of axes
6 against the tangled branches of trees, then they smashed all its carvings with
7 pick and hatchet; they burned Your Sanctuary down to the ground; they
8 desecrated Your name's dwelling place. They said in their hearts, "We will
9 crush them completely," and burned all God's meeting places in the land. No
signs appear for us, no prophets are left, and none of us know for how long.
10 For how long, God, will the foe blaspheme? Will the enemy revile Your name
11 forever? Why do You hold back Your right hand? Thrust it out from Your
12 bosom! Yet You, God, are my King of old, bringing salvation throughout the
13 land. In Your might You tore the sea to shreds and smashed the heads of sea
14 monsters on the waters. You shattered the head of Leviathan[85] and fed him
15 to the desert peoples. You split open spring and stream; You dried up surging
16 rivers. Yours is the day; Yours, too, is the night; You fashioned luminary and

---

83 | Literally "I was pierced in my kidneys."

84 | Literally "lift up your feet."

85 | The mythological sea beast; cf., e.g., 104:26; Isaiah 27:1; Job 40:25.

ד ה אֶרְאֶה: כִּי אֵין חַרְצֻבּוֹת לְמוֹתָם וּבָרִיא אוּלָם: בַּעֲמַל אֱנוֹשׁ אֵינֵמוֹ
ו ז וְעִם־אָדָם לֹא יְנֻגָּעוּ: לָכֵן עֲנָקַתְמוֹ גַאֲוָה יַעֲטָף־שִׁית חָמָס לָמוֹ: יָצָא
ח מֵחֵלֶב עֵינֵמוֹ עָבְרוּ מַשְׂכִּיּוֹת לֵבָב: יָמִיקוּ ׀ וִידַבְּרוּ בְרָע עֹשֶׁק מִמָּרוֹם
ט י יְדַבֵּרוּ: שַׁתּוּ בַשָּׁמַיִם פִּיהֶם וּלְשׁוֹנָם תִּהֲלַךְ בָּאָרֶץ: לָכֵן ׀ יָשִׁיב עַמּוֹ יָשׁוּב
יא הֲלֹם וּמֵי מָלֵא יִמָּצוּ לָמוֹ: וְאָמְרוּ אֵיכָה יָדַע־אֵל וְיֵשׁ דֵּעָה בְעֶלְיוֹן:
יב יג הִנֵּה־אֵלֶּה רְשָׁעִים וְשַׁלְוֵי עוֹלָם הִשְׂגּוּ־חָיִל: אַךְ־רִיק זִכִּיתִי לְבָבִי
יד טו וָאֶרְחַץ בְּנִקָּיוֹן כַּפָּי: וָאֱהִי נָגוּעַ כָּל־הַיּוֹם וְתוֹכַחְתִּי לַבְּקָרִים: אִם־
טז אָמַרְתִּי אֲסַפְּרָה כְמוֹ הִנֵּה דוֹר בָּנֶיךָ בָגָדְתִּי: וָאֲחַשְּׁבָה לָדַעַת זֹאת
יז יח עָמָל הִיא בְעֵינָי: עַד־אָבוֹא אֶל־מִקְדְּשֵׁי־אֵל אָבִינָה לְאַחֲרִיתָם: אַךְ הוּא
יט בַּחֲלָקוֹת תָּשִׁית לָמוֹ הִפַּלְתָּם לְמַשּׁוּאוֹת: אֵיךְ הָיוּ לְשַׁמָּה כְרָגַע סָפוּ
כ כא תַמּוּ מִן־בַּלָּהוֹת: כַּחֲלוֹם מֵהָקִיץ אֲדֹנָי בָּעִיר ׀ צַלְמָם תִּבְזֶה: כִּי
כב יִתְחַמֵּץ לְבָבִי וְכִלְיוֹתַי אֶשְׁתּוֹנָן: וַאֲנִי־בַעַר וְלֹא אֵדָע בְּהֵמוֹת הָיִיתִי
כג כד עִמָּךְ: וַאֲנִי תָמִיד עִמָּךְ אָחַזְתָּ בְּיַד־יְמִינִי: בַּעֲצָתְךָ תַנְחֵנִי וְאַחַר כָּבוֹד
כה כו תִּקָּחֵנִי: מִי־לִי בַשָּׁמָיִם וְעִמְּךָ לֹא־חָפַצְתִּי בָאָרֶץ: כָּלָה שְׁאֵרִי וּלְבָבִי
כז צוּר־לְבָבִי וְחֶלְקִי אֱלֹהִים לְעוֹלָם: כִּי־הִנֵּה רְחֵקֶיךָ יֹאבֵדוּ הִצְמַתָּה
כח כָּל־זוֹנֶה מִמֶּךָּ: וַאֲנִי ׀ קִרֲבַת אֱלֹהִים לִי טוֹב שַׁתִּי ׀ בַּאדֹנָי יֱהֹוִה מַחְסִי
לְסַפֵּר כָּל־מַלְאֲכוֹתֶיךָ:

עד א מַשְׂכִּיל לְאָסָף לָמָה אֱלֹהִים זָנַחְתָּ לָנֶצַח יֶעְשַׁן אַפְּךָ בְּצֹאן מַרְעִיתֶךָ:
ב זְכֹר עֲדָתְךָ ׀ קָנִיתָ קֶּדֶם גָּאַלְתָּ שֵׁבֶט נַחֲלָתֶךָ הַר־צִיּוֹן זֶה ׀ שָׁכַנְתָּ בּוֹ:
ג ד הָרִימָה פְעָמֶיךָ לְמַשֻּׁאוֹת נֶצַח כָּל־הֵרַע אוֹיֵב בַּקֹּדֶשׁ: שָׁאֲגוּ צֹרְרֶיךָ
ה בְּקֶרֶב מוֹעֲדֶךָ שָׂמוּ אוֹתֹתָם אֹתוֹת: יִוָּדַע כְּמֵבִיא לְמָעְלָה בִּסְבָךְ־עֵץ
ו ז קַרְדֻּמּוֹת: וְעַתָּה פִּתּוּחֶיהָ יָּחַד בְּכַשִּׁיל וְכֵילַפֹּת יַהֲלֹמוּן: שִׁלְחוּ בָאֵשׁ
ח מִקְדָּשֶׁךָ לָאָרֶץ חִלְּלוּ מִשְׁכַּן־שְׁמֶךָ: אָמְרוּ בְלִבָּם נִינָם יָחַד שָׂרְפוּ
ט כָל־מוֹעֲדֵי־אֵל בָּאָרֶץ: אוֹתֹתֵינוּ לֹא רָאִינוּ אֵין־עוֹד נָבִיא וְלֹא־אִתָּנוּ
י יֹדֵעַ עַד־מָה: עַד־מָתַי אֱלֹהִים יְחָרֶף צָר יְנָאֵץ אוֹיֵב שִׁמְךָ לָנֶצַח:
יא יב לָמָּה תָשִׁיב יָדְךָ וִימִינֶךָ מִקֶּרֶב חוקך כַלֵּה: וֵאלֹהִים מַלְכִּי מִקֶּדֶם חֵיקְךָ
יג פֹּעֵל יְשׁוּעוֹת בְּקֶרֶב הָאָרֶץ: אַתָּה פוֹרַרְתָּ בְעָזְּךָ יָם שִׁבַּרְתָּ רָאשֵׁי
יד תַנִּינִים עַל־הַמָּיִם: אַתָּה רִצַּצְתָּ רָאשֵׁי לִוְיָתָן תִּתְּנֶנּוּ מַאֲכָל לְעָם
טו טז לְצִיִּים: אַתָּה בָקַעְתָּ מַעְיָן וָנָחַל אַתָּה הוֹבַשְׁתָּ נַהֲרוֹת אֵיתָן: לְךָ יוֹם

17 sun. You set all the boundaries of the earth; summer and winter – You made
18 them. Remember this, LORD, when the enemy taunts, when a brutish people
19 revile Your name. Do not give up Your dove to the wild beasts or forget Your
20 lowly flock forever. Look to the covenant – for the land's dark crevasses are
21 haunted with violence. Do not let the downtrodden turn away in disgrace;
22 let the lowly and needy praise Your name. Arise, O God! Defend Your cause;
23 remember how brutes taunt You all day long. Do not forget the voice of Your
foes, the ever-rising din of those against You.

75 1 2 *To the lead singer,* al tashḥet[86] – *a psalm of Asaf, a song.* We praise You, God;
3 we praise You, and Your name is near. They tell of Your wonders. "At the
4 appointed time I set, I will judge with equity. When the earth and all its
5 dwellers dissolve, it is I who hold its pillars firm" – Selah. I warn the brazen,
6 "Do not be brazen," and the wicked, "Do not raise your horn – do not raise
7 your horn up high, preening with a haughty neck," for neither from the east
8 nor from the west nor from the wilderness is anyone raised up. God alone
9 is the judge; it is He who brings down or raises up, for in the LORD's hand
there is a cup of foaming wine, laced and brimming; from this He will pour,
10 and all the wicked of the earth will drink and drain it to its very dregs. As for
11 me, I will declare it forever; I will sing praises to the God of Yaakov. "I will
hack off all the horns of the wicked, while the horns of the righteous will be
raised up."

76 1 2 *To the lead singer, accompanied by music – a psalm of Asaf, a song.* God is
3 renowned in Yehuda; in Israel His name is great; His tent is set in Salem,[87]
4 His abode in Zion. There He shattered the bow's fiery shafts, the shield and
5 sword and weapons of war – Selah. Dazzling You were, mightier than the
6 mountains of prey. The fiercest of heart were plundered, lulled into a trance;
7 the most powerful of warriors could not lift their hands. At Your onslaught,
8 God of Yaakov, horse and chariot were stunned. You – O You are fearsome.
9 Who can stand before You once Your anger is roused? From the heavens You
10 sounded Your decree; the earth was stilled with fright when God arose for
11 judgment to save all the lowly of the earth – Selah. Human fury serves only
12 to praise You when You gird the last of Your fury. Make vows and fulfill them
to the LORD your God; all around Him will bring tribute to the Fearsome
13 One. He humbles the spirits of princes; He strikes fear in the kings of the
earth.

77 1 2 *To the lead singer, for Yedutun*[88] *– a psalm of Asaf.* My voice cries out to God –
3 my voice to God that He might hear me. On the day of my distress I seek
the Lord; at night my hand reaches out unceasingly; my soul refuses to
4 be comforted. I call God to mind and sigh in longing; I reflect, and my
5 spirit grows faint – Selah. You hold my eyelids open; I am anguished and
6 7 cannot speak. I think about the olden days, the years long gone. I recall my
contemplation by night – I reflect within my heart; I search within my soul.

86 | See note on 57:1.

87 | Another name for Jerusalem; cf. Genesis 14:18.

88 | See note on 39:1.

יז אַף־לְךָ לָיְלָה אַתָּה הֲכִינוֹתָ מָאוֹר וָשָׁמֶשׁ: אַתָּה הִצַּבְתָּ כׇּל־גְּבוּלוֹת
יח אָרֶץ קַיִץ וָחֹרֶף אַתָּה יְצַרְתָּם: זְכׇר־זֹאת אוֹיֵב חֵרֵף ׀ יהוה וְעַם־
יט נָבָל נִאֲצוּ שְׁמֶךָ: אַל־תִּתֵּן לְחַיַּת נֶפֶשׁ תּוֹרֶךָ חַיַּת עֲנִיֶּיךָ אַל־תִּשְׁכַּח
כ כא לָנֶצַח: הַבֵּט לַבְּרִית כִּי־מָלְאוּ מַחֲשַׁכֵּי־אֶרֶץ נְאוֹת חָמָס: אַל־יָשֹׁב
כב דַּךְ נִכְלָם עָנִי וְאֶבְיוֹן יְהַלְלוּ שְׁמֶךָ: קוּמָה אֱלֹהִים רִיבָה רִיבֶךָ זְכֹר
כג חֶרְפָּתְךָ מִנִּי־נָבָל כׇּל־הַיּוֹם: אַל־תִּשְׁכַּח קוֹל צֹרְרֶיךָ שְׁאוֹן קָמֶיךָ
עֹלֶה תָמִיד:
עה א ב לַמְנַצֵּחַ אַל־תַּשְׁחֵת מִזְמוֹר לְאָסָף שִׁיר: הוֹדִינוּ לְּךָ ׀ אֱלֹהִים הוֹדִינוּ
ג וְקָרוֹב שְׁמֶךָ סִפְּרוּ נִפְלְאוֹתֶיךָ: כִּי אֶקַּח מוֹעֵד אֲנִי מֵישָׁרִים אֶשְׁפֹּט:
ד ה נְמֹגִים אֶרֶץ וְכׇל־יֹשְׁבֶיהָ אָנֹכִי תִכַּנְתִּי עַמּוּדֶיהָ סֶּלָה: אָמַרְתִּי לַהוֹלְלִים
ו אַל־תָּהֹלּוּ וְלָרְשָׁעִים אַל־תָּרִימוּ קָרֶן: אַל־תָּרִימוּ לַמָּרוֹם קַרְנְכֶם
ז תְּדַבְּרוּ בְצַוָּאר עָתָק: כִּי לֹא מִמּוֹצָא וּמִמַּעֲרָב וְלֹא מִמִּדְבַּר הָרִים:
ח ט כִּי־אֱלֹהִים שֹׁפֵט זֶה יַשְׁפִּיל וְזֶה יָרִים: כִּי כוֹס בְּיַד־יהוה וְיַיִן חָמַר ׀
י מָלֵא מֶסֶךְ וַיַּגֵּר מִזֶּה אַךְ־שְׁמָרֶיהָ יִמְצוּ יִשְׁתּוּ כֹּל רִשְׁעֵי־אָרֶץ: וַאֲנִי
יא אַגִּיד לְעֹלָם אֲזַמְּרָה לֵאלֹהֵי יַעֲקֹב: וְכׇל־קַרְנֵי רְשָׁעִים אֲגַדֵּעַ תְּרוֹמַמְנָה
קַרְנוֹת צַדִּיק:
עו א ב לַמְנַצֵּחַ בִּנְגִינֹת מִזְמוֹר לְאָסָף שִׁיר: נוֹדָע בִּיהוּדָה אֱלֹהִים בְּיִשְׂרָאֵל
ג ד גָּדוֹל שְׁמוֹ: וַיְהִי בְשָׁלֵם סוּכּוֹ וּמְעוֹנָתוֹ בְצִיּוֹן: שָׁמָּה שִׁבַּר רִשְׁפֵי־קָשֶׁת
ה ו מָגֵן וְחֶרֶב וּמִלְחָמָה סֶלָה: נָאוֹר אַתָּה אַדִּיר מֵהַרְרֵי־טָרֶף: אֶשְׁתּוֹלְלוּ ׀
ז אַבִּירֵי לֵב נָמוּ שְׁנָתָם וְלֹא־מָצְאוּ כׇל־אַנְשֵׁי־חַיִל יְדֵיהֶם: מִגַּעֲרָתְךָ
ח אֱלֹהֵי יַעֲקֹב נִרְדָּם וְרֶכֶב וָסוּס: אַתָּה ׀ נוֹרָא אַתָּה וּמִי־יַעֲמֹד לְפָנֶיךָ
ט מֵאָז אַפֶּךָ: מִשָּׁמַיִם הִשְׁמַעְתָּ דִּין אֶרֶץ יָרְאָה וְשָׁקָטָה: בְּקוּם־לַמִּשְׁפָּט
י יא אֱלֹהִים לְהוֹשִׁיעַ כׇּל־עַנְוֵי־אֶרֶץ סֶלָה: כִּי־חֲמַת אָדָם תּוֹדֶךָּ שְׁאֵרִית
יב חֵמֹת תַּחְגֹּר: נִדְרוּ וְשַׁלְּמוּ לַיהוה אֱלֹהֵיכֶם כׇּל־סְבִיבָיו יֹבִילוּ שַׁי
יג לַמּוֹרָא: יִבְצֹר רוּחַ נְגִידִים נוֹרָא לְמַלְכֵי־אָרֶץ:
עז א ב לַמְנַצֵּחַ עַל־ידיתון לְאָסָף מִזְמוֹר: קוֹלִי אֶל־אֱלֹהִים וְאֶצְעָקָה קוֹלִי יְדוּתוּן
ג אֶל־אֱלֹהִים וְהַאֲזִין אֵלָי: בְּיוֹם צָרָתִי אֲדֹנָי דָּרָשְׁתִּי יָדִי ׀ לַיְלָה נִגְּרָה
ד וְלֹא תָפוּג מֵאֲנָה הִנָּחֵם נַפְשִׁי: אֶזְכְּרָה אֱלֹהִים וְאֶהֱמָיָה אָשִׂיחָה ׀
ה ו וְתִתְעַטֵּף רוּחִי סֶלָה: אָחַזְתָּ שְׁמֻרוֹת עֵינָי נִפְעַמְתִּי וְלֹא אֲדַבֵּר: חִשַּׁבְתִּי
ז יָמִים מִקֶּדֶם שְׁנוֹת עוֹלָמִים: אֶזְכְּרָה נְגִינָתִי בַּלָּיְלָה עִם־לְבָבִי אָשִׂיחָה

8 9 Will the Lord forsake us forever and never again show favor? Is His loyalty
10 gone forever, His promise ended for all generations? Has God forgotten to
11 show grace and in His wrath, curbed His compassion? – Selah. And I said, "I
12 am grieved that the Most High's right hand has changed." I will call to mind
13 the LORD's acts; I will recall Your wonders of old. I will contemplate all Your
14 works and reflect upon Your acts. God, Your way is holy. What god is as great
15 as our God? You are the God who performs wonders; You show Your might
16 to the nations. You redeemed Your people with Your own arm, the children
17 of Yaakov and Yosef – Selah. When the waters saw You, God, when the waters
18 saw You, they shivered; the very depths shuddered. The clouds streamed
19 with water; the skies sounded with thunder; Your bolts, too, flashed; The
sound of Your thunder rattled like wheels; lightning lit up the world; the earth
20 trembled and shook. You made Your way through the sea, Your path through
21 the mighty waters, and Your footsteps left no trace. You led Your people like
a flock by the hands of Moshe and Aharon.
78 1 2 *A maskil of Asaf.* Hear my teaching, O my people; lend Your ear to what I say. I
3 will open my mouth with a metaphor, I will disclose an ancient mystery – what
4 we have heard, what we know, and what our ancestors have told us we will not
hide from their children; to the next generation we will sing the LORD's praises
5 and the mighty deeds and wonders He has done. He established a decree in
Yaakov and founded the teaching in Israel, charging our ancestors to teach
6 it to their children so that the next generation would know it, the children
7 yet unborn, and tell it, in turn, to their own children and place their trust in
8 God and not forget God's acts but keep His commandments instead of being
like their ancestors, a wayward, rebellious generation, a generation not firm
9 of heart, its spirit unfaithful to God. The men of Efrayim, armed wielders of
10 bows, turned and fled on the day of battle. They did not keep God's covenant
11 and refused to follow His teaching; they forgot His acts and the wonders that
12 He showed them; before their ancestors He worked wonders, in the land of
13 Egypt, in the fields of Tzoan: He split the sea and led them across and stood
14 the waters like a wall; He guided them with cloud by day, with firelight all
15 through the night; He split rocks open in the wilderness and gave them drink
16 as from the great deep; He brought out streams from stone and made water
17 run down like rivers. Yet they continued to sin against Him, to defy the Most
18 High in the desert. They were determined to test God by demanding food for
19 themselves; they spoke out against God, saying, "Can God spread a table in
20 the wilderness? Yes, He struck a rock and water flowed and streams gushed
forth, but can He give us bread as well? Can He provide meat for His people?"
21 When the LORD heard this, He grew furious; fire flared out against Yaakov;
22 wrath blazed against Israel, for they did not believe in God and did not trust
23 in His salvation, but He commanded the skies above and opened the doors of
24 heaven; He rained down manna upon them for food and gave them the grain
25 of heaven. Each one ate a mighty feast; He sent down abundant fare for them;
26 He stirred up the east wind across the heavens and drove the south wind with
27 His might and rained down meat on them like dust, winged fowl like ocean

ח ט וְיְחַפֵּשׂ רוּחִי׃ הַלְעוֹלָמִים יִזְנַח ׀ אֲדֹנָי וְלֹא־יֹסִיף לִרְצוֹת עוֹד׃ הֶאָפֵס
י לָנֶצַח חַסְדּוֹ גָּמַר אֹמֶר לְדֹר וָדֹר׃ הֲשָׁכַח חַנּוֹת אֵל אִם־קָפַץ בְּאַף
יא יב רַחֲמָיו סֶלָה׃ וָאֹמַר חַלּוֹתִי הִיא שְׁנוֹת יְמִין עֶלְיוֹן׃ אזכיר מַעַלְלֵי־יָהּ אֶזְכּוֹר
יג כִּי־אֶזְכְּרָה מִקֶּדֶם פִּלְאֶךָ׃ וְהָגִיתִי בְכָל־פָּעֳלֶךָ וּבַעֲלִילוֹתֶיךָ אָשִׂיחָה׃
יד טו אֱלֹהִים בַּקֹּדֶשׁ דַּרְכֶּךָ מִי־אֵל גָּדוֹל כֵּאלֹהִים׃ אַתָּה הָאֵל עֹשֵׂה פֶלֶא
טז יז הוֹדַעְתָּ בָעַמִּים עֻזֶּךָ׃ גָּאַלְתָּ בִּזְרוֹעַ עַמֶּךָ בְּנֵי־יַעֲקֹב וְיוֹסֵף סֶלָה׃ רָאוּךָ
יח מַּיִם ׀ אֱלֹהִים רָאוּךָ מַּיִם יָחִילוּ אַף יִרְגְּזוּ תְהֹמוֹת׃ זֹרְמוּ מַיִם ׀ עָבוֹת
יט קוֹל נָתְנוּ שְׁחָקִים אַף־חֲצָצֶיךָ יִתְהַלָּכוּ׃ קוֹל רַעַמְךָ ׀ בַּגַּלְגַּל הֵאִירוּ
כ בְרָקִים תֵּבֵל רָגְזָה וַתִּרְעַשׁ הָאָרֶץ׃ בַּיָּם דַּרְכֶּךָ ושביליך בְּמַיִם רַבִּים וּשְׁבִילְךָ
כא וְעִקְּבוֹתֶיךָ לֹא נֹדָעוּ׃ נָחִיתָ כַצֹּאן עַמֶּךָ בְּיַד־מֹשֶׁה וְאַהֲרֹן׃

עח
א ב מַשְׂכִּיל לְאָסָף הַאֲזִינָה עַמִּי תּוֹרָתִי הַטּוּ אָזְנְכֶם לְאִמְרֵי־פִי׃ אֶפְתְּחָה
ג בְמָשָׁל פִּי אַבִּיעָה חִידוֹת מִנִּי־קֶדֶם׃ אֲשֶׁר שָׁמַעְנוּ וַנֵּדָעֵם וַאֲבוֹתֵינוּ
ד סִפְּרוּ־לָנוּ׃ לֹא נְכַחֵד ׀ מִבְּנֵיהֶם לְדוֹר אַחֲרוֹן מְסַפְּרִים תְּהִלּוֹת יְהוָה
ה וֶעֱזוּזוֹ וְנִפְלְאוֹתָיו אֲשֶׁר עָשָׂה׃ וַיָּקֶם עֵדוּת ׀ בְּיַעֲקֹב וְתוֹרָה שָׂם בְּיִשְׂרָאֵל
ו אֲשֶׁר צִוָּה אֶת־אֲבוֹתֵינוּ לְהוֹדִיעָם לִבְנֵיהֶם׃ לְמַעַן יֵדְעוּ ׀ דּוֹר אַחֲרוֹן
ז בָּנִים יִוָּלֵדוּ יָקֻמוּ וִיסַפְּרוּ לִבְנֵיהֶם׃ וְיָשִׂימוּ בֵאלֹהִים כִּסְלָם וְלֹא יִשְׁכְּחוּ
ח מַעַלְלֵי־אֵל וּמִצְוֺתָיו יִנְצֹרוּ׃ וְלֹא יִהְיוּ ׀ כַּאֲבוֹתָם דּוֹר סוֹרֵר וּמֹרֶה דּוֹר
ט לֹא־הֵכִין לִבּוֹ וְלֹא־נֶאֶמְנָה אֶת־אֵל רוּחוֹ׃ בְּנֵי־אֶפְרַיִם נוֹשְׁקֵי רוֹמֵי־
י קֶשֶׁת הָפְכוּ בְּיוֹם קְרָב׃ לֹא שָׁמְרוּ בְּרִית אֱלֹהִים וּבְתוֹרָתוֹ מֵאֲנוּ
יא יב לָלֶכֶת׃ וַיִּשְׁכְּחוּ עֲלִילוֹתָיו וְנִפְלְאוֹתָיו אֲשֶׁר הֶרְאָם׃ נֶגֶד אֲבוֹתָם עָשָׂה
יג פֶלֶא בְּאֶרֶץ מִצְרַיִם שְׂדֵה־צֹעַן׃ בָּקַע יָם וַיַּעֲבִירֵם וַיַּצֶּב־מַיִם כְּמוֹ־נֵד׃
יד טו וַיַּנְחֵם בֶּעָנָן יוֹמָם וְכָל־הַלַּיְלָה בְּאוֹר אֵשׁ׃ יְבַקַּע צֻרִים בַּמִּדְבָּר וַיַּשְׁקְ
טז יז כִּתְהֹמוֹת רַבָּה׃ וַיּוֹצִא נוֹזְלִים מִסָּלַע וַיּוֹרֶד כַּנְּהָרוֹת מָיִם׃ וַיּוֹסִיפוּ
יח עוֹד לַחֲטֹא־לוֹ לַמְרוֹת עֶלְיוֹן בַּצִּיָּה׃ וַיְנַסּוּ־אֵל בִּלְבָבָם לִשְׁאׇל־אֹכֶל
יט כ לְנַפְשָׁם׃ וַיְדַבְּרוּ בֵּאלֹהִים אָמְרוּ הֲיוּכַל אֵל לַעֲרֹךְ שֻׁלְחָן בַּמִּדְבָּר׃ הֵן
הִכָּה־צוּר ׀ וַיָּזוּבוּ מַיִם וּנְחָלִים יִשְׁטֹפוּ הֲגַם־לֶחֶם יוּכַל תֵּת אִם־יָכִין
כא שְׁאֵר לְעַמּוֹ׃ לָכֵן ׀ שָׁמַע יְהוָה וַיִּתְעַבָּר וְאֵשׁ נִשְּׂקָה בְיַעֲקֹב וְגַם־אַף
כב כג עָלָה בְיִשְׂרָאֵל׃ כִּי לֹא הֶאֱמִינוּ בֵּאלֹהִים וְלֹא בָטְחוּ בִּישׁוּעָתוֹ׃ וַיְצַו
כד שְׁחָקִים מִמָּעַל וְדַלְתֵי שָׁמַיִם פָּתָח׃ וַיַּמְטֵר עֲלֵיהֶם מָן לֶאֱכֹל וּדְגַן־
כה כו שָׁמַיִם נָתַן לָמוֹ׃ לֶחֶם אַבִּירִים אָכַל אִישׁ צֵידָה שָׁלַח לָהֶם לָשֹׂבַע׃ יַסַּע
כז קָדִים בַּשָּׁמָיִם וַיְנַהֵג בְּעֻזּוֹ תֵימָן׃ וַיַּמְטֵר עֲלֵיהֶם כֶּעָפָר שְׁאֵר וּכְחוֹל

28 29 sand; He made them fall inside His camp, all around His dwelling place, so
30 they ate and ate their fill; He brought them what they craved, but before they
31 tired of their cravings, while their food still filled their mouths, God's wrath
flared up against them. He killed the strongest ones among them; He brought
32 down the young men of Israel. Despite all this they went on sinning and did
33 not believe in His wonders, so He wasted their days like breath and their years
34 in dismay. When He killed them, they sought Him out; they came back and
35 desperately sought God. They remembered that God was their Rock, God
36 Most High their redeemer, but they betrayed Him with their lips, and with
37 their tongues they lied to Him; their hearts were not firmly with Him; they
38 were not faithful to His covenant, but He is merciful; He forgives offense and
does not destroy. He suppresses His anger again and again and never rouses
39 His full fury. He remembers that they are but flesh, a passing breath that never
40 returns. How often they defied Him in the wilderness, aggrieving Him in the
41 wasteland; they tested God again and again, provoking the Holy One of Israel.
42 They did not recall His power on the day He redeemed them from the foe,
43 when He set out His signs in Egypt and His wonders in the fields of Tzoan.
44 45 He turned their rivers to blood, their streams undrinkable; He unleashed
46 swarms to consume them and frogs to destroy them; He gave their crops
47 to blight, their produce to the locust; He killed their vines with hail, their
48 sycamores with frost; He abandoned their livestock to the hail, their cattle to
49 bolts of lightning; He unleashed against them His blazing fury, wrath, rage,
50 and misery, a legion of destroying angels. He leveled a path for His fury; He
did not spare their souls from death but abandoned their lives to the plague.
51 He struck down every firstborn in Egypt, the first fruits of manhood in the
52 tents of Ham, then He led His people on like sheep, guiding them like a flock
53 through the wilderness. He led them in safety; they did not fear, while the sea
54 covered their enemies. He brought them to His holy realm, to the mountain
55 His right hand had won. He dispossessed nations before them, allotted
56 them shares of inheritance, and settled the tribes of Israel in their tents, but
57 they tested and defied God Most High and did not keep His decrees. They
turned back and rebelled like their ancestors, treacherous as a faulty bow;
58 they angered Him with their high shrines and aroused His jealousy with their
59 60 idols. God heard and grew furious and utterly rejected Israel. He abandoned
61 the Sanctuary of Shiloh, the tent where He dwelled among humanity. He let
62 His might fall captive, His beauty into enemy hands;[89] He abandoned His
63 people to the sword, so furious with His share was He. His young men were
64 consumed by fire; His maidens had no wedding songs. His priests fell by the
65 sword; their widows never lamented them, then the Lord awoke as if from
66 sleep, like a warrior shaking off wine, and beat back His foes, subjecting them
67 to lasting shame. Yet He rejected the tent of Yosef and did not choose the
68 tribe of Efrayim; He chose the tribe of Yehuda, Mount Zion that He loves.
69 He built His Sanctuary like the high heavens, like the earth that He founded

89 | See 1 Samuel, chapter 4.

כח כט ימים עוף כנף: ויפל בקרב מחנהו סביב למשכנתיו: ויאכלו וישבעו
ל מאד ותאותם יבא להם: לא־זרו מתאותם עוד אכלם בפיהם:
לא ואף אלהים | עלה בהם ויהרג במשמניהם ובחורי ישראל הכריע:
לב לג בכל־זאת חטאו־עוד ולא האמינו בנפלאותיו: ויכל־בהבל ימיהם
לד לה ושנותם בבהלה: אם־הרגם ודרשוהו ושבו ושחרו־אל: ויזכרו
לו כי־אלהים צורם ואל עליון גאלם: ויפתוהו בפיהם ובלשונם יכזבו־
לז לח לו: ולבם לא־נכון עמו ולא נאמנו בבריתו: והוא רחום | יכפר עון יא
לט ולא־ישחית והרבה להשיב אפו ולא־יעיר כל־חמתו: ויזכר כי־בשר
מ המה רוח הולך ולא ישוב: כמה ימרוהו במדבר יעציבוהו בישימון:
מא מב וישובו וינסו אל וקדוש ישראל התוו: לא־זכרו את־ידו יום אשר־
מג פדם מני־צר: אשר־שם במצרים אתותיו ומופתיו בשדה־צען:
מד מה ויהפך לדם יאריהם ונזליהם בל־ישתיון: ישלח בהם ערב ויאכלם
מו מז וצפרדע ותשחיתם: ויתן לחסיל יבולם ויגיעם לארבה: יהרג בברד
מח גפנם ושקמותם בחנמל: ויסגר לברד בעירם ומקניהם לרשפים:
מט נ ישלח־בם | חרון אפו עברה וזעם וצרה משלחת מלאכי רעים: יפלס
נא נתיב לאפו לא־חשך ממות נפשם וחיתם לדבר הסגיר: ויך כל־בכור
נב במצרים ראשית אונים באהלי־חם: ויסע כצאן עמו וינהגם כעדר
נג נד במדבר: וינחם לבטח ולא פחדו ואת־אויביהם כסה הים: ויביאם
נה אל־גבול קדשו הר־זה קנתה ימינו: ויגרש מפניהם | גוים ויפילם
נו בחבל נחלה וישכן באהליהם שבטי ישראל: וינסו וימרו את־אלהים
נז עליון ועדותיו לא שמרו: ויסגו ויבגדו כאבותם נהפכו כקשת רמיה:
נח נט ויכעיסוהו בבמותם ובפסיליהם יקניאוהו: שמע אלהים ויתעבר
ס סא וימאס מאד בישראל: ויטש משכן שלו אהל שכן באדם: ויתן
סב לשבי עזו ותפארתו ביד־צר: ויסגר לחרב עמו ובנחלתו התעבר:
סג סד בחוריו אכלה־אש ובתולתיו לא הוללו: כהניו בחרב נפלו ואלמנתיו
סה סו לא תבכינה: ויקץ כישן | אדני כגבור מתרונן מיין: ויך־צריו אחור
סז חרפת עולם נתן למו: וימאס באהל יוסף ובשבט אפרים לא בחר:
סח סט ויבחר את־שבט יהודה את־הר ציון אשר אהב: ויבן כמו־רמים

70 forever, and He chose David, His servant, taking him from the sheepfolds.
71 From among the ewes He brought Him to tend to Yaakov, His people, and
72 Israel, His share. He tended them with a sound heart and guided them with
a skillful hand.
79 1 *A psalm of Asaf.* God, the nations have invaded Your heritage, defiled Your
2 holy Temple, and turned Jerusalem into ruins. They have left Your servants'
corpses as food for the fowl of the heavens, the flesh of Your devoted ones
3 for the beasts of the earth. They have spilled their blood like water all around
4 Jerusalem, with none to bury them. We have become the scorn of our
5 neighbors, the laughingstock of those around us.[90] How long, LORD? Will
6 You show Your anger forever, Your indignation blazing like fire?[91] Pour out
Your fury on the nations that do not know You, on the kingdoms that do not
7 invoke Your name – for they have devoured Yaakov and laid his homeland
8 waste.[92] Do not hold our ancestors' sins against us; let Your mercy rush toward
9 us, for we have sunk so low. Help us, God of our salvation, for Your name's
10 glory; Deliver us and forgive our sins for the sake of Your name. Why should
the nations say, "Where is their God?" Let the vengeance of Your servants'
11 spilled blood be known among the nations before our own eyes. Let the
captives' groans come before You; with Your arm's great strength, preserve
12 those on the brink of death. Pay back our neighbors sevenfold with the very
13 scorn they showed You, Lord, then we, Your people and the flock You tend,
will give thanks to You forever; throughout the generations we will sing Your
praise.
80 1 2 *To the lead singer, set to* shoshanim edut,[93] *a psalm of Asaf.* Shepherd of Israel,
give ear; You who lead Yosef like a flock, You who are enthroned on the
3 cherubim, shine forth. Before Efrayim, Binyamin, and Menashe, stir Your
4 strength and come to save us. God, bring us back; let Your presence shine,
5 that we may be saved. O LORD, God of Hosts, how long will You fume at
6 Your people's prayers? You have fed them tear-soaked bread and made them
7 drink tears by the bowlful. You have set us in strife with our neighbors, and
8 our enemies mock us. God of Hosts, bring us back; let Your presence shine
9 so that we may be saved. You carried a vine out of Egypt; You drove out
10 the nations and planted it. You cleared the ground for it; it took deep root
11 and filled the land. The hills were covered by its shade, mighty cedars by its
12 branches. Its boughs reached as far as the sea, its shoots as far as the river.
13 Why have You broken through its walls so that any passerby can pluck its
14 15 fruit? The wild forest boars gnaw at it; the field creatures graze at it. God of
Hosts, come back; Look down from heaven and see; take note of this vine,
16 this seedling Your right hand planted, this shoot[94] You nurtured as Your own –
17 now burnt by fire, chopped down, destroyed by the blast of Your presence.

---

90 | Cf. 44:14.
91 | Cf. 89:47.
92 | Cf. Jeremiah 10:25.
93 | See note on 60:1.
94 | Literally "son."

ע מִקְדָּשׁוֹ כְּאֶרֶץ יְסָדָהּ לְעוֹלָם: וַיִּבְחַר בְּדָוִד עַבְדּוֹ וַיִּקָּחֵהוּ מִמִּכְלְאֹת
עא צֹאן: מֵאַחַר עָלוֹת הֱבִיאוֹ לִרְעוֹת בְּיַעֲקֹב עַמּוֹ וּבְיִשְׂרָאֵל נַחֲלָתוֹ:
עב וַיִּרְעֵם כְּתֹם לְבָבוֹ וּבִתְבוּנוֹת כַּפָּיו יַנְחֵם:
עט א מִזְמוֹר לְאָסָף אֱלֹהִים בָּאוּ גוֹיִם ׀ בְּנַחֲלָתֶךָ טִמְּאוּ אֶת־הֵיכַל קָדְשֶׁךָ
ב שָׂמוּ אֶת־יְרוּשָׁלִַם לְעִיִּים: נָתְנוּ אֶת־נִבְלַת עֲבָדֶיךָ מַאֲכָל לְעוֹף
ג הַשָּׁמָיִם בְּשַׂר חֲסִידֶיךָ לְחַיְתוֹ־אָרֶץ: שָׁפְכוּ דָמָם ׀ כַּמַּיִם סְבִיבוֹת
ד יְרוּשָׁלִָם וְאֵין קוֹבֵר: הָיִינוּ חֶרְפָּה לִשְׁכֵנֵינוּ לַעַג וָקֶלֶס לִסְבִיבוֹתֵינוּ:
ה ו עַד־מָה יְהוָה תֶּאֱנַף לָנֶצַח תִּבְעַר כְּמוֹ־אֵשׁ קִנְאָתֶךָ: שְׁפֹךְ חֲמָתְךָ ׀
אֶל־הַגּוֹיִם אֲשֶׁר לֹא־יְדָעוּךָ וְעַל מַמְלָכוֹת אֲשֶׁר בְּשִׁמְךָ לֹא קָרָאוּ:
ז ח כִּי אָכַל אֶת־יַעֲקֹב וְאֶת־נָוֵהוּ הֵשַׁמּוּ: אַל־תִּזְכָּר־לָנוּ עֲוֺנֹת רִאשֹׁנִים
ט מַהֵר יְקַדְּמוּנוּ רַחֲמֶיךָ כִּי דַלּוֹנוּ מְאֹד: עָזְרֵנוּ ׀ אֱלֹהֵי יִשְׁעֵנוּ עַל־
י דְּבַר כְּבוֹד־שְׁמֶךָ וְהַצִּילֵנוּ וְכַפֵּר עַל־חַטֹּאתֵינוּ לְמַעַן שְׁמֶךָ: לָמָּה ׀
יֹאמְרוּ הַגּוֹיִם אַיֵּה אֱלֹהֵיהֶם יִוָּדַע בגיים לְעֵינֵינוּ נִקְמַת דַּם־עֲבָדֶיךָ בַּגּוֹיִם
יא הַשָּׁפוּךְ: תָּבוֹא לְפָנֶיךָ אֶנְקַת אָסִיר כְּגֹדֶל זְרוֹעֲךָ הוֹתֵר בְּנֵי תְמוּתָה:
יב וְהָשֵׁב לִשְׁכֵנֵינוּ שִׁבְעָתַיִם אֶל־חֵיקָם חֶרְפָּתָם אֲשֶׁר חֵרְפוּךָ אֲדֹנָי:
יג וַאֲנַחְנוּ עַמְּךָ ׀ וְצֹאן מַרְעִיתֶךָ נוֹדֶה לְּךָ לְעוֹלָם לְדֹר וָדֹר נְסַפֵּר
תְּהִלָּתֶךָ:
פ א ב לַמְנַצֵּחַ אֶל־שֹׁשַׁנִּים עֵדוּת לְאָסָף מִזְמוֹר: רֹעֵה יִשְׂרָאֵל ׀ הַאֲזִינָה נֹהֵג
ג כַּצֹּאן יוֹסֵף יֹשֵׁב הַכְּרוּבִים הוֹפִיעָה: לִפְנֵי אֶפְרַיִם ׀ וּבִנְיָמִן וּמְנַשֶּׁה
ד עוֹרְרָה אֶת־גְּבוּרָתֶךָ וּלְכָה לִישֻׁעָתָה לָּנוּ: אֱלֹהִים הֲשִׁיבֵנוּ וְהָאֵר
ה פָּנֶיךָ וְנִוָּשֵׁעָה: יְהוָה אֱלֹהִים צְבָאוֹת עַד־מָתַי עָשַׁנְתָּ בִּתְפִלַּת עַמֶּךָ:
ו ז הֶאֱכַלְתָּם לֶחֶם דִּמְעָה וַתַּשְׁקֵמוֹ בִּדְמָעוֹת שָׁלִישׁ: תְּשִׂימֵנוּ מָדוֹן
ח לִשְׁכֵנֵינוּ וְאֹיְבֵינוּ יִלְעֲגוּ־לָמוֹ: אֱלֹהִים צְבָאוֹת הֲשִׁיבֵנוּ וְהָאֵר פָּנֶיךָ
ט י וְנִוָּשֵׁעָה: גֶּפֶן מִמִּצְרַיִם תַּסִּיעַ תְּגָרֵשׁ גּוֹיִם וַתִּטָּעֶהָ: פִּנִּיתָ לְפָנֶיהָ
יא וַתַּשְׁרֵשׁ שָׁרָשֶׁיהָ וַתְּמַלֵּא־אָרֶץ: כָּסּוּ הָרִים צִלָּהּ וַעֲנָפֶיהָ אַרְזֵי־אֵל:
יב יג תְּשַׁלַּח קְצִירֶהָ עַד־יָם וְאֶל־נָהָר יוֹנְקוֹתֶיהָ: לָמָּה פָּרַצְתָּ גְדֵרֶיהָ וְאָרוּהָ
יד טו כָּל־עֹבְרֵי דָרֶךְ: יְכַרְסְמֶנָּה חֲזִיר מִיָּעַר וְזִיז שָׂדַי יִרְעֶנָּה: אֱלֹהִים צְבָאוֹת
טז שׁוּב נָא הַבֵּט מִשָּׁמַיִם וּרְאֵה וּפְקֹד גֶּפֶן זֹאת: וְכַנָּה אֲשֶׁר־נָטְעָה יְמִינֶךָ
יז וְעַל־בֵּן אִמַּצְתָּה לָּךְ: שְׂרֻפָה בָאֵשׁ כְּסוּחָה מִגַּעֲרַת פָּנֶיךָ יֹאבֵדוּ:

18 Let Your hand rest on the person at Your right hand, the person You nurtured
19 as Your own, then we will not turn away from You. Give us life, and we will
20 invoke Your name. LORD, God of Hosts, bring us back; let Your presence
shine so that we may be saved.

81 1 2 *To the lead singer, on the* gittit[95] – *of Asaf.* Sing for joy to God, our might; shout
3 out to the God of Yaakov. Raise a song, beat the drum, and play the sweet harp
4 and lyre. Sound the ram's horn on the New Moon, on our feast day when the
5 moon is full, for it is a statute for Israel, an ordinance of the God of Yaakov.
6 He established it as a decree for Yosef when He rose against the land of Egypt,
7 where I heard a language that I did not know. I relieved his shoulders of the
8 burden; his hands were freed from the builder's basket. In distress you called,
and I rescued you; I answered you from the secret place of thunder; I tested
9 you at the waters of Meriva – Selah. Hear, My people, and I will warn you,
10 Israel, if you would only listen to Me! Let there be no strange god among
11 you; do not bow to an alien god. I am the LORD your God who brought you
12 out of the land of Egypt – open your mouth wide, and I will fill it. Yet My
13 people would not heed My voice; Israel would not submit to Me, so I left
14 them to their stubborn hearts, letting them follow their own devices. If only
15 My people would listen to Me, if Israel would walk in My ways, I would soon
16 subdue their enemies and turn My hand against their foes. Those who hate
the LORD would come cringing before Him; their doom would last forever.
17 He would feed Israel[96] with the finest wheat; with honey from the rock I
would satisfy you.

82 1 *A psalm of Asaf.* God stands in the divine assembly; among divine beings
2 He delivers judgment. How long will you judge unjustly, showing favor to
3 the wicked? Selah. Do justice to the weak and the orphaned; vindicate the
4 poor and destitute; rescue the weak and needy; save them from the hand of
5 the wicked. They do not know, nor do they understand; they walk about in
6 darkness while all the earth's foundations shudder. I once thought, "You are
7 divine beings; all of you are children of the Most High," but you shall die like
8 mere men; you will fall like any prince. Arise, O God; judge the earth, for all
the nations are Your possession.

83 1 2 *A song, a psalm of Asaf.* God, do not remain silent; be not deaf to me; be not
3 still, O God, for look – Your enemies bustle; Your haters have raised their
4 heads; they devise sly schemes against Your people; they conspire against
5 Your sheltered ones. They say, "Let us go and obliterate them as a nation,
6 and Israel's name will be mentioned no more." Yes, their hearts conspire
7 as one; they have formed a pact against You: the tents of Edom and the
8 Ishmaelites, Moav and the Hagrites, Geval, Amon and Amalek, Philistia,
9 and the people of Tyre; Assyria, too, has joined them, giving aid to the sons
10 of Lot – Selah. Treat them as You did Midyan[97] – and Sisera and Yavin at
11 Kishon Stream, who perished at Ein Dor, who turned into dung for the soil.

95 | See note on 8:1.
96 | Literally "him."
97 | For all the following events, see Judges, chapters 4, 6–8.

יח יט תְּהִי־יָדְךָ עַל־אִישׁ יְמִינֶךָ עַל־בֶּן־אָדָם אִמַּצְתָּ לָּךְ׃ וְלֹא־נָסוֹג מִמֶּךָּ
כ תְּחַיֵּנוּ וּבְשִׁמְךָ נִקְרָא׃ יְהוָה אֱלֹהִים צְבָאוֹת הֲשִׁיבֵנוּ הָאֵר פָּנֶיךָ
וְנִוָּשֵׁעָה׃
פא א ב לַמְנַצֵּחַ ׀ עַל־הַגִּתִּית לְאָסָף׃ הַרְנִינוּ לֵאלֹהִים עוּזֵּנוּ הָרִיעוּ לֵאלֹהֵי
ג ד יַעֲקֹב׃ שְׂאוּ־זִמְרָה וּתְנוּ־תֹף כִּנּוֹר נָעִים עִם־נָבֶל׃ תִּקְעוּ בַחֹדֶשׁ שׁוֹפָר
ה ו בַּכֶּסֶה לְיוֹם חַגֵּנוּ׃ כִּי חֹק לְיִשְׂרָאֵל הוּא מִשְׁפָּט לֵאלֹהֵי יַעֲקֹב׃ עֵדוּת ׀
בִּיהוֹסֵף שָׂמוֹ בְּצֵאתוֹ עַל־אֶרֶץ מִצְרָיִם שְׂפַת לֹא־יָדַעְתִּי אֶשְׁמָע׃
ז ח הֲסִירוֹתִי מִסֵּבֶל שִׁכְמוֹ כַּפָּיו מִדּוּד תַּעֲבֹרְנָה׃ בַּצָּרָה קָרָאתָ וָאֲחַלְּצֶךָּ
ט אֶעֶנְךָ בְּסֵתֶר רַעַם אֶבְחָנְךָ עַל־מֵי מְרִיבָה סֶלָה׃ שְׁמַע עַמִּי וְאָעִידָה
י בָּךְ יִשְׂרָאֵל אִם־תִּשְׁמַע־לִי׃ לֹא־יִהְיֶה בְךָ אֵל זָר וְלֹא תִשְׁתַּחֲוֶה
יא לְאֵל נֵכָר׃ אָנֹכִי ׀ יְהוָה אֱלֹהֶיךָ הַמַּעַלְךָ מֵאֶרֶץ מִצְרָיִם הַרְחֶב־פִּיךָ
יב יג וַאֲמַלְאֵהוּ׃ וְלֹא־שָׁמַע עַמִּי לְקוֹלִי וְיִשְׂרָאֵל לֹא־אָבָה לִי׃ וָאֲשַׁלְּחֵהוּ
יד בִּשְׁרִירוּת לִבָּם יֵלְכוּ בְּמוֹעֲצוֹתֵיהֶם׃ לוּ עַמִּי שֹׁמֵעַ לִי יִשְׂרָאֵל בִּדְרָכַי
טו טז יְהַלֵּכוּ׃ כִּמְעַט אוֹיְבֵיהֶם אַכְנִיעַ וְעַל־צָרֵיהֶם אָשִׁיב יָדִי׃ מְשַׂנְאֵי
יז יְהוָה יְכַחֲשׁוּ־לוֹ וִיהִי עִתָּם לְעוֹלָם׃ וַיַּאֲכִילֵהוּ מֵחֵלֶב חִטָּה וּמִצּוּר
דְּבַשׁ אַשְׂבִּיעֶךָ׃
פב א ב מִזְמוֹר לְאָסָף אֱלֹהִים נִצָּב בַּעֲדַת־אֵל בְּקֶרֶב אֱלֹהִים יִשְׁפֹּט׃ עַד־מָתַי
ג תִּשְׁפְּטוּ־עָוֶל וּפְנֵי רְשָׁעִים תִּשְׂאוּ־סֶלָה׃ שִׁפְטוּ־דַל וְיָתוֹם עָנִי וָרָשׁ
ד ה הַצְדִּיקוּ׃ פַּלְּטוּ־דַל וְאֶבְיוֹן מִיַּד רְשָׁעִים הַצִּילוּ׃ לֹא יָדְעוּ ׀ וְלֹא יָבִינוּ
ו בַּחֲשֵׁכָה יִתְהַלָּכוּ יִמּוֹטוּ כָּל־מוֹסְדֵי אָרֶץ׃ אֲנִי־אָמַרְתִּי אֱלֹהִים אַתֶּם
ז ח וּבְנֵי עֶלְיוֹן כֻּלְּכֶם׃ אָכֵן כְּאָדָם תְּמוּתוּן וּכְאַחַד הַשָּׂרִים תִּפֹּלוּ׃ קוּמָה
אֱלֹהִים שָׁפְטָה הָאָרֶץ כִּי־אַתָּה תִנְחַל בְּכָל־הַגּוֹיִם׃
פג א ב שִׁיר מִזְמוֹר לְאָסָף׃ אֱלֹהִים אַל־דֳּמִי־לָךְ אַל־תֶּחֱרַשׁ וְאַל־תִּשְׁקֹט
ג ד אֵל׃ כִּי־הִנֵּה אוֹיְבֶיךָ יֶהֱמָיוּן וּמְשַׂנְאֶיךָ נָשְׂאוּ רֹאשׁ׃ עַל־עַמְּךָ יַעֲרִימוּ
ה סוֹד וְיִתְיָעֲצוּ עַל־צְפוּנֶיךָ׃ אָמְרוּ לְכוּ וְנַכְחִידֵם מִגּוֹי וְלֹא־יִזָּכֵר שֵׁם־
ו ז יִשְׂרָאֵל עוֹד׃ כִּי נוֹעֲצוּ לֵב יַחְדָּו עָלֶיךָ בְּרִית יִכְרֹתוּ׃ אָהֳלֵי אֱדוֹם
ח וְיִשְׁמְעֵאלִים מוֹאָב וְהַגְרִים׃ גְּבָל וְעַמּוֹן וַעֲמָלֵק פְּלֶשֶׁת עִם־יֹשְׁבֵי
ט י צוֹר׃ גַּם־אַשּׁוּר נִלְוָה עִמָּם הָיוּ זְרוֹעַ לִבְנֵי־לוֹט סֶלָה׃ עֲשֵׂה־לָהֶם
יא כְּמִדְיָן כְּסִיסְרָא כְיָבִין בְּנַחַל קִישׁוֹן׃ נִשְׁמְדוּ בְעֵין־דֹּאר הָיוּ דֹּמֶן

12 Render their nobles like Orev and Ze'ev, all their princes like Zevaḥ and
13 14 Tzalmuna, who said, "We will seize possession of God's meadows." My
15 God, make them like thistledown, like straw before the wind. As fire burns
16 up forests, as flame sets the hills ablaze, so shall You chase them with Your
17 storm and terrify them with Your whirlwind. Fill their faces with humiliation
18 until they seek Your name, LORD. May they ever be shamed and terrified; let
19 them be reviled; let them perish. Then they will know that Your name, Yours
alone, is the LORD, Most High over all the earth.
84 1 2 *To the lead singer, on the* gittit[98] *– a psalm of the sons of Koraḥ.*[99] How lovely
3 is Your dwelling place, O LORD of Hosts. My soul longs and pines for the
4 LORD's courtyards; my heart and my body sing out to the living God. Even
the bird makes a home for herself, the swallow a nest where she lays her
5 young – near Your altars, LORD of Hosts, my King and my God. Happy are
6 those who dwell in Your house; they will ever praise You – Selah. Happy are
7 those whose strength is in You, the paths ahead are in their hearts, those who
pass through the Valley of the Baca make it into a spring as if the early rain
8 cloaks it with blessing, so they go from rampart to rampart and appear before
9 God in Zion. O LORD, God of Hosts, listen to my prayer; Give ear, O God of
10 Yaakov – Selah. See our shield, God, and look upon the face of Your anointed
11 one, for a single day in Your courtyards is better than a thousand elsewhere;
I would rather remain at the threshold of the House of my God than dwell in
12 tents of wickedness, for the LORD God is sun and shield; the LORD will grant
grace and glory; He will not withhold good from those who walk blamelessly.
13 O LORD of Hosts, happy are those who trust in You.
85 1 2 *To the lead singer – a psalm of the sons of Koraḥ.* You showed favor to Your land,
3 LORD; You restored Yaakov's fortune. You forgave Your people's offense and
4 covered over all their sins – Selah. You gathered up all Your anger and turned
5 back from Your blazing fury. Bring us back, God of our salvation; retract Your
6 wrath against us. Will You show Your anger against us forever, drawing out
7 Your fury throughout the generations? Will You not give us life once more
8 so that Your people may rejoice in You? Show us Your loyalty, LORD; grant
9 us Your salvation. I wish to hear what God, the LORD, will speak when He
speaks of peace for His people and devoted ones – may they not turn back
10 to foolishness, for His salvation is close to those who fear Him – so that His
11 glory will dwell in our land. Loyalty and truth will meet; justice and peace
12 will kiss. Truth will sprout up from the earth, and justice will gaze down from
13 heaven. Yes, the LORD will grant goodness, and our land will yield its fruit.
14 Justice will walk before Him, marking a path for His steps.
86 1 *A prayer of David.* Lend Your ear to me, LORD, and answer me, for I am poor
2 and needy. Preserve my life, for I am devoted. You are my God; save Your
3 servant who trusts in You. Show me grace, Lord, for to You I call all day
4 long. Bring joy to the soul of Your servant, for to You, Lord, I lift up my soul,

---

98 | See note on 8:1.
99 | See note on 42:1.

יב לְאַדְמָה׃ שִׁיתֵמוֹ נְדִיבֵמוֹ כְּעֹרֵב וְכִזְאֵב וּכְזֶבַח וּכְצַלְמֻנָּע כָּל־נְסִיכֵמוֹ׃
יג יד אֲשֶׁר אָמְרוּ נִירֲשָׁה לָּנוּ אֵת נְאוֹת אֱלֹהִים׃ אֱלֹהַי שִׁיתֵמוֹ כַגַּלְגַּל כְּקַשׁ
טו טז לִפְנֵי־רוּחַ׃ כְּאֵשׁ תִּבְעַר־יָעַר וּכְלֶהָבָה תְּלַהֵט הָרִים׃ כֵּן תִּרְדְּפֵם
יז בְּסַעֲרֶךָ וּבְסוּפָתְךָ תְבַהֲלֵם׃ מַלֵּא פְנֵיהֶם קָלוֹן וִיבַקְשׁוּ שִׁמְךָ יְהוָה׃
יח יט יֵבֹשׁוּ וְיִבָּהֲלוּ עֲדֵי־עַד וְיַחְפְּרוּ וְיֹאבֵדוּ׃ וְיֵדְעוּ כִּי־אַתָּה שִׁמְךָ יְהוָה
לְבַדֶּךָ עֶלְיוֹן עַל־כָּל־הָאָרֶץ׃

פד א ב לַמְנַצֵּחַ עַל־הַגִּתִּית לִבְנֵי־קֹרַח מִזְמוֹר׃ מַה־יְּדִידוֹת מִשְׁכְּנוֹתֶיךָ יְהוָה
ג צְבָאוֹת׃ נִכְסְפָה וְגַם־כָּלְתָה ׀ נַפְשִׁי לְחַצְרוֹת יְהוָה לִבִּי וּבְשָׂרִי יְרַנְּנוּ
ד אֶל אֵל־חָי׃ גַּם־צִפּוֹר ׀ מָצְאָה בַיִת וּדְרוֹר ׀ קֵן ׀ לָהּ אֲשֶׁר־שָׁתָה
ה אֶפְרֹחֶיהָ אֶת־מִזְבְּחוֹתֶיךָ יְהוָה צְבָאוֹת מַלְכִּי וֵאלֹהָי׃ אַשְׁרֵי יוֹשְׁבֵי
ו בֵיתֶךָ עוֹד יְהַלְלוּךָ סֶּלָה׃ אַשְׁרֵי אָדָם עוֹז־לוֹ בָךְ מְסִלּוֹת בִּלְבָבָם׃
ז ח עֹבְרֵי ׀ בְּעֵמֶק הַבָּכָא מַעְיָן יְשִׁיתוּהוּ גַּם־בְּרָכוֹת יַעְטֶה מוֹרֶה׃ יֵלְכוּ
ט מֵחַיִל אֶל־חָיִל יֵרָאֶה אֶל־אֱלֹהִים בְּצִיּוֹן׃ יְהוָה אֱלֹהִים צְבָאוֹת שִׁמְעָה
י תְפִלָּתִי הַאֲזִינָה אֱלֹהֵי יַעֲקֹב סֶלָה׃ מָגִנֵּנוּ רְאֵה אֱלֹהִים וְהַבֵּט פְּנֵי
יא מְשִׁיחֶךָ׃ כִּי טוֹב־יוֹם בַּחֲצֵרֶיךָ מֵאָלֶף בָּחַרְתִּי הִסְתּוֹפֵף בְּבֵית אֱלֹהַי
יב מִדּוּר בְּאָהֳלֵי־רֶשַׁע׃ כִּי שֶׁמֶשׁ ׀ וּמָגֵן יְהוָה אֱלֹהִים חֵן וְכָבוֹד יִתֵּן
יג יְהוָה לֹא יִמְנַע־טוֹב לַהֹלְכִים בְּתָמִים׃ יְהוָה צְבָאוֹת אַשְׁרֵי אָדָם יב
בֹּטֵחַ בָּךְ׃

פה א ב לַמְנַצֵּחַ לִבְנֵי־קֹרַח מִזְמוֹר׃ רָצִיתָ יְהוָה אַרְצֶךָ שַׁבְתָּ שבות יַעֲקֹב׃ שְׁבִית
ג ד נָשָׂאתָ עֲוֺן עַמֶּךָ כִּסִּיתָ כָל־חַטָּאתָם סֶלָה׃ אָסַפְתָּ כָל־עֶבְרָתֶךָ הֱשִׁיבוֹתָ
ה ו מֵחֲרוֹן אַפֶּךָ׃ שׁוּבֵנוּ אֱלֹהֵי יִשְׁעֵנוּ וְהָפֵר כַּעַסְךָ עִמָּנוּ׃ הַלְעוֹלָם תֶּאֱנַף־
ז בָּנוּ תִּמְשֹׁךְ אַפְּךָ לְדֹר וָדֹר׃ הֲלֹא־אַתָּה תָּשׁוּב תְּחַיֵּנוּ וְעַמְּךָ יִשְׂמְחוּ־
ח ט בָךְ׃ הַרְאֵנוּ יְהוָה חַסְדֶּךָ וְיֶשְׁעֲךָ תִּתֶּן־לָנוּ׃ אֶשְׁמְעָה מַה־יְדַבֵּר הָאֵל ׀
יְהוָה כִּי ׀ יְדַבֵּר שָׁלוֹם אֶל־עַמּוֹ וְאֶל־חֲסִידָיו וְאַל־יָשׁוּבוּ לְכִסְלָה׃
י יא אַךְ קָרוֹב לִירֵאָיו יִשְׁעוֹ לִשְׁכֹּן כָּבוֹד בְּאַרְצֵנוּ׃ חֶסֶד־וֶאֱמֶת נִפְגָּשׁוּ
יב יג צֶדֶק וְשָׁלוֹם נָשָׁקוּ׃ אֱמֶת מֵאֶרֶץ תִּצְמָח וְצֶדֶק מִשָּׁמַיִם נִשְׁקָף׃ גַּם־
יד יְהוָה יִתֵּן הַטּוֹב וְאַרְצֵנוּ תִּתֵּן יְבוּלָהּ׃ צֶדֶק לְפָנָיו יְהַלֵּךְ וְיָשֵׂם לְדֶרֶךְ
פְּעָמָיו׃

פו א ב תְּפִלָּה לְדָוִד הַטֵּה־יְהוָה אָזְנְךָ עֲנֵנִי כִּי־עָנִי וְאֶבְיוֹן אָנִי׃ שָׁמְרָה נַפְשִׁי
ג כִּי־חָסִיד אָנִי הוֹשַׁע עַבְדְּךָ אַתָּה אֱלֹהַי הַבּוֹטֵחַ אֵלֶיךָ׃ חָנֵּנִי אֲדֹנָי
ד כִּי־אֵלֶיךָ אֶקְרָא כָּל־הַיּוֹם׃ שַׂמֵּחַ נֶפֶשׁ עַבְדֶּךָ כִּי־אֵלֶיךָ אֲדֹנָי נַפְשִׁי

5 for You, Lord, are good and forgiving, abounding in loyalty to all who call
6 7 to You. Give ear, LORD, to my prayer; listen to the sound of my plea. On the
8 day of my distress I call to You, for You will answer me. There are none like
9 You, Lord, among the gods, and no works like Yours. All the nations You
have made will come and bow before You, Lord, adding glory to Your name,
10 11 for You are great and work wonders; You alone are God. Teach me Your way,
LORD; I will walk in Your truth. Make my heart whole to revere Your name.
12 I will praise You, Lord my God, with all my heart, and give glory to Your
13 name forever, for Your loyalty to me is great; You have saved my soul from the
14 depths of Sheol. God, the insolent have risen against me; a cruel mob seeks
15 my life – they have no regard for You,[100] but You, Lord, are a compassionate
16 and gracious God, slow to anger and abounding in kindness and truth.[101] Turn
to me and show me grace; grant Your might to Your servant; save the child
17 of Your handmaid. Show me a sign of favor so that my haters will see and be
shamed when You, LORD, give me help and comfort.

87 1 *Of the sons of Koraḥ – a psalm, a song.* His foundation on the holy mountains –
2 3 the LORD loves the gates of Zion more than all of Yaakov's dwellings. Glorious
4 things are said of you, O city of God – Selah. Among those who know me I
mention Rahav[102] and Babylon, Philistia, Tyre, or Kush – "This one was born
5 there" – but of Zion it is said, "One and all were born there," and the Most
6 High Himself has established her. The LORD will keep count in the record
7 of peoples: "This one was born there" – Selah. They will dance and sing, "All
my springs well from you!"

88 1 *A song, a psalm of the sons of Koraḥ – to the lead singer,* maḥalat le'annot[103] – *a*
2 maskil *of Heiman the Ezrahite.*[104] O LORD, God of my salvation, I cried out by
3 day and before You by night. Let my prayer come before You; lend Your ear
4 to my plea, for my soul is glutted with misery; my life hovers on the brink of
5 Sheol; I am counted among those down in the Pit. I am like one drained of
6 vitality, abandoned[105] among the dead like corpses lying in the grave whom
7 You no longer recall, cut off from Your care. You have set me in the deepest
8 pit, in the darkness, in the depths; Your wrath weighs down upon me with
9 all Your overwhelming waves. You have distanced my friends from me; You
10 made me a horror to them; I am trapped with no way out. My eyes are sore
from suffering; I call out to You, LORD, each day; I stretch my hands out to
11 You. Will You work wonders for the dead? Will the shades rise up and praise
12 You? – Selah. Is Your loyalty mentioned in the grave, Your faithfulness in
13 the realm of destruction? Are Your wonders known in the darkness, Your
14 righteousness in the land of oblivion? As for me – to You, O LORD, I cry
15 out; my prayers greet You each morning. Why, O LORD, have You forsaken

---

100 | Cf. 54:5.
101 | Cf. Exodus 34:6.
102 | A mythical beast, here a symbolic designation for Egypt; cf. Isaiah 30:7.
103 | An unknown musical phrase; cf. 53:1.
104 | A famed Temple musician. See 1 Chronicles 15:17, 19, 25:4–6.
105 | Literally "freed."

ה ו אשא: כי־אתה אדני טוב וסלח ורב־חסד לכל־קראיך: האזינה יהוה
ז תפלתי והקשיבה בקול תחנונותי: ביום צרתי אקראך כי תענני:
ח ט אין־כמוך באלהים | אדני ואין כמעשיך: כל־גוים | אשר עשית
י יבואו | וישתחוו לפניך אדני ויכבדו לשמך: כי־גדול אתה ועשה
יא נפלאות אתה אלהים לבדך: הורני יהוה | דרכך אהלך באמתך יחד
יב לבבי ליראה שמך: אודך | אדני אלהי בכל־לבבי ואכבדה שמך
יג יד לעולם: כי־חסדך גדול עלי והצלת נפשי משאול תחתיה: אלהים |
טו זדים קמו־עלי ועדת עריצים בקשו נפשי ולא שמוך לנגדם: ואתה
טז אדני אל־רחום וחנון ארך אפים ורב־חסד ואמת: פנה אלי וחנני
יז תנה־עזך לעבדך והושיעה לבן־אמתך: עשה־עמי אות לטובה
ויראו שנאי ויבשו כי־אתה יהוה עזרתני ונחמתני:

פז א ב לבני־קרח מזמור שיר יסודתו בהררי־קדש: אהב יהוה שערי ציון
ג ד מכל משכנות יעקב: נכבדות מדבר בך עיר האלהים סלה: אזכיר |
ה רהב ובבל לידעי הנה פלשת וצור עם־כוש זה ילד־שם: ולציון |
ו יאמר איש ואיש ילד־בה והוא יכוננה עליון: יהוה יספר בכתוב
ז עמים זה ילד־שם סלה: ושרים כחללים כל־מעיני בך:

פח א שיר מזמור לבני קרח למנצח על־מחלת לענות משכיל להימן
ב ג האזרחי: יהוה אלהי ישועתי יום־צעקתי בלילה נגדך: תבוא לפניך
ד תפלתי הטה אזנך לרנתי: כי־שבעה ברעות נפשי וחיי לשאול
ה ו הגיעו: נחשבתי עם־יורדי בור הייתי כגבר אין־איל: במתים חפשי
כמו חללים | שכבי קבר אשר לא זכרתם עוד והמה מידך נגזרו:
ז ח שתני בבור תחתיות במחשכים במצלות: עלי סמכה חמתך וכל־
ט משבריך עניתה סלה: הרחקת מידעי ממני שתני תועבות למו כלא
י ולא אצא: עיני דאבה מני עני קראתיך יהוה בכל־יום שטחתי אליך
יא יב כפי: הלמתים תעשה־פלא אם־רפאים יקומו | יודוך סלה: היספר
יג בקבר חסדך אמונתך באבדון: היודע בחשך פלאך וצדקתך בארץ
יד טו נשיה: ואני | אליך יהוה שועתי ובבקר תפלתי תקדמך: למה יהוה

16 me; why do You hide Your face from me? Since my youth I have been poor,
17 wasting away, bearing Your terrors wherever I turn. Your fury has washed
18 over me; Your agonies devastate me. They surround me like water all day
19 long, completely encircling me. You have distanced me from loved one and
friend; those who know me are but darkness.

89 1 2 *A maskil of Eitan the Ezrahite.*[106] Let me sing of the LORD's loyalty forever;
3 I will spread word of Your faithfulness for all generations, for I thought,
Eternal loyalty has been built, constant as the heavens You established with
4 Your faithfulness – "I have formed a covenant with My chosen one; I have
5 sworn to My servant David. I will establish your seed forever; I have built
6 your throne for all generations" – Selah. The heavens praise Your wonders,
7 LORD, Your faithfulness among the holy assembly, for who in the skies can
compare with the LORD? Who is like the LORD among the heavenly beings,
8 9 a God so dreaded in the holy council, fearsome to all around Him? O LORD,
God of Hosts, who is as powerful as You, LORD? Your faithfulness surrounds
10 You. You rule over the surging sea – when its waves mount high, it is You who
11 stills them. It is You who crushed Rahav[107] to a corpse; with Your mighty
12 arm You scattered Your enemies. Yours are the heavens; Yours, too, is the
13 earth – You founded the world and all that fills it. The north and the south
14 were created by You; Tavor and Ḥermon[108] sing for joy of Your name. Yours
is an arm endowed with strength; Your hand is mighty; Your right hand is
15 raised high. Righteousness and justice form the base of Your throne; loyalty
16 and truth go before You. Happy are the people who know the joyful shout,
17 LORD; they walk in the light of Your presence. They rejoice in Your name all
18 day long, raised up through Your righteousness, for You are their beauty and
19 might, and our horn is raised high by Your favor, for our shield belongs to
20 the LORD, our king to the Holy One of Israel. Once in a vision You spoke to
Your devoted ones, saying, "I have granted help for a hero; I have raised up a
21 chosen one from the people. I have found David, My servant, and with My
22 holy oil anointed him so that My hand will be ready to help him, My arm to
23 24 give him strength. No enemy shall harm him, no wicked one oppress him; I
25 will cut down his foes before him and strike down his haters. My faithfulness
26 and loyalty are with him; his horn will be raised up in My name. I will set
27 his hand upon the sea, his right hand over the rivers. He will say to me, 'You
28 are my father, My God, the Rock of my salvation,' and I will make him my
29 firstborn, most high over kings of the earth. I will ever keep My loyalty for
30 him, My covenant ever faithful to him; I will appoint his seed forever, his
31 throne as lasting as the heavens. But if his children forsake My teaching and
32 do not follow in My laws, if they violate My statutes and do not keep My
33 commandments, I will punish their transgressions with the rod, their offenses
34 with wounds, but I will never withdraw from him My loyalty, nor betray
35 My faithfulness; I will not violate My covenant, nor alter what My lips have

---

106 | See 1 Chronicles 15:17, 19.

107 | See note on 87:4; cf. Isaiah 51:9; Job 26:12.

108 | Prominent mountains in the Galilee and Golan regions, respectively.

טז תִּזְנַח נַפְשִׁי תַּסְתִּיר פָּנֶיךָ מִמֶּנִּי׃ עָנִי אֲנִי וְגֹוֵעַ מִנֹּעַר נָשָׂאתִי אֵמֶיךָ
יז יח אָפוּנָה׃ עָלַי עָבְרוּ חֲרוֹנֶיךָ בִּעוּתֶיךָ צִמְּתוּתֻנִי׃ סַבּוּנִי כַמַּיִם כׇּל־הַיּוֹם
יט הִקִּיפוּ עָלַי יָחַד׃ הִרְחַקְתָּ מִמֶּנִּי אֹהֵב וָרֵעַ מְיֻדָּעַי מַחְשָׁךְ׃
פט א ב מַשְׂכִּיל לְאֵיתָן הָאֶזְרָחִי׃ חַסְדֵי יהוה עוֹלָם אָשִׁירָה לְדֹר וָדֹר ׀ אוֹדִיעַ
ג אֱמוּנָתְךָ בְּפִי׃ כִּי־אָמַרְתִּי עוֹלָם חֶסֶד יִבָּנֶה שָׁמַיִם ׀ תָּכִן אֱמוּנָתְךָ בָהֶם׃
ד ה כָּרַתִּי בְרִית לִבְחִירִי נִשְׁבַּעְתִּי לְדָוִד עַבְדִּי׃ עַד־עוֹלָם אָכִין זַרְעֶךָ וּבָנִיתִי
ו לְדֹר־וָדוֹר כִּסְאֲךָ סֶלָה׃ וְיוֹדוּ שָׁמַיִם פִּלְאֲךָ יהוה אַף־אֱמוּנָתְךָ בִּקְהַל
ז ח קְדֹשִׁים׃ כִּי מִי בַשַּׁחַק יַעֲרֹךְ לַיהוה יִדְמֶה לַיהוה בִּבְנֵי אֵלִים׃ אֵל
ט נַעֲרָץ בְּסוֹד־קְדֹשִׁים רַבָּה וְנוֹרָא עַל־כׇּל־סְבִיבָיו׃ יהוה ׀ אֱלֹהֵי צְבָאוֹת
י מִי־כָמוֹךָ חֲסִין ׀ יָהּ וֶאֱמוּנָתְךָ סְבִיבוֹתֶיךָ׃ אַתָּה מוֹשֵׁל בְּגֵאוּת הַיָּם
יא בְּשׂוֹא גַלָּיו אַתָּה תְשַׁבְּחֵם׃ אַתָּה דִכִּאתָ כֶחָלָל רָהַב בִּזְרוֹעַ עֻזְּךָ
יב פִּזַּרְתָּ אוֹיְבֶיךָ׃ לְךָ שָׁמַיִם אַף־לְךָ אָרֶץ תֵּבֵל וּמְלֹאָהּ אַתָּה יְסַדְתָּם׃
יג יד צָפוֹן וְיָמִין אַתָּה בְרָאתָם תָּבוֹר וְחֶרְמוֹן בְּשִׁמְךָ יְרַנֵּנוּ׃ לְךָ זְרוֹעַ עִם־
טו גְּבוּרָה תָּעֹז יָדְךָ תָּרוּם יְמִינֶךָ׃ צֶדֶק וּמִשְׁפָּט מְכוֹן כִּסְאֶךָ חֶסֶד וֶאֱמֶת
טז יְקַדְּמוּ פָנֶיךָ׃ אַשְׁרֵי הָעָם יוֹדְעֵי תְרוּעָה יהוה בְּאוֹר־פָּנֶיךָ יְהַלֵּכוּן׃
יז יח בְּשִׁמְךָ יְגִילוּן כׇּל־הַיּוֹם וּבְצִדְקָתְךָ יָרוּמוּ׃ כִּי־תִפְאֶרֶת עֻזָּמוֹ אָתָּה
יט כ וּבִרְצוֹנְךָ תרים קַרְנֵנוּ׃ כִּי לַיהוה מָגִנֵּנוּ וְלִקְדוֹשׁ יִשְׂרָאֵל מַלְכֵּנוּ׃ אָז תָּרוּם
דִּבַּרְתָּ בְחָזוֹן לַחֲסִידֶיךָ וַתֹּאמֶר שִׁוִּיתִי עֵזֶר עַל־גִּבּוֹר הֲרִימוֹתִי בָחוּר
כא כב מֵעָם׃ מָצָאתִי דָּוִד עַבְדִּי בְּשֶׁמֶן קׇדְשִׁי מְשַׁחְתִּיו׃ אֲשֶׁר יָדִי תִּכּוֹן עִמּוֹ
כג כד אַף־זְרוֹעִי תְאַמְּצֶנּוּ׃ לֹא־יַשִּׁא אוֹיֵב בּוֹ וּבֶן־עַוְלָה לֹא יְעַנֶּנּוּ׃ וְכַתּוֹתִי
כה מִפָּנָיו צָרָיו וּמְשַׂנְאָיו אֶגּוֹף׃ וֶאֱמוּנָתִי וְחַסְדִּי עִמּוֹ וּבִשְׁמִי תָּרוּם קַרְנוֹ׃
כו כז וְשַׂמְתִּי בַיָּם יָדוֹ וּבַנְּהָרוֹת יְמִינוֹ׃ הוּא יִקְרָאֵנִי אָבִי אָתָּה אֵלִי וְצוּר
כח כט יְשׁוּעָתִי׃ אַף־אָנִי בְּכוֹר אֶתְּנֵהוּ עֶלְיוֹן לְמַלְכֵי־אָרֶץ׃ לְעוֹלָם אשמור־לוֹ אֶשְׁמׇר־
ל לא חַסְדִּי וּבְרִיתִי נֶאֱמֶנֶת לוֹ׃ וְשַׂמְתִּי לָעַד זַרְעוֹ וְכִסְאוֹ כִּימֵי שָׁמָיִם׃ אִם־
לב יַעַזְבוּ בָנָיו תּוֹרָתִי וּבְמִשְׁפָּטַי לֹא יֵלֵכוּן׃ אִם־חֻקֹּתַי יְחַלֵּלוּ וּמִצְוֺתַי
לג לד לֹא יִשְׁמֹרוּ׃ וּפָקַדְתִּי בְשֵׁבֶט פִּשְׁעָם וּבִנְגָעִים עֲוֺנָם׃ וְחַסְדִּי לֹא־אָפִיר
לה מֵעִמּוֹ וְלֹא־אֲשַׁקֵּר בֶּאֱמוּנָתִי׃ לֹא־אֲחַלֵּל בְּרִיתִי וּמוֹצָא שְׂפָתַי לֹא

36 uttered. I have sworn by My holiness once and for all – I will never be false
37 to David. His seed will continue forever, His throne before Me like the sun,
38 established forever like the moon, that faithful witness in the sky" – Selah.
39 But You – You have forsaken, You have spurned, You grew furious at Your
40 anointed. You renounced Your servant's covenant and defiled his crown in the
41 42 dust. You broke down all his walls, and turned his fortresses to ruins. All who
43 pass by plunder him, and he has become his neighbors' scorn. You raised the
44 right hand of his foes and delighted all his enemies. You even turned back the
45 blade of his sword, and did not bolster him in battle. You brought his glory
46 to an end and hurled his throne to the ground. You cut short the days of his
47 prime and cloaked him with shame – Selah. How long, LORD? Will You hide
48 Yourself forever, Your wrath blazing like fire? Remember how brief my life
49 is – did You create humanity for naught? Who can live without seeing death
50 or save himself from Sheol's grasp? – Selah. Where are Your loyalties of old,
51 Lord, when You faithfully swore to David? Remember, Lord, the taunts Your
52 servants bore, what I bore from so many people, the taunts of Your enemies,
53 LORD, who taunted Your anointed at every step. Blessed is the LORD forever,
Amen and Amen.

BOOK FOUR

90 1 *A prayer of Moshe, the man of God.* Lord, You have been our shelter in every
2 generation. Before the mountains were born, before You brought forth the
3 earth and the world, from eternity to eternity, You are God. You turn mortals
4 back into dust, saying, "Return, you children of men," for a thousand years
in Your sight are like yesterday that has passed, like a brief watch in the night.
5 You sweep them away like a fleeting dream; in the morning they are like grass
6 newly grown – in the morning it sprouts and flourishes; by evening it withers
7 8 and dries up, for we are consumed by Your anger, terrified by Your fury. You
have set our iniquities before Yourself, our secret sins in the light of Your
9 presence. All our days pass away in Your wrath; we spend our years like a sigh.
10 The span of our life is seventy years – perhaps eighty, if we are strong – but
the best of them are toil and sorrow, for they are soon gone, and we fly away.
11 Who can know the force of Your anger? Your wrath matches the reverence
12 due to You. Teach us to count our days rightly, that our hearts may grow wise.
13 Relent, O LORD! How much longer? Show compassion for Your servants.
14 Nourish us each morning with Your loving-kindness so that we may sing and
15 rejoice all our days. Repay us with joy for the pain You inflicted upon us, for
16 all the years we saw suffering. Let Your deeds be seen by Your servants and
17 Your glory by their children. May the Lord our God's sweetness be upon us.
Grant us success through our efforts, and may our efforts succeed!
91 1 He who lives in the shelter of the Most High dwells in the shadow of Shaddai.
2 I say of the LORD, "My refuge and stronghold, my God in whom I trust,"
3 4 for He will save you from the fowler's snare, from deadly plague. With His
pinions He will cover you; beneath His wings you will find shelter; His loyalty
5 is an encircling shield. You need not fear terror by night, nor the arrow that
6 flies by day, nor the plague that stalks in darkness, nor disease that ravages

לו לז אֲשַׁנֶּה: אַחַת נִשְׁבַּעְתִּי בְקׇדְשִׁי אִם־לְדָוִד אֲכַזֵּב: זַרְעוֹ לְעוֹלָם יִהְיֶה
לח לט וְכִסְאוֹ כַשֶּׁמֶשׁ נֶגְדִּי: כְּיָרֵחַ יִכּוֹן עוֹלָם וְעֵד בַּשַּׁחַק נֶאֱמָן סֶלָה: וְאַתָּה
מ זָנַחְתָּ וַתִּמְאָס הִתְעַבַּרְתָּ עִם־מְשִׁיחֶךָ: נֵאַרְתָּה בְּרִית עַבְדֶּךָ חִלַּלְתָּ
מא מב לָאָרֶץ נִזְרוֹ: פָּרַצְתָּ כׇל־גְּדֵרֹתָיו שַׂמְתָּ מִבְצָרָיו מְחִתָּה: שַׁסֻּהוּ כׇּל־
מג עֹבְרֵי דָרֶךְ הָיָה חֶרְפָּה לִשְׁכֵנָיו: הֲרִימוֹתָ יְמִין צָרָיו הִשְׂמַחְתָּ כׇּל־
מד מה אוֹיְבָיו: אַף־תָּשִׁיב צוּר חַרְבּוֹ וְלֹא הֲקֵמֹתוֹ בַּמִּלְחָמָה: הִשְׁבַּתָּ מִטְּהָרוֹ
מו וְכִסְאוֹ לָאָרֶץ מִגַּרְתָּה: הִקְצַרְתָּ יְמֵי עֲלוּמָיו הֶעֱטִיתָ עָלָיו בּוּשָׁה
מז מח סֶלָה: עַד־מָה יְהוָה תִּסָּתֵר לָנֶצַח תִּבְעַר כְּמוֹ־אֵשׁ חֲמָתֶךָ: זְכׇר־
מט אֲנִי מֶה־חָלֶד עַל־מַה־שָּׁוְא בָּרָאתָ כׇל־בְּנֵי־אָדָם: מִי גֶבֶר יִחְיֶה וְלֹא
נ יִרְאֶה־מָּוֶת יְמַלֵּט נַפְשׁוֹ מִיַּד־שְׁאוֹל סֶלָה: אַיֵּה ׀ חֲסָדֶיךָ הָרִאשֹׁנִים ׀
נא אֲדֹנָי נִשְׁבַּעְתָּ לְדָוִד בֶּאֱמוּנָתֶךָ: זְכֹר אֲדֹנָי חֶרְפַּת עֲבָדֶיךָ שְׂאֵתִי בְחֵיקִי
נב כׇּל־רַבִּים עַמִּים: אֲשֶׁר חֵרְפוּ אוֹיְבֶיךָ ׀ יְהוָה אֲשֶׁר חֵרְפוּ עִקְּבוֹת
נג מְשִׁיחֶךָ: בָּרוּךְ יְהוָה לְעוֹלָם אָמֵן ׀ וְאָמֵן:

ספר רביעי
צ א תְּפִלָּה לְמֹשֶׁה אִישׁ־הָאֱלֹהִים אֲדֹנָי מָעוֹן אַתָּה הָיִיתָ לָּנוּ בְּדֹר וָדֹר:
ב בְּטֶרֶם ׀ הָרִים יֻלָּדוּ וַתְּחוֹלֵל אֶרֶץ וְתֵבֵל וּמֵעוֹלָם עַד־עוֹלָם אַתָּה
ג ד אֵל: תָּשֵׁב אֱנוֹשׁ עַד־דַּכָּא וַתֹּאמֶר שׁוּבוּ בְנֵי־אָדָם: כִּי אֶלֶף שָׁנִים
ה בְּעֵינֶיךָ כְּיוֹם אֶתְמוֹל כִּי יַעֲבֹר וְאַשְׁמוּרָה בַלָּיְלָה: זְרַמְתָּם שֵׁנָה יִהְיוּ
ו ז בַּבֹּקֶר כֶּחָצִיר יַחֲלֹף: בַּבֹּקֶר יָצִיץ וְחָלָף לָעֶרֶב יְמוֹלֵל וְיָבֵשׁ: כִּי־כָלִינוּ
ח בְאַפֶּךָ וּבַחֲמָתְךָ נִבְהָלְנוּ: שַׁתָּ עֲוֺנֹתֵינוּ לְנֶגְדֶּךָ עֲלֻמֵנוּ לִמְאוֹר פָּנֶיךָ:
ט י כִּי כׇל־יָמֵינוּ פָּנוּ בְעֶבְרָתֶךָ כִּלִּינוּ שָׁנֵינוּ כְמוֹ־הֶגֶה: יְמֵי־שְׁנוֹתֵינוּ בָהֶם
שִׁבְעִים שָׁנָה וְאִם בִּגְבוּרֹת ׀ שְׁמוֹנִים שָׁנָה וְרׇהְבָּם עָמָל וָאָוֶן כִּי־גָז
יא יב חִישׁ וַנָּעֻפָה: מִי־יוֹדֵעַ עֹז אַפֶּךָ וּכְיִרְאָתְךָ עֶבְרָתֶךָ: לִמְנוֹת יָמֵינוּ כֵּן
יג הוֹדַע וְנָבִא לְבַב חׇכְמָה: שׁוּבָה יְהוָה עַד־מָתָי וְהִנָּחֵם עַל־עֲבָדֶיךָ:
יד טו שַׂבְּעֵנוּ בַבֹּקֶר חַסְדֶּךָ וּנְרַנְּנָה וְנִשְׂמְחָה בְּכׇל־יָמֵינוּ: שַׂמְּחֵנוּ כִּימוֹת
טז עִנִּיתָנוּ שְׁנוֹת רָאִינוּ רָעָה: יֵרָאֶה אֶל־עֲבָדֶיךָ פׇעֳלֶךָ וַהֲדָרְךָ עַל־
יז בְּנֵיהֶם: וִיהִי ׀ נֹעַם אֲדֹנָי אֱלֹהֵינוּ עָלֵינוּ וּמַעֲשֵׂה יָדֵינוּ כּוֹנְנָה עָלֵינוּ יג
וּמַעֲשֵׂה יָדֵינוּ כּוֹנְנֵהוּ:
צא א ב יֹשֵׁב בְּסֵתֶר עֶלְיוֹן בְּצֵל שַׁדַּי יִתְלוֹנָן: אֹמַר לַיהוָה מַחְסִי וּמְצוּדָתִי
ג ד אֱלֹהַי אֶבְטַח־בּוֹ: כִּי הוּא יַצִּילְךָ מִפַּח יָקוּשׁ מִדֶּבֶר הַוּוֹת: בְּאֶבְרָתוֹ ׀
ה יָסֶךְ לָךְ וְתַחַת־כְּנָפָיו תֶּחְסֶה צִנָּה וְסֹחֵרָה אֲמִתּוֹ: לֹא־תִירָא מִפַּחַד
ו לָיְלָה מֵחֵץ יָעוּף יוֹמָם: מִדֶּבֶר בָּאֹפֶל יַהֲלֹךְ מִקֶּטֶב יָשׁוּד צׇהֳרָיִם:

7 at noon. A thousand may fall beside you, ten thousand at your right hand,
8 but it will not come near you. You will only look with your eyes and see the
9 punishment of the wicked. For you – "the LORD is my Refuge" – you have
10 made the Most High your abode. No harm will befall you; no sickness will
11 come near your home, for He will command His angels about you to guard
12 you in all your ways. They will lift you in their hands lest your foot stumble
13 on a stone. You will tread over lions and vipers; you will trample on young
14 lions and snakes. "Because he loves Me, I will rescue him; I will protect him
15 because he acknowledges My name. When he calls on Me, I will answer him;
16 I will be with him in distress; I will rescue him and bring him honor. With
long life I will satisfy him and show him My salvation."

92 1 2 *A psalm, a song for the Sabbath day.* It is good to thank the LORD, to sing
3 psalms to Your name, Most High, to sing of Your loving-kindness in the
4 morning and Your devotion at night to the music of the ten-stringed lyre, to
5 the melody of the harp. For Your work delights me, O LORD; I sing for joy
6 at the deeds of Your hands. How great are Your deeds, LORD; how profound
7 8 Your thoughts! A boor cannot know this, nor can a fool understand: though
the wicked may spring up like grass and all evildoers seem to flourish, they
9 10 will be destroyed for all eternity, but You, LORD, are exalted forever, for
Your enemies, O LORD – why, Your enemies will perish; all evildoers will be
11 scattered. You raise up my horn like the wild ox; I am anointed with fresh oil.
12 My eyes will see my enemies' downfall; my ears will hear my wicked attackers'
13 doom. The righteous will flourish like a palm tree; they will grow tall like a
14 cedar in Lebanon. Planted in the LORD's House, they will blossom in the
15 courtyards of our God. Even in old age, they will still bear fruit, always lush
16 and fresh, proclaiming that the LORD is upright. He is my Rock, in whom
there is no wrong.

93 1 The LORD reigns, robed in majesty; the LORD is robed, girded with strength –
2 the world stands firm; it will never be shaken. Your throne has always stood
3 firm; You are of eternity. The rivers rise up, O LORD; the river sounds surge;
4 the rivers surge and swell and crash. More powerful than the sounds of many
5 waters, than the mighty waves of the sea, is the LORD on high. Your decrees
are most faithful; holiness adorns Your House, LORD, for evermore.

94 1 2 O God of retribution, LORD – O God of retribution, shine forth! Rise up,
3 judge of the earth; treat the arrogant as they deserve. For how long, LORD,
4 for how long shall the wicked triumph? They pour out insolent words; all the
5 evildoers are full of boasting. They crush Your people, LORD, and oppress
6 Your own heritage. They kill the widow and the stranger; they murder the
7 orphaned, saying, "The LORD does not see; the God of Yaakov pays no heed."
8 Take heed, you most brutish people; you fools, when will you grow wise?
9 Will He who implants the ear fail to hear? Will He who forms the eye fail to
10 see? Will He who disciplines nations, He who teaches man knowledge, fail
11 to punish? The LORD knows that the thoughts of man are but mere fleeting
12 breath. Happy is the person whom You discipline, LORD, whom You instruct
13 in Your teaching, lending him peace in times of trouble until a pit is dug for the

ז ח יִפֹּל מִצִּדְּךָ ׀ אֶלֶף וּרְבָבָה מִימִינֶךָ אֵלֶיךָ לֹא יִגָּשׁ׃ רַק בְּעֵינֶיךָ תַבִּיט
ט וְשִׁלֻּמַת רְשָׁעִים תִּרְאֶה׃ כִּי־אַתָּה יְהֹוָה מַחְסִי עֶלְיוֹן שַׂמְתָּ מְעוֹנֶךָ׃
י יא לֹא־תְאֻנֶּה אֵלֶיךָ רָעָה וְנֶגַע לֹא־יִקְרַב בְּאָהֳלֶךָ׃ כִּי מַלְאָכָיו יְצַוֶּה־
יב לָּךְ לִשְׁמָרְךָ בְּכׇל־דְּרָכֶיךָ׃ עַל־כַּפַּיִם יִשָּׂאוּנְךָ פֶּן־תִּגֹּף בָּאֶבֶן רַגְלֶךָ׃
יג יד עַל־שַׁחַל וָפֶתֶן תִּדְרֹךְ תִּרְמֹס כְּפִיר וְתַנִּין׃ כִּי בִי חָשַׁק וַאֲפַלְּטֵהוּ
טו אֲשַׂגְּבֵהוּ כִּי־יָדַע שְׁמִי׃ יִקְרָאֵנִי ׀ וְאֶעֱנֵהוּ עִמּוֹ־אָנֹכִי בְצָרָה אֲחַלְּצֵהוּ
טז וַאֲכַבְּדֵהוּ׃ אֹרֶךְ יָמִים אַשְׂבִּיעֵהוּ וְאַרְאֵהוּ בִּישׁוּעָתִי׃
צב א ב מִזְמוֹר שִׁיר לְיוֹם הַשַּׁבָּת׃ טוֹב לְהֹדוֹת לַיהֹוָה וּלְזַמֵּר לְשִׁמְךָ עֶלְיוֹן׃
ג ד לְהַגִּיד בַּבֹּקֶר חַסְדֶּךָ וֶאֱמוּנָתְךָ בַּלֵּילוֹת׃ עֲלֵי־עָשׂוֹר וַעֲלֵי־נָבֶל עֲלֵי
ה ו הִגָּיוֹן בְּכִנּוֹר׃ כִּי שִׂמַּחְתַּנִי יְהֹוָה בְּפׇעֳלֶךָ בְּמַעֲשֵׂי יָדֶיךָ אֲרַנֵּן׃ מַה־גָּדְלוּ
ז מַעֲשֶׂיךָ יְהֹוָה מְאֹד עָמְקוּ מַחְשְׁבֹתֶיךָ׃ אִישׁ־בַּעַר לֹא יֵדָע וּכְסִיל
ח לֹא־יָבִין אֶת־זֹאת׃ בִּפְרֹחַ רְשָׁעִים ׀ כְּמוֹ עֵשֶׂב וַיָּצִיצוּ כׇּל־פֹּעֲלֵי אָוֶן
ט י לְהִשָּׁמְדָם עֲדֵי־עַד׃ וְאַתָּה מָרוֹם לְעֹלָם יְהֹוָה׃ כִּי הִנֵּה אֹיְבֶיךָ יְהֹוָה
יא כִּי־הִנֵּה אֹיְבֶיךָ יֹאבֵדוּ יִתְפָּרְדוּ כׇּל־פֹּעֲלֵי אָוֶן׃ וַתָּרֶם כִּרְאֵים קַרְנִי
יב בַּלֹּתִי בְּשֶׁמֶן רַעֲנָן׃ וַתַּבֵּט עֵינִי בְּשׁוּרָי בַּקָּמִים עָלַי מְרֵעִים תִּשְׁמַעְנָה
יג יד אׇזְנָי׃ צַדִּיק כַּתָּמָר יִפְרָח כְּאֶרֶז בַּלְּבָנוֹן יִשְׂגֶּה׃ שְׁתוּלִים בְּבֵית יְהֹוָה
טו בְּחַצְרוֹת אֱלֹהֵינוּ יַפְרִיחוּ׃ עוֹד יְנוּבוּן בְּשֵׂיבָה דְּשֵׁנִים וְרַעֲנַנִּים יִהְיוּ׃
טז לְהַגִּיד כִּי־יָשָׁר יְהֹוָה צוּרִי וְלֹא־עַלְתָה בּוֹ׃ עוֹלָתָה
צג א יְהֹוָה מָלָךְ גֵּאוּת לָבֵשׁ לָבֵשׁ יְהֹוָה עֹז הִתְאַזָּר אַף־תִּכּוֹן תֵּבֵל בַּל־
ב ג תִּמּוֹט׃ נָכוֹן כִּסְאֲךָ מֵאָז מֵעוֹלָם אָתָּה׃ נָשְׂאוּ נְהָרוֹת ׀ יְהֹוָה נָשְׂאוּ
ד נְהָרוֹת קוֹלָם יִשְׂאוּ נְהָרוֹת דׇּכְיָם׃ מִקֹּלוֹת ׀ מַיִם רַבִּים אַדִּירִים מִשְׁבְּרֵי־
ה יָם אַדִּיר בַּמָּרוֹם יְהֹוָה׃ עֵדֹתֶיךָ ׀ נֶאֶמְנוּ מְאֹד לְבֵיתְךָ נַאֲוָה־קֹדֶשׁ
יְהֹוָה לְאֹרֶךְ יָמִים׃
צד א ב אֵל־נְקָמוֹת יְהֹוָה אֵל נְקָמוֹת הוֹפִיעַ׃ הִנָּשֵׂא שֹׁפֵט הָאָרֶץ הָשֵׁב גְּמוּל
ג ד עַל־גֵּאִים׃ עַד־מָתַי רְשָׁעִים ׀ יְהֹוָה עַד־מָתַי רְשָׁעִים יַעֲלֹזוּ׃ יַבִּיעוּ
ה יְדַבְּרוּ עָתָק יִתְאַמְּרוּ כׇּל־פֹּעֲלֵי אָוֶן׃ עַמְּךָ יְהֹוָה יְדַכְּאוּ וְנַחֲלָתְךָ יְעַנּוּ׃
ו ז אַלְמָנָה וְגֵר יַהֲרֹגוּ וִיתוֹמִים יְרַצֵּחוּ׃ וַיֹּאמְרוּ לֹא יִרְאֶה־יָּהּ וְלֹא־יָבִין
ח ט אֱלֹהֵי יַעֲקֹב׃ בִּינוּ בֹּעֲרִים בָּעָם וּכְסִילִים מָתַי תַּשְׂכִּילוּ׃ הֲנֹטַע אֹזֶן
י הֲלֹא יִשְׁמָע אִם־יֹצֵר עַיִן הֲלֹא יַבִּיט׃ הֲיֹסֵר גּוֹיִם הֲלֹא יוֹכִיחַ הַמְלַמֵּד
יא יב אָדָם דָּעַת׃ יְהֹוָה יֹדֵעַ מַחְשְׁבוֹת אָדָם כִּי־הֵמָּה הָבֶל׃ אַשְׁרֵי ׀ הַגֶּבֶר
יג אֲשֶׁר־תְּיַסְּרֶנּוּ יָּהּ וּמִתּוֹרָתְךָ תְלַמְּדֶנּוּ׃ לְהַשְׁקִיט לוֹ מִימֵי רָע עַד יִכָּרֶה

14 wicked, for the LORD will not forsake His people, nor abandon His heritage.
15 Judgment shall again accord with justice, and all the true-hearted will follow
16 it. Who will protect me against the wicked? Who will stand up for me against
17 evildoers? Had the LORD not been my help, I would soon have dwelt in
18 death's silence. When I felt my foot was slipping, Your loving-kindness, LORD,
19 gave me support. When my dread rose within me, Your consolations soothed
20 my soul. Can a corrupt throne be allied with You, a throne that brings misery
21 through its law? They join forces against the life of the righteous and condemn
22 the innocent to death, but the LORD is my stronghold; my God is the Rock of
23 my refuge. He will return their own evil back upon them and with their own
corruption destroy them – the LORD our God will destroy them.
95 1 Come, let us sing for joy to the LORD and shout out to the Rock of our
2 salvation. Let us greet Him with thanksgiving and shout out to Him with
3 songs of praise, for the LORD is the great God, the great King, above all divine
4 beings. The depths of the earth are in His hand; the mountain peaks are
5 His; the sea is His, for He made it; the dry land too, for His hands formed it.
6 7 Come, let us bow in worship and kneel before the LORD our Maker, for He
is our God, and we are the people of His pasture, the flock He tends – today,
8 if you would heed His voice. Do not harden your hearts as you did at Meriva,
9 as you did then at Masa in the desert[109] when your ancestors tested Me and
10 tried Me though they had seen My deeds. For forty years I was riled by that
generation. I said, "They are a people whose hearts go astray, and they will
11 not acknowledge My ways," so I swore in My anger, "They will not enter My
place of rest."
96 1 2 Sing to the LORD a new song;[110] sing to the LORD, all the earth; sing to the
3 LORD, bless His name; proclaim his salvation day by day. Declare His glory
4 among the nations, His wonders among all peoples, for the LORD is great,
5 of highest praise, to be held in awe above all divine beings, for all the gods of
6 the peoples are mere idols – it was the LORD who made the heavens. Majesty
7 and splendor are before Him; strength and beauty fill His Sanctuary. Render
to the LORD, O families of the peoples, render to the LORD glory and might.
8 Render to the LORD the glory due His name; bring an offering, and come
9 into His courts. Bow to the LORD in the splendor of holiness;[111] tremble
10 before Him, all the earth. Say among the nations, "The LORD is King." The
world stands firm; it will never be shaken. He will judge the peoples with
11 equity. Let the heavens rejoice and the earth exult; let the sea roar, and all
12 that fills it; let the fields revel, and all they contain, then all the trees of the
13 forest will sing for joy before the LORD, for He is coming; He is coming to
judge the earth. He will judge the world with justice and the peoples with
His faithfulness.[112]
97 1 2 The LORD is King; let the earth exult; let the many islands rejoice. Clouds

109 | See Exodus 17:7; Deuteronomy 33:8.
110 | Cf. 1 Chronicles 16:23–33.
111 | Cf. 29:1–2.
112 | Cf. verse 9.

יד טו לְרָשָׁע שָׁחַת: כִּי ׀ לֹא־יִטֹּשׁ יהוה עַמּוֹ וְנַחֲלָתוֹ לֹא יַעֲזֹב: כִּי־עַד־
טז צֶדֶק יָשׁוּב מִשְׁפָּט וְאַחֲרָיו כָּל־יִשְׁרֵי־לֵב: מִי־יָקוּם לִי עִם־מְרֵעִים מִי־
יז יִתְיַצֵּב לִי עִם־פֹּעֲלֵי אָוֶן: לוּלֵי יהוה עֶזְרָתָה לִּי כִּמְעַט ׀ שָׁכְנָה
יח יט דוּמָה נַפְשִׁי: אִם־אָמַרְתִּי מָטָה רַגְלִי חַסְדְּךָ יהוה יִסְעָדֵנִי: בְּרֹב
כ שַׂרְעַפַּי בְּקִרְבִּי תַּנְחוּמֶיךָ יְשַׁעַשְׁעוּ נַפְשִׁי: הַיְחָבְרְךָ כִּסֵּא הַוּוֹת יֹצֵר
כא כב עָמָל עֲלֵי־חֹק: יָגוֹדּוּ עַל־נֶפֶשׁ צַדִּיק וְדָם נָקִי יַרְשִׁיעוּ: וַיְהִי יהוה
כג לִי לְמִשְׂגָּב וֵאלֹהַי לְצוּר מַחְסִי: וַיָּשֶׁב עֲלֵיהֶם ׀ אֶת־אוֹנָם וּבְרָעָתָם
יַצְמִיתֵם יַצְמִיתֵם יהוה אֱלֹהֵינוּ:

צה א ב לְכוּ נְרַנְּנָה לַיהוה נָרִיעָה לְצוּר יִשְׁעֵנוּ: נְקַדְּמָה פָנָיו בְּתוֹדָה בִּזְמִרוֹת
ג ד נָרִיעַ לוֹ: כִּי אֵל גָּדוֹל יהוה וּמֶלֶךְ גָּדוֹל עַל־כָּל־אֱלֹהִים: אֲשֶׁר בְּיָדוֹ
ה מֶחְקְרֵי־אָרֶץ וְתוֹעֲפוֹת הָרִים לוֹ: אֲשֶׁר־לוֹ הַיָּם וְהוּא עָשָׂהוּ וְיַבֶּשֶׁת
ו ז יָדָיו יָצָרוּ: בֹּאוּ נִשְׁתַּחֲוֶה וְנִכְרָעָה נִבְרְכָה לִפְנֵי־יהוה עֹשֵׂנוּ: כִּי הוּא
ח אֱלֹהֵינוּ וַאֲנַחְנוּ ׀ עַם מַרְעִיתוֹ וְצֹאן יָדוֹ הַיּוֹם אִם־בְּקֹלוֹ תִשְׁמָעוּ: אַל־
ט תַּקְשׁוּ לְבַבְכֶם כִּמְרִיבָה כְּיוֹם מַסָּה בַּמִּדְבָּר: אֲשֶׁר נִסּוּנִי אֲבוֹתֵיכֶם
י בְּחָנוּנִי גַּם־רָאוּ פָעֳלִי: אַרְבָּעִים שָׁנָה ׀ אָקוּט בְּדוֹר וָאֹמַר עַם תֹּעֵי
יא לֵבָב הֵם וְהֵם לֹא־יָדְעוּ דְרָכָי: אֲשֶׁר־נִשְׁבַּעְתִּי בְאַפִּי אִם־יְבֹאוּן אֶל־
מְנוּחָתִי:

צו א ב שִׁירוּ לַיהוה שִׁיר חָדָשׁ שִׁירוּ לַיהוה כָּל־הָאָרֶץ: שִׁירוּ לַיהוה בָּרְכוּ
ג שְׁמוֹ בַּשְּׂרוּ מִיּוֹם־לְיוֹם יְשׁוּעָתוֹ: סַפְּרוּ בַגּוֹיִם כְּבוֹדוֹ בְּכָל־הָעַמִּים
ד נִפְלְאוֹתָיו: כִּי גָדוֹל יהוה וּמְהֻלָּל מְאֹד נוֹרָא הוּא עַל־כָּל־אֱלֹהִים:
ה ו כִּי ׀ כָּל־אֱלֹהֵי הָעַמִּים אֱלִילִים וַיהוה שָׁמַיִם עָשָׂה: הוֹד־וְהָדָר לְפָנָיו
ז עֹז וְתִפְאֶרֶת בְּמִקְדָּשׁוֹ: הָבוּ לַיהוה מִשְׁפְּחוֹת עַמִּים הָבוּ לַיהוה כָּבוֹד
ח ט וָעֹז: הָבוּ לַיהוה כְּבוֹד שְׁמוֹ שְׂאוּ־מִנְחָה וּבֹאוּ לְחַצְרוֹתָיו: הִשְׁתַּחֲווּ
י לַיהוה בְּהַדְרַת־קֹדֶשׁ חִילוּ מִפָּנָיו כָּל־הָאָרֶץ: אִמְרוּ בַגּוֹיִם ׀ יהוה
יא מָלָךְ אַף־תִּכּוֹן תֵּבֵל בַּל־תִּמּוֹט יָדִין עַמִּים בְּמֵישָׁרִים: יִשְׂמְחוּ הַשָּׁמַיִם
יב וְתָגֵל הָאָרֶץ יִרְעַם הַיָּם וּמְלֹאוֹ: יַעֲלֹז שָׂדַי וְכָל־אֲשֶׁר־בּוֹ אָז יְרַנְּנוּ
יג כָּל־עֲצֵי־יָעַר: לִפְנֵי יהוה ׀ כִּי בָא כִּי בָא לִשְׁפֹּט הָאָרֶץ יִשְׁפֹּט־תֵּבֵל
בְּצֶדֶק וְעַמִּים בֶּאֱמוּנָתוֹ:

צז א ב יהוה מָלָךְ תָּגֵל הָאָרֶץ יִשְׂמְחוּ אִיִּים רַבִּים: עָנָן וַעֲרָפֶל סְבִיבָיו צֶדֶק

and deep mist surround Him; righteousness and justice form the base of
3 4 His throne. Fire blazes before Him, burning His enemies on every side. His
5 lightning lights up the world; the earth sees and trembles. Mountains melt like
6 wax before the LORD, before the Master of all the earth. The heavens proclaim
7 His righteousness, and all the peoples see His glory. All who worship images
8 and boast of idols are put to shame; all divine beings bow down to Him. Zion
hears and rejoices; let the towns of Yehuda be glad because of Your judgments,
9 LORD, for You, LORD, are supreme over all the earth; You are exalted far above
10 all heavenly powers. O lovers of the LORD, hate evil, for He protects the lives
11 of his devoted ones, delivering them from the hand of the wicked. Light is
12 sown for the righteous, and joy for the upright of heart. Rejoice in the LORD,
righteous ones; give thanks to His holy name.
98 1 *A psalm.* Sing a new song to the LORD, for He has done wondrous things;
2 His right hand and His holy arm have brought about victory. The LORD has
made His salvation known, displaying His righteousness before the eyes
3 of the nations. He has remembered His loving-kindness and loyalty to the
House of Israel; all the ends of the earth have seen the victory of our God.
4 Shout for joy to the LORD, all the earth; burst into song, sing with joy, make
5 6 music. Make music to the LORD on the harp; sing along with the harp with
trumpets and the sound of the ram's horn; shout for joy before the LORD,
7 the King! Let the sea roar, and all that fills it, the world and all who live in it.
8 9 Let the rivers clap their hands and the mountains sing together for joy before
the LORD, for He is coming to judge the earth. He will judge the world with
justice and the peoples with equity.[113]
99 1 The LORD reigns – let the peoples tremble; He sits enthroned on the cherubim –
2 let the earth quake. Great is the LORD in Zion; He is exalted over all the
3 4 peoples. Let them praise Your great and awesome name. He is holy! O mighty
King who loves justice, You have established equity; justice and righteousness
5 in Yaakov is Your doing. Exalt the LORD our God and bow at His footstool.
6 He is holy! Moshe and Aharon of His priests, Samuel of those who called on
7 His name – they called on the LORD, and He answered them. He spoke to
them in a pillar of cloud; they observed His decrees and the statutes He gave
8 them. LORD our God, You answered them. You were for them a forgiving God
9 though You punished their misdeeds. Exalt the LORD our God and bow at
His holy mountain, for the LORD our God is holy.
100 1 2 *A psalm of thanksgiving.* Shout out to the LORD, all the earth! Serve the LORD
3 with joy; come before Him in glad song. Know that the LORD is God; He
4 made us, and we are His; we are His people, the flock He tends. Enter His
gates with thanksgiving, His courts with praise; thank Him and bless His
5 name, for the LORD is good; His loving-kindness is forever, His faithfulness
for all generations.
101 1 *Of David – a psalm.* I will sing of loyalty and justice; to You, LORD, I will sing
2 praise. I contemplate the way of the blameless – when shall I reach it? I walk
3 about with a blameless heart within my own home. I will not set any depravity

113 | Cf. 96:13.

ג ד וּמִשְׁפָּט מְכוֹן כִּסְאוֹ: אֵשׁ לְפָנָיו תֵּלֵךְ וּתְלַהֵט סָבִיב צָרָיו: הֵאִירוּ
ה בְרָקָיו תֵּבֵל רָאֲתָה וַתָּחֵל הָאָרֶץ: הָרִים כַּדּוֹנַג נָמַסּוּ מִלִּפְנֵי יְהוָה
ו מִלִּפְנֵי אֲדוֹן כָּל־הָאָרֶץ: הִגִּידוּ הַשָּׁמַיִם צִדְקוֹ וְרָאוּ כָל־הָעַמִּים כְּבוֹדוֹ:
ז יֵבֹשׁוּ ׀ כָּל־עֹבְדֵי פֶסֶל הַמִּתְהַלְלִים בָּאֱלִילִים הִשְׁתַּחֲווּ־לוֹ כָּל־אֱלֹהִים:
ח שָׁמְעָה וַתִּשְׂמַח ׀ צִיּוֹן וַתָּגֵלְנָה בְּנוֹת יְהוּדָה לְמַעַן מִשְׁפָּטֶיךָ יְהוָה:
ט כִּי־אַתָּה יְהוָה עֶלְיוֹן עַל־כָּל־הָאָרֶץ מְאֹד נַעֲלֵיתָ עַל־כָּל־אֱלֹהִים:
י אֹהֲבֵי יְהוָה שִׂנְאוּ רָע שֹׁמֵר נַפְשׁוֹת חֲסִידָיו מִיַּד רְשָׁעִים יַצִּילֵם:
יא יב אוֹר זָרֻעַ לַצַּדִּיק וּלְיִשְׁרֵי־לֵב שִׂמְחָה: שִׂמְחוּ צַדִּיקִים בַּיהוָה וְהוֹדוּ
לְזֵכֶר קָדְשׁוֹ:

צח א מִזְמוֹר שִׁירוּ לַיהוָה ׀ שִׁיר חָדָשׁ כִּי־נִפְלָאוֹת עָשָׂה הוֹשִׁיעָה־לּוֹ יְמִינוֹ
ב ג וּזְרוֹעַ קָדְשׁוֹ: הוֹדִיעַ יְהוָה יְשׁוּעָתוֹ לְעֵינֵי הַגּוֹיִם גִּלָּה צִדְקָתוֹ: זָכַר
חַסְדּוֹ ׀ וֶאֱמוּנָתוֹ לְבֵית יִשְׂרָאֵל רָאוּ כָל־אַפְסֵי־אָרֶץ אֵת יְשׁוּעַת
ד ה אֱלֹהֵינוּ: הָרִיעוּ לַיהוָה כָּל־הָאָרֶץ פִּצְחוּ וְרַנְּנוּ וְזַמֵּרוּ: זַמְּרוּ לַיהוָה
ו בְּכִנּוֹר בְּכִנּוֹר וְקוֹל זִמְרָה: בַּחֲצֹצְרוֹת וְקוֹל שׁוֹפָר הָרִיעוּ לִפְנֵי ׀ הַמֶּלֶךְ
ז ח יְהוָה: יִרְעַם הַיָּם וּמְלֹאוֹ תֵּבֵל וְיֹשְׁבֵי בָהּ: נְהָרוֹת יִמְחֲאוּ־כָף יַחַד
ט הָרִים יְרַנֵּנוּ: לִפְנֵי־יְהוָה כִּי בָא לִשְׁפֹּט הָאָרֶץ יִשְׁפֹּט־תֵּבֵל בְּצֶדֶק
וְעַמִּים בְּמֵישָׁרִים:

צט א ב יְהוָה מָלָךְ יִרְגְּזוּ עַמִּים יֹשֵׁב כְּרוּבִים תָּנוּט הָאָרֶץ: יְהוָה בְּצִיּוֹן גָּדוֹל
ג ד וְרָם הוּא עַל־כָּל־הָעַמִּים: יוֹדוּ שִׁמְךָ גָּדוֹל וְנוֹרָא קָדוֹשׁ הוּא: וְעֹז
מֶלֶךְ מִשְׁפָּט אָהֵב אַתָּה כּוֹנַנְתָּ מֵישָׁרִים מִשְׁפָּט וּצְדָקָה בְּיַעֲקֹב ׀ אַתָּה
ה ו עָשִׂיתָ: רוֹמְמוּ יְהוָה אֱלֹהֵינוּ וְהִשְׁתַּחֲווּ לַהֲדֹם רַגְלָיו קָדוֹשׁ הוּא: מֹשֶׁה
וְאַהֲרֹן ׀ בְּכֹהֲנָיו וּשְׁמוּאֵל בְּקֹרְאֵי שְׁמוֹ קֹרִאים אֶל־יְהוָה וְהוּא יַעֲנֵם:
ז ח בְּעַמּוּד עָנָן יְדַבֵּר אֲלֵיהֶם שָׁמְרוּ עֵדֹתָיו וְחֹק נָתַן־לָמוֹ: יְהוָה אֱלֹהֵינוּ
ט אַתָּה עֲנִיתָם אֵל נֹשֵׂא הָיִיתָ לָהֶם וְנֹקֵם עַל־עֲלִילוֹתָם: רוֹמְמוּ יְהוָה
אֱלֹהֵינוּ וְהִשְׁתַּחֲווּ לְהַר קָדְשׁוֹ כִּי־קָדוֹשׁ יְהוָה אֱלֹהֵינוּ:

ק א ב מִזְמוֹר לְתוֹדָה הָרִיעוּ לַיהוָה כָּל־הָאָרֶץ: עִבְדוּ אֶת־יְהוָה בְּשִׂמְחָה בֹּאוּ
ג לְפָנָיו בִּרְנָנָה: דְּעוּ כִּי־יְהוָה הוּא אֱלֹהִים הוּא עָשָׂנוּ ולא אֲנַחְנוּ עַמּוֹ וְלוֹ
ד וְצֹאן מַרְעִיתוֹ: בֹּאוּ שְׁעָרָיו ׀ בְּתוֹדָה חֲצֵרֹתָיו בִּתְהִלָּה הוֹדוּ לוֹ בָּרְכוּ
ה שְׁמוֹ: כִּי־טוֹב יְהוָה לְעוֹלָם חַסְדּוֹ וְעַד־דֹּר וָדֹר אֱמוּנָתוֹ:

קא א ב לְדָוִד מִזְמוֹר חֶסֶד־וּמִשְׁפָּט אָשִׁירָה לְךָ יְהוָה אֲזַמֵּרָה: אַשְׂכִּילָה ׀ בְּדֶרֶךְ יד
ג תָּמִים מָתַי תָּבוֹא אֵלָי אֶתְהַלֵּךְ בְּתָם־לְבָבִי בְּקֶרֶב בֵּיתִי: לֹא־אָשִׁית ׀

before my eyes. I despise shifty dealing – such things will not cling to me.
4 Perverse hearts will keep away from me; I will have nothing to do with evil.
5 Those who slander their fellows in secret I will destroy; those of haughty eyes
6 and proud hearts I cannot bear. My eyes are on the faithful ones of the land to
have them dwell with me. Those whose ways are blameless, they will serve me.
7 There shall not dwell within my house anyone who practices deceit; No one
8 who speaks lies shall endure before my eyes. Morning after morning I destroy
all the wicked of the land, ridding the LORD's city of all evildoers.
102 1 *A prayer for the lowly when they grow overwhelmed and pour out their lament*
2 3 *before the LORD.* O LORD, listen to my prayer; let my cry reach You. Do not
hide Your face from me on the day of my distress; lend Your ear to me on
4 the day that I call – hurry, answer me! – for my days dissipate like smoke;
5 my bones are scorched as in a furnace; my heart is trampled and withered
6 like grass; I neglect to eat my food. From the noise of my groans, my bones
7 cleave to my flesh. I have become like a desert owl, like an owl among ruins;
8 9 I lie awake; I have become like a lonely bird upon a rooftop. All day long my
10 enemies taunt me; my revilers use my name as a curse, for I eat ashes for bread
11 and mingle my drink with tears because of Your fury and wrath, because You
12 raised me up and flung me down. My days are like lengthening shadows, and
13 I wither away like grass, but You, LORD, are enthroned forever; Your name
14 endures for all generations.[114] Rise up and have mercy on Zion; the time has
15 come to grant her grace; the hour has arrived, for Your servants love her very
16 stones; they even cherish her dust. Then the nations will fear the name of the
17 LORD, all the kings of the earth Your glory – when the LORD rebuilds Zion
18 and appears in His glory. He turns to the prayer of the destitute and does
19 not show contempt for their prayers. May this be inscribed for a generation
20 to come, that people yet unborn will praise the LORD. For the LORD gazes
21 down from His holy heights; He looks down from heaven to earth to hear the
22 groans of captives, to free those doomed to death; so that the LORD's name
23 may be proclaimed in Zion and in Jerusalem His praise when peoples gather
24 together, as well as kingdoms, to serve the LORD. He has sapped my strength
25 in midcourse and shortened my days. I say, "O my God, do not take me away
when only half my days are done – You whose years span the generations."
26 27 You founded the earth long ago; the heavens are Your handiwork. When they
are long gone, You will still stand; they will all wear out like a garment; You
28 change them like clothing, and they fade away, but You are always the same –
29 Your years never end. May Your servants' children dwell in peace and their
own seed be established in Your presence.
103 1 2 *Of David.* Bless the LORD, my soul, His holy name with all my being; bless
3 the LORD, my soul; forget none of His benefits – He forgives all your sins,
4 He heals all your ills, He redeems your life from the Pit, He crowns you with
5 love and compassion, and He sates you with good in your prime so that your
6 youth is renewed like the eagle's. The LORD executes righteousness and brings

114 | Cf. Lamentations 5:19.

ד לנגד עיני דבר־בליעל עשה־סטים שנאתי לא ידבק בי: לבב עקש
ה יסור ממני רע לא אדע: מלושני בסתר ׀ רעהו אותו אצמית גבה־ מלשני
ו עינים ורחב לבב אתו לא אוכל: עיני ׀ בנאמני־ארץ לשבת עמדי
ז הלך בדרך תמים הוא ישרתני: לא־ישב ׀ בקרב ביתי עשה רמיה
ח דבר שקרים לא־יכון לנגד עיני: לבקרים אצמית כל־רשעי־ארץ
להכרית מעיר־יהוה כל־פעלי און:

קב א ב תפלה לעני כי־יעטף ולפני יהוה ישפך שיחו: יהוה שמעה תפלתי
ג ושועתי אליך תבוא: אל־תסתר פניך ׀ ממני ביום צר לי הטה־אלי
ד אזנך ביום אקרא מהר ענני: כי־כלו בעשן ימי ועצמותי כמוקד
ה ו נחרו: הוכה כעשב ויבש לבי כי־שכחתי מאכל לחמי: מקול אנחתי
ז דבקה עצמי לבשרי: דמיתי לקאת מדבר הייתי ככוס חרבות:
ח ט שקדתי ואהיה כצפור בודד על־גג: כל־היום חרפוני אויבי מהוללי
י יא בי נשבעו: כי־אפר כלחם אכלתי ושקוי בבכי מסכתי: מפני־זעמך
יב יג וקצפך כי נשאתני ותשליכני: ימי כצל נטוי ואני כעשב איבש: ואתה
יד יהוה לעולם תשב וזכרך לדר ודר: אתה תקום תרחם ציון כי־עת
טו לחננה כי־בא מועד: כי־רצו עבדיך את־אבניה ואת־עפרה יחננו:
טז יז וייראו גוים את־שם יהוה וכל־מלכי הארץ את־כבודך: כי־בנה יהוה
יח ציון נראה בכבודו: פנה אל־תפלת הערער ולא־בזה את־תפלתם:
יט כ תכתב זאת לדור אחרון ועם נברא יהלל־יה: כי־השקיף ממרום
כא קדשו יהוה משמים ׀ אל־ארץ הביט: לשמע אנקת אסיר לפתח
כב כג בני תמותה: לספר בציון שם יהוה ותהלתו בירושלם: בהקבץ
כד עמים יחדו וממלכות לעבד את־יהוה: ענה בדרך כחו קצר ימי: כחי
כה כו אמר אלי אל־תעלני בחצי ימי בדור דורים שנותיך: לפנים הארץ
כז יסדת ומעשה ידיך שמים: המה ׀ יאבדו ואתה תעמד וכלם כבגד
כח כט יבלו כלבוש תחליפם ויחלפו: ואתה־הוא ושנותיך לא יתמו: בני־
עבדיך ישכונו וזרעם לפניך יכון:

קג א ב לדוד ׀ ברכי נפשי את־יהוה וכל־קרבי את־שם קדשו: ברכי נפשי
ג את־יהוה ואל־תשכחי כל־גמוליו: הסלח לכל־עונכי הרפא לכל־
ד ה תחלואיכי: הגואל משחת חייכי המעטרכי חסד ורחמים: המשביע
ו בטוב עדיך תתחדש כנשר נעוריכי: עשה צדקות יהוה ומשפטים

7 justice to all the oppressed. He revealed His ways to Moshe, His deeds to
8 the people of Israel. The LORD is compassionate and gracious, slow to anger,
9 abounding in kindness.[115] He does not contend for long or bear a grudge
10 forever; He has not treated us according to our sins or repaid us according to
11 our misdeeds, for as high as the heavens reach above the earth is the strength
12 of His love for those who fear Him; as far as the east is from the west He
13 has distanced our transgressions from us. As a father has compassion on his
14 children, so the LORD has compassion on those who fear Him, for He knows
15 how we are formed; He remembers that we are dust. Like grass are the days
16 of mortals, who spring up like wildflowers; with a mere gust of wind they are
17 gone, leaving no trace behind them, but the LORD's loyalty endures forever
18 for those who fear Him, His righteousness for their children's children, for
19 those who keep His covenant and remember to obey His laws. The LORD
20 has established His throne in heaven; His kingdom rules over all. Bless the
LORD, you His angels, those mighty in power who do His bidding, who obey
21 His word. Bless the LORD, all you His host, you ministers who do His will;
22 bless the LORD and all His works in every part of His dominion. Bless the
LORD, my soul.

104 1 Bless the LORD, my soul. O LORD my God, You are exceedingly great, clothed
2 in majesty and splendor; cloaked in a robe of light, You have spread out the
3 heavens like a tent. He roofs His upper chambers with water; He harnesses
4 the clouds as His chariot and rides on wings of wind. He makes the winds
5 His messengers, flames of fire His ministers. He has fixed the earth on its
6 foundations so that it will never be shaken. You covered it with the deep
7 like a cloak; the waters stood above the mountains. At Your onslaught they
8 fled; at the sound of Your thunder they rushed away, flowing over the hills,
9 streaming down into the valleys to the place You determined for them. You
set a boundary they were not to pass so that they would never cover the earth
10 again. He makes springs flow in the valleys; they make their way between
11 the hills, watering all the beasts of the field; the wild donkeys quench their
12 13 thirst. The birds of the sky roost above them, singing among the foliage. He
waters the mountains from His upper chambers; the earth is sated with the
14 fruit of Your work. He makes grass grow for the cattle and plants for human
15 use to bring forth food from the earth, wine to cheer people's hearts, oil to
16 make their faces shine, bread to sustain people's hearts. The trees of the LORD
17 drink their fill, the cedars of Lebanon that He planted. There birds build their
18 nests; the stork makes its home in the cypresses. High hills are for the wild
19 goats; rocky crags are shelter for the hyraxes. He made the moon to mark
20 the seasons; the sun knows when to set. You cast darkness, night falls, and
21 all the forest creatures stir. The young lions roar for prey; they seek their food
22 from God. When the sun rises, they slink away and settle down in their lairs.
23 24 People go out to their work, to their labor until evening. How many are Your
works, LORD; You made them all in wisdom; the earth is full of Your creations.
25 There is the vast, immeasurable sea teeming with countless creatures, living

115 | Cf. Exodus 34:6.

ז ח לְכׇל־עֲשׁוּקִים׃ יוֹדִיעַ דְּרָכָיו לְמֹשֶׁה לִבְנֵי יִשְׂרָאֵל עֲלִילוֹתָיו׃ רַחוּם
ט וְחַנּוּן יהוה אֶרֶךְ אַפַּיִם וְרַב־חָסֶד׃ לֹא־לָנֶצַח יָרִיב וְלֹא לְעוֹלָם יִטּוֹר׃
י יא לֹא כַחֲטָאֵינוּ עָשָׂה לָנוּ וְלֹא כַעֲוֺנֹתֵינוּ גָּמַל עָלֵינוּ׃ כִּי כִגְבֹהַּ שָׁמַיִם
יב עַל־הָאָרֶץ גָּבַר חַסְדּוֹ עַל־יְרֵאָיו׃ כִּרְחֹק מִזְרָח מִמַּעֲרָב הִרְחִיק מִמֶּנּוּ
יג יד אֶת־פְּשָׁעֵינוּ׃ כְּרַחֵם אָב עַל־בָּנִים רִחַם יהוה עַל־יְרֵאָיו׃ כִּי־הוּא
טו יָדַע יִצְרֵנוּ זָכוּר כִּי־עָפָר אֲנָחְנוּ׃ אֱנוֹשׁ כֶּחָצִיר יָמָיו כְּצִיץ הַשָּׂדֶה כֵּן
טז יז יָצִיץ׃ כִּי רוּחַ עָבְרָה־בּוֹ וְאֵינֶנּוּ וְלֹא־יַכִּירֶנּוּ עוֹד מְקוֹמוֹ׃ וְחֶסֶד יהוה ׀
יח מֵעוֹלָם וְעַד־עוֹלָם עַל־יְרֵאָיו וְצִדְקָתוֹ לִבְנֵי בָנִים׃ לְשֹׁמְרֵי בְרִיתוֹ
יט וּלְזֹכְרֵי פִקֻּדָיו לַעֲשׂוֹתָם׃ יהוה בַּשָּׁמַיִם הֵכִין כִּסְאוֹ וּמַלְכוּתוֹ בַּכֹּל
כ מָשָׁלָה׃ בָּרְכוּ יהוה מַלְאָכָיו גִּבֹּרֵי כֹחַ עֹשֵׂי דְבָרוֹ לִשְׁמֹעַ בְּקוֹל דְּבָרוֹ׃
כא כב בָּרְכוּ יהוה כׇּל־צְבָאָיו מְשָׁרְתָיו עֹשֵׂי רְצוֹנוֹ׃ בָּרְכוּ יהוה ׀ כׇּל־מַעֲשָׂיו
בְּכׇל־מְקֹמוֹת מֶמְשַׁלְתּוֹ בָּרְכִי נַפְשִׁי אֶת־יהוה׃
קד א בָּרְכִי נַפְשִׁי אֶת־יהוה יהוה אֱלֹהַי גָּדַלְתָּ מְאֹד הוֹד וְהָדָר לָבָשְׁתָּ׃
ב ג עֹטֶה־אוֹר כַּשַּׂלְמָה נוֹטֶה שָׁמַיִם כַּיְרִיעָה׃ הַמְקָרֶה בַמַּיִם עֲלִיּוֹתָיו
ד הַשָּׂם־עָבִים רְכוּבוֹ הַמְהַלֵּךְ עַל־כַּנְפֵי־רוּחַ׃ עֹשֶׂה מַלְאָכָיו רוּחוֹת
ה מְשָׁרְתָיו אֵשׁ לֹהֵט׃ יָסַד־אֶרֶץ עַל־מְכוֹנֶיהָ בַּל־תִּמּוֹט עוֹלָם וָעֶד׃
ו ז תְּהוֹם כַּלְּבוּשׁ כִּסִּיתוֹ עַל־הָרִים יַעַמְדוּ־מָיִם׃ מִן־גַּעֲרָתְךָ יְנוּסוּן מִן־
ח קוֹל רַעַמְךָ יֵחָפֵזוּן׃ יַעֲלוּ הָרִים יֵרְדוּ בְקָעוֹת אֶל־מְקוֹם זֶה ׀ יָסַדְתָּ
ט י לָהֶם׃ גְּבוּל־שַׂמְתָּ בַּל־יַעֲבֹרוּן בַּל־יְשׁוּבוּן לְכַסּוֹת הָאָרֶץ׃ הַמְשַׁלֵּחַ
יא מַעְיָנִים בַּנְּחָלִים בֵּין הָרִים יְהַלֵּכוּן׃ יַשְׁקוּ כׇּל־חַיְתוֹ שָׂדָי יִשְׁבְּרוּ פְרָאִים
יב יג צְמָאָם׃ עֲלֵיהֶם עוֹף־הַשָּׁמַיִם יִשְׁכּוֹן מִבֵּין עֳפָאיִם יִתְּנוּ־קוֹל׃ מַשְׁקֶה
יד הָרִים מֵעֲלִיּוֹתָיו מִפְּרִי מַעֲשֶׂיךָ תִּשְׂבַּע הָאָרֶץ׃ מַצְמִיחַ חָצִיר ׀ לַבְּהֵמָה
טו וְעֵשֶׂב לַעֲבֹדַת הָאָדָם לְהוֹצִיא לֶחֶם מִן־הָאָרֶץ׃ וְיַיִן ׀ יְשַׂמַּח לְבַב־
טז אֱנוֹשׁ לְהַצְהִיל פָּנִים מִשָּׁמֶן וְלֶחֶם לְבַב־אֱנוֹשׁ יִסְעָד׃ יִשְׂבְּעוּ עֲצֵי
יז יהוה אַרְזֵי לְבָנוֹן אֲשֶׁר נָטָע׃ אֲשֶׁר־שָׁם צִפֳּרִים יְקַנֵּנוּ חֲסִידָה בְּרוֹשִׁים
יח יט בֵּיתָהּ׃ הָרִים הַגְּבֹהִים לַיְּעֵלִים סְלָעִים מַחְסֶה לַשְׁפַנִּים׃ עָשָׂה יָרֵחַ
כ לְמוֹעֲדִים שֶׁמֶשׁ יָדַע מְבוֹאוֹ׃ תָּשֶׁת־חֹשֶׁךְ וִיהִי לָיְלָה בּוֹ־תִרְמֹשׂ כׇּל־
כא כב חַיְתוֹ־יָעַר׃ הַכְּפִירִים שֹׁאֲגִים לַטָּרֶף וּלְבַקֵּשׁ מֵאֵל אׇכְלָם׃ תִּזְרַח
כג הַשֶּׁמֶשׁ יֵאָסֵפוּן וְאֶל־מְעוֹנֹתָם יִרְבָּצוּן׃ יֵצֵא אָדָם לְפׇעֳלוֹ וְלַעֲבֹדָתוֹ
כד עֲדֵי־עָרֶב׃ מָה־רַבּוּ מַעֲשֶׂיךָ ׀ יהוה כֻּלָּם בְּחׇכְמָה עָשִׂיתָ מָלְאָה הָאָרֶץ
כה קִנְיָנֶךָ׃ זֶה ׀ הַיָּם גָּדוֹל וּרְחַב יָדָיִם שָׁם־רֶמֶשׂ וְאֵין מִסְפָּר חַיּוֹת קְטַנּוֹת

26 things great and small. There ships sail; You created that Leviathan[116] for Your
27 own pleasure. All of them look to You in hope, to give them their food when
28 it is due. They gather up what You give them; when You open Your hand,
29 they are sated with good. When You hide Your face, they grow terrified.
30 When You take away their breath, they die and return to dust. When You
emit Your breath, they are created, bringing new life to the face of the earth.
31 May the glory of the LORD last forever; may the LORD rejoice in His works.
32 When He looks at the earth, it trembles; when He touches the mountains,
33 they smoke. I will sing to the LORD all my life; I will sing to my God as long
34 35 as I live. May my reflections delight Him; I will rejoice in the LORD. May
sinners vanish from the earth and the wicked be no more. Bless the LORD,
my soul. *Halleluya!*[117]

105 1 Give thanks to the LORD; call on His name; [118] proclaim His acts among the
2 3 peoples. Sing to Him; make music to Him; tell of all His wonders. Glory
4 in His holy name; let the hearts of the LORD's seekers rejoice. Long for the
5 LORD and His might; seek out His presence always. Recall the wonders He
6 has done, the marvels and judgments He has pronounced, O seed of Avraham
7 His servant, O children of Yaakov, His chosen ones. He is the LORD, our God;
8 His judgments are throughout the land. He remembers His covenant forever,
9 His word of command for a thousand generations – which He formed with
10 Avraham, swore to Yisḥak,[119] and established with Yaakov as a statute, as an
11 eternal covenant for Israel – saying, "To you I will give the land of Canaan as
12 your share of inheritance" – when you were few in number, scarce, strangers
13 there, wandering from nation to nation, from one kingdom to another people.
14 Yet He let no one oppress them and rebuked kings for their sake, saying,
15 16 "Touch not My anointed ones, and do My prophets no harm." He summoned
17 famine to the land and cut off all supply of bread, but He sent a man before
18 them – Yosef, sold into slavery. They pressed his feet into fetters, and an iron
19 collar closed around his neck; until his words came to pass, the LORD's decree
20 purged him. The king sent and set him free; the ruler of peoples released him.
21 22 He made him master of his house, ruler over all he owned with the power to
23 imprison princes at will so that he could teach his elders wisdom. Then Israel
24 came to Egypt, and Yaakov settled in the land of Ḥam. He made His people
25 most fruitful, more numerous than their enemies. He changed their hearts
26 to hate His people, to conspire against His servants. He sent His servant
27 Moshe and Aharon, whom He had chosen, and they performed His signs
28 among them, wonders in the land of Ḥam. He sent darkness; it grew dark,
29 yet they still rebelled against His word. He turned their water into blood; He
30 killed their fish; their land teemed with frogs, even in their royal chambers.
31 32 He gave the word, and swarms came, and lice throughout their borders. He

---

116 | See note on 74:14.

117 | Literally "praise the LORD."

118 | For verses 1–15 of this psalm, cf. 1 Chronicles 16:8–22.

119 | A variant spelling of Yitzḥak. The verb "to laugh," on which the name is based, can itself appear in Biblical Hebrew both as *tzaḥak* and *saḥak*.

כו כז עִם־גְּדֹלוֹת: שָׁם אֳנִיּוֹת יְהַלֵּכוּן לִוְיָתָן זֶה־יָצַרְתָּ לְשַׂחֶק־בּוֹ: כֻּלָּם אֵלֶיךָ
כח יְשַׂבֵּרוּן לָתֵת אׇכְלָם בְּעִתּוֹ: תִּתֵּן לָהֶם יִלְקֹטוּן תִּפְתַּח יָדְךָ יִשְׂבְּעוּן
כט טוֹב: תַּסְתִּיר פָּנֶיךָ יִבָּהֵלוּן תֹּסֵף רוּחָם יִגְוָעוּן וְאֶל־עֲפָרָם יְשׁוּבוּן:
ל לא תְּשַׁלַּח רוּחֲךָ יִבָּרֵאוּן וּתְחַדֵּשׁ פְּנֵי אֲדָמָה: יְהִי כְבוֹד יְהוָה לְעוֹלָם
לב יִשְׂמַח יְהוָה בְּמַעֲשָׂיו: הַמַּבִּיט לָאָרֶץ וַתִּרְעָד יִגַּע בֶּהָרִים וְיֶעֱשָׁנוּ:
לג לד אָשִׁירָה לַיהוָה בְּחַיָּי אֲזַמְּרָה לֵאלֹהַי בְּעוֹדִי: יֶעֱרַב עָלָיו שִׂיחִי אָנֹכִי
לה אֶשְׂמַח בַּיהוָה: יִתַּמּוּ חַטָּאִים ׀ מִן־הָאָרֶץ וּרְשָׁעִים ׀ עוֹד אֵינָם בָּרְכִי
נַפְשִׁי אֶת־יְהוָה הַלְלוּיָהּ:

קה א ב הוֹדוּ לַיהוָה קִרְאוּ בִּשְׁמוֹ הוֹדִיעוּ בָעַמִּים עֲלִילוֹתָיו: שִׁירוּ־לוֹ זַמְּרוּ־
ג לוֹ שִׂיחוּ בְּכׇל־נִפְלְאוֹתָיו: הִתְהַלְלוּ בְּשֵׁם קׇדְשׁוֹ יִשְׂמַח לֵב ׀ מְבַקְשֵׁי
ד ה יְהוָה: דִּרְשׁוּ יְהוָה וְעֻזּוֹ בַּקְּשׁוּ פָנָיו תָּמִיד: זִכְרוּ נִפְלְאוֹתָיו אֲשֶׁר־עָשָׂה
ו ז מֹפְתָיו וּמִשְׁפְּטֵי־פִיו: זֶרַע אַבְרָהָם עַבְדּוֹ בְּנֵי יַעֲקֹב בְּחִירָיו: הוּא
ח יְהוָה אֱלֹהֵינוּ בְּכׇל־הָאָרֶץ מִשְׁפָּטָיו: זָכַר לְעוֹלָם בְּרִיתוֹ דָּבָר צִוָּה
ט י לְאֶלֶף דּוֹר: אֲשֶׁר כָּרַת אֶת־אַבְרָהָם וּשְׁבוּעָתוֹ לְיִשְׂחָק: וַיַּעֲמִידֶהָ
יא לְיַעֲקֹב לְחֹק לְיִשְׂרָאֵל בְּרִית עוֹלָם: לֵאמֹר לְךָ אֶתֵּן אֶת־אֶרֶץ־כְּנָעַן
יב יג חֶבֶל נַחֲלַתְכֶם: בִּהְיוֹתָם מְתֵי מִסְפָּר כִּמְעַט וְגָרִים בָּהּ: וַיִּתְהַלְּכוּ
יד מִגּוֹי אֶל־גּוֹי מִמַּמְלָכָה אֶל־עַם אַחֵר: לֹא־הִנִּיחַ אָדָם לְעׇשְׁקָם וַיּוֹכַח
טו טז עֲלֵיהֶם מְלָכִים: אַל־תִּגְּעוּ בִמְשִׁיחָי וְלִנְבִיאַי אַל־תָּרֵעוּ: וַיִּקְרָא רָעָב
יז עַל־הָאָרֶץ כׇּל־מַטֵּה־לֶחֶם שָׁבָר: שָׁלַח לִפְנֵיהֶם אִישׁ לְעֶבֶד נִמְכַּר
יח יט יוֹסֵף: עִנּוּ בַכֶּבֶל רגליו בַּרְזֶל בָּאָה נַפְשׁוֹ: עַד־עֵת בֹּא־דְבָרוֹ אִמְרַת רַגְלוֹ
כ כא יְהוָה צְרָפָתְהוּ: שָׁלַח מֶלֶךְ וַיַּתִּירֵהוּ מֹשֵׁל עַמִּים וַיְפַתְּחֵהוּ: שָׂמוֹ
כב אָדוֹן לְבֵיתוֹ וּמֹשֵׁל בְּכׇל־קִנְיָנוֹ: לֶאְסֹר שָׂרָיו בְּנַפְשׁוֹ וּזְקֵנָיו יְחַכֵּם:
כג כד וַיָּבֹא יִשְׂרָאֵל מִצְרָיִם וְיַעֲקֹב גָּר בְּאֶרֶץ־חָם: וַיֶּפֶר אֶת־עַמּוֹ מְאֹד
כה כו וַיַּעֲצִמֵהוּ מִצָּרָיו: הָפַךְ לִבָּם לִשְׂנֹא עַמּוֹ לְהִתְנַכֵּל בַּעֲבָדָיו: שָׁלַח מֹשֶׁה
כז עַבְדּוֹ אַהֲרֹן אֲשֶׁר בָּחַר־בּוֹ: שָׂמוּ־בָם דִּבְרֵי אֹתוֹתָיו וּמֹפְתִים בְּאֶרֶץ
כח כט חָם: שָׁלַח חֹשֶׁךְ וַיַּחְשִׁךְ וְלֹא־מָרוּ אֶת־דברו: הָפַךְ אֶת־מֵימֵיהֶם דְּבָרוֹ
ל לְדָם וַיָּמֶת אֶת־דְּגָתָם: שָׁרַץ אַרְצָם צְפַרְדְּעִים בְּחַדְרֵי מַלְכֵיהֶם:
לא לב אָמַר וַיָּבֹא עָרֹב כִּנִּים בְּכׇל־גְּבוּלָם: נָתַן גִּשְׁמֵיהֶם בָּרָד אֵשׁ לֶהָבוֹת

33 made their rain into hail, with flames of fire throughout their land. He struck
down their vines and figs and shattered the trees throughout their borders.
34 35 He gave the word, and the locusts came, grasshoppers without number; they
36 devoured all the grass in their land and devoured the fruits of their soil. He
struck down every firstborn in their land, all the first fruits of their manhood,
37 then He brought them out with silver and gold, and none among His tribes
38 did falter. Egypt rejoiced when they went out, for their terror had fallen upon
39 40 them. He spread out a cloud as a screen and fire to light up the night. They
41 asked, and He provided quail; He sated them with heavenly bread. He opened
42 up a rock, and water flowed out, running like a river in the parched land, for
43 He remembered His holy word to Avraham, His servant. He brought His
44 people out in joy, His chosen ones in glad song. He gave them the lands of
45 the nations; they took possession of the wealth of peoples so that they might
keep His statutes and observe His teachings. *Halleluya!*
106 1 *Halleluya!* Thank the Lord for He is good; His loving-kindness is forever.[120]
2 Who can articulate the Lord's mighty acts; who can express all His praise?
3 4 Happy are those who keep justice, who do what is right at all times. Remember
me, Lord, when You show Your people favor; keep me in mind for Your
5 salvation, that I may share in the good of Your chosen ones, rejoice in the
6 joy of Your own nation, and glory in Your heritage. We have sinned like our
7 ancestors; we have offended; we have done evil.[121] Our ancestors in Egypt
did not appreciate Your wonders, did not recall Your great loyalty – they
8 were defiant at the sea, at the Sea of Reeds, yet He saved them for the sake of
9 His name, to make known His mighty deeds. He blasted the Sea of Reeds,
10 and it dried up; He led them through the deep as through wilderness. He
saved them from the hands of haters and redeemed them from the hands
11 12 of enemies. The waters covered their foes; not one of them remained. They
13 had faith in His words and sang His praises, but they soon forgot what He
14 had done and would not await His counsel. They were seized with craving
15 in the wilderness and tested God in the wasteland. He granted what they
16 asked for but made them waste away. They grew envious of Moshe in the
17 camp, of Aharon, the Lord's holy one. The earth opened up and swallowed
18 Datan and closed over Aviram's mob, then fire burned up their mob; flame
19 set the wicked ones ablaze. They made a calf at Ḥorev and bowed to a molten
20 21 image, exchanging their Glory for a figure of a grass-eating ox. They forgot
22 God their savior, who had done great things in Egypt, wonders in the land
23 of Ham, awesome deeds at the Sea of Reeds. He would have wiped them
out were it not for Moshe, His chosen one, who stood in the breach before
24 Him to hold back His wrath from destroying them. They spurned the most
25 desirable land and did not have faith in His promise. They grumbled in their
26 tents and would not heed the Lord's voice, so He raised His hand against
27 them to cast them down in the wilderness, cast their seed among the nations,

120 | This verse is common in Psalms; cf. 107:1, 118:1, 29, 136:1.

121 | All the following events are recounted in the books of Exodus and Numbers.

לג לד בְּאַרְצָם: וַיַּךְ גַּפְנָם וּתְאֵנָתָם וַיְשַׁבֵּר עֵץ גְּבוּלָם: אָמַר וַיָּבֹא אַרְבֶּה
לה וְיֶלֶק וְאֵין מִסְפָּר: וַיֹּאכַל כָּל־עֵשֶׂב בְּאַרְצָם וַיֹּאכַל פְּרִי אַדְמָתָם:
לו לז וַיַּךְ כָּל־בְּכוֹר בְּאַרְצָם רֵאשִׁית לְכָל־אוֹנָם: וַיּוֹצִיאֵם בְּכֶסֶף וְזָהָב
לח וְאֵין בִּשְׁבָטָיו כּוֹשֵׁל: שָׂמַח מִצְרַיִם בְּצֵאתָם כִּי־נָפַל פַּחְדָּם עֲלֵיהֶם:
לט מ פָּרַשׂ עָנָן לְמָסָךְ וְאֵשׁ לְהָאִיר לָיְלָה: שָׁאַל וַיָּבֵא שְׂלָו וְלֶחֶם שָׁמַיִם
מא מב יַשְׂבִּיעֵם: פָּתַח צוּר וַיָּזוּבוּ מָיִם הָלְכוּ בַּצִּיּוֹת נָהָר: כִּי־זָכַר אֶת־דְּבַר
מג קָדְשׁוֹ אֶת־אַבְרָהָם עַבְדּוֹ: וַיּוֹצִא עַמּוֹ בְשָׂשׂוֹן בְּרִנָּה אֶת־בְּחִירָיו:
מד מה וַיִּתֵּן לָהֶם אַרְצוֹת גּוֹיִם וַעֲמַל לְאֻמִּים יִירָשׁוּ: בַּעֲבוּר ׀ יִשְׁמְרוּ חֻקָּיו טו
וְתוֹרֹתָיו יִנְצֹרוּ הַלְלוּיָהּ:

קו א ב הַלְלוּיָהּ ׀ הוֹדוּ לַיהוָה כִּי־טוֹב כִּי לְעוֹלָם חַסְדּוֹ: מִי יְמַלֵּל גְּבוּרוֹת
ג יהוה יַשְׁמִיעַ כָּל־תְּהִלָּתוֹ: אַשְׁרֵי שֹׁמְרֵי מִשְׁפָּט עֹשֵׂה צְדָקָה בְכָל־
ד ה עֵת: זָכְרֵנִי יהוה בִּרְצוֹן עַמֶּךָ פָּקְדֵנִי בִּישׁוּעָתֶךָ: לִרְאוֹת ׀ בְּטוֹבַת
ו בְּחִירֶיךָ לִשְׂמֹחַ בְּשִׂמְחַת גּוֹיֶךָ לְהִתְהַלֵּל עִם־נַחֲלָתֶךָ: חָטָאנוּ עִם־
ז אֲבוֹתֵינוּ הֶעֱוִינוּ הִרְשָׁעְנוּ: אֲבוֹתֵינוּ בְמִצְרַיִם ׀ לֹא־הִשְׂכִּילוּ נִפְלְאוֹתֶיךָ
ח לֹא זָכְרוּ אֶת־רֹב חֲסָדֶיךָ וַיַּמְרוּ עַל־יָם בְּיַם־סוּף: וַיּוֹשִׁיעֵם לְמַעַן שְׁמוֹ
ט לְהוֹדִיעַ אֶת־גְּבוּרָתוֹ: וַיִּגְעַר בְּיַם־סוּף וַיֶּחֱרָב וַיּוֹלִיכֵם בַּתְּהֹמוֹת
י יא כַּמִּדְבָּר: וַיּוֹשִׁיעֵם מִיַּד שׂוֹנֵא וַיִּגְאָלֵם מִיַּד אוֹיֵב: וַיְכַסּוּ־מַיִם צָרֵיהֶם
יב יג אֶחָד מֵהֶם לֹא נוֹתָר: וַיַּאֲמִינוּ בִדְבָרָיו יָשִׁירוּ תְּהִלָּתוֹ: מִהֲרוּ שָׁכְחוּ
יד מַעֲשָׂיו לֹא־חִכּוּ לַעֲצָתוֹ: וַיִּתְאַוּוּ תַאֲוָה בַּמִּדְבָּר וַיְנַסּוּ־אֵל בִּישִׁימוֹן:
טו טז וַיִּתֵּן לָהֶם שֶׁאֱלָתָם וַיְשַׁלַּח רָזוֹן בְּנַפְשָׁם: וַיְקַנְאוּ לְמֹשֶׁה בַּמַּחֲנֶה
יז לְאַהֲרֹן קְדוֹשׁ יהוה: תִּפְתַּח־אֶרֶץ וַתִּבְלַע דָּתָן וַתְּכַס עַל־עֲדַת
יח יט אֲבִירָם: וַתִּבְעַר־אֵשׁ בַּעֲדָתָם לֶהָבָה תְּלַהֵט רְשָׁעִים: יַעֲשׂוּ־עֵגֶל
כ בְּחֹרֵב וַיִּשְׁתַּחֲווּ לְמַסֵּכָה: וַיָּמִירוּ אֶת־כְּבוֹדָם בְּתַבְנִית שׁוֹר אֹכֵל
כא כב עֵשֶׂב: שָׁכְחוּ אֵל מוֹשִׁיעָם עֹשֶׂה גְדֹלוֹת בְּמִצְרָיִם: נִפְלָאוֹת בְּאֶרֶץ
כג חָם נוֹרָאוֹת עַל־יַם־סוּף: וַיֹּאמֶר לְהַשְׁמִידָם לוּלֵי מֹשֶׁה בְחִירוֹ עָמַד
כד בַּפֶּרֶץ לְפָנָיו לְהָשִׁיב חֲמָתוֹ מֵהַשְׁחִית: וַיִּמְאֲסוּ בְּאֶרֶץ חֶמְדָּה לֹא־
כה כו הֶאֱמִינוּ לִדְבָרוֹ: וַיֵּרָגְנוּ בְאָהֳלֵיהֶם לֹא שָׁמְעוּ בְּקוֹל יהוה: וַיִּשָּׂא יָדוֹ
כז לָהֶם לְהַפִּיל אוֹתָם בַּמִּדְבָּר: וּלְהַפִּיל זַרְעָם בַּגּוֹיִם וּלְזָרוֹתָם בָּאֲרָצוֹת:

28 and scattered them throughout the lands. They embraced Baal Peor and ate
29 sacrifices of the dead. Their practices provoked Him, and a plague broke out
30 among them, then Pinḥas took a stand and intervened, and the plague ceased.
31 32 This was counted to his merit for all generations forever. They moved Him
33 to fury at the waters of Meriva, and Moshe suffered because of them when
34 they defied his spirit, and he spoke rash words. They did not destroy the
35 peoples that the LORD bade them to destroy;[122] they mingled with the nations
36 and learned their ways. They served their idols, which became a snare for
37 38 them; they sacrificed their sons and their daughters to demons. They spilled
innocent blood, the blood of their sons and daughters; they sacrificed to the
39 idols of Canaan, and the land grew polluted with blood. They defiled with
40 their deeds, and strayed with their practices; the LORD's fury blazed against
41 His people, and He abhorred His share, so He handed them over to the
42 nations, and their haters ruled over them. Their enemies oppressed them,
43 and they were brought low by their power. Many times He saved them, but
44 they were defiant in their schemes and sank low in their guilt, yet He saw
45 their torment when He heard their cry. He remembered His covenant for
46 their sake, and He relented in His great loyalty. He stirred compassion for
47 them in the hearts of all their captors. Save us, LORD our God, and gather us
from the nations so that we may give thanks to Your holy name and glory in
48 Your praise. Blessed is the LORD, God of Israel, for ever and ever, and let all
the people say "Amen." *Halleluya!*[123]

107 1 2 Thank the LORD for He is good; His loving-kindness is forever;[124] let the BOOK FIVE
LORD's redeemed say this – those He redeemed from the enemy's hand,
3 those He gathered from the lands, from east and west, from north and south.
4 5 Some lost their way in desert wastelands, finding no inhabited towns; hungry
6 and thirsty, their will to live grew faint. They cried out to the LORD in their
7 torment; He rescued them from their distress; He led them by a straight path
8 to a town where they could settle. Let them thank the LORD for His loving-
9 kindness, for His wondrous deeds for humanity, for He quenches thirsty souls
10 and fills up hungry souls with goodness. Some sat in darkness and death-
11 shadow, bound in cruel iron chains, for they had defied God's words and
12 reviled the counsel of the Most High. He humbled their hearts with toil; they
13 stumbled, with none to help. They cried out to the LORD in their torment;
14 He saved them from their distress. He brought them out from darkness and
15 death-shadow and broke apart their bonds. Let them thank the LORD for His
16 loving-kindness, for His wondrous deeds for humanity, for He shattered gates
17 of bronze and cut their iron bars. Some were fools of sinful ways, suffering
18 because of their iniquities. They found all food repulsive and came close to the
19 gates of death. They cried out to the LORD in their torment; He saved them
20 from their distress. He sent His word and healed them and rescued them from

122 | See Judges. 2:1–5.
123 | Cf. 1 Chronicles 16:35–36.
124 | See note on 106:1.

כח כט וַיִּצָּמְדוּ לְבַעַל פְּעוֹר וַיֹּאכְלוּ זִבְחֵי מֵתִים׃ וַיַּכְעִיסוּ בְּמַעַלְלֵיהֶם וַתִּפְרׇץ־
ל לא בָּם מַגֵּפָה׃ וַיַּעֲמֹד פִּינְחָס וַיְפַלֵּל וַתֵּעָצַר הַמַּגֵּפָה׃ וַתֵּחָשֶׁב לוֹ לִצְדָקָה
לב לְדֹר וָדֹר עַד־עוֹלָם׃ וַיַּקְצִיפוּ עַל־מֵי מְרִיבָה וַיֵּרַע לְמֹשֶׁה בַּעֲבוּרָם׃
לג לד כִּי־הִמְרוּ אֶת־רוּחוֹ וַיְבַטֵּא בִּשְׂפָתָיו׃ לֹא־הִשְׁמִידוּ אֶת־הָעַמִּים אֲשֶׁר
לה לו אָמַר יְהוָה לָהֶם׃ וַיִּתְעָרְבוּ בַגּוֹיִם וַיִּלְמְדוּ מַעֲשֵׂיהֶם׃ וַיַּעַבְדוּ אֶת־
לז עֲצַבֵּיהֶם וַיִּהְיוּ לָהֶם לְמוֹקֵשׁ׃ וַיִּזְבְּחוּ אֶת־בְּנֵיהֶם וְאֶת־בְּנוֹתֵיהֶם
לח לַשֵּׁדִים׃ וַיִּשְׁפְּכוּ דָם נָקִי דַּם־בְּנֵיהֶם וּבְנוֹתֵיהֶם אֲשֶׁר זִבְּחוּ לַעֲצַבֵּי
לט כְנָעַן וַתֶּחֱנַף הָאָרֶץ בַּדָּמִים׃ וַיִּטְמְאוּ בְמַעֲשֵׂיהֶם וַיִּזְנוּ בְּמַעַלְלֵיהֶם׃
מ מא וַיִּחַר־אַף יְהוָה בְּעַמּוֹ וַיְתָעֵב אֶת־נַחֲלָתוֹ׃ וַיִּתְּנֵם בְּיַד־גּוֹיִם וַיִּמְשְׁלוּ
מב מג בָהֶם שֹׂנְאֵיהֶם׃ וַיִּלְחָצוּם אוֹיְבֵיהֶם וַיִּכָּנְעוּ תַּחַת יָדָם׃ פְּעָמִים רַבּוֹת
מד יַצִּילֵם וְהֵמָּה יַמְרוּ בַעֲצָתָם וַיָּמֹכּוּ בַּעֲוֺנָם׃ וַיַּרְא בַּצַּר לָהֶם בְּשׇׁמְעוֹ
מה מו אֶת־רִנָּתָם׃ וַיִּזְכֹּר לָהֶם בְּרִיתוֹ וַיִּנָּחֵם כְּרֹב חֲסָדָו׃ וַיִּתֵּן אוֹתָם לְרַחֲמִים
מז לִפְנֵי כׇּל־שׁוֹבֵיהֶם׃ הוֹשִׁיעֵנוּ ׀ יְהוָה אֱלֹהֵינוּ וְקַבְּצֵנוּ מִן־הַגּוֹיִם לְהֹדוֹת
מח לְשֵׁם קׇדְשֶׁךָ לְהִשְׁתַּבֵּחַ בִּתְהִלָּתֶךָ׃ בָּרוּךְ יְהוָה ׀ אֱלֹהֵי יִשְׂרָאֵל מִן־
הָעוֹלָם ׀ וְעַד הָעוֹלָם וְאָמַר כׇּל־הָעָם אָמֵן הַלְלוּיָהּ׃

ספר חמישי

קז א ב הֹדוּ לַיהוָה כִּי־טוֹב כִּי לְעוֹלָם חַסְדּוֹ׃ יֹאמְרוּ גְּאוּלֵי יְהוָה אֲשֶׁר גְּאָלָם
ג ד מִיַּד־צָר׃ וּמֵאֲרָצוֹת קִבְּצָם מִמִּזְרָח וּמִמַּעֲרָב מִצָּפוֹן וּמִיָּם׃ תָּעוּ בַמִּדְבָּר
ה בִּישִׁימוֹן דָּרֶךְ עִיר מוֹשָׁב לֹא מָצָאוּ׃ רְעֵבִים גַּם־צְמֵאִים נַפְשָׁם בָּהֶם
ו ז תִּתְעַטָּף׃ וַיִּצְעֲקוּ אֶל־יְהוָה בַּצַּר לָהֶם מִמְּצוּקוֹתֵיהֶם יַצִּילֵם׃ וַיַּדְרִיכֵם
ח בְּדֶרֶךְ יְשָׁרָה לָלֶכֶת אֶל־עִיר מוֹשָׁב׃ יוֹדוּ לַיהוָה חַסְדּוֹ וְנִפְלְאוֹתָיו
ט י לִבְנֵי אָדָם׃ כִּי־הִשְׂבִּיעַ נֶפֶשׁ שֹׁקֵקָה וְנֶפֶשׁ רְעֵבָה מִלֵּא־טוֹב׃ יֹשְׁבֵי
יא חֹשֶׁךְ וְצַלְמָוֶת אֲסִירֵי עֳנִי וּבַרְזֶל׃ כִּי־הִמְרוּ אִמְרֵי־אֵל וַעֲצַת עֶלְיוֹן
יב יג נָאָצוּ׃ וַיַּכְנַע בֶּעָמָל לִבָּם כָּשְׁלוּ וְאֵין עֹזֵר׃ וַיִּזְעֲקוּ אֶל־יְהוָה בַּצַּר לָהֶם
יד מִמְּצֻקוֹתֵיהֶם יוֹשִׁיעֵם׃ יוֹצִיאֵם מֵחֹשֶׁךְ וְצַלְמָוֶת וּמוֹסְרוֹתֵיהֶם יְנַתֵּק׃
טו טז יוֹדוּ לַיהוָה חַסְדּוֹ וְנִפְלְאוֹתָיו לִבְנֵי אָדָם׃ כִּי־שִׁבַּר דַּלְתוֹת נְחֹשֶׁת
יז יח וּבְרִיחֵי בַרְזֶל גִּדֵּעַ׃ אֱוִלִים מִדֶּרֶךְ פִּשְׁעָם וּמֵעֲוֺנֹתֵיהֶם יִתְעַנּוּ׃ כׇּל־אֹכֶל
יט תְּתַעֵב נַפְשָׁם וַיַּגִּיעוּ עַד־שַׁעֲרֵי מָוֶת׃ וַיִּזְעֲקוּ אֶל־יְהוָה בַּצַּר לָהֶם
כ מִמְּצֻקוֹתֵיהֶם יוֹשִׁיעֵם׃ יִשְׁלַח דְּבָרוֹ וְיִרְפָּאֵם וִימַלֵּט מִשְּׁחִיתוֹתָם׃

21 their destruction. Let them thank the Lord for His loving-kindness, for His
22 wondrous deeds for humanity; let them sacrifice thanksgiving offerings and
23 tell of His deeds with joy. Those who go down to the sea in ships, sailing across
24 the mighty waters – they have seen the works of the Lord, His wondrous
25 deeds in the deep. He spoke and stirred up a tempest that lifted up the waves;
26 they rose to the heavens and plunged down to the depths, their souls melted
27 in misery. They reeled and staggered like drunkards; all their skill was to no
28 avail. They cried out to the Lord in their torment; He brought them out from
29 their distress. He stilled the storm to a whisper, and the waves of the sea grew
30 calm. They rejoiced when all was quiet, then He guided them to their desired
31 harbor. Let them thank the Lord for His loving-kindness, for His wondrous
32 deeds for humanity. Let them exalt Him before the assembly and praise
33 Him in the council of the elders. He turns rivers into desert land, springs of
34 water into parched ground, fruitful land into salt-sown waste because of the
35 corruption of its people. He turns desert land into pools of water, wasteland
36 into flowing springs; He brings the hungry to live there, to build a town in
37 which to live. They sow fields and plant vineyards that yield a fruitful harvest;
38 He blesses them, and they flourish. He does not let their herds decrease,
39 40 but they shrink and languish under tyranny, cruelty, and sorrow. He pours
41 contempt on nobles and leads them astray into pathless chaos. He lifts the
42 destitute from poverty and increases their families like flocks. The upright see
43 and rejoice, while all wicked mouths are silenced. Let the wise keep all this in
mind; let them reflect on the Lord's loving-kindness.

108 1 2 *A song – a psalm of David.* My heart is sound, God; my heart is sound[125] – I
3 will sing and chant praises from my very soul. Stir, harp and lyre! I will stir
4 the dawn. I will praise You among the peoples, Lord; I will chant Your
5 praise among the nations, for Your loyalty is higher than the heavens; Your
6 truth reaches the skies. Rise up, God, over the heavens; unleash Your glory
7 over all the earth so that Your dear ones may be rescued; let Your right hand
8 bring victory – answer me! God promised in His Sanctuary that I would
triumph: I will divide up Shekhem and measure out the Valley of Sukkot;
9 Gilad and Menashe will be mine; Efrayim will be my chief stronghold, Yehuda
10 my scepter. Moav will be my washbasin; at Edom I'll fling my shoe; I will
11 crow over Philistia, but who will bring me to the fortified cities? Who will
12 lead me to Edom? Have You not forsaken us, God? God, You no longer
13 march out with our forces. Come to our aid against the enemy, for human
14 help is worthless. With God, we will triumph valiantly, and He will trample
our enemies.

109 1 *To the lead singer, of David – a psalm.* God of my praise, do not remain silent,
2 for wicked mouths, deceitful mouths have opened against me. They speak
3 to me with lying tongues; they surround me with words of hatred, attacking
4 me without cause. In return for my love they accuse me, yet I pray for them.[126]
5 6 They repay me with evil for good, with hatred for my love. "Station a wicked

125 | For verses 2–6 and 7–14, cf. 57:8–12 and 60:7–14, respectively.
126 | Literally "I am prayer."

כא כב יוֹדוּ לַיהוָה חַסְדּוֹ וְנִפְלְאוֹתָיו לִבְנֵי אָדָם: וְיִזְבְּחוּ זִבְחֵי תוֹדָה וִיסַפְּרוּ
כג מַעֲשָׂיו בְּרִנָּה: ׆ יוֹרְדֵי הַיָּם בָּאֳנִיּוֹת עֹשֵׂי מְלָאכָה בְּמַיִם
כד רַבִּים: ׆ הֵמָּה רָאוּ מַעֲשֵׂי יְהוָה וְנִפְלְאוֹתָיו
כה כו בִּמְצוּלָה: ׆ וַיֹּאמֶר וַיַּעֲמֵד רוּחַ סְעָרָה וַתְּרוֹמֵם גַּלָּיו: ׆ יַעֲלוּ
כז שָׁמַיִם יֵרְדוּ תְהוֹמוֹת נַפְשָׁם בְּרָעָה תִתְמוֹגָג: ׆ יָחוֹגּוּ וְיָנוּעוּ
כח כַּשִּׁכּוֹר וְכָל־חָכְמָתָם תִּתְבַּלָּע: ׆ וַיִּצְעֲקוּ אֶל־יְהוָה בַּצַּר לָהֶם
כט ל וּמִמְּצוּקֹתֵיהֶם יוֹצִיאֵם: יָקֵם סְעָרָה לִדְמָמָה וַיֶּחֱשׁוּ גַּלֵּיהֶם: וַיִּשְׂמְחוּ
לא כִי־יִשְׁתֹּקוּ וַיַּנְחֵם אֶל־מְחוֹז חֶפְצָם: יוֹדוּ לַיהוָה חַסְדּוֹ וְנִפְלְאוֹתָיו לִבְנֵי
לב לג אָדָם: וִירֹמְמוּהוּ בִּקְהַל־עָם וּבְמוֹשַׁב זְקֵנִים יְהַלְלוּהוּ: יָשֵׂם נְהָרוֹת
לד לְמִדְבָּר וּמֹצָאֵי מַיִם לְצִמָּאוֹן: אֶרֶץ פְּרִי לִמְלֵחָה מֵרָעַת יוֹשְׁבֵי בָהּ:
לה לו יָשֵׂם מִדְבָּר לַאֲגַם־מַיִם וְאֶרֶץ צִיָּה לְמֹצָאֵי מָיִם: וַיּוֹשֶׁב שָׁם רְעֵבִים
לז וַיְכוֹנְנוּ עִיר מוֹשָׁב: וַיִּזְרְעוּ שָׂדוֹת וַיִּטְּעוּ כְרָמִים וַיַּעֲשׂוּ פְּרִי תְבוּאָה:
לח לט וַיְבָרְכֵם וַיִּרְבּוּ מְאֹד וּבְהֶמְתָּם לֹא יַמְעִיט: וַיִּמְעֲטוּ וַיָּשֹׁחוּ מֵעֹצֶר רָעָה
מ מא וְיָגוֹן: ׆ שֹׁפֵךְ בּוּז עַל־נְדִיבִים וַיַּתְעֵם בְּתֹהוּ לֹא־דָרֶךְ: וַיְשַׂגֵּב
מב אֶבְיוֹן מֵעוֹנִי וַיָּשֶׂם כַּצֹּאן מִשְׁפָּחוֹת: יִרְאוּ יְשָׁרִים וְיִשְׂמָחוּ וְכָל־עַוְלָה
מג קָפְצָה פִּיהָ: מִי־חָכָם וְיִשְׁמָר־אֵלֶּה וְיִתְבּוֹנְנוּ חַסְדֵי יְהוָה:
קח א ב שִׁיר מִזְמוֹר לְדָוִד: נָכוֹן לִבִּי אֱלֹהִים אָשִׁירָה וַאֲזַמְּרָה אַף־כְּבוֹדִי:
ג ד עוּרָה הַנֵּבֶל וְכִנּוֹר אָעִירָה שָּׁחַר: אוֹדְךָ בָעַמִּים ׀ יְהוָה וַאֲזַמֶּרְךָ
ה ו בַּלְאֻמִּים: כִּי־גָדוֹל מֵעַל־שָׁמַיִם חַסְדֶּךָ וְעַד־שְׁחָקִים אֲמִתֶּךָ: רוּמָה
ז עַל־שָׁמַיִם אֱלֹהִים וְעַל כָּל־הָאָרֶץ כְּבוֹדֶךָ: לְמַעַן יֵחָלְצוּן יְדִידֶיךָ
ח הוֹשִׁיעָה יְמִינְךָ ועננו: אֱלֹהִים ׀ דִּבֶּר בְּקָדְשׁוֹ אֶעְלֹזָה אֲחַלְּקָה שְׁכֶם [וַעֲנֵנִי]
ט וְעֵמֶק סֻכּוֹת אֲמַדֵּד: לִי גִלְעָד ׀ לִי מְנַשֶּׁה וְאֶפְרַיִם מָעוֹז רֹאשִׁי יְהוּדָה
י מְחֹקְקִי: מוֹאָב ׀ סִיר רַחְצִי עַל־אֱדוֹם אַשְׁלִיךְ נַעֲלִי עֲלֵי־פְלֶשֶׁת
יא יב אֶתְרוֹעָע: מִי יֹבִלֵנִי עִיר מִבְצָר מִי נָחַנִי עַד־אֱדוֹם: הֲלֹא־אֱלֹהִים
יג זְנַחְתָּנוּ וְלֹא־תֵצֵא אֱלֹהִים בְּצִבְאֹתֵינוּ: הָבָה־לָּנוּ עֶזְרָת מִצָּר וְשָׁוְא
יד תְּשׁוּעַת אָדָם: בֵּאלֹהִים נַעֲשֶׂה־חָיִל וְהוּא יָבוּס צָרֵינוּ:
קט א ב לַמְנַצֵּחַ לְדָוִד מִזְמוֹר אֱלֹהֵי תְהִלָּתִי אַל־תֶּחֱרַשׁ: כִּי פִי רָשָׁע וּפִי־
ג מִרְמָה עָלַי פָּתָחוּ דִּבְּרוּ אִתִּי לְשׁוֹן שָׁקֶר: וְדִבְרֵי שִׂנְאָה סְבָבוּנִי
ד ה וַיִּלָּחֲמוּנִי חִנָּם: תַּחַת־אַהֲבָתִי יִשְׂטְנוּנִי וַאֲנִי תְפִלָּה: וַיָּשִׂימוּ עָלַי רָעָה
ו תַּחַת טוֹבָה וְשִׂנְאָה תַּחַת אַהֲבָתִי: הַפְקֵד עָלָיו רָשָׁע וְשָׂטָן יַעֲמֹד

7 person over him; let an adversary stand on his right.[127] When he is tried, let
8 him be found guilty; may his prayer count as offense. May his days be few;
9 may another seize his post. May his children become orphans, his wife a
10 widow; may his children wander and beg, foraging far from their ruined
11 12 homes. May a usurer seize all he owns and strangers plunder his wealth. May
13 no one show him any kindness and no one pity his orphans. May his posterity
14 be cut off, their name erased by the next generation. May the Lord recall his
15 fathers' offense, and may his mother's sin never be erased; may these ever
16 be before the Lord until He cuts off their name from the earth, for he was
never mindful of showing kindness but drove the poor, the needy, the heart
17 sore to death. He loved to curse – may curses come upon him – and showed
18 no desire for blessing – may it keep far away from him; he donned cursing as
19 his attire – may it seep inside him like water, like oil within his bones. May
20 it cloak him like a garment, always clasped around him like a belt." May this
be the due of my accusers from the Lord, of those who speak evil against
21 me, and may You, God my Lord, deal with me in keeping with Your name;
22 save me in Your good loyalty, for I am but poor and needy, and my heart is
23 pierced within me. I fade away like a lengthening shadow; I am shaken off
24 25 like a locust. My knees give way from fasting; my flesh is gaunt and lean. As
for me, I have become their scorn; when they see me, they shake their heads.
26 27 Help me, Lord my God; save me in keeping with Your loyalty, and they will
28 know that this is Your hand, that You, O Lord, have done this, so let them
curse, but You will bless; they will rise and be shamed while Your servant will
29 rejoice. My accusers will don disgrace; their shame will cloak them like a robe
30 while my mouth will declare great thanks to the Lord; I will praise Him in
31 the midst of the crowd, for He stands at the right hand of the needy to save
their lives from their condemners.

110 1 *Of David – a psalm.* The Lord has spoken to my lord: "Sit at My right hand
2 until I make your enemies a stool for your feet." Your mighty scepter the
3 Lord has sent forth from Zion; dominate your enemies. Your people offer
themselves willingly on your day of battle. In sacred splendor adored from
4 birth, yours is the dew bloom of youth. The Lord has sworn and will never
5 retract: "You are a priest forever by My decree, a rightful king." The Lord is at
6 your right hand, He who crushes kings on the day of His wrath. He executes
judgment upon the nations – so many corpses! – crushing heads far and wide.
7 He will drink from wayside streams and thus hold his head high.

111 1 *Halleluya!*[128] I will praise the Lord with all my heart in the gathered assembly
2 of the upright. Great are the Lord's works, sought by all who delight in them.
3 4 Majestic and splendid are His deeds; His righteousness stands forever. He
5 has won fame for His wonders; the Lord is gracious and compassionate. He
provides food for those who fear Him and forever remembers His covenant.

127 | Verses 6–19 are understood as either a curse pronounced by the speaker against his enemies or a quotation of his enemies' curse against him.

128 | This psalm and the next form alphabetical acrostics built on the first letters of every half or third of a verse.

ז ח עַל־יְמִינוֹ׃ בְּהִשָּׁפְטוֹ יֵצֵא רָשָׁע וּתְפִלָּתוֹ תִּהְיֶה לַחֲטָאָה׃ יִהְיוּ־יָמָיו
ט י מְעַטִּים פְּקֻדָּתוֹ יִקַּח אַחֵר׃ יִהְיוּ־בָנָיו יְתוֹמִים וְאִשְׁתּוֹ אַלְמָנָה׃ וְנוֹעַ
יא יָנוּעוּ בָנָיו וְשִׁאֵלוּ וְדָרְשׁוּ מֵחָרְבוֹתֵיהֶם׃ יְנַקֵּשׁ נוֹשֶׁה לְכָל־אֲשֶׁר־לוֹ
יב יג וְיָבֹזּוּ זָרִים יְגִיעוֹ׃ אַל־יְהִי־לוֹ מֹשֵׁךְ חָסֶד וְאַל־יְהִי חוֹנֵן לִיתוֹמָיו׃ יְהִי־
יד אַחֲרִיתוֹ לְהַכְרִית בְּדוֹר אַחֵר יִמַּח שְׁמָם׃ יִזָּכֵר ׀ עֲוֺן אֲבֹתָיו אֶל־יְהוָה
טו וְחַטַּאת אִמּוֹ אַל־תִּמָּח׃ יִהְיוּ נֶגֶד־יְהוָה תָּמִיד וְיַכְרֵת מֵאֶרֶץ זִכְרָם׃
טז יַעַן אֲשֶׁר ׀ לֹא זָכַר עֲשׂוֹת חָסֶד וַיִּרְדֹּף אִישׁ־עָנִי וְאֶבְיוֹן וְנִכְאֵה לֵבָב
יז לְמוֹתֵת׃ וַיֶּאֱהַב קְלָלָה וַתְּבוֹאֵהוּ וְלֹא־חָפֵץ בִּבְרָכָה וַתִּרְחַק מִמֶּנּוּ׃
יח יט וַיִּלְבַּשׁ קְלָלָה כְּמַדּוֹ וַתָּבֹא כַמַּיִם בְּקִרְבּוֹ וְכַשֶּׁמֶן בְּעַצְמוֹתָיו׃ תְּהִי־לוֹ
כ כְּבֶגֶד יַעְטֶה וּלְמֵזַח תָּמִיד יַחְגְּרֶהָ׃ זֹאת ׀ פְּעֻלַּת שֹׂטְנַי מֵאֵת יְהוָה
כא וְהַדֹּבְרִים רָע עַל־נַפְשִׁי׃ וְאַתָּה ׀ יְהוִה אֲדֹנָי עֲשֵׂה־אִתִּי לְמַעַן שְׁמֶךָ
כב כג כִּי־טוֹב חַסְדְּךָ הַצִּילֵנִי׃ כִּי־עָנִי וְאֶבְיוֹן אָנֹכִי וְלִבִּי חָלַל בְּקִרְבִּי׃ כְּצֵל
כד כִּנְטוֹתוֹ נֶהֱלָכְתִּי נִנְעַרְתִּי כָּאַרְבֶּה׃ בִּרְכַּי כָּשְׁלוּ מִצּוֹם וּבְשָׂרִי כָּחַשׁ
כה כו מִשָּׁמֶן׃ וַאֲנִי ׀ הָיִיתִי חֶרְפָּה לָהֶם יִרְאוּנִי יְנִיעוּן רֹאשָׁם׃ עָזְרֵנִי יְהוָה
כז אֱלֹהָי הוֹשִׁיעֵנִי כְחַסְדֶּךָ׃ וְיֵדְעוּ כִּי־יָדְךָ זֹּאת אַתָּה יְהוָה עֲשִׂיתָהּ׃
כח כט יְקַלְלוּ־הֵמָּה וְאַתָּה תְבָרֵךְ קָמוּ ׀ וַיֵּבֹשׁוּ וְעַבְדְּךָ יִשְׂמָח׃ יִלְבְּשׁוּ שׂוֹטְנַי
ל כְּלִמָּה וְיַעֲטוּ כַמְעִיל בָּשְׁתָּם׃ אוֹדֶה יְהוָה מְאֹד בְּפִי וּבְתוֹךְ רַבִּים
לא אֲהַלְלֶנּוּ׃ כִּי־יַעֲמֹד לִימִין אֶבְיוֹן לְהוֹשִׁיעַ מִשֹּׁפְטֵי נַפְשׁוֹ׃
קי א לְדָוִד מִזְמוֹר נְאֻם יְהוָה ׀ לַאדֹנִי שֵׁב לִימִינִי עַד־אָשִׁית אֹיְבֶיךָ הֲדֹם
ב ג לְרַגְלֶיךָ׃ מַטֵּה עֻזְּךָ יִשְׁלַח יְהוָה מִצִּיּוֹן רְדֵה בְּקֶרֶב אֹיְבֶיךָ׃ עַמְּךָ נְדָבֹת
ד בְּיוֹם חֵילֶךָ בְּהַדְרֵי־קֹדֶשׁ מֵרֶחֶם מִשְׁחָר לְךָ טַל יַלְדֻתֶךָ׃ נִשְׁבַּע יְהוָה ׀
ה וְלֹא יִנָּחֵם אַתָּה־כֹהֵן לְעוֹלָם עַל־דִּבְרָתִי מַלְכִּי־צֶדֶק׃ אֲדֹנָי עַל־יְמִינְךָ
ו מָחַץ בְּיוֹם־אַפּוֹ מְלָכִים׃ יָדִין בַּגּוֹיִם מָלֵא גְוִיּוֹת מָחַץ רֹאשׁ עַל־
ז אֶרֶץ רַבָּה׃ מִנַּחַל בַּדֶּרֶךְ יִשְׁתֶּה עַל־כֵּן יָרִים רֹאשׁ׃
קיא א ב הַלְלוּיָהּ ׀ אוֹדֶה יְהוָה בְּכָל־לֵבָב בְּסוֹד יְשָׁרִים וְעֵדָה׃ גְּדֹלִים מַעֲשֵׂי
ג יְהוָה דְּרוּשִׁים לְכָל־חֶפְצֵיהֶם׃ הוֹד־וְהָדָר פָּעֳלוֹ וְצִדְקָתוֹ עֹמֶדֶת לָעַד׃
ד ה זֵכֶר עָשָׂה לְנִפְלְאוֹתָיו חַנּוּן וְרַחוּם יְהוָה׃ טֶרֶף נָתַן לִירֵאָיו יִזְכֹּר לְעוֹלָם

6 He has revealed His powerful deeds to His people by granting them their
7 share of the nations. Truth and justice are His handiwork; all His decrees are
8 9 faithful, steady for all eternity, formed in truth and right. He sent freedom
to His people, ordaining His covenant forever; holy and awesome is His
10 name. Wisdom begins with fear of the LORD; good sense is gained by all who
practice it; His praise stands forever.

112 1 *Halleluya!* Happy are those who fear the LORD, who deeply delight in His
2 commandments. Their seed will be powerful in the land, a blessed upright
3 generation. Wealth and riches fill their homes; their righteousness stands
4 forever. Even in the darkness light glows for the upright; they are gracious,
5 compassionate, and just. All is well for those who lend graciously, who
6 conduct their affairs with justice, for they will never be shaken; the righteous
7 are remembered forever. They will fear no evil tidings; their hearts are firm;
8 they trust in the LORD. Their hearts are steady; they shall not fear; in the
9 end they will witness the fall of their foes. They give freely to the needy;
their righteousness stands forever; their horn will be raised up in glory.
10 The wicked shall see and grow furious, gnash their teeth, and shrink away;
the desire of the wicked shall perish.

113 1 *Halleluya!* Sing praise, servants of the LORD; praise the name of the LORD.
2 3 Blessed be the name of the LORD, now and for evermore. From sunrise
4 to sunset may the LORD's name be praised. The LORD is exalted above all
5 nations; His glory soars above the heavens. Who is like the LORD our God,
6 who sits enthroned so high yet looks down so low to see the heavens and
7 the earth? He lifts the poor from the dust, raises the needy from the refuse
8 9 heap, and seats them beside nobility, beside the nobles of His people.[129] He
settles the childless woman in her home as a joyous mother of children.
Halleluya!

114 1 When Israel came out of Egypt, the House of Yaakov from a people of foreign
2 3 tongue, Yehuda became His sanctuary, Israel His dominion. The sea saw and
4 fled; the Jordan turned back. The mountains skipped like rams, the hills like
5 lambs. What happened, sea, that you fled? Jordan, why did you turn back?
6 7 Why, mountains, did you skip like rams, you hills like lambs? Tremble, O
8 earth, in the Lord's presence, in the presence of the God of Yaakov – He
turned the rock into a pool of water, the flint into a flowing spring.

115 1 Not to us, LORD, not to us, but to Your name give glory for Your love, for Your
2 3 faithfulness. Why should the nations say, "Where, now, is their God?" Our
4 God is in heaven; He does as He pleases. Their idols are silver and gold, made
5 by human hands.[130] They have mouths but cannot speak, eyes but cannot see;
6 7 they have ears but cannot hear, noses but cannot smell; they have hands but
8 cannot feel, feet but cannot walk; no sound comes from their throat. Their
9 makers will become like them; so will all who trust in them. Israel, trust in
10 the LORD – He is their help and their shield. House of Aharon, trust in the
11 LORD – He is their help and their shield. You who fear the LORD, trust in

129 | Cf. 1 Samuel 2:8.

130 | For verses 4–11, cf. 135:15–20.

ו ז בְּרִיתֽוֹ׃ כֹּ֣חַ מַ֭עֲשָׂיו הִגִּ֣יד לְעַמּ֑וֹ לָתֵ֥ת לָ֝הֶ֗ם נַחֲלַ֥ת גּוֹיִֽם׃ מַעֲשֵׂ֣י יָ֭דָיו
ח אֱמֶ֣ת וּמִשְׁפָּ֑ט נֶ֝אֱמָנִ֗ים כׇּל־פִּקּוּדָֽיו׃ סְמוּכִ֣ים לָעַ֣ד לְעוֹלָ֑ם עֲ֝שׂוּיִ֗ם
ט בֶּאֱמֶ֥ת וְיָשָֽׁר׃ פְּד֤וּת ׀ שָׁ֘לַ֤ח לְעַמּ֗וֹ צִוָּֽה־לְעוֹלָ֥ם בְּרִית֑וֹ קָד֖וֹשׁ וְנוֹרָ֣א
טז י שְׁמֽוֹ׃ רֵ֘אשִׁ֤ית חׇכְמָ֡ה ׀ יִרְאַ֬ת יהוה שֵׂ֣כֶל ט֭וֹב לְכׇל־עֹשֵׂיהֶ֑ם תְּ֝הִלָּת֗וֹ
עֹמֶ֥דֶת לָעַֽד׃

קיב א ב הַלְלוּיָ֨הּ ׀ אַ֥שְֽׁרֵי־אִ֭ישׁ יָרֵ֣א אֶת־יהוה בְּ֝מִצְוֺתָ֗יו חָפֵ֥ץ מְאֹֽד׃ גִּבּ֣וֹר
ג בָּ֭אָרֶץ יִהְיֶ֣ה זַרְע֑וֹ דּ֖וֹר יְשָׁרִ֣ים יְבֹרָֽךְ׃ הוֹן־וָעֹ֥שֶׁר בְּבֵית֑וֹ וְ֝צִדְקָת֗וֹ
ד ה עֹמֶ֥דֶת לָעַֽד׃ זָ֘רַ֤ח בַּחֹ֣שֶׁךְ א֭וֹר לַיְשָׁרִ֑ים חַנּ֖וּן וְרַח֣וּם וְצַדִּֽיק׃ טֽוֹב־
ו אִ֭ישׁ חוֹנֵ֣ן וּמַלְוֶ֑ה יְכַלְכֵּ֖ל דְּבָרָ֣יו בְּמִשְׁפָּֽט׃ כִּֽי־לְעוֹלָ֥ם לֹֽא־יִמּ֑וֹט לְזֵ֥כֶר
ז ע֝וֹלָ֗ם יִהְיֶ֥ה צַדִּֽיק׃ מִשְּׁמוּעָ֣ה רָ֭עָה לֹ֣א יִירָ֑א נָכ֥וֹן לִ֝בּ֗וֹ בָּטֻ֥חַ בַּיהוה׃
ח ט סָמ֣וּךְ לִ֭בּוֹ לֹ֣א יִירָ֑א עַ֖ד אֲשֶׁר־יִרְאֶ֣ה בְצָרָֽיו׃ פִּזַּ֤ר ׀ נָ֘תַ֤ן לָאֶבְיֹנִ֗ים
י צִ֭דְקָתוֹ עֹמֶ֣דֶת לָעַ֑ד קַ֝רְנ֗וֹ תָּר֥וּם בְּכָבֽוֹד׃ רָשָׁ֤ע יִרְאֶ֨ה ׀ וְכָעָ֗ס שִׁנָּ֣יו
יַחֲרֹ֣ק וְנָמָ֑ס תַּאֲוַ֖ת רְשָׁעִ֣ים תֹּאבֵֽד׃

קיג א ב הַלְלוּיָ֨הּ ׀ הַ֭לְלוּ עַבְדֵ֣י יהוה הַ֝לְל֗וּ אֶת־שֵׁ֥ם יהוה׃ יְהִ֤י שֵׁ֣ם יהוה מְבֹרָ֑ךְ
ג ד מֵ֝עַתָּ֗ה וְעַד־עוֹלָֽם׃ מִמִּזְרַח־שֶׁ֥מֶשׁ עַד־מְבוֹא֑וֹ מְ֝הֻלָּ֗ל שֵׁ֣ם יהוה׃ רָ֭ם
ה עַל־כׇּל־גּוֹיִ֥ם ׀ יהוה עַ֖ל הַשָּׁמַ֣יִם כְּבוֹדֽוֹ׃ מִ֭י כַּיהוה אֱלֹהֵ֑ינוּ הַֽמַּגְבִּיהִ֥י
ו ז לָשָֽׁבֶת׃ הַֽמַּשְׁפִּילִ֥י לִרְא֑וֹת בַּשָּׁמַ֥יִם וּבָאָֽרֶץ׃ מְקִֽימִ֣י מֵעָפָ֣ר דָּ֑ל מֵ֝אַשְׁפֹּ֗ת
ח ט יָרִ֥ים אֶבְיֽוֹן׃ לְהוֹשִׁ֥יבִי עִם־נְדִיבִ֑ים עִ֝֗ם נְדִיבֵ֥י עַמּֽוֹ׃ מֽוֹשִׁיבִ֨י ׀ עֲקֶ֬רֶת
הַבַּ֗יִת אֵֽם־הַבָּנִ֥ים שְׂמֵחָ֗ה הַֽלְלוּיָֽהּ׃

קיד א ב בְּצֵ֣את יִ֭שְׂרָאֵל מִמִּצְרָ֑יִם בֵּ֥ית יַ֝עֲקֹ֗ב מֵעַ֥ם לֹעֵֽז׃ הָיְתָ֣ה יְהוּדָ֣ה לְקׇדְשׁ֑וֹ
ג ד יִ֝שְׂרָאֵ֗ל מַמְשְׁלוֹתָֽיו׃ הַיָּ֣ם רָ֭אָה וַיָּנֹ֑ס הַ֝יַּרְדֵּ֗ן יִסֹּ֥ב לְאָחֽוֹר׃ הֶ֭הָרִים
ה רָקְד֣וּ כְאֵילִ֑ים גְּ֝בָע֗וֹת כִּבְנֵי־צֹֽאן׃ מַה־לְּךָ֣ הַ֭יָּם כִּ֣י תָנ֑וּס הַ֝יַּרְדֵּ֗ן תִּסֹּ֥ב
ו ז לְאָחֽוֹר׃ הֶ֭הָרִים תִּרְקְד֣וּ כְאֵילִ֑ים גְּ֝בָע֗וֹת כִּבְנֵי־צֹֽאן׃ מִלִּפְנֵ֣י אָ֭דוֹן
ח ח֣וּלִי אָ֑רֶץ מִ֝לִּפְנֵ֗י אֱל֣וֹהַּ יַעֲקֹֽב׃ הַהֹפְכִ֣י הַצּ֣וּר אֲגַם־מָ֑יִם חַ֝לָּמִ֗ישׁ
לְמַעְיְנוֹ־מָֽיִם׃

קטו א לֹ֤א לָ֥נוּ יהוה לֹ֫א לָ֥נוּ כִּֽי־לְ֭שִׁמְךָ תֵּ֣ן כָּב֑וֹד עַל־חַ֝סְדְּךָ֗ עַל־אֲמִתֶּֽךָ׃
ב ג לָ֭מָּה יֹאמְר֣וּ הַגּוֹיִ֑ם אַיֵּה־נָ֝֗א אֱלֹהֵיהֶֽם׃ וֵאלֹהֵ֥ינוּ בַשָּׁמָ֑יִם כֹּ֖ל אֲשֶׁר־
ד ה חָפֵ֣ץ עָשָֽׂה׃ עֲ֭צַבֵּיהֶם כֶּ֣סֶף וְזָהָ֑ב מַ֝עֲשֵׂ֗ה יְדֵ֣י אָדָֽם׃ פֶּֽה־לָ֭הֶם וְלֹ֣א
ו יְדַבֵּ֑רוּ עֵינַ֥יִם לָ֝הֶ֗ם וְלֹ֣א יִרְאֽוּ׃ אׇזְנַ֣יִם לָ֭הֶם וְלֹ֣א יִשְׁמָ֑עוּ אַ֥ף לָ֝הֶ֗ם וְלֹ֣א
ז יְרִיחֽוּן׃ יְדֵיהֶ֤ם ׀ וְלֹ֬א יְמִישׁ֗וּן רַ֭גְלֵיהֶם וְלֹ֣א יְהַלֵּ֑כוּ לֹֽא־יֶ֝הְגּ֗וּ בִּגְרוֹנָֽם׃
ח ט כְּ֭מוֹהֶם יִהְי֣וּ עֹשֵׂיהֶ֑ם כֹּ֖ל אֲשֶׁר־בֹּטֵ֣חַ בָּהֶֽם׃ יִ֭שְׂרָאֵל בְּטַ֣ח בַּיהוה עֶזְרָ֖ם
י יא וּמָגִנָּ֣ם הֽוּא׃ בֵּ֣ית אַ֭הֲרֹן בִּטְח֣וּ בַיהוה עֶזְרָ֖ם וּמָגִנָּ֣ם הֽוּא׃ יִרְאֵ֣י יהוה

12 the LORD – He is their help and their shield. The LORD remembers us and
will bless us – He will bless the House of Israel; He will bless the House of
13 14 Aharon; He will bless those who fear the LORD, small and great alike. May
15 the LORD grant you increase, you and your children. May you be blessed by
16 the LORD, Maker of heaven and earth. The heavens are the LORD's, but He
17 has granted the earth to mankind. It is not the dead who praise the LORD,
18 nor any of those who descend into silence, but we who will bless the LORD
now and forever. *Halleluya!*

116 1 2 I love the LORD, for He hears my voice, my pleas; He turns His ear to me
3 whenever I call. The bonds of death encompassed me; the pangs of the grave
4 came upon me; I was overcome by trouble and sorrow, then I called on the
5 name of the LORD: "LORD, I pray, save my life." Gracious is the LORD, and
6 righteous; our God is full of compassion. The LORD protects the simple-
7 hearted; when I was brought low, He saved me. Be at peace once more, my
8 soul, for the LORD has been good to you, for You have rescued me from
9 death, my eyes from weeping, my feet from stumbling. I shall walk in the
10 LORD's presence in the land of the living. I had faith even when I said, "I suffer
11 12 terribly," even when I said rashly, "All people are liars." How can I repay the
13 LORD for all His goodness to me? I will raise the cup of salvation and call on
14 the name of the LORD; I will fulfill my vows to the LORD in the presence of
15 16 all His people. The LORD grieves at the death of His devoted ones. Please, O
LORD, I am Your servant – I am Your servant, the child of Your handmaid;
17 You set me free from my chains. To You I will bring a thanksgiving offering
18 and call on the LORD by name. I will fulfill my vows to the LORD in the
19 presence of all His people, in the courts of the House of the LORD, in your
midst, Jerusalem. *Halleluya!*

117 1 2 Praise the LORD, all nations, laud Him, all you peoples, for His loving-kindness
overwhelms us, and the LORD's truth is everlasting. *Halleluya!*

118 1 2 Thank the LORD for He is good; His loving-kindness is forever.[131] Let Israel
3 say, "His loving-kindness is forever." Let the House of Aharon say, "His loving-
4 kindness is forever." Let those who fear the LORD say, "His loving-kindness is
5 forever." In my distress I called on the LORD; the LORD answered me and set
6 7 me free. The LORD is with me; I have no fear. What can man do to me? The
8 LORD is with me; He is my helper – I will see the downfall of my enemies. It
9 is better to take refuge in the LORD than to trust in man. It is better to take
10 refuge in the LORD than to trust in nobles. The nations all surrounded me,
11 but in the LORD's name I drove them off. They surrounded me on every side,
12 but in the LORD's name I drove them off. They surrounded me like bees, but
13 they burned like a fire of thorns – in the LORD's name I drove them off. You
14 pressed me so hard I nearly fell, but the LORD came to my aid. The LORD is
15 my strength and song[132] – and now my salvation. Sounds of song and salvation
resound in the tents of the righteous: "The LORD's right hand has done mighty
16 deeds; the LORD's right hand is lifted high; the LORD's right hand has done

131 | For the first and last verses in this psalm, see note on 106:1.

132 | Cf. Exodus 15:2.

יב בִּטְחוּ בַיהוָה עֶזְרָם וּמָגִנָּם הוּא: יְהוָה זְכָרָנוּ יְבָרֵךְ יְבָרֵךְ אֶת־בֵּית
יג יִשְׂרָאֵל יְבָרֵךְ אֶת־בֵּית אַהֲרֹן: יְבָרֵךְ יִרְאֵי יְהוָה הַקְּטַנִּים עִם־הַגְּדֹלִים:
יד טו יֹסֵף יְהוָה עֲלֵיכֶם עֲלֵיכֶם וְעַל־בְּנֵיכֶם: בְּרוּכִים אַתֶּם לַיהוָה עֹשֵׂה
טז יז שָׁמַיִם וָאָרֶץ: הַשָּׁמַיִם שָׁמַיִם לַיהוָה וְהָאָרֶץ נָתַן לִבְנֵי־אָדָם: לֹא
יח הַמֵּתִים יְהַלְלוּ־יָהּ וְלֹא כׇּל־יֹרְדֵי דוּמָה: וַאֲנַחְנוּ ׀ נְבָרֵךְ יָהּ מֵעַתָּה
וְעַד־עוֹלָם הַלְלוּיָהּ:
קטז א ב אָהַבְתִּי כִּי־יִשְׁמַע ׀ יְהוָה אֶת־קוֹלִי תַּחֲנוּנָי: כִּי־הִטָּה אׇזְנוֹ לִי וּבְיָמַי
ג אֶקְרָא: אֲפָפוּנִי ׀ חֶבְלֵי־מָוֶת וּמְצָרֵי שְׁאוֹל מְצָאוּנִי צָרָה וְיָגוֹן אֶמְצָא:
ד ה וּבְשֵׁם־יְהוָה אֶקְרָא אָנָּה יְהוָה מַלְּטָה נַפְשִׁי: חַנּוּן יְהוָה וְצַדִּיק וֵאלֹהֵינוּ
ו ז מְרַחֵם: שֹׁמֵר פְּתָאיִם יְהוָה דַּלֹּתִי וְלִי יְהוֹשִׁיעַ: שׁוּבִי נַפְשִׁי לִמְנוּחָיְכִי
ח כִּי־יְהוָה גָּמַל עָלָיְכִי: כִּי חִלַּצְתָּ נַפְשִׁי מִמָּוֶת אֶת־עֵינִי מִן־דִּמְעָה
ט י אֶת־רַגְלִי מִדֶּחִי: אֶתְהַלֵּךְ לִפְנֵי יְהוָה בְּאַרְצוֹת הַחַיִּים: הֶאֱמַנְתִּי כִּי
יא יב אֲדַבֵּר אֲנִי עָנִיתִי מְאֹד: אֲנִי אָמַרְתִּי בְחׇפְזִי כׇּל־הָאָדָם כֹּזֵב: מָה־
יג אָשִׁיב לַיהוָה כׇּל־תַּגְמוּלוֹהִי עָלָי: כּוֹס־יְשׁוּעוֹת אֶשָּׂא וּבְשֵׁם יְהוָה
יד טו אֶקְרָא: נְדָרַי לַיהוָה אֲשַׁלֵּם נֶגְדָה־נָּא לְכׇל־עַמּוֹ: יָקָר בְּעֵינֵי יְהוָה
טז הַמָּוְתָה לַחֲסִידָיו: אָנָּה יְהוָה כִּי־אֲנִי עַבְדֶּךָ אֲנִי־עַבְדְּךָ בֶּן־אֲמָתֶךָ
יז יח פִּתַּחְתָּ לְמוֹסֵרָי: לְךָ־אֶזְבַּח זֶבַח תּוֹדָה וּבְשֵׁם יְהוָה אֶקְרָא: נְדָרַי
יט לַיהוָה אֲשַׁלֵּם נֶגְדָה־נָּא לְכׇל־עַמּוֹ: בְּחַצְרוֹת ׀ בֵּית יְהוָה בְּתוֹכֵכִי
יְרוּשָׁלָ͏ִם הַלְלוּיָהּ:
קיז א ב הַלְלוּ אֶת־יְהוָה כׇּל־גּוֹיִם שַׁבְּחוּהוּ כׇּל־הָאֻמִּים: כִּי גָבַר עָלֵינוּ ׀ חַסְדּוֹ
וֶאֱמֶת־יְהוָה לְעוֹלָם הַלְלוּיָהּ:
קיח א ב הוֹדוּ לַיהוָה כִּי־טוֹב כִּי לְעוֹלָם חַסְדּוֹ: יֹאמַר־נָא יִשְׂרָאֵל כִּי לְעוֹלָם
ג ד חַסְדּוֹ: יֹאמְרוּ־נָא בֵית־אַהֲרֹן כִּי לְעוֹלָם חַסְדּוֹ: יֹאמְרוּ־נָא יִרְאֵי יְהוָה
ה ו כִּי לְעוֹלָם חַסְדּוֹ: מִן־הַמֵּצַר קָרָאתִי יָּהּ עָנָנִי בַמֶּרְחָב יָהּ: יְהוָה לִי לֹא
ז ח אִירָא מַה־יַּעֲשֶׂה לִי אָדָם: יְהוָה לִי בְּעֹזְרָי וַאֲנִי אֶרְאֶה בְשֹׂנְאָי: טוֹב
ט לַחֲסוֹת בַּיהוָה מִבְּטֹחַ בָּאָדָם: טוֹב לַחֲסוֹת בַּיהוָה מִבְּטֹחַ בִּנְדִיבִים:
י יא כׇּל־גּוֹיִם סְבָבוּנִי בְּשֵׁם יְהוָה כִּי אֲמִילַם: סַבּוּנִי גַם־סְבָבוּנִי בְּשֵׁם יְהוָה
יב כִּי אֲמִילַם: סַבּוּנִי כִדְבוֹרִים דֹּעֲכוּ כְּאֵשׁ קוֹצִים בְּשֵׁם יְהוָה כִּי אֲמִילַם:
יג יד דַּחֹה דְחִיתַנִי לִנְפֹּל וַיהוָה עֲזָרָנִי: עׇזִּי וְזִמְרָת יָהּ וַיְהִי־לִי לִישׁוּעָה:
טו טז קוֹל ׀ רִנָּה וִישׁוּעָה בְּאׇהֳלֵי צַדִּיקִים יְמִין יְהוָה עֹשָׂה חָיִל: יְמִין יְהוָה

17 18 mighty deeds." I will not die but live, and I will tell of the LORD's deeds. The
LORD has chastened me severely, but He has not given me over to death.
19 Open for me the gates of righteousness that I may enter them and thank the
20 LORD. This is the gateway to the LORD; through it, the righteous shall enter.
21 22 I will thank You, for You answered me and became my salvation. The stone
23 the builders rejected has become the main cornerstone. This was from the
24 LORD; it is wondrous in our eyes. This is the day the LORD has made; let us
25 rejoice and be glad in it. LORD, please save us; LORD, please grant us success.
26 Blessed is the one who comes in the name of the LORD; we bless you from
27 the House of the LORD. The LORD is God; He has given us light. Bind the
28 festival offering with thick cords to the horns of the altar! You are my God,
29 and I will thank You; You are my God, and I will exalt You. Thank the LORD
for He is good; His loving-kindness is forever.
119 1 Happy are those whose way is blameless,[133] who walk in the LORD's teaching.
2 Happy are those who keep His decrees, who seek Him with all their heart,
3 4 who have done no wrong and walk in His ways. You have commanded that
5 Your decrees be carefully upheld. If only my ways were firm in upholding Your
6 statutes, then I would not be ashamed when I behold all Your commandments.
7 8 I thank You with a sincere heart as I learn Your just laws. I will uphold Your
statutes; do not utterly forsake me.
9 10 How can youths keep their paths pure? – by upholding Your word. I sought
11 You out with all my heart; let me not stray from Your commandments. I keep
12 Your promise hidden in my heart so that I will not sin against You. Blessed are
13 You, LORD; teach me Your statutes. My own lips recount all the laws of Your
14 15 mouth. I rejoice in following Your decrees as if in great wealth. I reflect on
16 Your precepts and behold Your paths. I delight in Your statutes; I will never
forget Your word.
17 18 Be good to Your servant so that I may live to uphold Your word. Uncover my
19 eyes so that I may behold the wonders of Your teaching. I am but a stranger
20 on earth – do not hide Your commandments from me. My soul is shattered
21 with longing at all times for Your laws. You blast the cursed, the insolent
22 who stray from Your commandments. Divest me of scorn and contempt,
23 for I keep Your decrees. Even when princes sit to scheme against me, Your
24 servant reflects upon Your statutes. Yes, Your statutes are my delight; they
are my advisors.
25 26 My soul clings to the dust; give me life by Your word. I recounted my ways,
27 and You answered me; teach me Your statutes. Grant me insight to follow
28 Your precepts, and I will reflect upon Your wonders. My soul weeps with grief;
29 sustain me by Your word. Remove from me ways of falsehood, and grace me
30 with Your teaching. I have chosen ways of truth; I have set Your laws before
31 32 me. I cling to Your decrees; LORD, let me not be shamed. I rush to follow Your
commandments, for You broaden my heart.

---

133 | This psalm forms an alphabetical acrostic with twenty-two sections of eight verses. In each section, all the verses begin with the same letter.

יז רוממה ימין יהוה עשה חיל: לא־אמות כי־אחיה ואספר מעשי
יח יט יה: יסר יסרני יה ולמות לא נתנני: פתחו־לי שערי־צדק אבא־בם
כ כא אודה יה: זה־השער ליהוה צדיקים יבאו בו: אודך כי עניתני
כב כג ותהי־לי לישועה: אבן מאסו הבונים היתה לראש פנה: מאת
כד יהוה היתה זאת היא נפלאת בעינינו: זה־היום עשה יהוה נגילה
כה כו ונשמחה בו: אנא יהוה הושיעה נא אנא יהוה הצליחה נא: ברוך
כז הבא בשם יהוה ברכנוכם מבית יהוה: אל ׀ יהוה ויאר לנו אסרו־
כח חג בעבתים עד־קרנות המזבח: אלי אתה ואודך אלהי ארוממך:
כט הודו ליהוה כי־טוב כי לעולם חסדו:

קיט
א ב אשרי תמימי־דרך ההלכים בתורת יהוה: אשרי נצרי עדתיו בכל־
ג ד לב ידרשוהו: אף לא־פעלו עולה בדרכיו הלכו: אתה צויתה פקדיך
ה ו לשמר מאד: אחלי יכנו דרכי לשמר חקיך: אז לא־אבוש בהביטי
ז ח אל־כל־מצותיך: אודך בישר לבב בלמדי משפטי צדקך: את־
חקיך אשמר אל־תעזבני עד־מאד:

ט י במה יזכה־נער את־ארחו לשמר כדברך: בכל־לבי דרשתיך אל־
יא יב תשגני ממצותיך: בלבי צפנתי אמרתך למען לא אחטא־לך: ברוך
יג יד אתה יהוה למדני חקיך: בשפתי ספרתי כל משפטי־פיך: בדרך
טו עדותיך ששתי כעל כל־הון: בפקודיך אשיחה ואביטה ארחתיך:
טז בחקתיך אשתעשע לא אשכח דברך:

יז יח גמל על־עבדך אחיה ואשמרה דברך: גל־עיני ואביטה נפלאות
יט כ מתורתך: גר אנכי בארץ אל־תסתר ממני מצותיך: גרסה נפשי
כא לתאבה אל־משפטיך בכל־עת: גערת זדים ארורים השגים
כב כג ממצותיך: גל מעלי חרפה ובוז כי עדתיך נצרתי: גם ישבו
כד שרים בי נדברו עבדך ישיח בחקיך: גם־עדתיך שעשעי אנשי
עצתי:

כה כו דבקה לעפר נפשי חיני כדברך: דרכי ספרתי ותענני למדני חקיך:
כז כח דרך־פקודיך הבינני ואשיחה בנפלאותיך: דלפה נפשי מתוגה
כט ל קימני כדברך: דרך־שקר הסר ממני ותורתך חנני: דרך־אמונה
לא לב בחרתי משפטיך שויתי: דבקתי בעדותיך יהוה אל־תבישני: דרך־
מצותיך ארוץ כי תרחיב לבי:

33 Teach me the ways of Your statutes, LORD, and I will keep to them to the end.
34 Grant me insight to keep Your teaching, and I will uphold it with all my heart.
35 36 Guide me along the path of Your commandments, for that is my desire. Turn
37 my heart to Your decrees and not to gain. Divert my eyes from false visions;
38 give me life through Your ways. Fulfill for Your servant Your promise, which
39 is for those who fear You. Remove the taunts I dread, for Your laws are good.
40 See how I long for Your precepts; in Your righteousness give me life.
41 42 Let Your loyalty come to me, LORD, Your salvation, as You promised. I will
43 have a retort for those who taunt me, for I trust in Your word. Do not utterly
44 strip the truth from my mouth, for in Your laws I place my hope. I will always
45 uphold Your teaching, for ever and ever. I will walk about freely, for I seek out
46 Your precepts. I speak of Your decrees in the presence of kings without shame.
47 48 I delight in Your commandments, which I love. I reach out my hands to Your
commandments, which I love, and reflect upon Your statutes.
49 50 Recall to Your servant Your word, by which You have given me hope; it is
51 my comfort in my suffering that Your promise gives me life. The insolent
52 mock me bitterly, but I do not turn away from Your teaching. I call to mind
53 Your eternal judgments, LORD, and I am comforted. Scorching rage at the
54 wicked grips me, at those who abandon Your teaching. Your laws are music
55 to me wherever I dwell. At night I recall Your name, LORD, and I uphold Your
56 teaching; It is my very own, for I keep Your precepts.
57 58 The LORD is my share; I promised to uphold Your word. I implore You with
59 all my heart: show me grace as You promised. I have considered my ways,
60 and my feet have turned back to Your decrees. I rush – and never delay – to
61 uphold Your commandments. The ropes of the wicked ensnare me, but I do
62 not forget Your teaching. At midnight I rise to give thanks to You for Your just
63 laws. I am a friend to all who fear You, to those who uphold Your precepts.
64 Your loyalty, LORD, fills the earth; teach me Your statutes.
65 66 You have shown Your servant favor according to Your word, LORD. Teach me
67 good sense and knowledge, for I believe in Your commandments. Before my
68 suffering I went astray, but now I uphold Your promise. You are good and do
69 good; teach me Your statutes. Though the insolent falsely accuse me, I will
70 keep Your precepts with all my heart. Their hearts are thick like fat, whereas
71 I delight in Your teaching. My suffering was good for me so that I might learn
72 Your statutes. For me, the teaching of Your mouth is better than thousands of
pieces of gold and silver.
73 Your hands formed me and firmed me; grant me insight, and I will learn Your
74 commandments. Let those who fear You see me and rejoice, for in Your word
75 I place my hope. I know, LORD, that Your laws are just and that You made me
76 suffer in faithfulness. Now may Your loyalty comfort me as You promised
77 Your servant. Let Your mercy come to me that I may live, for Your teaching is
78 my delight. Let the insolent be ashamed for wronging me without cause as I

לג לד הוֹרֵנִי יְהוָה דֶּרֶךְ חֻקֶּיךָ וְאֶצְּרֶנָּה עֵקֶב: הֲבִינֵנִי וְאֶצְּרָה תוֹרָתֶךָ
לה לו וְאֶשְׁמְרֶנָּה בְכָל־לֵב: הַדְרִיכֵנִי בִּנְתִיב מִצְוֺתֶיךָ כִּי־בוֹ חָפָצְתִּי: הַט־לִבִּי
לז אֶל־עֵדְוֺתֶיךָ וְאַל אֶל־בָּצַע: הַעֲבֵר עֵינַי מֵרְאוֹת שָׁוְא בִּדְרָכֶךָ חַיֵּנִי:
לח לט הָקֵם לְעַבְדְּךָ אִמְרָתֶךָ אֲשֶׁר לְיִרְאָתֶךָ: הַעֲבֵר חֶרְפָּתִי אֲשֶׁר יָגֹרְתִּי כִּי
מ מִשְׁפָּטֶיךָ טוֹבִים: הִנֵּה תָּאַבְתִּי לְפִקֻּדֶיךָ בְּצִדְקָתְךָ חַיֵּנִי:
מא מב וִיבֹאֻנִי חֲסָדֶךָ יְהוָה תְּשׁוּעָתְךָ כְּאִמְרָתֶךָ: וְאֶעֱנֶה חֹרְפִי דָבָר כִּי־בָטַחְתִּי
מג בִּדְבָרֶךָ: וְאַל־תַּצֵּל מִפִּי דְבַר־אֱמֶת עַד־מְאֹד כִּי לְמִשְׁפָּטֶךָ יִחָלְתִּי:
מד מה וְאֶשְׁמְרָה תוֹרָתְךָ תָמִיד לְעוֹלָם וָעֶד: וְאֶתְהַלְּכָה בָרְחָבָה כִּי פִקֻּדֶיךָ
מו מז דָרָשְׁתִּי: וַאֲדַבְּרָה בְעֵדֹתֶיךָ נֶגֶד מְלָכִים וְלֹא אֵבוֹשׁ: וְאֶשְׁתַּעֲשַׁע
מח בְּמִצְוֺתֶיךָ אֲשֶׁר אָהָבְתִּי: וְאֶשָּׂא־כַפַּי אֶל־מִצְוֺתֶיךָ אֲשֶׁר אָהָבְתִּי
וְאָשִׂיחָה בְחֻקֶּיךָ:
מט נ זְכָר־דָּבָר לְעַבְדֶּךָ עַל אֲשֶׁר יִחַלְתָּנִי: זֹאת נֶחָמָתִי בְעָנְיִי כִּי אִמְרָתְךָ
נא נב חִיָּתְנִי: זֵדִים הֱלִיצֻנִי עַד־מְאֹד מִתּוֹרָתְךָ לֹא נָטִיתִי: זָכַרְתִּי מִשְׁפָּטֶיךָ
נג מֵעוֹלָם ׀ יְהוָה וָאֶתְנֶחָם: זַלְעָפָה אֲחָזַתְנִי מֵרְשָׁעִים עֹזְבֵי תּוֹרָתֶךָ:
נד נה זְמִרוֹת הָיוּ־לִי חֻקֶּיךָ בְּבֵית מְגוּרָי: זָכַרְתִּי בַלַּיְלָה שִׁמְךָ יְהוָה וָאֶשְׁמְרָה
נו תּוֹרָתֶךָ: זֹאת הָיְתָה־לִּי כִּי פִקֻּדֶיךָ נָצָרְתִּי:
נז נח חֶלְקִי יְהוָה אָמַרְתִּי לִשְׁמֹר דְּבָרֶיךָ: חִלִּיתִי פָנֶיךָ בְכָל־לֵב חָנֵּנִי
נט ס כְּאִמְרָתֶךָ: חִשַּׁבְתִּי דְרָכָי וָאָשִׁיבָה רַגְלַי אֶל־עֵדֹתֶיךָ: חַשְׁתִּי וְלֹא
סא הִתְמַהְמָהְתִּי לִשְׁמֹר מִצְוֺתֶיךָ: חֶבְלֵי רְשָׁעִים עִוְּדֻנִי תּוֹרָתְךָ לֹא
סב סג שָׁכָחְתִּי: חֲצוֹת־לַיְלָה אָקוּם לְהוֹדוֹת לָךְ עַל מִשְׁפְּטֵי צִדְקֶךָ: חָבֵר
סד אָנִי לְכָל־אֲשֶׁר יְרֵאוּךָ וּלְשֹׁמְרֵי פִּקּוּדֶיךָ: חַסְדְּךָ יְהוָה מָלְאָה הָאָרֶץ
חֻקֶּיךָ לַמְּדֵנִי:
סה סו טוֹב עָשִׂיתָ עִם־עַבְדְּךָ יְהוָה כִּדְבָרֶךָ: טוּב טַעַם וָדַעַת לַמְּדֵנִי כִּי
סז בְמִצְוֺתֶיךָ הֶאֱמָנְתִּי: טֶרֶם אֶעֱנֶה אֲנִי שֹׁגֵג וְעַתָּה אִמְרָתְךָ שָׁמָרְתִּי:
סח סט טוֹב־אַתָּה וּמֵטִיב לַמְּדֵנִי חֻקֶּיךָ: טָפְלוּ עָלַי שֶׁקֶר זֵדִים אֲנִי בְּכָל־
ע עא לֵב ׀ אֱצֹּר פִּקּוּדֶיךָ: טָפַשׁ כַּחֵלֶב לִבָּם אֲנִי תּוֹרָתְךָ שִׁעֲשָׁעְתִּי: טוֹב־
עב לִי כִי־עֻנֵּיתִי לְמַעַן אֶלְמַד חֻקֶּיךָ: טוֹב־לִי תוֹרַת־פִּיךָ מֵאַלְפֵי זָהָב יז
וָכָסֶף:
עג עד יָדֶיךָ עָשׂוּנִי וַיְכוֹנְנוּנִי הֲבִינֵנִי וְאֶלְמְדָה מִצְוֺתֶיךָ: יְרֵאֶיךָ יִרְאוּנִי וְיִשְׂמָחוּ
עה כִּי לִדְבָרְךָ יִחָלְתִּי: יָדַעְתִּי יְהוָה כִּי־צֶדֶק מִשְׁפָּטֶיךָ וֶאֱמוּנָה עִנִּיתָנִי:
עו עז יְהִי־נָא חַסְדְּךָ לְנַחֲמֵנִי כְּאִמְרָתְךָ לְעַבְדֶּךָ: יְבֹאוּנִי רַחֲמֶיךָ וְאֶחְיֶה כִּי־
עח תוֹרָתְךָ שַׁעֲשֻׁעָי: יֵבֹשׁוּ זֵדִים כִּי־שֶׁקֶר עִוְּתוּנִי אֲנִי אָשִׂיחַ בְּפִקּוּדֶיךָ:

79 reflect upon Your precepts. May those who fear You come back to me, those
80 who know Your decrees. May my heart be soundly committed to Your laws
so that I will never be ashamed.

81 82 My soul pines for Your salvation; in Your word I place my hope. My eyes pine
83 for Your promise, saying, "Oh, when will You comfort me?" Though I am
84 like a wine skin shriveled in smoke, Your statutes I have not forgotten. How
many days does Your servant have left? When will You execute judgment on
85 my pursuers? The insolent have dug pits for me in defiance of Your teaching.
86 All Your commandments are faithful, but men pursue me without cause –
87 help me! They almost swept me off the earth, but I never abandoned Your
88 precepts. In keeping with Your loyalty, give me life, and I will uphold Your
mouth's decrees.

89 90 Forever, Lord, Your word endures in the heavens; Your faithfulness endures
91 throughout the generations; You made the earth firm, and it stands. By Your
92 laws they stand today, for all are Your servants. Were Your teaching not my
93 delight, I would have perished in suffering. I will never forget Your precepts,
94 for through them You give me life. I am Yours – save me, for I seek out
95 Your precepts. The wicked hoped to destroy me, but I contemplate Your
96 decrees. I have seen that everything, however perfect, has a limit, but Your
commandments are boundless.

97 98 How I love Your teaching! All day long I reflect upon it. Your commandments
99 make me wiser than my enemies, for they are mine forever. I have gained
100 understanding from all my teachers, for I reflect upon Your decrees. I have
101 attained more insight than some elders, for I keep Your precepts. I hold my
102 feet back from every evil path so that I may uphold Your word. I have not
103 turned away from Your laws, for You Yourself have taught me. How sweet
104 Your promise is to my palate, sweeter than honey to my mouth. I gain insight
from Your precepts, so I despise all paths of falsehood.

105 106 Your word is a lamp for my feet, a light for my path. I have sworn – and I
107 will keep my word – to uphold Your just laws. I have suffered gravely; Lord,
108 give me life in keeping with Your word. Accept, Lord, what my mouth
109 offers, and teach me Your laws. My life is constantly in danger, but I do not
110 forget Your teaching. The wicked have set a trap for me, yet I do not stray
111 from Your precepts. Your decrees are my everlasting share, for they are the
112 joy of my heart. I have set my heart on fulfilling Your statutes forever, to the
end.

113 114 Hypocrisy I despise, and Your teaching I love. You are my shelter and shield;
115 in Your word I place my hope. Turn away from me, evil ones, so that I may
116 keep the commandments of my God. Sustain me as You promised, and I will
117 live; do not crush my hopes. Care for me, and I will be saved; I will ever heed
118 Your statutes. You reject all who stray from Your statutes, for their deception
119 is only false. You discard like dross all the wicked of the land, so I love Your
120 decrees. My flesh creeps from dread of You, and Your laws I fear.
121 I have done what is just and right; do not abandon me to my oppressors.
122 Secure the good of Your servant; let me not be oppressed by the insolent.

עט פ יָשׁוּבוּ לִי יְרֵאֶיךָ וידעו עֵדֹתֶיךָ: יְהִי־לִבִּי תָמִים בְּחֻקֶּיךָ לְמַעַן לֹא וְיֹדְעֵי
אֵבוֹשׁ:
פא פב כָּלְתָה לִתְשׁוּעָתְךָ נַפְשִׁי לִדְבָרְךָ יִחָלְתִּי: כָּלוּ עֵינַי לְאִמְרָתֶךָ לֵאמֹר מָתַי
פג פד תְּנַחֲמֵנִי: כִּי־הָיִיתִי כְּנֹאד בְּקִיטוֹר חֻקֶּיךָ לֹא שָׁכָחְתִּי: כַּמָּה יְמֵי־עַבְדֶּךָ
פה מָתַי תַּעֲשֶׂה בְרֹדְפַי מִשְׁפָּט: כָּרוּ־לִי זֵדִים שִׁיחוֹת אֲשֶׁר לֹא כְתוֹרָתֶךָ:
פו פז כָּל־מִצְוֺתֶיךָ אֱמוּנָה שֶׁקֶר רְדָפוּנִי עָזְרֵנִי: כִּמְעַט כִּלּוּנִי בָאָרֶץ וַאֲנִי
פח לֹא־עָזַבְתִּי פִקֻּדֶיךָ: כְּחַסְדְּךָ חַיֵּנִי וְאֶשְׁמְרָה עֵדוּת פִּיךָ:
פט צ לְעוֹלָם יְהוָה דְּבָרְךָ נִצָּב בַּשָּׁמָיִם: לְדֹר וָדֹר אֱמוּנָתֶךָ כּוֹנַנְתָּ אֶרֶץ
צא צב וַתַּעֲמֹד: לְמִשְׁפָּטֶיךָ עָמְדוּ הַיּוֹם כִּי הַכֹּל עֲבָדֶיךָ: לוּלֵי תוֹרָתְךָ שַׁעֲשֻׁעָי
צג צד אָז אָבַדְתִּי בְעָנְיִי: לְעוֹלָם לֹא־אֶשְׁכַּח פִּקּוּדֶיךָ כִּי־בָם חִיִּיתָנִי: לְךָ־אֲנִי
צה הוֹשִׁיעֵנִי כִּי פִקּוּדֶיךָ דָרָשְׁתִּי: לִי קִוּוּ רְשָׁעִים לְאַבְּדֵנִי עֵדֹתֶיךָ אֶתְבּוֹנָן:
צו לְכָל־תִּכְלָה רָאִיתִי קֵץ רְחָבָה מִצְוָתְךָ מְאֹד:
צז צח מָה־אָהַבְתִּי תוֹרָתֶךָ כָּל־הַיּוֹם הִיא שִׂיחָתִי: מֵאֹיְבַי תְּחַכְּמֵנִי מִצְוֺתֶךָ
צט כִּי לְעוֹלָם הִיא־לִי: מִכָּל־מְלַמְּדַי הִשְׂכַּלְתִּי כִּי עֵדְוֺתֶיךָ שִׂיחָה לִי:
ק קא מִזְּקֵנִים אֶתְבּוֹנָן כִּי פִקּוּדֶיךָ נָצָרְתִּי: מִכָּל־אֹרַח רָע כָּלִאתִי רַגְלָי לְמַעַן
קב קג אֶשְׁמֹר דְּבָרֶךָ: מִמִּשְׁפָּטֶיךָ לֹא־סָרְתִּי כִּי־אַתָּה הוֹרֵתָנִי: מַה־נִּמְלְצוּ
קד לְחִכִּי אִמְרָתֶךָ מִדְּבַשׁ לְפִי: מִפִּקּוּדֶיךָ אֶתְבּוֹנָן עַל־כֵּן שָׂנֵאתִי | כָּל־
אֹרַח שָׁקֶר:
קה קו נֵר־לְרַגְלִי דְבָרֶךָ וְאוֹר לִנְתִיבָתִי: נִשְׁבַּעְתִּי וָאֲקַיֵּמָה לִשְׁמֹר מִשְׁפְּטֵי
קז קח צִדְקֶךָ: נַעֲנֵיתִי עַד־מְאֹד יְהוָה חַיֵּנִי כִדְבָרֶךָ: נִדְבוֹת פִּי רְצֵה־נָא יְהוָה
קט קי וּמִשְׁפָּטֶיךָ לַמְּדֵנִי: נַפְשִׁי בְכַפִּי תָמִיד וְתוֹרָתְךָ לֹא שָׁכָחְתִּי: נָתְנוּ
קיא רְשָׁעִים פַּח לִי וּמִפִּקּוּדֶיךָ לֹא תָעִיתִי: נָחַלְתִּי עֵדְוֺתֶיךָ לְעוֹלָם כִּי־
קיב שְׂשׂוֹן לִבִּי הֵמָּה: נָטִיתִי לִבִּי לַעֲשׂוֹת חֻקֶּיךָ לְעוֹלָם עֵקֶב:
קיג קיד סֵעֲפִים שָׂנֵאתִי וְתוֹרָתְךָ אָהָבְתִּי: סִתְרִי וּמָגִנִּי אָתָּה לִדְבָרְךָ יִחָלְתִּי:
קטו קטז סוּרוּ מִמֶּנִּי מְרֵעִים וְאֶצְּרָה מִצְוֺת אֱלֹהָי: סָמְכֵנִי כְאִמְרָתְךָ וְאֶחְיֶה וְאַל־
קיז קיח תְּבִישֵׁנִי מִשִּׂבְרִי: סְעָדֵנִי וְאִוָּשֵׁעָה וְאֶשְׁעָה בְחֻקֶּיךָ תָמִיד: סָלִיתָ כָּל־
קיט שׁוֹגִים מֵחֻקֶּיךָ כִּי־שֶׁקֶר תַּרְמִיתָם: סִגִים הִשְׁבַּתָּ כָל־רִשְׁעֵי־אָרֶץ לָכֵן
קכ אָהַבְתִּי עֵדֹתֶיךָ: סָמַר מִפַּחְדְּךָ בְשָׂרִי וּמִמִּשְׁפָּטֶיךָ יָרֵאתִי:
קכא קכב עָשִׂיתִי מִשְׁפָּט וָצֶדֶק בַּל־תַּנִּיחֵנִי לְעֹשְׁקָי: עֲרֹב עַבְדְּךָ לְטוֹב אַל־

123 124 My eyes pine for Your salvation, for Your righteous promise. Deal loyally
125 with Your servant, and teach me Your statutes. I am Your servant – grant me
126 insight so that I may know Your decrees. It is time for the LORD to act[134] – they
127 have violated Your teaching! Yes, I love Your commandments more than gold,
128 more than finest gold. Yes, I keep in line with all Your precepts, and I despise
all paths of falsehood.
129 130 Wondrous are Your decrees, so I keep them. Your words shine light as they
131 unfold, granting insight to the simple. My lips part to draw deep breath, for I
132 crave Your commandments. Turn to me and show me grace as You always do
133 for those who love Your name. Firm up my footsteps with Your promise, and
134 let no evil rule over me. Free me from human oppression, and I will uphold
135 Your precepts. Shine Your face upon Your servant, and teach me Your statutes.
136 Streams of water flow down from my eyes because they do not uphold Your
teaching.
137 138 You are righteous, LORD, and Your laws are upright. You impose Your decrees
139 with justice, in deep faithfulness. My fervor consumes me, for my foes have
140 forgotten Your words. Your promise is deeply pure, and Your servant loves it.
141 142 I am trivial and scorned, but I never forget Your precepts. Your righteousness
143 is ever just, and Your teaching is truth. Danger and despair have found me,
144 but Your commandments are my delight. Your decrees are ever just; grant me
insight, and I will live.
145 I call with all my heart – answer me, O LORD, so that I may keep Your statutes.
146 147 I call out to You to save me so that I may uphold Your decrees. I greet the dawn
148 and cry out; in Your word I place my hope. My eyes greet every watch of the
149 night, reflecting upon Your promise. Hear my voice through Your loyalty;
150 LORD, through Your laws You give me life. Pursuers of filth draw near – far
151 away from Your teaching. You draw close, LORD, and all Your commandments
152 are truth. I have long known of Your decrees, for You established them
forever.
153 See my suffering and rescue me, for I have never forgotten Your teaching.
154 Contend on my behalf and redeem me; give me life through Your promise.
155 Salvation is far from the wicked, for they do not seek out Your statutes.
156 157 Your mercy is abundant, LORD; give me life through Your laws. Though my
158 pursuers and foes are many, I have not strayed from Your decrees. When I see
159 traitors I am disgusted – those who do not uphold Your promise. See how
160 I love Your precepts, LORD; in keeping with Your loyalty give me life. The
essence of Your word is truth; all Your just laws last forever.
161 162 Princes pursue me without cause, but it is Your word that my heart dreads. I
163 rejoice over Your promise like one who finds great wealth. I despise and abhor
164 falsehood; Your teaching I love. Seven times a day I praise You for Your just
165 laws. Lovers of Your teaching enjoy great peace; no obstacles hold them back.
166 167 I hope for Your salvation, LORD, and I fulfill Your commandments. I uphold
168 Your decrees and love them dearly. I uphold Your precepts and decrees, for
all my ways are before You.

134 | Or, "It is time to act for the LORD."

קכג קכד יַעַשְׁקֻנִי זֵדִים: עֵינַי כָּלוּ לִישׁוּעָתֶךָ וּלְאִמְרַת צִדְקֶךָ: עֲשֵׂה עִם־עַבְדְּךָ
קכה קכו כְחַסְדֶּךָ וְחֻקֶּיךָ לַמְּדֵנִי: עַבְדְּךָ־אָנִי הֲבִינֵנִי וְאֵדְעָה עֵדֹתֶיךָ: עֵת לַעֲשׂוֹת
קכז קכח לַיהוָה הֵפֵרוּ תּוֹרָתֶךָ: עַל־כֵּן אָהַבְתִּי מִצְוֹתֶיךָ מִזָּהָב וּמִפָּז: עַל־כֵּן ׀
כָּל־פִּקּוּדֵי כֹל יִשָּׁרְתִּי כָּל־אֹרַח שֶׁקֶר שָׂנֵאתִי:
קכט קל פְּלָאוֹת עֵדְוֺתֶיךָ עַל־כֵּן נְצָרָתַם נַפְשִׁי: פֵּתַח־דְּבָרֶיךָ יָאִיר מֵבִין פְּתָיִים:
קלא קלב פִּי־פָעַרְתִּי וָאֶשְׁאָפָה כִּי לְמִצְוֺתֶיךָ יָאָבְתִּי: פְּנֵה־אֵלַי וְחָנֵּנִי כְּמִשְׁפָּט
קלג קלד לְאֹהֲבֵי שְׁמֶךָ: פְּעָמַי הָכֵן בְּאִמְרָתֶךָ וְאַל־תַּשְׁלֶט־בִּי כָל־אָוֶן: פְּדֵנִי
קלה מֵעֹשֶׁק אָדָם וְאֶשְׁמְרָה פִּקּוּדֶיךָ: פָּנֶיךָ הָאֵר בְּעַבְדֶּךָ וְלַמְּדֵנִי אֶת־
קלו חֻקֶּיךָ: פַּלְגֵי־מַיִם יָרְדוּ עֵינָי עַל לֹא־שָׁמְרוּ תוֹרָתֶךָ:
קלז קלח צַדִּיק אַתָּה יְהוָה וְיָשָׁר מִשְׁפָּטֶיךָ: צִוִּיתָ צֶדֶק עֵדֹתֶיךָ וֶאֱמוּנָה מְאֹד:
קלט קמ צִמְּתַתְנִי קִנְאָתִי כִּי־שָׁכְחוּ דְבָרֶיךָ צָרָי: צְרוּפָה אִמְרָתְךָ מְאֹד וְעַבְדְּךָ
קמא קמב אֲהֵבָהּ: צָעִיר אָנֹכִי וְנִבְזֶה פִּקֻּדֶיךָ לֹא שָׁכָחְתִּי: צִדְקָתְךָ צֶדֶק לְעוֹלָם
קמג קמד וְתוֹרָתְךָ אֱמֶת: צַר־וּמָצוֹק מְצָאוּנִי מִצְוֺתֶיךָ שַׁעֲשֻׁעָי: צֶדֶק עֵדְוֺתֶיךָ
לְעוֹלָם הֲבִינֵנִי וְאֶחְיֶה:
קמה קמו קָרָאתִי בְכָל־לֵב עֲנֵנִי יְהוָה חֻקֶּיךָ אֶצֹּרָה: קְרָאתִיךָ הוֹשִׁיעֵנִי וְאֶשְׁמְרָה
קמז קמח עֵדֹתֶיךָ: קִדַּמְתִּי בַנֶּשֶׁף וָאֲשַׁוֵּעָה לדבריך יִחָלְתִּי: קִדְּמוּ עֵינַי אַשְׁמֻרוֹת לִדְבָרְךָ
קמט קנ לָשִׂיחַ בְּאִמְרָתֶךָ: קוֹלִי שִׁמְעָה כְחַסְדֶּךָ יְהוָה כְּמִשְׁפָּטֶךָ חַיֵּנִי: קָרְבוּ
קנא רֹדְפֵי זִמָּה מִתּוֹרָתְךָ רָחָקוּ: קָרוֹב אַתָּה יְהוָה וְכָל־מִצְוֺתֶיךָ אֱמֶת:
קנב קֶדֶם יָדַעְתִּי מֵעֵדֹתֶיךָ כִּי לְעוֹלָם יְסַדְתָּם:
קנג קנד רְאֵה־עָנְיִי וְחַלְּצֵנִי כִּי־תוֹרָתְךָ לֹא שָׁכָחְתִּי: רִיבָה רִיבִי וּגְאָלֵנִי לְאִמְרָתְךָ
קנה קנו חַיֵּנִי: רָחוֹק מֵרְשָׁעִים יְשׁוּעָה כִּי־חֻקֶּיךָ לֹא דָרָשׁוּ: רַחֲמֶיךָ רַבִּים ׀
קנז קנח יְהוָה כְּמִשְׁפָּטֶיךָ חַיֵּנִי: רַבִּים רֹדְפַי וְצָרָי מֵעֵדְוֺתֶיךָ לֹא נָטִיתִי: רָאִיתִי
קנט בֹגְדִים וָאֶתְקוֹטָטָה אֲשֶׁר אִמְרָתְךָ לֹא שָׁמָרוּ: רְאֵה כִּי־פִקּוּדֶיךָ
קס אָהָבְתִּי יְהוָה כְּחַסְדְּךָ חַיֵּנִי: רֹאשׁ־דְּבָרְךָ אֱמֶת וּלְעוֹלָם כָּל־מִשְׁפַּט
צִדְקֶךָ:
קסא קסב שָׂרִים רְדָפוּנִי חִנָּם ומדבריך פָּחַד לִבִּי: שָׂשׂ אָנֹכִי עַל־אִמְרָתֶךָ כְּמוֹצֵא וּמִדְּבָרְךָ
קסג קסד שָׁלָל רָב: שֶׁקֶר שָׂנֵאתִי וַאֲתַעֵבָה תּוֹרָתְךָ אָהָבְתִּי: שֶׁבַע בַּיּוֹם הִלַּלְתִּיךָ
קסה עַל מִשְׁפְּטֵי צִדְקֶךָ: שָׁלוֹם רָב לְאֹהֲבֵי תוֹרָתֶךָ וְאֵין־לָמוֹ מִכְשׁוֹל:
קסו קסז שִׂבַּרְתִּי לִישׁוּעָתְךָ יְהוָה וּמִצְוֺתֶיךָ עָשִׂיתִי: שָׁמְרָה נַפְשִׁי עֵדֹתֶיךָ וָאֹהֲבֵם
קסח מְאֹד: שָׁמַרְתִּי פִקּוּדֶיךָ וְעֵדֹתֶיךָ כִּי כָל־דְּרָכַי נֶגְדֶּךָ:

169 Let my plea reach You, LORD; grant me insight in accordance with Your word.
170 171 Let my supplication come before You; deliver me as You promised. My lips
172 shall stream with praise, for You teach me Your statutes. My tongue shall sing
173 of Your promise, for all Your commandments are just. Let Your hand be my
174 help, for I have chosen Your precepts. I crave Your salvation, LORD, and in
175 Your teaching I delight. Let me live so that I can praise You, and may Your
176 laws help me. I have strayed like a lost sheep – come and seek Your servant,
for I have never forgotten Your commandments.

120 1 *A song of ascents.*[135] I called to the LORD in my distress, and He answered me.
2 3 "LORD, save me from lying lips, from a deceitful tongue." What will be done
4 to you, and what will you gain, O deceitful tongue? – only a warrior's sharp
5 arrows and hot broomwood coals. Woe to me that I dwell in Meshekh, that
6 I live among the tents of Kedar. I have lived too long among those who hate
7 peace. I am for peace, but whenever I speak of it, they are for war.

121 1 *A song of ascents.* I lift my eyes up to the hills; where will my help come
2 3 from? My help comes from the LORD, Maker of heaven and earth. He will
4 not let your foot slip; He who guards you does not slumber. Behold – the
5 Guardian of Israel neither slumbers nor sleeps. The LORD is your guardian;
6 the LORD is your shade at your right hand. The sun will not strike you by
7 day, nor the moon by night. The LORD will guard you from all harm; He will
8 guard your life. The LORD will guard your going and coming, now and for
evermore.

122 1 *A song of ascents – of David.* I rejoiced when they said to me, "Let us go to the
2 3 House of the LORD." Our feet stood within your gates, Jerusalem: Jerusalem,
4 built as a city joined together. There the tribes went up, the tribes of the LORD,
5 as a decree to Israel, to give thanks to the LORD's name, for there the thrones
6 of justice were set, the thrones of the House of David. Pray for the peace of
7 Jerusalem: "May those who love you prosper. May there be peace within your
8 ramparts, tranquility in your citadels." For the sake of my brothers and my
9 friends, I shall say, "Peace be within you." For the sake of the House of the
LORD our God, I shall seek your good.

123 1 2 *A song of ascents.* To You, enthroned in heaven, I lift my eyes. As the eyes of
slaves turn to their master's hand, as the eyes of a slave-girl to her mistress's
3 hand, so our eyes turn to the LORD our God, awaiting His favor. Show us
favor, LORD, show us favor, for we have suffered more than enough contempt.
4 Too long have we suffered the scorn of the complacent, the contempt of the
arrogant.

124 1 *A song of ascents – of David.* Had the LORD not been on our side – let Israel
2 say it – had the LORD not been on our side when men rose up against us,
3 4 they would have swallowed us alive when their anger raged against us. The
5 waters would have engulfed us; the torrent would have swept over us; over us
6 would have swept the raging waters. Blessed be the LORD, who did not leave
7 us as prey for their teeth. We escaped like a bird from the fowler's snare – the

---

135 | The next fifteen psalms carry the same superscription. "Ascents" perhaps denotes a musical instruction, a literary structure, or the physical ascents to the Temple or from exile.

קסט קע תקרב רנתי לפניך יהוה כדברך הבינני: תבוא תחנתי לפניך
קעא קעב כאמרתך הצילני: תבענה שפתי תהלה כי תלמדני חקיך: תען
קעג לשוני אמרתך כי כל־מצותיך צדק: תהי־ידך לעזרני כי פקודיך
קעד קעה בחרתי: תאבתי לישועתך יהוה ותורתך שעשעי: תחי־נפשי
קעו ותהללך ומשפטך יעזרני: תעיתי כשה אבד בקש עבדך כי מצותיך
לא שכחתי:

קכ א ב שיר המעלות אל־יהוה בצרתה לי קראתי ויענני: יהוה הצילה נפשי
ג משפת־שקר מלשון רמיה: מה־יתן לך ומה־יסיף לך לשון רמיה:
ד ה חצי גבור שנונים עם גחלי רתמים: אויה־לי כי־גרתי משך שכנתי
ו ז עם־אהלי קדר: רבת שכנה־לה נפשי עם שונא שלום: אני־שלום
וכי אדבר המה למלחמה:

קכא א ב שיר למעלות אשא עיני אל־ההרים מאין יבא עזרי: עזרי מעם יהוה
ג ד עשה שמים וארץ: אל־יתן למוט רגלך אל־ינום שמרך: הנה לא־
ה ינום ולא יישן שומר ישראל: יהוה שמרך יהוה צלך על־יד ימינך:
ו ז יומם השמש לא־יככה וירח בלילה: יהוה ישמרך מכל־רע ישמר
ח את־נפשך: יהוה ישמר־צאתך ובואך מעתה ועד־עולם:

קכב א ב שיר המעלות לדוד שמחתי באמרים לי בית יהוה נלך: עמדות
ג היו רגלינו בשעריך ירושלם: ירושלם הבנויה כעיר שחברה־לה
ד יחדו: ששם עלו שבטים שבטי־יה עדות לישראל להדות לשם
ה ו יהוה: כי שמה | ישבו כסאות למשפט כסאות לבית דוד: שאלו
ז שלום ירושלם ישליו אהביך: יהי־שלום בחילך שלוה בארמנותיך:
ח ט למען אחי ורעי אדברה־נא שלום בך: למען בית־יהוה אלהינו
אבקשה טוב לך:

קכג א ב שיר המעלות אליך נשאתי את־עיני הישבי בשמים: הנה כעיני
עבדים אל־יד אדוניהם כעיני שפחה אל־יד גברתה כן עינינו אל־
ג ד יהוה אלהינו עד שיחננו: חננו יהוה חננו כי־רב שבענו בוז: רבת
שבעה־לה נפשנו הלעג השאננים הבוז לגאיונים: לגאי יונים

קכד א ב שיר המעלות לדוד לולי יהוה שהיה לנו יאמר־נא ישראל: לולי
ג יהוה שהיה לנו בקום עלינו אדם: אזי חיים בלעונו בחרות אפם
ד ה בנו: אזי המים שטפונו נחלה עבר על־נפשנו: אזי עבר על־נפשנו
ו ז המים הזידונים: ברוך יהוה שלא נתננו טרף לשניהם: נפשנו כצפור

8 snare broke, and we escaped. Our help is in the name of the LORD, Maker of
heaven and earth.
125 1 *A song of ascents.* Those who trust in the LORD are like Mount Zion, which
2 cannot be shaken, which stands firm forever. As hills surround Jerusalem, so
3 the LORD surrounds His people, now and forever. The scepter of the wicked
shall not rest on the land allotted to the righteous, so the righteous shall
4 not set their hand to wrongdoing. Do good, LORD, to those who are good,
5 to those who are upright in heart. As for those who turn aside to crooked
ways, may the LORD make them wander the ways of evildoers. Peace be on
Israel!
126 1 *A song of ascents.* When the LORD brought back the exiles of Zion, we were
2 like dreamers – then were our mouths filled with laughter, our tongues with
songs of joy; then was it said among the nations, "The LORD has done great
3 things for them." The LORD has done great things for us, and we rejoiced.
4 5 Bring back our exiles, LORD, like streams in the Negev. May those who sowed
6 in tears reap in joy; may those who go out weeping, carrying a sack of seed,
come back in glad song, carrying their sheaves.
127 1 *A song of ascents – of Shlomo.* Unless the LORD builds the house, its builders
labor in vain. Unless the LORD guards the city, the guard keeps watch in vain.
2 In vain do you rise early and stay up late, you who eat hard-earned bread –
3 He provides for His loved ones while they sleep. Children are a gift from
4 the LORD, the fruit of the womb His reward. Like arrows in a warrior's hand
5 are the children of one's youth. Happy are those who fill their quivers with
them; they shall not be put to shame when they contend with the enemy at
the gate.
128 1 2 *A song of ascents.* Happy are all who fear the LORD, who walk in His ways. You
3 shall eat the fruit of your labor; You shall be happy and thriving. Your wife
shall be like a fruitful vine within your home, your children like olive saplings
4 5 around your table; thus shall one who fears the LORD be blessed. May the
LORD bless you from Zion; may you see Jerusalem thrive all the days of your
6 life; may you live to see your children's children. Peace be on Israel!
129 1 *A song of ascents.* I have suffered so much torment since my youth – let Israel
2 say it – I have suffered so much torment since my youth, but my tormentors
3 have never overcome me. Plowmen plowed across my back, making long
4 5 furrows, but the LORD is just; He has cut the bonds of the wicked. Let all who
6 hate Zion be driven back in shame; let them be like weeds on rooftops that
7 wither before they are pulled up, that will never fill a reaper's hand or yield an
8 armful for the gatherer of sheaves. No passersby will say to them: "The LORD's
blessing be upon you; we bless you in the name of the LORD."
130 1 2 *A song of ascents.* From the depths I have called out to You, O LORD. Lord, hear
3 my voice; let Your ears be attuned to the sound of my plea. If You, LORD, keep
4 account of sins, O Lord, who could stand? But with You there is forgiveness;

ח נִמְלְטָה מִפַּח יוֹקְשִׁים הַפַּח נִשְׁבָּר וַאֲנַחְנוּ נִמְלָטְנוּ: עֶזְרֵנוּ בְּשֵׁם יהוה
עֹשֵׂה שָׁמַיִם וָאָרֶץ:
קכה א שִׁיר הַמַּעֲלוֹת הַבֹּטְחִים בַּיהוה כְּהַר־צִיּוֹן לֹא־יִמּוֹט לְעוֹלָם יֵשֵׁב:
ב יְרוּשָׁלַםִ הָרִים סָבִיב לָהּ וַיהוה סָבִיב לְעַמּוֹ מֵעַתָּה וְעַד־עוֹלָם:
ג כִּי לֹא יָנוּחַ שֵׁבֶט הָרֶשַׁע עַל גּוֹרַל הַצַּדִּיקִים לְמַעַן לֹא־יִשְׁלְחוּ
ד הַצַּדִּיקִים ׀ בְּעַוְלָתָה יְדֵיהֶם: הֵיטִיבָה יהוה לַטּוֹבִים וְלִישָׁרִים
ה בְּלִבּוֹתָם: וְהַמַּטִּים עֲקַלְקַלּוֹתָם יוֹלִיכֵם יהוה אֶת־פֹּעֲלֵי הָאָוֶן שָׁלוֹם
עַל־יִשְׂרָאֵל:
קכו א ב שִׁיר הַמַּעֲלוֹת בְּשׁוּב יהוה אֶת־שִׁיבַת צִיּוֹן הָיִינוּ כְּחֹלְמִים: אָז יִמָּלֵא
שְׂחוֹק פִּינוּ וּלְשׁוֹנֵנוּ רִנָּה אָז יֹאמְרוּ בַגּוֹיִם הִגְדִּיל יהוה לַעֲשׂוֹת עִם־
ג ד אֵלֶּה: הִגְדִּיל יהוה לַעֲשׂוֹת עִמָּנוּ הָיִינוּ שְׂמֵחִים: שׁוּבָה יהוה אֶת־
ה ו שבותנו כַּאֲפִיקִים בַּנֶּגֶב: הַזֹּרְעִים בְּדִמְעָה בְּרִנָּה יִקְצֹרוּ: הָלוֹךְ יֵלֵךְ ׀ שְׁבִיתֵנוּ
וּבָכֹה נֹשֵׂא מֶשֶׁךְ־הַזָּרַע בֹּא־יָבֹא בְרִנָּה נֹשֵׂא אֲלֻמֹּתָיו:
קכז א שִׁיר הַמַּעֲלוֹת לִשְׁלֹמֹה אִם־יהוה ׀ לֹא־יִבְנֶה בַיִת שָׁוְא עָמְלוּ
ב בוֹנָיו בּוֹ אִם־יהוה לֹא־יִשְׁמָר־עִיר שָׁוְא ׀ שָׁקַד שׁוֹמֵר: שָׁוְא לָכֶם ׀
מַשְׁכִּימֵי קוּם מְאַחֲרֵי־שֶׁבֶת אֹכְלֵי לֶחֶם הָעֲצָבִים כֵּן יִתֵּן לִידִידוֹ שֵׁנָא:
ג ד הִנֵּה נַחֲלַת יהוה בָּנִים שָׂכָר פְּרִי הַבָּטֶן: כְּחִצִּים בְּיַד־גִּבּוֹר כֵּן בְּנֵי
ה הַנְּעוּרִים: אַשְׁרֵי הַגֶּבֶר אֲשֶׁר מִלֵּא אֶת־אַשְׁפָּתוֹ מֵהֶם לֹא־יֵבֹשׁוּ כִּי־
יְדַבְּרוּ אֶת־אוֹיְבִים בַּשָּׁעַר:
קכח א ב שִׁיר הַמַּעֲלוֹת אַשְׁרֵי כָּל־יְרֵא יהוה הַהֹלֵךְ בִּדְרָכָיו: יְגִיעַ כַּפֶּיךָ כִּי
ג תֹאכֵל אַשְׁרֶיךָ וְטוֹב לָךְ: אֶשְׁתְּךָ ׀ כְּגֶפֶן פֹּרִיָּה בְּיַרְכְּתֵי בֵיתֶךָ בָּנֶיךָ
ד כִּשְׁתִלֵי זֵיתִים סָבִיב לְשֻׁלְחָנֶךָ: הִנֵּה כִי־כֵן יְבֹרַךְ גָּבֶר יְרֵא יהוה:
ה ו יְבָרֶכְךָ יהוה מִצִּיּוֹן וּרְאֵה בְּטוּב יְרוּשָׁלָםִ כֹּל יְמֵי חַיֶּיךָ: וּרְאֵה־בָנִים יח
לְבָנֶיךָ שָׁלוֹם עַל־יִשְׂרָאֵל:
קכט א ב שִׁיר הַמַּעֲלוֹת רַבַּת צְרָרוּנִי מִנְּעוּרַי יֹאמַר־נָא יִשְׂרָאֵל: רַבַּת צְרָרוּנִי
ג מִנְּעוּרָי גַּם לֹא־יָכְלוּ לִי: עַל־גַּבִּי חָרְשׁוּ חֹרְשִׁים הֶאֱרִיכוּ למענותם: לְמַעֲנִיתָם
ד ה יהוה צַדִּיק קִצֵּץ עֲבוֹת רְשָׁעִים: יֵבֹשׁוּ וְיִסֹּגוּ אָחוֹר כֹּל שֹׂנְאֵי צִיּוֹן:
ו ז יִהְיוּ כַּחֲצִיר גַּגּוֹת שֶׁקַּדְמַת שָׁלַף יָבֵשׁ: שֶׁלֹּא מִלֵּא כַפּוֹ קוֹצֵר וְחִצְנוֹ
ח מְעַמֵּר: וְלֹא אָמְרוּ ׀ הָעֹבְרִים בִּרְכַּת־יהוה אֲלֵיכֶם בֵּרַכְנוּ אֶתְכֶם
בְּשֵׁם יהוה:
קל א ב שִׁיר הַמַּעֲלוֹת מִמַּעֲמַקִּים קְרָאתִיךָ יהוה: אֲדֹנָי שִׁמְעָה בְקוֹלִי תִּהְיֶינָה
ג ד אָזְנֶיךָ קַשֻּׁבוֹת לְקוֹל תַּחֲנוּנָי: אִם־עֲוֺנוֹת תִּשְׁמָר־יָהּ אֲדֹנָי מִי יַעֲמֹד: כִּי־

5 therefore You may be revered. I wait for the LORD – my soul waits – in His
6 word I put my hope. My soul waits for the Lord more than watchmen for the
7 morning, more than watchmen for the morning. Israel, put your hope in the
LORD, for loving-kindness is the LORD's, and great is His power to redeem.
8 It is He who will redeem Israel from all their sins.
131 1 *A song of ascents – of David.* LORD – my heart is not proud, my eyes not raised
2 too high. I do not concern myself with great affairs or things beyond me, but
I have made my soul calm and quiet like a soothed child against his mother;
3 like a soothed child is my soul within me. Israel, put your hope in the LORD,
now and for evermore.
132 1 2 *A song of ascents.* LORD, remember David and all his suffering. He swore an
3 oath to the LORD and made a vow to the Mighty One of Yaakov: "I will not
4 enter my house or go to bed, I will not let my eyes sleep or let my eyelids close,
5 until I find a place for the LORD, a dwelling for the Mighty One of Yaakov."[136]
6 7 We heard of it in Efrat; we found it in the fields of Yaar.[137] Let us enter His
8 dwelling; let us worship at His footstool. Advance, LORD, to Your resting
9 place, You and Your mighty Ark. Your priests are robed in righteousness;
10 Your devoted ones sing for joy. For the sake of Your servant David, do not
11 reject Your anointed one.[138] The LORD swore to David a firm oath that He
will not revoke: "One of your own descendants I will set upon your throne.
12 If your children keep My covenant and My decrees that I teach them, then
13 their children, too, for evermore shall sit upon your throne," for the LORD
14 has chosen Zion; He desired it for His home: "This is My resting place for
15 all time; here I will dwell, for that is My desire. I will amply bless its store of
16 food; its poor I will sate with bread. I will clothe its priests with salvation; its
17 devoted ones shall sing for joy. There I will make David's horn flourish; I will
18 prepare a lamp for My anointed one. I will clothe his enemies with shame,
but on him will rest a shining crown."
133 1 *A song of ascents – of David.* How good and pleasant it is when brothers dwell
2 together – like fragrant oil on the head flowing down onto the beard, Aharon's
3 beard that flows down over the collar of his robes, like the dew of Ḥermon
that flows down the mountains of Zion. There the LORD bestows His blessing,
life for evermore.
134 1 *A song of ascents.* Come bless the LORD, all you servants of the LORD, you
2 who nightly stand in the House of the LORD. Lift up your hands toward the
3 Sanctuary and bless the LORD. May the LORD – Maker of heaven and earth –
bless you from Zion!
135 1 *Halleluya!* Praise the name of the LORD; praise Him, you servants of the
2 LORD who stand in the LORD's House, in the courtyards of the House of
3 our God. Praise the LORD, for the LORD is good; sing praises to His name,
4 for it is lovely, for the LORD has chosen Yaakov as His own, Israel as his
5 treasure, for I know that the LORD is great, that our Lord is above all gods.

136 | See II Samuel, chapter 7.

137 | Kiryat Ye'arim, the previous home of the Ark; see I Chronicles 13:5.

138 | Cf. II Chronicles 6:41–42.

ה עִמְּךָ הַסְּלִיחָה לְמַעַן תִּוָּרֵא: קִוִּיתִי יהוה קִוְּתָה נַפְשִׁי וְלִדְבָרוֹ הוֹחָלְתִּי:
ו ז נַפְשִׁי לַאדֹנָי מִשֹּׁמְרִים לַבֹּקֶר שֹׁמְרִים לַבֹּקֶר: יַחֵל יִשְׂרָאֵל אֶל־יהוה
ח כִּי־עִם־יהוה הַחֶסֶד וְהַרְבֵּה עִמּוֹ פְדוּת: וְהוּא יִפְדֶּה אֶת־יִשְׂרָאֵל
מִכֹּל עֲוֺנֹתָיו:
קלא א שִׁיר הַמַּעֲלוֹת לְדָוִד יהוה ׀ לֹא־גָבַהּ לִבִּי וְלֹא־רָמוּ עֵינַי וְלֹא־הִלַּכְתִּי ׀
ב בִּגְדֹלוֹת וּבְנִפְלָאוֹת מִמֶּנִּי: אִם־לֹא שִׁוִּיתִי ׀ וְדוֹמַמְתִּי נַפְשִׁי כְּגָמֻל
ג עֲלֵי אִמּוֹ כַּגָּמֻל עָלַי נַפְשִׁי: יַחֵל יִשְׂרָאֵל אֶל־יהוה מֵעַתָּה וְעַד־
עוֹלָם:
קלב א ב שִׁיר הַמַּעֲלוֹת זְכוֹר־יהוה לְדָוִד אֵת כָּל־עֻנּוֹתוֹ: אֲשֶׁר נִשְׁבַּע לַיהוה
ג נָדַר לַאֲבִיר יַעֲקֹב: אִם־אָבֹא בְּאֹהֶל בֵּיתִי אִם־אֶעֱלֶה עַל־עֶרֶשׂ
ד ה יְצוּעָי: אִם־אֶתֵּן שְׁנַת לְעֵינָי לְעַפְעַפַּי תְּנוּמָה: עַד־אֶמְצָא מָקוֹם
ו לַיהוה מִשְׁכָּנוֹת לַאֲבִיר יַעֲקֹב: הִנֵּה־שְׁמַעֲנוּהָ בְאֶפְרָתָה מְצָאנוּהָ
ז ח בִּשְׂדֵי־יָעַר: נָבוֹאָה לְמִשְׁכְּנוֹתָיו נִשְׁתַּחֲוֶה לַהֲדֹם רַגְלָיו: קוּמָה יהוה
ט לִמְנוּחָתֶךָ אַתָּה וַאֲרוֹן עֻזֶּךָ: כֹּהֲנֶיךָ יִלְבְּשׁוּ־צֶדֶק וַחֲסִידֶיךָ יְרַנֵּנוּ:
י יא בַּעֲבוּר דָּוִד עַבְדֶּךָ אַל־תָּשֵׁב פְּנֵי מְשִׁיחֶךָ: נִשְׁבַּע־יהוה ׀ לְדָוִד
יב אֱמֶת לֹא־יָשׁוּב מִמֶּנָּה מִפְּרִי בִטְנְךָ אָשִׁית לְכִסֵּא־לָךְ: אִם־יִשְׁמְרוּ
בָנֶיךָ ׀ בְּרִיתִי וְעֵדֹתִי זוֹ אֲלַמְּדֵם גַּם־בְּנֵיהֶם עֲדֵי־עַד יֵשְׁבוּ לְכִסֵּא־
יג יד לָךְ: כִּי־בָחַר יהוה בְּצִיּוֹן אִוָּהּ לְמוֹשָׁב לוֹ: זֹאת־מְנוּחָתִי עֲדֵי־עַד פֹּה
טו טז אֵשֵׁב כִּי אִוִּתִיהָ: צֵידָהּ בָּרֵךְ אֲבָרֵךְ אֶבְיוֹנֶיהָ אַשְׂבִּיעַ לָחֶם: וְכֹהֲנֶיהָ
יז אַלְבִּישׁ יֶשַׁע וַחֲסִידֶיהָ רַנֵּן יְרַנֵּנוּ: שָׁם אַצְמִיחַ קֶרֶן לְדָוִד עָרַכְתִּי נֵר
יח לִמְשִׁיחִי: אוֹיְבָיו אַלְבִּישׁ בֹּשֶׁת וְעָלָיו יָצִיץ נִזְרוֹ:
קלג א שִׁיר הַמַּעֲלוֹת לְדָוִד הִנֵּה מַה־טּוֹב וּמַה־נָּעִים שֶׁבֶת אַחִים גַּם־יָחַד:
ב כַּשֶּׁמֶן הַטּוֹב ׀ עַל־הָרֹאשׁ יֹרֵד עַל־הַזָּקָן זְקַן־אַהֲרֹן שֶׁיֹּרֵד עַל־פִּי
ג מִדּוֹתָיו: כְּטַל־חֶרְמוֹן שֶׁיֹּרֵד עַל־הַרְרֵי צִיּוֹן כִּי שָׁם ׀ צִוָּה יהוה אֶת־
הַבְּרָכָה חַיִּים עַד־הָעוֹלָם:
קלד א שִׁיר הַמַּעֲלוֹת הִנֵּה ׀ בָּרְכוּ אֶת־יהוה כָּל־עַבְדֵי יהוה הָעֹמְדִים בְּבֵית־
ב ג יהוה בַּלֵּילוֹת: שְׂאוּ־יְדֵכֶם קֹדֶשׁ וּבָרְכוּ אֶת־יהוה: יְבָרֶכְךָ יהוה מִצִּיּוֹן
עֹשֵׂה שָׁמַיִם וָאָרֶץ:
קלה א ב הַלְלוּיָהּ ׀ הַלְלוּ אֶת־שֵׁם יהוה הַלְלוּ עַבְדֵי יהוה: שֶׁעֹמְדִים בְּבֵית
ג יהוה בְּחַצְרוֹת בֵּית אֱלֹהֵינוּ: הַלְלוּיָהּ כִּי־טוֹב יהוה זַמְּרוּ לִשְׁמוֹ כִּי
ד ה נָעִים: כִּי־יַעֲקֹב בָּחַר לוֹ יָהּ יִשְׂרָאֵל לִסְגֻלָּתוֹ: כִּי אֲנִי יָדַעְתִּי כִּי־גָדוֹל

6 Whatever pleases the LORD, He does in heaven and on earth, in the seas
7 and all the depths. He raises clouds from the ends of the earth; He makes
lightning bolts with the rain; He brings out the wind from His storehouses.
8 9 He struck down the firstborn of Egypt, humans and animals alike. He sent
signs and wonders into your midst, Egypt – against Pharaoh and all his
10 11 servants. He struck down many nations and slew mighty kings: Siḥon, king
12 of the Amorites, Og, king of Bashan, and all the kingdoms of Canaan, and He
13 gave their land as a heritage, a heritage for His people Israel. Your name, LORD,
14 endures forever; Your renown, LORD, for all generations. For the LORD will
15 vindicate His people, bring solace to His servants. The idols of the nations are
16 silver and gold, made by human hands.[139] They have mouths but cannot speak;
17 eyes but cannot see. They have ears but cannot hear; there is no breath in their
18 mouths. Their makers will become like them; so will all who trust in them.
19 20 House of Israel – bless the LORD! House of Aharon – bless the LORD! House
21 of Levi – bless the LORD! You who fear the LORD – bless the LORD! Blessed
is the LORD from Zion, He who dwells in Jerusalem. *Halleluya!*

136 1 2 Thank the LORD for He is good – His loving-kindness is forever.[140] Thank
3 the God of gods – His loving-kindness is forever. Thank the Lord of lords –
4 His loving-kindness is forever; the One who alone works great wonders –
5 His loving-kindness is forever; who made the heavens with wisdom – His
6 loving-kindness is forever; who spread the earth upon the waters – His
7 loving-kindness is forever; who made the great lights – His loving-kindness is
8 9 forever; the sun to rule by day – His loving-kindness is forever; the moon and
10 the stars to rule by night – His loving-kindness is forever; who struck Egypt
11 through their firstborn – His loving-kindness is forever; and brought out
12 Israel from their midst – His loving-kindness is forever; with a strong hand
13 and outstretched arm – His loving-kindness is forever; who split apart the
14 Sea of Reeds – His loving-kindness is forever; and made Israel pass through
15 it – His loving-kindness is forever; and hurled Pharaoh and his army into the
16 Sea of Reeds – His loving-kindness is forever; who led His people through the
17 wilderness – His loving-kindness is forever; who struck down great kings –
18 His loving-kindness is forever; and slew mighty kings – His loving-kindness
19 20 is forever; Siḥon, king of the Amorites – His loving-kindness is forever; and
21 Og, king of Bashan – His loving-kindness is forever;[141] and gave their land as
22 a heritage – His loving-kindness is forever; a heritage for His servant Israel –
23 His loving-kindness is forever; who remembered us in our lowly state – His
24 loving-kindness is forever; and rescued us from our tormentors – His loving-
25 kindness is forever; who gives food to all flesh – His loving-kindness is forever.
26 Give thanks to the God of heaven – His loving-kindness is forever.

137 1 2 By the rivers of Babylon, there we sat and wept as we remembered Zion. There
3 on the willow trees we hung up our harps, for there our captors asked us for
songs, our tormentors for amusement: "Sing us one of the songs of Zion!"

---

139 | For verses 15–20, cf. 115:4–11.

140 | See note on 106:1.

141 | See Numbers 21:21–35.

ו יהוה ואדנינו מכל־אלהים: כל אשר־חפץ יהוה עשה בשמים
ז ובארץ בימים וכל־תהמות: מעלה נשאים מקצה הארץ ברקים
ח למטר עשה מוצא־רוח מאוצרותיו: שהכה בכורי מצרים מאדם
ט עד־בהמה: שלח ׀ אתת ומפתים בתוככי מצרים בפרעה ובכל־
י יא עבדיו: שהכה גוים רבים והרג מלכים עצומים: לסיחון ׀ מלך האמרי
יב ולעוג מלך הבשן ולכל ממלכות כנען: ונתן ארצם נחלה נחלה
יג יד לישראל עמו: יהוה שמך לעולם יהוה זכרך לדר־ודר: כי־ידין
טו יהוה עמו ועל־עבדיו יתנחם: עצבי הגוים כסף וזהב מעשה ידי
טז יז אדם: פה־להם ולא ידברו עינים להם ולא יראו: אזנים להם ולא
יח יאזינו אף אין־יש־רוח בפיהם: כמוהם יהיו עשיהם כל אשר־בטח
יט כ בהם: בית ישראל ברכו את־יהוה בית אהרן ברכו את־יהוה: בית
כא הלוי ברכו את־יהוה יראי יהוה ברכו את־יהוה: ברוך יהוה ׀ מציון
שכן ירושלם הללויה:

קלו א ב הודו ליהוה כי־טוב כי לעולם חסדו: הודו לאלהי האלהים כי לעולם
ג ד חסדו: הודו לאדני האדנים כי לעולם חסדו: לעשה נפלאות גדלות
ה לבדו כי לעולם חסדו: לעשה השמים בתבונה כי לעולם חסדו:
ו ז לרקע הארץ על־המים כי לעולם חסדו: לעשה אורים גדלים כי
ח ט לעולם חסדו: את־השמש לממשלת ביום כי לעולם חסדו: את־
י הירח וכוכבים לממשלות בלילה כי לעולם חסדו: למכה מצרים
יא בבכוריהם כי לעולם חסדו: ויוצא ישראל מתוכם כי לעולם חסדו:
יב יג ביד חזקה ובזרוע נטויה כי לעולם חסדו: לגזר ים־סוף לגזרים כי
יד טו לעולם חסדו: והעביר ישראל בתוכו כי לעולם חסדו: ונער פרעה
טז וחילו בים־סוף כי לעולם חסדו: למוליך עמו במדבר כי לעולם
יז יח חסדו: למכה מלכים גדלים כי לעולם חסדו: ויהרג מלכים אדירים
יט כ כי לעולם חסדו: לסיחון מלך האמרי כי לעולם חסדו: ולעוג מלך
כא כב הבשן כי לעולם חסדו: ונתן ארצם לנחלה כי לעולם חסדו: נחלה
כג לישראל עבדו כי לעולם חסדו: שבשפלנו זכר לנו כי לעולם חסדו:
כד כה ויפרקנו מצרינו כי לעולם חסדו: נתן לחם לכל־בשר כי לעולם
כו חסדו: הודו לאל השמים כי לעולם חסדו:

קלז א ב על־נהרות ׀ בבל שם ישבנו גם־בכינו בזכרנו את־ציון: על־ערבים
ג בתוכה תלינו כנרותינו: כי שם ׀ שאלונו שובינו דברי־שיר ותוללינו

4 5 How can we sing the LORD's song on foreign soil? If I forget you, O Jerusalem,
6 may my right hand forget its skill. May my tongue cling to the roof of my
mouth if I do not remember you, if I do not set Jerusalem above my highest
7 joy. Remember, LORD, what the Edomites did on the day Jerusalem fell.
8 They said, "Tear it down; tear it down to its very foundations!"[142] Daughter
of Babylon, doomed to destruction, happy are those who pay you back for
9 what you have done to us; happy are those who seize your infants and dash
them against the rocks.
138 1 *Of David.* I thank You with all my heart; before the divine beings I sing Your
2 praise. I bow down toward Your holy Sanctuary and give thanks to Your name
for Your loyalty and truth, for You have exalted Your name and Your word
3 above all. On the day I called You answered me; You made my soul swell with
4 might. All kings of the earth will thank You, LORD, for they have heard the
5 words of Your mouth, and they will sing of the LORD's ways, for great is the
6 glory of the LORD. For the LORD is high up, yet He sees the lowly; aloft, He
7 discerns them from afar. Though I walk among foes, You preserve my life; You
thrust out Your hand against my enemies' wrath, and Your right hand saves
8 me. The LORD will fulfill His purpose for me; Your loyalty, LORD, is forever;
never forsake Your handiwork.
139 1 *To the lead singer, of David – a psalm.* O LORD, You have searched me, and You
2 know – You know when I sit and when I rise; You understand my thoughts
3 from afar. You trace my going out and lying down; You are familiar with all
4 5 my ways. Even before a word is on my tongue, You, LORD, know it all. You
keep close guard behind and before me; You have laid Your hand upon me.
6 Knowledge so wonderful is beyond me, so high that it is above my reach.
7 Where can I escape from Your spirit? Where can I flee from Your presence?
8 If I climb to heaven, You are there; if I make my bed in the underworld, there
9 You are. If I rise on the wings of the dawn, if I settle on the far side of the sea,
10 11 even there Your hand will guide me; Your right hand will hold me fast. Were I
to say, "Surely the darkness will hide me and light become night around me,"
12 to You the darkness would not be dark; night is light as day; to You dark and
13 light are one, for You created my innermost being;[143] You knit me together
14 in my mother's womb. I praise You because I am awesomely, wondrously
15 made; wonderful are Your works; I know that full well. My frame was not
hidden from You when I was formed in a secret place, woven in the depths
16 of the earth. Your eyes saw my unformed substance; in Your book it was all
inscribed when each part would be formed before any of them came to be.
17 How precious to me are Your thoughts, God; how vast in number they are.
18 Were I to count them, they would outnumber the grains of the sand, and when
19 I wake again, I am still with You! God, if only You would slay the wicked –
20 away from me, you men of blood! They speak of You with evil intent; Your
21 adversaries misuse Your name. Do I not hate those who hate You, LORD, and
22 loathe those who rise up against You? I have nothing but hatred for them; I

142 | See Obadiah 1:11–14.
143 | Literally "my kidneys."

ד שִׂמְחָה שִׁירוּ לָנוּ מִשִּׁיר צִיּוֹן׃ אֵיךְ נָשִׁיר אֶת־שִׁיר־יהוה עַל אַדְמַת
ה ו נֵכָר׃ אִם־אֶשְׁכָּחֵךְ יְרוּשָׁלָ͏ִם תִּשְׁכַּח יְמִינִי׃ תִּדְבַּק לְשׁוֹנִי ׀ לְחִכִּי אִם־
ז לֹא אֶזְכְּרֵכִי אִם־לֹא אַעֲלֶה אֶת־יְרוּשָׁלַ͏ִם עַל רֹאשׁ שִׂמְחָתִי׃ זְכֹר
יהוה ׀ לִבְנֵי אֱדוֹם אֵת יוֹם יְרוּשָׁלָ͏ִם הָאֹמְרִים עָרוּ ׀ עָרוּ עַד הַיְסוֹד
ח בָּהּ׃ בַּת־בָּבֶל הַשְּׁדוּדָה אַשְׁרֵי שֶׁיְשַׁלֶּם־לָךְ אֶת־גְּמוּלֵךְ שֶׁגָּמַלְתְּ לָנוּ׃
ט אַשְׁרֵי ׀ שֶׁיֹּאחֵז וְנִפֵּץ אֶת־עֹלָלַיִךְ אֶל־הַסָּלַע׃
קלח א ב לְדָוִד ׀ אוֹדְךָ בְכָל־לִבִּי נֶגֶד אֱלֹהִים אֲזַמְּרֶךָּ׃ אֶשְׁתַּחֲוֶה אֶל־הֵיכַל
קָדְשְׁךָ וְאוֹדֶה אֶת־שְׁמֶךָ עַל־חַסְדְּךָ וְעַל־אֲמִתֶּךָ כִּי־הִגְדַּלְתָּ עַל־כָּל־
ג ד שִׁמְךָ אִמְרָתֶךָ׃ בְּיוֹם קָרָאתִי וַתַּעֲנֵנִי תַּרְהִבֵנִי בְנַפְשִׁי עֹז׃ יוֹדוּךָ יהוה
ה כָּל־מַלְכֵי־אָרֶץ כִּי שָׁמְעוּ אִמְרֵי־פִיךָ׃ וְיָשִׁירוּ בְּדַרְכֵי יהוה כִּי־גָדוֹל
ו ז כְּבוֹד יהוה׃ כִּי־רָם יהוה וְשָׁפָל יִרְאֶה וְגָבֹהַּ מִמֶּרְחָק יְיֵדָע׃ אִם־אֵלֵךְ ׀
ח בְּקֶרֶב צָרָה תְּחַיֵּנִי עַל אַף אֹיְבַי תִּשְׁלַח יָדֶךָ וְתוֹשִׁיעֵנִי יְמִינֶךָ׃ יהוה
יִגְמֹר בַּעֲדִי יהוה חַסְדְּךָ לְעוֹלָם מַעֲשֵׂי יָדֶיךָ אַל־תֶּרֶף׃
קלט א ב לַמְנַצֵּחַ לְדָוִד מִזְמוֹר יהוה חֲקַרְתַּנִי וַתֵּדָע׃ אַתָּה יָדַעְתָּ שִׁבְתִּי וְקוּמִי
ג ד בַּנְתָּה לְרֵעִי מֵרָחוֹק׃ אָרְחִי וְרִבְעִי זֵרִיתָ וְכָל־דְּרָכַי הִסְכַּנְתָּה׃ כִּי אֵין
ה מִלָּה בִּלְשׁוֹנִי הֵן יהוה יָדַעְתָּ כֻלָּהּ׃ אָחוֹר וָקֶדֶם צַרְתָּנִי וַתָּשֶׁת עָלַי
ו ז כַּפֶּכָה׃ פלאיה דַעַת מִמֶּנִּי נִשְׂגְּבָה לֹא־אוּכַל לָהּ׃ אָנָה אֵלֵךְ מֵרוּחֶךָ פְּלִיאָה
ח וְאָנָה מִפָּנֶיךָ אֶבְרָח׃ אִם־אֶסַּק שָׁמַיִם שָׁם אָתָּה וְאַצִּיעָה שְּׁאוֹל הִנֶּךָּ׃
ט י אֶשָּׂא כַנְפֵי־שָׁחַר אֶשְׁכְּנָה בְּאַחֲרִית יָם׃ גַּם־שָׁם יָדְךָ תַנְחֵנִי וְתֹאחֲזֵנִי
יא יב יְמִינֶךָ׃ וָאֹמַר אַךְ־חֹשֶׁךְ יְשׁוּפֵנִי וְלַיְלָה אוֹר בַּעֲדֵנִי׃ גַּם־חֹשֶׁךְ לֹא־
יג יַחְשִׁיךְ מִמֶּךָ וְלַיְלָה כַּיּוֹם יָאִיר כַּחֲשֵׁיכָה כָּאוֹרָה׃ כִּי־אַתָּה קָנִיתָ כִלְיֹתָי
יד תְּסֻכֵּנִי בְּבֶטֶן אִמִּי׃ אוֹדְךָ עַל כִּי נוֹרָאוֹת נִפְלֵיתִי נִפְלָאִים מַעֲשֶׂיךָ
טו וְנַפְשִׁי יֹדַעַת מְאֹד׃ לֹא־נִכְחַד עָצְמִי מִמֶּךָּ אֲשֶׁר־עֻשֵּׂיתִי בַסֵּתֶר רֻקַּמְתִּי
טז בְּתַחְתִּיּוֹת אָרֶץ׃ גָּלְמִי ׀ רָאוּ עֵינֶיךָ וְעַל־סִפְרְךָ כֻּלָּם יִכָּתֵבוּ יָמִים
יז יֻצָּרוּ ולא אֶחָד בָּהֶם׃ וְלִי מַה־יָּקְרוּ רֵעֶיךָ אֵל מֶה עָצְמוּ רָאשֵׁיהֶם׃ וְלוֹ
יח יט אֶסְפְּרֵם מֵחוֹל יִרְבּוּן הֱקִיצֹתִי וְעוֹדִי עִמָּךְ׃ אִם־תִּקְטֹל אֱלוֹהַּ ׀ רָשָׁע
כ וְאַנְשֵׁי דָמִים סוּרוּ מֶנִּי׃ אֲשֶׁר יֹמְרוּךָ לִמְזִמָּה נָשֻׂא לַשָּׁוְא עָרֶיךָ׃
כא כב הֲלוֹא־מְשַׂנְאֶיךָ יהוה ׀ אֶשְׂנָא וּבִתְקוֹמְמֶיךָ אֶתְקוֹטָט׃ תַּכְלִית שִׂנְאָה

23 count them my enemies. Search me, God, and know my heart; test me and
24 know my innermost thoughts. See if there is any grievous way within me, and
lead me in the everlasting way.
140 1 2 *To the lead singer – a psalm of David.* Rescue me, LORD, from evil people;
3 keep me from violent people who plot evil in their hearts, who incite war
4 day after day. Their tongues are sharpened like a serpent's; spider venom is
5 beneath their lips – Selah. Watch over me, LORD; keep me from the grasp of
6 the wicked; from violent people who plot to trip me up. The haughty have
laid a trap for me; they spread out a net of ropes by my path; they have set
7 snares for me – Selah. I said to the LORD, "You are my God; give ear, LORD,
8 to the sound of my plea." O GOD, Lord, my saving might, shield my head
9 when weapons clash. O LORD, do not grant the desires of the wicked; do
10 not let them fulfill their schemes lest they exalt themselves – Selah. May the
heads of those surrounding me be overwhelmed by their own treacherous
11 lips. May fiery coals rain down on them; may He cast them into the fire, into
12 chasms, never to rise. Let no slanderer stand firm in the land; may evil hound
13 the violent, blow upon blow. I know that the LORD will uphold justice for the
14 lowly, the cause of the needy. Yes, the righteous will give thanks to Your name;
the upright will dwell in Your presence.
141 1 *A psalm of David.* I call to You, LORD – rush to me; give ear to my voice
2 when I call You. Accept my prayer like incense before You, my lifted hands
3 like the evening offering. Set a guard, LORD, over my mouth, a keeper at the
4 door of my lips; do not let my heart turn to anything evil or deal in deeds
5 of wickedness with evildoers – let me not feast on their decadence. Let the
righteous strike me, in loyalty reproach me. Let not fine oil distract my head,
6 but set my prayers ever against their evil deeds. May their judges be felled by a
7 rock so that they will listen to my words, for they are sweet. As a person plows
8 and breaks up the earth, so our bones are scattered at the mouth of Sheol, for
my eyes are on You, GOD my Lord; in You I take refuge – do not let my life ebb
9 away. Guard me from the snare they laid for me, from the traps of evildoers.
10 May the wicked fall into their own nets while I alone move on.
142 1 2 A maskil *of David while he was in the cave*[144] *– a prayer.* My voice cries to the
3 LORD; my voice pleads with the LORD. I will pour out my lament before Him,
4 tell my troubles to Him when my spirit grows faint within me. You know my
5 path – along the way I walk they have laid a trap for me. Look to the right and
6 witness – I have not one friend; I have nowhere to flee; no one cares for me. I
cry out to You, LORD – I say, "You are my refuge, my share in the land of the
7 living." Listen to my plea, for I have sunk so low; save me from my pursuers,
8 for they are too strong for me. Set me free from this confinement so that I
may give thanks to Your name; the righteous will gather around me when
You are good to me.
143 1 *A psalm of David.* LORD, hear my prayer; give ear to my pleas; in Your
2 faithfulness answer me, in Your righteousness. Do not visit judgment on Your

144 | See 1 Samuel 24:3–4.

כג שְׂנֵאתִים לְאוֹיְבִים הָיוּ לִי: חׇקְרֵנִי אֵל וְדַע לְבָבִי בְּחָנֵנִי וְדַע שַׂרְעַפָּי:
כד וּרְאֵה אִם־דֶּרֶךְ־עֹצֶב בִּי וּנְחֵנִי בְּדֶרֶךְ עוֹלָם:
קמ א ב לַמְנַצֵּחַ מִזְמוֹר לְדָוִד: חַלְּצֵנִי יְהֹוָה מֵאָדָם רָע מֵאִישׁ חֲמָסִים תִּנְצְרֵנִי:
ג ד אֲשֶׁר חָשְׁבוּ רָעוֹת בְּלֵב כׇּל־יוֹם יָגוּרוּ מִלְחָמוֹת: שָׁנְנוּ לְשׁוֹנָם כְּמוֹ־
ה נָחָשׁ חֲמַת עַכְשׁוּב תַּחַת שְׂפָתֵימוֹ סֶלָה: שׇׁמְרֵנִי יְהֹוָה ׀ מִידֵי רָשָׁע
ו מֵאִישׁ חֲמָסִים תִּנְצְרֵנִי אֲשֶׁר חָשְׁבוּ לִדְחוֹת פְּעָמָי: טָמְנוּ־גֵאִים ׀ פַּח
ז לִי וַחֲבָלִים פָּרְשׂוּ רֶשֶׁת לְיַד־מַעְגָּל מֹקְשִׁים שָׁתוּ־לִי סֶלָה: אָמַרְתִּי
ח לַיהֹוָה אֵלִי אָתָּה הַאֲזִינָה יְהֹוָה קוֹל תַּחֲנוּנָי: יֱהֹוִה אֲדֹנָי עֹז יְשׁוּעָתִי
ט סַכֹּתָה לְרֹאשִׁי בְּיוֹם נָשֶׁק: אַל־תִּתֵּן יְהֹוָה מַאֲוַיֵּי רָשָׁע זְמָמוֹ אַל־
י יא תָּפֵק יָרוּמוּ סֶלָה: רֹאשׁ מְסִבָּי עֲמַל שְׂפָתֵימוֹ יכסומו: ימיטו עֲלֵיהֶם יְכַסֵּמוֹ: יִמּוֹטוּ
יב גֶּחָלִים בָּאֵשׁ יַפִּלֵם בְּמַהֲמֹרוֹת בַּל־יָקוּמוּ: אִישׁ לָשׁוֹן בַּל־יִכּוֹן בָּאָרֶץ
יג אִישׁ־חָמָס רָע יְצוּדֶנּוּ לְמַדְחֵפֹת: יָדַעְתָּ כִּי־יַעֲשֶׂה יְהֹוָה דִּין עָנִי מִשְׁפַּט
יד אֶבְיֹנִים: אַךְ צַדִּיקִים יוֹדוּ לִשְׁמֶךָ יֵשְׁבוּ יְשָׁרִים אֶת־פָּנֶיךָ: יט
קמא א ב מִזְמוֹר לְדָוִד יְהֹוָה קְרָאתִיךָ חוּשָׁה לִּי הַאֲזִינָה קוֹלִי בְּקׇרְאִי־לָךְ: תִּכּוֹן
ג תְּפִלָּתִי קְטֹרֶת לְפָנֶיךָ מַשְׂאַת כַּפַּי מִנְחַת־עָרֶב: שִׁיתָה יְהֹוָה שׇׁמְרָה
ד לְפִי נִצְּרָה עַל־דַּל שְׂפָתָי: אַל־תַּט־לִבִּי ׀ לְדָבָר ׀ רָע לְהִתְעוֹלֵל עֲלִלוֹת ׀
ה בְּרֶשַׁע אֶת־אִישִׁים פֹּעֲלֵי־אָוֶן וּבַל־אֶלְחַם בְּמַנְעַמֵּיהֶם: יֶהֶלְמֵנִי צַדִּיק ׀
חֶסֶד וְיוֹכִיחֵנִי שֶׁמֶן רֹאשׁ אַל־יָנִי רֹאשִׁי כִּי־עוֹד וּתְפִלָּתִי בְּרָעוֹתֵיהֶם:
ו ז נִשְׁמְטוּ בִידֵי־סֶלַע שֹׁפְטֵיהֶם וְשָׁמְעוּ אֲמָרַי כִּי נָעֵמוּ: כְּמוֹ פֹלֵחַ וּבֹקֵעַ
ח בָּאָרֶץ נִפְזְרוּ עֲצָמֵינוּ לְפִי שְׁאוֹל: כִּי אֵלֶיךָ ׀ יֱהֹוִה אֲדֹנָי עֵינָי בְּכָה
ט חָסִיתִי אַל־תְּעַר נַפְשִׁי: שׇׁמְרֵנִי מִידֵי פַח יָקְשׁוּ לִי וּמֹקְשׁוֹת פֹּעֲלֵי
י אָוֶן: יִפְּלוּ בְמַכְמֹרָיו רְשָׁעִים יַחַד אָנֹכִי עַד־אֶעֱבוֹר:
קמב א ב מַשְׂכִּיל לְדָוִד בִּהְיוֹתוֹ בַמְּעָרָה תְפִלָּה: קוֹלִי אֶל־יְהֹוָה אֶזְעָק קוֹלִי
ג ד אֶל־יְהֹוָה אֶתְחַנָּן: אֶשְׁפֹּךְ לְפָנָיו שִׂיחִי צָרָתִי לְפָנָיו אַגִּיד: בְּהִתְעַטֵּף
ה עָלַי ׀ רוּחִי וְאַתָּה יָדַעְתָּ נְתִיבָתִי בְּאֹרַח־זוּ אֲהַלֵּךְ טָמְנוּ פַח לִי: הַבֵּיט
ו יָמִין ׀ וּרְאֵה וְאֵין־לִי מַכִּיר אָבַד מָנוֹס מִמֶּנִּי אֵין דּוֹרֵשׁ לְנַפְשִׁי: זָעַקְתִּי
ז אֵלֶיךָ יְהֹוָה אָמַרְתִּי אַתָּה מַחְסִי חֶלְקִי בְּאֶרֶץ הַחַיִּים: הַקְשִׁיבָה ׀ אֶל־
ח רִנָּתִי כִּי־דַלּוֹתִי מְאֹד הַצִּילֵנִי מֵרֹדְפַי כִּי אָמְצוּ מִמֶּנִּי: הוֹצִיאָה מִמַּסְגֵּר ׀
נַפְשִׁי לְהוֹדוֹת אֶת־שְׁמֶךָ בִּי יַכְתִּרוּ צַדִּיקִים כִּי תִגְמֹל עָלָי:
קמג א מִזְמוֹר לְדָוִד יְהֹוָה ׀ שְׁמַע תְּפִלָּתִי הַאֲזִינָה אֶל־תַּחֲנוּנַי בֶּאֱמֻנָתְךָ
ב עֲנֵנִי בְּצִדְקָתֶךָ: וְאַל־תָּבוֹא בְמִשְׁפָּט אֶת־עַבְדֶּךָ כִּי לֹא־יִצְדַּק לְפָנֶיךָ

3 servant, for no living thing can be justified before You, for the enemy hunted
me down, trampled my life to the ground, forced me to dwell in darkness
4 like those long dead, so my spirit is faint within me; my heart is stunned
5 inside me. I recall days of old; I contemplate all Your works; I reflect upon
6 Your handiwork. I spread out my hands to You; my soul thirsts for You like a
7 weary land – Selah. Swiftly answer me, LORD; my spirit pines away. Do not
8 hide Your face from me, or I shall be like those who plummet to the Pit. Let
me hear Your loyalty in the morning, for in You I trust; let me know the way
9 to go, for to You I lift up my life. Deliver me from my enemies, LORD; in You
10 I take cover. Teach me to do Your will, for You are my God; Your good spirit
11 will guide me along level ground. For the sake of Your name, LORD, let me
12 live; in Your righteousness bring me out of danger, and in Your loyalty destroy
my enemies; make all my mortal foes perish, for I am Your servant.

144 1 *Of David.* Blessed is the LORD, my Rock, who trains my hands for war, my
2 fingers for battle. He is my benefactor, my fortress, my stronghold, and my
3 refuge, my shield in whom I trust, He who subdues nations under me. LORD,
what is humanity that You care for it; what are mortals that You think of
4 them? Humanity is no more than a breath, its days like a fleeting shadow.
5 LORD, bend Your heavens and come down; touch the mountains so that they
6 pour forth smoke; flash forth lightning and scatter them; shoot Your arrows
7 and panic them. Reach out Your hand from on high; deliver me and rescue
8 me from the mighty waters, from the hands of foreigners whose every word
9 is worthless, whose right hands are raised in falsehood. To You, God, I will
10 sing a new song; to You I will play music on a ten-stringed harp. He who
gives salvation to kings, who saves His servant David from the cruel sword,
11 may He deliver me and rescue me from the hands of foreigners whose every
12 word is worthless, whose right hands are raised in falsehood. Then our sons
will be like saplings, well nurtured in their youth; our daughters will be like
13 sculpted pillars, fit to adorn a palace; our barns will be filled with every kind
of provision; our sheep will increase by thousands, even tens of thousands, in
14 our fields; our oxen will draw heavy loads. There will be no breach in the walls,
15 no going into captivity, no cries of distress in our streets. Happy are the people
for whom this is so; happy are the people whose God is the LORD.

145 1 *A song of praise of David.*[145] I will exalt You, my God, the King, and bless Your
2 name for ever and all time. Every day I will bless You and praise Your name
3 for ever and all time. Great is the LORD, of highest praise; His greatness is
4 unfathomable. One generation will praise Your works to the next and tell of
5 Your mighty deeds. On the glorious splendor of Your majesty and on the acts
6 of Your wonders, I will reflect. They shall talk of the power of Your awesome
7 deeds, and I will tell of Your greatness. They shall celebrate the fame of Your
8 great goodness and sing with joy of Your righteousness. The LORD is gracious
9 and compassionate, slow to anger and great in kindness. The LORD is good
10 to all, and His compassion extends to all His works. All Your works shall
11 thank You, LORD, and Your devoted ones shall bless You. They shall talk of

145 | This psalm takes the form of an alphabetical acrostic.

ג כָּל־חָי׃ כִּי רָדַף אוֹיֵב ׀ נַפְשִׁי דִּכָּא לָאָרֶץ חַיָּתִי הוֹשִׁיבַנִי בְמַחֲשַׁכִּים
ד ה כְּמֵתֵי עוֹלָם׃ וַתִּתְעַטֵּף עָלַי רוּחִי בְּתוֹכִי יִשְׁתּוֹמֵם לִבִּי׃ זָכַרְתִּי יָמִים ׀
ו מִקֶּדֶם הָגִיתִי בְכָל־פָּעֳלֶךָ בְּמַעֲשֵׂה יָדֶיךָ אֲשׂוֹחֵחַ׃ פֵּרַשְׂתִּי יָדַי אֵלֶיךָ
ז נַפְשִׁי ׀ כְּאֶרֶץ־עֲיֵפָה לְךָ סֶלָה׃ מַהֵר עֲנֵנִי ׀ יהוה כָּלְתָה רוּחִי אַל־
ח תַּסְתֵּר פָּנֶיךָ מִמֶּנִּי וְנִמְשַׁלְתִּי עִם־יֹרְדֵי בוֹר׃ הַשְׁמִיעֵנִי בַבֹּקֶר ׀ חַסְדֶּךָ
ט כִּי־בְךָ בָטָחְתִּי הוֹדִיעֵנִי דֶּרֶךְ־זוּ אֵלֵךְ כִּי־אֵלֶיךָ נָשָׂאתִי נַפְשִׁי׃ הַצִּילֵנִי
י מֵאֹיְבַי ׀ יהוה אֵלֶיךָ כִסִּתִי׃ לַמְּדֵנִי ׀ לַעֲשׂוֹת רְצוֹנֶךָ כִּי־אַתָּה אֱלוֹהָי
יא רוּחֲךָ טוֹבָה תַּנְחֵנִי בְּאֶרֶץ מִישׁוֹר׃ לְמַעַן־שִׁמְךָ יהוה תְּחַיֵּנִי בְּצִדְקָתְךָ ׀
יב תּוֹצִיא מִצָּרָה נַפְשִׁי׃ וּבְחַסְדְּךָ תַּצְמִית אֹיְבָי וְהַאֲבַדְתָּ כָּל־צֹרְרֵי נַפְשִׁי
כִּי אֲנִי עַבְדֶּךָ׃
קמד א לְדָוִד ׀ בָּרוּךְ יהוה ׀ צוּרִי הַמְלַמֵּד יָדַי לַקְרָב אֶצְבְּעוֹתַי לַמִּלְחָמָה׃
ב חַסְדִּי וּמְצוּדָתִי מִשְׂגַּבִּי וּמְפַלְטִי לִי מָגִנִּי וּבוֹ חָסִיתִי הָרוֹדֵד עַמִּי תַחְתָּי׃
ג ד יהוה מָה־אָדָם וַתֵּדָעֵהוּ בֶּן־אֱנוֹשׁ וַתְּחַשְּׁבֵהוּ׃ אָדָם לַהֶבֶל דָּמָה יָמָיו
ה ו כְּצֵל עוֹבֵר׃ יהוה הַט־שָׁמֶיךָ וְתֵרֵד גַּע בֶּהָרִים וְיֶעֱשָׁנוּ׃ בְּרוֹק בָּרָק
ז וּתְפִיצֵם שְׁלַח חִצֶּיךָ וּתְהֻמֵּם׃ שְׁלַח יָדֶיךָ מִמָּרוֹם פְּצֵנִי וְהַצִּילֵנִי מִמַּיִם
ח ט רַבִּים מִיַּד בְּנֵי נֵכָר׃ אֲשֶׁר פִּיהֶם דִּבֶּר־שָׁוְא וִימִינָם יְמִין שָׁקֶר׃ אֱלֹהִים
י שִׁיר חָדָשׁ אָשִׁירָה לָּךְ בְּנֵבֶל עָשׂוֹר אֲזַמְּרָה־לָּךְ׃ הַנּוֹתֵן תְּשׁוּעָה
יא לַמְּלָכִים הַפּוֹצֶה אֶת־דָּוִד עַבְדּוֹ מֵחֶרֶב רָעָה׃ פְּצֵנִי וְהַצִּילֵנִי מִיַּד בְּנֵי־
יב נֵכָר אֲשֶׁר פִּיהֶם דִּבֶּר־שָׁוְא וִימִינָם יְמִין שָׁקֶר׃ אֲשֶׁר בָּנֵינוּ ׀ כִּנְטִעִים
יג מְגֻדָּלִים בִּנְעוּרֵיהֶם בְּנוֹתֵינוּ כְזָוִיֹּת מְחֻטָּבוֹת תַּבְנִית הֵיכָל׃ מְזָוֵינוּ
מְלֵאִים מְפִיקִים מִזַּן אֶל זַן צֹאונֵנוּ מַאֲלִיפוֹת מְרֻבָּבוֹת בְּחוּצוֹתֵינוּ׃
יד טו אַלּוּפֵינוּ מְסֻבָּלִים אֵין פֶּרֶץ וְאֵין יוֹצֵאת וְאֵין צְוָחָה בִּרְחֹבֹתֵינוּ׃ אַשְׁרֵי
הָעָם שֶׁכָּכָה לּוֹ אַשְׁרֵי הָעָם שֶׁיהוה אֱלֹהָיו׃
קמה א תְּהִלָּה לְדָוִד אֲרוֹמִמְךָ אֱלוֹהַי הַמֶּלֶךְ וַאֲבָרְכָה שִׁמְךָ לְעוֹלָם וָעֶד׃
ב ג בְּכָל־יוֹם אֲבָרְכֶךָּ וַאֲהַלְלָה שִׁמְךָ לְעוֹלָם וָעֶד׃ גָּדוֹל יהוה וּמְהֻלָּל
ד מְאֹד וְלִגְדֻלָּתוֹ אֵין חֵקֶר׃ דּוֹר לְדוֹר יְשַׁבַּח מַעֲשֶׂיךָ וּגְבוּרֹתֶיךָ יַגִּידוּ׃
ה ו הֲדַר כְּבוֹד הוֹדֶךָ וְדִבְרֵי נִפְלְאוֹתֶיךָ אָשִׂיחָה׃ וֶעֱזוּז נוֹרְאֹתֶיךָ יֹאמֵרוּ
ז ח וגדלותיך אֲסַפְּרֶנָּה׃ זֵכֶר רַב־טוּבְךָ יַבִּיעוּ וְצִדְקָתְךָ יְרַנֵּנוּ׃ חַנּוּן וְרַחוּם וּגְדוּלָּתְךָ
ט יהוה אֶרֶךְ אַפַּיִם וּגְדָל־חָסֶד׃ טוֹב־יהוה לַכֹּל וְרַחֲמָיו עַל־כָּל־מַעֲשָׂיו׃
י יא יוֹדוּךָ יהוה כָּל־מַעֲשֶׂיךָ וַחֲסִידֶיךָ יְבָרְכוּכָה׃ כְּבוֹד מַלְכוּתְךָ יֹאמֵרוּ

12 the glory of Your kingship and speak of Your might, revealing to humanity
13 His mighty deeds and the glorious majesty of His kingship. Your kingdom
14 is an everlasting kingdom, and Your reign is for all generations. The Lord
15 supports all who fall and raises all who are bowed down. All raise their eyes to
16 You in hope, and You give them their food in due time. You open Your hand
17 and satisfy the needs of every living thing. The Lord is righteous in all His
18 ways and devoted in all He does. The Lord is close to all who call on Him,
19 to all who truly call on Him. He fulfills the will of those who revere Him; He
20 hears their cry and saves them. The Lord guards all who love Him, but all the
21 wicked He will destroy. My mouth shall speak the praise of the Lord, and all
creatures shall bless His holy name for ever and all time.

146 1 2 *Halleluya!* Praise the Lord, my soul. I will praise the Lord all my life; I will
3 sing to my God as long as I live. Put not your trust in nobles, in mortal man
4 who cannot save. His breath expires; he returns to the earth; on that day his
5 plans come to an end. Happy are those whose help is the God of Yaakov,
6 whose hope is in the Lord their God, who made heaven and earth, the seas
7 and all they contain – He who keeps faith forever. He secures justice for the
8 oppressed; He gives food to the hungry; the Lord sets captives free. The
Lord gives sight to the blind; the Lord raises those bowed down; the Lord
9 loves the righteous. The Lord protects the stranger; He gives courage to the
10 orphan and widow and thwarts the way of the wicked. The Lord shall reign
forever – He is your God, Zion, for all generations. *Halleluya!*

147 1 *Halleluya!* How good it is to make music to our God; how sweet it is to
2 sing glorious praise. The Lord rebuilds Jerusalem; He gathers the scattered
3 exiles of Israel. He heals the brokenhearted and binds up their wounds.
4 5 He counts the number of the stars, calling each by name. Great is our Lord
6 and mighty in power; His understanding has no limit. The Lord gives
7 courage to the humble but casts the wicked to the ground. Sing to the Lord
8 in thanks; make music to our God on the harp. He covers the sky with
clouds; He provides the earth with rain and makes grass grow on the hills.
9 10 He gives food to the beasts, to young ravens when they cry. He does not
take delight in the strength of horses or pleasure in the fleetness[146] of man.
11 The Lord takes pleasure in those who fear Him, who put their hope in His
12 13 loyalty. Praise the Lord, Jerusalem; sing to your God, Zion! – for He has
strengthened the bars of your gates and blessed your children in your midst.
14 He has brought peace to your borders and satisfied you with the finest wheat.
15 16 He sends His commandment to earth; swiftly runs His word. He spreads
17 snow like fleece, sprinkles frost like ashes, scatters hail like crumbs. Who
18 can withstand His cold? He sends His word and melts them; He stirs up His
19 wind, and the waters flow. He has declared His words to Yaakov, His statutes
20 and laws to Israel. He has done this for no other nation; such laws they do
not know. *Halleluya!*

146 | Literally "thighs."

יב וּגְבוּרָתְךָ יְדַבֵּרוּ: לְהוֹדִיעַ | לִבְנֵי הָאָדָם גְּבוּרֹתָיו וּכְבוֹד הֲדַר מַלְכוּתוֹ:
יג יד מַלְכוּתְךָ מַלְכוּת כָּל־עֹלָמִים וּמֶמְשַׁלְתְּךָ בְּכָל־דּוֹר וָדֹר: סוֹמֵךְ יְהוָה
טו לְכָל־הַנֹּפְלִים וְזוֹקֵף לְכָל־הַכְּפוּפִים: עֵינֵי־כֹל אֵלֶיךָ יְשַׂבֵּרוּ וְאַתָּה
טז נוֹתֵן־לָהֶם אֶת־אָכְלָם בְּעִתּוֹ: פּוֹתֵחַ אֶת־יָדֶךָ וּמַשְׂבִּיעַ לְכָל־חַי
יז יח רָצוֹן: צַדִּיק יְהוָה בְּכָל־דְּרָכָיו וְחָסִיד בְּכָל־מַעֲשָׂיו: קָרוֹב יְהוָה לְכָל־
יט קֹרְאָיו לְכֹל אֲשֶׁר יִקְרָאֻהוּ בֶאֱמֶת: רְצוֹן־יְרֵאָיו יַעֲשֶׂה וְאֶת־שַׁוְעָתָם
כ יִשְׁמַע וְיוֹשִׁיעֵם: שׁוֹמֵר יְהוָה אֶת־כָּל־אֹהֲבָיו וְאֵת כָּל־הָרְשָׁעִים
כא יַשְׁמִיד: תְּהִלַּת יְהוָה יְדַבֶּר פִּי וִיבָרֵךְ כָּל־בָּשָׂר שֵׁם קָדְשׁוֹ לְעוֹלָם
וָעֶד:

קמו א ב הַלְלוּיָהּ הַלְלִי נַפְשִׁי אֶת־יְהוָה: אֲהַלְלָה יְהוָה בְּחַיָּי אֲזַמְּרָה לֵאלֹהַי
ג ד בְּעוֹדִי: אַל־תִּבְטְחוּ בִנְדִיבִים בְּבֶן־אָדָם | שֶׁאֵין לוֹ תְשׁוּעָה: תֵּצֵא
ה רוּחוֹ יָשֻׁב לְאַדְמָתוֹ בַּיּוֹם הַהוּא אָבְדוּ עֶשְׁתֹּנֹתָיו: אַשְׁרֵי שֶׁאֵל יַעֲקֹב
ו בְּעֶזְרוֹ שִׂבְרוֹ עַל־יְהוָה אֱלֹהָיו: עֹשֶׂה | שָׁמַיִם וָאָרֶץ אֶת־הַיָּם וְאֶת־
ז כָּל־אֲשֶׁר־בָּם הַשֹּׁמֵר אֱמֶת לְעוֹלָם: עֹשֶׂה מִשְׁפָּט | לָעֲשׁוּקִים נֹתֵן
ח לֶחֶם לָרְעֵבִים יְהוָה מַתִּיר אֲסוּרִים: יְהוָה | פֹּקֵחַ עִוְרִים יְהוָה זֹקֵף
ט כְּפוּפִים יְהוָה אֹהֵב צַדִּיקִים: יְהוָה | שֹׁמֵר אֶת־גֵּרִים יָתוֹם וְאַלְמָנָה
י יְעוֹדֵד וְדֶרֶךְ רְשָׁעִים יְעַוֵּת: יִמְלֹךְ יְהוָה | לְעוֹלָם אֱלֹהַיִךְ צִיּוֹן לְדֹר
וָדֹר הַלְלוּיָהּ:

קמז א ב הַלְלוּיָהּ | כִּי־טוֹב זַמְּרָה אֱלֹהֵינוּ כִּי־נָעִים נָאוָה תְהִלָּה: בּוֹנֵה יְרוּשָׁלַםִ
ג יְהוָה נִדְחֵי יִשְׂרָאֵל יְכַנֵּס: הָרֹפֵא לִשְׁבוּרֵי לֵב וּמְחַבֵּשׁ לְעַצְּבוֹתָם:
ד ה מוֹנֶה מִסְפָּר לַכּוֹכָבִים לְכֻלָּם שֵׁמוֹת יִקְרָא: גָּדוֹל אֲדוֹנֵינוּ וְרַב־כֹּחַ
ו לִתְבוּנָתוֹ אֵין מִסְפָּר: מְעוֹדֵד עֲנָוִים יְהוָה מַשְׁפִּיל רְשָׁעִים עֲדֵי־אָרֶץ:
ז ח עֱנוּ לַיהוָה בְּתוֹדָה זַמְּרוּ לֵאלֹהֵינוּ בְכִנּוֹר: הַמְכַסֶּה שָׁמַיִם | בְּעָבִים
ט הַמֵּכִין לָאָרֶץ מָטָר הַמַּצְמִיחַ הָרִים חָצִיר: נוֹתֵן לִבְהֵמָה לַחְמָהּ לִבְנֵי
י עֹרֵב אֲשֶׁר יִקְרָאוּ: לֹא בִגְבוּרַת הַסּוּס יֶחְפָּץ לֹא־בְשׁוֹקֵי הָאִישׁ יִרְצֶה:
יא יב רוֹצֶה יְהוָה אֶת־יְרֵאָיו אֶת־הַמְיַחֲלִים לְחַסְדּוֹ: שַׁבְּחִי יְרוּשָׁלַםִ אֶת־
יג יְהוָה הַלְלִי אֱלֹהַיִךְ צִיּוֹן: כִּי־חִזַּק בְּרִיחֵי שְׁעָרָיִךְ בֵּרַךְ בָּנַיִךְ בְּקִרְבֵּךְ:
יד טו הַשָּׂם־גְּבוּלֵךְ שָׁלוֹם חֵלֶב חִטִּים יַשְׂבִּיעֵךְ: הַשֹּׁלֵחַ אִמְרָתוֹ אָרֶץ עַד־
טז יז מְהֵרָה יָרוּץ דְּבָרוֹ: הַנֹּתֵן שֶׁלֶג כַּצָּמֶר כְּפוֹר כָּאֵפֶר יְפַזֵּר: מַשְׁלִיךְ
יח קַרְחוֹ כְפִתִּים לִפְנֵי קָרָתוֹ מִי יַעֲמֹד: יִשְׁלַח דְּבָרוֹ וְיַמְסֵם יַשֵּׁב רוּחוֹ
יט כ יִזְּלוּ־מָיִם: מַגִּיד דְּבָרָו לְיַעֲקֹב חֻקָּיו וּמִשְׁפָּטָיו לְיִשְׂרָאֵל: לֹא עָשָׂה
כֵן | לְכָל־גּוֹי וּמִשְׁפָּטִים בַּל־יְדָעוּם הַלְלוּיָהּ:

148 1 *Halleluya!* Praise the Lord from the heavens; praise Him in the heights.
2 3 Praise Him, all His angels; praise Him, all His hosts. Praise Him, sun and
4 moon; praise Him, all shining stars. Praise Him, highest heavens and the
5 waters above the heavens. Let them praise the name of the Lord, for He
6 commanded, and they were created. He established them for ever and all
7 time, issuing a decree that will never change. Praise the Lord from the earth:
8 sea monsters and all the deep seas; fire and hail, snow, and mist, storm winds
9 10 that obey His word; mountains and all hills, fruit trees and all cedars; wild
11 animals and all cattle, creeping things and winged birds; kings of the earth
12 and all nations, princes and all judges on earth; youths and maidens alike,
13 old and young together. Let them praise the name of the Lord, for His name
14 alone is sublime; His majesty is above earth and heaven. He has raised the
horn of His people, glory for all His devoted ones, for the children of Israel,
the people close to Him. *Halleluya!*

149 1 *Halleluya!* Sing to the Lord a new song, His praise in the assembly of the
2 devoted. Let Israel rejoice in its Maker; let the children of Zion exult in their
3 King. Let them praise His name with dancing, sing praises to Him with
4 timbrel and harp, for the Lord delights in His people; He adorns the humble
5 with salvation. Let the devoted revel in glory; let them sing for joy on their
6 beds. Let high praises of God be in their throats and two-edged swords in
7 their hands to impose retribution on the nations, punishment on the peoples,
8 9 binding their kings with chains, their nobles with iron fetters, carrying
out the judgment written against them. This is the glory of all His devoted
ones. *Halleluya!*

150 1 *Halleluya!* Praise God in His Sanctuary; praise Him in His powerful skies.
2 Praise Him for His mighty deeds; praise Him for His surpassing greatness.
3 Praise Him with blasts of the ram's horn; praise Him with the harp and lyre.
4 5 Praise Him with timbrel and dance; praise Him with strings and flute. Praise
6 Him with clashing cymbals; praise Him with resounding cymbals. Let all that
breathe praise the Lord. *Halleluya!*

קמח א ב הַלְלוּיָהּ ׀ הַלְלוּ אֶת־יְהוָה מִן־הַשָּׁמַיִם הַלְלוּהוּ בַּמְּרוֹמִים׃ הַלְלוּהוּ
ג כָל־מַלְאָכָיו הַלְלוּהוּ כָּל־צְבָאָו׃ הַלְלוּהוּ שֶׁמֶשׁ וְיָרֵחַ הַלְלוּהוּ כָּל־
ד ה כּוֹכְבֵי אוֹר׃ הַלְלוּהוּ שְׁמֵי הַשָּׁמָיִם וְהַמַּיִם אֲשֶׁר ׀ מֵעַל הַשָּׁמָיִם׃ יְהַלְלוּ
ו אֶת־שֵׁם יְהוָה כִּי הוּא צִוָּה וְנִבְרָאוּ׃ וַיַּעֲמִידֵם לָעַד לְעוֹלָם חָק־נָתַן
ז ח וְלֹא יַעֲבוֹר׃ הַלְלוּ אֶת־יְהוָה מִן־הָאָרֶץ תַּנִּינִים וְכָל־תְּהֹמוֹת׃ אֵשׁ
ט וּבָרָד שֶׁלֶג וְקִיטוֹר רוּחַ סְעָרָה עֹשָׂה דְבָרוֹ׃ הֶהָרִים וְכָל־גְּבָעוֹת עֵץ
י יא פְּרִי וְכָל־אֲרָזִים׃ הַחַיָּה וְכָל־בְּהֵמָה רֶמֶשׂ וְצִפּוֹר כָּנָף׃ מַלְכֵי־אֶרֶץ
יב וְכָל־לְאֻמִּים שָׂרִים וְכָל־שֹׁפְטֵי אָרֶץ׃ בַּחוּרִים וְגַם־בְּתוּלוֹת זְקֵנִים
יג עִם־נְעָרִים׃ יְהַלְלוּ ׀ אֶת־שֵׁם יְהוָה כִּי־נִשְׂגָּב שְׁמוֹ לְבַדּוֹ הוֹדוֹ עַל־
יד אֶרֶץ וְשָׁמָיִם׃ וַיָּרֶם קֶרֶן ׀ לְעַמּוֹ תְּהִלָּה לְכָל־חֲסִידָיו לִבְנֵי יִשְׂרָאֵל
עַם קְרֹבוֹ הַלְלוּיָהּ׃

קמט א ב הַלְלוּיָהּ ׀ שִׁירוּ לַיהוָה שִׁיר חָדָשׁ תְּהִלָּתוֹ בִּקְהַל חֲסִידִים׃ יִשְׂמַח
ג יִשְׂרָאֵל בְּעֹשָׂיו בְּנֵי־צִיּוֹן יָגִילוּ בְמַלְכָּם׃ יְהַלְלוּ שְׁמוֹ בְמָחוֹל בְּתֹף וְכִנּוֹר
ד ה יְזַמְּרוּ־לוֹ׃ כִּי־רוֹצֶה יְהוָה בְּעַמּוֹ יְפָאֵר עֲנָוִים בִּישׁוּעָה׃ יַעְלְזוּ חֲסִידִים
ו בְּכָבוֹד יְרַנְּנוּ עַל־מִשְׁכְּבוֹתָם׃ רוֹמְמוֹת אֵל בִּגְרוֹנָם וְחֶרֶב פִּיפִיּוֹת
ז ח בְּיָדָם׃ לַעֲשׂוֹת נְקָמָה בַּגּוֹיִם תּוֹכֵחֹת בַּלְאֻמִּים׃ לֶאְסֹר מַלְכֵיהֶם
ט בְּזִקִּים וְנִכְבְּדֵיהֶם בְּכַבְלֵי בַרְזֶל׃ לַעֲשׂוֹת בָּהֶם ׀ מִשְׁפָּט כָּתוּב הָדָר
הוּא לְכָל־חֲסִידָיו הַלְלוּיָהּ׃

קנ א ב הַלְלוּיָהּ ׀ הַלְלוּ־אֵל בְּקָדְשׁוֹ הַלְלוּהוּ בִּרְקִיעַ עֻזּוֹ׃ הַלְלוּהוּ בִגְבוּרֹתָיו
ג הַלְלוּהוּ כְּרֹב גֻּדְלוֹ׃ הַלְלוּהוּ בְּתֵקַע שׁוֹפָר הַלְלוּהוּ בְּנֵבֶל וְכִנּוֹר׃
ד ה הַלְלוּהוּ בְתֹף וּמָחוֹל הַלְלוּהוּ בְּמִנִּים וְעוּגָב׃ הַלְלוּהוּ בְצִלְצְלֵי־שָׁמַע
ו הַלְלוּהוּ בְּצִלְצְלֵי תְרוּעָה׃ כֹּל הַנְּשָׁמָה תְּהַלֵּל יָהּ הַלְלוּיָהּ׃

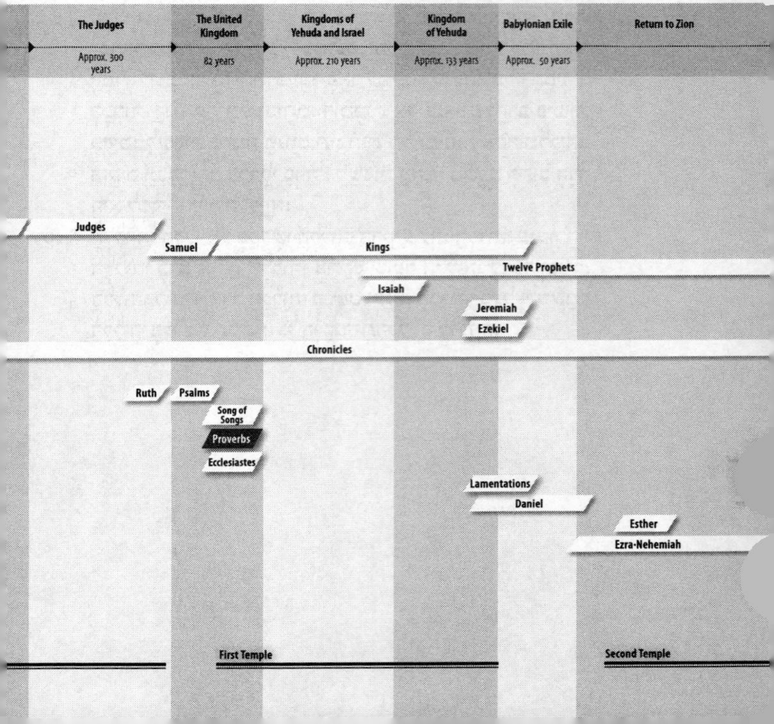
The Judges
The United Kingdom
Kingdoms of Yehuda and Israel
Kingdom of Yehuda
Babylonian Exile
Return to Zion
Approx. 300 years
82 years
Approx. 210 years
Approx. 133 years
Approx. 50 years
Judges
Samuel
Kings
Twelve Prophets
Isaiah
Jeremiah
Ezekiel
Chronicles
Ruth
Psalms
Song of Songs
Proverbs
Ecclesiastes
Lamentations
Daniel
Esther
Ezra-Nehemiah
First Temple
Second Temple

משלי

MISHLEI / PROVERBS

PROVERBS					
	The proverbs of Shlomo, king of Israel	Proverbs of Shlomo relating to the individual and the family	Words of wisdom	Proverbs of Shlomo that Ḥizkiya's people recorded	Statements of Agur, Aluka, and Lemuel
	Chs. 1–9	10:1–22:16	22:17–24:34	25–29	30–31

1 1 2 The proverbs of Shlomo son of David, king of Israel: To become familiar
3 with wisdom and instruction, to comprehend intelligent sayings, to gain
4 sensible instruction – righteousness, justice, and fairness, to provide
5 cleverness to the naive, knowledge and counsel to the youth. Let the wise
6 hear and profit further and the intelligent person acquire stratagems by
comprehending both proverb and adage, the words of the wise and their
7 riddles.[1] Fear of the Lord is the beginning of knowledge; fools scorn
wisdom and instruction.
8 Heed, my son, your father's instruction, and do not forsake your mother's
9 teaching. For they are like decorative ribbons for your head, and like
10 11 necklaces for your throat. My son, if sinners tempt you do not consent. If
they say, "Come along with us; let us lie in hiding in order to shed blood;
12 let us ambush the innocent for no reason. Let us swallow them alive
13 like Sheol,[2] the blameless like those who descend to the grave. We will
14 discover every sort of precious treasure and fill our homes with loot. Cast
15 your lot among us; there will be but one pocket for us all." My son, do not
16 go with them; divert your foot from their path. For their feet race toward
17 evil, and they rush to spill blood.[3] For in the view of every winged creature,
18 the snare is spread for naught.[4] Yet they lie in order to ambush their own
19 blood and hide in order to take their own lives. So it is with everyone who
lusts for gain, which eventually takes the life of its possessor.
20 Wisdom will sing out in public and give forth her voice in the squares.
21 From atop the crowded streets she will call; at the entrance to the gates,
22 in the city, she will speak her message. How long, you naive ones, will you
cherish naivete, you scoffers, the scoffing that you so desire? Fools, how
23 much longer will you despise knowledge? Respond to my rebuke. Look,
I will express my sentiments to you. I will inform you of my message.
24 Because I called and you refused, I extended my hand, but no one listened.
25 26 You abrogated my counsel, and you refused my rebuke. I too will laugh at
27 your fate; I will sneer when what you feared overtakes you. When what
you feared overtakes you like a disaster and your fate arrives like a storm,
28 when trouble and woe come upon you, then you will call for me, but I will
29 not answer. You will seek me, but you will not find me. All this because
30 they despised knowledge and did not choose the fear of the Lord. They
31 did not consent to my counsel, and they spurned all my rebukes. So now
they will eat the fruits of their ways, and they will be sated with their
32 own schemes. For the nonchalance of the naive will kill them, and the
33 indifference of the foolish will do them in. But he who heeds me shall
dwell securely, relieved of the fear of catastrophe.

---

1 | These are pedagogical devices for conveying wisdom.
2 | The netherworld.
3 | Cf. Isaiah 59:7.
4 | Birds, like criminals, do not think they will be caught.

א
א ב מִשְׁלֵי שְׁלֹמֹה בֶן־דָּוִד מֶלֶךְ יִשְׂרָאֵל: לָדַעַת חָכְמָה וּמוּסָר לְהָבִין
ג ד אִמְרֵי בִינָה: לָקַחַת מוּסַר הַשְׂכֵּל צֶדֶק וּמִשְׁפָּט וּמֵשָׁרִים: לָתֵת
ה לִפְתָאיִם עׇרְמָה לְנַעַר דַּעַת וּמְזִמָּה: יִשְׁמַע חָכָם וְיוֹסֶף לֶקַח וְנָבוֹן
ו ז תַּחְבֻּלוֹת יִקְנֶה: לְהָבִין מָשָׁל וּמְלִיצָה דִּבְרֵי חֲכָמִים וְחִידֹתָם: יִרְאַת
יְהוָה רֵאשִׁית דָּעַת חׇכְמָה וּמוּסָר אֱוִילִים בָּזוּ:
ח ט שְׁמַע בְּנִי מוּסַר אָבִיךָ וְאַל־תִּטֹּשׁ תּוֹרַת אִמֶּךָ: כִּי ׀ לִוְיַת חֵן הֵם
י לְרֹאשֶׁךָ וַעֲנָקִים לְגַרְגְּרֹתֶךָ: בְּנִי אִם־יְפַתּוּךָ חַטָּאִים אַל־תֹּבֵא:
יא יב אִם־יֹאמְרוּ לְכָה אִתָּנוּ נֶאֶרְבָה לְדָם נִצְפְּנָה לְנָקִי חִנָּם: נִבְלָעֵם
יג כִּשְׁאוֹל חַיִּים וּתְמִימִים כְּיוֹרְדֵי בוֹר: כׇּל־הוֹן יָקָר נִמְצָא נְמַלֵּא בָתֵּינוּ
יד טו שָׁלָל: גּוֹרָלְךָ תַּפִּיל בְּתוֹכֵנוּ כִּיס אֶחָד יִהְיֶה לְכֻלָּנוּ: בְּנִי אַל־תֵּלֵךְ
טז בְּדֶרֶךְ אִתָּם מְנַע רַגְלְךָ מִנְּתִיבָתָם: כִּי רַגְלֵיהֶם לָרַע יָרוּצוּ וִימַהֲרוּ
יז יח לִשְׁפׇּךְ־דָּם: כִּי־חִנָּם מְזֹרָה הָרָשֶׁת בְּעֵינֵי כׇּל־בַּעַל כָּנָף: וְהֵם לְדָמָם
יט יֶאֱרֹבוּ יִצְפְּנוּ לְנַפְשֹׁתָם: כֵּן אׇרְחוֹת כׇּל־בֹּצֵעַ בָּצַע אֶת־נֶפֶשׁ בְּעָלָיו
יִקָּח:
כ כא חׇכְמוֹת בַּחוּץ תָּרֹנָּה בָּרְחֹבוֹת תִּתֵּן קוֹלָהּ: בְּרֹאשׁ הֹמִיּוֹת תִּקְרָא
כב בְּפִתְחֵי שְׁעָרִים בָּעִיר אֲמָרֶיהָ תֹאמֵר: עַד־מָתַי ׀ פְּתָיִם תְּאֵהֲבוּ פֶתִי
כג וְלֵצִים לָצוֹן חָמְדוּ לָהֶם וּכְסִילִים יִשְׂנְאוּ־דָעַת: תָּשׁוּבוּ לְתוֹכַחְתִּי
כד הִנֵּה אַבִּיעָה לָכֶם רוּחִי אוֹדִיעָה דְבָרַי אֶתְכֶם: יַעַן קָרָאתִי וַתְּמָאֵנוּ
כה נָטִיתִי יָדִי וְאֵין מַקְשִׁיב: וַתִּפְרְעוּ כׇל־עֲצָתִי וְתוֹכַחְתִּי לֹא אֲבִיתֶם:
כו כז גַּם־אֲנִי בְּאֵידְכֶם אֶשְׂחָק אֶלְעַג בְּבֹא פַחְדְּכֶם: בְּבֹא כשאוה ׀ פַּחְדְּכֶם כְּשׁוֹאָה
כח וְאֵידְכֶם כְּסוּפָה יֶאֱתֶה בְּבֹא עֲלֵיכֶם צָרָה וְצוּקָה: אָז יִקְרָאֻנְנִי וְלֹא
כט אֶעֱנֶה יְשַׁחֲרֻנְנִי וְלֹא יִמְצָאֻנְנִי: תַּחַת כִּי־שָׂנְאוּ דָעַת וְיִרְאַת יְהוָה
ל לא לֹא בָחָרוּ: לֹא־אָבוּ לַעֲצָתִי נָאֲצוּ כׇּל־תּוֹכַחְתִּי: וְיֹאכְלוּ מִפְּרִי דַרְכָּם
לב וּמִמֹּעֲצֹתֵיהֶם יִשְׂבָּעוּ: כִּי מְשׁוּבַת פְּתָיִם תַּהַרְגֵם וְשַׁלְוַת כְּסִילִים
לג תְּאַבְּדֵם: וְשֹׁמֵעַ לִי יִשְׁכׇּן־בֶּטַח וְשַׁאֲנַן מִפַּחַד רָעָה:

2 1 My son, if you will accept my sayings and keep my precepts close to you,
2 to listen attentively to wisdom and bend your heart toward discernment;
3 indeed, if you will summon understanding and give your voice over to
4 discernment, if you will seek it like silver and search for it like buried
5 treasure, then you will understand the fear of the LORD and achieve
6 knowledge of God. For the LORD grants wisdom; from His mouth come
7 knowledge and comprehension. He preserves guidance for the upright
8 and shields those who walk in perfectness, so as to protect the paths of
9 justice and guard the way of His righteous ones. Then you will understand
10 righteousness, justice, and rectitude – every good pathway. When wisdom
11 and knowledge enter your heart, your soul will be pleased. Forethought
12 will watch over you; comprehension will protect you to rescue you
13 from an evil way, from men who speak perversions, who desert paths
14 of rectitude to follow roads of darkness; who are happy to perform evil
15 and rejoice in wicked perversions – their ways are crooked, and they are
16 misguided in their pathways – to save you from the strange woman,[5] from
17 the exotic woman who polishes her words, who abandons the companion
18 of her youth and forgets the covenant with her God – she inclines toward
19 death, her home; her footsteps lead to ghostly spirits; those who approach
20 her shall not return and will never regain the paths of life – so that you
will follow the way of good people and keep to the paths of the righteous.
21 For the upright will dwell in the land, and perfect ones will remain there,
22 but the wicked will be cut off from the land, and the treacherous will be
excised from it.

3 1 My son, do not forget my teaching, and let your heart guard my precepts.
2 3 For they will add longevity, years of vitality, and bring peace to you. May
loving-kindness and truth never leave you; tie them around your neck;
4 inscribe them upon the tablet of your heart. Find favor and approval in
the eyes of God and humans.

5 Trust in the LORD with all your heart; do not rely upon your own
6 understanding. In all matters acknowledge Him, and He will make your
7 paths straight. Do not be wise in your own eyes; rather, fear the LORD and
8 avoid evil. That will be a cure for your flesh and a healing potion for your
9 bones. Honor the LORD more than your wealth and more than the best
10 of all your produce. Then your barns will be filled with plenty, and your
vats will burst with new wine.

11 My son, do not scorn the LORD's discipline, and do not despise His
12 rebuke. For the LORD rebukes whom He loves, as a father does a son he
13 likes. Fortunate is the person who has attained wisdom; so is the person
14 who has attained comprehension. For its worth is better than the worth
15 of silver, and greater than gold is its value. It is more precious than pearls,

5 | Hebrew *zara*, a foreigner or outsider.

ב א ב בְּנִי אִם־תִּקַּח אֲמָרָי וּמִצְוֺתַי תִּצְפֹּן אִתָּךְ׃ לְהַקְשִׁיב לַחָכְמָה אָזְנֶךָ
ג ד תַּטֶּה לִבְּךָ לַתְּבוּנָה׃ כִּי אִם לַבִּינָה תִקְרָא לַתְּבוּנָה תִּתֵּן קוֹלֶךָ׃ אִם־
ה תְּבַקְשֶׁנָּה כַכָּסֶף וְכַמַּטְמוֹנִים תַּחְפְּשֶׂנָּה׃ אָז תָּבִין יִרְאַת יְהוָה וְדַעַת
ו ז אֱלֹהִים תִּמְצָא׃ כִּי־יְהוָה יִתֵּן חָכְמָה מִפִּיו דַּעַת וּתְבוּנָה׃ וצפן לַיְשָׁרִים יִצְפֹּן
ח תּוּשִׁיָּה מָגֵן לְהֹלְכֵי תֹם׃ לִנְצֹר אָרְחוֹת מִשְׁפָּט וְדֶרֶךְ חֲסִידָו יִשְׁמֹר׃
ט י אָז תָּבִין צֶדֶק וּמִשְׁפָּט וּמֵישָׁרִים כָּל־מַעְגַּל־טוֹב׃ כִּי־תָבוֹא חָכְמָה
יא בְלִבֶּךָ וְדַעַת לְנַפְשְׁךָ יִנְעָם׃ מְזִמָּה תִּשְׁמֹר עָלֶיךָ תְּבוּנָה תִנְצְרֶכָּה׃
יב יג לְהַצִּילְךָ מִדֶּרֶךְ רָע מֵאִישׁ מְדַבֵּר תַּהְפֻּכוֹת׃ הַעֹזְבִים אָרְחוֹת יֹשֶׁר
יד לָלֶכֶת בְּדַרְכֵי־חֹשֶׁךְ׃ הַשְּׂמֵחִים לַעֲשׂוֹת רָע יָגִילוּ בְּתַהְפֻּכוֹת רָע׃
טו טז אֲשֶׁר אָרְחֹתֵיהֶם עִקְּשִׁים וּנְלוֹזִים בְּמַעְגְּלוֹתָם׃ לְהַצִּילְךָ מֵאִשָּׁה זָרָה
יז מִנָּכְרִיָּה אֲמָרֶיהָ הֶחֱלִיקָה׃ הַעֹזֶבֶת אַלּוּף נְעוּרֶיהָ וְאֶת־בְּרִית אֱלֹהֶיהָ
יח יט שָׁכֵחָה׃ כִּי שָׁחָה אֶל־מָוֶת בֵּיתָהּ וְאֶל־רְפָאִים מַעְגְּלֹתֶיהָ׃ כָּל־בָּאֶיהָ
כ לֹא יְשׁוּבוּן וְלֹא־יַשִּׂיגוּ אָרְחוֹת חַיִּים׃ לְמַעַן תֵּלֵךְ בְּדֶרֶךְ טוֹבִים
כא וְאָרְחוֹת צַדִּיקִים תִּשְׁמֹר׃ כִּי־יְשָׁרִים יִשְׁכְּנוּ־אָרֶץ וּתְמִימִים יִוָּתְרוּ
כב בָהּ׃ וּרְשָׁעִים מֵאֶרֶץ יִכָּרֵתוּ וּבוֹגְדִים יִסְּחוּ מִמֶּנָּה׃

ג א ב בְּנִי תּוֹרָתִי אַל־תִּשְׁכָּח וּמִצְוֺתַי יִצֹּר לִבֶּךָ׃ כִּי אֹרֶךְ יָמִים וּשְׁנוֹת חַיִּים
ג וְשָׁלוֹם יוֹסִיפוּ לָךְ׃ חֶסֶד וֶאֱמֶת אַל־יַעַזְבֻךָ קָשְׁרֵם עַל־גַּרְגְּרוֹתֶיךָ כָּתְבֵם
ד עַל־לוּחַ לִבֶּךָ׃ וּמְצָא־חֵן וְשֵׂכֶל־טוֹב בְּעֵינֵי אֱלֹהִים וְאָדָם׃
ה ו בְּטַח אֶל־יְהוָה בְּכָל־לִבֶּךָ וְאֶל־בִּינָתְךָ אַל־תִּשָּׁעֵן׃ בְּכָל־דְּרָכֶיךָ
ז דָעֵהוּ וְהוּא יְיַשֵּׁר אֹרְחֹתֶיךָ׃ אַל־תְּהִי חָכָם בְּעֵינֶיךָ יְרָא אֶת־יְהוָה
ח ט וְסוּר מֵרָע׃ רִפְאוּת תְּהִי לְשָׁרֶּךָ וְשִׁקּוּי לְעַצְמוֹתֶיךָ׃ כַּבֵּד אֶת־יְהוָה
י מֵהוֹנֶךָ וּמֵרֵאשִׁית כָּל־תְּבוּאָתֶךָ׃ וְיִמָּלְאוּ אֲסָמֶיךָ שָׂבָע וְתִירוֹשׁ
יְקָבֶיךָ יִפְרֹצוּ׃
יא יב מוּסַר יְהוָה בְּנִי אַל־תִּמְאָס וְאַל־תָּקֹץ בְּתוֹכַחְתּוֹ׃ כִּי אֶת אֲשֶׁר יֶאֱהַב
יג יְהוָה יוֹכִיחַ וּכְאָב אֶת־בֵּן יִרְצֶה׃ אַשְׁרֵי אָדָם מָצָא חָכְמָה וְאָדָם יָפִיק
יד טו תְּבוּנָה׃ כִּי טוֹב סַחְרָהּ מִסְּחַר־כָּסֶף וּמֵחָרוּץ תְּבוּאָתָהּ׃ יְקָרָה הִיא

16 and all your possessions cannot equal it. Long life is in its right hand; in
17 its left hand is wealth and honor. Its ways are the ways of pleasantness,
18 and all of its paths are peaceful. It is a tree of life for those who grasp it;
those who hold fast to it are fortunate.
19 The Lord founded the earth with wisdom. He established the heavens
20 with discernment. With His knowledge were the depths carved out, and
21 the sky dropped dew. My son, do not allow them to elude your eyes.
22 Adhere to guidance and forethought. They will be a source of life for
23 your soul, a charming decoration around your neck. Then you will walk
24 securely on your way, and your foot will not stumble. If you lie down, you
25 will not fear; when you lie down, your sleep will be sweet for you. Fear
26 neither sudden fright nor the suffering of the wicked when it comes. For
the Lord will be your hope, and He will protect your foot from the snare.
27 Do not withhold benefit from its owner when it is in your power to act.
28 Do not say to your fellow, "Go, then come back, and tomorrow I will give
29 it to you," when you have it with you. Do not plot evil against your fellow
30 when he dwells trustingly with you. Do not quarrel with a person without
31 cause unless he has done you harm. Do not envy the criminal, and do
32 not adopt any of his ways. For the crooked are loathed by the Lord, but
33 with the upright He is intimate. The Lord's curse is in the house of the
34 wicked, but He blesses the abode of the righteous. At scoffers He scoffs,
35 but upon the humble He bestows grace. The wise inherit honor, whereas
fools receive disgrace.
4 1 Hear, sons, a father's instruction. Listen well and become familiar with
2 understanding, for I give you a valuable lesson. Do not abandon my
3 teachings. I was a son to my father, delicate and favored by my mother.
4 He taught me and said to me: "Let your heart uphold my words; guard
5 my precepts and thrive. Acquire wisdom, acquire understanding; do not
6 forget, and do not veer from the words of my mouth. Do not abandon
7 her, and she will watch over you. Love her, and she will protect you. The
beginning of wisdom: acquire wisdom, and, with all your acquisitions,
8 acquire understanding. Caress her and she will exalt you; she will honor
9 you when you embrace her. She will place upon your head a charming
10 ornament and reward you with a crown of glory." Hear, my son, and
11 accept my words; they will make many the years of life. I taught you
12 wisdom's way; I guided you along pathways of rectitude. When you walk,
your footsteps will not be constrained, and should you run, you will not
13 stumble. Hold fast to instruction; do not let go. Guard her, for she is your
14 life. Do not enter the path of the wicked, and do not tread in the way of evil
15 16 ones. Avoid it; do not traverse it; swerve and pass by. For they are unable
to sleep if they have not done harm; sleep is stolen from them if they
17 have not misled others. For they eat the bread of wickedness and drink
18 the wine of lawlessness. The path of the righteous is like a shining light;

טז מפניים וְכׇל־חֲפָצֶיךָ לֹא יִשְׁווּ־בָהּ: אֹרֶךְ יָמִים בִּימִינָהּ בִּשְׂמֹאולָהּ — מִפְּנִינִים
יז יח עֹשֶׁר וְכָבוֹד: דְּרָכֶיהָ דַרְכֵי־נֹעַם וְכׇל־נְתִיבוֹתֶיהָ שָׁלוֹם: עֵץ־חַיִּים הִיא
לַמַּחֲזִיקִים בָּהּ וְתֹמְכֶיהָ מְאֻשָּׁר:
יט כ יְהֹוָה בְּחׇכְמָה יָסַד־אָרֶץ כּוֹנֵן שָׁמַיִם בִּתְבוּנָה: בְּדַעְתּוֹ תְּהוֹמוֹת נִבְקָעוּ
כא כב וּשְׁחָקִים יִרְעֲפוּ־טָל: בְּנִי אַל־יָלֻזוּ מֵעֵינֶיךָ נְצֹר תֻּשִׁיָּה וּמְזִמָּה: וְיִהְיוּ
כג חַיִּים לְנַפְשֶׁךָ וְחֵן לְגַרְגְּרֹתֶיךָ: אָז תֵּלֵךְ לָבֶטַח דַּרְכֶּךָ וְרַגְלְךָ לֹא תִגּוֹף:
כד כה אִם־תִּשְׁכַּב לֹא־תִפְחָד וְשָׁכַבְתָּ וְעָרְבָה שְׁנָתֶךָ: אַל־תִּירָא מִפַּחַד
כו פִּתְאֹם וּמִשֹּׁאַת רְשָׁעִים כִּי תָבֹא: כִּי־יְהֹוָה יִהְיֶה בְכִסְלֶךָ וְשָׁמַר רַגְלְךָ
כז כח מִלָּכֶד: אַל־תִּמְנַע־טוֹב מִבְּעָלָיו בִּהְיוֹת לְאֵל ידיך לַעֲשׂוֹת: אַל־ — יָדְךָ
כט תֹּאמַר לרעיך ׀ לֵךְ וָשׁוּב וּמָחָר אֶתֵּן וְיֵשׁ אִתָּךְ: אַל־תַּחֲרֹשׁ עַל־רֵעֲךָ — לְרֵעֲךָ
ל רָעָה וְהוּא־יוֹשֵׁב לָבֶטַח אִתָּךְ: אַל־תרוב עִם־אָדָם חִנָּם אִם־לֹא גְמָלְךָ — תָּרִיב
לא לב רָעָה: אַל־תְּקַנֵּא בְּאִישׁ חָמָס וְאַל־תִּבְחַר בְּכׇל־דְּרָכָיו: כִּי תוֹעֲבַת
לג יְהֹוָה נָלוֹז וְאֶת־יְשָׁרִים סוֹדוֹ: מְאֵרַת יְהֹוָה בְּבֵית רָשָׁע וּנְוֵה צַדִּיקִים
לד לה יְבָרֵךְ: אִם־לַלֵּצִים הוּא־יָלִיץ ולעניים יִתֶּן־חֵן: כָּבוֹד חֲכָמִים יִנְחָלוּ — וְלַעֲנָוִים
וּכְסִילִים מֵרִים קָלוֹן:

ד א ב שִׁמְעוּ בָנִים מוּסַר אָב וְהַקְשִׁיבוּ לָדַעַת בִּינָה: כִּי לֶקַח טוֹב נָתַתִּי
ג לָכֶם תּוֹרָתִי אַל־תַּעֲזֹבוּ: כִּי־בֵן הָיִיתִי לְאָבִי רַךְ וְיָחִיד לִפְנֵי אִמִּי:
ד ה וַיֹּרֵנִי וַיֹּאמֶר לִי יִתְמָךְ־דְּבָרַי לִבֶּךָ שְׁמֹר מִצְוֺתַי וֶחְיֵה: קְנֵה חׇכְמָה
ו קְנֵה בִינָה אַל־תִּשְׁכַּח וְאַל־תֵּט מֵאִמְרֵי־פִי: אַל־תַּעַזְבֶהָ וְתִשְׁמְרֶךָּ
ז אֱהָבֶהָ וְתִצְּרֶךָּ: רֵאשִׁית חׇכְמָה קְנֵה חׇכְמָה וּבְכׇל־קִנְיָנְךָ קְנֵה בִינָה:
ח ט סַלְסְלֶהָ וּתְרוֹמְמֶךָּ תְּכַבֵּדְךָ כִּי תְחַבְּקֶנָּה: תִּתֵּן לְרֹאשְׁךָ לִוְיַת־חֵן
י עֲטֶרֶת תִּפְאֶרֶת תְּמַגְּנֶךָּ: שְׁמַע בְּנִי וְקַח אֲמָרָי וְיִרְבּוּ לְךָ שְׁנוֹת
יא יב חַיִּים: בְּדֶרֶךְ חׇכְמָה הֹרֵתִיךָ הִדְרַכְתִּיךָ בְּמַעְגְּלֵי־יֹשֶׁר: בְּלֶכְתְּךָ
יג לֹא־יֵצַר צַעֲדֶךָ וְאִם־תָּרוּץ לֹא תִכָּשֵׁל: הַחֲזֵק בַּמּוּסָר אַל־תֶּרֶף
יד נִצְּרֶהָ כִּי־הִיא חַיֶּיךָ: בְּאֹרַח רְשָׁעִים אַל־תָּבֹא וְאַל־תְּאַשֵּׁר בְּדֶרֶךְ
טו טז רָעִים: פְּרָעֵהוּ אַל־תַּעֲבׇר־בּוֹ שְׂטֵה מֵעָלָיו וַעֲבוֹר: כִּי לֹא יִשְׁנוּ אִם־
יז לֹא יָרֵעוּ וְנִגְזְלָה שְׁנָתָם אִם־לֹא יכשולו: כִּי לָחֲמוּ לֶחֶם רֶשַׁע וְיֵין — יַכְשִׁילוּ
יח חֲמָסִים יִשְׁתּוּ: וְאֹרַח צַדִּיקִים כְּאוֹר נֹגַהּ הוֹלֵךְ וָאוֹר עַד־נְכוֹן הַיּוֹם:

19 it increases its light until high noon, whereas the way of the wicked is like
20 darkness; they know not over what they will stumble. My son,
21 listen well to my words; bend your ear to my sayings. Do not allow your
22 eyes to be diverted from them; guard them within your heart. For they are
a source of life for him who has discovered them, healing for all his flesh.
23 More than all else that you guard, guard your heart, for from it life grows.
24 25 Eliminate perverse speech, and distance yourself from crooked lips. Let
26 your eyes gaze directly in front of you, your eyelids straight ahead. Align
27 the pathways upon which you walk, and let all your ways be righteous. Do
not veer to the right or to the left; withdraw your foot from evil.
5 1 2 My son, listen well to my wisdom; bend your ear to my understanding in
order to observe prudent thoughts so that your lips will guard discretion.
3 For honey drips from the lips of the strange woman whose palate is
4 smoother than oil, but her end is as bitter as wormwood, as sharp as a
5 double-edged sword. Her feet descend to Death; her footsteps hold open
6 Sheol. She does not aim toward a path of life; her ways wander she knows
not where.
7 Now, sons, hear me, and do not veer from the sayings of my mouth.
8 Distance your way from her; do not draw near to the door of her home
9 lest you give away your glory to others and your years to a merciless
10 man; lest strangers derive satisfaction from your strength, your efforts
11 consumed in an alien's house. In your final moments you will wail as your
12 flesh and frame decay. You will say, "How I did hate instruction, and my
13 heart despised rebuke! I did not hear the voice of my teachers, and to my
14 tutors I did not bend my ear. I was very nearly completely evil, exposed
15 before congregation and community." Drink water from your own cistern
16 and running water from your own well.[6] Your wellsprings will burst
17 outward, streams of water flowing in the squares. They will be yours, yours
18 alone; no strangers will share them with you. Your fount will be blessed,
19 and you will rejoice with the wife of your youth. An amorous doe, an
alluring gazelle, her breasts will sustain you at all times. Indulge in her
20 love always. Why indulge, my son, with a strange woman? Why embrace
21 an exotic woman's bosom? For a man's ways are before the Lord's eyes,
22 and He assesses all his footsteps. His sins will ensnare the evil person!
23 He will be fettered by the bonds of his transgression. He will die for not
6 1 taking instruction, and for indulging in his many follies. My son, if you
guaranteed a loan for your friend or extended your hand[7] on behalf of a
2 stranger, you have been ensnared by the words of your own mouth; you
3 have been trapped by the words of your own mouth. Do this, then, my
son, and save yourself, now that you have fallen into your friend's hand.
4 Quickly debase yourself and flatter your friend. Do not allow your eyes

---

6 | Metaphors for the man's wife; see verse 18.

7 | That is, put up surety.

יט כ דֶּרֶךְ רְשָׁעִים כָּאֲפֵלָה לֹא יָדְעוּ בַּמֶּה יִכָּשֵׁלוּ: בְּנִי
כא לִדְבָרַי הַקְשִׁיבָה לַאֲמָרַי הַט־אָזְנֶךָ: אַל־יַלִּיזוּ מֵעֵינֶיךָ שָׁמְרֵם בְּתוֹךְ
כב כג לְבָבֶךָ: כִּי־חַיִּים הֵם לְמֹצְאֵיהֶם וּלְכָל־בְּשָׂרוֹ מַרְפֵּא: מִכָּל־מִשְׁמָר
כד נְצֹר לִבֶּךָ כִּי־מִמֶּנּוּ תּוֹצְאוֹת חַיִּים: הָסֵר מִמְּךָ עִקְּשׁוּת פֶּה וּלְזוּת
כה כו שְׂפָתַיִם הַרְחֵק מִמֶּךָּ: עֵינֶיךָ לְנֹכַח יַבִּיטוּ וְעַפְעַפֶּיךָ יַיְשִׁרוּ נֶגְדֶּךָ: פַּלֵּס
כז מַעְגַּל רַגְלֶךָ וְכָל־דְּרָכֶיךָ יִכֹּנוּ: אַל־תֵּט־יָמִין וּשְׂמֹאול הָסֵר רַגְלְךָ
מֵרָע:
ה א ב בְּנִי לְחָכְמָתִי הַקְשִׁיבָה לִתְבוּנָתִי הַט־אָזְנֶךָ: לִשְׁמֹר מְזִמּוֹת וְדַעַת
ג ד שְׂפָתֶיךָ יִנְצֹרוּ: כִּי נֹפֶת תִּטֹּפְנָה שִׂפְתֵי זָרָה וְחָלָק מִשֶּׁמֶן חִכָּהּ: וְאַחֲרִיתָהּ
ה מָרָה כַלַּעֲנָה חַדָּה כְּחֶרֶב פִּיּוֹת: רַגְלֶיהָ יֹרְדוֹת מָוֶת שְׁאוֹל צְעָדֶיהָ
ו יִתְמֹכוּ: אֹרַח חַיִּים פֶּן־תְּפַלֵּס נָעוּ מַעְגְּלֹתֶיהָ לֹא תֵדָע:
ז ח וְעַתָּה בָנִים שִׁמְעוּ־לִי וְאַל־תָּסוּרוּ מֵאִמְרֵי־פִי: הַרְחֵק מֵעָלֶיהָ דַרְכֶּךָ
ט וְאַל־תִּקְרַב אֶל־פֶּתַח בֵּיתָהּ: פֶּן־תִּתֵּן לַאֲחֵרִים הוֹדֶךָ וּשְׁנֹתֶיךָ לְאַכְזָרִי:
י יא פֶּן־יִשְׂבְּעוּ זָרִים כֹּחֶךָ וַעֲצָבֶיךָ בְּבֵית נָכְרִי: וְנָהַמְתָּ בְאַחֲרִיתֶךָ בִּכְלוֹת
יב יג בְּשָׂרְךָ וּשְׁאֵרֶךָ: וְאָמַרְתָּ אֵיךְ שָׂנֵאתִי מוּסָר וְתוֹכַחַת נָאַץ לִבִּי: וְלֹא־
יד שָׁמַעְתִּי בְּקוֹל מוֹרָי וְלִמְלַמְּדַי לֹא־הִטִּיתִי אָזְנִי: כִּמְעַט הָיִיתִי בְכָל־רָע
טו טז בְּתוֹךְ קָהָל וְעֵדָה: שְׁתֵה־מַיִם מִבּוֹרֶךָ וְנֹזְלִים מִתּוֹךְ בְּאֵרֶךָ: יָפוּצוּ
יז מַעְיְנֹתֶיךָ חוּצָה בָּרְחֹבוֹת פַּלְגֵי־מָיִם: יִהְיוּ־לְךָ לְבַדֶּךָ וְאֵין לְזָרִים אִתָּךְ:
יח יט יְהִי־מְקוֹרְךָ בָרוּךְ וּשְׂמַח מֵאֵשֶׁת נְעוּרֶךָ: אַיֶּלֶת אֲהָבִים וְיַעֲלַת־חֵן ב
כ דַּדֶּיהָ יְרַוֻּךָ בְכָל־עֵת בְּאַהֲבָתָהּ תִּשְׁגֶּה תָמִיד: וְלָמָּה תִשְׁגֶּה בְנִי בְזָרָה
כא וּתְחַבֵּק חֵק נָכְרִיָּה: כִּי נֹכַח ׀ עֵינֵי יְהוָה דַּרְכֵי־אִישׁ וְכָל־מַעְגְּלֹתָיו
כב כג מְפַלֵּס: עֲווֹנֹתָיו יִלְכְּדֻנוֹ אֶת־הָרָשָׁע וּבְחַבְלֵי חַטָּאתוֹ יִתָּמֵךְ: הוּא
ו א יָמוּת בְּאֵין מוּסָר וּבְרֹב אִוַּלְתּוֹ יִשְׁגֶּה: בְּנִי אִם־עָרַבְתָּ לְרֵעֶךָ תָּקַעְתָּ
ב ג לַזָּר כַּפֶּיךָ: נוֹקַשְׁתָּ בְאִמְרֵי־פִיךָ נִלְכַּדְתָּ בְּאִמְרֵי־פִיךָ: עֲשֵׂה זֹאת
ד אֵפוֹא ׀ בְּנִי וְהִנָּצֵל כִּי בָאתָ בְכַף־רֵעֶךָ לֵךְ הִתְרַפֵּס וּרְהַב רֵעֶיךָ: אַל־

5 to sleep, nor your eyelids to slumber. Save yourself as would a deer from
the hunter's hand, as would a bird from the hand of the trapper.
6 7 Take note of the ant, lazy one; observe her ways and grow wise. She has
8 no captain, no overseer, and no commander, yet she prepares her bread
9 in the summer and stores up her food at harvest time. How long, lazy one,
10 will you lie idle? When will you get up from your sleep? A little sleep, a
11 little dozing, a little lying there with folded hands, and poverty will arrive
like a sudden intruder, privation like a soldier bearing a shield.
12 13 The knave, the schemer, he proceeds with a twisted mouth. He winks his
14 eyes, stomps his feet, signals with his fingers. Perversions are in his heart.
15 He plots evil at every opportunity. He incites strife. Therefore he will
suddenly meet his fate. Unexpectedly he will collapse, beyond cure.
16 Six there are that the Lord despises, and a seventh[8] which is anathema to
17 Him: haughty eyes, a false tongue, and hands that shed innocent blood;
18 a heart that devises wicked schemes; feet that hasten to race toward evil;
19 he who expresses deceptions, the false witness; and he who incites strife
20 among brothers. Guard, my son, your father's precepts; do not
21 forsake your mother's teachings. Bind them always within your heart;
22 wind them as an ornament around your neck. When you walk about, she
will guide you; when you lie down, she will watch over you; and when
23 you awake, she will converse with you. For the precept is like a lamp, the
teaching like light itself. The admonishments of instruction are the road
24 to life: to keep you away from the evil woman, from the smooth tongue
25 of the foreign woman. Do not lust for her beauty in your heart, and do
26 not let her entice you with her eyelids. Because, in exchange for a whore,
a man will yield his last loaf of bread, and a married woman will ensnare
27 even an honorable person. Can a man fetch fire in his lap and not burn
28 29 his clothing? Can a man walk on coals and not scorch his feet? So it is
with him who comes near his neighbor's wife; none who touches her will
30 remain unpunished. They do not abhor the thief who steals to satisfy his
31 hunger when he is starving. When discovered he might pay sevenfold and
32 even have to give away all his family's possessions. But the adulterer is a
33 mindless man; only one who wishes to destroy himself will do this. He
34 will find only illness and shame; his disgrace will never be erased. Envy
will stimulate the husband's wrath, so that he will show no pity in the day
35 of vengeance. He will accept no ransom whatsoever and will not consent
7 1 to your most excessive bribe. My son, guard my words, and keep
2 my precepts close to you. Guard my precepts and live – my teachings as
3 you would the pupil of your eyes. Bind them upon your fingers; inscribe
4 them upon the tablet of your heart. Say to Wisdom, "You are my sister!"
5 and call understanding a kinsman. This will protect you from the strange

---

8 | The formulations "six ... and a seventh" and "three ... and a fourth" are familiar mnemonic devices; cf., e.g., 30:15; Amos, chapters 1–2.

ה תתן שנה לעיניך ותנומה לעפעפיך: הנצל כצבי מיד וכצפור מיד
יקוש:
ו ז לך־אל־נמלה עצל ראה דרכיה וחכם: אשר אין־לה קצין שטר
ח ט ומשל: תכין בקיץ לחמה אגרה בקציר מאכלה: עד־מתי עצל ׀
י תשכב מתי תקום משנתך: מעט שנות מעט תנומות מעט ׀ חבק
יא ידים לשכב: ובא־כמהלך ראשך ומחסרך כאיש מגן:
יב יג אדם בליעל איש און הולך עקשות פה: קרץ בעינו מלל ברגלו
יד מרה באצבעתיו: תהפכות ׀ בלבו חרש רע בכל־עת מדנים ישלח: מדינים
טו על־כן פתאם יבוא אידו פתע ישבר ואין מרפא:
טז יז שש־הנה שנא יהוה ושבע תועבות נפשו: עינים רמות לשון תועבת
יח שקר וידים שפכות דם־נקי: לב חרש מחשבות און רגלים
יט ממהרות לרוץ לרעה: יפיח כזבים עד שקר ומשלח מדנים בין
כ אחים: נצר בני מצות אביך ואל־תטש תורת אמך:
כא כב קשרם על־לבך תמיד ענדם על־גרגרתך: בהתהלכך ׀ תנחה אתך
כג בשכבך תשמר עליך והקיצות היא תשיחך: כי נר מצוה ותורה אור
כד ודרך חיים תוכחות מוסר: לשמרך מאשת רע מחלקת לשון נכריה:
כה כו אל־תחמד יפיה בלבבך ואל־תקחך בעפעפיה: כי בעד־אשה זונה
כז עד־ככר לחם ואשת איש נפש יקרה תצוד: היחתה איש אש בחיקו
כח ובגדיו לא תשרפנה: אם־יהלך איש על־הגחלים ורגליו לא תכוינה:
כט ל כן הבא אל־אשת רעהו לא ינקה כל־הנגע בה: לא־יבוזו לגנב כי
לא יגנוב למלא נפשו כי ירעב: ונמצא ישלם שבעתים את־כל־הון ביתו
לב לג יתן: נאף אשה חסר־לב משחית נפשו הוא יעשנה: נגע־וקלון ימצא
לד לה וחרפתו לא תמחה: כי־קנאה חמת־גבר ולא־יחמול ביום נקם: לא־
ז א ישא פני כל־כפר ולא־יאבה כי תרבה־שחד: בני
ב שמר אמרי ומצותי תצפן אתך: שמר מצותי וחיה ותורתי כאישון
ג ד עיניך: קשרם על־אצבעתיך כתבם על־לוח לבך: אמר לחכמה
ה אחתי את ומדע לבינה תקרא: לשמרך מאשה זרה מנכריה אמריה

6 woman, the exotic woman who smooths her words.[9] From the window of
7 my home, through the lattice I peered. I saw among a group of innocents,
8 I discerned among the youngsters a mindless lad. He was passing through
the marketplace near her corner, marching along the road to her home –
9 10 in the dimness of dusk, in the darkness of nightfall, pitch-black. Suddenly
a woman stands opposite him; she poses as a harlot with seductive intent.
11 12 She is wild and wanton; her feet do not stay put in her own home. One
time outside the city, another time in the city squares, she lurks near every
13 14 corner. She seizes him, kisses him, and brazenly says to him: "I owed a
15 sacrificial peace offering; today I fulfilled my vow.[10] That is why I went out
16 toward you, to search for you, and I found you! I spread my couch with
17 quilts woven from Egyptian linen cords. I have perfumed my bed with
18 myrrh, aloes, and cinnamon. Come, let us gratify our lust until dawn;
19 let us make love playfully. For the man of the house is not home; he has
20 gone far away on the road. He took with him a purse filled with silver; he
21 will not return home until the full moon." She has misled him with her
22 countless persuasions; with her smooth lips she has led him astray. He
follows her unwittingly; he comes like an ox to the slaughter, prancing
23 into a halter until an arrow pierces his liver. He is like a bird rushing to
the trap, unaware that his life is at stake.
24 25 Now, sons, hear me; listen well to the words of my mouth. Let your
26 heart not stray toward her ways; do not wander into her paths, for she
27 has turned many into corpses, and numerous are her victims. Her home
8 1 is on the way to Sheol, descending to the chambers of death. Does not
2 wisdom call out; does not understanding raise her voice? Atop high
3 places, at the roadside, by the house at the crossroads she stands. Beside
the gates, at the city's entry, at the entrance to the portals she sings
4 5 out. To you, gentlemen, I call. I raise my voice to all humanity. Let the
ignorant understand prudence; let fools bring understanding to their
6 hearts. Hear me, for I speak noble words, and my lips open with words
7 of rectitude. My palate pronounces truth; wickedness is anathema to
8 my lips. In righteousness are spoken all the words of my mouth; there is
9 neither crookedness nor distortion in them. They are all convincing to
the contemplative person; they are accurate for those who would find
10 knowledge. Accept my instruction, not silver; accept knowledge rather
11 than refined gold. For wisdom is better than pearls; all prized possessions
12 do not compare to her. I, Wisdom, reside with cleverness; I have achieved
13 the ability to think ahead. Fear of the LORD is hatred of evil: arrogance,
14 pride, and the path of wrongdoing. I despise a perverse mouth. Counsel
and guidance are mine. I am the essence of understanding. Courage is
15 16 mine. By me do kings reign, and chieftains legislate righteousness. By

---

9 | A married woman seeking to seduce a young man.

10 | Therefore she has meat for a meal to which she invites the lad.

ו ז החליקה: כי בחלון ביתי בעד אשנבי נשקפתי: וארא בפתאים
ח אבינה בבנים נער חסר־לב: עבר בשוק אצל פנה ודרך ביתה יצעד:
ט י בנשף־בערב יום באישון לילה ואפלה: והנה אשה לקראתו שית
יא יב זונה ונצרת לב: המיה היא וסררת בביתה לא־ישכנו רגליה: פעם ׀
יג בחוץ פעם ברחבות ואצל כל־פנה תארב: והחזיקה בו ונשקה לו
יד טו העזה פניה ותאמר לו: זבחי שלמים עלי היום שלמתי נדרי: על־
טז כן יצאתי לקראתך לשחר פניך ואמצאך: מרבדים רבדתי ערשי
יז יח חטבות אטון מצרים: נפתי משכבי מר אהלים וקנמון: לכה נרוה
יט דדים עד־הבקר נתעלסה באהבים: כי אין האיש בביתו הלך בדרך
כ כא מרחוק: צרור־הכסף לקח בידו ליום הכסא יבא ביתו: הטתו ברב
כב לקחה בחלק שפתיה תדיחנו: הולך אחריה פתאם כשור אל־טבח
כג יבא וכעכס אל־מוסר אויל: עד יפלח חץ כבדו כמהר צפור אל־פח
ולא־ידע כי־בנפשו הוא:
כד כה ועתה בנים שמעו־לי והקשיבו לאמרי־פי: אל־ישט אל־דרכיה
כו לבך אל־תתע בנתיבותיה: כי־רבים חללים הפילה ועצמים כל־
ח כז א הרגיה: דרכי שאול ביתה ירדות אל־חדרי־מות: הלא־חכמה
ב תקרא ותבונה תתן קולה: בראש־מרמים עלי־דרך בית נתיבות
ג ד נצבה: ליד־שערים לפי־קרת מבוא פתחים תרנה: אליכם אישים
ה אקרא וקולי אל־בני אדם: הבינו פתאים ערמה וכסילים הבינו לב:
ו ז שמעו כי־נגידים אדבר ומפתח שפתי מישרים: כי־אמת יהגה חכי
ח ותועבת שפתי רשע: בצדק כל־אמרי־פי אין בהם נפתל ועקש:
ט י כלם נכחים למבין וישרים למצאי דעת: קחו־מוסרי ואל־כסף ודעת
יא מחרוץ נבחר: כי־טובה חכמה מפנינים וכל־חפצים לא ישוו־בה:
יב יג אני־חכמה שכנתי ערמה ודעת מזמות אמצא: יראת יהוה שנאת
יד רע גאה וגאון ׀ ודרך רע ופי תהפכות שנאתי: לי־עצה ותושיה
טו טז אני בינה לי גבורה: בי מלכים ימלכו ורזנים יחקקו צדק: בי שרים

17 me do rulers rule, and noblemen: all who judge righteously. I will love
18 those who love me. Those who search for me will surely find me. Wealth
19 and honor are with me, abundant riches rightfully obtained. My fruit is
20 better than the finest gold, my produce better than refined silver. On the
21 path of righteousness will I walk among the ways of justice. To bequeath
substance to those whom I love, I will fill their storehouses.
22 The Lord created me at the beginning of His path before His other deeds
23 long ago. From eternity I was formed, from the start, from the earliest
24 times on earth. When there were yet no depths, I was born, when there
25 were yet no wellsprings heavy with water. Before the mountains were
26 set down, before the hills I was born: when He had not yet made land
27 and outdoors, nor the beginning of the world's soil. As He firmed up the
heavens, there I was: when He engraved the horizon on the surface of
28 the deep, when He fortified the clouds up above, when strengthening
29 the fountains of the deep, when He set for the sea its limits so that water
would not transgress His command, when He carved out the earth's
30 foundations, I was a disciple by His side. I became a source of delight
31 day by day, bringing pleasure to Him all the time, bringing pleasure to the
world, His land, and my delight to all humanity.
32 33 Now, children, hear me. Fortunate are those who keep to my path. Obey
34 my instruction and become wise; do not disregard it. Fortunate is the
person who heeds me, persisting at my doors day by day, staying at the
35 doorposts of my doorways. For he who finds me finds life and gains favor
36 from the Lord. But he who turns away from me deprives himself; all who
hate me love death.
9 1 2 Wisdom built her house; she sculpted its pillars, seven of them. She
3 prepared a feast of meat, mixed her wine, and even set her table. She
sent her maidservants to call out from the ramparts upon the heights of
4 the city: "Whoever is ignorant, let him turn here." And to the mindless
5 one she said: "Come, partake of my bread and drink the wine that I
6 have mixed. Abandon ignorance and live well. Walk down the road to
7 understanding." He who preaches to a scoffer gains shame for himself;
8 the same goes for someone who rebukes a wicked person for his fault. Do
not rebuke a scoffer lest he hate you; rebuke a wise man, and he will love
9 you. Teach a wise man, and he will become yet wiser; inform a righteous
10 person, and he will add to his learning. The prerequisite for wisdom is
fear of the Lord; knowledge of the Holy One leads to understanding.
11 For through me you will increase your days, and years will be added to
12 your life. If you become wise, your wisdom will benefit you, but if you
13 scoff, you will suffer alone. The foolish woman squawks nonsense; she
14 knows nothing. She sits by the doorway of her house or upon a seat on
15 the city's heights to call out to passersby who walk along straight paths:
16 "Whoever is ignorant, let him turn aside here." The mindless one, she says

יז יָשֹׂרוּ וּנְדִיבִים כׇּל־שֹׁפְטֵי צֶדֶק׃ אֲנִי אהביה אֵהָב וּמְשַׁחֲרַי יִמְצָאֻנְנִי׃ אֹהֲבַי
יח יט עֹשֶׁר־וְכָבוֹד אִתִּי הוֹן עָתֵק וּצְדָקָה׃ טוֹב פִּרְיִי מֵחָרוּץ וּמִפָּז וּתְבוּאָתִי
כ כא מִכֶּסֶף נִבְחָר׃ בְּאֹרַח־צְדָקָה אֲהַלֵּךְ בְּתוֹךְ נְתִיבוֹת מִשְׁפָּט׃ לְהַנְחִיל
אֹהֲבַי ׀ יֵשׁ וְאֹצְרֹתֵיהֶם אֲמַלֵּא׃
כב כג יְהוָה קָנָנִי רֵאשִׁית דַּרְכּוֹ קֶדֶם מִפְעָלָיו מֵאָז׃ מֵעוֹלָם נִסַּכְתִּי מֵרֹאשׁ
כד מִקַּדְמֵי־אָרֶץ׃ בְּאֵין־תְּהֹמוֹת חוֹלָלְתִּי בְּאֵין מַעְיָנוֹת נִכְבַּדֵּי־מָיִם׃
כה כו בְּטֶרֶם הָרִים הׇטְבָּעוּ לִפְנֵי גְבָעוֹת חוֹלָלְתִּי׃ עַד־לֹא עָשָׂה אֶרֶץ וְחוּצוֹת
כז וְרֹאשׁ עַפְרוֹת תֵּבֵל׃ בַּהֲכִינוֹ שָׁמַיִם שָׁם אָנִי בְּחוּקוֹ חוּג עַל־פְּנֵי תְהוֹם׃
כח כט בְּאַמְּצוֹ שְׁחָקִים מִמָּעַל בַּעֲזוֹז עִינוֹת תְּהוֹם׃ בְּשׂוּמוֹ לַיָּם ׀ חֻקּוֹ וּמַיִם
ל לֹא יַעַבְרוּ־פִיו בְּחוּקוֹ מוֹסְדֵי אָרֶץ׃ וָאֶהְיֶה אֶצְלוֹ אָמוֹן וָאֶהְיֶה
לא שַׁעֲשֻׁעִים יוֹם ׀ יוֹם מְשַׂחֶקֶת לְפָנָיו בְּכׇל־עֵת׃ מְשַׂחֶקֶת בְּתֵבֵל אַרְצוֹ
וְשַׁעֲשֻׁעַי אֶת־בְּנֵי אָדָם׃
לב לג וְעַתָּה בָנִים שִׁמְעוּ־לִי וְאַשְׁרֵי דְּרָכַי יִשְׁמֹרוּ׃ שִׁמְעוּ מוּסָר וַחֲכָמוּ וְאַל־
לד תִּפְרָעוּ׃ אַשְׁרֵי אָדָם שֹׁמֵעַ לִי לִשְׁקֹד עַל־דַּלְתֹתַי יוֹם ׀ יוֹם לִשְׁמֹר
לה לו מְזוּזֹת פְּתָחָי׃ כִּי מֹצְאִי מצאי חַיִּים וַיָּפֶק רָצוֹן מֵיְהוָה׃ וְחֹטְאִי חֹמֵס מָצָא
נַפְשׁוֹ כׇּל־מְשַׂנְאַי אָהֲבוּ מָוֶת׃
ט א ב חׇכְמוֹת בָּנְתָה בֵיתָהּ חָצְבָה עַמּוּדֶיהָ שִׁבְעָה׃ טָבְחָה טִבְחָהּ מָסְכָה
ג יֵינָהּ אַף עָרְכָה שֻׁלְחָנָהּ׃ שָׁלְחָה נַעֲרֹתֶיהָ תִקְרָא עַל־גַּפֵּי מְרֹמֵי קָרֶת׃
ד ה מִי־פֶתִי יָסֻר הֵנָּה חֲסַר־לֵב אָמְרָה לּוֹ׃ לְכוּ לַחֲמוּ בְלַחֲמִי וּשְׁתוּ בְּיַיִן
ו ז מָסָכְתִּי׃ עִזְבוּ פְתָאיִם וִחְיוּ וְאִשְׁרוּ בְּדֶרֶךְ בִּינָה׃ יֹסֵר ׀ לֵץ לֹקֵחַ לוֹ
ח קָלוֹן וּמוֹכִיחַ לְרָשָׁע מוּמוֹ׃ אַל־תּוֹכַח לֵץ פֶּן־יִשְׂנָאֶךָּ הוֹכַח לְחָכָם
ט י וְיֶאֱהָבֶךָּ׃ תֵּן לְחָכָם וְיֶחְכַּם־עוֹד הוֹדַע לְצַדִּיק וְיוֹסֶף לֶקַח׃ תְּחִלַּת
יא חׇכְמָה יִרְאַת יְהוָה וְדַעַת קְדֹשִׁים בִּינָה׃ כִּי־בִי יִרְבּוּ יָמֶיךָ וְיוֹסִיפוּ ג
יב יג לְךָ שְׁנוֹת חַיִּים׃ אִם־חָכַמְתָּ חָכַמְתָּ לָּךְ וְלַצְתָּ לְבַדְּךָ תִשָּׂא׃ אֵשֶׁת
יד כְּסִילוּת הֹמִיָּה פְּתַיּוּת וּבַל־יָדְעָה מָּה׃ וְיָשְׁבָה לְפֶתַח בֵּיתָהּ עַל־כִּסֵּא
טו טז מְרֹמֵי קָרֶת׃ לִקְרֹא לְעֹבְרֵי־דָרֶךְ הַמְיַשְּׁרִים אֹרְחוֹתָם׃ מִי־פֶתִי יָסֻר

17 to him: "Stolen waters are sweet, and bread eaten secretly is pleasant."
18 He is unaware that the spirits of the dead are there; those to whom she
beckons are in Sheol's depths.
10 1 The proverbs of Shlomo: A wise son brings joy to his father; a foolish son
2 is his mother's misery. Treasures achieved by wickedness are of no benefit,
3 but righteousness rescues anyone from death. The LORD will not allow
the righteous to go hungry, but He will deny the wicked what they crave.
4 A fraudulent scale causes poverty, but the hand of the diligent grows rich.
5 The intelligent son stores away in the summer, but the son who slumbers
6 at harvest time brings shame. Blessings envelop the head of the righteous,
7 but lawlessness covers the mouth of the wicked. The mention of the
8 righteous is a blessing, but the name of the wicked will rot. The wise of
heart will seize precepts, but the foolish of lips will become bewildered.
9 He who walks in perfectness will walk securely, but whoever makes his
10 ways crooked will be crushed. He who winks his eye begets heartbreak,
11 and the foolish of lips will become bewildered. The mouth of the righteous
12 is a fount of life, but lawlessness covers the mouth of the wicked. Hatred
13 awakens disputes, but love covers over all wrongs. Wisdom is found on
the lips of the intelligent man, but a rod is for the back of a mindless man.
14 The wise conserve their knowledge, but the mouth of the fool is a disaster
15 in the making. The rich man considers his wealth his city of strength;
16 poverty is the poor man's disaster. The righteous man's wages lead to life;
17 the produce of the wicked leads to want. The path to life is for the one
18 who heeds instruction; he who shuns a rebuke misleads himself. He who
19 conceals enmity has lying lips; he who spreads slander is a fool. With too
many words, no one can avoid wrongdoing. He who restrains his lips is
20 intelligent. The righteous man's tongue is like refined silver; the heart of
21 the wicked is of little worth. The lips of the righteous sustain a multitude,
22 but fools die because of their mindlessness. It is the LORD's blessing
23 that enriches; it is not accompanied by disappointment. For the fool,
immorality is but play, but wisdom is play for the man of intelligence.
24 That which the wicked man dreads will befall him, but He will grant the
25 righteous their desire. As a sudden storm passes, so is the wicked man
26 gone, but the righteous man stands firm forever. Like vinegar to the teeth
and smoke to the eyes, so is the lazy man to those who commission him.
27 Fear of the LORD increases a person's days, but the years of the wicked are
28 shortened. The righteous can look forward to joy, but the hope of the
29 wicked is lost. The LORD's way is a sanctuary of strength for the innocent,
30 but it is a disaster for those who wreak evil. The righteous man will never
31 ever falter, but the wicked will not long dwell on earth. The mouth of the
32 righteous will utter wisdom, but the perverse tongue will be severed. The
lips of the righteous know to win favor, but the mouths of the wicked
11 1 know only perversity. False scales are anathema to the LORD; an accurate

יז הֵנָּה וַחֲסַר־לֵב וְאָמְרָה לּוֹ: מַיִם־גְּנוּבִים יִמְתָּקוּ וְלֶחֶם סְתָרִים יִנְעָם:
יח וְלֹא־יָדַע כִּי־רְפָאִים שָׁם בְּעִמְקֵי שְׁאוֹל קְרֻאֶיהָ:
י א ב מִשְׁלֵי שְׁלֹמֹה בֵּן חָכָם יְשַׂמַּח־אָב וּבֵן כְּסִיל תּוּגַת אִמּוֹ: לֹא־יוֹעִילוּ
ג אוֹצְרוֹת רֶשַׁע וּצְדָקָה תַּצִּיל מִמָּוֶת: לֹא־יַרְעִיב יְהוָה נֶפֶשׁ צַדִּיק וְהַוַּת
ד ה רְשָׁעִים יֶהְדֹּף: רָאשׁ עֹשֶׂה כַף־רְמִיָּה וְיַד חָרוּצִים תַּעֲשִׁיר: אֹגֵר בַּקַּיִץ
ו בֵּן מַשְׂכִּיל נִרְדָּם בַּקָּצִיר בֵּן מֵבִישׁ: בְּרָכוֹת לְרֹאשׁ צַדִּיק וּפִי רְשָׁעִים
ז ח יְכַסֶּה חָמָס: זֵכֶר צַדִּיק לִבְרָכָה וְשֵׁם רְשָׁעִים יִרְקָב: חֲכַם־לֵב יִקַּח
ט מִצְוֹת וֶאֱוִיל שְׂפָתַיִם יִלָּבֵט: הוֹלֵךְ בַּתֹּם יֵלֶךְ בֶּטַח וּמְעַקֵּשׁ דְּרָכָיו
י יא יִוָּדֵעַ: קֹרֵץ עַיִן יִתֵּן עַצָּבֶת וֶאֱוִיל שְׂפָתַיִם יִלָּבֵט: מְקוֹר חַיִּים פִּי צַדִּיק
יב וּפִי רְשָׁעִים יְכַסֶּה חָמָס: שִׂנְאָה תְּעוֹרֵר מְדָנִים וְעַל כָּל־פְּשָׁעִים תְּכַסֶּה
יג יד אַהֲבָה: בְּשִׂפְתֵי נָבוֹן תִּמָּצֵא חָכְמָה וְשֵׁבֶט לְגֵו חֲסַר־לֵב: חֲכָמִים
טו יִצְפְּנוּ־דָעַת וּפִי־אֱוִיל מְחִתָּה קְרֹבָה: הוֹן עָשִׁיר קִרְיַת עֻזּוֹ מְחִתַּת
טז יז דַּלִּים רֵישָׁם: פְּעֻלַּת צַדִּיק לְחַיִּים תְּבוּאַת רָשָׁע לְחַטָּאת: אֹרַח לְחַיִּים
יח שׁוֹמֵר מוּסָר וְעוֹזֵב תּוֹכַחַת מַתְעֶה: מְכַסֶּה שִׂנְאָה שִׂפְתֵי־שָׁקֶר וּמוֹצִא
יט דִבָּה הוּא כְסִיל: בְּרֹב דְּבָרִים לֹא יֶחְדַּל־פָּשַׁע וְחֹשֵׂךְ שְׂפָתָיו מַשְׂכִּיל:
כ כא כֶּסֶף נִבְחָר לְשׁוֹן צַדִּיק לֵב רְשָׁעִים כִּמְעָט: שִׂפְתֵי צַדִּיק יִרְעוּ רַבִּים
כב וֶאֱוִילִים בַּחֲסַר־לֵב יָמוּתוּ: בִּרְכַּת יְהוָה הִיא תַעֲשִׁיר וְלֹא־יוֹסִף עֶצֶב
כג כד עִמָּהּ: כִּשְׂחוֹק לִכְסִיל עֲשׂוֹת זִמָּה וְחָכְמָה לְאִישׁ תְּבוּנָה: מְגוֹרַת
כה רָשָׁע הִיא תְבוֹאֶנּוּ וְתַאֲוַת צַדִּיקִים יִתֵּן: כַּעֲבוֹר סוּפָה וְאֵין רָשָׁע
כו וְצַדִּיק יְסוֹד עוֹלָם: כַּחֹמֶץ ׀ לַשִּׁנַּיִם וְכֶעָשָׁן לָעֵינָיִם כֵּן הֶעָצֵל לְשֹׁלְחָיו:
כז כח יִרְאַת יְהוָה תּוֹסִיף יָמִים וּשְׁנוֹת רְשָׁעִים תִּקְצֹרְנָה: תּוֹחֶלֶת צַדִּיקִים
כט שִׂמְחָה וְתִקְוַת רְשָׁעִים תֹּאבֵד: מָעוֹז לַתֹּם דֶּרֶךְ יְהוָה וּמְחִתָּה לְפֹעֲלֵי
ל לא אָוֶן: צַדִּיק לְעוֹלָם בַּל־יִמּוֹט וּרְשָׁעִים לֹא יִשְׁכְּנוּ־אָרֶץ: פִּי־צַדִּיק
לב יָנוּב חָכְמָה וּלְשׁוֹן תַּהְפֻּכוֹת תִּכָּרֵת: שִׂפְתֵי צַדִּיק יֵדְעוּן רָצוֹן וּפִי
יא א רְשָׁעִים תַּהְפֻּכוֹת: מֹאזְנֵי מִרְמָה תּוֹעֲבַת יְהוָה וְאֶבֶן שְׁלֵמָה רְצוֹנוֹ:

2 weight is His desire. When arrogance comes, then comes disgrace, but
3 with modest men comes wisdom. The integrity of the upright guides
4 them, but the deviance of the treacherous ruins them. Wealth will not
help on the day of wrath, but righteousness rescues anyone from death.
5 The righteousness of the blameless man will make straight his ways; the
6 wicked man will fall by his own wickedness. The righteousness of upright
men saves them, but treacherous men are ensnared in their own mischief.
7 Hope is gone with the death of a wicked man; the sinner's expectation
8 comes to naught. The righteous man is rescued from woe; the wicked
9 man suffers in his stead. The liar destroys his fellow with his mouth, but
10 the righteous will be rescued through their knowledge. When it goes well
for the righteous, the city rejoices; with the downfall of the wicked, there
11 is song. By the blessing of the upright the city is uplifted; by the mouth
12 of the wicked it is ruined. A mindless man degrades his neighbor; a man
13 of discretion remains silent. The talebearer reveals secrets; the trustworthy
14 spirit conceals the matter. Without strategies a people falls; salvation
15 stems from abundant counsel. Broken is the person who guaranteed a
16 loan for a stranger, while a person who detests pledges is secure. A
17 compassionate woman seizes honor; ruthless men seize wealth. A kind
18 man does himself good, but a cruel man tears his own flesh. The wicked
man earns false wages, while he who sows righteousness earns a true
19 reward. Truly, righteousness assures life, but he who pursues evil ensures
20 his own death. The crooked of heart are anathema to the Lord; His
21 pleasure is in those whose ways are blameless. The wicked person will not
be forgiven, even for a moment, but even the descendants of the righteous
22 will be spared. Like a golden ring in a pig's snout is a beautiful woman
23 who lacks sense. The righteous desire only good; the wicked can hope
24 only for wrath. Some give freely and gain more thereby; others refrain
25 from generosity only to suffer loss. He who is himself a blessing will
26 prosper; someone who sustains others, he too will be sustained. The
nation will curse the one who withholds grain, but blessing will come
27 upon the head of the one who provides. He who searches for the good
28 seeks favor; he who pursues evil, evil will befall him. He who trusts in his
29 wealth will fall, but the righteous will flourish like a leaf. He who neglects
his family inherits the wind; the fool becomes a slave to the wise of heart.
30 The fruit of the righteous is a tree of life; he who draws others to him is
31 wise. If the righteous person is repaid on earth, certainly the wicked and
12 1 the sinner will be. The lover of instruction loves knowledge; he who
2 despises rebuke remains ignorant. The good man obtains favor from the
3 Lord; the scheming man corrupts others. A man cannot endure in
4 wickedness, but the righteous man's roots will not be shaken. A meritorious
woman is her husband's crown; a vulgar woman is like rot in his bones.
5 The thoughts of the righteous are of justice; the plans of the wicked are

ב ג בָּא־זָדוֹן וַיָּבֹא קָלוֹן וְאֶת־צְנוּעִים חׇכְמָה׃ תֻּמַּת יְשָׁרִים תַּנְחֵם וְסֶלֶף
ד ה בֹּגְדִים ושדם׃ לֹא־יוֹעִיל הוֹן בְּיוֹם עֶבְרָה וּצְדָקָה תַּצִּיל מִמָּוֶת׃ צִדְקַת יְשָׁדֵּם
ו תָּמִים תְּיַשֵּׁר דַּרְכּוֹ וּבְרִשְׁעָתוֹ יִפֹּל רָשָׁע׃ צִדְקַת יְשָׁרִים תַּצִּילֵם וּבְהַוַּת
ז בֹּגְדִים יִלָּכֵדוּ׃ בְּמוֹת אָדָם רָשָׁע תֹּאבַד תִּקְוָה וְתוֹחֶלֶת אוֹנִים אָבָדָה׃
ח ט צַדִּיק מִצָּרָה נֶחֱלָץ וַיָּבֹא רָשָׁע תַּחְתָּיו׃ בְּפֶה חָנֵף יַשְׁחִת רֵעֵהוּ וּבְדַעַת
י צַדִּיקִים יֵחָלֵצוּ׃ בְּטוּב צַדִּיקִים תַּעֲלֹץ קִרְיָה וּבַאֲבֹד רְשָׁעִים רִנָּה׃
יא יב בְּבִרְכַּת יְשָׁרִים תָּרוּם קָרֶת וּבְפִי רְשָׁעִים תֵּהָרֵס׃ בָּז־לְרֵעֵהוּ חֲסַר־
יג לֵב וְאִישׁ תְּבוּנוֹת יַחֲרִישׁ׃ הוֹלֵךְ רָכִיל מְגַלֶּה־סּוֹד וְנֶאֱמַן־רוּחַ מְכַסֶּה
יד טו דָבָר׃ בְּאֵין תַּחְבֻּלוֹת יִפׇּל־עָם וּתְשׁוּעָה בְּרֹב יוֹעֵץ׃ רַע־יֵרוֹעַ כִּי־עָרַב
טז זָר וְשֹׂנֵא תֹקְעִים בּוֹטֵחַ׃ אֵשֶׁת־חֵן תִּתְמֹךְ כָּבוֹד וְעָרִיצִים יִתְמְכוּ־
יז יח עֹשֶׁר׃ גֹּמֵל נַפְשׁוֹ אִישׁ חָסֶד וְעֹכֵר שְׁאֵרוֹ אַכְזָרִי׃ רָשָׁע עֹשֶׂה פְעֻלַּת־
יט שָׁקֶר וְזֹרֵעַ צְדָקָה שֶׂכֶר אֱמֶת׃ כֵּן־צְדָקָה לְחַיִּים וּמְרַדֵּף רָעָה לְמוֹתוֹ׃
כ כא תּוֹעֲבַת יְהוָה עִקְּשֵׁי־לֵב וּרְצוֹנוֹ תְּמִימֵי דָרֶךְ׃ יָד לְיָד לֹא־יִנָּקֶה רָּע
כב וְזֶרַע צַדִּיקִים נִמְלָט׃ נֶזֶם זָהָב בְּאַף חֲזִיר אִשָּׁה יָפָה וְסָרַת טָעַם׃
כג כד תַּאֲוַת צַדִּיקִים אַךְ־טוֹב תִּקְוַת רְשָׁעִים עֶבְרָה׃ יֵשׁ מְפַזֵּר וְנוֹסָף עוֹד
כה וְחוֹשֵׂךְ מִיֹּשֶׁר אַךְ־לְמַחְסוֹר׃ נֶפֶשׁ־בְּרָכָה תְדֻשָּׁן וּמַרְוֶה גַּם־הוּא יוֹרֶא׃
כו כז מֹנֵעַ בָּר יִקְּבֻהוּ לְאוֹם וּבְרָכָה לְרֹאשׁ מַשְׁבִּיר׃ שֹׁחֵר טוֹב יְבַקֵּשׁ רָצוֹן
כח וְדֹרֵשׁ רָעָה תְבוֹאֶנּוּ׃ בּוֹטֵחַ בְּעָשְׁרוֹ הוּא יִפֹּל וְכֶעָלֶה צַדִּיקִים יִפְרָחוּ׃
כט ל עוֹכֵר בֵּיתוֹ יִנְחַל־רוּחַ וְעֶבֶד אֱוִיל לַחֲכַם־לֵב׃ פְּרִי־צַדִּיק עֵץ חַיִּים וְלֹקֵחַ
יב לא א נְפָשׁוֹת חָכָם׃ הֵן צַדִּיק בָּאָרֶץ יְשֻׁלָּם אַף כִּי־רָשָׁע וְחוֹטֵא׃ אֹהֵב מוּסָר
ב אֹהֵב דָּעַת וְשֹׂנֵא תוֹכַחַת בָּעַר׃ טוֹב יָפִיק רָצוֹן מֵיְהוָה וְאִישׁ מְזִמּוֹת
ג ד יַרְשִׁיעַ׃ לֹא־יִכּוֹן אָדָם בְּרֶשַׁע וְשֹׁרֶשׁ צַדִּיקִים בַּל־יִמּוֹט׃ אֵשֶׁת־חַיִל
ה עֲטֶרֶת בַּעְלָהּ וּכְרָקָב בְּעַצְמוֹתָיו מְבִישָׁה׃ מַחְשְׁבוֹת צַדִּיקִים מִשְׁפָּט

6 of deceit. The words of the wicked are a deadly ambush, but the mouth
7 of the upright will save them. Turn over the wicked, and they are gone,
8 but the house of the righteous will stand. A man will be praised according
9 to his intelligence, but a twisted mind will be a mockery. Better the modest
10 person with a servant than the pretentious one who lacks bread. The
righteous man knows his beast's needs; the "compassion" of the wicked
11 is but cruelty. He who works his land will be sated with bread, but he
12 who trails idlers is mindless. The wicked person covets the bastion of evil
13 men, but the root of the righteous will bear fruit. In the treachery of lips
14 lurks a terrible pitfall; the righteous man avoids trouble. From the fruits
of a man's mouth he will be satisfied with good; the recompense of a
15 man's hands will come back to him. The fool's way is correct in his own
16 eyes, but the wise man heeds counsel. The fool's anger becomes known
17 in a day, but the clever man conceals his disgrace. One who breathes
faithfulness will testify truthfully, but a testimony of untruths is deceitful.
18 Some utter words like the stabs of a sword, but the tongue of the wise is
19 healing. Truthful speech endures forever, but lying language lasts but a
20 moment. Deceit is in the heart of those who plot evil, but for those who
21 counsel peace there is joy. No misfortune shall befall the righteous, but
22 the wicked are loaded with harm. Lying lips are anathema to the LORD,
23 but those who act in faithfulness do His wish. The clever man conceals
24 his knowledge; the heart of a fool proclaims nonsense. The hand of the
25 industrious will dominate; the indolent will be subservient. When worry
enters a man's heart, he should suppress it and gladden it with a good
26 word. The righteous man shows his fellow the way, but the way of the
27 wicked misleads them. The cheat has no time to singe his quarry, but
28 the wealth of an honorable man is earned by diligence. In the way of
righteousness is life; its path leads to immortality.
13 1 The wise son – the father's instruction. The scoffer – he heard no rebuke.
2 A man enjoys good from the fruits of his mouth; treacherous men enjoy
3 lawlessness. He who restrains his mouth protects himself; he who spreads
4 wide his lips prepares his downfall. The indolent person craves but has
5 nothing; the industrious soul will have plenty. The righteous man hates
6 falsehood; the wicked man defames and shames. Righteousness guards
7 the one whose way is blameless; wickedness perverts the sinner. Some
pretend to be wealthy but have nothing; others feign poverty but possess
8 great treasure. Wealth is a ransom for a man's life, but only if the poor man
9 hears no taunt. The light of the righteous glows; wicked men's candles
10 sputter. With arrogance comes strife; wisdom abides with those who take
11 counsel. Wealth achieved through duplicity dwindles; he who gathers
12 little by little will increase. Lengthy longing is a heartbreak; fulfilled
13 desire is a tree of life. He who despises a commandment will meet with
14 harm; he who reveres a precept will be at peace. The wise man's teaching

ו תַּחְבֻּלוֹת רְשָׁעִים מִרְמָה: דִּבְרֵי רְשָׁעִים אֱרׇב־דָּם וּפִי יְשָׁרִים יַצִּילֵם:
ז ח הָפוֹךְ רְשָׁעִים וְאֵינָם וּבֵית צַדִּיקִים יַעֲמֹד: לְפִי־שִׂכְלוֹ יְהֻלַּל־אִישׁ
ט וְנַעֲוֵה־לֵב יִהְיֶה לָבוּז: טוֹב נִקְלֶה וְעֶבֶד לוֹ מִמִּתְכַּבֵּד וַחֲסַר־לָחֶם:
י יא יוֹדֵעַ צַדִּיק נֶפֶשׁ בְּהֶמְתּוֹ וְרַחֲמֵי רְשָׁעִים אַכְזָרִי: עֹבֵד אַדְמָתוֹ יִשְׂבַּע־
יב לָחֶם וּמְרַדֵּף רֵיקִים חֲסַר־לֵב: חָמַד רָשָׁע מְצוֹד רָעִים וְשֹׁרֶשׁ צַדִּיקִים
יג יד יִתֵּן: בְּפֶשַׁע שְׂפָתַיִם מוֹקֵשׁ רָע וַיֵּצֵא מִצָּרָה צַדִּיק: מִפְּרִי פִי־אִישׁ
טו יִשְׂבַּע־טוֹב וּגְמוּל יְדֵי־אָדָם ישוב לוֹ: דֶּרֶךְ אֱוִיל יָשָׁר בְּעֵינָיו וְשֹׁמֵעַ יָשִׁיב
טז יז לְעֵצָה חָכָם: אֱוִיל בַּיּוֹם יִוָּדַע כַּעְסוֹ וְכֹסֶה קָלוֹן עָרוּם: יָפִיחַ אֱמוּנָה יַגִּיד
יח צֶדֶק וְעֵד שְׁקָרִים מִרְמָה: יֵשׁ בּוֹטֶה כְּמַדְקְרוֹת חָרֶב וּלְשׁוֹן חֲכָמִים
יט כ מַרְפֵּא: שְׂפַת־אֱמֶת תִּכּוֹן לָעַד וְעַד־אַרְגִּיעָה לְשׁוֹן שָׁקֶר: מִרְמָה
כא בְּלֶב־חֹרְשֵׁי רָע וּלְיֹעֲצֵי שָׁלוֹם שִׂמְחָה: לֹא־יְאֻנֶּה לַצַּדִּיק כׇּל־אָוֶן
כב וּרְשָׁעִים מָלְאוּ רָע: תּוֹעֲבַת יהוה שִׂפְתֵי־שָׁקֶר וְעֹשֵׂי אֱמוּנָה רְצוֹנוֹ:
כג כד אָדָם עָרוּם כֹּסֶה דָּעַת וְלֵב כְּסִילִים יִקְרָא אִוֶּלֶת: יַד־חָרוּצִים תִּמְשׁוֹל
כה כו וּרְמִיָּה תִּהְיֶה לָמַס: דְּאָגָה בְלֶב־אִישׁ יַשְׁחֶנָּה וְדָבָר טוֹב יְשַׂמְּחֶנָּה: יָתֵר
כז מֵרֵעֵהוּ צַדִּיק וְדֶרֶךְ רְשָׁעִים תַּתְעֵם: לֹא־יַחֲרֹךְ רְמִיָּה צֵידוֹ וְהוֹן־אָדָם
כח יָקָר חָרוּץ: בְּאֹרַח־צְדָקָה חַיִּים וְדֶרֶךְ נְתִיבָה אַל־מָוֶת:
יג א ב בֵּן חָכָם מוּסַר אָב וְלֵץ לֹא־שָׁמַע גְּעָרָה: מִפְּרִי פִי־אִישׁ יֹאכַל טוֹב
ג וְנֶפֶשׁ בֹּגְדִים חָמָס: נֹצֵר פִּיו שֹׁמֵר נַפְשׁוֹ פֹּשֵׂק שְׂפָתָיו מְחִתָּה־לוֹ:
ד ה מִתְאַוָּה וָאַיִן נַפְשׁוֹ עָצֵל וְנֶפֶשׁ חָרֻצִים תְּדֻשָּׁן: דְּבַר־שֶׁקֶר יִשְׂנָא צַדִּיק
ו וְרָשָׁע יַבְאִישׁ וְיַחְפִּיר: צְדָקָה תִּצֹּר תָּם־דָּרֶךְ וְרִשְׁעָה תְּסַלֵּף חַטָּאת:
ז ח יֵשׁ מִתְעַשֵּׁר וְאֵין כֹּל מִתְרוֹשֵׁשׁ וְהוֹן רָב: כֹּפֶר נֶפֶשׁ־אִישׁ עׇשְׁרוֹ וְרָשׁ
ט י לֹא־שָׁמַע גְּעָרָה: אוֹר־צַדִּיקִים יִשְׂמָח וְנֵר רְשָׁעִים יִדְעָךְ: רַק־בְּזָדוֹן
יא יִתֵּן מַצָּה וְאֶת־נוֹעָצִים חׇכְמָה: הוֹן מֵהֶבֶל יִמְעָט וְקֹבֵץ עַל־יָד יַרְבֶּה:
יב יג תּוֹחֶלֶת מְמֻשָּׁכָה מַחֲלָה־לֵב וְעֵץ חַיִּים תַּאֲוָה בָאָה: בָּז לְדָבָר יֵחָבֶל
יד לוֹ וִירֵא מִצְוָה הוּא יְשֻׁלָּם: תּוֹרַת חָכָם מְקוֹר חַיִּים לָסוּר מִמֹּקְשֵׁי

15 is a fount of life; it averts the snares of death. Good sense wins favor; the
16 way of the treacherous is unyielding. Every clever man acts thoughtfully;
17 a fool displays folly. The wicked messenger falls into trouble; the faithful
18 envoy delivers healing. Poverty and disgrace are for one who disregards
19 instruction, but whoever heeds rebuke will be honored. A gratified desire
20 is pleasant; the anathema of fools is to turn away from evil. He who walks
21 with the wise will become wise, but the companion of fools will fail. Evil
will pursue those steeped in sin; as for the righteous, He will repay them
22 with good. The good man bequeaths to his sons' sons, and the wealth of
23 the sinner is hidden away for the righteous. Abundant food may issue
from poor men's plowing, but many a field is barren because of improper
24 care. He who withholds the rod hates his child; he who loves him will
25 discipline him early. The righteous man eats till he is satisfied; the belly
14 1 of the wicked will want food. The wise among women builds her house;
2 the foolish woman tears it down with her own hands. He who follows
the correct path fears the LORD; the errant in his ways derides Him.
3 In the mouth of the fool is the staff of pride; the lips of the wise will
4 protect them. Without oxen the trough is bare; abundant grain requires
5 the ox's strength. A trustworthy witness does not lie; a false witness
6 breathes lies. The scoffer seeks wisdom but finds none, but knowledge
7 comes easily to the intelligent man. Stay far away from the foolish man;
8 otherwise, you will never know wise speech. The wisdom of the clever
man is that he considers his course; the folly of fools leads to delusion.
9 10 Fools discuss sinfulness; upright men, goodwill. The heart knows its own
11 bitterness; no outsider can share in its joy.[11] The house of the wicked will
12 be demolished; the tent of the upright will blossom. At times, the path
13 before a man seems straight, but it ends in paths of death. At times, even
14 laughter pains the heart, and joy ends in misery. The unrefined heart is
15 satisfied with his conduct, but the good man avoids him. The simpleton
16 believes everything; the clever man considers his footsteps. The wise man
fears God and averts evil; the fool assures himself and feels confident.
17 The short-tempered man will act foolishly; the schemer will be despised.
18 Simpletons inherit foolishness; the clever are crowned with knowledge.
19 Evil men will bow before good men; so too will the wicked at the gates
20 of the righteous. Even his neighbor will despise the pauper, but many are
21 the friends of the rich. He who derides his fellow is a sinner, but he who
22 shows favor to the lowly is fortunate. Surely those who plot evil will go
23 astray while those who plan good will find kindness and faithfulness. For
24 every manner of toil there is gain, but for mere talk there is only loss. The
25 wise wear their wealth as a crown, but the folly of fools is idiocy. A truthful
26 witness saves lives; he who breathes lies abets deceit. In fear of the LORD

---

11 | In other words, no one really knows what another person is feeling.

טו טז מָוֶת: שֵׂכֶל־טוֹב יִתֶּן־חֵן וְדֶרֶךְ בֹּגְדִים אֵיתָן: כָּל־עָרוּם יַעֲשֶׂה בְדָעַת
יז יח וּכְסִיל יִפְרֹשׂ אִוֶּלֶת: מַלְאָךְ רָשָׁע יִפֹּל בְּרָע וְצִיר אֱמוּנִים מַרְפֵּא: רֵישׁ
יט וְקָלוֹן פּוֹרֵעַ מוּסָר וְשׁוֹמֵר תּוֹכַחַת יְכֻבָּד: תַּאֲוָה נִהְיָה תֶּעֱרַב לְנָפֶשׁ
כ וְתוֹעֲבַת כְּסִילִים סוּר מֵרָע: הלוך אֶת־חֲכָמִים וחכם וְרֹעֶה כְסִילִים הוֹלֵךְ | יֶחְכָּם
כא כב יֵרוֹעַ: חַטָּאִים תְּרַדֵּף רָעָה וְאֶת־צַדִּיקִים יְשַׁלֶּם־טוֹב: טוֹב יַנְחִיל
כג בְּנֵי־בָנִים וְצָפוּן לַצַּדִּיק חֵיל חוֹטֵא: רָב־אֹכֶל נִיר רָאשִׁים וְיֵשׁ נִסְפֶּה
כד כה בְּלֹא מִשְׁפָּט: חוֹשֵׂךְ שִׁבְטוֹ שׂוֹנֵא בְנוֹ וְאֹהֲבוֹ שִׁחֲרוֹ מוּסָר: צַדִּיק
יד א אֹכֵל לְשֹׂבַע נַפְשׁוֹ וּבֶטֶן רְשָׁעִים תֶּחְסָר: חַכְמוֹת נָשִׁים בָּנְתָה בֵיתָהּ
ב וְאִוֶּלֶת בְּיָדֶיהָ תֶהֶרְסֶנּוּ: הוֹלֵךְ בְּיָשְׁרוֹ יְרֵא יְהוָה וּנְלוֹז דְּרָכָיו בּוֹזֵהוּ:
ג ד בְּפִי־אֱוִיל חֹטֶר גַּאֲוָה וְשִׂפְתֵי חֲכָמִים תִּשְׁמוּרֵם: בְּאֵין אֲלָפִים אֵבוּס ד
ה בָּר וְרָב־תְּבוּאוֹת בְּכֹחַ שׁוֹר: עֵד אֱמוּנִים לֹא יְכַזֵּב וְיָפִיחַ כְּזָבִים עֵד
ו ז שָׁקֶר: בִּקֶּשׁ־לֵץ חָכְמָה וָאָיִן וְדַעַת לְנָבוֹן נָקָל: לֵךְ מִנֶּגֶד לְאִישׁ כְּסִיל
ח וּבַל־יָדַעְתָּ שִׂפְתֵי־דָעַת: חָכְמַת עָרוּם הָבִין דַּרְכּוֹ וְאִוֶּלֶת כְּסִילִים
ט י מִרְמָה: אֱוִלִים יָלִיץ אָשָׁם וּבֵין יְשָׁרִים רָצוֹן: לֵב יוֹדֵעַ מָרַּת נַפְשׁוֹ
יא וּבְשִׂמְחָתוֹ לֹא־יִתְעָרַב זָר: בֵּית רְשָׁעִים יִשָּׁמֵד וְאֹהֶל יְשָׁרִים יַפְרִיחַ:
יב יג יֵשׁ דֶּרֶךְ יָשָׁר לִפְנֵי־אִישׁ וְאַחֲרִיתָהּ דַּרְכֵי־מָוֶת: גַּם־בִּשְׂחוֹק יִכְאַב־לֵב
יד וְאַחֲרִיתָהּ שִׂמְחָה תוּגָה: מִדְּרָכָיו יִשְׂבַּע סוּג לֵב וּמֵעָלָיו אִישׁ טוֹב:
טו טז פֶּתִי יַאֲמִין לְכָל־דָּבָר וְעָרוּם יָבִין לַאֲשֻׁרוֹ: חָכָם יָרֵא וְסָר מֵרָע וּכְסִיל
יז יח מִתְעַבֵּר וּבוֹטֵחַ: קְצַר־אַפַּיִם יַעֲשֶׂה אִוֶּלֶת וְאִישׁ מְזִמּוֹת יִשָּׂנֵא: נָחֲלוּ
יט פְתָאיִם אִוֶּלֶת וַעֲרוּמִים יַכְתִּרוּ דָעַת: שַׁחוּ רָעִים לִפְנֵי טוֹבִים וּרְשָׁעִים
כ כא עַל־שַׁעֲרֵי צַדִּיק: גַּם־לְרֵעֵהוּ יִשָּׂנֵא רָשׁ וְאֹהֲבֵי עָשִׁיר רַבִּים: בָּז־
כב לְרֵעֵהוּ חוֹטֵא וּמְחוֹנֵן עניים אַשְׁרָיו: הֲלוֹא־יִתְעוּ חֹרְשֵׁי רָע וְחֶסֶד עֲנָוִים
כג וֶאֱמֶת חֹרְשֵׁי טוֹב: בְּכָל־עֶצֶב יִהְיֶה מוֹתָר וּדְבַר־שְׂפָתַיִם אַךְ־לְמַחְסוֹר:
כד כה עֲטֶרֶת חֲכָמִים עָשְׁרָם אִוֶּלֶת כְּסִילִים אִוֶּלֶת: מַצִּיל נְפָשׁוֹת עֵד אֱמֶת
כו וְיָפִחַ כְּזָבִים מִרְמָה: בְּיִרְאַת יְהוָה מִבְטַח־עֹז וּלְבָנָיו יִהְיֶה מַחְסֶה:

there is a fortress of strength; even a devout man's children will find a
27 28 refuge. Fear of the LORD is a fount of life; it averts the snares of death. A
large population is a king's grandeur; the lack of subjects is a disaster for
29 the ruler. Patience leads to great knowledge, but impatience promotes
30 31 folly. A healing heart bring life to the flesh; envy is rot in the bones. He
who oppresses the poor blasphemes his Maker; the one who shows pity to
32 the pauper honors Him. The wicked man is felled by his wickedness; the
33 righteous man finds refuge even in his death. In the heart of the intelligent
34 man wisdom rests quietly; among fools it makes noise. Righteousness
exalts a nation, and the kindness of peoples is a purification offering.
35 A king shows favor to a capable servant, but he shows his wrath to one
15 1 who causes shame. A gentle response dispels wrath; a worrisome word
2 provokes anger. The tongue of the wise enhances knowledge; the mouths
3 of fools spout folly. The eyes of the LORD are everywhere, watching both
4 the evil and the good. A healing tongue is a tree of life; a distortion in
5 it makes for a broken spirit. The fool repels his father's instruction; he
6 who heeds rebuke grows clever. In the house of the righteous there is
7 great treasure; in the wicked man's crop there is ruin. The lips of the wise
8 disseminate knowledge; not so the hearts of fools. Wicked men's offerings
9 are anathema to the LORD; the prayer of the upright is His desire. The
way of the wicked is anathema to the LORD; He loves the pursuer of
10 righteousness. Instruction is harsh for anyone who forsakes the path; he
11 who hates rebuke shall perish. Sheol and the netherworld are open before
12 the LORD; how much more so are the hearts of humans. The scoffer
13 dislikes receiving rebuke; he will not call upon the wise. A happy heart
14 cheers the face; with a sad heart comes a crushed spirit. The heart of the
intelligent man seeks knowledge; the mouth of a fool keeps company with
15 folly. The poor man is miserable every day, but the contented heart feasts
16 always. Better a little, with fear of the LORD, than a great storehouse where
17 there is turmoil. Better a meal of greens with love present than a fattened
18 ox where hatred dwells. The hot-tempered man incites strife; the patient
19 man calms a quarrel. To the indolent, the way is a hedge of thorns; to the
upright, the path is paved.
20 A wise son brings joy to his father; a foolish man shames his mother.
21 Folly is a joy to the mindless, but the man of intelligence walks straight.
22 Without consultation, plans come to naught; with many advisors, they
23 succeed. A man's response brings him joy; how good is a timely word!
24 For the thinking man, the path of life is ever upward so that he will avert
25 Sheol below. The LORD will extirpate the house of the haughty, but He
26 will secure the widow's boundary stone.[12] Evil thoughts are anathema

12 | Protecting her property from encroachment.

כז כח יִרְאַת יְהוָה מְקוֹר חַיִּים לָסוּר מִמֹּקְשֵׁי מָוֶת׃ בְּרָב־עָם הַדְרַת־מֶלֶךְ
כט וּבְאֶפֶס לְאֹם מְחִתַּת רָזוֹן׃ אֶרֶךְ אַפַּיִם רַב־תְּבוּנָה וּקְצַר־רוּחַ מֵרִים
ל לא אִוֶּלֶת׃ חַיֵּי בְשָׂרִים לֵב מַרְפֵּא וּרְקַב עֲצָמוֹת קִנְאָה׃ עֹשֵׁק דָּל חֵרֵף
לב עֹשֵׂהוּ וּמְכַבְּדוֹ חֹנֵן אֶבְיוֹן׃ בְּרָעָתוֹ יִדָּחֶה רָשָׁע וְחֹסֶה בְמוֹתוֹ צַדִּיק׃
לג לד בְּלֵב נָבוֹן תָּנוּחַ חָכְמָה וּבְקֶרֶב כְּסִילִים תִּוָּדֵעַ׃ צְדָקָה תְרוֹמֵם־גּוֹי
לה וְחֶסֶד לְאֻמִּים חַטָּאת׃ רְצוֹן־מֶלֶךְ לְעֶבֶד מַשְׂכִּיל וְעֶבְרָתוֹ תִּהְיֶה
טו א ב מֵבִישׁ׃ מַעֲנֶה־רַּךְ יָשִׁיב חֵמָה וּדְבַר־עֶצֶב יַעֲלֶה־אָף׃ לְשׁוֹן חֲכָמִים
ג תֵּיטִיב דָּעַת וּפִי כְסִילִים יַבִּיעַ אִוֶּלֶת׃ בְּכָל־מָקוֹם עֵינֵי יְהוָה צֹפוֹת
ד ה רָעִים וְטוֹבִים׃ מַרְפֵּא לָשׁוֹן עֵץ חַיִּים וְסֶלֶף בָּהּ שֶׁבֶר בְּרוּחַ׃ אֱוִיל
ו יִנְאַץ מוּסַר אָבִיו וְשֹׁמֵר תּוֹכַחַת יַעְרִם׃ בֵּית צַדִּיק חֹסֶן רָב וּבִתְבוּאַת
ז ח רָשָׁע נֶעְכָּרֶת׃ שִׂפְתֵי חֲכָמִים יְזָרוּ דָעַת וְלֵב כְּסִילִים לֹא־כֵן׃ זֶבַח
ט רְשָׁעִים תּוֹעֲבַת יְהוָה וּתְפִלַּת יְשָׁרִים רְצוֹנוֹ׃ תּוֹעֲבַת יְהוָה דֶּרֶךְ
י רָשָׁע וּמְרַדֵּף צְדָקָה יֶאֱהָב׃ מוּסָר רָע לְעֹזֵב אֹרַח שׂוֹנֵא תוֹכַחַת
יא יב יָמוּת׃ שְׁאוֹל וַאֲבַדּוֹן נֶגֶד יְהוָה אַף כִּי־לִבּוֹת בְּנֵי־אָדָם׃ לֹא־יֶאֱהַב לֵץ
יג הוֹכֵחַ לוֹ אֶל־חֲכָמִים לֹא יֵלֵךְ׃ לֵב שָׂמֵחַ יֵיטִב פָּנִים וּבְעַצְּבַת־לֵב רוּחַ
יד טו נְכֵאָה׃ לֵב נָבוֹן יְבַקֶּשׁ־דָּעַת ופני כְסִילִים יִרְעֶה אִוֶּלֶת׃ כָּל־יְמֵי עָנִי וּפִי
טז רָעִים וְטוֹב־לֵב מִשְׁתֶּה תָמִיד׃ טוֹב־מְעַט בְּיִרְאַת יְהוָה מֵאוֹצָר רָב
יז וּמְהוּמָה בוֹ׃ טוֹב אֲרֻחַת יָרָק וְאַהֲבָה־שָׁם מִשּׁוֹר אָבוּס וְשִׂנְאָה־בוֹ׃
יח יט אִישׁ חֵמָה יְגָרֶה מָדוֹן וְאֶרֶךְ אַפַּיִם יַשְׁקִיט רִיב׃ דֶּרֶךְ עָצֵל כִּמְשֻׂכַת
חָדֶק וְאֹרַח יְשָׁרִים סְלֻלָה׃
כ כא בֵּן חָכָם יְשַׂמַּח־אָב וּכְסִיל אָדָם בּוֹזֶה אִמּוֹ׃ אִוֶּלֶת שִׂמְחָה לַחֲסַר־לֵב
כב וְאִישׁ תְּבוּנָה יְיַשֶּׁר־לָכֶת׃ הָפֵר מַחֲשָׁבוֹת בְּאֵין סוֹד וּבְרֹב יוֹעֲצִים
כג כד תָּקוּם׃ שִׂמְחָה לָאִישׁ בְּמַעֲנֵה־פִיו וְדָבָר בְּעִתּוֹ מַה־טּוֹב׃ אֹרַח חַיִּים
כה לְמַעְלָה לְמַשְׂכִּיל לְמַעַן סוּר מִשְּׁאוֹל מָטָּה׃ בֵּית גֵּאִים יִסַּח ׀ יְהוָה
כו וְיַצֵּב גְּבוּל אַלְמָנָה׃ תּוֹעֲבַת יְהוָה מַחְשְׁבוֹת רָע וּטְהֹרִים אִמְרֵי־נֹעַם׃

27 to the Lord, but pure are words of pleasantness. The man who pursues
28 ill-gotten profit ruins his home, but he who detests gifts will thrive. The
righteous man's heart reflects upon its response, but the mouth of the
29 wicked spouts evil. The Lord is distant from the wicked, but He hears
30 the prayers of the righteous. What brightens the eyes, gladdens the heart;
31 good tidings fatten the bones. The ear that heeds a life-giving rebuke
32 resides among the wise. He who disregards instruction despises himself;
33 he who heeds a rebuke acquires an understanding heart. Fear of the Lord
16 1 is wisdom's instruction; before honor comes humility. A person arranges
2 the thoughts of his heart, but the response comes from the Lord.[13] A
man's ways are all virtuous in his eyes, but it is the Lord who assesses
3 intentions. Rely upon the Lord in all that you do, and your plans will be
4 secured. The Lord made everything for His purpose, even the wicked for
5 his day of disaster. Every haughty person is anathema to the Lord; not
6 for a moment will he be deemed innocent. With kindness and truth, sin is
7 forgiven; with fear of the Lord, evil is avoided. When the Lord approves
8 of a man's ways, He will cause his enemies to make peace with him. Better
9 a little righteously attained than great bounty gained unjustly. If the heart
10 of man scrutinizes his way, the Lord will guide his footsteps. There is
magic upon the king's lips – in judgment, his mouth will betray no one.
11 Just scales and balances are the Lord's; all weights of the purse are His
12 work. Committing evil is anathema to kings, for only with righteousness
13 is a throne secured. The wish of a king is for righteous lips; he will love a
14 person who speaks honestly. A king's wrath is like death's messengers, but
15 the wise man can placate it. A king's bright face signals life; his approval
16 is like a late winter rain cloud. Acquiring wisdom is much better than
17 refined gold; acquiring understanding is superior to silver. The path of
the upright avoids evil; he who would keep himself from harm will guard
18 his way. Before collapse comes pride! Before failure, haughtiness of spirit!
19 Better a lowly spirit among the humble than dividing spoils with the
20 mighty. He who thinks matters over will discover good; he who trusts in
21 the Lord is fortunate. The wise of heart will be proclaimed intelligent;
22 sweet speech will increase learning. A fount of life is intelligence to
23 the one who has it; the fools' instruction is folly. The wise man's mind
24 informs his mouth; it adds instruction to his lips. Pleasant words are like
25 honeycomb: sweet to the soul and healing to the bones. At times, the
26 path before a man seems straight, but its end is in the paths of death. The
toiling person toils for himself, for when his mouth makes its demands.
27 28 The villain mines for malice; upon his lips is a scorching fire. The perverse
person incites strife; the quarrelsome person alienates his companion.
29 The lawless man misleads his fellow; he leads him along a base path.

13 | A person plans what he wants to say, but God determines what comes out of his mouth.

כז כח עֹכֵר בֵּיתוֹ בּוֹצֵעַ בָּצַע וְשׂוֹנֵא מַתָּנֹת יִחְיֶה: לֵב צַדִּיק יֶהְגֶּה לַעֲנוֹת וּפִי
כט רְשָׁעִים יַבִּיעַ רָעוֹת: רָחוֹק יהוה מֵרְשָׁעִים וּתְפִלַּת צַדִּיקִים יִשְׁמָע:
ל לא מְאוֹר־עֵינַיִם יְשַׂמַּח־לֵב שְׁמוּעָה טוֹבָה תְּדַשֶּׁן־עָצֶם: אֹזֶן שֹׁמַעַת
לב תּוֹכַחַת חַיִּים בְּקֶרֶב חֲכָמִים תָּלִין: פּוֹרֵעַ מוּסָר מוֹאֵס נַפְשׁוֹ וְשׁוֹמֵעַ
טז לג א תּוֹכַחַת קוֹנֶה לֵּב: יִרְאַת יהוה מוּסַר חָכְמָה וְלִפְנֵי כָבוֹד עֲנָוָה: לְאָדָם
ב מַעַרְכֵי־לֵב וּמֵיהוה מַעֲנֵה לָשׁוֹן: כָּל־דַּרְכֵי־אִישׁ זַךְ בְּעֵינָיו וְתֹכֵן
ג ד רוּחוֹת יהוה: גֹּל אֶל־יהוה מַעֲשֶׂיךָ וְיִכֹּנוּ מַחְשְׁבֹתֶיךָ: כֹּל פָּעַל יהוה
ה לַמַּעֲנֵהוּ וְגַם־רָשָׁע לְיוֹם רָעָה: תּוֹעֲבַת יהוה כָּל־גְּבַהּ־לֵב יָד לְיָד לֹא
ו ז יִנָּקֶה: בְּחֶסֶד וֶאֱמֶת יְכֻפַּר עָוֹן וּבְיִרְאַת יהוה סוּר מֵרָע: בִּרְצוֹת יהוה
ח דַּרְכֵי־אִישׁ גַּם־אוֹיְבָיו יַשְׁלִם אִתּוֹ: טוֹב מְעַט בִּצְדָקָה מֵרֹב תְּבוּאוֹת
ט בְּלֹא מִשְׁפָּט: לֵב אָדָם יְחַשֵּׁב דַּרְכּוֹ וַיהוה יָכִין צַעֲדוֹ: קֶסֶם ׀ עַל־
יא שִׂפְתֵי־מֶלֶךְ בְּמִשְׁפָּט לֹא יִמְעַל־פִּיו: פֶּלֶס ׀ וּמֹאזְנֵי מִשְׁפָּט לַיהוה
יב מַעֲשֵׂהוּ כָּל־אַבְנֵי־כִיס: תּוֹעֲבַת מְלָכִים עֲשׂוֹת רֶשַׁע כִּי בִצְדָקָה
יג יד יִכּוֹן כִּסֵּא: רְצוֹן מְלָכִים שִׂפְתֵי־צֶדֶק וְדֹבֵר יְשָׁרִים יֶאֱהָב: חֲמַת־מֶלֶךְ
טו מַלְאֲכֵי־מָוֶת וְאִישׁ חָכָם יְכַפְּרֶנָּה: בְּאוֹר־פְּנֵי־מֶלֶךְ חַיִּים וּרְצוֹנוֹ כְּעָב
טז מַלְקוֹשׁ: קְנֹה־חָכְמָה מַה־טּוֹב מֵחָרוּץ וּקְנוֹת בִּינָה נִבְחָר מִכָּסֶף:
יז יח מְסִלַּת יְשָׁרִים סוּר מֵרָע שֹׁמֵר נַפְשׁוֹ נֹצֵר דַּרְכּוֹ: לִפְנֵי־שֶׁבֶר גָּאוֹן וְלִפְנֵי
יט כִשָּׁלוֹן גֹּבַהּ רוּחַ: טוֹב שְׁפַל־רוּחַ אֶת־עניים מֵחַלֵּק שָׁלָל אֶת־גֵּאִים: עֲנָוִים
כ כא מַשְׂכִּיל עַל־דָּבָר יִמְצָא־טוֹב וּבוֹטֵחַ בַּיהוה אַשְׁרָיו: לַחֲכַם־לֵב יִקָּרֵא
כב נָבוֹן וּמֶתֶק שְׂפָתַיִם יֹסִיף לֶקַח: מְקוֹר חַיִּים שֵׂכֶל בְּעָלָיו וּמוּסַר אֱוִלִים
כג כד אִוֶּלֶת: לֵב חָכָם יַשְׂכִּיל פִּיהוּ וְעַל־שְׂפָתָיו יֹסִיף לֶקַח: צוּף־דְּבַשׁ אִמְרֵי־
כה נֹעַם מָתוֹק לַנֶּפֶשׁ וּמַרְפֵּא לָעָצֶם: יֵשׁ דֶּרֶךְ יָשָׁר לִפְנֵי־אִישׁ וְאַחֲרִיתָהּ
כו כז דַּרְכֵי־מָוֶת: נֶפֶשׁ עָמֵל עָמְלָה לּוֹ כִּי־אָכַף עָלָיו פִּיהוּ: אִישׁ בְּלִיַּעַל
כח כֹּרֶה רָעָה וְעַל־שפתיו כְּאֵשׁ צָרָבֶת: אִישׁ תַּהְפֻּכוֹת יְשַׁלַּח מָדוֹן שְׂפָתוֹ
כט וְנִרְגָּן מַפְרִיד אַלּוּף: אִישׁ חָמָס יְפַתֶּה רֵעֵהוּ וְהוֹלִיכוֹ בְּדֶרֶךְ לֹא־טוֹב:

30 He closes his eyes as he devises perversions; he purses his lips as he
31 executes evil. Gray hair is a crown of glory; it can be acquired through
32 the way of righteousness. Better a patient man than a mighty one; better
33 he who controls his mood than he who conquers a city. Lots may be cast
17 1 in a person's bosom, but all decision is from the LORD. Better dry bread
2 with tranquility than a house full of feasts with contention. A competent
servant will dominate a son who causes shame and will share in the
3 inheritance with the brothers. A crucible is for silver and a furnace for
4 gold; it is the LORD who tests the heart. The wicked man listens to sinful
5 lips; the liar gives ear to the tongue that speaks calamity. He who mocks
the pauper blasphemes his Maker; he who rejoices over misfortune will
6 not be deemed innocent. Grandchildren are the crown of the aged; the
7 glory of children is their parents. Exaggerated speech is unbecoming of a
8 knave; how much worse is false speech by a noble person. A bribe is like
a gemstone in the eyes of its possessor; he will justify it to whomever
9 he turns. He who overlooks an offense seeks friendship; he who repeats
10 the matter alienates a companion. One scolding will frighten a man of
11 understanding more than a hundred blows will a fool. Surely the rebel
12 courts disaster; a cruel messenger will be sent against him. Better that a
13 man encounter a bereaved bear, and not a fool in his folly. A person who
14 returns evil for good – evil will never depart from his house. He who
15 initiates strife opens floodgates; before the quarrel spreads, leave! He
who acquits the guilty, and he who condemns the innocent – both are
16 anathema to the LORD. Of what use is money given to a fool to acquire
17 wisdom when he has no mind for it? A good friend is always loving; he
18 is like a brother when trouble occurs. A mindless man extends his hand;
19 he guarantees loans on behalf of another. He who loves to offend loves
20 dispute; he who raises high his doorway invites collapse. The crooked
heart meets with no good; he whose tongue is duplicitous will fall into
21 evil. He who begets a fool knows misery; the father of the knave will never
22 rejoice. The happy heart enhances healing; the crushed spirit dries up
23 the marrow of the bone. Bribes are taken from the lap of a wicked man to
pervert the paths of justice.
24 Wisdom is in front of the man of understanding; in the eyes of the
25 fool it is at the ends of the earth. The foolish son causes his father pain,
26 and bitterness to her who bore him. Surely, it is not good to punish the
27 righteous or flog noble men for their rectitude. He who restrains his
words appreciates knowledge; he for whom speech is precious is a man
28 of understanding. Even a fool who keeps silent is deemed wise, and he
18 1 who shuts his lips, intelligent. The loner follows his passions; he rebuffs
2 all guidance. The fool does not desire understanding; he wishes only
3 to disclose his own thoughts. When the wicked man comes, derision
4 comes, along with shame and disgrace. The words of a person's mouth

ל לא עֹצֶה עֵינָיו לַחְשֹׁב תַּהְפֻּכוֹת קֹרֵץ שְׂפָתָיו כִּלָּה רָעָה׃ עֲטֶרֶת תִּפְאֶרֶת
לב שֵׂיבָה בְּדֶרֶךְ צְדָקָה תִּמָּצֵא׃ טוֹב אֶרֶךְ אַפַּיִם מִגִּבּוֹר וּמֹשֵׁל בְּרוּחוֹ
יז לג א מִלֹּכֵד עִיר׃ בַּחֵיק יוּטַל אֶת־הַגּוֹרָל וּמֵיְהוָה כָּל־מִשְׁפָּטוֹ׃ טוֹב פַּת
ב חֲרֵבָה וְשַׁלְוָה־בָהּ מִבַּיִת מָלֵא זִבְחֵי־רִיב׃ עֶבֶד־מַשְׂכִּיל יִמְשֹׁל בְּבֵן
ג מֵבִישׁ וּבְתוֹךְ אַחִים יַחֲלֹק נַחֲלָה׃ מַצְרֵף לַכֶּסֶף וְכוּר לַזָּהָב וּבֹחֵן לִבּוֹת
ד ה יְהוָה׃ מֵרַע מַקְשִׁיב עַל־שְׂפַת־אָוֶן שֶׁקֶר מֵזִין עַל־לְשׁוֹן הַוֹּת׃ לֹעֵג
ו לָרָשׁ חֵרֵף עֹשֵׂהוּ שָׂמֵחַ לְאֵיד לֹא יִנָּקֶה׃ עֲטֶרֶת זְקֵנִים בְּנֵי בָנִים
ז וְתִפְאֶרֶת בָּנִים אֲבוֹתָם׃ לֹא־נָאוָה לְנָבָל שְׂפַת־יֶתֶר אַף כִּי־לְנָדִיב
ח שְׂפַת־שָׁקֶר׃ אֶבֶן־חֵן הַשֹּׁחַד בְּעֵינֵי בְעָלָיו אֶל־כָּל־אֲשֶׁר יִפְנֶה יַשְׂכִּיל׃
ט י מְכַסֶּה־פֶּשַׁע מְבַקֵּשׁ אַהֲבָה וְשֹׁנֶה בְדָבָר מַפְרִיד אַלּוּף׃ תֵּחַת גְּעָרָה
יא בְמֵבִין מֵהַכּוֹת כְּסִיל מֵאָה׃ אַךְ־מְרִי יְבַקֶּשׁ־רָע וּמַלְאָךְ אַכְזָרִי יְשֻׁלַּח־
יב יג בּוֹ׃ פָּגוֹשׁ דֹּב שַׁכּוּל בְּאִישׁ וְאַל־כְּסִיל בְּאִוַּלְתּוֹ׃ מֵשִׁיב רָעָה תַּחַת
יד טוֹבָה לֹא־תמיש רָעָה מִבֵּיתוֹ׃ פּוֹטֵר מַיִם רֵאשִׁית מָדוֹן וְלִפְנֵי הִתְגַּלַּע תָמוּשׁ
טו הָרִיב נְטוֹשׁ׃ מַצְדִּיק רָשָׁע וּמַרְשִׁיעַ צַדִּיק תּוֹעֲבַת יְהוָה גַּם־שְׁנֵיהֶם׃
טז יז לָמָּה־זֶּה מְחִיר בְּיַד־כְּסִיל לִקְנוֹת חָכְמָה וְלֶב־אָיִן׃ בְּכָל־עֵת אֹהֵב
יח הָרֵעַ וְאָח לְצָרָה יִוָּלֵד׃ אָדָם חֲסַר־לֵב תּוֹקֵעַ כָּף עֹרֵב עֲרֻבָּה לִפְנֵי
יט כ רֵעֵהוּ׃ אֹהֵב פֶּשַׁע אֹהֵב מַצָּה מַגְבִּיהַּ פִּתְחוֹ מְבַקֶּשׁ־שָׁבֶר׃ עִקֶּשׁ־לֵב
כא לֹא יִמְצָא־טוֹב וְנֶהְפָּךְ בִּלְשׁוֹנוֹ יִפּוֹל בְּרָעָה׃ יֹלֵד כְּסִיל לְתוּגָה לוֹ
כב וְלֹא־יִשְׂמַח אֲבִי נָבָל׃ לֵב שָׂמֵחַ יֵיטִב גֵּהָה וְרוּחַ נְכֵאָה תְּיַבֶּשׁ־גָּרֶם׃
כג שֹׁחַד מֵחֵק רָשָׁע יִקָּח לְהַטּוֹת אָרְחוֹת מִשְׁפָּט׃
כד כה אֶת־פְּנֵי מֵבִין חָכְמָה וְעֵינֵי כְסִיל בִּקְצֵה־אָרֶץ׃ כַּעַס לְאָבִיו בֵּן כְּסִיל
כו וּמֶמֶר לְיוֹלַדְתּוֹ׃ גַּם עֲנוֹשׁ לַצַּדִּיק לֹא־טוֹב לְהַכּוֹת נְדִיבִים עַל־יֹשֶׁר׃
כז כח חוֹשֵׂךְ אֲמָרָיו יוֹדֵעַ דָּעַת וקַר־רוּחַ אִישׁ תְּבוּנָה׃ גַּם אֱוִיל מַחֲרִישׁ חָכָם יְקַר־
יח א יֵחָשֵׁב אֹטֵם שְׂפָתָיו נָבוֹן׃ לְתַאֲוָה יְבַקֵּשׁ נִפְרָד בְּכָל־תּוּשִׁיָּה יִתְגַּלָּע׃
ב ג לֹא־יַחְפֹּץ כְּסִיל בִּתְבוּנָה כִּי אִם־בְּהִתְגַּלּוֹת לִבּוֹ׃ בְּבוֹא־רָשָׁע בָּא
ד גַם־בּוּז וְעִם־קָלוֹן חֶרְפָּה׃ מַיִם עֲמֻקִּים דִּבְרֵי פִי־אִישׁ נַחַל נֹבֵעַ מְקוֹר

5 are deep waters; a fount of wisdom is like a bubbling brook. Tolerating
the guilty is not good; no more than subverting the innocent's judgment.
6 7 The lips of the fool cause disputes; his mouth invites violence. The mouth
8 of the fool is its own pitfall; his lips are his fatal snare. The words of an
9 argumentative person are like blows; they pierce the belly's chambers. The
person who is careless in his work – he, too, is brother to the destructive
10 man. The LORD's name is a tower of strength; the righteous person runs
11 there and is safe. The rich man's wealth is his city of strength; in his mind
12 it is like a mighty wall. Before collapse, a person's heart is haughty; before
13 honor comes humility. He who responds before he has listened – this is
14 folly for him, and shame. The brave person's spirit sustains him during
15 his illness, but a weak spirit, who can bear it? An intelligent man's heart
16 acquires knowledge; the ear of the wise seeks knowledge. A person's
generosity widens his path; it leads him into the presence of the great.
17 The first to present his case seems innocent until his fellow comes and
18 interrogates him. Casting lots can quiet quarrels and even separate
19 powerful adversaries. A brother wronged is like a fortified city; such
20 quarrels are like the bolts of a fortress. A man fills his stomach by the
21 fruits of his mouth; he will be satisfied by the harvest of his lips. Death
and life are in the power of the tongue; he who treats it lovingly will eat
22 its fruit. He who finds a wife finds what is good and has derived favor
23 from the LORD. A poor person speaks beseechingly, but the rich person
24 responds with impudence. A friendly man seeks many companions, but
19 1 one close friend is more loyal than a brother. Better a pauper who walks in
2 innocence than a person with perverse lips who is a fool. Ignorance, too,
3 is of no benefit to a person; he who hurries his footsteps sins. A person's
4 own folly distorts his path, yet he takes out his anger on the LORD. A
person with wealth accumulates many friends, but the pauper is separated
5 from his friends. He who testifies falsely will not be judged innocent; he
6 who spouts lies will not escape. Many court the noble person; all befriend
7 the generous person. The poor person's brothers all hate him; his friends
avoid him even more. He pursues them with words, but they are futile.
8 He who acquires a mind loves himself; he preserves understanding and
9 will find success. He who testifies falsely will not be judged innocent; he
who spouts lies will be doomed.
10 Luxury is unseemly for a fool; it is yet worse for a slave to rule his masters.
11 A person's forbearance reflects his intelligence, and it is to his glory that
12 he overlooks offense. Like a lion's roar is a king's rage; his favor is like dew
13 upon grass. A foolish son is a father's heartbreak; a wife's squabbles are
14 like annoying drops of water. Property and possessions are an ancestral
15 inheritance; an intelligent wife is from the LORD. Laziness induces
16 slumber; an idle person will starve. He who guards a precept guards
17 himself; he who abuses His ways will perish. He who is kind to a pauper

ה ו חָכְמָה: שְׂאֵת פְּנֵי־רָשָׁע לֹא־טוֹב לְהַטּוֹת צַדִּיק בַּמִּשְׁפָּט: שִׂפְתֵי כְסִיל
ז יָבֹאוּ בְרִיב וּפִיו לְמַהֲלֻמוֹת יִקְרָא: פִּי־כְסִיל מְחִתָּה־לוֹ וּשְׂפָתָיו מוֹקֵשׁ
ח ט נַפְשׁוֹ: דִּבְרֵי נִרְגָּן כְּמִתְלַהֲמִים וְהֵם יָרְדוּ חַדְרֵי־בָטֶן: גַּם מִתְרַפֶּה
י בִמְלַאכְתּוֹ אָח הוּא לְבַעַל מַשְׁחִית: מִגְדַּל־עֹז שֵׁם יהוה בּוֹ־יָרוּץ צַדִּיק ה
יא יב וְנִשְׂגָּב: הוֹן עָשִׁיר קִרְיַת עֻזּוֹ וּכְחוֹמָה נִשְׂגָּבָה בְּמַשְׂכִּיתוֹ: לִפְנֵי־שֶׁבֶר
יג יִגְבַּהּ לֵב־אִישׁ וְלִפְנֵי כָבוֹד עֲנָוָה: מֵשִׁיב דָּבָר בְּטֶרֶם יִשְׁמָע אִוֶּלֶת
יד הִיא־לוֹ וּכְלִמָּה: רוּחַ־אִישׁ יְכַלְכֵּל מַחֲלֵהוּ וְרוּחַ נְכֵאָה מִי יִשָּׂאֶנָּה:
טו טז לֵב נָבוֹן יִקְנֶה־דָּעַת וְאֹזֶן חֲכָמִים תְּבַקֶּשׁ־דָּעַת: מַתָּן אָדָם יַרְחִיב לוֹ
יז יח וְלִפְנֵי גְדֹלִים יַנְחֶנּוּ: צַדִּיק הָרִאשׁוֹן בְּרִיבוֹ יבא־רֵעֵהוּ וַחֲקָרוֹ: מִדְיָנִים וּבָא־
יט יַשְׁבִּית הַגּוֹרָל וּבֵין עֲצוּמִים יַפְרִיד: אָח נִפְשָׁע מִקִּרְיַת־עֹז ומדונים וּמִדְיָנִים
כ כִּבְרִיחַ אַרְמוֹן: מִפְּרִי פִי־אִישׁ תִּשְׂבַּע בִּטְנוֹ תְּבוּאַת שְׂפָתָיו יִשְׂבָּע:
כא כב מָוֶת וְחַיִּים בְּיַד־לָשׁוֹן וְאֹהֲבֶיהָ יֹאכַל פִּרְיָהּ: מָצָא אִשָּׁה מָצָא טוֹב
כג כד וַיָּפֶק רָצוֹן מֵיהוה: תַּחֲנוּנִים יְדַבֶּר־רָשׁ וְעָשִׁיר יַעֲנֶה עַזּוֹת: אִישׁ
יט א רֵעִים לְהִתְרֹעֵעַ וְיֵשׁ אֹהֵב דָּבֵק מֵאָח: טוֹב רָשׁ הוֹלֵךְ בְּתֻמּוֹ מֵעִקֵּשׁ
ב שְׂפָתָיו וְהוּא כְסִיל: גַּם בְּלֹא־דַעַת נֶפֶשׁ לֹא־טוֹב וְאָץ בְּרַגְלַיִם חוֹטֵא:
ג ד אִוֶּלֶת אָדָם תְּסַלֵּף דַּרְכּוֹ וְעַל־יהוה יִזְעַף לִבּוֹ: הוֹן יֹסִיף רֵעִים רַבִּים
ה וְדָל מֵרֵעֵהוּ יִפָּרֵד: עֵד שְׁקָרִים לֹא יִנָּקֶה וְיָפִיחַ כְּזָבִים לֹא יִמָּלֵט:
ו ז רַבִּים יְחַלּוּ פְנֵי־נָדִיב וְכָל־הָרֵעַ לְאִישׁ מַתָּן: כָּל אֲחֵי־רָשׁ ׀ שְׂנֵאֻהוּ
ח אַף כִּי מְרֵעֵהוּ רָחֲקוּ מִמֶּנּוּ מְרַדֵּף אֲמָרִים לא־הֵמָּה: קֹנֶה־לֵּב אֹהֵב לוֹ־
ט נַפְשׁוֹ שֹׁמֵר תְּבוּנָה לִמְצֹא־טוֹב: עֵד שְׁקָרִים לֹא יִנָּקֶה וְיָפִיחַ כְּזָבִים
יֹאבֵד:
י יא לֹא־נָאוֶה לִכְסִיל תַּעֲנוּג אַף כִּי־לְעֶבֶד ׀ מְשֹׁל בְּשָׂרִים: שֵׂכֶל אָדָם
יב הֶאֱרִיךְ אַפּוֹ וְתִפְאַרְתּוֹ עֲבֹר עַל־פָּשַׁע: נַהַם כַּכְּפִיר זַעַף מֶלֶךְ וּכְטַל
יג יד עַל־עֵשֶׂב רְצוֹנוֹ: הַוֺּת לְאָבִיו בֵּן כְּסִיל וְדֶלֶף טֹרֵד מִדְיְנֵי אִשָּׁה: בַּיִת
טו וָהוֹן נַחֲלַת אָבוֹת וּמֵיהוה אִשָּׁה מַשְׂכָּלֶת: עַצְלָה תַּפִּיל תַּרְדֵּמָה וְנֶפֶשׁ
טז יז רְמִיָּה תִרְעָב: שֹׁמֵר מִצְוָה שֹׁמֵר נַפְשׁוֹ בּוֹזֵה דְרָכָיו יומת: מַלְוֵה יהוה יָמוּת

18 lends to the LORD; He will repay him his kindness. Discipline your son
19 while there is yet hope; do not be dissuaded by his weeping. But excessive
wrath pays a penalty; spare him your wrath but continue your discipline.
20 Heed counsel and accept instruction; you will then be wise in the end.
21 Many are the thoughts in the heart of man, but it is the LORD's plan that
22 will prevail. What people seek from a person is his kindness; better a poor
23 man than one who lies. Fear of the LORD leads a person to life: he will
24 endure in satisfaction and not be visited by misfortune. The lazy man
25 buries his hand in the bowl but will not even return it to his mouth. Strike
the scoffer, and he will awaken from his ignorance; rebuke an intelligent
26 man, and he will advance his knowledge. The son who embarrasses and
27 disgraces does violence to his father and drives his mother away. My son,
28 stop listening to instruction that misinterprets words of knowledge. A
villainous witness scoffs at justice; the mouth of the wicked conceals
29 iniquity. Punishments are readied for scoffers and blows for the backs of
20 1 fools. Wine is a scoffer; beer is boisterous; those who go astray with them
2 will never be wise. A king's terror is like a lion's roar; he who provokes him
3 endangers his life. It is honorable for a man to refrain from dispute, yet
4 every fool gets entangled. The lazy man does not plow in winter;[14] he begs
5 at harvest time, but there is nothing. A plan in a man's mind is like deep
6 water; the thinking man will draw it out. Many people are called faithful,
7 but the truly trustworthy person is rare. The righteous man walks with
8 perfectness; fortunate are his children after him. The king who sits firmly
9 upon the throne of justice disperses evil with his gaze. Who can say "I
10 have cleansed my heart; I am pure of my sin"? False weights, inaccurate
11 measures: both are anathema to the LORD. A child may make himself
strange while at play but nevertheless be innocent and upright in his
12 conduct. An attentive ear and a discriminating eye – the LORD made them
13 both. Do not cherish sleep lest you become impoverished; keep your eyes
14 open, and you will be sated with bread. "Bad! Bad!" says the buyer, but
15 when he departs, he praises it. There are many pearls and much gold, but
16 lips of knowledge are a rare vessel. Take his garment, for he has put up
security for a stranger; if he did so on behalf of an alien woman – seize it!
17 The bread of betrayal tastes sweet to a man, but afterward his mouth fills
18 with gravel. Plans will succeed if advice is taken; therefore, wage war with
19 great forethought. He who reveals secrets is a talebearer; do not mingle
20 with a chatterer. The lamp of him who curses his father and mother will
21 dim as darkness descends. An inheritance initially obtained in haste will
22 not be blessed in the end. Do not say, "I will repay evil." Trust in the LORD;
23 He will help you. Fraudulent weights are anathema to the LORD; false
24 scales are wicked. A person's footsteps derive from the LORD; what can

14 | Winter is the rainy season, when the ground is prepared for planting.

יח חונן דל וגמלו ישלם־לו: יסר בנך כי־יש תקוה ואל־המיתו אל־
יט כ תשא נפשך: גרל־חמה נשא ענש כי אם־תציל ועוד תוסף: שמע גדל־
כא עצה וקבל מוסר למען תחכם באחריתך: רבות מחשבות בלב־
כב איש ועצת יהוה היא תקום: תאות אדם חסדו וטוב־רש מאיש
כג כד כזב: יראת יהוה לחיים ושבע ילין בל־יפקד רע: טמן עצל ידו
כה בצלחת גם־אל־פיהו לא ישיבנה: לץ תכה ופתי יערם והוכיח לנבון
כו כז יבין דעת: משדד־אב יבריח אם בן מביש ומחפיר: חדל־בני לשמע
כח מוסר לשגות מאמרי־דעת: עד בליעל יליץ משפט ופי רשעים
כ כט א יבלע־און: נכונו ללצים שפטים ומהלמות לגו כסילים: לץ היין
ב המה שכר וכל־שגה בו לא יחכם: נהם ככפיר אימת מלך מתעברו
ג ד חוטא נפשו: כבוד לאיש שבת מריב וכל־אויל יתגלע: מחרף עצל
ה לא־יחרש ישאל בקציר ואין: מים עמקים עצה בלב־איש ואיש ושאל
ו תבונה ידלנה: רב־אדם יקרא איש חסדו ואיש אמונים מי ימצא:
ז ח מתהלך בתמו צדיק אשרי בניו אחריו: מלך יושב על־כסא־דין
ט י מזרה בעיניו כל־רע: מי־יאמר זכיתי לבי טהרתי מחטאתי: אבן
יא ואבן איפה ואיפה תועבת יהוה גם־שניהם: גם במעלליו יתנכר־
יב נער אם־זך ואם־ישר פעלו: אזן שמעת ועין ראה יהוה עשה גם־
יג יד שניהם: אל־תאהב שנה פן־תורש פקח עיניך שבע־לחם: רע רע
טו יאמר הקונה ואזל לו אז יתהלל: יש זהב ורב־פנינים וכלי יקר
טז יז שפתי־דעת: לקח־בגדו כי־ערב זר ובעד נכרים חבלהו: ערב לאיש נכריה
יח לחם שקר ואחר ימלא־פיהו חצץ: מחשבות בעצה תכון ובתחבלות
יט עשה מלחמה: גולה־סוד הולך רכיל ולפתה שפתיו לא תתערב:
כ כא מקלל אביו ואמו ידעך נרו באישון חשך: נחלה מבחלת בראשונה באשון מבהלת
כב ואחריתה לא תברך: אל־תאמר אשלמה־רע קוה ליהוה וישע לך:
כג כד תועבת יהוה אבן ואבן ומאזני מרמה לא־טוב: מיהוה מצעדי־גבר

25 anyone know about where he is headed? It is man's failing to blurt out
26 sacred vows and consider them only afterward. The wise king disperses
27 the wicked; he rolls the wheel upon them.[15] The LORD's lamp is a person's
28 life; it searches out all the belly's chambers.[16] Kindness and truth will
29 protect a king; kindness will maintain his throne. The splendor of youth
30 is their strength; the grandeur of the old is their gray hair. Welts and
bruises are cleansing salves for the wicked as are blows to the belly's
21 1 chambers. The heart of a king is but a stream of water in the hand of the
2 LORD: to wherever He desires He directs it. A man's ways are all correct
in his eyes; it is the LORD who holds him to account for his intentions.
3 Pursuing righteousness and justice pleases the LORD more than sacrifice.
4 5 Lofty eyes and a haughty heart: the schemes of the wicked are sinful. The
thoughts of the diligent lead only to gain; all who are hasty only suffer
6 loss. Treasures achieved by a false tongue are like a fleeting breath in
7 search of death. The violence of the wicked will drag them down, for they
8 refuse to do what is just. Tortuous is the way of some men, and bizarre;
9 the pure person's actions are proper. Better to sit on the corner of a roof[17]
10 than with a quarrelsome wife in the home of friends. The wicked man
11 craves evil; even his comrade will not find favor in his eyes. When a scoffer
is punished, the simpleton grows wise; when a wise man is taught, he[18]
12 gains knowledge.[19] The righteous man contemplates the wicked man's
13 house and consigns the wicked to evil. He that stuffs his ear so as not to
14 hear the cry of the poor, he too will call out and not be answered. Alms
given in secret will subdue anger; a bribe in the bosom, fierce wrath.
15 Justice done is a joy for the righteous, but it is the downfall of those who
16 wreak evil. A man who strays from the path of reason will find rest in the
17 company of ghosts. He that loves luxury will become a needy man; he
18 that loves wine and oil does not get rich. A wicked man ransoms the
19 righteous; the traitor redeems the upright.[20] Better sit in a desert land than
20 with a quarrelsome wife and with anger. Delightful treasure and oil are in
21 the wise man's abode, but the foolish man swallows it up. He that pursues
22 righteousness and kindness finds life, virtue, and honor. A wise man
ascended to the fortress of the mighty and brought down the strength of
23 its fortress. He that guards his mouth and his tongue guards himself from
24 troubles. The arrogant villain – "scoffer" is his name – commits villainy
25 in a fit of rage. A lazy man's craving will kill him, for his hands refuse to

---

15 | A wheel rolled over wheat to separate the kernel from the chaff. Or, perhaps a chariot wheel rolled over the enemy.

16 | In other words, one's innermost thoughts.

17 | In isolation; see verse 19.

18 | Referring to the simpleton, when he sees the wise man being instructed. This follows *Mikra LeYisrael*.

19 | The simple person learns a lesson when he sees the scoffer punished and when he sees the wise person being taught.

20 | The wicked will serve as a ransom for the righteous and the traitor for the upright. Cf. 11:8.

כה וְאָדָם מַה־יָּבִין דַּרְכּוֹ: מוֹקֵשׁ אָדָם יָלַע קֹדֶשׁ וְאַחַר נְדָרִים לְבַקֵּר:
כו כז מְזָרֶה רְשָׁעִים מֶלֶךְ חָכָם וַיָּשֶׁב עֲלֵיהֶם אוֹפָן: נֵר יְהוָה נִשְׁמַת אָדָם
כח חֹפֵשׂ כָּל־חַדְרֵי־בָטֶן: חֶסֶד וֶאֱמֶת יִצְּרוּ־מֶלֶךְ וְסָעַד בַּחֶסֶד כִּסְאוֹ:
כט ל תִּפְאֶרֶת בַּחוּרִים כֹּחָם וַהֲדַר זְקֵנִים שֵׂיבָה: חַבֻּרוֹת פֶּצַע תמריק בְּרָע תַּמְרוּק
כא א וּמַכּוֹת חַדְרֵי־בָטֶן: פַּלְגֵי־מַיִם לֶב־מֶלֶךְ בְּיַד־יְהוָה עַל־כָּל־אֲשֶׁר יַחְפֹּץ
ב ג יַטֶּנּוּ: כָּל־דֶּרֶךְ־אִישׁ יָשָׁר בְּעֵינָיו וְתֹכֵן לִבּוֹת יְהוָה: עֲשֹׂה צְדָקָה
ד וּמִשְׁפָּט נִבְחָר לַיהוָה מִזָּבַח: רוּם־עֵינַיִם וּרְחַב־לֵב נִר רְשָׁעִים חַטָּאת:
ה ו מַחְשְׁבוֹת חָרוּץ אַךְ־לְמוֹתָר וְכָל־אָץ אַךְ־לְמַחְסוֹר: פֹּעַל אֹצָרוֹת
ז בִּלְשׁוֹן שָׁקֶר הֶבֶל נִדָּף מְבַקְשֵׁי־מָוֶת: שֹׁד־רְשָׁעִים יְגוֹרֵם כִּי מֵאֲנוּ
ח ט לַעֲשׂוֹת מִשְׁפָּט: הֲפַכְפַּךְ דֶּרֶךְ אִישׁ וָזָר וְזַךְ יָשָׁר פָּעֳלוֹ: טוֹב לָשֶׁבֶת
י עַל־פִּנַּת־גָּג מֵאֵשֶׁת מדונים וּבֵית חָבֶר: נֶפֶשׁ רָשָׁע אִוְּתָה־רָע לֹא־יֻחַן מִדְיָנִים
יא בְּעֵינָיו רֵעֵהוּ: בַּעֲנָשׁ־לֵץ יֶחְכַּם־פֶּתִי וּבְהַשְׂכִּיל לְחָכָם יִקַּח־דָּעַת:
יב יג מַשְׂכִּיל צַדִּיק לְבֵית רָשָׁע מְסַלֵּף רְשָׁעִים לָרָע: אֹטֵם אָזְנוֹ מִזַּעֲקַת־דָּל
יד גַּם־הוּא יִקְרָא וְלֹא יֵעָנֶה: מַתָּן בַּסֵּתֶר יִכְפֶּה־אָף וְשֹׁחַד בַּחֵק חֵמָה
טו טז עַזָּה: שִׂמְחָה לַצַּדִּיק עֲשׂוֹת מִשְׁפָּט וּמְחִתָּה לְפֹעֲלֵי אָוֶן: אָדָם תּוֹעֶה
יז מִדֶּרֶךְ הַשְׂכֵּל בִּקְהַל רְפָאִים יָנוּחַ: אִישׁ מַחְסוֹר אֹהֵב שִׂמְחָה אֹהֵב
יח יט יַיִן־וָשֶׁמֶן לֹא יַעֲשִׁיר: כֹּפֶר לַצַּדִּיק רָשָׁע וְתַחַת יְשָׁרִים בּוֹגֵד: טוֹב
כ שֶׁבֶת בְּאֶרֶץ־מִדְבָּר מֵאֵשֶׁת מדונים וָכָעַס: אוֹצָר ׀ נֶחְמָד וָשֶׁמֶן בִּנְוֵה מִדְיָנִים
כא חָכָם וּכְסִיל אָדָם יְבַלְּעֶנּוּ: רֹדֵף צְדָקָה וָחָסֶד יִמְצָא חַיִּים צְדָקָה וְכָבוֹד:
כב כג עִיר גִּבֹּרִים עָלָה חָכָם וַיֹּרֶד עֹז מִבְטֶחָה: שֹׁמֵר פִּיו וּלְשׁוֹנוֹ שֹׁמֵר
כד כה מִצָּרוֹת נַפְשׁוֹ: זֵד יָהִיר לֵץ שְׁמוֹ עוֹשֶׂה בְּעֶבְרַת זָדוֹן: תַּאֲוַת עָצֵל

26 work. All day he craves and craves, but the righteous man gives and does
27 not withhold. The sacrifice of the wicked is anathema, all the more so if
28 brought with nefarious intent. The lying witness is doomed; the man who
29 listens speaks for eternity. The wicked man's brazenness is upon his face;
30 the upright carefully considers his conduct. There is neither wisdom nor
31 understanding nor counsel against the LORD.[21] The horse may be prepared
22 1 for the day of battle, but deliverance is the LORD's. A good name is
2 preferable to great wealth; good grace is better than silver and gold. Rich
3 man and poor man meet – it is the LORD who made them both. The clever
man saw danger and hid; the ignorant continued onward and suffered.
4 The result of humility is fear of the LORD – wealth, honor, and life itself.
5 There are thorns and snares upon the crooked path; he who protects
6 himself keeps far from them. Train a youth in the way that befits him, then
7 even as he ages he will not turn away from it. The rich man rules the
8 destitute; the borrower is slave to the lender. He who sows injustice
9 reaps naught, and his rod of wrath will vanish. The generous man will be
10 blessed; he gave of his own bread to the pauper. Expel the scoffer, and
11 strife departs; gone are discord and disgrace. The pure-hearted friend with
12 gracious lips – a king is his companion. The eyes of the LORD watch over
13 the man of knowledge but disrupt the traitor's plans. The lazy man says,
14 "There is a lion out there! If I venture into the streets I will be killed!" The
mouth of a promiscuous woman is like a deep pit; he who is scorned by
15 the LORD will fall into it. Folly is bound up in the heart of a youth; the
16 rod of instruction will expel it far from him. He who enriches the pauper
17 will gain thereby; he who bestows gifts upon the rich will only lose. Bend
your ear and listen to the words of the wise; direct your heart to my
18 knowledge. It is pleasant that you preserve them in your belly and that
19 they stand firmly together on your lips. That you put your trust in the
20 LORD – this I have demanded of you today – yes, you! I have written these
21 threefold with great counsel and with forethought, to inform you of the
validity of these words of truth so that you can respond with truthful
22 words to those who sent you. Do not steal from a pauper,
23 thinking that he is helpless; do not crush the poor man at the gate. For
the LORD will plead his cause and confiscate the life of the one who
24 confiscated his. Do not befriend him who has a temper, and do not even
25 approach an irascible man, lest you learn his ways and set a trap for
26 yourself. Do not be among those who extend their hands as guarantors
27 for loans, for if you are unable to pay, why should he take your bed from
28 under you? Do not encroach upon the age-old boundary marker that was
29 set up by your ancestors. If you see a man adept at his work, he will one
23 1 day serve kings; he will not serve commoners. When you sit down to

---

21 | No amount of wisdom will avail if God does not wish it.

כו תְמִיתֶנּוּ כִּי־מֵאֲנוּ יָדָיו לַעֲשׂוֹת׃ כָּל־הַיּוֹם הִתְאַוָּה תַאֲוָה וְצַדִּיק יִתֵּן
כז כח וְלֹא יַחְשֹׂךְ׃ זֶבַח רְשָׁעִים תּוֹעֵבָה אַף כִּי־בְזִמָּה יְבִיאֶנּוּ׃ עֵד־כְּזָבִים
כט יֹאבֵד וְאִישׁ שׁוֹמֵעַ לָנֶצַח יְדַבֵּר׃ הֵעֵז אִישׁ רָשָׁע בְּפָנָיו וְיָשָׁר הוּא ׀
ל לא יכין דרכיו׃ אֵין חָכְמָה וְאֵין תְּבוּנָה וְאֵין עֵצָה לְנֶגֶד יהוה׃ סוּס מוּכָן יָבִין דַּרְכּוֹ
כב א לְיוֹם מִלְחָמָה וְלַיהוה הַתְּשׁוּעָה׃ נִבְחָר שֵׁם מֵעֹשֶׁר רָב מִכֶּסֶף וּמִזָּהָב
ב ג חֵן טוֹב׃ עָשִׁיר וָרָשׁ נִפְגָּשׁוּ עֹשֵׂה כֻלָּם יהוה׃ עָרוּם ׀ רָאָה רָעָה ויסתר וְנִסְתָּר
ד וּפְתָיִים עָבְרוּ וְנֶעֱנָשׁוּ׃ עֵקֶב עֲנָוָה יִרְאַת יהוה עֹשֶׁר וְכָבוֹד וְחַיִּים׃
ה ו צִנִּים פַּחִים בְּדֶרֶךְ עִקֵּשׁ שׁוֹמֵר נַפְשׁוֹ יִרְחַק מֵהֶם׃ חֲנֹךְ לַנַּעַר עַל־
ז פִּי דַרְכּוֹ גַּם כִּי־יַזְקִין לֹא־יָסוּר מִמֶּנָּה׃ עָשִׁיר בְּרָשִׁים יִמְשׁוֹל וְעֶבֶד
ח לֹוֶה לְאִישׁ מַלְוֶה׃ זוֹרֵעַ עַוְלָה יקצור־אָוֶן וְשֵׁבֶט עֶבְרָתוֹ יִכְלֶה׃ יִקְצָר־
ט י טוֹב־עַיִן הוּא יְבֹרָךְ כִּי־נָתַן מִלַּחְמוֹ לַדָּל׃ גָּרֵשׁ לֵץ וְיֵצֵא מָדוֹן וְיִשְׁבֹּת
יא יב דִּין וְקָלוֹן׃ אֹהֵב טהור־לֵב חֵן שְׂפָתָיו רֵעֵהוּ מֶלֶךְ׃ עֵינֵי יהוה נָצְרוּ טְהָר־
יג דָעַת וַיְסַלֵּף דִּבְרֵי בֹגֵד׃ אָמַר עָצֵל אֲרִי בַחוּץ בְּתוֹךְ רְחֹבוֹת אֵרָצֵחַ׃
יד טו שׁוּחָה עֲמֻקָּה פִּי זָרוֹת זְעוּם יהוה יפול־שָׁם׃ אִוֶּלֶת קְשׁוּרָה בְלֶב־נָעַר יִפָּל־
טז שֵׁבֶט מוּסָר יַרְחִיקֶנָּה מִמֶּנּוּ׃ עֹשֵׁק דָּל לְהַרְבּוֹת לוֹ נֹתֵן לְעָשִׁיר אַךְ־
יז יח לְמַחְסוֹר׃ הַט אָזְנְךָ וּשְׁמַע דִּבְרֵי חֲכָמִים וְלִבְּךָ תָּשִׁית לְדַעְתִּי׃ כִּי־
יט נָעִים כִּי־תִשְׁמְרֵם בְּבִטְנֶךָ יִכֹּנוּ יַחְדָּו עַל־שְׂפָתֶיךָ׃ לִהְיוֹת בַּיהוה
כ מִבְטַחֶךָ הוֹדַעְתִּיךָ הַיּוֹם אַף־אָתָּה׃ הֲלֹא כָתַבְתִּי לְךָ שלשום שָׁלִישִׁים
כא בְּמֹעֵצוֹת וָדָעַת׃ לְהוֹדִיעֲךָ קֹשְׁטְ אִמְרֵי אֱמֶת לְהָשִׁיב אֲמָרִים אֱמֶת
כב לְשֹׁלְחֶיךָ׃ אַל־תִּגְזָל־דָּל כִּי דַל־הוּא וְאַל־תְּדַכֵּא עָנִי
כג כד בַשָּׁעַר׃ כִּי־יהוה יָרִיב רִיבָם וְקָבַע אֶת־קֹבְעֵיהֶם נָפֶשׁ׃ אַל־תִּתְרַע
כה אֶת־בַּעַל אָף וְאֶת־אִישׁ חֵמוֹת לֹא תָבוֹא׃ פֶּן־תֶּאֱלַף אֹרְחֹתָו וְלָקַחְתָּ
כו כז מוֹקֵשׁ לְנַפְשֶׁךָ׃ אַל־תְּהִי בְתֹקְעֵי־כָף בַּעֹרְבִים מַשָּׁאוֹת׃ אִם־אֵין־לְךָ
כח לְשַׁלֵּם לָמָּה יִקַּח מִשְׁכָּבְךָ מִתַּחְתֶּיךָ׃ אַל־תַּסֵּג גְּבוּל עוֹלָם אֲשֶׁר עָשׂוּ
כט אֲבוֹתֶיךָ׃ חָזִיתָ אִישׁ ׀ מָהִיר בִּמְלַאכְתּוֹ לִפְנֵי־מְלָכִים יִתְיַצָּב בַּל־יִתְיַצֵּב
כג א לִפְנֵי חֲשֻׁכִּים׃ כִּי־תֵשֵׁב לִלְחוֹם אֶת־מוֹשֵׁל בִּין תָּבִין אֶת־אֲשֶׁר לְפָנֶיךָ׃

2 break bread with a ruler, consider well what is before you. If you are a
3 glutton, put a knife to your throat. Do not crave his delicacies; they are
4 the bread of lies. Do not exhaust yourself in order to get rich; follow your
5 understanding – desist! Blink your eyes at it; it is gone. It has grown wings;
6 like an eagle it flies heavenward. Do not eat a stingy man's bread; do not
7 crave his delicacies. For he silently measures. He will say to you, "Eat!
8 Drink!" But he does not mean it. You will vomit the bread you ate, and
9 you will have wasted your pleasant words. Do not address a fool; he will
10 ridicule the wisdom of your words. Do not move the age-old boundary
11 marker; do not encroach upon the orphans' fields, for their Redeemer is
12 strong, and He will take up their cause against you. Apply your heart
13 toward instruction and your ears to knowledgeable sayings. Do not
withhold instruction from a youth; if you strike him with the rod he will
14 not die. You will strike him with the rod and thereby save him from Sheol.
15 My son, if your heart has grown wise, my heart rejoices along with yours.
16 17 My mind[22] takes delight when your lips speak words of rectitude. Do not
envy sinners in your heart; envy only those who fear the LORD constantly.
18 19 Indeed there is a future; your hope will not be cut off. You, my son, listen
20 and grow wise; let your heart march along the proper road. Do not
associate with those who guzzle wine, who gorge themselves on meat.
21 For the drunkard and the glutton become impoverished; drowsiness
22 clothes them in tatters. Listen to your father who begot you; do not
23 disdain your mother when she is old. Buy truth; do not sell it. Buy
24 wisdom, instruction, and understanding. The father of the righteous man
25 will be glad, and he who begets a wise man will rejoice. Your father and
26 your mother will rejoice, and she who raised you will be glad. My son,
27 give your heart to me, and let your eyes watch my ways. For the harlot is
28 like a deep pit, and the alien woman is like a narrow well. Like a beast of
prey, she too lies in ambush; she destroys the betrayers among men.
29 To whom is there woe, to whom wailing? To whom quarrel, to whom
30 delusion, to whom needless wounds? To whom bloodshot eyes? To those
31 who linger late for wine and come in search of mixed drinks. Do not gaze
at wine so red, for he who keeps his eye upon the cup thinks he is walking
32 the straight and narrow. But in the end, it is as if he is bitten by a snake or
33 stung by a viper. Your eyes will see hallucinations; your heart will speak
34 distortions. You will be like one who lies in the midst of the sea or like
35 one who lies upon the ship's prow. "They struck me, but I felt no pain!
They pounded me, but I was unaware! Whenever I wake up, I will pursue
24 1 it all the more!" Do not envy men of evil; do not crave their company.
2 3 For their hearts contemplate violence, and their lips speak harm. With
4 wisdom will a house be built; with understanding it will hold firm. With

22 | Literally "my kidneys."

ב ג וְשַׂמְתָּ שַׂכִּין בְּלֹעֶךָ אִם־בַּעַל נֶפֶשׁ אָתָּה: אַל־תִּתְאָו לְמַטְעַמּוֹתָיו
ד ה וְהוּא לֶחֶם כְּזָבִים: אַל־תִּיגַע לְהַעֲשִׁיר מִבִּינָתְךָ חֲדָל: התעוף עֵינֶיךָ הֲתָעִיף
ו בּוֹ וְאֵינֶנּוּ כִּי עָשֹׂה יַעֲשֶׂה־לּוֹ כְנָפַיִם כְּנֶשֶׁר ועיף הַשָּׁמָיִם: אַל־תִּלְחַם יָעוּף
ז אֶת־לֶחֶם רַע עָיִן וְאַל־תִּתְאָו לְמַטְעַמֹּתָיו: כִּי ׀ כְּמוֹ־שָׁעַר בְּנַפְשׁוֹ כֶּן
ח הוּא אֱכוֹל וּשְׁתֵה יֹאמַר לָךְ וְלִבּוֹ בַּל־עִמָּךְ: פִּתְּךָ־אָכַלְתָּ תְקִיאֶנָּה
ט וְשִׁחַתָּ דְּבָרֶיךָ הַנְּעִימִים: בְּאָזְנֵי כְסִיל אַל־תְּדַבֵּר כִּי־יָבוּז לְשֵׂכֶל מִלֶּיךָ:
י יא אַל־תַּסֵּג גְּבוּל עוֹלָם וּבִשְׂדֵי יְתוֹמִים אַל־תָּבֹא: כִּי־גֹאֲלָם חָזָק הוּא־
יב יָרִיב אֶת־רִיבָם אִתָּךְ: הָבִיאָה לַמּוּסָר לִבֶּךָ וְאָזְנֶךָ לְאִמְרֵי־דָעַת:
יג יד אַל־תִּמְנַע מִנַּעַר מוּסָר כִּי־תַכֶּנּוּ בַשֵּׁבֶט לֹא יָמוּת: אַתָּה בַּשֵּׁבֶט תַּכֶּנּוּ
טו טז וְנַפְשׁוֹ מִשְּׁאוֹל תַּצִּיל: בְּנִי אִם־חָכַם לִבֶּךָ יִשְׂמַח לִבִּי גַם־אָנִי: וְתַעְלֹזְנָה
יז כִלְיוֹתָי בְּדַבֵּר שְׂפָתֶיךָ מֵישָׁרִים: אַל־יְקַנֵּא לִבְּךָ בַּחַטָּאִים כִּי אִם־
יח בְּיִרְאַת־יְהוָה כָּל־הַיּוֹם: כִּי אִם־יֵשׁ אַחֲרִית וְתִקְוָתְךָ לֹא תִכָּרֵת:
יט כ שְׁמַע־אַתָּה בְנִי וַחֲכָם וְאַשֵּׁר בַּדֶּרֶךְ לִבֶּךָ: אַל־תְּהִי בְסֹבְאֵי־יָיִן בְּזֹלְלֵי
כא כב בָשָׂר לָמוֹ: כִּי־סֹבֵא וְזוֹלֵל יִוָּרֵשׁ וּקְרָעִים תַּלְבִּישׁ נוּמָה: שְׁמַע לְאָבִיךָ
כג זֶה יְלָדֶךָ וְאַל־תָּבוּז כִּי־זָקְנָה אִמֶּךָ: אֱמֶת קְנֵה וְאַל־תִּמְכֹּר חָכְמָה גִּיל יָגִיל
כד כה וּמוּסָר וּבִינָה: גול יגול אֲבִי צַדִּיק יולד חָכָם וישמח בּוֹ: יִשְׂמַח־אָבִיךָ וְיוֹלֵד | יִשְׂמַח
כו כז וְאִמֶּךָ וְתָגֵל יוֹלַדְתֶּךָ: תְּנָה־בְנִי לִבְּךָ לִי וְעֵינֶיךָ דְּרָכַי תרצנה: כִּי־ תִּצֹּרְנָה
כח שׁוּחָה עֲמֻקָּה זוֹנָה וּבְאֵר צָרָה נָכְרִיָּה: אַף־הִיא כְּחֶתֶף תֶּאֱרֹב וּבוֹגְדִים
כט בְּאָדָם תּוֹסִף: לְמִי אוֹי לְמִי אֲבוֹי לְמִי מדונים ׀ לְמִי שִׂיחַ לְמִי פְּצָעִים מִדְיָנִים
ל חִנָּם לְמִי חַכְלִלוּת עֵינָיִם: לַמְאַחֲרִים עַל־הַיָּיִן לַבָּאִים לַחְקֹר מִמְסָךְ:
לא אַל־תֵּרֶא יַיִן כִּי יִתְאַדָּם כִּי־יִתֵּן בכיס עֵינוֹ יִתְהַלֵּךְ בְּמֵישָׁרִים: בַּכּוֹס
לב לג אַחֲרִיתוֹ כְּנָחָשׁ יִשָּׁךְ וּכְצִפְעֹנִי יַפְרִשׁ: עֵינֶיךָ יִרְאוּ זָרוֹת וְלִבְּךָ יְדַבֵּר
לד לה תַּהְפֻּכוֹת: וְהָיִיתָ כְּשֹׁכֵב בְּלֶב־יָם וּכְשֹׁכֵב בְּרֹאשׁ חִבֵּל: הִכּוּנִי בַל־
כד א חָלִיתִי הֲלָמוּנִי בַּל־יָדָעְתִּי מָתַי אָקִיץ אוֹסִיף אֲבַקְשֶׁנּוּ עוֹד: אַל־תְּקַנֵּא
ב בְּאַנְשֵׁי רָעָה וְאַל־תִּתְאָו לִהְיוֹת אִתָּם: כִּי־שֹׁד יֶהְגֶּה לִבָּם וְעָמָל
ג ד שִׂפְתֵיהֶם תְּדַבֵּרְנָה: בְּחָכְמָה יִבָּנֶה בָּיִת וּבִתְבוּנָה יִתְכּוֹנָן: וּבְדַעַת

knowledge its chambers will be filled with every sort of precious and
5 pleasant treasure. A wise man stands strong; a man of reason conserves
6 his resources. For only with plans can you wage war; victory is won with
7 abundant counsel. Wisdom is far removed from the fool; at the gate of
8 the wise he has nothing to say. He who but considers doing evil –
9 him they will call "master of schemes." Foolish thoughts are sinful; men
10 deem a scoffer anathema. Because you weakened yourself on the day of
11 another's distress, your own strength will diminish. If you failed to rescue
12 those being taken to their death, destined for slaughter – you will object,
"But, we didn't know of this!" – He who assesses men's hearts discerns;
He who guards your life knows; He will repay each man as he deserves.
13 My son, just as eating honey is as good as sweet droplets upon your palate,
14 so too is striving to achieve wisdom for yourself. If you succeed, there is
15 a future; your hope will not be cut off. Wicked one! Do not ambush the
16 righteous man's abode; do not do violence to his place of rest. Although
the righteous man falls seven times, he rises, but the wicked falter under
17 duress. Do not rejoice when your enemy falls; let your heart not be glad
18 when he falters, lest the Lord take notice and be displeased and remove
His wrath from him.
19 20 Do not compete with evildoers; do not envy the wicked. For there is no
21 future for evil; the lamp of the wicked will be dimmed. Fear the Lord,
22 my son, and the king; do not mingle with those who are disobedient. For
their day of retribution arrives suddenly, and the decrees of both – who
knows when?!
23 These too are sayings of the wise: Showing partiality in justice is not
24 good. He who says to the guilty, "You are innocent!"– nations will curse
25 him; peoples will condemn him. Those who offer rebuke will enjoy
26 pleasantness; the blessing of good fortune will come upon them. He
27 kisses with lips, does the one who replies with forthright words.[23] Prepare
your outdoor work; ready your field for yourself. Afterward, build your
house.
28 Do not offer unfounded testimony against your fellow; you will crush him
29 with your lips. Do not say, "I will do to him as he did to me; I will repay
the man as he deserves."
30 I passed by the field of a lazy man, by the vineyard of a mindless person;
31 it had become entirely overgrown with thorns, its surface covered with
32 weeds, its stone fence demolished. I observed and took it to heart; I noted,
33 and I took instruction. A little sleep, a little dozing, a little lying there with
34 folded hands, and poverty will come like a sudden intruder, privation like
a soldier bearing a shield.
25 1 These too are among the proverbs of Shlomo; they were transcribed by

23 | Forthright words (even if they are critical) are like giving a kiss.

ה חֲדָרִים יִמָּלְאוּ כָּל־הוֹן יָקָר וְנָעִים: גֶּבֶר־חָכָם בַּעוֹז וְאִישׁ־דַּעַת מְאַמֶּץ־
ו ז כֹּחַ: כִּי בְתַחְבֻּלוֹת תַּעֲשֶׂה־לְּךָ מִלְחָמָה וּתְשׁוּעָה בְּרֹב יוֹעֵץ: רָאמוֹת
ח לֶאֱוִיל חָכְמוֹת בַּשַּׁעַר לֹא יִפְתַּח־פִּיהוּ: מְחַשֵּׁב לְהָרֵעַ לוֹ בַּעַל־
ט י מְזִמּוֹת יִקְרָאוּ: זִמַּת אִוֶּלֶת חַטָּאת וְתוֹעֲבַת לְאָדָם לֵץ: הִתְרַפִּיתָ
יא בְּיוֹם צָרָה צַר כֹּחֶכָה: הַצֵּל לְקֻחִים לַמָּוֶת וּמָטִים לַהֶרֶג אִם־תַּחְשׂוֹךְ:
יב כִּי־תֹאמַר הֵן לֹא־יָדַעְנוּ זֶה הֲלֹא־תֹכֵן לִבּוֹת ׀ הוּא־יָבִין וְנֹצֵר נַפְשְׁךָ
יג הוּא יֵדָע וְהֵשִׁיב לְאָדָם כְּפָעֳלוֹ: אֱכָל־בְּנִי דְבַשׁ כִּי־טוֹב וְנֹפֶת מָתוֹק
יד עַל־חִכֶּךָ: כֵּן ׀ דְּעֶה חָכְמָה לְנַפְשֶׁךָ אִם־מָצָאתָ וְיֵשׁ אַחֲרִית וְתִקְוָתְךָ
טו טז לֹא תִכָּרֵת: אַל־תֶּאֱרֹב רָשָׁע לִנְוֵה צַדִּיק אַל־תְּשַׁדֵּד רִבְצוֹ: כִּי שֶׁבַע ׀
יז יִפּוֹל צַדִּיק וָקָם וּרְשָׁעִים יִכָּשְׁלוּ בְרָעָה: בִּנְפֹל אויביך אַל־תִּשְׂמָח אֹיִבְךָ
יח וּבִכָּשְׁלוֹ אַל־יָגֵל לִבֶּךָ: פֶּן־יִרְאֶה יְהוָה וְרַע בְּעֵינָיו וְהֵשִׁיב מֵעָלָיו
אַפּוֹ:
יט כ אַל־תִּתְחַר בַּמְּרֵעִים אַל־תְּקַנֵּא בָּרְשָׁעִים: כִּי ׀ לֹא־תִהְיֶה אַחֲרִית
כא לָרָע נֵר רְשָׁעִים יִדְעָךְ: יְרָא־אֶת־יְהוָה בְּנִי וָמֶלֶךְ עִם־שׁוֹנִים אַל־
כב תִּתְעָרָב: כִּי־פִתְאֹם יָקוּם אֵידָם וּפִיד שְׁנֵיהֶם מִי יוֹדֵעַ:
כג כד גַּם־אֵלֶּה לַחֲכָמִים הַכֵּר־פָּנִים בְּמִשְׁפָּט בַּל־טוֹב: אֹמֵר ׀ לְרָשָׁע צַדִּיק
כה אַתָּה יִקְּבֻהוּ עַמִּים יִזְעָמוּהוּ לְאֻמִּים: וְלַמּוֹכִיחִים יִנְעָם וַעֲלֵיהֶם תָּבוֹא
כו כז בִּרְכַּת־טוֹב: שְׂפָתַיִם יִשָּׁק מֵשִׁיב דְּבָרִים נְכֹחִים: הָכֵן בַּחוּץ ׀ מְלַאכְתֶּךָ
וְעַתְּדָהּ בַּשָּׂדֶה לָךְ אַחַר וּבָנִיתָ בֵיתֶךָ:
כח כט אַל־תְּהִי עֵד־חִנָּם בְּרֵעֶךָ וַהֲפִתִּיתָ בִּשְׂפָתֶיךָ: אַל־תֹּאמַר כַּאֲשֶׁר
עָשָׂה־לִי כֵּן אֶעֱשֶׂה־לּוֹ אָשִׁיב לָאִישׁ כְּפָעֳלוֹ:
ל לא עַל־שְׂדֵה אִישׁ־עָצֵל עָבַרְתִּי וְעַל־כֶּרֶם אָדָם חֲסַר־לֵב: וְהִנֵּה עָלָה כֻלּוֹ ׀
לב קִמְּשֹׂנִים כָּסּוּ פָנָיו חֲרֻלִּים וְגֶדֶר אֲבָנָיו נֶהֱרָסָה: וָאֶחֱזֶה אָנֹכִי אָשִׁית
לג לִבִּי רָאִיתִי לָקַחְתִּי מוּסָר: מְעַט שֵׁנוֹת מְעַט תְּנוּמוֹת מְעַט ׀ חִבֻּק
לד יָדַיִם לִשְׁכָּב: וּבָא־מִתְהַלֵּךְ רֵישֶׁךָ וּמַחְסֹרֶיךָ כְּאִישׁ מָגֵן:
כה א גַּם־אֵלֶּה מִשְׁלֵי שְׁלֹמֹה אֲשֶׁר הֶעְתִּיקוּ אַנְשֵׁי ׀ חִזְקִיָּה מֶלֶךְ־יְהוּדָה:

2 the men of Ḥizkiya, king of Yehuda: The glory of God is that He conceals
3 things; the glory of kings is that they search things out. As high as the
4 heavens, as deep as the earth, the minds of kings are unknowable. As dross
5 is removed from silver so that a vessel emerges for the silversmith, so too
must the wicked man be removed from the king's presence so that his
6 throne will be established in righteousness. Do not flaunt yourself before
7 a king; do not stand in the place of great men. For it is better that it be said
to you, "Step up here," than to be humiliated before the nobleman – this
8 your own eyes have surely observed. Do not enter into a dispute hastily,
9 for what will you do if your fellow puts you to shame in the end? Dispute
10 with him if you must, but do not reveal another's secret, lest a listener
11 reproach you and you be unable to retract your slander. Like golden apples
12 in silver settings, so are words spoken in proper sequence. Like a golden
earring or an ornament of pure gold, so does a wise man offer a rebuke
to a listening ear.
13 Like the coolness of snow on a summer harvest day, so is a messenger who
is faithful to his senders. He soothes his master's spirits.
14 Clouds and wind, but no rain! So is the man who praises himself for gifts
15 not given. With patience even a tyrant can be won over; a soft tongue can
16 break a bone. Have you found honey? Consume no more than you need,
17 lest you eat your fill and vomit it up. So too, set foot in your friend's home
18 but rarely, lest he have his fill of you and come to hate you. Like a club, a
sword, and a sharpened arrow is the man who bears false witness against
19 his fellow. Like a rotten tooth and a wobbly foot is trust in a traitor in times
20 of trouble. A tattered garment on a cold day is like vinegar upon natron[24]
21 or like songs sung to a despondent heart. If your foe is hungry, feed him
22 bread; if thirsty, give him water. For you will be shoveling coals upon his
23 head, and the Lord will reward you. The north wind produces rain; a
24 secretive tongue produces a scowling face. Better to sit on the corner of a
roof than with a quarrelsome wife in the home of friends.
25 Like cool waters upon a thirsty throat are glad tidings from a distant land.
26 Like a muddied spring and a ruined fountain is the righteous man who
27 bends before a wicked one. Eating too much honey is not good, and
28 searching for honor is not honorable. Like a breached city with no wall is a
26 1 man who has no control over his emotions. Like snow in the summer and
2 rain at harvest time, so is honor unseemly for a fool. As a sparrow wanders
and a swallow flies, so will an undeserved curse come back to him who
3 uttered it. Like a whip for a horse and a bridle for a donkey, so is a rod
4 for the backs of fools. Do not answer a fool according to his folly, lest you
5 become his equal. Answer a fool according to his folly, lest he consider
6 himself wise. It is like cutting off your feet or drinking down violence

24 |Natron is sodium bicarbonate (baking soda), used in biblical times as a cleanser. When mixed with vinegar, the solution froths and then quickly dissipates.

ב ג כְּבֹד אֱלֹהִים הַסְתֵּר דָּבָר וּכְבֹד מְלָכִים חֲקֹר דָּבָר׃ שָׁמַיִם לָרוּם וָאָרֶץ
ד לָעֹמֶק וְלֵב מְלָכִים אֵין חֵקֶר׃ הָגוֹ סִיגִים מִכָּסֶף וַיֵּצֵא לַצֹּרֵף כֶּלִי׃
ה ו הָגוֹ רָשָׁע לִפְנֵי־מֶלֶךְ וְיִכּוֹן בַּצֶּדֶק כִּסְאוֹ׃ אַל־תִּתְהַדַּר לִפְנֵי־מֶלֶךְ
ז וּבִמְקוֹם גְּדֹלִים אַל־תַּעֲמֹד׃ כִּי טוֹב אֲמָר־לְךָ עֲלֵה הֵנָּה מֵהַשְׁפִּילְךָ
ח לִפְנֵי נָדִיב אֲשֶׁר רָאוּ עֵינֶיךָ׃ אַל־תֵּצֵא לָרִב מַהֵר פֶּן מַה־תַּעֲשֶׂה
ט בְּאַחֲרִיתָהּ בְּהַכְלִים אֹתְךָ רֵעֶךָ׃ רִיבְךָ רִיב אֶת־רֵעֶךָ וְסוֹד אַחֵר אַל־
י יא תְּגָל׃ פֶּן־יְחַסֶּדְךָ שֹׁמֵעַ וְדִבָּתְךָ לֹא תָשׁוּב׃ תַּפּוּחֵי זָהָב בְּמַשְׂכִּיּוֹת
יב כָּסֶף דָּבָר דָּבֻר עַל־אָפְנָיו׃ נֶזֶם זָהָב וַחֲלִי־כָתֶם מוֹכִיחַ חָכָם עַל־אֹזֶן
שֹׁמָעַת׃
יג כְּצִנַּת־שֶׁלֶג ׀ בְּיוֹם קָצִיר צִיר נֶאֱמָן לְשֹׁלְחָיו וְנֶפֶשׁ אֲדֹנָיו יָשִׁיב׃ ז
יד טו נְשִׂיאִים וְרוּחַ וְגֶשֶׁם אָיִן אִישׁ מִתְהַלֵּל בְּמַתַּת־שָׁקֶר׃ בְּאֹרֶךְ אַפַּיִם
טז יְפֻתֶּה קָצִין וְלָשׁוֹן רַכָּה תִּשְׁבָּר־גָּרֶם׃ דְּבַשׁ מָצָאתָ אֱכֹל דַּיֶּךָּ פֶּן־
יז יח תִּשְׂבָּעֶנּוּ וַהֲקֵאתוֹ׃ הֹקַר רַגְלְךָ מִבֵּית רֵעֶךָ פֶּן־יִשְׂבָּעֲךָ וּשְׂנֵאֶךָ׃ מֵפִיץ
יט וְחֶרֶב וְחֵץ שָׁנוּן אִישׁ־עֹנֶה בְרֵעֵהוּ עֵד שָׁקֶר׃ שֵׁן רֹעָה וְרֶגֶל מוּעָדֶת
כ מִבְטָח בּוֹגֵד בְּיוֹם צָרָה׃ מַעֲדֶה־בֶּגֶד ׀ בְּיוֹם קָרָה חֹמֶץ עַל־נָתֶר
כא וְשָׁר בַּשִּׁרִים עַל לֶב־רָע׃ אִם־רָעֵב שֹׂנַאֲךָ הַאֲכִלֵהוּ לָחֶם וְאִם־
כב צָמֵא הַשְׁקֵהוּ מָיִם׃ כִּי גֶחָלִים אַתָּה חֹתֶה עַל־רֹאשׁוֹ וַיהוָה יְשַׁלֶּם־
כג כד לָךְ׃ רוּחַ צָפוֹן תְּחוֹלֵל גָּשֶׁם וּפָנִים נִזְעָמִים לְשׁוֹן סָתֶר׃ טוֹב שֶׁבֶת
עַל־פִּנַּת־גָּג מֵאֵשֶׁת מדונים וּבֵית חָבֶר׃ מִדְיָנִים
כה כו מַיִם קָרִים עַל־נֶפֶשׁ עֲיֵפָה וּשְׁמוּעָה טוֹבָה מֵאֶרֶץ מֶרְחָק׃ מַעְיָן נִרְפָּשׂ
כז וּמָקוֹר מָשְׁחָת צַדִּיק מָט לִפְנֵי־רָשָׁע׃ אָכֹל דְּבַשׁ הַרְבּוֹת לֹא־טוֹב
כח וְחֵקֶר כְּבֹדָם כָּבוֹד׃ עִיר פְּרוּצָה אֵין חוֹמָה אִישׁ אֲשֶׁר אֵין מַעְצָר
כו א לְרוּחוֹ׃ כַּשֶּׁלֶג ׀ בַּקַּיִץ וְכַמָּטָר בַּקָּצִיר כֵּן לֹא־נָאוֶה לִכְסִיל כָּבוֹד׃
ב ג כַּצִּפּוֹר לָנוּד כַּדְּרוֹר לָעוּף כֵּן קִלְלַת חִנָּם לא תָבֹא׃ שׁוֹט לַסּוּס מֶתֶג לוֹ
ד לַחֲמוֹר וְשֵׁבֶט לְגֵו כְּסִילִים׃ אַל־תַּעַן כְּסִיל כְּאִוַּלְתּוֹ פֶּן־תִּשְׁוֶה־לּוֹ גַם־
ה ו אָתָּה׃ עֲנֵה כְסִיל כְּאִוַּלְתּוֹ פֶּן־יִהְיֶה חָכָם בְּעֵינָיו׃ מְקַצֶּה רַגְלַיִם חָמָס

7 to send messages in the hand of a fool. Like removing the crutches[25]
8 from a cripple, so is a proverb in the mouth of a fool. Like binding a
9 pebble in a sling, so is granting honor to a fool. As a thorn comes into the
10 hand of a drunkard, so is a proverb in the mouth of a fool. The
quarrelsome man harms it all; he hires both the fool and the disobedient.
11 12 As a dog returns to his vomit, so does a fool repeat his folly. You observed
a man who is wise in his own eyes? There is more hope for a fool than
13 for him. The lazy man says, "There is a young lion on the road; a lion is
14 in the midst of the streets."[26] Just as a door twists on its hinges, so does
15 the lazy man on his bed. The lazy man buries his hand in the bowl, too
16 tired to bring it to his mouth. The lazy man is wiser in his own eyes than
17 seven sensible advisors. Like someone who grasps a dog's ears is he who
18 angrily intercedes in a dispute not his. Like someone acting as a madman,
19 shooting firebrands and deadly arrows, so is the man who cheats his fellow
20 and says, "I was only joking." Without wood, the fire will go out. Without
21 an argumentative man, strife is silenced. As charcoal for embers and wood
for a fire, so does a quarrelsome person ignite dispute.
22 The words of an argumentative man are like blows; they pierce the belly's
23 chambers. Like cheap silver covering an earthen vessel, so are enticing
24 lips with evil intentions. The foe disguises himself with his lips; inside,
25 he plots treachery. His voice may sound gracious, but do not trust him:
26 he has seven abominations in his heart. Hatred may be hidden in deep
27 deception, but its evil is exposed in public. He who digs a ditch will fall
28 into it; he who rolls a stone will find it rolls back on him. The false tongue
hates those whom it oppresses; the smooth tongue produces calamity.
27 1 Boast not about tomorrow, for you do not know what might yet occur
2 today. Let another person praise you, not your own mouth; a stranger, not
3 your own lips. Stone's weight, sand's burden – the aggravation caused by
4 a fool is heavier than both. Wrath's cruelty, fury's torrent – but who can
5 6 withstand jealousy? Better open rebuke than concealed love. A friend's
7 bruises are well intended; a foe's kisses are excessive. A satisfied person
tramples even honey; to a hungry person everything bitter tastes sweet.
8 Like a sparrow that wanders from its nest, so is a man who wanders from
9 his home. Oil and incense gladden the heart; better a friend's sweetness
10 than your own advice. Forsake neither your friend nor your father's
friend. Enter not your brother's home at the time of your misfortune; a
11 close neighbor is better than a distant brother. My son, become wise and
12 gladden my heart; I will then be able to respond to my critics. The clever
man saw danger and hid; the ignorant continued onward and suffered.
13 Take his garment, for he has put up security for a stranger. If he did so
14 on behalf of a foreign woman – seize it! He who blesses his fellow in a

---

25 | This admittedly unusual translation of a very obscure phrase is suggested by *Daat Mikra*.
26 | An excuse for not going out; cf. 22:13.

ז שֹׁתֶה שֹׁלֵחַ דְּבָרִים בְּיַד־כְּסִיל׃ דַּלְיוּ שֹׁקַיִם מִפִּסֵּחַ וּמָשָׁל בְּפִי כְסִילִים׃
ח ט כִּצְרוֹר אֶבֶן בְּמַרְגֵּמָה כֵּן־נוֹתֵן לִכְסִיל כָּבוֹד׃ חוֹחַ עָלָה בְיַד־שִׁכּוֹר
י וּמָשָׁל בְּפִי כְסִילִים׃ רַב מְחוֹלֵל־כֹּל וְשֹׂכֵר
יא יב כְּסִיל וְשֹׂכֵר עֹבְרִים׃ כְּכֶלֶב שָׁב עַל־קֵאוֹ כְּסִיל שׁוֹנֶה בְאִוַּלְתּוֹ׃ רָאִיתָ
יג אִישׁ חָכָם בְּעֵינָיו תִּקְוָה לִכְסִיל מִמֶּנּוּ׃ אָמַר עָצֵל שַׁחַל בַּדָּרֶךְ אֲרִי בֵּין
יד טו הָרְחֹבוֹת׃ הַדֶּלֶת תִּסּוֹב עַל־צִירָהּ וְעָצֵל עַל־מִטָּתוֹ׃ טָמַן עָצֵל יָדוֹ
טז בַּצַּלָּחַת נִלְאָה לַהֲשִׁיבָהּ אֶל־פִּיו׃ חָכָם עָצֵל בְּעֵינָיו מִשִּׁבְעָה מְשִׁיבֵי
יז יח טָעַם׃ מַחֲזִיק בְּאָזְנֵי־כָלֶב עֹבֵר מִתְעַבֵּר עַל־רִיב לֹּא־לוֹ׃ כְּמִתְלַהְלֵהַּ
יט הַיֹּרֶה זִקִּים חִצִּים וָמָוֶת׃ כֵּן־אִישׁ רִמָּה אֶת־רֵעֵהוּ וְאָמַר הֲלֹא־מְשַׂחֵק
כ כא אָנִי׃ בְּאֶפֶס עֵצִים תִּכְבֶּה־אֵשׁ וּבְאֵין נִרְגָּן יִשְׁתֹּק מָדוֹן׃ פֶּחָם לְגֶחָלִים
וְעֵצִים לְאֵשׁ וְאִישׁ מדונים לְחַרְחַר־רִיב׃ מִדְיָנִים
כב כג דִּבְרֵי נִרְגָּן כְּמִתְלַהֲמִים וְהֵם יָרְדוּ חַדְרֵי־בָטֶן׃ כֶּסֶף סִיגִים מְצֻפֶּה עַל־
כד חָרֶשׂ שְׂפָתַיִם דֹּלְקִים וְלֶב־רָע׃ בִּשְׂפָתָו יִנָּכֵר שׂוֹנֵא וּבְקִרְבּוֹ יָשִׁית
כה כו מִרְמָה׃ כִּי־יְחַנֵּן קוֹלוֹ אַל־תַּאֲמֶן־בּוֹ כִּי שֶׁבַע תּוֹעֵבוֹת בְּלִבּוֹ׃ תִּכַּסֶּה
כז שִׂנְאָה בְּמַשָּׁאוֹן תִּגָּלֶה רָעָתוֹ בְקָהָל׃ כֹּרֶה־שַּׁחַת בָּהּ יִפֹּל וְגֹלֵל אֶבֶן
כז כח א אֵלָיו תָּשׁוּב׃ לְשׁוֹן־שֶׁקֶר יִשְׂנָא דַכָּיו וּפֶה חָלָק יַעֲשֶׂה מִדְחֶה׃ אַל־
ב תִּתְהַלֵּל בְּיוֹם מָחָר כִּי לֹא־תֵדַע מַה־יֵּלֶד יוֹם׃ יְהַלֶּלְךָ זָר וְלֹא־פִיךָ
ג נָכְרִי וְאַל־שְׂפָתֶיךָ׃ כֹּבֶד־אֶבֶן וְנֵטֶל הַחוֹל וְכַעַס אֱוִיל כָּבֵד מִשְּׁנֵיהֶם׃
ד ה אַכְזְרִיּוּת חֵמָה וְשֶׁטֶף אָף וּמִי יַעֲמֹד לִפְנֵי קִנְאָה׃ טוֹבָה תּוֹכַחַת מְגֻלָּה
ו מֵאַהֲבָה מְסֻתָּרֶת׃ נֶאֱמָנִים פִּצְעֵי אוֹהֵב וְנַעְתָּרוֹת נְשִׁיקוֹת שׂוֹנֵא׃
ז ח נֶפֶשׁ שְׂבֵעָה תָּבוּס נֹפֶת וְנֶפֶשׁ רְעֵבָה כָּל־מַר מָתוֹק׃ כְּצִפּוֹר נוֹדֶדֶת
ט מִן־קִנָּהּ כֵּן־אִישׁ נוֹדֵד מִמְּקוֹמוֹ׃ שֶׁמֶן וּקְטֹרֶת יְשַׂמַּח־לֵב וּמֶתֶק רֵעֵהוּ
י מֵעֲצַת־נָפֶשׁ׃ רֵעֲךָ ורעה אָבִיךָ אַל־תַּעֲזֹב וּבֵית אָחִיךָ אַל־תָּבוֹא בְּיוֹם וְרֵעַ
יא אֵידֶךָ טוֹב שָׁכֵן קָרוֹב מֵאָח רָחוֹק׃ חֲכַם בְּנִי וְשַׂמַּח לִבִּי וְאָשִׁיבָה
יב יג חֹרְפִי דָבָר׃ עָרוּם רָאָה רָעָה נִסְתָּר פְּתָאיִם עָבְרוּ נֶעֱנָשׁוּ׃ קַח־בִּגְדוֹ
יד כִּי־עָרַב זָר וּבְעַד נָכְרִיָּה חַבְלֵהוּ׃ מְבָרֵךְ רֵעֵהוּ ׀ בְּקוֹל גָּדוֹל בַּבֹּקֶר

15 loud voice early in the morning – it will be reckoned to him as a curse. A
16 quarrelsome wife is akin to an annoying drip on a rainy day. Confining
her is like confining the wind; he will have to call for the muscles of his
17 right hand. As iron sharpens iron, so is a man gladdened by the presence
18 of another. He who tends to the fig tree shall eat its fruit; he who takes
19 care of his master shall be honored. As water reflects the face shown to it,
20 so does one man's heart reciprocate another's. Sheol and destruction are
never satisfied; human eyes, too, are never satisfied.

21 Silver is tested in a crucible and gold in a furnace; so too can a man be
22 tested by praise of him. Even if you crush a fool with a mortar and pestle
together with grain, his folly will not depart from him.

23 24 Know well the appearance of your sheep; pay attention to your flocks, for
wealth does not last forever, nor is a crown always passed from generation
25 to generation. Grass is gone; fresh grass is revealed, and the mountains'
26 greenery accumulates. Lamb's wool will be your clothing, and your male
27 goats will earn a field's price. There will be enough goats' milk to provide
food for you and your household and sustenance for your maidservants.

28 1 The wicked flee though there is no pursuer; the righteous rest securely
2 like a lion. When the land is rebellious, its rulers are many; with a man of
3 understanding and knowledge, stability endures. A pauper who oppresses
4 the poor is like a driving rain that leaves no food. Those who forsake
instruction praise the wicked; those who observe instruction combat
5 them. Evildoers cannot understand justice; those who seek the Lord
understand it all.

6 Better a pauper who walks in innocence than a man who is crooked in his
7 ways but rich. A wise son holds fast to instruction, but a companion of
8 gluttons shames his father. He who amasses wealth by usury and interest
9 gathers it for the one who is kind to the poor. He who turns his ear to
10 avoid hearing instruction renders even his prayers an anathema. He who
misleads the upright along an evil path will fall into his own trap, but the
11 innocent will inherit goodness. A rich man is wise in his own eyes, but an
12 insightful poor man will expose him. When the righteous celebrate, there
13 is great glory, but when the wicked arise, people must hide. He who would
cover up his sins will not succeed, but he who confesses and forsakes them
14 will find compassion. Fortunate is the person who is always cautious; he
15 who is obstinate will fall into disaster. Like a roaring lion and a prowling
bear is a wicked tyrant over a helpless people;
16 so is the senseless prince who is oppressive. He who hates sinful gain will
prolong his days.

17 A person desperate because he has murdered another – even if he flees
18 to the pit, do not assist him. He who walks in perfectness will be saved,
19 but he who is crooked in his ways will fall at once. He who works his land
will be sated with bread; he who trails idlers will have plenty of poverty.

טו הַשְׁכֵּים קְלָלָה תֵּחָשֶׁב לוֹ: דֶּלֶף טוֹרֵד בְּיוֹם סַגְרִיר וְאֵשֶׁת מדונים מִדְיָנִים
טז יז נִשְׁתָּוָה: צֹפְנֶיהָ צָפַן־רוּחַ וְשֶׁמֶן יְמִינוֹ יִקְרָא: בַּרְזֶל בְּבַרְזֶל יָחַד וְאִישׁ
יח יט יַחַד פְּנֵי־רֵעֵהוּ: נֹצֵר תְּאֵנָה יֹאכַל פִּרְיָהּ וְשֹׁמֵר אֲדֹנָיו יְכֻבָּד: כַּמַּיִם
כ הַפָּנִים לַפָּנִים כֵּן לֵב הָאָדָם לָאָדָם: שְׁאוֹל וַאֲבַדֹּה לֹא תִשְׂבַּעְנָה וְעֵינֵי
הָאָדָם לֹא תִשְׂבַּעְנָה:
כא כב מַצְרֵף לַכֶּסֶף וְכוּר לַזָּהָב וְאִישׁ לְפִי מַהֲלָלוֹ: אִם־תִּכְתּוֹשׁ אֶת־הָאֱוִיל ׀
בַּמַּכְתֵּשׁ בְּתוֹךְ הָרִיפוֹת בַּעֱלִי לֹא־תָסוּר מֵעָלָיו אִוַּלְתּוֹ:
כג כד יָדֹעַ תֵּדַע פְּנֵי צֹאנֶךָ שִׁית לִבְּךָ לַעֲדָרִים: כִּי לֹא לְעוֹלָם חֹסֶן וְאִם־נֵזֶר
כה כו לְדוֹר דור: גָּלָה חָצִיר וְנִרְאָה־דֶשֶׁא וְנֶאֶסְפוּ עִשְּׂבוֹת הָרִים: כְּבָשִׂים וָדוֹר
כז לִלְבוּשֶׁךָ וּמְחִיר שָׂדֶה עַתּוּדִים: וְדֵי ׀ חֲלֵב עִזִּים לְלַחְמְךָ לְלֶחֶם בֵּיתֶךָ
כח א ב וְחַיִּים לְנַעֲרוֹתֶיךָ: נָסוּ וְאֵין־רֹדֵף רָשָׁע וְצַדִּיקִים כִּכְפִיר יִבְטָח: בְּפֶשַׁע
ג אֶרֶץ רַבִּים שָׂרֶיהָ וּבְאָדָם מֵבִין יֹדֵעַ כֵּן יַאֲרִיךְ: גֶּבֶר רָשׁ וְעֹשֵׁק דַּלִּים
ד מָטָר סֹחֵף וְאֵין לָחֶם: עֹזְבֵי תוֹרָה יְהַלְלוּ רָשָׁע וְשֹׁמְרֵי תוֹרָה יִתְגָּרוּ
ה בָם: אַנְשֵׁי־רָע לֹא־יָבִינוּ מִשְׁפָּט וּמְבַקְשֵׁי יְהוָה יָבִינוּ כֹל:
ו ז טוֹב־רָשׁ הוֹלֵךְ בְּתֻמּוֹ מֵעִקֵּשׁ דְּרָכַיִם וְהוּא עָשִׁיר: נוֹצֵר תּוֹרָה בֵּן
ח מֵבִין וְרֹעֶה זוֹלְלִים יַכְלִים אָבִיו: מַרְבֶּה הוֹנוֹ בְּנֶשֶׁךְ ובתרבית לְחוֹנֵן וְתַרְבִּית
ט י דַּלִּים יִקְבְּצֶנּוּ: מֵסִיר אָזְנוֹ מִשְּׁמֹעַ תּוֹרָה גַּם־תְּפִלָּתוֹ תּוֹעֵבָה: מַשְׁגֶּה
יא יְשָׁרִים ׀ בְּדֶרֶךְ רָע בִּשְׁחוּתוֹ הוּא־יִפּוֹל וּתְמִימִים יִנְחֲלוּ־טוֹב: חָכָם
יב בְּעֵינָיו אִישׁ עָשִׁיר וְדַל מֵבִין יַחְקְרֶנּוּ: בַּעֲלֹץ צַדִּיקִים רַבָּה תִפְאָרֶת
יג וּבְקוּם רְשָׁעִים יְחֻפַּשׂ אָדָם: מְכַסֶּה פְשָׁעָיו לֹא יַצְלִיחַ וּמוֹדֶה וְעֹזֵב
יד טו יְרֻחָם: אַשְׁרֵי אָדָם מְפַחֵד תָּמִיד וּמַקְשֶׁה לִבּוֹ יִפּוֹל בְּרָעָה: אֲרִי־נֹהֵם
וְדֹב שׁוֹקֵק מוֹשֵׁל רָשָׁע עַל עַם־דָּל:
טז נָגִיד חֲסַר תְּבוּנוֹת וְרַב מַעֲשַׁקּוֹת שנאי בֶּצַע יַאֲרִיךְ יָמִים: ח שֹׂנֵא
יז יח אָדָם עָשֻׁק בְּדַם־נָפֶשׁ עַד־בּוֹר יָנוּס אַל־יִתְמְכוּ־בוֹ: הוֹלֵךְ תָּמִים
יט יִוָּשֵׁעַ וְנֶעְקַשׁ דְּרָכַיִם יִפּוֹל בְּאֶחָת: עֹבֵד אַדְמָתוֹ יִשְׂבַּע־לָחֶם וּמְרַדֵּף

20 A trustworthy man has many blessings; he who rushes to get rich will not
21 escape the consequences. Showing partiality is not right, or that a man[27]
22 should sin for a slice of bread. Distracted by his wealth is the miser; he
23 is unaware that want will come upon him. He who reproves a man will
24 eventually find more favor than someone who offers flattery. He who
robs his father and mother and insists that he has not sinned is a vandal's
25 accomplice. The selfish man incites strife; he who trusts in the LORD
26 will be enriched. He who trusts his own heart is a fool; he who walks
27 in wisdom will be safe. He who gives to the poor will not lose thereby;
28 he who looks away will receive many curses. When the wicked arise,
a man had better hide; with their destruction the righteous increase.
29 1 He who stiffens his neck when often rebuked will collapse suddenly,
2 beyond cure. When the righteous ascend to greatness, the people rejoice;
3 when a wicked man reigns, the people lament. A man who loves wisdom
brings joy to his father; he who keeps company with harlots squanders
4 his fortune. With justice, a king sustains the land; the gift-seeking man
lays it waste. The man who flatters his fellow spreads a net for his own
5
6 feet. The wicked man's sins are his own trap; the righteous man sings and
7 rejoices. The righteous man knows the poor man's plight; the wicked
8 man does not understand such knowledge. Scoffers inflame a city, but the
9 wise turn wrath away. A wise man in a legal dispute with a fool – he may
10 show anger or he may smile, but there is never satisfaction. Murderers
11 hate the innocent; the upright seek to protect him. The fool lets out all
12 his anger; the wise man calmly restrains it. A ruler who listens to lies –
13 all of his servants become wicked. The pauper and the scheming man
14 meet; the LORD illuminates the eyes of both. A king who judges the
15 poor truthfully – his throne will be firm forever. Rod and rebuke will
16 yield wisdom; a youth uncontrolled will disgrace his mother. When the
wicked ascend to greatness, sin increases, but the righteous will witness
17 their downfall. Discipline your child; he will bring you comfort and give
you delight.
18 Without a vision the people become mutinous; anyone who observes
19 instruction is fortunate. A slave cannot be controlled by words alone;
20 although he understands, he gives no response.[28] Have you seen a man
21 who hurries his speech? There is more hope for a fool than for him! He
who pampers his slave from an early age in the end will make him the
22 master. An angry man provokes conflict; with a hot-tempered man there
23 is much sin. A man's pride will bring him down; he who is lowly in spirit
24 will grasp honor. He who shares with a thief hates himself; he will hear
25 the oath but not testify. A man's panic becomes a trap, but he who trusts
26 in the LORD shall be lifted up. Many seek an audience with the ruler, but

27 | Meaning the judge.

28 | The implication is that a slave can be controlled only by beating him. See also Exodus 21:20–21, 26–27.

כ רֵיקִים יִשְׂבַּע־רִישׁ: אִישׁ אֱמוּנוֹת רַב־בְּרָכוֹת וְאָץ לְהַעֲשִׁיר לֹא
כא כב יִנָּקֶה: הַכֵּר־פָּנִים לֹא־טוֹב וְעַל־פַּת־לֶחֶם יִפְשַׁע־גָּבֶר: נִבְהָל לַהוֹן
כג אִישׁ רַע עָיִן וְלֹא־יֵדַע כִּי־חֶסֶר יְבֹאֶנּוּ: מוֹכִיחַ אָדָם אַחֲרַי חֵן יִמְצָא
כד מִמַּחֲלִיק לָשׁוֹן: גּוֹזֵל ׀ אָבִיו וְאִמּוֹ וְאֹמֵר אֵין־פָּשַׁע חָבֵר הוּא לְאִישׁ
כה כו מַשְׁחִית: רְחַב־נֶפֶשׁ יְגָרֶה מָדוֹן וּבוֹטֵחַ עַל־יְהוָה יְדֻשָּׁן: בּוֹטֵחַ בְּלִבּוֹ
כז הוּא כְסִיל וְהוֹלֵךְ בְּחָכְמָה הוּא יִמָּלֵט: נוֹתֵן לָרָשׁ אֵין מַחְסוֹר וּמַעְלִים
כח עֵינָיו רַב־מְאֵרוֹת: בְּקוּם רְשָׁעִים יִסָּתֵר אָדָם וּבְאָבְדָם יִרְבּוּ צַדִּיקִים:
כט א ב אִישׁ תּוֹכָחוֹת מַקְשֶׁה־עֹרֶף פֶּתַע יִשָּׁבֵר וְאֵין מַרְפֵּא: בִּרְבוֹת צַדִּיקִים
ג יִשְׂמַח הָעָם וּבִמְשֹׁל רָשָׁע יֵאָנַח עָם: אִישׁ־אֹהֵב חָכְמָה יְשַׂמַּח אָבִיו
ד וְרֹעֶה זוֹנוֹת יְאַבֶּד־הוֹן: מֶלֶךְ בְּמִשְׁפָּט יַעֲמִיד אָרֶץ וְאִישׁ תְּרוּמוֹת
ה ו יֶהֶרְסֶנָּה: גֶּבֶר מַחֲלִיק עַל־רֵעֵהוּ רֶשֶׁת פּוֹרֵשׂ עַל־פְּעָמָיו: בְּפֶשַׁע
ז אִישׁ רָע מוֹקֵשׁ וְצַדִּיק יָרוּן וְשָׂמֵחַ: יֹדֵעַ צַדִּיק דִּין דַּלִּים רָשָׁע לֹא־
ח ט יָבִין דָּעַת: אַנְשֵׁי לָצוֹן יָפִיחוּ קִרְיָה וַחֲכָמִים יָשִׁיבוּ אָף: אִישׁ־חָכָם
י נִשְׁפָּט אֶת־אִישׁ אֱוִיל וְרָגַז וְשָׂחַק וְאֵין נָחַת: אַנְשֵׁי דָמִים יִשְׂנְאוּ־תָם
יא וִישָׁרִים יְבַקְשׁוּ נַפְשׁוֹ: כָּל־רוּחוֹ יוֹצִיא כְסִיל וְחָכָם בְּאָחוֹר יְשַׁבְּחֶנָּה:
יב יג מֹשֵׁל מַקְשִׁיב עַל־דְּבַר־שָׁקֶר כָּל־מְשָׁרְתָיו רְשָׁעִים: רָשׁ וְאִישׁ תְּכָכִים
יד נִפְגָּשׁוּ מֵאִיר־עֵינֵי שְׁנֵיהֶם יְהוָה: מֶלֶךְ שׁוֹפֵט בֶּאֱמֶת דַּלִּים כִּסְאוֹ לָעַד
טו טז יִכּוֹן: שֵׁבֶט וְתוֹכַחַת יִתֵּן חָכְמָה וְנַעַר מְשֻׁלָּח מֵבִישׁ אִמּוֹ: בִּרְבוֹת
יז רְשָׁעִים יִרְבֶּה־פָּשַׁע וְצַדִּיקִים בְּמַפַּלְתָּם יִרְאוּ: יַסֵּר בִּנְךָ וִינִיחֶךָ וְיִתֵּן
מַעֲדַנִּים לְנַפְשֶׁךָ:
יח יט בְּאֵין חָזוֹן יִפָּרַע עָם וְשֹׁמֵר תּוֹרָה אַשְׁרֵהוּ: בִּדְבָרִים לֹא־יִוָּסֶר עָבֶד
כ כִּי־יָבִין וְאֵין מַעֲנֶה: חָזִיתָ אִישׁ אָץ בִּדְבָרָיו תִּקְוָה לִכְסִיל מִמֶּנּוּ:
כא כב מְפַנֵּק מִנֹּעַר עַבְדּוֹ וְאַחֲרִיתוֹ יִהְיֶה מָנוֹן: אִישׁ־אַף יְגָרֶה מָדוֹן וּבַעַל
כג כד חֵמָה רַב־פָּשַׁע: גַּאֲוַת אָדָם תַּשְׁפִּילֶנּוּ וּשְׁפַל־רוּחַ יִתְמֹךְ כָּבוֹד: חוֹלֵק
כה עִם־גַּנָּב שׂוֹנֵא נַפְשׁוֹ אָלָה יִשְׁמַע וְלֹא יַגִּיד: חֶרְדַּת אָדָם יִתֵּן מוֹקֵשׁ
כו וּבוֹטֵחַ בַּיהוָה יְשֻׂגָּב: רַבִּים מְבַקְשִׁים פְּנֵי־מוֹשֵׁל וּמֵיְהוָה מִשְׁפַּט־אִישׁ:

27 a man's judgment is from the LORD. An unjust man is an abomination
to the righteous; he who walks a straight path is an abomination to the
wicked.

30 1 The words of Agur[29] son of Yakeh, the Masaite; the oration spoken by this
2 man[30] to Itiel – to Itiel and to Ukhal:[31] I am more ignorant than any other
3 man; I lack human understanding. I never studied wisdom, nor do I have
4 knowledge of holy beings. Who rose to the heavens and descended? Who
gathered the wind in the hollow of his hands? Who wrapped water in a
cloak? Who erected the ends of the earth? What is his name or his son's
5 name, if you know? Every word of God is pure; He is a shield to those
6 who take refuge in him. Do not add to His words, lest He rebuke you,
7 and you be exposed as a liar. Two things I request of You; do not
8 deny them to me before I die. Keep emptiness and falsehood far from me;
give me neither poverty nor wealth; nourish me with my fixed portion
9 of bread, lest I become sated and deny and say, "Who is the LORD?" And
lest I become impoverished and steal and thereby defile the name of my
10 God. Do not malign a slave to his master lest he curse you and
11 you be found guilty. There is a generation that curses its father and does
12 not bless its mother. A generation pure in its own eyes but not cleansed
13 of its filth. A generation – how haughty are its eyes, its eyelids raised ever
14 upward![32] A generation whose teeth are swords and whose jaws are knives
ready to devour the poor from the earth – the neediest of mankind.
15 The leech has two daughters: "Give" and "Give." There are three[33] that are
16 never satisfied and four that never say, "Enough!" Sheol; the barren womb;
17 the earth is never satisfied with water; and fire never says, "Enough!" The
eye that mocks its father and belittles its mother's guidance – ravens of the
18 creek shall peck it out, and eagles shall devour it. Three things
19 are too wondrous for me; four I cannot know: the way of the eagle in the
heavens, the way of the serpent upon the rock, the way of a ship in the
20 midst of the sea, the way of a man with a young woman. So too, the way
of an adulterous woman: she eats,[34] wipes her mouth, and says, "I have
done no wrong!"

21 The earth shudders because of three things, and because of four it cannot
22 carry on: because of a slave who reigns, because of a knave who is sated
23 with bread, because of a hated wife who gains authority, and because of a
slave girl who displaces her mistress.

24 There are four that are the smallest on earth, yet they are exceedingly
25 wise: Ants are not a strong species, yet they prepare their food in summer.

29 | Agur is an otherwise unknown foreign sage.
30 | Cf. Numbers 24:3.
31 | Perhaps Agur's sons.
32 | Raised eyes are a sign of arrogance.
33 | See note on 6:16.
34 | A euphemism for sexual relations.

כז תּוֹעֲבַת צַדִּיקִים אִישׁ עָוֶל וְתוֹעֲבַת רָשָׁע יְשַׁר־דָּרֶךְ׃
ל א דִּבְרֵי ׀ אָגוּר בִּן־יָקֶה הַמַּשָּׂא נְאֻם הַגֶּבֶר לְאִיתִיאֵל לְאִיתִיאֵל וְאֻכָל׃
ב ג כִּי בַעַר אָנֹכִי מֵאִישׁ וְלֹא־בִינַת אָדָם לִי׃ וְלֹא־לָמַדְתִּי חָכְמָה וְדַעַת
ד קְדֹשִׁים אֵדָע׃ מִי עָלָה־שָׁמַיִם ׀ וַיֵּרַד מִי אָסַף־רוּחַ ׀ בְּחָפְנָיו מִי צָרַר־
מַיִם ׀ בַּשִּׂמְלָה מִי הֵקִים כָּל־אַפְסֵי־אָרֶץ מַה־שְּׁמוֹ וּמַה־שֶּׁם־בְּנוֹ כִּי
ה ו תֵדָע׃ כָּל־אִמְרַת אֱלוֹהַּ צְרוּפָה מָגֵן הוּא לַחֹסִים בּוֹ׃ אַל־תּוֹסְףְּ עַל־
ז דְּבָרָיו פֶּן־יוֹכִיחַ בְּךָ וְנִכְזָבְתָּ׃ שְׁתַּיִם שָׁאַלְתִּי מֵאִתָּךְ
ח אַל־תִּמְנַע מִמֶּנִּי בְּטֶרֶם אָמוּת׃ שָׁוְא ׀ וּדְבַר־כָּזָב הַרְחֵק מִמֶּנִּי רֵאשׁ
ט וָעֹשֶׁר אַל־תִּתֶּן־לִי הַטְרִיפֵנִי לֶחֶם חֻקִּי׃ פֶּן־אֶשְׂבַּע ׀ וְכִחַשְׁתִּי וְאָמַרְתִּי
י מִי יְהוָה וּפֶן־אִוָּרֵשׁ וְגָנַבְתִּי וְתָפַשְׂתִּי שֵׁם אֱלֹהָי׃ אַל־
יא תַּלְשֵׁן עֶבֶד אֶל־אֲדֹנָו פֶּן־יְקַלֶּלְךָ וְאָשָׁמְתָּ׃ דּוֹר אָבִיו יְקַלֵּל וְאֶת־אִמּוֹ
יב יג לֹא יְבָרֵךְ׃ דּוֹר טָהוֹר בְּעֵינָיו וּמִצֹּאָתוֹ לֹא רֻחָץ׃ דּוֹר מָה־רָמוּ עֵינָיו
יד וְעַפְעַפָּיו יִנָּשֵׂאוּ׃ דּוֹר ׀ חֲרָבוֹת שִׁנָּיו וּמַאֲכָלוֹת מְתַלְּעֹתָיו לֶאֱכֹל עֲנִיִּים
מֵאֶרֶץ וְאֶבְיוֹנִים מֵאָדָם׃
טו לַעֲלוּקָה ׀ שְׁתֵּי בָנוֹת הַב ׀ הַב שָׁלוֹשׁ הֵנָּה לֹא תִשְׂבַּעְנָה אַרְבַּע לֹא־
טז אָמְרוּ הוֹן׃ שְׁאוֹל וְעֹצֶר רָחַם אֶרֶץ לֹא־שָׂבְעָה מַּיִם וְאֵשׁ לֹא־אָמְרָה
יז הוֹן׃ עַיִן ׀ תִּלְעַג לְאָב וְתָבוּז לִיקְּהַת־אֵם יִקְּרוּהָ עֹרְבֵי־נַחַל וְיֹאכְלוּהָ
יח בְנֵי־נָשֶׁר׃ שְׁלֹשָׁה הֵמָּה נִפְלְאוּ מִמֶּנִּי וְאַרְבָּעָ לֹא
יט יְדַעְתִּים׃ דֶּרֶךְ הַנֶּשֶׁר ׀ בַּשָּׁמַיִם דֶּרֶךְ נָחָשׁ עֲלֵי צוּר דֶּרֶךְ־אֳנִיָּה בְלֶב־
כ יָם וְדֶרֶךְ גֶּבֶר בְּעַלְמָה׃ כֵּן ׀ דֶּרֶךְ אִשָּׁה מְנָאָפֶת אָכְלָה וּמָחֲתָה פִיהָ
וְאָמְרָה לֹא־פָעַלְתִּי אָוֶן׃
כא כב תַּחַת שָׁלוֹשׁ רָגְזָה אֶרֶץ וְתַחַת אַרְבַּע לֹא־תוּכַל שְׂאֵת׃ תַּחַת עֶבֶד
כג כִּי יִמְלוֹךְ וְנָבָל כִּי יִשְׂבַּע־לָחֶם׃ תַּחַת שְׂנוּאָה כִּי תִבָּעֵל וְשִׁפְחָה כִּי־
תִירַשׁ גְּבִרְתָּהּ׃
כד כה אַרְבָּעָה הֵם קְטַנֵּי־אָרֶץ וְהֵמָּה חֲכָמִים מְחֻכָּמִים׃ הַנְּמָלִים עַם לֹא־

26 Hyraxes are not a mighty species, yet they make their home in the rock.
27 28 The locust has no king, yet he marches forth as a troop. You can catch the
lizard with your hands, yet it resides in the palaces of kings.
29 30 There are three who are adept at marching and four at walking: The lion
31 is the mightiest of beasts, before nothing will he retreat; the hunter's
32 swift hound; the he-goat; the king whom none will challenge. If you are
insulted, maintain your dignity; if you consider otherwise, put your hand
33 to your mouth. Churning milk produces butter; a churning nose produces
31 1 blood; churning anger produces strife. The words to Lemuel,
2 king;[35] the oration with which his mother admonished him: What? My
3 son! What? Child of my womb! What? Child of my vows! Do not waste
your strength on women; do not pursue the paths of kingly pleasures.
4 This is not for kings, Lemuel. It is not for kings to drink wine, nor for
5 noblemen to ask, "Where is aged wine?" Lest he drink and forget what is
6 inscribed and subvert the cause of all the downtrodden. Leave aged wine
7 for the bereaved and wine for embittered souls. Let him drink and forget
8 his poverty and never again remember his plight. Speak up for the mute
9 and for the rights of all mortals. Speak up; judge righteously; advocate
the cause of the poor and needy.
10 An exemplary woman who can find? She is more valuable than pearls.
11 12 Her husband's heart trusts in her; he will lack no benefit. She will repay
13 his favors, not his insults, in all of her life's circumstances. She searches
14 for wool and flax,[36] and her hands work adroitly. She becomes like the
15 merchant ships; she brings her bread from afar.[37] She rises while it is
yet night; she gives sustenance to her household and portions to her
16 maidservants. When she sets her mind upon a field she buys it; with the
17 fruits of her labor she plants a vineyard. She girds herself with strength
18 and vigorously exerts her limbs.[38] When she discerns that her wares are
19 good, her lamp is not extinguished by night. She sets her hands to the
20 distaff, and her palms grasp the spinning rod. She stretches out her palm
21 to the poor and extends her hands to the needy. She need not fear for
her household because of snow, for her entire household is clothed in
22 scarlet.[39] She makes bedcoverings for herself; linen and purple is her
23 garment. Her husband is well known in the city gates[40] as he sits among
24 the elders of the land. She makes clothing and sells it and offers belts to the
25 merchant. Strength and beauty are her garment; she smiles as she faces the
26 future. She opens her mouth with wisdom, and the teaching of kindness

35 | Identified by some commentators as Shlomo.

36 | Wool for winter wear and linen for summer.

37 | She resourcefully acquires imported food and other goods.

38 | In hard work.

39 | The finest clothing will protect her family from the cold. Scarlet and especially purple (verse 22) were expensive dyes.

40 | The legal and commercial gathering place of the city.

כו עָז וַיָּכִינוּ בַקַּיִץ לַחְמָם: שְׁפַנִּים עַם לֹא־עָצוּם וַיָּשִׂימוּ בַסֶּלַע בֵּיתָם:
כז כח מֶלֶךְ אֵין לָאַרְבֶּה וַיֵּצֵא חֹצֵץ כֻּלּוֹ: שְׂמָמִית בְּיָדַיִם תְּתַפֵּשׂ וְהִיא
בְּהֵיכְלֵי מֶלֶךְ:
כט ל שְׁלֹשָׁה הֵמָּה מֵיטִיבֵי צָעַד וְאַרְבָּעָה מֵיטִבֵי לָכֶת: לַיִשׁ גִּבּוֹר בַּבְּהֵמָה
לא לב וְלֹא־יָשׁוּב מִפְּנֵי־כֹל: זַרְזִיר מָתְנַיִם אוֹ־תָיִשׁ וּמֶלֶךְ אַלְקוּם עִמּוֹ: אִם־
לג נָבַלְתָּ בְהִתְנַשֵּׂא וְאִם־זַמּוֹתָ יָד לְפֶה: כִּי מִיץ חָלָב יוֹצִיא חֶמְאָה
לא א וּמִיץ־אַף יוֹצִיא דָם וּמִיץ אַפַּיִם יוֹצִיא רִיב: דִּבְרֵי
ב לְמוּאֵל מֶלֶךְ מַשָּׂא אֲשֶׁר־יִסְּרַתּוּ אִמּוֹ: מַה־בְּרִי וּמַה־בַּר־בִּטְנִי
ג ד וּמֶה בַּר־נְדָרָי: אַל־תִּתֵּן לַנָּשִׁים חֵילֶךָ וּדְרָכֶיךָ לַמְחוֹת מְלָכִין: אַל
ה לַמְלָכִים ׀ לְמוֹאֵל אַל לַמְלָכִים שְׁתוֹ־יָיִן וּלְרוֹזְנִים או שֵׁכָר: פֶּן־ אֵי
ו יִשְׁתֶּה וְיִשְׁכַּח מְחֻקָּק וִישַׁנֶּה דִּין כָּל־בְּנֵי־עֹנִי: תְּנוּ־שֵׁכָר לְאוֹבֵד
ז ח וְיַיִן לְמָרֵי נָפֶשׁ: יִשְׁתֶּה וְיִשְׁכַּח רִישׁוֹ וַעֲמָלוֹ לֹא יִזְכָּר־עוֹד: פְּתַח־
ט פִּיךָ לְאִלֵּם אֶל־דִּין כָּל־בְּנֵי חֲלוֹף: פְּתַח־פִּיךָ שְׁפָט־צֶדֶק וְדִין עָנִי
וְאֶבְיוֹן:
י יא אֵשֶׁת־חַיִל מִי יִמְצָא וְרָחֹק מִפְּנִינִים מִכְרָהּ: בָּטַח בָּהּ לֵב בַּעְלָהּ
יב יג וְשָׁלָל לֹא יֶחְסָר: גְּמָלַתְהוּ טוֹב וְלֹא־רָע כֹּל יְמֵי חַיֶּיהָ: דָּרְשָׁה צֶמֶר
יד וּפִשְׁתִּים וַתַּעַשׂ בְּחֵפֶץ כַּפֶּיהָ: הָיְתָה כָּאֳנִיּוֹת סוֹחֵר מִמֶּרְחָק תָּבִיא
טו לַחְמָהּ: וַתָּקָם ׀ בְּעוֹד לַיְלָה וַתִּתֵּן טֶרֶף לְבֵיתָהּ וְחֹק לְנַעֲרֹתֶיהָ:
טז יז זָמְמָה שָׂדֶה וַתִּקָּחֵהוּ מִפְּרִי כַפֶּיהָ נָטַע כָּרֶם: חָגְרָה בְעוֹז מָתְנֶיהָ
יח וַתְּאַמֵּץ זְרוֹעֹתֶיהָ: טָעֲמָה כִּי־טוֹב סַחְרָהּ לֹא־יִכְבֶּה בַלַּיִל נֵרָהּ:
יט כ יָדֶיהָ שִׁלְּחָה בַכִּישׁוֹר וְכַפֶּיהָ תָּמְכוּ פָלֶךְ: כַּפָּהּ פָּרְשָׂה לֶעָנִי וְיָדֶיהָ
כא שִׁלְּחָה לָאֶבְיוֹן: לֹא־תִירָא לְבֵיתָהּ מִשָּׁלֶג כִּי כָל־בֵּיתָהּ לָבֻשׁ
כב כג שָׁנִים: מַרְבַדִּים עָשְׂתָה־לָּהּ שֵׁשׁ וְאַרְגָּמָן לְבוּשָׁהּ: נוֹדָע בַּשְּׁעָרִים
כד בַּעְלָהּ בְּשִׁבְתּוֹ עִם־זִקְנֵי־אָרֶץ: סָדִין עָשְׂתָה וַתִּמְכֹּר וַחֲגוֹר נָתְנָה
כה כו לַכְּנַעֲנִי: עֹז־וְהָדָר לְבוּשָׁהּ וַתִּשְׂחַק לְיוֹם אַחֲרוֹן: פִּיהָ פָּתְחָה בְחָכְמָה

27 is upon her tongue. She watches over the conduct of her household,
28 and she does not eat the bread of indolence. Her children rise up and
29 extol her; so does her husband praise her: "Many women have excelled,
30 but you have surpassed them all." Charm is false and beauty – empty
31 breath; a woman who fears the Lord, she is praiseworthy. Commend
her for the fruit of her hands, and let her deeds praise her in the city gates.

כז וְתֽוֹרַת־חֶ֝סֶד עַל־לְשׁוֹנָֽהּ׃ צ֭וֹפִיָּה הֲלִיכ֣וֹת בֵּיתָ֑הּ וְלֶ֥חֶם עַ֝צְל֗וּת לֹ֣א הֲלִיכ֣וֹת
כח כט תֹאכֵֽל׃ קָ֣מוּ בָ֭נֶיהָ וַֽיְאַשְּׁר֑וּהָ בַּ֝עְלָ֗הּ וַֽיְהַֽלְלָֽהּ׃ רַבּ֣וֹת בָּ֭נוֹת עָ֣שׂוּ חָ֑יִל
ל וְ֝אַ֗תְּ עָלִ֥ית עַל־כֻּלָּֽנָה׃ שֶׁ֣קֶר הַ֭חֵן וְהֶ֣בֶל הַיֹּ֑פִי אִשָּׁ֥ה יִרְאַת־יְ֝הוָ֗ה
לא הִ֣יא תִתְהַלָּֽל׃ תְּנוּ־לָ֭הּ מִפְּרִ֣י יָדֶ֑יהָ וִֽיהַלְל֖וּהָ בַשְּׁעָרִ֣ים מַעֲשֶֽׂיהָ׃

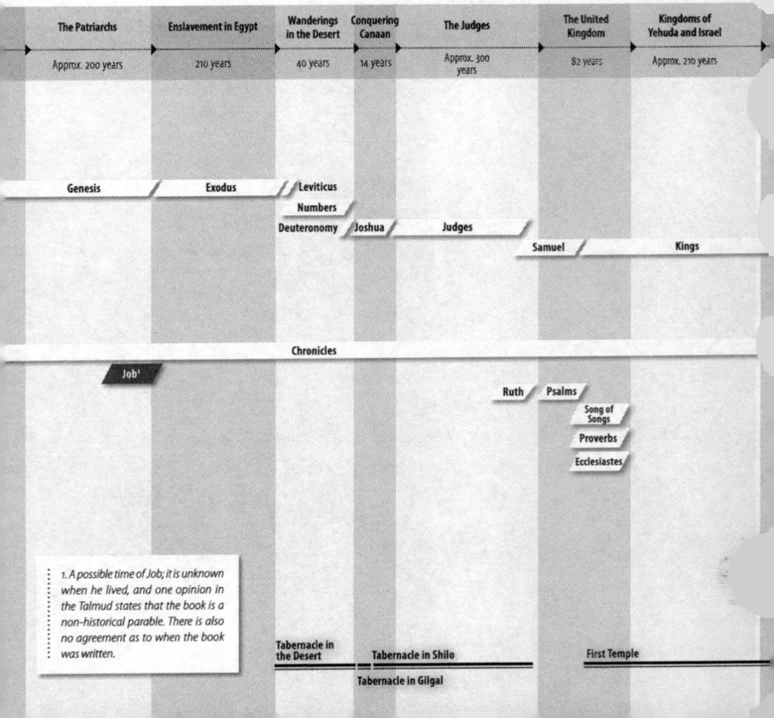

1. *A possible time of Job; it is unknown when he lived, and one opinion in the Talmud states that the book is a non-historical parable. There is also no agreement as to when the book was written.*

איוב
IYOV/JOB

JOB	Iyov's tragedies and his response to them	Discussion between Iyov and his friends regarding the reasons for the tragedies	Elihu's response to the discussion	God's response to Iyov	Iyov's response to God, and the end of the story
	Chs. 1–2	3–31	32–37	38–41	42

1 1 Once there was a man in the land of Utz,[1] and his name was Iyov. He was
2 innocent, honest, God-fearing, and always turned away from evil. He had
3 seven sons and three daughters. His livestock numbered seven thousand
sheep, three thousand camels, five hundred pairs of oxen, and five hundred
donkeys, and he had many workers. He was the greatest of the people of the
4 East. Now, his sons would hold a feast, each one at his house on his set day;
5 they would send for their sisters to come eat and drink with them. And when
the cycle of feast days had come full circle, Iyov would send a messenger to
his children and warn them to purify themselves. He would get up early in the
morning and offer as many sacrifices as he had children. For Iyov said, "Maybe
my children have sinned and cursed God in their hearts." This is what Iyov did
6 all of those days. And the day came: The heavenly entourage came to
stand in position before the LORD, and the Adversary,[2] too, was among them.
7 Then the LORD said to the Adversary, "Where are you coming from?" And the
Adversary answered the LORD, "I was wandering the world, walking to and
8 fro upon it." The LORD said to the Adversary, "Have you noticed My servant,
Iyov? For there is no one like him in the whole world – an innocent, honest,
9 God-fearing man, who always turns away from evil." "Is Iyov God-fearing
10 for nothing?" the Adversary replied to the LORD. "Have You not sheltered
him and his house and everything that is his, everything surrounding him?
You have blessed the labor of his hands, and his cattle bursts forth upon the
11 land. But if You would cast forth Your hand and lay it upon all that he has, I
12 swear he would curse You to Your face." The LORD said to the Adversary, "I
give everything that is his into your hands, only do not lay a hand on him."
13 So the Adversary departed from before the LORD. And the day came: His
sons and daughters were eating and drinking wine in the house of their oldest
14 brother, when a messenger came to Iyov. He said, "The cattle were plowing,
15 and the donkeys were grazing nearby, when a band from Sheba fell upon
them and stole them. They slaughtered the young men. I alone have escaped
16 to tell you." He was still speaking when another arrived and said, "A fire
from God fell from the heavens and engulfed the sheep and the young men.
17 It consumed them. I alone have escaped to tell you." He was still speaking
when another arrived and said, "The Chaldeans[3] split into three groups and
raided the camels. They stole them and slaughtered the young men. I alone
18 have escaped to tell you." He was still speaking when another arrived and
said, "Your sons and daughters were eating and drinking wine in the house
19 of their oldest brother. Suddenly a great wind blew from beyond the desert.
It slammed into all four sides of the house, and the house collapsed upon the
20 young people and they died. I alone have escaped to tell you." Iyov got up
and tore his coat, he pulled out the hair on his head and fell to the ground
21 and bowed down.[4] He said, "I emerged naked from my mother's womb, and

---

1 | In Transjordan (see Jer. 25:20; Lam. 4:21).
2 | Amember of the heavenly court (see Zech. 3:1).
3 | A tribe from Babylonia.
4 | Acts of mourning.

א א אִישׁ הָיָה בְאֶרֶץ־עוּץ אִיּוֹב שְׁמוֹ וְהָיָה ׀ הָאִישׁ הַהוּא תָּם וְיָשָׁר וִירֵא א
ב ג אֱלֹהִים וְסָר מֵרָע׃ וַיִּוָּלְדוּ לוֹ שִׁבְעָה בָנִים וְשָׁלוֹשׁ בָּנוֹת׃ וַיְהִי מִקְנֵהוּ
שִׁבְעַת אַלְפֵי־צֹאן וּשְׁלֹשֶׁת אַלְפֵי גְמַלִּים וַחֲמֵשׁ מֵאוֹת צֶמֶד־בָּקָר
וַחֲמֵשׁ מֵאוֹת אֲתוֹנוֹת וַעֲבֻדָּה רַבָּה מְאֹד וַיְהִי הָאִישׁ הַהוּא גָּדוֹל
ד מִכָּל־בְּנֵי־קֶדֶם׃ וְהָלְכוּ בָנָיו וְעָשׂוּ מִשְׁתֶּה בֵּית אִישׁ יוֹמוֹ וְשָׁלְחוּ
ה וְקָרְאוּ לִשְׁלֹשֶׁת אַחְיֹתֵיהֶם לֶאֱכֹל וְלִשְׁתּוֹת עִמָּהֶם׃ וַיְהִי כִּי הִקִּיפוּ יְמֵי
הַמִּשְׁתֶּה וַיִּשְׁלַח אִיּוֹב וַיְקַדְּשֵׁם וְהִשְׁכִּים בַּבֹּקֶר וְהֶעֱלָה עֹלוֹת מִסְפַּר
כֻּלָּם כִּי אָמַר אִיּוֹב אוּלַי חָטְאוּ בָנַי וּבֵרְכוּ אֱלֹהִים בִּלְבָבָם כָּכָה יַעֲשֶׂה
ו אִיּוֹב כָּל־הַיָּמִים׃ וַיְהִי הַיּוֹם וַיָּבֹאוּ בְּנֵי הָאֱלֹהִים לְהִתְיַצֵּב
ז עַל־יְהוָה וַיָּבוֹא גַם־הַשָּׂטָן בְּתוֹכָם׃ וַיֹּאמֶר יְהוָה אֶל־הַשָּׂטָן מֵאַיִן
תָּבֹא וַיַּעַן הַשָּׂטָן אֶת־יְהוָה וַיֹּאמַר מִשּׁוּט בָּאָרֶץ וּמֵהִתְהַלֵּךְ בָּהּ׃
ח וַיֹּאמֶר יְהוָה אֶל־הַשָּׂטָן הֲשַׂמְתָּ לִבְּךָ עַל־עַבְדִּי אִיּוֹב כִּי אֵין כָּמֹהוּ
ט בָּאָרֶץ אִישׁ תָּם וְיָשָׁר יְרֵא אֱלֹהִים וְסָר מֵרָע׃ וַיַּעַן הַשָּׂטָן אֶת־יְהוָה
י וַיֹּאמַר הַחִנָּם יָרֵא אִיּוֹב אֱלֹהִים׃ הֲלֹא־אַתָּ שַׂכְתָּ בַעֲדוֹ וּבְעַד־בֵּיתוֹ
וּבְעַד כָּל־אֲשֶׁר־לוֹ מִסָּבִיב מַעֲשֵׂה יָדָיו בֵּרַכְתָּ וּמִקְנֵהוּ פָּרַץ בָּאָרֶץ׃
יא וְאוּלָם שְׁלַח־נָא יָדְךָ וְגַע בְּכָל־אֲשֶׁר־לוֹ אִם־לֹא עַל־פָּנֶיךָ יְבָרְכֶךָּ׃
יב וַיֹּאמֶר יְהוָה אֶל־הַשָּׂטָן הִנֵּה כָל־אֲשֶׁר־לוֹ בְּיָדֶךָ רַק אֵלָיו אַל־תִּשְׁלַח
יג יָדֶךָ וַיֵּצֵא הַשָּׂטָן מֵעִם פְּנֵי יְהוָה׃ וַיְהִי הַיּוֹם וּבָנָיו וּבְנֹתָיו אֹכְלִים
יד וְשֹׁתִים יַיִן בְּבֵית אֲחִיהֶם הַבְּכוֹר׃ וּמַלְאָךְ בָּא אֶל־אִיּוֹב וַיֹּאמַר הַבָּקָר
טו הָיוּ חֹרְשׁוֹת וְהָאֲתֹנוֹת רֹעוֹת עַל־יְדֵיהֶם׃ וַתִּפֹּל שְׁבָא וַתִּקָּחֵם וְאֶת־
טז הַנְּעָרִים הִכּוּ לְפִי־חָרֶב וָאִמָּלְטָה רַק־אֲנִי לְבַדִּי לְהַגִּיד לָךְ׃ עוֹד ׀ זֶה
מְדַבֵּר וְזֶה בָּא וַיֹּאמַר אֵשׁ אֱלֹהִים נָפְלָה מִן־הַשָּׁמַיִם וַתִּבְעַר בַּצֹּאן
יז וּבַנְּעָרִים וַתֹּאכְלֵם וָאִמָּלְטָה רַק־אֲנִי לְבַדִּי לְהַגִּיד לָךְ׃ עוֹד ׀ זֶה מְדַבֵּר
וְזֶה בָּא וַיֹּאמַר כַּשְׂדִּים שָׂמוּ ׀ שְׁלֹשָׁה רָאשִׁים וַיִּפְשְׁטוּ עַל־הַגְּמַלִּים
וַיִּקָּחוּם וְאֶת־הַנְּעָרִים הִכּוּ לְפִי־חָרֶב וָאִמָּלְטָה רַק־אֲנִי לְבַדִּי לְהַגִּיד
יח לָךְ׃ עַד זֶה מְדַבֵּר וְזֶה בָּא וַיֹּאמַר בָּנֶיךָ וּבְנוֹתֶיךָ אֹכְלִים וְשֹׁתִים יַיִן
יט בְּבֵית אֲחִיהֶם הַבְּכוֹר׃ וְהִנֵּה רוּחַ גְּדוֹלָה בָּאָה ׀ מֵעֵבֶר הַמִּדְבָּר וַיִּגַּע
בְּאַרְבַּע פִּנּוֹת הַבַּיִת וַיִּפֹּל עַל־הַנְּעָרִים וַיָּמוּתוּ וָאִמָּלְטָה רַק־אֲנִי לְבַדִּי
כ לְהַגִּיד לָךְ׃ וַיָּקָם אִיּוֹב וַיִּקְרַע אֶת־מְעִלוֹ וַיָּגָז אֶת־רֹאשׁוֹ וַיִּפֹּל אַרְצָה
כא וַיִּשְׁתָּחוּ׃ וַיֹּאמֶר עָרֹם יָצָתִי מִבֶּטֶן אִמִּי וְעָרֹם אָשׁוּב שָׁמָה יְהוָה נָתַן

naked I will return there.[5] The LORD has given, the LORD has taken. May
22 the LORD's name be blessed." Despite all this, Iyov did not sin, nor accuse
2 1 God of wrongdoing. And the day came. The heavenly entourage came to
stand in position before the LORD, and the Adversary, too, was among them
2 standing in position before the LORD. Then the LORD said to the Adversary,
"Where are you coming from?" And the Adversary answered the LORD, "I
3 was wandering the world, walking to and fro upon it." The LORD said to the
Adversary, "Have you noticed My servant, Iyov? For there is no one like him
in the whole world – an innocent, honest, God-fearing man, who always turns
away from evil. He still holds on to his innocence, though you incited Me
4 against him so that I would destroy him for nothing." The Adversary replied
to the LORD and said, "As flesh against flesh, a man will give everything he
5 has to save his own soul. But if You would cast Your hand and lay it upon him
6 and his flesh, I swear he would curse You to Your face." The LORD said to the
7 Adversary, "He is in your hands, only do not kill him." Then the Adversary
departed from before the LORD, and he struck Iyov with terrible boils from
8 his heel to his head. He took a shard of pottery to scratch himself with, and
9 sat down in the dust. His wife said to him, "Are you still holding on to your
10 innocence? Curse God and die." He replied to her, "You are speaking like a
fool. Will we accept the good from God and not the bad?" And in spite of
everything, Iyov did not sin in his speech.
11 Now, three friends of Iyov – Elifaz the Temanite, Bildad the Shuhite, and
Tzofar the Naamatite – heard of the evil that had befallen him, and they
came, each from his home, and met together to nod in sorrow with him and
12 comfort him. They raised their eyes from afar and did not recognize him, and
they raised their voices and cried. They each tore their coat and threw dust
13 into the sky, letting it fall on their heads. They sat with him on the ground for
seven days and seven nights. And no one spoke a word to him, for they saw
3 1 how great was his pain. After this, Iyov opened his mouth and cursed the day
he was born.
2 3 Iyov spoke up and said: "Blot out the day of my birth and the night that
4 proclaimed: A male has been conceived! Darken that day! May God want
5 nothing of it; may no glimmer of it ever appear. May death-dark defile it, cloud
6 cover abide above it in bleak and bitter terror; may black oblivion take that
7 night and no day of the year, no month ever claim it. Make that night barren;
8 may no joy arise in its midst. Let them damn that night, those sorcerers who
9 know how to wake Leviathan.[6] Snuff out its first stars! Let it hope for light
10 and find none and never behold the eyelids of dawn, for it refused to lock
11 that womb[7] and hide agony from my eyes. Why couldn't I have died straight
12 out of the belly? Why did knees come to meet me; of what use the breasts
13 that nursed me? For now I would be lying in quiet repose, asleep and at rest,
14 15 with kings and advisors who build up ruins for themselves, among nobles

5 | That is, I will be buried naked of possessions.
6 | Leviathan is a crocodile or a mythical water creature.
7 | Iyov wishes he had been stillborn.

כב וַיהוָה לָקָח יְהִי שֵׁם יְהוָה מְבֹרָךְ׃ בְּכָל־זֹאת לֹא־חָטָא אִיּוֹב וְלֹא־נָתַן
ב א תִּפְלָה לֵאלֹהִים׃ וַיְהִי הַיּוֹם וַיָּבֹאוּ בְּנֵי הָאֱלֹהִים לְהִתְיַצֵּב עַל־יְהוָה
ב וַיָּבוֹא גַם־הַשָּׂטָן בְּתֹכָם לְהִתְיַצֵּב עַל־יְהוָה׃ וַיֹּאמֶר יְהוָה אֶל־הַשָּׂטָן
אֵי מִזֶּה תָּבֹא וַיַּעַן הַשָּׂטָן אֶת־יְהוָה וַיֹּאמַר מִשֻּׁט בָּאָרֶץ וּמֵהִתְהַלֵּךְ
ג בָּהּ׃ וַיֹּאמֶר יְהוָה אֶל־הַשָּׂטָן הֲשַׂמְתָּ לִבְּךָ אֶל־עַבְדִּי אִיּוֹב כִּי אֵין
כָּמֹהוּ בָּאָרֶץ אִישׁ תָּם וְיָשָׁר יְרֵא אֱלֹהִים וְסָר מֵרָע וְעֹדֶנּוּ מַחֲזִיק
ד בְּתֻמָּתוֹ וַתְּסִיתֵנִי בוֹ לְבַלְּעוֹ חִנָּם׃ וַיַּעַן הַשָּׂטָן אֶת־יְהוָה וַיֹּאמַר עוֹר
ה בְּעַד־עוֹר וְכֹל אֲשֶׁר לָאִישׁ יִתֵּן בְּעַד נַפְשׁוֹ׃ אוּלָם שְׁלַח־נָא יָדְךָ וְגַע
ו אֶל־עַצְמוֹ וְאֶל־בְּשָׂרוֹ אִם־לֹא אֶל־פָּנֶיךָ יְבָרְכֶךָּ׃ וַיֹּאמֶר יְהוָה אֶל־
ז הַשָּׂטָן הִנּוֹ בְיָדֶךָ אַךְ אֶת־נַפְשׁוֹ שְׁמֹר׃ וַיֵּצֵא הַשָּׂטָן מֵאֵת פְּנֵי יְהוָה וַיַּךְ
ח אֶת־אִיּוֹב בִּשְׁחִין רָע מִכַּף רַגְלוֹ עַד קָדְקֳדוֹ׃ וַיִּקַּח־לוֹ חֶרֶשׂ לְהִתְגָּרֵד וְעַד
ט בּוֹ וְהוּא יֹשֵׁב בְּתוֹךְ־הָאֵפֶר׃ וַתֹּאמֶר לוֹ אִשְׁתּוֹ עֹדְךָ מַחֲזִיק בְּתֻמָּתֶךָ
י בָּרֵךְ אֱלֹהִים וָמֻת׃ וַיֹּאמֶר אֵלֶיהָ כְּדַבֵּר אַחַת הַנְּבָלוֹת תְּדַבֵּרִי גַּם
אֶת־הַטּוֹב נְקַבֵּל מֵאֵת הָאֱלֹהִים וְאֶת־הָרָע לֹא נְקַבֵּל בְּכָל־זֹאת
לֹא־חָטָא אִיּוֹב בִּשְׂפָתָיו׃
יא וַיִּשְׁמְעוּ שְׁלֹשֶׁת ׀ רֵעֵי אִיּוֹב אֵת כָּל־הָרָעָה הַזֹּאת הַבָּאָה עָלָיו וַיָּבֹאוּ
אִישׁ מִמְּקֹמוֹ אֱלִיפַז הַתֵּימָנִי וּבִלְדַּד הַשּׁוּחִי וְצוֹפַר הַנַּעֲמָתִי וַיִּוָּעֲדוּ
יב יַחְדָּו לָבוֹא לָנוּד־לוֹ וּלְנַחֲמוֹ׃ וַיִּשְׂאוּ אֶת־עֵינֵיהֶם מֵרָחוֹק וְלֹא הִכִּירֻהוּ
וַיִּשְׂאוּ קוֹלָם וַיִּבְכּוּ וַיִּקְרְעוּ אִישׁ מְעִלוֹ וַיִּזְרְקוּ עָפָר עַל־רָאשֵׁיהֶם
יג הַשָּׁמָיְמָה׃ וַיֵּשְׁבוּ אִתּוֹ לָאָרֶץ שִׁבְעַת יָמִים וְשִׁבְעַת לֵילוֹת וְאֵין־דֹּבֵר
ג א אֵלָיו דָּבָר כִּי רָאוּ כִּי־גָדַל הַכְּאֵב מְאֹד׃ אַחֲרֵי־כֵן פָּתַח אִיּוֹב אֶת־פִּיהוּ
וַיְקַלֵּל אֶת־יוֹמוֹ׃
ב ג ד וַיַּעַן אִיּוֹב וַיֹּאמַר׃ יֹאבַד יוֹם אִוָּלֶד בּוֹ וְהַלַּיְלָה אָמַר הֹרָה גָבֶר׃ הַיּוֹם
הַהוּא יְהִי חֹשֶׁךְ אַל־יִדְרְשֵׁהוּ אֱלוֹהַּ מִמָּעַל וְאַל־תּוֹפַע עָלָיו נְהָרָה׃
ה ו יִגְאָלֻהוּ חֹשֶׁךְ וְצַלְמָוֶת תִּשְׁכָּן־עָלָיו עֲנָנָה יְבַעֲתֻהוּ כִּמְרִירֵי יוֹם׃ הַלַּיְלָה
הַהוּא יִקָּחֵהוּ אֹפֶל אַל־יִחַדְּ בִּימֵי שָׁנָה בְּמִסְפַּר יְרָחִים אַל־יָבֹא׃
ז ח הִנֵּה הַלַּיְלָה הַהוּא יְהִי גַלְמוּד אַל־תָּבֹא רְנָנָה בוֹ׃ יִקְּבֻהוּ אֹרְרֵי־יוֹם
ט הָעֲתִידִים עֹרֵר לִוְיָתָן׃ יֶחְשְׁכוּ כּוֹכְבֵי נִשְׁפּוֹ יְקַו־לְאוֹר וָאַיִן וְאַל־יִרְאֶה
י יא בְּעַפְעַפֵּי־שָׁחַר׃ כִּי לֹא סָגַר דַּלְתֵי בִטְנִי וַיַּסְתֵּר עָמָל מֵעֵינָי׃ לָמָּה לֹּא
יב מֵרֶחֶם אָמוּת מִבֶּטֶן יָצָאתִי וְאֶגְוָע׃ מַדּוּעַ קִדְּמוּנִי בִרְכָּיִם וּמַה־שָּׁדַיִם
יג יד כִּי אִינָק׃ כִּי־עַתָּה שָׁכַבְתִּי וְאֶשְׁקוֹט יָשַׁנְתִּי אָז ׀ יָנוּחַ לִי׃ עִם־מְלָכִים
טו וְיֹעֲצֵי אָרֶץ הַבֹּנִים חֳרָבוֹת לָמוֹ׃ אוֹ עִם־שָׂרִים זָהָב לָהֶם הַמְמַלְאִים

16 endowed with gold, their houses heaped with silver – or alongside a buried
17 stillbirth, an infant who never glimpsed the light. There the fearful cease to
18 tremble; there the weary rest. Captives are at ease and ignore the oppressor's
19 20 voice. Meek and mighty are equals; the slave is freed from his master. Why
21 does He waste light on the sufferer or life on the embittered, who wait for
22 death in vain, who seek it like a treasure, who gleefully rejoice, glad to reach
23 the grave; on a man whose path is hidden because God has blocked his view?
24 25 My groaning is my bread; my wails are rushing water. What I feared has come
26 to be; what I dreaded has overwhelmed me. I had no peace nor quiet nor rest;
and anguish has come."

4 1 2 Then Elifaz the Temanite spoke up and said: "If someone ventures a word
3 with you, could you bear it? But who can hold back? See, you have taught
4 many and have strengthened weak hands; your words could lift the stumbling
5 and brace buckling knees. But now that it's your turn, you falter; calamity
6 strikes and you quail. Isn't your piety your strength, your integrity your con-
7 fidence? What guiltless man has ever fallen to ruin? Since when are
8 the virtuous destroyed? From what I have seen, men who plow sin, sow sor-
9 row – reap them. At the breath of God, they are gone; one gust from His
10 nostrils and they die. The lion may roar, and he may howl, but his teeth will
11 break. He will succumb for lack of prey, and his cubs, abandoned, will waste
12 13 away. A word came to me in secret – my ear caught only a trace amid night-
14 thoughts and visions as slumber began to descend: terror came, and a shud-
15 der – my bones trembled, a wind rushed past my face – each hair on my flesh
16 stood on end. There it was – I could hardly make him out – a figure before
17 my eyes. Silence, then a voice: 'Will God acquit a mere mortal? What man is
18 pure before his Maker? If He cannot count on His own servants and finds
19 error even in His angels, what then of people whose homes are clay, whose
20 origins are dust, who are crushed like moths? By evening they are shattered,
21 gone forever, and no one will know. Their tent cords severed, they die, having

5 1 never grown wise.' Go ahead, cry out! But who will answer? To which angel
2 3 will you turn? After all, rage kills the fool, and passion destroys the feeble. I
4 remember seeing a fool taking root, and at once I cursed his home. His chil-
5 dren now are defenseless, helpless, rejected at the gate. The hungry feast on
his harvest, making off with it in baskets, and the thirsty lap up his riches.
6 Remember, affliction doesn't grow from the ground, and sin doesn't spring
7 up from the earth. For man is born to suffer as surely as arrows, flashing, whiz
8 9 upward. As for me, I would look to God; it is to God I'd state my case – who
10 does great, unfathomable things, wondrous deeds without number; who
11 lavishes rain upon the earth, sends water across pastures; who lifts up the
12 lowly and brings the bereaved to safety. He thwarts the plans of the cunning,
13 sets victory out of their reach, traps the wily in their designs, for rash advice
14 fails fast. The day is dark wherever they turn; by noon, they grope as if it were

טז יז בָּתֵּיהֶם כָּסֶף׃ אוֹ כְנֵפֶל טָמוּן לֹא אֶהְיֶה כְּעֹלְלִים לֹא־רָאוּ אוֹר׃ שָׁם
יח רְשָׁעִים חָדְלוּ רֹגֶז וְשָׁם יָנוּחוּ יְגִיעֵי כֹחַ׃ יַחַד אֲסִירִים שַׁאֲנָנוּ לֹא שָׁמְעוּ
יט כ קוֹל נֹגֵשׂ׃ קָטֹן וְגָדוֹל שָׁם הוּא וְעֶבֶד חָפְשִׁי מֵאֲדֹנָיו׃ לָמָּה יִתֵּן לְעָמֵל
כא אוֹר וְחַיִּים לְמָרֵי נָפֶשׁ׃ הַמְחַכִּים לַמָּוֶת וְאֵינֶנּוּ וַיַּחְפְּרֻהוּ מִמַּטְמוֹנִים׃
כב כג הַשְּׂמֵחִים אֱלֵי־גִיל יָשִׂישׂוּ כִּי יִמְצְאוּ־קָבֶר׃ לְגֶבֶר אֲשֶׁר־דַּרְכּוֹ נִסְתָּרָה
כד כה וַיָּסֶךְ אֱלוֹהַ בַּעֲדוֹ׃ כִּי־לִפְנֵי לַחְמִי אַנְחָתִי תָבֹא וַיִּתְּכוּ כַמַּיִם שַׁאֲגֹתָי׃ כִּי
כו פַחַד פָּחַדְתִּי וַיֶּאֱתָיֵנִי וַאֲשֶׁר יָגֹרְתִּי יָבֹא לִי׃ לֹא שָׁלַוְתִּי | וְלֹא שָׁקַטְתִּי
וְלֹא־נָחְתִּי וַיָּבֹא רֹגֶז׃

ד א ב וַיַּעַן אֱלִיפַז הַתֵּימָנִי וַיֹּאמַר׃ הֲנִסָּה דָבָר אֵלֶיךָ תִּלְאֶה וַעְצֹר בְּמִלִּין מִי
ג ד יוּכָל׃ הִנֵּה יִסַּרְתָּ רַבִּים וְיָדַיִם רָפוֹת תְּחַזֵּק׃ כּוֹשֵׁל יְקִימוּן מִלֶּיךָ וּבִרְכַּיִם
ה כֹּרְעוֹת תְּאַמֵּץ׃ כִּי עַתָּה | תָּבוֹא אֵלֶיךָ וַתֵּלֶא תִּגַּע עָדֶיךָ וַתִּבָּהֵל׃
ו ז הֲלֹא יִרְאָתְךָ כִּסְלָתֶךָ תִּקְוָתְךָ וְתֹם דְּרָכֶיךָ׃ זְכָר־נָא מִי הוּא נָקִי אָבָד
ח וְאֵיפֹה יְשָׁרִים נִכְחָדוּ׃ כַּאֲשֶׁר רָאִיתִי חֹרְשֵׁי אָוֶן וְזֹרְעֵי עָמָל יִקְצְרֻהוּ׃
ט י מִנִּשְׁמַת אֱלוֹהַ יֹאבֵדוּ וּמֵרוּחַ אַפּוֹ יִכְלוּ׃ שַׁאֲגַת אַרְיֵה וְקוֹל שָׁחַל וְשִׁנֵּי
יא יב כְפִירִים נִתָּעוּ׃ לַיִשׁ אֹבֵד מִבְּלִי־טָרֶף וּבְנֵי לָבִיא יִתְפָּרָדוּ׃ וְאֵלַי דָּבָר
יג יְגֻנָּב וַתִּקַּח אָזְנִי שֵׁמֶץ מֶנְהוּ׃ בִּשְׂעִפִּים מֵחֶזְיֹנוֹת לָיְלָה בִּנְפֹל תַּרְדֵּמָה
יד טו עַל־אֲנָשִׁים׃ פַּחַד קְרָאַנִי וּרְעָדָה וְרֹב עַצְמוֹתַי הִפְחִיד׃ וְרוּחַ עַל־פָּנַי
טז יַחֲלֹף תְּסַמֵּר שַׂעֲרַת בְּשָׂרִי׃ יַעֲמֹד | וְלֹא־אַכִּיר מַרְאֵהוּ תְּמוּנָה לְנֶגֶד
יז עֵינָי דְּמָמָה וָקוֹל אֶשְׁמָע׃ הַאֱנוֹשׁ מֵאֱלוֹהַ יִצְדָּק אִם מֵעֹשֵׂהוּ יִטְהַר־
יח יט גָּבֶר׃ הֵן בַּעֲבָדָיו לֹא יַאֲמִין וּבְמַלְאָכָיו יָשִׂים תָּהֳלָה׃ אַף | שֹׁכְנֵי בָתֵּי־
כ חֹמֶר אֲשֶׁר־בֶּעָפָר יְסוֹדָם יְדַכְּאוּם לִפְנֵי־עָשׁ׃ מִבֹּקֶר לָעֶרֶב יֻכַּתּוּ מִבְּלִי
כא ה א מֵשִׂים לָנֶצַח יֹאבֵדוּ׃ הֲלֹא־נִסַּע יִתְרָם בָּם יָמוּתוּ וְלֹא בְחָכְמָה׃ קְרָא־
ב נָא הֲיֵשׁ עוֹנֶךָּ וְאֶל־מִי מִקְּדֹשִׁים תִּפְנֶה׃ כִּי־לֶאֱוִיל יַהֲרָג־כָּעַשׂ וּפֹתֶה
ג ד תָּמִית קִנְאָה׃ אֲנִי־רָאִיתִי אֱוִיל מַשְׁרִישׁ וָאֶקּוֹב נָוֵהוּ פִתְאֹם׃ יִרְחֲקוּ
ה בָנָיו מִיֶּשַׁע וְיִדַּכְּאוּ בַשַּׁעַר וְאֵין מַצִּיל׃ אֲשֶׁר קְצִירוֹ | רָעֵב יֹאכֵל וְאֶל־
ו מִצִּנִּים יִקָּחֵהוּ וְשָׁאַף צַמִּים חֵילָם׃ כִּי | לֹא־יֵצֵא מֵעָפָר אָוֶן וּמֵאֲדָמָה
ז ח לֹא־יִצְמַח עָמָל׃ כִּי־אָדָם לְעָמָל יוּלָּד וּבְנֵי־רֶשֶׁף יַגְבִּיהוּ עוּף׃ אוּלָם
ט אֲנִי אֶדְרֹשׁ אֶל־אֵל וְאֶל־אֱלֹהִים אָשִׂים דִּבְרָתִי׃ עֹשֶׂה גְדֹלוֹת וְאֵין
י חֵקֶר נִפְלָאוֹת עַד־אֵין מִסְפָּר׃ הַנֹּתֵן מָטָר עַל־פְּנֵי־אָרֶץ וְשֹׁלֵחַ מַיִם
יא יב עַל־פְּנֵי חוּצוֹת׃ לָשׂוּם שְׁפָלִים לְמָרוֹם וְקֹדְרִים שָׂגְבוּ יֶשַׁע׃ מֵפֵר
יג מַחְשְׁבוֹת עֲרוּמִים וְלֹא־תַעֲשֶׂינָה יְדֵיהֶם תּוּשִׁיָּה׃ לֹכֵד חֲכָמִים בְּעָרְמָם
יד וַעֲצַת נִפְתָּלִים נִמְהָרָה׃ יוֹמָם יְפַגְּשׁוּ־חֹשֶׁךְ וְכַלַּיְלָה יְמַשְׁשׁוּ בַצָּהֳרָיִם׃

15 night! But He saves the defenseless from the sword and the poor from the
16 powerful, so there is hope for the wretched, and injustice will shut its mouth.
17 See, happy is the man whom God reproves! Do not scorn Shaddai's rebuke.
18 He injures but binds up the wound. He strikes, but His hands heal. From six
19 20 disasters He will save you, and even from the seventh you'll be spared. He
21 will deliver you from famine, and in war will save you from the sword. You
22 will be sheltered from treacherous tongues and have no fear of plunder; you
23 will laugh off scourge and pestilence, stand fearless before wild animals, and
24 in a pact with the stones of the field, be at peace with all creatures. You will
have tranquility in your tent, look around your dwelling and find you lack
25 nothing. Rest assured – you will have bountiful seed, offspring like grass
26 across the earth, and will be buried at a ripe old age like grain in the season's
27 fullness. We have probed this and know it to be true. Now take it to heart,
6 1 and you will know it, too." 2 Then Iyov spoke up and said: "If somehow
3 my agony could be weighed, if my calamity were placed on a scale, it would
4 be heavier than all the sand of the sea. That is why I have not held back. For
Shaddai's arrows are all about me; my spirit drinks their poison; God has set
5 His terrors against me. Does a wild ass bray over grass and an ox bellow over
6 his fodder? Who can stomach unsalted food? Why drink flavorless juice? I
7 8 refuse to touch such nauseating fare! If only my plea were answered, if God
9 would grant my wish, agree to crush me, lift His hand and pierce me – still I
10 would be consoled, even while writhing in relentless agony: I have never
11 hidden the Holy One's words. What strength do I have left to hope? And
12 when is my end? How long do I have? Am I solid as stone? Is my flesh made
13 of bronze? Is there no help from within? Has all counsel been driven from
14 me? Shame on him who fails his friend and forsakes the fear of God! My
15 brothers have betrayed me like a wadi, a channel where streams once coursed;
16 the streams are dark with ice, hidden by a covering of snow. As soon as it's
17 18 dry, they vanish; heat strikes, and at once they are gone. Their paths wind
about, come upon wasteland, and vanish. Tema's caravans[8] seek them out;
19 20 bands of Shebans look to them – but their hopes are thwarted; they arrive
and are dismayed. You are nothing to me! You see my terror and stand aghast.
21 22 When ever have I said: 'Give me! Pay a bribe on my behalf! Save me from
23 24 my enemy; pay some tyrant my ransom'? Teach me, and I will be quiet. Just
show me where I am wrong! Indeed, honest words are provocative, but what
25 26 good is your reproach? Who are you to come out with rebuke while brushing
27 off a despairing man's words? You would bargain for an orphan; you would
28 barter off your friend! Now, if you will be so kind as to turn toward me, I swear
29 I will not lie to you. Please, turn back; there is no wrong in me. Come
30 back – I remain in the right. Is there error on my tongue? Am I unable to
7 1 discern lies? Isn't a man's life a term of hard service, his days the days of a hired
2 hand? He is like a slave longing for shade, a worker waiting for his wage. I have
3 4 inherited empty months; nights of toil are now my lot. When I lie down, I
ask, 'When can I rise?' Night drags on, and sleeplessness sates me till dawn.

8 | Desert nomads.

טו טז וַיֹּשַׁע מֵחֶרֶב מִפִּיהֶם וּמִיַּד חָזָק אֶבְיוֹן׃ וַתְּהִי לַדַּל תִּקְוָה וְעֹלָתָה קָפְצָה
יז יח פִּיהָ׃ הִנֵּה אַשְׁרֵי אֱנוֹשׁ יוֹכִחֶנּוּ אֱלוֹהַּ וּמוּסַר שַׁדַּי אַל־תִּמְאָס׃ כִּי הוּא
יט יַכְאִיב וְיֶחְבָּשׁ יִמְחַץ וְיָדָו תִּרְפֶּינָה׃ בְּשֵׁשׁ צָרוֹת יַצִּילֶךָּ וּבְשֶׁבַע ׀ לֹא־
כ כא יִגַּע בְּךָ רָע׃ בְּרָעָב פָּדְךָ מִמָּוֶת וּבְמִלְחָמָה מִידֵי חָרֶב׃ בְּשׁוֹט לָשׁוֹן
כב תֵּחָבֵא וְלֹא־תִירָא מִשֹּׁד כִּי יָבוֹא׃ לְשֹׁד וּלְכָפָן תִּשְׂחָק וּמֵחַיַּת הָאָרֶץ
כג אַל־תִּירָא׃ כִּי עִם־אַבְנֵי הַשָּׂדֶה בְרִיתֶךָ וְחַיַּת הַשָּׂדֶה הָשְׁלְמָה־לָךְ׃
כד כה וְיָדַעְתָּ כִּי־שָׁלוֹם אָהֳלֶךָ וּפָקַדְתָּ נָוְךָ וְלֹא תֶחֱטָא׃ וְיָדַעְתָּ כִּי־רַב זַרְעֶךָ
כו וְצֶאֱצָאֶיךָ כְּעֵשֶׂב הָאָרֶץ׃ תָּבוֹא בְכֶלַח אֱלֵי־קָבֶר כַּעֲלוֹת גָּדִישׁ בְּעִתּוֹ׃
כז ו א הִנֵּה־זֹאת חֲקַרְנוּהָ כֶּן־הִיא שְׁמָעֶנָּה וְאַתָּה דַע־לָךְ׃ וַיַּעַן ב
ב ג אִיּוֹב וַיֹּאמַר׃ לוּ שָׁקוֹל יִשָּׁקֵל כַּעְשִׂי וְהַיָּתִי בְּמֹאזְנַיִם יִשְׂאוּ־יָחַד׃ כִּי־ וְהַוָּתִי
ד עַתָּה מֵחוֹל יַמִּים יִכְבָּד עַל־כֵּן דְּבָרַי לָעוּ׃ כִּי חִצֵּי שַׁדַּי עִמָּדִי אֲשֶׁר
ה חֲמָתָם שֹׁתָה רוּחִי בִּעוּתֵי אֱלוֹהַּ יַעַרְכוּנִי׃ הֲיִנְהַק־פֶּרֶא עֲלֵי־דֶשֶׁא
ו אִם יִגְעֶה־שּׁוֹר עַל־בְּלִילוֹ׃ הֲיֵאָכֵל תָּפֵל מִבְּלִי־מֶלַח אִם־יֶשׁ־טַעַם
ז ח בְּרִיר חַלָּמוּת׃ מֵאֲנָה לִנְגּוֹעַ נַפְשִׁי הֵמָּה כִּדְוֵי לַחְמִי׃ מִי־יִתֵּן תָּבוֹא
ט שֶׁאֱלָתִי וְתִקְוָתִי יִתֵּן אֱלוֹהַּ׃ וְיֹאֵל אֱלוֹהַּ וִידַכְּאֵנִי יַתֵּר יָדוֹ וִיבַצְּעֵנִי׃
י וּתְהִי עוֹד ׀ נֶחָמָתִי וַאֲסַלְּדָה בְחִילָה לֹא יַחְמוֹל כִּי־לֹא כִחַדְתִּי אִמְרֵי
יא יב קָדוֹשׁ׃ מַה־כֹּחִי כִי־אֲיַחֵל וּמַה־קִּצִּי כִּי־אַאֲרִיךְ נַפְשִׁי׃ אִם־כֹּחַ אֲבָנִים
יג יד כֹּחִי אִם־בְּשָׂרִי נָחוּשׁ׃ הַאִם אֵין עֶזְרָתִי בִי וְתֻשִׁיָּה נִדְּחָה מִמֶּנִּי׃ לַמָּס
טו מֵרֵעֵהוּ חָסֶד וְיִרְאַת שַׁדַּי יַעֲזוֹב׃ אַחַי בָּגְדוּ כְמוֹ־נָחַל כַּאֲפִיק נְחָלִים
טז יז יַעֲבֹרוּ׃ הַקֹּדְרִים מִנִּי־קָרַח עָלֵימוֹ יִתְעַלֶּם־שָׁלֶג׃ בְּעֵת יְזֹרְבוּ נִצְמָתוּ
יח בְּחֻמּוֹ נִדְעֲכוּ מִמְּקוֹמָם׃ יִלָּפְתוּ אָרְחוֹת דַּרְכָּם יַעֲלוּ בַתֹּהוּ וְיֹאבֵדוּ׃
יט כ הִבִּיטוּ אָרְחוֹת תֵּמָא הֲלִיכֹת שְׁבָא קִוּוּ־לָמוֹ׃ בֹּשׁוּ כִּי־בָטָח בָּאוּ עָדֶיהָ
כא כב וַיֶּחְפָּרוּ׃ כִּי־עַתָּה הֱיִיתֶם לוֹ תִּרְאוּ חֲתַת וַתִּירָאוּ׃ הֲכִי־אָמַרְתִּי הָבוּ
כג לִי וּמִכֹּחֲכֶם שִׁחֲדוּ בַעֲדִי׃ וּמַלְּטוּנִי מִיַּד־צָר וּמִיַּד עָרִיצִים תִּפְדּוּנִי׃
כד כה הוֹרוּנִי וַאֲנִי אַחֲרִישׁ וּמַה־שָּׁגִיתִי הָבִינוּ לִי׃ מַה־נִּמְרְצוּ אִמְרֵי־יֹשֶׁר
כו וּמַה־יּוֹכִיחַ הוֹכֵחַ מִכֶּם׃ הַלְהוֹכַח מִלִּים תַּחְשֹׁבוּ וּלְרוּחַ אִמְרֵי נֹאָשׁ׃
כז כח אַף־עַל־יָתוֹם תַּפִּילוּ וְתִכְרוּ עַל־רֵיעֲכֶם׃ וְעַתָּה הוֹאִילוּ פְנוּ־בִי וְעַל־
כט פְּנֵיכֶם אִם־אֲכַזֵּב׃ שֻׁבוּ־נָא אַל־תְּהִי עַוְלָה וְשֻׁבִי־עוֹד צִדְקִי־בָהּ׃ וְשׁוּבוּ
ל ז א הֲיֵשׁ־בִּלְשׁוֹנִי עַוְלָה אִם־חִכִּי לֹא־יָבִין הַוּוֹת׃ הֲלֹא־צָבָא לֶאֱנוֹשׁ עֲלֵי־
ב ג אָרֶץ וְכִימֵי שָׂכִיר יָמָיו׃ כְּעֶבֶד יִשְׁאַף־צֵל וּכְשָׂכִיר יְקַוֶּה פָעֳלוֹ׃ כֵּן
ד הָנְחַלְתִּי לִי יַרְחֵי־שָׁוְא וְלֵילוֹת עָמָל מִנּוּ־לִי׃ אִם־שָׁכַבְתִּי וְאָמַרְתִּי

5 6 My flesh is covered in maggots and earth, my skin is blistered and oozing. My
days pass more quickly than a weaver's shuttle carrying through the last thread
7 of hope.[9] Remember, my life is just a breath; my eye will never again see
8 goodness. The eye that sees me will see me no more; you will look, but I
9 will no longer be here. As a cloud fades and vanishes, he who descends into
10 Sheol[10] will not return; he will never go home again; the place will know him
11 no more. I will not hold back, either! I will speak from the agony of my spirit,
12 bemoan the bitterness of my soul: Am I Yam or the sea monster?[11] Why do
13 You place me under guard? I tell myself, my couch will comfort me, my bed
14 will share my burden, while You terrorize me with nightmares, horrify me
15 16 with visions, until I would choose strangulation, death, over these bones! I
17 am utterly spent. I will not live forever! Let me be. My days are vapor.[12] What
is man that You make so much of him, that You pay him so much attention,
18 scrutinizing him every morning, testing him every second? When will You
19 20 turn away from me long enough for me to swallow my spit? If I have sinned,
what have I done to You, warden of man? Why have You made me Your target,
21 a burden to myself? Why will You not pardon my crime and forgive my error?
Soon enough, I will be lying in the dust; You will look for me – but I will be
8 1 gone." 2 And Bildad the Shuhite answered and said: "How long will
3 you prattle on like this? The words of your mouth are one big wind! Does
4 God distort judgment, and Shaddai – would He pervert justice? When your
5 sons sinned against Him, He rightly did away with them. But if you seek God
6 and implore Shaddai, if you are pure and steadfast, He will come to your
7 protection and restore your righteous home. How humble your beginnings
8 will seem when in the end you are flourishing! Just ask those who came before
9 you and heed our ancestors' inquiries, for we were born yesterday and know
10 nothing; our lives are but shadows on this earth. Surely they would teach you,
11 surely they would tell you and bring these words from their hearts: 'Can
12 papyrus grow without a marsh? Will reeds flourish without water?' Even
13 while in flower, not yet plucked, they'll wither faster than the brush. That is
the fate of one who forgets God: the hope of the brazen comes to nothing.
14 His trust hangs on a thread; he relies on a spider's web. Lean on his house – it
15 16 will not stand! Hold onto it – it will not last! As for the righteous: moist in
17 the sun, shoots crop up in the garden, winding around a heap of roots and
18 piercing through a bed of rocks. Even if it's swallowed up then and there – the
19 place denying it: 'I have never seen you!' – it will continue on its way and
20 spring up from other soil. Remember, God does not abandon the blameless
21 and will not avail evil hands. In time, He will fill your mouth with laughter
22 and your lips with cries of joy. Your enemies will be clothed in shame, and
9 1 the tent of the wicked will cease to exist." And Iyov answered and

9 | A play on words: *tikva* means "hope" and also "thread" (cf. Josh. 2:18).

10 | The netherworld.

11 | Yam was the Canaanite sea-god. According to an ancient myth, God restrained the primeval sea monsters, the waters of chaos (cf. Is. 51:9–10).

12 | Fleeting and without substance (cf. Eccl. 1:2).

ה מָתַי אָקוּם וּמִדַּד־עָרֶב וְשָׂבַעְתִּי נְדֻדִים עֲדֵי־נָשֶׁף׃ לָבַשׁ בְּשָׂרִי רִמָּה
ו וגיש עָפָר עוֹרִי רָגַע וַיִּמָּאֵס׃ יָמַי קַלּוּ מִנִּי־אָרֶג וַיִּכְלוּ בְּאֶפֶס תִּקְוָה׃ וְגוּשׁ
ז ח זְכֹר כִּי־רוּחַ חַיָּי לֹא־תָשׁוּב עֵינִי לִרְאוֹת טוֹב׃ לֹא־תְשׁוּרֵנִי עֵין רֹאִי
ט י עֵינֶיךָ בִּי וְאֵינֶנִּי׃ כָּלָה עָנָן וַיֵּלַךְ כֵּן יוֹרֵד שְׁאוֹל לֹא יַעֲלֶה׃ לֹא־יָשׁוּב
יא עוֹד לְבֵיתוֹ וְלֹא־יַכִּירֶנּוּ עוֹד מְקֹמוֹ׃ גַּם־אֲנִי לֹא אֶחֱשָׂךְ פִּי אֲדַבְּרָה
יב בְּצַר רוּחִי אָשִׂיחָה בְּמַר נַפְשִׁי׃ הֲיָם־אָנִי אִם־תַּנִּין כִּי־תָשִׂים עָלַי
יג יד מִשְׁמָר׃ כִּי־אָמַרְתִּי תְּנַחֲמֵנִי עַרְשִׂי יִשָּׂא בְשִׂיחִי מִשְׁכָּבִי׃ וְחִתַּתַּנִי
טו בַחֲלֹמוֹת וּמֵחֶזְיֹנוֹת תְּבַעֲתַנִּי׃ וַתִּבְחַר מַחֲנָק נַפְשִׁי מָוֶת מֵעַצְמוֹתָי׃
טז יז מָאַסְתִּי לֹא־לְעֹלָם אֶחְיֶה חֲדַל מִמֶּנִּי כִּי־הֶבֶל יָמָי׃ מָה־אֱנוֹשׁ כִּי
יח תְגַדְּלֶנּוּ וְכִי־תָשִׁית אֵלָיו לִבֶּךָ׃ וַתִּפְקְדֶנּוּ לִבְקָרִים לִרְגָעִים תִּבְחָנֶנּוּ׃
יט כ כַּמָּה לֹא־תִשְׁעֶה מִמֶּנִּי לֹא־תַרְפֵּנִי עַד־בִּלְעִי רֻקִּי׃ חָטָאתִי מָה אֶפְעַל
כא לָךְ נֹצֵר הָאָדָם לָמָה שַׂמְתַּנִי לְמִפְגָּע לָךְ וָאֶהְיֶה עָלַי לְמַשָּׂא׃ וּמֶה
לֹא־תִשָּׂא פִשְׁעִי וְתַעֲבִיר אֶת־עֲוֺנִי כִּי־עַתָּה לֶעָפָר אֶשְׁכָּב וְשִׁחֲרְתַּנִי
ח א ב וְאֵינֶנִּי׃ וַיַּעַן בִּלְדַּד הַשּׁוּחִי וַיֹּאמַר׃ עַד־אָן תְּמַלֶּל־אֵלֶּה
ג וְרוּחַ כַּבִּיר אִמְרֵי־פִיךָ׃ הַאֵל יְעַוֵּת מִשְׁפָּט וְאִם־שַׁדַּי יְעַוֵּת־צֶדֶק׃
ד ה אִם־בָּנֶיךָ חָטְאוּ־לוֹ וַיְשַׁלְּחֵם בְּיַד־פִּשְׁעָם׃ אִם־אַתָּה תְּשַׁחֵר אֶל־אֵל
ו וְאֶל־שַׁדַּי תִּתְחַנָּן׃ אִם־זַךְ וְיָשָׁר אָתָּה כִּי־עַתָּה יָעִיר עָלֶיךָ וְשִׁלַּם נְוַת
ז ח צִדְקֶךָ׃ וְהָיָה רֵאשִׁיתְךָ מִצְעָר וְאַחֲרִיתְךָ יִשְׂגֶּה מְאֹד׃ כִּי־שְׁאַל־נָא
ט לְדֹר רִישׁוֹן וְכוֹנֵן לְחֵקֶר אֲבוֹתָם׃ כִּי־תְמוֹל אֲנַחְנוּ וְלֹא נֵדָע כִּי צֵל
י יָמֵינוּ עֲלֵי־אָרֶץ׃ הֲלֹא־הֵם יוֹרוּךָ יֹאמְרוּ לָךְ וּמִלִּבָּם יוֹצִאוּ מִלִּים׃
יא יב הֲיִגְאֶה־גֹּמֶא בְּלֹא בִצָּה יִשְׂגֶּה־אָחוּ בְלִי־מָיִם׃ עֹדֶנּוּ בְאִבּוֹ לֹא יִקָּטֵף
יג וְלִפְנֵי כָל־חָצִיר יִיבָשׁ׃ כֵּן אָרְחוֹת כָּל־שֹׁכְחֵי אֵל וְתִקְוַת חָנֵף תֹּאבֵד׃
יד טו אֲשֶׁר־יָקוֹט כִּסְלוֹ וּבֵית עַכָּבִישׁ מִבְטַחוֹ׃ יִשָּׁעֵן עַל־בֵּיתוֹ וְלֹא יַעֲמֹד
טז יַחֲזִיק בּוֹ וְלֹא יָקוּם׃ רָטֹב הוּא לִפְנֵי־שָׁמֶשׁ וְעַל־גַּנָּתוֹ יֹנַקְתּוֹ תֵצֵא׃
יז יח עַל־גַּל שָׁרָשָׁיו יְסֻבָּכוּ בֵּית אֲבָנִים יֶחֱזֶה׃ אִם־יְבַלְּעֶנּוּ מִמְּקֹמוֹ וְכִחֶשׁ
יט כ בּוֹ לֹא רְאִיתִיךָ׃ הֶן־הוּא מְשׂוֹשׂ דַּרְכּוֹ וּמֵעָפָר אַחֵר יִצְמָחוּ׃ הֶן־אֵל
כא לֹא יִמְאַס־תָּם וְלֹא־יַחֲזִיק בְּיַד־מְרֵעִים׃ עַד־יְמַלֵּה שְׂחוֹק פִּיךָ וּשְׂפָתֶיךָ
ט כב א תְרוּעָה׃ שֹׂנְאֶיךָ יִלְבְּשׁוּ־בֹשֶׁת וְאֹהֶל רְשָׁעִים אֵינֶנּוּ׃ וַיַּעַן

2 3 said: "Of course, I know it is so: man is no match for God. Challenge Him?
4 The chance of getting an answer is one in a thousand. A person may be
shrewd, he may be strong – but who has taken Him on and come out whole?
5 6 He moves mountains without their knowing, upturns them in His wrath; He
7 jolts the earth from its place – its pillars, they quake. At His command, the
8 sun will not rise, and the stars will seal themselves shut. Alone, He spreads
9 out the heavens and strides across Yam's back.[13] He makes the Bear, Orion,
10 the Pleiades, and the chambers of the South. He does great, unfathomable
11 things! Wondrous deeds without number! Sure, He passes me, but I don't
12 see Him; He goes by, but I am oblivious. He takes away – who can stop Him?
13 Who can ask, 'What are You doing?' God does not avert His anger. Even
14 Rahav's[14] cohorts surrender beneath Him. Who am I, then, to speak up to
15 Him, to carefully choose my words, when, even if I am right, I will get no
16 response as I stand pleading before my judge? If I call and He answers, I doubt
17 He would listen to me: He will strike me down in a storm and go on wounding
18 me for no reason. He will not let me breathe; He has filled me with poison.
19 If it's a matter of might – it is all His! And if justice – who will set my hearing?
20 If I am in the right, my mouth will convict me; if I am innocent, He will prove
21 22 me wrong. I am blameless! I do not care about myself; I despise my life. It is
all the same, anyway, so I say: He destroys the righteous along with the
23 wicked. If a sudden scourge strikes, He will scoff while the guiltless suffer.
24 The earth has been given to the wicked – He covers the judges' faces – if not
25 He, then who? Now my days sprint by like runners; they flee and see no joy.
26 27 They rush by like reed-boats, like a vulture swooping toward his prey. If I say,
28 'I will forget my claim, be free of this sorrow once and for all,' knowing You
29 will not clear me, I would fear all my pain. I will be found guilty. Why toil,
30 then, in vain? Even if I bathed in liquid snow, and were pure down to my
31 hands, You would plunge me into the Pit until even my clothes detested me.
32 For He is not a man, like me, to whom I can say, 'Come, let's take it to court!'
33 34 If only someone would arbitrate, place his hand on both of us, take His rod
35 off my back so that His terror would not haunt me, I could speak my mind
10 1 without fear, for I have been untrue here to myself. I loathe my life. I will say
2 it, then, loud and clear, and speak from the bitterness of my soul. I will say to
3 God: 'Do not condemn me! Just tell me what Your accusation is! Do You take
pleasure in oppressing man; do You so despise the work of Your hands that
4 You favor the advice of the wicked? Do You have the eyes of flesh and blood?
5 Do You see as humans see? Are Your days the days of mere mortals, Your years
6 the years of a man, in that You seek my iniquity and search out my every sin?
7 8 You know I have done nothing wrong; still there is no escape from You! Your
9 hands have shaped and made me, yet You ravage every part of me. Remember,
10 You kneaded me like clay,[15] and You will return me to dust. It was You who

13 | See note on 7:12.
14 | Another mythical sea monster.
15 | Created me (cf. Gen. 2:7).

ב ג אִיּוֹב וַיֹּאמַר: אָמְנָם יָדַעְתִּי כִי־כֵן וּמַה־יִּצְדַּק אֱנוֹשׁ עִם־אֵל: אִם־יַחְפֹּץ
ד לָרִיב עִמּוֹ לֹא־יַעֲנֶנּוּ אַחַת מִנִּי־אָלֶף: חֲכַם לֵבָב וְאַמִּיץ כֹּחַ מִי־הִקְשָׁה
ה ו אֵלָיו וַיִּשְׁלָם: הַמַּעְתִּיק הָרִים וְלֹא יָדָעוּ אֲשֶׁר הֲפָכָם בְּאַפּוֹ: הַמַּרְגִּיז
ז אֶרֶץ מִמְּקוֹמָהּ וְעַמּוּדֶיהָ יִתְפַלָּצוּן: הָאֹמֵר לַחֶרֶס וְלֹא יִזְרָח וּבְעַד
ח ט כּוֹכָבִים יַחְתֹּם: נֹטֶה שָׁמַיִם לְבַדּוֹ וְדוֹרֵךְ עַל־בָּמֳתֵי יָם: עֹשֶׂה־עָשׁ
י כְּסִיל וְכִימָה וְחַדְרֵי תֵמָן: עֹשֶׂה גְדֹלוֹת עַד־אֵין חֵקֶר וְנִפְלָאוֹת עַד־
יא יב אֵין מִסְפָּר: הֵן יַעֲבֹר עָלַי וְלֹא אֶרְאֶה וְיַחֲלֹף וְלֹא־אָבִין לוֹ: הֵן יַחְתֹּף
יג מִי יְשִׁיבֶנּוּ מִי־יֹאמַר אֵלָיו מַה־תַּעֲשֶׂה: אֱלוֹהַּ לֹא־יָשִׁיב אַפּוֹ תַּחְתָּו
יד טו שָׁחֲחוּ עֹזְרֵי רָהַב: אַף כִּי־אָנֹכִי אֶעֱנֶנּוּ אֶבְחֲרָה דְבָרַי עִמּוֹ: אֲשֶׁר אִם־
טז צָדַקְתִּי לֹא אֶעֱנֶה לִמְשֹׁפְטִי אֶתְחַנָּן: אִם־קָרָאתִי וַיַּעֲנֵנִי לֹא־אַאֲמִין
יז יח כִּי־יַאֲזִין קוֹלִי: אֲשֶׁר־בִּשְׂעָרָה יְשׁוּפֵנִי וְהִרְבָּה פְצָעַי חִנָּם: לֹא־יִתְּנֵנִי
יט הָשֵׁב רוּחִי כִּי יַשְׂבִּעַנִי מַמְּרֹרִים: אִם־לְכֹחַ אַמִּיץ הִנֵּה וְאִם־לְמִשְׁפָּט
כ כא מִי יוֹעִידֵנִי: אִם־אֶצְדָּק פִּי יַרְשִׁיעֵנִי תָּם־אָנִי וַיַּעְקְשֵׁנִי: תָּם־אָנִי לֹא־אֵדַע
כב נַפְשִׁי אֶמְאַס חַיָּי: אַחַת הִיא עַל־כֵּן אָמַרְתִּי תָּם וְרָשָׁע הוּא מְכַלֶּה:
כג כד אִם־שׁוֹט יָמִית פִּתְאֹם לְמַסַּת נְקִיִּם יִלְעָג: אֶרֶץ ׀ נִתְּנָה בְיַד־רָשָׁע פְּנֵי־
כה שֹׁפְטֶיהָ יְכַסֶּה אִם־לֹא אֵפוֹא מִי־הוּא: וְיָמַי קַלּוּ מִנִּי־רָץ בָּרְחוּ לֹא־רָאוּ
כו כז טוֹבָה: חָלְפוּ עִם־אֳנִיּוֹת אֵבֶה כְּנֶשֶׁר יָטוּשׂ עֲלֵי־אֹכֶל: אִם־אָמְרִי
כח אֶשְׁכְּחָה שִׂיחִי אֶעֶזְבָה פָנַי וְאַבְלִיגָה: יָגֹרְתִּי כָל־עַצְּבֹתָי יָדַעְתִּי כִּי־לֹא
כט ל תְנַקֵּנִי: אָנֹכִי אֶרְשָׁע לָמָּה־זֶּה הֶבֶל אִיגָע: אִם־הִתְרָחַצְתִּי בְמוֹ־שָׁלֶג בְּמֵי־
לא לב וַהֲזִכּוֹתִי בְּבֹר כַּפָּי: אָז בַּשַּׁחַת תִּטְבְּלֵנִי וְתִעֲבוּנִי שַׂלְמוֹתָי: כִּי־לֹא־
לג אִישׁ כָּמֹנִי אֶעֱנֶנּוּ נָבוֹא יַחְדָּו בַּמִּשְׁפָּט: לֹא יֵשׁ־בֵּינֵינוּ מוֹכִיחַ יָשֵׁת
לד לה יָדוֹ עַל־שְׁנֵינוּ: יָסֵר מֵעָלַי שִׁבְטוֹ וְאֵמָתוֹ אַל־תְּבַעֲתַנִּי: אֲדַבְּרָה וְלֹא
י א אִירָאֶנּוּ כִּי לֹא־כֵן אָנֹכִי עִמָּדִי: נָקְטָה נַפְשִׁי בְּחַיָּי אֶעֶזְבָה עָלַי שִׂיחִי
ב אֲדַבְּרָה בְּמַר נַפְשִׁי: אֹמַר אֶל־אֱלוֹהַּ אַל־תַּרְשִׁיעֵנִי הוֹדִיעֵנִי עַל מַה־
ג תְּרִיבֵנִי: הֲטוֹב לְךָ ׀ כִּי־תַעֲשֹׁק כִּי־תִמְאַס יְגִיעַ כַּפֶּיךָ וְעַל־עֲצַת רְשָׁעִים
ד ה הוֹפָעְתָּ: הַעֵינֵי בָשָׂר לָךְ אִם־כִּרְאוֹת אֱנוֹשׁ תִּרְאֶה: הֲכִימֵי אֱנוֹשׁ יָמֶיךָ
ו ז אִם־שְׁנוֹתֶיךָ כִּימֵי גָבֶר: כִּי־תְבַקֵּשׁ לַעֲוֺנִי וּלְחַטָּאתִי תִדְרוֹשׁ: עַל־
ח דַּעְתְּךָ כִּי־לֹא אֶרְשָׁע וְאֵין מִיָּדְךָ מַצִּיל: יָדֶיךָ עִצְּבוּנִי וַיַּעֲשׂוּנִי יַחַד
ט י סָבִיב וַתְּבַלְּעֵנִי: זְכָר־נָא כִּי־כַחֹמֶר עֲשִׂיתָנִי וְאֶל־עָפָר תְּשִׁיבֵנִי: הֲלֹא

11 poured me out like milk and like cheese congealed me.[16] You have clothed
12 me in skin and flesh, woven bone and sinew; You have granted me life and
13 kindness and kept my spirit under Your charge. Yet these things You have
14 hidden in Your heart – I know how You operate – when I sin, You will be
15 watching! You will not acquit me. I will take the blame if I have done wrong!
But even if cleared I will not lift my head. Enough of my disgrace now! Look
16 at my suffering. Something to be proud of – hunting me like a lion, then
17 coming back to work on me Your wonders. You stir up Your hostilities toward
18 me, Your rage and fury mounting, army after army upon me. Why did You
19 take me out of the womb? I could have died, no eye having seen me. If only
20 I could never have been – brought straight from belly to grave! Are my days
21 not numbered as it is? Let me be, turn away, allow me some relief before I go,
22 never to return, to a land of gloom and death-dark, a land whose brightness
11 1 is like murk, a land of death-dark, disorder, black light ablaze.'" Then
2 Tzofar the Naamatite answered and said: "Will a rant like yours go unan-
3 swered? Is a smooth talker always in the right? Will you keep on silencing
4 people, prattling on as you do, unrefuted? You have said, 'My teaching is pure;
5 in Your eyes, I am blameless!' But if only God were to speak up and open His
6 lips for you to hear, He would share with you wisdom's secrets, for its mysteries are twofold,[17] and you would know God has made you forget your sins.
7 Can you fathom the essence of God? Can you plumb the reaches of Shaddai?
8 It is higher than the heavens! What can you do? It is deeper than Sheol! What
9 can you know? It is longer than the earth and wider than the seas. If He takes
10 a man or delivers him to his enemy, if He hems him in – who can reverse it?
11 For He knows duplicity when He sees it; He spots falsehood and deceit. A
12
13 hollow man will have a brain when a wild ass gives birth to a human! But if
14 you direct your heart and spread out your hands toward Him – if there is sin
15 on those hands, cast it away, and let no evil lodge in your tents – then you will
16 lift your unblemished face, enduring and unafraid, and you will forget all your
17 suffering as if it were water flowing through. Your future will be brighter than
18 noon, and you will be radiant like daybreak; sure that there is hope, you will
19 burrow in and rest secure.[18] You will lie down fearing nothing, and multitudes
20 will seek your favor while the wicked pine away with nowhere in sight to run,
12 1 their hopes undone by despair." And Iyov answered and said: "You
2
3 are the last of the wise, all right – and with you, wisdom dies. See, I too have
4 a mind and am no less than you. Who has not grasped these things? My
friends have made a fool out of me, a righteous man – now a laughingstock.
5 When they call to God, He answers them! What pleasure the smug take in
6 calamity, too steady to stumble! Their tents are calm when bandits come; they
7 are secure among the brazen – all this by the very hand of God! Ask the
Behemoth,[19] and it will instruct you, or a bird in the sky – it will tell you.

---

16 | As an embryo gestating in the womb.

17 | There is wisdom known to humans and wisdom known only to God.

18 | The terms "burrow in" and "lie down" (v. 19) typically describe animals at rest.

19 | A mythical land animal, sometimes translated as "hippopotamus" (see 40:15).

יא כֶּחָלָב תַּתִּיכֵנִי וְכַגְּבִנָּה תַּקְפִּיאֵנִי: עוֹר וּבָשָׂר תַּלְבִּישֵׁנִי וּבַעֲצָמוֹת
יב וְגִידִים תְּסֹכְכֵנִי: חַיִּים וָחֶסֶד עָשִׂיתָ עִמָּדִי וּפְקֻדָּתְךָ שָׁמְרָה רוּחִי:
יג יד וְאֵלֶּה צָפַנְתָּ בִלְבָבֶךָ יָדַעְתִּי כִּי־זֹאת עִמָּךְ: אִם־חָטָאתִי וּשְׁמַרְתָּנִי
טו וּמֵעֲוֺנִי לֹא תְנַקֵּנִי: אִם־רָשַׁעְתִּי אַלְלַי לִי וְצָדַקְתִּי לֹא־אֶשָּׂא רֹאשִׁי
טז שְׂבַע קָלוֹן וּרְאֵה עָנְיִי: וְיִגְאֶה כַּשַּׁחַל תְּצוּדֵנִי וְתָשֹׁב תִּתְפַּלָּא בִי:
יז יח תְּחַדֵּשׁ עֵדֶיךָ ׀ נֶגְדִּי וְתֶרֶב כַּעַשְׂךָ עִמָּדִי חֲלִיפוֹת וְצָבָא עִמִּי: וְלָמָּה
יט מֵרֶחֶם הֹצֵאתָנִי אֶגְוַע וְעַיִן לֹא־תִרְאֵנִי: כַּאֲשֶׁר לֹא־הָיִיתִי אֶהְיֶה מִבֶּטֶן
כ כא לַקֶּבֶר אוּבָל: הֲלֹא־מְעַט יָמַי יחדל ישית מִמֶּנִּי וְאַבְלִיגָה מְּעָט: בְּטֶרֶם וַחֲדָל וְשִׁית
כב אֵלֵךְ וְלֹא אָשׁוּב אֶל־אֶרֶץ חֹשֶׁךְ וְצַלְמָוֶת: אֶרֶץ עֵיפָתָה ׀ כְּמוֹ אֹפֶל
יא א צַלְמָוֶת וְלֹא סְדָרִים וַתֹּפַע כְּמוֹ־אֹפֶל: וַיַּעַן צֹפַר הַנַּעֲמָתִי
ב ג וַיֹּאמַר: הֲרֹב דְּבָרִים לֹא יֵעָנֶה וְאִם־אִישׁ שְׂפָתַיִם יִצְדָּק: בַּדֶּיךָ מְתִים
ד יַחֲרִישׁוּ וַתִּלְעַג וְאֵין מַכְלִם: וַתֹּאמֶר זַךְ לִקְחִי וּבַר הָיִיתִי בְעֵינֶיךָ:
ה ו וְאוּלָם מִי־יִתֵּן אֱלוֹהַּ דַּבֵּר וְיִפְתַּח שְׂפָתָיו עִמָּךְ: וְיַגֶּד־לְךָ ׀ תַּעֲלֻמוֹת
ז חָכְמָה כִּי־כִפְלַיִם לְתוּשִׁיָּה וְדַע ׀ כִּי־יַשֶּׁה לְךָ אֱלוֹהַּ מֵעֲוֺנֶךָ: הַחֵקֶר
ח אֱלוֹהַּ תִּמְצָא אִם עַד־תַּכְלִית שַׁדַּי תִּמְצָא: גָּבְהֵי שָׁמַיִם מַה־תִּפְעָל
ט י עֲמֻקָּה מִשְּׁאוֹל מַה־תֵּדָע: אֲרֻכָּה מֵאֶרֶץ מִדָּהּ וּרְחָבָה מִנִּי־יָם: אִם־
יא יַחֲלֹף וְיַסְגִּיר וְיַקְהִיל וּמִי יְשִׁיבֶנּוּ: כִּי־הוּא יָדַע מְתֵי־שָׁוְא וַיַּרְא־אָוֶן
יב יג וְלֹא יִתְבּוֹנָן: וְאִישׁ נָבוּב יִלָּבֵב וְעַיִר פֶּרֶא אָדָם יִוָּלֵד: אִם־אַתָּה הֲכִינוֹתָ
יד לִבֶּךָ וּפָרַשְׂתָּ אֵלָיו כַּפֶּךָ: אִם־אָוֶן בְּיָדְךָ הַרְחִיקֵהוּ וְאַל־תַּשְׁכֵּן בְּאֹהָלֶיךָ
טו טז עַוְלָה: כִּי־אָז ׀ תִּשָּׂא פָנֶיךָ מִמּוּם וְהָיִיתָ מֻצָק וְלֹא תִירָא: כִּי־אַתָּה
יז עָמָל תִּשְׁכָּח כְּמַיִם עָבְרוּ תִזְכֹּר: וּמִצָּהֳרַיִם יָקוּם חָלֶד תָּעֻפָה כַּבֹּקֶר
יח יט תִּהְיֶה: וּבָטַחְתָּ כִּי־יֵשׁ תִּקְוָה וְחָפַרְתָּ לָבֶטַח תִּשְׁכָּב: וְרָבַצְתָּ וְאֵין ג
כ מַחֲרִיד וְחִלּוּ פָנֶיךָ רַבִּים: וְעֵינֵי רְשָׁעִים תִּכְלֶינָה וּמָנוֹס אָבַד מִנְהֶם
יב א ב וְתִקְוָתָם מַפַּח־נָפֶשׁ: וַיַּעַן אִיּוֹב וַיֹּאמַר: אָמְנָם כִּי
ג אַתֶּם־עָם וְעִמָּכֶם תָּמוּת חָכְמָה: גַּם־לִי לֵבָב ׀ כְּמוֹכֶם לֹא־נֹפֵל אָנֹכִי
ד מִכֶּם וְאֶת־מִי־אֵין כְּמוֹ־אֵלֶּה: שְׂחֹק לְרֵעֵהוּ ׀ אֶהְיֶה קֹרֵא לֶאֱלוֹהַּ
ה וַיַּעֲנֵהוּ שְׂחוֹק צַדִּיק תָּמִים: לַפִּיד בּוּז לְעַשְׁתּוּת שַׁאֲנָן נָכוֹן לְמוֹעֲדֵי
ו רָגֶל: יִשְׁלָיוּ אֹהָלִים ׀ לְשֹׁדְדִים וּבַטֻּחוֹת לְמַרְגִּיזֵי אֵל לַאֲשֶׁר הֵבִיא
ז אֱלוֹהַּ בְּיָדוֹ: וְאוּלָם שְׁאַל־נָא בְהֵמוֹת וְתֹרֶךָּ וְעוֹף הַשָּׁמַיִם וְיַגֶּד־לָךְ:

8 Just speak to the earth, and it will teach you; the fish of the sea, they'll explain!
9 10 Who doesn't know these things: 'The LORD's hand has made all this,[20] in
whose hand is the soul of every living being and the breath of all humankind;
11 12 can't the ear discern words the way the palate tastes food? Wisdom belongs
13 to the old, and acumen comes with longevity. He has wisdom and might! He
14 has counsel and insight! Indeed, what He destroys will not be rebuilt; who-
15 ever He imprisons will not be freed. When He stops the waters, there is
16 drought; when He sets them loose, they overturn the earth. Strength and
17 wisdom are His; deceived and deceiver under His sway. He leads wise men
18 away naked[21] and turns judges into fools; He undoes the belts of kings and
19 removes the sash around their loins; priests He leads away naked, ousting the
20 21 devoted; He strips orators of their words, rids elders of all sense; He pours
22 contempt on nobles and undoes the belts of conquerors; He draws mysteries
23 out of darkness and brings death-dark to light. He exalts nations, then oblit-
24 erates them; expands nations – then exiles them. He confounds the leaders
25 of the land, sending them to wander a pathless wilderness where they grope
13 1 in the dark with no light and stagger like drunkards.' All this I have seen with
2 my own eyes; my ears have heard and understood. What you know, I know,
3 too. I am no less than any of you. As for myself, I would rather speak to
4 Shaddai – I prefer to take it up with God – but you are spreaders of lies and
5 worthless healers, all of you. If only you would just be quiet – then you would
6 7 be wise! Now, please hear me out and listen to my charges. Will you lie to
8 God's face? Do you deceive on His behalf? Will you be taking His side? Do
9 you plan to speak for Him? Would it go well if He examined you? Or would
10 you delude Him, too? You can be sure He will set you straight if you secretly
11 play favorites. Would His splendor not terrify you and fear of Him not seize
12 13 you? Your aphorisms would turn to ash, your answers to lumps of clay. Quiet
14 now! Let me speak, come what may. Come what may, I will take my flesh in
15 my teeth and put my life in my own hands! Let Him kill me! I will wait for
16 Him.[22] I will argue my case before Him. This, too, will be my salvation: that
17 blasphemers dare not come near Him. Heed carefully my words; let my
18 declaration reach your ears. I hereby present my case; I know I am in the right.
19 20 Who dares contend with me? I will hold my peace and die! Just spare me
21 these two things, and I will not hide from You: take Your hand off me, and
22 that Your terror would not haunt me. Then call, and I will answer, or I will
23 speak and You will reply. Just how many are my sins and offenses? Show them
24 25 to me! Why do You hide Your face as if I am Your enemy? Would You chase
26 a driven leaf and hunt down dry straw? You sentence me to poison and hold
27 against me my boyhood sins; You have set my feet in lime[23] so You can follow

20 | This section, in single quotation marks, is Iyov's parody of his friends' parroting of the Wisdom tradition.

21 | A sign of madness.

22 | This reading is based on the vocalized version, the *keri*. *Ketiv* (the written version) is "though I have no hope."

23 | Lime stuck to the bottom of one's feet makes footprints that can be tracked.

ח ט אוֹ שִׂיחַ לָאָרֶץ וְתֹרֶךָּ וִיסַפְּרוּ לְךָ דְּגֵי הַיָּם: מִי לֹא־יָדַע בְּכָל־אֵלֶּה כִּי
י יַד־יהוה עָשְׂתָה זֹּאת: אֲשֶׁר בְּיָדוֹ נֶפֶשׁ כָּל־חָי וְרוּחַ כָּל־בְּשַׂר־אִישׁ:
יא יב הֲלֹא־אֹזֶן מִלִּין תִּבְחָן וְחֵךְ אֹכֶל יִטְעַם־לוֹ: בִּישִׁישִׁים חָכְמָה וְאֹרֶךְ
יג יד יָמִים תְּבוּנָה: עִמּוֹ חָכְמָה וּגְבוּרָה לוֹ עֵצָה וּתְבוּנָה: הֵן יַהֲרוֹס וְלֹא
טו יִבָּנֶה יִסְגֹּר עַל־אִישׁ וְלֹא יִפָּתֵחַ: הֵן יַעְצֹר בַּמַּיִם וְיִבָשׁוּ וִישַׁלְּחֵם
טז יז וְיַהַפְכוּ־אָרֶץ: עִמּוֹ עֹז וְתוּשִׁיָּה לוֹ שֹׁגֵג וּמַשְׁגֶּה: מוֹלִיךְ יוֹעֲצִים שׁוֹלָל
יח יט וְשֹׁפְטִים יְהוֹלֵל: מוּסַר מְלָכִים פִּתֵּחַ וַיֶּאְסֹר אֵזוֹר בְּמָתְנֵיהֶם: מוֹלִיךְ
כ כֹּהֲנִים שׁוֹלָל וְאֵתָנִים יְסַלֵּף: מֵסִיר שָׂפָה לְנֶאֱמָנִים וְטַעַם זְקֵנִים יִקָּח:
כא כב שׁוֹפֵךְ בּוּז עַל־נְדִיבִים וּמְזִיחַ אֲפִיקִים רִפָּה: מְגַלֶּה עֲמֻקוֹת מִנִּי־חֹשֶׁךְ
כג כד וַיֹּצֵא לָאוֹר צַלְמָוֶת: מַשְׂגִּיא לַגּוֹיִם וַיְאַבְּדֵם שֹׁטֵחַ לַגּוֹיִם וַיַּנְחֵם: מֵסִיר
כה לֵב רָאשֵׁי עַם־הָאָרֶץ וַיַּתְעֵם בְּתֹהוּ לֹא־דָרֶךְ: יְמַשְׁשׁוּ־חֹשֶׁךְ וְלֹא־אוֹר
יג א ב וַיַּתְעֵם כַּשִּׁכּוֹר: הֶן־כֹּל רָאֲתָה עֵינִי שָׁמְעָה אָזְנִי וַתָּבֶן לָהּ: כְּדַעְתְּכֶם
ג יָדַעְתִּי גַם־אָנִי לֹא־נֹפֵל אָנֹכִי מִכֶּם: אוּלָם אֲנִי אֶל־שַׁדַּי אֲדַבֵּר וְהוֹכֵחַ
ד ה אֶל־אֵל אֶחְפָּץ: וְאוּלָם אַתֶּם טֹפְלֵי־שָׁקֶר רֹפְאֵי אֱלִל כֻּלְּכֶם: מִי־יִתֵּן
ו הַחֲרֵשׁ תַּחֲרִישׁוּן וּתְהִי לָכֶם לְחָכְמָה: שִׁמְעוּ־נָא תוֹכַחְתִּי וְרִבוֹת
ז ח שְׂפָתַי הַקְשִׁיבוּ: הַלְאֵל תְּדַבְּרוּ עַוְלָה וְלוֹ תְּדַבְּרוּ רְמִיָּה: הֲפָנָיו תִּשָּׂאוּן
ט אִם־לָאֵל תְּרִיבוּן: הֲטוֹב כִּי־יַחְקֹר אֶתְכֶם אִם־כְּהָתֵל בֶּאֱנוֹשׁ תְּהָתֵלּוּ
י יא בוֹ: הוֹכֵחַ יוֹכִיחַ אֶתְכֶם אִם־בַּסֵּתֶר פָּנִים תִּשָּׂאוּן: הֲלֹא שְׂאֵתוֹ תְּבַעֵת
יב אֶתְכֶם וּפַחְדּוֹ יִפֹּל עֲלֵיכֶם: זִכְרֹנֵיכֶם מִשְׁלֵי־אֵפֶר לְגַבֵּי־חֹמֶר גַּבֵּיכֶם:
יג יד הַחֲרִישׁוּ מִמֶּנִּי וַאֲדַבְּרָה־אָנִי וְיַעֲבֹר עָלַי מָה: עַל־מָה | אֶשָּׂא בְשָׂרִי
טו בְשִׁנָּי וְנַפְשִׁי אָשִׂים בְּכַפִּי: הֵן יִקְטְלֵנִי לֹא אֲיַחֵל אַךְ־דְּרָכַי אֶל־פָּנָיו לוֹ
טז יז אוֹכִיחַ: גַּם־הוּא־לִי לִישׁוּעָה כִּי־לֹא לְפָנָיו חָנֵף יָבוֹא: שִׁמְעוּ שָׁמוֹעַ
יח מִלָּתִי וְאַחֲוָתִי בְּאָזְנֵיכֶם: הִנֵּה־נָא עָרַכְתִּי מִשְׁפָּט יָדַעְתִּי כִּי־אֲנִי
יט כ אֶצְדָּק: מִי־הוּא יָרִיב עִמָּדִי כִּי־עַתָּה אַחֲרִישׁ וְאֶגְוָע: אַךְ־שְׁתַּיִם אַל־
כא תַּעַשׂ עִמָּדִי אָז מִפָּנֶיךָ לֹא אֶסָּתֵר: כַּפְּךָ מֵעָלַי הַרְחַק וְאֵמָתְךָ אַל־
כב כג תְּבַעֲתַנִּי: וּקְרָא וְאָנֹכִי אֶעֱנֶה אוֹ־אֲדַבֵּר וַהֲשִׁיבֵנִי: כַּמָּה לִי עֲוֺנוֹת
כד וְחַטָּאוֹת פִּשְׁעִי וְחַטָּאתִי הֹדִיעֵנִי: לָמָּה־פָנֶיךָ תַסְתִּיר וְתַחְשְׁבֵנִי לְאוֹיֵב
כה כו לָךְ: הֶעָלֶה נִדָּף תַּעֲרוֹץ וְאֶת־קַשׁ יָבֵשׁ תִּרְדֹּף: כִּי־תִכְתֹּב עָלַי מְרֹרוֹת
כז וְתוֹרִישֵׁנִי עֲוֺנוֹת נְעוּרָי: וְתָשֵׂם בַּסַּד | רַגְלַי וְתִשְׁמוֹר כָּל־אָרְחֹתָי עַל־

28 my every step, tracking me all the time: he will rot away like a wine skin, like
14 1 a moth-eaten shirt. Man, who is born of woman, he is glutted with anguish;
2 his days are few. Like a flower, he blossoms, then withers; like a shadow, he
3 flees and cannot stay. Why do You hound such a creature, calling him to
4 5 account? Who can purify the defiled? No one! His days are determined: You
6 have set the number of his months and drawn the line he may not cross. Turn
away from him and let him be! Let him, like a hired hand, finish his day's work.
7 See, even a tree has hope: if chopped down, it will sprout again – its shoots
8 will not relent – and if its roots grow old in the earth, if its stump succumbs
9 to the dust, a whiff of water and it will flower, bursting forth like a new sapling.
10 11 But a man dies and wastes away; he perishes, and where is he then? Like water
12 drained from the sea, like a river scorched, run dry, a man lies down, never
13 again to rise; until the skies fall he will not wake; he will not be roused. If only
You would hide me in Sheol, keep me there until Your wrath has passed, set
14 a time, then call me to mind. If a man has already died, can he live again? I
15 will wait my entire term until my relief[24] comes: You will call, and I will
16 answer You. You will long for the work of Your hands. When You follow my
17 every step, You won't search out my sin; You will bundle and seal my wrong-
18 doing and plaster over my iniquity. Yet, as a mountain falls and crumbles and
19 a rock is dislodged from its place, as water wears away stones, its torrents
20 scouring the soil, You ravage a man's hope: You crush him forever, and he
21 vanishes; You mangle his face and banish him. If his sons are revered, he will
22 never know; if they come to ruin, he will not notice. Only his own flesh will
15 1 feel the pain; only his own spirit will grieve." Then Elifaz the
2 Temanite spoke up and said: "Quite the wise man, spouting empty opinions,
3 belly bursting with hot air from the east,[25] uttering worthless reproofs and
4 words that benefit no one. What is worse, you do away with all piety and
5 sabotage any prayer to God. Your mouth is schooled in sin, so you make
6 shrewd formulations. It's your mouth that gives you away, not me – your lips
7 testify against you. Are you the first ever to have been born? Were you created
8 before the hills? Do you eavesdrop on God's council, hoarding all His wisdom
9 for yourself? What do you know that we do not? What understanding do you
10 have that we lack? There is a gray-haired man in our midst, a man even older
11 than your father! Are these consolations insufficient? Are the words too softly
12 spoken? Where are your thoughts taking you, and what is that look in your
13 eye that you unleash your rage against God and let such words escape your
14 mouth? Since when do mortals deserve to be acquitted? Born of woman, how
15 can they be right? If God cannot even trust His angels, and even the heavens
16 are impure in His eyes, how much more loathsome and corrupt, then, is a
17 man who drinks iniquity like water? I will tell you! Listen to me: I will relay
18 exactly what I have seen, what wise men have not withheld but passed down
19 from our fathers, to whom alone the land was given; no stranger ever passed
20 among them. All his days, the wicked man trembles, the oppressor – in the

24 | To take my place in Sheol.
25 | The east wind is hot and dry.

כח יד א שָׁרְשֵׁי רַגְלַי תִּתְחַקֶּה׃ וְהוּא כְּרָקָב יִבְלֶה כְּבֶגֶד אֲכָלוֹ עָשׁ׃ אָדָם יְלוּד
ב אִשָּׁה קְצַר יָמִים וּשְׂבַע־רֹגֶז׃ כְּצִיץ יָצָא וַיִּמָּל וַיִּבְרַח כַּצֵּל וְלֹא יַעֲמוֹד׃
ג ד אַף־עַל־זֶה פָּקַחְתָּ עֵינֶךָ וְאֹתִי תָבִיא בְמִשְׁפָּט עִמָּךְ׃ מִי־יִתֵּן טָהוֹר
ה מִטָּמֵא לֹא אֶחָד׃ אִם־חֲרוּצִים ׀ יָמָיו מִסְפַּר־חֳדָשָׁיו אִתָּךְ חֻקָּו עָשִׂיתָ
ו ז וְלֹא יַעֲבֹר׃ שְׁעֵה מֵעָלָיו וְיֶחְדָּל עַד־יִרְצֶה כְּשָׂכִיר יוֹמוֹ׃ כִּי יֵשׁ לָעֵץ
ח תִּקְוָה אִם־יִכָּרֵת וְעוֹד יַחֲלִיף וְיֹנַקְתּוֹ לֹא תֶחְדָּל׃ אִם־יַזְקִין בָּאָרֶץ
ט שָׁרְשׁוֹ וּבֶעָפָר יָמוּת גִּזְעוֹ׃ מֵרֵיחַ מַיִם יַפְרִחַ וְעָשָׂה קָצִיר כְּמוֹ־נָטַע׃
י יא וְגֶבֶר יָמוּת וַיֶּחֱלָשׁ וַיִּגְוַע אָדָם וְאַיּוֹ׃ אָזְלוּ־מַיִם מִנִּי־יָם וְנָהָר יֶחֱרַב
יב וְיָבֵשׁ׃ וְאִישׁ שָׁכַב וְלֹא־יָקוּם עַד־בִּלְתִּי שָׁמַיִם לֹא יָקִיצוּ וְלֹא־יֵעֹרוּ
יג מִשְּׁנָתָם׃ מִי יִתֵּן ׀ בִּשְׁאוֹל תַּצְפִּנֵנִי תַּסְתִּירֵנִי עַד־שׁוּב אַפֶּךָ תָּשִׁית לִי
יד חֹק וְתִזְכְּרֵנִי׃ אִם־יָמוּת גֶּבֶר הֲיִחְיֶה כָּל־יְמֵי צְבָאִי אֲיַחֵל עַד־בּוֹא
טו טז חֲלִיפָתִי׃ תִּקְרָא וְאָנֹכִי אֶעֱנֶךָּ לְמַעֲשֵׂה יָדֶיךָ תִכְסֹף׃ כִּי־עַתָּה צְעָדַי
יז תִּסְפּוֹר לֹא־תִשְׁמֹר עַל־חַטָּאתִי׃ חָתֻם בִּצְרוֹר פִּשְׁעִי וַתִּטְפֹּל עַל־
יח יט עֲוֹנִי׃ וְאוּלָם הַר־נוֹפֵל יִבּוֹל וְצוּר יֶעְתַּק מִמְּקֹמוֹ׃ אֲבָנִים ׀ שָׁחֲקוּ מַיִם
כ תִּשְׁטֹף־סְפִיחֶיהָ עֲפַר־אָרֶץ וְתִקְוַת אֱנוֹשׁ הֶאֱבַדְתָּ׃ תִּתְקְפֵהוּ לָנֶצַח
כא וַיַּהֲלֹךְ מְשַׁנֶּה פָנָיו וַתְּשַׁלְּחֵהוּ׃ יִכְבְּדוּ בָנָיו וְלֹא יֵדָע וְיִצְעֲרוּ וְלֹא־יָבִין
כב טו א לָמוֹ׃ אַךְ־בְּשָׂרוֹ עָלָיו יִכְאָב וְנַפְשׁוֹ עָלָיו תֶּאֱבָל׃ וַיַּעַן אֱלִיפַז
ב ג הַתֵּימָנִי וַיֹּאמַר׃ הֶחָכָם יַעֲנֶה דַעַת־רוּחַ וִימַלֵּא קָדִים בִּטְנוֹ׃ הוֹכֵחַ
ד בְּדָבָר לֹא יִסְכּוֹן וּמִלִּים לֹא־יוֹעִיל בָּם׃ אַף־אַתָּה תָּפֵר יִרְאָה וְתִגְרַע
ה ו שִׂיחָה לִפְנֵי־אֵל׃ כִּי יְאַלֵּף עֲוֺנְךָ פִיךָ וְתִבְחַר לְשׁוֹן עֲרוּמִים׃ יַרְשִׁיעֲךָ
ז פִיךָ וְלֹא־אָנִי וּשְׂפָתֶיךָ יַעֲנוּ־בָךְ׃ הֲרִאישׁוֹן אָדָם תִּוָּלֵד וְלִפְנֵי גְבָעוֹת
ח ט חוֹלָלְתָּ׃ הַבְסוֹד אֱלוֹהַּ תִּשְׁמָע וְתִגְרַע אֵלֶיךָ חָכְמָה׃ מַה־יָּדַעְתָּ וְלֹא
י נֵדָע תָּבִין וְלֹא־עִמָּנוּ הוּא׃ גַּם־שָׂב גַּם־יָשִׁישׁ בָּנוּ כַּבִּיר מֵאָבִיךָ יָמִים׃
יא יב הַמְעַט מִמְּךָ תַּנְחֻמוֹת אֵל וְדָבָר לָאַט עִמָּךְ׃ מַה־יִּקָּחֲךָ לִבֶּךָ וּמַה־
יג יד יִּרְזְמוּן עֵינֶיךָ׃ כִּי־תָשִׁיב אֶל־אֵל רוּחֶךָ וְהֹצֵאתָ מִפִּיךָ מִלִּין׃ מָה־אֱנוֹשׁ
טו כִּי־יִזְכֶּה וְכִי־יִצְדַּק יְלוּד אִשָּׁה׃ הֵן בִּקְדֹשָׁו לֹא יַאֲמִין וְשָׁמַיִם לֹא־זַכּוּ
טז יז בְעֵינָיו׃ אַף כִּי־נִתְעָב וְנֶאֱלָח אִישׁ־שֹׁתֶה כַמַּיִם עַוְלָה׃ אֲחַוְךָ שְׁמַע־
יח לִי וְזֶה־חָזִיתִי וַאֲסַפֵּרָה׃ אֲשֶׁר־חֲכָמִים יַגִּידוּ וְלֹא כִחֲדוּ מֵאֲבוֹתָם׃
יט כ לָהֶם לְבַדָּם נִתְּנָה הָאָרֶץ וְלֹא־עָבַר זָר בְּתוֹכָם׃ כָּל־יְמֵי רָשָׁע הוּא

21 years he has left. The sound of terror is in his ears; when it's quiet, robbers
22 come near. He cannot hope to escape the darkness; he is fated for the sword.
23 24 He is cast out, food for vultures, knowing his day of darkness is near. Distress
25 and anguish terrorize him, like a king before battle, for he has stretched out
26 his arm against God and presumes to spar with Shaddai, charging toward
27 Him, neck raised behind his thick, embossed shields, for he has padded his
28 face with fat[26] and covered his loins with blubber. He will live in plundered
29 towns, in houses long abandoned, fated to become heaps of rubble. He will
30 have no riches, no enduring fortune, no wealth extending across the land. He
will never escape the darkness. Flame will shrivel his stalk, and the wind of
31 His mouth will sweep him away. May no man be led astray by falsehood, for
32 falsehood will be his reward. Withering before his time, his branches never
33 to be green again, he is like a vine shedding unripe fruit, like an olive tree
34 casting off buds. Remember, the brazen end up barren; homes built on bribes
35 burn down. Pregnant with treachery, they breed sin,[27] and their bellies con-
16 1 2 ceive deceit." Then Iyov spoke up and said: "I have heard such talk
3 before, tormenting comforters that you are! 'Is there an end to words of wind?
4 What pains you so, that you go on and on?'[28] I, too, could talk like you were
you in my shoes, composing fine phrases against you, shaking my head at your
5 plight. With my mouth, I would urge you on and spare you my consolations!
6 Speaking up would spare me no pain, and holding back, what would I lose?
7 8 But now, He has worn me out. You have laid waste to all I know. You have
shriveled me up – quite the sight to behold – my emaciation testifying against
9 me! His rage has ravaged me, made me His prey. How He bares His teeth!
10 My persecutor's gaze shoots through me. Men gape at me open-mouthed,
11 strike my cheek in scorn, band together against me. God hands me over to
12 evil men, hurls me into the grip of the wicked. I was at ease before He crushed
13 me, took hold of my neck, shattered me and made me into His target. His
bowmen surrounded me; He coldly sliced through my kidneys, poured my
14 juices out onto the ground; He broke through me, gash by gash, charging at
15 me like a warrior. I have sewn sackcloth onto my skin and dug my horns into
16 the dust.[29] My face is red from weeping, and death-dark covers my eyes,
17 18 though there is no wrongdoing on my hands, and my prayer is pure: 'Earth!
19 Do not cover up my blood! Let my cry find no resting place!' Even now, my
20 witness is in heaven; my defender is on high. My intermediaries, my derid-
21 ers – it is to God my eyes shed tears. A man may as well argue with God as
22 he would with his companions, for in only a few years I will go down that
17 1 path of no return. My spirit is crushed, my days have been snuffed out, the
2 3 graveyard awaits. All about are people who jeer; my eyes cannot bear it. Be
4 now my guarantor! Who else will pledge on my behalf? You cannot be exalted
5 for You have hidden reason from their hearts. Who invites friends to a feast

26 | A metaphor for rebelliousness (cf. Deut. 32:15).
27 | Cf. Psalms 7:15; Isaiah 59:4.
28 | Paraphrasing Elifaz in 15:2.
29 | A sign of defeat. Raised horns signify victory (cf., e.g., 1 Sam. 2:1, 10).

כא מִתְחוֹלֵל וּמִסְפַּר שָׁנִים נִצְפְּנוּ לֶעָרִיץ׃ קוֹל־פְּחָדִים בְּאׇזְנָיו בַּשָּׁלוֹם
כב כג שׁוֹדֵד יְבוֹאֶנּוּ׃ לֹא־יַאֲמִין שׁוּב מִנִּי־חֹשֶׁךְ וְצָפוּ הוּא אֱלֵי־חָרֶב׃ נֹדֵד וְצָפוּי
כד הוּא לַלֶּחֶם אַיֵּה יָדַע ׀ כִּי־נָכוֹן בְּיָדוֹ יוֹם־חֹשֶׁךְ׃ יְבַעֲתֻהוּ צַר וּמְצוּקָה
כה תִּתְקְפֵהוּ כְּמֶלֶךְ ׀ עָתִיד לַכִּידוֹר׃ כִּי־נָטָה אֶל־אֵל יָדוֹ וְאֶל־שַׁדַּי
כו כז יִתְגַּבָּר׃ יָרוּץ אֵלָיו בְּצַוָּאר בַּעֲבִי גַּבֵּי מָגִנָּיו׃ כִּי־כִסָּה פָנָיו בְּחֶלְבּוֹ וַיַּעַשׂ
כח פִּימָה עֲלֵי־כָסֶל׃ וַיִּשְׁכּוֹן ׀ עָרִים נִכְחָדוֹת בָּתִּים לֹא־יֵשְׁבוּ לָמוֹ אֲשֶׁר
כט הִתְעַתְּדוּ לְגַלִּים׃ לֹא־יֶעְשַׁר וְלֹא־יָקוּם חֵילוֹ וְלֹא־יִטֶּה לָאָרֶץ מִנְלָם׃
ל לא לֹא־יָסוּר ׀ מִנִּי־חֹשֶׁךְ יֹנַקְתּוֹ תְּיַבֵּשׁ שַׁלְהָבֶת וְיָסוּר בְּרוּחַ פִּיו׃ אַל־
לב יַאֲמֵן בַּשָּׁו נִתְעָה כִּי־שָׁוְא תִּהְיֶה תְמוּרָתוֹ׃ בְּלֹא־יוֹמוֹ תִּמָּלֵא וְכִפָּתוֹ
לג לד לֹא רַעֲנָנָה׃ יַחְמֹס כַּגֶּפֶן בִּסְרוֹ וְיַשְׁלֵךְ כַּזַּיִת נִצָּתוֹ׃ כִּי־עֲדַת חָנֵף
לה גַּלְמוּד וְאֵשׁ אָכְלָה אׇהֳלֵי־שֹׁחַד׃ הָרֹה עָמָל וְיָלֹד אָוֶן וּבִטְנָם תָּכִין
טז א ב מִרְמָה׃ וַיַּעַן אִיּוֹב וַיֹּאמַר׃ שָׁמַעְתִּי כְאֵלֶּה רַבּוֹת
ג מְנַחֲמֵי עָמָל כֻּלְּכֶם׃ הֲקֵץ לְדִבְרֵי־רוּחַ אוֹ מַה־יַּמְרִיצְךָ כִּי תַעֲנֶה׃
ד גַּם ׀ אָנֹכִי כָּכֶם אֲדַבֵּרָה לוּ־יֵשׁ נַפְשְׁכֶם תַּחַת נַפְשִׁי אַחְבִּירָה עֲלֵיכֶם
ה בְּמִלִּים וְאָנִיעָה עֲלֵיכֶם בְּמוֹ רֹאשִׁי׃ אֲאַמִּצְכֶם בְּמוֹ־פִי וְנִיד שְׂפָתַי
ו ז יַחְשֹׂךְ׃ אִם־אֲדַבְּרָה לֹא־יֵחָשֵׂךְ כְּאֵבִי וְאַחְדְּלָה מַה־מִּנִּי יַהֲלֹךְ׃ אַךְ־
ח עַתָּה הֶלְאָנִי הֲשִׁמּוֹתָ כׇּל־עֲדָתִי׃ וַתִּקְמְטֵנִי לְעֵד הָיָה וַיָּקׇם בִּי כַחֲשִׁי
ט בְּפָנַי יַעֲנֶה׃ אַפּוֹ טָרַף ׀ וַיִּשְׂטְמֵנִי חָרַק עָלַי בְּשִׁנָּיו צָרִי ׀ יִלְטוֹשׁ עֵינָיו
י יא לִי׃ פָּעֲרוּ עָלַי ׀ בְּפִיהֶם בְּחֶרְפָּה הִכּוּ לְחָיָי יַחַד עָלַי יִתְמַלָּאוּן׃ יַסְגִּירֵנִי
יב אֵל אֶל עֲוִיל וְעַל־יְדֵי רְשָׁעִים יִרְטֵנִי׃ שָׁלֵו הָיִיתִי ׀ וַיְפַרְפְּרֵנִי וְאָחַז
יג בְּעׇרְפִּי וַיְפַצְפְּצֵנִי וַיְקִימֵנִי לוֹ לְמַטָּרָה׃ יָסֹבּוּ עָלַי ׀ רַבָּיו יְפַלַּח כִּלְיוֹתַי
יד וְלֹא יַחְמֹל יִשְׁפֹּךְ לָאָרֶץ מְרֵרָתִי׃ יִפְרְצֵנִי פֶרֶץ עַל־פְּנֵי־פָרֶץ יָרֻץ עָלַי
טו טז כְּגִבּוֹר׃ שַׂק תָּפַרְתִּי עֲלֵי גִלְדִּי וְעֹלַלְתִּי בֶעָפָר קַרְנִי׃ פָּנַי חֳמַרְמְרָה חֳמַרְמְרוּ
יז יח מִנִּי־בֶכִי וְעַל עַפְעַפַּי צַלְמָוֶת׃ עַל לֹא־חָמָס בְּכַפָּי וּתְפִלָּתִי זַכָּה׃ אֶרֶץ
יט אַל־תְּכַסִּי דָמִי וְאַל־יְהִי מָקוֹם לְזַעֲקָתִי׃ גַּם־עַתָּה הִנֵּה־בַשָּׁמַיִם עֵדִי
כ כא וְשָׂהֲדִי בַּמְּרוֹמִים׃ מְלִיצַי רֵעָי אֶל־אֱלוֹהַּ דָּלְפָה עֵינִי׃ וְיוֹכַח לְגֶבֶר
כב עִם־אֱלוֹהַּ וּבֶן־אָדָם לְרֵעֵהוּ׃ כִּי־שְׁנוֹת מִסְפָּר יֶאֱתָיוּ וְאֹרַח לֹא־אָשׁוּב
יז א ב אֶהֱלֹךְ׃ רוּחִי חֻבָּלָה יָמַי נִזְעָכוּ קְבָרִים לִי׃ אִם־לֹא הֲתֻלִים עִמָּדִי
ג וּבְהַמְּרוֹתָם תָּלַן עֵינִי׃ שִׂימָה־נָּא עׇרְבֵנִי עִמָּךְ מִי הוּא לְיָדִי יִתָּקֵעַ׃
ד ה כִּי־לִבָּם צָפַנְתָּ מִּשָּׂכֶל עַל־כֵּן לֹא תְרֹמֵם׃ לְחֵלֶק יַגִּיד רֵעִים וְעֵינֵי בָנָיו

6 while his children look on, starving?[30] An exemplum, an epithet for all to
7 behold, that's what He has made me – a thing to spit at! My eyes have grown
8 dim from grief, and all my limbs are like a shadow. Decent people are outraged
9 by this, and the pure rise up against the godless. The righteous man will hold
10 fast to his path, and those with clean hands will be strengthened. But all of
11 you, please come back! Not a single one of you is wise! My days are over; my
12 plans, my heart's desires, are severed. They pretend that night is day, that light
13 is closer than the dark. If I have set up my home in Sheol, if I have laid out my
14 bed in darkness, called to the Pit: 'Father!' and to the worm: 'My mother, my
15 16 sister!' where, then, will be my hope? My hope – who can see it? As it descends
18 1 into Sheol, together we will go down into the dust." And Bildad the
2 Shuhite answered and said: "'How long will you all go on? Enough with
3 words! Think first. Then we can talk.'[31] Why make us into beasts? Do we strike
4 you as that stupid? How he ravages his soul in rage! Will the earth be aban-
5 doned, mountains moved, just for you? The light of the wicked dissipates,
6 and the flame of his fire dies down; in his tent, light turns to darkness, and his
7 lamp goes out on him. His proud stride is diminished; his own advice does
8 9 him in; his foot gets caught in a net, and he heads straight into snares. A trap
10 grips him by the heel; it tightens in knots around him; a rope hides on the
11 ground, and his pitfall waits along the way. On every side horrors terrify him,
12 and his feet falter. His children are sure to starve, calamity steadfast at his side;
13 14 disease ravages his skin, and Death's firstborn devours his limbs. Ripped from
15 the safety of his tent, he is brought before the King of Terrors;[32] he lives in a
16 home not his own, brimstone scattered across his estate. Underneath, his
17 roots wither; up above, his branches rot. His memory vanishes from across
18 the land, and his good name vanishes.[33] Thrust from light to darkness, he is
19 cast out of the world. He leaves no child, no offspring, not a single survivor
20 where he sojourned; in the West they are appalled by his fate; in the East they
21 are seized with terror. That is the abode of the wicked, the place for him who
19 1 2 does not know God." Then Iyov spoke up and said: "How
3 long will you go on afflicting me, crushing me with words? Ten times you
4 have taunted me shamelessly, full of disdain. If I have erred, that is my con-
5 cern! But if you have the gall to speak out, holding my disgrace against me,
6 then know, at least, that God has done me wrong, trapping me inside His net.
7 8 I cry foul but am never answered; I call out but there is no justice. He has
blocked my way – I cannot get through – He throws darkness on my path.
9 10 He has stripped me of my honor and knocked the crown off my head. From
11 all sides He beats me down, uproots my hope as He would a tree. He has set
12 His wrath ablaze, considers me an enemy; His troops move forward as one,
13 building their siege ramp against me, and set up camp around my tent. He
14 has pushed my brothers away, alienating all who knew me. My family never

30 | Iyov's friends offer much advice but do not take it themselves.

31 | Bildad here is paraphrasing Iyov's earlier statements back to him (see 13:13, 16:3).

32 | Perhaps King of the Netherworld.

33 | Literally "he has no name"; his good reputation has disappeared.

ו ז תִּכְלֶנָה: וְהִצִּגַנִי לִמְשֹׁל עַמִּים וְתֹפֶת לְפָנִים אֶהְיֶה: וַתֵּכַהּ מִכַּעַשׂ
ח עֵינִי וִיצֻרַי כַּצֵּל כֻּלָּם: יָשֹׁמּוּ יְשָׁרִים עַל־זֹאת וְנָקִי עַל־חָנֵף יִתְעֹרָר:
ט י וְיֹאחֵז צַדִּיק דַּרְכּוֹ וּטְהָר־יָדַיִם יֹסִיף אֹמֶץ: וְאוּלָם כֻּלָּם תָּשֻׁבוּ וּבֹאוּ ד
יא יב נָא וְלֹא־אֶמְצָא בָכֶם חָכָם: יָמַי עָבְרוּ זִמֹּתַי נִתְּקוּ מוֹרָשֵׁי לְבָבִי: לַיְלָה
יג לְיוֹם יָשִׂימוּ אוֹר קָרוֹב מִפְּנֵי־חֹשֶׁךְ: אִם־אֲקַוֶּה שְׁאוֹל בֵּיתִי בַּחֹשֶׁךְ
יד טו רִפַּדְתִּי יְצוּעָי: לַשַּׁחַת קָרָאתִי אָבִי אָתָּה אִמִּי וַאֲחֹתִי לָרִמָּה: וְאַיֵּה
טז אֵפוֹ תִקְוָתִי וְתִקְוָתִי מִי יְשׁוּרֶנָּה: בַּדֵּי שְׁאֹל תֵּרַדְנָה אִם־יַחַד עַל־עָפָר
יח א ב נָחַת: וַיַּעַן בִּלְדַּד הַשֻּׁחִי וַיֹּאמַר: עַד־אָנָה ׀ תְּשִׂימוּן
ג קִנְצֵי לְמִלִּין תָּבִינוּ וְאַחַר נְדַבֵּר: מַדּוּעַ נֶחְשַׁבְנוּ כַבְּהֵמָה נִטְמִינוּ
ד בְּעֵינֵיכֶם: טֹרֵף נַפְשׁוֹ בְּאַפּוֹ הַלְמַעַנְךָ תֵּעָזַב אָרֶץ וְיֶעְתַּק־צוּר מִמְּקֹמוֹ:
ה ו גַּם אוֹר רְשָׁעִים יִדְעָךְ וְלֹא־יִגַּהּ שְׁבִיב אִשּׁוֹ: אוֹר חָשַׁךְ בְּאָהֳלוֹ וְנֵרוֹ
ז ח עָלָיו יִדְעָךְ: יֵצְרוּ צַעֲדֵי אוֹנוֹ וְתַשְׁלִיכֵהוּ עֲצָתוֹ: כִּי־שֻׁלַּח בְּרֶשֶׁת
ט י בְּרַגְלָיו וְעַל־שְׂבָכָה יִתְהַלָּךְ: יֹאחֵז בְּעָקֵב פָּח יַחֲזֵק עָלָיו צַמִּים: טָמוּן
יא בָּאָרֶץ חַבְלוֹ וּמַלְכֻּדְתּוֹ עֲלֵי נָתִיב: סָבִיב בִּעֲתֻהוּ בַלָּהוֹת וֶהֱפִיצֻהוּ
יב יג לְרַגְלָיו: יְהִי־רָעֵב אֹנוֹ וְאֵיד נָכוֹן לְצַלְעוֹ: יֹאכַל בַּדֵּי עוֹרוֹ יֹאכַל בַּדָּיו
יד טו בְּכוֹר מָוֶת: יִנָּתֵק מֵאָהֳלוֹ מִבְטַחוֹ וְתַצְעִדֵהוּ לְמֶלֶךְ בַּלָּהוֹת: תִּשְׁכּוֹן
טז בְּאָהֳלוֹ מִבְּלִי־לוֹ יְזֹרֶה עַל־נָוֵהוּ גָפְרִית: מִתַּחַת שָׁרָשָׁיו יִבָשׁוּ וּמִמַּעַל
יז יח יִמַּל קְצִירוֹ: זִכְרוֹ־אָבַד מִנִּי־אָרֶץ וְלֹא־שֵׁם לוֹ עַל־פְּנֵי־חוּץ: יֶהְדְּפֻהוּ
יט מֵאוֹר אֶל־חֹשֶׁךְ וּמִתֵּבֵל יְנִדֻּהוּ: לֹא נִין לוֹ וְלֹא־נֶכֶד בְּעַמּוֹ וְאֵין שָׂרִיד
כ כא בִּמְגוּרָיו: עַל־יוֹמוֹ נָשַׁמּוּ אַחֲרֹנִים וְקַדְמֹנִים אָחֲזוּ שָׂעַר: אַךְ־אֵלֶּה
יט א מִשְׁכְּנוֹת עַוָּל וְזֶה מְקוֹם לֹא־יָדַע־אֵל: וַיַּעַן אִיּוֹב וַיֹּאמַר:
ב ג עַד־אָנָה תּוֹגְיוּן נַפְשִׁי וּתְדַכְּאוּנַנִי בְמִלִּים: זֶה עֶשֶׂר פְּעָמִים תַּכְלִימוּנִי
ד ה לֹא־תֵבֹשׁוּ תַּהְכְּרוּ־לִי: וְאַף־אָמְנָם שָׁגִיתִי אִתִּי תָּלִין מְשׁוּגָתִי: אִם־
ו אָמְנָם עָלַי תַּגְדִּילוּ וְתוֹכִיחוּ עָלַי חֶרְפָּתִי: דְּעוּ־אֵפוֹ כִּי־אֱלוֹהַּ עִוְּתָנִי
ז וּמְצוּדוֹ עָלַי הִקִּיף: הֵן אֶצְעַק חָמָס וְלֹא אֵעָנֶה אֲשַׁוַּע וְאֵין מִשְׁפָּט:
ח ט אָרְחִי גָדַר וְלֹא אֶעֱבוֹר וְעַל־נְתִיבוֹתַי חֹשֶׁךְ יָשִׂים: כְּבוֹדִי מֵעָלַי
י הִפְשִׁיט וַיָּסַר עֲטֶרֶת רֹאשִׁי: יִתְּצֵנִי סָבִיב וָאֵלַךְ וַיַּסַּע כָּעֵץ תִּקְוָתִי:
יא יב וַיַּחַר עָלַי אַפּוֹ וַיַּחְשְׁבֵנִי לוֹ כְצָרָיו: יַחַד ׀ יָבֹאוּ גְדוּדָיו וַיָּסֹלּוּ עָלַי דַּרְכָּם
יג יד וַיַּחֲנוּ סָבִיב לְאָהֳלִי: אַחַי מֵעָלַי הִרְחִיק וְיֹדְעַי אַךְ־זָרוּ מִמֶּנִּי: חָדְלוּ

15 comes; my friends are gone. I am a stranger, now, alien to my maidservants,
16 my household. I call to my manservant, but he does not answer. With my own
17 mouth I implore him. My wife is nauseated by my breath; my own brothers
18 can't stomach my stench. Even hoodlums despise me, defaming me behind
19 my back. Close friends are repulsed by me; my loved ones have turned against
20 21 me. My bones cling to my skin and flesh; my teeth are cemented shut. Pity
22 me, pity me, my friends! Look how God's hand has struck me down! Why
23 do you go after me like God, tearing me to shreds?[34] If only my words were
24 written, then engraved in bronze with a stylus of iron and lead, carved in stone
25 for eternity! As for myself, I know my Redeemer lives, and He will rise from
26 the dust at last.[35] And though they flay my skin, from within this flesh I will
27 see God. I will see Him for myself with my own eyes and no one else's. My
28 very kidneys will pine.[36] If you say, 'How will we pursue him? How will we
29 uproot him?'[37] – you would be wise to fear the sword, for wrath is sure to be
20 1 avenged. Beware, then, of justice." Then Tzofar the Naamatite spoke
2 up and said: "Thanks to my inner sense of things, my thoughts bid me to reply.
3 4 When I hear a biting reproach, I am inclined from within to respond. Don't
you know that from the beginning, ever since people were placed on earth,
5 the revelry of the wicked lasts but a moment, and the joy of the defiant is gone
6 in a flash? A person may tower up into the skies, and his head might graze the
7 clouds, but he vanishes forever like dung. Onlookers wonder, 'Where did he
8 go?' He will fly away like a dream, never to be found, chased off like a night
9 vision. The eyes that glimpsed him never will again! His home beholds him
10 no more. Poverty will crush his sons when his own hands return his wealth.[38]
11 12 His bones – full of vigor, robust – will lie down with him in the dust. Though
13 he hides evil, sweet there under his tongue, and, craving it, holds onto it, loath
14 15 to let it go, the food in his bowels turns to asp venom within. He swallows his
16 wealth then spews it out; God hurls it from his belly. It is poison of asps he
17 sucks, the viper's tongue that will kill him! He will never see streams, gleaming
18 rivers of honey and curd. His profits? He will not keep them, and any earnings
19 he will not enjoy, for he has crushed what belongs to the poor, robbed them
20 of their homes and not rebuilt them. Because his belly knows no quiet, he
21 will not escape with his pleasures. No one will be left to enjoy his bounty;
22 nothing good of his will last! Just when he is satisfied, calamity will strike: the
23 oppressed will overtake him. The moment he is about to fill his belly, the fire
24 of God's fury will let loose, warfare raining down on him. He flees from a
25 weapon made of iron? A bronze bow will pierce him. A blade is drawn?
26 It comes out his back, shooting through his bile. Terror descends! Thick
darkness awaits his treasured ones. Unfanned flames eat them alive, devouring

34 | Literally "never satiated with my flesh." "Devouring the flesh" of a victim is an idiom for slander; cf. 31:31; Psalms 27:2; Daniel 3:8.

35 | God will ultimately stand up to vindicate Iyov during his lifetime.

36 | The kidneys are the seat of the emotions.

37 | Literally "me." This translation accords with the manuscript variant "him."

38 | In other words, when the wicked person is forced to give up his ill-gotten wealth.

טו קְרוֹבָי וּמְיֻדָּעַי שְׁכֵחוּנִי׃ גָּרֵי בֵיתִי וְאַמְהֹתַי לְזָר תַּחְשְׁבֻנִי נָכְרִי הָיִיתִי
טז יז בְעֵינֵיהֶם׃ לְעַבְדִּי קָרָאתִי וְלֹא יַעֲנֶה בְּמוֹ־פִי אֶתְחַנֶּן־לוֹ׃ רוּחִי זָרָה
יח לְאִשְׁתִּי וְחַנֹּתִי לִבְנֵי בִטְנִי׃ גַּם־עֲוִילִים מָאֲסוּ בִי אָקוּמָה וַיְדַבְּרוּ־
יט כ בִי׃ תִּעֲבוּנִי כָּל־מְתֵי סוֹדִי וְזֶה־אָהַבְתִּי נֶהְפְּכוּ־בִי׃ בְּעוֹרִי וּבִבְשָׂרִי
כא דָּבְקָה עַצְמִי וָאֶתְמַלְּטָה בְּעוֹר שִׁנָּי׃ חָנֻּנִי חָנֻּנִי אַתֶּם רֵעָי כִּי יַד־אֱלוֹהַּ
כב כג נָגְעָה בִּי׃ לָמָּה תִּרְדְּפֻנִי כְמוֹ־אֵל וּמִבְּשָׂרִי לֹא תִשְׂבָּעוּ׃ מִי־יִתֵּן אֵפוֹ
כד וְיִכָּתְבוּן מִלָּי מִי־יִתֵּן בַּסֵּפֶר וְיֻחָקוּ׃ בְּעֵט־בַּרְזֶל וְעֹפָרֶת לָעַד בַּצּוּר
כה כו יֵחָצְבוּן׃ וַאֲנִי יָדַעְתִּי גֹּאֲלִי חָי וְאַחֲרוֹן עַל־עָפָר יָקוּם׃ וְאַחַר עוֹרִי
כז נִקְּפוּ־זֹאת וּמִבְּשָׂרִי אֶחֱזֶה אֱלוֹהַּ׃ אֲשֶׁר אֲנִי ׀ אֶחֱזֶה־לִּי וְעֵינַי רָאוּ
כח וְלֹא־זָר כָּלוּ כִלְיֹתַי בְּחֵקִי׃ כִּי תֹאמְרוּ מַה־נִּרְדָּף־לוֹ וְשֹׁרֶשׁ דָּבָר
כט נִמְצָא־בִי׃ גּוּרוּ לָכֶם ׀ מִפְּנֵי־חֶרֶב כִּי־חֵמָה עֲוֺנוֹת חָרֶב לְמַעַן תֵּדְעוּן
כ א ב שַׁדִּין׃ וַיַּעַן צֹפַר הַנַּעֲמָתִי וַיֹּאמַר׃ לָכֵן שְׂעִפַּי יְשִׁיבוּנִי שַׁדּוּן
ג ד וּבַעֲבוּר חוּשִׁי בִי׃ מוּסַר כְּלִמָּתִי אֶשְׁמָע וְרוּחַ מִבִּינָתִי יַעֲנֵנִי׃ הֲזֹאת
ה יָדַעְתָּ מִנִּי־עַד מִנִּי שִׂים אָדָם עֲלֵי־אָרֶץ׃ כִּי רִנְנַת רְשָׁעִים מִקָּרוֹב
ו וְשִׂמְחַת חָנֵף עֲדֵי־רָגַע׃ אִם־יַעֲלֶה לַשָּׁמַיִם שִׂיאוֹ וְרֹאשׁוֹ לָעָב יַגִּיעַ׃
ז ח כְּגֶלְלוֹ לָנֶצַח יֹאבֵד רֹאָיו יֹאמְרוּ אַיּוֹ׃ כַּחֲלוֹם יָעוּף וְלֹא יִמְצָאֻהוּ וְיֻדַּד
ט י כְּחֶזְיוֹן לָיְלָה׃ עַיִן שְׁזָפַתּוּ וְלֹא תוֹסִיף וְלֹא־עוֹד תְּשׁוּרֶנּוּ מְקוֹמוֹ׃ בָּנָיו
יא יְרַצּוּ דַלִּים וְיָדָיו תָּשֵׁבְנָה אוֹנוֹ׃ עַצְמוֹתָיו מָלְאוּ עֲלוּמָו וְעִמּוֹ עַל־עָפָר
יב יג תִּשְׁכָּב׃ אִם־תַּמְתִּיק בְּפִיו רָעָה יַכְחִידֶנָּה תַּחַת לְשׁוֹנוֹ׃ יַחְמֹל עָלֶיהָ
יד וְלֹא יַעַזְבֶנָּה וְיִמְנָעֶנָּה בְּתוֹךְ חִכּוֹ׃ לַחְמוֹ בְּמֵעָיו נֶהְפָּךְ מְרוֹרַת פְּתָנִים
טו טז בְּקִרְבּוֹ׃ חַיִל בָּלַע וַיְקִאֶנּוּ מִבִּטְנוֹ יֹרִשֶׁנּוּ אֵל׃ רֹאשׁ־פְּתָנִים יִינָק
יז תַּהַרְגֵהוּ לְשׁוֹן אֶפְעֶה׃ אַל־יֵרֶא בִפְלַגּוֹת נַהֲרֵי נַחֲלֵי דְּבַשׁ וְחֶמְאָה׃
יח יט מֵשִׁיב יָגָע וְלֹא יִבְלָע כְּחֵיל תְּמוּרָתוֹ וְלֹא יַעֲלֹס׃ כִּי־רִצַּץ עָזַב דַּלִּים
כ בַּיִת גָּזַל וְלֹא יִבֶנֵהוּ׃ כִּי ׀ לֹא־יָדַע שָׁלֵו בְּבִטְנוֹ בַּחֲמוּדוֹ לֹא יְמַלֵּט׃
כא כב אֵין־שָׂרִיד לְאָכְלוֹ עַל־כֵּן לֹא־יָחִיל טוּבוֹ׃ בִּמְלֹאות שִׂפְקוֹ יֵצֶר לוֹ
כג כָּל־יַד עָמֵל תְּבֹאֶנּוּ׃ יְהִי ׀ לְמַלֵּא בִטְנוֹ יְשַׁלַּח־בּוֹ חֲרוֹן אַפּוֹ וְיַמְטֵר
כד כה עָלֵימוֹ בִּלְחוּמוֹ׃ יִבְרַח מִנֵּשֶׁק בַּרְזֶל תַּחְלְפֵהוּ קֶשֶׁת נְחוּשָׁה׃ שָׁלַף
כו וַיֵּצֵא מִגֵּוָה וּבָרָק מִמְּרֹרָתוֹ יַהֲלֹךְ עָלָיו אֵמִים׃ כָּל־חֹשֶׁךְ טָמוּן לִצְפּוּנָיו

27 the last survivor in his tent. The heavens lay bare his guilt, and the earth rises
28 up against him. Waves surge into his house, floods on the day of wrath.
29 And that is what has been prepared for the wicked, their God-given por-
21 1 2 tion." Then Iyov spoke up and said: "Hear now what I have to say,
3 and let that be your consolation! Bear with me as I speak; afterward, deride
4 me. Is my grievance against a mere mortal? Why shouldn't my patience wear
5 6 thin? Turn toward me and be still; put your hands on your mouths. The
7 thought of it horrifies me; my flesh is seized with trembling. Why do the
8 wicked survive, grow old and prosper, their children right by their side, their
9 children's children ever before their eyes? Their homes are untroubled, at
10 peace, and they are spared God's rod. Their bulls breed without fail; their
11 cows give birth and do not miscarry; they send their young to frolic like
12 sheep; their children hop and skip, singing with the drum and lyre, rejoicing
13 to the sounds of the pipe. They happily live out their days and go down
14 peacefully to Sheol. They say to God, 'Turn away from us! We have no use
15 for Your ways! Who is Shaddai that we should serve Him? What would we
16 gain by praying to Him?' But their joy is not of their making.[39] It is beyond
17 me, the wicked man's thinking! How often does the lamp of the wicked
go out and disaster overtake them?! When does God, in His wrath, bring
18 calamity? How often are they like straw in the wind, like chaff swept up in a
19 storm?! When does God store up punishment for his sons, pay retribution
20 so he will know, so he will witness his ruin with his own eyes, drink down
21 the venom of Shaddai? What will he care about the fate of his family when
22 the months allotted him are running out? Who presumes to impart divine
23 mysteries to God, who judges on high? One man dies in perfect health, at
24 ease and tranquil; his pails are full of milk, the marrow of his bones moist.
25 26 Another dies a bitter soul, never having tasted prosperity. Both lie down
27 in the dust under a blanket of worms. Oh, I know your thoughts and the
28 schemes you plot against me. You say, 'Where, then, is the noble man's house,
29 and where the tent of the wicked?'[40] But haven't you asked those passing
30 through? You cannot deny their testimony: on doomsday the wicked man is
31 spared; on the day of wrath he is delivered! Who will confront him to his
32 face? Who will make him pay for what he has done, tell him he will be carried
33 to the grave, that a watch will be kept at the mound, that clods of earth from
the wadi will be his comfort, that others will come after him, that innumerable
34 are those who precede him? What are they for, these hollow consolations?
22 1 All that's left of your answers is betrayal." And Elifaz the Temanite
2 spoke up and said: "Who is to say a man is of any use to God, that the wise
3 could be of help to Him? What does Shaddai gain from your righteousness?
4 Does He profit from your blameless ways? Would He litigate because He fears
5 you? Is that why He has brought you to judgment? Clearly, your wickedness
6 is immense, your transgressions boundless! You demand pledges from others
7 without cause and strip the naked of their clothes. You withhold water from

39 |The undeserved happiness of the wicked is given freely by God.
40 |You claim that all receive their just deserts.

כז תְּאָכְלֵהוּ אֵשׁ לֹא־נֻפָּח יֵרַע שָׂרִיד בְּאָהֳלוֹ: יְגַלּוּ שָׁמַיִם עֲוֺנוֹ וְאֶרֶץ
כח כט מִתְקוֹמָמָה לוֹ: יִגֶל יְבוּל בֵּיתוֹ נִגָּרוֹת בְּיוֹם אַפּוֹ: זֶה ׀ חֵלֶק־אָדָם רָשָׁע
כא א ב מֵאֱלֹהִים וְנַחֲלַת אִמְרוֹ מֵאֵל: וַיַּעַן אִיּוֹב וַיֹּאמַר: שִׁמְעוּ שָׁמוֹעַ
ג מִלָּתִי וּתְהִי־זֹאת תַּנְחוּמֹתֵיכֶם: שָׂאוּנִי וְאָנֹכִי אֲדַבֵּר וְאַחַר דַּבְּרִי
ד ה תַלְעִיג: הֶאָנֹכִי לְאָדָם שִׂיחִי וְאִם־מַדּוּעַ לֹא־תִקְצַר רוּחִי: פְּנוּ־אֵלַי
ו וְהָשַׁמּוּ וְשִׂימוּ יָד עַל־פֶּה: וְאִם־זָכַרְתִּי וְנִבְהָלְתִּי וְאָחַז בְּשָׂרִי פַּלָּצוּת:
ז ח מַדּוּעַ רְשָׁעִים יִחְיוּ עָתְקוּ גַּם־גָּבְרוּ חָיִל: זַרְעָם נָכוֹן לִפְנֵיהֶם עִמָּם
ט וְצֶאֱצָאֵיהֶם לְעֵינֵיהֶם: בָּתֵּיהֶם שָׁלוֹם מִפָּחַד וְלֹא שֵׁבֶט אֱלוֹהַּ עֲלֵיהֶם:
י יא שׁוֹרוֹ עִבַּר וְלֹא יַגְעִל תְּפַלֵּט פָּרָתוֹ וְלֹא תְשַׁכֵּל: יְשַׁלְּחוּ כַצֹּאן עֲוִילֵיהֶם
יב יג וְיַלְדֵיהֶם יְרַקֵּדוּן: יִשְׂאוּ כְּתֹף וְכִנּוֹר וְיִשְׂמְחוּ לְקוֹל עוּגָב: יבלו בַטּוֹב יְכַלּוּ
יד יְמֵיהֶם וּבְרֶגַע שְׁאוֹל יֵחָתּוּ: וַיֹּאמְרוּ לָאֵל סוּר מִמֶּנּוּ וְדַעַת דְּרָכֶיךָ לֹא
טו טז חָפָצְנוּ: מַה־שַׁדַּי כִּי־נַעַבְדֶנּוּ וּמַה־נּוֹעִיל כִּי נִפְגַּע־בּוֹ: הֵן לֹא בְיָדָם
יז טוּבָם עֲצַת רְשָׁעִים רָחֲקָה מֶנִּי: כַּמָּה ׀ נֵר־רְשָׁעִים יִדְעָךְ וְיָבֹא עָלֵימוֹ
יח אֵידָם חֲבָלִים יְחַלֵּק בְּאַפּוֹ: יִהְיוּ כְּתֶבֶן לִפְנֵי־רוּחַ וּכְמֹץ גְּנָבַתּוּ סוּפָה:
יט כ אֱלוֹהַּ יִצְפֹּן־לְבָנָיו אוֹנוֹ יְשַׁלֵּם אֵלָיו וְיֵדָע: יִרְאוּ עֵינָו כִּידוֹ וּמֵחֲמַת שַׁדַּי
כא כב יִשְׁתֶּה: כִּי מַה־חֶפְצוֹ בְּבֵיתוֹ אַחֲרָיו וּמִסְפַּר חֳדָשָׁיו חֻצָּצוּ: הַלְאֵל
כג יְלַמֶּד־דָּעַת וְהוּא רָמִים יִשְׁפּוֹט: זֶה יָמוּת בְּעֶצֶם תֻּמּוֹ כֻּלּוֹ שַׁלְאֲנַן
כד כה וְשָׁלֵיו: עֲטִינָיו מָלְאוּ חָלָב וּמֹחַ עַצְמוֹתָיו יְשֻׁקֶּה: וְזֶה יָמוּת בְּנֶפֶשׁ
כו מָרָה וְלֹא־אָכַל בַּטּוֹבָה: יַחַד עַל־עָפָר יִשְׁכָּבוּ וְרִמָּה תְּכַסֶּה עֲלֵיהֶם:
כז כח הֵן יָדַעְתִּי מַחְשְׁבוֹתֵיכֶם וּמְזִמּוֹת עָלַי תַּחְמֹסוּ: כִּי תֹאמְרוּ אַיֵּה בֵית־
כט נָדִיב וְאַיֵּה אֹהֶל ׀ מִשְׁכְּנוֹת רְשָׁעִים: הֲלֹא שְׁאֶלְתֶּם עוֹבְרֵי דָרֶךְ
ל וְאֹתֹתָם לֹא תְנַכֵּרוּ: כִּי לְיוֹם אֵיד יֵחָשֶׂךְ רָע לְיוֹם עֲבָרוֹת יוּבָלוּ:
לא לב מִי־יַגִּיד עַל־פָּנָיו דַּרְכּוֹ וְהוּא־עָשָׂה מִי יְשַׁלֶּם־לוֹ: וְהוּא לִקְבָרוֹת
לג יוּבָל וְעַל־גָּדִישׁ יִשְׁקוֹד: מָתְקוּ־לוֹ רִגְבֵי נָחַל וְאַחֲרָיו כָּל־אָדָם
לד יִמְשׁוֹךְ וּלְפָנָיו אֵין מִסְפָּר: וְאֵיךְ תְּנַחֲמוּנִי הָבֶל וּתְשׁוּבֹתֵיכֶם נִשְׁאַר־
כב א ב מָעַל: וַיַּעַן אֱלִיפַז הַתֵּמָנִי וַיֹּאמַר: הַלְאֵל יִסְכָּן־גָּבֶר כִּי־יִסְכֹּן
ג עָלֵימוֹ מַשְׂכִּיל: הַחֵפֶץ לְשַׁדַּי כִּי תִצְדָּק וְאִם־בֶּצַע כִּי־תַתֵּם דְּרָכֶיךָ:
ד ה הֲמִיִּרְאָתְךָ יֹכִיחֶךָ יָבוֹא עִמְּךָ בַּמִּשְׁפָּט: הֲלֹא רָעָתְךָ רַבָּה וְאֵין־קֵץ
ו ז לַעֲוֺנֹתֶיךָ: כִּי־תַחְבֹּל אַחֶיךָ חִנָּם וּבִגְדֵי עֲרוּמִּים תַּפְשִׁיט: לֹא־מַיִם

8 the thirsty and deny the famished their bread. The land belongs to the strong,
9 and those He favors settle it.[41] You have sent widows away empty-handed and
10 shoved away the arms of orphans. That is why traps surround you and why
11 you are suddenly struck by fear! You cannot even see the darkness; many
12 waters blanket you. Is God not in the highest heavens? Can He not glimpse
13 the topmost stars? You said, 'What does God know? How could He judge
14 through the fog? Clouds hide Him, and He does not see, circling the rim of
15 heaven.' Haven't you noticed the ways of the world that sinners have long
16 trod – who are cut off before their time, their foundations washed away in a
17 18 river? They tell God, 'Turn away from us! What can Shaddai do, after all?' But
He filled their houses with joy. It is beyond me, the wicked man's thinking![42]
19 20 The righteous will see and delight, and the pure are sure to scoff: 'You see!
21 They were obliterated; fire has devoured their wealth!' Make amends with
22 Him and be at one again. Then – good things will find you. Accept the teach-
23 ings of His mouth, and place His words in your heart. If you return to Shaddai,
24 you will be restored. If you banish iniquity from your tent, if gold is like dust
25 to you and Ofir[43] like stones in a stream; if Shaddai will be your gold, your
26 27 shining silver, if you entreat Shaddai and lift your face to God, when you
28 implore Him – He will hear you, and you will pay your vows in full.[44] When
29 you make a decree, it will come to pass. Light will shine on your paths, for
30 God humbles the boastful but delivers the lowly. He rescues the innocent, so
23 1 you too will be delivered by the purity of your hands." And Iyov
2 spoke up and said: "Even now my complaint is bitter; His hand weighs down
3 on my moans. If only I knew where to find Him, if only I could approach His
4 throne, I would lay out my case before Him and fill my mouth with my
5 charges. I would know how He would answer me and understand what He
6 tells me. Would He come at me with force? No! He would put forward His
7 case. There the righteous would be heard, and I would escape my Judge for-
8 ever. But I go east, and He isn't there, then west, but I cannot discern Him;
9 He hides in the north, but I cannot catch Him; He cloaks Himself in the
10 south, but I do not see Him. He knows my ways; if He tested me, I would
11 emerge as pure as gold. My feet have followed in His tracks; I have held to
12 His path and have not strayed. Never diverging from the commandments of
13 His lips, I have held His words in my breast. But He is of one mind. Who can
14 turn Him back? He does as He wishes. When He carries out His decree,
15 He comes up with more of the same. That is why I would shudder at His
16 presence; I would behold and dread Him. God has weakened my heart;
17 Shaddai makes me shudder, yet I am not annihilated by the darkness; gloom
24 1 does not shroud my face. Why has Shaddai not set times for
2 judgment? Why can't those who know Him foresee His days?[45] Some take

41 |This parodies Iyov's statement in 9:24.
42 |Echoing 21:13–16.
43 |The gold of Ofir was especially fine.
44 |You will fulfill the vows made when entreating God once He has responded favorably.
45 |Days of wrath and judgment (see 20:28).

ח עָיֵף תַּשְׁקֶה וּמֵרָעֵב תִּמְנַע־לָחֶם׃ וְאִישׁ זְרוֹעַ לוֹ הָאָרֶץ וּנְשׂוּא פָנִים
ט י יֵשֶׁב בָּהּ׃ אַלְמָנוֹת שִׁלַּחְתָּ רֵיקָם וּזְרֹעוֹת יְתֹמִים יְדֻכָּא׃ עַל־כֵּן
יא סְבִיבוֹתֶיךָ פַחִים וִיבַהֶלְךָ פַּחַד פִּתְאֹם׃ אוֹ־חֹשֶׁךְ לֹא־תִרְאֶה וְשִׁפְעַת־
יב מַיִם תְּכַסֶּךָּ׃ הֲלֹא־אֱלוֹהַּ גֹּבַהּ שָׁמָיִם וּרְאֵה רֹאשׁ כּוֹכָבִים כִּי־רָמּוּ׃
יג יד וְאָמַרְתָּ מַה־יָּדַע אֵל הַבְעַד עֲרָפֶל יִשְׁפּוֹט׃ עָבִים סֵתֶר־לוֹ וְלֹא יִרְאֶה
טו וְחוּג שָׁמַיִם יִתְהַלָּךְ׃ הַאֹרַח עוֹלָם תִּשְׁמֹר אֲשֶׁר דָּרְכוּ מְתֵי־אָוֶן׃
טז יז אֲשֶׁר־קֻמְּטוּ וְלֹא־עֵת נָהָר יוּצַק יְסוֹדָם׃ הָאֹמְרִים לָאֵל סוּר מִמֶּנּוּ
יח וּמַה־יִּפְעַל שַׁדַּי לָמוֹ׃ וְהוּא מִלֵּא בָתֵּיהֶם טוֹב וַעֲצַת רְשָׁעִים רָחֲקָה
יט כ מֶנִּי׃ יִרְאוּ צַדִּיקִים וְיִשְׂמָחוּ וְנָקִי יִלְעַג־לָמוֹ׃ אִם־לֹא נִכְחַד קִימָנוּ
כא כב וְיִתְרָם אָכְלָה אֵשׁ׃ הַסְכֶּן־נָא עִמּוֹ וּשְׁלָם בָּהֶם תְּבוֹאַתְךָ טוֹבָה׃ קַח־
כג נָא מִפִּיו תּוֹרָה וְשִׂים אֲמָרָיו בִּלְבָבֶךָ׃ אִם־תָּשׁוּב עַד־שַׁדַּי תִּבָּנֶה
כד תַּרְחִיק עַוְלָה מֵאָהֳלֶךָ׃ וְשִׁית־עַל־עָפָר בָּצֶר וּבְצוּר נְחָלִים אוֹפִיר׃
כה כו וְהָיָה שַׁדַּי בְּצָרֶיךָ וְכֶסֶף תּוֹעָפוֹת לָךְ׃ כִּי־אָז עַל־שַׁדַּי תִּתְעַנָּג וְתִשָּׂא
כז כח אֶל־אֱלוֹהַּ פָּנֶיךָ׃ תַּעְתִּיר אֵלָיו וְיִשְׁמָעֶךָּ וּנְדָרֶיךָ תְשַׁלֵּם׃ וְתִגְזַר־אֹמֶר
כט וְיָקָם לָךְ וְעַל־דְּרָכֶיךָ נָגַהּ אוֹר׃ כִּי־הִשְׁפִּילוּ וַתֹּאמֶר גֵּוָה וְשַׁח עֵינַיִם
ל כג א יוֹשִׁעַ׃ יְמַלֵּט אִי־נָקִי וְנִמְלַט בְּבֹר כַּפֶּיךָ׃ וַיַּעַן אִיּוֹב ה
ב ג וַיֹּאמַר׃ גַּם־הַיּוֹם מְרִי שִׂחִי יָדִי כָּבְדָה עַל־אַנְחָתִי׃ מִי־יִתֵּן יָדַעְתִּי
ד וְאֶמְצָאֵהוּ אָבוֹא עַד־תְּכוּנָתוֹ׃ אֶעֶרְכָה לְפָנָיו מִשְׁפָּט וּפִי אֲמַלֵּא
ה ו תוֹכָחוֹת׃ אֵדְעָה מִלִּים יַעֲנֵנִי וְאָבִינָה מַה־יֹּאמַר לִי׃ הַבְּרָב־כֹּחַ יָרִיב
ז עִמָּדִי לֹא אַךְ־הוּא יָשִׂם בִּי׃ שָׁם יָשָׁר נוֹכָח עִמּוֹ וַאֲפַלְּטָה לָנֶצַח
ח ט מִשֹּׁפְטִי׃ הֵן קֶדֶם אֶהֱלֹךְ וְאֵינֶנּוּ וְאָחוֹר וְלֹא־אָבִין לוֹ׃ שְׂמֹאול בַּעֲשֹׂתוֹ
י וְלֹא־אָחַז יַעְטֹף יָמִין וְלֹא אֶרְאֶה׃ כִּי־יָדַע דֶּרֶךְ עִמָּדִי בְּחָנַנִי כַּזָּהָב
יא יב אֵצֵא׃ בַּאֲשֻׁרוֹ אָחֲזָה רַגְלִי דַּרְכּוֹ שָׁמַרְתִּי וְלֹא־אָט׃ מִצְוַת שְׂפָתָיו
יג וְלֹא אָמִישׁ מֵחֻקִּי צָפַנְתִּי אִמְרֵי־פִיו׃ וְהוּא בְאֶחָד וּמִי יְשִׁיבֶנּוּ וְנַפְשׁוֹ
יד טו אִוְּתָה וַיָּעַשׂ׃ כִּי יַשְׁלִים חֻקִּי וְכָהֵנָּה רַבּוֹת עִמּוֹ׃ עַל־כֵּן מִפָּנָיו אֶבָּהֵל
טז יז אֶתְבּוֹנֵן וְאֶפְחַד מִמֶּנּוּ׃ וְאֵל הֵרַךְ לִבִּי וְשַׁדַּי הִבְהִילָנִי׃ כִּי־לֹא נִצְמַתִּי
כד א מִפְּנֵי־חֹשֶׁךְ וּמִפָּנַי כִּסָּה־אֹפֶל׃ מַדּוּעַ מִשַּׁדַּי לֹא־
ב נִצְפְּנוּ עִתִּים וְיֹדְעוֹ לֹא־חָזוּ יָמָיו׃ גְּבֻלוֹת יַשִּׂיגוּ עֵדֶר גָּזְלוּ וַיִּרְעוּ׃

3 boundary stones,[46] steal flocks, lead them off to graze. They'll drive away an
4 orphan's donkey; they'll pawn a widow's ox as a pledge. They shove the needy
5 off the road, force the wretched of the earth into hiding. They go about their
work like wild donkeys in a wasteland, foraging for meat; the wilderness
6 sustains their young. They harvest from fields not their own and gather from
7 the vineyards of the wicked. They lie down naked, unclothed, with nothing
8 to cover them in the cold. They are soaked from mountain rains, cling to
9 a stone for lack of shelter; the wicked snatch orphans from breasts, pawn
10 the babies of the poor as pledges! They have no clothes, go naked; though
11 famished, they must carry sheaves.[47] As the olives drop they make oil; while
12 thirsty, they must tread grapes. In town, people wail; the throats of the dying
13 cry out, but God pays no heed. They rebel against the light! They do not know
14 His ways; they have not held to His paths. The murderer rises in the evening;
15 he slays the needy and impoverished like a robber in the night. The eye of the
adulterer, too, waits till dusk, thinking, 'No eye will glimpse me.' He hides his
16 face. In the dark, they break into homes. By day, they seal themselves up; they
17 are not fond of light. For them, daybreak is death-dark; they will know the
18 terror of death-dark! May they float across the face of the waters; may their
19 plot of earth be cursed, and may they never find refuge in vineyards.[48] As heat
20 and drought carry away snow-waters, let Sheol take those sinners. May the
womb forget such a man, a delicacy for maggots; may he be forever forgotten
21 and corruption break like wood. May his wife be barren, never to give birth,
22 his widow deprived of anything good. Though he may draw in the mighty by
23 force and stand firm – may he have no trust in life. Still, God keeps them safe;
24 they rely on that, and His eyes watch over their paths. If only He looked up,
they would cease to exist! If He looked down, they would be gone; they would
25 wither like the tops of the stalks. If this isn't the truth, prove me wrong! Who
25 1 can refute what I have said?" Then Bildad the Shuhite spoke up and
2 said: "Dominion and dread are His; He makes peace in His heights. Could
3
4 His armies be counted? On whom does His light not shine? How can mere
5 mortals do right by God? Born of woman, how can they be cleared? If even
6 the moon has no luster and the stars are impure in His eyes, what then of a
26 1 mortal, a worm, a human being, a maggot?" Then Iyov spoke up and
2 said: "What a help you are to the powerless, your feeble arm coming to the
3 rescue! What use is advice devoid of wisdom, clever insights freely bestowed?
4 Who put these words in your mouth? Whose breath just came out of you?
5
6 The shades tremble under the waters and their denizens! Sheol lies naked
7 before Him; Avaddon's abyss is unveiled.[49] It is He who hangs the earth over
8 nothingness, who stretches Tzafon[50] across the chaos, who bundles water into
9 clouds, yet no billow bursts its seams; He who covers the face of the full

46 | That is, steal land.
47 | They must work for others while starving themselves.
48 | For vineyards as a hiding place, see Judges 21:20–21.
49 | Sheol and Abaddon are names for the netherworld.
50 | A mountain near the north Syrian coast.

ג ד חמור יתומים ינהגו יחבלו שור אלמנה: יטו אבינים מדרך יחד
ה חבאו ענוי־ארץ: הן פראים ׀ במדבר יצאו בפעלם משחרי לטרף עניי־
ו ערבה לו לחם לנערים: בשדה בלילו יקצירו וכרם רשע ילקשו: יקצורו
ז ח ערום ילינו מבלי לבוש ואין כסות בקרה: מזרם הרים ירטבו ומבלי
ט י מחסה חבקו־צור: יגזלו משד יתום ועל־עני יחבלו: ערום הלכו
יא בלי לבוש ורעבים נשאו עמר: בין־שורתם יצהירו יקבים דרכו
יב ויצמאו: מעיר מתים ׀ ינאקו ונפש־חללים תשוע ואלוה לא־ישים
יג תפלה: המה ׀ היו במרדי אור לא־הכירו דרכיו ולא ישבו בנתיבתיו:
יד טו לאור יקום רוצח יקטל־עני ואביון ובלילה יהי כגנב: ועין נאף ׀
טז שמרה נשף לאמר לא־תשורני עין וסתר פנים ישים: חתר בחשך
יז בתים יומם חתמו־למו לא־ידעו אור: כי יחדו ׀ בקר למו צלמות
יח כי־יכיר בלהות צלמות: קל־הוא ׀ על־פני־מים תקלל חלקתם
יט בארץ לא־יפנה דרך כרמים: ציה גם־חם יגזלו מימי־שלג שאול
כ חטאו: ישכחהו רחם ׀ מתקו רמה עוד לא־יזכר ותשבר כעץ עולה:
כא כב רעה עקרה לא תלד ואלמנה לא ייטיב: ומשך אבירים בכחו
כג יקום ולא־יאמין בחיין: יתן־לו לבטח וישען ועיניהו על־דרכיהם:
כד כה רומו מעט ׀ ואיננו והמכו ככל יקפצון וכראש שבלת ימלו: ואם־
לא אפו מי יכזיבני וישם לאל מלתי:
כה א ויען בלדד
ב ג השחי ויאמר: המשל ופחד עמו עשה שלום במרומיו: היש מספר
ד לגדודיו ועל־מי לא־יקום אורהו: ומה־יצדק אנוש עם־אל ומה־
ה יזכה ילוד אשה: הן עד־ירח ולא יאהיל וכוכבים לא־זכו בעיניו:
ו אף כי־אנוש רמה ובן־אדם תולעה:
כו א ויען איוב
ב ג ויאמר: מה־עזרת ללא־כח הושעת זרוע לא־עז: מה־יעצת ללא
ד חכמה ותשיה לרב הודעת: את־מי הגדת מלין ונשמת־מי יצאה
ה ו ממך: הרפאים יחוללו מתחת מים ושכניהם: ערום שאול נגדו ואין
ז ח כסות לאבדון: נטה צפון על־תהו תלה ארץ על־בלימה: צרר מים
ט בעביו ולא־נבקע ענן תחתם: מאחז פני־כסה פרשז עליו עננו:

10 moon, spreading His cloud over it, He who delineates the waters' surface at
11 the edge between dark and light. The pillars of heaven quake from the shock
12 of His roar. With His might He strikes Yam; by His guile He crushes Rahav.[51]
13 By His breath the heavens are bright; His hand pierces through the fleeing
14 serpent. These are but hints of His ways, mere whispers; who can hear them?
27 1 Who can fathom His mighty thunder?" Iyov took up his theme again
2 and said: "By God, who has stripped me of justice, and Shaddai, who has
3 embittered my spirit, so long as my life is in me and God's breath is in my
4 5 nostrils, my lips will speak no wrong, nor will my tongue utter deceit. Heaven
6 forbid I say you are right! I will stand up for my integrity till the day I die. I
have held fast to my righteousness; I will not let go; my heart has never blas-
7 phemed: 'May my enemy end up like the wicked, my assailant like evildoers.'
8 9 [52] What hope will the brazen man have when he petitions God? Will God
10 hear his cry when calamity strikes? Will he be able to entreat Shaddai, to call
11 out to God at any time? I will teach you what is in God's hand and will not
12 hide what belongs to Shaddai: you all have seen it, so why do you prattle on:
13 'This is the God-given portion of the wicked, the tyrant's heritage, straight
14 from Shaddai. Say he has many sons: they are marked for the sword; his
15 descendants will never have enough bread; those who survive will be buried
16 by a plague; their widows will not mourn. If he accumulates silver like dust
17 and amasses clothing like clay, the righteous will wear what he's kept, and his
18 silver will go to the pure. His house is like a moth's, or like the booth a watch-
19 man makes. He may lie down a wealthy man, but not for long: when he wakes,
20 that man will be gone. Horror overtakes him like a torrent; a storm makes off
21 with him by night. The east wind carries him off and away; it hurls him from
22 his place. Unrelentingly He shoots at him; he flees, how he flees from His
23 28 1 hand! Hands clap all about him; he hears hissing from afar.' Now, silver has
2 its source, and gold – a place where it is refined. Iron is pulled from the earth,
3 and copper drawn from stone. He[53] cordons off the darkness, probes the
4 farthest reaches – rock, gloom, death-dark. He forges streams in far-off places
5 forgotten by wayfarers, where few have stepped foot, where the earth teems
6 with sustenance though it convulses like fire from below, where stones are
7 sapphire and gold dust abounds. No vulture knows the way there; the buz-
8 zard's eye has not glimpsed it. Not a single beast has reached it, nor has the
9 lion passed through. He reaches down into flint, upturning mountains at
10 their roots. He carves channels through rocks; His eye sees every precious
11 thing; He binds up the rivers' flow and brings that which they hide to
12 light. But where will wisdom be found, and where is the place
13 of understanding? Mortals cannot surmise where it lies; it will not be found
14 in the land of the living. The deep says: It is not in me! The sea says: Nor is it
15 16 with me! It cannot be bartered for gold, nor can it be weighed in silver; it
can't be exchanged for the gold of Ofir, precious rock crystal, or sapphire.

---

51 | See notes on 9:8, 13.

52 | Iyov has never cursed his enemies, even in his thoughts.

53 | God.

י יא חֹק־חָג עַל־פְּנֵי־מָיִם עַד־תַּכְלִית אוֹר עִם־חֹשֶׁךְ: עַמּוּדֵי שָׁמַיִם יְרוֹפָפוּ
יב יג וְיִתְמְהוּ מִגַּעֲרָתוֹ: בְּכֹחוֹ רָגַע הַיָּם ובתובנתו מָחַץ רָהַב: בְּרוּחוֹ שָׁמַיִם וּבִתְבוּנָתוֹ
יד שִׁפְרָה חֹלְלָה יָדוֹ נָחָשׁ בָּרִחַ: הֶן־אֵלֶּה ׀ קְצוֹת דְּרָכָו וּמַה־שֵּׁמֶץ דָּבָר
כז א נִשְׁמַע־בּוֹ וְרַעַם גְּבוּרֹתָו מִי יִתְבּוֹנָן: וַיֹּסֶף אִיּוֹב
ב ג שְׂאֵת מְשָׁלוֹ וַיֹּאמַר: חַי־אֵל הֵסִיר מִשְׁפָּטִי וְשַׁדַּי הֵמַר נַפְשִׁי: כִּי־כָל־
ד עוֹד נִשְׁמָתִי בִי וְרוּחַ אֱלוֹהַּ בְּאַפִּי: אִם־תְּדַבֵּרְנָה שְׂפָתַי עַוְלָה וּלְשׁוֹנִי
ה אִם־יֶהְגֶּה רְמִיָּה: חָלִילָה לִּי אִם־אַצְדִּיק אֶתְכֶם עַד־אֶגְוָע לֹא־אָסִיר
ו תֻּמָּתִי מִמֶּנִּי: בְּצִדְקָתִי הֶחֱזַקְתִּי וְלֹא אַרְפֶּהָ לֹא־יֶחֱרַף לְבָבִי מִיָּמָי:
ז ח יְהִי כְרָשָׁע אֹיְבִי וּמִתְקוֹמְמִי כְעַוָּל: כִּי מַה־תִּקְוַת חָנֵף כִּי יִבְצָע כִּי
ט י יֵשֶׁל אֱלוֹהַּ נַפְשׁוֹ: הֲצַעֲקָתוֹ יִשְׁמַע ׀ אֵל כִּי־תָבוֹא עָלָיו צָרָה: אִם־
יא עַל־שַׁדַּי יִתְעַנָּג יִקְרָא אֱלוֹהַּ בְּכָל־עֵת: אוֹרֶה אֶתְכֶם בְּיַד־אֵל אֲשֶׁר
יב עִם־שַׁדַּי לֹא אֲכַחֵד: הֵן־אַתֶּם כֻּלְּכֶם חֲזִיתֶם וְלָמָּה־זֶּה הֶבֶל תֶּהְבָּלוּ:
יג יד זֶה ׀ חֵלֶק־אָדָם רָשָׁע ׀ עִם־אֵל וְנַחֲלַת עָרִיצִים מִשַּׁדַּי יִקָּחוּ: אִם־יִרְבּוּ
טו בָנָיו לְמוֹ־חָרֶב וְצֶאֱצָאָיו לֹא יִשְׂבְּעוּ־לָחֶם: שְׂרִידָיו בַּמָּוֶת יִקָּבֵרוּ
טז וְאַלְמְנֹתָיו לֹא תִבְכֶּינָה: אִם־יִצְבֹּר כֶּעָפָר כָּסֶף וְכַחֹמֶר יָכִין מַלְבּוּשׁ:
יז יח יָכִין וְצַדִּיק יִלְבָּשׁ וְכֶסֶף נָקִי יַחֲלֹק: בָּנָה כָעָשׁ בֵּיתוֹ וּכְסֻכָּה עָשָׂה נֹצֵר:
יט כ עָשִׁיר יִשְׁכַּב וְלֹא יֵאָסֵף עֵינָיו פָּקַח וְאֵינֶנּוּ: תַּשִּׂיגֵהוּ כַמַּיִם בַּלָּהוֹת
כא כב לַיְלָה גְּנָבַתּוּ סוּפָה: יִשָּׂאֵהוּ קָדִים וְיֵלַךְ וִישָׂעֲרֵהוּ מִמְּקֹמוֹ: וְיַשְׁלֵךְ
כג עָלָיו וְלֹא יַחְמֹל מִיָּדוֹ בָּרוֹחַ יִבְרָח: יִשְׂפֹּק עָלֵימוֹ כַפֵּימוֹ וְיִשְׁרֹק עָלָיו
כח א ב מִמְּקֹמוֹ: כִּי יֵשׁ לַכֶּסֶף מוֹצָא וּמָקוֹם לַזָּהָב יָזֹקּוּ: בַּרְזֶל מֵעָפָר יֻקָּח
ג וְאֶבֶן יָצוּק נְחוּשָׁה: קֵץ ׀ שָׂם לַחֹשֶׁךְ וּלְכָל־תַּכְלִית הוּא חוֹקֵר אֶבֶן
ד אֹפֶל וְצַלְמָוֶת: פָּרַץ נַחַל ׀ מֵעִם־גָּר הַנִּשְׁכָּחִים מִנִּי־רָגֶל דַּלּוּ מֵאֱנוֹשׁ
ה ו נָעוּ: אֶרֶץ מִמֶּנָּה יֵצֵא־לָחֶם וְתַחְתֶּיהָ נֶהְפַּךְ כְּמוֹ־אֵשׁ: מְקוֹם־סַפִּיר
ז אֲבָנֶיהָ וְעַפְרֹת זָהָב לוֹ: נָתִיב לֹא־יְדָעוֹ עָיִט וְלֹא שְׁזָפַתּוּ עֵין אַיָּה:
ח ט לֹא־הִדְרִיכֻהוּ בְנֵי־שָׁחַץ לֹא־עָדָה עָלָיו שָׁחַל: בַּחַלָּמִישׁ שָׁלַח יָדוֹ
י יא הָפַךְ מִשֹּׁרֶשׁ הָרִים: בַּצּוּרוֹת יְאֹרִים בִּקֵּעַ וְכָל־יְקָר רָאֲתָה עֵינוֹ: מִבְּכִי
יב נְהָרוֹת חִבֵּשׁ וְתַעֲלֻמָהּ יֹצִא אוֹר: וְהַחָכְמָה מֵאַיִן תִּמָּצֵא
יג וְאֵי זֶה מְקוֹם בִּינָה: לֹא־יָדַע אֱנוֹשׁ עֶרְכָּהּ וְלֹא תִמָּצֵא בְּאֶרֶץ הַחַיִּים:
יד טו תְּהוֹם אָמַר לֹא בִי־הִיא וְיָם אָמַר אֵין עִמָּדִי: לֹא־יֻתַּן סְגוֹר תַּחְתֶּיהָ
טז וְלֹא יִשָּׁקֵל כֶּסֶף מְחִירָהּ: לֹא־תְסֻלֶּה בְּכֶתֶם אוֹפִיר בְּשֹׁהַם יָקָר וְסַפִּיר:

17 It will not be measured in gold and glass nor traded for fine golden vessels.
18 It cannot be mentioned with coral or crystal; wisdom's worth is beyond
19 pearls. It will not be measured in Kush's topaz nor weighed against the purest
20 gold. But from where will wisdom come, and where is the place of
21 understanding? For it is concealed from the eyes of every living being and
22 hidden from the birds of the sky. Abaddon[54] and Death say, 'Our ears have
23 24 heard rumor of it!' God knows the way to it, knows where it lies, for He looks
25 to the ends of the earth; He sees beneath all the skies. When He gave the
26 winds their weight and the water its measure, when He meted out the rain
27 and set a path for the thundercloud, He saw and appraised it, measured and
28 examined it. He said to man, 'Now see that fear of the Lord is wisdom, and
29 1 turning from evil is understanding.'" Iyov took up his theme again
2 and said: "If only I were as in months gone by, the days God watched over
3 me, when He shone His lamp over my head, when I walked by its light
4 through darkness, when I was young, in my prime, and my tent knew God's
5 protection, when Shaddai was still with me, when my servants surrounded
6 me, when He bathed my feet in cream and the Rock poured streams of oil
7 over me, when I would go out to the city gates and take my seat in the square.
8 9 On seeing me, young men would step back; elders got up to stand. Princes
10 held back from speaking and placed their hands on their mouths. Nobles'
11 voices turned to a hush, tongues cleaving to palates. When an ear heard and
12 extolled me – the eye that saw bore witness – when I rescued the poor who
13 cried out and the helpless orphan, when I received a beggar's blessing and
14 brought joy to the widow's heart, when I wore righteousness and it clothed
15 me – justice was my robe and diadem – when I was the blind man's eyes, the
16 lame man's legs, when I was father to the destitute and took up a stranger's
17 cause, I shattered the fangs of the wicked and plucked the prey from his teeth!
18 I said to myself, I will die surrounded by family and my days will be numerous
19 as the sand; my roots will be open to the waters, and dew will lie along my
20 21 branches. My wealth will be restored and the bow refreshed in my hand. They
22 listened to me eagerly, kept silent at my counsel. After I spoke, they said
23 nothing; my words poured down on them. How they waited for my rainfall,
24 mouths open wide to receive it! They would look my way when I smiled; they
25 never failed me when I showed them favor. I set them on their path and took
charge, dwelt among them like a king over his troops, like one who comforts
30 1 mourners. But now they mock me, men half my age whose fathers I wouldn't
2 deign to place with the dogs tending my flock! Of what use were their robust
3 hands? Thanks to them, the harvest was lost. Wasted by want and famine,
4 they flee to the wilderness – to gloom, ruin, and desolation; left to pick from
5 mallow bushes,[55] broom roots are their bread. Banished from society, howled
6 at like thieves, settling in the gullies of riverbeds, in crannies of earth and rock,
7 8 braying in bushes, huddling under nettles, rogues, nameless, they are cut off
9 10 from the land. Now I'm the butt of their taunt-songs, a ridiculous jingle – they

54 | See note on 26:6.

55 | Whose flowers are inedible.

יז יח לֹא־יַעַרְכֶנָּה זָהָב וּזְכוֹכִית וּתְמוּרָתָהּ כְּלִי־פָז׃ רָאמוֹת וְגָבִישׁ לֹא יִזָּכֵר
יט וּמֶשֶׁךְ חָכְמָה מִפְּנִינִים׃ לֹא־יַעַרְכֶנָּה פִּטְדַת־כּוּשׁ בְּכֶתֶם טָהוֹר לֹא
כ כא תְסֻלֶּה׃ וְהַחָכְמָה מֵאַיִן תָּבוֹא וְאֵי זֶה מְקוֹם בִּינָה׃ וְנֶעֶלְמָה
כב מֵעֵינֵי כָל־חָי וּמֵעוֹף הַשָּׁמַיִם נִסְתָּרָה׃ אֲבַדּוֹן וָמָוֶת אָמְרוּ בְּאָזְנֵינוּ
כג כד שָׁמַעְנוּ שִׁמְעָהּ׃ אֱלֹהִים הֵבִין דַּרְכָּהּ וְהוּא יָדַע אֶת־מְקוֹמָהּ׃ כִּי־הוּא
כה לִקְצוֹת־הָאָרֶץ יַבִּיט תַּחַת כָּל־הַשָּׁמַיִם יִרְאֶה׃ לַעֲשׂוֹת לָרוּחַ מִשְׁקָל
כו כז וּמַיִם תִּכֵּן בְּמִדָּה׃ בַּעֲשֹׂתוֹ לַמָּטָר חֹק וְדֶרֶךְ לַחֲזִיז קֹלוֹת׃ אָז רָאָהּ
כח וַיְסַפְּרָהּ הֱכִינָהּ וְגַם־חֲקָרָהּ׃ וַיֹּאמֶר ׀ לָאָדָם הֵן יִרְאַת אֲדֹנָי הִיא חָכְמָה
כט א ב וְסוּר מֵרָע בִּינָה׃ וַיֹּסֶף אִיּוֹב שְׂאֵת מְשָׁלוֹ וַיֹּאמַר׃ מִי־יִתְּנֵנִי
ג כְיַרְחֵי־קֶדֶם כִּימֵי אֱלוֹהַּ יִשְׁמְרֵנִי׃ בְּהִלּוֹ נֵרוֹ עֲלֵי רֹאשִׁי לְאוֹרוֹ אֵלֶךְ
ד ה חֹשֶׁךְ׃ כַּאֲשֶׁר הָיִיתִי בִּימֵי חָרְפִּי בְּסוֹד אֱלוֹהַּ עֲלֵי אָהֳלִי׃ בְּעוֹד שַׁדַּי
ו עִמָּדִי סְבִיבוֹתַי נְעָרָי׃ בִּרְחֹץ הֲלִיכַי בְּחֵמָה וְצוּר יָצוּק עִמָּדִי פַּלְגֵי־
ז ח שָׁמֶן׃ בְּצֵאתִי שַׁעַר עֲלֵי־קָרֶת בָּרְחוֹב אָכִין מוֹשָׁבִי׃ רָאוּנִי נְעָרִים
ט וְנֶחְבָּאוּ וִישִׁישִׁים קָמוּ עָמָדוּ׃ שָׂרִים עָצְרוּ בְמִלִּים וְכַף יָשִׂימוּ לְפִיהֶם׃
י יא קוֹל־נְגִידִים נֶחְבָּאוּ וּלְשׁוֹנָם לְחִכָּם דָּבֵקָה׃ כִּי אֹזֶן שָׁמְעָה וַתְּאַשְּׁרֵנִי
יב יג וְעַיִן רָאֲתָה וַתְּעִידֵנִי׃ כִּי־אֲמַלֵּט עָנִי מְשַׁוֵּעַ וְיָתוֹם וְלֹא־עֹזֵר לוֹ׃ בִּרְכַּת
יד אֹבֵד עָלַי תָּבֹא וְלֵב אַלְמָנָה אַרְנִן׃ צֶדֶק לָבַשְׁתִּי וַיִּלְבָּשֵׁנִי כִמְעִיל ו
טו טז וְצָנִיף מִשְׁפָּטִי׃ עֵינַיִם הָיִיתִי לַעִוֵּר וְרַגְלַיִם לַפִּסֵּחַ אָנִי׃ אָב אָנֹכִי
יז לָאֶבְיוֹנִים וְרִב לֹא־יָדַעְתִּי אֶחְקְרֵהוּ׃ וָאֲשַׁבְּרָה מְתַלְּעוֹת עַוָּל וּמִשִּׁנָּיו
יח יט אַשְׁלִיךְ טָרֶף׃ וָאֹמַר עִם־קִנִּי אֶגְוָע וְכַחוֹל אַרְבֶּה יָמִים׃ שָׁרְשִׁי פָתוּחַ
כ אֱלֵי־מָיִם וְטַל יָלִין בִּקְצִירִי׃ כְּבוֹדִי חָדָשׁ עִמָּדִי וְקַשְׁתִּי בְּיָדִי תַחֲלִיף׃
כא כב לִי־שָׁמְעוּ וְיִחֵלּוּ וְיִדְּמוּ לְמוֹ עֲצָתִי׃ אַחֲרֵי דְבָרִי לֹא יִשְׁנוּ וְעָלֵימוֹ
כג כד תִּטֹּף מִלָּתִי׃ וְיִחֲלוּ כַמָּטָר לִי וּפִיהֶם פָּעֲרוּ לְמַלְקוֹשׁ׃ אֶשְׂחַק אֲלֵהֶם
כה לֹא יַאֲמִינוּ וְאוֹר פָּנַי לֹא יַפִּילוּן׃ אֶבְחַר דַּרְכָּם וְאֵשֵׁב רֹאשׁ וְאֶשְׁכּוֹן
ל א כְּמֶלֶךְ בַּגְּדוּד כַּאֲשֶׁר אֲבֵלִים יְנַחֵם׃ וְעַתָּה ׀ שָׂחֲקוּ עָלַי צְעִירִים מִמֶּנִּי
ב לְיָמִים אֲשֶׁר־מָאַסְתִּי אֲבוֹתָם לָשִׁית עִם־כַּלְבֵי צֹאנִי׃ גַּם־כֹּחַ יְדֵיהֶם
ג לָמָּה לִּי עָלֵימוֹ אָבַד כָּלַח׃ בְּחֶסֶר וּבְכָפָן גַּלְמוּד הַעֹרְקִים צִיָּה אֶמֶשׁ
ד שׁוֹאָה וּמְשֹׁאָה׃ הַקֹּטְפִים מַלּוּחַ עֲלֵי־שִׂיחַ וְשֹׁרֶשׁ רְתָמִים לַחְמָם׃
ה ו מִן־גֵּו יְגֹרָשׁוּ יָרִיעוּ עָלֵימוֹ כַּגַּנָּב׃ בַּעֲרוּץ נְחָלִים לִשְׁכֹּן חֹרֵי עָפָר וְכֵפִים׃
ז ח בֵּין־שִׂיחִים יִנְהָקוּ תַּחַת חָרוּל יְסֻפָּחוּ׃ בְּנֵי־נָבָל גַּם־בְּנֵי בְלִי־שֵׁם נִכְּאוּ
ט י מִן־הָאָרֶץ׃ וְעַתָּה נְגִינָתָם הָיִיתִי וָאֱהִי לָהֶם לְמִלָּה׃ תִּעֲבוּנִי רָחֲקוּ

11 abhor me, avoid me, and do not hesitate to spit in my face. Because He has
undone those belts and afflicted me, they have loosened the bit from my face.
12 To my right the young mob rises, sending me reeling, building their siege
13 ramp against me. They break up my path, increase my calamity; no one holds
14 them back. In a torrent they burst through, coursing across the barren land.
15 Terrors turned loose on me chase off my nobility like the wind; my dignity
16 vanishes like a cloud. Now my spirit is emptied out; days of affliction have
17 18 taken hold. Night gnaws at my limbs; my sinews know no rest. Changing my
19 clothes takes all my strength; they bind me, tight as a collar! I am thrown into
20 the mire; I have become dust and ashes. I call out to You, but You do not
21 answer. I wait – but You reflect. You have turned cruel to me; with all Your
22 might You block my way. You sweep me up, cast me to the wind, and cun-
23 ningly diffuse me. I know You will send me off to death, the meeting house
24 of all the living. If a poor man reached out his hand to me, if in his misfortune
25 he entreated me… I swear I wept for the downtrodden! I despaired over the
26 needy! I hoped for good, but evil came; I longed for light, but darkness
27 arrived. My bowels seethe, refuse to be still. Days of suffering come to meet
28 29 me. I walk, blackened, bereft of sun; I rise up in the crowd and cry out; I have
30 been a brother to jackals, a companion to ostriches;[56] my skin is blackened,
31 singed off, my bones charred by the searing heat. My lyre is given over to
31 1 mourning and my pipe to the sounds of weeping.[57] I had forged a covenant
2 with my eyes never to gaze upon a young woman,[58] yet what was my God-
3 given portion from above, my inheritance from Shaddai on high? Isn't calam-
4 ity reserved for the wicked, disaster for those who do evil? Isn't it true He
5 watches my ways and counts my every step? I swear I never walked with
6 falsehood; my feet have never rushed to deceive. Let Him weigh me on honest
7 scales; God will know I am innocent, and if my feet have strayed off course,
if my heart has chased after my eyes, if any blemish has clung to my hands,
8 9 then may I sow while another eats and my crops be uprooted! If my heart has
been seduced by another woman, if I ever lurked around my neighbor's door,
10 then may my wife grind at the millstone for someone else, and may others
11 12 bend over her![59] For this is an abomination, a heinous crime, a fire blazing all
13 the way to Abaddon, ravaging all my grain! Have I ever scorned my servants,
14 man or woman, in their disputes with me? What then will I do when God
15 judges me? When He calls me to account, what will I say? Didn't He who
formed me in the womb form them as well? Were we not fashioned in the
16 selfsame womb? If I have withheld from the poor their desires, let a widow's
17 18 eyes pine away, eaten my bread alone and let no orphan partake of it – from
the time I was young, I raised him as if I were his father; from my mother's
19 womb I counseled her![60] – if ever I glimpsed a wretched man unclothed or a

56 | These animals lived in the wasteland and were considered despicable.
57 | Such instruments were normally used on joyful occasions.
58 | God punished Iyov despite his chastity.
59 | Meaning, have sexual relations with her.
60 | The word "him" refers to the orphan and "her" to the widow.

יא מֶנִּי וּמִפָּנַי לֹא־חָשְׂכוּ רֹק: כִּי־יתרו פִתַּח וַיְעַנֵּנִי וְרֶסֶן מִפָּנַי שִׁלֵּחוּ: יִתְרִי
יב יג עַל־יָמִין פִּרְחַח יָקוּמוּ רַגְלַי שִׁלֵּחוּ וַיָּסֹלּוּ עָלַי אָרְחוֹת אֵידָם: נָתְסוּ
יד נְתִיבָתִי לְהַיָּתִי יֹעִילוּ לֹא עֹזֵר לָמוֹ: כְּפֶרֶץ רָחָב יֶאֱתָיוּ תַּחַת שֹׁאָה לְהַוָּתִי
טו הִתְגַּלְגָּלוּ: הָהְפַּךְ עָלַי בַּלָּהוֹת תִּרְדֹּף כָּרוּחַ נְדִבָתִי וּכְעָב עָבְרָה
טז יז יְשֻׁעָתִי: וְעַתָּה עָלַי תִּשְׁתַּפֵּךְ נַפְשִׁי יֹאחֲזוּנִי יְמֵי־עֹנִי: לַיְלָה עֲצָמַי נִקַּר
יח מֵעָלָי וְעֹרְקַי לֹא יִשְׁכָּבוּן: בְּרָב־כֹּחַ יִתְחַפֵּשׂ לְבוּשִׁי כְּפִי כֻתָּנְתִּי יַאַזְרֵנִי:
יט כ הֹרָנִי לַחֹמֶר וָאֶתְמַשֵּׁל כֶּעָפָר וָאֵפֶר: אֲשַׁוַּע אֵלֶיךָ וְלֹא תַעֲנֵנִי עָמַדְתִּי
כא כב וַתִּתְבֹּנֶן בִּי: תֵּהָפֵךְ לְאַכְזָר לִי בְּעֹצֶם יָדְךָ תִשְׂטְמֵנִי: תִּשָּׂאֵנִי אֶל־רוּחַ
כג תַּרְכִּיבֵנִי וּתְמֹגְגֵנִי תשוה: כִּי־יָדַעְתִּי מָוֶת תְּשִׁיבֵנִי וּבֵית מוֹעֵד לְכָל־ תֻּשִׁיָּה
כד כה חָי: אַךְ לֹא־בְעִי יִשְׁלַח־יָד אִם־בְּפִידוֹ לָהֶן שׁוּעַ: אִם־לֹא בָכִיתִי
כו לִקְשֵׁה־יוֹם עָגְמָה נַפְשִׁי לָאֶבְיוֹן: כִּי טוֹב קִוִּיתִי וַיָּבֹא רָע וַאֲיַחֲלָה
כז כח לְאוֹר וַיָּבֹא אֹפֶל: מֵעַי רֻתְּחוּ וְלֹא־דָמּוּ קִדְּמֻנִי יְמֵי־עֹנִי: קֹדֵר הִלַּכְתִּי
כט בְּלֹא חַמָּה קַמְתִּי בַקָּהָל אֲשַׁוֵּעַ: אָח הָיִיתִי לְתַנִּים וְרֵעַ לִבְנוֹת יַעֲנָה:
ל לא עוֹרִי שָׁחַר מֵעָלָי וְעַצְמִי־חָרָה מִנִּי־חֹרֶב: וַיְהִי לְאֵבֶל כִּנֹּרִי וְעֻגָבִי
לא א ב לְקוֹל בֹּכִים: בְּרִית כָּרַתִּי לְעֵינָי וּמָה אֶתְבּוֹנֵן עַל־בְּתוּלָה: וּמֶה ׀ חֵלֶק
ג אֱלוֹהַּ מִמָּעַל וְנַחֲלַת שַׁדַּי מִמְּרֹמִים: הֲלֹא־אֵיד לְעַוָּל וְנֵכֶר לְפֹעֲלֵי
ד ה אָוֶן: הֲלֹא־הוּא יִרְאֶה דְרָכָי וְכָל־צְעָדַי יִסְפּוֹר: אִם־הָלַכְתִּי עִם־שָׁוְא
ו וַתַּחַשׁ עַל־מִרְמָה רַגְלִי: יִשְׁקְלֵנִי בְמֹאזְנֵי־צֶדֶק וְיֵדַע אֱלוֹהַּ תֻּמָּתִי:
ז אִם־תִּטֶּה אַשֻּׁרִי מִנִּי הַדָּרֶךְ וְאַחַר עֵינַי הָלַךְ לִבִּי וּבְכַפַּי דָּבַק מאוּם:
ח ט אֶזְרְעָה וְאַחֵר יֹאכֵל וְצֶאֱצָאַי יְשֹׁרָשׁוּ: אִם־נִפְתָּה לִבִּי עַל־אִשָּׁה וְעַל־
י יא פֶּתַח רֵעִי אָרָבְתִּי: תִּטְחַן לְאַחֵר אִשְׁתִּי וְעָלֶיהָ יִכְרְעוּן אֲחֵרִין: כִּי־הוא הִיא
יב זִמָּה והיא עָוֺן פְּלִילִים: כִּי אֵשׁ הִיא עַד־אֲבַדּוֹן תֹּאכֵל וּבְכָל־תְּבוּאָתִי וְהוּא
יג יד תְשָׁרֵשׁ: אִם־אֶמְאַס מִשְׁפַּט עַבְדִּי וַאֲמָתִי בְּרִבָם עִמָּדִי: וּמָה אֶעֱשֶׂה
טו כִּי־יָקוּם אֵל וְכִי־יִפְקֹד מָה אֲשִׁיבֶנּוּ: הֲלֹא־בַבֶּטֶן עֹשֵׂנִי עָשָׂהוּ וַיְכֻנֶנּוּ
טז יז בָּרֶחֶם אֶחָד: אִם־אֶמְנַע מֵחֵפֶץ דַּלִּים וְעֵינֵי אַלְמָנָה אֲכַלֶּה: וְאֹכַל
יח פִּתִּי לְבַדִּי וְלֹא־אָכַל יָתוֹם מִמֶּנָּה: כִּי מִנְּעוּרַי גְּדֵלַנִי כְאָב וּמִבֶּטֶן
יט אִמִּי אַנְחֶנָּה: אִם־אֶרְאֶה אוֹבֵד מִבְּלִי לְבוּשׁ וְאֵין כְּסוּת לָאֶבְיוֹן:

20 beggar lying uncovered, if his loins did not bless me as he warmed himself
21 with my sheep's fleece, if I ever lifted my hand against an orphan when I saw
22 my allies at the gate, then may my shoulder fall out of its socket and my elbow
23 break off at its joint, for I am haunted by God's terror. I cannot bear His maj-
24 25 esty! If I have placed my faith in gold, if I pronounced, 'In you I trust,' if I
26 rejoiced in my opulence, for my hand has found abundance, if I ever gazed at
27 the shimmering light, the moon, magisterial in its course, if my heart ever
28 strayed in secret, if I kissed my own hand,[61] this too would be criminal, for it
29 would mean I had denied God on high. I swear I never rejoiced in my enemy's
30 downfall, or exulted when evil found him, or let my mouth sin, wishing his
31 death with a curse. I swear no one in my vicinity ever exclaimed, 'Oh, how I'd
32 love to tear him to shreds!'[62] No stranger ever slept outside; I opened my
33 doors to the wayfarer. I swear I never hid my sins like Adam or concealed
34 iniquity in my breast because I feared a teeming mob, felt terrified by slan-
35 derous clans, or stood petrified at my doorstep. If only I had a hearing – take
36 my signature! May Shaddai answer – or let my rival write the indictment! I
37 would wear it on my shoulder, tie it around me like a wreath. I would tell Him
38 of my every step, approach Him as a prince. If the land has ever cried out
39 against me or its furrows joined together to weep, if I have eaten of its fruits
40 without paying or driven its rightful owners to despair, then may nettles
sprout up in place of wheat, stinkweed instead of barley! Iyov's words have
reached their end."

32 1 Then the three men stopped answering Iyov, for he thought himself
2 righteous. But Elihu son of Barakhel the Buzite, of the Ram family,
became incensed.[63] He was angry at Iyov for justifying himself before God.
3 He was also angry at Iyov's three friends for not being able to find an answer
4 and for condemning Iyov. But Elihu waited for Iyov to finish speaking, for the
5 men were older than he. Yet when he saw that the three men had no reply, he
6 grew angry. So Elihu the son of Barakhel the Buzite replied and said:
"Me, I am young; you, you are elders. That is why I have been perturbed,
7 afraid of expressing my argument among you. I said, let the wise speak; let
8 the many-yeared herald wisdom. But wisdom is a spirit within mortals, and
9 it is the breath of Shaddai that teaches them insight.[64] Not many become wise,
10 nor do many elders understand justice. So I say, hear me out; let me, too,
11 express my argument. Yes, I have been waiting for your words, I have listened
12 for your insights; as you examined the remarks, I have studied you. No one
13 has refuted Iyov. None of you can reply to his claims. Perhaps you say, we have
14 found a strategy: It is God who assails him, not a man. But it is not against
me that he contended with words; I will not reply to him by repeating what
15 you have said. They were dismayed and did not respond. Words fled from
16 17 them. I have waited for them to be quiet, not to speak, not to respond. Now,

61 | A gesture of worship (see, e.g., 1 Kings 19:18).

62 | That is, defame him; see 19:22 and note there.

63 | A fourth friend, not mentioned before, enters the conversation.

64 | Every person, not only the wise elders, has the capacity to understand.

כ כא אִם־לֹא בֵרְכוּנִי חֲלָצָו וּמִגֵּז כְּבָשַׂי יִתְחַמָּם׃ אִם־הֲנִיפוֹתִי עַל־יָתוֹם יָדִי
כב כִּי־אֶרְאֶה בַשַּׁעַר עֶזְרָתִי׃ כְּתֵפִי מִשִּׁכְמָה תִפּוֹל וְאֶזְרֹעִי מִקָּנָה תִשָּׁבֵר׃
כג כד כִּי־פַחַד אֵלַי אֵיד אֵל וּמִשְּׂאֵתוֹ לֹא אוּכָל׃ אִם־שַׂמְתִּי זָהָב כִּסְלִי
כה וְלַכֶּתֶם אָמַרְתִּי מִבְטַחִי׃ אִם־אֶשְׂמַח כִּי־רַב חֵילִי וְכִי־כַבִּיר מָצְאָה
כו כז יָדִי׃ אִם־אֶרְאֶה אוֹר כִּי יָהֵל וְיָרֵחַ יָקָר הֹלֵךְ׃ וַיִּפְתְּ בַּסֵּתֶר לִבִּי וַתִּשַּׁק
כח כט יָדִי לְפִי׃ גַּם־הוּא עָוֺן פְּלִילִי כִּי־כִחַשְׁתִּי לָאֵל מִמָּעַל׃ אִם־אֶשְׂמַח
ל בְּפִיד מְשַׂנְאִי וְהִתְעֹרַרְתִּי כִּי־מְצָאוֹ רָע׃ וְלֹא־נָתַתִּי לַחֲטֹא חִכִּי לִשְׁאֹל
לא בְּאָלָה נַפְשׁוֹ׃ אִם־לֹא אָמְרוּ מְתֵי אָהֳלִי מִי־יִתֵּן מִבְּשָׂרוֹ לֹא נִשְׂבָּע׃
לב לג בַּחוּץ לֹא־יָלִין גֵּר דְּלָתַי לָאֹרַח אֶפְתָּח׃ אִם־כִּסִּיתִי כְאָדָם פְּשָׁעָי
לד לִטְמוֹן בְּחֻבִּי עֲוֺנִי׃ כִּי אֶעֱרוֹץ ׀ הָמוֹן רַבָּה וּבוּז־מִשְׁפָּחוֹת יְחִתֵּנִי וָאֶדֹּם
לה לֹא־אֵצֵא פָתַח׃ מִי יִתֶּן־לִי ׀ שֹׁמֵעַ לִי הֶן־תָּוִי שַׁדַּי יַעֲנֵנִי וְסֵפֶר כָּתַב
לו לז אִישׁ רִיבִי׃ אִם־לֹא עַל־שִׁכְמִי אֶשָּׂאֶנּוּ אֶעֶנְדֶנּוּ עֲטָרוֹת לִי׃ מִסְפַּר
לח צְעָדַי אַגִּידֶנּוּ כְּמוֹ־נָגִיד אֲקָרְבֶנּוּ׃ אִם־עָלַי אַדְמָתִי תִזְעָק וְיַחַד תְּלָמֶיהָ
לט מ יִבְכָּיוּן׃ אִם־כֹּחָהּ אָכַלְתִּי בְלִי־כָסֶף וְנֶפֶשׁ בְּעָלֶיהָ הִפָּחְתִּי׃ תַּחַת חִטָּה ׀
יֵצֵא חוֹחַ וְתַחַת־שְׂעֹרָה בָאְשָׁה תַּמּוּ דִּבְרֵי אִיּוֹב׃
לב א וַיִּשְׁבְּתוּ שְׁלֹשֶׁת הָאֲנָשִׁים הָאֵלֶּה מֵעֲנוֹת אֶת־אִיּוֹב כִּי הוּא צַדִּיק
ב בְּעֵינָיו׃ וַיִּחַר אַף ׀ אֱלִיהוּא בֶן־בַּרַכְאֵל הַבּוּזִי מִמִּשְׁפַּחַת
ג רָם בְּאִיּוֹב חָרָה אַפּוֹ עַל־צַדְּקוֹ נַפְשׁוֹ מֵאֱלֹהִים׃ וּבִשְׁלֹשֶׁת רֵעָיו חָרָה
ד אַפּוֹ עַל אֲשֶׁר לֹא־מָצְאוּ מַעֲנֶה וַיַּרְשִׁיעוּ אֶת־אִיּוֹב׃ וֶאֱלִיהוּ חִכָּה
ה אֶת־אִיּוֹב בִּדְבָרִים כִּי זְקֵנִים־הֵמָּה מִמֶּנּוּ לְיָמִים׃ וַיַּרְא אֱלִיהוּא כִּי אֵין
ו מַעֲנֶה בְּפִי שְׁלֹשֶׁת הָאֲנָשִׁים וַיִּחַר אַפּוֹ׃ וַיַּעַן ׀ אֱלִיהוּא
בֶן־בַּרַכְאֵל הַבּוּזִי וַיֹּאמַר צָעִיר אֲנִי לְיָמִים וְאַתֶּם יְשִׁישִׁים עַל־כֵּן
ז זָחַלְתִּי וָאִירָא ׀ מֵחַוֺּת דֵּעִי אֶתְכֶם׃ אָמַרְתִּי יָמִים יְדַבֵּרוּ וְרֹב שָׁנִים
ח ט יֹדִיעוּ חָכְמָה׃ אָכֵן רוּחַ־הִיא בֶאֱנוֹשׁ וְנִשְׁמַת שַׁדַּי תְּבִינֵם׃ לֹא־רַבִּים
י יֶחְכָּמוּ וּזְקֵנִים יָבִינוּ מִשְׁפָּט׃ לָכֵן אָמַרְתִּי שִׁמְעָה־לִּי אֲחַוֶּה דֵעִי אַף־
יא אָנִי׃ הֵן הוֹחַלְתִּי ׀ לְדִבְרֵיכֶם אָזִין עַד־תְּבוּנֹתֵיכֶם עַד־תַּחְקְרוּן מִלִּין׃
יב יג וְעָדֵיכֶם אֶתְבּוֹנָן וְהִנֵּה אֵין לְאִיּוֹב מוֹכִיחַ עוֹנֶה אֲמָרָיו מִכֶּם׃ פֶּן־
יד תֹּאמְרוּ מָצָאנוּ חָכְמָה אֵל יִדְּפֶנּוּ לֹא־אִישׁ׃ וְלֹא־עָרַךְ אֵלַי מִלִּין
טו וּבְאִמְרֵיכֶם לֹא אֲשִׁיבֶנּוּ׃ חַתּוּ לֹא־עָנוּ עוֹד הֶעְתִּיקוּ מֵהֶם מִלִּים׃
טז יז וְהוֹחַלְתִּי כִּי־לֹא יְדַבֵּרוּ כִּי עָמְדוּ לֹא־עָנוּ עוֹד׃ אַעֲנֶה אַף־אֲנִי חֶלְקִי

18 I too will say my part; I too will express my argument, for I am full of words;
19 my stomach clenches with them. It is like unopened wine rupturing new
20 wineskins. So let me speak and find relief; let me open my mouth to reply,
21 22 but may I never turn my face toward any man nor favor any title.[65] May my
33 1 Maker take me from this world if I show favor. And yet, listen to my words
2 now, Iyov; hearken to all I say. Now I have opened my mouth; my tongue
3 speaks from within my palate. My words are the honesty of my heart, and my
4 lips have conveyed my argument in earnest. The spirit of God made me, and
5 Shaddai's breath gave me life, so if you can, reply to me. Set your contentions
6 7 before me. I am like you before God; I too was cut from clay.[66] My dread will
8 not terrorize you, and my hand upon you will not weigh you down, but
9 what you said rings in my ears, and I hear the sound of your words: 'I am
10 pure, without transgression, I am innocent, without iniquity, yet He comes
11 up with pretexts against me; He thinks me an enemy. He has set my feet in
12 lime so that He can follow my every step.'[67] My reply to you: in this you are
13 not right, for God is greater than humanity. Why do you seek a suit against
14 Him, saying, 'He does not reply to all mankind's charges'? For God speaks
15 one way, and two for those who cannot perceive it: in a dream, a night vision,
16 when slumber falls upon men, as they sleep in their beds, He opens their ears
17 to understanding, and issues His directives to turn them away from their
18 misdeeds, to conceal man's arrogance, to save his soul from the grave and his
19 life from the sword. He is chastened with pain, bedridden, his every limb
20 shivering mightily. His palate will be revolted by bread and his throat by
21 22 delectable foods. His flesh will putrefy out of sight, his skeleton laid bare. He
23 will approach the grave, his life the place of the dead. If for him there is a
championing angel, one out of a thousand who can testify to his uprightness
24 and have mercy upon him, saying, 'Save him from descending into the grave;
25 I have found his ransom,' then his flesh will be healthy as it was in his
26 childhood, restored, as in the days of his youth. He will then beseech his God,
God will long for him, and he will see His face and shout with joy. He will
27 return to him what he deserves. He will look upon people, and he will say, 'I
have sinned; I have accused the Upright One of a crime, and it was of no
28 benefit to me. God redeemed me from the grave, and my life takes in the light.'
29 30 Yes, this is how God intervenes two or three times with a man – to bring him
31 back from the grave to be lit with the light of life. Hearken, Iyov. Hear me. Be
32 silent and I will speak. If you have words, respond to me; speak, for I desire
33 your acquittal. But if not, you will listen to me. Be silent, and I will teach you
34 1 2 wisdom." Then Elihu continued and said: "Wise ones, listen to my
3 words; those who understand, lend an ear. Just as the ear discerns words, and
4 the palate the taste of food, let us examine this case so that between us, we
5 will know what is sweet. For Iyov has said, 'I am innocent, but God has
6 stripped me of justice. I am betrayed by those charges; the arrows are fatal

65 | Speak deferentially or show partiality.

66 | See Genesis 2:7.

67 | Cf. 13:27.

יח יט אֲחַוֶּה דֵעִי אַף־אָנִי׃ כִּי מָלֵתִי מִלִּים הֱצִיקַתְנִי רוּחַ בִּטְנִי׃ הִנֵּה בִטְנִי
כ כְּיַיִן לֹא־יִפָּתֵחַ כְּאֹבוֹת חֲדָשִׁים יִבָּקֵעַ׃ אֲדַבְּרָה וְיִרְוַח־לִי אֶפְתַּח שְׂפָתַי
כא כב וְאֶעֱנֶה׃ אַל־נָא אֶשָּׂא פְנֵי־אִישׁ וְאֶל־אָדָם לֹא אֲכַנֶּה׃ כִּי לֹא יָדַעְתִּי
לג א אֲכַנֶּה כִּמְעַט יִשָּׂאֵנִי עֹשֵׂנִי׃ וְאוּלָם שְׁמַע־נָא אִיּוֹב מִלָּי וְכָל־דְּבָרַי
ב ג הַאֲזִינָה׃ הִנֵּה־נָא פָּתַחְתִּי פִי דִּבְּרָה לְשׁוֹנִי בְחִכִּי׃ יֹשֶׁר־לִבִּי אֲמָרָי
ד ה וְדַעַת שְׂפָתַי בָּרוּר מִלֵּלוּ׃ רוּחַ־אֵל עָשָׂתְנִי וְנִשְׁמַת שַׁדַּי תְּחַיֵּנִי׃ אִם־
ו תּוּכַל הֲשִׁיבֵנִי עֶרְכָה לְפָנַי הִתְיַצָּבָה׃ הֵן־אֲנִי כְפִיךָ לָאֵל מֵחֹמֶר קֹרַצְתִּי
ז ח גַם־אָנִי׃ הִנֵּה אֵימָתִי לֹא תְבַעֲתֶךָּ וְאַכְפִּי עָלֶיךָ לֹא־יִכְבָּד׃ אַךְ אָמַרְתָּ
ט י בְאָזְנָי וְקוֹל מִלִּין אֶשְׁמָע׃ זַךְ אֲנִי בְּלִי פָשַׁע חַף אָנֹכִי וְלֹא עָוֺן לִי׃ הֵן
יא תְּנוּאוֹת עָלַי יִמְצָא יַחְשְׁבֵנִי לְאוֹיֵב לוֹ׃ יָשֵׂם בַּסַּד רַגְלָי יִשְׁמֹר כָּל־
יב יג אָרְחֹתָי׃ הֶן־זֹאת לֹא־צָדַקְתָּ אֶעֱנֶךָּ כִּי־יִרְבֶּה אֱלוֹהַּ מֵאֱנוֹשׁ׃ מַדּוּעַ
יד אֵלָיו רִיבוֹתָ כִּי כָל־דְּבָרָיו לֹא־יַעֲנֶה׃ כִּי־בְאַחַת יְדַבֶּר־אֵל וּבִשְׁתַּיִם
טו לֹא יְשׁוּרֶנָּה׃ בַּחֲלוֹם ׀ חֶזְיוֹן לַיְלָה בִּנְפֹל תַּרְדֵּמָה עַל־אֲנָשִׁים בִּתְנוּמוֹת
טז יז עֲלֵי מִשְׁכָּב׃ אָז יִגְלֶה אֹזֶן אֲנָשִׁים וּבְמֹסָרָם יַחְתֹּם׃ לְהָסִיר אָדָם מַעֲשֶׂה
יח יט וְגֵוָה מִגֶּבֶר יְכַסֶּה׃ יַחְשֹׂךְ נַפְשׁוֹ מִנִּי־שָׁחַת וְחַיָּתוֹ מֵעֲבֹר בַּשָּׁלַח׃ וְהוּכַח
כ בְּמַכְאוֹב עַל־מִשְׁכָּבוֹ וריב עֲצָמָיו אֵתָן׃ וְזִהֲמַתּוּ חַיָּתוֹ לָחֶם וְנַפְשׁוֹ וְרוֹב
כא כב מַאֲכַל תַּאֲוָה׃ יִכֶל בְּשָׂרוֹ מֵרֹאִי ושפי עַצְמוֹתָיו לֹא רֻאּוּ׃ וַתִּקְרַב לַשַּׁחַת וְשֻׁפּוּ
כג נַפְשׁוֹ וְחַיָּתוֹ לַמְמִתִים׃ אִם־יֵשׁ עָלָיו ׀ מַלְאָךְ מֵלִיץ אֶחָד מִנִּי־אָלֶף
כד לְהַגִּיד לְאָדָם יָשְׁרוֹ׃ וַיְחֻנֶּנּוּ וַיֹּאמֶר פְּדָעֵהוּ מֵרֶדֶת שָׁחַת מָצָאתִי כֹפֶר׃
כה כו רֻטֲפַשׁ בְּשָׂרוֹ מִנֹּעַר יָשׁוּב לִימֵי עֲלוּמָיו׃ יֶעְתַּר אֶל־אֱלוֹהַּ ׀ וַיִּרְצֵהוּ
כז וַיַּרְא פָּנָיו בִּתְרוּעָה וַיָּשֶׁב לֶאֱנוֹשׁ צִדְקָתוֹ׃ יָשֹׁר ׀ עַל־אֲנָשִׁים וַיֹּאמֶר
כח חָטָאתִי וְיָשָׁר הֶעֱוֵיתִי וְלֹא־שָׁוָה לִי׃ פָּדָה נפשי מֵעֲבֹר בַּשָּׁחַת וחיתי נַפְשׁוֹ | וְחַיָּתוֹ
כט ל בָּאוֹר תִּרְאֶה׃ הֶן־כָּל־אֵלֶּה יִפְעַל־אֵל פַּעֲמַיִם שָׁלוֹשׁ עִם־גָּבֶר׃ לְהָשִׁיב
לא נַפְשׁוֹ מִנִּי־שָׁחַת לֵאוֹר בְּאוֹר הַחַיִּים׃ הַקְשֵׁב אִיּוֹב שְׁמַע־לִי הַחֲרֵשׁ
לב לג וְאָנֹכִי אֲדַבֵּר׃ אִם־יֵשׁ־מִלִּין הֲשִׁיבֵנִי דַּבֵּר כִּי־חָפַצְתִּי צַדְּקֶךָּ׃ אִם־אַיִן ז
לד א אַתָּה שְׁמַע־לִי הַחֲרֵשׁ וַאֲאַלֶּפְךָ חָכְמָה׃ וַיַּעַן אֱלִיהוּא
ב ג וַיֹּאמַר׃ שִׁמְעוּ חֲכָמִים מִלָּי וְיֹדְעִים הַאֲזִינוּ לִי׃ כִּי־אֹזֶן מִלִּין תִּבְחָן
ד ה וְחֵךְ יִטְעַם לֶאֱכֹל׃ מִשְׁפָּט נִבְחֲרָה־לָּנוּ נֵדְעָה בֵינֵינוּ מַה־טּוֹב׃ כִּי־
ו אָמַר אִיּוֹב צָדַקְתִּי וְאֵל הֵסִיר מִשְׁפָּטִי׃ עַל־מִשְׁפָּטִי אֲכַזֵּב אָנוּשׁ חִצִּי

7 though I have not sinned.' Oh, who is a man like Iyov, who drinks mockery
8 like water, whose path is with those who do evil and who consorts with
9 wicked folk? For he has said, 'What use is it to man to do the will of God?'
10 So, men of wisdom, listen to me: far be it from God to do evil, from Shaddai
11 to carry out injustice. He repays a man according to his actions, and according
12 to his conduct He will provide for him. This is the truth: God does no evil,
13 and Shaddai does not distort justice. Who entrusted the earth to Him? Who
14 placed the world in His charge? If He turns his attention to him, He will take
15 back his spirit and soul; then all flesh will perish together, and humanity
16 will return to dust. If you want to understand, hear this; listen to the meaning
17 of my words: Would the hater of justice bind wounds? Will you vilify the
18 Perfectly Righteous? Would He say of the king that he is base; would He call
19 nobles evil, He who does not favor princes nor acknowledge the ruler over
20 the poor, for they are all the works of His hands? They die in a moment; in
the middle of the night they pass away. The people are shaken, because the
21 mighty have been deposed, but not at the hand of man. His eyes are upon the
22 ways of man, and He sees all his steps. There is no darkness, no death-dark,
23 that could hide evildoers. After all, it is not for man to make a case, to come
24 before God in judgment. He destroys the endlessly strong and appoints
25 others in their places. Because He knows their actions, they are crushed when
26 the night is over. He strikes them among evil men, before everyone's eyes,
27 28 because they turned away from Him and did not learn all His ways, bringing
upon Him the screams of the poor, for He hears the howls of the destitute.
29 He makes silence; who can breach it? He hides His face; who can see Him?
30 He sees nation and man as one to hinder the rule of the evil, of those who
31 would snare the nation. For to God, a person should say, 'I will bear it; I will
32 not remove the yoke. What I cannot see, show me, and if I have done evil, I
33 will do it no longer.' Did you think He should repay you as you see fit, despite
your rejection? Did you think it was up to you and not Him? Speak what you
34 35 know. Men of wisdom will tell me, and wise men will hear me. Iyov does not
36 speak with knowledge, and his words are not wise. May Iyov be tested forever,
37 dealt with as evil men are, for he continually increases his sin, his iniquity
35 1 among us is abundant, and he speaks too much against God." Then
2 Elihu continued and said: "Is this what you thought in your suit, saying, 'I am
3 more righteous than God'? For you have asked what benefit you receive:
4 'What use is there in my not sinning?' I will reply to you with words, you and
5 your friends as well. Look up at the sky and observe; peer into the
6 heavens – they are higher than you. If you sin, do you affect Him at all? Even
7 as your iniquities multiply, do you do anything to Him? If you are in the right,
8 what do you give Him; what does He accept from you? Your sin affects men
9 like you, and your goodness, humanity. They scream out of conflict and
10 oppression, cry out under the fists of many persecutors, but do not say,
11 'Where is God, my Maker, the One who gives strength in the night?'[68] But
He has taught us more than the animals of the earth, and He, more than the

68 | The oppressed fail to call upon God for help.

ז ח בְלִי־פָשַׁע: מִי־גֶבֶר כְּאִיּוֹב יִשְׁתֶּה־לַּעַג כַּמָּיִם: וְאָרַח לְחֶבְרָה עִם־פֹּעֲלֵי
ט אָוֶן וְלָלֶכֶת עִם־אַנְשֵׁי־רֶשַׁע: כִּי־אָמַר לֹא יִסְכָּן־גָּבֶר בִּרְצֹתוֹ עִם־
י אֱלֹהִים: לָכֵן ׀ אַנְשֵׁי לֵבָב שִׁמְעוּ לִי חָלִלָה לָאֵל מֵרֶשַׁע וְשַׁדַּי מֵעָוֶל:
יא יב כִּי פֹעַל אָדָם יְשַׁלֶּם־לוֹ וּכְאֹרַח אִישׁ יַמְצִאֶנּוּ: אַף־אָמְנָם אֵל לֹא־
יג יַרְשִׁיעַ וְשַׁדַּי לֹא־יְעַוֵּת מִשְׁפָּט: מִי־פָקַד עָלָיו אָרְצָה וּמִי שָׂם תֵּבֵל
יד טו כֻּלָּהּ: אִם־יָשִׂים אֵלָיו לִבּוֹ רוּחוֹ וְנִשְׁמָתוֹ אֵלָיו יֶאֱסֹף: יִגְוַע כָּל־בָּשָׂר
טז יָחַד וְאָדָם עַל־עָפָר יָשׁוּב: וְאִם־בִּינָה שִׁמְעָה־זֹּאת הַאֲזִינָה לְקוֹל
יז יח מִלָּי: הַאַף שׂוֹנֵא מִשְׁפָּט יַחֲבוֹשׁ וְאִם־צַדִּיק כַּבִּיר תַּרְשִׁיעַ: הַאֲמֹר
יט לְמֶלֶךְ בְּלִיָּעַל רָשָׁע אֶל־נְדִיבִים: אֲשֶׁר לֹא־נָשָׂא ׀ פְּנֵי שָׂרִים וְלֹא
כ נִכַּר־שׁוֹעַ לִפְנֵי־דָל כִּי־מַעֲשֵׂה יָדָיו כֻּלָּם: רֶגַע ׀ יָמֻתוּ וַחֲצוֹת לָיְלָה
כא יְגֹעֲשׁוּ עָם וְיַעֲבֹרוּ וְיָסִירוּ אַבִּיר לֹא בְיָד: כִּי־עֵינָיו עַל־דַּרְכֵי־אִישׁ
כב כג וְכָל־צְעָדָיו יִרְאֶה: אֵין־חֹשֶׁךְ וְאֵין צַלְמָוֶת לְהִסָּתֶר שָׁם פֹּעֲלֵי אָוֶן: כִּי
כד לֹא עַל־אִישׁ יָשִׂים עוֹד לַהֲלֹךְ אֶל־אֵל בַּמִּשְׁפָּט: יָרֹעַ כַּבִּירִים לֹא־
כה חֵקֶר וַיַּעֲמֵד אֲחֵרִים תַּחְתָּם: לָכֵן יַכִּיר מַעְבָּדֵיהֶם וְהָפַךְ לַיְלָה וְיִדַּכָּאוּ:
כו כז תַּחַת־רְשָׁעִים סְפָקָם בִּמְקוֹם רֹאִים: אֲשֶׁר עַל־כֵּן סָרוּ מֵאַחֲרָיו וְכָל־
כח דְּרָכָיו לֹא הִשְׂכִּילוּ: לְהָבִיא עָלָיו צַעֲקַת־דָּל וְצַעֲקַת עֲנִיִּים יִשְׁמָע:
כט וְהוּא יַשְׁקִט ׀ וּמִי יַרְשִׁעַ וְיַסְתֵּר פָּנִים וּמִי יְשׁוּרֶנּוּ וְעַל־גּוֹי וְעַל־
ל לא אָדָם יָחַד: מִמְּלֹךְ אָדָם חָנֵף מִמֹּקְשֵׁי עָם: כִּי אֶל־אֵל הֶאָמַר נָשָׂאתִי
לב לֹא אֶחְבֹּל: בִּלְעֲדֵי אֶחֱזֶה אַתָּה הֹרֵנִי אִם־עָוֶל פָּעַלְתִּי לֹא אֹסִיף:
לג הֲמֵעִמְּךָ יְשַׁלְּמֶנָּה ׀ כִּי־מָאַסְתָּ כִּי־אַתָּה תִבְחַר וְלֹא־אָנִי וּמַה־יָּדַעְתָּ
לד לה דַבֵּר: אַנְשֵׁי לֵבָב יֹאמְרוּ לִי וְגֶבֶר חָכָם שֹׁמֵעַ לִי: אִיּוֹב לֹא־בְדַעַת
לו יְדַבֵּר וּדְבָרָיו לֹא בְהַשְׂכֵּיל: אָבִי יִבָּחֵן אִיּוֹב עַד־נֶצַח עַל־תְּשֻׁבֹת
לז בְּאַנְשֵׁי־אָוֶן: כִּי יֹסִיף עַל־חַטָּאתוֹ פֶשַׁע בֵּינֵינוּ יִסְפּוֹק וְיִרֶב אֲמָרָיו
לה א ב לָאֵל: וַיַּעַן אֱלִיהוּ וַיֹּאמַר: הֲזֹאת חָשַׁבְתָּ לְמִשְׁפָּט
ג אָמַרְתָּ צִדְקִי מֵאֵל: כִּי־תֹאמַר מַה־יִּסְכָּן־לָךְ מָה־אֹעִיל מֵחַטָּאתִי:
ד ה אֲנִי אֲשִׁיבְךָ מִלִּין וְאֶת־רֵעֶיךָ עִמָּךְ: הַבֵּט שָׁמַיִם וּרְאֵה וְשׁוּר שְׁחָקִים
ו גָּבְהוּ מִמֶּךָּ: אִם־חָטָאתָ מַה־תִּפְעָל־בּוֹ וְרַבּוּ פְשָׁעֶיךָ מַה־תַּעֲשֶׂה־לּוֹ:
ז ח אִם־צָדַקְתָּ מַה־תִּתֶּן־לוֹ אוֹ מַה־מִיָּדְךָ יִקָּח: לְאִישׁ־כָּמוֹךָ רִשְׁעֶךָ
ט י וּלְבֶן־אָדָם צִדְקָתֶךָ: מֵרֹב עֲשׁוּקִים יַזְעִיקוּ יְשַׁוְּעוּ מִזְּרוֹעַ רַבִּים: וְלֹא־
יא אָמַר אַיֵּה אֱלוֹהַּ עֹשָׂי נֹתֵן זְמִרוֹת בַּלָּיְלָה: מַלְּפֵנוּ מִבַּהֲמוֹת אֶרֶץ

12 birds of heaven, has made us wise.[69] When they shout, they will not be
13 answered because of their arrogance. God will not listen to lies, and Shaddai
14 will not see them, and though you say that He will not see it, the case is before
15 Him; wait for Him. Now that there is deceit, He has grown angry and knows
16 no rest. Iyov opens his mouth with false arguments and without knowledge
36 1 2 talks too much." Then Elihu spoke again and said: "Wait for me a
3 bit, and I will teach you, for God still has words: 'I will raise My argument
4 from afar, and I will give justice to My creatures.' In truth, my words are not
5 false; my arguments with you are earnest. Yes, God is mighty – and He does
6 not despise the mighty, strong of heart. He does not let evildoers live but gives
7 the poor their due. He does not take His eyes off the righteous. He places
8 kings on the throne and ensconces them there. He raises them up. But should
9 He bind them in fetters, seize them in torturous ropes, then He will tell them
10 of their actions and their sins, which have multiplied. He reveals rebuke to
11 their ears and says, 'If they return from wrongdoing, if they listen and serve,
12 they will end their days well, their years peacefully. But if they do not listen,
13 the sword will overtake them; they will die for lack of knowledge.' The
evildoers turn up their noses; they do not call out even after He has bound
14 15 them. They die in their youth among the male prostitutes.[70] He will save the
16 poor from their poverty, and through distress opens their ears. He has even
distanced you from agony, from the bottomless chasm. Your table is laden
17 with rich food. Though you are beset by the evildoer's case, law and judgment
18 will support you. Beware: do not let affluence seduce you, nor a high ransom
19 20 sway you. Can you achieve salvation painlessly, without great effort? Hope
21 neither through the night nor for nations to rise from where they are. Take
22 care; do not turn toward evil as you have in times of trouble. Yes, God is
23 exalted in His strength; who is the Master like Him? Who appointed His rule,
24 and who can tell Him, 'You have done wrong'? Remember to declare that His
25 deeds are great, those that are recognized by man. All of mankind has seen
26 them; humanity has gazed on them from afar. Yes, God is unknowably great;
27 His days are innumerable. He rains down drops of water that pour down in
28 a stream; they flow down from the heights, showering a multitude of people.
29 Can anyone understand the spreading of the clouds, the thunder of His foggy
30 31 veil? He spreads His lightning over it, covering the very roots of the sea. With
32 these He judges nations, gives an abundance of food. Lightning covers over
33 the clouds; at His command it meets its mark. Its thunder proclaims Him, as
37 1 an angry blast rising upward. At this my heart quakes and falters in its place.
2 Hear His thunder with trembling, the rumble coming from His mouth.
3 4 Under all of heaven He flashes his lightning to the ends of the earth. After
this He roars with His thunder, rumbles in His loud voice. He does not hold
5 back; He makes His thunder heard. God thunders in His voice wondrously.
6 He does great things, unfathomable to us. He tells the snow, 'Fall upon the
7 earth,' the rain and the storm, His mighty torrential rains. He seals man in so

69 | Cf. 12:7.

70 | The depraved (see Deut. 23:18; 1 Kings 14:24).

יב יג וּמֵעוֹף הַשָּׁמַיִם יְחַכְּמֵנוּ׃ שָׁם יִצְעֲקוּ וְלֹא יַעֲנֶה מִפְּנֵי גְּאוֹן רָעִים׃ אַךְ־
יד שָׁוְא לֹא־יִשְׁמַע ׀ אֵל וְשַׁדַּי לֹא יְשׁוּרֶנָּה׃ אַף כִּי־תֹאמַר לֹא תְשׁוּרֶנּוּ
טו דִּין לְפָנָיו וּתְחוֹלֵל לוֹ׃ וְעַתָּה כִּי־אַיִן פָּקַד אַפּוֹ וְלֹא־יָדַע בַּפַּשׁ מְאֹד׃
טז לו א וְאִיּוֹב הֶבֶל יִפְצֶה־פִּיהוּ בִּבְלִי־דַעַת מִלִּין יַכְבִּר׃ וַיֹּסֶף
ב ג אֱלִיהוּא וַיֹּאמַר׃ כַּתַּר־לִי זְעֵיר וַאֲחַוֶּךָּ כִּי־עוֹד לֶאֱלוֹהַּ מִלִּים׃ אֶשָּׂא
ד דֵעִי לְמֵרָחוֹק וּלְפֹעֲלִי אֶתֵּן־צֶדֶק׃ כִּי־אָמְנָם לֹא־שֶׁקֶר מִלָּי תְּמִים
ה ו דֵּעוֹת עִמָּךְ׃ הֶן־אֵל כַּבִּיר וְלֹא יִמְאָס כַּבִּיר כֹּחַ לֵב׃ לֹא־יְחַיֶּה רָשָׁע
ז וּמִשְׁפַּט עֲנִיִּים יִתֵּן׃ לֹא־יִגְרַע מִצַּדִּיק עֵינָיו וְאֶת־מְלָכִים לַכִּסֵּא וַיֹּשִׁיבֵם
ח ט לָנֶצַח וַיִּגְבָּהוּ׃ וְאִם־אֲסוּרִים בַּזִּקִּים יִלָּכְדוּן בְּחַבְלֵי־עֹנִי׃ וַיַּגֵּד לָהֶם
י פָּעֳלָם וּפִשְׁעֵיהֶם כִּי יִתְגַּבָּרוּ׃ וַיִּגֶל אָזְנָם לַמּוּסָר וַיֹּאמֶר כִּי־יְשֻׁבוּן
יא יב מֵאָוֶן׃ אִם־יִשְׁמְעוּ וְיַעֲבֹדוּ יְכַלּוּ יְמֵיהֶם בַּטּוֹב וּשְׁנֵיהֶם בַּנְּעִימִים׃ וְאִם־
יג לֹא יִשְׁמְעוּ בְּשֶׁלַח יַעֲבֹרוּ וְיִגְוְעוּ בִּבְלִי־דָעַת׃ וְחַנְפֵי־לֵב יָשִׂימוּ אָף
יד טו לֹא יְשַׁוְּעוּ כִּי אֲסָרָם׃ תָּמֹת בַּנֹּעַר נַפְשָׁם וְחַיָּתָם בַּקְּדֵשִׁים׃ יְחַלֵּץ
טז עָנִי בְעָנְיוֹ וְיִגֶל בַּלַּחַץ אָזְנָם׃ וְאַף הֲסִיתְךָ ׀ מִפִּי־צָר רַחַב לֹא־מוּצָק
יז תַּחְתֶּיהָ וְנַחַת שֻׁלְחָנְךָ מָלֵא דָשֶׁן׃ וְדִין־רָשָׁע מָלֵאתָ דִּין וּמִשְׁפָּט
יח יט יִתְמֹכוּ׃ כִּי־חֵמָה פֶּן־יְסִיתְךָ בְשָׂפֶק וְרָב־כֹּפֶר אַל־יַטֶּךָּ׃ הֲיַעֲרֹךְ שׁוּעֲךָ
כ לֹא בְצָר וְכֹל מַאֲמַצֵּי־כֹחַ׃ אַל־תִּשְׁאַף הַלָּיְלָה לַעֲלוֹת עַמִּים תַּחְתָּם׃
כא כב הִשָּׁמֶר אַל־תֵּפֶן אֶל־אָוֶן כִּי עַל־זֶה בָּחַרְתָּ מֵעֹנִי׃ הֶן־אֵל יַשְׂגִּיב בְּכֹחוֹ
כג כד מִי כָמֹהוּ מוֹרֶה׃ מִי־פָקַד עָלָיו דַּרְכּוֹ וּמִי־אָמַר פָּעַלְתָּ עַוְלָה׃ זְכֹר
כה כִּי־תַשְׂגִּיא פָעֳלוֹ אֲשֶׁר שֹׁרְרוּ אֲנָשִׁים׃ כָּל־אָדָם חָזוּ־בוֹ אֱנוֹשׁ יַבִּיט
כו כז מֵרָחוֹק׃ הֶן־אֵל שַׂגִּיא וְלֹא נֵדָע מִסְפַּר שָׁנָיו וְלֹא־חֵקֶר׃ כִּי יְגָרַע נִטְפֵי־
כח כט מָיִם יָזֹקּוּ מָטָר לְאֵדוֹ׃ אֲשֶׁר־יִזְּלוּ שְׁחָקִים יִרְעֲפוּ עֲלֵי ׀ אָדָם רָב׃ אַף
ל אִם־יָבִין מִפְרְשֵׂי־עָב תְּשֻׁאוֹת סֻכָּתוֹ׃ הֵן־פָּרַשׂ עָלָיו אוֹרוֹ וְשָׁרְשֵׁי הַיָּם
לא לב כִּסָּה׃ כִּי־בָם יָדִין עַמִּים יִתֶּן־אֹכֶל לְמַכְבִּיר׃ עַל־כַּפַּיִם כִּסָּה־אוֹר וַיְצַו
לג לז א עָלֶיהָ בְמַפְגִּיעַ׃ יַגִּיד עָלָיו רֵעוֹ מִקְנֶה אַף עַל־עוֹלֶה׃ אַף־לְזֹאת יֶחֱרַד
ב ג לִבִּי וְיִתַּר מִמְּקוֹמוֹ׃ שִׁמְעוּ שָׁמוֹעַ בְּרֹגֶז קֹלוֹ וְהֶגֶה מִפִּיו יֵצֵא׃ תַּחַת־
ד כָּל־הַשָּׁמַיִם יִשְׁרֵהוּ וְאוֹרוֹ עַל־כַּנְפוֹת הָאָרֶץ׃ אַחֲרָיו ׀ יִשְׁאַג־קוֹל
ה יַרְעֵם בְּקוֹל גְּאוֹנוֹ וְלֹא יְעַקְּבֵם כִּי־יִשָּׁמַע קוֹלוֹ׃ יַרְעֵם אֵל בְּקוֹלוֹ
ו נִפְלָאוֹת עֹשֶׂה גְדֹלוֹת וְלֹא נֵדָע׃ כִּי לַשֶּׁלֶג ׀ יֹאמַר הֱוֵא אָרֶץ וְגֶשֶׁם
ז מָטָר וְגֶשֶׁם מִטְרוֹת עֻזּוֹ׃ בְּיַד־כָּל־אָדָם יַחְתּוֹם לָדַעַת כָּל־אַנְשֵׁי

8 that all men know His work. Even the animals retreat to their shelters and
9 curl up in their dens. From the chamber comes the storm,[71] and from the
10 constellations, the biting cold. With the breath of God, He brings ice; many
11 waters He turns solid; He weighs down the fog with moisture, and the clouds
12 scatter His lightning. It whirls and tumbles in accordance with His directives,
13 whatever they are commanded to do over all the settled lands. He provides
14 for His land, whether for punishment or favor. Hear this, Iyov; be silent, and
15 carefully contemplate God's wonders. Do you know when God commands
16 them and lightning shines in His cloud? Do you know the formation of fog,
17 the wonders of Him whose knowledge is perfect? Why do your clothes grow
18 warm as the land is stilled by the south wind? Have you beaten flat[72] the
19 heavens with Him, making them strong as a molten mirror? Tell us what to
20 say to Him; wrapped in darkness we cannot argue in our ignorance. When I
21 speak, is He told of it? Could a man so mired in confusion say anything? And
yet, even if the sun is unseen, obscured high up in the heavens, a wind passes
22 and sweeps the clouds away; golden rays from the north cover God in His
23 awesome glory. Shaddai cannot be reached; great in strength, great in justice,
24 mighty in righteousness, He does not afflict. Therefore He is revered by men;
38 1 even the wise of heart cannot see Him." Then the LORD answered
2 Iyov from the whirlwind and said: "Who dares darken wisdom with words
3 that know nothing? Now, gird your loins like a man; I will ask and you will
4 tell Me. Where were you when I laid the earth's foundations? Speak if you
5 have any understanding! Who fixed its dimensions? Do you know? Who
6 stretched a measuring line across it? On what ground were its pillars set; who
7 laid the cornerstone? When the morning stars sang as one and all the divine
8 beings cried out for joy, who barred Yam with double doors[73] as it gushed
9 10 forth from the womb, as I clothed it in cloud, swaddled it in fog, and held to
11 My boundary, bolting up its double doors, saying, 'Just this far and no more!
12 Here your proud torrents will stop.' Have you ever commanded the daybreak,
13 marked the spot where dawn would rise so that it could hold the edges of the
14 earth and shake the wicked out of it?[74] Like clay whose mold has been lifted,[75]
15 the wicked catch the eye like a garment – their light is lost, their upraised arm
16 broken at last. Have you traveled as far as the sea's depths, walked through
17 them, plumbing the abyss? Were the Gates of Death revealed to you? The
18 gates of death-dark, have you seen them? Have you gazed hard at the earth's
19 expanse? Say so, if you know all! Where is that path where light dwells? And
20 darkness, where is its place? Can you take it to its limits? Do you know
21 the way there? Of course you know – you were alive then! You have lived so
22 23 long![76] Have you reached the stores of snow, the treasuries of hail, which I

71 | The storms are kept in a chamber or vault until God lets them loose (cf. 38:22; Ps. 135:7).

72 | Hebrew *tarkia*, mirroring the description of the heavens as a metal sheet (*rakia*) in Genesis 1:6.

73 | See 7:12.

74 | The wicked are exposed in the daylight.

75 | The features of the earth can be seen, like an impression of a clay seal.

76 | This is said sarcastically.

ח ט מַעֲשֵׂהוּ: וַתָּבוֹא חַיָּה בְמוֹ־אָרֶב וּבִמְעוֹנֹתֶיהָ תִשְׁכֹּן: מִן־הַחֶדֶר תָּבוֹא
י סוּפָה וּמִמְּזָרִים קָרָה: מִנִּשְׁמַת־אֵל יִתֶּן־קָרַח וְרֹחַב מַיִם בְּמוּצָק:
יא יב אַף־בְּרִי יַטְרִיחַ עָב יָפִיץ עֲנַן אוֹרוֹ: וְהוּא מְסִבּוֹת ׀ מִתְהַפֵּךְ בְּתַחְבּוּלֹתָו
יג לְפָעֳלָם כֹּל אֲשֶׁר יְצַוֵּם ׀ עַל־פְּנֵי תֵבֵל אָרְצָה: אִם־לְשֵׁבֶט אִם־לְאַרְצוֹ
יד אִם־לְחֶסֶד יַמְצִאֵהוּ: הַאֲזִינָה זֹּאת אִיּוֹב עֲמֹד וְהִתְבּוֹנֵן ׀ נִפְלְאוֹת אֵל:
טו טז הֲתֵדַע בְּשׂוּם־אֱלוֹהַּ עֲלֵיהֶם וְהוֹפִיעַ אוֹר עֲנָנוֹ: הֲתֵדַע עַל־מִפְלְשֵׂי־
יז עָב מִפְלְאוֹת תְּמִים דֵּעִים: אֲשֶׁר־בְּגָדֶיךָ חַמִּים בְּהַשְׁקִט אֶרֶץ מִדָּרוֹם:
יח יט תַּרְקִיעַ עִמּוֹ לִשְׁחָקִים חֲזָקִים כִּרְאִי מוּצָק: הוֹדִיעֵנוּ מַה־נֹּאמַר לוֹ
כ לֹא־נַעֲרֹךְ מִפְּנֵי־חֹשֶׁךְ: הַיְסֻפַּר־לוֹ כִּי אֲדַבֵּר אִם־אָמַר אִישׁ כִּי יְבֻלָּע:
כא וְעַתָּה ׀ לֹא רָאוּ אוֹר בָּהִיר הוּא בַּשְּׁחָקִים וְרוּחַ עָבְרָה וַתְּטַהֲרֵם:
כב כג מִצָּפוֹן זָהָב יֶאֱתֶה עַל־אֱלוֹהַּ נוֹרָא הוֹד: שַׁדַּי לֹא־מְצָאנֻהוּ שַׂגִּיא־
כד כֹחַ וּמִשְׁפָּט וְרֹב־צְדָקָה לֹא יְעַנֶּה: לָכֵן יְרֵאוּהוּ אֲנָשִׁים לֹא־יִרְאֶה
לח א כָּל־חַכְמֵי־לֵב: וַיַּעַן־יהוה אֶת־אִיּוֹב מנה סערה — מִן ׀ הַסְּעָרָה
ב ג וַיֹּאמַר: מִי זֶה ׀ מַחְשִׁיךְ עֵצָה בְמִלִּין בְּלִי־דָעַת: אֱזָר־נָא כְגֶבֶר
ד חֲלָצֶיךָ וְאֶשְׁאָלְךָ וְהוֹדִיעֵנִי: אֵיפֹה הָיִיתָ בְּיָסְדִי־אָרֶץ הַגֵּד אִם־
ה יָדַעְתָּ בִינָה: מִי־שָׂם מְמַדֶּיהָ כִּי תֵדָע אוֹ מִי־נָטָה עָלֶיהָ קָּו:
ו ז עַל־מָה אֲדָנֶיהָ הָטְבָּעוּ אוֹ מִי־יָרָה אֶבֶן פִּנָּתָהּ: בְּרָן־יַחַד כּוֹכְבֵי
ח בֹקֶר וַיָּרִיעוּ כָּל־בְּנֵי אֱלֹהִים: וַיָּסֶךְ בִּדְלָתַיִם יָם בְּגִיחוֹ מֵרֶחֶם יֵצֵא:
ט י בְּשׂוּמִי עָנָן לְבֻשׁוֹ וַעֲרָפֶל חֲתֻלָּתוֹ: וָאֶשְׁבֹּר עָלָיו חֻקִּי וָאָשִׂים בְּרִיחַ
יא וּדְלָתָיִם: וָאֹמַר עַד־פֹּה תָבוֹא וְלֹא תֹסִיף וּפֹא־יָשִׁית בִּגְאוֹן גַּלֶּיךָ:
יב יג הֲמִיָּמֶיךָ צִוִּיתָ בֹּקֶר יִדַּעְתָּה שַׁחַר מְקֹמוֹ: לֶאֱחֹז בְּכַנְפוֹת הָאָרֶץ וְיִנָּעֲרוּ — הַשַּׁחַר
יד טו רְשָׁעִים מִמֶּנָּה: תִּתְהַפֵּךְ כְּחֹמֶר חוֹתָם וְיִתְיַצְּבוּ כְּמוֹ לְבוּשׁ: וְיִמָּנַע
טז מֵרְשָׁעִים אוֹרָם וּזְרוֹעַ רָמָה תִּשָּׁבֵר: הֲבָאתָ עַד־נִבְכֵי־יָם וּבְחֵקֶר
יז תְּהוֹם הִתְהַלָּכְתָּ: הֲנִגְלוּ לְךָ שַׁעֲרֵי־מָוֶת וְשַׁעֲרֵי צַלְמָוֶת תִּרְאֶה:
יח יט הִתְבֹּנַנְתָּ עַד־רַחֲבֵי־אָרֶץ הַגֵּד אִם־יָדַעְתָּ כֻלָּהּ: אֵי־זֶה הַדֶּרֶךְ יִשְׁכָּן־
כ אוֹר וְחֹשֶׁךְ אֵי־זֶה מְקֹמוֹ: כִּי תִקָּחֶנּוּ אֶל־גְּבוּלוֹ וְכִי תָבִין נְתִיבוֹת בֵּיתוֹ:
כא כב יָדַעְתָּ כִּי־אָז תִּוָּלֵד וּמִסְפַּר יָמֶיךָ רַבִּים: הֲבָאתָ אֶל־אֹצְרוֹת שָׁלֶג
כג וְאֹצְרוֹת בָּרָד תִּרְאֶה: אֲשֶׁר־חָשַׂכְתִּי לְעֶת־צָר לְיוֹם קְרָב וּמִלְחָמָה:

24 have kept for times of trouble, for days of war, for battle? Where is that path
25 where lightning strikes, scattering the east wind across the earth? Who cleft
26 a channel for the cascading waters, a path for the thundercloud bringing rain
27 to uninhabited lands, to wilderness no one enters, to saturate a desolate
28 wasteland and make grass sprout from the ground? Who fathered the rain?
29 Who gave birth to the beads of dew? From whose belly did the ice emerge?
30 The frosts of the heavens, who birthed them? The waters fuse into stone: the
31 surface of the deep is frozen solid. Can you bind the chains of the Pleiades or
32 let loose the reins of Orion? Can you bring Canis Major and Minor in their
33 season, the Bear with her cubs – will you guide them? Do you know the
34 laws of heaven? Will you establish its earthly dominion? Can you lift your
35 voice to the clouds and make a gush of water rush over you? Can you send
36 off lightning bolts so that they call to you: 'Here we are!' Who has hidden
37 wisdom deep inside, endowed the heart with understanding? Who colors
38 the skies blue with wisdom, tilts the pitchers of heaven? Do you know how
39 dust solidifies, how clods of earth amass? Do you hunt the lioness's prey, and
40 can you satisfy a lion's craving as he crouches in his den, poised to ambush
41 from the thicket? Who gives the raven its prey when its young cry out to
39 1 God and wander about with nothing to eat? Do you know the season the
2 mountain goats give birth? Do you watch as gazelles calve? Can you count
3 the months they fill; do you know the time of their birth? They crouch down,
4 bring forth their young, and cast away their offspring. Their progeny thrive,
5 grow in the wild; once they leave, they never come back. Who set the
6 wild ass free? Who cut the reins of the onager, whose home I made in the
7 wilderness, whose dwellings lie in salt lands? He scoffs at the clamoring city
8 and does not hear the taskmaster's shouts. He roams the mountain pastures
9 in search of anything green. Would the wild ox agree to serve you? Would he
10 lodge by your feeding trough? Can you fetter him to the furrow? Would he
11 plow the valleys behind you? Can you trust him to bring you a great yield?
12 Would you leave your hard labor to him? Could you count on him to come
13 back, to gather your seed and harvest? As for the ostrich – does her wing
14 joyously beat? Does she fly like the stork and falcon? She leaves her eggs
15 on the ground, warming them in the dust, forgetting a foot may crush
16 them, a wild beast could trample them. She is harsh with her children as if
17 they weren't her own. She doesn't care that her efforts are in vain,[77] for God
has deprived her of wisdom; He has not endowed her with understanding.
18 19 Otherwise she would soar on high, scoffing at the horse and its rider. Did you
20 endow the horse with his valor? Did you clothe his neck with a mane? Do
21 you make him rumble like locusts, neigh in majestic terror? He strikes the
22 earth, reveling in his power when he charges toward battle. He laughs off fear
23 and never recoils; he does not flinch at the sword. A quiverful of arrows
24 whizzes past him, the spear's blade and the lance. Raging and trembling he
25 gallops; he does not swerve as the horn sounds: at its blast he cries 'Aha!'
From afar he catches a whiff of war, the thundering of captains, battle cries.

77 | Ostriches were thought to be uncaring (cf. Lam. 4:3).

כד כה אי־זה הדרך יחלק אור יפץ קדים עלי־ארץ: מי־פלג לשטף תעלה
כו ודרך לחזיז קלות: להמטיר על־ארץ לא־איש מדבר לא־אדם בו:
כז כח להשביע שאה ומשאה ולהצמיח מצא דשא: היש־למטר אב או
כט מי־הוליד אגלי־טל: מבטן מי יצא הקרח וכפר שמים מי ילדו:
ל לא כאבן מים יתחבאו ופני תהום יתלכדו: התקשר מעדנות כימה
לב או־משכות כסיל תפתח: התציא מזרות בעתו ועיש על־בניה
לג לד תנחם: הידעת חקות שמים אם־תשים משטרו בארץ: התרים
לה לעב קולך ושפעת־מים תכסך: התשלח ברקים וילכו ויאמרו לך ח
לו לז הננו: מי־שת בטחות חכמה או מי־נתן לשכוי בינה: מי־יספר
לח שחקים בחכמה ונבלי שמים מי ישכיב: בצקת עפר למוצק ורגבים
לט מ ידבקו: התצוד ללביא טרף וחית כפירים תמלא: כי־ישחו במעונות
מא ישבו בסכה למו־ארב: מי יכין לערב צידו כי־ילדו אל־אל ישועו
לט א יתעו לבלי־אכל: הידעת עת לדת יעלי־סלע חלל אילות תשמר:
ב ג תספר ירחים תמלאנה וידעת עת לדתנה: תכרענה ילדיהן תפלחנה
ד חבליהם תשלחנה: יחלמו בניהם ירבו בבר יצאו ולא־שבו למו:
ה ו מי־שלח פרא חפשי ומסרות ערוד מי פתח: אשר־שמתי ערבה
ז ביתו ומשכנותיו מלחה: ישחק להמון קריה תשאות נוגש לא
ח ט ישמע: יתור הרים מרעהו ואחר כל־ירוק ידרוש: היאבה רים עבדך
י אם־ילין על־אבוסך: התקשר־רים בתלם עבתו אם־ישדד עמקים
יא יב אחריך: התבטח־בו כי־רב כחו ותעזב אליו יגיעך: התאמין בו
יג כי־ישוב זרעך וגרנך יאסף: כנף־רננים נעלסה אם־אברה חסידה ישיב
יד טו ונצה: כי־תעזב לארץ בציה ועל־עפר תחמם: ותשכח כי־רגל תזורה
טז וחית השדה תדושה: הקשיח בניה ללא־לה לריק יגיעה בלי־פחד:
יז יח כי־השה אלוה חכמה ולא־חלק לה בבינה: כעת במרום תמריא
יט תשחק לסוס ולרכבו: התתן לסוס גבורה התלביש צוארו רעמה:
כ כא התרעישנו כארבה הוד נחרו אימה: יחפרו בעמק וישיש בכח יצא
כב כג לקראת־נשק: ישחק לפחד ולא יחת ולא־ישוב מפני־חרב: עליו
כד תרנה אשפה להב חנית וכידון: ברעש ורגז יגמא־ארץ ולא־יאמין
כה כי־קול שופר: בדי שפר ׀ יאמר האח ומרחוק יריח מלחמה רעם

26 27 Is it by your wisdom the hawk flies, spreading his wings to head south? Does
28 the vulture soar at your bidding? Is that why he builds his nest on high? He
29 makes his home in the rock, on steep crags, a fortress. From there he seeks
30 out his food; his eyes gaze out from afar. His young gulp down blood; where
40 1 the dead are, he will be found." Then the LORD spoke up to Iyov and
2 said, "Should he who argues make claims against Shaddai? Should God reply
3 to one who accuses Him?" Iyov answered the LORD and
4 said, "I have been held worthless. What can I answer? I will hold my hand to
5 my mouth;[78] I've spoken once and will say no more; now twice. That is
6 enough." Then the LORD answered Iyov out of the whirlwind and
7 8 said: "Now gird your loins like a man; I will ask and you will tell Me. Do you
dare eschew My justice? Would you dare indict Me so that you can be in the
9 10 right? Do you have an arm like God's? Can your voice thunder like His? Then
deck yourself in majesty, magnificence; robe yourself in grandeur and glory!
11 Scatter your rage far and wide; behold all the prideful – bring them low.
12 Behold the prideful and humble them; trample the wicked wherever they
13 14 are! Bury them all in the dust; shroud their faces in oblivion. Then even I
15 would praise you for the deliverance won by your right hand. Consider
Behemoth;[79] I made him as I made you. He devours grass as cattle do.
16 17 Behold – how strong his loins, how mighty the muscles of his belly! His tail
18 stands erect like a cedar; the tendons of his thighs are woven together. His
19 limbs are bronze conduits, his bones like iron bars. He is the first of God's
20 works; only his Maker can draw a sword against him. The mountains bring
21 him their harvest; all beasts of the field frolic there. He lies down under the
22 lotuses, under the cover of the marsh's reeds. A thicket of lotus covers him;
23 the stream's willows surround him. If a river rushes over him, he will have no
24 fear, steady while the Jordan gushes into his mouth. Under his watchful
25 eyes, who can take him or run a grapnel through his nose? Can you pull out
26 Leviathan[80] with a hook, tie up his tongue with a rope? Can you wrap a
27 bulrush around his nose, pierce through his jaw with a prong? Would he
28 profusely plead with you? Would he speak soft words to you? Would he forge
29 a pact with you to forever be your slave? Would you be able to play with him
30 like a bird, tie him down for your maids? Will merchants bargain over him?
31 Will traders divvy him up? Could you fill his skin with barbs, his head with
41 32 1 harpoons? Lay a hand on him, and you will forget what war is! You see, in his
midst any hope will be crushed; all fall to their knees at the sight of him;
2 no one is fierce enough to confront him; who then can stand up to Me?
3 Whoever comes forward to take him on – I will reward him! Everything
4 under heaven is Mine. I refuse to keep quiet about him, his bravery, his
5 indomitable prowess! Who can strip away his outer trappings? The folds of
6 his jowls – who can delve inside? Who can wrest open the gates of his face?

78 | I will be silent.

79 | See note on 12:7.

80 | See note on 3:8.

כו כז שָׂרִים וּתְרוּעָה׃ הֲמִבִּינָתְךָ יַאֲבֶר־נֵץ יִפְרֹשׂ כְּנָפָו לְתֵימָן׃ אִם־עַל־
כח פִּיךָ יַגְבִּיהַּ נָשֶׁר וְכִי יָרִים קִנּוֹ׃ סֶלַע יִשְׁכֹּן וְיִתְלֹנָן עַל־שֶׁן־סֶלַע וּמְצוּדָה׃
כט ל מִשָּׁם חָפַר־אֹכֶל לְמֵרָחוֹק עֵינָיו יַבִּיטוּ׃ וְאֶפְרֹחָו יְעַלְעוּ־דָם וּבַאֲשֶׁר
מ א ב חֲלָלִים שָׁם הוּא׃ וַיַּעַן יְהוָה אֶת־אִיּוֹב וַיֹּאמַר׃ הֲרֹב
ג עִם־שַׁדַּי יִסּוֹר מוֹכִיחַ אֱלוֹהַּ יַעֲנֶנָּה׃ וַיַּעַן אִיּוֹב אֶת־
ד ה יְהוָה וַיֹּאמַר׃ הֵן קַלֹּתִי מָה אֲשִׁיבֶךָּ יָדִי שַׂמְתִּי לְמוֹ־פִי׃ אַחַת דִּבַּרְתִּי
ו וְלֹא אֶעֱנֶה וּשְׁתַּיִם וְלֹא אוֹסִיף׃ וַיַּעַן־יְהוָה אֶת־
ז אִיּוֹב מנסערה וַיֹּאמַר׃ אֱזָר־נָא כְגֶבֶר חֲלָצֶיךָ אֶשְׁאָלְךָ וְהוֹדִיעֵנִי׃ מִן ׀ סְעָרָה
ח ט הַאַף תָּפֵר מִשְׁפָּטִי תַּרְשִׁיעֵנִי לְמַעַן תִּצְדָּק׃ וְאִם־זְרוֹעַ כָּאֵל ׀ לָךְ
י יא וּבְקוֹל כָּמֹהוּ תַרְעֵם׃ עֲדֵה־נָא גָאוֹן וָגֹבַהּ וְהוֹד וְהָדָר תִּלְבָּשׁ׃ הָפֵץ
יב עֶבְרוֹת אַפֶּךָ וּרְאֵה כָל־גֵּאֶה וְהַשְׁפִּילֵהוּ׃ רְאֵה כָל־גֵּאֶה הַכְנִיעֵהוּ
יג יד וַהֲדֹךְ רְשָׁעִים תַּחְתָּם׃ טָמְנֵם בֶּעָפָר יָחַד פְּנֵיהֶם חֲבֹשׁ בַּטָּמוּן׃ וְגַם־
טו אֲנִי אוֹדֶךָּ כִּי־תוֹשִׁעַ לְךָ יְמִינֶךָ׃ הִנֵּה־נָא בְהֵמוֹת אֲשֶׁר־עָשִׂיתִי עִמָּךְ
טז יז חָצִיר כַּבָּקָר יֹאכֵל׃ הִנֵּה־נָא כֹחוֹ בְמָתְנָיו וְאֹנוֹ בִּשְׁרִירֵי בִטְנוֹ׃ יַחְפֹּץ
יח זְנָבוֹ כְמוֹ־אָרֶז גִּידֵי פַחֲדָו יְשֹׂרָגוּ׃ עֲצָמָיו אֲפִיקֵי נְחוּשָׁה גְּרָמָיו כִּמְטִיל
יט כ בַּרְזֶל׃ הוּא רֵאשִׁית דַּרְכֵי־אֵל הָעֹשׂוֹ יַגֵּשׁ חַרְבּוֹ׃ כִּי־בוּל הָרִים יִשְׂאוּ־
כא לוֹ וְכָל־חַיַּת הַשָּׂדֶה יְשַׂחֲקוּ־שָׁם׃ תַּחַת־צֶאֱלִים יִשְׁכָּב בְּסֵתֶר קָנֶה
כב כג וּבִצָּה׃ יְסֻכֻּהוּ צֶאֱלִים צִלְלוֹ יְסֻבּוּהוּ עַרְבֵי־נָחַל׃ הֵן יַעֲשֹׁק נָהָר וְלֹא
כד יַחְפּוֹז יִבְטַח ׀ כִּי־יָגִיחַ יַרְדֵּן אֶל־פִּיהוּ׃ בְּעֵינָיו יִקָּחֶנּוּ בְּמוֹקְשִׁים יִנְקָב־
כה כו אָף׃ תִּמְשֹׁךְ לִוְיָתָן בְּחַכָּה וּבְחֶבֶל תַּשְׁקִיעַ לְשֹׁנוֹ׃ הֲתָשִׂים אַגְמֹן
כז בְּאַפּוֹ וּבְחוֹחַ תִּקֹּב לֶחֱיוֹ׃ הֲיַרְבֶּה אֵלֶיךָ תַּחֲנוּנִים אִם־יְדַבֵּר אֵלֶיךָ
כח כט רַכּוֹת׃ הֲיִכְרֹת בְּרִית עִמָּךְ תִּקָּחֶנּוּ לְעֶבֶד עוֹלָם׃ הַתְשַׂחֶק־בּוֹ כַּצִּפּוֹר
ל לא וְתִקְשְׁרֶנּוּ לְנַעֲרוֹתֶיךָ׃ יִכְרוּ עָלָיו חַבָּרִים יֶחֱצוּהוּ בֵּין כְּנַעֲנִים׃ הַתְמַלֵּא
לב בְשֻׂכּוֹת עוֹרוֹ וּבְצִלְצַל דָּגִים רֹאשׁוֹ׃ שִׂים־עָלָיו כַּפֶּךָ זְכֹר מִלְחָמָה
מא א ב אַל־תּוֹסַף׃ הֵן־תֹּחַלְתּוֹ נִכְזָבָה הֲגַם אֶל־מַרְאָיו יֻטָל׃ לֹא־אַכְזָר כִּי
ג יְעוּרֶנּוּ וּמִי הוּא לְפָנַי יִתְיַצָּב׃ מִי הִקְדִּימַנִי וַאֲשַׁלֵּם תַּחַת כָּל־הַשָּׁמַיִם
ד ה לִי־הוּא׃ לא־אַחֲרִישׁ בַּדָּיו וּדְבַר־גְּבוּרוֹת וְחִין עֶרְכּוֹ׃ מִי־גִלָּה פְּנֵי לוֹ־
ו לְבוּשׁוֹ בְּכֶפֶל רִסְנוֹ מִי יָבוֹא׃ דַּלְתֵי פָנָיו מִי פִתֵּחַ סְבִיבוֹת שִׁנָּיו אֵימָה׃

7 Sheer terror – the curve of his teeth! His back is made of layers of shields[81]
8 locked shut and sealed. Each is flush with the next; not a breath can penetrate
9 10 them, each cleaving to the other, interlocked and conjoined. His sneezes are
11 flashes of light; his eyes are like the gleaming dawn. Out of his mouth come
12 flaming torches! Burning sparks escape. From his nostrils, smoke surges as if
13 from a steaming, boiling pot. His breath ignites coals; flames shoot from
14 15 his mouth. Strength abides in his neck; his power rushes before him. His
16 cascading flesh clings together, hard and immutable. His heart is hard as rock,
17 hard as the lower millstone.[82] Divine beings recoil before his majesty; waves
18 turn white at the devastation he brings. He who approaches with a sword is
19 doomed to fail – so too with a spear, dart, or lance. To him iron is straw;
20 bronze – rotted wood. No arrow can drive him away; slingstones look like
21 22 stubble. For him clubs are straw; he scoffs at the rushing dart. His underbelly
23 is sharp as shards, a threshing sledge across the mud. He makes the depths
24 boil like a pot; he turns the sea into a seething cauldron. He leaves behind
25 him a gleaming wake; the waters of the deep turn white. No one on earth can
26 overcome him; no one was made so fearless. He looks down at towering
42 1 creatures; he is king over every wild beast." Iyov answered and said
2 to the LORD: "I know that You can do anything, that no plan is beyond You.
3 'Who dares obscure wisdom when he himself knows nothing?' Indeed, I have
spoken but did not understand. There are wonders beyond me I did not know.
4 5 'Hear now, and I will speak; I will ask, and You will tell me...'[83] I have heard
6 You with my ears, but now I see You with my eyes: and so, I am utterly spent.
I take pity on dust and ashes."
7 After the LORD spoke these words to Iyov, the LORD said to Elifaz the
Temanite, "I am angry at you and your two friends, for you have not spoken
8 truthfully about Me, unlike My servant Iyov. Now take seven bulls and seven
rams, and go to My servant Iyov. Sacrifice them as a burnt offering on your
behalf, and Iyov My servant will pray for you. For I will accept his prayer
and will not commit any outrage against you, though you have not spoken
9 truthfully of Me, unlike My servant Iyov." Then Elifaz the Temanite and
Bildad the Shuhite and Tzofar the Naamatite went and did as the LORD had
10 told them. And the LORD lifted Iyov's face. Then the LORD restored what
Iyov had lost, for he prayed on behalf of his friends. And the LORD doubled
11 all that Iyov had. And all his brothers and sisters and all those who knew him
previously came to break bread with him at his house; they grieved with him
and comforted him for all the suffering that the LORD had brought upon
12 him. Each person gave him one *kesita*[84] and one ring of gold. The LORD
blessed Iyov's later days more than his early days. He came to have fourteen
thousand sheep, six thousand camels, one thousand pairs of oxen, and one

---

81 | Hard scales.

82 | The heavy base of the mill on which the upper millstone turns to grind the grain.

83 | Echoing God's statement in 38:3.

84 | Apparently a unit of silver.

ז ח גַּאֲוָה אֲפִיקֵי מָגִנִּים סָגוּר חוֹתָם צָר׃ אֶחָד בְּאֶחָד יִגַּשׁוּ וְרוּחַ לֹא־יָבוֹא
ט י בֵינֵיהֶם׃ אִישׁ־בְּאָחִיהוּ יְדֻבָּקוּ יִתְלַכְּדוּ וְלֹא יִתְפָּרָדוּ׃ עֲטִישֹׁתָיו תָּהֶל
יא אוֹר וְעֵינָיו כְּעַפְעַפֵּי־שָׁחַר׃ מִפִּיו לַפִּידִים יַהֲלֹכוּ כִּידוֹדֵי אֵשׁ יִתְמַלָּטוּ׃
יב יג מִנְּחִירָיו יֵצֵא עָשָׁן כְּדוּד נָפוּחַ וְאַגְמֹן׃ נַפְשׁוֹ גֶּחָלִים תְּלַהֵט וְלַהַב מִפִּיו
יד טו יֵצֵא׃ בְּצַוָּארוֹ יָלִין עֹז וּלְפָנָיו תָּדוּץ דְּאָבָה׃ מַפְּלֵי בְשָׂרוֹ דָבֵקוּ יָצוּק
טז יז עָלָיו בַּל־יִמּוֹט׃ לִבּוֹ יָצוּק כְּמוֹ־אָבֶן וְיָצוּק כְּפֶלַח תַּחְתִּית׃ מִשֵּׂתוֹ
יח יָגוּרוּ אֵלִים מִשְּׁבָרִים יִתְחַטָּאוּ׃ מַשִּׂיגֵהוּ חֶרֶב בְּלִי תָקוּם חֲנִית מַסָּע
יט כ וְשִׁרְיָה׃ יַחְשֹׁב לְתֶבֶן בַּרְזֶל לְעֵץ רִקָּבוֹן נְחוּשָׁה׃ לֹא־יַבְרִיחֶנּוּ בֶן־
כא קָשֶׁת לְקַשׁ נֶהְפְּכוּ־לוֹ אַבְנֵי־קָלַע׃ כְּקַשׁ נֶחְשְׁבוּ תוֹתָח וְיִשְׂחַק לְרַעַשׁ
כב כג כִּידוֹן׃ תַּחְתָּיו חַדּוּדֵי חָרֶשׂ יִרְפַּד חָרוּץ עֲלֵי־טִיט׃ יַרְתִּיחַ כַּסִּיר מְצוּלָה
כד כה יָם יָשִׂים כַּמֶּרְקָחָה׃ אַחֲרָיו יָאִיר נָתִיב יַחְשֹׁב תְּהוֹם לְשֵׂיבָה׃ אֵין־
כו עַל־עָפָר מָשְׁלוֹ הֶעָשׂוּ לִבְלִי־חָת׃ אֵת־כָּל־גָּבֹהַּ יִרְאֶה הוּא מֶלֶךְ
מב א ב עַל־כָּל־בְּנֵי־שָׁחַץ׃ וַיַּעַן אִיּוֹב אֶת־יְהוָה וַיֹּאמַר׃ יָדַעְתָּ
ג כִּי־כֹל תּוּכָל וְלֹא־יִבָּצֵר מִמְּךָ מְזִמָּה׃ מִי זֶה ׀ מַעְלִים עֵצָה בְּלִי דָעַת
ד לָכֵן הִגַּדְתִּי וְלֹא אָבִין נִפְלָאוֹת מִמֶּנִּי וְלֹא אֵדָע׃ שְׁמַע־נָא וְאָנֹכִי אֲדַבֵּר
ה ו אֶשְׁאָלְךָ וְהוֹדִיעֵנִי׃ לְשֵׁמַע־אֹזֶן שְׁמַעְתִּיךָ וְעַתָּה עֵינִי רָאָתְךָ׃ עַל־כֵּן
אֶמְאַס וְנִחַמְתִּי עַל־עָפָר וָאֵפֶר׃

ז וַיְהִי אַחַר דִּבֶּר יְהוָה אֶת־הַדְּבָרִים הָאֵלֶּה אֶל־אִיּוֹב וַיֹּאמֶר יְהוָה
אֶל־אֱלִיפַז הַתֵּימָנִי חָרָה אַפִּי בְךָ וּבִשְׁנֵי רֵעֶיךָ כִּי לֹא דִבַּרְתֶּם אֵלַי
ח נְכוֹנָה כְּעַבְדִּי אִיּוֹב׃ וְעַתָּה קְחוּ־לָכֶם שִׁבְעָה־פָרִים וְשִׁבְעָה אֵילִים
וּלְכוּ ׀ אֶל־עַבְדִּי אִיּוֹב וְהַעֲלִיתֶם עוֹלָה בַּעַדְכֶם וְאִיּוֹב עַבְדִּי יִתְפַּלֵּל
עֲלֵיכֶם כִּי אִם־פָּנָיו אֶשָּׂא לְבִלְתִּי עֲשׂוֹת עִמָּכֶם נְבָלָה כִּי לֹא דִבַּרְתֶּם
ט אֵלַי נְכוֹנָה כְּעַבְדִּי אִיּוֹב׃ וַיֵּלְכוּ אֱלִיפַז הַתֵּימָנִי וּבִלְדַּד הַשּׁוּחִי צֹפַר
הַנַּעֲמָתִי וַיַּעֲשׂוּ כַּאֲשֶׁר דִּבֶּר אֲלֵיהֶם יְהוָה וַיִּשָּׂא יְהוָה אֶת־פְּנֵי אִיּוֹב׃
י וַיהוָה שָׁב אֶת־שְׁבִית אִיּוֹב בְּהִתְפַּלְלוֹ בְּעַד רֵעֵהוּ וַיֹּסֶף יְהוָה אֶת־כָּל־ שְׁבוּת
יא אֲשֶׁר לְאִיּוֹב לְמִשְׁנֶה׃ וַיָּבֹאוּ אֵלָיו כָּל־אֶחָיו וְכָל־אַחְיֹתָיו וְכָל־יֹדְעָיו
לְפָנִים וַיֹּאכְלוּ עִמּוֹ לֶחֶם בְּבֵיתוֹ וַיָּנֻדוּ לוֹ וַיְנַחֲמוּ אֹתוֹ עַל כָּל־הָרָעָה
אֲשֶׁר־הֵבִיא יְהוָה עָלָיו וַיִּתְּנוּ־לוֹ אִישׁ קְשִׂיטָה אֶחָת וְאִישׁ נֶזֶם זָהָב
יב אֶחָד׃ וַיהוָה בֵּרַךְ אֶת־אַחֲרִית אִיּוֹב מֵרֵאשִׁתוֹ וַיְהִי־לוֹ אַרְבָּעָה עָשָׂר
אֶלֶף צֹאן וְשֵׁשֶׁת אֲלָפִים גְּמַלִּים וְאֶלֶף צֶמֶד־בָּקָר וְאֶלֶף אֲתוֹנוֹת׃

13 thousand she-donkeys. He came to have seven sons and three daughters:
14 one was called Yemima, the second was called Ketzia, and the third, Keren
15 Hapukh. Women more beautiful than Iyov's daughters could not be found
in the whole land. Their father gave them inheritances just as he did their
16 brothers. After all this, Iyov lived for one hundred and forty years. He saw
17 his children and grandchildren – four generations. Iyov died in old age, old
and full in days.

יג יד וַיְהִי־לוֹ שִׁבְעָנָה בָנִים וְשָׁלוֹשׁ בָּנוֹת: וַיִּקְרָא שֵׁם־הָאַחַת יְמִימָה וְשֵׁם
טו הַשֵּׁנִית קְצִיעָה וְשֵׁם הַשְּׁלִישִׁית קֶרֶן הַפּוּךְ: וְלֹא נִמְצָא נָשִׁים יָפוֹת
כִּבְנוֹת אִיּוֹב בְּכָל־הָאָרֶץ וַיִּתֵּן לָהֶם אֲבִיהֶם נַחֲלָה בְּתוֹךְ אֲחֵיהֶם:
טז וַיְחִי אִיּוֹב אַחֲרֵי־זֹאת מֵאָה וְאַרְבָּעִים שָׁנָה וַיַּרְא אֶת־בָּנָיו וְאֶת־בְּנֵי
יז בָנָיו אַרְבָּעָה דֹּרוֹת: וַיָּמָת אִיּוֹב זָקֵן וּשְׂבַע יָמִים:

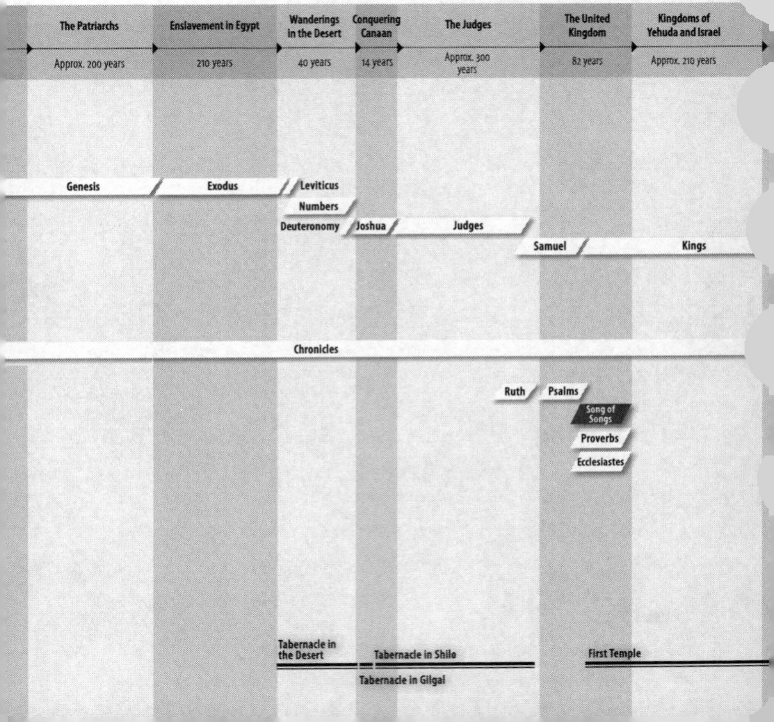
The Patriarchs
Approx. 200 years
Enslavement in Egypt
210 years
Wanderings in the Desert
40 years
Conquering Canaan
14 years
The Judges
Approx. 300 years
The United Kingdom
82 years
Kingdoms of Yehuda and Israel
Approx. 210 years
Genesis
Exodus
Leviticus
Numbers
Deuteronomy
Joshua
Judges
Samuel
Kings
Chronicles
Ruth
Psalms
Song of Songs
Proverbs
Ecclesiastes
Tabernacle in the Desert
Tabernacle in Shilo
Tabernacle in Gilgal
First Temple

שיר השירים

SHIR HASHIRIM / SONG OF SONGS

SONG OF SONGS	Song of yearning	Song of the wedding	Song of the missed opportunity and the desperate search	Song of the reunification
	Chs. 1–2	3:1–5:1	5:2–6:12	7–8

1 1 2 *Shlomo's Song of Songs.* [*She*] Would that he would kiss me with that mouth.
3 Better than any wine is your love, the fragrance of your oils finer; your very
name flows forth like fragrant oil;[1] what wonder that all the maidens love you?
4 Come, draw me after you; come, let us run – the king has brought me into
his chambers. In you our joy, our happiness: your love possesses us more than
5 any wine; flowing freely falls this love. [*She*] I am dark yet fair,
daughters of Jerusalem, like the tents of Kedar,[2] like the curtains of Shlomo.
6 Do not look at me: I am scorched black; the sun has stared at me. My mother's
sons were furious: they made me a keeper of the vineyards; my own vineyard
7 I did not keep. Tell me, you whom I have loved, where will you pasture; where
will you rest your flock at noon? Do not make me swathe my face and wander
8 among all the herds of your friends. [*He*] If you do not know, most beautiful
of women, go out in the tracks of the flock; bring your own young goats to
9 pasture beside the shepherds' huts. [*He*] A mare among Pharaoh's
10 chariots, that is what you are to me, my love, your cheeks fair in their strands
11 of beads, your neck bejeweled; I would make you strands of gold – with silver
12 flecks. [*She*] As long as my king[3] reclined to drink, my musk root gave its
13 14 scent, my beloved a bundle of myrrh to me, resting between my breasts; my
15 beloved a cluster of henna to me in the vineyards of Ein Gedi. [*He*]
16 How beautiful you are, my love, how beautiful, your eyes like doves. [*She*]
How beautiful you are, beloved, and how good. Our bed is green, luscious;
17 2 1 our house is roofed with cedars; its rafters are juniper trees. I am a dune flower
2 of the coast, I am a lily of the valleys. [*He*] A lily among thorn weeds is my
3 love among maidens. [*She*] An apple tree in the forest is my beloved among
young men. I yearn for his shade; there I rest, and his fruit fills my mouth with
4 sweetness. [*She*] He has brought me to the wine house, and his ensign flying
5 over me is love. Sustain me with raisin cakes; spread a bed for me among
6 apples – for I am sick with love. My head rests in his left arm; his right
7 embraces me. Swear to me, daughters of Jerusalem, by the she-gazelles, by
the does of the field, swear that you will not waken, will not rouse, this love
8 before its time. The voice of my beloved – I hear him coming,
9 springing over the hills, leaping the slopes; he is like a gazelle, my beloved;
he is like a young deer – here he stands behind our wall, gazing through the
10 windows, catching glimpses through every gap. My beloved spoke; he said
11 to me, "Come, rise, my love, my beautiful one, let us leave. Winter is over; the
12 rains have passed and left us. On the land, buds have appeared. The songbirds'
13 time has come, and the turtle dove's call sounds over our land. The fig has put
out her buds, and the flowering vines give scent – so come, rise, my love, my
14 beautiful one, let us leave." [*He*] My dove in the rock's cleft, in the
cliff's shadow – show me your face; let me hear your voice, for lovely is your
15 voice; your face so fair. [*She*] Catch the foxes, the little foxes ravaging
16 the vineyards just as our vineyard is in flower. My beloved is mine, and I am

---

1 | "Oil" (*shemen*) echoes "name" (*shem*); cf. Ecclesiastes 7:1.

2 | The tents of the tribes of Kedar were made from black goat hair.

3 | The beloved.

א א ב שִׁיר הַשִּׁירִים אֲשֶׁר לִשְׁלֹמֹה: יִשָּׁקֵנִי מִנְּשִׁיקוֹת פִּיהוּ כִּי־טוֹבִים דֹּדֶיךָ
ג מִיָּיִן: לְרֵיחַ שְׁמָנֶיךָ טוֹבִים שֶׁמֶן תּוּרַק שְׁמֶךָ עַל־כֵּן עֲלָמוֹת אֲהֵבוּךָ:
ד מָשְׁכֵנִי אַחֲרֶיךָ נָּרוּצָה הֱבִיאַנִי הַמֶּלֶךְ חֲדָרָיו נָגִילָה וְנִשְׂמְחָה בָּךְ
ה נַזְכִּירָה דֹדֶיךָ מִיַּיִן מֵישָׁרִים אֲהֵבוּךָ: שְׁחוֹרָה אֲנִי וְנָאוָה
ו בְּנוֹת יְרוּשָׁלָםִ כְּאָהֳלֵי קֵדָר כִּירִיעוֹת שְׁלֹמֹה: אַל־תִּרְאוּנִי שֶׁאֲנִי
שְׁחַרְחֹרֶת שֶׁשְּׁזָפַתְנִי הַשָּׁמֶשׁ בְּנֵי אִמִּי נִחֲרוּ־בִי שָׂמֻנִי נֹטֵרָה אֶת־
ז הַכְּרָמִים כַּרְמִי שֶׁלִּי לֹא נָטָרְתִּי: הַגִּידָה לִּי שֶׁאָהֲבָה נַפְשִׁי אֵיכָה
תִרְעֶה אֵיכָה תַּרְבִּיץ בַּצָּהֳרָיִם שַׁלָּמָה אֶהְיֶה כְּעֹטְיָה עַל עֶדְרֵי חֲבֵרֶיךָ:
ח אִם־לֹא תֵדְעִי לָךְ הַיָּפָה בַּנָּשִׁים צְאִי־לָךְ בְּעִקְבֵי הַצֹּאן וּרְעִי אֶת־
ט גְּדִיֹּתַיִךְ עַל מִשְׁכְּנוֹת הָרֹעִים: לְסֻסָתִי בְּרִכְבֵי פַרְעֹה
י יא דִּמִּיתִיךְ רַעְיָתִי: נָאווּ לְחָיַיִךְ בַּתֹּרִים צַוָּארֵךְ בַּחֲרוּזִים: תּוֹרֵי זָהָב
יב נַעֲשֶׂה־לָּךְ עִם נְקֻדּוֹת הַכָּסֶף: עַד־שֶׁהַמֶּלֶךְ בִּמְסִבּוֹ נִרְדִּי נָתַן רֵיחוֹ:
יג יד צְרוֹר הַמֹּר ׀ דּוֹדִי לִי בֵּין שָׁדַי יָלִין: אֶשְׁכֹּל הַכֹּפֶר ׀ דּוֹדִי לִי בְּכַרְמֵי
טו טז עֵין גֶּדִי: הִנָּךְ יָפָה רַעְיָתִי הִנָּךְ יָפָה עֵינַיִךְ יוֹנִים: הִנְּךָ יָפֶה
יז דוֹדִי אַף נָעִים אַף־עַרְשֵׂנוּ רַעֲנָנָה: קֹרוֹת בָּתֵּינוּ אֲרָזִים רחיטנו רָהִיטֵנוּ
ב א ב בְּרוֹתִים: אֲנִי חֲבַצֶּלֶת הַשָּׁרוֹן שׁוֹשַׁנַּת הָעֲמָקִים: כְּשׁוֹשַׁנָּה בֵּין הַחוֹחִים
ג כֵּן רַעְיָתִי בֵּין הַבָּנוֹת: כְּתַפּוּחַ בַּעֲצֵי הַיַּעַר כֵּן דּוֹדִי בֵּין הַבָּנִים בְּצִלּוֹ
ד חִמַּדְתִּי וְיָשַׁבְתִּי וּפִרְיוֹ מָתוֹק לְחִכִּי: הֱבִיאַנִי אֶל־בֵּית הַיָּיִן וְדִגְלוֹ עָלַי
ה אַהֲבָה: סַמְּכוּנִי בָּאֲשִׁישׁוֹת רַפְּדוּנִי בַּתַּפּוּחִים כִּי־חוֹלַת אַהֲבָה
ו ז אָנִי: שְׂמֹאלוֹ תַּחַת לְרֹאשִׁי וִימִינוֹ תְּחַבְּקֵנִי: הִשְׁבַּעְתִּי אֶתְכֶם בְּנוֹת
יְרוּשָׁלַםִ בִּצְבָאוֹת אוֹ בְּאַיְלוֹת הַשָּׂדֶה אִם־תָּעִירוּ ׀ וְאִם־תְּעוֹרְרוּ
ח אֶת־הָאַהֲבָה עַד שֶׁתֶּחְפָּץ: קוֹל דּוֹדִי הִנֵּה־זֶה בָּא מְדַלֵּג
ט עַל־הֶהָרִים מְקַפֵּץ עַל־הַגְּבָעוֹת: דּוֹמֶה דוֹדִי לִצְבִי אוֹ לְעֹפֶר הָאַיָּלִים
הִנֵּה־זֶה עוֹמֵד אַחַר כָּתְלֵנוּ מַשְׁגִּיחַ מִן־הַחַלֹּנוֹת מֵצִיץ מִן־הַחֲרַכִּים:
י יא עָנָה דוֹדִי וְאָמַר לִי קוּמִי לָךְ רַעְיָתִי יָפָתִי וּלְכִי־לָךְ: כִּי־הִנֵּה הַסְּתָו
יב עָבָר הַגֶּשֶׁם חָלַף הָלַךְ לוֹ: הַנִּצָּנִים נִרְאוּ בָאָרֶץ עֵת הַזָּמִיר הִגִּיעַ וְקוֹל
יג הַתּוֹר נִשְׁמַע בְּאַרְצֵנוּ: הַתְּאֵנָה חָנְטָה פַגֶּיהָ וְהַגְּפָנִים ׀ סְמָדַר נָתְנוּ
יד רֵיחַ קוּמִי לכי רַעְיָתִי יָפָתִי וּלְכִי־לָךְ: יוֹנָתִי בְּחַגְוֵי הַסֶּלַע לָךְ
בְּסֵתֶר הַמַּדְרֵגָה הַרְאִינִי אֶת־מַרְאַיִךְ הַשְׁמִיעִנִי אֶת־קוֹלֵךְ כִּי־קוֹלֵךְ
טו עָרֵב וּמַרְאֵיךְ נָאוֶה: אֶחֱזוּ־לָנוּ שׁוּעָלִים שׁוּעָלִים קְטַנִּים
טז מְחַבְּלִים כְּרָמִים וּכְרָמֵינוּ סְמָדַר: דּוֹדִי לִי וַאֲנִי לוֹ הָרֹעֶה בַּשּׁוֹשַׁנִּים:

17 his who pastures among lilies. Until the day has breathed its last and the
shadows have flown, turn like a gazelle, my beloved, turn like a young deer to
3 1 the riven hills. Upon my bed at night[4] I sought the one I love;
2 I sought him, I did not find him. I shall rise, I shall go all around the town –
through the streets, across the squares – searching for the one I love. I
3 searched for him but did not find him. The guards found me, those who go
4 around the town: "The one I love – have you seen him?" I had scarcely moved
away from them when I found the one I love. I caught hold of him; I will not
let him go until I have brought him to my mother's house, to the chamber
5 where I was conceived. Swear to me, daughters of Jerusalem, by the she-
gazelles, by the does of the field, swear that you will not waken, will not rouse,
6 this love before its time. [*Friends*] Who is this rising from the
wilderness like plumes of smoke, perfumed with myrrh and frankincense
7 more fragrant than all the merchants' powders? Here is Shlomo's bed, sixty
8 soldiers all around it, heroes of Israel, each bearing his sword, each schooled
9 in war, each with his sword at his thigh for fear at night. King Shlomo
10 built a palanquin of Lebanon wood; he ordered its pillars of silver, its seat of
gold; its cushions are purple, its space is lined with love by the daughters of
11 Jerusalem. Go out now and see, daughters of Zion; look at Shlomo the king,
at the crown his mother gave him on this his wedding day, on the day his heart
4 1 rejoiced. [*He*] How beautiful you are, my love, how beautiful, your
eyes like doves seen through your tresses; your hair like a flock of goats
2 flowing down Mount Gilad. Your teeth are like a perfect flock rising up from
3 washing: each mother ewe bore twins, not one among them lost.[5] Your lips
are a scarlet ribbon, and your speech is fair; your forehead like a pomegranate
4 glows through your tresses. Your neck is like the Tower of David, built in
5 splendor, a thousand shields adorning it, the shields of all the heroes. Your
6 two breasts are like young twins of a she-gazelle, pasturing in lilies. Until the
day has breathed its last, and the shadows have flown, I am going to the hill
7 of myrrh, to the slopes of frankincense. And all of you is beauty, my love, is
8 flawless, wholly. Come with me from Lebanon, bride; come down
with me from Lebanon; from the peak of Amana come, from the peaks of
9 Senir and Ḥermon,[6] from the lions' haunts, the leopards' hills. You have taken
my heart, my sister,[7] my bride; one glance of your eyes could take my heart,
10 any strand of the necklace you wear. How beautiful your love is, my sister, my
bride; how much better than wine your love, and finer than all perfumes the
11 scent of your oils. Your lips drip nectar, my bride; honey and milk lie under
12 your tongue, and on your dress lingers Lebanon's scent. A locked
13 garden is my sister, my bride, a locked well, a spring sealed up – yet your dry
ground is a pomegranate grove of sweetest fruits, henna plants, musk root;
14 musk root and saffron, calamus, cinnamon, fragrant trees of every kind, with

---

4 | Meaning in a dream.
5 | That is, your teeth are white and none is missing.
6 | In the Anti-Lebanon mountain range.
7 | A term of endearment.

יז עַד שֶׁיָּפוּחַ הַיּוֹם וְנָסוּ הַצְּלָלִים סֹב דְּמֵה־לְךָ דוֹדִי לִצְבִי אוֹ לְעֹפֶר
ג א הָאַיָּלִים עַל־הָרֵי בָתֶר: עַל־מִשְׁכָּבִי בַּלֵּילוֹת בִּקַּשְׁתִּי
ב אֵת שֶׁאָהֲבָה נַפְשִׁי בִּקַּשְׁתִּיו וְלֹא מְצָאתִיו: אָקוּמָה נָּא וַאֲסוֹבְבָה
בָעִיר בַּשְּׁוָקִים וּבָרְחֹבוֹת אֲבַקְשָׁה אֵת שֶׁאָהֲבָה נַפְשִׁי בִּקַּשְׁתִּיו וְלֹא
ג מְצָאתִיו: מְצָאוּנִי הַשֹּׁמְרִים הַסֹּבְבִים בָּעִיר אֵת שֶׁאָהֲבָה נַפְשִׁי
ד רְאִיתֶם: כִּמְעַט שֶׁעָבַרְתִּי מֵהֶם עַד שֶׁמָּצָאתִי אֵת שֶׁאָהֲבָה נַפְשִׁי
אֲחַזְתִּיו וְלֹא אַרְפֶּנּוּ עַד־שֶׁהֲבֵיאתִיו אֶל־בֵּית אִמִּי וְאֶל־חֶדֶר הוֹרָתִי:
ה הִשְׁבַּעְתִּי אֶתְכֶם בְּנוֹת יְרוּשָׁלִַם בִּצְבָאוֹת אוֹ בְּאַיְלוֹת הַשָּׂדֶה אִם־
ו תָּעִירוּ | וְאִם־תְּעוֹרְרוּ אֶת־הָאַהֲבָה עַד שֶׁתֶּחְפָּץ: מִי
זֹאת עֹלָה מִן־הַמִּדְבָּר כְּתִימְרוֹת עָשָׁן מְקֻטֶּרֶת מֹר וּלְבוֹנָה מִכֹּל
ז אַבְקַת רוֹכֵל: הִנֵּה מִטָּתוֹ שֶׁלִּשְׁלֹמֹה שִׁשִּׁים גִּבֹּרִים סָבִיב לָהּ מִגִּבֹּרֵי
ח יִשְׂרָאֵל: כֻּלָּם אֲחֻזֵי חֶרֶב מְלֻמְּדֵי מִלְחָמָה אִישׁ חַרְבּוֹ עַל־יְרֵכוֹ מִפַּחַד
ט בַּלֵּילוֹת: אַפִּרְיוֹן עָשָׂה לוֹ הַמֶּלֶךְ שְׁלֹמֹה מֵעֲצֵי הַלְּבָנוֹן:
י עַמּוּדָיו עָשָׂה כֶסֶף רְפִידָתוֹ זָהָב מֶרְכָּבוֹ אַרְגָּמָן תּוֹכוֹ רָצוּף אַהֲבָה
יא מִבְּנוֹת יְרוּשָׁלִָם: צְאֶינָה | וּרְאֶינָה בְּנוֹת צִיּוֹן בַּמֶּלֶךְ שְׁלֹמֹה בָּעֲטָרָה
ד א שֶׁעִטְּרָה־לּוֹ אִמּוֹ בְּיוֹם חֲתֻנָּתוֹ וּבְיוֹם שִׂמְחַת לִבּוֹ: הִנָּךְ
יָפָה רַעְיָתִי הִנָּךְ יָפָה עֵינַיִךְ יוֹנִים מִבַּעַד לְצַמָּתֵךְ שַׂעְרֵךְ כְּעֵדֶר הָעִזִּים
ב שֶׁגָּלְשׁוּ מֵהַר גִּלְעָד: שִׁנַּיִךְ כְּעֵדֶר הַקְּצוּבוֹת שֶׁעָלוּ מִן־הָרַחְצָה שֶׁכֻּלָּם
ג מַתְאִימוֹת וְשַׁכֻּלָה אֵין בָּהֶם: כְּחוּט הַשָּׁנִי שִׂפְתֹתַיִךְ וּמִדְבָּרֵיךְ נָאוֶה
ד כְּפֶלַח הָרִמּוֹן רַקָּתֵךְ מִבַּעַד לְצַמָּתֵךְ: כְּמִגְדַּל דָּוִיד צַוָּארֵךְ בָּנוּי
ה לְתַלְפִּיּוֹת אֶלֶף הַמָּגֵן תָּלוּי עָלָיו כֹּל שִׁלְטֵי הַגִּבֹּרִים: שְׁנֵי שָׁדַיִךְ כִּשְׁנֵי
ו עֳפָרִים תְּאוֹמֵי צְבִיָּה הָרוֹעִים בַּשּׁוֹשַׁנִּים: עַד שֶׁיָּפוּחַ הַיּוֹם וְנָסוּ הַצְּלָלִים
ז אֵלֶךְ לִי אֶל־הַר הַמּוֹר וְאֶל־גִּבְעַת הַלְּבוֹנָה: כֻּלָּךְ יָפָה רַעְיָתִי וּמוּם
ח אֵין בָּךְ: אִתִּי מִלְּבָנוֹן כַּלָּה אִתִּי מִלְּבָנוֹן תָּבוֹאִי תָּשׁוּרִי |
מֵרֹאשׁ אֲמָנָה מֵרֹאשׁ שְׂנִיר וְחֶרְמוֹן מִמְּעֹנוֹת אֲרָיוֹת מֵהַרְרֵי נְמֵרִים:
ט לִבַּבְתִּנִי אֲחֹתִי כַלָּה לִבַּבְתִּנִי באחד מֵעֵינַיִךְ בְּאַחַד עֲנָק מִצַּוְּרֹנָיִךְ: בְּאַחַת
י מַה־יָּפוּ דֹדַיִךְ אֲחֹתִי כַלָּה מַה־טֹּבוּ דֹדַיִךְ מִיַּיִן וְרֵיחַ שְׁמָנַיִךְ מִכָּל־
יא בְּשָׂמִים: נֹפֶת תִּטֹּפְנָה שִׂפְתוֹתַיִךְ כַּלָּה דְּבַשׁ וְחָלָב תַּחַת לְשׁוֹנֵךְ וְרֵיחַ
יב שַׂלְמֹתַיִךְ כְּרֵיחַ לְבָנוֹן: גַּן | נָעוּל אֲחֹתִי כַלָּה גַּל נָעוּל מַעְיָן
יג חָתוּם: שְׁלָחַיִךְ פַּרְדֵּס רִמּוֹנִים עִם פְּרִי מְגָדִים כְּפָרִים עִם־נְרָדִים:
יד נֵרְדְּ | וְכַרְכֹּם קָנֶה וְקִנָּמוֹן עִם כָּל־עֲצֵי לְבוֹנָה מֹר וַאֲהָלוֹת עִם כָּל־

15 myrrh plants and aloe, with all the finest spices, with a spring to water gardens,
16 a well of living waters, waters flowing down from Lebanon. [*She*] Wake
now, north wind; south wind, come; breathe life into my garden; let its
perfumes flow. Let my beloved come to his garden and eat his sweetest
5 1 fruits. [*He*] I have come into my garden, my sister, my bride; I have gathered
my myrrh and my balsam; I have eaten my honeycomb with honey; I have
drunk my wine with milk. [*Friends*] Eat, loved ones, eat; drink, drink deep of
2 love. [*She*] I am asleep; my heart is awake – my beloved's voice, he
is knocking – "Open for me, my sister, my love, my dove, my perfection, for
3 my head is covered with dew, my locks with drops of the night." "I have taken
off my dress; how can I put it on again? I have already washed my feet; how
4 can I dirty them?" My beloved withdrew his hand from the door, and my
5 being longed for him. I rose to open the door for my beloved; my hands were
dripping with myrrh, my fingers streaming myrrh oil over the handles of the
6 latch. I opened for my beloved – he had slipped away, gone. I fainted for him
as he spoke – I searched for him but could not find him; I called out but he
7 did not answer. The guards found me, those who go around the town; they
beat me, they wounded me, they pulled my shawl from me, those guardians
8 of the walls. Swear to me, daughters of Jerusalem: if you find my beloved,
9 swear that you will tell him – tell him I am sick with love. [*Friends*] What
makes your lover more than other lovers, most beautiful of women? What
makes your lover more than other men, that this is what you have us swear?
10 [*She*] He is bright, my beloved; he is glowing; you would know him among
11 ten thousand. His head shines like gold, fine gold, his hair cascading curls,
12 raven black; his eyes are like doves at springs of water, washed in milk, at rest
13 by the stream. His cheeks are like beds of balsam, like towers of perfume
14 herbs. His lips smell like lilies flowing with myrrh oil. His arms are like golden
bars set with aquamarine stones, his stomach like solid ivory inlaid with lapis
15 lazuli. His legs stand firm as marble pillars fixed on gold foundations. To see
16 him is like looking upon Lebanon, and he is as choice as its cedars. His mouth
is filled with sweetness; for all of him my longing. This is my beloved, this is
6 1 my love, daughters of Jerusalem. [*Friends*] Where has your beloved gone,
most beautiful of women? Where has your beloved turned? We shall search
2 for him with you. [*She*] My beloved has gone to his garden, down to the beds
3 of balsam to pasture in the gardens, to gather in lilies. I am my beloved's – my
beloved is mine – who pastures among lilies.
4 [*He*] My love, you are as beautiful as Tirtza,[8] as lovely as Jerusalem, as
5 terrifying as the ensigned armies. Turn your eyes from me for they have
overwhelmed me. Your hair is like a flock of goats streaming down from
6 Gilad. Your teeth are like a flock of ewes rising up from washing; each mother
7 ewe bore twins, not one among them lost. Your forehead like a pomegranate
8 glows through your tresses. Queens there are sixty, eighty concubines, and
9 maidens there are without number. But my dove, my perfection, is one –
one, unique to her mother – the shining one she bore. All the girls gaze at

8 | Capital of the Northern Kingdom before Shomron.

טו טז רָאשֵׁי בְשָׂמִים: מַעְיַן גַּנִּים בְּאֵר מַיִם חַיִּים וְנֹזְלִים מִן־לְבָנוֹן: עוּרִי
צָפוֹן וּבוֹאִי תֵימָן הָפִיחִי גַנִּי יִזְּלוּ בְשָׂמָיו יָבֹא דוֹדִי לְגַנּוֹ וְיֹאכַל פְּרִי
ה א מְגָדָיו: בָּאתִי לְגַנִּי אֲחֹתִי כַלָּה אָרִיתִי מוֹרִי עִם־בְּשָׂמִי אָכַלְתִּי
יַעְרִי עִם־דִּבְשִׁי שָׁתִיתִי יֵינִי עִם־חֲלָבִי אִכְלוּ רֵעִים שְׁתוּ וְשִׁכְרוּ
ב דּוֹדִים: אֲנִי יְשֵׁנָה וְלִבִּי עֵר קוֹל ׀ דּוֹדִי דוֹפֵק פִּתְחִי־לִי
אֲחֹתִי רַעְיָתִי יוֹנָתִי תַמָּתִי שֶׁרֹּאשִׁי נִמְלָא־טָל קְוֻצּוֹתַי רְסִיסֵי לָיְלָה:
ג פָּשַׁטְתִּי אֶת־כֻּתָּנְתִּי אֵיכָכָה אֶלְבָּשֶׁנָּה רָחַצְתִּי אֶת־רַגְלַי אֵיכָכָה
ד ה אֲטַנְּפֵם: דּוֹדִי שָׁלַח יָדוֹ מִן־הַחֹר וּמֵעַי הָמוּ עָלָיו: קַמְתִּי אֲנִי לִפְתֹּחַ
ו לְדוֹדִי וְיָדַי נָטְפוּ־מוֹר וְאֶצְבְּעֹתַי מוֹר עֹבֵר עַל כַּפּוֹת הַמַּנְעוּל: פָּתַחְתִּי
אֲנִי לְדוֹדִי וְדוֹדִי חָמַק עָבָר נַפְשִׁי יָצְאָה בְדַבְּרוֹ בִּקַּשְׁתִּיהוּ וְלֹא
ז מְצָאתִיהוּ קְרָאתִיו וְלֹא עָנָנִי: מְצָאֻנִי הַשֹּׁמְרִים הַסֹּבְבִים בָּעִיר הִכּוּנִי
ח פְצָעוּנִי נָשְׂאוּ אֶת־רְדִידִי מֵעָלַי שֹׁמְרֵי הַחֹמוֹת: הִשְׁבַּעְתִּי אֶתְכֶם
בְּנוֹת יְרוּשָׁלָם אִם־תִּמְצְאוּ אֶת־דּוֹדִי מַה־תַּגִּידוּ לוֹ שֶׁחוֹלַת אַהֲבָה
ט אָנִי: מַה־דּוֹדֵךְ מִדּוֹד הַיָּפָה בַּנָּשִׁים מַה־דּוֹדֵךְ מִדּוֹד שֶׁכָּכָה הִשְׁבַּעְתָּנוּ:
י יא דּוֹדִי צַח וְאָדוֹם דָּגוּל מֵרְבָבָה: רֹאשׁוֹ כֶּתֶם פָּז קְוֻצּוֹתָיו תַּלְתַּלִּים
יב שְׁחֹרוֹת כָּעוֹרֵב: עֵינָיו כְּיוֹנִים עַל־אֲפִיקֵי מָיִם רֹחֲצוֹת בֶּחָלָב יֹשְׁבוֹת
יג עַל־מִלֵּאת: לְחָיָו כַּעֲרוּגַת הַבֹּשֶׂם מִגְדְּלוֹת מֶרְקָחִים שִׂפְתוֹתָיו
יד שׁוֹשַׁנִּים נֹטְפוֹת מוֹר עֹבֵר: יָדָיו גְּלִילֵי זָהָב מְמֻלָּאִים בַּתַּרְשִׁישׁ מֵעָיו
טו עֶשֶׁת שֵׁן מְעֻלֶּפֶת סַפִּירִים: שׁוֹקָיו עַמּוּדֵי שֵׁשׁ מְיֻסָּדִים עַל־אַדְנֵי־פָז
טז מַרְאֵהוּ כַּלְּבָנוֹן בָּחוּר כָּאֲרָזִים: חִכּוֹ מַמְתַקִּים וְכֻלּוֹ מַחֲמַדִּים זֶה דוֹדִי
ו א וְזֶה רֵעִי בְּנוֹת יְרוּשָׁלָם: אָנָה הָלַךְ דּוֹדֵךְ הַיָּפָה בַּנָּשִׁים אָנָה פָּנָה דוֹדֵךְ
ב וּנְבַקְשֶׁנּוּ עִמָּךְ: דּוֹדִי יָרַד לְגַנּוֹ לַעֲרֻגוֹת הַבֹּשֶׂם לִרְעוֹת בַּגַּנִּים וְלִלְקֹט
ג שׁוֹשַׁנִּים: אֲנִי לְדוֹדִי וְדוֹדִי לִי הָרֹעֶה בַּשּׁוֹשַׁנִּים:
ד ה יָפָה אַתְּ רַעְיָתִי כְּתִרְצָה נָאוָה כִּירוּשָׁלָם אֲיֻמָּה כַּנִּדְגָּלוֹת: הָסֵבִּי
עֵינַיִךְ מִנֶּגְדִּי שֶׁהֵם הִרְהִיבֻנִי שַׂעְרֵךְ כְּעֵדֶר הָעִזִּים שֶׁגָּלְשׁוּ מִן־
ו הַגִּלְעָד: שִׁנַּיִךְ כְּעֵדֶר הָרְחֵלִים שֶׁעָלוּ מִן־הָרַחְצָה שֶׁכֻּלָּם מַתְאִימוֹת
ז ח וְשַׁכֻּלָה אֵין בָּהֶם: כְּפֶלַח הָרִמּוֹן רַקָּתֵךְ מִבַּעַד לְצַמָּתֵךְ: שִׁשִּׁים הֵמָּה
ט מְלָכוֹת וּשְׁמֹנִים פִּילַגְשִׁים וַעֲלָמוֹת אֵין מִסְפָּר: אַחַת הִיא יוֹנָתִי תַמָּתִי

her – declare that she is blessed – the queens and concubines – and speak her
10 praise. Who is this, like dawn to gaze upon, beautiful as the moon,
11 shining like the sun, as terrifying as the ensigned armies? [*She*] I went down
to the nut garden to see the spring growth by the stream, to see whether
12 the vines were in flower, whether the pomegranate buds had burst. I did
not know myself – I found myself amid the chariots of my princely people.
7 1 [*He*] Turn, turn back, Shulamite;[9] turn back, turn; let us see you. Why do you
2 gaze at the Shulamite as if she were a Maḥanayim[10] dancer? How lovely are
your steps in sandals, prince's daughter; the turn of your thighs like jewelry,
3 work of the artist's hands; your navel a circular bowl – may it never want for
4 wine; your belly curved like baled wheat, bounded round with lilies. Your
5 two breasts are like young twins of a she-gazelle, your neck an ivory tower,
your eyes like pools in Ḥeshbon,[11] like pools by the Bat Rabim Gate,[12] your
6 nose like the Tower of Lebanon gazing out to Damascus, your head rising
from you like the Carmel; its curls shine like purple – a king is tangled up
7 among its tresses. How beautiful you are, how good; love with all its joys.
8 9 Your bearing is like a date palm, your breasts its clustered fruits, but I said, "I
shall climb the date palm; I shall take hold of its branches," and your breasts
10 will be like clustered grapes, your breath the scent of apples. And your mouth
is like good wine, inside – [*She*] It is for my beloved, flowing freely, bringing
11 12 words to sleeping lips. I am my beloved's, and his longing is for me. Come,
13 my beloved, let us go to the fields; let us lodge in the villages; we will get up
early and go to the vineyards and see if the vine has flowered, if its blossoms
have opened out, and if the pomegranate buds have burst; there I shall give
14 you my love. The mandrakes impart their scent, and on our own doorstep
the sweetest of fruits, new and old; my beloved, I have hoarded them for you.
8 1 If only you could have been my brother, could have suckled at my mother's
breast. I would find you outside, I would kiss you, yet none would shame me.[13]
2 I would lead you; I would bring you to my mother's house; you would teach
me. I would give you to drink spiced wine, nectar of my pomegranate tree.
3 4 My head rests on his left arm, his right embraces me. Swear to me, daughters
of Jerusalem; tell me, why do you seek to waken, why to rouse, this love
5 before its time? [*Friends*] Who is this rising from the wilderness,
entwined with her beloved? [*She*] Beneath the apple tree I roused you where
6 your mother bore you, where in suffering she gave you birth. Set me like a
seal upon your heart, like the seal upon your arm – for love is as powerful as
death itself, and jealousy unyielding as Sheol;[14] it burns with sparks of fire,
7 with the LORD's own flame. Great waters cannot quench love, nor torrents

---

9 | Possibly a woman from the town of Shunem, or, alternatively, a feminine version of the name Shlomo.

10 | Literally "two camps," Maḥanayim may be the name of a place or a dance.

11 | East of Jerusalem, a place of fertile fields and vineyards (Is. 16:8–10) and the capital of the kingdom of the Amorite king Siḥon.

12 | An unknown location, perhaps in Ḥeshbon.

13 | The lover wishes for a natural closeness to her beloved that would not be considered indecent.

14 | The netherworld.

אַחַת הִיא לְאִמָּהּ בָּרָה הִיא לְיֽוֹלַדְתָּהּ רָאוּהָ בָנוֹת וַֽיְאַשְּׁרוּהָ מְלָכוֹת
י וּפִֽילַגְשִׁים וַֽיְהַלְלֽוּהָ׃ מִי־זֹאת הַנִּשְׁקָפָה כְּמוֹ־שָׁחַר יָפָה
יא כַלְּבָנָה בָּרָה כַּֽחַמָּה אֲיֻמָּה כַּנִּדְגָּלֽוֹת׃ אֶל־גִּנַּת אֱגוֹז יָרַדְתִּי לִרְאוֹת
יב בְּאִבֵּי הַנָּחַל לִרְאוֹת הֲפָֽרְחָה הַגֶּפֶן הֵנֵצוּ הָֽרִמֹּנִֽים׃ לֹא יָדַעְתִּי נַפְשִׁי
ז א שָׂמַתְנִי מַרְכְּבוֹת עַמִּי נָדִֽיב׃ שׁוּבִי שׁוּבִי הַשּֽׁוּלַמִּית שׁוּבִי שׁוּבִי וְנֶחֱזֶה־
ב בָּךְ מַה־תֶּֽחֱזוּ בַּשּֽׁוּלַמִּית כִּמְחֹלַת הַֽמַּחֲנָֽיִם׃ מַה־יָּפוּ פְעָמַיִךְ בַּנְּעָלִים
ג בַּת־נָדִיב חַמּוּקֵי יְרֵכַיִךְ כְּמוֹ חֲלָאִים מַעֲשֵׂה יְדֵי אָמָּֽן׃ שָׁרְרֵךְ אַגַּן
ד הַסַּהַר אַל־יֶחְסַר הַמָּזֶג בִּטְנֵךְ עֲרֵמַת חִטִּים סוּגָה בַּשּׁוֹשַׁנִּֽים׃ שְׁנֵי
ה שָׁדַיִךְ כִּשְׁנֵי עֳפָרִים תָּאֳמֵי צְבִיָּֽה׃ צַוָּארֵךְ כְּמִגְדַּל הַשֵּׁן עֵינַיִךְ בְּרֵכוֹת
בְּחֶשְׁבּוֹן עַל־שַׁעַר בַּת־רַבִּים אַפֵּךְ כְּמִגְדַּל הַלְּבָנוֹן צוֹפֶה פְּנֵי דַמָּֽשֶׂק׃
ו רֹאשֵׁךְ עָלַיִךְ כַּכַּרְמֶל וְדַלַּת רֹאשֵׁךְ כָּֽאַרְגָּמָן מֶלֶךְ אָסוּר בָּֽרְהָטִֽים׃
ז ח מַה־יָּפִית וּמַה־נָּעַמְתְּ אַהֲבָה בַּֽתַּעֲנוּגִֽים׃ זֹאת קוֹמָתֵךְ דָּֽמְתָה לְתָמָר
ט וְשָׁדַיִךְ לְאַשְׁכֹּלֽוֹת׃ אָמַרְתִּי אֶעֱלֶה בְתָמָר אֹֽחֲזָה בְּסַנְסִנָּיו וְיִֽהְיוּ־נָא
י שָׁדַיִךְ כְּאֶשְׁכְּלוֹת הַגֶּפֶן וְרֵיחַ אַפֵּךְ כַּתַּפּוּחִֽים׃ וְחִכֵּךְ כְּיֵין הַטּוֹב הוֹלֵךְ
יא לְדוֹדִי לְמֵישָׁרִים דּוֹבֵב שִׂפְתֵי יְשֵׁנִֽים׃ אֲנִי לְדוֹדִי וְעָלַי תְּשׁוּקָתֽוֹ׃
יב יג לְכָה דוֹדִי נֵצֵא הַשָּׂדֶה נָלִינָה בַּכְּפָרִֽים׃ נַשְׁכִּימָה לַכְּרָמִים נִרְאֶה
אִם־פָּֽרְחָה הַגֶּפֶן פִּתַּח הַסְּמָדַר הֵנֵצוּ הָֽרִמּוֹנִים שָׁם אֶתֵּן אֶת־דֹּדַי לָֽךְ׃
יד הַֽדּוּדָאִים נָֽתְנוּ־רֵיחַ וְעַל־פְּתָחֵינוּ כָּל־מְגָדִים חֲדָשִׁים גַּם־יְשָׁנִים דּוֹדִי
ח א צָפַנְתִּי לָֽךְ׃ מִי יִתֶּנְךָ כְּאָח לִי יוֹנֵק שְׁדֵי אִמִּי אֶמְצָֽאֲךָ בַחוּץ אֶשָּׁקְךָ
ב גַּם לֹא־יָבֻזוּ לִֽי׃ אֶנְהָֽגְךָ אֲבִיאֲךָ אֶל־בֵּית אִמִּי תְּלַמְּדֵנִי אַשְׁקְךָ מִיַּיִן
ג ד הָרֶקַח מֵעֲסִיס רִמֹּנִֽי׃ שְׂמֹאלוֹ תַּחַת רֹאשִׁי וִימִינוֹ תְּחַבְּקֵֽנִי׃ הִשְׁבַּעְתִּי
אֶתְכֶם בְּנוֹת יְרוּשָׁלִָם מַה־תָּעִירוּ ׀ וּֽמַה־תְּעֹֽרְרוּ אֶת־הָאַהֲבָה עַד
ה שֶׁתֶּחְפָּֽץ׃ מִי זֹאת עֹלָה מִן־הַמִּדְבָּר מִתְרַפֶּקֶת עַל־דּוֹדָהּ
תַּחַת הַתַּפּוּחַ עֽוֹרַרְתִּיךָ שָׁמָּה חִבְּלַתְךָ אִמֶּךָ שָׁמָּה חִבְּלָה יְלָדַֽתְךָ׃
ו שִׂימֵנִי כַֽחוֹתָם עַל־לִבֶּךָ כַּֽחוֹתָם עַל־זְרוֹעֶךָ כִּֽי־עַזָּה כַמָּוֶת אַהֲבָה
ז קָשָׁה כִשְׁאוֹל קִנְאָה רְשָׁפֶיהָ רִשְׁפֵּי אֵשׁ שַׁלְהֶבֶתְיָֽה׃ מַיִם רַבִּים לֹא

sweep it by. If a man offered all his wealth for love – they would laugh him
8 to shame. [*Brothers*] We have a little sister; her breasts are not yet
9 grown. What shall we do for our sister when a suitor comes for her? If she is a
wall, we will build a silver watchtower; if a door, we will bar her up with cedar.
10 [*She*] But I am a wall; my breasts are like towers. It was then that I found peace
11 in his eyes. [*He*] Once, Shlomo had a vineyard at Baal Hamon.[15] He gave the
vineyard over to the keepers; each keeper brought him in a thousand in silver
12 from the fruits. My vineyard stands before me, my own: Shlomo, keep your
13 thousand; pay two hundred to the keepers of the fruits. "You who still sit in
14 the gardens, friends listen for your voice. Have me hear." [*She*] Away with you,
my beloved, like a gazelle or a young deer over perfumed hills.

---

15 | An unidentified place meaning "master of wealth," perhaps hinting at Shlomo's riches.

יוּכְלוּ לְכַבּוֹת אֶת־הָאַהֲבָה וּנְהָרוֹת לֹא יִשְׁטְפוּהָ אִם־יִתֵּן אִישׁ אֶת־
ח כָּל־הוֹן בֵּיתוֹ בָּאַהֲבָה בּוֹז יָבוּזוּ לוֹ׃ אָחוֹת לָנוּ קְטַנָּה
ט וְשָׁדַיִם אֵין לָהּ מַה־נַּעֲשֶׂה לַאֲחוֹתֵנוּ בַּיּוֹם שֶׁיְּדֻבַּר־בָּהּ׃ אִם־חוֹמָה
י הִיא נִבְנֶה עָלֶיהָ טִירַת כָּסֶף וְאִם־דֶּלֶת הִיא נָצוּר עָלֶיהָ לוּחַ אָרֶז׃ אֲנִי
יא חוֹמָה וְשָׁדַי כַּמִּגְדָּלוֹת אָז הָיִיתִי בְעֵינָיו כְּמוֹצְאֵת שָׁלוֹם׃ כֶּרֶם הָיָה
לִשְׁלֹמֹה בְּבַעַל הָמוֹן נָתַן אֶת־הַכֶּרֶם לַנֹּטְרִים אִישׁ יָבִא בְּפִרְיוֹ אֶלֶף
יב כָּסֶף׃ כַּרְמִי שֶׁלִּי לְפָנָי הָאֶלֶף לְךָ שְׁלֹמֹה וּמָאתַיִם לְנֹטְרִים אֶת־פִּרְיוֹ׃
יג יד הַיּוֹשֶׁבֶת בַּגַּנִּים חֲבֵרִים מַקְשִׁיבִים לְקוֹלֵךְ הַשְׁמִיעִנִי׃ בְּרַח ׀ דּוֹדִי
וּדְמֵה־לְךָ לִצְבִי אוֹ לְעֹפֶר הָאַיָּלִים עַל הָרֵי בְשָׂמִים׃

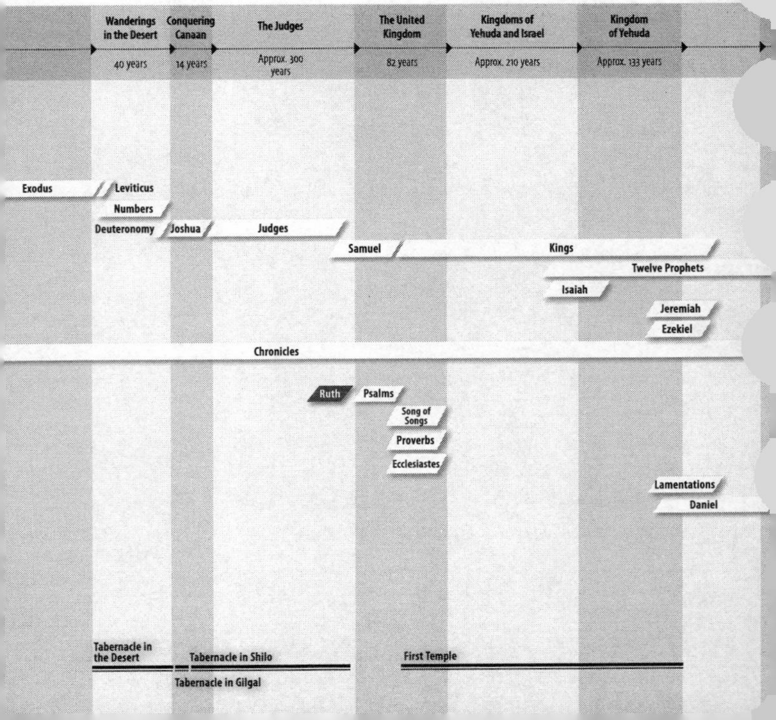

Wanderings in the Desert
40 years
Conquering Canaan
14 years
The Judges
Approx. 300 years
The United Kingdom
82 years
Kingdoms of Yehuda and Israel
Approx. 210 years
Kingdom of Yehuda
Approx. 133 years
Exodus
Leviticus
Numbers
Deuteronomy
Joshua
Judges
Samuel
Kings
Twelve Prophets
Isaiah
Jeremiah
Ezekiel
Chronicles
Ruth
Psalms
Song of Songs
Proverbs
Ecclesiastes
Lamentations
Daniel
Tabernacle in the Desert
Tabernacle in Shilo
Tabernacle in Gilgal
First Temple

רות
RUT/RUTH

RUTH			
	Naomi's family: Death, crisis, and alienation	Boaz and Ruth: Promises of sustenance and marriage	Naomi's family: Acceptance, marriage, and birth
	Ch. 1	2–3	4
	Approx. 10 years		

1 1 Once, in the days when the judges ruled,[1] there was a famine in the land. One
man set out from Beit Leḥem of Yehuda and journeyed to live for a while in
2 the land of Moav, and his wife and two sons came with him. This man's name
was Elimelekh, his wife's was Naomi, and his two sons' names were Maḥlon
and Kilyon, all Efratites[2] from Beit Leḥem of Yehuda. They duly arrived
3 in the fields of Moav, and there they stayed. But then Elimelekh, Naomi's
4 husband, died, and she was left there with her two sons. Both of them married
Moabite women – the first was called Orpa, the second Ruth – and they
5 lived on there for some ten years. After that, the two of them – Maḥlon and
Kilyon – died as well, and the woman was left bereaved of both her children
6 and her husband. She got up, her daughters-in-law with her, to return from
the land of Moav, for word had reached her in the land of Moav that the Lord
7 had brought His people to mind and granted them bread. So she left the place
where she had been, both of her daughters-in-law with her, and set off along
8 the way back to the land of Yehuda. But to her two daughters-in-law she said,
"Go on now, turn back, each to your mother's home, and may the Lord show
9 you that kindness that you have shown the dead and me. The Lord grant that
you find a place of rest, each in your husband's home." As she kissed them,
10 they wept aloud and said, "No. We shall return with you to your people."
11 Said Naomi, "Turn back, daughters; why would you come with me? Have
12 I still sons in my womb who could be husbands to you? Turn back, my
daughters – go; I am too old to be with a man. Even were I to say, 'There is
hope for me still,' were I even this night to be married, even if I could bear
13 sons again, are you to wait for them as they grow? Would you be chained to
them, never to be with another man? No, daughters, for your presence is most
14 bitter to me now, for the hand of the Lord has beaten me." Aloud they wept
15 still more, then Orpa kissed her mother-in-law – but Ruth clung to her. And
Naomi said, "Your sister-in-law has turned back to her people, to her gods.
16 Turn back after your sister-in-law." But Ruth replied, "Do not entreat me to
leave you, to turn back, not to walk after you. For wherever you walk, I shall
walk, and wherever you stay, there I stay. Your people is my people; your God
17 is my God. Wherever you die, there I die, and there shall I be buried. So may
the Lord do to me – and more – for death alone will separate me from you."
18 Naomi saw that Ruth was determined to come with her, and she spoke to her
19 no more. The two of them walked on until they came to Beit Leḥem, and
when they arrived at Beit Leḥem, the whole town crowded around as the
20 women asked, "Can this be Naomi?" She said to the women, "Call me not
21 Naomi. Call me Mara,[3] for Shaddai has made my life bitter beyond words. I
was full when I left this place, and empty has the Lord returned me. Why
call me, 'Naomi'? the Lord has spoken up against me; Shaddai has ruined
22 me." This is how Naomi, returning from the land of Moav with her daughter-
in-law, Ruth the Moabite, returned. They arrived at Beit Leḥem just as the

---

1 | Before the establishment of the monarchy.

2 | Efrat is another name for Beit Leḥem.

3 | Naomi means "pleasantness"; Mara means "bitterness."

א א וַיְהִי בִּימֵי שְׁפֹט הַשֹּׁפְטִים וַיְהִי רָעָב בָּאָרֶץ וַיֵּלֶךְ אִישׁ מִבֵּית לֶחֶם
ב יְהוּדָה לָגוּר בִּשְׂדֵי מוֹאָב הוּא וְאִשְׁתּוֹ וּשְׁנֵי בָנָיו: וְשֵׁם הָאִישׁ אֱלִימֶלֶךְ
וְשֵׁם אִשְׁתּוֹ נָעֳמִי וְשֵׁם שְׁנֵי־בָנָיו | מַחְלוֹן וְכִלְיוֹן אֶפְרָתִים מִבֵּית לֶחֶם
ג יְהוּדָה וַיָּבֹאוּ שְׂדֵי־מוֹאָב וַיִּהְיוּ־שָׁם: וַיָּמָת אֱלִימֶלֶךְ אִישׁ נָעֳמִי
ד וַתִּשָּׁאֵר הִיא וּשְׁנֵי בָנֶיהָ: וַיִּשְׂאוּ לָהֶם נָשִׁים מֹאֲבִיּוֹת שֵׁם הָאַחַת
ה עָרְפָּה וְשֵׁם הַשֵּׁנִית רוּת וַיֵּשְׁבוּ שָׁם כְּעֶשֶׂר שָׁנִים: וַיָּמֻתוּ גַם־שְׁנֵיהֶם
ו מַחְלוֹן וְכִלְיוֹן וַתִּשָּׁאֵר הָאִשָּׁה מִשְּׁנֵי יְלָדֶיהָ וּמֵאִישָׁהּ: וַתָּקָם הִיא
וְכַלֹּתֶיהָ וַתָּשָׁב מִשְּׂדֵי מוֹאָב כִּי שָׁמְעָה בִּשְׂדֵה מוֹאָב כִּי־פָקַד יהוה
ז אֶת־עַמּוֹ לָתֵת לָהֶם לָחֶם: וַתֵּצֵא מִן־הַמָּקוֹם אֲשֶׁר הָיְתָה־שָׁמָּה וּשְׁתֵּי
ח כַלֹּתֶיהָ עִמָּהּ וַתֵּלַכְנָה בַדֶּרֶךְ לָשׁוּב אֶל־אֶרֶץ יְהוּדָה: וַתֹּאמֶר נָעֳמִי
לִשְׁתֵּי כַלֹּתֶיהָ לֵכְנָה שֹּׁבְנָה אִשָּׁה לְבֵית אִמָּהּ יַעֲשֶׂה יהוה עִמָּכֶם חֶסֶד יַעַשׂ
ט כַּאֲשֶׁר עֲשִׂיתֶם עִם־הַמֵּתִים וְעִמָּדִי: יִתֵּן יהוה לָכֶם וּמְצֶאןָ מְנוּחָה
י אִשָּׁה בֵּית אִישָׁהּ וַתִּשַּׁק לָהֶן וַתִּשֶּׂאנָה קוֹלָן וַתִּבְכֶּינָה: וַתֹּאמַרְנָה־לָּהּ
יא כִּי־אִתָּךְ נָשׁוּב לְעַמֵּךְ: וַתֹּאמֶר נָעֳמִי שֹׁבְנָה בְנֹתַי לָמָּה תֵלַכְנָה עִמִּי
יב הַעוֹד־לִי בָנִים בְּמֵעַי וְהָיוּ לָכֶם לַאֲנָשִׁים: שֹׁבְנָה בְנֹתַי לֵכְןָ כִּי זָקַנְתִּי
מִהְיוֹת לְאִישׁ כִּי אָמַרְתִּי יֶשׁ־לִי תִקְוָה גַּם הָיִיתִי הַלַּיְלָה לְאִישׁ וְגַם
יג יָלַדְתִּי בָנִים: הֲלָהֵן | תְּשַׂבֵּרְנָה עַד אֲשֶׁר יִגְדָּלוּ הֲלָהֵן תֵּעָגֵנָה לְבִלְתִּי
הֱיוֹת לְאִישׁ אַל בְּנֹתַי כִּי־מַר־לִי מְאֹד מִכֶּם כִּי־יָצְאָה בִי יַד־יהוה:
יד וַתִּשֶּׂנָה קוֹלָן וַתִּבְכֶּינָה עוֹד וַתִּשַּׁק עָרְפָּה לַחֲמוֹתָהּ וְרוּת דָּבְקָה
טו בָּהּ: וַתֹּאמֶר הִנֵּה שָׁבָה יְבִמְתֵּךְ אֶל־עַמָּהּ וְאֶל־אֱלֹהֶיהָ שׁוּבִי אַחֲרֵי
טז יְבִמְתֵּךְ: וַתֹּאמֶר רוּת אַל־תִּפְגְּעִי־בִי לְעָזְבֵךְ לָשׁוּב מֵאַחֲרָיִךְ כִּי אֶל־
יז אֲשֶׁר תֵּלְכִי אֵלֵךְ וּבַאֲשֶׁר תָּלִינִי אָלִין עַמֵּךְ עַמִּי וֵאלֹהַיִךְ אֱלֹהָי: בַּאֲשֶׁר
תָּמוּתִי אָמוּת וְשָׁם אֶקָּבֵר כֹּה יַעֲשֶׂה יהוה לִי וְכֹה יֹסִיף כִּי הַמָּוֶת
יח יַפְרִיד בֵּינִי וּבֵינֵךְ: וַתֵּרֶא כִּי־מִתְאַמֶּצֶת הִיא לָלֶכֶת אִתָּהּ וַתֶּחְדַּל
יט לְדַבֵּר אֵלֶיהָ: וַתֵּלַכְנָה שְׁתֵּיהֶם עַד־בֹּאָנָה בֵּית לָחֶם וַיְהִי כְּבֹאָנָה
כ בֵּית לֶחֶם וַתֵּהֹם כָּל־הָעִיר עֲלֵיהֶן וַתֹּאמַרְנָה הֲזֹאת נָעֳמִי: וַתֹּאמֶר
אֲלֵיהֶן אַל־תִּקְרֶאנָה לִי נָעֳמִי קְרֶאןָ לִי מָרָא כִּי־הֵמַר שַׁדַּי לִי מְאֹד:
כא אֲנִי מְלֵאָה הָלַכְתִּי וְרֵיקָם הֱשִׁיבַנִי יהוה לָמָּה תִקְרֶאנָה לִי נָעֳמִי וַיהוה
כב עָנָה בִי וְשַׁדַּי הֵרַע־לִי: וַתָּשָׁב נָעֳמִי וְרוּת הַמּוֹאֲבִיָּה כַלָּתָהּ עִמָּהּ
הַשָּׁבָה מִשְּׂדֵי מוֹאָב וְהֵמָּה בָּאוּ בֵּית לֶחֶם בִּתְחִלַּת קְצִיר שְׂעֹרִים:

2 1 barley harvest began. Naomi had a relative from her husband Elimelekh's
2 family, a man of substance and great strength: his name was Boaz. Ruth the
Moabite said to Naomi, "I shall go to the field and gather the fallen grains,[4]
and follow after anyone who should show me favor." Naomi said, "Go, then,
3 my daughter," and so she went. She came and started to gather in the field
after the harvestmen, and it chanced to be the field plot of Boaz that she
4 came to – that man of Elimelekh's family. And there came Boaz himself,
arriving from Beit Leḥem and saying to the harvestmen, "The Lord be with
5 you." "The Lord bless you," they replied. "Whose is that young woman
6 over there?" asked Boaz of his servant in charge of the harvestmen. "That is
some Moabite girl," replied the servant in charge of the harvestmen, "the one
7 who came back with Naomi from the land of Moav. She said, 'Let me come
gleaning, gathering among the sheaves where the harvestmen have been,' and
so she came. She has been standing out here from early morning until now
8 and hardly sat at all in the shelter." Boaz went to Ruth and said, "Daughter,
take heed. Do not go gleaning in any other field, and do not leave this one;
9 cling close by my young women. Keep your eyes on the field they are
harvesting from and follow after them. I have instructed the young men by
no means to touch you. When you are thirsty, go to the jugs and drink of the
10 water the young men have drawn." Ruth fell upon her face, bowing low, and
she asked him, "Why is it that I have found favor in your eyes, that you give
11 me recognition such as this when I am a stranger?" Boaz said, "I have heard
of all you have done for your mother-in-law ever since your husband died, of
how you left your father, your mother, the land of your birth, and came to a
12 people you knew not the day before. May the Lord repay your labors; may
your reward be full at the hand of the Lord, God of Israel, under whose
13 mantle you come to take shelter." "Sir," she said, "I hope to find favor in your
eyes, for you give me solace, for you have spoken to your servant's heart
14 though I am not fit to be your servant." When the time came for eating, Boaz
said to her, "Come here; eat of this food and dip your bread in the vinegar."
She sat down beside the harvestmen, and he served her roasted grains, and
15 she ate and had her fill with more left over. And when she stood up to begin
gleaning again, Boaz instructed his workers, "Let her glean among the sheaves
16 as well; do not disgrace her. Drop some ears from the bundles as well; leave
17 them, let her glean them, and do not reproach her." Ruth carried on gleaning
in the field until evening, then threshed what she had gleaned; it was almost
18 an ephah of barley.[5] She lifted it up and came into the town. Her mother-in-
law saw what she had gleaned; she produced all that was left after she had
19 eaten her fill and gave it to her. "Where did you gather today," she asked, "and
where did you work? Bless whoever recognized you so." So Ruth told her
mother-in-law under whose patronage she had worked: "The man's name is
20 Boaz, with whom I worked today." Said Naomi to her daughter-in-law, "The

4 | These grains were always left for the poor; see Leviticus 19:9–10.

5 | An ephah is about 21 quarts (19.87 liters), a very large measure for one person to glean and carry home.

ב א וּלְנָעֳמִי מידע לְאִישָׁהּ אִישׁ גִּבּוֹר חַיִל מִמִּשְׁפַּחַת אֱלִימֶלֶךְ וּשְׁמוֹ מוֹדַע
ב בֹּעַז׃ וַתֹּאמֶר רוּת הַמּוֹאֲבִיָּה אֶל־נָעֳמִי אֵלְכָה־נָּא הַשָּׂדֶה וַאֲלַקֳטָה
ג בַשִּׁבֳּלִים אַחַר אֲשֶׁר אֶמְצָא־חֵן בְּעֵינָיו וַתֹּאמֶר לָהּ לְכִי בִתִּי׃ וַתֵּלֶךְ
וַתָּבוֹא וַתְּלַקֵּט בַּשָּׂדֶה אַחֲרֵי הַקֹּצְרִים וַיִּקֶר מִקְרֶהָ חֶלְקַת הַשָּׂדֶה
ד לְבֹעַז אֲשֶׁר מִמִּשְׁפַּחַת אֱלִימֶלֶךְ׃ וְהִנֵּה־בֹעַז בָּא מִבֵּית לֶחֶם וַיֹּאמֶר
ה לַקּוֹצְרִים יהוה עִמָּכֶם וַיֹּאמְרוּ לוֹ יְבָרֶכְךָ יהוה׃ וַיֹּאמֶר בֹּעַז לְנַעֲרוֹ
ו הַנִּצָּב עַל־הַקּוֹצְרִים לְמִי הַנַּעֲרָה הַזֹּאת׃ וַיַּעַן הַנַּעַר הַנִּצָּב עַל־
הַקּוֹצְרִים וַיֹּאמַר נַעֲרָה מוֹאֲבִיָּה הִיא הַשָּׁבָה עִם־נָעֳמִי מִשְּׂדֵה מוֹאָב׃
ז וַתֹּאמֶר אֲלַקֳטָה־נָּא וְאָסַפְתִּי בָעֳמָרִים אַחֲרֵי הַקּוֹצְרִים וַתָּבוֹא
ח וַתַּעֲמוֹד מֵאָז הַבֹּקֶר וְעַד־עַתָּה זֶה שִׁבְתָּהּ הַבַּיִת מְעָט׃ וַיֹּאמֶר בֹּעַז
אֶל־רוּת הֲלוֹא שָׁמַעַתְּ בִּתִּי אַל־תֵּלְכִי לִלְקֹט בְּשָׂדֶה אַחֵר וְגַם לֹא
ט תַעֲבוּרִי מִזֶּה וְכֹה תִדְבָּקִין עִם־נַעֲרֹתָי׃ עֵינַיִךְ בַּשָּׂדֶה אֲשֶׁר־יִקְצֹרוּן
וְהָלַכְתְּ אַחֲרֵיהֶן הֲלוֹא צִוִּיתִי אֶת־הַנְּעָרִים לְבִלְתִּי נָגְעֵךְ וְצָמִת וְהָלַכְתְּ
י אֶל־הַכֵּלִים וְשָׁתִית מֵאֲשֶׁר יִשְׁאֲבוּן הַנְּעָרִים׃ וַתִּפֹּל עַל־פָּנֶיהָ וַתִּשְׁתַּחוּ
אָרְצָה וַתֹּאמֶר אֵלָיו מַדּוּעַ מָצָאתִי חֵן בְּעֵינֶיךָ לְהַכִּירֵנִי וְאָנֹכִי נָכְרִיָּה׃
יא וַיַּעַן בֹּעַז וַיֹּאמֶר לָהּ הֻגֵּד הֻגַּד לִי כֹּל אֲשֶׁר־עָשִׂית אֶת־חֲמוֹתֵךְ אַחֲרֵי
מוֹת אִישֵׁךְ וַתַּעַזְבִי אָבִיךְ וְאִמֵּךְ וְאֶרֶץ מוֹלַדְתֵּךְ וַתֵּלְכִי אֶל־עַם אֲשֶׁר
יב לֹא־יָדַעַתְּ תְּמוֹל שִׁלְשׁוֹם׃ יְשַׁלֵּם יהוה פָּעֳלֵךְ וּתְהִי מַשְׂכֻּרְתֵּךְ שְׁלֵמָה
יג מֵעִם יהוה אֱלֹהֵי יִשְׂרָאֵל אֲשֶׁר־בָּאת לַחֲסוֹת תַּחַת־כְּנָפָיו׃ וַתֹּאמֶר
אֶמְצָא־חֵן בְּעֵינֶיךָ אֲדֹנִי כִּי נִחַמְתָּנִי וְכִי דִבַּרְתָּ עַל־לֵב שִׁפְחָתֶךָ וְאָנֹכִי
יד לֹא אֶהְיֶה כְּאַחַת שִׁפְחֹתֶיךָ׃ וַיֹּאמֶר לָהּ בֹעַז לְעֵת הָאֹכֶל גֹּשִׁי הֲלֹם
וְאָכַלְתְּ מִן־הַלֶּחֶם וְטָבַלְתְּ פִּתֵּךְ בַּחֹמֶץ וַתֵּשֶׁב מִצַּד הַקֹּצְרִים וַיִּצְבָּט־
טו לָהּ קָלִי וַתֹּאכַל וַתִּשְׂבַּע וַתֹּתַר׃ וַתָּקָם לְלַקֵּט וַיְצַו בֹּעַז אֶת־נְעָרָיו
טז לֵאמֹר גַּם בֵּין הָעֳמָרִים תְּלַקֵּט וְלֹא תַכְלִימוּהָ׃ וְגַם שֹׁל־תָּשֹׁלּוּ לָהּ
יז מִן־הַצְּבָתִים וַעֲזַבְתֶּם וְלִקְּטָה וְלֹא תִגְעֲרוּ־בָהּ׃ וַתְּלַקֵּט בַּשָּׂדֶה עַד־
יח הָעָרֶב וַתַּחְבֹּט אֵת אֲשֶׁר־לִקֵּטָה וַיְהִי כְּאֵיפָה שְׂעֹרִים׃ וַתִּשָּׂא וַתָּבוֹא
הָעִיר וַתֵּרֶא חֲמוֹתָהּ אֵת אֲשֶׁר־לִקֵּטָה וַתּוֹצֵא וַתִּתֶּן־לָהּ אֵת אֲשֶׁר־
יט הוֹתִרָה מִשָּׂבְעָהּ׃ וַתֹּאמֶר לָהּ חֲמוֹתָהּ אֵיפֹה לִקַּטְתְּ הַיּוֹם וְאָנָה עָשִׂית
יְהִי מַכִּירֵךְ בָּרוּךְ וַתַּגֵּד לַחֲמוֹתָהּ אֵת אֲשֶׁר־עָשְׂתָה עִמּוֹ וַתֹּאמֶר שֵׁם
כ הָאִישׁ אֲשֶׁר עָשִׂיתִי עִמּוֹ הַיּוֹם בֹּעַז׃ וַתֹּאמֶר נָעֳמִי לְכַלָּתָהּ בָּרוּךְ הוּא

Lord bless him, for he has not abandoned his kindness to the living or the
dead," and Naomi told her, "The man is our relative, one of our redeemers."
21 "He said to me as well," said Ruth the Moabite, "'Cling by my young men until
22 they finish all my harvest,'" and Naomi told her daughter-in-law Ruth, "That
is well, my daughter. Go out with his young women; do not go and come to
23 harm in other fields." So it was that she clung by Boaz's young women to glean
until the barley harvest was over, and then the wheat, and after that she sat at
3 1 home with her mother-in-law. "Daughter," said her mother-in-law Naomi to
her, "do I not wish I could find you a resting place that would be good for you?
2 Now there is Boaz, our relative, whose young women you were with, and he
3 will be doing his winnowing at the threshing floor tonight. You are going to
wash yourself and anoint yourself and put on your dress and go down to that
threshing floor. Do not let the man know that you are there until he has
4 finished eating and drinking. And when he lies down, take note of the place
where he lies, and afterward go there, uncover his feet, and lie down also – he
5 will tell you what to do next." "I shall do," said Ruth, "all that you tell me to
6 do." She went down to the threshing floor and did exactly as her mother-in-
7 law had instructed her. Boaz ate and drank and was happy, and he went and
lay down beside the heap of grain. Then she came to him silently, uncovered
8 his feet, and lay herself down. At midnight the man started and turned
9 over – there was a woman lying at his feet! "Who are you?" he said, and she
answered, "I am your maidservant Ruth – spread your mantle over your
10 maidservant, for you are a redeemer." And he replied, "The Lord bless you,
daughter, for this last kindness is yet greater than your first, for you have not
11 gone after the young men, poor or rich. Now, daughter, do not be afraid. I
shall do all that you ask, for all within my people's gate know well that you are
12 a woman of great strength, and I am indeed a redeemer to you, but there is a
13 redeemer still closer than me. Stay on here tonight, and in the morning, if he
wishes to redeem you, good: let him redeem. And if he cares not to redeem
14 you, I shall redeem you myself, as the Lord lives – stay until morning." So
she lay at his feet until morning and left before one person could recognize
another. "Let not a soul know there was a woman at the threshing floor," said
15 he. And then, "Give me the wrap that you are wearing; hold it out." She did,
and he measured six measures of barley into it; he placed it upon her and
16 went out into the city. She came to her mother-in-law, "Who are you, my
daughter?"[6] she said. And Ruth told her all that the man had done for her.
17 "He gave me these six measures of barley," she said. "He said to me, 'Do not
18 go back to your mother-in-law empty-handed.'" Said Naomi, "Sit down now,
daughter, until you find out how the matter will fall, for that man will not rest
4 1 unless the matter is settled today." Boaz went up to the city gate and sat down,
and the very redeemer of whom he had spoken passed by. "Peloni Almoni,"
2 said Boaz, "come here and be seated," and he turned aside and sat down. Then
Boaz took ten men from among the elders of the city, "Be seated here," he
3 said, and they too sat. Then he said to the redeemer, "Naomi, who came back

6 | Meaning "how are you?" or "what transpired?"

לַיהוָה אֲשֶׁר לֹא־עָזַב חַסְדּוֹ אֶת־הַחַיִּים וְאֶת־הַמֵּתִים וַתֹּאמֶר לָהּ
כא נָעֳמִי קָרוֹב לָנוּ הָאִישׁ מִגֹּאֲלֵנוּ הוּא: וַתֹּאמֶר רוּת הַמּוֹאֲבִיָּה גַּם ׀
כִּי־אָמַר אֵלַי עִם־הַנְּעָרִים אֲשֶׁר־לִי תִּדְבָּקִין עַד אִם־כִּלּוּ אֵת כָּל־
כב הַקָּצִיר אֲשֶׁר־לִי: וַתֹּאמֶר נָעֳמִי אֶל־רוּת כַּלָּתָהּ טוֹב בִּתִּי כִּי תֵצְאִי
כג עִם־נַעֲרוֹתָיו וְלֹא יִפְגְּעוּ־בָךְ בְּשָׂדֶה אַחֵר: וַתִּדְבַּק בְּנַעֲרוֹת בֹּעַז לְלַקֵּט
ג א עַד־כְּלוֹת קְצִיר־הַשְּׂעֹרִים וּקְצִיר הַחִטִּים וַתֵּשֶׁב אֶת־חֲמוֹתָהּ: וַתֹּאמֶר
ב לָהּ נָעֳמִי חֲמוֹתָהּ בִּתִּי הֲלֹא אֲבַקֶּשׁ־לָךְ מָנוֹחַ אֲשֶׁר יִיטַב־לָךְ: וְעַתָּה
הֲלֹא בֹעַז מֹדַעְתָּנוּ אֲשֶׁר הָיִית אֶת־נַעֲרוֹתָיו הִנֵּה־הוּא זֹרֶה אֶת־גֹּרֶן
ג הַשְּׂעֹרִים הַלָּיְלָה: וְרָחַצְתְּ ׀ וָסַכְתְּ וְשַׂמְתְּ שמלתך עָלַיִךְ וירדתי הַגֹּרֶן שִׂמְלֹתַיִךְ וְיָרַדְתְּ
ד אַל־תִּוָּדְעִי לָאִישׁ עַד כַּלֹּתוֹ לֶאֱכֹל וְלִשְׁתּוֹת: וִיהִי בְשָׁכְבוֹ וְיָדַעַתְּ
אֶת־הַמָּקוֹם אֲשֶׁר יִשְׁכַּב־שָׁם וּבָאת וְגִלִּית מַרְגְּלֹתָיו ושכבתי וְהוּא וְשָׁכָבְתְּ
ה יַגִּיד לָךְ אֵת אֲשֶׁר תַּעֲשִׂין: וַתֹּאמֶר אֵלֶיהָ כֹּל אֲשֶׁר־תֹּאמְרִי אֶעֱשֶׂה: אֵלַי
ו ז וַתֵּרֶד הַגֹּרֶן וַתַּעַשׂ כְּכֹל אֲשֶׁר־צִוַּתָּה חֲמוֹתָהּ: וַיֹּאכַל בֹּעַז וַיֵּשְׁתְּ וַיִּיטַב
לִבּוֹ וַיָּבֹא לִשְׁכַּב בִּקְצֵה הָעֲרֵמָה וַתָּבֹא בַלָּט וַתְּגַל מַרְגְּלֹתָיו וַתִּשְׁכָּב:
ח וַיְהִי בַּחֲצִי הַלַּיְלָה וַיֶּחֱרַד הָאִישׁ וַיִּלָּפֵת וְהִנֵּה אִשָּׁה שֹׁכֶבֶת מַרְגְּלֹתָיו:
ט וַיֹּאמֶר מִי־אָתְּ וַתֹּאמֶר אָנֹכִי רוּת אֲמָתֶךָ וּפָרַשְׂתָּ כְנָפֶךָ עַל־אֲמָתְךָ
י כִּי גֹאֵל אָתָּה: וַיֹּאמֶר בְּרוּכָה אַתְּ לַיהוָה בִּתִּי הֵיטַבְתְּ חַסְדֵּךְ הָאַחֲרוֹן
יא מִן־הָרִאשׁוֹן לְבִלְתִּי־לֶכֶת אַחֲרֵי הַבַּחוּרִים אִם־דַּל וְאִם־עָשִׁיר: וְעַתָּה
בִּתִּי אַל־תִּירְאִי כֹּל אֲשֶׁר־תֹּאמְרִי אֶעֱשֶׂה־לָּךְ כִּי יוֹדֵעַ כָּל־שַׁעַר עַמִּי
יב כִּי אֵשֶׁת חַיִל אָתְּ: וְעַתָּה כִּי אָמְנָם כִּי אם גֹאֵל אָנֹכִי וְגַם יֵשׁ גֹּאֵל
יג קָרוֹב מִמֶּנִּי: לִינִי ׀ הַלַּיְלָה וְהָיָה בַבֹּקֶר אִם־יִגְאָלֵךְ טוֹב יִגְאָל וְאִם־לֹא
יד יַחְפֹּץ לְגָאֳלֵךְ וּגְאַלְתִּיךְ אָנֹכִי חַי־יְהוָה שִׁכְבִי עַד־הַבֹּקֶר: וַתִּשְׁכַּב
מרגלותו עַד־הַבֹּקֶר וַתָּקָם בטרום יַכִּיר אִישׁ אֶת־רֵעֵהוּ וַיֹּאמֶר בְּטֶרֶם
טו אַל־יִוָּדַע כִּי־בָאָה הָאִשָּׁה הַגֹּרֶן: וַיֹּאמֶר הָבִי הַמִּטְפַּחַת אֲשֶׁר־
עָלַיִךְ וְאֶחֳזִי־בָהּ וַתֹּאחֶז בָּהּ וַיָּמָד שֵׁשׁ־שְׂעֹרִים וַיָּשֶׁת עָלֶיהָ וַיָּבֹא
טז הָעִיר: וַתָּבוֹא אֶל־חֲמוֹתָהּ וַתֹּאמֶר מִי־אַתְּ בִּתִּי וַתַּגֶּד־לָהּ אֵת כָּל־
יז אֲשֶׁר עָשָׂה־לָהּ הָאִישׁ: וַתֹּאמֶר שֵׁשׁ־הַשְּׂעֹרִים הָאֵלֶּה נָתַן לִי כִּי
יח אָמַר אַל־תָּבוֹאִי רֵיקָם אֶל־חֲמוֹתֵךְ: וַתֹּאמֶר שְׁבִי בִתִּי עַד אֲשֶׁר אֵלַי
תֵּדְעִין אֵיךְ יִפֹּל דָּבָר כִּי לֹא יִשְׁקֹט הָאִישׁ כִּי־אִם־כִּלָּה הַדָּבָר הַיּוֹם:
ד א וּבֹעַז עָלָה הַשַּׁעַר וַיֵּשֶׁב שָׁם וְהִנֵּה הַגֹּאֵל עֹבֵר אֲשֶׁר דִּבֶּר־בֹּעַז וַיֹּאמֶר
ב סוּרָה שְׁבָה־פֹּה פְּלֹנִי אַלְמֹנִי וַיָּסַר וַיֵּשֵׁב: וַיִּקַּח עֲשָׂרָה אֲנָשִׁים מִזִּקְנֵי
ג הָעִיר וַיֹּאמֶר שְׁבוּ־פֹה וַיֵּשֵׁבוּ: וַיֹּאמֶר לַגֹּאֵל חֶלְקַת הַשָּׂדֶה אֲשֶׁר

4 from the land of Moav, must sell the field plot of our kinsman Elimelekh. I
said I would let you know of it, inviting you to buy it in the presence of those
sitting here, in the presence of the elders of my people. If you wish to redeem
this, redeem; and if you will not redeem it, tell me: let me know, for there is
none before you to redeem, and I am next in line to you." "I shall redeem," he
5 said. "On the day you buy that field from Naomi," said Boaz, "and from Ruth
the Moabite, you will have bought the wife of a dead man with it, to restore
6 the dead man's name on his estate." Said the redeemer, "Such a redemption I
could not perform; it could be the ruin of my estate.[7] You redeem in my place;
7 I cannot redeem." In those long-ago days in Israel, a redemption or
exchange – anything to be officially enacted – was completed as follows.
One man would take off his shoe and would hand it to the other: that was the
8 bond then recognized among Israel. Now this redeemer said to Boaz, "Take
9 possession," and he took off his shoe. "You are my witnesses this day," said
Boaz to the elders and to all the people present, "that I take possession of all
that was Elimelekh's and all that was Kilyon's and Maḥlon's, from Naomi's
10 hand. And with it I take Ruth the Moabite, Maḥlon's wife, to be mine, to
rebuild the name of the dead on his estate. And the dead man's name will not
be cut off from among his brothers, from the gate of his own city – you are
11 my witnesses this day." And all the people at the gate and the elders said, "We
bear witness. May the Lord make the woman who is joining your house like
Raḥel and like Leah, who together built the House of Israel; may you go from
strength to strength in Efrata and your name be ever spoken in Beit Leḥem.
12 May your house be as the house of Peretz, whom Tamar bore to Yehuda,
growing from the seed that the Lord will give you from this young woman."
13 And so it was that Boaz took Ruth, and she became his wife, and he came to
14 her; the Lord granted her conception, and she bore a son. And the women
said to Naomi, "Blessed be the Lord, who has not withheld your redeemer
15 on this day – may the child's name be spoken in all Israel. May he restore your
spirit and sustain your old age, for your daughter-in-law, who loves you, she
16 has borne him, she who is better to you than seven sons could be." Naomi
17 took the child and placed him in her bosom and became his nurse. And her
neighbors named him, saying, "A son is born for Naomi!" They called him
Oved. And that was Oved the father of Yishai the father of David.
18 19 This is the line of Peretz: Peretz was the father of Ḥetzron. Ḥetzron was the
20 father of Ram; Ram was the father of Aminadav. Aminadav was the father of
21 Naḥshon; Naḥshon was the father of Salma. Salma was the father of Boaz;
22 Boaz was the father of Oved. Oved was the father of Yishai – and Yishai was
the father of David.

---

7 | Since a son born to Ruth and the redeemer would be considered Maḥlon's son, the field the redeemer stood to purchase would pass out of his estate.

ד לְאָחִינוּ לֶאֱלִימֶלֶךְ מָכְרָה נָעֳמִי הַשָּׁבָה מִשְּׂדֵה מוֹאָב׃ וַאֲנִי אָמַרְתִּי
אֶגְלֶה אָזְנְךָ לֵאמֹר קְנֵה נֶגֶד הַיֹּשְׁבִים וְנֶגֶד זִקְנֵי עַמִּי אִם־תִּגְאַל גְּאָל
וְאִם־לֹא יִגְאַל הַגִּידָה לִּי וְאֵדְעָ כִּי אֵין זוּלָתְךָ לִגְאוֹל וְאָנֹכִי אַחֲרֶיךָ
ה וַיֹּאמֶר אָנֹכִי אֶגְאָל׃ וַיֹּאמֶר בֹּעַז בְּיוֹם־קְנוֹתְךָ הַשָּׂדֶה מִיַּד נָעֳמִי וּמֵאֵת
רוּת הַמּוֹאֲבִיָּה אֵשֶׁת־הַמֵּת קניתי לְהָקִים שֵׁם־הַמֵּת עַל־נַחֲלָתוֹ׃ קָנִיתָ
ו וַיֹּאמֶר הַגֹּאֵל לֹא אוּכַל לגאול־לִי פֶּן־אַשְׁחִית אֶת־נַחֲלָתִי גְּאַל־לְךָ לִגְאָל־
ז אַתָּה אֶת־גְּאֻלָּתִי כִּי לֹא־אוּכַל לִגְאֹל׃ וְזֹאת לְפָנִים בְּיִשְׂרָאֵל עַל־
הַגְּאוּלָּה וְעַל־הַתְּמוּרָה לְקַיֵּם כָּל־דָּבָר שָׁלַף אִישׁ נַעֲלוֹ וְנָתַן לְרֵעֵהוּ
ח וְזֹאת הַתְּעוּדָה בְּיִשְׂרָאֵל׃ וַיֹּאמֶר הַגֹּאֵל לְבֹעַז קְנֵה־לָךְ וַיִּשְׁלֹף נַעֲלוֹ׃
ט וַיֹּאמֶר בֹּעַז לַזְּקֵנִים וְכָל־הָעָם עֵדִים אַתֶּם הַיּוֹם כִּי קָנִיתִי אֶת־כָּל־
י אֲשֶׁר לֶאֱלִימֶלֶךְ וְאֵת כָּל־אֲשֶׁר לְכִלְיוֹן וּמַחְלוֹן מִיַּד נָעֳמִי׃ וְגַם אֶת־
רוּת הַמֹּאֲבִיָּה אֵשֶׁת מַחְלוֹן קָנִיתִי לִי לְאִשָּׁה לְהָקִים שֵׁם־הַמֵּת
עַל־נַחֲלָתוֹ וְלֹא־יִכָּרֵת שֵׁם־הַמֵּת מֵעִם אֶחָיו וּמִשַּׁעַר מְקוֹמוֹ עֵדִים
יא אַתֶּם הַיּוֹם׃ וַיֹּאמְרוּ כָּל־הָעָם אֲשֶׁר־בַּשַּׁעַר וְהַזְּקֵנִים עֵדִים יִתֵּן יהוה
אֶת־הָאִשָּׁה הַבָּאָה אֶל־בֵּיתֶךָ כְּרָחֵל ׀ וּכְלֵאָה אֲשֶׁר בָּנוּ שְׁתֵּיהֶם אֶת־
יב בֵּית יִשְׂרָאֵל וַעֲשֵׂה־חַיִל בְּאֶפְרָתָה וּקְרָא־שֵׁם בְּבֵית לָחֶם׃ וִיהִי בֵיתְךָ
כְּבֵית פֶּרֶץ אֲשֶׁר־יָלְדָה תָמָר לִיהוּדָה מִן־הַזֶּרַע אֲשֶׁר יִתֵּן יהוה לְךָ
יג מִן־הַנַּעֲרָה הַזֹּאת׃ וַיִּקַּח בֹּעַז אֶת־רוּת וַתְּהִי־לוֹ לְאִשָּׁה וַיָּבֹא אֵלֶיהָ
יד וַיִּתֵּן יהוה לָהּ הֵרָיוֹן וַתֵּלֶד בֵּן׃ וַתֹּאמַרְנָה הַנָּשִׁים אֶל־נָעֳמִי בָּרוּךְ
טו יהוה אֲשֶׁר לֹא הִשְׁבִּית לָךְ גֹּאֵל הַיּוֹם וְיִקָּרֵא שְׁמוֹ בְּיִשְׂרָאֵל׃ וְהָיָה
לָךְ לְמֵשִׁיב נֶפֶשׁ וּלְכַלְכֵּל אֶת־שֵׂיבָתֵךְ כִּי כַלָּתֵךְ אֲשֶׁר־אֲהֵבַתֶךְ יְלָדַתּוּ
טז אֲשֶׁר־הִיא טוֹבָה לָךְ מִשִּׁבְעָה בָּנִים׃ וַתִּקַּח נָעֳמִי אֶת־הַיֶּלֶד וַתְּשִׁתֵהוּ
יז בְחֵיקָהּ וַתְּהִי־לוֹ לְאֹמֶנֶת׃ וַתִּקְרֶאנָה לוֹ הַשְּׁכֵנוֹת שֵׁם לֵאמֹר יֻלַּד־בֵּן
לְנָעֳמִי וַתִּקְרֶאנָה שְׁמוֹ עוֹבֵד הוּא אֲבִי־יִשַׁי אֲבִי דָוִד׃
יח יט וְאֵלֶּה תּוֹלְדוֹת פָּרֶץ פֶּרֶץ הוֹלִיד אֶת־חֶצְרוֹן׃ וְחֶצְרוֹן הוֹלִיד אֶת־רָם
כ וְרָם הוֹלִיד אֶת־עַמִּינָדָב׃ וְעַמִּינָדָב הוֹלִיד אֶת־נַחְשׁוֹן וְנַחְשׁוֹן הוֹלִיד
כא כב אֶת־שַׂלְמָה׃ וְשַׂלְמוֹן הוֹלִיד אֶת־בֹּעַז וּבֹעַז הוֹלִיד אֶת־עוֹבֵד׃ וְעֹבֵד
הוֹלִיד אֶת־יִשָׁי וְיִשַׁי הוֹלִיד אֶת־דָּוִד׃

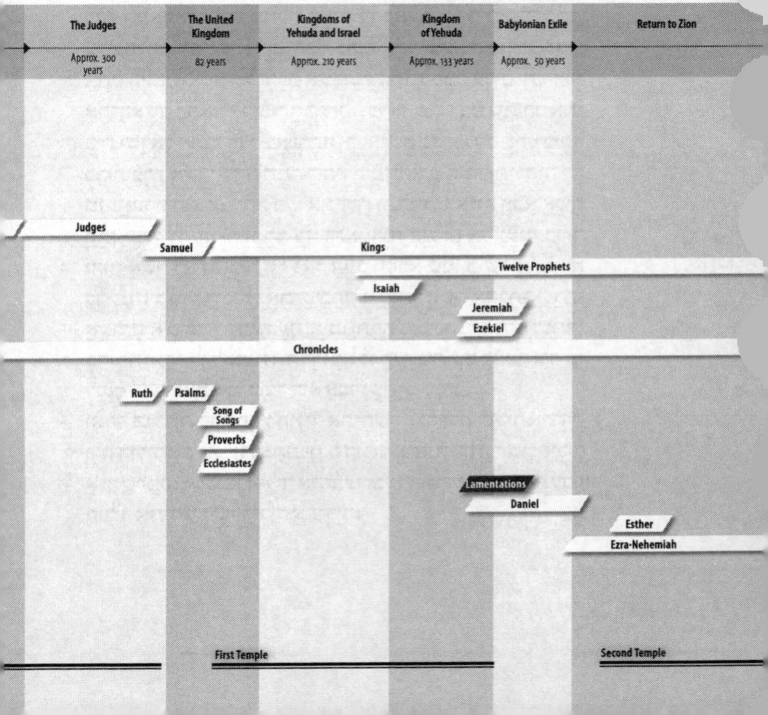

The Judges
The United Kingdom
Kingdoms of Yehuda and Israel
Kingdom of Yehuda
Babylonian Exile
Return to Zion
Approx. 300 years
82 years
Approx. 210 years
Approx. 133 years
Approx. 50 years
Judges
Samuel
Kings
Twelve Prophets
Isaiah
Jeremiah
Ezekiel
Chronicles
Ruth
Psalms
Song of Songs
Proverbs
Ecclesiastes
Lamentations
Daniel
Esther
Ezra-Nehemiah
First Temple
Second Temple

איכה

EIKHA/LAMENTATIONS

LAMENTATIONS	Zion alone	Destruction and anger	Lamentation of "the man"	Horrors of the destruction	Petition and lament
	Ch. 1	2	3	4	5

1 1 How the city that overflowed with people sits alone,[1] become like a widow;
she who was great among nations, princess of states, now a forced laborer.
2 She weeps, weeps through the nights; on her cheeks, tears. Of all her lovers
none console her; all her friends have betrayed her, become enemies to her.
3 Oppression has exiled Yehuda, oppression and the harshness of her labor.
Confined among nations, she finds no resting place; all her pursuers caught
4 up with her in the narrow spaces. The streets of Zion are grieving – no one
coming for the festival. All her gates are desolate; her priests are groaning; her
5 innocent girls are sorrowful, and she – her life is bitter. Her foes form the head
of this beast now, her enemies serene; for the LORD has brought her suffering
6 for all her crimes. Her little children walked away, captives, before foes. It is
gone from daughter Zion – all her splendor gone. Her princes have become
7 like stags that find no pasture, fleeing without strength before pursuers. She
remembers, Jerusalem, in her days of oppression and wandering, all that
she treasured that was hers long ago, how her people fell at the foe's hands
with none to help her; they see her now, these enemies, and laugh at her
8 downfall. She has sinned – Jerusalem sinned and so has become an outcast.
All who once respected her abase her: they have seen her naked. Now she
9 too is groaning, sits apart. Her impurity stains her skirts; she forgot what her
end would be. Her fall was startling; none console her. "LORD, witness my
10 oppression; the enemy grew strong." A foe has spread his hand over all that
she treasured. The nations saw her; they came to her Temple. Those that You
11 commanded must never enter Your assembly. All her nation groans: they
are seeking bread. They gave up their treasures for food, grasping at life. "See
12 this, LORD; look on – I am abased. May this never come to you, all you who
cross my path. Look on now and see – is there any pain like mine? Like that
which was done to me, like the suffering the LORD sent me on the day His
13 rage burned? From above He sent down fire through my bones and broke
them all. He spread a net for my feet, sent me backward. He rendered me
14 desolate all the day, ailing. The yoke of my crimes, bound together, the ropes
twisted in His hand, were raised to my neck and brought my strength down.
15 My Lord has given me over to those I cannot rise from. He cast all my heroes
aside – the Lord in my midst. He summoned forces forth to break my young
16 men. The LORD trod red the winepress of the virgin daughter Yehuda. For
these things I weep; my eyes, my eyes stream water, for the one who could
console me is far away from me, the one who would restore my life to me.
17 My children became desolate when the enemy mastered." Zion spreads her
hands – there is none to console her. The LORD commanded enemies against
18 Yaakov all around, Jerusalem an outcast among them, bleeding. She says, "The
LORD is just: I had refused His word. Listen, please, all peoples; witness this
19 pain. My young girls and youths have gone off in captivity. I called out to
my suitors; they have deceived me. My priests and my elders have starved in
20 the city; they sought bread for themselves to restore their lives. See, LORD,

1 | All chapters of Lamentations save the last are alphabetical acrostics.

א

א אֵיכָה ׀ יָשְׁבָה בָדָד הָעִיר רַבָּתִי עָם הָיְתָה כְּאַלְמָנָה רַבָּתִי בַגּוֹיִם
ב שָׂרָתִי בַּמְּדִינוֹת הָיְתָה לָמַס: בָּכוֹ תִבְכֶּה בַּלַּיְלָה וְדִמְעָתָהּ עַל לֶחֱיָהּ
ג אֵין־לָהּ מְנַחֵם מִכָּל־אֹהֲבֶיהָ כָּל־רֵעֶיהָ בָּגְדוּ בָהּ הָיוּ לָהּ לְאֹיְבִים:
גָּלְתָה יְהוּדָה מֵעֹנִי וּמֵרֹב עֲבֹדָה הִיא יָשְׁבָה בַגּוֹיִם לֹא מָצְאָה מָנוֹחַ
ד כָּל־רֹדְפֶיהָ הִשִּׂיגוּהָ בֵּין הַמְּצָרִים: דַּרְכֵי צִיּוֹן אֲבֵלוֹת מִבְּלִי בָּאֵי מוֹעֵד
כָּל־שְׁעָרֶיהָ שׁוֹמֵמִין כֹּהֲנֶיהָ נֶאֱנָחִים בְּתוּלֹתֶיהָ נּוּגוֹת וְהִיא מַר־לָהּ:
ה הָיוּ צָרֶיהָ לְרֹאשׁ אֹיְבֶיהָ שָׁלוּ כִּי־יְהוָה הוֹגָהּ עַל־רֹב פְּשָׁעֶיהָ עוֹלָלֶיהָ
ו הָלְכוּ שְׁבִי לִפְנֵי־צָר: וַיֵּצֵא מן בת־צִיּוֹן כָּל־הֲדָרָהּ הָיוּ שָׂרֶיהָ כְּאַיָּלִים מִבַּת־
ז לֹא־מָצְאוּ מִרְעֶה וַיֵּלְכוּ בְלֹא־כֹחַ לִפְנֵי רוֹדֵף: זָכְרָה יְרוּשָׁלַםִ יְמֵי עָנְיָהּ
וּמְרוּדֶיהָ כֹּל מַחֲמֻדֶיהָ אֲשֶׁר הָיוּ מִימֵי קֶדֶם בִּנְפֹל עַמָּהּ בְּיַד־צָר וְאֵין
ח עוֹזֵר לָהּ רָאוּהָ צָרִים שָׂחֲקוּ עַל־מִשְׁבַּתֶּהָ: חֵטְא חָטְאָה יְרוּשָׁלַםִ
עַל־כֵּן לְנִידָה הָיָתָה כָּל־מְכַבְּדֶיהָ הִזִּילוּהָ כִּי־רָאוּ עֶרְוָתָהּ גַּם־הִיא
ט נֶאֶנְחָה וַתָּשָׁב אָחוֹר: טֻמְאָתָהּ בְּשׁוּלֶיהָ לֹא זָכְרָה אַחֲרִיתָהּ וַתֵּרֶד
י פְּלָאִים אֵין מְנַחֵם לָהּ רְאֵה יְהוָה אֶת־עָנְיִי כִּי הִגְדִּיל אוֹיֵב: יָדוֹ פָּרַשׂ
צָר עַל כָּל־מַחֲמַדֶּיהָ כִּי־רָאֲתָה גוֹיִם בָּאוּ מִקְדָּשָׁהּ אֲשֶׁר צִוִּיתָה לֹא־
יא יָבֹאוּ בַקָּהָל לָךְ: כָּל־עַמָּהּ נֶאֱנָחִים מְבַקְּשִׁים לֶחֶם נָתְנוּ מחמודיהם מַחֲמַדֵּיהֶם
יב בְּאֹכֶל לְהָשִׁיב נָפֶשׁ רְאֵה יְהוָה וְהַבִּיטָה כִּי הָיִיתִי זוֹלֵלָה: לוֹא אֲלֵיכֶם
כָּל־עֹבְרֵי דֶרֶךְ הַבִּיטוּ וּרְאוּ אִם־יֵשׁ מַכְאוֹב כְּמַכְאֹבִי אֲשֶׁר עוֹלַל לִי
יג אֲשֶׁר הוֹגָה יְהוָה בְּיוֹם חֲרוֹן אַפּוֹ: מִמָּרוֹם שָׁלַח־אֵשׁ בְּעַצְמֹתַי וַיִּרְדֶּנָּה
יד פָּרַשׂ רֶשֶׁת לְרַגְלַי הֱשִׁיבַנִי אָחוֹר נְתָנַנִי שֹׁמֵמָה כָּל־הַיּוֹם דָּוָה: נִשְׂקַד
עֹל פְּשָׁעַי בְּיָדוֹ יִשְׂתָּרְגוּ עָלוּ עַל־צַוָּארִי הִכְשִׁיל כֹּחִי נְתָנַנִי אֲדֹנָי
טו בִּידֵי לֹא־אוּכַל קוּם: סִלָּה כָל־אַבִּירַי ׀ אֲדֹנָי בְּקִרְבִּי קָרָא עָלַי מוֹעֵד
טז לִשְׁבֹּר בַּחוּרָי גַּת דָּרַךְ אֲדֹנָי לִבְתוּלַת בַּת־יְהוּדָה: עַל־אֵלֶּה ׀ אֲנִי
בוֹכִיָּה עֵינִי ׀ עֵינִי יֹרְדָה מַּיִם כִּי־רָחַק מִמֶּנִּי מְנַחֵם מֵשִׁיב נַפְשִׁי הָיוּ בָנַי
יז שׁוֹמֵמִים כִּי גָבַר אוֹיֵב: פֵּרְשָׂה צִיּוֹן בְּיָדֶיהָ אֵין מְנַחֵם לָהּ צִוָּה יְהוָה
יח לְיַעֲקֹב סְבִיבָיו צָרָיו הָיְתָה יְרוּשָׁלַםִ לְנִדָּה בֵּינֵיהֶם: צַדִּיק הוּא יְהוָה
כִּי פִיהוּ מָרִיתִי שִׁמְעוּ־נָא כָל־עמים וּרְאוּ מַכְאֹבִי בְּתוּלֹתַי וּבַחוּרַי הָעַמִּים
יט הָלְכוּ בַשֶּׁבִי: קָרָאתִי לַמְאַהֲבַי הֵמָּה רִמּוּנִי כֹּהֲנַי וּזְקֵנַי בָּעִיר גָּוָעוּ
כ כִּי־בִקְשׁוּ אֹכֶל לָמוֹ וְיָשִׁיבוּ אֶת־נַפְשָׁם: רְאֵה יְהוָה כִּי־צַר־לִי מֵעַי

I am anguished. My stomach churns. My heart turns within me, for I have
21 refused You. Outside the sword bereaves me; at home it is like death. Hear
me – I am groaning; there is none to console me. My enemies heard of my
suffering – they rejoice: You have done this. When You bring the day You
22 called for, then they will be like me. Let all their evil come before You, and
do to them everything that You have done to me for all my crimes. My groans
compound; my heart is ailing."
2 1 How in His rage the Lord darkens the skies of daughter Zion; He has flung
from heaven down to earth all of Israel's splendor. He had no thought for
2 His footstool[2] on the day of His rage. The Lord devoured, showed no mercy
for the sheepfolds of Yaakov, devoured in His great rage daughter Yehuda's
fortresses – down they came to earth and brought low kingdoms, princes;
3 with burning rage He hacked off the horn of Israel's pride, held back His right
hand to let the enemy come. He burnt like flames of fire in Yaakov, consuming
4 on all sides. He trod[3] His bow like the enemy; like a foe He raised His right
hand and killed all those the eye treasured. In the tent of daughter Zion He
5 poured out rage like fire. It was as if He were the enemy. The Lord devoured
Israel, devoured all her palaces, razed her fortresses; in daughter Yehuda He
6 caused much moaning, mourning. He uprooted His Shelter like a garden,
destroyed His Tent of Meeting. The LORD erased the memory in Zion of
7 festival and Sabbath. He debased, in His flaming rage, king and priest. The
Lord shunned His altar, renounced His own Temple, gave over the walls of
her palaces into the enemy's hands. They called aloud in the LORD's House as
8 if it were a festival. The LORD planned demolition for daughter Zion's walls.
He stretched out the plumb line, devoured, did not hold back. Now boundary
9 and wall are grieving, pitiful. Her gates are sunk into the earth, their bars
broken and gone. Her king and ministers gone away among the nations, there
10 is no teaching. Even her prophets find no vision of the LORD. The elders in
daughter Zion sit on the ground and are silent. They lift up dust upon their
heads, wrap themselves in sacking; the young girls of Jerusalem lower their
11 heads to the ground. I have wept my eyes away; my stomach churns; my
marrow is poured onto the earth over my maiden nation's breaking, as little
12 ones, infants, faint in the town squares – they say to their mothers, "Where
are grain and wine?" as they faint away like the fallen in the city squares, as
13 their lives are poured out into their mothers' laps. How can I bear witness,
to what can I liken you, daughter Jerusalem? What can I compare you to and
comfort you, O virgin daughter Zion? Your breaking as vast as the ocean, who
14 will heal you? Your prophets brought you visions – empty, meaningless – but
did not uncover your sins to restore your fortunes. They envisioned worthless
15 delusions for you; they misled you. All who cross your path slap their hands
now in dismay. They whistle and shake their heads over daughter Jerusalem.
"Can this really be that city that was called 'Perfect Beauty,' 'Delight of all the

---

2 | The Temple, where the Divine Presence rested.

3 | God, pictured as the enemy, bends His bow and positions His arrows to shoot at Israel. See also 3:12.

חֳמַרְמָרוּ נֶהְפַּךְ לִבִּי בְּקִרְבִּי כִּי מָרוֹ מָרִיתִי מִחוּץ שִׁכְּלָה־חֶרֶב בַּבַּיִת
כא כַּמָּוֶת׃ שָׁמְעוּ כִּי נֶאֱנָחָה אָנִי אֵין מְנַחֵם לִי כָּל־אֹיְבַי שָׁמְעוּ רָעָתִי
כב שָׂשׂוּ כִּי אַתָּה עָשִׂיתָ הֵבֵאתָ יוֹם־קָרָאתָ וְיִהְיוּ כָמוֹנִי׃ תָּבֹא כָל־רָעָתָם
לְפָנֶיךָ וְעוֹלֵל לָמוֹ כַּאֲשֶׁר עוֹלַלְתָּ לִי עַל כָּל־פְּשָׁעָי כִּי־רַבּוֹת אַנְחֹתַי
וְלִבִּי דַוָּי׃

ב א אֵיכָה יָעִיב בְּאַפּוֹ ׀ אֲדֹנָי אֶת־בַּת־צִיּוֹן הִשְׁלִיךְ מִשָּׁמַיִם אֶרֶץ תִּפְאֶרֶת
ב יִשְׂרָאֵל וְלֹא־זָכַר הֲדֹם־רַגְלָיו בְּיוֹם אַפּוֹ׃ בִּלַּע אֲדֹנָי לֹא חָמַל אֵת וְלֹא
כָּל־נְאוֹת יַעֲקֹב הָרַס בְּעֶבְרָתוֹ מִבְצְרֵי בַת־יְהוּדָה הִגִּיעַ לָאָרֶץ חִלֵּל
ג מַמְלָכָה וְשָׂרֶיהָ׃ גָּדַע בָּחֳרִי־אַף כֹּל קֶרֶן יִשְׂרָאֵל הֵשִׁיב אָחוֹר יְמִינוֹ
ד מִפְּנֵי אוֹיֵב וַיִּבְעַר בְּיַעֲקֹב כְּאֵשׁ לֶהָבָה אָכְלָה סָבִיב׃ דָּרַךְ קַשְׁתּוֹ
כְּאוֹיֵב נִצָּב יְמִינוֹ כְּצָר וַיַּהֲרֹג כֹּל מַחֲמַדֵּי־עָיִן בְּאֹהֶל בַּת־צִיּוֹן שָׁפַךְ
ה כָּאֵשׁ חֲמָתוֹ׃ הָיָה אֲדֹנָי ׀ כְּאוֹיֵב בִּלַּע יִשְׂרָאֵל בִּלַּע כָּל־אַרְמְנוֹתֶיהָ
ו שִׁחֵת מִבְצָרָיו וַיֶּרֶב בְּבַת־יְהוּדָה תַּאֲנִיָּה וַאֲנִיָּה׃ וַיַּחְמֹס כַּגַּן שֻׂכּוֹ שִׁחֵת
מוֹעֲדוֹ שִׁכַּח יְהוָה ׀ בְּצִיּוֹן מוֹעֵד וְשַׁבָּת וַיִּנְאַץ בְּזַעַם־אַפּוֹ מֶלֶךְ וְכֹהֵן׃
ז זָנַח אֲדֹנָי ׀ מִזְבְּחוֹ נִאֵר מִקְדָּשׁוֹ הִסְגִּיר בְּיַד־אוֹיֵב חוֹמֹת אַרְמְנוֹתֶיהָ
ח קוֹל נָתְנוּ בְּבֵית־יְהוָה כְּיוֹם מוֹעֵד׃ חָשַׁב יְהוָה ׀ לְהַשְׁחִית חוֹמַת בַּת־
צִיּוֹן נָטָה קָו לֹא־הֵשִׁיב יָדוֹ מִבַּלֵּעַ וַיַּאֲבֶל־חֵל וְחוֹמָה יַחְדָּו אֻמְלָלוּ׃
ט טָבְעוּ בָאָרֶץ שְׁעָרֶיהָ אִבַּד וְשִׁבַּר בְּרִיחֶיהָ מַלְכָּהּ וְשָׂרֶיהָ בַגּוֹיִם אֵין
י תּוֹרָה גַּם־נְבִיאֶיהָ לֹא־מָצְאוּ חָזוֹן מֵיְהוָה׃ יֵשְׁבוּ לָאָרֶץ יִדְּמוּ זִקְנֵי
בַת־צִיּוֹן הֶעֱלוּ עָפָר עַל־רֹאשָׁם חָגְרוּ שַׂקִּים הוֹרִידוּ לָאָרֶץ רֹאשָׁן
יא בְּתוּלֹת יְרוּשָׁלִָם׃ כָּלוּ בַדְּמָעוֹת עֵינַי חֳמַרְמְרוּ מֵעַי נִשְׁפַּךְ לָאָרֶץ
יב כְּבֵדִי עַל־שֶׁבֶר בַּת־עַמִּי בֵּעָטֵף עוֹלֵל וְיוֹנֵק בִּרְחֹבוֹת קִרְיָה׃ לְאִמֹּתָם
יֹאמְרוּ אַיֵּה דָּגָן וָיָיִן בְּהִתְעַטְּפָם כֶּחָלָל בִּרְחֹבוֹת עִיר בְּהִשְׁתַּפֵּךְ נַפְשָׁם
יג אֶל־חֵיק אִמֹּתָם׃ מָה־אֲעוּדֵךְ מָה אֲדַמֶּה־לָּךְ הַבַּת יְרוּשָׁלִַם מָה אֲעִידֵךְ
אַשְׁוֶה־לָּךְ וַאֲנַחֲמֵךְ בְּתוּלַת בַּת־צִיּוֹן כִּי־גָדוֹל כַּיָּם שִׁבְרֵךְ מִי יִרְפָּא־
יד לָךְ׃ נְבִיאַיִךְ חָזוּ לָךְ שָׁוְא וְתָפֵל וְלֹא־גִלּוּ עַל־עֲוֹנֵךְ לְהָשִׁיב שביתך שְׁבוּתֵךְ
טו וַיֶּחֱזוּ לָךְ מַשְׂאוֹת שָׁוְא וּמַדּוּחִים׃ סָפְקוּ עָלַיִךְ כַּפַּיִם כָּל־עֹבְרֵי דֶרֶךְ
שָׁרְקוּ וַיָּנִעוּ רֹאשָׁם עַל־בַּת יְרוּשָׁלִָם הֲזֹאת הָעִיר שֶׁיֹּאמְרוּ כְּלִילַת

16 world'?" All your enemies gape their snarling mouths at you. They whistle
and grate their teeth; they say, "We have devoured them: this is the very day
17 we hoped for – we have done it, seen it."[4] The LORD has completed what He
planned to do. He has carried out His word, His command of long ago. He
destroyed and showed no mercy, brought the enemy joy over you; He raised
18 your foes' proud horn. The heart cries out toward the Lord. O wall of daughter
Zion, draw down, like a stream, your tears; day and night do not allow yourself
19 rest; let your eyes never be silenced. Get up, give voice in the night as every
watch begins; pour out your heart like water in the presence of the Lord.
Lift up your palms to Him over the lives of your little ones, fainting away
20 from hunger at the end of every street. See this, LORD, look on – to whom
have You done this? Can women eat their own children, the little ones they
nurtured? Can priest and prophet be murdered in the Temple of the Lord?
21 On the ground, lying down in the streets – youths, old men. My own young
girls and youths have fallen to the sword. You have killed on the day of Your
22 rage, have slaughtered, shown no compassion. You call those living around
me to come as if it were a festival. But there is no refugee or remnant on the
day of the LORD's rage. All those I nurtured and raised, my enemy disposed of.
3 1 2 I am the man who has seen oppression[5] through the staff of His rage. It is I
3 that He led, that He guided into the darkness, not light. It is to me alone that
4 He returns, turns His hand again against me all the day. He has made my flesh
5 and skin decay; He has broken my bones. He built a siege wall round me of
6 wormwood and of hardship. He sat me down in darkness like those forever
7 dead. He fenced me around – no escape; made heavy the bronze that holds
8 9 me. Even as I cry out to be saved, He has blocked my prayer. He fenced off
10 my way with hewn stone and twisted my paths. He is a bear lying in wait
11 for me, a lion in hiding. He turns me from my path, gashes me, renders me
12 desolate. He has trod His bow[6] and made me stand the target to His arrow.
13 14 Into my very heart He shot His quiver's load. I am the laughingstock of all
15 my people, their mocking song all the day. He has glutted me with bitterness
16 and quenched me with wormwood. He crushed my teeth in grit, trod me
17 into the ashes. Peace has deserted me: I have forgotten what goodness is.
18 19 I said, "My endurance is lost, and my hope of the LORD." Keep in mind
20 my affliction and wandering, wormwood, venom. Keep, keep in mind my
21 22 life, bowed low. I make this reply to my heart, and so I wait on. The LORD's
23 kindness – it is not finished; His compassion is not spent. New with each new
24 morning, how great is His faithfulness. I said to myself, the LORD is what I
25 have and so I shall yet wait for Him. The LORD is good to those who hope
26 for Him, to those who search for Him. To hope is good in silence for the
27 LORD to come, to rescue. It is good for a man to bear the yoke in his youth.

4 | In the acrostics of chapters 2–4, the *peh* and *ayin* are reversed.

5 | This chapter is a triple alphabetic acrostic, with twenty-two sets of three verses beginning with the same Hebrew letter.

6 | See 2:4.

טז יֳפִי מָשׂוֹשׂ לְכָל־הָאָרֶץ׃ פָּצוּ עָלַיִךְ פִּיהֶם כָּל־אוֹיְבַיִךְ שָׁרְקוּ וַיַּחַרְקוּ־שֵׁן
יז אָמְרוּ בִּלָּעְנוּ אַךְ זֶה הַיּוֹם שֶׁקִּוִּינֻהוּ מָצָאנוּ רָאִינוּ׃ עָשָׂה יהוה אֲשֶׁר
זָמָם בִּצַּע אֶמְרָתוֹ אֲשֶׁר צִוָּה מִימֵי־קֶדֶם הָרַס וְלֹא חָמָל וַיְשַׂמַּח עָלַיִךְ
יח אוֹיֵב הֵרִים קֶרֶן צָרָיִךְ׃ צָעַק לִבָּם אֶל־אֲדֹנָי חוֹמַת בַּת־צִיּוֹן הוֹרִידִי
כַנַּחַל דִּמְעָה יוֹמָם וָלַיְלָה אַל־תִּתְּנִי פוּגַת לָךְ אַל־תִּדֹּם בַּת־עֵינֵךְ׃
יט קוּמִי ׀ רֹנִּי בַלַּיִל לְרֹאשׁ אַשְׁמֻרוֹת שִׁפְכִי כַמַּיִם לִבֵּךְ נֹכַח פְּנֵי אֲדֹנָי
שְׂאִי אֵלָיו כַּפַּיִךְ עַל־נֶפֶשׁ עוֹלָלַיִךְ הָעֲטוּפִים בְּרָעָב בְּרֹאשׁ כָּל־חוּצוֹת׃
כ רְאֵה יהוה וְהַבִּיטָה לְמִי עוֹלַלְתָּ כֹּה אִם־תֹּאכַלְנָה נָשִׁים פִּרְיָם עֹלְלֵי
כא טִפֻּחִים אִם־יֵהָרֵג בְּמִקְדַּשׁ אֲדֹנָי כֹּהֵן וְנָבִיא׃ שָׁכְבוּ לָאָרֶץ חוּצוֹת
נַעַר וְזָקֵן בְּתוּלֹתַי וּבַחוּרַי נָפְלוּ בֶחָרֶב הָרַגְתָּ בְּיוֹם אַפֶּךָ טָבַחְתָּ לֹא
כב חָמָלְתָּ׃ תִּקְרָא כְיוֹם מוֹעֵד מְגוּרַי מִסָּבִיב וְלֹא הָיָה בְּיוֹם אַף־יהוה
פָּלִיט וְשָׂרִיד אֲשֶׁר־טִפַּחְתִּי וְרִבִּיתִי אֹיְבִי כִלָּם׃
ג א ב אֲנִי הַגֶּבֶר רָאָה עֳנִי בְּשֵׁבֶט עֶבְרָתוֹ׃ אוֹתִי נָהַג וַיֹּלַךְ חֹשֶׁךְ וְלֹא־אוֹר׃
ג ד אַךְ בִּי יָשֻׁב יַהֲפֹךְ יָדוֹ כָּל־הַיּוֹם׃ בִּלָּה בְשָׂרִי וְעוֹרִי שִׁבַּר עַצְמוֹתָי׃
ה ו בָּנָה עָלַי וַיַּקַּף רֹאשׁ וּתְלָאָה׃ בְּמַחֲשַׁכִּים הוֹשִׁיבַנִי כְּמֵתֵי עוֹלָם׃
ז ח גָּדַר בַּעֲדִי וְלֹא אֵצֵא הִכְבִּיד נְחָשְׁתִּי׃ גַּם כִּי אֶזְעַק וַאֲשַׁוֵּעַ שָׂתַם
ט י תְּפִלָּתִי׃ גָּדַר דְּרָכַי בְּגָזִית נְתִיבֹתַי עִוָּה׃ דֹּב אֹרֵב הוּא לִי אריה אֲרִי
יא יב בְּמִסְתָּרִים׃ דְּרָכַי סוֹרֵר וַיְפַשְּׁחֵנִי שָׂמַנִי שֹׁמֵם׃ דָּרַךְ קַשְׁתּוֹ וַיַּצִּיבֵנִי
יג יד כַּמַּטָּרָא לַחֵץ׃ הֵבִיא בְּכִלְיוֹתָי בְּנֵי אַשְׁפָּתוֹ׃ הָיִיתִי שְּׂחֹק לְכָל־עַמִּי
טו טז נְגִינָתָם כָּל־הַיּוֹם׃ הִשְׂבִּיעַנִי בַמְּרוֹרִים הִרְוַנִי לַעֲנָה׃ וַיַּגְרֵס בֶּחָצָץ
יז יח שִׁנָּי הִכְפִּישַׁנִי בָּאֵפֶר׃ וַתִּזְנַח מִשָּׁלוֹם נַפְשִׁי נָשִׁיתִי טוֹבָה׃ וָאֹמַר אָבַד
יט כ נִצְחִי וְתוֹחַלְתִּי מֵיהוה׃ זְכָר־עָנְיִי וּמְרוּדִי לַעֲנָה וָרֹאשׁ׃ זָכוֹר תִּזְכּוֹר
כא כב ותשיח עָלַי נַפְשִׁי׃ זֹאת אָשִׁיב אֶל־לִבִּי עַל־כֵּן אוֹחִיל׃ חַסְדֵי יהוה וְתָשׁוֹחַ
כג כִּי לֹא־תָמְנוּ כִּי לֹא־כָלוּ רַחֲמָיו׃ חֲדָשִׁים לַבְּקָרִים רַבָּה אֱמוּנָתֶךָ׃
כד כה חֶלְקִי יהוה אָמְרָה נַפְשִׁי עַל־כֵּן אוֹחִיל לוֹ׃ טוֹב יהוה לְקֹוָו לְנֶפֶשׁ
כו כז תִּדְרְשֶׁנּוּ׃ טוֹב וְיָחִיל וְדוּמָם לִתְשׁוּעַת יהוה׃ טוֹב לַגֶּבֶר כִּי־יִשָּׂא עֹל

28 29 He should sit alone and be silent: this was inflicted on him. Let him sink his
30 teeth into the dust – perhaps there is hope. Let him offer his cheek to the one
31 who beats him. Let him be glutted with insult. For the Lord will not shun him
32 through all eternity. For if He brings sorrow, He must, in His great kindness,
33 have compassion. He does not oppress from the heart to bring men sorrow,
34 35 to trample underfoot all the captives of this earth, to twist a man's claim
36 before the Most High, to let one's case be twisted – and yet my Lord not
37 38 see. Who ever *spoke and it was so* if the Lord did not command it? Do not all
39 evils and good emerge from the mouth of the Most High? How can a living
40 man protest; why should he protest his own sins? Let us seek out our ways,
41 understand them, and come back to the LORD. Let us raise our hearts with the
42 palms of our hands to God in heaven. *We rebelled and refused You – but You did*
43 *not forgive.* You covered us in rage and pursued us. You killed; You showed no
44 45 compassion. You covered Yourself in a cloud beyond the reach of prayers. You
46 have made us filth and loathing among nations. They gaped snarling mouths
47 at us, all our enemies. Terror and snare were with us; devastation, breaking.
48 49 Rivers of water ran from my eyes at my maiden nation's breaking. My eyes
50 pour out and will not stop, no respite until the LORD shall look down and see
51 52 us from heaven. My eyes torment me over all the daughters of my city. He
53 hunted me down like a bird, my enemy, for no cause. They closed off my life in
54 a pit; they laid the stone over me. The waters came up over my head; I said, "I
55 56 am condemned." LORD, I called Your name from the very lowest of pits. You
57 have heard my voice; do not close Your ears to my need, to my pleading. You
58 once were close when I called You, would tell me, "Do not fear." You would
59 fight my fight, my Lord, redeem my life. See, LORD, this twisted justice; judge
60 61 my case. Witness all their vengefulness, all that they plan to do to me. Hear
62 their insults, LORD, and all their plans for me, my attackers' mouthings, their
63 mutterings against me all the day. Watch them as they sit or rise: I am their
64 65 mocking song. LORD, return them payment for all that they have done. Bring
66 them heartache, Your curse on them. Pursue them with rage and annihilate
them from under the skies of the LORD.

4 1 How dull gold has become; how that finest gold has changed, the sacred
2 stones poured out at the end of every street. Precious children of Zion, worth
their very weight in gold – how they are considered now like cheap clay jars,
3 work of the potter's hands. Even jackals offer udders, give their cubs to suck.
4 My maiden people is cruel like desert ostriches. The tongues of infants cling
to their mouths' roofs with thirst. Little children beg for bread; none break it
5 for them. Those who once ate the finest foods sit desolate in the streets. Those
6 brought up in clothes of scarlet now embrace the trash heaps. My people's
punishment is greater even than that of Sedom, which was overturned all in
7 a moment; no hand touched it. Jerusalem's leaders were cleaner than snow
once, brighter than milk, glowing redder than carnelians from within, cut
8 as finely as sapphires. Now they are darker than pitch, unrecognized on the
9 streets, skin shriveled against bones, dry as wood. Better to be killed by the
sword than killed by hunger. The slain at least flow where they are stabbed, do

כח כט בִּנְעוּרָיו׃ יֵשֵׁב בָּדָד וְיִדֹּם כִּי נָטַל עָלָיו׃ יִתֵּן בֶּעָפָר פִּיהוּ אוּלַי יֵשׁ תִּקְוָה׃
ל לא לב יִתֵּן לְמַכֵּהוּ לֶחִי יִשְׂבַּע בְּחֶרְפָּה׃ כִּי לֹא יִזְנַח לְעוֹלָם אֲדֹנָי׃ כִּי אִם־
לג לד הוֹגָה וְרִחַם כְּרֹב חֲסָדָו׃ כִּי לֹא עִנָּה מִלִּבּוֹ וַיַּגֶּה בְּנֵי־אִישׁ׃ לְדַכֵּא תַּחַת
לה לו רַגְלָיו כֹּל אֲסִירֵי אָרֶץ׃ לְהַטּוֹת מִשְׁפַּט־גָּבֶר נֶגֶד פְּנֵי עֶלְיוֹן׃ לְעַוֵּת אָדָם
לז לח בְּרִיבוֹ אֲדֹנָי לֹא רָאָה׃ מִי זֶה אָמַר וַתֶּהִי אֲדֹנָי לֹא צִוָּה׃ מִפִּי עֶלְיוֹן לֹא
לט מ תֵצֵא הָרָעוֹת וְהַטּוֹב׃ מַה־יִּתְאוֹנֵן אָדָם חָי גֶּבֶר עַל־חֲטָאו׃ נַחְפְּשָׂה
מא דְרָכֵינוּ וְנַחְקֹרָה וְנָשׁוּבָה עַד־יהוה׃ נִשָּׂא לְבָבֵנוּ אֶל־כַּפָּיִם אֶל־אֵל
מב מג בַּשָּׁמָיִם׃ נַחְנוּ פָשַׁעְנוּ וּמָרִינוּ אַתָּה לֹא סָלָחְתָּ׃ סַכֹּתָה בָאַף וַתִּרְדְּפֵנוּ
מד מה הָרַגְתָּ לֹא חָמָלְתָּ׃ סַכּוֹתָה בֶעָנָן לָךְ מֵעֲבוֹר תְּפִלָּה׃ סְחִי וּמָאוֹס
מו מז תְּשִׂימֵנוּ בְּקֶרֶב הָעַמִּים׃ פָּצוּ עָלֵינוּ פִּיהֶם כָּל־אֹיְבֵינוּ׃ פַּחַד וָפַחַת
מח הָיָה לָנוּ הַשֵּׁאת וְהַשָּׁבֶר׃ פַּלְגֵי־מַיִם תֵּרַד עֵינִי עַל־שֶׁבֶר בַּת־עַמִּי׃
מט נ עֵינִי נִגְּרָה וְלֹא תִדְמֶה מֵאֵין הֲפֻגוֹת׃ עַד־יַשְׁקִיף וְיֵרֶא יהוה מִשָּׁמָיִם׃
נא נב עֵינִי עוֹלְלָה לְנַפְשִׁי מִכֹּל בְּנוֹת עִירִי׃ צוֹד צָדוּנִי כַּצִּפּוֹר אֹיְבַי חִנָּם׃
נג נד צָמְתוּ בַבּוֹר חַיָּי וַיַּדּוּ־אֶבֶן בִּי׃ צָפוּ־מַיִם עַל־רֹאשִׁי אָמַרְתִּי נִגְזָרְתִּי׃
נה נו קָרָאתִי שִׁמְךָ יהוה מִבּוֹר תַּחְתִּיּוֹת׃ קוֹלִי שָׁמָעְתָּ אַל־תַּעְלֵם אָזְנְךָ
נז נח לְרַוְחָתִי לְשַׁוְעָתִי׃ קָרַבְתָּ בְּיוֹם אֶקְרָאֶךָּ אָמַרְתָּ אַל־תִּירָא׃ רַבְתָּ
נט אֲדֹנָי רִיבֵי נַפְשִׁי גָּאַלְתָּ חַיָּי׃ רָאִיתָה יהוה עַוָּתָתִי שָׁפְטָה מִשְׁפָּטִי׃
ס סא רָאִיתָה כָּל־נִקְמָתָם כָּל־מַחְשְׁבֹתָם לִי׃ שָׁמַעְתָּ חֶרְפָּתָם יהוה כָּל־
סב סג מַחְשְׁבֹתָם עָלָי׃ שִׂפְתֵי קָמַי וְהֶגְיוֹנָם עָלַי כָּל־הַיּוֹם׃ שִׁבְתָּם וְקִימָתָם
סד הַבִּיטָה אֲנִי מַנְגִּינָתָם׃ תָּשִׁיב לָהֶם גְּמוּל יהוה כְּמַעֲשֵׂה יְדֵיהֶם׃
סה סו תִּתֵּן לָהֶם מְגִנַּת־לֵב תַּאֲלָתְךָ לָהֶם׃ תִּרְדֹּף בְּאַף וְתַשְׁמִידֵם מִתַּחַת
שְׁמֵי יהוה׃

ד א אֵיכָה יוּעַם זָהָב יִשְׁנֶא הַכֶּתֶם הַטּוֹב תִּשְׁתַּפֵּכְנָה אַבְנֵי־קֹדֶשׁ בְּרֹאשׁ
ב כָּל־חוּצוֹת׃ בְּנֵי צִיּוֹן הַיְקָרִים הַמְסֻלָּאִים בַּפָּז אֵיכָה נֶחְשְׁבוּ לְנִבְלֵי־
ג חֶרֶשׂ מַעֲשֵׂה יְדֵי יוֹצֵר׃ גַּם־תַּנִּין חָלְצוּ שַׁד הֵינִיקוּ גּוּרֵיהֶן בַּת־עַמִּי תַּנִּים
ד לְאַכְזָר כִּי עֲנִים בַּמִּדְבָּר׃ דָּבַק לְשׁוֹן יוֹנֵק אֶל־חִכּוֹ בַּצָּמָא עוֹלָלִים כַּיְעֵנִים
ה שָׁאֲלוּ לֶחֶם פֹּרֵשׂ אֵין לָהֶם׃ הָאֹכְלִים לְמַעֲדַנִּים נָשַׁמּוּ בַּחוּצוֹת
ו הָאֱמֻנִים עֲלֵי תוֹלָע חִבְּקוּ אַשְׁפַּתּוֹת׃ וַיִּגְדַּל עֲוֺן בַּת־עַמִּי מֵחַטַּאת
ז סְדֹם הַהֲפוּכָה כְמוֹ־רָגַע וְלֹא־חָלוּ בָהּ יָדָיִם׃ זַכּוּ נְזִירֶיהָ מִשֶּׁלֶג צַחוּ
ח מֵחָלָב אָדְמוּ עֶצֶם מִפְּנִינִים סַפִּיר גִּזְרָתָם׃ חָשַׁךְ מִשְּׁחוֹר תָּאֳרָם לֹא
ט נִכְּרוּ בַּחוּצוֹת צָפַד עוֹרָם עַל־עַצְמָם יָבֵשׁ הָיָה כָעֵץ׃ טוֹבִים הָיוּ

10 not starve for the yield of meadows. The hands of loving women have cooked
their own children; these have become their nourishment in my maiden
11 nation's breaking. The LORD burned all His anger, poured out all His flaming
12 rage. He set fire blazing in Zion; it consumed all her foundations. The kings
of the world did not believe it – not anyone living on earth – that a foe and
13 enemy could come and enter Jerusalem's gates – for the sins of her prophets,
her priests' offenses, who within her midst pour out the blood of righteous
14 people. They drift, blind, through the streets, disgusting with blood; no one
15 could possibly touch those clothes. "Keep away, impure," they cry out; "away,
away, do not touch," floating, drifting away. It is said among the nations, "They
16 may stay no longer here. It is the LORD's face that divides them. He will look
17 on them no more." They granted priests no honor and elders no favor. And
we: our eyes are worn out watching for our mirage of assistance, waiting,
18 ever waiting for a nation that knows no rescue. They stalked our very steps,
stopped us walking across our squares. Our end comes close, our days are
19 done, our end has come. Our pursuers came swifter than the eagles of the sky.
20 They pursued us over mountains; in the steppes they lay in ambush. Our life's
breath, the LORD's anointed, was caught up in our slaughter, the one whose
21 shade we said we would live in among nations. Rejoice, be merry, daughter
Edom, sitting there in the land of Utz. The cup will come to you in turn; you
22 will get drunk and be laid bare. Your offenses are done with, daughter Zion;
He will exile you no more. Your offenses are noted, daughter Edom; your
sins have been exposed.

5 1 Remember, LORD, what has become of us. See; witness our abjection:
2 3 our homeland turned over to strangers, our homes to foreign men. We are
4 orphans now, fatherless, our mothers are widows. We pay to drink our water;
5 our wood comes at a price. At our throats, they chase us; we labor; they give
6 7 us no respite. We hold out a hand to Egypt, to Assyria, for bread. Our fathers
8 sinned – they are gone now – we bear their offenses. Slaves now rule over
9 us; none will release us from their hands. We risk our lives for bread under
10 the sword in desert lands. Our skin burns like an oven with the fevers of
11 starvation. They raped women in Zion, virgin girls in the towns of Yehuda.
12 13 Princes were hung up by their hands; no regard was shown to elders. Young
14 men bear the millstone; boys stumble under loads of wood. No more elders
15 at the gates or young men lost in song. No more delight in our hearts; our
16 dance has turned to mourning. The crown of our heads has fallen, woe is
17 to us: we have sinned. For these things our hearts are ailing; for this our
18 19 eyes grow dark, for Mount Zion, desolate – foxes wander there. But You,
20 LORD, are enthroned forever; Your rule endures for all generations. Why
21 would You forever forget us, desert us, for days without end? Bring us back
22 to You, LORD, and we will come. Renew our days to be as they once were;
even if You leave and loathe us now, rage against us with a great passion.

Bring us back to You, Lord, and we will come.
Renew our days to be as they once were.

י חַלְלֵי־חֶרֶב מֵחַלְלֵי רָעָב שֶׁהֵם יָזֻבוּ מְדֻקָּרִים מִתְּנוּבוֹת שָׂדָי: יְדֵי
יא נָשִׁים רַחֲמָנִיּוֹת בִּשְּׁלוּ יַלְדֵיהֶן הָיוּ לְבָרוֹת לָמוֹ בְּשֶׁבֶר בַּת־עַמִּי: כִּלָּה
יב יהוה אֶת־חֲמָתוֹ שָׁפַךְ חֲרוֹן אַפּוֹ וַיַּצֶּת־אֵשׁ בְּצִיּוֹן וַתֹּאכַל יְסוֹדֹתֶיהָ: לֹא
הֶאֱמִינוּ מַלְכֵי־אֶרֶץ וכל יֹשְׁבֵי תֵבֵל כִּי יָבֹא צַר וְאוֹיֵב בְּשַׁעֲרֵי יְרוּשָׁלִָם: כֹּל
יג יד מֵחַטֹּאת נְבִיאֶיהָ עֲוֺנוֹת כֹּהֲנֶיהָ הַשֹּׁפְכִים בְּקִרְבָּהּ דַּם צַדִּיקִים: נָעוּ
טו עִוְרִים בַּחוּצוֹת נְגֹאֲלוּ בַּדָּם בְּלֹא יוּכְלוּ יִגְּעוּ בִּלְבֻשֵׁיהֶם: סוּרוּ טָמֵא
קָרְאוּ לָמוֹ סוּרוּ סוּרוּ אַל־תִּגָּעוּ כִּי נָצוּ גַּם־נָעוּ אָמְרוּ בַּגּוֹיִם לֹא יוֹסִפוּ
טז לָגוּר: פְּנֵי יהוה חִלְּקָם לֹא יוֹסִיף לְהַבִּיטָם פְּנֵי כֹהֲנִים לֹא נָשָׂאוּ זקנים וּזְקֵנִים
יז לֹא חָנָנוּ: עודינה תִּכְלֶינָה עֵינֵינוּ אֶל־עֶזְרָתֵנוּ הָבֶל בְּצִפִּיָּתֵנוּ צִפִּינוּ עוֹדֵינוּ
יח אֶל־גּוֹי לֹא יוֹשִׁעַ: צָדוּ צְעָדֵינוּ מִלֶּכֶת בִּרְחֹבֹתֵינוּ קָרַב קִצֵּנוּ מָלְאוּ
יט יָמֵינוּ כִּי־בָא קִצֵּנוּ: קַלִּים הָיוּ רֹדְפֵינוּ מִנִּשְׁרֵי שָׁמָיִם עַל־הֶהָרִים דְּלָקֻנוּ
כ בַּמִּדְבָּר אָרְבוּ לָנוּ: רוּחַ אַפֵּינוּ מְשִׁיחַ יהוה נִלְכַּד בִּשְׁחִיתוֹתָם אֲשֶׁר
כא אָמַרְנוּ בְּצִלּוֹ נִחְיֶה בַגּוֹיִם: שִׂישִׂי וְשִׂמְחִי בַּת־אֱדוֹם יושבתי בְּאֶרֶץ יוֹשֶׁבֶת
כב עוּץ גַּם־עָלַיִךְ תַּעֲבָר־כּוֹס תִּשְׁכְּרִי וְתִתְעָרִי: תַּם־עֲוֺנֵךְ בַּת־צִיּוֹן לֹא
יוֹסִיף לְהַגְלוֹתֵךְ פָּקַד עֲוֺנֵךְ בַּת־אֱדוֹם גִּלָּה עַל־חַטֹּאתָיִךְ:
ה א ב זְכֹר יהוה מֶה־הָיָה לָנוּ הַבִּיטָ וּרְאֵה אֶת־חֶרְפָּתֵנוּ: נַחֲלָתֵנוּ נֶהֶפְכָה
ג לְזָרִים בָּתֵּינוּ לְנָכְרִים: יְתוֹמִים הָיִינוּ אין אָב אִמֹּתֵינוּ כְּאַלְמָנוֹת: וְאֵין
ד ה מֵימֵינוּ בְּכֶסֶף שָׁתִינוּ עֵצֵינוּ בִּמְחִיר יָבֹאוּ: עַל צַוָּארֵנוּ נִרְדָּפְנוּ יָגַעְנוּ
ו ז לא הוּנַח־לָנוּ: מִצְרַיִם נָתַנּוּ יָד אַשּׁוּר לִשְׂבֹּעַ לָחֶם: אֲבֹתֵינוּ חָטְאוּ וְלֹא
ח אינם אנחנו עֲוֺנֹתֵיהֶם סָבָלְנוּ: עֲבָדִים מָשְׁלוּ בָנוּ פֹּרֵק אֵין מִיָּדָם: וְאֵינָם וַאֲנַחְנוּ
ט י בְּנַפְשֵׁנוּ נָבִיא לַחְמֵנוּ מִפְּנֵי חֶרֶב הַמִּדְבָּר: עוֹרֵנוּ כְּתַנּוּר נִכְמָרוּ
יא יב מִפְּנֵי זַלְעֲפוֹת רָעָב: נָשִׁים בְּצִיּוֹן עִנּוּ בְּתֻלֹת בְּעָרֵי יְהוּדָה: שָׂרִים
יג בְּיָדָם נִתְלוּ פְּנֵי זְקֵנִים לֹא נֶהְדָּרוּ: בַּחוּרִים טְחוֹן נָשָׂאוּ וּנְעָרִים בָּעֵץ
יד טו כָּשָׁלוּ: זְקֵנִים מִשַּׁעַר שָׁבָתוּ בַּחוּרִים מִנְּגִינָתָם: שָׁבַת מְשׂוֹשׂ לִבֵּנוּ
טז נֶהְפַּךְ לְאֵבֶל מְחֹלֵנוּ: נָפְלָה עֲטֶרֶת רֹאשֵׁנוּ אוֹי־נָא לָנוּ כִּי חָטָאנוּ:
יז יח עַל־זֶה הָיָה דָוֶה לִבֵּנוּ עַל־אֵלֶּה חָשְׁכוּ עֵינֵינוּ: עַל הַר־צִיּוֹן שֶׁשָּׁמֵם
יט כ שׁוּעָלִים הִלְּכוּ־בוֹ: אַתָּה יהוה לְעוֹלָם תֵּשֵׁב כִּסְאֲךָ לְדֹר וָדוֹר: לָמָּה
כא לָנֶצַח תִּשְׁכָּחֵנוּ תַּעַזְבֵנוּ לְאֹרֶךְ יָמִים: הֲשִׁיבֵנוּ יהוה ׀ אֵלֶיךָ וְנָשׁוּבָ
כב חַדֵּשׁ יָמֵינוּ כְּקֶדֶם: כִּי אִם־מָאֹס מְאַסְתָּנוּ קָצַפְתָּ עָלֵינוּ עַד־מְאֹד:

השיבנו יהוה אליך ונשובה
חדש ימינו כקדם

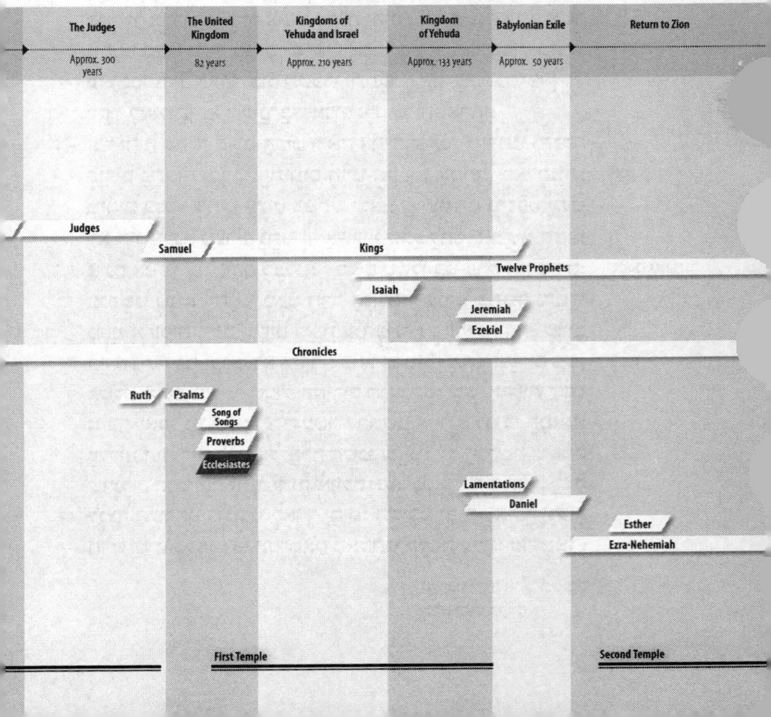

The Judges
The United Kingdom
Kingdoms of Yehuda and Israel
Kingdom of Yehuda
Babylonian Exile
Return to Zion
Approx. 300 years
82 years
Approx. 210 years
Approx. 133 years
Approx. 50 years
Judges
Samuel
Kings
Twelve Prophets
Isaiah
Jeremiah
Ezekiel
Chronicles
Ruth
Psalms
Song of Songs
Proverbs
Ecclesiastes
Lamentations
Daniel
Esther
Ezra-Nehemiah
First Temple
Second Temple

קהלת

KOHELET/ECCLESIASTES

ECCLESIASTES	Opening	Questioning and experimenting	Insights and counsel	Conclusion
	Chs. 1:1–11	1:12–6:12	7:1–12:7	12:8–14

1 1 2 The sayings of Kohelet son of David, king of Israel in Jerusalem.[1] Fleeting
3 breath, Kohelet said: Fleeting breath – it is all mere breath.[2] What profit
4 remains for all the labor one toils over beneath the sun? One generation
5 leaves, another comes; the earth remains forever. The sun rises, the sun sets;
6 it heaves toward its place and there it rises. Blowing south, turning north,
turning, turning, blows the wind, circling then turning, the wind returns.
7 All streams flow into the sea, yet the sea is not full. To the places where the
8 streams first flowed they return to flow again. Everything is burdensome. One
can say nothing, the eye can never see enough; the ear is never filled with
9 hearing. What has been is what will be, what was done will again be done,
10 and there is nothing new beneath the sun. Some thing may make a person say,
"Look at this: it is new!" – it already existed in all the eons that came before
11 us. The people of old left no memory behind, and those yet to come will leave
no more memorial for those who will come after.
12 13 I, Kohelet, was king of Israel in Jerusalem. And I set my mind to studying and
exploring with wisdom all that is done beneath the sky – a wretched
14 occupation, that one, given by God to mortal man to oppress himself with. I
saw everything that is done beneath the sky. It is nothing but fleeting breath,
15 nothing but courting the wind. What is crooked can never be straightened;
16 what is wanting can never be counted. I said to my mind, I have gathered and
built up more wisdom than anyone who has ruled over Jerusalem before, and
17 my mind has seen much of wisdom and insight. And I gave my mind over to
understand wisdom, to discern delirium and folly. I know that too is but
18 courting the wind. For in great wisdom lies great bitterness; and one who
2 1 gathers insight gathers pain. I said to my mind, Come, let me quench myself
with joy; let me sate myself with good living. I found that, too, but fleeting
2 3 breath. "Delirium," I called laughter; asked of joy, "What comes of this?" And
so I explored with my mind, steeping my body in wine, and grasping folly,
while my mind at the helm remained wise – that I might finally see what path
is good for mortal man to follow beneath the sky for as long as he should live.
4 5 I amassed a great estate. I built myself houses, planted vineyards, acquired
gardens and orchards for myself and planted them with every kind of fruit
6 tree. I ordered pools of water to be dug to irrigate a forest burgeoning with
7 trees. I bought slaves and maidservants, and others were born in my house;
I had livestock also, herds and flocks, more than anyone else who came before
8 me in Jerusalem. I collected silver and gold and the treasures of kings and
foreign lands; I brought in singers, male and female, and all the delights of
9 mankind; I took a woman, many women.[3] I grew great and gathered more
than anyone who had come before me in Jerusalem, while my wisdom still
10 stood by me. I withheld from my eyes nothing that they sought, nor did I

1 | Presumably Shlomo, who is also associated with the books of Proverbs and Song of Songs.

2 | Transient and insubstantial, or incapable of being explained rationally. This language recurs throughout the book.

3 | Following Ibn Ezra. The word *shidda* occurs only here in Tanakh.

א א ב דִּבְרֵי קֹהֶלֶת בֶּן־דָּוִד מֶלֶךְ בִּירוּשָׁלִָם׃ הֲבֵל הֲבָלִים אָמַר קֹהֶלֶת א
ג הֲבֵל הֲבָלִים הַכֹּל הָבֶל׃ מַה־יִּתְרוֹן לָאָדָם בְּכָל־עֲמָלוֹ שֶׁיַּעֲמֹל תַּחַת
ד ה הַשָּׁמֶשׁ׃ דּוֹר הֹלֵךְ וְדוֹר בָּא וְהָאָרֶץ לְעוֹלָם עֹמָדֶת׃ וְזָרַח הַשֶּׁמֶשׁ
ו וּבָא הַשָּׁמֶשׁ וְאֶל־מְקוֹמוֹ שׁוֹאֵף זוֹרֵחַ הוּא שָׁם׃ הוֹלֵךְ אֶל־דָּרוֹם
וְסוֹבֵב אֶל־צָפוֹן סוֹבֵב ׀ סֹבֵב הוֹלֵךְ הָרוּחַ וְעַל־סְבִיבֹתָיו שָׁב הָרוּחַ׃
ז כָּל־הַנְּחָלִים הֹלְכִים אֶל־הַיָּם וְהַיָּם אֵינֶנּוּ מָלֵא אֶל־מְקוֹם שֶׁהַנְּחָלִים
ח הֹלְכִים שָׁם הֵם שָׁבִים לָלָכֶת׃ כָּל־הַדְּבָרִים יְגֵעִים לֹא־יוּכַל אִישׁ לְדַבֵּר
ט לֹא־תִשְׂבַּע עַיִן לִרְאוֹת וְלֹא־תִמָּלֵא אֹזֶן מִשְּׁמֹעַ׃ מַה־שֶּׁהָיָה הוּא
שֶׁיִּהְיֶה וּמַה־שֶּׁנַּעֲשָׂה הוּא שֶׁיֵּעָשֶׂה וְאֵין כָּל־חָדָשׁ תַּחַת הַשָּׁמֶשׁ׃
י יֵשׁ דָּבָר שֶׁיֹּאמַר רְאֵה־זֶה חָדָשׁ הוּא כְּבָר הָיָה לְעֹלָמִים אֲשֶׁר הָיָה
יא מִלְּפָנֵנוּ׃ אֵין זִכְרוֹן לָרִאשֹׁנִים וְגַם לָאַחֲרֹנִים שֶׁיִּהְיוּ לֹא־יִהְיֶה לָהֶם
זִכָּרוֹן עִם שֶׁיִּהְיוּ לָאַחֲרֹנָה׃
יב יג אֲנִי קֹהֶלֶת הָיִיתִי מֶלֶךְ עַל־יִשְׂרָאֵל בִּירוּשָׁלִָם׃ וְנָתַתִּי אֶת־לִבִּי לִדְרוֹשׁ
וְלָתוּר בַּחָכְמָה עַל כָּל־אֲשֶׁר נַעֲשָׂה תַּחַת הַשָּׁמָיִם הוּא ׀ עִנְיַן רָע נָתַן
יד אֱלֹהִים לִבְנֵי הָאָדָם לַעֲנוֹת בּוֹ׃ רָאִיתִי אֶת־כָּל־הַמַּעֲשִׂים שֶׁנַּעֲשׂוּ
טו תַּחַת הַשָּׁמֶשׁ וְהִנֵּה הַכֹּל הֶבֶל וּרְעוּת רוּחַ׃ מְעֻוָּת לֹא־יוּכַל לִתְקֹן
טז וְחֶסְרוֹן לֹא־יוּכַל לְהִמָּנוֹת׃ דִּבַּרְתִּי אֲנִי עִם־לִבִּי לֵאמֹר אֲנִי הִנֵּה
הִגְדַּלְתִּי וְהוֹסַפְתִּי חָכְמָה עַל כָּל־אֲשֶׁר־הָיָה לְפָנַי עַל־יְרוּשָׁלִָם וְלִבִּי
יז רָאָה הַרְבֵּה חָכְמָה וָדָעַת׃ וָאֶתְּנָה לִבִּי לָדַעַת חָכְמָה וְדַעַת הוֹלֵלוֹת
יח וְשִׂכְלוּת יָדַעְתִּי שֶׁגַּם־זֶה הוּא רַעְיוֹן רוּחַ׃ כִּי בְּרֹב חָכְמָה רָב־כָּעַס
ב א וְיוֹסִיף דַּעַת יוֹסִיף מַכְאוֹב׃ אָמַרְתִּי אֲנִי בְּלִבִּי לְכָה־נָּא אֲנַסְּכָה
ב בְשִׂמְחָה וּרְאֵה בְטוֹב וְהִנֵּה גַם־הוּא הָבֶל׃ לִשְׂחוֹק אָמַרְתִּי מְהוֹלָל
ג וּלְשִׂמְחָה מַה־זֹּה עֹשָׂה׃ תַּרְתִּי בְלִבִּי לִמְשׁוֹךְ בַּיַּיִן אֶת־בְּשָׂרִי וְלִבִּי
נֹהֵג בַּחָכְמָה וְלֶאֱחֹז בְּסִכְלוּת עַד אֲשֶׁר־אֶרְאֶה אֵי־זֶה טוֹב לִבְנֵי הָאָדָם
ד אֲשֶׁר יַעֲשׂוּ תַּחַת הַשָּׁמַיִם מִסְפַּר יְמֵי חַיֵּיהֶם׃ הִגְדַּלְתִּי מַעֲשָׂי בָּנִיתִי
ה לִי בָּתִּים נָטַעְתִּי לִי כְּרָמִים׃ עָשִׂיתִי לִי גַּנּוֹת וּפַרְדֵּסִים וְנָטַעְתִּי בָהֶם
ו עֵץ כָּל־פֶּרִי׃ עָשִׂיתִי לִי בְּרֵכוֹת מָיִם לְהַשְׁקוֹת מֵהֶם יַעַר צוֹמֵחַ עֵצִים׃
ז קָנִיתִי עֲבָדִים וּשְׁפָחוֹת וּבְנֵי־בַיִת הָיָה לִי גַּם מִקְנֶה בָקָר וָצֹאן הַרְבֵּה
ח הָיָה לִי מִכֹּל שֶׁהָיוּ לְפָנַי בִּירוּשָׁלִָם׃ כָּנַסְתִּי לִי גַּם־כֶּסֶף וְזָהָב וּסְגֻלַּת
מְלָכִים וְהַמְּדִינוֹת עָשִׂיתִי לִי שָׁרִים וְשָׁרוֹת וְתַעֲנוּגֹת בְּנֵי הָאָדָם שִׁדָּה
ט וְשִׁדּוֹת׃ וְגָדַלְתִּי וְהוֹסַפְתִּי מִכֹּל שֶׁהָיָה לְפָנַי בִּירוּשָׁלִָם אַף חָכְמָתִי
י עָמְדָה לִּי׃ וְכֹל אֲשֶׁר שָׁאֲלוּ עֵינַי לֹא אָצַלְתִּי מֵהֶם לֹא־מָנַעְתִּי אֶת־לִבִּי

withhold any joy from myself. For my mind rejoiced in the fruits of my labor,
11 and that was my reward for all my toil. And then I turned to look at all my
works, at the work of my hands, at all that I had labored to achieve – and this
is what I saw: all is but fleeting breath, nothing but courting the wind, and
12 there is no true profit beneath the sun. And I turned to compare wisdom with
delirium and folly, for who is the man who will criticize the king after he has
13 done what he has done? And I saw that there is some advantage to wisdom
14 over foolishness, like the advantage of light over darkness. For "the wise man
has eyes in his head while the fool walks in darkness";[4] yet still I know, the
15 same fate awaits them both. I said to my mind, the fate of the fool awaits me
also; why then should I become wiser? And I told my mind that this too is
16 empty breath. For the wise man, like the fool, leaves no lasting memory. As
soon as the coming days arrive, all is forgotten. How can it be that the wise
17 man dies like the fool? I hated life; this that is done beneath the sun is evil to
18 me. Nothing but fleeting breath, nothing but courting the wind. And I hated
all the toil of my labors beneath the sun; all to be left to some person who will
19 come after me. Who knows whether he will be wise or foolish; either way, he
will lord it over all that I toiled for wisely beneath the sun; that too is empty
20 breath. And I turned toward despair over all the labor which I had toiled at
21 beneath the sun. For so often a person labors with wisdom and insight and
skill – and then bequeaths his share to someone who has not labored; this too
22 is as empty as breath, and a great evil. For what remains to a person of
all the labor and of all the thought that he has expended beneath the sky?
3 All his days are pain, his occupation bitterness, and even at night his mind
24 does not rest – and this too is empty breath. There is nothing better for a
person to do than to eat and drink and reap some good from his labor; this
25 I saw to be a gift from God. For who will eat, who will hasten to satisfy
26 my craving if not I? He gave wisdom and insight and joy to those who
are satisfied with what they have, but to the misdirected He gave a
preoccupation with gathering and collecting, only to turn it all over to someone
who pleases God. This too is empty breath; it is courting the wind.

3 1 "Everything has its moment; a time for every action beneath the sky."

2 There is a time for birth — and a time for death;
a time to plant — and a time to uproot.
3 A time to kill, — a time to heal;
a time to tear down — and a time to build up.
4 A time to weep, — a time to laugh;
a time for eulogy — and a time for dance.
5 A time to cast away stones, — a time to gather them up;[5]
a time to embrace — and a time to hold back from embracing.

---

4 | Kohelet sometimes quotes known sayings, here indicated by quotation marks, and then refutes them.

5 | This may refer to demolishing and constructing a building, or ruining a planting field by throwing stones into it.

מִכׇּל־שִׂמְחָה כִּי־לִבִּי שָׂמֵחַ מִכׇּל־עֲמָלִי וְזֶה־הָיָה חֶלְקִי מִכׇּל־עֲמָלִי׃
יא וּפָנִיתִי אֲנִי בְּכׇל־מַעֲשַׂי שֶׁעָשׂוּ יָדַי וּבֶעָמָל שֶׁעָמַלְתִּי לַעֲשׂוֹת וְהִנֵּה
יב הַכֹּל הֶבֶל וּרְעוּת רוּחַ וְאֵין יִתְרוֹן תַּחַת הַשָּׁמֶשׁ׃ וּפָנִיתִי אֲנִי לִרְאוֹת
חׇכְמָה וְהוֹלֵלוֹת וְסִכְלוּת כִּי ׀ מֶה הָאָדָם שֶׁיָּבוֹא אַחֲרֵי הַמֶּלֶךְ אֵת
יג אֲשֶׁר־כְּבָר עָשׂוּהוּ׃ וְרָאִיתִי אָנִי שֶׁיֵּשׁ יִתְרוֹן לַחׇכְמָה מִן־הַסִּכְלוּת
יד כִּיתְרוֹן הָאוֹר מִן־הַחֹשֶׁךְ׃ הֶחָכָם עֵינָיו בְּרֹאשׁוֹ וְהַכְּסִיל בַּחֹשֶׁךְ
טו הוֹלֵךְ וְיָדַעְתִּי גַם־אָנִי שֶׁמִּקְרֶה אֶחָד יִקְרֶה אֶת־כֻּלָּם׃ וְאָמַרְתִּי אֲנִי
בְּלִבִּי כְּמִקְרֵה הַכְּסִיל גַּם־אֲנִי יִקְרֵנִי וְלָמָּה חָכַמְתִּי אֲנִי אָז יֹתֵר
טז וְדִבַּרְתִּי בְלִבִּי שֶׁגַּם־זֶה הָבֶל׃ כִּי אֵין זִכְרוֹן לֶחָכָם עִם־הַכְּסִיל
לְעוֹלָם בְּשֶׁכְּבָר הַיָּמִים הַבָּאִים הַכֹּל נִשְׁכָּח וְאֵיךְ יָמוּת הֶחָכָם
יז עִם־הַכְּסִיל׃ וְשָׂנֵאתִי אֶת־הַחַיִּים כִּי רַע עָלַי הַמַּעֲשֶׂה שֶׁנַּעֲשָׂה
יח תַּחַת הַשָּׁמֶשׁ כִּי־הַכֹּל הֶבֶל וּרְעוּת רוּחַ׃ וְשָׂנֵאתִי אֲנִי אֶת־כׇּל־עֲמָלִי
יט שֶׁאֲנִי עָמֵל תַּחַת הַשָּׁמֶשׁ שֶׁאַנִּיחֶנּוּ לָאָדָם שֶׁיִּהְיֶה אַחֲרָי׃ וּמִי יוֹדֵעַ
הֶחָכָם יִהְיֶה אוֹ סָכָל וְיִשְׁלַט בְּכׇל־עֲמָלִי שֶׁעָמַלְתִּי וְשֶׁחָכַמְתִּי תַּחַת
כ הַשָּׁמֶשׁ גַּם־זֶה הָבֶל׃ וְסַבּוֹתִי אֲנִי לְיַאֵשׁ אֶת־לִבִּי עַל כׇּל־הֶעָמָל
כא שֶׁעָמַלְתִּי תַּחַת הַשָּׁמֶשׁ׃ כִּי־יֵשׁ אָדָם שֶׁעֲמָלוֹ בְּחׇכְמָה וּבְדַעַת
וּבְכִשְׁרוֹן וּלְאָדָם שֶׁלֹּא עָמַל־בּוֹ יִתְּנֶנּוּ חֶלְקוֹ גַּם־זֶה הֶבֶל וְרָעָה רַבָּה׃
כב כִּי מֶה־הֹוֶה לָאָדָם בְּכׇל־עֲמָלוֹ וּבְרַעְיוֹן לִבּוֹ שֶׁהוּא עָמֵל תַּחַת הַשָּׁמֶשׁ׃
כג כִּי כׇל־יָמָיו מַכְאֹבִים וָכַעַס עִנְיָנוֹ גַּם־בַּלַּיְלָה לֹא־שָׁכַב לִבּוֹ גַּם־זֶה
כד הֶבֶל הוּא׃ אֵין־טוֹב בָּאָדָם שֶׁיֹּאכַל וְשָׁתָה וְהֶרְאָה אֶת־נַפְשׁוֹ טוֹב
כה בַּעֲמָלוֹ גַּם־זֹה רָאִיתִי אָנִי כִּי מִיַּד הָאֱלֹהִים הִיא׃ כִּי מִי יֹאכַל וּמִי
כו יָחוּשׁ חוּץ מִמֶּנִּי׃ כִּי לְאָדָם שֶׁטּוֹב לְפָנָיו נָתַן חׇכְמָה וְדַעַת וְשִׂמְחָה
וְלַחוֹטֶא נָתַן עִנְיָן לֶאֱסֹף וְלִכְנוֹס לָתֵת לְטוֹב לִפְנֵי הָאֱלֹהִים גַּם־
ג א זֶה הֶבֶל וּרְעוּת רוּחַ׃ לַכֹּל זְמָן וְעֵת לְכׇל־חֵפֶץ תַּחַת הַשָּׁמָיִם׃
ב עֵת לָלֶדֶת וְעֵת לָמוּת
עֵת לָטַעַת וְעֵת לַעֲקוֹר נָטוּעַ׃
ג עֵת לַהֲרוֹג וְעֵת לִרְפּוֹא
עֵת לִפְרוֹץ וְעֵת לִבְנוֹת׃
ד עֵת לִבְכּוֹת וְעֵת לִשְׂחוֹק
עֵת סְפוֹד וְעֵת רְקוֹד׃
ה עֵת לְהַשְׁלִיךְ אֲבָנִים וְעֵת כְּנוֹס אֲבָנִים
עֵת לַחֲבוֹק וְעֵת לִרְחֹק מֵחַבֵּק׃

6 A time to seek, a time to lose;
a time to keep and a time to cast aside.
7 A time to tear, a time to sew;
a time for silence and a time for speech.
8 A time to love, a time to hate;
a time for war and a time for peace.
9 10 What profit then does he who toils gain from all his labor? I have seen the
11 occupation that God gave mortal man to torment himself with. He made
everything right in its proper time; He placed all the world in their minds;
yet no one ever fathoms what it is that God is forming from beginning to end.
12 And so I know that there is nothing better for them than to be happy and to
13 do what is good in their lifetimes. And if a man eats and drinks and reaps some
14 enjoyment from all his labor – that is a gift from God. And I know that
whatever God has made will exist forever. There is no adding to it, there is no
15 taking away; and God has made quite sure that He be feared. That which has
been is already here, and that which will be has already been. And God is
16 seeking after the pursued. Another thing that I saw beneath the sun: in the
place of justice – there is the evil; where righteousness is – there evil is found.
17 I said to my mind: God will judge both the righteous and the wicked, for the
18 time will come for every deed, for all that is done; there. And I said to my
mind, as regards mankind: God set them apart only to find that they are
19 nothing but cattle. For the fate of man is the fate of cattle: the same fate awaits
them both, the death of one is like the death of the other, their spirit is the
same, and the preeminence of man over beast is nothing, for it is all no more
20 than empty breath. All end up in the same place; all emerge from dust, and
21 all go back to dust. Who can say that the spirit of man rises on high while the
22 spirit of a beast sinks into the ground? I saw that there is nothing better for a
man than to take pleasure in his work, for that is his lot. For who will show
4 1 him what will become of it all when he is gone? I turned again and saw all
those made victims beneath the sun. There they were: the victims' tears and
none to console them; power in the hands of their oppressors and none to
2 console them. And I praise the dead, who have died already, more than the
3 living who yet live. But better than either are those who are yet to be, for they
4 have seen none of the evil that is wrought beneath the sun. And I saw that all
the striving and all the skill: it is all but one man's jealousy of another. This
5 too is empty breath and courting the wind. "The fool crosses his hands and
6 eats his own flesh." But better a handful gained peacefully, than two hands

ו עֵת לְבַקֵּשׁ וְעֵת לְאַבֵּד
עֵת לִשְׁמוֹר וְעֵת לְהַשְׁלִיךְ:
ז עֵת לִקְרוֹעַ וְעֵת לִתְפּוֹר
עֵת לַחֲשׁוֹת וְעֵת לְדַבֵּר:
ח עֵת לֶאֱהֹב וְעֵת לִשְׂנֹא
עֵת מִלְחָמָה וְעֵת שָׁלוֹם:
ט י מַה־יִּתְרוֹן הָעוֹשֶׂה בַּאֲשֶׁר הוּא עָמֵל: רָאִיתִי אֶת־הָעִנְיָן אֲשֶׁר נָתַן
יא אֱלֹהִים לִבְנֵי הָאָדָם לַעֲנוֹת בּוֹ: אֶת־הַכֹּל עָשָׂה יָפֶה בְעִתּוֹ גַּם אֶת־
הָעֹלָם נָתַן בְּלִבָּם מִבְּלִי אֲשֶׁר לֹא־יִמְצָא הָאָדָם אֶת־הַמַּעֲשֶׂה אֲשֶׁר־
יב עָשָׂה הָאֱלֹהִים מֵרֹאשׁ וְעַד־סוֹף: יָדַעְתִּי כִּי אֵין טוֹב בָּם כִּי אִם־
יג לִשְׂמוֹחַ וְלַעֲשׂוֹת טוֹב בְּחַיָּיו: וְגַם כָּל־הָאָדָם שֶׁיֹּאכַל וְשָׁתָה וְרָאָה ב
יד טוֹב בְּכָל־עֲמָלוֹ מַתַּת אֱלֹהִים הִיא: יָדַעְתִּי כִּי כָּל־אֲשֶׁר יַעֲשֶׂה
הָאֱלֹהִים הוּא יִהְיֶה לְעוֹלָם עָלָיו אֵין לְהוֹסִיף וּמִמֶּנּוּ אֵין לִגְרֹעַ
טו וְהָאֱלֹהִים עָשָׂה שֶׁיִּרְאוּ מִלְּפָנָיו: מַה־שֶּׁהָיָה כְּבָר הוּא וַאֲשֶׁר לִהְיוֹת
טז כְּבָר הָיָה וְהָאֱלֹהִים יְבַקֵּשׁ אֶת־נִרְדָּף: וְעוֹד רָאִיתִי תַּחַת הַשָּׁמֶשׁ
יז מְקוֹם הַמִּשְׁפָּט שָׁמָּה הָרֶשַׁע וּמְקוֹם הַצֶּדֶק שָׁמָּה הָרָשַׁע: אָמַרְתִּי
אֲנִי בְּלִבִּי אֶת־הַצַּדִּיק וְאֶת־הָרָשָׁע יִשְׁפֹּט הָאֱלֹהִים כִּי־עֵת לְכָל־
יח חֵפֶץ וְעַל כָּל־הַמַּעֲשֶׂה שָׁם: אָמַרְתִּי אֲנִי בְּלִבִּי עַל־דִּבְרַת בְּנֵי הָאָדָם
יט לְבָרָם הָאֱלֹהִים וְלִרְאוֹת שְׁהֶם־בְּהֵמָה הֵמָּה לָהֶם: כִּי מִקְרֶה בְנֵי־
הָאָדָם וּמִקְרֶה הַבְּהֵמָה וּמִקְרֶה אֶחָד לָהֶם כְּמוֹת זֶה כֵּן מוֹת זֶה וְרוּחַ
כ אֶחָד לַכֹּל וּמוֹתַר הָאָדָם מִן־הַבְּהֵמָה אָיִן כִּי הַכֹּל הָבֶל: הַכֹּל הוֹלֵךְ
כא אֶל־מָקוֹם אֶחָד הַכֹּל הָיָה מִן־הֶעָפָר וְהַכֹּל שָׁב אֶל־הֶעָפָר: מִי יוֹדֵעַ
רוּחַ בְּנֵי הָאָדָם הָעֹלָה הִיא לְמָעְלָה וְרוּחַ הַבְּהֵמָה הַיֹּרֶדֶת הִיא לְמַטָּה
כב לָאָרֶץ: וְרָאִיתִי כִּי אֵין טוֹב מֵאֲשֶׁר יִשְׂמַח הָאָדָם בְּמַעֲשָׂיו כִּי־
א הוּא חֶלְקוֹ כִּי מִי יְבִיאֶנּוּ לִרְאוֹת בְּמֶה שֶׁיִּהְיֶה אַחֲרָיו: וְשַׁבְתִּי אֲנִי ד
וָאֶרְאֶה אֶת־כָּל־הָעֲשֻׁקִים אֲשֶׁר נַעֲשִׂים תַּחַת הַשָּׁמֶשׁ וְהִנֵּה ׀ דִּמְעַת
הָעֲשֻׁקִים וְאֵין לָהֶם מְנַחֵם וּמִיַּד עֹשְׁקֵיהֶם כֹּחַ וְאֵין לָהֶם מְנַחֵם:
ב וְשַׁבֵּחַ אֲנִי אֶת־הַמֵּתִים שֶׁכְּבָר מֵתוּ מִן־הַחַיִּים אֲשֶׁר הֵמָּה חַיִּים עֲדֶנָה:
ג וְטוֹב מִשְּׁנֵיהֶם אֵת אֲשֶׁר־עֲדֶן לֹא הָיָה אֲשֶׁר לֹא־רָאָה אֶת־הַמַּעֲשֶׂה
ד הָרָע אֲשֶׁר נַעֲשָׂה תַּחַת הַשָּׁמֶשׁ: וְרָאִיתִי אֲנִי אֶת־כָּל־עָמָל וְאֵת כָּל־
כִּשְׁרוֹן הַמַּעֲשֶׂה כִּי הִיא קִנְאַת־אִישׁ מֵרֵעֵהוּ גַּם־זֶה הֶבֶל וּרְעוּת רוּחַ:
ה ו הַכְּסִיל חֹבֵק אֶת־יָדָיו וְאֹכֵל אֶת־בְּשָׂרוֹ: טוֹב מְלֹא כַף נָחַת מִמְּלֹא

7 full of labor and courting the wind. I turned again and saw empty breath
8 beneath the sun. It happens that a man may be alone, with no fellow, no child
even, no brother, yet there is no end to all his labor. His eye, too, will never
see enough of riches; yet he never asks himself, "For whom, after all, am I
laboring and denying myself goodness?" This too is empty breath and a
9 wretched business. Two are better than one for they have good return for all
10 their labor. For if one falls down, the other will raise him; but pity the one
11 who falls alone, for who will ever raise him? Two people lying down together
12 are warm, but how can one ever be warm alone? If one man should assault
another, two can stand against him, and a three-stranded thread is not readily
13 broken. Better a poor but clever youth than an old and foolish king, who does
14 not know how to take heed anymore. For he may come straight out of debtor's
15 prison to rule, though he was born poor in the old reign. Yes, I saw all of life
moving about beneath the sun, with the next child who will stand in his place.[6]
16 There is no end to this people, to all who came before them, and those who
come after them will likewise never rejoice in him.[7] This too is empty breath,
17 is courting the wind. Watch your step when you go to the House of God.
Better to take heed than to bring a fool's offering, for they know not what
5 1 doing wrong means.[8] Do not hasten your lips, do not hurry your heart to make
a vow in the presence of God – for God is in heaven while you are here on
2 earth; so let your words be few. For as dreams come of too much preoccupation,
3 so is a fool's voice known by too many words. If you make a vow to God, do
not delay in fulfilling it, for there is no use being a fool – whatever you vow,
4 5 fulfill. Better not to vow than to vow and not fulfill. Do not let your mouth
lead your flesh to sin, and do not tell the messenger that it was a mistake; why
should you have God rage at your words and destroy the work of your hands?
6 For so many dreams and so much empty breath, so many words – better only
7 to fear God. If you see oppression of a poor person or any perversion of law
and justice in the province, do not wonder at the fact, for every watchman
8 has a watchman over him, and there are higher ones yet above.[9] Yet the earth
9 below has the advantage over all; even a king is enslaved to the field.[10] One
who loves money will never be satisfied with money, nor one who loves
10 abundance, with produce: that too is fleeting breath. As good things multiply,
so do those who would consume them; and what advantage does it bring its
11 master but longing eyes? The sleep of a worker is sweet whether he eats much
12 or little, but the rich man's abundance will not let him sleep in peace. I have
seen a sickly evil beneath the sun: wealth hoarded by its owner, only to harm
13 him. For the wealth is lost in some ill venture, and a child is born to him when
14 he has nothing to his name. Naked as he emerged from his mother's womb,

---

6 | The clever youth who will succeed the foolish king.

7 | The new king, even if he is wise and just, will not be acclaimed by the multitude of past or future generations.

8 | They do not understand that it is better to act well than to sin and atone with a meaningless sacrifice.

9 | Have faith that higher authorities will correct injustices.

10 | The meaning of this verse is unclear, perhaps referring to the need or value of cultivating fields.

ז ח חפנים עמל ורעות רוח: ושבתי אני ואראה הבל תחת השמש: יש
אחד ואין שני גם בן ואח אין־לו ואין קץ לכל־עמלו גם־עינו לא־ עינו
תשבע עשר ולמי | אני עמל ומחסר את־נפשי מטובה גם־זה הבל
ט וענין רע הוא: טובים השנים מן־האחד אשר יש־להם שכר טוב
י בעמלם: כי אם־יפלו האחד יקים את־חברו ואילו האחד שיפול
יא ואין שני להקימו: גם אם־ישכבו שנים וחם להם ולאחד איך יחם:
יב ואם־יתקפו האחד השנים יעמדו נגדו והחוט המשלש לא במהרה
יג ינתק: טוב ילד מסכן וחכם ממלך זקן וכסיל אשר לא־ידע להזהר
יד טו עוד: כי־מבית הסורים יצא למלך כי גם במלכותו נולד רש: ראיתי
את־כל־החיים המהלכים תחת השמש עם הילד השני אשר יעמד
טז תחתיו: אין־קץ לכל־העם לכל אשר־היה לפניהם גם האחרונים
יז לא ישמחו־בו כי־גם־זה הבל ורעיון רוח: שמור רגליך כאשר תלך רגלך
אל־בית האלהים וקרוב לשמע מתת הכסילים זבח כי־אינם יודעים
ה א לעשות רע: אל־תבהל על־פיך ולבך אל־ימהר להוציא דבר לפני
האלהים כי האלהים בשמים ואתה על־הארץ על־כן יהיו דבריך
ב ג מעטים: כי בא החלום ברב ענין וקול כסיל ברב דברים: כאשר
תדר נדר לאלהים אל־תאחר לשלמו כי אין חפץ בכסילים את
ד ה אשר־תדר שלם: טוב אשר לא־תדר משתדור ולא תשלם: אל־
תתן את־פיך לחטיא את־בשרך ואל־תאמר לפני המלאך כי שגגה
ו היא למה יקצף האלהים על־קולך וחבל את־מעשה ידיך: כי ברב
ז חלמות והבלים ודברים הרבה כי את־האלהים ירא: אם־עשק רש
וגזל משפט וצדק תראה במדינה אל־תתמה על־החפץ כי גבה
ח מעל גבה שמר וגבהים עליהם: ויתרון ארץ בכל היא מלך לשדה הוא
ט נעבד: אהב כסף לא־ישבע כסף ומי־אהב בהמון לא תבואה גם־זה
י הבל: ברבות הטובה רבו אוכליה ומה־כשרון לבעליה כי אם־ראית ראות
יא עיניו: מתוקה שנת העבד אם־מעט ואם־הרבה יאכל והשבע
יב לעשיר איננו מניח לו לישון: יש רעה חולה ראיתי תחת השמש
יג עשר שמור לבעליו לרעתו: ואבד העשר ההוא בענין רע והוליד
יד בן ואין בידו מאומה: כאשר יצא מבטן אמו ערום ישוב ללכת

naked will he return.[11] And not the slightest thing from all his labor will he
15 retain to take with him. This too is a sickly evil; just as a person comes, so
16 shall he leave again. And what profit does he gain for toiling in the wind? All
17 his days he eats in darkness with great bitterness, and sickness, and fury. This
is what I have seen that is good: to eat and to drink and gain satisfaction from
all the labor at which you toil beneath the sun all the days of the life God has
18 given you – for this is your share. For if God gives any man wealth and
belongings and grants him the power to eat of them, to take hold of what is
19 his, to take pleasure in the fruits of his labors – that is a gift from God. For he
will not much remember the hard days of his life; for God has given him the
6 1 joy of his heart to occupy him. There is an evil I have seen beneath the sun,
2 and the harm it does people is great. There will be a man to whom God gives
wealth and possessions and honor so that he lacks nothing his heart desires.
And then God will not grant him the power to partake of it, and a stranger
3 will consume it all; this is empty breath and an evil sickness. A man may have
a hundred children and live for many years, and as many as his years may be,
if he is never satisfied with all that goodness – lacking even a burial[12] – I say a
4 stillborn child is better off than he. For he comes with a breath and leaves in
5 darkness, and in darkness is his name covered over. That child will never see
sunlight, will never know a thing, and yet he has more peace than such a man.
6 If a person lives a thousand years twice over and sees no pleasure – well, do
7 we not all go to the same place in the end? All of man's labor is only for his
8 mouth; and still his throat is never sated. What advantage does a wise man
hold over a fool? And what does an oppressed man profit from knowing how
9 to walk through life? Is it better for the eyes to see than for the spirit to enjoy?
10 This too is empty breath and courting the wind. Whatever has been is already
named – and it is known by now that this is but a man, who cannot contend
11 with one more powerful than he. There are so many things, such bountiful
12 production of empty breath, and what profit do they bring to man? For who
knows what is good for a man in his lifetime, during the numbered days of
his breath that he lives as a shadow; for who can tell what his fate will be
7 1 beneath the sun? "Better a good name than fine oil." Better the day
2 of death than of birth. Better to frequent a house of mourning than a feast,
3 for that is the end of all men, and the living do well to keep that in mind. Better
bitterness than laughter, for while the face is troubled, the mind is bettering
4 itself. A wise man's heart is in the house of mourning, and a fool's in the house
5 of celebration. Better to heed the rebuke of the wise than to hear the song of
6 fools. For fools' cackling is like the crackling of thorns under the pot. That
7 too is empty breath. Lucre turns a wise man delirious, and a gift makes him
8 lose his wisdom. The end of a thing is better than its beginning. Patience is
9 better than pride. Do not be so quick to anger, for anger lies in the lap of the
10 fool. Do not say, "What went wrong, that times gone by were better than

---

11 | See Job 1:21.

12 | The placement of this phrase is problematic. It may refer to the man's burial or to the fact that the stillborn did not receive burials.

טו כְּשֶׁבָּא וּמְאוּמָה לֹא־יִשָּׂא בַעֲמָלוֹ שֶׁיֹּלֵךְ בְּיָדוֹ: וְגַם־זֹה רָעָה חוֹלָה
טז כָּל־עֻמַּת שֶׁבָּא כֵּן יֵלֵךְ וּמַה־יִּתְרוֹן לוֹ שֶׁיַּעֲמֹל לָרוּחַ: גַּם כָּל־יָמָיו
יז בַּחֹשֶׁךְ יֹאכֵל וְכָעַס הַרְבֵּה וְחָלְיוֹ וָקָצֶף: הִנֵּה אֲשֶׁר־רָאִיתִי אָנִי טוֹב
אֲשֶׁר־יָפֶה לֶאֱכוֹל־וְלִשְׁתּוֹת וְלִרְאוֹת טוֹבָה בְּכָל־עֲמָלוֹ ׀ שֶׁיַּעֲמֹל
תַּחַת־הַשֶּׁמֶשׁ מִסְפַּר יְמֵי־חַיָּו אֲשֶׁר־נָתַן־לוֹ הָאֱלֹהִים כִּי־הוּא חֶלְקוֹ:
יח גַּם כָּל־הָאָדָם אֲשֶׁר נָתַן־לוֹ הָאֱלֹהִים עֹשֶׁר וּנְכָסִים וְהִשְׁלִיטוֹ לֶאֱכֹל
יט מִמֶּנּוּ וְלָשֵׂאת אֶת־חֶלְקוֹ וְלִשְׂמֹחַ בַּעֲמָלוֹ זֹה מַתַּת אֱלֹהִים הִיא: כִּי
ו א לֹא הַרְבֵּה יִזְכֹּר אֶת־יְמֵי חַיָּיו כִּי הָאֱלֹהִים מַעֲנֶה בְּשִׂמְחַת לִבּוֹ: יֵשׁ
ב רָעָה אֲשֶׁר רָאִיתִי תַּחַת הַשָּׁמֶשׁ וְרַבָּה הִיא עַל־הָאָדָם: אִישׁ אֲשֶׁר
יִתֶּן־לוֹ הָאֱלֹהִים עֹשֶׁר וּנְכָסִים וְכָבוֹד וְאֵינֶנּוּ חָסֵר לְנַפְשׁוֹ ׀ מִכֹּל אֲשֶׁר־
יִתְאַוֶּה וְלֹא־יַשְׁלִיטֶנּוּ הָאֱלֹהִים לֶאֱכֹל מִמֶּנּוּ כִּי אִישׁ נָכְרִי יֹאכְלֶנּוּ זֶה
ג הֶבֶל וָחֳלִי רָע הוּא: אִם־יוֹלִיד אִישׁ מֵאָה וְשָׁנִים רַבּוֹת יִחְיֶה וְרַב ׀
שֶׁיִּהְיוּ יְמֵי־שָׁנָיו וְנַפְשׁוֹ לֹא־תִשְׂבַּע מִן־הַטּוֹבָה וְגַם־קְבוּרָה לֹא־הָיְתָה
ד לּוֹ אָמַרְתִּי טוֹב מִמֶּנּוּ הַנָּפֶל: כִּי־בַהֶבֶל בָּא וּבַחֹשֶׁךְ יֵלֵךְ וּבַחֹשֶׁךְ שְׁמוֹ
ה ו יְכֻסֶּה: גַּם־שֶׁמֶשׁ לֹא־רָאָה וְלֹא יָדָע נַחַת לָזֶה מִזֶּה: וְאִלּוּ חָיָה אֶלֶף
ז שָׁנִים פַּעֲמַיִם וְטוֹבָה לֹא רָאָה הֲלֹא אֶל־מָקוֹם אֶחָד הַכֹּל הוֹלֵךְ: כָּל־
ח עֲמַל הָאָדָם לְפִיהוּ וְגַם־הַנֶּפֶשׁ לֹא תִמָּלֵא: כִּי מַה־יּוֹתֵר לֶחָכָם מִן־
ט הַכְּסִיל מַה־לֶּעָנִי יוֹדֵעַ לַהֲלֹךְ נֶגֶד הַחַיִּים: טוֹב מַרְאֵה עֵינַיִם מֵהֲלָךְ־
י נָפֶשׁ גַּם־זֶה הֶבֶל וּרְעוּת רוּחַ: מַה־שֶּׁהָיָה כְּבָר נִקְרָא שְׁמוֹ וְנוֹדָע
יא אֲשֶׁר־הוּא אָדָם וְלֹא־יוּכַל לָדִין עִם שֶׁהתקיף מִמֶּנּוּ: כִּי יֵשׁ־דְּבָרִים שֶׁתַּקִּיף
יב הַרְבֵּה מַרְבִּים הָבֶל מַה־יֹּתֵר לָאָדָם: כִּי מִי־יוֹדֵעַ מַה־טּוֹב לָאָדָם
בַּחַיִּים מִסְפַּר יְמֵי־חַיֵּי הֶבְלוֹ וְיַעֲשֵׂם כַּצֵּל אֲשֶׁר מִי־יַגִּיד לָאָדָם מַה־
ז א יִּהְיֶה אַחֲרָיו תַּחַת הַשָּׁמֶשׁ: טוֹב שֵׁם מִשֶּׁמֶן טוֹב וְיוֹם ג
ב הַמָּוֶת מִיּוֹם הִוָּלְדוֹ: טוֹב לָלֶכֶת אֶל־בֵּית־אֵבֶל מִלֶּכֶת אֶל־בֵּית מִשְׁתֶּה
ג בַּאֲשֶׁר הוּא סוֹף כָּל־הָאָדָם וְהַחַי יִתֵּן אֶל־לִבּוֹ: טוֹב כַּעַס מִשְּׂחֹק
ד כִּי־בְרֹעַ פָּנִים יִיטַב לֵב: לֵב חֲכָמִים בְּבֵית אֵבֶל וְלֵב כְּסִילִים בְּבֵית
ה ו שִׂמְחָה: טוֹב לִשְׁמֹעַ גַּעֲרַת חָכָם מֵאִישׁ שֹׁמֵעַ שִׁיר כְּסִילִים: כִּי כְקוֹל
ז הַסִּירִים תַּחַת הַסִּיר כֵּן שְׂחֹק הַכְּסִיל וְגַם־זֶה הָבֶל: כִּי הָעֹשֶׁק יְהוֹלֵל
ח חָכָם וִיאַבֵּד אֶת־לֵב מַתָּנָה: טוֹב אַחֲרִית דָּבָר מֵרֵאשִׁיתוֹ טוֹב אֶרֶךְ־
ט רוּחַ מִגְּבַהּ רוּחַ: אַל־תְּבַהֵל בְּרוּחֲךָ לִכְעוֹס כִּי כַעַס בְּחֵיק כְּסִילִים
י יָנוּחַ: אַל־תֹּאמַר מֶה הָיָה שֶׁהַיָּמִים הָרִאשֹׁנִים הָיוּ טוֹבִים מֵאֵלֶּה כִּי

11 these?" It is not wisdom that leads you to ask. Wisdom is better with an estate,
12 though it profits all who see the sun. For then a man is in the shade of wisdom
and the shade of money too. But the profit of understanding is greater, for
13 wisdom brings life to those who master it. Consider the acts of God – for
14 nobody can straighten what He has made crooked. On a good day, enjoy the
good, and on a bad day consider: God made both, one alongside the other;
15 and no man can afterward find fault with Him. I have seen it all in the few
days of my breath: righteous men who die in their righteousness, and wicked
16 ones who live long in their wickedness. So do not be too righteous, and do
17 not seek more wisdom, for why should you become desolate? Do not be too
18 wicked, and never be a fool, for why should you die before your time? Better
to hold the one, never loosening your hand upon the other, for a God-fearing
19 man will heed both warnings. Wisdom gives the wise man more power than
20 ten leaders wield in a city. Yes, there is no one in this world so righteous that
21 he only does good and never sins. Do not take to heart all the words you hear
22 said; do not hear your slave when he insults you. For many times, as your
23 heart well knows, you yourself have insulted others. I tried all this with my
24 wisdom. I said, "I shall be wiser"; but it was far away from me. All that has
25 ever been is far away, deep beyond fathoming. I turned my mind to understand
and to explore, to seek wisdom and reason; and to know the wickedness of
26 foolishness, to know folly and delirium. And this is what I found: woman is
more bitter than death, for she is all traps, with nets laid in her heart; her arms
are a prison; the man favored by God escapes her while a sinner becomes
27 entrapped. See what I found, said Kohelet, searching one by one to find
28 account. This too my soul sought and did not find: one righteous man in a
29 thousand I found, but among those few even one such woman I did not. Yes,
all that I found is this: that God created man straightforward; but men go
8 1 seeking endless accounts.[13] Who is like a wise man able to see meaning? The
2 wisdom a person has lights up his face, and his countenance is changed. Obey
3 the king's word, I say, and the word of your oath to God. Do not take flight;
walk clear away; do not be present when evil is brewing, for a king will do
4 what it pleases him to do. For a king's word rules, and who can say to him,
5 "What is it that you do?" One who heeds commands will know no harm, and
6 a wise mind remembers the time of judgment. For every thing has its time
7 and its judgment – and great is the evil man must suffer – for man cannot
8 know what will be, for when it comes who will tell him? Man has no power
over the wind – he cannot cage up the wind; no one rules on the day of death,
no one will take your place in that battle, and evil provides no escape for its
9 masters. All this have I seen, and I took it to heart: all that is done here beneath
10 the sun, wherever man wields power over man to harm him. As I looked
around, I saw wicked men coming from the holy place and buried honorably,
while those who acted with decency are forgotten by the town – here again:

---

13 | That is, reasons or schemes.

יא לֹא מֵחָכְמָה שָׁאַלְתָּ עַל־זֶה׃ טוֹבָה חָכְמָה עִם־נַחֲלָה וְיֹתֵר לְרֹאֵי
יב הַשָּׁמֶשׁ׃ כִּי בְּצֵל הַחָכְמָה בְּצֵל הַכָּסֶף וְיִתְרוֹן דַּעַת הַחָכְמָה תְּחַיֶּה
יג בְעָלֶיהָ׃ רְאֵה אֶת־מַעֲשֵׂה הָאֱלֹהִים כִּי מִי יוּכַל לְתַקֵּן אֵת אֲשֶׁר עִוְּתוֹ׃
יד בְּיוֹם טוֹבָה הֱיֵה בְטוֹב וּבְיוֹם רָעָה רְאֵה גַּם אֶת־זֶה לְעֻמַּת־זֶה עָשָׂה
טו הָאֱלֹהִים עַל־דִּבְרַת שֶׁלֹּא יִמְצָא הָאָדָם אַחֲרָיו מְאוּמָה׃ אֶת־הַכֹּל
רָאִיתִי בִּימֵי הֶבְלִי יֵשׁ צַדִּיק אֹבֵד בְּצִדְקוֹ וְיֵשׁ רָשָׁע מַאֲרִיךְ בְּרָעָתוֹ׃
טז יז אַל־תְּהִי צַדִּיק הַרְבֵּה וְאַל־תִּתְחַכַּם יוֹתֵר לָמָּה תִּשּׁוֹמֵם׃ אַל־תִּרְשַׁע
יח הַרְבֵּה וְאַל־תְּהִי סָכָל לָמָּה תָמוּת בְּלֹא עִתֶּךָ׃ טוֹב אֲשֶׁר תֶּאֱחֹז בָּזֶה
יט וְגַם־מִזֶּה אַל־תַּנַּח אֶת־יָדֶךָ כִּי־יְרֵא אֱלֹהִים יֵצֵא אֶת־כֻּלָּם׃ הַחָכְמָה
כ תָּעֹז לֶחָכָם מֵעֲשָׂרָה שַׁלִּיטִים אֲשֶׁר הָיוּ בָּעִיר׃ כִּי אָדָם אֵין צַדִּיק
כא בָּאָרֶץ אֲשֶׁר יַעֲשֶׂה־טּוֹב וְלֹא יֶחֱטָא׃ גַּם לְכָל־הַדְּבָרִים אֲשֶׁר יְדַבֵּרוּ
כב אַל־תִּתֵּן לִבֶּךָ אֲשֶׁר לֹא־תִשְׁמַע אֶת־עַבְדְּךָ מְקַלְלֶךָ׃ כִּי גַּם־פְּעָמִים
כג רַבּוֹת יָדַע לִבֶּךָ אֲשֶׁר גַּם־אַתָּ קִלַּלְתָּ אֲחֵרִים׃ כָּל־זֹה נִסִּיתִי בַחָכְמָה
כד אָמַרְתִּי אֶחְכָּמָה וְהִיא רְחוֹקָה מִמֶּנִּי׃ רָחוֹק מַה־שֶּׁהָיָה וְעָמֹק ׀ עָמֹק
כה מִי יִמְצָאֶנּוּ׃ סַבּוֹתִי אֲנִי וְלִבִּי לָדַעַת וְלָתוּר וּבַקֵּשׁ חָכְמָה וְחֶשְׁבּוֹן
כו וְלָדַעַת רֶשַׁע כֶּסֶל וְהַסִּכְלוּת הוֹלֵלוֹת׃ וּמוֹצֶא אֲנִי מַר מִמָּוֶת אֶת־
הָאִשָּׁה אֲשֶׁר־הִיא מְצוֹדִים וַחֲרָמִים לִבָּהּ אֲסוּרִים יָדֶיהָ טוֹב לִפְנֵי
כז הָאֱלֹהִים יִמָּלֵט מִמֶּנָּה וְחוֹטֵא יִלָּכֶד בָּהּ׃ רְאֵה זֶה מָצָאתִי אָמְרָה
כח קֹהֶלֶת אַחַת לְאַחַת לִמְצֹא חֶשְׁבּוֹן׃ אֲשֶׁר עוֹד־בִּקְשָׁה נַפְשִׁי וְלֹא
מָצָאתִי אָדָם אֶחָד מֵאֶלֶף מָצָאתִי וְאִשָּׁה בְכָל־אֵלֶּה לֹא מָצָאתִי׃
כט לְבַד רְאֵה־זֶה מָצָאתִי אֲשֶׁר עָשָׂה הָאֱלֹהִים אֶת־הָאָדָם יָשָׁר וְהֵמָּה
ח א בִקְשׁוּ חִשְּׁבֹנוֹת רַבִּים׃ מִי כְּהֶחָכָם וּמִי יוֹדֵעַ פֵּשֶׁר דָּבָר חָכְמַת אָדָם
ב תָּאִיר פָּנָיו וְעֹז פָּנָיו יְשֻׁנֶּא׃ אֲנִי פִּי־מֶלֶךְ שְׁמֹר וְעַל דִּבְרַת שְׁבוּעַת
ג אֱלֹהִים׃ אַל־תִּבָּהֵל מִפָּנָיו תֵּלֵךְ אַל־תַּעֲמֹד בְּדָבָר רָע כִּי כָּל־אֲשֶׁר
ד יַחְפֹּץ יַעֲשֶׂה׃ בַּאֲשֶׁר דְּבַר־מֶלֶךְ שִׁלְטוֹן וּמִי יֹאמַר־לוֹ מַה־תַּעֲשֶׂה׃
ה ו שׁוֹמֵר מִצְוָה לֹא יֵדַע דָּבָר רָע וְעֵת וּמִשְׁפָּט יֵדַע לֵב חָכָם׃ כִּי לְכָל־
ז חֵפֶץ יֵשׁ עֵת וּמִשְׁפָּט כִּי־רָעַת הָאָדָם רַבָּה עָלָיו׃ כִּי־אֵינֶנּוּ יֹדֵעַ מַה־
ח שֶּׁיִּהְיֶה כִּי כַּאֲשֶׁר יִהְיֶה מִי יַגִּיד לוֹ׃ אֵין אָדָם שַׁלִּיט בָּרוּחַ לִכְלוֹא
אֶת־הָרוּחַ וְאֵין שִׁלְטוֹן בְּיוֹם הַמָּוֶת וְאֵין מִשְׁלַחַת בַּמִּלְחָמָה וְלֹא־
ט יְמַלֵּט רֶשַׁע אֶת־בְּעָלָיו׃ אֶת־כָּל־זֶה רָאִיתִי וְנָתוֹן אֶת־לִבִּי לְכָל־
מַעֲשֶׂה אֲשֶׁר נַעֲשָׂה תַּחַת הַשָּׁמֶשׁ עֵת אֲשֶׁר שָׁלַט הָאָדָם בְּאָדָם לְרַע
י לוֹ׃ וּבְכֵן רָאִיתִי רְשָׁעִים קְבֻרִים וָבָאוּ וּמִמְּקוֹם קָדוֹשׁ יְהַלֵּכוּ וְיִשְׁתַּכְּחוּ

11 empty breath. For it is not soon that judgment is passed after evil; and so a
12 person's mind fills up with thoughts of doing evil. A sinner does a hundred
evil deeds and is granted long years for it. Yes, I know that good will come to
13 those who fear God – for fearing Him. And good will not come to an evil
man, and he will not live long – he passes like a shadow, for he does not fear
14 God. Yet see this thing of breath that happens on this earth: the righteous
who suffers the same fate as the wicked; and the wicked who enjoy the same
15 fate as the righteous – and I say: here again is empty breath. And so I praise
joy – for there is nothing as good for man beneath the sun as to eat and drink
and be happy. This is what he has to accompany him in his labors throughout
16 the life that God has given him beneath the sun. When I set my mind to
knowing wisdom, to seeing what it is that is done upon this earth – and all
17 day, all night, no sleep do our eyes see – I saw all the work of God; I saw that
no man can fathom the work that is done beneath the sun. A person labors
to seek it out and will never find it. If a wise man says he knows – no! And
9 1 never will he be able to discover it. All this I took into my mind, trying to
understand all this: that the righteous and the wise and all their actions – all
are in the hand of God. Their love, their hate, none of it is known; it all just
2 unfolds before them. All is as it is for all. The same fate awaits the righteous
and the wicked, the good and the pure and the impure, the one who brings
offerings and the one who does not. For a good man just as for a sinner, for
3 the one who swears falsely along with the one who fears his oath. This is the
evil in all that is done beneath the sun: the same fate attends everyone.
Therefore the hearts of man contemplate evil; delirium clouds their minds
4 all their lives – and then they go to join the dead. For anyone still bound to
life has something to rely upon: "Better to be a living dog than a dead lion."
5 For the living know at least that they must die, while the dead know nothing.
6 No longer rewarded for their actions, their names are forgotten. Their loves,
their hates, their passions – all are already lost. No longer have they any share,
7 any part in what is done beneath the sun. Go, eat your bread in joy, drink your
8 wine with a satisfied heart, for God has accepted your deeds. Let your clothes
9 at all times be clean; let your head never lack oil. Enjoy life with the woman
you love all the days of fleeting breath He has given you here beneath the sun,
for this is your share in life, your due for all your toil, all your labor beneath
10 the sun. Whatever you find it in your hands to do – do that with all your
strength. For there is no action or thought, no understanding or wisdom,
11 in Sheol,[14] where you are going. Then I turned again and saw beneath the
sun – that the race is not won by the swift, nor the war by the mighty; bread

14 | The netherworld.

יא בָעִיר אֲשֶׁר כֵּן־עָשׂוּ גַּם־זֶה הָבֶל: אֲשֶׁר אֵין־נַעֲשָׂה פִתְגָם מַעֲשֵׂה
יב הָרָעָה מְהֵרָה עַל־כֵּן מָלֵא לֵב בְּנֵי־הָאָדָם בָּהֶם לַעֲשׂוֹת רָע: אֲשֶׁר
חֹטֶא עֹשֶׂה רָע מְאַת וּמַאֲרִיךְ לוֹ כִּי גַּם־יוֹדֵעַ אָנִי אֲשֶׁר יִהְיֶה־טּוֹב
יג לְיִרְאֵי הָאֱלֹהִים אֲשֶׁר יִירְאוּ מִלְּפָנָיו: וְטוֹב לֹא־יִהְיֶה לָרָשָׁע וְלֹא־
יד יַאֲרִיךְ יָמִים כַּצֵּל אֲשֶׁר אֵינֶנּוּ יָרֵא מִלִּפְנֵי אֱלֹהִים: יֶשׁ־הֶבֶל אֲשֶׁר
נַעֲשָׂה עַל־הָאָרֶץ אֲשֶׁר ׀ יֵשׁ צַדִּיקִים אֲשֶׁר מַגִּיעַ אֲלֵהֶם כְּמַעֲשֵׂה
הָרְשָׁעִים וְיֵשׁ רְשָׁעִים שֶׁמַּגִּיעַ אֲלֵהֶם כְּמַעֲשֵׂה הַצַּדִּיקִים אָמַרְתִּי
טו שֶׁגַּם־זֶה הָבֶל: וְשִׁבַּחְתִּי אֲנִי אֶת־הַשִּׂמְחָה אֲשֶׁר אֵין־טוֹב לָאָדָם
תַּחַת הַשֶּׁמֶשׁ כִּי אִם־לֶאֱכוֹל וְלִשְׁתּוֹת וְלִשְׂמוֹחַ וְהוּא יִלְוֶנּוּ בַעֲמָלוֹ
טז יְמֵי חַיָּיו אֲשֶׁר־נָתַן־לוֹ הָאֱלֹהִים תַּחַת הַשָּׁמֶשׁ: כַּאֲשֶׁר נָתַתִּי אֶת־לִבִּי
לָדַעַת חָכְמָה וְלִרְאוֹת אֶת־הָעִנְיָן אֲשֶׁר נַעֲשָׂה עַל־הָאָרֶץ כִּי גַם בַּיּוֹם
יז וּבַלַּיְלָה שֵׁנָה בְּעֵינָיו אֵינֶנּוּ רֹאֶה: וְרָאִיתִי אֶת־כָּל־מַעֲשֵׂה הָאֱלֹהִים
כִּי לֹא יוּכַל הָאָדָם לִמְצוֹא אֶת־הַמַּעֲשֶׂה אֲשֶׁר נַעֲשָׂה תַחַת־הַשֶּׁמֶשׁ
בְּשֶׁל אֲשֶׁר יַעֲמֹל הָאָדָם לְבַקֵּשׁ וְלֹא יִמְצָא וְגַם אִם־יֹאמַר הֶחָכָם
ט א לָדַעַת לֹא יוּכַל לִמְצֹא: כִּי אֶת־כָּל־זֶה נָתַתִּי אֶל־לִבִּי וְלָבוּר אֶת־כָּל־
זֶה אֲשֶׁר הַצַּדִּיקִים וְהַחֲכָמִים וַעֲבָדֵיהֶם בְּיַד הָאֱלֹהִים גַּם־אַהֲבָה
ב גַם־שִׂנְאָה אֵין יוֹדֵעַ הָאָדָם הַכֹּל לִפְנֵיהֶם: הַכֹּל כַּאֲשֶׁר לַכֹּל מִקְרֶה
אֶחָד לַצַּדִּיק וְלָרָשָׁע לַטּוֹב וְלַטָּהוֹר וְלַטָּמֵא וְלַזֹּבֵחַ וְלַאֲשֶׁר אֵינֶנּוּ
ג זֹבֵחַ כַּטּוֹב כַּחֹטֶא הַנִּשְׁבָּע כַּאֲשֶׁר שְׁבוּעָה יָרֵא: זֶה ׀ רָע בְּכֹל אֲשֶׁר־
נַעֲשָׂה תַּחַת הַשֶּׁמֶשׁ כִּי־מִקְרֶה אֶחָד לַכֹּל וְגַם לֵב בְּנֵי־הָאָדָם מָלֵא־רָע
ד וְהוֹלֵלוֹת בִּלְבָבָם בְּחַיֵּיהֶם וְאַחֲרָיו אֶל־הַמֵּתִים: כִּי־מִי אֲשֶׁר יבחר יְחֻבַּר
אֶל כָּל־הַחַיִּים יֵשׁ בִּטָּחוֹן כִּי־לְכֶלֶב חַי הוּא טוֹב מִן־הָאַרְיֵה הַמֵּת:
ה כִּי הַחַיִּים יוֹדְעִים שֶׁיָּמֻתוּ וְהַמֵּתִים אֵינָם יוֹדְעִים מְאוּמָה וְאֵין־עוֹד
ו לָהֶם שָׂכָר כִּי נִשְׁכַּח זִכְרָם: גַּם אַהֲבָתָם גַּם־שִׂנְאָתָם גַּם־קִנְאָתָם כְּבָר
אָבָדָה וְחֵלֶק אֵין־לָהֶם עוֹד לְעוֹלָם בְּכֹל אֲשֶׁר־נַעֲשָׂה תַּחַת הַשָּׁמֶשׁ:
ז לֵךְ אֱכֹל בְּשִׂמְחָה לַחְמֶךָ וּשֲׁתֵה בְלֶב־טוֹב יֵינֶךָ כִּי כְבָר רָצָה הָאֱלֹהִים ד
ח אֶת־מַעֲשֶׂיךָ: בְּכָל־עֵת יִהְיוּ בְגָדֶיךָ לְבָנִים וְשֶׁמֶן עַל־רֹאשְׁךָ אַל־יֶחְסָר:
ט רְאֵה חַיִּים עִם־אִשָּׁה אֲשֶׁר־אָהַבְתָּ כָּל־יְמֵי חַיֵּי הֶבְלֶךָ אֲשֶׁר נָתַן־לְךָ
תַּחַת הַשֶּׁמֶשׁ כֹּל יְמֵי הֶבְלֶךָ כִּי הוּא חֶלְקְךָ בַּחַיִּים וּבַעֲמָלְךָ אֲשֶׁר־
י אַתָּה עָמֵל תַּחַת הַשָּׁמֶשׁ: כֹּל אֲשֶׁר תִּמְצָא יָדְךָ לַעֲשׂוֹת בְּכֹחֲךָ עֲשֵׂה
כִּי אֵין מַעֲשֶׂה וְחֶשְׁבּוֹן וְדַעַת וְחָכְמָה בִּשְׁאוֹל אֲשֶׁר אַתָּה הֹלֵךְ שָׁמָּה:
יא שַׁבְתִּי וְרָאֹה תַחַת־הַשֶּׁמֶשׁ כִּי לֹא לַקַּלִּים הַמֵּרוֹץ וְלֹא לַגִּבּוֹרִים

is not promised to the wise, nor to the intelligent, wealth, nor to the knowing,
12 favor, for time and misfortune come to them all. And man never knows when
his time will come: as fish are entrapped in the deadly net, as birds are trapped
in the snare, so too are people caught at that time of harm that falls upon them
13 without warning. This too I saw of wisdom beneath the sun – great beyond
14 my understanding. A small town. Few people in it. A great king came and
15 surrounded it and built great siege works all around. And one poor wise man
was there to be found, able to save the whole town by his wisdom. And not
16 a soul remembered that poor man. And I said: Wisdom is better than might,
17 but the wisdom of a poor man is scorned, his words go unheeded. The quiet
words of the wise are heeded more than the shout of a ruler among fools.
18 Better wisdom than weaponry – yet one misjudgment can destroy much that
10 1 is good. Dead flies ferment and putrefy much perfume; more costly than
2 wisdom, than honor, is one small dose of foolishness. A wise man's mind is
3 to his right as the mind of a fool is to his left. Even as he walks his chosen path
4 his mind is lacking, telling every passerby that he is a fool. If a ruler's spirit
turns against you, do not leave your place, for appeasement can lay great sins
5 to rest.[15] Here is an evil I have seen beneath the sun like an error coming forth
6 from the ruler's mouth: fools are raised to the greatest heights while rich men
7 sit in the gutter. I have seen slaves riding on horseback and princes walking
8 like slaves upon the ground. He who digs the pit may fall into it, and he who
9 tears down walls – a snake may bite him. He who quarries the stone will come
10 to grief by it, and he who chops the tree may by that tree be harmed. If the
ax grows blunt and is not polished, then the one who wields it must add force;
11 for skill yields profit only through wisdom. If the snake bites before he is
12 charmed, there is no profit to the charmer. The words of the wise bring favor
13 while the mouth of a fool will swallow him up. His speech begins with
14 foolishness and ends with evil delirium, yet the fool speaks on and on. Man
15 does not know what will be; yes, who may tell him what will come after? The
16 labor of fools exhausts them; they do not even know the way to town. I pity
you, the land whose king is a lad,[16] whose princes feast from the morning.
17 Happy the land whose king is a nobleman and whose princes eat at the right
18 time, like the brave, without drunkenness. "The roof caves in from much
19 laziness, and hands laid down spring leaks in the house." Feasts are made for
laughter, and wine fills life with joy – and money will answer for everything.
20 Never curse a king, not even in your mind, nor a rich man, even in your
bedchamber, for a bird of the sky will carry that voice; a winged creature will
11 1 repeat the word. Cast your bread out onto the waters, for in the long passage
2 of days you will find it again. Give of what is yours to seven, to eight, for on
3 this earth you cannot know what evil may yet come. If the clouds fill with
rain, they must empty it onto the earth. If a tree falls to the south, to the
4 north – wherever that tree falls, there it will lie. One who waits for the wind

---

15 | Calmness can pacify the ruler.
16 | A servant, not fit to rule.

הַמִּלְחָמָה וְגַם לֹא לַחֲכָמִים לֶחֶם וְגַם לֹא לַנְּבֹנִים עֹשֶׁר וְגַם לֹא לַיֹּדְעִים
יב חֵן כִּי־עֵת וָפֶגַע יִקְרֶה אֶת־כֻּלָּם: כִּי גַּם לֹא־יֵדַע הָאָדָם אֶת־עִתּוֹ
כַּדָּגִים שֶׁנֶּאֱחָזִים בִּמְצוֹדָה רָעָה וְכַצִּפֳּרִים הָאֲחֻזוֹת בַּפָּח כָּהֵם יוּקָשִׁים
יג בְּנֵי הָאָדָם לְעֵת רָעָה כְּשֶׁתִּפּוֹל עֲלֵיהֶם פִּתְאֹם: גַּם־זֹה רָאִיתִי חָכְמָה
יד תַּחַת הַשָּׁמֶשׁ וּגְדוֹלָה הִיא אֵלָי: עִיר קְטַנָּה וַאֲנָשִׁים בָּהּ מְעָט וּבָא־
טו אֵלֶיהָ מֶלֶךְ גָּדוֹל וְסָבַב אֹתָהּ וּבָנָה עָלֶיהָ מְצוֹדִים גְּדֹלִים: וּמָצָא בָהּ
אִישׁ מִסְכֵּן חָכָם וּמִלַּט־הוּא אֶת־הָעִיר בְּחָכְמָתוֹ וְאָדָם לֹא זָכַר אֶת־
טז הָאִישׁ הַמִּסְכֵּן הַהוּא: וְאָמַרְתִּי אָנִי טוֹבָה חָכְמָה מִגְּבוּרָה וְחָכְמַת
יז הַמִּסְכֵּן בְּזוּיָה וּדְבָרָיו אֵינָם נִשְׁמָעִים: דִּבְרֵי חֲכָמִים בְּנַחַת נִשְׁמָעִים
יח מִזַּעֲקַת מוֹשֵׁל בַּכְּסִילִים: טוֹבָה חָכְמָה מִכְּלֵי קְרָב וְחוֹטֶא אֶחָד יְאַבֵּד
י א טוֹבָה הַרְבֵּה: זְבוּבֵי מָוֶת יַבְאִישׁ יַבִּיעַ שֶׁמֶן רוֹקֵחַ יָקָר מֵחָכְמָה מִכָּבוֹד
ב ג סִכְלוּת מְעָט: לֵב חָכָם לִימִינוֹ וְלֵב כְּסִיל לִשְׂמֹאלוֹ: וְגַם־בַּדֶּרֶךְ
ד כשהסכל הֹלֵךְ לִבּוֹ חָסֵר וְאָמַר לַכֹּל סָכָל הוּא: אִם־רוּחַ הַמּוֹשֵׁל כְּשֶׁסָּכָל
ה תַּעֲלֶה עָלֶיךָ מְקוֹמְךָ אַל־תַּנַּח כִּי מַרְפֵּא יַנִּיחַ חֲטָאִים גְּדוֹלִים: יֵשׁ
ו רָעָה רָאִיתִי תַּחַת הַשָּׁמֶשׁ כִּשְׁגָגָה שֶׁיֹּצָא מִלִּפְנֵי הַשַּׁלִּיט: נִתַּן הַסֶּכֶל
ז בַּמְּרוֹמִים רַבִּים וַעֲשִׁירִים בַּשֵּׁפֶל יֵשֵׁבוּ: רָאִיתִי עֲבָדִים עַל־סוּסִים
ח וְשָׂרִים הֹלְכִים כַּעֲבָדִים עַל־הָאָרֶץ: חֹפֵר גּוּמָּץ בּוֹ יִפּוֹל וּפֹרֵץ גָּדֵר
ט י יִשְּׁכֶנּוּ נָחָשׁ: מַסִּיעַ אֲבָנִים יֵעָצֵב בָּהֶם בּוֹקֵעַ עֵצִים יִסָּכֶן בָּם: אִם־קֵהָה
הַבַּרְזֶל וְהוּא לֹא־פָנִים קִלְקַל וַחֲיָלִים יְגַבֵּר וְיִתְרוֹן הַכְשֵׁיר חָכְמָה:
יא יב אִם־יִשֹּׁךְ הַנָּחָשׁ בְּלוֹא־לָחַשׁ וְאֵין יִתְרוֹן לְבַעַל הַלָּשׁוֹן: דִּבְרֵי פִי־חָכָם
יג חֵן וְשִׂפְתוֹת כְּסִיל תְּבַלְּעֶנּוּ: תְּחִלַּת דִּבְרֵי־פִיהוּ סִכְלוּת וְאַחֲרִית פִּיהוּ
יד הוֹלֵלוּת רָעָה: וְהַסָּכָל יַרְבֶּה דְבָרִים לֹא־יֵדַע הָאָדָם מַה־שֶּׁיִּהְיֶה וַאֲשֶׁר
טו יִהְיֶה מֵאַחֲרָיו מִי יַגִּיד לוֹ: עֲמַל הַכְּסִילִים תְּיַגְּעֶנּוּ אֲשֶׁר לֹא־יָדַע לָלֶכֶת
טז יז אֶל־עִיר: אִי־לָךְ אֶרֶץ שֶׁמַּלְכֵּךְ נָעַר וְשָׂרַיִךְ בַּבֹּקֶר יֹאכֵלוּ: אַשְׁרֵיךְ
אֶרֶץ שֶׁמַּלְכֵּךְ בֶּן־חוֹרִים וְשָׂרַיִךְ בָּעֵת יֹאכֵלוּ בִּגְבוּרָה וְלֹא בַשְּׁתִי:
יח יט בַּעֲצַלְתַּיִם יִמַּךְ הַמְּקָרֶה וּבְשִׁפְלוּת יָדַיִם יִדְלֹף הַבָּיִת: לִשְׂחוֹק עֹשִׂים
כ לֶחֶם וְיַיִן יְשַׂמַּח חַיִּים וְהַכֶּסֶף יַעֲנֶה אֶת־הַכֹּל: גַּם בְּמַדָּעֲךָ מֶלֶךְ אַל־
תְּקַלֵּל וּבְחַדְרֵי מִשְׁכָּבְךָ אַל־תְּקַלֵּל עָשִׁיר כִּי עוֹף הַשָּׁמַיִם יוֹלִיךְ
יא א אֶת־הַקּוֹל וּבַעַל הכנפים יַגִּיד דָּבָר: שַׁלַּח לַחְמְךָ עַל־פְּנֵי הַמָּיִם כִּי־ כְּנָפַיִם
ב בְרֹב הַיָּמִים תִּמְצָאֶנּוּ: תֶּן־חֵלֶק לְשִׁבְעָה וְגַם לִשְׁמוֹנָה כִּי לֹא תֵדַע
ג מַה־יִּהְיֶה רָעָה עַל־הָאָרֶץ: אִם־יִמָּלְאוּ הֶעָבִים גֶּשֶׁם עַל־הָאָרֶץ יָרִיקוּ
ד וְאִם־יִפּוֹל עֵץ בַּדָּרוֹם וְאִם בַּצָּפוֹן מְקוֹם שֶׁיִּפּוֹל הָעֵץ שָׁם יְהוּא: שֹׁמֵר

5 will never sow; one who gazes at the clouds will never reap.[17] And just as you
know not the way of the wind, nor what frame fills a pregnant woman's womb,
6 so you cannot know the work of God; and everything is His work. Sow your
seeds in the morning, and come evening do not lay your hands to rest – for
you do not know which will prove fit, these seeds or those, or whether the
7 two are as good as one another. There is a sweetness in the light; it is good
8 for the eyes to see the sun. And should a man live many years, he should
rejoice in all of them, remembering, too, the days of darkness, for there will
9 be many. All that comes is but a breath. Young man, rejoice now in your youth;
let your heart give you pleasure while you are young. Follow your heart where
it leads you, your eyes where they allure you – and know that God will bring
10 you to judgment for all this. So clear your heart of bitterness and free your
12 1 flesh of pain, for youth and dark-haired days pass by like breath. And remember
your Creator in these days of your youth before the days of despair, before
2 years come when you shall say, "There is nothing here that I desire." Before
the sun is darkened and the light, the moon and stars and clouds return again
3 after the rain.[18] The day when the guards of the house will shake and the
soldiers buckle, when the grinders sit idle, grown few, and the women at the
4 windows sit in darkness. When all the doors in the street are closed as the
millstone falls silent, and a man starts up at the sound of a bird, but the singing
5 girls' voices drop low. And a man lives in terror of the heights and all the
pitfalls on the road. The almond blossoms, the grasshopper bears its burden,
the caper fruit breaks asunder, but man is departing for his final home, and
6 the mourners turn and turn about the streets. Remember – before the silver
cord snaps and the golden ball plunges downward, the jug breaks on the
7 edge of the spring, the basin is smashed against the well, the dust returns
8 to the earth where it began, and the spirit returns to God who gave it. Fleeting
9 breath, says Kohelet. It is all mere breath. More – as Kohelet was wise, he
also taught the people understanding; and he weighed and explored and
10 assembled many wise sayings. Kohelet sought out choicest words and
11 wrote honest words of truth. The words of the wise are like goads; like pointed
12 nails are the scholars' sayings. One shepherd gave them all. And further
than this, my son, take heed; there is no end to the making of books, and
13 much study wearies the flesh. The final word: it has all been said. Hold
14 God in awe, and heed His commands, for that is all man has. And all that is
done – God shall bring it to judgment; all that is hidden, the good and the bad.

The final word: it has all been said.
Hold God in awe, and heed His commands, for that is all man has.

---

17 | A farmer who waits for perfect weather will never plant or harvest.

18 | These verses may describe, metaphorically, the decline of the body in old age till death and burial.

ה רוּחַ לֹא יִזְרָע וְרֹאֶה בֶעָבִים לֹא יִקְצוֹר: כַּאֲשֶׁר אֵינְךָ יוֹדֵעַ מַה־דֶּרֶךְ
הָרוּחַ כַּעֲצָמִים בְּבֶטֶן הַמְּלֵאָה כָּכָה לֹא תֵדַע אֶת־מַעֲשֵׂה הָאֱלֹהִים
ו אֲשֶׁר יַעֲשֶׂה אֶת־הַכֹּל: בַּבֹּקֶר זְרַע אֶת־זַרְעֶךָ וְלָעֶרֶב אַל־תַּנַּח יָדֶךָ
כִּי אֵינְךָ יוֹדֵעַ אֵי זֶה יִכְשַׁר הֲזֶה אוֹ־זֶה וְאִם־שְׁנֵיהֶם כְּאֶחָד טוֹבִים:
ז ח וּמָתוֹק הָאוֹר וְטוֹב לַעֵינַיִם לִרְאוֹת אֶת־הַשָּׁמֶשׁ: כִּי אִם־שָׁנִים הַרְבֵּה
יִחְיֶה הָאָדָם בְּכֻלָּם יִשְׂמָח וְיִזְכֹּר אֶת־יְמֵי הַחֹשֶׁךְ כִּי־הַרְבֵּה יִהְיוּ
ט כָּל־שֶׁבָּא הָבֶל: שְׂמַח בָּחוּר בְּיַלְדוּתֶךָ וִיטִיבְךָ לִבְּךָ בִּימֵי בְחוּרוֹתֶךָ
וְהַלֵּךְ בְּדַרְכֵי לִבְּךָ ובמראי עֵינֶיךָ וְדָע כִּי עַל־כָּל־אֵלֶּה יְבִיאֲךָ הָאֱלֹהִים וּבְמַרְאֵה
י בַּמִּשְׁפָּט: וְהָסֵר כַּעַס מִלִּבֶּךָ וְהַעֲבֵר רָעָה מִבְּשָׂרֶךָ כִּי־הַיַּלְדוּת
יב א וְהַשַּׁחֲרוּת הָבֶל: וּזְכֹר אֶת־בּוֹרְאֶיךָ בִּימֵי בְּחוּרֹתֶיךָ עַד אֲשֶׁר לֹא־יָבֹאוּ
ב יְמֵי הָרָעָה וְהִגִּיעוּ שָׁנִים אֲשֶׁר תֹּאמַר אֵין־לִי בָהֶם חֵפֶץ: עַד אֲשֶׁר
לֹא־תֶחְשַׁךְ הַשֶּׁמֶשׁ וְהָאוֹר וְהַיָּרֵחַ וְהַכּוֹכָבִים וְשָׁבוּ הֶעָבִים אַחַר
ג הַגָּשֶׁם: בַּיּוֹם שֶׁיָּזֻעוּ שֹׁמְרֵי הַבַּיִת וְהִתְעַוְּתוּ אַנְשֵׁי הֶחָיִל וּבָטְלוּ
ד הַטֹּחֲנוֹת כִּי מִעֵטוּ וְחָשְׁכוּ הָרֹאוֹת בָּאֲרֻבּוֹת: וְסֻגְּרוּ דְלָתַיִם בַּשּׁוּק
ה בִּשְׁפַל קוֹל הַטַּחֲנָה וְיָקוּם לְקוֹל הַצִּפּוֹר וְיִשַּׁחוּ כָּל־בְּנוֹת הַשִּׁיר: גַּם
מִגָּבֹהַּ יִרָאוּ וְחַתְחַתִּים בַּדֶּרֶךְ וְיָנֵאץ הַשָּׁקֵד וְיִסְתַּבֵּל הֶחָגָב וְתָפֵר
הָאֲבִיּוֹנָה כִּי־הֹלֵךְ הָאָדָם אֶל־בֵּית עוֹלָמוֹ וְסָבְבוּ בַשּׁוּק הַסֹּפְדִים:
ו עַד אֲשֶׁר לֹא־ירחק חֶבֶל הַכֶּסֶף וְתָרֻץ גֻּלַּת הַזָּהָב וְתִשָּׁבֶר כַּד עַל־ יֵרָתֵק
ז הַמַּבּוּעַ וְנָרֹץ הַגַּלְגַּל אֶל־הַבּוֹר: וְיָשֹׁב הֶעָפָר עַל־הָאָרֶץ כְּשֶׁהָיָה
ח וְהָרוּחַ תָּשׁוּב אֶל־הָאֱלֹהִים אֲשֶׁר נְתָנָהּ: הֲבֵל הֲבָלִים אָמַר הַקּוֹהֶלֶת
ט הַכֹּל הָבֶל: וְיֹתֵר שֶׁהָיָה קֹהֶלֶת חָכָם עוֹד לִמַּד־דַּעַת אֶת־הָעָם וְאִזֵּן
י וְחִקֵּר תִּקֵּן מְשָׁלִים הַרְבֵּה: בִּקֵּשׁ קֹהֶלֶת לִמְצֹא דִּבְרֵי־חֵפֶץ וְכָתוּב
יא יֹשֶׁר דִּבְרֵי אֱמֶת: דִּבְרֵי חֲכָמִים כַּדָּרְבֹנוֹת וּכְמַשְׂמְרוֹת נְטוּעִים בַּעֲלֵי
יב אֲסֻפּוֹת נִתְּנוּ מֵרֹעֶה אֶחָד: וְיֹתֵר מֵהֵמָּה בְּנִי הִזָּהֵר עֲשׂוֹת סְפָרִים
יג הַרְבֵּה אֵין קֵץ וְלַהַג הַרְבֵּה יְגִעַת בָּשָׂר: סוֹף דָּבָר הַכֹּל נִשְׁמָע
יד אֶת־הָאֱלֹהִים יְרָא וְאֶת־מִצְוֺתָיו שְׁמוֹר כִּי־זֶה כָּל־הָאָדָם: כִּי אֶת־
כָּל־מַעֲשֶׂה הָאֱלֹהִים יָבִא בְמִשְׁפָּט עַל כָּל־נֶעְלָם אִם־טוֹב וְאִם־רָע:

סוף דבר הכל נשמע
את האלהים ירא ואת מצותיו שמור כי זה כל האדם

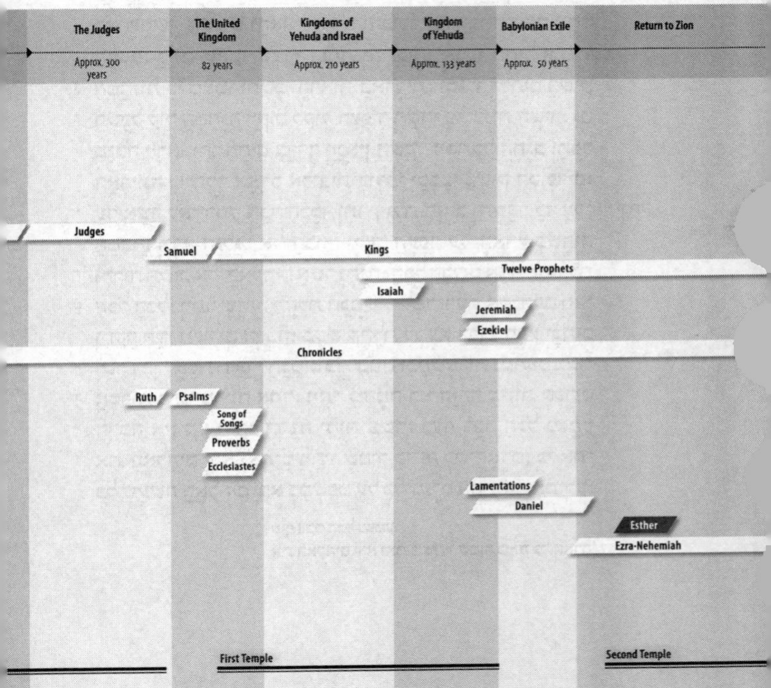

The Judges
The United Kingdom
Kingdoms of Yehuda and Israel
Kingdom of Yehuda
Babylonian Exile
Return to Zion
Approx. 300 years
82 years
Approx. 210 years
Approx. 133 years
Approx. 50 years
Judges
Samuel
Kings
Twelve Prophets
Isaiah
Jeremiah
Ezekiel
Chronicles
Ruth
Psalms
Song of Songs
Proverbs
Ecclesiastes
Lamentations
Daniel
Esther
Ezra-Nehemiah
First Temple
Second Temple

אסתר
ESTER/ESTHER

ESTHER	Aḥashverosh's party	Choosing a queen to replace Vashti	Haman's decree	Salvation
	Ch. 1	2	3–5	6–10

1 1 It happened in the days of Aḥashverosh – Aḥashverosh who ruled 127
2 provinces from Hodu to Kush. At that time, when King Aḥashverosh sat upon
3 his royal throne in the imperial city of Shushan[1] in the third year of his rule,
he made a feast for his ministers and courtiers, the elite of Persia and Media,
4 all his noblemen and the ministers of his provinces. There, for many days – 180
days in all – he displayed all the wealth of his noble reign and the dazzling
5 glory of his greatness. When that time had passed, the king held a feast for all
the people of the imperial city of Shushan, from the greatest to the lowliest,
6 in the courtyard of the king's palace garden. There, swaths of fine fabric – of
precious white cotton and sky-blue wool – were caught up with cords of the
finest linen and purple and draped over silver bars and columns of marble;
and couches of gold and silver were arranged on a terrace paved with alabaster
7 and marble, with mother of pearl and black onyx. And the guests were served
drinks in vessels of gold, vessels unlike any other – royal wine, abundant as
8 the king's largesse. And the drinking followed a rule of no duress, for the king
had thus instructed all the overseers of his home: honor the wishes of each
9 and every man. Meanwhile Vashti the queen made a feast of her own,
10 a women's feast in King Aḥashverosh's royal palace. And on the seventh day,
when the king had grown merry with wine, he instructed Mehuman, Bizta,
Ḥarvona, Bigta and Avagta, Zetar and Karkas – the seven eunuchs who
11 attended King Aḥashverosh – to bring Vashti the queen before the king in her
royal crown, to show the peoples and the ministers her charms, for she was
12 beautiful indeed. But Queen Vashti refused to come at the king's word,
conveyed through the eunuchs. So fury engulfed the king, and his rage blazed
13 inside him. Now the king addressed the wise men, those well versed
in procedure – for it was the king's practice to consult with those who knew
14 the law and the statutes; and those closest to him were Karshena, Shetar,
Admata, Tarshish, Meres, Marsena, and Memukhan, the seven ministers of
Persia and Media who came freely into the king's presence and occupied the
15 highest positions in the realm. What, he asked, would the law have them do
with Queen Vashti for refusing to obey the word of King Aḥashverosh as
16 conveyed to her by the eunuchs? And Memukhan replied before the
king and the ministers: "It is not only the king that Vashti the queen has
wronged, but all the ministers and all the peoples in all the provinces of King
17 Aḥashverosh. For this tale of the queen will go out to all the women, who will
cast their husbands into their contempt when they say, 'King Aḥashverosh
commanded Vashti the queen to be brought before him, but she did not
18 come!' Yes, this very day, all the ministers' wives of Persia and Media, who
have heard what the queen did, will tell all the king's ministers, and there will
19 be no end to the contempt and the fury. If, then, it so please the king, let a
royal declaration be sent out from him and be written among the laws of
Persia and Media, never to be contravened – that Vashti shall come no more
before King Aḥashverosh and that the king shall give her royal position to a

1 | Shushan (Susa) was the main administrative capital of the Persian Empire. The imperial city (*bira*) of Shushan is the acropolis, and the "town of Shushan" (3:15) is the lower city.

א א ויהי בימי אחשורוש הוא אחשורוש המלך מהדו ועד־כוש שבע א
ב ועשרים ומאה מדינה: בימים ההם כשבת ׀ המלך אחשורוש על
ג כסא מלכותו אשר בשושן הבירה: בשנת שלוש למלכו עשה
משתה לכל־שריו ועבדיו חיל ׀ פרס ומדי הפרתמים ושרי המדינות
ד לפניו: בהראתו את־עשר כבוד מלכותו ואת־יקר תפארת גדולתו
ה ימים רבים שמונים ומאת יום: ובמלואת ׀ הימים האלה עשה המלך
לכל־העם הנמצאים בשושן הבירה למגדול ועד־קטן משתה
ו שבעת ימים בחצר גנת ביתן המלך: חור ׀ כרפס ותכלת אחוז
בחבלי־בוץ וארגמן על־גלילי כסף ועמודי שש מטות ׀ זהב וכסף
ז על רצפת בהט־ושש ודר וסחרת: והשקות בכלי זהב וכלים מכלים
ח שונים ויין מלכות רב כיד המלך: והשתיה כדת אין אנס כי־כן ׀ יסד
ט המלך על כל־רב ביתו לעשות כרצון איש־ואיש: גם ושתי
המלכה עשתה משתה נשים בית המלכות אשר למלך אחשורוש:
י ביום השביעי כטוב לב־המלך ביין אמר למהומן בזתא חרבונא
בגתא ואבגתא זתר וכרכס שבעת הסריסים המשרתים את־פני
יא המלך אחשורוש: להביא את־ושתי המלכה לפני המלך בכתר
מלכות להראות העמים והשרים את־יפיה כי־טובת מראה היא:
יב ותמאן המלכה ושתי לבוא בדבר המלך אשר ביד הסריסים ויקצף
יג המלך מאד וחמתו בערה בו: ויאמר המלך לחכמים
יד ידעי העתים כי־כן דבר המלך לפני כל־ידעי דת ודין: והקרב אליו
כרשנא שתר אדמתא תרשיש מרס מרסנא ממוכן שבעת שרי ׀
טו פרס ומדי ראי פני המלך הישבים ראשנה במלכות: כדת מה־
לעשות במלכה ושתי על ׀ אשר לא־עשתה את־מאמר המלך
טז אחשורוש ביד הסריסים: ויאמר מומכן לפני המלך ממוכן
והשרים לא על־המלך לבדו עותה ושתי המלכה כי על־כל־השרים
יז ועל־כל־העמים אשר בכל־מדינות המלך אחשורוש: כי־יצא דבר־
המלכה על־כל־הנשים להבזות בעליהן בעיניהן באמרם המלך
יח אחשורוש אמר להביא את־ושתי המלכה לפניו ולא־באה: והיום
הזה תאמרנה ׀ שרות פרס־ומדי אשר שמעו את־דבר המלכה לכל
יט שרי המלך וכדי בזיון וקצף: אם־על־המלך טוב יצא דבר־מלכות
מלפניו ויכתב בדתי פרס־ומדי ולא יעבור אשר לא־תבוא ושתי
לפני המלך אחשורוש ומלכותה יתן המלך לרעותה הטובה ממנה:

20 woman who is better than she. And the royal decree that the king will issue
shall be heard in all his empire, vast as it is: that all women must honor their
21 husbands, from the greatest of them to the least." The proposal pleased the
22 king and the ministers, and the king accepted Memukhan's word. He sent
scrolls to all the king's provinces – province by province, each in its script,
and people by people, each in its language – ruling that every man must be
2 1 master in his home, speaking the language of his own people. Some
time later, when King Aḥashverosh's rage had subsided, he remembered
2 Vashti, and what she had done, and what had been decreed against her. The
king's attendants, those who served him closely, said, "Let beautiful young
3 virgins be sought for the king; let the king appoint officers in all the provinces
of his realm to gather every beautiful young virgin to the imperial city of
Shushan, to the harem, into the charge of Hegeh, the king's eunuch, the keeper
4 of the maidens, to be given their ointments there. Whichever young woman
the king likes best – let her become queen in Vashti's place!" The suggestion
5 pleased the king, and that is what he did. Now there was a Jewish
man in the imperial city of Shushan, and his name was Mordekhai son of Yair
6 son of Shimi son of Kish of the tribe of Binyamin. He had been exiled from
Jerusalem among the exiles expelled with Yekhonya, king of Yehuda – exiled
7 by Nevukhadnetzar, king of Babylon.[2] And Mordekhai was guardian to
Hadasa – Esther – his uncle's daughter, for she had no father or mother. The
girl was lovely and beautiful, and when her father and mother had died,
8 Mordekhai had adopted her as his own child. When the king's word and his
law were heard, and vast numbers of young women were gathered in the
imperial city of Shushan into the charge of Hegai, Esther too was taken to the
9 king's palace into the charge of Hegai, the keeper of the women. The young
woman pleased him, and she carried kindness with her, and he hastened to
give her all her ointments and meals and the seven young maids from the
king's palace to whom she was entitled; and he moved her and her maids to
10 the best quarters in the royal maidens' quarters. And Esther made no mention
of her people or her birth, for Mordekhai had instructed her strictly not to
11 reveal them. But every single day Mordekhai would walk around before the
harem courtyard to find out whether Esther was well and what was being
12 done with her. As each young woman would reach her turn to come before
King Aḥashverosh – after twelve months following her beauty regime, for that
was how many the days of their ointments were: six months in myrrh oil and
13 six months in perfumes and the women's ointments – the young woman
would come before the king. All that she asked for would be given her to bring
14 with her from the royal harem to the palace of the king. She would enter in
the evening, and in the morning she would return to the royal harem, passing
into the charge of Shaashgaz, the king's eunuch, keeper of the concubines.
Then she would come no more before the king unless he desired her and
15 she was called for by name. When the time came for Esther daughter of

2 | See II Kings 24:8–17.

כ וְנִשְׁמַע פִּתְגָם הַמֶּלֶךְ אֲשֶׁר־יַעֲשֶׂה בְּכָל־מַלְכוּתוֹ כִּי רַבָּה הִיא וְכָל־
כא הַנָּשִׁים יִתְּנוּ יְקָר לְבַעְלֵיהֶן לְמִגָּדוֹל וְעַד־קָטָן: וַיִּיטַב הַדָּבָר בְּעֵינֵי
כב הַמֶּלֶךְ וְהַשָּׂרִים וַיַּעַשׂ הַמֶּלֶךְ כִּדְבַר מְמוּכָן: וַיִּשְׁלַח סְפָרִים אֶל־כָּל־
מְדִינוֹת הַמֶּלֶךְ אֶל־מְדִינָה וּמְדִינָה כִּכְתָבָהּ וְאֶל־עַם וָעָם כִּלְשׁוֹנוֹ
ב א לִהְיוֹת כָּל־אִישׁ שֹׂרֵר בְּבֵיתוֹ וּמְדַבֵּר כִּלְשׁוֹן עַמּוֹ: אַחַר
הַדְּבָרִים הָאֵלֶּה כְּשֹׁךְ חֲמַת הַמֶּלֶךְ אֲחַשְׁוֵרוֹשׁ זָכַר אֶת־וַשְׁתִּי וְאֵת
ב אֲשֶׁר־עָשָׂתָה וְאֵת אֲשֶׁר־נִגְזַר עָלֶיהָ: וַיֹּאמְרוּ נַעֲרֵי־הַמֶּלֶךְ מְשָׁרְתָיו
ג יְבַקְשׁוּ לַמֶּלֶךְ נְעָרוֹת בְּתוּלוֹת טוֹבוֹת מַרְאֶה: וְיַפְקֵד הַמֶּלֶךְ פְּקִידִים
בְּכָל־מְדִינוֹת מַלְכוּתוֹ וְיִקְבְּצוּ אֶת־כָּל־נַעֲרָה־בְתוּלָה טוֹבַת מַרְאֶה
אֶל־שׁוּשַׁן הַבִּירָה אֶל־בֵּית הַנָּשִׁים אֶל־יַד הֵגֶא סְרִיס הַמֶּלֶךְ שֹׁמֵר
ד הַנָּשִׁים וְנָתוֹן תַּמְרוּקֵיהֶן: וְהַנַּעֲרָה אֲשֶׁר תִּיטַב בְּעֵינֵי הַמֶּלֶךְ תִּמְלֹךְ
ה תַּחַת וַשְׁתִּי וַיִּיטַב הַדָּבָר בְּעֵינֵי הַמֶּלֶךְ וַיַּעַשׂ כֵּן: אִישׁ ב
יְהוּדִי הָיָה בְּשׁוּשַׁן הַבִּירָה וּשְׁמוֹ מָרְדֳּכַי בֶּן יָאִיר בֶּן־שִׁמְעִי בֶּן־קִישׁ
ו אִישׁ יְמִינִי: אֲשֶׁר הָגְלָה מִירוּשָׁלַיִם עִם־הַגֹּלָה אֲשֶׁר הָגְלְתָה עִם יְכָנְיָה
ז מֶלֶךְ־יְהוּדָה אֲשֶׁר הֶגְלָה נְבוּכַדְנֶאצַּר מֶלֶךְ בָּבֶל: וַיְהִי אֹמֵן אֶת־הֲדַסָּה
הִיא אֶסְתֵּר בַּת־דֹּדוֹ כִּי אֵין לָהּ אָב וָאֵם וְהַנַּעֲרָה יְפַת־תֹּאַר וְטוֹבַת
ח מַרְאֶה וּבְמוֹת אָבִיהָ וְאִמָּהּ לְקָחָהּ מָרְדֳּכַי לוֹ לְבַת: וַיְהִי בְּהִשָּׁמַע
דְּבַר־הַמֶּלֶךְ וְדָתוֹ וּבְהִקָּבֵץ נְעָרוֹת רַבּוֹת אֶל־שׁוּשַׁן הַבִּירָה אֶל־יַד
ט הֵגָי וַתִּלָּקַח אֶסְתֵּר אֶל־בֵּית הַמֶּלֶךְ אֶל־יַד הֵגַי שֹׁמֵר הַנָּשִׁים: וַתִּיטַב
הַנַּעֲרָה בְעֵינָיו וַתִּשָּׂא חֶסֶד לְפָנָיו וַיְבַהֵל אֶת־תַּמְרוּקֶיהָ וְאֶת־מָנוֹתֶהָ
לָתֶת לָהּ וְאֵת שֶׁבַע הַנְּעָרוֹת הָרְאֻיוֹת לָתֶת־לָהּ מִבֵּית הַמֶּלֶךְ וַיְשַׁנֶּהָ
י וְאֶת־נַעֲרוֹתֶיהָ לְטוֹב בֵּית הַנָּשִׁים: לֹא־הִגִּידָה אֶסְתֵּר אֶת־עַמָּהּ וְאֶת־
יא מוֹלַדְתָּהּ כִּי מָרְדֳּכַי צִוָּה עָלֶיהָ אֲשֶׁר לֹא־תַגִּיד: וּבְכָל־יוֹם וָיוֹם מָרְדֳּכַי
מִתְהַלֵּךְ לִפְנֵי חֲצַר בֵּית־הַנָּשִׁים לָדַעַת אֶת־שְׁלוֹם אֶסְתֵּר וּמַה־יֵּעָשֶׂה
יב בָּהּ: וּבְהַגִּיעַ תֹּר נַעֲרָה וְנַעֲרָה לָבוֹא ׀ אֶל־הַמֶּלֶךְ אֲחַשְׁוֵרוֹשׁ מִקֵּץ
הֱיוֹת לָהּ כְּדָת הַנָּשִׁים שְׁנֵים עָשָׂר חֹדֶשׁ כִּי כֵּן יִמְלְאוּ יְמֵי מְרוּקֵיהֶן
שִׁשָּׁה חֳדָשִׁים בְּשֶׁמֶן הַמֹּר וְשִׁשָּׁה חֳדָשִׁים בַּבְּשָׂמִים וּבְתַמְרוּקֵי
יג הַנָּשִׁים: וּבָזֶה הַנַּעֲרָה בָּאָה אֶל־הַמֶּלֶךְ אֵת כָּל־אֲשֶׁר תֹּאמַר יִנָּתֵן לָהּ
יד לָבוֹא עִמָּהּ מִבֵּית הַנָּשִׁים עַד־בֵּית הַמֶּלֶךְ: בָּעֶרֶב ׀ הִיא בָאָה וּבַבֹּקֶר
הִיא שָׁבָה אֶל־בֵּית הַנָּשִׁים שֵׁנִי אֶל־יַד שַׁעַשְׁגַז סְרִיס הַמֶּלֶךְ שֹׁמֵר
הַפִּילַגְשִׁים לֹא־תָבוֹא עוֹד אֶל־הַמֶּלֶךְ כִּי אִם־חָפֵץ בָּהּ הַמֶּלֶךְ וְנִקְרְאָה
טו בְשֵׁם: וּבְהַגִּיעַ תֹּר־אֶסְתֵּר בַּת־אֲבִיחַיִל ׀ דֹּד מָרְדֳּכַי אֲשֶׁר לָקַח־

Aviḥayil – Mordekhai's uncle – whom Mordekhai had adopted as his own
child, to come before the king, she did not ask for anything except for
what Hegai, the king's eunuch, keeper of the women, told her to bring. Yet
16 Esther carried grace in the eyes of all who saw her. Esther was taken to King
Aḥashverosh, to his royal palace, in the tenth month, the month of Tevet, in
17 the seventh year of his reign. And the king loved Esther more than all the
other women, and she pleased him and carried grace and kindness with her,
more so than all the other virgins; and he placed a royal crown upon her head
18 and made her queen in Vashti's place. And the king made a great feast for all
his ministers and courtiers: the feast of Esther. And he granted the provinces
19 both a remission of their dues and gifts as vast as the king's largesse. As the
virgins were gathered in for a second time, Mordekhai was sitting at the King's
20 Gate. Esther had not told of her birth or of her people, just as Mordekhai had
instructed her; for Esther still heeded Mordekhai's words, just as she had
21 when she had lived under his care. As Mordekhai sat at the
King's Gate at that time, fury engulfed Bigtan and Teresh, two of the king's
eunuchs, guards of the threshold, and they plotted to lay their hands on King
22 Aḥashverosh. But Mordekhai learned of the plot and conveyed the knowledge
23 to Queen Esther, and Esther told the king in Mordekhai's name. The matter
was investigated and found to be true, and the two men were hung from a
post;[3] and the story was written down before the king in the scroll of the
3 1 chronicles. Some time after this, King Aḥashverosh promoted Haman
son of Hamedata the Agagite,[4] raising him to a seat above those of all his
2 fellow ministers. And all the king's courtiers serving at the King's Gate would
kneel and bow before Haman, for so had the king instructed, but Mordekhai
3 would neither kneel nor bow down. So the king's courtiers serving at the
King's Gate would ask Mordekhai, "Why do you not obey the king's
4 command?" When, day after day, they said this to him and he paid no
attention, they reported the matter to Haman, interested to see whether
5 Mordekhai's word would stand – for he had explained that he was a Jew. And
Haman noticed that Mordekhai, indeed, did not kneel or bow down before
6 him, and it filled Haman with rage. The thought of laying his hands only on
Mordekhai filled him with contempt, for they had told him who Mordekhai's
people were. No, Haman sought to destroy all of the Jews, all of Mordekhai's
7 people, all across the empire of Aḥashverosh. And so in the first month, the
month of Nisan, of the twelfth year of King Aḥashverosh's reign, a *pur* – lots,
in other words – was cast before Haman, day for day and month for month,
8 and it fell to the twelfth month, the month of Adar. Haman then
spoke to King Aḥashverosh: "There is one people, scattered and dispersed
among the peoples across all the provinces of your realm, whose laws are
different from those of all the other peoples, and who do not obey the king's
9 own laws, and it really is not worth the king's while to leave them so. If it so
please the king, let it be decreed in writing to destroy them, and I shall weigh

3 | The Persians "hung up" or impaled executed corpses for public display; cf. Deuteronomy 21:22–23.
4 | Descended from Amalek (see 1 Sam., ch. 15).

לוֹ לְבַת לָבוֹא אֶל־הַמֶּלֶךְ לֹא בִקְשָׁה דָּבָר כִּי אִם אֶת־אֲשֶׁר יֹאמַר
הֵגַי סְרִיס־הַמֶּלֶךְ שֹׁמֵר הַנָּשִׁים וַתְּהִי אֶסְתֵּר נֹשֵׂאת חֵן בְּעֵינֵי כָּל־
טז רֹאֶיהָ׃ וַתִּלָּקַח אֶסְתֵּר אֶל־הַמֶּלֶךְ אֲחַשְׁוֵרוֹשׁ אֶל־בֵּית מַלְכוּתוֹ בַּחֹדֶשׁ
יז הָעֲשִׂירִי הוּא־חֹדֶשׁ טֵבֵת בִּשְׁנַת־שֶׁבַע לְמַלְכוּתוֹ׃ וַיֶּאֱהַב הַמֶּלֶךְ
אֶת־אֶסְתֵּר מִכָּל־הַנָּשִׁים וַתִּשָּׂא־חֵן וָחֶסֶד לְפָנָיו מִכָּל־הַבְּתוּלוֹת
יח וַיָּשֶׂם כֶּתֶר־מַלְכוּת בְּרֹאשָׁהּ וַיַּמְלִיכֶהָ תַּחַת וַשְׁתִּי׃ וַיַּעַשׂ הַמֶּלֶךְ
מִשְׁתֶּה גָדוֹל לְכָל־שָׂרָיו וַעֲבָדָיו אֵת מִשְׁתֵּה אֶסְתֵּר וַהֲנָחָה לַמְּדִינוֹת
יט עָשָׂה וַיִּתֵּן מַשְׂאֵת כְּיַד הַמֶּלֶךְ׃ וּבְהִקָּבֵץ בְּתוּלוֹת שֵׁנִית וּמָרְדֳּכַי יֹשֵׁב
כ בְּשַׁעַר־הַמֶּלֶךְ׃ אֵין אֶסְתֵּר מַגֶּדֶת מוֹלַדְתָּהּ וְאֶת־עַמָּהּ כַּאֲשֶׁר צִוָּה
עָלֶיהָ מָרְדֳּכָי וְאֶת־מַאֲמַר מָרְדֳּכַי אֶסְתֵּר עֹשָׂה כַּאֲשֶׁר הָיְתָה בְאָמְנָה
כא אִתּוֹ׃ בַּיָּמִים הָהֵם וּמָרְדֳּכַי יֹשֵׁב בְּשַׁעַר־הַמֶּלֶךְ קָצַף בִּגְתָן
וָתֶרֶשׁ שְׁנֵי־סָרִיסֵי הַמֶּלֶךְ מִשֹּׁמְרֵי הַסַּף וַיְבַקְשׁוּ לִשְׁלֹחַ יָד בַּמֶּלֶךְ
כב אֲחַשְׁוֵרֹשׁ׃ וַיִּוָּדַע הַדָּבָר לְמָרְדֳּכַי וַיַּגֵּד לְאֶסְתֵּר הַמַּלְכָּה וַתֹּאמֶר אֶסְתֵּר
כג לַמֶּלֶךְ בְּשֵׁם מָרְדֳּכָי׃ וַיְבֻקַּשׁ הַדָּבָר וַיִּמָּצֵא וַיִּתָּלוּ שְׁנֵיהֶם עַל־עֵץ
ג א וַיִּכָּתֵב בְּסֵפֶר דִּבְרֵי הַיָּמִים לִפְנֵי הַמֶּלֶךְ׃ אַחַר ׀ הַדְּבָרִים
הָאֵלֶּה גִּדַּל הַמֶּלֶךְ אֲחַשְׁוֵרוֹשׁ אֶת־הָמָן בֶּן־הַמְּדָתָא הָאֲגָגִי וַיְנַשְּׂאֵהוּ
ב וַיָּשֶׂם אֶת־כִּסְאוֹ מֵעַל כָּל־הַשָּׂרִים אֲשֶׁר אִתּוֹ׃ וְכָל־עַבְדֵי הַמֶּלֶךְ
אֲשֶׁר־בְּשַׁעַר הַמֶּלֶךְ כֹּרְעִים וּמִשְׁתַּחֲוִים לְהָמָן כִּי־כֵן צִוָּה־לוֹ הַמֶּלֶךְ
ג וּמָרְדֳּכַי לֹא יִכְרַע וְלֹא יִשְׁתַּחֲוֶה׃ וַיֹּאמְרוּ עַבְדֵי הַמֶּלֶךְ אֲשֶׁר־בְּשַׁעַר
ד הַמֶּלֶךְ לְמָרְדֳּכָי מַדּוּעַ אַתָּה עוֹבֵר אֵת מִצְוַת הַמֶּלֶךְ׃ וַיְהִי באמרם   כְּאָמְרָם
אֵלָיו יוֹם וָיוֹם וְלֹא שָׁמַע אֲלֵיהֶם וַיַּגִּידוּ לְהָמָן לִרְאוֹת הֲיַעַמְדוּ דִּבְרֵי
ה מָרְדֳּכַי כִּי־הִגִּיד לָהֶם אֲשֶׁר־הוּא יְהוּדִי׃ וַיַּרְא הָמָן כִּי־אֵין מָרְדֳּכַי כֹּרֵעַ
ו וּמִשְׁתַּחֲוֶה לוֹ וַיִּמָּלֵא הָמָן חֵמָה׃ וַיִּבֶז בְּעֵינָיו לִשְׁלֹחַ יָד בְּמָרְדֳּכַי
לְבַדּוֹ כִּי־הִגִּידוּ לוֹ אֶת־עַם מָרְדֳּכָי וַיְבַקֵּשׁ הָמָן לְהַשְׁמִיד אֶת־כָּל־
ז הַיְּהוּדִים אֲשֶׁר בְּכָל־מַלְכוּת אֲחַשְׁוֵרוֹשׁ עַם מָרְדֳּכָי׃ בַּחֹדֶשׁ הָרִאשׁוֹן
הוּא־חֹדֶשׁ נִיסָן בִּשְׁנַת שְׁתֵּים עֶשְׂרֵה לַמֶּלֶךְ אֲחַשְׁוֵרוֹשׁ הִפִּיל פּוּר
הוּא הַגּוֹרָל לִפְנֵי הָמָן מִיּוֹם ׀ לְיוֹם וּמֵחֹדֶשׁ לְחֹדֶשׁ שְׁנֵים־עָשָׂר הוּא־
ח חֹדֶשׁ אֲדָר׃ וַיֹּאמֶר הָמָן לַמֶּלֶךְ אֲחַשְׁוֵרוֹשׁ יֶשְׁנוֹ עַם־ ג
אֶחָד מְפֻזָּר וּמְפֹרָד בֵּין הָעַמִּים בְּכֹל מְדִינוֹת מַלְכוּתֶךָ וְדָתֵיהֶם שֹׁנוֹת
מִכָּל־עָם וְאֶת־דָּתֵי הַמֶּלֶךְ אֵינָם עֹשִׂים וְלַמֶּלֶךְ אֵין־שֹׁוֶה לְהַנִּיחָם׃
ט אִם־עַל־הַמֶּלֶךְ טוֹב יִכָּתֵב לְאַבְּדָם וַעֲשֶׂרֶת אֲלָפִים כִּכַּר־כֶּסֶף אֶשְׁקוֹל

out ten thousand talents of silver into the hands of the administrators, to be
10 delivered to the king's treasury." The king removed the ring from his finger
11 and gave it to Haman son of Hamedata the Agagite, enemy of the Jews. And
the king said to Haman, "The silver is yours, and so is the people: do with
12 them as you will." The king's scribes were called on the thirteenth day of
the first month, and all that Haman commanded the king's viceroys, the
administrators of every single province and the ministers of every single
people, was written to province by province, each in its script, to people by
people, each in its language – written in the name of King Aḥashverosh and
13 sealed with the king's ring. Scrolls were sent out with the runners to all the
provinces of the king ruling that they kill, destroy, and annihilate all the Jews,
young and old, children and women alike, all in one day – the thirteenth day
of the twelfth month, which is the month of Adar – and seize the plunder.
14 The text of that letter was to be laid down as law in each and every province,
15 displayed for every people to see, to make them ready for that day. The
runners rushed out at the king's word, and the law was laid down in the
imperial city of Shushan. The king and Haman sat down to drink – and the
4 1 town of Shushan stood aghast. Mordekhai understood all that had
happened, and he tore his clothes and dressed himself in sackcloth and ashes;
and he walked out to the middle of the town, crying out, a loud and bitter cry.
2 He came as far as the entrance to the King's Gate, for no one may enter the
3 King's Gate dressed in sackcloth. And in every single province, wherever the
king's word and law extended, deep mourning prevailed among the Jews,
fasting and weeping and grief; the multitudes lay down upon sackcloth and
4 ashes. Esther's young maids and her eunuchs came and told her of this, and
the queen's whole body shook. She sent clothes for Mordekhai to put on,
to lay aside the sackcloth he was wearing, but he would not accept them.
5 So Esther called Hatakh, one of the king's eunuchs assigned to her, and
instructed him to go and speak to Mordekhai to find out what all this was and
6 why. Hatakh went out to Mordekhai, to the town square before the King's
7 Gate, and Mordekhai told him all that had happened to him, and all about
the silver that Haman had promised to have weighed out to the king's treasury
8 in return for the right to destroy the Jews. And he gave him the text of the
decree that had been issued in Shushan to annihilate them, telling him to
show it to Esther and to speak to her, instructing her strictly to go to the king
9 and plead with him, to implore him to help her people. Hatakh came and told
10 Esther what Mordekhai had said. And Esther told Hatakh, instructing him to
11 repeat her words to Mordekhai: "All the king's courtiers and all the people of
his provinces know that there is only one law for any man or woman who
comes before the king, into the inner courtyard, without being called: to be
killed. Unless, that is, the king extends the golden scepter toward him so that
he may live on. As for me – I have not been called to come before the king
12 these thirty days past." And they told Mordekhai what Esther had said.

י עַל־יְדֵי עֹשֵׂי הַמְּלָאכָה לְהָבִיא אֶל־גִּנְזֵי הַמֶּלֶךְ: וַיָּסַר הַמֶּלֶךְ אֶת־
טַבַּעְתּוֹ מֵעַל יָדוֹ וַיִּתְּנָהּ לְהָמָן בֶּן־הַמְּדָתָא הָאֲגָגִי צֹרֵר הַיְּהוּדִים:
יא וַיֹּאמֶר הַמֶּלֶךְ לְהָמָן הַכֶּסֶף נָתוּן לָךְ וְהָעָם לַעֲשׂוֹת בּוֹ כַּטּוֹב בְּעֵינֶיךָ:
יב וַיִּקָּרְאוּ סֹפְרֵי הַמֶּלֶךְ בַּחֹדֶשׁ הָרִאשׁוֹן בִּשְׁלוֹשָׁה עָשָׂר יוֹם בּוֹ וַיִּכָּתֵב
כְּכָל־אֲשֶׁר־צִוָּה הָמָן אֶל אֲחַשְׁדַּרְפְּנֵי־הַמֶּלֶךְ וְאֶל־הַפַּחוֹת אֲשֶׁר ׀
עַל־מְדִינָה וּמְדִינָה וְאֶל־שָׂרֵי עַם וָעָם מְדִינָה וּמְדִינָה כִּכְתָבָהּ וְעַם
וָעָם כִּלְשׁוֹנוֹ בְּשֵׁם הַמֶּלֶךְ אֲחַשְׁוֵרֹשׁ נִכְתָּב וְנֶחְתָּם בְּטַבַּעַת הַמֶּלֶךְ:
יג וְנִשְׁלוֹחַ סְפָרִים בְּיַד הָרָצִים אֶל־כָּל־מְדִינוֹת הַמֶּלֶךְ לְהַשְׁמִיד לַהֲרֹג
וּלְאַבֵּד אֶת־כָּל־הַיְּהוּדִים מִנַּעַר וְעַד־זָקֵן טַף וְנָשִׁים בְּיוֹם אֶחָד
בִּשְׁלוֹשָׁה עָשָׂר לְחֹדֶשׁ שְׁנֵים־עָשָׂר הוּא־חֹדֶשׁ אֲדָר וּשְׁלָלָם לָבוֹז:
יד פַּתְשֶׁגֶן הַכְּתָב לְהִנָּתֵן דָּת בְּכָל־מְדִינָה וּמְדִינָה גָּלוּי לְכָל־הָעַמִּים
טו לִהְיוֹת עֲתִדִים לַיּוֹם הַזֶּה: הָרָצִים יָצְאוּ דְחוּפִים בִּדְבַר הַמֶּלֶךְ וְהַדָּת
נִתְּנָה בְּשׁוּשַׁן הַבִּירָה וְהַמֶּלֶךְ וְהָמָן יָשְׁבוּ לִשְׁתּוֹת וְהָעִיר שׁוּשָׁן
ד א נָבוֹכָה: וּמָרְדֳּכַי יָדַע אֶת־כָּל־אֲשֶׁר נַעֲשָׂה וַיִּקְרַע מָרְדֳּכַי
אֶת־בְּגָדָיו וַיִּלְבַּשׁ שַׂק וָאֵפֶר וַיֵּצֵא בְּתוֹךְ הָעִיר וַיִּזְעַק זְעָקָה גְדֹלָה
ב וּמָרָה: וַיָּבוֹא עַד לִפְנֵי שַׁעַר־הַמֶּלֶךְ כִּי אֵין לָבוֹא אֶל־שַׁעַר הַמֶּלֶךְ
ג בִּלְבוּשׁ שָׂק: וּבְכָל־מְדִינָה וּמְדִינָה מְקוֹם אֲשֶׁר דְּבַר־הַמֶּלֶךְ וְדָתוֹ
מַגִּיעַ אֵבֶל גָּדוֹל לַיְּהוּדִים וְצוֹם וּבְכִי וּמִסְפֵּד שַׂק וָאֵפֶר יֻצַּע לָרַבִּים:
ד וַתָּבוֹאינָה נַעֲרוֹת אֶסְתֵּר וְסָרִיסֶיהָ וַיַּגִּידוּ לָהּ וַתִּתְחַלְחַל הַמַּלְכָּה וַתָּבוֹאנָה
מְאֹד וַתִּשְׁלַח בְּגָדִים לְהַלְבִּישׁ אֶת־מָרְדֳּכַי וּלְהָסִיר שַׂקּוֹ מֵעָלָיו וְלֹא
ה קִבֵּל: וַתִּקְרָא אֶסְתֵּר לַהֲתָךְ מִסָּרִיסֵי הַמֶּלֶךְ אֲשֶׁר הֶעֱמִיד לְפָנֶיהָ
ו וַתְּצַוֵּהוּ עַל־מָרְדֳּכָי לָדַעַת מַה־זֶּה וְעַל־מַה־זֶּה: וַיֵּצֵא הֲתָךְ אֶל־
ז מָרְדֳּכָי אֶל־רְחוֹב הָעִיר אֲשֶׁר לִפְנֵי שַׁעַר־הַמֶּלֶךְ: וַיַּגֶּד־לוֹ מָרְדֳּכַי אֵת
כָּל־אֲשֶׁר קָרָהוּ וְאֵת ׀ פָּרָשַׁת הַכֶּסֶף אֲשֶׁר אָמַר הָמָן לִשְׁקוֹל עַל־גִּנְזֵי
ח הַמֶּלֶךְ ביהודיים לְאַבְּדָם: וְאֶת־פַּתְשֶׁגֶן כְּתָב־הַדָּת אֲשֶׁר־נִתַּן בְּשׁוּשָׁן בַּיְּהוּדִים
לְהַשְׁמִידָם נָתַן לוֹ לְהַרְאוֹת אֶת־אֶסְתֵּר וּלְהַגִּיד לָהּ וּלְצַוּוֹת עָלֶיהָ
ט לָבוֹא אֶל־הַמֶּלֶךְ לְהִתְחַנֶּן־לוֹ וּלְבַקֵּשׁ מִלְּפָנָיו עַל־עַמָּהּ: וַיָּבוֹא הֲתָךְ
י וַיַּגֵּד לְאֶסְתֵּר אֵת דִּבְרֵי מָרְדֳּכָי: וַתֹּאמֶר אֶסְתֵּר לַהֲתָךְ וַתְּצַוֵּהוּ אֶל־
יא מָרְדֳּכָי: כָּל־עַבְדֵי הַמֶּלֶךְ וְעַם מְדִינוֹת הַמֶּלֶךְ יֹדְעִים אֲשֶׁר כָּל־אִישׁ
וְאִשָּׁה אֲשֶׁר־יָבוֹא אֶל־הַמֶּלֶךְ אֶל־הֶחָצֵר הַפְּנִימִית אֲשֶׁר לֹא־יִקָּרֵא
אַחַת דָּתוֹ לְהָמִית לְבַד מֵאֲשֶׁר יוֹשִׁיט־לוֹ הַמֶּלֶךְ אֶת־שַׁרְבִיט הַזָּהָב
יב וְחָיָה וַאֲנִי לֹא נִקְרֵאתִי לָבוֹא אֶל־הַמֶּלֶךְ זֶה שְׁלוֹשִׁים יוֹם: וַיַּגִּידוּ

13 Mordekhai sent back his reply to Esther: "Do not imagine that you can escape
14 to the king's palace from the fate of all the Jews. For if you keep your silence
at this time, relief and salvation will come forth for the Jews from some other
place, but you and your father's house will be lost forever. And who can say;
15 could it not be for just such a time as this that you came into royalty?" Esther
16 sent back word to Mordekhai: "Go – gather all the Jews in Shushan and fast
for me: do not eat and do not drink for three whole days, day or night; I and
my maids will fast also. So shall I come before the king in defiance of the
17 law – and if I am lost, I am lost." Mordekhai walked away; and he did all that
5 1 Esther had instructed him to do. On the third day, Esther dressed herself in
royalty and came to stand in the inner courtyard of the king's palace, facing
the king's palace, while the king sat upon his royal throne in the great hall,
2 facing the palace entrance. When the king noticed Queen Esther standing in
the courtyard, she carried grace in his eyes, so the king extended the golden
scepter in his hand toward Esther, and Esther came forward and touched the
3 scepter's end. And the king said to her, "What brings you, Esther, my queen?
4 And what would you ask? Be it even half my kingdom, it shall be yours." Esther
said, "If it so please the king, may the king and Haman come today to the feast
5 that I have prepared for him." And the king called out, "Make Haman hurry
to carry out Esther's word!" And the king and Haman came to the feast that
6 Esther had prepared. At that drinking feast, the king said to Esther, "What is
your desire, then? It shall be yours. What would you ask? Be it even half my
7 kingdom, it shall be done." And Esther answered: "This is my desire and my
8 request," she said. "If I have the king's favor, and if it so please the king to grant
what I desire, to honor my request – let the king and Haman come again to
the feast that I shall prepare for them. And tomorrow I shall do as the king
9 asks." Haman went out on that day, happy and buoyant of heart. But when he
saw Mordekhai at the King's Gate, and when Mordekhai did not stand up and
10 did not tremble in his presence, Haman was filled with rage against him. Yet
Haman restrained himself until he reached his home, and then he sent for all
11 his friends and for his wife, Zeresh. And Haman told them of his glorious
wealth and the great number of his sons and all the ways the king had elevated
him and raised him above all the other ministers and courtiers of the king.
12 Finally Haman said, "And Esther brought no one else but me with the king
to the feast that she made, and tomorrow too I am invited to her along with
13 the king. Yet all this is worth nothing to me whenever I see that Jew Mordekhai
14 sitting there at the King's Gate." Zeresh his wife replied, along with all his
friends: "Let a post be erected full fifty cubits high. In the morning, say the
word to the king, and Mordekhai shall be hung up from it. Then you will go
happy to the feast with the king." The idea pleased Haman, and he erected the

יג למרדכי את דברי אסתר: ויאמר מרדכי להשיב אל־אסתר אל־
יד תדמי בנפשך להמלט בית־המלך מכל־היהודים: כי אם־החרש
תחרישי בעת הזאת רוח והצלה יעמוד ליהודים ממקום אחר ואת
ובית־אביך תאבדו ומי יודע אם־לעת כזאת הגעת למלכות:
טו טז ותאמר אסתר להשיב אל־מרדכי: לך כנוס את־כל־היהודים
הנמצאים בשושן וצומו עלי ואל־תאכלו ואל־תשתו שלשת ימים
לילה ויום גם־אני ונערתי אצום כן ובכן אבוא אל־המלך אשר לא־
יז כדת וכאשר אבדתי אבדתי: ויעבר מרדכי ויעש ככל אשר־צותה
ה א עליו אסתר: ויהי ׀ ביום השלישי ותלבש אסתר מלכות ותעמד
בחצר בית־המלך הפנימית נכח בית המלך והמלך יושב על־כסא
ב מלכותו בבית המלכות נכח פתח הבית: ויהי כראות המלך את־
אסתר המלכה עמדת בחצר נשאה חן בעיניו ויושט המלך לאסתר
את־שרביט הזהב אשר בידו ותקרב אסתר ותגע בראש השרביט:
ג ויאמר לה המלך מה־לך אסתר המלכה ומה־בקשתך עד־חצי
ד המלכות וינתן לך: ותאמר אסתר אם־על־המלך טוב יבוא המלך
ה והמן היום אל־המשתה אשר־עשיתי לו: ויאמר המלך מהרו
את־המן לעשות את־דבר אסתר ויבא המלך והמן אל־המשתה
ו אשר־עשתה אסתר: ויאמר המלך לאסתר במשתה היין מה־
ז שאלתך וינתן לך ומה־בקשתך עד־חצי המלכות ותעש: ותען
ח אסתר ותאמר שאלתי ובקשתי: אם־מצאתי חן בעיני המלך ואם־
על־המלך טוב לתת את־שאלתי ולעשות את־בקשתי יבוא המלך
והמן אל־המשתה אשר אעשה להם ומחר אעשה כדבר המלך:
ט ויצא המן ביום ההוא שמח וטוב לב וכראות המן את־מרדכי בשער
י המלך ולא־קם ולא־זע ממנו וימלא המן על־מרדכי חמה: ויתאפק
המן ויבוא אל־ביתו וישלח ויבא את־אהביו ואת־זרש אשתו:
יא ויספר להם המן את־כבוד עשרו ורב בניו ואת כל־אשר גדלו המלך
יב ואת אשר נשאו על־השרים ועבדי המלך: ויאמר המן אף לא־
הביאה אסתר המלכה עם־המלך אל־המשתה אשר־עשתה כי
יג אם־אותי וגם־למחר אני קרוא־לה עם־המלך: וכל־זה איננו שוה
לי בכל־עת אשר אני ראה את־מרדכי היהודי יושב בשער המלך:
יד ותאמר לו זרש אשתו וכל־אהביו יעשו־עץ גבה חמשים אמה
ובבקר ׀ אמר למלך ויתלו את־מרדכי עליו ובא עם־המלך אל־

6 1 post. The king slept fitfully that night. He called for the scroll of the
records, the chronicles, to be brought to him, and they were read aloud before
2 him. There it was found written that Mordekhai had reported Bigtan and
Teresh, two of the king's eunuchs, guards of the threshold, who had planned
3 to lay hands upon King Aḥashverosh. The king said, "What honor or greatness
has been granted Mordekhai for doing this?" and the king's pages, those who
4 were attending him, said, "Nothing at all has been done for him." "Who is in
the courtyard?" asked the king. Haman had come to the outer courtyard of
the king's palace to speak to the king about hanging Mordekhai on the post
5 he had prepared for him. The king's pages said to him, "Ah, there is Haman
6 standing in the courtyard," and the king said, "Show him in!" In Haman came,
and the king asked him, "What should be done for a man the king wishes to
honor?" Said Haman to himself, "Whom could the king wish to honor more
7 8 than me?" So Haman told the king: "The man the king wishes to honor – let
the clothes of royalty be brought forth, clothes that the king himself has worn,
9 and a horse on which the king has ridden, on its head a royal crown; and let
these clothes and this horse be entrusted to one of the king's noble ministers
to dress the man the king wishes to honor. And let him lead that man, riding
on the horse, across the town square, crying out before him as they go, 'This
10 is what is done for the man whom the king wishes to honor!'" "Hurry!" said
the king to Haman. "Take the clothes and the horse as you have said, and do
just that for Mordekhai the Jew, who sits at the King's Gate – let no detail fall
11 short of what you have described!" So Haman took the clothes and the horse
and dressed Mordekhai and led him across the town square, crying out before
him as they went, "This is what is done for the man whom the king wishes to
12 honor!" Then Mordekhai returned to the King's Gate, and Haman rushed
13 back to his house grief stricken, covering his face. Haman told his wife Zeresh
and all his friends all that had happened to him, and his wise men with his
wife Zeresh said, "If this Mordekhai before whom you have begun to fall is
of Jewish blood, you will not overcome him; you will fall, you must fall before
14 him –" they were still speaking when the king's eunuchs arrived to fetch
7 1 Haman, with fearful haste, to the feast that Esther had prepared. So the king
2 and Haman arrived to drink with Queen Esther. On that second day also, at
the drinking feast, the king said to Esther, "What is your desire, Esther, my
queen? It shall be yours. What would you ask? Be it even half my kingdom, it
3 shall be done." And Queen Esther answered: "If I have your favor, my king,"
she said, "and if it so please the king – let me have my life as my desire, my
4 people as my request. For we have been sold, my people and I, to be killed,
destroyed, and annihilated. Had we but been sold as slaves and bondwomen,
I would have kept my silence, for that anguish is not worth any loss to the
5 king." King Aḥashverosh spoke; he said to Esther the queen: "Who is

ו א הַמִּשְׁתֶּה שָׂמֵחַ וַיִּיטַב הַדָּבָר לִפְנֵי הָמָן וַיַּעַשׂ הָעֵץ׃ בַּלַּיְלָה
הַהוּא נָדְדָה שְׁנַת הַמֶּלֶךְ וַיֹּאמֶר לְהָבִיא אֶת־סֵפֶר הַזִּכְרֹנוֹת דִּבְרֵי
ב הַיָּמִים וַיִּהְיוּ נִקְרָאִים לִפְנֵי הַמֶּלֶךְ׃ וַיִּמָּצֵא כָתוּב אֲשֶׁר הִגִּיד מָרְדֳּכַי
עַל־בִּגְתָנָא וָתֶרֶשׁ שְׁנֵי סָרִיסֵי הַמֶּלֶךְ מִשֹּׁמְרֵי הַסַּף אֲשֶׁר בִּקְשׁוּ לִשְׁלֹחַ
ג יָד בַּמֶּלֶךְ אֲחַשְׁוֵרוֹשׁ׃ וַיֹּאמֶר הַמֶּלֶךְ מַה־נַּעֲשָׂה יְקָר וּגְדוּלָּה לְמָרְדֳּכַי
ד עַל־זֶה וַיֹּאמְרוּ נַעֲרֵי הַמֶּלֶךְ מְשָׁרְתָיו לֹא־נַעֲשָׂה עִמּוֹ דָּבָר׃ וַיֹּאמֶר
הַמֶּלֶךְ מִי בֶחָצֵר וְהָמָן בָּא לַחֲצַר בֵּית־הַמֶּלֶךְ הַחִיצוֹנָה לֵאמֹר לַמֶּלֶךְ
ה לִתְלוֹת אֶת־מָרְדֳּכַי עַל־הָעֵץ אֲשֶׁר־הֵכִין לוֹ׃ וַיֹּאמְרוּ נַעֲרֵי הַמֶּלֶךְ
ו אֵלָיו הִנֵּה הָמָן עֹמֵד בֶּחָצֵר וַיֹּאמֶר הַמֶּלֶךְ יָבוֹא׃ וַיָּבוֹא הָמָן וַיֹּאמֶר
לוֹ הַמֶּלֶךְ מַה־לַּעֲשׂוֹת בָּאִישׁ אֲשֶׁר הַמֶּלֶךְ חָפֵץ בִּיקָרוֹ וַיֹּאמֶר הָמָן
ז בְּלִבּוֹ לְמִי יַחְפֹּץ הַמֶּלֶךְ לַעֲשׂוֹת יְקָר יוֹתֵר מִמֶּנִּי׃ וַיֹּאמֶר הָמָן אֶל־
ח הַמֶּלֶךְ אִישׁ אֲשֶׁר הַמֶּלֶךְ חָפֵץ בִּיקָרוֹ׃ יָבִיאוּ לְבוּשׁ מַלְכוּת אֲשֶׁר
לָבַשׁ־בּוֹ הַמֶּלֶךְ וְסוּס אֲשֶׁר רָכַב עָלָיו הַמֶּלֶךְ וַאֲשֶׁר נִתַּן כֶּתֶר מַלְכוּת
ט בְּרֹאשׁוֹ׃ וְנָתוֹן הַלְּבוּשׁ וְהַסּוּס עַל־יַד־אִישׁ מִשָּׂרֵי הַמֶּלֶךְ הַפַּרְתְּמִים
וְהִלְבִּשׁוּ אֶת־הָאִישׁ אֲשֶׁר הַמֶּלֶךְ חָפֵץ בִּיקָרוֹ וְהִרְכִּיבֻהוּ עַל־הַסּוּס
בִּרְחוֹב הָעִיר וְקָרְאוּ לְפָנָיו כָּכָה יֵעָשֶׂה לָאִישׁ אֲשֶׁר הַמֶּלֶךְ חָפֵץ
י בִּיקָרוֹ׃ וַיֹּאמֶר הַמֶּלֶךְ לְהָמָן מַהֵר קַח אֶת־הַלְּבוּשׁ וְאֶת־הַסּוּס כַּאֲשֶׁר
דִּבַּרְתָּ וַעֲשֵׂה־כֵן לְמָרְדֳּכַי הַיְּהוּדִי הַיּוֹשֵׁב בְּשַׁעַר הַמֶּלֶךְ אַל־תַּפֵּל
יא דָּבָר מִכֹּל אֲשֶׁר דִּבַּרְתָּ׃ וַיִּקַּח הָמָן אֶת־הַלְּבוּשׁ וְאֶת־הַסּוּס וַיַּלְבֵּשׁ ד
אֶת־מָרְדֳּכָי וַיַּרְכִּיבֵהוּ בִּרְחוֹב הָעִיר וַיִּקְרָא לְפָנָיו כָּכָה יֵעָשֶׂה לָאִישׁ
יב אֲשֶׁר הַמֶּלֶךְ חָפֵץ בִּיקָרוֹ׃ וַיָּשָׁב מָרְדֳּכַי אֶל־שַׁעַר הַמֶּלֶךְ וְהָמָן נִדְחַף
יג אֶל־בֵּיתוֹ אָבֵל וַחֲפוּי רֹאשׁ׃ וַיְסַפֵּר הָמָן לְזֶרֶשׁ אִשְׁתּוֹ וּלְכָל־אֹהֲבָיו
אֵת כָּל־אֲשֶׁר קָרָהוּ וַיֹּאמְרוּ לוֹ חֲכָמָיו וְזֶרֶשׁ אִשְׁתּוֹ אִם מִזֶּרַע הַיְּהוּדִים
מָרְדֳּכַי אֲשֶׁר הַחִלּוֹתָ לִנְפֹּל לְפָנָיו לֹא־תוּכַל לוֹ כִּי־נָפוֹל תִּפּוֹל לְפָנָיו׃
יד עוֹדָם מְדַבְּרִים עִמּוֹ וְסָרִיסֵי הַמֶּלֶךְ הִגִּיעוּ וַיַּבְהִלוּ לְהָבִיא אֶת־הָמָן
ז א אֶל־הַמִּשְׁתֶּה אֲשֶׁר־עָשְׂתָה אֶסְתֵּר׃ וַיָּבֹא הַמֶּלֶךְ וְהָמָן לִשְׁתּוֹת עִם־
ב אֶסְתֵּר הַמַּלְכָּה׃ וַיֹּאמֶר הַמֶּלֶךְ לְאֶסְתֵּר גַּם בַּיּוֹם הַשֵּׁנִי בְּמִשְׁתֵּה הַיַּיִן
מַה־שְּׁאֵלָתֵךְ אֶסְתֵּר הַמַּלְכָּה וְתִנָּתֵן לָךְ וּמַה־בַּקָּשָׁתֵךְ עַד־חֲצִי
ג הַמַּלְכוּת וְתֵעָשׂ׃ וַתַּעַן אֶסְתֵּר הַמַּלְכָּה וַתֹּאמַר אִם־מָצָאתִי חֵן בְּעֵינֶיךָ
הַמֶּלֶךְ וְאִם־עַל־הַמֶּלֶךְ טוֹב תִּנָּתֶן־לִי נַפְשִׁי בִּשְׁאֵלָתִי וְעַמִּי בְּבַקָּשָׁתִי׃
ד כִּי נִמְכַּרְנוּ אֲנִי וְעַמִּי לְהַשְׁמִיד לַהֲרוֹג וּלְאַבֵּד וְאִלּוּ לַעֲבָדִים וְלִשְׁפָחוֹת
ה נִמְכַּרְנוּ הֶחֱרַשְׁתִּי כִּי אֵין הַצָּר שֹׁוֶה בְּנֵזֶק הַמֶּלֶךְ׃ וַיֹּאמֶר

6 it – which one – who put it into his heart to do such a thing?!" "It is a foe, an
enemy," said Esther, "this vicious man: Haman!" And Haman was suddenly
7 terrified before the king and the queen. The king rose up in his rage and left
the wine feast for the palace garden as Haman stood up to entreat for his life
with Esther the queen, for he saw that the king was already set upon his
8 downfall. By the time the king came back from the palace garden to the
feasting chamber, Haman had thrown himself onto Esther's couch – "What!"
said the king. "Would you take the queen too, and with me in the palace?!"
The words came forth from the king's mouth, and Haman's face was covered
9 over. One of the eunuchs, Ḥarvona, said to the king, "You know, the post
Haman prepared for Mordekhai, who spoke up so well for the king, is
standing now in Haman's house, fifty cubits high." And the king said, "Hang
10 him from it!" Thus was Haman hung up from the very post he had prepared
8 1 for Mordekhai – and the king's rage subsided. On that day, King
Aḥashverosh granted Queen Esther the entire estate of Haman, enemy of the
Jews, and Mordekhai came before the king, for Esther had finally revealed
2 what he was to her. The king took off the very ring that he had once given to
Haman and gave it instead to Mordekhai, and Esther appointed Mordekhai
3 to govern Haman's estate. But then Esther spoke to the king again,
falling down at his feet, weeping and pleading with him to overturn the
wickedness of Haman the Agagite and the plot that he had thought up against
4 the Jews. The king extended his golden scepter to Esther, and Esther raised
5 herself up and stood before the king. She said, "If it so please the king, and if
I have his favor, and if it seems right to the king and I am pleasing in his
eyes – let the decree be written to revoke the scrolls that were the plot of
Haman son of Hamedata the Agagite, who wrote to destroy all the Jews in all
6 the king's provinces. For how can I live to see the evil that will come upon my
7 people; how can I live to see the loss of those I am born of?" King
Aḥashverosh said to Queen Esther and to Mordekhai the Jew, "Look, I have
given Esther Haman's estate, and he has been hung from the post for laying
8 hands upon the Jews. Now, write whatever you like about the Jews in the
king's name and seal it with the king's ring – but no writing that has been
written in the name of the king and sealed with the king's ring can ever be
9 revoked." So at that time, the king's scribes were called – on the twenty-third
day of the third month, the month of Sivan – and they wrote down all that
Mordekhai dictated, to the Jews and to the viceroys, the administrators, and
the ministers of all the provinces from Hodu to Kush, 127 provinces, to
province by province, each in its script, to people by people, each in its

הַמֶּלֶךְ אֲחַשְׁוֵרוֹשׁ וַיֹּאמֶר לְאֶסְתֵּר הַמַּלְכָּה מִי הוּא זֶה וְאֵי־זֶה הוּא
ו אֲשֶׁר־מְלָאוֹ לִבּוֹ לַעֲשׂוֹת כֵּן: וַתֹּאמֶר אֶסְתֵּר אִישׁ צַר וְאוֹיֵב הָמָן
ז הָרָע הַזֶּה וְהָמָן נִבְעַת מִלִּפְנֵי הַמֶּלֶךְ וְהַמַּלְכָּה: וְהַמֶּלֶךְ קָם בַּחֲמָתוֹ
מִמִּשְׁתֵּה הַיַּיִן אֶל־גִּנַּת הַבִּיתָן וְהָמָן עָמַד לְבַקֵּשׁ עַל־נַפְשׁוֹ מֵאֶסְתֵּר
ח הַמַּלְכָּה כִּי רָאָה כִּי־כָלְתָה אֵלָיו הָרָעָה מֵאֵת הַמֶּלֶךְ: וְהַמֶּלֶךְ שָׁב
מִגִּנַּת הַבִּיתָן אֶל־בֵּית ׀ מִשְׁתֵּה הַיַּיִן וְהָמָן נֹפֵל עַל־הַמִּטָּה אֲשֶׁר
אֶסְתֵּר עָלֶיהָ וַיֹּאמֶר הַמֶּלֶךְ הֲגַם לִכְבּוֹשׁ אֶת־הַמַּלְכָּה עִמִּי בַּבָּיִת
ט הַדָּבָר יָצָא מִפִּי הַמֶּלֶךְ וּפְנֵי הָמָן חָפוּ: וַיֹּאמֶר חַרְבוֹנָה אֶחָד מִן־
הַסָּרִיסִים לִפְנֵי הַמֶּלֶךְ גַּם הִנֵּה־הָעֵץ אֲשֶׁר־עָשָׂה הָמָן לְמָרְדֳּכַי אֲשֶׁר
דִּבֶּר־טוֹב עַל־הַמֶּלֶךְ עֹמֵד בְּבֵית הָמָן גָּבֹהַּ חֲמִשִּׁים אַמָּה וַיֹּאמֶר
י הַמֶּלֶךְ תְּלֻהוּ עָלָיו: וַיִּתְלוּ אֶת־הָמָן עַל־הָעֵץ אֲשֶׁר־הֵכִין לְמָרְדֳּכָי
ח א וַחֲמַת הַמֶּלֶךְ שָׁכָכָה: בַּיּוֹם הַהוּא נָתַן הַמֶּלֶךְ אֲחַשְׁוֵרוֹשׁ
לְאֶסְתֵּר הַמַּלְכָּה אֶת־בֵּית הָמָן צֹרֵר היהודיים וּמָרְדֳּכַי בָּא לִפְנֵי הַיְּהוּדִים
ב הַמֶּלֶךְ כִּי־הִגִּידָה אֶסְתֵּר מַה הוּא־לָהּ: וַיָּסַר הַמֶּלֶךְ אֶת־טַבַּעְתּוֹ אֲשֶׁר
הֶעֱבִיר מֵהָמָן וַיִּתְּנָהּ לְמָרְדֳּכָי וַתָּשֶׂם אֶסְתֵּר אֶת־מָרְדֳּכַי עַל־בֵּית
ג הָמָן: וַתּוֹסֶף אֶסְתֵּר וַתְּדַבֵּר לִפְנֵי הַמֶּלֶךְ וַתִּפֹּל לִפְנֵי רַגְלָיו
וַתֵּבְךְּ וַתִּתְחַנֶּן־לוֹ לְהַעֲבִיר אֶת־רָעַת הָמָן הָאֲגָגִי וְאֵת מַחֲשַׁבְתּוֹ
ד אֲשֶׁר חָשַׁב עַל־הַיְּהוּדִים: וַיּוֹשֶׁט הַמֶּלֶךְ לְאֶסְתֵּר אֵת שַׁרְבִט הַזָּהָב
ה וַתָּקָם אֶסְתֵּר וַתַּעֲמֹד לִפְנֵי הַמֶּלֶךְ: וַתֹּאמֶר אִם־עַל־הַמֶּלֶךְ טוֹב
וְאִם־מָצָאתִי חֵן לְפָנָיו וְכָשֵׁר הַדָּבָר לִפְנֵי הַמֶּלֶךְ וְטוֹבָה אֲנִי בְּעֵינָיו
יִכָּתֵב לְהָשִׁיב אֶת־הַסְּפָרִים מַחֲשֶׁבֶת הָמָן בֶּן־הַמְּדָתָא הָאֲגָגִי אֲשֶׁר
ו כָּתַב לְאַבֵּד אֶת־הַיְּהוּדִים אֲשֶׁר בְּכָל־מְדִינוֹת הַמֶּלֶךְ: כִּי אֵיכָכָה
אוּכַל וְרָאִיתִי בָּרָעָה אֲשֶׁר־יִמְצָא אֶת־עַמִּי וְאֵיכָכָה אוּכַל וְרָאִיתִי
ז בְּאָבְדַן מוֹלַדְתִּי: וַיֹּאמֶר הַמֶּלֶךְ אֲחַשְׁוֵרֹשׁ לְאֶסְתֵּר הַמַּלְכָּה
וּלְמָרְדֳּכַי הַיְּהוּדִי הִנֵּה בֵית־הָמָן נָתַתִּי לְאֶסְתֵּר וְאֹתוֹ תָּלוּ עַל־הָעֵץ
ח עַל אֲשֶׁר־שָׁלַח יָדוֹ ביהודיים: וְאַתֶּם כִּתְבוּ עַל־הַיְּהוּדִים כַּטּוֹב בַּיְּהוּדִים
בְּעֵינֵיכֶם בְּשֵׁם הַמֶּלֶךְ וְחִתְמוּ בְּטַבַּעַת הַמֶּלֶךְ כִּי־כְתָב אֲשֶׁר־נִכְתָּב
ט בְּשֵׁם־הַמֶּלֶךְ וְנַחְתּוֹם בְּטַבַּעַת הַמֶּלֶךְ אֵין לְהָשִׁיב: וַיִּקָּרְאוּ סֹפְרֵי־
הַמֶּלֶךְ בָּעֵת־הַהִיא בַּחֹדֶשׁ הַשְּׁלִישִׁי הוּא־חֹדֶשׁ סִיוָן בִּשְׁלוֹשָׁה
וְעֶשְׂרִים בּוֹ וַיִּכָּתֵב כְּכָל־אֲשֶׁר־צִוָּה מָרְדֳּכַי אֶל־הַיְּהוּדִים וְאֶל
הָאֲחַשְׁדַּרְפְּנִים וְהַפַּחוֹת וְשָׂרֵי הַמְּדִינוֹת אֲשֶׁר ׀ מֵהֹדּוּ וְעַד־כּוּשׁ שֶׁבַע
וְעֶשְׂרִים וּמֵאָה מְדִינָה מְדִינָה וּמְדִינָה כִּכְתָבָהּ וְעַם וָעָם כִּלְשֹׁנוֹ וְאֶל־

10 language, and to the Jews in their script and in their language. It was written
in the name of King Aḥashverosh and sealed with the king's ring, and the
scrolls were sent with the horseback runners, riding the swift horses of the
11 royal stable, the offspring of the royal mares, to convey that the king had
granted the Jews in every single town the right to come together to stand up
and defend their lives, to kill, destroy, and annihilate all the armed hordes
of the peoples and provinces who threatened them, even the children and
12 women, and to loot plunder, all on one day, the thirteenth day of the twelfth
13 month – the month of Adar – in all the provinces of King Aḥashverosh. The
text of that decree was to lay down the law in every single province, displayed
for every people to see, that the Jews should make themselves ready for that
14 day to wreak vengeance on their enemies. The runners, riding the swift horses
of the royal service, galloped out at great speed, spurred on at the king's word,
15 and the law was laid down in the imperial city of Shushan. So
Mordekhai left the king's presence in royal clothes of sky-blue wool and fine
white fabric, wearing a great coronet of gold and a mantle of finest linen and
purple, and the town of Shushan was filled with jubilation and happiness.
16 17 And the Jews basked in light and happiness, joy and great honor. And in each
and every province, in each and every town, as far as the king's word and law
reached, happiness and joy touched the Jews, with feasting and a holiday;
and many of the local people joined the Jews, for awe of the Jews had
9 1 overwhelmed them. On the thirteenth day of the twelfth month, the month
of Adar, when the king's word and his law were to come into effect, on the day
when the Jews' enemies had hoped to overcome them – it all was turned
2 around, as the Jews themselves overcame those who hated them. The Jews
came together in their cities throughout the provinces of King Aḥashverosh
to lay hands upon those who sought their harm, and no man could stand
3 before them, for fear of them had fallen upon all nations. And the ministers
of the provinces, the viceroys and the governors, and the administrators of
the king's court, all promoted the Jews, for fear of Mordekhai had fallen on
4 them. For Mordekhai was great now in the king's palace, and word of him was
spreading to all the provinces: this man, this Mordekhai, was becoming ever
5 greater. The Jews dealt all their enemies a terrible blow, of sword and slaughter
6 and destruction; they did whatever they pleased to those who hated them. In
the imperial city of Shushan the Jews killed and destroyed five hundred men,
7 and they killed
Parshandata and
Dalfon and
8 Aspata and
Porata and
Adalya and
9 Aridata and

י הַיְּהוּדִים כִּכְתָבָם וְכִלְשׁוֹנָם: וַיִּכְתֹּב בְּשֵׁם הַמֶּלֶךְ אֲחַשְׁוֵרֹשׁ וַיַּחְתֹּם
בְּטַבַּעַת הַמֶּלֶךְ וַיִּשְׁלַח סְפָרִים בְּיַד הָרָצִים בַּסּוּסִים רֹכְבֵי הָרֶכֶשׁ
יא הָאֲחַשְׁתְּרָנִים בְּנֵי הָרַמָּכִים: אֲשֶׁר נָתַן הַמֶּלֶךְ לַיְּהוּדִים ׀ אֲשֶׁר ׀ בְּכָל־
עִיר וָעִיר לְהִקָּהֵל וְלַעֲמֹד עַל־נַפְשָׁם לְהַשְׁמִיד וְלַהֲרֹג וּלְאַבֵּד אֶת־
יב כָּל־חֵיל עַם וּמְדִינָה הַצָּרִים אֹתָם טַף וְנָשִׁים וּשְׁלָלָם לָבוֹז: בְּיוֹם אֶחָד
בְּכָל־מְדִינוֹת הַמֶּלֶךְ אֲחַשְׁוֵרוֹשׁ בִּשְׁלוֹשָׁה עָשָׂר לְחֹדֶשׁ שְׁנֵים־עָשָׂר
יג הוּא־חֹדֶשׁ אֲדָר: פַּתְשֶׁגֶן הַכְּתָב לְהִנָּתֵן דָּת בְּכָל־מְדִינָה וּמְדִינָה גָּלוּי
לְכָל־הָעַמִּים וְלִהְיוֹת היהודיים עתודים לַיּוֹם הַזֶּה לְהִנָּקֵם מֵאֹיְבֵיהֶם: הַיְּהוּדִים עֲתִידִים
יד הָרָצִים רֹכְבֵי הָרֶכֶשׁ הָאֲחַשְׁתְּרָנִים יָצְאוּ מְבֹהָלִים וּדְחוּפִים בִּדְבַר
טו הַמֶּלֶךְ וְהַדָּת נִתְּנָה בְּשׁוּשַׁן הַבִּירָה: וּמָרְדֳּכַי יָצָא ׀ מִלִּפְנֵי
הַמֶּלֶךְ בִּלְבוּשׁ מַלְכוּת תְּכֵלֶת וָחוּר וַעֲטֶרֶת זָהָב גְּדוֹלָה וְתַכְרִיךְ בּוּץ
טז וְאַרְגָּמָן וְהָעִיר שׁוּשָׁן צָהֲלָה וְשָׂמֵחָה: לַיְּהוּדִים הָיְתָה אוֹרָה וְשִׂמְחָה ה
יז וְשָׂשֹׂן וִיקָר: וּבְכָל־מְדִינָה וּמְדִינָה וּבְכָל־עִיר וָעִיר מְקוֹם אֲשֶׁר דְּבַר־
הַמֶּלֶךְ וְדָתוֹ מַגִּיעַ שִׂמְחָה וְשָׂשׂוֹן לַיְּהוּדִים מִשְׁתֶּה וְיוֹם טוֹב וְרַבִּים
ט א מֵעַמֵּי הָאָרֶץ מִתְיַהֲדִים כִּי־נָפַל פַּחַד־הַיְּהוּדִים עֲלֵיהֶם: וּבִשְׁנֵים
עָשָׂר חֹדֶשׁ הוּא־חֹדֶשׁ אֲדָר בִּשְׁלוֹשָׁה עָשָׂר יוֹם בּוֹ אֲשֶׁר הִגִּיעַ דְּבַר־
הַמֶּלֶךְ וְדָתוֹ לְהֵעָשׂוֹת בַּיּוֹם אֲשֶׁר שִׂבְּרוּ אֹיְבֵי הַיְּהוּדִים לִשְׁלוֹט בָּהֶם
ב וְנַהֲפוֹךְ הוּא אֲשֶׁר יִשְׁלְטוּ הַיְּהוּדִים הֵמָּה בְּשֹׂנְאֵיהֶם: נִקְהֲלוּ הַיְּהוּדִים
בְּעָרֵיהֶם בְּכָל־מְדִינוֹת הַמֶּלֶךְ אֲחַשְׁוֵרוֹשׁ לִשְׁלֹחַ יָד בִּמְבַקְשֵׁי רָעָתָם
ג וְאִישׁ לֹא־עָמַד לִפְנֵיהֶם כִּי־נָפַל פַּחְדָּם עַל־כָּל־הָעַמִּים: וְכָל־שָׂרֵי
הַמְּדִינוֹת וְהָאֲחַשְׁדַּרְפְּנִים וְהַפַּחוֹת וְעֹשֵׂי הַמְּלָאכָה אֲשֶׁר לַמֶּלֶךְ
ד מְנַשְּׂאִים אֶת־הַיְּהוּדִים כִּי־נָפַל פַּחַד־מָרְדֳּכַי עֲלֵיהֶם: כִּי־גָדוֹל מָרְדֳּכַי
בְּבֵית הַמֶּלֶךְ וְשָׁמְעוֹ הוֹלֵךְ בְּכָל־הַמְּדִינוֹת כִּי־הָאִישׁ מָרְדֳּכַי הוֹלֵךְ
ה וְגָדוֹל: וַיַּכּוּ הַיְּהוּדִים בְּכָל־אֹיְבֵיהֶם מַכַּת־חֶרֶב וְהֶרֶג וְאַבְדָן וַיַּעֲשׂוּ
ו בְשֹׂנְאֵיהֶם כִּרְצוֹנָם: וּבְשׁוּשַׁן הַבִּירָה הָרְגוּ הַיְּהוּדִים וְאַבֵּד חֲמֵשׁ מֵאוֹת
ז אִישׁ: וְאֵת ׀
פַּרְשַׁנְדָּתָא וְאֵת ׀
דַּלְפוֹן וְאֵת ׀
ח אַסְפָּתָא: וְאֵת ׀
פּוֹרָתָא וְאֵת ׀
אֲדַלְיָא וְאֵת ׀
ט אֲרִידָתָא: וְאֵת ׀

Parmashta and
Arisai and
Aridai and
10 Vayzata, the ten
sons of Haman son of Hamedata, enemy of the Jews – but they did not touch
11 the plunder. On that same day, the number of those killed in the imperial city
12 of Shushan was brought to the king, and the king said to Queen Esther, "The
Jews have killed five hundred men in the imperial city of Shushan alone, as
well as Haman's ten sons – what must they have done in the rest of the king's
provinces? And now, what is your desire? It shall be yours. What would you
13 ask further? It shall be done." Esther said, "If it so please the king, may the
Jews of Shushan be granted tomorrow also to do as they did today, and let
14 Haman's ten sons be hung from the post." Thus the king commanded; the law
15 was laid down in Shushan, and Haman's ten sons were hung up. And the Jews
of Shushan gathered on the fourteenth day of Adar also and killed three
16 hundred men in Shushan, never once touching the plunder. Meanwhile, the
rest of the Jews in the king's provinces, having come together and stood
up to defend their lives, found rest from their enemies, killing seventy-five
thousand of those who hated them, though they did not touch the plunder.
17 That was on the thirteenth day of the month of Adar. On the fourteenth day
18 they rested, and they made it a day of feasting and happiness. The Jews who
were in Shushan came together both on the thirteenth and on the fourteenth,
and rested on the fifteenth, and made that a day of feasting and happiness.
19 Thus it came about that provincial Jews living in unwalled towns make the
fourteenth day of the month of Adar a day of happiness, of feasting and
20 festivity, and of sending one another good things to eat. Mordekhai wrote
all this down and sent scrolls to all the Jews in all the provinces of King
21 Aḥashverosh, near and far, to establish among them that they should mark
22 the fourteenth and fifteenth days of Adar every single year: the days when the
Jews rested from their enemies and the month that was turned for them from
sorrow to happiness, from mourning to celebration – to make them days of
feasting, happiness, sending one another good things to eat, and giving gifts
23 to the poor. And so the Jews accepted upon themselves what they had already
24 begun to perform and all that Mordekhai had written to them. For Haman
son of Hamedata the Agagite, enemy of all the Jews, had plotted against the
Jews to destroy them, and had drawn the *pur* – lots – to consume and to
25 destroy them. When this came before the king, he declared by the scroll that
the evil plot Haman had hatched against the Jews must come down upon his

פַּרְמַ֙שְׁתָּא֙ וְאֵ֣ת ׀
אֲרִיסַ֔י וְאֵ֣ת ׀
אֲרִידַ֖י וְאֵ֣ת ׀
י וַיְזָתָֽא׃ עֲשֶׂ֗רֶת
בְּנֵ֨י הָמָ֧ן בֶּֽן־הַמְּדָ֛תָא צֹרֵ֥ר הַיְּהוּדִ֖ים הָרָ֑גוּ וּבַּבִּזָּ֕ה לֹ֥א שָֽׁלְח֖וּ אֶת־יָדָֽם׃
יא יב בַּיּ֣וֹם הַה֗וּא בָּ֣א מִסְפַּ֧ר הַהֲרוּגִ֛ים בְּשׁוּשַׁ֥ן הַבִּירָ֖ה לִפְנֵ֥י הַמֶּֽלֶךְ׃ וַיֹּ֨אמֶר
הַמֶּ֜לֶךְ לְאֶסְתֵּ֣ר הַמַּלְכָּ֗ה בְּשׁוּשַׁ֣ן הַבִּירָ֡ה הָרְגוּ֩ הַיְּהוּדִ֨ים וְאַבֵּ֜ד חֲמֵ֧שׁ
מֵא֣וֹת אִ֗ישׁ וְאֵת֙ עֲשֶׂ֣רֶת בְּנֵי־הָמָ֔ן בִּשְׁאָ֛ר מְדִינ֥וֹת הַמֶּ֖לֶךְ מֶ֣ה עָשׂ֑וּ
יג וּמַה־שְּׁאֵלָתֵךְ֙ וְיִנָּ֣תֵֽן לָ֔ךְ וּמַה־בַּקָּשָׁתֵ֥ךְ ע֖וֹד וְתֵעָֽשׂ׃ וַתֹּ֤אמֶר אֶסְתֵּר֙
אִם־עַל־הַמֶּ֣לֶךְ ט֔וֹב יִנָּתֵ֣ן גַּם־מָ֗חָר לַיְּהוּדִים֙ אֲשֶׁ֣ר בְּשׁוּשָׁ֔ן לַעֲשׂ֖וֹת
יד כְּדָ֣ת הַיּ֑וֹם וְאֵ֛ת עֲשֶׂ֥רֶת בְּנֵֽי־הָמָ֖ן יִתְל֥וּ עַל־הָעֵֽץ׃ וַיֹּ֤אמֶר הַמֶּ֙לֶךְ֙
טו לְהֵֽעָשׂ֣וֹת כֵּ֔ן וַתִּנָּתֵ֥ן דָּ֖ת בְּשׁוּשָׁ֑ן וְאֵ֛ת עֲשֶׂ֥רֶת בְּנֵֽי־הָמָ֖ן תָּלֽוּ׃ וַיִּקָּ֨הֲל֜וּ
היהודיים אֲשֶׁר־בְּשׁוּשָׁ֗ן גַּ֠ם בְּי֨וֹם אַרְבָּעָ֤ה עָשָׂר֙ לְחֹ֣דֶשׁ אֲדָ֔ר וַיַּֽהַרְג֣וּ הַיְּהוּדִ֨ים
טז בְשׁוּשָׁ֔ן שְׁלֹ֥שׁ מֵא֖וֹת אִ֑ישׁ וּבַ֨בִּזָּ֔ה לֹ֥א שָֽׁלְח֖וּ אֶת־יָדָֽם׃ וּשְׁאָ֣ר הַיְּהוּדִ֡ים
אֲשֶׁר֩ בִּמְדִינ֨וֹת הַמֶּ֜לֶךְ נִקְהֲל֣וּ ׀ וְעָמֹ֣ד עַל־נַפְשָׁ֗ם וְנ֙וֹחַ֙ מֵאֹ֣יְבֵיהֶ֔ם וְהָרוֹג֙
יז בְּשֹׂ֣נְאֵיהֶ֔ם חֲמִשָּׁ֥ה וְשִׁבְעִ֖ים אָ֑לֶף וּבַ֨בִּזָּ֔ה לֹ֥א שָֽׁלְח֖וּ אֶת־יָדָֽם׃ בְּיוֹם־
שְׁלֹשָׁ֥ה עָשָׂ֖ר לְחֹ֣דֶשׁ אֲדָ֑ר וְנ֗וֹחַ בְּאַרְבָּעָ֤ה עָשָׂר֙ בּ֔וֹ וְעָשֹׂ֣ה אֹת֔וֹ י֖וֹם
יח מִשְׁתֶּ֥ה וְשִׂמְחָֽה׃ והיהודיים אֲשֶׁר־בְּשׁוּשָׁ֗ן נִקְהֲלוּ֙ בִּשְׁלֹשָׁ֤ה עָשָׂר֙ בּ֔וֹ וְהַיְּהוּדִ֣ים
וּבְאַרְבָּעָ֥ה עָשָׂ֖ר בּ֑וֹ וְנ֗וֹחַ בַּחֲמִשָּׁ֤ה עָשָׂר֙ בּ֔וֹ וְעָשֹׂ֣ה אֹת֔וֹ י֖וֹם מִשְׁתֶּ֥ה
יט וְשִׂמְחָֽה׃ עַל־כֵּ֞ן הַיְּהוּדִ֣ים הפרוזים הַיֹּשְׁבִים֮ בְּעָרֵ֣י הַפְּרָזוֹת֒ עֹשִׂ֗ים הַפְּרָזִ֗ים
אֵ֣ת י֤וֹם אַרְבָּעָה֙ עָשָׂר֙ לְחֹ֣דֶשׁ אֲדָ֔ר שִׂמְחָ֥ה וּמִשְׁתֶּ֖ה וְי֣וֹם ט֑וֹב וּמִשְׁלֹ֥חַ
כ מָנ֖וֹת אִ֥ישׁ לְרֵעֵֽהוּ׃ וַיִּכְתֹּ֣ב מָרְדֳּכַ֔י אֶת־הַדְּבָרִ֖ים הָאֵ֑לֶּה וַיִּשְׁלַ֨ח סְפָרִ֜ים
אֶל־כָּל־הַיְּהוּדִ֗ים אֲשֶׁר֙ בְּכָל־מְדִינוֹת֙ הַמֶּ֣לֶךְ אֲחַשְׁוֵר֔וֹשׁ הַקְּרוֹבִ֖ים
כא וְהָרְחוֹקִֽים׃ לְקַיֵּם֮ עֲלֵיהֶם֒ לִהְי֣וֹת עֹשִׂ֗ים אֵ֣ת י֤וֹם אַרְבָּעָה֙ עָשָׂר֙ לְחֹ֣דֶשׁ
כב אֲדָ֔ר וְאֵ֛ת יוֹם־חֲמִשָּׁ֥ה עָשָׂ֖ר בּ֑וֹ בְּכָל־שָׁנָ֖ה וְשָׁנָֽה׃ כַּיָּמִ֗ים אֲשֶׁר־נָ֨חוּ
בָהֶ֤ם הַיְּהוּדִים֙ מֵא֣וֹיְבֵיהֶ֔ם וְהַחֹ֗דֶשׁ אֲשֶׁר֩ נֶהְפַּ֨ךְ לָהֶ֤ם מִיָּגוֹן֙ לְשִׂמְחָ֔ה
וּמֵאֵ֖בֶל לְי֣וֹם ט֑וֹב לַעֲשׂ֣וֹת אוֹתָ֗ם יְמֵי֙ מִשְׁתֶּ֣ה וְשִׂמְחָ֔ה וּמִשְׁלֹ֤חַ מָנוֹת֙
כג אִ֣ישׁ לְרֵעֵ֔הוּ וּמַתָּנ֖וֹת לָאֶבְיֹנִֽים׃ וְקִבֵּל֙ הַיְּהוּדִ֔ים אֵ֥ת אֲשֶׁר־הֵחֵ֖לּוּ
כד לַעֲשׂ֑וֹת וְאֵ֛ת אֲשֶׁר־כָּתַ֥ב מָרְדֳּכַ֖י אֲלֵיהֶֽם׃ כִּי֩ הָמָ֨ן בֶּֽן־הַמְּדָ֜תָא הָֽאֲגָגִ֗י
צֹרֵר֙ כָּל־הַיְּהוּדִ֔ים חָשַׁ֥ב עַל־הַיְּהוּדִ֖ים לְאַבְּדָ֑ם וְהִפִּ֥ל פּוּר֙ ה֣וּא הַגּוֹרָ֔ל
כה לְהֻמָּ֖ם וּֽלְאַבְּדָֽם׃ וּבְבֹאָהּ֮ לִפְנֵ֣י הַמֶּלֶךְ֒ אָמַ֣ר עִם־הַסֵּ֔פֶר יָשׁ֞וּב מַחֲשַׁבְתּ֧וֹ
הָֽרָעָ֛ה אֲשֶׁר־חָשַׁ֥ב עַל־הַיְּהוּדִ֖ים עַל־רֹאשׁ֑וֹ וְתָל֥וּ אֹת֛וֹ וְאֶת־בָּנָ֖יו עַל־

26 own head, and that he and his sons must be hung from the post. So these
days were named Purim after the *pur*. So, following the words of the letter
27 and what they had seen and what had befallen them, they established and
accepted, for themselves and for their children, and for all who would ever
come to join their ranks, that they would keep these two days, never to be
neglected, as they are prescribed and at the right times, every single year.
28 Indeed, these days are remembered and marked in every single generation,
family by family, province upon province, town upon town; and these days
of Purim will never be neglected by the Jews, nor will their memory ever cease
29 to be among their children. And Queen Esther daughter of Aviḥayil,
together with Mordekhai the Jew, wrote with all their authority to confirm
30 this second letter of Purim. They sent out scrolls to all the Jews across 127
31 provinces – all of Aḥashverosh's realm – words of peace and truth. The scrolls
were to confirm these days of Purim in their times just as Mordekhai the
Jew and Esther the queen had fixed them, and indeed as they had all fixed
32 their fast days and entreaties, for themselves and for their children. Esther's
words confirmed this practice of Purim, and it was written down in the
10 1 scroll. As for King Aḥashverosh, he levied a tribute from the
2 people of all the land and of the islands of the sea. And the full account of his
authority and might, and all the greatness of Mordekhai, whom the king
exalted – are they not already written in the scroll of the chronicles of the
3 kings of Media and Persia? For Mordekhai the Jew was second in command
to King Aḥashverosh and revered too among the Jews – beloved of all the
multitudes of his brothers, working for the good of his people, and speaking
words of peace for all his children.

כו הָעֵץ: עַל־כֵּן קָרְאוּ לַיָּמִים הָאֵלֶּה פוּרִים עַל־שֵׁם הַפּוּר עַל־כֵּן עַל־
כז כָּל־דִּבְרֵי הָאִגֶּרֶת הַזֹּאת וּמָה־רָאוּ עַל־כָּכָה וּמָה הִגִּיעַ אֲלֵיהֶם: קִיְּמוּ
וְקִבְּלֻ הַיְּהוּדִים ׀ עֲלֵיהֶם ׀ וְעַל־זַרְעָם וְעַל כָּל־הַנִּלְוִים עֲלֵיהֶם וְלֹא
יַעֲבוֹר לִהְיוֹת עֹשִׂים אֵת־שְׁנֵי הַיָּמִים הָאֵלֶּה כִּכְתָבָם וְכִזְמַנָּם בְּכָל־
כח שָׁנָה וְשָׁנָה: וְהַיָּמִים הָאֵלֶּה נִזְכָּרִים וְנַעֲשִׂים בְּכָל־דּוֹר וָדוֹר מִשְׁפָּחָה
וּמִשְׁפָּחָה מְדִינָה וּמְדִינָה וְעִיר וָעִיר וִימֵי הַפּוּרִים הָאֵלֶּה לֹא יַעַבְרוּ
כט מִתּוֹךְ הַיְּהוּדִים וְזִכְרָם לֹא־יָסוּף מִזַּרְעָם: וַתִּכְתֹּב
אֶסְתֵּר הַמַּלְכָּה בַת־אֲבִיחַיִל וּמָרְדֳּכַי הַיְּהוּדִי אֶת־כָּל־תֹּקֶף לְקַיֵּם אֵת
ל אִגֶּרֶת הַפֻּרִים הַזֹּאת הַשֵּׁנִית: וַיִּשְׁלַח סְפָרִים אֶל־כָּל־הַיְּהוּדִים אֶל־
שֶׁבַע וְעֶשְׂרִים וּמֵאָה מְדִינָה מַלְכוּת אֲחַשְׁוֵרוֹשׁ דִּבְרֵי שָׁלוֹם וֶאֱמֶת:
לא לְקַיֵּם אֶת־יְמֵי הַפֻּרִים הָאֵלֶּה בִּזְמַנֵּיהֶם כַּאֲשֶׁר קִיַּם עֲלֵיהֶם מָרְדֳּכַי
הַיְּהוּדִי וְאֶסְתֵּר הַמַּלְכָּה וְכַאֲשֶׁר קִיְּמוּ עַל־נַפְשָׁם וְעַל־זַרְעָם דִּבְרֵי
לב הַצּוֹמוֹת וְזַעֲקָתָם: וּמַאֲמַר אֶסְתֵּר קִיַּם דִּבְרֵי הַפֻּרִים הָאֵלֶּה וְנִכְתָּב
י א בַּסֵּפֶר: וַיָּשֶׂם הַמֶּלֶךְ אחשרש ׀ מַס עַל־הָאָרֶץ וְאִיֵּי הַיָּם: אֲחַשְׁוֵרוֹשׁ
ב וְכָל־מַעֲשֵׂה תָקְפּוֹ וּגְבוּרָתוֹ וּפָרָשַׁת גְּדֻלַּת מָרְדֳּכַי אֲשֶׁר גִּדְּלוֹ הַמֶּלֶךְ
ג הֲלוֹא־הֵם כְּתוּבִים עַל־סֵפֶר דִּבְרֵי הַיָּמִים לְמַלְכֵי מָדַי וּפָרָס: כִּי ׀
מָרְדֳּכַי הַיְּהוּדִי מִשְׁנֶה לַמֶּלֶךְ אֲחַשְׁוֵרוֹשׁ וְגָדוֹל לַיְּהוּדִים וְרָצוּי לְרֹב
אֶחָיו דֹּרֵשׁ טוֹב לְעַמּוֹ וְדֹבֵר שָׁלוֹם לְכָל־זַרְעוֹ:

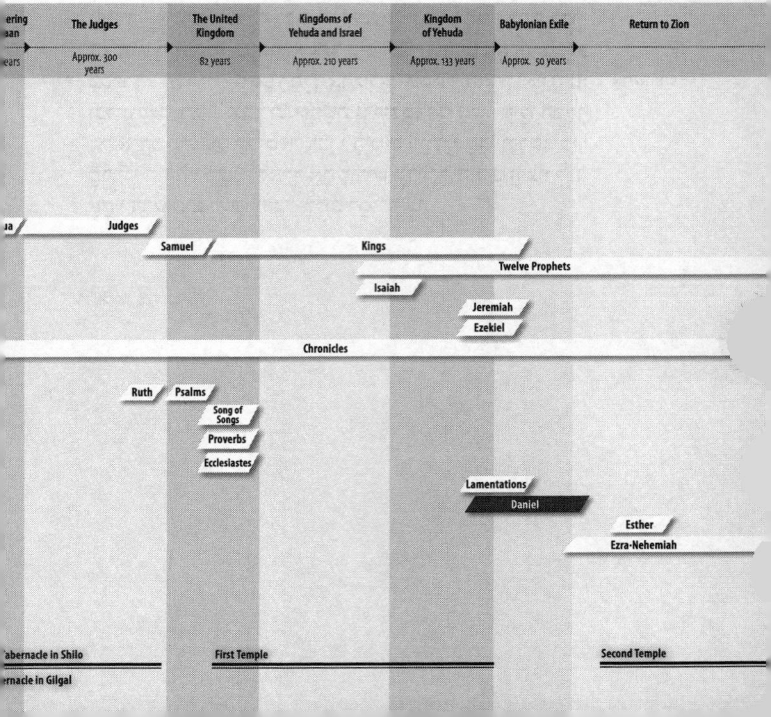

ering
aan
ears
The Judges
Approx. 300 years
The United Kingdom
82 years
Kingdoms of Yehuda and Israel
Approx. 210 years
Kingdom of Yehuda
Approx. 133 years
Babylonian Exile
Approx. 50 years
Return to Zion
ua
Judges
Samuel
Kings
Twelve Prophets
Isaiah
Jeremiah
Ezekiel
Chronicles
Ruth
Psalms
Song of Songs
Proverbs
Ecclesiastes
Lamentations
Daniel
Esther
Ezra-Nehemiah
abernacle in Shilo
ernacle in Gilgal
First Temple
Second Temple

דניאל
DANIEL

DANIEL	Daniel, Ḥananya, Mishael, and Azarya in the Babylonian exile	Daniel and his friends entangled with the kings Nevukhadnetzar, Belshatzar, and Daryavesh	Daniel's visions and his prayer
	Ch. 1	2–7	8–12

1 1 In the third year of the reign of Yehoyakim, the king of Yehuda,
Nevukhadnetzar, the king of Babylon, came to Jerusalem and besieged it.
2 The Lord handed Yehoyakim, the king of Yehuda, over to him, along with
some of the vessels of the House of God, which he then carried off to the
land of Shinar,[1] to the temple of his god, and he brought the vessels to the
3 treasury of his god. The king told Ashpenaz, his chief eunuch, to bring some
4 Israelites, some of royal lineage and some of the nobility – youths without
blemish, attractive, and adept in all wisdoms, who are lovers of knowledge
and astute in understanding, and disciplined enough to serve in the king's
palace – and to teach them the literature and language of the Chaldeans.
5 The king allotted them a daily portion of the king's food and of the wine that
he drank, and three years to train them, at the end of which some of them
6 would serve the king. Now among them were some Jews: Daniel, Ḥananya,
7 Mishael, and Azarya. The chief of the eunuchs renamed them: He called
Daniel Belteshatzar; Ḥananya, Shadrakh; Mishael, Meishakh; and Azarya
8 became Aved Nego. Daniel resolved in his heart not to defile himself with
the king's food or with the wine that he drank. He requested permission
9 from the chief of the eunuchs that he not defile himself. Now God had given
10 Daniel the kindness and sympathy of the chief of the eunuchs. The chief of
the eunuchs said to Daniel, "I am afraid of my lord the king, who has allotted
your food and drink. If he should notice that you look more wretched in
comparison with the other youths your age, you would be endangering my
11 head with the king." Daniel said to the steward whom the chief of the eunuchs
12 had appointed over Daniel, Ḥananya, Mishael, and Azarya: "Please, test your
servants for ten days. Let them give us vegetables to eat and water to drink.
13 Then compare our appearance and the appearance of the youths who eat from
the king's food. In accordance with what you observe, so shall you treat your
14 15 servants." He acceded to their request and tested them for ten days. And at
the end of ten days they looked better and healthier in appearance than all
16 the youths who had been eating the king's food. So the steward would take
away the royal food and the wine they were supposed to drink and would give
17 them vegetables. As for all of these four youths, God gave them knowledge
and proficiency in all literature and wisdom, and Daniel understood every
18 kind of vision as well as dreams. Now at the end of the time the king had
allotted to bring them forth, the chief of the eunuchs brought them before
19 Nevukhadnetzar. The king spoke with them, and out of all of them, not one
was found to compare with Daniel, Ḥananya, Mishael, and Azarya. They
20 served in the king's presence. And in every matter of wise understanding
that the king sought from them, he found them ten times better than all the
21 magicians and exorcists throughout his kingdom. Daniel remained there
2 1 until the first year of King Koresh. And in the second year of the
reign of Nevukhadnetzar, Nevukhadnetzar dreamed dreams; his spirit was
2 troubled, and sleep was a struggle for him. The king gave orders to summon

1 | Referring to Babylon; see Genesis 11:2.

א א בִּשְׁנַת שָׁלוֹשׁ לְמַלְכוּת יְהוֹיָקִים מֶלֶךְ־יְהוּדָה בָּא נְבוּכַדְנֶאצַּר מֶלֶךְ־
ב בָּבֶל יְרוּשָׁלַםִ וַיָּצַר עָלֶיהָ׃ וַיִּתֵּן אֲדֹנָי בְּיָדוֹ אֶת־יְהוֹיָקִים מֶלֶךְ־יְהוּדָה
וּמִקְצָת כְּלֵי בֵית־הָאֱלֹהִים וַיְבִיאֵם אֶרֶץ־שִׁנְעָר בֵּית אֱלֹהָיו וְאֶת־
ג הַכֵּלִים הֵבִיא בֵּית אוֹצַר אֱלֹהָיו׃ וַיֹּאמֶר הַמֶּלֶךְ לְאַשְׁפְּנַז רַב סָרִיסָיו
ד לְהָבִיא מִבְּנֵי יִשְׂרָאֵל וּמִזֶּרַע הַמְּלוּכָה וּמִן־הַפַּרְתְּמִים׃ יְלָדִים אֲשֶׁר
אֵין־בָּהֶם כָּל־מאוּם וְטוֹבֵי מַרְאֶה וּמַשְׂכִּילִים בְּכָל־חָכְמָה וְיֹדְעֵי דַעַת
וּמְבִינֵי מַדָּע וַאֲשֶׁר כֹּחַ בָּהֶם לַעֲמֹד בְּהֵיכַל הַמֶּלֶךְ וּלְלַמְּדָם סֵפֶר
ה וּלְשׁוֹן כַּשְׂדִּים׃ וַיְמַן לָהֶם הַמֶּלֶךְ דְּבַר־יוֹם בְּיוֹמוֹ מִפַּת־בַּג הַמֶּלֶךְ וּמִיֵּין
ו מִשְׁתָּיו וּלְגַדְּלָם שָׁנִים שָׁלוֹשׁ וּמִקְצָתָם יַעַמְדוּ לִפְנֵי הַמֶּלֶךְ׃ וַיְהִי בָהֶם
ז מִבְּנֵי יְהוּדָה דָּנִיֵּאל חֲנַנְיָה מִישָׁאֵל וַעֲזַרְיָה׃ וַיָּשֶׂם לָהֶם שַׂר הַסָּרִיסִים
שֵׁמוֹת וַיָּשֶׂם לְדָנִיֵּאל בֵּלְטְשַׁאצַּר וְלַחֲנַנְיָה שַׁדְרַךְ וּלְמִישָׁאֵל מֵישַׁךְ
ח וְלַעֲזַרְיָה עֲבֵד נְגוֹ׃ וַיָּשֶׂם דָּנִיֵּאל עַל־לִבּוֹ אֲשֶׁר לֹא־יִתְגָּאַל בְּפַת־בַּג
ט הַמֶּלֶךְ וּבְיֵין מִשְׁתָּיו וַיְבַקֵּשׁ מִשַּׂר הַסָּרִיסִים אֲשֶׁר לֹא יִתְגָּאָל׃ וַיִּתֵּן
י הָאֱלֹהִים אֶת־דָּנִיֵּאל לְחֶסֶד וּלְרַחֲמִים לִפְנֵי שַׂר הַסָּרִיסִים׃ וַיֹּאמֶר שַׂר
הַסָּרִיסִים לְדָנִיֵּאל יָרֵא אֲנִי אֶת־אֲדֹנִי הַמֶּלֶךְ אֲשֶׁר מִנָּה אֶת־מַאֲכַלְכֶם
וְאֶת־מִשְׁתֵּיכֶם אֲשֶׁר לָמָּה יִרְאֶה אֶת־פְּנֵיכֶם זֹעֲפִים מִן־הַיְלָדִים אֲשֶׁר
יא כְּגִילְכֶם וְחִיַּבְתֶּם אֶת־רֹאשִׁי לַמֶּלֶךְ׃ וַיֹּאמֶר דָּנִיֵּאל אֶל־הַמֶּלְצַר אֲשֶׁר
יב מִנָּה שַׂר הַסָּרִיסִים עַל־דָּנִיֵּאל חֲנַנְיָה מִישָׁאֵל וַעֲזַרְיָה׃ נַס־נָא אֶת־
עֲבָדֶיךָ יָמִים עֲשָׂרָה וְיִתְּנוּ־לָנוּ מִן־הַזֵּרֹעִים וְנֹאכְלָה וּמַיִם וְנִשְׁתֶּה׃
יג וְיֵרָאוּ לְפָנֶיךָ מַרְאֵינוּ וּמַרְאֵה הַיְלָדִים הָאֹכְלִים אֵת פַּת־בַּג הַמֶּלֶךְ
יד וְכַאֲשֶׁר תִּרְאֵה עֲשֵׂה עִם־עֲבָדֶיךָ׃ וַיִּשְׁמַע לָהֶם לַדָּבָר הַזֶּה וַיְנַסֵּם
טו יָמִים עֲשָׂרָה׃ וּמִקְצָת יָמִים עֲשָׂרָה נִרְאָה מַרְאֵיהֶם טוֹב וּבְרִיאֵי בָּשָׂר
טז מִן־כָּל־הַיְלָדִים הָאֹכְלִים אֵת פַּת־בַּג הַמֶּלֶךְ׃ וַיְהִי הַמֶּלְצַר נֹשֵׂא אֶת־
יז פַּת־בָּגָם וְיֵין מִשְׁתֵּיהֶם וְנֹתֵן לָהֶם זֵרְעֹנִים׃ וְהַיְלָדִים הָאֵלֶּה אַרְבַּעְתָּם
נָתַן לָהֶם הָאֱלֹהִים מַדָּע וְהַשְׂכֵּל בְּכָל־סֵפֶר וְחָכְמָה וְדָנִיֵּאל הֵבִין בְּכָל־
יח חָזוֹן וַחֲלֹמוֹת׃ וּלְמִקְצָת הַיָּמִים אֲשֶׁר־אָמַר הַמֶּלֶךְ לַהֲבִיאָם וַיְבִיאֵם
יט שַׂר הַסָּרִיסִים לִפְנֵי נְבֻכַדְנֶצַּר׃ וַיְדַבֵּר אִתָּם הַמֶּלֶךְ וְלֹא נִמְצָא מִכֻּלָּם
כ כְּדָנִיֵּאל חֲנַנְיָה מִישָׁאֵל וַעֲזַרְיָה וַיַּעַמְדוּ לִפְנֵי הַמֶּלֶךְ׃ וְכֹל דְּבַר חָכְמַת
בִּינָה אֲשֶׁר־בִּקֵּשׁ מֵהֶם הַמֶּלֶךְ וַיִּמְצָאֵם עֶשֶׂר יָדוֹת עַל כָּל־הַחַרְטֻמִּים
כא הָאַשָּׁפִים אֲשֶׁר בְּכָל־מַלְכוּתוֹ׃ וַיְהִי דָּנִיֵּאל עַד־שְׁנַת אַחַת לְכוֹרֶשׁ
הַמֶּלֶךְ׃

ב א וּבִשְׁנַת שְׁתַּיִם לְמַלְכוּת נְבֻכַדְנֶצַּר חָלַם נְבֻכַדְנֶצַּר
ב חֲלֹמוֹת וַתִּתְפָּעֶם רוּחוֹ וּשְׁנָתוֹ נִהְיְתָה עָלָיו׃ וַיֹּאמֶר הַמֶּלֶךְ לִקְרֹא

the magicians and the exorcists and the sorcerers and the Chaldeans to tell the
3 king about his dreams. They arrived and stood before the king. The king said
to them, "I dreamed a dream and my spirit was troubled to understand the
4 dream." The Chaldeans spoke to the king in Aramaic:[2] "O king, live forever!
5 Tell the dream to your servants and we will reveal its interpretation." The king
answered and said to the Chaldeans: "This matter is decided as far as I am
concerned: unless you make known to me the dream and its interpretation,
6 you shall be dismembered and your houses turned into wreckage. But if you
tell the dream and its interpretation, you shall receive gifts and rewards and
7 great honor from me, so tell me the dream and its meaning." They answered
a second time and said, "Let the king tell the dream to his servants and we
8 will reveal its interpretation." The king answered and said, "I know for sure
that you are buying time, since you see that the matter is already decided as
9 far as I am concerned: unless you make the dream known to me, there is one
verdict for all of you, for you have conspired to utter false and corrupt words
before me until time passes. Therefore, tell me the dream so that I can know
10 that you can tell me its interpretation." The Chaldeans answered the king and
said: "There is no man on earth who could address the king's concern, nor
has any great or mighty king asked such a thing of any magician, exorcist, or
11 Chaldean. And the thing that the king asks is difficult; there is no one else
who could tell it before the king except the gods, whose dwelling place is not
12 with flesh." In response to this, the king became enraged and very furious
13 and he commanded that all the wise men of Babylon be slain. And the decree
went forth and the wise men were about to be killed, and Daniel and his
14 companions were about to be killed. To this Daniel responded with
advice and reason to Aryokh, the chief executioner of the king, who had gone
15 forth to kill the wise men of Babylon. He spoke and asked Aryokh, the king's
officer, "Why this cruel decree from the king?" Then Aryokh made the matter
16 known to Daniel. So Daniel came and requested of the king that he be given
17 time to tell the interpretation to the king. Then Daniel went to his
house and made the matter known to his companions Ḥananya, Mishael, and
18 Azarya, so they might seek mercy from the God of the heavens concerning
this mystery, so that they would not kill Daniel and his companions along
19 with the rest of the wise men of Babylon. Then the secret was revealed to
Daniel in a night vision, after which Daniel blessed the God of the heavens.
20 Daniel spoke and said: "May the name of God be blessed from always to
21 forevermore, for wisdom and power are His. He changes the seasons and
times, He deposes kings and enthrones kings. He gives wisdom to the wise
22 and knowledge to insightful knowers. He reveals deep and hidden things. He
23 knows what is in the darkness, and light dwells with Him. To You, O God of
my fathers, I give thanks and praise, for now You have given me wisdom and
power, for You have made known to me that which we asked of You, for You

2 | At this point the text switches from Hebrew to Aramaic until chapter 8.

לַחַרְטֻמִּים וְלָאַשָּׁפִים וְלַמְכַשְּׁפִים וְלַכַּשְׂדִּים לְהַגִּיד לַמֶּלֶךְ חֲלֹמֹתָיו
ג וַיָּבֹאוּ וַיַּעַמְדוּ לִפְנֵי הַמֶּלֶךְ׃ וַיֹּאמֶר לָהֶם הַמֶּלֶךְ חֲלוֹם חָלָמְתִּי וַתִּפָּעֶם
ד רוּחִי לָדַעַת אֶת־הַחֲלוֹם׃ וַיְדַבְּרוּ הַכַּשְׂדִּים לַמֶּלֶךְ אֲרָמִית מַלְכָּא
ה לְעָלְמִין חֱיִי אֱמַר חֶלְמָא לעבדיך וּפִשְׁרָא נְחַוֵּא׃ עָנֵה מַלְכָּא וְאָמַר לְעַבְדָּךְ
לכשדיא מִלְּתָה מִנִּי אַזְדָּא הֵן לָא תְהוֹדְעוּנַּנִי חֶלְמָא וּפִשְׁרֵהּ הַדָּמִין לְכַשְׂדָּאֵי
ו תִּתְעַבְדוּן וּבָתֵּיכוֹן נְוָלִי יִתְּשָׂמוּן׃ וְהֵן חֶלְמָא וּפִשְׁרֵהּ תְּהַחֲוֺן מַתְּנָן
ז וּנְבִזְבָּה וִיקָר שַׂגִּיא תְּקַבְּלוּן מִן־קֳדָמָי לָהֵן חֶלְמָא וּפִשְׁרֵהּ הַחֲוֺנִי׃ עֲנוֹ
ח תִנְיָנוּת וְאָמְרִין מַלְכָּא חֶלְמָא יֵאמַר לְעַבְדוֹהִי וּפִשְׁרָה נְהַחֲוֵה׃ עָנֵה
מַלְכָּא וְאָמַר מִן־יַצִּיב יָדַע אֲנָה דִּי עִדָּנָא אַנְתּוּן זָבְנִין כָּל־קֳבֵל דִּי
ט חֲזֵיתוּן דִּי אַזְדָּא מִנִּי מִלְּתָא׃ דִּי הֵן־חֶלְמָא לָא תְהוֹדְעֻנַּנִי חֲדָה־הִיא
דָתְכוֹן וּמִלָּה כִדְבָה וּשְׁחִיתָה והזמנתון לְמֵאמַר קָדָמַי עַד דִּי עִדָּנָא הִזְדְּמִנְתּוּן
י יִשְׁתַּנֵּא לָהֵן חֶלְמָא אֱמַרוּ לִי וְאִנְדַּע דִּי פִשְׁרֵהּ תְּהַחֲוֻנַּנִי׃ עֲנוֹ כשדיא כַשְׂדָּאֵי
קֳדָם־מַלְכָּא וְאָמְרִין לָא־אִיתַי אֱנָשׁ עַל־יַבֶּשְׁתָּא דִּי מִלַּת מַלְכָּא
יוּכַל לְהַחֲוָיָה כָּל־קֳבֵל דִּי כָּל־מֶלֶךְ רַב וְשַׁלִּיט מִלָּה כִדְנָה לָא שְׁאֵל
יא לְכָל־חַרְטֹּם וְאָשַׁף וְכַשְׂדָּי׃ וּמִלְּתָא דִי־מַלְכָּה שָׁאֵל יַקִּירָה וְאָחֳרָן לָא
אִיתַי דִּי יְחַוִּנַּהּ קֳדָם מַלְכָּא לָהֵן אֱלָהִין דִּי מְדָרְהוֹן עִם־בִּשְׂרָא לָא
יב אִיתוֹהִי׃ כָּל־קֳבֵל דְּנָה מַלְכָּא בְּנַס וּקְצַף שַׂגִּיא וַאֲמַר לְהוֹבָדָה לְכֹל
יג חַכִּימֵי בָבֶל׃ וְדָתָא נֶפְקַת וְחַכִּימַיָּא מִתְקַטְּלִין וּבְעוֹ דָּנִיֵּאל וְחַבְרוֹהִי
יד לְהִתְקְטָלָה׃ בֵּאדַיִן דָּנִיֵּאל הֲתִיב עֵטָא וּטְעֵם לְאַרְיוֹךְ
טו רַב־טַבָּחַיָּא דִּי מַלְכָּא דִּי נְפַק לְקַטָּלָה לְחַכִּימֵי בָּבֶל׃ עָנֵה וְאָמַר
לְאַרְיוֹךְ שַׁלִּיטָא דִי־מַלְכָּא עַל־מָה דָתָא מְהַחְצְפָה מִן־קֳדָם מַלְכָּא
טז אֱדַיִן מִלְּתָא הוֹדַע אַרְיוֹךְ לְדָנִיֵּאל׃ וְדָנִיֵּאל עַל וּבְעָא מִן־מַלְכָּא דִּי
יז זְמָן יִנְתֵּן־לֵהּ וּפִשְׁרָא לְהַחֲוָיָה לְמַלְכָּא׃ אֱדַיִן דָּנִיֵּאל
יח לְבַיְתֵהּ אֲזַל וְלַחֲנַנְיָה מִישָׁאֵל וַעֲזַרְיָה חַבְרוֹהִי מִלְּתָא הוֹדַע׃ וְרַחֲמִין
לְמִבְעֵא מִן־קֳדָם אֱלָהּ שְׁמַיָּא עַל־רָזָה דְּנָה דִּי לָא יְהֹבְדוּן דָּנִיֵּאל
יט וְחַבְרוֹהִי עִם־שְׁאָר חַכִּימֵי בָבֶל׃ אֱדַיִן לְדָנִיֵּאל בְּחֶזְוָא דִי־לֵילְיָא רָזָא
כ גְּלִי אֱדַיִן דָּנִיֵּאל בָּרִךְ לֶאֱלָהּ שְׁמַיָּא׃ עָנֵה דָנִיֵּאל וְאָמַר לֶהֱוֵא שְׁמֵהּ
דִּי־אֱלָהָא מְבָרַךְ מִן־עָלְמָא וְעַד־עָלְמָא דִּי חָכְמְתָא וּגְבוּרְתָא דִּי לֵהּ
כא הִיא׃ וְהוּא מְהַשְׁנֵא עִדָּנַיָּא וְזִמְנַיָּא מְהַעְדֵּה מַלְכִין וּמְהָקֵים מַלְכִין
כב יָהֵב חָכְמְתָא לְחַכִּימִין וּמַנְדְּעָא לְיָדְעֵי בִינָה׃ הוּא גָּלֵא עַמִּיקָתָא
כג וּמְסַתְּרָתָא יָדַע מָה בַחֲשׁוֹכָא ונהירא עִמֵּהּ שְׁרֵא׃ לָךְ ׀ אֱלָהּ אֲבָהָתִי וּנְהוֹרָא
מְהוֹדֵא וּמְשַׁבַּח אֲנָה דִּי חָכְמְתָא וּגְבוּרְתָא יְהַבְתְּ לִי וּכְעַן הוֹדַעְתַּנִי

24 have made known to us the dream matter of the king." Thereupon Daniel went
to Aryokh, whom the king had appointed to kill the wise men of Babylon; he
went and said this to him: "Do not kill the wise men of Babylon. Bring me
before the king and I will tell him the interpretation."
25 So Aryokh, in great haste, brought Daniel before the king and this is what he
said to him: "I have found a man from the exiles of Yehuda who can make
26 known the interpretation to the king." The king responded and said to Daniel,
whose name was Belteshatzar, "Are you able to make known to me the dream
27 that I saw and its interpretation?" Daniel answered the king and said: "The
secret that the king demands is one that no wise man, exorcist, magician, or
28 diviner can tell the king, but there is a God in heaven who reveals secrets, and
He has made known to the king Nevukhadnetzar what will come to pass at
the end of days. Your dream and the vision in your head while in bed is as
29 follows: You, O king, your thoughts arose when you were in bed,
about what will come to pass hereafter, and He who reveals secrets has made
30 known to you that which shall come to pass. But as for me, it is not because
of any wisdom that I have beyond other living things that this secret was
revealed to me; rather it was so that the interpretation be made known to the
31 king, so that you know the thoughts of your heart. You, O king, were
looking, and – behold! – there was a huge figure. This figure was great and its
brightness was extraordinary. It was standing facing you, and its appearance
32 was terrifying. The head of this figure was of fine gold, its breast and its arms
33 were of silver, and its belly and thighs were of bronze, its legs were of iron, its
34 feet were partly of iron and partly of clay. As you watched, a stone was carved
out – not by hands – and it smote the figure on its iron and clay feet, and
35 smashed them into pieces. Then, all at once, the iron, the clay, the brass, the
silver, and the gold shattered and became like the chaff of a summer's
threshing floor; and the wind carried them off, and no trace of them was
found anywhere. And the stone that smote the figure became a great mountain
36 and filled the whole earth. This is the dream; now we will relate its meaning
37 before the king. You, O king, king of kings, to whom the God of the
38 heavens has given a kingdom of strength, power, and prestige, and wherever
dwell human beings, the beasts of the field and the birds of the sky, He has
39 put them in your hand and made you ruler of them all: you are the head of
39 gold. And after you shall arise another kingdom, inferior to you, and another,
40 third kingdom of bronze, which will rule the whole earth. And the fourth
kingdom will be as strong as iron, in the way that iron smashes and pulverizes
everything; and just as iron shatters all other materials, so shall this kingdom
41 shatter and crush. And as for your having seen that the feet and toes were
partly of potter's clay and partly of iron: it shall be a divided kingdom, but
some resilience of iron shall be in it, just as you saw there was iron mixed into

דִּי־בְעֵינָא מִנָּךְ דִּי־מִלַּת מַלְכָּא הוֹדַעְתֶּנָא׃ כָּל־קֳבֵל דְּנָה דָּנִיֵּאל עַל כד
עַל־אַרְיוֹךְ דִּי מַנִּי מַלְכָּא לְהוֹבָדָא לְחַכִּימֵי בָבֶל אֲזַל ׀ וְכֵן אֲמַר־
לֵהּ לְחַכִּימֵי בָבֶל אַל־תְּהוֹבֵד הַעֵלְנִי קֳדָם מַלְכָּא וּפִשְׁרָא לְמַלְכָּא
אֲחַוֵּא׃
כה אֱדַיִן אַרְיוֹךְ בְּהִתְבְּהָלָה הַנְעֵל לְדָנִיֵּאל קֳדָם מַלְכָּא וְכֵן אֲמַר־לֵהּ
דִּי־הַשְׁכַּחַת גְּבַר מִן־בְּנֵי גָלוּתָא דִּי יְהוּד דִּי פִשְׁרָא לְמַלְכָּא יְהוֹדַע׃
כו עָנֵה מַלְכָּא וְאָמַר לְדָנִיֵּאל דִּי שְׁמֵהּ בֵּלְטְשַׁאצַּר האיתיך כָּהֵל הַאִיתָךְ
כז לְהוֹדָעֻתַנִי חֶלְמָא דִי־חֲזֵית וּפִשְׁרֵהּ׃ עָנֵה דָנִיֵּאל קֳדָם מַלְכָּא וְאָמַר
רָזָא דִּי־מַלְכָּא שָׁאֵל לָא חַכִּימִין אָשְׁפִין חַרְטֻמִּין גָּזְרִין יָכְלִין לְהַחֲוָיָה
כח לְמַלְכָּא׃ בְּרַם אִיתַי אֱלָהּ בִּשְׁמַיָּא גָּלֵא רָזִין וְהוֹדַע לְמַלְכָּא נְבוּכַדְנֶצַּר
מָה דִּי לֶהֱוֵא בְּאַחֲרִית יוֹמַיָּא חֶלְמָךְ וְחֶזְוֵי רֵאשָׁךְ עַל־מִשְׁכְּבָךְ דְּנָה
כט הוּא׃ אנתה מַלְכָּא רעיוניך עַל־מִשְׁכְּבָךְ סְלִקוּ מָה דִּי אַנְתְּ | רַעְיוֹנָךְ
ל לֶהֱוֵא אַחֲרֵי דְנָה וְגָלֵא רָזַיָּא הוֹדְעָךְ מָה־דִי לֶהֱוֵא׃ וַאֲנָה לָא בְחָכְמָה
דִּי־אִיתַי בִּי מִן־כָּל־חַיַּיָּא רָזָא דְנָה גֱּלִי לִי לָהֵן עַל־דִּבְרַת דִּי פִשְׁרָא
לא לְמַלְכָּא יְהוֹדְעוּן וְרַעְיוֹנֵי לִבְבָךְ תִּנְדַּע׃ אנתה מַלְכָּא אַנְתְּ
חָזֵה הֲוַיְתָ וַאֲלוּ צְלֵם חַד שַׂגִּיא צַלְמָא דִּכֵּן רַב וְזִיוֵהּ יַתִּיר קָאֵם לְקָבְלָךְ
לב וְרֵוֵהּ דְּחִיל׃ הוּא צַלְמָא רֵאשֵׁהּ דִּי־דְהַב טָב חֲדוֹהִי וּדְרָעוֹהִי דִּי כְסַף
לג מְעוֹהִי וְיַרְכָתֵהּ דִּי נְחָשׁ׃ שָׁקוֹהִי דִּי פַרְזֶל רַגְלוֹהִי מנהון דִּי פַרְזֶל מִנְּהֵן
לד ומנהון דִּי חֲסַף׃ חָזֵה הֲוַיְתָ עַד דִּי הִתְגְּזֶרֶת אֶבֶן דִּי־לָא בִידַיִן וּמְחָת וּמִנְּהֵן
לה לְצַלְמָא עַל־רַגְלוֹהִי דִּי פַרְזְלָא וְחַסְפָּא וְהַדֶּקֶת הִמּוֹן׃ בֵּאדַיִן דָּקוּ ב
כַחֲדָה פַּרְזְלָא חַסְפָּא נְחָשָׁא כַּסְפָּא וְדַהֲבָא וַהֲווֹ כְּעוּר מִן־אִדְּרֵי־קַיִט
וּנְשָׂא הִמּוֹן רוּחָא וְכָל־אֲתַר לָא־הִשְׁתֲּכַח לְהוֹן וְאַבְנָא ׀ דִּי־מְחָת
לו לְצַלְמָא הֲוָת לְטוּר רַב וּמְלָאת כָּל־אַרְעָא׃ דְּנָה חֶלְמָא וּפִשְׁרֵהּ נֵאמַר
לז קֳדָם־מַלְכָּא׃ אנתה מַלְכָּא מֶלֶךְ מַלְכַיָּא דִּי אֱלָהּ אַנְתְּ
לח שְׁמַיָּא מַלְכוּתָא חִסְנָא וְתָקְפָּא וִיקָרָא יְהַב־לָךְ׃ וּבְכָל־דִּי דארין דָּיְרִין
בְּנֵי־אֲנָשָׁא חֵיוַת בָּרָא וְעוֹף־שְׁמַיָּא יְהַב בִּידָךְ וְהַשְׁלְטָךְ בְּכָלְּהוֹן
לט אנתה הוּא רֵאשָׁה דִּי דַהֲבָא׃ וּבָתְרָךְ תְּקוּם מַלְכוּ אָחֳרִי ארעא מִנָּךְ אַנְתְּ | אֲרַע
מ וּמַלְכוּ תליתיא אָחֳרִי דִּי נְחָשָׁא דִּי תִשְׁלַט בְּכָל־אַרְעָא׃ וּמַלְכוּ תְּלִיתָאָה
רביעיה תֶּהֱוֵא תַקִּיפָה כְּפַרְזְלָא כָּל־קֳבֵל דִּי פַרְזְלָא מְהַדֵּק וְחָשֵׁל רְבִיעָאָה
מא כֹּלָּא וּכְפַרְזְלָא דִּי־מְרָעַע כָּל־אִלֵּין תַּדִּק וְתֵרֹעַ׃ וְדִי־חֲזַיְתָה רַגְלַיָּא
וְאֶצְבְּעָתָא מנהון חֲסַף דִּי־פֶחָר ומנהון פַּרְזֶל מַלְכוּ פְלִיגָה תֶּהֱוֵה מִנְּהֵן | וּמִנְּהֵן
וּמִן־נִצְבְּתָא דִּי־פַרְזְלָא לֶהֱוֵא־בַהּ כָּל־קֳבֵל דִּי חֲזַיְתָה פַּרְזְלָא מְעָרַב

42 the muddy clay. And just as the toes of the feet were part iron and part clay,
43 the kingdom will be partly strong and partly brittle. And as for your having
seen the iron mixed into muddy clay, the parts will mingle via procreation but
44 they will not hold fast together, just as iron does not mix into clay. And during
the days of these kings, the God of the heavens shall set up a kingdom which
shall never be destroyed, and this kingdom will never be abandoned to the
rule of any other nation; rather it will smash and put an end to all these
45 kingdoms, and it will last forever, in the way that you saw a stone being carved
out of the mountain without hands it smashed the iron, the bronze, the clay,
the silver, and the gold. A great God has made known to the king what will
happen hereafter. And the dream is certain and its interpretation is
46 precise." Then the king Nevukhadnetzar fell upon his
face and paid homage to Daniel, and commanded that grain and wine
47 offerings be proffered to him. The king responded to Daniel and said, "Truly
your God is the God of gods and the ruler of kings and the revealer of secrets,
48 for you have been able to reveal this secret." Then the king exalted Daniel and
gave him many great gifts and made him ruler over the whole province of
49 Babylon and the chief officer of all the wise men of Babylon. Then Daniel
made a request of the king, so he appointed Shadrakh, Meishakh, and Aved
Nego over administration throughout Babylon, but Daniel remained at the
3 1 royal court. Nevukhadnetzar the king made a figure of gold: its
height was sixty cubits and its width six cubits. He erected it in the Dura Valley
2 in the province of Babylon. Then Nevukhadnetzar the king sent messengers
to assemble the satraps, the prefects and the governors, the counselors, the
treasurers, the justices, the magistrates, and all the officials of the provinces
to come to the dedication of the figure which Nevukhadnetzar the king had
3 erected. Then the satraps, the prefects and the governors, the counselors, the
treasurers, the justices, the magistrates, and all the rulers of the provinces
assembled for the dedication of the figure which Nevukhadnetzar had erected,
4 and they stood facing the figure which Nevukhadnetzar had erected. Then a
herald proclaimed loudly: "You are commanded, O peoples, nations, and
5 speakers of various languages, when you hear the sound of the horn, the pipe,
the zither, the sambuca, the harp, the double flute, and all kinds of music, you
shall fall down and worship the golden figure that Nevukhadnetzar the king
6 has erected, and anyone who does not fall down and worship will be thrown
7 at once into the midst of the fiery furnace." As a result, at the moment that all
the people heard the sound of the horn, the pipe, the zither, the sambuca, the
harp, the double flute, and all kinds of music, all the peoples, nations, and
speakers of various languages fell down and worshipped the golden figure
8 that Nevukhadnetzar the king had erected. And then, at that very moment,
9 some Chaldeans came forward and slandered the Jews. They spoke and said
10 to Nevukhadnetzar the king, "O king, may you live forever! You, O king, have
issued a decree that every person who hears the sound of the horn, the pipe,

מב בַּחֲסַף טִינָא: וְאֶצְבְּעָת רַגְלַיָּא מִנְּהוֹן פַּרְזֶל וּמִנְּהוֹן חֲסַף מִן־קְצָת מִנְּהֵין | וּמִנְּהֵין
מג מַלְכוּתָא תֶּהֱוֵה תַקִּיפָה וּמִנַּהּ תֶּהֱוֵא תְבִירָה: דִּי חֲזַיְתָ פַּרְזְלָא מְעָרַב וְדִי
בַּחֲסַף טִינָא מִתְעָרְבִין לֶהֱוֺן בִּזְרַע אֲנָשָׁא וְלָא־לֶהֱוֺן דָּבְקִין דְּנָה עִם־
מד דְּנָה הֵא־כְדִי פַרְזְלָא לָא מִתְעָרַב עִם־חַסְפָּא: וּבְיוֹמֵיהוֹן דִּי מַלְכַיָּא
אִנּוּן יְקִים אֱלָהּ שְׁמַיָּא מַלְכוּ דִּי לְעָלְמִין לָא תִתְחַבַּל וּמַלְכוּתָה לְעַם
אָחֳרָן לָא תִשְׁתְּבִק תַּדִּק וְתָסֵיף כָּל־אִלֵּין מַלְכְוָתָא וְהִיא תְּקוּם
מה לְעָלְמַיָּא: כָּל־קֳבֵל דִּי־חֲזַיְתָ דִּי מִטּוּרָא אִתְגְּזֶרֶת אֶבֶן דִּי־לָא בִידַיִן
וְהַדֶּקֶת פַּרְזְלָא נְחָשָׁא חַסְפָּא כַּסְפָּא וְדַהֲבָא אֱלָהּ רַב הוֹדַע לְמַלְכָּא
מו מָה דִּי לֶהֱוֵא אַחֲרֵי דְנָה וְיַצִּיב חֶלְמָא וּמְהֵימַן פִּשְׁרֵהּ: בֵּאדַיִן
מַלְכָּא נְבוּכַדְנֶצַּר נְפַל עַל־אַנְפּוֹהִי וּלְדָנִיֵּאל סְגִד וּמִנְחָה וְנִיחֹחִין אֲמַר
מז לְנַסָּכָה לֵהּ: עָנֵה מַלְכָּא לְדָנִיֵּאל וְאָמַר מִן־קְשֹׁט דִּי אֱלָהֲכוֹן הוּא
מח אֱלָהּ אֱלָהִין וּמָרֵא מַלְכִין וְגָלֵה רָזִין דִּי יְכֵלְתָּ לְמִגְלֵא רָזָה דְנָה: אֱדַיִן
מַלְכָּא לְדָנִיֵּאל רַבִּי וּמַתְּנָן רַבְרְבָן שַׂגִּיאָן יְהַב־לֵהּ וְהַשְׁלְטֵהּ עַל כָּל־
מט מְדִינַת בָּבֶל וְרַב־סִגְנִין עַל כָּל־חַכִּימֵי בָבֶל: וְדָנִיֵּאל בְּעָא מִן־מַלְכָּא
וּמַנִּי עַל עֲבִידְתָּא דִּי מְדִינַת בָּבֶל לְשַׁדְרַךְ מֵישַׁךְ וַעֲבֵד נְגוֹ וְדָנִיֵּאל
ג א בִּתְרַע מַלְכָּא: נְבוּכַדְנֶצַּר מַלְכָּא עֲבַד צְלֵם דִּי־דְהַב רוּמֵהּ
אַמִּין שִׁתִּין פְּתָיֵהּ אַמִּין שִׁת אֲקִימֵהּ בְּבִקְעַת דּוּרָא בִּמְדִינַת בָּבֶל:
ב וּנְבוּכַדְנֶצַּר מַלְכָּא שְׁלַח לְמִכְנַשׁ ׀ לַאֲחַשְׁדַּרְפְּנַיָּא סִגְנַיָּא וּפַחֲוָתָא
אֲדַרְגָּזְרַיָּא גְדָבְרַיָּא דְּתָבְרַיָּא תִּפְתָּיֵא וְכֹל שִׁלְטֹנֵי מְדִינָתָא לְמֵתֵא
ג לַחֲנֻכַּת צַלְמָא דִּי הֲקֵים נְבוּכַדְנֶצַּר מַלְכָּא: בֵּאדַיִן מִתְכַּנְּשִׁין
אֲחַשְׁדַּרְפְּנַיָּא סִגְנַיָּא וּפַחֲוָתָא אֲדַרְגָּזְרַיָּא גְדָבְרַיָּא דְּתָבְרַיָּא תִּפְתָּיֵא
וְכֹל שִׁלְטֹנֵי מְדִינָתָא לַחֲנֻכַּת צַלְמָא דִּי הֲקֵים נְבוּכַדְנֶצַּר מַלְכָּא
ד וְקָאמִין לָקֳבֵל צַלְמָא דִּי הֲקֵים נְבֻכַדְנֶצַּר: וְכָרוֹזָא קָרֵא בְחָיִל לְכוֹן וְקָיְמִין
ה אָמְרִין עַמְמַיָּא אֻמַּיָּא וְלִשָּׁנַיָּא: בְּעִדָּנָא דִּי־תִשְׁמְעוּן קָל קַרְנָא
מַשְׁרוֹקִיתָא קִיתָרֹס סַבְּכָא פְסַנְתֵּרִין סוּמְפֹּנְיָה וְכֹל זְנֵי זְמָרָא תִּפְּלוּן קַתְרוֹס
ו וְתִסְגְּדוּן לְצֶלֶם דַּהֲבָא דִּי הֲקֵים נְבוּכַדְנֶצַּר מַלְכָּא: וּמַן־דִּי־לָא יִפֵּל
ז וְיִסְגֻּד בַּהּ־שַׁעֲתָא יִתְרְמֵא לְגוֹא־אַתּוּן נוּרָא יָקִדְתָּא: כָּל־קֳבֵל דְּנָה
בֵּהּ זִמְנָא כְּדִי שָׁמְעִין כָּל־עַמְמַיָּא קָל קַרְנָא מַשְׁרוֹקִיתָא קִיתָרֹס קַתְרוֹס
שַׂבְּכָא פְּסַנְטֵרִין וְכֹל זְנֵי זְמָרָא נָפְלִין כָּל־עַמְמַיָּא אֻמַּיָּא וְלִשָּׁנַיָּא
ח סָגְדִין לְצֶלֶם דַּהֲבָא דִּי הֲקֵים נְבוּכַדְנֶצַּר מַלְכָּא: כָּל־קֳבֵל דְּנָה בֵּהּ
ט זִמְנָא קְרִבוּ גֻּבְרִין כַּשְׂדָּאִין וַאֲכַלוּ קַרְצֵיהוֹן דִּי יְהוּדָיֵא: עֲנוֹ וְאָמְרִין
י לִנְבוּכַדְנֶצַּר מַלְכָּא מַלְכָּא לְעָלְמִין חֱיִי: אַנְתְּ מַלְכָּא שָׂמְתָּ טְּעֵם דִּי אַנְתְּ

the zither, the sambuca, the harp, the double flute, and all kinds of music shall
11 fall down and worship the golden figure, and anyone who does not fall down
12 and worship shall be thrown into the midst of the fiery furnace. There are
some Jews whom you have appointed over the administration of Babylon:
Shadrakh, Meishakh, and Aved Nego. These men have not paid attention to
you, O king. They do not serve your god or worship the gold figure you
13 erected." Thereupon Nevukhadnetzar, in fury and rage, gave
an order to bring Shadrakh, Meishakh, and Aved Nego. So these men were
14 brought before the king. Nevukhadnetzar spoke and said to them, "Is it true,
Shadrakh, Meishakh, and Aved Nego, that you do not serve my god and that
15 you do not worship the golden figure I have erected? Now if you are prepared
to fall down and worship the figure I have made when you hear the sound of
the horn, the pipe, the zither, the sambuca, the harp, the double flute, and all
kinds of music then all will be well with you, but if you do not worship, at that
very moment you shall be thrown into the midst of the fiery furnace, and what
16 god can rescue you from my hand?" Shadrakh, Meishakh, and Aved Nego
replied and said to the king, "O Nevukhadnetzar, we do not need to answer
17 you at all about this matter. Behold, if He wishes, our God, whom we worship,
is able to rescue us. He can rescue us from the fiery furnace as well as from
18 your hand, O king. But even if He does not choose to save us, let it be known
to you, O king, that we will not serve your god and we will not worship the
19 golden figure you have erected." Then Nevukhadnetzar became
filled with fury, and the look on his face changed toward Shadrakh, Meishakh,
and Aved Nego. He spoke and ordered to heat up the furnace seven times
20 more than it was usually heated. And he commanded the mightiest men in
his army to tie up Shadrakh, Meishakh, and Aved Nego and to throw them
21 into the fiery furnace. So those men were tied up still wearing their mantles,
tunics, hats, and clothes and were thrown into the midst of the fiery furnace.
22 Because the king's command was urgent and the furnace was heated to excess,
the flame of the fire killed those men who lifted Shadrakh, Meishakh, and
23 Aved Nego into it. And those three men, Shadrakh, Meishakh, and Aved
24 Nego, fell down tied up into the midst of the fiery furnace. Then
Nevukhadnetzar the king was amazed and rose in haste; he turned and said
to his advisors, "Didn't we just throw three men tied up into the midst of the
25 fire?" They answered and said to the king, "That is true, O king." He replied
and said, "But I see four men, unbound, walking in the midst of the fire, and
none of them are injured! And the appearance of the fourth one is like an
26 angel." Then Nevukhadnetzar approached the opening of
the fiery furnace and spoke and said, "Shadrakh, Meishakh, and Aved Nego,

כָּל־אֱנָשׁ דִּי־יִשְׁמַע קָל קַרְנָא מַשְׁרֹקִיתָא קיתרס שַׂבְּכָא פְּסַנְתֵּרִין קַתְרוֹס
יא וסיפניה וְכֹל זְנֵי זְמָרָא יִפֵּל וְיִסְגֻּד לְצֶלֶם דַּהֲבָא: וּמַן־דִּי־לָא יִפֵּל וְיִסְגֻּד וְסוּפֹּנְיָה
יב יִתְרְמֵא לְגוֹא־אַתּוּן נוּרָא יָקִדְתָּא: אִיתַי גֻּבְרִין יְהוּדָאיִן דִּי־מַנִּיתָ
יָתְהוֹן עַל־עֲבִידַת מְדִינַת בָּבֶל שַׁדְרַךְ מֵישַׁךְ וַעֲבֵד נְגוֹ גֻּבְרַיָּא אִלֵּךְ
לָא־שָׂמוּ עליך מַלְכָּא טְעֵם לאלהיך לָא פָלְחִין וּלְצֶלֶם דַּהֲבָא דִּי עֲלָךְ | לֵאלָהָךְ
יג הֲקֵימְתָּ לָא סָגְדִין: בֵּאדַיִן נְבוּכַדְנֶצַּר בִּרְגַז וַחֲמָא אֲמַר
לְהַיְתָיָה לְשַׁדְרַךְ מֵישַׁךְ וַעֲבֵד נְגוֹ בֵּאדַיִן גֻּבְרַיָּא אִלֵּךְ הֵיתָיוּ קֳדָם
יד מַלְכָּא: עָנֵה נְבוּכַדְנֶצַּר וְאָמַר לְהוֹן הַצְדָּא שַׁדְרַךְ מֵישַׁךְ וַעֲבֵד נְגוֹ
טו לֵאלָהַי לָא אִיתֵיכוֹן פָּלְחִין וּלְצֶלֶם דַּהֲבָא דִּי הֲקֵימֶת לָא סָגְדִין: כְּעַן
הֵן אִיתֵיכוֹן עֲתִידִין דִּי בְעִדָּנָא דִּי־תִשְׁמְעוּן קָל קַרְנָא מַשְׁרוֹקִיתָא
קיתרס שַׂבְּכָא פְּסַנְתֵּרִין וְסוּמְפֹּנְיָה וְכֹל | זְנֵי זְמָרָא תִּפְּלוּן וְתִסְגְּדוּן קַתְרוֹס
לְצַלְמָא דִּי־עַבְדֵת וְהֵן לָא תִסְגְּדוּן בַּהּ־שַׁעֲתָה תִתְרְמוֹן לְגוֹא־
טז אַתּוּן נוּרָא יָקִדְתָּא וּמַן־הוּא אֱלָהּ דִּי יְשֵׁיזְבִנְכוֹן מִן־יְדָי: עֲנוֹ שַׁדְרַךְ
מֵישַׁךְ וַעֲבֵד נְגוֹ וְאָמְרִין לְמַלְכָּא נְבוּכַדְנֶצַּר לָא־חַשְׁחִין אֲנַחְנָה
יז עַל־דְּנָה פִּתְגָם לַהֲתָבוּתָךְ: הֵן אִיתַי אֱלָהַנָא דִּי־אֲנַחְנָא פָלְחִין יָכִל
יח לְשֵׁיזָבוּתַנָא מִן־אַתּוּן נוּרָא יָקִדְתָּא וּמִן־יְדָךְ מַלְכָּא יְשֵׁיזִב: וְהֵן לָא
יְדִיעַ לֶהֱוֵא־לָךְ מַלְכָּא דִּי לאלהיך לָא־איתנא פָלְחִין וּלְצֶלֶם דַּהֲבָא לֵאלָהָךְ
יט דִּי הֲקֵימְתָּ לָא נִסְגֻּד: בֵּאדַיִן נְבוּכַדְנֶצַּר הִתְמְלִי חֱמָא
וּצְלֵם אַנְפּוֹהִי אשתנו עַל־שַׁדְרַךְ מֵישַׁךְ וַעֲבֵד נְגוֹ עָנֵה וְאָמַר לְמֵזֵא אֶשְׁתַּנִּי
כ לְאַתּוּנָא חַד־שִׁבְעָה עַל דִּי חֲזֵה לְמֵזְיֵהּ: וּלְגֻבְרִין גִּבָּרֵי־חַיִל דִּי
בְחַיְלֵהּ אֲמַר לְכַפָּתָה לְשַׁדְרַךְ מֵישַׁךְ וַעֲבֵד נְגוֹ לְמִרְמֵא לְאַתּוּן נוּרָא
כא יָקִדְתָּא: בֵּאדַיִן גֻּבְרַיָּא אִלֵּךְ כְּפִתוּ בְּסַרְבָּלֵיהוֹן פטישיהון וְכַרְבְּלָתְהוֹן פַּטְּשֵׁיהוֹן
כב וּלְבֻשֵׁיהוֹן וּרְמִיו לְגוֹא־אַתּוּן נוּרָא יָקִדְתָּא: כָּל־קֳבֵל דְּנָה מִן־דִּי
מִלַּת מַלְכָּא מַחְצְפָה וְאַתּוּנָא אֵזֵה יַתִּירָה גֻּבְרַיָּא אִלֵּךְ דִּי הַסִּקוּ
כג לְשַׁדְרַךְ מֵישַׁךְ וַעֲבֵד נְגוֹ קַטִּל הִמּוֹן שְׁבִיבָא דִּי נוּרָא: וְגֻבְרַיָּא אִלֵּךְ
תְּלָתֵּהוֹן שַׁדְרַךְ מֵישַׁךְ וַעֲבֵד נְגוֹ נְפַלוּ לְגוֹא־אַתּוּן־נוּרָא יָקִדְתָּא
כד מְכַפְּתִין: אֱדַיִן נְבוּכַדְנֶצַּר מַלְכָּא תְּוַהּ וְקָם בְּהִתְבְּהָלָה
עָנֵה וְאָמַר לְהַדָּבְרוֹהִי הֲלָא גֻבְרִין תְּלָתָה רְמֵינָא לְגוֹא־נוּרָא מְכַפְּתִין
כה עָנַיִן וְאָמְרִין לְמַלְכָּא יַצִּיבָא מַלְכָּא: עָנֵה וְאָמַר הָא־אֲנָה חָזֵה גֻּבְרִין
אַרְבְּעָה שְׁרַיִן מַהְלְכִין בְּגוֹא־נוּרָא וַחֲבָל לָא־אִיתַי בְּהוֹן וְרֵוֵהּ דִּי
כו רביעיא דָּמֵה לְבַר־אֱלָהִין: בֵּאדַיִן קְרֵב נְבוּכַדְנֶצַּר לִתְרַע רְבִיעָאָה
אַתּוּן נוּרָא יָקִדְתָּא עָנֵה וְאָמַר שַׁדְרַךְ מֵישַׁךְ וַעֲבֵד־נְגוֹ עַבְדוֹהִי דִּי־

servants of the Most High God, come out and come here." Then Shadrakh,
27 Meishakh, and Aved Nego came out of the midst of the fire. And the satraps,
the prefects, the governors, and the king's advisors gathered round, looking
at these men over whose bodies the fire had no power: and the hair of their
heads was not singed, nor were their mantles damaged and not even a scent
28 of fire came from them. Then Nevukhadnetzar spoke and said, "Blessed be
the God of Shadrakh, Meishakh, and Aved Nego, who has sent His angel and
rescued His servants who trusted in Him and defied the edict of the king,
yielding their bodies rather than serve or worship any god except their own
29 God. I decree that persons of any people, nation, or language who blaspheme
against the God of Shadrakh, Meishakh, and Aved Nego will be dismembered
and their houses reduced to refuse, because there is no other god who is able
30 to rescue like Him." Then the king promoted Shadrakh, Meishakh, and Aved
31 Nego in the province of Babylon. Nevukhadnetzar the king,
addressing all the peoples, nations, and speakers of various languages who
32 dwell in all the earth: "May your peace abound. It is pleasing to me to tell of
33 the signs and wonders that the Most High God has performed with me. How
great are His signs and how powerful are His wonders! His kingdom is an
4 1 eternal kingdom, and His rule is over every generation. I, Nevukhadnetzar,
2 was at peace in my house, relaxed in my palace. I saw a dream that frightened
3 me, and my thoughts in my bed and the visions in my head upset me. Then I
issued a command to bring all the wise men of Babylon so they would
4 make known to me the meaning of the dream. When the magicians, the
soothsayers, the Chaldeans, and the astrologers arrived, I recited the dream
5 before them but they could not make its meaning known to me. And finally,
Daniel, whose name is Belteshatzar like the name of my god, and who has the
spirit of the holy gods within him, came before me, and I recited the dream
6 before him: O Belteshatzar, chief magician, about whom I know that the spirit
of the holy gods is within you and that no mystery can conquer you, tell the
7 interpretation of the vision I saw in my dream. There were visions in my head
while I was lying in my bed: I was looking and – behold! – there was a tree in
8 the midst of the earth and its height was colossal. The tree grew and became
strong, and its height reached the heavens and it was visible to the ends of all
9 the earth. Its foliage was beautiful and its fruit abundant, and it had food for
all. Wild beasts were taking shade under it, and in its branches were nesting
10 the birds of the heavens, and from it all flesh was being nourished. "I was
looking at the visions in my head as I lay in bed and – behold! – a holy angel
11 was coming down from the heavens. He called out forcefully and thus did he
speak: 'Cut down the tree and chop off its branches, bring down its foliage
and scatter its fruit. Let the beasts beneath it flee, as well as the birds from its
12 branches. However, leave the stump with its roots in the earth, chained in a
fetter of iron and bronze in the wild grass; let him be drenched by the dew of
13 the heavens; let his lot be with the beasts in the grassland. Let his heart be

אֱלָהָא עליא פְּקוּ וֶאֱתוֹ בֵּאדַיִן נָפְקִין שַׁדְרַךְ מֵישַׁךְ וַעֲבֵד נְגוֹ מִן־גּוֹא עִלָּאָה
כז נוּרָא׃ וּמִֽתְכַּנְּשִׁין אֲחַשְׁדַּרְפְּנַיָּא סִגְנַיָּא וּפַחֲוָתָא וְהַדָּבְרֵי מַלְכָּא חָזַיִן
לְגֻבְרַיָּא אִלֵּךְ דִּי לָא־שְׁלֵט נוּרָא בגשמיהון וּשְׂעַר רֵאשְׁהוֹן לָא בְּגֶשְׁמְהוֹן
כח הִתְחָרַךְ וְסָרְבָּלֵיהוֹן לָא שְׁנוֹ וְרֵיחַ נוּר לָא עֲדָת בְּהוֹן׃ עָנֵה נְבוּכַדְנֶצַּר
וְאָמַר בְּרִיךְ אֱלָהֲהוֹן דִּֽי־שַׁדְרַךְ מֵישַׁךְ וַעֲבֵד נְגוֹ דִּֽי־שְׁלַח מַלְאֲכֵהּ
וְשֵׁיזִב לְעַבְדוֹהִי דִּי הִתְרְחִצוּ עֲלוֹהִי וּמִלַּת מַלְכָּא שַׁנִּיו וִיהַבוּ גשמיהון גֶּשְׁמְהוֹן
כט דִּי לָא־יִפְלְחוּן וְלָא־יִסְגְּדוּן לְכָל־אֱלָהּ לָהֵן לֵאלָהֲהוֹן׃ וּמִנִּי שִׂים טְעֵם
דִּי כָל־עַם אֻמָּה וְלִשָּׁן דִּֽי־יֵאמַר שלה עַל־אֱלָהֲהוֹן דִּֽי־שַׁדְרַךְ מֵישַׁךְ שָׁלוּ
וַעֲבֵד נְגוֹא הַדָּמִין יִתְעֲבֵד וּבַיְתֵהּ נְוָלִי יִשְׁתַּוֵּה כָּל־קֳבֵל דִּי לָא אִיתַי
ג ל אֱלָהּ אָחֳרָן דִּֽי־יִכֻּל לְהַצָּלָה כִּדְנָה׃ בֵּאדַיִן מַלְכָּא הַצְלַח לְשַׁדְרַךְ
לא מֵישַׁךְ וַעֲבֵד נְגוֹ בִּמְדִינַת בָּבֶל׃ נְבוּכַדְנֶצַּר מַלְכָּא
לְכָל־עַמְמַיָּא אֻמַיָּא וְלִשָּׁנַיָּא דִּֽי־דארין בְּכָל־אַרְעָא שְׁלָמְכוֹן יִשְׂגֵּא׃ דָּיְרִין
לב אָתַיָּא וְתִמְהַיָּא דִּי עֲבַד עִמִּי אֱלָהָא עליא שְׁפַר קָדָמַי לְהַחֲוָיָה׃ עִלָּאָה
לג אָתוֹהִי כְּמָה רַבְרְבִין וְתִמְהוֹהִי כְּמָה תַקִּיפִין מַלְכוּתֵהּ מַלְכוּת עָלַם
ד א וְשָׁלְטָנֵהּ עִם־דָּר וְדָר׃ אֲנָה נְבוּכַדְנֶצַּר שְׁלֵה הֲוֵית בְּבֵיתִי וְרַעְנַן
ב בְּהֵיכְלִי׃ חֵלֶם חֲזֵית וִידַחֲלִנַּנִי וְהַרְהֹרִין עַל־מִשְׁכְּבִי וְחֶזְוֵי רֵאשִׁי
ג יְבַהֲלֻנַּנִי׃ וּמִנִּי שִׂים טְעֵם לְהַנְעָלָה קָדָמַי לְכֹל חַכִּימֵי בָבֶל דִּֽי־פְשַׁר
ד חֶלְמָא יְהוֹדְעֻנַּנִי׃ בֵּאדַיִן עללין חַרְטֻמַּיָּא אָשְׁפַיָּא כשדיא וְגָזְרַיָּא עָלִּין | כַּשְׂדָּאֵי
ה וְחֶלְמָא אָמַר אֲנָה קֳדָמֵיהוֹן וּפִשְׁרֵהּ לָא־מְהוֹדְעִין לִי׃ וְעַד אָחֳרֵין
עַל קָדָמַי דָּנִיֵּאל דִּֽי־שְׁמֵהּ בֵּלְטְשַׁאצַּר כְּשֻׁם אֱלָהִי וְדִי רוּחַ־אֱלָהִין
ו קַדִּישִׁין בֵּהּ וְחֶלְמָא קָדָמוֹהִי אַמְרֵת׃ בֵּלְטְשַׁאצַּר רַב חַרְטֻמַּיָּא דִּי
אֲנָה יִדְעֵת דִּי רוּחַ אֱלָהִין קַדִּישִׁין בָּךְ וְכָל־רָז לָא־אָנֵס לָךְ חֶזְוֵי חֶלְמִי
ז דִּֽי־חֲזֵית וּפִשְׁרֵהּ אֱמַר׃ וְחֶזְוֵי רֵאשִׁי עַל־מִשְׁכְּבִי חָזֵה הֲוֵית וַאֲלוּ אִילָן
ח בְּגוֹא אַרְעָא וְרוּמֵהּ שַׂגִּיא׃ רְבָה אִילָנָא וּתְקִף וְרוּמֵהּ יִמְטֵא לִשְׁמַיָּא
ט וַחֲזוֹתֵהּ לְסוֹף כָּל־אַרְעָא׃ עָפְיֵהּ שַׁפִּיר וְאִנְבֵּהּ שַׂגִּיא וּמָזוֹן לְכֹלָּא־בֵהּ
תְּחֹתוֹהִי תַּטְלֵל ׀ חֵיוַת בָּרָא וּבְעַנְפוֹהִי ידרון צִפֲּרֵי שְׁמַיָּא וּמִנֵּהּ יִתְּזִין יְדוּרָן
י כָּל־בִּשְׂרָא׃ חָזֵה הֲוֵית בְּחֶזְוֵי רֵאשִׁי עַל־מִשְׁכְּבִי וַאֲלוּ עִיר וְקַדִּישׁ
יא מִן־שְׁמַיָּא נָחִת׃ קָרֵא בְחַיִל וְכֵן אָמַר גֹּדּוּ אִילָנָא וְקַצִּצוּ עַנְפוֹהִי
אַתַּרוּ עָפְיֵהּ וּבַדַּרוּ אִנְבֵּהּ תְּנֻד חֵיוְתָא מִן־תַּחְתּוֹהִי וְצִפְּרַיָּא מִן־
יב עַנְפוֹהִי׃ בְּרַם עִקַּר שָׁרְשׁוֹהִי בְּאַרְעָא שְׁבֻקוּ וּבֶאֱסוּר דִּֽי־פַרְזֶל וּנְחָשׁ
בְּדִתְאָא דִּי בָרָא וּבְטַל שְׁמַיָּא יִצְטַבַּע וְעִם־חֵיוְתָא חֲלָקֵהּ בַּעֲשַׂב
יג אַרְעָא׃ לִבְבֵהּ מִן־אנושא יְשַׁנּוֹן וּלְבַב חֵיוָא יִתְיְהִב לֵהּ וְשִׁבְעָה עִדָּנִין אֲנָשָׁא

changed from a human one, and let him be given a beast's heart, and seven
14 seasons will pass over him. This proclamation is by decree of the angels and
the matter is by order of the holy ones, in order that everyone alive know that
the Most High rules the kingdom of man and He gives it to whomever He
15 wishes, and He can appoint over it the lowest of men.' This is the dream I saw,
I, King Nevukhadnetzar; and you, Belteshatzar, speak its interpretation, since
all the wise men of my kingdom are unable to make it known to me; but you
16 are, for the spirit of the holy gods is within you." Then Daniel, whose name
was Belteshatzar, was perplexed for a while, his thoughts upsetting him. The
king spoke up, saying, "Belteshatzar, do not let the dream and its meaning
upset you." Belteshatzar responded and said, "My lord, may the dream be for
17 your enemies, and its interpretation for your foes. The tree that you saw,
which grew and became strong until its height reached the heavens and it
18 became visible to the whole earth, and its foliage was beautiful and its fruit
abundant and it had food for all; beneath it wild beasts dwelled and in its
19 branches nested the birds of heaven – it is you, O king, who has grown great
and become strong, and your greatness grew greater and reached the heavens,
20 and your dominion to the edge of the earth. And whereas the king saw a holy
angel descend from the heavens and say, 'Cut down the tree and destroy it,
but leave the stump with its roots in the earth, chained in a fetter of iron and
bronze in the wild grass, and let him be drenched by the dew of the heavens
and let his lot be with the beasts of the field until seven seasons pass over him.'
21 This is the interpretation, O king, and it is the decree of the Most High which
22 has come upon my lord the king. You will be driven out of human society,
and your dwelling place shall be with the wild beasts, and you will be fed grass,
like cattle, and be drenched by the dew of the heavens, and seven seasons will
pass over you, until you know that the Most High rules the kingdom of
23 man and He gives it to whomever He wishes. And whereas they said to leave
the stump with the roots of the tree, your kingdom awaits you as soon as
24 you come to know that the heavens rule. Therefore, O king, may my advice
please you: redeem your sins by giving charity and your iniquities by acting
mercifully toward the poor; perhaps your peacefulness will be prolonged."
25 26 All this happened to Nevukhadnetzar the king. Twelve months
27 later, he was strolling on the roof of the royal palace in Babylon. The king
spoke and said, "Behold, this is the great Babylon, which I have built into the
28 royal seat by the force of my might and in honor of my splendor!" The word
was still in the king's mouth when a voice came down from the heavens:
"Regarding you it is decreed, Nevukhadnetzar the king: your kingdom has
29 been taken from you. And you shall be driven out of human society, and your
dwelling place will be with the beasts of the field; you will be fed grass like
cattle and seven seasons will pass over you, until you know that the Most High
30 rules the kingdom of man and He gives it to whomever He wishes." At that
very moment, the word about Nevukhadnetzar was fulfilled, and he was
chased out of human society and he ate grass, as cattle do, and his body was
drenched by the dew of the heavens until his hair grew long like eagle feathers

יד יחלפון עלוהי: בגזרת עירין פתגמא ומאמר קדישין שאלתא עד־
דברת די ינדעון חייא די־שליט עליא במלכות אנושא ולמן־די עלאה | אנשא
טו יצבא יתננה ושפל אנשים יקים עליה: דנה חלמא חזית אנה מלכא עלה
נבוכדנצר ואנתה בלטשאצר פשרא אמר כל־קבל די | כל־חכימי ואנת | פשרה
מלכותי לא־יכלין פשרא להודעותני ואנתה כהל די רוח־אלהין ואנת
טז קדישין בך: אדין דניאל די־שמה בלטשאצר אשתומם כשעה
חדה ורעינהי יבהלנה ענה מלכא ואמר בלטשאצר חלמא ופשרא ופשרה
אל־יבהלך ענה בלטשאצר ואמר מראי חלמא לשנאיך ופשרה לשנאך
יז לעריך: אילנא די חזית די רבה ותקף ורומה ימטא לשמיא וחזותה לערך
יח לכל־ארעא: ועפיה שפיר ואנבה שגיא ומזון לכלא־בה תחתוהי
יט תדור חיות ברא ובענפוהי ישכנן צפרי שמיא: אנתה־הוא מלכא אנת־
די רבית ותקפת ורבותך רבת ומטת לשמיא ושלטנך לסוף ארעא: רבת
כ ודי חזה מלכא עיר וקדיש נחת | מן־שמיא ואמר גדו אילנא
וחבלוהי ברם עקר שרשוהי בארעא שבקו ובאסור די־פרזל ונחש
בדתאא די ברא ובטל שמיא יצטבע ועם־חיות ברא חלקה עד
כא די־שבעה עדנין יחלפון עלוהי: דנה פשרא מלכא וגזרת עליא היא עלאה
כב די מטת על־מראי מלכא: ולך טרדין מן־אנשא ועם־חיות ברא
להוה מדרך ועשבא כתורין | לך יטעמון ומטל שמיא לך מצבעין
ושבעה עדנין יחלפון עליך עד די־תנדע די־שליט עליא במלכות עלך | עלאה
כג אנשא ולמן־די יצבא יתננה: ודי אמרו למשבק עקר שרשוהי די
כד אילנא מלכותך לך קימה מן־די תנדע די שלטן שמיא: להן מלכא
מלכי ישפר עליך וחטיך בצדקה פרק ועויתך במחן ענין הן תהוה עלך וחטאך
כה
כו ארכה לשלותך: כלא מטא על־נבוכדנצר מלכא: לקצת
כז ירחין תרי־עשר על־היכל מלכותא די בבל מהלך הוה: ענה מלכא
ואמר הלא דא־היא בבל רבתא די־אנה בניתה לבית מלכו בתקף
כח חסני וליקר הדרי: עוד מלתא בפם מלכא קל מן־שמיא נפל לך
כט אמרין נבוכדנצר מלכא מלכותא עדת מנך: ומן־אנשא לך טרדין
ועם־חיות ברא מדרך עשבא כתורין לך יטעמון ושבעה עדנין
יחלפון עליך עד די־תנדע די־שליט עליא במלכות אנשא ולמן־די עלך | עלאה
ל יצבא יתננה: בה־שעתא מלתא ספת על־נבוכדנצר ומן־אנשא
טריד ועשבא כתורין יאכל ומטל שמיא גשמה יצטבע עד די שערה

31 and his nails like bird claws. "And when the designated time period ended, I,
Nevukhadnetzar, raised my eyes to the heavens, and my wits returned to me,
and I blessed the Most High, and I praised and glorified the One who lives
forever, whose reign is an eternal reign and whose sovereignty endures from
32 generation to generation. And all who inhabit earth count as nothing in
comparison; and He does as He wishes with the hosts of the heavens and the
inhabitants of earth and there is no one who can protest His power and say
33 to Him, 'What are You doing?' At that very time my wits returned to me, and
for the honor of my kingdom, my splendor and my radiance returned to me.
And I was sought by my advisors and my noblemen, and I was reestablished
34 over my kingdom, and even more greatness was accorded to me. Now I,
Nevukhadnetzar, praise and exalt and give glory to the King of the heavens,
whose every deed is true, and whose ways are just, and who can humble those
who act arrogantly."

5 1 Beleshatzar the king made a great banquet for his one thousand nobles
2 and was drinking wine facing those thousand. Under the wine's influence,
Beleshatzar gave orders to bring the vessels of gold and silver which his
father, Nevukhadnetzar, had removed from the Temple in Jerusalem, so
that the king and his nobles, his wives and his concubines might use them
3 to drink. So they brought the vessels of gold which they had removed from
the Temple, the House of God which is in Jerusalem, and the king and his
4 nobles, his wives and his concubines drank from them. They drank the wine
and toasted their gods of gold and silver, of bronze, iron, wood, and stone.
5 Just then the fingers of a human hand emerged and were writing across from
the candelabra on the plastered wall of the king's palace, such that the king
6 could see the back of the hand that was writing. Then the king's face blanched,
and his thoughts frightened him, and the joints of his loins loosened, and
7 his knees knocked against each other. The king cried out loudly to bring the
soothsayers, the Chaldeans, and the astrologers. The king sent word to the
wise ones of Babylon and said, "Whoever of you will read this writing and
tell me its meaning shall wear royal purple and have a golden chain on his
8 neck and shall rule as the third in power in the kingdom." Then all
the wise ones of the king arrived, but they were not able to read the writing
9 or make its meaning known to the king. Then King Beleshatzar became very
10 agitated and his face blanched and his ministers were bewildered. The queen
mother, in response to the words of the king and his ministers, entered the
banquet hall and spoke up, saying, "O king, live forever! Do not let your
11 thoughts upset you or let your healthy look change. There is a man in your
kingdom in whom there is the spirit of the holy gods, and in your father's day
he was found to have insight and intelligence, and a wisdom like the wisdom
of the gods. And King Nevukhadnetzar, your father, appointed him to be the
chief of the magicians, soothsayers, Chaldeans, and astrologers – your father
12 the king! Since an extraordinary spirit and knowledge and intelligence – the
ability to interpret dreams and solve puzzles and resolve problems – were
found in this Daniel, whom the king named Belteshatzar, now let Daniel be

לא כְּנִשְׁרִין רְבָה וְטִפְרוֹהִי כְצִפְּרִין: וְלִקְצָת יוֹמַיָּה אֲנָה נְבוּכַדְנֶצַּר עַיְנַי ׀
לִשְׁמַיָּא נִטְלֵת וּמַנְדְּעִי עֲלַי יְתוּב ולעליא בָּרְכֵת וּלְחַי עָלְמָא שַׁבְּחֵת וּלְעִלָּאָה
לב וְהַדְּרֵת דִּי שָׁלְטָנֵהּ שָׁלְטָן עָלַם וּמַלְכוּתֵהּ עִם־דָּר וְדָר: וְכָל־דארי דָּיְרֵי
אַרְעָא כְּלָה חֲשִׁיבִין וּכְמִצְבְּיֵהּ עָבֵד בְּחֵיל שְׁמַיָּא ודארי אַרְעָא וְלָא וְדָיְרֵי
לג אִיתַי דִּי־יְמַחֵא בִידֵהּ וְיֵאמַר לֵהּ מָה עֲבַדְתְּ: בֵּהּ־זִמְנָא מַנְדְּעִי ׀ יְתוּב
עֲלַי וְלִיקַר מַלְכוּתִי הַדְרִי וְזִוִי יְתוּב עֲלַי וְלִי הַדָּבְרַי וְרַבְרְבָנַי יְבַעוֹן
לד וְעַל־מַלְכוּתִי הָתְקְנַת וּרְבוּ יַתִּירָה הוּסְפַת לִי: כְּעַן אֲנָה נְבֻכַדְנֶצַּר
מְשַׁבַּח וּמְרוֹמֵם וּמְהַדַּר לְמֶלֶךְ שְׁמַיָּא דִּי כָל־מַעֲבָדוֹהִי קְשֹׁט
וְאֹרְחָתֵהּ דִּין וְדִי מַהְלְכִין בְּגֵוָה יָכִל לְהַשְׁפָּלָה:
ה א בֵּלְשַׁאצַּר מַלְכָּא עֲבַד לְחֶם רַב לְרַבְרְבָנוֹהִי אֲלַף וְלָקֳבֵל אַלְפָּא
ב חַמְרָא שָׁתֵה: בֵּלְשַׁאצַּר אֲמַר ׀ בִּטְעֵם חַמְרָא לְהַיְתָיָה לְמָאנֵי דַּהֲבָא
וְכַסְפָּא דִּי הַנְפֵּק נְבוּכַדְנֶצַּר אֲבוּהִי מִן־הֵיכְלָא דִּי בִירוּשְׁלֶם וְיִשְׁתּוֹן
ג בְּהוֹן מַלְכָּא וְרַבְרְבָנוֹהִי שֵׁגְלָתֵהּ וּלְחֵנָתֵהּ: בֵּאדַיִן הַיְתִיו מָאנֵי דַהֲבָא
דִּי הַנְפִּקוּ מִן־הֵיכְלָא דִּי־בֵית אֱלָהָא דִּי בִירוּשְׁלֶם וְאִשְׁתִּיו בְּהוֹן
ד מַלְכָּא וְרַבְרְבָנוֹהִי שֵׁגְלָתֵהּ וּלְחֵנָתֵהּ: אִשְׁתִּיו חַמְרָא וְשַׁבַּחוּ לֵאלָהֵי
ה דַּהֲבָא וְכַסְפָּא נְחָשָׁא פַרְזְלָא אָעָא וְאַבְנָא: בַּהּ־שַׁעֲתָה נפקו אֶצְבְּעָן נְפַקָה
דִּי יַד־אֱנָשׁ וְכָתְבָן לָקֳבֵל נֶבְרַשְׁתָּא עַל־גִּירָא דִּי־כְתַל הֵיכְלָא דִּי
ו מַלְכָּא וּמַלְכָּא חָזֵה פַּס יְדָה דִּי כָתְבָה: אֱדַיִן מַלְכָּא זִיוֺהִי שְׁנוֹהִי
וְרַעְיֹנֹהִי יְבַהֲלוּנֵּהּ וְקִטְרֵי חַרְצֵהּ מִשְׁתָּרַיִן וְאַרְכֻבָּתֵהּ דָּא לְדָא נָקְשָׁן:
ז קָרֵא מַלְכָּא בְּחַיִל לְהֶעָלָה לְאָשְׁפַיָּא כשדיא וְגָזְרַיָּא עָנֵה מַלְכָּא כַּשְׂדָּאֵי
וְאָמַר ׀ לְחַכִּימֵי בָבֶל דִּי כָל־אֱנָשׁ דִּי־יִקְרֵה כְּתָבָה דְנָה וּפִשְׁרֵהּ יְחַוִּנַּנִי
ארגונא יִלְבַּשׁ והמונכא דִי־דַהֲבָא עַל־צַוְּארֵהּ וְתַלְתִּי בְמַלְכוּתָא וְהַמְנִיכָא
ח יִשְׁלַט: אֱדַיִן עללין כֹּל חַכִּימֵי מַלְכָּא וְלָא־כָהֲלִין כְּתָבָא עָלִּין
ט לְמִקְרֵא ופשרא לְהוֹדָעָה לְמַלְכָּא: אֱדַיִן מַלְכָּא בֵלְשַׁאצַּר שַׂגִּיא וּפִשְׁרֵהּ
י מִתְבָּהַל וְזִיוֺהִי שָׁנַיִן עֲלוֹהִי וְרַבְרְבָנוֹהִי מִשְׁתַּבְּשִׁין: מַלְכְּתָא לָקֳבֵל
מִלֵּי מַלְכָּא וְרַבְרְבָנוֹהִי לְבֵית מִשְׁתְּיָא עללת עֲנָת מַלְכְּתָא וַאֲמֶרֶת עַלַּת
יא מַלְכָּא לְעָלְמִין חֱיִי אַל־יְבַהֲלוּךְ רַעְיוֹנָךְ וזיויך אַל־יִשְׁתַּנּוֹ: אִיתַי גְּבַר וְזִיוָךְ
בְּמַלְכוּתָךְ דִּי רוּחַ אֱלָהִין קַדִּישִׁין בֵּהּ וּבְיוֹמֵי אֲבוּךְ נַהִירוּ וְשָׂכְלְתָנוּ
וְחָכְמָה כְּחָכְמַת־אֱלָהִין הִשְׁתְּכַחַת בֵּהּ וּמַלְכָּא נְבֻכַדְנֶצַּר אֲבוּךְ רַב
יב חַרְטֻמִּין אָשְׁפִין כַּשְׂדָּאִין גָּזְרִין הֲקִימֵהּ אֲבוּךְ מַלְכָּא: כָּל־קֳבֵל דִּי רוּחַ ׀ ד
יַתִּירָה וּמַנְדַּע וְשָׂכְלְתָנוּ מְפַשַּׁר חֶלְמִין וַאַחֲוָיַת אֲחִידָן וּמְשָׁרֵא קִטְרִין
הִשְׁתְּכַחַת בֵּהּ בְדָנִיֵּאל דִּי־מַלְכָּא שָׂם־שְׁמֵהּ בֵּלְטְשַׁאצַּר כְּעַן דָּנִיֵּאל

13 summoned and he will make the meaning known." So Daniel was
brought before the king. The king spoke and said to Daniel, "You are Daniel,
one of the exiles of Yehuda whom my father the king brought here from
14 Yehuda. And I have heard about you that the spirit of the gods is within you,
and that extraordinary insight and intelligence and wisdom has been found
15 within you. And just now there have been brought before me the wise ones,
the soothsayers, to read this writing so as to tell me its meaning, but they
16 could not tell me the meaning of the thing. And I have heard about you, that
you are able to interpret meaning and resolve problems. Now if you can read
the writing and make its meaning known to me, you shall wear royal purple,
a golden chain will be placed on your neck, and you will rule as the third in
17 power in the kingdom." Then Daniel responded and spoke before
the king, "Let your gifts remain yours, and give your presents to another,
but I shall read the writing for the king and I shall make its meaning known
18 to him. Regarding you, O king: the Most High God gave sovereignty and
19 greatness and honor and glory to Nevukhadnetzar, your father. And because
of the greatness that He gave him, all nations, peoples, and speakers of all
languages trembled in terror before him. He would kill whomever he wished,
and let live whomever he wished. He would exalt whomever he wished,
20 and debase whomever he wished. And when he became haughty and his
inclination to act wickedly became powerful, he was deposed from his royal
21 throne and his honor was taken away. And he was driven from human society
and his heart was made like a beast's. His dwelling place was with the wild
asses, and he was fed grass, like cattle, and his body was drenched by the
dew of the heavens, until he recognized that the Most High God rules the
22 kingdom of man and that He appoints over it whomever He wishes. And
you, Beleshatzar his son, have not humbled your own heart even though
23 you know all this. And you exalted yourself above the Lord of the heavens,
and you had the vessels of His House brought before you, and you and your
nobles, your wives and your concubines drank wine from them, and you
toasted your gods of silver and gold, of bronze, iron, wood, and stone, who
cannot see and cannot hear and cannot know. And the God who holds your
24 soul in His power and who owns all your paths you did not honor. So there
25 was sent from Him the back of a hand and this writing was inscribed. And
26 this is the writing which was inscribed: *Meneh, meneh tekel ufarsin.* This is
the interpretation of the message: *Meneh*; God has counted[3] your kingdom
27 and brought it to completion. *Tekel*; you have been weighed[4] in the scales
28 and been found wanting. *Peres*; your kingdom has been divided[5] and given
29 to Media and Persia." Then Beleshatzar gave an order, and they robed Daniel
in royal purple, and a chain of gold was placed on his neck, and they publicly
30 declared he would rule as third in power in the kingdom. That very night,
Beleshatzar, the Chaldean king, was killed.

---

3 | Aramaic *mena.*
4 | Aramaic *tekilta.*
5 | Aramaic *perisat.*

יג יִתְקְרֵי וּפִשְׁרָה יְהַחֲוֵה׃ בֵּאדַיִן דָּנִיֵּאל הֻעַל קֳדָם מַלְכָּא
עָנֵה מַלְכָּא וְאָמַר לְדָנִיֵּאל אנתה־הוּא דָנִיֵּאל דִּי־מִן־בְּנֵי גָלוּתָא דִּי אַנְתְּ־
יד יְהוּד דִּי הַיְתִי מַלְכָּא אַבִי מִן־יְהוּד׃ וְשִׁמְעֵת עליך דִּי רוּחַ אֱלָהִין בָּךְ עֲלָךְ
טו וְנַהִירוּ וְשָׂכְלְתָנוּ וְחָכְמָה יַתִּירָה הִשְׁתְּכַחַת בָּךְ׃ וּכְעַן הֻעַלּוּ קָדָמַי
חַכִּימַיָּא אָשְׁפַיָּא דִּי־כְתָבָה דְנָה יִקְרוֹן וּפִשְׁרֵהּ לְהוֹדָעֻתַנִי וְלָא־כָהֲלִין
טז פְּשַׁר־מִלְּתָא לְהַחֲוָיָה׃ וַאֲנָה שִׁמְעֵת עליך דִּי־תוכל פִּשְׁרִין לְמִפְשַׁר עֲלָךְ | תִּכֻּל
וְקִטְרִין לְמִשְׁרֵא כְּעַן הֵן תוכל כְּתָבָא לְמִקְרֵא וּפִשְׁרֵהּ לְהוֹדָעֻתַנִי תִּכֻּל
אַרְגְּוָנָא תִלְבַּשׁ והמונכא דִּי־דַהֲבָא עַל־צַוְּארָךְ וְתַלְתָּא בְמַלְכוּתָא וְהַמְנִיכָא
יז תִּשְׁלַט׃ בֵּאדַיִן עָנֵה דָנִיֵּאל וְאָמַר קֳדָם מַלְכָּא מַתְּנָתָךְ
לָךְ לֶהֶוְיָן וּנְבִזְבְּיָתָךְ לְאָחֳרָן הַב בְּרַם כְּתָבָא אֶקְרֵא לְמַלְכָּא וּפִשְׁרָא
יח אֲהוֹדְעִנֵּהּ׃ אנתה מַלְכָּא אֱלָהָא עליא מַלְכוּתָא וּרְבוּתָא וִיקָרָא אַנְתְּ | עִלָּאָה
יט וְהַדְרָא יְהַב לִנְבֻכַדְנֶצַּר אֲבוּךְ׃ וּמִן־רְבוּתָא דִּי יְהַב־לֵהּ כֹּל עַמְמַיָּא
אֻמַיָּא וְלִשָּׁנַיָּא הֲווֹ זאעין וְדָחֲלִין מִן־קֳדָמוֹהִי דִּי־הֲוָא צָבֵא הֲוָה קָטֵל זָיְעִין
וְדִי־הֲוָה צָבֵא הֲוָה מַחֵא וְדִי־הֲוָה צָבֵא הֲוָה מָרִים וְדִי־הֲוָא צָבֵא
כ הֲוָא מַשְׁפִּל׃ וּכְדִי רִם לִבְבֵהּ וְרוּחֵהּ תִּקְפַת לַהֲזָדָה הָנְחַת מִן־כָּרְסֵא
כא מַלְכוּתֵהּ וִיקָרָה הֶעְדִּיו מִנֵּהּ׃ וּמִן־בְּנֵי אֲנָשָׁא טְרִיד וְלִבְבֵהּ ׀ עִם־חֵיוְתָא
שוי וְעִם־עֲרָדַיָּא מְדוֹרֵהּ עִשְׂבָּא כְתוֹרִין יְטַעֲמוּנֵּהּ וּמִטַּל שְׁמַיָּא גִּשְׁמֵהּ שַׁוִּיו
יִצְטַבַּע עַד דִּי־יְדַע דִּי־שַׁלִּיט אֱלָהָא עליא בְּמַלְכוּת אֲנָשָׁא וּלְמַן־ עִלָּאָה
כב דִּי יִצְבֵּא יְהָקֵים עליה׃ ואנתה בְּרֵהּ בֵּלְשַׁאצַּר לָא הַשְׁפֵּלְתְּ לִבְבָךְ עֲלַהּ׃ וְאַנְתְּ
כג כָּל־קֳבֵל דִּי כָל־דְּנָה יְדַעְתָּ׃ וְעַל מָרֵא־שְׁמַיָּא ׀ הִתְרוֹמַמְתָּ וּלְמָאנַיָּא
דִּי־בַיְתֵהּ הַיְתִיו קדמיך ואנתה ורברבניך שֵׁגְלָתָךְ וּלְחֵנָתָךְ חַמְרָא קֳדָמָךְ וְאַנְתְּ וְרַבְרְבָנָךְ
שָׁתַיִן בְּהוֹן וְלֵאלָהֵי כַסְפָּא־וְדַהֲבָא נְחָשָׁא פַרְזְלָא אָעָא וְאַבְנָא דִּי
לָא־חָזַיִן וְלָא־שָׁמְעִין וְלָא יָדְעִין שַׁבַּחְתָּ וְלֵאלָהָא דִּי־נִשְׁמְתָךְ בִּידֵהּ
כד וְכָל־אֹרְחָתָךְ לֵהּ לָא הַדַּרְתָּ׃ בֵּאדַיִן מִן־קֳדָמוֹהִי שְׁלִיחַ פַּסָּא דִי־יְדָא
כה וּכְתָבָא דְנָה רְשִׁים׃ וּדְנָה כְתָבָא דִּי רְשִׁים מְנֵא מְנֵא תְּקֵל וּפַרְסִין׃
כו כז דְּנָה פְּשַׁר מִלְּתָא מְנֵא מְנָה־אֱלָהָא מַלְכוּתָךְ וְהַשְׁלְמַהּ׃ תְּקֵל תְּקִילְתָּה
כח בְמֹאזַנְיָא וְהִשְׁתְּכַחַתְּ חַסִּיר׃ פְּרֵס פְּרִיסַת מַלְכוּתָךְ וִיהִיבַת לְמָדַי
כט וּפָרָס׃ בֵּאדַיִן ׀ אֲמַר בֵּלְשַׁאצַּר וְהַלְבִּשׁוּ לְדָנִיֵּאל אַרְגְּוָנָא והמונכא דִּי־ וְהַמְנִיכָא
דַהֲבָא עַל־צַוְּארֵהּ וְהַכְרִזוּ עֲלוֹהִי דִּי־לֶהֱוֵא שַׁלִּיט תַּלְתָּא בְּמַלְכוּתָא׃
ל בֵּהּ בְּלֵילְיָא קְטִיל בֵּלְאשַׁצַּר מַלְכָּא כשדיא׃ כַּשְׂדָּאָה

6 1 And Daryavesh the Mede received the kingdom when he was about sixty-two
2 years old. Daryavesh decided to appoint one hundred twenty governors over
3 his kingdom, to be located throughout his kingdom. And above them were
three ministers, of whom Daniel was one, to whom the governors would
4 give an accounting, so that the royal treasury not be burdened. Now the
aforementioned Daniel surpassed the ministers and the governors because of
his extraordinary spirit, and the king intended to appoint him over the whole
5 kingdom. Then the ministers and governors sought to find a fault against
Daniel regarding affairs of state, but they could find no fault or corruption
because he was faithful, so no error or corruption was found regarding him.
6 Then those men said, "We will not find any fault against this Daniel unless
7 we find it in the law of his God." Then these ministers and governors
excitedly mobbed the king and said to him, "O Daryavesh the king, live
8 forever! All the ministers of the kingdom, the supervisors and the governors,
the counselors and the administrators have resolved together that the king
should enact a royal ordinance and binding obligation that for thirty days,
whosoever shall make any request of any god or any man other than you, O
9 king, shall be thrown into the lions' den. Now, O king, enact the obligation
and issue a written decree that cannot be changed, as a law of Media and
10 Persia that cannot be annulled." Consenting to all this, King Daryavesh
11 issued the obligation in a written decree. Now when Daniel learned that
this law had been issued in a written decree, he went to his house where he
had open windows in his attic facing Jerusalem, where three times a day he
would kneel down and pray and give thanks before his God, just as he had
12 always done before this. Then those men formed an excited mob and found
13 Daniel petitioning and supplicating his God. Then they approached the king
and said, concerning the king's edict, "Did you not issue an obligation in a
written decree that for thirty days, any man who makes a request from any
god or man other than you, O king, would be thrown into the lions' den?"
The king answered and said, "This matter is valid as a law of Media and Persia,
14 which cannot be annulled." Thereupon they answered and said before the
king, "Daniel, who is of the exiles of Yehuda, has not paid attention to you,
O king, nor to the obligation that you issued as a written decree, and three
15 times a day he makes his petitions." The moment the king heard about the
matter he was very displeased, and he made up his mind to rescue Daniel, and
16 until sunset he made efforts to save him. At that point those men excitedly
mobbed the king and said to the king, "Know, O king, that the law of Media
and Persia is that no obligation and ordinance which the king enacts can be
17 changed." Then the king issued a command, and they brought Daniel, and
threw him into the lions' den. The king spoke and said to Daniel, "May your

ו א ב וְדָרְיָוֶשׁ מדיא קַבֵּל מַלְכוּתָא כְּבַר שְׁנִין שִׁתִּין וְתַרְתֵּין׃ שְׁפַר קֳדָם מָדָאָה
דָּרְיָוֶשׁ וַהֲקִים עַל־מַלְכוּתָא לַאֲחַשְׁדַּרְפְּנַיָּא מְאָה וְעֶשְׂרִין דִּי לֶהֱוֺן
ג בְּכָל־מַלְכוּתָא׃ וְעֵלָּא מִנְּהוֺן סָרְכִין תְּלָתָה דִּי דָנִיֵּאל חַד מִנְּהוֺן דִּי־
לֶהֱוֺן אֲחַשְׁדַּרְפְּנַיָּא אִלֵּין יָהֲבִין לְהוֺן טַעְמָא וּמַלְכָּא לָא־לֶהֱוֵא נָזִק׃
ד אֱדַיִן דָּנִיֵּאל דְּנָה הֲוָא מִתְנַצַּח עַל־סָרְכַיָּא וַאֲחַשְׁדַּרְפְּנַיָּא כָּל־קֳבֵל
דִּי רוּחַ יַתִּירָא בֵּהּ וּמַלְכָּא עֲשִׁית לַהֲקָמוּתֵהּ עַל־כָּל־מַלְכוּתָא׃
ה אֱדַיִן סָרְכַיָּא וַאֲחַשְׁדַּרְפְּנַיָּא הֲווֺ בָעַיִן עִלָּה לְהַשְׁכָּחָה לְדָנִיֵּאל מִצַּד
מַלְכוּתָא וְכָל־עִלָּה וּשְׁחִיתָה לָא־יָכְלִין לְהַשְׁכָּחָה כָּל־קֳבֵל דִּי־מְהֵימַן
ו הוּא וְכָל־שָׁלוּ וּשְׁחִיתָה לָא הִשְׁתְּכַחַת עֲלוֺהִי׃ אֱדַיִן גֻּבְרַיָּא אִלֵּךְ
אָמְרִין דִּי לָא נְהַשְׁכַּח לְדָנִיֵּאל דְּנָה כָּל־עִלָּא לָהֵן הַשְׁכַּחְנָא עֲלוֺהִי
ז בְּדָת אֱלָהֵהּ׃ אֱדַיִן סָרְכַיָּא וַאֲחַשְׁדַּרְפְּנַיָּא אִלֵּן הַרְגִּשׁוּ
ח עַל־מַלְכָּא וְכֵן אָמְרִין לֵהּ דָּרְיָוֶשׁ מַלְכָּא לְעָלְמִין חֱיִי׃ אִתְיָעַטוּ כֹּל ׀
סָרְכֵי מַלְכוּתָא סִגְנַיָּא וַאֲחַשְׁדַּרְפְּנַיָּא הַדָּבְרַיָּא וּפַחֲוָתָא לְקַיָּמָה קְיָם
מַלְכָּא וּלְתַקָּפָה אֱסָר דִּי כָל־דִּי־יִבְעֵה בָעוּ מִן־כָּל־אֱלָהּ וֶאֱנָשׁ עַד־
ט יוֺמִין תְּלָתִין לָהֵן מִנָּךְ מַלְכָּא יִתְרְמֵא לְגֹב אַרְיָוָתָא׃ כְּעַן מַלְכָּא תְּקִים
אֱסָרָא וְתִרְשֻׁם כְּתָבָא דִּי לָא לְהַשְׁנָיָה כְּדָת־מָדַי וּפָרַס דִּי־לָא תֶעְדֵּא׃
י יא כָּל־קֳבֵל דְּנָה מַלְכָּא דָּרְיָוֶשׁ רְשַׁם כְּתָבָא וֶאֱסָרָא׃ וְדָנִיֵּאל כְּדִי יְדַע ה
דִּי־רְשִׁים כְּתָבָא עַל לְבַיְתֵהּ וְכַוִּין פְּתִיחָן לֵהּ בְּעִלִּיתֵהּ נֶגֶד יְרוּשְׁלֶם
וְזִמְנִין תְּלָתָה בְיוֺמָא הוּא ׀ בָּרֵךְ עַל־בִּרְכוֺהִי וּמְצַלֵּא וּמוֺדֵא קֳדָם
יב אֱלָהֵהּ כָּל־קֳבֵל דִּי־הֲוָא עָבֵד מִן־קַדְמַת דְּנָה׃ אֱדַיִן גֻּבְרַיָּא אִלֵּךְ
יג הַרְגִּשׁוּ וְהַשְׁכַּחוּ לְדָנִיֵּאל בָּעֵא וּמִתְחַנַּן קֳדָם אֱלָהֵהּ׃ בֵּאדַיִן קְרִבוּ
וְאָמְרִין קֳדָם־מַלְכָּא עַל־אֱסָר מַלְכָּא הֲלָא אֱסָר רְשַׁמְתָּ דִּי כָל־אֱנָשׁ
דִּי־יִבְעֵא מִן־כָּל־אֱלָהּ וֶאֱנָשׁ עַד־יוֺמִין תְּלָתִין לָהֵן מִנָּךְ מַלְכָּא יִתְרְמֵא
לְגוֺב אַרְיָוָתָא עָנֵה מַלְכָּא וְאָמַר יַצִּיבָא מִלְּתָא כְּדָת־מָדַי וּפָרַס דִּי־
יד לָא תֶעְדֵּא׃ בֵּאדַיִן עֲנוֺ וְאָמְרִין קֳדָם מַלְכָּא דִּי דָנִיֵּאל דִּי מִן־בְּנֵי
גָלוּתָא דִּי יְהוּד לָא־שָׂם עליך מַלְכָּא טְעֵם וְעַל־אֱסָרָא דִּי רְשַׁמְתָּ עֲלָךְ
טו וְזִמְנִין תְּלָתָה בְּיוֺמָא בָּעֵא בָּעוּתֵהּ׃ אֱדַיִן מַלְכָּא כְּדִי מִלְּתָא שְׁמַע
שַׂגִּיא בְּאֵשׁ עֲלוֺהִי וְעַל דָּנִיֵּאל שָׂם בָּל לְשֵׁיזָבוּתֵהּ וְעַד מֶעָלֵי שִׁמְשָׁא
טז הֲוָא מִשְׁתַּדַּר לְהַצָּלוּתֵהּ׃ בֵּאדַיִן גֻּבְרַיָּא אִלֵּךְ הַרְגִּשׁוּ עַל־מַלְכָּא
וְאָמְרִין לְמַלְכָּא דַּע מַלְכָּא דִּי־דָת לְמָדַי וּפָרַס דִּי־כָל־אֱסָר וּקְיָם
יז דִּי־מַלְכָּא יְהָקֵים לָא לְהַשְׁנָיָה׃ בֵּאדַיִן מַלְכָּא אֲמַר וְהַיְתִיו לְדָנִיֵּאל
וּרְמוֺ לְגֻבָּא דִּי אַרְיָוָתָא עָנֵה מַלְכָּא וְאָמַר לְדָנִיֵּאל אֱלָהָךְ דִּי אנתה אַנְתְּ

18 God, whom you serve constantly, rescue you." And a stone was brought and
placed on the opening of the den, which the king sealed with his own ring
and with the rings of his nobles so that nothing could be changed with regard
19 to Daniel. Then the king went to his palace and spent the night fasting. They
20 brought him no diversions, and sleep escaped him. In the morning the king
21 rose at the break of day and hurriedly went to the lions' den. When he came
near the den, he called out to Daniel in a pained voice. The king spoke and
said, "Daniel, servant of the living God, was your God, whom you serve
22 constantly, able to save you from the lions?" Then Daniel spoke to the king,
23 "O king, live forever! My God sent His angel, who shut the mouth of the lions
so they could not harm me, for I have been found innocent before Him, and
24 before you, O king, I have done no wrong." Then the king was overjoyed, and
commanded that Daniel be brought out of the den. And Daniel was brought
out of the den, and no injury was found on him because he had faith in his
25 God. And at the king's command they brought those men who had slandered
Daniel and threw them into the lions' den, along with their children and their
wives. Even before they reached the bottom of the den, the lions overpowered
26 them and shattered all their bones. Then Daryavesh the king wrote to all
peoples, nations, and speakers of all languages inhabiting the whole earth,
27 "May your peace abound! I have decreed that throughout the domain of my
kingdom people should fear and tremble before the God of Daniel, for He is
the living God, and He endures forever. His kingdom is indestructible and
28 His dominion is everlasting. He is rescuer and deliverer, and He makes signs
and wonders in the heavens and on earth; it is He who rescued Daniel from
29 the lions." And this Daniel prospered during the reign of Daryavesh and the
reign of Koresh the Persian.

7 1 In the first year of Beleshatzar, king of Babylon, Daniel saw a dream, and
visions in his head while in bed; then he wrote down the dream. He began
2 to speak. Thus Daniel spoke and said, "I was seeing my vision at nighttime
and – behold! – the four winds of the heavens were pounding the great sea.
3 And four powerful beasts arose from the sea, each different from the next.
4 The first one was like a lion that had the wings of an eagle. As I was watching,
its wings were plucked and it was lifted from the earth and raised onto two
5 legs like a man, and a human heart was given to it. And – behold! – there was
another, second beast like a bear. It was raised up on one side, and there were
three ribs in its mouth between its teeth. And this is what it was told: 'Arise!
6 Devour much flesh.' After this, I kept watching and – behold! – another,
looking like a leopard. It had four wings of a bird on its back, and the beast
7 had four heads! And it was given dominion. After this, I kept watching the
visions of the night and – behold! – a fourth beast, terrible and terrifying
and exceedingly powerful, and it had enormous iron teeth! It devoured and

יח פלח־לה בתדירא הוא ישיזבנך: והיתית אבן חדה ושמת על־פם
גבא וחתמה מלכא בעזקתה ובעזקת רברבנוהי די לא־תשנא
יט צבו בדניאל: אדין אזל מלכא להיכלה ובת טות ודחון לא־הנעל
כ קדמוהי ושנתה נדת עלוהי: באדין מלכא בשפרפרא יקום בנגהא
כא ובהתבהלה לגבא די־אריותא אזל: וכמקרבה לגבא לדניאל בקל
עציב זעק ענה מלכא ואמר לדניאל דניאל עבד אלהא חיא אלהך
כב די אנתה פלח־לה בתדירא היכל לשיזבותך מן־אריותא: אדין (אנת)
כג דניאל עם־מלכא מלל מלכא לעלמין חיי: אלהי שלח מלאכה וסגר
פם אריותא ולא חבלוני כל־קבל די קדמוהי זכו השתכחת לי ואף
כד קדמיך מלכא חבולה לא עבדת: באדין מלכא שגיא טאב עלוהי (קדמך)
ולדניאל אמר להנסקה מן־גבא והסק דניאל מן־גבא וכל־חבל
כה לא־השתכח בה די הימן באלהה: ואמר מלכא והיתיו גבריא אלך
די־אכלו קרצוהי די דניאל ולגב אריותא רמו אנון בניהון ונשיהון
ולא־מטו לארעית גבא עד די־שלטו בהון אריותא וכל־גרמיהון
כו הדקו: באדין דריוש מלכא כתב לכל־עממיא אמיא ולשניא די־
כז דארין בכל־ארעא שלמכון ישגא: מן־קדמי שים טעם די | בכל־ (דירין)
שלטן מלכותי להון זאעין ודחלין מן־קדם אלהה די־דניאל די־ (זיעין)
הוא | אלהא חיא וקים לעלמין ומלכותה די־לא תתחבל ושלטנה
כח עד־סופא: משיזב ומצל ועבד אתין ותמהין בשמיא ובארעא די
כט שיזב לדניאל מן־יד אריותא: ודניאל דנה הצלח במלכות דריוש
ובמלכות כורש פרסיא: (פרסאה)
ז א בשנת חדה לבלאשצר מלך בבל דניאל חלם חזה וחזוי ראשה
ב על־משכבה באדין חלמא כתב ראש מלין אמר: ענה דניאל ואמר
חזה הוית בחזוי עם־ליליא וארו ארבע רוחי שמיא מגיחן לימא
ג ד רבא: וארבע חיון רברבן סלקן מן־ימא שנין דא מן־דא: קדמיתא
כאריה וגפין די־נשר לה חזה הוית עד די־מריטו גפיה ונטילת מן־ (גפה)
ה ארעא ועל־רגלין כאנש הקימת ולבב אנש יהיב לה: וארו חיוה
אחרי תנינה דמיה לדב ולשטר־חד הקמת ותלת עלעין בפמה
ו בין שניה וכן אמרין לה קומי אכלי בשר שגיא: באתר דנה חזה (שנה)
הוית וארו אחרי כנמר ולה גפין ארבע די־עוף על־גביה וארבעה (גבה)
ז ראשין לחיותא ושלטן יהיב לה: באתר דנה חזה הוית בחזוי ליליא
וארו חיוה רביעיא דחילה ואימתני ותקיפא יתירה ושנין די־פרזל (רביעאה)

crushed and then trampled what remained with its feet. And it was different
8 from all the beasts that preceded it, and it had ten horns! I kept looking at
the horns and – behold! – another, small horn sprouted in their midst. And
three of the earlier horns were uprooted in front of it, and – behold! – this
9 horn had eyes like human eyes and a mouth speaking boastful things. I kept
watching as thrones were set out and the Ancient of Days sat. His clothes were
white as snow and the hair of His head like clean wool. His throne was sparks
10 of fire, its wheels flaming fire. A river of fire was streaming and flowing forth
before Him. Thousands of thousands were ministering to Him, and many
tens of thousands stood before Him. The court was sitting and the books
11 were opened. I kept watching. Then, during the sound of the boastful words
that the horn was speaking, I kept watching as the beast was slain and its body
12 destroyed and given over to the burning fire. And the rest of the beasts were
stripped of their dominion, and an extension of life was given to them until a
13 time and a season. I was seeing visions of the night and – behold! – along with
the clouds in the heavens, one like a human being was coming and reached the
14 Ancient of Days and was presented before Him. And he was given dominion
and honor and kingship, and all the nations and peoples and speakers of all
languages will serve him. His dominion is everlasting dominion that will not
15 be removed, and his kingdom will not be destroyed. My spirit – I,
Daniel – suffered within its vessel, my body, and the visions in my head
16 troubled me. I approached one of the attendants, seeking the truth from him
about all this, and he spoke to me and made the meaning of the things known
17 to me: 'These enormous beasts, of which there are four: four kingdoms will
18 arise from the earth. Holy ones of the Most High will receive the kingdom
19 and will inherit the kingdom for ever and ever.' Then I wished to be certain
about the fourth beast, which was different from all of them: exceedingly
fearsome, with teeth of iron and claws of bronze. It devoured and crushed
20 and then trampled what remained with its feet. And I wished to be certain
about the ten horns that were on its head and the other one that sprouted,
with three falling before it, that horn that had eyes in it and a mouth speaking
21 boastful things, and whose appearance was more powerful than the others. I
kept looking, and that horn was waging war against holy ones and prevailing
22 over them until the Ancient of Days arrived and judgment was passed in favor
of the holy ones of the Most High. And the time arrived, and holy ones took
23 possession of the kingdom. This is what he said: 'The fourth beast means
there will be a fourth kingdom in the land that will be different from all the
kingdoms. And it will devour the whole earth and will crush it and trample
24 it. And the ten horns mean that from that kingdom, ten kings will arise. Then
another will rise after them, and he will be different from the first ones, and
25 he will bring about the downfall of three kings. He will speak words against
the Most High, and he will afflict the holy ones of the Most High and plan to
change the times and the Law. They will be handed over to him for a time and
26 times, and half a time. And the court will sit in judgment and do away with
27 his dominion, devastating and destroying it to finality. And the kingship and

לַהּ רַבְרְבָן אָכְלָה וּמַדְּקָה וּשְׁאָרָא ברגליה רָפְסָה וְהִיא מְשַׁנְּיָה בְּרַגְלַהּ
ח מִן־כָּל־חֵיוָתָא דִּי קדמיה וְקַרְנַיִן עֲשַׂר לַהּ׃ מִשְׂתַּכַּל הֲוֵית בְּקַרְנַיָּא קָדָמַהּ
וַאֲלוּ קֶרֶן אָחֳרִי זְעֵירָה סִלְקָת ביניהון וּתְלָת מִן־קַרְנַיָּא קַדְמָיָתָא בֵּינֵיהֵן
אתעקרו מִן־קדמיה וַאֲלוּ עַיְנִין כְּעַיְנֵי אֲנָשָׁא בְּקַרְנָא־דָא וּפֻם מְמַלִּל אֶתְעֲקַרָה קֳדָמַהּ
ט רַבְרְבָן׃ חָזֵה הֲוֵית עַד דִּי כָרְסָוָן רְמִיו וְעַתִּיק יוֹמִין יְתִב לְבוּשֵׁהּ
כִּתְלַג חִוָּר וּשְׂעַר רֵאשֵׁהּ כַּעֲמַר נְקֵא כָּרְסְיֵהּ שְׁבִיבִין דִּי־נוּר גַּלְגִּלּוֹהִי
י נוּר דָּלִק׃ נְהַר דִּי־נוּר נָגֵד וְנָפֵק מִן־קֳדָמוֹהִי אֶלֶף אלפים יְשַׁמְּשׁוּנֵּהּ אַלְפִין
יא ורבו רבון קֳדָמוֹהִי יְקוּמוּן דִּינָא יְתִב וְסִפְרִין פְּתִיחוּ׃ חָזֵה הֲוֵית בֵּאדַיִן רִבְבָן
מִן־קָל מִלַּיָּא רַבְרְבָתָא דִּי קַרְנָא מְמַלֱּלָא חָזֵה הֲוֵית עַד דִּי קְטִילַת
יב חֵיוְתָא וְהוּבַד גִּשְׁמַהּ וִיהִיבַת לִיקֵדַת אֶשָּׁא׃ וּשְׁאָר חֵיוָתָא הֶעְדִּיו
יג שָׁלְטָנְהוֹן וְאַרְכָה בְחַיִּין יְהִיבַת לְהוֹן עַד־זְמַן וְעִדָּן׃ חָזֵה הֲוֵית בְּחֶזְוֵי
לֵילְיָא וַאֲרוּ עִם־עֲנָנֵי שְׁמַיָּא כְּבַר אֱנָשׁ אָתֵה הֲוָא וְעַד־עַתִּיק יוֹמַיָּא
יד מְטָה וּקְדָמוֹהִי הַקְרְבוּהִי׃ וְלֵהּ יְהִב שָׁלְטָן וִיקָר וּמַלְכוּ וְכֹל עַמְמַיָּא
אֻמַיָּא וְלִשָּׁנַיָּא לֵהּ יִפְלְחוּן שָׁלְטָנֵהּ שָׁלְטָן עָלַם דִּי־לָא יֶעְדֵּה וּמַלְכוּתֵהּ
טו דִּי־לָא תִתְחַבַּל׃ אֶתְכְּרִיַּת רוּחִי אֲנָה דָנִיֵּאל בְּגוֹא נִדְנֶה
טז וְחֶזְוֵי רֵאשִׁי יְבַהֲלֻנַּנִי׃ קִרְבֵת עַל־חַד מִן־קָאֲמַיָּא וְיַצִּיבָא אֶבְעֵא־מִנֵּהּ
יז עַל־כָּל־דְּנָה וַאֲמַר־לִי וּפְשַׁר מִלַּיָּא יְהוֹדְעִנַּנִי׃ אִלֵּין חֵיוָתָא רַבְרְבָתָא
יח דִּי אִנִּין אַרְבַּע אַרְבְּעָה מַלְכִין יְקוּמוּן מִן־אַרְעָא׃ וִיקַבְּלוּן מַלְכוּתָא
קַדִּישֵׁי עֶלְיוֹנִין וְיַחְסְנוּן מַלְכוּתָא עַד־עָלְמָא וְעַד עָלַם עָלְמַיָּא׃
יט אֱדַיִן צְבִית לְיַצָּבָא עַל־חֵיוְתָא רְבִיעָיְתָא דִּי־הֲוָת שָׁנְיָה מִן־כלהון כָּלְּהֵין
דְּחִילָה יַתִּירָה שניה דִּי־פַרְזֶל וטפריה דִּי־נְחָשׁ אָכְלָה מַדְּקָה וּשְׁאָרָא שִׁנַּהּ | וְטִפְרַהּ
כ ברגליה רָפְסָה׃ וְעַל־קַרְנַיָּא עֲשַׂר דִּי בְרֵאשַׁהּ וְאָחֳרִי דִּי סִלְקַת בְּרַגְלַהּ
ונפלו מִן־קדמיה תְּלָת וְקַרְנָא דִכֵּן וְעַיְנִין לַהּ וּפֻם מְמַלִּל רַבְרְבָן וְחֶזְוַהּ וּנְפַלָה | קֳדָמַהּ
כא רַב מִן־חַבְרָתַהּ׃ חָזֵה הֲוֵית וְקַרְנָא דִכֵּן עָבְדָה קְרָב עִם־קַדִּישִׁין
כב וְיָכְלָה לְהוֹן׃ עַד דִּי־אֲתָה עַתִּיק יוֹמַיָּא וְדִינָא יְהִב לְקַדִּישֵׁי עֶלְיוֹנִין
כג וְזִמְנָא מְטָה וּמַלְכוּתָא הֶחֱסִנוּ קַדִּישִׁין׃ כֵּן אֲמַר חֵיוְתָא רְבִיעָיְתָא
מלכו רביעיה תֶּהֱוֵא בְאַרְעָא דִּי תִשְׁנֵא מִן־כָּל־מַלְכְוָתָא וְתֵאכֻל רְבִיעָאָה
כד כָּל־אַרְעָא וּתְדוּשִׁנַּהּ וְתַדְּקִנַּהּ׃ וְקַרְנַיָּא עֲשַׂר מִנַּהּ מַלְכוּתָה עַשְׂרָה
מַלְכִין יְקֻמוּן וְאָחֳרָן יְקוּם אַחֲרֵיהֹן וְהוּא יִשְׁנֵא מִן־קַדְמָיֵא וּתְלָתָה
כה מַלְכִין יְהַשְׁפִּל׃ וּמִלִּין לְצַד עליא יְמַלִּל וּלְקַדִּישֵׁי עֶלְיוֹנִין יְבַלֵּא וְיִסְבַּר עִלָּאָה
כו לְהַשְׁנָיָה זִמְנִין וְדָת וְיִתְיַהֲבוּן בִּידֵהּ עַד־עִדָּן וְעִדָּנִין וּפְלַג עִדָּן׃ וְדִינָא
כז יִתִּב וְשָׁלְטָנֵהּ יְהַעְדּוֹן לְהַשְׁמָדָה וּלְהוֹבָדָה עַד־סוֹפָא׃ וּמַלְכוּתָא

the dominion and the grandeur of the kingdoms underneath all the heavens
will be given to the nation of the holy ones of the Most High. Their kingdom
28 is an eternal kingdom, and all rulers will serve and obey it.'" Here the account
concluded. I, Daniel, was very alarmed by my thoughts, and my face blanched,
but I kept the matter to myself.
8 1 In the third year[6] of the reign of King Beleshatzar, a vision came to me – I,
2 Daniel – after the one that was first shown me. I was looking at the vision
and while I watched, it was me in Shushan the imperial city, which is in the
3 province of Eilam. And I saw in the vision that I was beside the river Ulai. I
raised my eyes and saw – behold! – there was a ram standing near the river and
it had two horns. Now the horns were tall, but one was taller than the other;
4 the taller one rose up last. I saw the ram goring westward and northward
and southward, and none of the animals could withstand it and there was no
5 rescue from its power; it did whatever it pleased and grew bigger. And as I
was watching intently – behold! – a young he-goat came from the west over
the whole earth without touching the ground, and the goat had a prominent
6 horn between its eyes. The goat approached the ram with two horns that I
7 had seen standing near the river, and rushed toward it with furious force. And
I saw it reaching the ram and attacking with savage fury, and it smote the ram
and broke both of its horns. And the ram had no power to withstand it; the
he-goat threw it down to the ground, trampling it. And there was no one to
8 rescue the ram from its might. And the he-goat grew to enormity, but, at the
peak of its power, its great horn was shattered, and there arose to prominence
9 four in its place, facing the four winds of the heavens. And from one of them
there emerged one small one; it grew exceedingly great toward the south and
10 toward the east and toward the beautiful land. It grew great, up to the host of
the heavens, knocking some of the host of stars down to earth and trampling
11 upon them. It even grew to challenge the prince of the host of heaven, who
was deprived of the daily sacrifice and whose Sanctuary foundation was
12 thrown down. And the army was set against the daily sacrifice because of
13 sin. It threw truth to the ground, acting and succeeding. I heard a holy one
speaking, and another holy one said to whomever it was who was speaking,
"How long will this last, this vision of the removal of the daily sacrifice and
this sin-producing desolation and the giving over of the Sanctuary and the
14 multitudes for trampling?" He said to me, "For two thousand three hundred
15 evenings and mornings, then the Sanctuary will be made right again." While
I, Daniel, was seeing that vision, seeking understanding – behold! – standing
16 across from me was a man-like figure. I heard a human voice from between
the banks of the Ulai calling out. It said, "Gavriel, explain the vision to this
17 one." He approached where I was standing and when he came near I was
overwhelmed and fell prostrate. He said to me, "Understand, O mortal, that
18 the vision refers to the end-time." And as he was speaking to me, I fell asleep
19 as I lay prostrate on the ground. He touched me and he stood me up. He said,
"Behold, I am informing you about that which will come to be at the end of

6 | At this point the text switches from Aramaic back to Hebrew.

וְשָׁלְטָנָא וּרְבוּתָא דִּי מַלְכְוָת תְּחוֹת כָּל־שְׁמַיָּא יְהִיבַת לְעַם קַדִּישֵׁי
עֶלְיוֹנִין מַלְכוּתֵהּ מַלְכוּת עָלַם וְכֹל שָׁלְטָנַיָּא לֵהּ יִפְלְחוּן וְיִשְׁתַּמְּעוּן׃
כח עַד־כָּה סוֹפָא דִי־מִלְּתָא אֲנָה דָנִיֵּאל שַׂגִּיא ׀ רַעְיוֹנַי יְבַהֲלֻנַּנִי וְזִיוַי
יִשְׁתַּנּוֹן עֲלַי וּמִלְּתָא בְּלִבִּי נִטְרֵת׃
ח א בִּשְׁנַת שָׁלוֹשׁ לְמַלְכוּת בֵּלְאשַׁצַּר הַמֶּלֶךְ חָזוֹן נִרְאָה אֵלַי אֲנִי דָנִיֵּאל
ב אַחֲרֵי הַנִּרְאָה אֵלַי בַּתְּחִלָּה׃ וָאֶרְאֶה בֶּחָזוֹן וַיְהִי בִּרְאֹתִי וַאֲנִי בְּשׁוּשַׁן
הַבִּירָה אֲשֶׁר בְּעֵילָם הַמְּדִינָה וָאֶרְאֶה בֶּחָזוֹן וַאֲנִי הָיִיתִי עַל־אוּבַל
ג אוּלָי׃ וָאֶשָּׂא עֵינַי וָאֶרְאֶה וְהִנֵּה ׀ אַיִל אֶחָד עֹמֵד לִפְנֵי הָאֻבָל וְלוֹ
קְרָנָיִם וְהַקְּרָנַיִם גְּבֹהוֹת וְהָאַחַת גְּבֹהָה מִן־הַשֵּׁנִית וְהַגְּבֹהָה עֹלָה
ד בָּאַחֲרֹנָה׃ רָאִיתִי אֶת־הָאַיִל מְנַגֵּחַ יָמָּה וְצָפוֹנָה וָנֶגְבָּה וְכָל־חַיּוֹת
ה לֹא־יַעַמְדוּ לְפָנָיו וְאֵין מַצִּיל מִיָּדוֹ וְעָשָׂה כִרְצֹנוֹ וְהִגְדִּיל׃ וַאֲנִי ׀ הָיִיתִי
מֵבִין וְהִנֵּה צְפִיר־הָעִזִּים בָּא מִן־הַמַּעֲרָב עַל־פְּנֵי כָל־הָאָרֶץ וְאֵין נוֹגֵעַ
ו בָּאָרֶץ וְהַצָּפִיר קֶרֶן חָזוּת בֵּין עֵינָיו׃ וַיָּבֹא עַד־הָאַיִל בַּעַל הַקְּרָנַיִם
ז אֲשֶׁר רָאִיתִי עֹמֵד לִפְנֵי הָאֻבָל וַיָּרָץ אֵלָיו בַּחֲמַת כֹּחוֹ׃ וּרְאִיתִיו
מַגִּיעַ אֵצֶל הָאַיִל וַיִּתְמַרְמַר אֵלָיו וַיַּךְ אֶת־הָאַיִל וַיְשַׁבֵּר אֶת־שְׁתֵּי
קְרָנָיו וְלֹא־הָיָה כֹחַ בָּאַיִל לַעֲמֹד לְפָנָיו וַיַּשְׁלִיכֵהוּ אַרְצָה וַיִּרְמְסֵהוּ
ח וְלֹא־הָיָה מַצִּיל לָאַיִל מִיָּדוֹ׃ וּצְפִיר הָעִזִּים הִגְדִּיל עַד־מְאֹד וּכְעָצְמוֹ
נִשְׁבְּרָה הַקֶּרֶן הַגְּדוֹלָה וַתַּעֲלֶנָה חָזוּת אַרְבַּע תַּחְתֶּיהָ לְאַרְבַּע רוּחוֹת
ט הַשָּׁמָיִם׃ וּמִן־הָאַחַת מֵהֶם יָצָא קֶרֶן־אַחַת מִצְּעִירָה וַתִּגְדַּל־יֶתֶר
י אֶל־הַנֶּגֶב וְאֶל־הַמִּזְרָח וְאֶל־הַצֶּבִי׃ וַתִּגְדַּל עַד־צְבָא הַשָּׁמָיִם וַתַּפֵּל
יא אַרְצָה מִן־הַצָּבָא וּמִן־הַכּוֹכָבִים וַתִּרְמְסֵם׃ וְעַד שַׂר־הַצָּבָא הִגְדִּיל
יב וּמִמֶּנּוּ הֵרִים הַתָּמִיד וְהֻשְׁלַךְ מְכוֹן מִקְדָּשׁוֹ׃ וְצָבָא תִּנָּתֵן עַל־הַתָּמִיד הוּרַם
יג בְּפָשַׁע וְתַשְׁלֵךְ אֱמֶת אַרְצָה וְעָשְׂתָה וְהִצְלִיחָה׃ וָאֶשְׁמְעָה אֶחָד־
קָדוֹשׁ מְדַבֵּר וַיֹּאמֶר אֶחָד קָדוֹשׁ לַפַּלְמוֹנִי הַמְדַבֵּר עַד־מָתַי הֶחָזוֹן
יד הַתָּמִיד וְהַפֶּשַׁע שֹׁמֵם תֵּת וְקֹדֶשׁ וְצָבָא מִרְמָס׃ וַיֹּאמֶר אֵלַי עַד עֶרֶב
טו בֹּקֶר אַלְפַּיִם וּשְׁלֹשׁ מֵאוֹת וְנִצְדַּק קֹדֶשׁ׃ וַיְהִי בִּרְאֹתִי אֲנִי דָנִיֵּאל
טז אֶת־הֶחָזוֹן וָאֲבַקְשָׁה בִינָה וְהִנֵּה עֹמֵד לְנֶגְדִּי כְּמַרְאֵה־גָבֶר׃ וָאֶשְׁמַע
קוֹל־אָדָם בֵּין אוּלָי וַיִּקְרָא וַיֹּאמַר גַּבְרִיאֵל הָבֵן לְהַלָּז אֶת־הַמַּרְאֶה׃
יז וַיָּבֹא אֵצֶל עָמְדִי וּבְבֹאוֹ נִבְעַתִּי וָאֶפְּלָה עַל־פָּנָי וַיֹּאמֶר אֵלַי הָבֵן בֶּן־
יח אָדָם כִּי לְעֶת־קֵץ הֶחָזוֹן׃ וּבְדַבְּרוֹ עִמִּי נִרְדַּמְתִּי עַל־פָּנַי אָרְצָה וַיִּגַּע־בִּי
יט וַיַּעֲמִידֵנִי עַל־עָמְדִי׃ וַיֹּאמֶר הִנְנִי מוֹדִיעֲךָ אֵת אֲשֶׁר־יִהְיֶה בְּאַחֲרִית

20 the time of wrath, for that period has an end. The two-horned ram that you
21 saw represents the kings of Media and Persia. The he-goat symbolizes the
22 king of Ionia,[7] and the large horn between its eyes is the first king. And that
broken horn and the four that rose in its place signify four kingdoms that will
23 issue from that nation, but not one of them with its strength. And at the end
of their reign, when the sinners have reached full measure, there will arise a
24 fierce-faced king, one who is skilled at intrigue. His power will grow strong,
though not by his own might; he will bring about amazing ruin and succeed
in his activity. He will devastate powerful peoples and the nation of holy ones.
25 He will succeed by his cunning, with deceit in his hand. He will boast in his
heart and destroy many by stealth. But when he stands against the prince of
26 princes he will be broken without a human hand being raised. The vision of
the evenings and the mornings that has been told is true. And as for you, keep
27 the vision undisclosed, for it is far in the future." And I, Daniel, became weak
and was ill for days. Then I arose and dealt with the king's affairs, but I was in
shock over the vision and not understanding it.

9 1 It was the first year of Daryavesh son of Aḥashverosh, of Median stock, who
2 was made king over the kingdom of the Chaldeans. In year one of his reign,
I, Daniel, studied the books concerning the number of years that the Lord
told Yirmeya the prophet it would take to fulfill the desolation of Jerusalem:
3 seventy years.[8] I turned my face unto the Lord God to petition Him with
4 prayer and entreaties, with fasting, sackcloth, and ashes. I prayed to the Lord
my God and I confessed, saying, "O Lord, the great and awesome God, who
keeps the covenant and the love with those who love Him and keep His
5 commandments. We have sinned, offended, done evil, and rebelled, straying
6 from Your commandments and Your laws. We did not obey Your servants,
the prophets, who spoke in Your name to our kings, our princes, and our
7 fathers and to all the people of the land. Justice is Yours, O Lord, and ours is
shamefacedness, even unto this day, for the men of Yehuda, the inhabitants
of Jerusalem and all of Israel, near and far, in all the lands to which You have
8 scattered them, because of the treachery with which they betrayed You. Lord!
Shamefacedness is ours, belonging to our kings, our princes, and our fathers
9 because we have sinned against You. To the Lord our God belong mercy and
10 pardon, even though we have rebelled against Him and did not heed the voice
of our Lord God to walk according to His teachings which He set before us
11 through His servants, the prophets. And all of Israel transgressed against Your
Law and turned away, not heeding Your voice; the curse of breaking the oath
that was written in the teaching of Moshe, servant of God, was poured out
12 upon us because we sinned against Him. He fulfilled His word, that which
He had spoken regarding us and our judges who judged us, to bring upon us
a great evil the likes of which has never been done beneath all the heavens as
13 it was done in Jerusalem. Just as is written in the teaching of Moshe, all this

7 | Ionia was a region in Asia Minor inhabitant by Hellenic (Greek-speaking) peoples; the name Yavan eventually came to refer in Hebrew to the Greek lands and peoples in general.

8 | See Jeremiah 25:11–12, 29:10.

כ הזעם כי למועד קץ: האיל אשר־ראית בעל הקרנים מלכי מדי
כא ופרס: והצפיר השעיר מלך יון והקרן הגדולה אשר בין־עיניו הוא
כב המלך הראשון: והנשברת ותעמדנה ארבע תחתיה ארבע מלכיות
כג מגוי יעמדנה ולא בכחו: ובאחרית מלכותם כהתם הפשעים יעמד
כד מלך עז־פנים ומבין חידות: ועצם כחו ולא בכחו ונפלאות ישחית
כה והצליח ועשה והשחית עצומים ועם־קדשים: ועל־שכלו והצליח
מרמה בידו ובלבבו יגדיל ובשלוה ישחית רבים ועל שר־שרים
כו יעמד ובאפס יד ישבר: ומראה הערב והבקר אשר נאמר אמת
כז הוא ואתה סתם החזון כי לימים רבים: ואני דניאל נהייתי ונחליתי
ימים ואקום ואעשה את־מלאכת המלך ואשתומם על־המראה
ואין מבין:

ט א בשנת אחת לדריוש בן־אחשורוש מזרע מדי אשר המלך על
ב מלכות כשדים: בשנת אחת למלכו אני דניאל בינתי בספרים
מספר השנים אשר היה דבר־יהוה אל־ירמיה הנביא למלאות
ג לחרבות ירושלם שבעים שנה: ואתנה את־פני אל־אדני האלהים
ד לבקש תפלה ותחנונים בצום ושק ואפר: ואתפללה ליהוה אלהי ו
ואתודה ואמרה אנא אדני האל הגדול והנורא שמר הברית והחסד
ה לאהביו ולשמרי מצותיו: חטאנו ועוינו והרשענו ומרדנו וסור הרשענו
ו ממצותך וממשפטיך: ולא שמענו אל־עבדיך הנביאים אשר דברו
ז בשמך אל־מלכינו שרינו ואבתינו ואל כל־עם הארץ: לך אדני
הצדקה ולנו בשת הפנים כיום הזה לאיש יהודה ולישבי ירושלם
ולכל־ישראל הקרבים והרחקים בכל־הארצות אשר הדחתם שם
ח במעלם אשר מעלו־בך: יהוה לנו בשת הפנים למלכינו לשרינו
ט ולאבתינו אשר חטאנו לך: לאדני אלהינו הרחמים והסלחות כי
י מרדנו בו: ולא שמענו בקול יהוה אלהינו ללכת בתורתיו אשר נתן
יא לפנינו ביד עבדיו הנביאים: וכל־ישראל עברו את־תורתך וסור
לבלתי שמוע בקלך ותתך עלינו האלה והשבעה אשר כתובה
יב בתורת משה עבד־האלהים כי חטאנו לו: ויקם את־דבריו | אשר־ דברו
דבר עלינו ועל־שפטינו אשר שפטונו להביא עלינו רעה גדלה
אשר לא־נעשתה תחת כל־השמים כאשר נעשתה בירושלם:
יג כאשר כתוב בתורת משה את כל־הרעה הזאת באה עלינו ולא־

evil came upon us, and we did not seek to appease the Lord our God by
14 turning back from our sins and seeking to know Your truth. The Lord kept
watch over the evil and brought it upon us, for the Lord our God is just in
15 all His deeds that He has done, for we did not listen to His voice. And now,
O Lord our God, who took Your people out of the land of Egypt with mighty
power and have made a name for Yourself to this day – we have sinned; we have
16 behaved wickedly. Lord! In keeping with Your just acts, let Your anger and Your
fury be turned away from Your city Jerusalem, Your holy mountain. For due
to our sins and the transgressions of our fathers, Jerusalem and Your people
17 have become a disgrace to all around us. And now, let our God listen to the
prayer of Your servant and to his entreaties, and let Your face shine upon Your
18 desolate Temple, for the Lord's sake. Incline your ear, O my God, and listen;
open Your eyes to see our ruins and the city which is called by Your name, for
we are not relying on our righteousness in our entreaties to You, but on Your
19 great mercy. Lord, hear! Lord, forgive! Lord, pay attention and act! Do not
delay! For Your sake, O my God, because Your city and Your people are called
20 by Your name." And I was still speaking and praying and confessing my sin and
the sin of my people Israel and pouring out my entreaty before the Lord my
21 God about my God's holy mountain. And I was still speaking my prayer when
the man Gavriel, whom I had seen at the start of the vision, approached me,
22 soaring in flight at the time of the evening offering. He gave me understanding
as he instructed me, saying, "Daniel, I have now come forth to teach you
23 understanding. At the very start of your entreaties, a word came forth, and I
have come to tell it because you are beloved. Understand the word, and grasp
24 the meaning of the vision. Seventy cycles of a week of years are decreed upon
your people and on your holy city to complete the transgressions, to finish the
sins and to atone for iniquity, and to bring everlasting justice, to validate the
25 vision and the prophet, and to anoint a holy of holies. You must know and be
aware of this: from the utterance of the word to restore and build Jerusalem
until there is an anointed leader will be seven cycles of seven years, and during
sixty-two cycles of seven years it will be rebuilt with a plaza and a moat, albeit
26 in times of distress. And after the sixty-two cycles of seven years the anointed
one will disappear; there will be none, and the army of the next ruler will
destroy the city and the Sanctuary. But his end will be in a flood, and until the
27 end of the decreed war there will be desolations. He will make a strong alliance
with the multitude for one seven-year cycle, then for half of a seven-year cycle
he will ban sacrifices and grain offerings; and on the place they were brought
will be desolating abominations until the annihilation ordained is poured out
upon the desolator."
10 1 In the third year of Koresh, king of Persia, a word was revealed to Daniel, who
had been named Belteshatzar. And the word was certain to come true and
involved a great army. He understood the word and gained understanding
2 3 from his vision. In those days, I, Daniel, was mourning for three full weeks. I
did not eat baked delicacies, neither meat nor wine entered my mouth, and I
did not anoint myself with oil until the completion of three full weeks.

חִלִּינוּ אֶת־פְּנֵי ׀ יְהוָה אֱלֹהֵינוּ לָשׁוּב מֵעֲוֺנֵנוּ וּלְהַשְׂכִּיל בַּאֲמִתֶּךָ׃
יד וַיִּשְׁקֹד יְהוָה עַל־הָרָעָה וַיְבִיאֶהָ עָלֵינוּ כִּי־צַדִּיק יְהוָה אֱלֹהֵינוּ עַל־
טו כָּל־מַעֲשָׂיו אֲשֶׁר עָשָׂה וְלֹא שָׁמַעְנוּ בְּקֹלוֹ׃ וְעַתָּה ׀ אֲדֹנָי אֱלֹהֵינוּ אֲשֶׁר
הוֹצֵאתָ אֶת־עַמְּךָ מֵאֶרֶץ מִצְרַיִם בְּיָד חֲזָקָה וַתַּעַשׂ־לְךָ שֵׁם כַּיּוֹם הַזֶּה
טז חָטָאנוּ רָשָׁעְנוּ׃ אֲדֹנָי כְּכָל־צִדְקֹתֶךָ יָשָׁב־נָא אַפְּךָ וַחֲמָתְךָ מֵעִירְךָ
יְרוּשָׁלִַם הַר־קָדְשֶׁךָ כִּי בַחֲטָאֵינוּ וּבַעֲוֺנוֹת אֲבֹתֵינוּ יְרוּשָׁלִַם וְעַמְּךָ
יז לְחֶרְפָּה לְכָל־סְבִיבֹתֵינוּ׃ וְעַתָּה ׀ שְׁמַע אֱלֹהֵינוּ אֶל־תְּפִלַּת עַבְדְּךָ
יח וְאֶל־תַּחֲנוּנָיו וְהָאֵר פָּנֶיךָ עַל־מִקְדָּשְׁךָ הַשָּׁמֵם לְמַעַן אֲדֹנָי׃ הַטֵּה
אֱלֹהַי ׀ אָזְנְךָ וּשְׁמָע פקחה עֵינֶיךָ וּרְאֵה שֹׁמְמֹתֵינוּ וְהָעִיר אֲשֶׁר־נִקְרָא פְּקַח
שִׁמְךָ עָלֶיהָ כִּי ׀ לֹא עַל־צִדְקֹתֵינוּ אֲנַחְנוּ מַפִּילִים תַּחֲנוּנֵינוּ לְפָנֶיךָ
יט כִּי עַל־רַחֲמֶיךָ הָרַבִּים׃ אֲדֹנָי ׀ שְׁמָעָה אֲדֹנָי ׀ סְלָחָה אֲדֹנָי הַקֲשִׁיבָה
וַעֲשֵׂה אַל־תְּאַחַר לְמַעַנְךָ אֱלֹהַי כִּי־שִׁמְךָ נִקְרָא עַל־עִירְךָ וְעַל־עַמֶּךָ׃
כ וְעוֹד אֲנִי מְדַבֵּר וּמִתְפַּלֵּל וּמִתְוַדֶּה חַטָּאתִי וְחַטַּאת עַמִּי יִשְׂרָאֵל
כא וּמַפִּיל תְּחִנָּתִי לִפְנֵי יְהוָה אֱלֹהַי עַל הַר־קֹדֶשׁ אֱלֹהָי׃ וְעוֹד אֲנִי מְדַבֵּר
בַּתְּפִלָּה וְהָאִישׁ גַּבְרִיאֵל אֲשֶׁר רָאִיתִי בֶחָזוֹן בַּתְּחִלָּה מֻעָף בִּיעָף נֹגֵעַ
כב אֵלַי כְּעֵת מִנְחַת־עָרֶב׃ וַיָּבֶן וַיְדַבֵּר עִמִּי וַיֹּאמַר דָּנִיֵּאל עַתָּה יָצָאתִי
כג לְהַשְׂכִּילְךָ בִינָה׃ בִּתְחִלַּת תַּחֲנוּנֶיךָ יָצָא דָבָר וַאֲנִי בָּאתִי לְהַגִּיד כִּי
כד חֲמוּדוֹת אָתָּה וּבִין בַּדָּבָר וְהָבֵן בַּמַּרְאֶה׃ שָׁבֻעִים שִׁבְעִים נֶחְתַּךְ
עַל־עַמְּךָ ׀ וְעַל־עִיר קָדְשֶׁךָ לְכַלֵּא הַפֶּשַׁע ולחתם חטאות וּלְכַפֵּר וּלְהָתֵם חַטָּאת
עָוֺן וּלְהָבִיא צֶדֶק עֹלָמִים וְלַחְתֹּם חָזוֹן וְנָבִיא וְלִמְשֹׁחַ קֹדֶשׁ קָדָשִׁים׃
כה וְתֵדַע וְתַשְׂכֵּל מִן־מֹצָא דָבָר לְהָשִׁיב וְלִבְנוֹת יְרוּשָׁלִַם עַד־מָשִׁיחַ
נָגִיד שָׁבֻעִים שִׁבְעָה וְשָׁבֻעִים שִׁשִּׁים וּשְׁנַיִם תָּשׁוּב וְנִבְנְתָה רְחוֹב
כו וְחָרוּץ וּבְצוֹק הָעִתִּים׃ וְאַחֲרֵי הַשָּׁבֻעִים שִׁשִּׁים וּשְׁנַיִם יִכָּרֵת מָשִׁיחַ
וְאֵין לוֹ וְהָעִיר וְהַקֹּדֶשׁ יַשְׁחִית עַם נָגִיד הַבָּא וְקִצּוֹ בַשֶּׁטֶף וְעַד קֵץ
כז מִלְחָמָה נֶחֱרֶצֶת שֹׁמֵמוֹת׃ וְהִגְבִּיר בְּרִית לָרַבִּים שָׁבוּעַ אֶחָד וַחֲצִי
הַשָּׁבוּעַ יַשְׁבִּית ׀ זֶבַח וּמִנְחָה וְעַל כְּנַף שִׁקּוּצִים מְשֹׁמֵם וְעַד־כָּלָה
וְנֶחֱרָצָה תִּתַּךְ עַל־שֹׁמֵם׃
י א בִּשְׁנַת שָׁלוֹשׁ לְכוֹרֶשׁ מֶלֶךְ פָּרַס דָּבָר נִגְלָה לְדָנִיֵּאל אֲשֶׁר־נִקְרָא
שְׁמוֹ בֵּלְטְשַׁאצַּר וֶאֱמֶת הַדָּבָר וְצָבָא גָדוֹל וּבִין אֶת־הַדָּבָר וּבִינָה
ב לוֹ בַּמַּרְאֶה׃ בַּיָּמִים הָהֵם אֲנִי דָנִיֵּאל הָיִיתִי מִתְאַבֵּל שְׁלֹשָׁה שָׁבֻעִים
ג יָמִים׃ לֶחֶם חֲמֻדוֹת לֹא אָכַלְתִּי וּבָשָׂר וָיַיִן לֹא־בָא אֶל־פִּי וְסוֹךְ לֹא־
סָכְתִּי עַד־מְלֹאת שְׁלֹשֶׁת שָׁבֻעִים יָמִים׃

4 And it was the twenty-fourth day of the first month, and I was standing
5 alongside the great river, the Tigris. I raised my eyes and looked, and –
behold! – there was a man dressed in linen, and his waist was belted with fine
6 gold. And his torso was like aquamarine, and his face shone like lightning,
and his eyes were like fiery torches, and his arms and legs were like burnished
7 bronze, and the sound of his speech was like the sound of a multitude. And
only I, Daniel, saw this vision; and the people who were with me did not see
8 the vision, but a great terror fell over them, and they ran away to hide; and I
alone remained. And I looked at this great vision, and there was no strength
9 left in me; and my smile turned into ugliness, and I became powerless. I heard
the sound of his words, and while I listened to the sound of his words, I was
10 in a dream state, prostrate, my face to the ground. And – behold! – a hand
11 touched me and rocked me onto my knees and the palms of my hands. He
said to me, "Daniel, beloved man, understand the words that I am speaking
to you and stand up in place, for I have been sent to you now." And when he
12 said this to me I stood up trembling. He said to me, "Do not be afraid, Daniel,
for from the first day you set your heart on understanding and humbling
yourself before your God your words have been heard, so I came in response
13 to your words, but the prince of the kingdom of Persia stood opposing me
for twenty-one days, and then Mikhael, one of the chief princes, came to help
14 me after I had remained there with the kings of Persia. And I have come to
help you understand what will happen to your people in the end of days, for
15 there is another vision for those days." And as he spoke the words to me, I
16 turned my face to the ground and became dumb. And – behold! – something
like a human form was touching my lips, and I opened my mouth and spoke,
and I said to the one standing in front of me, "My lord, during the vision I
17 was seized by sudden pain, and I became powerless. And how is this servant
of my lord able to speak with you, my lord? As for me, from now on I have
18 no strength to sustain me, and no breath is left in me." The man-like one
19 touched me again and strengthened me. He said, "Do not be afraid, beloved
man, you are safe; grow stronger and stronger." And as he spoke to me I did
become stronger, and I said, "Let my lord speak, for you have strengthened
20 me." He said, "Do you know why I came to you? And now I must return to
fight with the prince of Persia, and when I leave, the prince of Ionia will
21 arrive. Nonetheless, I shall tell you what is written in the book of truth, and
there is no one who supports me against these except for Mikhael, your
11 1 prince, and I, in the first year of Daryavesh the Mede, was serving
2 as his strengthener and his refuge. And now I will tell you the truth: There
are three more kings in line to rule Persia, and the fourth will accumulate the
most wealth of all; and, empowered by his riches, he will stir up everyone
3 against the kingdom of Ionia. A mighty king will arise and rule a vast domain,
4 accomplishing whatever he desires. But when he reaches full stature, his
kingdom will be shattered and scattered to the four winds of heaven. It
will not belong to his descendants, nor will it be comparable to his vast
domain, for his kingdom will be torn apart and belong to others, not to them.

ד וּבְיוֹם עֶשְׂרִים וְאַרְבָּעָה לַחֹדֶשׁ הָרִאשׁוֹן וַאֲנִי הָיִיתִי עַל־יַד הַנָּהָר
ה הַגָּדוֹל הוּא חִדָּקֶל: וָאֶשָּׂא אֶת־עֵינַי וָאֵרֶא וְהִנֵּה אִישׁ־אֶחָד לָבוּשׁ
ו בַּדִּים וּמָתְנָיו חֲגֻרִים בְּכֶתֶם אוּפָז: וּגְוִיָּתוֹ כְתַרְשִׁישׁ וּפָנָיו כְּמַרְאֵה
בָרָק וְעֵינָיו כְּלַפִּידֵי אֵשׁ וּזְרֹעֹתָיו וּמַרְגְּלֹתָיו כְּעֵין נְחֹשֶׁת קָלָל וְקוֹל
ז דְּבָרָיו כְּקוֹל הָמוֹן: וְרָאִיתִי אֲנִי דָנִיֵּאל לְבַדִּי אֶת־הַמַּרְאָה וְהָאֲנָשִׁים
אֲשֶׁר הָיוּ עִמִּי לֹא רָאוּ אֶת־הַמַּרְאָה אֲבָל חֲרָדָה גְדֹלָה נָפְלָה עֲלֵיהֶם
ח וַיִּבְרְחוּ בְּהֵחָבֵא: וַאֲנִי נִשְׁאַרְתִּי לְבַדִּי וָאֶרְאֶה אֶת־הַמַּרְאָה הַגְּדֹלָה
הַזֹּאת וְלֹא נִשְׁאַר־בִּי כֹּחַ וְהוֹדִי נֶהְפַּךְ עָלַי לְמַשְׁחִית וְלֹא עָצַרְתִּי כֹּחַ:
ט וָאֶשְׁמַע אֶת־קוֹל דְּבָרָיו וּכְשָׁמְעִי אֶת־קוֹל דְּבָרָיו וַאֲנִי הָיִיתִי נִרְדָּם
י עַל־פָּנַי וּפָנַי אָרְצָה: וְהִנֵּה־יָד נָגְעָה בִּי וַתְּנִיעֵנִי עַל־בִּרְכַּי וְכַפּוֹת יָדָי:
יא וַיֹּאמֶר אֵלַי דָּנִיֵּאל אִישׁ־חֲמֻדוֹת הָבֵן בַּדְּבָרִים אֲשֶׁר אָנֹכִי דֹּבֵר אֵלֶיךָ
וַעֲמֹד עַל־עָמְדֶךָ כִּי עַתָּה שֻׁלַּחְתִּי אֵלֶיךָ וּבְדַבְּרוֹ עִמִּי אֶת־הַדָּבָר הַזֶּה
יב עָמַדְתִּי מַרְעִיד: וַיֹּאמֶר אֵלַי אַל־תִּירָא דָנִיֵּאל כִּי | מִן־הַיּוֹם הָרִאשׁוֹן
אֲשֶׁר נָתַתָּ אֶת־לִבְּךָ לְהָבִין וּלְהִתְעַנּוֹת לִפְנֵי אֱלֹהֶיךָ נִשְׁמְעוּ דְבָרֶיךָ
יג וַאֲנִי בָאתִי בִּדְבָרֶיךָ: וְשַׂר | מַלְכוּת פָּרַס עֹמֵד לְנֶגְדִּי עֶשְׂרִים וְאֶחָד
יוֹם וְהִנֵּה מִיכָאֵל אַחַד הַשָּׂרִים הָרִאשֹׁנִים בָּא לְעָזְרֵנִי וַאֲנִי נוֹתַרְתִּי
יד שָׁם אֵצֶל מַלְכֵי פָרָס: וּבָאתִי לַהֲבִינְךָ אֵת אֲשֶׁר־יִקְרָה לְעַמְּךָ בְּאַחֲרִית
טו הַיָּמִים כִּי־עוֹד חָזוֹן לַיָּמִים: וּבְדַבְּרוֹ עִמִּי כַּדְּבָרִים הָאֵלֶּה נָתַתִּי פָנַי
טז אַרְצָה וְנֶאֱלָמְתִּי: וְהִנֵּה כִּדְמוּת בְּנֵי אָדָם נֹגֵעַ עַל־שְׂפָתָי וָאֶפְתַּח־פִּי
וָאֲדַבְּרָה וָאֹמְרָה אֶל־הָעֹמֵד לְנֶגְדִּי אֲדֹנִי בַּמַּרְאָה נֶהֶפְכוּ צִירַי עָלַי
יז וְלֹא עָצַרְתִּי כֹּחַ: וְהֵיךְ יוּכַל עֶבֶד אֲדֹנִי זֶה לְדַבֵּר עִם־אֲדֹנִי זֶה וַאֲנִי
יח מֵעַתָּה לֹא־יַעֲמָד־בִּי כֹחַ וּנְשָׁמָה לֹא נִשְׁאֲרָה־בִי: וַיֹּסֶף וַיִּגַּע־בִּי כְּמַרְאֵה
יט אָדָם וַיְחַזְּקֵנִי: וַיֹּאמֶר אַל־תִּירָא אִישׁ־חֲמֻדוֹת שָׁלוֹם לָךְ חֲזַק וַחֲזָק
כ וּכְדַבְּרוֹ עִמִּי הִתְחַזַּקְתִּי וָאֹמְרָה יְדַבֵּר אֲדֹנִי כִּי חִזַּקְתָּנִי: וַיֹּאמֶר הֲיָדַעְתָּ
לָמָּה־בָּאתִי אֵלֶיךָ וְעַתָּה אָשׁוּב לְהִלָּחֵם עִם־שַׂר פָּרָס וַאֲנִי יוֹצֵא וְהִנֵּה
כא שַׂר־יָוָן בָּא: אֲבָל אַגִּיד לְךָ אֶת־הָרָשׁוּם בִּכְתָב אֱמֶת וְאֵין אֶחָד ז
יא א מִתְחַזֵּק עִמִּי עַל־אֵלֶּה כִּי אִם־מִיכָאֵל שַׂרְכֶם: וַאֲנִי בִּשְׁנַת
ב אַחַת לְדָרְיָוֶשׁ הַמָּדִי עָמְדִי לְמַחֲזִיק וּלְמָעוֹז לוֹ: וְעַתָּה אֱמֶת אַגִּיד
לָךְ הִנֵּה־עוֹד שְׁלֹשָׁה מְלָכִים עֹמְדִים לְפָרַס וְהָרְבִיעִי יַעֲשִׁיר עֹשֶׁר־
ג גָּדוֹל מִכֹּל וּכְחֶזְקָתוֹ בְעָשְׁרוֹ יָעִיר הַכֹּל אֵת מַלְכוּת יָוָן: וְעָמַד מֶלֶךְ
ד גִּבּוֹר וּמָשַׁל מִמְשָׁל רַב וְעָשָׂה כִּרְצוֹנוֹ: וּכְעָמְדוֹ תִּשָּׁבֵר מַלְכוּתוֹ וְתֵחָץ
לְאַרְבַּע רוּחוֹת הַשָּׁמָיִם וְלֹא לְאַחֲרִיתוֹ וְלֹא כְמָשְׁלוֹ אֲשֶׁר מָשָׁל כִּי

5 The king of the south will become strong, but one of his princes will be
6 stronger than he and govern a great domain. After a number of years they will
become allies, and the daughter of the king of the south will come to the king
of the north to manifest their peacemaking through marriage, but she will not
retain her military power, nor shall her father's power and army suffice, but
she shall be given over to death along with those who brought her and him
7 who begot her and strengthened her in those times. But from a sprouting of
her roots one will rise in his place. He will fight against the army and will enter
the fortress city of the king of the north and will act against them and prevail.
8 And he will also take captive their gods, with their molten images and their
precious vessels of silver and gold, bringing them to Egypt. Then he will leave
9 the king of the north alone for years. The king of the north will invade the
10 kingdom of the king of the south but then return to his own land. But his sons
will become stirred up and assemble a multitude of mighty forces. He will
penetrate, invading, sweeping through and passing beyond. Then he will turn
around, stirred up to attack again, until he reaches the fortress of the king of
11 the south. The king of the south will become bitterly angry and come forth
to make war with him, with the king of the north. The king of the south will
assemble a great multitude, and the multitude of the king of the north will be
12 given over to him. And as the multitude of captives are carried away, his heart
will become haughty. He will fell tens of thousands, but his triumph will not
13 last. For the king of the north shall again raise a multitude even greater than
the first and after a number of years will penetrate and invade with an
14 enormous army and plentiful supplies. And in those times, many will stand
against the king of the south. And renegade sons of your people will exalt
15 themselves to give substance to a vision and fail. And the king of the north
shall invade and pour out mounds of earthen siege works to capture a
reinforced city. And the forces of the south will not withstand the attack, not
16 even his elite troops, for they will have no strength to withstand it. And the
one who invaded it will do as he wishes, and no one will stand against him.
17 He will rule the land of beauty by his power of destruction. First he will be
determined to invade with the force of his whole kingdom, then he will act
as if he is behaving peacefully, and he will give him the daughter of one of his
wives to destroy the kingdom. But this plot will not succeed, and the kingdom
18 of the south will not become his. Then he will aim himself against the islands,
and capture many of them, but a military chief will put a stop to his insult,
19 returning insult to him. He will then turn back toward the fortresses of his
20 own land, but he will stumble and fall and never be found. And in his place
there will arise a person who transfers there a collector of tax for the splendor
of the kingdom, but within a few days he will be broken, and not in anger, nor
21 in war. And there will arise in his place a despicable person to whom royal
splendor was not given. He will come in peaceably but will seize the kingdom
22 with deceitful trickery. Armed forces will be swept away before him and
23 broken, even the prince of the covenant. And from the moment of forming
an alliance he will act deceitfully and will attack and overpower the ally with

ה תִּנָּתֵשׁ מַלְכוּתוֹ וְלַאֲחֵרִים מִלְּבַד־אֵלֶּה: וְיֶחֱזַק מֶלֶךְ־הַנֶּגֶב וּמִן־שָׂרָיו
ו וְיֶחֱזַק עָלָיו וּמָשָׁל מִמְשָׁל רַב מֶמְשַׁלְתּוֹ: וּלְקֵץ שָׁנִים יִתְחַבָּרוּ וּבַת
מֶלֶךְ־הַנֶּגֶב תָּבוֹא אֶל־מֶלֶךְ הַצָּפוֹן לַעֲשׂוֹת מֵישָׁרִים וְלֹא־תַעְצֹר כּוֹחַ
הַזְּרוֹעַ וְלֹא יַעֲמֹד וּזְרֹעוֹ וְתִנָּתֵן הִיא וּמְבִיאֶיהָ וְהַיֹּלְדָהּ וּמַחֲזִקָהּ
ז בָּעִתִּים: וְעָמַד מִנֵּצֶר שָׁרָשֶׁיהָ כַּנּוֹ וְיָבֹא אֶל־הַחַיִל וְיָבֹא בְּמָעוֹז מֶלֶךְ
ח הַצָּפוֹן וְעָשָׂה בָהֶם וְהֶחֱזִיק: וְגַם אֱלֹהֵיהֶם עִם־נְסִכֵיהֶם עִם־כְּלֵי
חֶמְדָּתָם כֶּסֶף וְזָהָב בַּשְּׁבִי יָבִא מִצְרָיִם וְהוּא שָׁנִים יַעֲמֹד מִמֶּלֶךְ
ט י הַצָּפוֹן: וּבָא בְּמַלְכוּת מֶלֶךְ הַנֶּגֶב וְשָׁב אֶל־אַדְמָתוֹ: וּבָנָו יִתְגָּרוּ וְאָסְפוּ
הֲמוֹן חֲיָלִים רַבִּים וּבָא בוֹא וְשָׁטַף וְעָבָר וְיָשֹׁב ויתגרו עַד־מָעֻזֹּה: וְיִתְגָּרֶה
יא וְיִתְמַרְמַר מֶלֶךְ הַנֶּגֶב וְיָצָא וְנִלְחַם עִמּוֹ עִם־מֶלֶךְ הַצָּפוֹן וְהֶעֱמִיד
יב הָמוֹן רָב וְנִתַּן הֶהָמוֹן בְּיָדוֹ: וְנִשָּׂא הֶהָמוֹן ירום לְבָבוֹ וְהִפִּיל רִבֹּאוֹת וְרָם
יג וְלֹא יָעוֹז: וְשָׁב מֶלֶךְ הַצָּפוֹן וְהֶעֱמִיד הָמוֹן רַב מִן־הָרִאשׁוֹן וּלְקֵץ
יד הָעִתִּים שָׁנִים יָבוֹא בוֹא בְּחַיִל גָּדוֹל וּבִרְכוּשׁ רָב: וּבָעִתִּים הָהֵם
רַבִּים יַעַמְדוּ עַל־מֶלֶךְ הַנֶּגֶב וּבְנֵי ׀ פָּרִיצֵי עַמְּךָ יִנַּשְּׂאוּ לְהַעֲמִיד חָזוֹן
טו וְנִכְשָׁלוּ: וְיָבֹא מֶלֶךְ הַצָּפוֹן וְיִשְׁפֹּךְ סוֹלְלָה וְלָכַד עִיר מִבְצָרוֹת וּזְרֹעוֹת
טז הַנֶּגֶב לֹא יַעֲמֹדוּ וְעַם מִבְחָרָיו וְאֵין כֹּחַ לַעֲמֹד: וְיַעַשׂ הַבָּא אֵלָיו
יז כִּרְצוֹנוֹ וְאֵין עוֹמֵד לְפָנָיו וְיַעֲמֹד בְּאֶרֶץ־הַצְּבִי וְכָלָה בְיָדוֹ: וְיָשֵׂם ׀ פָּנָיו
לָבוֹא בְּתֹקֶף כָּל־מַלְכוּתוֹ וִישָׁרִים עִמּוֹ וְעָשָׂה וּבַת הַנָּשִׁים יִתֶּן־
יח לוֹ לְהַשְׁחִיתָהּ וְלֹא תַעֲמֹד וְלֹא־לוֹ תִהְיֶה: וישב ׀ פָּנָיו לְאִיִּים וְלָכַד וְיָשֵׂם
יט רַבִּים וְהִשְׁבִּית קָצִין חֶרְפָּתוֹ לוֹ בִּלְתִּי חֶרְפָּתוֹ יָשִׁיב לוֹ: וְיָשֵׁב פָּנָיו
כ לְמָעוּזֵּי אַרְצוֹ וְנִכְשַׁל וְנָפַל וְלֹא יִמָּצֵא: וְעָמַד עַל־כַּנּוֹ מַעֲבִיר נוֹגֵשׂ
הֶדֶר מַלְכוּת וּבְיָמִים אֲחָדִים יִשָּׁבֵר וְלֹא בְאַפַּיִם וְלֹא בְמִלְחָמָה:
כא וְעָמַד עַל־כַּנּוֹ נִבְזֶה וְלֹא־נָתְנוּ עָלָיו הוֹד מַלְכוּת וּבָא בְשַׁלְוָה וְהֶחֱזִיק
כב מַלְכוּת בַּחֲלַקְלַקּוֹת: וּזְרֹעוֹת הַשֶּׁטֶף יִשָּׁטְפוּ מִלְּפָנָיו וְיִשָּׁבֵרוּ וְגַם נְגִיד
כג בְּרִית: וּמִן־הִתְחַבְּרוּת אֵלָיו יַעֲשֶׂה מִרְמָה וְעָלָה וְעָצַם בִּמְעַט־גּוֹי:

24 a small party. He will peaceably enter even the prosperous places in the
province and do that which his fathers never did, nor his grandfathers: he will
distribute spoils, booty, and riches to them. And he will devise plots against
25 strongholds for another time. And he will summon his might and his courage
against the king of the south with a great army. And the king of the south will
be roused to war with a great and exceedingly powerful army, but he will not
26 endure because plots will be devised against him. Those who eat bread from
his table will destroy him, and his army will be swept away and many shall fall
27 slain. And both of these kings' hearts will be oriented toward evil; they will
sit at one table and exchange lies, but it will not succeed, because it is not yet
28 the appointed end-time. Then he will return to his land with great riches and
his heart set against the holy covenant. He will accomplish what he wants,
29 then return to his own land. At the appointed time, he will return and come
to the south, but it will not be the same at the latter time as it was in the former.
30 When the ships of Kitim come at him, he will lose heart and retreat and rage
against the holy covenant. And he will act: he will turn to and ally with those
31 who have forsaken the holy covenant. Armed forces will rise at his command;
they will desecrate the Sanctuary stronghold, and abolish the daily sacrifice,
32 and set up the desolating abomination. And those who act wickedly against
the covenant he will seduce by flatteries, but the people who know their God
33 will be strong and act. The nation's wise ones will instruct many, though for
34 a time they will fall by the sword, by flame, by captivity, by plunder. And when
they fall, only a few will help them, but many will join them with deceitful
35 trickery. And of the wise ones, some will fall, in order to refine, cleanse, and
36 purify them until the end-time, which is still appointed to come. And the king
will do as he pleases, exalting himself and making himself greater than any
god. He will utter astonishing things against the God of gods. He will prosper
37 until the fury is complete, for that which is determined must take place. He
will have no regard for the gods of his ancestors or for the one in whom
women delight. He will have no regard for any god because he will make
38 himself greater than all. Instead, he will honor the god of strongholds. A god
whom his fathers did not know will he honor with gold, silver, precious
39 stones, and treasured things. And he will build cities for defense of the
strongholds, each with images of his god. He will provide abundant honor to
those who will acknowledge him; he will appoint them as rulers over the
40 many and distribute land for a price. And at the end-time, the king of the
south will try to lock horns with him, but the king of the north will storm
over him with chariots and with horsemen and with many ships. He will
41 invade countries, despoil them, and move on. He will also invade the land of
beauty, and many cities will fall, but these will escape his power: Edom and
42 Moav, Yevus and the choicest land of the sons of Amon. And he will attack
43 and destroy countries, and the land of Egypt will not escape. And he will have
power over the treasures of gold and silver, and over all the precious things
44 of Egypt, and the Libyans and Kushites will follow his entourage. But rumors
from the east and the north will alarm him, so he will go forth in a huge fury

כד בְּשַׁלְוָה וּבְמִשְׁמַנֵּי מְדִינָה יָבוֹא וְעָשָׂה אֲשֶׁר לֹא־עָשׂוּ אֲבֹתָיו וַאֲבוֹת
אֲבֹתָיו בִּזָּה וְשָׁלָל וּרְכוּשׁ לָהֶם יִבְזוֹר וְעַל מִבְצָרִים יְחַשֵּׁב מַחְשְׁבֹתָיו
כה וְעַד־עֵת: וְיָעֵר כֹּחוֹ וּלְבָבוֹ עַל־מֶלֶךְ הַנֶּגֶב בְּחַיִל גָּדוֹל וּמֶלֶךְ הַנֶּגֶב
יִתְגָּרֶה לַמִּלְחָמָה בְּחַיִל־גָּדוֹל וְעָצוּם עַד־מְאֹד וְלֹא יַעֲמֹד כִּי־יַחְשְׁבוּ
כו עָלָיו מַחֲשָׁבוֹת: וְאֹכְלֵי פַת־בָּגוֹ יִשְׁבְּרוּהוּ וְחֵילוֹ יִשְׁטוֹף וְנָפְלוּ חֲלָלִים
כז רַבִּים: וּשְׁנֵיהֶם הַמְּלָכִים לְבָבָם לְמֵרָע וְעַל־שֻׁלְחָן אֶחָד כָּזָב יְדַבֵּרוּ
כח וְלֹא תִצְלָח כִּי־עוֹד קֵץ לַמּוֹעֵד: וְיָשֹׁב אַרְצוֹ בִּרְכוּשׁ גָּדוֹל וּלְבָבוֹ עַל־
כט בְּרִית קֹדֶשׁ וְעָשָׂה וְשָׁב לְאַרְצוֹ: לַמּוֹעֵד יָשׁוּב וּבָא בַנֶּגֶב וְלֹא־תִהְיֶה
ל כָרִאשֹׁנָה וְכָאַחֲרֹנָה: וּבָאוּ בוֹ צִיִּים כִּתִּים וְנִכְאָה וְשָׁב וְזָעַם עַל־
לא בְּרִית־קוֹדֶשׁ וְעָשָׂה וְשָׁב וְיָבֵן עַל־עֹזְבֵי בְּרִית קֹדֶשׁ: וּזְרֹעִים מִמֶּנּוּ
יַעֲמֹדוּ וְחִלְּלוּ הַמִּקְדָּשׁ הַמָּעוֹז וְהֵסִירוּ הַתָּמִיד וְנָתְנוּ הַשִּׁקּוּץ מְשֹׁמֵם:
לב וּמַרְשִׁיעֵי בְרִית יַחֲנִיף בַּחֲלַקּוֹת וְעַם יֹדְעֵי אֱלֹהָיו יַחֲזִקוּ וְעָשׂוּ:
לג וּמַשְׂכִּילֵי עָם יָבִינוּ לָרַבִּים וְנִכְשְׁלוּ בְּחֶרֶב וּבְלֶהָבָה בִּשְׁבִי וּבְבִזָּה יָמִים:
לד לה וּבְהִכָּשְׁלָם יֵעָזְרוּ עֵזֶר מְעָט וְנִלְווּ עֲלֵיהֶם רַבִּים בַּחֲלַקְלַקּוֹת: וּמִן־
הַמַּשְׂכִּילִים יִכָּשְׁלוּ לִצְרוֹף בָּהֶם וּלְבָרֵר וְלַלְבֵּן עַד־עֵת קֵץ כִּי־עוֹד
לו לַמּוֹעֵד: וְעָשָׂה כִרְצוֹנוֹ הַמֶּלֶךְ וְיִתְרוֹמֵם וְיִתְגַּדֵּל עַל־כָּל־אֵל וְעַל אֵל
אֵלִים יְדַבֵּר נִפְלָאוֹת וְהִצְלִיחַ עַד־כָּלָה זַעַם כִּי נֶחֱרָצָה נֶעֱשָׂתָה:
לז וְעַל־אֱלֹהֵי אֲבֹתָיו לֹא יָבִין וְעַל־חֶמְדַּת נָשִׁים וְעַל־כָּל־אֱלוֹהַּ לֹא יָבִין
לח כִּי עַל־כֹּל יִתְגַּדָּל: וְלֶאֱלֹהַּ מָעֻזִּים עַל־כַּנּוֹ יְכַבֵּד וְלֶאֱלוֹהַּ אֲשֶׁר לֹא־
לט יְדָעֻהוּ אֲבֹתָיו יְכַבֵּד בְּזָהָב וּבְכֶסֶף וּבְאֶבֶן יְקָרָה וּבַחֲמֻדוֹת: וְעָשָׂה
לְמִבְצְרֵי מָעֻזִּים עִם־אֱלוֹהַּ נֵכָר אֲשֶׁר הכיר יַרְבֶּה כָבוֹד וְהִמְשִׁילָם יַכִּיר
מ בָּרַבִּים וַאֲדָמָה יְחַלֵּק בִּמְחִיר: וּבְעֵת קֵץ יִתְנַגַּח עִמּוֹ מֶלֶךְ הַנֶּגֶב
וְיִשְׂתָּעֵר עָלָיו מֶלֶךְ הַצָּפוֹן בְּרֶכֶב וּבְפָרָשִׁים וּבָאֳנִיּוֹת רַבּוֹת וּבָא
מא בַאֲרָצוֹת וְשָׁטַף וְעָבָר: וּבָא בְּאֶרֶץ הַצְּבִי וְרַבּוֹת יִכָּשֵׁלוּ וְאֵלֶּה יִמָּלְטוּ
מב מִיָּדוֹ אֱדוֹם וּמוֹאָב וְרֵאשִׁית בְּנֵי עַמּוֹן: וְיִשְׁלַח יָדוֹ בַּאֲרָצוֹת וְאֶרֶץ
מג מִצְרַיִם לֹא תִהְיֶה לִפְלֵיטָה: וּמָשַׁל בְּמִכְמַנֵּי הַזָּהָב וְהַכֶּסֶף וּבְכֹל
מד חֲמֻדוֹת מִצְרָיִם וְלֻבִים וְכֻשִׁים בְּמִצְעָדָיו: וּשְׁמֻעוֹת יְבַהֲלֻהוּ מִמִּזְרָח

45 to destroy and to exterminate many peoples. And he will set up splendid
greeting pavilions between the seas and the beautiful holy mountain. There
12 1 he will arrive at his own end, and no one will help him. And at that time,
Mikhael will arise, the great prince, guardian of the children of your people.
And there will be a time of great trouble, the likes of which has not happened
since nations came to be until that time. And at that time, your people will
2 escape, all of them found written in the book.[9] And many of those sleeping
in the dust of the earth will awaken, some to everlasting life and some to
3 humiliations and eternal degradation. And those who are wise will shine like
the radiance of the sky, and those who lead the many to a righteous path will
4 shine like stars forever. But you, Daniel, keep the words secret and
seal the book until the end-time. Many will search here and there, and
5 knowledge will increase." Then I, Daniel, looked and – behold! – there stood
two others, one on this bank of the river and one on that bank of the river.
6 One of them said to the man dressed in linen, who was above the waters of
7 the river, "Until when shall this wondrous time last?" I could hear the man
dressed in linen who was above the waters of the river. He lifted his right hand
and his left toward the heavens. He swore by the Eternal One that it will be
for a time, times, and a half. And that when the shattering of the holy people's
8 power is complete, all these things will come to an end. Now I heard, but I
did not understand, so I said, "My lord, what will come after these things?"
9 He said, "Go on your way, Daniel, for the things are secret and sealed until
10 the end-time. Many people will become refined, cleansed, and purified, but
wicked people will do wicked things, and none of the wicked will understand.
11 But the wise will understand. And from the time that the daily sacrifice will
be taken away and the desolating abomination is set up there will be 1,290
12 13 days. Happy is he who waits and reaches 1,335 days. But you, go to your end
and rest, and you will arise to your destiny at the end of days."

---

9 | Meaning the book of life.

מה וּמִצָּפוֹן וְיָצָא בְּחֵמָא גְדֹלָה לְהַשְׁמִיד וּלְהַחֲרִים רַבִּים: וְיִטַּע אָהֳלֵי
יב א אַפַּדְנוֹ בֵּין יַמִּים לְהַר־צְבִי־קֹדֶשׁ וּבָא עַד־קִצּוֹ וְאֵין עוֹזֵר לוֹ: וּבָעֵת
הַהִיא יַעֲמֹד מִיכָאֵל הַשַּׂר הַגָּדוֹל הָעֹמֵד עַל־בְּנֵי עַמֶּךָ וְהָיְתָה עֵת
צָרָה אֲשֶׁר לֹא־נִהְיְתָה מִהְיוֹת גּוֹי עַד הָעֵת הַהִיא וּבָעֵת הַהִיא יִמָּלֵט
ב עַמְּךָ כָּל־הַנִּמְצָא כָּתוּב בַּסֵּפֶר: וְרַבִּים מִיְּשֵׁנֵי אַדְמַת־עָפָר יָקִיצוּ אֵלֶּה
ג לְחַיֵּי עוֹלָם וְאֵלֶּה לַחֲרָפוֹת לְדִרְאוֹן עוֹלָם: וְהַמַּשְׂכִּלִים יַזְהִרוּ כְּזֹהַר
ד הָרָקִיעַ וּמַצְדִּיקֵי הָרַבִּים כַּכּוֹכָבִים לְעוֹלָם וָעֶד: וְאַתָּה
דָנִיֵּאל סְתֹם הַדְּבָרִים וַחֲתֹם הַסֵּפֶר עַד־עֵת קֵץ יְשֹׁטְטוּ רַבִּים וְתִרְבֶּה
ה הַדָּעַת: וְרָאִיתִי אֲנִי דָנִיֵּאל וְהִנֵּה שְׁנַיִם אֲחֵרִים עֹמְדִים אֶחָד הֵנָּה
ו לִשְׂפַת הַיְאֹר וְאֶחָד הֵנָּה לִשְׂפַת הַיְאֹר: וַיֹּאמֶר לָאִישׁ לְבוּשׁ הַבַּדִּים
ז אֲשֶׁר מִמַּעַל לְמֵימֵי הַיְאֹר עַד־מָתַי קֵץ הַפְּלָאוֹת: וָאֶשְׁמַע אֶת־
הָאִישׁ | לְבוּשׁ הַבַּדִּים אֲשֶׁר מִמַּעַל לְמֵימֵי הַיְאֹר וַיָּרֶם יְמִינוֹ וּשְׂמֹאלוֹ
אֶל־הַשָּׁמַיִם וַיִּשָּׁבַע בְּחֵי הָעוֹלָם כִּי לְמוֹעֵד מוֹעֲדִים וָחֵצִי וּכְכַלּוֹת
ח נַפֵּץ יַד־עַם־קֹדֶשׁ תִּכְלֶינָה כָל־אֵלֶּה: וַאֲנִי שָׁמַעְתִּי וְלֹא אָבִין וָאֹמְרָה
ט אֲדֹנִי מָה אַחֲרִית אֵלֶּה: וַיֹּאמֶר לֵךְ דָּנִיֵּאל כִּי־סְתֻמִים וַחֲתֻמִים
י הַדְּבָרִים עַד־עֵת קֵץ: יִתְבָּרְרוּ וְיִתְלַבְּנוּ וְיִצָּרְפוּ רַבִּים וְהִרְשִׁיעוּ רְשָׁעִים
יא וְלֹא יָבִינוּ כָּל־רְשָׁעִים וְהַמַּשְׂכִּלִים יָבִינוּ: וּמֵעֵת הוּסַר הַתָּמִיד וְלָתֵת
יב שִׁקּוּץ שֹׁמֵם יָמִים אֶלֶף מָאתַיִם וְתִשְׁעִים: אַשְׁרֵי הַמְחַכֶּה וְיַגִּיעַ לְיָמִים
יג אֶלֶף שְׁלֹשׁ מֵאוֹת שְׁלֹשִׁים וַחֲמִשָּׁה: וְאַתָּה לֵךְ לַקֵּץ וְתָנוּחַ וְתַעֲמֹד
לְגֹרָלְךָ לְקֵץ הַיָּמִין:

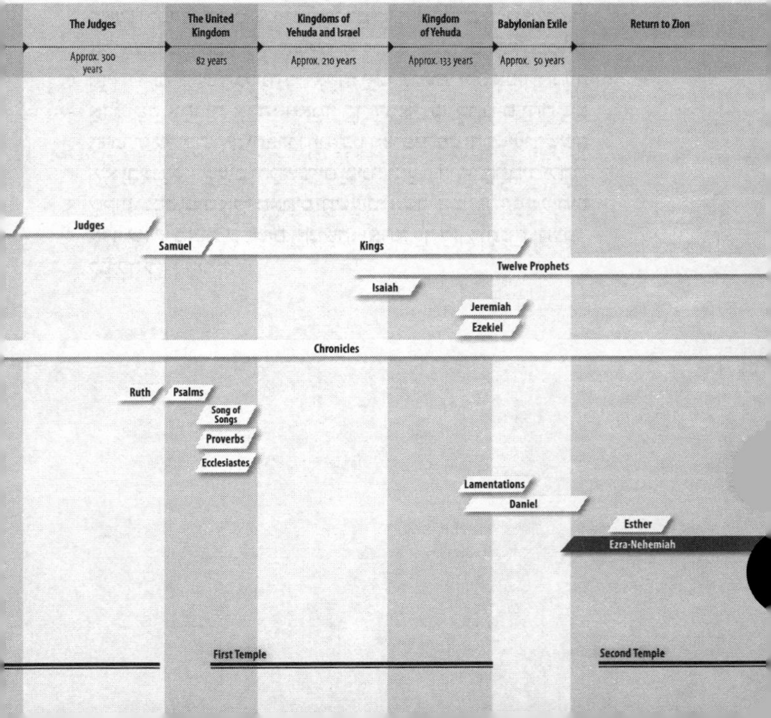
The Judges
The United Kingdom
Kingdoms of Yehuda and Israel
Kingdom of Yehuda
Babylonian Exile
Return to Zion
Approx. 300 years
82 years
Approx. 210 years
Approx. 133 years
Approx. 50 years
Judges
Samuel
Kings
Twelve Prophets
Isaiah
Jeremiah
Ezekiel
Chronicles
Ruth
Psalms
Song of Songs
Proverbs
Ecclesiastes
Lamentations
Daniel
Esther
Ezra-Nehemiah
First Temple
Second Temple

עזרא · נחמיה

EZRA · NEḤEMYA/NEHEMIAH

EZRA · NEHEMIAH	Koresh's declaration, those who ascended the land as a result and their actions	Ezra's ascendance and his actions	Neḥemya's ascendance and his determined action	Neḥemya's second ascent: Attempts to repair the crisis
	Ezra, chs. 1–6	Ezra 7–10	Nehemiah 1–12	Nehemiah 13
			12 years	

1 1 In the first year of Koresh, king of Persia, when the Lord's word pronounced
by Yirmeyahu had come to pass,[1] the Lord stirred the spirit of Koresh, king
of Persia, and he issued a proclamation throughout his kingdom, by word
2 of mouth and written word as well:[2] "Thus says Koresh, king of Persia: The
Lord, God of the heavens, has granted me all the kingdoms of the earth, and
3 He has charged me to build Him a House in Jerusalem, in Yehuda. Whoever
is among you from all His people, may his God be with him, and let him
go up to Jerusalem, in Yehuda, and build the House of the Lord, God of
4 Israel, who is the God in Jerusalem – and may his God be with him. As for
anyone left behind in the place where he lives, his townsmen shall aid him
with silver, gold, supplies, and beasts of burden, as well as gifts for the House
5 of God in Jerusalem." So all of the heads of the ancestral Houses of Yehuda
and Binyamin and the priests and the Levites, and all those whose spirit had
been stirred by God, prepared to go up and to build the House of the Lord,
6 in Jerusalem. And their neighbors supported them with vessels of silver, gold,
supplies, beasts of burden, and precious goods, aside from gifts which had
been donated.
7 King Koresh took out the vessels of the House of the Lord that Nevukhadnetzar had removed from Jerusalem and placed in the house of his gods.
8 Koresh, king of Persia, had them taken out by Mitredat, keeper of the trea-
9 sures, who counted them for Sheshbatzar, prince of Yehuda. And
this is an account of them: thirty golden dishes, one thousand silver dishes,
10 and twenty-nine knives; thirty golden bowls, four hundred ten double silver
11 bowls, and one thousand other vessels. All vessels of gold and silver were five
thousand four hundred in number; all were taken by Sheshbatzar when the
returning exiles were brought out from Babylonia to Jerusalem.
2 1 And these are the people of the province, coming up from the captivity of
the exile, that Nevukhadnetzar, king of Babylon, had exiled to Babylon. They
2 returned to Jerusalem and Judea, each to his own town. Those who came with
Zerubavel, Yeshua, Neḥemya, Seraya, Re'elaya, Mordekhai, Bilshan, Mispar,
Bigvai, Reḥum, Baana – the people of the nation of Israel – numbered as
3, 4, 5 follows: The sons of Parosh: 2,172. The sons of Shefatya: 372. The sons of
6 Araḥ: 775. The sons of Paḥat Moav – the sons of Yeshua and Yoav: 2,812.
7, 8, 9, 10 The sons of Eilam: 1,254. The sons of Zatu: 945. The sons of Zakai: 760. The
11, 12, 13 sons of Bani: 642. The sons of Bevai: 623. The sons of Azgad: 1,222. The sons
14, 15, 16 of Adonikam: 666. The sons of Bigvai: 2,056. The sons of Adin: 454. The

1 | See Jeremiah 25:11–12.
2 | Cf. II Chronicles 36:22–23.

א א וּבִשְׁנַת אַחַת לְכוֹרֶשׁ מֶלֶךְ פָּרַס לִכְלוֹת דְּבַר־יְהוָה מִפִּי יִרְמְיָה הֵעִיר א
יְהוָה אֶת־רוּחַ כֹּרֶשׁ מֶלֶךְ־פָּרַס וַיַּעֲבֶר־קוֹל בְּכָל־מַלְכוּתוֹ וְגַם־בְּמִכְתָּב
ב לֵאמֹר׃ כֹּה אָמַר כֹּרֶשׁ מֶלֶךְ פָּרַס כֹּל מַמְלְכוֹת הָאָרֶץ נָתַן לִי יְהוָה אֱלֹהֵי
הַשָּׁמָיִם וְהוּא־פָקַד עָלַי לִבְנוֹת־לוֹ בַיִת בִּירוּשָׁלִַם אֲשֶׁר בִּיהוּדָה׃
ג מִי־בָכֶם מִכָּל־עַמּוֹ יְהִי אֱלֹהָיו עִמּוֹ וְיַעַל לִירוּשָׁלִַם אֲשֶׁר בִּיהוּדָה
וְיִבֶן אֶת־בֵּית יְהוָה אֱלֹהֵי יִשְׂרָאֵל הוּא הָאֱלֹהִים אֲשֶׁר בִּירוּשָׁלִָם׃
ד וְכָל־הַנִּשְׁאָר מִכָּל־הַמְּקֹמוֹת אֲשֶׁר הוּא גָר־שָׁם יְנַשְּׂאוּהוּ אַנְשֵׁי מְקֹמוֹ
בְּכֶסֶף וּבְזָהָב וּבִרְכוּשׁ וּבִבְהֵמָה עִם־הַנְּדָבָה לְבֵית הָאֱלֹהִים אֲשֶׁר
ה בִּירוּשָׁלִָם׃ וַיָּקוּמוּ רָאשֵׁי הָאָבוֹת לִיהוּדָה וּבִנְיָמִן וְהַכֹּהֲנִים וְהַלְוִיִּם
לְכֹל הֵעִיר הָאֱלֹהִים אֶת־רוּחוֹ לַעֲלוֹת לִבְנוֹת אֶת־בֵּית יְהוָה אֲשֶׁר
ו בִּירוּשָׁלִָם׃ וְכָל־סְבִיבֹתֵיהֶם חִזְּקוּ בִידֵיהֶם בִּכְלֵי־כֶסֶף בַּזָּהָב בָּרְכוּשׁ
וּבַבְּהֵמָה וּבַמִּגְדָּנוֹת לְבַד עַל־כָּל־הִתְנַדֵּב׃
ז וְהַמֶּלֶךְ כּוֹרֶשׁ הוֹצִיא אֶת־כְּלֵי בֵית־יְהוָה אֲשֶׁר הוֹצִיא נְבוּכַדְנֶצַּר
ח מִירוּשָׁלִַם וַיִּתְּנֵם בְּבֵית אֱלֹהָיו׃ וַיּוֹצִיאֵם כּוֹרֶשׁ מֶלֶךְ פָּרַס עַל־יַד
ט מִתְרְדָת הַגִּזְבָּר וַיִּסְפְּרֵם לְשֵׁשְׁבַּצַּר הַנָּשִׂיא לִיהוּדָה׃ וְאֵלֶּה
מִסְפָּרָם אֲגַרְטְלֵי זָהָב שְׁלֹשִׁים אֲגַרְטְלֵי־כֶסֶף אָלֶף מַחֲלָפִים תִּשְׁעָה
י וְעֶשְׂרִים׃ כְּפוֹרֵי זָהָב שְׁלֹשִׁים כְּפוֹרֵי כֶסֶף מִשְׁנִים אַרְבַּע מֵאוֹת
יא וַעֲשָׂרָה כֵּלִים אֲחֵרִים אָלֶף׃ כָּל־כֵּלִים לַזָּהָב וְלַכֶּסֶף חֲמֵשֶׁת אֲלָפִים
וְאַרְבַּע מֵאוֹת הַכֹּל הֶעֱלָה שֵׁשְׁבַּצַּר עִם הֵעָלוֹת הַגּוֹלָה מִבָּבֶל
לִירוּשָׁלִָם׃

ב א וְאֵלֶּה ׀ בְּנֵי הַמְּדִינָה הָעֹלִים מִשְּׁבִי הַגּוֹלָה אֲשֶׁר הֶגְלָה נבוכדנצור נְבוּכַדְנֶצַּר
ב מֶלֶךְ־בָּבֶל לְבָבֶל וַיָּשׁוּבוּ לִירוּשָׁלִַם וִיהוּדָה אִישׁ לְעִירוֹ׃ אֲשֶׁר־בָּאוּ
עִם־זְרֻבָּבֶל יֵשׁוּעַ נְחֶמְיָה שְׂרָיָה רְעֵלָיָה מָרְדֳּכַי בִּלְשָׁן מִסְפָּר בִּגְוַי
ג רְחוּם בַּעֲנָה מִסְפַּר אַנְשֵׁי עַם יִשְׂרָאֵל׃ בְּנֵי פַרְעֹשׁ אַלְפַּיִם מֵאָה שִׁבְעִים
ד ה וּשְׁנָיִם׃ בְּנֵי שְׁפַטְיָה שְׁלֹשׁ מֵאוֹת שִׁבְעִים וּשְׁנָיִם׃ בְּנֵי אָרַח שְׁבַע מֵאוֹת
ו חֲמִשָּׁה וְשִׁבְעִים׃ בְּנֵי־פַחַת מוֹאָב לִבְנֵי יֵשׁוּעַ יוֹאָב אַלְפַּיִם שְׁמֹנֶה
ז ח מֵאוֹת וּשְׁנֵים עָשָׂר׃ בְּנֵי עֵילָם אֶלֶף מָאתַיִם חֲמִשִּׁים וְאַרְבָּעָה׃ בְּנֵי
ט זַתּוּא תְּשַׁע מֵאוֹת וְאַרְבָּעִים וַחֲמִשָּׁה׃ בְּנֵי זַכָּי שְׁבַע מֵאוֹת וְשִׁשִּׁים׃
י יא בְּנֵי בָנִי שֵׁשׁ מֵאוֹת אַרְבָּעִים וּשְׁנָיִם׃ בְּנֵי בֵבָי שֵׁשׁ מֵאוֹת עֶשְׂרִים
יב יג וּשְׁלֹשָׁה׃ בְּנֵי עַזְגָּד אֶלֶף מָאתַיִם עֶשְׂרִים וּשְׁנָיִם׃ בְּנֵי אֲדֹנִיקָם שֵׁשׁ
יד טו מֵאוֹת שִׁשִּׁים וְשִׁשָּׁה׃ בְּנֵי בִגְוָי אַלְפַּיִם חֲמִשִּׁים וְשִׁשָּׁה׃ בְּנֵי עָדִין
טז אַרְבַּע מֵאוֹת חֲמִשִּׁים וְאַרְבָּעָה׃ בְּנֵי־אָטֵר לִיחִזְקִיָּה תִּשְׁעִים וּשְׁמֹנָה׃

17, 18 sons of Ater of Yeḥizkiya: 98. The sons of Betzai: 323. The sons of Yora: 112.
19, 20, 21 The sons of Ḥashum: 223. The sons of Gibar: 95. The sons of Beit Leḥem: 123.
22, 23, 24 The people of Netofa: 56. The people of Anatot: 128. The sons of Azmavet: 42.
25, 26 The sons of Kiryat Arim, Kefira, and Be'erot: 743. The sons of the Rama and
27, 28 of Gava: 621. The people of Mikhmas: 122. The people of Beit El and Ai: 223.
29, 30, 31 The sons of Nevo: 52. The sons of Magbish: 156. The sons of the other Eilam:
32, 33, 34 1,254. The sons of Ḥarim: 320. The sons of Lod, Ḥadid, and Ono: 725. The
35, 36 sons of Yeriḥo: 345. The sons of Senaa: 3,630. The priests, sons of Yedaya, of
37, 38 the house of Yeshua: 973. The sons of Imer: 1,052. The sons of Pashḥur: 1,247.
39, 40 The sons of Ḥarim: 1,017. The Levites, sons of Yeshua and Kadmiel, of the
41, 42 sons of Hodavya: 74. The singers, the sons of Asaf: 128. The sons of the
gatekeepers – the sons of Shalum, the sons of Ater, the sons of Talmon,
43 the sons of Akuv, the sons of Ḥatita, the sons of Shovai – totaling 139. The
44 Netinim[3] – the sons of Tziḥa, the sons of Ḥasufa, the sons of Tabaot. The
45 sons of Keros, the sons of Siaha, the sons of Padon. The sons of Levana, the
46 sons of Ḥagava, the sons of Akuv. The sons of Ḥagav, the sons of Shalmai, the
47, 48 sons of Ḥanan. The sons of Gidel, the sons of Gaḥar, the sons of Re'aya. The
49 sons of Retzin, the sons of Nekoda, the sons of Gazam. The sons of Uza, the
50 sons of Pase'aḥ, the sons of Besai. The sons of Asna, the sons of Meunites,
51 the sons of Nefusim The sons of Bakbuk, the sons of Ḥakufa, the sons of
52, 53 Ḥarḥur. The sons of Batzlut, the sons of Meḥida, the sons of Ḥarsha. The
54 sons of Barkos, the sons of Sisra, the sons of Tamaḥ. The sons of Netziaḥ, the
55 sons of Ḥatifa. The sons of Shlomo's servants – the sons of Sotai, the sons of
56 HaSoferet,[4] the sons of Peruda. The sons of Yaela, the sons of Darkon, the
57 sons of Gidel. The sons of Shefatya, the sons of Ḥatil, the sons of Pokheret
58 HaTzevayim,[5] the sons of Ami. The Netinim and Shlomo's servants totaled
59 392. And these are those who came up from Tel Melaḥ, Tel Ḥarsha,
Keruv, Adan, Imer – but could not prove whether their ancestral house or
60 descent were of Israel: the sons of Delaya, the sons of Toviya, and the sons of
61 Nekoda: 652. And of the sons of the priests: the sons of Ḥavaya, the
sons of Hakotz, the sons of Barzilai – he who married one of the daughters
62 of Barzilai the Gileadite and was called by their name. These sought the
written record of their genealogy, which could not be found, and they were
63 therefore repudiated from the priesthood. The governor instructed them that
they must not eat from the holiest offerings until the advent of a priest for the

---

3 | A group of Temple servants, whose origins and precise role in the Temple are not entirely clear (see Josh. 9:27; 1 Chr. 9:2).

4 | Literally "the scribe," this name may have denoted the clan's profession.

5 | Literally "gazelle hunters," again perhaps the clan's vocation.

יז יח בְּנֵי בֵצָי שְׁלֹשׁ מֵאוֹת עֶשְׂרִים וּשְׁלֹשָׁה: בְּנֵי יוֹרָה מֵאָה וּשְׁנֵים עָשָׂר:
יט, כ כא בְּנֵי חָשֻׁם מָאתַיִם עֶשְׂרִים וּשְׁלֹשָׁה: בְּנֵי גִבָּר תִּשְׁעִים וַחֲמִשָּׁה: בְּנֵי
כב כג בֵית־לָחֶם מֵאָה עֶשְׂרִים וּשְׁלֹשָׁה: אַנְשֵׁי נְטֹפָה חֲמִשִּׁים וְשִׁשָּׁה: אַנְשֵׁי
כד כה עֲנָתוֹת מֵאָה עֶשְׂרִים וּשְׁמֹנָה: בְּנֵי עַזְמָוֶת אַרְבָּעִים וּשְׁנָיִם: בְּנֵי קִרְיַת
כו עָרִים כְּפִירָה וּבְאֵרוֹת שְׁבַע מֵאוֹת וְאַרְבָּעִים וּשְׁלֹשָׁה: בְּנֵי הָרָמָה
כז וָגָבַע שֵׁשׁ מֵאוֹת עֶשְׂרִים וְאֶחָד: אַנְשֵׁי מִכְמָס מֵאָה עֶשְׂרִים וּשְׁנָיִם:
כח כט אַנְשֵׁי בֵית־אֵל וְהָעָי מָאתַיִם עֶשְׂרִים וּשְׁלֹשָׁה: בְּנֵי נְבוֹ חֲמִשִּׁים
ל לא וּשְׁנָיִם: בְּנֵי מַגְבִּישׁ מֵאָה חֲמִשִּׁים וְשִׁשָּׁה: בְּנֵי עֵילָם אַחֵר אֶלֶף מָאתַיִם
לב לג חֲמִשִּׁים וְאַרְבָּעָה: בְּנֵי חָרִם שְׁלֹשׁ מֵאוֹת וְעֶשְׂרִים: בְּנֵי־לֹד חָדִיד
לד וְאוֹנוֹ שְׁבַע מֵאוֹת עֶשְׂרִים וַחֲמִשָּׁה: בְּנֵי יְרֵחוֹ שְׁלֹשׁ מֵאוֹת אַרְבָּעִים
לה לו וַחֲמִשָּׁה: בְּנֵי סְנָאָה שְׁלֹשֶׁת אֲלָפִים וְשֵׁשׁ מֵאוֹת וּשְׁלֹשִׁים: הַכֹּהֲנִים
לז בְּנֵי יְדַעְיָה לְבֵית יֵשׁוּעַ תְּשַׁע מֵאוֹת שִׁבְעִים וּשְׁלֹשָׁה: בְּנֵי אִמֵּר אֶלֶף
לח לט חֲמִשִּׁים וּשְׁנָיִם: בְּנֵי פַשְׁחוּר אֶלֶף מָאתַיִם אַרְבָּעִים וְשִׁבְעָה: בְּנֵי חָרִם
מ אֶלֶף וְשִׁבְעָה עָשָׂר: הַלְוִיִּם בְּנֵי־יֵשׁוּעַ וְקַדְמִיאֵל לִבְנֵי הוֹדַוְיָה שִׁבְעִים
מא מב וְאַרְבָּעָה: הַמְשֹׁרְרִים בְּנֵי אָסָף מֵאָה עֶשְׂרִים וּשְׁמֹנָה: בְּנֵי הַשֹּׁעֲרִים
בְּנֵי־שַׁלּוּם בְּנֵי־אָטֵר בְּנֵי־טַלְמוֹן בְּנֵי־עַקּוּב בְּנֵי חֲטִיטָא בְּנֵי שֹׁבָי הַכֹּל
מג מֵאָה שְׁלֹשִׁים וְתִשְׁעָה: הַנְּתִינִים בְּנֵי־צִיחָא בְנֵי־חֲשׂוּפָא בְּנֵי טַבָּעוֹת:
מד מה בְּנֵי־קֵרֹס בְּנֵי־סִיעֲהָא בְּנֵי פָדוֹן: בְּנֵי־לְבָנָה בְנֵי־חֲגָבָה בְּנֵי עַקּוּב:
מו, מז מח בְּנֵי־חָגָב בְּנֵי־שמלי בְּנֵי חָנָן: בְּנֵי־גִדֵּל בְּנֵי־גַחַר בְּנֵי רְאָיָה: בְּנֵי־רְצִין שַׁלְמָי
מט נ בְּנֵי־נְקוֹדָא בְּנֵי גַזָּם: בְּנֵי־עֻזָּא בְנֵי־פָסֵחַ בְּנֵי בֵסָי: בְּנֵי־אַסְנָה בְנֵי־
נא נב מְעוּנִים בְּנֵי נפיסים: בְּנֵי־בַקְבּוּק בְּנֵי־חֲקוּפָא בְּנֵי חַרְחוּר: בְּנֵי־ נְפוּסִים
נג בַצְלוּת בְּנֵי־מְחִידָא בְּנֵי חַרְשָׁא: בְּנֵי־בַרְקוֹס בְּנֵי־סִיסְרָא בְּנֵי־תָמַח:
נד נה בְּנֵי נְצִיחַ בְּנֵי חֲטִיפָא: בְּנֵי עַבְדֵי שְׁלֹמֹה בְּנֵי־סֹטַי בְּנֵי־הַסֹּפֶרֶת בְּנֵי
נו נז פְרוּדָא: בְּנֵי־יַעְלָה בְנֵי־דַרְקוֹן בְּנֵי גִדֵּל: בְּנֵי שְׁפַטְיָה בְנֵי־חַטִּיל בְּנֵי
נח פֹּכֶרֶת הַצְּבָיִים בְּנֵי אָמִי: כָּל־הַנְּתִינִים וּבְנֵי עַבְדֵי שְׁלֹמֹה שְׁלֹשׁ מֵאוֹת
נט תִּשְׁעִים וּשְׁנָיִם: וְאֵלֶּה הָעֹלִים מִתֵּל מֶלַח תֵּל
חַרְשָׁא כְּרוּב אַדָּן אִמֵּר וְלֹא יָכְלוּ לְהַגִּיד בֵּית־אֲבוֹתָם וְזַרְעָם אִם
ס מִיִּשְׂרָאֵל הֵם: בְּנֵי־דְלָיָה בְנֵי־טוֹבִיָּה בְּנֵי נְקוֹדָא שֵׁשׁ מֵאוֹת חֲמִשִּׁים
סא וּשְׁנָיִם: וּמִבְּנֵי הַכֹּהֲנִים בְּנֵי חֳבַיָּה בְּנֵי הַקּוֹץ בְּנֵי
בַרְזִלַּי אֲשֶׁר לָקַח מִבְּנוֹת בַּרְזִלַּי הַגִּלְעָדִי אִשָּׁה וַיִּקָּרֵא עַל־שְׁמָם:
סב אֵלֶּה בִּקְשׁוּ כְתָבָם הַמִּתְיַחְשִׂים וְלֹא נִמְצָאוּ וַיְגֹאֲלוּ מִן־הַכְּהֻנָּה:
סג וַיֹּאמֶר הַתִּרְשָׁתָא לָהֶם אֲשֶׁר לֹא־יֹאכְלוּ מִקֹּדֶשׁ הַקֳּדָשִׁים עַד עֲמֹד

64 Urim and the Tumim.[6] The entire community altogether numbered 42,360.
65 Aside from their male and female slaves of whom there were 7,337, they also
66 67 had 200 male and female singers. Their horses – 736; their mules – 245. Their
68 camels – 435; donkeys – 6,720. Some of the clan leaders, when they
arrived at the House of the LORD in Jerusalem, willingly contributed to fix
69 the House of God back on its foundations. Each giving what they could,
they donated to the project treasury sixty-one thousand gold drachmas,
70 five thousand silver mina, and one hundred priestly robes. And
the priests, Levites, and others of the people, the singers, gatekeepers,
and the Netinim, settled in their towns, so that all Israel were in their
3 1 towns. After the Israelites had settled in their towns, the seventh
2 month arrived, and the people assembled in Jerusalem as one. Then Yeshua
son of Yotzadak and his brothers the priests, and Zerubavel son of She'altiel
and his brothers, rose up and built an altar for the God of Israel, to present
3 burnt offerings as prescribed in the Torah of Moshe, man of God. They
established the altar upon its original foundations, for they were fearful of
the peoples of the land, and presented burnt offerings upon it to the LORD,
4 morning and evening. The people celebrated the Festival of Tabernacles
as prescribed, performing the designated number of daily offerings each
5 day in accordance with the law for each day.[7] Thereafter, they continued
to present the regular offerings, the offerings of the New Month and all of
the LORD's sacred assemblies, and the voluntary offerings brought for the
6 LORD. On the first day of the seventh month, the priests began to present
burnt offerings to the LORD, though the foundation of the LORD's Sanctuary
7 had not yet been laid. And the leaders paid the hewers and stone masons in
silver, and the Sidonians and Tyreans were given food and drink and oil to
bring cedar wood from Lebanon to the Sea of Jaffa,[8] in accordance with the
8 permission granted to them by Koresh, king of Persia. In the second
year of their arrival in Jerusalem, for the House of God, in the second month,
Zerubavel son of She'altiel and Yeshua son of Yotzadak and the rest of their
brothers – the priests and the Levites, and all those who had come from the
exile to Jerusalem – began by appointing the Levites, twenty years of age
9 and above, to supervise the work of constructing the LORD's House. Then
Yeshua, his sons and brothers, and Kadmiel and his sons, and the sons of
Yehuda, rose up as one to supervise the builders of the House of God, along
10 with the sons of Ḥenadad, their sons, and their brothers the Levites. After
the builders had laid the foundation for the Temple of the LORD, the priests
took up their positions in their vestments with trumpets, and the Levites, the
sons of Asaf, with cymbals, to praise the LORD as David, king of Israel, had
11 ordained. The Levites chanted hymns of praise thanking the LORD, "For He

6 | An oracle worn by the High Priest (see Ex. 28:30; Lev. 8:8) which by this time was evidently no longer extant.

7 | See Numbers 29:12–38.

8 | Cf. the construction of Shlomo's Temple in 1 Kings 5:16–32.

סד כֹּהֵן לְאוּרִים וּלְתֻמִּים: כָּל־הַקָּהָל כְּאֶחָד אַרְבַּע רִבּוֹא אַלְפַּיִם שְׁלֹשׁ־
סה מֵאוֹת שִׁשִּׁים: מִלְּבַד עַבְדֵיהֶם וְאַמְהֹתֵיהֶם אֵלֶּה שִׁבְעַת אֲלָפִים שְׁלֹשׁ
סו מֵאוֹת שְׁלֹשִׁים וְשִׁבְעָה וְלָהֶם מְשֹׁרְרִים וּמְשֹׁרְרוֹת מָאתָיִם: סוּסֵיהֶם
שְׁבַע מֵאוֹת שְׁלֹשִׁים וְשִׁשָּׁה פִּרְדֵיהֶם מָאתַיִם אַרְבָּעִים וַחֲמִשָּׁה:
סז גְּמַלֵּיהֶם אַרְבַּע מֵאוֹת שְׁלֹשִׁים וַחֲמִשָּׁה חֲמֹרִים שֵׁשֶׁת אֲלָפִים שְׁבַע
סח מֵאוֹת וְעֶשְׂרִים: וּמֵרָאשֵׁי הָאָבוֹת בְּבוֹאָם לְבֵית יְהוָה
סט אֲשֶׁר בִּירוּשָׁלִָם הִתְנַדְּבוּ לְבֵית הָאֱלֹהִים לְהַעֲמִידוֹ עַל־מְכוֹנוֹ: כְּכֹחָם
נָתְנוּ לְאוֹצַר הַמְּלָאכָה זָהָב דַּרְכְּמוֹנִים שֶׁשׁ־רִבֹּאות וָאָלֶף וְכֶסֶף מָנִים
ע חֲמֵשֶׁת אֲלָפִים וְכָתְנֹת כֹּהֲנִים מֵאָה: וַיֵּשְׁבוּ הַכֹּהֲנִים
וְהַלְוִיִּם וּמִן־הָעָם וְהַמְשֹׁרְרִים וְהַשּׁוֹעֲרִים וְהַנְּתִינִים בְּעָרֵיהֶם וְכָל־
ג א יִשְׂרָאֵל בְּעָרֵיהֶם: וַיִּגַּע הַחֹדֶשׁ הַשְּׁבִיעִי וּבְנֵי יִשְׂרָאֵל
ב בֶּעָרִים וַיֵּאָסְפוּ הָעָם כְּאִישׁ אֶחָד אֶל־יְרוּשָׁלִָם: וַיָּקָם יֵשׁוּעַ בֶּן־יוֹצָדָק
וְאֶחָיו הַכֹּהֲנִים וּזְרֻבָּבֶל בֶּן־שְׁאַלְתִּיאֵל וְאֶחָיו וַיִּבְנוּ אֶת־מִזְבַּח אֱלֹהֵי
יִשְׂרָאֵל לְהַעֲלוֹת עָלָיו עֹלוֹת כַּכָּתוּב בְּתוֹרַת מֹשֶׁה אִישׁ־הָאֱלֹהִים:
ג וַיָּכִינוּ הַמִּזְבֵּחַ עַל־מְכוֹנֹתָיו כִּי בְּאֵימָה עֲלֵיהֶם מֵעַמֵּי הָאֲרָצוֹת וַיַּעַל
ד עָלָיו עֹלוֹת לַיהוָה עֹלוֹת לַבֹּקֶר וְלָעָרֶב: וַיַּעֲשׂוּ אֶת־חַג הַסֻּכּוֹת כַּכָּתוּב
ה וְעֹלַת יוֹם בְּיוֹם בְּמִסְפָּר כְּמִשְׁפַּט דְּבַר־יוֹם בְּיוֹמוֹ: וְאַחֲרֵי־כֵן עֹלַת
תָּמִיד וְלֶחֳדָשִׁים וּלְכָל־מוֹעֲדֵי יְהוָה הַמְקֻדָּשִׁים וּלְכֹל מִתְנַדֵּב נְדָבָה
ו לַיהוָה: מִיּוֹם אֶחָד לַחֹדֶשׁ הַשְּׁבִיעִי הֵחֵלּוּ לְהַעֲלוֹת עֹלוֹת לַיהוָה
ז וְהֵיכַל יְהוָה לֹא יֻסָּד: וַיִּתְּנוּ־כֶסֶף לַחֹצְבִים וְלֶחָרָשִׁים וּמַאֲכָל וּמִשְׁתֶּה
וָשֶׁמֶן לַצִּדֹנִים וְלַצֹּרִים לְהָבִיא עֲצֵי אֲרָזִים מִן־הַלְּבָנוֹן אֶל־יָם יָפוֹא
ח כְּרִשְׁיוֹן כּוֹרֶשׁ מֶלֶךְ־פָּרַס עֲלֵיהֶם: וּבַשָּׁנָה הַשֵּׁנִית
לְבוֹאָם אֶל־בֵּית הָאֱלֹהִים לִירוּשָׁלִַם בַּחֹדֶשׁ הַשֵּׁנִי הֵחֵלּוּ זְרֻבָּבֶל
בֶּן־שְׁאַלְתִּיאֵל וְיֵשׁוּעַ בֶּן־יוֹצָדָק וּשְׁאָר אֲחֵיהֶם ׀ הַכֹּהֲנִים וְהַלְוִיִּם
וְכָל־הַבָּאִים מֵהַשְּׁבִי יְרוּשָׁלִַם וַיַּעֲמִידוּ אֶת־הַלְוִיִּם מִבֶּן עֶשְׂרִים
ט שָׁנָה וָמַעְלָה לְנַצֵּחַ עַל־מְלֶאכֶת בֵּית־יְהוָה: וַיַּעֲמֹד יֵשׁוּעַ בָּנָיו
וְאֶחָיו קַדְמִיאֵל וּבָנָיו בְּנֵי־יְהוּדָה כְּאֶחָד לְנַצֵּחַ עַל־עֹשֵׂה הַמְּלָאכָה
י בְּבֵית הָאֱלֹהִים בְּנֵי חֵנָדָד בְּנֵיהֶם וַאֲחֵיהֶם הַלְוִיִּם: וְיִסְּדוּ הַבֹּנִים אֶת־
הֵיכַל יְהוָה וַיַּעֲמִידוּ הַכֹּהֲנִים מְלֻבָּשִׁים בַּחֲצֹצְרוֹת וְהַלְוִיִּם בְּנֵי־אָסָף
יא בַּמְצִלְתַּיִם לְהַלֵּל אֶת־יְהוָה עַל־יְדֵי דָּוִיד מֶלֶךְ־יִשְׂרָאֵל: וַיַּעֲנוּ בְּהַלֵּל
וּבְהוֹדֹת לַיהוָה כִּי טוֹב כִּי־לְעוֹלָם חַסְדּוֹ עַל־יִשְׂרָאֵל וְכָל־הָעָם הֵרִיעוּ

is good; for His kindness to Israel is forever."[9] And all the people raised a great
shout in praise of the LORD, for the House of the LORD had been established.
12 But when many of the older priests, Levites, and family heads who had seen
the first House upon its foundations laid their eyes on this House, they wept
13 with loud voices,[10] while the crowds raised their voices in a shout of joy. The
people could not distinguish the sound of the shout of joy from the voices
of those who wept; for the people raised a great shout, and the sound was
heard from afar.
4 1 The adversaries of Yehuda and Binyamin heard that the returned exiles
2 were building a Sanctuary for the LORD, God of Israel. So they approached
Zerubavel and the family heads and said to them: "Let us join you in building
it, for we too worship your God and have been sacrificing to Him ever since
3 the days of Esar Ḥadon,[11] king of Assyria, who brought us here." But Zerubavel
and Yeshua and the rest of the family heads of Israel replied: "You shall
have no part with us building a House for our God; rather, it is our people
who, alone, shall build a House for the LORD, God of Israel, as Koresh,
4 king of Persia, has commanded us to do." And so the people of the land
5 undermined the people of Yehuda, and made them afraid to build. They
employed advisors to foil their plans throughout the reign of Koresh, king of
6 Persia, and through the reign of Daryavesh, king of Persia. During the reign
of Aḥashverosh, at the outset of his reign, they wrote an accusation against
7 the people of Yehuda and Jerusalem. And in the days of Artaḥshasta,
Bishlam, Mitredat, Tavel, and the rest of his associates wrote to Artaḥshasta,
king of Persia; the roll of letters was written in Aramaic and translated into
8 Aramaic.[12] Reḥum the chancellor and Shimshai the secretary wrote
9 a letter to King Artaḥshasta on the matter of Jerusalem as follows: Reḥum
the chancellor and Shimshai the secretary and their associates: the men of
Din-sharru, Afaresatekh, Tarpel, Persia, Erekh, Babylon, Shushan, Dahav, and
10 Elam,[13] and all the other nations whom great, esteemed Asenapar[14] exiled and
sent to settle in the city of Shomron and in the rest of the province beyond
11 the River:[15] And now, this is the copy of the letter which they sent to
him: "To King Artaḥshasta, from your servants, the people of the province
12 beyond the River. And now, let it be known to the king that the Jews
who arose from your midst have come to us, to Jerusalem. They are rebuilding
the rebellious, evil city. They are close to completing the construction of the
13 walls and have laid the foundations. Now, let it be known to the king that
should this city be rebuilt and its walls completed – no tributes, head taxes,
or property taxes will be paid, and in the end, the interests of the kingdom

9 | This phrase is common in Tanakh. Cf., e.g., Psalms 100:5, 106:1, 136:1; II Chronicles 5:13, 7:3.
10 | See Haggai 2:3.
11 | The successor of Sanḥeriv, who had exiled the ten tribes (see II Kings 19:37).
12 | As it presents these official letters, the text switches from Hebrew to Aramaic (until 6:18). Some of these letters may have been written in Old Persian and hence "translated into Aramaic."
13 | Verses 9–10 list the senders of the letter.
14 | Generally identified with Ashurbanipal (669–ca. 627 BCE), son of Esar Ḥadon.
15 | That is, east of the Euphrates River.

יב תְרוּעָה גְדוֹלָה בְהַלֵּל לַיהוָה עַל הוּסַד בֵּית־יְהוָה׃ וְרַבִּים מֵהַכֹּהֲנִים
וְהַלְוִיִּם וְרָאשֵׁי הָאָבוֹת הַזְּקֵנִים אֲשֶׁר רָאוּ אֶת־הַבַּיִת הָרִאשׁוֹן בְּיָסְדוֹ
זֶה הַבַּיִת בְּעֵינֵיהֶם בֹּכִים בְּקוֹל גָּדוֹל וְרַבִּים בִּתְרוּעָה בְשִׂמְחָה לְהָרִים
יג קוֹל׃ וְאֵין הָעָם מַכִּירִים קוֹל תְּרוּעַת הַשִּׂמְחָה לְקוֹל בְּכִי הָעָם כִּי ב
הָעָם מְרִיעִים תְּרוּעָה גְדוֹלָה וְהַקּוֹל נִשְׁמַע עַד־לְמֵרָחוֹק׃
ד א וַיִּשְׁמְעוּ צָרֵי יְהוּדָה וּבִנְיָמִן כִּי־בְנֵי הַגּוֹלָה בּוֹנִים הֵיכָל לַיהוָה אֱלֹהֵי
ב יִשְׂרָאֵל׃ וַיִּגְּשׁוּ אֶל־זְרֻבָּבֶל וְאֶל־רָאשֵׁי הָאָבוֹת וַיֹּאמְרוּ לָהֶם נִבְנֶה
עִמָּכֶם כִּי כָכֶם נִדְרוֹשׁ לֵאלֹהֵיכֶם ולא ׀ אֲנַחְנוּ זֹבְחִים מִימֵי אֵסַר חַדֹּן וְלוֹ ׀
ג מֶלֶךְ אַשּׁוּר הַמַּעֲלֶה אֹתָנוּ פֹּה׃ וַיֹּאמֶר לָהֶם זְרֻבָּבֶל וְיֵשׁוּעַ וּשְׁאָר
רָאשֵׁי הָאָבוֹת לְיִשְׂרָאֵל לֹא־לָכֶם וָלָנוּ לִבְנוֹת בַּיִת לֵאלֹהֵינוּ כִּי אֲנַחְנוּ
יַחַד נִבְנֶה לַיהוָה אֱלֹהֵי יִשְׂרָאֵל כַּאֲשֶׁר צִוָּנוּ הַמֶּלֶךְ כּוֹרֶשׁ מֶלֶךְ־
ד פָּרָס׃ וַיְהִי עַם־הָאָרֶץ מְרַפִּים יְדֵי עַם־יְהוּדָה ומבלהים אוֹתָם לִבְנוֹת׃ וּמְבַהֲלִים
ה וְסֹכְרִים עֲלֵיהֶם יוֹעֲצִים לְהָפֵר עֲצָתָם כָּל־יְמֵי כּוֹרֶשׁ מֶלֶךְ פָּרַס וְעַד־
ו מַלְכוּת דָּרְיָוֶשׁ מֶלֶךְ־פָּרָס׃ וּבְמַלְכוּת אֲחַשְׁוֵרוֹשׁ בִּתְחִלַּת מַלְכוּתוֹ
ז כָּתְבוּ שִׂטְנָה עַל־יֹשְׁבֵי יְהוּדָה וִירוּשָׁלִָם׃ וּבִימֵי
אַרְתַּחְשַׁשְׂתָּא כָּתַב בִּשְׁלָם מִתְרְדָת טָבְאֵל וּשְׁאָר כְּנָוֺתָו עַל־
אַרְתַּחְשַׁשְׂתָּא מֶלֶךְ פָּרָס וּכְתָב הַנִּשְׁתְּוָן כָּתוּב אֲרָמִית וּמְתֻרְגָּם
ח אֲרָמִית׃ רְחוּם בְּעֵל־טְעֵם וְשִׁמְשַׁי סָפְרָא כְּתַבוּ
ט אִגְּרָה חֲדָה עַל־יְרוּשְׁלֶם לְאַרְתַּחְשַׁשְׂתָּא מַלְכָּא כְּנֵמָא׃ אֱדַיִן רְחוּם
בְּעֵל־טְעֵם וְשִׁמְשַׁי סָפְרָא וּשְׁאָר כְּנָוָתְהוֹן דִּינָיֵא וַאֲפַרְסַתְכָיֵא
י טַרְפְּלָיֵא אֲפָרְסָיֵא אַרְכְּוָי בָבְלָיֵא שׁוּשַׁנְכָיֵא דהוא עֵלְמָיֵא׃ וּשְׁאָר דֶּהָיֵא
אֻמַיָּא דִּי הַגְלִי אָסְנַפַּר רַבָּא וְיַקִּירָא וְהוֹתֵב הִמּוֹ בְּקִרְיָה דִּי שָׁמְרָיִן
יא וּשְׁאָר עֲבַר־נַהֲרָה וּכְעֶנֶת׃ דְּנָה פַּרְשֶׁגֶן אִגַּרְתָּא דִּי
שְׁלַחוּ עֲלוֹהִי עַל־אַרְתַּחְשַׁשְׂתָּא מַלְכָּא עבדיך אֱנָשׁ עֲבַר־נַהֲרָה עַבְדָךְ
יב וּכְעֶנֶת׃ יְדִיעַ לֶהֱוֵא לְמַלְכָּא דִּי יְהוּדָיֵא דִּי סְלִקוּ מִן־
לְוָתָךְ עֲלֶינָא אֲתוֹ לִירוּשְׁלֶם קִרְיְתָא מָרָדְתָּא וּבִאישְׁתָּא בָּנַיִן וְשׁוּרַיָּ
יג אשכללו וְאֻשַּׁיָּא יַחִיטוּ׃ כְּעַן יְדִיעַ לֶהֱוֵא לְמַלְכָּא דִּי הֵן קִרְיְתָא דָךְ שַׁכְלִלוּ
תִתְבְּנֵא וְשׁוּרַיָּא יִשְׁתַּכְלְלוּן מִנְדָּה־בְלוֹ וַהֲלָךְ לָא יִנְתְּנוּן וְאַפְּתֹם

14 shall suffer. And now, since we consume the king's salt, and do not wish to see
anything unseemly occur to the king, we saw fit to send this letter to inform
15 the king, suggesting that you, O king, refer to the scrolls of the records of your
predecessors. In those scrolls you will discover and learn that this city has a
history of being rebellious and has inflicted harm upon kings and provinces;
from time immemorial, insurrections have wreaked havoc within it – this is
16 why this city was destroyed. We hereby forewarn the king that if this city is
built and its walls completed, you shall cease to rule over the province beyond
17 the River." The king sent this edict: "To Reḥum the chancellor and
Shimshai the secretary and all their associates residing in Shomron and
18 elsewhere in the province beyond the River: Peace. And now: The letter you
19 sent to us has been read before me in translation. I commissioned a search,
and it has indeed been found that this city has, from time immemorial,
risen up against kings, and rebellions and insurrections have wreaked havoc
20 within it. Mighty kings have ruled over Jerusalem and the entire province
beyond the River, and these kings were paid their tributes, head taxes, and
21 property taxes. Now issue a decree commanding these people to remain idle,
so that this city is not rebuilt until another edict to that effect is issued by me.
22 Take care not to err in this matter so as not to aggravate the damage to the
23 king." The moment King Artaḥshasta's letter was read before Reḥum
and Shimshai the secretary and their associates, they made haste and went
to Jerusalem, to oppose the Jews. They made them stop their work, using
24 belligerent force. Then[16] the work of building the House of God in
Jerusalem ceased and remained at a standstill until the second year of the
reign of Daryavesh, king of Persia.
5 1 And the prophets Ḥagai the prophet and Zekharya son of Ido prophesied
2 to the Jews in Yehuda and Jerusalem in the name of the God of Israel. So
Zerubavel son of She'altiel and Yeshua son of Yotzadak arose and began
to rebuild the House of God in Jerusalem with God's prophets supporting
them.
3 At that very time they were approached by Tattenai, governor of the province
beyond the River, and Shetar Bozenai and their associates, who asked them:
4 "Who authorized you to build this House and to perfect these goods?" Then
they[17] said to them: "What are the names of the men who are involved in
5 the construction?" But the providence of their God rested upon the elders
of Yehuda, so their adversaries did not stop them, waiting until their report
6 reached Daryavesh and a dispatch received. The following is
the copy of the letter sent to King Daryavesh by Tattenai, governor of the
province beyond the River, and Shetar Bozenai and his associates, the officials
7 of the province beyond the River. They sent him a report, which reads as
8 follows: "To King Daryavesh, all peace be with you. Let it be known to the
king that we went to the province of Yehuda, to the House of the great God.

16 | This verse returns to the original conflict in 4:1–3 regarding the construction of the Second Temple.
17 | Literally "we."

יד מַלְכִ֖ים תְּהַנְזִֽק׃ כְּעַ֗ן כָּל־קֳבֵל֙ דִּֽי־מְלַ֤ח הֵֽיכְלָא֙ מְלַ֔חְנָא וְעַרְוַ֣ת מַלְכָּ֔א
טו לָ֥א אֲרִ֖יךְ לַ֣נָא לְמֶחֱזֵ֑א עַל־דְּנָה֙ שְׁלַ֔חְנָא וְהוֹדַ֖עְנָא לְמַלְכָּֽא׃ דִּ֡י
יְבַקַּר֩ בִּסְפַ֨ר דָּכְרָנַיָּ֜א דִּ֣י אֲבָהָתָ֗ךְ וּתְהַשְׁכַּ֨ח בִּסְפַ֣ר דָּכְרָנַיָּא֮ וְתִנְדַּע֒ דִּ֣י
קִרְיְתָ֣א דָ֗ךְ קִרְיָ֤א מָֽרָדָא֙ וּמְהַנְזְקַ֤ת מַלְכִין֙ וּמְדִנָ֔ן וְאֶשְׁתַּדּוּר֙ עָבְדִ֣ין
טז בְּגַוַּ֔הּ מִן־יוֹמָ֖ת עָלְמָ֑א עַל־דְּנָ֖ה קִרְיְתָ֥א דָ֖ךְ הָֽחָרְבַֽת׃ מְהוֹדְעִ֤ין אֲנַ֙חְנָה֙
לְמַלְכָּ֔א דִּ֣י הֵ֤ן קִרְיְתָא֙ דָ֣ךְ תִּתְבְּנֵ֔א וְשׁוּרַיָּ֖ה יִשְׁתַּכְלְל֑וּן לָקֳבֵ֣ל דְּנָ֔ה
יז חֲלָק֙ בַּעֲבַ֣ר נַהֲרָ֔א לָ֥א אִיתַ֖י לָֽךְ׃ פִּתְגָמָ֞א שְׁלַ֣ח מַלְכָּ֗א עַל־
רְח֤וּם בְּעֵל־טְעֵם֙ וְשִׁמְשַׁ֣י סָפְרָ֔א וּשְׁאָר֙ כְּנָוָ֣תְה֔וֹן דִּ֥י יָתְבִ֖ין בְּשָׁמְרָ֑יִן
יח וּשְׁאָ֧ר עֲבַֽר־נַהֲרָ֛ה שְׁלָ֖ם וּכְעֶֽת׃ נִשְׁתְּוָנָ֕א דִּ֥י שְׁלַחְתּ֖וּן עֲלֶ֑ינָא מְפָרַ֥שׁ
יט קֱרִ֖י קָדָמָֽי׃ וּמִנִּי֮ שִׂ֣ים טְעֵם֒ וּבַקַּ֣רוּ וְהַשְׁכַּ֔חוּ דִּ֚י קִרְיְתָ֣א דָ֔ךְ מִן־יוֹמָת֙
כ עָֽלְמָ֔א עַל־מַלְכִ֖ין מִֽתְנַשְּׂאָ֑ה וּמְרַ֥ד וְאֶשְׁתַּדּ֖וּר מִתְעֲבֶד־בַּֽהּ׃ וּמַלְכִ֣ין
תַּקִּיפִ֗ין הֲווֹ֙ עַל־יְר֣וּשְׁלֶ֔ם וְשַׁ֨לִּיטִ֔ין בְּכֹ֖ל עֲבַ֣ר נַהֲרָ֑ה וּמִדָּ֥ה בְל֛וֹ וַהֲלָ֖ךְ
כא מִתְיְהֵ֥ב לְהֽוֹן׃ כְּעַן֙ שִׂ֣ימוּ טְעֵ֔ם לְבַטָּלָ֖א גֻּבְרַיָּ֣א אִלֵּ֑ךְ וְקִרְיְתָ֤א דָךְ֙ לָ֣א
כב תִתְבְּנֵ֔א עַד־מִנִּ֖י טַעְמָ֥א יִתְּשָֽׂם׃ וּזְהִירִ֥ין הֱו֛וֹ שָׁל֖וּ לְמֶעְבַּ֣ד עַל־דְּנָ֑ה
כג לְמָה֙ יִשְׂגֵּ֣א חֲבָלָ֔א לְהַנְזָקַ֖ת מַלְכִֽין׃ אֱדַ֗יִן מִן־דִּ֞י פַּרְשֶׁ֣גֶן
נִשְׁתְּוָנָא֮ דִּי֮ אַרְתַּחְשַׁ֣שְׂתְּא מַלְכָּא֒ קֱרִ֥י קֳדָם־רְח֖וּם וְשִׁמְשַׁ֣י סָפְרָ֑א
וּכְנָוָ֣תְה֗וֹן אֲזַ֨לוּ בִבְהִיל֤וּ לִירוּשְׁלֶם֙ עַל־יְה֣וּדָיֵ֔א וּבַטִּ֥לוּ הִמּ֖וֹ בְּאֶדְרָ֥ע
כד וְחָֽיִל׃ בֵּאדַ֗יִן בְּטֵלַת֙ עֲבִידַ֣ת בֵּית־אֱלָהָ֔א דִּ֖י בִּירוּשְׁלֶ֑ם וַהֲוָת֙
בָּֽטְלָ֔א עַ֚ד שְׁנַ֣ת תַּרְתֵּ֔ין לְמַלְכ֖וּת דָּרְיָ֥וֶשׁ מֶלֶךְ־פָּרָֽס׃

ה א וְהִתְנַבִּ֞י חַגַּ֣י נביאה וּזְכַרְיָ֤ה בַר־עִדּוֹא֙ נְבִיַּ֣איָּ֔א עַל־יְה֣וּדָיֵ֔א דִּ֥י בִיה֖וּד נְבִיָּ֣א
ב וּבִירוּשְׁלֶ֑ם בְּשֻׁ֛ם אֱלָ֥הּ יִשְׂרָאֵ֖ל עֲלֵיהֽוֹן׃ בֵּאדַ֡יִן קָ֠מוּ זְרֻבָּבֶ֨ל בַּר־
שְׁאַלְתִּיאֵ֜ל וְיֵשׁ֣וּעַ בַּר־יוֹצָדָ֗ק וְשָׁרִ֣יו לְמִבְנֵ֔א בֵּ֥ית אֱלָהָ֖א דִּ֣י בִירוּשְׁלֶ֑ם
וְעִמְּה֛וֹן נְבִיַּאיָּ֥א דִי־אֱלָהָ֖א מְסָעֲדִ֥ין לְהֽוֹן׃
ג בֵּהּ־זִמְנָא֙ אֲתָ֣א עֲלֵיה֗וֹן תַּתְּנַ֞י פַּחַ֧ת עֲבַֽר־נַהֲרָ֛ה וּשְׁתַ֥ר בּוֹזְנַ֖י וּכְנָוָתְה֑וֹן
וְכֵן֙ אָמְרִ֣ין לְהֹ֔ם מַן־שָׂ֨ם לְכֹ֜ם טְעֵ֗ם בַּיְתָ֤א דְנָה֙ לִבְּנֵ֔א וְאֻשַּׁרְנָ֥א דְנָ֖ה
ד לְשַׁכְלָלָֽה׃ אֱדַ֙יִן֙ כְּנֵ֣מָא אֲמַ֣רְנָא לְּהֹ֔ם מַן־אִנּ֣וּן שְׁמָהָ֔ת גֻּבְרַיָּ֕א דִּֽי־דְנָ֥ה
ה בִנְיָנָ֖א בָּנַֽיִן׃ וְעֵ֣ין אֱלָֽהֲהֹ֗ם הֲוָת֙ עַל־שָׂבֵ֣י יְהוּדָיֵ֔א וְלָא־בַטִּ֣לוּ הִמּ֔וֹ עַד־
ו טַעְמָ֖א לְדָרְיָ֣וֶשׁ יְהָ֑ךְ וֶאֱדַ֛יִן יְתִיב֥וּן נִשְׁתְּוָנָ֖א עַל־דְּנָֽה׃ פַּרְשֶׁ֣גֶן
אִ֠גַּרְתָּא דִּֽי־שְׁלַ֞ח תַּתְּנַ֣י ׀ פַּחַ֣ת עֲבַֽר־נַהֲרָ֗ה וּשְׁתַ֤ר בּוֹזְנַי֙ וּכְנָ֣וָתֵ֔הּ
ז אֲפַרְסְכָיֵ֔א דִּ֖י בַּעֲבַ֣ר נַהֲרָ֑ה עַל־דָּרְיָ֖וֶשׁ מַלְכָּֽא׃ פִּתְגָמָ֖א שְׁלַ֣חוּ עֲל֑וֹהִי
ח וְכִדְנָה֙ כְּתִ֣יב בְּגַוֵּ֔הּ לְדָרְיָ֥וֶשׁ מַלְכָּ֖א שְׁלָמָ֥א כֹֽלָּא׃ יְדִ֣יעַ ׀ לֶהֱוֵ֣א לְמַלְכָּ֗א
דִּֽי־אֲזַ֜לְנָא לִיה֣וּד מְדִֽינְתָּא֮ לְבֵית֮ אֱלָהָ֣א רַבָּא֒ וְה֤וּא מִתְבְּנֵא֙ אֶ֣בֶן

It is being built with smoothed stones and wood is being embedded within
its walls. This work is progressing diligently and is enjoying great success.
9 We demanded of their elders: 'Who authorized you to rebuild this House
10 and to perfect these goods?' We even asked for their names, so that we could
11 write and inform you of the names of the men who are their leaders. And this
was their reply to us: 'We are the servants of the God of the heavens and the
earth. We are rebuilding the House which was built many years ago; a great
12 king of Israel built it and completed it. But because our ancestors angered the
God of the heavens, He placed them in the power of Nevukhadnetzar, the
Chaldean, king of Babylon, who destroyed the House and exiled the people
13 to Babylon. However, in the first year of the reign of Koresh, king of
Babylon, King Koresh issued an edict that this Temple should be rebuilt.
14 Furthermore, regarding the silver and gold vessels of the House of God
that Nevukhadnetzar had taken away from the Sanctuary in Jerusalem and
brought to the sanctuary in Babylon – King Koresh released them from the
sanctuary in Babylon and handed them over to a man named Sheshbatzar
15 whom he appointed governor. And he said to him: "These are the vessels.
Take them, carry them with you, and place them in the Temple in Jerusalem,
16 and the House of God shall be rebuilt at its original site." Then
that Sheshbatzar came and laid the foundation of the House of God in
Jerusalem; and ever since, it has been under construction but has not been
17 completed.' Now, if it pleases the king, let a search be conducted there in the
royal archives in Babylon, to clarify whether an edict permitting the building
of the House of God in Jerusalem was indeed issued by King Koresh. Let
6 1 the king notify us what he wishes to do in this matter." So King
Daryavesh issued an edict, and they searched in the archive in Babylon where
2 the treasures were stored. But it was in the citadel of Aḥmeta, in the province
of Media, that one scroll was found, and this is what was written therein: "A
3 memorandum: In the first year of the reign of King Koresh,
King Koresh issued an edict regarding the House of God in Jerusalem. He
ordered that the House be rebuilt – a place where sacrifices are offered – its
foundations shall be fortified. Its height shall be sixty cubits and its width
4 sixty cubits. It shall have three courses of smoothed stones and one course of
5 wood, and the cost shall be paid out of the king's coffers. Additionally, the
gold and silver vessels of the House of God that Nevukhadnetzar had taken
from the Sanctuary in Jerusalem and brought to Babylon shall be returned.
Each one shall be replaced in the Temple in Jerusalem; you shall deposit it in
6 the House of God. Now, Tattenai, governor of the province beyond
the River, and Shetar Bozenai and associates, the surveyors of the province
7 beyond the River: keep your distance from there. Stop interfering with the
work of this House of God; let the governor of the Jews and their elders build
8 this House of God on its original site. I hereby issue a decree listing what you
must do to help these elders of these Jews rebuild this House of God; the
expense will be paid out of the king's coffers, from the taxes of the province

גְּלָל וְאָע מִתְּשָׂם בְּכֻתְלַיָּא וַעֲבִידְתָּא דָךְ אָסְפַּרְנָא מִתְעַבְדָא וּמַצְלַח
ט בִּידְהֹם׃ אֱדַיִן שְׁאֵלְנָא לְשָׂבַיָּא אִלֵּךְ כְּנֵמָא אֲמַרְנָא לְּהֹם מַן־שָׂם לְכֹם
י טְעֵם בַּיְתָא דְנָה לְמִבְנְיָה וְאֻשַּׁרְנָא דְנָה לְשַׁכְלָלָה׃ וְאַף שְׁמָהָתְהֹם
יא שְׁאֵלְנָא לְהֹם לְהוֹדָעוּתָךְ דִּי נִכְתֻּב שֻׁם־גֻּבְרַיָּא דִּי בְרָאשֵׁיהֹם׃ וּכְנֵמָא
פִתְגָמָא הֲתִיבוּנָא לְמֵמַר אֲנַחְנָא הִמּוֹ עַבְדוֹהִי דִי־אֱלָהּ שְׁמַיָּא
וְאַרְעָא וּבָנַיִן בַּיְתָא דִּי־הֲוָא בְנֵה מִקַּדְמַת דְּנָה שְׁנִין שַׂגִּיאָן וּמֶלֶךְ
יב לְיִשְׂרָאֵל רַב בְּנָהִי וְשַׁכְלְלֵהּ׃ לָהֵן מִן־דִּי הַרְגִּזוּ אֲבָהֳתַנָא לֶאֱלָהּ
שְׁמַיָּא יְהַב הִמּוֹ בְּיַד נְבוּכַדְנֶצַּר מֶלֶךְ־בָּבֶל כסדיא וּבַיְתָה דְנָה סַתְרֵהּ [כַּסְדָּאָה]
יג וְעַמָּה הַגְלִי לְבָבֶל׃ בְּרַם בִּשְׁנַת חֲדָה לְכוֹרֶשׁ מַלְכָּא
יד דִּי בָבֶל כּוֹרֶשׁ מַלְכָּא שָׂם טְעֵם בֵּית־אֱלָהָא דְנָה לִבְּנֵא׃ וְאַף מָאנַיָּא
דִי־בֵית־אֱלָהָא דִּי דַהֲבָה וְכַסְפָּא דִּי נְבוּכַדְנֶצַּר הַנְפֵּק מִן־הֵיכְלָא דִּי
בִירוּשְׁלֶם וְהֵיבֵל הִמּוֹ לְהֵיכְלָא דִּי בָבֶל הַנְפֵּק הִמּוֹ כּוֹרֶשׁ מַלְכָּא מִן־
טו הֵיכְלָא דִּי בָבֶל וִיהִיבוּ לְשֵׁשְׁבַּצַּר שְׁמֵהּ דִּי פֶחָה שָׂמֵהּ׃ וַאֲמַר־לֵהּ ׀
אלה מָאנַיָּא שֵׂא אֵזֶל־אֲחֵת הִמּוֹ בְּהֵיכְלָא דִּי בִירוּשְׁלֶם וּבֵית אֱלָהָא [אֵל]
טז יִתְבְּנֵא עַל־אַתְרֵהּ׃ אֱדַיִן שֵׁשְׁבַּצַּר דֵּךְ אֲתָא יְהַב אֻשַּׁיָּא
דִּי־בֵית אֱלָהָא דִּי בִירוּשְׁלֶם וּמִן־אֱדַיִן וְעַד־כְּעַן מִתְבְּנֵא וְלָא שְׁלִם׃
יז וּכְעַן הֵן עַל־מַלְכָּא טָב יִתְבַּקַּר בְּבֵית גִּנְזַיָּא דִּי־מַלְכָּא תַמָּה דִּי בְּבָבֶל
הֵן אִיתַי דִּי־מִן־כּוֹרֶשׁ מַלְכָּא שִׂים טְעֵם לְמִבְנֵא בֵּית־אֱלָהָא דֵךְ
ו א בִּירוּשְׁלֶם וּרְעוּת מַלְכָּא עַל־דְּנָה יִשְׁלַח עֲלֶינָא׃ בֵּאדַיִן
דָּרְיָוֶשׁ מַלְכָּא שָׂם טְעֵם וּבַקַּרוּ ׀ בְּבֵית סִפְרַיָּא דִּי גִנְזַיָּא מְהַחֲתִין תַּמָּה
ב בְּבָבֶל׃ וְהִשְׁתְּכַח בְּאַחְמְתָא בְּבִירְתָא דִּי בְּמָדַי מְדִינְתָּה מְגִלָּה חֲדָה
ג וְכֵן־כְּתִיב בְּגַוַּהּ דִּכְרוֹנָה׃ בִּשְׁנַת חֲדָה לְכוֹרֶשׁ מַלְכָּא כּוֹרֶשׁ
מַלְכָּא שָׂם טְעֵם בֵּית־אֱלָהָא בִירוּשְׁלֶם בַּיְתָא יִתְבְּנֵא אֲתַר דִּי־דָבְחִין
ד דִּבְחִין וְאֻשּׁוֹהִי מְסוֹבְלִין רוּמֵהּ אַמִּין שִׁתִּין פְּתָיֵהּ אַמִּין שִׁתִּין׃ נִדְבָּכִין
דִּי־אֶבֶן גְּלָל תְּלָתָא וְנִדְבָּךְ דִּי־אָע חֲדַת וְנִפְקְתָא מִן־בֵּית מַלְכָּא
ה תִּתְיְהִב׃ וְאַף מָאנֵי בֵית־אֱלָהָא דִּי דַהֲבָה וְכַסְפָּא דִּי נְבוּכַדְנֶצַּר הַנְפֵּק
מִן־הֵיכְלָא דִי־בִירוּשְׁלֶם וְהֵיבֵל לְבָבֶל יַהֲתִיבוּן וִיהָךְ לְהֵיכְלָא דִי־
ו בִירוּשְׁלֶם לְאַתְרֵהּ וְתַחֵת בְּבֵית אֱלָהָא׃ כְּעַן תַּתְּנַי פַּחַת
עֲבַר־נַהֲרָה שְׁתַר בּוֹזְנַי וּכְנָוָתְהוֹן אֲפַרְסְכָיֵא דִּי בַּעֲבַר נַהֲרָה רַחִיקִין
ז הֲווֹ מִן־תַּמָּה׃ שְׁבֻקוּ לַעֲבִידַת בֵּית־אֱלָהָא דֵךְ פַּחַת יְהוּדָיֵא וּלְשָׂבֵי
ח יְהוּדָיֵא בֵּית־אֱלָהָא דֵךְ יִבְנוֹן עַל־אַתְרֵהּ׃ וּמִנִּי שִׂים טְעֵם לְמָא דִי־
תַעַבְדוּן עִם־שָׂבֵי יְהוּדָיֵא אִלֵּךְ לְמִבְנֵא בֵּית־אֱלָהָא דֵךְ וּמִנִּכְסֵי מַלְכָּא

beyond the River. These funds shall be given to these men diligently so that
9 the work is not discontinued. And all that is needed: bulls, rams, and sheep
for offerings to the God of the heavens; wheat, salt, wine, and oil – whatever
is requested by the priests in Jerusalem – shall be provided to them daily,
10 without delay, so that they might offer fragrant sacrifices to the God of the
11 heavens and pray for the life of the king and his children. I hereby decree that
if anyone deviates from this edict, a beam shall be removed from his house,
12 and he will be impaled on it; his house shall be made into a ruin for this. May
the God who has established His name there overthrow any king or nation
who dares deviate thereupon by harming this House of God in Jerusalem. I,
13 Daryavesh, have issued this edict; let it be implemented in full." So
Tattenai, governor of the province beyond the River, and Shetar Bozenai and
14 their associates followed Daryavesh's edict in full. And the elders of the Jews
went on with the building successfully encouraged by the prophecy of Ḥagai
the prophet and Zekharya son of Ido; they built the House and completed it
according to the command of the God of Israel and in keeping with the edict
15 of Koresh, Daryavesh, and King Artaḥshasta of Persia. The construction of
this House was completed by the thirteenth day of the month of Adar, in the
16 sixth year of the reign of King Daryavesh. The Israelites, the priests
and the Levites, and all the other returning exiles celebrated the dedication
17 of the House of God with joy. In honor of the dedication of the House of
God, they offered one hundred bulls, two hundred rams, four hundred lambs
as well as goats to atone for all of Israel. There were twelve goats representing
18 the twelve tribes of Israel. They established the shifts of the priests and the
divisions of the Levites for the worship in the Temple in Jerusalem as
19 prescribed in the book of Moshe. The[18] returning exiles sacrificed
20 the Passover offering on the fourteenth day of the first month. For the priests
and the Levites had all purified themselves; every one of them was pure. They
slaughtered the Passover offering for all the returning exiles, and for their
21 brothers the priests, and for themselves. The Israelites who returned from the
exile partook of it, along with all those who separated themselves from the
impurity of the nations of the land and came to worship the LORD, God of
22 Israel. They celebrated the Festival of Unleavened Bread for seven days with
joy, for the LORD had brought them joy, by causing the king of Assyria[19] to
change his heart, supporting their construction of the House of the God of
7 1 Israel. Some time after this, during the reign of Artaḥshasta, king of
2 Persia, came Ezra, son of Seraya, son of Azarya, son of Ḥilkiya, son of Shalum,
3 son of Tzadok, son of Aḥituv, son of Amarya, son of Azarya, son of Merayot,
4 5 son of Zeraḥya, son of Uzi, son of Buki, son of Avishua, son of Pinḥas, son of
6 Elazar, son of Aharon the High Priest; this Ezra ascended from Babylon. He
was a scholar,[20] expert in the Torah of Moshe given by the LORD, God of
Israel; the king granted him his every wish, for the hand of the LORD, his God,

18 | Starting with this verse, the text reverts from Aramaic to Hebrew.
19 | Daryavesh.
20 | Literally "scribe."

דִּי מִדַּת עֲבַר נַהֲרָה אָסְפַּרְנָא נִפְקְתָא תֶּהֱוֵא מִתְיַהֲבָא לְגֻבְרַיָּא אִלֵּךְ
ט דִּי־לָא לְבַטָּלָא׃ וּמָה חַשְׁחָן וּבְנֵי תוֹרִין וְדִכְרִין וְאִמְּרִין ׀ לַעֲלָוָן ׀
לֶאֱלָהּ שְׁמַיָּא חִנְטִין מְלַח ׀ חֲמַר וּמְשַׁח כְּמֵאמַר כָּהֲנַיָּא דִי־בִירוּשְׁלֶם
י לֶהֱוֵא מִתְיְהֵב לְהֹם יוֹם ׀ בְּיוֹם דִּי־לָא שָׁלוּ׃ דִּי־לֶהֱוֺן מְהַקְרְבִין נִיחוֹחִין
יא לֶאֱלָהּ שְׁמַיָּא וּמְצַלַּיִן לְחַיֵּי מַלְכָּא וּבְנוֹהִי׃ וּמִנִּי שִׂים טְעֵם דִּי כָל־אֱנָשׁ
דִּי יְהַשְׁנֵא פִּתְגָמָא דְנָה יִתְנְסַח אָע מִן־בַּיְתֵהּ וּזְקִיף יִתְמְחֵא עֲלֹהִי
יב וּבַיְתֵהּ נְוָלוּ יִתְעֲבֵד עַל־דְּנָה׃ וֵאלָהָא דִּי שַׁכִּן שְׁמֵהּ תַּמָּה יְמַגַּר
כָּל־מֶלֶךְ וְעַם דִּי ׀ יִשְׁלַח יְדֵהּ לְהַשְׁנָיָה לְחַבָּלָה בֵּית־אֱלָהָא דֵךְ דִּי
יג בִירוּשְׁלֶם אֲנָה דָרְיָוֶשׁ שָׂמֶת טְעֵם אָסְפַּרְנָא יִתְעֲבִד׃ אֱדַיִן
תַּתְּנַי פַּחַת עֲבַר־נַהֲרָה שְׁתַר בּוֹזְנַי וּכְנָוָתְהוֹן לָקֳבֵל דִּי־שְׁלַח דָּרְיָוֶשׁ
יד מַלְכָּא כְּנֵמָא אָסְפַּרְנָא עֲבַדוּ׃ וְשָׂבֵי יְהוּדָיֵא בָּנַיִן וּמַצְלְחִין בִּנְבוּאַת
חַגַּי נביאה וּזְכַרְיָה בַּר־עִדּוֹא וּבְנוֹ וְשַׁכְלִלוּ מִן־טַעַם אֱלָהּ יִשְׂרָאֵל נְבִיָּא
טו וּמִטְּעֵם כּוֹרֶשׁ וְדָרְיָוֶשׁ וְאַרְתַּחְשַׁשְׂתְּא מֶלֶךְ פָּרָס׃ וְשֵׁיצִיא בַּיְתָה
דְנָה עַד יוֹם תְּלָתָה לִירַח אֲדָר דִּי־הִיא שְׁנַת־שֵׁת לְמַלְכוּת דָּרְיָוֶשׁ
טז מַלְכָּא׃ וַעֲבַדוּ בְנֵי־יִשְׂרָאֵל כָּהֲנַיָּא וְלֵוָיֵא וּשְׁאָר בְּנֵי־גָלוּתָא
יז חֲנֻכַּת בֵּית־אֱלָהָא דְנָה בְּחֶדְוָה׃ וְהַקְרִבוּ לַחֲנֻכַּת בֵּית־אֱלָהָא דְנָה
תּוֹרִין מְאָה דִּכְרִין מָאתַיִן אִמְּרִין אַרְבַּע מְאָה וּצְפִירֵי עִזִּין לחטיא לְחַטָּאָה
יח עַל־כָּל־יִשְׂרָאֵל תְּרֵי־עֲשַׂר לְמִנְיָן שִׁבְטֵי יִשְׂרָאֵל׃ וַהֲקִימוּ כָהֲנַיָּא ג
בִּפְלֻגָּתְהוֹן וְלֵוָיֵא בְּמַחְלְקָתְהוֹן עַל־עֲבִידַת אֱלָהָא דִּי בִירוּשְׁלֶם
יט כִּכְתָב סְפַר מֹשֶׁה׃ וַיַּעֲשׂוּ בְנֵי־הַגּוֹלָה אֶת־הַפָּסַח בְּאַרְבָּעָה
כ עָשָׂר לַחֹדֶשׁ הָרִאשׁוֹן׃ כִּי הִטַּהֲרוּ הַכֹּהֲנִים וְהַלְוִיִּם כְּאֶחָד כֻּלָּם
טְהוֹרִים וַיִּשְׁחֲטוּ הַפֶּסַח לְכָל־בְּנֵי הַגּוֹלָה וְלַאֲחֵיהֶם הַכֹּהֲנִים וְלָהֶם׃
כא וַיֹּאכְלוּ בְנֵי־יִשְׂרָאֵל הַשָּׁבִים מֵהַגּוֹלָה וְכֹל הַנִּבְדָּל מִטֻּמְאַת גּוֹיֵ־
כב הָאָרֶץ אֲלֵהֶם לִדְרֹשׁ לַיהוה אֱלֹהֵי יִשְׂרָאֵל׃ וַיַּעֲשׂוּ חַג־מַצּוֹת שִׁבְעַת
יָמִים בְּשִׂמְחָה כִּי ׀ שִׂמְּחָם יהוה וְהֵסֵב לֵב מֶלֶךְ־אַשּׁוּר עֲלֵיהֶם לְחַזֵּק
ז א יְדֵיהֶם בִּמְלֶאכֶת בֵּית־הָאֱלֹהִים אֱלֹהֵי יִשְׂרָאֵל׃ וְאַחַר
הַדְּבָרִים הָאֵלֶּה בְּמַלְכוּת אַרְתַּחְשַׁסְתְּא מֶלֶךְ־פָּרָס עֶזְרָא בֶּן־שְׂרָיָה
ב ג בֶּן־עֲזַרְיָה בֶּן־חִלְקִיָּה׃ בֶּן־שַׁלּוּם בֶּן־צָדוֹק בֶּן־אֲחִיטוּב׃ בֶּן־אֲמַרְיָה
ד ה בֶן־עֲזַרְיָה בֶן־מְרָיוֹת׃ בֶּן־זְרַחְיָה בֶן־עֻזִּי בֶן־בֻּקִּי׃ בֶּן־אֲבִישׁוּעַ בֶּן־
ו פִּינְחָס בֶּן־אֶלְעָזָר בֶּן־אַהֲרֹן הַכֹּהֵן הָרֹאשׁ׃ הוּא עֶזְרָא עָלָה מִבָּבֶל
וְהוּא־סֹפֵר מָהִיר בְּתוֹרַת מֹשֶׁה אֲשֶׁר־נָתַן יהוה אֱלֹהֵי יִשְׂרָאֵל וַיִּתֶּן־

7 was upon him. In the seventh year of the reign of Artaḥshasta, some
of the Israelites, priests, Levites, singers, gatekeepers, and Netinim ascended
8 to Jerusalem, arriving in Jerusalem in the fifth month, during the seventh year
9 of the king's reign. It was on the first day of the first month that the pilgrims
met up to begin their journey from Babylon, arriving in Jerusalem on the first
10 day of the fifth month, for the good hand of his God was upon him. For Ezra
had set his heart on expounding the LORD's Torah and observing it; he wished
11 to teach Israel its laws and precepts. This is the copy of the letter
given by King Artaḥshasta to Ezra the priest, the scholar: an authority of the
12 LORD's commandments and His laws to Israel.[21] "From
Artaḥshasta, king of kings, to Ezra the priest, scholar of the law of the God
13 of the heavens, and so forth. And now, I hereby issue an edict that any man
in my kingdom who is of the nation of Israel or its priests or Levites who is
14 ready to go to Jerusalem, may go there with you. Whereas, by the order of the
king and his seven ministers, you are hereby sent to supervise Yehuda and
15 Jerusalem, in accordance with the law of your God which you uphold. And
to transport the silver and gold donated by the king and his ministers to
16 the God of Israel whose Temple is in Jerusalem, along with any silver and
gold you may acquire anywhere in the province of Babylonia, as well as the
donations of the people and the priests to the House of their God in Jerusalem.
17 Therefore, act diligently and purchase offerings with this money: bulls, rams,
lambs, and their required grain offerings and wine libations, and offer them
18 upon the altar of the House of your God in Jerusalem. The rest of the silver
and gold may be put to use as you and your brothers see fit, according to the
19 will of your God. The vessels you are hereby entrusted with for the service
of the House of your God must be brought undamaged to the God of
20 Jerusalem. Whatever else is needed for the House of your God, that which
21 you are responsible to provide, may be charged to the king's coffers. I, King
Artaḥshasta, have issued an edict to all Keepers of the Treasures in the
province beyond the River, ordering them to diligently grant every request
22 of Ezra, the priest, scribe of the law of the God of the heavens, up to the sum
of one hundred *kikar* of silver, one hundred *kor* of wheat, one hundred *bat*
23 of wine, one hundred *bat* of oil, and an unlimited amount of salt. All that is
required by the law of the God of the heavens shall be provided assiduously
for the House of the God of the Heavens, so that His rage does not lash
24 out upon the realm of the king and his sons. We also inform you that no
priest, Levite, singer, gatekeeper, Natin, or any other person employed at
the House of this God shall be subject to the payment of tributes, head
25 taxes, or property taxes. And you, Ezra, use the wisdom of your God to
appoint judges and magistrates who will dispense judgment to all the
people in the province beyond the River, men with knowledge of the
laws of your God; you shall provide instruction to those who do not know
26 them. Anyone who fails to obey the laws of your God and the laws of the
king shall be sentenced promptly to death, corporal punishment, fine, or

21 | The entire text of this letter (7:12–26) is in Aramaic rather than Hebrew.

ז לוֹ הַמֶּלֶךְ כְּיַד־יְהוָה אֱלֹהָיו עָלָיו כֹּל בַּקָּשָׁתוֹ׃ וַיַּעֲלוּ מִבְּנֵי־
יִשְׂרָאֵל וּמִן־הַכֹּהֲנִים וְהַלְוִיִּם וְהַמְשֹׁרְרִים וְהַשֹּׁעֲרִים וְהַנְּתִינִים אֶל־
ח יְרוּשָׁלִָם בִּשְׁנַת־שֶׁבַע לְאַרְתַּחְשַׁסְתְּא הַמֶּלֶךְ׃ וַיָּבֹא יְרוּשָׁלִַם בַּחֹדֶשׁ
ט הַחֲמִישִׁי הִיא שְׁנַת הַשְּׁבִיעִית לַמֶּלֶךְ׃ כִּי בְּאֶחָד לַחֹדֶשׁ הָרִאשׁוֹן הוּא
יְסֻד הַמַּעֲלָה מִבָּבֶל וּבְאֶחָד לַחֹדֶשׁ הַחֲמִישִׁי בָּא אֶל־יְרוּשָׁלִַם כְּיַד־
י אֱלֹהָיו הַטּוֹבָה עָלָיו׃ כִּי עֶזְרָא הֵכִין לְבָבוֹ לִדְרֹשׁ אֶת־תּוֹרַת יְהוָה
יא וְלַעֲשֹׂת וּלְלַמֵּד בְּיִשְׂרָאֵל חֹק וּמִשְׁפָּט׃ וְזֶה ׀ פַּרְשֶׁגֶן הַנִּשְׁתְּוָן
אֲשֶׁר נָתַן הַמֶּלֶךְ אַרְתַּחְשַׁסְתְּא לְעֶזְרָא הַכֹּהֵן הַסֹּפֵר סֹפֵר דִּבְרֵי
יב מִצְוֺת־יְהוָה וְחֻקָּיו עַל־יִשְׂרָאֵל׃ אַרְתַּחְשַׁסְתְּא מֶלֶךְ מַלְכַיָּא
יג לְעֶזְרָא כָהֲנָא סָפַר דָּתָא דִּי־אֱלָהּ שְׁמַיָּא גְּמִיר וּכְעֶנֶת׃ מִנִּי שִׂים
טְעֵם דִּי כָל־מִתְנַדַּב בְּמַלְכוּתִי מִן־עַמָּה יִשְׂרָאֵל וְכָהֲנוֹהִי וְלֵוָיֵא
יד לִמְהָךְ לִירוּשְׁלֶם עִמָּךְ יְהָךְ׃ כָּל־קֳבֵל דִּי מִן־קֳדָם מַלְכָּא וְשִׁבְעַת
יָעֲטֹהִי שְׁלִיחַ לְבַקָּרָא עַל־יְהוּד וְלִירוּשְׁלֶם בְּדָת אֱלָהָךְ דִּי בִידָךְ׃
טו וּלְהֵיבָלָה כְּסַף וּדְהַב דִּי־מַלְכָּא וְיָעֲטוֹהִי הִתְנַדַּבוּ לֶאֱלָהּ יִשְׂרָאֵל דִּי
טז בִירוּשְׁלֶם מִשְׁכְּנֵהּ׃ וְכֹל כְּסַף וּדְהַב דִּי תְהַשְׁכַּח בְּכֹל מְדִינַת בָּבֶל
עִם הִתְנַדָּבוּת עַמָּא וְכָהֲנַיָּא מִתְנַדְּבִין לְבֵית אֱלָהֲהֹם דִּי בִירוּשְׁלֶם׃
יז כָּל־קֳבֵל דְּנָה אָסְפַּרְנָא תִקְנֵא בְּכַסְפָּא דְנָה תּוֹרִין ׀ דִּכְרִין אִמְּרִין
וּמִנְחָתְהוֹן וְנִסְכֵּיהוֹן וּתְקָרֵב הִמּוֹ עַל־מַדְבְּחָה דִּי בֵּית אֱלָהֲכֹם דִּי
יח בִירוּשְׁלֶם׃ וּמָה דִי עליך וְעַל־אחיך יִיטַב בִּשְׁאָר כַּסְפָּא וְדַהֲבָה עֲלָךְ | אֶחָךְ
יט לְמֶעְבַּד כִּרְעוּת אֱלָהֲכֹם תַּעַבְדוּן׃ וּמָאנַיָּא דִּי־מִתְיַהֲבִין לָךְ לְפָלְחָן
כ בֵּית אֱלָהָךְ הַשְׁלֵם קֳדָם אֱלָהּ יְרוּשְׁלֶם׃ וּשְׁאָר חַשְׁחוּת בֵּית אֱלָהָךְ
כא דִּי יִפֶּל־לָךְ לְמִנְתַּן תִּנְתֵּן מִן־בֵּית גִּנְזֵי מַלְכָּא׃ וּמִנִּי אֲנָה אַרְתַּחְשַׁסְתְּא
מַלְכָּא שִׂים טְעֵם לְכֹל גִּזַּבְרַיָּא דִּי בַּעֲבַר נַהֲרָה דִּי כָל־דִּי יִשְׁאֲלֶנְכוֹן
כב עֶזְרָא כָהֲנָה סָפַר דָּתָא דִּי־אֱלָהּ שְׁמַיָּא אָסְפַּרְנָא יִתְעֲבִד׃ עַד־כְּסַף
כַּכְּרִין מְאָה וְעַד־חִנְטִין כּוֹרִין מְאָה וְעַד־חֲמַר בַּתִּין מְאָה וְעַד־בַּתִּין
כג מְשַׁח מְאָה וּמְלַח דִּי־לָא כְתָב׃ כָּל־דִּי מִן־טַעַם אֱלָהּ שְׁמַיָּא יִתְעֲבֵד
אַדְרַזְדָּא לְבֵית אֱלָהּ שְׁמַיָּא דִּי־לְמָה לֶהֱוֵא קְצַף עַל־מַלְכוּת מַלְכָּא
כד וּבְנוֹהִי׃ וּלְכֹם מְהוֹדְעִין דִּי כָל־כָּהֲנַיָּא וְלֵוָיֵא זַמָּרַיָּא תָרָעַיָּא נְתִינַיָּא
וּפָלְחֵי בֵּית אֱלָהָא דְנָה מִנְדָּה בְלוֹ וַהֲלָךְ לָא שַׁלִּיט לְמִרְמֵא עֲלֵיהֹם׃
כה וְאַנְתְּ עֶזְרָא כְּחָכְמַת אֱלָהָךְ דִּי־בִידָךְ מֶנִּי שָׁפְטִין וְדַיָּנִין דִּי־לֶהֱוֺן
דאנין לְכָל־עַמָּה דִּי בַּעֲבַר נַהֲרָה לְכָל־יָדְעֵי דָּתֵי אֱלָהָךְ וְדִי לָא יָדַע דָּיְנִין
כו תְּהוֹדְעוּן׃ וְכָל־דִּי־לָא לֶהֱוֵא עָבֵד דָּתָא דִּי־אֱלָהָךְ וְדָתָא דִּי מַלְכָּא

27 imprisonment." Blessed is the LORD, God of our ancestors, for
turning the king's heart toward the cause of beautifying the House of the
28 LORD in Jerusalem. And for showing me kindness in the eyes of the king and
his ministers and all his valiant officers. So, by the grace of the LORD my God,
I gathered courage and assembled leaders from Israel to ascend to the land
with me.

8 1 These are the heads of families – along with their family lines – who came
2 up with me from Babylon during the reign of King Artahshasta. From the
family of Pinhas: Gershom; from the family of Itamar: Daniel; from the family
3 of David: Ḥatush, a descendant of Shekhanya. From the family of Parosh:
4 Zekharya; along with him were 150 men whose lineage was recorded. From
the family of Paḥat Moav: Elyeho'einai son of Zeraḥya; along with him were
5 two hundred men. From the family of Shekhanya, the son of Yaḥaziel; along
6 with him were three hundred men. And from the family of Adin: Eved son of
7 Yonatan, of the sons of Adin; along with him were fifty men; from the family
8 of Eilam: Yeshaya son of Atalya; along with him were seventy men. And from
the family of Shefatya: Zevadya son of Mikhael; along with him were eighty
9 men. From the family of Yoav: Ovadya son of Yeḥiel; along with him were two
10 hundred eighteen men; from the family of Shlomit: Ben Yosifya; along with
11 him were one hundred sixty men; from the family of Bevai: Zekharya son
12 of Bevai; along with him were twenty-eight men; from the family of Azgad:
13 Yoḥanan son of Hakatan; along with him were one hundred ten men; and
from the family of Adonikam, the last ones,[22] and these were their names:
14 Elifelet, Ye'iel, and Shemaya; along with them were sixty men. And from the
family of Bigvai: Utai and Zakur; along with them were seventy men.
15 I assembled them at the river that flows to Ahava, and we encamped there
for three days; I noted the presence of Israelites and priests, but I did not find
16 any of the Levites there. So I called upon Eliezer, Ariel, Shemaya, Elnatan,
Yariv, Elnatan, Natan, Zekharya, and Meshulam, who were leaders, as well
17 as Yoyariv and Elnatan, who were teachers. I charged them with the task of
approaching Ido, the master of a place called Kasifya. I placed words in their
mouths to relay to Ido and his brother, Netinim[23] in Kasifya, requesting that
18 they send us men to serve in the House of our God. And God's good hand
was upon us; they sent us a wise man who was descended from Maḥli son
of Levi, the son of Yisrael, namely Shereveya and his sons and brothers,
19 eighteen men. And also Ḥashavya, along with Yeshaya who was from the
20 family of Merari and his brothers and their sons, twenty men; As
well as two hundred twentyof the Netinim who had been dedicated to the
21 service of the Levites by David and his ministers, all listed by name. I then
proclaimed a fast there, upon the Ahava River, so that we might abstain from
sustenance before our God, asking Him for a smooth journey for ourselves,
22 for our small children, and for all of our possessions. For I was ashamed
to ask the king for a detachment of soldiers and cavalry to protect us from

22 | Likely the last members of the family to leave Babylon.

23 | See note on 2:43.

אָסְפַּרְנָא דִּינָה לֶהֱוֵא מִתְעֲבֵד מִנֵּהּ הֵן לְמוֹת הֵן לשרשו הֵן־לַעֲנָשׁ לִשְׁרֹשִׁי
כז נִכְסִין וְלֶאֱסוּרִין׃ בָּרוּךְ יְהוָה אֱלֹהֵי אֲבוֹתֵינוּ אֲשֶׁר
כח נָתַן כָּזֹאת בְּלֵב הַמֶּלֶךְ לְפָאֵר אֶת־בֵּית יְהוָה אֲשֶׁר בִּירוּשָׁלָםִ׃ וְעָלַי
הִטָּה־חֶסֶד לִפְנֵי הַמֶּלֶךְ וְיוֹעֲצָיו וּלְכָל־שָׂרֵי הַמֶּלֶךְ הַגִּבֹּרִים וַאֲנִי
הִתְחַזַּקְתִּי כְּיַד־יְהוָה אֱלֹהַי עָלַי וָאֶקְבְּצָה מִיִּשְׂרָאֵל רָאשִׁים לַעֲלוֹת
עִמִּי׃

ח א וְאֵלֶּה רָאשֵׁי אֲבֹתֵיהֶם וְהִתְיַחְשָׂם הָעֹלִים עִמִּי בְּמַלְכוּת אַרְתַּחְשַׁסְתְּא
ב הַמֶּלֶךְ מִבָּבֶל׃ מִבְּנֵי פִינְחָס גֵּרְשֹׁם מִבְּנֵי אִיתָמָר דָּנִיֵּאל מִבְּנֵי דָוִיד
ג חַטּוּשׁ׃ מִבְּנֵי שְׁכַנְיָה מִבְּנֵי פַרְעֹשׁ זְכַרְיָה וְעִמּוֹ הִתְיַחֵשׂ לִזְכָרִים מֵאָה
ד וַחֲמִשִּׁים׃ מִבְּנֵי פַּחַת מוֹאָב אֶלְיְהוֹעֵינַי בֶּן־זְרַחְיָה וְעִמּוֹ מָאתַיִם
ה ו הַזְּכָרִים׃ מִבְּנֵי שְׁכַנְיָה בֶּן־יַחֲזִיאֵל וְעִמּוֹ שְׁלֹשׁ מֵאוֹת הַזְּכָרִים׃ וּמִבְּנֵי
ז עָדִין עֶבֶד בֶּן־יוֹנָתָן וְעִמּוֹ חֲמִשִּׁים הַזְּכָרִים׃ וּמִבְּנֵי עֵילָם יְשַׁעְיָה בֶּן־
ח עֲתַלְיָה וְעִמּוֹ שִׁבְעִים הַזְּכָרִים׃ וּמִבְּנֵי שְׁפַטְיָה זְבַדְיָה בֶּן־מִיכָאֵל וְעִמּוֹ
ט שְׁמֹנִים הַזְּכָרִים׃ מִבְּנֵי יוֹאָב עֹבַדְיָה בֶּן־יְחִיאֵל וְעִמּוֹ מָאתַיִם וּשְׁמֹנָה
י עָשָׂר הַזְּכָרִים׃ וּמִבְּנֵי שְׁלוֹמִית בֶּן־יוֹסִפְיָה וְעִמּוֹ מֵאָה וְשִׁשִּׁים הַזְּכָרִים׃
יא יב וּמִבְּנֵי בֵבַי זְכַרְיָה בֶּן־בֵּבָי וְעִמּוֹ עֶשְׂרִים וּשְׁמֹנָה הַזְּכָרִים׃ וּמִבְּנֵי עַזְגָּד
יג יוֹחָנָן בֶּן־הַקָּטָן וְעִמּוֹ מֵאָה וַעֲשָׂרָה הַזְּכָרִים׃ וּמִבְּנֵי אֲדֹנִיקָם אַחֲרֹנִים
וְאֵלֶּה שְׁמוֹתָם אֱלִיפֶלֶט יְעִיאֵל וּשְׁמַעְיָה וְעִמָּהֶם שִׁשִּׁים הַזְּכָרִים׃
יד וּמִבְּנֵי בִּגְוַי עוּתַי וזבוד וְעִמָּהֶם שִׁבְעִים הַזְּכָרִים׃ וְזַכּוּר
טו וָאֶקְבְּצֵם אֶל־הַנָּהָר הַבָּא אֶל־אַהֲוָא וַנַּחֲנֶה שָׁם יָמִים שְׁלֹשָׁה וָאָבִינָה
טז בָעָם וּבַכֹּהֲנִים וּמִבְּנֵי לֵוִי לֹא־מָצָאתִי שָׁם׃ וָאֶשְׁלְחָה לֶאֱלִיעֶזֶר לַאֲרִיאֵל
לִשְׁמַעְיָה וּלְאֶלְנָתָן וּלְיָרִיב וּלְאֶלְנָתָן וּלְנָתָן וְלִזְכַרְיָה וְלִמְשֻׁלָּם רָאשִׁים
יז וּלְיוֹיָרִיב וּלְאֶלְנָתָן מְבִינִים׃ ואוצאה אוֹתָם עַל־אִדּוֹ הָרֹאשׁ בְּכָסִפְיָא וָאֲצַוֶּה
הַמָּקוֹם וָאָשִׂימָה בְּפִיהֶם דְּבָרִים לְדַבֵּר אֶל־אִדּוֹ אָחִיו הנתונים הַנְּתִינִים
יח בְּכָסִפְיָא הַמָּקוֹם לְהָבִיא־לָנוּ מְשָׁרְתִים לְבֵית אֱלֹהֵינוּ׃ וַיָּבִיאוּ לָנוּ
כְּיַד־אֱלֹהֵינוּ הַטּוֹבָה עָלֵינוּ אִישׁ שֶׂכֶל מִבְּנֵי מַחְלִי בֶּן־לֵוִי בֶּן־יִשְׂרָאֵל
יט וְשֵׁרֵבְיָה וּבָנָיו וְאֶחָיו שְׁמֹנָה עָשָׂר׃ וְאֶת־חֲשַׁבְיָה וְאִתּוֹ יְשַׁעְיָה מִבְּנֵי
כ מְרָרִי אֶחָיו וּבְנֵיהֶם עֶשְׂרִים׃ וּמִן־הַנְּתִינִים שֶׁנָּתַן
דָּוִיד וְהַשָּׂרִים לַעֲבֹדַת הַלְוִיִּם נְתִינִים מָאתַיִם וְעֶשְׂרִים כֻּלָּם נִקְּבוּ
כא בְשֵׁמוֹת׃ וָאֶקְרָא שָׁם צוֹם עַל־הַנָּהָר אַהֲוָא לְהִתְעַנּוֹת לִפְנֵי אֱלֹהֵינוּ
כב לְבַקֵּשׁ מִמֶּנּוּ דֶּרֶךְ יְשָׁרָה לָנוּ וּלְטַפֵּנוּ וּלְכָל־רְכוּשֵׁנוּ׃ כִּי בֹשְׁתִּי לִשְׁאוֹל

enemies on the journey, since we had already said to the king: "The hand of
our God is upon those who seek Him in their favor, but His fierce wrath is
23 upon all those who forsake Him." So we fasted and implored our God for
24 this, and He granted our plea. Then I set aside twelve of the leading priests
in addition to Shereveya and Ḥashavya and the ten kinsmen who were with
25 them. I weighed the silver and gold and vessels for them: all that the king
and his ministers and advisors and all the Israelites who had been present
26 had donated to the House of our God. These are the amounts I weighed for
them: six hundred fifty talents of silver and an additional one hundred silver
27 vessels worth one talent each; one hundred talents of gold; twenty golden
bowls worth one thousand gold darics,[24] and two vessels of brightly gleaming
28 copper as precious as gold. And I said to them: "You are holy to the Lord,
and the vessels are holy, and the silver and gold are a gift to the Lord, God
29 of your ancestors. Be vigilant and safeguard them until you weigh them in
the presence of the leaders of the priests and the Levites and the heads of the
fathers' households of Israel in Jerusalem, in the chambers of the House of
30 the Lord." So the priests and the Levites took it upon themselves to transport
the entire amount of silver, gold, and vessels to Jerusalem, to the House of our
31 God. We journeyed from the Ahava River on the twelfth day of the
first month, heading for Jerusalem; the providence of our God was upon us,
and He saved us from falling into the hands of enemies and from ambushes
32 33 on the road. We arrived in Jerusalem and rested there for three days. On
the fourth day, the silver and gold and vessels were weighed in the House
of our God and entrusted to Meremot, son of Uriya the priest, along with
Elazar son of Pinḥas; also present were the Levites, Yozavad son of Yeshua
34 and Noadya son of Binui. Everything was counted out and weighed, and the
35 weight of the lot was recorded in writing on that occasion. Those
who returned from the captivity, the exiles, presented burnt offerings to the
God of Israel: twelve bulls representing all of Israel, ninety-six rams, seventy-
seven sheep, and twelve goats for atonement; all of these a burnt offering to
36 the Lord. And they delivered the king's orders to the king's viceroys and to
the governors of the province beyond the River, who held the people and
9 1 the House of God in great esteem. When all of this was over, the
leaders approached me and said: "The people Israel, and even the priests
and Levites, have failed to separate themselves from the people of the land.
They engage in abominations in the manner of the Canaanites, the Hittites,
the Perizzites, the Jebusites, the Amonites, the Moabites, the Egyptians,
2 and the Amorites. For they have taken some of their daughters as wives for
themselves and for their sons, and the holy seed has been mixed up with that
of the people of the land; the leaders and the officials have led the way in this
3 unfaithfulness." When I heard this, I rent my garment and my mantle, tore
4 out hair from my head and beard, and sat down, dumbfounded. And those
who feared the word of the God of Israel gathered around me because of the
unfaithfulness of the returned exiles. I myself sat there dumbfounded until

24 | A Persian currency.

מִן־הַמֶּלֶךְ חַיִל וּפָרָשִׁים לְעָזְרֵנוּ מֵאוֹיֵב בַּדָּרֶךְ כִּי־אָמַרְנוּ לַמֶּלֶךְ לֵאמֹר
כג יַד־אֱלֹהֵינוּ עַל־כָּל־מְבַקְשָׁיו לְטוֹבָה וְעֻזּוֹ וְאַפּוֹ עַל כָּל־עֹזְבָיו׃ וַנָּצוּמָה
כד וַנְּבַקְשָׁה מֵאֱלֹהֵינוּ עַל־זֹאת וַיֵּעָתֵר לָנוּ׃ וָאַבְדִּילָה מִשָּׂרֵי הַכֹּהֲנִים
כה שְׁנֵים עָשָׂר לְשֵׁרֵבְיָה חֲשַׁבְיָה וְעִמָּהֶם מֵאֲחֵיהֶם עֲשָׂרָה׃ ואשקולה וָאֶשְׁקֳלָה
לָהֶם אֶת־הַכֶּסֶף וְאֶת־הַזָּהָב וְאֶת־הַכֵּלִים תְּרוּמַת בֵּית־אֱלֹהֵינוּ
כו הַהֵרִימוּ הַמֶּלֶךְ וְיֹעֲצָיו וְשָׂרָיו וְכָל־יִשְׂרָאֵל הַנִּמְצָאִים׃ וָאֶשְׁקֲלָה עַל־
יָדָם כֶּסֶף כִּכָּרִים שֵׁשׁ־מֵאוֹת וַחֲמִשִּׁים וּכְלֵי־כֶסֶף מֵאָה לְכִכָּרִים זָהָב
כז מֵאָה כִכָּר׃ וּכְפֹרֵי זָהָב עֶשְׂרִים לַאֲדַרְכֹנִים אָלֶף וּכְלֵי נְחֹשֶׁת מֻצְהָב
כח טוֹבָה שְׁנַיִם חֲמוּדֹת כַּזָּהָב׃ וָאֹמְרָה אֲלֵהֶם אַתֶּם קֹדֶשׁ לַיהוה וְהַכֵּלִים
כט קֹדֶשׁ וְהַכֶּסֶף וְהַזָּהָב נְדָבָה לַיהוה אֱלֹהֵי אֲבֹתֵיכֶם׃ שִׁקְדוּ וְשִׁמְרוּ עַד־
תִּשְׁקְלוּ לִפְנֵי שָׂרֵי הַכֹּהֲנִים וְהַלְוִיִּם וְשָׂרֵי־הָאָבוֹת לְיִשְׂרָאֵל בִּירוּשָׁלִָם
ל הַלִּשְׁכוֹת בֵּית יהוה׃ וְקִבְּלוּ הַכֹּהֲנִים וְהַלְוִיִּם מִשְׁקַל הַכֶּסֶף וְהַזָּהָב
לא וְהַכֵּלִים לְהָבִיא לִירוּשָׁלִַם לְבֵית אֱלֹהֵינוּ׃ וַנִּסְעָה מִנְּהַר
אַהֲוָא בִּשְׁנֵים עָשָׂר לַחֹדֶשׁ הָרִאשׁוֹן לָלֶכֶת יְרוּשָׁלִָם וְיַד־אֱלֹהֵינוּ
לב הָיְתָה עָלֵינוּ וַיַּצִּילֵנוּ מִכַּף אוֹיֵב וְאוֹרֵב עַל־הַדָּרֶךְ׃ וַנָּבוֹא יְרוּשָׁלִָם
לג וַנֵּשֶׁב שָׁם יָמִים שְׁלֹשָׁה׃ וּבַיּוֹם הָרְבִיעִי נִשְׁקַל הַכֶּסֶף וְהַזָּהָב וְהַכֵּלִים
בְּבֵית אֱלֹהֵינוּ עַל יַד־מְרֵמוֹת בֶּן־אוּרִיָּה הַכֹּהֵן וְעִמּוֹ אֶלְעָזָר בֶּן־
לד פִּינְחָס וְעִמָּהֶם יוֹזָבָד בֶּן־יֵשׁוּעַ וְנוֹעַדְיָה בֶן־בִּנּוּי הַלְוִיִּם׃ בְּמִסְפָּר
לה בְּמִשְׁקָל לַכֹּל וַיִּכָּתֵב כָּל־הַמִּשְׁקָל בָּעֵת הַהִיא׃ הַבָּאִים ד
מֵהַשְּׁבִי בְנֵי־הַגּוֹלָה הִקְרִיבוּ עֹלוֹת ׀ לֵאלֹהֵי יִשְׂרָאֵל פָּרִים שְׁנֵים־עָשָׂר
עַל־כָּל־יִשְׂרָאֵל אֵילִים ׀ תִּשְׁעִים וְשִׁשָּׁה כְּבָשִׂים שִׁבְעִים וְשִׁבְעָה
לו צְפִירֵי חַטָּאת שְׁנֵים עָשָׂר הַכֹּל עוֹלָה לַיהוה׃ וַיִּתְּנוּ ׀ אֶת־דָּתֵי הַמֶּלֶךְ
לַאֲחַשְׁדַּרְפְּנֵי הַמֶּלֶךְ וּפַחֲווֹת עֵבֶר הַנָּהָר וְנִשְּׂאוּ אֶת־הָעָם וְאֶת־בֵּית
ט א הָאֱלֹהִים׃ וּכְכַלּוֹת אֵלֶּה נִגְּשׁוּ אֵלַי הַשָּׂרִים לֵאמֹר לֹא־
נִבְדְּלוּ הָעָם יִשְׂרָאֵל וְהַכֹּהֲנִים וְהַלְוִיִּם מֵעַמֵּי הָאֲרָצוֹת כְּתֹעֲבֹתֵיהֶם
ב לַכְּנַעֲנִי הַחִתִּי הַפְּרִזִּי הַיְבוּסִי הָעַמֹּנִי הַמֹּאָבִי הַמִּצְרִי וְהָאֱמֹרִי׃ כִּי־
נָשְׂאוּ מִבְּנֹתֵיהֶם לָהֶם וְלִבְנֵיהֶם וְהִתְעָרְבוּ זֶרַע הַקֹּדֶשׁ בְּעַמֵּי הָאֲרָצוֹת
ג וְיַד הַשָּׂרִים וְהַסְּגָנִים הָיְתָה בַּמַּעַל הַזֶּה רִאשׁוֹנָה׃ וּכְשָׁמְעִי אֶת־
הַדָּבָר הַזֶּה קָרַעְתִּי אֶת־בִּגְדִי וּמְעִילִי וָאֶמְרְטָה מִשְּׂעַר רֹאשִׁי וּזְקָנִי
ד וָאֵשְׁבָה מְשׁוֹמֵם׃ וְאֵלַי יֵאָסְפוּ כֹּל חָרֵד בְּדִבְרֵי אֱלֹהֵי־יִשְׂרָאֵל עַל מַעַל

5 it was time for the afternoon offering. At the time of the evening offering, I
rose up from my fast, with my garment and mantle torn. I knelt down on my
6 knees and spread out my hands to the LORD my God. And I said: "My God!
I am utterly mortified to face You, my God, for our sins have increased so
much that they have piled up above our heads, and our guilt has mounted up
7 to the heavens. Ever since the days of our ancestors, we have been entrenched
in great guilt, until this very day. Because of our sins, we and our kings and
priests have been handed over to foreign kings, to the sword, to captivity, to
8 pillage, and to shamefacedness, from which we suffer to this very day. But now,
for a short moment we have been granted a pardon by the LORD our God,
who has left us a remnant and has given us a stake in His holy place. Our God
has rekindled the light in our eyes, allowing us to sustain ourselves a little in
9 our bondage. For indeed, we are slaves, but in our bondage, our God has not
forsaken us. He has shown us kindness through the kings of Persia, allowing
us to sustain ourselves, to exalt the House of our God and rebuild its ruins;
10 He has built us a wall in Yehuda and Jerusalem. And now, O our God, what
11 can we say after this? Indeed, we have forsaken Your commandments, which
You gave through Your servants, the prophets, who said:[25] The land that you
are coming into to possess is an impure land, polluted by the people of the
land whom, with their abominations, have filled it with their impurity from
12 end to end. And now, you shall not give your daughters to their sons, and
you shall not take their daughters for your sons, and you shall not seek their
peace or welfare, ever. Thus, you will be strong and partake of the best of the
13 land and bequeath it to your children forever. After all that has befallen us
due to our evil deeds and our great guilt, You, our God, have punished us for
14 less than the worth of our sins, having given us this remnant. Shall we then
disobey Your commandments yet again by intermarrying with these peoples
who are replete with these abominations? Would You not rage against us to
15 the end, not leaving a remnant or a trace? O LORD, God of Israel,
You have dealt with us righteously, for we are a mere remnant on this day; here
we are before You with our guilt, though we are unworthy of standing before
10 1 You." As Ezra prayed and confessed, weeping as he knelt down on
his knees before the House of God, a very large crowd of Israelites gathered
around him: men, women, and children, weeping a great deal.
2 Then Shekhanya son of Yeḥiel, of the sons of Eilam, spoke up, saying to Ezra:
"We have indeed been unfaithful to our God by marrying foreign women of
the peoples of the land; even so, there is still hope for Israel in this matter.
3 Now, let us make a covenant with our God to send away all these women
and their offspring, according to the counsel of the Lord and of those who
4 fear our God's commandments; everyone shall abide by the law. Rise up, for
it is your duty to take care of this matter; we will be with you. Be strong and
5 take action." So Ezra rose up and made the leaders of the priests
and the Levites and all of Israel take an oath that they would act upon this,

25 | See Leviticus, chapter 18.

ה הַגּוֹלָה וַאֲנִי יֹשֵׁב מְשׁוֹמֵם עַד לְמִנְחַת הָעָרֶב: וּבְמִנְחַת הָעֶרֶב קַמְתִּי
מִתַּעֲנִיתִי וּבְקָרְעִי בִגְדִי וּמְעִילִי וָאֶכְרְעָה עַל־בִּרְכַּי וָאֶפְרְשָׂה כַפַּי אֶל־
ו יְהוָה אֱלֹהָי: וָאֹמְרָה אֱלֹהַי בֹּשְׁתִּי וְנִכְלַמְתִּי לְהָרִים אֱלֹהַי פָּנַי אֵלֶיךָ
ז כִּי עֲוֺנֹתֵינוּ רָבוּ לְמַעְלָה רֹּאשׁ וְאַשְׁמָתֵנוּ גָדְלָה עַד לַשָּׁמָיִם: מִימֵי
אֲבֹתֵינוּ אֲנַחְנוּ בְּאַשְׁמָה גְדֹלָה עַד הַיּוֹם הַזֶּה וּבַעֲוֺנֹתֵינוּ נִתַּנּוּ אֲנַחְנוּ
מְלָכֵינוּ כֹהֲנֵינוּ בְּיַד ׀ מַלְכֵי הָאֲרָצוֹת בַּחֶרֶב בַּשְּׁבִי וּבַבִּזָּה וּבְבֹשֶׁת פָּנִים
ח כְּהַיּוֹם הַזֶּה: וְעַתָּה כִּמְעַט־רֶגַע הָיְתָה תְחִנָּה מֵאֵת ׀ יְהוָה אֱלֹהֵינוּ
לְהַשְׁאִיר לָנוּ פְּלֵיטָה וְלָתֶת־לָנוּ יָתֵד בִּמְקוֹם קָדְשׁוֹ לְהָאִיר עֵינֵינוּ
ט אֱלֹהֵינוּ וּלְתִתֵּנוּ מִחְיָה מְעַט בְּעַבְדֻתֵנוּ: כִּי־עֲבָדִים אֲנַחְנוּ וּבְעַבְדֻתֵנוּ
לֹא עֲזָבָנוּ אֱלֹהֵינוּ וַיַּט־עָלֵינוּ חֶסֶד לִפְנֵי מַלְכֵי פָרַס לָתֶת־לָנוּ מִחְיָה
לְרוֹמֵם אֶת־בֵּית אֱלֹהֵינוּ וּלְהַעֲמִיד אֶת־חָרְבֹתָיו וְלָתֶת־לָנוּ גָדֵר
י בִּיהוּדָה וּבִירוּשָׁלִָם: וְעַתָּה מַה־נֹּאמַר אֱלֹהֵינוּ אַחֲרֵי־זֹאת כִּי עָזַבְנוּ
יא מִצְוֺתֶיךָ: אֲשֶׁר צִוִּיתָ בְּיַד עֲבָדֶיךָ הַנְּבִיאִים לֵאמֹר הָאָרֶץ אֲשֶׁר אַתֶּם
בָּאִים לְרִשְׁתָּהּ אֶרֶץ נִדָּה הִיא בְּנִדַּת עַמֵּי הָאֲרָצוֹת בְּתוֹעֲבֹתֵיהֶם
יב אֲשֶׁר מִלְאוּהָ מִפֶּה אֶל־פֶּה בְּטֻמְאָתָם: וְעַתָּה בְּנוֹתֵיכֶם אַל־תִּתְּנוּ
לִבְנֵיהֶם וּבְנֹתֵיהֶם אַל־תִּשְׂאוּ לִבְנֵיכֶם וְלֹא־תִדְרְשׁוּ שְׁלֹמָם וְטוֹבָתָם
עַד־עוֹלָם לְמַעַן תֶּחֶזְקוּ וַאֲכַלְתֶּם אֶת־טוּב הָאָרֶץ וְהוֹרַשְׁתֶּם לִבְנֵיכֶם
יג עַד־עוֹלָם: וְאַחֲרֵי כָּל־הַבָּא עָלֵינוּ בְּמַעֲשֵׂינוּ הָרָעִים וּבְאַשְׁמָתֵנוּ
הַגְּדֹלָה כִּי ׀ אַתָּה אֱלֹהֵינוּ חָשַׂכְתָּ לְמַטָּה מֵעֲוֺנֵנוּ וְנָתַתָּה לָּנוּ פְּלֵיטָה
יד כָּזֹאת: הֲנָשׁוּב לְהָפֵר מִצְוֺתֶיךָ וּלְהִתְחַתֵּן בְּעַמֵּי הַתֹּעֵבוֹת הָאֵלֶּה
טו הֲלוֹא תֶאֱנַף־בָּנוּ עַד־כַּלֵּה לְאֵין שְׁאֵרִית וּפְלֵיטָה: יְהוָה
אֱלֹהֵי יִשְׂרָאֵל צַדִּיק אַתָּה כִּי־נִשְׁאַרְנוּ פְלֵיטָה כְּהַיּוֹם הַזֶּה הִנְנוּ לְפָנֶיךָ
י א בְּאַשְׁמָתֵינוּ כִּי אֵין לַעֲמוֹד לְפָנֶיךָ עַל־זֹאת: וּכְהִתְפַּלֵּל
עֶזְרָא וּכְהִתְוַדֹּתוֹ בֹּכֶה וּמִתְנַפֵּל לִפְנֵי בֵּית הָאֱלֹהִים נִקְבְּצוּ אֵלָיו
מִיִּשְׂרָאֵל קָהָל רַב־מְאֹד אֲנָשִׁים וְנָשִׁים וִילָדִים כִּי־בָכוּ הָעָם הַרְבֵּה
בֶכֶה:
ב וַיַּעַן שְׁכַנְיָה בֶן־יְחִיאֵל מִבְּנֵי עוֹלָם וַיֹּאמֶר לְעֶזְרָא אֲנַחְנוּ מָעַלְנוּ עֵילָם
בֵאלֹהֵינוּ וַנֹּשֶׁב נָשִׁים נָכְרִיּוֹת מֵעַמֵּי הָאָרֶץ וְעַתָּה יֵשׁ־מִקְוֶה לְיִשְׂרָאֵל
ג עַל־זֹאת: וְעַתָּה נִכְרָת־בְּרִית לֵאלֹהֵינוּ לְהוֹצִיא כָל־נָשִׁים וְהַנּוֹלָד
ד מֵהֶם בַּעֲצַת אֲדֹנָי וְהַחֲרֵדִים בְּמִצְוַת אֱלֹהֵינוּ וְכַתּוֹרָה יֵעָשֶׂה: קוּם כִּי־
ה עָלֶיךָ הַדָּבָר וַאֲנַחְנוּ עִמָּךְ חֲזַק וַעֲשֵׂה: וַיָּקָם עֶזְרָא
וַיַּשְׁבַּע אֶת־שָׂרֵי הַכֹּהֲנִים הַלְוִיִּם וְכָל־יִשְׂרָאֵל לַעֲשׂוֹת כַּדָּבָר הַזֶּה

6 and they took the oath. Then Ezra left his place before the House of God and
went to the chamber of Yoḥanan son of Elyashiv. He went there, all the while
abstaining from eating bread and drinking water, for he was still mourning the
7 unfaithfulness of the returned exiles. A proclamation was made throughout
Yehuda and Jerusalem calling all the returned exiles to assemble in Jerusalem,
8 warning that anyone who did not come within three days as prescribed by
the leaders and elders would have all his property confiscated and would be
shunned from the assembly of the exiles.
9 So all the people of Yehuda and Binyamin assembled in Jerusalem within
three days; it was the twentieth day of the ninth month. All of the people sat
in the plaza in front of the House of God, trembling because of the affair and
10 due to the heavy rains. Ezra the priest stood up and addressed them: "You
have been unfaithful by marrying foreign women, thus increasing the guilt of
11 Israel. But now, make your confession to the Lord, God of your ancestors,
and perform His will by separating yourselves from the peoples of the land
12 and from the foreign women." The whole assembly responded
13 loudly: "Indeed, we should do as you say. But there are many people, and it
is the rainy season so we cannot go on standing outdoors. In any event, the
task cannot be completed in a day or two, since we have sinned greatly in this
14 matter. Let our leaders stand in for the whole assembly: Every man in any of
our towns who has married a foreign woman shall come at his designated
time along with the elders and judges of that town until God's rage over this
15 affair has been turned away from us." Only Yonatan son of Asael, and Yaḥzeya
son of Tikva, objected to this, supported by Meshulam and Shabtai the Levite.
16 So that is what the returned exiles did. Ezra the priest and men who were
heads of families sequestered themselves to represent their families, all listed
by name. They convened on the first day of the tenth month to investigate the
17 matter. They concluded the investigation regarding the men who had married
18 foreign women on the first day of the first month. From
the families of the priests they found that those who had married foreign
women were: From the family of Yeshua son of Yotzadak, and his brothers:
19 Maaseya, Eliezer, Yariv, and Gedalya. They pledged to send away their
wives; the guilty parties vowed to bring rams of the flock for their guilt.
20 21 From the family of Imer: Ḥanani and Zevadya. From the family of Ḥarim:
22 Maaseya, Eliya, Shemaya, Yeḥiel, and Uziya. And from the family of Pashḥur:
23 Elyo'einai, Maaseya, Yishmael, Netanel, Yozavad, and Elasa. And of the
Levites: Yozavad, Shimi, and Kelaya – that is, Kelita – Petaḥya, Yehuda, and
24 Eliezer. And of the singers: Elyashiv; of the gatekeepers, Shalum, Telem, and
25 Uri. And of the Israelites: Of the sons of Parosh: Ramya, Yiziya, Malkiya,
26 Miyamin, Elazar, Malkiya, and Benaya. From the family of Eilam: Matanya,
27 Zekharya, Yeḥiel, Avdi, Yeremot, and Eliya. From the family of Zatu:
28 Elyo'einai, Elyashiv, Matanya, Yeremot, Zavad, and Aziza. From the family of
29 Bevai: Yehoḥanan, Ḥananya, Zabai, and Atlai. From the family of Bani:
30 Meshulam, Malukh, Adaya, Yashuv, She'al, and Ramot. From the family of

ו וַיִּשָּׁבֵעוּ: וַיָּקׇם עֶזְרָא מִלִּפְנֵי בֵּית הָאֱלֹהִים וַיֵּלֶךְ אֶל־לִשְׁכַּת יְהוֹחָנָן
בֶּן־אֶלְיָשִׁיב וַיֵּלֶךְ שָׁם לֶחֶם לֹא־אָכַל וּמַיִם לֹא־שָׁתָה כִּי מִתְאַבֵּל
ז עַל־מַעַל הַגּוֹלָה: וַיַּעֲבִירוּ קוֹל בִּיהוּדָה וִירוּשָׁלַ͏ִם לְכֹל בְּנֵי הַגּוֹלָה
ח לְהִקָּבֵץ יְרוּשָׁלָ͏ִם: וְכֹל אֲשֶׁר לֹא־יָבוֹא לִשְׁלֹשֶׁת הַיָּמִים כַּעֲצַת הַשָּׂרִים
וְהַזְּקֵנִים יׇחֳרַם כׇּל־רְכוּשׁוֹ וְהוּא יִבָּדֵל מִקְּהַל הַגּוֹלָה:
ט וַיִּקָּבְצוּ כׇל־אַנְשֵׁי־יְהוּדָה וּבִנְיָמִן ׀ יְרוּשָׁלַ͏ִם לִשְׁלֹשֶׁת הַיָּמִים הוּא חֹדֶשׁ
הַתְּשִׁיעִי בְּעֶשְׂרִים בַּחֹדֶשׁ וַיֵּשְׁבוּ כׇל־הָעָם בִּרְחוֹב בֵּית הָאֱלֹהִים
י מַרְעִידִים עַל־הַדָּבָר וּמֵהַגְּשָׁמִים: וַיָּקׇם עֶזְרָא הַכֹּהֵן וַיֹּאמֶר אֲלֵהֶם
אַתֶּם מְעַלְתֶּם וַתֹּשִׁיבוּ נָשִׁים נׇכְרִיּוֹת לְהוֹסִיף עַל־אַשְׁמַת יִשְׂרָאֵל:
יא וְעַתָּה תְּנוּ תוֹדָה לַיהֹוָה אֱלֹהֵי־אֲבֹתֵיכֶם וַעֲשׂוּ רְצוֹנוֹ וְהִבָּדְלוּ מֵעַמֵּי
יב הָאָרֶץ וּמִן־הַנָּשִׁים הַנׇּכְרִיּוֹת: וַיַּעֲנוּ כׇל־הַקָּהָל וַיֹּאמְרוּ
יג קוֹל גָּדוֹל כֵּן כדבריך עָלֵינוּ לַעֲשׂוֹת: אֲבָל הָעָם רָב וְהָעֵת גְּשָׁמִים כִּדְבָרְךָ
וְאֵין כֹּחַ לַעֲמוֹד בַּחוּץ וְהַמְּלָאכָה לֹא־לְיוֹם אֶחָד וְלֹא לִשְׁנַיִם כִּי־
יד הִרְבִּינוּ לִפְשֹׁעַ בַּדָּבָר הַזֶּה: יַעַמְדוּ־נָא שָׂרֵינוּ לְכׇל־הַקָּהָל וְכֹל ׀ אֲשֶׁר
בֶּעָרֵינוּ הַהֹשִׁיב נָשִׁים נׇכְרִיּוֹת יָבֹא לְעִתִּים מְזֻמָּנִים וְעִמָּהֶם זִקְנֵי־עִיר
וָעִיר וְשֹׁפְטֶיהָ עַד לְהָשִׁיב חֲרוֹן אַף־אֱלֹהֵינוּ מִמֶּנּוּ עַד לַדָּבָר הַזֶּה:
טו אַךְ יוֹנָתָן בֶּן־עֲשָׂהאֵל וְיַחְזְיָה בֶן־תִּקְוָה עָמְדוּ עַל־זֹאת וּמְשֻׁלָּם
טז וְשַׁבְּתַי הַלֵּוִי עֲזָרֻם: וַיַּעֲשׂוּ־כֵן בְּנֵי הַגּוֹלָה וַיִּבָּדְלוּ עֶזְרָא הַכֹּהֵן אֲנָשִׁים
רָאשֵׁי הָאָבוֹת לְבֵית אֲבֹתָם וְכֻלָּם בְּשֵׁמוֹת וַיֵּשְׁבוּ בְּיוֹם אֶחָד לַחֹדֶשׁ
יז הָעֲשִׂירִי לְדַרְיוֹשׁ הַדָּבָר: וַיְכַלּוּ בַכֹּל אֲנָשִׁים הַהֹשִׁיבוּ נָשִׁים נׇכְרִיּוֹת
יח עַד יוֹם אֶחָד לַחֹדֶשׁ הָרִאשׁוֹן: וַיִּמָּצֵא מִבְּנֵי הַכֹּהֲנִים
אֲשֶׁר הֹשִׁיבוּ נָשִׁים נׇכְרִיּוֹת מִבְּנֵי יֵשׁוּעַ בֶּן־יוֹצָדָק וְאֶחָיו מַעֲשֵׂיָה
יט וֶאֱלִיעֶזֶר וְיָרִיב וּגְדַלְיָה: וַיִּתְּנוּ יָדָם לְהוֹצִיא נְשֵׁיהֶם וַאֲשֵׁמִים אֵיל־צֹאן
כ כא עַל־אַשְׁמָתָם: וּמִבְּנֵי אִמֵּר חֲנָנִי וּזְבַדְיָה: וּמִבְּנֵי חָרִם מַעֲשֵׂיָה וְאֵלִיָּה
כב וּשְׁמַעְיָה וִיחִיאֵל וְעֻזִּיָּה: וּמִבְּנֵי פַּשְׁחוּר אֶלְיוֹעֵינַי מַעֲשֵׂיָה יִשְׁמָעֵאל
כג נְתַנְאֵל יוֹזָבָד וְאֶלְעָשָׂה: וּמִן־הַלְוִיִּם יוֹזָבָד וְשִׁמְעִי וְקֵלָיָה הוּא קְלִיטָא
כד פְּתַחְיָה יְהוּדָה וֶאֱלִיעֶזֶר: וּמִן־הַמְשֹׁרְרִים אֶלְיָשִׁיב וּמִן־הַשֹּׁעֲרִים
כה שַׁלֻּם וָטֶלֶם וְאוּרִי: וּמִיִּשְׂרָאֵל מִבְּנֵי פַרְעֹשׁ רַמְיָה וְיִזִּיָּה וּמַלְכִּיָּה וּמִיָּמִן
כו וְאֶלְעָזָר וּמַלְכִּיָּה וּבְנָיָה: וּמִבְּנֵי עֵילָם מַתַּנְיָה זְכַרְיָה וִיחִיאֵל וְעַבְדִּי
כז וִירֵמוֹת וְאֵלִיָּה: וּמִבְּנֵי זַתּוּא אֶלְיוֹעֵנַי אֶלְיָשִׁיב מַתַּנְיָה וִירֵמוֹת וְזָבָד
כח כט וַעֲזִיזָא: וּמִבְּנֵי בֵּבָי יְהוֹחָנָן חֲנַנְיָה זַבַּי עַתְלָי: וּמִבְּנֵי בָּנִי מְשֻׁלָּם מַלּוּךְ
ל וַעֲדָיָה יָשׁוּב וּשְׁאָל ירמות: וּמִבְּנֵי פַּחַת מוֹאָב עַדְנָא וּכְלָל בְּנָיָה וְרָמוֹת

Paḥat Moav: Adna, Kelal, Benaya, Maaseya, Matanya, Betzalel, Binui, and
31 Menashe. From the family of Ḥarim: Eliezer, Yishiya, Malkiya, Shemaya,
32, 33 Shimon; Binyamin, Malukh, and Shemarya. From the family of Ḥashum:
34 Matnai, Matata, Zavad, Elifelet, Yeremai, Menashe, and Shimi. From the
35, 36 family of Bani: Maadai, Amram, and U'el; Benaya, Bedya, Keluhu; Vanya,
37, 38 Meremot, Elyashiv, Matanya, Matnai, and Yaasai; Bani, Binui, and Shimi;
39, 40, 41 Shelemya, Natan, and Adaya; Makhnadvai, Shashai, Sharai; Azarel,
42, 43 Shelemyahu, Shemarya; Shalum, Amarya, Yosef. And from the family
44 of Nevo: Ye'iel, Matitya, Zavad, Zevina, Yadai, Yoel, and Benaya. All
these men had married foreign women, some of whom had produced
1 1 offspring.

NEḤEMYA / NEHEMIAH

The words of Neḥemya son of Ḥakhalya: In the
month of Kislev in the twentieth year,[1] I was in the citadel of Shushan.[2]
2 There came Ḥanani, one of my brothers, he and men from Yehuda whom I
questioned about the Jews, those survivors remaining from the captivity,[3]
3 and about Jerusalem. And they told me, "Those remaining from the captivity
in the province are degraded and in dire distress while Jerusalem's wall has
been everywhere broken through, and her gates have been put to the torch."
4 Upon hearing these tidings, I sat down and wept, mourning for days while
5 fasting and praying before the God of the heavens. I said,[4] "Please, LORD,
God of the heavens, the great and awesome God, who keeps His covenant of
6 love with those who love Him and keep His commandments, please, may
Your ear heed and Your eyes be open to hear Your servant's prayer that I am
now praying before You day and night on behalf of the Israelites Your servants,
while confessing the sins of the Israelites that we have sinned against You; I
7 and my father's house have also sinned. We have injured You grievously
and have not kept the commandments, statutes, and laws with which You
8 charged Moshe, Your servant. Remember, please, what You charged Moshe,
Your servant, saying,[5] 'You will break faith; I will disperse you among the
9 nations – yet you will return to Me; you will keep My commandments and
observe them. If you should be expelled to the farthest of horizons, even from
there I will gather them, bringing them to the place where I have chosen
10 to house My name,' for they are Your servants, Your people, whom You
11 redeemed by Your great power and Your strong hand. Please, O Lord – may
Your ear heed Your servant's prayer and the prayer of Your servants, eager to
revere Your name. Please let Your servant succeed today and grant him the
2 1 mercy of this man" – for I was official cupbearer to the king. It was
in the month of Nisan in the twentieth year of King Artaḥshasta, while wine
was before him, that I bore the wine and gave it to the king, whom I did not
2 displease. The king said to me, "Why is your face downcast? Since you are

1 | The twentieth year of the reign of Artaḥshasta I, king of Persia, was 445 BCE, several decades after Koresh first issued his proclamation allowing the Jews to return to the land of Israel.

2 | A royal capital that was also the setting for most of the book of Esther.

3 | This phrase likely refers to the Jewish community of returnees from Babylonia.

4 | The language of this prayer parallels several other passages (cf. 9:32, and Deut. 7:9; I Kings 8:23–52; Dan. 9:4; and II Chr. 6:14–40).

5 | See, e.g., Deuteronomy 4:25–30, 12:11, 30:1–6.

לא מַעֲשֵׂיָה מַתַּנְיָה בְּצַלְאֵל וּבִנּוּי וּמְנַשֶּׁה׃ וּבְנֵי חָרִם אֱלִיעֶזֶר יִשִּׁיָּה מַלְכִּיָּה
לב,לג שְׁמַעְיָה שִׁמְעוֹן׃ בִּנְיָמִן מַלּוּךְ שְׁמַרְיָה׃ מִבְּנֵי חָשֻׁם מַתְּנַי מַתַּתָּה זָבָד
לד,לה אֱלִיפֶלֶט יְרֵמַי מְנַשֶּׁה שִׁמְעִי׃ מִבְּנֵי בָנִי מַעֲדַי עַמְרָם וְאוּאֵל׃ בְּנָיָה
לו,לז,לח בֵדְיָה כלוהי׃ וַנְיָה מְרֵמוֹת אֶלְיָשִׁיב׃ מַתַּנְיָה מַתְּנַי ויעשו׃ וּבָנִי וּבִנּוּי כְּלוּהוּ | וַיַּעֲשָׂי
לט,מ,מא שִׁמְעִי׃ וְשֶׁלֶמְיָה וְנָתָן וַעֲדָיָה׃ מַכְנַדְבַי שָׁשַׁי שָׁרָי׃ עֲזַרְאֵל וְשֶׁלֶמְיָהוּ
מב,מג שְׁמַרְיָה׃ שַׁלּוּם אֲמַרְיָה יוֹסֵף׃ מִבְּנֵי נְבוֹ יְעִיאֵל מַתִּתְיָה זָבָד זְבִינָא
מד ידו וְיוֹאֵל בְּנָיָה׃ כָּל־אֵלֶּה נשאי נָשִׁים נָכְרִיּוֹת וְיֵשׁ מֵהֶם נָשִׁים וַיָּשִׂימוּ יַדַּי | נָשְׂאוּ
א א בָּנִים׃ דִּבְרֵי נְחֶמְיָה בֶּן־חֲכַלְיָה וַיְהִי בְחֹדֶשׁ־כִּסְלֵו נחמיה
ב שְׁנַת עֶשְׂרִים וַאֲנִי הָיִיתִי בְּשׁוּשַׁן הַבִּירָה׃ וַיָּבֹא חֲנָנִי אֶחָד מֵאַחַי הוּא
וַאֲנָשִׁים מִיהוּדָה וָאֶשְׁאָלֵם עַל־הַיְּהוּדִים הַפְּלֵיטָה אֲשֶׁר־נִשְׁאֲרוּ מִן־
ג הַשֶּׁבִי וְעַל־יְרוּשָׁלִָם׃ וַיֹּאמְרוּ לִי הַנִּשְׁאָרִים אֲשֶׁר נִשְׁאֲרוּ מִן־הַשְּׁבִי
שָׁם בַּמְּדִינָה בְּרָעָה גְדֹלָה וּבְחֶרְפָּה וְחוֹמַת יְרוּשָׁלִַם מְפֹרָצֶת וּשְׁעָרֶיהָ
ד נִצְּתוּ בָאֵשׁ׃ וַיְהִי כְּשָׁמְעִי ׀ אֶת־הַדְּבָרִים הָאֵלֶּה יָשַׁבְתִּי וָאֶבְכֶּה
ה וָאֶתְאַבְּלָה יָמִים וָאֱהִי צָם וּמִתְפַּלֵּל לִפְנֵי אֱלֹהֵי הַשָּׁמָיִם׃ וָאֹמַר אָנָּא
יְהוָה אֱלֹהֵי הַשָּׁמַיִם הָאֵל הַגָּדוֹל וְהַנּוֹרָא שֹׁמֵר הַבְּרִית וָחֶסֶד לְאֹהֲבָיו
ו וּלְשֹׁמְרֵי מִצְוֺתָיו׃ תְּהִי נָא אָזְנְךָ־קַשֶּׁבֶת וְעֵינֶיךָ פְתוּחוֹת לִשְׁמֹעַ אֶל־
תְּפִלַּת עַבְדְּךָ אֲשֶׁר אָנֹכִי מִתְפַּלֵּל לְפָנֶיךָ הַיּוֹם יוֹמָם וָלַיְלָה עַל־בְּנֵי
יִשְׂרָאֵל עֲבָדֶיךָ וּמִתְוַדֶּה עַל־חַטֹּאות בְּנֵי־יִשְׂרָאֵל אֲשֶׁר חָטָאנוּ לָךְ
ז וַאֲנִי וּבֵית־אָבִי חָטָאנוּ׃ חֲבֹל חָבַלְנוּ לָךְ וְלֹא־שָׁמַרְנוּ אֶת־הַמִּצְוֺת
ח וְאֶת־הַחֻקִּים וְאֶת־הַמִּשְׁפָּטִים אֲשֶׁר צִוִּיתָ אֶת־מֹשֶׁה עַבְדֶּךָ׃ זְכָר־נָא
אֶת־הַדָּבָר אֲשֶׁר צִוִּיתָ אֶת־מֹשֶׁה עַבְדְּךָ לֵאמֹר אַתֶּם תִּמְעָלוּ אֲנִי
ט אָפִיץ אֶתְכֶם בָּעַמִּים׃ וְשַׁבְתֶּם אֵלַי וּשְׁמַרְתֶּם מִצְוֺתַי וַעֲשִׂיתֶם אֹתָם
אִם־יִהְיֶה נִדַּחֲכֶם בִּקְצֵה הַשָּׁמַיִם מִשָּׁם אֲקַבְּצֵם והבואתים אֶל־ וַהֲבִיאוֹתִים
י הַמָּקוֹם אֲשֶׁר בָּחַרְתִּי לְשַׁכֵּן אֶת־שְׁמִי שָׁם׃ וְהֵם עֲבָדֶיךָ וְעַמֶּךָ אֲשֶׁר
יא פָּדִיתָ בְּכֹחֲךָ הַגָּדוֹל וּבְיָדְךָ הַחֲזָקָה׃ אָנָּא אֲדֹנָי תְּהִי נָא אָזְנְךָ־קַשֶּׁבֶת ה
אֶל־תְּפִלַּת עַבְדְּךָ וְאֶל־תְּפִלַּת עֲבָדֶיךָ הַחֲפֵצִים לְיִרְאָה אֶת־שְׁמֶךָ
וְהַצְלִיחָה־נָּא לְעַבְדְּךָ הַיּוֹם וּתְנֵהוּ לְרַחֲמִים לִפְנֵי הָאִישׁ הַזֶּה וַאֲנִי
ב א הָיִיתִי מַשְׁקֶה לַמֶּלֶךְ׃ וַיְהִי ׀ בְּחֹדֶשׁ נִיסָן שְׁנַת עֶשְׂרִים
לְאַרְתַּחְשַׁסְתְּא הַמֶּלֶךְ יַיִן לְפָנָיו וָאֶשָּׂא אֶת־הַיַּיִן וָאֶתְּנָה לַמֶּלֶךְ וְלֹא־
ב הָיִיתִי רַע לְפָנָיו׃ וַיֹּאמֶר לִי הַמֶּלֶךְ מַדּוּעַ ׀ פָּנֶיךָ רָעִים וְאַתָּה אֵינְךָ

3 not sick – it must be ill-heartedness." And I was filled with trepidation. Then
I said to the king, "May the king live forever! Why should my face not be
downcast when the city that houses my ancestral tombs lies in ruins with her
4 gates consumed by fire?" The king said to me, "What is it that you
5 ask?" I prayed to the God of the heavens, and then I said to the king, "If it
pleases the king, and if your servant pleases you, send me to Yehuda, to the
6 city of my ancestral tombs, and I will rebuild her." And the king said to me, as
the queen consort[6] sat with him, "How long will you be away, and when will
you return?" It pleased the king to send me, and we settled upon a time frame.
7 Then I said to the king, "If it pleases the king, let me be given missives to the
governors beyond the River granting me passage so that I may come to
8 Yehuda. Likewise a missive to Asaf, the royal forester, so that he will provide
me with timber to roof the gates of the citadel of the House,[7] the city wall,
and the residence to which I will come." The king endowed me in accordance
9 with the good hand of my God upon me. So I came to the governors beyond
the River and presented to them the king's missives; with me the king sent
10 army captains and cavalry. When Sanvalat the Horonite and
Toviya the Amonite servant heard of this, they took it exceedingly ill that
11 someone had come seeking the good of the Israelites. I arrived in Jerusalem
12 and was there for three days. Then I rose at night, I and a few people with me,
telling no one what my God was instilling in my heart to accomplish for
13 Jerusalem and taking no animals with me except the one I rode. That night I
exited through the Valley Gate facing Ein HaTanin and the Dung Gate, all the
while surveying the walls of Jerusalem that are everywhere broken through
14 and her gates consumed by fire. I passed on to the Spring Gate and the King's
15 pool, but there was no room for the animal beneath me to pass. So instead
that night I went up the streambed, still surveying the wall, then turned back,
16 reentered through the Valley Gate, and so returned. The officials did not know
where I had gone or what I was doing, and I had not yet told the Jews: the
17 priests, the nobles and officials, and the other participants in the project. Then
I said to them, "You see our dismal state with Jerusalem in ruins and her gates
having been put to the torch. Come – let us together rebuild Jerusalem's wall
18 and no longer be degraded!" I then revealed to them how my God's hand had
favored me and the things the king had said to me. They declared, "We will
19 arise and rebuild," their hands strengthened for the good. Hearing
of this, Sanvalat the Horonite, Toviya the Amonite servant, and Geshem the
Arab mocked and derided us, saying, "What do you think you are doing? Are
20 you rebelling against the king?" But I responded to them, saying, "It is the
God of heavens who will grant us success. We His servants will arise and

6 | Cf. Psalms 45:10.
7 | This likely refers to a fortified section of Jerusalem surrounding the Temple.

ג חוֹלֶה אֵין זֶה כִּי־אִם רֹעַ לֵב וָאִירָא הַרְבֵּה מְאֹד׃ וָאֹמַר לַמֶּלֶךְ הַמֶּלֶךְ
לְעוֹלָם יִחְיֶה מַדּוּעַ לֹא־יֵרְעוּ פָנַי אֲשֶׁר הָעִיר בֵּית־קִבְרוֹת אֲבֹתַי
ד חֲרֵבָה וּשְׁעָרֶיהָ אֻכְּלוּ בָאֵשׁ׃ וַיֹּאמֶר לִי הַמֶּלֶךְ עַל־מַה־
ה זֶּה אַתָּה מְבַקֵּשׁ וָאֶתְפַּלֵּל אֶל־אֱלֹהֵי הַשָּׁמָיִם׃ וָאֹמַר לַמֶּלֶךְ אִם־עַל־
הַמֶּלֶךְ טוֹב וְאִם־יִיטַב עַבְדְּךָ לְפָנֶיךָ אֲשֶׁר תִּשְׁלָחֵנִי אֶל־יְהוּדָה
ו אֶל־עִיר קִבְרוֹת אֲבֹתַי וְאֶבְנֶנָּה׃ וַיֹּאמֶר לִי הַמֶּלֶךְ וְהַשֵּׁגַל ׀ יוֹשֶׁבֶת
אֶצְלוֹ עַד־מָתַי יִהְיֶה מַהֲלָכְךָ וּמָתַי תָּשׁוּב וַיִּיטַב לִפְנֵי־הַמֶּלֶךְ וַיִּשְׁלָחֵנִי
ז וָאֶתְּנָה לוֹ זְמָן׃ וָאוֹמַר לַמֶּלֶךְ אִם־עַל־הַמֶּלֶךְ טוֹב אִגְּרוֹת יִתְּנוּ־לִי
עַל־פַּחֲווֹת עֵבֶר הַנָּהָר אֲשֶׁר יַעֲבִירוּנִי עַד אֲשֶׁר־אָבוֹא אֶל־יְהוּדָה׃
ח וְאִגֶּרֶת אֶל־אָסָף שֹׁמֵר הַפַּרְדֵּס אֲשֶׁר לַמֶּלֶךְ אֲשֶׁר יִתֶּן־לִי עֵצִים
לְקָרוֹת אֶת־שַׁעֲרֵי הַבִּירָה אֲשֶׁר־לַבַּיִת וּלְחוֹמַת הָעִיר וְלַבַּיִת אֲשֶׁר־
ט אָבוֹא אֵלָיו וַיִּתֶּן־לִי הַמֶּלֶךְ כְּיַד־אֱלֹהַי הַטּוֹבָה עָלָי׃ וָאָבוֹא אֶל־פַּחֲווֹת
עֵבֶר הַנָּהָר וָאֶתְּנָה לָהֶם אֵת אִגְּרוֹת הַמֶּלֶךְ וַיִּשְׁלַח עִמִּי הַמֶּלֶךְ שָׂרֵי
י חַיִל וּפָרָשִׁים׃ וַיִּשְׁמַע סַנְבַלַּט הַחֹרֹנִי וְטוֹבִיָּה הָעֶבֶד
הָעַמֹּנִי וַיֵּרַע לָהֶם רָעָה גְדֹלָה אֲשֶׁר־בָּא אָדָם לְבַקֵּשׁ טוֹבָה לִבְנֵי
יא יב יִשְׂרָאֵל׃ וָאָבוֹא אֶל־יְרוּשָׁלִָם וָאֱהִי־שָׁם יָמִים שְׁלֹשָׁה׃ וָאָקוּם ׀ לַיְלָה
אֲנִי וַאֲנָשִׁים ׀ מְעַט עִמִּי וְלֹא־הִגַּדְתִּי לְאָדָם מָה אֱלֹהַי נֹתֵן אֶל־לִבִּי
לַעֲשׂוֹת לִירוּשָׁלִָם וּבְהֵמָה אֵין עִמִּי כִּי אִם־הַבְּהֵמָה אֲשֶׁר אֲנִי רֹכֵב
יג בָּהּ׃ וָאֵצְאָה בְשַׁעַר־הַגַּיְא לַיְלָה וְאֶל־פְּנֵי עֵין הַתַּנִּין וְאֶל־שַׁעַר
הָאַשְׁפֹּת וָאֱהִי שֹׂבֵר בְּחוֹמֹת יְרוּשָׁלִַם אֲשֶׁר־המפרוצים וּשְׁעָרֶיהָ הֵם ׀ פְּרוּצִים
יד אֻכְּלוּ בָאֵשׁ׃ וָאֶעֱבֹר אֶל־שַׁעַר הָעַיִן וְאֶל־בְּרֵכַת הַמֶּלֶךְ וְאֵין־מָקוֹם
טו לַבְּהֵמָה לַעֲבֹר תַּחְתָּי׃ וָאֱהִי עֹלֶה בַנַּחַל לַיְלָה וָאֱהִי שֹׂבֵר בַּחוֹמָה
טז וָאָשׁוּב וָאָבוֹא בְּשַׁעַר הַגַּיְא וָאָשׁוּב׃ וְהַסְּגָנִים לֹא יָדְעוּ אָנָה הָלַכְתִּי
וּמָה אֲנִי עֹשֶׂה וְלַיְּהוּדִים וְלַכֹּהֲנִים וְלַחֹרִים וְלַסְּגָנִים וּלְיֶתֶר עֹשֵׂה
יז הַמְּלָאכָה עַד־כֵּן לֹא הִגַּדְתִּי׃ וָאוֹמַר אֲלֵהֶם אַתֶּם רֹאִים הָרָעָה אֲשֶׁר
אֲנַחְנוּ בָהּ אֲשֶׁר יְרוּשָׁלִַם חֲרֵבָה וּשְׁעָרֶיהָ נִצְּתוּ בָאֵשׁ לְכוּ וְנִבְנֶה אֶת־
יח חוֹמַת יְרוּשָׁלִַם וְלֹא־נִהְיֶה עוֹד חֶרְפָּה׃ וָאַגִּיד לָהֶם אֶת־יַד אֱלֹהַי
אֲשֶׁר־הִיא טוֹבָה עָלַי וְאַף־דִּבְרֵי הַמֶּלֶךְ אֲשֶׁר אָמַר־לִי וַיֹּאמְרוּ נָקוּם
יט וּבָנִינוּ וַיְחַזְּקוּ יְדֵיהֶם לַטּוֹבָה׃ וַיִּשְׁמַע סַנְבַלַּט הַחֹרֹנִי
וְטֹבִיָּה ׀ הָעֶבֶד הָעַמּוֹנִי וְגֶשֶׁם הָעַרְבִי וַיַּלְעִגוּ לָנוּ וַיִּבְזוּ עָלֵינוּ וַיֹּאמְרוּ
כ מָה־הַדָּבָר הַזֶּה אֲשֶׁר אַתֶּם עֹשִׂים הַעַל הַמֶּלֶךְ אַתֶּם מֹרְדִים׃ וָאָשִׁיב

rebuild, while for you there is neither a share nor a right nor any memory in
Jerusalem."
3 1 Then Elyashiv the High Priest and his brother priests arose and built the
Sheep Gate, consecrating it and erecting its doors. They consecrated from the
2 Tower of the Hundred up to the Tower of Ḥananel. The people of Yeriḥo built
3 next, and Zakur son of Imri built next. The Fish Gate was built by the sons
4 of HaSenaa:[8] they roofed it and erected its doors, bolts, and bars. Meremot
son of Uriya son of HaKotz made repairs next to them, then Meshulam son
5 of Berekhya son of Mesheizavel made repairs, then Tzadok son of Baana. The
Tekoites made repairs next to them, and their chieftains did not bend their
6 necks to the yoke of their lords.[9] The Old Gate was repaired by Yehoyada
son of Pase'aḥ and Meshulam son of Besodeya, who roofed it and erected
7 its doors, bolts, and bars. Melatya the Gibeonite and Yadon the Meronite
were repairing next to them along with men of Givon and the Mitzpa, of
8 the province beyond the River. Uziel son of Ḥarhaya, of the smiths, made
repairs next to them, as did Ḥananya of the perfumers – and they plastered
9 throughout Jerusalem up to the Wide Wall. Refaya son of Ḥur, commissioner
10 of a half district of Jerusalem, made repairs next to them. And Yedaya son
of Ḥarumaf made repairs next to them as well as opposite his home while
11 Ḥatush son of Ḥashavneya made repairs next to him. Malkiya son of Ḥarim
repaired a second segment as did Ḥashuv, son of Paḥat Moav, including
12 the Tower of Furnaces. Next, Shalum son of HaLoḥesh, commissioner of
13 a half district of Jerusalem, made repairs, together with his daughters. The
Valley Gate was repaired by Ḥanun and the residents of Zanoaḥ. They built
it, erecting its doors, bars, and bolts as well as one thousand cubits of the
14 wall up to the Dung Gate. The Dung Gate was repaired by Malkiya son
of Rekhav, commissioner of the Beit HaKerem district. He alone built it,
15 erecting its doors, bolts, and bars. The Spring Gate was repaired by Shalun
son of Kol Ḥozeh, commissioner of the Mitzpa district, who built it
himself, constructing its ceiling and erecting its doors, bolts, and bars in
addition to the wall of the Shelaḥ pool in the king's garden up to the stairs
16 descending from Ir David. Neḥemya son of Azbuk, half-district commissioner
of Beit Tzur, followed, repairing up to and opposite the tombs of David
17 and up to the artificial pool and the house of warriors. Following him, the
Levites made repairs: Reḥum son of Bani and next to him Ḥashavya, a half-
18 district commissioner of Ke'ila, made repairs along with his district. Their
kinsmen followed in making repairs: Bavai son of Ḥenadad, a half-district
19 commissioner of Ke'ila, and Ezer son of Yeshua, commissioner of the Mitzpa,
who repaired a second segment next to him opposite the elevated armory in
20 the inner corner. Barukh son of Zakai followed, fervently repairing a second
segment from the inner corner up to the entrance to the house of the High

8 | Cf. the list of returnees in Ezra, chapter 2.

9 | This can be understood as a criticism of the chieftains for failing to participate in the reconstruction: They "did not bend their [*own*] necks to the yoke of their lords," i.e., the officials in charge of the construction.

אַתֶּם דָּבָר וָאוֹמַר לָהֶם אֱלֹהֵי הַשָּׁמַיִם הוּא יַצְלִיחַ לָנוּ וַאֲנַחְנוּ עֲבָדָיו
נָקוּם וּבָנִינוּ וְלָכֶם אֵין־חֵלֶק וּצְדָקָה וְזִכָּרוֹן בִּירוּשָׁלִָם׃
ג א וַיָּקָם אֶלְיָשִׁיב הַכֹּהֵן הַגָּדוֹל וְאֶחָיו הַכֹּהֲנִים וַיִּבְנוּ אֶת־שַׁעַר הַצֹּאן
הֵמָּה קִדְּשׁוּהוּ וַיַּעֲמִידוּ דַּלְתֹתָיו וְעַד־מִגְדַּל הַמֵּאָה קִדְּשׁוּהוּ עַד
ב מִגְדַּל חֲנַנְאֵל׃ וְעַל־יָדוֹ בָנוּ אַנְשֵׁי יְרֵחוֹ וְעַל־יָדוֹ בָּנָה זַכּוּר בֶּן־
ג אִמְרִי׃ וְאֵת שַׁעַר הַדָּגִים בָּנוּ בְּנֵי הַסְּנָאָה הֵמָּה קֵרוּהוּ וַיַּעֲמִידוּ
ד דַּלְתֹתָיו מַנְעוּלָיו וּבְרִיחָיו׃ וְעַל־יָדָם הֶחֱזִיק מְרֵמוֹת בֶּן־אוּרִיָּה בֶּן־
הַקּוֹץ וְעַל־יָדָם הֶחֱזִיק מְשֻׁלָּם בֶּן־בֶּרֶכְיָה בֶּן־מְשֵׁיזַבְאֵל וְעַל־יָדָם
ה הֶחֱזִיק צָדוֹק בֶּן־בַּעֲנָא׃ וְעַל־יָדָם הֶחֱזִיקוּ הַתְּקוֹעִים וְאַדִּירֵיהֶם
ו לֹא־הֵבִיאוּ צַוָּרָם בַּעֲבֹדַת אֲדֹנֵיהֶם׃ וְאֵת שַׁעַר הַיְשָׁנָה הֶחֱזִיקוּ יוֹיָדָע
בֶּן־פָּסֵחַ וּמְשֻׁלָּם בֶּן־בְּסוֹדְיָה הֵמָּה קֵרוּהוּ וַיַּעֲמִידוּ דַּלְתֹתָיו וּמַנְעֻלָיו
ז וּבְרִיחָיו׃ וְעַל־יָדָם הֶחֱזִיק מְלַטְיָה הַגִּבְעֹנִי וְיָדוֹן הַמֵּרֹנֹתִי אַנְשֵׁי גִבְעוֹן
ח וְהַמִּצְפָּה לְכִסֵּא פַּחַת עֵבֶר הַנָּהָר׃ עַל־יָדוֹ הֶחֱזִיק עֻזִּיאֵל בֶּן־חַרְהֲיָה
צוֹרְפִים וְעַל־יָדוֹ הֶחֱזִיק חֲנַנְיָה בֶּן־הָרַקָּחִים וַיַּעַזְבוּ יְרוּשָׁלִַם עַד
ט הַחוֹמָה הָרְחָבָה׃ וְעַל־יָדָם הֶחֱזִיק רְפָיָה בֶן־חוּר שַׂר חֲצִי פֶּלֶךְ
י יְרוּשָׁלִָם׃ וְעַל־יָדָם הֶחֱזִיק יְדָיָה בֶן־חֲרוּמַף וְנֶגֶד בֵּיתוֹ וְעַל־יָדוֹ הֶחֱזִיק
יא חַטּוּשׁ בֶּן־חֲשַׁבְנְיָה׃ מִדָּה שֵׁנִית הֶחֱזִיק מַלְכִּיָּה בֶן־חָרִם וְחַשּׁוּב בֶּן־
יב פַּחַת מוֹאָב וְאֵת מִגְדַּל הַתַּנּוּרִים׃ וְעַל־יָדוֹ הֶחֱזִיק שַׁלּוּם בֶּן־הַלּוֹחֵשׁ
יג שַׂר חֲצִי פֶּלֶךְ יְרוּשָׁלִָם הוּא וּבְנוֹתָיו׃ אֵת שַׁעַר הַגַּיְא הֶחֱזִיק חָנוּן וְיֹשְׁבֵי
זָנוֹחַ הֵמָּה בָנוּהוּ וַיַּעֲמִידוּ דַּלְתֹתָיו מַנְעֻלָיו וּבְרִיחָיו וְאֶלֶף אַמָּה בַּחוֹמָה
יד עַד שַׁעַר הַשְׁפוֹת׃ וְאֵת ׀ שַׁעַר הָאַשְׁפּוֹת הֶחֱזִיק מַלְכִּיָּה בֶן־רֵכָב שַׂר
טו פֶּלֶךְ בֵּית־הַכָּרֶם הוּא יִבְנֶנּוּ וְיַעֲמִיד דַּלְתֹתָיו מַנְעֻלָיו וּבְרִיחָיו׃ וְאֵת
שַׁעַר הָעַיִן הֶחֱזִיק שַׁלּוּן בֶּן־כָּל־חֹזֶה שַׂר פֶּלֶךְ הַמִּצְפָּה הוּא יִבְנֶנּוּ
וִיטַלְלֶנּוּ ויעמידו דַּלְתֹתָיו מַנְעֻלָיו וּבְרִיחָיו וְאֵת חוֹמַת בְּרֵכַת הַשֶּׁלַח וְיַעֲמִיד
טז לְגַן־הַמֶּלֶךְ וְעַד־הַמַּעֲלוֹת הַיּוֹרְדוֹת מֵעִיר דָּוִיד׃ אַחֲרָיו הֶחֱזִיק נְחֶמְיָה
בֶן־עַזְבּוּק שַׂר חֲצִי פֶּלֶךְ בֵּית־צוּר עַד־נֶגֶד קִבְרֵי דָוִיד וְעַד־הַבְּרֵכָה
יז הָעֲשׂוּיָה וְעַד בֵּית הַגִּבֹּרִים׃ אַחֲרָיו הֶחֱזִיקוּ הַלְוִיִּם רְחוּם בֶּן־בָּנִי
יח עַל־יָדוֹ הֶחֱזִיק חֲשַׁבְיָה שַׂר־חֲצִי־פֶלֶךְ קְעִילָה לְפִלְכּוֹ׃ אַחֲרָיו הֶחֱזִיקוּ
יט אֲחֵיהֶם בַּוַּי בֶּן־חֵנָדָד שַׂר חֲצִי פֶּלֶךְ קְעִילָה׃ וַיְחַזֵּק עַל־יָדוֹ עֵזֶר בֶּן־
כ יֵשׁוּעַ שַׂר הַמִּצְפָּה מִדָּה שֵׁנִית מִנֶּגֶד עֲלֹת הַנֶּשֶׁק הַמִּקְצֹעַ׃ אַחֲרָיו
הֶחֱרָה הֶחֱזִיק בָּרוּךְ בֶּן־זבי מִדָּה שֵׁנִית מִן־הַמִּקְצוֹעַ עַד־פֶּתַח בֵּית זַכַּי

21 Priest Elyashiv. Meremot son of Uriya son of HaKotz followed, repairing
a second segment from the entrance of Elyashiv's house up to the edge of
22 Elyashiv's house. Following him, the priests, men of the vale,[10] made repairs.
23 Binyamin and Ḥashuv followed, making repairs opposite their homes,
followed by Azarya son of Maaseya son of Ananeya, who made repairs near
24 his own home. Binui son of Ḥenadad followed, repairing a second segment
from the house of Azarya to the inner corner all the way to the outer corner.
25 Then came Palal son of Uzai, opposite the inner corner and the Jutting Tower
of the upper royal residence of the Court of the Guard, followed by Pedaya
26 son of Parosh. The Netinim residing in the Ofel[11] made repairs up to the
27 Water Gate to the east and the Jutting Tower. The Tekoites followed, repairing
a second segment opposite the Great Jutting Tower extending to the Ofel
28 Wall. Above the Horse Gate, the priests made repairs, each opposite his
29 home. Tzadok son of Imer followed, repairing opposite his home, followed
in repairing by Shemaya son of Shekhanya, guardian of the East Gate.
30 Ḥananya son of Shelemya and Ḥanun the sixth son of Tzalaf followed,
repairing a second segment, followed by Meshulam son of Berekhya, who
31 made repairs opposite his own chamber. Malkiya son of HaTzorfi followed,
making the repairs up to the house of the Netinim and the Traders – opposite
32 the Muster Gate and the Corner Ascent. The smiths and the traders made
33 repairs between the Corner Ascent and the Sheep Gate. When
Sanvalat heard that we were rebuilding the wall, he was furious; enraged, he
34 jeered at the Jews. Speaking before his kinsmen and the Samaritan forces,
he said, "What are the miserable Jews doing? Will they plaster, offer the
consecration sacrifices, and reach the completion day? Will they revive
35 the stones from the rubble heaps after they have been burned?" Toviya the
Amonite, who was with him, said, "So what if they are building? A climbing
36 jackal could break through their stone wall!" Hear, our God, how we are
shamed! Heap their derision on their own heads, rendering them spoils in a
37 land of captivity. Do not cover their crimes. Do not erase their sin from Your
38 presence, for they have incited anger against the builders. So we built the wall
and the entire wall was joined together up to its halfway point, and the people
acted with a willing heart.

4 1 But when Sanvalat and Toviya and the Arabs, Amonites, and Ashdodites
heard that the walls of Jerusalem were being rejuvenated as the breaks began
2 to be filled, they were incensed. They all then joined together to wage war
3 upon Jerusalem and cause confusion there. But we prayed to our God and
4 meanwhile set up a watch over the walls, day and night, against them. Yehuda
was saying, "The bearers' strength is sapped; the rubble has no end – we are
5 simply unable to build the wall." Our enemies declared, "They will neither
know nor see until we come among them and slaughter them – ending the
6 entire endeavor." But when the Jews living among them came, they told us

10 | Perhaps the Jordan Valley.

11 | The Ofel was an elevated, fortified portion of Jerusalem, located to the south of the Temple Mount.

כא אלישיב הכהן הגדול: אחריו החזיק מרמות בן־אוריה בן־הקוץ
כב מדה שנית מפתח בית אלישיב ועד־תכלית בית אלישיב: ואחריו
כג החזיקו הכהנים אנשי הככר: אחריו החזיק בנימן וחשוב נגד ביתם
כד אחריו החזיק עזריה בן־מעשיה בן־ענניה אצל ביתו: אחריו החזיק
בנוי בן־חנדד מדה שנית מבית עזריה עד־המקצוע ועד־הפנה:
כה פלל בן־אוזי מנגד המקצוע והמגדל היוצא מבית המלך העליון
כו אשר לחצר המטרה אחריו פדיה בן־פרעש: והנתינים היו ישבים
כז בעפל עד נגד שער המים למזרח והמגדל היוצא: אחריו החזיקו
התקעים מדה שנית מנגד המגדל הגדול היוצא ועד חומת העפל:
כח כט מעל | שער הסוסים החזיקו הכהנים איש לנגד ביתו: אחריו החזיק
צדוק בן־אמר נגד ביתו ואחריו החזיק שמעיה בן־שכניה שמר
ל שער המזרח: אחרי החזיק חנניה בן־שלמיה וחנון בן־צלף הששי (אחריו)
לא מדה שני אחריו החזיק משלם בן־ברכיה נגד נשכתו: אחרי החזיק (אחריו)
מלכיה בן־הצרפי עד־בית הנתינים והרכלים נגד שער המפקד
לב ועד עלית הפנה: ובין עלית הפנה לשער הצאן החזיקו הצרפים
לג והרכלים: ויהי כאשר שמע סנבלט כי־אנחנו בונים
לד את־החומה ויחר לו ויכעס הרבה וילעג על־היהודים: ויאמר | לפני
אחיו וחיל שמרון ויאמר מה היהודים האמללים עשים היעזבו
להם היזבחו היכלו ביום היחיו את־האבנים מערמות העפר והמה
לה שרופות: וטוביה העמני אצלו ויאמר גם אשר־הם בונים אם־
לו יעלה שועל ופרץ חומת אבניהם: שמע אלהינו כי־היינו בוזה
לז והשב חרפתם אל־ראשם ותנם לבזה בארץ שביה: ואל־תכס
על־עונם וחטאתם מלפניך אל־תמחה כי הכעיסו לנגד הבונים:
לח ונבנה את־החומה ותקשר כל־החומה עד־חציה ויהי לב לעם ו
לעשות:
ד א ויהי | כאשר שמע סנבלט וטוביה והערבים והעמנים והאשדודים
כי־עלתה ארוכה לחמות ירושלם כי־החלו הפרצים להסתם ויחר
ב להם מאד: ויקשרו כלם יחדו לבוא להלחם בירושלם ולעשות
ג לו תועה: ונתפלל אל־אלהינו ונעמיד משמר עליהם יומם ולילה
ד מפניהם: ויאמר יהודה כשל כח הסבל והעפר הרבה ואנחנו לא
ה נוכל לבנות בחומה: ויאמרו צרינו לא ידעו ולא יראו עד אשר־
ו נבוא אל־תוכם והרגנום והשבתנו את־המלאכה: ויהי כאשר־באו

ten times that at the places to which we always return, they will come upon
7 us.[12] Therefore, in the lower places behind the wall, within the crags, I arrayed
8 the people, arranging them in families with their swords, lances, and bows. I
looked out, then got to my feet, saying to the nobles and officials and the rest
of the people, "Fear them not; remember the great and awe-inspiring Lord,
and fight for your kinsmen, for your sons and daughters, your wives, and your
9 homes." And when our enemies heard that we had been informed
and that God had thus foiled their plan, we all returned to the wall, each of us
10 to our tasks. From that day on, half my men engaged in the work while half
bore the lances, shields, bows, and armor, with the officers following behind
11 all the House of Yehuda. They built the wall, and the bearers loaded – with
12 one hand doing the work and the other holding a weapon. The builders each
had their swords strapped at their hips as they built, and the horn blower was
13 by my side. For I had said to the nobles and officials and the rest of the people,
"The work is extensive and widely scattered as long as we are spread along
14 the wall, far away from each other. Wherever you hear the sound
15 of the horn, gather to us there – our God will fight for us." So we engaged
in the work, with half holding lances from the break of dawn until the stars
16 showed. At the same time I also said to the people, "Each of you and your
men must sleep in Jerusalem, serving as a watch by night and a workforce by
17 day." Neither I, nor my brothers nor my men nor the watchmen following me
ever undressed – each with his weapon even at the water.[13]
5 1 There was a vehement outcry by the people and their wives against their
2 fellow Jews. Some said, "We have so many sons and daughters that we need
3 to buy grain in order to eat and so stay alive." Others said, "We must mortgage
our fields, our vineyards, and our homes to buy grain to stave off starvation."
4 And there were some who said, "We have had to borrow money against our
5 fields and vineyards to pay the king's levy. Is our brothers' flesh not like ours?
Their sons akin to our own? And yet we must force our sons and daughters
into servitude, and some of our daughters have already been forced in that way
6 while we stand helplessly by. Our fields and vineyards have gone to others." I
7 was incensed when I heard of their cries and of these events. Taking counsel
from my heart, I upbraided the nobles and officials, saying to them, "You are
exacting exorbitant payments from your own brothers!" Then I summoned
8 them to a large assembly, and I said to them, "Insofar as we could afford to,
we have been buying back our brother Jews who were sold to other nations,[14]
but now you will sell your brothers to be sold back to us?" And they were
9 silenced and could find nothing to say. Then I said, "What you are doing is not
right. You should walk in fear of our God and of the derision of our enemies,

12 | That is, they warned us of the impending attack.
13 | In other words, we were armed at all times, vigilant for potential threats.
14 | See Leviticus 25:47–49.

הַיְּהוּדִים הַיֹּשְׁבִים אֶצְלָם וַיֹּאמְרוּ לָנוּ עֶשֶׂר פְּעָמִים מִכָּל־הַמְּקֹמוֹת
ז אֲשֶׁר־תָּשׁוּבוּ עָלֵינוּ׃ וָאַעֲמִיד מִתַּחְתִּיּוֹת לַמָּקוֹם מֵאַחֲרֵי לַחוֹמָה
בצחחיים וָאַעֲמִיד אֶת־הָעָם לְמִשְׁפָּחוֹת עִם־חַרְבֹתֵיהֶם רָמְחֵיהֶם בַּצְּחִיחִים
ח וְקַשְּׁתֹתֵיהֶם׃ וָאֵרֶא וָאָקוּם וָאֹמַר אֶל־הַחֹרִים וְאֶל־הַסְּגָנִים וְאֶל־יֶתֶר
הָעָם אַל־תִּירְאוּ מִפְּנֵיהֶם אֶת־אֲדֹנָי הַגָּדוֹל וְהַנּוֹרָא זְכֹרוּ וְהִלָּחֲמוּ עַל־
ט אֲחֵיכֶם בְּנֵיכֶם וּבְנֹתֵיכֶם נְשֵׁיכֶם וּבָתֵּיכֶם׃ וַיְהִי כַּאֲשֶׁר
שָׁמְעוּ אוֹיְבֵינוּ כִּי־נוֹדַע לָנוּ וַיָּפֶר הָאֱלֹהִים אֶת־עֲצָתָם ונשוב כֻּלָּנוּ וַנָּשָׁב
י אֶל־הַחוֹמָה אִישׁ אֶל־מְלַאכְתּוֹ׃ וַיְהִי ׀ מִן־הַיּוֹם הַהוּא חֲצִי נְעָרַי עֹשִׂים
בַּמְּלָאכָה וְחֶצְיָם מַחֲזִיקִים וְהָרְמָחִים הַמָּגִנִּים וְהַקְּשָׁתוֹת וְהַשִּׁרְיֹנִים
יא וְהַשָּׂרִים אַחֲרֵי כָּל־בֵּית יְהוּדָה׃ הַבּוֹנִים בַּחוֹמָה וְהַנֹּשְׂאִים בַּסֶּבֶל
יב עֹמְשִׂים בְּאַחַת יָדוֹ עֹשֶׂה בַמְּלָאכָה וְאַחַת מַחֲזֶקֶת הַשָּׁלַח׃ וְהַבּוֹנִים
יג אִישׁ חַרְבּוֹ אֲסוּרִים עַל־מָתְנָיו וּבוֹנִים וְהַתּוֹקֵעַ בַּשּׁוֹפָר אֶצְלִי׃ וָאֹמַר
אֶל־הַחֹרִים וְאֶל־הַסְּגָנִים וְאֶל־יֶתֶר הָעָם הַמְּלָאכָה הַרְבֵּה וּרְחָבָה
יד וַאֲנַחְנוּ נִפְרָדִים עַל־הַחוֹמָה רְחוֹקִים אִישׁ מֵאָחִיו׃ בִּמְקוֹם
אֲשֶׁר תִּשְׁמְעוּ אֶת־קוֹל הַשּׁוֹפָר שָׁמָּה תִּקָּבְצוּ אֵלֵינוּ אֱלֹהֵינוּ יִלָּחֶם
טו לָנוּ׃ וַאֲנַחְנוּ עֹשִׂים בַּמְּלָאכָה וְחֶצְיָם מַחֲזִיקִים בָּרְמָחִים מֵעֲלוֹת
טז הַשַּׁחַר עַד צֵאת הַכּוֹכָבִים׃ גַּם בָּעֵת הַהִיא אָמַרְתִּי לָעָם אִישׁ וְנַעֲרוֹ
יז יָלִינוּ בְּתוֹךְ יְרוּשָׁלִָם וְהָיוּ־לָנוּ הַלַּיְלָה מִשְׁמָר וְהַיּוֹם מְלָאכָה׃ וְאֵין אֲנִי
וְאַחַי וּנְעָרַי וְאַנְשֵׁי הַמִּשְׁמָר אֲשֶׁר אַחֲרַי אֵין־אֲנַחְנוּ פֹשְׁטִים בְּגָדֵינוּ
אִישׁ שִׁלְחוֹ הַמָּיִם׃

ה א ב וַתְּהִי צַעֲקַת הָעָם וּנְשֵׁיהֶם גְּדוֹלָה אֶל־אֲחֵיהֶם הַיְּהוּדִים׃ וְיֵשׁ אֲשֶׁר
ג אֹמְרִים בָּנֵינוּ וּבְנֹתֵינוּ אֲנַחְנוּ רַבִּים וְנִקְחָה דָגָן וְנֹאכְלָה וְנִחְיֶה׃ וְיֵשׁ
אֲשֶׁר אֹמְרִים שְׂדֹתֵינוּ וּכְרָמֵינוּ וּבָתֵּינוּ אֲנַחְנוּ עֹרְבִים וְנִקְחָה דָגָן
ד בָּרָעָב׃ וְיֵשׁ אֲשֶׁר אֹמְרִים לָוִינוּ כֶסֶף לְמִדַּת הַמֶּלֶךְ שְׂדֹתֵינוּ וּכְרָמֵינוּ׃
ה וְעַתָּה כִּבְשַׂר אַחֵינוּ בְּשָׂרֵנוּ כִּבְנֵיהֶם בְּנֵינוּ וְהִנֵּה אֲנַחְנוּ כֹבְשִׁים
אֶת־בָּנֵינוּ וְאֶת־בְּנֹתֵינוּ לַעֲבָדִים וְיֵשׁ מִבְּנֹתֵינוּ נִכְבָּשׁוֹת וְאֵין לְאֵל
ו יָדֵנוּ וּשְׂדֹתֵינוּ וּכְרָמֵינוּ לַאֲחֵרִים׃ וַיִּחַר לִי מְאֹד כַּאֲשֶׁר שָׁמַעְתִּי אֶת־
ז זַעֲקָתָם וְאֵת הַדְּבָרִים הָאֵלֶּה׃ וַיִּמָּלֵךְ לִבִּי עָלַי וָאָרִיבָה אֶת־הַחֹרִים
וְאֶת־הַסְּגָנִים וָאֹמְרָה לָהֶם מַשָּׁא אִישׁ־בְּאָחִיו אַתֶּם נשאים וָאֶתֵּן נֹשִׁים
ח עֲלֵיהֶם קְהִלָּה גְדוֹלָה׃ וָאֹמְרָה לָהֶם אֲנַחְנוּ קָנִינוּ אֶת־אַחֵינוּ הַיְּהוּדִים
הַנִּמְכָּרִים לַגּוֹיִם כְּדֵי בָנוּ וְגַם־אַתֶּם תִּמְכְּרוּ אֶת־אֲחֵיכֶם וְנִמְכְּרוּ־לָנוּ
ט וַיַּחֲרִישׁוּ וְלֹא מָצְאוּ דָּבָר׃ ויאמר לֹא־טוֹב הַדָּבָר אֲשֶׁר־אַתֶּם עֹשִׂים וָאֹמַר

10 the nations. And yes, I too, my brothers, and my men have been demanding
11 money and grain in repayment of debt. Let us now end this exaction! Will you
not return to them this very day their fields, their vineyards, their olive groves,
and their homes and also forgo the money – be it even one hundred silver
coins – and the grain, wine, and olive oil that you are exacting from them?"
12 And they said, "We will restore it all and demand no more of them. We will
do just as you say." Whereupon I summoned the priests and had them swear
13 to act accordingly. I then shook out my pocket, declaring, "So may God shake
out of his home and possessions anyone who does not act accordingly; just so
may he be shaken out and left empty." The entire congregation said "Amen"
14 and praised the LORD – and the people acted accordingly. From the day he
invested me as governor of the land of Yehuda – from the twentieth to the
thirty-second year of King Artaḥshasta – twelve years – neither my kinsmen
15 nor I partook of the governor's food tribute, for the governors preceding
me burdened the people heavily, taking bread and wine from them as well
as forty silver shekel while their men lorded over the people. But I did not
16 do so because of fear of God. I also supported the work on the wall, and we
did not acquire any fields;[15] rather, all my men were gathered there for that
17 enterprise. At my table were one hundred fifty men from the Jews and the
18 officials as well as those joining us from the surrounding nations. One ox, six
choice sheep, and poultry were made for me each day – that was one day's
provision – and every ten days there was an abundant supply of wine. Yet even
so, I did not claim the governors' food tribute because the service burdened
19 this people too heavily. Remember me favorably, my God, for everything
6 1 I did on behalf of this people. Now Sanvalat, Toviya, Geshem the
Arab, and our other enemies heard that I had rebuilt the wall and that not a
single break remained, although at that time I had not yet erected doors in the
2 gates. Then Sanvalat and Geshem sent to me, saying, "Come, let us convene
3 together in Kefirim, in Bikat Ono," all the while intending to do me harm. I
sent them messengers saying, "I am engaged in an epic enterprise and cannot
come down lest the project cease while I withdraw to come down to you."
4 They sent to me in this manner four times, and I replied to them accordingly.
5 Then Sanvalat sent his man to me for the fifth time in this fashion, but with an
6 open missive in his hand. In it was written, "It is rumored among the nations
and confirmed by Gashmu[16] that you and the Jews plan to rebel, and that
is why you are building the wall, intending to be their king, and additional
7 such reports. Furthermore, you have set up prophets to proclaim of you in
Jerusalem, 'A king in Yehuda.' Now the king will hear such reports! Come,
8 let us deliberate together." But I sent back to him, saying, "These reports you

15 | I did not seize land from the poor as payment or collateral for financial support.
16 | Gashmu is a variant of Geshem.

י הֲלוֹא בְּיִרְאַת אֱלֹהֵינוּ תֵּלֵכוּ מֵחֶרְפַּת הַגּוֹיִם אוֹיְבֵינוּ: וְגַם־אֲנִי אַחַי
יא וּנְעָרַי נֹשִׁים בָּהֶם כֶּסֶף וְדָגָן נַעַזְבָה־נָּא אֶת־הַמַּשָּׁא הַזֶּה: הָשִׁיבוּ נָא
לָהֶם כְּהַיּוֹם שְׂדֹתֵיהֶם כַּרְמֵיהֶם זֵיתֵיהֶם וּבָתֵּיהֶם וּמְאַת הַכֶּסֶף וְהַדָּגָן
יב הַתִּירוֹשׁ וְהַיִּצְהָר אֲשֶׁר אַתֶּם נֹשִׁים בָּהֶם: וַיֹּאמְרוּ נָשִׁיב וּמֵהֶם לֹא
נְבַקֵּשׁ כֵּן נַעֲשֶׂה כַּאֲשֶׁר אַתָּה אוֹמֵר וָאֶקְרָא אֶת־הַכֹּהֲנִים וָאַשְׁבִּיעֵם
יג לַעֲשׂוֹת כַּדָּבָר הַזֶּה: גַּם־חָצְנִי נָעַרְתִּי וָאֹמְרָה כָּכָה יְנַעֵר הָאֱלֹהִים אֶת־
כָּל־הָאִישׁ אֲשֶׁר לֹא־יָקִים אֶת־הַדָּבָר הַזֶּה מִבֵּיתוֹ וּמִיגִיעוֹ וְכָכָה יִהְיֶה
נָעוּר וָרֵק וַיֹּאמְרוּ כָל־הַקָּהָל אָמֵן וַיְהַלְלוּ אֶת־יהוה וַיַּעַשׂ הָעָם כַּדָּבָר
יד הַזֶּה: גַּם מִיּוֹם ׀ אֲשֶׁר־צִוָּה אֹתִי לִהְיוֹת פֶּחָם בְּאֶרֶץ יְהוּדָה מִשְּׁנַת
עֶשְׂרִים וְעַד שְׁנַת שְׁלֹשִׁים וּשְׁתַּיִם לְאַרְתַּחְשַׁסְתְּא הַמֶּלֶךְ שָׁנִים שְׁתֵּים
טו עֶשְׂרֵה אֲנִי וְאַחַי לֶחֶם הַפֶּחָה לֹא אָכַלְתִּי: וְהַפַּחוֹת הָרִאשֹׁנִים אֲשֶׁר־
לְפָנַי הִכְבִּידוּ עַל־הָעָם וַיִּקְחוּ מֵהֶם בְּלֶחֶם וָיַיִן אַחַר כֶּסֶף־שְׁקָלִים
אַרְבָּעִים גַּם נַעֲרֵיהֶם שָׁלְטוּ עַל־הָעָם וַאֲנִי לֹא־עָשִׂיתִי כֵן מִפְּנֵי יִרְאַת
טז אֱלֹהִים: וְגַם בִּמְלֶאכֶת הַחוֹמָה הַזֹּאת הֶחֱזַקְתִּי וְשָׂדֶה לֹא קָנִינוּ וְכָל־
יז נְעָרַי קְבוּצִים שָׁם עַל־הַמְּלָאכָה: וְהַיְּהוּדִים וְהַסְּגָנִים מֵאָה וַחֲמִשִּׁים
יח אִישׁ וְהַבָּאִים אֵלֵינוּ מִן־הַגּוֹיִם אֲשֶׁר־סְבִיבֹתֵינוּ עַל־שֻׁלְחָנִי: וַאֲשֶׁר
הָיָה נַעֲשֶׂה לְיוֹם אֶחָד שׁוֹר אֶחָד צֹאן שֵׁשׁ־בְּרֻרוֹת וְצִפֳּרִים נַעֲשׂוּ־לִי
וּבֵין עֲשֶׂרֶת יָמִים בְּכָל־יַיִן לְהַרְבֵּה וְעִם־זֶה לֶחֶם הַפֶּחָה לֹא בִקַּשְׁתִּי
יט כִּי־כָבְדָה הָעֲבֹדָה עַל־הָעָם הַזֶּה: זָכְרָה־לִּי אֱלֹהַי לְטוֹבָה כֹּל אֲשֶׁר־
ו א עָשִׂיתִי עַל־הָעָם הַזֶּה: וַיְהִי כַאֲשֶׁר נִשְׁמַע לְסַנְבַלַּט
וְטוֹבִיָּה וּלְגֶשֶׁם הָעַרְבִי וּלְיֶתֶר אֹיְבֵינוּ כִּי בָנִיתִי אֶת־הַחוֹמָה וְלֹא־
נוֹתַר בָּהּ פָּרֶץ גַּם עַד־הָעֵת הַהִיא דְּלָתוֹת לֹא־הֶעֱמַדְתִּי בַשְּׁעָרִים:
ב וַיִּשְׁלַח סַנְבַלַּט וְגֶשֶׁם אֵלַי לֵאמֹר לְכָה וְנִוָּעֲדָה יַחְדָּו בַּכְּפִירִים בְּבִקְעַת
ג אוֹנוֹ וְהֵמָּה חֹשְׁבִים לַעֲשׂוֹת לִי רָעָה: וָאֶשְׁלְחָה עֲלֵיהֶם מַלְאָכִים
לֵאמֹר מְלָאכָה גְדוֹלָה אֲנִי עֹשֶׂה וְלֹא אוּכַל לָרֶדֶת לָמָּה תִשְׁבַּת
ד הַמְּלָאכָה כַּאֲשֶׁר אַרְפֶּהָ וְיָרַדְתִּי אֲלֵיכֶם: וַיִּשְׁלְחוּ אֵלַי כַּדָּבָר הַזֶּה
ה אַרְבַּע פְּעָמִים וָאָשִׁיב אוֹתָם כַּדָּבָר הַזֶּה: וַיִּשְׁלַח אֵלַי סַנְבַלַּט כַּדָּבָר
ו הַזֶּה פַּעַם חֲמִישִׁית אֶת־נַעֲרוֹ וְאִגֶּרֶת פְּתוּחָה בְּיָדוֹ: כָּתוּב בָּהּ בַּגּוֹיִם
נִשְׁמָע וְגַשְׁמוּ אֹמֵר אַתָּה וְהַיְּהוּדִים חֹשְׁבִים לִמְרוֹד עַל־כֵּן אַתָּה
ז בוֹנֶה הַחוֹמָה וְאַתָּה הֹוֶה לָהֶם לְמֶלֶךְ כַּדְּבָרִים הָאֵלֶּה: וְגַם־נְבִיאִים
הֶעֱמַדְתָּ לִקְרֹא עָלֶיךָ בִירוּשָׁלִַם לֵאמֹר מֶלֶךְ בִּיהוּדָה וְעַתָּה יִשָּׁמַע
ח לַמֶּלֶךְ כַּדְּבָרִים הָאֵלֶּה וְעַתָּה לְכָה וְנִוָּעֲצָה יַחְדָּו: וָאֶשְׁלְחָה אֵלָיו

speak of never were, for it is from your own heart that you are fabricating
9 them." They are all trying to intimidate us, saying, "They will withdraw their
hands from the task, leaving it undone." Now may my hands grow in strength!
10 Then I came to the house of Shemaya son of Delaya son of Meheitavel, who
was in seclusion, and he said, "Let us meet in the House of God, inside the
Sanctuary, while shutting the Sanctuary doors – for they are coming to kill
11 you. At night they are coming to kill you." But I said, "Should a man like
myself run away? And who am I to enter the Sanctuary and live? No! I will
12 not come in." Then I realized that it was not God who had sent him – his
13 prophecy about me was because Toviya and Sanvalat had hired him. He
was hired so that I would take fright and act in this way, sinning, so that they
14 could then defame and disgrace me. My God, remember Toviya and
Sanvalat for these actions of theirs, as well as Noadya the prophetess and the
15 other prophets who tried to intimidate me. But the wall was completed on
16 the twenty-fifth of Elul after fifty-two days. When all our enemies
heard, all the surrounding nations were afraid and sank low in their own eyes,
17 recognizing that this endeavor was brought about by our God. Yet throughout
this time the nobles of the Jews frequently sent letters to Toviya while those
18 from Toviya came to them. For many in Yehuda were sworn to him as he was
the son-in-law of Shekhanya son of Araḥ, and his own son Yehoḥanan had
19 married the daughter of Meshulam son of Berekhya. Accordingly, they would
mention his good deeds to me while divulging my words to him, and all the
while, Toviya was sending out letters to intimidate me.
7 1 Once the wall had been built and I had erected the doors, the gatekeepers,
2 singers, and Levites were counted. Then I put my brother Ḥanani and
Ḥananya, commander of the citadel, in command of Jerusalem, for he was
3 widely known as a true and God-fearing man. I gave orders to them: "Let
the gates of Jerusalem not be opened until the sun heats up, and while
still stationed there, close the doors and bar them shut. Furthermore, let
the inhabitants of Jerusalem be assigned to guard shifts, each to his watch
4 or opposite his home." Now while the city was large and extensive, her
5 population was sparse, and the rebuilt houses were few.[17] Then my God
inspired me to gather the nobles and officials and the people to register their
genealogy, and I found the genealogical record of those who first came up.[18] In
6 it I found written: These are the people of the province, coming
up from the captivity of the exile, that Nevukhadnetzar, king of Babylon, had
7 exiled. They returned to Jerusalem and Judea, each to his own town. Those
coming with Zerubavel, Yeshua, Neḥemya, Azarya, Raamya, Naḥamani,
Mordekhai, Bilshan, Misperet, Bigvai, Neḥum, Baana – the people of the
8, 9 nation of Israel – numbered as follows: The sons of Parosh: 2,172. The sons
10, 11 of Shefatya: 372. The sons of Araḥ: 652. The sons of Paḥat Moav – the sons

17 | Literally "no houses had been built," but the context implies that the housing was inadequate rather than nonexistent.

18 | This genealogical record also appears in Ezra, chapter 2, with minor variations.

לֵאמֹר לֹא נִהְיָה כַּדְּבָרִים הָאֵלֶּה אֲשֶׁר אַתָּה אוֹמֵר כִּי מִלִּבְּךָ אַתָּה
ט בוֹדָאם: כִּי כֻלָּם מְיָרְאִים אוֹתָנוּ לֵאמֹר יִרְפּוּ יְדֵיהֶם מִן־הַמְּלָאכָה
י וְלֹא תֵעָשֶׂה וְעַתָּה חַזֵּק אֶת־יָדָי: וַאֲנִי־בָאתִי בֵּית שְׁמַעְיָה בֶן־דְּלָיָה
בֶּן־מְהֵיטַבְאֵל וְהוּא עָצוּר וַיֹּאמֶר נִוָּעֵד אֶל־בֵּית הָאֱלֹהִים אֶל־תּוֹךְ
הַהֵיכָל וְנִסְגְּרָה דַּלְתוֹת הַהֵיכָל כִּי בָּאִים לְהָרְגֶךָ וְלַיְלָה בָּאִים לְהָרְגֶךָ:
יא וָאֹמְרָה הַאִישׁ כָּמוֹנִי יִבְרָח וּמִי כָמוֹנִי אֲשֶׁר־יָבוֹא אֶל־הַהֵיכָל וָחָי לֹא
יב אָבוֹא: וָאַכִּירָה וְהִנֵּה לֹא־אֱלֹהִים שְׁלָחוֹ כִּי הַנְּבוּאָה דִּבֶּר עָלַי וְטוֹבִיָּה
יג וְסַנְבַלַּט שְׂכָרוֹ: לְמַעַן שָׂכוּר הוּא לְמַעַן־אִירָא וְאֶעֱשֶׂה־כֵּן וְחָטָאתִי
יד וְהָיָה לָהֶם לְשֵׁם רָע לְמַעַן יְחָרְפוּנִי: זָכְרָה אֱלֹהַי לְטוֹבִיָּה
וּלְסַנְבַלַּט כְּמַעֲשָׂיו אֵלֶּה וְגַם לְנוֹעַדְיָה הַנְּבִיאָה וּלְיֶתֶר הַנְּבִיאִים
טו אֲשֶׁר הָיוּ מְיָרְאִים אוֹתִי: וַתִּשְׁלַם הַחוֹמָה בְּעֶשְׂרִים וַחֲמִשָּׁה לֶאֱלוּל ז
טז לַחֲמִשִּׁים וּשְׁנַיִם יוֹם: וַיְהִי כַּאֲשֶׁר שָׁמְעוּ כָּל־אוֹיְבֵינוּ וַיִּרְאוּ
כָּל־הַגּוֹיִם אֲשֶׁר סְבִיבֹתֵינוּ וַיִּפְּלוּ מְאֹד בְּעֵינֵיהֶם וַיֵּדְעוּ כִּי מֵאֵת אֱלֹהֵינוּ
יז נֶעֶשְׂתָה הַמְּלָאכָה הַזֹּאת: גַּם ׀ בַּיָּמִים הָהֵם מַרְבִּים חֹרֵי יְהוּדָה
יח אִגְּרֹתֵיהֶם הוֹלְכוֹת עַל־טוֹבִיָּה וַאֲשֶׁר לְטוֹבִיָּה בָּאוֹת אֲלֵיהֶם: כִּי־
רַבִּים בִּיהוּדָה בַּעֲלֵי שְׁבוּעָה לוֹ כִּי־חָתָן הוּא לִשְׁכַנְיָה בֶן־אָרַח וִיהוֹחָנָן
יט בְּנוֹ לָקַח אֶת־בַּת־מְשֻׁלָּם בֶּן בֶּרֶכְיָה: גַּם טוֹבֹתָיו הָיוּ אֹמְרִים לְפָנַי
וּדְבָרַי הָיוּ מוֹצִיאִים לוֹ אִגְּרוֹת שָׁלַח טוֹבִיָּה לְיָרְאֵנִי:
ז א וַיְהִי כַּאֲשֶׁר נִבְנְתָה הַחוֹמָה וָאַעֲמִיד הַדְּלָתוֹת וַיִּפָּקְדוּ הַשּׁוֹעֲרִים
ב וְהַמְשֹׁרְרִים וְהַלְוִיִּם: וָאֲצַוֶּה אֶת־חֲנָנִי אָחִי וְאֶת־חֲנַנְיָה שַׂר הַבִּירָה
ג עַל־יְרוּשָׁלָ͏ִם כִּי־הוּא כְּאִישׁ אֱמֶת וְיָרֵא אֶת־הָאֱלֹהִים מֵרַבִּים: ויאמר וָאֹמַר
לָהֶם לֹא יִפָּתְחוּ שַׁעֲרֵי יְרוּשָׁלַ͏ִם עַד־חֹם הַשֶּׁמֶשׁ וְעַד הֵם עֹמְדִים יָגִיפוּ
הַדְּלָתוֹת וֶאֱחֹזוּ וְהַעֲמֵיד מִשְׁמְרוֹת יֹשְׁבֵי יְרוּשָׁלַ͏ִם אִישׁ בְּמִשְׁמָרוֹ
ד וְאִישׁ נֶגֶד בֵּיתוֹ: וְהָעִיר רַחֲבַת יָדַיִם וּגְדֹלָה וְהָעָם מְעַט בְּתוֹכָהּ וְאֵין
ה בָּתִּים בְּנוּיִם: וַיִּתֵּן אֱלֹהַי אֶל־לִבִּי וָאֶקְבְּצָה אֶת־הַחֹרִים וְאֶת־הַסְּגָנִים
וְאֶת־הָעָם לְהִתְיַחֵשׂ וָאֶמְצָא סֵפֶר הַיַּחַשׂ הָעוֹלִים בָּרִאשׁוֹנָה וָאֶמְצָא
ו כָּתוּב בּוֹ: אֵלֶּה ׀ בְּנֵי הַמְּדִינָה הָעֹלִים מִשְּׁבִי הַגּוֹלָה אֲשֶׁר
הֶגְלָה נְבוּכַדְנֶצַּר מֶלֶךְ בָּבֶל וַיָּשׁוּבוּ לִירוּשָׁלַ͏ִם וְלִיהוּדָה אִישׁ לְעִירוֹ:
ז הַבָּאִים עִם־זְרֻבָּבֶל יֵשׁוּעַ נְחֶמְיָה עֲזַרְיָה רַעַמְיָה נַחֲמָנִי מָרְדֳּכַי בִּלְשָׁן
ח מִסְפֶּרֶת בִּגְוַי נְחוּם בַּעֲנָה מִסְפַּר אַנְשֵׁי עַם יִשְׂרָאֵל: בְּנֵי פַרְעֹשׁ אַלְפַּיִם
ט י מֵאָה וְשִׁבְעִים וּשְׁנָיִם: בְּנֵי שְׁפַטְיָה שְׁלֹשׁ מֵאוֹת שִׁבְעִים וּשְׁנָיִם: בְּנֵי
יא אָרַח שֵׁשׁ מֵאוֹת חֲמִשִּׁים וּשְׁנָיִם: בְּנֵי־פַחַת מוֹאָב לִבְנֵי יֵשׁוּעַ וְיוֹאָב

12, 13 of Yeshua and Yoav – 2,818. The sons of Eilam: 1,254. The sons of Zatu: 845.
14, 15, 16, 17 The sons of Zakai: 760. The sons of Binui: 648. The sons of Bevai: 628. The
18, 19 sons of Azgad: 2,322. The sons of Adonikam: 667. The sons of Bigvai: 2,067.
20, 21, 22 The sons of Adin: 655. The sons of Ater, with Ḥizkiya: 98. The sons of Ḥashum:
23, 24, 25 328. The sons of Betzai: 324. The sons of Ḥarif: 112. The sons of Givon: 95.
26, 27, 28 The people of Beit Leḥem and Netofa: 188. The people of Anatot: 128. The
29 people of Beit Azmavet: 42. The people of Kiryat Ye'arim, Kefira, and Be'erot:
30, 31, 32 743. The people of the Rama and Gava: 621. The people of Mikhmas: 122. The
33, 34 people of Beit El and Ai: 123. The people of the other Nevo: 52. The sons of
35, 36, 37 the other Eilam: 1,254. The sons of Ḥarim: 320. The sons of Yeriḥo: 345. The
38, 39 sons of Lod, Ḥadid, and Ono: 721. The sons of Senaa: 3,930. The priests – sons
40, 41 of Yedaya, of the house of Yeshua: 973. The sons of Imer: 1,052. The sons of
42, 43 Pashḥur: 1,247. The sons of Ḥarim: 1,017. The Levites – the sons of Yeshua and
44, 45 Kadmiel, of the sons of Hodva: 74. The singers, the sons of Asaf: 148. The
gatekeepers – the sons of Shalum, the sons of Ater, the sons of Talmon, the
46 sons of Akuv, the sons of Ḥatita, the sons of Shovai: 138. The Netinim – the
47, 48 sons of Tziḥa, the sons of Ḥasufa, the sons of Tabaot, the sons of Keros,
the sons of Sia, the sons of Padon, the sons of Levana, the sons of Ḥagava,
49 the sons of Shalmai the sons of Ḥanan, the sons of Gidel, the sons of
50, 51, 52 Gaḥar, the sons of Re'aya, the sons of Retzin, the sons of Nekoda, the
sons of Gazam, the sons of Uza, the sons of Pase'aḥ, the sons of Besai, the
53 sons of Meunites, the sons of Nefishsim, the sons of Bakbuk, the sons of
54 Ḥakufa, the sons of Ḥarḥur, the sons of Batzlit, the sons of Meḥida, the
55 sons of Ḥarsha, the sons of Barkos, the sons of Sisera, the sons of Tamaḥ,
56, 57 the sons of Netziaḥ, and the sons of Ḥatifa. The sons of Shlomo's servants –
58 the sons of Sotai, the sons of Soferet, the sons of Perida, the sons of Yaala,
59 the sons of Darkon, the sons of Gidel, the sons of Shefatya, the sons of Ḥatil,
60 the sons of Pokheret HaTzvayim, and the sons of Amon. The Netinim and
61 Shlomo's servants totaled 392. And these are those who came
up from Tel Melaḥ, Tel Ḥarsha, Keruv, Adon, and Imer but could not prove

יב אַלְפַּיִם וּשְׁמֹנֶה מֵאוֹת שְׁמֹנָה עָשָׂר׃ בְּנֵי עֵילָם אֶלֶף מָאתַיִם חֲמִשִּׁים
יג יד וְאַרְבָּעָה׃ בְּנֵי זַתּוּא שְׁמֹנֶה מֵאוֹת אַרְבָּעִים וַחֲמִשָּׁה׃ בְּנֵי זַכָּי שְׁבַע
טו טז מֵאוֹת וְשִׁשִּׁים׃ בְּנֵי בִנּוּי שֵׁשׁ מֵאוֹת אַרְבָּעִים וּשְׁמֹנָה׃ בְּנֵי בֵבָי שֵׁשׁ
יז מֵאוֹת עֶשְׂרִים וּשְׁמֹנָה׃ בְּנֵי עַזְגָּד אַלְפַּיִם שְׁלֹשׁ מֵאוֹת עֶשְׂרִים וּשְׁנָיִם׃
יח יט בְּנֵי אֲדֹנִיקָם שֵׁשׁ מֵאוֹת שִׁשִּׁים וְשִׁבְעָה׃ בְּנֵי בִגְוָי אַלְפַּיִם שִׁשִּׁים
כ כא וְשִׁבְעָה׃ בְּנֵי עָדִין שֵׁשׁ מֵאוֹת חֲמִשִּׁים וַחֲמִשָּׁה׃ בְּנֵי־אָטֵר לְחִזְקִיָּה
כב כג תִּשְׁעִים וּשְׁמֹנָה׃ בְּנֵי חָשֻׁם שְׁלֹשׁ מֵאוֹת עֶשְׂרִים וּשְׁמֹנָה׃ בְּנֵי בֵצָי
כד כה שְׁלֹשׁ מֵאוֹת עֶשְׂרִים וְאַרְבָּעָה׃ בְּנֵי חָרִיף מֵאָה שְׁנֵים עָשָׂר׃ בְּנֵי גִבְעוֹן
כו כז תִּשְׁעִים וַחֲמִשָּׁה׃ אַנְשֵׁי בֵית־לֶחֶם וּנְטֹפָה מֵאָה שְׁמֹנִים וּשְׁמֹנָה׃ אַנְשֵׁי
כח עֲנָתוֹת מֵאָה עֶשְׂרִים וּשְׁמֹנָה׃ אַנְשֵׁי בֵית־עַזְמָוֶת אַרְבָּעִים וּשְׁנָיִם׃
כט אַנְשֵׁי קִרְיַת יְעָרִים כְּפִירָה וּבְאֵרוֹת שְׁבַע מֵאוֹת אַרְבָּעִים וּשְׁלֹשָׁה׃
ל לא אַנְשֵׁי הָרָמָה וָגָבַע שֵׁשׁ מֵאוֹת עֶשְׂרִים וְאֶחָד׃ אַנְשֵׁי מִכְמָס מֵאָה
לב לג וְעֶשְׂרִים וּשְׁנָיִם׃ אַנְשֵׁי בֵית־אֵל וְהָעָי מֵאָה עֶשְׂרִים וּשְׁלֹשָׁה׃ אַנְשֵׁי נְבוֹ
לד אַחֵר חֲמִשִּׁים וּשְׁנָיִם׃ בְּנֵי עֵילָם אַחֵר אֶלֶף מָאתַיִם חֲמִשִּׁים וְאַרְבָּעָה׃
לה לו בְּנֵי חָרִם שְׁלֹשׁ מֵאוֹת וְעֶשְׂרִים׃ בְּנֵי יְרֵחוֹ שְׁלֹשׁ מֵאוֹת אַרְבָּעִים
לז לח וַחֲמִשָּׁה׃ בְּנֵי־לֹד חָדִיד וְאוֹנוֹ שְׁבַע מֵאוֹת וְעֶשְׂרִים וְאֶחָד׃ בְּנֵי סְנָאָה
לט שְׁלֹשֶׁת אֲלָפִים תְּשַׁע מֵאוֹת וּשְׁלֹשִׁים׃ הַכֹּהֲנִים בְּנֵי יְדַעְיָה לְבֵית
מ יֵשׁוּעַ תְּשַׁע מֵאוֹת שִׁבְעִים וּשְׁלֹשָׁה׃ בְּנֵי אִמֵּר אֶלֶף חֲמִשִּׁים וּשְׁנָיִם׃
מא מב בְּנֵי פַשְׁחוּר אֶלֶף מָאתַיִם אַרְבָּעִים וְשִׁבְעָה׃ בְּנֵי חָרִם אֶלֶף שִׁבְעָה
מג עָשָׂר׃ הַלְוִיִּם בְּנֵי־יֵשׁוּעַ לְקַדְמִיאֵל לִבְנֵי לְהוֹדְוָה שִׁבְעִים וְאַרְבָּעָה׃
מד מה הַמְשֹׁרְרִים בְּנֵי אָסָף מֵאָה אַרְבָּעִים וּשְׁמֹנָה׃ הַשֹּׁעֲרִים בְּנֵי־שַׁלֻּם בְּנֵי־
אָטֵר בְּנֵי־טַלְמֹן בְּנֵי־עַקּוּב בְּנֵי חֲטִיטָא בְּנֵי שֹׁבָי מֵאָה שְׁלֹשִׁים וּשְׁמֹנָה׃
מו מז הַנְּתִינִים בְּנֵי־צִחָא בְנֵי־חֲשֻׂפָא בְּנֵי טַבָּעוֹת׃ בְּנֵי־קֵירֹס בְּנֵי־סִיעָא בְּנֵי
מח מט פָדוֹן׃ בְּנֵי־לְבָנָה בְנֵי־חֲגָבָא בְּנֵי שַׁלְמָי׃ בְּנֵי־חָנָן בְּנֵי־גִדֵּל בְּנֵי־גָחַר׃
נ,נא נב בְּנֵי־רְאָיָה בְנֵי־רְצִין בְּנֵי נְקוֹדָא׃ בְּנֵי־גַזָּם בְּנֵי־עֻזָּא בְּנֵי פָסֵחַ׃ בְּנֵי־בֵסַי
נג בְּנֵי־מְעוּנִים בְּנֵי נְפוּשְׁסִים׃ בְּנֵי־בַקְבּוּק בְּנֵי־חֲקוּפָא בְּנֵי חַרְחוּר׃ נְפִישְׁסִים
נד נה בְּנֵי־בַצְלִית בְּנֵי־מְחִידָא בְּנֵי חַרְשָׁא׃ בְּנֵי־בַרְקוֹס בְּנֵי־סִיסְרָא בְּנֵי־
נו נז תָמַח׃ בְּנֵי נְצִיחַ בְּנֵי חֲטִיפָא׃ בְּנֵי עַבְדֵי שְׁלֹמֹה בְּנֵי־סוֹטַי בְּנֵי־סֹפֶרֶת
נח נט בְּנֵי פְרִידָא׃ בְּנֵי־יַעְלָא בְנֵי־דַרְקוֹן בְּנֵי גִדֵּל׃ בְּנֵי שְׁפַטְיָה בְנֵי־חַטִּיל
ס בְּנֵי פֹּכֶרֶת הַצְּבָיִים בְּנֵי אָמוֹן׃ כָּל־הַנְּתִינִים וּבְנֵי עַבְדֵי שְׁלֹמֹה שְׁלֹשׁ
סא מֵאוֹת תִּשְׁעִים וּשְׁנָיִם׃ וְאֵלֶּה הָעוֹלִים מִתֵּל מֶלַח תֵּל
חַרְשָׁא כְּרוּב אַדּוֹן וְאִמֵּר וְלֹא יָכְלוּ לְהַגִּיד בֵּית־אֲבוֹתָם וְזַרְעָם אִם

62 whether their ancestral houses or descent were of Israel: the sons of Delaya,
63 the sons of Toviya, and the sons of Nekoda: 642. Of the priests: the
sons of Ḥavaya, the sons of HaKotz, and the sons of Barzilai – he who married
one of the daughters of Barzilai the Gileadite and was called by their name.
64 These sought the written record of their genealogy, which could not be found,
65 and were therefore repudiated from the priesthood. The governor instructed
them that they must not eat from the holiest offerings until the advent of the
66 priest for the Urim and Tumim.[19] The entire community together numbered
67 42,360. Aside from their male and female slaves, of whom there were 7,337,
they also had 245 male and female singers. (*Their horses – 736; their mules – 245.) *In a few versions it is written:
68 69 Camels: 435; donkeys: 6,720. A few of the clan leaders
donated toward the work. His Excellency the governor donated gold to the
treasury – one thousand drachmas and fifty basins – as well as five hundred
70 thirty priestly robes. Some of the clan leaders also donated to the
project treasury – twenty thousand gold drachmas and two thousand two
71 hundred silver mina – while the rest of the people gave twenty thousand gold
72 drachmas, two thousand silver mina, and sixty-seven priestly robes. And the
priests, Levites, gatekeepers, singers, others of the people, and the Netinim
settled in their towns, so that all Israel were in their towns. Now
8 1 the seventh month arrived, and the Israelites were in their towns.[20] All the
people assembled together in the open plaza opposite the Water Gate, calling
upon Ezra the scholar[21] to bring out the scroll of the Torah of Moshe: the
2 LORD's command to Israel. So Ezra the priest brought the Torah before the
congregation – men and women and all who could understand what they
3 heard – on the first day of the seventh month. He read it from the first light
until midday in the plaza facing the Water Gate before the men and the
women and all who understood, and the ears of all the people were attuned
4 to the Torah scroll. Ezra the scholar was standing upon a wooden platform
erected for the occasion. Next to him, on his right, stood Matitya, Shema,
Anaya, Uriya, Ḥilkiya, and Maaseya, and on his left were Pedaya, Mishael,
5 Malkiya, Ḥashum, Ḥashbadana, Zekharya, and Meshulam. Then
Ezra, who was elevated above all the people, opened the scroll before the
6 entire people, and as he did so, the people all stood up. Then Ezra blessed
the LORD, the almighty God, and the people answered, "Amen, Amen," while
lifting up their hands. They bowed and prostrated themselves before the
7 LORD, faces down to the ground, then Yeshua and Bani and Shereveya, Yamin,
Akuv, Shabtai, Hodiya, Maaseya, Kelita, Azarya, Yozavad, Ḥanan, Pelaya, and
the Levites explained the Torah to the people, who all the while remained

19 | An oracle worn by the High Priest (see Ex. 28:30; Lev. 8:8), which by this time was evidently no longer extant.

20 | Cf. Ezra 3:1.

21 | See note on Ezra 7:6.

סב מִיִּשְׂרָאֵל הֵם: בְּנֵי־דְלָיָה בְנֵי־טוֹבִיָּה בְּנֵי נְקוֹדָא שֵׁשׁ מֵאוֹת וְאַרְבָּעִים
סג וּשְׁנָיִם: וּמִן־הַכֹּהֲנִים בְּנֵי חֳבַיָּה בְּנֵי הַקּוֹץ בְּנֵי בַרְזִלַּי
סד אֲשֶׁר לָקַח מִבְּנוֹת בַּרְזִלַּי הַגִּלְעָדִי אִשָּׁה וַיִּקָּרֵא עַל־שְׁמָם: אֵלֶּה בִּקְשׁוּ
סה כְתָבָם הַמִּתְיַחְשִׂים וְלֹא נִמְצָא וַיְגֹאֲלוּ מִן־הַכְּהֻנָּה: וַיֹּאמֶר הַתִּרְשָׁתָא
לָהֶם אֲשֶׁר לֹא־יֹאכְלוּ מִקֹּדֶשׁ הַקֳּדָשִׁים עַד עֲמֹד הַכֹּהֵן לְאוּרִים וְתֻמִּים:
סו סז כָּל־הַקָּהָל כְּאֶחָד אַרְבַּע רִבּוֹא אַלְפַּיִם שְׁלֹשׁ־מֵאוֹת וְשִׁשִּׁים: מִלְּבַד
עַבְדֵיהֶם וְאַמְהֹתֵיהֶם אֵלֶּה שִׁבְעַת אֲלָפִים שְׁלֹשׁ מֵאוֹת שְׁלֹשִׁים
וְשִׁבְעָה וְלָהֶם מְשֹׁרְרִים וּמְשֹׁרְרוֹת מָאתַיִם וְאַרְבָּעִים וַחֲמִשָּׁה:
*סוּסֵיהֶם שְׁבַע מֵאוֹת שְׁלֹשִׁים וְשִׁשָּׁה פִּרְדֵיהֶם מָאתַיִם אַרְבָּעִים וַחֲמִשָּׁה: * בקצת ספרים כתוב כאן:
סח גְּמַלִּים אַרְבַּע מֵאוֹת שְׁלֹשִׁים וַחֲמִשָּׁה חֲמֹרִים שֵׁשֶׁת אֲלָפִים שְׁבַע
סט מֵאוֹת וְעֶשְׂרִים: וּמִקְצָת רָאשֵׁי הָאָבוֹת נָתְנוּ לַמְּלָאכָה
הַתִּרְשָׁתָא נָתַן לָאוֹצָר זָהָב דַּרְכְּמֹנִים אֶלֶף מִזְרָקוֹת חֲמִשִּׁים כָּתְנוֹת
ע כֹּהֲנִים שְׁלֹשִׁים וַחֲמֵשׁ מֵאוֹת: וּמֵרָאשֵׁי הָאָבוֹת נָתְנוּ
לְאוֹצַר הַמְּלָאכָה זָהָב דַּרְכְּמוֹנִים שְׁתֵּי רִבּוֹת וְכֶסֶף מָנִים אַלְפַּיִם
עא וּמָאתָיִם: וַאֲשֶׁר נָתְנוּ שְׁאֵרִית הָעָם זָהָב דַּרְכְּמֹנִים שְׁתֵּי רִבּוֹא
עב וְכֶסֶף מָנִים אַלְפָּיִם וְכָתְנֹת כֹּהֲנִים שִׁשִּׁים וְשִׁבְעָה: וַיֵּשְׁבוּ הַכֹּהֲנִים
וְהַלְוִיִּם וְהַשּׁוֹעֲרִים וְהַמְשֹׁרְרִים וּמִן־הָעָם וְהַנְּתִינִים וְכָל־יִשְׂרָאֵל
בְּעָרֵיהֶם וַיִּגַּע הַחֹדֶשׁ הַשְּׁבִיעִי וּבְנֵי יִשְׂרָאֵל בְּעָרֵיהֶם:
ח א וַיֵּאָסְפוּ כָל־הָעָם כְּאִישׁ אֶחָד אֶל־הָרְחוֹב אֲשֶׁר לִפְנֵי שַׁעַר־הַמָּיִם
וַיֹּאמְרוּ לְעֶזְרָא הַסֹּפֵר לְהָבִיא אֶת־סֵפֶר תּוֹרַת מֹשֶׁה אֲשֶׁר־צִוָּה יְהוָה
ב אֶת־יִשְׂרָאֵל: וַיָּבִיא עֶזְרָא הַכֹּהֵן אֶת־הַתּוֹרָה לִפְנֵי הַקָּהָל מֵאִישׁ
ג וְעַד־אִשָּׁה וְכֹל מֵבִין לִשְׁמֹעַ בְּיוֹם אֶחָד לַחֹדֶשׁ הַשְּׁבִיעִי: וַיִּקְרָא־בוֹ
לִפְנֵי הָרְחוֹב אֲשֶׁר ׀ לִפְנֵי שַׁעַר־הַמַּיִם מִן־הָאוֹר עַד־מַחֲצִית הַיּוֹם נֶגֶד
ד הָאֲנָשִׁים וְהַנָּשִׁים וְהַמְּבִינִים וְאָזְנֵי כָל־הָעָם אֶל־סֵפֶר הַתּוֹרָה: וַיַּעֲמֹד
עֶזְרָא הַסֹּפֵר עַל־מִגְדַּל־עֵץ אֲשֶׁר עָשׂוּ לַדָּבָר וַיַּעֲמֹד אֶצְלוֹ מַתִּתְיָה
וְשֶׁמַע וַעֲנָיָה וְאוּרִיָּה וְחִלְקִיָּה וּמַעֲשֵׂיָה עַל־יְמִינוֹ וּמִשְּׂמֹאלוֹ פְּדָיָה
ה וּמִישָׁאֵל וּמַלְכִּיָּה וְחָשֻׁם וְחַשְׁבַּדָּנָה זְכַרְיָה מְשֻׁלָּם: וַיִּפְתַּח
עֶזְרָא הַסֵּפֶר לְעֵינֵי כָל־הָעָם כִּי־מֵעַל כָּל־הָעָם הָיָה וּכְפִתְחוֹ עָמְדוּ
ו כָל־הָעָם: וַיְבָרֶךְ עֶזְרָא אֶת־יְהוָה הָאֱלֹהִים הַגָּדוֹל וַיַּעֲנוּ כָל־הָעָם
אָמֵן ׀ אָמֵן בְּמֹעַל יְדֵיהֶם וַיִּקְּדוּ וַיִּשְׁתַּחֲוֻּ לַיהוָה אַפַּיִם אָרְצָה:
ז וְיֵשׁוּעַ וּבָנִי וְשֵׁרֵבְיָה ׀ יָמִין עַקּוּב שַׁבְּתַי ׀ הוֹדִיָּה מַעֲשֵׂיָה קְלִיטָא
עֲזַרְיָה יוֹזָבָד חָנָן פְּלָאיָה וְהַלְוִיִּם מְבִינִים אֶת־הָעָם לַתּוֹרָה וְהָעָם

8 standing. They read from the scroll of God's Torah while explaining and
9 clarifying each detail to render the readings understandable. Then
Neḥemya, His Excellency the governor, along with Ezra the priest and scholar
and the Levites teaching the people, said to all the people, "Today is sacred to
the LORD, your God.[22] You should neither mourn nor weep" – for the people
10 were all weeping as they listened to the words of the Torah. Then he told
them, "Now go and feast on delicacies, drink sweet things, and send servings
of food to those who have none – for this day is sacred to our Lord. Do not
11 be sorrowful, for rejoicing in the LORD is your strength and shelter." And the
Levites quieted all the people, saying: "Hush! This day is sacred – do not be
12 sorrowful!" So all the people went to dine and drink and to send servings of
food to one another and to make merry, for they understood what they had
13 been taught. And on the second day, all the clan leaders of the people
gathered with the priests and Levites around Ezra the scholar to ponder the
14 words of the Torah. And in the Torah they found written that the LORD had
commanded at the hands of Moshe that the Israelites should dwell in booths
15 during the festival of the seventh month and that they should announce and
have proclaimed throughout their towns and in Jerusalem, "Go out to the
hills and bring back leafy branches of olive, pine, myrtle, and date, thickly
16 leaved branches to construct booths as prescribed."[23] So the people went out
and brought branches and built booths for themselves – on their rooftops or
in their courtyards and in the courtyards of God's House and in the plaza of
17 the Water Gate and in the plaza of the Efrayim Gate. The entire community
who had returned from the captivity constructed booths and dwelt in those
booths, which the Israelites had not done since the days of Yeshua bin Nun
18 until that day. There was jubilant rejoicing. And he read from the scroll of
God's Torah every day from the first day until the last. They held the festival
for seven days and on the eighth day, a sacred assembly, as ordained by law.
9 1 Then on the twenty-fourth of that month, the Israelites convened, fasting and
2 in sackcloth with earth on themselves. The seed of Israel separated themselves
from all those of foreign descent. Standing, they confessed their sins and the
3 wrongdoings of their ancestors. While still standing in their places, they read
from the scroll of the LORD their God's Torah for a quarter of the day, and
for another quarter-day they confessed and prostrated themselves before
4 the LORD, their God. Standing on the Levites' platform Yeshua and
Bani, Kadmiel, Shevanya, Buni, Shereveya, Bani, and Kenani cried out in loud
5 voices to the LORD, their God. Then Yeshua and Kadmiel, Bani, Ḥashavneya,
Shereveya, Hodiya, Shevanya, and Petaḥya, the Levites, declared, "Rise and
bless the LORD your God from this world to eternity. May they bless Your
6 glorious name – exalted above any blessing or praise." You alone are the
LORD – You created the heavens, the highest heavens with all their hosts,

22 | See Leviticus 23:23–25.
23 | Leviticus 23:33–43.

ח עַל־עׇמְדָם׃ וַיִּקְרְאוּ בַסֵּפֶר בְּתוֹרַת הָאֱלֹהִים מְפֹרָשׁ וְשׂוֹם שֶׂכֶל
ט וַיָּבִינוּ בַּמִּקְרָא׃ וַיֹּאמֶר נְחֶמְיָה הוּא הַתִּרְשָׁתָא וְעֶזְרָא
הַכֹּהֵן ׀ הַסֹּפֵר וְהַלְוִיִּם הַמְּבִינִים אֶת־הָעָם לְכׇל־הָעָם הַיּוֹם קָדֹשׁ־הוּא
לַיהוה אֱלֹהֵיכֶם אַל־תִּתְאַבְּלוּ וְאַל־תִּבְכּוּ כִּי בוֹכִים כׇּל־הָעָם כְּשׇׁמְעָם
י אֶת־דִּבְרֵי הַתּוֹרָה׃ וַיֹּאמֶר לָהֶם לְכוּ אִכְלוּ מַשְׁמַנִּים וּשְׁתוּ מַמְתַקִּים ח
וְשִׁלְחוּ מָנוֹת לְאֵין נָכוֹן לוֹ כִּי־קָדוֹשׁ הַיּוֹם לַאֲדֹנֵינוּ וְאַל־תֵּעָצֵבוּ
יא כִּי־חֶדְוַת יהוה הִיא מָעֻזְּכֶם׃ וְהַלְוִיִּם מַחְשִׁים לְכׇל־הָעָם לֵאמֹר
יב הַסּוּ כִּי הַיּוֹם קָדֹשׁ וְאַל־תֵּעָצֵבוּ׃ וַיֵּלְכוּ כׇל־הָעָם לֶאֱכֹל וְלִשְׁתּוֹת
וּלְשַׁלַּח מָנוֹת וְלַעֲשׂוֹת שִׂמְחָה גְדוֹלָה כִּי הֵבִינוּ בַּדְּבָרִים אֲשֶׁר הוֹדִיעוּ
יג לָהֶם׃ וּבַיּוֹם הַשֵּׁנִי נֶאֶסְפוּ רָאשֵׁי הָאָבוֹת לְכׇל־הָעָם
הַכֹּהֲנִים וְהַלְוִיִּם אֶל־עֶזְרָא הַסֹּפֵר וּלְהַשְׂכִּיל אֶל־דִּבְרֵי הַתּוֹרָה׃
יד וַיִּמְצְאוּ כָּתוּב בַּתּוֹרָה אֲשֶׁר צִוָּה יהוה בְּיַד־מֹשֶׁה אֲשֶׁר יֵשְׁבוּ בְנֵי־
טו יִשְׂרָאֵל בַּסֻּכּוֹת בֶּחָג בַּחֹדֶשׁ הַשְּׁבִיעִי׃ וַאֲשֶׁר יַשְׁמִיעוּ וְיַעֲבִירוּ קוֹל
בְּכׇל־עָרֵיהֶם וּבִירוּשָׁלַם לֵאמֹר צְאוּ הָהָר וְהָבִיאוּ עֲלֵי־זַיִת וַעֲלֵי־עֵץ
שֶׁמֶן וַעֲלֵי הֲדַס וַעֲלֵי תְמָרִים וַעֲלֵי עֵץ עָבֹת לַעֲשֹׂת סֻכֹּת כַּכָּתוּב׃
טז וַיֵּצְאוּ הָעָם וַיָּבִיאוּ וַיַּעֲשׂוּ לָהֶם סֻכּוֹת אִישׁ עַל־גַּגּוֹ וּבְחַצְרֹתֵיהֶם
וּבְחַצְרוֹת בֵּית הָאֱלֹהִים וּבִרְחוֹב שַׁעַר הַמַּיִם וּבִרְחוֹב שַׁעַר אֶפְרָיִם׃
יז וַיַּעֲשׂוּ כׇל־הַקָּהָל הַשָּׁבִים מִן־הַשְּׁבִי ׀ סֻכּוֹת וַיֵּשְׁבוּ בַסֻּכּוֹת כִּי לֹא־
עָשׂוּ מִימֵי יֵשׁוּעַ בִּן־נוּן כֵּן בְּנֵי יִשְׂרָאֵל עַד הַיּוֹם הַהוּא וַתְּהִי שִׂמְחָה
יח גְּדוֹלָה מְאֹד׃ וַיִּקְרָא בְּסֵפֶר תּוֹרַת הָאֱלֹהִים יוֹם ׀ בְּיוֹם מִן־הַיּוֹם
הָרִאשׁוֹן עַד הַיּוֹם הָאַחֲרוֹן וַיַּעֲשׂוּ־חָג שִׁבְעַת יָמִים וּבַיּוֹם הַשְּׁמִינִי
עֲצֶרֶת כַּמִּשְׁפָּט׃
ט א וּבְיוֹם עֶשְׂרִים וְאַרְבָּעָה לַחֹדֶשׁ הַזֶּה נֶאֶסְפוּ בְנֵי־יִשְׂרָאֵל בְּצוֹם וּבְשַׂקִּים
ב וַאֲדָמָה עֲלֵיהֶם׃ וַיִּבָּדְלוּ זֶרַע יִשְׂרָאֵל מִכֹּל בְּנֵי נֵכָר וַיַּעַמְדוּ וַיִּתְוַדּוּ עַל־
ג חַטֹּאתֵיהֶם וַעֲוֺנוֹת אֲבֹתֵיהֶם׃ וַיָּקוּמוּ עַל־עׇמְדָם וַיִּקְרְאוּ בְּסֵפֶר תּוֹרַת
יהוה אֱלֹהֵיהֶם רְבִעִית הַיּוֹם וּרְבִעִית מִתְוַדִּים וּמִשְׁתַּחֲוִים לַיהוה
ד אֱלֹהֵיהֶם׃ וַיָּקׇם עַל־מַעֲלֵה הַלְוִיִּם יֵשׁוּעַ וּבָנִי קַדְמִיאֵל
שְׁבַנְיָה בֻּנִּי שֵׁרֵבְיָה בָּנִי כְנָנִי וַיִּזְעֲקוּ בְּקוֹל גָּדוֹל אֶל־יהוה אֱלֹהֵיהֶם׃
ה וַיֹּאמְרוּ הַלְוִיִּם יֵשׁוּעַ וְקַדְמִיאֵל בָּנִי חֲשַׁבְנְיָה שֵׁרֵבְיָה הוֹדִיָּה שְׁבַנְיָה
פְתַחְיָה קוּמוּ בָּרְכוּ אֶת־יהוה אֱלֹהֵיכֶם מִן־הָעוֹלָם עַד־הָעוֹלָם וִיבָרְכוּ
ו שֵׁם כְּבֹדֶךָ וּמְרוֹמַם עַל־כׇּל־בְּרָכָה וּתְהִלָּה׃ אַתָּה־הוּא יהוה לְבַדֶּךָ
אַתָּ עָשִׂיתָ אֶת־הַשָּׁמַיִם שְׁמֵי הַשָּׁמַיִם וְכׇל־צְבָאָם הָאָרֶץ וְכׇל־אֲשֶׁר

the earth and all upon it, and the seas with all that they contain. You give life
7 to them all, and the hosts of heaven prostrate themselves before You.[24] You
are the LORD God who chose Avram, bringing him out of Ur Kasdim and
8 changing his name to Avraham. Finding his heart faithful to You, You forged
a covenant with him to give his seed the land of the Canaanites, Hittites,
Amorites, Perizzites, Jebusites, and Girgashites, and You kept Your word
9 because You are just. You saw our ancestors suffering oppression in Egypt;
10 You heard their cries at the Sea of Reeds. You performed signs and wonders
against Pharaoh, all his servants, and all the people of his land because You
knew with what cruel wickedness they had treated them, thus making a
11 name for Yourself to this day. You split the sea for them so that they passed
through it on dry ground, but You hurled their pursuers into the depths like
12 a stone into raging waters. You guided them with a column of cloud by day
and with a column of fire at night to illuminate the way for them to walk.
13 You descended on Mount Sinai and spoke to them from heaven, giving them
14 just laws and true teachings, goodly statutes and commandments. You made
Your holy Sabbath known to them and charged them with commandments,
15 statutes, and teachings through the hand of Your servant Moshe. For their
hunger You gave them food from heaven and for their thirst extracted water
for them from the rock. You told them to enter and inherit the land that You
16 had raised Your hand in oath to give to them. But they and our fathers acted
in willful wickedness, stiffening their necks and disobeying Your commands.
17 Refusing to listen, they did not remember Your marvels which You performed
for them. They stiffened their necks and rebelliously turned their heads
to return to their slavery. But you are a God of forgiveness – compassionate
and gracious, slow to anger, abounding in kindness – and did not forsake
18 them. Even though they made themselves a molten calf, declaring, "This
19 is your god who brought you out of Egypt," and aroused great anger, You
in Your infinite compassion did not forsake them in the wilderness. The
cloud column did not cease guiding the way by day, nor did the nocturnal
20 fire column cease illuminating the way for them to walk. You conferred Your
good spirit upon them for enlightenment, and You did not withhold Your
21 manna from their mouths while giving them water to slake their thirst. For
forty years You provided for them in the desert – they lacked for nothing:
22 their clothes did not wear out, nor did their feet swell. You bestowed upon
them kingdoms and peoples whom You then dispersed to the far reaches.
They inherited Siḥon's land, the realm of Ḥeshbon's king, and the land of
23 Og, king of the Bashan. You multiplied their descendants like the celestial
stars and brought them to the land that You had told their ancestors to come
24 to and possess. Then the sons came and took possession of the land, for You
subdued the Canaanite inhabitants before them, delivering them into their
25 hands – their rulers and the land's peoples – to do with as they willed. They
captured fortified cities and a rich fertile land, inheriting houses full of all

---

24 | This passage contains allusions to many other biblical verses and episodes, especially in the Torah. Verse 6 parallels Psalms 148.

עָלֶיהָ הַיַּמִּים וְכָל־אֲשֶׁר בָּהֶם וְאַתָּה מְחַיֶּה אֶת־כֻּלָּם וּצְבָא הַשָּׁמַיִם לְךָ
ז מִשְׁתַּחֲוִים: אַתָּה הוּא יהוה הָאֱלֹהִים אֲשֶׁר בָּחַרְתָּ בְּאַבְרָם וְהוֹצֵאתוֹ
ח מֵאוּר כַּשְׂדִּים וְשַׂמְתָּ שְּׁמוֹ אַבְרָהָם: וּמָצָאתָ אֶת־לְבָבוֹ נֶאֱמָן לְפָנֶיךָ
וְכָרוֹת עִמּוֹ הַבְּרִית לָתֵת אֶת־אֶרֶץ הַכְּנַעֲנִי הַחִתִּי הָאֱמֹרִי וְהַפְּרִזִּי
וְהַיְבוּסִי וְהַגִּרְגָּשִׁי לָתֵת לְזַרְעוֹ וַתָּקֶם אֶת־דְּבָרֶיךָ כִּי צַדִּיק אָתָּה:
ט וַתֵּרֶא אֶת־עֳנִי אֲבֹתֵינוּ בְּמִצְרָיִם וְאֶת־זַעֲקָתָם שָׁמַעְתָּ עַל־יַם־סוּף:
י וַתִּתֵּן אֹתֹת וּמֹפְתִים בְּפַרְעֹה וּבְכָל־עֲבָדָיו וּבְכָל־עַם אַרְצוֹ כִּי יָדַעְתָּ
יא כִּי הֵזִידוּ עֲלֵיהֶם וַתַּעַשׂ־לְךָ שֵׁם כְּהַיּוֹם הַזֶּה: וְהַיָּם בָּקַעְתָּ לִפְנֵיהֶם
וַיַּעַבְרוּ בְתוֹךְ־הַיָּם בַּיַּבָּשָׁה וְאֶת־רֹדְפֵיהֶם הִשְׁלַכְתָּ בִמְצוֹלֹת כְּמוֹ־
יב אֶבֶן בְּמַיִם עַזִּים: וּבְעַמּוּד עָנָן הִנְחִיתָם יוֹמָם וּבְעַמּוּד אֵשׁ לַיְלָה
יג לְהָאִיר לָהֶם אֶת־הַדֶּרֶךְ אֲשֶׁר יֵלְכוּ־בָהּ: וְעַל הַר־סִינַי יָרַדְתָּ וְדַבֵּר
עִמָּהֶם מִשָּׁמָיִם וַתִּתֵּן לָהֶם מִשְׁפָּטִים יְשָׁרִים וְתוֹרוֹת אֱמֶת חֻקִּים
יד וּמִצְוֹת טוֹבִים: וְאֶת־שַׁבַּת קָדְשְׁךָ הוֹדַעְתָּ לָהֶם וּמִצְוֹת וְחֻקִּים וְתוֹרָה
טו צִוִּיתָ לָהֶם בְּיַד מֹשֶׁה עַבְדֶּךָ: וְלֶחֶם מִשָּׁמַיִם נָתַתָּה לָהֶם לִרְעָבָם וּמַיִם
מִסֶּלַע הוֹצֵאתָ לָהֶם לִצְמָאָם וַתֹּאמֶר לָהֶם לָבוֹא לָרֶשֶׁת אֶת־הָאָרֶץ
טז אֲשֶׁר־נָשָׂאתָ אֶת־יָדְךָ לָתֵת לָהֶם: וְהֵם וַאֲבֹתֵינוּ הֵזִידוּ וַיַּקְשׁוּ אֶת־
יז עָרְפָּם וְלֹא שָׁמְעוּ אֶל־מִצְוֹתֶיךָ: וַיְמָאֲנוּ לִשְׁמֹעַ וְלֹא־זָכְרוּ נִפְלְאֹתֶיךָ
אֲשֶׁר עָשִׂיתָ עִמָּהֶם וַיַּקְשׁוּ אֶת־עָרְפָּם וַיִּתְּנוּ־רֹאשׁ לָשׁוּב לְעַבְדֻתָם
בְּמִרְיָם וְאַתָּה אֱלוֹהַּ סְלִיחוֹת חַנּוּן וְרַחוּם אֶרֶךְ־אַפַּיִם וְרַב־וחסד חֶסֶד
יח וְלֹא עֲזַבְתָּם: אַף כִּי־עָשׂוּ לָהֶם עֵגֶל מַסֵּכָה וַיֹּאמְרוּ זֶה אֱלֹהֶיךָ אֲשֶׁר
יט הֶעֶלְךָ מִמִּצְרָיִם וַיַּעֲשׂוּ נֶאָצוֹת גְּדֹלוֹת: וְאַתָּה בְּרַחֲמֶיךָ הָרַבִּים לֹא
עֲזַבְתָּם בַּמִּדְבָּר אֶת־עַמּוּד הֶעָנָן לֹא־סָר מֵעֲלֵיהֶם בְּיוֹמָם לְהַנְחֹתָם
בְּהַדֶּרֶךְ וְאֶת־עַמּוּד הָאֵשׁ בְּלַיְלָה לְהָאִיר לָהֶם וְאֶת־הַדֶּרֶךְ אֲשֶׁר
כ יֵלְכוּ־בָהּ: וְרוּחֲךָ הַטּוֹבָה נָתַתָּ לְהַשְׂכִּילָם וּמַנְךָ לֹא־מָנַעְתָּ מִפִּיהֶם
כא וּמַיִם נָתַתָּה לָהֶם לִצְמָאָם: וְאַרְבָּעִים שָׁנָה כִּלְכַּלְתָּם בַּמִּדְבָּר לֹא
כב חָסֵרוּ שַׂלְמֹתֵיהֶם לֹא בָלוּ וְרַגְלֵיהֶם לֹא בָצֵקוּ: וַתִּתֵּן לָהֶם מַמְלָכוֹת
וַעֲמָמִים וַתַּחְלְקֵם לְפֵאָה וַיִּירְשׁוּ אֶת־אֶרֶץ סִיחוֹן וְאֶת־אֶרֶץ מֶלֶךְ
כג חֶשְׁבּוֹן וְאֶת־אֶרֶץ עוֹג מֶלֶךְ־הַבָּשָׁן: וּבְנֵיהֶם הִרְבִּיתָ כְּכֹכְבֵי הַשָּׁמָיִם
כד וַתְּבִיאֵם אֶל־הָאָרֶץ אֲשֶׁר־אָמַרְתָּ לַאֲבֹתֵיהֶם לָבוֹא לָרָשֶׁת: וַיָּבֹאוּ
הַבָּנִים וַיִּירְשׁוּ אֶת־הָאָרֶץ וַתַּכְנַע לִפְנֵיהֶם אֶת־יֹשְׁבֵי הָאָרֶץ הַכְּנַעֲנִים
וַתִּתְּנֵם בְּיָדָם וְאֶת־מַלְכֵיהֶם וְאֶת־עַמְמֵי הָאָרֶץ לַעֲשׂוֹת בָּהֶם כִּרְצוֹנָם:
כה וַיִּלְכְּדוּ עָרִים בְּצֻרוֹת וַאֲדָמָה שְׁמֵנָה וַיִּירְשׁוּ בָּתִּים מְלֵאִים־כָּל־טוּב

good things – hewn cisterns and vineyards, olive groves, and plentiful fruit
orchards. They ate and were satisfied, growing rich and fat, luxuriating in Your
26 great goodness. Yet they disobeyed and rebelled against You, casting Your
Torah behind their backs and slaughtering Your prophets who admonished
27 them so as to return them to You, thus arousing great anger. So You gave them
into the hands of their oppressors, who indeed oppressed them. Then, in the
time of their oppression, they cried out to You, and hearing from heaven, You
in Your infinite compassion sent them liberators, who delivered them from
28 the hands of their oppressors. But as soon as they were again at ease, they
continued committing wrongs against You – so You abandoned them to their
enemies, who tyrannized them. Then they returned, crying out to You, and
You, hearing from heaven, rescued them out of Your compassion time and
29 again. You admonished them so that they would turn back to Your teaching,
but they acted wickedly, disobeying Your commands while transgressing
Your laws – those by which a person shall live. Instead, turning a stubborn
30 shoulder, they stiffened their necks and would not listen. You bore with
them for many years, admonishing them at the hands of Your prophets
through Your spirit. They still would not listen, so You delivered them into
31 the hands of the peoples of the lands. But in Your infinite mercy you did not
annihilate them or forsake them, for You are a compassionate and gracious
32 God. Now, our God, the great, mighty, and awe-inspiring God, keeper of
the covenant and the love, do not deem as trivial all that hardship we have
encountered – our kings, princes, priests and prophets, our ancestors, and
33 all Your people – from the days of the Assyrian kings until today. You have
been just throughout all that has come upon us, for You have dealt in truth
34 while we have committed evil. Our kings and our princes, our priests, and
our ancestors did not act according to Your Torah; they heeded neither
Your commands nor the warnings through which You admonished them.
35 Despite their sovereign rule and the bountiful goodness You had bestowed
upon them in the expansive and rich land You had given them, they did
36 not serve You, nor did they repent or turn away from their evil deeds. Now
here we are – subjugated – and it is in this land that You bestowed upon our
ancestors so that they could partake of her fruits and her bounty that we are
37 now subjugated. She yields abundant crops – for the kings whom You have set
over us for our sins. They reign as they will over our bodies and our livestock.
We are indeed in dire trouble and distress.

10 1 Yet amid all this we commit to a faithful covenant and put it in writing under
2 the seal of our leaders, Levites, and priests. These are the signatories: His
3 Excellency the governor, Neḥemya son of Ḥakhalya, and Tzidkiya, Seraya,
4 5 Azarya, Yirmeya, Pashḥur, Amarya, Malkiya, Ḥatush, Shevanya, Malukh,
6, 7 8 Ḥarim, Meremot, Ovadya, Daniel, Gineton, Barukh, Meshulam, Aviya,
9 10 Miyamin, Maazya, Bilgai, and Shemaya – these are the priests; of the Levites:
11 Yeshua son of Azanya, Binui, a descendant of Ḥenadad and Kadmiel;their
12 brothers: Shevanya, Hodiya, Kelita, Pelaya, Ḥanan, Mikha, Reḥov, Ḥashavya,

בָּרוֹת חֲצוּבִים כְּרָמִים וְזֵיתִים וְעֵץ מַאֲכָל לָרֹב וַיֹּאכְלוּ וַיִּשְׂבְּעוּ וַיַּשְׁמִינוּ
כו וַיִּתְעַדְּנוּ בְּטוּבְךָ הַגָּדוֹל׃ וַיַּמְרוּ וַיִּמְרְדוּ בָּךְ וַיַּשְׁלִכוּ אֶת־תּוֹרָתְךָ אַחֲרֵי
גַוָּם וְאֶת־נְבִיאֶיךָ הָרָגוּ אֲשֶׁר־הֵעִידוּ בָם לַהֲשִׁיבָם אֵלֶיךָ וַיַּעֲשׂוּ נֶאָצוֹת
כז גְּדוֹלֹת׃ וַתִּתְּנֵם בְּיַד צָרֵיהֶם וַיָּצֵרוּ לָהֶם וּבְעֵת צָרָתָם יִצְעֲקוּ אֵלֶיךָ
וְאַתָּה מִשָּׁמַיִם תִּשְׁמָע וּכְרַחֲמֶיךָ הָרַבִּים תִּתֵּן לָהֶם מוֹשִׁיעִים וְיוֹשִׁיעוּם
כח מִיַּד צָרֵיהֶם׃ וּכְנוֹחַ לָהֶם יָשׁוּבוּ לַעֲשׂוֹת רַע לְפָנֶיךָ וַתַּעַזְבֵם בְּיַד
אֹיְבֵיהֶם וַיִּרְדּוּ בָהֶם וַיָּשׁוּבוּ וַיִּזְעָקוּךָ וְאַתָּה מִשָּׁמַיִם תִּשְׁמַע וְתַצִּילֵם
כט כְּרַחֲמֶיךָ רַבּוֹת עִתִּים׃ וַתָּעַד בָּהֶם לַהֲשִׁיבָם אֶל־תּוֹרָתֶךָ וְהֵמָּה הֵזִידוּ
וְלֹא־שָׁמְעוּ לְמִצְוֺתֶיךָ וּבְמִשְׁפָּטֶיךָ חָטְאוּ־בָם אֲשֶׁר־יַעֲשֶׂה אָדָם וְחָיָה
ל בָהֶם וַיִּתְּנוּ כָתֵף סוֹרֶרֶת וְעָרְפָּם הִקְשׁוּ וְלֹא שָׁמֵעוּ׃ וַתִּמְשֹׁךְ עֲלֵיהֶם
שָׁנִים רַבּוֹת וַתָּעַד בָּם בְּרוּחֲךָ בְּיַד־נְבִיאֶיךָ וְלֹא הֶאֱזִינוּ וַתִּתְּנֵם בְּיַד
לא עַמֵּי הָאֲרָצֹת׃ וּבְרַחֲמֶיךָ הָרַבִּים לֹא־עֲשִׂיתָם כָּלָה וְלֹא עֲזַבְתָּם כִּי אֵל־
לב חַנּוּן וְרַחוּם אָתָּה׃ וְעַתָּה אֱלֹהֵינוּ הָאֵל הַגָּדוֹל הַגִּבּוֹר וְהַנּוֹרָא שׁוֹמֵר
הַבְּרִית וְהַחֶסֶד אַל־יִמְעַט לְפָנֶיךָ אֵת כָּל־הַתְּלָאָה אֲשֶׁר־מְצָאַתְנוּ
לִמְלָכֵינוּ לְשָׂרֵינוּ וּלְכֹהֲנֵינוּ וְלִנְבִיאֵנוּ וְלַאֲבֹתֵינוּ וּלְכָל־עַמֶּךָ מִימֵי
לג מַלְכֵי אַשּׁוּר עַד הַיּוֹם הַזֶּה׃ וְאַתָּה צַדִּיק עַל כָּל־הַבָּא עָלֵינוּ כִּי־אֱמֶת
לד עָשִׂיתָ וַאֲנַחְנוּ הִרְשָׁעְנוּ׃ וְאֶת־מְלָכֵינוּ שָׂרֵינוּ כֹּהֲנֵינוּ וַאֲבֹתֵינוּ לֹא עָשׂוּ
לה תּוֹרָתֶךָ וְלֹא הִקְשִׁיבוּ אֶל־מִצְוֺתֶיךָ וּלְעֵדְוֺתֶיךָ אֲשֶׁר הַעִידֹתָ בָּהֶם׃ וְהֵם
בְּמַלְכוּתָם וּבְטוּבְךָ הָרָב אֲשֶׁר־נָתַתָּ לָהֶם וּבְאֶרֶץ הָרְחָבָה וְהַשְּׁמֵנָה
לו אֲשֶׁר־נָתַתָּ לִפְנֵיהֶם לֹא עֲבָדוּךָ וְלֹא־שָׁבוּ מִמַּעַלְלֵיהֶם הָרָעִים׃ הִנֵּה
אֲנַחְנוּ הַיּוֹם עֲבָדִים וְהָאָרֶץ אֲשֶׁר־נָתַתָּה לַאֲבֹתֵינוּ לֶאֱכֹל אֶת־פִּרְיָהּ
לז וְאֶת־טוּבָהּ הִנֵּה אֲנַחְנוּ עֲבָדִים עָלֶיהָ׃ וּתְבוּאָתָהּ מַרְבָּה לַמְּלָכִים
אֲשֶׁר־נָתַתָּה עָלֵינוּ בְּחַטֹּאותֵינוּ וְעַל גְּוִיֹּתֵינוּ מֹשְׁלִים וּבִבְהֶמְתֵּנוּ
כִּרְצוֹנָם וּבְצָרָה גְדוֹלָה אֲנָחְנוּ׃
י א וּבְכָל־זֹאת אֲנַחְנוּ כֹּרְתִים אֲמָנָה וְכֹתְבִים וְעַל הֶחָתוּם שָׂרֵינוּ לְוִיֵּנוּ ט
ב כֹּהֲנֵינוּ׃ וְעַל הַחֲתוּמִים נְחֶמְיָה הַתִּרְשָׁתָא בֶּן־חֲכַלְיָה וְצִדְקִיָּה׃
ג,ד,ה שְׂרָיָה עֲזַרְיָה יִרְמְיָה׃ פַּשְׁחוּר אֲמַרְיָה מַלְכִּיָּה׃ חַטּוּשׁ שְׁבַנְיָה מַלּוּךְ׃
ו,ז,ח חָרִם מְרֵמוֹת עֹבַדְיָה׃ דָּנִיֵּאל גִּנְּתוֹן בָּרוּךְ׃ מְשֻׁלָּם אֲבִיָּה מִיָּמִן׃
ט,י מַעַזְיָה בִלְגַּי שְׁמַעְיָה אֵלֶּה הַכֹּהֲנִים׃ וְהַלְוִיִּם וְיֵשׁוּעַ בֶּן־אֲזַנְיָה בִּנּוּי
יא מִבְּנֵי חֵנָדָד קַדְמִיאֵל׃ וַאֲחֵיהֶם שְׁבַנְיָה הוֹדִיָּה קְלִיטָא פְּלָאיָה חָנָן׃

13, 14, 15 Zakur, Shereveya, Shevanya, Hodiya, Bani, and Beninu; the leaders of the
16, 17 people: Parosh, Paḥat Moav, Eilam, Zatu, Bani, Buni, Azgad, Bevai, Adoniya,
18, 19, 20 Bigvai, Adin, Ater, Ḥizkiya, Azur, Hodiya, Ḥashum, Betzai, Ḥarif, Anatot,
21, 22, 23 Neivai, Magpiash, Meshulam, Ḥezir, Mesheizavel, Tzadok, Yadua, Pelatya,
24, 25, 26, 27 Ḥanan, Anaya, Hoshe'a, Ḥananya, Ḥashuv, Haloḥesh, Pilḥa, Shovek, Reḥum,
28, 29 Ḥashavena, Maaseya, Aḥiya, Ḥanan, Anan, Malukh, Ḥarim, and Baana; and
the rest of the people and the priests, Levites, gatekeepers, singers, and
Netinim, and all those who had separated themselves from the peoples of
the lands to be with God's Torah, with their wives, their sons, and their
30 daughters – all those able to understand – all these supported their kinsmen,
their lords, binding themselves by an oath, under the penalty of a curse, to
follow in the way of God's teaching as given into the hand of God's servant
Moshe and to keep and observe all the commandments of the LORD our
31 Master and His laws and precepts. So we will neither give our daughters to
32 the peoples of the land nor take their daughters for our sons.[25] And those
peoples of the land who bring the merchandise and assorted foods to sell on
the Sabbath day – we will not buy from them on the Sabbath or on any holy
day. In the seventh year we will forgo[26] the crops as well as each person's debt.
33 We took certain charges upon ourselves, imposing upon ourselves a third of
34 a shekel yearly toward the service of the House of our God: for the column
bread,[27] for the regular daily grain offering and the regular daily burnt offering,
for the Sabbaths, for the New Months, for the appointed times, for the
designated sacred offerings, for the purification offerings to atone for Israel,
35 and for all the labor of our God's House. We cast lots for the wood
offering that the priests, the Levites, and the people would bring to the House
of our God at fixed times each and every year, to be burned on the altar of the
36 LORD our God, as is written in the Torah.[28] Also to bring to the House of the
LORD[29] the first fruits of our land and all the first fruits of all trees each and
37 every year; also the firstborn of our sons and of our animals – as written in
the Torah[30] – while the firstborn of our cattle and sheep will be brought to the
38 House of our God, to the priests serving in our God's House.[31] The initial
offering of our dough and our donations of the fruit of all trees, and the wine
and olive oil, we will bring to the priests, to the chambers of the House of our
God, and the tenth from our lands to the Levites, those Levites receiving the
39 tithes in all our farming towns. The priest, descendant of Aharon, will be with
the Levites when the Levites tithe, and the Levites will bring the tithed

---

25 | See Deuteronomy 7:3. Ezra addressed this sin immediately upon his arrival in Jerusalem; see Ezra, chapters 9–10.

26 | Although this verse explicitly mentions only the obligation to forgive debt in the seventh year (Deut. 15:2), the Hebrew verb *natash* (literally "abandon") further alludes to Exodus 23:11, which employs the same verb to demand that farmers leave their land fallow during the seventh year.

27 | See Leviticus 24:5–9.

28 | See Leviticus 6:5–6.

29 | See Exodus 23:19; Deuteronomy 26:1–11.

30 | See Exodus 13:13; Numbers 18:15.

31 | See, e.g., Deuteronomy 12:17.

יב,יג יד,טו מִיכָא רְחוֹב חֲשַׁבְיָה׃ זַכּוּר שֵׁרֵבְיָה שְׁבַנְיָה׃ הוֹדִיָּה בָנִי בְּנִינוּ׃ רָאשֵׁי
טז יז הָעָם פַּרְעֹשׁ פַּחַת מוֹאָב עֵילָם זַתּוּא בָּנִי׃ בֻּנִּי עַזְגָּד בֵּבָי׃ אֲדֹנִיָּה
יח,יט כ בִגְוַי עָדִין׃ אָטֵר חִזְקִיָּה עַזּוּר׃ הוֹדִיָּה חָשֻׁם בֵּצָי׃ חָרִיף עֲנָתוֹת נובי׃ נֵיבָי
כא,כב כג מַגְפִּיעָשׁ מְשֻׁלָּם חֵזִיר׃ מְשֵׁיזַבְאֵל צָדוֹק יַדּוּעַ׃ פְּלַטְיָה חָנָן עֲנָיָה׃
כד,כה כו הוֹשֵׁעַ חֲנַנְיָה חַשּׁוּב׃ הַלּוֹחֵשׁ פִּלְחָא שׁוֹבֵק׃ רְחוּם חֲשַׁבְנָה מַעֲשֵׂיָה׃
כט אֲחִיָּה חָנָן עָנָן׃ מַלּוּךְ חָרִם בַּעֲנָה׃ וּשְׁאָר הָעָם הַכֹּהֲנִים הַלְוִיִּם
הַשּׁוֹעֲרִים הַמְשֹׁרְרִים הַנְּתִינִים וְכָל־הַנִּבְדָּל מֵעַמֵּי הָאֲרָצוֹת אֶל־תּוֹרַת
ל הָאֱלֹהִים נְשֵׁיהֶם בְּנֵיהֶם וּבְנֹתֵיהֶם כֹּל יוֹדֵעַ מֵבִין׃ מַחֲזִקִים עַל־אֲחֵיהֶם
אַדִּירֵיהֶם וּבָאִים בְּאָלָה וּבִשְׁבוּעָה לָלֶכֶת בְּתוֹרַת הָאֱלֹהִים אֲשֶׁר
נִתְּנָה בְּיַד מֹשֶׁה עֶבֶד־הָאֱלֹהִים וְלִשְׁמוֹר וְלַעֲשׂוֹת אֶת־כָּל־מִצְוֺת
לא יְהוָה אֲדֹנֵינוּ וּמִשְׁפָּטָיו וְחֻקָּיו׃ וַאֲשֶׁר לֹא־נִתֵּן בְּנֹתֵינוּ לְעַמֵּי הָאָרֶץ
לב וְאֶת־בְּנֹתֵיהֶם לֹא נִקַּח לְבָנֵינוּ׃ וְעַמֵּי הָאָרֶץ הַמְבִיאִים אֶת־הַמַּקָּחוֹת
וְכָל־שֶׁבֶר בְּיוֹם הַשַּׁבָּת לִמְכּוֹר לֹא־נִקַּח מֵהֶם בַּשַּׁבָּת וּבְיוֹם קֹדֶשׁ
לג וְנִטֹּשׁ אֶת־הַשָּׁנָה הַשְּׁבִיעִית וּמַשָּׁא כָל־יָד׃ וְהֶעֱמַדְנוּ עָלֵינוּ מִצְוֺת
לד לָתֵת עָלֵינוּ שְׁלִשִׁית הַשֶּׁקֶל בַּשָּׁנָה לַעֲבֹדַת בֵּית אֱלֹהֵינוּ׃ לְלֶחֶם
הַמַּעֲרֶכֶת וּמִנְחַת הַתָּמִיד וּלְעוֹלַת הַתָּמִיד הַשַּׁבָּתוֹת הֶחֳדָשִׁים
לַמּוֹעֲדִים וְלַקֳּדָשִׁים וְלַחַטָּאוֹת לְכַפֵּר עַל־יִשְׂרָאֵל וְכֹל מְלֶאכֶת בֵּית־
לה אֱלֹהֵינוּ׃ וְהַגּוֹרָלוֹת הִפַּלְנוּ עַל־קֻרְבַּן הָעֵצִים הַכֹּהֲנִים
הַלְוִיִּם וְהָעָם לְהָבִיא לְבֵית אֱלֹהֵינוּ לְבֵית־אֲבֹתֵינוּ לְעִתִּים מְזֻמָּנִים
לו שָׁנָה בְשָׁנָה לְבַעֵר עַל־מִזְבַּח יְהוָה אֱלֹהֵינוּ כַּכָּתוּב בַּתּוֹרָה׃ וּלְהָבִיא
אֶת־בִּכּוּרֵי אַדְמָתֵנוּ וּבִכּוּרֵי כָּל־פְּרִי כָל־עֵץ שָׁנָה בְשָׁנָה לְבֵית יְהוָה׃
לז וְאֶת־בְּכֹרוֹת בָּנֵינוּ וּבְהֶמְתֵּנוּ כַּכָּתוּב בַּתּוֹרָה וְאֶת־בְּכוֹרֵי בְקָרֵינוּ
וְצֹאנֵינוּ לְהָבִיא לְבֵית אֱלֹהֵינוּ לַכֹּהֲנִים הַמְשָׁרְתִים בְּבֵית אֱלֹהֵינוּ׃
לח וְאֶת־רֵאשִׁית עֲרִיסֹתֵינוּ וּתְרוּמֹתֵינוּ וּפְרִי כָל־עֵץ תִּירוֹשׁ וְיִצְהָר נָבִיא
לַכֹּהֲנִים אֶל־לִשְׁכוֹת בֵּית־אֱלֹהֵינוּ וּמַעְשַׂר אַדְמָתֵנוּ לַלְוִיִּם וְהֵם הַלְוִיִּם
לט הַמְעַשְּׂרִים בְּכֹל עָרֵי עֲבֹדָתֵנוּ׃ וְהָיָה הַכֹּהֵן בֶּן־אַהֲרֹן עִם־הַלְוִיִּם

40 tenths up to the House of our God – to the chambers, to the treasury. For it
is to those chambers that the Israelites and the descendants of Levi will
bring the donations of the grain, wine, and olive oil, where the Temple
vessels are, as are the serving priests, gatekeepers, and singers – we will not
11 1 forsake the House of our God. The ranking officers of the people settled in
Jerusalem, and the rest of the people cast lots: one in ten was to come settle
in Jerusalem, the holy city, while the other nine-tenths remained in the
2 rural towns. And the people blessed all those who volunteered to settle in
3 Jerusalem. These are the leaders of the province who settled in
Jerusalem, while in the towns of Yehuda, everyone settled on their own
holdings, each in their own towns[32] – Israel, the priests, the Levites, the
4 Netinim, and the descendants of Shlomo's servants. In Jerusalem resided
some descendants of Yehuda and some descendants of Binyamin. Among the
descendants of Yehuda were Ataya son of Uziya son of Zekharya son of
5 Amarya son of Shefatya son of Mahalalel, of the line of Peretz, and Masseya
son of Barukh son of Kol Ḥozeh son of Ḥazaya son of Adaya son of Yoyariv
6 son of Zekharya of the family of Shela. Altogether, the descendants of Peretz
7 living in Jerusalem numbered 468 skilled fighters. These are
the descendants of Binyamin: Salu son of Meshulam son of Yoed son of
8 Pedaya son of Kolaya son of Maaseya son of Itiel son of Yeshaya followed by
9 Gabai and Salai – 928, with Yoel son of Zikhri as their superior officer and
10 Yehuda son of Hasenua as second-in-command over the city. Of the
11 priests: Yedaya son of Yoyariv, Yakhin, Seraya son of Ḥilkiya son of Meshulam
son of Tzadok son of Merayot son of Aḥituv in charge of the House of God,
12 and their kinsmen acting in the service of the House – 822, along with
Adaya son of Yeroḥam son of Pelalya son of Amtzi son of Zekharya son of
13 Pashḥur son of Malkiya and his brothers, leaders of clans – 242, along with
14 Amashsai son of Azarel son of Aḥzai son of Meshilemot son of Imer and their
kinsmen, powerful men – 128, and their superior officer was Zavdiel, of high
15 lineage. Of the Levites: Shemaya son of Ḥashuv son of Azrikam
16 son of Ḥashavya son of Buni. Shabetai and Yozavad of the Levite leaders
17 oversaw the external duties[33] of the House of God. Matanya son of Mikha
son of Zavdi son of Asaf was the first to open the prayers with thanks and
gratitude, seconded by Bakbukya from among his kinsmen and also by Avda
18 son of Shamua son of Galal son of Yedutun. All of the Levites in the holy city
19 numbered 284. And the gatekeepers – Akuv, Talmon, and their
20 kinsmen, who guard the gates – 172. Now the rest of Israel, the priests, and
the Levites were throughout the towns of Yehuda – each one in his inherited
21 property. The Netinim resided in the Ofel, and Tziḥa and Gishpa oversaw the
22 Netinim. Uzi son of Bani son of Ḥashavya son of Matanya son of
Mikha was the superior officer of the Levites in Jerusalem. He was one of the

32 | This list contains many parallels to 1 Chronicles, chapter 9.

33 | This service contrasts with the sacred rituals performed inside the Temple, perhaps including some combination of maintenance work, financial management, religious instruction, and bringing supplies to the Temple.

בַּעְשַׂר הַלְוִיִּם וְהַלְוִיִּם יַעֲלוּ אֶת־מַעֲשַׂר הַמַּעֲשֵׂר לְבֵית אֱלֹהֵינוּ אֶל־
מ הַלְּשָׁכוֹת לְבֵית הָאוֹצָר׃ כִּי אֶל־הַלְּשָׁכוֹת יָבִיאוּ בְנֵי־יִשְׂרָאֵל וּבְנֵי
הַלֵּוִי אֶת־תְּרוּמַת הַדָּגָן הַתִּירוֹשׁ וְהַיִּצְהָר וְשָׁם כְּלֵי הַמִּקְדָּשׁ וְהַכֹּהֲנִים
יא א הַמְשָׁרְתִים וְהַשּׁוֹעֲרִים וְהַמְשֹׁרְרִים וְלֹא נַעֲזֹב אֶת־בֵּית אֱלֹהֵינוּ׃ וַיֵּשְׁבוּ
שָׂרֵי־הָעָם בִּירוּשָׁלִָם וּשְׁאָר הָעָם הִפִּילוּ גוֹרָלוֹת לְהָבִיא ׀ אֶחָד מִן־
ב הָעֲשָׂרָה לָשֶׁבֶת בִּירוּשָׁלִַם עִיר הַקֹּדֶשׁ וְתֵשַׁע הַיָּדוֹת בֶּעָרִים׃ וַיְבָרְכוּ
ג הָעָם לְכֹל הָאֲנָשִׁים הַמִּתְנַדְּבִים לָשֶׁבֶת בִּירוּשָׁלִָם׃ וְאֵלֶּה
רָאשֵׁי הַמְּדִינָה אֲשֶׁר יָשְׁבוּ בִּירוּשָׁלִָם וּבְעָרֵי יְהוּדָה יָשְׁבוּ אִישׁ
בַּאֲחֻזָּתוֹ בְּעָרֵיהֶם יִשְׂרָאֵל הַכֹּהֲנִים וְהַלְוִיִּם וְהַנְּתִינִים וּבְנֵי עַבְדֵי
ד שְׁלֹמֹה׃ וּבִירוּשָׁלִַם יָשְׁבוּ מִבְּנֵי יְהוּדָה וּמִבְּנֵי בִנְיָמִן מִבְּנֵי יְהוּדָה עֲתָיָה
בֶּן־עֻזִּיָּה בֶּן־זְכַרְיָה בֶן־אֲמַרְיָה בֶּן־שְׁפַטְיָה בֶן־מַהֲלַלְאֵל מִבְּנֵי פָרֶץ׃
ה וּמַעֲשֵׂיָה בֶן־בָּרוּךְ בֶּן־כָּל־חֹזֶה בֶּן־חֲזָיָה בֶן־עֲדָיָה בֶן־יוֹיָרִיב בֶּן־זְכַרְיָה
ו בֶּן־הַשִּׁלֹנִי׃ כָּל־בְּנֵי־פֶרֶץ הַיֹּשְׁבִים בִּירוּשָׁלִָם אַרְבַּע מֵאוֹת שִׁשִּׁים
ז וּשְׁמֹנָה אַנְשֵׁי־חָיִל׃ וְאֵלֶּה בְּנֵי בִנְיָמִן סַלֻּא בֶּן־מְשֻׁלָּם בֶּן־
ח יוֹעֵד בֶּן־פְּדָיָה בֶּן־קוֹלָיָה בֶּן־מַעֲשֵׂיָה בֶּן־אִיתִיאֵל בֶּן־יְשַׁעְיָה׃ וְאַחֲרָיו
ט גַּבַּי סַלָּי תְּשַׁע מֵאוֹת עֶשְׂרִים וּשְׁמֹנָה׃ וְיוֹאֵל בֶּן־זִכְרִי פָּקִיד עֲלֵיהֶם
י וִיהוּדָה בֶן־הַסְּנוּאָה עַל־הָעִיר מִשְׁנֶה׃ מִן־הַכֹּהֲנִים
יא יְדַעְיָה בֶן־יוֹיָרִיב יָכִין׃ שְׂרָיָה בֶן־חִלְקִיָּה בֶּן־מְשֻׁלָּם בֶּן־צָדוֹק בֶּן־
יב מְרָיוֹת בֶּן־אֲחִיטוּב נְגִד בֵּית הָאֱלֹהִים׃ וַאֲחֵיהֶם עֹשֵׂה הַמְּלָאכָה
לַבַּיִת שְׁמֹנֶה מֵאוֹת עֶשְׂרִים וּשְׁנָיִם וַעֲדָיָה בֶּן־יְרֹחָם בֶּן־פְּלַלְיָה
יג בֶּן־אַמְצִי בֶּן־זְכַרְיָה בֶּן־פַּשְׁחוּר בֶּן־מַלְכִּיָּה׃ וְאֶחָיו רָאשִׁים לְאָבוֹת
מָאתַיִם אַרְבָּעִים וּשְׁנָיִם וַעֲמַשְׁסַי בֶּן־עֲזַרְאֵל בֶּן־אַחְזַי בֶּן־מְשִׁלֵּמוֹת
יד בֶּן־אִמֵּר׃ וַאֲחֵיהֶם גִּבֹּרֵי חַיִל מֵאָה עֶשְׂרִים וּשְׁמֹנָה וּפָקִיד עֲלֵיהֶם
טו זַבְדִּיאֵל בֶּן־הַגְּדוֹלִים׃ וּמִן־הַלְוִיִּם שְׁמַעְיָה בֶן־חַשּׁוּב בֶּן־
טז עַזְרִיקָם בֶּן־חֲשַׁבְיָה בֶּן־בּוּנִּי׃ וְשַׁבְּתַי וְיוֹזָבָד עַל־הַמְּלָאכָה הַחִיצֹנָה
יז לְבֵית הָאֱלֹהִים מֵרָאשֵׁי הַלְוִיִּם׃ וּמַתַּנְיָה בֶן־מִיכָא בֶן־זַבְדִּי בֶן־אָסָף
רֹאשׁ הַתְּחִלָּה יְהוֹדֶה לַתְּפִלָּה וּבַקְבֻּקְיָה מִשְׁנֶה מֵאֶחָיו וְעַבְדָּא בֶּן־
יח שַׁמּוּעַ בֶּן־גָּלָל בֶּן־ידיתון׃ כָּל־הַלְוִיִּם בְּעִיר הַקֹּדֶשׁ מָאתַיִם שְׁמֹנִים יְדוּתוּן
יט וְאַרְבָּעָה׃ וְהַשּׁוֹעֲרִים עַקּוּב טַלְמוֹן וַאֲחֵיהֶם הַשֹּׁמְרִים
כ בַּשְּׁעָרִים מֵאָה שִׁבְעִים וּשְׁנָיִם׃ וּשְׁאָר יִשְׂרָאֵל הַכֹּהֲנִים הַלְוִיִּם בְּכָל־
כא עָרֵי יְהוּדָה אִישׁ בְּנַחֲלָתוֹ׃ וְהַנְּתִינִים יֹשְׁבִים בָּעֹפֶל וְצִיחָא וְגִשְׁפָּא
כב עַל־הַנְּתִינִים׃ וּפְקִיד הַלְוִיִּם בִּירוּשָׁלִַם עֻזִּי בֶן־בָּנִי בֶּן־

descendants of Asaf, those singers who accompanied the service of the House
23 of God in accordance with the king's command[34] and the singers' faithful
24 commitment.[35] Petaḥya son of Mesheizavel, of the descendants of
Zeraḥ son of Yehuda, was at the king's hand for all matters concerning the
25 people. As for the unwalled villages with their outlying fields, the descendants
of Yehuda resided in Kiryat Arba and its satellites, in Divon and its satellites,
26 27 in Yekavtze'el and its villages, in Yeshua, in Molada, in Beit Pelet, in Ḥatzar
28 Shual, in Be'er Sheva and its satellites, in Tziklag and Mekhona and its
29 30 satellites, in Ein Rimon, in Tzora, and in Yarmut, Zanoaḥ, and Adulam and
their villages, Lakhish and its fields, and Azeka and its satellites. Thus they
31 settled from Be'er Sheva to the Valley of Ben Hinom. And the descendants of
Binyamin – from Gava, Mikhmas, and Aya, and Beit El and its satellites,
32, 33 34 Anatot, Nov, Ananeya, Ḥatzor, Rama, Gitayim, Ḥadid, Tzevoyim, Nevalat,
35 36 Lod and Ono and the Valley of the Smiths. The Levite divisions were found
12 1 throughout Yehuda and Binyamin. These are the priests and the
Levites who came up with Zerubavel son of She'altiel and Yeshua: Seraya,
2, 3 4, 5 Yirmeya, Ezra, Amarya, Malukh, Ḥatush, Shekhanya, Reḥum, Meremot, Ido,
6 7 Ginetoi, Aviya, Miyamin, Maadya, Bilga, Shemaya and Yoyariv, Yedaya, Salu,
Amok, Ḥilkiya, Yedaya – these were the leaders of the priests and their
8 kinsmen in the days of Yeshua. The Levites: Yeshua, Binui, Kadmiel,
Shereveya, Yehuda, and Matanya along with his kinsmen – in charge of the
9 songs of thanksgiving – with Bakbukya and Uni their kinsmen in shifts
10 alongside them. Now Yeshua[36] fathered Yoyakim, Yoyakim fathered Elyashiv,
11 and Elyashiv – Yoyada. Yoyada fathered Yonatan, and Yonatan fathered
12 Yadua. In the days of Yoyakim, these priests were clan chiefs: for Seraya,
13 Meraya; for Yirmeya, Ḥananya; for Ezra, Meshulam; for Amarya, Yehoḥanan;
14 15 for Melikhu, Yonatan; for Shevanya, Yosef; for Ḥarim, Adna; for Merayot,
16 17 Ḥelki; for Ido, Zekharya; for Gineton, Meshulam; for Aviya, Zikhri; for
18 Minyamin and Moadya, Piltai; for Bilga, Shamua; for Shemaya, Yehonatan;
19, 20 21 for Yoyariv, Matnai; for Yedaya, Uzi; for Salai, Kalai; for Amok, Ever; for
22 Ḥilkiya, Ḥashavya; and for Yedaya, Netanel. In the days of Elyashiv, Yoyada
and Yoḥanan, and Yadua, the Levites were recorded according to their clan
23 chiefs, as were the priests of the reign of Daryavesh the Persian. For
Levi's line, the patriarchal clans are written in the book of Chronicles[37] up to
24 the days of Yoḥanan son of Elyashiv. The leaders of the Levites: Ḥashavya,
Shereveya, and Yeshua son of Kadmiel alongside their kinsmen to praise
and give thanks as commanded by David, the man of God – one shift
25 opposite another. Matanya and Bakbukya, Ovadya, Meshulam, Talmon, and

---

34 | This refers either to a command of the current Persian king or to rules originally established by King David for the First Temple.

35 | Perhaps a financial stipend that the king ordered be allotted to them or, more broadly, a "contract" regarding their responsibilities.

36 | This Yeshua is the first High Priest of the Second Temple (Ezra 3:2), not Yeshua the Levite mentioned two verses earlier.

37 | Based on the juxtaposition to the previous verse, this book was probably a chronicle from the days of King Daryavesh.

חֲשַׁבְיָה בֶּן־מַתַּנְיָה בֶּן־מִיכָא מִבְּנֵי אָסָף הַמְשֹׁרְרִים לְנֶגֶד מְלֶאכֶת
כג בֵּית־הָאֱלֹהִים׃ כִּי־מִצְוַת הַמֶּלֶךְ עֲלֵיהֶם וַאֲמָנָה עַל־הַמְשֹׁרְרִים דְּבַר־
כד יוֹם בְּיוֹמוֹ׃ וּפְתַחְיָה בֶּן־מְשֵׁיזַבְאֵל מִבְּנֵי־זֶרַח בֶּן־יְהוּדָה
כה לְיַד הַמֶּלֶךְ לְכָל־דָּבָר לָעָם׃ וְאֶל־הַחֲצֵרִים בִּשְׂדֹתָם מִבְּנֵי יְהוּדָה
יָשְׁבוּ בְּקִרְיַת הָאַרְבַּע וּבְנֹתֶיהָ וּבְדִיבֹן וּבְנֹתֶיהָ וּבִיקַּבְצְאֵל וַחֲצֵרֶיהָ׃
כו כז וּבְיֵשׁוּעַ וּבְמֹלָדָה וּבְבֵית־פָּלֶט׃ וּבַחֲצַר שׁוּעָל וּבִבְאֵר שֶׁבַע וּבְנֹתֶיהָ׃
כח, כט ל וּבְצִקְלַג וּבִמְכֹנָה וּבִבְנֹתֶיהָ׃ וּבְעֵין רִמּוֹן וּבְצָרְעָה וּבְיַרְמוּת׃ זָנֹחַ עֲדֻלָּם
וְחַצְרֵיהֶם לָכִישׁ וּשְׂדֹתֶיהָ עֲזֵקָה וּבְנֹתֶיהָ וַיַּחֲנוּ מִבְּאֵר־שֶׁבַע עַד־גֵּיא
לא לב הִנֹּם׃ וּבְנֵי בִנְיָמִן מִגָּבַע מִכְמָשׂ וְעַיָּה וּבֵית־אֵל וּבְנֹתֶיהָ׃ עֲנָתוֹת נֹב
לג, לד לה עֲנָנְיָה׃ חָצוֹר ׀ רָמָה גִּתָּיִם׃ חָדִיד צְבֹעִים נְבַלָּט׃ לֹד וְאוֹנוֹ גֵּי הַחֲרָשִׁים׃
לו יב א וּמִן־הַלְוִיִּם מַחְלְקוֹת יְהוּדָה לְבִנְיָמִין׃ וְאֵלֶּה הַכֹּהֲנִים
וְהַלְוִיִּם אֲשֶׁר עָלוּ עִם־זְרֻבָּבֶל בֶּן־שְׁאַלְתִּיאֵל וְיֵשׁוּעַ שְׂרָיָה יִרְמְיָה
ב, ג ד עֶזְרָא׃ אֲמַרְיָה מַלּוּךְ חַטּוּשׁ׃ שְׁכַנְיָה רְחֻם מְרֵמֹת׃ עִדּוֹא גִנְּתוֹי
ה, ו ז אֲבִיָּה׃ מִיָּמִין מַעַדְיָה בִּלְגָּה׃ שְׁמַעְיָה וְיוֹיָרִיב יְדַעְיָה׃ סַלּוּ עָמוֹק
ח חִלְקִיָּה יְדַעְיָה אֵלֶּה רָאשֵׁי הַכֹּהֲנִים וַאֲחֵיהֶם בִּימֵי יֵשׁוּעַ׃ וְהַלְוִיִּם
יֵשׁוּעַ בִּנּוּי קַדְמִיאֵל שֵׁרֵבְיָה יְהוּדָה מַתַּנְיָה עַל־הֻיְּדוֹת הוּא וְאֶחָיו׃
ט, י וּבַקְבֻּקְיָה וְעֻנּו אֲחֵיהֶם לְנֶגְדָּם לְמִשְׁמָרוֹת׃ וְיֵשׁוּעַ הוֹלִיד אֶת־יוֹיָקִים וְעֻנִּי
יא וְיוֹיָקִים הוֹלִיד אֶת־אֶלְיָשִׁיב וְאֶלְיָשִׁיב אֶת־יוֹיָדָע׃ וְיוֹיָדָע הוֹלִיד אֶת־
יב יוֹנָתָן וְיוֹנָתָן הוֹלִיד אֶת־יַדּוּעַ׃ וּבִימֵי יוֹיָקִים הָיוּ כֹהֲנִים רָאשֵׁי הָאָבוֹת
יג לִשְׂרָיָה מְרָיָה לְיִרְמְיָה חֲנַנְיָה׃ לְעֶזְרָא מְשֻׁלָּם לַאֲמַרְיָה יְהוֹחָנָן׃
יד, טו טז למלוכי יוֹנָתָן לִשְׁבַנְיָה יוֹסֵף׃ לְחָרִם עַדְנָא לִמְרָיוֹת חֶלְקָי׃ לעדיא לִמְלִיכוּ לְעִדּוֹא
יז יח זְכַרְיָה לְגִנְּתוֹן מְשֻׁלָּם׃ לַאֲבִיָּה זִכְרִי לְמִנְיָמִין לְמוֹעַדְיָה פִּלְטָי׃ לְבִלְגָּה
יט כ שַׁמּוּעַ לִשְׁמַעְיָה יְהוֹנָתָן׃ וּלְיוֹיָרִיב מַתְּנַי לִידַעְיָה עֻזִּי׃ לְסַלַּי קַלָּי
כא כב לְעָמוֹק עֵבֶר׃ לְחִלְקִיָּה חֲשַׁבְיָה לִידַעְיָה נְתַנְאֵל׃ הַלְוִיִּם בִּימֵי אֶלְיָשִׁיב
יוֹיָדָע וְיוֹחָנָן וְיַדּוּעַ כְּתוּבִים רָאשֵׁי אָבוֹת וְהַכֹּהֲנִים עַל־מַלְכוּת דָּרְיָוֶשׁ
כג הַפָּרְסִי׃ בְּנֵי לֵוִי רָאשֵׁי הָאָבוֹת כְּתוּבִים עַל־סֵפֶר דִּבְרֵי
כד הַיָּמִים וְעַד־יְמֵי יוֹחָנָן בֶּן־אֶלְיָשִׁיב׃ וְרָאשֵׁי הַלְוִיִּם חֲשַׁבְיָה שֵׁרֵבְיָה
וְיֵשׁוּעַ בֶּן־קַדְמִיאֵל וַאֲחֵיהֶם לְנֶגְדָּם לְהַלֵּל לְהוֹדוֹת בְּמִצְוַת דָּוִיד
כה אִישׁ־הָאֱלֹהִים מִשְׁמָר לְעֻמַּת מִשְׁמָר׃ מַתַּנְיָה וּבַקְבֻּקְיָה עֹבַדְיָה

26 Akuv – guards and gatekeepers in shifts, stationed at the gate posterns. These
were in the days of Yoyakim son of Yeshua son of Yotzadak and in the days
27 of Neḥemya the governor and Ezra the priest and scholar. At the
dedication of Jerusalem's wall, they sought out the Levites in all of their
dwelling places to bring them to Jerusalem in order to celebrate the dedication
28 joyously with thanksgiving and music, with cymbals, harps, and lyres. The
clans of the singers assembled from the plain around Jerusalem and from the
29 villages of Netofa and from Beit HaGilgal and from the fields of Geva and
30 Azmavet – for the singers had built themselves villages around Jerusalem. The
priests and the Levites purified themselves, then purified the people and the
31 gates and the wall. I then brought the leaders of the Jews to the top of the wall,
having arranged two sizable choirs of thanksgiving and a procession to the
32 right atop the wall toward the Dung Gate. Hoshaya followed them with half
33 34 the ranking officers of Yehuda, and Azarya, Ezra, and Meshulam, Yehuda and
Binyamin, and Shemaya and Yirmeya.
35 Some of the descendants of the priests were accompanying on the trumpets;
Zekharya son of Yonatan son of Shemaya son of Matanya son of Mikhaya
36 son of Zakur son of Asaf and his kinsmen – Shemaya and Azarel, Milalai,
Gilalai, Maai, Netanel, Yehuda, Ḥanani – were accompanying on the musical
instruments assigned by David, the man of God. Ezra the scribe preceded
37 them. At the Spring Gate and opposite them, some climbed the steps of the
City of David, ascending the wall above David's palace up to the Water Gate
38 to the east. Meanwhile, the second thanksgiving choir walked in the opposite
direction, and I followed, with half the people, on top of the wall, over the
39 Tower of the Furnaces up to the Wide Wall and over the Efrayim Gate and the
Old Gate and the Fish Gate and the Tower of Ḥananel and the Tower of the
40 Hundred up to the Sheep Gate, then stood at the Gate of the Guard. So the
two processions came to a standstill in the House of God – as did I and with
41 me half of the officials. The priests – Elyakim, Maaseya, Minyamin, Mikhaya,
42 Elyo'einai, Zekharya, Ḥananya – accompanied on the trumpets. Maaseya
and Shemaya and Elazar and Uzi and Yehoḥanan and Malkiya and Eilam
43 and Azer – the singers made music with Yizraḥya as their officer. On that day,
they offered many communal sacrifices and rejoiced, for God had filled them
with elation, and the women and children also rejoiced, and the jubilation of
44 Jerusalem was heard from afar. On that day, men were appointed to supervise
the chambers, to collect within them the stores of the contributions, the firsts
and the tithes from the village fields – those portions allotted by the Torah to
the priests and Levites – for Yehuda rejoiced in the priests and Levites who
45 stood and served and who carried out the ritual duties of their God, the ritual
duties of purity and those of the singers and the gatekeepers, as charged by
46 David and his son Shlomo. For in the days of old, of David and Asaf, there
were already leaders of the singers and songs of praise and thanksgiving to
47 God. And during the days of Zerubavel and of Neḥemya, all Israel provided
the daily portions allotted for the singers and gatekeepers and dedicated

כו מְשֻׁלָּם טַלְמֹן עַקּוּב שֹׁמְרִים שׁוֹעֲרִים מִשְׁמָר בַּאֲסֻפֵּי הַשְּׁעָרִים׃ אֵלֶּה
בִּימֵי יוֹיָקִים בֶּן־יֵשׁוּעַ בֶּן־יוֹצָדָק וּבִימֵי נְחֶמְיָה הַפֶּחָה וְעֶזְרָא הַכֹּהֵן
כז הַסּוֹפֵר׃ וּבַחֲנֻכַּת חוֹמַת יְרוּשָׁלַ͏ִם בִּקְשׁוּ אֶת־הַלְוִיִּם
מִכָּל־מְקוֹמֹתָם לַהֲבִיאָם לִירוּשָׁלָ͏ִם לַעֲשֹׂת חֲנֻכָּה וְשִׂמְחָה וּבְתוֹדוֹת
כח וּבְשִׁיר מְצִלְתַּיִם נְבָלִים וּבְכִנֹּרוֹת׃ וַיֵּאָסְפוּ בְּנֵי הַמְשֹׁרְרִים וּמִן־הַכִּכָּר
כט סְבִיבוֹת יְרוּשָׁלַ͏ִם וּמִן־חַצְרֵי נְטֹפָתִי׃ וּמִבֵּית הַגִּלְגָּל וּמִשְּׂדוֹת גֶּבַע
ל וְעַזְמָוֶת כִּי חֲצֵרִים בָּנוּ לָהֶם הַמְשֹׁרְרִים סְבִיבוֹת יְרוּשָׁלָ͏ִם׃ וַיִּטַּהֲרוּ
הַכֹּהֲנִים וְהַלְוִיִּם וַיְטַהֲרוּ אֶת־הָעָם וְאֶת־הַשְּׁעָרִים וְאֶת־הַחוֹמָה׃
לא וָאַעֲלֶה אֶת־שָׂרֵי יְהוּדָה מֵעַל לַחוֹמָה וָאַעֲמִידָה שְׁתֵּי תוֹדֹת גְּדוֹלֹת
לב וְתַהֲלֻכֹת לַיָּמִין מֵעַל לַחוֹמָה לְשַׁעַר הָאַשְׁפֹּת׃ וַיֵּלֶךְ אַחֲרֵיהֶם הוֹשַׁעְיָה
לג לד וַחֲצִי שָׂרֵי יְהוּדָה׃ וַעֲזַרְיָה עֶזְרָא וּמְשֻׁלָּם׃ יְהוּדָה וּבִנְיָמִן וּשְׁמַעְיָה
וְיִרְמְיָה׃
לה וּמִבְּנֵי הַכֹּהֲנִים בַּחֲצֹצְרוֹת זְכַרְיָה בֶן־יוֹנָתָן בֶּן־שְׁמַעְיָה בֶּן־מַתַּנְיָה
לו בֶּן־מִיכָיָה בֶּן־זַכּוּר בֶּן־אָסָף׃ וְאֶחָיו שְׁמַעְיָה וַעֲזַרְאֵל מִלֲלַי גִּלֲלַי
מָעַי נְתַנְאֵל וִיהוּדָה חֲנָנִי בִּכְלֵי־שִׁיר דָּוִיד אִישׁ הָאֱלֹהִים וְעֶזְרָא
לז הַסּוֹפֵר לִפְנֵיהֶם׃ וְעַל שַׁעַר הָעַיִן וְנֶגְדָּם עָלוּ עַל־מַעֲלוֹת עִיר דָּוִיד
לח בַּמַּעֲלֶה לַחוֹמָה מֵעַל לְבֵית דָּוִיד וְעַד שַׁעַר הַמַּיִם מִזְרָח׃ וְהַתּוֹדָה
הַשֵּׁנִית הַהוֹלֶכֶת לְמוֹאל וַאֲנִי אַחֲרֶיהָ וַחֲצִי הָעָם מֵעַל לְהַחוֹמָה מֵעַל
לט לְמִגְדַּל הַתַּנּוּרִים וְעַד הַחוֹמָה הָרְחָבָה׃ וּמֵעַל לְשַׁעַר־אֶפְרַיִם וְעַל־
שַׁעַר הַיְשָׁנָה וְעַל־שַׁעַר הַדָּגִים וּמִגְדַּל חֲנַנְאֵל וּמִגְדַּל הַמֵּאָה וְעַד
מ שַׁעַר הַצֹּאן וְעָמְדוּ בְּשַׁעַר הַמַּטָּרָה׃ וַתַּעֲמֹדְנָה שְׁתֵּי הַתּוֹדֹת בְּבֵית
מא הָאֱלֹהִים וַאֲנִי וַחֲצִי הַסְּגָנִים עִמִּי׃ וְהַכֹּהֲנִים אֶלְיָקִים מַעֲשֵׂיָה מִנְיָמִין
מב מִיכָיָה אֶלְיוֹעֵינַי זְכַרְיָה חֲנַנְיָה בַּחֲצֹצְרוֹת׃ וּמַעֲשֵׂיָה וּשְׁמַעְיָה וְאֶלְעָזָר
וְעֻזִּי וִיהוֹחָנָן וּמַלְכִּיָּה וְעֵילָם וָעָזֶר וַיַּשְׁמִיעוּ הַמְשֹׁרְרִים וְיִזְרַחְיָה
מג הַפָּקִיד׃ וַיִּזְבְּחוּ בַיּוֹם הַהוּא זְבָחִים גְּדוֹלִים וַיִּשְׂמָחוּ כִּי הָאֱלֹהִים
שִׂמְּחָם שִׂמְחָה גְדוֹלָה וְגַם הַנָּשִׁים וְהַיְלָדִים שָׂמֵחוּ וַתִּשָּׁמַע שִׂמְחַת
מד יְרוּשָׁלַ͏ִם מֵרָחוֹק׃ וַיִּפָּקְדוּ בַיּוֹם הַהוּא אֲנָשִׁים עַל־הַנְּשָׁכוֹת לָאוֹצָרוֹת
לַתְּרוּמוֹת לָרֵאשִׁית וְלַמַּעַשְׂרוֹת לִכְנוֹס בָּהֶם לִשְׂדֵי הֶעָרִים מְנָאוֹת
הַתּוֹרָה לַכֹּהֲנִים וְלַלְוִיִּם כִּי שִׂמְחַת יְהוּדָה עַל־הַכֹּהֲנִים וְעַל־הַלְוִיִּם
מה הָעֹמְדִים׃ וַיִּשְׁמְרוּ מִשְׁמֶרֶת אֱלֹהֵיהֶם וּמִשְׁמֶרֶת הַטָּהֳרָה וְהַמְשֹׁרְרִים
מו וְהַשֹּׁעֲרִים כְּמִצְוַת דָּוִיד שְׁלֹמֹה בְנוֹ׃ כִּי־בִימֵי דָוִיד וְאָסָף מִקֶּדֶם רָאשֵׁ
מז הַמְשֹׁרְרִים וְשִׁיר־תְּהִלָּה וְהֹדוֹת לֵאלֹהִים׃ וְכָל־יִשְׂרָאֵל בִּימֵי זְרֻבָּבֶל

portions for the Levites, while the Levites in turn dedicated portions for the
13 1 descendants of Aharon. On that day the book of Moshe was read
aloud to the listening people, and in it was found written that no Amonite
2 or Moabite shall be admitted to the congregation of God,[38] because they
would not greet the Israelites with food and water and hired Bilam to curse
3 them – but our God turned his curse into a blessing. And when they heard
4 the Torah, they separated all those of mixed lineage from Israel. Previously,
Elyashiv the priest had occupied a chamber of our God's House, and he was
5 connected to Toviya,[39] to whom he had assigned a substantial chamber, one
in which they had previously stored the grain offerings, the incense, and
the vessels as well as the tithes of grain, new wine, and olive oil, assigned by
decree to the Levites, the singers, and the gatekeepers, as well as the dedicated
6 donations for the priests. Throughout this period I was not in Jerusalem, for
in the thirty-second year of Artaḥshasta, king of Babylon, I came to the king;
7 after some time I requested leave from the king, then came to Jerusalem
and recognized the evil that Elyashiv had committed on behalf of Toviya,
8 assigning him a chamber in the courtyards of God's House. I was appalled
9 and cast out all the vessels of the house of Toviya from the chamber. I gave
orders, and they purified the chambers to which I then returned the vessels
10 of God's House and the grain offerings and the incense. I also discovered
that the portions allotted to the Levites had not been provided and that the
Levites and singers who performed the ritual duties had fled, each to his
11 field. I then upbraided the officials, demanding, "Why has God's House been
12 forsaken?!" I then reassembled them and restationed them at their posts. And
all Yehuda brought the tithes of grain, wine, and olive oil to the storerooms.
13 I then appointed treasurers over these stores: Shelemya the priest, Tzadok
the scribe, and Pedaya of the Levites, along with Ḥanan son of Zakur son of
Matanya, for they were considered trustworthy, and they were the ones who
14 were to distribute the shares to their kinsmen. My God, remember
me for this and do not erase my loyal actions which I have performed for the
15 House of my God and its shifts of service. In those very days in Yehuda I saw
treading in winepresses on the Sabbath and those bringing heaps of produce
and loading the donkeys with wine, grapes, figs, and all kinds of burdens, then
bringing them to Jerusalem on the Sabbath day – and I admonished them on
16 that day when they were selling the food.[40] And the Tyreans dwelling there
would bring fish and all manner of merchandise and sell it on the Sabbath to
17 the Jews, and in Jerusalem itself. I upbraided the nobles of Yehuda, demanding
of them, "What is this evil thing you are doing, desecrating the Sabbath
18 day? Your ancestors acted just like this, so that our God brought all this evil
upon us and upon this city,[41] and now you are stoking anger against Israel by

38 | This prohibition and its rationale appear in Deuteronomy 23:4–7; see also Ezra 9:1–2, 12.

39 | Perhaps by familial ties (cf. 6:17–18 above) or a friendship or alliance. Regardless, Toviya's Amonite lineage (see 2:10) was problematic.

40 | See 10:32 above.

41 | This behavior is described in Jeremiah 17:19–27.

וּבִימֵי נְחֶמְיָה נֹתְנִים מְנָיוֹת הַמְשֹׁרְרִים וְהַשֹּׁעֲרִים דְּבַר־יוֹם בְּיוֹמוֹ
יג א וּמַקְדִּשִׁים לַלְוִיִּם וְהַלְוִיִּם מַקְדִּשִׁים לִבְנֵי אַהֲרֹן׃ בַּיּוֹם הַהוּא
נִקְרָא בְּסֵפֶר מֹשֶׁה בְּאָזְנֵי הָעָם וְנִמְצָא כָּתוּב בּוֹ אֲשֶׁר לֹא־יָבוֹא עַמֹּנִי
ב וּמֹאָבִי בִּקְהַל הָאֱלֹהִים עַד־עוֹלָם׃ כִּי לֹא קִדְּמוּ אֶת־בְּנֵי יִשְׂרָאֵל
בַּלֶּחֶם וּבַמָּיִם וַיִּשְׂכֹּר עָלָיו אֶת־בִּלְעָם לְקַלְלוֹ וַיַּהֲפֹךְ אֱלֹהֵינוּ הַקְּלָלָה
ג ד לִבְרָכָה׃ וַיְהִי כְּשָׁמְעָם אֶת־הַתּוֹרָה וַיַּבְדִּילוּ כָל־עֵרֶב מִיִּשְׂרָאֵל׃ וְלִפְנֵי
ה מִזֶּה אֶלְיָשִׁיב הַכֹּהֵן נָתוּן בְּלִשְׁכַּת בֵּית־אֱלֹהֵינוּ קָרוֹב לְטוֹבִיָּה׃ וַיַּעַשׂ
לוֹ לִשְׁכָּה גְדוֹלָה וְשָׁם הָיוּ לְפָנִים נֹתְנִים אֶת־הַמִּנְחָה הַלְּבוֹנָה וְהַכֵּלִים
וּמַעְשַׂר הַדָּגָן הַתִּירוֹשׁ וְהַיִּצְהָר מִצְוַת הַלְוִיִּם וְהַמְשֹׁרְרִים וְהַשֹּׁעֲרִים
ו וּתְרוּמַת הַכֹּהֲנִים׃ וּבְכָל־זֶה לֹא הָיִיתִי בִּירוּשָׁלָ͏ִם כִּי בִּשְׁנַת שְׁלֹשִׁים
וּשְׁתַּיִם לְאַרְתַּחְשַׁסְתְּא מֶלֶךְ־בָּבֶל בָּאתִי אֶל־הַמֶּלֶךְ וּלְקֵץ יָמִים
ז נִשְׁאַלְתִּי מִן־הַמֶּלֶךְ׃ וָאָבוֹא לִירוּשָׁלָ͏ִם וָאָבִינָה בָרָעָה אֲשֶׁר עָשָׂה
ח אֶלְיָשִׁיב לְטוֹבִיָּה לַעֲשׂוֹת לוֹ נִשְׁכָּה בְּחַצְרֵי בֵּית הָאֱלֹהִים׃ וַיֵּרַע
לִי מְאֹד וָאַשְׁלִיכָה אֶת־כָּל־כְּלֵי בֵית־טוֹבִיָּה הַחוּץ מִן־הַלִּשְׁכָּה׃
ט וָאֹמְרָה וַיְטַהֲרוּ הַלְּשָׁכוֹת וָאָשִׁיבָה שָּׁם כְּלֵי בֵּית הָאֱלֹהִים אֶת־
י הַמִּנְחָה וְהַלְּבוֹנָה׃ וָאֵדְעָה כִּי־מְנָיוֹת הַלְוִיִּם לֹא נִתָּנָה וַיִּבְרְחוּ אִישׁ־
יא לְשָׂדֵהוּ הַלְוִיִּם וְהַמְשֹׁרְרִים עֹשֵׂי הַמְּלָאכָה׃ וָאָרִיבָה אֶת־הַסְּגָנִים
וָאֹמְרָה מַדּוּעַ נֶעֱזַב בֵּית־הָאֱלֹהִים וָאֶקְבְּצֵם וָאַעֲמִדֵם עַל־עָמְדָם׃
יב יג וְכָל־יְהוּדָה הֵבִיאוּ מַעְשַׂר הַדָּגָן וְהַתִּירוֹשׁ וְהַיִּצְהָר לָאוֹצָרוֹת׃ וָאוֹצְרָה
עַל־אוֹצָרוֹת שֶׁלֶמְיָה הַכֹּהֵן וְצָדוֹק הַסּוֹפֵר וּפְדָיָה מִן־הַלְוִיִּם וְעַל־
יָדָם חָנָן בֶּן־זַכּוּר בֶּן־מַתַּנְיָה כִּי נֶאֱמָנִים נֶחְשָׁבוּ וַעֲלֵיהֶם לַחֲלֹק
יד לַאֲחֵיהֶם׃ זָכְרָה־לִּי אֱלֹהַי עַל־זֹאת וְאַל־תֶּמַח חֲסָדַי
טו אֲשֶׁר עָשִׂיתִי בְּבֵית אֱלֹהַי וּבְמִשְׁמָרָיו׃ בַּיָּמִים הָהֵמָּה רָאִיתִי בִיהוּדָה ׀
דֹּרְכִים־גִּתּוֹת ׀ בַּשַּׁבָּת וּמְבִיאִים הָעֲרֵמוֹת וְעֹמְסִים עַל־הַחֲמֹרִים וְאַף־
יַיִן עֲנָבִים וּתְאֵנִים וְכָל־מַשָּׂא וּמְבִיאִים יְרוּשָׁלַ͏ִם בְּיוֹם הַשַּׁבָּת וָאָעִיד
טז בְּיוֹם מִכְרָם צָיִד׃ וְהַצֹּרִים יָשְׁבוּ בָהּ מְבִיאִים דָּאג וְכָל־מֶכֶר וּמֹכְרִים
יז בַּשַּׁבָּת לִבְנֵי יְהוּדָה וּבִירוּשָׁלָ͏ִם׃ וָאָרִיבָה אֵת חֹרֵי יְהוּדָה וָאֹמְרָה לָהֶם
מָה־הַדָּבָר הָרָע הַזֶּה אֲשֶׁר אַתֶּם עֹשִׂים וּמְחַלְּלִים אֶת־יוֹם הַשַּׁבָּת׃
יח הֲלוֹא כֹה עָשׂוּ אֲבֹתֵיכֶם וַיָּבֵא אֱלֹהֵינוּ עָלֵינוּ אֵת כָּל־הָרָעָה הַזֹּאת

19 desecrating the Sabbath." Then, when the shadows darkened the
gates of Jerusalem before the Sabbath, I ordered the doors shut, declaring that
they should not be opened until after the Sabbath. And I stationed some of my
20 men at the gates so that no loads could be brought in on the Sabbath. Once
or twice the traders and vendors of various goods camped overnight outside
21 Jerusalem. I warned them, saying: "Why are you camping outside the wall?
If you ever do this again, I will use violence against you!" From then on they
22 stopped coming on the Sabbath. Then I ordered the Levites to come, once
they had purified themselves, to guard the gates so as to sanctify the Sabbath
day. My God, remember this too on my behalf, and be merciful to me in Your
23 abundant kindness. In those days I also saw those Jews who had
24 brought home Ashdodite, Amonite, and Moabite wives. As for their children,
some spoke Ashdodite and could not even speak Hebrew, and so it was for
25 each people in their native tongue. I upbraided them, cursed them, struck
some of the men and ripped out their hair, and made them swear an oath to
God – that you shall never give your daughters to their sons or marry their
26 daughters to your sons or to yourselves. Was it not with these that Shlomo,
king of Israel, sinned? Among all the many nations there was no king like him,
he was beloved by his God, and God made him king over all of Israel – yet
27 even he was led astray by the foreign women.[42] Shall we then listen to you
to commit all this great evil, breaking faith with our God by bringing home
28 foreign wives?! Even one of the sons of Yoyada son of Elyashiv the High Priest
29 was a son-in-law to Sanvalat the Horonite – and I made him flee from me. My
God, remember this against them – the defilement of the priesthood and the
30 covenant of the priesthood and the Levites. But I purified them of all foreign
elements and established duty shifts for the priests and the Levites – each for
31 his official tasks – also for the first fruits and for the wood offerings at fixed
times. Remember me favorably, O my God.

42 | See 1 Kings 11:1–11.

וְעַל הָעִיר הַזֹּאת וְאַתֶּם מוֹסִיפִים חָרוֹן עַל־יִשְׂרָאֵל לְחַלֵּל אֶת־
יט הַשַּׁבָּת: וַיְהִי כַּאֲשֶׁר צָלֲלוּ שַׁעֲרֵי יְרוּשָׁלַ͏ִם לִפְנֵי הַשַּׁבָּת
וָאֹמְרָה וַיִּסָּגְרוּ הַדְּלָתוֹת וָאֹמְרָה אֲשֶׁר לֹא יִפְתָּחוּם עַד אַחַר הַשַּׁבָּת
כ וּמִנְּעָרַי הֶעֱמַדְתִּי עַל־הַשְּׁעָרִים לֹא־יָבוֹא מַשָּׂא בְּיוֹם הַשַּׁבָּת: וַיָּלִינוּ
כא הָרֹכְלִים וּמֹכְרֵי כָל־מִמְכָּר מִחוּץ לִירוּשָׁלָ͏ִם פַּעַם וּשְׁתָּיִם: וָאָעִידָה
בָהֶם וָאֹמְרָה אֲלֵיהֶם מַדּוּעַ אַתֶּם לֵנִים נֶגֶד הַחוֹמָה אִם־תִּשְׁנוּ יָד
כב אֶשְׁלַח בָּכֶם מִן־הָעֵת הַהִיא לֹא בָאוּ בַּשַּׁבָּת: וָאֹמְרָה לַלְוִיִּם אֲשֶׁר
יִהְיוּ מִטַּהֲרִים וּבָאִים שֹׁמְרִים הַשְּׁעָרִים לְקַדֵּשׁ אֶת־יוֹם הַשַּׁבָּת
כג גַּם־זֹאת זָכְרָה־לִּי אֱלֹהַי וְחוּסָה עָלַי כְּרֹב חַסְדֶּךָ: גַּם ׀
בַּיָּמִים הָהֵם רָאִיתִי אֶת־הַיְּהוּדִים הֹשִׁיבוּ נָשִׁים אשדודיות עמוניות
כד מוֹאֲבִיּוֹת: וּבְנֵיהֶם חֲצִי מְדַבֵּר אַשְׁדּוֹדִית וְאֵינָם מַכִּירִים לְדַבֵּר
כה יְהוּדִית וְכִלְשׁוֹן עַם וָעָם: וָאָרִיב עִמָּם וָאֲקַלְלֵם וָאַכֶּה מֵהֶם אֲנָשִׁים
וָאֶמְרְטֵם וָאַשְׁבִּיעֵם בֵּאלֹהִים אִם־תִּתְּנוּ בְנֹתֵיכֶם לִבְנֵיהֶם וְאִם־תִּשְׂאוּ
כו מִבְּנֹתֵיהֶם לִבְנֵיכֶם וְלָכֶם: הֲלוֹא עַל־אֵלֶּה חָטָא־שְׁלֹמֹה מֶלֶךְ־יִשְׂרָאֵל
וּבַגּוֹיִם הָרַבִּים לֹא־הָיָה מֶלֶךְ כָּמֹהוּ וְאָהוּב לֵאלֹהָיו הָיָה וַיִּתְּנֵהוּ
אֱלֹהִים מֶלֶךְ עַל־כָּל־יִשְׂרָאֵל גַּם־אוֹתוֹ הֶחֱטִיאוּ הַנָּשִׁים הַנָּכְרִיּוֹת:
כז וְלָכֶם הֲנִשְׁמַע לַעֲשֹׂת אֵת כָּל־הָרָעָה הַגְּדוֹלָה הַזֹּאת לִמְעֹל בֵּאלֹהֵינוּ
כח לְהֹשִׁיב נָשִׁים נָכְרִיּוֹת: וּמִבְּנֵי יוֹיָדָע בֶּן־אֶלְיָשִׁיב הַכֹּהֵן הַגָּדוֹל חָתָן
כט לְסַנְבַלַּט הַחֹרֹנִי וָאַבְרִיחֵהוּ מֵעָלָי: זָכְרָה לָהֶם אֱלֹהָי עַל־גָּאֳלֵי הַכְּהֻנָּה
ל וּבְרִית הַכְּהֻנָּה וְהַלְוִיִּם: וְטִהַרְתִּים מִכָּל־נֵכָר וָאַעֲמִידָה מִשְׁמָרוֹת
לא לַכֹּהֲנִים וְלַלְוִיִּם אִישׁ בִּמְלַאכְתּוֹ: וּלְקֻרְבַּן הָעֵצִים בְּעִתִּים מְזֻמָּנוֹת
וְלַבִּכּוּרִים זָכְרָה־לִּי אֱלֹהַי לְטוֹבָה:

אַשְׁדֳּדִיּוֹת
עַמֳּנִיּוֹת

CHRONICLES	Geneological tables	End of Sha'ul's reign and David's reign in Jerusalem	End of David's reign and preparations for Shlomo's reign	Shlomo's reign	First kings of Yehuda: Reḥavam, Aviya, Asa, and Yehoshafat
	I Chronicles chs. 1–9	I Chronicles 10–21	I Chronicles 22–29	II Chronicles 1–9	II Chronicles 10–20
		33 years		40 years	86 years

Family of the dynasty of Aḥav: Reigns of Yehoram, Aḥazya, and Atalya	The downfall of Aram and ascendance of Assyria: Reigns of Yoash, Amatzya, Uziya, Yotam, and Aḥaz	From the downfall of Assyria to the ascendance of Babylonia: Reigns of Ḥizkiya, Menashe, Amon, and Yoshiya	Final kings of Yehuda: Yehoaḥaz, Yehoyakim, Yehoyakhin, and Tzidkiya
II Chronicles 21–22	II Chronicles 23–28	II Chronicles 29–35	II Chronicles 36
15 years	153 years	117 years	22 years

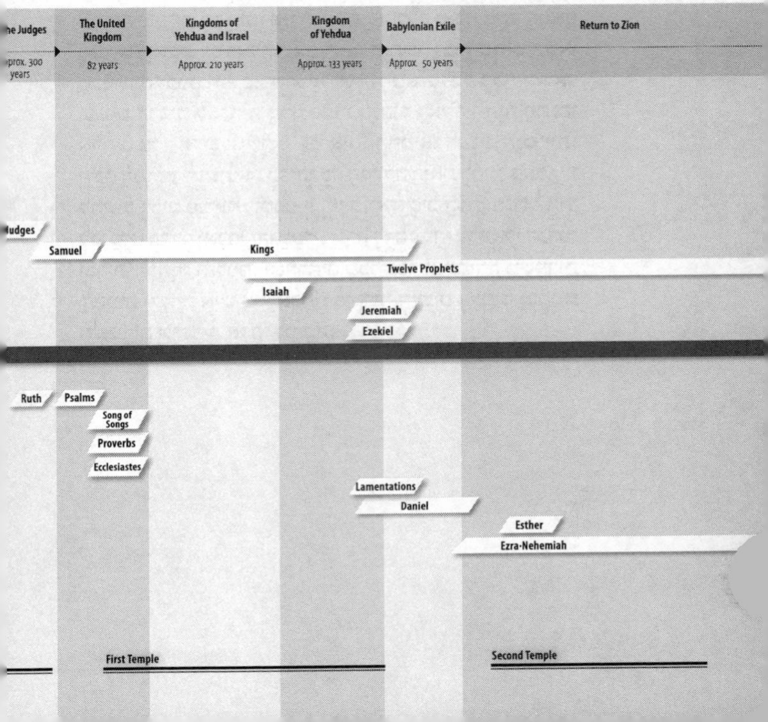

דברי הימים
DIVREI HAYAMIM/ CHRONICLES

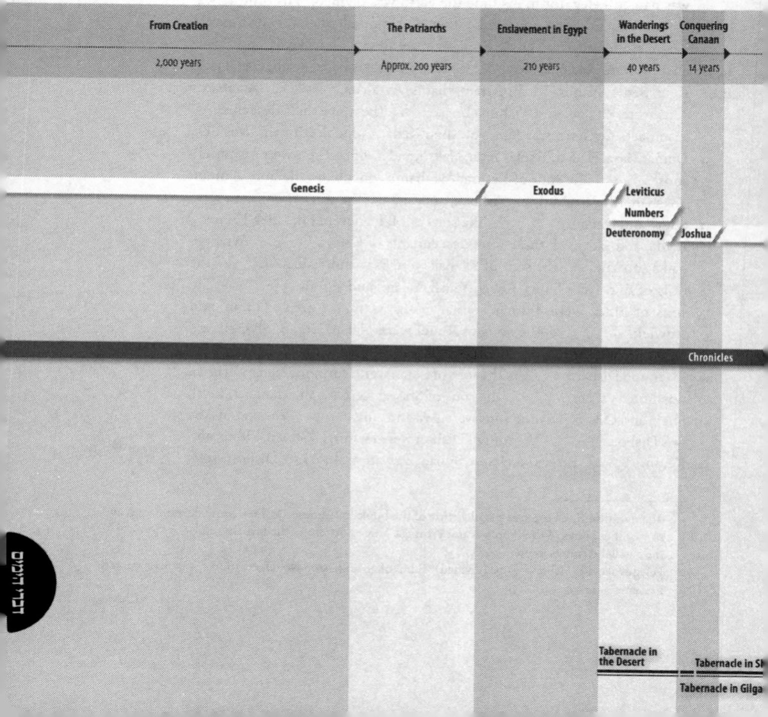

1 1, 2, 3 Adam, Shet, Enosh;[1] Keinan, Mahalalel, Yered; Ḥanokh, Metushelaḥ,
4 5 Lemekh; Noaḥ, Shem, Ḥam, and Yefet. Yefet's sons were Gomer, Magog,
6 Madai, Yavan, Tuval, Meshekh, and Tiras. The sons of Gomer were Ashkenaz,
7 Difat, and Togarma. The sons of Yavan were Elisha, Tarshish, Kitim, and
8 Rodanim. The sons of Ḥam were Kush, Mitzrayim, Put, and
9 Kenaan. The sons of Kush were Seva, Ḥavila, Savta, Raama, and Savtekha.
10 The sons of Raama were Sheva and Dedan. Kush was the father of Nimrod,
11 the first mighty warrior on earth. Mitzrayim was the father of the
12 Ludim, Anamim, Lehavim, and Naftuḥim, Patrusim, Kasluḥim – from whom
13 the Philistines descended – and the Kaftorim. Kenaan was the
14 father of Tzidon, his firstborn, and Ḥet, and the Jebusites, Amorites, and
15 16 Girgashites, the Hivites, Arkites, and Sinites, the Arvadites, Zemarites, and
17 Hamatites. Shem's sons were Elam, Ashur, Arpakhshad, Lud, Aram,
18 Utz, Ḥul, Geter, and Meshekh. Arpakhshad was the father of
19 Shelaḥ, and Shelaḥ was the father of Ever. To Ever, two sons were born. One
was named Peleg, for in his time the earth was divided.[2] His brother was
20 named Yoktan. Yoktan was the father of Almodad, Shelef, Ḥatzarmavet,
21, 22, 23 Yeraḥ, Hadoram, Uzal, Dikla, Eival, Avimael, Sheva, Ofir, Ḥavila, and Yovav;
24, 25 all these were Yoktan's sons. Shem, Arpakhshad, Shelaḥ; Ever, Peleg,
26, 27, 28 Reu; Serug, Naḥor, Teraḥ; Avram, that is, Avraham. Avraham's
29 sons were Yitzḥak and Yishmael. These are their descendants:
30 Yishmael's firstborn was Nevayot, then Kedar, Adbe'el, Mivsam, Mishma,
31 Duma, Masa, Ḥadad, Teima, Yetur, Nafish, and Kedma. These were Yishmael's
32 sons. The sons of Ketura, Avraham's concubine: she bore Zimran,
Yokshan, Medan, Midyan, Yishbak, and Shuaḥ. The sons of Yokshan were
33 Sheva and Dedan. The sons of Midyan were Eifa, Efer, Ḥanokh,
34 Avida, and Eldaa: all these were descendants of Ketura. Avraham
35 had a son Yitzḥak. The sons of Yitzḥak were Esav and Yisrael. The
36 sons of Esav were Elifaz, Reuel, Yeush, Yalam, and Koraḥ. The
sons of Elifaz were Teiman, Omar, Tzefi, Gatam, Kenaz, Timna, and
37 Amalek. The sons of Reuel were Naḥat, Zeraḥ, Shama, and
38 Miza. The sons of Se'ir were Lotan, Shoval, Tzivon, Ana, Dishon,
39 Etzer, and Dishan. The sons of Lotan were Ḥori and Homam. Timna
40 was Lotan's sister. The sons of Shoval were Alyan, Manaḥat, Eival,
41 Shefi, and Onam. Tzivon's sons were Aya and Ana. The son of Ana
was Dishon. The sons of Dishon were Ḥemran, Eshban, Yitran, and
42 Keran. Etzer's sons were Bilhan, Zaavan, and Yaakan. Dishon's sons

1 | The narrative in Chronicles parallels that of the books of Genesis, Joshua, Samuel, and Kings, and some other books of the Prophets and Writings. Large portions of the text are similar or identical to the parallel accounts in these books.

2 | Peleg evokes the Hebrew *niflega* (divided). This is often understood to refer to the dispersion recounted in Genesis 11:1–9.

א

א ב ג אָדָם שֵׁת אֱנוֹשׁ׃ קֵינָן מַהֲלַלְאֵל יָרֶד׃ חֲנוֹךְ מְתוּשֶׁלַח לָמֶךְ׃ א
ד ה נֹחַ שֵׁם חָם וָיָפֶת׃ בְּנֵי יֶפֶת גֹּמֶר וּמָגוֹג וּמָדַי וְיָוָן וְתֻבָל וּמֶשֶׁךְ וְתִירָס׃
ו ז וּבְנֵי גֹּמֶר אַשְׁכְּנַז וְדִיפַת וְתוֹגַרְמָה׃ וּבְנֵי יָוָן אֱלִישָׁה וְתַרְשִׁישָׁה כִּתִּים
ח ט וְרוֹדָנִים׃ בְּנֵי חָם כּוּשׁ וּמִצְרַיִם פּוּט וּכְנָעַן׃ וּבְנֵי כוּשׁ
י סְבָא וַחֲוִילָה וְסַבְתָּא וְרַעְמָא וְסַבְתְּכָא וּבְנֵי רַעְמָא שְׁבָא וּדְדָן׃ וְכוּשׁ
יא יָלַד אֶת־נִמְרוֹד הוּא הֵחֵל לִהְיוֹת גִּבּוֹר בָּאָרֶץ׃ וּמִצְרַיִם
יב יָלַד אֶת־לוּדִיים וְאֶת־עֲנָמִים וְאֶת־לְהָבִים וְאֶת־נַפְתֻּחִים׃ וְאֶת־ לוּדִים
פַּתְרֻסִים וְאֶת־כַּסְלֻחִים אֲשֶׁר יָצְאוּ מִשָּׁם פְּלִשְׁתִּים וְאֶת־
יג יד כַּפְתֹּרִים׃ וּכְנַעַן יָלַד אֶת־צִידוֹן בְּכֹרוֹ וְאֶת־חֵת׃ וְאֶת־
טו הַיְבוּסִי וְאֶת־הָאֱמֹרִי וְאֵת הַגִּרְגָּשִׁי׃ וְאֶת־הַחִוִּי וְאֶת־הַעַרְקִי וְאֶת־
טז יז הַסִּינִי׃ וְאֶת־הָאַרְוָדִי וְאֶת־הַצְּמָרִי וְאֶת־הַחֲמָתִי׃ בְּנֵי
שֵׁם עֵילָם וְאַשּׁוּר וְאַרְפַּכְשַׁד וְלוּד וַאֲרָם וְעוּץ וְחוּל וְגֶתֶר
יח וָמֶשֶׁךְ׃ וְאַרְפַּכְשַׁד יָלַד אֶת־שָׁלַח וְשֶׁלַח יָלַד אֶת־עֵבֶר׃
יט וּלְעֵבֶר יֻלַּד שְׁנֵי בָנִים שֵׁם הָאֶחָד פֶּלֶג כִּי בְיָמָיו נִפְלְגָה הָאָרֶץ וְשֵׁם
כ אָחִיו יָקְטָן׃ וְיָקְטָן יָלַד אֶת־אַלְמוֹדָד וְאֶת־שָׁלֶף וְאֶת־חֲצַרְמָוֶת
כא כב וְאֶת־יָרַח׃ וְאֶת־הֲדוֹרָם וְאֶת־אוּזָל וְאֶת־דִּקְלָה׃ וְאֶת־עֵיבָל וְאֶת־
כג אֲבִימָאֵל וְאֶת־שְׁבָא׃ וְאֶת־אוֹפִיר וְאֶת־חֲוִילָה וְאֶת־יוֹבָב כָּל־אֵלֶּה
כד כה בְּנֵי יָקְטָן׃ שֵׁם ׀ אַרְפַּכְשַׁד שָׁלַח׃ עֵבֶר פֶּלֶג רְעוּ׃ שְׂרוּג
כו כז כח נָחוֹר תָּרַח׃ אַבְרָם הוּא אַבְרָהָם׃ בְּנֵי אַבְרָהָם יִצְחָק
כט וְיִשְׁמָעֵאל׃ אֵלֶּה תֹּלְדוֹתָם בְּכוֹר יִשְׁמָעֵאל נְבָיוֹת וְקֵדָר
ל לא וְאַדְבְּאֵל וּמִבְשָׂם׃ מִשְׁמָע וְדוּמָה מַשָּׂא חֲדַד וְתֵימָא׃ יְטוּר נָפִישׁ
לב וָקֵדְמָה אֵלֶּה הֵם בְּנֵי יִשְׁמָעֵאל׃ וּבְנֵי קְטוּרָה פִּילֶגֶשׁ
אַבְרָהָם יָלְדָה אֶת־זִמְרָן וְיָקְשָׁן וּמְדָן וּמִדְיָן וְיִשְׁבָּק וְשׁוּחַ וּבְנֵי יָקְשָׁן
לג שְׁבָא וּדְדָן׃ וּבְנֵי מִדְיָן עֵיפָה וָעֵפֶר וַחֲנוֹךְ וַאֲבִידָע וְאֶלְדָּעָה
לד כָּל־אֵלֶּה בְּנֵי קְטוּרָה׃ וַיּוֹלֶד אַבְרָהָם אֶת־יִצְחָק בְּנֵי יִצְחָק
לה עֵשָׂו וְיִשְׂרָאֵל׃ בְּנֵי עֵשָׂו אֱלִיפַז רְעוּאֵל וִיעוּשׁ וְיַעְלָם
לו וְקֹרַח׃ בְּנֵי אֱלִיפַז תֵּימָן וְאוֹמָר צְפִי וְגַעְתָּם קְנַז וְתִמְנָע
לז לח וַעֲמָלֵק׃ בְּנֵי רְעוּאֵל נַחַת זֶרַח שַׁמָּה וּמִזָּה׃ וּבְנֵי
לט שֵׂעִיר לוֹטָן וְשׁוֹבָל וְצִבְעוֹן וַעֲנָה וְדִישֹׁן וְאֵצֶר וְדִישָׁן׃ וּבְנֵי
מ לוֹטָן חֹרִי וְהוֹמָם וַאֲחוֹת לוֹטָן תִּמְנָע׃ בְּנֵי שׁוֹבָל עַלְיָן
מא וּמָנַחַת וְעֵיבָל שְׁפִי וְאוֹנָם וּבְנֵי צִבְעוֹן אַיָּה וַעֲנָה׃ בְּנֵי עֲנָה
מב דִּישׁוֹן וּבְנֵי דִישׁוֹן חַמְרָן וְאֶשְׁבָּן וְיִתְרָן וּכְרָן׃ בְּנֵי־

43 were Utz and Aran. These were the kings who reigned in Edom
before any king reigned over the Israelites: Bela son of Beor. His city was
44 named Dinhava. When Bela died, Yovav son of Zeraḥ from Botzra succeeded
45 him as king. When Yovav died, Ḥusham from the land of the Temanites
46 succeeded him as king. When Ḥusham died, Hadad son of Bedad, who
defeated Midyan in the country of Moav, succeeded him as king. His city was
47 named Avit. When Hadad died, Samla from Masreka succeeded him as king.
48 When Samla died, Sha'ul from Reḥovot HaNahar succeeded him as king.
49 50 When Sha'ul died, Baal Ḥanan son of Akhbor succeeded him as king. When
Baal Ḥanan died, Hadad succeeded him as king. His city was named Pa'i, and
his wife's name was Meheitavel, daughter of Matred, daughter of Mei Zahav.
51, 52 And Hadad died. The chiefs of Edom were Timna, Alva, Yetet, Oholivama,
53, 54 Ela, Pinon, Kenaz, Teiman, Mivtzar, Magdiel, and Iram; these are the chiefs
2 1 of Edom. These are the sons of Yisrael: Reuven, Shimon, Levi,
2 Yehuda, Yissakhar, Zevulun, Dan, Yosef, Binyamin, Naftali, Gad, and
3 Asher. The sons of Yehuda were Er, Onan, and Shela; these three
were born to him from Shua's daughter, the Canaanite. Er, Yehuda's firstborn,
4 was wicked in the LORD's sight, and He took his life. Tamar, his daughter-in-
5 law, bore him Peretz and Zeraḥ. Yehuda's sons were five in all. The sons of
6 Peretz were Ḥetzron and Ḥamul. The sons of Zeraḥ were Zimri,
7 Eitan, Heiman, Kalkol, and Dara, five in all. Karmi's son was Akhar,
8 the scourge of Israel, who broke the ban,[3] and Eitan's son was
9 Azarya. The sons of Ḥetzron that were born to him were Yeraḥme'el,
10 Ram, and Keluvai. Ram was the father of Aminadav; Aminadav was the father
11 of Naḥshon, leader of the sons of Yehuda. Naḥshon was the father of Salma;
12 Salma was the father of Boaz. Boaz was the father of Oved; Oved was the
13 father of Yishai. Ishai was the father of his firstborn Eliav, Avinadav second,
14, 15 Shima third, Netanel fourth, Radai fifth, Otzem sixth, David seventh;
16 their sisters were Tzeruya and Avigayil. The sons of Tzeruya: Avshai, Yoav,
17 and Asael – three. Avigayil bore Amasa, and the father of Amasa was Yeter
18 the Ishmaelite. Kalev son of Ḥetzron had children by his wife Azuva
19 and by Yeriot; these were her sons: Yesher, Shovav, and Ardon. When Azuva
20 died, Kalev married Efrat, who bore him Ḥur. Ḥur was the father of Uri, and
21 Uri was the father of Betzalel. Later, Ḥetzron came to the daughter
of Makhir, father of Gilad – he married her when he was sixty years old – and
22 she bore him Seguv. Seguv was the father of Yair, who acquired twenty-three

---

3 | See Joshua 7:16–26.

מג אֵצֶר בִּלְהָן וְזַעֲוָן יַעֲקָן בְּנֵי דִישׁוֹן עוּץ וַאֲרָן׃ וְאֵלֶּה הַמְּלָכִים
אֲשֶׁר מָלְכוּ בְּאֶרֶץ אֱדוֹם לִפְנֵי מְלָךְ־מֶלֶךְ לִבְנֵי יִשְׂרָאֵל בֶּלַע בֶּן־בְּעוֹר
מד וְשֵׁם עִירוֹ דִּנְהָבָה׃ וַיָּמָת בָּלַע וַיִּמְלֹךְ תַּחְתָּיו יוֹבָב בֶּן־זֶרַח מִבָּצְרָה׃
מה מו וַיָּמָת יוֹבָב וַיִּמְלֹךְ תַּחְתָּיו חוּשָׁם מֵאֶרֶץ הַתֵּימָנִי׃ וַיָּמָת חוּשָׁם וַיִּמְלֹךְ
תַּחְתָּיו הֲדַד בֶּן־בְּדַד הַמַּכֶּה אֶת־מִדְיָן בִּשְׂדֵה מוֹאָב וְשֵׁם עִירוֹ עיות׃ עֲוִית
מז מח וַיָּמָת הֲדָד וַיִּמְלֹךְ תַּחְתָּיו שַׂמְלָה מִמַּשְׂרֵקָה׃ וַיָּמָת שַׂמְלָה וַיִּמְלֹךְ
מט תַּחְתָּיו שָׁאוּל מֵרְחֹבוֹת הַנָּהָר׃ וַיָּמָת שָׁאוּל וַיִּמְלֹךְ תַּחְתָּיו בַּעַל חָנָן
נ בֶּן־עַכְבּוֹר׃ וַיָּמָת בַּעַל חָנָן וַיִּמְלֹךְ תַּחְתָּיו הֲדַד וְשֵׁם עִירוֹ פָּעִי וְשֵׁם
נא אִשְׁתּוֹ מְהֵיטַבְאֵל בַּת־מַטְרֵד בַּת מֵי זָהָב׃ וַיָּמָת הֲדָד וַיִּהְיוּ אַלּוּפֵי
נב אֱדוֹם אַלּוּף תִּמְנָע אַלּוּף עליה אַלּוּף יְתֵת׃ אַלּוּף אָהֳלִיבָמָה אַלּוּף עַלְוָה
נג נד אֵלָה אַלּוּף פִּינֹן׃ אַלּוּף קְנַז אַלּוּף תֵּימָן אַלּוּף מִבְצָר׃ אַלּוּף מַגְדִּיאֵל
ב א אַלּוּף עִירָם אֵלֶּה אַלּוּפֵי אֱדוֹם׃ אֵלֶּה בְּנֵי יִשְׂרָאֵל רְאוּבֵן
ב שִׁמְעוֹן לֵוִי וִיהוּדָה יִשָּׂשכָר וּזְבֻלוּן׃ דָּן יוֹסֵף וּבִנְיָמִן נַפְתָּלִי גָּד
ג וְאָשֵׁר׃ בְּנֵי יְהוּדָה עֵר וְאוֹנָן וְשֵׁלָה שְׁלוֹשָׁה נוֹלַד לוֹ מִבַּת־
ד שׁוּעַ הַכְּנַעֲנִית וַיְהִי עֵר ׀ בְּכוֹר יְהוּדָה רַע בְּעֵינֵי יְהוָה וַיְמִיתֵהוּ׃ וְתָמָר
ה כַּלָּתוֹ יָלְדָה לּוֹ אֶת־פֶּרֶץ וְאֶת־זָרַח כָּל־בְּנֵי יְהוּדָה חֲמִשָּׁה׃ בְּנֵי פֶרֶץ
ו חֶצְרוֹן וְחָמוּל׃ וּבְנֵי זֶרַח זִמְרִי וְאֵיתָן וְהֵימָן וְכַלְכֹּל וָדָרַע
ז כֻּלָּם חֲמִשָּׁה׃ וּבְנֵי כַּרְמִי עָכָר עוֹכֵר יִשְׂרָאֵל אֲשֶׁר מָעַל
ח ט בַּחֵרֶם׃ וּבְנֵי אֵיתָן עֲזַרְיָה׃ וּבְנֵי חֶצְרוֹן אֲשֶׁר
י נוֹלַד־לוֹ אֶת־יְרַחְמְאֵל וְאֶת־רָם וְאֶת־כְּלוּבָי׃ וְרָם הוֹלִיד אֶת־עַמִּינָדָב
יא וְעַמִּינָדָב הוֹלִיד אֶת־נַחְשׁוֹן נְשִׂיא בְּנֵי יְהוּדָה׃ וְנַחְשׁוֹן הוֹלִיד אֶת־
יב שַׂלְמָא וְשַׂלְמָא הוֹלִיד אֶת־בֹּעַז׃ וּבֹעַז הוֹלִיד אֶת־עוֹבֵד וְעוֹבֵד
יג הוֹלִיד אֶת־יִשָׁי׃ וְאִישַׁי הוֹלִיד אֶת־בְּכֹרוֹ אֶת־אֱלִיאָב וַאֲבִינָדָב
יד טו הַשֵּׁנִי וְשִׁמְעָא הַשְּׁלִישִׁי׃ נְתַנְאֵל הָרְבִיעִי רַדַּי הַחֲמִישִׁי׃ אֹצֶם הַשִּׁשִּׁי
טז דָּוִיד הַשְּׁבִעִי׃ וְאַחְיֹתֵיהֶם צְרוּיָה וַאֲבִיגָיִל וּבְנֵי צְרוּיָה אַבְשַׁי וְיוֹאָב
יז וַעֲשָׂה־אֵל שְׁלֹשָׁה׃ וַאֲבִיגַיִל יָלְדָה אֶת־עֲמָשָׂא וַאֲבִי עֲמָשָׂא יֶתֶר
יח הַיִּשְׁמְעֵאלִי׃ וְכָלֵב בֶּן־חֶצְרוֹן הוֹלִיד אֶת־עֲזוּבָה אִשָּׁה
יט וְאֶת־יְרִיעוֹת וְאֵלֶּה בָנֶיהָ יֵשֶׁר וְשׁוֹבָב וְאַרְדּוֹן׃ וַתָּמָת עֲזוּבָה וַיִּקַּח־לוֹ
כ כָלֵב אֶת־אֶפְרָת וַתֵּלֶד לוֹ אֶת־חוּר׃ וְחוּר הוֹלִיד אֶת־אוּרִי וְאוּרִי
כא הוֹלִיד אֶת־בְּצַלְאֵל׃ וְאַחַר בָּא חֶצְרוֹן אֶל־בַּת־מָכִיר
אֲבִי גִלְעָד וְהוּא לְקָחָהּ וְהוּא בֶּן־שִׁשִּׁים שָׁנָה וַתֵּלֶד לוֹ אֶת־שְׂגוּב׃
כב וּשְׂגוּב הוֹלִיד אֶת־יָאִיר וַיְהִי־לוֹ עֶשְׂרִים וְשָׁלוֹשׁ עָרִים בְּאֶרֶץ

23 cities in the land of Gilad. But Geshur and Aram seized the hamlets
of Yair from them, Kenat and its dependencies, sixty towns. All these were
24 the sons of Makhir, father of Gilad. After the death of Ḥetzron in Kalev Efrata,
25 Aviya, Ḥetzron's wife, bore Ashḥur, the father of Tekoa. The sons of Yeraḥme'el,
Ḥetzron's firstborn: Ram his firstborn, Buna, Oren, Otzem, and Aḥiya.
26 Yeraḥme'el had another wife, whose name was Atara; she was the mother of
27 Onam. The sons of Ram, Yeraḥme'el's firstborn: Maatz, Yamin,
28 and Eker. The sons of Onam: Shamai and Yada. The sons of Shamai: Nadav
29 and Avishur. The name of Avishur's wife was Avihayil, and she bore him
30 Aḥban and Molid. The sons of Nadav: Seled and Apayim; Seled died
31 childless. The sons of Apayim: Yishi. The sons of Yishi: Sheshan.
32 The sons of Sheshan: Aḥlai. The sons of Yada, Shamai's brother:
33 Yeter and Yonatan; Yeter died childless. The sons of Yonatan: Pelet
34 and Zaza. These were the sons of Yeraḥme'el. Sheshan had no sons, only
35 daughters. Sheshan had an Egyptian slave whose name was Yarḥa. Sheshan
36 gave his daughter in marriage to Yarḥa his servant, and she bore him Atai. Atai
37 was the father of Natan, Natan was the father of Zavad, Zavad was the father
38 of Eflal, Eflal was the father of Oved, Oved was the father of Yehu, Yehu was
39 the father of Azarya, Azarya was the father of Ḥeletz, Ḥeletz was the father
40 of Elasa, Elasa was the father of Sisemai, Sisemai was the father of Shalum,
41 Shalum was the father of Yekamya, and Yekamya was the father of
42 Elishama. The sons of Kalev, brother of Yeraḥme'el: Meisha his
firstborn was the father of Zif and the people of Maresha, father of Ḥevron.
43 44 The sons of Ḥevron: Koraḥ, Tapuaḥ, Rekem, and Shema. Shema was the
father of Raḥam the father of Yorke'am, and Rekem was the father of Shamai.
45 46 The son of Shamai: Maon, and Maon was the father of Beit Tzur. Eifa, Kalev's
concubine, bore Ḥaran, Motza, and Gazez; Ḥaran was the father of
47 Gazez. The sons of Yodai: Regem, Yotam, Geishan, Pelet, Eifa, and
48 49 Shaaf. Kalev's concubine, Maakha, bore Shever and Tirḥana, and she bore
Shaaf father of Madmana, Sheva father of Makhbena and father of Giva;
50 Kalev's daughter was Akhsa. These were the sons of Kalev son of Ḥur, the
51 firstborn of Efrata: Shoval father of Kiryat Ye'arim, Salma father of Beit
52 Leḥem, Ḥaref father of Beit Gader. Shoval father of Kiryat Ye'arim had sons:
53 Haroeh,[4] half of the Menuḥot. The families of Kiryat Ye'arim: the Itrites, the
Putites, the Shumatites, and the Mishraites; from these came the Zoratites
54 and the Eshtaolites. The sons of Salma: Beit Leḥem, the Netofatites,
55 Atrot Beit Yoav, and half of the Manahatites, the Zorites. The scribal families
that dwelt at Yabetz: the Tiratites, the Shimeatites, and the Sucatites; these
3 1 are the Kinites who came from Ḥamat, father of Beit Rekhav. These
were the sons of David that were born to him at Ḥevron: the firstborn Amnon

4 | The descendants of Haroeh populated half of the city of Menuḥot, likely a variant name for Manaḥat; cf. verse 54.

כג הַגִּלְעָד׃ וַיִּקַּח גְּשׁוּר־וַאֲרָם אֶת־חַוֺּת יָאִיר מֵאִתָּם אֶת־קְנָת
כד וְאֶת־בְּנֹתֶיהָ שִׁשִּׁים עִיר כׇּל־אֵלֶּה בְּנֵי מָכִיר אֲבִי־גִלְעָד׃ וְאַחַר מוֹת־
חֶצְרוֹן בְּכָלֵב אֶפְרָתָה וְאֵשֶׁת חֶצְרוֹן אֲבִיָּה וַתֵּלֶד לוֹ אֶת־אַשְׁחוּר אֲבִי
כה תְקוֹעַ׃ וַיִּהְיוּ בְנֵי־יְרַחְמְאֵל בְּכוֹר חֶצְרוֹן הַבְּכוֹר ׀ רָם וּבוּנָה וָאֹרֶן
כו וָאֹצֶם אֲחִיָּה׃ וַתְּהִי אִשָּׁה אַחֶרֶת לִירַחְמְאֵל וּשְׁמָהּ עֲטָרָה הִיא אֵם
כז אוֹנָם׃ וַיִּהְיוּ בְנֵי־רָם בְּכוֹר יְרַחְמְאֵל מַעַץ וְיָמִין וָעֵקֶר׃
כח כט וַיִּהְיוּ בְנֵי־אוֹנָם שַׁמַּי וְיָדָע וּבְנֵי שַׁמַּי נָדָב וַאֲבִישׁוּר׃ וְשֵׁם אֵשֶׁת אֲבִישׁוּר
ל אֲבִיהָיִל וַתֵּלֶד לוֹ אֶת־אַחְבָּן וְאֶת־מוֹלִיד׃ וּבְנֵי נָדָב סֶלֶד וְאַפָּיִם וַיָּמָת
לא סֶלֶד לֹא בָנִים׃ וּבְנֵי אַפַּיִם יִשְׁעִי וּבְנֵי יִשְׁעִי שֵׁשָׁן וּבְנֵי שֵׁשָׁן
לב אַחְלָי׃ וּבְנֵי יָדָע אֲחִי שַׁמַּי יֶתֶר וְיוֹנָתָן וַיָּמָת יֶתֶר לֹא
לג לד בָנִים׃ וּבְנֵי יוֹנָתָן פֶּלֶת וְזָזָא אֵלֶּה הָיוּ בְּנֵי יְרַחְמְאֵל׃ וְלֹא־
לה הָיָה לְשֵׁשָׁן בָּנִים כִּי אִם־בָּנוֹת וּלְשֵׁשָׁן עֶבֶד מִצְרִי וּשְׁמוֹ יַרְחָע׃ וַיִּתֵּן
לו שֵׁשָׁן אֶת־בִּתּוֹ לְיַרְחָע עַבְדּוֹ לְאִשָּׁה וַתֵּלֶד לוֹ אֶת־עַתָּי׃ וְעַתַּי הוֹלִיד
לז אֶת־נָתָן וְנָתָן הוֹלִיד אֶת־זָבָד׃ וְזָבָד הוֹלִיד אֶת־אֶפְלָל וְאֶפְלָל הוֹלִיד
לח לט אֶת־עוֹבֵד׃ וְעוֹבֵד הוֹלִיד אֶת־יֵהוּא וְיֵהוּא הוֹלִיד אֶת־עֲזַרְיָה׃ וַעֲזַרְיָה
מ הֹלִיד אֶת־חָלֶץ וְחֶלֶץ הֹלִיד אֶת־אֶלְעָשָׂה׃ וְאֶלְעָשָׂה הֹלִיד אֶת־סִסְמָי
מא וְסִסְמַי הֹלִיד אֶת־שַׁלּוּם׃ וְשַׁלּוּם הוֹלִיד אֶת־יְקַמְיָה וִיקַמְיָה הֹלִיד
מב אֶת־אֱלִישָׁמָע׃ וּבְנֵי כָלֵב אֲחִי יְרַחְמְאֵל מֵישָׁע בְּכֹרוֹ הוּא
מג אֲבִי־זִיף וּבְנֵי מָרֵשָׁה אֲבִי חֶבְרוֹן׃ וּבְנֵי חֶבְרוֹן קֹרַח וְתַפֻּחַ וְרֶקֶם וָשָׁמַע׃
מד מה וְשֶׁמַע הוֹלִיד אֶת־רַחַם אֲבִי יָרְקֳעָם וְרֶקֶם הוֹלִיד אֶת־שַׁמָּי׃ וּבֶן־שַׁמַּי
מו מָעוֹן וּמָעוֹן אֲבִי בֵית־צוּר׃ וְעֵיפָה פִּילֶגֶשׁ כָּלֵב יָלְדָה אֶת־חָרָן וְאֶת־
מז מוֹצָא וְאֶת־גָּזֵז וְחָרָן הֹלִיד אֶת־גָּזֵז׃ וּבְנֵי יָהְדָּי רֶגֶם וְיוֹתָם
מח וְגֵישָׁן וָפֶלֶט וְעֵיפָה וָשָׁעַף׃ פִּלֶגֶשׁ כָּלֵב מַעֲכָה יָלַד שֶׁבֶר וְאֶת־תִּרְחֲנָה׃
מט וַתֵּלֶד שַׁעַף אֲבִי מַדְמַנָּה אֶת־שְׁוָא אֲבִי מַכְבֵּנָה וַאֲבִי גִבְעָא וּבַת־כָּלֵב
נ עַכְסָה׃ אֵלֶּה הָיוּ בְּנֵי כָלֵב בֶּן־חוּר בְּכוֹר אֶפְרָתָה שׁוֹבָל אֲבִי קִרְיַת
נא נב יְעָרִים׃ שַׂלְמָא אֲבִי בֵית־לָחֶם חָרֵף אֲבִי בֵית־גָּדֵר׃ וַיִּהְיוּ בָנִים
נג לְשׁוֹבָל אֲבִי קִרְיַת יְעָרִים הָרֹאֶה חֲצִי הַמְּנֻחוֹת׃ וּמִשְׁפְּחוֹת קִרְיַת
יְעָרִים הַיִּתְרִי וְהַפּוּתִי וְהַשֻּׁמָתִי וְהַמִּשְׁרָעִי מֵאֵלֶּה יָצְאוּ הַצָּרְעָתִי
נד וְהָאֶשְׁתָּאֻלִי׃ בְּנֵי שַׂלְמָא בֵּית לֶחֶם וּנְטוֹפָתִי עַטְרוֹת
נה בֵּית יוֹאָב וַחֲצִי הַמָּנַחְתִּי הַצָּרְעִי׃ וּמִשְׁפְּחוֹת סֹפְרִים ישבו יַעְבֵּץ יֹשְׁבֵי
תִּרְעָתִים שִׁמְעָתִים שׂוּכָתִים הֵמָּה הַקִּינִים הַבָּאִים מֵחַמַּת אֲבִי בֵית־
ג א רֵכָב׃ וְאֵלֶּה הָיוּ בְּנֵי דָוִיד אֲשֶׁר נוֹלַד־לוֹ בְּחֶבְרוֹן הַבְּכוֹר ׀

2 to Aḥinoam the Jezreelite; the second, Daniel to Avigayil the Carmelite; the
third, Avshalom son of Maakha daughter of King Talmai of Geshur; the
3 fourth, Adoniya son of Ḥagit; the fifth, Shefatya, to Avital; and the sixth,
4 Yitre'am, to his wife Egla. Six were born to him in Ḥevron, and he reigned
there for seven years and six months, and for thirty-three years he reigned in
5 Jerusalem. And these were born to him in Jerusalem: Shima, Shovav,
6 Natan, and Shlomo – four to Batshua daughter of Amiel; then Yivḥar,
7 8 Elishama, Elifelet, Noga, Nefeg, Yafia, Elishama, Elyada, and Elifelet – nine,
9 all David's sons beyond the sons of the concubines and Tamar, their
10 sister. The sons of Shlomo: Reḥavam, his son Aviya, his son Asa, his
11 12 son Yehoshafat, his son Yoram, his son Aḥazyahu, his son Yoash, his son
13 Amatzyahu, his son Azarya, his son Yotam, his son Aḥaz, his son Ḥizkiyahu,
14 15 his son Menashe,his son Amon, and his son Yoshiyahu. The sons of
Yoshiyahu: the firstborn Yoḥanan; the second, Yehoyakim; the third,
16 Tzidkiyahu; and the fourth, Shalum. The sons of Yehoyakim: his son Yekhonya
17 and his son Tzidkiya. The sons of Yekhonya, the captive: his sons She'altiel,
18 19 Malkiram, Pedaya, Shenatzar, Yekamya, Hoshama, and Nedavya. The sons
of Pedaya: Zerubavel and Shimi; the sons of Zerubavel: Meshulam and
20 Ḥananya and their sister Shlomit, and Ḥashuva, Ohel, Berekhya, Ḥasdaya,
21 and Yushav Ḥesed – five. The sons of Ḥananya: Pelatya and Yeshaya, his son
22 Refaya, his son Arnan, his son Ovadya, and his son Shekhanya. The
son of Shekhanya: Shemaya; the sons of Shemaya: Ḥatush, Yigal, Bariaḥ,
23 Ne'arya, and Shafat – six.[5] The sons of Ne'arya: Elyo'einai, Ḥizkiya, and
24 Azrikam – three. And the sons of Elyo'einai: Hodavyahu, Elyashiv, Pelaya,
4 1 Akuv, Yoḥanan, Delaya, and Anani – seven. The sons of Yehuda:
2 Peretz, Ḥetzron, Karmi, Ḥur, and Shoval. Re'aya son of Shoval was the father
of Yaḥat, and Yaḥat was the father of Aḥumai and Lahad; these were the
3 families of the Zoratites. These were of the father of Eitam: Yizre'el,
4 Yishma, and Yidbash; their sister's name was Hatzlelponi; Penuel was the
father of Gedor, and Ezer the father of Ḥusha. These were the sons of Ḥur,
5 the firstborn of Efrata, the father of Beit Leḥem. Ashḥur the father of Tekoa
6 had two wives, Ḥela and Naara; Naara bore him Aḥuzam, Ḥefer, Teimeni,
7 and Aḥashtari; these were the sons of Naara. The sons of Ḥela: Tzeret, Tzoḥar,
8 and Etnan. Kotz was the father of Anuv, Tzoveva, and the families of Aḥarḥel
9 son of Harum. Yabetz was the most honorable of his brothers; his mother
10 named him Yabetz, "for I bore him in pain."[6] Yabetz called out to the God of
Israel, saying, "O, that You would bless me and increase my borders, and that
Your hand might be with me so that You might keep me from harm to prevent
11 my pain." And God granted what he asked. Keluv the brother of

---

5 | Some propose that one name has fallen out of the text; others explain that Shemaya is counted among the six immediate descendants of Shekhanya enumerated here.

6 | The root letters *ayin-bet-tzadi* in the name Yabetz mirror those of *etzev*, "pain."

ב אַמְנֹן לַאֲחִינֹעַם הַיִּזְרְעֵאלִית שֵׁנִי דָּנִיֵּאל לַאֲבִיגַיִל הַכַּרְמְלִית׃ הַשְּׁלִשִׁי
לְאַבְשָׁלוֹם בֶּן־מַעֲכָה בַּת־תַּלְמַי מֶלֶךְ גְּשׁוּר הָרְבִיעִי אֲדֹנִיָּה בֶן־חַגִּית׃
ג ד הַחֲמִישִׁי שְׁפַטְיָה לַאֲבִיטָל הַשִּׁשִּׁי יִתְרְעָם לְעֶגְלָה אִשְׁתּוֹ׃ שִׁשָּׁה
נוֹלַד־לוֹ בְחֶבְרוֹן וַיִּמְלָךְ־שָׁם שֶׁבַע שָׁנִים וְשִׁשָּׁה חֳדָשִׁים וּשְׁלֹשִׁים
ה וְשָׁלוֹשׁ שָׁנָה מָלַךְ בִּירוּשָׁלִָם׃ וְאֵלֶּה נוּלְּדוּ־לוֹ
בִּירוּשָׁלָיִם שִׁמְעָא וְשׁוֹבָב וְנָתָן וּשְׁלֹמֹה אַרְבָּעָה לְבַת־שׁוּעַ בַּת־
ו ז עַמִּיאֵל׃ וְיִבְחָר וֶאֱלִישָׁמָע וֶאֱלִיפָלֶט׃ וְנֹגַהּ וְנֶפֶג וְיָפִיעַ׃ וֶאֱלִישָׁמָע
ח ט וְאֶלְיָדָע וֶאֱלִיפֶלֶט תִּשְׁעָה׃ כֹּל בְּנֵי דָוִיד מִלְּבַד בְּנֵי־פִילַגְשִׁים וְתָמָר
י אֲחוֹתָם׃ וּבֶן־שְׁלֹמֹה רְחַבְעָם אֲבִיָּה בְנוֹ אָסָא בְנוֹ יְהוֹשָׁפָט
יא יב בְּנוֹ׃ יוֹרָם בְּנוֹ אֲחַזְיָהוּ בְנוֹ יוֹאָשׁ בְּנוֹ׃ אֲמַצְיָהוּ בְנוֹ עֲזַרְיָה בְנוֹ יוֹתָם
יג יד טו בְּנוֹ׃ אָחָז בְּנוֹ חִזְקִיָּהוּ בְנוֹ מְנַשֶּׁה בְנוֹ׃ אָמוֹן בְּנוֹ יֹאשִׁיָּהוּ בְנוֹ׃ וּבְנֵי
יֹאשִׁיָּהוּ הַבְּכוֹר יוֹחָנָן הַשֵּׁנִי יְהוֹיָקִים הַשְּׁלִשִׁי צִדְקִיָּהוּ הָרְבִיעִי שַׁלּוּם׃
טז יז וּבְנֵי יְהוֹיָקִים יְכָנְיָה בְנוֹ צִדְקִיָּה בְנוֹ׃ וּבְנֵי יְכָנְיָה אַסִּר שְׁאַלְתִּיאֵל בְּנוֹ׃
יח יט וּמַלְכִּירָם וּפְדָיָה וְשֶׁנְאַצַּר יְקַמְיָה הוֹשָׁמָע וּנְדַבְיָה׃ וּבְנֵי פְדָיָה זְרֻבָּבֶל
כ וְשִׁמְעִי וּבֶן־זְרֻבָּבֶל מְשֻׁלָּם וַחֲנַנְיָה וּשְׁלֹמִית אֲחוֹתָם׃ וַחֲשֻׁבָה וָאֹהֶל
כא וּבֶרֶכְיָה וַחֲסַדְיָה יוּשַׁב חֶסֶד חָמֵשׁ׃ וּבֶן־חֲנַנְיָה פְּלַטְיָה וִישַׁעְיָה בְּנֵי
כב רְפָיָה בְּנֵי אַרְנָן בְּנֵי עֹבַדְיָה בְּנֵי שְׁכַנְיָה׃ וּבְנֵי שְׁכַנְיָה שְׁמַעְיָה
כג וּבְנֵי שְׁמַעְיָה חַטּוּשׁ וְיִגְאָל וּבָרִיחַ וּנְעַרְיָה וְשָׁפָט שִׁשָּׁה׃ וּבֶן־נְעַרְיָה
כד אֶלְיוֹעֵינַי וְחִזְקִיָּה וְעַזְרִיקָם שְׁלֹשָׁה׃ וּבְנֵי אֶלְיוֹעֵינַי הודיוהו וְאֶלְיָשִׁיב [הוֹדַוְיָהוּ]
ד א וּפְלָיָה וְעַקּוּב וְיוֹחָנָן וּדְלָיָה וַעֲנָנִי שִׁבְעָה׃ בְּנֵי יְהוּדָה פֶּרֶץ
ב חֶצְרוֹן וְכַרְמִי וְחוּר וְשׁוֹבָל׃ וּרְאָיָה בֶן־שׁוֹבָל הוֹלִיד אֶת־יַחַת וְיַחַת
ג הוֹלִיד אֶת־אֲחוּמַי וְאֶת־לָהַד אֵלֶּה מִשְׁפְּחוֹת הַצָּרְעָתִי׃ וְאֵלֶּה
ד אֲבִי עֵיטָם יִזְרְעֶאל וְיִשְׁמָא וְיִדְבָּשׁ וְשֵׁם אֲחוֹתָם הַצְלֶלְפּוֹנִי׃ וּפְנוּאֵל
אֲבִי גְדֹר וְעֵזֶר אֲבִי חוּשָׁה אֵלֶּה בְנֵי־חוּר בְּכוֹר אֶפְרָתָה אֲבִי בֵּית
ה ו לָחֶם׃ וּלְאַשְׁחוּר אֲבִי תְקוֹעַ הָיוּ שְׁתֵּי נָשִׁים חֶלְאָה וְנַעֲרָה׃ וַתֵּלֶד לוֹ
נַעֲרָה אֶת־אֲחֻזָּם וְאֶת־חֵפֶר וְאֶת־תֵּימְנִי וְאֶת־הָאֲחַשְׁתָּרִי אֵלֶּה בְּנֵי
ז ח נַעֲרָה׃ וּבְנֵי חֶלְאָה צֶרֶת יצחר וְאֶתְנָן׃ וְקוֹץ הוֹלִיד אֶת־עָנוּב וְאֶת־ [וְצֹחַר]
ט הַצֹּבֵבָה וּמִשְׁפְּחוֹת אֲחַרְחֵל בֶּן־הָרוּם׃ וַיְהִי יַעְבֵּץ נִכְבָּד מֵאֶחָיו וְאִמּוֹ
י קָרְאָה שְׁמוֹ יַעְבֵּץ לֵאמֹר כִּי יָלַדְתִּי בְּעֹצֶב׃ וַיִּקְרָא יַעְבֵּץ לֵאלֹהֵי [ב]
יִשְׂרָאֵל לֵאמֹר אִם־בָּרֵךְ תְּבָרְכֵנִי וְהִרְבִּיתָ אֶת־גְּבוּלִי וְהָיְתָה יָדְךָ
עִמִּי וְעָשִׂיתָ מֵּרָעָה לְבִלְתִּי עָצְבִּי וַיָּבֵא אֱלֹהִים אֶת־אֲשֶׁר
יא שָׁאָל׃ וּכְלוּב אֲחִי־שׁוּחָה הוֹלִיד אֶת־מְחִיר הוּא אֲבִי

12 Shuḥa was the father of Meḥir, who was the father of Eshton. Eshton was the
father of Beit Rafa, Pase'aḥ, and Teḥina father of Ir Naḥash; these were the
13 people of Rekha. The sons of Kenaz: Otniel and Seraya; and the
14 sons of Otniel: Ḥatat and Meonotai, who was the father of Ofra. Seraya was
the father of Yoav father of Gei Ḥarashim, called thus because they were
15 craftsmen.[7] The sons of Kalev son of Yefuneh: Iru, Ela, and Naam;
16 and the sons of Ela: Kenaz. The sons of Yehalelel: Zif, Zifa, Tireya, and Asarel.
17 The sons of Ezra: Yeter, Mered, Efer, and Yalon. She conceived Miriam,
18 Shamai, and Yishbaḥ father of Eshtemoa, while his Judahite wife bore Yered
father of Gedor, Ḥever father of Sokho, and Yekutiel father of Zanoaḥ.
These were the sons of Bitya daughter of Pharaoh, whom Mered
19 married. The sons of the Judahite wife, sister of Naḥam, were the
20 fathers of Ke'ila the Garmite and Eshtemoa the Maakhatite. The sons of
Shimon: Amnon, Rina, Ben Ḥanan, and Tilon. The sons of Yishi: Zoḥet and
21 Ben Zoḥet. The sons of Shela son of Yehuda: Er father of Lekha, Lada father
22 of Maresha, the families of the house of the linen work at Beit Ashbe'a, Yokim,
the men of Kozeva, Yoash, Saraf who married into Moav, and Yashuvi
23 Leḥem – the records are ancient. These were the potters and residents of
24 Neta'im and Gedera; they lived there with the king in his service. The
25 sons of Shimon: Nemuel, Yamin, Yariv, Zeraḥ, Sha'ul, his son Shalum, his son
26 Mibsam, and his son Mishma. The sons of Mishma: his son Ḥamuel, his son
27 Zakur, and his son Shimi. Shimi had sixteen sons and six daughters, but his
brothers did not have many children; none of their family grew as the
28, 29 Judahites did. They lived in Be'er Sheva, Molada, Ḥatzar Shual, Bilha, Etzem,
30, 31 Tolad, Betuel, Ḥorma, Tziklag, Beit Markabot, Ḥatzar Susim, Beit Biri, and
32 Shaarayim. These were their towns until David's reign, along with their
33 villages: Eitam, Ayin, Rimon, Tokhen, and Ashan – five towns along with all
their settlements that surrounded these towns as far as Baal. These were their
34 abodes, and they kept genealogical records: Meshovav, Yamlekh, Yosha son
35 of Amatzya, and Yoel, and Yehu son of Yoshivya son of Seraya son of Asiel.
36 37 Elyo'einai, Yaakova, Yeshoḥaya, Asaya, Adiel, Yesimiel, Benaya, and Ziza son
38 of Shifri son of Alon son of Yedaya son of Shimri son of Shemaya. These, listed
by name, were the leaders of their clans, and their ancestral houses spread far
39 and wide. They journeyed to the entrance of Gedor and up to the eastern side
40 of the valley in search of pastureland for their flock. They found good, rich
pasture; the land was vast, calm, and tranquil, for the previous dwellers were
41 from Ḥam. Those recorded by name arrived in King Yeḥizkiyahu's time. They
attacked their tents and the Meunites who were found there; they utterly
destroyed them – to this day – and settled in their place, for there was
42 pastureland for their flock there. Some of them, of the Simeonites, journeyed
to the mountains of Se'ir – five hundred men with Pelatya, Ne'arya, Refaya,

7 | *Ḥarashim* is Hebrew for "craftsmen."

יב אֶשְׁתּוֹן: וְאֶשְׁתּוֹן הוֹלִיד אֶת־בֵּית רָפָא וְאֶת־פָּסֵחַ וְאֶת־תְּחִנָּה אֲבִי
יג עִיר־נָחָשׁ אֵלֶּה אַנְשֵׁי רֵכָה: וּבְנֵי קְנַז עָתְנִיאֵל וּשְׂרָיָה וּבְנֵי
יד עָתְנִיאֵל חֲתַת: וּמְעוֹנֹתַי הוֹלִיד אֶת־עָפְרָה וּשְׂרָיָה הוֹלִיד אֶת־יוֹאָב
טו אֲבִי גֵּיא חֲרָשִׁים כִּי חֲרָשִׁים הָיוּ: וּבְנֵי כָּלֵב בֶּן־יְפֻנֶּה עִירוּ
טז אֵלָה וָנָעַם וּבְנֵי אֵלָה וּקְנַז: וּבְנֵי יְהַלֶּלְאֵל זִיף וְזִיפָה תִּירְיָא וַאֲשַׂרְאֵל:
יז וּבֶן־עֶזְרָה יֶתֶר וּמֶרֶד וְעֵפֶר וְיָלוֹן וַתַּהַר אֶת־מִרְיָם וְאֶת־שַׁמַּי וְאֶת־
יח יִשְׁבָּח אֲבִי אֶשְׁתְּמֹעַ: וְאִשְׁתּוֹ הַיְהֻדִיָּה יָלְדָה אֶת־יֶרֶד אֲבִי גְדוֹר
וְאֶת־חֶבֶר אֲבִי שׂוֹכוֹ וְאֶת־יְקוּתִיאֵל אֲבִי זָנוֹחַ וְאֵלֶּה בְּנֵי בִּתְיָה בַת־
יט פַּרְעֹה אֲשֶׁר לָקַח מָרֶד: וּבְנֵי אֵשֶׁת הוֹדִיָּה אֲחוֹת נַחַם אֲבִי
כ קְעִילָה הַגַּרְמִי וְאֶשְׁתְּמֹעַ הַמַּעֲכָתִי: וּבְנֵי שִׁימוֹן אַמְנוֹן וְרִנָּה בֶּן־חָנָן
כא ותולון וּבְנֵי יִשְׁעִי זוֹחֵת וּבֶן־זוֹחֵת: בְּנֵי שֵׁלָה בֶן־יְהוּדָה עֵר אֲבִי לֵכָה וְתִילוֹן
כב וְלַעְדָּה אֲבִי מָרֵשָׁה וּמִשְׁפְּחוֹת בֵּית־עֲבֹדַת הַבֻּץ לְבֵית אַשְׁבֵּעַ: וְיוֹקִים
וְאַנְשֵׁי כֹזֵבָא וְיוֹאָשׁ וְשָׂרָף אֲשֶׁר־בָּעֲלוּ לְמוֹאָב וְיָשֻׁבִי לָחֶם וְהַדְּבָרִים
כג עַתִּיקִים: הֵמָּה הַיּוֹצְרִים וְיֹשְׁבֵי נְטָעִים וּגְדֵרָה עִם־הַמֶּלֶךְ בִּמְלַאכְתּוֹ
כד יָשְׁבוּ שָׁם: בְּנֵי שִׁמְעוֹן נְמוּאֵל וְיָמִין יָרִיב זֶרַח שָׁאוּל:
כה כו שַׁלֻּם בְּנוֹ מִבְשָׂם בְּנוֹ מִשְׁמָע בְּנוֹ: וּבְנֵי מִשְׁמָע חַמּוּאֵל בְּנוֹ זַכּוּר בְּנוֹ
כז שִׁמְעִי בְנוֹ: וּלְשִׁמְעִי בָּנִים שִׁשָּׁה עָשָׂר וּבָנוֹת שֵׁשׁ וּלְאֶחָיו אֵין בָּנִים
כח רַבִּים וְכֹל מִשְׁפַּחְתָּם לֹא הִרְבּוּ עַד־בְּנֵי יְהוּדָה: וַיֵּשְׁבוּ בִּבְאֵר־שֶׁבַע
כט ל וּמוֹלָדָה וַחֲצַר שׁוּעָל: וּבְבִלְהָה וּבְעֶצֶם וּבְתוֹלָד: וּבִבְתוּאֵל וּבְחָרְמָה
לא וּבְצִיקְלַג: וּבְבֵית מַרְכָּבוֹת וּבַחֲצַר סוּסִים וּבְבֵית בִּרְאִי וּבְשַׁעֲרָיִם אֵלֶּה
לב עָרֵיהֶם עַד־מְלֹךְ דָּוִיד: וְחַצְרֵיהֶם עֵיטָם וָעַיִן רִמּוֹן וְתֹכֶן וְעָשָׁן עָרִים
לג חָמֵשׁ: וְכָל־חַצְרֵיהֶם אֲשֶׁר סְבִיבוֹת הֶעָרִים הָאֵלֶּה עַד־בָּעַל זֹאת
לד לה מוֹשְׁבֹתָם וְהִתְיַחְשָׂם לָהֶם: וּמְשׁוֹבָב וְיַמְלֵךְ וְיוֹשָׁה בֶּן־אֲמַצְיָה: וְיוֹאֵל
לו וְיֵהוּא בֶּן־יוֹשִׁבְיָה בֶּן־שְׂרָיָה בֶּן־עֲשִׂיאֵל: וְאֶלְיוֹעֵינַי וְיַעֲקֹבָה וִישׁוֹחָיָה
לז וַעֲשָׂיָה וַעֲדִיאֵל וִישִׂימִאֵל וּבְנָיָה: וְזִיזָא בֶן־שִׁפְעִי בֶן־אַלּוֹן בֶּן־יְדָיָה
לח בֶּן־שִׁמְרִי בֶּן־שְׁמַעְיָה: אֵלֶּה הַבָּאִים בְּשֵׁמוֹת נְשִׂיאִים בְּמִשְׁפְּחוֹתָם
לט וּבֵית אֲבוֹתֵיהֶם פָּרְצוּ לָרוֹב: וַיֵּלְכוּ לִמְבוֹא גְדֹר עַד לְמִזְרַח הַגָּיְא
מ לְבַקֵּשׁ מִרְעֶה לְצֹאנָם: וַיִּמְצְאוּ מִרְעֶה שָׁמֵן וָטוֹב וְהָאָרֶץ רַחֲבַת יָדַיִם
מא וְשֹׁקֶטֶת וּשְׁלֵוָה כִּי מִן־חָם הַיֹּשְׁבִים שָׁם לְפָנִים: וַיָּבֹאוּ אֵלֶּה הַכְּתוּבִים
בְּשֵׁמוֹת בִּימֵי ׀ יְחִזְקִיָּהוּ מֶלֶךְ־יְהוּדָה וַיַּכּוּ אֶת־אָהֳלֵיהֶם וְאֶת־המעינים הַמְּעוּנִים
אֲשֶׁר נִמְצְאוּ־שָׁמָּה וַיַּחֲרִימֻם עַד־הַיּוֹם הַזֶּה וַיֵּשְׁבוּ תַּחְתֵּיהֶם כִּי־מִרְעֶה
מב לְצֹאנָם שָׁם: וּמֵהֶם ׀ מִן־בְּנֵי שִׁמְעוֹן הָלְכוּ לְהַר שֵׂעִיר אֲנָשִׁים חֲמֵשׁ

43 and Uziel, sons of Yishi, at their head. They struck down the last remnant of
5 1 Amalek and settled there to this day. The sons of Reuven, the
firstborn of Yisrael – for he was Yisrael's firstborn, but when he defiled his
father's bed, his birthright was granted to the sons of Yosef son of Yisrael, and
2 he was no longer recorded as the firstborn. Though Yehuda was the most
powerful of his brothers, and a ruler came from him, the birthright belonged
3 to Yosef. The sons of Reuven the firstborn of Yisrael: Ḥanokh, Palu,
4 Ḥetzron, and Karmi. The sons of Yoel: his son Shemaya, his son Gog, his son
5 6 Shimi, his son Mikha, his son Re'aya, and his son Baal; his son Be'era, who
was exiled by King Tilegat Pilne'eser of Assyria, was the leader of the
7 Reubenites. And his kinsmen, by their families, according to their
8 genealogical records: Ye'iel the head, Zekharyahu, and Bela son of Azaz son
9 of Shema son of Yoel; he lived in Aroer up to Nevo and Baal Meon. And on
the eastern side, he lived up to the outskirts of the wilderness on this side of
10 the Euphrates, for their cattle had increased in the land of Gilad. In Sha'ul's
time, they waged war with the Hagrites, who fell by their hand, and they
11 pitched their tents all over the region to the east of Gilad. The sons
12 of Gad lived across from them in the land of the Bashan up to Salkha; Yoel
was the head and Shafam the second-in-command, with Yanai and Shafat in
13 the Bashan. Their kinsmen by their ancestral houses: Mikhael, Meshulam,
14 Sheva, Yorai, Yakan, Zia, and Ever – seven. These were the sons
of Aviḥayil son of Ḥuri son of Yaroaḥ son of Gilad son of Mikhael son of
15 Yeshishai son of Yaḥdo son of Buz; Aḥi son of Avdiel son of Guni was the
16 head of their ancestral house. They lived in Gilad in the Bashan and its
17 dependencies and in all the pasturelands of the Sharon to their limits. All
these were recorded in genealogies during the time of King Yotam of Yehuda
18 and the time of King Yorovam of Israel. The Reubenites, the Gadites,
and half the tribe of Menashe were seasoned warriors: bow drawers and
bearers of shield and sword experienced in warfare, 44,760 ready for war.
19 20 They waged war with the Hagrites: Yetur, Nafish, and Nodav. They
overpowered them, and the Hagrites and all their allies were delivered into
their hands, for they cried out to God in battle; He answered their pleas
21 because they placed their trust in Him. They captured their livestock: 50,000
22 camels, 250,000 sheep, 2,000 donkeys, and 100,000 human captives; many
had fallen slain because the war was from God, and they settled in their place
23 until the exile. The descendants of half the tribe of Menashe
lived in the region; from the Bashan up to Baal Ḥermon, Senir, and Mount
24 Ḥermon, they were numerous. These are the heads of their ancestral houses:
Efer, Yishi, Eliel, Azriel, Yirmeya, Hodavya, and Yaḥdiel, powerful men, men
25 of renown, the heads of their ancestral houses. But they broke faith
with the God of their ancestors and lusted after the gods of the people of the
26 land whom God had destroyed before them. And the God of Israel stirred

מג מֵאוֹת וּפְלַטְיָה וּנְעַרְיָה וּרְפָיָה וְעֻזִּיאֵל בְּנֵי יִשְׁעִי בְּרֹאשָׁם: וַיַּכּוּ אֶת־
ה א שְׁאֵרִית הַפְּלֵטָה לַעֲמָלֵק וַיֵּשְׁבוּ שָׁם עַד הַיּוֹם הַזֶּה: וּבְנֵי
רְאוּבֵן בְּכוֹר־יִשְׂרָאֵל כִּי הוּא הַבְּכוֹר וּבְחַלְּלוֹ יְצוּעֵי אָבִיו נִתְּנָה בְּכֹרָתוֹ
ב לִבְנֵי יוֹסֵף בֶּן־יִשְׂרָאֵל וְלֹא לְהִתְיַחֵשׂ לַבְּכֹרָה: כִּי יְהוּדָה גָּבַר בְּאֶחָיו
ג וּלְנָגִיד מִמֶּנּוּ וְהַבְּכֹרָה לְיוֹסֵף: בְּנֵי רְאוּבֵן בְּכוֹר יִשְׂרָאֵל
ד חֲנוֹךְ וּפַלּוּא חֶצְרוֹן וְכַרְמִי: בְּנֵי יוֹאֵל שְׁמַעְיָה בְנוֹ גּוֹג בְּנוֹ שִׁמְעִי בְנוֹ:
ה ו מִיכָה בְנוֹ רְאָיָה בְנוֹ בַּעַל בְּנוֹ: בְּאֵרָה בְנוֹ אֲשֶׁר הֶגְלָה תִּלְּגַת פִּלְנְאֶסֶר
ז מֶלֶךְ אַשֻּׁר הוּא נָשִׂיא לָראוּבֵנִי: וְאֶחָיו לְמִשְׁפְּחֹתָיו בְּהִתְיַחֵשׂ
ח לְתֹלְדוֹתָם הָרֹאשׁ יְעִיאֵל וּזְכַרְיָהוּ: וּבֶלַע בֶּן־עָזָז בֶּן־שֶׁמַע בֶּן־יוֹאֵל
ט הוּא יוֹשֵׁב בַּעֲרֹעֵר וְעַד־נְבוֹ וּבַעַל מְעוֹן: וְלַמִּזְרָח יָשַׁב עַד־לְבוֹא
י מִדְבָּרָה לְמִן־הַנָּהָר פְּרָת כִּי מִקְנֵיהֶם רָבוּ בְּאֶרֶץ גִּלְעָד: וּבִימֵי שָׁאוּל
עָשׂוּ מִלְחָמָה עִם־הַהַגְרִאִים וַיִּפְּלוּ בְּיָדָם וַיֵּשְׁבוּ בְּאָהֳלֵיהֶם עַל־כָּל־
יא פְּנֵי מִזְרָח לַגִּלְעָד: וּבְנֵי־גָד לְנֶגְדָּם יָשְׁבוּ בְּאֶרֶץ הַבָּשָׁן
יב יג עַד־סַלְכָה: יוֹאֵל הָרֹאשׁ וְשָׁפָם הַמִּשְׁנֶה וְיַעְנַי וְשָׁפָט בַּבָּשָׁן: וַאֲחֵיהֶם
לְבֵית אֲבוֹתֵיהֶם מִיכָאֵל וּמְשֻׁלָּם וְשֶׁבַע וְיוֹרַי וְיַעְכָּן וְזִיעַ וָעֵבֶר
יד שִׁבְעָה: אֵלֶּה ׀ בְּנֵי אֲבִיחַיִל בֶּן־חוּרִי בֶּן־יָרוֹחַ בֶּן־גִּלְעָד
טו בֶּן־מִיכָאֵל בֶּן־יְשִׁישַׁי בֶּן־יַחְדּוֹ בֶּן־בּוּז: אֲחִי בֶּן־עַבְדִּיאֵל בֶּן־גּוּנִי רֹאשׁ
טז לְבֵית אֲבוֹתָם: וַיֵּשְׁבוּ בַּגִּלְעָד בַּבָּשָׁן וּבִבְנֹתֶיהָ וּבְכָל־מִגְרְשֵׁי שָׁרוֹן
יז עַל־תּוֹצְאוֹתָם: כֻּלָּם הִתְיַחְשׂוּ בִּימֵי יוֹתָם מֶלֶךְ־יְהוּדָה וּבִימֵי יָרָבְעָם
יח מֶלֶךְ־יִשְׂרָאֵל: בְּנֵי־רְאוּבֵן וְגָדִי וַחֲצִי שֵׁבֶט־מְנַשֶּׁה מִן־בְּנֵי־
חַיִל אֲנָשִׁים נֹשְׂאֵי מָגֵן וְחֶרֶב וְדֹרְכֵי קֶשֶׁת וּלְמוּדֵי מִלְחָמָה אַרְבָּעִים
יט וְאַרְבָּעָה אֶלֶף וּשְׁבַע־מֵאוֹת וְשִׁשִּׁים יֹצְאֵי צָבָא: וַיַּעֲשׂוּ מִלְחָמָה עִם־
כ הַהַגְרִיאִים וִיטוּר וְנָפִישׁ וְנוֹדָב: וַיֵּעָזְרוּ עֲלֵיהֶם וַיִּנָּתְנוּ בְיָדָם הַהַגְרִיאִים
וְכֹל שֶׁעִמָּהֶם כִּי לֵאלֹהִים זָעֲקוּ בַּמִּלְחָמָה וְנַעְתּוֹר לָהֶם כִּי־בָטְחוּ בוֹ:
כא וַיִּשְׁבּוּ מִקְנֵיהֶם גְּמַלֵּיהֶם חֲמִשִּׁים אֶלֶף וְצֹאן מָאתַיִם וַחֲמִשִּׁים אֶלֶף
כב וַחֲמוֹרִים אַלְפָּיִם וְנֶפֶשׁ אָדָם מֵאָה אָלֶף: כִּי־חֲלָלִים רַבִּים נָפָלוּ כִּי
כג מֵהָאֱלֹהִים הַמִּלְחָמָה וַיֵּשְׁבוּ תַחְתֵּיהֶם עַד־הַגֹּלָה: וּבְנֵי
חֲצִי שֵׁבֶט מְנַשֶּׁה יָשְׁבוּ בָּאָרֶץ מִבָּשָׁן עַד־בַּעַל חֶרְמוֹן וּשְׂנִיר וְהַר־
כד חֶרְמוֹן הֵמָּה רָבוּ: וְאֵלֶּה רָאשֵׁי בֵית־אֲבוֹתָם וְעֵפֶר וְיִשְׁעִי וֶאֱלִיאֵל
וְעַזְרִיאֵל וְיִרְמְיָה וְהוֹדַוְיָה וְיַחְדִּיאֵל אֲנָשִׁים גִּבּוֹרֵי חַיִל אַנְשֵׁי שֵׁמוֹת
כה רָאשִׁים לְבֵית אֲבוֹתָם: וַיִּמְעֲלוּ בֵּאלֹהֵי אֲבֹתֵיהֶם וַיִּזְנוּ
כו אַחֲרֵי אֱלֹהֵי עַמֵּי־הָאָרֶץ אֲשֶׁר־הִשְׁמִיד אֱלֹהִים מִפְּנֵיהֶם: וַיָּעַר אֱלֹהֵי

the spirit of King Pul of Assyria – the spirit of King Tilegat Pilneser of
Assyria – and he exiled the Reubenites, the Gadites, and half the tribe of
Menashe and led them away to Ḥelaḥ, Ḥavor, Hara, and the Gozan River to
27 28 this day. The sons of Levi: Gershon, Kehat, and Merari. The sons of
29 Kehat: Amram, Yitzhar, Ḥevron, and Uziel. The children of Amram:
Aharon, Moshe, and Miriam. The sons of Aharon: Nadav, Avihu, Elazar, and
30 Itamar. Elazar was the father of Pinḥas, Pinḥas was the father of Avishua,
31 32 Avishua was the father of Buki, Buki was the father of Uzi, Uzi was the father
33 of Zeraḥya, Zeraḥya was the father of Merayot, Merayot was the father of
34 Amarya, Amarya was the father of Aḥituv, Aḥituv was the father of Tzadok,
35 Tzadok was the father of Aḥimaatz, Aḥimaatz was the father of Azarya, Azarya
36 was the father of Yoḥanan, and Yoḥanan was the father of Azarya – he was
the one who served as priest in the House that Shlomo built in Jerusalem.
37 38 Azarya fathered Amarya, Amarya was the father of Aḥituv, Aḥituv was the
39 father of Tzadok, Tzadok was the father of Shalum, Shalum was the father of
40 Ḥilkiya, Ḥilkiya was the father of Azarya, Azarya was the father of Seraya,
41 and Seraya was the father of Yehotzadak. Yehotzadak went into exile
with the Lord's exile of Yehuda and Jerusalem at the hand of
6 1 Nevukhadnetzar. The sons of Levi: Gershom, Kehat, and Merari.
2 3 These are the names of the sons of Gershom: Livni and Shimi. The sons of
4 Kehat: Amram, Yitzhar, Ḥevron, and Uziel. The sons of Merari: Maḥli and
5 Mushi. These are the families of the Levites according to their ancestors – of
6 Gershom: his son Livni, his son Yaḥat, his son Zima, his son Yoaḥ, his son
7 Ido, his son Zeraḥ, and his son Ye'aterai. The sons of Kehat: his son Aminadav,
8 9 his son Koraḥ, his son Asir, his son Elkana, his son Evyasaf, his son Asir, his
10 son Taḥat, his son Uriel, his son Uziya, and his son Sha'ul. The sons of Elkana:
11 12 Amasai and Aḥimot, his son Elkana, his son Tzofai, his son Naḥat, his son
13 Eliav, his son Yeroḥam, and his son Elkana. The sons of Shmuel: his firstborn
14 Vashni and Aviya. The son of Merari: Maḥli, his son Livni, his son Shimi, his
15 16 son Uza, his son Shima, his son Ḥagiya, and his son Asaya. These are the ones
whom David appointed over the singing in the House of the Lord once the
17 Ark came to rest. They served with song in the Tabernacle of the Tent of
Meeting until Shlomo built the House of the Lord in Jerusalem; they
18 performed their service as they were bid. These are the men who performed
along with their sons: the Kehatites, Heiman the singer son of Yoel son of
19 20 Shmuel son of Elkana son of Yeroḥam son of Eliel son of Toaḥ son of Tzuf
21 son of Elkana son of Maḥat son of Amasai son of Elkana son of Yoel son of
22 Azarya son of Tzefanya son of Taḥat son of Asir son of Evyasaf son of Koraḥ
23 24 son of Yitzhar son of Kehat son of Levi son of Yisrael; his kinsman Asaf,
25 who stood on his right, that is, Asaf son of Berekhyahu son of Shima son of

יִשְׂרָאֵל אֶת־רוּחַ ׀ פּוּל מֶלֶךְ־אַשּׁוּר וְאֶת־רוּחַ תִּלְּגַת פִּלְנֶסֶר מֶלֶךְ
אַשּׁוּר וַיַּגְלֵם לָרְאוּבֵנִי וְלַגָּדִי וְלַחֲצִי שֵׁבֶט מְנַשֶּׁה וַיְבִיאֵם לַחְלַח וְחָבוֹר
כז וְהָרָא וּנְהַר גּוֹזָן עַד הַיּוֹם הַזֶּה׃ בְּנֵי לֵוִי גֵּרְשׁוֹן קְהָת וּמְרָרִי׃
כח כט וּבְנֵי קְהָת עַמְרָם יִצְהָר וְחֶבְרוֹן וְעֻזִּיאֵל׃ וּבְנֵי עַמְרָם אַהֲרֹן
ל וּמֹשֶׁה וּמִרְיָם וּבְנֵי אַהֲרֹן נָדָב וַאֲבִיהוּא אֶלְעָזָר וְאִיתָמָר׃ אֶלְעָזָר
לא הוֹלִיד אֶת־פִּינְחָס פִּינְחָס הֹלִיד אֶת־אֲבִישׁוּעַ׃ וַאֲבִישׁוּעַ הוֹלִיד
לב אֶת־בֻּקִּי וּבֻקִּי הוֹלִיד אֶת־עֻזִּי׃ וְעֻזִּי הוֹלִיד אֶת־זְרַחְיָה וּזְרַחְיָה הוֹלִיד
לג אֶת־מְרָיוֹת׃ מְרָיוֹת הוֹלִיד אֶת־אֲמַרְיָה וַאֲמַרְיָה הוֹלִיד אֶת־אֲחִיטוּב׃
לד לה וַאֲחִיטוּב הוֹלִיד אֶת־צָדוֹק וְצָדוֹק הוֹלִיד אֶת־אֲחִימָעַץ׃ וַאֲחִימַעַץ
לו הוֹלִיד אֶת־עֲזַרְיָה וַעֲזַרְיָה הוֹלִיד אֶת־יוֹחָנָן׃ וְיוֹחָנָן הוֹלִיד אֶת־עֲזַרְיָה
לז הוּא אֲשֶׁר כִּהֵן בַּבַּיִת אֲשֶׁר־בָּנָה שְׁלֹמֹה בִּירוּשָׁלִָם׃ וַיּוֹלֶד עֲזַרְיָה
לח אֶת־אֲמַרְיָה וַאֲמַרְיָה הוֹלִיד אֶת־אֲחִיטוּב׃ וַאֲחִיטוּב הוֹלִיד
לט אֶת־צָדוֹק וְצָדוֹק הוֹלִיד אֶת־שַׁלּוּם׃ וְשַׁלּוּם הוֹלִיד אֶת־חִלְקִיָּה
מ וְחִלְקִיָּה הוֹלִיד אֶת־עֲזַרְיָה׃ וַעֲזַרְיָה הוֹלִיד אֶת־שְׂרָיָה וּשְׂרָיָה הוֹלִיד
מא אֶת־יְהוֹצָדָק׃ וִיהוֹצָדָק הָלַךְ בְּהַגְלוֹת יְהוָה אֶת־יְהוּדָה וִירוּשָׁלִַם בְּיַד
ו א ב נְבֻכַדְנֶאצַּר׃ בְּנֵי לֵוִי גֵּרְשֹׁם קְהָת וּמְרָרִי׃ וְאֵלֶּה שְׁמוֹת
ג בְּנֵי־גֵרְשׁוֹם לִבְנִי וְשִׁמְעִי׃ וּבְנֵי קְהָת עַמְרָם וְיִצְהָר וְחֶבְרוֹן וְעֻזִּיאֵל׃
ד ה בְּנֵי מְרָרִי מַחְלִי וּמֻשִׁי וְאֵלֶּה מִשְׁפְּחוֹת הַלֵּוִי לַאֲבֹתֵיהֶם׃ לְגֵרְשׁוֹם
ו לִבְנִי בְנוֹ יַחַת בְּנוֹ זִמָּה בְנוֹ׃ יוֹאָח בְּנוֹ עִדּוֹ בְנוֹ זֶרַח בְּנוֹ יְאָתְרַי בְּנוֹ׃
ז ח בְּנֵי קְהָת עַמִּינָדָב בְּנוֹ קֹרַח בְּנוֹ אַסִּיר בְּנוֹ׃ אֶלְקָנָה בְנוֹ וְאֶבְיָסָף בְּנוֹ
ט י וְאַסִּיר בְּנוֹ׃ תַּחַת בְּנוֹ אוּרִיאֵל בְּנוֹ עֻזִּיָּה בְנוֹ וְשָׁאוּל בְּנוֹ׃ וּבְנֵי אֶלְקָנָה
יא יב עֲמָשַׂי וַאֲחִימוֹת׃ אֶלְקָנָה בְּנוֹ אֶלְקָנָה צוֹפַי בְּנוֹ וְנַחַת בְּנוֹ׃ אֱלִיאָב בְּנֵי
יג יד בְּנוֹ יְרֹחָם בְּנוֹ אֶלְקָנָה בְנוֹ׃ וּבְנֵי שְׁמוּאֵל הַבְּכֹר וַשְׁנִי וַאֲבִיָּה׃ בְּנֵי מְרָרִי
טו מַחְלִי לִבְנִי בְנוֹ שִׁמְעִי בְנוֹ עֻזָּה בְנוֹ׃ שִׁמְעָא בְנוֹ חַגִּיָּה בְנוֹ עֲשָׂיָה בְנוֹ׃
טז וְאֵלֶּה אֲשֶׁר הֶעֱמִיד דָּוִיד עַל־יְדֵי־שִׁיר בֵּית יְהוָה מִמְּנוֹחַ הָאָרוֹן׃
יז וַיִּהְיוּ מְשָׁרְתִים לִפְנֵי מִשְׁכַּן אֹהֶל־מוֹעֵד בַּשִּׁיר עַד־בְּנוֹת שְׁלֹמֹה אֶת־
יח בֵּית יְהוָה בִּירוּשָׁלִָם וַיַּעַמְדוּ כְמִשְׁפָּטָם עַל־עֲבוֹדָתָם׃ וְאֵלֶּה הָעֹמְדִים
יט וּבְנֵיהֶם מִבְּנֵי הַקְּהָתִי הֵימָן הַמְשׁוֹרֵר בֶּן־יוֹאֵל בֶּן־שְׁמוּאֵל׃ בֶּן־אֶלְקָנָה
כ בֶּן־יְרֹחָם בֶּן־אֱלִיאֵל בֶּן־תּוֹחַ׃ בֶּן־צִיף בֶּן־אֶלְקָנָה בֶּן־מַחַת בֶּן־עֲמָשָׂי׃ צוּף
כא כב בֶּן־אֶלְקָנָה בֶּן־יוֹאֵל בֶּן־עֲזַרְיָה בֶּן־צְפַנְיָה׃ בֶּן־תַּחַת בֶּן־אַסִּיר בֶּן־
כג כד אֶבְיָסָף בֶּן־קֹרַח׃ בֶּן־יִצְהָר בֶּן־קְהָת בֶּן־לֵוִי בֶּן־יִשְׂרָאֵל׃ וְאָחִיו אָסָף
כה הָעֹמֵד עַל־יְמִינוֹ אָסָף בֶּן־בֶּרֶכְיָהוּ בֶּן־שִׁמְעָא׃ בֶּן־מִיכָאֵל בֶּן־בַּעֲשֵׂיָה

26 Mikhael son of Baaseya son of Malkiya son of Etni son of Zeraḥ son of Adaya
27 28 son of Eitan son of Zima son of Shimi son of Yaḥat son of Gershom son of
29 Levi; with their kinsmen, the sons of Merari, on the left: Eitan
30 son of Kishi son of Avdi son of Malukh son of Ḥashavya, son of Amatzya son
31 32 of Ḥilkiya son of Amtzi son of Bani son of Shemer son of Maḥli son of Mushi
33 son of Merari son of Levi. Their kinsmen, the Levites, were on
34 duty for all the service of the Tabernacle of the House of God. Aharon and
his sons made offerings on the altar of burnt offerings and on the incense altar,
performing all the work of the Holy of Holies and atoning for Israel according
35 to all that Moshe, God's servant, had commanded. These are the
36 sons of Aharon: his son Elazar, his son Pinḥas, his son Avishua, his son Buki,
37 his son Uzi, his son Zeraḥya, his son Merayot, his son Amarya, his son Aḥituv,
38 39 his son Tzadok, and his son Aḥimaatz. These are their dwelling
places throughout their encampments within their borders: to the sons of
40 Aharon of the families of Kehatites, for the lot fell to them, they assigned
41 Ḥevron in the land of Yehuda and its surrounding pasturelands, but
they assigned the fields of the city and its villages to Kalev son of
42 Yefuneh. To the sons of Aharon they gave the cities of refuge:
Ḥevron, Livna with its pasturelands, Yatir, Eshtemoa with its pasturelands,
43 44 Ḥilez with its pasturelands, Devir with its pasturelands, Ashan with its
45 pasturelands, and Beit Shemesh with its pasturelands. From the tribe of
Binyamin: Geva with its pasturelands, Alemet with its pasture-lands,
and Anatot with its pasturelands; in all, thirteen cities for their
46 families. To the remaining families of Kehatites of the tribe, ten
47 cities were assigned by lot to half the tribe of Menashe. To the
Gershomites according to their families from the tribe of Yissakhar, the tribe
of Asher, the tribe of Naftali, and the tribe of Menashe in the Bashan – thirteen
48 cities. To the Merarites according to their families from the tribe
of Reuven, the tribe of Gad, and the tribe of Zevulun, twelve cities
49 were assigned by lot. The Israelites gave the Levites cities and their
50 pasturelands. They assigned by lot these cities, mentioned by name,
to the tribe of the Judahites, the tribe of the Simeonites, and the tribe of the
51 Benjaminites. Some of the Kehatite families had the cities of their
52 territory from the tribe of Efrayim. They gave them the cities of refuge:
Shekhem with its pasturelands in the hill country of Efrayim, Gezer with
53 its pasturelands, Yokme'am with its pasturelands, Beit Ḥoron with its
54 pasturelands, Ayalon with its pasturelands, and Gat Rimon with its
55 pasturelands. For the remaining families of Kehatites from half the
tribe of Menashe: Aner with its pasturelands and Bilam with its

כו כז בֶּן־מַלְכִּיָּה׃ בֶּן־אֶתְנִי בֶן־זֶרַח בֶּן־עֲדָיָה׃ בֶּן־אֵיתָן בֶּן־זִמָּה בֶּן־שִׁמְעִי׃
כח כט בֶּן־יַחַת בֶּן־גֵּרְשֹׁם בֶּן־לֵוִי׃ וּבְנֵי מְרָרִי אֲחֵיהֶם עַל־
ל הַשְּׂמֹאול אֵיתָן בֶּן־קִישִׁי בֶּן־עַבְדִּי בֶּן־מַלּוּךְ׃ בֶּן־חֲשַׁבְיָה בֶן־אֲמַצְיָה
לא לב בֶּן־חִלְקִיָּה׃ בֶּן־אַמְצִי בֶן־בָּנִי בֶּן־שָׁמֶר׃ בֶּן־מַחְלִי בֶּן־מוּשִׁי בֶּן־מְרָרִי
לג בֶּן־לֵוִי׃ וַאֲחֵיהֶם הַלְוִיִּם נְתוּנִים לְכָל־עֲבוֹדַת מִשְׁכַּן בֵּית
לד הָאֱלֹהִים׃ וְאַהֲרֹן וּבָנָיו מַקְטִירִים עַל־מִזְבַּח הָעוֹלָה וְעַל־מִזְבַּח ג
הַקְּטֹרֶת לְכֹל מְלֶאכֶת קֹדֶשׁ הַקֳּדָשִׁים וּלְכַפֵּר עַל־יִשְׂרָאֵל כְּכֹל אֲשֶׁר־
לה צִוָּה מֹשֶׁה עֶבֶד הָאֱלֹהִים׃ וְאֵלֶּה בְּנֵי אַהֲרֹן אֶלְעָזָר בְּנוֹ
לו לז פִּינְחָס בְּנוֹ אֲבִישׁוּעַ בְּנוֹ׃ בֻּקִּי בְנוֹ עֻזִּי בְנוֹ זְרַחְיָה בְנוֹ׃ מְרָיוֹת בְּנוֹ
לח לט אֲמַרְיָה בְנוֹ אֲחִיטוּב בְּנוֹ׃ צָדוֹק בְּנוֹ אֲחִימַעַץ בְּנוֹ׃ וְאֵלֶּה
מוֹשְׁבוֹתָם לְטִירוֹתָם בִּגְבוּלָם לִבְנֵי אַהֲרֹן לְמִשְׁפַּחַת הַקְּהָתִי כִּי
מ לָהֶם הָיָה הַגּוֹרָל׃ וַיִּתְּנוּ לָהֶם אֶת־חֶבְרוֹן בְּאֶרֶץ יְהוּדָה וְאֶת־מִגְרָשֶׁיהָ
מא סְבִיבֹתֶיהָ׃ וְאֶת־שְׂדֵה הָעִיר וְאֶת־חֲצֵרֶיהָ נָתְנוּ לְכָלֵב בֶּן־
מב יְפֻנֶּה׃ וְלִבְנֵי אַהֲרֹן נָתְנוּ אֶת־עָרֵי הַמִּקְלָט אֶת־חֶבְרוֹן
וְאֶת־לִבְנָה וְאֶת־מִגְרָשֶׁיהָ וְאֶת־יַתִּר וְאֶת־אֶשְׁתְּמֹעַ וְאֶת־מִגְרָשֶׁיהָ׃
מג מד וְאֶת־חִילֵז וְאֶת־מִגְרָשֶׁיהָ אֶת־דְּבִיר וְאֶת־מִגְרָשֶׁיהָ׃ וְאֶת־עָשָׁן וְאֶת־
מה מִגְרָשֶׁיהָ וְאֶת־בֵּית שֶׁמֶשׁ וְאֶת־מִגְרָשֶׁיהָ׃ וּמִמַּטֵּה בִנְיָמִן אֶת־גֶּבַע
וְאֶת־מִגְרָשֶׁיהָ וְאֶת־עָלֶמֶת וְאֶת־מִגְרָשֶׁיהָ וְאֶת־עֲנָתוֹת וְאֶת־מִגְרָשֶׁיהָ
מו כָּל־עָרֵיהֶם שְׁלֹשׁ־עֶשְׂרֵה עִיר בְּמִשְׁפְּחוֹתֵיהֶם׃ וְלִבְנֵי
קְהָת הַנּוֹתָרִים מִמִּשְׁפַּחַת הַמַּטֶּה מִמַּחֲצִית מַטֵּה חֲצִי מְנַשֶּׁה בַּגּוֹרָל
מז עָרִים עָשֶׂר׃ וְלִבְנֵי גֵרְשׁוֹם לְמִשְׁפְּחוֹתָם מִמַּטֵּה יִשָּׂשכָר
וּמִמַּטֵּה אָשֵׁר וּמִמַּטֵּה נַפְתָּלִי וּמִמַּטֵּה מְנַשֶּׁה בַּבָּשָׁן עָרִים שְׁלֹשׁ
מח עֶשְׂרֵה׃ לִבְנֵי מְרָרִי לְמִשְׁפְּחוֹתָם מִמַּטֵּה רְאוּבֵן וּמִמַּטֵּה־
מט גָד וּמִמַּטֵּה זְבוּלֻן בַּגּוֹרָל עָרִים שְׁתֵּים עֶשְׂרֵה׃ וַיִּתְּנוּ בְנֵי־יִשְׂרָאֵל
נ לַלְוִיִּם אֶת־הֶעָרִים וְאֶת־מִגְרְשֵׁיהֶם׃ וַיִּתְּנוּ בַגּוֹרָל מִמַּטֵּה
בְנֵי־יְהוּדָה וּמִמַּטֵּה בְנֵי־שִׁמְעוֹן וּמִמַּטֵּה בְּנֵי בִנְיָמִן אֵת הֶעָרִים הָאֵלֶּה
נא אֲשֶׁר־יִקְרְאוּ אֶתְהֶם בְּשֵׁמוֹת׃ וּמִמִּשְׁפְּחוֹת בְּנֵי קְהָת וַיְהִי
נב עָרֵי גְבוּלָם מִמַּטֵּה אֶפְרָיִם׃ וַיִּתְּנוּ לָהֶם אֶת־עָרֵי הַמִּקְלָט אֶת־שְׁכֶם
נג וְאֶת־מִגְרָשֶׁיהָ בְּהַר אֶפְרָיִם וְאֶת־גֶּזֶר וְאֶת־מִגְרָשֶׁיהָ׃ וְאֶת־יָקְמְעָם
נד וְאֶת־מִגְרָשֶׁיהָ וְאֶת־בֵּית חוֹרוֹן וְאֶת־מִגְרָשֶׁיהָ׃ וְאֶת־אַיָּלוֹן וְאֶת־
נה מִגְרָשֶׁיהָ וְאֶת־גַּת־רִמּוֹן וְאֶת־מִגְרָשֶׁיהָ׃ וּמִמַּחֲצִית מַטֵּה מְנַשֶּׁה אֶת־
עָנֵר וְאֶת־מִגְרָשֶׁיהָ וְאֶת־בִּלְעָם וְאֶת־מִגְרָשֶׁיהָ לְמִשְׁפַּחַת לִבְנֵי־

56 pasturelands. To the Gershomites from half the tribe of Menashe:
Golan in Bashan with its pasturelands and Ashtarot with its
57 pasturelands; from the tribe of Yissakhar: Kedesh with its
58 pasturelands, Dovrat with its pasturelands, Ramot with its pasturelands, and
59 Anem with its pasturelands; from the tribe of Asher: Mashal with
60 its pasturelands, Avdon with its pasturelands, Ḥukok with its pasturelands,
61 and Reḥov with its pasturelands; from the tribe of Naftali: Kedesh
in Galilee with its pasturelands, Ḥamon with its pasturelands, and Kiryatayim
62 with its pasturelands. To the remaining Merarites from the tribe of
Zevulun: Rimono with its pasturelands and Tavor with its pasturelands.
63 Beyond the Jordan at Yeriḥo, on the east side of the Jordan, from the tribe of
Reuven: Betzer in the wilderness with its pasturelands, Yahtza with its
64 pasturelands, Kedemot with its pasturelands, and Meifaat with its
65 pasturelands. From the tribe of Gad: Ramot in Gilad with its
66 pasturelands, Maḥanayim with its pasturelands, Ḥeshbon with its
7 1 pasturelands, and Yazeir with its pasturelands. The sons of Yissakhar:
2 Tola, Puah, Yashuv, and Shimron – four. The sons of Tola: Uzi, Refaya, Yeriel,
Yaḥmai, Ivsam, and Shmuel; heads of their ancestral houses of Tola, they were
powerful men in their generation. In David's time, they numbered
3 22,600. The son of Uzi: Yizraḥya. The sons of Yizraḥya: Mikhael,
4 Ovadya, Yoel, and Yishiya – five, all of them heads. And with them by their
generations, according to their ancestral houses, were military battle
5 units – 36,000, for they had many wives and sons. Their kinsmen, belonging
to all the families of Yissakhar, powerful warriors, were 87,000 in all according
6 to their genealogical record. Binyamin: Bela, Bekher, and
7 Yediael – three. The sons of Bela: Etzbon, Uzi, Uziel, Yerimot, and Iri – five,
heads of ancestral houses, powerful warriors; according to the genealogical
8 records, they were 22,034. The sons of Bekher: Zemira, Yoash,
Eliezer, Elyo'einai, Omri, Yeremot, Aviya, Anatot, and Alemet; all these were
9 the sons of Bekher. According to their genealogical record by their
generations, heads of their ancestral houses, powerful warriors, they were
10 20,200. The son of Yediael: Bilhan; the sons of Bilhan: Yeush,
11 Binyamin, Ehud, Kenaana, Zeitan, Tarshish, and Aḥishaḥar. All these were
the sons of Yediael, heads of the fathers, seasoned warriors, a force of 17,200
12 ready for war. Shupim and Ḥupim were the sons of Ir; Ḥushim the son of
13 Aḥer. The sons of Naftali: Yaḥatziel, Guni, Yetzer, and Shalum, the
14 descendants of Bilha. The sons of Menashe: Asriel, whom his

נו קְהָת הַנּוֹתָרִים׃ לִבְנֵי גֵּרְשׁוֹם מִמִּשְׁפַּחַת חֲצִי מַטֵּה
מְנַשֶּׁה אֶת־גּוֹלָן בַּבָּשָׁן וְאֶת־מִגְרָשֶׁהָ וְאֶת־עַשְׁתָּרוֹת וְאֶת־
נז מִגְרָשֶׁיהָ׃ וּמִמַּטֵּה יִשָּׂשכָר אֶת־קֶדֶשׁ וְאֶת־מִגְרָשֶׁהָ
נח אֶת־דָּבְרַת וְאֶת־מִגְרָשֶׁהָ׃ וְאֶת־רָאמוֹת וְאֶת־מִגְרָשֶׁהָ וְאֶת־עָנֵם
נט וְאֶת־מִגְרָשֶׁהָ׃ וּמִמַּטֵּה אָשֵׁר אֶת־מָשָׁל וְאֶת־מִגְרָשֶׁהָ
ס וְאֶת־עַבְדּוֹן וְאֶת־מִגְרָשֶׁהָ׃ וְאֶת־חוּקֹק וְאֶת־מִגְרָשֶׁהָ וְאֶת־רְחֹב
סא וְאֶת־מִגְרָשֶׁהָ׃ וּמִמַּטֵּה נַפְתָּלִי אֶת־קֶדֶשׁ בַּגָּלִיל
וְאֶת־מִגְרָשֶׁהָ וְאֶת־חַמּוֹן וְאֶת־מִגְרָשֶׁהָ וְאֶת־קִרְיָתַיִם וְאֶת־
סב מִגְרָשֶׁהָ׃ לִבְנֵי מְרָרִי הַנּוֹתָרִים מִמַּטֵּה זְבוּלֻן אֶת־רִמּוֹנוֹ
סג וְאֶת־מִגְרָשֶׁהָ אֶת־תָּבוֹר וְאֶת־מִגְרָשֶׁהָ׃ וּמֵעֵבֶר לְיַרְדֵּן יְרֵחוֹ לְמִזְרַח
הַיַּרְדֵּן מִמַּטֵּה רְאוּבֵן אֶת־בֶּצֶר בַּמִּדְבָּר וְאֶת־מִגְרָשֶׁהָ וְאֶת־יַהְצָה
סד וְאֶת־מִגְרָשֶׁהָ׃ וְאֶת־קְדֵמוֹת וְאֶת־מִגְרָשֶׁהָ וְאֶת־מֵיפַעַת וְאֶת־
סה מִגְרָשֶׁהָ׃ וּמִמַּטֵּה־גָד אֶת־רָאמוֹת בַּגִּלְעָד וְאֶת־מִגְרָשֶׁהָ
סו וְאֶת־מַחֲנַיִם וְאֶת־מִגְרָשֶׁהָ׃ וְאֶת־חֶשְׁבּוֹן וְאֶת־מִגְרָשֶׁהָ וְאֶת־יַעְזֵיר
ז א וְאֶת־מִגְרָשֶׁהָ׃ וְלִבְנֵי יִשָּׂשכָר תּוֹלָע וּפוּאָה ישיב וְשִׁמְרוֹן יָשׁוּב
ב אַרְבָּעָה׃ וּבְנֵי תוֹלָע עֻזִּי וּרְפָיָה וִירִיאֵל וְיַחְמַי וְיִבְשָׂם וּשְׁמוּאֵל רָאשִׁים
לְבֵית־אֲבוֹתָם לְתוֹלָע גִּבּוֹרֵי חַיִל לְתֹלְדוֹתָם מִסְפָּרָם בִּימֵי דָוִיד
ג עֶשְׂרִים־וּשְׁנַיִם אֶלֶף וְשֵׁשׁ מֵאוֹת׃ וּבְנֵי עֻזִּי יִזְרַחְיָה וּבְנֵי
ד יִזְרַחְיָה מִיכָאֵל וְעֹבַדְיָה וְיוֹאֵל יִשִּׁיָּה חֲמִשָּׁה רָאשִׁים כֻּלָּם׃ וַעֲלֵיהֶם
לְתוֹלְדוֹתָם לְבֵית אֲבוֹתָם גְּדוּדֵי צְבָא מִלְחָמָה שְׁלֹשִׁים וְשִׁשָּׁה אָלֶף
ה כִּי־הִרְבּוּ נָשִׁים וּבָנִים׃ וַאֲחֵיהֶם לְכֹל מִשְׁפְּחוֹת יִשָּׂשכָר גִּבּוֹרֵי חֲיָלִים
ו שְׁמוֹנִים וְשִׁבְעָה אֶלֶף הִתְיַחְשָׂם לַכֹּל׃ בִּנְיָמִן בֶּלַע וָבֶכֶר
ז וִידִיעֲאֵל שְׁלֹשָׁה׃ וּבְנֵי בֶלַע אֶצְבּוֹן וְעֻזִּי וְעֻזִּיאֵל וִירִימוֹת וְעִירִי
חֲמִשָּׁה רָאשֵׁי בֵּית אָבוֹת גִּבּוֹרֵי חֲיָלִים וְהִתְיַחְשָׂם עֶשְׂרִים וּשְׁנַיִם
ח אֶלֶף וּשְׁלֹשִׁים וְאַרְבָּעָה׃ וּבְנֵי בֶכֶר זְמִירָה וְיוֹעָשׁ וֶאֱלִיעֶזֶר
וְאֶלְיוֹעֵינַי וְעָמְרִי וִירֵמוֹת וַאֲבִיָּה וַעֲנָתוֹת וְעָלָמֶת כָּל־אֵלֶּה בְּנֵי־בָכֶר׃
ט וְהִתְיַחְשָׂם לְתֹלְדוֹתָם רָאשֵׁי בֵּית אֲבוֹתָם גִּבּוֹרֵי חָיִל עֶשְׂרִים אֶלֶף
י וּמָאתָיִם׃ וּבְנֵי יְדִיעֲאֵל בִּלְהָן וּבְנֵי בִלְהָן יעיש וּבִנְיָמִן יְעוּשׁ
יא וְאֵהוּד וּכְנַעֲנָה וְזֵיתָן וְתַרְשִׁישׁ וַאֲחִישָׁחַר׃ כָּל־אֵלֶּה בְּנֵי יְדִיעֲאֵל
לְרָאשֵׁי הָאָבוֹת גִּבּוֹרֵי חֲיָלִים שִׁבְעָה־עָשָׂר אֶלֶף וּמָאתַיִם יֹצְאֵי צָבָא
יב יג לַמִּלְחָמָה׃ וְשֻׁפִּם וְחֻפִּם בְּנֵי עִיר חֻשִׁם בְּנֵי אַחֵר׃ בְּנֵי נַפְתָּלִי
יד יַחֲצִיאֵל וְגוּנִי וְיֵצֶר וְשַׁלּוּם בְּנֵי בִלְהָה׃ בְּנֵי מְנַשֶּׁה אַשְׂרִיאֵל

15 Aramean concubine bore; she bore Makhir the father of Gilad. And Makhir
took wives for Ḥupim and for Shupim. The name of his sister was Maakha,
16 and the name of the second was Tzelofḥad; Tzelofḥad had daughters. Maakha
the wife of Makhir bore a son, and she named him Peresh. The name of his
17 brother was Sheresh, and his sons were Ulam and Rekem. The son of Ulam:
18 Bedan. These were the sons of Gilad son of Makhir son of Menashe. His sister
19 Hamolekhet bore Ish Hod, Aviezer, and Maḥla. The sons of Shemida were
20 Aḥyan, Shekhem, Likḥi, and Aniam. The sons of Efrayim: Shutalaḥ,
21 his son Bered, his son Taḥat, his son Elada, his son Taḥat, his son Zavad, and
his son Shutelaḥ as well as Ezer and Elad; the men of Gat, who were born in
22 the land, killed them because they went down to raid their cattle. Their father
23 Efrayim mourned for a long time, and his brothers came to comfort him. He
was intimate with his wife, she conceived and bore a son, and he named him
24 Beria because evil had befallen his house.[8] His daughter was She'era, who
25 built lower and upper Beit Ḥoron and Uzen She'era. Also his son Refaḥ, his
26 sons Reshef and Telaḥ, his son Taḥan, his son Ladan, his son Amihud, his son
27 28 Elishama, his son Non, and his son Yehoshua. Their property and
settlements were Beit El and its dependencies, on the east Naaran, on the west
Gezer and its dependencies, and Shekhem and its dependencies up to Aya
29 and its dependencies. Next to the descendants of Menashe: Beit She'an
and its dependencies, Ta'nakh and its dependencies, Megiddo and its
dependencies, Dor and its dependencies; in these lived the sons of Yosef son
30 of Yisrael. The sons of Asher: Imna, Yishva, Yishvi, and Beria, and
31 Seraḥ their sister. The sons of Beria: Ḥever and Malkiel, who was the father
32 of Birzayit. Ḥever was the father of Yaflet, Shomer, and Ḥotam and their sister
33 Shua. The sons of Yaflet: Pasakh, Bimhal, and Ashvat; these were the sons of
34 35 Yaflet. The sons of Shemer: Aḥi, Roga, Ḥuba, and Aram. The sons of Helem,
36 his brother: Tzofaḥ, Imna, Shelesh, and Amal. The sons of Tzofaḥ: Suaḥ,
37 Ḥarnefer, Shual, Beri, Yimra, Betzer, Hod, Shama, Shilsha, Yitran, and Be'era.
38 39 The sons of Yeter: Yefuneh, Pispa, and Ara. The sons of Ula: Araḥ, Ḥaniel,
40 and Ritzya. All these sons of Asher were heads of the ancestral house and
elite, powerful warriors. According to their genealogical record, the number
of their fighting force was 26,000.

8 1 Binyamin was the father of Bela, his firstborn, Ashbel the second, Aḥraḥ the
2, 3 third, Noḥa the fourth, and Rafa the fifth. Bela had sons: Adar, Gera, Avihud,
4, 5, 6 Avishua, Naaman, Aḥoaḥ, Gera, Shefufan, and Ḥuram. These were the sons
of Eḥud; they were the ancestral heads of the inhabitants of Geva, and they
7 were exiled to Manaḥat: Naaman, Aḥiya, and Gera – he exiled them and was
8 the father of Uza and Aḥiḥud. Shaḥarayim was the father of children in the
9 country of Moav after he had sent away Ḥushim and Baara his wives; he

8 | "Beria" evokes the Hebrew *beraa*, "in evil."

טו אֲשֶׁר יָלָדָה פִּילַגְשׁוֹ הָאֲרַמִּיָּה יָלְדָה אֶת־מָכִיר אֲבִי גִלְעָד׃ וּמָכִיר
לָקַח אִשָּׁה לְחֻפִּים וּלְשֻׁפִּים וְשֵׁם אֲחֹתוֹ מַעֲכָה וְשֵׁם הַשֵּׁנִי צְלָפְחָד
טז וַתִּהְיֶנָה לִצְלָפְחָד בָּנוֹת׃ וַתֵּלֶד מַעֲכָה אֵשֶׁת־מָכִיר בֵּן וַתִּקְרָא שְׁמוֹ
יז פֶּרֶשׁ וְשֵׁם אָחִיו שָׁרֶשׁ וּבָנָיו אוּלָם וָרָקֶם׃ וּבְנֵי אוּלָם בְּדָן אֵלֶּה בְּנֵי
יח גִלְעָד בֶּן־מָכִיר בֶּן־מְנַשֶּׁה׃ וַאֲחֹתוֹ הַמֹּלֶכֶת יָלְדָה אֶת־אִישׁ הוֹד
יט וְאֶת־אֲבִיעֶזֶר וְאֶת־מַחְלָה׃ וַיִּהְיוּ בְּנֵי שְׁמִידָע אַחְיָן וָשֶׁכֶם וְלִקְחִי
כ וַאֲנִיעָם׃ וּבְנֵי אֶפְרַיִם שׁוּתָלַח וּבֶרֶד בְּנוֹ וְתַחַת בְּנוֹ וְאֶלְעָדָה
כא בְנוֹ וְתַחַת בְּנוֹ׃ וְזָבָד בְּנוֹ וְשׁוּתֶלַח בְּנוֹ וְעֵזֶר וְאֶלְעָד וַהֲרָגוּם אַנְשֵׁי־גַת
כב הַנּוֹלָדִים בָּאָרֶץ כִּי יָרְדוּ לָקַחַת אֶת־מִקְנֵיהֶם׃ וַיִּתְאַבֵּל אֶפְרַיִם אֲבִיהֶם
כג יָמִים רַבִּים וַיָּבֹאוּ אֶחָיו לְנַחֲמוֹ׃ וַיָּבֹא אֶל־אִשְׁתּוֹ וַתַּהַר וַתֵּלֶד בֵּן
כד וַיִּקְרָא אֶת־שְׁמוֹ בְּרִיעָה כִּי בְרָעָה הָיְתָה בְּבֵיתוֹ׃ וּבִתּוֹ שֶׁאֱרָה וַתִּבֶן
כה אֶת־בֵּית־חוֹרוֹן הַתַּחְתּוֹן וְאֶת־הָעֶלְיוֹן וְאֵת אֻזֵּן שֶׁאֱרָה׃ וְרֶפַח בְּנוֹ
כו וְרֶשֶׁף וְתֶלַח בְּנוֹ וְתַחַן בְּנוֹ׃ לַעְדָּן בְּנוֹ עַמִּיהוּד בְּנוֹ אֱלִישָׁמָע בְּנוֹ׃
כז כח נוֹן בְּנוֹ יְהוֹשֻׁעַ בְּנוֹ׃ וַאֲחֻזָּתָם וּמֹשְׁבוֹתָם בֵּית־אֵל וּבְנֹתֶיהָ
וְלַמִּזְרָח נַעֲרָן וְלַמַּעֲרָב גֶּזֶר וּבְנֹתֶיהָ וּשְׁכֶם וּבְנֹתֶיהָ עַד־עַיָּה וּבְנֹתֶיהָ׃
כט וְעַל־יְדֵי בְנֵי־מְנַשֶּׁה בֵּית־שְׁאָן וּבְנֹתֶיהָ תַּעְנַךְ וּבְנֹתֶיהָ מְגִדּוֹ וּבְנוֹתֶיהָ
ל דּוֹר וּבְנוֹתֶיהָ בְּאֵלֶּה יָשְׁבוּ בְּנֵי יוֹסֵף בֶּן־יִשְׂרָאֵל׃ בְּנֵי אָשֵׁר
לא יִמְנָה וְיִשְׁוָה וְיִשְׁוִי וּבְרִיעָה וְשֶׂרַח אֲחוֹתָם׃ וּבְנֵי בְרִיעָה חֶבֶר וּמַלְכִּיאֵל
לב הוּא אֲבִי ברזות׃ וְחֶבֶר הוֹלִיד אֶת־יַפְלֵט וְאֶת־שׁוֹמֵר וְאֶת־חוֹתָם בִּרְזָיִת
לג וְאֵת שׁוּעָא אֲחוֹתָם׃ וּבְנֵי יַפְלֵט פָּסַךְ וּבִמְהָל וְעַשְׁוָת אֵלֶּה בְּנֵי יַפְלֵט׃
לד לה וּבְנֵי שָׁמֶר אֲחִי ורוהגה יחבה וַאֲרָם׃ וּבֶן־הֵלֶם אָחִיו צוֹפַח וְיִמְנָע וְרָהְגָּה וְחֻבָּה
לו לז וְשֵׁלֶשׁ וְעָמָל׃ בְּנֵי צוֹפַח סוּחַ וְחַרְנֶפֶר וְשׁוּעָל וּבֵרִי וְיִמְרָה׃ בֶּצֶר וָהוֹד
לח לט וְשַׁמָּא וְשִׁלְשָׁה וְיִתְרָן וּבְאֵרָא׃ וּבְנֵי יֶתֶר יְפֻנֶּה וּפִסְפָּה וַאֲרָא׃ וּבְנֵי
מ עֻלָּא אָרַח וְחַנִּיאֵל וְרִצְיָא׃ כָּל־אֵלֶּה בְנֵי־אָשֵׁר רָאשֵׁי בֵית־הָאָבוֹת
בְּרוּרִים גִּבּוֹרֵי חֲיָלִים רָאשֵׁי הַנְּשִׂיאִים וְהִתְיַחְשָׂם בַּצָּבָא בַּמִּלְחָמָה
מִסְפָּרָם אֲנָשִׁים עֶשְׂרִים וְשִׁשָּׁה אָלֶף׃
ח א ב וּבִנְיָמִן הוֹלִיד אֶת־בֶּלַע בְּכֹרוֹ אַשְׁבֵּל הַשֵּׁנִי וְאַחְרַח הַשְּׁלִישִׁי׃ נוֹחָה
ג הָרְבִיעִי וְרָפָא הַחֲמִישִׁי׃ וַיִּהְיוּ בָנִים לְבֶלַע אַדָּר וְגֵרָא וַאֲבִיהוּד׃
ד ה ו וַאֲבִישׁוּעַ וְנַעֲמָן וַאֲחוֹחַ׃ וְגֵרָא וּשְׁפוּפָן וְחוּרָם׃ וְאֵלֶּה בְּנֵי אֵחוּד אֵלֶּה
ז הֵם רָאשֵׁי אָבוֹת לְיוֹשְׁבֵי גֶבַע וַיַּגְלוּם אֶל־מָנַחַת׃ וְנַעֲמָן וַאֲחִיָּה וְגֵרָא
ח הוּא הֶגְלָם וְהוֹלִיד אֶת־עֻזָּא וְאֶת־אֲחִיחֻד׃ וְשַׁחֲרַיִם הוֹלִיד בִּשְׂדֵה
ט מוֹאָב מִן־שִׁלְחוֹ אֹתָם חוּשִׁים וְאֶת־בַּעֲרָא נָשָׁיו׃ וַיּוֹלֶד מִן־חֹדֶשׁ

10 fathered sons by his wife Ḥodesh: Yovav, Tzivya, Mesha, Malkam, Yeutz,
11 Sakheya, and Mirma; these were his sons, ancestral heads. Through
12 Ḥushim, he also fathered Avituv and Elpaal. The sons of Elpaal: Ever,
13 Misham, Shemed – who built Ono and Lod with its dependencies Beriya
and Shema – they were the ancestral heads of the inhabitants of Ayalon,
14 who drove away the inhabitants of Gat – Aḥyo, Shashak, and Yeremot.
15, 16, 17 Zevadya, Arad, Eder, Mikhael, Yishpa, and Yoḥa were sons of Beria. Zevadya,
18 Meshulam, Ḥizki, Ḥever, Yishmerai, Yizlia, and Yovav were the sons of Elpaal.
19, 20, 21 Yakim, Zikhri, Zavdi, Elienai, Tziletai, Eliel, Adaya, Beraya, and Shimrat were
22, 23, 24 the sons of Shimi. Yishpan, Ever, Eliel, Avdon, Zikhri, Ḥanan, Ḥananya,
25, 26 Eilam, Antotiya, Yifdeya, and Penuel were the sons of Shashak. Shamsherai,
27 Sheḥarya, Atalya, Yaareshya, Eliya, and Zikhri were the sons of Yeroḥam.
28 These were the ancestral heads, heads of their generations; these resided
29 in Jerusalem. The father of Givon lived in Givon, and the name of
30 his wife was Maakha; his firstborn son was Avdon, then Tzur, Kish, Baal,
31 32 Nadav, Gedor, Aḥyo, and Zekher. Miklot was the father of Shima, and
they too lived in Jerusalem alongside their kinsmen, together with their
33 kinsmen.[9] Ner was the father of Kish, Kish was the father of Sha'ul,
and Sha'ul was the father of Yehonatan, Malkishua, Avinadav, and Eshbaal.
34 35 Yonatan's son was Meriv Baal, and Meriv Baal was the father of Mikha. The
36 sons of Mikha: Piton, Melekh, Taare'a, and Aḥaz. Aḥaz was the father of
Yehoada, Yehoada was the father of Alemet, Azmavet, and Zimri, and Zimri
37 was the father of Motza. Motza was the father of Bina, his son Rafa, his
38 son Elasa, and his son Atzel. Atzel had six sons, and these are their names:
Azrikam, Bokheru, Yishmael, She'arya, Ovadya, and Ḥanan; all these were
39 the sons of Atzel. The sons of his brother Eshek: his firstborn Ulam, Yeush
40 the second, and Elifelet the third. The sons of Ulam were powerful warriors
of Ulam – bow drawers and men of substance who had many children and
9 1 grandchildren – 150; all these were descendants of Binyamin. All
of Israel were registered by genealogy; they are recorded in the book of
the Kings of Israel. And Yehuda was exiled to Babylon because they broke
2 faith. The first to settle on their own holdings, in their own towns, were
3 Israel, the priests, the Levites, and the Netinim.[10] In Jerusalem resided some
4 Judahites, Benjaminites, Efraimites, and Manassites: Utai son of Amihud son
of Omri son of Imri son of Bani, of the descendants of Peretz son of Yehuda;
5 6 of the Shilonites, the firstborn Asaya and his sons; and of the descendants
7 of Zeraḥ, Yeuel and their kinsmen – 690. Of the Benjaminites: Salu son of
8 Meshulam son of Hodavya son of Hasenua, Yivneya son of Yeroḥam, Ela son
of Uzi son of Mikhri, Meshulam son of Shefatya son of Reuel son of Yivneya,

---

9 | Both the descendants of Miklot and the descendants of Yeroḥam mentioned in verses 26–28 shared Jerusalem with their kinsmen from other tribes; cf. 9:3.

10 | A group of servants in the Temple, apparently of non-Jewish extraction, whose origins are not fully known.

י אִשְׁתּוֹ אֶת־יוֹבָב וְאֶת־צִבְיָא וְאֶת־מֵישָׁא וְאֶת־מַלְכָּם: וְאֶת־יְעוּץ
יא וְאֶת־שָׂכְיָה וְאֶת־מִרְמָה אֵלֶּה בָנָיו רָאשֵׁי אָבוֹת: וּמֵחֻשִׁים הוֹלִיד
יב אֶת־אֲבִיטוּב וְאֶת־אֶלְפָּעַל: וּבְנֵי אֶלְפַּעַל עֵבֶר וּמִשְׁעָם וָשָׁמֶד הוּא
יג בָּנָה אֶת־אוֹנוֹ וְאֶת־לֹד וּבְנֹתֶיהָ: וּבְרִעָה וָשֶׁמַע הֵמָּה רָאשֵׁי הָאָבוֹת
יד לְיוֹשְׁבֵי אַיָּלוֹן הֵמָּה הִבְרִיחוּ אֶת־יוֹשְׁבֵי גַת: וְאַחְיוֹ שָׁשַׁק וִירֵמוֹת:
טו טז יז וּזְבַדְיָה וַעֲרָד וָעָדֶר: וּמִיכָאֵל וְיִשְׁפָּה וְיוֹחָא בְּנֵי בְרִיעָה: וּזְבַדְיָה
יח יט וּמְשֻׁלָּם וְחִזְקִי וָחָבֶר: וְיִשְׁמְרַי וְיִזְלִיאָה וְיוֹבָב בְּנֵי אֶלְפָּעַל: וְיָקִים וְזִכְרִי
כ כא וְזַבְדִּי: וֶאֱלִיעֵינַי וְצִלְּתַי וֶאֱלִיאֵל: וַעֲדָיָה וּבְרָאיָה וְשִׁמְרָת בְּנֵי שִׁמְעִי:
כב כג כד וְיִשְׁפָּן וָעֵבֶר וֶאֱלִיאֵל: וְעַבְדּוֹן וְזִכְרִי וְחָנָן: וַחֲנַנְיָה וְעֵילָם וְעַנְתֹתִיָּה:
כה כו כז וְיִפְדְיָה ופניאל בְּנֵי שָׁשָׁק: וְשַׁמְשְׁרַי וּשְׁחַרְיָה וַעֲתַלְיָה: וְיַעֲרֶשְׁיָה וּפְנוּאֵל
כח וְאֵלִיָּה וְזִכְרִי בְּנֵי יְרֹחָם: אֵלֶּה רָאשֵׁי אָבוֹת לְתֹלְדוֹתָם רָאשִׁים אֵלֶּה
כט יָשְׁבוּ בִירוּשָׁלָם: וּבְגִבְעוֹן יָשְׁבוּ אֲבִי גִבְעוֹן וְשֵׁם אִשְׁתּוֹ
ל לא מַעֲכָה: וּבְנוֹ הַבְּכוֹר עַבְדּוֹן וְצוּר וְקִישׁ וּבַעַל וְנָדָב: וּגְדוֹר וְאַחְיוֹ וָזָכֶר:
לב וּמִקְלוֹת הוֹלִיד אֶת־שִׁמְאָה וְאַף־הֵמָּה נֶגֶד אֲחֵיהֶם יָשְׁבוּ בִירוּשָׁלַם
לג עִם־אֲחֵיהֶם: וְנֵר הוֹלִיד אֶת־קִישׁ וְקִישׁ הוֹלִיד אֶת־
שָׁאוּל וְשָׁאוּל הוֹלִיד אֶת־יְהוֹנָתָן וְאֶת־מַלְכִּי־שׁוּעַ וְאֶת־אֲבִינָדָב וְאֶת־
לד לה אֶשְׁבָּעַל: וּבֶן־יְהוֹנָתָן מְרִיב בָּעַל וּמְרִי בַעַל הוֹלִיד אֶת־מִיכָה: וּבְנֵי
לו מִיכָה פִּיתוֹן וָמֶלֶךְ וְתַאְרֵעַ וְאָחָז: וְאָחָז הוֹלִיד אֶת־יְהוֹעַדָּה וִיהוֹעַדָּה
הוֹלִיד אֶת־עָלֶמֶת וְאֶת־עַזְמָוֶת וְאֶת־זִמְרִי וְזִמְרִי הוֹלִיד אֶת־מוֹצָא:
לז לח וּמוֹצָא הוֹלִיד אֶת־בִּנְעָא רָפָה בְנוֹ אֶלְעָשָׂה בְנוֹ אָצֵל בְּנוֹ: וּלְאָצֵל
שִׁשָּׁה בָנִים וְאֵלֶּה שְׁמוֹתָם עַזְרִיקָם ׀ בֹּכְרוּ וְיִשְׁמָעֵאל וּשְׁעַרְיָה
לט וְעֹבַדְיָה וְחָנָן כָּל־אֵלֶּה בְּנֵי אָצֵל: וּבְנֵי עֵשֶׁק אָחִיו אוּלָם בְּכֹרוֹ
מ יְעוּשׁ הַשֵּׁנִי וֶאֱלִיפֶלֶט הַשְּׁלִשִׁי: וַיִּהְיוּ בְנֵי־אוּלָם אֲנָשִׁים גִּבֹּרֵי־חַיִל ד
דֹּרְכֵי קֶשֶׁת וּמַרְבִּים בָּנִים וּבְנֵי בָנִים מֵאָה וַחֲמִשִּׁים כָּל־אֵלֶּה מִבְּנֵי
ט א בִנְיָמִן: וְכָל־יִשְׂרָאֵל הִתְיַחְשׂוּ וְהִנָּם כְּתוּבִים עַל־סֵפֶר מַלְכֵי
ב יִשְׂרָאֵל וִיהוּדָה הָגְלוּ לְבָבֶל בְּמַעֲלָם: וְהַיּוֹשְׁבִים הָרִאשֹׁנִים אֲשֶׁר
ג בַּאֲחֻזָּתָם בְּעָרֵיהֶם יִשְׂרָאֵל הַכֹּהֲנִים הַלְוִיִּם וְהַנְּתִינִים: וּבִירוּשָׁלִַם
ד יָשְׁבוּ מִן־בְּנֵי יְהוּדָה וּמִן־בְּנֵי בִנְיָמִן וּמִן־בְּנֵי אֶפְרַיִם וּמְנַשֶּׁה: עוּתַי
ה בֶּן־עַמִּיהוּד בֶּן־עָמְרִי בֶּן־אִמְרִי בֶן־בנימן־בְּנֵי־פֶרֶץ בֶּן־יְהוּדָה: וּמִן־ בְּנֵי מִן־
ו הַשִּׁילוֹנִי עֲשָׂיָה הַבְּכוֹר וּבָנָיו: וּמִן־בְּנֵי זֶרַח יְעוּאֵל וַאֲחֵיהֶם שֵׁשׁ־מֵאוֹת
ז וְתִשְׁעִים: וּמִן־בְּנֵי בִּנְיָמִן סַלּוּא בֶּן־מְשֻׁלָּם בֶּן־הוֹדַוְיָה בֶּן־הַסְּנֻאָה:
ח וְיִבְנְיָה בֶּן־יְרֹחָם וְאֵלָה בֶן־עֻזִּי בֶּן־מִכְרִי וּמְשֻׁלָּם בֶּן־שְׁפַטְיָה בֶּן־

9 and their kinsmen by their generations – 956. All these men were heads of
10 their ancestral houses. Of the priests: Yedaya, Yehoyariv, Yakhin,
11 Azarya son of Ḥilkiya son of Meshulam son of Tzadok son of Merayot son
12 of Aḥituv in charge of the House of God; Adaya son of Yeroḥam
son of Pashḥur son of Malkiya, and Maasai son of Adiel son of Yaḥzera son
13 of Meshulam son of Meshilemit son of Imer, together with their kinsmen,
heads of their ancestral houses – 1,760 powerful men for the work of the
14 service of the House of God. Of the Levites: Shemaya son of Ḥashuv son of
15 Azrikam son of Ḥashavya; of the descendants of Merari, Bakbakar, Ḥeresh,
16 Galal, and Matanya son of Mikha son of Zikhri son of Asaf, Ovadya son of
Shemaya son of Galal son of Yedutun, and Berekhya son of Asa son of Elkana,
17 who lived in the villages of the Netofatites. And the gatekeepers: Shalum,
18 Akub, Talmon, and Aḥiman, and their kinsman Shalum was the head; they
had previously been stationed at the king's gate toward the east – these were
19 the gatekeepers of the Levite camp. Shalum son of Koreh son of Evyasaf son
of Koraḥ and his kinsmen of the Korahite ancestral house were in charge
of the work of the service, keepers of the Tent threshold. Their ancestors
20 had been in charge of the Tent of the Lord, keepers of the entrance. Pinḥas
son of Elazar had been their ruler in times past; the Lord was with him.
21 Zekharya son of Meshelemya was the gatekeeper of the entrance to the
22 Tent of Meeting. In all, 212 were selected to be gatekeepers of the threshold;
they were listed by genealogy in their villages. David and Shmuel the seer
23 had established them in permanent office, and they and their descendants
guarded the gates of the House of the Lord and of the House of the Tent;
24 25 the gatekeepers stood at all four sides: east, west, north, and south. Their
kin from their villages were to come in every seven days to be with them in
26 turn, for the four chief gatekeepers – who were Levites – were on permanent
duty; they were in charge of the chambers and the treasuries of the House
27 of God. They lodged near the House of God, for they were responsible for
28 guard duty and for unlocking it every morning. Some of them were in charge
of the service vessels, of bringing in a certain number and bringing out a
29 certain number; some of them were in charge of the vessels, including all the
sacred vessels, and of the fine flour, the wine, the oil, the frankincense, and
30 31 the spices. Some of the priests prepared mixtures of the spices. Matitya of
the Levites, the firstborn of Shalum the Korahite, was in permanent charge
32 of the pan-bread preparation while some of their Kehatite kinsmen were in
33 charge of the showbread, making them every Sabbath. Then there
were the singers, the ancestral heads of the Levites; they lived in the chambers
34 exempt from other duties because they worked day and night. These were the
ancestral heads of the Levites according to their generations; these resided
in Jerusalem.

ט רְעוּאֵל בֶּן־יִבְנִיָּה: וַאֲחֵיהֶם לְתֹלְדוֹתָם תְּשַׁע מֵאוֹת וַחֲמִשִּׁים וְשִׁשָּׁה
י כָּל־אֵלֶּה אֲנָשִׁים רָאשֵׁי אָבוֹת לְבֵית אֲבֹתֵיהֶם: וּמִן־
יא הַכֹּהֲנִים יְדַעְיָה וִיהוֹיָרִיב וְיָכִין: וַעֲזַרְיָה בֶּן־חִלְקִיָּה בֶּן־מְשֻׁלָּם בֶּן־
יב צָדוֹק בֶּן־מְרָיוֹת בֶּן־אֲחִיטוּב נְגִיד בֵּית הָאֱלֹהִים: וַעֲדָיָה
בֶּן־יְרֹחָם בֶּן־פַּשְׁחוּר בֶּן־מַלְכִּיָּה וּמַעְשַׂי בֶּן־עֲדִיאֵל בֶּן־יַחְזֵרָה בֶּן־
יג מְשֻׁלָּם בֶּן־מְשִׁלֵּמִית בֶּן־אִמֵּר: וַאֲחֵיהֶם רָאשִׁים לְבֵית אֲבוֹתָם אֶלֶף
וּשְׁבַע מֵאוֹת וְשִׁשִּׁים גִּבּוֹרֵי חֵיל מְלֶאכֶת עֲבוֹדַת בֵּית־הָאֱלֹהִים:
יד וּמִן־הַלְוִיִּם שְׁמַעְיָה בֶן־חַשּׁוּב בֶּן־עַזְרִיקָם בֶּן־חֲשַׁבְיָה מִן־בְּנֵי מְרָרִי:
טו טז וּבַקְבַּקַּר חֶרֶשׁ וְגָלָל וּמַתַּנְיָה בֶּן־מִיכָא בֶּן־זִכְרִי בֶּן־אָסָף: וְעֹבַדְיָה
בֶּן־שְׁמַעְיָה בֶּן־גָּלָל בֶּן־יְדוּתוּן וּבֶרֶכְיָה בֶן־אָסָא בֶּן־אֶלְקָנָה הַיּוֹשֵׁב
יז בְּחַצְרֵי נְטוֹפָתִי: וְהַשֹּׁעֲרִים שַׁלּוּם וְעַקּוּב וְטַלְמֹן וַאֲחִימָן וַאֲחִיהֶם
יח שַׁלּוּם הָרֹאשׁ: וְעַד־הֵנָּה בְּשַׁעַר הַמֶּלֶךְ מִזְרָחָה הֵמָּה הַשֹּׁעֲרִים
יט לְמַחֲנוֹת בְּנֵי לֵוִי: וְשַׁלּוּם בֶּן־קוֹרֵא בֶּן־אֶבְיָסָף בֶּן־קֹרַח וְאֶחָיו לְבֵית־
אָבִיו הַקָּרְחִים עַל מְלֶאכֶת הָעֲבוֹדָה שֹׁמְרֵי הַסִּפִּים לָאֹהֶל וַאֲבֹתֵיהֶם
כ עַל־מַחֲנֵה יְהוָה שֹׁמְרֵי הַמָּבוֹא: וּפִינְחָס בֶּן־אֶלְעָזָר נָגִיד הָיָה עֲלֵיהֶם
כא לְפָנִים יְהוָה ׀ עִמּוֹ: זְכַרְיָה בֶּן מְשֶׁלֶמְיָה שֹׁעֵר פֶּתַח לְאֹהֶל מוֹעֵד:
כב כֻּלָּם הַבְּרוּרִים לְשֹׁעֲרִים בַּסִּפִּים מָאתַיִם וּשְׁנֵים עָשָׂר הֵמָּה בְחַצְרֵיהֶם
כג הִתְיַחְשָׂם הֵמָּה יִסַּד דָּוִיד וּשְׁמוּאֵל הָרֹאֶה בֶּאֱמוּנָתָם: וְהֵם וּבְנֵיהֶם
כד עַל־הַשְּׁעָרִים לְבֵית־יְהוָה לְבֵית הָאֹהֶל לְמִשְׁמָרוֹת: לְאַרְבַּע רוּחוֹת
כה יִהְיוּ הַשֹּׁעֲרִים מִזְרָח יָמָּה צָפוֹנָה וָנֶגְבָּה: וַאֲחֵיהֶם בְּחַצְרֵיהֶם לָבוֹא
כו לְשִׁבְעַת הַיָּמִים מֵעֵת אֶל־עֵת עִם־אֵלֶּה: כִּי בֶאֱמוּנָה הֵמָּה אַרְבַּעַת
גִּבֹּרֵי הַשֹּׁעֲרִים הֵם הַלְוִיִּם וְהָיוּ עַל־הַלְּשָׁכוֹת וְעַל־הָאֹצְרוֹת בֵּית
כז הָאֱלֹהִים: וּסְבִיבוֹת בֵּית־הָאֱלֹהִים יָלִינוּ כִּי־עֲלֵיהֶם מִשְׁמֶרֶת וְהֵם
כח עַל־הַמַּפְתֵּחַ וְלַבֹּקֶר לַבֹּקֶר: וּמֵהֶם עַל־כְּלֵי הָעֲבוֹדָה כִּי־בְמִסְפָּר
כט יְבִיאוּם וּבְמִסְפָּר יוֹצִיאוּם: וּמֵהֶם מְמֻנִּים עַל־הַכֵּלִים וְעַל כָּל־כְּלֵי
ל הַקֹּדֶשׁ וְעַל־הַסֹּלֶת וְהַיַּיִן וְהַשֶּׁמֶן וְהַלְּבוֹנָה וְהַבְּשָׂמִים: וּמִן־בְּנֵי
לא הַכֹּהֲנִים רֹקְחֵי הַמִּרְקַחַת לַבְּשָׂמִים: וּמַתִּתְיָה מִן־הַלְוִיִּם הוּא הַבְּכוֹר
לב לְשַׁלֻּם הַקָּרְחִי בֶּאֱמוּנָה עַל מַעֲשֵׂה הַחֲבִתִּים: וּמִן־בְּנֵי הַקְּהָתִי מִן־
לג אֲחֵיהֶם עַל־לֶחֶם הַמַּעֲרָכֶת לְהָכִין שַׁבַּת שַׁבָּת: וְאֵלֶּה
הַמְשֹׁרְרִים רָאשֵׁי אָבוֹת לַלְוִיִּם בַּלְּשָׁכֹת פטירים כִּי־יוֹמָם וָלַיְלָה [פְּטוּרִים]
לד עֲלֵיהֶם בַּמְּלָאכָה: אֵלֶּה רָאשֵׁי הָאָבוֹת לַלְוִיִּם לְתֹלְדוֹתָם רָאשִׁים
אֵלֶּה יָשְׁבוּ בִירוּשָׁלָם:

35 In Givon lived the father of Givon, Ye'iel, and the name of his wife was Maakha.
36 37 His firstborn son was Avdon, then Tzur, Kish, Baal, Ner, Nadav, Gedor,
38 Aḥyo, Zekharya, and Miklot; Miklot was the father of Shimam, and they too,
39 opposite their kinsmen, lived in Jerusalem with their kinsmen. Ner
was the father of Kish, Kish was the father of Sha'ul, and Sha'ul was the father
40 of Yehonatan, Malkishua, Avinadav, and Eshbaal. Yehonatan's son was Meriv
41 Baal, and Meriv Baal was the father of Mikha. The sons of Mikha: Piton,
42 Melekh, and Taḥare'a. Aḥaz was the father of Yara, Yara was the father of
43 Alemet, Azmavet, and Zimri, and Zimri was the father of Motza. Motza was
44 the father of Bina, his son Refaya, his son Elasa, and his son Atzel. Atzel had
six sons, and these are their names: Azrikam, Bokheru, Yishmael, She'arya,
Ovadya, and Ḥanan; these were the sons of Atzel.

10 1 The Philistines fought against Israel; the men of Israel fled before the
2 Philistines and fell slain on Mount Gilboa. And the Philistines closed in
on Sha'ul and his sons; the Philistines struck down Yonatan, Avinadav, and
3 Malkishua, the sons of Sha'ul. And the battle weighed heavily upon Sha'ul,
4 and when the archers found him, he shook, frightened by the archers. "Draw
your sword and stab me with it," Sha'ul said to his arms bearer, "lest these
heathens come and torture me." But his arms bearer was not willing due
5 to his great reverence, so Sha'ul took the sword and fell upon it. When his
arms bearer saw that Sha'ul was dead, he too fell on the sword and died.
6 7 Sha'ul, his three sons, and all his house died together on that day. When all
the men of Israel in the valley and on the other side of the Jordan realized
that Sha'ul and his sons had fled and died, they abandoned their cities and
8 fled. And Philistines came and settled in them. The next day, when
Philistines came to strip the corpses, they found Sha'ul and his sons fallen on
9 Mount Gilboa. They stripped him, carried off his head and his armor, and
sent word throughout the land of the Philistines, bringing tidings to their
10 idols and to the people. They deposited his armor in the temple of their gods
11 and fastened his skull in the temple of Dagon. Now when all the
people of Yavesh Gilad heard of everything that the Philistines did to Sha'ul,
12 all their boldest men set out, carried off Sha'ul's corpse and the corpses of
his sons, and brought them to Yavesh. They buried their bones beneath the
13 terebinth in Yavesh and fasted for seven days. Thus Sha'ul died for breaking
faith with the LORD, for failing to keep the LORD's word, and for inquiring of
14 a necromancer; he did not inquire of the LORD, so He put him to death and
turned the kingship over to David son of Yishai.

11 1 Now all the tribes of Israel gathered to David at Ḥevron. "Look, we are your

לה לו וּבְגִבְע֛וֹן יָשְׁב֥וּ אֲבִֽי־גִבְע֖וֹן יעואל וְשֵׁ֥ם אִשְׁתּ֖וֹ מַעֲכָֽה׃ וּבְנ֥וֹ הַבְּכ֖וֹר יְעִיאֵ֑ל
לז עַבְדּ֑וֹן וְצ֣וּר וְקִ֔ישׁ וּבַ֖עַל וְנֵ֥ר וְנָדָֽב׃ וּגְד֥וֹר וְאַחְי֖וֹ וּזְכַרְיָ֥ה וּמִקְלֽוֹת׃
לח וּמִקְל֖וֹת הוֹלִ֣יד אֶת־שִׁמְאָ֑ם וְאַף־הֵ֗ם נֶ֧גֶד אֲחֵיהֶ֛ם יָשְׁב֥וּ בִירוּשָׁלִַ֖ם
לט עִם־אֲחֵיהֶֽם׃ וְנֵר֙ הוֹלִ֣יד אֶת־קִ֔ישׁ וְקִ֖ישׁ הוֹלִ֣יד אֶת־שָׁא֑וּל
וְשָׁא֗וּל הוֹלִ֤יד אֶת־יְהֽוֹנָתָן֙ וְאֶת־מַלְכִּי־שׁ֔וּעַ וְאֶת־אֲבִֽינָדָ֖ב וְאֶת־
מ מא אֶשְׁבָּֽעַל׃ וּבֶן־יְהוֹנָתָ֖ן מְרִ֣יב בָּ֑עַל וּמְרִי־בַ֖עַל הוֹלִ֥יד אֶת־מִיכָֽה׃ וּבְנֵ֖י
מב מִיכָ֑ה פִּית֥וֹן וָמֶ֖לֶךְ וְתַחְרֵֽעַ׃ וְאָחָז֙ הוֹלִ֣יד אֶת־יַעְרָ֔ה וְיַעְרָ֗ה הוֹלִ֛יד
מג אֶת־עָלֶ֥מֶת וְאֶת־עַזְמָ֖וֶת וְאֶת־זִמְרִ֑י וְזִמְרִ֖י הוֹלִ֥יד אֶת־מוֹצָֽא׃ וּמוֹצָ֖א
מד הוֹלִ֣יד אֶת־בִּנְעָ֑א וּרְפָיָ֥ה בְנ֛וֹ אֶלְעָשָׂ֥ה בְנ֖וֹ אָצֵ֥ל בְּנֽוֹ׃ וּלְאָצֵ֣ל שִׁשָּׁ֣ה
בָנִים֮ וְאֵ֣לֶּה שְׁמוֹתָם֒ עַזְרִיקָ֣ם ׀ בֹּכְר֡וּ וְיִשְׁמָעֵאל֩ וּשְׁעַרְיָ֨ה וְעֹבַדְיָ֜ה וְחָנָ֗ן
אֵ֛לֶּה בְּנֵ֥י אָצַֽל׃
י א וּפְלִשְׁתִּ֖ים נִלְחֲמ֣וּ בְיִשְׂרָאֵ֑ל וַיָּ֨נָס אִֽישׁ־יִשְׂרָאֵ֜ל מִפְּנֵ֣י פְלִשְׁתִּ֗ים וַיִּפְּל֥וּ
ב חֲלָלִ֖ים בְּהַ֥ר גִּלְבֹּֽעַ׃ וַיַּדְבְּק֣וּ פְלִשְׁתִּ֔ים אַחֲרֵ֥י שָׁא֖וּל וְאַחֲרֵ֣י בָנָ֑יו וַיַּכּ֣וּ
ג פְלִשְׁתִּ֗ים אֶת־יוֹנָתָ֛ן וְאֶת־אֲבִֽינָדָ֥ב וְאֶת־מַלְכִּי־שׁ֖וּעַ בְּנֵ֥י שָׁאֽוּל׃ וַתִּכְבַּ֤ד
הַמִּלְחָמָה֙ עַל־שָׁא֔וּל וַיִּמְצָאֻ֥הוּ הַמּוֹרִ֖ים בַּקָּ֑שֶׁת וַיָּ֖חֶל מִן־הַיּוֹרִֽים׃
ד וַיֹּ֣אמֶר שָׁא֣וּל אֶל־נֹשֵׂ֪א כֵלָיו֩ שְׁלֹ֨ף חַרְבְּךָ֜ ׀ וְדָקְרֵ֣נִי בָ֗הּ פֶּן־יָ֜בֹאוּ הָעֲרֵלִ֤ים
הָאֵ֙לֶּה֙ וְהִתְעַלְּלוּ־בִ֔י וְלֹ֤א אָבָה֙ נֹשֵׂ֣א כֵלָ֔יו כִּ֥י יָרֵ֖א מְאֹ֑ד וַיִּקַּ֤ח שָׁאוּל֙ אֶת־
ה הַחֶ֔רֶב וַיִּפֹּ֖ל עָלֶֽיהָ׃ וַיַּ֥רְא נֹשֵֽׂא־כֵלָ֖יו כִּ֣י מֵ֣ת שָׁא֑וּל וַיִּפֹּ֥ל גַּם־ה֛וּא עַל־
ו ז הַחֶ֖רֶב וַיָּמֹֽת׃ וַיָּ֣מָת שָׁא֗וּל וּשְׁלֹ֤שֶׁת בָּנָיו֙ וְכָל־בֵּית֔וֹ יַחְדָּ֖ו מֵֽתוּ׃ וַיִּרְא֞וּ
כָּל־אִ֨ישׁ יִשְׂרָאֵ֤ל אֲשֶׁר־בָּעֵ֙מֶק֙ כִּ֣י נָ֔סוּ וְכִי־מֵ֖תוּ שָׁא֣וּל וּבָנָ֑יו וַיַּעַזְב֤וּ
ח עָרֵיהֶם֙ וַיָּנֻ֔סוּ וַיָּבֹ֣אוּ פְלִשְׁתִּ֔ים וַיֵּשְׁב֖וּ בָּהֶֽם׃ וַֽיְהִי֙ מִֽמָּחֳרָ֔ת
וַיָּבֹ֥אוּ פְלִשְׁתִּ֖ים לְפַשֵּׁ֣ט אֶת־הַחֲלָלִ֑ים וַֽיִּמְצְא֤וּ אֶת־שָׁאוּל֙ וְאֶת־בָּנָ֔יו
ט נֹפְלִ֖ים בְּהַ֥ר גִּלְבֹּֽעַ׃ וַיַּפְשִׁיטֻ֕הוּ וַיִּשְׂא֥וּ אֶת־רֹאשׁ֖וֹ וְאֶת־כֵּלָ֑יו וַֽיְשַׁלְּח֨וּ
י בְאֶֽרֶץ־פְּלִשְׁתִּ֜ים סָבִ֗יב לְבַשֵּׂ֛ר אֶת־עֲצַבֵּיהֶ֖ם וְאֶת־הָעָֽם׃ וַיָּשִׂ֙ימוּ֙ אֶת־
יא כֵּלָ֔יו בֵּ֖ית אֱלֹהֵיהֶ֑ם וְאֶת־גֻּלְגָּלְתּ֥וֹ תָקְע֖וּ בֵּ֥ית דָּגֽוֹן׃ וַֽיִּשְׁמְע֔וּ
יב כֹּ֖ל יָבֵ֣ישׁ גִּלְעָ֑ד אֵ֛ת כָּל־אֲשֶׁר־עָשׂ֥וּ פְלִשְׁתִּ֖ים לְשָׁאֽוּל׃ וַיָּק֜וּמוּ כָּל־אִ֣ישׁ
חַ֗יִל וַיִּשְׂא֞וּ אֶת־גּוּפַ֤ת שָׁאוּל֙ וְאֵת֙ גּוּפֹ֣ת בָּנָ֔יו וַיְבִיא֖וּם יָבֵ֑ישָׁה וַֽיִּקְבְּר֨וּ
יג אֶת־עַצְמֽוֹתֵיהֶ֜ם תַּ֤חַת הָֽאֵלָה֙ בְּיָבֵ֔שׁ וַיָּצ֖וּמוּ שִׁבְעַ֥ת יָמִֽים׃ וַיָּ֣מָת שָׁא֗וּל
בְּמַֽעֲלוֹ֙ אֲשֶׁ֤ר מָעַל֙ בַּֽיהוָ֔ה עַל־דְּבַ֥ר יְהוָ֖ה אֲשֶׁ֣ר לֹא־שָׁמָ֑ר וְגַם־לִשְׁא֥וֹל
יד בָּא֖וֹב לִדְרֽוֹשׁ׃ וְלֹֽא־דָרַ֣שׁ בַּֽיהוָ֔ה וַיְמִיתֵ֑הוּ וַיַּסֵּב֙ אֶת־הַמְּלוּכָ֔ה לְדָוִ֖יד
בֶּן־יִשָֽׁי׃
יא א וַיִּקָּבְצ֧וּ כָֽל־יִשְׂרָאֵ֛ל אֶל־דָּוִ֖יד חֶבְר֣וֹנָה לֵאמֹ֑ר הִנֵּ֛ה עַצְמְךָ֥ וּבְשָׂרְךָ֖

2 own flesh and blood. All along, even when Sha'ul was king, you were the one
who led Israel out and brought them back. And the LORD your God said to
you, 'You shall shepherd My people Israel, and you shall be ruler over Israel.'"
3 All the elders of Israel came to the king at Ḥevron; David formed a covenant
with them at Ḥevron before the LORD, and they anointed David as king over
4 Israel, fulfilling the word of the LORD through Shmuel. David and
all Israel went to Jerusalem, that is, Yevus, where the Jebusites had settled
5 the land. The people of Yevus said to David, "You shall not enter here." But
6 David captured the stronghold of Zion, that is, the City of David. Then David
said, "Whoever is the first to attack the Jebusites will be made a leader and
an officer." The first to go up was Yoav son of Tzeruya, and he was made the
7 leader. David settled in the stronghold, and for that reason it was called the
8 City of David. He built up the city all around in a complete circuit from the
9 Milo while Yoav repaired the rest of the city. And David grew in greatness;
the LORD of Hosts was with him.
10 These are the leaders among David's warriors who gave him great support in
his kingdom, together with all of Israel, to appoint him as king in accordance
11 with the LORD's word about Israel. This is an account of David's
warriors: Yoshovam son of Ḥakhmoni was the head of the Thirty; he wielded
12 his spear against three hundred victims at one time. Next in rank was Elazar
13 son of Dodo the Ahohite; he was among the warriors of the Three. He was
with David in Pas Damim where the Philistines had gathered for war. There
14 was a plot of land full of barley, and the troops fled from the Philistines. But
they took their stand in the middle of the plot, defended it, and defeated the
15 Philistines; the LORD saved them with a great victory. Once, the chief three
of the Thirty went down to the rock to David in the cave of Adulam, when an
16 army of Philistines was encamped in the Refaim Valley. At the time, David
was in the stronghold while the Philistines were then stationed at Beit Leḥem.
17 David was seized with a craving and said, "Oh – if only someone could give
18 me water to drink from the well of Beit Leḥem by the gate." So the three
warriors infiltrated the Philistine camp, drew water from the Beit Leḥem
well by the gate, and carried it back. But when they brought it to David, he
19 would not drink it and poured it out in a libation to the LORD. "The Lord
forbid that I do such a thing!" he said. "Shall I drink the lifeblood of men who
risked their very lives by going?" And he would not drink it. These were the
20 feats of the three warriors. Avshai, the brother of Yoav, was the head
of these three. He wielded his spear against three hundred victims. He was
21 famous among the three. Of the three in the second rank he was the most
honored and so became their leader, though he never reached the rank of
22 the Three. Benaya son of Yehoyada, from Kavtze'el, was a powerful
man who achieved great feats. He defeated the two leonine warriors of Moav,

ב אַנְחְנוּ: גַּם־תְּמוֹל גַּם־שִׁלְשׁוֹם גַּם בִּהְיוֹת שָׁאוּל מֶלֶךְ אַתָּה הַמּוֹצִיא
וְהַמֵּבִיא אֶת־יִשְׂרָאֵל וַיֹּאמֶר יְהוָה אֱלֹהֶיךָ לְךָ אַתָּה תִרְעֶה אֶת־
ג עַמִּי אֶת־יִשְׂרָאֵל וְאַתָּה תִּהְיֶה נָגִיד עַל עַמִּי יִשְׂרָאֵל: וַיָּבֹאוּ כָּל־
זִקְנֵי יִשְׂרָאֵל אֶל־הַמֶּלֶךְ חֶבְרוֹנָה וַיִּכְרֹת לָהֶם דָּוִיד בְּרִית בְּחֶבְרוֹן
לִפְנֵי יְהוָה וַיִּמְשְׁחוּ אֶת־דָּוִיד לְמֶלֶךְ עַל־יִשְׂרָאֵל כִּדְבַר יְהוָה בְּיַד־
ד שְׁמוּאֵל: וַיֵּלֶךְ דָּוִיד וְכָל־יִשְׂרָאֵל יְרוּשָׁלִַם הִיא יְבוּס
ה וְשָׁם הַיְבוּסִי יֹשְׁבֵי הָאָרֶץ: וַיֹּאמְרוּ יֹשְׁבֵי יְבוּס לְדָוִיד לֹא תָבוֹא הֵנָּה
ו וַיִּלְכֹּד דָּוִיד אֶת־מְצֻדַת צִיּוֹן הִיא עִיר דָּוִיד: וַיֹּאמֶר דָּוִיד כָּל־מַכֵּה
יְבוּסִי בָּרִאשׁוֹנָה יִהְיֶה לְרֹאשׁ וּלְשָׂר וַיַּעַל בָּרִאשׁוֹנָה יוֹאָב בֶּן־צְרוּיָה
ז ח וַיְהִי לְרֹאשׁ: וַיֵּשֶׁב דָּוִיד בַּמְצָד עַל־כֵּן קָרְאוּ־לוֹ עִיר דָּוִיד: וַיִּבֶן הָעִיר
ט מִסָּבִיב מִן־הַמִּלּוֹא וְעַד־הַסָּבִיב וְיוֹאָב יְחַיֶּה אֶת־שְׁאָר הָעִיר: וַיֵּלֶךְ ה
דָּוִיד הָלוֹךְ וְגָדוֹל וַיהוָה צְבָאוֹת עִמּוֹ:
י וְאֵלֶּה רָאשֵׁי הַגִּבּוֹרִים אֲשֶׁר לְדָוִיד הַמִּתְחַזְּקִים עִמּוֹ בְמַלְכוּתוֹ עִם־
יא כָּל־יִשְׂרָאֵל לְהַמְלִיכוֹ כִּדְבַר יְהוָה עַל־יִשְׂרָאֵל: וְאֵלֶּה מִסְפַּר
הַגִּבֹּרִים אֲשֶׁר לְדָוִיד יָשָׁבְעָם בֶּן־חַכְמוֹנִי רֹאשׁ השלושים הוּא־עוֹרֵר הַשָּׁלִישִׁים
יב אֶת־חֲנִיתוֹ עַל־שְׁלֹשׁ־מֵאוֹת חָלָל בְּפַעַם אֶחָת: וְאַחֲרָיו אֶלְעָזָר בֶּן־
יג דּוֹדוֹ הָאֲחוֹחִי הוּא בִּשְׁלוֹשָׁה הַגִּבֹּרִים: הוּא־הָיָה עִם־דָּוִיד בַּפַּס דַּמִּים
וְהַפְּלִשְׁתִּים נֶאֶסְפוּ־שָׁם לַמִּלְחָמָה וַתְּהִי חֶלְקַת הַשָּׂדֶה מְלֵאָה שְׂעוֹרִים
יד וְהָעָם נָסוּ מִפְּנֵי פְלִשְׁתִּים: וַיִּתְיַצְּבוּ בְתוֹךְ־הַחֶלְקָה וַיַּצִּילוּהָ וַיַּכּוּ אֶת־
טו פְּלִשְׁתִּים וַיּוֹשַׁע יְהוָה תְּשׁוּעָה גְדוֹלָה: וַיֵּרְדוּ שְׁלוֹשָׁה מִן־הַשְּׁלוֹשִׁים
רֹאשׁ עַל־הַצֻּר אֶל־דָּוִיד אֶל־מְעָרַת עֲדֻלָּם וּמַחֲנֵה פְלִשְׁתִּים חֹנָה
טז בְּעֵמֶק רְפָאִים: וְדָוִיד אָז בַּמְּצוּדָה וּנְצִיב פְּלִשְׁתִּים אָז בְּבֵית לָחֶם:
יז וַיִּתְאָו דָּוִיד וַיֹּאמַר מִי יַשְׁקֵנִי מַיִם מִבּוֹר בֵּית־לֶחֶם אֲשֶׁר בַּשָּׁעַר:
יח וַיִּבְקְעוּ הַשְּׁלֹשָׁה בְּמַחֲנֵה פְלִשְׁתִּים וַיִּשְׁאֲבוּ־מַיִם מִבּוֹר בֵּית־לֶחֶם
אֲשֶׁר בַּשַּׁעַר וַיִּשְׂאוּ וַיָּבִאוּ אֶל־דָּוִיד וְלֹא־אָבָה דָוִיד לִשְׁתּוֹתָם וַיְנַסֵּךְ
יט אֹתָם לַיהוָה: וַיֹּאמֶר חָלִילָה לִּי מֵאֱלֹהַי מֵעֲשׂוֹת זֹאת הֲדַם הָאֲנָשִׁים
הָאֵלֶּה אֶשְׁתֶּה בְנַפְשׁוֹתָם כִּי בְנַפְשׁוֹתָם הֱבִיאוּם וְלֹא אָבָה לִשְׁתּוֹתָם
כ אֵלֶּה עָשׂוּ שְׁלֹשֶׁת הַגִּבּוֹרִים: וְאַבְשַׁי אֲחִי־יוֹאָב הוּא
הָיָה רֹאשׁ הַשְּׁלוֹשָׁה וְהוּא עוֹרֵר אֶת־חֲנִיתוֹ עַל־שְׁלֹשׁ מֵאוֹת חָלָל
כא ולא־שֵׁם בַּשְּׁלוֹשָׁה: מִן־הַשְּׁלוֹשָׁה בַשְּׁנַיִם נִכְבָּד וַיְהִי לָהֶם לְשָׂר וְלוֹ־
כב וְעַד־הַשְּׁלוֹשָׁה לֹא־בָא: בְּנָיָה בֶן־יְהוֹיָדָע בֶּן־אִישׁ־חַיִל
רַב־פְּעָלִים מִן־קַבְצְאֵל הוּא הִכָּה אֵת שְׁנֵי אֲרִיאֵל מוֹאָב וְהוּא יָרַד

23 and he climbed down into a pit and overpowered a lion on a snowy day. He
defeated an Egyptian man of formidable proportions, five cubits tall. The
Egyptian held a spear like a weaver's beam, but he charged down at him with
a pole, snatched the spear from the Egyptian's hand, and killed him with his
24 own spear. These were the feats of Benayahu son of Yehoyada, and he was
25 famous among the three warriors. He was among the most honored of the
Thirty, though he never reached the rank of the Three, and David appointed
26 him over his bodyguard. The most valiant of the warriors were: Asael
27 brother of Yoav, Elḥanan son of Dodo from Beit Leḥem, Shamot the
28 Harorite, Ḥeletz the Pelonite, Ira son of Ikesh the Tekoite, Aviezer the
29 30 Anatotite, Sibekhai the Hushatite, Ilai the Ahohite, Mahrai
31 the Netofatite, Ḥeled son of Baana the Netofatite, Itai son of Rivai
32 from Giva of the Benjaminites, Benaya of Pirathon, Ḥurai of Naḥalei
33 Gaash, Aviel the Arbatite, Azmavet the Bahrumite, Elyaḥba the
34 Shaalbonite, the sons of Hashem the Gizonite, Yonatan son of
35 Shageh the Hararite, Aḥiam son of Sakhar the Hararite, Elifal son of
36 37 Ur, Ḥefer the Mekheratite, Aḥiya the Pelonite, Ḥetzro the
38 Carmelite, Naarai son of Ezbai, Yoel brother of Natan, Mivḥar son of
39 Hagri, Tzelek the Amonite, Naḥrai the Berotite, the arms bearer of
40 41 Yoav son of Tzeruya, Ira the Itrite, Garev the Yitrite, Uriya
42 the Hittite, Zavad son of Aḥlai, Adina son of Shiza the Reubenite, a
43 leader of the Reubenites, and thirty with him. Ḥanan son of Maakha,
44 Yoshafat the Mitnite, Uziya the Ashteratite, Shama and Ye'iel, sons
45 of Ḥotam the Aroerite, Yediael son of Shimri and his brother Yoḥa
46 the Tizite, Eliel the Mahavite, Yeribai and Yoshavya, sons of Elnaam,
47 Yitma the Moabite, Eliel, Oved, and Yaasiel the Mezobaite.
12 1 These people came to David in Tziklag while he was still held in check by
2 Sha'ul son of Kish; they joined his warriors, his allies in battle: archers who
could use both their right and left hands for slinging stones and shooting
3 arrows – they were of Sha'ul's kin from Binyamin. At the head were Aḥiezer
and Yoash, sons of Shema'a of Giva; Yeziel and Pelet, sons of Azmavet;
4 Berakha and Yehu of Anatot; Yishmaya of Givon, a warrior of the thirty in
5 charge of the Thirty; Yirmeya, Yaḥaziel, Yoḥanan, and Yozavad of Gedera;
6 7 Eluzai, Yerimot, Be'alya, Shemaryahu, and Shefatyahu the Ḥarufite; Elkana,
8 Yishyahu, Azarel, Yoezer, and Yoshovam the Korahites; and Yoela and
9 Zevadya sons of Yeroḥam of Gedor. Warriors of the Gadites defected to

כג וְהִכָּה אֶת־הָאֲרִי בְּתוֹךְ הַבּוֹר בְּיוֹם הַשָּׁלֶג׃ וְהֽוּא הִכָּה אֶת־הָאִישׁ
הַמִּצְרִי אִישׁ מִדָּה ׀ חָמֵשׁ בָּאַמָּה וּבְיַד הַמִּצְרִי חֲנִית כִּמְנוֹר אֹרְגִים
וַיֵּרֶד אֵלָיו בַּשָּׁבֶט וַיִּגְזֹל אֶת־הַחֲנִית מִיַּד הַמִּצְרִי וַיַּהַרְגֵהוּ בַּחֲנִיתוֹ׃
כד כה אֵלֶּה עָשָׂה בְּנָיָהוּ בֶּן־יְהוֹיָדָע וְלוֹ־שֵׁם בִּשְׁלוֹשָׁה הַגִּבֹּרִים׃ מִן־
הַשְּׁלוֹשִׁים הִנּוֹ נִכְבָּד הוּא וְאֶל־הַשְּׁלֹשָׁה לֹא־בָא וַיְשִׂימֵהוּ דָוִיד
כו עַל־מִשְׁמַעְתּוֹ׃ וְגִבּוֹרֵי הַחֲיָלִים עֲשָׂהאֵל אֲחִי יוֹאָב אֶלְחָנָן
כז בֶּן־דּוֹדוֹ מִבֵּית לָחֶם׃ שַׁמּוֹת הַהֲרוֹרִי חֶלֶץ
כח הַפְּלוֹנִי׃ עִירָא בֶן־עִקֵּשׁ הַתְּקוֹעִי אֲבִיעֶזֶר
כט ל הָעַנְּתוֹתִי׃ סִבְּכַי הַחֻשָׁתִי עִילַי הָאֲחוֹחִי׃ מַהְרַי
לא הַנְּטֹפָתִי חֵלֶד בֶּן־בַּעֲנָה הַנְּטוֹפָתִי׃ אִיתַי בֶּן־רִיבַי
לב מִגִּבְעַת בְּנֵי בִנְיָמִן בְּנָיָה הַפִּרְעָתֹנִי׃ חוּרַי מִנַּחֲלֵי
לג גָעַשׁ אֲבִיאֵל הָעַרְבָתִי׃ עַזְמָוֶת הַבַּחֲרוּמִי
לד אֶלְיַחְבָּא הַשַּׁעַלְבֹנִי׃ בְּנֵי הָשֵׁם הַגִּזוֹנִי יוֹנָתָן בֶּן־שָׁגֵה
לה הַהֲרָרִי׃ אֲחִיאָם בֶּן־שָׂכָר הַהֲרָרִי אֱלִיפַל בֶּן־
לו לז אוּר׃ חֵפֶר הַמְּכֵרָתִי אֲחִיָּה הַפְּלֹנִי׃ חֶצְרוֹ
לח הַכַּרְמְלִי נַעֲרַי בֶּן־אֶזְבָּי׃ יוֹאֵל אֲחִי נָתָן מִבְחָר בֶּן־
לט הַגְרִי׃ צֶלֶק הָעַמּוֹנִי נַחְרַי הַבֵּרֹתִי נֹשֵׂא כְּלֵי יוֹאָב בֶּן־
מ מא צְרוּיָה׃ עִירָא הַיִּתְרִי גָּרֵב הַיִּתְרִי׃ אוּרִיָּה
מב הַחִתִּי זָבָד בֶּן־אַחְלָי׃ עֲדִינָא בֶן־שִׁיזָא הָרְאוּבֵנִי
מג רֹאשׁ לָרְאוּבֵנִי וְעָלָיו שְׁלוֹשִׁים׃ חָנָן בֶּן־מַעֲכָה
מד וְיוֹשָׁפָט הַמִּתְנִי׃ עֻזִּיָּא הָעַשְׁתְּרָתִי שָׁמָע ויעואל בְּנֵי וִיעִיאֵל
מה חוֹתָם הָעֲרֹעֵרִי׃ יְדִיעֲאֵל בֶּן־שִׁמְרִי וְיֹחָא אָחִיו
מו הַתִּיצִי׃ אֱלִיאֵל הַמַּחֲוִים וִירִיבַי וְיוֹשַׁוְיָה בְּנֵי אֶלְנָעַם וְיִתְמָה
מז הַמּוֹאָבִי׃ אֱלִיאֵל וְעוֹבֵד וְיַעֲשִׂיאֵל הַמְּצֹבָיָה׃
יב א וְאֵלֶּה הַבָּאִים אֶל־דָּוִיד לְצִיקְלַג עוֹד עָצוּר מִפְּנֵי שָׁאוּל בֶּן־קִישׁ
ב וְהֵמָּה בַּגִּבּוֹרִים עֹזְרֵי הַמִּלְחָמָה׃ נֹשְׁקֵי קֶשֶׁת מַיְמִינִים וּמַשְׂמִאלִים
ג בָּאֲבָנִים וּבַחִצִּים בַּקָּשֶׁת מֵאֲחֵי שָׁאוּל מִבִּנְיָמִן׃ הָרֹאשׁ אֲחִיעֶזֶר
וְיוֹאָשׁ בְּנֵי הַשְּׁמָעָה הַגִּבְעָתִי ויזואל וָפֶלֶט בְּנֵי עַזְמָוֶת וּבְרָכָה וְיֵהוּא וִיזִיאֵל
ד ה הָעַנְּתֹתִי׃ וְיִשְׁמַעְיָה הַגִּבְעוֹנִי גִּבּוֹר בַּשְּׁלֹשִׁים וְעַל־הַשְּׁלֹשִׁים׃ וְיִרְמְיָה
ו וְיַחֲזִיאֵל וְיוֹחָנָן וְיוֹזָבָד הַגְּדֵרָתִי׃ אֶלְעוּזַי וִירִימוֹת וּבְעַלְיָה וּשְׁמַרְיָהוּ
ז וּשְׁפַטְיָהוּ החריפי׃ אֶלְקָנָה וְיִשִּׁיָּהוּ וַעֲזַרְאֵל וְיוֹעֶזֶר וְיָשָׁבְעָם הַקָּרְחִים׃ הַחֲרוּפִי
ח ט וְיוֹעֵאלָה וּזְבַדְיָה בְּנֵי יְרֹחָם מִן־הַגְּדוֹר׃ וּמִן־הַגָּדִי נִבְדְּלוּ אֶל־דָּוִיד

David in his wilderness stronghold, experienced men of war who wielded
shield and spear – their faces were like the faces of lions, and they could
10 race over the hills like deer. At the head was Ezer, with Ovadya the
11 12 second, Eliav the third, Mishmana the fourth, Yirmeyahu the fifth, Atai the
13 14 sixth, Eliel the seventh, Yoḥanan the eighth, Elzabad the ninth, Yirmeyahu the
15 tenth, and Makhbanai the eleventh. These were heads of the army
from the Gadites; the least of them was worth a hundred, and the greatest
16 a thousand. These are the ones who crossed the Jordan in the first month
when all its banks were overflowing; they drove away all those in the valleys
17 to the east and to the west. Some of the Benjaminites and Judahites
18 came to David at his stronghold. David went out to meet them in response.
"If you came to me in peace to help me," he said to them, "my heart will be
bound to yours; but if you came to betray me to my enemies though my
hands have done no wrong, may the God of our ancestors see and condemn
19 you!" Suddenly the spirit seized Amasai, the head of the thirty: "We
are yours, David. We are with you, son of Yishai – peace! Peace to you and
peace to all who help you, for it is God who helps you." So David accepted
20 them and assigned them as heads of the force. Some of Menashe
defected to David when he came with the Philistines to fight against Sha'ul,
but he did not help the Philistines because their chieftains took counsel
and sent him away, saying, "At the cost of our heads, he will defect to his
21 master Sha'ul." As he went to Tziklag, some of Menashe defected to him:
Adnaḥ, Yozavad, Yediael, Mikhael, Yozavad, Elihu, and Ziletai, heads of the
22 clans of Menashe. They helped David against the raiders, for they were all
23 valiant warriors, and they became officers of the army. Day by day, men kept
coming to David to support him until his forces were as great as the heavenly
24 forces. These are the numbers of the divisions of the armed troops
who came over to David in Ḥevron to transfer Sha'ul's kingship to him in
25 accordance with the word of the Lord. The Judahites, bearing
26 shield and spear, 6,800 armed troops; of the Simeonites, warriors
27 28 ready for battle, 7,100; of the Levites, 4,600; Yehoyada,
29 leader of the house of Aharon, and 3,700 with him; Tzadok, a
30 valiant young warrior, and 22 officers from his father's house; of the
Benjaminites, Sha'ul's own kin, 3,000 – even now, most of them kept their
31 allegiance to the house of Sha'ul. Of the Efraimites, 20,800 warriors,
32 famous throughout their ancestral houses; from half of the tribe of
Menashe, 18,000 who were singled out by name to come and make David
33 king; of the Issacharites, men who understood the times and knew
what Israel would do, 200 at their head, and all their brothers were at their

לַמְצַד מִדְבָּרָה גִּבֹּרֵי הַחַיִל אַנְשֵׁי צָבָא לַמִּלְחָמָה עֹרְכֵי צִנָּה וָרֹמַח
י וּפְנֵי אַרְיֵה פְּנֵיהֶם וְכִצְבָאיִם עַל־הֶהָרִים לְמַהֵר: עֵזֶר הָרֹאשׁ
יא עֹבַדְיָה הַשֵּׁנִי אֱלִיאָב הַשְּׁלִשִׁי: מִשְׁמַנָּה הָרְבִיעִי יִרְמְיָה הַחֲמִשִׁי:
יג יד עַתַּי הַשִּׁשִּׁי אֱלִיאֵל הַשְּׁבִעִי: יוֹחָנָן הַשְּׁמִינִי אֶלְזָבָד הַתְּשִׁיעִי: יִרְמְיָהוּ
טו הָעֲשִׂירִי מַכְבַּנַּי עַשְׁתֵּי עָשָׂר: אֵלֶּה מִבְּנֵי־גָד רָאשֵׁי הַצָּבָא
טז אֶחָד לְמֵאָה הַקָּטָן וְהַגָּדוֹל לְאָלֶף: אֵלֶּה הֵם אֲשֶׁר עָבְרוּ אֶת־הַיַּרְדֵּן
בַּחֹדֶשׁ הָרִאשׁוֹן וְהוּא מְמַלֵּא עַל־כׇּל־גדיתיו וַיַּבְרִיחוּ אֶת־כׇּל־ גְּדוֹתָיו
יז הָעֲמָקִים לַמִּזְרָח וְלַמַּעֲרָב: וַיָּבֹאוּ מִן־בְּנֵי בִנְיָמִן וִיהוּדָה
יח עַד־לַמְצַד לְדָוִיד: וַיֵּצֵא דָוִיד לִפְנֵיהֶם וַיַּעַן וַיֹּאמֶר לָהֶם אִם־לְשָׁלוֹם
בָּאתֶם אֵלַי לְעׇזְרֵנִי יִהְיֶה־לִּי עֲלֵיכֶם לֵבָב לְיָחַד וְאִם־לְרַמּוֹתֵנִי לְצָרַי
יט בְּלֹא חָמָס בְּכַפַּי יֵרֶא אֱלֹהֵי אֲבוֹתֵינוּ וְיוֹכַח: וְרוּחַ לָבְשָׁה
אֶת־עֲמָשַׂי רֹאשׁ השלושים לְךָ דָוִיד וְעִמְּךָ בֶן־יִשַׁי שָׁלוֹם ׀ שָׁלוֹם הַשָּׁלִישִׁים
לְךָ וְשָׁלוֹם לְעֹזְרֶךָ כִּי עֲזָרְךָ אֱלֹהֶיךָ וַיְקַבְּלֵם דָּוִיד וַיִּתְּנֵם בְּרָאשֵׁי
כ הַגְּדוּד: וּמִמְּנַשֶּׁה נָפְלוּ עַל־דָּוִיד בְּבֹאוֹ עִם־פְּלִשְׁתִּים עַל־
שָׁאוּל לַמִּלְחָמָה וְלֹא עֲזָרֻם כִּי בְעֵצָה שִׁלְּחֻהוּ סַרְנֵי פְלִשְׁתִּים לֵאמֹר
כא בְּרָאשֵׁינוּ יִפּוֹל אֶל־אֲדֹנָיו שָׁאוּל: בְּלֶכְתּוֹ אֶל־צִיקְלַג נָפְלוּ עָלָיו ׀
מִמְּנַשֶּׁה עַדְנַח וְיוֹזָבָד וִידִיעֲאֵל וּמִיכָאֵל וְיוֹזָבָד וֶאֱלִיהוּא וְצִלְּתָי רָאשֵׁי
כב הָאֲלָפִים אֲשֶׁר לִמְנַשֶּׁה: וְהֵמָּה עָזְרוּ עִם־דָּוִיד עַל־הַגְּדוּד כִּי־גִבּוֹרֵי
כג חַיִל כֻּלָּם וַיִּהְיוּ שָׂרִים בַּצָּבָא: כִּי לְעֶת־יוֹם בְּיוֹם יָבֹאוּ עַל־דָּוִיד לְעׇזְרוֹ
כד עַד־לְמַחֲנֶה גָדוֹל כְּמַחֲנֵה אֱלֹהִים: וְאֵלֶּה מִסְפְּרֵי רָאשֵׁי
הֶחָלוּץ לַצָּבָא בָּאוּ עַל־דָּוִיד חֶבְרוֹנָה לְהָסֵב מַלְכוּת שָׁאוּל אֵלָיו
כה כְּפִי יְהוָה: בְּנֵי יְהוּדָה נֹשְׂאֵי צִנָּה וָרֹמַח שֵׁשֶׁת אֲלָפִים
כו וּשְׁמוֹנֶה מֵאוֹת חֲלוּצֵי צָבָא: מִן־בְּנֵי שִׁמְעוֹן גִּבּוֹרֵי חַיִל
כז לַצָּבָא שִׁבְעַת אֲלָפִים וּמֵאָה: מִן־בְּנֵי הַלֵּוִי אַרְבַּעַת אֲלָפִים
כח וְשֵׁשׁ מֵאוֹת: וִיהוֹיָדָע הַנָּגִיד לְאַהֲרֹן וְעִמּוֹ שְׁלֹשֶׁת אֲלָפִים
כט וּשְׁבַע מֵאוֹת: וְצָדוֹק נַעַר גִּבּוֹר חָיִל וּבֵית־אָבִיו שָׂרִים
ל עֶשְׂרִים וּשְׁנָיִם: וּמִן־בְּנֵי בִנְיָמִן אֲחֵי שָׁאוּל שְׁלֹשֶׁת אֲלָפִים
לא וְעַד־הֵנָּה מַרְבִּיתָם שֹׁמְרִים מִשְׁמֶרֶת בֵּית שָׁאוּל: וּמִן־בְּנֵי
אֶפְרַיִם עֶשְׂרִים אֶלֶף וּשְׁמוֹנֶה מֵאוֹת גִּבּוֹרֵי חַיִל אַנְשֵׁי שֵׁמוֹת לְבֵית
לב אֲבוֹתָם: וּמֵחֲצִי מַטֵּה מְנַשֶּׁה שְׁמוֹנָה עָשָׂר אָלֶף אֲשֶׁר נִקְּבוּ
לג בְּשֵׁמוֹת לָבוֹא לְהַמְלִיךְ אֶת־דָּוִיד: וּמִבְּנֵי יִשָּׂשכָר יוֹדְעֵי
בִינָה לָעִתִּים לָדַעַת מַה־יַּעֲשֶׂה יִשְׂרָאֵל רָאשֵׁיהֶם מָאתַיִם וְכׇל־אֲחֵיהֶם

34 command; of Zevulun, 50,000 seasoned warriors, ready for battle
35 with all weapons of war, giving support with undivided loyalty; of
36 Naftali, 1,000 officers along with 37,000 with shield and spear; of the
37 Danites, 28,600 ready for battle; of Asher, 40,000 seasoned warriors
38 ready for battle. From across the Jordan, from the Reubenites,
39 Gadites, and half the tribe of Menashe – 120,000, with all weapons of war. All
these men of war, offering support with all their hearts, came to Ḥevron to
make David king over all of Israel, and all the rest of Israel as well were of one
40 heart: to make David king. They stayed with David for three days, feasting
41 and drinking, for their brothers had prepared for them. And those who were
nearby, as far as Yissakhar, Zevulun, and Naftali, brought food on donkeys,
camels, mules, and cattle: baked goods, cakes of figs and raisins, wine, oil, and
13 1 an abundance of cattle and sheep, for there was joy in Israel. David
took counsel with the officers of thousands and hundreds, with every leader.
2 And David said to all the assembly of Israel: "If you approve, and if it is the
will of the Lord our God, let us send word far and wide to our brothers who
remain in all the lands of Israel, together with the priests and Levites in the
3 cities of their pasturelands, so they may gather to us. Then we will bring the
Ark of our God back to us, for we did not seek it out in the days of Sha'ul."
4 And all of the assembly agreed to do so, for the idea seemed right in the eyes
5 of all the people. So David assembled all of Israel – from Shiḥor of Egypt
6 to Levo Ḥamat – to bring the Ark of God from Kiryat Ye'arim. David went
up with all of Israel to Baala of Kiryat Ye'arim of Yehuda, to bring up from
there the Ark of God, of the Lord Enthroned upon the Cherubim, which
7 is called by the Name. They mounted the Ark of God onto a new cart from
8 the house of Avinadav, with Uza and Aḥyo driving the cart and David and
all of Israel reveling before God with all their might, with song and with lyre,
9 with harp and with timbrel, with cymbal and with trumpet. When they came
to the threshing floor of Kidon, Uza reached out his hand to grasp hold of
10 the Ark, for the oxen had stumbled. And the Lord's rage flared up against
Uza; He struck him down for having reached out his hand toward the Ark,
11 and he died there before God. David was enraged that the Lord had burst
12 out against Uza, so that place has been called Peretz Uza[11] to this day. David
feared God on that day, and he said, "How will I bring the Ark of the Lord to
13 me?" David did not remove the Ark of the Lord to him in the City of David;
14 he had it redirected to the house of Oved Edom the Gittite. The Ark of God

11 | Literally "outburst of Uza."

לד עַל־פִּיהֶם׃ מִזְּבֻלוּן יוֹצְאֵי צָבָא עֹרְכֵי מִלְחָמָה בְּכָל־כְּלֵי
לה מִלְחָמָה חֲמִשִּׁים אָלֶף וְלַעֲדֹר בְּלֹא־לֵב וָלֵב׃ וּמִנַּפְתָּלִי שָׂרִים
לו אָלֶף וְעִמָּהֶם בְּצִנָּה וַחֲנִית שְׁלֹשִׁים וְשִׁבְעָה אָלֶף׃ וּמִן־הַדָּנִי
לז עֹרְכֵי מִלְחָמָה עֶשְׂרִים־וּשְׁמוֹנָה אֶלֶף וְשֵׁשׁ מֵאוֹת׃ וּמֵאָשֵׁר
לח יוֹצְאֵי צָבָא לַעֲרֹךְ מִלְחָמָה אַרְבָּעִים אָלֶף׃ וּמֵעֵבֶר לַיַּרְדֵּן
מִן־הָרְאוּבֵנִי וְהַגָּדִי וַחֲצִי ׀ שֵׁבֶט מְנַשֶּׁה בְּכֹל כְּלֵי צְבָא מִלְחָמָה מֵאָה
לט וְעֶשְׂרִים אָלֶף׃ כָּל־אֵלֶּה אַנְשֵׁי מִלְחָמָה עֹדְרֵי מַעֲרָכָה בְּלֵבָב שָׁלֵם
בָּאוּ חֶבְרוֹנָה לְהַמְלִיךְ אֶת־דָּוִיד עַל־כָּל־יִשְׂרָאֵל וְגַם כָּל־שֵׁרִית
מ יִשְׂרָאֵל לֵב אֶחָד לְהַמְלִיךְ אֶת־דָּוִיד׃ וַיִּהְיוּ־שָׁם עִם־דָּוִיד יָמִים שְׁלוֹשָׁה
מא אֹכְלִים וְשׁוֹתִים כִּי־הֵכִינוּ לָהֶם אֲחֵיהֶם׃ וְגַם הַקְּרוֹבִים־אֲלֵיהֶם עַד־ ו
יִשָּׂשכָר וּזְבֻלוּן וְנַפְתָּלִי מְבִיאִים לֶחֶם בַּחֲמוֹרִים וּבַגְּמַלִּים וּבַפְּרָדִים ׀
וּבַבָּקָר מַאֲכָל קֶמַח דְּבֵלִים וְצִמּוּקִים וְיַיִן וְשֶׁמֶן וּבָקָר וְצֹאן לָרֹב כִּי
יג א שִׂמְחָה בְּיִשְׂרָאֵל׃ וַיִּוָּעַץ דָּוִיד עִם־שָׂרֵי הָאֲלָפִים וְהַמֵּאוֹת
ב לְכָל־נָגִיד׃ וַיֹּאמֶר דָּוִיד לְכֹל ׀ קְהַל יִשְׂרָאֵל אִם־עֲלֵיכֶם טוֹב וּמִן־
יְהוָה אֱלֹהֵינוּ נִפְרְצָה נִשְׁלְחָה עַל־אַחֵינוּ הַנִּשְׁאָרִים בְּכֹל אַרְצוֹת
יִשְׂרָאֵל וְעִמָּהֶם הַכֹּהֲנִים וְהַלְוִיִּם בְּעָרֵי מִגְרְשֵׁיהֶם וְיִקָּבְצוּ אֵלֵינוּ׃
ג ד וְנָסֵבָּה אֶת־אֲרוֹן אֱלֹהֵינוּ אֵלֵינוּ כִּי־לֹא דְרַשְׁנֻהוּ בִּימֵי שָׁאוּל׃ וַיֹּאמְרוּ
ה כָל־הַקָּהָל לַעֲשׂוֹת כֵּן כִּי־יָשַׁר הַדָּבָר בְּעֵינֵי כָל־הָעָם׃ וַיַּקְהֵל דָּוִיד
אֶת־כָּל־יִשְׂרָאֵל מִן־שִׁיחוֹר מִצְרַיִם וְעַד־לְבוֹא חֲמָת לְהָבִיא אֶת־
ו אֲרוֹן הָאֱלֹהִים מִקִּרְיַת יְעָרִים׃ וַיַּעַל דָּוִיד וְכָל־יִשְׂרָאֵל בַּעֲלָתָה
אֶל־קִרְיַת יְעָרִים אֲשֶׁר לִיהוּדָה לְהַעֲלוֹת מִשָּׁם אֵת אֲרוֹן הָאֱלֹהִים ׀
ז יְהוָה יוֹשֵׁב הַכְּרוּבִים אֲשֶׁר־נִקְרָא שֵׁם׃ וַיַּרְכִּיבוּ אֶת־אֲרוֹן הָאֱלֹהִים
ח עַל־עֲגָלָה חֲדָשָׁה מִבֵּית אֲבִינָדָב וְעֻזָּא וְאַחְיוֹ נֹהֲגִים בָּעֲגָלָה׃ וְדָוִיד
וְכָל־יִשְׂרָאֵל מְשַׂחֲקִים לִפְנֵי הָאֱלֹהִים בְּכָל־עֹז וּבְשִׁירִים וּבְכִנֹּרוֹת
ט וּבִנְבָלִים וּבְתֻפִּים וּבִמְצִלְתַּיִם וּבַחֲצֹצְרוֹת׃ וַיָּבֹאוּ עַד־גֹּרֶן כִּידֹן וַיִּשְׁלַח
י עֻזָּא אֶת־יָדוֹ לֶאֱחֹז אֶת־הָאָרוֹן כִּי שָׁמְטוּ הַבָּקָר׃ וַיִּחַר־אַף יְהוָה בְּעֻזָּא
יא וַיַּכֵּהוּ עַל אֲשֶׁר־שָׁלַח יָדוֹ עַל־הָאָרוֹן וַיָּמָת שָׁם לִפְנֵי אֱלֹהִים׃ וַיִּחַר
לְדָוִיד כִּי־פָרַץ יְהוָה פֶּרֶץ בְּעֻזָּא וַיִּקְרָא לַמָּקוֹם הַהוּא פֶּרֶץ עֻזָּא עַד
יב הַיּוֹם הַזֶּה׃ וַיִּירָא דָוִיד אֶת־הָאֱלֹהִים בַּיּוֹם הַהוּא לֵאמֹר הֵיךְ אָבִיא
יג אֵלַי אֵת אֲרוֹן הָאֱלֹהִים׃ וְלֹא־הֵסִיר דָּוִיד אֶת־הָאָרוֹן אֵלָיו אֶל־עִיר
יד דָּוִיד וַיַּטֵּהוּ אֶל־בֵּית עֹבֵד־אֱדֹם הַגִּתִּי׃ וַיֵּשֶׁב אֲרוֹן הָאֱלֹהִים עִם־בֵּית

remained at the house of Oved Edom the Gittite for three months, and the
Lord blessed the house of Oved Edom and all that was his.
14 1 King Ḥiram of Tyre sent envoys to David, and cedar logs, stonemasons,
2 and carpenters to build him a house. And David knew that the Lord had
established him as king over Israel and that the kingship had been exalted for
3 the sake of His people Israel. David took more wives in Jerusalem,
4 and David fathered more sons and daughters. These are the names of those
5 born to him in Jerusalem: Shamua, Shovav, Natan, and Shlomo; Yivḥar,
6 7 Elishua, and Elpelet; Noga, Nefeg, and Yafia; Elishama, Be'elyada, and
8 Elifelet. When the Philistines heard that David had been appointed as king
over Israel, all the Philistines marched in to hunt David down. When David
9 heard, he marched out to preempt them. The Philistines came and raided the
10 Refaim Valley. David inquired of the Lord, "Shall I go up to the Philistines?
Will You deliver them into my hands?" "Go up," the Lord replied to him, "for
11 I will surely deliver the Philistines into your hands." They marched up to Baal
Peratzim, and there David defeated them. And David said, "God has blasted
my enemies away by my hand like a blast of water," so he named that place
12 Baal Peratzim.[12] They abandoned their idols there, and David gave orders to
13 burn them with fire. But the Philistines returned once more and
14 went raiding in the valley. David inquired of God once more, and God said,
"Do not go up after them; turn around to go behind them and advance upon
15 them opposite the baca trees. As soon as you hear the sound of marching
echoing across the tops of the baca trees, go out to attack, for then God
16 will go out before you to strike down the Philistine force." And David did
as God commanded him, and he defeated the Philistine force from Givon
17 up to Gezer. David's fame grew throughout the lands, and the Lord spread
15 1 fear of him throughout the nations. David made himself houses in the City
of David. He prepared a place for the Ark of God and pitched a tent for it.
2 Then David declared, "No one should bear the Ark of God except for the
Levites, for the Lord has chosen them to bear the Ark of the Lord and to
3 serve Him forever." David assembled all of Israel to Jerusalem
4 to bring up the Ark of the Lord to the place he had prepared for it. Then
5 David gathered all the descendants of Aharon and the Levites: Of
6 the Kehatites, the leader Uriel and his kin, 120; of the Merarites,
7 the leader Asaya and his kin, 220; of the Gershomites, the leader
8 Yoel and his kin, 130; of the sons of Elitzafan, the leader Shemaya
9 and his kin, 200; of the sons of Ḥevron, the leader Eliel and
10 his kin, 80; of the sons of Uziel, the leader Aminadav and his

12 | From the Hebrew *peretz*, meaning "bursting out" or "blast"; cf. 13:11.

עֹבֵד אֱדֹם בְּבֵיתוֹ שְׁלֹשָׁה חֳדָשִׁים וַיְבָרֶךְ יְהוָה אֶת־בֵּית עֹבֵד־אֱדֹם
וְאֶת־כָּל־אֲשֶׁר־לוֹ:
יד א וַיִּשְׁלַח חירם מֶלֶךְ־צֹר מַלְאָכִים אֶל־דָּוִיד וַעֲצֵי אֲרָזִים וְחָרָשֵׁי חוּרָם
ב קִיר וְחָרָשֵׁי עֵצִים לִבְנוֹת לוֹ בָּיִת: וַיֵּדַע דָּוִיד כִּי־הֱכִינוֹ יְהוָה
לְמֶלֶךְ עַל־יִשְׂרָאֵל כִּי־נִשֵּׂאת לְמַעְלָה מַלְכוּתוֹ בַּעֲבוּר עַמּוֹ
ג יִשְׂרָאֵל: וַיִּקַּח דָּוִיד עוֹד נָשִׁים בִּירוּשָׁלִָם וַיּוֹלֶד דָּוִיד
ד עוֹד בָּנִים וּבָנוֹת: וְאֵלֶּה שְׁמוֹת הַיְלוּדִים אֲשֶׁר הָיוּ־לוֹ בִּירוּשָׁלִָם שַׁמּוּעַ
ה ו וְשׁוֹבָב נָתָן וּשְׁלֹמֹה: וְיִבְחָר וֶאֱלִישׁוּעַ וְאֶלְפָּלֶט: וְנֹגַהּ וְנֶפֶג וְיָפִיעַ:
ז ח וֶאֱלִישָׁמָע וּבְעֶלְיָדָע וֶאֱלִיפָלֶט: וַיִּשְׁמְעוּ פְלִשְׁתִּים כִּי־נִמְשַׁח דָּוִיד
לְמֶלֶךְ עַל־כָּל־יִשְׂרָאֵל וַיַּעֲלוּ כָל־פְּלִשְׁתִּים לְבַקֵּשׁ אֶת־דָּוִיד וַיִּשְׁמַע
ט י דָּוִיד וַיֵּצֵא לִפְנֵיהֶם: וּפְלִשְׁתִּים בָּאוּ וַיִּפְשְׁטוּ בְּעֵמֶק רְפָאִים: וַיִּשְׁאַל
דָּוִיד בֵּאלֹהִים לֵאמֹר הַאֶעֱלֶה עַל־פלשתיים וּנְתַתָּם בְּיָדִי וַיֹּאמֶר פְלִשְׁתִּים
יא לוֹ יְהוָה עֲלֵה וּנְתַתִּים בְּיָדֶךָ: וַיַּעֲלוּ בְּבַעַל־פְּרָצִים וַיַּכֵּם שָׁם דָּוִיד
וַיֹּאמֶר דָּוִיד פָּרַץ הָאֱלֹהִים אֶת־אוֹיְבַי בְּיָדִי כְּפֶרֶץ מָיִם עַל־כֵּן קָרְאוּ
יב שֵׁם־הַמָּקוֹם הַהוּא בַּעַל פְּרָצִים: וַיַּעַזְבוּ־שָׁם אֶת־אֱלֹהֵיהֶם וַיֹּאמֶר
יג דָּוִיד וַיִּשָּׂרְפוּ בָּאֵשׁ: וַיֹּסִיפוּ עוֹד פְּלִשְׁתִּים וַיִּפְשְׁטוּ בָּעֵמֶק:
יד וַיִּשְׁאַל עוֹד דָּוִיד בֵּאלֹהִים וַיֹּאמֶר לוֹ הָאֱלֹהִים לֹא תַעֲלֶה אַחֲרֵיהֶם
טו הָסֵב מֵעֲלֵיהֶם וּבָאתָ לָהֶם מִמּוּל הַבְּכָאִים: וִיהִי כְּשָׁמְעֲךָ אֶת־קוֹל
הַצְּעָדָה בְּרָאשֵׁי הַבְּכָאִים אָז תֵּצֵא בַמִּלְחָמָה כִּי־יָצָא הָאֱלֹהִים לְפָנֶיךָ
טז לְהַכּוֹת אֶת־מַחֲנֵה פְלִשְׁתִּים: וַיַּעַשׂ דָּוִיד כַּאֲשֶׁר צִוָּהוּ הָאֱלֹהִים
יז וַיַּכּוּ אֶת־מַחֲנֵה פְלִשְׁתִּים מִגִּבְעוֹן וְעַד־גָּזְרָה: וַיֵּצֵא שֵׁם־דָּוִיד בְּכָל־
טו א הָאֲרָצוֹת וַיהוָה נָתַן אֶת־פַּחְדּוֹ עַל־כָּל־הַגּוֹיִם: וַיַּעַשׂ־לוֹ בָתִּים בְּעִיר
ב דָּוִיד וַיָּכֶן מָקוֹם לַאֲרוֹן הָאֱלֹהִים וַיֶּט־לוֹ אֹהֶל: אָז אָמַר דָּוִיד לֹא
לָשֵׂאת אֶת־אֲרוֹן הָאֱלֹהִים כִּי אִם־הַלְוִיִּם כִּי־בָם ׀ בָּחַר יְהוָה לָשֵׂאת
ג אֶת־אֲרוֹן יְהוָה וּלְשָׁרְתוֹ עַד־עוֹלָם: וַיַּקְהֵל דָּוִיד אֶת־כָּל־
יִשְׂרָאֵל אֶל־יְרוּשָׁלִָם לְהַעֲלוֹת אֶת־אֲרוֹן יְהוָה אֶל־מְקוֹמוֹ אֲשֶׁר־
ד ה הֵכִין לוֹ: וַיֶּאֱסֹף דָּוִיד אֶת־בְּנֵי אַהֲרֹן וְאֶת־הַלְוִיִּם: לִבְנֵי
ו קְהָת אוּרִיאֵל הַשָּׂר וְאֶחָיו מֵאָה וְעֶשְׂרִים: לִבְנֵי מְרָרִי
ז עֲשָׂיָה הַשָּׂר וְאֶחָיו מָאתַיִם וְעֶשְׂרִים: לִבְנֵי גֵרְשׁוֹם
ח יוֹאֵל הַשָּׂר וְאֶחָיו מֵאָה וּשְׁלֹשִׁים: לִבְנֵי אֱלִיצָפָן שְׁמַעְיָה
ט הַשָּׂר וְאֶחָיו מָאתָיִם: לִבְנֵי חֶבְרוֹן אֱלִיאֵל הַשָּׂר וְאֶחָיו
י שְׁמוֹנִים: לִבְנֵי עֻזִּיאֵל עַמִּינָדָב הַשָּׂר וְאֶחָיו מֵאָה וּשְׁנֵים

11 kin, 112. David summoned the priests Tzadok and Evyatar and the
12 Levites Uriel, Asaya, Yoel, Shemaya, Eliel, and Aminadav and told them,
"You are the ancestral heads of the Levites; you and your kin must sanctify
yourselves. Then you will bring up the Ark of the Lord, God of Israel, to
13 the place I have prepared for it. Because it was not you the first time, the
Lord our God burst out against us, for we did not seek Him in the right
14 way." The priests and Levites sanctified themselves to bring up the Ark of
15 the Lord, God of Israel, and the Levites carried the Ark of God as Moshe
had commanded according to the word of the Lord: bearing poles upon
16 their shoulders. David ordered the Levite leaders to position their
brothers the singers with musical instruments – lyres, harps, and cymbals – to
play out loud, raising sounds of joy.
17 So the Levites appointed Heiman son of Yoel, and of his kinsmen Asaf son of
18 Berekhyahu, and of their Merarite kin Eitan son of Kushayahu, along with their
kinsmen within the second order: Zekharyahu, Ben, Yaaziel, Shemiramot,
Yeḥiel, Uni, Eliav, Benayahu, Maaseyahu, Matityahu, Elifelehu, Mikneyahu,
19 Oved Edom, and Ye'iel, the gatekeepers. The singers Heiman, Asaf, and
20 Eitan played on cymbals of bronze; Zekharya, Yaaziel, Shemiramot, Yeḥiel,
21 Uni, Eliav, Maaseyahu, and Benayahu played the *alamot*[13] on harps while
Matityahu, Elifelehu, Mikneyahu, Oved Edom, Ye'iel, and Azazyahu led with
22 the *sheminit* on lyres. Kenanyahu, the chief musician of the Levites, conducted
23 the music, for he was skilled. Berekhya and Elkana were gatekeepers for the
24 Ark while Shevanyahu, Yoshafat, Netanel, Amasai, Zekharyahu, Benayahu,
and Eliezer the priests sounded the trumpets before the Ark of God, with
25 Oved Edom and Yeḥiya as gatekeepers for the Ark. Thus David, the elders
of Israel, and the officers of thousands went with joy to bring up the Ark of
26 the Lord's Covenant from the house of Oved Edom. Because God
supported the Levites who carried the Ark of the Lord's Covenant, they
27 sacrificed seven bulls and seven rams. David was clad in a robe of fine linen,
as were all the Levites who carried the Ark, the musicians, and Kenanya,
28 the chief musician of the singers; David also wore a linen ephod.[14] And all
of Israel brought up the Ark of the Lord's Covenant with joyous shouting,
with the sound of the ram's horn and trumpets and cymbals, and the music
29 of lyres and harps. As the Ark of the Lord's Covenant reached the City of
David, Mikhal, Sha'ul's daughter, was watching through the window, and
when she saw David – the king! – dancing and reveling, she felt a rush of
16 1 contempt for him. They brought the Ark of God, set it up within the
tent that David had pitched for it, and offered up burnt offerings and peace
2 offerings before God. When David had finished offering the burnt offering

13 | *Alamot* and *sheminit* (v. 21) are musical terms of uncertain meaning; cf. Psalms 6:1, 46:1.
14 | An outer garment worn by the priests (see Ex., ch. 28).

יא עָשָׂר׃ וַיִּקְרָא דָוִיד לְצָדוֹק וּלְאֶבְיָתָר הַכֹּהֲנִים וְלַלְוִיִּם
יב לְאוּרִיאֵל עֲשָׂיָה וְיוֹאֵל שְׁמַעְיָה וֶאֱלִיאֵל וְעַמִּינָדָב׃ וַיֹּאמֶר לָהֶם אַתֶּם
רָאשֵׁי הָאָבוֹת לַלְוִיִּם הִתְקַדְּשׁוּ אַתֶּם וַאֲחֵיכֶם וְהַעֲלִיתֶם אֵת אֲרוֹן
יג יהוה אֱלֹהֵי יִשְׂרָאֵל אֶל־הֲכִינוֹתִי לוֹ׃ כִּי לְמַבָּרִאשׁוֹנָה לֹא אַתֶּם
יד פָּרַץ יהוה אֱלֹהֵינוּ בָּנוּ כִּי־לֹא דְרַשְׁנֻהוּ כַּמִּשְׁפָּט׃ וַיִּתְקַדְּשׁוּ הַכֹּהֲנִים
טו וְהַלְוִיִּם לְהַעֲלוֹת אֶת־אֲרוֹן יהוה אֱלֹהֵי יִשְׂרָאֵל׃ וַיִּשְׂאוּ בְנֵי־הַלְוִיִּם
אֵת אֲרוֹן הָאֱלֹהִים כַּאֲשֶׁר צִוָּה מֹשֶׁה כִּדְבַר יהוה בִּכְתֵפָם בַּמֹּטוֹת
טז עֲלֵיהֶם׃ וַיֹּאמֶר דָּוִיד לְשָׂרֵי הַלְוִיִּם לְהַעֲמִיד אֶת־אֲחֵיהֶם
הַמְשֹׁרְרִים בִּכְלֵי־שִׁיר נְבָלִים וְכִנֹּרוֹת וּמְצִלְתָּיִם מַשְׁמִיעִים לְהָרִים־
בְּקוֹל לְשִׂמְחָה׃
יז וַיַּעֲמִידוּ הַלְוִיִּם אֵת הֵימָן בֶּן־יוֹאֵל וּמִן־אֶחָיו אָסָף בֶּן־בֶּרֶכְיָהוּ וּמִן־בְּנֵי
יח מְרָרִי אֲחֵיהֶם אֵיתָן בֶּן־קוּשָׁיָהוּ׃ וְעִמָּהֶם אֲחֵיהֶם הַמִּשְׁנִים זְכַרְיָהוּ בֵּן
וְיַעֲזִיאֵל וּשְׁמִירָמוֹת וִיחִיאֵל ׀ וְעֻנִּי אֱלִיאָב וּבְנָיָהוּ וּמַעֲשֵׂיָהוּ וּמַתִּתְיָהוּ
יט וֶאֱלִיפְלֵהוּ וּמִקְנֵיָהוּ וְעֹבֵד אֱדֹם וִיעִיאֵל הַשֹּׁעֲרִים׃ וְהַמְשֹׁרְרִים הֵימָן
כ אָסָף וְאֵיתָן בִּמְצִלְתַּיִם נְחֹשֶׁת לְהַשְׁמִיעַ׃ וּזְכַרְיָה וַעֲזִיאֵל וּשְׁמִירָמוֹת
כא וִיחִיאֵל וְעֻנִּי וֶאֱלִיאָב וּמַעֲשֵׂיָהוּ וּבְנָיָהוּ בִּנְבָלִים עַל־עֲלָמוֹת׃ וּמַתִּתְיָהוּ
וֶאֱלִיפְלֵהוּ וּמִקְנֵיָהוּ וְעֹבֵד אֱדֹם וִיעִיאֵל וַעֲזַזְיָהוּ בְּכִנֹּרוֹת עַל־הַשְּׁמִינִית
כב כג לְנַצֵּחַ׃ וּכְנַנְיָהוּ שַׂר־הַלְוִיִּם בְּמַשָּׂא יָסֹר בַּמַּשָּׂא כִּי מֵבִין הוּא׃ וּבֶרֶכְיָה
כד וְאֶלְקָנָה שֹׁעֲרִים לָאָרוֹן׃ וּשְׁבַנְיָהוּ וְיוֹשָׁפָט וּנְתַנְאֵל וַעֲמָשַׂי וּזְכַרְיָהוּ
וּבְנָיָהוּ וֶאֱלִיעֶזֶר הַכֹּהֲנִים מחצצרים בַּחֲצֹצְרוֹת לִפְנֵי אֲרוֹן הָאֱלֹהִים מַחְצְרִים
כה וְעֹבֵד אֱדֹם וִיחִיָּה שֹׁעֲרִים לָאָרוֹן׃ וַיְהִי דָוִיד וְזִקְנֵי יִשְׂרָאֵל וְשָׂרֵי
הָאֲלָפִים הַהֹלְכִים לְהַעֲלוֹת אֶת־אֲרוֹן בְּרִית־יהוה מִן־בֵּית עֹבֵד־אֱדֹם
כו בְּשִׂמְחָה׃ וַיְהִי בֶּעְזֹר הָאֱלֹהִים אֶת־הַלְוִיִּם נֹשְׂאֵי אֲרוֹן
כז בְּרִית־יהוה וַיִּזְבְּחוּ שִׁבְעָה־פָרִים וְשִׁבְעָה אֵילִים׃ וְדָוִיד מְכֻרְבָּל ׀
בִּמְעִיל בּוּץ וְכָל־הַלְוִיִּם הַנֹּשְׂאִים אֶת־הָאָרוֹן וְהַמְשֹׁרְרִים וּכְנַנְיָה הַשַּׂר
כח הַמַּשָּׂא הַמְשֹׁרְרִים וְעַל־דָּוִיד אֵפוֹד בָּד׃ וְכָל־יִשְׂרָאֵל מַעֲלִים אֶת־
אֲרוֹן בְּרִית־יהוה בִּתְרוּעָה וּבְקוֹל שׁוֹפָר וּבַחֲצֹצְרוֹת וּבִמְצִלְתָּיִם
כט מַשְׁמִעִים בִּנְבָלִים וְכִנֹּרוֹת׃ וַיְהִי אֲרוֹן בְּרִית יהוה בָּא עַד־עִיר דָּוִיד
וּמִיכַל בַּת־שָׁאוּל נִשְׁקְפָה ׀ בְּעַד הַחַלּוֹן וַתֵּרֶא אֶת־הַמֶּלֶךְ דָּוִיד מְרַקֵּד
טז א וּמְשַׂחֵק וַתִּבֶז לוֹ בְּלִבָּהּ׃ וַיָּבִיאוּ אֶת־אֲרוֹן הָאֱלֹהִים וַיַּצִּיגוּ
אֹתוֹ בְּתוֹךְ הָאֹהֶל אֲשֶׁר נָטָה־לוֹ דָּוִיד וַיַּקְרִיבוּ עֹלוֹת וּשְׁלָמִים לִפְנֵי
ב הָאֱלֹהִים׃ וַיְכַל דָּוִיד מֵהַעֲלוֹת הָעֹלָה וְהַשְּׁלָמִים וַיְבָרֶךְ אֶת־הָעָם

3 and the peace offerings, he blessed the people in the name of the Lord. He
then distributed a loaf of bread, a share of meat, and a cake of raisins to all
4 the people of Israel, every single man and woman. He appointed some of the
Levites as attendants before the Ark of the Lord to invoke, thank, and praise
5 the Lord, God of Israel: Asaf was the head, Zekharya his second,
Ye'iel, Shemiramot, Yeḥiel, Matitya, Eliav, Benayahu, Oved Edom, and Ye'iel
6 with lyres and harps, Asaf sounding the cymbals, and the priests Benayahu
and Yaḥaziel with trumpets continually before the Ark of God's Covenant.
7 On that day, for the first time, David gave thanksgiving to the Lord through
Asaf and his kinsmen:
8 Give thanks to the Lord; call on His name;[15] proclaim His acts among the
9 10 peoples. Sing to Him, make music to Him, tell of all His wonders. Glory in
11 His holy name; let the hearts of the Lord's seekers rejoice. Long for the Lord
12 and His might; seek out His presence always. Recall the wonders He has
13 done, the marvels and judgments He has pronounced. O seed of Yisrael His
14 servant, O children of Yaakov, His chosen ones. He is the Lord, our God;
15 His judgments are throughout the land. Remember His covenant forever,
16 His word of command for a thousand generations – which He formed with
17 Avraham, swore to Yitzḥak, and established with Yaakov as a statute, as an
18 eternal covenant for Israel, saying, "To you I will give the land of Canaan as
19 your share of inheritance," when you were few in number, scarce, strangers
20 there, wandering from nation to nation, from one kingdom to another people.
21 Yet He let no one oppress them and rebuked kings for their sake, saying,
22 23 "Touch not My anointed ones, and do My prophets no harm." Sing to the
24 Lord, all the earth;[16] proclaim His salvation day by day; declare His glory
25 among the nations, His wonders among all peoples, for the Lord is great, of
26 highest praise, to be held in awe above all divine beings – for all the gods of
27 the peoples are mere idols; it was the Lord who made the heavens. Majesty
28 and splendor are before Him, might and joy in His place. Render to the Lord,
29 O families of the peoples – render to the Lord glory and might – render to
the Lord the glory due His name. Bring an offering and come before Him;
30 bow down to the Lord in the splendor of holiness. Tremble before Him, all
31 the earth – the world stands firm; it will never be shaken. Let the heavens
rejoice and the earth exult; let them say among the nations, "The Lord is
32 King." Let the sea roar, and all that fills it; let the fields revel, and all they
33 contain; then the trees of the forest will sing for joy before the Lord, for He
34 is coming to judge the earth. Thank the Lord for He is good; His loving-
35 kindness is forever. Say, "Save us, God of our salvation; gather us and rescue
us from the nations, so that we may give thanks to Your holy name and glory
36 in Your praise." Blessed is the Lord, God of Israel, for ever and ever. And all
37 the people said, "Amen," and "Praise the Lord!" He then left Asaf
and his kinsmen there before the Ark of the Lord's Covenant in constant
38 daily service before the Ark. Oved Edom and his kin numbered sixty-eight;

15 | Cf. Psalms 105:1–15.
16 | Cf. Psalms 96:1–13.

ג בשם יהוה: ויחלק לכל־איש ישראל מאיש ועד־אשה לאיש ככר־
ד לחם ואשפר ואשישה: ויתן לפני ארון יהוה מן־הלוים משרתים
ה ולהזכיר ולהודות ולהלל ליהוה אלהי ישראל: אסף
הראש ומשנהו זכריה יעיאל ושמירמות ויחיאל ומתתיה ואליאב
ובניהו ועבד אדם ויעיאל בכלי נבלים ובכנרות ואסף במצלתים
ו משמיע: ובניהו ויחזיאל הכהנים בחצצרות תמיד לפני ארון ברית־
ז האלהים: ביום ההוא אז נתן דויד בראש להדות ליהוה ביד־אסף
ואחיו:
ח ט הודו ליהוה קראו בשמו הודיעו בעמים עלילתיו: שירו לו זמרו־לו
י שיחו בכל־נפלאתיו: התהללו בשם קדשו ישמח לב מבקשי יהוה:
יא יב דרשו יהוה ועזו בקשו פניו תמיד: זכרו נפלאתיו אשר עשה מפתיו
יג יד ומשפטי־פיהו: זרע ישראל עבדו בני יעקב בחיריו: הוא יהוה
טו אלהינו בכל־הארץ משפטיו: זכרו לעולם בריתו דבר צוה לאלף
טז יז דור: אשר כרת את־אברהם ושבועתו ליצחק: ויעמידה ליעקב
יח לחק לישראל ברית עולם: לאמר לך אתן ארץ־כנען חבל נחלתכם:
יט כ בהיותכם מתי מספר כמעט וגרים בה: ויתהלכו מגוי אל־גוי
כא וממממלכה אל־עם אחר: לא־הניח לאיש לעשקם ויוכח עליהם
כב כג מלכים: אל־תגעו במשיחי ובנביאי אל־תרעו: שירו ליהוה כל־
כד הארץ בשרו מיום־אל־יום ישועתו: ספרו בגוים את־כבודו בכל־
כה העמים נפלאתיו: כי גדול יהוה ומהלל מאד ונורא הוא על־כל־
כו כז אלהים: כי כל־אלהי העמים אלילים ויהוה שמים עשה: הוד והדר
כח לפניו עז וחדוה במקמו: הבו ליהוה משפחות עמים הבו ליהוה
כט כבוד ועז: הבו ליהוה כבוד שמו שאו מנחה ובאו לפניו השתחוו
ל ליהוה בהדרת־קדש: חילו מלפניו כל־הארץ אף־תכון תבל בל־
לא לב תמוט: ישמחו השמים ותגל הארץ ויאמרו בגוים יהוה מלך: ירעם
לג הים ומלואו יעלץ השדה וכל־אשר־בו: אז ירננו עצי היער מלפני
לד יהוה כי־בא לשפוט את־הארץ: הודו ליהוה כי טוב כי לעולם
לה חסדו: ואמרו הושיענו אלהי ישענו וקבצנו והצילנו מן־הגוים
לו להדות לשם קדשך להשתבח בתהלתך: ברוך יהוה אלהי ז
ישראל מן־העולם ועד־העלם ויאמרו כל־העם אמן והלל
לז ליהוה: ויעזב־שם לפני ארון ברית־יהוה לאסף ולאחיו
לח לשרת לפני הארון תמיד לדבר־יום ביומו: ועבד אדם ואחיהם

39 Oved Edom son of Yeditun and Ḥosa were to be gatekeepers. Tzadok the
priest and his kin, the priests, remained in the presence of the LORD's
40 Tabernacle at the high shrine at Givon to offer up burnt offerings regularly
to the LORD, morning and evening, on the altar of burnt offering in accordance with all that is written in the LORD's Law that He commanded Israel
41 to follow. With them were Heiman and Yedutun and the rest of the chosen
who were singled out by name to give thanks to the LORD, for His loving-
42 kindness lasts forever; Heiman and Yedutun accompanied them with
trumpets and cymbals and played instruments for the sacred song. Yedutun's
43 sons were posted at the gate. Then all the people went back home, and David
17 1 turned around to bless his own house. Once he had settled in his
palace, David said to the prophet Natan, "Here I am dwelling in a cedarwood
2 palace while the Ark of the Lord's Covenant is dwelling beneath tents." "Do
whatever you have in mind," Natan said to David, "for God is with
3 4 you." But that same night, the word of God came to Natan: "Go and
say to My servant David: Thus says the LORD: You shall not be the one to
5 build a house for Me to dwell in. For I have not dwelt in a house from the day
I brought the Israelites out to this day; I have gone from tent to tent, from
6 Tabernacle to Tabernacle. But wherever I roamed throughout Israel, have I
ever spoken a word to any of the judges of Israel whom I charged to shepherd
7 My people, saying, 'Why have you not built Me a cedarwood palace?' Now,
you shall say so to My servant David: Thus says the LORD of Hosts: I took
you out of the pasture, from following the sheep, to be ruler over My people
8 Israel. I have been with you wherever you went, and I have cut down all your
enemies before you. I will make for you a name – one of the greatest names
9 on earth. I will set aside a place for My people Israel and let them take root
and settle down within it, and they will be disturbed no longer; violent men
10 will no longer wear them down as they once did in the days when I appointed
judges over My people Israel. I will subdue all of your enemies; moreover, I
11 declare that the LORD will establish a house for you. For it will be when your
days are done and you must go the way of your ancestors, I will raise up your
own seed after you – among your own sons – and I will establish his kingship.
12 13 He will build Me a house, and I will firmly establish his throne forever. I will
be a Father to him, and he will be a son to Me; My loyalties will never stray
14 from him, as I removed them from him who was before you. I will set him in
My house and in My kingship forever, and his throne will be secure forever."
15 16 Natan related all these words and all this vision to David. Now King
David came and sat before the LORD. "Who am I, O LORD God, and who is
17 my house," he said, "that you have brought me so far? And yet even this is
small in Your eyes, God, as You also speak of Your servant's house in the
18 distant future and perceive me as a worthy man, O LORD God. But what more

לט שִׁשִּׁים וּשְׁמוֹנָה וְעֹבֵד אֱדֹם בֶּן־יְדִיתוּן וְחֹסָה לְשֹׁעֲרִים׃ וְאֵת ׀ צָדוֹק
מ הַכֹּהֵן וְאֶחָיו הַכֹּהֲנִים לִפְנֵי מִשְׁכַּן יְהוָה בַּבָּמָה אֲשֶׁר בְּגִבְעוֹן׃ לְהַעֲלוֹת
עֹלוֹת לַיהוָה עַל־מִזְבַּח הָעֹלָה תָּמִיד לַבֹּקֶר וְלָעָרֶב וּלְכָל־הַכָּתוּב
מא בְּתוֹרַת יְהוָה אֲשֶׁר צִוָּה עַל־יִשְׂרָאֵל׃ וְעִמָּהֶם הֵימָן וִידוּתוּן וּשְׁאָר
מב הַבְּרוּרִים אֲשֶׁר נִקְּבוּ בְּשֵׁמוֹת לְהֹדוֹת לַיהוָה כִּי לְעוֹלָם חַסְדּוֹ׃ וְעִמָּהֶם
הֵימָן וִידוּתוּן חֲצֹצְרוֹת וּמְצִלְתַּיִם לְמַשְׁמִיעִים וּכְלֵי שִׁיר הָאֱלֹהִים
מג וּבְנֵי יְדוּתוּן לַשָּׁעַר׃ וַיֵּלְכוּ כָל־הָעָם אִישׁ לְבֵיתוֹ וַיִּסֹּב דָּוִיד לְבָרֵךְ
יז א אֶת־בֵּיתוֹ׃ וַיְהִי כַּאֲשֶׁר יָשַׁב דָּוִיד בְּבֵיתוֹ וַיֹּאמֶר דָּוִיד אֶל־
נָתָן הַנָּבִיא הִנֵּה אָנֹכִי יוֹשֵׁב בְּבֵית הָאֲרָזִים וַאֲרוֹן בְּרִית־יְהוָה תַּחַת
ב יְרִיעוֹת׃ וַיֹּאמֶר נָתָן אֶל־דָּוִיד כֹּל אֲשֶׁר בִּלְבָבְךָ עֲשֵׂה כִּי הָאֱלֹהִים
ג עִמָּךְ׃ וַיְהִי בַּלַּיְלָה הַהוּא וַיְהִי דְּבַר־אֱלֹהִים אֶל־נָתָן לֵאמֹר׃
ד לֵךְ וְאָמַרְתָּ אֶל־דָּוִיד עַבְדִּי כֹּה אָמַר יְהוָה לֹא אַתָּה תִּבְנֶה־לִּי הַבַּיִת
ה לָשָׁבֶת׃ כִּי לֹא יָשַׁבְתִּי בְּבַיִת מִן־הַיּוֹם אֲשֶׁר הֶעֱלֵיתִי אֶת־יִשְׂרָאֵל עַד
ו הַיּוֹם הַזֶּה וָאֶהְיֶה מֵאֹהֶל אֶל־אֹהֶל וּמִמִּשְׁכָּן׃ בְּכֹל אֲשֶׁר־הִתְהַלַּכְתִּי
בְּכָל־יִשְׂרָאֵל הֲדָבָר דִּבַּרְתִּי אֶת־אַחַד שֹׁפְטֵי יִשְׂרָאֵל אֲשֶׁר צִוִּיתִי
ז לִרְעוֹת אֶת־עַמִּי לֵאמֹר לָמָּה לֹא־בְנִיתֶם לִי בֵּית אֲרָזִים׃ וְעַתָּה כֹּה־
תֹאמַר לְעַבְדִּי לְדָוִיד כֹּה אָמַר יְהוָה צְבָאוֹת אֲנִי לְקַחְתִּיךָ מִן־הַנָּוֶה
ח מִן־אַחֲרֵי הַצֹּאן לִהְיוֹת נָגִיד עַל עַמִּי יִשְׂרָאֵל׃ וָאֶהְיֶה עִמְּךָ בְּכֹל אֲשֶׁר
הָלַכְתָּ וָאַכְרִית אֶת־כָּל־אוֹיְבֶיךָ מִפָּנֶיךָ וְעָשִׂיתִי לְךָ שֵׁם כְּשֵׁם הַגְּדוֹלִים
ט אֲשֶׁר בָּאָרֶץ׃ וְשַׂמְתִּי מָקוֹם לְעַמִּי יִשְׂרָאֵל וּנְטַעְתִּיהוּ וְשָׁכַן תַּחְתָּיו
וְלֹא יִרְגַּז עוֹד וְלֹא־יוֹסִיפוּ בְנֵי־עַוְלָה לְבַלֹּתוֹ כַּאֲשֶׁר בָּרִאשׁוֹנָה׃
י וּלְמִיָּמִים אֲשֶׁר צִוִּיתִי שֹׁפְטִים עַל־עַמִּי יִשְׂרָאֵל וְהִכְנַעְתִּי אֶת־כָּל־
יא אוֹיְבֶיךָ וָאַגִּד לָךְ וּבַיִת יִבְנֶה־לְּךָ יְהוָה׃ וְהָיָה כִּי־מָלְאוּ יָמֶיךָ לָלֶכֶת
עִם־אֲבֹתֶיךָ וַהֲקִימוֹתִי אֶת־זַרְעֲךָ אַחֲרֶיךָ אֲשֶׁר יִהְיֶה מִבָּנֶיךָ וַהֲכִינוֹתִי
יב יג אֶת־מַלְכוּתוֹ׃ הוּא יִבְנֶה־לִּי בָּיִת וְכֹנַנְתִּי אֶת־כִּסְאוֹ עַד־עוֹלָם׃ אֲנִי
אֶהְיֶה־לּוֹ לְאָב וְהוּא יִהְיֶה־לִּי לְבֵן וְחַסְדִּי לֹא־אָסִיר מֵעִמּוֹ כַּאֲשֶׁר
יד הֲסִירוֹתִי מֵאֲשֶׁר הָיָה לְפָנֶיךָ׃ וְהַעֲמַדְתִּיהוּ בְּבֵיתִי וּבְמַלְכוּתִי עַד־
טו הָעוֹלָם וְכִסְאוֹ יִהְיֶה נָכוֹן עַד־עוֹלָם׃ כְּכֹל הַדְּבָרִים הָאֵלֶּה וּכְכֹל הֶחָזוֹן
טז הַזֶּה כֵּן דִּבֶּר נָתָן אֶל־דָּוִיד׃ וַיָּבֹא הַמֶּלֶךְ דָּוִיד וַיֵּשֶׁב לִפְנֵי
יְהוָה וַיֹּאמֶר מִי־אֲנִי יְהוָה אֱלֹהִים וּמִי בֵיתִי כִּי הֲבִיאֹתַנִי עַד־הֲלֹם׃
יז וַתִּקְטַן זֹאת בְּעֵינֶיךָ אֱלֹהִים וַתְּדַבֵּר עַל־בֵּית־עַבְדְּךָ לְמֵרָחוֹק וּרְאִיתַנִי
יח כְּתוֹר הָאָדָם הַמַּעֲלָה יְהוָה אֱלֹהִים׃ מַה־יּוֹסִיף עוֹד דָּוִיד אֵלֶיךָ לְכָבוֹד

could David add, for the honor You have given Your servant? You know Your
19 servant. It is for the sake of Your servant, O Lord, and Your own will, that
20 You brought about this greatness, to make all this greatness known. O Lord,
there is no one like You and no god besides You, as we have heard all along.
21 And who is like Your people Israel – the only nation on earth God went to
redeem as His own people, making a name for Yourself of greatness and
wondrous deeds by driving out nations before the people You redeemed for
22 Yourself from Egypt. You have made Your people Israel Your own people
23 forever, and You, O Lord, have become their God. Now, O Lord, let the
promise You made regarding Your servant and regarding his house endure
24 forever; do as You have pro-mised. May Your name endure and be exalted
forever; let them say, 'The Lord of Hosts, God of Israel, is the one God of
25 Israel,' and may the House of David be established before You. As You, My
God, have revealed to Your servant that You will build him a house, Your
26 servant has been moved to pray before You. And now, O Lord – You are
27 God, and You have promised this grace to Your servant. And now – may it
please You to bless Your servant's house to be before You forever, for You, O
18 1 Lord, have blessed it and are blessed forever." Some time later,
David defeated the Philistines, and subjugated them, and seized Gat and its
2 dependencies from the hand of the Philistines. He defeated Moav, and Moav
3 became tribute-bearing vassals to David. David defeated King Hadadezer of
Tzova near Ḥamat as he set out to establish his rule by the River Euphrates;
4 David captured 1,000 chariots, 7,000 riders, and 20,000 infantrymen from
5 him and hamstrung all the chariot horses, retaining 100 chariot horses. Aram
of Damascus came to King Hadadezer of Tzova's aid, but David struck down
6 22,000 of Aram's men. David then took over Aram of Damascus, and the
Arameans became David's tribute-bearing vassals. And the Lord granted
7 victory to David wherever he went. David took the golden quivers that were
8 with Hadadezer's officials and brought them to Jerusalem. And from Tivḥat
and Kun, Hadadezer's cities, David confiscated vast amounts of bronze,
which Shlomo used to make the bronze sea, the pillars, and the bronze
9 vessels. When To'u, king of Ḥamat, heard that David had defeated
10 the entire force of King Hadadezer of Tzova, he sent his son Hadoram to King
David to greet him and congratulate him for having conquered Hadadezer in
battle, for Hadadezer had been at war with To'u. With him was a vast array of
11 gold and silver and bronze vessels. King David devoted those, too, to the
Lord, in addition to all the silver and gold he had carried off from all the
12 nations of Edom, Moav, the Amonites, the Philistines, and Amalek. Avshai
13 son of Tzeruya struck down 18,000 of Edom in the Valley of Salt. He stationed
governors in Edom, and all Edom became David's vassals. And the Lord

יט אֶת־עַבְדְּךָ֥ וְאַתָּ֖ה אֶת־עַבְדְּךָ֥ יָדָֽעְתָּ׃ יְהוָ֕ה בַּעֲב֤וּר עַבְדְּךָ֙ וּֽכְלִבְּךָ֔
כ עָשִׂ֕יתָ אֵ֥ת כָּל־הַגְּדוּלָּ֖ה הַזֹּ֑את לְהֹדִ֖יעַ אֶת־כָּל־הַגְּדֻלּֽוֹת׃ יְהוָה֙ אֵ֣ין
כא כָּמ֔וֹךָ וְאֵ֥ין אֱלֹהִ֖ים זֽוּלָתֶ֑ךָ בְּכֹ֥ל אֲשֶׁר־שָׁמַ֖עְנוּ בְּאָזְנֵֽינוּ׃ וּמִי֙ כְּעַמְּךָ֣
יִשְׂרָאֵ֔ל גּ֥וֹי אֶחָ֖ד בָּאָ֑רֶץ אֲשֶׁר֩ הָלַ֨ךְ הָאֱלֹהִ֜ים לִפְדּ֧וֹת ל֣וֹ עָ֗ם לָשׂ֤וּם
לְךָ֙ שֵׁ֚ם גְּדֻלּ֣וֹת וְנֹרָא֔וֹת לְגָרֵ֗שׁ מִפְּנֵ֤י עַמְּךָ֙ אֲשֶׁר־פָּדִ֣יתָ מִמִּצְרַ֔יִם גּוֹיִֽם׃
כב וַתִּתֵּ֞ן אֶת־עַמְּךָ֧ יִשְׂרָאֵ֛ל ׀ לְךָ֥ לְעָ֖ם עַד־עוֹלָ֑ם וְאַתָּ֣ה יְהוָ֔ה הָיִ֥יתָ לָהֶ֖ם
כג לֵאלֹהִֽים׃ וְעַתָּ֣ה יְהוָ֔ה הַדָּבָ֗ר אֲשֶׁ֨ר דִּבַּ֤רְתָּ עַֽל־עַבְדְּךָ֙ וְעַל־בֵּית֔וֹ יֵאָמֵ֖ן
כד עַד־עוֹלָ֑ם וַעֲשֵׂ֖ה כַּאֲשֶׁ֥ר דִּבַּֽרְתָּ׃ וְיֵאָמֵ֡ן וְיִגְדַּל֩ שִׁמְךָ֨ עַד־עוֹלָ֜ם לֵאמֹ֗ר
יְהוָ֤ה צְבָאוֹת֙ אֱלֹהֵ֣י יִשְׂרָאֵ֔ל אֱלֹהִ֖ים לְיִשְׂרָאֵ֑ל וּבֵית־דָּוִ֥יד עַבְדְּךָ֖ נָכ֥וֹן
כה לְפָנֶֽיךָ׃ כִּ֣י ׀ אַתָּ֣ה אֱלֹהַ֗י גָּלִ֙יתָ֙ אֶת־אֹ֣זֶן עַבְדְּךָ֔ לִבְנ֥וֹת ל֖וֹ בָּ֑יִת עַל־כֵּן֙
כו מָצָ֣א עַבְדְּךָ֔ לְהִתְפַּלֵּ֖ל לְפָנֶֽיךָ׃ וְעַתָּ֣ה יְהוָ֔ה אַתָּה־ה֖וּא הָאֱלֹהִ֑ים
כז וַתְּדַבֵּר֙ עַֽל־עַבְדְּךָ֔ הַטּוֹבָ֖ה הַזֹּֽאת׃ וְעַתָּ֗ה הוֹאַ֙לְתָּ֙ לְבָרֵךְ֙ אֶת־
בֵּ֣ית עַבְדְּךָ֔ לִהְי֥וֹת לְעוֹלָ֖ם לְפָנֶ֑יךָ כִּֽי־אַתָּ֤ה יְהוָה֙ בֵּרַ֔כְתָּ וּמְבֹרָ֖ךְ
יח א לְעוֹלָֽם׃ וַיְהִי֙ אַחֲרֵי־כֵ֔ן וַיַּ֥ךְ דָּוִ֛יד אֶת־פְּלִשְׁתִּ֖ים וַיַּכְנִיעֵ֑ם
ב וַיִּקַּ֛ח אֶת־גַּ֥ת וּבְנֹתֶ֖יהָ מִיַּ֥ד פְּלִשְׁתִּֽים׃ וַיַּ֖ךְ אֶת־מוֹאָ֑ב וַיִּהְי֤וּ מוֹאָב֙
ג עֲבָדִ֣ים לְדָוִ֔יד נֹשְׂאֵ֖י מִנְחָֽה׃ וַיַּ֥ךְ דָּוִ֛יד אֶת־הֲדַדְעֶ֥זֶר מֶֽלֶךְ־צוֹבָ֖ה חֲמָ֑תָה
ד בְּלֶכְתּ֕וֹ לְהַצִּ֥יב יָד֖וֹ בִּנְהַר פְּרָֽת׃ וַיִּלְכֹּ֨ד דָּוִ֜יד מִמֶּ֨נּוּ אֶ֣לֶף רֶ֗כֶב וְשִׁבְעַ֤ת
אֲלָפִים֙ פָּֽרָשִׁ֔ים וְעֶשְׂרִ֥ים אֶ֖לֶף אִ֣ישׁ רַגְלִ֑י וַיְעַקֵּ֤ר דָּוִיד֙ אֶת־כָּל־הָרֶ֔כֶב
ה וַיּוֹתֵ֥ר מִמֶּ֖נּוּ מֵ֥אָה רָֽכֶב׃ וַיָּבֹא֙ אֲרַ֣ם דַּרְמֶ֔שֶׂק לַעְז֕וֹר לַהֲדַדְעֶ֖זֶר מֶ֣לֶךְ
ו צוֹבָ֑ה וַיַּ֣ךְ דָּוִיד֙ בַּאֲרָ֔ם עֶשְׂרִֽים־וּשְׁנַ֥יִם אֶ֖לֶף אִֽישׁ׃ וַיָּ֨שֶׂם דָּוִ֜יד בַּאֲרַ֣ם
דַּרְמֶ֗שֶׂק וַיְהִ֤י אֲרָם֙ לְדָוִ֔יד עֲבָדִ֖ים נֹשְׂאֵ֣י מִנְחָ֑ה וַיּ֤וֹשַׁע יְהוָה֙ לְדָוִ֔יד
ז בְּכֹ֖ל אֲשֶׁ֥ר הָלָֽךְ׃ וַיִּקַּ֣ח דָּוִ֗יד אֵ֚ת שִׁלְטֵ֣י הַזָּהָ֔ב אֲשֶׁ֣ר הָי֔וּ עַ֖ל עַבְדֵ֣י
ח הֲדַדְעָ֑זֶר וַיְבִיאֵ֖ם יְרוּשָׁלִָֽם׃ וּמִטִּבְחַ֤ת וּמִכּוּן֙ עָרֵ֣י הֲדַדְעֶ֔זֶר לָקַ֥ח דָּוִ֖יד
נְחֹ֣שֶׁת רַבָּ֣ה מְאֹ֑ד בָּ֣הּ ׀ עָשָׂ֣ה שְׁלֹמֹ֗ה אֶת־יָ֤ם הַנְּחֹ֙שֶׁת֙ וְאֶת־הָֽעַמּוּדִ֔ים
ט וְאֵ֖ת כְּלֵ֥י הַנְּחֹֽשֶׁת׃ וַיִּשְׁמַ֕ע תֹּ֖עוּ מֶ֣לֶךְ חֲמָ֑ת כִּ֚י הִכָּ֣ה דָוִ֔יד
י אֶֽת־כָּל־חֵ֖יל הֲדַדְעֶ֥זֶר מֶֽלֶךְ־צוֹבָֽה׃ וַיִּשְׁלַ֣ח אֶת־הֲדוֹרָֽם־בְּנ֣וֹ אֶל־הַמֶּֽלֶךְ־
דָּ֠וִיד לשאול־לוֹ לְשָׁל֞וֹם וּֽלְבָרְכ֗וֹ עַל֩ אֲשֶׁ֨ר נִלְחַ֤ם בַּהֲדַדְעֶ֙זֶר֙ וַיַּכֵּ֔הוּ לִשְׁאָל־
כִּֽי־אִ֛ישׁ מִלְחֲמ֥וֹת תֹּ֖עוּ הָיָ֣ה הֲדַדְעָ֑זֶר וְכֹ֗ל כְּלֵ֛י זָהָ֥ב וָכֶ֖סֶף וּנְחֹֽשֶׁת׃
יא גַּם־אֹתָ֗ם הִקְדִּ֞ישׁ הַמֶּ֤לֶךְ דָּוִיד֙ לַֽיהוָ֔ה עִם־הַכֶּ֙סֶף֙ וְהַזָּהָ֔ב אֲשֶׁ֥ר נָשָׂ֖א
מִכָּל־הַגּוֹיִ֑ם מֵאֱד֤וֹם וּמִמּוֹאָב֙ וּמִבְּנֵ֣י עַמּ֔וֹן וּמִפְּלִשְׁתִּ֖ים וּמֵעֲמָלֵֽק׃
יב וְאַבְשַׁ֣י בֶּן־צְרוּיָ֗ה הִכָּ֤ה אֶת־אֱדוֹם֙ בְּגֵ֣יא הַמֶּ֔לַח שְׁמוֹנָ֥ה עָשָׂ֖ר אָֽלֶף׃
יג וַיָּ֤שֶׂם בֶּאֱדוֹם֙ נְצִיבִ֔ים וַיִּהְי֥וּ כָל־אֱד֖וֹם עֲבָדִ֣ים לְדָוִ֑יד וַיּ֤וֹשַׁע יְהוָה֙ אֶת־

14 granted victory to David wherever he went. David reigned over all of Israel,
15 upholding justice and righteousness for all his people. Yoav son of Tzeruya
was the commander of his army; Yehoshafat son of Aḥilud was royal herald;
16 Tzadok son of Aḥituv, and Avimelekh son of Evyatar, were priests; Shavsha
17 was royal scribe; Benayahu son of Yehoyada commanded the Keretites and
Peletites; and David's sons were chief ministers to the king.
19 1 Some time later, King Naḥash of the Amonites died, and his son reigned in
2 his place. "I will show loyalty to Ḥanun son of Naḥash," said David, "just as
his father showed loyalty to me." David sent messengers to offer condolences
for his father, and David's officials reached the land of the Amonites to offer
3 condolences to Ḥanun. But the ministers of the Amonites said to Ḥanun, "Do
you really think that David honors your father because he sent you condolences? No – his officials came to you to scout and spy out the city to
4 overthrow it." So Ḥanun had David's officials seized; he shaved them, cut off
5 half of their uniforms – up to their hips – and sent them off. When David was
informed about the men, he sent word out to them, for the men were utterly
humiliated. "Remain in Yeriḥo until your beards grow," said the king, "and
6 then return." When the Amonites realized that they had become
odious to David, Ḥanun and the Amonites sent a thousand talents of silver
to hire chariots and riders from Aram Naharayim, Aram Maakha, and Tzova.
7 They hired 32,000 chariots along with the king of Maakha and his men, who
came and set up camp before Meideva while the Amonites gathered from
8 their towns and arrived for battle. When David heard, he sent Yoav
9 together with his entire military force. The Amonites advanced and deployed
for battle by the city entrance, while the kings who had come were stationed
10 separately, in the open field. Yoav saw that he was faced with battle before him
and behind him, so he selected all of Israel's elite troops and deployed against
11 Aram. He handed command of the remaining troops to his brother Avshai
12 and deployed them against the Amonites. "If Aram overpowers me, come to
my aid," he said, "and if the Amonites overpower you, I will come to your aid.
13 Let us be strong and remain strong for the sake of our people and for the sake
14 of the cities of our God, and may the Lord do as He sees fit." Then Yoav and
all the troops with him charged out to battle against Aram, who fled before
15 them. When the Amonites saw that Aram had fled, they too fled before Yoav's
16 brother Avshai and entered the city; thus Yoav came to Jerusalem. But
when Aram saw that they had been defeated by Israel, they sent messengers
and summoned the Arameans who were across the Euphrates, with Shofakh,
17 Hadadezer's army commander, at their head. When this was reported to
David, he mustered all of Israel and crossed the Jordan to reach them, and he
drew up his forces against them. When David drew up his forces against Aram
18 in battle, they fought back against him, but still Aram fled before Israel, and
David killed 7,000 riders and 40,000 infantrymen from Aram. And as for

יד דָּוִיד בְּכֹל אֲשֶׁר הָלָךְ: וַיִּמְלֹךְ דָּוִיד עַל־כָּל־יִשְׂרָאֵל וַיְהִי עֹשֶׂה מִשְׁפָּט
טו וּצְדָקָה לְכָל־עַמּוֹ: וְיוֹאָב בֶּן־צְרוּיָה עַל־הַצָּבָא וִיהוֹשָׁפָט בֶּן־אֲחִילוּד
טז מַזְכִּיר: וְצָדוֹק בֶּן־אֲחִיטוּב וַאֲבִימֶלֶךְ בֶּן־אֶבְיָתָר כֹּהֲנִים וְשַׁוְשָׁא סוֹפֵר:
יז וּבְנָיָהוּ בֶּן־יְהוֹיָדָע עַל־הַכְּרֵתִי וְהַפְּלֵתִי וּבְנֵי־דָוִיד הָרִאשֹׁנִים לְיַד
הַמֶּלֶךְ:
יט א ב וַיְהִי אַחֲרֵי־כֵן וַיָּמָת נָחָשׁ מֶלֶךְ בְּנֵי־עַמּוֹן וַיִּמְלֹךְ בְּנוֹ תַּחְתָּיו: וַיֹּאמֶר
דָּוִיד אֶעֱשֶׂה־חֶסֶד ׀ עִם־חָנוּן בֶּן־נָחָשׁ כִּי־עָשָׂה אָבִיו עִמִּי חֶסֶד וַיִּשְׁלַח
דָּוִיד מַלְאָכִים לְנַחֲמוֹ עַל־אָבִיו וַיָּבֹאוּ עַבְדֵי דָוִיד אֶל־אֶרֶץ בְּנֵי־עַמּוֹן
ג אֶל־חָנוּן לְנַחֲמוֹ: וַיֹּאמְרוּ שָׂרֵי בְנֵי־עַמּוֹן לְחָנוּן הַמְכַבֵּד דָּוִיד אֶת־
אָבִיךָ בְּעֵינֶיךָ כִּי־שָׁלַח לְךָ מְנַחֲמִים הֲלֹא בַּעֲבוּר לַחְקֹר וְלַהֲפֹךְ וּלְרַגֵּל
ד הָאָרֶץ בָּאוּ עֲבָדָיו אֵלֶיךָ: וַיִּקַּח חָנוּן אֶת־עַבְדֵי דָוִיד וַיְגַלְּחֵם וַיִּכְרֹת
ה אֶת־מַדְוֵיהֶם בַּחֵצִי עַד־הַמִּפְשָׂעָה וַיְשַׁלְּחֵם: וַיֵּלְכוּ וַיַּגִּידוּ לְדָוִיד עַל־
הָאֲנָשִׁים וַיִּשְׁלַח לִקְרָאתָם כִּי־הָיוּ הָאֲנָשִׁים נִכְלָמִים מְאֹד וַיֹּאמֶר
ו הַמֶּלֶךְ שְׁבוּ בִירֵחוֹ עַד אֲשֶׁר־יְצַמַּח זְקַנְכֶם וְשַׁבְתֶּם: וַיִּרְאוּ
בְּנֵי עַמּוֹן כִּי הִתְבָּאֲשׁוּ עִם־דָּוִיד וַיִּשְׁלַח חָנוּן וּבְנֵי עַמּוֹן אֶלֶף כִּכַּר־כֶּסֶף
לִשְׂכֹּר לָהֶם מִן־אֲרַם נַהֲרַיִם וּמִן־אֲרַם מַעֲכָה וּמִצּוֹבָה רֶכֶב וּפָרָשִׁים:
ז וַיִּשְׂכְּרוּ לָהֶם שְׁנַיִם וּשְׁלֹשִׁים אֶלֶף רֶכֶב וְאֶת־מֶלֶךְ מַעֲכָה וְאֶת־
עַמּוֹ וַיָּבֹאוּ וַיַּחֲנוּ לִפְנֵי מֵידְבָא וּבְנֵי עַמּוֹן נֶאֶסְפוּ מֵעָרֵיהֶם וַיָּבֹאוּ
ח לַמִּלְחָמָה: וַיִּשְׁמַע דָּוִיד וַיִּשְׁלַח אֶת־יוֹאָב וְאֵת כָּל־צָבָא
ט הַגִּבּוֹרִים: וַיֵּצְאוּ בְּנֵי עַמּוֹן וַיַּעַרְכוּ מִלְחָמָה פֶּתַח הָעִיר וְהַמְּלָכִים
י אֲשֶׁר־בָּאוּ לְבַדָּם בַּשָּׂדֶה: וַיַּרְא יוֹאָב כִּי־הָיְתָה פְנֵי־הַמִּלְחָמָה אֵלָיו
יא פָּנִים וְאָחוֹר וַיִּבְחַר מִכָּל־בָּחוּר בְּיִשְׂרָאֵל וַיַּעֲרֹךְ לִקְרַאת אֲרָם: וְאֵת
יב יֶתֶר הָעָם נָתַן בְּיַד אַבְשַׁי אָחִיו וַיַּעַרְכוּ לִקְרַאת בְּנֵי עַמּוֹן: וַיֹּאמֶר
אִם־תֶּחֱזַק מִמֶּנִּי אֲרָם וְהָיִיתָ לִּי לִתְשׁוּעָה וְאִם־בְּנֵי עַמּוֹן יֶחֶזְקוּ מִמְּךָ
יג וְהוֹשַׁעְתִּיךָ: חֲזַק וְנִתְחַזְּקָה בְּעַד־עַמֵּנוּ וּבְעַד עָרֵי אֱלֹהֵינוּ וַיהוָה ח
יד הַטּוֹב בְּעֵינָיו יַעֲשֶׂה: וַיִּגַּשׁ יוֹאָב וְהָעָם אֲשֶׁר־עִמּוֹ לִפְנֵי אֲרָם לַמִּלְחָמָה
טו וַיָּנוּסוּ מִפָּנָיו: וּבְנֵי עַמּוֹן רָאוּ כִּי־נָס אֲרָם וַיָּנוּסוּ גַם־הֵם מִפְּנֵי אַבְשַׁי
טז אָחִיו וַיָּבֹאוּ הָעִירָה וַיָּבֹא יוֹאָב יְרוּשָׁלִָם: וַיַּרְא אֲרָם כִּי
נִגְּפוּ לִפְנֵי יִשְׂרָאֵל וַיִּשְׁלְחוּ מַלְאָכִים וַיּוֹצִיאוּ אֶת־אֲרָם אֲשֶׁר מֵעֵבֶר
יז הַנָּהָר וְשׁוֹפַךְ שַׂר־צְבָא הֲדַדְעֶזֶר לִפְנֵיהֶם: וַיֻּגַּד לְדָוִיד וַיֶּאֱסֹף אֶת־
כָּל־יִשְׂרָאֵל וַיַּעֲבֹר הַיַּרְדֵּן וַיָּבֹא אֲלֵהֶם וַיַּעֲרֹךְ אֲלֵהֶם וַיַּעֲרֹךְ דָּוִיד
יח לִקְרַאת אֲרָם מִלְחָמָה וַיִּלָּחֲמוּ עִמּוֹ: וַיָּנָס אֲרָם מִלִּפְנֵי יִשְׂרָאֵל וַיַּהֲרֹג

19 Shofakh, their army commander, he put him to death. When all those who
were subject to Hadadezer realized that they had been routed before Israel,
they surrendered to David and became subject to him. And Aram was not
20 1 willing to come to the Amonites' aid again. The next spring – when
kings launch campaigns – Yoav led the army forces and ravaged the land of
the Amonites; he came and laid siege to Raba while David stayed in
2 Jerusalem. Yoav defeated Raba and destroyed it. David took their king's crown
from upon his head and found that it weighed a talent of gold and was set
with jewels, and it was placed on David's head. And he brought out great
3 masses of spoil from the city. As for its people, he brought them out and set
them to work with saws and iron picks and axes; David did the same thing
for all the Amonite towns. Then David and all the troops returned to
4 Jerusalem. Some time later, battle broke out with the Philistines at
Gezer; this time, Sibekhai the Hushatite defeated Sipai, a descendant of the
5 Refaim,[17] and they were subdued. Yet another war broke out against
the Philistines, and Elḥanan son of Yair defeated Laḥmi, brother of Golyat
6 the Gittite, whose spear shaft was like a weaver's beam. Yet another
war broke out, in Gat. There was a man of gigantic proportions who had six
fingers and six toes on his hands and feet, twenty-four in all; he, too, was
7 descended from the Rafa. When he taunted Israel, Yehonatan son of Shima,
8 David's brother, struck him down. All these were descendants of the Rafa in
21 1 Gat, and they fell at the hand of David and his subjects. An adversary[18]
2 rose up against Israel and incited David to number Israel. "Go and count Israel
from Be'er Sheva to Dan," said David to Yoav and the officers of the people,
3 "then report back to me so that I will know their number." "May the Lord
increase His people a hundred times over," said Yoav, "but my lord the king,
they are all my lord's subjects – why should my lord make such a request?
4 Why should he bring guilt to Israel?" But the king's word prevailed against
5 Yoav, and Yoav set out, traveled all around Israel, and came to Jerusalem. Yoav
delivered the census figures of the population to David: in all of Israel there
were 1,100,000 sword-drawing men, while in Yehuda there were 470,000
6 sword-drawing men – but he did not count Levi and Binyamin among them,
7 for the king's order was abhorrent to Yoav. This affair was grave in the eyes of
8 God, and He struck against Israel. "I have sinned grievously by doing
this thing," David said to God. "Now please excuse Your servant's offense, for
9 I have been so foolish." The Lord spoke to Gad, David's seer. "Go
10 and tell David – thus says the Lord – I am holding three things over you;
11 choose one of them, and I will bring it upon you." Gad came to David and

17 | A race of giants. See, e.g., Deuteronomy 2:11.

18 | A member of the celestial host. Cf. 1 Samuel 24:1, and see also Zechariah 3:1–2; Job, chapters 1–2.

דָּוִיד מֵאֲרָם שִׁבְעַת אֲלָפִים רֶכֶב וְאַרְבָּעִים אֶלֶף אִישׁ רַגְלִי וְאֵת שׁוֹפַךְ
יט שַׂר־הַצָּבָא הֵמִית: וַיִּרְאוּ עַבְדֵי הֲדַדְעֶזֶר כִּי נִגְּפוּ לִפְנֵי יִשְׂרָאֵל
וַיַּשְׁלִימוּ עִם־דָּוִיד וַיַּעַבְדֻהוּ וְלֹא־אָבָה אֲרָם לְהוֹשִׁיעַ אֶת־בְּנֵי־עַמּוֹן
כ א עוֹד: וַיְהִי לְעֵת תְּשׁוּבַת הַשָּׁנָה לְעֵת | צֵאת הַמְּלָכִים
וַיִּנְהַג יוֹאָב אֶת־חֵיל הַצָּבָא וַיַּשְׁחֵת | אֶת־אֶרֶץ בְּנֵי־עַמּוֹן וַיָּבֹא וַיָּצַר
ב אֶת־רַבָּה וְדָוִיד יֹשֵׁב בִּירוּשָׁלִָם וַיַּךְ יוֹאָב אֶת־רַבָּה וַיֶּהֶרְסֶהָ: וַיִּקַּח
דָּוִיד אֶת־עֲטֶרֶת־מַלְכָּם מֵעַל רֹאשׁוֹ וַיִּמְצָאָהּ | מִשְׁקַל כִּכַּר־זָהָב וּבָהּ
אֶבֶן יְקָרָה וַתְּהִי עַל־רֹאשׁ דָּוִיד וּשְׁלַל הָעִיר הוֹצִיא הַרְבֵּה מְאֹד:
ג וְאֶת־הָעָם אֲשֶׁר־בָּהּ הוֹצִיא וַיָּשַׂר בַּמְּגֵרָה וּבַחֲרִיצֵי הַבַּרְזֶל
וּבַמְּגֵרוֹת וְכֵן יַעֲשֶׂה דָוִיד לְכֹל עָרֵי בְנֵי־עַמּוֹן וַיָּשָׁב דָּוִיד וְכָל־הָעָם
ד יְרוּשָׁלִָם: וַיְהִי אַחֲרֵי־כֵן וַתַּעֲמֹד מִלְחָמָה בְּגֶזֶר
עִם־פְּלִשְׁתִּים אָז הִכָּה סִבְּכַי הַחֻשָׁתִי אֶת־סִפַּי מִילִדֵי הָרְפָאִים
ה וַיִּכָּנֵעוּ: וַתְּהִי־עוֹד מִלְחָמָה אֶת־פְּלִשְׁתִּים וַיַּךְ
אֶלְחָנָן בֶּן־יָעוּר אֶת־לַחְמִי אֲחִי גָּלְיָת הַגִּתִּי וְעֵץ חֲנִיתוֹ כִּמְנוֹר יָעִיר
ו אֹרְגִים: וַתְּהִי־עוֹד מִלְחָמָה בְּגַת וַיְהִי | אִישׁ מִדָּה
ז וְאֶצְבְּעֹתָיו שֵׁשׁ־וָשֵׁשׁ עֶשְׂרִים וְאַרְבַּע וְגַם־הוּא נוֹלַד לְהָרָפָא: וַיְחָרֵף
ח אֶת־יִשְׂרָאֵל וַיַּכֵּהוּ יְהוֹנָתָן בֶּן־שִׁמְעָא אֲחִי דָוִיד: אֵל נוּלְּדוּ לְהָרָפָא
כא א בְּגַת וַיִּפְּלוּ בְיַד־דָּוִיד וּבְיַד־עֲבָדָיו: וַיַּעֲמֹד שָׂטָן עַל־
ב יִשְׂרָאֵל וַיָּסֶת אֶת־דָּוִיד לִמְנוֹת אֶת־יִשְׂרָאֵל: וַיֹּאמֶר דָּוִיד אֶל־יוֹאָב
וְאֶל־שָׂרֵי הָעָם לְכוּ סִפְרוּ אֶת־יִשְׂרָאֵל מִבְּאֵר שֶׁבַע וְעַד־דָּן וְהָבִיאוּ
ג אֵלַי וְאֵדְעָה אֶת־מִסְפָּרָם: וַיֹּאמֶר יוֹאָב יוֹסֵף יְהוָה עַל־עַמּוֹ | כָּהֵם
מֵאָה פְעָמִים הֲלֹא אֲדֹנִי הַמֶּלֶךְ כֻּלָּם לַאדֹנִי לַעֲבָדִים לָמָּה יְבַקֵּשׁ
ד זֹאת אֲדֹנִי לָמָּה יִהְיֶה לְאַשְׁמָה לְיִשְׂרָאֵל: וּדְבַר־הַמֶּלֶךְ חָזַק עַל־יוֹאָב
ה וַיֵּצֵא יוֹאָב וַיִּתְהַלֵּךְ בְּכָל־יִשְׂרָאֵל וַיָּבֹא יְרוּשָׁלִָם: וַיִּתֵּן יוֹאָב אֶת־מִסְפַּר
מִפְקַד־הָעָם אֶל־דָּוִיד וַיְהִי כָל־יִשְׂרָאֵל אֶלֶף אֲלָפִים וּמֵאָה אֶלֶף אִישׁ
ו שֹׁלֵף חֶרֶב וִיהוּדָה אַרְבַּע מֵאוֹת וְשִׁבְעִים אֶלֶף אִישׁ שֹׁלֵף חָרֶב: וְלֵוִי
ז וּבִנְיָמִן לֹא פָקַד בְּתוֹכָם כִּי־נִתְעַב דְּבַר־הַמֶּלֶךְ אֶת־יוֹאָב: וַיֵּרַע בְּעֵינֵי
ח הָאֱלֹהִים עַל־הַדָּבָר הַזֶּה וַיַּךְ אֶת־יִשְׂרָאֵל: וַיֹּאמֶר דָּוִיד אֶל־
הָאֱלֹהִים חָטָאתִי מְאֹד אֲשֶׁר עָשִׂיתִי אֶת־הַדָּבָר הַזֶּה וְעַתָּה הַעֲבֶר־
ט נָא אֶת־עֲוֺן עַבְדְּךָ כִּי נִסְכַּלְתִּי מְאֹד: וַיְדַבֵּר יְהוָה אֶל־גָּד
י חֹזֵה דָוִיד לֵאמֹר: לֵךְ וְדִבַּרְתָּ אֶל־דָּוִיד לֵאמֹר כֹּה אָמַר יְהוָה שָׁלוֹשׁ
יא אֲנִי נֹטֶה עָלֶיךָ בְּחַר־לְךָ אַחַת מֵהֵנָּה וְאֶעֱשֶׂה־לָּךְ: וַיָּבֹא גָד אֶל־דָּוִיד

12 said to him, "Thus says the Lord: Make your choice: either three years of
famine, or three months of devastation by your foe while your enemy's sword
overwhelms you, or three days of the Lord's sword – that is, sickness in the
land, with the angel of the Lord bringing destruction within every border
of Israel. Now consider what reply I should bring back to Him who sent
13 me." "I am in grave torment," David said to Gad. "Let me fall into
the hand of the Lord, for His mercy is exceedingly great; do not let me fall
14 into human hands." The Lord sent a sickness against Israel, and 70,000
15 people in Israel fell. God sent an angel to destroy Jerusalem, but as he was
about to wreak destruction, the Lord looked down and relented from the
evil. "Enough," He said to the destroying angel. "Now stay your hand."
And the angel of the Lord halted by the threshing floor of Ornan the
16 Jebusite. David looked up and saw the Lord's angel standing
between earth and heaven with his sword drawn in his hand, stretched forth
against Jerusalem. And David and the elders, covered in sackcloth, fell upon
17 their faces. "I am the one who said to number the people," David said to
God. "I am the one who sinned, and I have committed grave evil. But this
flock – what have they done? O Lord, my God, let Your hand move against
me and my father's house, but upon Your people, let there be no
18 plague." Then an angel of the Lord charged Gad to say to David,
"Go up and erect an altar to the Lord by the threshing floor of Ornan the
19 Jebusite," and David went up at Gad's word, which he spoke in the Lord's
20 name. As Ornan turned back, he saw the angel, and his four sons with him
21 hid – Ornan had been threshing wheat. As David approached Ornan, Ornan
looked out and saw David, and he came out of the threshing floor and bowed
22 to David with his face to the ground. "Give me the site of the threshing floor
so that I may build an altar to the Lord upon it," David said to Ornan. "Give
it to me for the full price so that the plague will cease among the people."
23 "Take it," Ornan said to David, "and let my lord the king do as he sees fit.
Look, I will provide you with the oxen for burnt offerings and threshing
boards for wood and wheat for a grain offering – I will provide everything."
24 "No," said King David to Ornan, "for I must purchase it at the full price – I
will not bring what is yours to the Lord and offer a burnt offering at no cost."
25 26 So David paid Ornan six hundred shekel of gold for the site, and David built
an altar there for the Lord and sacrificed burnt offerings and peace offerings.
He called out to the Lord, and He answered him with heavenly fire upon the
27 altar of burnt offerings. Then the Lord commanded the angel, and
28 he placed his sword back in its sheath. At that time, when David saw that the
Lord had answered him at the threshing floor of Ornan the Jebusite, he
29 offered his sacrifices there because the Lord's Tabernacle that Moshe had
made in the wilderness and the altar of burnt offerings were at the high
30 shrine in Givon at the time. David could not go before it to inquire of God
22 1 because he was terrified of the Lord's angel's sword. "This is the House
of the Lord God," said David, "and this is the altar for Israel's burnt

יב וַיֹּאמֶר לוֹ כֹּה־אָמַר יְהוָה קַבֶּל־לָךְ: אִם־שָׁלוֹשׁ שָׁנִים רָעָב וְאִם־שְׁלֹשָׁה
חֳדָשִׁים נִסְפֶּה מִפְּנֵי־צָרֶיךָ וְחֶרֶב אוֹיְבֶיךָ | לְמַשֶּׂגֶת וְאִם־שְׁלֹשֶׁת יָמִים
חֶרֶב יְהוָה | וְדֶבֶר בָּאָרֶץ וּמַלְאַךְ יְהוָה מַשְׁחִית בְּכָל־גְּבוּל יִשְׂרָאֵל
יג וְעַתָּה רְאֵה מָה־אָשִׁיב אֶת־שֹׁלְחִי דָּבָר: וַיֹּאמֶר דָּוִיד אֶל־
גָּד צַר־לִי מְאֹד אֶפְּלָה־נָּא בְיַד־יְהוָה כִּי־רַבִּים רַחֲמָיו מְאֹד וּבְיַד־אָדָם
יד אַל־אֶפֹּל: וַיִּתֵּן יְהוָה דֶּבֶר בְּיִשְׂרָאֵל וַיִּפֹּל מִיִּשְׂרָאֵל שִׁבְעִים אֶלֶף אִישׁ:
טו וַיִּשְׁלַח הָאֱלֹהִים | מַלְאָךְ | לִירוּשָׁלִַם לְהַשְׁחִיתָהּ וּכְהַשְׁחִית רָאָה
יְהוָה וַיִּנָּחֶם עַל־הָרָעָה וַיֹּאמֶר לַמַּלְאָךְ הַמַּשְׁחִית רַב עַתָּה הֶרֶף יָדֶךָ
טז וּמַלְאַךְ יְהוָה עֹמֵד עִם־גֹּרֶן אָרְנָן הַיְבוּסִי: וַיִּשָּׂא דָוִיד אֶת־
עֵינָיו וַיַּרְא אֶת־מַלְאַךְ יְהוָה עֹמֵד בֵּין הָאָרֶץ וּבֵין הַשָּׁמַיִם וְחַרְבּוֹ
שְׁלוּפָה בְּיָדוֹ נְטוּיָה עַל־יְרוּשָׁלִָם וַיִּפֹּל דָּוִיד וְהַזְּקֵנִים מְכֻסִּים
יז בַּשַּׂקִּים עַל־פְּנֵיהֶם: וַיֹּאמֶר דָּוִיד אֶל־הָאֱלֹהִים הֲלֹא אֲנִי אָמַרְתִּי
לִמְנוֹת בָּעָם וַאֲנִי־הוּא אֲשֶׁר־חָטָאתִי וְהָרֵעַ הֲרֵעוֹתִי וְאֵלֶּה הַצֹּאן
מֶה עָשׂוּ יְהוָה אֱלֹהַי תְּהִי נָא יָדְךָ בִּי וּבְבֵית אָבִי וּבְעַמְּךָ לֹא
יח לְמַגֵּפָה: וּמַלְאַךְ יְהוָה אָמַר אֶל־גָּד לֵאמֹר לְדָוִיד כִּי | יַעֲלֶה
יט דָוִיד לְהָקִים מִזְבֵּחַ לַיהוָה בְּגֹרֶן אָרְנָן הַיְבֻסִי: וַיַּעַל דָּוִיד בִּדְבַר־גָּד
כ אֲשֶׁר דִּבֶּר בְּשֵׁם יְהוָה: וַיָּשָׁב אָרְנָן וַיַּרְא אֶת־הַמַּלְאָךְ וְאַרְבַּעַת בָּנָיו
כא עִמּוֹ מִתְחַבְּאִים וְאָרְנָן דָּשׁ חִטִּים: וַיָּבֹא דָוִיד עַד־אָרְנָן וַיַּבֵּט אָרְנָן
כב וַיַּרְא אֶת־דָּוִיד וַיֵּצֵא מִן־הַגֹּרֶן וַיִּשְׁתַּחוּ לְדָוִיד אַפַּיִם אָרְצָה: וַיֹּאמֶר
דָּוִיד אֶל־אָרְנָן תְּנָה־לִּי מְקוֹם הַגֹּרֶן וְאֶבְנֶה־בּוֹ מִזְבֵּחַ לַיהוָה בְּכֶסֶף
כג מָלֵא תְּנֵהוּ לִי וְתֵעָצַר הַמַּגֵּפָה מֵעַל הָעָם: וַיֹּאמֶר אָרְנָן אֶל־דָּוִיד
קַח־לָךְ וְיַעַשׂ אֲדֹנִי הַמֶּלֶךְ הַטּוֹב בְּעֵינָיו רְאֵה נָתַתִּי הַבָּקָר לָעֹלוֹת
כד וְהַמּוֹרִגִּים לָעֵצִים וְהַחִטִּים לַמִּנְחָה הַכֹּל נָתָתִּי: וַיֹּאמֶר הַמֶּלֶךְ דָּוִיד
לְאָרְנָן לֹא כִּי־קָנֹה אֶקְנֶה בְּכֶסֶף מָלֵא כִּי לֹא־אֶשָּׂא אֲשֶׁר־לְךָ לַיהוָה
כה וְהַעֲלוֹת עוֹלָה חִנָּם: וַיִּתֵּן דָּוִיד לְאָרְנָן בַּמָּקוֹם שִׁקְלֵי זָהָב מִשְׁקַל שֵׁשׁ
כו מֵאוֹת: וַיִּבֶן שָׁם דָּוִיד מִזְבֵּחַ לַיהוָה וַיַּעַל עֹלוֹת וּשְׁלָמִים וַיִּקְרָא אֶל־
כז יְהוָה וַיַּעֲנֵהוּ בָאֵשׁ מִן־הַשָּׁמַיִם עַל מִזְבַּח הָעֹלָה: וַיֹּאמֶר
כח יְהוָה לַמַּלְאָךְ וַיָּשֶׁב חַרְבּוֹ אֶל־נְדָנָהּ: בָּעֵת הַהִיא בִּרְאוֹת דָּוִיד כִּי־
כט עָנָהוּ יְהוָה בְּגֹרֶן אָרְנָן הַיְבוּסִי וַיִּזְבַּח שָׁם: וּמִשְׁכַּן יְהוָה אֲשֶׁר־עָשָׂה
ל מֹשֶׁה בַמִּדְבָּר וּמִזְבַּח הָעוֹלָה בָּעֵת הַהִיא בַּבָּמָה בְּגִבְעוֹן: וְלֹא־יָכֹל
דָּוִיד לָלֶכֶת לְפָנָיו לִדְרֹשׁ אֱלֹהִים כִּי נִבְעַת מִפְּנֵי חֶרֶב מַלְאַךְ יְהוָה:
כב א וַיֹּאמֶר דָּוִיד זֶה הוּא בֵּית יְהוָה הָאֱלֹהִים וְזֶה־מִּזְבֵּחַ לְעֹלָה

2 offerings." Then David gave orders to assemble all the foreigners who
lived in the land of Israel, and he appointed masons to cut hewn stones for
3 the construction of God's House. David prepared vast amounts of iron for
nails for the gate doors and for clamps, as well as immeasurable amounts of
4 bronze and countless cedar logs, for the Sidonians and Tyrians had brought
5 vast amounts of cedarwood to David. "My son Shlomo is young and
inexperienced," said David, "and the House to be built for the LORD must be
incomparably magnificent, of fame and glory throughout all lands – I will
now make preparations for it." And so David made many preparations before
6 his death, and he summoned his son Shlomo and commanded him to build
7 a House for the LORD, God of Israel. "My son," David said to Shlomo,
"I set my heart upon building a House for the name of the LORD my God.
8 But the word of the LORD came to me, saying, 'You have shed much blood
and waged mighty wars – you will not build a House for My name, for you
9 have shed too much blood upon the earth before Me. Now a son has been
born to you; he will be a man of peace. I will give him rest from all his
surrounding enemies, for Shlomo will be his name,[19] and I will grant peace
10 and calm to Israel in his time. He will build a House in My name; he will be
a son to Me, and I a Father to him, and I will establish his royal throne over
11 Israel forever.' Now, my son, may the LORD be with you so that you may
succeed in building the House of the LORD your God, as He spoke of you.
12 But may the LORD grant you wisdom and understanding and appoint you
13 over Israel in order to keep the Torah of the LORD your God. You will prosper
if you take care to keep the laws and rulings that the LORD commanded
14 Moshe for Israel. Be strong and brave; do not quake or cower. Here I have
struggled to prepare for the House of the LORD: a hundred thousand talents
of gold, a million talents of silver, and immeasurably vast amounts of bronze
15 and iron. I have prepared wood and stone which you will supplement. With
you are many craftsmen: masons, cutters of stone and wood, and experts in
16 every craft. The gold, silver, bronze, and iron cannot be counted; arise and
17 take action, and may the LORD be with you." David then commanded all the
18 officials of Israel to assist his son Shlomo: "The LORD your God is with you,
and He has granted you rest on every side, for He gave the people of the land
into my hands, and the land lies conquered before the LORD and His people.
19 Now set your hearts and souls to seeking out the LORD your God; arise and
build the Temple of the LORD God in order to bring the Ark of the LORD's
Covenant and the sacred vessels of God into the House to be built for the
LORD's name."

23 1 When David was old and full of days, he made his son Shlomo king over
2 Israel. He assembled all of Israel's officials, priests, and Levites. The
3 Levites of thirty years old and up were counted, and they numbered 38,000

---

19 | The name Shlomo evokes the Hebrew *shalom* (peace).

ב לְיִשְׂרָאֵל׃ וַיֹּאמֶר דָּוִיד לִכְנוֹס אֶת־הַגֵּרִים אֲשֶׁר בְּאֶרֶץ
יִשְׂרָאֵל וַיַּעֲמֵד חֹצְבִים לַחְצוֹב אַבְנֵי גָזִית לִבְנוֹת בֵּית הָאֱלֹהִים׃
ג וּבַרְזֶל ׀ לָרֹב לַמִּסְמְרִים לְדַלְתוֹת הַשְּׁעָרִים וְלַמְחַבְּרוֹת הֵכִין דָּוִיד
ד וּנְחֹשֶׁת לָרֹב אֵין מִשְׁקָל׃ וַעֲצֵי אֲרָזִים לְאֵין מִסְפָּר כִּי־הֵבִיאוּ הַצִּידֹנִים
ה וְהַצֹּרִים עֲצֵי אֲרָזִים לָרֹב לְדָוִיד׃ וַיֹּאמֶר דָּוִיד שְׁלֹמֹה בְנִי
נַעַר וָרָךְ וְהַבַּיִת לִבְנוֹת לַיהוָה לְהַגְדִּיל ׀ לְמַעְלָה לְשֵׁם וּלְתִפְאֶרֶת
ו לְכָל־הָאֲרָצוֹת אָכִינָה נָּא לוֹ וַיָּכֶן דָּוִיד לָרֹב לִפְנֵי מוֹתוֹ׃ וַיִּקְרָא לִשְׁלֹמֹה
ז בְנוֹ וַיְצַוֵּהוּ לִבְנוֹת בַּיִת לַיהוָה אֱלֹהֵי יִשְׂרָאֵל׃ וַיֹּאמֶר דָּוִיד
ח לִשְׁלֹמֹה בנו אֲנִי הָיָה עִם־לְבָבִי לִבְנוֹת בַּיִת לְשֵׁם יְהוָה אֱלֹהָי׃ וַיְהִי בְּנִי
עָלַי דְּבַר־יְהוָה לֵאמֹר דָּם לָרֹב שָׁפַכְתָּ וּמִלְחָמוֹת גְּדֹלוֹת עָשִׂיתָ לֹא־
ט תִבְנֶה בַיִת לִשְׁמִי כִּי דָּמִים רַבִּים שָׁפַכְתָּ אַרְצָה לְפָנָי׃ הִנֵּה־בֵן נוֹלָד
לָךְ הוּא יִהְיֶה אִישׁ מְנוּחָה וַהֲנִיחוֹתִי לוֹ מִכָּל־אוֹיְבָיו מִסָּבִיב כִּי שְׁלֹמֹה
י יִהְיֶה שְׁמוֹ וְשָׁלוֹם וָשֶׁקֶט אֶתֵּן עַל־יִשְׂרָאֵל בְּיָמָיו׃ הוּא־יִבְנֶה בַיִת
לִשְׁמִי וְהוּא יִהְיֶה־לִּי לְבֵן וַאֲנִי־לוֹ לְאָב וַהֲכִינוֹתִי כִּסֵּא מַלְכוּתוֹ עַל־
יא יִשְׂרָאֵל עַד־עוֹלָם׃ עַתָּה בְנִי יְהִי יְהוָה עִמָּךְ וְהִצְלַחְתָּ וּבָנִיתָ בֵּית
יב יְהוָה אֱלֹהֶיךָ כַּאֲשֶׁר דִּבֶּר עָלֶיךָ׃ אַךְ יִתֶּן־לְּךָ יְהוָה שֵׂכֶל וּבִינָה וִיצַוְּךָ
יג עַל־יִשְׂרָאֵל וְלִשְׁמוֹר אֶת־תּוֹרַת יְהוָה אֱלֹהֶיךָ׃ אָז תַּצְלִיחַ אִם־תִּשְׁמוֹר
לַעֲשׂוֹת אֶת־הַחֻקִּים וְאֶת־הַמִּשְׁפָּטִים אֲשֶׁר צִוָּה יְהוָה אֶת־מֹשֶׁה
יד עַל־יִשְׂרָאֵל חֲזַק וֶאֱמָץ אַל־תִּירָא וְאַל־תֵּחָת׃ וְהִנֵּה בְעָנְיִי הֲכִינוֹתִי
לְבֵית־יְהוָה זָהָב כִּכָּרִים מֵאָה־אֶלֶף וְכֶסֶף אֶלֶף אֲלָפִים כִּכָּרִים וְלַנְּחֹשֶׁת
וְלַבַּרְזֶל אֵין מִשְׁקָל כִּי לָרֹב הָיָה וְעֵצִים וַאֲבָנִים הֲכִינוֹתִי וַעֲלֵיהֶם
טו תּוֹסִיף׃ וְעִמְּךָ לָרֹב עֹשֵׂי מְלָאכָה חֹצְבִים וְחָרָשֵׁי אֶבֶן וָעֵץ וְכָל־חָכָם
טז בְּכָל־מְלָאכָה׃ לַזָּהָב לַכֶּסֶף וְלַנְּחֹשֶׁת וְלַבַּרְזֶל אֵין מִסְפָּר קוּם וַעֲשֵׂה
יז וִיהִי יְהוָה עִמָּךְ׃ וַיְצַו דָּוִיד לְכָל־שָׂרֵי יִשְׂרָאֵל לַעְזֹר לִשְׁלֹמֹה בְנוֹ׃
יח הֲלֹא יְהוָה אֱלֹהֵיכֶם עִמָּכֶם וְהֵנִיחַ לָכֶם מִסָּבִיב כִּי ׀ נָתַן בְּיָדִי אֵת יֹשְׁבֵי
יט הָאָרֶץ וְנִכְבְּשָׁה הָאָרֶץ לִפְנֵי יְהוָה וְלִפְנֵי עַמּוֹ׃ עַתָּה תְּנוּ לְבַבְכֶם ט
וְנַפְשְׁכֶם לִדְרוֹשׁ לַיהוָה אֱלֹהֵיכֶם וְקוּמוּ וּבְנוּ אֶת־מִקְדַּשׁ יְהוָה
הָאֱלֹהִים לְהָבִיא אֶת־אֲרוֹן בְּרִית־יְהוָה וּכְלֵי קֹדֶשׁ הָאֱלֹהִים לַבַּיִת
הַנִּבְנֶה לְשֵׁם־יְהוָה׃

כג א וְדָוִיד זָקֵן וְשָׂבַע יָמִים וַיַּמְלֵךְ אֶת־שְׁלֹמֹה בְנוֹ עַל־
ב יִשְׂרָאֵל׃ וַיֶּאֱסֹף אֶת־כָּל־שָׂרֵי יִשְׂרָאֵל וְהַכֹּהֲנִים וְהַלְוִיִּם׃
ג וַיִּסָּפְרוּ הַלְוִיִּם מִבֶּן שְׁלֹשִׁים שָׁנָה וָמָעְלָה וַיְהִי מִסְפָּרָם לְגֻלְגְּלֹתָם

4 men. "Of these, 24,000 shall oversee the work of the House of the Lord,
5 6,000 shall be officers and judges, 4,000 shall be gatekeepers, and 4,000 are
6 to praise the Lord with instruments that I have made for praise." David
then organized them into divisions according to the sons of
7 Levi – Gershon, Kehat, and Merari. The Gershonites: Ladan and
8 Shimi. The sons of Ladan: the head was Yeḥiel, then Zetam and
9 Yoel – three. The sons of Shimi: Shelomot, Ḥaziel, and Haran –
10 three. These were the ancestral heads of Ladan. The sons of Shimi:
11 Yaḥat, Zina, Yeush, and Beria; these were the sons of Shimi – four. Yaḥat was
the head, and Ziza was the second, but Yeush and Beria did not have many
12 children, so they were counted as a single ancestral house. The sons
13 of Kehat: Amram, Yitzhar, Ḥevron, and Uziel – four. The sons of
Amram were Aharon and Moshe. Aharon was set apart to be sanctified for
the holiest of holies, he and his sons forever – to sacrifice before the Lord, to
14 serve Him, and to bless in His name forever. As for Moshe, the man of God,
15 his sons were associated with the tribe of Levi. The sons of Moshe:
16 17 Gershom and Eliezer. Of the sons of Gershom, Shevuel was the head. As for
the sons of Eliezer, Reḥavya was the head, and Eliezer had no other sons, but
18 the sons of Reḥavya were very many. Of the sons of Yitzhar, Shlomit
19 was the head. The sons of Ḥevron: Yeriyahu was the head, Amarya
20 the second, Yaḥaziel the third, and Yekamam the fourth. The sons
21 of Uziel: Mikha was the head and Yishiya the second. The sons
22 of Merari: Maḥli and Mushi. The sons of Maḥli: Elazar and Kish. Elazar
died with no sons, only daughters, and the sons of Kish, their kin, married
23 24 them. The sons of Mushi: Maḥli, Eder, and Yeremot – three. These are the
descendants of Levi according to their ancestral houses, the ancestral heads
as listed by name and by the number of sons who performed the work for
25 the service of the House of the Lord from twenty years old and up. For
David said, "The Lord, God of Israel, has granted rest to His people, and
26 He will dwell in Jerusalem forever, so the Levites no longer need to carry
27 the Tabernacle and all the vessels for its service." Therefore, one of the final
28 acts of David was to count the sons of Levi twenty years old and up, for their
station was beside the sons of Aharon for the service of Lord's House – to
oversee the courtyards, the chambers, the purification of all that was sacred,
29 and any work for the service of God's House: the showbread, the fine flour
for grain offerings, the unleavened wafers, the pan offerings, the offerings
30 mixed with oil, and all quantities and measurements. They were also to
stand each morning to give thanks and sing praise to the Lord, as well as
31 in the evening, and whenever burnt offerings were offered up to the Lord
on the Sabbath, New Moons, and festivals in accordance with the required
32 number – continually in the Lord's presence. They were to keep watch

ד לִגְבָרִים שְׁלֹשִׁים וּשְׁמוֹנָה אָלֶף׃ מֵאֵלֶּה לְנַצֵּחַ עַל־מְלֶאכֶת בֵּית־יְהוָה
ה עֶשְׂרִים וְאַרְבָּעָה אָלֶף וְשֹׁטְרִים וְשֹׁפְטִים שֵׁשֶׁת אֲלָפִים׃ וְאַרְבַּעַת
אֲלָפִים שֹׁעֲרִים וְאַרְבַּעַת אֲלָפִים מְהַלְלִים לַיהוָה בַּכֵּלִים אֲשֶׁר עָשִׂיתִי
ו לְהַלֵּל׃ וַיֶּחָלְקֵם דָּוִיד מַחְלְקוֹת לִבְנֵי לֵוִי לְגֵרְשׁוֹן קְהָת
ז ח וּמְרָרִי׃ לַגֵּרְשֻׁנִּי לַעְדָּן וְשִׁמְעִי׃ בְּנֵי לַעְדָּן הָרֹאשׁ
ט יְחִיאֵל וְזֵתָם וְיוֹאֵל שְׁלֹשָׁה׃ בְּנֵי שִׁמְעִי שְׁלֹמוֹת וַחֲזִיאֵל שְׁלֹמִית
י וְהָרָן שְׁלֹשָׁה אֵלֶּה רָאשֵׁי הָאָבוֹת לְלַעְדָּן׃ וּבְנֵי שִׁמְעִי יַחַת
יא זִינָא וִיעוּשׁ וּבְרִיעָה אֵלֶּה בְנֵי־שִׁמְעִי אַרְבָּעָה׃ וַיְהִי־יַחַת הָרֹאשׁ
וְזִיזָה הַשֵּׁנִי וִיעוּשׁ וּבְרִיעָה לֹא־הִרְבּוּ בָנִים וַיִּהְיוּ לְבֵית אָב לִפְקֻדָּה
יב אֶחָת׃ בְּנֵי קְהָת עַמְרָם יִצְהָר חֶבְרוֹן וְעֻזִּיאֵל
יג אַרְבָּעָה׃ בְּנֵי עַמְרָם אַהֲרֹן וּמֹשֶׁה וַיִּבָּדֵל אַהֲרֹן לְהַקְדִּישׁוֹ
קֹדֶשׁ קָדָשִׁים הוּא־וּבָנָיו עַד־עוֹלָם לְהַקְטִיר לִפְנֵי יְהוָה לְשָׁרְתוֹ וּלְבָרֵךְ
יד בִּשְׁמוֹ עַד־עוֹלָם׃ וּמֹשֶׁה אִישׁ הָאֱלֹהִים בָּנָיו יִקָּרְאוּ עַל־שֵׁבֶט
טו טז הַלֵּוִי׃ בְּנֵי מֹשֶׁה גֵּרְשׁוֹם וֶאֱלִיעֶזֶר׃ בְּנֵי גֵרְשׁוֹם שְׁבוּאֵל
יז הָרֹאשׁ׃ וַיִּהְיוּ בְנֵי־אֱלִיעֶזֶר רְחַבְיָה הָרֹאשׁ וְלֹא־הָיָה לֶאֱלִיעֶזֶר בָּנִים
יח אֲחֵרִים וּבְנֵי רְחַבְיָה רָבוּ לְמָעְלָה׃ בְּנֵי יִצְהָר שְׁלֹמִית
יט הָרֹאשׁ׃ בְּנֵי חֶבְרוֹן יְרִיָּהוּ הָרֹאשׁ אֲמַרְיָה הַשֵּׁנִי יַחֲזִיאֵל
כ הַשְּׁלִישִׁי וִיקַמְעָם הָרְבִיעִי׃ בְּנֵי עֻזִּיאֵל מִיכָה הָרֹאשׁ וְיִשִּׁיָּה
כא הַשֵּׁנִי׃ בְּנֵי מְרָרִי מַחְלִי וּמוּשִׁי בְּנֵי מַחְלִי אֶלְעָזָר וְקִישׁ׃
כב וַיָּמָת אֶלְעָזָר וְלֹא־הָיוּ לוֹ בָּנִים כִּי אִם־בָּנוֹת וַיִּשָּׂאוּם בְּנֵי־קִישׁ אֲחֵיהֶם׃
כג כד בְּנֵי מוּשִׁי מַחְלִי וְעֵדֶר וִירֵמוֹת שְׁלֹשָׁה׃ אֵלֶּה בְנֵי־לֵוִי לְבֵית אֲבֹתֵיהֶם
רָאשֵׁי הָאָבוֹת לִפְקוּדֵיהֶם בְּמִסְפַּר שֵׁמוֹת לְגֻלְגְּלֹתָם עֹשֵׂה הַמְּלָאכָה
כה לַעֲבֹדַת בֵּית יְהוָה מִבֶּן עֶשְׂרִים שָׁנָה וָמָעְלָה׃ כִּי אָמַר דָּוִיד הֵנִיחַ
כו יְהוָה אֱלֹהֵי־יִשְׂרָאֵל לְעַמּוֹ וַיִּשְׁכֹּן בִּירוּשָׁלַם עַד־לְעוֹלָם׃ וְגַם לַלְוִיִּם
כז אֵין־לָשֵׂאת אֶת־הַמִּשְׁכָּן וְאֶת־כָּל־כֵּלָיו לַעֲבֹדָתוֹ׃ כִּי בְדִבְרֵי דָוִיד
כח הָאַחֲרוֹנִים הֵמָּה מִסְפַּר בְּנֵי־לֵוִי מִבֶּן עֶשְׂרִים שָׁנָה וּלְמָעְלָה׃ כִּי
מַעֲמָדָם לְיַד־בְּנֵי אַהֲרֹן לַעֲבֹדַת בֵּית יְהוָה עַל־הַחֲצֵרוֹת וְעַל־
הַלְּשָׁכוֹת וְעַל־טָהֳרַת לְכָל־קֹדֶשׁ וּמַעֲשֵׂה עֲבֹדַת בֵּית הָאֱלֹהִים׃
כט וּלְלֶחֶם הַמַּעֲרֶכֶת וּלְסֹלֶת לְמִנְחָה וְלִרְקִיקֵי הַמַּצּוֹת וְלַמַּחֲבַת
ל וְלַמֻּרְבֶּכֶת וּלְכָל־מְשׂוּרָה וּמִדָּה׃ וְלַעֲמֹד בַּבֹּקֶר בַּבֹּקֶר לְהֹדוֹת וּלְהַלֵּל
לא לַיהוָה וְכֵן לָעָרֶב׃ וּלְכֹל הַעֲלוֹת עֹלוֹת לַיהוָה לַשַּׁבָּתוֹת לֶחֳדָשִׁים
לב וְלַמֹּעֲדִים בְּמִסְפָּר כְּמִשְׁפָּט עֲלֵיהֶם תָּמִיד לִפְנֵי יְהוָה׃ וְשָׁמְרוּ אֶת־

over the Tent of Meeting, over what was sacred, and to attend the sons of
24 1 Aharon, their kin, for the service of the House of the Lord. As for
the division of the sons of Aharon, the sons of Aharon were Nadav, Avihu,
2 Elazar, and Itamar. Nadav and Avihu died before their father, and they had
3 no children, so Elazar and Itamar served as priests. David, Tzadok of the sons
of Elazar, and Aḥimelekh of the sons of Itamar divided them up into offices
4 of their service. It was found that there were more male heads of the sons of
Elazar than of the sons of Itamar, and they divided them up accordingly: the
sons of Elazar with sixteen heads of ancestral houses and the sons of Itamar
5 with eight ancestral houses. They divided them by lot, equally, for there were
both officers of the Sanctuary and officers of God among the sons of Elazar
6 and the sons of Itamar. Then Shemaya son of Netanel, the scribe
from Levi, recorded them in the presence of the king, the officers, the priest
Tzadok, Aḥimelekh son of Evyatar, and the ancestral heads of the priests and
Levites: for every ancestral house selected for Itamar, two ancestral houses
7 were selected for Elazar. The first lot fell to Yehoyariv, the second to
8, 9 Yedaya, the third to Ḥarim, the fourth to Seorim, the fifth to Malkiya, the sixth
10, 11 to Miyamin, the seventh to Hakotz, the eighth to Aviya, the ninth to Yeshua,
12 the tenth to Shekhanyahu, the eleventh to Elyashiv, the twelfth to Yakim,
13, 14 the thirteenth to Ḥupa, the fourteenth to Yeshevav, the fifteenth to Bilga, the
15, 16 sixteenth to Imer, the seventeenth to Ḥezir, the eighteenth to Hapitzetz, the
17 nineteenth to Petaḥya, the twentieth to Yeḥezkel, the twenty-first to Yakhin,
18 the twenty-second to Gamul, the twenty-third to Delayahu, and the twenty-
19 fourth to Maazyahu. Their duties for their service were to come
to the House of the Lord according to the requirements of their ancestor
20 Aharon as the Lord, God of Israel, had commanded him. The rest of the
21 sons of Levi: the son of Amram, Shuvael; the sons of Shuvael, Yeḥdeyahu and
22 Reḥavyahu; and the son of Reḥavyahu, Yishiya, the head. Of the Izharites:
23 Shelomot and the son of Shelomot, Yaḥat. The sons of:[20] Yeriyahu, Amaryahu
24 the second, Yaḥaziel the third, and Yekamam the fourth. The son of Uziel,
25 Mikha and the son of Mikha, Shamir. The brother of Mikha, Yishiya and the
26 son of Yishiya, Zekharyahu. The sons of Merari: Maḥli and Mushi. The sons
27 of Yaaziyahu, his son – that is, the sons of Merari through his son Yaaziyahu:
28 Shoham, Zakur, and Ivri. Of Maḥli: Elazar, who had no sons. Of Kish: the
29 30 son of Kish, Yeraḥme'el. The sons of Mushi: Maḥli, Eder, and Yerimot. These
31 were the sons of Levi according to their ancestral clans. Like their brothers,
the sons of Aharon, they too cast lots in the presence of King David, Tzadok,
Aḥimelekh, and the ancestral heads of the priests and Levites – each ancestral
25 1 head and his younger brother. David and the army officers singled
out the sons of Asaf, Heiman, and Yedutun for service: they were to play in

20 | The sons of Ḥevron. "Ḥevron" is not explicit in the Hebrew, but cf. 23:19.

מִשְׁמֶרֶת אֹהֶל־מוֹעֵד וְאֵת מִשְׁמֶרֶת הַקֹּדֶשׁ וּמִשְׁמֶרֶת בְּנֵי אַהֲרֹן
כד א אֲחֵיהֶם לַעֲבֹדַת בֵּית יְהוָה׃ וְלִבְנֵי אַהֲרֹן מַחְלְקוֹתָם בְּנֵי
ב אַהֲרֹן נָדָב וַאֲבִיהוּא אֶלְעָזָר וְאִיתָמָר׃ וַיָּמָת נָדָב וַאֲבִיהוּא לִפְנֵי אֲבִיהֶם
ג וּבָנִים לֹא־הָיוּ לָהֶם וַיְכַהֲנוּ אֶלְעָזָר וְאִיתָמָר׃ וַיֶּחָלְקֵם דָּוִיד וְצָדוֹק
ד מִן־בְּנֵי אֶלְעָזָר וַאֲחִימֶלֶךְ מִן־בְּנֵי אִיתָמָר לִפְקֻדָּתָם בַּעֲבֹדָתָם׃ וַיִּמָּצְאוּ
בְנֵי־אֶלְעָזָר רַבִּים לְרָאשֵׁי הַגְּבָרִים מִן־בְּנֵי אִיתָמָר וַיַּחְלְקוּם לִבְנֵי
אֶלְעָזָר רָאשִׁים לְבֵית־אָבוֹת שִׁשָּׁה עָשָׂר וְלִבְנֵי אִיתָמָר לְבֵית אֲבוֹתָם
ה שְׁמוֹנָה׃ וַיַּחְלְקוּם בְּגוֹרָלוֹת אֵלֶּה עִם־אֵלֶּה כִּי־הָיוּ שָׂרֵי־קֹדֶשׁ וְשָׂרֵי
ו הָאֱלֹהִים מִבְּנֵי אֶלְעָזָר וּבִבְנֵי אִיתָמָר׃ וַיִּכְתְּבֵם שְׁמַעְיָה
בֶן־נְתַנְאֵל הַסּוֹפֵר מִן־הַלֵּוִי לִפְנֵי הַמֶּלֶךְ וְהַשָּׂרִים וְצָדוֹק הַכֹּהֵן
וַאֲחִימֶלֶךְ בֶּן־אֶבְיָתָר וְרָאשֵׁי הָאָבוֹת לַכֹּהֲנִים וְלַלְוִיִּם בֵּית־אָב אֶחָד
ז אָחֻז לְאֶלְעָזָר וְאָחֻז ׀ אָחֻז לְאִיתָמָר׃ וַיֵּצֵא הַגּוֹרָל הָרִאשׁוֹן
ח ט לִיהוֹיָרִיב לִידַעְיָה הַשֵּׁנִי׃ לְחָרִם הַשְּׁלִשִׁי לִשְׂעֹרִים הָרְבִעִי׃ לְמַלְכִּיָּה
י יא הַחֲמִישִׁי לְמִיָּמִן הַשִּׁשִּׁי׃ לְהַקּוֹץ הַשְּׁבִעִי לַאֲבִיָּה הַשְּׁמִינִי׃ לְיֵשׁוּעַ
יב הַתְּשִׁעִי לִשְׁכַנְיָהוּ הָעֲשִׂרִי׃ לְאֶלְיָשִׁיב עַשְׁתֵּי עָשָׂר לְיָקִים שְׁנֵים עָשָׂר׃
יג יד לְחֻפָּה שְׁלֹשָׁה עָשָׂר לְיֶשֶׁבְאָב אַרְבָּעָה עָשָׂר׃ לְבִלְגָּה חֲמִשָּׁה עָשָׂר
טו לְאִמֵּר שִׁשָּׁה עָשָׂר׃ לְחֵזִיר שִׁבְעָה עָשָׂר לְהַפִּצֵּץ שְׁמוֹנָה עָשָׂר׃
טז יז לִפְתַחְיָה תִּשְׁעָה עָשָׂר לִיחֶזְקֵאל הָעֶשְׂרִים׃ לְיָכִין אֶחָד וְעֶשְׂרִים
יח לְגָמוּל שְׁנַיִם וְעֶשְׂרִים׃ לִדְלָיָהוּ שְׁלֹשָׁה וְעֶשְׂרִים לְמַעַזְיָהוּ אַרְבָּעָה
יט וְעֶשְׂרִים׃ אֵלֶּה פְקֻדָּתָם לַעֲבֹדָתָם לָבוֹא לְבֵית־יְהוָה
כ כְּמִשְׁפָּטָם בְּיַד אַהֲרֹן אֲבִיהֶם כַּאֲשֶׁר צִוָּהוּ יְהוָה אֱלֹהֵי יִשְׂרָאֵל׃ וְלִבְנֵי
כא לֵוִי הַנּוֹתָרִים לִבְנֵי עַמְרָם שׁוּבָאֵל לִבְנֵי שׁוּבָאֵל יֶחְדְּיָהוּ׃ לִרְחַבְיָהוּ
כב לִבְנֵי רְחַבְיָהוּ הָרֹאשׁ יִשִּׁיָּה׃ לַיִּצְהָרִי שְׁלֹמוֹת לִבְנֵי שְׁלֹמוֹת יָחַת׃
כג כד וּבָנַי יְרִיָּהוּ אֲמַרְיָהוּ הַשֵּׁנִי יַחֲזִיאֵל הַשְּׁלִישִׁי יְקַמְעָם הָרְבִיעִי׃ בְּנֵי
כה עֻזִּיאֵל מִיכָה לִבְנֵי מִיכָה שמור׃ אֲחִי מִיכָה יִשִּׁיָּה לִבְנֵי יִשִּׁיָּה זְכַרְיָהוּ׃ שָׁמִיר
כו כז בְּנֵי מְרָרִי מַחְלִי וּמוּשִׁי בְּנֵי יַעֲזִיָּהוּ בְנוֹ׃ בְּנֵי מְרָרִי לְיַעֲזִיָּהוּ בְנוֹ וְשֹׁהַם
כח כט וְזַכּוּר וְעִבְרִי׃ לְמַחְלִי אֶלְעָזָר וְלֹא־הָיָה לוֹ בָּנִים׃ לְקִישׁ בְּנֵי־קִישׁ
ל יְרַחְמְאֵל׃ וּבְנֵי מוּשִׁי מַחְלִי וְעֵדֶר וִירִימוֹת אֵלֶּה בְּנֵי הַלְוִיִּם לְבֵית
לא אֲבֹתֵיהֶם׃ וַיַּפִּילוּ גַם־הֵם גּוֹרָלוֹת לְעֻמַּת ׀ אֲחֵיהֶם בְּנֵי־אַהֲרֹן לִפְנֵי
דָּוִיד הַמֶּלֶךְ וְצָדוֹק וַאֲחִימֶלֶךְ וְרָאשֵׁי הָאָבוֹת לַכֹּהֲנִים וְלַלְוִיִּם אָבוֹת
כה א הָרֹאשׁ לְעֻמַּת אָחִיו הַקָּטָן׃ וַיַּבְדֵּל דָּוִיד וְשָׂרֵי
הַצָּבָא לַעֲבֹדָה לִבְנֵי אָסָף וְהֵימָן וִידוּתוּן הנביאים בְּכִנֹּרוֹת בִּנְבָלִים הַנִּבְּאִים

prophetic ecstasy on lyres, harps, and cymbals. The list of skilled men who
2 performed this service: Of the sons of Asaf: Zakur, Yosef, Netanya, and
Asarela – Asaf's sons charged by Asaf, who prophesied by the king's orders.
3 Of Yedutun: the sons of Yedutun: Gedalyahu, Zeri, Yeshayahu, Ḥashavyahu,
and Matityahu – six[21] charged by their father Yedutun, who played on the
4 harp in prophetic ecstasy, giving thanks and praising the Lord. Of
Heiman: the sons of Heiman: Bukiyahu, Matanyahu, Uziel, Shevuel, Yerimot,
Ḥananya, Ḥanani, Eliata, Gidalti, Romamti Ezer, Yoshbekasha, Maloti, Hotir,
5 and Maḥaziot; all these were sons of Heiman, the king's seer, in accordance
with God's promise to exalt him – God gave Heiman fourteen sons and three
6 daughters. All these were charged by their father with the music in the House
of the Lord, with cymbals, harps, and lyres for the service of the House of
God. Directly charged by the king
7 were Asaf, Yedutun, and Heiman. Together with their brothers who
were trained in making music for the Lord, the total number of skilled
8 players was 288. They cast lots to determine shifts for small and great alike,
9 for skilled player together with student. The first
lot fell for Asaf – to Yosef; the second to Gedalyahu, he and his brothers
10 and sons – twelve; the third to Zakur,
11 his sons, and his brothers – twelve; the fourth to Yitzri,
12 his sons, and his brothers – twelve; the fifth to Netanyahu,
13 his sons, and his brothers – twelve; the sixth to Bukiyahu,
14 his sons, and his brothers – twelve; the seventh to Yesarela,
15 his sons, and his brothers – twelve; the eighth to Yeshayahu,
16 his sons, and his brothers – twelve; the ninth to Matanyahu,
17 his sons, and his brothers – twelve; the tenth to Shimi,
18 his sons, and his brothers – twelve; the eleventh to Azarel,
19 his sons, and his brothers – twelve; the twelfth to Ḥashavya,
20 his sons, and his brothers – twelve; the thirteenth to Shuvael,
21 his sons, and his brothers – twelve; the fourteenth to Matityahu,
22 his sons, and his brothers – twelve; the fifteenth to Yeremot,
23 his sons, and his brothers – twelve; the sixteenth to Ḥananyahu,
24 his sons, and his brothers – twelve; the seventeenth to Yoshbekasha,
25 his sons, and his brothers – twelve; the eighteenth to Ḥanani,
26 his sons, and his brothers – twelve; the nineteenth to Maloti,
27 his sons, and his brothers – twelve; the twentieth to Eliyata,
28 his sons, and his brothers – twelve; the twenty-first to Hotir,

21 | Verse 17 indicates that the sixth son is Shimi.

ב וּבִמְצִלְתַּיִם וַיְהִי מִסְפָּרָם אַנְשֵׁי מְלָאכָה לַעֲבֹדָתָם: לִבְנֵי אָסָף זַכּוּר
וְיוֹסֵף וּנְתַנְיָה וַאֲשַׂרְאֵלָה בְּנֵי אָסָף עַל יַד־אָסָף הַנִּבָּא עַל־יְדֵי הַמֶּלֶךְ:
ג לִידוּתוּן בְּנֵי יְדוּתוּן גְּדַלְיָהוּ וּצְרִי וִישַׁעְיָהוּ חֲשַׁבְיָהוּ וּמַתִּתְיָהוּ
שִׁשָּׁה עַל יְדֵי אֲבִיהֶם יְדוּתוּן בַּכִּנּוֹר הַנִּבָּא עַל־הֹדוֹת וְהַלֵּל
ד לַיהוָה: לְהֵימָן בְּנֵי הֵימָן בֻּקִּיָּהוּ מַתַּנְיָהוּ עֻזִּיאֵל שְׁבוּאֵל
וִירִימוֹת חֲנַנְיָה חֲנָנִי אֱלִיאָתָה גִדַּלְתִּי וְרֹמַמְתִּי עֶזֶר יָשְׁבְּקָשָׁה מַלּוֹתִי
ה הוֹתִיר מַחֲזִיאוֹת: כָּל־אֵלֶּה בָנִים לְהֵימָן חֹזֵה הַמֶּלֶךְ בְּדִבְרֵי הָאֱלֹהִים
לְהָרִים קָרֶן וַיִּתֵּן הָאֱלֹהִים לְהֵימָן בָּנִים אַרְבָּעָה עָשָׂר וּבָנוֹת שָׁלוֹשׁ:
ו כָּל־אֵלֶּה עַל־יְדֵי אֲבִיהֶם בַּשִּׁיר בֵּית יְהוָה בִּמְצִלְתַּיִם נְבָלִים וְכִנֹּרוֹת
לַעֲבֹדַת בֵּית הָאֱלֹהִים עַל יְדֵי הַמֶּלֶךְ
ז אָסָף וִידוּתוּן וְהֵימָן: וַיְהִי מִסְפָּרָם עִם־אֲחֵיהֶם מְלֻמְּדֵי־שִׁיר לַיהוָה
ח כָּל־הַמֵּבִין מָאתַיִם שְׁמוֹנִים וּשְׁמוֹנָה: וַיַּפִּילוּ גּוֹרָלוֹת מִשְׁמֶרֶת לְעֻמַּת
ט כַּקָּטֹן כַּגָּדוֹל מֵבִין עִם־תַּלְמִיד: וַיֵּצֵא הַגּוֹרָל הָרִאשׁוֹן לְאָסָף
י לְיוֹסֵף גְּדַלְיָהוּ הַשֵּׁנִי הוּא־וְאֶחָיו וּבָנָיו שְׁנֵים עָשָׂר: הַשְּׁלִשִׁי זַכּוּר
יא הָרְבִיעִי לַיִּצְרִי בָּנָיו וְאֶחָיו שְׁנֵים עָשָׂר:
יב הַחֲמִישִׁי נְתַנְיָהוּ בָּנָיו וְאֶחָיו שְׁנֵים עָשָׂר:
יג הַשִּׁשִּׁי בֻּקִּיָּהוּ בָּנָיו וְאֶחָיו שְׁנֵים עָשָׂר:
יד הַשְּׁבִיעִי יְשַׂרְאֵלָה בָּנָיו וְאֶחָיו שְׁנֵים עָשָׂר:
טו הַשְּׁמִינִי יְשַׁעְיָהוּ בָּנָיו וְאֶחָיו שְׁנֵים עָשָׂר:
טז הַתְּשִׁיעִי מַתַּנְיָהוּ בָּנָיו וְאֶחָיו שְׁנֵים עָשָׂר:
יז הָעֲשִׂירִי שִׁמְעִי בָּנָיו וְאֶחָיו שְׁנֵים עָשָׂר:
יח עַשְׁתֵּי־עָשָׂר עֲזַרְאֵל בָּנָיו וְאֶחָיו שְׁנֵים עָשָׂר:
יט הַשְּׁנֵים עָשָׂר לַחֲשַׁבְיָה בָּנָיו וְאֶחָיו שְׁנֵים עָשָׂר:
כ לִשְׁלֹשָׁה עָשָׂר שׁוּבָאֵל בָּנָיו וְאֶחָיו שְׁנֵים עָשָׂר:
כא לְאַרְבָּעָה עָשָׂר מַתִּתְיָהוּ בָּנָיו וְאֶחָיו שְׁנֵים עָשָׂר:
כב לַחֲמִשָּׁה עָשָׂר לִירֵמוֹת בָּנָיו וְאֶחָיו שְׁנֵים עָשָׂר:
כג לְשִׁשָּׁה עָשָׂר לַחֲנַנְיָהוּ בָּנָיו וְאֶחָיו שְׁנֵים עָשָׂר:
כד לְשִׁבְעָה עָשָׂר לְיָשְׁבְּקָשָׁה בָּנָיו וְאֶחָיו שְׁנֵים עָשָׂר:
כה לִשְׁמוֹנָה עָשָׂר לַחֲנָנִי בָּנָיו וְאֶחָיו שְׁנֵים עָשָׂר:
כו לְתִשְׁעָה עָשָׂר לְמַלּוֹתִי בָּנָיו וְאֶחָיו שְׁנֵים עָשָׂר:
כז לְעֶשְׂרִים לֶאֱלִיָּתָה בָּנָיו וְאֶחָיו שְׁנֵים עָשָׂר:
כח לְאֶחָד וְעֶשְׂרִים לְהוֹתִיר בָּנָיו וְאֶחָיו שְׁנֵים עָשָׂר:

29 his sons, and his brothers – twelve; the twenty-second to Gidalti,
30 his sons, and his brothers – twelve; the twenty-third to Maḥaziot,
31 his sons, and his brothers – twelve; the twenty-fourth to Romamti Ezer,
26 1 his sons, and his brothers – twelve. As for the divisions of gatekeepers:
Of the Korahites: Meshelemyahu son of Koreh of the sons of Asaf.
2 Meshelemyahu's sons: Zekharyahu the firstborn, Yediael the second,
3 Zevadyahu the third, Yatniel the fourth, Eilam the fifth, Yehoḥanan the sixth,
4 and Eleiho'einai the seventh. Oved Edom's sons: Shemaya the firstborn,
Yehozavad the second, Yoaḥ the third, Sakhar the fourth, Netanel the fifth,
5 Amiel the sixth, Yissakhar the seventh, and Peuletai the eighth – for God
6 had blessed him. The sons born to Shemaya were dominant
7 in their father's house, for they were worthy men. The sons of
Shemaya: Otni, Refael, Oved, and Elzavad; his worthy brothers were Elihu
8 and Semakhyahu. All these sons of Oved Edom's – they and their sons and
brothers – were worthy men with a strong capacity for work; sixty-two
9 from Oved Edom. Meshelemyahu's sons and brothers were worthy, able
10 men – eighteen. Ḥosah of the Merarites' sons: Shimri the head was
11 not the firstborn, but his father designated him as chief; Ḥilkiyahu the second,
Tevalyahu the third, and Zekharyahu the fourth. The sons and brothers
12 of Ḥosa were thirteen in all. These divisions of gatekeepers by their chief
13 men had shifts just like their kin who served in the House of the Lord. For
each gate they cast lots for small and great alike according to their ancestral
14 houses. The lot for the east fell to Shelemyahu, and when they cast
lots for his son Zekharyahu, a wise counselor, his lot came out for the north.
15 16 For Oved Edom the south, and for his sons the storehouse. For Shupim
and Ḥosa the west, with the Shalekhet Gate by the ascending road. Watch
17 corresponded to watch: on the east were six Levites; on the north, four each
18 day; on the south, four each day as well as two and two at the storehouse; for
19 the vestibule to the west, four for the road and two for the vestibule. These
20 were the divisions of gatekeepers among the Korahites and the Merarites. Of
the Levites, Aḥiya was in charge of the treasuries of the House of the Lord
and the treasuries of the dedicated items.
21 The sons of Ladan, the sons of the Gershonites belonging to Ladan, were the
22 ancestral heads of Ladan the Gershonite: Yeḥieli. The sons of Yeḥieli, Zetam
and his brother Yoel, who were in charge of the treasuries of the House of the
23 Lord. Of the Amramites, the Izharites, the Hebronites, and the Uzielites:
24 25 Shevuel son of Gershom son of Moshe was chief officer of the treasuries. His
kin, of Eliezer, were his son Reḥavyahu, his son Yeshayahu, his son Yoram,
26 his son Zikhri, and his son Shlomit; this Shlomit and his brothers were in
charge of all the treasuries of items that had been dedicated by King David,

כט בָּנָיו וְאֶחָיו שְׁנֵים עָשָׂר׃ לִשְׁנַיִם וְעֶשְׂרִים לְגִדַּלְתִּי
ל בָּנָיו וְאֶחָיו שְׁנֵים עָשָׂר׃ לִשְׁלֹשָׁה וְעֶשְׂרִים לְמַחֲזִיאוֹת
לא בָּנָיו וְאֶחָיו שְׁנֵים עָשָׂר׃ לְאַרְבָּעָה וְעֶשְׂרִים לְרוֹמַמְתִּי עָזֶר
כו א בָּנָיו וְאֶחָיו שְׁנֵים עָשָׂר׃ לְמַחְלְקוֹת לְשֹׁעֲרִים
ב לַקָּרְחִים מְשֶׁלֶמְיָהוּ בֶן־קֹרֵא מִן־בְּנֵי אָסָף׃ וְלִמְשֶׁלֶמְיָהוּ בָּנִים זְכַרְיָהוּ
ג הַבְּכוֹר יְדִיעֲאֵל הַשֵּׁנִי זְבַדְיָהוּ הַשְּׁלִישִׁי יַתְנִיאֵל הָרְבִיעִי׃ עֵילָם
ד הַחֲמִישִׁי יְהוֹחָנָן הַשִּׁשִּׁי אֶלְיְהוֹעֵינַי הַשְּׁבִיעִי׃ וּלְעֹבֵד אֱדֹם בָּנִים
שְׁמַעְיָה הַבְּכוֹר יְהוֹזָבָד הַשֵּׁנִי יוֹאָח הַשְּׁלִשִׁי וְשָׂכָר הָרְבִיעִי וּנְתַנְאֵל
ה הַחֲמִישִׁי׃ עַמִּיאֵל הַשִּׁשִּׁי יִשָּׂשכָר הַשְּׁבִיעִי פְּעֻלְּתַי הַשְּׁמִינִי כִּי בֵרְכוֹ
ו אֱלֹהִים׃ וְלִשְׁמַעְיָה בְנוֹ נוֹלַד בָּנִים הַמִּמְשָׁלִים לְבֵית
ז אֲבִיהֶם כִּי־גִבּוֹרֵי חַיִל הֵמָּה׃ בְּנֵי שְׁמַעְיָה עָתְנִי וּרְפָאֵל
ח וְעוֹבֵד אֶלְזָבָד אֶחָיו בְּנֵי־חָיִל אֱלִיהוּ וּסְמַכְיָהוּ׃ כָּל־אֵלֶּה מִבְּנֵי ׀
עֹבֵד אֱדֹם הֵמָּה וּבְנֵיהֶם וַאֲחֵיהֶם אִישׁ־חַיִל בַּכֹּחַ לַעֲבֹדָה שִׁשִּׁים
ט וּשְׁנַיִם לְעֹבֵד אֱדֹם׃ וְלִמְשֶׁלֶמְיָהוּ בָּנִים וְאַחִים בְּנֵי־חָיִל שְׁמוֹנָה
י עָשָׂר׃ וּלְחֹסָה מִן־בְּנֵי־מְרָרִי בָּנִים שִׁמְרִי הָרֹאשׁ כִּי לֹא־
יא הָיָה בְכוֹר וַיְשִׂימֵהוּ אָבִיהוּ לְרֹאשׁ׃ חִלְקִיָּהוּ הַשֵּׁנִי טְבַלְיָהוּ הַשְּׁלִשִׁי
יב זְכַרְיָהוּ הָרְבִעִי כָּל־בָּנִים וְאַחִים לְחֹסָה שְׁלֹשָׁה עָשָׂר׃ לְאֵלֶּה מַחְלְקוֹת
הַשֹּׁעֲרִים לְרָאשֵׁי הַגְּבָרִים מִשְׁמָרוֹת לְעֻמַּת אֲחֵיהֶם לְשָׁרֵת
יג בְּבֵית יְהוָה׃ וַיַּפִּילוּ גוֹרָלוֹת כַּקָּטֹן כַּגָּדוֹל לְבֵית אֲבוֹתָם לְשַׁעַר
יד וָשָׁעַר׃ וַיִּפֹּל הַגּוֹרָל מִזְרָחָה לְשֶׁלֶמְיָהוּ וּזְכַרְיָהוּ בְנוֹ יוֹעֵץ
טו בְּשֶׂכֶל הִפִּילוּ גוֹרָלוֹת וַיֵּצֵא גוֹרָלוֹ צָפוֹנָה׃ לְעֹבֵד אֱדֹם נֶגְבָּה וּלְבָנָיו
טז בֵּית הָאֲסֻפִּים׃ לְשֻׁפִּים וּלְחֹסָה לַמַּעֲרָב עִם שַׁעַר שַׁלֶּכֶת בַּמְסִלָּה
יז הָעוֹלָה מִשְׁמָר לְעֻמַּת מִשְׁמָר׃ לַמִּזְרָח הַלְוִיִּם שִׁשָּׁה לַצָּפוֹנָה לַיּוֹם
יח אַרְבָּעָה לַנֶּגְבָּה לַיּוֹם אַרְבָּעָה וְלָאֲסֻפִּים שְׁנַיִם שְׁנָיִם׃ לַפַּרְבָּר לַמַּעֲרָב
יט אַרְבָּעָה לַמְסִלָּה שְׁנַיִם לַפַּרְבָּר׃ אֵלֶּה מַחְלְקוֹת הַשֹּׁעֲרִים לִבְנֵי הַקָּרְחִי
כ וְלִבְנֵי מְרָרִי׃ וְהַלְוִיִּם אֲחִיָּה עַל־אוֹצְרוֹת בֵּית הָאֱלֹהִים וּלְאֹצְרוֹת
הַקֳּדָשִׁים׃
כא בְּנֵי לַעְדָּן בְּנֵי הַגֵּרְשֻׁנִּי לְלַעְדָּן רָאשֵׁי הָאָבוֹת לְלַעְדָּן הַגֵּרְשֻׁנִּי יְחִיאֵלִי׃
כב כג בְּנֵי יְחִיאֵלִי זֵתָם וְיוֹאֵל אָחִיו עַל־אֹצְרוֹת בֵּית יְהוָה׃ לַעַמְרָמִי לַיִּצְהָרִי
כד לַחֶבְרוֹנִי לָעָזִּיאֵלִי׃ וּשְׁבֻאֵל בֶּן־גֵּרְשׁוֹם בֶּן־מֹשֶׁה נָגִיד עַל־הָאֹצָרוֹת׃
כה וְאֶחָיו לֶאֱלִיעֶזֶר רְחַבְיָהוּ בְנוֹ וִישַׁעְיָהוּ בְנוֹ וְיֹרָם בְּנוֹ וְזִכְרִי בְנוֹ ושלמות וּשְׁלֹמִית
כו בְּנוֹ׃ הוּא שְׁלֹמוֹת וְאֶחָיו עַל כָּל־אֹצְרוֹת הַקֳּדָשִׁים אֲשֶׁר הִקְדִּישׁ

the ancestral heads of the officers of thousands and hundreds, and the army
27 officers – they had dedicated part of the spoils of war for the maintenance of
28 the House of the Lord. All that Shmuel the seer, Sha'ul son of Kish, Avner
son of Ner, and Yoav son of Tzeruya had dedicated – and all that anyone else
29 had dedicated – was under the charge of Shlomit and his brothers. Of
the Izharites, Kenanyahu and his sons were appointed for external duties in
30 Israel, as officials and judges. Of the Hebronites, Ḥashavyahu and
his kin – 1,700 worthy men – were in charge of Israel on the west bank of the
31 Jordan for all the work of the Lord and the king's service. Among the
Hebronites, Yeriya was the leader of the Hebronites according to the
genealogy of his father's house: in the fortieth year of David's reign, worthy
32 men were sought out and found in Yazeir of Gilad. King David appointed him
and his kin, 2,700 worthy men, over the Reubenites, the Gadites, and half the
tribe of Menashe, for anything concerning the word of God and the king's
27 1 orders. This is the list of the Israelites, the ancestral heads, the officers
of thousands and hundreds, and their officials who served the king in all
matters concerning the divisions that marched back and forth every month
2 of the year. Each division had 24,000. Yoshovam son of Zavdiel was
in charge of the first division for the first month, and there were 24,000 in his
3 division. Descended from Peretz, he was the leader of all the army comman-
4 ders during the first month. Dodai the Ahohite was in charge of the
division for the second month; Miklot was chief officer of his division, and
5 in his division were 24,000. The third army commander for
the third month was the leader Benayahu son of Yehoyada the priest; in his
6 division were 24,000. This same Benayahu was a warrior of the Thirty who
7 led the Thirty, and his son Amizavad was in his division. The fourth
for the fourth month was Asael brother of Yoav and his son Zevadya after
8 him; in his division were 24,000. The fifth for the fifth month was
9 the officer Shamhut the Izrahite; in his division were 24,000. The
sixth for the sixth month was Ira son of Ikesh the Tekoaite; in his division
10 were 24,000. The seventh for the seventh month was Ḥeletz the
11 Pelonite, descended from Efrayim; in his division were 24,000. The
eighth for the eighth month was Sibekhai the Hushatite, of the Zerahites; in
12 his division were 24,000. The ninth for the ninth month was
13 Aviezer the Anatotite, of Binyamin; in his division were 24,000. The
tenth for the tenth month was Mahrai the Netofatite, of Zeraḥ; in his division

דָּוִ֣יד הַמֶּ֑לֶךְ וְרָאשֵׁ֣י הָאָב֗וֹת לְשָׂרֵי־הָאֲלָפִ֛ים וְהַמֵּא֖וֹת וְשָׂרֵ֥י הַצָּבָֽא׃
כז כח מִן־הַמִּלְחָמ֛וֹת וּמִן־הַשָּׁלָ֖ל הִקְדִּ֑ישׁוּ לְחַזֵּ֖ק לְבֵ֥ית יְהוָֽה׃ וְכֹ֗ל
הַהִקְדִּ֜ישׁ שְׁמוּאֵ֣ל הָֽרֹאֶ֗ה וְשָׁא֤וּל בֶּן־קִישׁ֙ וְאַבְנֵ֣ר בֶּן־נֵ֔ר וְיוֹאָ֖ב
כט בֶּן־צְרוּיָ֑ה כֹּל֙ הַמַּקְדִּ֔ישׁ עַ֥ל יַד־שְׁלֹמִ֖ית וְאֶחָֽיו׃ לַיִּצְהָרִ֗י
כְּנַנְיָ֤הוּ וּבָנָיו֙ לַמְּלָאכָ֣ה הַחִיצוֹנָ֔ה עַל־יִשְׂרָאֵ֖ל לְשֹׁטְרִ֥ים
ל וּלְשֹׁפְטִֽים׃ לַֽחֶבְרוֹנִ֗י חֲשַׁבְיָ֨הוּ וְאֶחָ֜יו בְּנֵי־חַ֗יִל אֶ֚לֶף וּשְׁבַע־
מֵא֔וֹת עַ֚ל פְּקֻדַּ֣ת יִשְׂרָאֵ֔ל מֵעֵ֥בֶר לַיַּרְדֵּ֖ן מַעְרָ֑בָה לְכֹל֙ מְלֶ֣אכֶת יְהוָ֔ה
לא וְלַעֲבֹדַ֖ת הַמֶּֽלֶךְ׃ לַֽחֶבְרוֹנִי֙ יְרִיָּ֣ה הָרֹ֔אשׁ לַֽחֶבְרוֹנִ֥י לְתֹלְדֹתָ֖יו לְאָב֑וֹת
בִּשְׁנַ֨ת הָאַרְבָּעִ֜ים לְמַלְכ֤וּת דָּוִיד֙ נִדְרָ֔שׁוּ וַיִּמָּצֵ֥א בָהֶ֛ם גִּבּ֥וֹרֵי חַ֖יִל בְּיַעְזֵ֥יר
לב גִּלְעָֽד׃ וְאֶחָיו֙ בְּנֵי־חַ֔יִל אַלְפַּ֥יִם וּשְׁבַ֛ע מֵא֖וֹת רָאשֵׁ֣י הָאָב֑וֹת וַיַּפְקִידֵ֞ם
דָּוִ֣יד הַמֶּ֗לֶךְ עַל־הָרֽאוּבֵנִ֤י וְהַגָּדִי֙ וַחֲצִי֙ שֵׁ֣בֶט הַֽמְנַשִּׁ֔י לְכָל־דְּבַ֥ר
כז א הָאֱלֹהִ֖ים וּדְבַ֥ר הַמֶּֽלֶךְ׃ וּבְנֵ֨י יִשְׂרָאֵ֜ל ׀ לְמִסְפָּרָ֗ם רָאשֵׁ֨י
הָאָב֜וֹת ׀ וְשָׂרֵ֣י הָאֲלָפִ֗ים ׀ וְהַמֵּא֡וֹת וְשֹׁטְרֵיהֶם֩ הַמְשָׁרְתִ֨ים אֶת־הַמֶּ֜לֶךְ
לְכֹ֣ל ׀ דְּבַ֣ר הַֽמַּחְלְק֗וֹת הַבָּאָ֤ה וְהַיֹּצֵאת֙ חֹ֣דֶשׁ בְּחֹ֔דֶשׁ לְכֹ֖ל חָדְשֵׁ֣י
ב הַשָּׁנָ֑ה הַמַּחֲלֹ֙קֶת֙ הָֽאַחַ֔ת עֶשְׂרִ֥ים וְאַרְבָּעָ֖ה אָֽלֶף׃ עַ֞ל
הַמַּחֲלֹ֣קֶת הָרִֽאשׁוֹנָ֗ה לַחֹ֙דֶשׁ֙ הָֽרִאשׁ֔וֹן יָשָׁבְעָ֖ם בֶּן־זַבְדִּיאֵ֑ל וְעַל֙
ג מַחֲלֻקְתּ֔וֹ עֶשְׂרִ֥ים וְאַרְבָּעָ֖ה אָֽלֶף׃ מִן־בְּנֵי־פֶ֖רֶץ הָרֹ֣אשׁ לְכָל־שָׂרֵ֣י
ד הַצְּבָא֑וֹת לַחֹ֖דֶשׁ הָרִאשֽׁוֹן׃ וְעַ֞ל מַחֲלֹ֣קֶת ׀ הַחֹ֣דֶשׁ הַשֵּׁנִ֗י
דּוֹדַ֤י הָאֲחוֹחִי֙ וּמַ֣חֲלֻקְתּ֔וֹ וּמִקְל֖וֹת הַנָּגִ֑יד וְעַל֙ מַחֲלֻקְתּ֔וֹ עֶשְׂרִ֥ים
ה וְאַרְבָּעָ֖ה אָֽלֶף׃ שַׂ֣ר הַצָּבָ֤א הַשְּׁלִישִׁי֙ לַחֹ֣דֶשׁ הַשְּׁלִישִׁ֔י
בְּנָיָ֧הוּ בֶן־יְהוֹיָדָ֛ע הַכֹּהֵ֖ן רֹ֑אשׁ וְעַל֙ מַחֲלֻקְתּ֔וֹ עֶשְׂרִ֥ים וְאַרְבָּעָ֖ה אָֽלֶף׃
ו ה֧וּא בְנָיָ֛הוּ גִּבּ֥וֹר הַשְּׁלֹשִׁ֖ים וְעַל־הַשְּׁלֹשִׁ֑ים וּמַ֣חֲלֻקְתּ֔וֹ עַמִּֽיזָבָ֖ד
ז בְּנֽוֹ׃ הָרְבִיעִ֞י לַחֹ֣דֶשׁ הָרְבִיעִ֗י עֲשָׂהאֵל֙ אֲחִ֣י יוֹאָ֔ב וּזְבַדְיָ֥ה
ח בְנ֖וֹ אַחֲרָ֑יו וְעַל֙ מַחֲלֻקְתּ֔וֹ עֶשְׂרִ֥ים וְאַרְבָּעָ֖ה אָֽלֶף׃ הַחֲמִישִׁ֗י
לַחֹ֤דֶשׁ הַחֲמִישִׁי֙ הַשַּׂ֣ר שַׁמְה֔וּת הַיִּזְרָ֑ח וְעַל֙ מַחֲלֻקְתּ֔וֹ עֶשְׂרִ֥ים וְאַרְבָּעָ֖ה
ט אָֽלֶף׃ הַשִּׁשִּׁי֙ לַחֹ֣דֶשׁ הַשִּׁשִּׁ֔י עִירָ֥א בֶן־עִקֵּ֖שׁ הַתְּקוֹעִ֑י וְעַל֙
י מַחֲלֻקְתּ֔וֹ עֶשְׂרִ֥ים וְאַרְבָּעָ֖ה אָֽלֶף׃ הַשְּׁבִיעִי֙ לַחֹ֣דֶשׁ
הַשְּׁבִיעִ֔י חֶ֥לֶץ הַפְּלוֹנִ֖י מִן־בְּנֵ֣י אֶפְרָ֑יִם וְעַל֙ מַחֲלֻקְתּ֔וֹ עֶשְׂרִ֥ים וְאַרְבָּעָ֖ה
יא אָֽלֶף׃ הַשְּׁמִינִי֙ לַחֹ֣דֶשׁ הַשְּׁמִינִ֔י סִבְּכַ֖י הַחֻשָׁתִ֑י לַזַּרְחִ֔י וְעַל֙
יב מַחֲלֻקְתּ֔וֹ עֶשְׂרִ֥ים וְאַרְבָּעָ֖ה אָֽלֶף׃ הַתְּשִׁיעִי֙ לַחֹ֣דֶשׁ
הַתְּשִׁיעִ֔י אֲבִיעֶ֥זֶר הָֽעַנְּתֹתִ֖י לַבִּנְיָמִינִ֑י וְעַל֙ מַחֲלֻקְתּ֔וֹ עֶשְׂרִ֥ים וְאַרְבָּעָ֖ה לַבֶּן ׀ יְמִינִי
יג אָֽלֶף׃ הָעֲשִׂירִי֙ לַחֹ֣דֶשׁ הָעֲשִׂירִ֔י מַהְרַ֥י הַנְּטֽוֹפָתִ֖י לַזַּרְחִ֑י

14 were 24,000. The eleventh for the eleventh month was Benaya the
15 Piratonite, of the Efraimites; in his division were 24,000. The twelfth
for the twelfth month was Ḥeldai the Netofatite, of Otniel; in his division
16 were 24,000. In charge of the tribes of Israel: over Reuven, the
chief officer was Eliezer son of Zikhri. Over Shimon, Shefatya son of
17 Maakha. Over Levi, Ḥashavya son of Kemuel. Over Aharon,
18 Tzadok. Over Yehuda, Elihu, of the brothers of David. Over
19 Yissakhar, Omri son of Mikhael. Over Zevulun, Yishmayahu son of
20 Ovadyahu. Over Naftali, Yerimot son of Azriel. Over the Efraimites,
Hoshe'a son of Azazyahu. Over half the tribe of Menashe, Yoel son of
21 Pedayahu; over half of Menashe in Gilad, Ido son of Zekharyahu.
22 Over Binyamin, Yaasiel son of Avner. Over Dan, Azarel son of
23 Yeroḥam. These were the officers of the tribes of Israel. David did not take a
census of those under twenty years old because the LORD promised to
24 increase Israel like the stars of the heavens. Yoav son of Tzeruya began to
number them – although he did not finish; for this, wrath rose against
Israel, and the count was not entered into the account in King David's
25 chronicles. The royal treasuries were overseen by Azmavet son of
Adiel, while over the treasuries of the fields, cities, villages, and towers was
26 Yehonatan son of Uziyahu. Over the field preparation for
27 agriculture, Ezri son of Keluv; over the vineyards, Shimi the
Ramatite, while over the vineyard produce for the wine cellars, Zavdi the
28 Shifmite. Over the olive groves and sycamore trees in the plains,
29 Baal Ḥanan the Gederite; over the oil stores, Yoash. Over the cattle
grazing in the Sharon, Shirtai the Sharonite; over the cattle in the valleys,
30 Shafat son of Adlai. Over the camels, Ovil the Ishmaelite; over the
31 donkeys, Yeḥdeyahu the Meronotite; over the flocks, Yaziz the
Hagarite. All these were the officials who managed the property that belonged
32 to King David. Yehonatan, David's uncle, was a wise advisor and
33 scribe; and Yeḥiel the Hakhmonite was with the king's sons. Aḥitofel was the
34 king's advisor, while Ḥushai the Arkite was Friend of the King. After Aḥitofel
was Yehoyada son of Benayahu and Evyatar, and the king's army commander
28 1 was Yoav. David assembled in Jerusalem all the officers of Israel – the
officers of the tribes, the officers of the divisions that served the king, the
officers of thousands and the officers of hundreds, and the officers of all the
property that belonged to the king and his sons – along with the officials, the
2 warriors, and all the powerful men. King David rose to his feet and said: "Hear
me, my brothers and my people – I had my heart set on building a resting

יד וְעַל֙ מַחֲלֻקְתּ֔וֹ עֶשְׂרִ֥ים וְאַרְבָּעָ֖ה אָֽלֶף׃ עַשְׁתֵּֽי־עָשָׂ֣ר
לְעַשְׁתֵּֽי עָשָׂ֣ר הַחֹ֔דֶשׁ בְּנָיָ֥ה הַפִּרְעָתוֹנִ֖י מִן־בְּנֵ֣י אֶפְרָ֑יִם וְעַל֙ מַחֲלֻקְתּ֔וֹ
טו עֶשְׂרִ֥ים וְאַרְבָּעָ֖ה אָֽלֶף׃ הַשְּׁנֵ֨ים עָשָׂ֜ר לִשְׁנֵ֤ים עָשָׂר֙
הַחֹ֔דֶשׁ חֶלְדַּ֥י הַנְּטוֹפָתִ֖י לְעָתְנִיאֵ֑ל וְעַל֙ מַחֲלֻקְתּ֔וֹ עֶשְׂרִ֥ים וְאַרְבָּעָ֖ה
טז אָֽלֶף׃ וְעַל֙ שִׁבְטֵ֣י יִשְׂרָאֵ֔ל לָרְאוּבֵנִ֣י נָגִ֔יד אֱלִיעֶ֖זֶר בֶּן־זִכְרִ֑י
יז לַשִּׁמְעוֹנִ֕י שְׁפַטְיָ֖הוּ בֶּן־מַעֲכָֽה׃ לְלֵוִ֕י חֲשַׁבְיָ֖ה בֶן־קְמוּאֵ֑ל
יח לְאַהֲרֹ֖ן צָדֽוֹק׃ לִֽיהוּדָ֕ה אֱלִיה֖וּ מֵאֲחֵ֣י דָוִ֑יד לְיִשָּׂשכָ֕ר
יט עָמְרִ֖י בֶּן־מִיכָאֵֽל׃ לִזְבוּלֻ֕ן יִשְׁמַעְיָ֖הוּ בֶּן־עֹבַדְיָ֑הוּ
כ לְנַ֨פְתָּלִ֔י יְרִימ֖וֹת בֶּן־עַזְרִיאֵֽל׃ לִבְנֵ֣י אֶפְרַ֔יִם הוֹשֵׁ֖עַ בֶּן־
כא עֲזַזְיָ֑הוּ לַחֲצִי֙ שֵׁ֣בֶט מְנַשֶּׁ֔ה יוֹאֵ֖ל בֶּן־פְּדָיָֽהוּ׃ לַחֲצִ֤י הַֽמְנַשֶּׁה֙
כב גִּלְעָ֔דָה יִדּ֖וֹ בֶּן־זְכַרְיָ֑הוּ לְבִנְיָמִ֕ן יַעֲשִׂיאֵ֖ל בֶּן־אַבְנֵֽר׃ לְדָ֕ן
כג עֲזַרְאֵ֖ל בֶּן־יְרֹחָ֑ם אֵ֕לֶּה שָׂרֵ֖י שִׁבְטֵ֥י יִשְׂרָאֵֽל׃ וְלֹֽא־נָשָׂ֤א דָוִיד֙ מִסְפָּרָ֔ם
לְמִבֶּ֛ן עֶשְׂרִ֥ים שָׁנָ֖ה וּלְמָ֑טָּה כִּ֚י אָמַ֣ר יהוה לְהַרְבּ֥וֹת אֶת־יִשְׂרָאֵ֖ל
כד כְּכוֹכְבֵ֥י הַשָּׁמָֽיִם׃ יוֹאָ֨ב בֶּן־צְרוּיָ֜ה הֵחֵ֤ל לִמְנוֹת֙ וְלֹ֣א כִלָּ֔ה וַיְהִ֥י בָזֹ֛את
קֶ֖צֶף עַל־יִשְׂרָאֵ֑ל וְלֹ֣א עָלָ֗ה הַמִּסְפָּר֙ בְּמִסְפַּ֣ר דִּבְרֵֽי הַיָּמִ֔ים לַמֶּ֖לֶךְ
כה דָּוִֽיד׃ וְעַל֙ אֹצְר֣וֹת הַמֶּ֔לֶךְ עַזְמָ֖וֶת בֶּן־עֲדִיאֵ֑ל
וְעַ֣ל הָאֹצָר֡וֹת בַּשָּׂדֶ֜ה בֶּעָרִ֣ים וּבַכְּפָרִ֗ים וּבַמִּגְדָּלוֹת֙ יְהוֹנָתָ֣ן בֶּן־
כו עֻזִּיָּֽהוּ׃ וְעַ֕ל עֹשֵׂ֖י מְלֶ֣אכֶת הַשָּׂדֶ֑ה לַעֲבֹדַ֖ת הָאֲדָמָ֑ה עֶזְרִ֖י
כז בֶּן־כְּלֽוּב׃ וְעַֽל־הַכְּרָמִ֔ים שִׁמְעִ֖י הָרָמָתִ֑י וְעַ֤ל שֶׁבַּכְּרָמִים֙
כח לְאֹצְר֣וֹת הַיַּ֔יִן זַבְדִּ֖י הַשִּׁפְמִֽי׃ וְעַל־הַזֵּיתִ֤ים וְהַשִּׁקְמִים֙ אֲשֶׁ֣ר
כט בַּשְּׁפֵלָ֔ה בַּ֥עַל חָנָ֖ן הַגְּדֵרִ֑י וְעַל־אֹצְר֥וֹת הַשֶּׁ֖מֶן יוֹעָֽשׁ׃ וְעַל־
הַבָּקָר֙ הָרֹעִ֣ים בַּשָּׁר֔וֹן שטרי הַשָּׁרוֹנִ֑י וְעַל־הַבָּקָר֙ בָּעֲמָקִ֔ים שָׁפָ֖ט שִׁרְטַ֣י
ל בֶּן־עַדְלָֽי׃ וְעַל־הַ֨גְּמַלִּ֔ים אוֹבִ֖יל הַיִּשְׁמְעֵאלִ֑י וְעַל־הָ֣אֲתֹנ֔וֹת
לא יֶחְדְּיָ֖הוּ הַמֵּרֹנֹתִֽי׃ וְעַל־הַצֹּ֖אן יָזִ֣יז הַהַגְרִ֑י כָּל־אֵ֨לֶּה֙ שָׂרֵ֣י
לב הָרְכ֔וּשׁ אֲשֶׁ֖ר לַמֶּ֥לֶךְ דָּוִֽיד׃ וִיהוֹנָתָ֤ן דּוֹד־דָּוִיד֙ יוֹעֵ֔ץ אִֽישׁ־
לג מֵבִ֥ין וְסוֹפֵ֖ר ה֑וּא וִיחִיאֵ֥ל בֶּן־חַכְמוֹנִ֖י עִם־בְּנֵ֥י הַמֶּֽלֶךְ׃ וַאֲחִיתֹ֖פֶל יוֹעֵ֣ץ
לד לַמֶּ֑לֶךְ וְחוּשַׁ֥י הָאַרְכִּ֖י רֵ֥עַ הַמֶּֽלֶךְ׃ וְאַחֲרֵ֨י אֲחִיתֹ֜פֶל יְהוֹיָדָ֤ע בֶּן־בְּנָיָ֙הוּ֙
כח א וְאֶבְיָתָ֔ר וְשַׂר־צָבָ֥א לַמֶּ֖לֶךְ יוֹאָֽב׃ וַיַּקְהֵ֣ל דָּ֠וִיד אֶת־כָּל־שָׂרֵ֨י
יִשְׂרָאֵ֜ל שָׂרֵ֣י הַשְּׁבָטִ֗ים וְשָׂרֵ֨י הַֽמַּחְלְק֜וֹת הַמְשָׁרְתִ֣ים אֶת־הַמֶּ֗לֶךְ וְשָׂרֵ֨י
הָאֲלָפִ֜ים וְשָׂרֵ֣י הַמֵּא֗וֹת וְשָׂרֵ֣י כָל־רְכֽוּשׁ־וּמִקְנֶ֣ה ׀ לַמֶּ֣לֶךְ וּלְבָנָ֗יו עִם־
ב הַסָּרִיסִ֛ים וְהַגִּבּוֹרִ֖ים וּלְכָל־גִּבּ֣וֹר חָ֑יִל אֶל־יְרוּשָׁלִָֽם׃ וַיָּ֨קָם דָּוִ֤יד הַמֶּ֙לֶךְ֙
עַל־רַגְלָ֔יו וַיֹּ֕אמֶר שְׁמָע֖וּנִי אַחַ֣י וְעַמִּ֑י אֲנִ֣י עִם־לְבָבִ֗י לִבְנוֹת֩ בֵּ֨ית מְנוּחָ֜ה

place for the Ark of the LORD's Covenant and for the footstool of our God,
3 and I made preparations for building. But God said to me, 'You will not build
4 a House for My name, for you are a man of war, and you have shed blood.' Yet
the LORD, God of Israel, chose me out of all my father's house to be king over
Israel forever, for He chose Yehuda as ruler, and within the House of Yehuda,
my father's house; and out of my father's sons, it was me He wished to make
5 king over all Israel. And out of all my sons – for the LORD has granted me
many sons – He has chosen my son Shlomo to sit on the throne of the LORD's
6 royal dominion over Israel. And He said to me, 'Your son Shlomo will be the
one to build My House and My courtyards, for I have chosen him as My son,
7 and I will be his Father. I will establish his kingdom forever so long as he
8 adheres firmly to My commandments and rulings as he does now.' And now,
before the eyes of all Israel, the LORD's assembly, and in the hearing of our
God: keep and seek out all the commandments of the LORD your God so that
you will inherit the good land and leave it to your children after you forever.
9 As for you, my son Shlomo, know the God of your father and serve Him with
a full heart and a willing soul, for the LORD searches all hearts and understands the design of all thoughts. If you search for Him, He will be there for
10 you, but if you forsake Him, He will abandon you forever. Look now, for the
LORD has chosen you to build a House for the Sanctuary – be strong and take
11 action." Then David gave to his son Shlomo the design for the Hall,
its buildings, its upper chambers, its inner chambers, and the place for the
12 Ark and its covering; all his inspired designs for the courts of the House of
the LORD, for all its surrounding chambers, for the treasuries of the House of
13 God, and for the treasuries of the dedicated items; along with the divisions
of priests and Levites and all the work of the service of the House of the LORD
14 and all the vessels for the service of the House of the LORD; the weight of
gold for all golden vessels for each and every kind of service and the weight
15 of silver for all vessels for each and every kind of service; the weight of the
gold candelabra and their golden lamps, with the weight needed for each
candelabrum and its lamps and the weight of silver needed for each
candelabrum and its lamps in accordance with the use of each candelabrum;
16 the weight of gold needed for the tables for showbread for each table, and
17 silver for the silver tables; pure gold for the forks, basins, and pitchers; the
weight of gold needed for every bowl and the weight of silver needed for every
18 bowl; the weight of refined gold needed for the incense altar; and gold for the
design of the chariot – the cherubim that spread their wings to shelter
19 the Ark of the LORD's Covenant. "All is written down, under the inspiration
of the LORD given me to understand – all the work of the building
20 design," David said to his son Shlomo. "Be strong and brave – do
not quake or cower, for the LORD God, my God, is with you. He will never
let you go or leave you until all the work for the service of the House of the
21 LORD is complete. Look – here are the divisions of priests and Levites for all
the service of the House of God; skilled, willing men will be with you for

ג לַאֲרוֹן בְּרִית־יהוה וְלַהֲדֹם רַגְלֵי אֱלֹהֵינוּ וַהֲכִינוֹתִי לִבְנוֹת: וְהָאֱלֹהִים
אָמַר לִי לֹא־תִבְנֶה בַיִת לִשְׁמִי כִּי אִישׁ מִלְחָמוֹת אַתָּה וְדָמִים שָׁפָכְתָּ:
ד וַיִּבְחַר יהוה אֱלֹהֵי יִשְׂרָאֵל בִּי מִכֹּל בֵּית־אָבִי לִהְיוֹת לְמֶלֶךְ עַל־יִשְׂרָאֵל
לְעוֹלָם כִּי בִיהוּדָה בָּחַר לְנָגִיד וּבְבֵית יְהוּדָה בֵּית אָבִי וּבִבְנֵי אָבִי בִּי
ה רָצָה לְהַמְלִיךְ עַל־כָּל־יִשְׂרָאֵל: וּמִכָּל־בָּנַי כִּי רַבִּים בָּנִים נָתַן לִי יהוה
וַיִּבְחַר בִּשְׁלֹמֹה בְנִי לָשֶׁבֶת עַל־כִּסֵּא מַלְכוּת יהוה עַל־יִשְׂרָאֵל:
ו וַיֹּאמֶר לִי שְׁלֹמֹה בִנְךָ הוּא־יִבְנֶה בֵיתִי וַחֲצֵרוֹתָי כִּי־בָחַרְתִּי בוֹ לִי לְבֵן
ז וַאֲנִי אֶהְיֶה־לּוֹ לְאָב: וַהֲכִינוֹתִי אֶת־מַלְכוּתוֹ עַד־לְעוֹלָם אִם־יֶחֱזַק
ח לַעֲשׂוֹת מִצְוֹתַי וּמִשְׁפָּטַי כַּיּוֹם הַזֶּה: וְעַתָּה לְעֵינֵי כָל־יִשְׂרָאֵל קְהַל־
יהוה וּבְאָזְנֵי אֱלֹהֵינוּ שִׁמְרוּ וְדִרְשׁוּ כָּל־מִצְוֹת יהוה אֱלֹהֵיכֶם לְמַעַן
תִּירְשׁוּ אֶת־הָאָרֶץ הַטּוֹבָה וְהִנְחַלְתֶּם לִבְנֵיכֶם אַחֲרֵיכֶם עַד־עוֹלָם:
ט וְאַתָּה שְׁלֹמֹה־בְנִי דַּע אֶת־אֱלֹהֵי אָבִיךָ וְעָבְדֵהוּ בְּלֵב שָׁלֵם וּבְנֶפֶשׁ
חֲפֵצָה כִּי כָל־לְבָבוֹת דּוֹרֵשׁ יהוה וְכָל־יֵצֶר מַחֲשָׁבוֹת מֵבִין אִם־
י תִּדְרְשֶׁנּוּ יִמָּצֵא לָךְ וְאִם־תַּעַזְבֶנּוּ יַזְנִיחֲךָ לָעַד: רְאֵה ׀ עַתָּה כִּי־יהוה יא
יא בָּחַר בְּךָ לִבְנוֹת־בַּיִת לַמִּקְדָּשׁ חֲזַק וַעֲשֵׂה: וַיִּתֵּן דָּוִיד
לִשְׁלֹמֹה בְנוֹ אֶת־תַּבְנִית הָאוּלָם וְאֶת־בָּתָּיו וְגַנְזַכָּיו וַעֲלִיֹּתָיו וַחֲדָרָיו
יב הַפְּנִימִים וּבֵית הַכַּפֹּרֶת: וְתַבְנִית כֹּל אֲשֶׁר הָיָה בָרוּחַ עִמּוֹ לְחַצְרוֹת
בֵּית־יהוה וּלְכָל־הַלְּשָׁכוֹת סָבִיב לְאֹצְרוֹת בֵּית הָאֱלֹהִים וּלְאֹצְרוֹת
יג הַקֳּדָשִׁים: וּלְמַחְלְקוֹת הַכֹּהֲנִים וְהַלְוִיִּם וּלְכָל־מְלֶאכֶת עֲבוֹדַת בֵּית־
יד יהוה וּלְכָל־כְּלֵי עֲבוֹדַת בֵּית־יהוה: לַזָּהָב בַּמִּשְׁקָל לַזָּהָב לְכָל־כְּלֵי
עֲבוֹדָה וַעֲבוֹדָה לְכֹל כְּלֵי הַכֶּסֶף בְּמִשְׁקָל לְכָל־כְּלֵי עֲבוֹדָה וַעֲבוֹדָה:
טו וּמִשְׁקָל לִמְנֹרוֹת הַזָּהָב וְנֵרֹתֵיהֶם זָהָב בְּמִשְׁקַל־מְנוֹרָה וּמְנוֹרָה
וְנֵרֹתֶיהָ וְלִמְנֹרוֹת הַכֶּסֶף בְּמִשְׁקָל לִמְנוֹרָה וְנֵרֹתֶיהָ כַּעֲבוֹדַת מְנוֹרָה
טז וּמְנוֹרָה: וְאֶת־הַזָּהָב מִשְׁקָל לְשֻׁלְחֲנוֹת הַמַּעֲרֶכֶת לְשֻׁלְחַן וְשֻׁלְחָן
יז וְכֶסֶף לְשֻׁלְחֲנוֹת הַכָּסֶף: וְהַמִּזְלָגוֹת וְהַמִּזְרָקוֹת וְהַקְּשָׂווֹת זָהָב טָהוֹר
וְלִכְפוֹרֵי הַזָּהָב בְּמִשְׁקָל לִכְפוֹר וּכְפוֹר וְלִכְפוֹרֵי הַכֶּסֶף בְּמִשְׁקָל לִכְפוֹר
יח וּכְפוֹר: וּלְמִזְבַּח הַקְּטֹרֶת זָהָב מְזֻקָּק בַּמִּשְׁקָל וּלְתַבְנִית הַמֶּרְכָּבָה
יט הַכְּרֻבִים זָהָב לְפֹרְשִׂים וְסֹכְכִים עַל־אֲרוֹן בְּרִית־יהוה: הַכֹּל בִּכְתָב
כ מִיַּד יהוה עָלַי הִשְׂכִּיל כֹּל מַלְאֲכוֹת הַתַּבְנִית: וַיֹּאמֶר
דָּוִיד לִשְׁלֹמֹה בְנוֹ חֲזַק וֶאֱמַץ וַעֲשֵׂה אַל־תִּירָא וְאַל־תֵּחָת כִּי יהוה
אֱלֹהִים אֱלֹהַי עִמָּךְ לֹא יַרְפְּךָ וְלֹא יַעַזְבֶךָּ עַד־לִכְלוֹת כָּל־מְלֶאכֶת
כא עֲבוֹדַת בֵּית־יהוה: וְהִנֵּה מַחְלְקוֹת הַכֹּהֲנִים וְהַלְוִיִּם לְכָל־עֲבוֹדַת

every job and task; and the officers and all the people are at your every
29 1 command." King David said to the whole assembly, "Shlomo my
son, whom God has singled out, is young and inexperienced, but the task at
2 hand is great – for the palace is not for man but for the Lord God. With all
my might I have made preparations for the House of my God – the necessary
gold, silver, bronze, iron, and wood, as well as stones of rock crystal and stones
for setting, stones of antimony, colored stones, all kinds of precious stones,
3 and vast quantities of marble. What is more, out of my devotion to the House
of my God, I have given over my own private treasure of gold and silver to the
4 House of my God in addition to all that I prepared for the Holy House: three
thousand talents of gold – Ofir gold – and seven thousand talents of refined
5 silver to overlay the walls of the buildings, the necessary gold and silver for
all the work of the craftsmen. Who, then, is willing to offer freely and devote
6 himself today to the Lord?" Then the leaders of the ancestral houses, the
officers of the tribes, the officers of thousands and hundreds, and the officers
7 of the king's service made willing donations: for the work of God's House
they gave five thousand talents and ten thousand darics of gold, ten thousand
talents of silver, eighteen thousand talents of bronze, and one hundred
8 thousand talents of iron. Whoever had precious stones with him gave them
to the treasury of the House of the Lord in the care of Yeḥiel the Gershonite.
9 The people rejoiced over the donations they made so willingly, for they had
offered freely to the Lord with whole hearts. King David, too, was stirred
10 with great joy. David blessed the Lord in front of the entire assembly,
and David said, "Blessed are You, O Lord God of Israel, our Father for ever
11 and ever. Yours, O Lord, is the greatness and the might, the glory and the
fame and the splendor. Yes, all that is in heaven and earth is Yours; Yours, O
12 Lord, is the kingdom; You are exalted as head above all. Wealth and honor
come from You, and You rule over all; in Your hand is power and might; Your
13 hand gives greatness and strength to all. Now, our God, we thank You and
14 praise Your glorious name, for who am I, and who are my people, that we
should have the power to offer so freely? For all is from You, and we have
15 given You only what is Yours. For to You we are but pas-sersby, mere
transients like all our ancestors; our days are like shadows over the earth –
16 there is no hope. O Lord our God, all this abundance we have prepared, to
17 build You a house for Your holy name, is from Your hand, and all is Yours. I
know, my God, that You search hearts and desire what is upright; I, with an
upright heart, willingly offer all this. And now I see Your people, who are
18 present here, offering freely and joyously to You. O Lord, God of Avraham,
Yitzḥak, and Yisrael our ancestors, keep such desires and thoughts in the
19 hearts of Your people forever; direct their hearts to You. And grant that
my son Shlomo will keep Your commandments, decrees, and laws with a
whole heart and do all these things and build the palace for which I have

בֵּית הָאֱלֹהִים וְעִמְּךָ בְכָל־מְלָאכָה לְכָל־נָדִיב בַּחׇכְמָה לְכָל־עֲבוֹדָה
כט א וְהַשָּׂרִים וְכׇל־הָעָם לְכׇל־דְּבָרֶיךָ׃ וַיֹּאמֶר דָּוִיד הַמֶּלֶךְ
לְכׇל־הַקָּהָל שְׁלֹמֹה בְנִי אֶחָד בָּחַר־בּוֹ אֱלֹהִים נַעַר וָרָךְ וְהַמְּלָאכָה
ב גְדוֹלָה כִּי לֹא לְאָדָם הַבִּירָה כִּי לַיהֹוָה אֱלֹהִים׃ וּכְכׇל־כֹּחִי הֲכִינוֹתִי
לְבֵית־אֱלֹהַי הַזָּהָב ׀ לַזָּהָב וְהַכֶּסֶף לַכֶּסֶף וְהַנְּחֹשֶׁת לַנְּחֹשֶׁת הַבַּרְזֶל
לַבַּרְזֶל וְהָעֵצִים לָעֵצִים אַבְנֵי־שֹׁהַם וּמִלּוּאִים אַבְנֵי־פוּךְ וְרִקְמָה וְכֹל
ג אֶבֶן יְקָרָה וְאַבְנֵי־שַׁיִשׁ לָרֹב׃ וְעוֹד בִּרְצוֹתִי בְּבֵית אֱלֹהַי יֶשׁ־לִי סְגֻלָּה
זָהָב וָכָסֶף נָתַתִּי לְבֵית־אֱלֹהַי לְמַעְלָה מִכׇּל־הֲכִינוֹתִי לְבֵית הַקֹּדֶשׁ׃
ד שְׁלֹשֶׁת אֲלָפִים כִּכְּרֵי זָהָב מִזְּהַב אוֹפִיר וְשִׁבְעַת אֲלָפִים כִּכַּר־כֶּסֶף
ה מְזֻקָּק לָטוּחַ קִירוֹת הַבָּתִּים׃ לַזָּהָב לַזָּהָב וְלַכֶּסֶף לַכֶּסֶף וּלְכׇל־מְלָאכָה
ו בְּיַד חָרָשִׁים וּמִי מִתְנַדֵּב לְמַלֹּאות יָדוֹ הַיּוֹם לַיהֹוָה׃ וַיִּתְנַדְּבוּ שָׂרֵי
הָאָבוֹת וְשָׂרֵי ׀ שִׁבְטֵי יִשְׂרָאֵל וְשָׂרֵי הָאֲלָפִים וְהַמֵּאוֹת וּלְשָׂרֵי מְלֶאכֶת
ז הַמֶּלֶךְ׃ וַיִּתְּנוּ לַעֲבוֹדַת בֵּית־הָאֱלֹהִים זָהָב כִּכָּרִים חֲמֵשֶׁת־אֲלָפִים
וַאֲדַרְכֹנִים רִבּוֹ וְכֶסֶף כִּכָּרִים עֲשֶׂרֶת אֲלָפִים וּנְחֹשֶׁת רִבּוֹ וּשְׁמוֹנַת
ח אֲלָפִים כִּכָּרִים וּבַרְזֶל מֵאָה־אֶלֶף כִּכָּרִים׃ וְהַנִּמְצָא אִתּוֹ אֲבָנִים
ט נָתְנוּ לְאוֹצַר בֵּית־יְהֹוָה עַל יַד־יְחִיאֵל הַגֵּרְשֻׁנִּי׃ וַיִּשְׂמְחוּ הָעָם עַל־
הִתְנַדְּבָם כִּי בְּלֵב שָׁלֵם הִתְנַדְּבוּ לַיהֹוָה וְגַם דָּוִיד הַמֶּלֶךְ שָׂמַח שִׂמְחָה
י גְדוֹלָה׃ וַיְבָרֶךְ דָּוִיד אֶת־יְהֹוָה לְעֵינֵי כׇּל־הַקָּהָל וַיֹּאמֶר
יא דָּוִיד בָּרוּךְ אַתָּה יְהֹוָה אֱלֹהֵי יִשְׂרָאֵל אָבִינוּ מֵעוֹלָם וְעַד־עוֹלָם׃ לְךָ
יְהֹוָה הַגְּדֻלָּה וְהַגְּבוּרָה וְהַתִּפְאֶרֶת וְהַנֵּצַח וְהַהוֹד כִּי־כֹל בַּשָּׁמַיִם
יב וּבָאָרֶץ לְךָ יְהֹוָה הַמַּמְלָכָה וְהַמִּתְנַשֵּׂא לְכֹל ׀ לְרֹאשׁ׃ וְהָעֹשֶׁר וְהַכָּבוֹד
מִלְּפָנֶיךָ וְאַתָּה מוֹשֵׁל בַּכֹּל וּבְיָדְךָ כֹּחַ וּגְבוּרָה וּבְיָדְךָ לְגַדֵּל וּלְחַזֵּק
יג לַכֹּל׃ וְעַתָּה אֱלֹהֵינוּ מוֹדִים אֲנַחְנוּ לָךְ וּמְהַלְלִים לְשֵׁם תִּפְאַרְתֶּךָ׃
יד וְכִי מִי אֲנִי וּמִי עַמִּי כִּי־נַעְצֹר כֹּחַ לְהִתְנַדֵּב כָּזֹאת כִּי־מִמְּךָ הַכֹּל וּמִיָּדְךָ
טו נָתַנּוּ לָךְ׃ כִּי־גֵרִים אֲנַחְנוּ לְפָנֶיךָ וְתוֹשָׁבִים כְּכׇל־אֲבֹתֵינוּ כַּצֵּל ׀ יָמֵינוּ
טז עַל־הָאָרֶץ וְאֵין מִקְוֶה׃ יְהֹוָה אֱלֹהֵינוּ כֹּל הֶהָמוֹן הַזֶּה אֲשֶׁר הֲכִינֹנוּ
יז לִבְנוֹת־לְךָ בַיִת לְשֵׁם קׇדְשֶׁךָ מִיָּדְךָ היא וּלְךָ הַכֹּל׃ וְיָדַעְתִּי אֱלֹהַי כִּי הוּא
אַתָּה בֹּחֵן לֵבָב וּמֵישָׁרִים תִּרְצֶה אֲנִי בְּיֹשֶׁר לְבָבִי הִתְנַדַּבְתִּי כׇל־אֵלֶּה
יח וְעַתָּה עַמְּךָ הַנִּמְצְאוּ־פֹה רָאִיתִי בְשִׂמְחָה לְהִתְנַדֶּב־לָךְ׃ יְהֹוָה אֱלֹהֵי
אַבְרָהָם יִצְחָק וְיִשְׂרָאֵל אֲבֹתֵינוּ שׇׁמְרָה־זֹּאת לְעוֹלָם לְיֵצֶר מַחְשְׁבוֹת
יט לְבַב עַמֶּךָ וְהָכֵן לְבָבָם אֵלֶיךָ׃ וְלִשְׁלֹמֹה בְנִי תֵּן לֵבָב שָׁלֵם לִשְׁמוֹר
מִצְוֹתֶיךָ עֵדְוֹתֶיךָ וְחֻקֶּיךָ וְלַעֲשׂוֹת הַכֹּל וְלִבְנוֹת הַבִּירָה אֲשֶׁר־

20 prepared." Then David declared to the whole assembly, "Now bless
the LORD your God!" And the whole assembly blessed the LORD, God of
their ancestors, and bowed down low and prostrated themselves before the
21 LORD and the king. On the following day, they made sacrifices to the LORD
and offered up burnt offerings to the LORD: a thousand bulls, a thousand
rams, and a thousand sheep along with their libation offerings and sacrifices
22 in abundance for all of Israel. On that day they feasted and drank before the
LORD with great joy. They proclaimed Shlomo son of David as king once
23 more, anointing him before the LORD as prince and Tzadok as priest. And
Shlomo ascended the LORD's throne in his father David's place; he flourished,
24 and all of Israel obeyed him; all the officers and warriors as well as all of King
25 David's sons pledged their allegiance to King Shlomo. The LORD granted
Shlomo supreme greatness in the eyes of all Israel and endowed him with a
26 royal majesty beyond that of any king of Israel before him. Thus
27 David son of Yishai was king over all Israel. The length of time that he reigned
over Israel was forty years: he reigned in Ḥevron for seven years, and he
28 reigned in Jerusalem for thirty-three. He died at a ripe old age, full of days,
29 wealth, and honor, and his son Shlomo reigned in his place. The earlier and
later deeds of King David are recorded in the chronicles of the seer Shmuel,
30 the chronicles of the prophet Natan, and the chronicles of the seer Gad, along
with all the accounts of his rule, his might, and the events that befell him and
Israel and all the kingdoms of the land.

II CHRONICLES

1 1 Shlomo son of David gained power over his kingdom; the LORD his God was
2 with him, and He granted him supreme greatness. Shlomo gave orders to all
of Israel: to the officers of thousands and hundreds, to the judges, and to all
3 the leaders of all Israel, the ancestral heads. And Shlomo and all his assembly
went to the high shrine at Givon because the Tent of Meeting that Moshe, the
4 LORD's servant, had made in the wilderness was there – although David had
brought up the Ark of God from Kiryat Ye'arim to the place that David had
5 prepared for it, having pitched a tent for it in Jerusalem – and the bronze altar
that Betzalel son of Uri had made was there before the Sanctuary of the LORD,
6 and Shlomo and the assembly made inquiry at it. Shlomo went up there to
the bronze altar before the LORD at the Tent of Meeting, and he offered up
7 a thousand burnt offerings upon it. That night God appeared to
8 Shlomo and said to him, "Ask – what shall I give you?" And Shlomo said to
God, "You treated David my father with great loyalty and made me king in his
9 place. Now, O LORD God, let Your promise to my father David be fulfilled,
for You have made me king over a people as abundant as the dust of the earth.
10 Now grant me wisdom and knowledge so that I may lead this people out and
bring them back, for who will judge this great people of Yours?"

כ הֲכִינוֹתִי: וַיֹּאמֶר דָּוִיד לְכָל־הַקָּהָל בָּרְכוּ־נָא אֶת־יְהוָה
אֱלֹהֵיכֶם וַיְבָרְכוּ כָל־הַקָּהָל לַיהוָה אֱלֹהֵי אֲבֹתֵיהֶם וַיִּקְּדוּ וַיִּשְׁתַּחֲווּ
כא לַיהוָה וְלַמֶּלֶךְ: וַיִּזְבְּחוּ לַיהוָה ׀ זְבָחִים וַיַּעֲלוּ עֹלוֹת לַיהוָה לְמָחֳרַת
הַיּוֹם הַהוּא פָּרִים אֶלֶף אֵילִים אֶלֶף כְּבָשִׂים אֶלֶף וְנִסְכֵּיהֶם וּזְבָחִים לָרֹב
כב לְכָל־יִשְׂרָאֵל: וַיֹּאכְלוּ וַיִּשְׁתּוּ לִפְנֵי יְהוָה בַּיּוֹם הַהוּא בְּשִׂמְחָה גְדוֹלָה
וַיַּמְלִיכוּ שֵׁנִית לִשְׁלֹמֹה בֶן־דָּוִיד וַיִּמְשְׁחוּ לַיהוָה לְנָגִיד וּלְצָדוֹק לְכֹהֵן:
כג וַיֵּשֶׁב שְׁלֹמֹה עַל־כִּסֵּא יְהוָה ׀ לְמֶלֶךְ תַּחַת־דָּוִיד אָבִיו וַיַּצְלַח וַיִּשְׁמְעוּ
כד אֵלָיו כָּל־יִשְׂרָאֵל: וְכָל־הַשָּׂרִים וְהַגִּבֹּרִים וְגַם כָּל־בְּנֵי הַמֶּלֶךְ דָּוִיד
כה נָתְנוּ יָד תַּחַת שְׁלֹמֹה הַמֶּלֶךְ: וַיְגַדֵּל יְהוָה אֶת־שְׁלֹמֹה לְמַעְלָה לְעֵינֵי
כָּל־יִשְׂרָאֵל וַיִּתֵּן עָלָיו הוֹד מַלְכוּת אֲשֶׁר לֹא־הָיָה עַל־כָּל־מֶלֶךְ לְפָנָיו
כו עַל־יִשְׂרָאֵל: וְדָוִיד בֶּן־יִשָׁי מָלַךְ עַל־כָּל־יִשְׂרָאֵל:
כז וְהַיָּמִים אֲשֶׁר מָלַךְ עַל־יִשְׂרָאֵל אַרְבָּעִים שָׁנָה בְּחֶבְרוֹן מָלַךְ שֶׁבַע
כח שָׁנִים וּבִירוּשָׁלַם מָלַךְ שְׁלֹשִׁים וְשָׁלוֹשׁ: וַיָּמָת בְּשֵׂיבָה טוֹבָה שְׂבַע
כט יָמִים עֹשֶׁר וְכָבוֹד וַיִּמְלֹךְ שְׁלֹמֹה בְנוֹ תַּחְתָּיו: וְדִבְרֵי דָּוִיד הַמֶּלֶךְ
הָרִאשֹׁנִים וְהָאַחֲרֹנִים הִנָּם כְּתוּבִים עַל־דִּבְרֵי שְׁמוּאֵל הָרֹאֶה וְעַל־
ל דִּבְרֵי נָתָן הַנָּבִיא וְעַל־דִּבְרֵי גָּד הַחֹזֶה: עִם כָּל־מַלְכוּתוֹ וּגְבוּרָתוֹ
וְהָעִתִּים אֲשֶׁר עָבְרוּ עָלָיו וְעַל־יִשְׂרָאֵל וְעַל כָּל־מַמְלְכוֹת
א א הָאֲרָצוֹת: וַיִּתְחַזֵּק שְׁלֹמֹה בֶן־דָּוִיד עַל־מַלְכוּתוֹ וַיהוָה דברי הימים ב
ב אֱלֹהָיו עִמּוֹ וַיְגַדְּלֵהוּ לְמָעְלָה: וַיֹּאמֶר שְׁלֹמֹה לְכָל־יִשְׂרָאֵל לְשָׂרֵי
הָאֲלָפִים וְהַמֵּאוֹת וְלַשֹּׁפְטִים וּלְכֹל נָשִׂיא לְכָל־יִשְׂרָאֵל רָאשֵׁי הָאָבוֹת:
ג וַיֵּלְכוּ שְׁלֹמֹה וְכָל־הַקָּהָל עִמּוֹ לַבָּמָה אֲשֶׁר בְּגִבְעוֹן כִּי־שָׁם הָיָה אֹהֶל
ד מוֹעֵד הָאֱלֹהִים אֲשֶׁר עָשָׂה מֹשֶׁה עֶבֶד־יְהוָה בַּמִּדְבָּר: אֲבָל אֲרוֹן
הָאֱלֹהִים הֶעֱלָה דָוִיד מִקִּרְיַת יְעָרִים בַּהֵכִין לוֹ דָּוִיד כִּי נָטָה־לוֹ אֹהֶל
ה בִּירוּשָׁלָם: וּמִזְבַּח הַנְּחֹשֶׁת אֲשֶׁר עָשָׂה בְּצַלְאֵל בֶּן־אוּרִי בֶן־חוּר שָׂם
ו לִפְנֵי מִשְׁכַּן יְהוָה וַיִּדְרְשֵׁהוּ שְׁלֹמֹה וְהַקָּהָל: וַיַּעַל שְׁלֹמֹה שָׁם עַל־
מִזְבַּח הַנְּחֹשֶׁת לִפְנֵי יְהוָה אֲשֶׁר לְאֹהֶל מוֹעֵד וַיַּעַל עָלָיו עֹלוֹת
ז אָלֶף: בַּלַּיְלָה הַהוּא נִרְאָה אֱלֹהִים לִשְׁלֹמֹה וַיֹּאמֶר לוֹ שְׁאַל
ח מָה אֶתֶּן־לָךְ: וַיֹּאמֶר שְׁלֹמֹה לֵאלֹהִים אַתָּה עָשִׂיתָ עִם־דָּוִיד אָבִי
ט חֶסֶד גָּדוֹל וְהִמְלַכְתַּנִי תַּחְתָּיו: עַתָּה יְהוָה אֱלֹהִים יֵאָמֵן דְּבָרְךָ עִם
י דָּוִיד אָבִי כִּי אַתָּה הִמְלַכְתַּנִי עַל־עַם רַב כַּעֲפַר הָאָרֶץ: עַתָּה חָכְמָה
וּמַדָּע תֶּן־לִי וְאֵצְאָה לִפְנֵי הָעָם־הַזֶּה וְאָבוֹאָה כִּי־מִי יִשְׁפֹּט אֶת־עַמְּךָ
הַזֶּה הַגָּדוֹל:

11 "Because this was your desire," God said to Shlomo, "and you did not ask for
wealth, possessions, honor, or the lives of your enemies, nor did you ask for
a long life, but you asked instead for the wisdom and knowledge to judge My
12 people over whom I made you king, wisdom and knowledge are granted to
you, and I will give you wealth, possessions, and honor as well – such as kings
13 before you have never had and kings after you never will." So Shlomo came
down from the high shrine in Givon, from before the Tent of Meeting, to
14 Jerusalem, and he reigned over Israel. Shlomo amassed chariots and
horsemen; he had 1,400 chariots and 12,000 horsemen. He stationed them
15 in the chariot towns and with the king in Jerusalem. The king made silver as
common in Jerusalem as stones, while cedars were as common as sycamores
16 in the lowlands. Shlomo's horses were procured from Egypt and Keveh;
17 the king's traders would import them from Keveh at a set price. The cost of
importing a chariot from Egypt was 600 pieces of silver, while a horse was 150;
these, in turn, were exported to all the kings of the Hittites and all the kings
18 of Aram. And Shlomo gave orders to build a House for the LORD's name and
2 1 a royal house for himself. Shlomo designated 70,000 men as carriers, 80,000
men as quarriers in the mountains, and 3,600 to oversee them.
2 Shlomo then sent to King Ḥuram of Tyre, saying, "You once dealt with my
3 father David, sending him cedars to build a house to dwell in. I am now
building a House for the name of the LORD my God, devoting it to Him to
offer before Him fragrant incense, the daily showbread, and burnt offerings
each morning and evening, and on the Sabbaths and the New Moons and the
4 festivals of the LORD our God, as ordained for Israel forever. The House I am
5 building must be great, for the Lord our God is greater than any other god. Yet
who has the power to build Him a House when the heavens – even the highest
heavens – cannot contain Him? And who am I to build Him a House except
6 as a place to sacrifice before Him? Now send me a man skilled in working
with gold, silver, bronze, and iron; and with purple, crimson, and blue; one
who is skilled in the art of engraving to be with the skilled workers whom
7 my father David provided for me in Yehuda and Jerusalem. Send me cedar,
cypress, and sandalwood from Lebanon, for I know how skilled your servants
are at cutting cedar wood – now my own servants together with your servants
8 will prepare vast quantities of timber for me, for the House I am building will
9 be massive and magnificent. I will provide your servants, the woodcutters
who cut the timber, with twenty thousand *kor*[22] of beaten wheat, twenty
thousand *kor* of barley, twenty thousand *bat*[23] of wine, and twenty thousand
bat of oil."

---

22 | A dry measure equivalent to approximately 400 liters.

23 | A liquid measure equivalent to approximately 43 liters.

יא וַיֹּאמֶר אֱלֹהִים ׀ לִשְׁלֹמֹה יַעַן אֲשֶׁר הָיְתָה זֹאת עִם־לְבָבֶךָ וְלֹא־
שָׁאַלְתָּ עֹשֶׁר נְכָסִים וְכָבוֹד וְאֵת נֶפֶשׁ שֹׂנְאֶיךָ וְגַם־יָמִים רַבִּים לֹא
שָׁאָלְתָּ וַתִּשְׁאַל־לְךָ חָכְמָה וּמַדָּע אֲשֶׁר תִּשְׁפּוֹט אֶת־עַמִּי אֲשֶׁר
יב הִמְלַכְתִּיךָ עָלָיו: הַחָכְמָה וְהַמַּדָּע נָתוּן לָךְ וְעֹשֶׁר וּנְכָסִים וְכָבוֹד
אֶתֶּן־לָךְ אֲשֶׁר ׀ לֹא־הָיָה כֵן לַמְּלָכִים אֲשֶׁר לְפָנֶיךָ וְאַחֲרֶיךָ לֹא
יג יִהְיֶה־כֵּן: וַיָּבֹא שְׁלֹמֹה לַבָּמָה אֲשֶׁר־בְּגִבְעוֹן יְרוּשָׁלִַם מִלִּפְנֵי אֹהֶל
יד מוֹעֵד וַיִּמְלֹךְ עַל־יִשְׂרָאֵל: וַיֶּאֱסֹף שְׁלֹמֹה רֶכֶב וּפָרָשִׁים
וַיְהִי־לוֹ אֶלֶף וְאַרְבַּע־מֵאוֹת רֶכֶב וּשְׁנֵים־עָשָׂר אֶלֶף פָּרָשִׁים וַיַּנִּיחֵם
טו בְּעָרֵי הָרֶכֶב וְעִם־הַמֶּלֶךְ בִּירוּשָׁלִָם: וַיִּתֵּן הַמֶּלֶךְ אֶת־הַכֶּסֶף וְאֶת־
הַזָּהָב בִּירוּשָׁלִַם כָּאֲבָנִים וְאֵת הָאֲרָזִים נָתַן כַּשִּׁקְמִים אֲשֶׁר־בַּשְּׁפֵלָה
טז לָרֹב: וּמוֹצָא הַסּוּסִים אֲשֶׁר לִשְׁלֹמֹה מִמִּצְרָיִם וּמִקְוֵא סֹחֲרֵי הַמֶּלֶךְ
יז מִקְוֵא יִקְחוּ בִּמְחִיר: וַיַּעֲלוּ וַיּוֹצִיאוּ מִמִּצְרַיִם מֶרְכָּבָה בְּשֵׁשׁ מֵאוֹת
כֶּסֶף וְסוּס בַּחֲמִשִּׁים וּמֵאָה וְכֵן לְכָל־מַלְכֵי הַחִתִּים וּמַלְכֵי אֲרָם בְּיָדָם
יח יוֹצִיאוּ: וַיֹּאמֶר שְׁלֹמֹה לִבְנוֹת בַּיִת לְשֵׁם יהוה וּבַיִת לְמַלְכוּתוֹ:
ב א וַיִּסְפֹּר שְׁלֹמֹה שִׁבְעִים אֶלֶף אִישׁ סַבָּל וּשְׁמוֹנִים אֶלֶף אִישׁ חֹצֵב בָּהָר
וּמְנַצְּחִים עֲלֵיהֶם שְׁלֹשֶׁת אֲלָפִים וְשֵׁשׁ מֵאוֹת:
ב וַיִּשְׁלַח שְׁלֹמֹה אֶל־חוּרָם מֶלֶךְ־צֹר לֵאמֹר כַּאֲשֶׁר עָשִׂיתָ עִם־דָּוִיד
ג אָבִי וַתִּשְׁלַח־לוֹ אֲרָזִים לִבְנוֹת־לוֹ בַיִת לָשֶׁבֶת בּוֹ: הִנֵּה אֲנִי בוֹנֶה־ יב
בַיִת לְשֵׁם ׀ יהוה אֱלֹהָי לְהַקְדִּישׁ לוֹ לְהַקְטִיר לְפָנָיו קְטֹרֶת־סַמִּים
וּמַעֲרֶכֶת תָּמִיד וְעֹלוֹת לַבֹּקֶר וְלָעֶרֶב לַשַּׁבָּתוֹת וְלֶחֳדָשִׁים וּלְמוֹעֲדֵי
ד יהוה אֱלֹהֵינוּ לְעוֹלָם זֹאת עַל־יִשְׂרָאֵל: וְהַבַּיִת אֲשֶׁר־אֲנִי בוֹנֶה גָּדוֹל
ה כִּי־גָדוֹל אֱלֹהֵינוּ מִכָּל־הָאֱלֹהִים: וּמִי יַעֲצָר־כֹּחַ לִבְנוֹת־לוֹ בַיִת כִּי
הַשָּׁמַיִם וּשְׁמֵי הַשָּׁמַיִם לֹא יְכַלְכְּלֻהוּ וּמִי אֲנִי אֲשֶׁר אֶבְנֶה־לּוֹ בַיִת כִּי
ו אִם־לְהַקְטִיר לְפָנָיו: וְעַתָּה שְׁלַח־לִי אִישׁ־חָכָם לַעֲשׂוֹת בַּזָּהָב וּבַכֶּסֶף
וּבַנְּחֹשֶׁת וּבַבַּרְזֶל וּבָאַרְגְּוָן וְכַרְמִיל וּתְכֵלֶת וְיֹדֵעַ לְפַתֵּחַ פִּתּוּחִים
עִם־הַחֲכָמִים אֲשֶׁר עִמִּי בִּיהוּדָה וּבִירוּשָׁלִַם אֲשֶׁר הֵכִין דָּוִיד אָבִי:
ז וּשְׁלַח־לִי עֲצֵי אֲרָזִים בְּרוֹשִׁים וְאַלְגּוּמִּים מֵהַלְּבָנוֹן כִּי אֲנִי יָדַעְתִּי
אֲשֶׁר עֲבָדֶיךָ יוֹדְעִים לִכְרוֹת עֲצֵי לְבָנוֹן וְהִנֵּה עֲבָדַי עִם־עֲבָדֶיךָ:
ח ט וּלְהָכִין לִי עֵצִים לָרֹב כִּי הַבַּיִת אֲשֶׁר־אֲנִי בוֹנֶה גָּדוֹל וְהַפְלֵא: וְהִנֵּה
לַחֹטְבִים לְכֹרְתֵי הָעֵצִים נָתַתִּי חִטִּים ׀ מַכּוֹת לַעֲבָדֶיךָ כֹּרִים עֶשְׂרִים
אֶלֶף וּשְׂעֹרִים כֹּרִים עֶשְׂרִים אֶלֶף וְיַיִן בַּתִּים עֶשְׂרִים אֶלֶף וְשֶׁמֶן בַּתִּים
עֶשְׂרִים אָלֶף:

10 King Ḥuram of Tyre answered in writing and sent this to Shlomo: "Because
11 the Lord loves His people, He has made you king over them. Blessed is the
Lord, God of Israel, who made the heaven and earth," Ḥuram continued,
"for having granted King David a wise son, endowed with intelligence and
understanding, who will build a House for the Lord and a house for his
12 kingdom. Now I have sent a skilled man endowed with understanding –
13 Ḥuram Avi, the son of a Danite woman and a Tyrian father. He is skilled at
working with gold, silver, bronze, iron, stone, and wood; with purple, blue,
fine linen, and crimson; he can engrave anything and work with any kind of
medium he is given along with your own craftsmen and the craftsmen of my
14 lord, your father David. As for the wheat, barley, oil, and wine my lord has
15 spoken of – let him send it to his servants. We will cut down as many trees
from Lebanon as you need and bring them to you as rafts by sea to Jaffa, and
16 you will convey them up to Jerusalem." Shlomo then counted all the
foreigners in the land of Israel after the census his father David had taken:
17 153,600 were found. He assigned 70,000 of them as carriers, 80,000 as
3 1 quarriers, and 3,600 as overseers to set the people to work. Shlomo began to
build the House of the Lord in Jerusalem on Mount Moria where He had
appeared to his father David, on the site that David had prepared on the
2 threshold of Ornan the Jebusite. He began construction on the second day
3 of the second month in the fourth year of his reign. These are the foundations
that Shlomo laid for the construction of the House of God: its length in cubits
4 of the old standard was sixty cubits, and its width was twenty cubits. The
length of the Hall in front of the House was equal to the width of the House,
twenty cubits, and its height was one hundred twenty cubits. He overlaid the
5 interior with pure gold. He paneled the main part of the House with cypress
wood and overlaid that with fine gold, embossing it with shapes of palm trees
6 and chains, and he adorned the House with precious stones for splendor – the
7 gold was Parvayim gold. He paneled the House with gold – the beams,
the thresholds, its doors, and its walls – and engraved cherubim on the
8 walls. He made the place of the Holy of Holies; its length, along the
width of the House, was twenty cubits, and its width was twenty cubits, and
9 he paneled it with fine gold, using six hundred talents. The weight of the
nails was fifty shekel of gold, and he paneled the upper chambers with
10 gold. In the place of the Holy of Holies, he made two sculptured
11 cherubim and overlaid them with gold. The wings of the cherubim were
twenty cubits long: one wing, five cubits long, touched the wall of the House,
12 while the other wing, five cubits long, reached the other cherub's wing; the
other cherub's wing, five cubits long, reached the wall of the House, while the

י וַיֹּאמֶר חוּרָם מֶלֶךְ־צֹר בִּכְתָב וַיִּשְׁלַח אֶל־שְׁלֹמֹה בְּאַהֲבַת יהוה אֶת־
יא עַמּוֹ נְתָנְךָ עֲלֵיהֶם מֶלֶךְ: וַיֹּאמֶר חוּרָם בָּרוּךְ יהוה אֱלֹהֵי יִשְׂרָאֵל אֲשֶׁר
עָשָׂה אֶת־הַשָּׁמַיִם וְאֶת־הָאָרֶץ אֲשֶׁר נָתַן לְדָוִיד הַמֶּלֶךְ בֵּן חָכָם יוֹדֵעַ
יב שֵׂכֶל וּבִינָה אֲשֶׁר יִבְנֶה־בַּיִת לַיהוה וּבַיִת לְמַלְכוּתוֹ: וְעַתָּה שָׁלַחְתִּי
יג אִישׁ־חָכָם יוֹדֵעַ בִּינָה לְחוּרָם אָבִי: בֶּן־אִשָּׁה מִן־בְּנוֹת דָּן וְאָבִיו אִישׁ־
צֹרִי יוֹדֵעַ לַעֲשׂוֹת בַּזָּהָב־וּבַכֶּסֶף בַּנְּחֹשֶׁת בַּבַּרְזֶל בָּאֲבָנִים וּבָעֵצִים
בָּאַרְגָּמָן בַּתְּכֵלֶת וּבַבּוּץ וּבַכַּרְמִיל וּלְפַתֵּחַ כָּל־פִּתּוּחַ וְלַחְשֹׁב כָּל־
יד מַחֲשָׁבֶת אֲשֶׁר יִנָּתֶן־לוֹ עִם־חֲכָמֶיךָ וְחַכְמֵי אֲדֹנִי דָּוִיד אָבִיךָ: וְעַתָּה
הַחִטִּים וְהַשְּׂעֹרִים הַשֶּׁמֶן וְהַיַּיִן אֲשֶׁר אָמַר אֲדֹנִי יִשְׁלַח לַעֲבָדָיו:
טו וַאֲנַחְנוּ נִכְרֹת עֵצִים מִן־הַלְּבָנוֹן כְּכָל־צָרְכֶּךָ וּנְבִיאֵם לְךָ רַפְסֹדוֹת
טז עַל־יָם יָפוֹ וְאַתָּה תַּעֲלֶה אֹתָם יְרוּשָׁלָםִ: וַיִּסְפֹּר שְׁלֹמֹה
כָּל־הָאֲנָשִׁים הַגֵּיּוֹרִים אֲשֶׁר בְּאֶרֶץ יִשְׂרָאֵל אַחֲרֵי הַסְּפָר אֲשֶׁר סְפָרָם
דָּוִיד אָבִיו וַיִּמָּצְאוּ מֵאָה וַחֲמִשִּׁים אֶלֶף וּשְׁלֹשֶׁת אֲלָפִים וְשֵׁשׁ מֵאוֹת:
יז וַיַּעַשׂ מֵהֶם שִׁבְעִים אֶלֶף סַבָּל וּשְׁמֹנִים אֶלֶף חֹצֵב בָּהָר וּשְׁלֹשֶׁת אֲלָפִים
ג א וְשֵׁשׁ מֵאוֹת מְנַצְּחִים לְהַעֲבִיד אֶת־הָעָם: וַיָּחֶל שְׁלֹמֹה לִבְנוֹת אֶת־
בֵּית־יהוה בִּירוּשָׁלַםִ בְּהַר הַמּוֹרִיָּה אֲשֶׁר נִרְאָה לְדָוִיד אָבִיהוּ אֲשֶׁר
ב הֵכִין בִּמְקוֹם דָּוִיד בְּגֹרֶן אָרְנָן הַיְבוּסִי: וַיָּחֶל לִבְנוֹת בַּחֹדֶשׁ הַשֵּׁנִי
ג בַּשֵּׁנִי בִּשְׁנַת אַרְבַּע לְמַלְכוּתוֹ: וְאֵלֶּה הוּסַד שְׁלֹמֹה לִבְנוֹת אֶת־
בֵּית הָאֱלֹהִים הָאֹרֶךְ אַמּוֹת בַּמִּדָּה הָרִאשׁוֹנָה אַמּוֹת שִׁשִּׁים וְרֹחַב
ד אַמּוֹת עֶשְׂרִים: וְהָאוּלָם אֲשֶׁר עַל־פְּנֵי הָאֹרֶךְ עַל־פְּנֵי רֹחַב־הַבַּיִת
אַמּוֹת עֶשְׂרִים וְהַגֹּבַהּ מֵאָה וְעֶשְׂרִים וַיְצַפֵּהוּ מִפְּנִימָה זָהָב טָהוֹר:
ה וְאֵת ׀ הַבַּיִת הַגָּדוֹל חִפָּה עֵץ בְּרוֹשִׁים וַיְחַפֵּהוּ זָהָב טוֹב וַיַּעַל עָלָיו
ו תִּמֹרִים וְשַׁרְשְׁרוֹת: וַיְצַף אֶת־הַבַּיִת אֶבֶן יְקָרָה לְתִפְאָרֶת וְהַזָּהָב זְהַב
ז פַּרְוָיִם: וַיְחַף אֶת־הַבַּיִת הַקֹּרוֹת הַסִּפִּים וְקִירוֹתָיו וְדַלְתוֹתָיו זָהָב וּפִתַּח
ח כְּרוּבִים עַל־הַקִּירוֹת: וַיַּעַשׂ אֶת־בֵּית־קֹדֶשׁ הַקֳּדָשִׁים אָרְכּוֹ
עַל־פְּנֵי רֹחַב־הַבַּיִת אַמּוֹת עֶשְׂרִים וְרָחְבּוֹ אַמּוֹת עֶשְׂרִים וַיְחַפֵּהוּ זָהָב
ט טוֹב לְכִכָּרִים שֵׁשׁ מֵאוֹת: וּמִשְׁקָל לְמִסְמְרוֹת לִשְׁקָלִים חֲמִשִּׁים זָהָב
י וְהָעֲלִיּוֹת חִפָּה זָהָב: וַיַּעַשׂ בְּבֵית־קֹדֶשׁ הַקֳּדָשִׁים כְּרוּבִים
יא שְׁנַיִם מַעֲשֵׂה צַעֲצֻעִים וַיְצַפּוּ אֹתָם זָהָב: וְכַנְפֵי הַכְּרוּבִים אָרְכָּם אַמּוֹת
עֶשְׂרִים כְּנַף הָאֶחָד לְאַמּוֹת חָמֵשׁ מַגַּעַת לְקִיר הַבַּיִת וְהַכָּנָף הָאַחֶרֶת
יב אַמּוֹת חָמֵשׁ מַגִּיעַ לִכְנַף הַכְּרוּב הָאַחֵר: וּכְנַף הַכְּרוּב הָאֶחָד אַמּוֹת
חָמֵשׁ מַגִּיעַ לְקִיר הַבַּיִת וְהַכָּנָף הָאַחֶרֶת אַמּוֹת חָמֵשׁ דְּבֵקָה לִכְנַף

13 other wing, five cubits long, was joined to the wing of the other cherub. The
wings of these cherubim spanned twenty cubits; they stood on their feet
14 with their faces toward the House. He made the veil of blue,
purple, and crimson thread and fine linen and decorated it with
15 cherubim. He made two pillars, each thirty-five cubits high, at the
16 front of the House, with a capital five cubits high atop them. He
made chains in the Inner Sanctuary and set them on top of the pillars; he
17 fashioned one hundred pomegranates and placed them on the chains. He set
up the pillars in front of the Hall, one to the right and one to the left; he named
4 1 the one on the right Yakhin and the one on the left Boaz. He made
an altar of bronze twenty cubits long, twenty cubits wide, and ten cubits
2 high. He made the Molten Sea,[24] ten cubits across from rim to rim
and perfectly round. It was five cubits high and thirty cubits in circumference.
3 Figures of oxen[25] were beneath it all around it, clustered around the Sea ten
4 to a cubit; two rows of oxen were cast together with it. It stood upon twelve
oxen, three facing north, three facing west, three facing south, and three facing
5 east; the Sea was on top of them, and all their haunches turned inward. It was
a handbreadth thick, and its rim was like the rim of a cup, like the petals of a
6 lily; its capacity was three thousand *bat*. He made ten lavers, placing
five on the right and five on the left; these were for rinsing what was used for
7 the burnt offering, while the Sea was for the priests to wash in. He
made the ten golden candelabra as instructed and set them in the Sanctuary,
8 five on the right and five on the left. He made ten tables and placed
9 them in the Sanctuary, and he made a hundred basins of gold. He
made the priests' courtyard, the great court, and doors for the court; he
10 overlaid its doors with bronze. He placed the Sea on the right side, in the
11 southeast corner. Ḥuram crafted the pots and the shovels and the
basins. And so Ḥuram completed all the work for the House of God as
12 commissioned by King Shlomo: Two pillars and two globe-shaped capitals
for the pillar tops; two pieces of meshwork to cover the two globe-shaped
capitals for the pillar tops; and four hundred pomegranates for the two pieces
of meshwork – two rows of pomegranates for each piece of meshwork that
14 covered the two globe-shaped capitals on top of the pillars. He made the
15 stands and the lavers for the stands; one Sea with twelve oxen beneath it;
16 pots, shovels, and forks, and all their equipment that Ḥuram Avi crafted for

---

24 | A large tank made of cast metal.

25 | The parallel verse in 1 Kings 7:24 reads "bulb-shaped knobs" in place of "figures of oxen."

יג הַכְּרוּב הָאַחֵר: כַּנְפֵי הַכְּרוּבִים הָאֵלֶּה פֹּרְשִׂים אַמּוֹת עֶשְׂרִים וְהֵם
יד עֹמְדִים עַל־רַגְלֵיהֶם וּפְנֵיהֶם לַבָּיִת: וַיַּעַשׂ אֶת־הַפָּרֹכֶת
טו תְּכֵלֶת וְאַרְגָּמָן וְכַרְמִיל וּבוּץ וַיַּעַל עָלָיו כְּרוּבִים: וַיַּעַשׂ לִפְנֵי
הַבַּיִת עַמּוּדִים שְׁנַיִם אַמּוֹת שְׁלֹשִׁים וְחָמֵשׁ אֹרֶךְ וְהַצֶּפֶת אֲשֶׁר־עַל־
טז רֹאשׁוֹ אַמּוֹת חָמֵשׁ: וַיַּעַשׂ שַׁרְשְׁרוֹת בַּדְּבִיר וַיִּתֵּן עַל־רֹאשׁ
יז הָעַמֻּדִים וַיַּעַשׂ רִמּוֹנִים מֵאָה וַיִּתֵּן בַּשַּׁרְשְׁרוֹת: וַיָּקֶם אֶת־הָעַמּוּדִים
עַל־פְּנֵי הַהֵיכָל אֶחָד מִיָּמִין וְאֶחָד מֵהַשְּׂמֹאול וַיִּקְרָא שֵׁם־הימיני הַיְמָנִי
ד א יָכִין וְשֵׁם הַשְּׂמָאלִי בֹּעַז: וַיַּעַשׂ מִזְבַּח נְחֹשֶׁת עֶשְׂרִים אַמָּה
ב אָרְכּוֹ וְעֶשְׂרִים אַמָּה רָחְבּוֹ וְעֶשֶׂר אַמּוֹת קוֹמָתוֹ: וַיַּעַשׂ
אֶת־הַיָּם מוּצָק עֶשֶׂר בָּאַמָּה מִשְּׂפָתוֹ אֶל־שְׂפָתוֹ עָגוֹל ׀ סָבִיב וְחָמֵשׁ
ג בָּאַמָּה קוֹמָתוֹ וְקָו שְׁלֹשִׁים בָּאַמָּה יָסֹב אֹתוֹ סָבִיב: וּדְמוּת בְּקָרִים
תַּחַת לוֹ סָבִיב ׀ סָבִיב סוֹבְבִים אֹתוֹ עֶשֶׂר בָּאַמָּה מַקִּיפִים אֶת־הַיָּם
ד סָבִיב שְׁנַיִם טוּרִים הַבָּקָר יְצוּקִים בְּמֻצַקְתּוֹ: עוֹמֵד עַל־שְׁנֵים עָשָׂר
בָּקָר שְׁלֹשָׁה פֹנִים ׀ צָפוֹנָה וּשְׁלוֹשָׁה פֹנִים ׀ יָמָּה וּשְׁלֹשָׁה ׀ פֹּנִים נֶגְבָּה
וּשְׁלֹשָׁה פֹּנִים מִזְרָחָה וְהַיָּם עֲלֵיהֶם מִלְמָעְלָה וְכָל־אֲחֹרֵיהֶם בָּיְתָה:
ה וְעָבְיוֹ טֶפַח וּשְׂפָתוֹ כְּמַעֲשֵׂה שְׂפַת־כּוֹס פֶּרַח שׁוֹשַׁנָּה מַחֲזִיק בַּתִּים
ו שְׁלֹשֶׁת אֲלָפִים יָכִיל: וַיַּעַשׂ כִּיּוֹרִים עֲשָׂרָה וַיִּתֵּן חֲמִשָּׁה
מִיָּמִין וַחֲמִשָּׁה מִשְּׂמֹאול לְרָחְצָה בָהֶם אֶת־מַעֲשֵׂה הָעוֹלָה יָדִיחוּ בָם
ז וְהַיָּם לְרָחְצָה לַכֹּהֲנִים בּוֹ: וַיַּעַשׂ אֶת־מְנֹרוֹת הַזָּהָב עֶשֶׂר
ח כְּמִשְׁפָּטָם וַיִּתֵּן בַּהֵיכָל חָמֵשׁ מִיָּמִין וְחָמֵשׁ מִשְּׂמֹאול: וַיַּעַשׂ
שֻׁלְחָנוֹת עֲשָׂרָה וַיַּנַּח בַּהֵיכָל חֲמִשָּׁה מִיָּמִין וַחֲמִשָּׁה מִשְּׂמֹאול וַיַּעַשׂ
ט מִזְרְקֵי זָהָב מֵאָה: וַיַּעַשׂ חֲצַר הַכֹּהֲנִים וְהָעֲזָרָה הַגְּדוֹלָה
י וּדְלָתוֹת לָעֲזָרָה וְדַלְתוֹתֵיהֶם צִפָּה נְחֹשֶׁת: וְאֶת־הַיָּם נָתַן מִכֶּתֶף
יא הַיְמָנִית קֵדְמָה מִמּוּל נֶגְבָּה: וַיַּעַשׂ חוּרָם אֶת־הַסִּירוֹת
וְאֶת־הַיָּעִים וְאֶת־הַמִּזְרָקוֹת וַיְכַל חירם לַעֲשׂוֹת אֶת־הַמְּלָאכָה אֲשֶׁר חוּרָם
יב עָשָׂה לַמֶּלֶךְ שְׁלֹמֹה בְּבֵית הָאֱלֹהִים: עַמּוּדִים שְׁנַיִם וְהַגֻּלּוֹת וְהַכֹּתָרוֹת
עַל־רֹאשׁ הָעַמּוּדִים שְׁתָּיִם וְהַשְּׂבָכוֹת שְׁתַּיִם לְכַסּוֹת אֶת־שְׁתֵּי גֻּלּוֹת
יג הַכֹּתָרוֹת אֲשֶׁר עַל־רֹאשׁ הָעַמּוּדִים: וְאֶת־הָרִמּוֹנִים אַרְבַּע מֵאוֹת
לִשְׁתֵּי הַשְּׂבָכוֹת שְׁנַיִם טוּרִים רִמּוֹנִים לַשְּׂבָכָה הָאֶחָת לְכַסּוֹת אֶת־
יד שְׁתֵּי גֻּלּוֹת הַכֹּתָרוֹת אֲשֶׁר עַל־פְּנֵי הָעַמּוּדִים: וְאֶת־הַמְּכֹנוֹת עָשָׂה
טו וְאֶת־הַכִּיֹּרוֹת עָשָׂה עַל־הַמְּכֹנוֹת: אֶת־הַיָּם אֶחָד וְאֶת־הַבָּקָר שְׁנֵים־
טז עָשָׂר תַּחְתָּיו: וְאֶת־הַסִּירוֹת וְאֶת־הַיָּעִים וְאֶת־הַמִּזְלָגוֹת וְאֶת־כָּל־

17 King Shlomo, for the House of the Lord, were of burnished bronze. The king
had them cast in clay molds on the Jordan plain between Sukkot and
18 Tzeredata. Shlomo made such vast amounts of all of these vessels that the
19 weight of the bronze was not determined. Shlomo made all
the vessels for the House of God, the golden altar, and the tables for displaying
20 the showbread. The candelabra and their lamps, which were to burn as
21 instructed in front of the Inner Sanctuary, were of solid gold; the flowers, the
22 lamps, and the tongs were all of gold, of purest gold. The shears, basins,
spoons, and firepans were of solid gold; the doors at the entrance to the
innermost House, to the Holy of Holies, and the doors of the Hall of the
5 1 House, were of gold. When all the work that Shlomo did for the
House of the Lord was finished, Shlomo brought what David, his father, had
dedicated – the silver, the gold, and all the vessels – and placed them in the
2 treasury of the House of God. Then Shlomo assembled the elders
of Israel – all the heads of the tribes, the patriarchal ancestral leaders of the
Israelites – to Jerusalem, to bring up the Ark of the Lord's Covenant from
3 the City of David, which is Zion. All the men of Israel assembled before the
4 king in the seventh month during the festival.[26] When all the elders of Israel
5 had arrived, the Levites lifted up the Ark and brought up the Ark, and the
Tent of Meeting, and all the sacred vessels in the Tent. While the Levite
6 priests brought them up, King Shlomo and the whole community of Israel,
who had joined him before the Ark, sacrificed sheep and oxen – far too many
7 to number or count. The priests brought the Ark of the Lord's Covenant to
its place – to the House's Inner Sanctuary, the Holy of Holies, to under the
8 shade of the cherubim's wings. The cherubim's wings were spread over the
place of the Ark so that the cherubim covered the Ark and its poles from
9 above. The poles extended beyond the Ark so that the ends of the poles were
discernible from the Inner Sanctuary, but they could not be seen from the
10 outside, and they are there to this day. The Ark contained nothing but the
two tablets Moshe gave at Ḥorev when the Lord made a covenant with the
11 Israelites as they left Egypt. And as the priests left the Holy Place –
for all the priests present had sanctified themselves, regardless of their
12 divisions – all the Levite musicians – Asaf, Heiman, and Yedutun, their sons,
and their kin, dressed in fine linen – stood at the east end of the altar with
cymbals, harps, and lyres, while a hundred twenty priests sounded the
13 trumpets. The trumpet players and the singers joined together as one, playing
in unison, to praise and give thanks to the Lord. As they lifted up their voices,
with trumpets and cymbals and musical instruments, praising the Lord –
"For He is good, for His loving-kindness is forever" – the House, the House

26 | That is, Sukkot, the Festival of Tabernacles.

כְּלֵיהֶם עָשָׂה חוּרָם אָבִיו לַמֶּלֶךְ שְׁלֹמֹה לְבֵית יְהוָה נְחֹשֶׁת מָרוּק׃
יז בְּכִכַּר הַיַּרְדֵּן יְצָקָם הַמֶּלֶךְ בַּעֲבִי הָאֲדָמָה בֵּין סֻכּוֹת וּבֵין צְרֵדָתָה׃
יח וַיַּעַשׂ שְׁלֹמֹה כָּל־הַכֵּלִים הָאֵלֶּה לָרֹב מְאֹד כִּי לֹא נֶחְקַר מִשְׁקַל
יט הַנְּחֹשֶׁת׃ וַיַּעַשׂ שְׁלֹמֹה אֵת כָּל־הַכֵּלִים אֲשֶׁר בֵּית הָאֱלֹהִים
כ וְאֵת מִזְבַּח הַזָּהָב וְאֶת־הַשֻּׁלְחָנוֹת וַעֲלֵיהֶם לֶחֶם הַפָּנִים׃ וְאֶת־הַמְּנֹרוֹת
כא וְנֵרֹתֵיהֶם לְבַעֲרָם כַּמִּשְׁפָּט לִפְנֵי הַדְּבִיר זָהָב סָגוּר׃ וְהַפֶּרַח וְהַנֵּרוֹת
כב וְהַמֶּלְקַחַיִם זָהָב הוּא מִכְלוֹת זָהָב׃ וְהַמְזַמְּרוֹת וְהַמִּזְרָקוֹת וְהַכַּפּוֹת
וְהַמַּחְתּוֹת זָהָב סָגוּר וּפֶתַח הַבַּיִת דַּלְתוֹתָיו הַפְּנִימִיּוֹת לְקֹדֶשׁ
הַקֳּדָשִׁים וְדַלְתֵי הַבַּיִת לַהֵיכָל זָהָב׃
ה א וַתִּשְׁלַם כָּל־הַמְּלָאכָה אֲשֶׁר־עָשָׂה שְׁלֹמֹה לְבֵית יְהוָה וַיָּבֵא שְׁלֹמֹה
אֶת־קָדְשֵׁי ׀ דָּוִיד אָבִיו וְאֶת־הַכֶּסֶף וְאֶת־הַזָּהָב וְאֶת־כָּל־הַכֵּלִים נָתַן
ב בְּאֹצְרוֹת בֵּית הָאֱלֹהִים׃ אָז יַקְהֵיל שְׁלֹמֹה אֶת־זִקְנֵי יִשְׂרָאֵל
וְאֶת־כָּל־רָאשֵׁי הַמַּטּוֹת נְשִׂיאֵי הָאָבוֹת לִבְנֵי יִשְׂרָאֵל אֶל־יְרוּשָׁלָ͏ִם
ג לְהַעֲלוֹת אֶת־אֲרוֹן בְּרִית־יְהוָה מֵעִיר דָּוִיד הִיא צִיּוֹן׃ וַיִּקָּהֲלוּ אֶל־
ד הַמֶּלֶךְ כָּל־אִישׁ יִשְׂרָאֵל בֶּחָג הוּא הַחֹדֶשׁ הַשְּׁבִעִי׃ וַיָּבֹאוּ כֹּל זִקְנֵי
ה יִשְׂרָאֵל וַיִּשְׂאוּ הַלְוִיִּם אֶת־הָאָרוֹן׃ וַיַּעֲלוּ אֶת־הָאָרוֹן וְאֶת־אֹהֶל מוֹעֵד
ו וְאֶת־כָּל־כְּלֵי הַקֹּדֶשׁ אֲשֶׁר בָּאֹהֶל הֶעֱלוּ אֹתָם הַכֹּהֲנִים הַלְוִיִּם׃ וְהַמֶּלֶךְ
שְׁלֹמֹה וְכָל־עֲדַת יִשְׂרָאֵל הַנּוֹעָדִים עָלָיו לִפְנֵי הָאָרוֹן מְזַבְּחִים צֹאן
ז וּבָקָר אֲשֶׁר לֹא־יִסָּפְרוּ וְלֹא יִמָּנוּ מֵרֹב׃ וַיָּבִיאוּ הַכֹּהֲנִים אֶת־אֲרוֹן
בְּרִית־יְהוָה אֶל־מְקוֹמוֹ אֶל־דְּבִיר הַבַּיִת אֶל־קֹדֶשׁ הַקֳּדָשִׁים אֶל־תַּחַת
ח כַּנְפֵי הַכְּרוּבִים׃ וַיִּהְיוּ הַכְּרוּבִים פֹּרְשִׂים כְּנָפַיִם עַל־מְקוֹם הָאָרוֹן וַיְכַסּוּ
ט הַכְּרוּבִים עַל־הָאָרוֹן וְעַל־בַּדָּיו מִלְמָעְלָה׃ וַיַּאֲרִיכוּ הַבַּדִּים וַיֵּרָאוּ
רָאשֵׁי הַבַּדִּים מִן־הָאָרוֹן עַל־פְּנֵי הַדְּבִיר וְלֹא יֵרָאוּ הַחוּצָה וַיְהִי־שָׁם
י עַד הַיּוֹם הַזֶּה׃ אֵין בָּאָרוֹן רַק שְׁנֵי הַלֻּחוֹת אֲשֶׁר־נָתַן מֹשֶׁה בְּחֹרֵב
יא אֲשֶׁר כָּרַת יְהוָה עִם־בְּנֵי יִשְׂרָאֵל בְּצֵאתָם מִמִּצְרָיִם׃ וַיְהִי
בְּצֵאת הַכֹּהֲנִים מִן־הַקֹּדֶשׁ כִּי כָּל־הַכֹּהֲנִים הַנִּמְצְאִים הִתְקַדָּשׁוּ אֵין
יב לִשְׁמוֹר לְמַחְלְקוֹת׃ וְהַלְוִיִּם הַמְשֹׁרְרִים לְכֻלָּם לְאָסָף לְהֵימָן לִידֻתוּן
וְלִבְנֵיהֶם וְלַאֲחֵיהֶם מְלֻבָּשִׁים בּוּץ בִּמְצִלְתַּיִם וּבִנְבָלִים וְכִנֹּרוֹת עֹמְדִים
מִזְרָח לַמִּזְבֵּחַ וְעִמָּהֶם כֹּהֲנִים לְמֵאָה וְעֶשְׂרִים מחצררים בַּחֲצֹצְרוֹת׃ מַחְצְרִים
יג וַיְהִי כְאֶחָד למחצצרים וְלַמְשֹׁרְרִים לְהַשְׁמִיעַ קוֹל־אֶחָד לְהַלֵּל לְמַחְצְרִים
וּלְהֹדוֹת לַיהוָה וּכְהָרִים קוֹל בַּחֲצֹצְרוֹת וּבִמְצִלְתַּיִם וּבִכְלֵי הַשִּׁיר
וּבְהַלֵּל לַיהוָה כִּי טוֹב כִּי לְעוֹלָם חַסְדּוֹ וְהַבַּיִת מָלֵא עָנָן בֵּית יְהוָה׃

14 of the LORD, filled with cloud. The priests could not stand and serve
because of the cloud, for the glory of the LORD had filled the House of
6 1 God. Then Shlomo declared, "The LORD promised that He would
2 dwell in deep mist; I have built You an exalted House, a permanent place for
3 Your abode." The king turned his face and blessed the whole assembly of Israel
4 as the whole assembly of Israel stood. "Blessed is the LORD, God of Israel,"
he said, "who made a promise to my father David with His own mouth and
5 has now fulfilled it with His own hands, saying: 'From the day I brought My
people out of the land of Egypt, I never chose a city from among all the tribes
of Israel to build a House where My name would be, nor did I choose a man
6 as ruler over My people Israel. Then I chose Jerusalem as the place where My
7 name will be, and I chose David to be over My people Israel.' My father David
had his heart set on building a House for the name of the LORD, God of Israel.
8 But the LORD said to my father David, 'Though you have set your heart on
9 building a House for My name, and though you have set your heart well, you
will not be the one to build the House. But your son, the issue of your own
10 loins – he will be the one to build a House for My name.' The LORD has
fulfilled the promise He made; I have risen in my father's stead, and I sit upon
Israel's throne as the LORD promised. I have built the House for the name of
11 the LORD, God of Israel. And there I have placed the Ark, which contains the
12 covenant that the LORD formed with the Israelites." And he stood before the
Altar of the LORD, facing the whole assembly of Israel, and he raised his hands.
13 Shlomo had made a bronze laver that was five cubits long, five cubits wide,
and three cubits high and had placed it in the courtyard; now he stepped onto
it and knelt, facing the whole assembly of Israel, and raised his palms
14 heavenward. "O LORD, God of Israel," he cried, "there is no god like You in
heaven or on earth. O keeper of the covenant and the love for Your servants,
15 who walk before You with all their heart, You kept what You promised to my
father David; You made him a promise with Your own mouth, and You have
16 fulfilled it with Your own hand this very day. Now O LORD, God of Israel,
keep the promise You made to Your servant David, my father, saying, 'No one
of your lineage shall be cut off from sitting on the throne of Israel before Me,
but only if your sons keep to the path of My teaching, as you walked before
17 Me.' Now, O LORD, God of Israel, let the promise You made to Your servant
18 David be realized. For will God truly dwell with humanity on earth? If the
heavens – the highest heavens – cannot contain You, how will this House that
19 I have built? Yet, turn to the prayer of your servant, O LORD my God, and to
20 his plea; Listen to the cry and the prayer your servant offers before You. Let
Your eyes be open to this House day and night, to the place where You
determined to put Your name. Listen to the prayer Your servant offers at this

יד וְלֹא־יָכְלוּ הַכֹּהֲנִים לַעֲמוֹד לְשָׁרֵת מִפְּנֵי הֶעָנָן כִּי־מָלֵא כְבוֹד־יְהוָה יג
ו א אֶת־בֵּית הָאֱלֹהִים: אָז אָמַר שְׁלֹמֹה יְהוָה אָמַר לִשְׁכּוֹן
ב ג בָּעֲרָפֶל: וַאֲנִי בָּנִיתִי בֵית־זְבֻל לָךְ וּמָכוֹן לְשִׁבְתְּךָ עוֹלָמִים: וַיַּסֵּב הַמֶּלֶךְ
ד אֶת־פָּנָיו וַיְבָרֶךְ אֵת כָּל־קְהַל יִשְׂרָאֵל וְכָל־קְהַל יִשְׂרָאֵל עוֹמֵד: וַיֹּאמֶר
בָּרוּךְ יְהוָה אֱלֹהֵי יִשְׂרָאֵל אֲשֶׁר דִּבֶּר בְּפִיו אֵת דָּוִיד אָבִי וּבְיָדָיו מִלֵּא
ה לֵאמֹר: מִן־הַיּוֹם אֲשֶׁר הוֹצֵאתִי אֶת־עַמִּי מֵאֶרֶץ מִצְרַיִם לֹא־בָחַרְתִּי
בְעִיר מִכֹּל שִׁבְטֵי יִשְׂרָאֵל לִבְנוֹת בַּיִת לִהְיוֹת שְׁמִי שָׁם וְלֹא־בָחַרְתִּי
ו בְאִישׁ לִהְיוֹת נָגִיד עַל־עַמִּי יִשְׂרָאֵל: וָאֶבְחַר בִּירוּשָׁלִַם לִהְיוֹת שְׁמִי
ז שָׁם וָאֶבְחַר בְּדָוִיד לִהְיוֹת עַל־עַמִּי יִשְׂרָאֵל: וַיְהִי עִם־לְבַב דָּוִיד אָבִי
ח לִבְנוֹת בַּיִת לְשֵׁם יְהוָה אֱלֹהֵי יִשְׂרָאֵל: וַיֹּאמֶר יְהוָה אֶל־דָּוִיד אָבִי
יַעַן אֲשֶׁר הָיָה עִם־לְבָבְךָ לִבְנוֹת בַּיִת לִשְׁמִי הֱטִיבוֹתָ כִּי הָיָה עִם־
ט לְבָבֶךָ: רַק אַתָּה לֹא תִבְנֶה הַבָּיִת כִּי בִנְךָ הַיּוֹצֵא מֵחֲלָצֶיךָ הוּא־יִבְנֶה
י הַבַּיִת לִשְׁמִי: וַיָּקֶם יְהוָה אֶת־דְּבָרוֹ אֲשֶׁר דִּבֵּר וָאָקוּם תַּחַת דָּוִיד
אָבִי וָאֵשֵׁב ׀ עַל־כִּסֵּא יִשְׂרָאֵל כַּאֲשֶׁר דִּבֶּר יְהוָה וָאֶבְנֶה הַבַּיִת לְשֵׁם
יא יְהוָה אֱלֹהֵי יִשְׂרָאֵל: וָאָשִׂים שָׁם אֶת־הָאָרוֹן אֲשֶׁר שָׁם בְּרִית יְהוָה
יב אֲשֶׁר כָּרַת עִם־בְּנֵי יִשְׂרָאֵל: וַיַּעֲמֹד לִפְנֵי מִזְבַּח יְהוָה נֶגֶד כָּל־קְהַל
יג יִשְׂרָאֵל וַיִּפְרֹשׂ כַּפָּיו: כִּי־עָשָׂה שְׁלֹמֹה כִּיּוֹר נְחֹשֶׁת וַיִּתְּנֵהוּ בְּתוֹךְ
הָעֲזָרָה חָמֵשׁ אַמּוֹת אָרְכּוֹ וְחָמֵשׁ אַמּוֹת רָחְבּוֹ וְאַמּוֹת שָׁלוֹשׁ קוֹמָתוֹ
וַיַּעֲמֹד עָלָיו וַיִּבְרַךְ עַל־בִּרְכָּיו נֶגֶד כָּל־קְהַל יִשְׂרָאֵל וַיִּפְרֹשׂ כַּפָּיו
יד הַשָּׁמָיְמָה: וַיֹּאמַר יְהוָה אֱלֹהֵי יִשְׂרָאֵל אֵין־כָּמוֹךָ אֱלֹהִים בַּשָּׁמַיִם
וּבָאָרֶץ שֹׁמֵר הַבְּרִית וְהַחֶסֶד לַעֲבָדֶיךָ הַהֹלְכִים לְפָנֶיךָ בְּכָל־לִבָּם:
טו אֲשֶׁר שָׁמַרְתָּ לְעַבְדְּךָ דָּוִיד אָבִי אֵת אֲשֶׁר־דִּבַּרְתָּ לוֹ וַתְּדַבֵּר בְּפִיךָ
טז וּבְיָדְךָ מִלֵּאתָ כַּיּוֹם הַזֶּה: וְעַתָּה יְהוָה ׀ אֱלֹהֵי יִשְׂרָאֵל שְׁמֹר לְעַבְדְּךָ
דָוִיד אָבִי אֵת אֲשֶׁר דִּבַּרְתָּ לּוֹ לֵאמֹר לֹא־יִכָּרֵת לְךָ אִישׁ מִלְּפָנַי יוֹשֵׁב
עַל־כִּסֵּא יִשְׂרָאֵל רַק אִם־יִשְׁמְרוּ בָנֶיךָ אֶת־דַּרְכָּם לָלֶכֶת בְּתוֹרָתִי
יז כַּאֲשֶׁר הָלַכְתָּ לְפָנָי: וְעַתָּה יְהוָה אֱלֹהֵי יִשְׂרָאֵל יֵאָמֵן דְּבָרְךָ אֲשֶׁר
יח דִּבַּרְתָּ לְעַבְדְּךָ לְדָוִיד: כִּי הַאֻמְנָם יֵשֵׁב אֱלֹהִים אֶת־הָאָדָם עַל־הָאָרֶץ
הִנֵּה שָׁמַיִם וּשְׁמֵי הַשָּׁמַיִם לֹא יְכַלְכְּלוּךָ אַף כִּי־הַבַּיִת הַזֶּה אֲשֶׁר בָּנִיתִי:
יט וּפָנִיתָ אֶל־תְּפִלַּת עַבְדְּךָ וְאֶל־תְּחִנָּתוֹ יְהוָה אֱלֹהָי לִשְׁמֹעַ אֶל־הָרִנָּה
כ וְאֶל־הַתְּפִלָּה אֲשֶׁר עַבְדְּךָ מִתְפַּלֵּל לְפָנֶיךָ: לִהְיוֹת עֵינֶיךָ פְתֻחוֹת
אֶל־הַבַּיִת הַזֶּה יוֹמָם וָלַיְלָה אֶל־הַמָּקוֹם אֲשֶׁר אָמַרְתָּ לָשׂוּם שִׁמְךָ
שָׁם לִשְׁמוֹעַ אֶל־הַתְּפִלָּה אֲשֶׁר יִתְפַּלֵּל עַבְדְּךָ אֶל־הַמָּקוֹם הַזֶּה:

21 place. Listen to the pleas of Your servant and of Your people, Israel, who
pray at this place. Listen from Your heavenly abode; listen and forgive.
22 Should a person wrong another who then imposes an oath upon him, and
he thus becomes cursed, and he comes before Your altar in this House
23 with the curse – listen from the heavens, take action, and judge your
servant. Avenge the wicked by bringing his own ways upon his own
head, and vindicate the righteous by rewarding him as befits his
24 righteousness. Should Your people Israel be defeated by an enemy
because they have sinned against You, and they come back, acknowledging
25 Your name in prayer and pleading before You in this House – listen from the
heavens, forgive the sin of Your people Israel, and bring them back to the land
26 You gave to them and to their ancestors. When the heavens are
stopped up and there is no rain because they have sinned against You, and
they pray at this place and acknowledge Your name, repenting from their sins
27 so that You will answer them – listen from the heavens and forgive the sin of
Your servants and Your people Israel, having taught them the proper path to
follow. Shower rain upon the land You gave to Your people as their
28 share. Should there be famine in the land, should there be sickness,
should there be blight, mildew, locust, or larvae, should enemies harass them
29 in the land within their own gates – oh, any suffering or any disease! – and
anyone from Your people, Israel, offers any prayer or any plea, moved by his
30 own suffering and pain, and raises his palms toward this House – listen from
Your heavenly abode and forgive. Treat each person according to his ways,
31 for You know his heart – for You alone know the hearts of humanity – so that
they will revere You and follow in Your ways for as long as they live upon the
32 soil that You gave to our ancestors. Should the foreigner, too, not
of Your people Israel, come from a distant land for the sake of Your great name
and Your mighty hand and Your outstretched arm; should he come and pray
33 at this House – listen from Your heavenly abode and fulfill all that the
foreigner calls out to You. For then all the peoples of the land will know Your
name and revere You as Your people Israel does, for then they will know that
34 it is Your name that is proclaimed over this House. Should Your
people go out to war against their enemies, wherever You might send them,
and they pray toward this city You have chosen and the House I built for Your
35 name – listen from the heavens to their prayer and plea, and uphold their
36 cause. Should they sin against You – for there is no person who does not
sin – and You rage against them and deliver them over to their enemy, who
37 drags them off as captives to a land far or near, but they take it to heart in the
land where they are being held captive, and they repent and offer pleas to You

כא וְשָׁמַעְתָּ אֶל־תַּחֲנוּנֵי עַבְדְּךָ וְעַמְּךָ יִשְׂרָאֵל אֲשֶׁר יִתְפַּלְלוּ אֶל־הַמָּקוֹם
הַזֶּה וְאַתָּה תִּשְׁמַע מִמְּקוֹם שִׁבְתְּךָ מִן־הַשָּׁמַיִם וְשָׁמַעְתָּ וְסָלָחְתָּ׃
כב אִם־יֶחֱטָא אִישׁ לְרֵעֵהוּ וְנָשָׁא־בוֹ אָלָה לְהַאֲלֹתוֹ וּבָא אָלָה לִפְנֵי
כג מִזְבַּחֲךָ בַּבַּיִת הַזֶּה׃ וְאַתָּה ׀ תִּשְׁמַע מִן־הַשָּׁמַיִם וְעָשִׂיתָ וְשָׁפַטְתָּ
אֶת־עֲבָדֶיךָ לְהָשִׁיב לְרָשָׁע לָתֵת דַּרְכּוֹ בְּרֹאשׁוֹ וּלְהַצְדִּיק צַדִּיק לָתֶת
כד לוֹ כְּצִדְקָתוֹ׃ וְאִם־יִנָּגֵף עַמְּךָ יִשְׂרָאֵל לִפְנֵי אוֹיֵב כִּי יֶחֶטְאוּ־
לָךְ וְשָׁבוּ וְהוֹדוּ אֶת־שְׁמֶךָ וְהִתְפַּלְלוּ וְהִתְחַנְּנוּ לְפָנֶיךָ בַּבַּיִת הַזֶּה׃
כה וְאַתָּה תִּשְׁמַע מִן־הַשָּׁמַיִם וְסָלַחְתָּ לְחַטַּאת עַמְּךָ יִשְׂרָאֵל וַהֲשֵׁיבוֹתָם
כו אֶל־הָאֲדָמָה אֲשֶׁר־נָתַתָּה לָהֶם וְלַאֲבֹתֵיהֶם׃ בְּהֵעָצֵר
הַשָּׁמַיִם וְלֹא־יִהְיֶה מָטָר כִּי יֶחֶטְאוּ־לָךְ וְהִתְפַּלְלוּ אֶל־הַמָּקוֹם הַזֶּה
כז וְהוֹדוּ אֶת־שְׁמֶךָ מֵחַטָּאתָם יְשׁוּבוּן כִּי תַעֲנֵם׃ וְאַתָּה ׀ תִּשְׁמַע
הַשָּׁמַיִם וְסָלַחְתָּ לְחַטַּאת עֲבָדֶיךָ וְעַמְּךָ יִשְׂרָאֵל כִּי תוֹרֵם אֶל־הַדֶּרֶךְ
הַטּוֹבָה אֲשֶׁר יֵלְכוּ־בָהּ וְנָתַתָּה מָטָר עַל־אַרְצְךָ אֲשֶׁר־נָתַתָּה לְעַמְּךָ
כח לְנַחֲלָה׃ רָעָב כִּי־יִהְיֶה בָאָרֶץ דֶּבֶר כִּי־יִהְיֶה שִׁדָּפוֹן וְיֵרָקוֹן
אַרְבֶּה וְחָסִיל כִּי יִהְיֶה כִּי יָצַר־לוֹ אֹיְבָיו בְּאֶרֶץ שְׁעָרָיו כָּל־נֶגַע וְכָל־
כט מַחֲלָה׃ כָּל־תְּפִלָּה כָל־תְּחִנָּה אֲשֶׁר יִהְיֶה לְכָל־הָאָדָם וּלְכֹל עַמְּךָ
יִשְׂרָאֵל אֲשֶׁר יֵדְעוּ אִישׁ נִגְעוֹ וּמַכְאֹבוֹ וּפָרַשׂ כַּפָּיו אֶל־הַבַּיִת הַזֶּה׃
ל וְאַתָּה תִּשְׁמַע מִן־הַשָּׁמַיִם מְכוֹן שִׁבְתֶּךָ וְסָלַחְתָּ וְנָתַתָּה לָאִישׁ כְּכָל־
דְּרָכָיו אֲשֶׁר תֵּדַע אֶת־לְבָבוֹ כִּי־אַתָּה לְבַדְּךָ יָדַעְתָּ אֶת־לְבַב בְּנֵי
לא הָאָדָם׃ לְמַעַן יִירָאוּךָ לָלֶכֶת בִּדְרָכֶיךָ כָּל־הַיָּמִים אֲשֶׁר־הֵם חַיִּים
לב עַל־פְּנֵי הָאֲדָמָה אֲשֶׁר נָתַתָּה לַאֲבֹתֵינוּ׃ וְגַם אֶל־
הַנָּכְרִי אֲשֶׁר לֹא־מֵעַמְּךָ יִשְׂרָאֵל הוּא וּבָא ׀ מֵאֶרֶץ רְחוֹקָה לְמַעַן
שִׁמְךָ הַגָּדוֹל וְיָדְךָ הַחֲזָקָה וּזְרוֹעֲךָ הַנְּטוּיָה וּבָאוּ וְהִתְפַּלְלוּ אֶל־
לג הַבַּיִת הַזֶּה׃ וְאַתָּה תִּשְׁמַע מִן־הַשָּׁמַיִם מִמְּכוֹן שִׁבְתֶּךָ וְעָשִׂיתָ כְּכֹל
אֲשֶׁר־יִקְרָא אֵלֶיךָ הַנָּכְרִי לְמַעַן יֵדְעוּ כָל־עַמֵּי הָאָרֶץ אֶת־שְׁמֶךָ
וּלְיִרְאָה אֹתְךָ כְּעַמְּךָ יִשְׂרָאֵל וְלָדַעַת כִּי־שִׁמְךָ נִקְרָא עַל־הַבַּיִת הַזֶּה
לד אֲשֶׁר בָּנִיתִי׃ כִּי־יֵצֵא עַמְּךָ לַמִּלְחָמָה עַל־אוֹיְבָיו בַּדֶּרֶךְ אֲשֶׁר
תִּשְׁלָחֵם וְהִתְפַּלְלוּ אֵלֶיךָ דֶּרֶךְ הָעִיר הַזֹּאת אֲשֶׁר בָּחַרְתָּ בָּהּ וְהַבַּיִת
לה אֲשֶׁר־בָּנִיתִי לִשְׁמֶךָ׃ וְשָׁמַעְתָּ מִן־הַשָּׁמַיִם אֶת־תְּפִלָּתָם וְאֶת־תְּחִנָּתָם
לו וְעָשִׂיתָ מִשְׁפָּטָם׃ כִּי יֶחֶטְאוּ־לָךְ כִּי אֵין אָדָם אֲשֶׁר לֹא־יֶחֱטָא וְאָנַפְתָּ
בָם וּנְתַתָּם לִפְנֵי אוֹיֵב וְשָׁבוּם שׁוֹבֵיהֶם אֶל־אֶרֶץ רְחוֹקָה אוֹ קְרוֹבָה׃
לז וְהֵשִׁיבוּ אֶל־לְבָבָם בָּאָרֶץ אֲשֶׁר נִשְׁבּוּ־שָׁם וְשָׁבוּ ׀ וְהִתְחַנְּנוּ אֵלֶיךָ

in the land of their captivity, declaring, 'We have sinned and offended and
38 done evil,' and they come back to You with all their heart and all their soul in
the land of their captivity, and they pray toward their own land which You
gave to their ancestors, to the city that You chose and the House that I built
39 for Your name – listen from Your heavenly abode to their prayer and their
pleas, uphold their cause, and forgive Your people who sinned against You.
40 Now, my God, let Your eyes be open and Your ears be attuned to the prayers
41 of this place. And now, O LORD God, advance to Your resting place,
You and Your mighty Ark. Your priests, O LORD God, are robed in victory;
42 Your devoted ones will rejoice in goodness. O LORD God, do not reject Your
7 1 anointed one. Remember Your loyalty to Your servant David." As
Shlomo concluded his prayer, fire flared down from the heavens and
consumed the burnt offering and the sacrifices, and the LORD's glory filled
2 the House – the priests could not enter the LORD's House because of the
3 divine glory that filled the LORD's House. When all the Israelites saw the fire
and the LORD's glory descending to the House, they kneeled down on the
floor with their faces to the ground, bowed down, and gave thanks to the
4 LORD, "for He is good, for His loving-kindness is forever." And the king and
5 all the people offered sacrifices before the LORD; King Shlomo
offered a sacrifice of 22,000 cattle and 120,000 sheep – thus the king and all
6 of Israel dedicated the House of God. The priests stood at their posts as well
as the Levites with their instruments for the LORD's music, those that King
David had made to give thanks to the LORD – for His loving-kindness is
forever! – whenever David offered praise through them. The priests, facing
7 them, sounded the trumpets, and all of Israel stood by. On that day,
Shlomo consecrated the center of the courtyard in front of the House of the
LORD, for it was there that he prepared the burnt offerings and the fats of the
peace offerings. The bronze altar that he had made could not contain all of
8 the burnt offering, the grain offering, and the fats. At that same time, Shlomo
celebrated the festival for seven days together with all of Israel; they were a
9 massive assembly from Levo Ḥamat to the Ravine of Egypt. On the eighth
day they held an assembly, for they had celebrated the dedication of the altar
10 for seven days and the festival for seven days. And on the twenty-third day of
the seventh month he sent the people back to their homes, joyful and glad at
heart for the goodness the LORD had shown to David and Shlomo and His
11 people Israel. Shlomo had finished building the House of the LORD and the
king's own house. He managed to fulfill all that he had in mind for the House
12 of the LORD and his own house. Now the LORD appeared to Shlomo
by night and said to him, "I have heard your prayer, and I have chosen this
13 place as a place of sacrifice for Me. Should I stop up the heavens and there is
no rain, or command the locust to devour the land, or send forth disease

לח בְּאֶרֶץ שִׁבְיָם לֵאמֹר חָטָאנוּ הֶעֱוִינוּ וְרָשָׁעְנוּ: וְשָׁבוּ אֵלֶיךָ בְּכָל־לִבָּם
וּבְכָל־נַפְשָׁם בְּאֶרֶץ שִׁבְיָם אֲשֶׁר־שָׁבוּ אֹתָם וְהִתְפַּלְלוּ דֶּרֶךְ אַרְצָם
אֲשֶׁר נָתַתָּה לַאֲבוֹתָם וְהָעִיר אֲשֶׁר בָּחַרְתָּ וְלַבַּיִת אֲשֶׁר־בָּנִיתִי
לט לִשְׁמֶךָ: וְשָׁמַעְתָּ מִן־הַשָּׁמַיִם מִמְּכוֹן שִׁבְתְּךָ אֶת־תְּפִלָּתָם וְאֶת־
מ תְּחִנֹּתֵיהֶם וְעָשִׂיתָ מִשְׁפָּטָם וְסָלַחְתָּ לְעַמְּךָ אֲשֶׁר חָטְאוּ־לָךְ: עַתָּה
אֱלֹהַי יִהְיוּ־נָא עֵינֶיךָ פְּתֻחוֹת וְאָזְנֶיךָ קַשֻּׁבוֹת לִתְפִלַּת הַמָּקוֹם
מא הַזֶּה: וְעַתָּה קוּמָה יהוה אֱלֹהִים לְנוּחֶךָ אַתָּה
וַאֲרוֹן עֻזֶּךָ כֹּהֲנֶיךָ יהוה אֱלֹהִים יִלְבְּשׁוּ תְשׁוּעָה וַחֲסִידֶיךָ יִשְׂמְחוּ
מב בַטּוֹב: יהוה אֱלֹהִים אַל־תָּשֵׁב פְּנֵי מְשִׁיחֶךָ זָכְרָה לְחַסְדֵי דָּוִיד
ז א עַבְדֶּךָ: וּכְכַלּוֹת שְׁלֹמֹה לְהִתְפַּלֵּל וְהָאֵשׁ יָרְדָה מֵהַשָּׁמַיִם
ב וַתֹּאכַל הָעֹלָה וְהַזְּבָחִים וּכְבוֹד יהוה מָלֵא אֶת־הַבָּיִת: וְלֹא יָכְלוּ
הַכֹּהֲנִים לָבוֹא אֶל־בֵּית יהוה כִּי־מָלֵא כְבוֹד־יהוה אֶת־בֵּית יהוה:
ג וְכֹל ׀ בְּנֵי יִשְׂרָאֵל רֹאִים בְּרֶדֶת הָאֵשׁ וּכְבוֹד יהוה עַל־הַבָּיִת וַיִּכְרְעוּ
אַפַּיִם אַרְצָה עַל־הָרִצְפָה וַיִּשְׁתַּחֲווּ וְהוֹדוֹת לַיהוה כִּי טוֹב כִּי לְעוֹלָם
ד ה חַסְדּוֹ: וְהַמֶּלֶךְ וְכָל־הָעָם זֹבְחִים זֶבַח לִפְנֵי יהוה: וַיִּזְבַּח
הַמֶּלֶךְ שְׁלֹמֹה אֶת־זֶבַח הַבָּקָר עֶשְׂרִים וּשְׁנַיִם אֶלֶף וְצֹאן מֵאָה וְעֶשְׂרִים
ו אָלֶף וַיַּחְנְכוּ אֶת־בֵּית הָאֱלֹהִים הַמֶּלֶךְ וְכָל־הָעָם: וְהַכֹּהֲנִים עַל־
מִשְׁמְרוֹתָם עֹמְדִים וְהַלְוִיִּם בִּכְלֵי־שִׁיר יהוה אֲשֶׁר עָשָׂה דָּוִיד הַמֶּלֶךְ
לְהֹדוֹת לַיהוה כִּי־לְעוֹלָם חַסְדּוֹ בְּהַלֵּל דָּוִיד בְּיָדָם וְהַכֹּהֲנִים מחצצרים מַחְצְרִים
ז נֶגְדָּם וְכָל־יִשְׂרָאֵל עֹמְדִים: וַיְקַדֵּשׁ שְׁלֹמֹה אֶת־תּוֹךְ הֶחָצֵר
אֲשֶׁר לִפְנֵי בֵית־יהוה כִּי־עָשָׂה שָׁם הָעֹלוֹת וְאֵת חֶלְבֵי הַשְּׁלָמִים כִּי־
מִזְבַּח הַנְּחֹשֶׁת אֲשֶׁר־עָשָׂה שְׁלֹמֹה לֹא יָכוֹל לְהָכִיל אֶת־הָעֹלָה וְאֶת־
ח הַמִּנְחָה וְאֶת־הַחֲלָבִים: וַיַּעַשׂ שְׁלֹמֹה אֶת־הֶחָג בָּעֵת הַהִיא שִׁבְעַת
יָמִים וְכָל־יִשְׂרָאֵל עִמּוֹ קָהָל גָּדוֹל מְאֹד מִלְּבוֹא חֲמָת עַד־נַחַל מִצְרָיִם:
ט וַיַּעֲשׂוּ בַּיּוֹם הַשְּׁמִינִי עֲצָרֶת כִּי ׀ חֲנֻכַּת הַמִּזְבֵּחַ עָשׂוּ שִׁבְעַת יָמִים
י וְהֶחָג שִׁבְעַת יָמִים: וּבְיוֹם עֶשְׂרִים וּשְׁלֹשָׁה לַחֹדֶשׁ הַשְּׁבִיעִי שִׁלַּח
אֶת־הָעָם לְאָהֳלֵיהֶם שְׂמֵחִים וְטוֹבֵי לֵב עַל־הַטּוֹבָה אֲשֶׁר עָשָׂה יהוה
יא לְדָוִיד וְלִשְׁלֹמֹה וּלְיִשְׂרָאֵל עַמּוֹ: וַיְכַל שְׁלֹמֹה אֶת־בֵּית יהוה וְאֶת־בֵּית יד
הַמֶּלֶךְ וְאֵת כָּל־הַבָּא עַל־לֵב שְׁלֹמֹה לַעֲשׂוֹת בְּבֵית־יהוה וּבְבֵיתוֹ
יב הִצְלִיחַ: וַיֵּרָא יהוה אֶל־שְׁלֹמֹה בַּלָּיְלָה וַיֹּאמֶר לוֹ שָׁמַעְתִּי
יג אֶת־תְּפִלָּתֶךָ וּבָחַרְתִּי בַּמָּקוֹם הַזֶּה לִי לְבֵית זָבַח: הֵן אֶעֱצֹר הַשָּׁמַיִם
וְלֹא־יִהְיֶה מָטָר וְהֵן־אֲצַוֶּה עַל־חָגָב לֶאֱכוֹל הָאָרֶץ וְאִם־אֲשַׁלַּח דֶּבֶר

14 among My people – if My people, who are called by My name, humble
themselves and pray and seek My presence and turn back from their evil
ways – then I will listen from Heaven and forgive their sins and heal their land.
15 Now My eyes will be open and My ears attuned to the prayers of this place.
16 Now I have chosen to consecrate this House for My name to be there forever;
17 My eyes and My heart will be there for all time. As for you – if you walk before
Me as your father David did, fulfilling all I have commanded you, keeping
18 My laws and My rulings, then I will establish your royal throne in accordance
with My covenant with your father David: 'No one of your lineage will be cut
19 off from ruling over Israel.' But if you turn back from Me and abandon the
commandments and laws I set before you and serve other gods and worship
20 them, then I will uproot them from the land that I gave them and I will cast
this House – which I sanctified for My own name – from My presence, leaving
21 it as a proverb and a byword among all the nations. And whoever passes by
this once-exalted House will reel and say, 'Why did the Lord do this to this
22 land and this House?' And they will answer, 'Because they left the Lord, the
God of their ancestors, who brought them out of the land of Egypt, and they
embraced other gods and worshipped them and served them. For this, He
brought all this evil upon them.'"
8 1 At the end of the twenty years that Shlomo had spent building the House of
2 the Lord and the king's own house, Shlomo built up the cities that Ḥuram
3 had given to him, and he settled Israelites there. Shlomo went to Ḥamat Tzova
4 and seized it. He built Tadmor in the wilderness, and in Ḥamat he built all the
5 store towns. He built Upper Beit Ḥoron and Lower Beit Ḥoron and fortified
6 cities with walls, gates, and bars, as well as Baalat and all of Shlomo's store
towns, chariot towns, and cavalry towns – all that Shlomo desired to build
7 in Jerusalem, Lebanon, and throughout the land of his dominion. As for all
the people who remained among the Hittites, the Amorites, the Perizzites,
8 the Hivvites, and the Jebusites, who were not of the Israelites – some of their
remaining descendants, whom the Israelites had not destroyed, Shlomo
9 drafted them for forced labor to this day. Shlomo never reduced the Israelites
to slavery for his work, for they were military men, his commanding officers,
10 and the officers of his chariots and cavalry. These were King Shlomo's
11 ministers of prefects: two hundred fifty supervised the people. Shlomo
brought Pharaoh's daughter up from the City of David to the palace he had
built for her, saying, "My wife will not live in the house of King David of Israel,
for wherever the Ark of the Lord has been is holy."

יד בְּעַמִּי: וְיִכָּנְעוּ עַמִּי אֲשֶׁר נִקְרָא־שְׁמִי עֲלֵיהֶם וְיִתְפַּלְלוּ וִיבַקְשׁוּ פָנַי
וְיָשֻׁבוּ מִדַּרְכֵיהֶם הָרָעִים וַאֲנִי אֶשְׁמַע מִן־הַשָּׁמַיִם וְאֶסְלַח לְחַטָּאתָם
טו וְאֶרְפָּא אֶת־אַרְצָם: עַתָּה עֵינַי יִהְיוּ פְתֻחוֹת וְאָזְנַי קַשֻּׁבוֹת לִתְפִלַּת
טז הַמָּקוֹם הַזֶּה: וְעַתָּה בָּחַרְתִּי וְהִקְדַּשְׁתִּי אֶת־הַבַּיִת הַזֶּה לִהְיוֹת־שְׁמִי
יז שָׁם עַד־עוֹלָם וְהָיוּ עֵינַי וְלִבִּי שָׁם כָּל־הַיָּמִים: וְאַתָּה אִם־תֵּלֵךְ לְפָנַי
כַּאֲשֶׁר הָלַךְ דָּוִיד אָבִיךָ וְלַעֲשׂוֹת כְּכֹל אֲשֶׁר צִוִּיתִיךָ וְחֻקַּי וּמִשְׁפָּטַי
יח תִשְׁמוֹר: וַהֲקִימוֹתִי אֵת כִּסֵּא מַלְכוּתֶךָ כַּאֲשֶׁר כָּרַתִּי לְדָוִיד אָבִיךָ
יט לֵאמֹר לֹא־יִכָּרֵת לְךָ אִישׁ מוֹשֵׁל בְּיִשְׂרָאֵל: וְאִם־תְּשׁוּבוּן אַתֶּם
וַעֲזַבְתֶּם חֻקּוֹתַי וּמִצְוֺתַי אֲשֶׁר נָתַתִּי לִפְנֵיכֶם וַהֲלַכְתֶּם וַעֲבַדְתֶּם אֱלֹהִים
כ אֲחֵרִים וְהִשְׁתַּחֲוִיתֶם לָהֶם: וּנְתַשְׁתִּים מֵעַל אַדְמָתִי אֲשֶׁר־נָתַתִּי לָהֶם
וְאֶת־הַבַּיִת הַזֶּה אֲשֶׁר הִקְדַּשְׁתִּי לִשְׁמִי אַשְׁלִיךְ מֵעַל פָּנָי וְאֶתְּנֶנּוּ
כא לְמָשָׁל וְלִשְׁנִינָה בְּכָל־הָעַמִּים: וְהַבַּיִת הַזֶּה אֲשֶׁר הָיָה עֶלְיוֹן לְכָל־
עֹבֵר עָלָיו יִשֹּׁם וְאָמַר בַּמֶּה עָשָׂה יהוה כָּכָה לָאָרֶץ הַזֹּאת וְלַבַּיִת
כב הַזֶּה: וְאָמְרוּ עַל אֲשֶׁר עָזְבוּ אֶת־יהוה | אֱלֹהֵי אֲבֹתֵיהֶם אֲשֶׁר הוֹצִיאָם
מֵאֶרֶץ מִצְרַיִם וַיַּחֲזִיקוּ בֵּאלֹהִים אֲחֵרִים וַיִּשְׁתַּחֲווּ לָהֶם וַיַּעַבְדוּם
עַל־כֵּן הֵבִיא עֲלֵיהֶם אֵת כָּל־הָרָעָה הַזֹּאת:
ח א וַיְהִי מִקֵּץ | עֶשְׂרִים שָׁנָה אֲשֶׁר בָּנָה שְׁלֹמֹה אֶת־בֵּית יהוה וְאֶת־בֵּיתוֹ:
ב וְהֶעָרִים אֲשֶׁר נָתַן חוּרָם לִשְׁלֹמֹה בָּנָה שְׁלֹמֹה אֹתָם וַיּוֹשֶׁב שָׁם אֶת־
ג ד בְּנֵי יִשְׂרָאֵל: וַיֵּלֶךְ שְׁלֹמֹה חֲמָת צוֹבָה וַיֶּחֱזַק עָלֶיהָ: וַיִּבֶן אֶת־תַּדְמֹר
ה בַּמִּדְבָּר וְאֵת כָּל־עָרֵי הַמִּסְכְּנוֹת אֲשֶׁר בָּנָה בַּחֲמָת: וַיִּבֶן אֶת־בֵּית
חוֹרוֹן הָעֶלְיוֹן וְאֶת־בֵּית חוֹרוֹן הַתַּחְתּוֹן עָרֵי מָצוֹר חוֹמוֹת דְּלָתַיִם
ו וּבְרִיחַ: וְאֶת־בַּעֲלָת וְאֵת כָּל־עָרֵי הַמִּסְכְּנוֹת אֲשֶׁר־הָיוּ לִשְׁלֹמֹה וְאֵת
כָּל־עָרֵי הָרֶכֶב וְאֵת עָרֵי הַפָּרָשִׁים וְאֵת | כָּל־חֵשֶׁק שְׁלֹמֹה אֲשֶׁר חָשַׁק
ז לִבְנוֹת בִּירוּשָׁלִַם וּבַלְּבָנוֹן וּבְכֹל אֶרֶץ מֶמְשַׁלְתּוֹ: כָּל־הָעָם הַנּוֹתָר
מִן־הַחִתִּי וְהָאֱמֹרִי וְהַפְּרִזִּי וְהַחִוִּי וְהַיְבוּסִי אֲשֶׁר לֹא מִיִּשְׂרָאֵל הֵמָּה:
ח מִן־בְּנֵיהֶם אֲשֶׁר נוֹתְרוּ אַחֲרֵיהֶם בָּאָרֶץ אֲשֶׁר לֹא־כִלּוּם בְּנֵי יִשְׂרָאֵל
ט וַיַּעֲלֵם שְׁלֹמֹה לְמַס עַד הַיּוֹם הַזֶּה: וּמִן־בְּנֵי יִשְׂרָאֵל אֲשֶׁר לֹא־נָתַן
שְׁלֹמֹה לַעֲבָדִים לִמְלַאכְתּוֹ כִּי־הֵמָּה אַנְשֵׁי מִלְחָמָה וְשָׂרֵי שָׁלִישָׁיו
י וְשָׂרֵי רִכְבּוֹ וּפָרָשָׁיו: וְאֵלֶּה שָׂרֵי הנציבים אֲשֶׁר־לַמֶּלֶךְ שְׁלֹמֹה חֲמִשִּׁים הַנִּצָּבִים
יא וּמָאתַיִם הָרֹדִים בָּעָם: וְאֶת־בַּת־פַּרְעֹה הֶעֱלָה שְׁלֹמֹה מֵעִיר דָּוִיד
לַבַּיִת אֲשֶׁר בָּנָה־לָהּ כִּי אָמַר לֹא־תֵשֵׁב אִשָּׁה לִי בְּבֵית דָּוִיד מֶלֶךְ־
יִשְׂרָאֵל כִּי־קֹדֶשׁ הֵמָּה אֲשֶׁר־בָּאָה אֲלֵיהֶם אֲרוֹן יהוה:

12 At that time, Shlomo offered up burnt offerings to the Lord on the Lord's
13 altar that he had built in front of the Hall, performing the constant daily
service as the laws of Moshe dictated: on Sabbaths, New Moons, and the three
annual festivals: the Festival of Unleavened Bread, the Festival of Weeks, and
14 the Festival of Tabernacles. He maintained his father David's orders regarding
the division of priestly duties, the Levites' shifts to sing praise and serve
before the priests according to the constant daily service, and the division of
gatekeepers for each gate, following the orders of David, the man of God.
15 They did not deviate from any of the king's orders to the priests and the
16 Levites regarding these matters, or regarding the treasuries. Thus all Shlomo's
work was accomplished from the day the foundations of the Lord's House
were laid until its completion; the House of the Lord was completely
17 finished. Shlomo then went to Etzyon Gever and Eilot on the
18 seacoast in the land of Edom. Ḥuram sent him ships with his own servants,
who were familiar with the sea, and together with Shlomo's servants, they
traveled to Ofir. There they collected gold – 450 talents – and brought it to
9 1 King Shlomo. Now the Queen of Sheba had been hearing of
Shlomo's fame, and she came with a vast entourage to test him with riddles
in Jerusalem, with camels bearing spices, an immense wealth of gold, and
precious stones. She came to Shlomo and told him all that she had in mind.
2 Shlomo addressed all of her words; nothing remained hidden from Shlomo,
3 and there was nothing he failed to address. When the Queen of Sheba saw
4 Shlomo's wisdom and the House he had built, and the fare of his table and
how his subjects were seated, and his servants' attendance and attire and his
cupbearers and their attire, and the burnt offerings he offered up in the House
5 of the Lord, she was left breathless. "What I heard in my land about your
6 deeds and your wisdom is true," she said to the king. "I never believed their
words until I came and saw it with my own eyes – and I was not told even half
7 of your great wisdom; you have surpassed the rumors I heard. How fortunate
are your people, and how fortunate are these attendants of yours who are
8 always in your presence and hear your wisdom. Blessed be the Lord your
God, who delighted in you and set you upon His throne as king for the Lord
your God; because your God loves Israel and wishes to establish them forever,
9 He has made you king over them to uphold justice and righteousness." She
gave the king one hundred twenty talents of gold and a great wealth of spices
and precious stones; never again has there been a wealth of spices like the
10 Queen of Sheba's gift to King Shlomo – the servants of Ḥuram and Shlomo
who conveyed gold from Ofir had also brought sandalwood and precious
11 stones, and the king had the sandalwood made into banisters for the House
of the Lord and the royal house, and harps and lyres for the musicians, the
12 likes of which had never been seen before in the land of Yehuda – and he gave
the Queen of Sheba all that she desired, far more than she had brought to the

יב אָז הֶעֱלָה שְׁלֹמֹה עֹלוֹת לַיהוה עַל מִזְבַּח יהוה אֲשֶׁר בָּנָה לִפְנֵי הָאוּלָם:
יג וּבִדְבַר־יוֹם בְּיוֹם לְהַעֲלוֹת כְּמִצְוַת מֹשֶׁה לַשַּׁבָּתוֹת וְלֶחֳדָשִׁים
וְלַמּוֹעֲדוֹת שָׁלוֹשׁ פְּעָמִים בַּשָּׁנָה בְּחַג הַמַּצּוֹת וּבְחַג הַשָּׁבֻעוֹת וּבְחַג
יד הַסֻּכּוֹת: וַיַּעֲמֵד כְּמִשְׁפַּט דָּוִיד־אָבִיו אֶת־מַחְלְקוֹת הַכֹּהֲנִים עַל־
עֲבֹדָתָם וְהַלְוִיִּם עַל־מִשְׁמְרוֹתָם לְהַלֵּל וּלְשָׁרֵת נֶגֶד הַכֹּהֲנִים לִדְבַר־
יוֹם בְּיוֹמוֹ וְהַשּׁוֹעֲרִים בְּמַחְלְקוֹתָם לְשַׁעַר וָשָׁעַר כִּי כֵן מִצְוַת דָּוִיד
טו אִישׁ־הָאֱלֹהִים: וְלֹא סָרוּ מִצְוַת הַמֶּלֶךְ עַל־הַכֹּהֲנִים וְהַלְוִיִּם לְכָל־דָּבָר
טז וְלָאֹצָרוֹת: וַתִּכֹּן כָּל־מְלֶאכֶת שְׁלֹמֹה עַד־הַיּוֹם מוּסַד בֵּית־יהוה וְעַד־
יז כְּלֹתוֹ שָׁלֵם בֵּית יהוה: אָז הָלַךְ שְׁלֹמֹה לְעֶצְיוֹן־
יח גֶּבֶר וְאֶל־אֵילוֹת עַל־שְׂפַת הַיָּם בְּאֶרֶץ אֱדוֹם: וַיִּשְׁלַח־לוֹ חוּרָם בְּיַד־
עֲבָדָיו אוניות וַעֲבָדִים יוֹדְעֵי יָם וַיָּבֹאוּ עִם־עַבְדֵי שְׁלֹמֹה אוֹפִירָה אֳנִיּוֹת
וַיִּקְחוּ מִשָּׁם אַרְבַּע־מֵאוֹת וַחֲמִשִּׁים כִּכַּר זָהָב וַיָּבִיאוּ אֶל־הַמֶּלֶךְ
ט א שְׁלֹמֹה: וּמַלְכַּת־שְׁבָא שָׁמְעָה אֶת־שֵׁמַע שְׁלֹמֹה וַתָּבוֹא
לְנַסּוֹת אֶת־שְׁלֹמֹה בְחִידוֹת בִּירוּשָׁלַםִ בְּחַיִל כָּבֵד מְאֹד וּגְמַלִּים נֹשְׂאִים
בְּשָׂמִים וְזָהָב לָרֹב וְאֶבֶן יְקָרָה וַתָּבוֹא אֶל־שְׁלֹמֹה וַתְּדַבֵּר עִמּוֹ אֵת
ב כָּל־אֲשֶׁר הָיָה עִם־לְבָבָהּ: וַיַּגֶּד־לָהּ שְׁלֹמֹה אֶת־כָּל־דְּבָרֶיהָ וְלֹא־נֶעְלַם
ג דָּבָר מִשְּׁלֹמֹה אֲשֶׁר לֹא הִגִּיד לָהּ: וַתֵּרֶא מַלְכַּת־שְׁבָא אֵת חָכְמַת
ד שְׁלֹמֹה וְהַבַּיִת אֲשֶׁר בָּנָה: וּמַאֲכַל שֻׁלְחָנוֹ וּמוֹשַׁב עֲבָדָיו וּמַעֲמַד
מְשָׁרְתָיו וּמַלְבּוּשֵׁיהֶם וּמַשְׁקָיו וּמַלְבּוּשֵׁיהֶם וַעֲלִיָּתוֹ אֲשֶׁר יַעֲלֶה בֵּית
ה יהוה וְלֹא־הָיָה עוֹד בָּהּ רוּחַ: וַתֹּאמֶר אֶל־הַמֶּלֶךְ אֱמֶת הַדָּבָר אֲשֶׁר
ו שָׁמַעְתִּי בְּאַרְצִי עַל־דְּבָרֶיךָ וְעַל־חָכְמָתֶךָ: וְלֹא־הֶאֱמַנְתִּי לְדִבְרֵיהֶם
עַד אֲשֶׁר־בָּאתִי וַתִּרְאֶינָה עֵינַי וְהִנֵּה לֹא הֻגַּד־לִי חֲצִי מַרְבִּית חָכְמָתֶךָ
ז יָסַפְתָּ עַל־הַשְּׁמוּעָה אֲשֶׁר שָׁמָעְתִּי: אַשְׁרֵי אֲנָשֶׁיךָ וְאַשְׁרֵי עֲבָדֶיךָ
ח אֵלֶּה הָעֹמְדִים לְפָנֶיךָ תָּמִיד וְשֹׁמְעִים אֶת־חָכְמָתֶךָ: יְהִי יהוה אֱלֹהֶיךָ
בָּרוּךְ אֲשֶׁר חָפֵץ בְּךָ לְתִתְּךָ עַל־כִּסְאוֹ לְמֶלֶךְ לַיהוה אֱלֹהֶיךָ בְּאַהֲבַת
אֱלֹהֶיךָ אֶת־יִשְׂרָאֵל לְהַעֲמִידוֹ לְעוֹלָם וַיִּתֶּנְךָ עֲלֵיהֶם לְמֶלֶךְ לַעֲשׂוֹת
ט מִשְׁפָּט וּצְדָקָה: וַתִּתֵּן לַמֶּלֶךְ מֵאָה וְעֶשְׂרִים כִּכַּר זָהָב וּבְשָׂמִים לָרֹב
מְאֹד וְאֶבֶן יְקָרָה וְלֹא הָיָה כַּבֹּשֶׂם הַהוּא אֲשֶׁר נָתְנָה מַלְכַּת־שְׁבָא
י לַמֶּלֶךְ שְׁלֹמֹה: וְגַם עַבְדֵי חירם וְעַבְדֵי שְׁלֹמֹה אֲשֶׁר־הֵבִיאוּ זָהָב חוּרָם
יא מֵאוֹפִיר הֵבִיאוּ עֲצֵי אַלְגּוּמִּים וְאֶבֶן יְקָרָה: וַיַּעַשׂ הַמֶּלֶךְ אֶת־עֲצֵי
הָאַלְגּוּמִּים מְסִלּוֹת לְבֵית־יהוה וּלְבֵית הַמֶּלֶךְ וְכִנֹּרוֹת וּנְבָלִים לַשָּׁרִים
יב וְלֹא־נִרְאוּ כָהֵם לְפָנִים בְּאֶרֶץ יְהוּדָה: וְהַמֶּלֶךְ שְׁלֹמֹה נָתַן לְמַלְכַּת־

king. Then, together with her servants, she took her leave and journeyed back
13 to her own land. The weight of gold that Shlomo received in a
14 single year was 666 talents beside imports from traveling merchants and
traders; all the Arabian kings and the governors of the land would bring gold
15 and silver to Shlomo. King Shlomo made two hundred shields of beaten
16 gold – six hundred pieces of beaten gold went into each shield – and three
hundred bucklers of beaten gold – three hundred pieces of gold went into
each buckler – and the king placed them in the House of the Lebanon
17 Forest. The king made an enormous ivory throne and overlaid it
18 with pure gold. Six steps led up to the throne; a golden footstool was attached
to the throne, and there were armrests on both sides of the seat. Two lions
19 were positioned by the armrests, and twelve lions stood there on the six steps
20 on either side. Nothing like it was ever made in any other kingdom. All the
king's drinking vessels were of gold, and all the utensils of the House of the
Lebanon Forest were of solid gold. Silver counted for nothing in the days of
21 Shlomo, for the king's ships traveled to Tarshish with Ḥiram's servants; every
three years, the ships would come from Tarshish loaded with gold and silver,
22 ivory, monkeys, and peacocks. King Shlomo surpassed all the kings of the
23 earth in wealth and in wisdom; all the kings of the earth sought an audience
24 with Shlomo to hear the wisdom that God had granted him. And each one
brought his tribute: vessels of silver and vessels of gold, garments, weapons,
25 spices, horses, and mules according to the yearly due. Shlomo had
four thousand horse stables and chariots and twelve thousand horsemen. He
26 stationed them in the chariot towns and with the king in Jerusalem. He ruled
over all the kings from the River[27] to the land of the Philistines and up to the
27 border of Egypt. The king made silver as common in Jerusalem as stones,
28 while cedars were as common as sycamores in the lowlands. Shlomo's horses
29 were imported from Egypt and from all over the world. The rest of Shlomo's
history, earlier and later, is recorded in the chronicles of the prophet Natan,
the prophecy of Aḥiya the Shilonite, and the oracles of the Seer Yedo[28] about
30 Yorovam son of Nevat. Shlomo reigned in Jerusalem over all of Israel for
31 forty years. Then Shlomo slept with his ancestors, and they buried him
in the City of David, his father, and his son Reḥavam reigned in his
10 1 place. Reḥavam went to Shekhem, for all of Israel had come to
2 Shekhem for his coronation. Yorovam son of Nevat heard this when he was
in Egypt, for he had escaped from King Shlomo. Now Yorovam returned from
3 Egypt. They sent for and summoned him, and Yorovam came with all of Israel,

---

27 | The Euphrates.

28 | Believed to be the same as the prophet Ido mentioned in 12:15 and 13:22.

שְׁבָא אֶת־כָּל־חֶפְצָהּ אֲשֶׁר שָׁאָלָה מִלְּבַד אֲשֶׁר־הֵבִיאָה אֶל־הַמֶּלֶךְ
יג וַתַּהֲפֹךְ וַתֵּלֶךְ לְאַרְצָהּ הִיא וַעֲבָדֶיהָ׃ וַיְהִי מִשְׁקַל הַזָּהָב אֲשֶׁר־
יד בָּא לִשְׁלֹמֹה בְּשָׁנָה אֶחָת שֵׁשׁ מֵאוֹת וְשִׁשִּׁים וָשֵׁשׁ כִּכְּרֵי זָהָב׃ לְבַד
מֵאַנְשֵׁי הַתָּרִים וְהַסֹּחֲרִים מְבִיאִים וְכָל־מַלְכֵי עֲרַב וּפַחוֹת הָאָרֶץ
טו מְבִיאִים זָהָב וָכֶסֶף לִשְׁלֹמֹה׃ וַיַּעַשׂ הַמֶּלֶךְ שְׁלֹמֹה מָאתַיִם צִנָּה זָהָב
טז שָׁחוּט שֵׁשׁ מֵאוֹת זָהָב שָׁחוּט יַעֲלֶה עַל־הַצִּנָּה הָאֶחָת׃ וּשְׁלֹשׁ־מֵאוֹת
מָגִנִּים זָהָב שָׁחוּט שְׁלֹשׁ מֵאוֹת זָהָב יַעֲלֶה עַל־הַמָּגֵן הָאֶחָת וַיִּתְּנֵם
יז הַמֶּלֶךְ בְּבֵית יַעַר הַלְּבָנוֹן׃ וַיַּעַשׂ הַמֶּלֶךְ כִּסֵּא־שֵׁן גָּדוֹל
יח וַיְצַפֵּהוּ זָהָב טָהוֹר׃ וְשֵׁשׁ מַעֲלוֹת לַכִּסֵּא וְכֶבֶשׁ בַּזָּהָב לַכִּסֵּא מָאֳחָזִים
וְיָדוֹת מִזֶּה וּמִזֶּה עַל־מְקוֹם הַשָּׁבֶת וּשְׁנַיִם אֲרָיוֹת עֹמְדִים אֵצֶל הַיָּדוֹת׃
יט וּשְׁנֵים עָשָׂר אֲרָיוֹת עֹמְדִים שָׁם עַל־שֵׁשׁ הַמַּעֲלוֹת מִזֶּה וּמִזֶּה לֹא־
כ נַעֲשָׂה כֵן לְכָל־מַמְלָכָה׃ וְכֹל כְּלֵי מַשְׁקֵה הַמֶּלֶךְ שְׁלֹמֹה זָהָב וְכֹל כְּלֵי
בֵית־יַעַר הַלְּבָנוֹן זָהָב סָגוּר אֵין כֶּסֶף נֶחְשָׁב בִּימֵי שְׁלֹמֹה לִמְאוּמָה׃
כא כִּי־אֳנִיּוֹת לַמֶּלֶךְ הֹלְכוֹת תַּרְשִׁישׁ עִם עַבְדֵי חוּרָם אַחַת לְשָׁלוֹשׁ שָׁנִים
תָּבוֹאנָה ׀ אֳנִיּוֹת תַּרְשִׁישׁ נֹשְׂאוֹת זָהָב וָכֶסֶף שֶׁנְהַבִּים וְקוֹפִים וְתוּכִּיִּים׃
כב כג וַיִּגְדַּל הַמֶּלֶךְ שְׁלֹמֹה מִכֹּל מַלְכֵי הָאָרֶץ לְעֹשֶׁר וְחָכְמָה׃ וְכֹל מַלְכֵי
הָאָרֶץ מְבַקְשִׁים אֶת־פְּנֵי שְׁלֹמֹה לִשְׁמֹעַ אֶת־חָכְמָתוֹ אֲשֶׁר־נָתַן
כד הָאֱלֹהִים בְּלִבּוֹ׃ וְהֵם מְבִיאִים אִישׁ מִנְחָתוֹ כְּלֵי כֶסֶף וּכְלֵי זָהָב וּשְׂלָמוֹת טו
כה נֵשֶׁק וּבְשָׂמִים סוּסִים וּפְרָדִים דְּבַר־שָׁנָה בְּשָׁנָה׃ וַיְהִי
לִשְׁלֹמֹה אַרְבַּעַת אֲלָפִים אֻרְיוֹת סוּסִים וּמַרְכָּבוֹת וּשְׁנֵים־עָשָׂר אֶלֶף
כו פָּרָשִׁים וַיַּנִּיחֵם בְּעָרֵי הָרֶכֶב וְעִם־הַמֶּלֶךְ בִּירוּשָׁלָםִ׃ וַיְהִי מוֹשֵׁל בְּכָל־
כז הַמְּלָכִים מִן־הַנָּהָר וְעַד־אֶרֶץ פְּלִשְׁתִּים וְעַד גְּבוּל מִצְרָיִם׃ וַיִּתֵּן הַמֶּלֶךְ
אֶת־הַכֶּסֶף בִּירוּשָׁלַםִ כָּאֲבָנִים וְאֵת הָאֲרָזִים נָתַן כַּשִּׁקְמִים אֲשֶׁר־
כח בַּשְּׁפֵלָה לָרֹב׃ וּמוֹצִיאִים סוּסִים מִמִּצְרַיִם לִשְׁלֹמֹה וּמִכָּל־הָאֲרָצוֹת׃
כט וּשְׁאָר דִּבְרֵי שְׁלֹמֹה הָרִאשֹׁנִים וְהָאַחֲרוֹנִים הֲלֹא־הֵם כְּתוּבִים עַל־
דִּבְרֵי נָתָן הַנָּבִיא וְעַל־נְבוּאַת אֲחִיָּה הַשִּׁילוֹנִי וּבַחֲזוֹת יעדי הַחֹזֶה יֶעְדּוֹ
ל עַל־יָרָבְעָם בֶּן־נְבָט׃ וַיִּמְלֹךְ שְׁלֹמֹה בִּירוּשָׁלַםִ עַל־כָּל־יִשְׂרָאֵל אַרְבָּעִים
לא שָׁנָה׃ וַיִּשְׁכַּב שְׁלֹמֹה עִם־אֲבֹתָיו וַיִּקְבְּרֻהוּ בְּעִיר דָּוִיד אָבִיו וַיִּמְלֹךְ
י א רְחַבְעָם בְּנוֹ תַּחְתָּיו׃ וַיֵּלֶךְ רְחַבְעָם שְׁכֶמָה כִּי שְׁכֶם בָּאוּ
ב כָל־יִשְׂרָאֵל לְהַמְלִיךְ אֹתוֹ׃ וַיְהִי כִּשְׁמֹעַ יָרָבְעָם בֶּן־נְבָט וְהוּא בְמִצְרַיִם
ג אֲשֶׁר בָּרַח מִפְּנֵי שְׁלֹמֹה הַמֶּלֶךְ וַיָּשָׁב יָרָבְעָם מִמִּצְרָיִם׃ וַיִּשְׁלְחוּ
וַיִּקְרְאוּ־לוֹ וַיָּבֹא יָרָבְעָם וְכָל־יִשְׂרָאֵל וַיְדַבְּרוּ אֶל־רְחַבְעָם לֵאמֹר׃

4 who made the following speech to Reḥavam: "Your father made our yoke
heavy – now relieve the heavy workload and the harsh yoke your father placed
5 upon us, and we will serve you." "Leave for three days," he said to them, "and
6 then come back to me," and the people left. King Reḥavam consulted
with the elders who had served his father Shlomo during his lifetime. "How
7 would you advise to answer this people's request?" he said. "If you treat this
people kindly today," they told him, "and appease them by speaking kind
8 words, then they will become your servants forever." But he rejected the
advice that the elders gave him and consulted with the youngsters who had
9 grown up with him and who now served him. "What do you advise?" he asked
them. "How should we answer this people's request? They told me, 'Relieve
10 the yoke your father placed upon us.'" The youngsters who had grown up with
him said, "This is what you should say to the people who told you, 'Your father
made our yoke heavy – you should relieve us.' Tell them this: 'My little finger
11 is thicker than my father's loins. Now, my father burdened you with a heavy
yoke, but I will increase your yoke; my father flogged you with whips – I will
12 use scorpions.'" Yorovam and all the people came to Reḥavam on
the third day, just as the king had commanded them, saying, "Come back to
13 me on the third day." The king answered them harshly, rejecting the advice of
14 the elders. He answered them as the youngsters had advised, saying, "I will
burden you with a heavy yoke and make it even heavier; my father flogged
15 you with whips, but I will use scorpions!" The king would not listen to the
people, for it was part of God's plan in order to fulfill the promise that the
Lord had made to Yorovam son of Nevat through Aḥiyahu the Shilonite.
16 When all Israel saw that the king would not listen to them, the people retorted
to the king, "We have no part in David nor any share in the son of Yishai!
Every man to your tent, O Israel! Now look to your own house, O David!"
17 And all Israel went back to their tents. But as for the Israelites who
18 lived in the towns of Yehuda, Reḥavam ruled over them. King Reḥavam sent
out Hadoram, who was in charge of the forced labor, but Israelites pelted him
with stones, and he died. At that, Reḥavam forced his way onto his chariot,
19 to flee to Jerusalem. And the Israelites have rebelled against the
11 1 House of David ever since. When Reḥavam reached Jerusalem, he
assembled the House of Yehuda and Binyamin – 180,000 elite fighters – to
2 fight against Israel, to restore the kingship to Reḥavam. But the word
3 of the Lord came to Shemayahu, man of God: "Say to Reḥavam son of
Shlomo, king of Yehuda, and to all of Israel who live in Yehuda and Binyamin:
4 'Thus says the Lord: Do not advance, and do not fight with your brothers.
Let every man go back home, for it is through Me that this has come about.'"

ד אָבִיךָ הִקְשָׁה אֶת־עֻלֵּנוּ וְעַתָּה הָקֵל מֵעֲבֹדַת אָבִיךָ הַקָּשָׁה וּמֵעֻלּוֹ
ה הַכָּבֵד אֲשֶׁר־נָתַן עָלֵינוּ וְנַעַבְדֶךָּ: וַיֹּאמֶר אֲלֵהֶם עוֹד שְׁלֹשֶׁת יָמִים
ו וְשׁוּבוּ אֵלָי וַיֵּלֶךְ הָעָם: וַיִּוָּעַץ הַמֶּלֶךְ רְחַבְעָם אֶת־הַזְּקֵנִים
אֲשֶׁר־הָיוּ עֹמְדִים לִפְנֵי שְׁלֹמֹה אָבִיו בִּהְיֹתוֹ חַי לֵאמֹר אֵיךְ אַתֶּם
ז נוֹעָצִים לְהָשִׁיב לָעָם־הַזֶּה דָּבָר: וַיְדַבְּרוּ אֵלָיו לֵאמֹר אִם־תִּהְיֶה לְטוֹב
לְהָעָם הַזֶּה וּרְצִיתָם וְדִבַּרְתָּ אֲלֵהֶם דְּבָרִים טוֹבִים וְהָיוּ לְךָ עֲבָדִים
ח כָּל־הַיָּמִים: וַיַּעֲזֹב אֶת־עֲצַת הַזְּקֵנִים אֲשֶׁר יְעָצֻהוּ וַיִּוָּעַץ אֶת־הַיְלָדִים
ט אֲשֶׁר גָּדְלוּ אִתּוֹ הָעֹמְדִים לְפָנָיו: וַיֹּאמֶר אֲלֵהֶם מָה אַתֶּם נוֹעָצִים
וְנָשִׁיב דָּבָר אֶת־הָעָם הַזֶּה אֲשֶׁר דִּבְּרוּ אֵלַי לֵאמֹר הָקֵל מִן־הָעֹל
י אֲשֶׁר־נָתַן אָבִיךָ עָלֵינוּ: וַיְדַבְּרוּ אִתּוֹ הַיְלָדִים אֲשֶׁר גָּדְלוּ אִתּוֹ לֵאמֹר
כֹּה תֹאמַר לָעָם אֲשֶׁר־דִּבְּרוּ אֵלֶיךָ לֵאמֹר אָבִיךָ הִכְבִּיד אֶת־עֻלֵּנוּ
יא וְאַתָּה הָקֵל מֵעָלֵינוּ כֹּה תֹּאמַר אֲלֵהֶם קָטָנִּי עָבָה מִמָּתְנֵי אָבִי: וְעַתָּה
אָבִי הֶעְמִיס עֲלֵיכֶם עֹל כָּבֵד וַאֲנִי אֹסִיף עַל־עֻלְּכֶם אָבִי יִסַּר אֶתְכֶם
יב בַּשּׁוֹטִים וַאֲנִי בָּעַקְרַבִּים: וַיָּבֹא יָרָבְעָם וְכָל־הָעָם אֶל־
רְחַבְעָם בַּיּוֹם הַשְּׁלִשִׁי כַּאֲשֶׁר דִּבֶּר הַמֶּלֶךְ לֵאמֹר שׁוּבוּ אֵלַי בַּיּוֹם
יג הַשְּׁלִשִׁי: וַיַּעֲנֵם הַמֶּלֶךְ קָשָׁה וַיַּעֲזֹב הַמֶּלֶךְ רְחַבְעָם אֵת עֲצַת הַזְּקֵנִים:
יד וַיְדַבֵּר אֲלֵהֶם כַּעֲצַת הַיְלָדִים לֵאמֹר אַכְבִּיד אֶת־עֻלְּכֶם וַאֲנִי אֹסִיף
טו עָלָיו אָבִי יִסַּר אֶתְכֶם בַּשּׁוֹטִים וַאֲנִי בָּעַקְרַבִּים: וְלֹא־שָׁמַע הַמֶּלֶךְ
אֶל־הָעָם כִּי־הָיְתָה נְסִבָּה מֵעִם הָאֱלֹהִים לְמַעַן הָקִים יְהוָה אֶת־דְּבָרוֹ
טז אֲשֶׁר דִּבֶּר בְּיַד אֲחִיָּהוּ הַשִּׁלוֹנִי אֶל־יָרָבְעָם בֶּן־נְבָט: וְכָל־יִשְׂרָאֵל כִּי
לֹא־שָׁמַע הַמֶּלֶךְ לָהֶם וַיָּשִׁיבוּ הָעָם ׀ אֶת־הַמֶּלֶךְ ׀ לֵאמֹר מַה־לָּנוּ
חֵלֶק בְּדָוִיד וְלֹא־נַחֲלָה בְּבֶן־יִשַׁי אִישׁ לְאֹהָלֶיךָ יִשְׂרָאֵל עַתָּה רְאֵה
יז בֵיתְךָ דָּוִיד וַיֵּלֶךְ כָּל־יִשְׂרָאֵל לְאֹהָלָיו: וּבְנֵי יִשְׂרָאֵל הַיֹּשְׁבִים
יח בְּעָרֵי יְהוּדָה וַיִּמְלֹךְ עֲלֵיהֶם רְחַבְעָם: וַיִּשְׁלַח הַמֶּלֶךְ רְחַבְעָם אֶת־
הֲדֹרָם אֲשֶׁר עַל־הַמַּס וַיִּרְגְּמוּ־בוֹ בְנֵי־יִשְׂרָאֵל אֶבֶן וַיָּמֹת וְהַמֶּלֶךְ
יט רְחַבְעָם הִתְאַמֵּץ לַעֲלוֹת בַּמֶּרְכָּבָה לָנוּס יְרוּשָׁלִָם: וַיִּפְשְׁעוּ
יא א יִשְׂרָאֵל בְּבֵית דָּוִיד עַד הַיּוֹם הַזֶּה: וַיָּבֹא
רְחַבְעָם יְרוּשָׁלִַם וַיַּקְהֵל אֶת־בֵּית יְהוּדָה וּבִנְיָמִן מֵאָה וּשְׁמוֹנִים אֶלֶף
בָּחוּר עֹשֵׂה מִלְחָמָה לְהִלָּחֵם עִם־יִשְׂרָאֵל לְהָשִׁיב אֶת־הַמַּמְלָכָה
ב לִרְחַבְעָם: וַיְהִי דְּבַר־יְהוָה אֶל־שְׁמַעְיָהוּ אִישׁ־הָאֱלֹהִים
ג לֵאמֹר: אֱמֹר אֶל־רְחַבְעָם בֶּן־שְׁלֹמֹה מֶלֶךְ יְהוּדָה וְאֶל כָּל־יִשְׂרָאֵל
ד בִּיהוּדָה וּבִנְיָמִן לֵאמֹר: כֹּה אָמַר יְהוָה לֹא־תַעֲלוּ וְלֹא־תִלָּחֲמוּ עִם־

And they heeded the Lord's word and turned back from the campaign
5 against Yorovam. Reḥavam settled in Jerusalem and built fortified
6, 7 cities in Yehuda. He built up Beit Leḥem, Eitam, Tekoa, Beit Tzur, Sokho,
8, 9, 10 Adulam, Gat, Maresha, Zif, Adorayim, Lakhish, Azeka, Tzora, Ayalon,
11 and Ḥevron, which are in Yehuda and in Binyamin, as fortified towns. He
reinforced the fortresses and stationed commanders in them along with stores
12 of food, oil, and wine, and he supplied every city with shields and spears; by
greatly increasing their strength, he maintained control of Yehuda and
13 Binyamin. From all over Israel, the priests and the Levites left their
14 own borders and presented themselves to him; the Levites left their land and
their holdings and went to Yehuda and Jerusalem because Yorovam and his
15 sons prevented them from ministering to the Lord – he appointed his own
16 priests for the shrines and idols and for the calves that he had made – and they
were followed by all those of the tribes of Israel whose hearts were devoted
to seeking the Lord, God of Israel; they came to Jerusalem to offer sacrifice
17 to the Lord, the God of their ancestors. They strengthened the Judahite
kingship and supported Reḥavam son of Shlomo for three years, because for
18 three years they followed in David and Shlomo's path. Reḥavam
married Maḥalat, the daughter of Yerimot son of David, and of Aviḥayil the
19 daughter of Eliav son of Yishai. She bore him sons: Yeush, Shemarya, and
20 Zaham. After her, he married Maakha, daughter of Avshalom, and she bore
21 him Aviya, Atai, Ziza, and Shlomit. Out of all his wives and concubines,
Reḥavam loved Maakha, Avshalom's daughter, the most – he married eighteen
wives and sixty concubines and fathered twenty-eight sons and sixty
22 daughters – and Reḥavam designated Aviya son of Maakha as head and prince
23 over his brothers, for he intended to make him king. He strategically
positioned his sons in all the fortified cities throughout the regions of Yehuda
and Binyamin, provided them with ample food, and secured many wives for
12 1 them. As Reḥavam's kingdom grew stronger and more established, he
2 abandoned the teachings of the Lord, he and all Israel with him. In
the fifth year of Reḥavam's reign, because they broke faith with the Lord,
3 King Shishak of Egypt launched an attack on Jerusalem with 1,200 chariots,
60,000 riders, and countless troops that came with him from Egypt – Libyans,
4 Sukkites, and Kushites. He captured Yehuda's fortified cities and invaded as
5 far as Jerusalem. The prophet Shemaya came to Reḥavam and the
officers of Yehuda, who had assembled at Jerusalem because of Shishak, and
said to them, "Thus says the Lord: You abandoned Me, so I, too, have
6 abandoned you to the hands of Shishak." The officers of Israel and the king

אֲחֵיכֶם שׁוּבוּ אִישׁ לְבֵיתוֹ כִּי מֵאִתִּי נִהְיָה הַדָּבָר הַזֶּה וַיִּשְׁמְעוּ אֶת־
ה דִּבְרֵי יְהוָה וַיָּשֻׁבוּ מִלֶּכֶת אֶל־יָרָבְעָם: וַיֵּשֶׁב רְחַבְעָם
ו בִּירוּשָׁלָם וַיִּבֶן עָרִים לְמָצוֹר בִּיהוּדָה: וַיִּבֶן אֶת־בֵּית־לֶחֶם וְאֶת־עֵיטָם
ז ח וְאֶת־תְּקוֹעַ: וְאֶת־בֵּית־צוּר וְאֶת־שׂוֹכוֹ וְאֶת־עֲדֻלָּם: וְאֶת־גַּת וְאֶת־
ט י מָרֵשָׁה וְאֶת־זִיף: וְאֶת־אֲדוֹרַיִם וְאֶת־לָכִישׁ וְאֶת־עֲזֵקָה: וְאֶת־צָרְעָה
יא וְאֶת־אַיָּלוֹן וְאֶת־חֶבְרוֹן אֲשֶׁר בִּיהוּדָה וּבְבִנְיָמִן עָרֵי מְצֻרוֹת: וַיְחַזֵּק
יב אֶת־הַמְּצֻרוֹת וַיִּתֵּן בָּהֶם נְגִידִים וְאֹצְרוֹת מַאֲכָל וְשֶׁמֶן וָיָיִן: וּבְכָל־
עִיר וָעִיר צִנּוֹת וּרְמָחִים וַיְחַזְּקֵם לְהַרְבֵּה מְאֹד וַיְהִי־לוֹ יְהוּדָה
יג וּבִנְיָמִן: וְהַכֹּהֲנִים וְהַלְוִיִּם אֲשֶׁר בְּכָל־יִשְׂרָאֵל הִתְיַצְּבוּ
יד עָלָיו מִכָּל־גְּבוּלָם: כִּי־עָזְבוּ הַלְוִיִּם אֶת־מִגְרְשֵׁיהֶם וַאֲחֻזָּתָם וַיֵּלְכוּ
טו לִיהוּדָה וְלִירוּשָׁלָם כִּי־הִזְנִיחָם יָרָבְעָם וּבָנָיו מִכַּהֵן לַיהוָה: וַיַּעֲמֶד־לוֹ
טז כֹּהֲנִים לַבָּמוֹת וְלַשְּׂעִירִים וְלָעֲגָלִים אֲשֶׁר עָשָׂה: וְאַחֲרֵיהֶם מִכֹּל שִׁבְטֵי
יִשְׂרָאֵל הַנֹּתְנִים אֶת־לְבָבָם לְבַקֵּשׁ אֶת־יְהוָה אֱלֹהֵי יִשְׂרָאֵל בָּאוּ
יז יְרוּשָׁלַם לִזְבּוֹחַ לַיהוָה אֱלֹהֵי אֲבוֹתֵיהֶם: וַיְחַזְּקוּ אֶת־מַלְכוּת יְהוּדָה
וַיְאַמְּצוּ אֶת־רְחַבְעָם בֶּן־שְׁלֹמֹה לְשָׁנִים שָׁלוֹשׁ כִּי הָלְכוּ בְּדֶרֶךְ דָּוִיד
יח וּשְׁלֹמֹה לְשָׁנִים שָׁלוֹשׁ: וַיִּקַּח־לוֹ רְחַבְעָם אִשָּׁה אֶת־מָחֲלַת
יט בֶּן־יְרִימוֹת בֶּן־דָּוִיד אֲבִיהַיִל בַּת־אֱלִיאָב בֶּן־יִשָׁי: וַתֵּלֶד לוֹ בָּנִים בַּת־
כ אֶת־יְעוּשׁ וְאֶת־שְׁמַרְיָה וְאֶת־זָהַם: וְאַחֲרֶיהָ לָקַח אֶת־מַעֲכָה בַּת־
אַבְשָׁלוֹם וַתֵּלֶד לוֹ אֶת־אֲבִיָּה וְאֶת־עַתַּי וְאֶת־זִיזָא וְאֶת־שְׁלֹמִית:
כא וַיֶּאֱהַב רְחַבְעָם אֶת־מַעֲכָה בַת־אַבְשָׁלוֹם מִכָּל־נָשָׁיו וּפִילַגְשָׁיו כִּי
נָשִׁים שְׁמוֹנֶה־עֶשְׂרֵה נָשָׂא וּפִילַגְשִׁים שִׁשִּׁים וַיּוֹלֶד עֶשְׂרִים וּשְׁמוֹנָה
כב בָּנִים וְשִׁשִּׁים בָּנוֹת: וַיַּעֲמֵד לָרֹאשׁ רְחַבְעָם אֶת־אֲבִיָּה בֶן־מַעֲכָה
כג לְנָגִיד בְּאֶחָיו כִּי לְהַמְלִיכוֹ: וַיָּבֶן וַיִּפְרֹץ מִכָּל־בָּנָיו לְכָל־אַרְצוֹת יְהוּדָה
וּבִנְיָמִן לְכֹל עָרֵי הַמְּצֻרוֹת וַיִּתֵּן לָהֶם הַמָּזוֹן לָרֹב וַיִּשְׁאַל הֲמוֹן נָשִׁים:
יב א וַיְהִי כְּהָכִין מַלְכוּת רְחַבְעָם וּכְחֶזְקָתוֹ עָזַב אֶת־תּוֹרַת יְהוָה וְכָל־
ב יִשְׂרָאֵל עִמּוֹ: וַיְהִי בַּשָּׁנָה הַחֲמִישִׁית לַמֶּלֶךְ רְחַבְעָם עָלָה
ג שִׁישַׁק מֶלֶךְ־מִצְרַיִם עַל־יְרוּשָׁלָם כִּי מָעֲלוּ בַּיהוָה: בְּאֶלֶף וּמָאתַיִם
רֶכֶב וּבְשִׁשִּׁים אֶלֶף פָּרָשִׁים וְאֵין מִסְפָּר לָעָם אֲשֶׁר־בָּאוּ עִמּוֹ מִמִּצְרַיִם
ד לוּבִים סֻכִּיִּים וְכוּשִׁים: וַיִּלְכֹּד אֶת־עָרֵי הַמְּצֻרוֹת אֲשֶׁר לִיהוּדָה וַיָּבֹא
ה עַד־יְרוּשָׁלָם: וּשְׁמַעְיָה הַנָּבִיא בָּא אֶל־רְחַבְעָם וְשָׂרֵי יְהוּדָה
אֲשֶׁר־נֶאֶסְפוּ אֶל־יְרוּשָׁלַם מִפְּנֵי שִׁישָׁק וַיֹּאמֶר לָהֶם כֹּה־אָמַר יְהוָה
ו אַתֶּם עֲזַבְתֶּם אֹתִי וְאַף־אֲנִי עָזַבְתִּי אֶתְכֶם בְּיַד־שִׁישָׁק: וַיִּכָּנְעוּ שָׂרֵי־

7 humbled themselves and declared, "The Lord is right." When the Lord saw
that they had humbled themselves, the word of the Lord came to Shemaya:
"They have humbled themselves; I will not destroy them. I will grant them
some measure of deliverance, and My fury will not be poured out on
8 Jerusalem through Shishak. But they will become subjects to him so that they
will know the difference between service to Me and service to kingdoms of
9 other lands." King Shishak of Egypt attacked Jerusalem, and he
seized the treasures of the House of the Lord and the treasures of the royal
palace; he seized everything. He even seized the golden shields that Shlomo
10 had made. King Reḥavam had bronze shields made in their place and
entrusted them to the chief sentry who guarded the entrance of the palace.
11 Whenever the king went to the House of the Lord, the sentry would come
12 and carry them and then return them to the sentry armory. Once he had
humbled himself, the Lord's wrath subsided, and He did not inflict complete
13 destruction; some goodness was found in Yehuda. King Reḥavam
established a strong reign in Jerusalem. He was forty-one years old when he
became king, and for seventeen years he reigned in Jerusalem – the city where
the Lord had chosen to establish His name out of all the tribes of Israel. His
14 mother's name was Naama the Amonite. And he did what was evil, for he did
15 not set his heart on seeking out the Lord. The rest of Reḥavam's
history, earlier and later, is recorded in the chronicles of the prophet Shemaya
and of the seer Ido, in charge of genealogy. There was ongoing war between
16 Reḥavam and Yorovam. And Reḥavam slept with his ancestors, and he was
13 1 buried in the City of David. And his son Aviya reigned in his place. In
2 the eighteenth year of King Yorovam, Aviya became king over Yehuda. For
three years he reigned in Jerusalem, and his mother's name was Mikhayahu,
the daughter of Uriel of Giva. War continued between Aviya and Yorovam.
3 Aviya went out to battle with a military force of 400,000 elite
fighters while Yorovam drew up his battle lines against him with a
4 force of 800,000 elite warriors. Then Aviya stood up on the top of
Mount Tzemarayim, which is in the hill country of Efrayim. "Listen to me,
5 Yorovam and all of Israel," he said. "You certainly know that the Lord, God
of Israel, gave kingship over Israel to David forever, to him and his sons as a
6 covenant of salt. Yet Yorovam son of Nevat, Shlomo's servant, rose up and
7 rebelled against his master. And worthless, depraved men gathered about him
and defied Reḥavam son of Shlomo; Reḥavam was young and soft-willed,
8 and he could not withstand them. And now, you believe you are able to
withstand the kingdom of the Lord in the charge of David's descendants
because you are a vast multitude and because you have golden calves that
9 Yorovam made for you as gods? Have you not rejected the Lord's priests – the
sons of Aharon and the Levites? Like the peoples of other lands, you made
your own priests – whoever shows up for ordination with a young bull or

ז יִשְׂרָאֵל וְהַמֶּלֶךְ וַיֹּאמְרוּ צַדִּיק ׀ יְהוָה׃ וּבִרְאוֹת יְהוָה כִּי נִכְנָעוּ הָיָה
דְבַר־יְהוָה אֶל־שְׁמַעְיָה ׀ לֵאמֹר נִכְנְעוּ לֹא אַשְׁחִיתֵם וְנָתַתִּי לָהֶם
ח כִּמְעַט לִפְלֵיטָה וְלֹא־תִתַּךְ חֲמָתִי בִּירוּשָׁלִַם בְּיַד־שִׁישָׁק׃ כִּי יִהְיוּ־לוֹ
ט לַעֲבָדִים וְיֵדְעוּ עֲבוֹדָתִי וַעֲבוֹדַת מַמְלְכוֹת הָאֲרָצוֹת׃ וַיַּעַל
שִׁישַׁק מֶלֶךְ־מִצְרַיִם עַל־יְרוּשָׁלִַם וַיִּקַּח אֶת־אֹצְרוֹת בֵּית־יְהוָה וְאֶת־
אֹצְרוֹת בֵּית הַמֶּלֶךְ אֶת־הַכֹּל לָקָח וַיִּקַּח אֶת־מָגִנֵּי הַזָּהָב אֲשֶׁר עָשָׂה
י שְׁלֹמֹה׃ וַיַּעַשׂ הַמֶּלֶךְ רְחַבְעָם תַּחְתֵּיהֶם מָגִנֵּי נְחֹשֶׁת וְהִפְקִיד עַל־יַד
יא שָׂרֵי הָרָצִים הַשֹּׁמְרִים פֶּתַח בֵּית הַמֶּלֶךְ׃ וַיְהִי מִדֵּי־בוֹא הַמֶּלֶךְ בֵּית
טז יב יְהוָה בָּאוּ הָרָצִים וּנְשָׂאוּם וֶהֱשִׁבוּם אֶל־תָּא הָרָצִים׃ וּבְהִכָּנְעוֹ שָׁב
מִמֶּנּוּ אַף־יְהוָה וְלֹא לְהַשְׁחִית לְכָלָה וְגַם בִּיהוּדָה הָיָה דְּבָרִים
יג טוֹבִים׃ וַיִּתְחַזֵּק הַמֶּלֶךְ רְחַבְעָם בִּירוּשָׁלִַם וַיִּמְלֹךְ כִּי בֶן־
אַרְבָּעִים וְאַחַת שָׁנָה רְחַבְעָם בְּמָלְכוֹ וּשְׁבַע עֶשְׂרֵה שָׁנָה ׀ מָלַךְ
בִּירוּשָׁלִַם הָעִיר אֲשֶׁר־בָּחַר יְהוָה לָשׂוּם אֶת־שְׁמוֹ שָׁם מִכֹּל שִׁבְטֵי
יד יִשְׂרָאֵל וְשֵׁם אִמּוֹ נַעֲמָה הָעַמֹּנִית׃ וַיַּעַשׂ הָרָע כִּי לֹא הֵכִין לִבּוֹ לִדְרוֹשׁ
טו אֶת־יְהוָה׃ וְדִבְרֵי רְחַבְעָם הָרִאשֹׁנִים וְהָאַחֲרוֹנִים הֲלֹא־הֵם
כְּתוּבִים בְּדִבְרֵי שְׁמַעְיָה הַנָּבִיא וְעִדּוֹ הַחֹזֶה לְהִתְיַחֵשׂ וּמִלְחֲמוֹת
טז רְחַבְעָם וְיָרָבְעָם כָּל־הַיָּמִים׃ וַיִּשְׁכַּב רְחַבְעָם עִם־אֲבֹתָיו וַיִּקָּבֵר בְּעִיר
יג א דָּוִיד וַיִּמְלֹךְ אֲבִיָּה בְנוֹ תַּחְתָּיו׃ בִּשְׁנַת שְׁמוֹנֶה עֶשְׂרֵה
ב לַמֶּלֶךְ יָרָבְעָם וַיִּמְלֹךְ אֲבִיָּה עַל־יְהוּדָה׃ שָׁלוֹשׁ שָׁנִים מָלַךְ בִּירוּשָׁלִַם
וְשֵׁם אִמּוֹ מִיכָיָהוּ בַת־אוּרִיאֵל מִן־גִּבְעָה וּמִלְחָמָה הָיְתָה בֵּין אֲבִיָּה
ג וּבֵין יָרָבְעָם׃ וַיֶּאְסֹר אֲבִיָּה אֶת־הַמִּלְחָמָה בְּחַיִל גִּבּוֹרֵי מִלְחָמָה אַרְבַּע־
מֵאוֹת אֶלֶף אִישׁ בָּחוּר וְיָרָבְעָם עָרַךְ עִמּוֹ מִלְחָמָה בִּשְׁמוֹנֶה
ד מֵאוֹת אֶלֶף אִישׁ בָּחוּר גִּבּוֹר חָיִל׃ וַיָּקָם אֲבִיָּה מֵעַל לְהַר
ה צְמָרַיִם אֲשֶׁר בְּהַר אֶפְרָיִם וַיֹּאמֶר שְׁמָעוּנִי יָרָבְעָם וְכָל־יִשְׂרָאֵל׃ הֲלֹא
לָכֶם לָדַעַת כִּי יְהוָה ׀ אֱלֹהֵי יִשְׂרָאֵל נָתַן מַמְלָכָה לְדָוִיד עַל־יִשְׂרָאֵל
ו לְעוֹלָם לוֹ וּלְבָנָיו בְּרִית מֶלַח׃ וַיָּקָם יָרָבְעָם בֶּן־נְבָט עֶבֶד שְׁלֹמֹה בֶן־
ז דָּוִיד וַיִּמְרֹד עַל־אֲדֹנָיו׃ וַיִּקָּבְצוּ עָלָיו אֲנָשִׁים רֵקִים בְּנֵי בְלִיַּעַל וַיִּתְאַמְּצוּ
עַל־רְחַבְעָם בֶּן־שְׁלֹמֹה וּרְחַבְעָם הָיָה נַעַר וְרַךְ־לֵבָב וְלֹא הִתְחַזַּק
ח לִפְנֵיהֶם׃ וְעַתָּה ׀ אַתֶּם אֹמְרִים לְהִתְחַזֵּק לִפְנֵי מַמְלֶכֶת יְהוָה בְּיַד בְּנֵי
דָוִיד וְאַתֶּם הָמוֹן רָב וְעִמָּכֶם עֶגְלֵי זָהָב אֲשֶׁר עָשָׂה לָכֶם יָרָבְעָם
ט לֵאלֹהִים׃ הֲלֹא הִדַּחְתֶּם אֶת־כֹּהֲנֵי יְהוָה אֶת־בְּנֵי אַהֲרֹן וְהַלְוִיִּם וַתַּעֲשׂוּ
לָכֶם כֹּהֲנִים כְּעַמֵּי הָאֲרָצוֹת כָּל־הַבָּא לְמַלֵּא יָדוֹ בְּפַר בֶּן־בָּקָר וְאֵילִם

10 seven rams becomes a priest of non-gods. As for us – the LORD is our God,
and we have not abandoned Him; the priests ministering to the LORD are the
11 sons of Aharon, and the Levites are performing their service. They offer
sacrifices to the LORD – burnt offerings every morning and evening and
fragrant incense; they set rows of bread on the pure table; they light the
golden candelabrum with its lamps every evening, for we keep the charge of
12 the LORD our God while you have abandoned Him. Here, now, at our head
are God and His priests with their battle trumpets to sound the battle cry
against you! Do not fight with the LORD, the God of your ancestors, for you
13 cannot succeed!" Meanwhile, Yorovam had led the ambush around to attack
them from behind, so his men were in front of Yehuda, and his ambush was
14 behind them. When Yehuda turned around, battle suddenly raged before
them and behind them, and they cried out to the LORD as the priests blasted
15 the trumpets. The men of Yehuda raised the battle shout, and as they shouted
16 out, God defeated Yorovam and all of Israel before Aviya and Yehuda. The
17 Israelites fled before Yehuda, and God delivered them into their hands. Aviya
and his men dealt them a deadly blow, and 500,000 of Israel's elite warriors
18 fell slain. Thus Israel was defeated at that time while the Judahites grew strong
19 because they relied on the LORD, God of their ancestors. Aviya pursued
Yorovam and seized towns from him: Beit El with its villages, Yeshana with
20 its villages, and Efrayin with its villages. Yorovam never regained his power
21 in Aviyahu's time; the LORD struck him down, and he died. But
Aviyahu grew in strength; he married fourteen wives and fathered twenty-two
22 sons and sixteen daughters. The rest of Aviya's history, his ways and words,
23 are recorded in the tales of the prophet Ido. And Aviya slept with his ancestors
and was buried in the City of David, and his son Asa reigned in his place. In
14 1 his time, the land saw peace for ten years. Asa did what was good
2 and right in the eyes of the LORD his God. He removed the foreign altars and
3 the shrines; he razed the worship pillars and cut down the sacred trees.[29] And
he commanded Yehuda to seek the LORD, God of their ancestors, and to keep
4 the Torah and commandments. He removed the shrines and the sun altars
5 from all the towns of Yehuda, and the kingdom saw peace under his rule. He
built fortified cities in Yehuda, for the land was peaceful; there were no wars
6 during these years, for the LORD had granted him rest. He said to Yehuda,
"Let us build these cities and surround them with walls and towers, with gates
and bars. The land still stretches out before us, for we have sought the LORD
our God; we sought Him, and He granted us rest all around." So they built
7 and they flourished. Asa had an army of 300,000 from Yehuda,
armed with buckler and spear, and 280,000 from Binyamin, armed with shield
8 and bow; all these were powerful warriors. Zeraḥ the Kushite marched out

29 | Hebrew "*asherim*": trees, wooden posts, or images representing the Canaanite fertility goddess Ashera.

י שִׁבְעָה וְהָיָה כֹהֵן לְלֹא אֱלֹהִים: וַאֲנַחְנוּ יְהוָה אֱלֹהֵינוּ וְלֹא עֲזַבְנֻהוּ
יא וְכֹהֲנִים מְשָׁרְתִים לַיהוָה בְּנֵי אַהֲרֹן וְהַלְוִיִּם בַּמְלָאכֶת: וּמַקְטִרִים
לַיהוָה עֹלוֹת בַּבֹּקֶר־בַּבֹּקֶר וּבָעֶרֶב־בָּעֶרֶב וּקְטֹרֶת־סַמִּים וּמַעֲרֶכֶת
לֶחֶם עַל־הַשֻּׁלְחָן הַטָּהוֹר וּמְנוֹרַת הַזָּהָב וְנֵרֹתֶיהָ לְבָעֵר בָּעֶרֶב בָּעֶרֶב
כִּי־שֹׁמְרִים אֲנַחְנוּ אֶת־מִשְׁמֶרֶת יְהוָה אֱלֹהֵינוּ וְאַתֶּם עֲזַבְתֶּם אֹתוֹ:
יב וְהִנֵּה עִמָּנוּ בָרֹאשׁ הָאֱלֹהִים ׀ וְכֹהֲנָיו וַחֲצֹצְרוֹת הַתְּרוּעָה לְהָרִיעַ
עֲלֵיכֶם בְּנֵי יִשְׂרָאֵל אַל־תִּלָּחֲמוּ עִם־יְהוָה אֱלֹהֵי־אֲבֹתֵיכֶם כִּי־לֹא
יג תַצְלִיחוּ: וְיָרָבְעָם הֵסֵב אֶת־הַמַּאְרָב לָבוֹא מֵאַחֲרֵיהֶם וַיִּהְיוּ לִפְנֵי
יד יְהוּדָה וְהַמַּאְרָב מֵאַחֲרֵיהֶם: וַיִּפְנוּ יְהוּדָה וְהִנֵּה לָהֶם הַמִּלְחָמָה פָּנִים
טו וְאָחוֹר וַיִּצְעֲקוּ לַיהוָה וְהַכֹּהֲנִים מחצצרים בַּחֲצֹצְרוֹת: וַיָּרִיעוּ אִישׁ מַחְצְרִים
יְהוּדָה וַיְהִי בְּהָרִיעַ אִישׁ יְהוּדָה וְהָאֱלֹהִים נָגַף אֶת־יָרָבְעָם וְכָל־
טז יִשְׂרָאֵל לִפְנֵי אֲבִיָּה וִיהוּדָה: וַיָּנוּסוּ בְנֵי־יִשְׂרָאֵל מִפְּנֵי יְהוּדָה וַיִּתְּנֵם
יז אֱלֹהִים בְּיָדָם: וַיַּכּוּ בָהֶם אֲבִיָּה וְעַמּוֹ מַכָּה רַבָּה וַיִּפְּלוּ חֲלָלִים מִיִּשְׂרָאֵל
יח חֲמֵשׁ־מֵאוֹת אֶלֶף אִישׁ בָּחוּר: וַיִּכָּנְעוּ בְנֵי־יִשְׂרָאֵל בָּעֵת הַהִיא וַיֶּאֶמְצוּ
יט בְּנֵי יְהוּדָה כִּי נִשְׁעֲנוּ עַל־יְהוָה אֱלֹהֵי אֲבוֹתֵיהֶם: וַיִּרְדֹּף אֲבִיָּה אַחֲרֵי
יָרָבְעָם וַיִּלְכֹּד מִמֶּנּוּ עָרִים אֶת־בֵּית־אֵל וְאֶת־בְּנוֹתֶיהָ וְאֶת־יְשָׁנָה
כ וְאֶת־בְּנוֹתֶיהָ וְאֶת־עפרין וּבְנֹתֶיהָ: וְלֹא־עָצַר כֹּחַ־יָרָבְעָם עוֹד בִּימֵי עֶפְרָיִן
כא אֲבִיָּהוּ וַיִּגְּפֵהוּ יְהוָה וַיָּמֹת: וַיִּתְחַזֵּק אֲבִיָּהוּ וַיִּשָּׂא־לוֹ נָשִׁים
כב אַרְבַּע עֶשְׂרֵה וַיּוֹלֶד עֶשְׂרִים וּשְׁנַיִם בָּנִים וְשֵׁשׁ עֶשְׂרֵה בָּנוֹת: וְיֶתֶר
כג דִּבְרֵי אֲבִיָּה וּדְרָכָיו וּדְבָרָיו כְּתוּבִים בְּמִדְרַשׁ הַנָּבִיא עִדּוֹ: וַיִּשְׁכַּב
אֲבִיָּה עִם־אֲבֹתָיו וַיִּקְבְּרוּ אֹתוֹ בְּעִיר דָּוִיד וַיִּמְלֹךְ אָסָא בְנוֹ תַּחְתָּיו
יד א בְּיָמָיו שָׁקְטָה הָאָרֶץ עֶשֶׂר שָׁנִים: וַיַּעַשׂ אָסָא הַטּוֹב וְהַיָּשָׁר
ב בְּעֵינֵי יְהוָה אֱלֹהָיו: וַיָּסַר אֶת־מִזְבְּחוֹת הַנֵּכָר וְהַבָּמוֹת וַיְשַׁבֵּר אֶת־
ג הַמַּצֵּבוֹת וַיְגַדַּע אֶת־הָאֲשֵׁרִים: וַיֹּאמֶר לִיהוּדָה לִדְרוֹשׁ אֶת־יְהוָה
ד אֱלֹהֵי אֲבוֹתֵיהֶם וְלַעֲשׂוֹת הַתּוֹרָה וְהַמִּצְוָה: וַיָּסַר מִכָּל־עָרֵי יְהוּדָה
ה אֶת־הַבָּמוֹת וְאֶת־הַחַמָּנִים וַתִּשְׁקֹט הַמַּמְלָכָה לְפָנָיו: וַיִּבֶן עָרֵי מְצוּרָה
בִּיהוּדָה כִּי־שָׁקְטָה הָאָרֶץ וְאֵין־עִמּוֹ מִלְחָמָה בַּשָּׁנִים הָאֵלֶּה כִּי־הֵנִיחַ
ו יְהוָה לוֹ: וַיֹּאמֶר לִיהוּדָה נִבְנֶה ׀ אֶת־הֶעָרִים הָאֵלֶּה וְנָסֵב חוֹמָה
וּמִגְדָּלִים דְּלָתַיִם וּבְרִיחִים עוֹדֶנּוּ הָאָרֶץ לְפָנֵינוּ כִּי דָרַשְׁנוּ אֶת־יְהוָה
ז אֱלֹהֵינוּ דָּרַשְׁנוּ וַיָּנַח לָנוּ מִסָּבִיב וַיִּבְנוּ וַיַּצְלִיחוּ: וַיְהִי לְאָסָא
חַיִל נֹשֵׂא צִנָּה וָרֹמַח מִיהוּדָה שְׁלֹשׁ מֵאוֹת אֶלֶף וּמִבִּנְיָמִן נֹשְׂאֵי מָגֵן
ח וְדֹרְכֵי קֶשֶׁת מָאתַיִם וּשְׁמוֹנִים אֶלֶף כָּל־אֵלֶּה גִּבּוֹרֵי חָיִל: וַיֵּצֵא אֲלֵיהֶם

against them with an army of a million men and three hundred chariots, and
9 they came as far as Maresha. Asa marched out before him, and they drew up
10 their battle lines in the Valley of Tzefat at Maresha. Then Asa called out to the
Lord his God. "O Lord," he said, "to You there is no difference between
helping the powerful and the powerless. Help us, O Lord our God, for upon
You we rely, and in Your name we confront this multitude. O Lord, You are
11 our God; let no mortal prevail against You." And the Lord defeated
12 the Kushites before Asa and Yehuda, and the Kushites fled. Asa and his men
pursued them as far as Gerar, and the Kushites fell until none were left alive,
for they had been broken before the Lord and His army. The men of
13 Yehuda carried off masses of spoil; they ravaged all the towns around
Gerar – which had been seized with terror of the Lord – and they plundered
14 all the towns, for they were full of goods. They also ravaged livestock
enclosures and captured flocks of sheep and camels. Then they returned to
15 1 Jerusalem. The spirit of God came upon Azaryahu son of Oded. He
2 approached Asa and said to him, "Listen to me, Asa, and all Yehuda and
Binyamin: The Lord is with you so long as you are with Him; if you seek
Him, He will be there for you, but if you abandon Him, He will abandon
3 you. For a long time, Israel has been without a true God, without
4 guiding priests, without Torah, but in their distress they came back to the
5 Lord, God of Israel – they sought Him, and He was there for them. In those
times, traveling back and forth was not safe, for great turmoil stirred all the
6 people of the lands. Nation was crushed by nation, city by city, for God
7 frenzied them with a torrent of troubles. Now take courage, and do not let
8 your hands go limp – for your work shall be rewarded." When Asa
heard these words, the prophecy of the prophet Oded, he took courage. He
purged the abominations from all the land of Yehuda and Binyamin and the
towns he had taken over in the hill country of Efrayim, and he repaired the
9 Altar of the Lord in front of the Hall of the Lord. He gathered all of Yehuda
and Binyamin and those that lived among them from Efrayim, Menashe, and
Shimon, for there had been a mass immigration of Israelites when they saw
10 that the Lord his God was with him. They gathered in Jerusalem
11 in the third month in the fifteenth year of Asa's reign and offered sacrifices to
the Lord on that day from the spoil they had brought: seven hundred oxen
12 and seven thousand sheep. And they entered into a covenant to seek the
Lord, the God of their ancestors, with all their hearts and all their souls.
13 Whoever would not seek the Lord, God of Israel, would be put to death,
14 whether young or old, man or woman. They pronounced this oath to the
Lord in a loud voice, with shouting out, blasting the trumpets and rams'
15 horns. And all of Yehuda rejoiced over the oath, for they had sworn it with all
their hearts and sought Him with all their desire. And He was there for them,
16 and the Lord granted them rest on every side. King Asa even deposed his
mother Maakha from the position of queen mother because she had made a

זֶרַח הַכּוּשִׁי בְּחַיִל אֶלֶף אֲלָפִים וּמַרְכָּבוֹת שְׁלֹשׁ מֵאוֹת וַיָּבֹא עַד־
ט מָרֵשָׁה: וַיֵּצֵא אָסָא לְפָנָיו וַיַּעַרְכוּ מִלְחָמָה בְּגֵיא צְפַתָה לְמָרֵשָׁה:
י וַיִּקְרָא אָסָא אֶל־יהוה אֱלֹהָיו וַיֹּאמַר יהוה אֵין־עִמְּךָ לַעְזוֹר בֵּין רַב
לְאֵין כֹּחַ עָזְרֵנוּ יהוה אֱלֹהֵינוּ כִּי־עָלֶיךָ נִשְׁעַנּוּ וּבְשִׁמְךָ בָאנוּ עַל־הֶהָמוֹן
יא הַזֶּה יהוה אֱלֹהֵינוּ אַתָּה אַל־יַעְצֹר עִמְּךָ אֱנוֹשׁ: וַיִּגֹּף יהוה
יב אֶת־הַכּוּשִׁים לִפְנֵי אָסָא וְלִפְנֵי יְהוּדָה וַיָּנֻסוּ הַכֻּשִׁים: וַיִּרְדְּפֵם אָסָא
וְהָעָם אֲשֶׁר־עִמּוֹ עַד־לִגְרָר וַיִּפֹּל מִכּוּשִׁים לְאֵין לָהֶם מִחְיָה כִּי־נִשְׁבְּרוּ
יג לִפְנֵי־יהוה וְלִפְנֵי מַחֲנֵהוּ וַיִּשְׂאוּ שָׁלָל הַרְבֵּה מְאֹד: וַיַּכּוּ אֵת כָּל־הֶעָרִים
סְבִיבוֹת גְּרָר כִּי־הָיָה פַחַד־יהוה עֲלֵיהֶם וַיָּבֹזּוּ אֶת־כָּל־הֶעָרִים כִּי־בִזָּה
יד רַבָּה הָיְתָה בָהֶם: וְגַם־אָהֳלֵי מִקְנֶה הִכּוּ וַיִּשְׁבּוּ צֹאן לָרֹב וּגְמַלִּים
טו א וַיָּשֻׁבוּ יְרוּשָׁלָ͏ִם: וַעֲזַרְיָהוּ בֶּן־עוֹדֵד הָיְתָה עָלָיו רוּחַ
ב אֱלֹהִים: וַיֵּצֵא לִפְנֵי אָסָא וַיֹּאמֶר לוֹ שְׁמָעוּנִי אָסָא וְכָל־יְהוּדָה וּבִנְיָמִן
יהוה עִמָּכֶם בִּהְיוֹתְכֶם עִמּוֹ וְאִם־תִּדְרְשֻׁהוּ יִמָּצֵא לָכֶם וְאִם־תַּעַזְבֻהוּ
ג יַעֲזֹב אֶתְכֶם: וְיָמִים רַבִּים לְיִשְׂרָאֵל לְלֹא ׀ אֱלֹהֵי אֱמֶת
ד וּלְלֹא כֹּהֵן מוֹרֶה וּלְלֹא תוֹרָה: וַיָּשָׁב בַּצַּר־לוֹ עַל־יהוה אֱלֹהֵי יִשְׂרָאֵל
ה וַיְבַקְשֻׁהוּ וַיִּמָּצֵא לָהֶם: וּבָעִתִּים הָהֵם אֵין שָׁלוֹם לַיּוֹצֵא וְלַבָּא כִּי
ו מְהוּמֹת רַבּוֹת עַל כָּל־יוֹשְׁבֵי הָאֲרָצוֹת: וְכֻתְּתוּ גוֹי־בְּגוֹי וְעִיר בְּעִיר
ז כִּי־אֱלֹהִים הֲמָמָם בְּכָל־צָרָה: וְאַתֶּם חִזְקוּ וְאַל־יִרְפּוּ יְדֵיכֶם כִּי יֵשׁ
ח שָׂכָר לִפְעֻלַּתְכֶם: וְכִשְׁמֹעַ אָסָא הַדְּבָרִים הָאֵלֶּה וְהַנְּבוּאָה
עֹדֵד הַנָּבִיא הִתְחַזַּק וַיַּעֲבֵר הַשִּׁקּוּצִים מִכָּל־אֶרֶץ יְהוּדָה וּבִנְיָמִן
וּמִן־הֶעָרִים אֲשֶׁר לָכַד מֵהַר אֶפְרָיִם וַיְחַדֵּשׁ אֶת־מִזְבַּח יהוה אֲשֶׁר
ט לִפְנֵי אוּלָם יהוה: וַיִּקְבֹּץ אֶת־כָּל־יְהוּדָה וּבִנְיָמִן וְהַגָּרִים עִמָּהֶם
מֵאֶפְרַיִם וּמְנַשֶּׁה וּמִשִּׁמְעוֹן כִּי־נָפְלוּ עָלָיו מִיִּשְׂרָאֵל לָרֹב בִּרְאֹתָם
י כִּי־יהוה אֱלֹהָיו עִמּוֹ: וַיִּקָּבְצוּ יְרוּשָׁלַ͏ִם בַּחֹדֶשׁ הַשְּׁלִישִׁי
יא לִשְׁנַת חֲמֵשׁ־עֶשְׂרֵה לְמַלְכוּת אָסָא: וַיִּזְבְּחוּ לַיהוה בַּיּוֹם הַהוּא מִן־
יב הַשָּׁלָל הֵבִיאוּ בָּקָר שְׁבַע מֵאוֹת וְצֹאן שִׁבְעַת אֲלָפִים: וַיָּבֹאוּ בַבְּרִית
יג לִדְרוֹשׁ אֶת־יהוה אֱלֹהֵי אֲבוֹתֵיהֶם בְּכָל־לְבָבָם וּבְכָל־נַפְשָׁם: וְכֹל
אֲשֶׁר לֹא־יִדְרֹשׁ לַיהוה אֱלֹהֵי־יִשְׂרָאֵל יוּמָת לְמִן־קָטֹן וְעַד־גָּדוֹל
יד לְמֵאִישׁ וְעַד־אִשָּׁה: וַיִּשָּׁבְעוּ לַיהוה בְּקוֹל גָּדוֹל וּבִתְרוּעָה וּבַחֲצֹצְרוֹת
יז טו וּבְשׁוֹפָרוֹת: וַיִּשְׂמְחוּ כָל־יְהוּדָה עַל־הַשְּׁבוּעָה כִּי בְכָל־לְבָבָם נִשְׁבָּעוּ
טז וּבְכָל־רְצוֹנָם בִּקְשֻׁהוּ וַיִּמָּצֵא לָהֶם וַיָּנַח יהוה לָהֶם מִסָּבִיב: וְגַם־מַעֲכָה
אֵם ׀ אָסָא הַמֶּלֶךְ הֱסִירָהּ מִגְּבִירָה אֲשֶׁר־עָשְׂתָה לַאֲשֵׁרָה מִפְלָצֶת

monstrous image for Ashera;[30] Asa cut down her monstrous image, crushed
17 it, and burned it by the Kidron Valley. Though the high shrines were not
18 removed from Israel, Asa's heart was true all the days of his life. He brought
his father's sacred items and his own sacred items into the House of God:
19 silver, gold, and the vessels. And no war took place until the thirty-fifth year
16 1 of Asa's reign. In the thirty-sixth year of Asa's reign, Basha, king of
Israel, marched against Yehuda and fortified Rama to prevent Asa, king of
2 Yehuda, from marching out into battle. So Asa took silver and gold from the
treasuries of the House of the Lord and the royal palace and sent it to Ben
3 Hadad, king of Aram, who resided in Damascus, with this message: "There
is an alliance between me and you and between my father and your father.
Look, I have sent you silver and gold; go and break your alliance with Basha,
4 king of Israel, so that he will withdraw from me." Ben Hadad complied with
King Asa and sent his military officers to the towns of Israel; they attacked
5 Iyon, Dan, and Avel Mayim and all the store towns of Naftali. When Basha
6 heard, he ceased construction in Rama, halting his work. King Asa
then summoned all of Yehuda to seize the stones and wood that Basha had
been using to fortify Rama, and with them he in turn fortified Geva and
7 Mitzpa. Soon after, the seer Ḥanani came to King Asa of Yehuda
and said to him, "Because you relied on the king of Aram instead of relying
8 on the Lord your God, an army of the king of Aram has escaped you. The
Kushites and the Libyans were a mighty force indeed, with chariots and riders
abundant, but when you relied upon the Lord, He delivered them into your
9 hands, for the eyes of the Lord roam all over the land, giving strength to
those whose hearts are completely with Him. This time you have been foolish,
10 and from now on you will have war." Asa was angry at the seer, and in his rage
over this, he had him thrown into prison; Asa also dealt harshly with certain
11 people at the same time. Asa's history, earlier and later, is recorded in the book
12 of the Kings of Yehuda and Israel. In the thirty-ninth year of his reign, Asa
suffered from a foot disease, and his disease grew severe. Yet even in his illness
13 he did not seek help from the Lord but from healers. And Asa slept with his
14 ancestors; he died in the forty-first year of his reign. They buried him in the
tomb he had hewn for himself in the City of David. They laid him out on a
bier that had been covered with all kinds of spices and perfumes, artfully
17 1 prepared, and lit an enormous fire in his honor. His son Yehoshafat
2 reigned in his place, and he grew more powerful against Israel. He stationed
forces in all of Yehuda's fortified cities, and he stationed garrisons in the land
3 of Yehuda and in the towns of Efrayim that his father Asa had taken over. The
Lord was with Yehoshafat, for he followed in the ways of David as his father

30 | See note on 14:2.

יז וַיַּכְרֵת אָסָא אֶת־מִפְלַצְתָּהּ וַיָּדֶק וַיִּשְׂרֹף בְּנַחַל קִדְרוֹן׃ וְהַבָּמוֹת לֹא־
יח סָרוּ מִיִּשְׂרָאֵל רַק לְבַב־אָסָא הָיָה שָׁלֵם כָּל־יָמָיו׃ וַיָּבֵא אֶת־קָדְשֵׁי
יט אָבִיו וְקָדָשָׁיו בֵּית הָאֱלֹהִים כֶּסֶף וְזָהָב וְכֵלִים׃ וּמִלְחָמָה לֹא הָיָתָה
טז א עַד שְׁנַת־שְׁלֹשִׁים וְחָמֵשׁ לְמַלְכוּת אָסָא׃ בִּשְׁנַת שְׁלֹשִׁים
וָשֵׁשׁ לְמַלְכוּת אָסָא עָלָה בַּעְשָׁא מֶלֶךְ־יִשְׂרָאֵל עַל־יְהוּדָה וַיִּבֶן אֶת־
ב הָרָמָה לְבִלְתִּי תֵּת יוֹצֵא וָבָא לְאָסָא מֶלֶךְ יְהוּדָה׃ וַיֹּצֵא אָסָא כֶּסֶף
וְזָהָב מֵאֹצְרוֹת בֵּית יְהוָה וּבֵית הַמֶּלֶךְ וַיִּשְׁלַח אֶל־בֶּן־הֲדַד מֶלֶךְ אֲרָם
ג הַיּוֹשֵׁב בְּדַרְמֶשֶׂק לֵאמֹר׃ בְּרִית בֵּינִי וּבֵינֶךָ וּבֵין אָבִי וּבֵין אָבִיךָ הִנֵּה
שָׁלַחְתִּי לְךָ כֶּסֶף וְזָהָב לֵךְ הָפֵר בְּרִיתְךָ אֶת־בַּעְשָׁא מֶלֶךְ יִשְׂרָאֵל
ד וְיַעֲלֶה מֵעָלָי׃ וַיִּשְׁמַע בֶּן־הֲדַד אֶל־הַמֶּלֶךְ אָסָא וַיִּשְׁלַח אֶת־שָׂרֵי
הַחֲיָלִים אֲשֶׁר־לוֹ אֶל־עָרֵי יִשְׂרָאֵל וַיַּכּוּ אֶת־עִיּוֹן וְאֶת־דָּן וְאֵת אָבֵל
ה מָיִם וְאֵת כָּל־מִסְכְּנוֹת עָרֵי נַפְתָּלִי׃ וַיְהִי כִּשְׁמֹעַ בַּעְשָׁא וַיֶּחְדַּל מִבְּנוֹת
ו אֶת־הָרָמָה וַיַּשְׁבֵּת אֶת־מְלַאכְתּוֹ׃ וְאָסָא הַמֶּלֶךְ לָקַח
אֶת־כָּל־יְהוּדָה וַיִּשְׂאוּ אֶת־אַבְנֵי הָרָמָה וְאֶת־עֵצֶיהָ אֲשֶׁר בָּנָה בַּעְשָׁא
ז וַיִּבֶן בָּהֶם אֶת־גֶּבַע וְאֶת־הַמִּצְפָּה׃ וּבָעֵת הַהִיא בָּא
חֲנָנִי הָרֹאֶה אֶל־אָסָא מֶלֶךְ יְהוּדָה וַיֹּאמֶר אֵלָיו בְּהִשָּׁעֶנְךָ עַל־מֶלֶךְ
אֲרָם וְלֹא נִשְׁעַנְתָּ עַל־יְהוָה אֱלֹהֶיךָ עַל־כֵּן נִמְלַט חֵיל מֶלֶךְ־אֲרָם
ח מִיָּדֶךָ׃ הֲלֹא הַכּוּשִׁים וְהַלּוּבִים הָיוּ לְחַיִל ׀ לָרֹב לְרֶכֶב וּלְפָרָשִׁים
ט לְהַרְבֵּה מְאֹד וּבְהִשָּׁעֶנְךָ עַל־יְהוָה נְתָנָם בְּיָדֶךָ׃ כִּי יְהוָה עֵינָיו
מְשֹׁטְטוֹת בְּכָל־הָאָרֶץ לְהִתְחַזֵּק עִם־לְבָבָם שָׁלֵם אֵלָיו נִסְכַּלְתָּ עַל־
י זֹאת כִּי מֵעַתָּה יֵשׁ עִמְּךָ מִלְחָמוֹת׃ וַיִּכְעַס אָסָא אֶל־הָרֹאֶה וַיִּתְּנֵהוּ
בֵּית הַמַּהְפֶּכֶת כִּי־בְזַעַף עִמּוֹ עַל־זֹאת וַיְרַצֵּץ אָסָא מִן־הָעָם בָּעֵת
יא הַהִיא׃ וְהִנֵּה דִּבְרֵי אָסָא הָרִאשׁוֹנִים וְהָאַחֲרוֹנִים הִנָּם כְּתוּבִים עַל־
יב סֵפֶר הַמְּלָכִים לִיהוּדָה וְיִשְׂרָאֵל׃ וַיֶּחֱלֶא אָסָא בִּשְׁנַת שְׁלוֹשִׁים וָתֵשַׁע
לְמַלְכוּתוֹ בְּרַגְלָיו עַד־לְמַעְלָה חָלְיוֹ וְגַם־בְּחָלְיוֹ לֹא־דָרַשׁ אֶת־יְהוָה
יג כִּי בָּרֹפְאִים׃ וַיִּשְׁכַּב אָסָא עִם־אֲבֹתָיו וַיָּמָת בִּשְׁנַת אַרְבָּעִים וְאַחַת
יד לְמָלְכוֹ׃ וַיִּקְבְּרֻהוּ בְקִבְרֹתָיו אֲשֶׁר כָּרָה־לוֹ בְּעִיר דָּוִיד וַיַּשְׁכִּיבֻהוּ
בַּמִּשְׁכָּב אֲשֶׁר מִלֵּא בְּשָׂמִים וּזְנִים מְרֻקָּחִים בְּמִרְקַחַת מַעֲשֶׂה
יז א וַיִּשְׂרְפוּ־לוֹ שְׂרֵפָה גְּדוֹלָה עַד־לִמְאֹד׃ וַיִּמְלֹךְ יְהוֹשָׁפָט בְּנוֹ
ב תַּחְתָּיו וַיִּתְחַזֵּק עַל־יִשְׂרָאֵל׃ וַיִּתֶּן־חַיִל בְּכָל־עָרֵי יְהוּדָה הַבְּצֻרוֹת
ג וַיִּתֵּן נְצִיבִים בְּאֶרֶץ יְהוּדָה וּבְעָרֵי אֶפְרַיִם אֲשֶׁר לָכַד אָסָא אָבִיו׃ וַיְהִי
יְהוָה עִם־יְהוֹשָׁפָט כִּי הָלַךְ בְּדַרְכֵי דָּוִיד אָבִיו הָרִאשֹׁנִים וְלֹא דָרַשׁ

4 did at first, and he did not seek the Baalim. He sought his father's God and
5 followed His commandments – unlike the ways of Israel. And the Lord
established the kingdom firmly in his grasp. All Yehuda paid tribute to
6 Yehoshafat, and he had great wealth and honor. His heart soared with the
Lord's ways; moreover, he removed the high shrines and the sacred trees
7 from Yehuda. In the third year of his reign he sent his officials Ben
Ḥayil, Ovadya, Zekharya, Netanel, and Mikhayahu to teach in the towns of
8 Yehuda together with the Levites Shemayahu, Netanyahu, Zevadyahu, Asael,
Shemiramot, Yehonatan, Adoniyahu, Toviyahu, and Tov Adoniya, with the
9 priests Elishama and Yehoram accompanying the Levites. They taught in
Yehuda with the scroll of the Lord's Torah, making their way around all the
10 towns of Yehuda and teaching among the people. All the kingdoms of the
lands surrounding Yehuda were struck with fear of the Lord, and none made
11 war against Yehoshafat. Some of the Philistines offered gifts to Yehoshafat
and silver as tribute; the Arabians brought him 7,700 rams and 7,700
12 he-goats. Yehoshafat steadily rose in greatness. He built fortresses
13 and store towns in Yehuda; he led great industry in the towns of Yehuda and
14 a powerful military force in Jerusalem. They were enlisted this way
according to their ancestral houses: Yehuda's officer of thousands was the
15 officer Adna in charge of 300,000 warriors; next to him was the
16 officer Yehoḥanan in charge of 280,000; next to him was Amasya
son of Zikhri, a volunteer for the Lord's service, in charge of 200,000
17 warriors. From Binyamin the warrior Elyada in charge of 200,000
18 armed with bow and shield, and next to him Yehozavad in charge of
19 180,000 armed troops. These were in the king's service in addition
to those that the king had stationed in the fortified cities throughout
18 1 Yehuda. Yehoshafat had great wealth and honor, and he made a
2 marriage alliance with Aḥav. After some years, he went down to Aḥav in
Shomron. Aḥav had many sheep and oxen slaughtered for him and for the
3 people with him, and he persuaded him to march up to Ramot Gilad. Aḥav,
king of Israel, said to Yehoshafat, king of Yehuda, "Will you go with me to
Ramot Gilad?" "I am ready, as you are," he said to him. "My troops are your
4 own troops; we will accompany you in battle." Then Yehoshafat said to the
5 king of Israel, "Please, inquire of the Lord today." So the king of Israel
gathered the prophets, four hundred men, and said to them, "Shall we go to
battle over Ramot Gilad, or should I refrain?" "Advance!" they said, "and God
6 will deliver them to the king's hand." "Is there no other prophet of the Lord
7 here?" said Yehoshafat. "Let us inquire through him." "There is another man
through whom we could inquire of the Lord," the king of Israel said to
Yehoshafat, "but I despise him; he will not prophesy good for me, only evil

ד לַבְּעָלִים׃ כִּי לֵאלֹהֵי אָבִיו דָּרָשׁ וּבְמִצְוֺתָיו הָלָךְ וְלֹא כְּמַעֲשֵׂה יִשְׂרָאֵל׃
ה וַיָּכֶן יְהוָה אֶת־הַמַּמְלָכָה בְּיָדוֹ וַיִּתְּנוּ כָל־יְהוּדָה מִנְחָה לִיהוֹשָׁפָט
ו וַיְהִי־לוֹ עֹשֶׁר וְכָבוֹד לָרֹב׃ וַיִּגְבַּהּ לִבּוֹ בְּדַרְכֵי יְהוָה וְעוֹד הֵסִיר אֶת־
ז הַבָּמוֹת וְאֶת־הָאֲשֵׁרִים מִיהוּדָה׃ וּבִשְׁנַת שָׁלוֹשׁ לְמָלְכוֹ
שָׁלַח לְשָׂרָיו לְבֶן־חַיִל וּלְעֹבַדְיָה וְלִזְכַרְיָה וְלִנְתַנְאֵל וּלְמִיכָיָהוּ לְלַמֵּד
ח בְּעָרֵי יְהוּדָה׃ וְעִמָּהֶם הַלְוִיִּם שְׁמַעְיָהוּ וּנְתַנְיָהוּ וּזְבַדְיָהוּ וַעֲשָׂהאֵל
ושמרימות וִיהוֹנָתָן וַאֲדֹנִיָּהוּ וְטוֹבִיָּהוּ וְטוֹב אֲדוֹנִיָּה הַלְוִיִּם וְעִמָּהֶם וּשְׁמִירָמוֹת
ט אֱלִישָׁמָע וִיהוֹרָם הַכֹּהֲנִים׃ וַיְלַמְּדוּ בִּיהוּדָה וְעִמָּהֶם סֵפֶר תּוֹרַת יְהוָה
י וַיָּסֹבּוּ בְּכָל־עָרֵי יְהוּדָה וַיְלַמְּדוּ בָּעָם׃ וַיְהִי ׀ פַּחַד יְהוָה עַל כָּל־מַמְלְכוֹת
יא הָאֲרָצוֹת אֲשֶׁר סְבִיבוֹת יְהוּדָה וְלֹא נִלְחֲמוּ עִם־יְהוֹשָׁפָט׃ וּמִן־
פְּלִשְׁתִּים מְבִיאִים לִיהוֹשָׁפָט מִנְחָה וְכֶסֶף מַשָּׂא גַּם הָעַרְבִיאִים
מְבִיאִים לוֹ צֹאן אֵילִים שִׁבְעַת אֲלָפִים וּשְׁבַע מֵאוֹת וּתְיָשִׁים שִׁבְעַת
יב אֲלָפִים וּשְׁבַע מֵאוֹת׃ וַיְהִי יְהוֹשָׁפָט הֹלֵךְ וְגָדֵל עַד־לְמָעְלָה
יג וַיִּבֶן בִּיהוּדָה בִּירָנִיּוֹת וְעָרֵי מִסְכְּנוֹת׃ וּמְלָאכָה רַבָּה הָיָה לוֹ בְּעָרֵי
יד יְהוּדָה וְאַנְשֵׁי מִלְחָמָה גִּבּוֹרֵי חַיִל בִּירוּשָׁלִָם׃ וְאֵלֶּה פְקֻדָּתָם
לְבֵית אֲבוֹתֵיהֶם לִיהוּדָה שָׂרֵי אֲלָפִים עַדְנָה הַשָּׂר וְעִמּוֹ גִּבּוֹרֵי חַיִל
טו שְׁלֹשׁ מֵאוֹת אָלֶף׃ וְעַל־יָדוֹ יְהוֹחָנָן הַשָּׂר וְעִמּוֹ מָאתַיִם
טז וּשְׁמוֹנִים אָלֶף׃ וְעַל־יָדוֹ עֲמַסְיָה בֶן־זִכְרִי הַמִּתְנַדֵּב לַיהוָה
יז וְעִמּוֹ מָאתַיִם אֶלֶף גִּבּוֹר חָיִל׃ וּמִן־בִּנְיָמִן גִּבּוֹר חַיִל אֶלְיָדָע
יח וְעִמּוֹ נֹשְׁקֵי־קֶשֶׁת וּמָגֵן מָאתַיִם אָלֶף׃ וְעַל־יָדוֹ
יט יְהוֹזָבָד וְעִמּוֹ מֵאָה־וּשְׁמוֹנִים אֶלֶף חֲלוּצֵי צָבָא׃ אֵלֶּה
הַמְשָׁרְתִים אֶת־הַמֶּלֶךְ מִלְּבַד אֲשֶׁר־נָתַן הַמֶּלֶךְ בְּעָרֵי הַמִּבְצָר בְּכָל־
יח א יְהוּדָה׃ וַיְהִי לִיהוֹשָׁפָט עֹשֶׁר וְכָבוֹד לָרֹב וַיִּתְחַתֵּן לְאַחְאָב׃
ב וַיֵּרֶד לְקֵץ שָׁנִים אֶל־אַחְאָב לְשֹׁמְרוֹן וַיִּזְבַּח־לוֹ אַחְאָב צֹאן וּבָקָר לָרֹב
ג וְלָעָם אֲשֶׁר עִמּוֹ וַיְסִיתֵהוּ לַעֲלוֹת אֶל־רָמוֹת גִּלְעָד׃ וַיֹּאמֶר אַחְאָב
מֶלֶךְ־יִשְׂרָאֵל אֶל־יְהוֹשָׁפָט מֶלֶךְ יְהוּדָה הֲתֵלֵךְ עִמִּי רָמֹת גִּלְעָד וַיֹּאמֶר
ד לוֹ כָּמוֹנִי כָמוֹךָ וּכְעַמְּךָ עַמִּי וְעִמְּךָ בַּמִּלְחָמָה׃ וַיֹּאמֶר יְהוֹשָׁפָט אֶל־
ה מֶלֶךְ יִשְׂרָאֵל דְּרָשׁ־נָא כַיּוֹם אֶת־דְּבַר יְהוָה׃ וַיִּקְבֹּץ מֶלֶךְ־יִשְׂרָאֵל
אֶת־הַנְּבִאִים אַרְבַּע מֵאוֹת אִישׁ וַיֹּאמֶר אֲלֵהֶם הֲנֵלֵךְ אֶל־רָמֹת גִּלְעָד
ו לַמִּלְחָמָה אִם־אֶחְדָּל וַיֹּאמְרוּ עֲלֵה וְיִתֵּן הָאֱלֹהִים בְּיַד הַמֶּלֶךְ׃ וַיֹּאמֶר
ז יְהוֹשָׁפָט הַאֵין פֹּה נָבִיא לַיהוָה עוֹד וְנִדְרְשָׁה מֵאֹתוֹ׃ וַיֹּאמֶר מֶלֶךְ־
יִשְׂרָאֵל ׀ אֶל־יְהוֹשָׁפָט עוֹד אִישׁ־אֶחָד לִדְרוֹשׁ אֶת־יְהוָה מֵאֹתוֹ וַאֲנִי

all the time – he is Mikhayehu son of Yimla." "Do not say such a thing, O
8 king," said Yehoshafat. So the king of Israel summoned one of the eunuchs
9 and said, "Bring Mikhayehu son of Yimla at once." The king of Israel and
Yehoshafat, king of Yehuda, each sat upon their thrones attired in robes; they
sat by the threshing floor at the entrance of the gate of Shomron, and all the
10 prophets were prophesying before them. Tzidkiyahu son of Kenaana had
made himself horns of iron. "Thus says the LORD," he said, "with these you
11 shall gore Aram until their demise." And all the prophets echoed his prophecy:
"Advance to Ramot Gilad, and be victorious," they were saying. "The LORD
12 will deliver it to the king's hand." Then the messenger who had gone to
summon Mikhayehu told him, "Look here – the words of the prophets are
unanimous; they favor the king. May your words be like their words – speak
13 favorably." "As the LORD lives," said Mikhayehu, "I will speak only what my
14 God says to me." He came up to the king, and the king said to him,
"Mikha – shall we go to battle over Ramot Gilad, or should I refrain?"
"Advance and be victorious," he said, "and they will be delivered into your
15 hands." "How many times must I have you swear?" the king said to him. "You
16 must speak only the truth to me, by the name of the LORD." "I saw all of Israel
scattered over the hills," he said, "like sheep without a shepherd. And the
17 LORD said: These have no masters. Let each man return home in peace." "Did
I not tell you?" the king of Israel said to Yehoshafat. "He never prophesies
18 good for me – only evil!" "Therefore listen to the word of the LORD,"
he continued. "I saw the LORD sitting on His throne, with all the heavenly
19 hosts standing to His right and to His left. And the LORD said, 'Who will lure
Aḥav, king of Israel, so that he will advance and fall at Ramot Gilad?' This one
20 said this, and that one said that. Then a spirit came forward and stood before
21 the LORD and said, 'I will lure him.' 'How?' said the LORD. 'I will go out and
become a false spirit in the mouths of all his prophets,' it said. 'Lure him – you
22 will succeed,' He said. 'Go out and do so.' And now look – the LORD has
placed a false spirit in the mouths of these prophets of yours, and the LORD
23 has pronounced evil for you." Tzidkiyahu son of Kenaana came
forward and slapped Mikhayehu across the cheek. "Which way did the spirit
24 of the LORD pass from me to speak to you?" he said. "Oh, you will see on that
25 day," Mikhayehu said, "when you enter the innermost room to hide." "Seize
Mikhayehu!" said the king of Israel. "Hand him over to Amon, the city
26 governor, and to Yoash, the king's son, and say, 'Thus says the king: Put this
one in prison, and feed him only scant bread and scant water until my safe
27 return.'" "If you indeed return safely, then the LORD did not speak through
28 me," said Mikhayehu, and added, "Listen, all peoples!"[31] So the king

31 | Cf. Micah 1:2.

שְׂנֵאתִיהוּ כִּי אֵינֶנּוּ מִתְנַבֵּא עָלַי לְטוֹבָה כִּי כׇל־יָמָיו לְרָעָה הוּא
ח מִיכָיְהוּ בֶן־יִמְלָא וַיֹּאמֶר יְהוֹשָׁפָט אַל־יֹאמַר הַמֶּלֶךְ כֵּן׃ וַיִּקְרָא מֶלֶךְ
ט יִשְׂרָאֵל אֶל־סָרִיס אֶחָד וַיֹּאמֶר מַהֵר מיכהו בֶן־יִמְלָא׃ וּמֶלֶךְ יִשְׂרָאֵל מִיכָיְהוּ
וִיהוֹשָׁפָט מֶלֶךְ־יְהוּדָה יוֹשְׁבִים אִישׁ עַל־כִּסְאוֹ מְלֻבָּשִׁים בְּגָדִים
וְיֹשְׁבִים בְּגֹרֶן פֶּתַח שַׁעַר שֹׁמְרוֹן וְכׇל־הַנְּבִיאִים מִתְנַבְּאִים לִפְנֵיהֶם׃
י וַיַּעַשׂ לוֹ צִדְקִיָּהוּ בֶן־כְּנַעֲנָה קַרְנֵי בַרְזֶל וַיֹּאמֶר כֹּה־אָמַר יְהוָה בְּאֵלֶּה
יא תְּנַגַּח אֶת־אֲרָם עַד־כַּלּוֹתָם׃ וְכׇל־הַנְּבִאִים נִבְּאִים כֵּן לֵאמֹר עֲלֵה
יב רָמֹת גִּלְעָד וְהַצְלַח וְנָתַן יְהוָה בְּיַד הַמֶּלֶךְ׃ וְהַמַּלְאָךְ אֲשֶׁר־הָלַךְ ׀
לִקְרֹא לְמִיכָיְהוּ דִּבֶּר אֵלָיו לֵאמֹר הִנֵּה דִּבְרֵי הַנְּבִאִים פֶּה־אֶחָד טוֹב
יג אֶל־הַמֶּלֶךְ וִיהִי־נָא דְבָרְךָ כְּאַחַד מֵהֶם וְדִבַּרְתָּ טּוֹב׃ וַיֹּאמֶר מִיכָיְהוּ
יד חַי־יְהוָה כִּי אֶת־אֲשֶׁר־יֹאמַר אֱלֹהַי אֹתוֹ אֲדַבֵּר׃ וַיָּבֹא אֶל־הַמֶּלֶךְ
וַיֹּאמֶר הַמֶּלֶךְ אֵלָיו מִיכָה הֲנֵלֵךְ אֶל־רָמֹת גִּלְעָד לַמִּלְחָמָה אִם־אֶחְדָּל
טו וַיֹּאמֶר עֲלוּ וְהַצְלִיחוּ וְיִנָּתְנוּ בְּיֶדְכֶם׃ וַיֹּאמֶר אֵלָיו הַמֶּלֶךְ עַד־כַּמֶּה
פְעָמִים אֲנִי מַשְׁבִּיעֶךָ אֲשֶׁר לֹא־תְדַבֵּר אֵלַי רַק אֱמֶת בְּשֵׁם יְהוָה׃
טז וַיֹּאמֶר רָאִיתִי אֶת־כׇּל־יִשְׂרָאֵל נְפוֹצִים עַל־הֶהָרִים כַּצֹּאן אֲשֶׁר אֵין־
לָהֶן רֹעֶה וַיֹּאמֶר יְהוָה לֹא־אֲדֹנִים לָאֵלֶּה יָשׁוּבוּ אִישׁ־לְבֵיתוֹ בְּשָׁלוֹם׃
יז וַיֹּאמֶר מֶלֶךְ־יִשְׂרָאֵל אֶל־יְהוֹשָׁפָט הֲלֹא אָמַרְתִּי אֵלֶיךָ לֹא־יִתְנַבֵּא
יח עָלַי טוֹב כִּי אִם־לְרָע׃ וַיֹּאמֶר לָכֵן שִׁמְעוּ דְבַר־יְהוָה יח
רָאִיתִי אֶת־יְהוָה יוֹשֵׁב עַל־כִּסְאוֹ וְכׇל־צְבָא הַשָּׁמַיִם עֹמְדִים עַל־יְמִינוֹ
יט וּשְׂמֹאלוֹ׃ וַיֹּאמֶר יְהוָה מִי יְפַתֶּה אֶת־אַחְאָב מֶלֶךְ־יִשְׂרָאֵל וְיַעַל וְיִפֹּל
כ בְּרָמוֹת גִּלְעָד וַיֹּאמֶר זֶה אֹמֵר כָּכָה וְזֶה אֹמֵר כָּכָה׃ וַיֵּצֵא הָרוּחַ וַיַּעֲמֹד
כא לִפְנֵי יְהוָה וַיֹּאמֶר אֲנִי אֲפַתֶּנּוּ וַיֹּאמֶר יְהוָה אֵלָיו בַּמָּה׃ וַיֹּאמֶר אֵצֵא
וְהָיִיתִי לְרוּחַ שֶׁקֶר בְּפִי כׇּל־נְבִיאָיו וַיֹּאמֶר תְּפַתֶּה וְגַם־תּוּכַל צֵא
כב וַעֲשֵׂה־כֵן׃ וְעַתָּה הִנֵּה נָתַן יְהוָה רוּחַ שֶׁקֶר בְּפִי נְבִיאֶיךָ אֵלֶּה וַיהוָה
כג דִּבֶּר עָלֶיךָ רָעָה׃ וַיִּגַּשׁ צִדְקִיָּהוּ בֶן־כְּנַעֲנָה וַיַּךְ אֶת־מִיכָיְהוּ
עַל־הַלֶּחִי וַיֹּאמֶר אֵי זֶה הַדֶּרֶךְ עָבַר רוּחַ־יְהוָה מֵאִתִּי לְדַבֵּר אֹתָךְ׃
כד וַיֹּאמֶר מִיכָיְהוּ הִנְּךָ רֹאֶה בַּיּוֹם הַהוּא אֲשֶׁר תָּבוֹא חֶדֶר בְּחֶדֶר
כה לְהֵחָבֵא׃ וַיֹּאמֶר מֶלֶךְ יִשְׂרָאֵל קְחוּ אֶת־מִיכָיְהוּ וַהֲשִׁיבֻהוּ אֶל־אָמוֹן
כו שַׂר־הָעִיר וְאֶל־יוֹאָשׁ בֶּן־הַמֶּלֶךְ׃ וַאֲמַרְתֶּם כֹּה אָמַר הַמֶּלֶךְ שִׂימוּ זֶה
כז בֵּית הַכֶּלֶא וְהַאֲכִלֻהוּ לֶחֶם לַחַץ וּמַיִם לַחַץ עַד שׁוּבִי בְשָׁלוֹם׃ וַיֹּאמֶר
מִיכָיְהוּ אִם־שׁוֹב תָּשׁוּב בְּשָׁלוֹם לֹא־דִבֶּר יְהוָה בִּי וַיֹּאמֶר שִׁמְעוּ עַמִּים
כח כֻּלָּם׃ וַיַּעַל מֶלֶךְ־יִשְׂרָאֵל וִיהוֹשָׁפָט מֶלֶךְ־יְהוּדָה אֶל־רָמֹת

29 of Israel and Yehoshafat, king of Yehuda, advanced to Ramot Gilad. "I will
disguise myself and go into battle,"[32] the king of Israel said to Yehoshafat,
"while you should wear your robes." And the king of Israel disguised himself,
30 and they went into battle. Now the king of Aram had instructed his chariot
commanders as follows: "Do not attack anyone, great or small, except for the
31 king of Israel." When the chariot commanders saw Yehoshafat, they thought,
"He must be the king of Israel." They charged toward him to attack, but
Yehoshafat cried out, and the LORD came to his aid; God diverted them away
32 from him. When the chariot commanders realized that he was not the king
33 of Israel, they turned back away from him. But one man drew his bow at
random, and he struck the king of Israel in between the joints of his armor.
He called out to his chariot driver, "Steer back around and get me out of the
34 camp, for I am wounded." As the battle raged that day, the king was propped
up in his chariot facing Aram until the evening; he died as the sun was
19 1 setting. Yehoshafat, king of Yehuda, returned home safely to
2 Jerusalem. But the seer Yehu son of Ḥanani went out to meet him. "Should
you help the wicked and love those who hate the LORD?" he said to King
3 Yehoshafat. "For this, the LORD's wrath, is unleashed against you. Yet there is
still some goodness found within you, for you have purged the sacred trees
4 from the land, and you have set your heart on seeking God." Yehoshafat
dwelled in Jerusalem, and he went out again among the people – from Be'er
Sheva up to the hill country of Efrayim – to bring them back to the LORD,
5 God of their ancestors. He appointed judges in the land in all the fortified
6 cities of Yehuda, city by city. He said to the judges, "Consider what you do,
for you are judging not for the people's sake but for the LORD's, and He is with
7 you in judgment. Now, may fear of the LORD be upon you; act with care, for
there is no corruption with the LORD our God, or favoritism, or accepting
8 bribes." When they returned to Jerusalem, there too, Yehoshafat appointed
certain Levites, priests, and some of Israel's ancestral heads to pass judgment
9 for the LORD and to settle disputes. He commanded them, saying, "Thus you
10 shall act: with fear of the LORD, faithfully, and with whole hearts. Whenever
your brothers bring a case before you from their hometowns – whether it
concerns bloodshed, law and commandment, statutes, or rules – you must
instruct them so that they do not incur guilt before the LORD, bringing wrath
11 upon you and your brothers; if you act thus, you will not incur guilt. The head
priest Amaryahu is over you in all matters concerning the LORD, and
Zevadyahu son of Yishmael, the leader of the house of Yehuda, in all matters
concerning the king; the Levites shall serve as your officers. Act with courage,
and may the LORD be with the good."
20 1 Some time later, the Moabites and Amonites, together with some Amonites,[33]
2 advanced against Yehoshafat for battle. They came and told Yehoshafat, "A
vast multitude is advancing against you from across the sea, from Aram; they

---

32 | Literally "disguise yourself," but this must be understood as referring to the king of Israel himself.

33 | Hebrew *Amonim*. Radak understands the latter group to be the Meunites, as the terms *Amonim* and *Meunim* are interchangeable elsewhere; cf. 26:7–8.

כט גִּלְעָד: וַיֹּאמֶר מֶלֶךְ יִשְׂרָאֵל אֶל־יְהוֹשָׁפָט הִתְחַפֵּשׂ וָבוֹא בַמִּלְחָמָה
ל וְאַתָּה לְבַשׁ בְּגָדֶיךָ וַיִּתְחַפֵּשׂ מֶלֶךְ יִשְׂרָאֵל וַיָּבֹאוּ בַּמִּלְחָמָה: וּמֶלֶךְ
אֲרָם צִוָּה אֶת־שָׂרֵי הָרֶכֶב אֲשֶׁר־לוֹ לֵאמֹר לֹא תִּלָּחֲמוּ אֶת־הַקָּטֹן
לא אֶת־הַגָּדוֹל כִּי אִם־אֶת־מֶלֶךְ יִשְׂרָאֵל לְבַדּוֹ: וַיְהִי כִּרְאוֹת שָׂרֵי הָרֶכֶב
אֶת־יְהוֹשָׁפָט וְהֵמָּה אָמְרוּ מֶלֶךְ־יִשְׂרָאֵל הוּא וַיָּסֹבּוּ עָלָיו לְהִלָּחֵם
לב וַיִּזְעַק יְהוֹשָׁפָט וַיהוָה עֲזָרוֹ וַיְסִיתֵם אֱלֹהִים מִמֶּנּוּ: וַיְהִי כִּרְאוֹת שָׂרֵי
לג הָרֶכֶב כִּי לֹא־הָיָה מֶלֶךְ יִשְׂרָאֵל וַיָּשֻׁבוּ מֵאַחֲרָיו: וְאִישׁ מָשַׁךְ בַּקֶּשֶׁת
לְתֻמּוֹ וַיַּךְ אֶת־מֶלֶךְ יִשְׂרָאֵל בֵּין הַדְּבָקִים וּבֵין הַשִּׁרְיָן וַיֹּאמֶר לָרַכָּב
לד הֲפֹךְ יָדֶיךָ וְהוֹצֵאתַנִי מִן־הַמַּחֲנֶה כִּי הָחֳלֵיתִי: וַתַּעַל הַמִּלְחָמָה בַּיּוֹם יָדְךָ
הַהוּא וּמֶלֶךְ יִשְׂרָאֵל הָיָה מַעֲמִיד בַּמֶּרְכָּבָה נֹכַח אֲרָם עַד־הָעָרֶב
יט א וַיָּמָת לְעֵת בּוֹא הַשָּׁמֶשׁ: וַיָּשָׁב יְהוֹשָׁפָט מֶלֶךְ־יְהוּדָה
ב אֶל־בֵּיתוֹ בְּשָׁלוֹם לִירוּשָׁלִָם: וַיֵּצֵא אֶל־פָּנָיו יֵהוּא בֶן־חֲנָנִי הַחֹזֶה
וַיֹּאמֶר אֶל־הַמֶּלֶךְ יְהוֹשָׁפָט הֲלָרָשָׁע לַעְזֹר וּלְשֹׂנְאֵי יְהוָה תֶּאֱהָב
ג וּבָזֹאת עָלֶיךָ קֶּצֶף מִלִּפְנֵי יְהוָה: אֲבָל דְּבָרִים טוֹבִים נִמְצְאוּ עִמָּךְ
כִּי־בִעַרְתָּ הָאֲשֵׁרוֹת מִן־הָאָרֶץ וַהֲכִינוֹתָ לְבָבְךָ לִדְרֹשׁ הָאֱלֹהִים:
ד וַיֵּשֶׁב יְהוֹשָׁפָט בִּירוּשָׁלִָם וַיָּשָׁב וַיֵּצֵא בָעָם מִבְּאֵר שֶׁבַע עַד־הַר אֶפְרַיִם
ה וַיְשִׁיבֵם אֶל־יְהוָה אֱלֹהֵי אֲבוֹתֵיהֶם: וַיַּעֲמֵד שֹׁפְטִים בָּאָרֶץ בְּכָל־עָרֵי
ו יְהוּדָה הַבְּצֻרוֹת לְעִיר וָעִיר: וַיֹּאמֶר אֶל־הַשֹּׁפְטִים רְאוּ מָה־אַתֶּם
ז עֹשִׂים כִּי לֹא לְאָדָם תִּשְׁפְּטוּ כִּי לַיהוָה וְעִמָּכֶם בִּדְבַר מִשְׁפָּט: וְעַתָּה
יְהִי פַחַד־יְהוָה עֲלֵיכֶם שִׁמְרוּ וַעֲשׂוּ כִּי־אֵין עִם־יְהוָה אֱלֹהֵינוּ עַוְלָה
ח וּמַשֹּׂא פָנִים וּמִקַּח־שֹׁחַד: וְגַם בִּירוּשָׁלִַם הֶעֱמִיד יְהוֹשָׁפָט מִן־הַלְוִיִּם
וְהַכֹּהֲנִים וּמֵרָאשֵׁי הָאָבוֹת לְיִשְׂרָאֵל לְמִשְׁפַּט יְהוָה וְלָרִיב וַיָּשֻׁבוּ
ט יְרוּשָׁלִָם: וַיְצַו עֲלֵיהֶם לֵאמֹר כֹּה תַעֲשׂוּן בְּיִרְאַת יְהוָה בֶּאֱמוּנָה וּבְלֵבָב
י שָׁלֵם: וְכָל־רִיב אֲשֶׁר־יָבוֹא עֲלֵיכֶם מֵאֲחֵיכֶם ׀ הַיֹּשְׁבִים בְּעָרֵיהֶם בֵּין־
דָּם ׀ לְדָם בֵּין־תּוֹרָה לְמִצְוָה לְחֻקִּים וּלְמִשְׁפָּטִים וְהִזְהַרְתֶּם אֹתָם וְלֹא
יֶאְשְׁמוּ לַיהוָה וְהָיָה־קֶצֶף עֲלֵיכֶם וְעַל־אֲחֵיכֶם כֹּה תַעֲשׂוּן וְלֹא
יא תֶאְשָׁמוּ: וְהִנֵּה אֲמַרְיָהוּ כֹהֵן הָרֹאשׁ עֲלֵיכֶם לְכֹל ׀ דְּבַר יְהוָה וּזְבַדְיָהוּ
בֶן־יִשְׁמָעֵאל הַנָּגִיד לְבֵית־יְהוּדָה לְכֹל דְּבַר־הַמֶּלֶךְ וְשֹׁטְרִים הַלְוִיִּם
לִפְנֵיכֶם חִזְקוּ וַעֲשׂוּ וִיהִי יְהוָה עִם־הַטּוֹב:

כ א וַיְהִי אַחֲרֵי־כֵן בָּאוּ בְנֵי־מוֹאָב וּבְנֵי עַמּוֹן וְעִמָּהֶם ׀ מֵהָעַמּוֹנִים
ב עַל־יְהוֹשָׁפָט לַמִּלְחָמָה: וַיָּבֹאוּ וַיַּגִּידוּ לִיהוֹשָׁפָט לֵאמֹר בָּא עָלֶיךָ
הָמוֹן רָב מֵעֵבֶר לַיָּם מֵאֲרָם וְהִנָּם בְּחַצְצוֹן תָּמָר הִיא עֵין גֶּדִי:

3 are now in Ḥatzetzon Tamar" – that is, Ein Gedi. Yehoshafat was afraid, but
he was determined to seek the LORD, and he proclaimed a fast for all of
4 Yehuda. Yehuda gathered together to appeal to the LORD; they came from all
5 the towns of Yehuda to appeal to the LORD. Yehoshafat stood among the
assembly of Yehuda and Jerusalem in the House of the LORD before the new
6 courtyard. "O LORD, God of our ancestors," he said, "You are God in heaven,
and You rule over all the kingdoms of the nations. Power and might are in
7 Your hand; You cannot be overcome. You, our God, dispossessed the people
of this land before Your people Israel; You gave it to the seed of Avraham, who
8 loved You, forever. There they settled, and there they built a Sanctuary for
9 Your name, saying, 'Should evil come upon us, sword, judgment, disease, or
famine, we will stand before this House – before You, for Your name is on this
House – and we will cry out to You in our distress; You will hear, and You will
10 save.' And now, here are the people of Amon and Moav and Mount Se'ir; You
did not allow Israel to travel through them when they came from the land of
11 Egypt – they circumvented them and did not destroy them – but see how
they repay us; they come to drive us out from Your possession, which You
12 gave us as ours. Our God, will You not pass judgment against them? For we
are powerless against this vast multitude that advances toward us. We know
13 not what to do; our eyes are upon You." All of Yehuda stood before the LORD
14 with their little ones and wives and children. And in the midst of the
crowd, the spirit of the LORD came upon Yaḥaziel son of Zekaryahu son of
15 Benaya son of Ye'iel son of Matanya, a Levite of the sons of Asaf: "Listen, all
of Yehuda and the people of Jerusalem and King Yehoshafat," he said. "Thus
says the LORD to you: Do not be frightened or dismayed in the face of this
16 vast horde, for this battle is not yours, but God's. Tomorrow, charge down at
them as they ascend the Ascent of the Blossom; you will encounter them at
17 the end of the wadi before the wilderness of Yeruel. You will not need to fight
this battle – take your positions and stand still, and you will see the LORD's
victory among you, Yehuda and Jerusalem. Do not be frightened or dismayed;
18 tomorrow, go out before them, and the LORD will be with you." And
Yehoshafat bowed with his face to the ground, and all of Yehuda and the
people of Jerusalem flung themselves down before the LORD in worship of
19 the LORD. Then the Levites – of the Kehatites and the Korahites – stood up
20 to sing praise to the LORD, God of Israel, in loud, powerful voices. They rose
early in the morning and set out for the wilderness of Tekoa. As they set out,
Yehoshafat stood and said, "Listen to me, Yehuda and the people of Jerusalem:
have firm belief in the LORD your God, and you will stand firm; have firm
21 belief in His prophets, and you will succeed." When he had given counsel to
the people, he gave the cue to those who were to sing and give praise to the
LORD in the splendor of holiness as they went out before the army, declaring,
22 "Give praise to the LORD, for His loving-kindness is forever." And as they
burst into joyful song and praise, the LORD set ambushes against the people
of Amon, Moav, and Mount Se'ir, who were advancing against Yehuda, and
23 they were routed. The Amonites and Moabites rose against the people of

ג וַיִּרָא וַיִּתֵּן יְהוֹשָׁפָט אֶת־פָּנָיו לִדְרוֹשׁ לַיהוָה וַיִּקְרָא־צוֹם עַל־כָּל־
ד יְהוּדָה׃ וַיִּקָּבְצוּ יְהוּדָה לְבַקֵּשׁ מֵיְהוָה גַּם מִכָּל־עָרֵי יְהוּדָה בָּאוּ לְבַקֵּשׁ
ה אֶת־יְהוָה׃ וַיַּעֲמֹד יְהוֹשָׁפָט בִּקְהַל יְהוּדָה וִירוּשָׁלַ͏ִם בְּבֵית יְהוָה לִפְנֵי
ו הֶחָצֵר הַחֲדָשָׁה׃ וַיֹּאמַר יְהוָה אֱלֹהֵי אֲבֹתֵינוּ הֲלֹא אַתָּה־הוּא אֱלֹהִים
בַּשָּׁמַיִם וְאַתָּה מוֹשֵׁל בְּכֹל מַמְלְכוֹת הַגּוֹיִם וּבְיָדְךָ כֹּחַ וּגְבוּרָה וְאֵין
ז עִמְּךָ לְהִתְיַצֵּב׃ הֲלֹא ׀ אַתָּה אֱלֹהֵינוּ הוֹרַשְׁתָּ אֶת־יֹשְׁבֵי הָאָרֶץ הַזֹּאת
ח מִלִּפְנֵי עַמְּךָ יִשְׂרָאֵל וַתִּתְּנָהּ לְזֶרַע אַבְרָהָם אֹהַבְךָ לְעוֹלָם׃ וַיֵּשְׁבוּ־בָהּ
ט וַיִּבְנוּ לְךָ ׀ בָּהּ מִקְדָּשׁ לְשִׁמְךָ לֵאמֹר׃ אִם־תָּבוֹא עָלֵינוּ רָעָה חֶרֶב
שְׁפוֹט וְדֶבֶר וְרָעָב נַעַמְדָה לִפְנֵי הַבַּיִת הַזֶּה וּלְפָנֶיךָ כִּי שִׁמְךָ בַּבַּיִת
י הַזֶּה וְנִזְעַק אֵלֶיךָ מִצָּרָתֵנוּ וְתִשְׁמַע וְתוֹשִׁיעַ׃ וְעַתָּה הִנֵּה בְנֵי־עַמּוֹן
וּמוֹאָב וְהַר־שֵׂעִיר אֲשֶׁר לֹא־נָתַתָּה לְיִשְׂרָאֵל לָבוֹא בָהֶם בְּבֹאָם
יא מֵאֶרֶץ מִצְרָיִם כִּי סָרוּ מֵעֲלֵיהֶם וְלֹא הִשְׁמִידוּם׃ וְהִנֵּה־הֵם גֹּמְלִים
יב עָלֵינוּ לָבוֹא לְגָרְשֵׁנוּ מִיְּרֻשָּׁתְךָ אֲשֶׁר הוֹרַשְׁתָּנוּ׃ אֱלֹהֵינוּ הֲלֹא תִשְׁפָּט־
בָּם כִּי אֵין בָּנוּ כֹּחַ לִפְנֵי הֶהָמוֹן הָרָב הַזֶּה הַבָּא עָלֵינוּ וַאֲנַחְנוּ לֹא נֵדַע
יג מַה־נַּעֲשֶׂה כִּי עָלֶיךָ עֵינֵינוּ׃ וְכָל־יְהוּדָה עֹמְדִים לִפְנֵי יְהוָה גַּם־טַפָּם
יד נְשֵׁיהֶם וּבְנֵיהֶם׃ וְיַחֲזִיאֵל בֶּן־זְכַרְיָהוּ בֶּן־בְּנָיָה בֶּן־יְעִיאֵל
בֶּן־מַתַּנְיָה הַלֵּוִי מִן־בְּנֵי אָסָף הָיְתָה עָלָיו רוּחַ יְהוָה בְּתוֹךְ הַקָּהָל׃
טו וַיֹּאמֶר הַקְשִׁיבוּ כָל־יְהוּדָה וְיֹשְׁבֵי יְרוּשָׁלַ͏ִם וְהַמֶּלֶךְ יְהוֹשָׁפָט כֹּה־אָמַר
יְהוָה לָכֶם אַתֶּם אַל־תִּירְאוּ וְאַל־תֵּחַתּוּ מִפְּנֵי הֶהָמוֹן הָרָב הַזֶּה כִּי
טז לֹא לָכֶם הַמִּלְחָמָה כִּי לֵאלֹהִים׃ מָחָר רְדוּ עֲלֵיהֶם הִנָּם עֹלִים בְּמַעֲלֵה
יז הַצִּיץ וּמְצָאתֶם אֹתָם בְּסוֹף הַנַּחַל פְּנֵי מִדְבַּר יְרוּאֵל׃ לֹא לָכֶם לְהִלָּחֵם
בָּזֹאת הִתְיַצְּבוּ עִמְדוּ וּרְאוּ אֶת־יְשׁוּעַת יְהוָה עִמָּכֶם יְהוּדָה וִירוּשָׁלַ͏ִם
יח אַל־תִּירְאוּ וְאַל־תֵּחַתּוּ מָחָר צְאוּ לִפְנֵיהֶם וַיהוָה עִמָּכֶם׃ וַיִּקֹּד יְהוֹשָׁפָט
אַפַּיִם אָרְצָה וְכָל־יְהוּדָה וְיֹשְׁבֵי יְרוּשָׁלַ͏ִם נָפְלוּ לִפְנֵי יְהוָה לְהִשְׁתַּחֲוֹת
יט לַיהוָה׃ וַיָּקֻמוּ הַלְוִיִּם מִן־בְּנֵי הַקְּהָתִים וּמִן־בְּנֵי הַקָּרְחִים לְהַלֵּל לַיהוָה
כ אֱלֹהֵי יִשְׂרָאֵל בְּקוֹל גָּדוֹל לְמָעְלָה׃ וַיַּשְׁכִּימוּ בַבֹּקֶר וַיֵּצְאוּ לְמִדְבַּר
תְּקוֹעַ וּבְצֵאתָם עָמַד יְהוֹשָׁפָט וַיֹּאמֶר שְׁמָעוּנִי יְהוּדָה וְיֹשְׁבֵי יְרוּשָׁלַ͏ִם
כא הַאֲמִינוּ בַּיהוָה אֱלֹהֵיכֶם וְתֵאָמֵנוּ הַאֲמִינוּ בִנְבִיאָיו וְהַצְלִיחוּ׃ וַיִּוָּעַץ
אֶל־הָעָם וַיַּעֲמֵד מְשֹׁרְרִים לַיהוָה וּמְהַלְלִים לְהַדְרַת־קֹדֶשׁ בְּצֵאת
כב לִפְנֵי הֶחָלוּץ וְאֹמְרִים הוֹדוּ לַיהוָה כִּי לְעוֹלָם חַסְדּוֹ׃ וּבְעֵת הֵחֵלּוּ
בְרִנָּה וּתְהִלָּה נָתַן יְהוָה ׀ מְאָרְבִים עַל־בְּנֵי עַמּוֹן מוֹאָב וְהַר־שֵׂעִיר
כג הַבָּאִים לִיהוּדָה וַיִּנָּגֵפוּ׃ וַיַּעַמְדוּ בְּנֵי עַמּוֹן וּמוֹאָב עַל־יֹשְׁבֵי הַר־שֵׂעִיר

Mount Se'ir to destroy and annihilate them, and once they had finished off
24 the people of Se'ir, they proceeded to destroy one another. When Yehuda
reached the wilderness's vantage point, they looked out toward the hordes
and saw nothing but corpses sprawled all over the ground; none had escaped.
25 When Yehoshafat and his men advanced to seize the spoil, they found vast
quantities of goods and precious objects among the corpses; they loaded
themselves up until they could carry no more. It took them three days to carry
26 off the spoil, there was so much. On the fourth day they gathered at Berakha
Valley, for there they blessed the LORD – for this reason, that place is called
27 the Berakha Valley to this day. Then, with Yehoshafat at their head, all the
men of Yehuda and Jerusalem returned to Jerusalem with joy, for the LORD
28 had granted them joy over their enemies. They came to Jerusalem with harps
29 and lyres and trumpets to the House of the LORD. And fear of God was on
all the kingdoms of the lands, for they heard that the LORD had fought against
30 the enemies of Israel. So Yehoshafat's kingdom was at peace, for his God had
31 granted him rest on every side. Thus Yehoshafat reigned over
Yehuda. He was thirty-five years old when he became king, and for twenty-
five years he reigned in Jerusalem. His mother's name was Azuva daughter of
32 Shilḥi. He followed in the ways of his father Asa and did not turn away from
33 them, doing what was right in the eyes of the LORD. Only the high shrines
were not removed, and the hearts of the people were not devoted to the God
34 of their ancestors. The rest of Yehoshafat's history, earlier and later, is recorded
in the chronicles of Yehu son of Ḥanani, which were copied into the book of
35 the Kings of Israel. Later Yehoshafat, king of Yehuda, formed an alliance
36 with Aḥazya, king of Israel, whose ways were wicked. They joined forces to
build a fleet of ships to travel to Tarshish, and they built a fleet at Etzyon
37 Gever. But Eliezer son of Dodavahu of Mareshah prophesied
against him, saying, "When you joined forces with Aḥazyahu, the LORD burst
out against your work." And the ships were wrecked and not fit to sail to
21 1 Tarshish. And Yehoshafat slept with his ancestors and was buried with his
2 ancestors in the City of David. And his son Yehoram reigned in his place. He
had brothers, the sons of Yehoshafat: Azarya, Yeḥiel, Zekharyahu, Azaryahu,
Mikhael, and Shefatyahu; all these were sons of King Yehoshafat of Israel.
3 Their father gave them many gifts, silver and gold and precious things, along
with fortified cities in Yehuda, but he gave the kingship to Yehoram because
4 he was the firstborn. Once Yehoram had ascended his father's throne
and gained power, he had all his brothers killed by the sword along with some
5 of Israel's officials. Yehoram was thirty-two years old when he became king,
6 and for eight years he reigned in Jerusalem. He followed in the ways of the
kings of Israel, as the house of Aḥav had done, for Aḥav's daughter was his
7 wife, and he did what was evil in the eyes of the LORD. But the LORD was not
willing to destroy the House of David for the sake of the covenant He had
made with David, because He had promised to grant him and his descendants

לְהַחֲרִים וּלְהַשְׁמִיד וּכְכַלּוֹתָם בְּיוֹשְׁבֵי שֵׂעִיר עָזְרוּ אִישׁ בְּרֵעֵהוּ
כד לְמַשְׁחִית׃ וִיהוּדָה בָּא עַל־הַמִּצְפֶּה לַמִּדְבָּר וַיִּפְנוּ אֶל־הֶהָמוֹן וְהִנָּם
כה פְּגָרִים נֹפְלִים אַרְצָה וְאֵין פְּלֵיטָה׃ וַיָּבֹא יְהוֹשָׁפָט וְעַמּוֹ לָבֹז אֶת־
שְׁלָלָם וַיִּמְצְאוּ בָהֶם לָרֹב וּרְכוּשׁ וּפְגָרִים וּכְלֵי חֲמֻדוֹת וַיְנַצְּלוּ לָהֶם
כו לְאֵין מַשָּׂא וַיִּהְיוּ יָמִים שְׁלוֹשָׁה בֹּזְזִים אֶת־הַשָּׁלָל כִּי רַב־הוּא׃ וּבַיּוֹם
הָרְבִעִי נִקְהֲלוּ לְעֵמֶק בְּרָכָה כִּי שָׁם בֵּרְכוּ אֶת־יְהוָה עַל־כֵּן קָרְאוּ
כז אֶת־שֵׁם הַמָּקוֹם הַהוּא עֵמֶק בְּרָכָה עַד־הַיּוֹם׃ וַיָּשֻׁבוּ כָּל־אִישׁ יְהוּדָה
וִירוּשָׁלִַם וִיהוֹשָׁפָט בְּרֹאשָׁם לָשׁוּב אֶל־יְרוּשָׁלִַם בְּשִׂמְחָה כִּי־שִׂמְּחָם
כח יְהוָה מֵאוֹיְבֵיהֶם׃ וַיָּבֹאוּ יְרוּשָׁלִַם בִּנְבָלִים וּבְכִנֹּרוֹת וּבַחֲצֹצְרוֹת אֶל־
כט בֵּית יְהוָה׃ וַיְהִי פַּחַד אֱלֹהִים עַל כָּל־מַמְלְכוֹת הָאֲרָצוֹת בְּשָׁמְעָם כִּי
ל נִלְחַם יְהוָה עִם אוֹיְבֵי יִשְׂרָאֵל׃ וַתִּשְׁקֹט מַלְכוּת יְהוֹשָׁפָט וַיָּנַח לוֹ
לא אֱלֹהָיו מִסָּבִיב׃ וַיִּמְלֹךְ יְהוֹשָׁפָט עַל־יְהוּדָה בֶּן־שְׁלֹשִׁים יט
וְחָמֵשׁ שָׁנָה בְּמָלְכוֹ וְעֶשְׂרִים וְחָמֵשׁ שָׁנָה מָלַךְ בִּירוּשָׁלִָם וְשֵׁם אִמּוֹ
לב עֲזוּבָה בַּת־שִׁלְחִי׃ וַיֵּלֶךְ בְּדֶרֶךְ אָבִיו אָסָא וְלֹא־סָר מִמֶּנָּה לַעֲשׂוֹת
לג הַיָּשָׁר בְּעֵינֵי יְהוָה׃ אַךְ הַבָּמוֹת לֹא־סָרוּ וְעוֹד הָעָם לֹא־הֵכִינוּ לְבָבָם
לד לֵאלֹהֵי אֲבֹתֵיהֶם׃ וְיֶתֶר דִּבְרֵי יְהוֹשָׁפָט הָרִאשֹׁנִים וְהָאַחֲרֹנִים הִנָּם
כְּתוּבִים בְּדִבְרֵי יֵהוּא בֶן־חֲנָנִי אֲשֶׁר הֹעֲלָה עַל־סֵפֶר מַלְכֵי יִשְׂרָאֵל׃
לה וְאַחֲרֵי־כֵן אֶתְחַבַּר יְהוֹשָׁפָט מֶלֶךְ־יְהוּדָה עִם אֲחַזְיָה מֶלֶךְ־יִשְׂרָאֵל
לו הוּא הִרְשִׁיעַ לַעֲשׂוֹת׃ וַיְחַבְּרֵהוּ עִמּוֹ לַעֲשׂוֹת אֳנִיּוֹת לָלֶכֶת תַּרְשִׁישׁ
לז וַיַּעֲשׂוּ אֳנִיּוֹת בְּעֶצְיוֹן גָּבֶר׃ וַיִּתְנַבֵּא אֱלִיעֶזֶר בֶּן־דֹּדָוָהוּ
מִמָּרֵשָׁה עַל־יְהוֹשָׁפָט לֵאמֹר כְּהִתְחַבֶּרְךָ עִם־אֲחַזְיָהוּ פָּרַץ יְהוָה
כא א אֶת־מַעֲשֶׂיךָ וַיִּשָּׁבְרוּ אֳנִיּוֹת וְלֹא עָצְרוּ לָלֶכֶת אֶל־תַּרְשִׁישׁ׃ וַיִּשְׁכַּב
יְהוֹשָׁפָט עִם־אֲבֹתָיו וַיִּקָּבֵר עִם־אֲבֹתָיו בְּעִיר דָּוִיד וַיִּמְלֹךְ יְהוֹרָם בְּנוֹ
ב תַּחְתָּיו׃ וְלוֹ־אַחִים בְּנֵי יְהוֹשָׁפָט עֲזַרְיָה וִיחִיאֵל וּזְכַרְיָהוּ וַעֲזַרְיָהוּ
ג וּמִיכָאֵל וּשְׁפַטְיָהוּ כָּל־אֵלֶּה בְּנֵי יְהוֹשָׁפָט מֶלֶךְ יִשְׂרָאֵל׃ וַיִּתֵּן לָהֶם ׀
אֲבִיהֶם מַתָּנוֹת רַבּוֹת לְכֶסֶף וּלְזָהָב וּלְמִגְדָּנוֹת עִם־עָרֵי מְצֻרוֹת
ד בִּיהוּדָה וְאֶת־הַמַּמְלָכָה נָתַן לִיהוֹרָם כִּי־הוּא הַבְּכוֹר׃ וַיָּקָם
יְהוֹרָם עַל־מַמְלֶכֶת אָבִיו וַיִּתְחַזַּק וַיַּהֲרֹג אֶת־כָּל־אֶחָיו בֶּחָרֶב וְגַם
ה מִשָּׂרֵי יִשְׂרָאֵל׃ בֶּן־שְׁלֹשִׁים וּשְׁתַּיִם שָׁנָה יְהוֹרָם בְּמָלְכוֹ וּשְׁמוֹנֶה שָׁנִים
ו מָלַךְ בִּירוּשָׁלִָם׃ וַיֵּלֶךְ בְּדֶרֶךְ ׀ מַלְכֵי יִשְׂרָאֵל כַּאֲשֶׁר עָשׂוּ בֵּית אַחְאָב
ז כִּי בַּת־אַחְאָב הָיְתָה לּוֹ אִשָּׁה וַיַּעַשׂ הָרַע בְּעֵינֵי יְהוָה׃ וְלֹא־אָבָה
יְהוָה לְהַשְׁחִית אֶת־בֵּית דָּוִיד לְמַעַן הַבְּרִית אֲשֶׁר כָּרַת לְדָוִיד וְכַאֲשֶׁר

8 a lamp for all time. In his time Edom rebelled against Yehuda and appointed
9 their own king. Yehoram crossed over with his officers and all his chariots;
he advanced at night to attack Edom, who had surrounded him and his chariot
10 officers. Edom has rebelled against Yehuda ever since; it was also then that
Livna rebelled against his rule because he abandoned the Lord, God of his
11 ancestors. He even made high shrines in the hills of Yehuda, led the people
12 of Jerusalem astray, and corrupted Yehuda. A letter came to him
from the prophet Eliyahu saying, "Thus says the Lord, God of your father
David: Because you did not follow in the ways of your father Yehoshafat and
13 in the ways of Asa, king of Yehuda, but followed in the ways of the kings of
Israel and, like the house of Aḥav, led Yehuda and the people of Jerusalem
astray, and because you killed your brothers from your father's house, who
14 were better than you – the Lord is about to unleash a devastating plague
15 among your people, your sons and wives, and all your possessions. And you
yourself will suffer from severe sickness, from a bowel disease – until your
16 bowels slip out from sheer sickness, day by day." And the Lord stirred against
Yehoram the spirit of the Philistines and the Arabs who neighbored the
17 Kushites. They marched up against Yehuda, invaded them, and captured all
the possessions that were found around the royal palace, as well as his sons
and wives. The only son that was left to him was Yehoaḥaz, his youngest son.
18 19 After all this, the Lord struck him with an incurable bowel disease. Gradually,
his bowels slipped out from sheer sickness, and at the end of the second year
he died in gruesome agony. The people did not make a great fire in his honor
20 as they did for his ancestors. He was thirty-two years old when he became
king, and for eight years he reigned in Jerusalem. No one was sorry when he
died, and they buried him in the City of David, but not in the royal tombs.
22 1 The people of Jerusalem made Aḥazyahu, his youngest son, king in his place
because all the older sons had been killed by the raiders who infiltrated the
camp with the Arabs. Thus Aḥazyahu, son of King Yehoram of Yehuda,
2 became king. Aḥazyahu was forty-two years old when he became
king, and he reigned in Jerusalem for a single year; his mother's name was
3 Atalyahu daughter of Omri. He too followed in the ways of the house of Aḥav,
4 for his mother taught him wicked ways. Like the house of Aḥav he did what
was evil in the eyes of the Lord, for they had become his counselors after his
5 father's death, to his undoing. It was their counsel that he followed in
accompanying Yehoram son of Aḥav, king of Israel, to war against Ḥazael,
6 king of Aram, at Ramot Gilad where the Arameans defeated Yoram. He went
back to Yizre'el to recover from the wounds he had sustained in Rama when
fighting against Ḥazael, king of Aram. Azaryahu son of Yehoram, king of
Yehuda, went down to visit Yehoram son of Aḥav in Yizre'el while he was
7 injured. Through Aḥazyahu's visit to Yoram, God brought about his downfall,

ח אָמַר לָתֵת לוֹ נִיר וּלְבָנָיו כָּל־הַיָּמִים׃ בְּיָמָיו פָּשַׁע אֱדוֹם מִתַּחַת יַד־
ט יְהוּדָה וַיַּמְלִיכוּ עֲלֵיהֶם מֶלֶךְ׃ וַיַּעֲבֹר יְהוֹרָם עִם־שָׂרָיו וְכָל־הָרֶכֶב עִמּוֹ
י וַיְהִי קָם לַיְלָה וַיַּךְ אֶת־אֱדוֹם הַסּוֹבֵב אֵלָיו וְאֵת שָׂרֵי הָרָכֶב׃ וַיִּפְשַׁע
אֱדוֹם מִתַּחַת יַד־יְהוּדָה עַד הַיּוֹם הַזֶּה אָז תִּפְשַׁע לִבְנָה בָּעֵת הַהִיא
יא מִתַּחַת יָדוֹ כִּי עָזַב אֶת־יְהוָה אֱלֹהֵי אֲבֹתָיו׃ גַּם־הוּא עָשָׂה בָמוֹת
יב בְּהָרֵי יְהוּדָה וַיֶּזֶן אֶת־יֹשְׁבֵי יְרוּשָׁלִַם וַיַּדַּח אֶת־יְהוּדָה׃ וַיָּבֹא
אֵלָיו מִכְתָּב מֵאֵלִיָּהוּ הַנָּבִיא לֵאמֹר כֹּה ׀ אָמַר יְהוָה אֱלֹהֵי דָּוִיד אָבִיךָ
תַּחַת אֲשֶׁר לֹא־הָלַכְתָּ בְּדַרְכֵי יְהוֹשָׁפָט אָבִיךָ וּבְדַרְכֵי אָסָא מֶלֶךְ־
יג יְהוּדָה׃ וַתֵּלֶךְ בְּדֶרֶךְ מַלְכֵי יִשְׂרָאֵל וַתַּזְנֶה אֶת־יְהוּדָה וְאֶת־יֹשְׁבֵי
יְרוּשָׁלִַם כְּהַזְנוֹת בֵּית אַחְאָב וְגַם אֶת־אַחֶיךָ בֵית־אָבִיךָ הַטּוֹבִים מִמְּךָ
יד הָרָגְתָּ׃ הִנֵּה יְהוָה נֹגֵף מַגֵּפָה גְדוֹלָה בְּעַמֶּךָ וּבְבָנֶיךָ וּבְנָשֶׁיךָ וּבְכָל־
טו רְכוּשֶׁךָ׃ וְאַתָּה בָּחֳלָיִים רַבִּים בְּמַחֲלָה מֵעֶיךָ עַד־יֵצְאוּ מֵעֶיךָ מִן־
טז הַחֹלִי יָמִים עַל־יָמִים׃ וַיָּעַר יְהוָה עַל־יְהוֹרָם אֶת־רוּחַ הַפְּלִשְׁתִּים
יז וְהָעַרְבִים אֲשֶׁר עַל־יַד כּוּשִׁים׃ וַיַּעֲלוּ בִיהוּדָה וַיִּבְקָעוּהָ וַיִּשְׁבּוּ אֵת
כָּל־הָרְכוּשׁ הַנִּמְצָא לְבֵית־הַמֶּלֶךְ וְגַם־בָּנָיו וְנָשָׁיו וְלֹא נִשְׁאַר־לוֹ בֵּן
יח כִּי אִם־יְהוֹאָחָז קְטֹן בָּנָיו׃ וְאַחֲרֵי כָּל־זֹאת נְגָפוֹ יְהוָה ׀ בְּמֵעָיו לָחֳלִי
יט לְאֵין מַרְפֵּא׃ וַיְהִי לְיָמִים ׀ מִיָּמִים וּכְעֵת צֵאת הַקֵּץ לְיָמִים שְׁנַיִם
יָצְאוּ מֵעָיו עִם־חָלְיוֹ וַיָּמָת בְּתַחֲלֻאִים רָעִים וְלֹא־עָשׂוּ לוֹ עַמּוֹ שְׂרֵפָה
כ כִּשְׂרֵפַת אֲבֹתָיו׃ בֶּן־שְׁלֹשִׁים וּשְׁתַּיִם הָיָה בְמָלְכוֹ וּשְׁמוֹנֶה שָׁנִים
מָלַךְ בִּירוּשָׁלִָם וַיֵּלֶךְ בְּלֹא חֶמְדָּה וַיִּקְבְּרֻהוּ בְּעִיר דָּוִיד וְלֹא בְּקִבְרוֹת
כב א הַמְּלָכִים׃ וַיַּמְלִיכוּ יוֹשְׁבֵי יְרוּשָׁלִַם אֶת־אֲחַזְיָהוּ בְנוֹ הַקָּטֹן תַּחְתָּיו כִּי
כָּל־הָרִאשֹׁנִים הָרַג הַגְּדוּד הַבָּא בָעַרְבִים לַמַּחֲנֶה וַיִּמְלֹךְ אֲחַזְיָהוּ
ב בֶּן־יְהוֹרָם מֶלֶךְ יְהוּדָה׃ בֶּן־אַרְבָּעִים וּשְׁתַּיִם שָׁנָה
אֲחַזְיָהוּ בְמָלְכוֹ וְשָׁנָה אַחַת מָלַךְ בִּירוּשָׁלִָם וְשֵׁם אִמּוֹ עֲתַלְיָהוּ
ג בַּת־עָמְרִי׃ גַּם־הוּא הָלַךְ בְּדַרְכֵי בֵּית אַחְאָב כִּי אִמּוֹ הָיְתָה יוֹעַצְתּוֹ
ד לְהַרְשִׁיעַ׃ וַיַּעַשׂ הָרַע בְּעֵינֵי יְהוָה כְּבֵית אַחְאָב כִּי הֵמָּה הָיוּ־לוֹ יוֹעֲצִים
ה אַחֲרֵי מוֹת אָבִיו לְמַשְׁחִית לוֹ׃ גַּם בַּעֲצָתָם הָלַךְ וַיֵּלֶךְ אֶת־יְהוֹרָם
בֶּן־אַחְאָב מֶלֶךְ יִשְׂרָאֵל לַמִּלְחָמָה עַל־חֲזָאֵל מֶלֶךְ־אֲרָם בְּרָמוֹת
ו גִּלְעָד וַיַּכּוּ הָרַמִּים אֶת־יוֹרָם׃ וַיָּשָׁב לְהִתְרַפֵּא בְיִזְרְעֶאל כִּי הַמַּכִּים
אֲשֶׁר הִכֻּהוּ בָרָמָה בְּהִלָּחֲמוֹ אֶת־חֲזָהאֵל מֶלֶךְ אֲרָם וַעֲזַרְיָהוּ בֶן־
יְהוֹרָם מֶלֶךְ יְהוּדָה יָרַד לִרְאוֹת אֶת־יְהוֹרָם בֶּן־אַחְאָב בְּיִזְרְעֶאל
ז כִּי־חֹלֶה הוּא׃ וּמֵאֱלֹהִים הָיְתָה תְּבוּסַת אֲחַזְיָהוּ לָבוֹא אֶל־יוֹרָם

for when he arrived, he went out with Yehoram to meet Yehu son of Nimshi,
8 whom the LORD had anointed to destroy the house of Aḥav. As Yehu was
executing judgment on the house of Aḥav, he encountered the Judahite
officers and Aḥazyahu's nephews who attended Aḥazyahu, and he killed them.
9 He then sought out Aḥazyahu and had him captured as he was hiding in
Shomron, and he was brought to Yehu. He put him to death and buried him,
for they said, "He was the son of Yehoshafat, who sought the LORD with all
his heart." The house of Aḥazyahu was not powerful enough to rule the
10 kingdom. When Atalyahu, the mother of Aḥazyahu, saw that her
son was dead, she swiftly assassinated all those of royal descent in the house
11 of Yehuda. But Yehoshavat, the daughter of the king, took Yoash, Aḥazyahu's
son, stole him away from where the princes were being put to death, and
placed him in the bed-chamber together with his nurse. Because Yehoshavat,
King Yehoram's daughter and the wife of the priest Yehoyada, was Aḥazyahu's
12 sister, she hid him from Atalyahu so that she would not put him to death. He
stayed with them in the House of God, hiding for six years, while Atalya
23 1 reigned over the land. By the seventh year, Yehoyada had gained
power, and he formed a pact with the officers of hundreds – Azaryahu son of
Yeroḥam, Yishmael son of Yehoḥanan, Azaryahu son of Oved, Maaseyahu
2 son of Adayahu, and Elishafat son of Zikhri. They made their way around
Yehuda and gathered the Levites and ancestral heads from all the towns of
3 Yehuda, then came to Jerusalem. Then all the assembly formed a covenant
with the king in the House of God. "Here is the king's son," he said to them.
4 "He shall reign as the LORD promised David's descendants would. This is
what you must do: out of the priests and Levites on weekly duty, a third of
5 you shall be gatekeepers, a third of you shall be stationed at the royal palace,
and a third at the Foundation Gate. All the people shall be in the courtyards
6 of the House of the LORD. No one must enter the House of the LORD except
for the priests and the Levites on duty; they may enter because they are
7 consecrated, but all the people must keep the LORD's charge. The Levites must
surround the king on all sides and make sure every man's weapon is poised,
and whoever enters the House must be killed. And stay with the king when
8 he goes or comes." The Levites and all of Yehuda did all that the priest
Yehoyada instructed them, and each took their men – those on weekly duty
and those off weekly duty, for the priest Yehoyada had not dismissed the
9 divisions. The priest Yehoyada then gave the officers of hundreds
David's own spears, shields, and quivers, which were in the House of God.
10 He then stationed all the people – each man with his weapon poised – from
the south end of the House to the north end of the House, by the altar and
11 the House, all around the king. They brought out the king's son, set the crown
and the royal insignia upon him, and declared him king. Yehoyada and his
12 sons anointed him and shouted, "Long live the king!" Atalyahu

וּבְבֹאוֹ יָצָא עִם־יְהוֹרָם אֶל־יֵהוּא בֶן־נִמְשִׁי אֲשֶׁר מְשָׁחוֹ יְהוָה לְהַכְרִית
ח אֶת־בֵּית אַחְאָב׃ וַיְהִי כְּהִשָּׁפֵט יֵהוּא עִם־בֵּית אַחְאָב וַיִּמְצָא אֶת־שָׂרֵי
ט יְהוּדָה וּבְנֵי אֲחֵי אֲחַזְיָהוּ מְשָׁרְתִים לַאֲחַזְיָהוּ וַיַּהַרְגֵם׃ וַיְבַקֵּשׁ אֶת־
אֲחַזְיָהוּ וַיִּלְכְּדֻהוּ וְהוּא מִתְחַבֵּא בְשֹׁמְרוֹן וַיְבִאֻהוּ אֶל־יֵהוּא וַיְמִתֻהוּ
וַיִּקְבְּרֻהוּ כִּי אָמְרוּ בֶּן־יְהוֹשָׁפָט הוּא אֲשֶׁר־דָּרַשׁ אֶת־יְהוָה בְּכָל־לְבָבוֹ
י וְאֵין לְבֵית אֲחַזְיָהוּ לַעְצֹר כֹּחַ לְמַמְלָכָה׃ וַעֲתַלְיָהוּ אֵם
אֲחַזְיָהוּ רָאֲתָה כִּי־מֵת בְּנָהּ וַתָּקָם וַתְּדַבֵּר אֶת־כָּל־זֶרַע הַמַּמְלָכָה
יא לְבֵית יְהוּדָה׃ וַתִּקַּח יְהוֹשַׁבְעַת בַּת־הַמֶּלֶךְ אֶת־יוֹאָשׁ בֶּן־אֲחַזְיָהוּ
וַתִּגְנֹב אֹתוֹ מִתּוֹךְ בְּנֵי־הַמֶּלֶךְ הַמּוּמָתִים וַתִּתֵּן אֹתוֹ וְאֶת־מֵינִקְתּוֹ
בַּחֲדַר הַמִּטּוֹת וַתַּסְתִּירֵהוּ יְהוֹשַׁבְעַת בַּת־הַמֶּלֶךְ יְהוֹרָם אֵשֶׁת יְהוֹיָדָע
הַכֹּהֵן כִּי הִיא הָיְתָה אֲחוֹת אֲחַזְיָהוּ מִפְּנֵי עֲתַלְיָהוּ וְלֹא הֱמִיתָתְהוּ׃
יב וַיְהִי אִתָּם בְּבֵית הָאֱלֹהִים מִתְחַבֵּא שֵׁשׁ שָׁנִים וַעֲתַלְיָה מֹלֶכֶת עַל־
כג א הָאָרֶץ׃ וּבַשָּׁנָה הַשְּׁבִעִית הִתְחַזַּק יְהוֹיָדָע וַיִּקַּח אֶת־שָׂרֵי
הַמֵּאוֹת לַעֲזַרְיָהוּ בֶן־יְרֹחָם וּלְיִשְׁמָעֵאל בֶּן־יְהוֹחָנָן וְלַעֲזַרְיָהוּ בֶן־עוֹבֵד
ב וְאֶת־מַעֲשֵׂיָהוּ בֶן־עֲדָיָהוּ וְאֶת־אֱלִישָׁפָט בֶּן־זִכְרִי עִמּוֹ בַבְּרִית׃ וַיָּסֹבּוּ
בִּיהוּדָה וַיִּקְבְּצוּ אֶת־הַלְוִיִּם מִכָּל־עָרֵי יְהוּדָה וְרָאשֵׁי הָאָבוֹת לְיִשְׂרָאֵל
ג וַיָּבֹאוּ אֶל־יְרוּשָׁלִָם׃ וַיִּכְרֹת כָּל־הַקָּהָל בְּרִית בְּבֵית הָאֱלֹהִים עִם־
הַמֶּלֶךְ וַיֹּאמֶר לָהֶם הִנֵּה בֶן־הַמֶּלֶךְ יִמְלֹךְ כַּאֲשֶׁר דִּבֶּר יְהוָה עַל־בְּנֵי
ד דָוִיד׃ זֶה הַדָּבָר אֲשֶׁר תַּעֲשׂוּ הַשְּׁלִשִׁית מִכֶּם בָּאֵי הַשַּׁבָּת לַכֹּהֲנִים
ה וְלַלְוִיִּם לְשֹׁעֲרֵי הַסִּפִּים׃ וְהַשְּׁלִשִׁית בְּבֵית הַמֶּלֶךְ וְהַשְּׁלִשִׁית בְּשַׁעַר
ו הַיְסוֹד וְכָל־הָעָם בְּחַצְרוֹת בֵּית יְהוָה׃ וְאַל־יָבוֹא בֵית־יְהוָה כִּי אִם־
הַכֹּהֲנִים וְהַמְשָׁרְתִים לַלְוִיִּם הֵמָּה יָבֹאוּ כִּי־קֹדֶשׁ הֵמָּה וְכָל־הָעָם
ז יִשְׁמְרוּ מִשְׁמֶרֶת יְהוָה׃ וְהִקִּיפוּ הַלְוִיִּם אֶת־הַמֶּלֶךְ סָבִיב אִישׁ וְכֵלָיו
בְּיָדוֹ וְהַבָּא אֶל־הַבַּיִת יוּמָת וִהְיוּ אֶת־הַמֶּלֶךְ בְּבֹאוֹ וּבְצֵאתוֹ׃
ח וַיַּעֲשׂוּ הַלְוִיִּם וְכָל־יְהוּדָה כְּכֹל אֲשֶׁר־צִוָּה יְהוֹיָדָע הַכֹּהֵן וַיִּקְחוּ אִישׁ
אֶת־אֲנָשָׁיו בָּאֵי הַשַּׁבָּת עִם יוֹצְאֵי הַשַּׁבָּת כִּי לֹא פָטַר יְהוֹיָדָע הַכֹּהֵן
ט אֶת־הַמַּחְלְקוֹת׃ וַיִּתֵּן יְהוֹיָדָע הַכֹּהֵן לְשָׂרֵי הַמֵּאוֹת אֶת־
הַחֲנִיתִים וְאֶת־הַמָּגִנּוֹת וְאֶת־הַשְּׁלָטִים אֲשֶׁר לַמֶּלֶךְ דָּוִיד אֲשֶׁר בֵּית
י הָאֱלֹהִים׃ וַיַּעֲמֵד אֶת־כָּל־הָעָם וְאִישׁ ׀ שִׁלְחוֹ בְיָדוֹ מִכֶּתֶף הַבַּיִת
הַיְמָנִית עַד־כֶּתֶף הַבַּיִת הַשְּׂמָאלִית לַמִּזְבֵּחַ וְלַבָּיִת עַל־הַמֶּלֶךְ סָבִיב׃
כ יא וַיּוֹצִיאוּ אֶת־בֶּן־הַמֶּלֶךְ וַיִּתְּנוּ עָלָיו אֶת־הַנֵּזֶר וְאֶת־הָעֵדוּת וַיַּמְלִיכוּ
יב אֹתוֹ וַיִּמְשָׁחֻהוּ יְהוֹיָדָע וּבָנָיו וַיֹּאמְרוּ יְחִי הַמֶּלֶךְ׃ וַתִּשְׁמַע

heard the sound of the people thronging and praising the king, and she came
13 to the people at the House of the LORD. When she looked up to find the king
standing on the platform by the entrance with officers with trumpets beside
the king, all the people of the land rejoicing and blowing the trumpets, and
singers with their instruments leading the celebration, Atalyahu rent her
14 clothes and shouted, "Treason! Treason!" But Yehoyada brought
out the officers of hundreds, the force commanders. "Take her out through
the ranks," he said to them, "and put anyone who follows to the sword," for
the priest thought, "They should not put her to death in the House of the
15 LORD." They cleared the way for her, and she entered the royal palace through
the Horse Gate, and there they put her to death.
16 Then Yehoyada forged a covenant between him and all the people, and with
17 the king, to be the LORD's people. All the people came to the temple of Baal
and tore it down, shattered its altars and images, and killed Matan, the priest of
18 Baal, in front of the altars. Yehoyada then assigned the duties of the House of
the LORD to the charge of the Levite priests that David had appointed over the
House of the LORD to offer the LORD's burnt offerings, as written in Moshe's
19 teaching, in joy and song as David set down. He appointed gatekeepers at
the gates of the House of the LORD to prevent the entry of anyone with any
20 kind of impurity. Then he had the officers of the hundreds, the nobility, the
leaders of the people, and all the people of the land escort the king down from
the House of the LORD. They came in through the upper gate of the royal
21 palace, and they set the king upon the royal throne. All the people of the land
rejoiced, and calm settled over the city. As for Atalyahu, they had put her to
24 1 death by sword. Yoash was seven years old when he became king,
and for forty years he reigned in Jerusalem. His mother's name was Tziya of
2 Be'er Sheva. Yoash did what was right in the eyes of the LORD all the days of
Yehoyada the priest.
3 Yehoyada arranged two wives for him, and he fathered sons and daughters.
4 5 After some time, Yoash decided to restore the House of the LORD. He
gathered the priests and the Levites and said to them, "Go out to the towns
of Yehuda and collect the money due annually from all of Israel to repair the
House of your God. Take care of it right away." But the Levites did not act
6 right away. The king summoned Yehoyada, the head, and said to him,
"Why have you not required the Levites to bring the tax imposed by Moshe,
the LORD's servant, from Yehuda and Jerusalem and from the assembly of
7 Israel for the Tent of Testimony?" For the followers of the wicked Atalyahu
had violently broken into the House of God and even used all the sacred
8 objects of the House of the LORD for the Baalim. At the king's command,
9 they made a chest and placed it outside the gate of the LORD's House. A
proclamation was issued in Yehuda and Jerusalem: to bring to the LORD the

עֲתַלְיָהוּ אֶת־קוֹל הָעָם הָרָצִים וְהַמְהַלְלִים אֶת־הַמֶּלֶךְ וַתָּבוֹא אֶל־
יג הָעָם בֵּית יְהוָה׃ וַתֵּרֶא וְהִנֵּה הַמֶּלֶךְ עוֹמֵד עַל־עַמּוּדוֹ בַּמָּבוֹא וְהַשָּׂרִים
וְהַחֲצֹצְרוֹת עַל־הַמֶּלֶךְ וְכָל־עַם הָאָרֶץ שָׂמֵחַ וְתוֹקֵעַ בַּחֲצֹצְרוֹת
וְהַמְשׁוֹרְרִים בִּכְלֵי הַשִּׁיר וּמוֹדִיעִים לְהַלֵּל וַתִּקְרַע עֲתַלְיָהוּ אֶת־בְּגָדֶיהָ
יד וַתֹּאמֶר קֶשֶׁר קָשֶׁר׃ וַיּוֹצֵא יְהוֹיָדָע הַכֹּהֵן
אֶת־שָׂרֵי הַמֵּאוֹת ׀ פְּקוּדֵי הַחַיִל וַיֹּאמֶר אֲלֵהֶם הוֹצִיאוּהָ אֶל־מִבֵּית
הַשְּׂדֵרוֹת וְהַבָּא אַחֲרֶיהָ יוּמַת בֶּחָרֶב כִּי אָמַר הַכֹּהֵן לֹא תְמִיתוּהָ בֵּית
טו יְהוָה׃ וַיָּשִׂימוּ לָהּ יָדַיִם וַתָּבוֹא אֶל־מְבוֹא שַׁעַר־הַסּוּסִים בֵּית הַמֶּלֶךְ
וַיְמִיתוּהָ שָׁם׃
טז וַיִּכְרֹת יְהוֹיָדָע בְּרִית בֵּינוֹ וּבֵין כָּל־הָעָם וּבֵין הַמֶּלֶךְ לִהְיוֹת לְעָם
יז לַיהוָה׃ וַיָּבֹאוּ כָל־הָעָם בֵּית־הַבַּעַל וַיִּתְּצֻהוּ וְאֶת־מִזְבְּחֹתָיו וְאֶת־
יח צְלָמָיו שִׁבֵּרוּ וְאֵת מַתָּן כֹּהֵן הַבַּעַל הָרְגוּ לִפְנֵי הַמִּזְבְּחוֹת׃ וַיָּשֶׂם
יְהוֹיָדָע פְּקֻדֹּת בֵּית יְהוָה בְּיַד הַכֹּהֲנִים הַלְוִיִּם אֲשֶׁר חָלַק דָּוִיד עַל־בֵּית
יְהוָה לְהַעֲלוֹת עֹלוֹת יְהוָה כַּכָּתוּב בְּתוֹרַת מֹשֶׁה בְּשִׂמְחָה וּבְשִׁיר עַל
יט יְדֵי דָוִיד׃ וַיַּעֲמֵד הַשּׁוֹעֲרִים עַל־שַׁעֲרֵי בֵּית יְהוָה וְלֹא־יָבוֹא טָמֵא
כ לְכָל־דָּבָר׃ וַיִּקַּח אֶת־שָׂרֵי הַמֵּאוֹת וְאֶת־הָאַדִּירִים וְאֶת־הַמּוֹשְׁלִים
בָּעָם וְאֵת ׀ כָּל־עַם הָאָרֶץ וַיּוֹרֶד אֶת־הַמֶּלֶךְ מִבֵּית יְהוָה וַיָּבֹאוּ
בְּתוֹךְ־שַׁעַר הָעֶלְיוֹן בֵּית הַמֶּלֶךְ וַיּוֹשִׁיבוּ אֶת־הַמֶּלֶךְ עַל כִּסֵּא
כא הַמַּמְלָכָה׃ וַיִּשְׂמְחוּ כָל־עַם־הָאָרֶץ וְהָעִיר שָׁקָטָה וְאֶת־עֲתַלְיָהוּ
כד א הֵמִיתוּ בֶחָרֶב׃ בֶּן־שֶׁבַע שָׁנִים יֹאָשׁ בְּמָלְכוֹ וְאַרְבָּעִים
ב שָׁנָה מָלַךְ בִּירוּשָׁלָ͏ִם וְשֵׁם אִמּוֹ צִבְיָה מִבְּאֵר שָׁבַע׃ וַיַּעַשׂ יוֹאָשׁ הַיָּשָׁר
בְּעֵינֵי יְהוָה כָּל־יְמֵי יְהוֹיָדָע הַכֹּהֵן׃
ג ד וַיִּשָּׂא־לוֹ יְהוֹיָדָע נָשִׁים שְׁתָּיִם וַיּוֹלֶד בָּנִים וּבָנוֹת׃ וַיְהִי אַחֲרֵי־כֵן הָיָה
ה עִם־לֵב יוֹאָשׁ לְחַדֵּשׁ אֶת־בֵּית יְהוָה׃ וַיִּקְבֹּץ אֶת־הַכֹּהֲנִים וְהַלְוִיִּם
וַיֹּאמֶר לָהֶם צְאוּ לְעָרֵי יְהוּדָה וְקִבְצוּ מִכָּל־יִשְׂרָאֵל כֶּסֶף לְחַזֵּק ׀ אֶת־
בֵּית אֱלֹהֵיכֶם מִדֵּי שָׁנָה בְּשָׁנָה וְאַתֶּם תְּמַהֲרוּ לַדָּבָר וְלֹא מִהֲרוּ
ו הַלְוִיִּם׃ וַיִּקְרָא הַמֶּלֶךְ לִיהוֹיָדָע הָרֹאשׁ וַיֹּאמֶר לוֹ מַדּוּעַ
לֹא־דָרַשְׁתָּ עַל־הַלְוִיִּם לְהָבִיא מִיהוּדָה וּמִירוּשָׁלַ͏ִם אֶת־מַשְׂאַת מֹשֶׁה
ז עֶבֶד־יְהוָה וְהַקָּהָל לְיִשְׂרָאֵל לְאֹהֶל הָעֵדוּת׃ כִּי עֲתַלְיָהוּ הַמִּרְשַׁעַת
בָּנֶיהָ פָרְצוּ אֶת־בֵּית הָאֱלֹהִים וְגַם כָּל־קָדְשֵׁי בֵית־יְהוָה עָשׂוּ לַבְּעָלִים׃
ח וַיֹּאמֶר הַמֶּלֶךְ וַיַּעֲשׂוּ אֲרוֹן אֶחָד וַיִּתְּנֻהוּ בְּשַׁעַר בֵּית־יְהוָה חוּצָה׃
ט וַיִּתְּנוּ־קוֹל בִּיהוּדָה וּבִירוּשָׁלַ͏ִם לְהָבִיא לַיהוָה מַשְׂאַת מֹשֶׁה עֶבֶד־

10 tax that Moshe, servant of God, imposed on Israel in the wilderness. And all
the officials and all the people brought it gladly, and they dropped it into the
11 chest until it was full. Whenever the Levites saw that there was a consi-derable
amount of money in the chest, they would bring it to the king's officers, and
the royal scribe and the chief priest's clerk would come and empty the chest,
then put it back in its place. They did this regularly and collected a large
12 amount of money. The king and Yehoyada gave it to those who oversaw the
work on the House of the LORD; they hired masons and carpenters to restore
the House of the LORD as well as smiths of iron and bronze to repair the
13 House of the LORD. The craftsmen did their work well, and they carried out
the repair work; they restored the House of God to its original condition and
14 made reinforcements. When they had finished, they brought the remaining
money to the king and Yehoyada, and it was made into vessels for the House
of the LORD: utensils for the service and the burnt offerings, spoons, and
vessels of gold and silver. Burnt offerings were offered up regularly in the
15 House of the LORD all the days of Yehoyada. Yehoyada grew old and
full of days, and he died; he was one hundred thirty years old when he died.
16 They buried him in the City of David among the kings because of the good
17 he had done in Israel and for God and His House. After the death
of Yehoyada, the officials of Yehuda came and pandered to the king, moving
18 the king to obey them. They abandoned the House of the LORD, the God of
their ancestors, and they worshipped sacred trees and idols; this offense
19 stirred up divine fury against Yehuda and Jerusalem. He sent prophets among
them to bring them back to the LORD, and they warned them, but they would
20 not pay any heed. Then the spirit of God seized Zekharya son of
Yehoyada the priest, and he stood above the people. "Thus says God," he said
to them. "Why do you transgress the LORD's commandments when you
cannot succeed? Because you have abandoned the LORD, He has abandoned
21 you." But they conspired against him, and at the king's command, they pelted
22 him with stones in the courtyard of the House of the LORD. Yoash would not
remember the loyalty his father Yehoyada had shown him, and he killed his
23 son. As he died he said, "May the LORD see and avenge." At the end
of the year, the Aramean army marched up against him. They invaded Yehuda
and Jerusalem and killed all the leaders of the people from among the people
24 and sent all their spoil to the king of Damascus. Though the Aramean army
had come with but few men, the LORD delivered a vast force into their hands,
for they had abandoned the LORD, God of their ancestors – and on Yoash,
25 they executed judgment. When they withdrew from him, leaving him gravely
wounded, his servants conspired against him for murdering the sons[34] of
Yehoyada the priest. They killed him in his bed, and he died. And they buried
26 him in the City of David, but they did not bury him in the royal tombs. These
were the ones who conspired against him: Zavad son of Shimat the Amonite
27 woman and Yehozavad son of Shimrit the Moabite woman. The accounts of

34 | Verses 20–21 above describe only the killing of Zekharya.

י הָאֱלֹהִים עַל־יִשְׂרָאֵל בַּמִּדְבָּר׃ וַיִּשְׂמְחוּ כָל־הַשָּׂרִים וְכָל־הָעָם וַיָּבִיאוּ
יא וַיַּשְׁלִיכוּ לָאָרוֹן עַד־לְכַלֵּה׃ וַיְהִי בְּעֵת יָבִיא אֶת־הָאָרוֹן אֶל־פְּקֻדַּת
הַמֶּלֶךְ בְּיַד הַלְוִיִּם וְכִרְאוֹתָם כִּי־רַב הַכֶּסֶף וּבָא סוֹפֵר הַמֶּלֶךְ וּפְקִיד
כֹּהֵן הָרֹאשׁ וִיעָרוּ אֶת־הָאָרוֹן וְיִשָּׂאֻהוּ וִישִׁבֻהוּ אֶל־מְקֹמוֹ כֹּה עָשׂוּ
יב לְיוֹם בְּיוֹם וַיַּאַסְפוּ־כֶסֶף לָרֹב׃ וַיִּתְּנֵהוּ הַמֶּלֶךְ וִיהוֹיָדָע אֶל־עוֹשֵׂה
מְלֶאכֶת עֲבוֹדַת בֵּית־יהוה וַיִּהְיוּ שֹׂכְרִים חֹצְבִים וְחָרָשִׁים לְחַדֵּשׁ
יג בֵּית יהוה וְגַם לְחָרָשֵׁי בַרְזֶל וּנְחֹשֶׁת לְחַזֵּק אֶת־בֵּית יהוה׃ וַיַּעֲשׂוּ
עֹשֵׂי הַמְּלָאכָה וַתַּעַל אֲרוּכָה לַמְּלָאכָה בְּיָדָם וַיַּעֲמִידוּ אֶת־בֵּית
יד הָאֱלֹהִים עַל־מַתְכֻּנְתּוֹ וַיְאַמְּצֻהוּ׃ וּכְכַלּוֹתָם הֵבִיאוּ לִפְנֵי הַמֶּלֶךְ
וִיהוֹיָדָע אֶת־שְׁאָר הַכֶּסֶף וַיַּעֲשֵׂהוּ כֵלִים לְבֵית־יהוה כְּלֵי שָׁרֵת וְהַעֲלוֹת
וְכַפּוֹת וּכְלֵי זָהָב וָכָסֶף וַיִּהְיוּ מַעֲלִים עֹלוֹת בְּבֵית־יהוה תָּמִיד כֹּל יְמֵי
טו יְהוֹיָדָע׃ וַיִּזְקַן יְהוֹיָדָע וַיִּשְׂבַּע יָמִים וַיָּמֹת בֶּן־מֵאָה וּשְׁלֹשִׁים
טז שָׁנָה בְּמוֹתוֹ׃ וַיִּקְבְּרֻהוּ בְעִיר־דָּוִיד עִם־הַמְּלָכִים כִּי־עָשָׂה טוֹבָה
יז בְּיִשְׂרָאֵל וְעִם־הָאֱלֹהִים וּבֵיתוֹ׃ וְאַחֲרֵי מוֹת יְהוֹיָדָע
יח בָּאוּ שָׂרֵי יְהוּדָה וַיִּשְׁתַּחֲווּ לַמֶּלֶךְ אָז שָׁמַע הַמֶּלֶךְ אֲלֵיהֶם׃ וַיַּעַזְבוּ
אֶת־בֵּית יהוה אֱלֹהֵי אֲבוֹתֵיהֶם וַיַּעַבְדוּ אֶת־הָאֲשֵׁרִים וְאֶת־הָעֲצַבִּים
יט וַיְהִי־קֶצֶף עַל־יְהוּדָה וִירוּשָׁלִַם בְּאַשְׁמָתָם זֹאת׃ וַיִּשְׁלַח בָּהֶם נְבִאִים
כ לַהֲשִׁיבָם אֶל־יהוה וַיָּעִידוּ בָם וְלֹא הֶאֱזִינוּ׃ וְרוּחַ אֱלֹהִים
לָבְשָׁה אֶת־זְכַרְיָה בֶּן־יְהוֹיָדָע הַכֹּהֵן וַיַּעֲמֹד מֵעַל לָעָם וַיֹּאמֶר לָהֶם
כֹּה ׀ אָמַר הָאֱלֹהִים לָמָה אַתֶּם עֹבְרִים אֶת־מִצְוֹת יהוה וְלֹא תַצְלִיחוּ
כא כִּי־עֲזַבְתֶּם אֶת־יהוה וַיַּעֲזֹב אֶתְכֶם׃ וַיִּקְשְׁרוּ עָלָיו וַיִּרְגְּמֻהוּ אֶבֶן
כב בְּמִצְוַת הַמֶּלֶךְ בַּחֲצַר בֵּית יהוה׃ וְלֹא־זָכַר יוֹאָשׁ הַמֶּלֶךְ הַחֶסֶד אֲשֶׁר
עָשָׂה יְהוֹיָדָע אָבִיו עִמּוֹ וַיַּהֲרֹג אֶת־בְּנוֹ וּכְמוֹתוֹ אָמַר יֵרֶא יהוה
כג וְיִדְרֹשׁ׃ וַיְהִי ׀ לִתְקוּפַת הַשָּׁנָה עָלָה עָלָיו חֵיל אֲרָם
וַיָּבֹאוּ אֶל־יְהוּדָה וִירוּשָׁלִַם וַיַּשְׁחִיתוּ אֶת־כָּל־שָׂרֵי הָעָם מֵעָם וְכָל־
כד שְׁלָלָם שִׁלְּחוּ לְמֶלֶךְ דַּרְמָשֶׂק׃ כִּי בְמִצְעַר אֲנָשִׁים בָּאוּ ׀ חֵיל אֲרָם
וַיהוה נָתַן בְּיָדָם חַיִל לָרֹב מְאֹד כִּי עָזְבוּ אֶת־יהוה אֱלֹהֵי אֲבוֹתֵיהֶם
כה וְאֶת־יוֹאָשׁ עָשׂוּ שְׁפָטִים׃ וּבְלֶכְתָּם מִמֶּנּוּ כִּי־עָזְבוּ אֹתוֹ בְּמַחֲלֻיִים
רַבִּים הִתְקַשְּׁרוּ עָלָיו עֲבָדָיו בִּדְמֵי בְּנֵי יְהוֹיָדָע הַכֹּהֵן וַיַּהַרְגֻהוּ עַל־
מִטָּתוֹ וַיָּמֹת וַיִּקְבְּרֻהוּ בְּעִיר דָּוִיד וְלֹא קְבָרֻהוּ בְּקִבְרוֹת הַמְּלָכִים׃
כו וְאֵלֶּה הַמִּתְקַשְּׁרִים עָלָיו זָבָד בֶּן־שִׁמְעָת הָעַמּוֹנִית וִיהוֹזָבָד בֶּן־
כז שִׁמְרִית הַמּוֹאָבִית׃ וּבָנָיו וְרֹב הַמַּשָּׂא עָלָיו וִיסוֹד בֵּית הָאֱלֹהִים יֶרֶב

his sons, the many pronouncements against him, and the restoration of the
House of God, are recorded in the annotations of the Book of Kings. And his
25 1 son Amatzyahu reigned in his place. Amatzyahu was twenty-five
years old when he became king, and for twenty-nine years he reigned in
2 Jerusalem. His mother's name was Yehoadan of Jerusalem. He did what was
3 right in the eyes of the LORD, though not with a whole heart. Once he had
the kingdom firmly in his grasp, he killed the officials who had struck down
4 the king, his father. But he did not execute their sons, in accordance with what
is written in the Torah, the book of Moshe, as the LORD commanded, "Parents
shall not die for their children, nor children for their parents. A person shall
5 die only for his own sin."[35] Amatzyahu gathered the men of Yehuda
and assigned all of Yehuda and Binyamin, according to ancestral house, under
officers of thousands and officers of hundreds. He mustered those who were
twenty years old and up and found that there were 300,000 men fit for military
6 service, able to wield spear and shield. Then he hired 100,000 from Israel for
7 one hundred talents of silver. But a man of God came to him and said, "O
king, the army of Israel must not accompany you, for the LORD is not with
8 Israel – not with any of the people of Efrayim. Unless you go by yourself and
battle fiercely, God will bring you down before the enemy, for God has the
9 power to aid or to overthrow." "But what of the hundred talents I gave for the
Israelite mercenaries?" Amatzyahu said to the man of God. "The LORD can
10 give you much more than that," said the man of God. So Amatzyahu
discharged the mercenaries who had come to him from Efrayim, sending
them back home; they were furious with Yehuda, and they went back home
11 in a fierce rage. Amatzyahu took courage and led his troops down to
12 the Valley of Salt, and he struck down ten thousand of the men of Se'ir. And
the men of Yehuda took another ten thousand captives alive; they brought
them to the clifftop and threw them down from the clifftop; they were all
13 dashed to pieces. But the mercenaries Amatzyahu had sent back
without letting them accompany him in battle attacked the towns of Yehuda
from Shomron to Beit Ḥoron, struck down three thousand people, and seized
14 large amounts of spoil. When Amatzyahu came back from
slaughtering the Edomites, he brought the gods of the people of Se'ir. He set
15 them up as his gods and bowed and offered sacrifices before them. Then the
LORD's fury raged against Amatzyahu, and he sent a prophet to him. "Why
did you seek out that people's gods when they could not save their own people
16 from your hands?" he said to him. "Who made you the king's counselor?" he
said, cutting him off. "Leave off! Why should you be struck down?" So the
prophet left off, but added, "I know that God has planned to destroy you
17 because you acted thus and would not listen to my counsel." Then
Amatzyahu, king of Yehuda, took counsel and sent to Yoash son of Yehoaḥaz
18 son of Yehu, king of Israel, saying, "Come, let us meet face to face." Yoash,
king of Israel, sent a response to Amatzyahu, king of Yehuda: "The thistle in

35 | Deuteronomy 24:16.

הִנָּם כְּתוּבִים עַל־מִדְרַשׁ סֵפֶר הַמְּלָכִים וַיִּמְלֹךְ אֲמַצְיָהוּ בְנוֹ
כה א תַּחְתָּיו׃ בֶּן־עֶשְׂרִים וְחָמֵשׁ שָׁנָה מָלַךְ אֲמַצְיָהוּ וְעֶשְׂרִים
ב וָתֵשַׁע שָׁנָה מָלַךְ בִּירוּשָׁלִָם וְשֵׁם אִמּוֹ יְהוֹעַדָּן מִירוּשָׁלִָם׃ וַיַּעַשׂ הַיָּשָׁר
ג בְּעֵינֵי יְהוָה רַק לֹא בְּלֵבָב שָׁלֵם׃ וַיְהִי כַּאֲשֶׁר חָזְקָה הַמַּמְלָכָה עָלָיו
ד וַיַּהֲרֹג אֶת־עֲבָדָיו הַמַּכִּים אֶת־הַמֶּלֶךְ אָבִיו׃ וְאֶת־בְּנֵיהֶם לֹא הֵמִית
כִּי כַכָּתוּב בַּתּוֹרָה בְּסֵפֶר מֹשֶׁה אֲשֶׁר־צִוָּה יְהוָה לֵאמֹר לֹא־יָמוּתוּ
אָבוֹת עַל־בָּנִים וּבָנִים לֹא־יָמוּתוּ עַל־אָבוֹת כִּי אִישׁ בְּחֶטְאוֹ
ה יָמוּתוּ׃ וַיִּקְבֹּץ אֲמַצְיָהוּ אֶת־יְהוּדָה וַיַּעֲמִידֵם לְבֵית־אָבוֹת
לְשָׂרֵי הָאֲלָפִים וּלְשָׂרֵי הַמֵּאוֹת לְכָל־יְהוּדָה וּבִנְיָמִן וַיִּפְקְדֵם לְמִבֶּן
עֶשְׂרִים שָׁנָה וָמַעְלָה וַיִּמְצָאֵם שְׁלֹשׁ־מֵאוֹת אֶלֶף בָּחוּר יוֹצֵא צָבָא
ו אֹחֵז רֹמַח וְצִנָּה׃ וַיִּשְׂכֹּר מִיִּשְׂרָאֵל מֵאָה אֶלֶף גִּבּוֹר חָיִל בְּמֵאָה כִכַּר־
ז כָּסֶף׃ וְאִישׁ הָאֱלֹהִים בָּא אֵלָיו לֵאמֹר הַמֶּלֶךְ אַל־יָבוֹא עִמְּךָ צְבָא
ח יִשְׂרָאֵל כִּי אֵין יְהוָה עִם־יִשְׂרָאֵל כֹּל בְּנֵי אֶפְרָיִם׃ כִּי אִם־בֹּא אַתָּה
עֲשֵׂה חֲזַק לַמִּלְחָמָה יַכְשִׁילְךָ הָאֱלֹהִים לִפְנֵי אוֹיֵב כִּי יֶשׁ־כֹּחַ בֵּאלֹהִים
ט לַעְזוֹר וּלְהַכְשִׁיל׃ וַיֹּאמֶר אֲמַצְיָהוּ לְאִישׁ הָאֱלֹהִים וּמַה־לַּעֲשׂוֹת
לִמְאַת הַכִּכָּר אֲשֶׁר נָתַתִּי לִגְדוּד יִשְׂרָאֵל וַיֹּאמֶר אִישׁ הָאֱלֹהִים יֵשׁ
י לַיהוָה לָתֶת לְךָ הַרְבֵּה מִזֶּה׃ וַיַּבְדִּילֵם אֲמַצְיָהוּ לְהַגְּדוּד אֲשֶׁר־בָּא
אֵלָיו מֵאֶפְרַיִם לָלֶכֶת לִמְקוֹמָם וַיִּחַר אַפָּם מְאֹד בִּיהוּדָה וַיָּשׁוּבוּ
יא לִמְקוֹמָם בָּחֳרִי־אָף׃ וַאֲמַצְיָהוּ הִתְחַזַּק וַיִּנְהַג אֶת־עַמּוֹ
יב וַיֵּלֶךְ גֵּיא הַמֶּלַח וַיַּךְ אֶת־בְּנֵי־שֵׂעִיר עֲשֶׂרֶת אֲלָפִים׃ וַעֲשֶׂרֶת אֲלָפִים
חַיִּים שָׁבוּ בְּנֵי יְהוּדָה וַיְבִיאוּם לְרֹאשׁ הַסָּלַע וַיַּשְׁלִיכוּם מֵרֹאשׁ הַסֶּלַע
יג וְכֻלָּם נִבְקָעוּ׃ וּבְנֵי הַגְּדוּד אֲשֶׁר הֵשִׁיב אֲמַצְיָהוּ מִלֶּכֶת עִמּוֹ
לַמִּלְחָמָה וַיִּפְשְׁטוּ בְּעָרֵי יְהוּדָה מִשֹּׁמְרוֹן וְעַד־בֵּית חוֹרוֹן וַיַּכּוּ מֵהֶם
יד שְׁלֹשֶׁת אֲלָפִים וַיָּבֹזּוּ בִּזָּה רַבָּה׃ וַיְהִי אַחֲרֵי בוֹא אֲמַצְיָהוּ
מֵהַכּוֹת אֶת־אֲדוֹמִים וַיָּבֵא אֶת־אֱלֹהֵי בְּנֵי שֵׂעִיר וַיַּעֲמִידֵם לוֹ לֵאלֹהִים
טו וְלִפְנֵיהֶם יִשְׁתַּחֲוֶה וְלָהֶם יְקַטֵּר׃ וַיִּחַר־אַף יְהוָה בַּאֲמַצְיָהוּ וַיִּשְׁלַח
אֵלָיו נָבִיא וַיֹּאמֶר לוֹ לָמָּה דָרַשְׁתָּ אֶת־אֱלֹהֵי הָעָם אֲשֶׁר לֹא־הִצִּילוּ
טז אֶת־עַמָּם מִיָּדֶךָ׃ וַיְהִי ׀ בְּדַבְּרוֹ אֵלָיו וַיֹּאמֶר לוֹ הַלְיוֹעֵץ לַמֶּלֶךְ נְתַנּוּךָ
חֲדַל־לְךָ לָמָּה יַכּוּךָ וַיֶּחְדַּל הַנָּבִיא וַיֹּאמֶר יָדַעְתִּי כִּי־יָעַץ אֱלֹהִים
יז לְהַשְׁחִיתֶךָ כִּי־עָשִׂיתָ זֹּאת וְלֹא שָׁמַעְתָּ לַעֲצָתִי׃ וַיִּוָּעַץ
אֲמַצְיָהוּ מֶלֶךְ יְהוּדָה וַיִּשְׁלַח אֶל־יוֹאָשׁ בֶּן־יְהוֹאָחָז בֶּן־יֵהוּא מֶלֶךְ
יח יִשְׂרָאֵל לֵאמֹר לְךָ נִתְרָאֶה פָנִים׃ וַיִּשְׁלַח יוֹאָשׁ מֶלֶךְ־יִשְׂרָאֵל אֶל־

Lebanon sent to the cedar in Lebanon, saying, 'Give your daughter as a wife
for my son.' But a wild beast in Lebanon passed by and trampled the thistle.
19 You boast that you have defeated Edom, and your arrogant heart craves more
glory. Now stay at home; why should you provoke disaster and fall down
20 together with Yehuda?" But Amatzyahu paid no heed, for God had
determined to hand them over because they had sought out the gods of
21 Edom. Yoash, king of Israel, marched up and met Amatzyahu, king of Yehuda,
22 face to face in Beit Shemesh of Yehuda. Yehuda was routed before Israel, and
23 every man fled back to his tent. As for Amatzyahu, king of Yehuda, the son of
Yoash son of Yehoaḥaz – Yoash, king of Israel, captured him in Beit Shemesh
and brought him to Jerusalem. He demolished four hundred cubits of the
24 Jerusalem wall from the Efrayim Gate to the Corner Gate. And with all the
gold and silver, all the vessels to be found in the House of God under
Oved Edom's care, the royal treasures, and hostages, he returned to
25 Shomron. Amatzyahu son of Yoash, king of Yehuda, lived on for
26 fifteen years after the death of Yoash son of Yehoaḥaz, king of Israel. As for
the rest of Amatzyahu's history, earlier and later, it is recorded in the Book of
27 Kings of Yehuda and Israel. From the time that Amatzyahu turned away from
the LORD, a conspiracy was formed against him in Jerusalem, and he fled to
28 Lakhish, but they sent after him to Lakhish and assassinated him there. They
conveyed his body back by horse and buried him with his ancestors in the
26 1 city of Yehuda. Then all the people of Yehuda took Uziyahu, who was sixteen
2 years old, and made him king in place of his father Amatzyahu. He was the
one who rebuilt Eilot and restored it to Yehuda once the king slept with his
ancestors.

3 Uziyahu was sixteen years old when he became king, and for fifty-two years
4 he reigned in Jerusalem. His mother's name was Yekholya of Jerusalem. He
did what was right in the eyes of the LORD just as his father Amatzyahu had
5 done. He was determined to seek God in the time of Zekharyahu, who
understood God's visions. As long as he sought the LORD, God made him
6 prosper. He went out to fight against the Philistines and breached the walls
of Gat, Yavneh, and Ashdod, and he built cities in Ashdod and among the
7 Philistines. God helped him against the Philistines, the Arabs who live in Gur
8 Baal, and the Meunites. The Amonites offered tribute to Uziyahu, and his
fame reached all the way to the border of Egypt, for he grew very powerful.
9 Uziyahu built towers in Jerusalem on the Corner Gate and the Valley Gate
10 and at the Angle,[36] and he reinforced them. He built towers in the wilderness
and dug many cisterns because he had a wealth of livestock in the lowlands

---

36 | A certain spot in the eastern wall.

אֲמַצְיָהוּ מֶלֶךְ־יְהוּדָה לֵאמֹר הַחוֹחַ אֲשֶׁר בַּלְּבָנוֹן שָׁלַח אֶל־הָאֶרֶז
אֲשֶׁר בַּלְּבָנוֹן לֵאמֹר תְּנָה־אֶת־בִּתְּךָ לִבְנִי לְאִשָּׁה וַתַּעֲבֹר חַיַּת הַשָּׂדֶה
יט אֲשֶׁר בַּלְּבָנוֹן וַתִּרְמֹס אֶת־הַחוֹחַ: אָמַרְתָּ הִנֵּה הִכִּיתָ אֶת־אֱדוֹם וּנְשָׂאֲךָ
לִבְּךָ לְהַכְבִּיד עַתָּה שְׁבָה בְּבֵיתֶךָ לָמָּה תִתְגָּרֶה בְּרָעָה וְנָפַלְתָּ אַתָּה
כ וִיהוּדָה עִמָּךְ: וְלֹא־שָׁמַע אֲמַצְיָהוּ כִּי מֵהָאֱלֹהִים הִיא לְמַעַן תִּתָּם
כא בְּיָד כִּי דָרְשׁוּ אֵת אֱלֹהֵי אֱדוֹם: וַיַּעַל יוֹאָשׁ מֶלֶךְ־יִשְׂרָאֵל וַיִּתְרָאוּ
כב פָנִים הוּא וַאֲמַצְיָהוּ מֶלֶךְ־יְהוּדָה בְּבֵית שֶׁמֶשׁ אֲשֶׁר לִיהוּדָה: וַיִּנָּגֶף
כג יְהוּדָה לִפְנֵי יִשְׂרָאֵל וַיָּנֻסוּ אִישׁ לְאֹהָלָיו: וְאֵת אֲמַצְיָהוּ מֶלֶךְ־יְהוּדָה
בֶּן־יוֹאָשׁ בֶּן־יְהוֹאָחָז תָּפַשׂ יוֹאָשׁ מֶלֶךְ־יִשְׂרָאֵל בְּבֵית שָׁמֶשׁ וַיְבִיאֵהוּ
יְרוּשָׁלִַם וַיִּפְרֹץ בְּחוֹמַת יְרוּשָׁלִַם מִשַּׁעַר אֶפְרַיִם עַד־שַׁעַר הַפּוֹנֶה
כד אַרְבַּע מֵאוֹת אַמָּה: וְכָל־הַזָּהָב וְהַכֶּסֶף וְאֵת כָּל־הַכֵּלִים הַנִּמְצְאִים
בְּבֵית־הָאֱלֹהִים עִם־עֹבֵד אֱדוֹם וְאֶת־אֹצְרוֹת בֵּית הַמֶּלֶךְ וְאֵת בְּנֵי
כה הַתַּעֲרֻבוֹת וַיָּשָׁב שֹׁמְרוֹן: וַיְחִי אֲמַצְיָהוּ בֶן־יוֹאָשׁ מֶלֶךְ
יְהוּדָה אַחֲרֵי מוֹת יוֹאָשׁ בֶּן־יְהוֹאָחָז מֶלֶךְ יִשְׂרָאֵל חֲמֵשׁ עֶשְׂרֵה שָׁנָה:
כו וְיֶתֶר דִּבְרֵי אֲמַצְיָהוּ הָרִאשֹׁנִים וְהָאַחֲרוֹנִים הֲלֹא הִנָּם כְּתוּבִים עַל־
כז סֵפֶר מַלְכֵי יְהוּדָה וְיִשְׂרָאֵל: וּמֵעֵת אֲשֶׁר־סָר אֲמַצְיָהוּ מֵאַחֲרֵי יְהוָה
וַיִּקְשְׁרוּ עָלָיו קֶשֶׁר בִּירוּשָׁלִַם וַיָּנָס לָכִישָׁה וַיִּשְׁלְחוּ אַחֲרָיו לָכִישָׁה
כח וַיְמִיתֻהוּ שָׁם: וַיִּשָּׂאֻהוּ עַל־הַסּוּסִים וַיִּקְבְּרוּ אֹתוֹ עִם־אֲבֹתָיו בְּעִיר
כו א יְהוּדָה: וַיִּקְחוּ כָּל־עַם יְהוּדָה אֶת־עֻזִּיָּהוּ וְהוּא בֶּן־שֵׁשׁ עֶשְׂרֵה שָׁנָה
ב וַיַּמְלִיכוּ אֹתוֹ תַּחַת אָבִיו אֲמַצְיָהוּ: הוּא בָּנָה אֶת־אֵילוֹת וַיְשִׁיבֶהָ כא
לִיהוּדָה אַחֲרֵי שְׁכַב־הַמֶּלֶךְ עִם־אֲבֹתָיו:
ג בֶּן־שֵׁשׁ עֶשְׂרֵה שָׁנָה עֻזִּיָּהוּ בְמָלְכוֹ וַחֲמִשִּׁים וּשְׁתַּיִם שָׁנָה מָלַךְ
ד בִּירוּשָׁלִָם וְשֵׁם אִמּוֹ יכיליה מִן־יְרוּשָׁלִָם: וַיַּעַשׂ הַיָּשָׁר בְּעֵינֵי יְהוָה יְכָלְיָה
ה כְּכֹל אֲשֶׁר־עָשָׂה אֲמַצְיָהוּ אָבִיו: וַיְהִי לִדְרֹשׁ אֱלֹהִים בִּימֵי זְכַרְיָהוּ
הַמֵּבִין בִּרְאֹת הָאֱלֹהִים וּבִימֵי דָּרְשׁוֹ אֶת־יְהוָה הִצְלִיחוֹ הָאֱלֹהִים:
ו וַיֵּצֵא וַיִּלָּחֶם בַּפְּלִשְׁתִּים וַיִּפְרֹץ אֶת־חוֹמַת גַּת וְאֵת חוֹמַת יַבְנֶה וְאֵת
ז חוֹמַת אַשְׁדּוֹד וַיִּבְנֶה עָרִים בְּאַשְׁדּוֹד וּבַפְּלִשְׁתִּים: וַיַּעְזְרֵהוּ הָאֱלֹהִים
ח עַל־פְּלִשְׁתִּים וְעַל־הָעַרְבִיִּים הַיֹּשְׁבִים בְּגוּר־בָּעַל וְהַמְּעוּנִים: וַיִּתְּנוּ הָעַרְבִים
הָעַמּוֹנִים מִנְחָה לְעֻזִּיָּהוּ וַיֵּלֶךְ שְׁמוֹ עַד־לְבוֹא מִצְרַיִם כִּי הֶחֱזִיק עַד־
ט לְמָעְלָה: וַיִּבֶן עֻזִּיָּהוּ מִגְדָּלִים בִּירוּשָׁלִַם עַל־שַׁעַר הַפִּנָּה וְעַל־שַׁעַר
י הַגַּיְא וְעַל־הַמִּקְצוֹעַ וַיְחַזְּקֵם: וַיִּבֶן מִגְדָּלִים בַּמִּדְבָּר וַיַּחְצֹב בֹּרוֹת רַבִּים
כִּי מִקְנֶה־רַב הָיָה לוֹ וּבַשְּׁפֵלָה וּבַמִּישׁוֹר אִכָּרִים וְכֹרְמִים בֶּהָרִים

and on the plain; he had farmers and vinedressers in the hills and the fertile
11 lands, for he had a deep love for the soil. Uziyahu had a military
force of soldiers ready for war, organized by divisions commanded by Ye'iel
the recruitment officer and Maaseyahu the captain under the direction of
12 Ḥananyahu, one of the royal officers. The ancestral heads in charge of the
13 fighting men numbered 2,600; they commanded an army of 307,500 ready
14 for war, a powerful force to support the king against the enemy. Uziyahu
provided shields and spears, helmets and mail, and bows and slingstones for
15 his entire army. In Jerusalem he invented ingenious devices that could shoot
arrows and large stones from the towers and corner defenses. And his fame
spread far and wide, for he had been miraculously helped until he grew
16 powerful. But as he grew powerful, his arrogant heart grew corrupt, and he
broke faith with the LORD his God: he entered the LORD's Sanctuary to offer
17 incense on the incense altar. Azaryahu the priest followed him with eighty of
18 the LORD's priests – powerful men – and confronted King Uziyahu. "It is not
for you, Uziyahu, to offer incense to the LORD," they said to him. "That is for
the priests, the descendants of Aharon, who have been consecrated to offer
incense. Leave the Sanctuary because you broke faith – it will bring you no
19 glory from the LORD God." Uziyahu – with the incense burner in his hand,
about to offer incense – flew into a rage, but as he raged at the priests, skin-
blight broke out on his forehead before the priests in the House of the LORD
20 by the incense altar. Azaryahu the head priest and all the priests turned to
him – and suddenly, he had skin-blight on his forehead! They rushed him out
21 of there, and he too was in a hurry to leave, for the LORD had struck him. King
Uziyahu remained a blighted man until his dying day. He remained in secluded
quarters, blighted, banned from the House of the LORD, while his son Yotam
22 took charge of the palace and governed the people of the land. As for the rest
of Uziyahu's history, earlier and later, it is recorded by the prophet Yeshayahu
23 son of Amotz. And Uziyahu slept with his ancestors, and they buried him
with his ancestors in the open field near the royal burial grounds, for they
27 1 said, "He is blighted." And his son Yotam reigned in his place. Yotam
was twenty-five years old when he became king, and for sixteen years he
reigned in Jerusalem. His mother's name was Yerusha daughter of Tzadok.
2 He did what was right in the eyes of the LORD just as his father Uziyahu had
done, but he did not enter the LORD's Sanctuary. And the people were still
3 corrupt. He built the upper gate of the House of the LORD and did extensive
4 construction on the Ofel Wall. He built towns in the hill country of Yehuda
5 and fortresses and towers in the woodland. He fought against the king of the
Amonites and overpowered them, and that year, the Amonites paid him one
hundred talents of silver, ten thousand *kor* of wheat, and ten thousand *kor* of
barley. The Amonites gave him the same amount in the second and third years
6 as well. And Yotam grew powerful, for he was committed to the ways

יא וּבַכַּרְמֶל כִּי־אֹהֵב אֲדָמָה הָיָה׃ וַיְהִי לְעֻזִּיָּהוּ חַיִל עֹשֵׂה
מִלְחָמָה יוֹצְאֵי צָבָא לִגְדוּד בְּמִסְפַּר פְּקֻדָּתָם בְּיַד יעואל הַסּוֹפֵר יְעִיאֵל
יב וּמַעֲשֵׂיָהוּ הַשּׁוֹטֵר עַל יַד־חֲנַנְיָהוּ מִשָּׂרֵי הַמֶּלֶךְ׃ כֹּל מִסְפַּר רָאשֵׁי
יג הָאָבוֹת לְגִבּוֹרֵי חָיִל אַלְפַּיִם וְשֵׁשׁ מֵאוֹת׃ וְעַל־יָדָם חֵיל צָבָא שְׁלֹשׁ
מֵאוֹת אֶלֶף וְשִׁבְעַת אֲלָפִים וַחֲמֵשׁ מֵאוֹת עוֹשֵׂי מִלְחָמָה בְּכֹחַ חָיִל
יד לַעְזֹר לַמֶּלֶךְ עַל־הָאוֹיֵב׃ וַיָּכֶן לָהֶם עֻזִּיָּהוּ לְכָל־הַצָּבָא מָגִנִּים וּרְמָחִים
טו וְכוֹבָעִים וְשִׁרְיֹנוֹת וּקְשָׁתוֹת וּלְאַבְנֵי קְלָעִים׃ וַיַּעַשׂ ׀ בִּירוּשָׁלִַם
חִשְּׁבֹנוֹת מַחֲשֶׁבֶת חוֹשֵׁב לִהְיוֹת עַל־הַמִּגְדָּלִים וְעַל־הַפִּנּוֹת לִירוֹא
בַּחִצִּים וּבָאֲבָנִים גְּדֹלוֹת וַיֵּצֵא שְׁמוֹ עַד־לְמֵרָחוֹק כִּי־הִפְלִיא לְהֵעָזֵר
טז עַד כִּי־חָזָק׃ וּכְחֶזְקָתוֹ גָּבַהּ לִבּוֹ עַד־לְהַשְׁחִית וַיִּמְעַל בַּיהוָה אֱלֹהָיו
יז וַיָּבֹא אֶל־הֵיכַל יְהוָה לְהַקְטִיר עַל־מִזְבַּח הַקְּטֹרֶת׃ וַיָּבֹא אַחֲרָיו
יח עֲזַרְיָהוּ הַכֹּהֵן וְעִמּוֹ כֹּהֲנִים ׀ לַיהוָה שְׁמוֹנִים בְּנֵי־חָיִל׃ וַיַּעַמְדוּ עַל־
עֻזִּיָּהוּ הַמֶּלֶךְ וַיֹּאמְרוּ לוֹ לֹא־לְךָ עֻזִּיָּהוּ לְהַקְטִיר לַיהוָה כִּי לַכֹּהֲנִים
בְּנֵי־אַהֲרֹן הַמְקֻדָּשִׁים לְהַקְטִיר צֵא מִן־הַמִּקְדָּשׁ כִּי מָעַלְתָּ וְלֹא־לְךָ
יט לְכָבוֹד מֵיְהוָה אֱלֹהִים׃ וַיִּזְעַף עֻזִּיָּהוּ וּבְיָדוֹ מִקְטֶרֶת לְהַקְטִיר וּבְזַעְפּוֹ
עִם־הַכֹּהֲנִים וְהַצָּרַעַת זָרְחָה בְמִצְחוֹ לִפְנֵי הַכֹּהֲנִים בְּבֵית יְהוָה מֵעַל
כ לְמִזְבַּח הַקְּטֹרֶת׃ וַיִּפֶן אֵלָיו עֲזַרְיָהוּ כֹהֵן הָרֹאשׁ וְכָל־הַכֹּהֲנִים וְהִנֵּה־
הוּא מְצֹרָע בְּמִצְחוֹ וַיַּבְהִלוּהוּ מִשָּׁם וְגַם־הוּא נִדְחַף לָצֵאת כִּי נִגְּעוֹ
כא יְהוָה׃ וַיְהִי עֻזִּיָּהוּ הַמֶּלֶךְ מְצֹרָע ׀ עַד־יוֹם מוֹתוֹ וַיֵּשֶׁב בֵּית החפשות הַחָפְשִׁית
מְצֹרָע כִּי נִגְזַר מִבֵּית יְהוָה וְיוֹתָם בְּנוֹ עַל־בֵּית הַמֶּלֶךְ שׁוֹפֵט אֶת־עַם
כב הָאָרֶץ׃ וְיֶתֶר דִּבְרֵי עֻזִּיָּהוּ הָרִאשֹׁנִים וְהָאַחֲרֹנִים כָּתַב יְשַׁעְיָהוּ בֶן־
כג אָמוֹץ הַנָּבִיא׃ וַיִּשְׁכַּב עֻזִּיָּהוּ עִם־אֲבֹתָיו וַיִּקְבְּרוּ אֹתוֹ עִם־אֲבֹתָיו
בִּשְׂדֵה הַקְּבוּרָה אֲשֶׁר לַמְּלָכִים כִּי אָמְרוּ מְצוֹרָע הוּא וַיִּמְלֹךְ יוֹתָם בְּנוֹ
כז א תַּחְתָּיו׃ בֶּן־עֶשְׂרִים וְחָמֵשׁ שָׁנָה יוֹתָם בְּמָלְכוֹ וְשֵׁשׁ־עֶשְׂרֵה
ב שָׁנָה מָלַךְ בִּירוּשָׁלִָם וְשֵׁם אִמּוֹ יְרוּשָׁה בַּת־צָדוֹק׃ וַיַּעַשׂ הַיָּשָׁר בְּעֵינֵי
יְהוָה כְּכֹל אֲשֶׁר־עָשָׂה עֻזִּיָּהוּ אָבִיו רַק לֹא־בָא אֶל־הֵיכַל יְהוָה וְעוֹד
ג הָעָם מַשְׁחִיתִים׃ הוּא בָּנָה אֶת־שַׁעַר בֵּית־יְהוָה הָעֶלְיוֹן וּבְחוֹמַת
ד הָעֹפֶל בָּנָה לָרֹב׃ וְעָרִים בָּנָה בְּהַר־יְהוּדָה וּבֶחֳרָשִׁים בָּנָה בִּירָנִיּוֹת
ה וּמִגְדָּלִים׃ וְהוּא נִלְחַם עִם־מֶלֶךְ בְּנֵי־עַמּוֹן וַיֶּחֱזַק עֲלֵיהֶם וַיִּתְּנוּ־לוֹ
בְנֵי־עַמּוֹן בַּשָּׁנָה הַהִיא מֵאָה כִּכַּר־כֶּסֶף וַעֲשֶׂרֶת אֲלָפִים כֹּרִים חִטִּים
וּשְׂעוֹרִים עֲשֶׂרֶת אֲלָפִים זֹאת הֵשִׁיבוּ לוֹ בְּנֵי עַמּוֹן וּבַשָּׁנָה הַשֵּׁנִית
ו וְהַשְּׁלִשִׁית׃ וַיִּתְחַזֵּק יוֹתָם כִּי הֵכִין דְּרָכָיו לִפְנֵי יְהוָה אֱלֹהָיו׃

7 of the Lord his God. The rest of Yotam's history, and all his wars and ways,
8 are recorded in the Book of Kings of Israel and Yehuda. He was twenty-five
years old when he became king, and for sixteen years, he reigned in Jerusalem.
9 And Yotam slept with his ancestors, and they buried him in the City of David.
28 1 And his son Aḥaz reigned in his place. Aḥaz was twenty years old when he
became king, and for sixteen years he reigned in Jerusalem. But he did not do
2 what was right in the eyes of the Lord like his ancestor David. He followed
3 in the ways of the kings of Israel and even made images for the Baalim; he
offered sacrifices in the Valley of Ben Hinom and burned his sons to death
in fire, imitating the abominations of the nations whom the Lord had
4 dispossessed before the Israelites. He made sacrifices and offerings at the high
5 shrines and on hilltops and under every shady tree. The Lord his God handed
him over to the king of Aram. He defeated him, took a great number of his
people captive, and led them to Damascus. He was also handed over to the
6 king of Israel, who dealt him a crushing blow. Pekaḥ son of
Remalyahu killed 120,000 of Yehuda in a single day, all powerful warriors, for
7 they had abandoned the Lord, God of their ancestors. Zikhri, a
warrior of Efrayim, killed Maaseyahu the king's son, and Azrikam the chief
8 officer of the palace, and Elkana, second to the king. And the
Israelites took 200,000 of their brothers captive – women, boys, and girls;
they also seized vast amounts of spoil from them, and they brought the spoil
9 to Shomron. But a prophet of the Lord by the name of Oded was
there, and he went out before the army arriving at Shomron. "Behold!" he
said to them. "In His wrath against Yehuda, the Lord, God of your ancestors,
has handed them over to you. But you have killed them in such anger that it
10 has reached the heavens. Do you now intend to subjugate the people of
Yehuda and Jerusalem as your own slaves and maidservants? Are you not
11 guilty of an offense against the Lord your God yourselves? Now listen to me:
send back those you took captive from among your brothers, for the Lord's
12 wrath rages against you." Certain leaders of Efrayim – Azaryahu
son of Yehoḥanan, Berekhyahu son of Meshilemot, Yeḥizkiyahu son of
13 Shalum, and Amasa son of Ḥadlai – then rose before the incoming army. "You
must not bring the captives here," they said to them. "It will only cause us to
offend the Lord. Do you wish to exacerbate our offense and our sins? For
14 our offense is already grave, and His wrath rages against Israel." So
the soldiers released the captives and the spoil in the presence of the officers
15 and the whole crowd. Then the aforementioned men took the captives, and
from the spoil they clothed all those who were naked. They provided them
with clothes, shoes, food, drink, and balm, helped the weak mount donkeys,
and led them to their kinsmen in Yeriḥo, city of palms. Then they went back
16 to Shomron. At that time, King Aḥaz sent to the kings of Assyria for

ז וְיֶתֶר דִּבְרֵי יוֹתָם וְכָל־מִלְחֲמֹתָיו וּדְרָכָיו הִנָּם כְּתוּבִים עַל־סֵפֶר מַלְכֵי
ח יִשְׂרָאֵל וִיהוּדָה׃ בֶּן־עֶשְׂרִים וְחָמֵשׁ שָׁנָה הָיָה בְמָלְכוֹ וְשֵׁשׁ־עֶשְׂרֵה
ט שָׁנָה מָלַךְ בִּירוּשָׁלִָם׃ וַיִּשְׁכַּב יוֹתָם עִם־אֲבֹתָיו וַיִּקְבְּרוּ אֹתוֹ בְּעִיר
כח א דָּוִיד וַיִּמְלֹךְ אָחָז בְּנוֹ תַּחְתָּיו׃ בֶּן־עֶשְׂרִים שָׁנָה אָחָז בְּמָלְכוֹ וְשֵׁשׁ־
עֶשְׂרֵה שָׁנָה מָלַךְ בִּירוּשָׁלִָם וְלֹא־עָשָׂה הַיָּשָׁר בְּעֵינֵי יְהוָה כְּדָוִיד
ב ג אָבִיו׃ וַיֵּלֶךְ בְּדַרְכֵי מַלְכֵי יִשְׂרָאֵל וְגַם מַסֵּכוֹת עָשָׂה לַבְּעָלִים׃ וְהוּא
הִקְטִיר בְּגֵיא בֶן־הִנֹּם וַיַּבְעֵר אֶת־בָּנָיו בָּאֵשׁ כְּתֹעֲבוֹת הַגּוֹיִם אֲשֶׁר
ד הֹרִישׁ יְהוָה מִפְּנֵי בְּנֵי יִשְׂרָאֵל׃ וַיְזַבֵּחַ וַיְקַטֵּר בַּבָּמוֹת וְעַל־הַגְּבָעוֹת
ה וְתַחַת כָּל־עֵץ רַעֲנָן׃ וַיִּתְּנֵהוּ יְהוָה אֱלֹהָיו בְּיַד מֶלֶךְ אֲרָם וַיַּכּוּ־בוֹ
וַיִּשְׁבּוּ מִמֶּנּוּ שִׁבְיָה גְדוֹלָה וַיָּבִיאוּ דַּרְמָשֶׂק וְגַם בְּיַד־מֶלֶךְ יִשְׂרָאֵל נִתָּן
ו וַיַּךְ־בּוֹ מַכָּה גְדוֹלָה׃ וַיַּהֲרֹג פֶּקַח בֶּן־רְמַלְיָהוּ
בִּיהוּדָה מֵאָה וְעֶשְׂרִים אֶלֶף בְּיוֹם אֶחָד הַכֹּל בְּנֵי־חָיִל בְּעָזְבָם אֶת־
ז יְהוָה אֱלֹהֵי אֲבוֹתָם׃ וַיַּהֲרֹג זִכְרִי ׀ גִּבּוֹר אֶפְרַיִם אֶת־
מַעֲשֵׂיָהוּ בֶּן־הַמֶּלֶךְ וְאֶת־עַזְרִיקָם נְגִיד הַבָּיִת וְאֶת־אֶלְקָנָה מִשְׁנֵה
ח הַמֶּלֶךְ׃ וַיִּשְׁבּוּ בְנֵי־יִשְׂרָאֵל מֵאֲחֵיהֶם מָאתַיִם אֶלֶף
נָשִׁים בָּנִים וּבָנוֹת וְגַם־שָׁלָל רָב בָּזְזוּ מֵהֶם וַיָּבִיאוּ אֶת־הַשָּׁלָל
ט לְשֹׁמְרוֹן׃ וְשָׁם הָיָה נָבִיא לַיהוָה עֹדֵד שְׁמוֹ וַיֵּצֵא לִפְנֵי
הַצָּבָא הַבָּא לְשֹׁמְרוֹן וַיֹּאמֶר לָהֶם הִנֵּה בַּחֲמַת יְהוָה אֱלֹהֵי־אֲבוֹתֵיכֶם
י עַל־יְהוּדָה נְתָנָם בְּיֶדְכֶם וַתַּהַרְגוּ־בָם בְּזַעַף עַד לַשָּׁמַיִם הִגִּיעַ׃ וְעַתָּה
בְּנֵי־יְהוּדָה וִירוּשָׁלִַם אַתֶּם אֹמְרִים לִכְבֹּשׁ לַעֲבָדִים וְלִשְׁפָחוֹת לָכֶם
יא הֲלֹא רַק־אַתֶּם עִמָּכֶם אֲשָׁמוֹת לַיהוָה אֱלֹהֵיכֶם׃ וְעַתָּה שְׁמָעוּנִי
וְהָשִׁיבוּ הַשִּׁבְיָה אֲשֶׁר שְׁבִיתֶם מֵאֲחֵיכֶם כִּי חֲרוֹן אַף־יְהוָה
יב עֲלֵיכֶם׃ וַיָּקֻמוּ אֲנָשִׁים מֵרָאשֵׁי בְנֵי־אֶפְרַיִם עֲזַרְיָהוּ בֶן־
יְהוֹחָנָן בֶּרֶכְיָהוּ בֶן־מְשִׁלֵּמוֹת וִיחִזְקִיָּהוּ בֶּן־שַׁלֻּם וַעֲמָשָׂא בֶּן־חַדְלָי
יג עַל־הַבָּאִים מִן־הַצָּבָא׃ וַיֹּאמְרוּ לָהֶם לֹא־תָבִיאוּ אֶת־הַשִּׁבְיָה הֵנָּה
כִּי לְאַשְׁמַת יְהוָה עָלֵינוּ אַתֶּם אֹמְרִים לְהֹסִיף עַל־חַטֹּאתֵנוּ וְעַל־
יד אַשְׁמָתֵנוּ כִּי־רַבָּה אַשְׁמָה לָנוּ וַחֲרוֹן אָף עַל־יִשְׂרָאֵל׃ וַיַּעֲזֹב
טו הֶחָלוּץ אֶת־הַשִּׁבְיָה וְאֶת־הַבִּזָּה לִפְנֵי הַשָּׂרִים וְכָל־הַקָּהָל׃ וַיָּקֻמוּ
הָאֲנָשִׁים אֲשֶׁר־נִקְּבוּ בְשֵׁמוֹת וַיַּחֲזִיקוּ בַשִּׁבְיָה וְכָל־מַעֲרֻמֵּיהֶם הִלְבִּישׁוּ
מִן־הַשָּׁלָל וַיַּלְבִּשׁוּם וַיַּנְעִלוּם וַיַּאֲכִלוּם וַיַּשְׁקוּם וַיְסֻכוּם וַיְנַהֲלוּם
בַּחֲמֹרִים לְכָל־כּוֹשֵׁל וַיְבִיאוּם יְרֵחוֹ עִיר־הַתְּמָרִים אֵצֶל אֲחֵיהֶם וַיָּשׁוּבוּ
טז שֹׁמְרוֹן׃ בָּעֵת הַהִיא שָׁלַח הַמֶּלֶךְ אָחָז עַל־מַלְכֵי אַשּׁוּר

17 aid. For the Edomites had invaded once more, defeating Yehuda and taking
captives, while the Philistines had raided the towns in the lowlands and the
18 Negev of Yehuda. They captured Beit Shemesh, Ayalon, Gederot, Sokho with
its villages, Timna with its villages, and Gimzo with its villages, and they
19 settled there. For the Lord had humbled Yehuda because of King Aḥaz of
Israel, for he had let Yehuda run wild and had broken faith with the Lord.
20 King Tilegat Pilne'eser of Assyria indeed came to him, but to oppress him,
21 not to support him. For Aḥaz had ransacked the House of the Lord and the
palace of the king and the officials and paid tribute to the king of Assyria – to
22 no avail. In his time of crisis, he still broke faith with the Lord, that King
23 Aḥaz. He sacrificed to the gods of those who had defeated them –
Damascus – thinking, "If the gods of the kings of Aram are helping them, I
will sacrifice to them, and they will help me." But they only led to his ruin and
24 to the ruin of all Israel. Aḥaz gathered all the vessels of the House of God,
broke them in pieces, and shut up the doors of the House of the Lord. And
25 he made himself altars in every corner of Jerusalem. In every town in Yehuda,
he built high shrines for sacrifices to other gods, angering the Lord, God of
26 his ancestors. The rest of his history and all his ways, earlier and later, are
27 recorded in the Book of Kings of Yehuda and Israel. And Aḥaz slept with his
ancestors, and they buried him in the city of Jerusalem, but they did not bring
him to the royal tombs of Israel. And his son Yeḥizkiyahu reigned in his
29 1 place. Yeḥizkiyahu became king at the age of twenty-five, and for
twenty-nine years he reigned in Jerusalem. His mother's name was Aviya
2 daughter of Zekharyahu. He did what was right in the eyes of the Lord just
3 as his ancestor David did. In the first month of the first year of his reign, he
4 opened the doors of the House of the Lord and repaired them. He brought
5 in the priests and the Levites and gathered them in the eastern square. "Listen
to me, Levites," he said to them. "Now sanctify yourselves and sanctify the
House of the Lord, God of your ancestors – remove the contamination from
6 the Holy Place. For our fathers have broken faith and done what is evil in the
eyes of the Lord our God. They abandoned Him and turned away from the
7 Lord's dwelling place; they turned their backs. They also shut the doors of
the Hall and put out the lamps; they never burned incense and never offered
8 up burnt offerings in the Sanctuary to the God of Israel. And the Lord grew
furious with Yehuda and Jerusalem, and He made them an object of shock, a
9 place of desolation and shrieking, as you see with your own eyes – our fathers
fell by the sword, and our sons and daughters and wives were taken captive
10 because of this. Now – I have set my heart on forming a covenant with the
11 Lord, God of Israel, so that His fierce anger will leave us. Now – my sons, do
not be passive, for the Lord has chosen you to stand and serve before Him,
12 to be His ministers and make offerings to Him." Then the Levites
arose: Maḥat son of Amasai and Yoel son of Azaryahu, of the sons of the

יז יח לַעְזֹר לוֹ: וְעוֹד אֲדוֹמִים בָּאוּ וַיַּכּוּ בִיהוּדָה וַיִּשְׁבּוּ־שֶׁבִי: וּפְלִשְׁתִּים
פָּשְׁטוּ בְּעָרֵי הַשְּׁפֵלָה וְהַנֶּגֶב לִיהוּדָה וַיִּלְכְּדוּ אֶת־בֵּית־שֶׁמֶשׁ וְאֶת־
אַיָּלוֹן וְאֶת־הַגְּדֵרוֹת וְאֶת־שׂוֹכוֹ וּבְנוֹתֶיהָ וְאֶת־תִּמְנָה וּבְנֹתֶיהָ וְאֶת־
יט גִּמְזוֹ וְאֶת־בְּנֹתֶיהָ וַיֵּשְׁבוּ שָׁם: כִּי־הִכְנִיעַ יהוה אֶת־יְהוּדָה בַּעֲבוּר אָחָז
כ מֶלֶךְ־יִשְׂרָאֵל כִּי הִפְרִיעַ בִּיהוּדָה וּמָעוֹל מַעַל בַּיהוה: וַיָּבֹא עָלָיו
כא תִּלְּגַת פִּלְנְאֶסֶר מֶלֶךְ אַשּׁוּר וַיָּצַר לוֹ וְלֹא חֲזָקוֹ: כִּי־חָלַק אָחָז אֶת־בֵּית
יהוה וְאֶת־בֵּית הַמֶּלֶךְ וְהַשָּׂרִים וַיִּתֵּן לְמֶלֶךְ אַשּׁוּר וְלֹא לְעֶזְרָה לוֹ:
כב כג וּבְעֵת הָצֵר לוֹ וַיּוֹסֶף לִמְעוֹל בַּיהוה הוּא הַמֶּלֶךְ אָחָז: וַיִּזְבַּח לֵאלֹהֵי
דַרְמֶשֶׂק הַמַּכִּים בּוֹ וַיֹּאמֶר כִּי אֱלֹהֵי מַלְכֵי־אֲרָם הֵם מַעְזְרִים אוֹתָם
כד לָהֶם אֲזַבֵּחַ וְיַעְזְרוּנִי וְהֵם הָיוּ־לוֹ לְהַכְשִׁילוֹ וּלְכָל־יִשְׂרָאֵל: וַיֶּאֱסֹף אָחָז
אֶת־כְּלֵי בֵית־הָאֱלֹהִים וַיְקַצֵּץ אֶת־כְּלֵי בֵית־הָאֱלֹהִים וַיִּסְגֹּר אֶת־
כה דַּלְתוֹת בֵּית־יהוה וַיַּעַשׂ לוֹ מִזְבְּחוֹת בְּכָל־פִּנָּה בִּירוּשָׁלִָם: וּבְכָל־עִיר
וָעִיר לִיהוּדָה עָשָׂה בָמוֹת לְקַטֵּר לֵאלֹהִים אֲחֵרִים וַיַּכְעֵס אֶת־יהוה
כו אֱלֹהֵי אֲבֹתָיו: וְיֶתֶר דְּבָרָיו וְכָל־דְּרָכָיו הָרִאשֹׁנִים וְהָאַחֲרוֹנִים הִנָּם
כז כְּתוּבִים עַל־סֵפֶר מַלְכֵי־יְהוּדָה וְיִשְׂרָאֵל: וַיִּשְׁכַּב אָחָז עִם־אֲבֹתָיו
וַיִּקְבְּרֻהוּ בָעִיר בִּירוּשָׁלִַם כִּי לֹא הֱבִיאֻהוּ לְקִבְרֵי מַלְכֵי יִשְׂרָאֵל וַיִּמְלֹךְ
כט א יְחִזְקִיָּהוּ בְנוֹ תַּחְתָּיו: יְחִזְקִיָּהוּ מָלַךְ בֶּן־עֶשְׂרִים
וְחָמֵשׁ שָׁנָה וְעֶשְׂרִים וָתֵשַׁע שָׁנָה מָלַךְ בִּירוּשָׁלִָם וְשֵׁם אִמּוֹ אֲבִיָּה
ב בַּת־זְכַרְיָהוּ: וַיַּעַשׂ הַיָּשָׁר בְּעֵינֵי יהוה כְּכֹל אֲשֶׁר־עָשָׂה דָּוִיד אָבִיו:
ג הוּא בַשָּׁנָה הָרִאשׁוֹנָה לְמָלְכוֹ בַּחֹדֶשׁ הָרִאשׁוֹן פָּתַח אֶת־דַּלְתוֹת
ד בֵּית־יהוה וַיְחַזְּקֵם: וַיָּבֵא אֶת־הַכֹּהֲנִים וְאֶת־הַלְוִיִּם וַיַּאַסְפֵם לִרְחוֹב
ה הַמִּזְרָח: וַיֹּאמֶר לָהֶם שְׁמָעוּנִי הַלְוִיִּם עַתָּה הִתְקַדְּשׁוּ וְקַדְּשׁוּ אֶת־בֵּית
ו יהוה אֱלֹהֵי אֲבֹתֵיכֶם וְהוֹצִיאוּ אֶת־הַנִּדָּה מִן־הַקֹּדֶשׁ: כִּי־מָעֲלוּ אֲבֹתֵינוּ
וְעָשׂוּ הָרַע בְּעֵינֵי יהוה־אֱלֹהֵינוּ וַיַּעַזְבֻהוּ וַיַּסֵּבּוּ פְנֵיהֶם מִמִּשְׁכַּן יהוה
ז וַיִּתְּנוּ־עֹרֶף: גַּם סָגְרוּ דַּלְתוֹת הָאוּלָם וַיְכַבּוּ אֶת־הַנֵּרוֹת וּקְטֹרֶת לֹא
ח הִקְטִירוּ וְעֹלָה לֹא־הֶעֱלוּ בַקֹּדֶשׁ לֵאלֹהֵי יִשְׂרָאֵל: וַיְהִי קֶצֶף יהוה
עַל־יְהוּדָה וִירוּשָׁלִָם וַיִּתְּנֵם לזועה לְשַׁמָּה וְלִשְׁרֵקָה כַּאֲשֶׁר אַתֶּם לְזַעֲוָה
ט רֹאִים בְּעֵינֵיכֶם: וְהִנֵּה נָפְלוּ אֲבוֹתֵינוּ בֶּחָרֶב וּבָנֵינוּ וּבְנוֹתֵינוּ וְנָשֵׁינוּ
י בַּשְּׁבִי עַל־זֹאת: עַתָּה עִם־לְבָבִי לִכְרוֹת בְּרִית לַיהוה אֱלֹהֵי יִשְׂרָאֵל
יא וְיָשֹׁב מִמֶּנּוּ חֲרוֹן אַפּוֹ: בָּנַי עַתָּה אַל־תִּשָּׁלוּ כִּי־בָכֶם בָּחַר יהוה לַעֲמֹד כב
יב לְפָנָיו לְשָׁרְתוֹ וְלִהְיוֹת לוֹ מְשָׁרְתִים וּמַקְטִרִים: וַיָּקֻמוּ הַלְוִיִּם
מַחַת בֶּן־עֲמָשַׂי וְיוֹאֵל בֶּן־עֲזַרְיָהוּ מִן־בְּנֵי הַקְּהָתִי וּמִן־בְּנֵי מְרָרִי קִישׁ

Kehatites; of the sons of Merari, Kish son of Avdi and Azaryahu son of
13 Yehalelel; of the Gershonites, Yoaḥ son of Zima and Eden son of Yoaḥ; of the
sons of Elitzafan, Shimri and Yei'el; of the sons of Asaf, Zekharyahu and
14 Matanyahu; of the sons of Heiman, Yeḥiel and Shimi; and of the
15 sons of Yedutun, Shemaya and Uziel. They gathered their kinsmen and
sanctified themselves, and as the king had commanded by the word of the
16 LORD, they went in to purify the House of the LORD. The priests went in to
purify the inner section of the House of the LORD, and they brought out all
the impurity that they found in the LORD's Sanctuary to the courtyard of the
House of the LORD; the Levites then took it and carried it out to Kidron
17 Valley. They began the sanctification on the first day of the first month, and
by the eighth day of the month they reached the Hall of the LORD; they
sanctified the House of the LORD in eight days, and by the sixteenth of the
18 first month, they had finished. They went in to King Ḥizkiyahu
and reported, "We have purified the entire House of the LORD, the altar of
burnt offerings and all its utensils, and the table for the showbread and all its
19 utensils. All the vessels that King Aḥaz despised when he broke faith during
his reign, we have restored and sanctified – and here they are before the Altar
20 of the LORD." King Yeḥizkiyahu rose early, gathered the city
21 officials, and went up to the House of the LORD. They brought seven bulls,
seven rams, seven lambs, and seven buck goats for a purification offering on
behalf of the kingdom, the Sanctuary, and Yehuda, and he ordered the
descendants of Aharon, the priests, to offer it up on the Altar of the LORD.
22 They slaughtered the bulls, and the priests received the blood and dashed it
against the altar; they slaughtered the rams and dashed the blood against the
23 altar; they slaughtered the lambs and dashed the blood against the altar. Then
they led the goats for the purification offering before the king and the
24 assembly, and they rested their hands upon them. The priests slaughtered
them and offered their blood as a purification offering on the altar to atone
for all of Israel, for the king had designated the burnt offering and the
25 purification offering on behalf of all Israel. He stationed the Levites at the
House of the LORD with cymbals, harps, and lyres, as ordered by David, the
seer Gad, and the prophet Natan, for the LORD's commandment was issued
through His prophets.
26 The Levites stood with David's instruments, the priest with
27 trumpets. Ḥizkiyahu then gave the order for the burnt offering to
be offered up on the altar, and as the burnt offering began, the song to the
LORD and the trumpets began as well, accompanied by the instruments of
28 David, king of Israel. The whole crowd worshipped as the singers sang and
29 the trumpets played on until the burnt offering was finished. Once the
offering was finished, the king and everyone in his presence kneeled and
30 worshipped. King Yeḥizkiyahu and the officials ordered the Levites to sing
praise to the LORD with the words of David and the seer Asaf, and they
31 praised them in sheer joy, knelt down low, and bowed. Then
Yeḥizkiyahu spoke up and said, "You have now consecrated yourselves to the

בֶּן־עַבְדִּי וַעֲזַרְיָהוּ בֶּן־יְהַלֶּלְאֵל וּמִן־הַגֵּרְשֻׁנִּי יוֹאָח בֶּן־זִמָּה וְעֵדֶן
יג בֶּן־יוֹאָח׃ וּמִן־בְּנֵי אֱלִיצָפָן שִׁמְרִי ויעואל וּמִן־בְּנֵי אָסָף זְכַרְיָהוּ וִיעִיאֵל
יד וּמַתַּנְיָהוּ׃ וּמִן־בְּנֵי הֵימָן יחואל וְשִׁמְעִי וּמִן־בְּנֵי יְחִיאֵל
טו יְדוּתוּן שְׁמַעְיָה וְעֻזִּיאֵל׃ וַיַּאַסְפוּ אֶת־אֲחֵיהֶם וַיִּתְקַדְּשׁוּ וַיָּבֹאוּ כְמִצְוַת־
טז הַמֶּלֶךְ בְּדִבְרֵי יְהוָה לְטַהֵר בֵּית יְהוָה׃ וַיָּבֹאוּ הַכֹּהֲנִים לִפְנִימָה בֵית־
יְהוָה לְטַהֵר וַיּוֹצִיאוּ אֵת כָּל־הַטֻּמְאָה אֲשֶׁר מָצְאוּ בְּהֵיכַל יְהוָה לַחֲצַר
יז בֵּית יְהוָה וַיְקַבְּלוּ הַלְוִיִּם לְהוֹצִיא לְנַחַל־קִדְרוֹן חוּצָה׃ וַיָּחֵלּוּ בְּאֶחָד
לַחֹדֶשׁ הָרִאשׁוֹן לְקַדֵּשׁ וּבְיוֹם שְׁמוֹנָה לַחֹדֶשׁ בָּאוּ לְאוּלָם יְהוָה
וַיְקַדְּשׁוּ אֶת־בֵּית־יְהוָה לְיָמִים שְׁמוֹנָה וּבְיוֹם שִׁשָּׁה עָשָׂר לַחֹדֶשׁ
יח הָרִאשׁוֹן כִּלּוּ׃ וַיָּבוֹאוּ פְנִימָה אֶל־חִזְקִיָּהוּ הַמֶּלֶךְ
וַיֹּאמְרוּ טִהַרְנוּ אֶת־כָּל־בֵּית יְהוָה אֶת־מִזְבַּח הָעוֹלָה וְאֶת־כָּל־כֵּלָיו
יט וְאֶת־שֻׁלְחַן הַמַּעֲרֶכֶת וְאֶת־כָּל־כֵּלָיו׃ וְאֵת כָּל־הַכֵּלִים אֲשֶׁר הִזְנִיחַ
הַמֶּלֶךְ אָחָז בְּמַלְכוּתוֹ בְּמַעֲלוֹ הֵכַנּוּ וְהִקְדָּשְׁנוּ וְהִנָּם לִפְנֵי מִזְבַּח
כ יְהוָה׃ וַיַּשְׁכֵּם יְחִזְקִיָּהוּ הַמֶּלֶךְ וַיֶּאֱסֹף אֵת שָׂרֵי הָעִיר וַיַּעַל
כא בֵּית יְהוָה׃ וַיָּבִיאוּ פָרִים־שִׁבְעָה וְאֵילִים שִׁבְעָה וּכְבָשִׂים שִׁבְעָה
וּצְפִירֵי עִזִּים שִׁבְעָה לְחַטָּאת עַל־הַמַּמְלָכָה וְעַל־הַמִּקְדָּשׁ וְעַל־יְהוּדָה
כב וַיֹּאמֶר לִבְנֵי אַהֲרֹן הַכֹּהֲנִים לְהַעֲלוֹת עַל־מִזְבַּח יְהוָה׃ וַיִּשְׁחֲטוּ הַבָּקָר
וַיְקַבְּלוּ הַכֹּהֲנִים אֶת־הַדָּם וַיִּזְרְקוּ הַמִּזְבֵּחָה וַיִּשְׁחֲטוּ הָאֵלִים וַיִּזְרְקוּ
כג הַדָּם הַמִּזְבֵּחָה וַיִּשְׁחֲטוּ הַכְּבָשִׂים וַיִּזְרְקוּ הַדָּם הַמִּזְבֵּחָה׃ וַיַּגִּישׁוּ אֶת־
כד שְׂעִירֵי הַחַטָּאת לִפְנֵי הַמֶּלֶךְ וְהַקָּהָל וַיִּסְמְכוּ יְדֵיהֶם עֲלֵיהֶם׃ וַיִּשְׁחָטוּם
הַכֹּהֲנִים וַיְחַטְּאוּ אֶת־דָּמָם הַמִּזְבֵּחָה לְכַפֵּר עַל־כָּל־יִשְׂרָאֵל כִּי לְכָל־
כה יִשְׂרָאֵל אָמַר הַמֶּלֶךְ הָעוֹלָה וְהַחַטָּאת׃ וַיַּעֲמֵד אֶת־הַלְוִיִּם בֵּית יְהוָה
בִּמְצִלְתַּיִם בִּנְבָלִים וּבְכִנֹּרוֹת בְּמִצְוַת דָּוִיד וְגָד חֹזֵה־הַמֶּלֶךְ וְנָתָן
הַנָּבִיא כִּי בְיַד־יְהוָה הַמִּצְוָה בְּיַד־נְבִיאָיו׃
כו כז וַיַּעַמְדוּ הַלְוִיִּם בִּכְלֵי דָוִיד וְהַכֹּהֲנִים בַּחֲצֹצְרוֹת׃ וַיֹּאמֶר
חִזְקִיָּהוּ לְהַעֲלוֹת הָעֹלָה לְהַמִּזְבֵּחַ וּבְעֵת הֵחֵל הָעוֹלָה הֵחֵל שִׁיר־
כח יְהוָה וְהַחֲצֹצְרוֹת וְעַל־יְדֵי כְּלֵי דָּוִיד מֶלֶךְ יִשְׂרָאֵל׃ וְכָל־הַקָּהָל
מִשְׁתַּחֲוִים וְהַשִּׁיר מְשׁוֹרֵר וְהַחֲצֹצְרוֹת מחצצרים הַכֹּל עַד לִכְלוֹת מַחְצְרִים
כט הָעֹלָה׃ וּכְכַלּוֹת לְהַעֲלוֹת כָּרְעוּ הַמֶּלֶךְ וְכָל־הַנִּמְצְאִים אִתּוֹ וַיִּשְׁתַּחֲווּ׃
ל וַיֹּאמֶר יְחִזְקִיָּהוּ הַמֶּלֶךְ וְהַשָּׂרִים לַלְוִיִּם לְהַלֵּל לַיהוָה בְּדִבְרֵי דָוִיד
לא וְאָסָף הַחֹזֶה וַיְהַלְלוּ עַד־לְשִׂמְחָה וַיִּקְּדוּ וַיִּשְׁתַּחֲווּ׃ וַיַּעַן
יְחִזְקִיָּהוּ וַיֹּאמֶר עַתָּה מִלֵּאתֶם יֶדְכֶם לַיהוָה גֹּשׁוּ וְהָבִיאוּ זְבָחִים

LORD. Come forth and bring sacrifices and thanksgiving offerings to the
House of the LORD!" And the crowd came bearing sacrifices and thanksgiving
32 offerings, and all those with a generous heart brought burnt offerings: the
number of burnt offerings that the crowd brought was seventy bulls, one
hundred rams, and two hundred lambs – all these were for burnt offerings to
33 the LORD. There were six hundred bulls and three thousand sheep for sacred
34 offerings, but the priests were too few to manage the flaying of all the burnt
offerings, so their Levite kinsmen assisted them until other priests had
sanctified themselves, and the work was done. The Levites were more
35 conscientious than the priests about sanctifying themselves. Besides the great
number of burnt offerings, there were also the fat from the peace offerings
and the libations for the burnt offerings. Thus the service of the House of the
36 LORD was reinstated. And Yeḥizkiyahu and all the people rejoiced over
what God had provided for the people, for it had come about so
30 1 suddenly. Yeḥizkiyahu sent to all Israel and Yehuda – he even wrote
letters to Efrayim and Menashe – to come to the House of the LORD in
2 Jerusalem to celebrate Passover before the LORD, God of Israel. The king and
his officials, together with all the assembly in Jerusalem, decided to celebrate
3 Passover in the second month – they were not able to celebrate on the usual
date because not enough priests had sanctified themselves, and the people
4 had not yet gathered to Jerusalem – and the plan seemed right to the king and
5 all the assembly.[37] So they issued a proclamation to spread the word
throughout Israel from Be'er Sheva to Dan to come and celebrate Passover
before the LORD, God of Israel, in Jerusalem, for they had rarely kept it as
6 prescribed. The couriers set out all over Israel and Yehuda with letters from
the king and his officials proclaiming the royal decree: "Israelites, come back
to the LORD, God of Avraham, Yitzḥak, and Yisrael, and He will come back
to the remnant of you who escaped from the hands of the kings of Assyria.
7 Do not be like your fathers and brothers who broke faith with the LORD, God
8 of their ancestors – He gave them up to desolation as you can see. Now – do
not stiffen your necks like your fathers; yield to the LORD and come to His
Sanctuary, which He has sanctified forever. Serve the LORD your God, and
9 His fierce wrath will turn away from you. If you come back to the LORD, your
brothers' and children's captors will show them mercy, and they will come
back to this land, for the LORD your God is gracious and merciful, and He
10 will not turn His face away from you if you come back to Him." As
the couriers passed from city to city in the land of Efrayim and Menashe and
11 up to Zevulun, they were ridiculed and mocked. Yet some people from Asher,
12 Menashe, and Zevulun humbled themselves and came to Jerusalem. In
Yehuda God's hand was upon them and made them one in heart to keep the
13 king's and the officials' order about the word of the LORD. So a multitude of
people gathered to Jerusalem to celebrate the Festival of Unleavened Bread
14 in the second month – a massive crowd. They set to work and removed the

37 | Cf. Numbers 9:6–13.

וְתוֹדוֹת לְבֵית יְהוָה וַיָּבִיאוּ הַקָּהָל זְבָחִים וְתוֹדוֹת וְכָל־נְדִיב לֵב עֹלוֹת׃
לב וַיְהִי מִסְפַּר הָעֹלָה אֲשֶׁר הֵבִיאוּ הַקָּהָל בָּקָר שִׁבְעִים אֵילִים מֵאָה
לג כְּבָשִׂים מָאתָיִם לְעֹלָה לַיהוָה כָּל־אֵלֶּה׃ וְהַקֳּדָשִׁים בָּקָר שֵׁשׁ מֵאוֹת
לד וְצֹאן שְׁלֹשֶׁת אֲלָפִים׃ רַק הַכֹּהֲנִים הָיוּ לִמְעָט וְלֹא יָכְלוּ לְהַפְשִׁיט
אֶת־כָּל־הָעֹלוֹת וַיְחַזְּקוּם אֲחֵיהֶם הַלְוִיִּם עַד־כְּלוֹת הַמְּלָאכָה וְעַד־
לה יִתְקַדְּשׁוּ הַכֹּהֲנִים כִּי הַלְוִיִּם יִשְׁרֵי לֵבָב לְהִתְקַדֵּשׁ מֵהַכֹּהֲנִים׃ וְגַם־עֹלָה
לָרֹב בְּחֶלְבֵי הַשְּׁלָמִים וּבַנְּסָכִים לָעֹלָה וַתִּכּוֹן עֲבוֹדַת בֵּית־יְהוָה׃
לו וַיִּשְׂמַח יְחִזְקִיָּהוּ וְכָל־הָעָם עַל הַהֵכִין הָאֱלֹהִים לָעָם כִּי בְּפִתְאֹם הָיָה
הַדָּבָר׃ וַיִּשְׁלַח יְחִזְקִיָּהוּ עַל־כָּל־יִשְׂרָאֵל וִיהוּדָה וְגַם־ ל א
אִגְּרוֹת כָּתַב עַל־אֶפְרַיִם וּמְנַשֶּׁה לָבוֹא לְבֵית־יְהוָה בִּירוּשָׁלִָם לַעֲשׂוֹת
ב פֶּסַח לַיהוָה אֱלֹהֵי יִשְׂרָאֵל׃ וַיִּוָּעַץ הַמֶּלֶךְ וְשָׂרָיו וְכָל־הַקָּהָל בִּירוּשָׁלִָם
ג לַעֲשׂוֹת הַפֶּסַח בַּחֹדֶשׁ הַשֵּׁנִי׃ כִּי לֹא יָכְלוּ לַעֲשֹׂתוֹ בָּעֵת הַהִיא כִּי
ד הַכֹּהֲנִים לֹא־הִתְקַדְּשׁוּ לְמַדַּי וְהָעָם לֹא־נֶאֶסְפוּ לִירוּשָׁלִָם׃ וַיִּישַׁר
ה הַדָּבָר בְּעֵינֵי הַמֶּלֶךְ וּבְעֵינֵי כָּל־הַקָּהָל׃ וַיַּעֲמִידוּ דָבָר לְהַעֲבִיר קוֹל
בְּכָל־יִשְׂרָאֵל מִבְּאֵר־שֶׁבַע וְעַד־דָּן לָבוֹא לַעֲשׂוֹת פֶּסַח לַיהוָה אֱלֹהֵי־
ו יִשְׂרָאֵל בִּירוּשָׁלִָם כִּי לֹא לָרֹב עָשׂוּ כַּכָּתוּב׃ וַיֵּלְכוּ הָרָצִים בָּאִגְּרוֹת
מִיַּד הַמֶּלֶךְ וְשָׂרָיו בְּכָל־יִשְׂרָאֵל וִיהוּדָה וּכְמִצְוַת הַמֶּלֶךְ לֵאמֹר בְּנֵי
יִשְׂרָאֵל שׁוּבוּ אֶל־יְהוָה אֱלֹהֵי אַבְרָהָם יִצְחָק וְיִשְׂרָאֵל וְיָשֹׁב אֶל־
ז הַפְּלֵיטָה הַנִּשְׁאֶרֶת לָכֶם מִכַּף מַלְכֵי אַשּׁוּר׃ וְאַל־תִּהְיוּ כַּאֲבוֹתֵיכֶם
וְכַאֲחֵיכֶם אֲשֶׁר מָעֲלוּ בַּיהוָה אֱלֹהֵי אֲבוֹתֵיהֶם וַיִּתְּנֵם לְשַׁמָּה כַּאֲשֶׁר
ח אַתֶּם רֹאִים׃ עַתָּה אַל־תַּקְשׁוּ עָרְפְּכֶם כַּאֲבוֹתֵיכֶם תְּנוּ־יָד לַיהוָה וּבֹאוּ
לְמִקְדָּשׁוֹ אֲשֶׁר הִקְדִּישׁ לְעוֹלָם וְעִבְדוּ אֶת־יְהוָה אֱלֹהֵיכֶם וְיָשֹׁב מִכֶּם
ט חֲרוֹן אַפּוֹ׃ כִּי בְשׁוּבְכֶם עַל־יְהוָה אֲחֵיכֶם וּבְנֵיכֶם לְרַחֲמִים לִפְנֵי
שׁוֹבֵיהֶם וְלָשׁוּב לָאָרֶץ הַזֹּאת כִּי־חַנּוּן וְרַחוּם יְהוָה אֱלֹהֵיכֶם וְלֹא־יָסִיר
י פָּנִים מִכֶּם אִם־תָּשׁוּבוּ אֵלָיו׃ וַיִּהְיוּ הָרָצִים עֹבְרִים מֵעִיר ׀
לָעִיר בְּאֶרֶץ־אֶפְרַיִם וּמְנַשֶּׁה וְעַד־זְבֻלוּן וַיִּהְיוּ מַשְׂחִיקִים עֲלֵיהֶם
יא וּמַלְעִגִים בָּם׃ אַךְ אֲנָשִׁים מֵאָשֵׁר וּמְנַשֶּׁה וּמִזְּבֻלוּן נִכְנְעוּ וַיָּבֹאוּ
יב לִירוּשָׁלִָם׃ גַּם בִּיהוּדָה הָיְתָה יַד הָאֱלֹהִים לָתֵת לָהֶם לֵב אֶחָד לַעֲשׂוֹת
יג מִצְוַת הַמֶּלֶךְ וְהַשָּׂרִים בִּדְבַר יְהוָה׃ וַיֵּאָסְפוּ יְרוּשָׁלִַם עַם־רָב לַעֲשׂוֹת
יד אֶת־חַג הַמַּצּוֹת בַּחֹדֶשׁ הַשֵּׁנִי קָהָל לָרֹב מְאֹד׃ וַיָּקֻמוּ וַיָּסִירוּ אֶת־

altars that were around Jerusalem; they removed all the incense altars and
15 cast them into the Kidron Valley. They slaughtered the Passover sacrifice on
the fourteenth of the second month. Having been ashamed, the priests and
the Levites had sanctified themselves and brought burnt offerings to the
16 House of the Lord. Now they took up their usual positions as dictated by
the teaching of Moshe, man of God, with the priests dashing the blood that
17 the Levites handed to them. Many among the crowd had not sanctified
themselves, and the Levites were in charge of slaughtering the Passover
sacrifice for all those who were impure so that it would be holy to the Lord.
18 Most of the people – many of them from Efrayim, Menashe, Yissakhar and
Zevulun – ate the Passover sacrifice without purifying themselves despite
what was prescribed. But Yeḥizkiyahu prayed on their behalf, saying, "May
19 the God Lord atone for all those who have set their heart on seeking
God the Lord, God of their ancestors, even if they are not purified for the
20 Sanctuary." The Lord heard Yeḥizkiyahu and forgave the
21 people. The Israelites who were in Jerusalem celebrated the
Festival of Unleavened Bread for seven days with great joy. Day by day, the
Levites and the priests sang praise to the Lord, playing to the Lord on
22 powerful instruments. Yeḥizkiyahu spoke encouragingly to all the
Levites who showed great promise in their service to the Lord. They ate the
food of the festival for seven days, sacrificing peace offerings and giving thanks
23 to the Lord, God of their ancestors. Then all the assembly agreed
together to celebrate for another seven days, and they celebrated for seven
24 days in joy, for Ḥizkiyahu king of Yehuda provided the assembly with a
thousand bulls and seven thousand sheep, the officials provided the assembly
with a thousand bulls and ten thousand sheep, and the priests had sanctified
25 themselves in great numbers. And there was rejoicing among all the assembly
of Yehuda, the priests, and the Levites, all the assembly that had come from
Israel, and the outsiders who had come from the land of Israel to live in
26 Yehuda – there was great joy in Jerusalem, for nothing like this had
happened in Jerusalem since the days of Shlomo son of David, king of
27 Israel. And the Levite priests rose and blessed the people;
their voices rang out, and their prayers reached His Holy abode in
31 1 heaven. When all of this was over, all Israel who were present went
out to the towns of Yehuda and tore down the worship pillars, cut down the
sacred trees, and razed the high shrines and the altars throughout Yehuda,
Binyamin, Efrayim, and Menashe, to the very last one. Then all the Israelites
2 went back, each to his own property in his own town. Yeḥizkiyahu
appointed the divisions of priests and Levites, division by division, each of
the priests and Levites according to their service: for burnt offerings and
peace offerings, to minister, and to give thanks and sing praise at the gates of
3 the Lord's courts. The king's contribution from his own possessions was for the burnt offerings: for the morning and evening burnt offerings
and for the burnt offerings for the Sabbaths, the New Moons, and the festivals,
4 as written in the Lord's Torah. And he ordered the people, the inhabitants

הַמְזַבְּחוֹת אֲשֶׁר בִּירוּשָׁלִַם וְאֵת כׇּל־הַמְקַטְּרוֹת הֵסִירוּ וַיַּשְׁלִיכוּ
טו לְנַחַל קִדְרוֹן׃ וַיִּשְׁחֲטוּ הַפֶּסַח בְּאַרְבָּעָה עָשָׂר לַחֹדֶשׁ הַשֵּׁנִי וְהַכֹּהֲנִים
טז וְהַלְוִיִּם נִכְלְמוּ וַיִּתְקַדְּשׁוּ וַיָּבִיאוּ עֹלוֹת בֵּית יְהוָה׃ וַיַּעַמְדוּ עַל־עׇמְדָם
כְּמִשְׁפָּטָם כְּתוֹרַת מֹשֶׁה אִישׁ־הָאֱלֹהִים הַכֹּהֲנִים זֹרְקִים אֶת־הַדָּם
יז מִיַּד הַלְוִיִּם׃ כִּי־רַבַּת בַּקָּהָל אֲשֶׁר לֹא־הִתְקַדָּשׁוּ וְהַלְוִיִּם עַל־שְׁחִיטַת
יח הַפְּסָחִים לְכֹל לֹא טָהוֹר לְהַקְדִּישׁ לַיהוָה׃ כִּי מַרְבִּית הָעָם רַבַּת
מֵאֶפְרַיִם וּמְנַשֶּׁה יִשָּׂשכָר וּזְבֻלוּן לֹא הִטֶּהָרוּ כִּי־אָכְלוּ אֶת־הַפֶּסַח
בְּלֹא כַכָּתוּב כִּי הִתְפַּלֵּל יְחִזְקִיָּהוּ עֲלֵיהֶם לֵאמֹר יְהוָה הַטּוֹב יְכַפֵּר
יט בְּעַד׃ כׇּל־לְבָבוֹ הֵכִין לִדְרוֹשׁ הָאֱלֹהִים ׀ יְהוָה אֱלֹהֵי אֲבוֹתָיו וְלֹא
כ כְּטׇהֳרַת הַקֹּדֶשׁ׃ וַיִּשְׁמַע יְהוָה אֶל־יְחִזְקִיָּהוּ וַיִּרְפָּא
כא אֶת־הָעָם׃ וַיַּעֲשׂוּ בְנֵי־יִשְׂרָאֵל הַנִּמְצְאִים בִּירוּשָׁלִַם אֶת־חַג
הַמַּצּוֹת שִׁבְעַת יָמִים בְּשִׂמְחָה גְדוֹלָה וּמְהַלְלִים לַיהוָה יוֹם ׀ בְּיוֹם
כב הַלְוִיִּם וְהַכֹּהֲנִים בִּכְלֵי־עֹז לַיהוָה׃ וַיְדַבֵּר יְחִזְקִיָּהוּ
עַל־לֵב כׇּל־הַלְוִיִּם הַמַּשְׂכִּילִים שֵׂכֶל־טוֹב לַיהוָה וַיֹּאכְלוּ אֶת־
הַמּוֹעֵד שִׁבְעַת הַיָּמִים מְזַבְּחִים זִבְחֵי שְׁלָמִים וּמִתְוַדִּים לַיהוָה אֱלֹהֵי
כג אֲבוֹתֵיהֶם׃ וַיִּוָּעֲצוּ כׇּל־הַקָּהָל לַעֲשׂוֹת שִׁבְעַת יָמִים אֲחֵרִים
כד וַיַּעֲשׂוּ שִׁבְעַת יָמִים שִׂמְחָה׃ כִּי חִזְקִיָּהוּ מֶלֶךְ־יְהוּדָה הֵרִים לַקָּהָל
אֶלֶף פָּרִים וְשִׁבְעַת אֲלָפִים צֹאן וְהַשָּׂרִים הֵרִימוּ לַקָּהָל פָּרִים אֶלֶף
כה וְצֹאן עֲשֶׂרֶת אֲלָפִים וַיִּתְקַדְּשׁוּ כֹהֲנִים לָרֹב׃ וַיִּשְׂמְחוּ ׀ כׇּל־קְהַל יְהוּדָה
וְהַכֹּהֲנִים וְהַלְוִיִּם וְכׇל־הַקָּהָל הַבָּאִים מִיִּשְׂרָאֵל וְהַגֵּרִים הַבָּאִים מֵאֶרֶץ
כו יִשְׂרָאֵל וְהַיּוֹשְׁבִים בִּיהוּדָה׃ וַתְּהִי שִׂמְחָה־גְדוֹלָה בִּירוּשָׁלִָם כִּי מִימֵי
כז שְׁלֹמֹה בֶן־דָּוִיד מֶלֶךְ יִשְׂרָאֵל לֹא כָזֹאת בִּירוּשָׁלִָם׃ וַיָּקֻמוּ
הַכֹּהֲנִים הַלְוִיִּם וַיְבָרְכוּ אֶת־הָעָם וַיִּשָּׁמַע בְּקוֹלָם וַתָּבוֹא תְפִלָּתָם
לא א לִמְעוֹן קׇדְשׁוֹ לַשָּׁמָיִם׃ וּכְכַלּוֹת כׇּל־זֹאת יָצְאוּ
כׇּל־יִשְׂרָאֵל הַנִּמְצְאִים לְעָרֵי יְהוּדָה וַיְשַׁבְּרוּ הַמַּצֵּבוֹת וַיְגַדְּעוּ
הָאֲשֵׁרִים וַיְנַתְּצוּ אֶת־הַבָּמוֹת וְאֶת־הַמִּזְבְּחֹת מִכׇּל־יְהוּדָה וּבִנְיָמִן
וּבְאֶפְרַיִם וּמְנַשֶּׁה עַד־לְכַלֵּה וַיָּשׁוּבוּ כׇּל־בְּנֵי יִשְׂרָאֵל אִישׁ לַאֲחֻזָּתוֹ
ב לְעָרֵיהֶם׃ וַיַּעֲמֵד יְחִזְקִיָּהוּ אֶת־מַחְלְקוֹת הַכֹּהֲנִים וְהַלְוִיִּם
עַל־מַחְלְקוֹתָם אִישׁ ׀ כְּפִי עֲבֹדָתוֹ לַכֹּהֲנִים וְלַלְוִיִּם לְעֹלָה וְלִשְׁלָמִים
ג לְשָׁרֵת וּלְהֹדוֹת וּלְהַלֵּל בְּשַׁעֲרֵי מַחֲנוֹת יְהוָה׃ וּמְנָת הַמֶּלֶךְ
מִן־רְכוּשׁוֹ לָעֹלוֹת לְעֹלוֹת הַבֹּקֶר וְהָעֶרֶב וְהָעֹלוֹת לַשַּׁבָּתוֹת וְלֶחֳדָשִׁים
ד וְלַמֹּעֲדִים כַּכָּתוּב בְּתוֹרַת יְהוָה׃ וַיֹּאמֶר לָעָם לְיוֹשְׁבֵי יְרוּשָׁלִַם לָתֵת

of Jerusalem, to give the portions due to the priests and the Levites in order
5 to encourage their devotion to the LORD's Torah. As soon as word spread, the
Israelites brought large amounts of their first grain, wine, oil, honey, and all
6 their produce – they brought generous tithes of everything. The people of
Israel and Yehuda living in the towns of Yehuda also brought tithes of cattle
and sheep and tithes of sacred items that they had consecrated to the LORD
7 their God, and they laid it out in many heaps. By the third month,
the heaps began to accumulate, and they were finished by the seventh
8 month. When Yeḥizkiyahu and the officials came and saw the
9 heaps, they blessed the LORD and His people Israel. Yeḥizkiyahu
10 questioned the priests and the Levites about the heaps, and the priest
Azaryahu, head of the house of Tzadok, answered him. "Since they began to
bring the contributions into the House of the LORD," he said, "we have eaten
our fill and had plenty left over, for the LORD has blessed His people, and this
11 great amount still remains." Yeḥizkiyahu then gave orders to arrange
12 store chambers in the House of the LORD, and they arranged them; they
faithfully brought in the contributions, the tithes, and the consecrated items.
The chief officer in charge of them was Kananyahu the Levite, with his brother
13 Shimi as second, while Yeḥiel, Azazyahu, Naḥat, Asael, Yerimot, Yozavad,
Eliel, Yismakhyahu, Maḥat, and Benayahu were overseers assisting
Kananyahu and his brother Shimi by appointment of King Yeḥizkiyahu and
14 of Azaryahu, the chief officer of the House of God. Koreh son of Yimna the
Levite, keeper of the east gate, was in charge of the freewill offerings to God,
of distributing the contribution reserved for the LORD, and of the most holy
15 offerings. Eden, Minyamin, Yeshua, Shemayahu, Amaryahu, and Shekhanyahu
were his loyal assistants in the priestly towns, distributing their kinsmen's
16 portions by division to great and small alike in addition to distributing the
daily rations to all males three years and up – registered by genealogy – who
came to the House of the LORD for service in shifts according to their
17 divisions. The priests were registered according to their ancestral houses
while Levites from twenty years and up were listed according to their offices
18 within their divisions. Both groups were registered by genealogy with all their
young children, their wives, their sons, and their daughters, for in their duty
19 they led lives of holiness. As for the priestly descendants of Aharon in the
fields of common land adjoining their cities, in every city the aforementioned
men distributed portions to every male priest and to every Levite who was
20 registered by genealogy. Yeḥizkiyahu instituted this throughout Yehuda; he
21 did what was good and right and true before the LORD his God. Every task
he undertook – for the service of the House of God, the Torah, and the
commandment of seeking his God – he did with all his heart, and he was
successful.

32 1 After these faithful deeds came Sanḥeriv, king of Assyria. He invaded Yehuda
and set up camp next to the fortified cities, intending to conquer them for
2 himself. When Yeḥizkiyahu saw that Sanḥeriv had come and was intent on
3 war over Jerusalem, he took counsel with his officials and warriors about

ה מנת הכהנים והלוים למען יחזקו בתורת יהוה: וכפרץ הדבר הרבו
בני־ישראל ראשית דגן תירוש ויצהר ודבש וכל תבואת שדה
ו ומעשר הכל לרב הביאו: ובני ישראל ויהודה היושבים בערי יהודה
גם־הם מעשר בקר וצאן ומעשר קדשים המקדשים ליהוה אלהיהם
ז הביאו ויתנו ערמות ערמות: בחדש השלשי
ח החלו הערמות ליסוד ובחדש השביעי כלו: ויבאו
יחזקיהו והשרים ויראו את־הערמות ויברכו את־יהוה ואת עמו
ט ישראל: וידרש יחזקיהו על־הכהנים והלוים על־
י הערמות: ויאמר אליו עזריהו הכהן הראש לבית צדוק ויאמר כג
מהחל התרומה לביא בית־יהוה אכול ושבוע והותר עד־לרוב כי
יא יהוה ברך את־עמו והנותר את־ההמון הזה: ויאמר
יב יחזקיהו להכין לשכות בבית יהוה ויכינו: ויביאו את־התרומה
והמעשר והקדשים באמונה ועליהם נגיד כונניהו הלוי ושמעי כנניהו
יג אחיהו משנה: ויחיאל ועזזיהו ונחת ועשהאל וירימות ויוזבד
ואליאל ויסמכיהו ומחת ובניהו פקידים מיד כונניהו ושמעי אחיו כנניהו
יד במפקד יחזקיהו המלך ועזריהו נגיד בית־האלהים: וקורא בן־ימנה
הלוי השוער למזרחה על נדבות האלהים לתת תרומת יהוה וקדשי
טו הקדשים: ועל־ידו עדן ומנימן וישוע ושמעיהו אמריהו ושכניהו
טז בערי הכהנים באמונה לתת לאחיהם במחלקות כגדול כקטן:
מלבד התיחשם לזכרים מבן שלוש שנים ולמעלה לכל־הבא לבית־
יז יהוה לדבר־יום ביומו לעבודתם במשמרותם כמחלקותיהם: ואת
התיחש הכהנים לבית אבותיהם והלוים מבן עשרים שנה ולמעלה
יח במשמרותיהם במחלקותיהם: ולהתיחש בכל־טפם נשיהם ובניהם
יט ובנותיהם לכל־קהל כי באמונתם יתקדשו־קדש: ולבני אהרן
הכהנים בשדי מגרש עריהם בכל־עיר ועיר אנשים אשר נקבו
כ בשמות לתת מנות לכל־זכר בכהנים ולכל־התיחש בלוים: ויעש
כזאת יחזקיהו בכל־יהודה ויעש הטוב והישר והאמת לפני יהוה
כא אלהיו: ובכל־מעשה אשר־החל | בעבודת בית־האלהים ובתורה
ובמצוה לדרש לאלהיו בכל־לבבו עשה והצליח:
לב א אחרי הדברים והאמת האלה בא סנחריב מלך־אשור ויבא ביהודה
ב ויחן על־הערים הבצרות ויאמר לבקעם אליו: וירא יחזקיהו כי־בא
ג סנחריב ופניו למלחמה על־ירושלם: ויועץ עם־שריו וגבריו לסתום

stopping the flow of springs that were outside the city, and they supported
4 him. A great crowd gathered, and they stopped up all the springs and the wadi
that flowed through the land, saying, "Why should the kings of Assyria come
5 and find water in abundance?" Determined, he repaired all the breaches in the
wall, raised up towers over it, and built another wall outside it. He reinforced
the Milo in the City of David, and he commissioned weapons and shields in
6 abundance. He appointed battle officers over the people and gathered them
to him by the square at the city gate to encourage them with these words:
7 "Be strong and determined; do not fear or hesitate in the face of the Assyrian
king and all the horde that accompany him, for what is with us is far greater
8 than what is with him. With him is but an arm of flesh; with us is the Lord
our God to help us and fight our battles." And the people were encouraged
9 by the words of King Yeḥizkiyahu of Yehuda. After this, King
Sanḥeriv of Assyria – who was stationed at Lakhish with all his forces – sent
his servants with this message to Jerusalem to King Yeḥizkiyahu of Yehuda
10 and to all the people of Yehuda who lived in Jerusalem: "Thus says Sanḥeriv,
king of Assyria: In what do you place your trust, that you remain under siege
11 in Jerusalem? Yeḥizkiyahu is misleading you – condemning you to die in
hunger and in thirst – by saying, 'The Lord our God will save us from the
12 king of Assyria's hand.' Is this not the same Yeḥizkiyahu who removed his
high shrines and altars and told Yehuda and Jerusalem, 'Before a single altar
13 you shall worship and offer sacrifices'? Are you unaware of what my ancestors
and I have done to all the peoples of other lands? Have the gods of the nations
14 of other lands managed to save their lands from my hand? Who among all
the gods of these nations utterly destroyed by my ancestors managed to save
their people from my hand, that your God will manage to save you from my
15 hand? Now do not let Ḥizkiyahu deceive you or mislead you thus; do not
believe him, for no god from any nation or any kingdom has managed to
save his people from my hand or the hand of my ancestors. Your God will
16 not manage to save you from my hand either." His servants continued to
17 disparage the Lord God and His servant Yeḥizkiyahu; he also wrote letters
that ridiculed the Lord, God of Israel, claiming about Him, "Just as the gods
of the nations of other lands failed to save their nations from my hand, the
18 God of Yeḥizkiyahu will fail to save His people from my hand." They shouted
out in Hebrew at the people of Jerusalem on the wall to frighten and intimi-
19 date them so as to capture the city. They spoke about the God of Jerusalem
as if they were speaking about the gods of the peoples of other lands, made by
20 human hands. Then King Yeḥizkiyahu and the prophet Yishayahu
21 son of Amotz prayed about this and cried out to heaven. And the
Lord sent an angel who annihilated every warrior, commander, and officer
in the camp of the king of Assyria, who then slunk back to his land in utter
disgrace. When he reached the temple of his gods, some of his very own sons

ד אֶת־מֵימֵי הָעֲיָנוֹת אֲשֶׁר מִחוּץ לָעִיר וַיַּעְזְרֻהוּ׃ וַיִּקָּבְצוּ עַם־רָב וַיִּסְתְּמוּ
אֶת־כׇּל־הַמַּעְיָנוֹת וְאֶת־הַנַּחַל הַשּׁוֹטֵף בְּתוֹךְ־הָאָרֶץ לֵאמֹר לָמָּה
ה יָבוֹאוּ מַלְכֵי אַשּׁוּר וּמָצְאוּ מַיִם רַבִּים׃ וַיִּתְחַזַּק וַיִּבֶן אֶת־כׇּל־הַחוֹמָה
הַפְּרוּצָה וַיַּעַל עַל־הַמִּגְדָּלוֹת וְלַחוּצָה הַחוֹמָה אַחֶרֶת וַיְחַזֵּק אֶת־
ו הַמִּלּוֹא עִיר דָּוִיד וַיַּעַשׂ שֶׁלַח לָרֹב וּמָגִנִּים׃ וַיִּתֵּן שָׂרֵי מִלְחָמוֹת עַל־
הָעָם וַיִּקְבְּצֵם אֵלָיו אֶל־רְחוֹב שַׁעַר הָעִיר וַיְדַבֵּר עַל־לְבָבָם לֵאמֹר׃
ז חִזְקוּ וְאִמְצוּ אַל־תִּירְאוּ וְאַל־תֵּחַתּוּ מִפְּנֵי מֶלֶךְ אַשּׁוּר וּמִלִּפְנֵי כׇּל־
ח הֶהָמוֹן אֲשֶׁר־עִמּוֹ כִּי־עִמָּנוּ רַב מֵעִמּוֹ׃ עִמּוֹ זְרוֹעַ בָּשָׂר וְעִמָּנוּ יְהוָה
אֱלֹהֵינוּ לְעׇזְרֵנוּ וּלְהִלָּחֵם מִלְחֲמֹתֵנוּ וַיִּסָּמְכוּ הָעָם עַל־דִּבְרֵי יְחִזְקִיָּהוּ
ט מֶלֶךְ־יְהוּדָה׃ אַחַר זֶה שָׁלַח סַנְחֵרִיב מֶלֶךְ־אַשּׁוּר עֲבָדָיו
יְרוּשָׁלַיְמָה וְהוּא עַל־לָכִישׁ וְכׇל־מֶמְשַׁלְתּוֹ עִמּוֹ עַל־יְחִזְקִיָּהוּ מֶלֶךְ
י יְהוּדָה וְעַל־כׇּל־יְהוּדָה אֲשֶׁר בִּירוּשָׁלַ͏ִם לֵאמֹר׃ כֹּה אָמַר סַנְחֵרִיב
יא מֶלֶךְ אַשּׁוּר עַל־מָה אַתֶּם בֹּטְחִים וְיֹשְׁבִים בְּמָצוֹר בִּירוּשָׁלָ͏ִם׃ הֲלֹא
יְחִזְקִיָּהוּ מַסִּית אֶתְכֶם לָתֵת אֶתְכֶם לָמוּת בְּרָעָב וּבְצָמָא לֵאמֹר יְהוָה
יב אֱלֹהֵינוּ יַצִּילֵנוּ מִכַּף מֶלֶךְ אַשּׁוּר׃ הֲלֹא־הוּא יְחִזְקִיָּהוּ הֵסִיר אֶת־
בָּמֹתָיו וְאֶת־מִזְבְּחֹתָיו וַיֹּאמֶר לִיהוּדָה וְלִירוּשָׁלַ͏ִם לֵאמֹר לִפְנֵי מִזְבֵּחַ
יג אֶחָד תִּשְׁתַּחֲווּ וְעָלָיו תַּקְטִירוּ׃ הֲלֹא תֵדְעוּ מֶה עָשִׂיתִי אֲנִי וַאֲבוֹתַי
לְכֹל עַמֵּי הָאֲרָצוֹת הֲיָכוֹל יָכְלוּ אֱלֹהֵי גּוֹיֵ הָאֲרָצוֹת לְהַצִּיל אֶת־אַרְצָם
יד מִיָּדִי׃ מִי בְּכׇל־אֱלֹהֵי הַגּוֹיִם הָאֵלֶּה אֲשֶׁר הֶחֱרִימוּ אֲבוֹתַי אֲשֶׁר יָכוֹל
טו לְהַצִּיל אֶת־עַמּוֹ מִיָּדִי כִּי יוּכַל אֱלֹהֵיכֶם לְהַצִּיל אֶתְכֶם מִיָּדִי׃ וְעַתָּה
אַל־יַשִּׁיא אֶתְכֶם חִזְקִיָּהוּ וְאַל־יַסִּית אֶתְכֶם כָּזֹאת וְאַל־תַּאֲמִינוּ לוֹ
כִּי־לֹא יוּכַל כׇּל־אֱלוֹהַּ כׇּל־גּוֹי וּמַמְלָכָה לְהַצִּיל עַמּוֹ מִיָּדִי וּמִיַּד אֲבוֹתָי
טז אַף כִּי אֱלֹהֵיכֶם לֹא־יַצִּילוּ אֶתְכֶם מִיָּדִי׃ וְעוֹד דִּבְּרוּ עֲבָדָיו עַל־יְהוָה
יז הָאֱלֹהִים וְעַל יְחִזְקִיָּהוּ עַבְדּוֹ׃ וּסְפָרִים כָּתַב לְחָרֵף לַיהוָה אֱלֹהֵי
יִשְׂרָאֵל וְלֵאמֹר עָלָיו לֵאמֹר כֵּאלֹהֵי גּוֹיֵ הָאֲרָצוֹת אֲשֶׁר לֹא־הִצִּילוּ
יח עַמָּם מִיָּדִי כֵּן לֹא־יַצִּיל אֱלֹהֵי יְחִזְקִיָּהוּ עַמּוֹ מִיָּדִי׃ וַיִּקְרְאוּ בְקוֹל־גָּדוֹל
יְהוּדִית עַל־עַם יְרוּשָׁלַ͏ִם אֲשֶׁר עַל־הַחוֹמָה לְיָרְאָם וּלְבַהֲלָם לְמַעַן
יט יִלְכְּדוּ אֶת־הָעִיר׃ וַיְדַבְּרוּ אֶל־אֱלֹהֵי יְרוּשָׁלָ͏ִם כְּעַל אֱלֹהֵי עַמֵּי הָאָרֶץ
כ מַעֲשֵׂה יְדֵי הָאָדָם׃ וַיִּתְפַּלֵּל יְחִזְקִיָּהוּ הַמֶּלֶךְ וִישַׁעְיָהוּ
כא בֶן־אָמוֹץ הַנָּבִיא עַל־זֹאת וַיִּזְעֲקוּ הַשָּׁמָיִם׃ וַיִּשְׁלַח יְהוָה
מַלְאָךְ וַיַּכְחֵד כׇּל־גִּבּוֹר חַיִל וְנָגִיד וְשָׂר בְּמַחֲנֵה מֶלֶךְ אַשּׁוּר וַיָּשׇׁב
בְּבֹשֶׁת פָּנִים לְאַרְצוֹ וַיָּבֹא בֵּית אֱלֹהָיו ומיציאו מֵעָיו שָׁם הִפִּילֻהוּ וּמִיצִיאֵי

22 struck him down by the sword. Thus the Lord saved Yeḥizkiyahu and the
people of Jerusalem from the hands of King Sanḥeriv of Assyria and everyone
23 else; He provided for them in every way. Many came to Jerusalem to offer
tribute to the Lord and treasures to Yeḥizkiyahu, king of Yehuda, and he was
exalted in the eyes of all the nations ever after.
24 At that time, Yeḥizkiyahu became ill, on the verge of death. He prayed to
25 the Lord, and He answered him and gave him a sign. But Yeḥizkiyahu did
not respond as would befit the favor he had been granted, for he had grown
26 arrogant, and wrath came upon him and upon Yehuda and Jerusalem. Then
Yeḥizkiyahu humbled himself because of his arrogant heart – he and the
people of Jerusalem – and the wrath of the Lord did not come upon them
27 in Yeḥizkiyahu's time. Yeḥizkiyahu had great riches and honor, and he made
himself treasuries for silver, gold, gems, spices, decorative shields, and all
28 kinds of precious objects, as well as storehouses for produce of grain, wine,
29 and oil, stalls for all kinds of animals, and stables for livestock. And he
acquired cities and vast flocks of sheep and cattle, for God had endowed him
30 with a wealth of possessions. This was the same Yeḥizkiyahu who dammed
the upper pool of the waters of Giḥon and directed them down to the western
31 side of the City of David. Yeḥizkiyahu was successful in all that he did. As for
the delegation of Babylonian officials that sent to him to inquire about the
sign that was in the land – God left him to his own devices to test him, to learn
32 all that was in his heart. The rest of Yeḥizkiyahu's history and his
loyal deeds are recorded in the vision of the prophet Yeshayahu son of Amotz
33 in the Book of Kings of Yehuda and Israel. And Yeḥizkiyahu slept with his
ancestors, and they buried him in the upper section of the tombs of David's
descendants; all of Yehuda and the people of Jerusalem honored him upon
33 1 his death. And his son Menashe reigned in his place. Menashe was
twelve years old when he became king, and for fifty-five years he reigned in
2 Jerusalem. He did what was evil in the eyes of the Lord, imitating the horrors
3 of the nations whom the Lord had dispossessed before the Israelites. He
rebuilt the high shrines that his father Yeḥizkiyahu had torn down, and he
erected altars for the Baalim, made sacred trees, and bowed down to all the
4 heavenly hosts and served them. He even built altars in the House of the
Lord, of which the Lord had said, "My name will be in Jerusalem forever."
5 He built altars for all the heavenly hosts in both courtyards of the House of the
6 Lord; he passed his sons through the fire in the Valley of Hinom; he practiced
augury, divination, and soothsaying, and consulted ghosts and spirits – he did
7 so much that was evil in the eyes of the Lord, angering Him. He placed a
carved idol that he had made in the House of God, of which God promised
to David and his son Shlomo: "In this House, and in Jerusalem, which I have
8 chosen out of all the tribes of Israel, I will establish My name forever. And
never again will I turn Israel's feet away from the land that I granted your
ancestors – so long as they carefully observe all that I commanded them, all

כב בַחָרֶב: וַיּוֹשַׁע יְהוָה אֶת־יְחִזְקִיָּהוּ וְאֵת ׀ יֹשְׁבֵי יְרוּשָׁלִַם מִיַּד סַנְחֵרִיב
כג מֶלֶךְ־אַשּׁוּר וּמִיַּד־כֹּל וַיְנַהֲלֵם מִסָּבִיב: וְרַבִּים מְבִיאִים מִנְחָה לַיהוָה
לִירוּשָׁלִַם וּמִגְדָּנוֹת לִיחִזְקִיָּהוּ מֶלֶךְ יְהוּדָה וַיִּנַּשֵּׂא לְעֵינֵי כָל־הַגּוֹיִם
מֵאַחֲרֵי־כֵן:
כד בַּיָּמִים הָהֵם חָלָה יְחִזְקִיָּהוּ עַד־לָמוּת וַיִּתְפַּלֵּל אֶל־יְהוָה וַיֹּאמֶר לוֹ
כה וּמוֹפֵת נָתַן לוֹ: וְלֹא־כִגְמֻל עָלָיו הֵשִׁיב יְחִזְקִיָּהוּ כִּי גָבַהּ לִבּוֹ וַיְהִי עָלָיו
כו קֶצֶף וְעַל־יְהוּדָה וִירוּשָׁלִָם: וַיִּכָּנַע יְחִזְקִיָּהוּ בְּגֹבַהּ לִבּוֹ הוּא וְיֹשְׁבֵי
כז יְרוּשָׁלִָם וְלֹא־בָא עֲלֵיהֶם קֶצֶף יְהוָה בִּימֵי יְחִזְקִיָּהוּ: וַיְהִי לִיחִזְקִיָּהוּ
עֹשֶׁר וְכָבוֹד הַרְבֵּה מְאֹד וְאוֹצָרוֹת עָשָׂה־לוֹ לְכֶסֶף וּלְזָהָב וּלְאֶבֶן
כח יְקָרָה וְלִבְשָׂמִים וּלְמָגִנִּים וּלְכֹל כְּלֵי חֶמְדָּה: וּמִסְכְּנוֹת לִתְבוּאַת דָּגָן
כט וְתִירוֹשׁ וְיִצְהָר וְאֻרָוֹת לְכָל־בְּהֵמָה וּבְהֵמָה וַעֲדָרִים לָאֲוֵרוֹת: וְעָרִים
עָשָׂה לוֹ וּמִקְנֵה־צֹאן וּבָקָר לָרֹב כִּי נָתַן־לוֹ אֱלֹהִים רְכוּשׁ רַב מְאֹד:
ל וְהוּא יְחִזְקִיָּהוּ סָתַם אֶת־מוֹצָא מֵימֵי גִיחוֹן הָעֶלְיוֹן ויישרם לְמַטָּה־ וַיַּשְּׁרֵם
לא מַּעְרָבָה לְעִיר דָּוִיד וַיַּצְלַח יְחִזְקִיָּהוּ בְּכָל־מַעֲשֵׂהוּ: וְכֵן בִּמְלִיצֵי ׀
שָׂרֵי בָּבֶל הַמְשַׁלְּחִים עָלָיו לִדְרֹשׁ הַמּוֹפֵת אֲשֶׁר הָיָה בָאָרֶץ עֲזָבוֹ
לב הָאֱלֹהִים לְנַסּוֹתוֹ לָדַעַת כָּל־בִּלְבָבוֹ: וְיֶתֶר דִּבְרֵי יְחִזְקִיָּהוּ
וַחֲסָדָיו הִנָּם כְּתוּבִים בַּחֲזוֹן יְשַׁעְיָהוּ בֶן־אָמוֹץ הַנָּבִיא עַל־סֵפֶר מַלְכֵי־
לג יְהוּדָה וְיִשְׂרָאֵל: וַיִּשְׁכַּב יְחִזְקִיָּהוּ עִם־אֲבֹתָיו וַיִּקְבְּרֻהוּ בְּמַעֲלֵה קִבְרֵי
בְנֵי־דָוִיד וְכָבוֹד עָשׂוּ־לוֹ בְמוֹתוֹ כָל־יְהוּדָה וְיֹשְׁבֵי יְרוּשָׁלִָם וַיִּמְלֹךְ
לג א מְנַשֶּׁה בְנוֹ תַּחְתָּיו: בֶּן־שְׁתֵּים עֶשְׂרֵה שָׁנָה מְנַשֶּׁה
ב בְמָלְכוֹ וַחֲמִשִּׁים וְחָמֵשׁ שָׁנָה מָלַךְ בִּירוּשָׁלִָם: וַיַּעַשׂ הָרַע בְּעֵינֵי יְהוָה
ג כְּתוֹעֲבוֹת הַגּוֹיִם אֲשֶׁר הוֹרִישׁ יְהוָה מִפְּנֵי בְּנֵי יִשְׂרָאֵל: וַיָּשָׁב וַיִּבֶן
אֶת־הַבָּמוֹת אֲשֶׁר נִתַּץ יְחִזְקִיָּהוּ אָבִיו וַיָּקֶם מִזְבְּחוֹת לַבְּעָלִים וַיַּעַשׂ
ד אֲשֵׁרוֹת וַיִּשְׁתַּחוּ לְכָל־צְבָא הַשָּׁמַיִם וַיַּעֲבֹד אֹתָם: וּבָנָה מִזְבְּחוֹת
ה בְּבֵית יְהוָה אֲשֶׁר אָמַר יְהוָה בִּירוּשָׁלִַם יִהְיֶה־שְּׁמִי לְעוֹלָם: וַיִּבֶן
ו מִזְבְּחוֹת לְכָל־צְבָא הַשָּׁמָיִם בִּשְׁתֵּי חַצְרוֹת בֵּית־יְהוָה: וְהוּא הֶעֱבִיר
אֶת־בָּנָיו בָּאֵשׁ בְּגֵי בֶן־הִנֹּם וְעוֹנֵן וְנִחֵשׁ וְכִשֵּׁף וְעָשָׂה אוֹב וְיִדְּעוֹנִי
ז הִרְבָּה לַעֲשׂוֹת הָרַע בְּעֵינֵי יְהוָה לְהַכְעִיסוֹ: וַיָּשֶׂם אֶת־פֶּסֶל הַסֶּמֶל
אֲשֶׁר עָשָׂה בְּבֵית הָאֱלֹהִים אֲשֶׁר אָמַר אֱלֹהִים אֶל־דָּוִיד וְאֶל־שְׁלֹמֹה
בְנוֹ בַּבַּיִת הַזֶּה וּבִירוּשָׁלִַם אֲשֶׁר בָּחַרְתִּי מִכֹּל שִׁבְטֵי יִשְׂרָאֵל אָשִׂים
ח אֶת־שְׁמִי לְעֵילוֹם: וְלֹא אוֹסִיף לְהָסִיר אֶת־רֶגֶל יִשְׂרָאֵל מֵעַל הָאֲדָמָה
אֲשֶׁר הֶעֱמַדְתִּי לַאֲבֹתֵיכֶם רַק ׀ אִם־יִשְׁמְרוּ לַעֲשׂוֹת אֵת כָּל־אֲשֶׁר

9 the Torah, statutes, and laws given through Moshe." But Menashe led Yehuda
and the people of Jerusalem astray to do even worse evil than the nations that
10 the LORD had destroyed before the Israelites. The LORD spoke to
11 Menashe and his people, but they would not listen. So the LORD brought
the army officers of the king of Assyria against them; they captured Menashe
12 with hooks, bound him with fetters, and led him to Babylon. In his distress,
he pleaded for the favor of the LORD his God and humbled himself deeply
13 before the God of his ancestors. He prayed to Him; He responded to his
prayer and heard his plea, and He returned him to his kingdom in Jerusalem.
14 Menashe recognized that the LORD is God. After that, he built an outer wall
for the City of David to the west of the Giḥon, in the wadi, reaching the Fish
Gate and encircling the Ofel; he raised it up high. And he appointed military
15 commanders in all the fortified cities in Yehuda. He removed the foreign gods
and the idol from the House of the LORD along with all the altars he built on
the hill of the House of the LORD and in Jerusalem, and he cast them outside
16 of the city. He restored the Altar of the LORD and sacrificed peace offerings
and thanksgiving offerings upon it, and he ordered Yehuda to serve the LORD,
17 God of Israel. The people still offered sacrifices upon the high shrines, but
18 only to the LORD their God. The rest of Menashe's history, his prayer to his
God, and the words of the seers who spoke to him in the name of the LORD,
19 God of Israel, are in the chronicles of the kings of Israel. His prayer and God's
response to it, all his sins and how he broke faith, and the places where he built
high shrines and set up sacred trees and idols before he humbled himself are
20 recorded in the chronicles of Ḥozai. And Menashe slept with his ancestors,
and he was buried by his palace. And his son Amon reigned in his place.
21 Amon was twenty-two years old when he became king, and for two years
22 he reigned in Jerusalem. He did what was evil in the eyes of the LORD, as his
father Menashe had done. He sacrificed to all the idols that his father Menashe
23 had made and worshipped them. But he did not humble himself before the
LORD as his father Menashe had humbled himself; instead, Amon incurred
24 more and more guilt. So his servants formed a conspiracy against him and
25 assassinated him in his palace. But the people of the land struck down all those
who had conspired against King Amon, and the people of the land made his
son Yoshiyahu king in his place.
34 1 Yoshiyahu was eight years old when he became king, and for thirty-one
2 years he reigned in Jerusalem. He did what was right in the eyes of the LORD,
following in the ways of his ancestor David; he strayed neither right nor left.
3 In the eighth year of his reign, though he was still young, he began to seek
out the God of his ancestor David; and in the twelfth year, he began to
purge Yehuda and Jerusalem of the high shrines and sacred trees and idols
4 and images. Under his supervision they smashed the altars of the Baalim,
cut down the sun altars that were built above them, razed the sacred trees,

ט צִוִּיתִים לְכׇל־הַתּוֹרָה וְהַחֻקִּים וְהַמִּשְׁפָּטִים בְּיַד־מֹשֶׁה: וַיֶּתַע מְנַשֶּׁה
אֶת־יְהוּדָה וְיֹשְׁבֵי יְרוּשָׁלָ͏ִם לַעֲשׂוֹת רָע מִן־הַגּוֹיִם אֲשֶׁר הִשְׁמִיד יְהֹוָה
י מִפְּנֵי בְּנֵי יִשְׂרָאֵל: וַיְדַבֵּר יְהֹוָה אֶל־מְנַשֶּׁה וְאֶל־עַמּוֹ וְלֹא
יא הִקְשִׁיבוּ: וַיָּבֵא יְהֹוָה עֲלֵיהֶם אֶת־שָׂרֵי הַצָּבָא אֲשֶׁר לְמֶלֶךְ אַשּׁוּר
וַיִּלְכְּדוּ אֶת־מְנַשֶּׁה בַּחֹחִים וַיַּאַסְרֻהוּ בַּנְחֻשְׁתַּיִם וַיּוֹלִיכֻהוּ בָּבֶלָה:
יב וּכְהָצֵר לוֹ חִלָּה אֶת־פְּנֵי יְהֹוָה אֱלֹהָיו וַיִּכָּנַע מְאֹד מִלִּפְנֵי אֱלֹהֵי אֲבֹתָיו:
יג וַיִּתְפַּלֵּל אֵלָיו וַיֵּעָתֶר לוֹ וַיִּשְׁמַע תְּחִנָּתוֹ וַיְשִׁיבֵהוּ יְרוּשָׁלַ͏ִם לְמַלְכוּתוֹ
יד וַיֵּדַע מְנַשֶּׁה כִּי יְהֹוָה הוּא הָאֱלֹהִים: וְאַחֲרֵי־כֵן בָּנָה חוֹמָה חִיצוֹנָה ׀
לְעִיר־דָּוִיד מַעְרָבָה לְגִיחוֹן בַּנַּחַל וְלָבוֹא בְשַׁעַר הַדָּגִים וְסָבַב לָעֹפֶל
טו וַיַּגְבִּיהֶהָ מְאֹד וַיָּשֶׂם שָׂרֵי־חַיִל בְּכׇל־הֶעָרִים הַבְּצֻרוֹת בִּיהוּדָה: וַיָּסַר
אֶת־אֱלֹהֵי הַנֵּכָר וְאֶת־הַסֶּמֶל מִבֵּית יְהֹוָה וְכׇל־הַמִּזְבְּחוֹת אֲשֶׁר בָּנָה
טז בְּהַר בֵּית־יְהֹוָה וּבִירוּשָׁלָ͏ִם וַיַּשְׁלֵךְ חוּצָה לָעִיר: וַיִּכֶן אֶת־מִזְבַּח יְהֹוָה וַיִּבֶן
וַיִּזְבַּח עָלָיו זִבְחֵי שְׁלָמִים וְתוֹדָה וַיֹּאמֶר לִיהוּדָה לַעֲבוֹד אֶת־יְהֹוָה
יז אֱלֹהֵי יִשְׂרָאֵל: אֲבָל עוֹד הָעָם זֹבְחִים בַּבָּמוֹת רַק לַיהֹוָה אֱלֹהֵיהֶם:
יח וְיֶתֶר דִּבְרֵי מְנַשֶּׁה וּתְפִלָּתוֹ אֶל־אֱלֹהָיו וְדִבְרֵי הַחֹזִים הַמְדַבְּרִים
אֵלָיו בְּשֵׁם יְהֹוָה אֱלֹהֵי יִשְׂרָאֵל הִנָּם עַל־דִּבְרֵי מַלְכֵי יִשְׂרָאֵל:
יט וּתְפִלָּתוֹ וְהֵעָתֶר־לוֹ וְכׇל־חַטָּאתוֹ וּמַעְלוֹ וְהַמְּקֹמוֹת אֲשֶׁר בָּנָה בָהֶם
בָּמוֹת וְהֶעֱמִיד הָאֲשֵׁרִים וְהַפְּסִלִים לִפְנֵי הִכָּנְעוֹ הִנָּם כְּתוּבִים עַל
כ דִּבְרֵי חוֹזָי: וַיִּשְׁכַּב מְנַשֶּׁה עִם־אֲבֹתָיו וַיִּקְבְּרֻהוּ בֵּיתוֹ וַיִּמְלֹךְ אָמוֹן
בְּנוֹ תַּחְתָּיו:
כא בֶּן־עֶשְׂרִים וּשְׁתַּיִם שָׁנָה אָמוֹן בְּמׇלְכוֹ וּשְׁתַּיִם שָׁנִים מָלַךְ בִּירוּשָׁלָ͏ִם:
כב וַיַּעַשׂ הָרַע בְּעֵינֵי יְהֹוָה כַּאֲשֶׁר עָשָׂה מְנַשֶּׁה אָבִיו וּלְכׇל־הַפְּסִילִים
כג אֲשֶׁר עָשָׂה מְנַשֶּׁה אָבִיו זִבַּח אָמוֹן וַיַּעַבְדֵם: וְלֹא נִכְנַע מִלִּפְנֵי יְהֹוָה
כד כְּהִכָּנַע מְנַשֶּׁה אָבִיו כִּי הוּא אָמוֹן הִרְבָּה אַשְׁמָה: וַיִּקְשְׁרוּ עָלָיו עֲבָדָיו
כה וַיְמִיתֻהוּ בְּבֵיתוֹ: וַיַּכּוּ עַם־הָאָרֶץ אֵת כׇּל־הַקֹּשְׁרִים עַל־הַמֶּלֶךְ אָמוֹן
וַיַּמְלִיכוּ עַם־הָאָרֶץ אֶת־יֹאשִׁיָּהוּ בְנוֹ תַּחְתָּיו:

לד א בֶּן־שְׁמוֹנֶה שָׁנִים יֹאשִׁיָּהוּ בְמׇלְכוֹ וּשְׁלֹשִׁים וְאַחַת שָׁנָה מָלַךְ
ב בִּירוּשָׁלָ͏ִם: וַיַּעַשׂ הַיָּשָׁר בְּעֵינֵי יְהֹוָה וַיֵּלֶךְ בְּדַרְכֵי דָּוִיד אָבִיו וְלֹא־סָר כד
יָמִין וּשְׂמֹאול:
ג וּבִשְׁמוֹנֶה שָׁנִים לְמׇלְכוֹ וְהוּא עוֹדֶנּוּ נַעַר הֵחֵל לִדְרוֹשׁ לֵאלֹהֵי דָּוִיד
אָבִיו וּבִשְׁתֵּים עֶשְׂרֵה שָׁנָה הֵחֵל לְטַהֵר אֶת־יְהוּדָה וִירוּשָׁלַ͏ִם מִן־
ד הַבָּמוֹת וְהָאֲשֵׁרִים וְהַפְּסִלִים וְהַמַּסֵּכוֹת: וַיְנַתְּצוּ לְפָנָיו אֵת מִזְבְּחוֹת

the idols, and the images, ground them to dust, and scattered them over
5 the graves of those who had sacrificed to them. He burned the bones of the
idolatrous priests on their own altars and thus purged Yehuda and Jerusalem.
6 In the towns of Menashe, Efrayim, Shimon, and as far as Naftali – with ruins
7 all around – he smashed the altars, ground the sacred trees and the idols to
dust, and cut down all the sun altars all over the land of Israel. Then he went
8 back to Jerusalem. In the eighteenth year of his reign, after purging
the land and the House, he sent Shafan son of Atzalyahu, Maaseyahu the city
governor, and Yoaḥ son of Yoaḥaz, the herald, to repair the House of the Lord
9 his God. They came to Ḥilkiyahu the High Priest and gave him the silver that
had been brought to the House of God – that which the Levite guardians of
the threshold had collected from Menashe, Efrayim, and all the remnant of
10 Israel, and from Yehuda, Binyamin, and the people of Jerusalem.[38] They gave
it to the foremen in charge of the House of the Lord, and they paid it out
to the workers in the House of the Lord who worked to keep the House in
11 repair, and they gave some to the carpenters and the builders to purchase
quarry stones and timber for binders and for roof beams for the buildings that
12 the kings of Yehuda had let fall into ruin. The people were honest
workers, and they were supervised by the Levites Yaḥat and Ovadyahu of the
sons of Merari, and Zekharya and Meshulam of the sons of Kehat, who were
13 in charge. Other Levites, all of them skilled with musical instruments, were in
charge of the porters, directing all those who worked at various tasks; other
14 Levites were scribes, officers, and gatekeepers. As they took out the money
that had been brought to the House of the Lord, Ḥilkiyahu the priest found
15 a scroll of the Lord's Torah given by Moshe. Ḥilkiyahu remarked to the
scribe Shafan, "I found a scroll of the teaching in the House of the Lord,"
16 and Ḥilkiyahu gave the book to Shafan. Shafan brought the book to the king
and further reported to the king: "Your servants are fulfilling all that has been
17 assigned to them. They have melted down the silver found in the House
of the Lord, and they have paid it out to the foremen and to the workers."
18 Then Shafan the scribe told the king, "The priest Ḥilkiyahu gave me a scroll,"
19 and Shafan read from it before the king. When the king heard the words of
20 the teaching, he rent his clothes. And the king gave orders to Ḥilkiyahu,
Aḥikam son of Shafan, Avdon son of Mikha, Shafan the scribe, and Asaya,
21 the king's servant: "Go, inquire of the Lord on my behalf and on behalf of
those who are left in Israel and Yehuda, about the words of this scroll that
has just been found. For great was the fury the Lord poured out on us when
our ancestors did not keep the Lord's word and do all that was prescribed
22 in this book." The priest Ḥilkiyahu and those sent by the king went

---

38 | See note on 19:8.

הַבְּעָלִים וְהַחַמָּנִים אֲשֶׁר־לְמַעְלָה מֵעֲלֵיהֶם גִּדֵּעַ וְהָאֲשֵׁרִים וְהַפְּסִלִים
ה וְהַמַּסֵּכוֹת שִׁבַּר וְהֵדַק וַיִּזְרֹק עַל־פְּנֵי הַקְּבָרִים הַזֹּבְחִים לָהֶם׃ וְעַצְמוֹת
ו כֹּהֲנִים שָׂרַף עַל־מזבחותים וַיְטַהֵר אֶת־יְהוּדָה וְאֶת־יְרוּשָׁלִָם׃ וּבְעָרֵי מִזְבְּחוֹתָם
ז מְנַשֶּׁה וְאֶפְרַיִם וְשִׁמְעוֹן וְעַד־נַפְתָּלִי בחר בתיהם סָבִיב׃ וַיְנַתֵּץ אֶת־ בְּחַרְבֹתֵיהֶם
הַמִּזְבְּחוֹת וְאֶת־הָאֲשֵׁרִים וְהַפְּסִלִים כִּתַּת לְהֵדַק וְכָל־הַחַמָּנִים גִּדַּע
ח בְּכָל־אֶרֶץ יִשְׂרָאֵל וַיָּשָׁב לִירוּשָׁלִָם׃ וּבִשְׁנַת שְׁמוֹנֶה
עֶשְׂרֵה לְמָלְכוֹ לְטַהֵר הָאָרֶץ וְהַבָּיִת שָׁלַח אֶת־שָׁפָן בֶּן־אֲצַלְיָהוּ
וְאֶת־מַעֲשֵׂיָהוּ שַׂר־הָעִיר וְאֵת יוֹאָח בֶּן־יוֹאָחָז הַמַּזְכִּיר לְחַזֵּק אֶת־
ט בֵּית יהוה אֱלֹהָיו׃ וַיָּבֹאוּ אֶל־חִלְקִיָּהוּ ׀ הַכֹּהֵן הַגָּדוֹל וַיִּתְּנוּ אֶת־
הַכֶּסֶף הַמּוּבָא בֵית־אֱלֹהִים אֲשֶׁר אָסְפוּ־הַלְוִיִּם שֹׁמְרֵי הַסַּף מִיַּד
מְנַשֶּׁה וְאֶפְרַיִם וּמִכֹּל שְׁאֵרִית יִשְׂרָאֵל וּמִכָּל־יְהוּדָה וּבִנְיָמִן וישבי וַיָּשֻׁבוּ
י יְרוּשָׁלִָם׃ וַיִּתְּנוּ עַל־יַד עֹשֵׂה הַמְּלָאכָה הַמֻּפְקָדִים בְּבֵית יהוה וַיִּתְּנוּ
אֹתוֹ עוֹשֵׂי הַמְּלָאכָה אֲשֶׁר עֹשִׂים בְּבֵית יהוה לִבְדּוֹק וּלְחַזֵּק הַבָּיִת׃
יא וַיִּתְּנוּ לֶחָרָשִׁים וְלַבֹּנִים לִקְנוֹת אַבְנֵי מַחְצֵב וְעֵצִים לַמְחַבְּרוֹת וּלְקָרוֹת
יב אֶת־הַבָּתִּים אֲשֶׁר הִשְׁחִיתוּ מַלְכֵי יְהוּדָה׃ וְהָאֲנָשִׁים עֹשִׂים
בֶּאֱמוּנָה בַּמְּלָאכָה וַעֲלֵיהֶם ׀ מֻפְקָדִים יַחַת וְעֹבַדְיָהוּ הַלְוִיִּם מִן־בְּנֵי
מְרָרִי וּזְכַרְיָה וּמְשֻׁלָּם מִן־בְּנֵי הַקְּהָתִים לְנַצֵּחַ וְהַלְוִיִּם כָּל־מֵבִין בִּכְלֵי־
יג שִׁיר׃ וְעַל הַסַּבָּלִים וּמְנַצְּחִים לְכֹל עֹשֵׂה מְלָאכָה לַעֲבוֹדָה וַעֲבוֹדָה
יד וּמֵהַלְוִיִּם סוֹפְרִים וְשֹׁטְרִים וְשׁוֹעֲרִים׃ וּבְהוֹצִיאָם אֶת־הַכֶּסֶף הַמּוּבָא
בֵּית יהוה מָצָא חִלְקִיָּהוּ הַכֹּהֵן אֶת־סֵפֶר תּוֹרַת־יהוה בְּיַד־מֹשֶׁה׃
טו וַיַּעַן חִלְקִיָּהוּ וַיֹּאמֶר אֶל־שָׁפָן הַסּוֹפֵר סֵפֶר הַתּוֹרָה מָצָאתִי בְּבֵית
טז יהוה וַיִּתֵּן חִלְקִיָּהוּ אֶת־הַסֵּפֶר אֶל־שָׁפָן׃ וַיָּבֵא שָׁפָן אֶת־הַסֵּפֶר אֶל־
הַמֶּלֶךְ וַיָּשֶׁב עוֹד אֶת־הַמֶּלֶךְ דָּבָר לֵאמֹר כֹּל אֲשֶׁר־נִתַּן בְּיַד־עֲבָדֶיךָ
יז הֵם עֹשִׂים׃ וַיַּתִּיכוּ אֶת־הַכֶּסֶף הַנִּמְצָא בְּבֵית־יהוה וַיִּתְּנוּהוּ עַל־יַד
יח הַמֻּפְקָדִים וְעַל־יַד עוֹשֵׂי הַמְּלָאכָה׃ וַיַּגֵּד שָׁפָן הַסּוֹפֵר לַמֶּלֶךְ לֵאמֹר
יט סֵפֶר נָתַן לִי חִלְקִיָּהוּ הַכֹּהֵן וַיִּקְרָא־בוֹ שָׁפָן לִפְנֵי הַמֶּלֶךְ׃ וַיְהִי כִּשְׁמֹעַ
כ הַמֶּלֶךְ אֵת דִּבְרֵי הַתּוֹרָה וַיִּקְרַע אֶת־בְּגָדָיו׃ וַיְצַו הַמֶּלֶךְ אֶת־חִלְקִיָּהוּ
וְאֶת־אֲחִיקָם בֶּן־שָׁפָן וְאֶת־עַבְדּוֹן בֶּן־מִיכָה וְאֵת ׀ שָׁפָן הַסּוֹפֵר וְאֵת
כא עֲשָׂיָה עֶבֶד־הַמֶּלֶךְ לֵאמֹר׃ לְכוּ דִרְשׁוּ אֶת־יהוה בַּעֲדִי וּבְעַד הַנִּשְׁאָר
בְּיִשְׂרָאֵל וּבִיהוּדָה עַל־דִּבְרֵי הַסֵּפֶר אֲשֶׁר נִמְצָא כִּי־גְדוֹלָה חֲמַת־
יהוה אֲשֶׁר נִתְּכָה בָנוּ עַל אֲשֶׁר לֹא־שָׁמְרוּ אֲבוֹתֵינוּ אֶת־דְּבַר יהוה
כב לַעֲשׂוֹת כְּכָל־הַכָּתוּב עַל־הַסֵּפֶר הַזֶּה׃ וַיֵּלֶךְ חִלְקִיָּהוּ

to Ḥulda the prophet, wife of Shalum son of Tok'hat son of Ḥasra, keeper of
the wardrobe – she lived in Jerusalem in the Mishneh[39] – and they spoke to
23 her about this. She said to them, "Thus says the LORD, God of Israel: Say to
the man who sent you to me:
24 Thus says the LORD: I am about to bring disaster upon this place and its
inhabitants – all the curses written in the scroll they read out before the king
25 of Yehuda. Because they left Me and made sacrifices to other gods to anger
Me with all their practices, My fury will be poured out on this place, and it
26 will not be extinguished. And to the king of Yehuda, who sent you to inquire
of the LORD, say this: Thus says the LORD, God of Israel: Concern-
27 ing the words that you heard, because you softened your heart and you
humbled yourself before God when you heard His promise about this place
and its people, and you humbled yourself before Me and rent your clothes
28 and wept before Me, I, too have heard. The LORD has spoken. I will gather
you to your ancestors, and you will be gathered to your grave peacefully; your
own eyes will not see all the disaster I will bring upon this place and its
29 inhabitants." And they reported back to the king. The king sent and
30 gathered all the elders of Yehuda and Jerusalem. And the king went up to the
House of the LORD along with all the men of Yehuda and the inhabitants of
Jerusalem, the priests and the Levites and all the people, great and small. And
in their hearing, he read out all the words of the scroll of the covenant that
31 had been found in the House of the LORD. The king stood in his place and
reinstated the covenant before the LORD: to follow the LORD and to keep His
commandments, decrees, and laws with all his heart and all his soul, to fulfill
32 the words of the covenant as written in this book. He then pledged all those
who were present in Jerusalem and Binyamin, and the people of Jerusalem
33 committed to the covenant of God, the God of their ancestors. Then
Yoshiyahu removed all the abominations from all the territory that belonged
to the Israelites and obliged all who were in Israel to worship the LORD, their
God; all his life, they did not stray from the LORD, God of their
35 1 ancestors. Yoshiyahu celebrated Passover for the LORD in Jerusalem;
they slaughtered the Passover sacrifice on the fourteenth of the first month.
2 He reappointed the priests to their shifts and encouraged them in the service
3 of the House of the LORD. And he instructed the Levites, who taught all Israel
and who were holy to the LORD, "Place the holy Ark in the House built by
Shlomo son of David, king of Israel; no longer shall you carry it on your
4 shoulders. Now serve the LORD your God and His people Israel; group
yourselves according to your ancestral houses in your divisions as instructed
5 by both David, king of Israel, and Shlomo his son. Take positions in the
Sanctuary grouped according to the ancestral houses of your kinsmen, the

39 | A quarter in the city.

וַאֲשֶׁר הַמֶּלֶךְ אֶל־חֻלְדָּה הַנְּבִיאָה אֵשֶׁת ׀ שַׁלֻּם בֶּן־תּוֹקְהַת בֶּן־חַסְרָה תָּקְהַת
שׁוֹמֵר הַבְּגָדִים וְהִיא יוֹשֶׁבֶת בִּירוּשָׁלִַם בַּמִּשְׁנֶה וַיְדַבְּרוּ אֵלֶיהָ כָּזֹאת׃
כג וַתֹּאמֶר לָהֶם כֹּה־אָמַר יְהוָה אֱלֹהֵי יִשְׂרָאֵל אִמְרוּ לָאִישׁ אֲשֶׁר־שָׁלַח
אֶתְכֶם אֵלָי׃
כד כֹּה אָמַר יְהוָה הִנְנִי מֵבִיא רָעָה עַל־הַמָּקוֹם הַזֶּה וְעַל־יוֹשְׁבָיו אֵת
כָּל־הָאָלוֹת הַכְּתוּבוֹת עַל־הַסֵּפֶר אֲשֶׁר קָרְאוּ לִפְנֵי מֶלֶךְ יְהוּדָה׃
כה תַּחַת ׀ אֲשֶׁר עֲזָבוּנִי ויקטירו לֵאלֹהִים אֲחֵרִים לְמַעַן הַכְעִיסֵנִי בְּכֹל וַיְקַטְּרוּ
כו מַעֲשֵׂי יְדֵיהֶם וְתִתַּךְ חֲמָתִי בַּמָּקוֹם הַזֶּה וְלֹא תִכְבֶּה׃ וְאֶל־מֶלֶךְ יְהוּדָה
הַשֹּׁלֵחַ אֶתְכֶם לִדְרוֹשׁ בַּיהוָה כֹּה תֹאמְרוּ אֵלָיו   כֹּה־אָמַר
כז יְהוָה אֱלֹהֵי יִשְׂרָאֵל הַדְּבָרִים אֲשֶׁר שָׁמָעְתָּ׃ יַעַן רַךְ־לְבָבְךָ וַתִּכָּנַע ׀
מִלִּפְנֵי אֱלֹהִים בְּשָׁמְעֲךָ אֶת־דְּבָרָיו עַל־הַמָּקוֹם הַזֶּה וְעַל־יֹשְׁבָיו
וַתִּכָּנַע לְפָנַי וַתִּקְרַע אֶת־בְּגָדֶיךָ וַתֵּבְךְּ לְפָנָי וְגַם־אֲנִי שָׁמַעְתִּי נְאֻם־
כח יְהוָה׃ הִנְנִי אֹסִפְךָ אֶל־אֲבֹתֶיךָ וְנֶאֱסַפְתָּ אֶל־קִבְרוֹתֶיךָ בְּשָׁלוֹם וְלֹא־
תִרְאֶינָה עֵינֶיךָ בְּכֹל הָרָעָה אֲשֶׁר אֲנִי מֵבִיא עַל־הַמָּקוֹם הַזֶּה וְעַל־
כט יֹשְׁבָיו וַיָּשִׁיבוּ אֶת־הַמֶּלֶךְ דָּבָר׃   וַיִּשְׁלַח הַמֶּלֶךְ וַיֶּאֱסֹף אֶת־
ל כָּל־זִקְנֵי יְהוּדָה וִירוּשָׁלִָם׃ וַיַּעַל הַמֶּלֶךְ בֵּית־יְהוָה וְכָל־אִישׁ יְהוּדָה
וְיֹשְׁבֵי יְרוּשָׁלִַם וְהַכֹּהֲנִים וְהַלְוִיִּם וְכָל־הָעָם מִגָּדוֹל וְעַד־קָטָן וַיִּקְרָא
לא בְאָזְנֵיהֶם אֶת־כָּל־דִּבְרֵי סֵפֶר הַבְּרִית הַנִּמְצָא בֵּית יְהוָה׃ וַיַּעֲמֹד
הַמֶּלֶךְ עַל־עָמְדוֹ וַיִּכְרֹת אֶת־הַבְּרִית לִפְנֵי יְהוָה לָלֶכֶת אַחֲרֵי יְהוָה
וְלִשְׁמוֹר אֶת־מִצְוֹתָיו וְעֵדְוֹתָיו וְחֻקָּיו בְּכָל־לְבָבוֹ וּבְכָל־נַפְשׁוֹ לַעֲשׂוֹת
לב אֶת־דִּבְרֵי הַבְּרִית הַכְּתוּבִים עַל־הַסֵּפֶר הַזֶּה׃ וַיַּעֲמֵד אֵת כָּל־הַנִּמְצָא
בִירוּשָׁלִַם וּבִנְיָמִן וַיַּעֲשׂוּ יֹשְׁבֵי יְרוּשָׁלִַם כִּבְרִית אֱלֹהִים אֱלֹהֵי
לג אֲבוֹתֵיהֶם׃ וַיָּסַר יֹאשִׁיָּהוּ אֶת־כָּל־הַתּוֹעֵבוֹת מִכָּל־הָאֲרָצוֹת אֲשֶׁר לִבְנֵי
יִשְׂרָאֵל וַיַּעֲבֵד אֵת כָּל־הַנִּמְצָא בְּיִשְׂרָאֵל לַעֲבוֹד אֶת־יְהוָה אֱלֹהֵיהֶם
לה א כָּל־יָמָיו לֹא סָרוּ מֵאַחֲרֵי יְהוָה אֱלֹהֵי אֲבוֹתֵיהֶם׃   וַיַּעַשׂ
יֹאשִׁיָּהוּ בִירוּשָׁלִַם פֶּסַח לַיהוָה וַיִּשְׁחֲטוּ הַפֶּסַח בְּאַרְבָּעָה עָשָׂר לַחֹדֶשׁ
ב הָרִאשׁוֹן׃ וַיַּעֲמֵד הַכֹּהֲנִים עַל־מִשְׁמְרוֹתָם וַיְחַזְּקֵם לַעֲבוֹדַת בֵּית
ג יְהוָה׃ וַיֹּאמֶר לַלְוִיִּם המבונים לְכָל־יִשְׂרָאֵל הַקְּדוֹשִׁים לַיהוָה תְּנוּ הַמְּבִינִים
אֶת־אֲרוֹן־הַקֹּדֶשׁ בַּבַּיִת אֲשֶׁר בָּנָה שְׁלֹמֹה בֶן־דָּוִיד מֶלֶךְ יִשְׂרָאֵל
אֵין־לָכֶם מַשָּׂא בַּכָּתֵף עַתָּה עִבְדוּ אֶת־יְהוָה אֱלֹהֵיכֶם וְאֵת עַמּוֹ
ד יִשְׂרָאֵל׃ והכונו לְבֵית־אֲבוֹתֵיכֶם כְּמַחְלְקוֹתֵיכֶם בִּכְתָב דָּוִיד מֶלֶךְ וְהָכִינוּ
ה יִשְׂרָאֵל וּבְמִכְתַּב שְׁלֹמֹה בְנוֹ׃ וְעִמְדוּ בַקֹּדֶשׁ לִפְלֻגּוֹת בֵּית הָאָבוֹת

6 common people, with the Levites divided by ancestral house. Slaughter the
Passover sacrifice once you have sanctified yourselves, and prepare it for your
7 kinsmen to fulfill the LORD's word given through Moshe." Yoshiyahu
donated flocks to the people for Passover sacrifices for all those present, a
total of 30,000 lambs and kid goats and 3,000 bulls; these were of the king's
8 own possessions. His officials also made a voluntary donation to the
people, the priests, and the Levites. Ḥilkiya, Zekharyahu, and Yeḥiel, the chief
officers of the House of God, gave 2,600 Passover sacrifices and 300 bulls to
9 the priests. Kananyahu and his brothers Shemayahu and Netanel, as well as
Ḥashavyahu, Ye'iel, and Yozavad, the officers of the Levites, donated 5,000
10 Passover sacrifices and 500 bulls to the Levites. When the preparations for
the service were complete, the priests stood in position and the Levites in
11 their divisions as the king had ordered. They slaughtered the Passover
sacrifice, and the priests dashed the blood they received, while the Levites
12 did the flaying. And they set aside the parts of the burnt offering, arranging
them according to the groups of the common people's ancestral houses, to
offer them to the LORD as written in the book of Moshe, and they did the
13 same for the bulls. They cooked the Passover sacrifice with fire, as required,
and they cooked the sacred offerings in pots, kettles, and pans, then carried
14 them quickly to all the people. After that, they made preparations for
themselves and for the priests; the priestly descendants of Aharon were busy
offering up the burnt offerings and the fats late into the night, so the Levites
made the preparations for themselves and for the priestly descendants of
15 Aharon. The singers, the sons of Asaf, were at their posts as ordered by David,
Asaf, Heiman, and Yedutun, the king's seer, while the gatekeepers were
stationed at every gate; they were not to neglect their duties, for their fellow
16 Levites made the preparations for them. Thus all the necessary preparations
for the LORD's service were completed on that day, the Passover was
celebrated, and the burnt offerings were offered up on the Altar of the LORD
17 as king Yoshiyahu had commanded. The Israelites who were present
celebrated Passover at that time and the Festival of Unleavened Bread for
18 seven days. There had not been such a Passover celebration in Israel since the
days of the prophet Shmuel; none of the kings of Israel ever celebrated
Passover as Yoshiyahu did with the priests, the Levites, all of Yehuda, the
19 Israelites who were present, and the people of Jerusalem. It was in
the eighteenth year of Yoshiyahu's reign that this Passover was celebrated.
20 After all this, after Yoshiyahu had set the House in order, King Nekho of Egypt
marched up to fight in Karkemish on the Euphrates, and Yoshiyahu went out
21 to meet him. He sent messengers out to meet him, saying, "What have I to
do with you, king of Yehuda? It is not you that I am marching against today,
but against my rival house, and God has bid me to make haste. Do not meddle
22 with God, who is with me, and He will not destroy you." But Yoshiyahu would
not turn away from him; instead, he donned his royal armor in order to fight
against him and did not heed the words that Nekho quoted from God. And
23 he joined the battle in the Valley of Megiddo. The archers shot King Yoshiyahu,

ו לַאֲחֵיכֶם בְּנֵי הָעָם וַחֲלֻקַּת בֵּית־אָב לַלְוִיִּם: וְשַׁחֲטוּ הַפָּסַח וְהִתְקַדְּשׁוּ כה
ז וְהָכִינוּ לַאֲחֵיכֶם לַעֲשׂוֹת כִּדְבַר־יְהוָה בְּיַד־מֹשֶׁה: וַיָּרֶם
יֹאשִׁיָּהוּ לִבְנֵי הָעָם צֹאן כְּבָשִׂים וּבְנֵי־עִזִּים הַכֹּל לַפְּסָחִים לְכָל־
הַנִּמְצָא לְמִסְפַּר שְׁלֹשִׁים אֶלֶף וּבָקָר שְׁלֹשֶׁת אֲלָפִים אֵלֶּה מֵרְכוּשׁ
ח הַמֶּלֶךְ: וְשָׂרָיו לִנְדָבָה לָעָם לַכֹּהֲנִים וְלַלְוִיִּם הֵרִימוּ חִלְקִיָּה
וּזְכַרְיָהוּ וִיחִיאֵל נְגִידֵי בֵּית הָאֱלֹהִים לַכֹּהֲנִים נָתְנוּ לַפְּסָחִים אַלְפַּיִם
ט וְשֵׁשׁ מֵאוֹת וּבָקָר שְׁלֹשׁ מֵאוֹת: וכונניהו וּשְׁמַעְיָהוּ וּנְתַנְאֵל אֶחָיו וְכָנַנְיָהוּ
וַחֲשַׁבְיָהוּ וִיעִיאֵל וְיוֹזָבָד שָׂרֵי הַלְוִיִּם הֵרִימוּ לַלְוִיִּם לַפְּסָחִים חֲמֵשֶׁת
י אֲלָפִים וּבָקָר חֲמֵשׁ מֵאוֹת: וַתִּכּוֹן הָעֲבוֹדָה וַיַּעַמְדוּ הַכֹּהֲנִים עַל־
יא עָמְדָם וְהַלְוִיִּם עַל־מַחְלְקוֹתָם כְּמִצְוַת הַמֶּלֶךְ: וַיִּשְׁחֲטוּ הַפָּסַח וַיִּזְרְקוּ
יב הַכֹּהֲנִים מִיָּדָם וְהַלְוִיִּם מַפְשִׁיטִים: וַיָּסִירוּ הָעֹלָה לְתִתָּם לְמִפְלַגּוֹת
לְבֵית־אָבוֹת לִבְנֵי הָעָם לְהַקְרִיב לַיהוָה כַּכָּתוּב בְּסֵפֶר מֹשֶׁה וְכֵן
יג לַבָּקָר: וַיְבַשְּׁלוּ הַפֶּסַח בָּאֵשׁ כַּמִּשְׁפָּט וְהַקֳּדָשִׁים בִּשְּׁלוּ בַּסִּירוֹת
יד וּבַדְּוָדִים וּבַצֵּלָחוֹת וַיָּרִיצוּ לְכָל־בְּנֵי הָעָם: וְאַחַר הֵכִינוּ לָהֶם וְלַכֹּהֲנִים
כִּי הַכֹּהֲנִים בְּנֵי אַהֲרֹן בְּהַעֲלוֹת הָעוֹלָה וְהַחֲלָבִים עַד־לָיְלָה וְהַלְוִיִּם
טו הֵכִינוּ לָהֶם וְלַכֹּהֲנִים בְּנֵי אַהֲרֹן: וְהַמְשֹׁרְרִים בְּנֵי־אָסָף עַל־מַעֲמָדָם
כְּמִצְוַת דָּוִיד וְאָסָף וְהֵימָן וִידֻתוּן חוֹזֵה הַמֶּלֶךְ וְהַשֹּׁעֲרִים לְשַׁעַר וָשָׁעַר
טז אֵין לָהֶם לָסוּר מֵעַל עֲבֹדָתָם כִּי־אֲחֵיהֶם הַלְוִיִּם הֵכִינוּ לָהֶם: וַתִּכּוֹן
כָּל־עֲבוֹדַת יְהוָה בַּיּוֹם הַהוּא לַעֲשׂוֹת הַפֶּסַח וְהַעֲלוֹת עֹלוֹת עַל מִזְבַּח
יז יְהוָה כְּמִצְוַת הַמֶּלֶךְ יֹאשִׁיָּהוּ: וַיַּעֲשׂוּ בְנֵי־יִשְׂרָאֵל הַנִּמְצְאִים אֶת־
יח הַפֶּסַח בָּעֵת הַהִיא וְאֶת־חַג הַמַּצּוֹת שִׁבְעַת יָמִים: וְלֹא־נַעֲשָׂה פֶסַח
כָּמֹהוּ בְּיִשְׂרָאֵל מִימֵי שְׁמוּאֵל הַנָּבִיא וְכָל־מַלְכֵי יִשְׂרָאֵל ׀ לֹא־עָשׂוּ
כַּפֶּסַח אֲשֶׁר־עָשָׂה יֹאשִׁיָּהוּ וְהַכֹּהֲנִים וְהַלְוִיִּם וְכָל־יְהוּדָה וְיִשְׂרָאֵל
יט הַנִּמְצָא וְיוֹשְׁבֵי יְרוּשָׁלִָם: בִּשְׁמוֹנֶה עֶשְׂרֵה שָׁנָה
כ לְמַלְכוּת יֹאשִׁיָּהוּ נַעֲשָׂה הַפֶּסַח הַזֶּה: אַחֲרֵי כָל־זֹאת אֲשֶׁר הֵכִין
יֹאשִׁיָּהוּ אֶת־הַבַּיִת עָלָה נְכוֹ מֶלֶךְ־מִצְרַיִם לְהִלָּחֵם בְּכַרְכְּמִישׁ
כא עַל־פְּרָת וַיֵּצֵא לִקְרָאתוֹ יֹאשִׁיָּהוּ: וַיִּשְׁלַח אֵלָיו מַלְאָכִים ׀ לֵאמֹר ׀
מַה־לִּי וָלָךְ מֶלֶךְ יְהוּדָה לֹא־עָלֶיךָ אַתָּה הַיּוֹם כִּי אֶל־בֵּית מִלְחַמְתִּי
וֵאלֹהִים אָמַר לְבַהֲלֵנִי חֲדַל־לְךָ מֵאֱלֹהִים אֲשֶׁר־עִמִּי וְאַל־יַשְׁחִיתֶךָ:
כב וְלֹא־הֵסֵב יֹאשִׁיָּהוּ פָנָיו מִמֶּנּוּ כִּי לְהִלָּחֶם־בּוֹ הִתְחַפֵּשׂ וְלֹא שָׁמַע
כג אֶל־דִּבְרֵי נְכוֹ מִפִּי אֱלֹהִים וַיָּבֹא לְהִלָּחֵם בְּבִקְעַת מְגִדּוֹ: וַיֹּרוּ הַיֹּרִים
לַמֶּלֶךְ יֹאשִׁיָּהוּ וַיֹּאמֶר הַמֶּלֶךְ לַעֲבָדָיו הַעֲבִירוּנִי כִּי הָחֳלֵיתִי מְאֹד:

and the king said to his servants, "Take me away, for I am gravely wounded."
24 His servants took him out of the chariot, transferred him to his deputy's
chariot, and conveyed him to Jerusalem, where he died. He was buried in the
tombs of his ancestors. And all of Yehuda and Jerusalem mourned for
25 Yoshiyahu. Yirmeyahu composed a lament for Yoshiyahu that all the
keening men and women sing in their laments for Yoshiyahu to this day; it
has become part of Israelite custom and was incorporated into the laments.
26 The rest of Yoshiyahu's history and his loyal deeds are recorded in the Lord's
27 teaching. And his history, earlier and later, is recorded in the Book of Kings
36 1 of Israel and Yehuda. The people of the land took Yehoaḥaz,
2 Yoshiyahu's son, and made him king in his father's place in Jerusalem. Yoaḥaz
was twenty-three years old when he became king, and for three months, he
3 reigned in Jerusalem. But the king of Egypt deposed him in Jerusalem and
imposed a fine on the land of one hundred talents of silver and one talent of
4 gold. The king of Egypt made his brother Elyakim king over Yehuda and
Jerusalem, and he changed his name to Yehoyakim. As for his brother Yoaḥaz,
5 Nekho took him and brought him to Egypt. Yehoyakim was twenty-
five years old when he became king, and for eleven years he reigned in
6 Jerusalem. He did what was evil in the eyes of the Lord his God. Then
Nevukhadnetzar, king of Babylon, marched up against him, and he bound
7 him in fetters to lead him to Babylon. Nevukhadnetzar brought some of the
vessels from the House of the Lord to Babylon, and he kept them in his
8 palace in Babylon. As for the rest of Yehoyakim's history and the horrors he
performed and what was found against him, they are recorded in the Book
of Kings of Israel and Yehuda. And his son Yehoyakhin reigned in his
9 place. Yehoyakhin was eight years old when he became king, and for
three months and ten days he reigned in Jerusalem. He did what was evil in
10 the eyes of the Lord. In the spring, King Nevukhadnetzar sent and had
him brought to Babylon along with the precious objects in the House of
the Lord, and he made his brother Tzidkiyahu king over Yehuda and
11 Jerusalem. Tzidkiyahu was twenty-one years old when he became
12 king, and for eleven years he reigned in Jerusalem. He did what was evil in
the eyes of the Lord his God, and he would not humble himself before the
13 prophet Yirmeyahu, who spoke for the Lord. He also rebelled against King
Nevukhadnetzar, who had made him swear by God.[40] He stiffened his neck
14 and set his heart against returning to the Lord, God of Israel. All the upper
classes of the priests and the people broke faith time and again, imitating all
the abominations of the nations; they defiled the House of the Lord that He
15 had consecrated in Jerusalem. The Lord, God of the ancestors, sent His
messengers to them time after time, for He had compassion on His people
16 and His dwelling place, but they continued to scorn God's messengers and
mock His words and ridicule His prophets until the Lord's wrath rose against
17 His people to the point of no return. He unleashed the king of the Chaldeans

40 | An oath of fealty.

כד וַיַּעֲבִירֻהוּ עֲבָדָיו מִן־הַמֶּרְכָּבָה וַיַּרְכִּיבֻהוּ עַל רֶכֶב הַמִּשְׁנֶה אֲשֶׁר־לוֹ
וַיּוֹלִיכֻהוּ יְרוּשָׁלַ͏ִם וַיָּמָת וַיִּקָּבֵר בְּקִבְרוֹת אֲבֹתָיו וְכָל־יְהוּדָה וִירוּשָׁלַ͏ִם
כה מִתְאַבְּלִים עַל־יֹאשִׁיָּהוּ׃ וַיְקוֹנֵן יִרְמְיָהוּ עַל־יֹאשִׁיָּהוּ
וַיֹּאמְרוּ כָל־הַשָּׁרִים ׀ וְהַשָּׁרוֹת בְּקִינוֹתֵיהֶם עַל־יֹאשִׁיָּהוּ עַד־הַיּוֹם
כו וַיִּתְּנוּם לְחֹק עַל־יִשְׂרָאֵל וְהִנָּם כְּתוּבִים עַל־הַקִּינוֹת׃ וְיֶתֶר דִּבְרֵי
כז יֹאשִׁיָּהוּ וַחֲסָדָיו כַּכָּתוּב בְּתוֹרַת יְהוָה׃ וּדְבָרָיו הָרִאשֹׁנִים וְהָאַחֲרֹנִים
לו א הִנָּם כְּתוּבִים עַל־סֵפֶר מַלְכֵי־יִשְׂרָאֵל וִיהוּדָה׃ וַיִּקְחוּ עַם־
הָאָרֶץ אֶת־יְהוֹאָחָז בֶּן־יֹאשִׁיָּהוּ וַיַּמְלִיכֻהוּ תַחַת־אָבִיו בִּירוּשָׁלָ͏ִם׃
ב בֶּן־שָׁלוֹשׁ וְעֶשְׂרִים שָׁנָה יוֹאָחָז בְּמָלְכוֹ וּשְׁלֹשָׁה חֳדָשִׁים מָלַךְ
ג בִּירוּשָׁלָ͏ִם׃ וַיְסִירֵהוּ מֶלֶךְ־מִצְרַיִם בִּירוּשָׁלָ͏ִם וַיַּעֲנֹשׁ אֶת־הָאָרֶץ מֵאָה
ד כִכַּר־כֶּסֶף וְכִכַּר זָהָב׃ וַיַּמְלֵךְ מֶלֶךְ־מִצְרַיִם אֶת־אֶלְיָקִים אָחִיו עַל־
יְהוּדָה וִירוּשָׁלַ͏ִם וַיַּסֵּב אֶת־שְׁמוֹ יְהוֹיָקִים וְאֶת־יוֹאָחָז אָחִיו לָקַח נְכוֹ
ה וַיְבִיאֵהוּ מִצְרָיְמָה׃ בֶּן־עֶשְׂרִים וְחָמֵשׁ שָׁנָה יְהוֹיָקִים
בְּמָלְכוֹ וְאַחַת עֶשְׂרֵה שָׁנָה מָלַךְ בִּירוּשָׁלָ͏ִם וַיַּעַשׂ הָרַע בְּעֵינֵי יְהוָה
ו אֱלֹהָיו׃ עָלָיו עָלָה נְבוּכַדְנֶאצַּר מֶלֶךְ בָּבֶל וַיַּאַסְרֵהוּ בַּנְחֻשְׁתַּיִם
ז לְהֹלִיכוֹ בָּבֶלָה׃ וּמִכְּלֵי בֵּית יְהוָה הֵבִיא נְבוּכַדְנֶאצַּר לְבָבֶל וַיִּתְּנֵם
ח בְּהֵיכָלוֹ בְּבָבֶל׃ וְיֶתֶר דִּבְרֵי יְהוֹיָקִים וְתֹעֲבֹתָיו אֲשֶׁר־עָשָׂה וְהַנִּמְצָא
עָלָיו הִנָּם כְּתוּבִים עַל־סֵפֶר מַלְכֵי יִשְׂרָאֵל וִיהוּדָה וַיִּמְלֹךְ יְהוֹיָכִין בְּנוֹ
ט תַּחְתָּיו׃ בֶּן־שְׁמוֹנֶה שָׁנִים יְהוֹיָכִין בְּמָלְכוֹ וּשְׁלֹשָׁה
חֳדָשִׁים וַעֲשֶׂרֶת יָמִים מָלַךְ בִּירוּשָׁלָ͏ִם וַיַּעַשׂ הָרַע בְּעֵינֵי יְהוָה׃
י וְלִתְשׁוּבַת הַשָּׁנָה שָׁלַח הַמֶּלֶךְ נְבוּכַדְנֶאצַּר וַיְבִאֵהוּ בָבֶלָה עִם־
כְּלֵי חֶמְדַּת בֵּית־יְהוָה וַיַּמְלֵךְ אֶת־צִדְקִיָּהוּ אָחִיו עַל־יְהוּדָה
יא וִירוּשָׁלָ͏ִם׃ בֶּן־עֶשְׂרִים וְאַחַת שָׁנָה צִדְקִיָּהוּ בְמָלְכוֹ וְאַחַת
יב עֶשְׂרֵה שָׁנָה מָלַךְ בִּירוּשָׁלָ͏ִם׃ וַיַּעַשׂ הָרַע בְּעֵינֵי יְהוָה אֱלֹהָיו לֹא נִכְנַע
יג מִלִּפְנֵי יִרְמְיָהוּ הַנָּבִיא מִפִּי יְהוָה׃ וְגַם בַּמֶּלֶךְ נְבוּכַדְנֶאצַּר מָרָד אֲשֶׁר
הִשְׁבִּיעוֹ בֵּאלֹהִים וַיֶּקֶשׁ אֶת־עָרְפּוֹ וַיְאַמֵּץ אֶת־לְבָבוֹ מִשּׁוּב אֶל־יְהוָה
יד אֱלֹהֵי יִשְׂרָאֵל׃ גַּם כָּל־שָׂרֵי הַכֹּהֲנִים וְהָעָם הִרְבּוּ למעול־מַעַל כְּכֹל לִמְעָל־
תֹּעֲבוֹת הַגּוֹיִם וַיְטַמְּאוּ אֶת־בֵּית יְהוָה אֲשֶׁר הִקְדִּישׁ בִּירוּשָׁלָ͏ִם׃
טו וַיִּשְׁלַח יְהוָה אֱלֹהֵי אֲבוֹתֵיהֶם עֲלֵיהֶם בְּיַד מַלְאָכָיו הַשְׁכֵּם וְשָׁלוֹחַ
טז כִּי־חָמַל עַל־עַמּוֹ וְעַל־מְעוֹנוֹ׃ וַיִּהְיוּ מַלְעִבִים בְּמַלְאֲכֵי הָאֱלֹהִים
וּבוֹזִים דְּבָרָיו וּמִתַּעְתְּעִים בִּנְבִאָיו עַד עֲלוֹת חֲמַת־יְהוָה בְּעַמּוֹ עַד־
יז לְאֵין מַרְפֵּא׃ וַיַּעַל עֲלֵיהֶם אֶת־מֶלֶךְ כשדיים וַיַּהֲרֹג בַּחוּרֵיהֶם בַּחֶרֶב כַּשְׂדִּים

against them, and he slew their young men by the sword in their Temple with
no pity for any young man or maiden, the old, or the frail – they were all
18 handed over to him. And every last vessel in the House of God, great and
small, and the treasuries of the House of the Lord and the treasuries of the
19 king and his officials – he brought everything to Babylon. They burned down
the House of God and tore down the wall of Jerusalem; they burned all its
20 palaces with fire and destroyed all its treasures. He exiled the remnant who
had survived the sword to Babylon, and they became slaves for him and his
21 sons until the Persian Empire rose to power – fulfilling the word of the Lord
as pronounced by Yirmeyahu: until the land had paid back its Sabbatical
years, it lay Sabbath-fallow all the days of its desolation until seventy years
22 were fulfilled. In the first year of Koresh, king of Persia, when the
Lord's word pronounced by Yirmeyahu had come to pass, the Lord stirred
the spirit of Koresh, king of Persia, and he issued a proclamation throughout
23 his kingdom by word of mouth and written word as well: "Thus says Koresh,
king of Persia: The Lord, God of the heavens, has granted me all the kingdoms
of the earth, and He has charged me to build Him a House in Jerusalem in
Yehuda. Whoever is among you from all His people, may the Lord his God
be with him, and let him go up!"

בְּבֵית מִקְדָּשָׁם וְלֹא חָמַל עַל־בָּחוּר וּבְתוּלָה זָקֵן וְיָשֵׁשׁ הַכֹּל נָתַן בְּיָדוֹ׃
יח וְכֹל כְּלֵי בֵּית הָאֱלֹהִים הַגְּדֹלִים וְהַקְּטַנִּים וְאֹצְרוֹת בֵּית יהוה וְאֹצְרוֹת
יט הַמֶּלֶךְ וְשָׂרָיו הַכֹּל הֵבִיא בָבֶל׃ וַיִּשְׂרְפוּ אֶת־בֵּית הָאֱלֹהִים וַיְנַתְּצוּ
אֵת חוֹמַת יְרוּשָׁלָ͏ִם וְכָל־אַרְמְנוֹתֶיהָ שָׂרְפוּ בָאֵשׁ וְכָל־כְּלֵי מַחֲמַדֶּיהָ
כ לְהַשְׁחִית׃ וַיֶּגֶל הַשְּׁאֵרִית מִן־הַחֶרֶב אֶל־בָּבֶל וַיִּהְיוּ־לוֹ וּלְבָנָיו
כא לַעֲבָדִים עַד־מְלֹךְ מַלְכוּת פָּרָס׃ לְמַלֹּאות דְּבַר־יהוה בְּפִי יִרְמְיָהוּ
עַד־רָצְתָה הָאָרֶץ אֶת־שַׁבְּתוֹתֶיהָ כָּל־יְמֵי הָשַּׁמָּה שָׁבָתָה לְמַלֹּאות
כב שִׁבְעִים שָׁנָה׃ וּבִשְׁנַת אַחַת לְכוֹרֶשׁ מֶלֶךְ פָּרַס לִכְלוֹת דְּבַר־
יהוה בְּפִי יִרְמְיָהוּ הֵעִיר יהוה אֶת־רוּחַ כּוֹרֶשׁ מֶלֶךְ־פָּרַס וַיַּעֲבֶר־קוֹל
כג בְּכָל־מַלְכוּתוֹ וְגַם־בְּמִכְתָּב לֵאמֹר׃ כֹּה־אָמַר כּוֹרֶשׁ ׀ מֶלֶךְ פָּרַס כָּל־
מַמְלְכוֹת הָאָרֶץ נָתַן לִי יהוה אֱלֹהֵי הַשָּׁמַיִם וְהוּא־פָקַד עָלַי לִבְנוֹת־
לוֹ בַיִת בִּירוּשָׁלַ͏ִם אֲשֶׁר בִּיהוּדָה מִי־בָכֶם מִכָּל־עַמּוֹ יהוה אֱלֹהָיו עִמּוֹ
וְיָעַל׃

REFERENCE MATERIAL

THE TEN COMMANDMENTS (*TAAM ELYON*)

The Ten Commandments can be read aloud using two systems of cantillation, the *Taam Elyon* ("High Cantillation") and *Taam Taḥton* ("Low Cantillation"). These systems also denote two different divisions of the passage into verses – in *Taam Elyon* each commandment represents one verse (although see below), while *Taam Taḥton* yields verses of more or less equal size. Because of the prodigious length of some of the verses in *Taam Elyon*, they contain an outsize number of the more ornate-sounding cantillation marks, such as *pazer* and *zarka-segol*, adding a dramatic flourish to the reading in this system. The distinct divisions also give rise to subtle differences in the vocalization of the words themselves, such as the exchange of a *kamatz* for a *pataḥ*, or the addition or subtraction of a *dagesh* in certain letters.

The system of division that originally held sway in the land of Israel was apparently *Taam Taḥton*, while *Taam Elyon* originated in a Babylonian tradition. Nevertheless, both systems can be found superimposed in the oldest biblical manuscripts, with the words written only once but each carrying two cantillation marks. This superimposition has led to a good deal of confusion and disagreement, especially regarding the first verse: The version of *Taam Elyon* presented here is that of Rabbi Yaakov Emden, which unites the first two commandments into a single verse. According to Rabbi Wolf Heidenheim, however, the first verse should end at the words מבית עבדים.

Rabbi Ḥizkiya ben Manoaḥ wrote (see *Ḥizkuni*, Exodus 20:14) that on the Festival of Shavuot the Ten Commandments should be read publicly using the *Taam Elyon*, while one should use *Taam Taḥton* whenever reading them as part of the normal order of the weekly Torah readings (in Parashat Yitro or Vaetḥanan). This is the custom of most Ashkenazic communities. On the other hand, Rabbi Menaḥem de Lonzano writes in *Or Torah* that *Taam Elyon* should be employed whenever the Ten Commandments are read publicly, whereas only individuals reading to themselves should make use of *Taam Taḥton*. This is the custom of Sephardic congregations. The Jews of Yemen, whose customs mirrored those of Babylonian Jewry, possessed only *Taam Elyon*.

עשרת הדברות שבפרשת יתרו
בטעם העליון

אָנֹכִי֙ יְהוָ֣ה אֱלֹהֶ֔יךָ אֲשֶׁ֧ר הוֹצֵאתִ֛יךָ
מֵאֶ֥רֶץ מִצְרַ֖יִם מִבֵּ֣ית עֲבָדִ֑ים לֹ֣א יִהְיֶ֣ה לְךָ֩ אֱלֹהִ֨ים אֲחֵרִ֜ים
עַל־פָּנַ֗י לֹ֣א תַעֲשֶׂ֣ה־לְךָ֣ פֶ֣סֶל ׀ וְכָל־תְּמוּנָ֡ה אֲשֶׁ֣ר בַּשָּׁמַ֣יִם ׀ מִמַּ֡עַל
וַאֲשֶׁר֩ בָּאָ֨רֶץ מִתַּ֜חַת וַאֲשֶׁ֣ר בַּמַּ֣יִם ׀ מִתַּ֣חַת לָאָ֗רֶץ לֹֽא־
תִשְׁתַּחֲוֶ֣ה לָהֶם֮ וְלֹ֣א תָעָבְדֵם֒ כִּ֣י אָנֹכִ֞י יְהוָ֤ה אֱלֹהֶ֙יךָ֙ אֵ֣ל קַנָּ֔א
פֹּ֠קֵד עֲוֺ֨ן אָבֹ֧ת עַל־בָּנִ֛ים עַל־שִׁלֵּשִׁ֥ים וְעַל־רִבֵּעִ֖ים לְשֹׂנְאָ֑י
וְעֹ֥שֶׂה חֶ֖סֶד לַאֲלָפִ֑ים לְאֹהֲבַ֖י וּלְשֹׁמְרֵ֥י מִצְוֺתָֽי׃ לֹ֥א
תִשָּׂ֛א אֶת־שֵׁם־יְהוָ֥ה אֱלֹהֶ֖יךָ לַשָּׁ֑וְא כִּ֣י לֹ֤א יְנַקֶּה֙ יְהוָ֔ה אֵ֛ת
אֲשֶׁר־יִשָּׂ֥א אֶת־שְׁמ֖וֹ לַשָּֽׁוְא׃
זָכ֞וֹר אֶת־י֤וֹם הַשַּׁבָּת֙ לְקַדְּשׁ֔וֹ שֵׁ֤שֶׁת יָמִים֙ תַּעֲבֹד֮ וְעָשִׂ֣יתָ כָל־
מְלַאכְתֶּךָ֒ וְי֙וֹם֙ הַשְּׁבִיעִ֜י שַׁבָּ֣ת ׀ לַיהוָ֣ה אֱלֹהֶ֗יךָ לֹ֣א תַעֲשֶׂ֣ה כָל־
מְלָאכָ֡ה אַתָּ֣ה ׀ וּבִנְךָ֣ וּ֠בִתֶּךָ עַבְדְּךָ֨ וַאֲמָתְךָ֜ וּבְהֶמְתֶּ֗ךָ וְגֵרְךָ֙ אֲשֶׁ֣ר
בִּשְׁעָרֶ֔יךָ כִּ֣י שֵֽׁשֶׁת־יָמִים֩ עָשָׂ֨ה יְהוָ֜ה אֶת־הַשָּׁמַ֣יִם וְאֶת־הָאָ֗רֶץ
אֶת־הַיָּם֙ וְאֶת־כָּל־אֲשֶׁר־בָּ֔ם וַיָּ֖נַח בַּיּ֣וֹם הַשְּׁבִיעִ֑י עַל־כֵּ֗ן בֵּרַ֧ךְ
יְהוָ֛ה אֶת־י֥וֹם הַשַּׁבָּ֖ת וַֽיְקַדְּשֵֽׁהוּ׃ כַּבֵּ֥ד אֶת־אָבִ֖יךָ
וְאֶת־אִמֶּ֑ךָ לְמַ֙עַן֙ יַאֲרִכ֣וּן יָמֶ֔יךָ עַ֚ל הָֽאֲדָמָ֔ה אֲשֶׁר־יְהוָ֥ה אֱלֹהֶ֖יךָ
נֹתֵ֥ן לָֽךְ׃ לֹ֥א תִרְצָֽח׃ לֹ֥א
תִנְאָֽף׃ לֹ֥א תִגְנֹֽב׃ לֹֽא־
תַעֲנֶ֥ה בְרֵעֲךָ֖ עֵ֥ד שָֽׁקֶר׃ לֹ֥א
תַחְמֹ֖ד בֵּ֣ית רֵעֶ֑ךָ לֹֽא־
תַחְמֹ֞ד אֵ֣שֶׁת רֵעֶ֗ךָ וְעַבְדּ֤וֹ וַאֲמָתוֹ֙ וְשׁוֹר֣וֹ וַחֲמֹר֔וֹ וְכֹ֖ל אֲשֶׁ֥ר
לְרֵעֶֽךָ׃

According to the Gr"a and Heidenheim, the first commandment until מִבֵּית עֲבָדִים should be read with the regular trop.

עשרת הדברות שבפרשת ואתחנן

בטעם העליון

אָנֹכִי יְהוָה אֱלֹהֶיךָ

אֲשֶׁר הוֹצֵאתִיךָ מֵאֶרֶץ מִצְרַיִם מִבֵּית עֲבָדִים לֹא יִהְיֶה לְךָ

אֱלֹהִים אֲחֵרִים עַל־פָּנַי לֹא תַעֲשֶׂה־לְךָ פֶסֶל ׀ כָּל־תְּמוּנָה

אֲשֶׁר בַּשָּׁמַיִם ׀ מִמַּעַל וַאֲשֶׁר בָּאָרֶץ מִתַּחַת וַאֲשֶׁר בַּמַּיִם ׀

מִתַּחַת לָאָרֶץ לֹא־תִשְׁתַּחְוֶה לָהֶם וְלֹא תָעָבְדֵם כִּי אָנֹכִי יְהוָה

אֱלֹהֶיךָ אֵל קַנָּא פֹּקֵד עֲוֺן אָבוֹת עַל־בָּנִים וְעַל־שִׁלֵּשִׁים

וְעַל־רִבֵּעִים לְשֹׂנְאָי וְעֹשֶׂה חֶסֶד לַאֲלָפִים לְאֹהֲבַי וּלְשֹׁמְרֵי

מצותו: לֹא תִשָּׂא אֶת־שֵׁם־יְהוָה אֱלֹהֶיךָ לַשָּׁוְא כִּי לֹא מִצְוֺתָי

יְנַקֶּה יְהוָה אֵת אֲשֶׁר־יִשָּׂא אֶת־שְׁמוֹ לַשָּׁוְא: שָׁמוֹר

אֶת־יוֹם הַשַּׁבָּת לְקַדְּשׁוֹ כַּאֲשֶׁר צִוְּךָ ׀ יְהוָה אֱלֹהֶיךָ שֵׁשֶׁת יָמִים

תַּעֲבֹד וְעָשִׂיתָ כָּל־מְלַאכְתֶּךָ וְיוֹם הַשְּׁבִיעִי שַׁבָּת ׀ לַיהוָה

אֱלֹהֶיךָ לֹא תַעֲשֶׂה כָל־מְלָאכָה אַתָּה וּבִנְךָ־וּבִתֶּךָ וְעַבְדְּךָ־

וַאֲמָתֶךָ וְשׁוֹרְךָ וַחֲמֹרְךָ וְכָל־בְּהֶמְתֶּךָ וְגֵרְךָ אֲשֶׁר בִּשְׁעָרֶיךָ לְמַעַן

יָנוּחַ עַבְדְּךָ וַאֲמָתְךָ כָּמוֹךָ וְזָכַרְתָּ כִּי־עֶבֶד הָיִיתָ ׀ בְּאֶרֶץ מִצְרַיִם

וַיֹּצִאֲךָ יְהוָה אֱלֹהֶיךָ מִשָּׁם בְּיָד חֲזָקָה וּבִזְרֹעַ נְטוּיָה עַל־כֵּן צִוְּךָ

יְהוָה אֱלֹהֶיךָ לַעֲשׂוֹת אֶת־יוֹם הַשַּׁבָּת: כַּבֵּד

אֶת־אָבִיךָ וְאֶת־אִמֶּךָ כַּאֲשֶׁר צִוְּךָ יְהוָה אֱלֹהֶיךָ לְמַעַן ׀ יַאֲרִיכֻן

יָמֶיךָ וּלְמַעַן יִיטַב לָךְ עַל הָאֲדָמָה אֲשֶׁר־יְהוָה אֱלֹהֶיךָ נֹתֵן

לָךְ: לֹא תִרְצָח: וְלֹא

תִנְאָף: וְלֹא תִגְנֹב: וְלֹא־

תַעֲנֶה בְרֵעֲךָ עֵד שָׁוְא: וְלֹא

תַחְמֹד אֵשֶׁת רֵעֶךָ וְלֹא

תִתְאַוֶּה בֵּית רֵעֶךָ שָׂדֵהוּ וְעַבְדּוֹ וַאֲמָתוֹ שׁוֹרוֹ וַחֲמֹרוֹ וְכֹל אֲשֶׁר

לְרֵעֶךָ:

According to the Gr"a and Heidenheim, the first commandment until מִבֵּית עֲבָדִים should be read with the regular trop.

TEXTUAL VARIANTS

In this list we have marked only those phrases which differ significantly from the version printed inside. Minor spelling and vowelization variants (*ḥataf pataḥ* in place of *shva*, etc.) which do not make a significant difference to reading or meaning are not listed.

The variants cited are only those with authoritative sources, gleaned from the attestants of tradition, the classical commentators and grammarians (Targum Yonatan, Rashi, Ibn Ezra, Radak, Minḥat Shai, Heidenheim, and others) or found in the majority of the manuscripts and early print editions.

בראשית ט, כט
במקום: וַיִּהְיֽ
בספרים אחרים: וַיִּהְיוּ

ויקרא
במקום: פרשה פתוחה: ז, כח
בספרים אחרים: פרשה פתוחה: ז, כב

דברים כג, ב
במקום: דַּכָּה
בספרים אחרים: דַּכָּא

יהושע ו, טו
במקום: כַּעֲלוֹת
בספרים אחרים: בעלות כתיב
כַּעֲלוֹת קרי

יהושע ח, כב
במקום: לוֹ
בספרים אחרים: לָהֶם

יהושע טו, נב
במקום: וְדוּמָה
בספרים אחרים: וְרוּמָה

שופטים כ, לד
במקום: מִנֶּגֶד
בספרים אחרים: מִנֶּגֶב

שמואל א ז, כב
במקום: בְּכֹל
בספרים אחרים: כְּכֹל

שמואל א ח, פעמים רבות
במקום: הֲדַדְעֶזֶר
בספרים אחרים: הֲדַרְעֶזֶר

שמואל א י, ה
במקום: גִּבְעַת
בספרים אחרים: אֶל־גִּבְעַת

שמואל א יד, ג
במקום: אִכָבוֹד ו
בספרים אחרים: אִי־כָבוֹד ו

שמואל א יד, מט
במקום: וּמַלְכִּי־שׁוּעַ
בספרים אחרים: וּמַלְכִּישׁוּעַ

שמואל א ל, ל
במקום: בְּכוֹר־עָשָׁן
בספרים אחרים: בְּבוֹר־עָשָׁן

שמואל א לא, ב
במקום: וְאֶת־מַלְכִּי־שׁוּעַ
בספרים אחרים: וְאֶת־מַלְכִּישׁוּעַ

שמואל ב ז, ח
במקום: לְדָוִד
בספרים אחרים: דָּוִד

שמואל ב ז, כב
במקום: בְּכֹל
בספרים אחרים: כְּכֹל

שמואל ב ח, פעמים רבות
במקום: הֲדַדְעֶזֶר
בספרים אחרים: הֲדַדְעֶזֶר

שמואל ב י, ה
במקום: בִּירֵחוֹ
בספרים אחרים: בִּירֵחוֹ

שמואל ב כג, לג
במקום: הָאֲרָרִי
בספרים אחרים: הָאֲרָרִי

מלכים א ח, א
במקום: אֶת־כָּל־רָאשֵׁי
בספרים אחרים: וְאֶת־כָּל־רָאשֵׁי

מלכים א ח, לא
במקום: וְנָשָׁא־
בספרים אחרים: וְנָשָׁא־

מלכים א יב, ב
במקום: הַמֶּלֶךְ שְׁלֹמֹה
בספרים אחרים: שְׁלֹמֹה הַמֶּלֶךְ

מלכים א טו, ט
במקום: עַל־יְהוּדָה
בספרים אחרים: מֶלֶךְ יְהוּדָה

מלכים ב יא, ב
במקום: הַמְּמוּתְתִים
בספרים אחרים: הַמּוּמָתִים

מלכים ב יב, כב
במקום: וִיוֹזָכָר
בספרים אחרים: וִיוֹזָבָד

מלכים ב טו, לו
במקום: וְכָל־אֲשֶׁר
בספרים אחרים: אֲשֶׁר

מלכים ב יט, לז
במקום: וְשַׂרְאֶצֶר
בספרים אחרים: וְשַׂרְאֶצֶר

מלכים ב כג, ד
במקום: הָעֲשׂוּיִם
בספרים אחרים: העשוום כתיב
הָעֲשׂוּיִם קרי

ישעיה ג, כג
במקום: הַגִּלְיֹנִים
בספרים אחרים: וְהַגִּלְיֹנִים

ישעיה ז, יד; ח, ח
במקום: עִמָּנוּאֵל
בספרים אחרים: עִמָּנוּ אֵל

ישעיה י, טו
במקום: וְאֶת־מְרִימָיו
בספרים אחרים: אֶת־מְרִימָיו

ישעיה לא, א
במקום: עַל־סוּסִים
בספרים אחרים: וְעַל־סוּסִים

ישעיה לד, יג
במקום: קִמּ֑וֹשׂ
בספרים אחרים: קִמּ֑וֹשׂ

ישעיה לז, לח
במקום: וְשַׂרְאֶ֫צֶר
בספרים אחרים: וְשַׂרְאֶ֫צֶר

ישעיה נד, ט
במקום: כִּי־מֵ֤י
בספרים אחרים: כִּימֵ֤י

ישעיה סג, יא
במקום: רֹעֵ֣ה
בספרים אחרים: רֹעֵ֣י

ירמיה כד, א
במקום: יְכָנְיָ֨הוּ
בספרים אחרים: יְכָנְיָ֨ה

ירמיה לט, פעמים רבות
במקום: שַׂרְאֶ֫צֶר
בספרים אחרים: שַׂרְאֶ֫צֶר

ירמיה נא, מו
במקום: מֹשֵׁ֑ל
בספרים אחרים: וּמֹשֵׁ֑ל

יחזקאל יד, ח
במקום: וַהֲשִׁמֹתִ֙יהוּ֙
בספרים אחרים: וַהֲשִׁמֹתִ֙יהוּ֙

יחזקאל טז, נג
במקום: שְׁבִ֣יתְהֶ֔ן
בספרים אחרים: שבִ֣ותהֶ֔ן כתיב
שְׁבִ֣יתְהֶ֔ן קרי

יחזקאל ל, ט
במקום: כְּי֥וֹם מִצְרַ֖יִם
בספרים אחרים: בְּי֥וֹם מִצְרַ֖יִם

יחזקאל לא, יא
במקום: בְּרִשְׁע֖וֹ
בספרים אחרים: כְּרִשְׁע֖וֹ

יחזקאל לו, כג
במקום: לְעֵֽינֵיהֶֽם
בספרים אחרים: לְעֵֽינֵיכֶֽם

יחזקאל לט, כח
במקום: אֶל־אַדְמָתָ֑ם
בספרים אחרים: עַל־אַדְמָתָ֑ם

הושע ט, ו
במקום: קִמּ֣וֹשׂ
בספרים אחרים: קִימּ֣וֹשׂ

מיכה ב, ב
במקום: וְאִ֥ישׁ
בספרים אחרים: אִ֥ישׁ

מיכה ב, י
במקום: טָמְאָ֑ה
בספרים אחרים: טָמְאָ֑ה, טָמְאָ֑ה

צפניה ג, טו
במקום: לֹֽא־תִֽירְאִ֥י
בספרים אחרים: לֹֽא־תִרְאִ֥י

חגי ב, י
במקום: בְּיַד־
בספרים אחרים: אֶל־

זכריה ז, ב
במקום: שַׂרְאֶ֫צֶר
בספרים אחרים: שַׂרְאֶ֫צֶר

תהלים ט, יד
במקום: חָנְנֵ֬נִי
בספרים אחרים: חַנְנֵ֬נִי

תהלים כד, ד

במקום: נפשׁוֹ כתיב נַפְשִׁי קרי

בספרים אחרים: נַפְשׁוֹ קרי וכתיב נַפְשׁוֹ

נַפְשִׁי קרי וכתיב

נפשִׁי כתיב נַפְשׁוֹ

תהלים מה, י

במקום: בְּיִקְּרוֹתֶיךָ

בספרים אחרים: בִּיקְּרוֹתֶיךָ

תהלים קיח, ה

במקום: בַּמֶּרְחָב יָהּ

בספרים אחרים: בַמֶּרְחַבְיָה

משלי ז, כה

במקום: אַל־תֵּתַע

בספרים אחרים: וְאַל־תֵּתַע

משלי ח, טז

במקום: צֶדֶק

בספרים אחרים: אָרֶץ משלי יז, כו

במקום: עֲלֵי־יֹשֶׁר

בספרים אחרים: עַל־יֹשֶׁר

משלי יז, כו

במקום: עֲלֵי־יֹשֶׁר

בספרים אחרים: עַל־יֹשֶׁר

משלי כד, לא

במקום: קִמְּשֹׂנִים

בספרים אחרים: קִמְּשׁוֹנִים

משלי כז, כ

במקום: וַאֲבַדֹּה

בספרים אחרים: וְאבדה כתיב

וַאֲבַדּוֹן קרי

איוב כא, יב

במקום: כְּתֹף

בספרים אחרים: בְּתֹף

איוב כח, יז

במקום: וּזְכוֹכִית

בספרים אחרים: וּזְכוֹכִית

איוב מ, יא

במקום: עַבְרוֹת

בספרים אחרים: עֶבְרוֹת

איוב מא, ב

במקום: יְעוּרֶנּוּ

בספרים אחרים: יְעִירֶנּוּ כתיב

יְעוּרֶנּוּ

קהלת יב, ד

במקום: וְיָקוּם

בספרים אחרים: וְיָקוּם

אסתר ח, יא

במקום: וְלַהֲרֹג

בספרים אחרים: לַהֲרֹגאסתר ט, ב

במקום: לִפְנֵיהֶם

בספרים אחרים: בִּפְנֵיהֶם

אסתר ט, ב

במקום: לִפְנֵיהֶם

בספרים אחרים: בִּפְנֵיהֶם

דניאל א, פעמים רבות

במקום: פַּת־בַּג

בספרים אחרים: פַּתְבַּג

דניאל יא, כו

במקום: פַּת־בָּגוֹ

בספרים אחרים: פַּתְבָּגוֹ

עזרא ד, יג

במקום: וְאַפְּתֹם

בספרים אחרים: וְאַפְּתֹם

עזרא ח, יד
במקום: וְעִמָּהֶם
בספרים אחרים: וְעִמּוֹ

נחמיה ז, מח
במקום: שַׁלְמָי
בספרים אחרים: שַׂלְמָי

נחמיה ז, נד
במקום: בַצְלִית
בספרים אחרים: בצלות כתיב
בַּצְלִית קרי

דברי הימים א ו, מג
במקום: חִילֵן
בספרים אחרים: חִילֵז

דברי הימים א ט, יג
במקום: חֵיל
בספרים אחרים: חֵיל

דברי הימים א יב, ח
במקום: הַגְּדוּר
בספרים אחרים: הַגְּדוּר, הַגְּדוּד

דברי הימים א יח, פעמים רבות
במקום: הֲדַדְעֶזֶר
בספרים אחרים: הֲדַרְעֶזֶר

דברי הימים א כב, י
במקום: כִּסֵּא
בספרים אחרים: אֶת־כִּסֵּא

דברי הימים א כד, כג
במקום: וּבְנֵי
בספרים אחרים: וּבְנֵי

דברי הימים ב ו, כב
במקום: וְנָשָׁא־
בספרים אחרים: וְנָשָׂא־

דברי הימים ב י, יד
במקום: אַכְבִּיד
בספרים אחרים: אָבִי הִכְבִּיד

דברי הימים ב י, טז
במקום: וְכָל־יִשְׂרָאֵל
בספרים אחרים: וְכָל־יִשְׂרָאֵל רָאוּ

דברי הימים ב כ, לז
במקום: כְּהִתְחַבֶּרְךָ
בספרים אחרים: בְּהִתְחַבֶּרְךָ

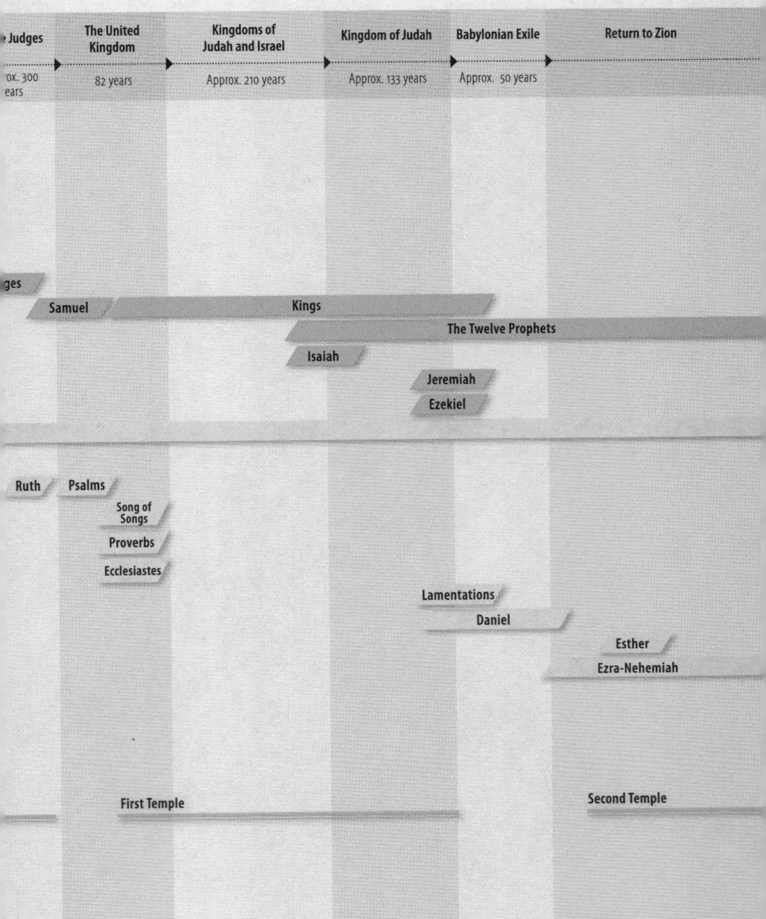

Judges
Approx. 300 years
The United Kingdom
82 years
Kingdoms of Judah and Israel
Approx. 210 years
Kingdom of Judah
Approx. 133 years
Babylonian Exile
Approx. 50 years
Return to Zion
Samuel
Kings
The Twelve Prophets
Isaiah
Jeremiah
Ezekiel
Ruth
Psalms
Song of Songs
Proverbs
Ecclesiastes
Lamentations
Daniel
Esther
Ezra-Nehemiah
First Temple
Second Temple

TIMELINE OF THE BOOKS OF TANAKH

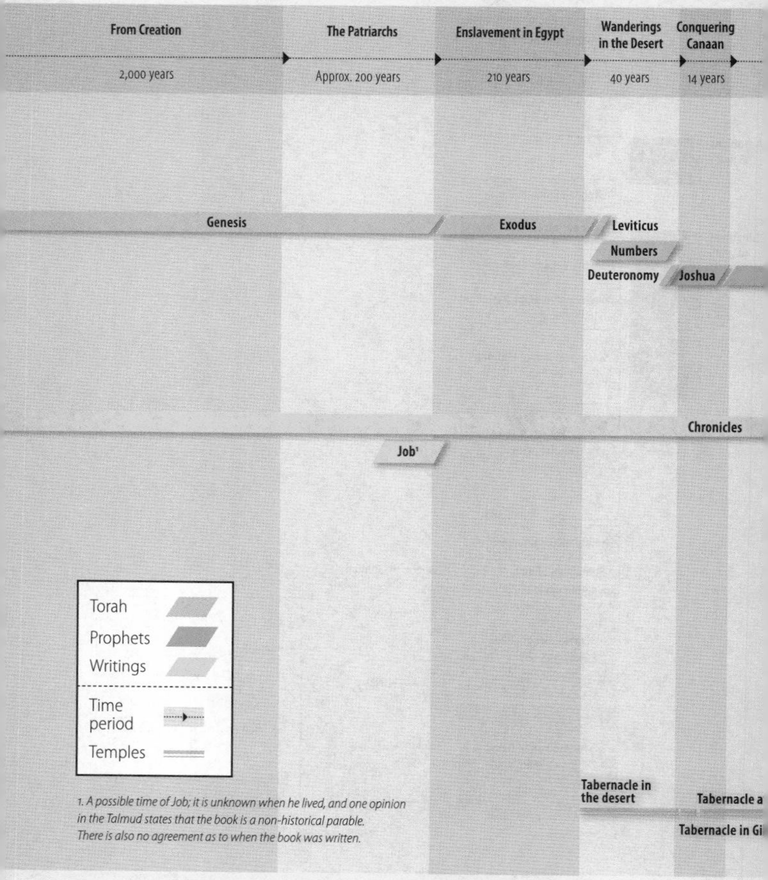

1. A possible time of Job; it is unknown when he lived, and one opinion in the Talmud states that the book is a non-historical parable. There is also no agreement as to when the book was written.

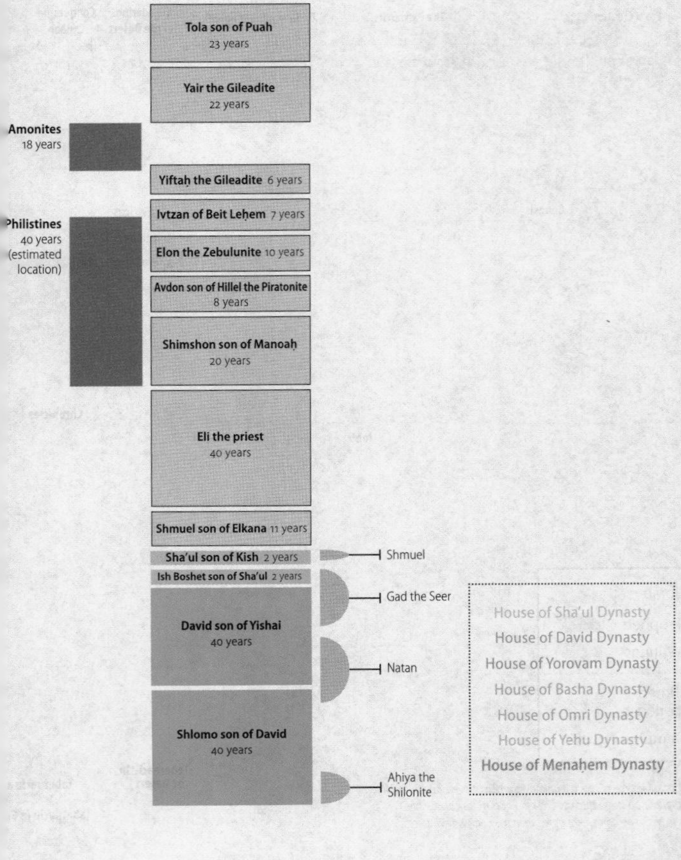
Tola son of Puah
23 years
Yair the Gileadite
22 years
Amonites
18 years
Yiftaḥ the Gileadite 6 years
Ivtzan of Beit Leḥem 7 years
Philistines
40 years
(estimated
location)
Elon the Zebulunite 10 years
Avdon son of Hillel the Piratonite
8 years
Shimshon son of Manoaḥ
20 years
Eli the priest
40 years
Shmuel son of Elkana 11 years
Sha'ul son of Kish 2 years
Shmuel
Ish Boshet son of Sha'ul 2 years
Gad the Seer
David son of Yishai
40 years
Natan
Shlomo son of David
40 years
Aḥiya the
Shilonite
House of Sha'ul Dynasty
House of David Dynasty
House of Yorovam Dynasty
House of Basha Dynasty
House of Omri Dynasty
House of Yehu Dynasty
House of Menaḥem Dynasty

LEADERS OF ISRAEL
(FROM ENTERING THE LAND OF ISRAEL TO THE DIVISION OF THE KINGDOM)

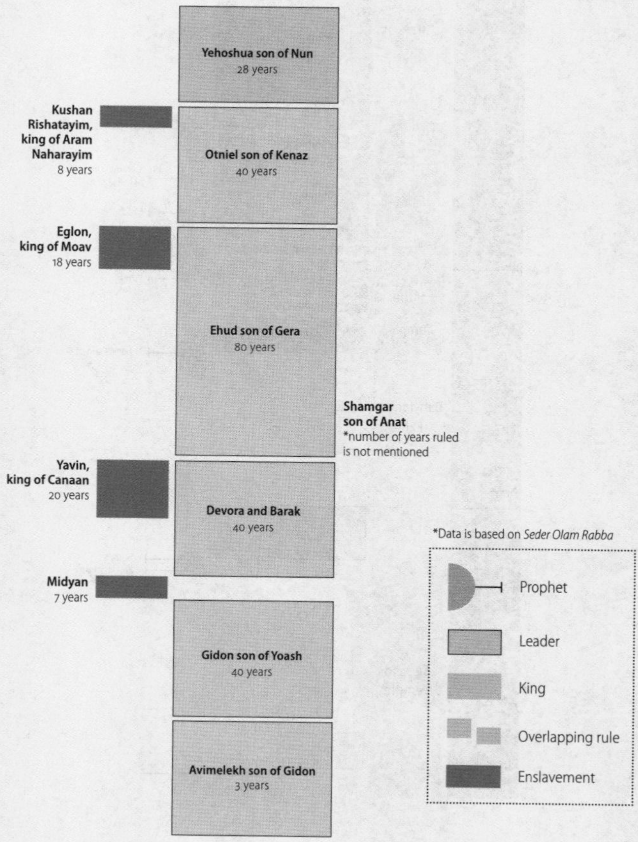

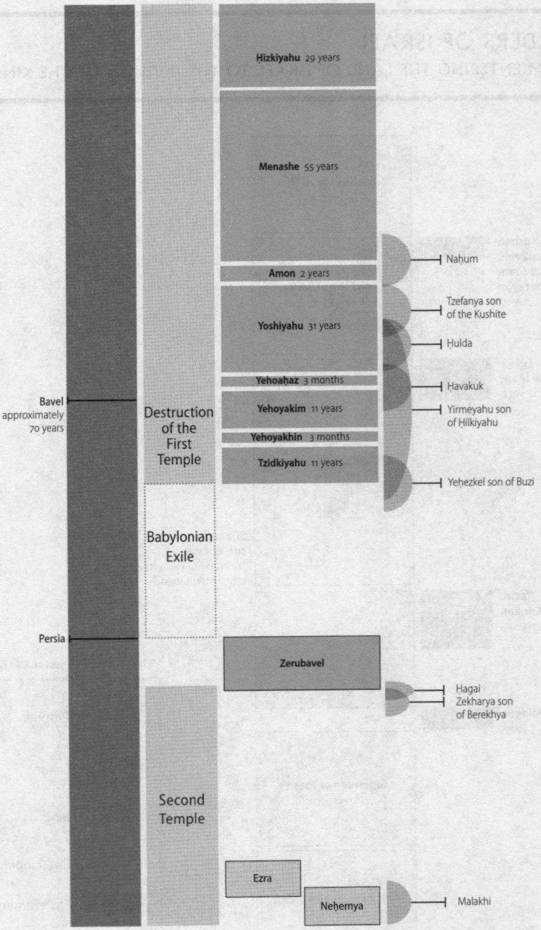

Ḥizkiyahu 29 years
Menashe 55 years
Amon 2 years
Yoshiyahu 31 years
Yehoaḥaz 3 months
Yehoyakim 11 years
Yehoyakhin 3 months
Tzidkiyahu 11 years
Nahum
Tzefanya son of the Kushite
Ḥulda
Ḥavakuk
Yirmeyahu son of Ḥilkiyahu
Yeḥezkel son of Buzi
Bavel
approximately 70 years
Destruction of the First Temple
Babylonian Exile
Persia
Zerubavel
Ḥagai
Zekharya son of Berekhya
Second Temple
Ezra
Neḥemya
Malakhi

LEADERS OF ISRAEL
(FROM THE DIVISION OF THE KINGDOM TO THE RETURN TO ZION)

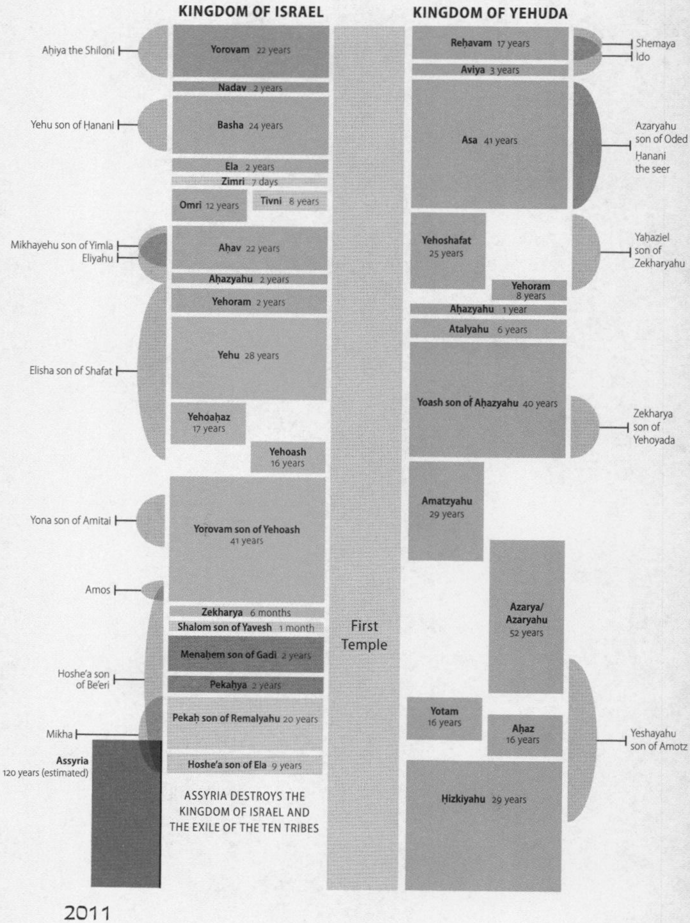

LISTINGS OF THE MAIN FAMILIES IN TANAKH

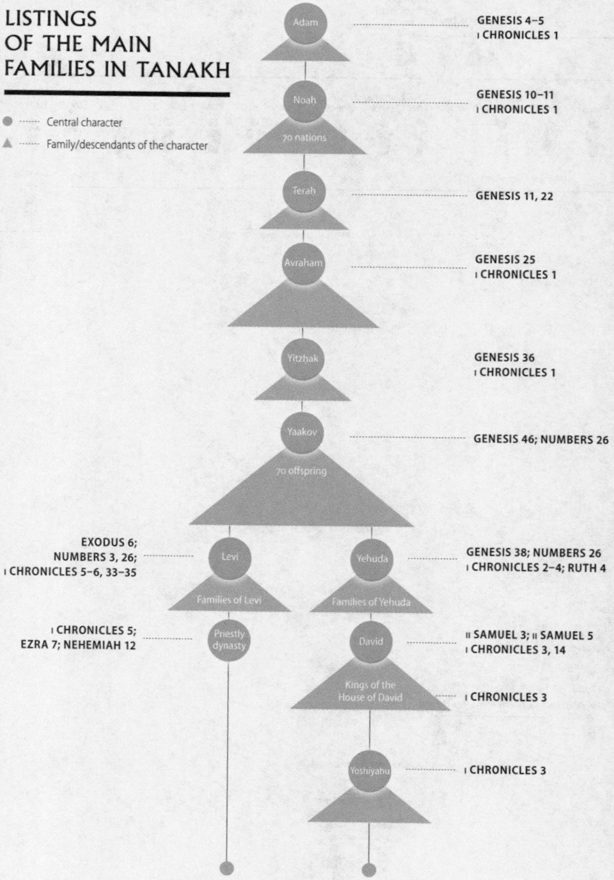

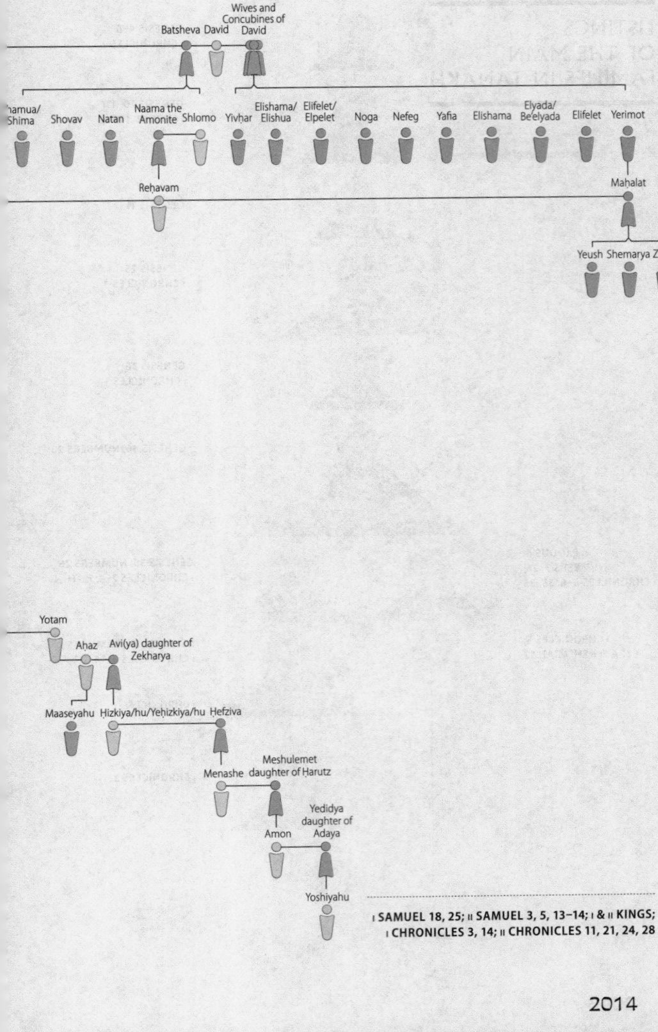

I SAMUEL 18, 25; II SAMUEL 3, 5, 13–14; I & II KINGS; I CHRONICLES 3, 14; II CHRONICLES 11, 21, 24, 28

DAVID'S DESCENDANTS

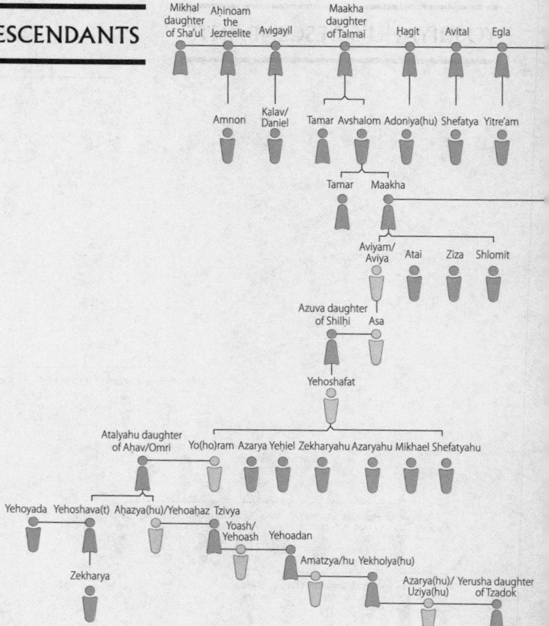

YOSHIYAHU'S DESCENDANTS

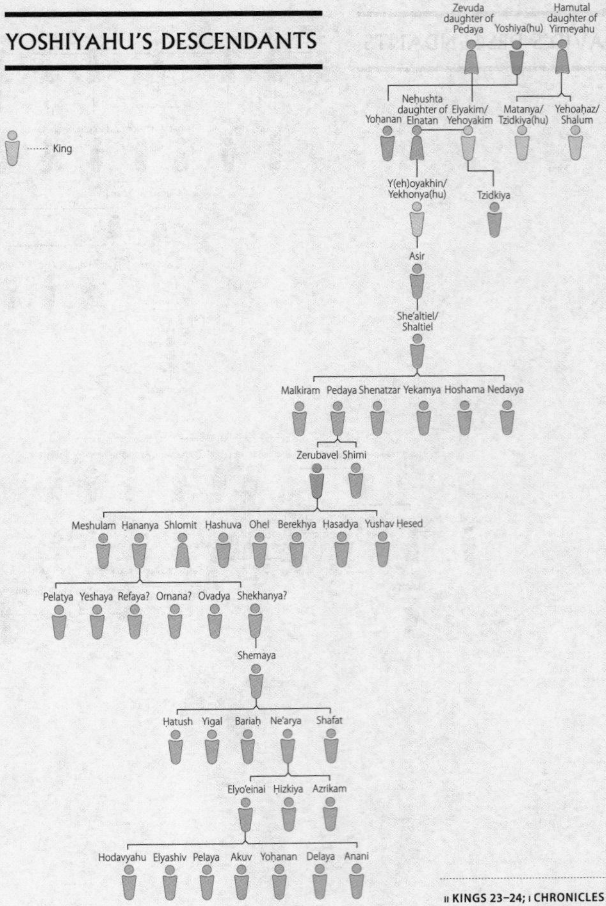

II KINGS 23–24; I CHRONICLES 3

1. THE WARS OF YEHOSHUA (JOSH. 6–11)

2. TRIBAL DIVISION OF LAND (JOSH. 13–19)

3. JUDGES

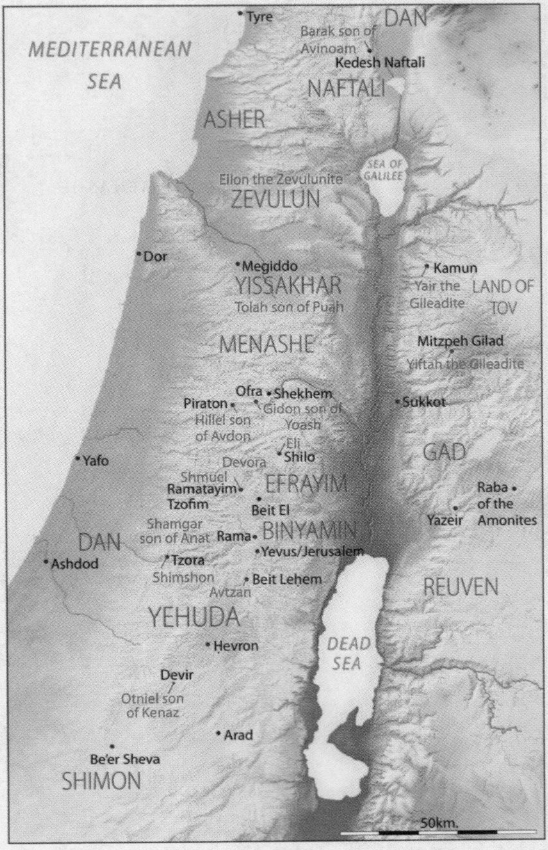
Tyre
DAN
Barak son of Avinoam
Kedesh Naftali
MEDITERRANEAN SEA
NAFTALI
ASHER
SEA OF GALILEE
Eilon the Zevulunite
ZEVULUN
Dor
Megiddo
Kamun
YISSAKHAR
Yair the Gileadite
LAND OF TOV
Tolah son of Puah
MENASHE
Mitzpeh Gilad
Yiftah the Gileadite
Ofra
Shekhem
Piraton
Gidon son of Yoash
Sukkot
Hillel son of Avdon
Eli
Shilo
Yafo
Devora
GAD
Shmuel
Ramatayim Tzofim
EFRAYIM
Raba of the Amonites
Beit El
Yazeir
Shamgar son of Anat
Rama
BINYAMIN
DAN
Yevus/Jerusalem
Ashdod
Tzora
Shimshon
Beit Leḥem
Avtzan
REUVEN
YEHUDA
Ḥevron
DEAD SEA
Devir
Otniel son of Kenaz
Arad
Be'er Sheva
SHIMON
50km.

4. PHILISTINE WARS AND THE WANDERINGS OF THE TRIBE OF DAN

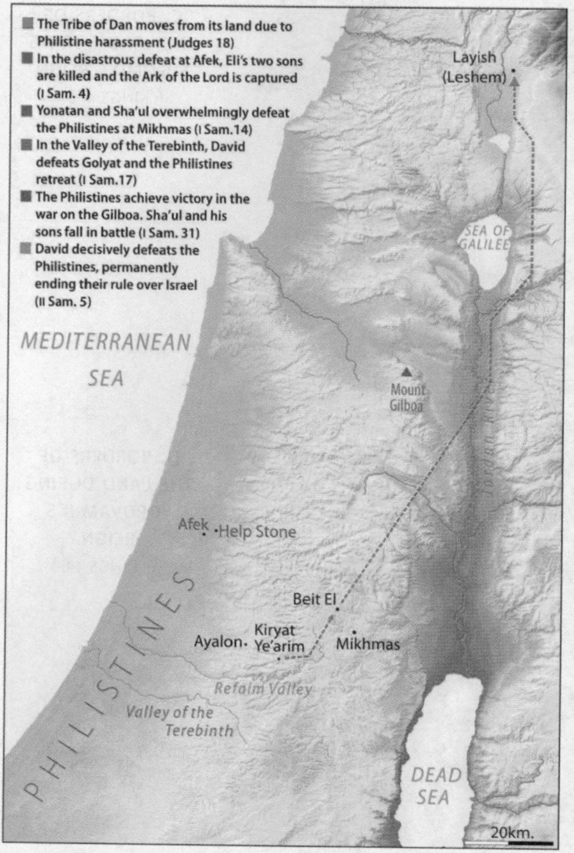

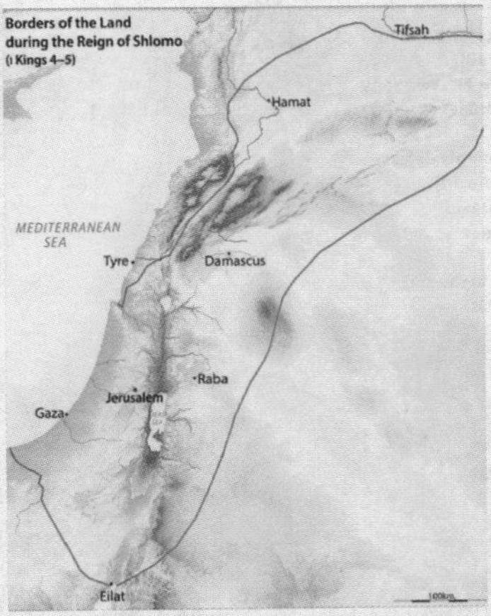

C. BORDERS OF THE LAND DURING SHLOMO'S REIGN

(I KINGS 4–5)

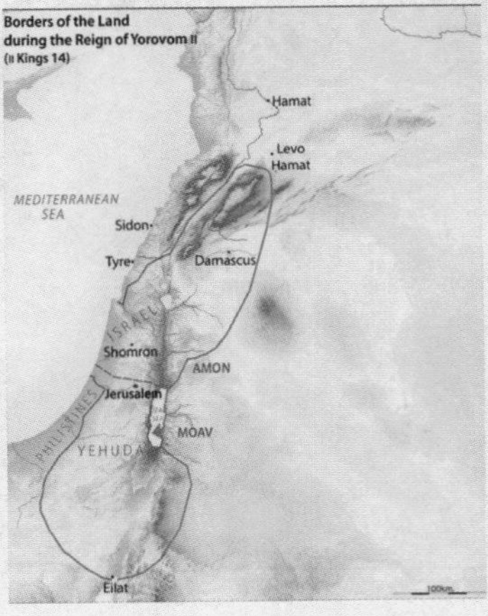

D. BORDERS OF THE LAND DURING YOROVAM II'S REIGN

(II KINGS 14)

5. BORDERS OF THE LAND OF ISRAEL

A. BORDERS OF THE LAND IN PARASHAT MASEI

(NUM. 34)

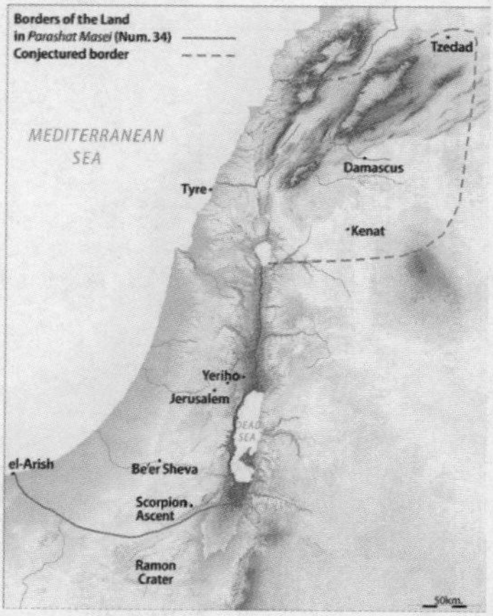

B. BORDERS OF THE LAND AT THE BEGINNING OF DAVID'S REIGN

(II SAM. 5:1–5)

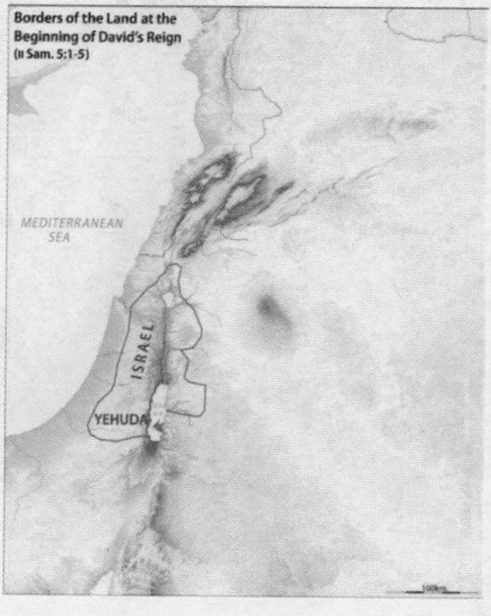

6. TRAVELS OF THE TABERNACLE AND THE ARK

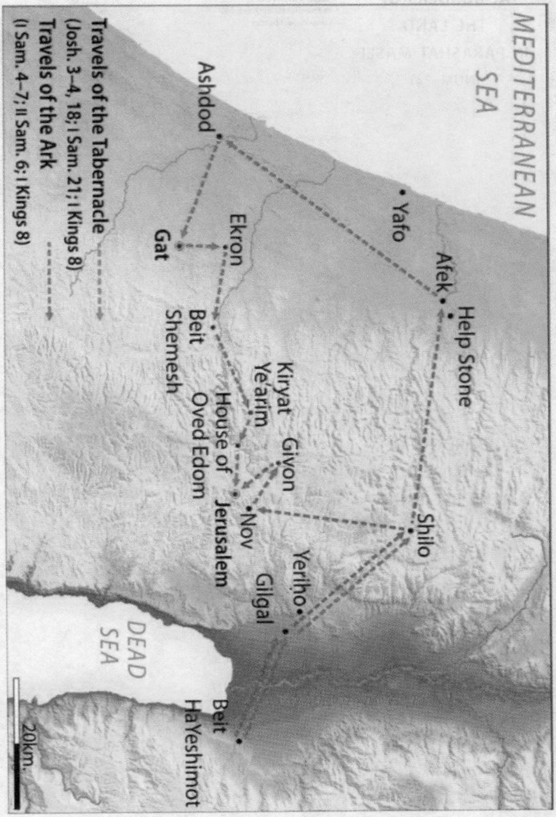

7. WALLS OF JERUSALEM

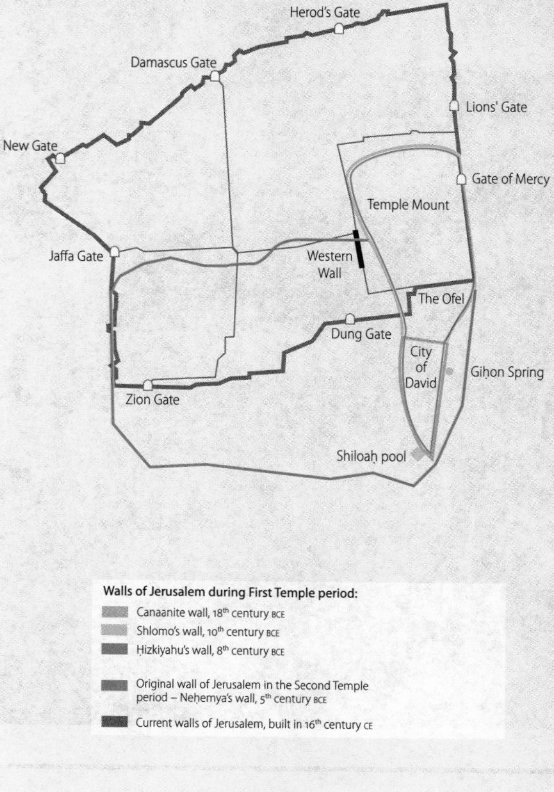

THE TABERNACLE IN THE DESERT

A – Holy of Holies
B – Curtain
C – Sanctuary
D – Screen
E – Laver
F – Sacrificial altar
G – Hangings

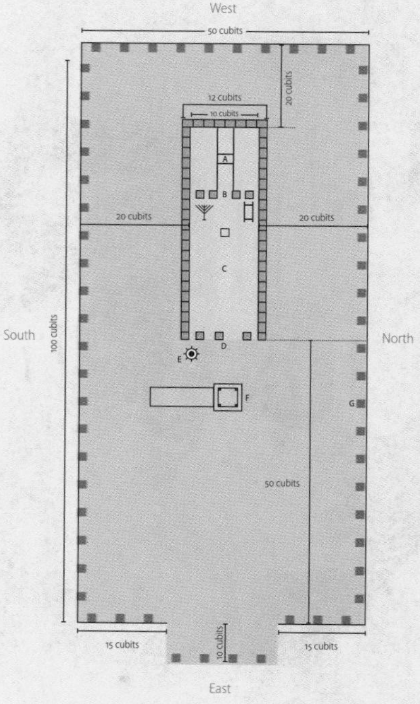

Temples – size comparison

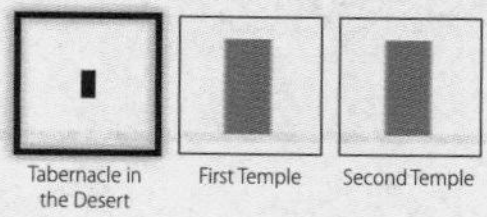

FIRST TEMPLE

A – Inner Sanctuary
B – Sanctuary
C – Hall
D – Laver
E – Sacrificial altar
F – Shlomo's Sea
G – Courtyard (estimated size)

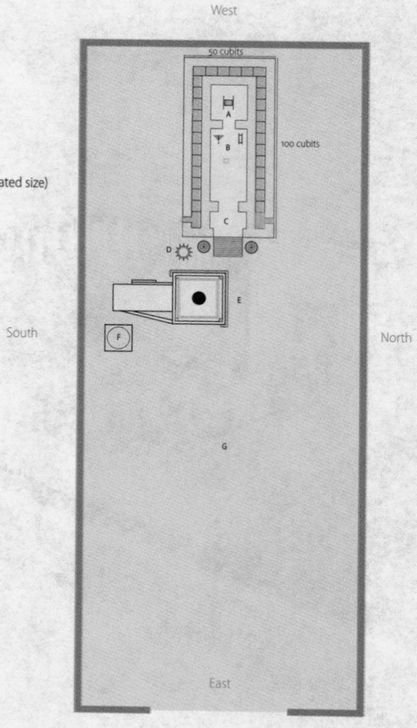

Temples – size comparison

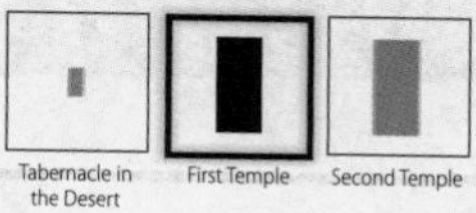

SECOND TEMPLE

A – Holy of Holies
B – Sanctuary
C – Hall
D – Rampart
E – Sacrificial altar
F – Priests' courtyard
G – Israelites' courtyard
H – Women's courtyard

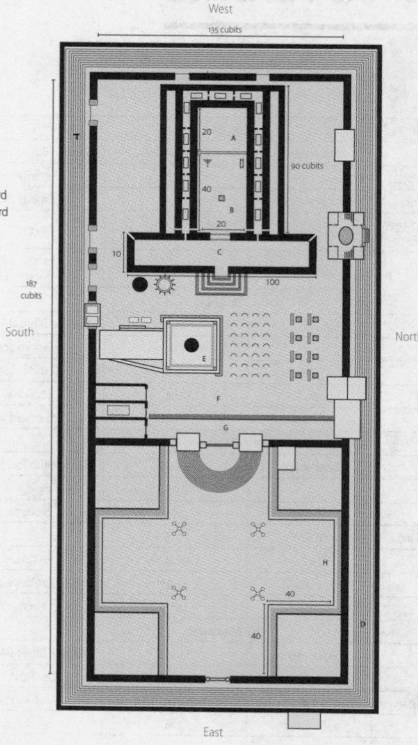

Temples – size comparison

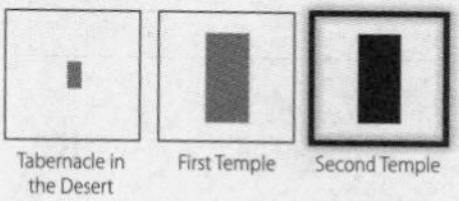

We have no information about the Temple built by those who ascended from Babylon. Therefore, we present here a diagram of Herod's Temple, on the assumption that the dimensions remained as they had been from the foundation of the Second Temple.

WEIGHTS AND MEASURES

Length			
Unit	**Equivalent**	**Centimeters**	**Sample Biblical Reference**
fingerbreadth		20 cm	Jeremiah 52:21
handbreadth	4 fingerbreadths	80 cm	Exodus 25:25
span (distance between thumb and little finger)	3 handbreadths	24 cm	Exodus 28:16
cubit	2 span	48 cm	Exodus 26:16 Judges 3:16

Weight			
Unit	**Equivalent**	**Grams**	**Sample Biblical Reference**
gerah		0.8	Exodus 30:13
shekel	20 gerah	19.2	Exodus 38:24
maneh	50 shekel	480	Ezekiel 45:12
talent	60 maneh	28,800	Exodus 25:39

Dry Measures			
Unit	**Equivalent**	**Liters**	**Sample Biblical Reference**
kab		1.38	II Kings 6:25
omer	1.8 kab	2.49	Exodus 16:16
(Rabbinic: tarkav)	1.66 omer	4.14	
se'a	2 tarkav	8.29	II Kings 7:1
ephah	3 se'a	24.88	Ezekiel 45:24
homer	10 ephah	248.9	Isaiah 5:10

Dry Measures			
Unit	**Equivalent**	**Liters**	**Sample Biblical Reference**
log		0.34	Leviticus 14:12
tenth of an ephah	7.2 log	2.49	Leviticus 14:12
hin	0.166 ephah	4.14	Exodus 30:24
(rabbinic: jug)	2 hin	8.29	
bat	3 jug	24.88	I Kings 7:26
kor	10 bat	248.9	Ezekiel 45:14